What the reviewers say about the ALL MUSIC GUIDE series:

"Delivers on the promise of _____ _____ _____ with knowledge."
_____ _ly

"This extremely valuable and _____ _____ _____ not only on recordings, but also style descriptions, history, profiles, reflective essays, music maps, and more."
—*The Christian Science Monitor*

"Anybody who owns a record collection should invest in the owners manual, *All Music Guide.*"
—*San Francisco Chronicle*

"I can't imagine a serious music lover, record store, radio station or library without a copy."
—*Whole Earth Review*

"Quite an amazing reference volume, invaluable for the record collector."
—*DISCoveries*

"Don't visit a record store without it."

—*Guitar Player*

"A dream come true for contemporary record collectors . . . this book ought to be in every home that has a resident music enthusiast."
—*San Francisco Examiner*

"The sheer scope of the enterprise makes this volume the one indispensable book in a music reference library."

—*Addicted to Noise*

"Any library or individual who doesn't cough up the very reasonable bucks to own this tome will remain musically illiterate."

—*Small Press*

"A massive piece of work, and a very good value for the money."
—*Living Blues*

"This is the best overall record guide."

—*The Beat*

"A number of guides have appeared to help the neophyte wade through the maze of recordings. *The All Music Guide* is by far the best of these books. . . . The result is an informed (and informative), candid, and literate production."

—*Dirty Linen*

"A valuable resource and well worth its reasonable cover price for the music fan trying to make sense of the plethora of reissues and new releases."
—*Illinois Entertainer*

"In its scope, Miller Freeman's *All Music Guide* is without peer."
—*Publishers Weekly*

"A powerful informational tool—very condensed and rarely wishy-washy. . . . Such succinct summings-up, along with terse chronologies of career phases, and discussions of genre styles, make the book a true bargain."

—Puncture

"A treasure trove of concise informative reviews . . . an essential addition to any music lover's library."

—The Ithaca Journal

"Highly recommended references for discriminating music buyers."

—Reviewer's Bookwatch

"[The *All Music Guide to Jazz*] is one fun book for any fan of jazz, new or old. . . . This book represents the informational cornerstone to an understanding and appreciation of the genre . . . . So grab yourself a copy, flip on some Miles, pour a martini, and settle in for some cool fun."

—BAM Magazine

"An entertaining, informative and easy to access format. . . . Will easily become your number one reference book, if not replace all others."

—Small Press

"Easily the best guide to hit the market both as an encyclopedia and as a tool to help readers pick discs for purchase. Everyone needs one of these on their shelf."

—Real Blues

"It's a definite must for any serious music collector."

—Country Song Roundup

"Heads above any other jazz guide available."

—Vintage Guitar Magazine

All Music Guide to

Rock

2nd Edition

The experts' guide to the best recordings in Rock, Pop, Soul, R&B, and Rap

Edited by
Michael Erlewine, Executive Editor
Vladimir Bogdanov, Database Design
Chris Woodstra, Editor-In-Chief
Stephen Thomas Erlewine, Senior Editor
Richie Unterberger, Senior Editor

●AMG All Music Guide Series

Miller
Freeman
Books

San Francisco

Published by Miller Freeman Books
600 Harrison Street, San Francisco, CA 94107
Publishers of *Guitar Player, Bass Player* and *Keyboard* magazines
Miller Freeman, Inc. is a United News and Media Company

 Miller Freeman
A United News & Media company

Distributed to the book trade in the U.S. and Canada by
Publishers Group West, P.O. Box 8843, Emeryville, CA 94662

Distributed to the music trade in the U.S. and Canada by
Hal Leonard Publishing, P.O. Box 13819, Milwaukee, WI 53213

ISBN 0-87930- 494-4

Cover Design: Nita Ybarra
Cover Photo: Jay Blakesberg

Production: Anna Hiller, Dorothy Cox, Matt Kelsey, and Wendy Davis

Printed in the United States of America
    99 00   5 4

CONTENTS

HOW TO USE THIS BOOK

ARTIST NAME   (Alternate name in parentheses)

VITAL STATISTICS   For groups, **f.** indicates date (and place) of formation; **db.** indicates date disbanded. For individual performers, date and place of birth (**b.**) and death (**d.**) are given, if known.

INSTRUMENT(S) / STYLE   For individual performers, major instruments are listed here, followed by one or more styles of music associated with each performer or group.

BIOGRAPHY   A quick view of the artist's life and musical career. For major performers, proportionately longer biographies are provided.

MAJOR ALBUMS   These are the albums selected and reviewed by our editors and contributors.

KEY TO SYMBOLS   ● ★ ☆

☆ ESSENTIAL COLLECTIONS   Albums marked with a star should be part of any good collection of the genre. Often, these are also a good first purchase (filled star). By hearing these albums, you can get a good overview of the entire genre. These are must-hear and must-have recordings. You can't go wrong with them.

● ★ FIRST PURCHASE   Albums marked with either a filled circle or a filled star should be your first purchase. This is where to begin to find out if you like this particular artist. These albums are representative of the best this artist has to offer. If you don't like these picks, chances are this artist is not for you. In the case of an artist who has a number of distinct periods, you will find an essential pick marked for each period. Albums are listed chronologically when possible.

ALBUM RATINGS: ✦ TO ✦✦✦✦✦   In addition to the stars and circles used to distinguish exceptionally noteworthy albums, as explained above, all albums are rated on a scale from one to five diamonds.

ALBUM TITLE   The name of the album is listed in bold as it appears on the original when possible. Very long titles have been abbreviated, or repeated in full as part of the review, where needed.

DATE   The date of an album's first release, if known.

RECORD LABEL   Record labels indicate the current (or most recent) release of this recording. Label numbers are not given because they change frequently.

REVIEWERS   The name of each review's author are given at the end of the review. "AMG" indicates a review written by the *All Music Guide* staff.

The English Beat

f. 1978, Birmingham, England, **db.** 1983
New Wave, Ska-Revival

One of the earliest and most important ska-revivalist groups, Birmingham's the Beat formed in 1978 (the band had to change its name to the English Beat in the US to avoid confusion with Paul Collins' band of the same name). The multiracial band carved a distinct sound through the use of alternating lead vocals by guitarist Dave Wakeling and punk-toaster/rapper Ranking Roger, supported by a tight band consisting of Andy Cox (guitar), Dave Steel (bass), and Everett Moreton (drums).

The addition of 50-year-old saxophonist Saxa, who originally played with Prince Buster and Desmond Dekker, gave the band credibility and fleshed out its sound. An opening spot for the Selecter led to the band's signing to 2-Tone, where they released the hit single "Tears of a Clown," a wonderful version of the Smokey Robinson classic.

In 1980 the band decided to form their own 2-Tone inspired label, Go-Feet (distributed by Arista). A string of hit singles followed in the UK, including "Mirror in the Bathroom." Their debut LP, *I Just Can't Stop It*, combined the early hits with other pop/ska-oriented material. "Stand Down Margaret," with its anti-Thatcher stance, found the band moving in a more political direction, leading to several benefit gigs for "radical" causes. Musically, the Beat slowed down the tempo for a more traditional reggae sound showcased on 1981's *Wha'ppen*. This direction failed to bring the chart success of its predecessor.

Featuring a more pop-oriented approach, 1982's *Special Beat Service* helped the band increase its US fan base through MTV exposure of "Save It for Later" and "I Confess," but the band members decided to call it quits later that same year. Wakeling and Ranking Roger went on to form General Public, and Cox and Steel formed Fine Young Cannibals. —*Chris Woodstra*

☆ **I Just Can't Stop It** / Oct. 1980 / IRS ✦✦✦✦✦
The Beat's debut is a true landmark of the period, perfectly blending intense politics with a playful, yet driving dance beat. While the sound could be mimicked by other revivalists, the top-notch songwriting represented on this album is what set them apart. *I Just Can't Stop It* plays like a Greatest Hits album (most of their hits are found here) and still holds up today. —*Chris Woodstra*

Wha'ppen? / Jun. 1981 / IRS ✦✦✦
After the nearly perfect debut, the Beat seem somewhat directionless on *Wha'ppen?* No longer instantly danceable, the tunes have slowed to sub-reggae tempo with more political content (though less focused this time around). The two unmemorable singles, "Drowning" and "Doors of Your Heart," failed to make an impact in the charts, and only "Dreamhome in N.Z." leaves any lasting impression. —*Chris Woodstra*

Special Beat Service / 1982 / IRS ✦✦✦✦
The final Beat album focuses less on politics and more on the subject of personal relationships. Their most polished effort, the band leaves behind their early ska influences in favor of jangly pop that, at times, delves into African and Latin rhythms. Includes the flawless singles "Save It for Later" and "I Confess." —*Chris Woodstra*

● **What Is Beat?** / 1983 / IRS ✦✦✦✦
While the best introduction to Beat is still the first album, *What Is Beat?* does a good job of collecting the hits from each of the three albums. The live tracks and remixes are a nice addition for completists but are generally unnecessary for anyone else. —*Chris Woodstra*

b.p.m: The Very Best of the Beat / Nov. 1995 / Arista ✦✦✦✦
b.p.m: The Very Best of the Beat nearly duplicates the original *What is Beat?* collection, covering all of the band's hit singles. Initial runs of the album came with an additional disc of remixes and dub versions, making it a nice, though not necessary, addition for fans and completists. —*Chris Woodstra*

ALL MUSIC GUIDE WEBSITE

The *All Music Guide* reference books offer just a taste of the wealth of information to be discovered at our website (http://allmusic.com/), the largest and most comprehensive site of its kind on the Internet. Along with the same detailed biographical entries and album reviews found in the books, the AMG website offers much more, touching base with the one-hit wonders, session players, novelty artists, and studio technicians whom, for reasons of space, the book cannot.

Of course, the site doesn't replace the books, it complements them; while the books compile overviews of the superstars, the cult heroes and the true innovators into one handy volume, the AMG homepage fills in the gaps, taking full advantage of the seemingly boundless scope of the web to offer exhaustive coverage of thousands of other, more obscure artists and albums. In addition, it features even more detailed information on music's landmark performers and records, including recording information and hyperlinks to related artists; a click on your mouse allows quick access from, for example, our Neil Young biography to both the Buffalo Springfield or CSNY entries as well as less obvious—but no less important—links to the likes of Pearl Jam (with whom Young cut the 1995 LP *Mirror Ball*). At the same time, the site affords one luxury that the print format cannot; while published books cannot be updated until the next edition, the AMG website evolves and changes along with the music industry; if your favorite band releases a new album, or their drummer quits, you'll find it noted on-line long before you'll see it mentioned in book form. Information can be accessed through the All Music Guide site in one of three easy ways: to find what you're looking for, simply type the name of the particular artist, album or song in the appropriate space, click on the "search" button, and the available data will appear. You can also click on regular features like our music maps, essays and glossaries, or even help us grow by suggesting new artists and albums to cover.

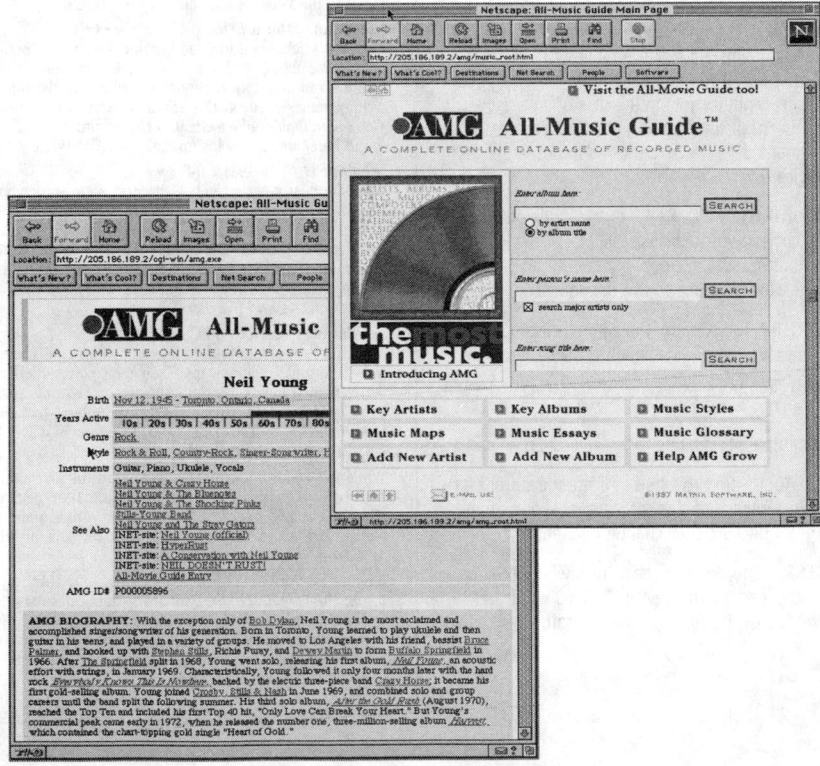

FOREWORD

Music is an essential part of my life and I am not alone in this. Tracking down the very best music is very time consuming—a fine art. Each hour of music takes an hour of life; there is no such thing as an abridged recording. A guide can be a great help. There is something wonderful about the discovery of a new genre, artist or a really great piece of new music by a favorite artist. That is what this book is all about—a concise guide to the very best in rock music.

AMG editors Chris Woodstra and Stephen Thomas Erlewine, with help from Richie Unterberger, Bruce Eder, Cub Koda, and Sean Cooper have done an outstanding job in compiling this book and in coordinating their work with that of over 100 additional free-lance writers.

Special thanks to Vladimir Bogdanov and Ludmilla Lobenko (and to AMG staff members Mark Donkers, Jason Ankeny, John Bush, Steve Huey and Jonathan Ball) for their unceasing efforts with the database and many other aspects of this project.

I would also like to thank my wife Margaret for her support and understanding. The organization and management of this kind of project does not respect evenings or weekends. There was a lot of midnight oil burned to put this book into your hands and the spirit of the editing team, from the outset, was first rate.

Michael Erlewine
Founder and Executive Editor
All Music Guides

ALL MUSIC GUIDE DATABASE

The All Music Guide is the most comprehensive database ever assembled and it is now available in many forms—books, kiosks, CD-ROMs, web sites, and commerical online services. The All Music Guide project continues to broaden its overall coverage and, at the same time, provide increasing detail for each artist. This book contains the most signficant subset of the database, the tip of the top (so to speak) of the very best country music of all time. We hope you will find it useful. The All Music Guide is also available in the following formats:

Books:
  All Music Guide (Miller Freeman Books, 3rd Edition, 1996)
  All Music Guide to Jazz (Miller Freeman Books, 2nd Edition, 1996)
  All Music Guide to the Blues (Miller Freeman Books, 1996)
  All Music Guide to Country (Miller Freeman Books, 1997)
  VideoHound & All-Movie Guide Stargazer (Visible Ink, 1995)

Electronic Formats:
  All Music Guide CD-ROM (Corel, release date to be announced)
  All-Movie Guide CD-ROM (Corel)
  MusicRoms (music and data) for Blues, Jazz, R&B, Latin, etc. (Selectware/Compton's)
  All Music Guide (hard disk version) (Great Bear Technology)
  World Beat CD-ROM (Medio)

In Store Kiosks:
  Musicland's Soundsite
  Sam Goody's

Internet AMG sites:
  ALLMUSIC.COM
  ALLMOVIE.COM
  THENEWAGE.COM

Since the All Music Guide is an ongoing project, we appreciate your feedback. Perhaps we have left out some of your favorite albums, and/or included ones that you don't consider essential. Let us know about it. We welcome criticism, suggestions, additions, and/or deletions. The All Music Guide is a work in progress. If you are knowledgeable on the recordings of a particular artist or group and would like to participate in future editions of the books and/or our larger electronic database, write or give us a call.

ALL MUSIC GUIDE
  407 N. State Street
  Big Rapids, MI 49307

  616-796-3437
  FAX 616-796-3060

  A division of Alliance Entertainment Corp.

ABOUT THE EDITORS

Michael Erlewine

All Music Guide editor Michael Erlewine helped form the Prime Movers Blues Band in Ann Arbor, Michigan in 1965. He was the lead singer and played amplified harmonica in this pace-setting band (the first of its kind). The original band included a number of now well-known musicians including Iggy Pop (drums), "Blue" Gene Tyranny (piano; now a well-known avant-garde classical composer); Jack Dawson (bass; became bass player for Siegel-Schwall Blues Band); and Michael's brother Dan Erlewine (lead guitar; now monthly columnist for *Guitar Player* magazine). Michael has extensively interviewed blues performers, both in video and audio, and, along with his band, helped to shape the first few Ann Arbor Blues festivals. Today Michael is a systems programmer and director of Matrix Software. Aside from the company's work in music and film data, Matrix is the largest center for astrological programming and research in North America. Michael has been a practicing astrologer for more than 30 years and has an international reputation in that field.

Michael is also very active in Tibetan Buddhism and serves as the director of the Heart Center Karma Thegsum Choling, one of the main centers in North America for the translation, transcription, and publication of psychological texts and teachings of the Karma Kagyu Lineage of Tibetan Buddhism. Michael has been married for 25 years, and he and his wife Margaret live in Big Rapids, Michigan. They have four children.

Vladimir Bogdanov

Russian mathematician and programmer Vladimir Bogdanov has been involved in the design and development of *All Music Guide* databases since 1991. Having experience in many different fields such as nuclear physics, psychology, social studies and ancient chronology he now applies his knowledge to the construction of unique music reference tools utilizing the latest computer technologies. His personal interest lies in applying artificial intelligence and other mathematical methods to areas with complex semantic structures, like music, film, literature. Vladimir's ultimate goal is to provide people with the means to find what they need, even if they don't know what they are looking for.

Chris Woodstra

Chris Woodstra has had a lifelong obsession with music and is an avid record collector. He has worked many years in music retail, he was a DJ, hosting programs in every genre of music, and has been a contributing editor for several local arts and entertainment magazines. Working as an editor for the *All Music Guide* database has given him the opportunity to combine his technical skills, a B.S. in Physics and Mathematics, and his love of music for the first time in his life. Being a perfectionist by nature, Chris makes sure that that any information that goes into the database has been carefully researched and verified.

Stephen Thomas Erlewine

Stephen Thomas Erlewine studied English at the University of Michigan and was the arts editor of the school's newspaper, The Michigan Daily. In addition to editing the *All Music Guide*, Erlewine is a freelance writer and musician.

Richie Unterberger

Richie Unterberger is a writer and editor who lives in San Francisco. He was the editor of the travel and music sections of *The Millenium Whole Earth Catalog* (Harper Collins, 1994). Between 1985 and 1991, he was the editor of *Option* magazine, the national publication devoted to coverage of all types of alternative and independently produced music. In his professional work, he is dedicated to enhancing the appreciation of the arts, culture, and history in as educational, entertaining, and affordable fashion as possible, in both multimedia technologies and more traditional print media. Since watching *A Hard Day's Night* at the age of four, his favorite group has been the Beatles.

ACKNOWLEDGMENTS

This book would not have been possible without the guidance of Andrew Gun McIver and Ven. Khenpo Karthar, Rinpoche. Special thanks to Richie Unterberger, Cub Koda, Bruce Eder, Carl Bierling, and Holland Compact Disc.

To our production staff. . .
Jason Ankeny, Jonathan Ball, Sherry Batchelder, Nancy Beilfuss, Sandra Brennan, John Bush, Julie Clark, Grace Concepcion, Mark Donkers, Brandy Lynn Ellison, Elizabeth Carey Erlewine, Margaret Louise Erlewine, Sarah Morgen Erlewine, Clarke Fountain, Kevin Fowler, Douglas Gabert, Yelena German, Yuriy German, Brenda Haney, Kristi Hassen, Mary Anne Henry, Will Holmes, Jeanna Hopkins, Steve Huey, Jennifer Hughes, Deborah Kirby, Katie Kuhns, Luda Lobenko, Jody Mitchell, Mary Prodger, Forest Ray, Bob Smith, Reuben Tucker

and to all the Matrix staff. . .
Kyle Alexander, Irene Baldwin, Richard Batchelder, Susan Brownlee, Stephanie Clement, Walter Crockett, Tricia Davis, Phillip Erlewine, Stephen Erlewine, Iotis Erlewine, Thomas Goyett, Jeffrey Jawer, Kurt Kemperman, Mary E. King, Michael King, Madeline Koperski, Teresa Swift-Eckert

All Music Guide to Rock

Editors

Michael Erlewine,
Executive Editor
Vladimir Bogdanov,
Database Design
Chris Woodstra,
Editor-in-Chief
Stephen Thomas Erlewine,
Senior Editor
Richie Unterberger,
Senior Editor

Contributors

Steve Aldrich
Jason Ankeny
Jonathan Ball
Ashley S. Battel
George Bedard
Vladimir Bogdanov
Myles Boisen
Ross Boissoneau
John Book
Rob Bowman
Rick A. Bueche
Scott Bultman
John Bush
Bil Carpenter
Phil Carter
Kenneth M. Cassidy
Darryl Cater
James Chrispell
Rick Clark
David Cleary
Sean Cooper
Bill Dahl
Hank Davis
Michael P. Dawson
Donna DiChario

John Dougan
Bruce Eder
Iotis Erlewine
Meredith Erlewine
Michael Erlewine
Stephen Thomas Erlewine
Colin Escott
John Floyd
Dan Forte
Michael Freedberg
James A. Gardner
Richard S. Ginell
Robert Gordon
Bob Gottlieb
Tom Graves
Brett Hartenbach
Dan Heilman
Alex Henderson
Steve Huey
Eddie Huffman
David Jehnzen
Julian Katz
Kit Kiefer
Cub Koda
Linda Kohanov
Paul Kohler
Larry Lapka
Jack Leaver
Kip Lornell
John Lowe
Decibel Dennis MacDonald
Brian Mansfield
Steven McDonald
Kembrew McLeood
Kevin McLeod
Richard Meyer
Tom Mitchell
Gary Mollica
Tomas Mureika
Michael G. Nastos

Jim O'Neal
Jas Obrecht
Christine Ohlman
Thom Owens
Richard Pack
Roch Parisien
Archie Patterson
Dan Pavlides
Jana Pendragon
Heather Phares
Matthew Plichta
J. Poet
Bob Porter
Jim Powers
Chip Renner
Michael Ribas
William Ruhlmann
Spaz Schnee
Ali Sinclair
Richard Skelly
Chris Slawecki
Leo Stanley
Peter Stepek
Denise Sullivan
David Szatmary
Jeff Tamarkin
"Blue" Gene Tyranny
Neal Umphred
Richie Unterberger
Barry Weber
Tony Wilds
Stephen Winick
Kurt Wolff
Chris Woodstra
Jim Worbois
Carol Wright
Ron Wynn
Scott Yanow

INTRODUCTION

Rock 'n' roll is entering its fifth decade of existence. In that time, stacks of worthwhile recordings have piled up, and while live rock 'n' roll is electrifying, the history of the music is, for better or worse, passed on through recordings. With that in mind, *The All Music Guide to Rock* doesn't attempt to tell the history of rock 'n' roll, it offers a guide to performers and their recordings. Like the previous books in the *All Music Guide* series, the intent of *The All Music Guide to Rock* is not to draw comparisons between the artists, but to provide a guide to the artists themselves. It helps readers find the best recordings by everyone from Pat Boone to Michael Bolton, from Elvis Presley to Madonna, judging each artist's music on its own terms.

Given our space limitations, certain artists had to be excluded, yet we included a broad range of musicians reflecting the wide range of stylistic variations rock 'n' roll has taken over the years. Stylistically, rock 'n' roll encompasses blues, R&B, country, traditional pop, folk, vaudeville, British music hall, electronica—nearly every form of music finds its way into rock 'n' roll, and every subgenre of rock 'n' roll has found its way into *The All Music Guide to Rock*. That doesn't mean every rockabilly or doo wop singer, or every heavy metal or punk band has been included. Nevertheless, you'll find scores of rockabilly, doo wop, metal, and punk records in here, along with psychedelia, garage rock, British Invasion, pub rock, lo-fi, post-punk, techno, house, Brill Building pop, Southern rock . . . the vast variety of styles that make popular music so intriguing.

What makes rock 'n' roll so interesting is the sheer amount of variety it offers. It's been a long road from Chuck Berry and Elvis Presley to the Wu-Tang Clan and Pavement, and all the side roads have something interesting to offer. It may be the songcraft of Neil Diamond or it could be the trance-inducing electronics of the Orb. It could be the driving heartland rock 'n' roll of Bob Seger and John Mellencamp or the minimalist rock of the Ramones, AC/DC and Unrest, who all take simplicity in different sonic directions. Is it all rock and roll? In the conventional sense it's not, but it is all popular music that owes its existence to rock 'n' roll. There's not an obvious link between Sonic Youth and Chuck Berry, yet there are links between Chuck Berry and the Velvet Underground, and the Velvets and Sonic Youth.

The All Music Guide to Rock tries to explain Sonic Youth to Chuck Berry fans and, just as importantly, Chuck Berry to Sonic Youth fans. In the meantime, the book explores unheralded subgenres like garage and surf rock that rarely get space in conventional rock books. It also spotlights cult figures from the Celibate Rifles to Scott Walker that may have never gotten popular recognition, yet they had a small impact in shaping popular music—or they simply made intriguing, interesting music. *The All Music Guide to Rock* may not explore every genre of rock 'n' roll in depth, yet it helps make sense of the ever-changing entity that is rock 'n' roll. If the book does anything, it should open you up to some terrific music you may not have heard before.

As the decades have passed, the music has changed and so have the recording formats. For the past decade, the compact disc has been the dominant medium, replacing the long-playing vinyl album. However, in the early years of rock 'n' roll, the single was the dominant format. Artists like Elvis Presley, Chuck Berry, Fats Domino, Buddy Holly, the Everly Brothers, and Jerry Lee Lewis didn't think in terms of making cohesive full-length albums—they were making their next hit single. Around 1966, long-playing albums became the dominant musical format in rock 'n' roll, with British Invasion bands like the Beatles and the Kinks crafting records that were tied together by both lyrical and musical themes. Soon, artists were putting more thought into making cohesive albums. Initially, this meant "concept albums"—records like The Who's *Tommy*, The Kinks' *Arthur*, or the Moody Blues' *Days of Future Passed* —that told specific stories with their songs. Concept albums gave way to a wave of progressive rock bands that wrote music that could only be told over the course of a full-length album. As the British Invasion groups explored conceptual records, American psychedelic bands like the Grateful Dead and Jefferson Airplane were making music that could not be confined to a three-minute single, so they also concentrated on full-length albums. Eventually, hard rock bands like Led Zeppelin had hit albums, not singles, which helped inaugurate the era of album-rock. Ever since the late '60s, the majority of rock bands focused their creative attentions on full-length albums and several groups had long, successful careers without the benefit of hit singles. Consequently, albums were more important to the careers of '70s rockers like David Bowie and Queen than they were to the careers of Duane Eddy or the Ventures, which explains why Bowie and Queen have more albums listed than Eddy or the Ventures. It's not a critical judgment about which band is more important, it's a reflection of their particular era.

Within the text are biographies and reviews of 2,500 artists. The goal of *The All Music Guide* is not to draw comparisons between Carpenters and Mötley Crüe albums, or pit the Beatles against the Clash. Rather, the intent of *The All Music Guide to Rock* is to provide a guide to the recordings of a particular artist, offering a biography and description of the music, as well as to capsule reviews of their albums. If the description of a musician intrigues you, the book also provides a starting point for each artist, in the form of a filled-in circle or star. Each entry in the book has a filled-in circle, with the possible exception of artists with only one album. Within each entry, to the right of the album's title, is a rating for the album itself, on a scale from one to five. These ratings are based on the artist themselves, not of their overall worth (for instance, a four-star Whitney Houston album is not necessarily the same as a four-star Nirvana album). The only global rating in the book is a star, which signals an album that is the best of its genre—in other words, it's essential listening.

Many of the artists included in *The All Music Guide to Rock* have a complete discography—on occasion, significant bootlegs and rarities have been included, as well—but some records were not reviewed because of space constraints. Similarly, some artists have selected listings, particularly acts that only had a handful of hits. On the other hand, musicians like James Brown and Elvis Presley have simply released too many albums for each album to be reviewed in our allotted space. In this case, all of their major records have been included, along with some interesting minor albums that illustrate the depth of their artistry. Also, hard-rock bands like Deep Purple and Black Sabbath, who continued to tour and record similar albums for nearly 30 years, have selected listings because their latter-day records proved the law of diminishing returns, both commercially and creatively. By listing the highlights, we are attempting to sort out the highlights in their lengthy, occasionally convoluted discography. When records haven't been reviewed, they have been rated, providing a guideline to the album's worth. By providing both an artist's biography and a reviewed discography, *The All Music Guide to Rock* provides enough information to satisfy both the curious and the collector. There's a wildly diverse selection of artists and records within the book, showcasing the unpredictable evolutions of rock 'n' roll over its 40 years of existence. No matter your taste, you'll find something of interest within the book, and if you don't, take a look at our internet site (www.allmusic.com), which provides thorough discographies and extensive biographies for an even larger variety of artists.

The All Music Guide to Rock has been culled from a much larger database that is available in several electronic formats as listed on the inside cover. The All Music Guide is constantly updated and corrected, so if you spot any mistakes or inconsistencies, please contact us.

A

ABBA

f. 1971, Stockholm, Sweden, **db.** 1983
Europop, Pop-Rock, Euro-Dance

The origins of the Swedish superstars ABBA, the most commercially successful pop group of the 1970s, date back to 1966, when keyboardist and vocalist Benny Andersson, a onetime member of the popular beat outfit the Hep Stars, first teamed with guitarist and vocalist Bjorn Ulvaeus, the leader of the folk-rock unit the Hootenanny Singers. The two performers began composing songs together and handling session and production work for Polar Music/Union Songs, a publishing company owned by Stig Anderson, himself a prolific songwriter throughout the 1950s and 1960s. At the same time, both Andersson and Ulvaeus worked on projects with their respective girlfriends; Andersson had become involved with vocalist Agnetha Faltskog, a performer with a recent No. 1 Swedish hit, "I Was So in Love," under her belt, while Ulvaeus began seeing Anni-Frid Lyngstad, a onetime jazz singer who rose to fame by winning a national talent contest.

In 1971 Andersson and Faltskog ventured into theatrical work. Faltskog accepted the role of Mary Magdalene in a production of Andrew Lloyd Webber's *Jesus Christ Superstar,* and her cover of the musical's "Don't Know How to Love Him" became a significant hit. The next year, the duo of Andersson and Ulvaeus scored a massive international hit with "People Need Love," which featured Faltskog and Lyngstad on backing vocals. The record's success earned them an invitation to enter the Swedish leg of the 1973 Eurovision song contest, where, under the unwieldy name of Bjorn, Benny, Agnetha & Frida, they submitted "Ring Ring," which proved extremely popular with audiences but placed only third in the judges' ballots.

The next year, rechristened ABBA (a suggestion from Stig Anderson and an acronym of the members' first names), the quartet submitted the single "Waterloo," and became the first Swedish act to win the Eurovision competition. The record proved to be the first of many international hits, although the group hit a slump after their initial success, as subsequent singles failed to chart. In 1975, however, ABBA issued "S.O.S.," a smash not only in America and Britain but in non-English speaking countries such as Spain, Germany, and the Benelux nations, where the group's success was unprecedented. A string of hits followed, including "Mamma Mia," "Fernando," and "Dancing Queen" (ABBA's sole US chart-topper), further honing their lush, buoyant sound. By the spring of 1976, they were in position to issue their first *Greatest Hits* collection.

ABBA's popularity continued in 1977, when both "Knowing Me, Knowing You" and "The Name of the Game" dominated airwaves. The group also starred in the feaure film *ABBA—The Movie,* which was released in 1978. That year Ulvaeus and Faltskog married, as had Andersson and Lyngstad in 1973, although the latter couple separated a few months later; in fact, romantic suffering was the subject of many songs on the quartet's next LP, 1979's *Voulez-Vous.* Shortly after the release of 1980's *Super Trouper,* Ulvaeus and Faltskog divorced as well, further straining the group dynamic. *The Visitors,* issued the following year, was the final LP of new ABBA material, and the foursome officially disbanded in late 1982.

Although all of the group's members soon embarked on new projects—both Lyngstad and Faltskog issued solo LPs, while Andersson and Ulvaeus collaborated with Tim Rice on the musical *Chess*—none proved as successful as the group's earlier work, largely because throughout much of the world, especially Europe and Australia, the ABBA phenomenon never went away. Repackaged hits compilations and live collections continued hitting the charts long after the group's demise, and new artists regularly pointed to the quartet's inspiration. While the British dance duo Erasure released a covers collection, *ABBA-esque,* an Australian group called Bjorn Again found success as ABBA

impersonators. In 1993, "Dancing Queen" became a staple of U2's "Zoo TV" tour—Andersson and Ulvaeus even joined the Irish superstars onstage in Stockholm—while the 1995 feature *Muriel's Wedding,* which won acclaim for its depiction of a lonely Australian girl who seeks refuge in ABBA's music, helped bring the group's work to the attention of a new generation of moviegoers and music fans. —*Jason Ankeny*

Ring Ring / 1973 / Polar ✦✦
This, the first album by the group later called ABBA (they were called Bjorn, Benny, Agnetha & Annifrid at the time), originally was released only in Sweden; England and America didn't show any interest until the group won the Eurovision Song Contest with "Waterloo" the following year, although "Ring Ring" had been a hit in several other countries. It's clear that this team has spent a lot of time listening to albums like *Abbey Road* and *Honky Chateau,* not to mention *Sweet Baby James.* But they've also been absorbing a range of the pop charts of the late '60s and early '70s. At the same time, they haven't put together the ABBA sound yet. For one thing, the men sing almost as much as the women, and for another, Benny Andersson and Bjorn Ulvaeus have underproduced the recordings, even as they have overarranged the music. (Eventually released in Europe, *Ring Ring* has not been released officially in the US, although import copies are available.) —*William Ruhlmann*

Waterloo / 1974 / Atlantic ✦✦
ABBA's second (and US debut) album contains the title track, an American Top Ten hit and UK chart-topper, as well as "Honey, Honey," a minor US hit, and "Ring Ring," a minor British hit co-written by the ABBA team of Benny Andersson, Stig Anderson, and Bjorn Ulvaeus with Neil Sedaka and Phil Cody. It is, however, an uneven collection, ranging from reggae to near-hard rock, demonstrating that ABBA had not yet got its pop assembly line fully into operation. —*William Ruhlmann*

ABBA / 1975 / Atlantic ✦✦✦
ABBA appears on the cover of this album sitting in the back of a limousine and drinking champagne, which may have been intended as an ironic comment on their one-hit wonder status at the time but became an apt reflection of their status after this record's success. The lead-off track is the irresistible "Mamma Mia," their second UK chart topper and a US Top 40 hit. Also included are the equally catchy "SOS" (Top Ten in Britain, Top 40 in America) and the minor UK hit "I Do, I Do, I Do, I Do, I Do," which actually did better in the US. —*William Ruhlmann*

Arrival / Jan. 1977 / Atlantic ✦✦✦✦
ABBA's titled fourth album of new material appeared after the group had "arrived" as major stars. It featured "Dancing Queen," a tame disco number that went to No. 1 in both the US and UK, as well as "Knowing Me, Knowing You" (another UK No. 1 that hit the Top 40 in the US) and a third single, "Money, Money, Money." —*William Ruhlmann*

The Album / Feb. 1978 / Atlantic ✦✦✦✦
ABBA's fifth new studio album continued its phenomenal international success, featuring the UK No. 1s "The Name of the Game" and "Take a Chance on Me," and achieving ABBA's highest—ever showing in the US LP charts; it reached the Top 20 and sold a million copies in six months. It was also musically ambitious, featuring "The Girl with the Golden Hair," described as "3 scenes from a mini-musical," which anticipated the theatrical ambitions Andersson and Ulvaeus would fulfill with *Chess* six years later. —*William Ruhlmann*

Voulez-Vous / Jun. 1979 / Polygram ✦✦
Internationally, it was business as usual for ABBA on its sixth studio album, which included the hits "Voulez-Vous," "I Have a Dream," "Angeleyes," "Does Your Mother Know," and "Chiquitita," all of which made the UK Top Five. But America had begun to lose interest; the album stopped at gold (500,000 copies), with only "Chiquitita" getting into the Top 40. —*William Ruhlmann*

Super Trouper / Dec. 1980 / Atlantic ✦✦

Always pop-savvy, ABBA took account of the passing of disco with this release and moved back toward the pop-rock sound more typical of their early albums with this, their seventh. They were rewarded with their last big US hit, "The Winner Takes It All," plus two more American chart entries and an uptick in album sales. In the UK, they continued to roll along, with the title track becoming their final No. 1 single. — *William Ruhlmann*

The Visitors / 1981 / Atlantic ✦✦✦

ABBA's swan song was also perhaps their most musically sophisticated album. Although it was short on big hits ("The Visitors" and "When All Is Said and Done" charted in the US, "One of Us" and "Head Over Heels" in the UK, with only "One of Us" making the Top Ten), it was a consistent record imbued with a sense of the pressures that were splitting the group (the title track was subtitled "Crackin' Up"). — *William Ruhlmann*

The Singles: The First Ten Years / 1982 / Atlantic ✦✦✦✦

This 23-track double LP contains 16 of ABBA's 20 US chart entries and 22 of their 25 UK hits. Especially notable are the group's final new single, "Under Attack," and the terrific ballad "The Day Before You Came," which had previously appeared in the US only as a non-LP B-side. This collection supersedes the previous *Greatest Hits* albums, and, since ABBA was a singles band, captures their essence. — *William Ruhlmann*

ABBA Live / 1986 / Atlantic ✦✦

ABBA turns in close copies of their studio hits in these live performances recorded between 1977 and 1981. For completists only. — *William Ruhlmann*

More ABBA Gold / Jun. 1, 1993 / Polydor ✦✦✦✦

All of the singles and important album tracks that aren't featured on *Gold* are available on *More ABBA Gold*. — *Stephen Thomas Erlewine*

★ **Gold: Greatest Hits** / Aug. 9, 1993 / Polydor ✦✦✦✦✦

A 19-track, 77-minute CD collection released in Europe in 1992 and in the US the following year to cash in on the resurgence of interest in ABBA, this is an excellent single-disc hits package, and, given that the group's catalog was sold to PolyGram in 1989, the only one that's available in the US, where the earlier *Greatest Hits; Greatest Hits, Vol. 2;* and *The Singles: The First Ten Years* (all originally released on LP by Atlantic) are out of print. — *William Ruhlmann*

Thank You for the Music [box] / Apr. 18, 1995 / Polydor ✦✦✦✦

Released in Europe in October 1994 and in the US six months later, *Thank You for the Music* is the ABBA box-set retrospective, tracing their 10 years of record making, 1972-1982, including 52 previously released tracks on the first three discs, plus a fourth disc of rarities. Listening to all the singles, plus scattered album tracks and B-sides, provides a clear picture of the group's development. Early on, there is considerable stylistic experimentation, as these pop dabblers ape everything from Phil Spector's "Wall of Sound" rock to big-band swing. But after "Dancing Queen," they find their niche in disco, and the second disc is loaded with hit songs anchored to the familiar bass-heavy walking beat and swooping synths-meant-to-sound-like-strings that defined that most '70s of genres. On the third disc, covering their last years, ABBA returns to the more propulsive pop-rock of early classics like "SOS" and "Mamma Mia," revving up the tempo in acknowledgment of the arrival of new wave. Wracked by romantic discord, they also achieve somewhat more meaningful lyrics before calling it a day. In the album's liner notes, the band members register mild protest at the inclusion of unreleased material on the fourth disc—what they finished and liked, they released, they note. Fair warning. Most prominent in a collection of alternate takes, miscellaneous B-sides, foreign-language recordings, and TV soundtracks is the 23-and-a-half-minute "ABBA Undeleted," a medley of 15 song fragments and Swedish studio chatter that suggests ABBA had a few more hits in them if they had found the time to finish them off. Nevertheless, this remains fan-only material. (This album is not to be confused with the 1983 compilation of the same title released by Epic Records in the UK.) — *William Ruhlmann*

ABC

f. 1980, Sheffield, England

Dance-Pop, New Wave, Pop-Rock, New Romantic, Synth-Pop

One of the more popular new wave bands of the early '80s, the British group ABC built upon the detached, synthesized R&B pop of David Bowie and Roxy Music, adding a self-conscious, campy sense of theatrics and style. Under the direction of vocalist Martin Fry, the group scored several catchy, synth-driven dance-pop hits in the early '80s, including "Poison Arrow," "Look of Love," and "Be Near Me."

During the late '70s, Fry ran his own fanzine, *Modern Drugs*, while he attended Sheffield University. ABC formed in 1980, after Fry interviewed the Vice Versa members Mark White (guitar) and Stephen Singleton (saxophone) for his fanzine. The two musicians asked Fry to join their band as a vocalist, and he soon became part of the group; the lineup also featured drummer David Robinson and bassist Mark Lick-

ley. Soon Fry had taken control of the electronic band, steering them in a more pop-oriented direction and renaming the group ABC. By the fall of 1981, the band had signed a record contract with Phonogram Records, which agreed to distribute ABC's own label, Neutron. ABC released their first single, "Tears Are Not Enough," in November; it peaked at No. 19 on the UK charts. Before they recorded their second single, Robinson left the band and was replaced by David Palmer in early 1982. Two singles, "Poison Arrow" and "The Look of Love," became British Top Ten hits in the spring, paving the way for their debut album, *The Lexicon of Love*, to enter the charts at No. 1. "All of My Heart" also became a Top Ten hit in the fall of 1982.

Toward the end of 1982, the group began concentrating on the United States. Their American success was helped by the fledgling MTV network, which aired videos for "The Look of Love" and "Poison Arrow" frequently, making both singles Top 25 hits in the spring of 1983. Palmer left the band in the summer of 1983, as ABC was recording their second album. Featuring a harder, rock sound driven by guitars, not keyboards, *Beauty Stab* was released late in 1983. Supported by the No. 18 single "That Was Then but This Is Now," the album didn't perform as well as the debut, peaking at No. 12; the record also was a commercial disappointment in the US. Late in 1984, ABC—now consisting solely of Fry and White, augmented by various session musicians—released "(How to Be A) Millionaire," which failed to put a halt to their commercial slide.

After its release, the duo moved to New York, where they added David Yarritu and Eden to the group; neither member could play or sing—they were added for the visual effect.

Released at the beginning of 1985, the light, catchy "Be Near Me" became a hit single in Britain, climbing to No. 26. Due to the single's success, *How to Be a . . . Zillionaire!* became a Top 30 hit in both the UK and US. "Be Near Me" was released as a US single toward the end of 1985, and it became the group's first American Top Ten hit. Even though they had a fair amount of success in 1985, ABC's subsequent singles stalled on the charts. Fry was also ill for most of the latter half of the year; he recovered in 1987 and began writing and recording with White. In the summer of 1987, ABC released "When Smokey Sings," which was a major hit, reaching No. 5 in the US and No. 11 in the UK *Alphabet City* followed that fall, peaking at No. 7 in the UK and No. 48 in the US. Two years later they released *Up*, which charted only in the UK. *Absolutely*, a greatest-hits collection, made it into the British Top Ten in 1990.

After the release of *Up*, Martin Fry took an extended break from the music industry, returning in 1997 with a revamped ABC and a new album, *Skyscraping*, which was released only in the UK. Shortly before ABC's comeback, England experienced a short-lived New Romantic revival called Romo, which increased Fry's exposure substantially, and which, in turn, helped *Skyscraping* earn good reviews and respectable sales. — *Stephen Thomas Erlewine*

● **The Lexicon of Love** / 1982 / Mercury ✦✦✦✦

ABC's stylish debut successfully melded the cool detachment of Bryan Ferry and David Bowie with a more pop-oriented production than either Roxy Music or Bowie. Even if the songs tended to blend over the course of the album, the record was successful, scoring two hits with "The Look of Love" and "Poison Arrow." — *Stephen Thomas Erlewine*

Beauty Stab / 1983 / Mercury ✦✦✦

For their second album, ABC toned down the synths and turned up the guitars, making an inconsistent set of rocking, Roxy-styled pop that does have its impressive moments, particularly the single "That Was Then but This Is Now." — *Stephen Thomas Erlewine*

How to Be a . . . Zillionaire! / 1985 / Mercury ✦✦✦✦

Moving away from the guitar histrionics of *Beauty Stab*, Martin Fry reduced ABC to a duo of himself and Mark White for 1985's danceable *How to Be a . . . Zillionaire!* Incorporating light hip-hop rhythms, ABC made sure *Zillionaire* sounded contemporary for mid-'80s dance clubs, and as a result, some of the record sounds stiff and dated. Stil, when Fry's sense of melody is on, as on the catchy single "Be Near Me," or when he trades in his vicious, cynical wit, as on "How to Be a Millionaire" and "So Hip It Hurts," the record rivals the peaks of *Lexicon of Love*. — *Stephen Thomas Erlewine*

Alphabet City / 1987 / Mercury ✦✦✦

Returning to the Motown and Northern Soul that provided the basis of their debut album, ABC turned to the pop songcraft on their fourth album, *Alphabet City*. The increased songcraft is certainly engaging, particularly on the hit "When Smokey Sings," but the songs are usually indistinguishable from each other, resulting in a sleek, stylish and thoroughly entertaining album that leaves no lasting memory. — *Stephen Thomas Erlewine*

Up / Oct. 30, 1989 / Mercury ✦✦

ABC's formula started to sound tired on their fifth album, which completed their contract with PolyGram, and unlike their first four, missed the charts in the US, while managing only one week in the UK. The singles "One Better World" and "The Real Thing" were, only minor hits in England and nonentities in America. — *William Ruhlmann*

Absolutely ABC: The Best of ABC / Aug. 1990 / Mercury ✦✦✦✦
Absolutely ABC: The Best of ABC is a terrific 13-track collection of the
synth-pop band's greatest hits, featuring all of the group's necessary singles. Without concentrating too heavily on any particular album, each of
the group's first five albums is represented by its highlights, so *Absolutely ABC* functions as a fine overview, containing every song a casual
fan could want ("Poison Arrow," "The Look of Love," "Tears Are Not
Enough," "That Was Then But This Is Now," "How to Be a Millionaire,"
"Be Near Me," "When Smokey Sings"), even if *The Lexicon of Love*
remains a better encapsulation of what the band was all about. [The CD
version of *Absolutely* contains four unnecessary remixes of four of the
group's biggest hits.] —*Stephen Thomas Erlewine*

Abracadabra / Oct. 1991 / MCA ✦✦
Abracadabra is a disheartening latter-day album from ABC, who are
attempting to stay modern by incorporating both house and smooth,
Philly soul flourishes to their sound. Occasionally the results sound supple and alluring, but the record is undone by a complete lack of strong,
melodic songs, as well as what sounds like Martin Fry's indifference to
the material. —*Stephen Thomas Erlewine*

Skyscraping / Mar. 1997 / Deconstruction ✦✦✦
After spending half the better part of a decade in semi-retirement, Martin Fry regrouped ABC for the surprisingly successful comeback *Skyscraping*. Instead of pursuing the dance-pop inclinations of ABC's late-
'80s records, Fry returns to the grandly theatrical new romantic pop of
Lexicon of Love, cutting it with some contemporary dance production
techniques. Collaborating with Heaven 17's Glenn Gregory, Fry constructs a number of shiny pop gems, highlighted by glammy guitars and
shining synthesizers. While *Skyscraping* isn't as consistently thrilling as
his best '80s singles, it has a number of fine moments and is ABC's best
record since *How to Be a Zillionaire*. —*Stephen Thomas Erlewine*

Paula Abdul

b. Jun. 19, 1962, Los Angeles, CA
*Vocals / Dance-Pop, Urban, Adult Contemporary, Pop-Rock, Club/
Dance*
In the wake of Madonna's success, many dance-pop divas filled the
charts, but out of them all, Paula Abdul was the only one who sustained
a career. The former Los Angeles Lakers cheerleader and choreographer
began to make inroads in pop music when she was hired as an assistant
dance director on the Jacksons' "Victory" tour, which led to a job choreographing Janet Jackson's videos for *Control*. Abdul's work on Jackson's
videos helped make the album a hit, making her a sought-after choreographer. After working on "The Tracy Ullman Show" and videos for ZZ
Top, Duran Duran, and the Pointer Sisters, Abdul began a recording
career, releasing her debut album, *Forever Your Girl*, in 1988. The first
two singles drawn from the record were moderate hits, but the release of
"Straight Up" at the end of the year made her a superstar. Staying at the
top of the charts for three weeks, "Straight Up" began a string of six No.
1 singles (with "The Way That You Love Me" recharting at No. 3 in 1989)
that ran through the summer of 1991.
    Abdul's singles were hits not because her singing was exceptional—
her voice is thin and transparent—but because she worked with savvy
producers who had a knack for picking songs with solid pop and dance
hooks. Abdul's spectacular big-budget videos helped push the sales of
Forever Your Girl past seven million in the US alone. While her second
album, 1991's *Spellbound*, wasn't as successful, it still sold over three
million copies and spent two weeks at No. 1. After *Spellbound*, Abdul
took a few years off. During that time, she successfully fought a lawsuit
filed by a former backup singer who alleged it was she, not Abdul, who
had sung on *Forever Your Girl*. Abdul released her third album, *Head
Over Heels*, in the summer of 1995. —*Stephen Thomas Erlewine*

● **Forever Your Girl** / Jun. 1988 / Virgin ✦✦✦✦
Choreographer-turned-diva Abdul debuts with this upbeat collection of
dance-pop that yielded a string of Top 40 hits, including four No. 1
smashes—"Straight Up," "Cold Hearted," "Opposites Attract," and "Forever Your Girl." —*Donna DiChario*

Spellbound / May 1991 / Captive/Virgin ✦✦✦
This fine sophomore set includes sweet pop-soul balladry ("Rush, Rush")
and dance tunes ("The Promise of a New Day"). —*Bil Carpenter*

Head over Heels / Jun. 13, 1995 / Captive/Virgin ✦✦
Four years after the release of *Spellbound*, Paula Abdul returned with
the sleek *Head Over Heels*. *Head Over Heels* doesn't sound all that different from her previous album; it incorporates a couple of current
dance trends without ever letting the beats dominate the accessible pop
melodies. Unfortunately, the songs are more well constructed than well
written—all of the arrangements hide the fact that the songs usually
lack strong hooks. That weakness is accentuated by the length of the
album. Approaching nearly 70 minutes, *Head Over Heels* spends too
much time with lesser songs. Abdul remains an engaging presence,
even with her limited vocal talents, and the record's best songs—the

slinky "My Love Is for Real," for instance—are more mature and seductive than her earlier works, showing that she has the possibility to grow
old gracefully. —*Stephen Thomas Erlewine*

AC/DC

f. 1973, Sydney, Australia
Hard Rock, Heavy Metal
AC/DC's mammoth power-chord roar became one of the most influential hard rock sounds of the '70s. In its own way, it was a reaction against
the pompous art rock and lumbering stadium rock of the early '70s. AC/
DC's rock was minimalist—no matter how huge and bludgeoning the
guitar chords were, there was a clear sense of space and restraint. Combined with Bon Scott's larynx-shredding vocals, the band spawned
countless imitators over the next two decades.
    AC/DC was formed in 1973 in Australia by guitarist Malcolm Young
after his band the Velvet Underground collapsed (Young's band has no
relation to the seminal American group). With his younger brother
Angus as lead guitarist, the band played some gigs around Sydney.
Angus was only 15 years old at the time, and his sister suggested that he
should wear his school uniform on stage; the look became the band's
visual trademark. While still in Sydney, the original lineup (featuring
singer Dave Evans) cut a single called "Can I Sit Next to You," with ex-
Easybeats Harry Vanda and George Young (Malcolm and Angus' older
brother) producing. The band moved to Melbourne the following year,
where drummer Phil Rudd and bassist Mark Evans joined the band. The
band's chauffeur, Bon Scott, became their lead vocalist when singer,
Dave Evans refused to go on stage.
    Previously Scott had been a drummer for the Australian pop bands
Fraternity and the Valentines. More importantly, he helped cement the
group's image as brutes; he had several convictions on minor criminal
offenses and was rejected by the Australian Army for being "socially
maladjusted." And AC/DC *was* socially maladjusted. Throughout their
career they favored crude double entendres and violent imagery, all
spiked with a mischievous sense of fun.
    The group released two albums—*High Voltage* and *TNT*—in Austra-
lia in 1974 and 1975. Material from the two records comprised the 1976
release *High Voltage* in the US and UK; the group also toured both
countries. *Dirty Deeds Done Dirt Cheap* followed at the end of the year.
Evans left the band at the beginning of 1977, with Cliff Williams taking
his place. In the fall of 1977 AC/DC released *Let There Be Rock*, which
became their first album to chart in the US. *Powerage*, released in
spring of 1978, expanded their audience even further, thanks in no small
part to their dynamic live shows (which were captured on 1978's live *If
You Want Blood, You've Got It*). What really broke the doors down for
the band was the following year's *Highway to Hell*, which hit No. 17 in
the US and No. 8 in the UK, becoming the group's first million-seller.
    AC/DC's train was derailed when Bon Scott died on February 20,
1980. The official coroner's report stated he had "drunk himself to
death." In March the band replaced Scott with Brian Johnson. The following month, the band recorded *Back in Black*, which would prove to
be their biggest album, selling over ten million copies in the US alone.
For the next few years, the band was one of the largest rock bands in the
world, with *For Those About to Rock We Salute You* topping the charts
in the US. In 1982 Rudd left the band; he was replaced by Simon Wright.
    After 1983's *Flick of the Switch*, the band's commercial standing
began to slip; they were able to reverse their slide with 1990's *The
Razor's Edge*, which spawned the hit "Thunderstruck." While they
haven't proved to be the commercial powerhouse they were during the
late '70s and early '80s, the '90s have seen them maintain their status as
a top international concert draw. In the fall of 1995, their sixteenth
album, *Ballbreaker*, was released. Produced by Rick Rubin, the album
received some of the most positive reviews of AC/DC's career. *Ballbreaker* entered the American charts at No. 4 and sold over a million
copies in its first six months of release. —*Stephen Thomas Erlewine*

High Voltage / Oct. 1976 / Atco ✦✦✦✦
AC/DC kicked things off properly by blowing away the girders with
their concussion bomb skronk. Raw, raunchy, and fun-o-plenty, its songs
include "The Jack," guaranteed to offend every woman in listening
radius. —*Tom Graves*

Let There Be Rock / Jun. 1977 / Atco ✦✦✦✦
A great follow-up, it proved these Aussies would be a nasty itch for a
long time. There's great meltdown boogie on songs like "Let There Be
Rock," "Problem Child," and "Whole Lotta Rosie." —*Tom Graves*

Powerage / May 1978 / Atco ✦✦✦
While the band still rocks with vicious authority, the quality of their
songwriting on *Powerage* is slightly weaker than on its predecessor, *Let
There Be Rock*. All of the musicians turn in strong performances—Angus and Malcolm Young sound wild, and Bon Scott is positively unhinged—but there aren't enough great riffs to make *Powerage*
one of the band's classics. —*Stephen Thomas Erlewine*

If You Want Blood You've Got It / Dec. 1978 / Atco ✦✦✦
Although the sound engineering is lacking, rock 'n' roll still ain't much more in your face than this. Fans had known what a great live band AC/DC was, and this was the album that proved it to everyone else. It collects the best tracks from the early years and spits them back louder than bejeezus. — *Tom Graves*

☆ **Highway to Hell** / Aug. 1979 / Atco ✦✦✦✦✦
This is a classic of hard rock-heavy metal—noise-grunge-skronk-pillage-and-burn. Earlier AC/DC albums had great riffs and killer chords, but *Highway to Hell* proved the boys could write, too. Not a clinker on this thudfest, and songs like "Highway to Hell" and "Girls Got Rhythm" have, appropriately, become rock staples. — *Tom Graves*

★ **Back in Black** / Aug. 1980 / Atco ✦✦✦✦✦
After Bon Scott's death, AC/DC came back with reinforcements and released another truly great hard-rock album. Brian Johnson ups the ante with his own tough-as-tacks vocals. Robert "Mutt" Lange's production on *Back in Black* remains one of the most powerful in all of hard rock. All in all, this is great diamond-hard, full-throttle rock 'n' roll. — *Tom Graves*

Dirty Deeds Done Dirt Cheap / Apr. 1981 / Atco ✦✦✦✦
An odds 'n' sods collection of earlier Bon Scott-era tracks, it's worth it for the unforgettable title track alone. — *Tom Graves*

For Those About to Rock We Salute You / Nov. 1981 / Atco ✦✦✦
For Those About to Rock We Salute You is another masterwork from the Brian Johnson period. The title song has become the group's signature track and is featured in AC/DC concerts with pyrotechnics galore. It's a must for those who don't mind staring into the face of deafness. — *Tom Graves*

Flick of the Switch / Aug. 1983 / Atco ✦✦

74 Jailbreak / 1984 / Atco ✦✦✦
Actually an EP of Bon Scott-period material, it's nonetheless some of AC/DC's best and most blistering blues. In particular the title song and an incendiary "Baby, Please Don't Go" are worth the admission. — *Tom Graves*

Fly on the Wall / Jul. 1985 / Atco ✦✦

Who Made Who / May 1986 / Atco ✦✦✦
On paper, *Who Made Who* is just a cheap soundtrack to a cheap movie (Stephen King's disastrous *Maximum Overdrive*), but it's actually much more than that. It serves as a ripping AC/DC retrospective, tearing through such classics as "You Shook Me All Night Long" and "For Those About to Rock," adding the pounding title track to their canon, and rescuing overlooked songs like "Sink the Pink" from otherwise mediocre albums. It's not a perfect retrospective—there's no "Back in Black," "Highway to Hell," or "Dirty Deeds Done Dirt Cheap"—but what is here is terrific. — *Stephen Thomas Erlewine*

Blow up Your Video / Feb. 1988 / Atco ✦✦✦
Blow Up Your Video shows signs of the band's breaking out of their mid-'80s slump. Angus Young's guitar lurches and growls throughout the album, coming to a blistering head on "This Means War" and "Heatseeker." Any record with moments this smashingly visceral deserves at least one listen. — *Stephen Thomas Erlewine*

The Razor's Edge / Sep. 1990 / Atco ✦✦✦
Although AC/DC's popularity had decreased by the early '90s, the band still had a lot of life left in it. Arguably the Australian headbangers' strongest album in more than half a decade, *Razor's Edge* is quintessential AC/DC—rowdy, abrasive, unapologetically fun metal full of blistering power chords, memorable hooks, and testosterone-driven lyrics. Lead singer Brian Johnson sounds more inspired than he had since 1983's *Flick of the Switch*, and lead guitarist Angus Young isn't about to take any prisoners on such hard-hitting material as "Shot of Love," the menacing title song, and the appropriately titled "Got You by the Balls." Although not quite in a class with *Back in Black*, *Highway to Hell*, or *Let There Be Rock*—all of which would, for novices, serve as fine introductions to the distinctive band—*Razor's Edge* was a welcome addition to AC/DC's catalog. — *Alex Henderson*

AC/DC Live / Oct. 27, 1992 / Atco ✦✦
Most of AC/DC's casual fans will be happy with the shorter, single-disc version, which includes all of the hits and eliminates all of the ten-minute-plus excesses that are proudly featured on the double-disc set. Hardcore fans will need the double-disc set. — *Stephen Thomas Erlewine*

Ballbreaker / Sep. 26, 1995 / East West ✦✦✦
In more than 20 years, AC/DC have never changed their minimalist, bone-crunching hard rock. During their first ten years, that wasn't a problem, since they were still finding ways to expand and subvert the pattern, but ever since *For Those About to Rock*, they've had trouble coming up with consistent material. Consequently, their performances tended to be a little lazy, and their records didn't deliver a reliable knockout punch. Released in 1990, *The Razor's Edge* showed some signs

of life, and their comeback culminated in the Rick Rubin-produced *Ballbreaker*. What makes *Ballbreaker* different from the albums AC/DC churned out during the '80s is simple—it's a matter of focus. Although "Hard as a Rock" comes close, there aren't any songs as immediately memorable as any of their '70s classics, or even "Money Talks." However, unlike any record since *Back in Black*, there are no bad songs on the album. Surprisingly, Rubin's production is a bit too dry, lacking the muscle needed to make the riffs sound truly earthshaking. Nevertheless, Angus Young's riffs are powerful and catchy, showcasing every element that makes him one of hard rock and heavy metal's greatest guitarists. Throughout the album, the band sounds committed and professional, making *Ballbreaker* the best late-period AC/DC album to date. — *Stephen Thomas Erlewine*

Ace

f. Dec. 1972, Sheffield, England, **db.** Jul. 1977
Pop-Rock, Pub Rock
Ace was one of the few pub-rock groups to enjoy success on the pop charts, largely due to the warm, soulful vocals of Paul Carrack. While Carrack's voice certainly had crossover appeal—as he would later prove with his own records, as well as his work with Squeeze and Roxy Music—the band was also less devoted to the three-chord boogie and country-rock that marked most pub-rock bands, favoring soulful R&B. And while they did have hits, their time in the spotlight was brief, and they fell apart shortly after Carrack left for a solo career.

Phil Harris (guitar) and Alan "Bam" King (guitar, vocals) formed Ace in 1972, recruiting Paul Carrack (keyboards, vocals), Terry "Tex" Comer (bass) and Steve Witherington (drums) over the course of the next year. Before the group began recording, they went through several drummers; Witherington was replaced by Chico Greenwood, who was later replaced by Fran Byrne in 1974. After developing a small but dedicated following on the pub-rock circuit, Ace signed with Anchor Records and recorded *Five-a-Side*. "How Long"—a song about Comer's leaving the band briefly to play with the Sutherland Brothers and Quiver, and his subsequent return—was released as the first single. Most listeners interpreted the song as an ode to a crumbling love affair, and it became a fluke hit in both the UK and the US. Ace released *Time for Another* in 1975, but it was generally ignored, especially since the popularity of pub-rock was declining rapidly.

Harris left the band in early 1976 and was replaced by Jon Woodhead. Later that year Ace opened unsuccessfully for Yes, and moved to Los Angeles, hoping that the US would prove more receptive to their music. It wasn't. Ace released a final album, *No Strings*, in 1977 and disbanded. Comer, Carrack, and Byrne joined Frankie Miller, but by 1979 Carrack left to sing with Roxy Music. After his time with Roxy, he launched a solo career, which he balanced with playing with artists like Squeeze, Nick Lowe and Mike & the Mechanics. — *Stephen Thomas Erlewine*

Five-A-Side / 1974 / Anchor ✦✦✦✦
Five-A-Side, Ace's debut album, is notable for introducing the world to the soulful singing talent of Paul Carrack, especially on the hit "How Long," which went to No. 1 on some charts in 1975. The band has a low-key style, frequently dominated by Carrack's piano and organ work, that is sometimes suggestive of Traffic and of the Tulsa country-rock sound of J.J. Cale, Delaney & Bonnie, and Leon Russell, although they never work up quite as much of a sweat as the last two. Already road-weary when they made this album, Ace, especially in Carrack's lyrics, comments extensively on the travails of being in a struggling rock 'n' roll band. Even "How Long," which sounds like the lament of a lover betrayed, is really about somebody's quitting the group. All of which makes the irony of the song's being their sole hit all the more acute. — *William Ruhlmann*

Time for Another / Dec. 1975 / Anchor ✦✦✦
Although Ace emphasized its Englishness and pub-rock origins by posing on the album cover in a pub, complete with dartboard and pints of beer in hand, their second album continued to bear the musical influence of America, specifically the Southwestern America of Tulsa's soulful Shelter Records label and people like Leon Russell and J.J. Cale. Theirs was a low-key, percolating approach that would be taken to mass success a few years down the line by Dire Straits. But *Time For Another* lacked the chief ingredient that had made its predecessor, *Five-A-Side*, successful: a hit on the order of "How Long." Keyboard player and vocalist Paul Carrack made a couple of valiant attempts, notably on the side-openers "I Think It's Gonna Last" and "No Future in Your Eyes." But Ace was a group of equals in creative participation, if not in talent, and much of the album was given over to the undistinguished contributions of other band members. With this album, the band was on its way to being a one-hit wonder. — *William Ruhlmann*

No Strings / Jan. 1977 / Anchor ✦✦
● **Best of Ace** / 1988 / See For Miles ✦✦✦✦
Best of Ace is a smartly assembled, 14-track collection that draws from each of the band's albums. Ace is best remembered for the ultra-slick

"How Long," but little of the collection bears resemblance to that hit. Instead, they're shown doing what they did best (and more often)—playing laidback, rootsy pub-rock. —*Chris Woodstra*

Ace of Base

f. 1990, Gothenburg, Sweden
Dance-Pop, Adult Contemporary, Euro-Dance, Club/Dance
Comprised of vocalists Jenny Berggren and Linn Berggren and keyboardists Jonas "Joker" Berggren and Ulf "Buddah" Ekberg, the Swedish quartet Ace of Base became a phenomenally popular international act with their 1993 debut album, *The Sign*. Ace of Base's simple, melodic Euro-disco was equally popular on radio and in the clubs, earning the quartet three US Top Ten singles—"All That She Wants," "Don't Turn Around," and "The Sign," which spent six weeks at No. 1.

Before the quartet formed in 1990, sisters Jenny and Malin Berggren sang in local church choirs in Gothenburg, Sweden. Their brother, Jonas, played synthesizers and wrote songs with Ulf Ekberg. Eventually Jonas and Ulf recruited Jenny and Linn to sing with them, and the quartet began playing dance music at local clubs in the late summer of 1990. Within a year, the group signed with Mega Records and released their debut single, "Wheel of Fortune," in 1992. By that time, the quartet had joined forces with John Ballard, who produced their recordings and wrote the majority of their songs; occasionally, Ballard co-wrote with Jonas Berggren. "Wheel of Fortune" became a hit across Scandinavia, and soon the German-based record label Metronome signed a European distribution deal with the group. "All That She Wants" was Ace of Base's first single in Europe and, thanks to heavy exposure on MTV, the song became a No. 1 hit in ten different countries. In the spring of 1993, Ace of Base released their European debut album, *Happy Nation*.

"All That She Wants" was released in America in the fall of 1993 and quickly went platinum, beginning a string of platinum Top Ten singles in the US. Released in the fall of 1993, Ace of Base's American debut album *The Sign*—a reconfigured version of *Happy Nation* featuring four new songs—quickly sold nearly two million copies in the US. Throughout 1994, Ace of Base dominated radio in America and Europe as "All That She Wants," "Don't Turn Around," and "The Sign" received heavy airplay on a number of radio formats, including Top 40, adult contemporary, urban, and, bizarrely, modern rock. By the end of the year, *The Sign* had sold over eight million copies in the US alone. Ace of Base was nominated for three Grammys that year, including Best New Artist. Ace of Base released their second album, *The Bridge*, in the fall of 1995. Although it went platinum in its first six months of release, the record failed to duplicate the remarkable multi-platinum success of *The Sign*. —*Stephen Thomas Erlewine*

● **The Sign** / Nov. 23, 1993 / Arista ✦✦✦✦
Ace of Base's strong point is not versatility—all of their hit singles have exactly the same beat. But that doesn't matter. On their debut album, *The Sign*, they managed to create a piece of melodic Euro-disco that was a huge hit all over the world, appealing to both dance clubs and pop radio. And with singles like "All That She Wants," "The Sign," and "Don't Turn Around," it's easy to see why they were hits—the beat is relentless, and the hooks are incessantly catchy. —*Stephen Thomas Erlewine*

Bridge / Nov. 21, 1995 / Arista ✦✦✦
Ace of Base's sequel to their multi-platinum debut *The Sign* sounds like the same record on the surface. There are the bouncy Euro-pop beats, ingratiatingly catchy melodies, and shiny production. However, underneath that gloss is songwriting. Ace of Base still might not be innovators, but they don't need to be. Instead, they turn out tightly constructed pop songs that are better written than they appear—songs like the hit "Beautiful Life" would sound good in different arrangements or performed acoustically. And the songs on *The Bridge* are, overall, better than the ones on *The Sign*. Ace of Base might not be able to replicate the phenomenal success of their debut, but they have managed to deliver an album that is just as satisfying. —*Stephen Thomas Erlewine*

Johnny Ace (John Alexander)

b. Jun. 9, 1929, Memphis, TN, d. Dec. 25, 1954, Houston, TX
Piano, Vocals / R&B
The senseless death of young pianist Johnny Ace while indulging in a round of Russian roulette backstage at Houston's City Auditorium on Christmas Day of 1954 tends to overshadow his relatively brief but illustrious recording career on Duke Records. That's a pity, for Ace's gentle, plaintive vocal balladry deserves reverence on its own merit, not because of the scandalous fallout resulting from his tragic demise.

John Marshall Alexander was a member in good standing of the Beale Streeters, a loosely knit crew of Memphis youngbloods that variously included B.B. King, Bobby Bland, and Earl Forest. Signing with local DJ David Mattis' fledgling Duke logo in 1952, the rechristened Ace hit the top of the R&B charts his very first time out with the mellow ballad "My Song." From then on, Ace could do no musical wrong, racking up hit after hit for Duke in the same smooth, urbane style. "Cross My

Heart," "The Clock," "Saving My Love for You," "Please Forgive Me," and "Never Let Me Go" all dented the uppermost reaches of the charts. And then, with one fatal gunshot, all that talent was lost forever (weepy tribute records quickly emerged by Frankie Ervin, Johnny Fuller, Varetta Dillard, and the Five Wings).

Ace scored his biggest hit of all posthumously. His haunting "Pledging My Love" (cut with the Johnny Otis orchestra in support) remained atop *Billboard*'s R&B lists for ten weeks in early 1955. One further hit, "Anymore," exhausted Duke's stockpile of Ace masters, so they tried to clone the late pianist's success by recruiting Johnny's younger brother (St. Clair Alexander) to record as Buddy Ace. When that didn't work out, Duke boss Don Robey took singer Jimmy Lee Land, renamed him Buddy Ace, and recorded him all the way into the late '60s. —*Bill Dahl*

● **Johnny Ace Memorial Album** / 1955 / Duke ✦✦✦✦
It's downright bizarre that Ace's catalog hasn't enjoyed a fresh reissue in 40 years. This 12-song CD is the exact same package that Don Robey rushed out after the pianist's death, with all the velvety hits ("Pledging My Love," "My Song," "The Clock," "Never Let Me Go") and a mere two blistering rockers, "How Can You Be So Mean" and "Don't You Know." A more thorough examination of Ace's discography is definitely in order! —*Bill Dahl*

David Ackles

b. Feb. 27, 1937, Little Rock, OH
Vocals, Guitar / Singer-Songwriter
Born in Rock Island, IL, David Ackles is a critically acclaimed but commerically ignored singer-songwriter who made four albums between 1968 and 1973, the most prominent of which was 1972's *American Gothic*, which was produced by lyricist Bernie Taupin, a big Ackles fan. Despite his obscurity, Ackles has exerted an influence on subsequent singer-songwriters, as acknowledged by Elvis Costello. —*William Ruhlmann*

The Road to Cairo / 1968 / Elektra ✦✦
David Ackles / 1968 / Elektra ✦✦
Subway to the Country / 1970 / Elektra ✦✦✦
● **American Gothic** / 1972 / Elektra ✦✦✦✦
The years have been only kind to the album considered David Ackles' masterpiece when it was released. Ackles combined an early '70s singer-songwriter sensibility with a theater music background that placed him as much in the tradition of Brecht-Weill and Jacques Brel as Bob Dylan. Not only are his songs fully realized, dramatic statements, but Ackles proves himself a warm, accomplished singer. When this album got no higher than No. 167 in the charts, Ackles' fans were heartbroken. Decades later, *American Gothic* remains one of those great albums that never found its audience. It waits to be rediscovered. —*William Ruhlmann*

Five & Dime / 1973 / Columbia ✦✦✦
American Gothic, the predecessor to *Five & Dime*, was David Ackles' ambitious portrait of American life, in its broad scope and geography and diversity of style. *Five & Dime* is more a collection of miniatures, still drawn with Ackles' customary eye for detail and sung in his rich, knowing voice. Its pleasures are more subtle than those in the expansive *American Gothic*, but no less real. (And "Surf's Down," complete with harmonies by Dean Torrance of Jan & Dean, is the wickedest beach music parody since "Back in the USSR.") This is music of wit, feeling, and sophistication that should be heard by fans of American songcraft from Stephen Foster and Irving Berlin to Randy Newman. Criminally, it was also David Ackles' last album. —*William Ruhlmann*

The Action

f. 1965, London, England, db. 1967
British Invasion, Garage Rock, Mod
In the mid-'60s, the Action had a strong grass-roots following among British mods. But despite the production services of George Martin, they never managed anything close to a hit record. The Action were the most soul-oriented of the mod groups, favoring guitar-oriented covers of Motown tunes and standard R&B dance numbers of the day like "Harlem Shuffle." Martin's production put the emphasis on Reggie King's rich blue-eyed soul vocals and the group's high vocal harmonies, with occasional horns. Their later original material shows an increased sophistication in both songwriting and production. The Action were akin to a more soul-oriented Small Faces, though they didn't match the Faces' energy or songwriting. —*Richie Unterberger*

● **The Ultimate Action** / 1981 / Edsel ✦✦✦✦
The Ultimate Action is indeed the ultimate compilation of this cult band. The 17 cuts (three were added to the CD reissue) include both sides of all five of their Parlophone singles, plus a batch of unreleased songs and obscure Continental-only singles. This respectable collection has its moments, especially their riveting cover of the Marvelettes' "I'll

Keep on Holding On" (a great lost hit-single-that-never-was) and the brooding mod lament "Wasn't It You." —*Richie Unterberger*

Bryan Adams

b. Nov. 5, 1959, Kingston, Ontario, Canada
Guitar, Vocals / Rock 'n' Roll, Adult Contemporary, Pop-Rock
Bryan Adams was one of the most popular mainstream rock 'n' rollers to emerge in the '80s, producing a series of platinum albums and Top Ten hits. Adams wasn't an innovator on the level of Bruce Springsteen, or even John Cougar Mellencamp. He followed in their footsteps, smoothing out their rougher edges while retaining a down-to-earth earnestness in both his straightforward rock 'n' roll and his husky voice. At the beginning of his career, he relied more on rock than pop, but as his career progressed, he became known for his ballads. But both his rockers and his slow numbers were the result of his craftsmanship, both as a writer and a performer; Adams never let anything obscure a good hook.

Born in Canada, Adams began his career as a songwriting partner of Jim Vallence, a former member of Prism. Vallence and Adams wrote songs for several Canadian rockers, including Loverboy and Bachman-Turner Overdrive, as well as Bonnie Tyler and Kiss. Adams landed a solo record contract with A&M Records in 1981, releasing an eponymous album by the end of year; it failed to make the charts. The following year, he released *You Want It, You Got It*, which managed to reach the US charts.

Bryan Adams' commercial breakthrough came in 1983 with *Cuts Like a Knife*. "Straight from the Heart," a ballad taken from the record, reached the Top Ten before the album was released. The album also made it into the Top Ten, while the title track peaked at No. 15; a third single, "This Time," reached No. 24.

Late in 1984 Adams returned with the surging, mid-tempo "Run to You," which became his second Top Ten single; it also became his first British hit, peaking at No. 11. *Reckless*, also released in late 1984, became a blockbuster success, spending two weeks at the top of the US album charts and selling over five million copies. Besides "Run to You," *Reckless* featured five other Top 15 singles, including the No. 1 "Heaven," "Summer of '69," "Somebody," "One Night Love Affair," and "It's Only Love," a duet with Tina Turner.

Released in 1987, *Into the Fire* proved to be a considerable commercial disappointment, spending 33 weeks on the charts, selling one million copies, and spawning only one Top Ten hit, "Heat of the Night." Four years later, Adams returned with "(Everything I Do) I Do It for You," the theme song for the movie *Robin Hood: Prince of Thieves*. The song became a huge hit, spending seven weeks at No. 1 in the US; in Britain, it was at the top of the charts for an astonishing 15 weeks, the longest stay at No. 1 since Frankie Laine's "I Believe" in 1953. The success of "(Everything I Do) I Do It for You" re-established Adams as a mainstream-rock commercial powerhouse, setting the stage for the triple-platinum *Waking Up the Neighbours*, released in the fall of 1991. *Waking Up the Neighbours* launched the No. 2 hit "Can't Stop This Thing We Started," the minor hit "There Will Never Be Another Tonight," and two Top 15 singles, "Thought I'd Died and Gone to Heaven" and "Do I Have to Say the Words?"

The following year, Bryan Adams released a greatest-hits collection, *So Far, So Good*, which featured a new track, "Please Forgive Me." The ballad became another Top Ten success, as did the similar-sounding "All for Love"—a collaboration with Rod Stewart and Sting taken from *The Three Musketeers*—which reached No. 1. In the summer of 1995, Adams had his fourth No. 1 single, "Have You Ever Really Loved a Woman?," taken from the *Don Juan DeMarco* soundtrack; the single spent five weeks at No. 1.

Bryan Adams released *18 'til I Die*, his first new studio album since 1991's *Waking Up the Neighbours*, in the summer of 1996. —*Stephen Thomas Erlewine*

Bryan Adams / 1980 / A&M ♦♦

You Want It You Got It / 1981 / A&M ♦♦♦
With its crystal-clear production, courtesy of Bob Clearmountain, *You Want It, You Got It* is state-of-the art nouveau rock 'n' roll of the post-Springsteen era. The guitars rev up, the bass drum is deeper than a well, the vocals are nasal and punky. The songs don't have the craft or commitment of Adams' peers/competitors—Springsteen, Petty, Mellencamp, et al.—but you may not know it for the first few spins, just because the sound is so hot and infectious, and by then it may not matter. Actually, this is a much more enjoyable record in many respects than the rock 'n' roll assembly-line products Adams constructed once he hit the arenas. As it was, with this one, he was on his way. All he did later was take this approach and make it slicker. —*William Ruhlmann*

Cuts Like a Knife / Jan. 1983 / A&M ♦♦♦♦
A Top Ten breakthrough album in the US for this Canadian rocker, it was carried by the strength of "Straight from the Heart." —*Donna DiChario*

Reckless / 1984 / A&M ♦♦♦♦
Radio-friendly and pop-rock driven by Adams' trademark gravelly vocals that spawned three Top Ten hits, including "Heaven," "Run to You," and a duet with Tina Turner on "It's Only Love." —*Donna DiChario*

Into the Fire / Mar. 1987 / A&M ♦♦
Adams keeps the fire burning with the Top Ten "Heat of the Night." —*Donna DiChario*

Waking up the Neighbours / Sep. 1991 / A&M ♦♦♦
After the disappointing *Into the Fire*, Adams returned to the top of the charts with *Waking Up the Neighbours*, thanks to the massive success of "(Everything I Do) I Do It for You." —*Stephen Thomas Erlewine*

● **So Far So Good** / Nov. 2, 1993 / A&M ♦♦♦♦
Eliminating the filler that tends to clutter his albums, *So Far, So Good* simply gathers all of Adams' big hits (including a new one, "Please Forgive Me") in one concise package, making it the one essential Bryan Adams album and the only one that can be listened to straight through from start to finish. —*Stephen Thomas Erlewine*

Live! Live! Live! / 1995 / A&M ♦♦
Bryan Adams' *Live! Live! Live!* is a straightforward live album, featuring his greatest hits replicated in concert. Adams' support band is professional, and he is in fine voice; but the record doesn't offer any new interpretations of the hits, nor does it have much energy. Consequently, it isn't necessary for anyone but the most dedicated fans. —*Stephen Thomas Erlewine*

18 'til I Die / Jun. 1996 / A&M ♦♦
After experiencing enormous success in the early '90s with a handful of soundtrack contributions, Bryan Adams returned in 1996 with *18 'til I Die*, his first full-length album in five years. Since 1991's "(Everything I Do) I Do It for You," Adams' biggest hits have been big, sweeping power ballads; evidently constrained by that middle-of-the-road persona, *18 'til I Die* attempts to return to the rockin' good times vibes of his earlier records. The sound is grunged up a little, and he appears on the album cover in a bizarrely glitzy mod suit—all meant to telegraph the message that even as Adams approaches 40, he remains a hip teen at heart. Of course, the music doesn't prove that to be true. He turns up the guitars for "The Only Thing That Looks Good on Me Is You," "Black Pearl," and "(I Wanna Be Your) Underwear," but that sort of raunch prevents the album from being much fun—he's simply trying too hard. On the effortless ballads, Adams remains a rock-solid adult contemporary craftsman, writing songs with embarassingly catchy hooks and melodies. Unfortunately, the ballads don't sit comfortably alongside the rockers—they sound like the work of two different artists, one trying to sing to baby boomers, the other desperately trying to connect with teens. And while Adams might believe he'll stay a teenager until the end, he's most honest when singing songs to adults like himself. —*Stephen Thomas Erlewine*

Barry Adamson

b. Jun. 1, 1958, Manchester, England
Bass / Alternative Pop-Rock, Film Music
Adamson's work as a bassist for Magazine and Nick Cave's Bad Seeds gave little indication of the complex, cinematic works he has composed as a solo artist. After leaving the Bad Seeds in 1987, Adamson decided to follow the path of film composers like John Barry, Ennio Morricone, and Bernard Herrmann, whose work had intrigued him since childhood. His first full-length album, 1989's *Moss Side Story* (he had released one previous EP in 1988), was a tour de force blending post-punk, industrial, spy guitar, and various classic movie composer quotes into a seamless 54-minute soundtrack to an ominous film noir that didn't exist. This recording led to Adamson's work on soundtracks for actual films in the early '90s, including *Delusion*, *Gas Food Lodging*, and *Shuttle Cock*. Adamson has also continued to compose quasi-cinematic recordings for imaginary films like 1996's *Oedipus Shmoedipus*, although none has matched the sustained excitement of *Moss Side Story*. —*Richie Unterberger*

● **Moss Side Story** / 1989 / Mute ♦♦♦♦
Adamson's first full-length album is still unequivocally his best. Elements of rock, voices from news reports, blood-curdling wordless female vocals (courtesy of experimental/punk diva Diamanda Galas), lounge keyboards, and swirling funereal ambient music are interwoven on this taut and compelling, almost continuous, imaginary "soundtrack." The result is a sinister and edgy soundscape that's as gripping as any black-and-white thriller. The CD adds three bonus cuts, including Adamson's updates of "The Man with the Golden Arm" and "Alfred Hitchcock Presents." —*Richie Unterberger*

Delusion / 1991 / Mute ♦♦
It's perhaps unsurprising that Adamson's eclectic compositional talent doesn't work nearly as well when he has to wed his vision to an actual film. This soundtrack for an obscure 1991 movie contains plenty of

interesting bits, elements, and pieces—somber Spanish guitar, haunting orchestral passages, *Phantom of the Opera* organ phrases, manic Latin music, and a too-brief, ominous update of the 1963 British instrumental hit "Diamonds." The problem is that it doesn't ebb and flow into a sum greater than its parts. In fact, the jarring bits of dialogue (which are meaningless without the context of the film) are often downright annoying and make the sum substantially less than whatever whole it might have formed. —*Richie Unterberger*

Soul Murder / 1992 / Mute ✦✦✦
Equally as ambitious as *Moss Side Story*, but this doesn't come off nearly as well. Apparently constructed to evoke similar underworld soundscapes, too much of this is built around simple, sparse (sometimes electronic) riffs. The production lacks force and density, and the pieces don't flow into each other with the cohesion that he's demonstrated in other work. Nifty bits of haunting orchestral ambience and lounge jazz keyboards remain, and it does hit a groove at times, especially with the goofy French pop song (with childish vocals) "Un Petit Miracle" and the brutal ska treatment of the James Bond theme. —*Richie Unterberger*

The Negro Inside / Oct. 19, 1993 / Mute ✦✦
Something of a holding pattern. On this six-song EP, Adamson extrapolates from contemporary Black dance beats, samples his American publicist's answering machine message and Jane Birkin's hit "Je T'Aime," and throws in lounge jazz piano bits and more. The pieces aren't that striking, and one gets the sense that he's tossing out ideas to play with in the interim between full-length scores/albums. —*Richie Unterberger*

Oedipus Shmoedipus / Aug. 7, 1996 / Mute ✦✦✦✦
After some releases with more of a pop, beat-heavy feel, Adamson moves back—sort of—into the land of noirish soundtrack. Unlike *Moss Side Story*, it's not really a soundtrack with repeated themes and motifs. A lot of pieces establish soundtrack-like moods, but the flow never builds up a momentum of its own. As individual soundscapes, though, the tracks (largely instrumental) are reasonably impressive, whether it's burlesque-type fare, a takeoff on Miles Davis, or lounge jazz. If noir is what you want, "It's Business as Usual" is especially creepy, with its neurotic answering machine messages nearly buried under waves of disquieting sounds; achieving a similar effect, in an entirely different manner, is "Vermillion Kisses," a fairytale narrative with a morbid ending. Nick Cave adds a guest vocal to (and co-writes) "The Sweetest Embrace"; Pulp's Jarvis Cocker can be heard on (and co-writes) another cut. Adamson's skill in layering and devising unusual sound textures still qualifies him as one of experimental rock's more imaginative composers and producers. But on the more rock-oriented pieces, he's using too many of those damn beat-boxes for his own good. —*Richie Unterberger*

The Adverts

f. 1976, London, England, **db.** 1980
Punk
With their raw, enthusiastic immaturity, the Adverts were a bright but short-lived light of the punk era, distinguished by the fact that their bassist, Gayle Advert, was one of the first female stars of punk rock. After they (barely) mastered one chord, the Adverts began playing at London's Roxy Club in 1976, where they quickly came to the attention of the Damned's guitarist Brian James. James offered the band an opening spot on the Damned's tour and directed them toward Stiff Records. Stiff released their self-deprecating debut single, "One Chord Wonders," in 1977, when the band could still barely play. But when they released their second single, the disturbingly funny "Gary Gilmore's Eyes," the group rocketed into the UK Top 20 in a storm of controversy. The Adverts' first album, *Crossing the Red Sea with the Adverts*, fulfilled the single's promise, but the second, 1979's *Cast of Thousands*, sounded as if they'd poured all of their musical ideas into their first album; the group broke up the following year. —*Stephen Thomas Erlewine*

● **Crossing the Red Sea with the Adverts** / Mar. 1978 / Bright ✦✦✦✦
Some will argue eloquently that the Adverts' debut is the great overlooked UK punk record of the late-'70s. I think it's X-Ray Spex's *Germ Free Adolescents*, but I'm willing to give the Adverts second place. From the moment they released their first single ("One Chord Wonders") up to and including the release of this album, the Adverts recorded great, arty, fast, and loud punk clamor rooted in anomie ("Bored Teenagers"), class consciousness ("Safety in Numbers"), and comic book horror ("Gary Gilmore's Eyes"). Led by the Rotten/Strummer-isms of frontman T.V. Smith, *Crossing the Red Sea* sounds as snotty, defiant, and liberating as it did 17 years ago. In fact, it sounds surprisingly relevant and more intelligent than I remember. An ignored masterpiece. —*John Dougan*

Cast of Thousands / Mar. 1980 / RCA ✦✦

Aerosmith

f. 1970, Boston, MA
Hard Rock, Pop-Rock, Heavy Metal
Aerosmith was one of the most popular hard-rock bands of the '70s, setting the style and sound of hard rock and heavy metal for the next two decades with their raunchy, bluesy swagger. The Boston-based quintet found the middle ground between the menace of the Rolling Stones and the campy, sleazy flamboyance of the New York Dolls, developing a lean, dirty riff-oriented boogie that was loose and swinging and as hard as a diamond.

In the meantime, they developed a prototype for power-ballads with "Dream On," a piano ballad that was orchestrated with strings and distorted guitars. Aerosmith's ability to pull off both ballads and rock 'n' roll made them extremely popular during the mid-'70s, when they had a string of gold and platinum albums. By the early '80s, the group's audience had declined as the band fell prey to drug and alcohol abuse. However, their career was far from over—in the late '80s, Aerosmith pulled off one of the most remarkable comebacks in rock history, returning to the top of the charts with a group of albums that equalled, if not surpassed, the popularity of their '70s albums.

In 1970 the first incarnation of Aerosmith formed when vocalist Steven Tyler met guitarist Joe Perry while working at a Sunapee, NH, ice cream parlor. Tyler, who originally was a drummer, and Perry decided to form a power trio with bassist Tom Hamilton. The group soon expanded to a quartet, adding a second guitarist called Ray Tabano; he was quickly replaced by Brad Whitford, a former member of Earth Inc. With the addition of drummer Joey Kramer, Tyler became the full-time lead singer by the end of year. Aerosmith relocated to Boston at the end of 1970.

After playing clubs in the Massachusetts and New York areas for two years, the group landed a record contract with Columbia Records in 1972. Aerosmith's self-titled debut album was released in the fall of 1973, climbing to No. 166. "Dream On" was released as the first single, and it was a minor hit, reaching No. 59. For the next year the band built a fan base by touring America, supporting groups as diverse as the Kinks, Mahavishnu Orchestra, Sha Na Na, and Mott the Hoople. The performance of *Get Your Wings* (1974), the group's second album and the first produced by Jack Douglas, benefitted from their constant touring, spending a total of 86 weeks on the chart.

Aerosmith's third record, 1975's *Toys in the Attic*, was their breakthrough album both commercially and artistically. By the time it was recorded, the band's sound had developed into a sleek, hard-driving hard rock powered by simple, almost brutal, blues-based riffs. Many critics at the time labelled the group as punk rockers, and it's easy to see why—instead of adhering to the world-music pretentions of Led Zeppelin or the prolonged gloomy mysticism of Black Sabbath, Aerosmith stripped heavy metal to its basic core, spitting out spare riffs that not only rocked, but rolled. Steven Tyler's lyrics were filled with double entendres and clever jokes, and the entire band had a streetwise charisma that separated them from the heavy, lumbering arena rockers of the era. *Toys in the Attic* captured the essence of the newly invigorated Aerosmith. "Sweet Emotion," the first single from *Toys in the Attic*, broke into the Top 40 in the summer of 1975, with the album reaching No. 11 shortly afterward. Its success prompted the re-release of the power ballad "Dream On," which shot into the Top Ten in early 1976. Both *Aerosmith* and *Get Your Wings* climbed back up the charts in the wake of *Toys in the Attic*. "Walk This Way," the final single from *Toys in the Attic*, was released around the time of the group's new 1976 album, *Rocks*. Although it didn't feature a Top Ten hit like "Walk This Way," *Rocks* went platinum quickly, peaking at No. 3.

In early 1977, Aerosmith took a break and prepared material for their fifth album. Released late in 1977, *Draw the Line* was another hit, climbing to No. 11 on the US charts, but it showed signs of exhaustion. In addition to another tour in 1978, the band appeared in the movie *Sgt. Pepper's Lonely Hearts Club Band*, performing "Come Together," which eventually became a No. 23 hit. *Live! Bootleg* appeared late in 1978 and became another success, reaching No. 13. Aerosmith recorded *Night in the Ruts* in 1979, releasing the record at the end of the year. By the time of its release, Joe Perry had left the band to form the Joe Perry Project. *Night in the Ruts* performed respectably, climbing to No. 14 and going gold, but it was the least successful Aerosmith record to date. Brad Whitford left the group in early 1980, forming the Whitford-St. Holmes Band with former Ted Nugent guitarist Derek St. Holmes.

As Aerosmith regrouped with new guitarists Jimmy Crespo and Rick Dufay, the band released *Aerosmith's Greatest Hits* in late 1980; the record would eventually sell over six million copies. The new lineup of Aerosmith released *Rock in a Hard Place* in 1982. Peaking at No. 32, it failed to match the performance of *Night in the Ruts*. Perry and Whitford returned to the band in 1984, and the group began a reunion tour dubbed "Back in the Saddle." Early in the tour, Tyler collapsed on stage, offering proof that the band hadn't conquered their notorious drug and alcohol addictions. The following year, Aerosmith released *Done with Mirrors*, the original lineup's first record since 1979 and their first for Geffen Records. Although it didn't perform as well as *Rock in a Hard Place*, the album showed that the band was revitalized.

After the release of *Done with Mirrors*, Tyler and Perry completed rehabilitation programs. In 1986 the pair appeared on Run D.M.C.'s cover of "Walk This Way" and appeared in the video. "Walk This Way" became a hit, reaching No. 4 and receiving saturation airplay on MTV. "Walk This Way" set the stage for the band's full-scale comeback effort, the Bruce Fairburn-produced *Permanent Vacation* (1987). Tyler and Perry collaborated with professional hard-rock songwriters like Holly Knight and Desmond Child, resulting in the hits "Dude (Looks Like a Lady)," "Rag Doll" and "Angel." *Permanent Vacation* peaked at No. 11 and sold over three million copies.

Pump, released in 1989, continued the band's winning streak, reaching No. 5, selling over four million copies, and spawning the Top Ten singles "Love in an Elevator," "Janie's Got a Gun," and "What It Takes." Aerosmith released *Get a Grip* in 1993. Like *Permanent Vacation* and *Pump*, *Get a Grip* was produced by Bruce Fairburn and featured significant contributions from professional songwriters. The album was as successful as the band's previous two records, featuring the hit singles "Livin' on the Edge," "Cryin'," and "Amazing." In 1994 Aerosmith released *Big Ones*, a compilation of hits from their Geffen years, which fulfilled their contract with the label; it went double platinum shortly after its release.

While Aerosmith was at the height of its revitalized popularity in the early '90s, the group signed a lucrative multi-million dollar contract with Columbia Records, even though they still owed Geffen two albums. It wasn't until 1995 that the band was able to begin working on their first record under the new contract—nearly five years after the contract was signed. The making of Aerosmith albums usually had been difficult, but the recording of *Nine Lives* was plagued with bad luck. The band went through a number of producers and songwriters before settling on Kevin Shirley in 1996. More damaging, however, was the dismissal of the band's manager, Tim Collins, who had been responsible for bringing the band from the brink of addiction. Upon his firing, Collins insinuated that Steven Tyler was using hard drugs again, an allegation that Aerosmith adamantly denied. Under such circumstances, recording became quite difficult, and when *Nine Lives* finally appeared in the spring of 1997, the initial reviews were mixed; even though album debuted at No. 1, it quickly fell down the charts. —*Stephen Thomas Erlewine*

Aerosmith / Jan. 1973 / Columbia ✦✦✦
The debut from this Boston band shows a sensitive side with their best-known ballad, "Dream On." But the focus remains on raw, aggressive garage rock style as amply displayed on "Mama Kin," "One Way Street," and "Make It." —*Donna DiChario*

Get Your Wings / Mar. 1974 / Columbia ✦✦✦✦
Aerosmith took the Yardbirds classic "Train Kept a Rollin'" and made it their own with Steven Tyler's blistering vocals and Joe Perry's ace guitar work. —*Donna DiChario*

☆ **Toys in the Attic** / Apr. 1975 / Columbia ✦✦✦✦✦
After nearly getting off the ground with *Get Your Wings*, Aerosmith finally perfected their mix of Stonesy raunch and Zeppelin-esque riffing with their third album, *Toys in the Attic*. The success of the album derives from a combination of an increased sense of songwriting skills and purpose. Not only does Joe Perry turn out indelible riffs like "Walk This Way," "Toys in the Attic," and "Sweet Emotion," Steven Tyler has fully embraced sleaziness as his artistic muse. Taking his cue from the old dirty blues "Big Ten Inch Record," Tyler writes with a gleeful impishness about sex throughout *Toys in the Attic*, whether it's the teenage heavy petting of "Walk This Way," the promiscuous "Sweet Emotion," or the double-entendres of "Uncle Salty" and "Adam's Apple." The rest of Aerosmith, led by Perry's dirty, exaggerated riffing, provide an appropriately greasy backing. Before *Toys in the Attic*, no other hard rock band sounded like this. Sure, Aerosmith cribbed heavily from the records of the Rolling Stones, New York Dolls, and Led Zeppelin, but they didn't have any of the menace of their influences, nor any of their mystique. Aerosmith was a gritty, street-wise hard-rock band who played their blues as blooze and in were in it for a good time, and *Toys in the Attic* crystalizes that attitude. —*Stephen Thomas Erlewine*

☆ **Rocks** / May 1976 / Columbia ✦✦✦✦✦
Although the hits ("Back in the Saddle" and "Last Child") weren't as big as "Sweet Emotion" and "Walk This Way," *Rocks* remains Aerosmith's finest moment, full of relentlessly sleazy rock powered by some of the dirtiest guitar riffs ever committed to tape. —*Stephen Thomas Erlewine*

Draw the Line / Dec. 1977 / Columbia ✦✦✦
Where the decadent celebration of *Rocks* was glorious, *Draw the Line* collapses in its own hedonism, mainly because the band didn't write enough songs that match even the worst of *Rocks* and *Toys in the Attic*. Only the title track and the pseudo-pomp rock of "Kings and Queens" stand out among the murk. —*Stephen Thomas Erlewine*

Live Bootleg / Oct. 1978 / Columbia ✦✦
While it has its moments, *Live Bootleg* is surprisingly devoid of energy, giving a false impression of the group in concert. —*Stephen Thomas Erlewine*

Night in the Ruts / Nov. 1979 / Columbia ✦
Night In The Ruts is the sound of Aerosmith near the bottom. They go through the hard rock motions, but there's no spark in the performances and no distinctiveness to the songwriting. The album's single was an anemic remake of the Shangri-Las' "Remember (Walking in the Sand)" that crept to No. 67. The album itself, although a Top 20 gold-seller, was Aerosmith's least successful to this point. Bad as things were, they proceeded to get worse: lead guitarist Joe Perry decamped after the recording of this album, and rhythm guitarist Brad Whitford soon followed. —*William Ruhlmann*

★ **Greatest Hits** / Oct. 1980 / Columbia ✦✦✦✦✦
Although Aerosmith was an album-rock band, they made only two essential albums—*Toys in the Attic* and *Rocks*. The rest of their albums were quite uneven, even though each had its individual stellar tracks. *Greatest Hits* collects all of the highlights from Aerosmith's '70s heyday, picking the best cuts from each record. Apart from a pair of relatively uninteresting obscurities ("Come Together," "Remember (Walking in the Sand)") tacked on to the end of the album, there is no fat on *Greatest Hits*—the hits, from "Dream On" to "Kings and Queens," keep piling up. This is the definitive sound of late-'70s hard rock—lean, mean, grinding boogie—and it provided the blueprint for legions of bands in the late '80s. —*Stephen Thomas Erlewine*

Rock in a Hard Place / Aug. 1982 / Columbia ✦
The only album that Aerosmith made in a six-year period between 1979 and 1985, *Rock in a Hard Place* is the work of original members Steven Tyler, Tom Hamilton, and Joey Kramer, with replacement guitarists Jimmy Crespo and Rick Dufay standing in for the departed Joe Perry and Brad Whitford. It has a more punk-oriented, less hard rock approach than typical Aerosmith, but it is far below their usual standard. When it proved a commercial disaster, Aerosmith parted company with Columbia Records and looked to be on its last legs. —*William Ruhlmann*

Done with Mirrors / Nov. 1985 / Geffen ✦✦✦✦
Joe Perry returned to the fold in 1985, and the band turned out their finest record since *Rocks*. Unlike the records that preceded it, *Done with Mirrors* was powered by the same smart-assed lyrics and filthy guitars that formed the core of Aerosmith's best songs. It didn't receive the commercial or critical attention that *Permanent Vacation* did two years later, but *Done with Mirrors* is the better album; it marks the beginning of their remarkable comeback. —*Stephen Thomas Erlewine*

Classics Live / Apr. 1986 / Columbia ✦✦
With Aerosmith on the way back up, Columbia Records assembled this album of live recordings from 1977 to 1983 in order to cash in. Both the original band and the interim edition with guitarists Jimmy Crespo and Rick Dufay are represented, some of the band's better known material is featured, and the result is a second-rate redundancy. Stick to *Live Bootleg* for live Aerosmith recordings. —*William Ruhlmann*

Classics Live 2 / Jun. 1987 / Columbia ✦✦✦
A rare case where the sequel surpasses the original release, *Classics Live 2* is the leanest, toughest, and best live album Aerosmith has released. —*Stephen Thomas Erlewine*

Permanent Vacation / Aug. 1987 / Geffen ✦✦✦
Apart from the strong singles—"Dude (Looks Like a Lady)," "Angel," and "Rag Doll"—*Permanent Vacation* isn't as consistent or rocking a record as *Done with Mirrors;* too often, it relies on slick, horn-spiked production instead of genuine grit, making the moments when Joe Perry's guitar does kick into overdrive all the more splendid. —*Stephen Thomas Erlewine*

Gems / 1988 / Columbia ✦✦✦✦
Gems is not a greatest-hits album. Instead, it's a collection of album tracks and AOR staples ("Mama Kin," "Lord of the Thighs," "Chip Away the Stone," "Rats in the Cellar") that may not make sense as a retrospective, but rocks harder, stronger, and longer than most albums they released during the 1970s. —*Stephen Thomas Erlewine*

Pump / Sep. 1989 / Geffen ✦✦✦✦
Where *Permanent Vacation* seemed a little overwhelmed by its pop concessions, *Pump* revels in them without ever losing sight of Aerosmith's dirty hard-rock core. Which doesn't mean the record is a sell-out—"What It Takes" has more emotion and grit than any of their other power ballads; "Janie's Got a Gun" tackles more complex territory than most previous songs; and "The Other Side" and "Love in an Elevator" rock relentlessly, no matter how many horns and synths fight with the guitars. Such ambition and successful musical eclecticism make *Pump* rank with *Rocks* and *Toys in the Attic*. —*Stephen Thomas Erlewine*

Pandora's Box / Nov. 1991 / Columbia ✦✦
A bare-bones three-CD box set concentrating on Aerosmith's glory days at Columbia during the 1970s, *Pandora's Box* has plenty of fine music but fails as a retrospective. All the hits are available in better singles collections (or more consistent original albums), and the rarities and the packaging are nothing special. Because of licensing restrictions, the set

isn't able to cover their startling 1980s comeback, so it's not comprehensive, either; it's for diehard fans only. —*Stephen Thomas Erlewine*

Get a Grip / Apr. 1993 / Geffen ✦✦✦
Coming on the heels of the commercially and artistically successful *Pump*, the fitfully entertaining *Get a Grip* pales against its predecessor's musical diversity. But it's not for lack of trying. In fact, Aerosmith tries too hard, making a stab at social commentary ("Livin' on the Edge"), while keeping adolescent fans in their corner with their trademark raunch-rock ("Get a Grip" and "Eat the Rich"), as well as having radio-ready hit ballads ("Cryin'," "Amazing," and "Crazy"). The problem is, it's a studied performance—it sounds like what an Aerosmith album *should* sound like. Most of the album *sounds* good; it's just that there isn't much beneath the surface. —*Stephen Thomas Erlewine*

• **Big Ones** / Nov. 1, 1994 / Geffen ✦✦✦✦
Big Ones serves up the hits and nothing but the hits; Aerosmith's excellent debut for Geffen, *Done with Mirrors*, is conveniently overlooked. So what's left is some of the finest mainstream hard rock of the late '80s and early '90s—the fruits of one of the most remarkable comebacks in rock 'n' roll history. Unfortunately, there's precious little of the classic Aerosmith raunch; in fact, the two new tracks are the hardest, slinkiest tracks here. Otherwise, the uptempo tracks bog down in overproduction ("Love in an Elevator"), and the frequently embarrassingly overwrought power ballads ("Angel" and "Crazy") dominate too much of the album. So what's left? The band's best stab at social commentary ("Janie's Got a Gun"), a sublime slinky throwaway ("Deuces Are Wild"), deliciously sleazy blues-rockers ("Rag Doll," "(Dude) Looks Like a Lady") and their best ballads ("What It Takes" and "Cryin' "). —*Stephen Thomas Erlewine*

Box of Fire / Nov. 22, 1994 / Columbia ✦✦✦✦
Box of Fire collects all of Aerosmith's Columbia albums in a deluxe box set, adding liner notes, but the actual discs themselves contain the same remastering and artwork as the regular releases. Consequently, the set is useful for fans replacing their entire collection, but other listeners might want to stick with the original albums. —*Stephen Thomas Erlewine*

Nine Lives / Mar. 18, 1997 / Sony ✦✦✦
Aerosmith signed a multi-million-dollar contract with Columbia Records before they had completed their deal with Geffen, which meant that a lot was riding on their Columbia debut, *Nine Lives*, when it was finally delivered in 1997. During recording, the band nearly broke up, and they worked with a number of producers—including Glen Ballard, the man behind Alanis Morissette—before settling on Kevin Shirley, an in-house producer responsible for Silverchair and Journey. Perhaps that's the reason *Nine Lives* sounds so calculated, as if it was assembled by a band trying to sound like Aerosmith. In a sense, it is—not one of the 13 songs was written without the assistance of professional songwriters. Of course, some of the best moments of *Pump* and *Permanent Vacation* were also written with professionals, but they had an appealing, slick surface that made them infectious. *Nine Lives*, in contrast, is over-labored, with Aerosmith making a conscious effort to sound hip and vibrant, which ironically simply makes them sound tired. Not only are the performances perfunctory, but the songs aren't catchy—no matter how hard it tries, "Fallin' in Love (Is Hard on the Knees)" never develops a hook, and it is not an exception. A handful of cuts approximate the raunchy appeal of prime Aerosmith, but *Nine Lives* is hardly the triumphant comeback it should have been. —*Stephen Thomas Erlewine*

Afghan Whigs

f. 1986, Cincinnati, OH
Alternative Pop-Rock
Evolving from a garage-punk band in the vein of the Replacements, Dinosaur Jr., and Mudhoney to a literate, pretentious, soul-inflected post-punk quartet, the Afghan Whigs were one of most critically acclaimed alternative bands of the early '90s. Although the band never broke into the mainstream, they developed a dedicated cult following, primarily because of lead singer-songwriter Greg Dulli's tortured, angst-ridden tales of broken relationships and self-loathing. The Afghan Whigs were one of the few alternative bands that formed in the late '80s to acknowledge R&B, attempting to create a fusion of soul and post-punk. The Afghan Whigs were formed when vocalist/rhythm guitarist Greg Dulli, bassist John Curley, lead guitarist Rick McCollum, and drummer Steve Earle were attending the University of Cincinnati. Dulli, who was raised in Hamilton, OH, was studying film at the university, where he met fellow students McCollum and Earle. Unlike the rest of the band, Curley didn't attend the University of Cincinnati. He arrived in the city to intern as a photographer at the *Cincinnati Enquirer*, a job that his father—who published *USA Today*—arranged for him. For the next few years, Curley continued to shoot pictures for the paper, quitting only when the band's schedule became too busy for him to work both jobs. Dulli happened to meet Curley when visiting a friend's apartment building. Eventually, the pair formed the Afghan Whigs in 1986, along with McCollum and Earle.

In 1988, the Afghan Whigs released their debut album, *Big Top Halloween*, on their independent record label, Ultrasuede. The album

received good word-of-mouth in underground music publications and college radio. A copy of the record worked its way to the influential Seattle-based independent record label Sub Pop, and the label arranged for the Whigs to release a one-off single. The single led to a full-blown record contract with Sub Pop. *Up in It*, their first Sub Pop album, was released in 1990. For the next two years, the Afghan Whigs toured America consistently, occasionally heading to Europe and England. In 1992 their third album, *Congregation*, was released to very positive reviews. After its release, the band was courted by a number of major labels. The band released one more record on Sub Pop, an EP of soul and R&B covers called *Uptown Avondale*, and signed to Elektra Records.

Gentlemen, the band's major-label debut, was released to considerable critical acclaim in the fall of 1993. "Debonair," the first single pulled from the album, received major play from MTV, and all of the reviews were positive. Nevertheless, the band wasn't able to ascend past cult status, and even all the critical praise engendered a backlash, most notably in the form of an anti-Whigs fanzine called *Fat Greg Dulli*. In the summer of 1994 the band released the *What Jail Is Like* EP to coincide with their American tour. Upon the completion of their international tour in the fall of 1994, the band took an extended break. Steve Earle left the band in the spring of 1995; he was replaced by Paul Buchignani just before the band entered the studio to record their fifth album. *Black Love*, their second album for Elektra, was released in the spring of 1996. Again, the album received positive reviews, but the band failed to break out of their cult status. —*Stephen Thomas Erlewine*

Big Top Halloween / 1988 / Ultrasuede ✦✦
Too often, Midwestern rock bands cannot escape being labeled Replacements clones, but the Afghan Whigs, although vocalist Greg Dulli was originally called a rougher Paul Westerberg, show on their extremely rare debut release that Midwestern rock doesn't necessarily have to overwhelm with its country influences. Although *Big Top Halloween* is sometimes too cluttered in its mix, the album delivers bits of beauty and evidence of the band's future brilliance. —*Matt Carlson*

Up in It / 1990 / Sub Pop ✦✦✦
Up in It was for Sub Pop the first release for a band outside of the Seattle area and was for the Afghan Whigs the first true step toward its own sound. Greg Dulli has always exhibited a stronger lyrical focus than his fellow Sub Pop brethren, and here he delivers intricate and lush stories from a rock singer's voice. Musically, the album still resembles the Replacements, but it is much stronger lyrically. —*Matt Carlson*

Congregation / Aug. 1991 / Sub Pop ✦✦✦✦
Dulli's songwriting continues to improve on their last full-length independent album, while the band itself sounds tougher and able to keep up with the twists in the songwriting. —*Stephen Thomas Erlewine*

Uptown Avondale / 1992 / Sub Pop ✦✦✦
The Whigs' final independent release was a scorching EP of soul and R&B covers and is arguably their finest moment. —*Stephen Thomas Erlewine*

• **Gentlemen** / Oct. 5, 1993 / Elektra ✦✦✦✦
With their major label debut, *Gentlemen*, the Afghan Whigs have finally come into their own. Throughout *Gentlemen*, the Whigs act as if they were Minneapolis punks ripping through the Stax songbook as written by Paul Westerberg. It's a riveting, original album, uncompromising in its honesty and punk/soul roots. In short, with this album the Afghan Whigs have fulfilled the promise of their earlier, independent records. —*Stephen Thomas Erlewine*

What Jail is Like / Aug. 9, 1994 / Elektra ✦✦
A release of the "Gentlemen" song with six bonus tracks. Live tracks make it worthwhile for fans, and covers including the Supremes' "My World Is Empty Without You" make it worthwhile for record collectors. Good sound quality. —*Matt Carlson*

Black Love / Mar. 12, 1996 / Elektra ✦✦✦
After the dense, pseudoliterary aspirations of *Gentlemen*, *Black Love* sounds nearly lighthearted. That doesn't mean it's a light record; lead singer-songwriter Greg Dulli has an overwhelming affection for the morose and the twisted. From the grinding guitars to the hardboiled lyrics, the Afghan Whigs revel in the dark side. The problem is, Dulli isn't a compelling enough melodicist to make the songs stick; furthermore, his lyrics frequently sound like posturing, as if they were learned from books and movies. When the Afghan Whigs are at their best, they create a soundscape that evokes the lyrical world Dulli tries so hard to conjure. Rooted in indie-guitar rock, the band blends in slight elements of early '70s soul and R&B, with an occasional country overtone. It reads better than it sounds; they play with organs and attempt to land in a groove, but it doesn't amount to genuine, gritty soul. Instead, their funk experiments add another thick layer of grunge. Combined with the clanging guitars and the willfully bleak lyrics, the result is an album so lumbering and unmelodic that it can only be admired, not enjoyed. —*Stephen Thomas Erlewine*

a-ha

f. 1977, Oslo, Norway
Synth-pop, Pop-Rock
For a short time in the summer of 1985, a-ha were superstars. Thanks to their groundbreaking video for "Take On Me"—a clever clip that combined pencil sketches with live-action footage of the attractive band members—the band had a huge hit single. Their pleasantly catchy brand of synthesized pop in the vein of Duran Duran wasn't what made the song a hit; it was the video. Consequently, the band wasn't able to score another big hit after "Take on Me," even though they tried valiantly several times ("The Sun Always Shines on T.V." made a small dent on the charts in the beginning of 1986). a-ha turned toward more moody, synth-based adult-contemporary pop with their 1988 album, *Stay on These Roads*; they have pursued the same musical direction ever since. —*Stephen Thomas Erlewine*

● **Hunting High and Low** / Jun. 1985 / Warner Brothers ✦✦✦✦
This is friendly synthesizer pop, fronted by the emotive, sometimes falsetto vocals of Morten Harket. But it was Harket's looks, as exhibited in the semi-animated video, that sent "Take on Me" to No. 1 in the summer of 1985. The album also contains the follow-up, "The Sun Always Shines on T.V." (No. 20). But so far, this million-selling debut is the beginning and end of a-ha as legitimate record makers in the US. (In the UK, by contrast, the album spawned four Top Ten hits, including the title track and "Train of Thought.") —*William Ruhlmann*

Scoundrel Days / 1986 / Warner Brothers ✦✦✦
In the US, this close copy of a-ha's debut album was a considerable disappointment, with only "Cry Wolf" getting as high as No. 50. But in England, it was a different story, as *Scoundrel Days* became a-ha's second straight album to peak at No. 2, and there were three Top 20 hits in "I've Been Losing You," "Cry Wolf," and "Manhattan Skyline." —*William Ruhlmann*

Stay on These Roads / 1988 / Warner Brothers ✦✦
The recording career of a-ha hit the skids in America with its third release. But in the UK, the album became the group's third straight to peak at No. 2, though it charted for a shorter period than the first two albums, and there were four Top 25 hits—the title track, "The Blood That Moves the Body," "Touchy!," and "You Are the One." (Included was a-ha's 1987 theme from the James Bond movie *The Living Daylights*, a UK No. 5 that missed the US charts.) Even in a country with a demonstrated affection for Scandinavians, however (remember ABBA?), that was a fall-off, even if the decline was more gradual; and three albums in, a-ha wasn't demonstrating any development from its first hit, just more of the same and a little less distinctive. —*William Ruhlmann*

East of the Sun, West of the Moon / 1990 / Warner Brothers ✦✦✦
A small surprise, too quickly destined for the cut-out bins considering the way their career finally went after *Hunting High and Low*. This is a nicely crafted collection of songs, performed and sung beautifully, with lots of echoes and suggestions tucked into the music. While not an album one can discuss at length, it's an album that's a pleasure to listen to and one that deserves a better reception than the one, unfortunately, that it seems to have received. —*Steven McDonald*

Memorial Beach / Apr. 1992 / Warner Brothers ✦
For its fifth album, a-ha varies its style somewhat, trying for a U2 approach on lead-off track "Dark Is the Night for All." This is a long way from the peppy appeal of "Take On Me," but just as far from an improvement. —*William Ruhlmann*

Air Liquide

f. Koln, Germany
Ambient, Techno, Acid, Electro-Techno, Electronica
Not to be confused with the international chemical company of the same name, the Koln-based duo of Cem Oral and Ingmar Koch (who go by the names Jammin' Unit and Walker, respectively) have been making hard-hitting experimental acid and techno as Air Liquide since the early '90s. Recording first for their own Structure label before signing with Rising High in 1993, the pair currently record for the New York-based Smile Communications, as well as in various side projects for labels such as DJungle Fever, Anodyne, Blue Angel, and Oral's own Pharma imprint. Although the pair have dabbled in everything from beatless ambient to back-breaking, nosebleed gabber, the bulk of their material has clustered around dirty, mid-tempo acid and breakbeat techno, with the focus on thick 303 lines and simple, minimal phrases. They've also increasingly moved to a more hip-hop-infused brand of caustic electro, with tracks appearing on Rising High's *Further Self-Evident Truths* label compilations and the Coldcut *Journeys by DJ* mixed CD.
Koch got his start in the music industry on the far side of the integrity line, pumping out assembly line house and hip-hop for the German Hype! and Technoline labels before the latter went bankrupt in the early '90s. He then headed for university, studying electronic composition and attempting to break the bad habits he'd picked up in mainstream pro-

duction. It was then that Koch met Oral, a member of the same German underground scene that included J. Berger, Mike Ink, and Biochip C.'s Martin Damm. Together the group consolidated their efforts toward assembling the influential Structure label group, which included the Structure, Monotone, Blue, and DJungle Fever imprints. With releases running the spectrum from ambient, house, and techno to acid and hardcore, Koch and Oral's work together began to coalesce into a coherent sound reflecting shared influences such as Chicago acid, early New York hip-hop, and '70s prog experimentalists such as Neu! and Can.
Soon after Structure dissolved into the various labels and projects of its key participants, Walker and Jammin' Unit signed the Air Liquide name to the English Rising High label, through which they released a number of well-received full- and EP-length albums, including *Liquid Air*, *Nephology*, and *Weather Machine*. The pair currently record for Smile. Walker continues to release material on his own Pharma label, as well as through DJungle Fever, Analog, and others. Oral released a solo album as Jammin' Unit, titled *Jammin' Unit Discovers Chemical Dub*, also through Rising High. —*Sean Cooper*

● **The Increased Difficulty of Concentration** / Oct. 25, 1994 / Smile Communications ✦✦✦✦
A sprawling two-CD compilation of tunes roughly separable into either ambient or experimental acid/techno. Although a bit simplistic at times, the material's as good as anything the duo released through Rising High, proving the move to Smile hasn't shaken their sound. Also in evidence is an increased predilection for breaks, which has continued to grow since this set's release. —*Sean Cooper*

Air Supply

f. 1976, Melbourne, Australia
Adult Contemporary, Soft Rock, Pop-Rock
With their heavily orchestrated, sweet ballads, the Australian soft-rock group Air Supply became a staple of early-'80s radio, scoring a string of seven straight Top Five singles. Air Supply, for most intents and purposes, was the duo of vocalists Russell Hitchcock and Graham Russell; other members came through the group over the years, yet they only functioned as backing musicians and added little to the group's sound. Hitchcock and Russell met while performing in a Sydney, Australia, production of *Jesus Christ Superstar* in 1976. The two singers formed a partnership, and with the addition of four supporting musicians—keyboardist Frank Esler-Smith, guitarist David Moyse, bassist David Green, and drummer Ralph Cooper—Air Supply was born.
For several years the group gained no attention outside of Australia, earning one significant hit single, "Love and Other Bruises." Their first international exposure came in the late '70s, when Rod Stewart had them as his opening act on a North American tour. Air Supply signed a record contract with Arista in 1980, releasing their first album by the end of the year. *Lost in Love*, their debut, was a major success in the US, selling over two million copies and spawning the hit singles "Lost in Love," "All Out of Love," and "Every Woman in the World." The following year they released their second album, *The One That You Love*. The title track became their only No. 1 hit and it featured two other Top Ten hits, "Here I Am (Just When I Thought I Was Over You)" and "Sweet Dreams." With their third album, 1982's *Now and Forever*, their popularity dipped slightly; it had only one Top Ten hit, "Even the Nights Are Better." The other two singles, "Young Love" and "Two Less Lonely People in the World," scraped the bottom of the Top 40. Air Supply released a *Greatest Hits* collection in 1983, featuring a new single, "Making Love Out of Nothing at All." The single spent two weeks at No. 2, while the album peaked at No. 7 and eventually sold over four million copies.
Two years later, they released *Air Supply*, their fourth album. It featured the No. 19 single "Just as I Am," but it was clear that their audience was shrinking; the album was their first not to go platinum. *Hearts in Motion* (1986) was even less successful, peaking at No. 84 and spending only nine weeks on the charts. After its disappointing performance, Air Supply broke up. Hitchcock and Russell reunited in 1991, releasing *Earth Is . . .*, but the album failed to make the charts as did 1993's *Vanishing Race* and 1995's *News from Nowhere*. —*Stephen Thomas Erlewine*

● **Greatest Hits** / 1988 / Arista ✦✦✦✦
This self-explanatory collection includes "Lost in Love" (No. 1), "The One That You Love" (No. 1), "Every Woman in the World" (No. 5), "All Out of Love" (No. 2), "Sweet Dreams" (No. 5), "Making Love Out of Nothing at All" (No. 2), "Even the Nights Are Better" (No. 5), and many more soft pop hits. —*Rick Clark*

The Alarm

f. 1981, Rhyl, Wales, **db.** 1992
Alternative Pop-Rock
Comparisons to U2 have dogged Welsh quartet the Alarm throughout their career, but in light of the Alarm's socially conscious lyrics, melodic rock anthems, and gravitation toward a mainstream alternative sound

over their career, perhaps the comparisons are justified. Lead singer and guitarist Mike Peters was actually inspired by U2's passion and commitment to form the group in 1981 with guitarist/vocalist David Sharp, bassist Eddie MacDonald, and drummer Nigel Twist. Their early sound was energetic and largely acoustic-based, while the group's stage look encompassed skintight leather pants, gaudy belts, and spiked hair. Their first of several UK hits was "68 Guns," but they didn't chart in America until 1987 with "Presence of Love," which reached No. 77 and proved to be the extent of their US singles chart success. By that point in their career, the group had adopted a more electric guitar-based sound and had gravitated more towards the mainstream, but since U2 had hit the big time, the Alarm seemed too much like a pale imitation. The band tried something different on 1989's *Change*, which featured more traditional Celtic influences and a guest appearance from the Welsh Symphony Orchestra, but it proved to be too little too late. The Alarm broke up early in the '90s, and Mike Peters embarked on a solo career. — *Steve Huey*

Declaration / 1984 / IRS ✦✦✦
The Alarm's first full-length album was, to a certain extent, a collection of the singles they had been releasing since October 1982: "Marching On," "The Stand," "Sixty-Eight Guns" (No. 17 UK), "Where Were You Hiding When the Storm Broke?" (No. 22 UK) and "The Deceiver" (No. 51 UK). As such, it had a strident, immediate appeal that was also somewhat relentless; The Alarm seemed to play every song as if it were the climax of their set. In the short term, that excited listeners, however; *Declaration* was a No. 6 hit in England and broke through to the Top 50 in the US. In retrospect, it's more smoke than fire. — *William Ruhlmann*

Strength / 1985 / IRS ✦✦✦✦
In addition to an improved sense of musicality and dynamics, *Strength* featured the Alarm's finest group of songs, making it their single best studio album. — *Stephen Thomas Erlewine*

Eye of the Hurricane / 1987 / IRS ✦✦✦
This should have been the album that put the Alarm on the path to major stardom; instead, it marked the limits of their appeal. From the early fervor of their punk/acoustic debut, the group had evolved into more of a mainstream rock act without ever getting out from under the shadow of their mentors, U2. In fact, here they sounded more like U2 than ever, and now that that group had ascended to superstardom, the comparison only hurt them. The signal hit here was "Rain in the Summertime," an overproduced leadoff track followed by "Rescue Me" and "Presence of Love." All three tracks got AOR radio play in the US, so you couldn't say the Alarm wasn't getting exposure, especially when they were touring with Bob Dylan. However, they weren't getting through. — *William Ruhlmann*

Change / 1989 / IRS ✦✦✦
Clearly, change was called for in the Alarm's career, and on their fourth album, the group achieved a tighter, hard rock sound by turning to producer Tony Visconti. Their extensive roadwork and promotional efforts had opened doors for them at AOR and college radio, which played "Sold Me down the River," "Devolution Workin' Man Blues," and "Love Don't Come Easy." "River" even became the Alarm's biggest US single, peaking at No. 50. But the album sold about the same as *Eye of the Hurricane*, indicating that all the hard work had only enabled them to run in place. The problem remained the same: the Alarm had calmed down from its early martial style and turned into a competent mainstream rock band, but they still sounded too much like U2, and the rock riffs and throaty vocals still didn't add up to memorable songs. — *William Ruhlmann*

● **Standards** / Dec. 1990 / IRS ✦✦✦✦
This solid anthology covers everything from early aggressive topical folk-rock anthems ("Marching On," "The Stand") to more mainstream rock hits like "Strength" and "Sold Me down the River." — *Rick Clark*

Raw / Apr. 1991 / IRS ✦✦
It's hard to avoid the conclusion that the Alarm's fifth new studio album, *Raw*, released six months after the career-summarizing hits collection *Standards*, was a contractual obligation record. Lacking promotion, it crept into the pop chart for a single week at No. 161, while the title track earned some AOR and college radio play. Despite that title, this was another competent mainstream rock collection, its unnecessary highlight a cover of Neil Young's "Rockin' in the Free World." "Moments in Time" presented a ballad-tempo history of the band, always a sure sign of an impending breakup (cf. "Creeque Alley," "The Ballad of Mott"). "Somewhere we got lost along the way," sings Mike Peters. Sad, but true. — *William Ruhlmann*

Arthur Alexander

b. 1942, Florence, AL, d. Jun. 9, 1993, Nashville, TN
Vocals / Soul, R&B
Alexander was one of the first true singing, songwriting stars of country-soul, a genre that wed Southern Black R&B singers to songs written in a

country format and played basically by white musicians. Alexander's "You Better Move On" (No. 24-1962) was the first hit to come out of Rick Hall's fledgling Muscle Shoals studio. Alexander's work was immediately appreciated by his peers in the business; those who have covered his tunes (self-penned or otherwise) read like a *Who's Who* from both sides of the Atlantic—"Anna" (Beatles); "Soldiers of Love" (Beatles and Marshall Crenshaw); "Burning Love" (Elvis Presley); "Set Me Free" (Joe Tex, Esther Phillips, Percy Sledge). The Rolling Stones' cover of "You Better Move On" led to valuable contacts for Rick Hall, and the resulting business enabled him to build the new FAME studio. It was the start of the whole Muscle Shoals sound, and Alexander's career was one of its cornerstones. He went on, after a brief retirement, to record for both Warner Brothers and Buddah.

"Anna (Go to Him)," one of Alexander's best-known tunes, epitomizes the anguished, haunting tone of his music. From the onset, the heavily echoed piano and tortured vocal set a mood that is soulful, mysterious, a little spooky, and totally mesmerizing. His work is essential to any country-soul collection.

As Alexander began a comeback in 1993, he died of a heart attack. However, the album he completed before his death, *Lonely Just Like Me*, is a gentle record that is a fine way to end his career. Warner Bros. issued an Arthur Alexander retrospective anthology in 1994 featuring the early-'70s LP he recorded for them, plus some unissued tracks. — *Christine Ohlman*

★ **The Ultimate Arthur Alexander** / Jun. 15, 1993 / Razor & Tie ✦✦✦✦✦
Alexander's songs are better known in versions by the Beatles, Elvis Presley, and the Rolling Stones, but no one recorded better versions than Alexander himself. *The Ultimate Arthur Alexander* truly lives up to its title, gathering the best songs (including "Anna [Go to Him]," "You Better Move On," and "Soldiers of Love") from Alexander's remarkably influential and underrated career. Absolutely essential for any R&B and soul collection. — *Stephen Thomas Erlewine*

Rainbow Road / Apr. 26, 1994 / Warner Archives ✦✦✦✦
Songwriter and vocalist Arthur Alexander was sorely neglected during his lifetime, despite possessing a stark, compelling voice and being among pop and soul's greatest storytellers. He remained on the outside, coming close but never attaining stardom. This CD features 15 fantastic songs, most from the great 1972 Warner Bros. album recorded in Memphis that Alexander thought would finally earn him that elusive smash. There are also some singles cut in Nashville as companion records to the Memphis session. The 15 tracks range from the hypnotic title cut and "In the Middle of It All" to the uptempo burners "You Got Me Knockin' " and "Burning Love." There's also a moving gospel number, "Thank God He Came." This disc is a wonderful tribute to an unjustly ignored artist. — *Ron Wynn*

Alice in Chains

f. 1987, Seattle, WA
Alternative Pop-Rock, Heavy Metal, Grunge
In many ways, Alice In Chains was the definitive heavy metal band of the early '90s. Drawing equally from the heavy riffing of post-Van Halen metal and the gloomy strains of post-punk, the band developed a bleak, nihilistic sound that balanced grinding hard rock with subtly textured acoustic numbers. They were hard enough for metal fans, but their dark subject matter and punky attack placed them among the front ranks of the Seattle-based grunge bands. While this dichotomy helped the group soar to multi-platinum status with their second album, 1992's *Dirt*, it also divided them. Guitarist Jerry Cantrell always leaned toward the mainstream, while vocalist Layne Staley was fascinated with the seamy underground. Such tension drove the band toward stardom in their early years, but after *Dirt*, Alice In Chains suffered from near-crippling internal tensions that kept the band off the road for the remainder of the '90s, and, consequently, the group never quite fulfilled their potential.

Layne Staley formed the initial incarnation of the band while in high school in the mid-'80s, naming the group Alice N Chains. Staley met Jerry Cantrell in 1987 at the Seattle rehearsal warehouse the Music Bank, and the two began working together, changing the group's name to Alice in Chains. Cantrell's friends Mike Starr (bass) and Sean Kinney (drums) rounded out the lineup, and the band began playing local Seattle clubs. Columbia Records signed the group in 1989, and the label quickly made the band a priority, targeting heavy metal audiences. Early in 1990 the label released the *We Die Young* EP as a promotional device, and the song became a hit on metal radio, setting the stage for the summer release of the group's debut, *Facelift*. Alice in Chains supported the album by opening for Van Halen, Poison, and Iggy Pop, and it became a hit, going gold by the end of the year. As the band prepared their second album, they released the largely acoustic EP *Sap* in 1991 to strong reviews.

Before the release of Alice in Chains' second album, Seattle became a media sensation, thanks to the surprise success of Nirvana. As a result, Alice was now marketed as an alternative band, not as a metal outfit, and the group landed a song, the menacing "Would?," on the *Singles* soundtrack during the summer of 1992. "Would?" helped build anticipation for *Dirt*, the group's relentlessly bleak second album that was released in the fall of 1992 to very good reviews. After its release, Starr left and was replaced by Mike Inez. *Dirt* went platinum by the end of 1992, but its gloomy lyrics launched many rumors that Layne Staley was addicted to heroin. Alice in Chains soldiered on in the face of such criticism, performing successfully on the third Lollapalooza tour in 1993, which helped *Dirt* reach sales of three million.

The band released the low-key EP *Jar of Flies* in early 1994. It debuted at No. 1 upon its release, becoming the first EP to top the album charts. Despite the band's continued success, they stayed off the road, which fueled speculation that Staley was mired in heroin addiction. Later that year, Staley did give a few concerts, as part of the Gacy Bunch—a Seattle supergroup also featuring Pearl Jam's Mike McCready, the Screaming Trees' Barrett Martin, and John Baker Saunders. The group subsequently renamed itself Mad Season and released *Above* in early 1995. Later that year Alice in Chains re-emerged with an eponymous third album, which debuted at No. 1 on the American charts. Again, the band chose not to tour, which launched yet another round of speculation that band was suffering from various addictions and was on the verge of disbanding. The group did give one concert—their first in three years—in 1996, performing for an episode of *MTV Unplugged*, which was released as an album that summer. Despite its success, the album did nothing to dispel doubts about the group's future, and neither did Jerry Cantrell's solo album in 1997. *—Stephen Thomas Erlewine*

Facelift / Aug. 1990 / Columbia ✦✦✦
Alice in Chains' first album earned them a strong following with its crunching, foreboding rock, including the singles "Man in the Box" and "We Die Young." *Facelift* might not have the grand thematic sweep of *Dirt*, but it makes up for it with sheer energy and muscular riffs. *—Stephen Thomas Erlewine*

Sap / Feb. 1992 / Columbia ✦✦✦✦
Before Alice in Chains delivered their second album, they released *Sap*, a five-song EP featuring acoustic-oriented material. For anyone who pigeonholed them as mere gloom-mongers after their debut, *Sap* was a shock; it showed that they were capable of playing quieter, more intricate music without losing any intensity. *—Stephen Thomas Erlewine*

● **Dirt** / Oct. 1992 / Columbia ✦✦✦✦
To say that *Dirt* is a dark album is something of an understatement. Alice in Chains conveys a stark, stoic beauty to the pain of their protagonists. The violence and disturbing elements (both musical and lyrical) are offset by a mantra-like feel of inner strength and acceptance. Musically, Alice in Chains' rhythm section lays down a heavy, doom-struck base over which twin guitars and double-tracked vocals slash appealingly. There are lots of interesting tempo and time-signature changes, with the band veering into progressive-rock territory on occasion. *—Roch Parisien*

Jar of Flies / Jan. 25, 1994 / Columbia ✦✦✦✦
Like *Sap* before it, *Jar of Flies* is a quieter, acoustic-oriented experimental EP released between full-length albums, but it also works well as a coda to the epochal *Dirt*. Although the songs are calmer, they are by no means gentle, providing harrowing examinations of loss. Thankfully, musical stretches like the instrumental "Whale & Wasp" and the swing-blues of "Swing on This" are successful, and the best material here ("I Stay Away" and "No Excuses") rivals the best tracks on *Dirt*. *—Stephen Thomas Erlewine*

Alice in Chains / Nov. 21, 1995 / Columbia ✦✦✦
Dispelling rumors of their demise due to Layne Staley's heroin addiction, *Alice in Chains* is an accomplished, detailed effort showcasing Jerry Cantrell's continually developing writing and songcrafting skills. The band relies less on metallic riffs and more on melody and complex, varying textures than their previous full-length albums, integrating some of the more delicate acoustic moods of their EPs. The lyrics deal with familiar AIC subject matter: despair, misery, loneliness, and disappointment, but in an understated fashion, making the endurance of Staley's characters more apparent than on *Dirt*. The thematic unity and consistent visceral impact *Alice in Chains* lacks in comparison to that album are more than made up for by songs like "Grind," "Brush Away," "Over Now," and the ballad "Heaven Beside You," which are easily among the band's best work. *—Steve Huey*

Unplugged / Jul. 1996 / Sony ✦✦✦
Between the end of 1993 and a performance for "MTV Unplugged" in the spring of 1996, Alice in Chains performed no concerts; they didn't even support the release of their eponymous third album with a minor tour. There's a variety of reasons for their inactivity—primarily it's due to the health of certain members—but the lack of concerts made the *Unplugged* performance seem special. During the concert, Alice in Chains drew from their three albums and two EPs, offering new, more reflective arrangements of harder songs like "Would?" and virtually recreating the original versions of "Got Me Wrong" and "No Excuses."

Throughout the album, the group sounds tight and professional; on the basis of this performance, it's hard to believe that they hadn't played together for nearly three years, but it doesn't offer anything that the albums don't already. The acoustic arrangements of the harder songs sound like novelties, and the rest sound like rehashes of their previous work, only without much energy. Again, it's a case of an *Unplugged* album that is designed for the band's core audience, which makes it a fairly entertaining effort that is essentially just an official bootleg. *—Stephen Thomas Erlewine*

Davie Allan

b. United States
Psychedelic, Film Music, Hot Rod
Providing the soundtrack to numerous biker and teen exploitation movies in the mid- and late '60s, Davie Allan & the Arrows bridged the surf and psychedelic eras. Their driving, basic instrumentals featured loads and loads of fuzz guitar, as well as generous dollops of tremulo bar waggling and wah-wah. The guitarist and his band first made their mark with the minor hit "Apache '65," a version of the Shadows/Jorgen Ingmann instrumental classic "Apache." Hooking up with notorious exploitation movie producer Mike Curb, the Arrows provided the soundtracks to numerous B-movies on the Tower and Sidewalk labels; their greatest success, "Blues Theme" (from *The Wild Angels*, starring Peter Fonda), made the Top 40 in 1967. When Curb abandoned racy movies for the Osmonds and purging MGM Records of its psychedelic acts, the Arrows' flight was over. *—Richie Unterberger*

● **King Fuzz** / 199? / Fuzzwalk ✦✦✦✦
The only compilation of Allan's numerous '60s recordings, condensing the highlights of his 1965-67 soundtracks, albums, and B-sides into 15 songs. For all but specialists, "Blues Theme" is all you need. The guitar pyrotechnics are occasionally impressive, but the repetitive fuzz-psychedelic riffs are numbing over the course of an entire LP. *—Richie Unterberger*

Lee Allen

b. Jul. 2, 1926, Sewanee, TN, **d.** Oct. 18, 1994, Los Angeles, CA
Saxophone / R&B, New Orleans R&B
The blasting tenor saxophone of Lee Allen was every bit as integral a factor in the sizzling sound of '50s New Orleans R&B as were the well-documented contributions of Fats Domino, Lloyd Price, and Little Richard. As a key member of the studio band at Cosimo's, Allen played searing solos that sparked hundreds of Crescent City classics. Allen's wallpaper-peeling sax solos are instantly identifiable—check out Richard's "Slippin' and Slidin'" and "Tutti Frutti" for irrefutably exciting evidence.

But despite his sax mastery, Allen failed to sustain a brief solo career. Signing with Al Silver's New York-based Ember label, he managed one decent-sized hit in 1958, the rocking instrumental "Walkin' with Mr. Lee," while the second-line scorcher "Boppin' at the Hop" inexplicably never received any national airplay.

When the New Orleans sound shifted to a funkier beat, Allen's muscular sound fell out of favor on the local recording scene. Nevertheless, Allen remained active until his death in 1994, touring extensively with Domino, as well as working with a variety of young rockers (including the Blasters) who revered his blistering sound. *—Bill Dahl*

● **Walkin' with Mr. Lee** / 1958 / Collectables ✦✦✦✦
The only solo album of New Orleans' leading tenor sax man during the '50s, this has some hot-rockin' instrumentals. *—Bill Dahl*

The Allman Brothers Band

f. 1969, Macon, GA
Blues-Rock, Southern Rock
The Allman Brothers Band was the major instigator of the Southern rock genre of the '70s and one of the major rock acts of the first half of that decade; it continues to be popular. In its original configuration, the group consisted of Duane Allman (b. Nov 20, 1946–d. Oct 29, 1971) on guitar; Gregg Allman (b. Dec 8, 1947) on organ and vocals; Dickey Betts (b. Dec 12, 1943) on guitar and vocals; Berry Oakley (b. Apr 4, 1948–d. Nov 11, 1971) on bass; and Butch Trucks and Jaimo (born John Lee Johnson, July 8, 1944) on drums. This sextet was a showcase for the twin-guitar work of Duane Allman and Dickey Betts and for the bluesy singing of Gregg Allman. It cut three albums between 1969 and 1971. *Live at the Fillmore East*, the Allmans' breakthrough third album, went gold four days before bandleader Duane Allman was killed in a motorcycle accident. The group continued as a quintet, finishing its fourth album, *Eat a Peach* (1972), which was a major success. After bassist Oakley was killed in a motorcycle accident, the group was augmented with bassist Lamar Williams (b. 1947–d. Jan 1983) and pianist Chuck Leavell to complete its fifth album, *Brothers and Sisters*, which topped the charts and spawned the No. 2 single "Ramblin' Man." The group split

up in acrimony after the release of *Win, Lose or Draw* in 1975.

The Allmans re-formed in 1978, this time returning to the sextet format, with Allman, Betts, Trucks, and Jaimo being joined by guitarist Dan Toler and bassist David Goldflies for the gold-selling *Enlightened Rogues* (1979). Two more albums, *Reach for the Sky* and *Brothers of the Road* (for which David Toler replaced Jaimo and Mike Lawler was added on piano), were released before the band split again.

After the release of a boxed-set retrospective, *Dreams*, in 1989, the Allmans again re-formed, with Warren Haynes on second lead guitar and Allen Woody on bass; to date they have released four more albums and toured extensively. — *William Ruhlmann*

The Allman Brothers Band / 1969 / Polydor ✦✦✦✦
The Allmans' aggressive synthesis of blues, rock, jazz, and gospel made an impressive entrance on this 1969 debut, with soon-to-be-standards like "Whipping Post" and the dynamic, moody "Dreams." Highlights like "Don't Want You No More," "It's Not My Cross to Bear," "Black Hearted Woman," and "Trouble No More" are further reasons why this was one of the greatest bands ever to emerge from the American South. — *Rick Clark*

Idlewild South / 1970 / Polydor ✦✦✦✦
The Allmans' second effort may not have been quite as strong as their powerful debut, but *Idlewild South* had more than a handful of gems with songs like the celebratory "Revival," the earthy "Midnight Rider," and the instrumental "In Memory of Elizabeth Reed," with its soaring twin-guitar counterpuntal melodies. — *Rick Clark*

☆ **Live at Fillmore East** / Mar. 1971 / Polydor ✦✦✦✦✦
The double-disc *Allman Brothers Band at Fillmore East* is one of rock's greatest live albums, featuring amazing interplay within highly dynamic arrangements. Most of the tracks exceed ten minutes, but the Allmans never stumble. "Hot 'lanta," "In Memory of Elizabeth Reed," and "Statesboro Blues" are highlights. Contrary to claims that these are untouched performances, *Fillmore East* actually was a skillfully edited document (courtesy of producer Tom Dowd) taken from a run of shows at Bill Graham's Fillmore. — *Rick Clark*

★ **Eat a Peach** / 1972 / Polydor ✦✦✦✦✦
Half of *Eat a Peach* consists of more fiery improvisations from the *Live at Fillmore* dates, in the form of the "Mountain Jam." Even though this was released after Duane Allman's fatal motorcycle accident, the studio sides include some tracks showcasing his soaring lead work. Creatively, the band was in peak form with great tracks like "Ain't Wastin' Time No More," "Melissa," "One Way Out," "Stand Back," "Blue Sky," and the delicate acoustic guitar instrumental "Little Martha." — *Rick Clark*

Brothers and Sisters / 1973 / Polydor ✦✦✦✦
In spite of the inclusion of Dickey Betts' "Ramblin' Man" and "Jessica," *Brothers and Sisters* is a noticeable comedown from the previous four albums. Muddy production doesn't help matters, either. — *Rick Clark*

Beginnings / 1973 / Polydor ✦✦✦✦
Beginnings is nothing more than the first two albums on a single disc. Since its release, Polygram has done a markedly improved remastering job, releasing each album separately. — *Rick Clark*

Win, Lose or Draw / 1975 / Polydor ✦✦
The Allman Brothers' sixth album was their final new studio effort before their first breakup, in 1976. It featured the minor hit singles "Nevertheless" and "Louisiana Lou and Three Card Monty John" and was a Top Five, gold-selling release, but that was just on momentum. In fact, it's a tired effort by a highly competent band that's going through the motions and repeating itself. — *William Ruhlmann*

Wipe the Windows, Check the Oil, Dollar Gas / 1976 / Polydor ✦✦✦
By the time this, the Allmans' second live album, was released in the fall of 1976, the band had suffered what appeared to be an irrevocable split, which cast a pall over the record and made it their lowest charting since their debut. In retrospect, it's an appealing effort, chronicling the version of the band that existed from the death of Berry Oakley to the first breakup (a one-guitar, two-keyboards lineup) and featuring concert versions of some of the better material from *Eat a Peach* and *Brothers and Sisters*. — *William Ruhlmann*

Enlightened Rogues / 1979 / Polydor ✦✦✦
After six years of spotty albums, the Allmans made a strong comeback with this Tom Dowd-produced effort. Gregg Allman is in fine voice, and the band kicks up some sparks throughout. Some of the material is a little weak, but "Crazy Love," a duet by Bonnie Bramlett and Dickie Betts, is a highlight. — *Rick Clark*

Reach for the Sky / 1980 / Arista ✦✦
The second album from *Allmans Mach Two* shows them holding their own, wearing their influences (especially gospel) a bit more on their sleeves, and even coming up with a minor single in "Angeline." — *William Ruhlmann*

Brothers of the Road / 1981 / Arista ✦✦
"Straight from the Heart" (No.39), written by Dickey Betts and Johnny

Cobb and sung by Gregg Allman, is one of the group's better accommodations to pop music, and on the whole, this is an accessible version of their trademark sound: call it Allmans Lite. The ruling influence here may be Arista president Clive Davis, who also oversaw the pop-oriented Grateful Dead albums of the same period. But the main duty of pop music is to sell, and when this album petered out at No. 44, the Allmans called it quits for the second time. — *William Ruhlmann*

Dreams / Jun. 1989 / Polydor ✦✦✦✦
This is a thoughtfully compiled box set, containing highlights throughout the Allman Brothers' entire career, as well as solo projects and early pre-Allman recordings. A booklet with generous annotation and photos is provided. The remastering is a noticeable improvement over initial CD releases of the Allman catalog. If you've got the bucks for a box set, this is a worthwhile acquisition for completists and those looking for a comprehensive introduction. — *Rick Clark*

Seven Turns / Oct. 1990 / Epic ✦✦✦✦
After a nine-year absence, the Allmans return with a vengeance on *Seven Turns*, with tracks like the hard-swinging opener "Good Clean Fun" and the powerful blues-rock workout "Gambler's Roll." The Dickey Betts-penned title track, a mystical take on life, is the album's spiritual highlight, while "True Gravity" is the musical peak, ranking with "In Memory of Elizabeth Reed" as one of the band's best instrumentals. Overall, *Seven Turns* is their strongest album since 1972's *Eat a Peach*. — *Rick Clark*

Live at Ludlow Garage: 1970 / 1991 / Polydor ✦✦✦✦
It's no *Fillmore East*, of course, but this archival release does present the classic lineup of the Allmans at their near-peak, and fans will be pleased to have more Duane on disc. — *William Ruhlmann*

Shades of Two Worlds / Jul. 1991 / Epic ✦✦✦
Weaker than *Seven Turns*, *Shades of Two Worlds* still has its moments, particularly the extended rave-up "Kind of Bird." "Bad Rain" and "Nobody Knows" are two other highlights. — *Rick Clark*

Decade of Hits 1969-1979 / Oct. 1991 / Polydor ✦✦✦✦
Decade of Hits 1969-1979 collects highlights from the Allman Brothers' first decade of existence and features many of their best-known songs; it provides a solid introduction to the definitive Southern rock band. — *Stephen Thomas Erlewine*

Evening with the Allman Brothers Band / Mar. 1992 / Epic ✦✦✦
Given that they scored their big breakthrough with *Fillmore East* and that their career has been based on concert work, it's surprising that the Allmans have released so few live albums. This one finds them in vintage form, playing extended versions of both recent tunes and old favorites. A second-set album was intended, but presumably it was cancelled after this record sold poorly. — *William Ruhlmann*

The Fillmore Concerts / Oct. 20, 1992 / Polydor ✦✦✦✦
Fillmore Concerts is an expanded version of the classic *Fillmore East*, featuring several songs that didn't make the original album, re-edited tracks that now run at their original length, and sterling remastered sound; for hardcore fans, it's the ultimate version of this landmark set. — *Stephen Thomas Erlewine*

Where It All Begins / May 3, 1994 / Epic ✦✦✦
Twenty-five years after their debut album, the Allman Brothers continue to make records in the same basic style, alternating Gregg Allman's bluesy (and increasingly craggy) vocals against Dickey Betts' more country-tinged ones and relying on extended song structures that leave plenty of room for high-pitched, melodic guitar runs by Betts and his current partner, Warren Haynes. There are no classics here, but this is a respectable recreation of Allman standard fare (much of it sounds familiar the first time you listen), which is why it is selling to their fan base and no one else. — *William Ruhlmann*

Marc Almond

b. Jul. 9, 1959, Southport, England
Vocals / Dance-Pop, New Wave, New Romantic, Synth-Pop

After disbanding Soft Cell, vocalist Marc Almond pursued a solo career that followed the same vaguely sleazy, electronic dance-pop his former group had made popular. Almond's strength was never his personality—his voice tends to waver around the notes instead of hitting them—it was the atmosphere he created with the synths and drum machines. Underneath all of the electronics and disco rhythms, Almond hearkened back to the days of cabaret singers, updating it with that sound for dance clubs of the '80s.

Before he properly started a solo career, Marc Almond formed Marc and the Mambas, a loose congregation that featured Matt Johnson of The The and Annie Hogan. *"Untitled"* (1983), the group's first album, featured covers of Lou Reed, Syd Barrett, and Jacques Brel; throughout his career, Almond would cover the songs of Brel, which he had learned from the records of Scott Walker. Like Walker, Almond used Brel's heavily orchestrated compositions and social ruminations as a starting point, both musically and lyrically—Almond added a self-conscious element of camp with his Euro-disco and occasionally sleazy lyrics. *Torment and Toreros* (1983), Marc and the Mambas' second album, explored this path in more detail than *"Untitled,"* only to an orchestral background. After its release, the group broke up.

Almond formed the backing group the Willing Sinners in 1984, releasing *Vermin in Ermine* in 1984. Almond began to hit his stride with this album, which fulfilled most of his campy cabaret fantasies. *Stories of Johnny*, released the following year, was more cohesive, spawning a British hit with the title song. Even though he maintained a cult following in England and various parts of Europe, his records were not being released in the US.

In 1987 Almond released *Mother Fist ... and Her Five Daughters*, his first proper solo album and his bleakest work to date; a compilation, *Singles 1984-1987*, appeared the same year. *Stars We Are*, released the following year, was a brighter, more welcoming album that revived his commercial career. In addition to a duet with Nico on "Your Kisses Burn," Almond duetted with Gene Pitney on Pitney's own "Something's Gotten Hold of My Heart," which became a No. 1 single. *Stars We Are* also became his first album released in the US since Soft Cell.

Almond followed the success of *The Stars We Are* in 1990 with the pet project *Jacques*, a collection of Brel songs. That same year he released *Enchanted*, which was more successful than *Jacques*, but it didn't reach the heights of *Stars We Are*. In 1991 he released *The Tenement Symphony* and in 1993 a live album entitled *Twelve Years of Tears* appeared. Two years later, *Treasure Box* was released. *—Stephen Thomas Erlewine*

● **Singles: 1984-1987** / 1987 / Some Bizarre ◆◆◆◆
Singles: 1984-1987 is a fine compilation of hits Marc Almond had immediately after the disbandment of Soft Cell, featuring such Almond classics as "The House is Haunted," "Stories of Johnny," and "Mother Fist." *—Stephen Thomas Erlewine*

Memorabilia / 1991 / Mercury ◆◆◆◆
Memorabilia is a fine, but far from perfect, overview of Marc Almond's entire career, from Soft Cell to his solo recordings. Concentrating primarily on accessible, pop-oriented material, the collection overlooks some of his most ambitious material, but that makes the record a good introduction for the curious. However, be forewarned that Almond re-cut the vocals for three Soft Cell songs, including the hit "Tainted Love" and the title track, for this compilation, thereby lessening the value of the record in the eyes of most casual fans, since these are not the familiar versions. *—Stephen Thomas Erlewine*

ALT

f. 1993, Dublin, Ireland
Folk-Rock
ALT is a side project (and supergroup of sorts) consisting of Andy White, Liam O Maonlai (Hothouse Flowers), and Tim Finn (ex-Split Enz); the name comes from the first letters of each of their first names. In 1993 the three began writing together informally in Dublin; one of the songs, "Many's the Time (in Dublin)," appeared on Finn's 1993 album, *Before & After*. In June 1994 they reconvened in Finn's Melbourne-based Periscope Studios, where they recorded their debut album, *Altitude*. *Altitude* was released by EMI-Australia in 1995 and in the US on Cooking Vinyl. *—Chris Woodstra*

Bootleg / 1995 / ALT Recordings ◆◆◆◆
This band-released official bootleg captures the group in an intimate live setting during their first tour of Australia and New Zealand. The band really can't be considered "tight" in the traditional musical sense, but that's not the point anyway—this is the work of a tight group of friends having fun with informal sing-alongs. In many ways, *Bootleg* is a stronger album than the proper release—wonderfully sloppy despite the fact that they know the songs better at this point, but probably capturing the spirit of the project better. Most of the songs from *Altitude* are performed, as well as "Many's the Time," the song from Tim Finn's *Before and After* which documents the band's formation, and the ever-charming Tim Finn's between-song stage banter is simply priceless. *—Chris Woodstra*

Bootleg / 1995 / ALT Recordings ◆◆◆◆
This band-released official bootleg captures the group in an intimate live setting during their first tour of Australia and New Zealand. The band really can't be considered "tight" in the traditional musical sense, but that's not the point anyway—this is the work of a tight group of friends having fun with informal sing-alongs. In many ways, *Bootleg* is a stronger album than the proper release—wonderfully sloppy despite the fact that they know the songs better at this point, but probably capturing the spirit of the project better. Most of the songs from *Altitude* are performed, as well as "Many's the Time," the song from Tim Finn's *Before and After* which documents the band's formation, and the ever-charming Tim Finn's between-song stage banter is simply priceless. *—Chris Woodstra*

● **Altitude** / Oct. 24, 1995 / ALT/Cooking Vinyl ◆◆◆◆
ALT is a side project of Andy White, Liam O'Maonlai (Hothouse Flowers), and Tim Finn (ex-Split Enz, Crowded House). *Altitude* represents the trio's post-pub jamming with the predictable result of an informal, at times sloppy, album filled with seemingly unfinished songs. While fans of the individual members may be put off by these qualities, there is a spirit to these sessions that not only overcomes the shortcomings in content but gives the record a rare warmth and charm. *—Chris Woodstra*

Altered Images

f. 1979, London, England, **db.** 1984
New Wave, Power Pop
Altered Images was a British power-pop group formed in 1979 and led by film actress Claire Grogan. The group lasted until 1984, their biggest success coming with the UK Top Three hit "Happy Birthday" in 1981. *— William Ruhlmann*

Happy Birthday / 1981 / Portrait ◆◆◆◆
The album *Happy Birthday* bears little resemblance to the cute and bubbly new wave pop of the title track for which they're best remembered. Instead of capitalizing on the brightness of the obvious hit single, producer Steve Severinson (of Siouxsie & the Banshees) pushed the band into moodier post-punk territory with minimalist arrangements and simple, driving rhythms. Clair Grogan's little-girl voice was probably better suited for pop, but the combination of the two extremes is certainly interesting, if not as fun and engaging as "Happy Birthday." *—Chris Woodstra*

Pinky Blue / 1982 / Portrait ◆◆
The band's follow-up is a slicker, though less interesting, affair. "I Could Be Happy" and "See Those Eyes" show that they can still pull off a couple of catchy singles, but a cover of Neil Diamond's "Song Sung Blue" is certainly a mistake. *—Chris Woodstra*

Bite / 1983 / Portrait ◆◆
Hopelessly out-of-touch and past her prime, Grogan takes on a more mature and sophisticated pose (as revealed on the album cover) and takes a stab at dance-pop. The results, of course, are uninteresting, with the exception of the single "Don't Talk to Me About Love," a UK Top Ten. *—Chris Woodstra*

● **I Could Be Happy: Best of Altered Images** / Apr. 22, 1997 / Sony ◆◆◆◆
I Could Be Happy: The Best of Altered Images is an excellent, thorough collection covering all of the highlights from the band's three albums, adding several non-LP singles for good measure. All of the group's hits—"Happy Birthday," "I Could Be Happy," "See Those Eyes," "Love and Kisses"—are presented, usually in their single versions, plus many fine album tracks, making *I Could Be Happy* a definitive retrospective. *— Stephen Thomas Erlewine*

Alternative TV

f. 1976, London, England
Punk, New Wave
Although a part (albeit a small part) of the early English punk-rock scene, Alternative TV is probably best known for the scabrous fanzine (*Sniffin' Glue*) published by lead singer Mark Perry (aka Mark P). Perry's 'zine embodied punk's tear-it-down ethos with a wonderfully petulant and sarcastic attitude, a fact that makes his transition to punk musician such a profound disappointment. Ironically, Perry's band turned out to be far less interesting than his mimeographed fanzine. Daringly attempting to add the space-rock influences of Can and the satirical art-rock damage of Frank Zappa to the primarily faster and louder punk zeitgeist, Perry fell from grace with a resounding thud. The music meandered, the lyrics sounded painfully overwritten and narcissistic, and Perry's tuneless "singing" didn't help at all. Oddly enough, Alternative TV did produce some worthwhile music and had a long career for a band so conspicuously lacking in talent. (Perry led a version of this band until 1990.) From 1979-1980, Perry led an equally mediocre band called the Good Missionaries, who had the good sense to call it a career after one record. *—John Dougan*

● **Splitting in 2** / 1989 / Anagram ◆◆◆◆
A handful of tracks from the first album and some outtakes and unreleased stuff make up the only consistently listenable album in the surprisingly large Alternative TV library. It's not that the irritating mannerisms aren't here, it's simply that they're more bearable; and some of the songs are, surprise, actually good. *—John Dougan*

Dave Alvin

b. 1955, Los Angeles, CA
Guitar, Vocals / Rock 'n' Roll, Rockabilly Revival, Singer-Songwriter, Roots-Rock, Americana
Former Blaster Dave Alvin has forged a singer-songwriter career since

the band's official breakup in the late '80s. He also served as temporary guitarist for X, was a member of their acoustic side project the Knitters, and formed his own all-star band, the Pleasure Barons, which at times included Mojo Nixon, Rosie Flores, and Country Dick Montana. Alvin comes from a strictly California perspective—but not that of sun and fun; rather, he is a champion of the blue-collar man. Born in 1955 in Los Angeles, Alvin is a lifelong California resident and takes his inspiration from the state's inland-scapes and his own heart. He deftly juxtaposes the hard content with sprightly rockabilly and traditional music. His 1987 Epic debut, *Romeo's Escape*, showed the promise of his writing when Dwight Yoakam later covered his "Long White Cadillac,"and X recorded "Fourth of July." That year Alvin also handled soundtrack chores for Allison Anders' first feature film, *Border Radio. Blue Blvd* (1991, Hightone) took it further on down the dusty road, while *Museum of the Heart* and *King of California* continued the thread of straight-ahead workingman's music from the Golden State. Country music also figures into the Alvin oeuvre, as he remains a devotee of Merle Haggard and Buck Owens; between records, he compiled an album of Haggard covers, *Tulare Dust*, in 1994. —*Denise Sullivan*

Every Night About This Time / 1987 / Demon ✦✦✦✦
This is Dave Alvin's solo debut, which was released initially in the UK, then picked up for US release by Epic Records, which changed the album title to *Romeo's Escape*. —*William Ruhlmann*

● **Romeo's Escape** / Dec. 1987 / Razor & Tie ✦✦✦✦
This is the quintessential California singer-songwriter album. Alvin comes out strong with "Fourth of July," "Long White Cadillac" (formerly recorded by the Blasters), along with "Every Night About This Time," and "Border Radio"— all standards in the contemporary canon. Aided by his friends and the best studio musicians available, there's nothing wrong with this record—a logical continuation of the Blasters' legacy and a stellar start on his solo career. —*Denise Sullivan*

Blue Blvd / Aug. 1991 / Hightone ✦✦✦
The only thing that mars this wonderful, rootsy singer-songwriter album is a heavy production hand and a drum sound attempting to give it a rock edge; consequently, some of the more beautiful songs like the title track suffer under the weight, but the final cut, "Dry River," is alone worth the price of the disc. Alvin's rock 'n' roll pals come out to play—Dwight Yoakam, David Hidalgo, saxophonist Lee Allen—making the record essential for anyone interested in the state of California roots music in the early '90s. —*Denise Sullivan*

Museum of Heart / Sep. 20, 1993 / Hightone ✦✦✦
Alvin's vision falters slightly, as none of the songs here is as instantly likable or classic as on previous outings. Perhaps stunted by more than half of the songs' being co-writes ("Between the Cracks" with Tom Russell), Alvin's normally clear and simple approach is muddled, but the instrumentation is flawless; and his regular all-star cast (John Doe, Syd Straw and Katy Moffatt) is present. —*Denise Sullivan*

King of California / May 1, 1994 / Hightone ✦✦✦
Dave Alvin makes an "unplugged" album, reprising many of his familiar tunes—"Fourth of July," "Every Night About This Time," and "Border Radio" among them—in an acoustic setting that wouldn't be foreign to Woody Guthrie. Neither would the lower class portraits of struggle that are Alvin's metier. The songs stand up well in this relatively unadorned, becalmed setting; in fact, some are even more poignant. —*William Ruhlmann*

Interstate City / Jul. 1996 / Hightone ✦✦✦✦
Recorded at the Continental Club in Austin, TX, with his backup band, the Guilty Men, *Interstate City* documents the nervy energy and gritty sound of Dave Alvin live in concert. Alvin tears through his back catalog with surprising gusto, touching on both the Blasters and his solo hits. Most enticing for fans, however, are the new songs he works into the set. Most of the newer numbers are on par with his finest material, and they are delivered with an intoxicating rush. *Interstate City* is one of the rare live albums that actually improves on the original recordings. —*Thom Owens*

Amazing Blondel

f. 1969, England
Art-Rock/Progressive-Rock
One of England's most unusual rock outfits of the 1970s, Amazing Blondel was a trio whose members played instruments dating from medieval to Elizabethan times, and songs styled to those periods. Named for Richard the Lionhearted's legendary favorite minstrel, Amazing Blondel consisted of three musicians from Scunthorpe, England: John David Gladwin (lute, oboe, cittern, double bass), Terry Wincott (pipe organ, harmonium, cittern, recorders, flute, crumhorn, tabor pipe, ocarina, guitar), and Edward Baird (guitar, guitern, percussion). Gladwin and Wincott founded the group as a duo after the breakup of the band Methuselah, of which both had been members. They'd wearied of playing shows where the instruments were so loud it was impossible to hear

themselves singing, and, as their acoustic set had gone over well with audiences, the duo moved in that direction. In 1970, with help from several musicians, including legendary British guitarist Big Jim Sullivan, they recorded an album entitled *Amazing Blondel*. By that time, Baird had joined Gladwin and Wincott to make a trio. Their first album was a collection of soft acoustic rock numbers that included one medieval-styled song that seemed to go over better than anything else, and that was the direction they aimed for in their future releases. Soon after, they were signed to Island Records and began refining their sound, both on stage and in the studio.

The trio became known for playing upwards of 40 instruments on stage, though without backup musicians—each song was simply planned for no more than three instruments at any one time. Although Gladwin and company were the first to admit that they were no virtuosos on their chosen instruments, their work sounded credible to modern ears, and their shows were fun despite the delicacy of the array of instruments, which required as much as five hours to get into tune; unlike most rock acts of the era, if they couldn't get them into tune, the group didn't perform.

Despite their reliance on acoustic instruments, the trio wasn't averse to composing extended suites that ran up to 25 minutes, and while some of the music had a repetitive quality, the best of it played off of achingly beautiful melodies. *England*, released in 1972, was the high point for the trio and got them their heaviest airplay to date in America if only modest sales. Gladwin left soon after its release, however, and the Amazing Blondel were reduced to a duo for their follow-up, *Blondel* (1973). It marked the last of their "period" material. On subsequent albums, beginning with *Mulgrave Street*, the group—supported by various rock musicians, including Mick Ralphs, Paul Rogers, and Steve Winwood—would aim for a harder, more contemporary sound vaguely resembling Steeleye Span. None of the records would succeed much outside of England, though they ultimately did record a live album in Japan. —*Bruce Eder*

Amazing Blondel / 1970 / Edsel ✦✦
The group's first album, recorded as a duo backed by top British session men Big Jim Sullivan and Clem Cattini. The sound is generally more mainstream rock (there are even a sitar and tabla noodling around on one track), a lot less elegant and a lot bluesier (especially "You Don't Want My Love") than anything they were later known for, and with horns (of the local marching band variety) around as well. The antique-style tracks ("Saxon Lady," "Season of the Year," "Shepherd's Song") worked best, and became the basis for what followed. This is the only Edsel reissue of the group's albums that has any sonic deficiencies; there's a little noise, owing to the fact that the master tapes are lost. Terry Wincott's notes are a welcome addition. —*Bruce Eder*

Evensong / 1970 / Edsel ✦✦✦
The trio's first fully realized album, a self-consciously archaic work built around medieval balladry and madrigals, and performed on period instruments. The group doesn't sound entirely at ease working in this style, but the crisp, folklike feel and the timbre and singing have great charm. The strongest songs are those such as "Willowood," closest to the group members' own experiences and dealing with Kent, from which they all hailed. The 1996 Edsel CD reissue contains new notes by the original group members and is very finely remastered. —*Bruce Eder*

Fantasia Lindum / 1971 / Island ✦✦✦✦
The concept album rears its head—and rears back about 500 years. While other progressive rock groups were doing album-length suites dealing with apocalyptic themes, Amazing Blondel was doing 20-minute-long multi-part pieces ("fantasia" is the best classical music term) about Kent, England, and songs depicting idealized love between men and women, man and nature, and man and God. It all plays a little like the Strawbs' work of this same era without the sardonic edge, and it is all achingly beautiful. The 1996 CD reissue is especially pleasing for eliminating the problem of surface noise that afflicted most copies of the original LP. —*Bruce Eder*

● **England** / 1972 / Island ✦✦✦✦
The group's best album, and their last as a trio, is a lyrical, gentle, yet very ambitious expansion of their sound into a richer vein, with a wider range of instrumentation, extending their basic medieval instruments and psychedelic effects. The mix radiates a compelling beauty that makes this record linger long in the memory. The sound is very elegant, but this time out the timing and editing are perfect. The 1997 compact disc reissue, a terrific-sounding transfer, recreates the original British album's packaging, complete with the lyrics and original photos. —*Bruce Eder*

Blondel / 1973 / Edsel ✦✦✦
The group—reduced to a duo—in its swan song for Island Records. The album lacks the panache of their previous albums, although it has a smoothness that makes each track a very easy listen. The antique sensibilities are beginning to give way to more modern songwriting techniques. —*Bruce Eder*

Mulgrave Street / 1974 / DJM ✦✦
Their first album for Beatles publisher Dick James' DJM Records shows Blondel, as they were now known, moving into more of a modern electric folk-rock idiom, with help from Paul Kossoff, Mick Ralphs, Paul Rodgers, Eddie Jobson, Simon Kirke, and other British rock alumni of the early-to-middle '70s. More contemporary than their earlier work, but nowhere near as distinctive. —*Bruce Eder*

Inspiration / 1975 / DJM ✦✦✦
A further effort at rocking up the folky sound, and so successful at it that one had to wonder why stick with the name or the image at all? —*Bruce Eder*

Englishe Musicke / 1993 / Edsel ✦✦✦✦
English Musicke is a 16-track collection that draws from the band's three prime-period albums—*Evensong* (1970), *Fantasia Lindum* (1971), and *England* (1972). Though most progressive rock doesn't translate well on collections due to its more album-oriented concept nature, *English Musicke* shows Amazing Blondel's music in a fair light. The songs work well as self-contained pieces, and the real concept—the medieval sound—is consistent throughout, making this a nice career overview and a pretty good introduction, though the converted will undoubtedly need the albums in their entirety. —*Chris Woodstra*

Live Abroad / 1996 / H.T.D. ✦✦✦✦
Not only a beautiful record, but an amazing find some 24 years after the fact—a live Amazing Blondel album, 71 minutes of concert recordings made in Europe by the group during 1972 and 1973. All of the tracks were written by John David Gladwin, the composing mainstay of the group, making this a kind of live "best-of" album, comprised of the best songs off the albums *England, Fantasia Lindum* (including the latter's 20-minute title track, in an astonishingly tight performance, better than the studio recording, marred only by some minor sound distortion toward the end), and *Evensong.* "Seascape," "Dolor Dolcis" (aka "Sweet Sorrow"), "Willowood," "Spring Air," and "Landscape" are among the highlights. The group acquits itself extremely well, with impeccable harmonies and gorgeous balance to the all-acoustic instruments that would've put most other English folk-rock groups to shame. Moreover, on tracks such as "Willowood," the musicianship is quite overpowering, as Gladwin displays a virtuosity on the lute that, four centuries ago, would've made him a star in his local county. The sound is remarkably clean, and the stereo separation gives a good sense of the intimacy of the performances. The joking around on stage—especially the account of the sound of the crumhorn by Terry Wincott—presents a light side of the group that their albums seldom displayed adequately. (The botched "Shepherd's Song" opening is also pretty funny, and the performance is beguilingly boisterous.) —*Bruce Eder*

The Amazing Rhythm Aces

f. 1974, Memphis, TN, db. 1981
Country-Rock
A mainstream country-rock band similar in execution (if not commercial success) to the Eagles, the Amazing Rhythm Aces were formed in Memphis in 1974 by bassist Jeff Davis and drummer Butch McDade, who had earlier recorded and toured with the great singer-songwriter Jesse Winchester. After striking out on their own, Davis and McDade enlisted vocalist/guitarist Russell Smith, keyboardist Billy Earhart III, dobro player Barry Burton, and pianist James Hooker to develop a sound composed of equal parts pop, country and blue-eyed soul.

Stacked Deck, the Amazing Rhythm Aces debut album, appeared in 1975; it produced two significant crossover hits, "Third Rate Romance" and "Amazing Grace (Used to Be Her Favorite Song)," the group's lone Top Ten country single. A year later, the hit "The End Is Not in Sight (The Cowboy Tune)," from the LP *Too Stuffed to Jump*, won the Aces a Grammy for Country Vocal Performance by a Group. Following the release of 1977's *Toucan Do It Too*, Burton left the group and was replaced by Duncan Cameron. In 1978, the Aces released *Burning the Ballroom Down*, followed a year later by a self-titled effort featuring cameos by Joan Baez, Tracy Nelson, and the Muscle Shoals Horns; both were met with critical approval, but sold poorly. They released one final record, *How the Hell Do You Spell Rhythum*, before disbanding. While Smith went on to become a successful songwriter, Earhart joined Hank Williams, Jr.'s Bama Band, and Cameron joined Sawyer Brown—a group which, ironically enough, would find significant chart success in the 1980s with a sound similar to what the Amazing Rhythm Aces had created a decade earlier.

After a hiatus of some 15 years, the Aces reformed in 1994. The group, now comprised of Smith, Davis, McDade, Earhart, Hooker, and new guitarist/mandolinist Danny Parks, marked their return to duty by releasing *Born Again*, a collection of newly-recorded renditions of their biggest hits. They also began composing new songs for a projected comeback album. —*Jason Ankeny*

● **Stacked Deck** / 1975 / ABC ✦✦✦✦
"Amazing" is certainly the word. In addition to "Third Rate Romance,"

which has been covered by artists as diverse as Earl Scruggs and Elvis Costello (and was a hit once again on the country chart in the mid-'90s), this album features a collection of amazing tunes by an incredibly hot band that sound fresh 20 years after they were recorded. Look for the single of "Third Rate Romance," which features the non-LP "Mystery Train" on the flip side. —*Jim Worbois*

Too Stuffed to Jump / 1976 / ABC ✦✦✦
Although *Too Stuffed to Jump* isn't quite as strong a record as the debut, the album features enough good material to recommend it. Some different influences come into play on this one, like the jazzy shuffle of "Same Ole Me." And who could not hear Leon Russell in "Typical American Boy"? —*Jim Worbois*

Toucan Do It Too / 1977 / ABC ✦✦
Compared to the first album, *Toucan Do It Too* just doesn't have life or joy. Still, it's a pleasant record from the Aces, and the title track is particularly memorable. —*Jim Worbois*

Burning the Ballroom Down / 1978 / ABC ✦✦✦
This record is a bit more focused than the last and, for that reason, stands up a bit better over time. With the song "I Pity the Mother and Father," Smith explores territory not often examined in popular music; it will speak to anyone with kids who are growing up way too fast. —*Jim Worbois*

The Amazing Rhythm Aces / 1978 / Columbia ✦✦✦
By 1979 the Aces' recording career was winding down, and their label folded. As a result, this record was released on both ABC and Columbia, with the only difference being the picture on the back cover. This album also saw the departure of guitarist/producer Barry Burton. Whatever the causes, this is their strongest album in some time. —*Jim Worbois*

How the Hell Do You Spell Rhythm? / 1980 / Warner Brothers ✦✦
The band goes out in tighter-than-tight style, covering "Further On down the Road," Delbert McClinton's "Object of My Affection," and Van Morrison's "Wild Night" and introducing the original version of "Big Ole Brew." —*Kit Kiefer*

Ambrosia

f. 1971, Los Angeles, CA, db. 1982
Art-Rock/Progressive-Rock, Soft Rock, Pop-Rock
Los Angeles quartet Ambrosia, whose founding members included guitarist/vocalist David Pack, bassist/vocalist Joe Puerta, keyboardist Christopher North, and drummer Burleigh Drummond, fused symphonic art rock with a slickly produced pop sound. The group was discovered in 1971 by Los Angeles Philharmonic conductor Zubin Mehta, who featured Ambrosia as part of a so-called All-American Dream Concert. However, it took them four more years to get a record contract; *Ambrosia* was released in 1975 and spawned the chart singles "Holdin' on to Yesterday" and "Nice, Nice, Very Nice." The latter was based on Kurt Vonnegut, Jr.'s *Cat's Cradle*. Ambrosia scored another hit in 1977 with a cover of the Beatles' "Magical Mystery Tour" from the film *All This and World War II*, in which they also appeared.

North left the group just before their biggest pop breakthrough in 1978 with the No. 3 hit "How Much I Feel." Ambrosia followed this success in 1980 with another No. 3 hit, "Biggest Part of Me," and the No. 13 follow-up "You're the Only Woman." Their next album failed, ending their run of chart success, and the group broke up; individual members are still active as session musicians and vocalists, as well as producers. —*Steve Huey*

Ambrosia / 1975 / 20th Century ✦✦✦✦
A wonderful debut album, that was engineered by Alan Parsons. Top-notch mid-'70s art rock, with great musicianship, it features "Holdin' On to Yesterday" and "Nice, Nice, Very Nice." —*Scott Bultman*

Somewhere I've Never Travelled / 1976 / Warner Brothers ✦✦✦
Their second album is more in the symphonic realm but just as good as their debut. —*Scott Bultman*

Life Beyond L.A. / 1978 / Warner Brothers ✦✦

One Eighty / 1980 / Warner Brothers ✦✦✦
It contains their biggest pop hits, "Biggest Part of Me" and "You're the Only Woman." —*Scott Bultman*

Road Island / 1982 / Warner Brothers ✦✦

● **Anthology** / May 20, 1997 / Warner Brothers ✦✦✦✦
For various legal reasons, no Ambrosia recordings were released on compact disc in America until 1997's *Anthology*, and while it's an imperfect collection, it does offer a reasonably thorough overview of the group's career. It only briefly touches on the band's early art-rock records, choosing to concentrate instead on their early '80s soft-rock hits like "Biggest Part of Me," "You're the Only Woman," and "How Much I Feel." As a result, dedicated prog-rock fans will find this collection inadequate, but for most casual listeners, it will contain everything they need and then some, since the disc is padded with three new songs that are pleasant but unremarkable. —*Stephen Thomas Erlewine*

America

f. 1967, London, England
Soft Rock, Pop-Rock

America was a light folk-rock act of the early '70s who had several Top Ten hits, including the No. 1s "A Horse with No Name" and "Sister Golden Hair." Vocalists/guitarists Dewey Bunnell, Dan Peak, and Gerry Beckley met while they were still in high school in the late '60s; all three were sons of US Air Force officers who were stationed in the UK. After they completed school in 1970, they formed an acoustic folk-rock quartet called Daze in London, which was soon pared down to the trio of Bunnell, Peak, and Beckley. Adopting the name America, the group landed a contract with Jeff Dexter, a promoter for the Roundhouse concert venue. Dexter had America open for several major artists, and the group soon signed with Warner Bros. Records. By the fall of 1970 the group was recording their debut album in London, with producers Ian Samwell and Jeff Dexter.

"A Horse with No Name," America's debut single, was released at the end of 1971. In January 1972, the song—which strongly recalled the acoustic numbers of Neil Young—became a No. 3 hit in the UK. The group's self-titled debut album followed the same stylistic pattern and became a hit as well, peaking at No. 14. After their British success, America returned to North America, beginning a supporting tour for the Everly Brothers. "A Horse with No Name" was released in the US that spring, where it soon became a No. 1 single, pushing Neil Young's "Heart of Gold" off the top of the charts; *America* followed the single to the top of the charts. "I Need You" became another Top Ten hit that summer, and the group began work on its second album with the Beatles' producer George Martin. "Ventura Highway," the first single released from this collaboration, became their third straight Top Ten hit in December of 1972. In the beginning of 1973, America won the Grammy award for Best New Artist of 1972.

Homecoming was released in January 1973, becoming a Top Ten hit in the US and peaking at No. 21 in the UK. Under Martin's direction, America's essential sound didn't change, it just became more polished. However, the hits stopped coming fairly soon—they had only one minor Top 40 hit in 1973. *Hat Trick*, the group's third album, was released toward the end of 1973; it failed to make it past No. 28 on the American charts. Released in the late fall of 1974, *Holiday* was the third record the group made with George Martin. *Holiday* returned America to the top of the charts, peaking at No. 3 and launching the hit singles "Tin Man" and "Lonely People." "Sister Golden Hair," pulled from 1975's *Hearts*, became their second No. 1 single. That same year the group released *History/America's Greatest Hits*, which would eventually sell over four million copies.

Although America's 1976 effort *Hideaway* went gold and peaked at No. 11, the group's audience was beginning to decline. At the end of 1976, Dan Peek left the group, deciding to become a Contemporary Christian recording artist. The group continued as a duo, releasing *Harbor* to a lukewarm reception. America's last Martin-produced record, *Silent Letter*, was released in 1979 to little attention. America returned to the Top Ten in 1982 with "You Can Do Magic," an adult-contemporary pop number that featured synthesizers along with their trademark harmonies. "The Border" became their last Top 40 hit in 1983, peaking at No. 33. America released their last album, *America in Concert*, in the summer of 1985. The group has continued to tour successfully into the '90s. *—Stephen Thomas Erlewine*

● **History: Greatest Hits** / 1975 / Warner Brothers ◆◆◆◆
A nice roundup of their peak years (1971-1975), it includes tracks like "A Horse with No Name," "I Need You," "Ventura Highway," "Tin Man," "Lonely People," "Sister Golden Hair," and more. *—Dan Heilman*

● **Encore: More Greatest Hits** / Jul. 1991 / Rhino ◆◆◆◆
This follow-up to their *Greatest Hits* contains "The Border," "Right Before Your Eyes," "Today's the Day," and "You Can Do Magic." The rest of the tracks are album sides or previously unreleased material. *—AMG*

American Flyer

f. United States
Country-Rock, Pop-Rock

American Flyer was a 1970s folk-rock quartet made up of former members of other groups: Craig Fuller was from Pure Prairie League, Eric Kaz had been a member of Blues Magoos, Steve Katz was in Blood, Sweat & Tears, and Doug Yule had played in the Velvet Underground. Together they charted with two albums on United Artists in the mid-'70s. *—William Ruhlmann*

● **American Flyer** / 1976 / United Artists ◆◆◆◆
American Flyer deserved better. Eric Kaz had written great love songs for Linda Ronstadt and Bonnie Raitt, and Craig Fuller was coming off his Top 40 hit "Amie" with Pure Prairie League. As it happened, Steve Katz's "Back In '57" turned out to be one of the album's highlights, but "Let Me Down Easy," by Kaz and Fuller, was a minor hit, and there was

also Kaz's classic co-composition, "Love Has No Pride." But those were just the cream of an excellent set produced by George Martin. Add it all up, and it should have meant more than a chart peak in the lower reaches of the Top 100, an early indication that, for whatever reasons, American Flyer was not destined to become the next Crosby, Stills, Nash & Young. *—William Ruhlmann*

● **Spirit of a Woman** / 1977 / United Artists ◆◆
Maybe there was room for only one really successful country-folk-rock group with good songs and strong harmonies in the mid-'70s, and the job had already been taken by the Eagles. Who knows? American Flyer's second and final album didn't have as many great songs as the debut, and some of them were swamped by strings, but it was a pleasant work, notably featuring a version of Eric Kaz's "I'm Blowin' Away," which Bonnie Raitt had covered a couple of years earlier. *—William Ruhlmann*

American Music Club

f. 1983, San Francisco, CA, **db.** 1995
Alternative Pop-Rock, Folk-Rock, Singer-Songwriter, Indie-Rock

Although chosen for its deliberately nondescript qualities, in retrospect the name American Music Club was the perfect moniker for the lauded San Francisco-based band led by singer-songwriter Mark Eitzel: over the course of seven acclaimed albums, the group tied together the disparate strands of the American musical fabric—rock, folk, country, punk, even lounge schmaltz—into a remarkably distinct and riveting whole, creating a brilliant and cohesive body of work dappled by moments of haunting beauty and impenetrable darkness.

Although born in California, Eitzel spent his formative years in Great Britain and Ohio before returning to the Bay Area in 1980 with the punk band the Naked Skinnies. After the band's break-up, he founded American Music Club in 1983 with guitarist Vudi (born Mark Pankler), bassist Dan Pearson, keyboardist Brad Johnson, and drummer Matt Norelli. Despite the skill and diversity of the other members, Eitzel quickly became the group's focal point. An evocative vocalist and gutter poet capable of composing songs of disquieting honesty and intensity, he was also frequently the band's worst enemy. Eitzel had been a heavy drinker since the age of 16, and AMC shows often disintegrated into surreal backdrops for his alcoholic rants and self-destructive showmanship; throughout the group's tumultuous career, his erratic behavior led him to briefly exit their ranks on numerous occasions.

Still, Eitzel quelled his demons long enough for AMC to record their 1985 debut, *The Restless Stranger;* later disowned by the group, the album does offer a rough outline of their increasingly eclectic sound, and it firmly established Eitzel's worldview, a harrowing vision of life as seen through the bottom of a shot glass. 1987's *Engine* honed the formula. The addition of producer Tom Mallon as a fulltime member expanded the group's sonic palette, while Eitzel's songs achieved new levels of intimacy as compositions like "Outside This Bar" and "Gary's Song" grappled with the realities of the drinking life.

While American Music Club languished in obscurity in their native country, they earned a solid European cult following on the strength of 1988's *California*, a frequently brilliant collection highlighted by the shimmering country and folk accoutrements that couched fractured love songs like "Firefly" and "Western Sky"; "Blue and Grey Shirt," Eitzel's most heartfelt and powerful composition to date, was the first in a series of devastating chronicles of friends lost to the AIDS epidemic. Still, the album garnered little notice, and their next LP, 1989's *United Kingdom*, appeared only in the nation that lent the record its name; another superb collection drawing on leftover material and live tracks, it featured "The Hula Maiden," the first recorded fruits of Eitzel's growing fascination with lounge crooning.

After a solo acoustic Eitzel release, 1991's *Songs of Love: Live in London*, American Music Club emerged with its masterpiece, *Everclear*, a remarkable song cycle released to phenomenal critical acclaim (and the usual negligible commercial interest). Still, the lavish praise heaped on *Everclear* (named in honor of a vicious, 180-proof transparent liquor) finally made the major labels take notice, and a bidding war ensued. After months of negotiations, AMC—now consisting of Eitzel, Vudi, Pearson, multi-instrumentalist Bruce Kaphan, and drummer Tim Mooney—signed with Reprise in the US and Virgin throughout the rest of the world, and entered the studio with acclaimed producer Mitchell Froom.

The result, 1993's *Mercury*, was a typically iconoclastic effort featuring unwieldy song titles like "What Godzilla Said to God When His Name Wasn't Found in the Book of Life" and "The Hopes and Dreams of Heaven's 10,000 Whores" resting uneasily against lush, obtuse gems like "If I Had a Hammer," "Apology for an Accident," and "Johnny Mathis' Feet." Despite glowing reviews, *Mercury* fared poorly on the charts and earned virtually no recognition from radio or MTV. In 1994 AMC issued *San Francisco*, an erratic collection that precariously balanced stark, moving confessions like "Fearless" and "The Thorn in My Side Is Gone" alongside slick pop constructs such as "Wish the World Away" and "Can You Help Me." When *San Francisco* failed to connect, American Music Club finally dissolved. In 1996 Eitzel issued his proper solo debut *60 Watt Silver Lining*, a collection of torch songs. At the end of the year, he and producer Peter Buck of R.E.M. returned to the studio to record 1997's *West*. —*Jason Ankeny*

The Restless Stranger / 1986 / Grifter ♦♦
The Restless Stranger is generally omitted from the official American Music Club discography; their first album, its existence was consistently disavowed by the band members in press releases, interviews, and the like. Although it is by far the weakest release in the AMC canon, the album does have its merits; while the production and arrangements never jell with Mark Eitzel's songs, there are fleeting moments here that hint at the eclectic brilliance to come. And already Eitzel is a sharp story-teller; years later he would reprise the opener, "Room Above the Bar," to heartbreaking effect in an a cappella version on his solo acoustic outing *Songs of Love: Live in London*. —*Jason Ankeny*

Engine / 1987 / Frontier ♦♦♦
AMC's sophomore release marks a significant advancement over *The Restless Stranger*, and it offers more than a few of the band's definitive moments. Much of the credit goes to producer Tom Mallon, who arranges the record with an intuitive grasp of the anatomical make-up of Mark Eitzel's burgeoning songcraft; the rest of the credit belongs to Eitzel himself, who offers up some of his first truly great compositions. Chief among them is "Outside This Bar," a chilling portrait of the her-metically sealed comforts of the drinking life. —*Jason Ankeny*

California / 1988 / Frontier ♦♦♦♦
With the erratic *California*, Mark Eitzel's songwriting skills blossom into full maturity. From the pedal-steel-inflected opener "Firefly" to the luminous "Western Sky," the best of his compositions reveal uncommon depth and emotional heft. "Somewhere" cuts with the savage humor of a master storyteller, while "Blue and Grey Shirt," a memoir of a friend's AIDS-related death, is simply devastating. A number of the cuts don't work at all—the muddy "Bad Liquor" is an indecipherable rant, while "Laughing Stock" is by-the-numbers melodrama—but those that do are nothing short of transcendent. —*Jason Ankeny*

United Kingdom / 1990 / Demon ♦♦♦♦
American Music Club's first indisputably great album, the import-only *United Kingdom* is also the band's most spare and unsettling work. Originally conceived as a collection of site-specific songs (hence the opener, "Here They Roll Down," which samples the sounds of a freeway off-ramp), the LP instead cobbles together leftover material and live tracks that fuse into a remarkably cohesive and balanced whole. Among the highlights: "Heaven in Your Hands" ranks firmly as one of Mark Eit-zel's most beautiful and unguarded love songs, while the lounge-fla-vored "Hula Maiden" finds the singer at his most perversely comic; the solo acoustic "Never Mind" details an emotional free-fall, while on the lush "Dreamers of the Dream," Eitzel clings to one of the record's few rays of hope as though his life depended on it. —*Jason Ankeny*

● **Everclear** / Oct. 1991 / Alias ♦♦♦♦
Put simply, *Everclear* is AMC's masterpiece. Benefitting immensely from improved production values, the album crystallizes the band's often erratic vision into a unified, endlessly complex whole. While the arrangements are typically diffuse—"Crabwalk" is shambling rockabilly, "Royal Cafe" is sweet country-pop, and "Rise" is anthemic alterna-rock—a consistency of tone and a sense of place that are absent from the band's other records run through these songs. Similarly, Mark Eitzel's compositions achieve an uncommon emotional balance, never once slipping into pathos or melodrama; the atmospheric "Miracle on 8th Street" and "The Confidential Agent" offer cinema-verite evocations of relationships at the breaking point, while the brute force of alcoholic laments like "Sick of Food" or the funereal "Why Won't You Stay" is stag-gering—never before or since has this loser been quite so beautiful. —*Jason Ankeny*

Mercury / Mar. 1993 / Reprise ♦♦♦♦
Leave it to American Music Club to make their major-label bow with the most perversely idiosyncratic record in their catalog. Produced with eccentric panache by Mitchell Froom, *Mercury* spotlights the band at their darkest and most eclectic, favoring odd rhythms, bizarre effects, and extreme arrangements ranging from the synthetic lounge grandeur of the worshipful "Johnny Mathis' Feet" to the swirling sonic maelstrom of the fatalistic "Challenger." Under the cover of defense-mechanism titles like "What Godzilla Said to God When His Name Wasn't Found in the Book of Life," "If I Had a Hammer" and "The Hopes and Dreams of Heaven's 10,000 Whores," Mark Eitzel paints some of his bleakest por-traits to date; even the most superficially upbeat tracks—"Keep Me Around," "Hollywood 4-5-92," "Over and Done"—are relentlessly grim at their core. A triumph of abject misery. —*Jason Ankeny*

San Francisco / Oct. 4, 1994 / Reprise ♦♦♦
Regrettably, with their final effort, *San Francisco*, American Music Club

went out with a whimper, not a bang. An undeveloped, erratic collection of songs, the record suffers under the weight of overly slick, commercial arrangements and production that renders tracks like "It's Your Birth-day," "Wish the World Away," and "Hello Amsterdam" as bland alterna-rock; only the effervescent "Can You Help Me?" manages to absorb and transcend its glossy pop veneer. Still, Mark Eitzel goes down swinging, conjuring a handful of haunting gems—the best cuts on *San Francisco*, from the luminous opener "Fearless" to the achingly tender "The Thorn in My Side Is Gone," are also the most simple. AMC never needed adornment, just a sympathetic ear. —*Jason Ankeny*

Tori Amos

b. Aug. 22, 1963, Newton, NC
Piano, Keyboards, Vocals / Singer-Songwriter, Alternative Pop-Rock
Tori Amos (b. Myra Ellen Amos) was one of several female singer-song-writers who combined the stark lyrical attack of alternative rock with a distinctly '70s musical approach. Her music falls between the orches-trated meditations of Kate Bush and the stripped-down poetics of Joni Mitchell. In addition to reviving the singer-songwriter traditions of the '70s, Amos revived the piano as a rock 'n' roll instrument. With her 1992 album *Little Earthquakes*, Amos built a dedicated following that contin-ued to expand with her second album, *Under the Pink*.
Born in North Carolina but raised in Maryland, Tori Amos was the daughter of a Methodist preacher. By the age of four, she was singing and playing piano in the church choir; she began writing her own songs shortly afterward. Amos won a scholarship to Baltimore's Peabody Con-servatory based on her instrumental prowess. While she was studying at Peabody, she became infatuated by rock 'n' roll, particularly the music of Led Zeppelin. She began writing pop ballads and performing in local bars. Amos moved to Los Angeles in her late teens to become a pop singer.
Atlantic records signed her in 1987, recording an uninspired pop-metal album called *Y Kant Tori Read* the following year. The record was a complete failure, attracting no attention from radio or press and sell-ing very few copies; nevertheless, she didn't lose her record contract. By 1990 Amos had adopted a new approach, singing spare, haunting semi-confessional piano ballads that were arranged like Kate Bush but had the melodies and lyrical approach of Joni Mitchell. Atlantic sponsored a trip to England in 1991, where she played a series of concerts in support of an EP, *Me and a Gun*.
The harrowing "Me and a Gun" was an autobiographical song, telling the tale of a rape. It gained positive reviews throughout the media, and both the EP and the concerts sold well. *Little Earthquakes*, Amos' first album as a singer-songwriter, was released in late 1991 and sold well in both the US and the UK. In 1992 she released the *Crucify* EP, which fea-tured three covers, including Nirvana's "Smells Like Teen Spirit" and Led Zeppelin's "Thank You." Delivered in early 1994, *Under the Pink*, the full-length follow-up to *Little Earthquakes*, was a bigger hit, selling over a million copies and launching the minor hit singles "God" and "Corn-flake Girl." Two years later, Amos delivered her third album, *Boys for Pele*. —*Stephen Thomas Erlewine*

● **Little Earthquakes** / 1991 / Atlantic ♦♦♦♦
Tori Amos garnered a devoted following with this haunting debut whose spare instrumentation and confessional, poetically quirky lyric invited close emotional connection. However, the album's intense inti macy is uncompromising and not always comforting; Amos' musing on religion, sexual relationships, and gender identity were just as likely to encompass rage, sarcasm, and self-reliant strength as pain, tender ness, and self-doubt. The album's most intimate moment is the harrow ing "Me and a Gun," where Amos strips the music down to only he voice and confronts the listener with the story of her own real-life rape The challenging emotional complexity and passionate soul-baring o *Little Earthquakes* make it Amos' best album to date. —*Steve Huey*

Crucify / 1992 / Atlantic ♦♦♦
Crucify is a five-song EP that builds upon the success of *Little Earth quakes*. Most notable among the songs is her voice/piano reading o Nirvana's "Smells Like Teen Spirit," showing what a fine songwrite Kurt Cobain was; the title song (a different mix than the version o *Earthquakes*) and versions of the Rolling Stones' "Angie" and Led Ze pelin's "Thank You" are noteworthy. —*Stephen Thomas Erlewine*

Under the Pink / Dec. 7, 1994 / Atlantic ♦♦♦♦
The proper follow-up to *Little Earthquakes* finds Amos stretching h compositions out a bit, expanding her arrangements, and playing up t prog-rock influence of Kate Bush. Overall, *Under the Pink* is slightly le consistent than its predecessor; the intimacy is there, but not quite so stunning, and some of her poetic imagery is a bit more obscure. How-ever, these are minor complaints; *Under the Pink* is still compelling and necessary for anyone who enjoyed *Little Earthquakes*. —*Steve Huey*

Boys for Pele / Jan. 23, 1996 / Atlantic ♦♦♦
Highly ambitious, challenging, idiosyncratic, and confounding, *Boys for Pele* expands on the more experimental and progressive tendencies of

Under the Pink. Amos frequently discards traditional song structures and employs wide-ranging, eclectic instrumentation in her music, while her lyrics seem to grow even more obscure, giving the album a very impressionistic feel. While there are certainly worthwhile moments, her experiments don't always work; some of the songs fail to stick, and it takes a few plays before many start to sink in. Ultimately, *Boys for Pele* is polarizing. Some Amos fans will only admire her more for taking the risks she does, while others may find to their disappointment that the intimacy and personal connection that helped Amos build her fan base are too difficult to detect. —*Steve Huey*

Laurie Anderson (Laura Phillips Anderson)

b. Jun. 5, 1947, Chicago, IL
Violin, Vocals / Experimental

With a background as a sculptor and a spoken-word performance artist who had worked with literary mavericks John Giorno and William Burroughs and Fluxus-inspired avant-garde artists and musicians, Laurie Anderson, at first blush, seemed too arty and too much of a cult figure to have a high-profile career as a pop-rock performer. Still, in the world of popular music, stranger things have happened. Her 1981 debut single, the sensational avant-garde pop song "O Superman" (originally released on the One Ten label, re-released on Warner Bros.), enthralled some critics, but clocking in at 11 mostly repetitive minutes with barely a hint of melody, it alienated many others. A hit in England, "O Superman," along with Anderson's considerable reputation as a force in the Lower East Side arts scene and the enthusiastic, early support she received from the New York music press, secured her a long, successful career as an interdisciplinary performer.

Since "O Superman" catapulted her into the "rock scene," Anderson has been as exciting and intriguing a performer as rock 'n' roll (or at least her permutation of it) has ever seen. Funny, challenging, haunting and often mesmerizing, Anderson's unique talents wipe away the notion that avant-garde proclivities have no place in pop music or are so intellectually rigorous as to be beyond the grasp of its audience. Not a musician in the traditional sense (another fact that raised the ire of her detractors), Anderson artfully and intelligently combines music, video, spoken word, and dance, creating both complex performance pieces and simple, unabashed pop songs, often in collaboration with such formidable musicians as Peter Gabriel, Bill Laswell, Adrian Belew, Lou Reed, and Nile Rodgers. Not as prolific a performer as her fans would like, she remains a continually fascinating and provocative artist who has since broadened her reach by successes in film (*Home of the Brave*) and publishing (*The Nerve Bible*). —*John Dougan*

● **Big Science** / 1982 / Warner Brothers ✦✦✦✦
Big Science is essentially a chunk of the more elaborate and difficult four-part multi-media performance piece *United States*. But, that said, *Big Science* never sounds like a portion; it is in fact a meal in itself. The music is moody and minimalistic, and Anderson's wry observations are perspicacious, smartalecky, and, at times, laugh-out-loud funny. There have been numerous artists attempting work like this since *Big Science;* few, however, equal Anderson's panache. Not your average pop record. Oh yeah, "O Superman" is here in all its glory. —*John Dougan*

United States Live / 1984 / Warner Brothers ✦✦✦
Once her popularity seemed assured, Warner Bros. felt safe releasing this five-record set (since reissued on four CDs) comprising *United States'* entire four-and-a-half hours. It's not the first place I'd recommend going to hear Anderson's work, but for those so inclined it's well worth the effort. Although live performances of *United States* included film segments that ran during some of her monologues, *United States* is about communication and how we interpret and use language. It's a bit pretentious, a tad long-winded, and its size makes it unwieldy to listen to in one sitting, but this is an important work loaded with enough insight, wit, and humanity to make relistening and re-evaluating worthwhile. —*John Dougan*

Mister Heartbreak / 1984 / Warner Brothers ✦✦✦✦
A more pop-oriented record (there are musicians here like Adrian Belew and Peter Gabriel), Anderson displays a functional singing voice that graces such wonderful songs as "Sharkey's Day" and "Excellent Birds" (a duet with Gabriel). More accessible than *Big Science*, but in some ways a record indicating that while she may not be a musician herself, Anderson certainly knows how to pick them, work with them, and challenge them. A thoroughly wonderful record. —*John Dougan*

Home of the Brave / 1986 / Warner Brothers ✦✦✦
The soundtrack to Anderson's film, containing older songs such as "Sharkey's Night" and new material, notably "Language Is a Virus." It suffers by being shortened for album length and missing the visual element, but it is still enjoyable. —*William Ruhlmann*

Strange Angels / Oct. 1989 / Warner Brothers ✦✦✦✦
Purists may disagree, but I think *Strange Angels* is Anderson's most stunning work. It may be due to its nearly giddy selection of pop songs (including the ecstatic "Babydoll"), but here Anderson sounds supremely confident as a pop singer-songwriter. Rather than weighing down her songs with avant-gardisms, *Strange Angels* positively luxuriates in this conflation of the avant-garde and the popular. Hence, there is a relentless joyfulness that imbues this record, but it never sacrifices intelligence one iota. A brilliantly conceived record, *Strange Angels* offers the best of both worlds to the benighted and aficionados. —*John Dougan*

Bright Red / Oct. 25, 1994 / Warner Brothers ✦✦✦
Almost six years after *Strange Angels*, Anderson's follow-up was the dark and foreboding *Bright Red*. A slight disappointment, Brian Eno's production heightens the almost amorphous quality of the material, which succeeds in fits and starts. Still, there are moments like "Speechless" and "Poison" that are as gripping as anything she's ever recorded. As with any artist this interesting, Anderson's prodigious talents are on display; you'll simply have to dig a little deeper for them to be revealed. —*John Dougan*

The Ugly One with the Jewels and Other Stories / Mar. 14, 1995 / Warner Brothers ✦✦✦✦
On her later albums, Laurie Anderson had moved from her earlier spoken word-plus-effects style to a more overtly musical approach, with less effective results. *The Ugly One with the Jewels*, a recording of a live performance of readings from her book *Stories from the Nerve Bible*, returned her to speaking instead of singing, and it was her best album since *Big Science*. The 18 stories reflected Anderson's extensive travels, including forays into the Third World and to convents, although she made Los Angeles and Houston sound just as exotic. In fact, telling her stories over sounds from birds to guitars to electronic beeps, she seemed an anthropologist from another world, always finding the natives friendly but strange. And she didn't fail to recognize that she could appear just as odd to them: "The Ugly One with the Jewels" was a name used by one of her subjects to describe her. —*William Ruhlmann*

The Angels

f. 1961, Orange, NJ, **db.** 1967
Girl-Group

The Angels' 1963 No. 1 hit, "My Boyfriend's Back," is one of the half-dozen or so archetypal girl-group classics. Handclap beats, sassy vocals, slightly campy lyrics, and an arrangement paced by wailing horns and street-corner harmonies—it was a surefire hit and one that the group could never live up to, although they continued to record for some time.

The Angels had actually been around for a while before "My Boyfriend's Back," making the Top 20 in 1961 with the ballad " 'Till," and the Top 40 with a follow-up, "Cry Baby Cry." Featuring sisters Barbara and Phyllis Allibut, along with lead singer Linda Jansen, the group were at this time more inclined toward lush doo wop, somewhat in the mold of Little Anthony & the Imperials. Jansen left near the end of 1962, to be replaced by Peggy Santiglia, who gave the trio a tougher sound. In 1963 they hooked up with the songwriting/production team of Feldman-Goldstein-Gottehrer (later to oversee the McCoys and the Strangeloves), who penned and produced material more in line with the Spectorian "wall of sound" gracing the airwaves at the peak of the girl-group era. "My Boyfriend's Back" was originally cut as a demo that music publishers hoped to shop to the Shirelles, but it turned out so well that it was released as an Angels single, after they had been freed from their prior contract to sign with Smash. Surprisingly, they would never make the Top 20 again, although they had minor hits with "Thank You and Goodnight," "I Adore Him," and "Wow Wow Wee (He's the Boy for Me)." They were decent, ebullient singers, the best of their efforts standing up well to other New York-produced groups like the Shirelles, but they could never latch on to a tune as sure-fire as "My Boyfriend's Back" again, despite (or maybe because of) a supply of material from the Feldman-Goldstein-Gottehrer consortium. They worked as session vocalists in the '60s, most notably on Lou Christie's "Lightnin' Strikes," and continued to record, unsuccessfully, throughout the '60s. —*Richie Unterberger*

● **Best of the Angels** / Jun. 18, 1996 / Polygram ✦✦✦✦
Twenty-one-song anthology of cuts from the early and mid-'60s, with all the hits, including the pre-"My Boyfriend's Back" charters "'Til" and "Cry Baby Cry." Despite the spirited vocals, accomplished production, and occasional highlights like "Why Don't the Boy Leave Me Alone?," "World Without Love" (not the Lennon-McCartney song), the ska-flavored "Jamaica Joe," and the James Bond riffs of "Boy from Crosstown," nothing here lights up the room like "My Boyfriend's Back." It's the best collection, though, for those who want to hear more from the group than what's available on oldies compilations. —*Richie Unterberger*

The Animals

f. 1964, Newcastle, England, **db.** 1968
Group / Rock 'n' Roll, Electric British Blues, British Invasion, Psychedelic, British Blues

One of the most important bands originating from England's R&B scene during the early '60s, the Animals were second only to the Rolling Stones in influence among R&B-based bands in the first wave of the British Invasion. The Animals had their origins in a Newcastle-based group called the Kansas City Five, whose membership included pianist Alan Price, drummer John Steel, and vocalist Eric Burdon. Price exited to join the Kontours in 1962, while Burdon went off to London. The Kontours, whose membership included Bryan "Chas" Chandler, eventually were transmuted into the Alan Price R&B Combo, with John Steel joining on drums. Burdon's return to Newcastle in early 1963 heralded his return to the lineup. The final member of the combo, guitarist Hilton Valentine, joined just in time for the recording of a self-produced EP under the band's new name, the Animals. That record alerted Graham Bond to the Animals; he was likely responsible for pointing impresario Giorgio Gomelsky to the group.

Gomelsky booked the band into his Crawdaddy Club in London, and they were subsequently signed by Mickie Most, an independent producer who secured a contract with EMI's Columbia imprint. A studio session in February 1964 yielded their Columbia debut single, "Baby Let Me Take You Home" (adapted from "Baby Let Me Follow You Down"), which rose to No. 21 on the British charts. For years it has been rumored incorrectly that the Animals got their next single, "House of the Rising Sun," from Bob Dylan's first album, but more recently it has been revealed that, like "Baby Let Me Take You Home," the song came to them courtesy of Josh White. In any event, the song—given a new guitar riff by Valentine and a soulful organ accompaniment devised by Price—shot to the top of the UK and US charts early that summer. This success led to a follow-up session that summer, yielding their first long-playing record, *The Animals*. Their third single, "I'm Crying," rose to No. 8 on the British charts. The group compiled an enviable record of Top Ten successes, including "Don't Let Me Be Misunderstood" and "We've Gotta Get Out of This Place," along with a second album, *Animal Tracks*.

In May of 1965, immediately after recording "We've Gotta Get Out of This Place," Alan Price left the band, citing fear of flying as the reason; subsequent biographies of the band have indicated that the reasons were less psychological. When "House of the Rising Sun" was recorded, using what was essentially a group arrangement, the management persuaded the band to put one person's name down as arranger. Price came up the lucky one, supposedly with the intention that the money from the arranger credit would be divided later on. The money was never divided, however, and as soon as it began rolling in, Price suddenly developed his fear of flying and exited the band. Others cite the increasing contentiousness between Burdon and Price over leadership of the group as the latter's reason for leaving. In any case, a replacement was recruited in the person of Dave Rowberry.

In the meantime, the group was growing increasingly unhappy with the material they were being given to record by manager Mickie Most. Not only were the majority of these songs much too commercial for their taste, but they represented a false image of the band, even if many were successful. "It's My Life," a No. 7 British hit and a similar smash in America, caused the Animals to terminate their association with Most and with EMI Records. They moved over to Decca/London Records and came up with a more forceful, powerful sound on their first album for the new label, *Animalisms*. The lineup shifts continued, however—Steel exited in 1966, after recording *Animalisms*, and was replaced by Barry Jenkins, formerly of the Nashville Teens. Chandler left in mid-1966 after recording "Don't Bring Me Down," and Valentine remained until the end of 1966, but essentially "Don't Bring Me Down" marked the end of the original Animals.

Burdon reformed the group under the aegis of Eric Burdon and the New Animals, with Jenkins on drums, John Weider on guitar and violin, Danny McCulloch on bass, and Vic Briggs on guitar. He remained officially a solo act for a time, releasing a collection of material called *Eric Is Here* in 1967. As soon as the contract with English Decca was up, Burdon signed with MGM directly for worldwide distribution, and the new lineup made their debut in mid-1967. Eric Burdon and the New Animals embraced psychedelia to the hilt amid the full bloom of The Summer of Love. By the end of 1968, Briggs and McCulloch were both replaced by Burdon's old friend, keyboard player/vocalist Zoot Money, and his longtime stablemate, guitarist Andy Summers, while Weider switched to bass. Finally, in 1969 Burdon pulled the plug on what was left of the Animals. He hooked up with a Los Angeles-based group called War, and started a subsequent solo career that continues to this day.

The original Animals reunited in 1976 for a superb album called *Before We Were So Rudely Interrupted*, which picked up right where *Animalisms* had left off a decade earlier and which was well received critically but failed to capture the public's attention. In 1983 a somewhat longer-lasting reunion came about between the original members, augmented with the presence of Zoot Money on keyboards. The resulting album, *Ark*, consisting of entirely new material, was well received by critics and charted surprisingly high, and a world tour followed. By the

end of the year and the heavy touring schedule, however, it was clear that this reunion was not going to be a lasting event. The quintet split up again, having finally let the other shoe drop on their careers and history, and walked away with some financial rewards, along with memories of two generations of rock fans cheering their every note. —*Bruce Eder*

The Animals [US] / 1964 / MGM ✦✦✦
Early blues-oriented material rounded out by a few more commercial tracks. This album is stronger than the British version, as it includes several more tracks from their singles. —*Bruce Eder*

The Animals [UK] / 1964 / Columbia ✦✦
The group's British debut long-player in England is a somewhat dry collection of blues and R&B covers, showing the group still trying to gain some confidence within the studio. Note: All material from this album appears on EMI's *Complete Animals* double-CD set. —*Bruce Eder*

The Animals on Tour / 1965 / MGM ✦✦
Lest anyone think this is a live album, don't be fooled by the title—MGM Records used the "On Tour" moniker for an album by Herman's Hermits as well, but that wasn't a live one either. The tracks are good ones, though, showing a lot more flash than their first long-player. —*Bruce Eder*

In the Beginning / 1965 / Sundazed ✦✦✦
Recorded in December 1963 at a live concert, this CD captures the Animals at their rawest and most animated on record, ripping ferociously through a bunch of standards (by Chuck Berry, James B. Odom, et al.), playing the crowd and making snide comments about their London rivals the Rolling Stones, all with Sonny Boy Williamson II hanging somewhere around the stage. Sundazed has actually found the original master to this oft-bootlegged piece of rock/blues history. —*Bruce Eder*

Animal Tracks [UK] / 1965 / Columbia ✦✦✦✦
The band's second British album displays far more energy and dexterity than its predecessor. Originals such as "For Miss Caulker" are paired with excellent covers like "Bright Lights Big City," "I Ain't Got You," and "Roadrunner," along with Ray Charles' "Hallelujah I Love Her So" and "I Believe to My Soul." Note: All tracks appearing on this album are available on EMI's *Complete Animals* double CD. —*Bruce Eder*

Animalization / 1966 / PolyGram ✦✦✦✦
The best of the group's early albums, mostly sophisticated blues-based rock which, for the first time on a long-player, managed to capture the spontaneity of their live sound while allowing them a chance to really stretch out in the studio. Around this time in the band's history, however, the albums get confusing: *Animalization*, released in September 1966 by MGM in America, was simply the British *Animalisms* with three tracks missing, and four other songs ("Don't Bring Me Down," "Cheating," "Inside Looking Out," and "See See Rider") added. But MGM's *Animalism*, released two months later, consisted of tracks recorded in America during the original group's final US tour that never saw the light of day in England. —*Bruce Eder*

Animalism [US] / 1966 / Decca ✦✦✦
The last gasp of the original Animals, albeit with Barry Jenkins on drums in place of John Steel and Dave Rowberry on the ivories in lieu of Alan Price. A superb collection of rock numbers, as advanced from the band's early classics as the Stones' *Aftermath* repertory was from "It's All Over Now." Loud, intense, well-focused, hard-rocking blues. —*Bruce Eder*

Animalisms / 1966 / Decca ✦✦✦✦
Very similar in lineup to the American *Animalization*, this is probably the group's best noncompilation album, with a finely developed R&B sound throughout and excellent playing, all yielding an incomparable collection of good, solid, bluesy, ballsy rock numbers, highlighted by "Gin House Blues" and "Don't Bring Me Down." —*Bruce Eder*

Winds of Change / 1967 / One Way ✦✦
This album marked the debut of Eric Burdon and the New Animals, a decidedly looser, more psychedelic outfit than any the blues-singing idol had previously been associated with. "San Franciscan Nights," "Paint It Black," and "Yes I'm Experienced" (Burdon's answer to Jimi Hendrix' "Are You Experienced?") were moody and pulsating and fiercely experimental. One can get a glimpse of this band at work in the D.A. Pennebaker movie *Monterey Pop*, doing "Paint It Black" on stage. It was a logical extension of the later work of the original Animals into the Summer of Love. —*Bruce Eder*

Eric Is Here / 1967 / One Way ✦✦
During the months after Eric Burdon and the remaining members of the original Animals split, the singer cut this album backed by an orchestra and doing songs by Randy Newman, Barry Mann, Cynthia Weill, and other pop-music fixtures—quite a turnaround for the blues purist Burdon, and also very effective as mainstream pop music, including the US hit "Help Me Girl." To add to the general confusion surrounding this material, some of it seems to have been recorded with the original Animals, or at sessions conducted while they were still together. Sev-

eral songs, including "Help Me Girl," show up on Sequel Records' *Inside Looking Out. —Bruce Eder*

Every One of Us / 1968 / One Way ♦♦
A rather spare and disappointing album, recorded amid the splintering of the original New Animals. Keyboard player Zoot Money arrived to fill up the lineup even as guitarist Vic Briggs and bassist Danny McCullough prepared to leave. —*Bruce Eder*

The Twain Shall Meet / 1968 / One Way ♦♦♦
Twain Shall Meet was a more lopsidedly experimental album; even its major hit, "Sky Pilot," a venture into anti-war politicking on an epic level, marked a new level of sophistication for the band, which played hard and became well known for their ability to jam on stage. —*Bruce Eder*

Love Is / 1968 / One Way ♦♦
One can get an idea of the confusion that fans must have felt by virtue of the fact that *Love Is* was the third album by Eric Burdon and the Animals to be issued in 1968, even with a major lineup change taking place. Future Police-man Andy Somers (aka Summers) arrived on guitar to join his longtime stablemate Zoot Money, while John Weider moved over to bass. This album marked the end of the Animals as a continuously operating music unit, and betrays an understandable lack of direction and enthusiasm. —*Bruce Eder*

The Best of Eric Burdon & the Animals, Vol. 2 / 1969 / MGM ♦♦♦
Actually the third Animals' hits LP to be released by MGM in the 1960s, this collection is the work of lead singer Eric Burdon with the backup group he assembled upon the breakup of the original Animals. The recordings all come from 1967 and 1968, Burdon's psychedelicized period, when he was penning praises of the Monterey Pop Festival ("Monterey," No. 15) and San Francisco ("San Franciscan Nights," No. 9). The only other Top 40 hit on the album was the antiwar epic "Sky Pilot" (No. 15), in its full seven-and-a-half-minute glory. Burdon had come a long way from his Newcastle roots and his blues records, and this was the last album in his second phase; in fact, the New Animals had split by the time it was released. —*William Ruhlmann*

Before We Were So Rudely Interrupted / 1976 / Jet ♦♦♦
The title says it all—returning to the studio a decade after their break-up, the original group lineup with Alan Price picks up right where *Animalization* and *Animalism* left off, with superb musicianship and a good if unspectacular selection of material. —*Bruce Eder*

Ark / 1983 / IRS ♦♦
The group's formal reunion, complete with a new repertory and a well-financed recording. The album has its dark, moody moments, and sometimes bogs down in the sheer heaviness of the sound and sensibilities, but where Burdon is on target as a singer, which is 70% of the time, the group sounds amazingly good. —*Bruce Eder*

Rip It to Shreds: Their Greatest Hits Live / 1984 / IRS ♦♦
A document of the group's 1983 reunion tour. They played better shows along this tour than the one they actually taped. Some of the balances (especially on the guitars) are a little off, and the band's sound and overall performance are somewhat creaky and anemic at times; but it is a fair representation of a largely successful attempt at recapturing past glories. —*Bruce Eder*

★ **The Best of the Animals** / 1988 / ABKCO ♦♦♦♦♦
The original Animals' American hits, including "House of the Rising Sun," "Don't Let Me Be Misunderstood," "It's My Life," and "We Gotta Get Out of This Place," in a compilation originally released in 1965. The lineup of songs is strong, but the sound is indifferent. The British *Complete Animals* covers the same territory and a lot more to much greater effect, at only twice the cost with three times the music and infinitely superior sound and notes. —*Bruce Eder*

Inside Looking Out: The 1965-1966 Sessions / 1990 / Sequel ♦♦♦♦
Together with the double-CD *The Complete Animals*, *Inside Looking Out* forms a retrospective of the great British Invasion band. This 22-song compilation features all of the essential recordings cut by the group in 1965 and 1966 after they broke with their original producer, Mickie Most, and before Eric Burdon dissolved the core of the original lineup to pursue solo stardom with an Animals group featuring entirely different musicians. These tracks were perhaps more soul-oriented than their previous recordings, but the group still burns on the hits "Inside Looking Out" and "Don't Bring Me Down." Despite the absence of original keyboardist Alan Price, the group continued to showcase Burdon's passionate vocals and burning, vibrant organ (by Price's replacement Dave Rowberry) on both renowned and obscure R&B tunes, with an occasional original thrown in. Besides the entirety of their final British LP *Animalisms* (from 1966) and the above-mentioned singles, the CD includes the hits "Help Me Girl" and "See See Rider" (credited to "Eric Burdon and the Animals," these were possibly Burdon solo records). The four tracks from their first release, an independently released 1963 EP featuring primitive R&B standards, are small but noteworthy bonus cuts that close this collection. —*Richie Unterberger*

Roadrunners! / 1990 / Raven ♦♦♦
A 19-track collection of otherwise unavailable live performances from 1966-1968, taken from shows in Melbourne, Stockholm, London, and the '67 Monterey Pop Festival, as well as radio and television broadcasts. Most of this dates from the psychedelic version of the band, which will disappoint those who are primarily interested in the group's rock/R&B prime. It's quite a good relic, though, with rough and ready execution by both Burdon and the band, and some unusual R&B and psychedelic material alongside the versions of hits like "Inside Looking Out," "Monterey," "San Franciscan Nights," and "When I Was Young." Sound ranges from fair to very good. —*Richie Unterberger*

★ **The Complete Animals** / Jul. 1990 / EMI ♦♦♦♦♦
The title is a bit of a misnomer; this double CD does include the complete sessions that the Animals recorded with producer Mickie Most in 1964 and 1965. The 40 songs capture the band at their peak, including most of their best and biggest hits: "House of the Rising Sun," "Don't Let Me Be Misunderstood," "Bring It On Home to Me," "We Gotta Get Out of This Place," "I'm Crying," "It's My Life," and "Boom Boom." Most of the rest of the tunes don't match the excellence of these smashes, though they're solid. The great majority are covers of vintage R&B/rock tunes by Chuck Berry, Fats Domino, and the like, which aren't quite as durable as reinterpretations from the same era by the Stones and Yardbirds. When they hit the mark, though, the Animals produced some great album tracks that have been mostly forgotten, such as "I'm Mad Again" (originally by John Lee Hooker), "Worried Life Blues," and "Bury My Body." After leaving Most, the group would maintain their peak for another year or so (this period is represented on the fine import collection *Inside Looking Out*) despite the departure of one of rock's all-time finest organists, Alan Price. This compilation has everything that Price recorded with the group, including four previously unreleased cuts and "I'm Gonna Change the World," the non-LP Eric Burdon original on the B-side of "It's My Life." —*Richie Unterberger*

Paul Anka

b. Jul. 30, 1941, Ottawa, Ontario, Canada
Vocals / Pop, Teen Idol, Brill Building Pop
Hugely successful vocalist from 1957 into the '80s, as well as writer of several venerable pop-music standards. The young native of Ottawa, Canada, took the US by storm in 1957 with his rock-slanted ballad "Diana," a No. 1 smash on ABC-Paramount Records. Dramatic renditions of "You Are My Destiny," "Lonely Boy," "Put Your Head on My Shoulder," and "Puppy Love" elevated the youth to teen-idol status over the next three years. Moving to RCA in 1962, the maturing Anka continued to chart regularly, although some of his most notable '60s copyrights were bequeathed to others; he wrote "My Way" for Frank Sinatra as well as the theme for TV's "The Tonight Show." Anka returned to the top pop slot in 1974 with the controversial million-seller "(You're) Having My Baby," cut in Muscle Shoals and issued on United Artists, and he enjoyed several follow-up smashes, many featuring vocalist Odia Coates. —*Bill Dahl*

● **30th Anniversary Collection** / Oct. 1989 / Rhino ♦♦♦♦
The best package of Anka's early teen-idol hits, featuring "Diana," "Puppy Love," "Put Your Head on My Shoulder," and "You Are My Destiny," as well as his '70s easy-listening hits ("My Way," "(You're) Having My Baby"). —*Cub Koda*

Adam Ant

b. Nov. 3, 1954, London, England
Keyboards, Vocals / New Wave, Pop-Rock, Post-Punk
One of the seminal figures of new wave, Adam Ant (born Stuart Leslie Goddard) had several distinct phases to his career. Initially, he explored a jagged, guitar-oriented post-punk with his group Adam and the Ants before giving way to a more pop-oriented, glam-tinged musical direction that brought him to the top of the charts. After that had run its course, he refashioned himself as a mainstream singer, which enabled him to stretch his career out for a couple of years. Once it seemed that his musical career had evaporated, he made an unexpected comeback in the early '90s as an adult alternative artist. During all this time, he recorded several great pop singles and had a surprisingly large impact on alternative rock.

Adam Ant formed Adam and the Ants with guitarist Lester Square, bassist Andy Warren, and drummer Paul Flanagan in London in 1977. The group's approach was more theatrical than most punk groups, incorporating sadomasochistic imagery into their concerts. During this time, the group's lineup was fairly unstable, with Square being replaced by Mark Gaumont. The band released their debut, *Dirk Wears White Sox*, on the independent label Do It in 1979. *Dirk* was an ambitious and somewhat dark album, filled with jerky rhythms, angular guitar riffs, and elements of glam rock in Adam's vocals; Adam reacquired the rights to the record in 1983, reissuing it in a resequenced and remixed form, with the tracks "Catholic Day" and "Day I Met God" replaced by

"Zerox" and "Kick," as well as including a new version of "Cartrouble."

At the time of its release, *Dirk Wears White Sox* wasn't a critical or commercial success, and the band felt the need to rework their image. Ant hired Malcolm McLaren, the manager of the Sex Pistols, to help redefine their image. McLaren dressed the band in pirate outfits and suggested a more accessible and pop-oriented, rhythmic variation on punk. Adam and the Ants followed his advice, preparing material for a new album. However, McLaren persuaded all of the Ants to leave Adam, using them as the core members of Bow Wow Wow. Adam Ant immediately formed a new version of the Ants, adding guitarist Marco Pirroni, bassist Kevin Mooney, and drummers Terry Lee Miall and Merrick (born Chris Hughes). Pirroni, in particular, became very important in the band's musical direction, co-writing the majority of the songs with Adam, thus beginning a collaboration between the duo that would continue into the '90s.

Driven by a relentless, driving beat and chanting melodies, the new band's first album, 1980's *Kings of the Wild Frontier*, became an enormous hit in the UK, launching three Top Ten hit singles, including the No. 2 "Ant Music." The band's success was helped by a series of visually enticing videos, prominently featuring the skinny, handsome Adam Ant decked out in pirate gear. *Prince Charming*, released the following year, retained the same formula as *Kings of the Wild Frontier*, spawning two No. 1 singles, "Stand and Deliver" and "Prince Charming." Even though the album was a commercial success, the formula was beginning to wear thin.

After *Prince Charming*, Adam Ant ditched the Ants for a solo career, retaining Marco Pirroni as a songwriting collaborator and a supporting musician. Adam's first solo album, *Friend or Foe*, was released in 1982 and featured the No. 1 single "Goody Two Shoes" and the Top Ten title track. Although his next album, 1983's *Strip*, had some highlights and hit singles, it marked the end of his reign as one of Britain's top pop stars.

Released in 1985, the Tony Visconti-produced *Vive le Rock* had some fun moments, but the performance was too studied and the record didn't earn any hit singles, so Adam Ant pursued a surprisingly successful career in acting. In 1990 Ant made a comeback with the catchy hit single "Room at the Top" from the *Manners & Physique* record, but the album failed to produce another hit single. For the next five years, Ant concentrated on acting.

By the time Adam Ant returned to recording in 1995, echoes of his music could be heard in the spiky singles of Elastica, the neo-goth industrial rock of Nine Inch Nails, and the pseudo-glam of Suede. Instead of capitalising on the burgeoning new wave revival, Adam Ant's 1995 comeback *Wonderful* had little to do with the stylish, intensely rhythmic music he made in the early '80s. Instead, the album repositioned him as a more mature pop-rocker, with crafted songs that featured acoustic guitars as prominently as electrics. The album was a moderate hit in the US and the UK, as was the single "Wonderful." —*Stephen Thomas Erlewine*

Dirk Wears White Sox / Dec. 1979 / Epic ✦✦✦✦
The original Ants line-up released only one LP, *Dirk Wears White Sox*, for Do It in 1979. The album finds a young Adam Ant exploring the sometimes awkward fusion of punk, glam, and minimalist post-punk with bizarre images and disturbing tales of alienation, sex, and brutality. And while the somewhat pretentious, overly-arty lyrics and inexperienced playing are a drawback, the album offers a fascinating look at the Ants' formative years, capturing a raw energy that would be sacrificed for more polish on subsequent releases. At the height of Antmania, Adam Ant acquired the rights to the album, re-mixing it, dropping a few tracks, and adding a couple of early tracks for reissue in 1983 with a different cover for Epic. In 1995, Sony Music UK released a hybrid version for CD, restoring the cover art, original mixes, and the previously dropped tracks but retaining the additions and running order of the reissue. Epic chose to keep the re-mixed version for CD release in the US. —*Chris Woodstra*

Kings of the Wild Frontier / 1980 / Epic ✦✦✦✦
Combining pounding tom-toms (from two drummers and drum kits), a guitar style adapted from Ennio Morricone movie soundtracks, and a visual motif borrowed from pirates and Native Americans, Adam and the Ants had a brief run as Britain's top band in the wake of the punk/power-pop days of the late '70s. This second album was their apex, featuring the signature tune "Antmusic." —*William Ruhlmann*

Prince Charming / 1981 / Epic ✦✦✦
The final album with the Ants is bland in comparison to the brilliant *Kings of the Wild Frontier*, with the band drifting dangerously close to "new romantic" territory. While "Stand and Deliver" is one of the high points of the band's career, the cringe-worthy "Ant Rap" is certainly the low point. The essential tracks can all be found on *Antics in the Forbidden Zone*, so only completists need bother. —*Chris Woodstra*

Friend or Foe / 1982 / Epic ✦✦✦
As a solo artist, Adam Ant struck gold in the US with this album, which

adopts the same musical style as that of the Ants and features the hit "Goody Two Shoes" and a version of the Doors' "Hello, I Love You." —*William Ruhlmann*

Strip / Nov. 1983 / Epic ✦✦
With this album, Adam Ant's musical career began to hit the skids. He was still popular enough in the UK to squeeze out one more Top Ten hit with "Puss 'n' Boots," but the album stopped at No. 20 after three straight Top Five hits. In the US, where Ant had peaked with his solo debut, *Friend or Foe*, the year before, this one got only to No. 65. And no wonder—the mixture of driving, danceable rock, and humor that had made *Kings of the Wild Frontier*, *Prince Charming*, and even some of *Friend or Foe* enjoyable had given way to a lighter pop approach and outright camp, especially on the title track, a minor singles chart entry produced by Phil Collins. Somehow, Ant had lost his appeal, and fast. —*William Ruhlmann*

Vive le Rock / 1985 / Epic ✦✦
Adam Ant adopted a '50s-style rock 'n' roll sound for his third solo album, achieving a pastiche with some of the effervescence, but none of the definition (or popularity), of Elton John's "Crocodile Rock." Producer Tony Visconti tried to give him some of the plastic rock legitimacy of *Ziggy Stardust* era David Bowie, but Ant was even goofier; especially with his vocals smothered in harmony and echo and buried in the mix, he wasn't so much transformed into a rocker manque as rendered anonymous on his own record. The best track was the year-old UK Top 40 hit "Apollo 9," which had some of the manic energy of the Adam and the Ants hits. If the rest of the album had recreated its dizzy spirit, Ant might have made the comeback he needed with *Vive le Rock*. Or maybe not. It's possible that his moment simply had passed. In any case, the album flopped on both sides of the Atlantic, Ant was dropped by his record label, and he didn't make another album for more than four years. (*Vive le Rock* was reissued in 1996 with the added track "Mohair Locker Room Pin-Up Boys.") —*William Ruhlmann*

Manners and Physique / Feb. 1990 / MCA ✦✦
For his comeback album and first new release in nearly five years, Adam Ant turned to old Prince crony Andre Cymone, who transformed him into a dance music singer, producing and playing all the instruments on contemporary dance tracks, over which Ant's long-time partner Marco Pirroni played lead guitar and Ant himself contributed appropriately rhythmic vocals. Some of the lyrics had his old flair for mockery, but, like most dance music singers, he came off as only a part of the production, rather than its focus. Nevertheless, the makeover was good for a UK/US Top 20 hit in "Room at the Top" and respectable chart peaks of No. 19 (England) and No. 57 (America), a big improvement over 1985, when he looked washed up. —*William Ruhlmann*

● **Antics in the Forbidden Zone** / Oct. 1990 / Epic ✦✦✦✦
The most comprehensive overview of the band. In 22 tracks, all of the hits are represented, as well as key album cuts and a rare B-side, "Beat My Guest." An essential part of any new wave collection. —*Chris Woodstra*

Peel Sessions / Jul. 1, 1991 / Dutch East India ✦✦✦
A nice collection of recordings made for John Peel's radio show from 1978 to 1979. This is probably the best documentation of the early days of the band, combining live-in-the-studio versions of material from *Dirk Wears White Sox*, early singles, and previously unreleased tracks. Essential for hardcore fans. —*Chris Woodstra*

B-Side Babies! / Sep. 27, 1994 / Epic/Legacy ✦✦✦✦
Since Adam Ant once had a group called the B-Sides, it makes sense that his singles, both as lead singer of Adam and the Ants and as a solo, would have non-LP B-sides. And since Ant was a hit in the UK before he made it in America, and was always bigger in Britain, many of those B-sides appeared only on English singles. This is a collection of songs recorded between 1980 and 1985 that gave Ant a chance to try novelty approaches, while the A-sides relentlessly beat out his trademark "Antmusic." In fact, songs like "Making History" do have that characteristic yodel and the Burundi-style drumming of Terry Miall and Merrick. But elsewhere, Ant tries different things, frequently light, slight things like "Juanito the Bandito." But fun was always one of his qualities, and it's here in abundance. —*William Ruhlmann*

Wonderful / Mar. 7, 1995 / Capitol ✦✦✦
Adam Ant recorded his first album in five years (and second in ten years) at Abbey Road Studio No. 2, where the Beatles recorded; and a Beatle sound wore off on the songs, which sounded like Beatle music of 1966-67, from the rhythmic cadences to the strummed acoustic guitars and backwards tape sounds. Ant was always better at image than music, whether he was mixing Native American and pirate gear or employing African-style drumming more for the look than the sound back in the Antmusic days. Since then, he hasn't had any musical compass, although he posed as a dance music frontman for 1990's *Manners and Physique*. Here he borrowed Madonna's photographer, Anton Corbijn, and her basic theme —sex-as-amusement/nourishment/salvation. He

succeeded in sounding horny, but that didn't make him seductive. — *William Ruhlmann*

Anthrax

f. Jun. 1981, New York, NY
Thrash, Heavy Metal, Speed Metal, Rap-Metal
Nearly as much as Metallica or Megadeth, Anthrax has been responsible for the emergence of speed and thrash metal. Combining the speed and fury of hardcore punk with the prominent guitars and vocals of heavy metal, Anthrax helped create a new subgenre of heavy metal on their early albums. Guitarists Scott Ian and Dan Spitz are a formidable pair, spitting out lightning-fast riffs and solos that never seem masturbatory. Unlike Metallica or Megadeth, they had the good sense to temper their often serious music with a healthy dose of humor and realism.

After their first album, *Fistful of Metal*, singer Joey Belladonna and bassist Frank Bello joined the lineup. Belladonna helped take the band further away from conventional metal clichés, and over the next five albums (with the exception of 1988's *State of Euphoria*, where the band sounded as if they were in a creative straight-jacket), Anthrax arguably became the leaders of speed metal.

As the '80s became the '90s, Anthrax began to increase their experiments with hip-hop, culminating in a tour with Public Enemy in 1991 and a joint re-recording of PE's classic "Bring the Noise."

After their peak period of the late '80s, Anthrax kicked Belladonna out of the band in 1992 and replaced him with ex-Armored Saint vocalist John Bush—a singer who was gruffer and deeper, fitting most metal conventions perfectly. Subsequently, their sound became less unique and their audience shrank slightly as a consequence, but it would be foolish to count Anthrax out—these guys are too clever to fade away. — *Stephen Thomas Erlewine*

Fistful of Metal / 1984 / Megaforce ✦✦
Anthrax' lineup had not yet solidified when they recorded their debut album, and neither had their style. Fans of the group's peak-period material are likely to find *Fistful of Metal* offputting, as the band sounds more like a Judas Priest knockoff with rather silly, stereotypical heavy metal lyrics than the thrash innovators they would become. Bassist Dan Lilker, who subsequently left to form Nuclear Assault, is present for this album, while vocalist Joey Belladonna is not. — *Steve Huey*

Armed and Dangerous / 1985 / Megaforce ✦✦✦
This EP featured the debut of Joey Belladonna (vocals) and Frank Bello (bass). — *John Book*

Spreading the Disease / 1985 / Megaforce ✦✦✦✦
Anthrax' first album with vocalist Joey Belladonna is a huge leap forward, featuring strongly rhythmic, pounding riffs and vocals that alternate between hardcore-type shouting and surprising amounts of melody. Two tracks left over from the Lilker days are here, as well. The traditional metal lyrical fare is more original, while also introducing a penchant for paying tribute to favorite fictional characters and pop-culture artifacts ("Lone Justice" and "Medusa" are prime examples).One of Anthrax' best efforts. — *Steve Huey*

● **Among the Living** / 1987 / Megaforce ✦✦✦✦
Generally considered the band's best album, *Among the Living* broadened the scope of Anthrax' subject matter with socially conscious lyrics addressing prejudice, violence, drug abuse ("Efilnikufesin [N.F.L.]," a rip on John Belushi), and the hollowness of the music business, as well as a politically correct ode to the "Indians." However, the band refuses to take itself too seriously, also recording tributes to Stephen King and Judge Dredd. Musically, the band delivers a powerful, aggressive roar driven by impossibly fast riffing and the changing tempos and collectively shouted vocals of hardcore, especially on the classic "Caught in a Mosh." The brutal rhythm guitar work of Scott Ian and the explosive drumming of Charlie Benante relentlessly push the songs along while still maintaining a solid groove, and more than make up for some lyrical awkwardness. — *Steve Huey*

I'm the Man / 1987 / Megaforce ✦✦✦✦
This EP features three versions of the title track, the group's pioneering fusion of rap and heavy metal, plus a cover of Black Sabbath's "Sabbath, Bloody Sabbath" and live perfomances of *Among the Living*'s "Caught in a Mosh" and "I Am the Law." While artists like the Beastie Boys and Run-D.M.C. had experimented with rock/rap fusion, Anthrax was the first band on the rock side of the equation to do so, and their take was naturally harder and heavier than anything that came before. Of course, the experiment wouldn't have worked if Anthrax' music hadn't already relied on strongly rhythmic grooves, and their playful sense of humor didn't hurt either. A must-hear. — *Steve Huey*

State of Euphoria / 1988 / Megaforce ✦✦✦
The proper follow-up to *Among the Living* was somewhat disappointing in its inconsistency. While there are some good moments—"Be All, End All" is one of the band's most melodic moments, and several other tracks catch fire—the best thing here is a cover of Trust's "Antisocial," and it

doesn't bode well when covers outshine original material. The lyrics continue the self-consciously intellectual, P.C. approach begun on *Among the Living*, but about half of the album is surprisingly dull. — *Steve Huey*

Persistence of Time / Aug. 1990 / Megaforce ✦✦✦✦
Persistence of Time rivals *Among the Living* as Anthrax' best album and might even be a clear-cut favorite if some of the songs had been trimmed a bit. The more cartoonish side of the band is missing here, trimmed in favor of a dark, uncompromising examination of society's dirty underbelly—nearly every song rails against hatred and prejudice, but without an excess of optimism. The standout track is, once again, a cover—Joe Jackson's "Got the Time"—but the rest of the album is strong enough to hold its own. This is the album for those who want Anthrax' serious side without any of the pop-culture references and tributes; others might miss those elements, particularly since there has always been a sort of clumsiness to some of the more intellectual lyrics. However, *Persistence of Time* is their most lyrically consistent album, and the music simply rages. — *Steve Huey*

Attack of the Killer B's / Jun. 1991 / Island ✦✦✦✦
Not just for devoted fans, this collection of B-sides, covers, rarities, and obscurities actually presents a surprisingly solid overview of the range and diversity of Anthrax' material in an engaging, entertaining manner. Listeners wanting to hear more of the band's sense of humor will be pleased with the bizarre "Milk (Ode to Billy)" (one of two S.O.D. songs redone here), the hilarious power-ballad satire "N.F.B.," and the anti-censorship tune "Startin' Up a Posse," which uses rather predictable tactics to make its point but has such a gleeful, idiotic bounce that it's difficult not to be amused. Two live songs from *Persistence of Time* are included, capturing the band's serious side, and their various influences are documented through covers of Trust, Discharge, Kiss, and even surf-rockers the Chantays. But the most important item here is the slamming (and highly influential) duet with Public Enemy on that group's classic "Bring the Noise," which paved the way for a host of other bands to mix the aggression and intensity of heavy metal with hip-hop. — *Steve Huey*

Sound of White Noise / May 1993 / Elektra ✦✦✦
With the addition of deep-voiced vocalist John Bush and a retooled sound attempting to keep up with the times after the alternative rock explosion, Anthrax sounds less distinctive on *Sound of White Noise*, tightening up their guitar riffs and song structures while making definite moves toward a grungier, Seattle-influenced sound. Anthrax' rhythm section, as always, takes no prisoners, making what might seem like a desperate attempt to follow new trends into another aggressive, pummeling effort that sounds anything but defeated; the intensity is still there. — *Steve Huey*

Live—the Island Years / Apr. 5, 1994 / Island ✦✦✦
This 70-minute concert recording from October 1991, issued after Anthrax had switched record labels, provides a good overview of the band's first seven years, including songs from the albums *Spreading the Disease*, *Among the Living*, *State of Euphoria*, *Persistence of Time*, and *Attack of the Killer Bs*. Public Enemy joins them for "Bring the Noise," and there are two tracks, the otherwise unavailable "Metal Thrashing Mad" and "In My World," recorded live in the studio in January 1992. — *William Ruhlmann*

Stomp 442 / Oct. 24, 1995 / Elektra ✦✦
Anthrax continued their downward spiral with *Stomp 442*, a generic collection of speed metal bombast. Previously the band had been able to save their weakest material by the sheer force of their personality, but by the time they recorded *Stomp 442*, they had lost a number of their key members. Instead of recharging the band, the new members make Anthrax seem somewhat unsure of where to go next ; they pull out their old bag of tricks, but none of their blistering riffs, thundering drums, or hip-hop experiments carries any excitement any more. A handful of tracks suggest that the band could save themselves, but *Stomp 442* is a disheartening experience for the band's dedicated followers. — *Stephen Thomas Erlewine*

The Anti-Nowhere League

f. 1980, Tunbridge Wells, England, **db.** 1987
Punk, Alternative Pop-Rock
There is an old expression about a blind pig finding a chestnut now and again, and that certainly rings true when addressing the overnight phenomenon known as the Anti-Nowhere League. Fronted by a codpiece-wearing goon of a lead singer with questionable personal hygiene who went by the name Animal, the League somehow managed to release one vulgar, loud, stupid, funny, thoroughly great EP, but hung around like a bunch of talentless louts who never got the message to clear off. Playing standard, raunchy, Sex Pistols-influenced punk rock, Animal cranked up the disgust factor either by uttering a string of obscenities or boasting about his indiscriminate taste in partners (including animals) in sexual intercourse. Like a punk parody worthy of Nick Lowe, the

League actually got a lot of press when it looked as though their record was going to be banned in England and, or so it was whispered at the time, the US. Fortunately, it wasn't, and the grubby glory of this group of shameless yobs became ours to cherish. They did record a few full-length albums (including a live one recorded in Yugoslavia), and all are worthless. —*John Dougan*

● **We Are... the League** / 1982 / WXYZ ✦✦✦✦
Featuring a thrash-and-bash version of Ralph McTell's "Streets of London" and the disgusting "So What," this is a refreshing blast of ignorance that revels in its own tastelessness the way pigs roll around in the mud. Lead singer Animal growls and tells of mighty sexual exploits, while guitarist Magoo coughs up hairball after hairball of distortion. Special treat is the hilariously dumb "I Hate . . . People." —*John Dougan*

Perfect Crime / 1987 / GWR ✦✦
In the five years it took them to make a second studio album, the Anti-Nowhere League evolved from its obscenity-laced, power chord punk sound to something more like such mainstream UK rock bands as the Stranglers and Big Country. This just made them more pretentious and less amusing, however. —*William Ruhlmann*

Best of the Anti-Nowhere League / Aug. 27, 1993 / Cleopatra ✦✦✦✦
The League were loud, obnoxious, hostile, vulgar, and, above all, stupid. Anything you'll ever need by this band is here, including their first five singles and the original, uncensored version of their ode to corruption and bestiality, "So What," which was brought to the attention of heavy metal fans when Metallica covered it on the B-side of their "Sad But True" single. —*Steve Huey*

Any Trouble

f. 1975, Manchester, England, **db.** Dec. 1984
Rock 'n' Roll, New Wave, Pub Rock
Any Trouble was an under-appreciated bright spot on Stiff Records, which had no shortage of talented artists. Bandleader Clive Gregson's appearance, hardened love songs, and vocal style may have led to comparisons to Elvis Costello, but they were no second-rate rip-off; each of their four albums revealed a songwriter of unique talent and a more-than-capable band to execute the songs.

Manchester-native Gregson formed the original band in 1975 while attending teaching school in Crewe, taking the group's name from a misquote from the Mel Brooks film *Blazing Saddles*. After a brief moment as a folky trio, by 1976 Any Trouble had changed to a four-piece rock group, speeding up their repertoire in response to the punk movement. By this point the lineup was Gregson (vocals/guitar), Chris Parks (guitar), Phil Barnes (bass), and Mel Harley (drums). They built a strong following playing the pub circuit and released their own single, catching the attention of Radio One's John Peel, who quickly took the band and played the song on his show. This exposure started a small-scale bidding war from several labels. By 1980, the group signed with Stiff Records.

Stiff enlisted John Wood, a renowned producer (Nick Drake, John Martyn, Richard Thompson) who had recently produced Squeeze, to produce Any Trouble's first album. *Where Are All the Nice Girls?*, which had all the makings of a new wave classic, was met with some rave reviews but failed to rack up the big sales that were expected of it. After the record failed commercially, Stiff suggested that Gregson drop the band and re-define himself as a solo artist à la Elvis Costello—Buddy Gregson. Gregson declined, deciding instead to replace the band's weak link, drummer Harley, with the more capable Martin Hughes. They began work on the follow-up immediately.

Wheels in Motion (1981), while certainly more accomplished, lacked the spark of the first album, and the record simply didn't catch on in the UK Any Trouble took a stab at Stateside success with a small promotional tour. Halfway through the tour, the band heard by word-of-mouth that they had been dropped by Stiff and were left stranded in America. Eventually they found their way back, but the stress of the situation broke up the band for about 18 months.

A new deal was arranged with EMI-America in 1982. Hughes left the band and was replaced by Andy Ebsworth, and Steve Gurl was added on keyboards. Chris Parks left shortly thereafter. Essentially a new band, the four-piece recorded *Any Trouble* in 1983. Again, the same story—should've been a hit, somehow overlooked. Gregson, knowing the band couldn't last much longer, talked EMI into letting them do a double album. As a parting shot, Gregson and company stretched out for *Wrong End of the Race*, a sprawling album that allowed them to show their diversity and influences over 25 tracks of new originals, remakes of earlier Any Trouble songs, and a few covers. In America, the album was distilled to a single record. "Baby Now That I Found You" saw some airplay on MTV; the reviews were good, but the band's cult status didn't change. In December of 1984, the band played their last gig and called it quits. Gregson went on to a distinguished, though still underappreciated, career both as a solo artist and as a collaborator with Christine Collister. —*Chris Woodstra*

● **Where Are All the Nice Girls?** / 1980 / Stiff ✦✦✦✦
The first album is a pure pub/pop rock delight. Leading off with the infectious "Second Choice" (one of the great "should have been hits") and ending up with the unlikely ABBA cover "Name of the Game," Gregson and company run though 12 tunes, almost all obsessed with love gone wrong. A cult favorite. —*Chris Woodstra*

Live at the Venue / 1981 / Line ✦✦✦✦
Originally released as a promo for radio, this live show from 1980 finds the band in its natural setting. The album provides the best picture of the band at its peak, playing with higher energy than in the studio. —*Chris Woodstra*

Wheels in Motion / Aug. 1981 / Stiff ✦✦✦
The playing on their sophomore effort is more sophisticated, and the production is cleaner; but it lacks some of the bite of the first album. Gregson's now-standard obsession makes an appearance on the album's highlight, "Trouble with Love." —*Chris Woodstra*

Any Trouble / 1983 / EMI ✦✦✦
The band's move from the Stiff label to EMI marked an attempt to crack the US market with a mainstream radio-ready album, a new lineup, and another batch of well-crafted songs from Clive Gregson. Unfortunately overlooked at the time, material from this album continued to be a part of Gregson's solo sets in the '90s. —*Chris Woodstra*

Wrong End of the Race / 1984 / Beat Goes On ✦✦✦
Issued as a double LP in England and a single LP in the US, *Wrong End of the Race* compiles unnecessary re-recordings of previously released songs, some new tracks, and a few interesting covers. Knowing that this would be their final album, Gregson attempted to assemble material that would show the band's diversity and their wide variety of influences. And while this does reveal some interesting sides to the band, ultimately the indulgence and mostly uninspired performances led to their weakest set. —*Chris Woodstra*

Aphex Twin

b. 1971, Cornwall, England
Synthesizer, Keyboards / Ambient Techno, Experimental, Electronica
Using synth gadgetry that he wires and manufactures himself, Richard D. James has explored the experimental possibilities of the two major movements in techno during the late '80s: acid and ambient-house. Though his first major single "Didgeridoo" was a piece of acid thrash designed to tire dancers during his DJ sets, the ambient-house genre later took him under its wing for his first volume of *Selected Ambient Works*. James reacted to the exposure with increasingly experimental and harsh works that portrayed an artist unwilling to become either pigeonholed or categorizable.

He was born in 1971 in Cornwall, England, and began taking apart electronics gear as a teenager. (Just do the math on the title *Selected Ambient Works 85-92*—his first recordings were made at the age of 14.) Inspired by acid-house in the late '80s, James began DJing raves around Cornwall. His first release—recorded with Tom Middleton and credited to Aphex Twin Featuring Schizophrenia—was the *Analogue Bubblebath 1* EP, which appeared on the Mighty Force label in September 1991. Middleton left later that year to form Global Communication, after which James recorded a second volume in the *Analogue Bubblebath* series. This release—the first to include "Digeridoo"—got some airplay on the London pirate radio-station KISS-FM, and prompted the Belgian R&S label to sign him early the following year. A re-recording of "Digeridoo" made No. 55 in the British charts just after its April 1992 release, and James followed with the *Xylem Tube* EP in June. He also co-formed (with Grant Wilson-Claridge) his own Rephlex label around this time, releasing the *Joyrex* series of singles as Caustic Window during mid-1992. These limited-edition recordings continued the cold acid precision of "Digeridoo."

The electronic climate had begun to warm in the early '90s, though; the Orb had proved the commercial viability of ambient-house in June 1992, and R&S scrambled to find useful material from its own artists. In November 1992, James acquiesced with *Selected Ambient Works 85-92*, an album of home material recorded during the past seven years. Simply stated, it became an ambient-house masterpiece, the genre's second work of brilliance after *The Orb's Adventures Beyond the Ultraworld*. As his star began to shine, several bands approached him to remix their work, and he complied, with mostly unrecognizable reworkings of tracks by St. Etienne, the Cure, Jesus Jones, Meat Beat Manifesto, and Curve.

Early in 1993 Richard James signed to Warp Records, the influential British label that introduced "electronic listening music" with the *Artificial Intelligence* series of albums by ambient-techno pioneers Black Dog, B12, FUSE (aka Richie Hawtin,) and Autechre, among others. James' release in the series, titled *Surfing on Sine Waves*, was recorded as Polygon Window and released in January 1993. The album charted a course between the raw muscle of James' nose-bleed techno and the understated minimalism of *Selected Ambient Works*. A deal between

Warp and TVT gave *Surfing on Sine Waves* an American release—James' first—by the summer of 1993. In December of 1993, the new single "On" resulted in James' highest chart placing, a No. 32 spot on the British charts. The resulting album, *Selected Ambient Works, Vol. 2*, appeared to be a joke on the ambient-house community. So minimal as to be barely conscious, the quadruple-album left most of the beats behind, with only tape loops of unsettling ambient noise remaining. The album struck out with critics, but hit No. 11 on the British charts and earned James a major-label American contract with Sire soon after.

James began 1995 with the January release of *Classics*, a compilation of his early R&S singles. Two months later, he put out the single "Ventolin," a harsh, appropriately wheezing ode to the asthma drug on which he relies. *I Care Because You Do* followed in April, pairing his ambient material with a form of techno experimentalism that allied itself both with his hardcore roots and the work of many post-classical composers—including Philip Glass, who arranged an orchestral version of the album's "Icct Hedral" on the single "Donkey Rhubarb." The fourth proper Aphex Twin album, *Richard D. James*, continued his forays into acid-jungle and experimental music. —*John Bush*

★ **Selected Ambient Recordings 85-92** / 1993 / R&S ✦✦✦✦✦
Selected Ambient Works is a desperately sparse album; thin percussion and several haunted-synth lines are the only components on most songs, and Richard D. James added only one vocal sample on the entire album ("We are the music makers, and we are the dreamers of dreams"). Also, the sound quality is relatively poor—it was recorded direct to cassette tape and reportedly suffered a mangling by a cat. All this belies the status of *Selected Ambient Works* as a watershed of ambient music. It reveals no influences and sounds unlike anything that preceded it, due in large part to the effects James managed to wrangle from his supply of home-manufactured contraptions. —*John Bush*

Analogue Bubblebath III / Mar. 1, 1994 / Rephlex ✦✦✦
His first full-length release, this long out-of-print album features James' early brand of techno, indebted to acid and trance but still of a distorted quality all its own. No song titles are provided on the CD version (which comes in a slimline case with only a sticker on the front), but the LP version (enclosed in a brown paper bag) lists long decimals as the titles. —*John Bush*

Selected Ambient Works, Vol. 2 / Apr. 1994 / Sire ✦✦✦
Selected Ambient Works, Vol. 2 is a more difficult and challenging album than the Aphex Twin's previous collection. The music is all texture; there are only the faintest traces of beats and forward movement. Instead, all of these untitled tracks are long, unsettling electronic soundscapes, alternately quiet and confrontational; although most of the music is rather subdued, it is never easy listening. While some listeners may find this double-disc album dull (the two discs run more than 70 minutes), many listeners will be intrigued and fascinated by the intricately detailed music of the Aphex Twin. —*Stephen Thomas Erlewine*

Classics / 1995 / R&S ✦✦✦
Given Richard D. James' popularity, R&S Records of Belgium decided to combine two singles recorded for the label, half of another single, two remixes, and a live track for the *Classics* album. At 13 tracks and 74 minutes, it's a good compilation of his early dark techno. —*John Bush*

I Care Because You Do / Apr. 25, 1995 / Sire ✦✦✦✦
James' most consistent work, *I Care* fuses his earlier hardcore techno days with the smooth rhythm and atmosphere of his ambient work, often on the same song. "Ventolin" is one of the harshest singles ever recorded; "Next Heap With" is the highlight of the album. —*John Bush*

Richard D. James Album / 1996 / Elektra ✦✦✦✦
Perhaps inspired by the experimental drum'n'bass being created by Squarepusher (a recent signee to his Rephlex label), Richard D. James' third major-label album as Aphex Twin was his first to work with jungle—though, to his credit, he had released the breakbeat EP *Hangable Auto Bulb* almost a year earlier. Contemporaries Orbital and Underworld were beginning to incorporate moderate use of drum'n'bass in their work as well, but this album was more extreme than virtually all jungle being made at the time. The beats are jackhammer quick and even more jarring, considering what is—for the most part—laid over the top: the same fragile, slow-moving melodies that characterized Aphex Twin's earlier ambient works. Most overtly disturbing is "Milkman," the first straightahead vocal track from Aphex Twin; the song is a child-like ode that gradually deteriorates into a bizarre fantasy concerning the milkman's wife. With all the Aphex Twin's curious idiosyncrasies, though, *Richard D. James Album* is a very listenable record and a worthy follow-up to *I Care Because You Do*. (The American issue features the English EP "Girl/Boy.") —*John Bush*

Fiona Apple

b. 1977, New York, NY
Piano, Vocals / Singer-Songwriter, Adult Alternative Pop-Rock
Singer-songwriter Fiona Apple gained a recording contract in 1995 as

one in a crop of mid-'90s female artists, but her confessional writing and throaty vocals made the teenager sound like much more than just the latest flavor. Born in 1977 in New York to singer Diana McAfee and actor Brandon Maggart, Fiona Apple began playing the piano at the age of eight and started composing her own songs just four years later, after the separation of her parents and her own brutal rape. After leaving high school at the age of 16, she journeyed to Los Angeles to see her father and make a demo tape of her songs. After several months of tape-passing, Sony Music signed Apple in 1995. After recording *Tidal* with producer Andrew Slater, she released the album in mid-1996 and began touring. Constant videoplay of the single "Shadowboxer" on both MTV and VH1 brought *Tidal* into the upper reaches of the album charts. —*John Bush*

● **Tidal** / Jul. 23, 1996 / Clean Slate ✦✦✦✦
Fiona Apple demonstrates considerable talent on her debut album, *Tidal*, but it is unformed, unfocused talent. Her voice is surprisingly rich and supple for a teenager, and her jazzy, sophisticated piano playing also belies her age. Given the right material, such talents could have flourished, but she has concentrated on her own compositions, which are nowhere near as impressive as her musicianship. Most of *Tidal* is comprised of confessional singer-songwriter material, and while they strive to say something deep and important, much of the lyrics settle for cliches. Apple does have a handful of impressive songs on *Tidal*, like the haunting "Shadowboxer" and "Sullen Girl," but the gap between her performing talents and songwriting skills is too large to make the album anything more than a promising, and very intriguing, debut. —*Stephen Thomas Erlewine*

Apples (in stereo)

f. 1993, Denver, CO
Lo-Fi, Indie Rock
The sunny pop band the Apples (in stereo) was one of the leading lights of the Elephant 6 Recording Company collective, a coterie of like-minded, lo-fi indie groups—including the Olivia Tremor Control, Neutral Milk Hotel, and Secret Square—who shared musicians, ideas, and sensibilities. They were led by singer-songwriter Robert Schneider, a native of the tiny town of Ruston, LA, also home to Jeff Mangum (later of Neutral Milk Hotel) as well as William Cullen Hart and Bill Doss (who formed the Olivia Tremor Control).

Throughout high school, the aspiring musicians—all influenced by the likes of the Beatles, the Zombies, Pink Floyd, and Sonic Youth—exchanged home recordings and played in each other's bands. After college, Schneider and Mangum relocated to Denver, where Schneider struck up a friendship with fellow Beach Boys fan and bass player Jim McIntyre; after enlisting drummer Hilarie Sidney and guitarist Robert Parfitt, they formed the Apples, and issued their self-titled debut EP on the Elephant 6 label. To avoid confusion with other similarly-named bands, they officially became the Apples (in stereo) for 1995's full-length debut *Fun Trick Noisemaker;* in 1996, Schneider produced the Olivia Tremor Control's *Music From the Unrealized Film Script "Dusk at Cubist Castle,"* and later in the year the Apples issued *Science Faire*, a collection of singles and rare material. —*Jason Ankeny*

Fun Trick Noisemaker / May 2, 1995 / spinART ✦✦✦✦
Childlike and effervescent, the debut LP from the Apples (in stereo) is a pure pop delight, a warm, fuzzy collection of chiming melodies and bubblegum attitudes. The songs—with their parade of references to GummiWorms, Saturday morning cartoons, Green Machines (the Big Wheel's bad-ass cousin), and the Phantom Zone—are wistfully nostalgic, but never naive or kitschy. A refeshingly simple and energetic collection of bright guitar-pop, *Fun Trick Noisemaker* more than lives up to its title. —*Jason Ankeny*

Science Faire / Sep. 1996 / spinART ✦✦✦✦
A collection of rarities cut between 1993 and 1995, *Science Faire* includes the group's 1993 debut seven-inch, recorded when they were simply the Apples, and features alternate versions of *Fun Trick Noisemaker's* "Tidal Wave" and "Glowworm," along with gems like "Haley." —*Jason Ankeny*

Archers of Loaf

f. 1991, Chapel Hill, NC
Alternative Pop-Rock, Indie Rock
Formed in the early '90s, the indie-rock quartet Archers of Loaf specialize in an off-kilter, noisy, and surprisingly tuneful brand of alternative rock. The Archers begin with Pavement's warped guitar-pop sensibilities, adding more sheets of pure white noise and more cryptic lyrics, and play with an often invigorating, reckless sense of fun. The band became a college/underground sensation when the single "Web in Front" became a hit on alternative and college radio in the summer of 1993. They followed it with the acclaimed debut *Icky Mettle* later in the year; it also received a sizable amount of airplay on college radio. In 1994 the

band released two EPs and worked on their second record, *Vee Vee*, which was released in early 1995; like its predecessor, *Vee Vee* was a college radio hit, securing the Archers of Loaf's place as one of the hippest indie-rock bands of the mid-'90s. Both the rarities collection *Speed of Cattle* and *All the Nation's Airports* followed in 1996. —*Stephen Thomas Erlewine*

● **Icky Mettle** / 1994 / Alias ✦✦✦✦
Icky Mettle, the Archers of Loaf's debut album, is filled with jagged guitars playing broken riffs, but they have enough melodic sense to tie it all together into memorable songs, as evidenced by the alternative rock hit "Web in Front." As that song's lyrics suggest ("All I ever wanted was to be your spine"), the group cherishes the obscure, but they are never weird for weirdness' sake; their fragmented poetry fits the cut-and-paste of the noisy music. —*Stephen Thomas Erlewine*

Vee Vee / Mar. 1995 / Alias ✦✦✦✦
Icky Mettle, the Archers' debut album, became just enough of an underground hit to scare the band away from most of their pop instincts. Filled with unexpected, jarring shards of noise and melodies that never quite manage to be catchy, *Vee Vee* relies more on attitude and energy than their previous records. It's an approach that works; for all their oblique song structures and overt noise, Archers of Loaf is a band that can rock hard. With the harder rhythms and jerky guitars, the group can usually obscure the elliptical hooks by just rocking out, which means the album is a bracing listen, yet not an engaging one. —*Stephen Thomas Erlewine*

The Speed of Cattle / Feb. 20, 1996 / Alias ✦✦✦

All the Nation's Airports / Sep. 24, 1996 / Alias/Elektra ✦✦✦

The Archies

f. 1968, Riverdale
Bubblegum
Not satisfied with his success with the Monkees, bubblegum pop manufacturer Don Kirshner formed this studio group based on the comic books and animated television show of the same name in the late '60s. Hiring an array of seasoned session musicians to support lead vocalists Ron Dante, Jeff Barry, and Ellie Greenwich, the Archies managed to produce several hits in the late '60s under the direction of Jeff Barry, including the massive hit single, "Sugar, Sugar." After a short spark of success, the group promptly vanished, leaving only nostalgic memories. —*Stephen Thomas Erlewine*

● **Great Archies** / RCA ✦✦✦✦
The Great Archies is an 18-track collection that features all of the fabricated pop group's biggest hits, including the No. 1 single "Sugar Sugar," the Top Ten "Jingle Jangle," and "Bang-Shang-a-Lang." The album is comprehensive, containing far more material than most fans could want. "Sugar Sugar" may be an infectious, guilty pleasure, but that doesn't mean re-writes of the song are enjoyable. Nevertheless, *The Great Archies* remains the definitive compilation. It is all the Archies you could ever need and more. —*Stephen Thomas Erlewine*

Argent

f. 1969, England, **db.** 1976
Art-Rock/Progressive-Rock, Pop-Rock
After the Zombies broke up, keyboardist/songwriter Rod Argent formed his own band in 1969, which incorporated more classical, jazz, and art-rock influences in accordance with Argent's musical training. The group's other members were guitarist/songwriter Russ Ballard, bassist Jim Rodford, and drummer Bob Henrit. Argent's first two albums, *Argent* and *Ring of Hands*, received a fair amount of critical acclaim, but their real breakthrough came with 1972's *All Together Now*, which contained the Top Five smash "Hold Your Head Up"; *In Deep* produced a minor hit with "God Gave Rock 'n' Roll to You," which was covered by Kiss in 1992. By 1974 Ballard had developed his songwriting talents enough to leave for a solo career (Three Dog Night had a Top Ten single in 1971 with his "Liar," from *Argent*), and was replaced by guitarist John Verity and string player John Grimaldi. Without Ballard, the group lost its focus and indulged its tendencies towards extended art-rock passages and improvisational solos to somewhat excessive levels. Argent broke up in 1976; Rodford joined the Kinks, while Argent himself recorded several solo albums and became a record producer, working with Tanita Tikaram, among others. —*Steve Huey*

Argent / 1969 / BGO ✦✦✦
With hindsight, it seems as if the Zombies didn't so much come to a halt as split off into two different directions. Colin Blunstone would take the band's poppiest, sweetest elements; Argent would take the gutsier ones, and appropriate the intricate keyboard arrangements (naturally enough, as keyboardist Rod Argent was the leader of both Argent and the Zombies). Neither Blunstone nor Argent would approach the majesty of the Zombies' prime, but they'd offer some pretty fair approximations. And that's what you get on Argent's self-titled debut—a fair

approximation of late-period Zombies, with a much heavier hard/progressive rock feel. There's nothing that's nearly as arresting as *Odessey and Oracle*, but it's not bad at all. Includes Russ Ballard's "Liar," the first Argent track to get heavy airplay in the US. —*Richie Unterberger*

All Together Now / 1972 / Epic ✦✦✦✦
Thanks to the hit single "Hold Your Head Up," *All Together Now* was Argent's most successful album, and in many ways, it's also their most consistent. Although it isn't quite as interesting as the debut, the band has perfected an anthemic rock that owes as much to hard rock and progressive rock. Cuts like "Be My Lover, Be My Friend," "I Am the Dance of Ages" and "Keep On Rollin'" will appeal to fans of "Hold Your Head Up," even if they lack the wild spark of *Argent*. —*Stephen Thomas Erlewine*

● **Anthology: The Best of Argent** / 1976 / Epic ✦✦✦✦
At eight tracks, *Anthology: The Best of Argent* might be a little skimpy, but it includes all of the band's biggest hits and choicest inclusions, including "Hold Your Head Up," "Liar," "God Gave Rock and Roll to You," and a reworking of Rod Argent's Zombies hit "Time of the Season." —*Stephen Thomas Erlewine*

Joan Armatrading

b. Dec. 9, 1950, Basseterre, St. Kitts, West Indies
Guitar, Piano, Vocals / Singer-Songwriter
Born on the island of St. Kitts, British singer-songwriter Joan Armatrading was her country's first Black woman to make commercial inroads into her chosen genre, spicing her take on folk with bits of soul and reggae, and has had a remarkably long, consistent career. Emigrating to England in 1958, Armatrading met lyricist Pam Nestor in a touring production of *Hair*, and the two began collaborating on material later featured on Armatrading's 1972 debut, *Whatever's for Us*. The two ended their partnership afterwards, and Armatrading resurfaced in 1975 with *Back to the Night*. Featuring former members of Fairport Convention, *Joan Armatrading* catapulted the singer into the UK Top 20 and produced her only Top Ten single, "Love and Affection." Armatrading's subsequent albums sold well in the UK to her newly established fan base, but only respectably in the US, where it took her until 1980 to have a real hit (the all-electric *Me Myself I*). *The Key* also did quite well, but Armatrading remained largely a cult artist with a small but devoted following in America, never quite achieving the stardom she had in Britain. Armatrading has been successful enough to record regularly up through the mid-'90s and continues to tour. —*Steve Huey*

Whatever's for Us / 1972 / A&M ✦✦
Joan Armatrading's debut album is all but co-credited to Pam Nestor, who co-wrote 11 of the 14 songs and whose picture and bio appear on the album jacket. (She doesn't perform on the record, however.) Since Armatrading dispensed with the collaboration on later albums, a comparison is instructive. On these relatively short songs (averaging about 2:45), Armatrading is more outward-looking than on her later songs. Much of her work is done in close-ups, but many of the songs on *Whatever's for Us* pull back from the "I-you" focus of subsequent efforts to take in the family, especially, and the world at large. Granted, when it is viewed positively, at least in the formal sense. For the album, Armatrading used some of Elton John's brain trust, and especially when she plays piano, the sound is not unlike an early John album such as *Tumbleweed Connection*. *Whatever's for Us* is a promising debut that, nevertheless, does not include any material that has proven to be memorable. —*William Ruhlmann*

Back to the Night / 1975 / A&M ✦✦✦
Even this early on, Armatrading's basic theme—the conflict between the need for romantic attachment and the need for independence—is in place in all its paradoxical glory. She revels in the joys of love and is repelled by the threat love represents to her identity. On this release, the message overwhelms the medium, however. Armatrading hasn't yet developed the musical structures to make her lyrical concerns memorable. —*William Ruhlmann*

Joan Armatrading / Sep. 1976 / A&M ✦✦✦✦
Her third album was the one most people fell in love with, attracted by her Caribbean-flavored singing of articulate romantic lyrics and Glyn Johns' tasteful folk-rock production, especially on "Love and Affection." —*William Ruhlmann*

Show Some Emotion / Oct. 1977 / A&M ✦✦✦
A companion piece to *Joan Armatrading*, this lovely album contains the title track, "Warm Love," and "Willow." —*William Ruhlmann*

To the Limit / Oct. 1978 / A&M ✦✦✦
She began to up the musical ante with a more rock-oriented approach, and her songs also took on a more argumentative tone, especially in the critical "Barefoot and Pregnant." —*William Ruhlmann*

Steppin' Out / 1979 / A&M ✦✦✦
In 1979 Armatrading's following in the US was not big enough to justify the release of this concert album, although it was recorded in North America. It demonstrates her rapport with her fans and her effective-

ness as a live performer and includes such favorites as "Love and Affection" and "You Rope You Tie Me." — *William Ruhlmann*

How Cruel / Nov. 1979 / A&M ✦✦✦
How Cruel is a four-song, one-sided, 12-inch EP released, according to the blurb on the cover, because the tunes were "so good they couldn't wait for an album!!!" (The title track had already appeared, albeit not in the US, on the live *Steppin' Out* album.) In fact, the songs are good, although the decision to release them probably had more to do with having something in the marketplace between the autumn 1978 release of *To the Limit* and the spring 1980 release of *Me Myself, I.* The best track is "How Cruel," a complaint about her career ("I had somebody say once I was way too Black/And someone answers she's not Black enough for me") with a terrific sax solo by Lon Price, although "He Wants Her," with a lazy reggae beat, also impresses. — *William Ruhlmann*

Me Myself, I / May 1980 / A&M ✦✦✦✦
On the trio of albums that made her reputation in 1976-1978,(*Joan Armatrading, Show Some Emotion,* and *To the Limit,*) Armatrading relied on the pristine production of Glyn Johns to underscore the sensitivity of her folk-based confessional songs. Here, on her first full-length album in two years, she turned to rock producer Richard Gottehrer and a session band that included Anton Fig, Chris Spedding, and members of the E Street Band, making her case for being a mainstream rocker. The songs were less serious, too, notably the title track, a UK hit. (The album's other British chart single was the ballad "All the Way from America," which was more in the style of her earlier work.) The result was the best-selling album Armatrading has ever had in either the US or UK. — *William Ruhlmann*

Walk Under Ladders / Sep. 1981 / A&M ✦✦✦
Dominant keyboard lines and the characteristic fat percussion approach of producer Steve Lillywhite completed Armatrading's transformation from folky to new wave diva on this album. Still, it was songs like "The Weakness in Me" to which old fans responded, although the UK hits were "I'm Lucky" and "No Love." Another British Top Ten, the album was less successful in the US, consolidating Armatrading's expanded following without propelling her to major stardom. — *William Ruhlmann*

The Key / Mar. 1983 / A&M ✦✦✦✦
The best of Armatrading's later albums, which took on a much harder rock edge. Steve Lillywhite produced, and Armatrading provided some good uptempo material, including "Drop the Pilot" and "(I Love It When You) Call Me Names." — *William Ruhlmann*

Track Record / Nov. 1983 / A&M ✦✦✦✦
Track Record was the first anthology of Joan Armatrading's '70s recordings to be assembled, and the 13-track collection remains an excellent sampler of her first eight albums, featuring such highlights as "Me Myself, I," "Love and Affection," "Show Some Emotion," and her only chart hit, "Drop the Pilot." — *Stephen Thomas Erlewine*

Secret Secrets / Feb. 1985 / A&M ✦✦✦
Mike Howlett, known for the dance-friendly, keyboard-dominated pop sheen of his productions for groups like A Flock of Seagulls and Berlin, gives a similar sound to Armatrading here (lots of echo on the vocals, lots of shimmering, horn-like synthesizer parts). It isn't really a good fit, though the record sold respectably and produced a minor UK chart hit in "Temptation." — *William Ruhlmann*

Sleight of Hand / May 1986 / A&M ✦✦
Armatrading becomes her own producer here (with Steve Lillywhite returning as mixer), and does herself no favors, continuing to overwhelm her songs with effects. By now, her cult was beginning to become disaffected, and she had failed to break through to the pop mainstream. At this point, she was selling fewer and fewer records and seemed destined to keep playing concerts to fans who would call out for "Love and Affection." — *William Ruhlmann*

The Shouting Stage / Jul. 1988 / A&M ✦✦
The good news is that, after several albums of flirting with rock and overproduction, Joan Armatrading has developed a spare sound, once again focusing on her songs and singing, backed by such tasteful accompanists as Dire Straits members Mark Knopfler and Alan Clark. The not-so-good news is that, lyrically, Armatrading seems trapped in a romantic cul-de-sac; when she doesn't have the object of her affections, she longs for him, but when she does have him, she argues with him and suspects him of infidelity, not to mention emotional abuse. There is a traditional sense of relationships mixed in with hints of the nascent "men just don't get it" flavor of '90s feminism. One is tempted to say that you can't have it both ways, but then Armatrading's emotional outpourings have always had more to do with contemporaneous honesty than long-term consistency. — *William Ruhlmann*

Hearts and Flowers / Jun. 1990 / A&M ✦✦
For much of her 12th new studio album, Joan Armatrading sounds as if she is ending a bad relationship, but by the last two songs she sounds as if she's beginning a good one. Still, she finds herself pledging herself to

someone she worries may not have the same commitment she does. Thus, perhaps the album's signal song (and Armatrading's first UK chart single in five years) is "More Than One Kind of Love," in which she touts the value of friendship over romance. "Good friendships seldom die," she sings, and we are painfully aware that, especially in Armatrading's world, even good love affairs seldom live. Still, this is less a revelation than an incremental development in the artist's work, and *Hearts and Flowers* doesn't contain any songs that rank among her best. — *William Ruhlmann*

Square the Circle / Jun. 23, 1992 / A&M ✦✦✦
Joan Armatrading, who has spent the better part of her career demanding greater commitment and fidelity from men than they seem willing to give her, turns the tables on her 13th album, abandoning herself to lust for "the wrong guy" and unfaithfulness to her beloved. The equation produces interesting, if not always successful, results, such as the characterstically convoluted "Can't Get Over (How I Broke Your Heart)," but makes a poor lead-in to the philosophical "If Women Ruled the World," which proves that sexism sounds just as lame-brained coming from a woman as it does coming from a man. "Not all men kill babies," Armatrading admits, which is certainly a relief to hear. But if women ruled the world, there would be "no more war, no more hate . . . no more sons dying young." This from a woman who lived under the Margaret Thatcher regime during the Falklands War. — *William Ruhlmann*

What's Inside / Oct. 10, 1995 / RCA ✦✦
Joan Armatrading's abandonment of A&M Records after two decades makes sense when you consider that the long-time independent had been swallowed by PolyGram. What doesn't make sense is where she went, the virtually moribund RCA, which managed to release this label debut as though it were a state secret. The album itself is an interesting mixture of the styles Armatrading has employed at various times in her career, from the spare, intimate approach associated with her "Love and Affection" phase to the pop-rock of "Me Myself, I." The coulda-been-a-hit is "Can't Stop Loving You." Many of the tracks are augmented by strings, courtesy of the London Metropolitan Orchestra, and the Kronos Quartet checks in for one track. Romance is the subject, as usual, and, as usual, it is treated in sometimes quirky ways, such as in "Shapes and Sizes," which advises that you express your love while you can, because "Obituary columns are full of love." Hmm. This is an album for the cult, which is appropriate, since they're the only ones likely to know of its existence. — *William Ruhlmann*

● **Greatest Hits** / Jun. 18, 1996 / A&M ✦✦✦✦
Greatest Hits features all of Joan Armatrading's biggest hits and best-known tracks, including "Love and Affection," "Show Some Emotion," and "Rosie," as well as the previously unreleased live track, "Kissin' and a Huggin'." The disc is a thorough retrospective and functions as an excellent introduction to the introspective singer-songwriter. — *Thom Owens*

Love and Affection / 1997 / A&M ✦✦✦✦
Love and Affection is a 38-track, double-disc retrospective of Joan Armatrading's entire 20-year history with A&M, containing nearly all of her best material, from hit singles like "Show Some Emotion" and the title track to important album tracks. For casual fans wanting a more detailed and comprehensive compilation than a single-disc greatest hits collection, *Love and Affection* is an excellent summation of Armatrading's many strengths. — *Stephen Thomas Erlewine*

Army of Lovers

f. 1987, Sweden
Europop, Euro-Dance
The flamboyant multi-cultural Swedish dance-pop group Army of Lovers formed in 1987, the brainchild of composer and producer Alexander Bard. Five years earlier Bard first emerged as a member of the short-lived trio Baard, best known for the single "Life in a Goldfish Bowl." In 1985—in drag, no less—he led Barbie, a band also comprising hairdresser Jean-Pierre Barda (alias Farouk), Yazmina Chantal, and model Camilla Henemark (a.k.a. Katanga); two years later, Bard, Barda, and Henemark (now performing under the name La Camilla) founded Army of Lovers, taking the name in honor of the 1970s cult movie *Armee der Liebenden* as well as a gay documentary titled *Army of Lovers, or Revolt of the Perverts.*

With the aid of designer and stylist Camilla Thulin, the group created an outrageously campy image, their wardrobe drawing heavily on religious imagery while also referencing history and folklore. Army of Lovers debuted in 1988 with the single "When the Night Is Cold," followed by the more dance-minded "Love Me Like a Loaded Gun." After scoring a 1989 hit with "Supernatural," the next year they issued their debut LP *Disco Extravaganza* (issued in the US as *Army of Lovers*). 1991's *Massive Luxury Overdose,* recorded with producer Anders Wollbeck, was their breakthrough; in tandem with a pair of lurid videos, the singles "Crucified" and "Obsession" became club hits, and the group became major stars in their native Scandinavia and throughout Eastern Europe.

In the wake of the record's success, however, La Camilla was fired and replaced by model and school teacher Michaela Dornonville de la Cour, who debuted on the single "Judgment Day." After recording music for the soundtrack to the film *Ha Ett Underbart Liv*, Army of Lovers recruited former phone-sex operator Dominika Peczynski and released 1993's *The Gods of Earth and Heaven;* the single "Israelism" became the subject of considerable controversy when it was accused of mocking Jewish culture, but ironically rose to the No. 1 spot on the Israeli pop charts. After 1994's *Glory Glamour and Gold,* de la Cour exited, paving the way for the return of La Camilla prior to the release of the 1996 *Les Greatest Hits.* With Army of Lovers on hiatus, Bard formed a new group, Vacuum, and issued 1997's *The Plutonium Cathedral;* La Camilla, meanwhile, mounted a solo career. —*Jason Ankeny*

Army of Lovers / Aug. 13, 1991 / Giant ✦✦✦
Originally titled *Disco Extravaganza* in its native Europe, Army of Lovers' debut relies significantly on sampled material, as well as worldbeat rhythms and other international influences. —*Jason Ankeny*

Massive Luxury Overdose / Mar. 17, 1992 / Giant ✦✦✦✦
Massive Luxury Overdose is Army of Lovers' breakthrough effort. Along with their over-the-top videos, the singles "Crucified" and "Obsession" became the group's biggest hits. —*Jason Ankeny*

Gods of Earth and Heaven / Jun. 1, 1993 / Alex ✦✦✦✦
Along with the controversial hit "Israelism," Army of Lovers' third LP *The Gods of Earth and Heaven* features the singles "La Plage de Saint Tropez" and "I Am." —*Jason Ankeny*

● **Les Greatest Hits** / 1995 / Ils International ✦✦✦✦
Les Greatest Hits remains the best introduction to Army of Lovers' music. Along with the singles "Supernatural," "Crucified," "Obsession," and "Israelism," it features the new tracks "Give My Life," "Venus and Mars," and "Requiem." —*Jason Ankeny*

P.P. Arnold

b. 1946, Los Angeles, CA
Vocals / Soul
A soul vocalist who came from a family of gospel singers, Pat (P.P.) Arnold began singing as a four-year-old. She got her start backing Bobby Day before being invited to join the Ikettes, backing Ike and Tina Turner. Arnold toured with them in the '60s, including one stint with the Rolling Stones. Mick Jagger persuaded her to remain in London, and she later recorded for the Immediate label (then run by the Stones' manager Andrew Loog-Oldham). Loog-Oldham, Jagger, and Mike Hurst produced Arnold's debut LP, *The First Lady of Immediate,* in 1967, which included the single "The First Cut Is the Deepest," written by Cat Stevens and later popularized by Rod Stewart. Arnold also had moderate success with the singles "The Time Has Come," "(If You Think) You're Groovy," and "Angel in the Morning" in the late '60s, though they were hits in England and Europe rather than America. Arnold was part of the cast for the play *Catch My Soul* in 1969 and subsequently acted in the television shows "Fame" and "Knots Landing," plus Andrew Lloyd Webber's *Starlight Express.* Arnold re-entered the music world in the mid-'80s. She sang lead on a Boy George song for the film *Electric Dreams* in 1984 while on 10 Records. She worked with Dexter Wansel and Loose Ends on the single "A Little Pain," which she recorded as Pat Arnold. She then had another English hit with the single "Burn It Up" on the Rhythm King label. The Beatmasters later produced her song "Dynamite." —*Ron Wynn*

● **P. P. Arnold Collection** / May 21, 1991 / Sony ✦✦✦✦
Transplanted American R&B singer hits it big with achingly soulful ballads. A '60s curio and more, especially "The First Cut Is the Deepest." —*Bruce Eder*

Arrested Development

f. 1988, Atlanta, GA, **db.** 1996
Hip Hop, Urban, Alternative Rap
One of the major success stories of 1992, Arrested Development is a progressive rap collective fusing soul, blues, hip-hop, and Sly and the Family Stone-influenced funk with political, socially conscious lyrics. The group was founded in the late '80s by rapper Speech (born Todd Thomas) and DJ Headliner (born Timothy Barnwell), who met while attending the Art Institute of Atlanta. The two formed a gangsta-rap outfit called Disciples of Lyrical Rebellion and later became Secret Society. After hearing Public Enemy, the two decided to make the transition to a more positive, Afrocentric viewpoint, and gradually picked up members such as dancers Montsho Eshe and Aerle Taree (the latter is Speech's cousin), percussionist Rasa Don, his fiancee, singer Dionne Farris, and spiritual adviser and theorist Baba Oje.

Arrested Development's debut album took its title from the amount of time it took the group to secure a record contract; *Three Years, Five Months and Two Days in the Life of . . .* produced the hit single "Ten-

nessee," a strongly spiritual track inspired by the deaths of Speech's brother and grandmother and partially based on summer visits to the latter's home in Ripley, TN, as a child. The album garnered rave reviews and sold over four million copies, while "Tennessee" went gold and hit the Top Ten; its two follow-ups, "People Everyday" (a rewrite of Sly's "Everyday People) and "Mr. Wendal," did likewise. Accolades poured in; Arrested Development won Grammys for Best Rap Album by a Duo or Group and Best New Artist (the first rap act to do so) and were named *Rolling Stone's* Band of the Year.

The band played on the 1993 Lollapalooza tour, released an *Unplugged* album, and also contributed the track "Revolution" to supporter Spike Lee's *Malcolm X.* However, there was dissension in the ranks; Farris, whose vocals were a big part of "Tennessee"'s success, left the group for a solo career, and Speech shook up the lineup, switching Headliner to a co-rapping slot and replacing him with DJ Kwesi Asuo, also adding bassist Foley, singer Nadirah, and dancer Ajile. Their second album, *Zingalamaduni* (Swahili for "beehive of culture"), was released in 1994; while some reviews hailed it as a major work, overall response from both critics and record buyers was more ambivalent. Speech, who writes a column on racial issues for his mother's newspaper, the *Milwaukee Community Journal,* and occasionally lectures on his political views, was criticized for allowing his politics to become heavy-handed, while he himself was portrayed as a control freak unable to work with others after Farris' departure. Those rumors were lent credence in 1996 when, contrary to Speech's earlier assertion that the group would be around for ten or twelve years, Arrested Development officially broke up. Speech went solo and recorded a debut album, which failed to make an impact. —*Steve Huey*

● **Three Years, Five Months & Two Days in the Life of . . .** / Mar. 24, 1992 / Chrysalis ✦✦✦✦
A crew that became one of 1992's sensations by infusing hip-hop with blues sensibility on their debut, *Three Years, Five Months & Two Days in the Life of . . . ,* especially on the single "Tennessee." —*Ron Wynn*

Unplugged / Mar. 1993 / Chrysalis ✦✦
Basically a live rerecording of *Three Years, Five Months, & Two Days in the Life of . . .* (minus their breakthrough hit, "Tennessee"), *Unplugged* breaks no new ground for Arrested Development. Eight of the 11 songs on the album are from their debut, and the three new tracks are slight. The album is filled out with remixes of seven tracks, which are the instrumental tracks with the vocals turned down but still slightly audible. Despite the fact that it doesn't offer anything new on *Three Years,* the album is an enjoyable listen. —*Stephen Thomas Erlewine*

Zingalamaduni / Jun. 14, 1994 / Chrysalis ✦✦✦
Arrested Development's proper follow-up to their smash debut doesn't stray too far from the rootsy Southern hip-hop that made *Three Years* a hit, but it doesn't ignite as frequently as its predecessor. While its best tracks, like "Mister Landlord" and "Praisin' U," are the equal of "Mr. Wendal" or "People Everyday," there is no statement of purpose on the level of "Tennessee." The album is too unfocused to be as impressive as the debut, but *Zingalamundi* shows that the group is more than a one-hit wonder. —*Stephen Thomas Erlewine*

The Art of Noise

f. Jan. 1984, London, England, **db.** 1990
New Wave, Experimental
Anne Dudley, Gary Lanagan, and J.J. Jeczalik were members of producer Trevor Horn's in-house studio band in the early '80s before they formed Art of Noise, a techno-pop group whose music was an amaglam of studio gimmickry, tape splicing, and synthesized beats. The Art of Noise took material from a variety of sources: hip-hop, rock, jazz, R&B, traditional pop, found sounds, and noise all worked their way into the group's distinctly post-modern soundscapes.

Dudley was the center of the group, having arranged and produced material for Frankie Goes to Hollywood, ABC, and Paul McCartney before forming the Art of Noise. The trio signed with Trevor Horn's ZTT label, releasing their first EP, *Into Battle with the Art of Noise,* in 1983. The following year, the group released the full-length (*Who's Afraid Of?) The Art of Noise!,* which featured the hit single "Close (To the Edit)."

After "Close (To the Edit)," the group parted ways with Horn and ZTT, releasing *In Visible Silence* in 1986; the album included the UK Top Ten hit "Peter Gunn," which featured Duane Eddy on guitar. *Re-works of the Art of Noise,* an album of remixes and live tracks, was released that same year. *In No Sense? Nonsense!,* released in 1987, saw the band experimenting with orchestras and choirs as well as horns and rock bands. The next year, the Art of Noise released a greatest-hits collection, *The Best of the Art of Noise,* which featured their collaboration with Tom Jones on Prince's "Kiss." *Below the Waste* (1990) captured the band experimenting with world music; it received a lukewarm critical and commercial reception. The following year, a low-key remix album directed by Killing Joke's Youth called *The Ambient Collection* appeared. Later in the year, the Art of Noise broke up; Dudley eventually worked with Killing Joke's Jaz Coleman and Phil Collins. —*Stephen Thomas Erlewine*

● **The Best of the Art of Noise** / 1988 / China ✦✦✦✦
All of the Art of Noise's best tracks are here, including "Close (To the Edit)," "Legacy," and a cover of Prince's "Kiss" with Tom Jones on lead vocals. —*Stephen Thomas Erlewine*

Ash

f. 1989, Ulster, Northern Island
Alternative Pop-Rock, Brit-Pop, Punk-Pop
Ash was one of the most successful post-Brit-pop bands of the mid-'90s, rocketing to the top of the UK charts with their infectious punk-pop. Like Nirvana, the trio combined pop melodies with an indie-punk rush and heavy guitars. What distinguished Ash was their youth—all three members were in their teens when the first recordings were released, and their music reverberated with emotions and obsessions of youth.

Guitarist/vocalist Tim Wheeler and bassist Mark Hamilton formed Ash in Ulster, Northern Ireland, in 1989, when they were 12 years old. Initially, the duo was inspired by heavy metal, but they eventually became infatuated with punk, indie, and pop music, largely due to the appearance of Nirvana's *Nevermind*. By the time Ash released their independent debut single, "Jack Named the Planets," in 1994, they had added drummer Rick McMurray. "Jack Named the Planets"—which was released as the group were studying for their A-Level exams—became an indie hit and earned the group a contract with Infectious Records.

In late 1994, the group released the mini-album *Trailer*, which featured the UK indie hit "Petrol." A reconfigured *Trailer* was released a year later in America. Throughout 1995, Ash supported a number of prestigious acts—including Suede, Dinosaur Jr. and Elastica—and racked up a string of singles, which culminated in the No. 11 hit "Girl from Mars" early in the summer; its success coincided with their graduation from high school. After playing the summer festivals in the UK, Ash headed toward America, where they signed with Reprise and spent three months touring the country; they frequently had to break the law in order to play in 21-and-over clubs. Produced by Owen Morris (Oasis, the Verve), Ash's debut album *1977* was released in May 1996. *1977* entered the UK charts at No. 1, becoming one of the most popular British albums of the year. Though the album didn't perform quite so well in the US, the group did manage to consolidate a cult following during the course of 1996. —*Stephen Thomas Erlewine*

Trailer / Oct. 1995 / Reprise ✦✦✦✦
Ash's debut album is a fairly standard piece of heavy guitar grunge blessed with ingratiating melodies. Since the band members were all in their teens when they recorded *Trailer*, it makes sense that they are more energetic than innovative; they tend to come up lacking in terms of original songs. Nevertheless, for fans of '90s heavy-guitar grunge-pop, *Trailer* serves up the goods. —*Stephen Thomas Erlewine*

● **1977** / May 1996 / Infectious/Reprise ✦✦✦✦
Two-thirds of Ash were born in 1977, which means that their latter-day punk-pop isn't very catholic. Instead of sticking to the rigid rules of American punk-pop—which means you can't stretch the song past three minutes—Ash takes a cinematic approach to their songs, throwing in elements of power pop, glam, post-Nirvana grunge, and post-Oasis rock. It's a melting pot of pop styles, basically because the members of the band are so young that they haven't conformed to the standards of the indie and punk subcultures. Sure, Ash still uses loud guitars—they're all over *1977*—but they create a distinctive, melodic, and energetic sound that's equal parts heavy grunge and light pop. And while they may indulge in jamming a bit too much, they remain a pop band at heart, capable of turning out epic guitar-pop like "Goldfinger," pop-punk like "Kung Fu," and the lovely but loud "Girl from Mars" with equal flair. —*Stephen Thomas Erlewine*

Live at the Wireless / Feb. 1997 / Death Star ✦✦✦
A limited-edition, semi-official bootleg released on Ash's own label, *Live at the Wireless* is a vigorous but curiously unengaging live recording that just misses its full potential. Recorded live in a radio studio during the group's 1996 Australian tour, the record does crackle with energy, but the lack of a studio audience is a mixed blessing. While the sound may be clearer than an audience recording, the lack of interaction with a crowd prevents the album from being truly transcendent. Even so, Ash is a powerful live band, and their exuberence is infectious, whether it's on hits like "Girl from Mars," "Goldfinger," and "Kung Fu," or their punked-up cover of Ween's "What the Deener Was Talking About." That alone makes *Live at the Wireless* worth seeking out for dedicated fans. —*Stephen Thomas Erlewine*

Ashford & Simpson

f. 1964, Harlem, NY
Vocals / Soul, Disco, R&B, Urban
Nickolas Ashford (b.May 4, 1942, Fairfield, SC) and Valerie Simpson

(b.Aug 26, 1946, New York City) have two careers, as songwriters and as performers, with the former seemingly more important than the latter until the mid-'80s. The two met in 1964 and scored their first songwriting hit in 1966 with Ray Charles' recording of their "Let's Go Get Stoned." After a period at Scepter Records, they moved to Motown, where they wrote hits for the duo of Marvin Gaye and Tammi Terrell ("Ain't Nothing Like the Real Thing," "You're All I Need to Get By"). When Diana Ross left the Supremes for a solo career, Ashford & Simpson wrote "Reach Out and Touch Somebody's Hand" for her.

Their own performing career was launched in 1973 with *Keep It Comin'* on Motown and *Gimme Something Real* on Warner Bros. Their first success came in 1977 with the gold-selling *Send It*, which contained the Top Ten R&B hit "Don't Cost You Nothing." *Is It Still Good to Ya*, a second gold album, contained the No. 2 R&B hit "It Seems to Hang On" in 1978. *Stay Free*, their third straight gold album, contained "Found a Cure," another R&B smash that also made the Top 40 on the pop chart. *A Musical Affair*, 1980, featured the hit "Love Don't Make It Right," but it was not as successful as previous efforts.

Meanwhile, A&S continued to work with other artists, scoring successes with Ross, Chaka Khan ("I'm Every Woman"), and Gladys Knight. Their own career saw a resurgence in 1984 with *Solid*, which went gold and produced the R&B No. 1 "Solid" (No. 12 on the pop charts), "Outta the World," and "Babies." During the late '80s and '90s, Ashford & Simpson continued to tour and record sporadically. —*William Ruhlmann*

● **Capitol Gold: The Best of Ashford & Simpson** / Jun. 21, 1993 / Capitol ✦✦✦✦
Ashford & Simpson scored 33 entries on the R&B singles charts between 1973 and 1990, all but one of them on Warner Bros. or Capitol. This compilation licenses the two biggest hits from the duo's tenure at Warner, "It Seems to Hang On" and "Found a Cure," both of which hit the Top Ten. It also features the eight Capitol titles that made the R&B Top 40: "Street Corner," "Love It Away," "High-Rise," "Solid," "Outta the World," "Babies," "Count Your Blessings," and "I'll Be There for You." There are also six tracks culled from the five Capitol albums, bringing the disc's time to over 71 minutes. In other words, this is about as comprehensive an overview of A&S's career as could be managed by one label on one disc. There are good biographical liner notes by compiler David Nathan. —*William Ruhlmann*

Gospel According to Ashford & Simpson / Oct. 29, 1996 / Capitol ✦✦✦✦
This 15-song sampler of their 1980s work leans far more heavily on tracks from the first half of the decade. It includes the hits "I'll Be There for You," "Count Your Blessings," "Street Opera," and "Solid," although one of their biggest, "Outta the World," is strangely absent. More than just about any other single-artist compilation you could name, this is a definitive representation of how mainstream soul often sounded in the 1980s. Which is to say, it often sounded more like adult contemporary pop than soul. —*Richie Unterberger*

Asia

f. Jan. 1981, Los Angeles, CA
Art-Rock/Progressive-Rock, Pop-Rock
When they appeared in the early '80s, Asia seemed to be a holdover from the '70s, when supergroups and self-important progressive rockers reigned supreme. Featuring members of such seminal art-rock bands as King Crimson (John Wetton), Emerson, Lake & Palmer (Carl Palmer), and Yes (Steve Howe), as well as Geoff Downes from the Buggles, Asia did feature stretches of indulgent instrumentals on their records. However, they also could be surprisingly poppy, and that is what brought them to the top of the charts with their debut album, *Asia*, and its hit single, "Heat of the Moment." *Alpha*, their second album, also had a couple of hits ("Don't Cry" and "The Smile Has Left Your Eyes"), but its follow-up, *Astra*, was a flop. The group disbanded in 1985, only to reunite in 1990 without John Wetton; Pat Thrall took his place. After churning out a couple of new songs for a greatest-hits collection, the band hit the road, including two sold-out dates in front of 20,000 fans in Moscow, of all places. Since then, they have toured sporadically and have released two albums, *Aqua* in 1992 and *Aria* in 1994. —*Stephen Thomas Erlewine*

Asia / 1982 / Geffen ✦✦✦✦
The debut release for this supergroup (featuring Steve Howe [Yes], John Wetton [UK], Carl Palmer [ELP], and Geoff Downes [Yes]) showcases their classy pop-rock, with several hits. —*Paul Kohler*

Alpha / 1983 / Geffen ✦✦✦
The follow-up album has the same lineup as the first. —*Paul Kohler*

Astra / Nov. 1985 / Geffen ✦✦
Asia was always a bland, derivative excuse for a dinosaur rock band, but when their debut album came out in 1982 and sold three million copies, they seemed like a repudiation of the new wave movement, the pop music equivalent of the Reagan revolution in politics. Like Ronnie, how-

ever, Asia ran out of gas around mid-decade. True, they were still constructing keyboard-dominated, heroic-voiced arena pop; but suddenly nobody cared anymore, or at least not enough customers to vault them into the Top Ten, and for this kind of band, it's platinum or don't bother. So, first, guitarist Steve Howe took his marbles and went home to Yes, and then the rest of the band packed it in, too. They'd be back, of course, when the money was right. —*William Ruhlmann*

● **Then & Now** / Aug. 1990 / Geffen ◆◆◆◆
This compilation includes all of their Top 40 hits—"Heat of the Moment," "Only Time Will Tell," "Don't Cry," and "The Smile Has Left Your Eyes"—as well as some unreleased tracks. —*AMG*

Aqua / 1992 / JRS ◆◆
Their latest release for a new label is noticeably missing the vocal work of former bassist John Wetton. Carl Palmer, Steve Howe, and Geoff Downes are still on hand, producing more of their brand of slick, smooth rock. It's reminiscent of the revamped Bad Company. —*Scott Bultman*

Aria / May 1994 / Mayhem ◆◆

Archives 1 / Feb. 4, 1997 / Pavement ◆◆◆
Archives 1 collects previously unreleased material from the arena-rockers Asia, including "Heart of Gold," "Tears," "The Mariner's Dream," "Reality," "I Can't Wait a Lifetime," and "Dusty Road." For fanatics only. —*Jason Ankeny*

The Associates

f. 1979, Edinburgh, Scotland, db. 1991
Pop-Rock, Dance-Pop, New Wave, Synth-Pop
Formed in Edinburgh, Scotland in 1979, the Associates comprised vocalist Billy Mackenzie and multi-instrumentalist Alan Rankine. Built on an eclectic mix of influences and interests ranging from art-rock to glam and disco, the group debuted with a manic cover of David Bowie's "Boys Keep Swinging," which earned them a contract with Fiction Records. Their 1980 debut LP, *The Affectionate Punch*, was a critically acclaimed work that expanded the duo's sound into both stark minimalism and melodramatic ballads, earning Mackenzie's powerful voice favorable comparisons to Scott Walker.

After jumping to the Situation Two label, the Associates released a series of singles that explored a continually diverse array of styles and textures. With 1982's "Party Fears Two," issued under their own Associates label imprint, the group finally hit the UK Top Ten, and the follow-up singles "Club Country" and "18 Carat Love Affair" both reached the Top 30. In 1982 *Sulk* was the group's definitive statement, a fascinating blend of lush, New Romantic popcraft and dark, surreal cabaret stylings.

After the LP's success, however, relations between Mackenzie and Rankine soured, and the latter left the group for a solo career, releasing the albums *The Day the World Became Her Age* (1986), *She Loves Me Not* (1987) and *The Big Picture Sucks* (1989). Undaunted, Mackenzie retained the Associates name and teamed with Martin Rushent to record an album that went unreleased, although a few of the tracks later emerged on 1985's *Perhaps*, fleshed out by keyboardist Howard Hughes and guitarist Steve Reid.

A long layoff followed, with another album, *The Glamour Chase*, recorded but rejected by label chiefs. In 1990 the Eurodisco-flavored *Wild and Lonely* emerged, and its lack of success effectively ended the Associates' story. In early 1997, while in the midst of preparing for a projected comeback, Mackenzie committed suicide. —*Jason Ankeny*

Affectionate Punch: Edition 1 / 1980 / Fiction ◆◆◆◆
A highly inspired debut, it picks up where late-'70s Bowie leaves off. —*Steve Aldrich*

Fourth Drawer Down / 1981 / Beggars Banquet ◆◆◆
Singles released between the *Punch* and *Sulk* LPs are collected here. —*Steve Aldrich*

Sulk: Edition 1 / 1982 / Associates ◆◆◆◆
A jarring, difficult, but richly rewarding album, it's a classic of early '80s UK pop and is well worth seeking out in this version. —*Steve Aldrich*

Perhaps / 1985 / WEA ◆◆

Wild and Lonely / Sep. 1990 / Charisma ◆◆

● **Popera: The Singles Collection** / Dec. 11, 1990 / Sire ◆◆◆◆

The Association

f. 1965, Los Angeles, CA, db. 1973
Pop-Rock
The smooth, soft pop harmonies and occasional light psychedelic touches of the Association resulted in several smash singles for the sextet from 1966 to 1968. The group was founded by keyboardist/multi-instrumentalist Terry Kirkman, along with lead vocalist Gary Alexander, guitarist/vocalists Russ Giguere and Jim Yester, bassist/vocalist Brian Coles, and drummer Ted Blueschel. After two flop singles, "Babe I'm

Gonna Leave You" and Bob Dylan's "One Two Many Mornings," the Association scored its first Top Ten hit with "Along Comes Mary," which received a major publicity boost from allegations that it contained coded references to marijuana. Kirkman's "Cherish" next became their first No. 1 hit, and the Association lent their lush, romantic harmonies to a string of Top Ten hits that included another No. 1, "Windy," "Never My Love," and "Everything That Touches You." However, their sales declined after 1968, with attempts to forge a more rock-oriented sound falling flat with the public. The group recorded a soundtrack for the film *Goodbye Columbus* in 1969 and a comeback album, *Waterbeds in Trinidad*, in 1972, but their popularity had hit bottom. Brian Coles died of a drug overdose in 1973, and the band broke up thereafter, reuniting occasionally for concerts and oldies shows. —*Steve Huey*

Association's Greatest Hits / 1968 / Warner Brothers ◆◆◆◆
Although *Association's Greatest Hits* contains only 13 tracks, the group's biggest hits—"Along Comes Mary," "Cherish," "Windy," "Never My Love," "Everything That Touches You"—are included, making the compilation satisfactory for casual listeners. —*Stephen Thomas Erlewine*

● **Songs That Made Them Famous** / 1986 / Pair ◆◆◆◆
Beyond the hits, all of which are included here ("Windy," "Cherish," "Along Comes Mary"), the Association made stunning orchestral folk-pop that still makes the listener feel good. —*Jeff Tamarkin*

The Association's Golden Heebie-Jeebies / 1987 / Edsel ◆◆
The liner notes make a game effort at presenting the Association as a band that could be meaningfully psychedelic when it wanted to be. Accordingly, this 15-song compilation draws from the trippier efforts of their first three albums (originally issued in 1966 and 1967). The fact of the matter is, though, that these guys offered about as much of a genuine psychedelic experience as smoking a banana peel. Being a pop-rock band in Southern California during this period, they couldn't help reflecting the era's wilder ethos in some modestly adventurous arrangements and slightly ambitious lyrics. Still, more often than not, this collection sounds like nothing so much as a psychedelic Four Freshmen, dominated by frothy harmonies that are as reliable an indication of substance as the whipped cream on a pie. The material is not downright obnoxious—it's somewhat pleasant—but with three exceptions, the songs pass from one ear to the other as easily as whipped cream goes through the digestive system. Two of those three exceptions, "Along Comes Mary" and "Windy," are available on any greatest hits collection; the other, the haunting raga-rocker (and minor hit single) "Pandora's Golden Heebie Jeebies," was reissued in much stronger company on Rhino's *Nuggets Volume 5*. —*Richie Unterberger*

The Astronauts

f. Boulder, CO
Surf
Along with Minnesota's Trashmen, the Astronauts (from Colorado) were the premier landlocked, Midwestern surf group of the 1960s. They recorded numerous singles and albums and achieved vast regional popularity, but they scored only one modest national hit, "Baja." With little material of their own, they judiciously tapped heavyweights like Lee Hazlewood (who wrote "Baja"), Roger Christian, and Gary Usher, as well as covering tunes by Dick Dale and Henry Mancini. The group shone brightest on the instrumentals, which used mounds of Fender reverb and two rhythm guitars; when they sang, the results were much less successful. —*Richie Unterberger*

● **Surf Party** / 1988 / RCA ◆◆◆◆
This compilation of 20 songs from their 1963-64 heyday features the best of their sleek instrumentals and raucous R&B-influenced numbers. "Competition Coupe" (written by surf scenesters Christian and Usher) stands up well to early numbers in the same vein by the Beach Boys and Jan & Dean, but covers of classics like "Around and Around," "Twist and Shout," and "Susie-Q" are lead-footed. And the group original "You Gotta Let Me Go" is a transparent ripoff of the Beatles' "I'll Be Back." The instrumentals on this collection have a gloriously supple power, though. Besides "Baja," highlights include the instrumental themes to the obscure films *Surf Party* and *Ride the Wild Surf*, the latter written by Roger Christian, Brian Wilson, and Jan Berry. —*Richie Unterberger*

Live / 1989 / Bear Family ◆◆◆
This CD combines their two live albums from the early '60s ("Everything Is A-OK" and "Astronauts Orbit Kampus") on one disc. As a premier American teen combo of the pre-Beatles era, this makes for unbelievably exciting, greasy, shake 'em on down rock 'n' roll from beginning to end. —*Cub Koda*

Atari Teenage Riot

f. 1992, Berlin, Germany
Experimental, Hardcore Techno, Jungle/Drum 'N Bass, Electronica
Berlin hardcore dissenters Atari Teenage Riot are among a new genera-

tion of German techno artists (including ATR's Alec Empire, EC80R, Speedfreak, DJ Bleed, etc.) seeking to reconnect music with political radicalism through ever more challenging, experimental hybrids, engaging everything from speed metal and acid to jungle and hardcore punk. Formed in 1992 by Empire, Hanin Elias, and Carl Crack, ATR's controversial first single, "Hunting for Nazis," was released by German techno stronghold Force Inc. that same year (Force Inc. owner Achim Szepanski is also known for his commitment to political radicalism). Since then the group has released a string of singles and full-lengths, all of them instantly recognizable for their brash, noisy fusions of brittle, 200+ bpm breaks, massive guitar riffs, and a good deal of shouting. Similar in motivation to Detroit's Underground Resistance or industrial dance group Consolidated, ATR has professed a concern with a general conservative shift in the Western political climate (particularly in Germany after the collapse of communism in Russia and Eastern Europe) and for the development of new, overtly political forms of youth culture by way of response.

Somewhat surprisingly, the group's early singles landed them a recording deal with UK major Phonogram in 1993, through whom they released a number of singles before skipping out on their contract (the label reportedly wanted more straight-ahead, commercial techno from the group). Using their Phonogram advance for the full-length album they never delivered, ATR formed Digital Hardcore Recordings (DHR) in 1994, the imprint under which they would release most of their subsequent material to date, including the full-lengths *Delete Yourself* and *The Future of War*, plus a number of singles and EPs. DHR has also expanded to include a number of up-and-coming German artists—including EC80R and Shizuo—with similar political leanings, and signed a domestic licensing deal with Beastie Boys label Grand Royal in 1996. Partly as a result of that deal and partly through the increasing popularity of ATR member Alec Empire (who's released a number of solo full-lengths and singles through Force Inc., Chrome, Mille Plateaux, and Riot Beats, as well as DHR), ATR has become one of the first new-school European techno groups to achieve success in America, with alternative radio and MTV picking up on the them in late 1996 and the release of an American album early the following year. —*Sean Cooper*

Delete Yourself / Mar. 1996 / DHR/Grand Royal ✦✦✦✦
Although *Delete Yourself* is a raucous, blustery advance of punk vigor—full of pissed-off shouting and loud, angry guitars—its backbone of gabber-core techno, sputtering, overdriven breakbeats, and sampled, scud-attack speed metal riffs means nailing the album down to any one style is an exercise in futility. Somewhat frail and ridiculous upon repeat listenings, the album is similar in tone, perhaps, to some late-'80s New York and Washington DC hardcore, lessening amazement that Atari Teenage Riot was given a contract by the Beastie Boys' imprint Grand Royal in 1997. —*Sean Cooper*

● **Burn, Berlin, Burn** / Apr. 22, 1997 / Grand Royal ✦✦✦✦
This American compilation of the group's first two import-only albums—including five tracks from 1995's *Delete Yourself* and nine from 1997's *The Future of War*—offers a fair selection of songs, including the extreme noise terror of "Deutschland (Has Gotta Die)" and "Into the Riot." If there is one drawback, it's that *Burn, Berlin, Burn* lacks the coherence and flow of Atari Teenage Riot's proper albums. Still, in lieu of forking over $50 for the imports, it's a much wiser purchase. —*John Bush*

Juan Atkins

b. Sep. 12, 1962, Detroit, MI
Techno, Club/Dance, Detroit Techno, Electronica
Widely proclaimed the Godfather of Techno, Detroit-native Juan Atkins began experimenting with synthesizers in the 1970s, eventually blending Parliament funk with early-'80s electro to record "Clear" in 1984, regarded as the beginning of techno proper.

Born the son of a Detroit concert promoter on September 12, 1962, Atkins attended Belleville High School and studied music and acting at Washtenaw Community College in nearby Ypsilanti. Of crucial importance to the rise of Atkins and the sound of minimalist-funk Detroit techno is local Detroit DJ Electrifying Mojo. His eclectic radio show introduced bands like Kraftwerk, Prince, Depeche Mode, and the B-52s to the Detroit pioneers and sparked their imaginations. Atkins soon began working for the Mojo, producing lengthy mix jams with partner Derrick May. Itching to make his own material, Atkins recorded two singles with Rick Davies; West Coast jazz and soul label Fantasy later gave the recordings a wide release, and the material also appeared on Detroit's Southbound label (as *Interface*). Though Atkins DJed with May as Deep Space and helped out on two early Derrick May singles (as Rhythim Is Rhythim), a falling out temporarily ended the relationship between the two revolutionaries. Atkins continued working throughout the '80s, pushing the now-crucial sound of Detroit techno (which mutated into acid-house) on singles recorded as Model 500 (collected on *Classics* [R&S]) as well as Infiniti. Into the '90s, Atkins continued to DJ

and record, hailed by the entire dance community as one of the founders of techno. —*John Bush*

● **Magic Tracks, Vol. 2** / Nov. 10, 1993 / Pow Wow ✦✦✦✦
Classics / 1995 / R&S ✦✦✦✦
Classics makes it all clear. Here are the roots of later developments such as techno-funk, acid-house, rave, and trance, recorded almost ten years before the forms became popular. —*John Bush*

Atlantic Starr

f. 1976, White Plains, NY
Soul, Disco, Urban, Adult Contemporary, Quiet Storm
New York-based Atlantic Starr began in 1976. Brothers David (guitar, vocals), Jonathan (trombone), and Wayne (keyboards) Lewis started a funk-soul band, adding lead vocalist Sharon Bryant, bassist Clifford Archer, drummer Porter Carroll, saxophonist Koran Daniels, percussionist/flutist Joseph Phillips, and trumpeter William Sudderth. They signed with A&M a couple of years later, staying through 1987 and landing several hits, among them "Gimme Your Lovin'," "Circles," "When Love Calls," "Stand Up," "Silver Shadow," "One Love," and the crossover hit "Secret Lovers." Their albums *Brilliance* and *As the Band Turns* were also Top 20 pop hits, their most successful A&M LPs. They switched to Warner Bros. in 1987, and their first release, *All in the Name of Love*, included another pop smash, "Always," the group's sole No. 1 pop and R&B hit. They enjoyed more R&B successes with Warner through the '80s. Sharon Bryant left in 1989 for Polydor; she was replaced by Barbara Weathers, who later left for a solo career as well. *Love Crazy*, in 1991, was their most recent release. —*Ron Wynn*

● **Secret Lovers: The Best of Atlantic Starr** / 1986 / A&M ✦✦✦✦
A nice anthology, although it emphasizes the ballad smashes and doesn't convey much of their earlier, harder flavor. Atlantic Starr moved to Warner Bros. in the late '80s, so their former label cranked out a greatest-hits LP to take advantage of their hit status. These songs were staples of '80s urban contemporary radio, and the ballads are still carried in the '90s on many Quiet Storm playlists. —*Ron Wynn*

Classics, Vol. 10 / 1987 / A&M ✦✦✦✦
This collection gathers their A&M hits, which include "Freak-a-Ristic," "Secret Lovers," and "If Your Heart Isn't in It." But the group scored its biggest smash after moving to Warner Bros., the R&B and pop chart-topping "Always." —*Ron Wynn*

The Atlantics

f. Australia
Surf
One of the greatest instrumental surf groups did not even hail from America. The Atlantics, despite their name, were an Australian combo that not only emulated the sound of California surf music, but ranked among its very best practitioners. Featuring a reverb-heavy, extremely "wet" sound, the Atlantics attacked original material, standards, and movie themes with a nervy blend of precision and over-the-top intensity. As in Dick Dale's music, touches of Middle Eastern influences can be detected. (Some members of the group claimed Greek and Egyptian heritage.) Their second single, "Bombora," went to the top of the Australian charts in 1963, and the follow-up "The Crusher" was also a big hit. But Beatlemania spelled commercial death for the Atlantics, as it did for US surf combos, in 1964 and 1965. After several albums and a few more equally fine instrumental singles, the Atlantics became a vocal group in the last half of the '60s, but they are most renowned for their instrumental recordings. Still regarded with respect in Australia and New Zealand, they remain virtually unknown elsewhere, except to fanatical surf music specialists. —*Richie Unterberger*

The Explosive Sound of the Atlantics / 199? / Repertoire ✦✦✦✦
This is a bit cornball compared to their best stuff. A few numbers are surfizations of standards like "Secret Love," and though most of the material is original, the allusions to folk melodies sometimes make this sound like the kind of surf band you'd find playing in a Greek restaurant. There's plenty of nifty guitar work, though, and only a couple of cuts are on *The CBS Singles Collection*, making this a good supplement to that compilation. The original Australian LP is harder to find than the German CD reissue, which adds bonus cuts. —*Richie Unterberger*

● **The CBS Singles Collection 1963-1965** / Canetoad ✦✦✦✦
Both sides of their first nine singles. Includes "Bombora," "The Crusher," strong originals, and hard-boiled overhauls of "Goldfinger" and "Peter Gunn." As essential as Dick Dale, though much more obscure. —*Richie Unterberger*

The Au Pairs

f. 1978, Birmingham, England, **db.** 1983
Post-Punk
Blasting into the post-punk consciousness with a tremendous debut

album, the Au Pairs, fronted by lesbian feminist Lesley Woods, played brittle, dissonant, guitar-based rock that shared political and musical kinship with the Mekons and (especially) the Gang of Four. The music was danceable, imbued with an almost petulant irony, and for a while, very hip and well-liked by critics. Unlike many bands of the moment, however, the Au Pairs (at least initially) backed it up with searing, confrontational songs celebrating sexuality from a woman's perspective. They also took swipes at the conservative political climate sweeping England after Margaret Thatcher's election as Prime Minister. Occasionally Wood's commitments to sexual and social politics made her sound inflexible, doctrinaire, and hectoring (especially on their OK second album), but at first blush, the Au Pairs were a mighty intimidating proposition, able to take on so much and deliver great music in the process. After a desultory live album in 1983 (*Au Pairs Live in Berlin*), the band split up, and Woods and her bandmates have maintained a low profile. —*John Dougan*

● **Playing with a Different Sex** / 1981 / RPM ✦✦✦✦
Opening with the tongue-in-cheek "We're So Cool," the Au Pairs' debut record is a stunner, from Lesley Woods' scratchy guitar and declamatory vocals to lead guitarist Paul Foad's brittle soloing. This is an uncompromising, defiant record that asks no quarter. Gender roles are turned upside down, hetero—and homo-sexual relationships put under a microscope, and theories about sex and sexuality turned upside down. Similarly, the tense political situation in Northern Ireland is harrowingly addressed in "Armagh," which details Tory-sanctioned torture and sexual abuse of wrongly imprisoned Irish women. An unflinching look at the world, *Playing with a Different Sex* is one of the great, and perhaps forgotten, post-punk records. The CD reissue on RPM adds eight significant bonus cuts from 1979-81 singles, which include different versions of tracks from the album and some songs that didn't make it onto the LP in any form. —*John Dougan*

Sense & Sensuality / 1982 / RPM ✦✦✦✦
On their second album, the Au Pairs were very much in tune with the growth pangs of the punk/new wave scene in the early 1980s. In stripping their music to a funkier, more rhythmic essence, and shifting the focus of their lyrics to the personal rather than the political, they lost some of the impact (and critical acclaim) of their debut. Musically, however, things were more interesting. The addition of horns and imaginative synthesizers allowed for more satisfying sonic diversity. The words were still confrontational, but more obscure in their intent. Although occasionally political (as in the blunt anti-Reagan screed "America"), they were more concerned with questioning sex/relationship roles (as in "Sex Without Stress," "Intact," and "Instant Touch"). The record didn't get as much attention as their first LP, but it's just as much a touchstone of post-punk. The CD reissue adds six pop-oriented bonus tracks (four from a BBC broadcast in 1983, and two from a 1983 demo) that were written for their never-completed third album. —*Richie Unterberger*

Live in Berlin / 1983 / AKA ✦✦✦

Equal But Different—BBC Sessions '79-'81 / 1994 / RPM ✦✦✦
Twenty tracks recorded for the BBC between 1979-1981, representing most of what the group performed on British radio. (Four other tracks from a 1983 session appear as bonus cuts on RPM's CD reissue of the *Sense & Sensuality* album.) It leans most heavily on the first LP and singles (in fact, versions of every single one of the debut album's tracks are here), though there are also a half-dozen songs from *Sense & Sensuality*. No big surprises, with the exception of a couple of otherwise-unavailable items, "Ideal Woman" and "Monogamy." The latter tune is the set's clear highlight, as it represents the band's only foray (and quite a good one) into all-out, straightforward, guitar-heavy punk rock. Much of the rest is too monochromatic for the unconverted, but fans should like this. It's a better representation of their live prime than the *Live in Berlin* album, and with 79 minutes' running time and meticulous liner notes, it offers terrific value. —*Richie Unterberger*

Patti Austin

b. Aug. 10, 1948, New York, NY
Vocals / Urban, Adult Contemporary
A professional since the age of five, Patti Austin was a protégé of Dinah Washington and Sammy Davis, Jr. A 1969 single for United Artists titled "Family Tree" cracked the R&B Top 50. Austin cut her debut LP, *End of a Rainbow*, for Creed Taylor's CTI label in 1976, followed by *Havana Candy* in 1977 and *Body Language* in 1980. She sang lead vocals for Japanese koto player Yutaka Yokokura on "Love Light" in 1978, did a duet with Michael Jackson on "It's the Falling in Love" for *Off the Wall*, and sang "The Closer I Get to You" on Tom Browne's album in 1979. Austin dueted with George Benson on "Moody's Mood for Love" in 1980. She sang backgrounds for sessions by Houston Person, Noel Pointer, Ralph McDonald, Angela Bofill, and Roberta Flack. Austin did vocals on Quincy Jones' *The Dude* LP in 1981, and was featured on the hit "Razzamatazz." She inked a solo deal on Jones' Qwest label, and her 1982 LP *Every Home Should Have One* included the No. 1 pop hit (No.

9 R&B) "Baby, Come to Me," which got widespread exposure via the ABC soap opera "General Hospital." The follow-up single, "How Do You Keep the Music Playing," was the theme for the film *Best Friends*. Both songs paired Austin with James Ingram. She continued recording for Jones' Qwest label through the '80s, but she couldn't recapture her pop or R&B success, despite working with several top producers, including Jam-Lewis in 1985. Austin switched to GRP in 1990 and recorded *Love Is Gonna Getcha*, with the singles "Through the Test of Time" and "Good in Love." She subsequently recorded *Carry On* and *Live, with Shelton Becton* in 1991 and 1992. —*Ron Wynn*

Live at the Bottom Line / 1979 / Epic ✦✦✦
Patti Austin came closest on this late '70s live set to transferring onto vinyl the qualities that make her an outstanding vocalist outside the studio. There's more spontaneity, emotion, and charisma in the vocals on this album than on almost all her other releases combined; perhaps the nightclub setting inspired her, or, more likely, Austin was free to sing without any agendas, marketing strategies, or producers' visions being factored into the process. —*Ron Wynn*

Every Home Should Have One / Sep. 1981 / Qwest ✦✦✦✦
Quincy Jones-produced pop album featuring "Baby, Come to Me," which became a belated hit when it was featured on "General Hospital" two years after the album came out. —*William Ruhlman*

Getting Away with Murder / Oct. 1985 / Qwest ✦✦✦
Patti Austin's third Qwest album was a success, making the Top 50 on the R&B chart and throwing off three R&B chart singles, "Honey for the Bees," "The Heat of Heat," and the title track. But you could tell it was supposed to do a lot better on the pop chart: five heavyweight producers (Russ Titelman, Tommy LiPuma, Monte Moir, and Jimmy Jam and Terry Lewis), plus 14 songwriters, contributed to what was doubtless a big-budget production, and that means label head Quincy Jones was looking for a lot more in the way of crossover than a low chart ranking for "The Heat of Heat." In retrospect, the fault lies with all that high-priced help, while Austin gives her all in any guise they devise for her—sultry balladeer, disco diva, pop princess. —*William Ruhlmann*

The Real Me / Aug. 1988 / Qwest ✦✦✦✦
And how! Austin tackles standards such as "Smoke Gets in Your Eyes" and "They Can't Take That Away from Me," and succeeds brilliantly. Her version of Comden, Green, and Bernstein's "I Can Cook, Too" is enough by itself to make this a pick. —*William Ruhlmann*

Love Is Gonna Getcha / Mar. 1990 / GRP ✦✦
Her debut for GRP included the somewhat cutesy but nicely done title track, a decent mix of fusion, light jazz, show biz, and pre-rock pop. Patti Austin can really sing anything, and unfortunately, on most of her albums, that's what happens; she gets everything shoved her way. The album did land her two mild hits, "Through the Test of Time" and "Good in Love." —*Ron Wynn*

That Secret Place / Apr. 1994 / GRP ✦✦
This is virtually a duet album between Patti Austin and guitarist Lee Ritenour, who produced, bringing with him a Who's Who of New York fusion players. It's a tasteful, well-constructed, consistently dull and lifeless effort. Here a reggae beat, there an actual duet with El DeBarge, and all devoid of any real fire. The closest anyone comes to life is when they cover Aretha Franklin's "Rock Steady" and Austin sneaks in elements of impersonation. But if during Austin's Qwest days they were trying to turn her into a soul-pop singer along the lines of Janet Jackson, now GRP is trying to make another Anita Baker out of her, and the fit is no better. —*William Ruhlmann*

● **Best Of** / Jun. 28, 1994 / Columbia ✦✦✦✦
The Best of Patti Austin isn't quite what it appears to be. Instead of compiling her big early-'80s hits like "Baby, Come to Me" and "How Do You Keep the Music Playing," the 16-track collection features her lesser-known late-'70s material for CTI Records, where she had only one notable hit in 1977 with "Say You Love Me." Despite the lack of hits, the compilation is actually quite enjoyable, featuring graceful versions of songs as diverse as "More Today Than Yesterday," "You Don't Have to Say You're Sorry," "Lost in the Stars," "We've Got Tonight," and "Another Nail for My Heart." It may not be the definitive Austin collection, but it remains a good introduction to her style. —*Stephen Thomas Erlewine*

The Ultimate Collection / Jun. 6, 1995 / GRP ✦✦✦✦

Australian Crawl

f. 1979, Melbourne, Australia, **db.** 1984
Punk, New Wave
From their emergence in 1979 through disbanding a scant five years later, Australian Crawl stood as a bizarre anomaly against the largely punk and political scene Down Under. Essentially sculpted as the Melbourne Beach Boys, the Crawl's songs ranged from odes to Errol Flynn and Resort Girls to rousing sing-alongs like "Hootchie Gucci Fiorucci Mama" and their mash cover of the Kingsmen's "Louie Louie." Consisting of James Reyne (lead vocals, piano), Guy McDonough (co-lead

vocals, rhythm guitar), Bill McDonough (drums, percussion), Simon Binks (lead/acoustic/slide guitar), Paul Williams (bass), and Brad Robinson (rhythm guitar), the Crawl appeared initially to be little more than hedonistic surfers—in Reyne's own words, "part of people's lives; a representation of the beach, the open air and good vibes". But their debut album, 1980's *The Boys Light Up*, also contained recountings of automobile accidents ("Indisposed") and vicious attacks against shallow materialists ("Beautiful People", the Crawl's first hit single). Their combination of light breezy tunes with significantly darker subtexts (not altogether unlike Brian Wilson's best material) left *The Boys Light Up* on the Aussie charts for no less than 104 weeks.

In 1981 the sophomore effort, *Sirocco*, did not mess much with their proven formula. Alongside hits like "Lakeside," "Things Don't Seem," and "Errol," the album produced their standard "Unpublished Critics," a Reyne rant later redone as a live track on the B-side of "Louie Louie." The follow-up *Sons of Beaches* added famed producer Mike Chapman to the mix, lending the proceedings a more polished sound, while much of the music remained the same (the hit "Shutdown" even borrowing its title from a Beach Boys classic). However, *Sons* also found Reyne starting to veer off into new territory, earmarked by the cryptic "Letter From Zimbabwe." Still entrenched in classic Crawl arrangements, hints began to emerge of Reyne's crucial shift in direction.

After a No. 1 12-inch EP, *Semantics*, the Crawl released their fourth and final studio album, *Phalanx*, at the end of 1983. (The American version of this album, released on Geffen in 1984, bore the title *Semantics*, and served as more of a compilation of the Crawl's career to date.) Aside from the cover of "Louie Louie," *Phalanx* contained the smash single "Reckless," a song Reyne would later redo for one of his solo ventures. Shortly before their demise, the Crawl served as opening act for Duran Duran on certain legs of the *Arena* tour. They would release a rare live album, *Final Wave*, and a posthumous singles collection, *Crawl File*, before Reyne jaunted off on a hugely successful solo career that continues even now to thrive in his native Australia.

Significantly, each of the Crawl's four studio albums and their EP all reached the Top Five on the Australian pop charts, granting them a level of fever-pitch success shared by only a handful of Aussie artists before or since. —*Tomas Mureika*

The Boys Light Up / 1980 / EMI ✦✦✦✦
Immensely popular (in Australia) debut platter from Beach-Boys-downunder features light hooks and catchy riffs with just a hint of the darkness to come. Highlights include the singles "Downhearted" and "Beautiful People," but James Reyne's automobile accident-inspired "Indisposed" is the strongest suggestion of what lay below the surface on these delicate pop structures. *Boys* remained on the Aussie pop charts for 104 weeks. —*Tomas Mureika*

Sirocco / 1981 / EMI ✦✦✦✦
Single-laden sophomore effort finds the Crawl mining the same territory as their debut, but with more polish and better hooks. "Things Don't Seem,""Unpublished Critics," and "Lakeside" (an ode to ogling at nudist beaches) all quickly became Crawl standards, while James Reyne's dedication to "Errol" (famed Australian actor Flynn, about whom Reyne decries, "I would give everything just to be like him") solidified both Flynn's and Reyne's epic stature in the Aussie mindset, pointing the way toward the Crawl frontman's lucrative solo career. Spent eight months in the Top 20. —*Tomas Mureika*

Sons of Beaches / 1982 / EMI ✦✦
Legendary producer Mike Chapman (Sweet, Blondie, Pat Benatar) is the lone variation on the Crawl's third offering. While most of the disc comprises standard Crawl fare (epitomized by the single, "Shutdown"), Reyne's oddball "Letter from Zimbabwe" stands out as a prototype for his later solo work. Slick production, some nice tunes, but ultimately a disappointing clone of the far superior *Sirocco*. —*Tomas Mureika*

Semantics / 1983 / EMI ✦✦✦
The Crawl achieved their highest chart-topping status with a No. 1 EP and follow-up album incorporating most of the former's tracks. Their smash cover of "Louie Louie" and the Simon Binks-penned "White Limbo" firmly established the Crawl as solid pub-rockers, while James Reyne's haunting "Restless" confirmed his own movement away from the rest of the group. (Reyne would later redo "Restless" for his third solo album.) While not an artistic triumph, the Crawl's final studio work provided them a commercial swansong of such proportions that it practically paved the way for Reyne's re-emergence at the end of the decade. —*Tomas Mureika*

● **Crawl File** / 1994 / EMI ✦✦✦✦
The requisite singles compilation, *Crawl File* actually culls most of the band's best work (all of the singles are present save "Louie Louie"). While seriously lacking in the liner note department, this is nonetheless a good overview of the bright but short life of a landmark Australian band, a genuine anomaly for its time. —*Tomas Mureika*

Final Wave / EMI ✦✦✦
This very rare live collection revived the Crawl's "Louie Louie" cover, but

it was regarded mainly as an attempt to cash in on the band's success before their glow faded. —*Tomas Mureika*

Autechre

f. 1991, England
Experimental, Electronica, Post-Rock/Experimental, Ambient Techno
Like the Orb, Aphex Twin, and mu-Ziq, Autechre are about as close to being techno superstars as the tenets of the genre and the limitations of its audience will allow. Through a series of full-length works and a smattering of EPs on Warp, Clear, and their own Skam label, the group has consistently garnered the praise of press and public alike. Unlike many of their more club-bound colleagues, however, Autechre's Sean Booth and Rob Brown have roots planted firmly in American electro, and though the more mood-based, sharply digital texture of their update may seem to speak otherwise, it was through early 12s like Egyptian Lover's "Egypt, Egypt," Grandmaster Flash's "Scorpio," and "Pretty" Tony Butler's "Get Some" that their combined aesthetic began to form.

Booth and Brown met through a mutual friend, trading junked-up pause-button mixtapes of their favorite singles. Happening onto some bargain-basement analog gear through questionable circumstances, the pair began experimenting with their own music before they were out of high school. After some disastrous experiences with a few small labels, the pair sent a tape to Warp records, whose releases by Sweet Exorcist, Nightmares on Wax, and B12 were announcing a new age in UK-based techno (and one in which Autechre would become a key component). Releasing a handful of singles through the label, Autechre's first stabs were collected on their debut full-length, *Incunabula*, as well as the ten-inch box-set remix EP *Basscadet*. Subsequent albums brought a wider audience through stateside reissue (through Wax Trax!/TVT). Although stylistically rooted, affectations for the ponderous extend beyond their name and track titles ("C/Pach," "Bronchusevenmx24"), with the basic premise of their approach being music without a whole lot of stylistic baggage. In addition to Autechre, Booth and Brown have released material as Gescom on their own Skam imprint and through the Clear label, most notably the *Sounds of Machines Our Parents Used* EP on the latter. The group has also provided a number of memorable remixes (often times more memorable than their original material) for trip-hoppers Palmskin Productions and Slowly, as well as Mick Harris' ambient dub project Scorn. —*Sean Cooper*

Incunabula / 1993 / Wax Trax! ✦✦✦✦
Although considered a close relative of UK techno, Booth and Brown do much to distance themselves from the dance floor, infusing their tracks with rhythmic complexity as well as subtle melodicism, to make *Incunabula* suitable for home listening. —*Sean Cooper*

Amber / 1994 / Warp ✦✦✦✦
Subtle, occasionally haunting, *Amber* takes the ambient stratagems of *Garbage* to their logical conclusion, simplifying the percussion and focusing more on theme and song development. The results are mixed, but provide ample proof of electronic music's capacity to engage the full range of emotions. —*Sean Cooper*

● **Tri Repetae** / 1995 / Warp ✦✦✦✦
A masterful collection of wheezing, clanking, utterly foreign post-techno, blending alternately up—and down-tempo, often crushing beats with subtle, occasionally tender melodies. The album is a far cry from the more listener—friendly earlier material, but is also less derivative, stepping up the electro influence into a digital environment as frightening as it is funky. TVT's reissue adds a second disc containing the two *Anvil Vapre* EPs and the ironically titled *Garbage*. —*Sean Cooper*

Chiastic Slide / Jan. 1997 / Warp ✦✦✦
After *Tri Repetae*, the stunning leap forward with which Autechre astounded the techno world, the duo's fourth proper album came as a disappointment to many. The waves of polar static and mechanic clicks that distinguished *Tri Repetae* make *Chiastic Slide* little more than a variation on a form. Even worse, the album has too few ideas for its near-70-minute length, and the duo seem content with short loops being repeated and repeated for up to ten minutes on a track. Though several songs are on a par with *Tri Repetae*—and that's being generous—*Chiastic Slide* just can't compare with Autechre's earlier work. —*John Bush*

The Auteurs

f. 1992, London, England, **db.** 1996
Alternative Pop-Rock
When the Auteurs' released their debut album in 1993, the British press linked them with the massively popular Suede as part of a "glam revival." While the band can blast out guitar-drenched rockers like Suede, the Auteurs come to life when they draw from the quiet side of such distinctively English guitar-pop bands like the Kinks, the Smiths, and George Harrison. Luke Haines, the group's guitarist, vocalist, and songwriter, writes highly melodic pop songs that combine the airy melodicism of Harrison with the cutting social observations of Davies;

they're sharp, intelligent songs, full of humor and gorgeous melancholy, even when they're loud rockers. With their two albums, *New Wave* and *Now I'm a Cowboy*, they've earned a devoted cult in the UK, without gathering much support in the United States. By the time the group released the Steve Albini-produced *After Murder Park* in early 1996, they had even lost most of their cult audience in the UK; accordingly, the album was a stiff, even on the indie charts. Before its release, Haines had dropped hints in interviews that the record may be the Auteurs' last. Six months after the release of *After Murder Park*, Haines released an album with his side project, Badder Meinhoff. —*Stephen Thomas Erlewine*

● **New Wave** / Mar. 1993 / Plan 9/Caroline ◆◆◆◆
The debut from the Auteurs hearkens back to the golden years of British pop. The auteur of the Auteurs, Luke Haines, is as acerbic and insightful about modern British life as Ray Davies, singing about marrying show-girls and the upper classes. Songs like "Junk Shop Clothes" and "Bailed Out" have a Merseybeat quality, while "Early Years" points the way to the group's angrier, harder sound. More than just pastiche artists, *New Wave* presents the Auteurs as a group with both wit and heart. —*Heather Phares*

Now I'm a Cowboy / May 31, 1994 / Capitol ◆◆◆◆
On the Auteurs' second album, the tunes are tighter, and the hooks and wit are even sharper. The band even rocks out (in a refined way, of course) on songs like "Lenny Valentino." Haines continues to write about the scheming rich and shabbily genteel, wrapping his words in loud guitars and sighing cellos. "New French Girlfriend" and "Chinese Bakery" are just two of the gems on *Now I'm a Cowboy*, proving that the Auteurs have plenty to say and a catchy way to say it. —*Heather Phares*

After Murder Park / Feb. 1996 / Hut ◆◆◆◆
On their third album, *After Murder Park*, the pretentiously monikered Auteurs fancy themselves the bridge between the thinking-man's Blur school of modern Brit-pop and a vintage proto-glam band. It is ulti-mately a contrived illusion. The band's creative processes are transpar-ent; "rather than let this chorus' conventional pop structure progress as expected, we'll throw in some dissonant twists to show how inventive we are." The seams are obvious: "Insert Odd Sounds Here" in bold aural lettering. Vocalist/guitarist Luke Haines comes on with disaffected swagger and attempted social import of a more contemporary Ray Davies by way of Steve Harley's Cockney Rebel, but his lyrics, while showing the occasional clever turn, are simply not up to the task. The further you delve into the disc, the more tiresome the effort gets, as the stage makeup peels away in great, greasy gobs. That being said, a couple of numbers come close to redeeming the project. "Unsolved Child Mur-der" and the title track actually work, with delicate, finely drawn melo-dies and a truly sad story. —*Roch Parisien*

Autosalvage

f. New York, NY
Psychedelic
One of the relatively few New York psychedelic groups to achieve national recognition, Autosalvage's day in the limelight was fairly dim and brief. The band included bassist Skip Boone, the brother of Lovin' Spoonful bassist Steve Boone, and Rick Turner, who contributed guitar to most of the tracks on Ian & Sylvia's 1966 album, *Play One More*. Autosalvage's self-titled 1968 album revealed a fairly large palette, with touches of folk, blues, and strings. The group's cheerful harmonies owed a bit to the Lovin' Spoonful, and Frank Zappa (perhaps impressed by their sometimes disjointed and improvisational material) was a fan, but their material was not strong enough to forge a distinctive identity. Boone and drummer Darius Davenport also appear on the obscure 1968 album by Bear, but otherwise Autosalvage's debut was also their curtain call. —*Richie Unterberger*

Autosalvage / 1968 / RCA ◆◆◆
Cuts like the opening track (titled, confusingly enough, "Auto Salvage") show the band at their best—strong melody, airy harmonies, a churning psychedelic arrangement. They didn't live up to that potential often on their only album, which is saddled by a fair amount of mediocre and rambling material. The British reissue on Edsel adds informative histor-ical liner notes. —*Richie Unterberger*

Frankie Avalon (Francis Avallone)

b. Sep. 18, 1939, Philadelphia, PA
Vocals / Pop, Teen Idol
At the end of the '50s and beginning of the '60s, Frankie Avalon was one of the biggest teen idols around, hitting the top of the charts consistently from 1958 until the end of 1960. Avalon didn't possess a terrific voice, but he did have material that was tailor-made for a receptive teen audi-ence. At the height of his popularity, he had five Top Ten hits in 1959, including "Dede Dinah," "Ginger Bread," "Why," and "Venus." When the '60s began in earnest, Avalon embarked on an acting career; he starred in a hugely successful series of beach movies with Annette Funicello.

After he began acting, Avalon didn't return to music throughout the decade. In the '70s Avalon began making occasional film and television appearances while he worked the nostalgia and club circuits; he contin-ues to sing and act in the '90s. —*Stephen Thomas Erlewine*

● **The Best of Frankie Avalon** / Apr. 11, 1995 / Varese Sarabande ◆◆◆◆
The definitive compilation, with the original versions of 18 songs from 1958-1962, all but one of them a chart hit of some sort. Has all the Top Ten smashes and a bunch of minor post-1959 singles that found him swinging toward pop crooner material with barely any relation to rock 'n' roll. —*Richie Unterberger*

The Avengers

f. 1977, San Francisco, CA, **db.** 1982
Punk
The Avengers were a San Francisco-based hardcore punk rock group formed in 1977, featuring Penelope Housten (vocals), Greg Westermark (guitar), Johnathan Postal (bass), and Danny Furious (drums). They had broken up by the time their only full-length album was released in 1983. —*William Ruhlmann*

● **Avengers** / 1983 / CD Presents ◆◆◆◆
Although it was released in 1983, this collection represents just about everything San Francisco's late, great Avengers recorded from 1977-78. By contemporary standards, it's by-the-book punk thrash: Greg Ingra-ham's guitar spews up hairball after hairball of distortion, while Pene-lope Houston snarls in her best impression of Johnny Rotten. However, contemporary standards diminish what great music this was and what a great band the Avengers were. Dozens of bands came in their wake, but few could recapture the excitement and ferocity of their sound. Houston, who re-emerged years later as a folk-rocker, is in full fury on these 14 tracks, especially the youth culture solidarity anthem "We Are the One" and the tale of desperation "Thin White Line." A few spins of this and you'll hear how the Avengers influenced everyone from Black Flag to X. Yes, they were that good. A forgotten classic. —*John Dougan*

The Average White Band

f. 1972, Scotland, **db.** 1990
Instrumental / Soul, Funk, Quiet Storm
The Average White Band had their name jokingly bestowed on them by Bonnie Bramlett of Delanie & Bonnie; during their prime, AWB's solid grooves and overall chemistry were anything but average. But the name did reflect their paradoxical position: they were an American-style soul band made up of native Scots. The group was formed in Glasgow, Scot-land, in early 1972 by Alan Gorrie (b. Jul. 19, 1946, Perth, Scotland) on bass and vocals; Michael Rosen (soon replaced by Hamish Stuart [b. Oct. 8, 1949, Glasgow, Scotland] on guitar and vocals; Onnie McIntyre (b. Sep. 25, 1945, Lennox Town, Scotland) on vocals and guitar; Robbie McIntosh (b. 1950, Scotland—d. Sep. 23, 1974, Los Angeles) on drums; Roger Ball (b. Jun. 4, 1944, Dundee, Scotland) on keyboards and saxo-phone; and Malcolm Duncan (b. Aug. 24, 1945, Montrose, Scotland) on saxophone. After their 1973 debut album, *Show Your Hand*, went unno-ticed, they hooked up with producer Arif Mardin to record *Average White Band* (frequently called *AWB* because of the initials on the cover). Released in August 1974, the album topped the charts and spawned the near-instrumental dance hit "Pick Up the Pieces," which also went to No. 1. Meanwhile, tragedy struck the band when drummer Robbie McIntosh died of a drug overdose; he was replaced by Steve Ferrone (b. Apr. 25, 1950, Brighton, England). AWB nearly replicated its success with the third album, *Cut the Cake*, and its title single, both of which reached the Top Ten. But the sameness of the group's approach and such side projects as an album with Ben E. King broke its momentum. Also, the rise of disco left its funky soul style sounding dated. AWB managed a couple more gold albums in *Person to Person* (January 1977) and *Warmer Communications* (March 1978), and its popularity lasted longer in the UK than in the US, but by the start of the '80s the band was permanently out of fashion. The band members have worked as session sidemen for artists ranging from Chaka Khan to Paul McCartney and Badfinger. —*Rick Clark & William Ruhlmann*

AWB / Aug. 1974 / Atlantic ◆◆◆◆
After debuting with 1973's excellent but neglected *Show Your Hand* (later reissued as *Put It Where You Want It*), the Average White Band switched from MCA to Atlantic and hit big with this self-titled gem. Upon first hearing gutsy, Tower of Power-influenced funk like "Person to Person" and the instrumental "Pick Up the Pieces" (a No. 1 R&B hit), many soul fans were shocked to learn that not only were they white—they were whites from Scotland. Like Teena Marie five years later, AWB embraced soul and funk with so much conviction that it was clear this was anything but an "average" white band. This album is full of treasures that weren't big hits but should have been—including the addictive "You Got It," the ominous "There's Always Someone Waiting," and a gutsy remake of the Isley Brothers' "Work to Do." When Rhino

reissued *AWB* on CD in 1995, an edited live version of "Pick Up the Pieces" recorded at the 1977 Montreux Jazz Festival was added. (The full-length version had been included on Rhino's 1994 reissue of *Warmer Communications.*) —*Alex Henderson*

Soul Searching / Jul. 1976 / Atlantic ✦✦✦✦
AWB's artistic winning streak continued with its outstanding fourth album, *Soul Searching*. Interestingly, this wasn't an album that enjoyed a great deal of publicity or contained a lot of major hits. In fact, its biggest single, the dreamy "Queen of My Soul," made it only to No. 21 on Billboard's R&B albums chart. But thanks to the devoted following AWB had acquired since signing with Atlantic in 1974, *Soul Searching* went gold. Indeed, AWB aficionados were quite receptive to first-rate material ranging from the invigorating "I'm the One" to the hauntingly romantic "A Love of Your Own." By zeroing in on their strengths—hard-hitting funk and delightfully melodic soul—AWB saw to it that *Soul Searching* was every bit as rewarding as its predecessors. —*Alex Henderson*

Warmer Communications . . . and More / 1978 / Hit Label ✦✦✦✦
When other soulsters were turning to flashy disco/pop arrangements in 1978, AWB wisely stuck with the type of smooth soul and unapologetically gritty funk that had put the band on the map. By 1980 AWB would, in fact, turn to straight-up disco. But on *Warmer Communications*, AWB's last truly great album, the funk still prevailed. From such sweaty funk as "Your Love Is a Miracle," "Big City Lights," and "Same Feeling, Different Song" to relaxed "slow jams" like "One Look over My Shoulder (Is This Really Goodbye?)" and the ethereal "She's a Dream," *Warmer Communications* is the work of a band that was still being true to itself. In 1994 Rhino reissued this classic on CD and added two instrumental bonus tracks: the driving "McEwan's Export" and an extended live version of "Pick Up the Pieces" (recorded at the 1977 Montreux Jazz Festival in Switzerland) that boasts improvisatory solos by jazz greats like trumpeter Randy Brecker, tenor sax man Michael Brecker, alto sax man Sonny Fortune, and flutist Herbie Mann. The inspired jam proves that the freedom of jazz and the immediacy of R&B can be a dynamic combination. —*Alex Henderson*

Feel No Fret . . . And More / 1979 / Rhino/Atlantic ✦✦✦
The once-magnificent Average White Band was suffering from both artistic and commercial decline by the end of the 1970s. Although decent, *Feel No Fret* is a mild disappointment when compared to such pearls as *Soul Searching* and *Cut the Cake*. There are some noteworthy songs here, including the congenial "Atlantic Avenue," the grinding "When Will You Be Mine," and a cover of "Walk On By" (previously recorded by Dionne Warwick, Isaac Hayes, and Gloria Gaynor). But on the whole, this CD (which boasts four likable but not essential bonus tracks first heard on the *Part VIII* LP) falls short of AWB's previously high standards. Only the more devoted AWB fans will want this album, the first AWB date since 1973's *Put It Where You Want It* (aka *Show Your Hand*) that didn't go gold. —*Alex Henderson*

● **Pickin' Up the Pieces: The Best of Average White Band (1974-1980)** / Sep. 1, 1992 / Rhino ✦✦✦✦
Anyone who is seriously interested in '70s soul and funk should own at least three or four Average White Band albums. But if a person insists on allotting himself/herself only one AWB CD, this is the logical choice. All of the essential hits—from the sweaty funk of "Cut the Cake," "Pick Up the Pieces," and "School Boy Crush" to the unapologetically romantic "If I Ever Lose This Heaven"—are included. Though most of the selections were recorded when AWB was still very much in its prime, a few were made after the Scottish band had peaked. "Let's Go Round Again" (1980) finds AWB taking a glossy pop/disco approach that's hardly in a class with its earlier triumphs, but is likable enough. Most of the selections, however, aren't simply decent; they are excellent. —*Alex Henderson*

Kevin Ayers

f. Aug. 16, 1945, Herne Bay, Kent, England
Bass, Guitar, Vocals / Art-Rock/Progressive-Rock
Kevin Ayers is one of rock's oddest and more likable enigmas, even if often he's seemed not to operate at his highest potential. Perhaps that's because he's never seemed to take his music too seriously—one of his essential charms *and* most aggravating limitations. Since the late '60s, he's released many albums with a distinctly British sensibility, making ordinary lyrical subjects seem extraordinary with his rich, low vocals; inventive wordplay; and bemused, relaxed attitude. Apt to flavor his songs with female backup choruses and exotic island rhythms, the singer-songwriter inspires the image of a sort of progressive-rock beach bum, writing about life's absurdities with a celebratory, relaxed detachment. Yet he is also one of progressive rock's more important (and more humane) innovators, helping to launch the Soft Machine as their original bassist, and working with noted European progressive musicians like Mike Oldfield, Lol Coxhill, and Steve Hillage.

Ayers early cultivated a taste for the bohemian lifestyle, spending much of his childhood in Majorca before he moved with his mother to Canterbury in the early '60s. There he fell in with the town's fermenting underground scene, which included future members of the Soft Machine and Caravan. For a while he sang with the Wilde Flowers, a group that included future Softs Robert Wyatt and Hugh Hopper. He left in 1965, met fellow freak Daevid Allen in Majorca, and returned to the UK in 1966 to found the first lineup of the Soft Machine with Allen, Wyatt, and Mike Ratledge.

Wyatt is usually regarded as the prime mover behind the Soft Machine, but Ayers' contributions carried equal weight in the early days. Besides playing bass, he wrote and sang much of their material. He can be heard on their 1967 demos and 1968 debut album, but by the end of 1968 he felt burned out and quit. Selling his bass to Mitch Mitchell of the Jimi Hendrix Experience, he began to write songs on guitar, leading to a contract with Harvest in 1969. His relationship with his ex-Soft Machine mates remained amiable; in fact, Wyatt and Ratledge (as well as Ayers' replacement, Hugh Hopper) guested on Ayers' 1969 debut.

Ayers' solo material reflected a folkier, lazier, and gentler bent than the Soft Machine. In some respects he was comparable to Syd Barrett without the madness—and without the ferocious heights of Barrett's most innovative work. Ayers was never less than enjoyable and original, though his albums were erratic right from the start, veering from sing-along ditties and pleasant, frothy folk ballads to dissonant improvisation. The more ambitious progressive rock elements came to the fore when he fronted the Whole World in the early '70s. The backing band included a teenage Mike Oldfield on guitar, Lol Coxhill on sax, and David Bedford on piano. But Ayers released only one album with them before they dissolved.

Ayers continued to release albums in a poppier vein at a regular pace throughout the '70s. As some critics have noted, this dependable output formed an ironic counterpoint to his lyrics, which often celebrated a life of leisure or even laziness. That lazy charm was often a dominant feature of his records, although Ayers kept things interesting with offbeat arrangements, occasionally singing in foreign tongues, and flavoring his production with unusual instruments and world-music rhythms. He (or Harvest) never gave up on the singles market, and indeed his best early-'70s efforts in that direction were accessible enough to have been hits with a little more push. Or a little less weirdness. Even Ayers at his most accessible and direct wasn't mainstream, a virtue that endeared him to his loyal cult. That cult was limited to the rock underground, and Ayers logically concentrated on albums throughout the 1970s. Almost always pleasant, eccentric, and catchy, they nonetheless started to sound like a cul-de-sac by the mid-'70s. Ayers pressed on without changing his approach, despite the dwindling audience for progressive rock and the oncoming train of punk and new wave. He's recorded only sporadically since 1980, though he remained active in the 1990s, mostly on the European continent. His recent work has had virtually no exposure in the States, where even at his peak he was known only by underground, progressive-rock enthusiasts. —*Richie Unterberger*

Joy of a Toy / Nov. 1969 / Beat Goes On ✦✦✦
As the Soft Machine's first bassist and original principal songwriter, Kevin Ayers was an overlooked force behind the group's groundbreaking recordings in 1967 and 1968. This, his solo debut, is so tossed-off and nonchalant that one gets the impression he wanted to take it easy after helping pilot the manic innovations of the Softs. Laissez-faire sloth has always been part of Ayers' persona, and this record's intermittent lazy charm helped establish it. That doesn't get around the fact, however, that this set of early progressive rock does not feature extremely strong material. Ayers' command of an assortment of instruments is impressive, and his deep bass vocals and playful, almost goofy song-sketches are affecting, but they don't really stick with the listener. It's no accident that some of the tracks recall early Soft Machine; Robert Wyatt drums on most of the songs, and "Song for Insane Times" is virtually a bonafide Soft Machine performance, featuring actual backing from the group itself. A likable but slight album that is at its best when Ayers is at his folkiest. —*Richie Unterberger*

Shooting at the Moon / Mar. 1970 / Beat Goes On ✦✦
Ayers put together a progressive-rock supergroup of sorts for his second album, including Lol Coxhill on sax, David Bedford on keyboards, and a 17-year-old Mike Oldfield on bass; all three musicians would go on to notable solo careers in progressive rock and experimental music. The success of this haphazard affair depends on your appetite for disjointed art rock. There's a not inconsiderable amount of challenging jams that owe a lot to avant-garde jazz and electronics. Ayers is better off when he sticks to his greatest strength: the sweet, folky ballads intoned in his unique bass voice, like "May I" and "The Oyster and the Flying Fish," though these eventually segue into discordant instrumental riffing. The title track is an update of an old song from the original Soft Machine repertoire that was performed more straightforwardly (and much more successfully) as "Jet-Propelled Photograph" on their 1967 demos (which have been reissued on numerous packages). —*Richie Unterberger*

Whatevershebringswesing / Jan. 1971 / Beat Goes On ✦✦✦✦
This album of songs about melancholy and solitude may seem like a

disparate collection. After a few listens, the essence of the song cycle becomes clear. The near-hit "Stranger in Blue Suede Shoes" and "Song from the Bottom of a Well" are among the standout tracks. —*Jim Powers*

Bananamour / May 1973 / Beat Goes On ✦✦✦
A solid, enjoyable collection of songs written from the point of view of Kevin Ayers' own particular brand of existentialism—self-conscious individualism sustained by plenty of wine. The American version of this album contains the near-hit "Caribbean Moon," as well as the Syd Barrett tribute "Oh Wot a Dream." —*Jim Powers*

June 1st 1974 / 1974 / Island ✦✦✦
Kevin Ayers' guests take over side one, with Eno turning in a powerful "Baby's On Fire," John Cale a harrowing "Heartbreak Hotel," and Nico an endless "The End." Ayers runs the show on side two, playing an engaging set of melodic folk-rock topped by his sturdy baritone. —*William Ruhlmann*

Confessions of Dr Dream / May 1974 / Beat Goes On ✦✦
Kevin Ayers' fifth album, *The Confessions of Doctor Dream and Other Stories*, is typical of his work. He sings in his distinctive deep voice with his cultured English accent (sounds a lot like John Cale) in songs set in a variety of pop styles, from hard rock to a music hall approach. He is frequently playful and engaging, although his songs don't ultimately add up to much. The album's second side contains an 18-minute suite called "The Confessions of Doctor Dream," featuring a cameo by Nico, which exemplifies Ayers' amiable, if unfocused appeal. —*William Ruhlmann*

Sweet Deceiver / Mar. 1975 / Beat Goes On ✦✦✦
One of Ayers' more mainstream efforts. Any album that has Elton John playing piano on a few tracks can't be too weird. That's not to say, though, that this is exactly mainstream in and of itself. Ayers continues to play his offhandedly charming miniatures, with occasional Caribbean rhythms and trademark droll, bemused lyrics. The problem is that while this has its charm when you're listening, little sticks or incites you to return. By this point in his career, Ayers was in danger of catching on a treadmill, restating his idiosyncratic concerns in familiar ways without amplifying them. —*Richie Unterberger*

● **Odd Ditties** / 1976 / Harvest ✦✦✦✦
It is an oddity that, for all the ambition of his albums, this collection of singles and unreleased outtakes may be Ayers' most satisfying LP. Why? Perhaps because when he's constrained within the 45 format, he taps his strongest and most endearing qualities—easygoing, singalong melodies; droll, nonchalant (even non sequitur) lyrics; good-natured sotto voce vocals; even female backup harmonies. There's little trace of the inaccessible, difficult (usually instrumental) passages that occupy much of the space on his early albums. Spanning 1969 to 1973, this includes eight tracks that wound up on flop singles, as well as six outtakes from the albums he recorded during this period, though there were no obvious reasons for their exclusion (too pop-oriented, perhaps?). These are "odd ditties": catchy, with occasional Caribbean rhythms and French lyrics, but way too goofball to be taken to heart by a mass audience, at times sounding like a more together Syd Barrett. Needless to say, none of these nifty tunes was anything close to a hit. —*Richie Unterberger*

Yes We Have No Mananas / Jul. 1976 / Beat Goes On ✦✦✦
Although the slick, nearly AOR-style production threatens to swamp the music on this album, the solid songwriting wins out in the end. Ayers has written several songs about achieving stardom; the pithy "Star" is a highlight. A cover of Marlene Dietrich's "Falling in Love with You" is this album's near-hit. —*Jim Powers*

Rainbow Takeaway / Apr. 1978 / Beat Goes On ✦✦
By the late '70s, Ayers was faced not only with the problem of increasingly redundant material, but also with the fact that the audience for his brand of weirdo progressive rock was shrinking precipitously, making him sound not just repetitious, but dated. There are still some good moments on this album: the chamber music arrangement of "Strange Song," the brief burst of singalong nonsense called "Hat Song." But it's one of his more faceless efforts, with anonymously laidback arrangements that are more prone to swirling keyboards than much of his previous output. And "Beware of the Dog" is so meandering in its attempt to be likably weird that it's virtually meaningless. —*Richie Unterberger*

● **Kevin Ayers Collection** / 1983 / See For Miles ✦✦✦✦
This hour-long chronological sampling of Ayers' Harvest and Island discs features several rare single sides (like "Puis-Je?," the French version of "May I?") in addition to some of his best album cuts. With an extensive biographical essay in the liner notes, this is the ideal place to get acquainted with Ayers' work. —*Jim Powers*

Aztec Camera

f. 1980, Glasgow, Scotland
Alternative Pop-Rock, New Wave, Pop-Rock
For most intents and purposes, Aztec Camera is Roddy Frame, a Scottish guitarist/vocalist/songwriter. Several other musicians have passed through the band over the years—including founding members Campbell Owens (bass) and Dave Mulholland (drums)—but the one constant has been Frame. Throughout his career he has created a sophisticated, lush, and nearly jazzy acoustic-oriented guitar pop, relying on gentle melodies and clever wordplay inspired by Elvis Costello.

Aztec Camera released their debut album, *High Land, Hard Rain*, in 1983. Before its release, Owens and Mulholland had left the group, leaving Frame to assemble the record himself. Upon its release, the album won significant critical praise for its well-crafted, multilayered pop. After releasing a stop-gap EP, *Oblivious*, the group's second full-length record, *Knife*, appeared in 1984. Produced by Mark Knopfler, the album was more polished and immediate than the debut, featuring horn arrangements and a slight R&B influence. Three years later Roddy Frame returned with *Love*, which featured musical support from several studio musicians. *Love* was a synthesized stab at pop-R&B, resulting in his greatest commercial success; the album launched four hit singles, including the Top Ten "Somewhere in My Heart."

Two years later Aztec Camera returned to a more guitar-oriented sound with *Stray*. It wasn't as commercially successful as *Love*, but it was a hit with fans who missed the chiming hooks of Frame's early work. *Dreamland*, released in 1993, followed the same pattern as *Stray* and achieved about the same amount of commercial and critical success. —*Stephen Thomas Erlewine*

● **High Land, Hard Rain** / Jun. 1983 / Sire ✦✦✦✦
This intelligent and detailed, if somewhat overambitious, debut showcases vocalist/songwriter Roddy Frame's catchy and wordy acoustic-based pop songs. Imagine a folky version of Elvis Costello, with better guitar chops, and you've got the picture here. None of the Camera's other albums have come close to matching this release. —*John Floyd*

Knife / Sep. 1984 / Sire ✦✦✦
Aztec Camera's second album cuts back the ethereal atmosphere, revealing a stripped-down, vaguely R&B-influenced pop sense. —*Stephen Thomas Erlewine*

Love / Nov. 1987 / Sire ✦✦
Roddy Frame dispensed with the previous members of Aztec Camera and turned to a group of American session musicians and high-powered producers (Russ Titelman, Tommy LiPuma) for his third full-length album, on which he also abandoned his singer-songwriter, folk-rock approach in favor of an American R&B style. It's a distinct step down from the ingenuity of his first couple of records, and was met with indifference in the US, which seemed to be its intended target. In the UK, the album belatedly took off after its second single, "Somewhere in My Heart," went to No. 3 and became Aztec Camera's only Top Ten LP. (Other UK chart singles were "How Men Are" [No. 25] and "Working in a Goldmine" [No. 31].) —*William Ruhlmann*

Stray / Jun. 1990 / Sire ✦✦✦✦
After a lukewarm stab at soul (*Love*), Roddy Frame returns to a brilliantly textured guitar pop on *Stray*, covering rock, soul, and jazzy pop in the space of one album. It's all tied together by Frame's intelligent, sometimes precious, lyrics and melodic pop sense; it's one of Aztec Camera's finest albums. —*Stephen Thomas Erlewine*

Dreamland / May 25, 1993 / Sire ✦✦✦✦
Aztec Camera's first album since 1990's *Stray* continues singer-songwriter Roddy Frame's return to form. Highlighted by the gorgeous Motown-Byrds hybrid single "Dream Sweet Dreams" and the lush, warm ballads "Valium Summer" and "Let Your Love Decide," *Dreamland* ranks among Aztec Camera's best. —*Stephen Thomas Erlewine*

Frestonia / Nov. 14, 1995 / Reprise ✦✦✦
Most of Aztec Camera's albums are similar to each other, featuring Roddy Frame's gently chiming guitars and laidback R&B. *Frestonia* is no exception to the rule. Throughout the album, Frame's meticulous production and sophisticated pop/R&B songwriting blend effortlessly, providing a seamless sequence of songs. There may not be much to distinguish the songs from each other—or from previous Aztec Camera albums, for that matter—but that just means the album succeeds in sustaining a warm, engaging atmosphere. —*Stephen Thomas Erlewine*

B

The B-52's

f. Oct. 1976, Athens, GA, db. 1994
Alternative Pop-Rock, New Wave
The first of many acts to define the college town of Athens, GA, as a hotbed of alternative music, the B-52's took their name from the Southern slang for the mile-high bouffant wigs sported by singers Kate Pierson and Cindy Wilson, a look emblematic of the band's campy, thrift-store aesthetic. The five-piece group, which included founding members Fred Schneider, guitarist Ricky Wilson (Cindy's older brother), and drummer Keith Strickland, formed in the mid-1970s after a drunken evening at a Chinese restaurant. The band members had little or no previous musical experience and performed most of their earliest shows with taped guitar and percussion accompaniment.

After pressing up a few thousand copies of the single "Rock Lobster," the B-52's traveled to the famed Max's Kansas City club for their first paying gig. Subsequent appearances at CBGB's brought the group to the attention of the New York press, and in 1979 they issued their self-titled debut album, a collection of manic, bizarre, and eminently danceable songs that scored an underground club hit with a reworked version of "Rock Lobster." The next year they issued *Wild Planet*, which reached the Top 20 on the US album charts; *Party Mix*, an EP's worth of reworked material from the band's first two proper outings, appeared in 1981.

In 1982 *Mesopotamia* arose out of a series of aborted sessions with producer David Byrne, which saw the B-52's largely abandon their trademark sense of humor, a situation rectified by the next year's *Whammy!*, a move into electronic territory. After a Schneider solo LP, 1984's *Fred Schneider and the Shake Society*, the group returned to the studio to record 1986's *Bouncing Off the Satellites*. On October 12, 1985, however, Ricky Wilson died; though originally his death was attributed to natural causes, it was later revealed that he had succumbed to AIDS. In light of Wilson's death, the group found it impossible to promote the new album, and they spent the next several years in seclusion.

In 1989 the B-52's finally returned with *Cosmic Thing*, their most commercially successful effort to date. Marked by Strickland's move from drums to guitar and club-friendly production from Don Was and Nile Rodgers, the album launched several hit singles, including the party smash "Love Shack," "Roam," and "Deadbeat Club." In 1990 Cindy Wilson retired from active duty, leaving the remaining trio to soldier on for 1992's *Good Stuff*. A year later, dubbed the BC-52's, they performed the theme song for Steven Spielberg's live-action feature *The Flintsones*. —*Jason Ankeny*

★ **The B-52's** / Jul. 1979 / Warner Brothers ✦✦✦✦✦
It's all here on the debut album: the "Secret Agent Man" drum/guitar tracks that compel the feet to dance, topped by shrill female vocals and the brash speak-singing of Fred Schneider giving forth with some of the strangest non sequiturs as though he were an overexcited carnival barker. Includes "Planet Claire" and the hit "Rock Lobster." —*William Ruhlmann*

Wild Planet / Sep. 1980 / Warner Brothers ✦✦✦
Conventional wisdom has it that all the B-52's' subsequent releases are highly inferior to their debut. While *Wild Planet* is not the rarefied wonder their first platter is, it's still darned good. The songs here are generally faster, tighter, and punchier than previously, though production values are not as wonderfully quirky and detailed; fewer songs here are as over-the-top crazy as the first album's "Rock Lobster" or "52 Girls." These formless selections continue to exhibit a cunning mix of girl-group, garage band, surf, and television theme song influences, all propelled by an itchy dance beat. "Give Me Back My Man" allows Cindy Wilson a unique opportunity to croon a broad, expressive melodic line. Fred Schneider parades his inimitably nervous vocals on chucklesome ditties like "Quiche Lorraine" and "Strobe Light." The best songs here are "Private Idaho," a wonderfully jittery number that employs a variant on the famous melodic snippet from the "Twilight Zone" theme music, and "Devil in My Car," a delightfully loopy hoot that lays the craziness on very thickly. Performances and sound quality are fine. This album is well worth hearing and is recommended. —*David Cleary*

Party Mix! / Jul. 1981 / Warner Brothers ✦✦
Party Mix! is a six-track mini-album that selects three tracks each from the B-52's' first two albums, *The B-52's* and *Wild Planet*, and presents them in dance mixes. Since the group's bouncy songs are already danceready, this makes for alternatives rather than real improvements, even from a dance floor perspective. —*William Ruhlmann*

Mesopotamia / Jan. 1982 / Warner Brothers ✦✦
After setting dance floors alight and funny bones aquiver with their first two albums, *The B-52's* and *Wild Planet* in 1979-1980, the B-52's seemed to run out of gas soon after, issuing a stop-gap remix mini-album, *Party Mix*, in 1981, and then turning in *another* stop-gap mini in this lackluster set, produced by David Byrne, who must have seemed like a good choice, although his sense of humor is less zany, if just as weird, as the B's. *Mesopotamia* is the sound of a band once on firm ground but now losing its footing. —*William Ruhlmann*

Whammy! / Apr. 1983 / Warner Brothers ✦✦✦
After the still-born *Mesopotamia*, *Whammy!* is a pleasing return to the classic fun-loving wackiness of the first album, even if some of the songs sound a little forced and self-conscious. —*Stephen Thomas Erlewine*

Bouncing off the Satellites / Sep. 1986 / Warner Brothers ✦✦
Released about a year after the death of guitarist Ricky Wilson, *Bouncing off the Satellites* is a disjointed, uneven record that starts off strong but collapses into a mess of studio slickness by the end of the album. —*Stephen Thomas Erlewine*

Cosmic Thing / Jun. 1989 / Reprise ✦✦✦✦
Belatedly, and despite the death of their musical leader Ricky Wilson, the B-52's found enormous commercial success with this album, which effectively recapitulates their zany virtues, especially on the two Top Ten hits "Love Shack" and "Roam." —*William Ruhlmann*

Dance This Mess Around: The Best of the B-52's / 1990 / Island ✦✦✦✦
The Best of the B-52's: Dance This Mess Around contains 13 tracks all culled from the group's first four albums. Most of the compilation concentrates on the band's first two albums, *The B-52's* and *Wild Planet*, while picking highlights from the more uneven *Mesopotamia* and *Whammy!* Though it hits most of the group's best songs, their eponymous debut remains the pinnacle of their achievements, as well as the best introduction to the band. —*Stephen Thomas Erlewine*

Party Mix/Mesopotamia / Feb. 1991 / Warner Brothers ✦✦
In 1981, The B-52's issued a six-track EP containing remixes of some of the most popular songs from their first two albums. In 1982, they released a new six-track EP produced by Talking Heads' David Byrne called *Mesopotamia*. Neither of them was essential, but both had their virtues, and they were put together on one CD after the group's big commercial breakthrough with *Cosmic Thing*. —*William Ruhlmann*

Good Stuff / Jun. 23, 1992 / Reprise ✦✦
If *Cosmic Thing* found them returned to most-favored party band status, this followup gamely soldiers on in similar fashion. Without Cindy Wilson, *Good Stuff* becomes Kate Pierson's showcase, while even Fred Schneider turns in his most purely musical performance to date. If the B-52's hit some dead ends while trying to stretch out a bit, be assured

there are enough classic bits to make this one worthwhile. —*Steve Aldrich*

Howie B

b. Glasgow, Scotland
Keyboards, Sampler, Synthesizer / Ambient, Trip-Hop
Howie B emerged from Britain's mid-'90s dance music scene as part of the so-called "Trip Hop" movement, which emphasized slow break beats, dub reggae-influenced soundscapes, and little-to-no vocals. After releasing a number of 12" singles (including the simple but hypnotic British hit "Birth"), remixing dozens of songs for other artists, and finishing his full-length CD *Music for Babies*, he began working with U2 on the *Passengers* record (in association with what is arguably one of his biggest influences, Brian Eno). That collaboration led to the more fruitful results of U2's *Pop*, on which he served as an informal producer, engineer, and "beat supervisor." His high-profile work with U2 has threatened to overshadow his innovative role as a DJ/producer/musician.

His only full-length, *Music for Babies* shows off his tendencies toward creating mostly subtle, but sometimes dramatic, washes of sound that de-emphasize any sort of beat. Similar in shape and form to the Future Sound of London's sound sculptures, *Music for Babies* most definitely evokes Brian Eno's ambient masterworks of the 1970s, as is evidenced by the title—which is a tribute to Eno's ambient "soundtracks" for non-existent movies such as *Music for Airports*. Whereas his full-length album represents his tendencies toward making free-floating sound paintings, his 12" singles highlight a steady, if not loping, beat. At the end of 1996, Howie B was spending less time on his own music and more time remixing and producing other artists' work. —*Kevin McLeod*

● **Music for Babies** / Aug. 6, 1996 / Polydor ✦✦✦✦
His full-length debut under his own name is something of a disappointment, lacking both the spacey out-ness of Skylab and the detail of his Mo' Wax and Pussyfoot material. Recorded as a document of his wife's first pregnancy, it sounds as if Howie was using the studio to catch up on lost sleep. In fairness, there's some good material here; "Allergy" and "How to Suckie" play beats and textures off one another amiably, where "Here Comes the Tooth" and the title track drag ambient a few yards left of subtlety. The vinyl version comes accompanied by a booklet of bizarre stories by author Mike Benson. —*Sean Cooper*

Babes in Toyland

f. 1987, Minneapolis, MN
Alternative Pop-Rock, Grunge, Riot Grrrl
Babes in Toyland are about as harsh as rock music gets. Guitarist Kat Bjelland screams and thrashes her guitar to the gut-pounding, throttling beat of bassist Maureen Herman and drummer Lorie Barbero. Over their two albums and two EPs, the all-female trio offer no escape from their strongly female-oriented, but not necessarily feminist, rock.

Bjelland formed Babes in Toyland in 1987 in Minneapolis, after playing around San Francisco for several years in bands that featured, at various times, Jennifer Finch of L7 and Courtney Love of Hole. After releasing a single on Sub Pop's singles club, Babes in Toyland came to the attention of Sonic Youth, who took them on a tour of Europe. Soon, they recorded their abrasive debut, *Spanking Machine*, with producer Jack Endino; one more independent EP followed before they signed to Reprise. In between labels, original bassist Michelle Leon left the group.

Sonic Youth's Lee Ranaldo produced their second album, *Fontanelle*, which showed no signs of concession to a major label. In early 1993, the band broke up for several days before re-forming to record the *Painkillers* EP and hitting the road with Lollapalooza 93.

Even though Lollapalooza offered the group a boost in public exposure, they chose not to capitalize on it; instead, it took them nearly two years to release a new record, *Nemesisters*, in April 1995. —*Stephen Thomas Erlewine*

Spanking Machine / 1990 / Twin/Tone ✦✦✦✦
A great one the first time out of the blocks. Kat Bjelland's guitar is a rampaging string machine, while her vocals pin you to the wall. Not for the weak or fainthearted. —*John Dougan*

To Mother / Jul. 1, 1991 / Twin/Tone ✦✦✦
An EP follow-up that's strong but not life-changing. —*John Dougan*

● **Fontanelle** / Aug. 11, 1992 / Reprise ✦✦✦✦
Fontanelle, Babes in Toyland's major-label debut, is stronger than *Spanking Machine*. The band has grown tighter and more vicious, making their anger sting even harder. Not to be missed is Kat Bjelland's attack on Courtney Love, "Bruise Violet," one of the harshest songs ever recorded. —*Stephen Thomas Erlewine*

Painkiller / Jun. 22, 1993 / Warner Brothers ✦✦✦
Painkiller features four solid new tracks, one re-recording, and one track that is a brutal, 35-minute live performance of the *Fontanelle* album. It's

a good introduction to the intense, loud punk rock of Babes in Toyland. —*AMG*

Nemesisters / May 9, 1995 / Reprise ✦✦
On *Nemesisters*, Babes in Toyland becomes a full-fledged heavy metal band. Most of the raw, slashing guitars of their early records are gone, replaced by a pulsing, plodding grind that never catches fire. Gone are the inspired, angry lyrics, replaced by jokes that just aren't that funny—the opener "Hello," the cheap puns of "Sweet 69," and the deconstructionist covers of "All by Myself" and "Deep Song," which are too obvious to be humorous. "Sweet 69" does have a pummelling heavy groove that makes its jokes forgivable, but the majority of the album is simply dull, recycled riffs and rhythms, and that is hard to forgive. —*Stephen Thomas Erlewine*

Baby Bird

f. Great Britain
Singer-Songwriter, Alternative Pop-Rock
Baby Bird began as the alias of Steven Jones, a prolific British singer-songwriter who initiated his performing career as a member of the Dogs in Honey "anti-theater" troupe. After buying a four-track machine, he began making his first lo-fi home recordings; over the next several years, he wrote some 400 eclectic pop songs, ranging in content from surreal, comic narratives to intensely personal meditations.

At the urging of friends, Jones sent out Baby Bird tapes to record companies, but his music was roundly rejected; however, Chrysalis Music did offer a publishing deal that Jones accepted, applying his earnings towards financing a series of independently released, limited-edition collections. The first disc of material culled from the vast Baby Bird archives, *I Was Born a Man*, appeared in early 1995; within the course of a year, three other acclaimed albums—*Bad Shave*, *Fatherhood*, and *The Happiest Man Alive*—followed and won Jones a contract with Echo Records.

Upon making the leap to a major label, Baby Bird mutated from a one-man project into a full band, as Jones assembled a backing group comprised of guitarist Luke Scott, bassist John Pedder, keyboardist Hugh Chadbourne, and drummer Rob Gregory. In its new incarnation, Baby Bird debuted in late 1996 with *Ugly Beautiful*, a lush, sparkling collection of re-recordings of favorite songs from Jones' back catalogue, all selected by fans by means of postcard ballots included in the first four albums. —*Jason Ankeny*

I Was Born a Man / Oct. 1995 / Baby Bird ✦✦✦
For his first Baby Bird collection *I Was Born a Man*, Steven Jones assembled more than 20 songs from his home recordings, thereby establishing his sound, style, and *modus operandi*. From the outset, Jones' records are devoted to mid-'80s British alternative rock; echoes of Echo & the Bunnymen, Robyn Hitchcock, and U2 can be heard throughout the album, but they are delivered in an endearingly primitive fashion, due to the lo-fi constraints of his home porta-studio. This works in his favor, as the poor songs sound as if they were recorded for a lark, and the best songs shine through the hissy songs. Still, Jones' apparent lack of quality control can make the lengthy mess of *I Was Born a Man* a trying experience, even for listeners accustomed to sifting through Sebadoh records. —*Stephen Thomas Erlewine*

Bad Shave / Oct. 1995 / Baby Bird ✦✦✦✦
By tightening his quality control considerably, Steven Jones makes a convincing case that he is a madly talented English eccentric with Baby Bird's second album, *Bad Shave*. About half of the album is devoted to full-fledged songs, several of which (including the title track) are genuinely eerie and haunting. The rest, of course, is comprised of lightweight material that sounds as if Jones was indulging his warped sense of humor, but in this context, where they're balanced by more substantial songs, they have greater impact. Although it still is a little too obscure for its own good, *Bad Shave* is an intriguing listen, and one that suggests Jones' talent may be too big to stay in the bedroom. —*Stephen Thomas Erlewine*

● **Fatherhood** / Jan. 1996 / Baby Bird ✦✦✦✦
Unlike the other early Baby Bird releases, the songs that comprise *Fatherhood* actually stake out some thematic unity—in this case, of course, paternity. Sporting a rather disconcerting cover featuring a faux-pregnant Steven Jones, *Fatherhood* is the strongest and most ambitious of the four initial collections of Baby Bird home recordings; from the Dylanesque wordplay of "Bad Blood" to the psychedelia of "Aluminium Beach" to the surreal Franco-pop of the closer "May We," these are complex, mature songs that belie their primitive four-track origins. —*Jason Ankeny*

Happiest Man Alive / Mar. 1996 / Baby Bird ✦✦
Baby Bird's *The Happiest Man Alive* is the fourth album Steven Jones has assembled from his home recordings in the span of just under a year. Given that fact, it shouldn't be entirely surprising that it is the weakest Baby Bird album to date. *The Happiest Man Alive* feels like

outtakes from *Bad Shave* and *Fatherhood*, and in a way they are. Jones recorded some 600 songs in his home on a Casio and cheap guitar over the course of six years and began assembling his records from these very tapes in 1995. Though there are literally hundreds of songs left in his collection, *The Happiest Man Alive* suggests that he picked all the best tracks for his first three albums. Occasionally, he has buried a gem within his kitschy, melancholy camp-cabaret, but the album is of interest only to fanatics and fetishists willing to dig through everything Jones has recorded. —*Stephen Thomas Erlewine*

Ugly Beautiful / Oct. 1996 / Echo ✦✦✦✦
Moving to a major label and switching to a full backing band for *Ugly Beautiful* is both a positive and negative development for Baby Bird. In the positive sense, Steven Jones's songs—including a handful of tracks that were on his indie releases—are given a clarity they were lacking in the past, and the full-bodied arrangements reveal songs like "Good Night" and "You're Gorgeous" as effortlessly catchy pop singles. However, the sonic clarity and the larger arrangements also reveal that Jones is neither as clever nor as strange as his lo-fi albums suggested. Indeed, he often sounds as if he's stuck in 1985, replicating the quirky charms of Robyn Hitchcock and Echo & the Bunnymen, and he has neither the wit nor the adventure of either artist. So *Ugly Beautiful* often treads close to cutesy nostalgia, of all things, but it's saved by the sporadic surfacing of his songcraft. Even in this radio-ready setting, "I Didn't Want to Wake You Up" has a disquieting power, and "You're Gorgeous" positively radiates with twisted sexuality. But the long, "ironic" jams and unfocused material that end the record suggest that, instead of representing the first flowering of his full talent, *Ugly Beautiful* may be the peak of it. —*Stephen Thomas Erlewine*

Babyface (Kenny Edmonds)

b. Apr. 10, 1959, Indianapolis, IN
Vocals, Keyboards / Urban, Adult Contemporary, Club/Dance
With his friend Antonio Reid, Babyface formed a Cincinnati-based band, the Deele, in the early '80s. They were introduced by members of Midnight Star to Solar Records executive Dick Griffey, who put them to work producing music for Carrie Lucas, the Whispers, and Dynasty. Since then, they've produced hits for Sheena Easton, Pebbles, Paula Abdul, and others.

During the '90s, Babyface's dominance has extended beyond the production arena and into the performing circle. A series of hit releases depicting him simultaneously as a vulnerable romantic and accomplished lover turned Babyface into arguably this decade's biggest urban male vocalist. The string actually began in the mid-'80s with the underrated *Lovers*, but picked up steam with *Tender Lover* in 1989. *Tender Lover* crossed over into pop territory and eventually sold more than two million copies, ending any doubts that Babyface would be a major solo star. The singles "Whip Appeal" and "It's No Crime" were Top Ten R&B and pop hits, and they remain staples on urban radio. He followed that with *A Closer Look* in 1991, and his most recent LP, *For the Cool in You*, earned another platinum certification and ranked among 1993's biggest R&B/urban albums.

Babyface hit his peak in 1995, as he produced hits for artists like Boyz II Men, Madonna, and Whitney Houston and coordinated the *Waiting to Exhale* soundtrack. In the fall of 1996 he released *Day*, his first solo album since 1993, to strong reviews, but the album failed to generate a hit single as large as any of his outside productions in the last two years. —*Bil Carpenter*

● **Tender Lover** / Jul. 1989 / Solar ✦✦✦✦
Babyface's second solo album yielded the first No. 1 R&B hit of the 1990s, while establishing Edmonds as a major personality and performer. He wrote or co-wrote much of the material and even played several instruments. It was a combination of slick production and nicely sung sentimental tributes and heartache ballads. —*Ron Wynn*

Lovers / Sep. 1989 / Solar ✦✦✦
On his solo debut, Babyface sings with just enough earnestness to be soulful and just enough sophistication and slickness to avoid sounding too much like a throwback. —*Ron Wynn*

A Closer Look / Nov. 19, 1991 / Solar ✦✦✦✦
Babyface has established himself as both a performing and production star in the '90s. His alternately innocent, hurt, and disillusioned vocals are this decade's equivalent of the soul/love songs of the '70s and '80s. He can sing sentimental material or tender tunes, or seem angry and confused. His lyrics get overly coy, but they've struck many responsive chords among women in particular. It's not soul, but that's what many who never heard Sam Cooke think it is. —*Ron Wynn*

For the Cool in You / Aug. 1993 / Epic ✦✦✦
Babyface has supplanted Luther Vandross as the reigning prince of vocal romanticism in Black popular music among the affluent crowd. His ability to sound poignant, vulnerable, and appealing, as well as write and produce catchy songs replete with hooks, has won him widespread

popularity and consistent commercial success. Such tracks as "For the Cool in You," "A Bit Old-Fashioned," and "I'll Always Love You" demonstrate his mastery of an ideal formula. Babyface sings with the right blend of authority, conviction, earnestness, and innocence, and if he's hardly a compelling pure singer, he's the right vocalist for the current era. —*Ron Wynn*

The Day / Oct. 29, 1996 / Sony ✦✦✦✦
The Day was the first album Babyface released after being elevated to a virtually guaranteed hit-maker in the mid-'90s through his work with Whitney Houston, Boyz II Men, Madonna, and Mariah Carey, among many others. The album confirms his skill for subtle, inventive songwriting and accessible, polished, yet soulful, production. Babyface can straddle the line between hip-hop and traditional soul better than nearly any other artist, as evidenced by the hits he has orchestrated for other artists. On his own, he is still compelling—his voice is as smooth as silk, and nearly as seductive—but it doesn't quite have the force of personality as his greatest productions. Nevertheless, *The Day* qualifies as state-of-the-art mid-'90s soul, featuring a handful of terrific songs and a lot of extremely pleasurable filler. —*Leo Stanley*

The Babys

f. 1976, London, England, db. 1981
Pop-Rock, Arena Rock
The Babys generated extensive hype upon formation in 1976 as one of mainstream pop-rock's brightest hopes for the future. While competent, their music never broke away from its Raspberries-meets-AOR style to develop its own distinctive sound. The group consisted of vocalist/bassist John Waite, guitarist Wally Stocker, former Spontaneous Combustion and Strider drummer Tony Brock, and keyboardist/guitarist Mike Corby, who was replaced by Jonathan Cain in 1978; bassist Ricky Phillips also joined later on. Overshadowed by the punk and new wave movement in their native UK, the band concentrated on the American market and did score two Top 20 singles with "Isn't It Time" and "Every Time I Think of You."

By 1981 the Babys' future didn't look so bright anymore, and the group disbanded, with Stocker joining Air Supply's road band. Waite went solo and finally broke through on the charts in 1984 with the No. 1 smash "Missing You," while Cain joined Journey; the two later reunited in the AOR supergroup Bad English. —*Steve Huey*

● **Anthology** / Oct. 1981 / Chrysalis ✦✦✦✦
Anthology is a fine ten-track collection featuring all of the Babys' biggest hits, including "If You've Got the Time," "Isn't It Time," "Every Time I Think of You," "Head First," "Back on My Feet Again" and "Turn and Walk Away." Since the band's records were generally uneven affairs, most fans will be satisfied with this reasonably comprehensive overview. —*Stephen Thomas Erlewine*

Burt Bacharach

b. May 12, 1928, Kansas City, MO
Pop, Brill Building Pop, Pop-Rock
With a hit-single track record spanning four decades, Burt Bacharach has become one of the most important composers of popular music in the late 20th century. Born May 12, 1928, in Kansas City, he studied cello, drums, and piano as a child, and was later transplanted to New York City by his father, a syndicated columnist. The time spent in New York gave him a chance to sneak into clubs to watch his bebop heroes Dizzy Gillespie and Charlie Parker; he also played in several jazz bands during the 1940s. Bacharach studied music theory and composition at the Mannes School in New York, at Berkshire Music Center, at the New School for Social Research (with Darius Milhaud), at Montreal's McGill University, and at the Music Academy of the West in Santa Barbara, CA. A period in the Army interrupted his concentrated music study, but even while serving in Germany, Bacharach arranged and played piano for a dance band. He also played in nightclubs and backed Steve Lawrence, the Ames Brothers, and Paula Stewart. Bacharach was discharged in 1952, and he married Stewart on December 22 of the next year.

On return to the US, he began writing songs for Lawrence, Patti Page, the Ames Brothers, and others, but his first hit came from Marty Robbins in late 1957 when Robbins took "The Story of My Life" to the American Top 20 and the No. 1 spot in England. The single was also notable for its co-composer, Hal David, who became Bacharach's songwriting partner and collaborated on most of his big hits. The Bacharach/David team followed up in January 1958 with Perry Como's "Magic Moments," another UK chart-topper and a Top Five entry in America. Bacharach's marriage dissolved in 1958, and he left for Europe to tour with Marlene Dietrich. He returned in 1961 and wrote several songs for the Drifters with Bob Hilliard (including "Mexican Divorce" and "Please Stay") before reuniting with Hal David. At an arranging session, he found the singer who became the ultimate vehicle for his songs: Dionne Warwick, who was working as a member of the Drifters' backup vocal group the Gospelaires.

By late 1962 Bacharach and David began focusing most of their composing energy on Warwick, who was the recipient of 15 Top 40 singles from 1962 to 1968 (including the Top Tens "Anyone Who Had a Heart," "Walk on By," "Message to Michael," "I Say a Little Prayer," "Valley of the Dolls" and "Do You Know the Way to San Jose?"). The duo also remained dominant in England, where Frankie Vaughan, Cilla Black, Sandie Shaw, the Walker Brothers, and Herb Alpert all hit No. 1 with Bacharach/David compositions. In the '60s, the songwriters contributed film scores for *What's New Pussycat?*, *Alfie*, and *Casino Royale*. Their most celebrated score, *Butch Cassidy and the Sundance Kid* (1969), won Oscars for Best Original Score and Best Theme Song for "Raindrops Keep Fallin' on My Head" (plus two non-musical Academy Awards). Bacharach and David began working on the musical *Promises, Promises* in the late '60s; it won a Tony and a Grammy Award (for cast album) during a popular three-year-run Broadway run. Bacharach hit the charts himself in 1969 with the show's "I'll Never Fall in Love Again" reaching the Top 100. Surprisingly, this was not his only foray into recording; Bacharach had reached No. 4 in the UK charts in May 1965 with "Trains and Boats and Planes," and he released several popular solo albums during the late '60s.

The beginning of the '70s looked bright for Burt Bacharach, as the Carpenters took "(They Long to Be) Close to You" to No. 1 in the US in July 1970. The forecast was premature, though, as three of his closest partners—Hal David, Dionne Warwick, and his second wife, Angie Dickinson—left him. He gathered several accolades for an eponymous 1971 album featuring renditions of his previous hit compositions, but later albums were disappointing, and Bacharach's next hit was more than a decade in coming. Finally in 1981 he collaborated with Christopher Cross, Carol Bayer Sager, and Peter Allen on the Oscar-winning "Arthur's Theme." Bacharach married Bayer Sager just one year later, and together they wrote Roberta Flack's Top 20 hit "Making Love," as well as "Heartlight," which Neil Diamond took to No. 5.

Once Bacharach resumed composing he began to hit, and 1986 was one of his finest years, with two American No. 1s: "That's What Friends Are For" (by an all-star group including Warwick, Elton John, Gladys Knight, and Stevie Wonder) and a duet by Patti LaBelle & Michael McDonald titled "On My Own." He divorced Sager in 1991, but worked with Dionne Warwick again two years later on "Sunny Weather Love," from her *Friends Can Be Lovers* album. Also in 1993 Bacharach contributed songs to James Ingram, Earth, Wind & Fire and Tevin Campbell. Around the same time, many alternative bands began name-checking the hit-maker as an influence, and Oasis frontman Noel Gallagher joined him on the stage of the Royal Albert Hall as well as including a picture of him on the cover of Oasis' *Definitely Maybe*. BBC-TV focused on Bacharach in a January 1996 documentary. —*John Bush*

★ **The Look of Love: The Classic Songs of Burt Bacharach** / 1996 / Polygram ✦✦✦✦✦
Although it doesn't contain every great song Burt Bacharach ever wrote, the various artists collection *The Look of Love: The Classic Songs of Burt Bacharach* is a wonderful sampling of his best moments. Over the course of 23 tracks, the album includes the most familiar Bacharach songs, all of them presented in their original hit versions, which means there is Dionne Warwick's "Walk on By," Dusty Springfield's "I Just Don't Know What to Do With Myself," the Walker Brothers' "Make It Easy on Yourself," Sandie Shaw's "(There's) Always Something There to Remind Me," Gene Pitney's "Twenty Four Hours from Tulsa," Aretha Franklin's "I Say a Little Prayer," BJ Thomas' "Raindrops Keep Fallin' on My Head," and the Carpenters' "(They Long to Be) Close to You," among many others. Perhaps the collection could have featured all the key moments over the course of two discs, but as it stands, *The Look of Love* is an indispensible sampler of one of the greatest pop music composers of the '60s. —*Stephen Thomas Erlewine*

Bachman-Turner Overdrive

f. 1972, Vancouver, British Columbia, db. 1979
Rock 'n' Roll, Pop-Rock, Arena Rock
After his 1970 departure from the Guess Who, guitarist Randy Bachman recorded a solo album (*Axe*) and planned a project with ex-Nice keyboardist Keith Emerson (later cancelled due to illness) before forming Bachman-Turner Overdrive in 1972. Originally called Brave Belt, the metal group was comprised of singer/guitarist Bachman, fellow Guess Who alum Chad Allan, bassist C.F. "Fred" Turner, and Randy's brother, drummer Robbie; after a pair of LPs (*Brave Belt I* and *Brave Belt II*), Allan was replaced by another Bachman brother, guitarist Tim, and in homage to the trucker's magazine *Overdrive*, the unit became BTO.

While their self-titled 1973 debut caused little impact in the US or the band's native Canada, *Bachman-Turner Overdrive II* was a smash, netting a hit single with the anthemic "Taking Care of Business." Before the release of 1974's *Not Fragile*, Tim Bachman exited the group to begin a

career in production and was replaced by Blair Thornton; the album was a chart-topping success and notched a No. 1 single with "You Ain't Seen Nothin' Yet."

After two more albums—*Four Wheel Drive* and *Head On*, both issued in 1975—Randy Bachman left the group for a solo career, releasing the LP *Survivor* before forming another group, Ironhorse. Bachman-Turner Overdrive continued in his absence with replacement Jim Clench for three more albums, *Freeways* (1977), *Street Action*, and *Rock n' Roll Nights* (both 1978), eventually changing their name to simply BTO. At the tail end of the decade, the band dissolved, but in the 1980s they regrouped to tour as both Bachman-Turner Overdrive (led by Randy) and BTO (led by Robbie); confusion triggered by the name game resulted in Randy Bachman's filing suit against his onetime bandmates for rights to the group's logo. —*Jason Ankeny*

● **Greatest Hits** / 1981 / Mercury ✦✦✦✦
All the essential hits are here on this good-sounding set. The lack of liner notes keeps this from being an informative place to start, but if you are looking for just the music, the high points are here. —*Rick Clark*

The Anthology / Jul. 20, 1993 / PolyGram ✦✦✦✦
This double-disc set features fine remastering from the original masters, plus extensive liner notes. This is an ideal choice for the *true* fan who is just converting to CD, and is looking for more than the basic hits package. Hit seekers will still find *BTO's Greatest Hits* more than adequate. —*Rick Clark*

Bad Brains

f. 1979, Washington, D.C., db. 1995
Alternative Pop-Rock, Hardcore Punk
By melding punk with reggae, Bad Brains became one of the definitive American hardcore punk groups of the early '80s. Although the group released only a handful of records during their peak, including the legendary cassette-only debut *Bad Brains*, they developed a dedicated following, many of whom would later form their own hardcore and alternative bands. As for the Bad Brains themselves, they continued to record and tour in varying lineups led by guitarist Dr. Know into the late '90s, yet never managed to break out of their cult status.

Dr. Know (b. Gary Miller), a former jazz fusion guitarist, formed Bad Brains in 1979, inspired by both the amateurish rage of the Sex Pistols and the political reggae of Bob Marley. Realizing that the lines between punk and reggae were already blurred in the UK, he set out to replicate that situation in the US, and he recruited several similarly minded musicians—vocalist H.R. (b. Paul D. Hudson), bassist Darryl Aaron Jenifer, and drummer Earl Hudson—to prove his point. Bad Brains quickly became one of the most popular punk bands on the East Coast, particularly in their hometown of Washington, DC. Their live performances were legendary, but their recordings were difficult to find. Their debut single "Pay to Cum" was pressed in limited numbers, and their 1982 debut album was issued only in cassette form by ROIR. In addition to the *Bad Brains* tape, the group released a handful of other EPs in 1982, finally moving to PVC for 1983's full-length debut *Rock for Light*, which was produced by Ric Ocasek.

The handful of indie recordings the Bad Brains left behind, as well as their live shows, made the band a legend in American hardcore, but few potential fans could actually hear the band because of poor distribution and erratic touring. The band took three years to deliver the follow-up to *Rock for Light*, finally releasing *I Against I* on SST in 1986. In those three years, the group developed more heavy metal leanings, and the resulting record received mixed reviews. More importantly, it divided the band, with Dr. Know and Jenifer wishing to continue to pursue heavy rock, and H.R. and Hudson wanting to devote themselves to reggae. Over the next three years, the latter pair frequently left the band to make reggae albums before finally departing in 1989. They were replaced by Israel Joseph-I (b. Dexter Pinto) and Mackie Jayson, respectively.

In the wake of the alternative rock boom of the early '90s, the Bad Brains were finally offered a major-label contract in 1993, releasing *Rise* on Epic later that year. The album bombed, and the group was dropped. Maverick Records offered the group a contract in 1995, provided that the original lineup reunited. They did so and released *God of Love* that summer, to mixed reviews and poor sales. H.R. and Hudson left the band shortly after the album's release, and the band was dropped by Maverick. —*Stephen Thomas Erlewine*

Bad Brains / Feb. 1982 / ROIR ✦✦✦✦
On their debut album, Bad Brains established their explosive mix of reggae and hardcore. At this stage, the fusion was a little tentative, with the band able to pull off the punk better than the reggae, but the band's sheer energy made the album successful. —*Stephen Thomas Erlewine*

Rock for Light / 1983 / Plan 9/Caroline ✦✦✦✦
On their Ric Ocasek-produced second album, Bad Brains were able to balance the hardcore and reggae elements more skillfully than they had on their debut, but *Rock for Light* suffers from a lack of cohesiveness.

Even if it is a little inconsistent, the unique power of their vision makes the album worthwhile. —*Stephen Thomas Erlewine*

● **I Against I** / 1986 / SST ✦✦✦✦
Slick production helped the Brains make the most satisfying metal/reggae record of their career. Dr. Know's guitar is pushed way up front in the mix, and the funkier backbeat (replacing the hardcore speed blur) kicks every track (especially "Return to Heaven") into high gear. —*John Dougan*

Live / 1988 / SST ✦✦✦
Compiled from a series of 1987 concerts, *Live* captures Bad Brains at the height of their onstage prowess. It is necessary listening for hardcore fans. —*Stephen Thomas Erlewine*

Attitude: The ROIR Session / 1989 / Ineffect ✦✦✦✦
Attitude is actually Bad Brains' eponymous cassette-only 1982 debut, re-titled and re-formatted for the CD age. A potent hybrid of Rastafarian reggae ("Leaving Babylon," "I Luv I Jah") and take-no-prisoners hardcore (a re-recorded "Pay to Cum," "Banned in D.C."), its fury and impact remain undimmed. —*Jason Ankeny*

Quickness / Sep. 1989 / Plan 9/Caroline ✦✦
Quickness was Bad Brains' most metal-oriented record to date, with the band eliminating most of the reggae numbers and concentrating on thick, driving rhythms accentuated by metallic, jazz-tinged leads by Dr. Know. —*Stephen Thomas Erlewine*

Youth Are Getting Restless: Live in Amsterdam / May 1990 / Plan 9/ Caroline ✦✦✦
Youth Are Getting Restless repeats some of the same material from *Live*, albeit in different versions. The album was culled from the same tour as *Live*, but it captures a blistering concert from Amsterdam instead of compiling various performances. Consequently, it's a tighter and more exciting album, their best live record. —*Stephen Thomas Erlewine*

Rise / Aug. 1993 / Epic ✦✦
Bad Brains took longer than most bands do to reach the majors (that is, among those who ever do), and by now they are very different from the group that made their debut with a self-titled cassette on ROIR in 1982. As heard on *Rise*, they are basically a thrash metal band with elements of rap and reggae. In other words, they're fairly trendy. Meanwhile, of course, they're now playing in a bigger league, and their competition includes everyone from Metallica to Public Enemy, against whom they come off as reasonable competition, but no more. Hope they got a big advance and didn't spend it all in one place. —*William Ruhlmann*

God of Love / May 23, 1995 / Maverick ✦✦
For *God of Love*, Bad Brains' first album for Madonna's label Maverick, the original lineup of the group reunited. Presumably, this was for the reported multi-million dollar record contract—which was offered after the success of Green Day and the Beastie Boys—and not because the band had any great love for each other; during the supporting tour, HR slugged their manager and left the group, only to return within a week. Ric Ocasek, the producer of their breakthrough *Rock for Light*, also returned to produce the record. However, just because all the original participants returned, it didn't mean the sound or the inspiration returned. *God of Love* was flat and unenergetic. It failed to have an impact and faded from view soon after its release. —*Stephen Thomas Erlewine*

Bad Company

f. 1973, England
Blues-Rock, Hard Rock, Arena Rock
Formed in 1973, the British hard-rock outfit Bad Company was a super-group comprised of ex-King Crimson bassist Boz Burrell, former Mott the Hoople guitarist Mick Ralphs, and singer Paul Rodgers and drummer Simon Kirke, both onetime members of Free. Powered by Rodgers' muscular vocals and Ralphs' blues-based guitar work, Bad Company was the first group signed to Led Zeppelin's vanity label Swan Song; their eponymously titled 1974 debut was an international hit that topped the US album charts and scored a No. 1 single with "Can't Get Enough of Your Love."
Straight Shooter, issued the following year, was another major success, notching the hit "Feel Like Makin' Love," while 1976's *Run with the Pack* was Bad Company's third consecutive million-selling record. After 1977's *Burnin' Sky*, the group recorded 1979's *Desolation Angels*, which embellished their sound with synthesizers and strings; a three-year hiatus followed before the release of *Rough Diamonds*, the group's final LP in its original incarnation.
In 1986 Ralphs and Kirke resurrected the Bad Company name, enlisting former Ted Nugent vocalist Brian Howe to replace Rodgers; the reconfigured unit's debut *From 10 to 6* was a commercial failure, but 1988's *Dangerous Age* was a minor hit. In 1990 *Holy Water* fared even better, as the power ballad "If You Needed Somebody" became a Top 20 success. *Here Comes Trouble*, issued in 1992, achieved platinum status,

and earned another Top 40 hit with "How About That." On their 20th anniversary, Bad Company expanded into a quintet with the addition of bassist Rick Wills and rhythm guitarist Dave Colwell, and released the live retrospective *The Best of Bad Company Live... What You Hear Is What You Get*. Two more LPs, 1995's *The Company of Strangers* and the next year's *Stories Told and Untold*, followed. —*Jason Ankeny*

Bad Company / Jun. 1974 / Swan Song ✦✦✦✦
This powerhouse debut includes "Can't Get Enough," "Ready for Love," and the title track. —*Dan Heilman*

Straight Shooter / Apr. 1975 / Swan Song ✦✦✦
Their hot streak continues on this fine follow-up, with "Feel like Makin' Love." —*Dan Heilman*

Run with the Pack / Jan. 1976 / Swan Song ✦✦
By this, their third album, it was becoming increasingly clear that Bad Company's music was a formula, and an unusually restrictive one. (They did try adding strings on the title track, which is one of the rewrites of the song "Bad Company.") With the band touring the world and momentum on their side, *Run with the Pack* shot up the charts, too, but it didn't get quite as high or stay quite as long as its predecessors, mostly because of the lack of really memorable material. The biggest single was a cover of the Coasters' hit "Young Blood." —*William Ruhlmann*

Burnin' Sky / Mar. 1977 / Swan Song ✦✦✦
The string finally ran out for Bad Company with its fourth album. Their approach was so simple that it almost inevitably became formulaic, and although Mick Ralphs continued to screech with his sparse guitar leads and Paul Rodgers continued to present his lust in a soulful voice—well, we had heard it several times. By its fourth album, Bad Company was getting sloppy around the edges, but the real reason this was the first Bad Company record to miss the Top Ten in the US and the UK is that there was no hit single. Clearly, it was time to try something new. —*William Ruhlmann*

Desolation Angels / Mar. 1979 / Swan Song ✦✦✦
After a couple of mediocre efforts, *Desolation Angels* marked a return to form for Bad Company. It was also the band's last consistent album, powered by "Rock 'n' Roll Fantasy" and "Gone, Gone, Gone." —*Stephen Thomas Erlewine*

Rough Diamonds / Aug. 1982 / Swan Song ✦✦
Instead of capitalizing on their "Rock 'n' Roll Fantasy" resurgence, Bad Company disappeared for another three years before trying it again with *Rough Diamonds*. Remember, it was not yet common in the music business for major groups to stay away from the marketplace that long. In Bad Company's case, the results were disastrous. The album didn't even make the Top 25 in the US or go gold, much less platinum, and the music was softer and less distinctive than on their earlier records. —*William Ruhlmann*

● **10 from 6** / Dec. 1985 / Swan Song ✦✦✦✦
10 from 6 means ten songs from six albums—namely, Bad Company's first six records, all of which were big hits on album-rock radio. This brief yet very effective collection gathers all of the group's best-known songs ("Can't Get Enough," "Feel like Makin' Love," "Shootin' Star," "Bad Company," "Rock 'n' Roll Fantasy," "Ready for Love") in one place. Although most album-oriented hard-rock acts are better heard on the original albums, Bad Company's records tended to be more uneven than those of their peers, making *10 from 6* a valuable collection for the group's casual fans, who will want to bypass the cluttered studio albums and just get the cream of the crop. —*Stephen Thomas Erlewine*

Bad Religion

f. 1980, Los Angeles, CA
Punk, Alternative Pop-Rock, Hardcore Punk
Out of all of the Southern Californian hardcore punk bands of the early '80s, Bad Religion stayed around the longest. For over a decade, they retained their underground credibility without turning out a series of indistinguishable records that all sound the same. Instead, the band refined their attack, adding inflections of psychedelia, heavy metal, and hard rock along the way, as well as a considerable dose of melody. Between their 1982 debut and their first major-label record, 1993's *Recipe for Hate*, Bad Religion stayed vital in the hardcore community by tightening their musical execution and keeping their lyrics complex and righteously angry.
Bad Religion formed in the northern suburbs of Los Angeles in 1980, comprising guitarist Brett Gurewitz, vocalist Greg Graffin, bassist Jay Bentley, and drummer Jay Lishrout. Gurewitz established his own record company, Epitaph, to release the band's records. Between their self-titled EP and their first full-length record, Pete Finestone replaced Lishrout as the group's drummer. *How Could Hell Be Any Worse (1980-1985)*, their debut album, was released in 1982 and gained them some attention on the national US hardcore scene. After its release, the group's lineup changed, as bassist Paul Dedona and drummer Davy Goldman joined the group. *Into the Unknown*, the group's second

album, appeared in 1983. Featuring a vaguely psychedelicized sound and several keyboards, the album was musically impressive; but it made many of their fans angry, and the band's following decreased dramatically.

In the meantime, the band's lineup was undergoing some more shakeups. Gurewitz had to take 1984 off to recover from various substance-abuse problems, leaving Graffin as the band's only original member. In addition to Graffin, the 1984 incarnation of the band featured former Circle Jerks guitarist Greg Hetson, bassist Tim Gallegos, and returning drummer Pete Finestone. Bad Religion's next release, the harder, punkier *Back to the Known* EP restored faith among the group's devoted fans. After its release, the group went on hiatus for three years.

When Bad Religion returned in 1987, the band featured Gurewitz, Graffin, Lishrout, Hetson, and Finestone. They released *Suffer* the following year, a record that re-established the group as prominent players in the US underground punk/hardcore scene. They followed with *No Control* (1989) and *Against the Grain* (1990). By the time of their 1993 album, *Recipe for Hate*, alternative rock had become popular with the mainstream; in addition, the band's following was quite large. These two factors contributed to Bad Religion's signing a major-label contract with Atlantic Records. *Recipe for Hate* was originally released on Epitaph, but it was soon re-released with the support of Atlantic. The group's first proper major-label album was 1994's *Stranger Than Fiction;* it was also Gurewitz' last album with the group. Before the release of *Stranger Than Fiction*, Epitaph had an unexpected hit with the Offspring's *Smash*, causing Gurewitz to spend more time at the label; reports also indicated that he was displeased with Bad Religion's major label contract. The group replaced Gurewitz for their supporting tour, which proved to be their least successful to date.

Bad Religion released their second major-label album, *The Gray Race*, in early 1996. *— Stephen Thomas Erlewine*

How Can Hell Be Any Worse (1980-1985) / 1982 / Epitaph ✦✦✦
A tremendous collection of early Bad Religion that covers most of their hardcore and early post-hardcore period, including their debut record, *How Could Hell Be Any Worse*. Graffin's snarl is prominently displayed, and the band rages through this anthology's 28 tracks, which include three takes of their signature theme "Bad Religion." Lots of tracks are suffused with a quasi-liberal, populist message (e.g., "Politics," "World War III," and "Oligarchy") and are more lyrically sophisticated than one might assume. An excellent introduction. *—John Dougan*

Into the Unknown / 1983 / Epitaph ✦✦✦✦
At a time when most L.A. bands were playing extremely fast, stripped-down rock, Bad Religion released this chunk of '70s-styled hard rock that anticipated the '70s revival by about a decade. It's a bit off-putting at first blush, mainly because the tempos are slower and more deliberate, and because of the use of swirling organs and pianos. But it's a terrific record that was perhaps more daring than anyone realized at the time of its release. An extremely influential and interesting record, one that any fan of hard rock should own. *—John Dougan*

Back to the Known / 1984 / Epitaph ✦✦
Apparently Bad Religion felt they had departed from their hardcore roots too much on *Into the Unknown*, so they returned immediately with the aptly titled EP, *Back to the Known*. As the title suggests, the band eliminated all the hints of psychedelia and keyboards that flowed throughout the previous album, concentrating on relentless punk rock. While it's a stylistic retreat, the band's strength is blistering hardcore punk, which is something *Back to the Known* delivers in spades. *— Stephen Thomas Erlewine*

Suffer / 1988 / Epitaph ✦✦✦✦
Featuring a reunited version of the original band, *Suffer* is a fast, stripped-down, blazing record that relentlessly tears through its songs. In terms of sheer sonic intensity, *Suffer* is their best record yet, even if it is lacking in musical diversity. *— Stephen Thomas Erlewine*

No Control / Dec. 1989 / Epitaph ✦✦✦✦
No Control is even more uncompromising than *Suffer*, except that this time, Bad Religion concentrated more on songwriting and melody, making the album their most impressive straight hardcore effort. *—Stephen Thomas Erlewine*

Against the Grain / 1990 / Epitaph ✦✦✦✦
After reuniting in 1988, Bad Religion went on a recording binge that saw the release of three records in two years. All are good, with *No Control* hands-down the best of the three. What's crucial at this point in their career is that the band was concerned with simply being a good rock band and less concerned with being aging punks. As a result the music doesn't sound retrograde or tossed-off, and Graffin, Gurewitz, and Co. never come off like a pathetic bunch of middle-age punks desperately attempting to sound young. This music takes maturity head-on and deals with it in a way that gets to the roots of living in society as opposed to dying before you get old—the former being much tougher than the latter. But even from the start, Bad Religion's music was never about

taking the easy way out, and these three releases are a testament to that attitude. *—John Dougan*

Generator / Mar. 13, 1992 / Epitaph ✦✦✦
Generator demonstrates an improved sense of melody from Greg Graffin, which doesn't mean Bad Religion has abandoned their blistering hardcore inclinations. Instead, the band has managed to incorporate melody within the framework, adding an increased depth to their already provocative songs. *—Stephen Thomas Erlewine*

Recipe for Hate / Sep. 21, 1993 / Atlantic ✦✦✦
Although it doesn't sound all that different from what X was doing ten years ago (and fairly close to the music they were making, too), the seminal L.A. punk rockers gained a larger audience with *Recipe for Hate*. Featuring guest spots from Eddie Vedder and Johnette Napolitano from Concrete Blonde, *Recipe for Hate* features a smoother version of punk. All of the trademark anger and guitars are still present, but some of the melodies, harmonies and riffs lean toward mainstream rock 'n' roll. Fortunately, this all works in Bad Religion's favor—their music is more accessible, but it doesn't lack integrity. *—Stephen Thomas Erlewine*

Stranger Than Fiction / Aug. 30, 1994 / Atlantic ✦✦✦
Paced by the terrific single "21st Century Digital Boy," and an equally terrific video, Bad Religion's biggest selling record to date comes a decade and a half after they decided to enter the rock 'n' roll sweepstakes. Few bands sound this good this far into a career, and it's a tribute to the talent of this quintet that they do. As expected, the production values have increased considerably since the days of *How Could Hell . . .*, and this record comfortably fits in both hard-rock and alternative rock formats, but that's not a knock against Bad Religion. More than anything, it's a compliment. *—John Dougan*

● **All Ages** / Nov. 7, 1995 / Epitaph ✦✦✦✦

Gray Race / Feb. 27, 1996 / Atlantic ✦✦
Under the direction of producer Ric Ocasek, Bad Religion continues to smooth out the rough edges in its sound, replacing tension with clean, powerful bombast. *Gray Race* is a more melodic effort than the previous *Stranger Than Fiction* and, in the process, it initially sounds more commercial. But beneath that melody is a typically confrontational, prickly set of songs that proudly flaunt the band's punk roots. With their radio-ready production and heavy guitars, Bad Religion may not sound much like a hardcore band anymore, but they haven't lost their edge and that is what makes *Gray Race* a fine set of punk-influenced, alternative hard rock. *—Stephen Thomas Erlewine*

Badfinger

f. 1968, England, **db.** 1983
Power Pop, Pop-Rock
Rarely has a recorded group had so much apparent opportunity and so much bad luck as Badfinger. Paul McCartney discovered Badfinger's demo and signed them to the Beatles' Apple label. McCartney penned their first hit, "Come and Get It," which was featured (along with a couple of their other songs) in the movie *The Magic Christian*, as well as on their debut, *Magic Christian Music*. With their follow-up, *No Dice*, Badfinger's image as a poor man's Beatles began to evaporate, due to the new sophistication found in the writing skills of all the band members. George Harrison and Todd Rundgren took turns producing their third album, *Straight Up*, which had two more international hits with "Baby Blue" and "Day After Day." Poised to take advantage of this great success, Badfinger lost momentum as Apple Records began to crumble under mismanagement and confusion.

In November 1973, Badfinger released *Ass*—a good album, but one that was a little rough around the edges. Only months later, Badfinger released a self-titled debut for Warner, who were eager to try to regain the momentum from *Straight Up*. The album was an improvement over *Ass*, but it still suffered from the hasty release. Determined to get it right, Badfinger went into the studio with Chris Thomas and produced some of their very best music in *Wish You Were Here*.

Upon discovering a questionable disappearance of monies from Badfinger's publishing escrow account, Warner pulled the record weeks after its release, in spite of glowing reviews. Undaunted but terribly upset by the situation, the band cut another album, *Head First*, which Warner also barred from release.

Depressed by personal and professional problems, Pete Ham (guitar, vocal, keys) hung himself in his garage on April 23, 1975. After a five-year break, Tom Evans (bass, vocals) and Joey Molland (guitar, vocals) regrouped and released the spotty *Airwaves* on Elektra; the subsequent *Say No More* was even weaker. In 1983 Evans, frustrated over not receiving proper royalty compensation and other endless band business problems, took his life. Molland sporadically continued with Badfinger during the rest of the '80s and '90s, hiring different sidemen for each tour, while also pursuing a solo career. *—Rick Clark*

Magic Christian Music / Feb. 16, 1970 / Capitol ✦✦✦
Magic Christian Music is Badfinger's uneven debut. The band hadn't

found their sound yet. Nevertheless, tracks like "Come and Get It" and "Maybe Tomorrow" gave power-pop fans a good taste of this band's potential. —*Rick Clark*

No Dice / Nov. 9, 1970 / Capitol ✦✦✦✦
Badfinger's distinctive melodic abilities, great vocals, and solid ensemble work on *No Dice* was a strong case that this quartet could stand on its own, apart from Apple's shadow. "I Can't Take It," "Midnight Caller," the beautifully romantic "We're for the Dark," and "No Matter What," (one of the greatest pop singles ever), are among *No Dice*'s many highlights. —*Rick Clark*

Straight Up / Dec. 13, 1971 / Capitol ✦✦✦✦
George Harrison and Todd Rundgren took turns producing Badfinger's third album, *Straight Up*, which produced two international hits with the gorgeous "Day After Day" and the wall-of-sound pop-rock masterpiece "Baby Blue." Badfinger forges a unique sound with their sweeping, strained high harmonies; thick, edgy rhythm-guitar parts; and a drumming style that featured an exaggerated hi-hat attack on the backbeat. Check out "Take It All," "Sometimes," and the powerful "It's Over" for examples. —*Rick Clark*

Ass / Nov. 26, 1973 / Apple ✦✦✦
Badfinger had seen genuine stardom slip out of its reach after Apple began to crumble, just as *Straight Up* and its singles "Baby Blue" and "Day After Day" scaled the charts. As a result, the band tried to recast themselves as blues-rockers on their final record for the label, perhaps in an attempt to compete with the burgeoning ranks of arena-rockers emerging on both sides of the Atlantic. By and large, the shift in direction was ill-advised, since they couldn't quite write riff-heavy songs or perform them with conviction. *Ass*, however, is not entirely a wash-out. When Badfinger abandons their hard-rocking pretensions, they still can write excellent, Beatlesque power-pop songs, as "When I Say," "I Can Love," "Icicles," and Pete Ham's lovely kiss-off to their label, "Apple of My Eye," indicate. Even with such highlights, though, *Ass* is a considerable disappointment after the flawless power-pop of *No Dice* and *Straight Up*. —*Stephen Thomas Erlewine*

Badfinger / Feb. 1974 / Warner Brothers ✦✦
Tentatively titled *For Love or Money*, this was an unfortunate rush job that, in spite of it all, generated a handful of fine songs. Produced by Chris Thomas (Beatles, Roxy Music, Pink Floyd), Joey Molland's darkly meditative "Give It Up," "Andy Norris," and "Island" are fine contributions. "Lonely You," "Shine On," and "Song for a Lost Friend" showcase Pete Ham's emotive lower tenor and his considerable melodic skills. On the down side, "Matted Spam" is a horrible attempt at marrying soul with their sound, and "I Miss You" has enough sugar on it to put Paul McCartney into a coma. Regardless of that, fans of the band will be glad to know that an import CD can be obtained. —*Rick Clark*

Wish You Were Here / Nov. 1974 / Warner Brothers ✦✦✦
After many professional and personal distractions, Badfinger refocused their creative energies and, with producer Chris Thomas, created one of their finest albums. The urgent fanfare of the opening track, "Just a Chance," sets the make-it-or-break-it undercurrent here. This features two impressive medleys, "In the Meantime/Some Other Time" and "Meanwhile Back at the Ranch/Should I Smoke," which features stately horn backing by the Average White Band. —*Rick Clark*

Airwaves / Mar. 1979 / Elektra ✦✦
Using the magic of overdubbing and a complement of star studio musicians, Tom Evans and Joey Molland take a respectable shot at recreating the three-part harmonies and pop sheen of the early '70s Badfinger. "I want to get back," Evans sings on the title track, and you would, too, if you had been reduced to manual labor after hobnobbing with the Beatles. Like early Badfinger, much of this evokes their old mentors, especially "Love Is Gonna Come at Last" (No. 69), their first singles chart hit in seven years. Often, however, the material is only pedestrian, and although this album actually did a little better commercially than the group's two Warner Bros. albums of 1974, it didn't make for a real comeback. —*William Ruhlmann*

Say No More / 1981 / Radio ✦✦
Badfinger lists itself as a quintet on this album, including long-time members Joey Molland and Tom Evans, plus keyboard player Tony Kaye, drummer Richard Bryans, and guitar player Glenn Sherba. Certainly, they sound more like a band on this record than they did on its predecessor, *Airwaves*, which was basically a Molland-Evans duo album, but that is not an improvement. They tend to rock out more here, downplaying the more folkish and melodic pop tendencies in their music. Sometimes, as on "Because I Love You," they sound like the Raspberries trying to sound like the Beatles. The hit, such as it was, was "Hold On," (No. 56), a shadow of former glories, and although this album charted briefly, it only confirmed that Badfinger was no longer a record seller. —*William Ruhlmann*

The Best of Badfinger, Vol. 2 / 1989 / Rhino ✦✦✦
A decent attempt at chronicling the last half of their career, which included one of the great lost pop-rock albums of the '70s, *Wish You Were Here*. With the exception of important tracks like Joey Molland's "Love Time" and Pete Ham's "Dennis," *Wish...* is well represented. Key tracks from the self-titled Warner debut are included, as well as several sides from the never-released *Head First*. Also included are the only two tracks worth having from their 1979 album *Airwaves*. Until the Warner albums get released on CD stateside (which is doubtful), this is the only place you can get these fine tracks. —*Rick Clark*

● **Come and Get It: The Best of Badfinger** / Apr. 1995 / Apple ✦✦✦✦
A well-chosen 21-track best-of, wisely emphasizing their melodic, tender side rather than their oft-pedestrian hard rockers, *Come and Get It* draws from all four of their late-'60s and early-'70s Apple albums, although the absence of "We're for the Dark" from *No Dice* is a significant omission. —*Richie Unterberger*

David Baerwald

b. 1960, Oxford, OH
Vocals, Guitar, Keyboards / Singer-Songwriter, Pop-Rock
After the quick dissolution of David + David in the mid-'80s, David Baerwald began a solo career, releasing his solo debut, *Bedtime Stories*, in 1990. As with David + David's sole album, it was an album of deceptively laidback pop; the calm production and subtle, memorable melodies hid the fact that Baerwald's characters were either inflicting or suffering from emotional pain. It was a triumph, winning raves from critics, but it sold very few copies. With his second album, 1993's *Triage*, Baerwald decided to have the music match the message, creating soundscapes that recalled a subdued, more pop-friendly Tom Waits. Again, the critical praise was substantial, but the record sold even less than the first. —*Stephen Thomas Erlewine*

● **Bedtime Stories** / May 1990 / A&M ✦✦✦✦
Sparse arrangements lay the foundation for Baerwald's thought-provoking musings and solid vocals. —*Donna DiCharlo*

Triage / Oct. 6, 1992 / A&M ✦✦✦
Like *Bedtime Stories*, *Triage* focuses on deceit and corruption, but this time the political and social are mixed with the personal. Baerwald's music fits his themes, with dark guitars and synthesizers covering the clanking percussion. It's a remarkably accomplished record, even if its pretensions sometimes overwhelm its accomplishments. —*Stephen Thomas Erlewine*

Joan Baez

b. Jan. 9, 1941, Staten Island, NY
Guitar, Vocals / Folk, Traditional Folk, Singer-Songwriter, Folk-Rock, Pop-Rock, Contemporary Folk
The most accomplished interpretive folksinger of the 1960s, Joan Baez has influenced nearly every aspect of popular music in a career still going strong after more than 35 years. Baez is possessed of a once-in-a-lifetime soprano, which, since the late '50s, she has put in the service of folk and pop music as well as a variety of political causes. Starting out in Boston, Baez first gained recognition at the 1959 Newport Folk Festival, then cut her debut album, *Joan Baez* (Oct. 1960), for Vanguard Records. It was made up of 13 traditional songs, some of them Child ballads, given near-definitive treatment. A moderate success on release, the album took off after the breakthrough of *Joan Baez, Vol. 2* (Sept. 1961), and both albums became huge hits, as did Baez' third album, *Joan Baez in Concert* (Sept. 1962). Each album went gold and stayed in the best-seller charts more than two years.

From 1962 to 1964, Baez was the popular face of folk music, headlining festivals and concert tours and singing at political events, including the August 1963 March on Washington. During this period, she began to champion the work of folk songwriter Bob Dylan, and gradually her repertoire moved from traditional material toward the socially conscious work of the emerging generation of '60s artists like Dylan. Her albums of this period were *Joan Baez in Concert, Part 2* (Nov. 1963) and *Joan Baez/5* (Oct. 1964), which contained her cover of Phil Ochs' "There But for Fortune," a Top Ten hit in the UK.

Like other popular folk performers, Baez was affected by the changes in popular music wrought by the appearance of the Beatles in the US in 1964 and Dylan's introduction of folk-rock in 1965, and she began to augment her simple acoustic guitar backing with other instruments, initially on *Farewell Angelina* (Oct. 1965). It was followed by a Christmas album, *Noel* (Oct. 1966), and *Joan* (Aug. 1967), albums on which she was accompanied by an orchestra conducted by Peter Schickele.

Baez continued to experiment in the late '60s, releasing *Baptism—A Journey Through Our Time* (June 1968), in which she recited poetry, and *Any Day Now* (Dec. 1968), a double album of Dylan songs done with country backing, which went gold. In March 1968, Baez married antiwar protest leader David Harris, who was imprisoned as a draft evader.

Harris was a country music fan, and Baez' turn toward country, which continued on *David's Album* (June 1969) and *One Day at a Time* (Mar. 1970), reflected his taste. *Blessed Are . . .* (Aug. 1971) was a gold-selling double album that spawned a gold Top Ten hit in Baez' cover of the Band's "The Night They Drove Old Dixie Down." It was followed by *Carry It On* (Dec. 1971), the soundtrack to a documentary about Baez and Harris. Baez switched record-label affiliation to A&M Records with *Come from the Shadows* (May 1972), which moved her in a more pop direction. *Where Are You Now, My Son?* (May 1973) included sounds taped during Baez' visit to Hanoi in December 1972.

In the late '60s and early '70s, Baez moved toward pop-rock music and began to write her own songs, culminating in the gold-selling *Diamonds & Rust* (Apr. 1975), which was followed by the entirely self-written *Gulf Winds* (Oct. 1976). Baez moved to the Portrait label of CBS (now Sony) Records with *Blowin' Away* (June 1977), but she left the label after *Honest Lullaby* (May 1979). Her next album, *European Tour* (1980), was released only outside the US. It was another seven years before she found an American record label, Gold Castle, for *Recently* (1987), which was followed by the live album *Diamonds & Rust in the Bullring* (Jan. 1989) and *Speaking of Dreams* (Oct. 1989). Baez moved to Virgin Records for *Play Me Backwards* (Aug. 1992). In 1993 Vanguard released *Rare, Live & Classic*, a three-CD boxed set retrospective. *Ring Them Bells*, a live album on which Baez was joined by musical descendants like Mary-Chapin Carpenter and Indigo Girls, came out on Guardian Records in 1995. —*William Ruhlmann*

☆ **Joan Baez** / 1960 / Vanguard ✦✦✦✦✦
Revelatory first album features Baez singing traditional folk songs. —*William Ruhlmann*

Joan Baez in Concert, Vol. 1 / 1962 / Vanguard ✦✦✦✦

Joan Baez in Concert, Part 2 / 1963 / Vanguard ✦✦✦
A superb followup to *Part 1*, with some more interesting material. —*Bruce Eder*

5 / 1964 / Vanguard ✦✦✦
A good folk set, from a variety of sources. —*Bruce Eder*

Farewell, Angelina / 1965 / Vanguard ✦✦✦
Baez moves toward contemporary work, with songs by Donovan and Woody Guthrie. She sings four songs by Bob Dylan, including the title track. —*William Ruhlmann*

Noel / 1966 / Vanguard ✦✦✦✦
An album of stately beauty, Baez' pure, soaring soprano is accompanied by a consort of recorders and viols, lute, harpsichord, baroque organ, winds, strings, and percussion. Her rendition of the "Coventry Carol" is stirring, and Baez pours her heart into "The Carol of the Birds." Considering Baez' politics, one would never know she recorded this album in the Vietnam War era. —*Decibel Dennis MacDonald*

Joan / 1967 / Vanguard ✦✦✦
Ornate, heavily orchestrated versions of other people's songs. Over-produced, but quite beautiful. —*Bruce Eder*

Any Day Now / 1968 / Vanguard ✦✦✦
Any Day Now is an all-Dylan album that includes a definitive performance of "Love Is Just a Four-Letter Word." —*William Ruhlmann*

● **The First Ten Years** / 1970 / Vanguard ✦✦✦✦
A nearly perfect cross-section of her most enduring work, both traditional and contemporary. —*Bruce Eder*

Come from the Shadows / 1972 / A&M ✦✦✦
After recording for the folk label Vanguard for more than a decade, Baez moved to A&M. On this label debut, she maintained her interest in country music, recording in Nashville with some of the city's session aces. She also continued to dedicate herself to radical politics, from her set opener "Prison Trilogy," which pledged, "We're gonna raze the prisons to the ground," to the closer, John Lennon's "Imagine." In between were her call on Bob Dylan to return to protest music ("To Bobby") and her sister Mimi Farina's touching tribute to Janis Joplin, "In the Quiet Morning." —*William Ruhlmann*

Hits the Greatest & Others / 1973 / Vanguard ✦✦✦
An alternate cross-section of Baez' Vanguard music, including her monster hit "The Night They Drove Old Dixie Down." —*Bruce Eder*

Where Are You Now, My Son? / 1973 / A&M ✦✦✦
Not only is this *not* the place to start listening to Joan Baez, it's the album that separates the true fans from the, um, fellow travelers. Side 2 is taken up by the title song, a musical account of Baez' trip to Hanoi over Christmas of 1972, complete with the sound of US bombs falling on the city. Side 1, on the other hand, contains one of Baez' best original songs, "A Young Gypsy," and two by her sister, "Mary Call" and "Best of Friends." —*William Ruhlmann*

★ **Diamonds and Rust** / 1975 / A&M ✦✦✦✦✦
Baez's peak as a songwriter (title track) and folk/rock interpreter, singing songs of Jackson Browne, John Prine, and Bob Dylan. —*William Ruhlmann*

Joan Baez in Concert / 1976 / Vanguard ✦✦✦
A vibrant concert recording with a radiant sound, humor, and topicality. —*Bruce Eder*

The Best of Joan Baez / 1977 / A&M ✦✦✦✦
Emotionally charged songs from her '70s albums on A&M. Not early Baez, this album of touching songs is probably too commercial for die-hard folk fans. Excellent. —*Michael Erlewine*

Honest Lullaby / 1979 / Portrait ✦✦✦
On her second album for CBS' Portrait label (and her last new album issued in the US for eight years), Baez was given a full-scale pop-rock production by veteran Barry Beckett and the studio band in Muscle Shoals, AL. The result, on songs that range from "Let Your Love Flow" to "Before the Deluge," is accessible but not particularly memorable '70s-style pop. If you always wanted to know what the words to "No Woman, No Cry" are, however, this is the place to find out. —*William Ruhlmann*

Very Early Joan Baez / 1983 / Vanguard ✦✦✦
A masterful raid on the vault, recapturing the purity and simplicity of her debut recording. —*Bruce Eder*

Live Europe 83: Children of the Eighties / 1983 / Ariola ✦✦✦✦
While Baez declined to record again in the US unless she could get on a major label, she did make several live albums in Europe in the interim. This is the best of them, mixing old favorites like "Farewell, Angelina" with new originals like her heartfelt "For the Children of the Eighties." (Import) —*William Ruhlmann*

Recently / 1988 / Gold Castle ✦✦✦✦
Baez returned to US record shops with a vengeance here, delivering her interpretations of songs by Dire Straits, Johnny Clegg, U2, and Peter Gabriel, performers whose political consciousness may have been formed by listening to old Joan Baez albums. And on the title track, a stunning original, she boldly answered ex-husband David Harris' downbeat memoir of the '60s, *Dreams Die Hard*, as well as other '80s revisionists. —*William Ruhlmann*

Rare, Live & Classic / Sep. 1993 / Vanguard ✦✦✦✦
Spanning three discs, the box set *Rare, Live & Classic* is an odd mix of Baez's best-known songs and rarities. For the hardcore collector, there are plenty of interesting items here, including previously unreleased duets with Bob Dylan, Donovan, Bill Wood, and Jeffrey Shurtleff, but there's too much material for casual fans; they would be better off with her original albums or single-disc compilations. —*Stephen Thomas Erlewine*

Greatest Hits / May 7, 1996 / A&M ✦✦✦✦
Greatest Hits is a reasonably comprehensive collection of Joan Baez's best-known songs, concentrating mainly on her crossover hits. Although it misses several fine items, the compilation remains an effective introduction for the curious listener. —*Stephen Thomas Erlewine*

Anita Baker

b. Dec. 20, 1957, Detroit, MI
Vocals / Soul, Urban, Adult Contemporary, Pop, Quiet Storm
Anita Baker's strong, sensual alto helped her break the doors down in the middle of the '80s. More than any other singer, she defined Quiet Storm—smooth, romantic soul for adults. Baker's music is sophisticated without being cold, romantic without being saccharine; besides soul, her singing has roots in jazz and classic pop, bringing a refined romanticism to her music. Although her 1983 debut, *The Songstress*, disappeared upon its release, her 1986 album, *Rapture*, was a modern classic that ushered in a new era of urban contemporary and modern pop singing. None of her following records was quite as good, but her singing remains impressive on each album, and she was one of the most popular urban/adult contemporary singers of the '80s and '90s. —*Stephen Thomas Erlewine*

The Songstress / Jun. 1983 / Elektra ✦✦✦✦
Trends in African-American music changed considerably between Anita Baker's first taste of national exposure in 1979 (when she was a member of Detroit soul band Chapter 8 and sang lead on the hit ballad "I Just Wanna Be Your Girl") and her debut solo album, *The Songstress*, in 1983. While 1979's Black music charts were full of large funk bands, standup vocal harmony groups, and disco divas, rappers, and techno-funksters like the System were very much in vogue in 1983. Instead of following trends, Baker excelled by doing what she does best: gospel-influenced, '70s-type soul/pop with jazz overtones. *The Songstress*, released by the small Beverly Glen label and reissued by Elektra in 1991, wasn't the mega-hit her next album, *Rapture*, would be. But the Sarah Vaughan-influenced singer began to build a following with such honest, heartfelt ballads and "slow jams" as "No More Tears," "You're the Best Thing Yet," and the caressing "Angel." A sweaty taste of gospel-drenched funk, the invigorating "Squeeze Me" is atypical of the ballad-oriented Baker, although she definitely shines at this faster tempo. Indeed, Baker's solo career was off to a most impressive start with *The*

Songstress. For those who savored *Rapture* and *Giving You the Best That I Got, The Songstress* is also essential listening. —*Alex Henderson*

● **Rapture** / Mar. 1986 / Elektra ✦✦✦✦
Though Anita Baker got some airplay out of *The Songstress*, that promising solo debut didn't bring her financial security. In fact, Baker was earning her living as a legal secretary in her native Detroit when she signed with Elektra in the mid-'80s. Elektra gave her a strong promotional push, and the equally superb *Rapture* became the megahit that *The Songstress* should have been. To its credit, Elektra made her a major star by focusing on Baker's strong point—romantic but gospel-influenced R&B/pop ballads and "slow jams," sometimes with jazz overtones—and letting her be true to herself. *Rapture* gave Baker one moving hit after another, including "Sweet Love," "Caught Up in the Rapture," "Same Ole Love" and "No One in This World." Praising Baker in a 1986 interview, veteran R&B critic Steve Ivory asserted, "To me, singers like Anita Baker and Frankie Beverly define what R&B or soul music is all about." Indeed, *Rapture's* tremendous success made it clear that there was still a sizeable market for adult-oriented, more traditional R&B singing. —*Alex Henderson*

Giving You the Best That I Got / Oct. 1988 / Elektra ✦✦✦✦
The sizeable following that Baker acquired with *Rapture* proved quite receptive to the only slightly less appealing *Giving You the Best That I Got*—an album that's quite similar to its predecessors. Though not quite on a par with *The Songstress* or *Rapture, Best* is far superior to most of 1988's uninspired R&B releases. Instead of tampering with *Rapture's* consistently romantic and mellow soul/pop approach, Elektra brought back that album's producer, Michael J. Powell, and kept her at the top of the charts with such sleek yet earthy fare as "Just Because" (whose harmonies bring to mind producers Jimmy Jam and Terry Lewis, but lack the hip-hop elements they're quick to employ), "Priceless," the haunting "Good Love," and the title song. Much of Baker's music has contained jazz overtones, but on the Brazilian-influenced, slightly bossa nova-ish "Good Enough," Sarah Vaughan's influence becomes even more apparent—and indicates that Baker is making a tremendous mistake by not recording outright jazz. —*Alex Henderson*

Compositions / Jun. 1990 / Elektra ✦✦✦
On *Rapture* and *Giving You the Best That I Got*, Baker embraced a blend of technology and "real instruments"—a definite contrast to the completely high-tech approach of so much '80s and '90s R&B. But on *Compositions*, producer Michael J. Powell moved even closer to a '70s-like approach to R&B—recording Baker's vocals live in the studio, employing a live rhythm section, and avoiding drum machines altogether. What stayed the same was the type of material. Once again, Baker rejects hip-hop, techno-funk, new jack swing, and other '80s/'90s Black music styles in favor of a consistently relaxed soul/pop mood. Though there's a lot to admire here—including "No One to Blame," "Soul Inspiration" and "Whatever It Takes," a song Baker wrote with Gerald Levert and Marc Gordon of Levert—Baker's approach was beginning to sound like a formula in 1990. Clearly blessed with a magnificent range and lots of soul, Baker needs to experiment and take more risks. And one way to go just might be jazz. The torchy and captivating "Lonely" shows that she has the ability to record a first-rate jazz album (if Elektra would okay such a project for her). Imagine Baker backed by James Moody, Tom Harrell, Chick Corea, Ray Brown, and Grady Tate! —*Alex Henderson*

Rhythm of Love / Sep. 13, 1994 / Elektra ✦✦✦
As the 1990s progressed, Anita Baker was sounding more and more contrived. One hoped that someone with so appealing a voice would challenge herself and try something different—perhaps recording more standards or exploring straightahead jazz (which she's obviously quite capable of doing). But instead of gambling with inspiration and risking a decline in sales, Baker tends to play it safe and offers a disc that often sounds like formula at work. Though *Rhythm of Love* is a generally decent album and even contains a few gems (including the dusky "Wrong Man," the torchy "Sometimes I Wonder Why," and heartfelt interpretations of "My Funny Valentine" and "The Look of Love"), Baker is capable of a lot more. The diva gives the impression that she desperately needs to follow Natalie Cole's lead and get away from catering to radio. —*Alex Henderson*

LaVern Baker

b. Nov. 11, 1929, Chicago, IL, **d.** Mar. 10, 1997
Vocals / R&B, Jump Blues
LaVern Baker was one of the sexiest divas gracing the mid-'50s rock 'n' roll circuit, boasting a brashly seductive vocal delivery tailor-made for belting the catchy novelties "Tweedlee Dee," "Bop-Ting-a-Ling," and "Tra La La" for Atlantic Records during rock's first wave of prominence.
Born Delores Williams, she was singing at the Club DeLisa on Chicago's South Side at age 17, decked out in raggedy attire and billed as "Little Miss Sharecropper" (the same handle that she used for her recording debut for RCA Victor with Eddie "Sugarman" Penigar's band

in 1949). She changed her name briefly to Bea Baker when recording for OKeh in 1951 with Maurice King's Wolverines, then settled on the first name of LaVern when she joined Todd Rhodes' band as featured vocalist in 1952. (She fronted Rhodes' aggregation on the impassioned ballad "Trying" for Cincinnati's King Records.)
LaVern signed with Atlantic as a solo in 1953, debuting with the incendiary "Soul on Fire." The coy, Latin-tempo "Tweedlee Dee" was a smash in 1955 on both the R&B and pop charts, although her impact on the latter was blunted when squeaky-clean Georgia Gibbs covered it for Mercury. An infuriated Baker filed suit over the whitewashing, but lost. By that time, though, her star had ascended; Baker's "Bop-Ting-a-Ling," "Play It Fair," "Still," and the rocking "Jim Dandy" all vaulted into the R&B Top Ten over the next couple of years.
Baker's statuesque figure and charismatic persona made her a natural for TV and movies. She co-starred on the historic R&B revue segment on Ed Sullivan's TV program in November 1955 and did memorable numbers in Alan Freed's rock movies *Rock, Rock, Rock* and *Mr. Rock & Roll*. Her Atlantic records remained popular throughout the decade—she hit big in 1958 with the ballad "I Cried a Tear," adopted a pseudosanctified bellow for the rousing Leiber & Stoller-penned gospel sendup "Saved" in 1960, and cut a Bessie Smith tribute album before leaving Atlantic in 1964. A brief stop at Brunswick Records (where she did a sassy duet with Jackie Wilson, "Think Twice") preceded a late-'60s jaunt to entertain the troops in Vietnam. She became seriously ill after the trip and was hospitalized, eventually settling far out of the limelight in the Philippines. She remained there for 22 years, running an NCO club on Subic Bay for the US government.
In 1988 Baker returned stateside to star in Atlantic's 40th anniversary bash at New York's Madison Square Garden. That led to a soundtrack appearance in the film *Dick Tracy*, a starring role in the Broadway musical *Black & Blue* (replacing her ex-Atlantic labelmate Ruth Brown), a nice comeback disc for DRG (*Woke Up This Mornin'*), and a memorable appearance at the Chicago Blues Festival. Baker died March 10, 1997. —*Bill Dahl*

Sings Bessie Smith / Jan. 27, 1958 / Atlantic ✦✦✦✦
This is an album that should not have worked. LaVern Baker (a fine R&B singer) was joined by all-stars from mainstream jazz (including trumpeter Buck Clayton, trombonist Vic Dickenson, tenor-saxophonist Paul Quinichette, and pianist Nat Pierce) for 12 songs associated with the great '20s blues singer Bessie Smith. Despite the potentially conflicting styles, this project is quite successful and often exciting. The arrangements by Phil Moore, Nat Pierce, and Ernie Wilkins do not attempt to recreate the original recordings. Baker sings in her own style (rather than trying to emulate Bessie Smith), and the hot solos work well with her vocals. —*Scott Yanow*

★ **Soul on Fire: The Best of LaVern Baker** / 1991 / Rhino ✦✦✦✦✦
The cream of this vivacious 1950s R&B belter's Atlantic catalog comprises this 20-track hits collection. Includes Baker's bouncy "Tweedlee Dee," the storming rockers "Jim Dandy" and "Bop-Ting-a-Ling," the pseudo-gospel raveup "Saved," and Baker's torchy blues ballads "Soul on Fire" and "I Cried a Tear." She imparts "See See Rider" with a lighthearted reading that contrasts starkly with Chuck Willis' Atlantic smash of a few years before. —*Bill Dahl*

Blues Side of Rock'n' Roll / 1993 / Star Club ✦✦✦✦
This import may be of slightly dubious origins (sounds like everything was dubbed from vinyl, though the sound quality is quite acceptable), but it delves a lot deeper into LaVern Baker's Atlantic discography (26 cuts) and picks up a few essential sides ignored by Atlantic's own CD: "Tra La La," "Voodoo Voodoo," "Hey Memphis" (Baker's sequel to Elvis' "Little Sister"), and a hellacious version of "He's a Real Gone Guy" sporting a vicious King Curtis sax break. —*Bill Dahl*

Mickey Baker

b. Oct. 15, 1925, Louisville, KY
Guitar / R&B, Rock 'n' Roll
Of all the guitarists who helped transform rhythm & blues into rock 'n' roll, Mickey Baker is one of the very most important, ranking almost on the level of Chuck Berry and Bo Diddley. The reason he isn't nearly as well known as those legends is that a great deal of his work wasn't issued under his own name, but as a backing guitarist for many R&B and rock 'n' roll musicians. Baker originally aspired to be a jazz musician, but he turned to calypso, mambo, and then R&B, where the most work could be found. In the early and mid-'50s, he did countless sessions for Atlantic, King, RCA, Decca, and OKeh, playing on such classics as the Drifters' "Money Honey" and "Such a Night," Joe Turner's "Shake Rattle & Roll," Ruth Brown's "Mama, He Treats Your Daughter Mean," and Big Maybelle's "Whole Lot of Shakin' Going On." He also released a few singles under his own name, and made a Latin jazz-tinged solo album, *Guitar Mambo.* Baker's best work, though, was recorded as half of the duo Mickey & Sylvia. Their hit "Love Is Strange," as well as several other unknown

but nearly equally strong tracks, featured Baker's keening, bluesy guitar riffs, which were gutsier and more piercing than 'most anything else around in the late '50s. Mickey & Sylvia split in the late '50s (though they recorded off and on until the middle of the next decade), and Baker recorded his best solo album, the all-instrumental *The Wildest Guitar*, around 1960. In 1961 he took the male spoken part (usually assumed to be Ike Turner) on Ike & Tina Turner's first hit, "It's Gonna Work out Fine." Shortly afterwards he moved to France, making a few hard-to-find solo records and working with a lot of French pop and rock performers, including Ronnie Bird, the best '60s French rock singer. He's recorded only sporadically since the mid-'60s. —*Richie Unterberger*

Wildest Guitar / 1959 / Atlantic ◆◆◆◆
Despite Baker's well-deserved reputation as one of the most influential guitar players of early rock 'n' roll, *The Wildest Guitar* was one of the few chances he got to really strut his stuff as a solo artist. This entirely instrumental set features keening, sharp, bluesy riffs in much the same distinctive style that gained him fame on "Love Is Strange" and other tunes with Mickey & Sylvia. The choice of material, though, is a bit surprising, favoring some cornball standards: "Third Man Theme," "Autumn Leaves," "Lullaby of the Leaves," and Cole Porter's "Night and Day." Baker (who also arranged the album) manages to invest all of these with a snazzy R&B feel and biting solos. And he does actually write four of the 12 tunes himself, on which he fashions the kind of straightforward R&B that one would be more likely to expect. This is a pretty good showcase to hear Baker's unadorned virtuosity. But he's really better appreciated within the context of stronger material, either as half of Mickey & Sylvia or on the innumerable '50s R&B cuts (many on Atlantic) that feature his session work. —*Richie Unterberger*

● **Rock with a Sock** / Jun. 28, 1994 / Bear Family ◆◆◆◆
This 28-cut single disc covers several early and mid-'50s tracks with Baker finding creative ways to perform on period-piece rock and R&B/novelty material. His playing is uniformly impressive, even when fitting into less-than-outstanding productions and compositions. There are five Mickey and Sylvia tracks that conclude the session; they range from the interesting "Hello Stranger" to the odd "Woe, Woe Is Me," but really take away from the disc's purpose—to showcase Mickey Baker the player and demonstrate why he has such a sterling reputation among guitar fans and musicians. —*Ron Wynn*

The Balancing Act

f. 1984, Los Angeles, CA, db. 1989
Group / Alternative Pop-Rock, Folk-Rock
Originally formed in 1984 to perform the songs of singer-songwriter/guitarist Jeff Davis, the L.A.-based Balancing Act was built around acoustic guitars, distinctive harmonies, intelligent, quirky songs, and an assorted array of instruments such as melodica, recorder, and even a shortwave radio. Even though the band forged its sound around acoustic-based songs, don't look for a typical folk-rock, singer-songwriter affair. Davis, along with guitarist Willie Aron, bassist Steve Wagner, and percussionist Robert Blackmon, employed touches of atonality and rhythmic twists, along with the songcraft that was at the heart of all their records. They also chose, in the studio and on stage, to reach outside the realms of the acoustic world for material by the likes of Captain Beefheart, Funkadelic, and Public Image Ltd.

The band, which by the time of the first record featured songs by Wagner and Aron as well as Davis, released an EP (originally in 1986 on their own Type A label) and two full-length records between 1987 and 1988 for IRS (the first two on its Primitive Man Recording Company subsidiary). The Balancing Act, despite showing growth with each recording, failed to make any waves commercially and disbanded after their third album, *Curtains*, which found the band at the top of its game. —*Brett Hartenbach*

New Campfire Songs / 1986 / Primitive Man ◆◆◆◆
Produced by singer-songwriter Peter Case and recorded in just over a week, the Balancing Act's acoustic-based debut EP contains five original tunes and a terrific cover of Captain Beefheart's *Zig Zag Wanderer* that are performed with a ragged charm. Songs such as Jeff Davis' *Wonderful World Tonight* and *Who Got the Pearls?* feature sly melodic, instrumental, and lyrical twists and turns, along with occasional bits of dissonance. *New Campfire Songs* proves to be a solid first outing that only gets stronger with repeated listenings. —*Brett Hartenbach*

● **Three Squares and a Roof** / 1987 / IRS ◆◆◆◆
The Balancing Act's sophomore effort includes the same mix of fine songs, harmonies, jumping rhythms, and atonal instrumental passages as their debut EP. The group's first full-length album is slightly more polished than its predecessor, although it's by no means slick. The CD version also contains the six tracks from *New Campfire Songs* and is recommended. —*Brett Hartenbach*

Curtains / 1988 / IRS ◆◆◆◆
Gang of Four's Andy Gill produced the third and final record from L.A.'s Balancing Act, which adds touches of jazz and jagged electric guitar to the band's eccentric folk-rock sound. The album boasts the group's best collection of songs, as well as a cover of Funkadelics' *Can You Get to That*, and in a close call is probably the first choice among the individual releases, although go for the *Three Squares/Campfire Songs* CD if you can find it. —*Brett Hartenbach*

Hank Ballard

b. Nov. 18, 1936, Detroit, MI
Vocals / R&B
Though born in Alabama, Ballard moved to Detroit at an early age, forming a doo wop group called the Royals by age 16. He signed to the King label in early 1953. Midsize chart hits followed, and the group's name was changed to the Midnighters to avoid confusion with labelmates the Five Royales when "Work with Me Annie" became a national hit. Banned because of "explicit" lyrics, the song spawned a flurry of answer records (some by Ballard himself), most of them hitting the R&B charts as well. The hits kept coming throughout the early '60s, but the flipside of one of them became a national hit when Chubby Checker re-recorded "The Twist," spawning a national craze. Ballard's best records are informed by gospel-style harmonies and gritty guitar work, usually played by Alonzo Tucker. —*Cub Koda*

★ **Sexy Ways: The Best of Hank Ballard & The Midnighters** / Nov. 16, 1993 / Rhino ◆◆◆◆◆
Hank Ballard & the Midnighters were the 2 Live Crew of the early '50s, burning up the airwaves and Black jukeboxes with lascivious-for-the-time period tunes like "Work with Me Annie," "Annie Had a Baby," and the title track. Although Ballard would go on to write dance hits, including the original version of "The Twist," the Midnighters at their best ("Open Up the Back Door") were doo wop at the end of a dark alley. Forget all previous compilations on these guys; this is the one. —*Cub Koda*

Afrika Bambaataa

b. Apr. 10, 1960, South Bronx, NY
Vocals / Hip Hop, Club/Dance, Electro-Funk, Electric Funk
A seminal Bronx DJ during the '70s, Afrika Bambaataa ascended to godfather-of-rap status (not to mention house and techno) with "Planet Rock," a 1982 hit single that blended the beats of hip-hop with techno futurism inspired by German pioneers Kraftwerk. Even before he began recording in 1980, though, Bambaataa was hip-hop's foremost DJ, an organizer and promoter of the large block parties during the mid-to-late-'70s that presaged the rise of rap. After the success of "Planet Rock," he recorded electro-oriented rap only sparingly, concentrating instead on fusion—exemplified by his singles with ex-Sex Pistol John Lydon and the Godfather of Soul, James Brown. Bambaataa had moved to the background by the late '80s (as far as hip-hop was concerned), but the rise of his Zulu Nation collective—including De La Soul, Queen Latifah, A Tribe Called Quest and the Jungle Brothers—found him once more being tipped as one of rap's founding fathers.

Born Kevin Donovan in the Bronx on April 10, 1960, Afrika Bambaataa Aasim took his name from a 19th-century Zulu chief. Beginning in 1977, Bambaataa began organizing block parties and break-dancing competitions around the Bronx. His excellent turntable techniques led many to proclaim him the best DJ in the business (though Grandmaster Flash and DJ Kool Herc were more innovative), and his record debut—as a producer—came in 1980 with Soul Sonic Force's "Zulu Nation Throwdown." The single was a rallying cry for the Zulu Nation, a group of like-minded Afrocentric musicians that gained fame only in the late '80s but had influenced the rise of hip-hop crews throughout the decade.

Aside from more production credits on several later singles during 1980-81, Afrika Bambaataa didn't become an actual recording artist until 1982. He signed with Tommy Boy Records and released his first single, "Jazzy Sensation," early that year. "Planet Rock" followed in June and quickly exploded. Recorded with the help of producer/dancefloor authority Arthur Baker and assimilating the melody of Kraftwerk's "Trans-Europe Express," the single hit No. 4 on the R&B charts (but missed the pop Top 40) and joined the Sugarhill Gang's "Rapper's Delight" as one of the early classics of hip-hop. (Grandmaster Flash's "The Message" followed just three months later.) In the single's wake came dozens of electro groups and recordings, though none touched the quality of "Planet Rock"—except, perhaps, Bambaataa's own follow-up, "Looking for the Perfect Beat." Out of those electro groups came several predominant dance styles of the 1980s and '90s: Detroit techno, Miami bass, and, to a more limited extent, Chicago house.

Freed somewhat by his new-found popularity, Afrika Bambaataa began branching out in 1984, recording "Unity" with help from James Brown and "World Destruction" with John Lydon (as Time Zone). That same year, Bambaataa delivered an album debut of sorts, *Shango Funk Theology*, recorded as Shango with Material personnel Bill Laswell and

Michael Beinhorn. A virtually LP-length single titled "Funk You!" appeared in 1985, after which Bambaataa recorded his proper album debut, *Beware (The Funk Is Everywhere)*. He left Tommy Boy in 1986, after an album compilation of "Planet Rock" mixes, and signed with Capitol. The first album release for the label was 1988's *The Light*, recorded as Afrika Bambaataa & the Family, which included contributions from George Clinton, UB40, Bootsy Collins, and Boy George. Three years later, Bambaataa's third album *1990-2000: Decade of Darkness* was released on Capitol, coinciding with his career retrospective *Time Zone*, released on his own Planet Rock Records. —*John Bush*

★ **Planet Rock—The Album** / 1986 / Tommy Boy ✦✦✦✦✦
All the important early 12-inchers from 1982-1984 are here, including "Planet Rock" and "Looking for the Perfect Beat," plus three previously unreleased tracks. (Recorded with Soulsonic Force) —*John Floyd*

Beware (The Funk Is Everywhere) / 1986 / Tommy Boy ✦✦✦✦
Another stunning assortment of singles is included, with heavier beats, thicker rhythms, and a blistering cover of the MC5's "Kick Out the Jams." —*John Floyd*

Banana Splits

f. 1967, Chicago, IL
Bubblegum
To a pre-teen generation for whom the concept of "free love" equalled unlimited hugs from mom and the notion of "getting high" meant nothing more than a breakfast cereal-induced sugar coma, the Banana Splits marked the apotheosis of such staples of late 1960s culture as psychedelia, pop art and, of course, music. Like the Archies and Josie & the Pussycats, the band was essentially a marketing front for a collective of faceless studio musicians; unlike their peers, however, in their own unique way the Banana Splits represented the acid culture's subtle encroachment into mainstream children's entertainment. By employing the kinds of camera techniques, surreal set designs and hallucinatory images more commonly associated with the era's underground filmmaking, their television series brought the lessons of the Summer of Love to Saturday mornings; not unlike the similarly subversive (and, not coincidentally, similarly structured) "Pee-Wee's Playhouse" two decades later, "the Banana Splits" freed children's minds as it captured their imaginations, and its lasting influence has proven remarkable.

The Banana Splits were the brainchild of Joseph Barbera, one half of the famed Hanna-Barbera animation team behind such characters as the Flintstones, the Jetsons, Yogi Bear, and Scooby Doo. In 1967 Barbera was approached by Lee Rich of the Leo Burnett Agency, a Chicago-based advertising firm, to create a program designed as a showcase for Kellogg's, the Battle Creek, MI, breakfast cereal magnate. Rich proposed that Barbera produce an hour-long Saturday morning children's show; Barbera countered that the show should break new ground, and suggested that instead of animated characters, its hosts might be costumed performers resembling giant puppets. Some time later, Barbera outlined his finished proposal to the Burnett staff and Kellogg's representatives, as well as Grant Tinker, an NBC televison executive who later became the network's president; to bring his ideas to life, Barbera introduced an actor dressed in a Yogi Bear costume, a move that proved instrumental in selling the series on the spot.

Essentially, the Banana Splits concept was like the Monkees once removed; clearly modeled on the exuberance and slapstick comedy of the Beatles' film *A Hard Day's Night*, the show also borrowed heavily from the bright, psychedelic image the Fab Four sported on the cover of *Sgt. Pepper's Lonely Hearts Club Band*. Like both the Beatles and the Monkees, the Splits were a four-piece pop band, and like the Monkees (and the Beatles in *Help!*), they even lived together in the same mod digs. Unlike their human predecessors, however, the Banana Splits were bizarre, anthropomorphic animals: rhythm guitarist Drooper was a lion, lead guitarist Fleegle was a dog, keyboardist Snorky was an elephant, and drummer Bingo was a monkey. The episodes consisted of skits, cartoons, a live-action cliffhanger serial called "Danger Island" (directed by Richard Donner, who went on to helm the *Superman* and *Lethal Weapon* films), and of course, musical performances. In total, some 23 bubblegum tunes were produced for the show; one was even written by soul crooner Barry White. In 1968, Decca issued an LP, *We're the Banana Splits*, collecting a dozen of the program's performances; the series' theme, "The Tra-La-La Song," even reached the Billboard Top 100 singles chart. In addition, Kellogg's issued an eight-song double EP pack, available only through the company for two cereal box tops and 50 cents.

"The Banana Splits" was a ratings blockbuster during the 1968-1969 television season, drawing an incredible 65 percent share of the Saturday morning audience. The second season, however, proved disastrous. While the Hanna-Barbera production staff filmed all new episodes, they did so without changing the backgrounds or any of the set designs, prompting young viewers to mistakenly believe that the new segments were reruns. Consequently, ratings plummeted, and "the Banana Splits"

was unceremoniously axed in 1970. The show went largely forgotten for much of the decade, but in the 1980s a resurgence began; first punk satirists the Dickies covered "The Tra-La-La Song," and then no less a figure than R.E.M. frontman Michael Stipe declared the Banana Splits a bigger influence on his work than even the Beatles. In the 1990s, the revival exploded: the acclaimed singer Liz Phair recorded her own rendition of "The Tra-La-La Song" for a tribute collection of Saturday morning themes, and more importantly, the original "Banana Splits" episodes went into heavy rotation on cable's Cartoon Network for an entirely new generation of viewers to enjoy. —*Jason Ankeny*

● **We're the Banana Splits** / 1985 / Decca ✦✦✦✦
We're the Banana Splits collects a dozen ace performances from the first season of the band's Saturday morning series. In addition to the oft-covered theme tune "The Tra-La-La" song—offered here in a longer version than heard over the opening credits—the set includes the buoyant "(You're the) Lovin' End" and "Gonna Find Me a Cave." —*Jason Ankeny*

Bananarama

f. 1981, London, England
Dance-Pop, New Wave, Pop-Rock
The most successful British girl-group in pop history, Bananarama formed in London in late 1981. Drawing equal inspiration for their name from the children's television program "The Banana Splits" and the Roxy Music song "Pyjamarama," the trio comprised lifelong friends Keren Woodward and Sarah Dallin, along with Siobhan Fahey, whom Dallin befriended at the London College of Fashion. After getting their start singing at friends' parties and at nightclubs (where they performed accompanied by backing tapes—none of the women played their own instruments), they came to the attention of ex-Sex Pistols drummer Paul Cook, who produced Bananarama's first single, a cover of Swahili Black Blood's "Aie A Mwana."

After the group backed Fun Boy Three on the single "It Ain't What You Do, It's the Way You Do It," the Three returned the favor for 1982's "He Was Really Sayin' Somethin'," a cover of the 1965 Velvelettes song that was the first of Bananarama's 26 UK chart smashes. While their initial hits, including "Shy Boy," "Na Na Hey Hey Kiss Him Goodbye," and "Cruel Summer" (their first US smash) were roundly dismissed as fluffy pop fare, the success of 1984's rape-themed release "Robert DeNiro's Waiting" convinced the group to tackle more serious topics; however, the follow-up single, "Rough Justice"—a song protesting political tensions in Northern Ireland—bombed, and the trio's career stalled.

In 1986 Bananarama's fortunes improved considerably when they joined forces with the production team of Stock/Aitken/Waterman, who produced the album *Wow!* The group's most successful outing to date, the LP's cover of the Shocking Blue's "Venus" was an international charttopper, and both "Love in the First Degree" and "I Heard a Rumour" were major hits as well.

In 1987 Fahey left the group after marrying Eurythmics' Dave Stewart; she later resurfaced as one half of the duo Shakespear's Sister. Woodward and Dallin, meanwhile, enlisted pal Jacquie O'Sullivan, formerly of the Sheilagh Sisters, to fill the void. After a long layoff, the revamped group teamed with new producer Youth to issue the 1991 album *Pop Life*, which featured a cover of the Doobie Brothers' "Long Train Running." Shortly after the album's release, O'Sullivan, too, exited, and Woodward and Dallin forged on as a duo for 1992's *Please Yourself* and 1995's *Ultra Violet*. —*Jason Ankeny*

Deep Sea Skiving / Mar. 1983 / London ✦✦✦✦
Although this was not their American breakthrough, it was their biggest UK success, hitting the Top Ten and featuring the hits "He Was Really Sayin' Somethin'," "Shy Boy," and "Na Na Hey Hey Kiss Him Goodbye." It establishes the formula for the group's success, with its untrained unison trio singing and pop exuberance. The amateurishness of the singers was what made them so appealing. —*William Ruhlmann*

Bananarama / May 1984 / London ✦✦✦
The group adopted a more glamorous fashion style for this album, which finally brought them US success with the Top Ten hit "Cruel Summer." Also included is "Robert De Niro's Waiting." —*William Ruhlmann*

True Confessions / Jul. 1986 / Razor & Tie ✦✦✦
Bananarama scored its biggest US hit with this third album, earning gold sales due to the No. 1 single "Venus." —*William Ruhlmann*

● **Greatest Hits Collection** / Nov. 1988 / London ✦✦✦✦
The Greatest Hits Collection is a 14-track overview of Bananarama's first four albums, drawing equally from their early new wave records and their late '80s dance-pop. As a result, it's a definitive retrospective and their most consistent record, featuring all of their hit singles—including "Shy Boy," "Robert DeNiro's Waiting," "Cruel Summer," "Venus," "I Heard a Rumour," "I Can't Help It"—and none of the filler that cluttered their records. —*Stephen Thomas Erlewine*

Pop Life / May 1991 / London ✦✦

Ultra Violet / Jan. 23, 1996 / Curb ✦✦
Attempting a comeback after five years, Karen Woodward and Sarah Dallin turned in a set of predictable Euro-NRG dance music, courtesy of producer Gary Miller. The perky amateurishness that had made the old Bananarama fun was replaced by slick, unfeeling efficiency, and the beats just weren't that new, which may be why this album disappeared without a trace upon release. —*William Ruhlmann*

The Band

f. 1967, Toronto, Ontario, db. Nov. 1976
Rock 'n' Roll, Country-Rock, Folk-Rock
Composed of four Canadians and one American, the Band first came together in Toronto in the early '60s as Ronnie Hawkins' backup group. Hawkins recorded nine 45s for Roulette between 1959 and 1963. Drummer Levon Helm plays on all nine, guitarist Robbie Robertson and bass player Rick Danko can be heard on the last three, pianist Richard Manuel is on the last two, and organist Garth Hudson plays on the final outing only. Leaving Hawkins collectively in early 1964, they called themselves the Levon Helm Sextet, Levon and the Hawks, and (for a brief spell) the Canadian Squires, releasing two singles before becoming Bob Dylan's backup ensemble for his crazed electric tour of North America, Australia, and Europe in the fall of 1965 through the spring of 1966. (After a couple of gigs, Levon headed back to Arkansas.)
    Playing with Dylan had a profound influence on the Band. Woodshedding for two years in Woodstock, NY, they released their debut album, *Music from Big Pink*, in the summer of 1968. Over the succeeding eight years, the Band stood completely apart from everything else happening in rock 'n' roll. There was no precedent for what they did. Ironically, given that they were four-fifths Canadian, their music embodied an essence of Americana that no one else in rock 'n' roll has approached. Chief writer Robbie Robertson wrote about the American South, the land, rural America, tradition, and the value and richness of heritage and blood ties. The settings for his songs included cornfields during the Civil War and carnivals at the edge of town. He was most concerned with displaced people and the passing of a way of life. Sonically, the Band was also unique. Hudson played accordion, sax, and organ; drummer Levon Helm doubled on mandolin and guitar; pianist Manuel drummed whenever Helm was out front; bassist Rick Danko played fiddle when they needed a rural or "old-timey" feel; guitarist Robbie Robertson had a pinched, economical style that kept one teetering on the edge with tension. As a unit, they quite consciously avoided any of the current trends. They didn't want their voices to blend, because that is what everyone else was doing; they wanted their piano to sound like a funky old upright, not like a brand-spanking-new Yamaha; and so on. In the process they created some of the most ethereal and evocative music imaginable. —*Rob Bowman*

☆ **Music from Big Pink** / Jul. 1, 1968 / Capitol ✦✦✦✦✦
Everything about the Band's debut album, *Music from Big Pink*, flew in the face of the current ethos of rock 'n' roll in 1968. For example, the disc opens in an unusual fashion, with a ballad, the Richard Manuel/Bob Dylan composition "Tears of Rage." There is not a guitar solo on the album, and this was a time when Jeff Beck, Eric Clapton, and Jimi Hendrix ruled the world. There was a lot of harmony singing that was deliberately ragged: together but not together, a community where the people that made up the community could be individuals. And then there were the songs, enigmatic tales such as "The Weight," "Chest Fever," and the first released version of Bob Dylan's "I Shall Be Released." An unbelievably strong debut. —*Rob Bowman*

★ **The Band** / Sep. 22, 1969 / Capitol ✦✦✦✦✦
Big Pink had been a fine, even superior debut; *The Band* was their masterpiece. Robbie Robertson's songwriting had grown by leaps and bounds. As players, all five musicians had reached a completely new level of ensemble cohesion. The sum was very much greater than the parts, and the parts were as good as any that existed. The album's single, "Up on Cripple Creek," became the Band's first and only Top 30 release. It was one of several songs on the album that had an old-timey feel. Other highlights on this masterpiece include "Rag Mama Rag," "The Night They Drove Old Dixie Down," and "King Harvest." —*Rob Bowman*

Stage Fright / Aug. 17, 1970 / Capitol ✦✦✦
Stage Fright was a reaction to a level of adulation that the Band members were unprepared for. It was conceived as a lighter, less serious, more rock 'n' roll type of album. The final product ended up somewhat darker, as the Band themselves were going through a number of changes. "The Shape I'm In" and "Stage Fright" tell the story well. Some of the original feeling manifests itself in romps such as "Strawberry Wine" and "W.S. Walcott Medicine Show." —*Rob Bowman*

Cahoots / Sep. 15, 1971 / Capitol ✦✦
Cahoots was the first album recorded at Albert Grossman's Bearsville Studios in Woodstock. The sessions were not easy, as the studio was still having the bugs worked out and the Band was experiencing internal

problems. Robertson's songs had become much more difficult; the structures, chord changes, and arrangements were increasingly complex. Despite these factors, the album has a number of gems, including "Life Is a Carnival," with its great Allen Toussaint horn arrangement; Dylan's "When I Paint My Masterpiece"; a duet between Richard Manuel and Van Morrison entitled "4% Pantomime"; "The River Hymn"; and "Where Do We Go from Here?" —*Rob Bowman*

Rock of Ages / Aug. 15, 1972 / Capitol ✦✦✦✦
Recorded on New Year's Eve 1971/1972, this was the Band's last gig for a year and a half. Allen Toussaint was brought in again to write horn arrangements for many of their classics. The results were inspired. Highlights are many, but of particular note are a cover of Marvin Gaye's "Baby Don't Do It" and a live recording of a track that had earlier been relegated to B-side status only, "Get Up Jake." —*Rob Bowman*

Moondog Matinee / Oct. 15, 1973 / Capitol ✦✦
The Band essentially went back to being the Hawks of the late '50s and early '60s on this album of cover tunes. They demonstrated considerable expertise on their versions of rock 'n' roll and R&B standards like Clarence "Frogman" Henry's "Ain't Got No Home," Chuck Berry's "The Promised Land," and Fats Domino's "I'm Ready," but of course that didn't do much to satisfy the audience they had established with their original material and that, two years after the disappointing *Cahoots*, was waiting for something in the same league with their first three albums. —*William Ruhlmann*

Northern Lights Southern Cross / Nov. 1, 1975 / Capitol ✦✦✦✦
The first studio album of Band originals in four years, in many respects *Northern Lights Southern Cross* was viewed as a comeback. It also can be seen as a swan song. The album was the Band's finest since their self-titled sophomore effort. On this album of eight songs, the Band explores new timbres, utilizing for the first time 24 tracks and what was (then) new synthesizer technology. "Acadian Driftwood" stands out as one of Robertson's finest compositions, the equal to anything else the Band ever recorded. —*Rob Bowman*

The Best of the Band / Jul. 15, 1976 / Capitol ✦✦✦✦
With this album, Capitol Records began the inevitable process of repackaging the music of the Band, which the company would do at increasing length without solving the fundamental problem that the Band, despite the quality of their individual songs, was not a singles act and was hard to summarize in a compilation. That said, for the real neophyte, this single-disc, 11-song album may be as good as anything. It contains the Band's two most famous songs, "The Weight" and "The Night They Drove Old Dixie Down," as well as the group's only Top 30 hit, "Up on Cripple Creek," and such songs as "Tears of Rage" and "Stage Fright" that they probably played at nearly every show they performed. It's true that if you really want to understand the Band, you have to hear all of *Music from Big Pink* and *The Band*. But if you just want a snapshot, here it is. —*William Ruhlmann*

Islands / Mar. 15, 1977 / Capitol ✦✦
Theoretically, even though the Band had given up touring as of Thanksgiving 1976, they were going to keep making records, and *Islands* was the first album released in the new era. Only, it wasn't; it was the album they scraped together to complete their ten-LP contract with Capitol Records and the last new full-length album the original five members ever made. The playing, as ever, was impeccable, and the record had its moments, notably a Richard Manuel vocal on the chestnut "Georgia on My Mind" that had been released as a single in 1976 to boost Georgia governor Jimmy Carter's successful run for the Presidency. But the songwriting quality was mediocre, and the Band had set such a standard for itself in that department that *Islands* couldn't help suffering enormously in comparison. —*William Ruhlmann*

Anthology / 1978 / Capitol ✦✦✦
Deciding 1976's *The Best of the Band* wasn't enough (or wanting to have a product out to compete with *The Last Waltz*), Capitol released the two-LP *Anthology*, a skimpy 20-track, two-LP set with liner notes by rock critic Robert Palmer. It's more complete than *The Best of the Band*, but shares the same problem—that the Band is best appreciated on their full-length albums rather than on any compilation. —*William Ruhlmann*

The Last Waltz / Apr. 1978 / Warner Brothers ✦✦✦✦
The Band's farewell gig was held at Winterland in San Francisco on Thanksgiving 1976. Guests from all periods of their career were invited to participate. The luminaries included Bob Dylan, Van Morrison, Neil Young, Joni Mitchell, Muddy Waters, Eric Clapton, and Paul Butterfield. The four-hour concert was one of the most spectacular in rock history. Two hours of it were released on this three-LP (now two-CD) set. Utilizing horns one more time, this was the gig of the Band's life and one of the greatest in rock history. —*Rob Bowman*

To Kingdom Come / Sep. 1989 / Capitol ✦✦✦✦
If (and only if) you have it in your budget for just *one* Band set, *To Kingdom Come (The Definitive Collection)* provides a good collection of

their best songs, presented in remastered form. Even though the sequencing is chronological, experiencing these songs out of the context of their original albums may be disconcerting for some. In other words, the best way to *hear* this great group is to start with their first two albums, then move on to *Rock of Ages*, and so on. Nevertheless, this is an exceptionally solid overview. —*Rick Clark*

Jericho / Nov. 2, 1993 / Rhino ✦✦✦
A full 17 years after *The Last Waltz*, the Band re-formed without Robbie Robertson (or the late Richard Manuel) and recorded *Jericho*. Far from being an embarrassment, *Jericho* is their strongest record since *Northern Lights Southern Cross* and arguably their best since *Stage Fright*. Without Robertson, the Band relies on a variety of sources for their material (including Bob Dylan, Bruce Springsteen, and Jules Shear) and proves that they can interpret nearly any song well. Musically, the Band can still juggle rock, folk, blues, and country effortlessly, producing a rootsy sound distinctly their own. It sounds like the heyday of the group, which is more than can be said of either of Robertson's solo albums. —*Stephen Thomas Erlewine*

Across the Great Divide / Nov. 15, 1994 / Capitol ✦✦✦
Capitol's 1989 Band compilation *To Kingdom Come* was subtitled "The Definitive Collection," so what is this? Well, the other one was only a two-disc set, and this is a three-disc set. As the CD reissue/box set boom goes on, record companies have taken to redoing acts they've already done, so even though the Band has one classy CD anthology (and a few tacky ones), Capitol gives us another. In this case, they've divided it into two discs' worth of the greatest hits, followed by a disc of rarities (some not so rare) and unreleased tracks including pre-Band recordings by the Hawks, collaborations with Bob Dylan, live tracks from the Woodstock and Watkins Glen festivals, and the like. All of which pushes this set up a price point or two from the earlier one without adding anything substantial. —*William Ruhlmann*

Live at Watkins Glen / Apr. 4, 1995 / Capitol ✦✦
Along with the Allman Brothers and the Grateful Dead, the Band was a featured act at the 1973 Watkins Glen festival, a half-forgotten event that attracted half a million spectators. This rather brief (ten-song) excerpt from their set may be of interest to Band fans, but it's really rather unnecessary in light of a much better live album (*Rock of Ages*) and the fact that the performance itself wasn't anything spectacular. It does have a couple of surprising covers (Chuck Berry's "Back to Memphis" and the Four Tops' "Loving You Is Sweeter Than Ever"), and a couple of jams, including one of Garth Hudson's patented strange instrumental organ interludes. —*Richie Unterberger*

High on the Hog / Feb. 27, 1996 / Rhino ✦✦
Jericho was a surprise. The reunited Band, minus guitarist Robbie Robertson, created an album that built on their strengths by using carefully selected contemporary songwriters and covers. Although it lacked the resonance of *Music from Big Pink* or even *Stage Fright*, the group sounded fresh, and it was a better album than most of the Band's solo records. *High on the Hog*, the second album by the reunited Band, isn't quite as good, but it has a number of stellar moments. The key to the album's success isn't the material—they're saddled with a couple of weak songs—but the group's interplay. By now the musicians have developed a sympathetic interaction that sounds ancient but still living, breathing, and vital. It's a joy to hear them play, and that's what carries *High on the Hog* over its rough spots. —*Stephen Thomas Erlewine*

The Bangles

f. 1981, Los Angeles, CA, db. Oct. 1989
Group / New Wave, Pop-Rock, Paisley Underground
Originally Colours, the Supersonic Bangs, and the Bangs, the all-singing/all-performing four-woman Bangles formed in 1981 and sprang from the Los Angeles Paisley Underground scene. Later they traded their garage band roots for a slick, heavily produced pop sound that turned them into one of the most successful chart groups of either gender during the '80s.

In the beginning, the group played original, '60's-based guitar-rock, and often covered Big Star, the Merry Go Round, and Love. Sisters Debbi and Vicki Peterson on drums and bass respectively and singer/guitarist Susanna Hoffs started the group when the Petersons responded to a want-ad placed by Hoffs; later they added Annette Zilinskas on bass.

The scruffy girl-group self-released the single "Getting Out of Hand," which sounded like a lost song by the Mamas and the Papas; they followed it with a loose, four-song pop EP on IRS before signing to Columbia. *All Over the Place* was produced by David Kahne and released in 1984, once the band had been given an all-over clean-up. By that time Zilinskas had left the fold to join Blood on the Saddle, and former Runaway Michael Steele was added to the line-up.

For the second album, 1985's *Different Light*, the band was aided by Prince (or Christopher, as he was known during that phase) with his song "Manic Monday," which charted at No. 2 and paved the way for the follow-up smash, "Walk Like an Egyptian," which went to No. 1 and sent

the album to the top of the charts. There was a sexist assumption among some critics that the successful female group couldn't really play and needed studio and live assistance, but as with any slick chart band, sessionmen were in fact credited, beginning on the second album. Future Black Crowes producer George Drakoulias was enlisted to play the guitar lead for their next single, a cover of Simon and Garfunkel's "Hazy Shade of Winter," from the *Less Than Zero* soundtrack that reached No. 1 in 1987. At the same time, Hoffs appeared in a B-movie, *The Allnighter*, and it garnered the band some undesirable attention; but the follow-up album, *Everything*, spawned another No. 1, "Eternal Flame," in 1988.

The band packed it in because of the usual artistic differences in 1989. The Petersons' sibling harmonies gave the group its unique sound; but singer Susanna Hoffs was often considered the focal point, and that contributed to the tension. Vicki Peterson sings with the Continental Drifters and filled in for Charlotte Caffey during 1994's Go-Gos reunion tour. Hoffs has recorded two solo albums since the band's break-up, *When You're a Boy* in 1991 and a self-titled record in 1996. Debbie Peterson and Steele continue to work with various alternative pop groups. —*Denise Sullivan*

Bangles / Jun. 1982 / Faulty ✦✦✦✦
The Bangles' debut EP is the perfect example of what was going on in Los Angeles' Paisley Underground during the early '80s. Singer Susanna Hoffs literally growls her way through "The Real World," a tight, uptempo pop song in the tradition of Love. The guitars ring out, and the layered, three-part harmonies recall the Mamas and the Papas and the Beatles. The Bangles later proved to be a garage band made good, but this early version produced arguably their best work and proves beyond a shadow of a doubt that they were never a girl-group creation but an entirely rocking, working band, schooled in the best traditions of '60s rock. —*Denise Sullivan*

All Over The Place / May 1984 / Columbia ✦✦✦✦
The Bangles' major label debut is an essential album in the band's catalog. Guitarist and vocalist Vicki Peterson penned most of the '60s and early '70s guitar-rock songs, like the mini-hit "Hero Takes a Fall" (it was rumored the hero in the title was Dream Syndicate's Steve Wynn). The record also includes covers of the obscure Merry Go Round hit "Live" and ex-Soft Boy Kimberley Rew's "Going Down to Liverpool." The band was polished a bit by producer David Kahne and the release capitalized on the pretty, all-girl-group angle rather than the band's actual raw talent, which might otherwise have been too rough and retro for radio at the time. Nonetheless, the band retained enough of the original spunk that made them appealing in the first place. —*Denise Sullivan*

Different Light / Jan. 1986 / Columbia ✦✦✦
The band's second album went to No. 1 on the strength of the first single, "Manic Monday," written especially for the band by Prince, and its follow-up, "Walk like an Egyptian," penned by '80s hit-making giant Liam Sternberg. Though even more polished than the debut, *Different Light* is a testament to the mid-'80s sound, replete with synthesizers (Mitchell Froom assisted); even on Jules Shear's magnificent "If She Knew What She Wants" and Alex Chilton's standard "September Gurls," the band's vocal strengths shine through the gloss, and their pop sensibilities are not completely lost. —*Denise Sullivan*

Everything / Oct. 1988 / Columbia ✦✦
The band really turned up the glamour meter for *Everything*, but the success of *Different Light* would have been hard to top. Yet again enlisting the aid of professional songwriters along the lines of Billy Steinberg and Tom Kelly, the band's original guitar-rock intent suffered at the hands of over-the-top song structures and production. Teaming the Bangles with such odd pairings as metal guitarist Vinnie Vincent and future Jane's Addiction/Red Hot Chili Peppers guitarist Dave Navarro was a very misguided concept. Although the record yielded the No. 1 hit "Eternal Flame" and another hit, "In Your Room," the group imploded a year later under the weight of diminished expectations and artistic differences. At that point, they could afford to retire. —*Denise Sullivan*

● **Greatest Hits** / May 1990 / Columbia ✦✦✦✦
Greatest Hits is just that, including a great version of Simon & Garfunkel's "Hazy Shade of Winter," a hit from the *Less Than Zero* soundtrack that's not found on their other albums. Another previously unreleased track is a reading of the Grass Roots chestnut "Where Were You When I Needed You." The highlights from their weakest album, *Everything*, are provided, rendering that album inconsequential. It would've been nice if Sony had utilized the space on CD to include more essential album tracks from their first two albums, like "September Gurls," "Live," and "James." As collections go, this is a place to start, but *All Over the Place* is their most appealing album. —*Rick Clark*

The Barbarians

f. 1965, Boston, MA
Garage Rock, Pop-Rock
With their appearances on the *Nuggets* compilation and the "T.A.M.I.

Show," the Barbarians are one of the best-remembered garage bands of the '60s. Not that it's easy to forget the sight of a one-handed drummer, complete with hook, driving his band through a garage-punk number in the company of the day's biggest British Invasion, soul, and surf stars. Moulty was hardly self-conscious; on the tiny hit single immortalized on *Nuggets* (titled, logically enough, "Moulty"), he tells the story of the triumph over his loss in no uncertain melodramatic terms. The band also managed a somewhat bigger hit single, the British Invasion-inspired novelty "Are You a Boy or Are You a Girl." —*Richie Unterberger*

● **Are You a Boy or Are You a Girl?** / 1966 / One Way ✦✦✦
While the Barbarians live up to a lot of people's vision of the classic garage band image-wise, their album is disappointing and thin-sounding; the material is average and doesn't even rock terribly hard. "Are You a Boy Or Are You a Girl" and "Moulty" are both here, but much of the rest of the songs are overdone standards ("House of the Rising Sun" is especially lame). "What the New Breed Say" is an okay anthem of rebellion, and "I'll Keep On Seeing You" a modestly touching ballad, but as songwriters the Barbarians were light-years behind their principal New England rivals, the Remains. Disappointingly, the LP doesn't include their best song, "Hey Little Bird" (which they performed on the *T.A.M.I. Show*). Die-hards are advised to track down the cut on the obscure garage band compilation reissue *The New England Teen Scene Vol. II*, although the studio version isn't as ferocious as their rendition on film. —*Richie Unterberger*

Barclay James Harvest

f. Sep. 1966, Oldham, England
Group / Art-Rock/Progressive-Rock, Folk-Rock
Barclay James Harvest was, for many years, one of the most hard-luck outfits in progressive rock. A quartet of solid rock musicians—John Lees, guitar, vocals; Les Holroyd, bass, vocals; Stuart "Woolly" Wolstenholme, keyboards, vocals; and Mel Pritchard, drums—with a knack for writing hook-laden songs built on pretty melodies, they harmonized like the Beatles and wrote extended songs with more of a beat than the Moody Blues. They were signed to EMI at the same time as Pink Floyd, and both bands moved over to the company's progressive rock-oriented Harvest imprint at the same time, but somehow Barclay James Harvest never managed to connect with public for a major hit in England, much less America.

The group was formed in September 1966 in Oldham, Lancashire. Lees and Wolstenholme were classmates who played together in a band called the Blues Keepers; that group soon merged with a band called the Wickeds, which included Holroyd and Pritchard. They became Barclay James Harvest in June 1967 and began rehearsing at an 18th century farmhouse in Lancashire. The psychedelic era was in full swing, and the era of progressive rock was about to begin; the Moody Blues, in particular, were beginning to cut a swath across the music world. BJH cut a series of demos late in the year, and by the spring of 1968 they were signed to EMI's Parlophone label; in April they issued their first single, a folky, faux-classical song called "Early Morning." The group got caught up a year later in a corporate change at EMI, and it was decided to move the more progressive-sounding groups on the label onto a new label—Harvest, taken from BJH's name. Their first release on the new label was the single "Brother Thrush."

In 1970 they released their first album, *Barclay James Harvest*, which included several of the early songs and displayed the group's strengths; filled with strong harmony singing, aggressive electric guitar, and swelling Mellotron parts, it set the pattern for their subsequent releases, with Lees and Holroyd handling most of the songwriting. The album failed to chart, and a subsequent tour was a financial disaster. Their second album, *Once Again* (1971), was an artistic letdown, made up of rather lethargic songs, although it did contain the superb "Mockingbird." The band recorded two more albums for Harvest, *Short Stories* (1971) and *Baby James Harvest* (1972), and spent much of 1972 on the road, including an unsuccessful tour of the US. They also released a pair of singles, "When the City Sleeps" and "Breathless," under the pseudonym "Bombadil" (a name taken from a J.R.R. Tolkien short story), all to no avail. In 1973 they parted company with EMI after one last single, "Rock and Roll Woman."

Later in 1973 the band signed with Polydor, and their fortunes began turning around, though only very gradually. Their first album for the new label, *Everyone Is Everybody Else*, seemed promising; it was a more powerful and coherent work than the group had ever released for EMI, with Lees' guitar dominating on songs like "Paper Wings" and "For No One." The album also presented the first example of the group's consciously paying tribute to (and satirizing) another group's hit song; "Great 1974 Mining Disaster" was a very heavy-sounding tribute/satire of the Bee Gees' "New York Mining Disaster 1941." (They would later do work in this vein involving the Moody Blues.) The album failed to chart, however, as did the single "Poor Boy Blues," with its gorgeous harmonies. It seemed at first as though BJH was locked once again into a cycle

of failure. Finally in late 1974 their double album *Barclay James Harvest Live* broke through to the public. The group was rewarded with Top 40 placement in England and more sales activity on the European continent than they'd previously seen. Their next album, *Time Honoured Ghosts*, recorded in San Francisco, continued this gradual breakthrough when it was released in 1975, reaching No. 32 in England. A year later *Octoberon* reached the Top 20. An EP containing live versions of "Rock 'n' Roll Star" and "Medicine Man" became another chart entry in the spring of 1977. By this time EMI had begun to take advantage of the success of the group's Polydor work, and released *A Major Fancy*, a John Lees' solo album that had been on the shelf for five years.

In 1977 they released *Gone to Earth*, their most accomplished album to date, and by the end of the year the group found themselves playing to arena-sized audiences. The release of *XII* in 1978—which managed to just miss the British Top 30—was followed by the group's first (and only) personnel shake-up. In June 1979, Wolstenholme announced his exit from the band in favor of a solo career; the group's final tour with Wolstenholme was recorded and later released by Polydor under the title *The Live Tapes*. He was replaced by two new members, singer-keyboardman-saxophonist Kevin McAlea and singer-guitarist-keyboardman Colin Browne. Wolstenholme released one solo album, 1979's *Maestro*, to little success, and then retired for a time from the music business.

Their 1979 album *Eyes of the Universe* was a modest hit in England, but its release marked a flashpoint in Barclay James Harvest's career in continental Europe, especially Germany; on August 30, 1980, the band performed a free concert in front of nearly 200,000 people at the Reichstag in Berlin, which was filmed and recorded. A subsequent live album, *Concert for the People*, became the group's biggest selling album in England, rising to No. 15 in 1982. *Turn of the Tide* (1981) and *Ring of Changes* (1983) were less successful, although the latter did spawn their last charting single, "Just a Day Away." Their subsequent Polydor albums, *Victims of Circumstance*, *Face to Face*, and *Welcome to the Show*, charted ever lower in England, even as the group's popularity grew in Europe. In 1988 they released a new live album, *Glasnost*, cut at a concert in East Berlin. The group marked the 25th anniversary with a concert in Liverpool and toured to support a British Polydor compilation, *The Best of Barclay James Harvest.* —*Bruce Eder*

Barclay James Harvest / Jun. 1970 / Sire ✦✦✦✦

Once Again / 1971 / Sire ✦✦✦

Other Short Stories / 1971 / Sire ✦✦✦

Baby James Harvest / 1972 / Harvest ✦✦✦✦

Everyone Is Everybody Else / Jun. 1974 / Polydor ✦✦
The group's first album for Polydor is several steps above their EMI work. Most of the psychedelic-era influences are softened here and broadened, and transmuted into something heavier and more serious, even as the Beatle-esque harmonies remain intact. The guitars sound real heavy, almost larger than life here, while the swelling Mellotron and synthesizer sounds give the music the feel of an orchestra. The group had also mastered by this time the Pink Floyd technique of playing pretty tunes really slowly, which made them sound incredibly profound (it's actually a technique that goes back, in different forms, to Gustav Mahler and Anton Bruckner). John Lees gives superb, virtuoso performances on lead guitar on "Paper Wings" and "For No One." Les Holroyd's gorgeous "Poor Boy Blues" sounded more like Crosby, Stills & Nash than CSN did in those days, and is almost worth the price of the CD. (British import) —*Bruce Eder*

Octoberon / 1976 / Polydor ✦✦✦
A strong follow-up to *Everyone Is Everybody Else*, with more of a mythic orientation to the music. (British import) —*Bruce Eder*

● **Best of Barclay James Harvest, Vol. 1** / 1977 / Harvest ✦✦✦✦

☆ **Gone to Earth** / 1977 / MCA ✦✦✦✦✦
The group's best album, featuring some of their most effective hard rock and their best tunes. John Lees' soaring, poetic "Hymn" became a major part of their stage act, but is still pretty powerful in its studio version, and Les Holroyd's "Hard Hearted Woman" also turned into a concert favorite. The real highlight, however, is John Lees' "Poor Man's Moody Blues," which manages to outdo the other band at their own game. (British import) —*Bruce Eder*

Live Tapes / 1978 / Polydor ✦✦
This double live CD, made on BJH's last tour with Woolly Wolstenholme, is one of the better live albums to come out of the progressive rock genre. Though not as exciting as *Genesis Live* or as majestic as *Yessongs*, it shows the group in excellent form, playing and harmonizing beautifully and doing many of their best songs, among them "Child of the Universe," "Rock 'n' Roll Star," "Poor Man's Moody Blues," "For No One," and "Mockingbird" (the latter never sounded more beautiful). All of the tracks work significantly better as live cuts than in their original studio form. Lees' guitar and Wolstenholme's keyboards work together very well on stage and within the songs. The only complaint one could

have is the price—for just under 80 minutes of music, the two CDs could have been combined on one disc. The sound is good, though there is no real audience "presence," except between songs. (British import) —*Bruce Eder*

Best of Barclay James Harvest, Vol. 2 / 1979 / Harvest ✦✦✦✦
Best of Barclay James Harvest, Vol. 3 / 1981 / Harvest ✦✦✦✦
The Harvest Years / Jun. 7, 1991 / EMI ✦✦✦✦
A double CD consisting of more than 30 songs culled from BJH's first six Harvest albums. In addition to excellent sound (the stuff has been treated with Sonic Solutions' "No Noise" process), this set also includes oddities for the hardcore collectors, such as lost quadraphonic mixes on various early-'70s tracks. At $30, it's the comprehensive collection to get on their Harvest material, but also maybe a bit of overkill for the casual fan. (British import) —*Bruce Eder*

The Best of Barclay James Harvest [Polydor] / 1992 / Polydor ✦✦✦✦
The highlights of their post-1974 Polydor history, good but not a substitute for their individual albums. —*Bruce Eder*

Barclay James Harvest/Once Again / Oct. 27, 1995 / One Way ✦✦✦✦
The Best of Barclay James Harvest [EMI] / 1996 / EMI ✦✦✦✦
This single-disc, 20-song collection is probably the best compilation of the group's early work for the neophyte or the casual fan, containing all of the essential tracks in excellent sound along with a thumbnail biographical sketch. It is certainly the place to start for any potential fan, showing off the strongest of their songs from six albums, including "Mockingbird," and various singles, along with the John Lees solo track "Child of the Universe." (British import) —*Bruce Eder*

The Bar-Kays
....

f. 1966, Memphis, TN
Soul, Funk
Even though four group founders were killed in a 1967 plane crash along with Otis Redding, the Bar-Kays came back to reign as one of the top R&B outfits of the '70s. The original Bar-Kays were a Memphis instrumental combo that scored an R&B hit in 1967 on Volt with the rousing "Soul Finger." Guitarist Jimmy King, organist Ronnie Caldwell, drummer Carl Cunningham, and saxist Phalon Jones perished with Redding, leaving trumpeter Ben Cauley and bassist James Alexander to re-form the group. After honing their chops with session work at Stax, the new Bar-Kays kicked off a long string of R&B smashes in 1976 with "Shake Your Rump to the Funk" on Mercury. —*Bill Dahl*

Soul Finger / 1967 / Rhino ✦✦✦✦
The Bar-Kays were being trained as a second generation Booker T & the MG's, largely by MG drummer Al Jackson. *Soul Finger* was their first album, coming off the success of their debut single, the group-written title cut. The album is in the classic Memphis-soul instrumental vein: sparse arrangements, accentuated low-end, walloping snare drum, and slightly delayed backbeat, with horns taking the place of vocals. *Soul Finger* was the only album made by this particular version of the group. —*Rob Bowman*

Gotta Groove / 1969 / Stax ✦✦✦
After the plane crash in December 1967, trumpeter Ben Cauley and bass player James Alexander regrouped, forming a second edition of the Bar-Kays. *Gotta Groove* was the new group's first release. Modeled on earlier Bar-Kays work, the album is totally instrumental, including covers of the Mar-Keys' "Grab This Thing" and the Beatles' "Yesterday" and "Hey Jude." No standout cuts but plenty of fine, hard-driving slices of Memphis instrumental soul. —*Rob Bowman*

Black Rock / Feb. 1971 / Volt ✦✦✦
As the title implies, the Bar-Kays were redefining both their image and their sound. Adding vocals for the first time, the group produced hardrock covers of Aretha Franklin's "Baby I Love You," Sam and Dave's "You Don't Know like I Know," and Sly's "Dance to the Music." The recording is an odd melange of Vanilla Fudge, Chicago, and Funkadelic. Appended at the end is an instrumental version of "Montego Bay" that was cut as a single between *Gotta Groove* and this album. Certainly dated, *Black Rock* will not be to everybody's taste. —*Rob Bowman*

Do You See What I See? / 1972 / Polydor ✦✦
Some vigorous funk and an occasional soulful ballad by the Bar-Kays, who were re-establishing their funk credentials and rebuilding after the '67 plane crash. This album included the title track and several other short, peppy vocal and instrumental numbers, although it wasn't as well-produced as some later '70s and '80s efforts. —*Ron Wynn*

Coldblooded / 1974 / Stax ✦✦✦
One of the albums that the Bar-Kays cut for Stax in the early '70s when they revamped the group after the disastrous late '60s plane crash that killed all but two of the originals. The new lineup featured guitarist Lloyd Smith, drummer Michael Beard, vocalist John Colbert, trumpeter Charles Allen, saxophonist Havery Henderson, and others. This was classic Southern funk, with gospel-tinged vocals, energetic horn tracks,

and lyrics that ranged from downhome musings to urban admonitions. —*Ron Wynn*

Too Hot to Stop / Oct. 1976 / Mercury ✦✦✦✦
One of their best '70s dates, the Bar-Kays were in overdrive throughout this one. The title track was a huge hit, and the other uptempo tunes were equally fast-paced and tightly played. The few slow songs provided enough changes of pace to keep things varied. The horn charts, production, and arrangements were funk personified, although they were starting to add synthesized elements in anticipation of changes on the urban front. —*Ron Wynn*

Flying High on Your Love / Nov. 1977 / Mercury ✦✦✦
The Bar-Kays were riding the crest as the top funk band in the South. This album didn't have any one standout track, but had several solid ones that got wide regional airplay and even a little national attention. They were beginning to modify their sound as well, peeling back the horns a bit and putting the bass/synthesizer underplay more to the front. —*Ron Wynn*

Money Talks / Oct. 1978 / Stax ✦✦✦
Prototype Southern funk and hot R&B licks. —*Ron Wynn*

Light of Life / Dec. 1978 / Mercury ✦✦
The second of two Bar-Kays albums that were issued in 1978, this one used similar horn charts and upbeat, fast-paced funk rhythms that the group had made popular. It didn't have as many slow numbers, either, and was more animated and exuberant than its predecessor. —*Ron Wynn*

Injoy / Oct. 1979 / Mercury ✦✦
The Bar-Kays debuted on Mercury at the end of the '70s and gradually altered their style. Horn funk was dying out in 1980, and while they weren't yet ready to disband their horn section, they were steadily reducing their role. They kept the same collective, half-sung, half-yelled vocals, but now the bass/drum/synthesizer interplay was at the center, with the horns in the background. —*Ron Wynn*

As One / Nov. 1980 / Mercury ✦✦✦✦
This was arguably their best Mercury album. It included "Move Your Boogie Body," plus their finest inspirational tune, "Deliver Us," and the title cut was a solid winner as well. They had found the ideal mix of horns, electronics, funk backbeats, and R&B/gospel vocals, and everything clicked on every selection. —*Ron Wynn*

Nightcruising / Nov. 1981 / Mercury ✦✦✦
Another fine early '80s album, with one of their biggest hits in the decade, the single "Hit and Run." The Bar-Kays were for a time the dominant funk band around, and were one of the few that had been able to survive into the '80s. The horns were still there, although they'd soon be purged from the arrangements. —*Ron Wynn*

Propositions / Nov. 1982 / Mercury ✦✦
Signs of decline begin to emerge with this album. They were now moving squarely away from the driving, horn-centered funk that had made their reputation, and trying to cope with a slimmer backbeat and more groove-oriented sound. They adapted the slinky, synthesized formula patented by Cameo and had some success, but they weren't singing with the same aggressiveness and confidence. —*Ron Wynn*

● **Best of [Stax]** / 1988 / Stax ✦✦✦✦
Stax's *The Best of the Bar-Kays* inexplicably leaves off "Soul Finger," as well as "Knucklehead" and "Give Everybody Some," concentrating instead on the group's early-'70s incarnation as a funk band. Although it is missing their soul instrumentals from the late '60s, the compilation remains a good overview of their early '70s work for Stax/Volt, featuring such songs as "Montego Bay," "Humpin'," "A.J. the Housefly" and the Top Ten R&B hit "Son of Shaft." —*Stephen Thomas Erlewine*

The Best of the Bar-Kays [Mercury] / May 18, 1993 / Mercury ✦✦✦✦
When the Bar-Kays joined Mercury Records in 1976, they shifted musical styles slightly, veering away from the goofy but funky soul instrumentals that defined their Stax singles and concentrating on loose, wild funk that was driven by fat bass lines and whining synthesizers. Mercury's *The Best of the Bar-Kays* captures the majority of the highlights from their '70s recordings for the label. Over the course of 16 tracks, the compilation features the majority of their Top Ten R&B hits—including "Shake Your Rump to the Funk," "Too Hot to Stop," "Move Your Boogie Body," and "Hit and Run"—as well as several fine album tracks like "Freakshow on the Dance Floor," "Shut the Funk Up," and "Sexomatic" that illustrate the depth of the group's musical skills. —*Stephen Thomas Erlewine*

Best of the Bar-Kays, Vol. 2 / May 21, 1996 / Mercury ✦✦✦
Another scoop of mid-'70s-mid-'80s material from the Mercury era, for those with an interest in the band's slicker phase. It's pretty formulaic but does include several R&B hits such as "Spellbound," "Do It," "Boogie Body Land," "Let's Have Some Fun," "Dirty Dancer," "Your Place or Mine," "Sexomatic," and "She Talks to Me with Her Body," whose the-

matic concerns can be easily gleaned from the titles. —*Richie Unterberger*

Syd Barrett

b. Jan. 6, 1946, Cambridge, England
Guitar, Vocals / Psychedelic
Like a supernova, Roger "Syd" Barrett burned briefly and brightly, leaving an indelible mark upon psychedelic and progressive rock as the founder and original singer, songwriter, and lead guitarist of Pink Floyd. Barrett was responsible for most of their brilliant first album, 1967's *The Piper at the Gates of Dawn*, but left or was fired from the band in early 1968 after his erratic behavior had made him too difficult to deal with. (He appears on a couple tracks on their second album, *A Saucerful of Secrets*.) Such was his stature within the original lineup that few observers thought the band could survive his departure; in fact, the original group's management decided to keep Syd on and leave the rest of the band to their own devices. Pink Floyd never recaptured the playful humor and mad energy of their work with Barrett.

After a period of hibernation, Barrett re-emerged in 1970 with a pair of albums, *The Madcap Laughs* and *Barrett*, which featured considerable support from his former bandmates (especially his replacement, David Gilmour, who produced most of the sessions). Members of the Soft Machine also play on these records, which have a ragged, unfinished, and folky feel. Barrett's eccentric humor, sly wordplay, and infectious melodies range from brilliant to chaotic on his solo work. Lacking the taut power of his recordings with the Floyd in 1967, they nevertheless remain fascinating and moving glimpses into a creative psyche gone awry after (it is theorized) too much fame and too many drugs too early. With increasing psychological problems, Barrett withdrew into seclusion after these albums. He never released any more material, and these days he rarely appears in public, let alone to play music.

Barrett's music and mystique continue to grow more than two decades later. Latter-day new wave psychedelic acts like Julian Cope, the Television Personalities, and (especially) Robyn Hitchcock acknowledge Barrett's tremendous influence on their work. The Barrett cult became large enough to warrant the release of an entire album of previously unreleased material and outtakes, *Opel*, in the late '80s, as well as his sessions for the BBC. —*Richie Unterberger*

● **The Madcap Laughs** / Jan. 1970 / Capitol ✦✦✦✦
While this collection bears similarities to the songs found on *The Piper at the Gates of Dawn*, the only Pink Floyd album Barrett contributed to significantly, it nevertheless comes across more as a session of runthroughs and demos than as a finished record. Its very roughness is its charm, undercutting the whimsy of the songs with Barrett's ultimate strangeness. — *William Ruhlmann*

Barrett / Nov. 1970 / Capitol ✦✦✦
On his second solo album, Barrett was joined by Humble Pie drummer Jerry Shirley and Pink Floyd members Rick Wright (organ) and Dave Gilmour (guitar). Gilmour and Wright acted as producers as well. Instrumentally, the result is a bit fuller and smoother than the first album, although it's since been revealed that Gilmour and Wright embellished these songs as best they could without much involvement from Barrett, who was often unable or unwilling to perfect his performance. The songs, however, are just as fractured as on his debut, if not more so. "Baby Lemonade," "Gigolo Aunt," and the nursery rhyming "Effervescing Elephant" rank among his peppiest and best-loved tunes. Elsewhere, the tone is darker and more meandering. It was regarded as something of a charming but unfocused throwaway at the time of its release, but Barrett's singularly whimsical and unsettling vision holds up well. —*Richie Unterberger*

Peel Sessions / 1987 / Dutch East India ✦✦
In February 1970, Syd Barrett performed five songs for John Peel's show on the BBC, accompanied by Jerry Shirley on drums and Dave Gilmour on guitar. Besides reprising "Terrapin" from his first album, the session featured three of the strongest tunes from his second LP, "Gigolo Aunt," "Baby Lemonade," and (a very brief) "Effervescing Elephant." This five-song EP also includes the bouncy, easygoing "Two of a Kind," which doesn't appear on any other release; it's since been claimed that this was actually a composition by Pink Floyd organist Rick Wright. The rest of the songs don't differ much from the officially released versions; they're somewhat sparer and looser. A decent if not absolutely essential relic for the Barrett/Floyd fan, with excellent sound. —*Richie Unterberger*

Opel / Apr. 1989 / Capitol ✦✦✦
For several years, the existence of "lost" material by Barrett had been speculated on by the singer's vociferous cult, fueled by numerous patchy bootlegs of intriguing outtakes. The release of *Opel* lived up to, and perhaps exceeded, fans' expectations. With 14 tracks spanning 1968 to 1970, including six alternate takes and eight songs that had never been officially released in any form, it is as essential as his two 1970 LPs. The tone is very much in keeping with his pair of solo albums: ragged, predominantly acoustic, melodic, and teetering on the edge of dementia. At

the same time, it's charming and lyrically pungent, with Barrett's inimitable sense of childlike whimsy. The production is generally more minimal than on his other albums, even bare-bones at times, but if anything, this adds to the music's stark power. Highlights are the lengthy brooding title track, the multi-layered swirl of "Swan Lee," the alternate take of "Dark Globe" (with much better, more restrained vocals than the previous version), and the exuberant, infectious "Milky Way." Meticulous liner notes and excellent sound complete this loving archival package. —*Richie Unterberger*

Octopus: The Best of Syd Barrett / May 29, 1992 / CEMA Special Markets ✦✦✦
A well-chosen, 14-track, single-disc compilation of Barrett's solo work, presumably discount-priced and aimed at the casual listener. But Barrett is such a specialized taste and has such a small body of work that one wonders why CEMA Special Markets (a division of EMI) would bother. — *William Ruhlmann*

Crazy Diamond / Apr. 19, 1994 / EMI ✦✦✦✦
A three-CD box set that enshrines Barrett's complete recorded legacy as a solo artist. Besides including his two 1970 albums, this collection includes the 1989 compilation of unreleased material, *Opel*. The chief attraction of this set for Barrett fans is no less than 19 previously unreleased alternate takes from throughout his quite brief solo career. All of those alternate takes, it's important to note, are alternate versions of songs that appear on the three previously available albums; no entirely unheard compositions were unearthed. Nonetheless, these alternate takes are more interesting listening than you might expect, for a couple of reasons. First, Barrett was so mercurial (and occasionally unfocused) in the studio that it was difficult to get him to play a song the same way twice. Second, the alternate takes are usually starker and more acoustic in nature than the official versions; they're not better, but have interesting different slants. With some of the songs repeated two, three, or even four times, this is definitely for the hardcore fan. But it's a beautifully produced document, with a meticulously detailed booklet, of a uniquely primitive visionary, and has many moments of charming and chilling power. It includes everything salvageable that he produced, with the exception of the *Peel Sessions*. It doesn't match his work with the original Pink Floyd, but the music continues to influence and be emulated (most notably by Robyn Hitchcock), though never equaled. —*Richie Unterberger*

Magnesium Proverbs [Bootleg] / The Gold Standard ✦✦✦
A 23-track compilation that some fans may find to promise more than it really delivers. First off, about two-thirds of this is actually stuff that Barrett recorded with Pink Floyd. While this material is undeniably interesting, it's appeared elsewhere (particularly on the fine Barrett-era Pink Floyd bootleg compilation *A Saucerful of Outtakes*). Some of the tracks are rare British singles that are available on official releases (although those releases may be inconvenient to locate or expensive to purchase). And the rarest items—three songs from a 1970 BBC session, and three live songs from Barrett's only concert appearance (also in 1970)—are dampened by very poor sound. The BBC cuts are transistor-radio quality; on the live ones, the vocals are hardly audible. If this is the only Barrett bootleg you can find, you'll still find things to enjoy, like the early '66 bluesy Floyd demos and the oft-booted hissy '67 Floyd BBC broadcasts. It doesn't change the fact that it's a very uneven listening experience. —*Richie Unterberger*

Rhamadam [Bootleg] / No Man's Land ✦✦
After the *Crazy Diamond* box set, the radio sessions, and the *Magnesium Proverbs* bootleg, could there possibly be anything left, from a guy who didn't record that much to begin with? Well, yes, and most of it's here on this collection of odds and ends from his work both with and without Pink Floyd. There are yet more alternate versions from his 1969 sessions; the otherwise unreleased 1968 percussion instrumental "Rhamadam"; guitar instrumental bits from a fruitless mid-'70s session; lo-fi live Floyd 1967 cuts; an instrumental outtake from Floyd's *Piper* LP; and a Canadian interview from 1967. The fidelity is pretty variable, the snippets of otherwise unavailable instrumentals really aren't proper songs, and the alternates are not remarkable variations on what you can find on the box set. So it's not an essential purchase, even for many Syd/Floyd fans. We're talking Syd Barrett here, though, an enigma that creates insatiable hunger for material within his cult, and committed fanatics will find it a worthwhile cache of material that's hard to find anywhere else. The unquestioned highlight is a throbbing, almost punky 15-minute version of "Interstellar Overdrive" from the Floyd days. The poppy, innocuous covers of "Why Do Fools Fall in Love" and "Don't Ask Me" have no Syd Barrett involvement at all; they're 1965 demos by Joker's Wild, Dave Gilmour's pre-Floyd outfit. —*Richie Unterberger*

Barry & the Remains

f. 1964, Boston, MA, **db.** 1966
Rock 'n' Roll, Pop-Rock
A strong contender for the finest overlooked American band of the mid-

'60s, the Remains (led by Barry Tashian) were the most notable Boston group of the era. But they never broke out nationally, despite signing to Epic and copping an opening slot on the Beatles' final American tour in 1966. Although they are sometimes described as a garage band, that designation isn't at all accurate; the Remains shared the same British Invasion influences as many American teen acts, but their straight-ahead attack and sharp songwriting had a lot of professional finesse, and they sometimes sounded like a fusion of the Beatles and the Zombies, with their energetic harmonies and guitar-electric keyboard blend.

Four fine singles for Epic found little action outside of the Northeast. Frustrated by the disparity they perceived between their studio work and their furious live show, they cut an audition tape for Capitol, although no offer from the label was forthcoming (the session was issued for collectors many years later). An uneven but solid debut album for Epic was released near the end of 1966, but by that time the Remains were breaking up, dispirited by the stalemate in which their career seemed to have been mired. Remains drummer N.D. Smart II played with Gram Parsons and Emmylou Harris; Tashian also played with Harris and today is a Nashville-based country-folk musician, often recording as a duo with his wife, Holly. *—Richie Unterberger*

● **The Remains** / 1966 / Epic/Legacy ✦✦✦✦
A fabulous reissue that shows the group as one of the finest, and possibly *the* finest, British Invasion-inspired American garage band of the mid-'60s. The Remains had it all, except success: their first-rate original material combined tight harmonies and tuneful melodies with brash energy. This 21-track disc repackages their entire 1966 LP and adds a wealth of bonus cuts, including all their non-LP singles and some excellent unreleased songs. *—Richie Unterberger*

Live in Boston / 1984 / Eva ✦✦
This live-in-the-studio demo was accorded raves by the few collectors who managed to hear it before its appearance on this LP. Although Remains leader Barry Tashian has said that it captures the band's prowess better than their studio material, it's a disappointment. Six of the seven songs are cover versions of very well-known rock hits—"Johnny B. Goode," "I'm a Man," "All Day and All of the Night," "Hang On Sloopy," "Like a Rolling Stone"—competently done, but hardly revelatory, as the Remains' chief strength was their excellent songwriting. The version of the original tune "Why Do I Cry" is indeed fine and powerful, but the Remains' legacy is best heard on the excellent, nearly all-original *The Remains* collection on Epic. *—Richie Unterberger*

Session with the Remains / Feb. 27, 1996 / Sundazed ✦✦✦
The first official release of their '66 live-in-the-studio Capitol demo, in considerably better sound quality than when it appeared on a French import of dubious legality. This has a very high reputation in collector circles, but in my opinion it is not the Remains at their best, principally because they recorded only one original ("Why Do I Cry"). The rest of the seven demos are high-energy run-throughs of live standards of the era, like "Hang On Sloopy," "I'm a Man," and "Johnny B. Goode." The CD is fleshed out with five previously unreleased demos of group originals (different versions of all of these appear on the Epic reissue), and a previously unknown demo of "Walkin' the Dog." Most listeners will be satisfied with Epic's excellent Remains retrospective, but this is a useful supplement for collectors who want a little more. *—Richie Unterberger*

Dave Bartholomew

b. Dec. 24, 1920, Edgard, LA
Trumpet / R&B, New Orleans R&B
A major contributor to New Orleans R&B, Dave Bartholomew was a pivotal figure as a writer, arranger, producer, and A&R man for Imperial. Bartholomew's productions helped make Fats Domino a major player in R&B and rock 'n' roll, and he assembled the great house band that backed Domino, Little Richard, Lloyd Price, Smiley Lewis, and several other Crescent City greats. This band included pianist Allen Toussaint, bassist Frank Fields, saxophonists Lee Allen, Alvin "Red" Tyler, and Herb Hardesty, and drummer Earl Palmer. Bartholomew recorded as a solo artist for King and others before taking over at Imperial, but his fame came from that stint. Bartholomew greatly reduced his activities after Domino left Imperial in the early '60s, but he occasionally resurfaced to conduct his band. *—Ron Wynn*

★ **The Spirit of New Orleans: The Genius of Dave Bartholomew** / 1993 / Capitol ✦✦✦✦✦
A two-disc set featuring 50 tracks and several artists (including Fats Domino, Smiley Lewis, T-Bone Walker, Shirley and Lee, and Earl King,) *The Spirit of New Orleans* conveys Bartholomew's groundbreaking achievements in R&B and rock 'n' roll. *—Stephen Thomas Erlewine*

Rob Base & DJ E-Z Rock

b. May 18, 1967, Harlem, NY
Vocals / Hip Hop
Best-known for his 1988 platinum classic "It Takes Two," Rob Base (with

DJ E-Z Rock) rode his hit onto R&B radio stations as well as danceclubs, providing a touchstone for the style known as hip-house. After leaping several hurdles—vicious rumours about his personal life and the legal action of Maze's Frankie Beverly after Base sampled Maze on his hit "Joy and Pain"—he responded in 1989 with *The Incredible Base*. None of the singles on his second album had the force of "It Takes Two," however, and Rob Base was largely forgotten several years later.

Born Robert Ginyard in Harlem, Rob Base began performing with a group called the Sureshot Seven in fifth grade. By the time of high school graduation, the only members left were Base and DJ E-Z Rock (b. Roney Bryce, Harlem, NY). The duo began recording, and their first single, "DJ Interview," appeared on the World to World label. They had gained a distribution deal with Profile by 1987. The first Profile release, the title-track single from their debut album *It Takes Two*, became a street sensation upon its release in mid-1988. Though the single just barely reached the R&B Top 20 and Pop Top 40, massive club airplay enhanced its impact considerably. Both the single and album eventually went platinum, and Rob Base & DJ E-Z Rock gained Single of the Year honors both in *Spin* and *The Village Voice*. The second single, "Get on the Dance Floor," continued Base's dance appeal, and his excellent rapping helped him retain his street credentials.

By the end of 1989, however, Rob Base was on his own; his only explanation for the disappearance of DJ E-Z Rock was "personal problems." The release of *The Incredible Base* in 1989 was a bit of a comedown; despite several interesting tracks—including a reworking of Edwin Starr's "War"—neither the album nor any singles connected with listeners. *—John Bush*

● **It Takes Two** / 1988 / Profile ✦✦✦✦
Without question, Rob Base & D.J. E-Z Rock had the party anthem of 1988 in "It Takes Two"—an insanely infectious rap/dance gem using a James Brown/Lyn Collins classic of the same name as a reference point. While the song was a major hit in dance music and club circles, Base won over hip-hop's hardcore with his strong technique as a rapper. Though most of this debut album falls short of that mega-hit's excellence, it's a generally decent effort that has both hip-hop and R&B appeal. A reflection on societal breakdown, the sobering "Times Are Gettin' Ill" is atypical of this album, which favors soul-flavored party music over social and political commentary. From Maze's "Joy & Pain" (which the duo used without Frankie Beverly's permission, inspiring him to threaten legal action) to the house-influenced "Get on the Dance Floor," *It Takes Two* thrives on strong hooks and unapologetic escapism. *—Alex Henderson*

The Incredible Base / Nov. 1989 / Profile ✦✦✦
Rob Base had parted company with DJ E-Z Rock by the time he recorded his second album, *The Incredible Base*, but his approach didn't change significantly. The New Yorker still favored party music over social or political commentary, and managed to appeal to both hardcore hip-hoppers and R&B fans who weren't necessarily big rap supporters. Though nothing here is in a class with the first album's unforgettable title song, this CD definitely has its strong points. On "War," Base samples Edwin Starr's Motown classic, not to make a political statement, but to question the feuds that were so prevalent in rap in the late '80s and early '90s. "If You Really Want to Party," "Turn It Out (Go Base)" and "Get Up and Have a Good Time" won't win any awards for profound lyrics, but they function quite well on the dance floor. Like so many rappers, Base couldn't count on longevity; by the mid-'90s, his popularity had faded considerably. *—Alex Henderson*

Break of Dawn / Sep. 13, 1994 / Warlock ✦✦

The Basement Wall

f. 1966, Baton Rouge, LA, **db.** 1968
Garage Rock
One of the more pop-oriented '60s garage bands, this Baton Rouge, LA, group had a big regional hit with "Never Existed" in 1967. Their sound contained elements of Texas punk; the bouncing Farfisa organ style of the Five Americans; and British Invasion harmonies. Likeable, if not terribly significant, they disbanded in 1968, and much of their unreleased material was issued in the mid-'80s. *—Richie Unterberger*

Incredible Sound Of . . . / 1985 / Cicadelic ✦✦✦
The documentation on this album is sketchy, but apparently many of these 14 songs were previously unissued. This competent punk-pop material spans 1966-1968. Ronnie Weiss of the fine Texas band Mouse & The Traps (whose "A Public Execution" was included on *Nuggets*) plays lead guitar on "Never Existed." *—Richie Unterberger*

Fontella Bass

b. Jul. 3, 1940, St. Louis, MO
Piano, Vocals / Soul
An explosive gospel and soul singer, Fontella Bass is the daughter of the great vocalist Martha Bass and sister of David Peaston, as well as ex-wife

of Art Ensemble of Chicago trumpeter Lester Bowie. But none of that family history means as much as her own skills, which include a tremendous voice, great range, and distinctive delivery. Bass, who is also a fine pianist and organist, sang in several church choirs, as her mother was a member of Clara Ward's gospel troupe. She later moved into R&B, singing in Oliver Sain's band and working with Little Milton in the early '60s. Bass teamed with Bobby McClure for two duets on Checker in 1965. "Don't Mess Up a Good Thing" reached No. 5 on the R&B charts and inched into the pop Top 30, while "You'll Miss Me When I'm Gone" got into the R&B Top 30. Bass' debut single as a solo act was her greatest; "Rescue Me" topped the R&B charts for a month, peaked at No. 4 on the pop charts, and was among the era's finest soul singles. The follow-up, "Recovery," was better than it has been credited, and reached No. 13. Bass never again attained soul stardom, but she has remained busy in the ensuing years. She later sang with Bowie's group, the Art Ensemble of Chicago, and was featured on the LP *Les Stances a Sophie*. She has also been part of the gospel group From the Root to the Source and has reunited with Bowie on occasional projects. —*Ron Wynn*

● **Rescued: The Best of Fontella Bass** / Mar. 10, 1992 / Chess ✦✦✦✦
"Rescue Me" might have been her only big hit, but Fontella Bass was a terrific gospel-influenced soul vocalist who cut several great sides for Checker/Chess Records in the mid-'60s. They might not have gotten the attention they deserved when they were released, but they have held up very well over the years. *Rescued: The Best of Fontella Bass* collects 16 of her finest tracks, including "Rescue Me," three duets with Bobby McClure, and a previously unreleased song; it makes a convincing case that she should have had more hit singles than she did. —*Stephen Thomas Erlewine*

The Bats

f. 1982, Christchurch, New Zealand
Alternative Pop-Rock
One of the shining stars of the fertile Flying Nun record label in New Zealand, the Bats were formed in 1982 in Christchurch by guitarist/vocalist Robert Scott from the Clean, bassist Paul Kean (ex-Toy Love), drummer Malcolm Grant (ex-Builders), and vocalist/multi-instrumentalist Kaye Woodward. With their fresh take on garagey folk-rock that flirts with power-pop, the band quickly became critics' favorites in the late '80s. After two generally overlooked (except by critics and specialists) albums for Communion Records, they signed to Mammoth Records in 1991, gaining only slightly more mainstream exposure. The Bats disbanded for 18 months in the mid-'90s, when Robert Scott rejoined the Clean for a reunion tour and album, but reformed in 1995, releasing their sixth album, *Couchmaster*, in the fall. —*Chris Woodstra*

Compiletely Bats / 1987 / Flying Nun ✦✦✦✦
Compiletely Bats collects the band's early output, including some non-LP rarities. —*Chris Woodstra*

● **Daddy's Highway** / 1987 / Communion ✦✦✦✦
The Bats' full-length debut immediately endears itself with the band's offbeat, at times frantic, version of jangly folk-rock with charmingly off-kilter harmonies. Robert Scott's effortless melodies and catchy hooks give an overall upbeat feeling despite a decidedly melancholy subject matter. —*Chris Woodstra*

The Law of Things / 1990 / Communion ✦✦✦
The Law of Things is essentially *Daddy's Highway, Part 2*, displaying their update on '60s pop sensibility in full force. The production is slightly slicker, but the songs continue in the same tradition that made the first album endlessly enjoyable. —*Chris Woodstra*

Fear of God / 1991 / Mammoth ✦✦✦
Though a bit redundant after the first two albums, *Fear of God* finds Robert Scott continuing his craftsmanlike songwriting without fail. The songs are perfect slices of pop, even if they aren't particularly memorable this time out. —*Chris Woodstra*

Silverbeet / Dec. 1992 / Mammoth ✦✦✦
"Courage," "Sighting the Sound," "No Time for Your Kind," "Half Way to Nowhere"—all heady songs delivered at power-pop pace with such overwhelming resolve as to leave the listener almost woozy . . . like OD'ing on midway rides after downing too much cotton candy. The Bats offer an occasional change of pace, such as the hypnotizing "Stay Away" and the doleful "Valley Floor." Soaring and somber, moody and frenetic, *Silverbeet* is not your usual confectionary. But let this stuff seep in for a few listens and you may find yourself converted. —*Roch Parisien*

Spill the Beans / Jul. 12, 1994 / Mammoth ✦✦

Couchmaster / Oct. 24, 1995 / Mammoth ✦✦✦

Bauhaus

f. 1978, Northampton, Northamptonshire, En, **db**. Jul. 5, 1983
Alternative Pop-Rock, Goth-Rock, Post-Punk
Bauhaus are the founding fathers of goth-rock, creating a minimalistic,

overbearingly gloomy style of post-punk rock driven by jagged guitar chords and cold, distant synthesizers. Throughout their brief career, the band explored all the variations on their bleak musical ideas, adding elements of glam rock, experimental electronic rock, funk, and heavy metal. While their following has never expanded beyond a cult, they kept their cult alive well into the '90s, a full decade after they disbanded.

The group formed in 1978 in Northampton, England. Guitarist/vocalist Daniel Ash, bassist/vocalist David Jay (born David Jay Haskins), and drummer Kevin Haskins had played together as a trio called the Craze before forming Bauhaus with vocalist Peter Murphy. Originally, the band was called Bauhaus 1919 after the German art movement; by 1979, they had dropped the 1919 from their name.

In August 1979 the group released their debut single, "Bela Lugosi's Dead," on the independent Small Wonder Records. Although it did not make the pop charts, it became the de facto goth-rock anthem, staying in the UK independent charts for years. Three months later, the group signed with Beggars Banquet's subsidiary label, 4AD. The group's second single, "Dark Entries," was released in January 1980. After their first European tour, Bauhaus released their third single, "Terror Couple Kill Colonel," in the summer of that year; it became a hit on the indie charts.

After touring America for the first time in September, the group released a version of T. Rex' "Telegram Sam." In October they released their debut album, *In the Flat Field*, which reached No. 1 on the independent charts and No. 72 on the pop charts. The success of the album led to their first hits on the pop charts; both "Kick in the Eye" and "The Passion of Lovers" made the UK Top 60 in 1981. In October they released their second album, *Mask*, which revealed a more ambitious musical direction; the new direction, which featured elements of metal and electronic sonic textures, made the music more accessible without abandoning the dark, foreboding core. *Mask* was a commercial success, peaking at No. 30 on the UK charts.

In March 1982 Bauhaus released the EP *Searching for Satori*, which reached No. 45 on the UK charts; another successful single, "Spirit," followed in the summer. That fall, the group had a No. 15 hit with their version of David Bowie's "Ziggy Stardust." The success of the single propelled their third album, *The Sky's Gone Out*, to No. 4 on the album charts.

Peter Murphy contracted pneumonia at the beginning of 1983, which prevented him from participating in the recording sessions for Bauhaus' fourth album, *Burning from the Inside*. Consequently, the record featured substantial contributions from Daniel Ash and David Jay, who both pursued more personal and atmospheric directions. After Murphy recovered, the band toured Japan and then returned to the UK to promote the summer release of *Burning from the Inside*. The album was another hit, peaking at No. 13. In July Bauhaus split up.

After Bauhaus' breakup, Murphy formed Dali's Car with Japan's Mick Karn and then pursued a solo career. Ash continued with Tones on Tail, a project he began in 1981; Kevin Haskins also joined the band after Bauhaus' split. David Jay made some solo records and joined the Jazz Butcher briefly. Ash, Haskins, and Jay formed Love and Rockets in 1985 after a proposed Bauhaus reunion fell apart because Peter Murphy wasn't interested in the project. —*Stephen Thomas Erlewine*

In the Flat Field / Dec. 1980 / 4AD/Beggars Banquet ✦✦✦
It captures the brooding bleakness of early Bauhaus. —*David Szatmary*

Mask / Oct. 1981 / Beggars Banquet ✦✦✦
In this follow-up to *In the Flat Field*, Bauhaus matures by creating an album that stands on its own rather than a collection of scattered hits strung together with not-so-strong fillers. Feedback-driven looped guitars, fuzz bass, and Peter Murphy's ever-haunting, commanding vocals help to create their best album. More raw than their later material, yet nicely refined next to their first, it includes "The Passion of Lovers" and "Kick in the Eye." —*Julian Katz*

The Sky's Gone Out / Oct. 1982 / A&M ✦✦✦
An upbeat, commercially successful Bauhaus album (No. 4 in the UK). It includes a remake of Bowie's "Ziggy Stardust" and a three-part mini-opera, "The Three Shadows." —*David Szatmary*

Burning from the Inside / Jul. 1983 / A&M ✦✦✦✦
During the recording sessions for Bauhaus' final album, *Burning from the Inside*, Peter Murphy suffered from pneumonia, leaving David J and Daniel Ash to complete most of the record themselves. The result is the band's most pop-oriented album; it's also their best, even if it is slightly incohesive. —*Stephen Thomas Erlewine*

● **Singles: 1979-1983** / Nov. 1985 / Beggars Banquet ✦✦✦✦
Essentially, Bauhaus was a singles band—all of their best moments were individual songs, not entire albums. And the double-disc *The Singles 1979-1983* collects them all, including some B-sides and album tracks, making it the one essential Bauhaus purchase. —*Stephen Thomas Erlewine*

Swing the Heartache: The BBC Sessions / Jul. 1989 / Beggars Banquet ✦✦✦✦
This is a posthumous collection of five sessions on English BBC, some

from John Peel's famous show, on which Bauhaus abandoned hits such as "Bela Lugosi" and "Dark Entries" to experiment with different songs and revamp certain prereleased material. The loose, live-recorded format suits this group, whose creative and skilled musicianship is highlighted on this recording. "God in an Alcove" and "Swing the Heartache" are rendered much better here.—*Julian Katz*

Bay City Rollers

f. 1967, Edinburgh, Scotland, **db.** 1978
Power Pop, Pop-Rock, Bubblegum
The Bay City Rollers were a Scottish pop-rock band of the '70s with a strong following among teenage girls. The origins of the group go back to the formation of the duo the Longmuir Brothers in the late '60s, consisting of drummer Derek Longmuir (b. Mar. 19, 1952, Edinburgh, Scotland) and his bass-playing brother Alan (b. June 20, 1953, Edinburgh). They eventually changed their name to Saxon, adding singer Nobby Clarke and John Devine. Then they changed their name again by pointing at random to a spot on a map of the United States: Bay City, MI. Their first hit was a cover of the Gentrys' "Keep On Dancing," which reached No. 9 in the UK in September 1971. In June 1972, guitarist Eric Faulkner (b. Oct. 21, 1954, Edinburgh) joined. In January 1973, singer Leslie McKeown (b. Nov. 12, 1955, Edinburgh), and guitarist Stuart Wood (b. Feb. 25, 1957, Edinburgh) replaced Clarke and Devine, stabilizing the quintet's lineup.

After flopping with three singles, they finally hit the Top Ten again in February 1974 with a cover of the Shangri-Las' "Remember (Walking in the Sand)." At this point, the Rollers became a teen sensation in Great Britain, with their good looks and tartan knickers, and they scored a series of Top Ten UK hits over the next two and a half years: "Shang-a-Lang," "Summerlove Sensation," "All of Me Loves All of You," "Bye Bye Baby" (a cover of the Four Seasons hit that went to No. 1), "Give a Little Love" (another No. 1), "Money Honey," "Love Me like I Love You," and "I Only Wanna Be with You" (a cover of the Dusty Springfield hit). Their albums *Rollin'*, *Once upon a Star*, *Wouldn't You Like It*, and *Dedication* were also Top Ten successes, with *Rollin'* and *Once upon a Star* getting to No. 1. They scored their first US hit with "Saturday Night," which was released in September 1975 and hit No. 1 in January 1976. It was followed by the Top Ten hits "Money Honey" and "You Made Me Believe in Magic." The Rollers also had five straight gold albums in the US: *Bay City Rollers*, *Rock 'n' Roll Love Letter*, *Dedication*, *It's a Game*, and *Greatest Hits*.

Alan Longmuir left the band in June 1976 and was replaced by Ian Mitchell (b. Aug. 22, 1958, Downpatrick, County Down, Northern Ireland) who was in turn replaced by Pat McGlynn (b. Mar. 31, 1958, Edinburgh) in June 1977. Longmuir returned in 1978, the same year that McKeown was replaced by Duncan Faure and Faulkner quit to go solo. But by then the Bay City Rollers had scored their last hits. — *William Ruhlmann*

● **Greatest Hits** / Nov. 1977 / Arista ✦✦✦✦
The Bay City Rollers never got their fair shake as a "legitimate" band, and this ten-track, no-frills collection proves it. Although it collects only their biggest, most overexposed hits, when removed from the hype, the Rollers' music has an enduring innocence and charm with enough catchy hooks and pure pop melodies to compete with other power-pop bands of the era. — *Chris Woodstra*

The Beach Boys

f. 1961, Hawthorne, CA
Rock 'n' Roll, Surf, Pop-Rock
The Beach Boys are the most successful and important American band of the rock music era. They were formed in 1961 in Hawthorne, CA, around the three Wilson brothers: Brian (b. June 20, 1942) (bass, piano, vocals), Dennis (b. Dec. 4, 1944–d. Dec. 28, 1983) (drums, vocals), and Carl (b. Dec. 21, 1946) (guitar, vocals). Additional members were Mike Love (b. Mar. 15, 1941) (vocals), the Wilsons' cousin, and Al Jardine (b. Sept. 3, 1942) (guitar, vocals). From the start, the focus of the group's music was Brian Wilson, who combined a fascination with vocal harmony in the Four Freshmen mold with a love of Chuck Berry-derived rock 'n' roll. Added to that was the subject matter of middle-class teenage life in Southern California—surfing, cars, and girls.

The result was massive popular success for the group during the first half of the 1960s, starting with their first chart entry, "Surfin'," in 1962. "Surfin' " was released on a local record label. Subsequently, the group signed to the major label Capitol Records, where they stayed for the rest of the '60s. But their early recordings have continued to turn up on one discount label after another ever since. To date, the most complete and best-quality version of the material is to be found on the 1991 DCC album *Lost and Found! (1961-62)*.

The Beach Boys' first Capitol single, "Surfin' Safari," was released in June 1962 and became their first Top 40 hit. It was followed in October by a debut album of the same name. Similarly, in March 1963, Capitol

released the single "Surfin' USA," which became the group's first Top Ten hit, and the *Surfin' USA* album, which went gold. They followed in July with "Surfer Girl," another Top Ten, and in September with a gold-selling *Surfer Girl* LP.

By this point, Brian Wilson, who was composing nearly all of the material (with lyrics by himself, Love, and others), had taken over production of the group's records as well. Given the accelerated recording schedule of the day, it was an awesome task when coupled with his onstage performing duties. This is illustrated by the release of the Beach Boys' fourth album, the million-selling *Little Deuce Coupe*, less than a month after *Surfer Girl*. The album featured a version of their latest Top Ten hit, "Be True to Your School."

The Beach Boys dominated the pop music of 1963, but in early 1964, the Beatles arrived in the US, followed by the rest of the British Invasion, and the Beach Boys felt the competition keenly. Unlike most American recording artists, however, the group did not suffer a drop-off in popularity. In fact, 1964 was another banner year for the Beach Boys, with the Top Ten singles "Fun, Fun, Fun," "When I Grow Up (To Be a Man)," and "Dance, Dance, Dance," as well as their first No. 1 single, the gold-selling "I Get Around," and three more gold albums, *Shut Down, Vol. 2* (*Vol. 1* had been a various artists album), *All Summer Long*, and their first No. 1 LP, *Beach Boys Concert*. (There was also a Beach Boys' *Christmas Album*.)

The strain of all that work caught up with Brian Wilson, however, and at the end of 1964, he retired from onstage work with the Beach Boys, retaining his composing and producing duties. The group eventually settled on Bruce Johnston (b. June 24, 1944) as his replacement.

The first product of this arrangement was the March 1965 album *The Beach Boys Today!*, which contained a version of their next No. 1 single, "Help Me, Rhonda," followed four months later by the group's eighth straight gold album, *Summer Days (And Summer Nights!!)* and its single, the Top Ten "California Girls." Such recordings gave evidence of the expansion of Brian Wilson's musical imagination, which found him taking longer to make records that were more ambitious than the group's early teen anthems.

While Wilson prepared his next opus, Capitol's release schedule was satisfied by *The Beach Boys' Party!* album, released in September, featuring a hit cover of "Barbara Ann." In March 1966 Wilson released "Caroline, No," which was billed as a solo single and made the Top 40. But he did not launch a full-fledged solo career at this time, instead completing the group's *Pet Sounds* LP (May 1966), which featured the Top Ten hits "Sloop John B" and "Wouldn't It Be Nice" and was universally hailed as one of the greatest rock albums of all time, though it did not sell as well as Beach Boys albums usually did.

Wilson trumped it with the No. 1 gold single "Good Vibrations," released in October. By this point, he was being hailed in the media as a genius as he prepared a new album tentatively titled *Smile*. The album never appeared, however. A single, "Heroes and Villains" (July 1967), offered tantalizing clues to what would become a legendary unheard, unfinished masterpiece. But Brian Wilson, whether because of the pressure to top himself and compete with the Beatles and others, internal disagreements within the group, psychological problems, or drug abuse, ceded leadership of the Beach Boys. Their next album, *Smiley Smile* (September 1967), was produced by the group as a whole.

At the same time, the Beach Boys suffered a commercial decline, and though they continued to release new albums—*Wild Honey* (December 1967), *Friends* (June 1968), *20/20* (February 1969)—and singles through the end of the decade, they ceased to be an important force in popular music. In 1970 the group switched to the Reprise subsidiary of Warner Bros. Records for a series of albums that sometimes drew critical approval without restoring their commercial appeal—*Sunflower* (August 1970), *Surf's Up* (August 1971), *Carl and the Passions: So Tough* (May 1972), initially packaged with a reissue of *Pet Sounds*, and *Holland* (January 1973).

The Beach Boys returned to prominence in the mid-'70s on a wave of nostalgia and a potent concert act that focused on their early hits. Capitol Records had repackaged their catalogue repeatedly, but *Endless Summer*, a June 1974 double LP compiling their early-'60s work, amazingly topped the charts, becoming their first gold album in seven years. In July 1976 the Beach Boys released *15 Big Ones*, their first new studio album in more than three years and their first album in a decade to credit Brian Wilson as producer. The album spawned a Top Ten hit in a cover of Chuck Berry's "Rock and Roll Music," but the group's commercial appeal, at least as far as new recordings, was temporary. Subsequent albums *The Beach Boys Love You* (April 1977) and *M.I.U. Album* (September 1978) sold less well. Brian Wilson's "comeback" also proved elusive after 1977.

The Beach Boys moved to their third major label with the release of *L.A. (Light Album)* on the Caribou subsidiary of CBS Records in March 1979. But neither that album nor its follow-up, *Keepin' the Summer Alive* (March 1980), did anything to change the group's commercial status. In December 1983 Dennis Wilson drowned. In June 1985 the group returned with *The Beach Boys*, their first new album in five years, which marked the end of their Caribou contract.

The Beach Boys recorded sporadically thereafter. In 1987 they scored a surprising hit cover of "Wipeout," co-billed with rap act the Fat Boys. In 1988, minus Brian Wilson, who finally launched a solo career, they returned to No. 1 with "Kokomo," from the hit film *Cocktail*. In 1992 they released their first new album in seven years, *Summer in Paradise*.

Especially with the dawn of the CD era, the extensive repackagings of Beach Boys material have continued apace. The year 1993 finally brought a five-CD boxed-set retrospective, *Good Vibrations: Thirty Years of the Beach Boys*. In 1995, after the resolution of various legal issues, lead singer Mike Love and Brian Wilson began working together again, but the partnership was quickly derailed by various tensions, and Wilson began collaborating with Van Dyke Parks and working on a new solo album. The next year, the Beach Boys released a collection of duets with country artists titled *Stars and Stripes, Vol. 1*, and there were plans for a box set chronicling the Pet Sounds sessions, but the compilation was delayed by disagreements within the Beach Boys camp. — *William Ruhlmann*

Surfin' Safari / Oct. 29, 1962 / Capitol ♦♦

The Beach Boys' debut album, recorded in an era in which little was expected of rock groups in the way of strong LP-length statements, is mostly thin and awkward in both songwriting and production. The title track, their first true smash, is great, as is its flipside ("409"), which was not only a hit in its own right, but was the first vocal hot rod classic. "Surfin," their debut single (and small national hit), is also good, and one of the few Beach Boys tracks that could be said to have a garage-like quality. Unfortunately, most of the other cuts (most of which are group originals) are sub-standard ditties, as Brian Wilson had a way to go in honing his compositional genius. It does, however, afford a glimpse of the group as they sounded when they were a true *band* in the studio, before most of their parts were played by session musicians. Two of the better cuts, "The Shift" and the instrumental "Moon Dawg," have a grittier-than-usual surf-rock base that would flower on 1963 hits like "Surfin' USA." A 1990 Capitol CD combines this and *Surfin' USA* on one disc, with the addition of three rare bonus cuts from the same era. (Note: In 1990 Capitol reissued all of the Beach Boys' 1960s albums in such "two-fer" packages that offered excellent value, adding rare/unreleased additional material and lengthy liner notes. These are now deleted and getting hard to find, but are infinitely preferable to the unadorned single-album reissues now in the catalog. Stick with the 1990 CD two-fers, if you can locate them.) — *Richie Unterberger*

Surfin' U.S.A. / Mar. 25, 1963 / Capitol ♦♦♦♦

The real breakthrough, as Brian Wilson asserts himself in the studio as both songwriter and arranger on a set of material that was much stronger than *Surfin' Safari*. Besides the hit title track and its popular dragracing flipside ("Shut Down"), this has a lovely, heartbreaking ballad ("Lonely Sea") and a couple of strong Brian Wilson originals ("The Noble Surfer" and "Farmer's Daughter"). There are also five instrumentals that demonstrate that, before session musicians took over most of the parts, the Beach Boys could play respectably gutsy surf-rock as a self-contained unit. Indeed, the album as a whole is the best they would make, prior to the late '60s, as a band that played most of their instruments, rather than as a vehicle for Brian Wilson's ideas. The LP was a huge hit, vital to launching surf music as a national craze, and one of the few truly strong records to be recorded by a self-contained American rock band before the British Invasion. A 1990 Capitol CD combines this and *Surfin' Safari* on one disc, with the addition of three rare bonus cuts from the same era. — *Richie Unterberger*

Surfer Girl / Sep. 23, 1963 / Capitol ♦♦♦

Capitol pushed the Beach Boys for too much material in too short a time for the group to maintain as much quality control as would have been desirable. Consequently, most of their pre-1965 albums contain a high degree of filler, and thus stack up poorly next to those of such contemporaries as the Beatles, who were able to maintain high standards on almost all of their LP tracks. *Surfer Girl* does have some great tunes, including the title song, the hot rod ditty "Little Deuce Coupe," and "Catch a Wave" (which could have been a substantial hit single on its own merits). Most significant of all is the gorgeous ballad "In My Room," which anticipated future Beach Boys releases both in its sophisticated production (strings, organ, dense harmonies) and its personal, solipsistic lyrics. The rest is surprisingly mediocre filler, especially as at this point they were restricting their lyrical themes to beach culture almost exclusively; "Your Summer Dream," with its unusual harmonies, is about the most interesting of the obscure tracks. If you're not a dedicated Beach Boys fan, though, you should pass, as you can find the first-rate tracks on best-of anthologies. A 1990 Capitol CD combines this and *Shut Down, Vol. 2* on one disc, adding the 45 version of "Fun, Fun, Fun," a German version of "In My Room," and the previously unreleased Brian Wilson composition "I Do." — *Richie Unterberger*

Little Deuce Coupe / Oct. 21, 1963 / Capitol ♦♦

Little Deuce Coupe was a concept album of sorts, in that most of the songs had something to do with cars and hot rod culture. That's a pretty thin train of thought to sustain for most of a record. What's worse, by the Beach Boys' own standards of hot rod tunes, most of the tracks are pretty trite and unimaginative, rating among their worst early material. Not only that, the three best cuts—"Little Deuce Coupe," "409," and "Shut Down"—had already been issued on LP. The most noteworthy of the other tracks was the Top Ten hit "Be True to Your School," whose fine tune and arrangement are marred by breathtakingly sappy lyrics of faith and loyalty to one's high school. (The album version, oddly, is different from the superior single, which had the Honeys adding female cheerleader chants.) "Spirit of America" and "A Young Man Is Gone" (a James Dean tribute with Four Freshmen-style vocals) are moderately interesting, but on the whole this is probably the worst early Beach Boys album, with the possible exception of *Surfin' Safari* (and their 1964 Christmas LP, which doesn't really count). A 1990 Capitol CD combines this and *All Summer Long* on one disc, adding the 45 version of "Be True to Your School," alternate takes of "Little Honda" and "Don't Back Down," and the previously unreleased "All Dressed Up for School." — *Richie Unterberger*

Shut Down, Vol. 2 / Mar. 23, 1964 / Capitol ♦♦♦

Another erratic early album from the Beach Boys; few other rock LPs have such a wide gap between the best and worst material. On the good side, you have absolute classics in the Chuck Berryish "Fun, Fun, Fun," and its superb B-side, "Don't Worry Baby," one of the most advanced pop productions of 1964 with its breathtaking harmonies and unusual lyric. "The Warmth of the Sun" is one of the most melodic (and melancholic) ballads they ever recorded, and "Why Do Fools Fall in Love" is one of their best oldies covers. Yet the rest reduces the oceanic scale of the classics to dishwater, whether they're throwaway hot rod tunes and instrumentals, innocuous high school romantic ditties, or a soulless cover of "Louie Louie." When this album hit the racks in early 1964, the Beatles were proving that you could make LPs that were all killer, no filler; the Beach Boys would soon be forced to up their ante. A 1990 Capitol CD combines this and *Surfer Girl* on one disc, adding the 45 version of "Fun, Fun, Fun," a German version of "In My Room," and the previously unreleased Brian Wilson composition "I Do." — *Richie Unterberger*

All Summer Long / Jul. 13, 1964 / Capitol ♦♦♦

The best pre-1965 Beach Boys album featured their brilliant No. 1 single "I Get Around," as well as other standout cuts in the beautifully sad "Wendy," "Little Honda" (one of their best hot rod tunes, covered by the Hondells for a hit), and their remake of the late-'50s doo-wop classic "Hushabye." The nostalgic "All Summer Long," another great production, seemed (whether intentionally or not) like a sort of farewell to the frivolous California beach culture that had supplied the lyrical grist for most of their music up to this point, with a longing, regretful chorus that was totally at odds with the bouncy arrangement. Other relatively little-known treasures are the sumptuous ballad "Girls on the Beach," with some of their best early harmonizing, and "Don't Back Down," with uncommonly anxious lyrics. You can't give a high rating, however, to an album that also contained such disposable filler as the "Our Favorite Recording Sessions" comedy bit and "Do You Remember?," a "let's-pay-tribute-to-rock's-early-days" number with a shit-eating grin wide enough to qualify as an oldies radio ID jingle. A 1990 Capitol CD combines this and *Little Deuce Coupe* on one disc, adding the 45 version of "Be True to Your School," alternate takes of "Little Honda" and "Don't Back Down," and the previously unreleased "All Dressed Up for School." — *Richie Unterberger*

The Beach Boys Concert / Oct. 19, 1964 / Capitol ♦♦

Recorded live in Sacramento in 1964, the Beach Boys run through several of their big early hits and a batch of covers that hadn't made it to record. The screaming, while not at a *Beatles at Hollywood Bowl* level, is loud enough to present a real problem as far as sonic clarity, especially given that the instruments aren't recorded too well, either. Even more crucially, the Beach Boys simply didn't play nearly as well onstage as on record, at least at this concert; the arrangements are thin, and the playing and singing are ragged, though the group is enthusiastic. None of this stopped it from becoming one of their biggest sellers; in fact, in topped the charts for four weeks, at the height of the British Invasion. It's also of interest in that it has several covers that they didn't release as studio recordings in the '60s, including "Johnny B. Goode," Jan & Dean's "The Little Old Lady from Pasadena," the dorky "Long Tall Texan," "Monster Mash," the Four Freshmen's "Graduation Day," and the Rivington's goofy doo wop raveup, "Papa-Oom-Mow-Mow." Everyone other than major Beach Boys fans should give it a miss. A 1990 Capitol CD combines this and *Live in London* (1968 live material that has also, confusingly, been issued as *Beach Boys '69*) on one disc, adding previously unreleased live versions of "Don't Worry Baby" (from 1964) and "Heroes and Villains" (from 1967). — *Richie Unterberger*

The Beach Boys Today! / Mar. 8, 1965 / Capitol ✦✦✦✦
Brian Wilson's retirement from performing to concentrate on studio recording and production reaped immediate dividends with *Today!*, the first Beach Boys album that is strong almost from start to finish. "Dance, Dance, Dance" and "Do You Wanna Dance" were upbeat hits with Spector-influenced arrangements, but Wilson began to deal with more sophisticated themes on another smash 45, "When I Grow Up," on which these eternal teenagers looked forward to the advancing years with fear and uncertainty. Surf/hot rod/beach themes were permanently retired in favor of late adolescent-early adult romance on this album, which included such decent outings in this vein as "She Knows Me Too Well," "Kiss Me Baby," and "In the Back of My Mind." The true gem is "Please Let Me Wonder," one of the group's most delicate mid-'60s works, with heartbreaking melodies and harmonies. Be aware that the version of "Help Me, Rhonda" found here is an inferior, earlier, and slower rendition; the familiar hit single take was on their next album, *Summer Days and Summer Nights*. A 1990 Capitol CD combines this and *Summer Days and Summer Nights* on one disc, adding alternate takes of "Dance, Dance, Dance," "I'm So Young," and "Let Him Run Wild," as well as a previously unreleased studio version of "Graduation Day." Most significantly, it also adds the non-LP single from late '65, "The Little Girl I Once Knew," which looked forward to *Pet Sounds* in its studio experimentation and lyrical themes. *—Richie Unterberger*

Summer Days (And Summer Nights!!) / Jul. 5, 1965 / Capitol ✦✦✦✦
Summer Days and Summer Nights was a bit of regression from the success of *Today*, lapsing into that distressing division between first-rate cuts and lightweight also-rans that characterized their pre-'65 albums. The difference is that the very best tracks were operating on a more sophisticated level than the '62-64 classics. "Help Me, Rhonda" was a No. 1 single and would be their last Top 40 exercise in sheer fun for a while. More impressive was "California Girls," with its symphonic arrangement, glorious harmonies, and archetypal statement of California lifestyle. On the other hand, subpar efforts like "Amusement Park USA." and "Salt Lake City," throwbacks to the emptyheaded summer filler of previous days, will necessitate that the CD remote button remain close at hand. The covers of "The Girl from New York City" and "Then I Kissed Her" are well done, but don't break new ground. Yet a couple of cuts are among their essential LP-only efforts. "Let Him Run Wild" is a soulful ballad with a great Brian Wilson falsetto vocal. "Girl Don't Tell Me," with its gorgeous melody, fine lead vocal debut from Carl Wilson, and subtle depiction of romantic rejection and disappointment, may be *the* best obscure pre-*Pet Sounds* Beach Boys track. A 1990 Capitol CD combines this and *The Beach Boys Today!* on one disc, adding alternate takes of "Dance, Dance, Dance," "I'm So Young," and "Let Him Run Wild," as well as a previously unreleased studio version of "Graduation Day." Most significantly, it also adds the non-LP single from late '65, "The Little Girl I Once Knew," which looked forward to *Pet Sounds* in its studio experimentation and lyrical themes. *—Richie Unterberger*

The Beach Boys Party! / Nov. 8, 1965 / Capitol ✦✦✦
Capitol, which had already released ten Beach Boys albums in three years, was bugging the group for product that it could release in time for the 1965 Christmas season. To buy time while Brian Wilson began conceiving the *Pet Sounds* masterpiece, the group issued a set of covers, mostly of the '50s rock and R&B they had listened to as schoolboys. Packaged as if it had been recorded at an actual party, it was in fact recorded in the studio, with friends and romantic partners adding sounds and vocals to create an informal atmosphere. With the exception of a bass guitar, all the instruments are acoustic; the acoustic guitar-and-bongo arrangements, in fact, give this a hootenanny campfire feel. In recent years, this album has gone up a few notches in critical esteem, praised for its loose, casual feel and insight into the group's influences. Realisically, though, its present-day appeal lies mostly with dedicated fans of the group, as fun and engaging as it is. Others will find the material shopworn in places, and the presentation too corny. It does have the massive hit "Barbara Ann," which actually features Dean Torrence (of Jan & Dean) on lead vocals; other highlights include "Mountain of Love," an unexpected version of "The Times They Are a-Changin'," and *three* Beatles covers. A 1990 Capitol CD combines this and *Stack-o-Tracks* on one disc, adding three previously unreleased backing tracks to the *Stack-o-Tracks* half of the program. *—Richie Unterberger*

☆ **Pet Sounds** / May 16, 1966 / Capitol ✦✦✦✦✦
The best Beach Boys album, and one of the best of the 1960s. The group here reached a whole new level in terms of both composition and production, layering tracks upon tracks of vocals and instruments to create a richly symphonic sound. Conventional keyboards and guitars were combined with exotic touches of orchestrated strings, bicycle bells, buzzing organs, harpsichords, flutes, the Theremin, Hawaiian-sounding string instruments, Coca-Cola cans, barking dogs, and more. It wouldn't have been a classic without great songs, and this has some of the group's most stunning melodies, as well as lyrical themes that evoke both the intensity of newly-born love affairs and the disappointment of failed

romance (add some general statements about loss of innocence and modern-day confusion as well). The spiritual quality of the material is enhanced by some of the most gorgeous upper-register male vocals (especially by Brian and Carl Wilson) ever heard on a rock record. "Wouldn't It Be Nice," "God Only Knows," "Caroline, No," and "Sloop John B" (the last of which wasn't originally intended to go on the album) are the well-known hits, but equally worthy are such cuts as "You Still Believe in Me," "Don't Talk," "I Know There's An Answer," and "I Just Wasn't Made for These Times." It's often said that this is more of a Brian Wilson album than a Beach Boys recording (session musicians played most of the parts), but it should be noted that the harmonies are pure Beach Boys (and some of their best). Massively influential upon its release (although it was a relatively low seller compared to their previous LPs), it immediately vaulted the band into the top level of rock innovators among the intelligentsia, especially in Britain, where it was a much bigger hit. The CD reissue adds a few interesting but inessential outtakes. *—Richie Unterberger*

Smile / 1967 / [Bootleg] ✦✦✦
In 1966 Brian Wilson began work on the *Smile* LP, which was intended as the ultimate pop/progressive/psychedelic record. Many vocal and instrumental tracks were recorded, but the project was abandoned in 1967 due to accumulated pressures from Wilson's family, fellow Beach Boys, and the record company, combined with Brian's own fragile and sensitive ego. In the ensuing years, *Smile* was accorded status as the most legendary unreleased album of all time, although the record was in fact never close to being finished. Many, though by no means all, of the tracks in progress were bootlegged in the 1980s; many, though by no means all, of these, in turn, finally surfaced on Capitol's *Good Vibrations* box set. Several bootlegs of the *Smile* sessions are still easily available, most featuring tracks that still haven't been officially released, or alternate takes and mixes of ones that did surface. A lot of these are interesting, to say the least, including the "Fire" part of the legendary "Elements" suite, the downright avant-garde "George Fell into His French Horn," and extended snippets of "Good Vibrations" and "Heroes in Villains" as works in progress. There are numerous exquisitely beautiful passages, great ensemble singing, and brilliant orchestral pop instrumentation to be found on these outtakes, but the fact is that Wilson somehow lacked the discipline to combine them into a pop masterpiece that was both brilliant and commercial. Search for the double-CD compilation versions of these outtakes, which, though expensive, are more thorough than the various single-disc versions available. *—Richie Unterberger*

Smiley Smile / Sep. 18, 1967 / Capitol ✦✦✦
After the collapse of the much-discussed, uncompleted *Smile* project—which was supposed to take the innovations of *Pet Sounds* to even grander heights—the Beach Boys released *Smiley Smile* in its place. (To clarify much confusion: *Smiley Smile* is an entirely different piece of work than *Smile* would have been, although some material that ended up on *Smiley Smile* would have most likely been used on *Smile*. Also, much of *Smiley Smile* was in fact recorded *after* the *Smile* sessions had ceased.) For fans expecting something along the lines of *Sgt. Pepper* (and there were many of them), *Smile* was a major disappointment, replacing psychedelic experimentation with spare, eccentric miniatures. Heard now, outside of such unrealistic expectations, it's a rather nifty, if slight, effort that's plenty weird—in fact, often downright goofy—despite Brian Wilson's retreat from both avant-pop and active leadership of the group. "Wind Chimes," "Wonderful," "Vegetables," and much of the rest is low-key psychedelic quirkiness, with abundant fine harmonies and unusual arrangements. The standouts, nonetheless, were two recent hit singles in which Brian Wilson's ambitions were still intact: the inscrutable mini-opera "Heroes and Villains," and the No. 1 hit "Good Vibrations," one of the few occasions where the group managed to be recklessly experimental and massively commercial at the same time. A 1990 Capitol CD combines this and *Wild Honey* on one disc, adding previously unreleased in-progress versions of "Good Vibrations" and "Heroes and Villains," the a cappella B-side "You're Welcome," a 1967 version of "Their Hearts Were Full of Spring," and an excellent outtake, "Can't Wait Too Long." *—Richie Unterberger*

Wild Honey / Dec. 18, 1967 / Capitol ✦✦✦
After the *Smile* sessions shut down, the Beach Boys became much more of a *band* than they had been in the mid-'60s. They began playing most of their own instruments on record for the first time since 1963, and Brian Wilson was no longer nearly as dominant a production mastermind. The problem was, as Wilson increasingly withdrew from a leadership role (and, subsequently, from the real world altogether), the Beach Boys were revealed as a group that, although capable of producing some fine and interesting music, were no longer innovators on the level of the Beatles and other figureheads. *Wild Honey* had a looser, funkier feel than any previous Beach Boys effort, at times approaching a kind of bleached-out white soul. The resulting music was often quite pleasant, for the great harmonies if nothing else, but the material and arrange-

ments were simply thinner than they had been for a long time. The record does feature a nice Top 20 hit in "Darlin'" (even if it was a rewrite of a song that had been composed four years earlier, and recorded by Sharon Marie). The small hit single "Wild Honey," with its seductive Theremin lines, was also a highlight, and "Here Comes the Night" (a group original, not the Them hit) also had a lot of appeal. Much of the rest was pleasing but insessential. A 1990 Capitol CD combines this and *Smiley Smile* on one disc, adding previously unreleased in-progress versions of "Good Vibrations" and "Heroes and Villains," the a cappella B-side "You're Welcome," a 1967 version of "Their Hearts Were Full of Spring," and an excellent outtake, "Can't Wait Too Long." —*Richie Unterberger*

Friends / Jun. 24, 1968 / Capitol ♦♦
Released when Cream and Jimi Hendrix were at their apex, the low-key pleasantries of *Friends* seemed downright irrelevant in mid-1968. Today it sounds better, but it's certainly one of the group's more minor efforts, as the members started to divide the songwriting more or less evenly among themselves, rather than letting Brian Wilson provide most of the material. The title track was a charming, if innocuous, minor hit. The bossa nova "Busy Doin' Nothin'" was a subtly subversive piece of rock muzak, though hindsight reveals a rather worrisome indolence in the lyrics, as penned by Wilson, who was starting to withdraw into his own world. The production and harmonies remained pleasantly idiosyncratic, but there was little substance at the heart of most of the songs. The irony was that *Smile* had collapsed, in part, because some of the Beach Boys felt that Wilson's increasingly avant-garde leanings would lose their pop audience; yet by the time of *Friends*, the Beach Boys had done a pretty good job of losing most of their audience by retreating to a less experimental, more group-based approach. A 1990 Capitol CD combines this and *20/20* on one disc, adding five bonus tracks also cut in the late '60s, highlighted by the minor hit "Break Away," Dennis Wilson's oddly spacy "Celebrate the News," and a cover of "Walk On By." —*Richie Unterberger*

Stack-O-Tracks / Aug. 1968 / Capitol ♦♦
One of the oddest albums released by a major rock group in the '60s, *Stack-O-Tracks* consisted of instrumental backing tracks to 15 of their more famous songs, stripped of their vocals to encourage karaoke-like singalongs. It's an indication of how low the Beach Boys' commercial stock had fallen at Capitol that the label was desperate enough to put out the kind of release that usually surfaces only via bootleg. It's thus of interest mostly to collectors and Beach Boys scholars who want to dig a little deeper into the instrumental tracks than they can otherwise (although on some of the tunes, you can hear some faint remnants of the vocal lines bleeding in). A 1990 Capitol CD combines this and *The Beach Boys Party!* on one disc, adding three previously unreleased backing tracks (of "Help Me Rhonda," "California Girls," and "Our Car Club") to the *Stack-O-Tracks* half of the program. —*Richie Unterberger*

20/20 / Feb. 3, 1969 / Capitol ♦♦♦
20/20 was not a proper album, being compiled from singles and left-overs in order to fulfill contractual obligations to Capitol. Nonetheless, it's one of their better post-*Pet Sounds* records, with a couple of good medium-sized late-'60s singles, "Do It Again" and "I Can Hear Music," that were fun retro sort of exercises. "Time to Get Alone," with its unusually shifting, jazzy melody, was one of Brian Wilson's last outstanding compositions. "Never Learn Not to Love" is far more notorious, not for the music (which is average), but for the fact that it was, according to some sources, composed by Charles Manson (although the song is credited to Dennis Wilson). The highlights, however, were a couple of *Smile* era tunes, especially "Cabinessence," a suite-like collaboration between Brian Wilson and Van Dyke Parks that gives some idea of the complex directions that were being explored during that ill-fated project. Therein lay the group's dilemma: as hard as they were trying to establish their identity as an integrated band in the late '60s, their new recordings were overshadowed by the bits and pieces of *Smile* that emerged at the time. A 1990 Capitol CD combines this and *Friends* on one disc, adding five bonus tracks also cut in the late '60s, highlighted by the minor hit "Break Away," Dennis Wilson's oddly spacy "Celebrate the News," and a cover of "Walk On By." —*Richie Unterberger*

Sunflower / Aug. 31, 1970 / Capitol ♦♦♦
The group's first new '70s album, and a highpoint for all concerned, from the transcendental doo wop music of "This Whole World" to the simple pleasantries of "Add Some Music." —*Bruce Eder*

Surf's Up [Caribou] / Aug. 30, 1971 / Caribou ♦♦♦♦
Its title notwithstanding, this album has less to do with surfing than with the band's coming to terms with aging and with changing audiences—environmentalism shares space alongside the title track, a poignant, serious masterpiece of modern pop music. —*Bruce Eder*

Carl and the Passions: So Tough / May 15, 1972 / Caribou ♦♦
For reasons best known to themselves, the Beach Boys chose to package their new 1972 album as a twofer with their 1966 masterpiece *Pet Sounds*. The new album inevitably suffered in comparison, but the

Brian Wilson tunes "You Need a Mess of Help to Stand Alone" and "Marcella" are standouts. —*William Ruhlmann*

Holland / Jan. 8, 1973 / Caribou ♦♦♦
The California sun mixed with mysticism and some outrageous sound experiments (all with a great beat). A failed effort to renew the group's sound with a change of venue (to Holland) that is salvaged largely by the presence of one great rock number ("Sail On Sailor") and a conceptual piece ("California Saga") that has a phenomenal middle section. —*Bruce Eder*

The Beach Boys in Concert / Nov. 19, 1973 / Caribou ♦♦♦
With virtually no audience presence on this live album, it's a good deal less exciting than either of their Capitol live recordings. But some of the concert renditions ("Don't Worry Baby") are superior to the studio originals, and the record as a whole is consistently rewarding. A farewell to the band's third golden era, with a big sound and an excellent cross-section of songs. —*Bruce Eder*

★ **Endless Summer** / Jun. 24, 1974 / Capitol ♦♦♦♦♦
A notable collection, as the record that sparked the commercial revival of the band's fortunes during the '70s, although all of the material on it has been remastered in superior form on other Capitol CDs. —*Bruce Eder*

Spirit of America / Apr. 14, 1975 / Capitol ♦♦♦
A followup to *Endless Summer*, much weaker in content (except for the inclusion of "Breakaway"), but its near-repeat success helped put the group back in the spotlight. —*Bruce Eder*

15 Big Ones / Jul. 5, 1976 / Caribou ♦♦
A return to simplicity and the group's roots, complete with a hit Chuck Berry cover ("Rock and Roll Music") and a lot of songs about beaches, babes, and amusement parks. It was a hit too. —*Bruce Eder*

Beach Boys '69 (Beach Boys Live in London) / Nov. 15, 1976 / Caribou ♦♦
First off, let's clear up some discographical confusion: this album was originally titled *Live in London* and released overseas in 1970. When it was issued in the States in 1976, the title was changed to *Beach Boys '69*. Further obfuscating matters, the performances were actually recorded in 1968. Brian Wilson is not present on these tracks, in which the group combines 1965-68 hits like "California Girls," "Good Vibrations," and "Darlin'" with much less celebrated songs from their late-'60s LPs. The Beach Boys were always far better in the studio than they were onstage. This record does demonstrate that they could recreate their music in a live setting with reasonable competence (though the singing outshines the playing). It is not, however, particularly exciting or essential stuff; the live arrangements, especially on the more complex numbers, can sound pretty pale when compared to the more familiar studio versions. A 1990 Capitol CD combines this (reverting to the *Live in London* title) and *The Beach Boys Concert* (from 1964) on one disc, adding previously unreleased live versions of "Don't Worry Baby" (from 1964) and "Heroes and Villains" (from 1967). —*Richie Unterberger*

Love You / Apr. 11, 1977 / Caribou ♦♦♦
The Beach Boys had hailed the return of Brian Wilson with their 1976 album *15 Big Ones*, but it was on this follow-up, produced by Wilson, who also wrote almost all of it as well, that he was heard in all his demented glory, singing with childlike wonder about Johnny Carson, among other topics. Strange, but fascinating, especially for longtime Wilson watchers. —*William Ruhlmann*

M.I.U. Album / Sep. 25, 1978 / Caribou ♦♦♦
The group's last halfway-good album, sparked by pleasant singing, some unexpected rock cover versions, and funny wordplay by Brian Wilson. —*Bruce Eder*

L.A. (Light Album) / Mar. 16, 1979 / Caribou ♦♦
The Beach Boys went into their outtakes archive for this cobbled-together collection, which features the lovely Brian and Carl Wilson collaboration "Good Timin'." Much of it is mediocre, however, and the nearly 11-minute disco version of "Here Comes the Night" is an embarrassment. —*William Ruhlmann*

Keepin' the Summer Alive / Mar. 17, 1980 / Caribou ♦
A low point. Bruce Johnston produces a Beach Boys soundalike album using the actual group, plus 22 other credited musicians, while Carl Wilson collaborates with Randy Bachman of Bachman-Turner Overdrive. —*William Ruhlmann*

The Beach Boys / Jun. 1985 / Caribou ♦♦
The Beach Boys' first all-new studio album in five years (and last for seven years) is a concerted attempt to regain old glories, which it did to an extent, selling better than any record since *15 Big Ones* (1976) and spinning off the Top 40 single "Getcha Back" and the chart entry "It's Gettin' Late." But despite the production sheen provided by Steve Levine (of Culture Club fame), this is another competent but uninspired effort. —*William Ruhlmann*

Still Cruisin' / Aug. 1989 / Capitol ✦✦
The Beach Boys' success with soundtracks, notably their No. 1 1988 hit with "Kokomo" from *Cocktail*, provides the rationale for this hodge-podge of oldies and one-off singles. Their new savior, producer Terry Melcher, helps them sound like a professional '60s cover band. Meanwhile, Brian Wilson has quietly disappeared. — *William Ruhlmann*

Lost and Found! (1961-62) / 1991 / DCC ✦✦
Before securing a deal with Capitol, the Beach Boys made their first inroads into the music business with recordings for several tiny L.A. labels in 1961 and 1962. This CD presents no less than 16 takes from these sessions, along with sundry studio chatter. Only a few of these cuts were issued at the time: their debut single "Surfin'" and a single issued under the pseudonym Kenny and the Cadets. This compilation is definitely for the serious fan; the sound is very basic and thin in comparison to their famous recordings, and there are multiple takes of most of the songs that can make for trying listening. That said, it is also at times a fascinating glimpse into history, showing the Beach Boys polishing their already impressive harmonies on early versions of "Surfer Girl" and "Surfin' Safari." Much of the rest of the material is a bit maudlin in nature, owing more to doo wop and teen idol balladry than the driving surf music that would make the group superstars in 1963. This compilation of mostly previously unissued material features songs from their very first recording session in October of 1961 and includes exhaustive liner notes. — *Richie Unterberger*

☆ **The Absolute Best, Vol. 1** / Jul. 1991 / Capitol ✦✦✦✦✦
The early hits and their best-known songs ("Surfin' USA," "Fun, Fun, Fun," etc.), and a good anthology from that standpoint—but none of all the really interesting stuff from the albums and B-sides. It's also a little too predictable, making it okay for the unadventurous. — *Bruce Eder*

☆ **The Absolute Best, Vol. 2** / Aug. 1991 / Capitol ✦✦✦✦✦
Absolute Best, Vol. 2 picks up where the first volume left off, beginning with "California Girls" and running through the early '70s. On the whole, the music on *Absolute Best, Vol. 2* is more adventurous than its predecessor, containing more studio experiments and layered arrangements. If you have the first volume, the second volume is equally necessary, considering it contains such classics as "Barbara Ann," "Caroline, No," "Sloop John B.," "Wouldn't It Be Nice," "God Only Knows," "Good Vibrations," and "Heroes and Villains." — *Stephen Thomas Erlewine*

Summer in Paradise / Aug. 3, 1992 / Brother ✦
What would The Beach Boys be like if Brian Wilson were banned and lead singer Mike Love ruled the roost? Like this—writing bad new songs, recording bad covers of old songs—a pointless parody of themselves. — *William Ruhlmann*

☆ **Good Vibrations: Thirty Years of the Beach Boys** / Jun. 21, 1993 / Capitol ✦✦✦✦✦
A five-CD box set, containing a whopping 142 tracks and covering the group's entire career, that manages to feel like too much and not enough at the same time. True, all of the key hits and most of their finest album tracks are here. The group's decline after 1966—and very sharp decline after 1970—is inescapable, and even though most of the material here is from the 1960s, the fourth disc especially (spanning the early 1970s to the late 1980s) is very rough sailing indeed. It's true that about 50 of these tracks are previously unreleased, but be warned that many of them are demos, backing tracks, and alternate versions of well-known songs that aren't a great deal different from the officially released versions. Also, some of the unreleased "tracks" are radio spots. That's not to say that these rare items aren't interesting for the fan; they are. It's just that it's too overwhelming a package for the non-fanatic, and a rather expensive, spotty one for the devoted fan (who will undoubtedly already have at least half the contents). By far, the most interesting unreleased tracks date from the legendary *Smile* sessions (nearly an album's worth). Never actually completed, they aren't quite the masterpiece that some have claimed, but are extremely interesting, often beautiful excursions into psychedelic production and songwriting that often resemble sound paintings more than songs. Comes with a 60-page booklet by Beach Boy historian David Leaf. — *Richie Unterberger*

Lei'd in Hawaii Rehearsal [bootleg] / 1994 / Vigotone ✦✦✦
Live Beach Boys bootlegs pale in comparison with the ones from studio sources, but this may be the most interesting, presenting a perfect-quality rehearsal tape from August 1967 (with Brian very much present). Spare, fragile versions of several of their '60s hits (one of these takes, "Surfer Girl," closed the official *Good Vibrations* box set, if you need a preview); Mike Love ruins "Heroes and Villains" with a corny narration. Includes a couple of interesting '60s outtakes ("We're Together Again," from 1968, and "Sherry She Needs Me," from 1965, although the vocals weren't added until 1976), and a good quality radio broadcast of four songs from a November 1963 show at the Hollywood Bowl. — *Richie Unterberger*

Mike Love, Not War [bootleg] / 1994 / Spank ✦✦
The first half of this CD is taken from a live Michigan concert from October 1966, the same one that yielded the version of "Good Vibrations" that appears on the official *Good Vibrations* box. The sound quality isn't quite as good on these 11 songs ("Good Vibrations" itself is not included), but it's still very good for an unauthorized live '60s tape. But there are a couple of major problems. Brian Wilson is absent, as he almost always was from the stage from 1965 onwards. Just as important, the Beach Boys, more than almost any other top-level rock group of the time, were inferior stage performers. The singing and playing are thin, awkward, tentative, and lacking in drive and energy. They play many of their best songs from the mid-'60s (including a few from *Pet Sounds*), but set against the magnificence of the studio recordings, they're downright anemic. Following this are nine songs from a November 1964 Swedish performance (with Brian in tow) that are gutsier, but still a pale reflection of the studio creations. There are a couple of songs ("Surfer Girl" and "Louie, Louie") that don't show up on the official *Concert* album, also recorded in 1964, but basically it's barely different from that set in sound and song selection. A cool, raucous "What'd I Say" from an early 1964 show in Sydney (also released officially on an import) closes out a release that's for collectors only, despite the relatively high audio quality. — *Richie Unterberger*

20 Good Vibrations—the Greatest Hits / Apr. 4, 1995 / Capitol ✦✦✦
Amazingly, given the number of Beach Boys compilations, there has yet to be a one-disc anthology presenting their biggest singles from "Surfin' Safari," which hit the Top Ten on some charts in 1962, to "Kokomo," a No. 1 hit in 1988. This album attempts to fill that gap. It includes those two, as well as such chart-toppers as "Surfin' USA," "I Get Around," "Barbara Ann," and "Good Vibrations." But it fails in its mission in a number of respects. For one thing, it's only 49 minutes long; another 25 minutes of hits could have been included. For another, the choices are somewhat idiosyncratic. "Catch a Wave" was never a single, much less a hit, but it's here, while "When I Grow Up (To Be a Man)," a Top Ten single, is not. All the tracks except "Kokomo" are Capitol recordings from 1962 to 1966, which means later hits on other labels, notably the Top Ten "Rock and Roll Music" (1976), are missing. And in a couple of instances, the hit versions are not included: "Be True to Your School" and "Help Me, Rhonda" are significantly different album tracks, not the original singles. Finally, the sequencing is not chronological, which makes the group's stylistic changes confusing. All in all, this is not the ideal hits collection, and unless you're a big fan of "Kokomo" who happens not to own the *Cocktail* soundtrack, you'd be better off sticking to one or both of the *Absolute Best* collections or *Endless Summer*. — *William Ruhlmann*

Stars & Stripes, Vol. 1 / Aug. 20, 1996 / A&M ✦✦
In a move that only the crassest marketing men (or Mike Love) could have imagined, the Beach Boys cashed in on the popular boom in country music in the early '90s with *Stars and Stripes, Vol. 1*. Instead of recording a country album themselves, they hired a batch of country vocalists—ranging from Toby Keith to Willie Nelson and Lorrie Morgan—to perform the group's old hits. As for the Beach Boys themselves, they just provide backing vocals. None of the songs translates particularly well to country settings, and the production has a canned, sterile ambience that sounds nothing like either country or surf-rock. Furthermore, the country vocalists don't sing with any true feeeling for the material; in attempts to personalize the songs, they knock the songs completely off-track. A handful of singers deliver good performances, but for the most part *Stars and Stripes, Vol. 1* is an unmitigated disaster and an outright embarrassment for all involved. — *Stephen Thomas Erlewine*

Time to Get Alone / [Bootleg] ✦✦✦
An expensive double CD of unreleased '60s material. The first disc puts their much-vaunted family psychodrama on display more nakedly than anywhere else, opening with a 40-minute (!) reel of rehearsals for "Help Me Rhonda" that finds dad Murry Wilson sitting in on the sessions. Perhaps drunk, Murry harps and hectors his sons' band on how to sing their lines, accusing them of big-headedness when the results aren't to his satisfaction; the boys put up with it as best they can. Disc one also has a half hour of outtakes and rehearsals from the *Party!* album, including a few songs ("Laugh at Me," "Ticket to Ride," "California Girls," "Little Deuce Coupe") that didn't make it onto the finished product. Disc two has marginally different versions and alternate mixes of songs from their *Today, Summer Days,* and *Pet Sounds* albums, along with reels of outtakes from the "Good Vibrations" and "Heroes And Villains" singles (themselves usually packaged with *Smile* bootlegs). Certainly *Time to Get Alone* is for fanatics only, but those fanatics will find it interesting and occasionally fascinating. — *Richie Unterberger*

Pet Sounds Rehearsals / [Bootleg] ✦✦✦
Almost an hour of rehearsal takes and backing tracks for some of *Pet Sounds'* best tracks. Like the Beatles' *Get Back* bootlegs, these are fascinating artifacts for scholars of the group, but pretty low on entertain-

ment value. The piano practices for "You Still Believe in Me" verge on low comedy at times with the constant grating mistakes, reminiscent of that Monty Python sketch where John Cleese, playing Beethoven, couldn't get the intro right to his Fifth Symphony. We also get to hear how many overzealous bicycle bells and horns were stripped from the final take, as well as a work-in-progress document of "I Just Wasn't Made for These Times" and basic tracks for "Wouldn't It Be Nice" and "I'm Waiting for the Day." —*Richie Unterberger*

Beastie Boys

f. 1979, New York, NY
Hip Hop, Alternative Pop-Rock, Hardcore Punk

As the first white rap group of any importance, the Beastie Boys received the scorn of critics and strident hip-hop musicians, who accused them of cultural pirating, especially since they began as a hardcore punk group in 1981. But the Beasties weren't pirating—they treated rap as part of a post-punk musical underground, where the do-it-yourself aesthetics of hip-hop and punk weren't that far apart. Of course, the exaggerated B-Boy and frat boy parodies of their unexpected hit debut album *Licensed to Ill* didn't help their cause. For much of the mid-'80s, the Beastie Boys were considered macho clowns, and while their ambitious, Dust Brothers-produced second album, *Paul's Boutique*, dismissed that theory, it was ignored by both the public and the press at the time. In retrospect, it was one of the first albums to predict the genre-bending, self-referential pop kaleidoscope of '90s pop. The Beasties refined their eclectic approach with 1992's *Check Your Head*, where they played their own instruments. *Check Your Head* brought the Beasties back to the top of the charts, and within a few years, they were considered one of the most influential and ambitious groups of the '90s, cultivating a musical community not only through their music, but with their record label, Grand Royal, and their magazine of the same name.

It was remarkable turn of events for a group that demonstrated no significant musical talent on their first records. All three members of the Beastie Boys—Mike D (b. Mike Diamond, Nov. 20, 1966), MCA (b. Adam Yauch, Aug. 5, 1965), and Ad-Rock (b. Adam Horovitz, Oct. 31, 1967)—came from wealthy middle-class Jewish families in New York and had become involved in the city's punk underground when they were teenagers in the early '80s. Diamond and Yauch formed the Beastie Boys with drummer Kate Schellenbach and guitarist John Berry in 1981, and the group began playing underground clubs around New York. The next year, the Beasties released the seven-inch EP *Polly Wog Stew* on the indie Rat Cage, to little attention. That year, the band met Horovitz, who had formed the hardcore group the Young and the Useless. By early 1983 Schellenbach and Berry had left the group—they would later join Luscious Jackson and Thwig, respectively—and Horovitz had joined the Beasties. The revamped group released the rap record "Cookie Puss" as a 12-inch single later in 1983. Based on a prank phone call the group made to Carvel Ice Cream, the single became an underground hit in New York, and by early 1984, they had abandoned punk and turned their attention to rap.

In 1984,the Beasties joined forces with producer Rick Rubin, a heavy metal and hip-hop fan who had recently founded Def Jam Records with his fellow New York University student Russell Simmons. Def Jam officially signed the Beastie Boys in 1985, and that year they had a hit single from the soundtrack to *Krush Groove* with "She's On It," a rap track that sampled AC/DC's "Back in Black" and suggested the approach of the group's forthcoming debut album. The Beasties received their first significant national exposure later in 1985, when they opened for Madonna on her *Virgin Tour*. The trio taunted the audience with profanity and were generally poorly received. One other major tour, as the openers for Run-D.M.C.'s ill-fated *Raisin' Hell* trek, followed before *License to Ill* was released late in 1986. An amalgam of street beats, metal riffs, B-boy jokes, and satire, *License to Ill* was interpreted as a mindless, obnoxious party record by many critics and conservative action groups, but that didn't stop the album from becoming the fastest-selling debut in Columbia Records' history, moving over 750,000 copies in its first six weeks. Much of that success was due to the single "Fight for Your Right (To Party)," which became a massive crossover success. In fact, *License to Ill* became the biggest-selling rap album of the '80s, which generated much criticism from certain hip-hop fans who believed that the Beasties were merely cultural pirates. On the other side of the coin, the group was being attacked from the right, who claimed their lyrics were violent and sexist and that their concerts—which featured female audience members dancing in go-go cages and a giant inflatable penis, similar to what the Stones used in their mid-'70s concerts—caused even more outrage. Throughout their 1987 tour, they were plagued with arrests and lawsuits and were accused of inciting crime.

While much of the Beasties' exaggerated obnoxious behavior started out as a joke, it became a self-parody by the end of 1987, so it wasn't a surprise that the group decided to revamp their sound and image during the next two years. During 1988 they became involved in a bitter lawsuit with Def Jam and Rick Rubin, who claimed he was responsible for the group's success and threatened to release outtakes as their second album. The group finally broke away by the end of the year, and they relocated to California, where they signed with Capitol Records. While in California, they met the production team the Dust Brothers, and they convinced the duo to use their prospective debut album as the basis for the Beasties' second album, *Paul's Boutique*. Densely layered with interweaving samples and pop culture references, the retro-funk-psychedelia of *Paul's Boutique* was entirely different from *License to Ill*, and many observers weren't quite sure what to make of it. Several publications gave it rave reviews, but when it failed to produce a single bigger than the No. 36 "Hey Ladies," it was quickly forgotten.

Despite its poor commercial performance, *Paul's Boutique* gained a cult following, and its cut-and-paste sample techniques would later be hailed as visionary, especially after the Dust Brothers altered the approach for Beck's acclaimed 1996 album *Odelay*. Still, the record was declared a disaster in the early '90s, but that didn't prevent the Beasties from building their own studio and founding their own record label, Grand Royal, for their next record, *Check Your Head*. Alternating between old school hip-hop, raw amateurish funk, and hardcore punk, *Check Your Head* was less accomplished than *Paul's Boutique*, but it was just as diverse. Furthermore, the burgeoning cult around the Beasties made the album a surprise Top 10 hit upon its spring 1992 release. "Jimmy James," "Pass the Mic," and "So Whatcha Want" were bigger hits on college and alternative rock radio than they were on rap radio, and the group suddenly became hip again. Early in 1994 they collected their early punk recordings on the compilation *Some Old Bullshit*, which was followed in June by their fourth album, *Ill Communication*. Essentially an extension of *Check Your Head*, the record debuted at No. 1 upon its release, and the singles "Sabotage" and "Sure Shot" helped send it to double-platinum status. During the summer of 1994 they co-headlined the fourth Lollapalooza festival with Smashing Pumpkins. That same year, Grand Royal became a full-fledged record label as it released Luscious Jackson's acclaimed debut album, *Natural Ingredients*. The Beasties' *Grand Royal* magazine was also launched that year.

Over the next few years, the Beasties remained quiet as they concentrated on political causes and their record label. In 1996 they released the hardcore EP *Aglio E Olio* and the instrumental soul-jazz and funk collection, *The In Sound from Way Out*. Also that year, Adam Yauch organized a two-day festival to raise awareness about and money for Tibet's plight under the Chinese government. As of the spring of 1997, the Beastie Boys were completing their fifth album. —*Stephen Thomas Erlewine*

☆ **Licensed to Ill** / 1986 / Def Jam ✦✦✦✦
The impact of this album in 1987 was about as subtle as a brick through a window. It was the first No. 1 hip-hop album, selling four million copies, and the first album from a white rap group. From the opening kick of John Bonham's drums (taken from "When the Levee Breaks"), the Beasties proceed to steal from every record they can get their hands on and rhyme about an absurd array of macho fantasies. Sure, it's obnoxious—but it's an act, and an insanely humorous one at that; no other rappers brag about being thrown out of White Castle, drinking Budweiser, or having "more rhymes than Phyllis Diller." Even if some of it sounds dated today, the sheer force of the music and the whiny rhymes still make this worth hearing. —*Stephen Thomas Erlewine*

★ **Paul's Boutique** / Jul. 1989 / Capitol ✦✦✦✦
Endlessly complex and relentlessly innovative, *Paul's Boutique* is the Beastie Boys' masterpiece. It's very dense, with samples from nearly every genre of music and clever, literate, absurd lyrics dropping references from Jack Kerouac to *Dragnet*. *Paul's Boutique* is a virtual catalog of pop culture, deeply rooted in the 1970s. As rappers, the Beasties have grown immeasurably, writing lyrics that are both smart-assed and smart. Musically, the album is much richer than *Ill*, covering everything from funk and pop to country and hip-hop, with several layers of samples and beats on each track. *Paul's Boutique* is a brilliant, visionary album, and hasn't aged a day since its release. —*Stephen Thomas Erlewine*

☆ **Check Your Head** / Apr. 21, 1992 / Capitol ✦✦✦✦
Check Your Head returned the Beastie Boys to the spotlight, although in the most unlikely manner possible. Refashioning themselves as a loose and gritty groove band, the Beasties picked up their instruments again and made an album of dirty Stax and New Orleans funk, tripped-out reggae, hard hip-hop, blistering hardcore punk, and scores of pop culture references and jokes. In its own way, *Check Your Head* is as trailblazing as *Paul's Boutique;* with its inspired amateurishness, it acknowledges no boundaries or limitations, creating a post-post-punk world where Eddie Harris, Bob Dylan, Cheap Trick, Groove Holmes, Spoonie Gee, and Biz Markie exist together as one music. And, strange as it may sound, it works. —*Stephen Thomas Erlewine*

Some Old Bullshit / Feb. 8, 1994 / Grand Royal/Capitol ✦✦
Sadly, the title is accurate. Even for die-hard Beastie fans, the early hard-core punk of *Pollywog Stew* wears thin quickly, and "Cooky Puss," while fairly interesting, only hints at their future inventiveness, leaving *Some Old Bullshit* for completists only. —*Stephen Thomas Erlewine*

Ill Communication / May 23, 1994 / Grand Royal ✦✦✦✦
More of a refinement and restatement of *Check Your Head* than a bold departure, *Ill Communication* still finds the Beastie Boys in prime form, adding more elements of jazz to their dense, surrealistic sound. From the scores of wah-wah guitars to the short hardcore punk songs, *Ill Communication* is firmly entrenched in '70s worship without ever once sounding like it's recycled. It may offer the same thing as *Check Your Head*, but *Ill Communication* never sounds formulaic or tired. —*Stephen Thomas Erlewine*

Root Down EP / May 23, 1995 / Grand Royal ✦✦
Released as the Beastie Boys were beginning a US arena tour in spring 1995, the *Root Down* EP features a handful of rote remixes and tepid live tracks that are of interest only to diehard fans. —*Stephen Thomas Erlewine*

Aglio E Olio EP / Nov. 13, 1995 / Grand Royal ✦✦

The In Sound from Way Out / Apr. 2, 1996 / Grand Royal/Capitol ✦✦✦
Originally released through the Beasties' French fan club, *The In Sound From Way Out* is a collection of the group's funky instrumentals from *Check Your Head* and *Ill Communication*, with a couple of new tracks thrown in. The Beasties have a flair for loose, gritty funk and soul-jazz, and the stuttering, greasy keyboards of Money Mark give the music an extra edge; he helps make the music sound as authentic as anything from the early '70s. Fans of the band's dynamic wordplay might find *The In Sound from Way Out* a disappointment, but anyone who grooved on the wildly eclectic fusions of *Check Your Head* and *Ill Communication* will find the album endlessly enjoyable. —*Stephen Thomas Erlewine*

The Beat

f. 1978, San Francisco, CA, db. 1983
New Wave, Power Pop
A Los Angeles-based power-pop outfit formed by Paul Collins (ex-Nerves), the Beat recorded its self-titled debut LP after signing to Columbia Records in 1979. Despite good reviews and some regional success, the album failed to make much impact. On a second attempt, 1982's *The Kids Are the Same* (this time credited to Paul Collins' Beat), also failed and effectively broke up the band. However, Collins returned the next year with a harder rocking lineup including Patti Smith Group drummer Jay Dee Daugherty. Their EP, *To Beat or Not to Beat*, was again ignored; it proved to be the band's last recording. While it seemed that the Beat's only claim to fame would be forcing the (English) Beat to change its name in the US, the band's albums are now seen as classic examples of power-pop. Paul Collins returned to a solo career in the '90s, signing to Wagon Wheel Records. —*Chris Woodstra*

● **The Beat** / 1979 / Columbia ✦✦✦✦
The Beat's great self-titled debut was produced by Bruce Botnick (the Doors), and is a must-own for lovers of melodic guitar-driven pop 'n' roll. Check out "Different Kind of Girl," "Don't Wait Up for Me," and "Walking Out on Love." Great tunes! —*Rick Clark*

The Kids Are the Same / 1982 / Columbia ✦✦✦

Beat Farmers

f. 1983, San Diego, CA, db. Nov. 11, 1995
Roots-Rock, Jangle-Pop
The Beat Farmers enjoyed a cult following throughout the 1980s and early 1990s until the untimely passing of lead singer/drummer/guitarist Country Dick Montana in November 1995. He was just 40, and he collapsed of a massive heart attack at the Long Horn, a bar in Whistler, British Columbia, in western Canada.

Montana, a former record store owner and past president of the Kinks Preservation Society fan club, formed the Beat Farmers in San Diego in 1983, influenced on the one hand by country and blues music, but on the other by the first wave of punk-rock bands to come out of Los Angeles. The group began to latch on to a following at San Diego and Los Angeles-area clubs, satisfying a need for roots-based rock 'n' roll before most people even knew the need existed. Over the years, Montana collaborated with a wide range of Los Angeles-based musicians and singers, including Mojo Nixon, John Doe from the group X, Rosie Flores, the Bangles, Los Lobos, Katy Moffatt, blues singer/pianist Candye Kane, and ex-Blasters guitarist Dave Alvin.

The Beat Farmers discography is more extensive than most people would think, because a number of recordings are hard to find or out of print. The original group consisted of Montana on drums, guitar, and

vocals; Jerry Raney on guitar and vocals; Buddy Blue on guitar and vocals; and Rolle Dexter on bass.

The Beat Farmers formed in August 1983 when they played a series of shows at the Spring Valley Inn in San Diego, and later played a local bar, Bodies. By March 1984 they were signed to Rhino Records for a one-off deal, and with a $4,000 budget, recorded *Tales of the New West*, their debut, which was released in January 1985. They began their first US tour and signed a seven- record deal with Curb Records. In December 1985 Buddy Blue left the band and was replaced by guitarist/mandolinist Joey Harris, who had worked earlier with Montana in a precursor to the Beat Farmers, Country Dick and the Snuggle Bunnies. Around the time of their first US tour, the band also began to tour in Europe, where the passion for blues-rock, roots-rock, and country-rock runs higher than in parts of the US. The group's album *Pursuit of Happiness* spurred the single "Make It Last," which got airplay on more than 40 country Western stations. But once country radio programmers had a chance to hear the rest of the album, they quickly dropped the single, since many of them felt the rest of the album was too rock 'n' roll-oriented.

In 1989 Montana and Harris joined Mojo Nixon and Dave Alvin from the Blasters to form the Pleasure Barons, a group that specialized in "lounge" music. A year later, Montana went into the hospital for thyroid surgery and continued to visit the doctor's office for cancer treatments. In the midst of all of this, the group grew dissatisfied with its relationship with Curb Records, and they attempted to get out of their seven-album contract around the same time they discovered a live album, *Loud and Plowed and . . . LIVE*, had been released without their knowledge. In between national tours, Montana occupied himself with other projects in the Los Angeles area, including the Incredible Hayseeds, Country Dick's Petting Zoo, Country Dick's Garage, and the Pleasure Barons.

In 1993 the Beat Farmers recorded their first album for Sector 2 Records (an Austin, TX, label), in Vancouver, Canada, *Viking Lullabys*. (sic) The record was released in August 1994, and the band toured in earnest once again to support their release. While working on a second album for Sector 2, Curb Records released a *Greatest Hits* album, again without the band's consent. The Beat Farmers' last album, *Manifold*, was released on Sept. 19, 1995, but was released two weeks earlier in San Diego to coincide with the Street Scene, an outdoor festival there. The group toured the US in September and October, playing venues in Texas, the Midwest, and New York City.

On Nov. 8, 1995, Montana suffered a massive heart attack three songs into the band's set at the Long Horn in Whistler, B.C. The remaining Beat Farmers decide to dissolve the band on Nov. 11, 1995.

Despite his risqué stage antics and bantering with his audiences, whom he often sprayed with beer, Country Dick Montana was a gentle soul who, after shows, would make his way around a club, shaking hands, signing autographs and chatting for a few minutes with all who took the time to say hello. Since Montana's death, guitarists Joey Harris and Jerry Raney have gone on to form their own bands, continuing to some extent the roots-rock tradition of the Beat Farmers. At their live shows, the group was unique for the way Montana would get out from behind his drum set to step out front and center and play guitar as well.

In 1996 Bar None Records of Hoboken, N.J., posthumously released *The Devil Lied to Me*, a long-awaited Country Dick Montana solo album. On this excellent and star-studded affair with regionally and nationally famous musicians from the Los Angeles area, Montana is joined by roots chanteuses Katy Moffatt and Rosie Flores, as well as talented live performers like Mojo Nixon and ex-Blasters guitarist Alvin. Highlights include Alvin's "Rich Man's Town," Paul Kamanski's "Indigo Rider," a cover of Tom Petty's "Listen to Her Heart," and the originals "King of the Hobos," as well as a tribute to amateur rappers—and there are many of both in San Diego—"Bum Rap." —*Richard Skelly*

Tales of the New West / May 1985 / Rhino ✦✦✦✦
Their debut, *Tales of the New West* features the basic blueprint the band would follow from that point on—straightahead country-rockers infused with fun and abandon instead of sterile reverence. While the band wasn't completely able to translate their sound in the studio at this point, the album is still worthwhile and one of their best studio albums. —*Chris Woodstra*

Glad 'n' Greasy / 1986 / Rhino ✦✦✦
Glad 'n' Greasy is a six-track EP recorded in the UK shortly after the first album. A cover of Neil Young's "Powderfinger" stands out as the highlight. Much of the EP has been appended to the import edition of *Tales of the West.* —*Chris Woodstra*

Van Go / Jun. 1986 / Curb ✦✦
For their second full-length album, recorded during a busy touring schedule, the Beat Farmers seem to have run out of steam and ideas, turning in a lackluster performance and generally uninspired album. "Riverside" was later used in an advertisement for Budweiser Beer. —*Chris Woodstra*

Pursuit of Happiness / Aug. 1987 / Curb ✦✦
Their most commercial sounding album to date. While the added gloss detracts from the band's true calling, they do seem more comfortable in the studio this time out. "Make It Last," the album's highpoint, nearly broke into country markets, but the rest of the album is just generic, rootsy rock 'n' roll. —*Chris Woodstra*

Poor & Famous / 1989 / Curb ✦✦

● **Loud and Plowed and . . . LIVE!!** / May 1990 / Curb ✦✦✦✦
Loud and Plowed and . . . LIVE!! is a "best of live" collection that shows the band at the height of their powers in their best environment. Since none of their studio albums was able to completely capture the raw energy and fun of the Beat Farmers, this remains the definative document of their career and is the best place to start. —*Chris Woodstra*

● **Best Of** / May 2, 1995 / Curb ✦✦✦✦
Best of the Beat Farmers is a skimpy, ten-track survey of the band's career that covers their best known songs. For those who just need a taste, the album works well as a basic introduction. Liner notes would have been nice. —*Chris Woodstra*

Manifold / Oct. 1995 / Sector 2 ✦✦
The Beat Farmers' reunion album shows that they still are tight musicians, but it lacks any standout songs, making *Manifold* an enjoyable genre exercise, but nothing more than that. —*David Jehnzen*

Beat Happening

f. 1982, Olympia, WA
Alternative Pop-Rock, Indie Rock
Beat Happening was among the truly seminal and influential American bands of the post-punk era, a paragon of pop minimalism, rebellious innocence, and indie defiance. The linchpin of the Olympia, WA,-based International Pop Underground, they adopted a stance in direct opposition to the accepted norms at the heart of rock music; ignoring all notions of pretense, professionalism, and stardom, Beat Happening created an unorthodox, raw sound that democratically rotated vocal, guitar, and drum duties between members while jettisoning bass altogether. Dropping their last names to further emphasize their everyman approach, members Calvin (Johnson), Heather (Lewis), and Bret (Lunsford) expressed simple truths and simple emotions with simple music, favoring off-key, tuneless vocals, and three-chord primitivism over slick, processed packaging. Implicit in their work was a rejection of major-label trappngs, as the group steadfastly remained with K Records, Calvin's self-owned imprint and a model of D.I.Y. indie success.

Beat Happening formed in the early 1980s. Calvin, a longtime fixture of the Olympia scene who also helped establish the original *Sub Pop* fanzine (the basis for the subsequent label), had already founded K, originally a cassette-only project started to release music no other company would touch. An alumnus of the short-lived Cool Rays, Calvin teamed with Heather and assorted friends in the first incarnation of Beat Happening, playing shows whenever and wherever they could as long as the performances were held at all-ages venues. His canyon-deep baritone quickly became as much a group trademark as their sardonic, even juvenile, songs. Bret joined in mid-1983, and Beat Happening issued a debut five-song cassette a year later. A sightseeing trip to Japan followed, and while in Tokyo, the trio recorded their second effort, 1984's *Three Tea Breakfast* EP. Their 1985 eponymous full-length debut, produced by the Wipers' Greg Sage, brought Beat Happening their first widespread exposure, as well as a number of comparisons to the burgeoning British twee-pop scene spearheaded by the Pastels. A long lay-off followed before release of 1988's remarkable *Jamboree*, co-produced by Mark Lanegan and Gary Lee Conner of the Screaming Trees.

The four-song joint release *Beat Happening/Screaming Trees* surfaced a few months later, trailed by 1989's *Black Candy*. With the release of 1991's *Dreamy*, Beat Happening's influence on the indie community became increasingly pronounced; not only did the blossoming cuddle-core movement owe the trio a huge debt, but in the summer of 1991 Calvin masterminded the International Pop Underground Festival, a now-legendary concert spotlighting more than 50 bands—among them Bikini Kill, Fugazi, Scrawl, the Fastbacks, L7, and Mecca Normal—all aligned in their opposition to corporate music. The sublime *You Turn Me On* followed, but apart from "Not a Care in the World," a track contributed to a 1992 Sub Pop sampler given away free to readers of *Sassy* magazine, Beat Happening spent much of the decade in limbo as Calvin focused on his Dub Narcotic Sound System project as well as the Halo Benders, a band founded with Built to Spill's Doug Martsch. Despite their absence from the stage and the studio, the trio maintained that they had not disbanded, and they reportedly continue practicing on a monthly basis. —*Jason Ankeny*

Beat Happening / 1985 / K ✦✦✦

Jamboree / 1988 / Sub Pop/K ✦✦✦✦
Co-produced by Steve Fisk and the Screaming Trees' Mark Lanegan and Gary Lee Conner, Beat Happening's brief, brilliant sophomore effort significantly expands the trio's horizons without sacrificing any of their naive charm. Sporting a fuller, more intricate sound and stronger songs than their debut, *Jamboree* crystallizes the trio's love-rock aesthetic in its embryonic stages; veering sharply from the idyllic drones of the perennial "Indian Summer" to the poignant crush-pop of "Cat Walk" to the indie-party classic "Midnight A Go-Go," each cut is a marvel of innocence and ingenuity. —*Jason Ankeny*

Black Candy / 1989 / Sub Pop/K ✦✦✦
As evidenced by its title, *Black Candy* is Beat Happening's darkest, most deliriously ominous album; clearly influenced by the Cramps, the record is dominated by Calvin Johnson's coffin-creak vocals, with Heather Lewis' breathy sweetness rarely in earshot to lighten the mood. A less developed batch of compositions than the previous *Jamboree*, it strives to evoke the mood of a grade-Z teen horror flick soundtrack, with faux-creepy songs ("Pajama Party in a Haunted Hive," "Gravedigger Blues," "Bonfire") and primal, drum-dominated production; less eclectic and nuanced than the trio's other LPs, *Black Candy* quickly grows tiresome, although the oft-covered highlight "Cast a Shadow" is a treat. —*Jason Ankeny*

1983-85 / 1990 / K ✦✦✦✦
1983-1985 compiles 27 early Beat Happening tracks, spanning the trio's eponymous debut LP, the *Three Tea Breakfast* EP, a handful of compilation appearances, singles, and a wealth of unreleased material. A portrait of the group at their most primitive, the fidelity is often poor, but the kinetic energy of the early sessions is palpable, and the wide-eyed charm of gems like "Look Around," "Foggy Eyes," "Fourteen," and the classic "Bad Seeds" is undeniable. —*Jason Ankeny*

Dreamy / 1991 / Sub Pop/K ✦✦✦✦
A stunning return to form, *Dreamy* reprises the dark aggression of the preceding *Black Candy*, but brings to the table a significantly stronger and more assured collection of songs. Measuring Calvin Johnson's increasingly menacing lead turns with Heather Lewis' more wistful contributions, the album strikes a careful balance between maturity and naivete. For all of their ragged minimalism, tracks like "Collide," "Revolution Come and Gone," and "Me Untamed" are remarkably sophisticated and assured. And in addition to the newfound sexiness of cuts like "Nancy Sin" and "Red Head Walking," there's a renewed sense of emotional urgency. Lewis' beguiling "Fortune Cookie Prize" is one of the group's most buoyant love songs, while the mournful "Cry for a Shadow" exposes the tenderness beneath Johnson's tough-guy veneer. —*Jason Ankeny*

● **You Turn Me On** / Oct. 2, 1992 / Sub Pop/K ✦✦✦✦
Beat Happening's (possibly) final LP is also their best. Concluding the emotional and musical progression begun with the minimalist innocence of their earliest work, *You Turn Me On* is a mature record of tremendous breadth and complexity. Where once the trio's songs were brief and bouncy, the nine tracks here are epic (several top out at over six minutes) and ambitious; produced in part by ex-Young Marble Giant Stuart Moxham (an obvious influence), the record's full, deep sound belies its bare-bones performances. "Teenage Caveman" sports booming, primal drums perfectly suited to its title, while the propulsive "Noise" manufactures the illusion of a bassline where none ever existed. The most democratic record in an output founded on egalitarian ideals, *You Turn Me On* offers Heather Lewis' strongest songs ever—her hypnotic nine-minute "Godsend" is the LP's heart and soul—and she and Calvin Johnson even trade verses on the closing "Bury the Hammer." As for Johnson himself, his solo contributions are exceptional; the spartan opener "Tiger Trap" is an evocative heartbreaker, and the title track is a fire-breathing corker. A masterpiece. —*Jason Ankeny*

Beat Rodeo

f. 1983, Minneapolis, MN
Alternative Pop-Rock, Roots-Rock
This '80s pop-rock quartet was led by singer-songwriter/guitarist Steve Almaas from Minneapolis (who had previously played bass in the Suicide Commandos) and featuring guitarist/singer Bill Schunk, bassist/vocalist Dan Prater, and drummer Mike Osborn. That lineup made the debut album, *Staying Out Late with Beat Rodeo*, first released on Zensor Records in Germany in July 1984, then picked up for US distribution by I.R.S. Records in 1985. By the time of the second album, *Home in the Heart of the Beat*, Lewis King had replaced Osborn, and George Usher had been added on keyboards. —*William Ruhlmann*

Staying out Late with . . . Beat Rodeo / Jul. 1984 / IRS ✦✦
Steve Almaas' Beat Rodeo proves to be a pleasant but rather weightless pop-rock band of the mid-'80s, neo-mid-'60s mode. A couple of decades have gone by, and so they faithfully recreate the earnest vocals, the bouncy beats, the bright, quickly strummed guitars. They are abetted by producers Don Dixon (it's his metier) and Richard Gottehrer, who gets a typically sharp sound on the two tracks he handled (added to the domestically released I.R.S. Records version of the album). All of this sounded

hipper in 1985, when the Blasters, Green on Red, and many others were playing "roots" or "retro" rock, but by now it sounds like an amusing curiosity. (Originally released, minus the Gottehrer tracks, on Zensor Records in Germany in July 1984.) — *William Ruhlmann*

● **Home in the Heart of the Beat** / 1986 / IRS ◆◆◆
Less overtly retro than *Staying Up Late*, Beat Rodeo's second album, produced by Scott Litt (R.E.M., etc.) rocked a little harder and at the same time, with the addition of keyboards (plus guest sax by Lenny Pickett and guest vocals by Syd Straw), was somewhat smoother as well. More important, Steve Almaas' songs were more substantial—lyrically more ambitious, lyrically more personal and direct. Beat Rodeo still didn't catch on, but *Home in the Heart of the Beat* demonstrated that they were a band with potential. — *William Ruhlmann*

The Beatles

f. 1960, Liverpool, England, **db.** 1970
Rock 'n' Roll, British Invasion, Psychedelic, Pop-Rock
The Beatles were the most popular and influential rock act of all time, but their significance cannot be measured solely in record sales (as impressive as those are). They synthesized all that was good about early rock 'n' roll and changed it into something original and even more exciting. They established the prototype for the self-contained rock group that wrote and performed their own material. As composers, their craft and melodic inventiveness were second to none, and key to the evolution of rock from its blues/R&B-based forms into a style that was far more eclectic, but equally visceral. As singers, both John Lennon and Paul McCartney were among the best and most expressive vocalists in rock; the group's harmonies were intricate and exhilarating. As performers, they were (at least until touring had ground them down) exciting and photogenic; when they retreated into the studio, they were instrumental in pioneering advanced techniques and multi-layered arrangements. They were also the first British rock group to achieve worldwide prominence, launching a British Invasion that made rock truly an international phenomenon.

Guitarist and teenage rebel John Lennon got hooked on rock 'n' roll in the mid-1950s and formed a band, the Quarrymen, at his Liverpool high school. Around mid-1957, the Quarrymen were joined by another guitarist, Paul McCartney, nearly two years Lennon's junior. A bit later they were joined by another guitarist, George Harrison, a friend of McCartney's. The Quarrymen would change lineups constantly in the late 1950s, eventually reducing to the core trio of guitarists.

The Quarrymen changed their name to the Silver Beatles in 1960, quickly dropping the "Silver" to become just the Beatles. Lennon's art college friend Stuart Sutcliffe joined on bass, but finding a permanent drummer was a vexing problem until Pete Best joined in the summer of 1960. He successfully auditioned for the combo just before they left for a several-month stint in Hamburg, Germany. When they returned to Liverpool at the end of 1960, the band—formerly also-rans on the exploding Liverpudlian "beat" scene—were suddenly the most exciting act on the local circuit. They consolidated their following in 1961 with constant gigging in the Merseyside area, most often at the legendary Cavern Club.

They also returned for engagements in Hamburg during 1961, although Sutcliffe dropped out of the band that year to concentrate on his art school studies there. McCartney took over on bass, Harrison settled in as lead guitarist, and Lennon had rhythm guitar; everyone sang. In mid-1961 the Beatles (minus Sutcliffe) made their first recordings in Germany, as a backup group to a British rock guitarist-singer based in Hamburg, Tony Sheridan. (Sutcliffe, tragically, would die of a brain hemorrhage in April 1962.)

Near the end of 1961, the Beatles' exploding local popularity caught the attention of local record store manager Brian Epstein, who was soon managing the band, as well. He used his contacts to swiftly acquire a January 1, 1962, audition at Decca Records that has been heavily bootlegged (some tracks were officially released in 1995). After weeks of deliberation, Decca turned them down, as did several other British labels. Epstein's perseverance was finally rewarded with an audition for producer George Martin at Parlophone, an EMI subsidiary; Martin signed the Beatles in mid-1962.

In August 1962 drummer Pete Best was kicked out of the group, a controversial decision that has been the cause of much speculation since. He was replaced by Ringo Starr (born Richard Starkey), drummer with another popular Merseyside outfit, Rory Storm and the Hurricanes. Starr had been in the Beatles for a few weeks when they recorded their first single, "Love Me Do"/"P.S. I Love You," in September 1962. Both sides of the 45 were Lennon-McCartney originals, and the songwriting team would be credited with most of the group's material throughout the Beatles' career.

The Beatles phenomenon didn't truly kick in until "Please Please Me," which topped the British charts in early 1963. This was *the* prototype British Invasion single—an infectious melody, charging guitars, and

positively exuberant harmonies. The same traits were evident on their third 45, "From Me to You" (a British No. 1), and their debut LP, *Please Please Me*. Although it was mostly recorded in a single day, *Please Please Me* topped the British charts for an astonishing 30 weeks, establishing the group as the most popular rock 'n' roll act ever seen in the UK.

The Beatles had taken the best elements of the rock and pop they loved and made them their own. Since the Quarrymen days, they had been steeped in the classic early rock of Elvis, Buddy Holly, Chuck Berry, Little Richard, Carl Perkins, and the Everly Brothers; they'd also kept an ear open to the early '60s sounds of Motown, Phil Spector, and the girl groups. They added an unmatched songwriting savvy (inspired by Brill Building teams such as Gerry Goffin and Carole King), a brash guitar-oriented attack, wildly enthusiastic vocals, and the embodiment of the youthful flair of their generation, ready to dispense with post-war austerity and claim a culture of their own. They were also unsurpassed in their eclecticism, willing to borrow from blues, popular standards, gospel, folk, or whatever seemed suitable for their musical vision. Producer George Martin was the perfect foil for the group, refining their ideas without tinkering with their essence. During the last half of their career, he was indispensable for his ability to translate their concepts into arrangements that required complex orchestration, innovative applications of recording technology, and an ever-widening array of instruments.

Just as crucially, the Beatles were never ones to stand still and milk formulas. All of their subsequent albums and singles would show remarkable artistic progression (though never at the expense of a catchy tune). Even on their second LP, *With the Beatles* (1963), it was evident that their talents as composers and instrumentalists were expanding furiously, as they devised ever more inventive melodies and harmonies, and boosted the fullness of their arrangements. The 1963 singles "She Loves You" and "I Want to Hold Your Hand" established the group not just as a successful pop act, but as a phenomenon never before seen in the British entertainment business, as each single sold over a million copies in the UK. After some celebrated national TV appearances, Beatlemania broke out across the British Isles in late 1963, the group generating screams and hysteria at all of their public appearances, musical or otherwise.

Capitol, which had first refusal of the Beatles' recordings in the United States, had declined to issue the group's first few singles, which ended up appearing on relatively small American independents. Capitol took up its option on "I Want to Hold Your Hand," which stormed to the top of the US charts within weeks of its release on December 26, 1963. The Beatles' television appearances on "The Ed Sullivan Show" in February 1964 launched Beatlemania (and the entire British Invasion) on an even bigger scale than it had reached in Britain. In the first week of April 1964, the Beatles had the top five best-selling singles in the US; they also had the top two slots on the album charts, as well as other entries throughout the *Billboard* Top 100. No one had ever dominated the market for popular music so heavily; it's doubtful than anyone ever will again. The Beatles themselves would continue to reach No. 1 with most of their singles and albums until their 1970 breakup.

A Hard Day's Night, 1964's cinema verite-style motion picture comedy/musical, cemented their image as the Fab Four—happy-go-lucky, individualistic, cheeky, funny lads with nonstop energy. The soundtrack was also a triumph, consisting entirely of Lennon-McCartney tunes, including such standards as the title tune, "And I Love Her," "If I Fell," "Can't Buy Me Love," and "Things We Said Today." Between riotous international tours in 1964 and 1965, the Beatles continued to pump out more chart-topping albums and singles. (Until 1967, the group's British albums were often truncated for release in the States; when their catalog was transferred to CD, the albums were released worldwide in their British configurations.) In retrospect, critics have judged *Beatles for Sale* (late 1964) and *Help!* (mid-1965) as the band's least impressive efforts. To some degree, that's true. Touring and an insatiable market placed heavy demands upon their songwriting, and some of the originals and covers on these records, while brilliant by many groups' standards, were filler in the context of the Beatles' best work. The best songs from this period, however, show the group continuing to move forward, especially the singles "I Feel Fine," "She's a Woman," "Ticket to Ride," and "Help!," which boast increasingly intricate guitar sounds and clever lyrics.

Although the Beatles' second film, *Help!*, was a much sillier and less sophisticated affair than their first feature, it too was a huge commercial success. By this time, though, the Beatles had nothing to prove in commercial terms; the remaining frontiers were artistic challenges that could only be met in the studio. They rose to the occasion at the end of 1965 with *Rubber Soul*, one of the classic folk-rock records. Lyrically, Lennon, McCartney, and even Harrison (who was now writing some tunes on his own) were evolving beyond boy-girl scenarios into complex, personal feelings. They were also pushing the limits of studio rock by devising new guitar and bass textures, experimenting with distortion and multi-tracking, and using unconventional (for rock) instruments like the sitar.

The "Paperback Writer"/"Rain" single found the group abandoning romantic themes entirely, boosting the bass to previously unknown levels, and fooling around with psychedelic imagery and backwards tapes on the B-side. Drugs (psychedelic and otherwise) were fueling their already fertile imaginations, but they felt creatively hindered by their touring obligations. *Revolver*, released in the summer of 1966, proved what the group could be capable of when allotted months of time in the studio. Hazy hard guitars and thicker vocal arrangements formed the bed of these increasingly imagistic, ambitious lyrics; the group's eclecticism now encompassed everything from singalong novelties ("Yellow Submarine") and string quartet-backed character sketches ("Eleanor Rigby") to Indian-influenced swirls of echo and backwards tapes ("Tomorrow Never Knows").

For the past couple of years, live performance had become a rote exercise for the group, tired of competing with thousands of screaming fans that drowned out most of their vocals and instruments. The final concert of their 1966 American tour (in San Francisco on August 29, 1966) would be their last in front of a paying audience, as the group decided to stop playing live in order to concentrate on their studio recordings. This was a radical (indeed, unprecedented) step in 1966, and the media were rife with speculation that the act was breaking up, especially after all four Beatles spent late 1966 engaged in separate personal and artistic pursuits. The appearance of the "Penny Lane"/"Strawberry Fields Forever" single in February 1967 squelched these concerns. Frequently cited as the strongest double-A-side ever, the Beatles were now pushing forward into unabashedly psychedelic territory in their use of orchestral arrangements and mellotron, without abandoning their grasp of memorable melody and immediately accessible lyrical messages.

Sgt. Pepper, released in June 1967 as the Summer of Love dawned, was the definitive psychedelic soundtrack. Or at least so it was perceived at the time; subsequent critics have painted the album as an uneven affair, given a conceptual unity via its brilliant multi-tracked overdubs, singalong melodies, and fairy tale-ish lyrics. Others remain convinced, as millions did at the time, that it represented pop's greatest triumph, or indeed an evolution of pop into art with a capital A. In addition to mining all manner of roots influences, the musicians were also picking up vibes from Indian music, avant-garde electronics, classical, music hall, and more. When the Beatles premiered their hippie anthem "All You Need Is Love" as part of a worldwide TV broadcast, they had been truly anointed as spokespersons for their generation (a role they had not actively sought), and it seemed they could do no wrong.

Musically, that would usually continue to be the case, but the group's strength began to unravel at a surprisingly quick pace. In August 1967, Brian Epstein—prone to suicidal depression over the past year—died of a drug overdose, leaving them without a manager. The group pressed on with their next film project, *Magical Mystery Tour*, directed by themselves; lacking focus or even basic professionalism, the picture bombed when it was premiered on BBC television in December 1967, giving the media the first real chance to roast the Beatles over a flame. (Another film, the animated feature *Yellow Submarine*, would appear in 1968, although the Beatles had little involvement with the project, either in terms of the movie or the soundtrack.)

Judged solely on musical merit, *The White Album*, a double LP released in late 1968, was a triumph. While largely abandoning their psychedelic instruments to return to guitar-based rock, they maintained their whimsical eclecticism, proving themselves masters of everything from blues-rock to vaudeville. It contains some of their finest work as individual songwriters (as does the brilliant non-LP single from this era, "Hey Jude"/"Revolution").

But by the *White Album*, it was clear (if only in retrospect) that each member was more concerned with his own expression than that of the collective group. In addition, George Harrison was becoming a more prolific and skilled composer, imbuing his own melodies (which were nearly the equal of those of his more celebrated colleagues) with a cosmic lightness. Harrison was beginning to resent his junior status, and the group began to bicker more openly in the studio. Ringo, whose solid drumming and good nature could usually be counted upon (as was evident in his infrequent lead vocals), actually quit for a couple of weeks in the midst of the *White Album* sessions. Apple Records, started by the group earlier in 1968 as a sort of utopian commercial enterprise, was becoming a financial and organizational nightmare.

These weren't ideal conditions under which to record a new album in January 1969, especially when McCartney was pushing the group to return to live performing, although none of the others seemed especially keen on the idea. They did agree to try and record a "back-to-basics," live-in-the-studio-type LP, the sessions being filmed for a television special. Harrison enlisted American soul keyboardist Billy Preston as kind of a fifth member on the sessions, both to beef up the arrangements and to alleviate the uncomfortable atmosphere. In order to provide a suitable concert-like experience for the film, the group did climb the roof of

their Apple headquarters in London to deliver an impromptu performance on January 30, 1969, before the police stopped it; this was their last live concert of any sort.

The album and film—at first titled *Get Back*, and later to emerge as *Let It Be*—remained in the can as the group tried to figure out how the projects should be mixed, packaged, and distributed. A couple of the best tracks, "Get Back"/"Don't Let Me Down," were issued as a single in the spring of 1969. By this time, the Beatles' quarrels were intensifying in a dispute over management; McCartney wanted their affairs to be handled by his new father-in-law, Lee Eastman, while the other members of the group favored a tough American businessman, Allen Klein.

It was something of a miracle, then, that the final album recorded by the group, *Abbey Road*, was one of their most unified efforts (even if, by this time, the musicians were recording many of their parts separately). It certainly boasted some of their most intricate melodies, harmonies, and instrumental arrangements. It also heralded the arrival of Harrison as a composer of equal talent to Lennon and McCartney, as George wrote the album's two most popular tunes, "Something" and "Here Comes the Sun." The Beatles were still progressing, but it turned out to be the end of the road, as their business disputes continued to grow. Lennon, who had begun releasing solo singles and performing with friends as the Plastic Ono Band, threatened to resign in late 1969, although he was dissuaded from making a public announcement.

Most of the early 1969 tapes remained unreleased, partially because the footage for the planned television broadcast of these sessions was now going to be produced as a documentary movie. For the accompanying soundtrack album, *Let It Be*, Lennon, Harrison, and Allen Klein decided to have celebrated American producer Phil Spector record some additional instrumentation and do some mixing. By the time it was released, the Beatles were no more.

In fact, there had been no recording done by the group as a four-man unit since August 1969, and each member of the band had begun to pursue serious outside professional interests independently via the Plastic Ono Band, Harrison's tour with Delaney and Bonnie, Starr's starring role in the *Magic Christian* film, and McCartney's first solo album. The outside world for the most part remained almost wholly unaware of the seriousness of the group's friction, making it a devastating shock for much of the world's youth when McCartney announced that he was leaving the Beatles on April 10, 1970. At the end of 1970, McCartney sued the rest of the Beatles to dissolve their partnership; the battle dragged through the courts for years, scotching any prospects of a group reunion.

In any case, each member of the band quickly established a viable solo career. Within a short time, it became apparent both that the Beatles were *not* going to settle their differences and reunite, and that their solo work could not compare with what they were capable of creating together. Despite periodic rumors of reunions throughout the 1970s, no group projects came close to materializing. Any hopes of a reunion vanished when Lennon was assassinated in New York City in December 1980. The Beatles continued their solo careers throughout the 1980s, but their releases became less frequent, and their commercial success gradually diminished, as listeners without first-hand memories of the combo created their own idols.

Legal wrangles at Apple prevented the official issue of previously unreleased Beatles material for over two decades (although much of it was bootlegged). The situation finally changed in the 1990s, after McCartney, Harrison, Starr, and Lennon's widow, Yoko Ono, settled their principal business disagreements. In 1994, this resulted in a double CD of BBC sessions from the early and mid-'60s. The next year, a much more ambitious project was undertaken: a multi-part film documentary, broadcast on network television in 1995, and then released (with double the length) for the home video market in 1996, with the active participation of the surviving Beatles.

To coincide with the *Anthology* documentary, three double CDs of previously unreleased/rare material were issued in 1995 and 1996. Additionally, McCartney, Harrison, and Starr (with some assistance from Jeff Lynne) embellished a couple of John Lennon demos from the 1970s with overdubs to create two new tracks ("Free as a Bird" and "Real Love") that were billed as actual Beatles recordings. Whether this constitutes the actual long-awaited "reunion" is the subject of much debate. Still, the massive commercial success of outtakes that had, after all, been recorded 25 to 30 years ago, spoke volumes about the unabated appeal the Beatles continue to exert worldwide. —*Richie Unterberger*

☆ **Please Please Me** / Mar. 22, 1963 / Capitol ◆◆◆◆◆
Thirty years after its release, the Beatles' first album still stands not only as a blueprint for what the group itself would accomplish in the next three years, but for what a large part of popular music would sound like from then on. Listening now, one revels anew in the songwriting of John Lennon and Paul McCartney (songs include "I Saw Her Standing There"), their remarkable harmonies and solo singing, and the encyclopedia of pop and rock they offer from other sources—especially light pop and hard R&B (like the show-stopping closer, Lennon's take on the

Isley Brothers' "Twist and Shout"). The CD reissue is in the original mono, but Mobile Fidelity has issued the album in stereo. — *William Ruhlmann*

☆ **With the Beatles** / Nov. 22, 1963 / Capitol ✦✦✦✦
In only a few months, and despite a torrid schedule, the Beatles demonstrated enormous growth on their second album (growth and change would be constants throughout their remarkable career). From the forceful "It Won't Be Long" to the bouncy "All My Loving," their original songs have made a leap, especially in ensemble playing, and the covers again offer a broad range, from Broadway show music ("Til There Was You" from *The Music Man*) to two great Motown songs ("You Really Got a Hold on Me" and "Money"). The CD reissue is in mono, while Mobile Fidelity has issued it in stereo. — *William Ruhlmann*

☆ **A Hard Day's Night [UK]** / Jul. 10, 1964 / Capitol ✦✦✦✦✦
Maybe it was all the success of the previous year, but on their third (UK) album, the Beatles sound positively triumphant, roaring through exciting songs like the title tune, "Can't Buy Me Love," and "Any Time at All." On their first album to be entirely self-written, it's the material (produced under incredible pressure) that continues to impress. "I Should Have Known Better," "If I Fell," "And I Love Her"—these are songs a generation can sing word-for-word decades later. At the same time, one can hear around the edges the beginnings of Lennon's darker side and individual voice, as more than once he refers to something he can't stand. "I'll Cry Instead" is almost bitter. *A Hard Day's Night's* freshness has not dated an hour. — *William Ruhlmann*

☆ **Beatles for Sale** / Dec. 4, 1964 / Capitol ✦✦✦✦✦
In a sense, this fourth UK album is a step back for the Beatles as they return to the eight-originals-with-six-covers formula of their first two albums. Fatigue is clearly setting in. But some of the originals are gems, especially Lennon's "No Reply" and "I'm a Loser," songs confirming his sense of anguish. The covers of Chuck Berry, Carl Perkins, and Little Richard are, once again, inspired recastings of formative material for the group. — *William Ruhlmann*

☆ **Help! [UK]** / Aug. 6, 1965 / Capitol ✦✦✦✦✦
The Beatles' fifth UK album contained seven songs used in their film plus seven other songs and marked a move to a softer, more reflective style. The lyrics are more prominent and thoughtful, and the sound more often features slow tempos, acoustic guitars, and other instruments. Lennon continued to cry for "Help!" and bitterly declared "You've Got to Hide Your Love Away" over a strummed acoustic. McCartney took a bluegrass/country turn in "I've Just Seen a Face" and achieved his biggest ballad with "Yesterday" (singing before a string quartet). Once again, the Beatles had exhibited remarkable growth and pointed the way for all of pop music to follow. — *William Ruhlmann*

☆ **Rubber Soul [UK]** / Dec. 3, 1965 / Capitol ✦✦✦✦
While the Beatles still largely stuck to love songs on *Rubber Soul,* the lyrics represented a quantum leap in terms of thoughtfulness, maturity, and complex ambiguities. Musically, too, it was a substantial leap forward, with intricate folk-rock arrangements that reflected the increasing influence of Dylan and the Byrds. The group and George Martin were also beginning to expand the conventional instrumental parameters of the rock group, using a sitar on "Norwegian Wood," Greek-like guitar lines on "Michelle" and "Girl," fuzz bass on "Think for Yourself," and a piano made to sound like a harpsichord on the instrumental break of "In My Life." While John and Paul were beginning to carve separate songwriting identities at this point, the album is full of great tunes, from "Norwegian Wood" and "Michelle" to "Girl," "I'm Looking Through You," "You Won't See Me," "Drive My Car," and "Nowhere Man" (the last of which was the first Beatle song to move beyond romantic themes entirely). George Harrison was also developing into a fine songwriter with his two contributions, "Think for Yourself" and the Byrdsish "If I Needed Someone." — *Richie Unterberger*

☆ **Revolver [UK]** / Aug. 5, 1966 / Capitol ✦✦✦✦
The three songs that were swiped for the US album *Yesterday . . . and Today* were the least of another astonishing leap in songwriting and production that introduced "Eleanor Rigby," "Yellow Submarine," "She Said, She Said," "Good Day Sunshine," "For No One," "Got to Get You into My Life," and "Tomorrow Never Knows." If McCartney was becoming a consummate pop craftsman with a command of horns and strings, Lennon was delving into a drugged psyche while experimenting with tape loops and strange sounds. And George Harrison, whose unprecedented three songs were led by "Taxman," was finally flowering into a first-rate songwriter. — *William Ruhlmann*

☆ **Sgt. Pepper's Lonely Hearts Club Band** / Jun. 1, 1967 / Capitol ✦✦✦✦✦
The Beatles' finest album is a song cycle full of childlike whimsy and irresistibly catchy songs. Its playfulness belies an amazingly fluid arrangement of melodies, lyrics, and sounds that flow together into a whole, creating its own magical world. An open-ended embrace of light pop, hard rock, Indian music, swing, classical music, and blues, the album makes the case for musical unity-in-diversity, seemingly gathering all that came before it into surprising yet perfect combinations. The Beatles only occasionally approached this achievement in isolated moments afterward, and nobody else even came close, then or since. — *William Ruhlmann*

☆ **Magical Mystery Tour** / Nov. 27, 1967 / Capitol ✦✦✦✦✦
The US version of the soundtrack for their ill-fated British television special embellished the six songs that were found on the British *Magical Mystery Tour* double EP with five other cuts from their 1967 singles. (The CD version of the record has now been standardized worldwide as the 11 tracks found on the American version.) The psychedelic sound is very much in the vein of *Sgt. Pepper,* and even spacier in parts (especially the sound collages of "I Am the Walrus"). Unlike *Sgt. Pepper,* there's no vague overall conceptual/thematic unity to the material, which has made *Magical Mystery Tour* suffer slightly in comparison. Still, the music is mostly great, and "Penny Lane," "Strawberry Fields Forever," "All You Need Is Love," and "Hello Goodbye" were all huge, glorious, and innovative singles. The ballad "The Fool in the Hill," though only a part of the *Magical Mystery Tour* soundtrack, is also one of the most popular Beatle tunes from the era. — *Richie Unterberger*

☆ **The Beatles [White Album]** / Nov. 22, 1968 / Capitol ✦✦✦✦✦
In their later recordings, the Beatles largely eschewed the elaborate arrangements and instrumentation of 1967 in favor of returning to the simpler sound of the four-piece band. They did not, however, return to the ensemble style of 1964, rather serving as backup to one of four leaders, depending on who wrote the song. On this sprawling double album, already apparent individual styles gain ascendency; likewise, musical styles are not so much combined as separated out in pastiche form—the Beach Boys pop of "Back in the USSR," the blues of "Yer Blues," the folk of "Rocky Raccoon," the hard rock of "Birthday," the schmaltzy pop of "Good Night." The musical facility is amazing but also seems near-parodic. — *William Ruhlmann*

Yellow Submarine / Jan. 13, 1969 / Capitol ✦✦✦
The only Beatles album that could really be classified as inessential, mostly because it wasn't really a proper album at all, but a soundtrack that used only four new Beatles songs. (The rest of the album was filled out with "Yellow Submarine," "All You Need Is Love," and a George Martin score that held little appeal to rock listeners.) What's more, the four new tracks were little more than pleasant throwaways that had been recorded during 1967 and early 1968. These aren't all that bad; "All Together Now" is a kiddieish singalong, "Hey Bulldog" has some mild Lennon nastiness, and Harrison's "It's All Too Much" is highlighted by some tidal waves of feedback guitar. It would have been a far better value if it had been released as a four-song EP (an idea the Beatles even considered at one point, with the addition of a bonus track in "Across the Universe," but ultimately discarded). — *Richie Unterberger*

☆ **Abbey Road** / Sep. 26, 1969 / Capitol ✦✦✦✦✦
The last Beatles album to be recorded (although *Let It Be* was the last to be released), *Abbey Road* is a fitting swan song for the group, echoing some of the faux-conceptual forms of *Sgt. Pepper,* but featuring stronger compositions and more rock-oriented ensemble work. The group were still pushing forward in all facets of their art, whether devising some of the greatest harmonies to be heard on any rock record (especially on "Because"), constructing a medley of songs/vignettes that covered much of side two, adding subtle touches of moog synthesizer, or crafting furious guitar-heavy rock (on "The End," "I Want You (She's So Heavy)," and "Come Together"). George Harrison also blossomed into a major songwriter with his contributions, the buoyant "Here Comes the Sun" and the supremely melodic ballad "Something," the latter of which became the first Harrison-penned Beatles hit. Whether or not it was the Beatles' best work, it was certainly the most immaculately produced (with the possible exception of *Sgt. Pepper's*) and most tightly constructed. — *Richie Unterberger*

In the Beginning: Early Tapes (Circa 1960) / May 4, 1970 / Polydor ✦✦
Before beginning their recording career, the Beatles recorded a few tracks in Hamburg in 1961 as the backing group for British singer Tony Sheridan. Reissued in countless different packages around the globe after the Beatles became famous, this should in no way be considered their first album; not only were their skills rudimentary, but Sheridan takes all but one of the lead vocals on this set of fairly tame covers of popular and early rock standards. Several tracks are of interest: "Ain't She Sweet," with a lead vocal by John Lennon, was a small American hit single in 1964; the driving instrumental "Cry for a Shadow" was written by Lennon and George Harrison; and "My Bonnie," with Paul McCartney's shouts clearly audible in the background, was responsible for bringing the group to the attention of Brian Epstein. — *Richie Unterberger*

☆ **Let It Be** / May 8, 1970 / Capitol ✦✦✦✦✦
The only Beatles album to occasion negative, even hostile reviews, there are few other rock records as controversial as *Let It Be.* First off, several

facts need to be explained. Although released in May 1970, this was *not* their final album, but recorded largely in early 1969, way before *Abbey Road*. Phil Spector was enlisted in early 1970 to do some post-production work, but did *not* work with the band as a unit, as George Martin and Glyn Johns had on the sessions themselves; Spector's work was limited to mixing and some overdubs. And, although his use of strings has generated much criticism, by and large he left the original performances to stand as is. Only "The Long and Winding Road" and (to a lesser degree) "Across the Universe" and "I Me Mine" get the wall-of-sound layers of strings and female choruses. Although most of the album, then, has a live-in-the-studio feel, the main problem was that the material wasn't uniformly strong, and that the Beatles themselves were in fairly lousy moods due to inter-group tension. All that said, the album is on the whole underrated, even discounting the fact that a sub-standard Beatles record is better than almost any other group's best work. McCartney in particular offers several gems: the gospelish "Let It Be," which has some of his best lyrics; "Get Back," one of his hardest rockers; and the melodic "The Long and Winding Road," ruined by Spector's heavy-handed overdubs (the superior string-less, choir-less version was finally released on *Anthology Vol. 3*). The folky "Two of Us," with John and Paul harmonizing, was also a highlight. Most of the rest of the material, by contrast, was going through the motions to some degree, although there are some good moments of straight hard rock in "I've Got a Feeling" and "Dig a Pony." As flawed and bumpy as it is, it's an album well worth having; when the Beatles were in top form here, they were as good as ever. —*Richie Unterberger*

● **1962-1966** / Apr. 2, 1973 / Capitol ✦✦✦✦
Assembling a compilation of the Beatles is a difficult task, not only because they had an enormous number of hits, but also because singles didn't tell the full story; many of their album tracks were as important as the singles, if not more so. The double-album *1962-1966*, commonly called the "Red Album," does the job surprisingly well, hitting most of the group's major early hits and adding important album tracks like "You've Got to Hide Your Love Away," "Drive My Car," "Norwegian Wood" and "In My Life." Naturally, there are many great songs missing from the 26-track *1962-1966* and perhaps it would have made more sense to include the *Revolver* cuts on its companion volume, *1967-1970*, yet the Red Album captures the essence of the Beatles' pre-*Sgt. Pepper* records. —*Stephen Thomas Erlewine*

● **1967-1970** / Apr. 2, 1973 / Capitol ✦✦✦✦
Picking up where *1962-1966* left off, the double-album compilation *1967-1970*, commonly called the "Blue Album," covers the Beatles' later records, from *Sgt. Pepper* through *Let It Be*. Like the Red Album, the Blue Album contains a mixture of hits, including singles like "Lady Madonna," "Hey Jude" and "Revolution" that were never included on an LP, plus important album tracks like "Lucy in the Sky with Diamonds," "A Day in the Life," "While My Guitar Gently Weeps" and "Come Together." Like its predecessor, *1967-1970* misses several great songs, but the compilation nevertheless does capture the essence of the Beatles' later recordings. —*Stephen Thomas Erlewine*

Live at the Hollywood Bowl / May 4, 1977 / Capitol ✦✦✦
Previously unreleased live performances culled from shows at the Hollywood Bowl in 1964 and 1965. The screaming never stops, but the group's musical talent and personal charm shine through. —*William Ruhlmann*

Live! At the Star-Club in Hamburg, Germany / Jun. 13, 1977 / Lingasong ✦✦
The historical interest of this album is considerable: The Beatles, on the precipice of fame, playing their last Hamburg club show on December 31, 1962 (contrary to the 1961 date given on some liner notes). The problem, from a latter-day perspective, was that the Beatles didn't play all that well, and, more importantly, the sound is not up to par in the least, as it was captured on a primitive portable recorder. That said, it's interesting to hear the Beatles as they were in their club days, with a set list (almost exclusively covers) of rock 'n' roll tunes, several of which never made their way onto any official Beatle release. Their primal energy does come through, despite the missed notes and faint vocals. The US and European versions of this double album differ slightly, and the album has been reissued, in its entirety and in piecemeal excerpts, numerous times since it first appeared. —*Richie Unterberger*

Beatles Rarities [U.K.] / Oct. 19, 1979 / Parlophone ✦✦✦
In 1978, Parlophone Records in the UK released *The Beatles Collection*, a boxed set containing the Beatles' 12 original UK albums. Since the British tendency in the 1960s was not to include singles on albums, this meant that the box did not contain more than 30 tracks that had only appeared in Britain on singles and EPs. To make up for that to some extent, Parlophone added to the box a *Rarities* album containing 17 of those stray tracks (in the US, the box was released in a limited edition with a slightly different *Rarities* album, not to be confused with the *Rarities* album released in the US in 1980, which is completely different.) The idea was to include the least easily available of the lost tracks, so

hits like "Hey Jude" weren't included. In 1979, Parlophone issued the *Rarities* album separate from the box, and heard on its own it comes across as a miscellaneous collection which demonstrates that even Beatles B-sides could be enjoyable performances. —*William Ruhlmann*

Rarities [U.S.] / Mar. 4, 1980 / Capitol ✦✦
A disappointment even to hardcore fans when it was released, this gathered a few stray non-LP tracks and alternate mixes/versions that were slightly different from commonly available takes. Most of the rare tracks have been reissued on the *Past Masters* or *Please Please Me* CDs; the only reason to seek this out is if you're determined to track down the marginally different versions of a half-dozen songs like "Help!," "Don't Pass Me By," "Penny Lane," and "I'm Only Sleeping." —*Richie Unterberger*

The Beatles Conquer America [bootleg] / 1985 / NEMS ✦✦✦
There are dozens of live bootlegs from the Beatlemania era, but this one stands out, if you're trying to collect some selectively. Over half of this double LP features their complete performances from the three Ed Sullivan shows they taped in February 1964. These weren't just great, electrifying performances, featuring most of their best early songs, and capturing the group's jubilance at a time when they had yet to tire of live concerts. These were also truly historic events in the history of rock 'n' roll, introducing the best group of the 1960s to the United States, and lighting a musical and cultural fire under much of America's youth. The sound is pretty good (the music is usually clearly more audible than the frenzied screaming), taken directly from the two-inch video tapes onto which the songs were recorded. As significant bonuses, it also includes their fourth and final Ed Sullivan appearance from September 1965, and three songs that were broadcast on *Shindig* in January 1965. Not easy to find, but worth tracking down. —*Richie Unterberger*

☆ **Past Masters, Vol. 1** / Mar. 7, 1988 / Capitol ✦✦✦✦✦
When EMI and Capitol released the Beatles' recordings on compact disc, it was decided to issue the albums in their original British formats in both the UK and the US. The British albums frequently did not contain singles released by the Beatles at the same time, and there were other odd tracks not included on albums. Thus two discs were necessary to gather the stray material (some of which included their biggest hits). This first volume, for example, running from 1962 to 1965, contains "She Loves You," "I Want to Hold Your Hand," and "I Feel Fine." —*William Ruhlmann*

☆ **Past Masters, Vol. 2** / Mar. 7, 1988 / Capitol ✦✦✦✦✦
Completing the CD release of the Beatles' complete EMI/Capitol catalog, this disc contains "We Can Work It Out," "Paperback Writer," "Lady Madonna," "Hey Jude," "Get Back," "Let It Be," and other later Beatles songs. —*William Ruhlmann*

/ 1990 / Chthonian ✦✦✦

Unsurpassed Demos / 1993 / Yellow Dog [Bootleg] ✦✦✦✦
In May 1968 the Beatles assembled at George Harrison's home to demo material for their upcoming *White Album* sessions. The results have been frequently bootlegged; this is the most comprehensive single-disc collection, including 24 tunes in all. Predominantly acoustic in arrangement, with minimal percussion (if Ringo is present, it's not immediately evident), this has a great informal, almost campfire spirit, despite the tensions so widely reported of the group in the subsequent studio sessions. Many of the songs are extremely close in arrangement to the final studio versions, but it's great to hear them approach their ultimate shape with a cameraderie and light, joyful tone that unavoidably got muted when they were ironed out in the control room. John's songs are the most interesting (great versions of "Revolution," "Julia," "I'm So Tired," and "Sexy Sadie" especially), with occasional added half-serious lyrics; there are good versions of "Back in the USSR" and "Blackbird" as well. Also interesting are the songs that didn't make it onto the album: Lennon's "Child of Nature" (changed into "Jealous Guy" for *Imagine*), McCartney's "Singalong Junk" (which would surface on his first solo LP), and Harrison's "Sour Milk Sea" (given to Jackie Lomax), "Not Guilty," and "Circles" (both of which he'd eventually release on solo albums). —*Richie Unterberger*

Get Back Sessions / 1993 / [Bootleg] ✦✦✦
Get Back was the original title of the *Let It Be* album, but the album was shelved for a year before it finally gained official release. Because the Beatles were filmed for hundreds of hours during the course of the sessions, more unreleased material dates from this juncture of their career than any other. Unfortunately, the bulk of this ranks among their worst unreleased stuff, consisting mostly of sloppy rehearsals and chaotic covers of dozens of rock 'n' roll oldies. An unbelievable number of different bootlegs have issued this material in varying configurations since 1969, and although the recent CDs feature vastly improved sound quality, not much can be done to salvage the performances, which after all were never intended for circulation. However, there are some excellent cuts to be found, particularly in several alternate takes of songs from *Let It Be* (especially the stringless "Long and Winding Road"), and even the lousy

stuff serves as a fascinating illustration of the group's vast array of influences, their working methods in the studio, and, at worst, the roots of the band's disintegration. It's impossible to recommend specific collections, as there are hundreds of different titles floating around, even some box sets, and they're always uncovering more outtakes. The non-completist should look for the *Get Back* album as it was originally mastered and sequenced (featuring nearly the same content as *Let It Be*, but adding a couple of different songs and containing much different, less elaborate, un-Spectorized mixes) and/or the rooftop session from the film's final sequence, which is an inspired live performance of most of the material from *Let It Be*. — *Richie Unterberger*

Shea!/Candlestick Park / 1994 / Spank ✦✦✦

Although this isn't one of the Beatles' more notable live bootlegs, it does combine two of their most famous gigs onto one disc: the August 15, 1965 performance that found them playing to over 50,000 fans at New York's Shea Stadium, and their final performance before a paying audience at San Francisco's Candlestick Park on August 29, 1966. Yes, the screams are overwhelming in their volume and hysteria, but the fidelity and performances are pretty good considering the circumstances. The Shea Stadium performance was filmed for television, and (although this wasn't discovered until over 25 years later) the Beatles secretly overdubbed some parts onto the soundtrack in early 1966, accounting in part for why the sound is beefier here than it is on tapes of many other Beatle shows from the same period. The album comes with a great 48-page booklet of photos from the shows and lengthy recollections of the concert by Beatle PR man Tony Barrow. — *Richie Unterberger*

Live at the BBC / Dec. 1994 / Apple/Capitol ✦✦✦✦

From 1962 to 1965, the Beatles made 52 appearances on the BBC, recording live-in-the-studio performances of both their official releases and several dozen songs that they never issued on disc. This magnificent two-disc compilation features 56 of these tracks, including 29 covers of early rock, R&B, soul, and pop tunes that never appeared on their official releases, as well as the Lennon-McCartney original "I'll Be on My Way," which they gave in 1963 to Billy J. Kramer rather than record it themselves. These performances are nothing less than electrifying, especially the previously unavailable covers, which feature quite a few versions of classics by Chuck Berry, Little Richard, Carl Perkins, and Elvis Presley. There are also off-the-beaten-path tunes by the Everly Brothers and Buddy Holly, on down to obscurities by the Jodimars, Chan Romero (a marvelous "Hippy Hippy Shake"), Eddie Fontaine, and Ann-Margret. The greatest gem is probably their fabulous version of Arthur Alexander's "Soldier of Love," which (like several of the tracks) would have easily qualified as a highlight of their early releases if they had issued it officially. Restored from existing tapes of various quality, the sound is mostly very good and never less than listenable. Unfortunately, they weren't able to include every single rarity that the Beatles recorded for the BBC; the absence of Carl Perkins' "Lend Me Your Comb," which has circulated on bootlegs in a high-fidelity version and is now available on *Anthology 1*, is especially mystifying. Minor quibbles aside, these performances, available on bootlegs for years, compose the major missing chapter in the Beatles' legacy, and it's great to have them easily obtainable in a first-rate package. — *Richie Unterberger*

Anthology 1 / Nov. 21, 1995 / Apple/Capitol ✦✦✦

The first in a series of three double-CD sets of previously unreleased and rare Beatles material, released in conjunction with the mammoth *Anthology* video documentary. This covers the late '50s to the end of 1964, mixing studio outtakes, live performances, primitive recordings from the Quarrymen/Silver Beatles days, excerpts from the famous 1962 Decca audition, the most notable 1961 Tony Sheridan-era recordings, and brief spoken bits from interviews. Although this material is undeniably of vast historical importance, it can't be placed in the same company as the Beatles' proper albums, in either cohesion or quality. For that matter, for many Beatle fanatics, a good 50 percent or so of the set is no revelation, as much of this stuff has been circulating on bootleg (in somewhat lesser audio fidelity) for quite a while. While the studio outtakes (many never even heard on bootleg) are the most enticing items, these are almost exclusively alternate versions of songs they placed on their official releases (the most notable exceptions being the 1964 R&B cover "Leave My Kitten Alone," the 1962 demo "How Do You Do It," and the unimpressive 1964 Harrison original, "You Know What to Do"). Sometimes the differences are quite interesting (a much more electric-oriented version of "And I Love Her," for example), but the alternates also illustrate how the group were virtually unerring in selecting the best arrangement and take of their songs for the final versions. The 1963-64 live material is excellent in both performance and sound quality, though offered in piecemeal extracts. The pre-1962 items are sometimes taken from private rehearsal tapes of primitive fidelity, and are really of archival value only. One could go on at great length about the many curiosities and finds unearthed by this compilation, but for most general consumers, two observations may suffice. It does not stand up to the Beat-

les' fully conceived albums (even *Live at the BBC*), but the Beatles' scraps and leavings are more interesting than over 95 percent of other performers' best work. By that standard, this must be judged a worthwhile collection, especially (but not solely) for dedicated Beatles fans. — *Richie Unterberger*

Anthology 2 / Mar. 19, 1996 / Apple/Capitol ✦✦✦

As expected, the second installment of the *Anthology* series reflects the Beatles' increasing use of the studio-as-laboratory during their "middle years." Some live material from 1965 to 1966 appears on the first disc, and the second "reunion" single ("Real Love") leads off the set. But the emphasis is upon alternate takes from early 1965 to early 1968, during which time the group rapidly evolved from post-Merseybeat through folk-rock to psychedelia. As with the first volume, this is nearly always interesting, but perhaps thinner on revelations that some might expect. The *Help!*-era outtakes "If You've Got Troubles" and "That Means a Lot" are on the light side but very fun, especially the latter, which Paul and the group perform much better than P.J. Proby (who covered the song shortly afterward). Some of the alternate takes are extremely different, and excellent performances on their own merits: the funkier version of "I'm Looking Through You," the less mellow arrangement of "Norwegian Wood," a wall-of-drugs reverb for "Tomorrow Never Knows," a very Byrds-like approach to "And Your Bird Can Sing" (with giggle-laden vocals), an acoustic demo of "Fool on the Hill." The earlier, much more acoustic version of "Strawberry Fields Forever" is the most notable gem. On the other hand, much of the material differs from the official cuts in fairly minute gradations and will be of greater interest to scholars than general listeners (although discoveries like a different solo on "Penny Lane" are fascinating). The seven live tracks on disc one, from the waning days of Beatlemania, are better than many would have assumed, showing the group still capable of generating heat onstage. — *Richie Unterberger*

Anthology 3 / Oct. 29, 1996 / Capitol ✦✦✦✦

The final installment of the *Anthology* series has two discs of previously unreleased material from the *White Album* era through the group's demise in early 1970. In terms of sheer listenability, this may be the strongest volume of the three, if only because it focuses almost solely upon studio recordings, rather than mixing live concerts/broadcasts and outtakes. Also, by this time the Beatles had perfected their approach to recording, meaning that even the early/alternate versions of many of their cuts were often of outstanding quality. There's some prime stuff here: "unplugged" *White Album* demos from mid-'68, radically different versions of "While My Guitar Gently Weeps" and "Helter Skelter," a stringless "The Long and Winding Road," three beautifully sung and played Harrison solo demos from early 1969, and several songs the Beatles never released, like "All Things Must Pass," "Not Guilty," "Teddy Boy," "Come and Get It," and "Junk." Not everything here is so great that the casual consumer would be fascinated, of course. As on previous *Anthology* sets, some of these alternates are only very slightly different from the official versions; the oldies covers from the *Let It Be* era are off-the-cuff jams that aren't up to the group's usual level of brilliance. It's still a fascinating collection, both for the insight it affords us into the group's creative process at the end of their career, and for the considerable excellence of the music itself. — *Richie Unterberger*

Decca Tapes / Yellow Dog [Bootleg] ✦✦

On January 1, 1962, nearly a full year before the release of their debut single, the Beatles unsuccessfully auditioned for Decca Records. The complete, 15-song tape of the session—including a dozen covers and three Lennon-McCartney originals—has been much bootlegged since the 1970s, and has periodically appeared on piecemeal semi-legal releases (always missing the Lennon/McCartney tunes), but is easily available in its entirety on several different packages. The historical significance of this tape is vast; it illustrates where the Beatles were at this crucial juncture of their career. Less flatteringly, it illustrates how vastly they improved between the time of this audition and their first official album release, *Please Please Me*, 15 months later. In comparison, the sound here is thin and awkward, rife with tentative guitar phrases, nervous lead vocals, and stiff drumming (by Pete Best, who was still in the band at this point). Keeping in mind that this was never intended for public release, in hindsight one finds a great deal of potential and charm, as well as outlines of their great harmonies. The group ended up reprising a lot of the covers, like "Money" and "Till There Was You," on their early albums and BBC broadcasts in much better versions; they also covered some odd popular standards ("September In The Rain," "Sheik Of Araby") that appear nowhere else. Especially fascinating are the three Lennon/McCartney tunes, "Hello Little Girl," "Love Of The Loved," and "Like Dreamers Do," which they never released on EMI, but ended up giving to the Fourmost, Cilla Black, and the Applejacks respectively; the Beatles' versions are much more rock-oriented and much better. Some of this material is now officially available on *Anthology 1*. — *Richie Unterberger*

Ultra Rare Trax/Back-Track/Unsurpassed Masters / [Bootleg] ◆◆◆
The release of the 13-song *Sessions* bootleg was followed a few years later by a veritable flood of EMI outtakes on the multi-volume series *Ultra Rare Trax*, which has appeared with further embellishments on the *Back-Track* and *Unsurpassed Masters* series. Besides reprising material from *Sessions*, these unearthed dozens of alternate takes of classic Beatles material spanning their entire career, ranging from nearly identical alternate mixes to radically different arrangements and versions. The latter are the most interesting, standouts being the vastly different, folkier (and great) earlier versions of "Strawberry Fields Forever" and a much different version of "Norwegian Wood." There are also considerably different takes of "She's A Woman," "From Me To You," "Can't Buy Me Love," "The Fool On The Hill," "I Saw Her Standing There," "A Hard Day's Night," and "Flying," as well as rehearsals and backing tracks which provide intimate glimpses of works-in-progress like "Help." The fidelity on these are usually outstanding, easily up to official standards, making these outtakes essential for serious Beatle scholars and many general Beatle fans. Some of this material is now available on the *Anthology* series. —*Richie Unterberger*

Live in Tokyo / [Bootleg] ◆◆◆
When the Beatles performed in Tokyo in 1966, they were filmed by Japanese television, resulting in one of the finest quality live tapes of the group from the Beatlemania era. The problem lies in the performances; by this time, they had tired of touring and were to a large degree going through the motions. So, despite the release-quality fidelity of this set, listeners may be taken aback by the fair number of flubbed notes, off-key harmonies, and indifferent vocals (on Harrison's "If I Needed Someone" in particular). All things considered, it could have been much worse; the group were struggling with jet-decibel-level screaming fans and primitive sound systems, after all, and they largely do manage to sing and play with reasonable conviction, especially McCartney, always the most committed onstage performer of the four. Includes many of their hits from the late-'64 to mid-'66 era; especially interesting is the stringless band version of "Yesterday," as none of the Beatles except Paul played on the studio recording. —*Richie Unterberger*

The Beau Brummels

f. 1964, San Francisco, CA, **db.** 1969
Country-Rock, Folk-Rock, Pop-Rock
Although they only had two big hits, the Beau Brummels were one of the most important and underrated American groups of the 1960s. They were the first US unit of any sort to successfully respond to the British Invasion. They were arguably the first folk-rock group, even predating the Byrds, and also anticipated some key elements of the San Francisco psychedelic sound with their soaring harmonies and exuberant melodies. Before they finally reached the end of the string, they were also among the first bands to record country-rock in the late '60s.

The axis of the band was formed by guitarist/songwriter Ron Elliott, who penned most of the Brummels' moody and melodious material, and singer Sal Valentino, owner of one of the finest voices in mid-'60s rock. Spotted by local DJ Tom Donahue in a club in San Mateo (just south of San Francisco), the group was signed to Donahue's small San Francisco-based label, Autumn Records, in 1964. With Sly Stewart (later Sly Stone) in the producer's chair, they made the Top 20 right off the bat with "Laugh, Laugh." The melancholy, minor-key original sounded so much like the British bands inundating the airwaves that many listeners initially mistook the Brummels for an English act. The followup single, "Just a Little," was another excellent, moody number that became their biggest hit, making the Top Ten.

The Beau Brummels made a couple of fine albums in 1965, dominated by strong original material and featuring the band's ringing guitars and multipart, mournful harmonies. The best of their early work is nearly as fine as the Byrds' first recordings, but the band was losing ground commercially, partially because Autumn, being such a small label, lacked promotional muscle. "You Tell Me Why" was their only other Top 40 hit, though "Sad Little Girl" and the Byrds knockoff "Don't Talk to Strangers" were excellent singles. The band also shuffled personnel a few times, and Ron Elliott was unable to stay on the road because of diabetes. Autumn was sold in 1966 to Warner, who made the lunk-headed move of forcing the band to record an entire album of Top 40 covers—ignoring the fact that original material was one of the Brummels' primary fortes.

Regrouping as a trio, the group recorded a critically acclaimed, more experimental album in 1967, *Triangle*. Their last Warner LP, *Bradley's Barn*, found the group branching into country-rock, a year or so before it became trendy. The Beau Brummels did re-form for an unimpressive reunion album in 1975, and although Ron Elliott and Sal Valentino continued to make music and work on various low-profile projects of their own, they've never made records on par with the Brummels' vintage work. —*Richie Unterberger*

Introducing the Beau Brummels / Apr. 1965 / Sundazed ◆◆◆◆
A much stronger debut than the norm for the era. Ten of the 12 cuts are Ron Elliott originals, including the hits "Laugh Laugh," "Still in Love with You Baby," and "Just a Little." The hard-rocking numbers are the weakest, but "Stick Like Glue" and "I Would Be Happy" are fine Beatlesque numbers, and "They'll Make You Cry" is a first-rate moody folk-rocker. The CD reissue adds two bonus tracks, a demo of "Just a Little," and the single "Good Time Music." —*Richie Unterberger*

The Beau Brummels, Vol. 2 / 1965 / Sundazed ◆◆◆
No big hits on this album, but it's the best LP by the Brummels' first lineup. The 12 original songs feature several fine Ron Elliott harmony folk-rockers that stand up well to the Byrds' material from the same era, including "I Want You," "You Tell Me Why," "Sad Little Girl," and the Byrds imitation "Don't Talk to Strangers." The CD reissue adds bonus alternate versions of "Woman" and "When It Comes to Your Love." —*Richie Unterberger*

Beau Brummels '66 / Jul. 1966 / Warner Brothers ◆◆
Picture this: it's 1966, you're a major label, and you've just acquired one of the best rock groups in America for your roster. Not only that, but one of the band's chief strengths is its excellent original material. So what do you have them do for the first album under your direction? Naturally, you have them record cover versions of some of the biggest rock and pop hits of the last year or so! It would be an unimaginably idiotic strategy today, but it was an idiotic strategy even then, when rock criticism was in its infancy, and such a marrow-headed move would pass unnoticed. The group clearly isn't putting too much of their heart and soul into covers of smashes by the Beatles, Byrds, and Mamas & Papas, along with ludicrous selections like "Mrs. Brown You've Got a Lovely Daughter" and "Bang Bang." It's not as bad as you think—Sal Valentino, as the cliche goes, could sing the telephone book and make it sound not half-bad. But it was a commercial and artistic disaster that, even more crucially, helped put the nail in the coffin of the group's original and best incarnation. —*Richie Unterberger*

Triangle / Jul. 1967 / Warner Brothers ◆◆◆◆
A beautiful venture by the surviving trio into a more authentic form of folk and country-rock, with a repertoire that recalls the more famous Everly Brothers classic, *Roots*. —*Bruce Eder*

Bradley's Barn / Oct. 1968 / Edsel ◆◆◆
Only vocalist Sal Valentino and guitarist/arranger Ron Elliott remained in the Beau Brummels by the time of their 1968 swan song, recorded at Owen Bradley's Nashville studios. While the album is influenced by country and Western, the Brummels haven't forsaken their pop roots either; unlike most crossovers, *Bradley's Barn* creates a workable fusion between the two, emphasizing the best qualities of each. —*Jason Ankeny*

From the Vaults / 1982 / Rhino ◆◆◆◆
A very solid collection of rare or previously unreleased material from the group's mid-'60s prime. Mostly Ron Elliott originals, they're easily up to the standard of the ones that made it onto their first two LPs, with "Gentle Wondering Ways," "She Loves Me," "She Sends Me," and "Love Is Just a Game" being standouts. Achingly tuneful folk-rock, it also includes an alternate, slower version of "Sad Little Girl," the silly dance-rock confection "The Jerk," and a few cuts that hint at the country-rock direction they would take in the late '60s. —*Richie Unterberger*

● **The Best of the Beau Brummels: Golden Archive Series** / 1987 / Rhino ◆◆◆◆
Probably the best (and best-sounding) anthology covering their golden years, although it lacks their brilliant, later country-based work at its best. —*Bruce Eder*

Autumn of Their Years / 1994 / Big Beat ◆◆◆
These underrated folk-rock pioneers cut a great number of unreleased outtakes/demos during their mid-'60s prime that didn't make it onto the albums they released for the tiny Autumn label during that period. Fourteen of those songs were released in the early 1980s by Rhino on the fine *From the Vaults* album. *Autumn of Their Years* reprises ten of those tunes and adds 16 previously unreleased cuts for a grand total of 26, all of which are group originals. There are a lot of fine moments here, but it's actually a bit much for all but hardcore fans. First off, the best cuts—ones like "She Sends Me," "Dream On," and "Love Is Just a Game," which display their supremely haunting folk-rock melodicism and minor-key harmonies—were already available on *From the Vaults*. The 16 newly found demos aren't as good, production-wise (several are acoustic sketches) or material-wise. Earlier demos of their hits "Laugh Laugh," "Just a Little," and "Still in Love with You Baby" are interesting in comparison to the originals, but not as good. And some strong cuts from *From the Vaults* are inexplicably omitted. Of the new vault finds, the highlight is "Tomorrow Is Another Day," an acoustic ballad showcasing Sal Valentino's rich and moving vocals. —*Richie Unterberger*

San Fran Sessions / Jun. 11, 1996 / Sundazed ✦✦✦
Be clear from the git-go: this three-CD, 60-song set, which consists *solely* of rarities, demos, alternate takes, and unissued performances from 1964-66, should be acquired only by serious fans of the band. It's not the place to start, and most listeners would be better served by picking up a greatest hits disc or the original Autumn albums. If you do love the band, though, it's an excellent journey through the backwaters of their early repertoire. The Brummels rarely wrote or recorded anything lousy, and this presents interesting, substantially different versions of officially released songs like "Laugh, Laugh" and "Just a Little"; obscure tracks that have been available only on out-of-print LPs or import collections; and quite a few demos that have never before seen the light. The beautifully sad harmonies and glittering guitar arrangements are usually present, and the compositions—even the totally unissued ones—are usually quite strong. From a historical viewpoint, it's interesting in that it presents a lot of previously unheard Sal Valentino-penned tunes. (Ron Elliott wrote most of the songs that ended up on official releases.) The sound is superb, as are the liner notes. —*Richie Unterberger*

The Beautiful South

f. 1989, Hull, England
Alternative Pop-Rock, Pop-Rock
After the British indie-pop group the Housemartins disbanded in 1989, vocalist Paul Heaton and drummer David Hemmingway formed the Beautiful South. Where their previous group relied on jazzy guitars and witty, wry lyrics, the Beautiful South boasted a more sophisticated, jazzy pop sound, layered with keyboards, R&B-inflected female backing vocals, and, occasionally, light orchestrations. Often, the group's relaxed, catchy songs contradicted the sarcastic, cynical thrust of the lyrics. Nevertheless, the band's pleasant arrangements often tempered whatever bitterness there was in Heaton's lyrics, and that's part of the reason the Beautiful South became quite popular within its native Britain during the '90s. Though the group never found a niche in America—by the middle of the decade, their records weren't even being released in the US—their string of melodic jazz-pop singles made them one of the most successful, if one of the least flashy, bands in Britain. Their popularity was confirmed by the astonishing success of their 1994 singles compilation, *Carry On up the Charts*, which became one of the biggest-selling albums in British history.

Heaton and Hemmingway formed the Beautiful South immediately after the breakup of the Housemartins, who were one of the most popular and well-reviewed British guitar-pop bands of the mid-'80s. The Housemartins had earned a reputation for being somewhat downbeat Northerners, so the duo chose the name Beautiful South sarcastically. To complete the lineup, the pair hired former Anthill Runaways vocalist Briana Corrigan, bassist Sean Welch, drummer David Stead (formerly a Housemartins roadie), and guitarist David Rotheray, who became Heaton's new collaborator. In the summer of 1989 they released their first single, "Song for Whoever," on the Housemartins' old record label, Go!. "Song for Whoever" climbed to No. 2, while its follow-up, "You Keep It All In," peaked at No. 8 in September 1989. A month later the group's debut, *Welcome to the Beautiful South*, was released to positive reviews.

"A Little Time," the first single from the group's second album *Choke*, became the group's first No. 1 single in the fall of 1990. *Choke* was also well received, even though it didn't quite match the performance of the debut, in terms of either sales or reviews. In particular, some critics complained that Heaton was becoming too clever and cynical for his own good. The Beautiful South released their third album, *0898*, in 1992; it was their first record not to be released in the United States, but it maintained their success in Britain. After the release of *0898*, Corrigan left the group, reportedly upset over some of Heaton's ironic lyrics. She was replaced by Jacqui Abbot, who made her first appearance on the band's fourth album, 1994's *Miaow.*

While both *0898* and *Miaow* were popular, they were only moderate successes. Their respectable chart performances in no way prepared any observers, including the band themselves, for the blockbuster success of *Carry On up the Charts*, a greatest-hits collection released at the end of 1994. *Carry On up the Charts* entered the charts at No. 1. It was one of the fastest-selling albums in UK history, and its success outlasted the Christmas season. The album stayed at No. 1 for several months, going platinum many times over and, in the process, becoming one of the most popular albums in British history. The album wasn't released in America until late 1995, after it broke several UK records. The Beautiful South released their follow-up to *Miaow, Blue Is the Colour*, in the fall of 1996. —*Stephen Thomas Erlewine*

Welcome to the Beautiful South / Oct. 1989 / Go! Discs ✦✦✦✦
The difference between the catchy light pop that constitutes the Beautiful South's music and the bitter, pessimistic lyrics innocently sung by Paul Heaton is so great it constitutes a kind of malevolent seduction. But

that's the point. Released in the US in January 1990. —*William Ruhlmann*

Choke / Nov. 1990 / Go! Discs ✦✦✦
The Beautiful South's second album conceals its bitter, mean cynicism in layers of lush, jazz-tinged pop, making all of the bile go down easily. —*Stephen Thomas Erlewine*

0898 / Apr. 1992 / Go! Discs ✦✦✦
There are no big poses or walls of crunchy guitars on *0898*. Instead, the group—which includes three lead vocalists—deals in fragile melodies and harmonies, soulful but low-key instrumentation, and lyrics full of subtle social commentary and humor. In North America, where mainstream audiences have been well trained to salivate to very obvious musical bells, the Beautiful South may be too clever for its own good. At times, the group even couches itself in the guise of a smooth lounge act, rebelling against current trends by having something to say while not making a racket about it. Producer John Kelly (Peter Gabriel) has contributed an incisive and full-bodied production to *0898*, a great improvement over the rather thin sound of the group's previous *Choke.* —*Roch Parisien*

Miaow / 1994 / Go! Discs ✦✦✦
The Beautiful South expanded upon the sound of *0898* with *Miaow*, another expertly crafted set of sophisticated, jazzy pop. Even with the addition of new vocalist Jacqueline Abbot, the band has not changed much between the two albums and what is different is subtle—the arrangements are more intricate and the melodies are more graceful. Though the album is slightly uneven, much of the music is excellent, highlighted by "Prettiest Eyes" and a cover of Fred Neil's "Everybody's Talkin." —*Stephen Thomas Erlewine*

● **Carry On up the Charts: The Best Of** / Nov. 16, 1994 / Go! Discs ✦✦✦✦
Carry On up the Charts: The Best of the Beautiful South was the surprise British hit of 1994, going platinum five times between its late fall release and the summer of 1995. The success was surprising, because while the band had been modestly popular, their last few albums were sliding down the charts. However, their hits collection, *Carry On up the Charts*, flew to No. 1 and stayed there for weeks. It's nothing more than all their singles, but compiled they make the most convincing case for the Beautiful South's sly, cynical sophisticated pop. *Carry On up the Charts* was finally released in the United States in the fall of 1995, with fewer tracks. —*Stephen Thomas Erlewine*

Blue is the Colour / Nov. 5, 1996 / Go! Discs ✦✦✦✦

Be Bop Deluxe

f. 1972, England, db. 1978
Art-Rock/Progressive-Rock
Be-Bop Deluxe was a 1970s British rock group led by guitarist Bill Nelson (b. Dec. 18, 1948, Wakefield, Yorkshire, England) that veered between glam-rock, pop, and heavy metal, with lots of demonstrations of Nelson's guitar prowess. After recording with Gentle Revolution and on his own, Nelson put together the first lineup of Be-Bop Deluxe in 1972: Ian Parkin (guitar); Robert Bryan (drums); and Nicholas Chatterton-Dew (drums). But after the release of the first album, *Axe Victim*, Nelson sacked the band. The second album, *Futurama*, featured Nelson with a rhythm section of bassist Charles Tumahai and drummer Simon Fox. Keyboard player Andrew Clark joined for the third album, *Sunburst Finish*, which contained the UK chart single "Ships in the Night." Be-Bop Deluxe released a fourth album, *Modern Music,*; a concert recording, *Live! In the Air Age*, that became their only UK Top Ten hit; and a fifth studio album, *Drastic Plastic*, before Nelson folded the enterprise, briefly tried another group, Red Noise, and went solo again in 1979. Since then he has recorded prolifically, if experimentally, and handled occasional production jobs. —*William Ruhlmann*

Axe Victim / 1974 / Harvest ✦✦✦
When Be-Bop Deluxe's first album was released during the glam-rock wave in 1974, and the band (then comprising Bill Nelson and Ian Parkin on guitars, Robert Bryan on bass, and Nicholas Chatterton-Dew on drums) turned up on the back of the record cover in heavy makeup, it was viewed as being in the David Bowie mold, which certainly took in Nelson's thin but confident tenor vocals and the uptempo rock approach, and even ballads like "Adventures in a Yorkshire Landscape" that sounded a lot like Bowie's "Rock 'n' Roll Suicide." But it was already obvious that Nelson was an unusually lyrical guitarslinger, and in fact the tunes often took a backseat to his sometimes jazzy, sometimes metallish excursions. He was, as he sang, "an axe victim," but at the same time, Be-Bop Deluxe's musical identity was uncertain. —*William Ruhlmann*

Futurama / Jul. 1975 / Harvest ✦✦
Bill Nelson sacked the rest of Be-Bop Deluxe after the release of *Axe Victim* and hired bassist Charles Tumahai and drummer Simon Fox to make *Futurama*. The back cover shows Nelson, decked out in a fool's

costume, chained and restrained by his new bandmates. But on the record, he lets his guitar playing free to dominate the proceedings even more than it did on Be-Bop's debut and constructs sometimes overly elaborate arrangements that overwhelm whatever substance the songs might otherwise have. — *William Ruhlmann*

Sunburst Finish / Jan. 1976 / Harvest ✦✦✦✦
Adding keyboard player Andrew Clark to make Be-Bop Deluxe a quartet, Bill Nelson finally found a balance between his virtuosic guitar playing and the demands of pop songwriting. The arrangements were still busy, but the humor of Nelson's music was on display as never before, and the songs frequently were catchy. For the first time, it began to seem that the group had a future beyond serving as a foundation for Nelson's splashy guitar work, as Be-Bop Deluxe charted in the US and the UK and even scored a Top 25 British hit with "Ships in the Night." — *William Ruhlmann*

Modern Music / Sep. 1976 / Harvest ✦✦✦
Things had changed for Be-Bop Deluxe by the time of its fourth album. The band that turned up in glam-rock regalia on its 1974 debut, *Axe Victim*, was in suit and tie on the cover of *Modern Music* in 1976. Inside, the band's transformation into a sophisticated pop group seemed complete. Arrangements were still ornate, but the songs were dominated by their highly imagistic lyrics, and as often as not, Nelson was borrowing ideas from the Beatles. It didn't quite work, despite pleasant numbers such as "Orphans of Babylon" and "Kiss of Light," perhaps because a true pop sensibility requires a gift for simplicity that Nelson has never exhibited. The album charted high in England and made the Top 100 in the US, but it was Be-Bop's peak, not its breakthrough. — *William Ruhlmann*

Drastic Plastic / Feb. 1978 / Harvest ✦✦✦
Guitarist/leader Bill Nelson has always had his head in a space that's defined by the 1950s World's Fair idea of the future—a world of monorails and strange machines. This is particularly evident here, with Nelson's affection for Japan competing for space with paeans to electrical communication. At times charming and even romantic, at other times outré, *Drastic Plastic* marked the end of the band and hinted at Nelson's musical experiments to come. — *Steven McDonald*

● **Raiding the Divine Archive: The Best of Be Bop Deluxe** / Aug. 1990 / Capitol ✦✦✦✦
The release is a smartly assembled overview of the arty-sci-fi-rock outfit (heavier on the rock), led by Bill Nelson, one of the most powerfully elegant lead guitarists of the '70s. The band was an early experimenter in techno-rock. Dense clinical production (sometimes recalling mid-period Roxy Music), further underscored by Nelson's cold detached vocals, does a poor job of drawing the listener into appreciating the band's real musical strengths. — *Rick Clark*

Beck

b. Jul. 8, 1970, Los Angeles, CA
Guitar, Vocals / Alternative Pop-Rock, Lo-Fi, Indie Rock
With his porta-studio, keyboard, drum machine, and guitar, singer-songwriter Beck (b. Beck Hansen) created music that celebrated the junk culture of the '90s. Beck's music drew from hip-hop, folk, experimental rock, psychedelia, pop, and rock 'n' roll, recycling everything into a colorful, messy, and willfully diverse brand of post-modern rock, filled with warped, satiric imagery and clumsy poetry. With all of his rootless eclecticism, Beck is distinctly a product of the '90s; all of his influences were processed through television and records, not real-life experiences. But that trashy, disposable quality is what makes his music unique.

Beck came to national attention in early 1994, when his folky hip-hop single "Loser" began to receive airplay on alternative rock stations across America. "Loser" was originally released independently on a California label in late 1993. The single became a club hit and quickly spread to underground and alternative radio stations. Beck became the center of a major-label bidding war; he eventually signed with DGC Records. Beck released his debut album, *Mellow Gold*, in early 1994. *Mellow Gold* received rave reviews and became a gold record as "Loser" climbed into the Top Ten. Beck's contract with DGC allows him to release records that he and the company deem uncommercial on indie labels. Consequently, the singer-songwriter released two new records by the summer of 1994, which were both recorded at roughly the same time as *Mellow Gold*. *Stereopathetic Soulmanure* was a noisy, more experimental album than his debut and was released on Flipside Records. *One Foot in the Grave* accentuated his folk roots and was released on K Records. Neither album sold on the level of *Mellow Gold*, but both sold respectably.

As he prepared his second album for DGC, Beck toured with Lollapalooza Five in the summer of 1995. Beck's second major-label album, *Odelay*, finally appeared in the summer of 1996; it was released to overwhelmingly positive reviews. Throughout 1996, word-of-mouth began to spread on *Odelay*, and it earned Album of the Year status from most major critics' polls and, even more surprisingly, it received several Grammy Nominations, including Album of the Year. — *Stephen Thomas Erlewine*

Mellow Gold / Mar. 1994 / DGC ✦✦✦✦
From its kaleidoscopic array of junk-culture musical styles to its assured, surrealistic wordplay, Beck's debut album *Mellow Gold* is a stunner. Throughout the record, Beck plays as if there are no divisions between musical genres, freely blending rock, rap, folk, psychedelia, and country. Although his inspired sense of humor occasionally plays as if he's a smirking, irony-addled hipster, his music is never kitschy, and his wordplay is constantly inspired. Since *Mellow Gold* was pieced together from home-recorded tapes, it lacks coherent production, functioning more as a stylistic sampler; there are the stoner raps of "Loser" and "Beercan," the urban folk of "Pay No Mind (Snoozer)," the mock-industrial onslaught of "Motherf—er," the garagey "F—-in' with My Head," the trancy acoustic "Blackhole," and the gently sardonic folk-rock of "Nitemare Hippy Girl." It's a dizzying demonstration of musical skills, but it's all tied together by a simple, yet clever, sense of songcraft and a truly original lyrical viewpoint, one that's basic but as colorful as free verse. By blending boundaries so thoroughly and intoxicatingly, *Mellow Gold* established a new vein of alternative rock, one that was fueled by ideas instead of attitude. — *Stephen Thomas Erlewine*

Stereopathetic Soulmanure / Apr. 1994 / Flipside ✦✦
Within months of the release of *Mellow Gold*, Beck released his second album, *Stereopathetic Soulmanure*, a schizophrenic collection of lo-fi recordings from between 1988 and 1993. Much of the music on the album draws from the noisy, experimental post-punk of Sonic Youth and the dirty, primitive junk-rock of Pussy Galore; his absurdist sense of humor surfaces only rarely, and only in the guise of such sophomoric cuts as "Jagermeister Pie" and "Satan Gave Me a Taco," while his sense of songcraft is inaudible. Essentially, the record was both a palate-cleanser, one designed to scare away the "Loser" fans, and a bid for indie credibility, since the music on *Stereopathetic* is as uncompromising and as unlistenable as Sonic Youth or their many imitators at their most extreme. — *Stephen Thomas Erlewine*

One Foot in the Grave / Aug. 1994 / K ✦✦✦✦
One Foot in the Grave appeared not long after the noisy freak-out of *Stereopathetic Soulmanure*, and its quiet, folky textures couldn't be more different from its predecessor, or the genre-bending *Mellow Gold*, for that matter. Recorded before *Mellow Gold*, the record showcases Beck as a post-modern folkie, and the results are revelatory. Stripped of the intoxicating production that dominated *Mellow Gold*, Beck's songs prove to be wonderful, vibrant tunes, teeming with emotion, haunting wordplay, and simple, memorable melodies. It's alternately haunting and jubilant, and Calvin Johnston's occasional harmonies lend the record an intimate warmth. It's a gentle record, and its collection of small gems is every bit as impressive as the songs on *Mellow Gold* or its 1996 follow-up, *Odelay*. — *Stephen Thomas Erlewine*

● **Odelay** / Jun. 18, 1996 / DGC ✦✦✦✦
Beck's debut, *Mellow Gold*, was a glorious sampler of musical styles, careening from lo-fi hip-hop to folk, moving back through garage rock and arty noise. It was an impressive album, but the parts didn't necessarily stick together. The two albums that followed within months of *Mellow Gold*—*Stereopathetic Soulmanure* and *One Foot in the Grave*—were specialist releases that disproved the idea that Beck was simply a one-hit wonder. But *Odelay*, the much-delayed proper follow-up to *Mellow Gold*, proves the depth and scope of his talents. *Odelay* fuses the disparate strands of Beck's music—folk, country, hip-hop, rock 'n' roll, blues, jazz, easy listening, rap, pop—into one dense sonic collage. Songs frequently morph from one genre to another, seemingly unrelated genres; bursts of noise give way to country songs with hip-hop beats, easy listening melodies transform into a weird fusion of pop, jazz and cinematic strings. It's genre-defying music that refuses to see boundaries. All of the songs on *Odelay* are rooted in simple forms—whether it's blues ("Devil's Haircut"), country ("Lord Only Knows," "Sissyneck"), soul ("Hotwax"), folk ("Ramshackle"), or rap ("High 5 (Rock the Catskills)," "Where It's At")—but they twist the conventions of the genre. "Where It's At" is peppered with soul, jazz, funk, and rap references, while "Novacane" slams from indie rock to funk and back to white noise. With the aid of the Dust Brothers, Beck has created a dense, endlessly intriguing album overflowing with ideas. Furthermore, it's an album that completely ignores the static, nihilistic trends of the American alternative/independent underground, creating a fluid, creative, and startlingly original work. — *Stephen Thomas Erlewine*

Jeff Beck

b. Jun. 24, 1944, Wallington, Surrey, England
Guitar / Rock 'n' Roll, Electric British Blues, Hard Rock, Fusion
While he was as innovative as Jimmy Page, as tasteful as Eric Clapton, and nearly as visionary as Jimi Hendrix, Jeff Beck never achieved the same commercial success as his contemporaries, primarily because of the haphazard way he approached his career. After Rod

Stewart left the Jeff Beck Group in 1971, Beck never worked with a charismatic lead singer who could have helped sell his music to a wide audience. Furthermore, he was simply too idiosyncratic, moving from heavy metal to jazz-fusion within a blink of an eye. As his career progressed, he became more fascinated by automobiles than guitars, releasing only one album during the course of the '90s. All the while, Beck retained the respect of fellow guitarists, who found his reclusiveness alluring.

Jeff Beck began his musical career after a short stint at London's Wimbledon Art College. He earned a reputation by supporting Lord Sutch, which helped him land the job as the Yardbirds' lead guitarist after the departure of Eric Clapton. Beck stayed with the Yardbirds for nearly two years, leaving in late 1966 on the pretext that he was retiring from music. He returned several months later with "Love Is Blue," a single he played poorly because he detested the song. Later in 1967 he formed the Jeff Beck Group with vocalist Rod Stewart, bassist Ron Wood, and drummer Aynsley Dunbar, who was quickly replaced by Mickey Waller; keyboardist Nicky Hopkins joined in early 1968. With their crushingly loud reworkings of blues songs and vocal and guitar interplay, the Jeff Beck Group established the template for heavy metal. Neither of the band's records, Truth (1968) nor Beck-Ola (a 1969 album that was recorded with new drummer Tony Newman), was particularly successful, and the band tended to fight regularly, especially on their frequent tours of the US. In 1970 Stewart and Wood left to join the Faces, and Beck broke up the group.

Beck had intended to form a power trio with Vanilla Fudge members Carmine Appice (drums) and Tim Bogert (bass), but those plans were derailed when he was in a serious car crash in 1970. By the time he recuperated in 1971, Bogart and Appice were playing in Cactus, so the guitarist formed a new version of the Jeff Beck Group. Featuring keyboardist Max Middleton, drummer Cozy Powell, bassist Clive Chaman, and vocalist Bobby Tench, the new band recorded Rough and Ready (1972) and The Jeff Beck Group (1973). Neither album attracted much attention. Cactus dissolved in late 1972, and Beck, Bogert, and Appice formed a power trio the next year. The group's lone studio album—a live record was released in Japan but never in the UK or US—was widely panned for its plodding arrangements and weak vocals, and the group disbanded the next year.

For about 18 months Beck remained quiet, re-emerging in 1975 with Blow by Blow. Produced by George Martin, Blow by Blow was an all-instrumental jazz-fusion album that received strong reviews. Beck collaborated with Jan Hammer, a former keyboardist for the Mahavishnu Orchestra, for 1976's Wired, and supported the album with a co-headlining tour with Hammer's band. The tour was documented on the 1977 album Jeff Beck with the Jan Hammer Group—Live.

After the Hammer tour, Beck retired to his estate outside London and remained quiet for three years. He returned in 1980 with There and Back, which featured contributions from Hammer. After the tour for There and Back, Beck retired again, returning five years later with the slick, Nile Rogers-produced Flash. A pop-rock album recorded with a variety of vocalists, Flash featured Beck's only hit single, the Stewart-sung "People Get Ready," and boasted "Escape," which won the Grammy for Best Rock Instrumental. During 1987 he played lead guitar on Mick Jagger's second solo album, Primitive Cool. There was another long wait between Flash and 1989's Jeff Beck's Guitar Shop with Terry Bozzio and Tony Hymas. Though the album sold only moderately well, Guitar Shop received uniformly strong reviews and won the Grammy for Best Rock Instrumental. Beck supported the album with a tour, this time co-headlining with guitarist Stevie Ray Vaughan. Again, Beck entered semi-retirement upon the completion of the tour.

In 1992 Beck played lead guitar on Roger Waters' comeback album, Amused to Death. A year later he released Crazy Legs, a tribute to Gene Vincent and his lead guitarist Cliff Gallup, which was recorded with the Big Town Playboys. Beck remained quiet after the album's release. — Stephen Thomas Erlewine

Truth / Aug. 1968 / Epic ✦✦✦✦
Along with Led Zeppelin's self-titled first album, Jeff Beck's Truth is considered the primo primer for what came to be known as heavy metal. Fusing the thunderous rhythm section of Ron Wood on bass and Mickey Waller on drums with his paint-blistering lead guitar and Rod Stewart's gravel-and-whiskey vocals, Beck's visionary approach to blues and rock 'n' roll influenced practically every rock band that followed on both sides of the Atlantic. Although Beck could be unpredictable and eclectic (witness his straightforward, acoustic reading of "Greensleeves"), Truth features the smoking "Beck's Bolero," "Rock My Plimsoul," and the wah-wah pièce de résistance, "I Ain't Superstitious." — Tom Graves

Beck-Ola / Jun. 1969 / Epic ✦✦✦✦
A year after Jeff Beck recorded Truth, he came back with the even heavier Beck-Ola. Although the songwriting seems diluted, and the addition of Nicky Hopkins on piano added spice in all the wrong places, Beck-Ola is still a gut-slamming good time. Notable tracks include "Spanish Boots" and "Plynth (Water Down the Drain)." — Tom Graves

Rough & Ready / Oct. 1971 / Epic ✦✦✦
After Jeff Beck nearly died in a car crash, he came back in 1971 with a new group and a new sound, reflecting his more introspective state of mind. Although the firepower and guitar blasts are still there, he burns cooler. With the help of the jazzy Max Middleton on piano, Beck created one of rock's most haunting set pieces, "Raynes Park Blues." Other highlights include the dynamic ballad "Jody" and the hard grinding rock groove of "I've Been Used." — Tom Graves & Rick Clark

Jeff Beck Group / Apr. 1972 / Epic ✦✦✦
Continuing with the same group lineup as on Rough & Ready, Jeff Beck Group was slagged off by critics for Steve Cropper's admittedly lazy production. However, several of the songs hold up masterfully, including the skronky "Ice Cream Cakes," the superlative redo of Don Nix's "Going Down," and the beautifully sad and wistful instrumental, "Definitely Maybe." Beware of early, poor-sounding versions. — Tom Graves

Blow by Blow / Mar. 1975 / Epic ✦✦✦✦
When Jeff Beck announced that he was working on an all-instrumental album, few but his legion of guitar fans could have predicted the far-reaching impact of this pivotal jazz-rock fusion album. Teamed with the Beatles' ex-producer George Martin, Beck singlehandedly created a new subtext for rock 'n' roll. With his virtuosity and taste at an all-time peak, Beck let loose with such unforgettable tracks as the Roy Buchanan-inspired "Cause We've Ended as Lovers" and the percolating "Freeway Jam." This is one of rock's great instrumental works. — Tom Graves

Wired / May 1976 / Epic ✦✦✦✦
Nearly Blow by Blow's equal, although Beck doesn't venture any further musically. Charles Mingus' "Goodbye Pork Pie Hat" alone is worth the price. (Available on Mobile Fidelity's Ultradisc) — Tom Graves

Live with the Jan Hammer Group / Mar. 1977 / Epic ✦✦
Jeff Beck toured to promote Wired, backed by a jazz-fusion group led by synthesizer player Jan Hammer. This straightforward live souvenir combines songs from Blow by Blow and Wired, plus a few other things, and while it features typically fiery playing from Beck, the backup is a bit too heavy-handed and the occasional vocals (by Hammer and drummer Tony Smith) are embarrassing. — William Ruhlmann

There & Back / Jun. 1980 / Epic ✦✦✦
Jeff Beck's first new studio album in four years found him moving from old keyboard partner Jan Hammer (three tracks) to new one Tony Hymas (five), which turned out to be the difference between competition and support. Hence, the second side of this instrumental album is more engaging and less of a funk-fusion extravaganza than most of the first. If it were anybody else, you'd say that this was a transitional album, but this was the only studio album Beck released between 1976 and 1985, which makes it more like an unexpected Christmas letter from an old friend: "Everything's fine, still playing guitar." — William Ruhlmann

Flash / Jul. 1985 / Epic ✦✦✦
Produced by Nile Rodgers and Arthur Baker, Flash is Beck's surprisingly successful stab at a pop album, featuring a fine performance from Rod Stewart on "People Get Ready." — Stephen Thomas Erlewine

Jeff Beck's Guitar Shop / Oct. 1989 / Epic ✦✦✦✦
A guitar hero in his prime, he's full of fury and finesse, with top-notch support from Terry Bozzio and Tony Hymas. — Jas Obrecht

Beckology / Nov. 19, 1991 / Epic ✦✦✦✦
Covering everything from his earliest (and terrific) tracks with the Tridents through his spot-on interpretation of Santo & Johnny's "Sleep Walk," Beckology features great remastering, smart packaging (resembling a vintage Fender tweed guitar case), and the essential Yardbirds and solo years material. The set (55 tracks in all) also collects the best material from weaker albums such as Flash and There & Back. A definitive overview of Beck's career would have included his work as a sideman with artists like Stevie Wonder, Rod Stewart, and Donovan; nevertheless, Beckology is as comprehensive a collection as one will find on this innovative guitarist. — Tom Graves & Rick Clark

Frankie's House / Jan. 5, 1992 / Epic ✦✦
Beck fans will find his playing here mesmerizing, surpassing the technical mastery of Guitar Shop. Apart from a sizzling instrumental version of "High Heeled Sneakers," less devoted listeners will find Frankie's House as captivating as most other incidental film music. — Stephen Thomas Erlewine

Crazy Legs / Jun. 29, 1993 / Epic ✦✦
Jeff Beck has made many strange albums, but none was ever quite as strange as this. With the Big Town Playboys offering support, Beck rips through 15 Gene Vincent numbers (not "Be-Bop-a-Lula," however), paying tribute to Vincent's guitarist, Cliff Gallup. Beck sounds terrific as he reconstructs Gallup's parts, but he doesn't add anything to the originals. Still, Crazy Legs is a fun listen and offers many insights into Beck's playing, if not Gallup's. — Stephen Thomas Erlewine

● **Best of Beck** / Aug. 15, 1995 / Epic ✦✦✦✦
Basically this record exists because the record company wanted to have

some product on the shelf while Beck was touring. The 14 tracks do contain some of his most often-played (by radio, at any rate) recordings, including "Shapes of Things," "Plynth," and "Beck's Bolero" from the original Jeff Beck Group days in the late '60s, and the vocoder showcase "She's a Woman" and fusion landmark "Freeway Jam" from *Blow by Blow*. It may do for casual listeners who want only one Beck CD, although more serious fans would be better off with the *Beckology* box. *—Richie Unterberger*

Best of Jeff Beck / Columbia ♦♦
The chief appeal of this European import, a skimpy nine-song survey of Beck's late-'60s work, is the inclusion of three tracks from rare solo singles that weren't featured on the first two Jeff Beck Group albums: "Hi Ho Silver Lining," "Tallyman," and "Love Is Blue." Beck takes lead vocals on the first two of these, and though "Hi Ho Silver Lining" actually made the British Top 20, Beck and/or those around him quickly realized that a strong lead vocal presence (i.e., someone other than Beck) was in order. These are typical British pop-rock tunes of the era, but the real curiosity is "Love Is Blue," a cheesy rendition of the Paul Mauriat megasmash that sets Beck's stinging guitar against a near-Muzak arrangement. *—Richie Unterberger*

The Bee Gees

f. 1958, Brisbane, Australia
Disco, Adult Contemporary, Soft Rock, Pop-Rock
One of the longest-lived acts in pop history, the Bee Gees also ranked among the most enduring and eclectic. Best known for a string of massive hits recorded at the peak of the disco era, they embraced the complete spectrum of popular music, moving from lush balladry to psychedelia to country to R&B—each phase a distinct point along an artistic continuum linked by the trio's trademark close, high harmonies and impeccable melodies.

The Bee Gees' name was an abbreviation of the Brothers Gibb; the oldest of the three siblings who comprised the group's core was vocalist/guitarist Barry Gibb, born September 1, 1947, in Manchester, England. His singing twin brothers Robin and Maurice were born December 22, 1949, on the Isle of Man. They were three of five children born to bandleader Hugh Gibb and his wife Barbara. The trio made their performing debut in 1955 as the Blue Cats, performing a brief set of Lonnie Donegan and Tommy Steele covers at the Manchester club where their father's group was headlining. In 1958 the Gibbs emigrated to Brisbane, Australia, where the boys regularly played at area talent shows and other amateur showcases, occasionally performing songs composed by Barry.

After adopting the name Brothers Gibb, quickly shortened to simply the Bee Gees, they were spotted in 1959 by disc jockey Bill Gates, who soon became the group's manager and played their demo tapes on his radio show. An 18-month residency as the house band at the Beachcomber Nightclub in Surfers Paradise allowed the group to hone a set of original material composed by Barry, and in 1962 they signed to Festival Records. A series of singles followed, but despite hosting their own weekly television series, the Bee Gees found little success outside the Brisbane area. After issuing their debut LP *Barry Gibb and the Bee Gees Sing and Play 14 Barry Gibb Songs* in 1965, they began making plans to return to England, and while relocating topped the Australian charts with the title track from 1966's *Spicks and Specks*.

Upon settling in London, the Bee Gees' ranks swelled to include bassist Vince Melouney and drummer Colin Peterson. After enlisting a new manager —Robert Stigwood, the director of NEMS Enterprises, the company owned by Beatles manager Brian Epstein—the group signed to Polydor to release the single "New York Mining Disaster 1941," a Top 20 hit in both Britain and the US in 1967. After issuing the somewhat deceptively titled *Bee Gees First* in 1967, the Bee Gees released the sublime ballad "To Love Somebody," followed by the shimmering "Massachusetts," their first UK chart-topper and the highlight of 1968's *Horizontal*.

After another 1968 effort, *Idea*, the Bee Gees followed the psychedelic lead of the Beatles and the Rolling Stones and mounted 1969's *Odessa*, an ambitious double LP that baffled most fans. When the subsequent double A-sided single "Jumbo"/"The Singer Not the Song" also failed, the group issued "I've Got to Get a Message to You," a poignant ballad that reached the No. 1 spot—the first of many career resurrections enjoyed during the Bee Gees' long history. The atmospheric "First of May" followed, and the brothers' Midas touch was further reaffirmed by "Only One Woman," a Top Ten hit penned by the group for the Marbles.

However, inner strife and problems with drugs and alcohol were quickly tearing the Bee Gees apart, and in the middle of 1969 Robin exited to begin a solo career, scoring a major hit with "Saved by the Bell." Barry and Maurice, the latter of whom had recently wed singer Lulu, forged on alone, working on the film *Cucumber Castle* while tackling country with the single "Don't Forget to Remember." Drummer Peterson soon departed as well, ultimately filing a lawsuit claiming

rights to the Bee Gees name; a year-long court battle ensued, during which time the group lost virtually all of its chart momentum. Both Barry and Maurice issued solo singles, although neither was a hit; finally in 1970 Robin returned to the fold, and although the brothers' career was in grave condition throughout Europe, their reunion yielded a pair of American hits, "Lonely Days" and the chart-topping "How Can You Mend a Broken Heart."

After the commercial failure of 1971's *Trafalgar* and 1972's *To Whom It May Concern*, the Bee Gees signed with Stigwood's new label RSO, and on his advice, they began adopting a more Americanized sound with 1973's *Life in a Tin Can*. Nevertheless, the record did not pull the group out of its slump, and they had been reduced to playing small clubs when Stigwood recruited producer Arif Mardin to helm 1974's *Mr. Natural*, an R&B-flavored effort recorded in Miami. Mardin returned for 1975's *Main Course*, on which the Bee Gees completely reinvented themselves as a dance unit defined by falsetto harmonies, slick melodies, and propulsive funk rhythms. The results were immediate, as the lead single "Jive Talkin'" hit No. 1 in the US and returned the trio to the Top Ten in Britain. The follow-up "Nights on Broadway" was also a major hit, and the group remained in Miami to record 1976's chart-topping *Children of the World*, which spawned the smashes "You Should Be Dancing" and "Love So Right."

Ironically, the New York underground disco scene was considered a thing of the recent past when the Bee Gees were contacted to contribute music to the soundtrack of the film *Saturday Night Fever*, a latter-day *Rebel Without a Cause* exploring the discotheque nightlife. In addition to writing and producing hits for Yvonne Elliman ("If I Can't Have You") and Tavares ("More Than a Woman"), the Bee Gees also recorded a number of new songs for *Saturday Night Fever*, including the opening theme "Stayin' Alive;" when the film premiered in 1977, not only did it establish the Hollywood career of star John Travolta, but it completely revitalized the disco scene, creating a national dance craze and influencing fashions for the duration of the 1970s. The soundtrack quickly emerged as the definitive document of the disco era, topping the charts for 24 weeks, and the Bee Gees became the music's brightest stars; the first single, "Stayin' Alive," was just one of their three No. 1 singles from the LP, followed by "How Deep Is Your Love" and the brilliant "Night Fever."

After a laughable misstep—starring in the film musical *Sgt. Pepper's Lonely Hearts Club Band*—the Bee Gees returned in 1979 with *Spirits Having Flown*, another No. 1 smash that generated three more chart-topping singles: "Tragedy," "Too Much Heaven," and "Love You Inside Out." However, 1981's *Living Eyes* failed even to crack the Top 40 as disco went bust. The group also became overshadowed by their youngest brother, Andy Gibb, who had become a major star in his own right at the end of the 1970s. Apart from contributing to the soundtrack of the 1983 *Saturday Night Fever* sequel *Stayin' Alive*, the Bee Gees spent much of the decade out of the spotlight, writing and producing hits for artists as diverse as Barbra Streisand, Diana Ross, Dionne Warwick, and the team of Kenny Rogers and Dolly Parton.

When the group finally returned in 1987 with the mature *ESP*, they were warmly received across the globe, and the LP and single "You Win Again" hit No. 1 virtually everywhere but the US, where the stigma of the Gibbs' disco-era excesses, both musical and otherwise, continued to overshadow their other achievements. After the death of brother Andy and Maurice's subsequent relapse into alcoholism, the Bee Gees briefly retired, but they resurfaced in 1989 with *One;* a success throughout Europe, its title track reached the Top Ten in America. After 1991's *High Civilization* and 1993's *Size Isn't Everything*, they again spent several years in hibernation before returning in 1997 with *Still Waters*, released to coincide with the trio's induction into the Rock and Roll Hall of Fame. *—Jason Ankeny*

The Bee Gee's First / Jul. 1967 / PolyGram ♦♦♦
The Bee Gees' latter-day success with disco and other superficial pop pap has caused many to forget that when they first achieved international prominence, they were accomplished and serious singers and songwriters. Robin and Barry Gibb (with occasional help from Maurice) penned all of the material on their first album they recorded after moving to England (they had already previously released quite a few records in Australia). The Bee Gees were both praised and denigrated for emulating the Beatles' harmonies; in fact their songs at this point were quite brooding, even melancholy at times. The string arrangements, skirting the boundary between melodrama and mock-rococo, highlighted the pensive nature of the material and Robin's verging-on-tears vocal delivery on this strong, at times ambitious set. *First* includes the hits "To Love Somebody," "New York Mining Disaster 1941" (which evoked the most Beatle copycat cries), and "Holiday," although "In My Own Time" and "I Can't See Nobody" are overlooked highlights of similar quality. *—Richie Unterberger*

Horizontal / Jan. 1968 / Polydor ♦♦♦
This album is a little more moody than *First*, with its use of minor chords and song structure. At the same time, the Bee Gees continue to

grow as songwriters, and there is no shortage of good songs. The hit "Massachusetts" pretty much sets the tone for the album; if you like that one, you're sure to like the rest of the album as well. —*Jim Worbois*

Idea / Aug. 1968 / Polydor ♦♦
On *Idea* the Bee Gees stretch out somewhat and, in addition to their usual fare, have a go at a Hollies-type song ("Kitty Can") and a jazzy number ("Kilburn Towers"). Not everything on the record works, but at least they weren't afraid to try something different. —*Jim Worbois*

Odessa / Jan. 1969 / Polydor ♦♦♦♦
Though it was recorded during times of great stress, *Odessa* was one of the Bee Gee's finest achievements. Originally conceived as a concept album, the record became a double album tied together only by its lavish sound. While the album failed to spin off any major hit singles, most of the songs on the record are excellent, highlighted by "Odessa (City on the Black Sea)," "Melody Fair," and "Black Diamond." —*Stephen Thomas Erlewine*

● **The Best of the Bee Gees, Vol. 1** / Jun. 1969 / Polydor ♦♦♦♦
The Best of the Bee Gees, Vol. 1 is a fine 12-track collection of the group's late-'60s hits, featuring such singles as "I Started a Joke," "To Love Somebody," "I've Gotta Get a Message to You," "Words," and "New York Mining Disaster." —*Stephen Thomas Erlewine*

Cucumber Castle / Apr. 1970 / Polydor ♦♦

Two Years on / Jan. 1971 / Polydor/Atco ♦♦♦♦
After a turbulent period in the late '60s, the Bee Gees temporarily packed it in. When they regrouped, the band consisted solely of the three brothers. What resulted was their largest commercial success to date. In addition to featuring "Lonely Days," the Bee Gees' highest-charting single to date and their first gold record, this is a fine record in its own right. It's as strong as any Bee Gees album from their early years and worth looking for. —*Jim Worbois*

Trafalgar / Sep. 1971 / Polydor ♦♦♦
Trafalgar's "How Can You Mend a Broken Heart?" was the Bee Gees' first No. 1 single. Despite this chart success, the record doesn't rate as highly as some of the other albums of this period, due to somewhat lackluster material. —*Jim Worbois*

To Whom It May Concern / 1972 / Polydor ♦♦

Life in a Tin Can / Jan. 1973 / Polydor ♦♦
The Bee Gees were now recording in the US (Los Angeles, to be exact) and, if anything, that proved to be a detriment. For the most part, this is a record of "sensitive" ballads, much like everything else coming out of Southern California at the time. For that reason, it doesn't stand up against much of their earlier work. —*Jim Worbois*

The Best of the Bee Gees, Vol. 2 / Jul. 1973 / Polydor ♦♦♦♦
The Best of the Bee Gees, Vol. 2 is a 14-song retrospective covering the group's early '70s hits, including not only pop classics like "How Can You Mend a Broken Heart" and "Lonely Days," but also lesser-known numbers like "I.O.I.O.," "Melody Fair," "Don't Wanna Live Inside Myself," "My World," "Run to Me," "Alive," and Robin Gibb's solo hit "Saved by the Bell." —*Stephen Thomas Erlewine*

Mr. Natural / May 1974 / Polydor ♦
With the assistence of producer Arif Mardin, the Bee Gees began to revamp their sound on *Mr. Natural*, moving closer toward Philly-soul and disco. Though the album didn't have any big hits, it did lay the foundation for the disco breakthrough of *Main Course* and "Jive Talkin'," and fans will find a number of fine moments on the album, including the failed singles "Charade," "Throw a Penny," and "Mr. Natural," as well as the pulsing "Down the Road." —*Stephen Thomas Erlewine*

Main Course / May 1975 / Polydor ♦♦♦♦
On *Main Course* the Bee Gees began incorporating soul into their well-constructed sound, inching the group closer to their watershed disco years. Like most Bee Gees' albums, the material is fairly inconsistent, but the strongest moments—including the hit singles "Jive Talkin'" and "Nights on Broadway"—rank with the group's best work. —*Stephen Thomas Erlewine*

Children of the World / Sep. 1976 / Polydor ♦♦

● **Bee Gees Gold, Vol. 1** / Oct. 1976 / Polydor ♦♦♦♦
The Bee Gees Gold, Vol. 1 compiles the group's biggest singles from their first five years of hit records, beginning with 1967's "New York Mining Disaster 1941" and ending with 1971's "How Can You Mend a Broken Heart." Although the compilation isn't presented in chronological order, it does contains all of their biggest hits ("To Love Somebody," "Holiday," "Lonely Days," "I've Got to Get a Message to You," "I Started a Joke"), making it a fine overview of the group's first heyday. —*Stephen Thomas Erlewine*

☆ **Saturday Night Fever** / Nov. 1977 / RSO ♦♦♦♦♦
One of the biggest-selling albums of all time, this double-disc soundtrack features the Bee Gees hits "Stayin' Alive," "Night Fever," and "How Deep Is Your Love"; Yvonne Elliman's "If I Can't Have You"; and a

selection of popular disco hits by Tavares, K.C. & the Sunshine Band, and others. This was not just the soundtrack to a film, it was the soundtrack to an era. That era is over, but it's evoked by the music. —*William Ruhlmann*

1963-1966: Birth of Brilliance / 1978 / Festival ♦♦♦♦
Thirty-two song double CD presents much of the best material from the domestic Excelsior compilations of their early years, as well as some songs (some of which are pretty good) that don't appear on those sets. Because of its better sound, this collection has the edge as the best compilation of their early work, though it's hard to find. —*Richie Unterberger*

Spirits Having Flown / Jan. 1979 / RSO ♦♦♦♦

● **Greatest** / Oct. 1979 / RSO ♦♦♦♦
Greatest is a double-album, 20-song retrospective of the Bee Gees' late '70s hits. All of the band's biggest disco-era hits—"Jive Talkin'," "Nights on Broadway," "Fanny (Be Tender with My Love)," "You Should Be Dancing," "Love So Right," "How Deep Is Your Love," "Stayin' Alive," "Night Fever," "Too Much Heaven," "Tragedy," "Love You Inside Out"—are included, as well as several fine album tracks and the group's version of Andy Gibb's "(Our Love) Don't Throw It All Away." Although it's a a little too long for some casual fans, it remains an excellent overview of the Bee Gees' most commercially successful era. —*Stephen Thomas Erlewine*

Living Eyes / 1981 / RSO ♦♦

Staying Alive / Jun. 1983 / RSO ♦♦♦
This sequel to *Saturday Night Fever* lacked the box office clout of the original, and the soundtrack album was likewise a disappointing seller, but it actually contains some of the better Bee Gees work of the '80s, notably the sad ballad "Someone Belonging to Someone." —*William Ruhlmann*

E.S.P. / Sep. 1987 / Warner Brothers ♦♦

One / Jul. 25, 1989 / Warner Brothers ♦♦♦
The Bee Gees made a commercial comeback outside the US with 1987's *E.S.P.* and its single, "You Win Again." *One*, on the other hand, had an improved chart showing in the US, but sales fell off elsewhere. The Bee Gees are remarkable pop craftsmen; "It's My Neighborhood" is a canny, if blatant, rewrite of Michael Jackson's "Beat It," for example, and it only reminds you that Jackson's falsetto whoops owe something to Barry Gibb. And, say what you will, "One" and "House Of Shame" are convincing pop music. ("One" was a Top Ten comeback hit that topped soft-rock radio playlists.) This stuff works as pop for the same reason "I've Gotta Get a Message to You" and "You Should Be Dancing" did; the melodies are catchy, the hooks are deathless, and the vocals convey emotion over meaning. It may be weightless, but it's polished. —*William Ruhlmann*

Tales from the Brothers Gibb / Oct. 1990 / Polydor ♦♦♦
Although the Bee Gees were a singles band, and consequently their hits compilations were frequently more consistent than their actual albums, the four-disc box set *Tales from the Brothers Gibb* is an example of a wasted opportunity. While all of the big hits are featured over the course of 71 tracks, the set is unevenly balanced, featuring more latter-day material than their generally more interesting early recordings. Also, it doesn't choose particularly well from the group's albums, overlooking several key tracks in favor of bland cuts from '80s records, and the rarities, including several live tracks and a demo of "E.S.P.," aren't of much worth. Consequently, *Tales from the Brothers Gibb* appeals to neither the collector, who will have the bulk of this material, nor the casual fan, since it contains too much mediocre material to sift through. —*Stephen Thomas Erlewine*

High Civilization / Apr. 1991 / Warner Brothers ♦♦
A misstep. The Bee Gees seem to have felt that, their comeback completed by the Top Ten success of "One," it was time to go really contemporary and take on, oh, say, Prince. Wrong. The techno-rock sounds silly with those near-Chipmunk harmonies, and it's all overdone. You can't really blame a band that has had recurring success by faithfully following contemporary pop trends for trying it, but you can blame them for failing. —*William Ruhlmann*

Size Isn't Everything / Nov. 1993 / Polydor ♦♦♦
These guys are persistent and they work hard for the money, carefully cloning current fashion. You can just hear them saying, "We did disco, we can do hip-hop," and you can hear them try on "Paying the Price of Love," with its heavy percussion track. But it wasn't their approximation of the Compton beat that got them (just barely) back in the pop charts, it was the hook, which wasn't all that different from "Massachusetts." —*William Ruhlmann*

To Be or Not to Be / Dec. 12, 1995 / Thunderbolt ♦♦♦
A 26-track, single-disc collection culled from the Bee Gee's mid-'60s recordings as Australian pop stars mimicking the styles and sound of the British Invasion, *To Be Or Not To Be* has many of the best songs from their early career, but it isn't the most comprehensive collection

available. Nevertheless, it is a solid sampler and has only four songs less than the definitive double-disc compilation, *1963-1966: Birth of Brilliance.* —*Stephen Thomas Erlewine*

Still Waters / May 6, 1997 / Polydor ◆◆◆
As if they finally realized that they couldn't quite compete with contemporary musical fashions any more, the Bee Gees moved firmly into "mature" territory with *Still Waters.* However, they are canny enough to realize that they shouldn't abandon the frothy disco that made them superstars in the late '70s—they should merely temper it with measured rhythms and tasteful melodies. Consequently, nothing on *Still Waters* is infectious, but it is pleasant, and while only a handful of singles stand out—"I Could Not Love You More" is a sweet ballad—it is still a fine, professional effort from these consummate professionals. —*Stephen Thomas Erlewine*

Bel Canto

f. 1985, Norway
Alternative Pop-Rock
The atmospheric, melancholy, somewhat medieval soundscapes of Bel Canto (Italian for "beautiful song") mix an essentially synth-based, chamber-rock sound with a wide range of orchestral and folk instruments and have been compared to the Cocteau Twins. The group hails from Norway and consists of ethereal vocalist Anneli Marian Drecker, plus Nils Johansen and Geir Jennsen. The group claims to draw its inspiration from powerful energy fields, including those of the female and the earth's gravitational pull; additionally, their compositions sometimes draw on world music and the ambient experiments of Brian Eno. Bel Canto released its first album, *White-Out Conditions,* in 1987. After 1989's *Birds of Passage,* they recorded 1992's *Shimmering, Warm and Bright* and 1996's *Magic Box.* —*Steve Huey*

White-Out Conditions / 1987 / Nettwerk ◆◆◆
Bel Canto's first album is refreshing and intriguing. Although it's uneven, it is definitely more than just a search for a new style. —*Vladimir Bogdanov*

● **Birds of Passage** / 1989 / Nettwerk ◆◆◆◆
With completely professional material, it is well composed and performed. —*Vladimir Bogdanov*

Shimmering, Warm & Bright / Sep. 22, 1992 / Dali ◆◆◆◆
The famous warm, "medieval electronic" sound of Bel Canto reaches the point of elaborate purity on this mature album. —*Vladimir Bogdanov*

Magic Box / Feb. 27, 1996 / Atlantic ◆◆◆

Bell Biv Devoe

f. 1988, Boston, MA
Urban, New Jack R&B
Bell Biv DeVoe was hatched in the minds of its members, New Edition's Ricky Bell, Michael Bivins, and Ronnie DeVoe, upon the departure of lead singer Bobby Brown in 1986. But it wasn't until after the group completed its supporting tour for the album *Heart Break* in 1988 that the trio gave in to the urgings of *Heart Break* producers Jimmy Jam and Terry Lewis and decided to chart its own course. Bell Biv DeVoe enlisted a variety of producers for its debut album, with Jam and Lewis and Public Enemy producers Hank and Keith Shocklee. The results were quite unlike anything in New Edition's repertoire. The beats were funkier, the lyrics and vocals were sexier, and the overall sound had a harder, hip-hop-tinged edge. The album's title track, "Poison," became a No. 3 smash, and it was followed by the equally successful "Do Me!" and the R&B hits "B.B.D. (I Thought It Was Me)," "When Will I See You Smile Again?," and "She's Dope." The album itself went on to sell over three million copies and was followed by a remix album the next year. Meanwhile, Bivins took some time off to assemble the so-called East Coast Family, discovering and producing debut albums for Another Bad Creation and Boyz II Men. *Hootie Mack,* Bell Biv DeVoe's second proper album, was released in 1993 but didn't make as much of an impact. In 1996 all three members of Bell Biv Devoe participated in a reunion of the New Edition. —*Steve Huey*

● **Poison** / Mar. 1990 / MCA ◆◆◆◆
With so many faceless, soundalike albums having come out of the "new jack swing" hybrid in the late '80s and early—to mid-'90s, it's important to give credit to the form's more creative and imaginative figures. Along with Guy and Bobby Brown, Bell Biv Devoe (a New Edition spinoff trio comprised of Ricky Bell, Michael Bivens, and Ronnie DeVoe) delivered some of "new jack swing's" most worthwhile material. A hard-edged, tough-minded blend of R&B/funk and hip-hop, *Poison* was (like Brown's *Don't Be Cruel*) a radical departure from the Jackson 5-influenced "bubble gum soul" New Edition was originally known for. Defined by their urgency, rawness, and vitality, "Poison," "BBD (I Thought It Was Me)," "She's Dope!" and "Do Me!" are considered "new jack swing" classics and are indeed among the best the style has to offer. Taking a break from the CD's overall aggression, BBD moves closer to

New Edition's sound with the decent, though far from outstanding, ballads "When Will I See You Again" and "I Do Need You." While other "new jacks" were content to simply emulate Guy, the distinctive BBD deserves applause for daring to stake out its own territory. —*Alex Henderson*

Hootie Mack / Jun. 1993 / MCA ◆◆◆
Hootie Mack not only keeps the same energetic vibe that made *Poison* a hit, but expands upon that base, adding a more street-oriented production that, at its best, is more sexy and funky than their debut. Unfortunately, the high points on this album aren't as numerous as those on *Poison;* not only that, but the good songs didn't receive much airplay, causing the album to drop off the charts quickly. —*Stephen Thomas Erlewine*

Archie Bell

b. Sep. 1, 1944, Henderson, TX
Vocals / Soul
Few groups offered good-time soul music as enjoyable, danceable, and high-spirited as Archie Bell & the Drells. The singer (from Houston, as he was eager to proclaim in the middle of some of his uptempo hits) had a left-field No. 1 smash with the limb-loosening "Tighten Up," which took off right after Bell was drafted. In 1968 Bell (who was able to fit in some recording and performing duties until his stint in the army was over) teamed with emerging Philadelphia soul mavens Kenneth Gamble and Leon Huff, who produced and wrote his material over the next couple of years. With sophisticated arrangements and punchy horn charts, dance hits like "I Can't Stop Dancing," "(There's Gonna Be a) Showdown," and "Do the Choo Choo" were instrumental in establishing the sound of Philadelphia as an artistic force. After a fallow period in the early '70s, Bell reunited with Gamble and Huff for a run of successful, disco-fied dance soul in the mid-'70s. —*Richie Unterberger*

● **Tightening It Up: The Best of Archie Bell & The Drells** / Aug. 16, 1994 / Rhino ◆◆◆◆
Twenty of the group's big and small hits, charting their course from Southern-fried soul through the sound of Philadelphia and disco. —*Richie Unterberger*

Chris Bell

b. Jan. 12, 1951, Memphis, TN, d. Dec. 27, 1978, Memphis, TN
Guitar, Vocals / Power Pop
Chris Bell was one of the unsung heroes of American pop music. Despite a life marked by tragedy and a career crippled by commercial indifference, the singer-songwriter's slim body of recorded work proved massively influential on the generations of indie rockers who emerged in his wake. Born January 12, 1951, in Memphis, Bell grew up enveloped by the city's indigenous soul sounds—typified by the prodigious output of the Stax label—but his first love was the music of the British Invasion. Inspired by the Beatles, he took up the guitar in his early teens. Within a few years, Bell was writing and performing his own songs with friends Richard Rosebrough and Terry Manning, but his Anglo-pop leanings set him squarely outside of the Memphis musical community.

In high school Bell struck up a friendship with another young performer named Alex Chilton, who occasionally jammed with Bell's band but turned down an invitation to join on a full-time basis. While Chilton soon rose to fame as the frontman of the Box Tops, Bell became a fixture at Memphis' famed Ardent Studios, where he worked as a part-time recording engineer and cut his earliest songs. While attending college, he roomed with former high school friend Andy Hummel, with whom Bell eventually returned to Memphis to form a new band with drummer Jody Stephens and, later, Chilton, who had grown frustrated with his role in the Box Tops and quit.

Together, the four musicians comprised the power-pop band Big Star. Their debut album, 1972's *No.1 Record,* eventually earned mythic status as an underground classic, but sabotaged by poor distribution, it was deemed a commercial failure at the time of release. Crushed, Bell became suicidal and left the band, although he did contribute his skills to a handful of tracks on the follow-up, *Radio City.* While Bell continued working on music, his depression worsened, and he became addicted to heroin; to help revitalize his career, his brother David led him to France's Chateau D'Herouville studios, where a batch of demos were cut for a planned album. After skipping over to London, the Bell brothers mixed the songs with Geoff Emerick, the engineer on the Beatles' final albums, at producer George Martin's Air Studios.

The completed tracks were roundly rejected, however, and Bell returned to Memphis, where he cut a few more songs with Big Star's Stephens and local musician Ken Woodley in 1974. He ultimately returned to Europe and played solo shows in folk clubs. After plans for a Big Star reunion tour fell through, Bell returned to the US and dropped out of music, taking a management position in his family's fast food chain. In 1977, however, the tiny New York label Car issued a remarkable single, "I Am the Cosmos," backed with "You and Your Sister," on which

Bell was supported by Chilton; the record was well received, and spurred him to form a new band. But on the morning of December 27, 1978, his speeding car hit a tree, and he was killed instantly. Over the course of the following decade, the legendary stature of Big Star continued to grow exponentially, and finally, Bell's long-unreleased demos were collected under the title *I Am the Cosmos* and released to wide acclaim in 1992. *—Jason Ankeny*

I Am the Cosmos / Feb. 21, 1992 / Rykodisc ✦✦✦✦
A collection of the late Chris Bell's solo work, it includes mostly demos. The title track is a brilliant downer (Big Star and Badfinger at half-speed) that opens the album. "You and Your Sister" is a gorgeous heart-breaker, rendered with delicate acoustic guitars and Mellotron and guest vocalist Alex Chilton. Not everything Bell undertakes is so fragile. "I Don't Know" (and its later, inferior incarnation, "Get Away"), "Make a Scene," and "Fight at the Table" are relentless rockers. Bell's voice may be an acquired taste for some, as it occasionally gets a little whiney. When it does connect with the music, the results can be quite affecting, particularly on "You and Your Sister," "Speed of Sound," and the title track. Ryko has done a great job remastering these tapes, and the packaging is a first-rate labor of love. *—Rick Clark*

William Bell (William Yarborough)

b. Jul. 16, 1937, Memphis, TN
Piano, Vocals / Soul
William Bell was one of the first artists signed to the Stax label during its fledgling years in Memphis, and he greatly influenced the "Stax sound" as both a performer and writer. His self-penned "You Don't Miss Your Water" (1961) almost defined the genre known as country-soul, with the unmistakable gospel feel of Bell's elegant, lilting vocal over a country-church piano figure. It was this perfect marriage of styles that became Bell's trademark at Stax and opened the door for others—most notably Otis Redding (who initially mined the same country-soul vein)—to follow. With the ascent of Redding, Bell's star began to fade somewhat. He continued to record (the beautiful, string-laden "I Forgot to Be Your Lover" in 1968) and, most importantly, to write (his own "Tribute to a King," written after Redding's death, and Albert King's "Born Under a Bad Sign," both co-written with Booker T. Jones). After Stax' collapse in 1975, Bell moved to Mercury, where he scored his first-ever million-seller with "Tryin' to Love Two." Bell continues to live and work in Memphis. *—Christine Ohlman*

The Soul of a Bell / 1967 / Stax ✦✦✦✦
William Bell's history illustrates just how singles-oriented soul was in the 1960s. Though he'd enjoyed a hit in 1961 with "You Don't Miss Your Water," it wasn't until 1967 that Stax finally released his first album, the magnificent *The Soul Of A Bell*. From that classic and Bell's moderate hits "Never Like This Before" and "Everybody Loves A Winner" to heart-felt versions of "Do Right Woman, Do Right Man" and "I've Been Loving You Too Long," everything on this album (reissued on CD in 1991) illustrates the gospel-drenched richness of Southern soul. Meanwhile, the influence of Motown and the Four Tops is hard to miss on the riveting single "Eloise (Hang On In There)," which should have been a major hit, but surprisingly, never even charted. *—Alex Henderson*

Duets / 1968 / Stax ✦✦✦
In the late '60s, Bell recorded a number of male/female duets with partners Judy Clay, Carla Thomas, and Mavis Staples; the ones with Clay were the most successful, "Private Number" and "My Baby Specializes" becoming modest R&B hits. All of his duet projects are assembled here, along with three solo sides that he cut in the 1970s. It's not among Bell's most striking work, but it's decent pop/soul, closer to Motown in feel than a lot of Stax material. I don't know what the deal is, but the version of "My Baby Specializes" here, though credited to Bell and Clay, seems to feature only Clay, unless that's Bell adding an odd backup grunt here and there. *—Richie Unterberger*

● **The Best of William Bell** / 1988 / Stax ✦✦✦✦
Post-Atlantic work from the late '60s and early '70s, it includes Bell's playful duets with Judy Clay. *—Bill Dahl*

A Little Something Extra / 1992 / Stax ✦✦✦
A fine collection of Stax outtakes from the 1960s, *Little Something Extra* features several tracks, including his smoldering version of "Will You Love Me Tomorrow?," that rival his original singles. *—Stephen Thomas Erlewine*

Greatest Hits, Vols. 1 & 2 / 1995 / Ichiban ✦✦✦✦

Belly

f. 1992, Providence, RI, **db.** 1996
Alternative Pop-Rock
After several years in the Throwing Muses, as well as a brief detour in the Breeders in 1990, Tanya Donelly formed her own band, Belly, in 1992. With Belly, Donelly expanded her dreamy pop hooks into more concise, catchy songs, as well as harder-edged rock. The band's

1993 debut, *Star*, became one of the first beneficiaries of the commercialization of alternative rock; it rode to gold status within its first year of release, as "Feed the Tree" made headway on mainstream pop radio. Despite their strong start, Belly never became genuine stars, and once their 1995 followup *King* bombed, Donelly disbanded the group.

Tanya Donelly (vocals, guitar) formed Belly with fellow ex-Muse Fred Abong (bass), drummer Chris Gorman, and his guitarist brother Tom. Donelly hired Pixies producer Gil Norton to work on the group's debut EP, *Slow Dust*, which confirmed that her dream-pop sensibilities had more hooks than many of her peers. *Slow Dust* reached No. 1 on the British indie charts in early 1992, and two other EPs followed that year, generating strong word of mouth. Belly's debut album, *Star*, was released in February 1993 to strong reviews, and its first single, "Feed the Tree," reached the UK Top 40, helping the album enter the British charts at No. 2. Shortly afterward, the single became a crossover hit in the US. The band added Gail Greenwood as bassist—Abong left the band during the recording of *Star*—that spring, and spent the remainder of 1993 on tour, helping send the album to gold status in America.

During 1994, Belly recorded their second album with classic rock producer Glyn Johns. The resulting record, *King*, was more rock-oriented than its predecessor, partially because of Johns' work and partially because of Greenwood, who was a harder rocker than Donelly. *King* was expected to be Belly's breakthrough into the mainstream, but it was greeted with mixed reviews upon its spring release and quickly fell off the charts. In the wake of its failure, Donelly disbanded Belly in 1996, releasing her first solo EP, *Sliding and Diving*, at the end of the year. Greenwood joined L7 by the end of the year. *—Stephen Thomas Erlewine*

● **Star** / Jan. 1993 / 4AD ✦✦✦✦
Tanya Donelly's songwriting began to blossom on the Throwing Muses' *The Real Ramona*, and Belly's debut, *Star*, is where it reaches fruition. Using the trancy harmonies of dream-pop as a foundation, Donelly expands the genre's boundaries, trimming away its pretensions and incorporating a flair for sweet, concise pop hooks and folk-rock inflections. She also spikes her airy melodies with disarmingly disturbing lyrics. Images of betrayal and death float throughout the album, but what hits home initially—and what stays after the album is finished—are the hooks, whether it's the rolling sing-along of "Gepetto," the surging "Slow Dog," the melancholy "Stay," or the cool, detached sexiness of "Feed the Tree." Occasionally, Donelly suffers from preciousness or unformed ideas, but *Star* remains an enchanting debut. *—Stephen Thomas Erlewine*

King / Feb. 14, 1995 / Sire/Reprise ✦✦✦
By developing a flair for tight, melodic hooks on *Star*, Tanya Donelly unexpectedly achieved the crossover success with Belly that eluded her with the Throwing Muses and Breeders. Evidently inspired by such success and eager to prove that Belly was a full-fledged band, not just a solo project, Donelly and company made a bid for stardom with their second album, *King*. Veteran producer Glyn Johns gives the band an appealingly punchy sheen, and with the assistance of Tom Gorman and new bassist Gail Greenwood, Donelly cuts away her remaining arty preciousness, concentrating solely on big pop songs. While some fans will miss the occasional detour into spacey dream-pop, Belly's makeover is quite convincing, and the cloaked stardom of "Super-Connected," the quirky hooks of "Now They'll Sleep," and the epic ballad of "Judas My Heart" are neglected gems of post-alternative modern rock. Ironically, such shiny hooks didn't make Belly stars; it lost them their original fan base, and by the time the record was released in 1995, modern rock radio was concentrating solely on harder guitar rock, so *King* was overlooked, and the band broke up shortly afterward. The album and the group deserved a better fate. *—Stephen Thomas Erlewine*

Jesse Belvin

b. Dec. 15, 1933, San Antonio, TX, **d.** Feb. 6, 1960, Fairhope, AR
Vocals / Soul, R&B
While not nearly as well remembered by the general public as either Sam Cooke or Otis Redding, singer Jesse Belvin was in many regards a performer of equal stature whose career was also cut far too short by tragedy. At the time of his death, Belvin was moving in much the same direction as Cooke (he was even on the same record label, although signed earlier), and was scoring and writing hits long before Redding ever cut a record.

Jesse Lorenzo Belvin was born in San Antonio, Texas, in 1932. When he was five, his family relocated to Los Angeles, and by age seven he was singing in church. He discovered R&B in his early teens, and in 1950 he joined jazz saxophonist Big Jay McNeely's backing vocal quartet Three Dots and a Dash. Belvin's falsetto was placed up front in his debut release, 1950's "All the Wine Is Gone"; the response was so strong that on the group's next record, his name was placed directly under McNeely's on the B-side, "Sad Story." In 1952 Belvin and bandmate Marvin Phillips signed to Specialty. They cut four singles: the first three—"Baby Don't Go," "One Little Blessing," and "Love of My Life"—were credited to Jesse Belvin, and all failed to chart. The last, "Dream Girl," which featured Belvin on piano and vocals with Phillips on saxophone, was credited to "Jesse & Marvin," and got to No. 2 on the R&B charts in 1953.

Unfortunately, just as it looked as if Belvin's career was going to take off, he was drafted. While home on leave, he wrote a song called "Earth Angel," inspired by a young white woman who lived near him. The song was subsequently recorded by a semi-professional doo-wop quartet called the Penguins and became one of the first rhythm-and-blues singles to cross over onto the pop charts, selling a million copies between late 1954 and early 1955. (A lawsuit later erupted over the authorship and origins of the song that took almost two years to settle; Belvin was awarded one-third credit for the song, alongside the Penguins' Curtis Williams and a third singer.)

Belvin was a prolific songwriter, but his business approach was rather cavalier. In a period in which millions of dollars were sometimes earned on a carefully protected copyright, Belvin wrote songs as a way of raising quick cash and often sold them outright to others for as little as $100. The result was dozens upon dozens of songs that Belvin was responsible for as writer and singer on the demo or guide track, few of which he actually received credit for. In 1956 he signed a longterm contract with Modern Records. He continued to sing for other labels under assumed names, working in the background with other artists. Some of the Modern releases were credited to the Cliques, which was really Jesse Belvin and Eugene Church, but most were credited to Belvin alone.

It was with Modern that he cut his most enduring record. "Goodnight My Love" had been written by producer George Motola ten years earlier, but he had never been able to finish it; Belvin provided the lines for the bridge that completed the song, but he asked for $400 in lieu of co-authorship credit. Motola didn't have it, but a colleague, John Marascalco, did, and put up the money, receiving co-authorship credit in the bargain. The song reached No. 7 on the R&B charts in 1956. Curiously, the pianist on the recording was an 11-year-old session player making his recording debut, Barry White, who would emerge as a giant in his own right about two decades later. More important at the time, "Goodnight My Love" became the outro theme to Alan Freed's rock 'n' roll radio show, heard by millions of young listeners every night.

Belvin cut ten singles for Modern, of which "Goodnight My Love" was far and away the most successful. In 1958 he was again on the move, recording for Knight, Class, and Jamie Records under his own name, as well as for the Alladin label in association with the Sharptones. His biggest success that year, however, came through a group called the Shields, which had been formed by George Motola to record on his own Tender label. Adding his voice to the mix, Belvin joined the group, which included Frankie Ervin on lead and Johnny "Guitar" Watson on guitar. The Shields' only record with Belvin was "You Cheated," which had already been cut by a white group called the Slades; the Shields' version was the more successful, reaching No. 15 on the pop charts in the summer of 1958.

Around this time, Belvin's career took a decided upswing, in part with help from his wife Jo Anne, a fine songwriter in her own right who became his manager and took charge of his career. One of the first results was getting him signed to RCA Records; his first big success for the new label came in April of 1959 with the Top 40 hit "Guess Who." He finished his first album, *Just Jesse Belvin*, later in the year, developing a more mature studio sound and a somewhat more sophisticated singing style as well. Like Sam Cooke, who would follow him to RCA with similar goals a short time later, Belvin began to realize that he had the potential to cross over to adult white audiences while keeping his original fans. For its part, RCA saw in Belvin the potential for another Nat 'King' Cole or Billy Eckstine. A powerful and charismatic performer, Belvin had acquired the nickname "Mr. Easy" for his way with the ballads that increasingly made up his live sets.

In late 1959, with the encouragement of his wife and the support of producer Dick Pierce and arranger/conductor Marty Paitch, Belvin went into the studio for three recording dates that yielded a dozen songs, among them intensely soulful covers of standards like "Blues in the Night," "In the Still of the Night," and "Makin' Whoopee." The band included Art Pepper on sax and clarinet and Jack Sheldon on trumpet, and the playing was extraordinary all the way around. Alas, Belvin never heard the finished album, *Mr. Easy.* On February 6, 1960, shortly after finishing a performance in Little Rock, AR, on a bill with Sam Cooke, Jackie Wilson, and Marv Johnson, Belvin and his wife were killed in a head-on auto collision. *Mr. Easy* was released later in 1960, his final testament and an enduring legacy. —*Bruce Eder*

Just Jesse Belvin / 1959 / RCA ✦✦✦
The next-to-last album made by R&B crooner/balladeer Jesse Belvin is part slick pop and part soulful R&B, although his sound has more Nat "King" Cole influence than gospel. Belvin's work merged the smooth,

sophisticated West Coast sound with the more earthy Southern approach. —*Ron Wynn*

Mr. Easy / 1960 / RCA ✦✦✦✦
Some would argue that this album (reissued on CD in 1995) isn't really representative of Jesse Belvin's sound, coming at the very end of his life, so that he couldn't follow it up, and displaying a final mix that he never got to hear. But *Mr. Easy* is about as fine an album as any R&B singer ever cut in search of a mainstream audience, and ought to be in every '50s vocal collection. Anyone who owns even one Sam Cooke CD should make it his business to buy it, and nobody who enjoys Nat King Cole, Frank Sinatra, or Billy Eckstine would be doing wrong, either. No, his voice wasn't as rich as Sinatra's or Cooke's at either's best, but he knew how to use it, and he went further with this material than anybody had a right to, straddling the worlds of soul and popular music magnificently. The closing number, "The Very Thought of You," is worth the price of the disc, and isn't much easier to listen to than Cooke's "A Change Is Gonna Come," even if it is a very different kind of song. (European import) —*Bruce Eder*

Jesse Belvin's Best / 1966 / Camden ✦✦✦✦
A good collection of '50s tracks by West Coast balladeer and light R&B vocalist Jesse Belvin. He had a silky, smooth style and was a top crooner. Belvin had a huge hit in 1956, "Goodnight My Love," and another pop success in 1958, "Guess Who." He worked in the same territory as Brook Benton, and was a bit removed from Billy Eckstine and Herb Jeffries, who were more jazz-oriented. —*Ron Wynn*

...But Not Forgotten / 196 / United ✦✦✦
Terrible sound quality, but this old LP features the balladeer's best-known mid-'50s work for Modern Records. —*Bill Dahl*

Yesterdays / 1975 / RCA ✦✦✦✦

Blues Balladeer / 1990 / Specialty ✦✦✦✦
Belvin's Specialty Records sides, cut during the early 1950's, just prior to his induction into the army, including all of his solo credited recordings and the Jesse & Marvin sides. —*Bruce Eder*

● **Goodnight My Love** / 1991 / Capitol ✦✦✦✦
Here's Jesse Belvin's Modern Records legacy, from 1955-57. The 25 songs (including an alternate take of "Goodnight My Love") include an undubbed version of "Beware," a pair of previously unheard songs ("What Can I Do Without You," "I'll Make a Bet"), a compelling soulful cover of Sam Cooke's "You Send Me," and the previously overlooked single version of "Sad and Lonesome," as well as a sample ("Summertime") of the kind of pop standard that he would later master. Whether he's doing doo wop or crooning, the voice is magnificent, and the overall sound is extremely powerful and points very much toward the sound that Belvin would arrive at before his death. This CD isn't easy to find—stores stock Flair/Virgin's B.B. King reissues more willingly—but it's worth tracking down or ordering. —*Bruce Eder*

Golden Classics / Apr. 22, 1997 / Collectables ✦✦✦✦
Twenty-six songs and 75 minutes of pure gold, all but two of which are drawn from his RCA period. Worth the price just for the song "Witchcraft." —*Bruce Eder*

My Last Goodbye / RCA ✦✦✦
Sentimental love songs, ballads, and some uptempo R&B from the great crooner Jesse Belvin, who was killed in a 1960 car crash in Arkansas. He was the ultimate romantic vocalist, and might have made similar inroads as Sam Cooke had he lived into the '60s. This is an overview of his material. —*Ron Wynn*

Pat Benatar (Pat Andrzejewski)

b. Jan. 10, 1953, Brooklyn, NY
Vocals / Pop-Rock, Arena Rock
Pat Benatar's polished mainstream pop-rock made her one of the more popular female vocalists of the early '80s. Although she came on like an arena rocker with her power chords, tough sexuality, and powerful vocals, her music was straight pop-rock underneath all the bluster.

Benatar began singing in New York in the late '70s; she was discovered by Rick Newman at his "Catch a Rising Star" club in 1979. Under the management of Newman, Benatar signed with Chrysalis Records, releasing her debut album, *In the Heat of the Night*, that same year. The record launched her string of hit singles with the No. 23 "Heartbreaker." Featuring the Top Ten hit "Hit Me with Your Best Shot," Benatar's second album, 1980's *Crimes of Passion*, had a greater success, selling over four million copies and winning the Grammy for Best Female Rock Vocal Performance. Her third album, *Precious Time* (1981), reached No. 1 on the album charts; a single from the album called "Fire and Ice" won Benatar another Grammy. She married her producer/guitarist Neil Geraldo in 1982, the same year the platinum *Get Nervous* was released. Benatar released a live album, *Live from Earth*, the next year; it contained one of her biggest hits, "Love Is a Battlefield." Although 1984's

Tropico contained her biggest hit "We Belong" (No. 5), the album was her lowest-charting to date.

"Invincible" (1985), taken from *The Legend of Billie Jean* soundtrack, was her last Top Ten hit. Even though it included the hit single "Sex as a Weapon," Benatar's *Seven the Hard Way* (1985) became her first album not to go platinum; it didn't even go gold. She took a couple of years off before returning with *Wide Awake in Dreamland* in 1988; it didn't chart as high as *Seven the Hard Way*, but it earned a gold record, as did *Best Shots*, a greatest-hits collection released the next year.

Benatar didn't record a new album until 1991, when she released the blues record *True Love*. It proved a critical and commercial disaster, prompting her to return to her mainstream rock on 1993's *Gravity's Rainbow;* nevertheless, the reversal in musical direction didn't return her to the top of the charts. *—Stephen Thomas Erlewine*

In the Heat of The Night / Sep. 1979 / Chrysalis ✦✦✦✦
This debut album features her trademark power-pop song "Heartbreaker." *—Donna DiChario*

Crimes of Passion / Aug. 1980 / Chrysalis ✦✦✦✦
The success of Pat Benatar's debut single "Heartbreaker" made it evident that listeners longed to hear the Long Islander rock out more often. Instead of stressing new wave-ish material as she generally did on *In the Heat of the Night*, Benatar cranked up the electric guitars the second time around and delivered the loudest, most aggressively rockin' album of her career. Both artistically and commercially, this change of direction paid off handsomely. In 1980, women who rocked forcefully were the exception instead of the rule, and Benatar was among the enjoyable exceptions. From "Out of Touch" to the celebrated "Hit Me with Your Best Shot," *Crimes of Passion* is a gritty hard rock gem that is as fun as it is loud. One song that definitely isn't escapist, however, is "Hell Is for Children"— a commentary on child abuse that is downright chilling. *—Alex Henderson*

Precious Time / Jul. 1981 / Chrysalis ✦✦✦
Pat Benatar's third album, *Precious Time*, was her only No. 1 record, but it wasn't as consistent as her previous two albums. While it follows the same polished arena rock formula of *In the Heat of the Night* and *Crimes of Passion, Precious Time* takes off only on the singles "Fire and Ice" and "Promises in the Dark," which exploit Benatar's powerful voice and her band's sleek variation on hard rock. *—Stephen Thomas Erlewine*

Get Nervous / Nov. 1982 / Chrysalis ✦✦✦
In interviews, Pat Benatar made it clear that she had no desire to be stereotyped as a hard rocker, often adding that she preferred new wave's melodic keyboards over hard rock and metal's crunching guitars. Indeed, *Get Nervous* was the most melodic album she'd done since *In the Heat of the Night*. This isn't to say that *Get Nervous* was a return to new wave-ish leanings; in fact, songs like "Anxiety (Get Nervous)," "The Victim," and "Silent Partners" are intense, forceful jewels that rock aggressively. But at the same time, the album's pop elements and strong emphasis on melody leave no doubt that the last thing on Benatar's mind was recording another *Crimes of Passion*. *—Alex Henderson*

Live from Earth / Oct. 1983 / Chrysalis ✦✦
As the title suggests, the bulk of *Live from Earth* is compiled from various concerts where Benatar faithfully recreates the sound of her albums. The remaining two songs were new studio tracks, including the single "Love Is a Battlefield," her best song since "Fire and Ice." Unfortunately, she didn't write it, nor did any of her band members. *—Stephen Thomas Erlewine*

Tropico / Nov. 1984 / Chrysalis ✦✦✦
On *Tropico*, Pat Benatar began moving toward a more middle-of-the-road sound, as evidenced by the hit single "We Belong." The change in direction revitalized the singer, resulting in her best album since *Precious Time*. *—Stephen Thomas Erlewine*

Seven the Hard Way / Nov. 1985 / Chrysalis ✦✦✦
Seven the Hard Way continues the slick pop approach of *Tropico* and is benefitted by a wealth of songs written by professional songwriters. At this point, Benatar and her band weren't coming up with material as catchy or memorable as "Invincible" and "Sex as a Weapon," so the presence of the pro songwriting was a blessing, not a curse. *—Stephen Thomas Erlewine*

Wide Awake in Dreamland / Jun. 1988 / Chrysalis ✦✦✦
Although it falls short of the excellence of *Crimes of Passion, Precious Time*, and *Get Nervous, Wide Awake in Dreamland* is a generally decent and respectable effort that has more pluses than minuses. Closer in spirit to *Tropico* than *Passion* or *Time*, the consistently melodic *Dreamland* stresses pop elements and steers clear of hard rock. The CD's most memorable offerings include the haunting and moody "Too Long a Soldier," the infectious "Lift Em On Up," and the disturbing commentary on child abuse "Suffer the Little Children." Unfortunately, Benatar's popularity was starting to decline in 1988 , and in the early—to-mid-'90s, she would receive little attention. *—Alex Henderson*

● **Best Shots** / Nov. 1989 / Chrysalis ✦✦✦✦
Multi-Grammy winner Benatar has vocal range to spare on this hits collection, including her rockers "Heartbreaker," "Fire and Ice," and "Hell Is for Children." *—Donna DiChario*

True Love / Apr. 1991 / Chrysalis ✦✦
A radical departure from the type of slick pop-rock she'd been embracing on albums like *Tropico* and *Wide Awake in Dreamland, True Love* found Pat Benatar embracing blues and early pre-rock R&B. Opting for less production and a much rawer approach, an inspired Benatar ditches the synthesizers and keyboards and sounds as if she's leading a bar band in a Chicago dive. From Albert King's "I Get Evil" to B.B. King's "Payin' the Cost to Be the Boss" to Charles Brown's "Please Come Home for Christmas," the results aren't breathtaking, but they are generally honest and soulful. Quite clearly, this was an album Benatar was anxious to make. *—Alex Henderson*

Gravity's Rainbow / Jun. 1, 1993 / Chrysalis ✦✦
Gravity's Rainbow marked Pat Benatar's return to arena rock after the dismal failure of her blues album, *True Love*. While it was well produced and carefully constructed, the album failed to capture an audience. Although she had returned to the sound that made her famous, both radio and the record-buying public had lost interest and the album slipped off the charts shortly after its release. *—Stephen Thomas Erlewine*

Very Best Of: All Fired Up / 1994 / Chrysalis ✦✦✦✦
A double-disc collection featuring all of her hits and popular album tracks, *All Fired Up: The Very Best of Pat Benatar* is the definitive collection of the popular mainstream rocker. It trims the fat from her spotty albums, leaving the best material she recorded throughout her career. Nevertheless, it features too much material for most listeners and is worthwhile only for dedicated fans. *—Stephen Thomas Erlewine*

16 Classic Performances / Jul. 9, 1996 / EMI ✦✦✦✦
If you're serious about your Benatar, you'll probably aim for the two-CD *All Fired Up* anthology. This 16-track single-disc compilation has many of her biggest hits (with some notable ones, like "Treat Me Right," omitted), and previously unreleased live versions of "Helter Skelter" and "Hit Me with Your Best Shot" from the early '80s. *—Richie Unterberger*

Brook Benton (Benjamin Franklin Peay)

b. Sep. 19, 1931, Camden, SC, **d.** Apr. 9, 1988, New York City, NY
Vocals / R&B, Soul

Silky smooth: that was Brook Benton's byword from his first record to his very last, as the singer parlayed his rich baritone pipes into seven No. 1 R&B hits and eight Top Ten items. Stints on the gospel circuit preceded Benton's first secular session for Okeh in 1953, but his career didn't begin to take off until he teamed with writer/producer Clyde Otis. Benton co-wrote and sang hundreds of demos for other artists before frequent collaborator Otis signed his friend to Mercury; together they pioneered a lush, violin-studded variation on the standard R&B sound, which beautifully showcased Benton's intimate vocals. Benton crashed the top spot on the R&B charts in early 1959 with his moving "It's Just a Matter of Time," then rapidly encored with three more R&B chart-toppers—"Thank You Pretty Baby," "So Many Ways," and "Kiddio." Pairing with Mercury labelmate Dinah Washington, their delightful repartee on "Baby (You've Got What It Takes)" and "A Rockin' Good Way" paced the R&B lists in 1960. The early '60s were a prolific period for Benton, but he left Mercury a few years later and bounced between labels before reemerging with the atmospheric Tony Joe White ballad "Rainy Night in Georgia" on Cotillion in 1970. Benton later made a halfhearted attempt to cash in on the disco craze, but his hitmaking reign was at an end long before his death in 1988. *—Bill Dahl*

● **Anthology** / 1986 / Rhino ✦✦✦✦
Rhino's Brook Benton *Anthology* is a 23-track collection that hits all of the high points, including not only songs from his tenure with Mercury—"It's Just a Matter of Time," "So Many Ways," "Kiddio," "Baby (You've Got What It Takes), "A Rockin' Good Way (To Mess Around and Fall in Love)," "The Boll Weevil Song," "Hotel Happiness"—but his later hits on Cotillion Records, including "Rainy Night in Georgia." It's the only collection that covers such a wide range of material. The terrific *40 Greatest Hits* features only his Mercury recordings, which admittedly are his best work—and thereby gives a good overview. But Rhino's *Anthology* is the only thoughtfully compiled retrospective of Benton's entire career. *—Stephen Thomas Erlewine*

40 Greatest Hits / 1989 / Mercury ✦✦✦✦
Everything you need to know about Benton's bluesy, sexy pop music is included here, in the duets with Dinah Washington. *—Hank Davis*

Berlin

f. 1982, Los Angeles, CA, **db.** 1987
Pop-Rock

This Los Angeles-based synth-pop group, founded by bassist John Crawford, singer Terri Nunn, and keyboard player David Diamond, made its first national impression with the provocative single "Sex (I'm A . . .)" from the gold-selling debut EP *Pleasure Victim* in 1983. The group was filled out by guitarist Ric Olsen, bassist player Matt Reid, and drummer Rob Brill. Berlin's first full-length LP was the gold *Love Life* in 1984. In 1985 the group was pared down to a trio of Crawford, Nunn, and Brill. Berlin topped the charts in 1986 with the single "Take My Breath Away," the love theme from the Tom Cruise movie *Top Gun.* Nunn left for a solo career in 1987, and Crawford and Brill teamed up in the Big F. — *William Ruhlmann*

Pleasure Victim / 1982 / Geffen ✦✦✦✦
Berlin pulled three dance-pop hits from this seven-track, 29-minute debut EP, which successfully combined synth-beats with the sexy vocals of Terri Nunn, especially on the uninhibited "Sex (I'm A . . .)." (*Pleasure Victim* was released by Enigma in September 1982 and reissued by Geffen in January 1983. An extra track was added when it was released on CD.) — *William Ruhlmann*

Love Life / 1984 / Geffen ✦✦✦
Berlin consolidated its position as synth-pop sex merchant (and thus the successor to Blondie) with this, its first full-length album. Mike (A Flock of Seagulls) Howlett produced most of the record, although disco producer Giorgio Moroder and his partner Richie Zito worked on two tracks, among them the Top 25 single "No More Words." The result was a gold-selling, Top 30 album of danceable pop. But this was Berlin's high-water mark. Reduced to a trio in 1985, they again teamed with Moroder for the ballad "Take My Breath Away" in 1986, but were history by 1987, as the sex/dance crown passed to Madonna. — *William Ruhlmann*

Count Three and Pray / 1986 / Geffen ✦✦✦✦
A major change of direction for Berlin, *Count Three and Pray* was an artistic triumph but a commercial disappointment. After making a name for itself playing very European-sounding synth-pop, the L.A. trio recruited producer Bob Ezrin (known for his work with Alice Cooper and others) and unveiled a more hard-edged, guitar-oriented sound. From the rockin' "Trash" (which features none other than Ted Nugent—the last person one would expect to work with Berlin!) to the ballad "Pink and Velvet" (a tale of two heroin addicts' romance that is as poignant as it is disturbing), *Count Three and Pray* leaves no doubt just how much lead singer Terri Nunn and her colleagues were enjoying this radical change. But sadly, record buyers weren't ready for it. Despite the inclusion of the hauntingly pretty No. 1 hit "Take My Breath Away" (included in the film *Top Gun*), the album didn't sell nearly as well as *Pleasure Victim* or *Love Life.* Geffen was bitterly disappointed, and Berlin soon broke up. — *Alex Henderson*

● **The Best of Berlin 1979-1988** / 1989 / Geffen ✦✦✦✦
All of Berlin's greatest hits and best material are included on this fine single-disc collection. — *Stephen Thomas Erlewine*

Chuck Berry (Charles Edward Anderson Berry)

b. Oct. 18, 1926, St Louis, MO
Guitar, Vocals / Rock 'n' Roll
Of all the early breakthrough rock 'n' roll artists, none is more important to the development of the music than Chuck Berry. He is its greatest songwriter, the main shaper of its instrumental voice, one of its greatest guitarists, and one of its greatest performers. Quite simply, without him, there would be no Beatles, Rolling Stones, Beach Boys, Bob Dylan, nor a myriad others. There would be no standard "Chuck Berry guitar intro," the instrument's clarion call to get the joint rockin' in any setting. The clippety-clop rhythms of rockabilly would not have been mainstreamed into the now standard 4/4 rock 'n' roll beat. There would be no obsessive wordplay by modern-day tunesmiths; in fact, the whole history (and artistic level) of rock 'n' roll songwriting would have been much poorer without him. As Brian Wilson said, he wrote "all of the great songs and came up with all the rock 'n' roll beats." Those who do not claim him as a seminal influence or profess a liking for his music and showmanship show their ignorance of rock's development, as well as his place as the music's first great creator. Elvis may have fueled rock 'n' roll's imagery, but Chuck Berry was its heartbeat and original mindset.

He was born Charles Edward Anderson Berry to a large family in St. Louis. A bright pupil, Berry developed a love for poetry and hard blues early on, winning a high school talent contest with a guitar and vocal rendition of Jay McShann's big band number, "Confessin' the Blues." With some local tutelage from the neighborhood barber, Chuck progressed from a four-string tenor guitar to an official six-string model and was soon working the local East St. Louis club scene, sitting in everywhere he could. He quickly found out that Black audiences liked a wide variety of music and set himself to the task of being able to reproduce as much of it as possible. What he found they *really* liked—besides the blues and Nat King Cole tunes—was the sight and sound of a Black man playing white hillbilly music, and Berry's showmanlike flair, coupled with his seemingly inexhaustible supply of fresh verses for old favorites, quickly made him a name on the circuit. In 1954 he ended up

taking over pianist Johnny Johnson's small combo, and a residency at the Cosmopolitan Club soon made the Chuck Berry Trio the top attraction in the Black community, with Ike Turner's Kings of Rhythm their only real competition.

But Berry had bigger ideas; he yearned to make records, and a trip to Chicago netted a two-minute conversation with his idol Muddy Waters, who encouraged him to approach Chess Records. Upon listening to Berry's homemade demo tape, label president Leonard Chess professed a liking for a hillbilly tune on it named "Ida Red" and quickly scheduled a session for May 21, 1955. During the session the title was changed to "Maybellene, and rock 'n' roll history was born. Although the record made it only to the mid-20s on the *Billboard* pop chart, its overall influence was massive and groundbreaking. Here was finally a Black rock 'n' roll record with across-the-board appeal, embraced by white teenagers and Southern hillbilly musicians (a young Elvis Presley—still a full year from national stardom—quickly added it to his stage show), that for once couldn't be successfully covered by a pop singer like Snooky Lanson on "Your Hit Parade." Part of the secret to its originality was Chuck's blazing 24-bar guitar solo in the middle of it, the imaginative rhyme schemes in the lyrics, and the sheer thump of the record, all signaling that rock 'n' roll had arrived and was no fad. Helping to put the record over to a white teenage audience was the highly influential New York disc jockey Alan Freed, who had been given part of the writers' credit by Chess in return for his spins and plugs. But to his credit, Freed was also the first white DJ-promoter to consistently use Berry on his rock 'n' roll stage show extravaganzas at the Brooklyn Fox and Paramount theaters (playing to predominantly white audiences). When Hollywood came calling a year or so later, Freed also made sure that Chuck appeared with him in *Rock! Rock! Rock!, Go, Johnny, Go!,* and *Mister Rock 'n' Roll.* Within a year's time, Chuck had gone from a local St. Louis blues picker making $15 a night to a sensation commanding over a hundred times that.

The hits started coming thick and fast over the next few years, every one of them about to become a classic of the genre: "Roll Over Beethoven," "Thirty Days," "Too Much Monkey Business," "Brown Eyed Handsome Man," "You Can't Catch Me," "School Day," "Carol," "Back in the USA," "Little Queenie," "Memphis, Tennessee," "Johnny B. Goode," and the tune that defined the moment perfectly, "Rock and Roll Music." Berry was not only in constant demand, touring the country on mixed package shows and appearing on television and in movies, but smart enough to know exactly what to do with the spoils of a suddenly successful show business career. He started investing heavily in St. Louis area real estate and, ever one to push the envelope, opened up a racially mixed nightspot called the Club Bandstand in 1958, to the consternation of uptight locals. *These* were not the plans of your average R&B singers who contented themselves with a wardrobe of flashy suits, a new Cadillac, and the nicest house in the Black section. Berry was smart, with plenty of business savvy, and was already making plans to open an amusement park in nearby Wentzville. When the St. Louis hierarchy found out that an underage hat-check girl Berry hired had also set up shop as a prostitute at a nearby hotel, trouble came down on Berry like a sledgehammer on a fly. Charged with transporting a minor over state lines (the Mann Act), Berry endured two trials and was sentenced to federal prison for two years as a result.

He emerged from prison a moody, embittered man. But two very important things had happened in his absence. First, British teenagers had discovered his music and were making his old songs hits all over again. Second, and perhaps most important, America had discovered the Beatles and the Rolling Stones, both of whom based their music on Berry's style, with the Stones' early albums looking like a Berry song list. Rather than being relegated to the has-been circuit, Berry found himself in the midst of a world-wide beat boom with his music as the centerpiece. He came back with a clutch of hits ("Nadine," "No Particular Place to Go," "You Never Can Tell"), toured Britain in triumph, and appeared on the big screen with his British disciples in the groundbreaking *T.A.M.I. Show* in 1964.

Berry had moved with the times and found a new audience in the bargain, and when the cries of yeah-yeah-yeah were replaced with peace signs, Chuck altered his live act to include a passel of slow blues and quickly became a fixture on the festival and hippie ballroom circuit. After a disastrous stint with Mercury Records, he returned to Chess in the early '70s and scored his last hit with a live version of the salacious nursery rhyme, "My Ding a Ling," yielding his first official gold record. By decade's end, he was as in demand as ever, working every oldies revival show, TV special, and festival that was thrown his way. But once again, troubles with the law reared their ugly head, and 1979 saw Berry headed back to prison, this time for income tax evasion. Upon release this time, the creative days of Chuck Berry seemed to have come to an end. He appeared as himself in the Alan Freed biopic, *American Hot Wax,* and was inducted into the Rock & Roll Hall of Fame, but steadfastly refused to record any new material or even issue a live album. His live performances became increasingly erratic, with Berry working with terrible backup bands and turning in sloppy, out-of-tune performances that did much to tarnish his reputation with younger fans and oldtimers alike. In 1987 he published his first book, *Chuck Berry: The Autobiography*, and the same year saw the film release of what will likely be his lasting legacy, the rockumentary *Hail! Hail! Rock 'n' Roll*, which included live footage from a 60th-birthday concert with Keith Richards as musical director and the usual bevy of superstars coming out for guest turns. But for all of his offstage exploits and seemingly ongoing troubles with the law, Chuck Berry remains the epitome of rock 'n' roll. Perhaps John Lennon said it best. "If you were going to give rock 'n' roll another name, you might call it 'Chuck Berry.'" —*Cub Koda*

After School Session / 1958 / Chess ✦✦✦✦
While Chuck Berry's first album, *After School Session*, featured only one hit single, the Top Ten "School Day," several of the songs became rock 'n' roll standards, including "Too Much Monkey Business," "No Money Down," and "Brown Eyed Handsome Man." *After School Session* also featured a couple of stylistic variations, including the calypso-flavored "Havana Moon" and the straight blues of "Wee, Wee Hours." —*Stephen Thomas Erlewine*

One Dozen Berrys / 1958 / Chess ✦✦✦✦
The core of *One Dozen Berrys*, Chuck Berry's second album, was formed by the hit single "Sweet Little Sixteen," "Oh, Baby Doll," and "Rock and Roll Music." Besides "Reelin' and Rockin'," which failed as a single, not many of the album tracks became rock 'n' roll standards, yet the overall quality of the record is quite high, with "It Don't Take but a Few Minutes" and "Low Feeling" being particularly strong. —*Stephen Thomas Erlewine*

Is on Top / 1959 / Chess ✦✦✦✦
Berry's best '50s Chess album (his third) features many of his biggest hits, plus atmospheric instrumentals like "Blues for Hawaiians." —*Cub Koda*

Rockin' at the Hops / 1960 / Chess ✦✦✦
Chuck Berry opens this, his fourth album, with "Bye Bye Johnny," a sequel to "Johnny B. Goode," and closes it with "Let It Rock," which makes for two classics out of 12 songs in less than 28 minutes. There are also two good minor songs, "Too Pooped to Pop" and "Betty Jean." The filler includes instrumentals, blues workouts, covers, the usual. The classics are available elsewhere. —*William Ruhlmann*

New Juke Box Hits / 1961 / Chess ✦✦✦
Chuck Berry's fifth Chess Records album, *New Juke Box Hits*, was recorded and released in the midst of the legal difficulties that would put him in jail the next year. That distraction seems to have kept him from composing top-flight material, and the attendant publicity adversely affected his record sales; the album contained no hits. The single was "I'm Talking About You," later successfully recorded by the Rolling Stones, and the album contained "Thirteen Question Method" and "Don't You Lie to Me," worthy minor entries in the Berry canon. Elsewhere, Berry filled out the record covering others' hits—Nat "King" Cole's "Route 66," B.B. King's "Sweet Sixteen," Little Richard's "Rip It Up." The result is a good rock 'n' roll set, but it's not in the same league with Berry's earlier albums. —*William Ruhlmann*

☆ **St. Louis to Liverpool** / 1964 / Chess ✦✦✦✦
Berry's first album recorded after his release from prison shows him doing more than just picking up where he left off. "No Particular Place to Go," "You Never Can Tell," "Promised Land," and "Little Marie" (his sequel to "Memphis") all charted during 1964 and present Berry doing a more mature brand of the sound he pioneered. As though aware of the British Invasion acts that were (in the cases of the Beatles and the Rolling Stones) covering his stuff extremely well, he rose to the occasion by delivering a group of more complex songs that still retain his classic sound. Those four singles and a brace of album originals make this one of Berry's most successful and enduring albums. —*Bruce Eder*

Golden Hits / 1967 / Mercury ✦✦
Berry's first release for Mercury Records was this collection of re-recordings—done at a faster tempo, and in stereo—of his Chess hits. The songs are fine, but that's the best that can be said for this release. The playing, though competent, lacks the rough road-house ambience of the originals, and the stereo sound is an unnecessary distraction. —*Bruce Eder*

The London Sessions / 1972 / Chess ✦✦✦
Half of this album is a studio recording featuring Ian McLagan and Kenny Jones of the Faces. The other half is a live recording from the Lancaster Arts Festival in Coventry, England, featuring performances of "My Ding-a-Ling" and "Reelin' and Rockin'" that, in edited form, became the first hit singles for Chuck Berry in many years. ("My Ding-a-Ling" went gold and hit No. 1.) This gold-selling, Top Ten album represents Berry's commercial, if not artistic, peak. —*William Ruhlmann*

★ **The Great Twenty-Eight** / 1982 / Chess ✦✦✦✦✦
A single-disc compilation of Berry's original Chess greats, every one a gem: "Maybellene," "Johnny B. Goode," "Roll Over Beethoven," "Sweet Little Sixteen," and "Little Queenie" are the music the Beatles and others cut their teeth on. Beyond essential. —*Cub Koda*

Rock 'n' Roll Rarities / 1986 / Chess ✦✦✦✦
On this follow-up to *The Great Twenty-Eight*, the songs are familiar, but the versions are not. Delving into the Chess Records archives, producer Steve Hoffman has come up with 20 tracks, many in unreleased or unusual versions. Some are demos, some are stereo recordings of songs usually heard in mono. Hoffman has remixed many of them, bringing up the '50s and '60s sound quality to near-'80s standards. Start with *The Great Twenty-Eight*, but come to this collection for interesting new ways to hear the old Berry favorites. —*William Ruhlmann*

More Rock 'n' Roll Rarities from the Golden Era of Chess Records / Aug. 1986 / Chess ✦✦✦
This second volume of producer Steve Hoffman's discoveries in the Chess Records vaults features some less prominent Chuck Berry tunes, again in the form of demos, unreleased alternate takes, and stereo remixes. We are getting into collector territory here, but there are still some enjoyable examples of the Berry repertoire. —*William Ruhlmann*

Hail! Hail! Rock 'n' Roll / 1987 / MCA ✦✦✦
This is the soundtrack to a documentary film chronicling a concert held to celebrate Chuck Berry's 60th birthday. The band was led by Keith Richards and featured Berry's regular pianist, Johnnie Johnson; Richards' regular pianist, Chuck Leavell; Rolling Stones sax player Bobby Keys; bassist Joey Spampinato from NRBQ; and drummer Steve Jordan from Richards' solo band. The guests included Robert Cray, Linda Ronstadt, Eric Clapton, Julian Lennon, and Etta James. Berry was ragged-voiced but enthusiastic, the band had spirit, and the guests, even if they were sometimes unlikely, were sincere. The best way to hear Berry's music is to get the original recordings, of course, but as a souvenir of the Taylor Hackford film, this is an enjoyable romp through the catalog. —*William Ruhlmann*

☆ **The Chess Box** / 1988 / Chess ✦✦✦✦✦
Over the course of three compact discs, *The Chess Box* contains all the highlights from Chuck Berry's career, including all of the hit singles. In addition to the familiar items, which are all included here, there are numerous tracks that are lesser-known but equally good. That's particularly true on the stellar first two discs, where album tracks, B-sides, and forgotten singles like "Downbound Train," "Drifting Heart," "Havana Moon," "Betty Jean," "Bye Bye Johnny," "Down the Road a Piece," and "The Thirteen Question Method" get space with "Maybellene," "Thirty Days," "No Money Down," "Roll Over Beethoven," "Too Much Monkey Business," "Brown Eyed Handsome Man," "School Day," "Rock and Roll Music," "Sweet Little Sixteen," "Johnny B. Goode," and "Carol." Toward the end of the set, the quality of the material begins to sag a bit, but there are still forgotten gems like "Tulane" that prove that Berry's songwriting hadn't completely dried up. *The Great Twenty-Eight* remains the definitive hits collection, but *The Chess Box* is an absolutely essential item for any serious fan, either of Chuck Berry or rock 'n' roll. —*Stephen Thomas Erlewine*

Missing Berries / Jul. 1990 / Chess ✦✦✦
The third and final collection of Chuck Berry rarities from the Chess Records vaults, *Missing Berries* concentrates on Berry's blues recordings, which were never quite as captivating as his rock 'n' roll, but they're fascinating for devoted fans. —*Stephen Thomas Erlewine*

★ **His Best, Vol. 1** / Mar. 25, 1997 / Chess ✦✦✦✦✦
Focusing on his single tracks in a chronological manner, this first of two volumes in MCA's Chess 50th Anniversary collection hits all the high spots of Berry's career up to 1958. It also serves as the first compilation to really showcase Berry's development as a songwriter over the first three years of his massive crossover success, including the seldom-anthologized "Downbound Train" (perhaps the darkest and most demonic ditty he ever recorded) juxtaposed against his car songs ("Maybellene," "You Can't Catch Me"), his calculated and carefully crafted instant classics for the 1950s teenage market ("Reelin' and Rockin,'" "Sweet Little Sixteen," "School Day") and his celebrations of the music itself ("Rock and Roll Music," "Johnny B. Goode," "Roll Over Beethoven"). There's a ton of great music here (with a second companion volume to complete the picture). For a big chunk of what makes Chuck Berry perhaps rock 'n' roll's original triple-threat package (singer, songwriter and its first guitar hero), there's much here to recommend this volume as a first-time purchase. Note: This collection and its companion volume now take the place of the single disc *The Great Twenty-Eight*, which is now out of print. —*Cub Koda*

☆ **His Best, Vol. 2** / May 20, 1997 / MCA ✦✦✦✦
Picking up where the first volume left off, *His Best, Vol. 2* runs through Chuck Berry's best-known singles in 1958 with "Sweet Little Rock and Roller" and had his first No. 1 record with "My Ding-A-Ling." In addition to hits like "Let It Rock," "Little Queenie," "Almost Grown," "Nadine," "No Particular Place to Go," "You Never Can Tell," and "Promised Land," there are lesser-known gems that make it more than just a greatest hits

collection. No matter how good the two-part *His Best* series is (and for fans who don't want to spring for *The Chess Box*, it's the best way to assemble a reasonably comprehensive Chuck collection), it's still a shame that Chess decided to delete the flawless single-disc compilation *The Great Twenty-Eight* in favor of this series. —*Stephen Thomas Erlewine*

Dave Berry (David Holgate Grundy)

b. Feb. 6, 1941, Woodhouse, Sheffield, Yorkshire,
Guitar, Vocals / British Invasion

Briefly a big star in Britain in the mid-'60s, Dave Berry faced the same dilemma as several other British teen idols of the era: R&B was obviously nearest and dearest to his heart, but he needed to record blatantly pop material to make the hit parade. It was also obvious that Berry was, in fact, much more suited towards pop ballads than rough 'n' tumble R&B, regardless of his personal preferences. At his peak, his output was divided between hard R&B/rockers and straight pop. Help from ace session players like Jimmy Page and John Paul Jones notwithstanding, his smooth voice was frankly ill-equipped to deliver the goods with anything close to the same panache as Mick Jagger or Eric Burdon on the bluesier items. He made rather a good go of it, on the other hand, with romantic pop-rock ballads, hitting the British Top Ten with "The Crying Game" (1964), Bobby Goldsboro's "Little Things" (1965), and the excruciatingly sentimental "Mama" (1966). "This Strange Effect," written by Ray Davies (though not released by the Kinks), was a huge European hit for him in 1965 as well.

Berry's voice was not exactly teeming with character, and he never made the slightest impression on the US market, but the best of his material is quite pleasant period fare. He remains well regarded in his homeland, where the Sex Pistols unexpectedly covered his toughest track, "Don't Gimme No Lip Child." Even more unexpectedly, "The Crying Game" brought Berry's voice to his biggest international audience ever in 1992, when it was used as the theme song for one of the year's most successful films. —*Richie Unterberger*

● **This Strange Effect** / 1986 / See For Miles ✦✦✦✦
All the Dave Berry you need, with all but one of the 20 tracks dating from his 1964-66 heyday. Sensibly divided into a ten-song R&B side and a ten-song pop side, it includes all his hit singles—"The Crying Game," "Little Things," "Memphis," the unfortunate "Mama"—as well as "This Strange Effect" and "Don't Gimme No Lip Child." Some of the R&B tracks are mediocre; others (especially "Gimme No Lip") growl along neatly. Some of the lesser-known pop numbers are pretty nifty as well, the highlight being "I'm Gonna Take You There," which was penned by Graham Gouldman (who also wrote hits for the Yardbirds and the Hollies in the mid-'60s). —*Richie Unterberger*

Richard Berry

b. Apr. 11, 1935, Extension, LA, **d.** Jan. 23, 1997, Los Angeles, CA
Vocals / R&B, Rock 'n' Roll

If for no other reason than that he was the original writer and performer of "Louie Louie" (itself based on "El Loca Cha Cha," by Rene Touzet), Richard Berry holds a permanent place of honor in the history of rock 'n' roll. Beyond that, though, Berry was an important, if secondary, figure of the early- and mid-'50s Los Angeles R&B scene. As a teenager, with the Flairs and as a solo act, Berry recorded quite a few singles that demonstrated his versatilty with ballads, novelty songs, and even Little Richard-styled numbers. His facility with deep-voiced, comic material was a clear forerunner of the Coasters, and he was the uncredited lead singer on Leiber & Stoller's "Riot in Cell Block No.9," recorded by the Robins, later to mutate into the Coasters. He took another uncredited vocal as Ella James' deep-voiced sparring partner on "Roll with Me, Henry," one of the biggest R&B hits of the mid-'50s. Berry originally recorded "Louie Louie" in 1956; the record was a regional hit in several West Coast cities, but no more than that.

Berry's recording career petered out in the late '50s, though he remained an active performer. In the early '60s, several Northwest bands seized upon "Louie Louie" as cover material, scoring sizable regional hits; finally, in 1963, the Kingsmen broke the song nationally, reaching No. 2. In the decades since then, "Louie Louie" has become one of the most oft-covered rock standards of all time; there are probably well over 1000 versions by now. The song was investigated by the FBI, and inspired parades and campaigns to adopt it as the official song of the State of Washington. The original version, ironically, remains extremely difficult to find, appearing only on obscure compilations (the Berry version on Rhino's *Louie Louie* anthology is a re-recording). For Berry, there was a happy ending; in the late '80s, he regained the rights to the song that he had lost many years ago. —*Richie Unterberger*

● **Get Out of the Car** / 1982 / Flair ✦✦✦✦
Twenty songs from the mid-'50s, both solo and with the Flairs. Berry wrote or co-wrote most of the tunes, which are solid if somewhat generic R&B on the verge of rock 'n' roll, occasionally treading into doo

wop territory. He's most memorable on the uptempo, comic jiving numbers, with a sardonic and sassy tone that pointed the way for the Coasters. This doesn't have "Louie Louie" or any of the late-'50s material he recorded for the Flip label, which is available on the hard-to-find Swedish import *Louie Louie*. —*Richie Unterberger*

Cindy Lee Berryhill

b. United States
Guitar, Vocals / Singer-Songwriter, Alternative Pop-Rock, Folk-Rock

Cindy Lee Berryhill is a folk-rock singer-songwriter who, although one hates to say it, plays better on paper than on record. Those who bemoan the decline of fresh singer-songwriter talent in the pop and rock mainstream have to admire her obvious respect for classic singer-songwriter values, and her determination to present them in a present-day context that doesn't merely ape the sound of the '60s and '70s. She has the desirable liberal and feminist politics, and is conscious of delivering these with a sense of humor. But her vocals and songwriting, not to mention that sense of humor, are not top-flight enough to make her more than a minor performer, if a periodically engaging one.

Berryhill has always identified herself with the alternative rock scene, playing in a punk rock band before going solo, and supporting such acts as Billy Bragg, the Smithereens, the Proclaimers, and X. Her music usually owes as much to folk as rock, though. The San Diegan's 1987 debut, *Who's Gonna Save the World*, may be her best simply because it is her most straightforward. Then, as now, she was most effective, ironically, at her most basic and serious. Her talking-blues and satirical numbers are not funny or biting enough, and when she adopts a jiving vocal tone, the results are much more awkward than when she just sings.

Berryhill does not lack ambition, moving to New York City in the late 1980s to become part of the non-starting "anti-folk" scene. It wouldn't be accurate to say that this hurt her career, as the movement wasn't wide enough to be perceived as a failure. But it didn't do much for her, either, although former Patti Smith guitarist (and Suzanne Vega producer) Lenny Kaye produced her second album.

Moving back to Southern California in the 1990s, she went for a much more unusual sound on 1994's *Garage Orchestra*, enlisting help from musicians who had worked with the San Diego Symphony and the Harry Partch Ensemble. Again, the combination looks more interesting than it sounds, though the ambition is certainly laudable. *Straight Outta Marysville* in 1996 settled between the extremes, going back to a folkier sound while retaining a wider range of instrumentation than the standard folk-rock unit. —*Richie Unterberger*

● **Who's Gonna Save the World?** / 1987 / Rhino ✦✦✦✦
A reasonably strong debut of a sassy and confident folk-rocker, ranging from rabble-rousing anthems to straight country-folk-rock to playing for laughs. "Looking Through Portholes" (which recalls vintage Ian & Sylvia) and the uncommonly pastoral "Cellaigh Green" are among the best songs she's ever done; the more playful narratives are less successful. —*Richie Unterberger*

Naked Movie Star / 1989 / Rhino ✦✦✦✦
This quirky, Los Angeles-based folkie, aided by a folk/rock production courtesy of Lenny Kaye, comments on life in Hollywood, Donald Trump, and other subjects with a sometimes flip, sometimes self-deprecating attitude. —*William Ruhlmann*

Garage Orchestra / Sep. 27, 1994 / Earth Music/Cargo ✦✦✦
Berryhill goes all out to create a sort of symphonic folk-rock sound here, augmenting the standard guitar-oriented lineup with vibraphone, tympani, cello, mandolin, and more. It's neither the glorious success nor the massive failure one would expect. It's just folk-rockish material with orchestral arrangements, and the songs are nice enough. But that's not sufficient to elevate this into anything approaching a major work. —*Richie Unterberger*

Straight Outta Marysville / Mar. 19, 1996 / Cargo ✦✦✦
Berryhill is like a baseball pitcher who tosses fine games every fourth or fifth outing. If you happen to see one of those games, you'd have no idea why the pitcher didn't perform like that all of the time. By the same token, if you heard only Berryhill's best tracks, you'd think she was a major singer-songwriter, or at least on the verge of becoming one. That's what happens here. When she cuts the schtick and concentrates on the heart of the matter, as on "California" or "Unwritten Love Song" (her most soulful vocal ever), she sounds like a real contender. The rest of the time she doesn't sing or write as well, making one wish she could turn on the juice more, or at least focus on singing expressively instead of dropping into her talky mannerisms so often. —*Richie Unterberger*

Bettie Serveert

f. 1990, Amsterdam, Holland
Alternative Pop-Rock, Indie Rock

Comprised of vocalist/guitarist Carol van Dijk, guitarist Peter Visser, bassist Herman Bunskoeke, and drummer Berend Dubbe, the Dutch guitar-pop quartet Bettie Serveert released their debut album, *Palomine*, in 1992. Bettie Serveert has jangly hooks and sweet melodies to spare, but the group can rock as hard as the Pretenders. Featuring the radio hits "Kid's Alright" and "Tom Boy," *Palomine* made the band alternative rock stars. The group's second album, *Lamprey*, was released in 1995 to favorable reviews, as was 1997's *Dust Bunnies*. — *Stephen Thomas Erlewine*

● **Palomine** / Jul. 1993 / Matador ✦✦✦✦
What makes *Palomine*, Bettie Serveert's debut album, such a wonderful record is the way the band balances the sweet guitar-pop of "Tom Boy" with yearning ballads like "Palomine" and gutsy garage-rockers like "Kid's Alright" without ever sounding forced or cliched. Instead, all of the band's music is tied together by their weaving guitars, pulsing rhythms, and especially Carol van Dijk's voice, which conveys more genuine emotion and grit than most vocalists in alternative rock. — *Stephen Thomas Erlewine*

Lamprey / Jan. 24, 1995 / Matador ✦✦
Lamprey, Bettie Serveert's second album, is a reprise of *Palomine*, down to the way Carol van Dijk's voice catches in her throat as she goes into the chorus of "Ray Ray Rain"—just as it did on "Palomine." *Lamprey* lacks the hooks of *Palomine*, substituting the winding guitar licks that enhanced the melodies of the first album for the melodies themselves. Though the group turns in a couple of affecting songs—"Ray Ray Rain" and "Crutches"—the album is essentially a rewrite of the first, only without the charm or the benefit of hard-rockers like "Kid's Alright." — *Stephen Thomas Erlewine*

Dust Bunnies / Mar. 25, 1997 / Capitol ✦✦✦
While *Dust Bunnies* is a tighter, more melodic album than Bettie Serveert's flawed second record *Lamprey*, it doesn't necessarily return the band to the heights of *Palomine*. Musically, *Dust Bunnies* is no different than its two predecessors, and the group's lack of development is a little bit eerie. It's one thing to have a distinctive sound and quite another to make two albums that sound like outtakes from your debut. Instead of developing or refining their sound, Bettie Serveert stay within their self-imposed boundaries, crafting small, simple jangle-pop songs that never rock too hard or sound too soft. Occasionally, as on "Co-Coward" and "Sugar the Pill," they create wonderful pop gems, but too often the music is nothing more than pleasant. — *Stephen Thomas Erlewine*

Paul Bevoir

b. England
Vocals, Guitar / Pop-Rock, Mod Revival
Paul Bevoir did his best to keep the British mod revival going well into the '80s as the main creative force behind the charmingly determined Jet Set and as the underground movement's leading songwriter, contributing perfectly crafted '60s-style pop songs to the Candees, Melvyn and the Smartys, and Dee Walker. After the Jet Set released their first LP, *There Goes the Neighborhood* in 1985, Bevoir released his first solo album, *The Happiest Days of Your Life*, backed by the Family Way. The album received some acclaim in the British press, but Bevoir kept his solo work in the background while he continued to push on with the Jet Set until they disbanded in 1988. Bevoir formed Smalltown Parade in 1990, releasing two albums before the group broke up. In 1994 Bevoir resurfaced, releasing *Dumb Angel* for the Tangerine Label. — *Chris Woodstra*

The Happiest Days of Your Life / 1985 / Tangerine ✦✦✦✦
● **Dumb Angel** / 1994 / Tangerine ✦✦✦✦

Big Audio Dynamite

f. 1984, London, England
Alternative Pop-Rock, Alternative Dance
After British guitarist/singer Mick Jones (b. June 26, 1955, Brixton, London, England) was fired from the punk rock group the Clash in 1983, he formed Big Audio Dynamite (B.A.D.) in 1984 with video artist Don Letts (effects and vocals), Greg Roberts (drums), Dan Donovan (keyboards), and Leo "E-Zee Kill" Williams (bass). B.A.D. debuted on record with the single "The Bottom Line" in September 1985. The group followed the more experimental funk elements of the Clash's *Combat Rock*, adding samplers, dance tracks, and found sounds to Jones' concise pop songwriting. Jones suffered from a near-fatal bout of pneumonia in 1988, but he bounced back with 1989's *Megatop Phoenix*. After that record, the band split at the end of 1989. Jones added Gary Stonadge (bass/vocals), Chris Kavanagh (drums/vocals), and Nick Hawkins (guitar/vocals) to form Big Audio Dynamite II, while Letts, Williams, and Roberts formed Screaming Target, and Donovan joined the Sisters of Mercy. Releasing *The Globe*, the first full-length album with the new lineup, in 1991, B.A.D. II experienced their greatest success yet with the American Top

40 hit single "Rush." In 1994 the band's name was truncated to Big Audio, and the album *Higher Power* was released.

After *Higher Power*, Big Audio parted ways with Epic Records, signing with Radioactive in early 1995. On *Punk* (1995), their first album for Radioactive, the group was renamed Big Audio Dynamite. — *Stephen Thomas Erlewine and William Ruhlmann*

This Is Big Audio Dynamite / Oct. 1985 / Columbia ✦✦✦
Since Mick Jones was the more melodic, pop force in the Clash, it was a surprise that the band he formed after being kicked out of that group was such an unusual mix of synthesized drumming and spoken-word tape inserts, although beneath all the gimmicky sounds (and perhaps accentuated by them) were Jones' often winning songs, among which were the UK Top 40 hits "E =MC2" and "Medicine Show." — *William Ruhlmann*

No. 10, Upping St. / Oct. 1986 / Columbia ✦✦✦✦
Temporarily reuniting with his former Clash partner Joe Strummer (who co-produced this album and co-wrote five songs), Mick Jones expands on the formula of the debut with Big Audio Dynamite's second album. *No. 10 Upping Street* features better songs that meld samples, found sounds, dance rhythms, and elements of hip-hop more completely and effectively than those on the first record. "C'mon Every Beatbox" and "V. Thirteen" made the UK singles chart. "Badrock City," added to the album after its initial release, made the US R&B singles chart. — *Stephen Thomas Erlewine and William Ruhlmann*

Tighten Up, Vol. '88 / Jun. 1988 / Columbia ✦✦
Mick Jones tightens the rather free-form structures of the previous B.A.D. albums on *Tighten Up, Vol. '88*. While he was aiming for a greater commercial success, the result was only partially successful; the best tracks didn't work as singles, and the singles didn't have the creative spark that marks the best of B.A.D.'s music. "Just Play Music!" made the UK singles chart. — *Stephen Thomas Erlewine*

Megatop Phoenix / Sep. 1989 / Columbia ✦✦✦
On *Megatop Phoenix*, Jones delves even further into a dance-influenced, cut-and-paste approach to pop music that manages to capture all of the inventiveness of late-'80s dance music without losing sight of the melodies that have always been his strength. — *Stephen Thomas Erlewine*

The Globe / Aug. 1991 / Columbia ✦✦✦✦
Although the second incarnation of Big Audio Dynamite doesn't sound all that different from the first, Mick Jones' songwriting and concepts are reinvigorated on *The Globe*, making it one of the best B.A.D. albums. It also ranked as their most commercially successful in the US, where "Rush" hit the Top 40, with the title track also charting. — *Stephen Thomas Erlewine*

Higher Power / Nov. 8, 1994 / Columbia ✦✦
Nine years and six albums on, Big Audio's formula of Mick Jones-penned pop tunes, hip-hop beats, and odd found sounds was beginning to sound worn. As indicated on such tracks as "Looking for a Song" and "Harrow Road," carrying on seemed to have become something of a burden for Jones, who increasingly turned to '60s-derived guitar riffs and simple pop melodies. The rhythm section remained too far down in the mix to induce dancing, and the tape inserts—well, Jones was still no Pink Floyd. Obviously, by whatever name they chose, Big Audio needed to rethink their approach. — *William Ruhlmann*

F-Punk / Jun. 20, 1995 / Radioactive ✦✦
For his first album for Radioactive, Mick Jones changed the name of his group back to Big Audio Dynamite and delivered *Punk*. While the name was a retreat to BAD's most creative and exciting days of the '80s, the music on *F-Punk* simply reiterated all of the ideas of their last few albums—which means that it restated the same themes as all of their previous records. Far from being "punk," with all its classic rock references and allusions to the glory days of 1977, the album sounds tied to the past. — *Stephen Thomas Erlewine*

● **Greatest Hits** / Sep. 12, 1995 / Columbia ✦✦✦✦
Big Audio Dynamite's albums have always been fairly inconsistent affairs, which makes *Greatest Hits* such a worthwhile purchase. Collecting 15 songs from their six albums at Columbia, when they were alternately called B.A.D. and B.A.D. II, the album contains hits like "Globe" and "Rush," as well as album tracks and college radio hits. — *Stephen Thomas Erlewine*

Big Black

f. 1982, Chicago, IL, **db.** 1988
Alternative Pop-Rock
Proudly and self-consciously abrasive, Big Black's music is polarizing; either you think that Steve Albini's relentlessly thin, metallic, emotionless guitar grind and distorted vocals are an uncompromising work of art or you think it's all self-indulgent crap. The band's clinical noise and grotesque, often misogynist, lyrics easily made them the most extreme, nihilistic band in the American underground in the mid-'80s. After recording three EPs with an unstable lineup, Big Black recorded its first

full album with Albini and Santiago Durango on guitar, Dave Lovering on bass, and a drum machine. None of their recordings show much musical progression; instead, the band gets harder, noisier, and nastier on each subsequent record. Before the band recorded their final and best album, 1987's *Songs About Fucking*, Durango left the group to study law; Albini pulled the plug on the band shortly afterward.

Although Big Black's lifespan was short, Albini's influence on the American independent music scene of the late '80s and '90s has been substantial. After Big Black's breakup he formed the equally uncompromising Rapeman, but Albini's real influence has been through his numerous productions. Over the years he has produced literally hundreds of bands; most of them are justifiably unknown, but some are quite famous—including the Pixies, the Breeders, Urge Overkill, PJ Harvey, and Nirvana. Albini's simple production functions as a type of photograph, capturing the band in an aural black and white; his production shows all of the band's strengths, as well as all of their faults. He frequently cuts the bass levels to a minimum, leaving only a harsh guitar grind, which makes his records a bit wearing to listen to. Many young bands of the '90s have embraced his signature guitar grind, as well as his strident punk-rock ethics, as a reaction to alternative music's move into the mainstream. —*Stephen Thomas Erlewine*

Atomizer / 1986 / Homestead ♦♦♦♦
Big Black was the brainchild of Chicago-based fanzine writer Steve Albini; *Atomizer* was the group's first full-length release after three EPs. This is an extremely bleak and disturbing album. The music is a grinding, assaultive brew (all of it built upon obsessively repeated riffs) that shows the noticeable influence of hardcore, noise, and heavy metal genres; over this, Albini shouts and spits rudimentary, sometimes scatological, lyrics about the darkest side of life and human nature. Parallels to groups such as Public Image Limited and Joy Division can be made, but the profound level of rage contained in this music is unique. Subjects include out-of-control boozing ("Stinking Drunk"), guns ("Bazooka Joe"), self-immolation and arson ("Kerosene"), slaughterhouses ("Cables"), and deviant sex ("Fists of Love" and "Bad Houses"). "Jordan, Minnesota" pushes the envelope even further; this combative number about child molestation closes with screamed distorted sounds that seemingly depict nonconsensual sex. Sound quality is sometimes squelched or lacking. Production values are not bad, though; while vocals are sometimes buried in the mix, instrumental textures are clearly defined. This chillingly nihilistic release is not a pleasant listen and may not hold up well once its initial shock value has worn away, though some folks may take to this album's desolate social commentary and angry music. —*David Cleary*

Hammer Party / 1986 / Homestead ♦♦♦
Combining Big Black's first two EPs, *Lungs* and *Bulldozer*, on one disc, *Hammer Party* shows the band evolving from Steve Albini's one-man guitar and drum machine aggro-fest to the fleshed-out, but no less insular, attack of the bassless trio. It's the band's sparest work, but also some of its most abrasive. For CD release, a third EP, *Racer-X*, was added to *The Hammer Party*. —*Stephen Thomas Erlewine*

The Rich Man's Eight-Track Tape / 1987 / Touch & Go ♦♦♦♦
Rich Man's Eight-Track combines the *Headache* EP and *Atomizer* album on one disc. *Atomizer*, the band's first full-length album, is a self-consciously aggressive and noxious onslaught of guitars and drums, wallowing in its own depravity; for the first time, Albini and Company achieve the sound they were aiming for. *Headache* isn't as good; it's a retread of *Atomizer* without any of the surprise. —*Stephen Thomas Erlewine*

● **Songs About Fucking** / 1987 / Touch & Go ♦♦♦♦
Easily the best album Big Black ever recorded. The bleak noise of *Songs About Fucking* matches the empty nihilism of Albini's ranting lyrics; for once, the sheer force of the music actually makes the band seem threatening, scary, and dangerous. —*Stephen Thomas Erlewine*

Big Bopper (Jiles Perry Richardson)

f. Oct. 24, 1930, Sabine Pass, TX, **db.** Feb. 3, 1959, Clear Lake, IA
Vocals / Rock 'n' Roll
Legendary as one of the three rock greats to die in the tragic 1959 Clear Lake, IA, plane crash that also claimed the lives of Buddy Holly and Ritchie Valens, the Big Bopper (born Jiles Perry Richardson) had just established himself as a rock hitmaker with the rollicking "Chantilly Lace." Born in the heart of Texas, Richardson grew up in Beaumont and changed his first name to Jape. He broke into show biz as a DJ over KTRM radio, where he coined the nickname "The Big Bopper." He began recording for Mercury in 1957, his animated baritone scaling pop playlists the next year with "Chantilly Lace"—easily his top seller—and the equally raucous novelty "Big Bopper's Wedding." Richardson wrote "White Lightning," a huge country hit for George Jones, and Johnny Preston's No. 1 smash "Running Bear." —*Bill Dahl*

● **Hellooo Baby!: Best of the Big Bopper, 1954-1959** / 1989 / Rhino ♦♦♦♦
Hellooo Baby!: Best of the Big Bopper, 1954-1959 is a single-CD compilation of the Bopper's finest, including "Chantilly Lace," "Little Red Riding Hood," and "The Big Bopper's Wedding." It's wild and fun. —*Cub Koda*

Big Brother & the Holding Company

f. 1965, San Francisco, CA, **db.** 1972
Blues-Rock, Psychedelic
Big Brother is remembered primarily as the group that gave Janis Joplin her start. There's no denying that Joplin was by far the band's most striking asset, and that Big Brother would never have made a significant impression if they hadn't been fortunate enough to add her to their lineup shortly after forming. But Big Brother also occupies a significant place in the history of San Francisco psychedelic rock, as one of the bands that best captured the era's loosest, most reckless and indulgent qualities in its high-energy mutations of blues and folk-rock.

Big Brother was formed in 1965 in Haight-Ashbury; by the time Joplin joined in mid-1966, the lineup was Sam Andrews and James Gurley on guitar, Peter Albin on bass, and David Getz on drums. Joplin, a recent arrival from Texas, entered the band at the instigation of Chet Helms, who (other than Bill Graham) was the most important San Francisco rock promoter. Big Brother, like the Grateful Dead and Quicksilver Messenger Service, were not great songwriters or singers. They didn't entirely welcome Joplin's presence at first, and Joplin did not dominate the group right away, sharing lead vocals with other members.

It soon became evident to both band and audience that Joplin's fiery wail—mature and emotionally wrenching, even at that early stage—had to be spotlighted to make Big Brother a contender. But Big Brother wasn't superfluous to the effort, interpreting folk and blues with an inventive (if sometimes sloppy) eclecticism that often gave way to distorted guitar jamming, and matching Joplin's passion with a high-spirited, anything-goes ethos of their own.

Big Brother catapulted into national attention with their performance at the Monterey Pop Festival in June 1967, particularly with Joplin's galvanizing interpretation of "Ball and Chain" (which was a highlight of the film of the event). High-powered management and record label bids rolled in immediately, but unfortunately the group had tied themselves up in a bad contract with the small Mainstream label, at a time where they were stranded on the road and needed cash. Their one Mainstream album (released in 1967) actually isn't bad at all, containing some of their stronger cuts, such as "Down on Me" and "Coo Coo." It didn't fully capture the band's strengths, and with the help of new high-powered manager Albert Grossman (also handler of Bob Dylan, the Band, and Peter, Paul & Mary), they extricated themselves from the Mainstream deal and signed with Columbia.

The one Big Brother album for Columbia that featured Joplin, *Cheap Thrills* (1968), wasn't completed without problems of its own. John Simon found the band so difficult to work with that he withdrew his production credit from the final LP, which was assembled from both studio sessions and live material (recorded for an aborted concert album). *Cheap Thrills* nonetheless went to No. 1 when it was finally released, and though it, too, was an erratic affair, it contained some of the best moments of acid rock's glory days, including "Ball and Chain," "Summertime," "Combination of the Two," and "Piece of My Heart."

Cheap Thrills made Big Brother superstars, a designation that was short-lived. By the end of 1968, Joplin had decided to go solo, a move from which neither she nor Big Brother ever fully recovered. That's putting matters too simply: Joplin never found a backing band as sympathetic, but she did record some excellent material in the remaining two years of her life. Big Brother, on the other hand, had the wind totally knocked out of their sails. Although they did re-form for a while in the early '70s with different singers (indeed, they continue to perform in watered-down variations today), nothing would ever be the same. —*Richie Unterberger*

Big Brother & the Holding Company / 1967 / Columbia ♦♦♦
Big Brother's debut LP was a low-budget quickie, but it included a Joplin classic in Top 50 hit "Down On Me" and was a good example of San Francisco psychedelia. —*William Ruhlmann*

★ **Cheap Thrills** / Aug. 1968 / Columbia ♦♦♦♦♦
Cheap Thrills, the major-label debut of Janis Joplin, was one of the most eagerly anticipated, and one of the most successful, albums of 1968. Joplin and Big Brother had earned extensive press notice ever since they played the Monterey Pop Festival in June 1967, but their only recorded work was a poorly produced, self-titled Mainstream album, and they spent a year getting out of their contract with Mainstream in order to sign with Columbia while demand built. When *Cheap Thrills* appeared in August 1968, it shot into the charts, reaching No. 1 and going gold within a couple of months, while "Piece of My Heart" became a Top 40 hit. Joplin, with her ear—(and vocal

cord) shredding voice, was the obvious standout. Nobody had ever heard singing as emotional, as desperate, as determined, as loud as Joplin's, and *Cheap Thrills* was her greatest moment. Big Brother's backup, typical of the guitar-dominated sound of San Francisco psychedelia, made up in enthusiasm what it lacked in precision. But everybody knew who the real star was, and Joplin played her last gig with Big Brother while the album was still on top of the charts. Neither she nor the band would ever equal it. Heard today, *Cheap Thrills* is a musical time capsule and remains a showcase for one of rock's most distinctive singers. — *William Ruhlmann*

Be a Brother / Oct. 1970 / Columbia ♦♦
Big Brother comes back as a sextet with the additions of guitarist David Schallock and singer-songwriter/producer Nick Gravenites. Of course, it's a different band without Janis Joplin, but that psychedelic sound is still in place, albeit with a Chicago blues edge, courtesy of Gravenites. There's also an amusing reply to Merle Haggard's "Okie From Muskogee," "I'll Change Your Flat Tire, Merle." — *William Ruhlmann*

Cheaper Thrills / 1984 / Made To Last ♦♦
Recorded on July 28, 1966, before the band had cut any studio material, this performance was one of Janis Joplin's first gigs with Big Brother. The sound is decent, with several famous staples of their repertoire already in place—"Down On Me," "Coo-Coo," "Ball and Chain." Yet in comparison with their best studio and live recordings from 1967 and 1968, this is a bit limp. Big Brother was never noted for polish, but made up for that with reckless bravado; however, that's largely missing at this juncture in their development, which finds them sounding somewhat tentative in their adaptation of R&B and garage-band ethos to heavy guitar arrangements. Big Brother was never noted for songwriting ability, either, and this set is pretty reliant on R&B staples like "Let the Good Times Roll" and "I Know You Rider"; the unabashedly psychedelic workout "Gutra's Garden" hasn't aged well at all. Joplin's vocals are fairly strong, but these early versions of "Down On Me" and, especially, "Ball and Chain" don't hold a candle to her performances of the same tunes at the 1967 Monterey Pop Festival. Other members of the band take the lead vocal on a few numbers, emphatically proving—as they always did when given a chance—that Joplin was necessary to put them on the map. This recording is an interesting glimpse into the group's formative days, though, and features eight songs not on their late-'60s albums. — *Richie Unterberger*

Big Country

f. 1981, Dunfermline, Scotland
New Wave, Pop-Rock
Scottish group Big Country burst onto the 1982 rock scene with a uniquely expansive twin-guitar sound (made by Stuart Adamson [b. Apr. 11, 1958, Manchester, England], formerly of the Skids, and Bruce Watson [b. Mar. 11, 1961, Timmins, Ontario, Canada]) that at times recalled bagpipes. Bassist Tony Butler [b. Feb. 13, 1957, London, England] (whose credits included the Pretenders and Pete Townshend) and drummer Mark Brzezicki (b. June 21, 1957, Slough, Buckinghamshire, England), who also worked with Townshend), provided an aggressively supple rhythmic foundation.

The Chris Thomas-produced debut effort "Harvest Home" didn't chart, but *The Crossing*, cinematically produced by the innovative Steve Lillywhite, captured the band's sonic vision perfectly. It contains the band's first (and only significant stateside) hit, "In a Big Country."

Big Country followed *The Crossing* with an EP containing the fine "Wonderland," which basically echoed the spirit of "In a Big Country." In England, meanwhile, Big Country scored a brief string of hits, gaining enough popularity to sell out two nights at London's Wembley Stadium in December 1984. The album *Steeltown* entered British charts at No. 1. After a 20-month layoff, Big Country released *The Seer*. "Look Away" was a 1986 British hit, but received only moderate attention on US rock radio. The rather generic *Peace in Our Time*, released in 1988 on a new label (Reprise), was a misguided redirection of their sound, ditching most of the qualities that made the band so appealing.

Big Country and Reprise then parted ways, and 1991's *No Place Like Home* was released only in the UK. Big Country resurfaced on Fox/RCA in 1993 with *The Buffalo Skinners*, which failed to chart in the US. — *Rick Clark*

The Crossing / Aug. 1983 / Mercury ♦♦♦♦
One of the most unusual and exciting debut rock releases of the early '80s, the album contains expansive hits, including "In a Big Country" and "Fields of Fire." Producer Steve Lillywhite (U2, Simple Minds) aided in the band's larger-than-life sound and grand themes. Other highlights are "Chance" and "Harvest Home." (*The Crossing* went gold in the US in January 1984.) — *Rick Clark*

Wonderland [EP] / Apr. 1984 / Mercury ♦♦♦
Big Country followed up its debut album, *The Crossing*, with this four-song EP, which contained the characteristically anthemic title track, a US chart single and UK Top Ten hit. Also included were "All Fall Together" and two UK B-sides, "Angle Park" and "The Crossing." None of these tracks turned up on a Big Country album in the US until 1994, when *The Best of Big Country* featured "Wonderland." Although out of print, this record provides an effective sampler of the Big Country sound. — *William Ruhlmann*

Steeltown / Nov. 1984 / Mercury ♦♦♦
Big Country came out of one of the less dominant parts of the United Kingdom with an anthemic sound and vaguely revolutionary-sounding lyrics to captivate the British listening public and interest Americans. Big Country continued their winning ways at home with this, its second album, which topped the charts and produced three Top 40 hits—"East of Eden," "Where the Rose Is Sown," and "Just a Shadow." But in the US, the album was perceived as proving that the band's sound, guitars-as-bagpipes, courtesy of the E-bow, was a one-time novelty, while Stuart Adamson's lyrics, full of British socialist working-class fervor, seemed jingoistic and pretentious. Nevertheless, much of the music, as on the first album, made for stirring rock 'n' roll. — *William Ruhlmann*

The Seer / Jul. 1986 / Mercury ♦♦♦
Continuing their trademark sound to a fine effect, it contains the hits "Look Away," "The Teacher," "One Great Thing," and "Hold the Heart." — *Rick Clark*

Peace in Our Time / Sep. 1988 / Reprise ♦♦
For its fourth album, Big Country made two changes seemingly intended to bolster its fortunes in America—switching from Mercury Records to Reprise and enlisting hot producer Peter Wolf. The bagpipe guitar sound was de-emphasized, along with the political lyrics, and Wolf treated singer Stuart Adamson as he had Starship singer Mickey Thomas, adding echo and backup harmonies to beef him up. On songs like the lead-off single "King of Emotion" (Top 20 in Britain, non-charting in the US), Wolf sought to retain Big Country's heroic quality while adding the widescreen dramatic style and cheerleader choral approach of Starship's "We Built This City." It was a brave try, but it didn't really suit the group, making *Peace in Our Time* Big Country's least representative and least interesting album. (Nevertheless, the title track made the UK Top 40, and "Broken Heart [Thirteen Valleys]" also charted.) — *William Ruhlmann*

The Buffalo Skinners / Sep. 14, 1993 / Fox ♦♦♦
Scotland's Big Country was never able to surpass the expectations set by the 1983 debut *The Crossing* and its fistful of rousing rock anthems like "In a Big Country" and "Fields of Fire." *The Buffalo Skinners* succeeds because it doesn't waste energy trying to top the past. One can sense a conscious effort here to restrain those elements that had become Big Country formula—guitars that sound like bagpipes, vocals dripping with drama, and the shouted "Hah's" that would seem to punctuate every BC chorus— with the complete abandonment found on 1988's misguided *Peace in Our Time*. There's no fluff, bluff or bluster on *Buffalo Skinners*—just a solid serving of earthy rock with integrity. — *Roch Parisien*

● **The Best of Big Country** / Feb. 22, 1994 / Mercury ♦♦♦♦
All the British chart hits are here, including the fine, otherwise unavailable (except for the 12-inch vinyl EP) 1984 single "Wonderland" and the 1990 singles "Save Me" (from the British compilation *Through a Big Country*) and "Heart of the World," plus "Republican Party Reptile," the only track from Big Country's UK-only 1991 album *No Place Like Home* to be released in the US. It includes good liner notes and release info. — *Rick Clark*

Why the Long Face / Jun. 5, 1995 / Tansatlantic ♦♦
Big Country's seventh studio album was released on an indie, reflecting the group's relative decline into obscurity and making the title ironic. Notwithstanding their low profile, the band actually put on a brave face here, turning in a set full of impassioned guitar-dominated rock that sometimes bordered on heavy metal. But no matter how loud the guitars got, they still took a back seat to Stuart Adamson's impassioned vocals, his lyrics conflating the anguish of romance with the anguish of social conditions. The band's career may have been embattled, but Adamson's conflicts were of a smaller, and a larger, nature. The CD version contained two bonus tracks, a cover of Lou Reed's "Vicious" and an "unplugged" version of the band's early hit, "In a Big Country." — *William Ruhlmann*

Big Head Todd & the Monsters

f. Colorado
Rock 'n' Roll, Blues-Rock, Folk-Rock
During the late '80s and early '90s, Big Head Todd & the Monsters (the Colorado-based trio of guitarist/keyboard player Todd Park Mohr, bass-

ist Rob Squires, and drummer Brian Nevin) built their audience through constant touring, playing college towns across the country. With these tours, they built a solid fan base before they had even signed to a major label. Although they have released several records, they haven't been able to completely transfer the live appeal of their laidback, slightly jazzy, blues-based pop to tape. Nevertheless, each of their records contains many fine moments, and 1993's *Sister Sweetly*, which went gold and stayed in the charts over a year, showed that they were continuing to improve their songwriting as well as their playing. It was followed by their second major label album, *Strategem*, in 1994; *Beautiful World* appeared in 1997. —*Stephen Thomas Erlewine*

Another Mayberry / 1989 / Big ✦✦✦
That big head of Todd Park Mohr's is full of country and folk guitar licks (played on electric guitar a la '60s folk-rock) that give his music a relentlessly familiar feel, even if he got his riffs secondhand off R.E.M. albums. Similarly, his husky voice and slightly slurred enunciation evoke generations of rock singers. So, his band's debut album, while pleasantly recognizable on first listen, also has trouble distinguishing itself. After a while, though, the subtlety of his lyrics becomes more apparent, and while the result isn't as impressive as, say, the Smiths, Mohr proves to have an individual world view beyond the chiming guitar chords. (Originally released in 1989 on the group's own Big Records label, *Another Mayberry* was reissued by Giant Records in 1994.) —*William Ruhlmann*

Midnight Radio / 1991 / Big ✦✦✦

● **Sister Sweetly** / Feb. 1993 / Giant ✦✦✦✦
There was a reason that *Sister Sweetly* expanded Big Head Todd's cult—it's their most consistent and satisfying album yet, full of acoustic charm, relaxed funk, and breezy blues. —*Stephen Thomas Erlewine*

Strategem / Sep. 27, 1994 / Giant ✦✦
The sleeper success of *Sister Sweetly*, which went gold without ever breaking the Top 100, held promise for this, Big Head Todd's second major label release. So far, the group had sold to its fan base and to a sympathetic wider audience that responded to its neo-'70s sound. Singer-songwriter/guitarist Todd Park Mohr is a near soundalike for the late Quicksilver Messenger Service leader Dino Valenti, and his band follows the cadences and blues-folk guitar lines of the San Francisco psychedelic bands and the Southern rock bands, especially Lynyrd Skynyrd. What *Strategem* needed was songwriting that could distinguish the group, consolidate its following, and advance its career. Instead, the album seems a step back, its songs ponderous, its performances too clipped and restrained. As a result, the album was on and off the charts in two months, and the band suddenly had to make up lost ground. —*William Ruhlmann*

Beautiful World / Feb. 11, 1997 / Warner Brothers ✦✦✦
Strategem was an unexpected failure, delivered exactly at the moment when Big Head & the Monsters could have broken into the mainstream. With its followup, *Beautiful World*, the group regains their musical strengths, but at the expense of the pop songs that could bring them to a wider audience. The Monsters jam with an expert grace throughout the record, particularly with guests John Lee Hooker and Bernie Worrell, and producer Jerry Harrison helps keep things focused. However, the group neglected to write hooks, which means *Beautiful World* is an album for the converted, not one to bring them a new audience. —*Stephen Thomas Erlewine*

Big Star

f. 1971, Memphis, TN, **db.** 1975
Power Pop, Pop-Rock
Next to the Velvet Underground, Memphis' Big Star is the grandaddy of all cult groups. The crisp, succinct pop found on their first two albums was ignored upon release in the early '70s, but by the '80s, Big Star's sound was everywhere. Everyone from the dB's, R.E.M. and the Replacements to Tommy Keene, Matthew Sweet, Teenage Fanclub, and Primal Scream has integrated Big Star's formula into their own styles, and this has turned Big Star cofounder Alex Chilton (b. Dec. 28, 1950, Memphis, Tennessee) into a cult icon. The group was formed by Chris Bell (b. Jan. 12, 1951, Memphis, TN, d. Dec. 27, 1978, Memphis, TN) in 1971 and, in addition to singer/guitarists Chilton and Bell, featured bassist Andy Hummell (b. Jan. 26, 1951, Memphis, TN) and drummer Jody Stephens (b. Oct. 4, 1952). Although Bell was living in the home of the blues and soul, it was the Anglo-pop stylings of the Beatles and the Kinks that rang his bell. Alex Chilton, former vocalist for the Box Tops, shared Bell's affection for Brit-pop and joined the group, rechristened Big Star after a local supermarket chain.

With producer Terry Manning, the group recorded *No.1 Record* in 1972, released on the studio's in-house Ardent label at a time when rock had become tediously pompous and self-indulgent. It was well received

in the press, and it seemed like a radio natural, but poor distribution squelched whatever hit potential it had.

Chris Bell, disappointed with the poor reception of his band's debut, struck out on his own in 1972. Bell, who shared vocal and writing credits on the first album, died in a car wreck before he was able to release his solo work. His sound was equally idiosyncratic, remaining distinctly flavored by the British sound. Most of his work has since been released on a Rykodisc collection called *I Am the Cosmos*.

Chilton was left to mastermind the blistering *Radio City*. The lush charm of *No.1 Record* was replaced by Chilton's slashing, skewered guitar runs and his mangy, stray-cat vocals. The album was loaded with would-be classics ("September Gurls," "Back of a Car," "You Get What You Deserve") but again, the album was poorly distributed and fell between the cracks.

Disenchanted with the politics of the music business, and suffering from drug and alcohol abuse, Chilton hooked up with Memphis producer Jim Dickinson and vented his spleen on *Third/Sister Lovers*, recorded in 1974 but shelved until 1978. More a Chilton solo project than a group effort, the album was an erratic but sometimes brilliant emotional outcry that balanced the beautiful ("Stroke It Noel," "Blue Light") with the horrific ("Holocaust," "Kangaroo").

With the demise of Big Star, lead singer Alex Chilton pursued a renegade solo career that has taken him full circle from untamed reckless garage rock to his earthy mid-Southern musical R&B roots.

The effervescent, near-perfect guitar pop found on *No.1 Record* and *Radio City* have maintained their vitality, making them legitimate rock classics that deserve more than their cult status. It is fair to say that, in spite of almost nonexistent commercial success, Big Star has been an important influence on many of the post-punk/power-pop bands since the late '70s. Among bands who owe a debt to Big Star are R.E.M., the Replacements, the Posies, Game Theory, the Bangles, Teenage Fanclub, and Primal Scream. —*Rick Clark*

 # 1 Record / 1972 / Ardent ✦✦✦✦
The problem with coming in late on an artwork lauded as "influential" is that you've probably encountered the work it influenced first, so its truly innovative qualities are lost. Thus, if you are hearing Big Star's debut album for the first time decades after its release (as, inevitably, most people must), you may be reminded of Tom Petty and the Heartbreakers or R.E.M., who came after—that is, if you don't think of the Byrds and the Beatles, circa 1965. What was remarkable about *No. 1 Record* in 1972 was that nobody except Big Star (and maybe Badfinger and the Raspberries) wanted to sound like this—simple, light pop with sweet harmonies and jangly guitars. Since then, dozens of bands have rediscovered those pleasures. But in a way, that's an advantage because, whatever freshness is lost across the years, Big Star's craft is only confirmed. These are sturdy songs, feelingly performed, and once you get beyond the style to the content, you'll still be impressed. —*William Ruhlmann*

Radio City / 1974 / Ardent ✦✦✦✦
Largely lacking co-leader Chris Bell, Big Star's second album also lacked something of the pop sweetness (especially the harmonies) of *No. 1 Record*. What it possessed was Alex Chilton's urgency (sometimes desperation) on songs that made his case as a genuine rock &roll eccentric. If *No.1 Record* had a certain pop perfection that brought everything together, *Radio City* was the sound of everything falling apart, which proved at least as compelling. —*William Ruhlmann*

☆ **Third/Sister Lovers** / 1978 / Rykodisc ✦✦✦✦✦
Basically an Alex Chilton solo project, it is aided by remaining bandmate Jody Stephens (drums) and a slew of Memphis players. Chilton, frustrated at the music biz and career let-downs, enlisted producer Jim Dickinson to aid in this creative tightrope-walk without a net. The result is a listening experience that's as uncompromisingly harrowing as Neil Young's *Tonight's the Night*. Not for the casual listener, it's still essential in any serious rock listener's collection. Never really finished, the album has been released several times under different titles and with different tracks since it first appeared under the name *Third* on PVC Records (7903) in 1978. The version currently in print, Rykodisc RCD-10220, was released February 21, 1992; it resequences the material and features more of it than any earlier version, including two previously unreleased tracks. —*Rick Clark and William Ruhlmann*

Big Star Live / Feb. 21, 1992 / Rykodisc ✦✦✦
A weak performance from a live radio special, it may be of interest to hardcore fans but it certainly is no place to start discovering Big Star. —*Rick Clark*

★ **# 1 Record/Radio City** / Jun. 10, 1992 / Stax ✦✦✦✦✦
Their first two albums (1972, 1974) were loaded with amazing songs and performances. Mid-period Beatles, Kinks, and Byrds turned inside out and regurgitated into a unique sound. A must-own for any lover of Anglo-pop-rock. —*Rick Clark*

Columbia: Live at Missouri University / Sep. 14, 1993 / Zoo ✦✦
This "reunion" of sorts features original Big Star members Alex Chilton and Jody Stephens augmented by Ken Stringfellow and Jonathan Auer, the two frontmen for the Posies. The performances are ragged but, for the most part, right. Once Chilton gets down to business, he delivers strong performances on "September Gurls" and Todd Rundgren's "Slut." Auer and Stringfellow particularly shine on Chris Bell's "I Am the Cosmos" and "Back of a Car." —*Rick Clark*

Bikini Kill

f. Oct. 1990, Olympia, WA
Alternative Pop-Rock, Indie Rock, Riot Grrrl
The point band of the early-'90s Riot Grrrl movement, Olympia, WA,'s Bikini Kill exploded onto the male-dominated indie rock scene by fusing the visceral power of punk with the impassioned ideals of feminism. Calling for "Revolution Girl Style Now," the group's fiercely polemical and anthemic music helped give rise to a newly empowered generation of women in rock, presaging the dominance female artists would enjoy throughout the decade. Bikini Kill formed in the late '80s at Olympia's liberal Evergreen College, where students Kathleen Hanna, Tobi Vail, and Kathi Wilcox first teamed to publish a feminist fanzine, also dubbed *Bikini Kill*. Seeking to bring the publication's agenda to life, they decided to form a band, enlisting guitarist Billy Boredom (born William Karren) to round out the lineup. Led by singer-songwriter Hanna, a former stripper, the group laced their incendiary live performances with aggressive political stances that challenged the accepted hierarchy of the underground music community; slam dancers were forced to mosh at the fringes of the stage so that women could remain at the front of the crowd, for example, and female audience members were often invited to take control of the microphone to openly discuss issues of sexual abuse and misconduct.

In 1991 Bikini Kill issued its first recording, *Revolution Girl Style Now,* an independently distributed demo cassette. For their first official release, the quartet signed with the aggressively independent Olympia-based label Kill Rock Stars; the *Bikini Kill* EP, produced by Fugazi's Ian Mackaye, consisted largely of reworked versions of material from the first cassette. In 1992 the band issued *Yeah, Yeah, Yeah,* a split 12-inch released with the British group Huggy Bear's *Our Troubled Youth* on its flipside; a subsequent UK tour with Huggy Bear in early 1993 raised the visibility of the Riot Grrrl groundswell to unprecedented heights, and the movement became the focus of many media outlets on both sides of the Atlantic. When Bikini Kill returned to the US, they joined forces with Joan Jett, whom the band held up as an early paragon of Riot Grrrl aesthetics. Jett produced the group's next single, the bracing "New Radio"/ "Rebel Girl," and Hanna returned the favor by co-writing the song "Spinster" for the Jett album *Pure and Simple*. In 1994 Bikini Kill released *Pussy Whipped;* their most potent effort to date, it featured the songwriting emergence of both Vail and Wilcox, a trend continued on 1996's *Reject All American*. —*Jason Ankeny*

Bikini Kill / 1992 / Kill Rock Stars ✦✦✦
The group's scabrous debut LP. Hanna's lyrics and singing are equally caustic, creating explosive songs like "Feels Blind" and the amusingly titled "Suck My Left One." This group has anger and intelligence on its side. —*Heather Phares*

● **Pussywhipped** / 1994 / Kill Rock Stars ✦✦✦✦
A more experimental follow-up from these punk rock furies. While there's still lots of vitriol, the songs are more varied and even catchy. "Rebel Girl" is a manifesto just waiting to be discovered, and the rest of the album sees the band occasionally adding fun to their recipe for punk chaos. A good starting point. —*Heather Phares*

Reject All American / Apr. 5, 1996 / Kill Rock Stars ✦✦✦
Bikini Kill delivered the second album just a little too late. By the time *Reject All American* hit the stores in 1996, the media's fascination with riot grrrl had passed, leaving the band the province of a small cult. Of course, they prefer it that way, but the insularity of their audience and their message is reflected in the music. *Reject All American* has the requisite raw production, blistering three-chord riffs, and Kathleen Hanna's gut-churning screams, but the result isn't necessarily entirely effective. The problem is the band is preaching to a converted audience—and their music doesn't have enough hooks to effectively sell their message. There are some good songs on the album, and on the whole it's a tighter album than their debut, but it doesn't capture the moment the way *Pussywhipped* did, and Bikini Kill is all about immediacy. Therefore, *Reject All American* is sort of irrelevant. —*Stephen Thomas Erlewine*

The Birthday Party

f. 1977, Melbourne, England, db. 1983
Post-Punk
The Birthday Party was one of the darkest and most challenging post-punk groups to emerge in the early '80s, creating bleak and noisy soundscapes that provided the perfect setting for vocalist Nick Cave's difficult, disturbing stories of religion, violence, and perversity. Under the direction of Cave and guitarist Rowland S. Howard, the band tore through reams of blues and rockabilly licks, spitting out hellacious feedback and noise at an unrelenting pace. As the band's career progressed, Cave's vision got darker, and their songs alternated between dirges and blistering sonic assaults.

Originally, the Australian band was called the Boys Next Door, comprising Cave, Howard, Mick Harvey (guitar, drums, organ, piano), bassist Tracy Pew, and drummer Phil Calvert. After the album *Door Door* and the EP *Hee Haw* under that name, the band moved to London and switched their name to the deceptively benign Birthday Party. Once they arrived in Britain, the group's demented, knotty post-punk began to gel. They released their first international album, *Prayers on Fire*, in 1981, earning critical praise in the UK and US. While the band was preparing to record the followup, Pew was jailed for drunk driving; former Magazine member Barry Adamson, Harry Howard, and Chris Walsh filled in for the absent Pew on 1982's *Junkyard*.

After the release of *Junkyard,* the band fired Calvert and moved to Germany, where they began collaborating with such experimental post-punk acts as Lydia Lunch and Einsturzende Neubaten. Harvey left the Birthday Party in the summer of 1983. The group briefly continued with drummer Des Heffner, but they soon disbanded after a final concert in Melbourne, Australia. Cave had the most successful solo career, recording a series of albums in the '80s and '90s that maintained his status as a popular cult figure; Harvey joined Cave's backing band, the Bad Seeds. Howard joined Crime and the City Solution, which also featured his brother Harry. —*Stephen Thomas Erlewine*

Prayers on Fire / 1981 / 4AD ✦✦✦✦
Howling, hellacious mangled art-noise. Surefire. —*John Dougan*

Drunk on the Pope's Blood / 1981 / 4AD ✦✦✦
An extremely harrowing live EP, with Lydia Lunch. —*John Dougan*

Junkyard / 1982 / 4AD ✦✦✦
Slightly less confrontational but no less disturbing. —*John Dougan*

A Collection / 1985 / Missing Link ✦✦✦✦
A Collection draws from the Birthday Party's *Junkyard* and *Prayers on Fire* albums, adding a few tracks from the *Hee Haw* EP and some alternate takes. The compilation has also been issued under the title *The Best and the Rarest* and provides an effective introduction to the band. —*Stephen Thomas Erlewine*

● **Hits** / Oct. 13, 1992 / 4AD ✦✦✦✦
As an album title, *Hits* is an intentionally ironic misnomer for one of Australia's most influential rock bands of the late '70s and early '80s. Having "hits" was the furthest thing from the Birthday Party's collective mind over the course of five tumultuous years that followed the group's move to England from Down Under; the members reviled anything that hinted at mainstream acceptance. Ten years on, the intensity of this music is still frightening. It's a dense, mutant hybrid that evolved from punk, progressive rock, funk, and improvisational jazz, without directly owning up to any of these base materials. Vocalist Nick Cave (who has gone on to an equally creative solo career) didn't just sing about society's dark, depraved underbelly, he lived the experience right there on disc and on stage. —*Roch Parisien*

Elvin Bishop

b. Oct. 21, 1942, Tulsa, OK
Guitar, Vocals / Blues-Rock, Southern Rock, Modern Electric Chicago Blues, Contemporary Electric Blues
Elvin Bishop grew up on a farm in Iowa with no electricity and no running water. His family moved to Oklahoma when he was ten. Raised in an all-white community, he had no exposure to Blacks or their music except though the radio, where he would listen to sounds from Mexico and blues stations in Shreveport, LA; in particular, the piercing sound of Jimmy Reed's harmonica got his attention. Bishop says it was like a crossword puzzle that he had to figure out. What is this music? Who makes it? Where and how do Black people live? What is this music all about? He put the pieces together.

But it was not until he won a National Merit Scholarship to the University of Chicago in 1959 that he found the real answers to his questions. Suddenly, there he was right in the heart of the Chicago blues scene. Live. It was a dream come true. "The first thing I did when I got there was to make friends with the Black guys working in the cafeteria. They took me to all the clubs. I sank myself totally in the blues life as quick as I could," says Bishop.

After two years of college, he dropped out and was into music full time. Howlin' Wolf guitarist Smokey Smothers befriended Bishop and taught him the basics of blues guitar. In the early '60s he met and teamed up with Paul Butterfield to become the core of the Butterfield Blues Band. He practiced day and night on the blues music that he loved. He and Butterfield played together in just about every place possible—campuses, houses, parks, and clubs. They began to become well known in 1963 when they took a job at Big John's on Chicago's North Side, and the Paul Butterfield Blues Band was born. Bishop helped to create and played on the first several Butterfield albums. (The Pigboy Crabshaw is Bishop's countrified persona referred to in the title of the third Butterfield album.)

When he left the Butterfield band after the *In My Own Dream* album (1968), Bishop settled in the San Francisco area, where he appeared often at the Filmore with artists like Eric Clapton, B. B. King, and Jimi Hendrix. He recorded for Epic (four albums) and later signed with Capricorn in 1974. His recording of "Traveling Shoes" (from the album *Let It Flow*) hit the charts, but he scored big with the lovely tune "Fooled Around and Fell in Love" (from his album *Struttin' My Stuff*) in 1976. He was (and is) famous for having fun on stage (putting on a great show) and letting the good times roll. Over the next few years the Elvin Bishop Group dissolved. He released his album *Best Of* in 1979 and was not heard from much until he signed with Alligator in 1988.

Bishop then released *Big Fun* (1988) and *Don't Let the Bossman Get You Down* (1991), which were well received. He also participated in Alligator's 1992 20th anniversary cross-country tour. His latest release is *Ace in the Hole* (1995). Over the years, Bishop has graced the albums of many great bluesmen, including Clifton Chenier and John Lee Hooker. He toured with B.B. King in 1995. Bishop is known for his sense of humor, his unique style of slide guitar, and fusion of blues, gospel, R&B, and country flavors. He lives with his wife and family in the San Francisco area, is a prodigious gardener, and continues to play dates in the US and abroad. — *Michael Erlewine*

Let It Flow / May 1974 / Capricorn ♦♦♦♦
For his fourth album, Elvin Bishop organized a new backup group and switched to Capricorn Records. Capricorn was known as the standard bearer of the Southern rock movement—the Allman Brothers Band, the Marshall Tucker Band, etc.—and Bishop was able to emphasize the country/blues aspects of his persona and his music in the move from Marin County, CA, to Macon, GA. The guest artists included the Allmans' Dickey Betts, Marshall Tucker's Toy Caldwell, Charlie Daniels, and Sly Stone, and Bishop turned in one of his best sets of songs, including "Travelin' Shoes" (with its Allmans-like twin lead guitar work), which became his first charting single, just as the album was his first to make the Top 100 LPs. — *William Ruhlmann*

Juke Joint Jump / Apr. 1975 / Capricorn ♦♦♦
Elvin Bishop's Macon takeover continued on his second Capricorn album, which had a slightly less country feel than *Let It Flow* but continued to be dominated by twin guitar playing (courtesy of Bishop and Johnny "V" Vernazza) and honky tonk piano playing (from Phil Aaberg). The song quality wasn't quite as consistent this time, but "Sure Feels Good" became Bishop's second singles chart entry. — *William Ruhlmann*

The Best of Elvin Bishop: Crabshaw Rising / Sep. 1975 / Epic ♦♦♦
In his first manifestation as a band leader (1969-1972), Elvin Bishop lived in Marin County, CA, and performed under the auspices of promoter Bill Graham. Not surprisingly, the three albums he cut in that period, two for Graham's Fillmore label and the third for its parent, Epic, fit into the soul-blues-rock style of post-psychedelic San Francisco, even to the point of featuring an extended instrumental, "Hogbottom," on which Bishop takes Carlos Santana's place fronting the Santana percussion section. This ten-track compilation selects from the albums *The Elvin Bishop Group*, *Feel It!*, and *Rock My Soul*, effectively summarizing this phase in Bishop's career. Long out of print, it was superseded in 1994 by the 18-track CD *The Best of Elvin Bishop: Tulsa Shuffle*, which contained nine of its selections. Then, oddly enough, it was reissued in 1996! — *William Ruhlmann*

Struttin' My Stuff / Dec. 1975 / Capricorn ♦♦♦
Features the hit single "Fooled Around and Fell in Love," sung by Mickey Thomas. — *William Ruhlmann*

Hometown Boy Makes Good! / Oct. 1976 / Capricorn ♦♦
Elvin Bishop broke the bank with the success of "Fooled Around and Fell in Love" in the spring of 1976, so when he returned with this album in the fall, he turned up on the cover holding bags of money. The question, of course, was whether the hit would turn out to be a breakthrough or a fluke. The nearest thing to a followup to "Fooled Around" was "Spend Some Time," a ballad on which Mickey Thomas again sang soulfully. But it barely scraped into the charts, and the rest was typical Bishop good-time boogie (along with trendy tastes of disco and reggae), the relatively thin songwriting reflecting a rushed recording schedule. This was Bishop's fourth new album in just over two-and-a-half years. — *William Ruhlmann*

Hog Heaven / 1978 / Capricorn ♦♦♦
Capricorn Records, having switched distribution from Warner Brothers to Phondisc, was on its way out by the time it released this, its sixth Elvin Bishop album, which may help explain why, only two years after he was in the Top Ten with "Fooled Around and Fell in Love," he didn't

even reach the charts with this album. It's also true that lead singer Mickey Thomas had decamped to join Jefferson Starship, leaving Bishop to reestablish his country blues boy persona. But Maria Muldaur had signed on (she sings lead on "True Love"), and with two years between studio albums, Bishop had found the time to write some good vehicles for his guitar work and Southern rock backup band. — *William Ruhlmann*

Big Fun / 1988 / Alligator ♦♦♦
In the ten years between the release of *Hog Heaven* and this comeback record, Elvin Bishop was represented in record stores by a *Best Of* on Capricorn and an album released only in Germany (*Is You Is or Is You Ain't My Baby?* on Line Records). Then he signed with Bruce Iglauer's independent blues label Alligator and made this record, which, naturally, emphasizes his more blues-oriented guitar playing, although without sacrificing his country boy identity. Dr. John tickles some of the ivories, and harmonica player Norton Buffalo (of Commander Cody and His Lost Planet Airmen) also guests. — *William Ruhlmann*

Don't Let the Bossman Get You Down! / Jul. 1, 1991 / Alligator ♦♦♦♦
On *Don't Let the Bossman Get You Down*, Bishop projects a good-natured, humorous persona in the extended spoken-word sections of his songs, but still finds time to play a lot of tasty blues guitar. — *William Ruhlmann*

● **Sure Feels Good: The Best of Elvin Bishop** / Jun. 9, 1992 / PolyGram ♦♦♦♦
A fine collection of the blues-rock guitarist's best moments, which covers more material than the earlier compilation, *Best of Elvin Bishop/Crabshaw Rising*. — *Stephen Thomas Erlewine*

The Best of Elvin Bishop: Tulsa Shuffle / May 10, 1994 / Epic/Legacy ♦♦♦♦
This 18-track compilation selects from the albums *The Elvin Bishop Group*, *Feel It!*, and *Rock My Soul*, effectively summarizing this phase in Bishop's career. The only thing wrong with it is that it would be easy to make the mistake of thinking that it covers all of his solo career rather than only the first four years, especially because there have now been four different albums released with the title *The Best of Elvin Bishop*. — *William Ruhlmann*

Ace in the Hole / Jul. 25, 1995 / Alligator ♦♦♦
On Elvin Bishop's third Alligator release, *Ace in the Hole*, his guitar playing remains as fiery as ever, but the overall quality of the songwriting has slipped somewhat, making it his least consistent effort on the label. — *Thom Owens*

Bjork

b. Oct. 21, 1965, Reykjavik, Iceland
Keyboards, Vocals / Alternative Pop-Rock, Club/Dance
Bjork first came to prominence as one of the lead vocalists of the avant-pop Icelandic sextet the Sugarcubes, but when she launched a solo career after the group's 1992 demise, she quickly eclipsed her old band's popularity. Instead of following in the Sugarcubes' arty guitar-rock pretentions, Bjork immersed herself in dance and club culture, working with many of the biggest names in the genre, including Nellee Hooper, Underworld, and Tricky. *Debut*, her first solo effort, not only established her new artistic direction, but became an international hit, making her one of the '90s' most unlikely stars.

Though the title of *Debut* implied that it was Bjork's first-ever solo project, she had actually been a professional vocalist since she was a child. When she was in elementary school in Reykjavik, she studied classical piano, and her teachers submitted a tape of her singing Tina Charles' "I Love to Love" to Iceland's Radio One. After "I Love to Love" was aired, a record label called Falkkin offered Bjork a record contract. At the age of 11, her eponymous first album was released; the record contained covers of several pop songs, including the Beatles' "Fool on the Hill," and boasted artwork from her mother and guitar work from her stepfather. *Bjork* became a hit within Iceland but was not released in any other country.

Bjork's musical tastes were changed by the punk revolution of the late '70s. In 1979 she formed a post-punk group called Exodus, and the next year she sang in Jam 80. In 1981 Bjork and Exodus bassist Jakob Magnusson formed Tappi Tikarrass, which released an EP, *Bitid Fast I Vitid*, on Spor later that year; it was followed by the full-length *Miranda* in 1983. After Tappi Takarrass, she formed the goth-tinged post-punk group KUKL with Einar Orn Benediktsson. KUKL released two albums, *The Eye* (1984) and *Holidays in Europe* (1986), on Crass Records before the band metamorphisized into the Sugarcubes in the summer of 1986.

The Sugarcubes became one of the rare Icelandic bands to break out of their native country when their debut album, *Life's Too Good*, became a British and American hit in 1988. For the next four years the group maintained a cult following in the UK and the US, while they were stars within Iceland. During 1990 Bjork recorded a set of jazz standards and originals with an Icelandic be-bop group called Trio Gud-mundar Ingolfssonar. The album, *Gling-Glo*, was released only in Ice-land. By 1992, tensions between Bjork and Einar had grown substantially, which resulted in the band's splitting.

Bjork moved to London, where she began pursuing a dance-oriented solo career. The previous year, she had sung on 808 State's "Ooops," which sparked her interest in club and house music. Bjork struck up a working relationship with Nellee Hooper, a producer who had formerly worked with Soul II Soul and Massive Attack. The first result of their partnership was "Human Behaviour," which was released in June 1993. "Human Behaviour" became a Top 40 hit in the UK, setting the stage for the surprising No. 3 debut of the full-length album *Debut*. Throughout 1993, Bjork had hit UK singles—including "Venus as a Boy," "Big Time Sensuality," and the non-LP "Play Dead," a collaboration with David Arnold taken from the film *Young Americans*—as well as modern rock radio hits in the US; in both countries, she earned rave reviews. *NME* named *Debut* the album of the year, and Bjork won International Female Solo Artist and Newcomer at the BRIT Awards. *Debut* went gold in the US and platinum in the UK.

During 1994 Bjork was relatively quiet, as she recorded her second album with Nellee Hooper, Tricky, 808 State's Graham Massey, and Howie B. of Mo' Wax Records; she also released a remix EP, co-wrote the title track for Madonna's *Bedtime Stories*, and performed on *MTV Unplugged* that same year. "Army of Me," the first single from Bjork's forthcoming album, was released as a teaser single in the spring of 1995; it debuted at No. 10 in the UK and became a moderate alternative rock hit in the US. *Post*, her second album, was released in June 1995 to positive reviews; it peaked at No. 2 in the UK and No. 32 in the US. *Post* matched its predecessor in terms of sales and praise, going gold in the US and helping her earn her second BRIT Award for Best International Female Artist. *Post* yielded the British hit singles "Isobel" (No. 23), "It's Oh So Quiet" (No. 4), and "Hyperballad" (No. 8), but her singles failed to make much headway on American radio or MTV. Late in 1996 Bjork released *Telegram*, an album comprised of radical remixes of the entire *Post* album; *Telegram* was released in America in January 1997. *—Stephen Thomas Erlewine*

● **Debut** / Jul. 1993 / Elektra ◆◆◆◆
Bjork's first album since the breakup of the Sugarcubes outshines any of her old group's albums. Covering everything from dance-pop and club music to jazzy torch songs, *Debut* reveals Bjork as a fine song-writer, capable of writing wrenching ("Like Someone in Love") and intoxicating pop songs ("There's More to Life Than This"). Throughout the record, Bjork's thin voice shows a surprising amount of versatility. *Debut* is one of the strongest, most musically varied and consistent dance records of the '90s. *—Stephen Thomas Erlewine*

Post / Jun. 13, 1995 / Elektra ◆◆◆◆
Debut was a worldwide success, raising the expectations for Bjork's sec-ond album, *Post*. Bjork doesn't depart from the innovations of *Debut*, she refines them, pushing the jazz/dance fusions into different territo-ries, like the big-band explosions of "It's Oh So Quiet" and the trancey "Possibly Maybe." While it's more subtle and not quite as infectious as *Debut*, the album is more accomplished and varied, switching from the menacing "Army of Me" to the graceful "Isobel" without seeming inco-herent. *—Stephen Thomas Erlewine*

Telegram / Jan. 14, 1997 / Elektra ◆◆◆◆
In theory, *Telegram* is a remixed album of all the songs from *Post*, but the arrangements are so different, it might as well be another record entirely. Bjork has re-recorded several of her vocals, handing the origi-nal backing tracks to a variety of producers and musicians—everyone from Photek to the Brodsky Quartet. While *Telegram* provides some of the most challenging listening yet heard on Bjork album, it is essentially because the new arrangements are radical; in terms of electronic dance music, the actual music and remixes are far from radical. Still, *Telegram* works as an excellent introduction to techno for alternative-pop fans unsure of where to begin exploring. *—Stephen Thomas Erlewine*

The Black Crowes

f. 1984, Atlanta, GA
Rock 'n' Roll, Hard Rock, Blues-Rock
At the time of their 1990 debut, the kind of rock 'n' roll the Black Crowes specialize in was out of style. Only Guns N' Roses came close to approx-imating a vintage Stones-style raunch, but they were too angry and jagged to pull it off completely. The Black Crowes replicated that Stonesy swagger and Faces boogie perfectly. Vocalist Chris Robinson appropriated the sound and style of vintage Rod Stewart, while guitarist Rich Robinson fused Keith Richards' lean attack with Ron Wood's messy rhythmic sense. At their best, the Black Crowes echo classic rock with-out slavishly imitating their influences.

The Robinson brothers originally formed the Black Crowes in Geor-gia in 1984. By the time of their 1990 debut, *Shake Your Money Maker*, the group comprised Chris Robinson (vocals), Rich Robinson (guitar),

Johnny Colt (bass), Jeff Cease (guitar), and Steve Gorman (drums). "Jeal-ous Again," the first single from *Shake Your Money Maker*, was a mod-erate hit, but it was the band's cover of Otis Redding's "Hard to Handle" that made the group a multi-platinum success. "Hard to Handle" climbed its way into the Top 40, propelling the album into the Top Ten. The acoustic ballad "She Talks to Angels" became the band's second Top 40 hit in the spring of 1991. *Shake Your Money Maker* would eventually sell over three million copies.

The Black Crowes delivered their second album, *The Southern Har-mony and Musical Companion*, in the spring of 1992. It entered the charts at No. 1, but it didn't have as many hit singles as the debut; none of the singles cracked the Top 40, and only "Remedy" and "Thorn in My Pride" made the Top 100. Nevertheless, the band established themselves as a popular concert attraction that summer, selling out theaters across America. During 1992 the band added keyboardist Eddie Hersch as a permanent member. The Black Crowes' third album, *Amorica*, arrived in late 1994. *Amorica* debuted in the Top Ten, but none of the singles from the album made the charts; even though the record went gold, it slipped off the charts in early 1995.

Three Snakes & One Charm, the group's fourth album, was released in July 1996. The album entered the charts at No. 15, but it quickly slipped out of the Top 50. Nevertheless, the album received the best reviews of any Crowes album since *The Southern Harmony and Musi-cal Companion*. *—Stephen Thomas Erlewine*

Shake Your Money Maker / Jan. 1990 / Def American ◆◆◆◆
The best ideas on the Crowes' debut are all about 20 years old, but when those ideas are replicas of vintage Stones and Faces, timeliness is not an issue. The mix of throttling rockers and acoustic ballads doesn't flow with the grace of *Beggar's Banquet*, but the best songs here—"Twice as Hard," "She Talks to Angels," "Could I've Been So Blind"—act as anchors for a strikingly confident debut. *—John Floyd*

● **The Southern Harmony and Musical Companion** / May 12, 1992 / Def American ◆◆◆◆
On *The Southern Harmony & Musical Companion* the Crowes avoid the sophomore slump by taking the best elements of their debut and fleshing them out (and giving the rhythm section and keyboards more room to breathe). The Stones/Faces/Humble Pie comparisons are still relevant, but the band's own identity flourishes on such songs as "Rem-edy," "Black Moon Creeping," and "Sting Me." *—John Floyd*

Amorica / Nov. 1, 1994 / American ◆◆◆◆
On *Amorica*, the Black Crowes finally come into their own, taking their cue from the most relaxed, groove-oriented tracks on their previous album. While the album contains no immediately obvious singles, the songs are the best the band has ever written, stretching out into a hard, jam-oriented, funky blues-rock. The Black Crowes' influences are still discernable—no band celebrates the glory days of rock culture quite as enthusiastically—but they use the music of the Stones, the Faces, and Little Feat much the same way the Stones used the music of Chuck Berry: it's a starting point that leads the band into a new direction, incor-porating different musical genres and making the music original. That sense of reinterpretation is what keeps *Amorica* fresh. *—Stephen Tho-mas Erlewine*

Three Snakes & One Charm / Jul. 23, 1996 / American ◆◆◆
With *Amorica*, the Black Crowes began developing a distinctive sound, shading their Stonesy Southern boogie with a variety of rootsy and psy-chedelic overtones. But where *Amorica* was rich with kaleidoscopic col-ors, *Three Snakes & One Charm* is stripped down and direct. Sure, it has a punchy, muscular sound that is, if anything, more eclectic than its pre-decessor, but the production is distressingly monotonous and the songs lack strong hooks. Even with its faults, *Three Snakes & One Charm* is a winning album, mainly because the Black Crowes' musicianship contin-ues to deepen—the musical fusions and eclecticism are seamless, partic-ularly from lead guitarist Rich Robinson. Their musicianship would be even more impressive if the songs were equal in quality. *—Stephen Tho-mas Erlewine*

The Black Dog

f. 1989, England
Ambient Techno, Electronica, Club/Dance
Taking their name from a British euphemism for imminent doom, the Black Dog (also appearing variously as Black Dog Productions, Balil, Xeper, and Plaid, among others) formed in the early '90s as the trio of Ken Downie, Ed Handley, and Andy Turner. Forging a challenging, relentless combination of early techno, electro, and hip-hop with a pen-chant for odd time signatures, high-tech atmospherics, and Egyptian ico-nography, the group immediately distinguished itself from the scores of disposable techno musicians covering familiar ground in the post-rave UK. Something of a closet phenomenon attracting the devotion of DJs who nonetheless refused to play their complicated brew for fear of being booed off the decks, Black Dog was immediately placed in the emerging "intelligent techno" category upon the release of the full-

length debut *Bytes*. A largely UK-media constituted phrase meant to peg music involving dance music compositional styles nonetheless intended for home listening, the term has since taken hold and is often applied to groups like Autechre, Aphex Twin, mu-Ziq, and As One. As Plaid, Ed Handley and Andy Turner had already released a handful of material (including an album) before meeting Downie, but the time spent in BDP was their most productive up to that point. In addition to the Dog's inclusion on the perhaps more high-profile *Artificial Intelligence* compilations on Warp and remixes for the likes of Bjork, Blondie, U.N.K.L.E., and Ned's Atomic Dustbin, the group released several full-length works as a group before Handley and Turner defected in 1995 to refocus on Plaid full-time. The pair released an EP on the Clear label in mid-1995 and are working on material for a Warp debut. Downie has continued with the Black Dog name, releasing the full-length *Music for Adverts* in 1996. —*Sean Cooper*

● **Bytes** / 1992 / Warp ✦✦✦✦
BDP's full-length debut was a sprawling deviation from techno-as-throwaway-dance floor-fare, weaving surprisingly engaging melodic and harmonic passages around complex rhythmic patterns and diverse, somewhat ambient atmospherics. Although all of the material was previously released in 12-inch or EP form, it holds up surprisingly well as a unified, coherent whole. With B12's *Electro Soma* and Autechre's *Incunabula*, it is one of the first and finest blasts in the European "intelligent techno" movement. —*Sean Cooper*

Temple of Transparent Balls / 1993 / GPR ✦✦✦
Black Dog's proper debut, this time for the GPR label. Includes probably the group's most well-known single track, "Cost II," released on 12-inch simultaneously with the album. —*Sean Cooper*

Parallel / 1995 / GPR ✦✦✦
A pre-*Bytes* collection of odd tracks released after the group had already parted. Some quality material, but without the integrated feel of their other full-length works. —*Sean Cooper*

Spanners / Apr. 25, 1995 / East West ✦✦✦✦
The group's last full-length work as a trio, *Spanners* steps even further afield of the dance floor, retaining many of traditional techno's stylistic characteristics while twisting and stretching them to more song-y lengths and shapes. Somewhat surprisingly, *Spanners* was licensed for domestic release by EastWest immediately after its release. —*Sean Cooper*

Music for Adverts (And Short Films) / 1996 / Warp ✦✦✦
With a cover thumbing its nose at Brian Eno's similarly titled series of albums from the 1970s and song titles ranging in reference from bad Hollywood films to washing powders, it would seem the Black Dog is engaged in a bit of a musical piss-take. Nothing of the sort, actually, as lone Dog Ken Downie's first solo work since the departure of partners Ed Handley and Andy Turner is a serious, often wistful collection of post-rave electronica, incorporating elements of techno, ambient, hip-hop, jungle, and jazz. Although lacking somewhat in complexity, Downie more than makes up for it in focus and emotional content. —*Sean Cooper*

Black Flag

f. 1977, Los Angeles, CA, **db.** 1986
Hardcore Punk
In many ways, Black Flag was the definitve Los Angeles hardcore punk band. Although their music flirted with heavy metal and experimental noise and jazz more than that of most hardcore bands, they defined the image and the aesthetic. Through their ceaseless touring, the band cultivated the American underground scene; every year, Black Flag played in every area of the US, influencing countless numbers of bands. Although their recording career was hampered by a draining lawsuit, which was followed by a seemingly endless stream of independently released records, the band was unquestionably one of the most infuential American post-punk bands. A full decade and a half before the fusion of punk and metal became popular, Black Flag created a ferocious, edgy, and ironic amalgam of underground aesthetics and gut-pounding metal. Their lyrics alluded to social criticism and a political viewpoint, but it was all conveyed as seething, cynical angst, which was occasionally very funny. Furthermore, Black Flag demonstrated an affection for bohemia—both in terms of musical experimentation and a fondness for poetry—that reiterated the band's underground roots and prevented it from becoming nothing but a heavy metal group. And it didn't matter who was in the band—throughout the years, the lineup changed numerous times—because the Black Flag name and four-bar logo became punk institutions.

Black Flag was formed in 1977 by guitarist Greg Ginn, a graduate of UCLA. Ginn formed the band with bassist Chuck Dukowski; the pair soon added drummer Brian Migdol and vocalist Keith Morris. At the same time, Ginn and Dukowski formed an independent record label, SST, which released the band's first EP, *Nervous Breakdown*, in 1978.

Morris and Migdol departed the next year—Morris went on to form the Circle Jerks—and they were respectively replaced with Chavo Pederast and Robo. By the release of 1980's *Jealous Again*, Black Flag had begun to tour the US relentlessly, building up a small, but dedicated, following of fans. After the release of *Jealous Again*, Black Flag went through another major lineup change. Pederast left the group and was replaced by Henry Rollins, a Washington DC fan who jumped on stage to sing with the band during a New York performance. At the same time, the band added a second guitarist, Dez Cadena, which gave the group a heavier sound.

Early in 1981 Black Flag signed a record contract with Unicorn Records, a subsidiary of MCA. The band delivered their first full-length album, *Damage*, to Unicorn; the label refused to release the record, claiming that the content was too dangerous and vulgar. Undaunted, Ginn released the album on SST Records. Upon its release, the album received considerable critical acclaim. Soon after the album appeared on the shelves, Unicorn sued Black Flag and SST over the release of *Damaged*. For the next two years, the band was prevented from using the name Black Flag or their logo on any records. During that time, the group continued to tour, and they surreptitiously released *Everything Went Black*, a double-album retrospective that contained no mention of the band, although it listed the names of the members on the front cover. The dispute ended in 1983, when Unicorn went bankrupt and the rights to the Black Flag name and logo reverted to the band.

As if to make up for lost time, Black Flag became impossibly prolific when it returned to recording in 1984. A new version of the group—featuring Ginn on guitar and bass (the latter was credited to the pseudonym Dale Nixon), bass, Rollins, and drummer Bill Stevenson—recorded the albums *My War* and *Family Man*. After those two albums were recorded, the group added bassist Kira Roessler and cut *Slip It In*, its third official album of 1984. In addition to those three albums, Black Flag released the cassette-only *Live '84* and the compilation *The First Four Years* in 1984, as well as reissuing *Everything Went Black* with all the proper credits restored. The group's touring and recording pace didn't slow in 1985; they released three records—*Loose Nut*, *The Process of Weeding Out*, and *In My Head*. By the end of the year, Anthony Martinez replaced Stevenson on drums.

After Black Flag released the live album *Who's Got the 10 ?* in early 1986, Greg Ginn broke up the band. Ginn recorded two albums with the more experimental Gone, but he concentrated on running SST Records, which had become one of the most important American independent labels of the era. By the time Black Flag broke up, SST had already released albums by such bands as Hüsker Dü, the Minutemen, Meat Puppets, and Sonic Youth. For most of the late '80s, Ginn retired from performing, choosing to operate SST Records instead; during this time, the label released early recordings from bands like Soundgarden, Dinosaur Jr., and Screaming Trees. Ginn returned to music in 1993, releasing a solo album on his new record label, Cruz.

After Black Flag's breakup, Henry Rollins formed the Rollins Band. For the rest of the '80s, he released music recorded with the Rollins Band on a variety of independent labels, as well as solo spoken-word recordings. In the early '90s, Rollins became one of the most recognizable figures of alternative music. —*Stephen Thomas Erlewine*

★ **Damaged** / 1981 / SST ✦✦✦✦✦
Perhaps the best album to emerge from the quagmire that was early-'80s California hardcore punk, the visceral, intensely physical presence of this record has yet to be equaled, although many bands have tried. Although Black Flag had been recording for three years before this release, the fact that Henry Rollins was now their lead singer made all the difference. His furious bellow and barely contained ferocity were the missing pieces the band needed to become great. Also, guitarist/mastermind Greg Ginn wrote a slew of great songs for this record that, while suffused with the usual punk conceits (alienation, boredom, disenfranchisement), were capable of making one laugh out loud, especially the proto-slacker satire "TV Party." Extremely controversial when it was released, *Damaged* endured the slings and arrows of outrageous criticism (some reacted as though this record alone would cause the fall of America's youth) to become and remain an important document of its time. —*John Dougan*

Everything Went Black / 1983 / SST ✦✦✦

Family Man / 1984 / SST ✦✦✦

The First Four Years / 1984 / SST ✦✦✦
The best collection of pre-Rollins era Black Flag. Much of *The First Four Years* finds the band in developmental mode, but the sonic anarchy and political vituperation met head-on more than once, creating a ferociously good time. Not simply for completists, this is an important recording of the then-burgeoning L.A. hardcore scene. —*John Dougan*

Live '84 / 1984 / SST ✦✦
Live '84 is a cassette-only release of a standard (for them anyway) Black Flag gig. Opening up with an eight-and-a-half minute hardcore/punk/jazz instrumental, "The Process of Weeding Out" (which came from an

earlier Black Flag instrumental EP of the same title), it was abundantly clear that Black Flag was no longer just another punk band; as much as they loved to kick out the jams, they also loved destroying the audience's preconceived notions of how punk bands were supposed to behave. Running at 70 minutes, this is a terrific live recording of Black Flag at their performing peak. —*John Dougan*

My War / 1984 / SST ✦✦
After a rancorous three-year legal battle with their label, Unicorn, that prevented their releasing any new material, Black Flag binged in the mid-'80s, releasing a flurry of records that had even the most devoted fans scrambling to keep up. They did, however, start this period somewhat inauspiciously with *My War*, a pretentious mess of a record with a totally worthless second side. Featuring three tracks of slower-than-Black Sabbath muck with Rollins howling like a caged animal, it was self-indulgence masquerading as inspiration and about as much fun as wading through a tar pit. Side one, however, was quite good, with the title track especially intimidating. —*John Dougan*

Slip It In / 1984 / SST ✦✦✦
Slip It In followed *My War* almost immediately, and while a bit better (fewer mega-volume angst drones), the band still wanders a bit, experimenting with expanding the breadth of hardcore into a newer hard rock/punk sound. This is especially true of Greg Ginn's guitar playing, which was becoming increasingly avant-garde and exciting. Rather than simply coughing up one cliched solo after another, he wandered up and down the fretboard as a jazz player like Blood Ulmer would, making the material more interesting than what most Black Flag-influenced bands were playing. —*John Dougan*

In My Head / 1985 / SST ✦✦✦✦
Hot on the heels of the live record came *Loose Nut* and *In My Head*, which showed significant improvement over *My War* and *Slip It In*. Rollins and Ginn were exploring by-now standard lyrical themes: hate, paranoia, loneliness, anomie, and violence, but framing them around music that was demanding, powerful and exciting. *In My Head* is the slightly better of the two, primarily because it's a little edgier and uncontrolled, but at this juncture, Black Flag was making some of the best contemporary rock music extant. —*John Dougan*

Loose Nut / 1985 / SST ✦✦✦✦
Despite being on top of their game, Black Flag called it a career in 1986, but did so in fine style. The live record *Who's Got the 10 ?* was recorded at a barn-burner of a gig with the band (especially Ginn) sounding as though they could take on the world. Extra points for a great version of the cautionary "Drinking and Driving." The cassette and CD contain an extra 30 minutes. —*John Dougan*

Wasted . . . Again / 1987 / SST ✦✦✦✦
Wasted . . . Again is a posthumous release that is an essential career summation. For those hearing the ear-searing sounds of early-'80s SoCal hardcore punk for the first time, *Wasted . . . Again* is an essential purchase. —*John Dougan*

Black Grape

f. 1993, Manchester, England
Alternative Pop-Rock, Brit-Pop
After the Happy Mondays disbanded in 1992, most observers would have guessed that the group's leader, vocalist Shaun Ryder, would succumb to the myriad of drug addictions that hastened the breakup of the group. Instead of dying, Ryder regained his strength and came back with a new band, Black Grape, in the summer of 1995. Black Grape was embraced by both the British public and press, making Shaun Ryder one of the more unexpected comebacks in rock 'n' roll history.

Ryder formed Black Grape in 1993, recruiting ex-Happy Monday Bez (dancing, percussion), rappers Kermit (b. Paul Leveridge) and Jed from the Ruthless Rap Assassins, and ex-Paris Angels guitarist Wags. Black Grape began recording demos only weeks after the implosion of the Happy Mondays. Over the course of recording and writing *It's Great When You're Straight*, Ryder recruited a number of musicians, most notably producer and bassist Danny Saber, keyboardist/producer Stephen Lironi, and former Bluebells and Smiths guitarist Gary Gannon. Black Grape's debut album was recorded over a period of seven weeks in late 1994 and early 1995; after it was completed, the band signed with Radioactive Records. The group's first single, "Reverend Black Grape," entered the Top Ten upon its release. The group's debut album, *It's Great When You're Straight . . . Yeah*, was released in August 1995. The album entered the UK charts at No. 1.

"In the Name of the Father" and "Kelly's Heroes" followed "Reverend Black Grape" into the Top 20 later in 1995. Toward the end of the year, Kermit suffered a severe case of septicemia, a form of blood poisoning caused by bad water he drank while in Mexico; although he came close to death—bits of his heart and liver were flaking off—he had recovered by the spring of 1996. Black Grape was prepared to head to America

early in 1996 when they were denied entry because of their prior drug convictions. After a couple of months the passports were cleared, and the band was admitted to the US. Because of his illness, Kermit had to miss the tour, and his spot was filled by Psycho, who became a permanent member of the band after the completion of the tour. Before Black Grape launched their US tour in spring of 1996, Bez left the band because of financial disagreements with the record company.

In May 1996, Black Grape returned with the single "Fat Neck," which entered the UK charts in the Top Ten; the song featured former Smiths member Johnny Marr on guitar. A month after the release of "Fat Neck," the group released their football anthem "England's Irie," which was recorded with Joe Strummer. Like "Fat Neck" before it, "England's Irie" became a Top Ten hit. —*Stephen Thomas Erlewine*

It's Great When You're Straight . . . Yeah / Oct. 10, 1995 / Radioactive ✦✦✦✦
When the Happy Mondays fell apart in 1992, most observers assumed that Shaun Ryder would never recover from his numerous drug addictions. No one could have ever predicted that he would return to the top of the charts three years later, relatively fit and healthy, with a new band that fulfilled all of the promises of his old group. Black Grape are what the Happy Mondays always were, only better. Leaving behind all of the stiff musicianship that plagued even the best Mondays records, Black Grape's debut *It's Great When You're Straight . . . Yeah* is a surreal, funky, profane and perversely joyous album, overflowing with casual eclecticism and giddy humor. Working with a band that is looser and grittier than the Mondays, Ryder sounds reinvigorated, creating bizarre rhymes that tie together junk culture, drug lingo, literary references, and utter nonsense. Ryder's lyrics have always been free-wheelingly impenetrable, but now he's working with Kermit, a rapper who is the equal of his skills. Even better, the music has deep grooves and catchy pop hooks that come straight out of left field. From the blaring harmonica of the triumphant "Reverend Black Grape" and the trippy sitars of "In the Name of the Father" to the seedy, rolling "Shake Your Money" and the stinging guitars of "Tramazi Parti," *It's Great* is filled with music that goes in unconventional directions without ever sounding forced. Not only is *It's Great When You're Straight* a triumphant return for Shaun Ryder and his sidekick Bez, it's the first album they have ever recorded that justifies all of the hype. —*Stephen Thomas Erlewine*

Black Oak Arkansas

f. 1970, Black Oak, AR, **db.** 1980
Hard Rock, Southern Rock, Boogie Rock
Southern-rock veterans Black Oak Arkansas never quite achieved the level of success enjoyed by contemporaries like Lynyrd Skynyrd and the Allman Brothers, but they have remained a cult band, thanks to their raw, primitive energy and the testosterone-fueled antics of lead vocalist/showman James "Big Jim Dandy" Mangrum. Named for Mangrum's hometown, Black Oak Arkansas eventually built up a solid following through incessant touring and enjoyed a run of ten charting albums between 1971 and 1976. The band also found itself with a Top 30 single in their raunchy cover of a LaVern Baker's R&B hit called "Jim Dandy to the Rescue," which became Mangrum's signature song. When album sales dried up, Mangrum re-formed the band with more musically skilled veteran players and continued to tour, although the group's glory days were past.

Black Oak Arkansas dates back to the mid-'60s, when a group of young, long-haired misfits headed by Jim Mangrum, unable to find work, turned to rock 'n' roll. However, the group was unable to purchase equipment and ended up being arrested for grand larceny after stealing items from the local school in order to get money. They were nearly run out of town and went to live in the nearby hills, locating and borrowing equipment where they could. The band moved to New Orleans in 1969 and called itself Knowbody Else, with a lineup of vocalist Mangrum; guitarists Ricky "Ricochet" Reynolds, Stanley "Goober" Knight, and Harvey "Burley" Jett; bassist Pat Daugherty; and drummer Wayne Evans. Knowbody Else recorded a self-titled album for Stax, which went nowhere; rethinking their approach, the band became interested in psychedelia and Eastern spirituality, which they filtered through their Southern Baptist upbringing. Changing their name to Black Oak Arkansas, the band secured a deal with Atlantic after several trips to Los Angeles and released its self-titled debut in 1971. While it wasn't a hit, the band toured extensively, building a reputation as a raw, incendiary live act that made up for occasional musical deficiencies with energy and the explicit sexuality of Mangrum, who flaunted his body at every opportunity and became known for such antics as miming sex with the washboard he used for musical accompaniment. The band's second album, *Keep the Faith*, was a noticeable improvement, as the band had honed its sound and material through numerous live gigs. *If an Angel Came to See You, Would You Make Her Feel at Home?* followed the same year, featuring new drummer Tommy Aldridge, but it was 1973's *Raunch 'n' Roll Live* that established the group as a commercial force. That year,

High on the Hog became their most commercially successful album, reaching No. 52 on the charts. It was buoyed by the Top 30 cover version of "Jim Dandy to the Rescue," which featured female vocalist Ruby Starr trading innuendoes with Jim "Dandy" Mangrum. Several more albums followed before the group parted ways with Atlantic in 1976. Jett left the band in 1975 and was replaced by Starr cohort James Henderson. Lineup shifts were rampant as the group switched to MCA; Aldridge left and was replaced by Joel Williams, while the guitar/bass axis was gutted and rebuilt around Greg Reding, Jack Holder, and bassist Andy Tanas. This lineup released *Race with the Devil* in 1977, after the band had one last taste of success with the "Strong Enough to Be Gentle" single. After several lackluster, straightforward Southern-rock albums, the band called it quits in 1980. After recovering from a heart attack, Mangrum reunited with Reynolds in 1984 for a solo album, *Ready as Hell. —Steve Huey*

● **Hot & Nasty: The Best of Black Oak Arkansas** / 1993 / Rhino ✦✦✦✦
Hot & Nasty: The Best of Black Oak Arkansas cherry-picks from all of the group's hit-and-miss albums, taking their two hit singles, "Jim Dandy" and "Strong Enough to Be Gentle," and most of their AOR favorites. —*Stephen Thomas Erlewine*

Black Sabbath

f. 1969, Birmingham, England
Heavy Metal
No band has come closer to embodying heavy metal than Black Sabbath. Over the years, their lineup may have changed, but their music hasn't—it has remained the same loud, methodical guitar-based heavy rock that it was in the early '70s. Their slow, sludgy attack was part design and part accident. Because of an accident that cut the tips of his fingers, Tony Iommi tuned his guitar down a half-step because he couldn't play comfortably unless the strings were slightly slack; the lower tuning made his mammoth riffs sound heavier. Bassist Geezer Butler's lyrics reveled in black magic, fantasy, drugs, mental illness, and the occult, but never sex; Ozzy Osbourne sang them in a flat, almost tuneless, banshee wail. Butler and drummer Bill Ward never had any flair for playing around with the rhythm, preferring to let the beat plod on and on. Their songwriting never strayed from one riff, a chorus, another riff, and a guitar solo, but that is part of their appeal. Taken together, the primitive musicianship, bad poetry, obsessive fantasy world, crawling tempos, and overpowering volume simultaneously represent everything good and bad about heavy metal.

Critics detested them when they were at the peak of their powers in the early '70s, and they still do. But critical acclaim was never essential to the band's success. Black Sabbath was, in many ways, an underground band—parents hated them, hippies hated them, self-respecting rockers hated them. Everybody hated them except teenagers. And those were the teenagers who grew up and formed bands, from Metallica to Soundgarden to Henry Rollins. Everybody from the heaviest of metal bands to the sludgiest of grunge bands listened to Black Sabbath when they were teenagers.

Of course, after Black Sabbath hit their peak, they stuck around way too long. Some of their first six albums were great, some of them merely had good tracks, but all of them had something to recommend them. Osbourne hung around for two more records before jumping ship for good. Former Rainbow lead vocalist Ronnie James Dio replaced him in 1979; the new lineup released their first record, *Heaven and Hell*, in 1980. It was a far cry from their best, but it sounded like *Paranoid* compared to what they would later release. Throughout the '80s, the band members kept shifting, with Iommi being the only member to remain in all of the lineups. At the end of the decade, he was the only original member left in the band. Not only was Black Sabbath suffering musically, but their credibility was being questioned by their devoted fans as well. In 1991, Iommi persuaded Butler and, for a brief time, Dio, to rejoin. Black Sabbath continues to lurch forward in the '90s, oblivious to the criticism and declining record sales, but their early records continue to inspire—as well as infuriate—whole new generations of listeners. —*Stephen Thomas Erlewine*

Black Sabbath / May 1970 / Warner Brothers ✦✦✦✦
Their debut album set the tone with the title cut, "The Wizard," "Wasp," and "Warning." —*Cub Koda*

★ **Paranoid** / Jan. 1971 / Warner Brothers ✦✦✦✦✦
Paranoid, released in the UK in September 1970 and held back from US release until January 1971 to avoid cutting off sales of the still-selling debut LP, became Black Sabbath's bestselling album ever. "Paranoid" and "Iron Man" (the latter released as a single a full year after the album) became Black Sabbath's only US singles-chart entries, and the album became their only UK chart-topper. Although the album was deplored by critics at the time, the reasons for its success are easy to hear now. Subtle, it ain't (listen to the way Ozzy Osbourne sings note-for-note the same simple melodies Tony Iommi plays), but that's the point. In

songs like "Paranoid" and "Iron Man," generations of teenagers heard their own insecurities writ large. —*William Ruhlmann*

☆ **Masters of Reality** / Aug. 1971 / Warner Brothers ✦✦✦✦✦
With *Paranoid*, Black Sabbath perfected the formula for their lumbering heavy metal. On its followup, *Masters of Reality*, the group merely repeated the formula, setting the stage for a career of recycling the same sounds and riffs. But on *Masters of Reality* Sabbath still were fresh and had a seemingly endless supply of crushingly heavy riffs to bludgeon their audiences into sweet, willing oblivion. If the album is a showcase for anyone, it is Tony Iommi, who keeps the album afloat with a series of slow, loud riffs, the best of which—"Sweet Leaf" and "Children of the Grave" among them—rank among his finest playing. Taken in tandem with the more consistent *Paranoid*, *Masters of Reality* forms the core of Sabbath's canon. There are a few stray necessary tracks scattered throughout the group's other early '70s albums, but *Masters of Reality* is the last time they delivered a consistent album and its influence can be heard throughout the generations of heavy metal bands that followed. —*Stephen Thomas Erlewine*

Black Sabbath, Vol. 4 / Sep. 1972 / Warner Brothers ✦✦✦✦
This is a surprisingly song-oriented set of cynical boogie. —*John Floyd*

Sabbath, Bloody Sabbath / Dec. 1973 / Warner Brothers ✦✦✦✦
Sabbath adds some synths to their sludge and comes up with a surprisingly solid album that manages to expand on their patented slow, gloomy sound. —*Stephen Thomas Erlewine*

Sabotage / Aug. 1975 / Warner Brothers ✦✦✦✦
On *Sabotage* the band was at their artiest, adding synths and found sounds that accentuated Iommi's tight solos and riffs. It may not be their best or most influential record, but *Sabotage* is certainly one of their most interesting. In fact, it was the last consistently impressive album they ever recorded. —*Stephen Thomas Erlewine*

We Sold Our Soul for Rock and Roll / Feb. 1976 / Warner Brothers ✦✦✦✦
Running over 70 minutes, *We Sold Our Soul for Rock and Roll* is a solid 16-track sampler from the band's first six albums, what you might call Sabbath's glory days. —*John Floyd & Cub Koda*

Technical Ecstasy / Oct. 1976 / Warner Brothers ✦✦
Never Say Die! / Oct. 1978 / Warner Brothers ✦✦
Never Say Die! was the last album Ozzy Osbourne recorded with Sabbath and it's easy to see why he left the group. Once, the band's plodding, gloomy riffs had a stately majesty to them—on *Never Say Die!* they simply sound lethargic. Osbourne doesn't sound like he cares much about the material, delivering his lines in a lazy, affected manner; he sings as if he had already left the group. —*Stephen Thomas Erlewine*

Heaven and Hell / May 1980 / Warner Brothers ✦✦✦
Black Sabbath's first album without Ozzy Osbourne sounds curiously revitalized. The band's return to form had something to do with their new vocalist, Ronnie James Dio, but it was mostly due to the fact the band had written a set of riffs that were fairly memorable. The result was their best record since *Sabotage*, and the only good record the group recorded in the '80s. —*Stephen Thomas Erlewine*

The Mob Rules / Nov. 1981 / Warner Brothers ✦✦
Mob Rules, Black Sabbath's second album with Ronnie James Dio, went gold, but that was a testament to the strength of the previous *Heaven and Hell*, not the merits of the new record. While it essentially reiterated the formula of *Heaven and Hell*, *Mob Rules* lacked the blunt, powerful riffs that made the former record a platinum success. —*Stephen Thomas Erlewine*

Under Wheels of Confusion (1970-87) / Nov. 6, 1996 / Castle ✦✦✦✦
An unwieldy four-disc, 52-track box set, *Under the Wheels of Confusion 1970-1987* nevertheless contains the bulk of Sabbath's best work, dipping considerably in quality during the second half of the set, when Ozzy Osbourne left the group and was replaced by Ronnie James Dio. Even though all of the stone-cold classics are here, as are all of Dio's best tracks, Sabbath remains best appreciated through their original albums, which capture the essence of the metal giants much better than this box. —*Stephen Thomas Erlewine*

Cilla Black (Priscilla Maria Veronica White)

b. May 27, 1943, Liverpool, England
Vocals / Pop-Rock, British Invasion, Girl-Group
Cilla Black was the hatcheck girl at the Cavern, the club in Liverpool where the Beatles played in their early days. Like them, she was signed to a management contract by Brian Epstein. Parlophone, the Beatles' label, released her first single, "Love of the Loved" (written by the Beatles' John Lennon and Paul McCartney), in September 1963. It was a Top 40 UK hit and was followed by the chart-topping "Anyone Who Had a Heart," a dramatic ballad by Burt Bacharach and Hal David that had been a US hit for Dionne Warwick and that set the pattern for Black's later recordings. Black's third single, "You're My World," was another UK

No. 1 and a Top 40 hit in the US in July 1964. In the US, Black scored only four more chart entries, "It's for You" (1964) (also by Lennon-McCartney), "He Won't Ask Me" (1964), "Alfie" (1966), and "Step Inside Love" (1968) (by McCartney). But she was much more popular in the UK, where her Top Ten hits included "It's for You," "You've Lost That Lovin' Feelin'" (1965), "Love's Just a Broken Heart" (1966), "Alfie," "Don't Answer Me" (1966), "Step Inside Love," "Surround Yourself with Sorrow" (1969), "Conversations" (1969), and "Something Tells Me (Something's Gonna Happen Tonight)" (1971). She also made the Top 40 with "I've Been Wrong Before" (1965) (by Randy Newman), "A Fool I Am" (1966), "What Good Am I" (1967), "I Only Live to Love" (1967), "Where Is Tomorrow" (1968), "If I Thought You'd Ever Change Your Mind" (1970), and "Baby We Can't Go Wrong" (1974). On the LP chart, *Cilla* (1965), *Cilla Sings a Rainbow* (1966), and *Sher-oo* (1968) all made the Top Ten; *The Best of Cilla Black* (1968) and *The Very Best of Cilla Black* (1983) hit the Top 40.

In 1968 she launched a television series on the BBC and went on to become a popular British TV entertainer in the 1970s. *—William Ruhlmann*

● **Best of Cilla** / Nov. 1968 / Parlophone ◆◆◆◆
By the fall of 1968, Cilla Black had scored 14 chart entries in the UK, of which eight had hit the Top Ten and two had gone to No. 1. This 14-track British compilation contains 11 of those songs, including all but one of the Top Tens. Her singles began with "Love of the Loved," a Beatles cast-off in their Merseybeat style, but she really hit her stride copying Dionne Warwick on "Anyone Who Had a Heart," and went on to score all her hits in a melodramatic ballad style, with lots of strings and heartbreak. She is thus in a category with contemporaries like Dusty Springfield and Lulu, but unlike them, she never showed much taste for rock or blues, instead moving unerringly to the middle of the road. As a result, today she seems not much more than a footnote in the history of the Beatles. *—William Ruhlmann*

Frank Black

b. 1965, Long Beach, CA
Guitar, Vocals / Alternative Pop-Rock
Inverting his stage name from Black Francis to Frank Black, the former Pixies lead singer-songwriter embarked on a solo career after he broke up the band in early 1993. Actually, he began recording his solo album *before* he told the band the news. Working with former Pere Ubu member Eric Drew Feldman, Black occasionally heads into the ferocious post-punk guitar territory that marked such landmark albums as *Surfer Rosa* and *Doolittle*, but more frequently he plays up his considerably underrated melodic side. His self-titled 1993 debut album was an adventurous sketchbook of pop styles ranging from surf rock to heavy metal, from Beatlesque pop to new wave.

Black's second album, 1994's *Teenager of the Year*, was a sprawling and diverse album that amplified all the best points of *Frank Black*. Although it received favorable reviews and had an alternative radio hit with "Headache," it slipped off the charts two weeks after its release. Black parted ways with Elektra and 4AD in early 1995, signing a new contract with American. Black released his first album for American, the hard-rocking *The Cult of Ray*, in January 1996. *—Stephen Thomas Erlewine*

Frank Black / Mar. 1993 / 4AD/Elektra ◆◆◆◆
On *Frank Black*, Charles Thompson (formerly Black Francis of the Pixies) brings the pop undercurrents that have always floated through his music to the forefront. The sonic onslaught of the Pixies is here in small doses (portions of "Los Angeles" and "Parry the Wind High, Low," "Czar," and the Iggy Pop tribute "Ten Percenter"), but there are more Lennon, Bowie, Brian Wilson, and surf-rock influences than Iggy; even the Ramones tribute is a lovely pop number. "Los Angeles" encapsulates all of the album into one track; it begins with an acoustic folk section, slams into a punkish verse, and ends with a gorgeous Beatlesque coda. That Thompson can pull it off all in one song *and* make it work says volumes for his talents. *—Stephen Thomas Erlewine*

● **Teenager of the Year** / May 24, 1994 / 4AD/Elektra ◆◆◆◆
Frank Black's second album is a wildly ambitious and eclectic piece of guitar-pop, ranging from the full-throttle roar of "Whatever Happened to Pong?" and "Thalassocracy" to the pure pop of "Headache" and the gorgeous, winding melodies of "Speedy Marie." It might be a little long, but *Teenager of the Year* is packed with thrilling, innovative pop. *—Stephen Thomas Erlewine*

The Cult of Ray / Jan. 30, 1996 / Warner Brothers ◆◆
Frank Black has never had a problem with being weird. He practically pioneered mixing bizarre lyrics about science fiction, sex, and religion with loud guitars when he led the Pixies to the outer limits of pop music in the '80s. So maybe it's in keeping that *The Cult of Ray*, his third solo album, is his weirdest yet. It's truly a strange record for Black—it flirts with the ordinary, something with which he's never had a relationship before. While there are still flashes of Black's normal eccentricity on

songs like "The Marsist," "Men in Black," and "The Creature Crawling," for the most part *The Cult of Ray* is subdued and stripped-down where his previous solo albums sound liberated in their wide-band weirdness. There are three songs about moshing, of all things, on *The Cult of Ray*, all of which have the same tired-sounding chugging punk guitars that lesser artists have made their bread and butter for years. And, oddly enough, there's an honest-to-goodness, straightforward love song called "I Don't Want to Hurt You (Every Single Time)," which sounds watered-down and forced compared to some of the unique and personal love songs he's created over the years with the Pixies and on his own. While *The Cult of Ray* isn't a disaster, it's certainly a disappointment. *—Heather Phares*

Otis Blackwell

b. 1931, Brooklyn, NY
Piano / R&B, Rock 'n' Roll, Urban Blues
Few 1950s rock 'n' roll tunesmiths were as prolifically talented as Otis Blackwell. His immortal compositions include Little Willie John's "Fever," Elvis Presley's "Don't Be Cruel" and "All Shook Up," Jerry Lee Lewis' "Great Balls of Fire" and "Breathless," and Jimmy Jones' "Handy Man" (just for starters).

Though he often collaborated with various partners on the thriving '50s New York R&B scene (Winfield Scott, Eddie Cooley and Jack Hammer, to name three), Blackwell's songwriting style is as identifiable as that of Willie Dixon or Jerry Leiber & Mike Stoller. He helped formulate the musical vocabulary of rock 'n' roll when the genre was barely breathing on its own.

Befitting a true innovator, Blackwell's early influences were a tad out of the ordinary. As a lad growing up in Brooklyn, he dug the Westerns that his favorite nearby cinema screened. At that point, Tex Ritter was Otis' main man. Smooth blues singers Chuck Willis and Larry Darnell also made an impression. By 1952, Blackwell parlayed a victory at an Apollo Theater talent show into a recording deal with veteran producer Joe Davis for RCA, switching to Davis' own Jay-Dee logo the next year. He was fairly prolific at Jay-Dee, enjoying success with the throbbing "Daddy Rollin' Stone" (later covered by the Who). From 1955 on, though, Blackwell concentrated primarily on songwriting (Atlantic, Date, Cub, and MGM later issued scattered Blackwell singles).

"Fever," co-written by Cooley, was Blackwell's first winner (he used the pen name of John Davenport, since he was still contractually obligated to Jay-Dee). Blackwell never met Elvis in person, but his material traveled a direct pipeline to the rock icon; "Return to Sender," "One Broken Heart for Sale," and "Easy Question" also came from his pen. Dee Clark ("Just Keep It Up" and "Hey Little Girl"), Thurston Harris, Wade Flemons, Clyde McPhatter, Brook Benton, Ben E. King, the Drifters, Bobby Darin, Ral Donner, Gene Vincent, and plenty more of rock's primordial royalty benefitted from Blackwell's compositional largesse before the British Invasion forever altered the Brill Building scene.

In 1977, Blackwell returned to recording with a Herb Abramson-produced set for Inner City comprised of his own renditions of the songs that made him famous. A 1991 stroke paralyzed the legendary songscribe, but his influence remains so enduring that it inspired *Brace Yourself!*, an all-star 1994 tribute album that included contributions by Dave Edmunds, Joe Ely, Deborah Harry, Chrissie Hynde, Kris Kristofferson, Graham Parker, and bluesman Joe Louis Walker. *—Bill Dahl*

● **Otis Blackwell 1953-55** / 1991 / Flyright ◆◆◆◆
The British Flyright logo has neatly compiled all 17 known titles that Blackwell cut for Jay-Dee, including "Daddy Rollin' Stone," the equally ominous "On That Power Line," and four sides with a killer New York combo featuring tenor sax wailer Sam "The Man" Taylor and guitarist Mickey Baker. *—Bill Dahl*

Blake Babies

f. 1986, Boston, MA, **db.** 1991
Alternative Pop-Rock, Jangle-Pop
While Blake Babies made several engaging records the late '80s and early '90s, they never broke out of the collegiate rock circles where they were adored. It wasn't until 1992 that their leader, Juliana Hatfield, began getting recognition as a songwriter in more mainstream publications, but that was after the group was broken up. Over their four albums, Hatfield's songwriting and thin, girlish singing improved drastically as the band's post-R.E.M. alternative pop grew more muscular, branching out into both punkier and folkier territories on each record. By the time of their last full-length album, 1990's *Sunburn*, guitarist John Strohm was emerging as an impressive songwriter in his own right. After a final EP in 1991, the band split, with Hatfield emerging as an alternative superstar and Strohm and drummer Freda Boner forming the acclaimed guitar-pop band Antenna. *—Stephen Thomas Erlewine*

Nicely, Nicely / 1987 / Mammoth ✦✦✦✦
The Blake Babies' debut album, released on their own record label. —*William Ruhlmann*

Earwig / 1989 / Mammoth ✦✦✦✦
On their first full-length album, the Blake Babies' knack for melodic, chiming guitar-pop became evident, with songs like "Outta My Head" and "Take Your Head off My Shoulder" leading a pack of fine original numbers. —*Stephen Thomas Erlewine*

Sunburn / 1990 / Mammoth ✦✦✦✦
Juliana Hatfield's songwriting began to blossom on the Blake Babies' second full-length album, *Sunburn*. Her melodies and hooks are direct and catchy while her lyrics are disarming in their casual honesty. This doesn't mean that John Strohm's songs don't amount to anything; in fact, his songs and lyrical contributions help balance Hatfield's tendency to be simplistic and childish. At their best, the duo made a surprisingly effective pop songwriting team. *Sunburn* features the band at their best. —*Stephen Thomas Erlewine*

Rosy Jack World / Jun. 21, 1991 / Mammoth ✦✦✦
● **Innocence and Experience** / Sep. 28, 1993 / Mammoth ✦✦✦✦
Featuring songs from all of their albums as well as a couple of rare tracks, *Innocence and Experience* is a fine collection of the Blake Babies' best work; it's a fine introduction to their ringing, R.E.M.-style guitar-pop. —*Stephen Thomas Erlewine*

The Blasters

f. 1979, Los Angeles, CA, **db.** 1987
Group / Rock 'n' Roll, Rockabilly Revival, Roots-Rock, New Wave
The all-American roots music band the Blasters were principally brothers Dave and Phil Alvin, whose first-hand experience with blues masters shaped their sound and turned them into contemporary singer-songwriters whose interest in roots rock has never waned.

The Alvins, along with Bill Bateman on drums and John Bazz on bass, grew up in Downey, CA, in the shadow of Disneyland. Their musical education involved hanging out with musicians like Lee Allen, Marcus Johnson, and T-Bone Walker, all of whom tipped the band to the ways of blues and R&B. Ironically, by the time they were ready to work in Los Angeles clubs, the punk rock explosion was in full swing, and they found an audience for their rough and ready sound among the punks, particularly fans of X, with whom they frequently shared the bill. *American Music* (1980) was a collection of roots covers and originals. Followed by *The Blasters* (1981, Slash), the band had added veteran pianist Gene Taylor, baritone saxophonist Steve Berlin, and mentor Allen on tenor sax. Amazingly, the album reached No. 36 on the charts. In 1982 they recorded the live EP *Over There* for Slash, followed by 1983's *Non-Fiction*. Less focused on rockabilly revivalism, Dave Alvin had become the band's chief cook and songwriter. Berlin had left the fold to join Los Lobos.

The Hard Line in 1985 was even more polished and featured the work of Ry Cooder and John Mellencamp, whose song "Colored Lights" had been written and produced with the band in mind. The band called it a day after that, but it continues to perform live as the Blasters sans Dave Alvin; Greg "Smokey" Hormel serves as his replacement. After joining X for a brief spell, Dave Alvin launched a career as a prolific solo recording artist; Phil Alvin released one solo album before heading back to school to pursue post-graduate work in mathematics. Taylor is also a solo recording artist. —*Denise Sullivan*

American Music / 1980 / Rollin' Rock✦✦✦✦
The Blasters / 1981 / Slash ✦✦✦✦
You might have thought the Blasters had been in suspended animation for 25 years when their major-label debut turned up in late 1981 sounding for all the world like something cut in the Sun Studios in Memphis in 1956. Dave Alvin knew all the licks and his brother Phil had the R&B/country wail down. Best of all, you couldn't tell the oldies from Dave's newly written classics. Welcome to the birth of rock 'n' roll, all over again. —*William Ruhlmann*

Over There [Live] / Oct. 1982 / Slash ✦✦✦
On this six-song EP, recorded May 22, 1982, at the Venue in London, the Blasters take on such '50s rock 'n' roll classics as Jerry Lee Lewis' "High School Confidential" and Little Richard's "Keep a-Knockin'." The band's fidelity to their influences does not dampen their enthusiasm—they may be looking back, but they're bringing the old sound back to life. Maybe the best way to experience this band was live, not on record, at least in their early days, and this recording catches them at a fiery peak. —*William Ruhlmann*

Non Fiction / 1983 / Slash ✦✦✦✦
An album of orginals by Dave Alvin, accompanied by the expanded lineup that included Steve Berlin and Lee Allen on sax, this is prime-time vintage Blasters. Opening with the crowd-pleasing love song "Red Rose," moving through "Barefoot Rock " (no doubt inspired by Jimmy McCracklin's "Georgia Slop," later covered by Los Lobos), on to one of

Alvin's finest hours as songwriter with "Long White Cadillac" (made famous by Dwight Yoakam), and winding down with "Boomtown," the Blasters are effective at retracing and reflecting the concerns of the common man and woman—a celebration of Americana, careful never to wallow in nostalgia. —*Denise Sullivan*

Hard Line / 1985 / Slash ✦✦
Somehow, the Blasters could never make up their minds whether they were neo or retro, whether they wanted to expand beyond their influences or just copy them. By the end of this confused, if earnest collection, they've covered John Mellencamp and declared "Rock and Roll Will Stand." It did, but the Blasters did not. —*William Ruhlmann*

● **The Blasters Collection** / Mar. 12, 1991 / Slash ✦✦✦✦
The Slash years are compiled here, along with three previously unreleased tracks, forming the perfect overview of the Blasters' short recording career devoted to blues, country, and R&B. From the outset of their career, from "Marie Marie" to "Border Radio," it was clear Dave Alvin would be a songwriter to be reckoned with—one for the ages. Tracing his development through "Long White Cadillac" (later recorded by Dwight Yoakam), "Trouble Bound" (with the Jordanaires on vocals), and the hard-country "Dark Night," brother Phil Alvin brings the necessary heart, soul, and authenticity to the work and the band are masters of their form. Few work or rock harder. —*Denise Sullivan*

Mary J. Blige

b. Jan. 11, 1971, Bronx, NY
Vocals / Hip Hop, Urban, Club/Dance
Crowned the new "Queen of Hip-Hop Soul," Mary J. Blige enjoyed a breakout year in 1992 with *What's the 411?* Such singles as "Reminisce" and "Real Love" thrust the Atlanta-born singer into the spotlight at age 21. She was raised in Yonkers and performed in local groups before making her debut for the Uptown label. The album went platinum, and a remixed version was later issued. The single "Reminisce" had a second life when it was reworked and redone in a rap version by the duo of Pete Rock and C.L. Smooth. After 1994's *My Life*, she released *Share My World* in 1997. —*Ron Wynn*

● **What's the 411?** / 1992 / Uptown/MCA ✦✦✦✦
Mary J. Blige's debut album, *What's the 411?*, was a revolution in disguise. Like her new-jack predecessors, Blige combined R&B with hip-hop, but unlike Guy and Bobby Brown, her music was seductive and sly. More importantly, she sounds grittier and more real than most new jack swingers or female R&B vocalists. Blige can slip between singing and rapping with ease, which is partially the reason why *What's the 411?* is so successful. It doesn't hurt that her collaborators, from Grand Puba to Sean "Puffy" Combs, help construct backing tracks that are melodic, relentlessly funky, and sexy. —*Stephen Thomas Erlewine*

My Life / 1994 / Suave/Relativity ✦✦✦✦
Share My World / Apr. 22, 1997 / MCA ✦✦✦✦
Mary J. Blige established herself as the leading female vocalist of street-smart, hip-hop urban soul with her first two albums; with *Share My World*, she relaxed a bit, as if she didn't have to prove herself quite so much anymore. The end result is less hip-hop and more R&B, and while that means the record is tamer than her first two albums, it is ultimately more seductive. Working with Babyface, R. Kelly, Mtume, and Jimmy Jam & Terry Lewis, Blige creates a seamless album of smooth soul underpinned with gritty hip-hop beats; the lead single "Love Is All We Need" epitomizes this approach, as her voice effortlessly intertwines with Nas, creating a minor classic. The remainder of the album is plagued a bit by uneven songwriting, but Blige's charismatic, sexy vocals and the professional production make *Share My World* another terrific album from one of the '90s' best urban soul vocalists. —*Leo Stanley*

Blind Faith

f. May 1969, England, **db.** Nov. 1969
Rock 'n' Roll, Blues-Rock, British Blues
The calculated grafting of ex-Cream members Eric Clapton (b. Mar. 30, 1945, Ripley, Surrey, England) on guitar and vocals, and Ginger Baker (b. Aug. 19, 1939, Lewisham, England) on percussion, to ex-Traffic member Steve Winwood (b. May 12, 1948, Birmingham, England) on keyboards, guitar, and vocals, and bassist/violinist Rick Grech (b. Nov. 1, 1945, Bordeaux, France; d. Mar. 17, 1990) of the popular British group Family brought the term "supergroup" to new levels of hype. The talent involved in this amalgamation was quite impressive, but the cynical marketing minds behind this appropriately named fabrication failed to consider natural group chemistry. The volatile personalities in the lineup helped ensure that Blind Faith would be nothing more than an interesting one-off. Blind Faith debuted with a free concert before 100,000 people in London's Hyde Park on June 7, 1969.

The band made an auspicious live US debut, selling out Madison Square Garden on July 12. But things soured quickly, with the members going their separate ways at the conclusion of their 20-concert, six-week US tour on August 24, and Blind Faith became yet another historical footnote in the ongoing marriage of commerce and artistic expression. In spite of unrealistic pressure to live up to fan expectations, Blind Faith delivered a single, self-titled album in July 1969 that at times almost made good on its perceived potential. It still holds up today as a listening experience, thanks to Clapton's inspiring "Presence of the Lord," Winwood's reading of Buddy Holly's "Well All Right," and his own plaintive "Can't Find My Way Home." — *Rick Clark*

● **Blind Faith** / Jul. 1969 / RSO ✦✦✦✦
More than a quarter century after the release of Blind Faith's first and last album, all the stories of hype and manipulation pall before the album's enduring appeal. Steve Winwood is especially impressive, contributing three compositions—"Had to Cry Today," "Can't Find My Way Home," and "Sea of Joy"—that continue to rank among his best, and singing with his usual soulfulness. Eric Clapton's "Presence of the Lord" is also a perennial in his repertoire, and his guitar playing throughout the record is distinctive and impressive. If Ginger Baker overplays somewhat for contemporary tastes (especially on his 15-minute showcase, "Do What You Like"), late-'60s tastes were more accommodating, and Baker nevertheless demonstrates why he is among the handful of great drummers in rock. And whatever you think of the hype, the album was a notable success. — *William Ruhlmann*

Blondie

f. Aug. 1974, New York, NY, **db.** Oct. 1982
Punk, New Wave, Pop-Rock, Dance-Pop, Club/Dance
Blondie was the most commercially successful band to emerge from the much vaunted punk/new wave movement of the late '70s. The group was formed in New York City in August 1974 by singer Deborah Harry (b. July 1, 1945, Miami), formerly of Wind in the Willows, and guitarist Chris Stein (b. Jan. 5, 1950, Brooklyn) out of the remnants of Harry's previous group, the Stilettos. The lineup fluctuated over the next year. Drummer Clement Burke (b. Nov. 24, 1955, New York) joined in May 1975. Bassist Gary Valentine joined in August. In October, keyboard player James Destri (b. Apr. 13, 1954) joined, to complete the initial permanent lineup. They released their first album, *Blondie*, on Private Stock Records in December 1976. In July 1977, Valentine was replaced by Frank Infante.

In August Chrysalis Records bought their contract from Private Stock and in October reissued *Blondie* and released the second album, *Plastic Letters*. Blondie expanded to a sextet in November with the addition of bassist Nigel Harrison (born Princes Risborough, Buckinghamshire, England), as Infante switched to guitar. Blondie broke commercially in the UK in March 1978, when their cover of Randy and the Rainbows' 1963 hit "Denise," renamed "Denis," became a Top Ten hit, as did *Plastic Letters*, followed by a second UK Top Ten, "(I'm Always Touched by Your) Presence, Dear."

Blondie turned to UK producer/songwriter Mike Chapman for their third album, *Parallel Lines*, which was released in September 1978 and eventually broke them worldwide. "Picture This" was a UK Top 40 hit, and "Hanging on the Telephone" made the UK Top Ten, but it was the album's third single, the disco-influenced "Heart of Glass," that took Blondie to No. 1 in both the UK and the US. Both "Sunday Girl" hit No. 1 in the UK in May, and "One Way or Another" hit the US Top 40 in August. Blondie followed with their fourth album, *Eat to the Beat*, in October. Its first single, "Dreaming," went Top Ten in the UK, Top 40 in the US. The second single, "Union City Blue," went Top 40. In March 1980, the third UK single from *Eat to the Beat*, "Atomic," became the group's third British No. 1. (It later made the US Top 40.)

Meanwhile, Harry was collaborating with German disco producer Giorgio Moroder on "Call Me," the theme from the movie *American Gigolo*. It became Blondie's second transatlantic chart topper. Blondie's fifth album, *Autoamerican*, was released in November 1980, and its first single was the reggaeish tune "The Tide Is High," which went to No. 1 in the US and UK. The second single was the rap-oriented "Rapture," which topped the US pop charts and went Top Ten in the UK. But the band's eclectic style reflected a diminished participation by its members—Infante sued, charging that he wasn't being used on the records, though he settled and stayed in the lineup.

But in 1981, the members of Blondie worked on individual projects, notably Harry's gold-selling solo album, *KooKoo*. *The Best of Blondie* was released in the fall of the year. *The Hunter*, Blondie's sixth and last new album, was released in July 1982, preceded by the single "Island of Lost Souls," a Top 40 hit in the US and UK. "War Child" also became a Top 40 hit in the UK, but *The Hunter* was a commercial disappointment. At the same time, Stein became seriously ill with the genetic disease pemphigus. As a result, Blondie broke up in October 1982, with Deborah Harry launching a part-time solo career while caring for Stein, who eventually recovered. — *William Ruhlmann*

Blondie / Dec. 1976 / Chrysalis ✦✦✦✦
If new wave was about reconfiguring and recontextualizing simple pop-rock forms of the '50s and '60s in new, ironic, and aggressive ways, then Blondie, which took the girl-group style of the early and mid-'60s and added a '70s archness, fit right in. True punksters may have deplored the group early on (they never had the hip cachet of Talking Heads or even the Ramones), but Blondie's secret weapon, which was deployed increasingly over their career, was a canny pop straddle—they sent the music up and celebrated it at the same time. So, for instance, songs like "X Offender" (their first single) and "In the Flesh" (their first hit, in Australia) had the tough-girl-with-a-tender-heart tone of the Shangri-Las (Brill Building songwriter Ellie Greenwich even sang backup on the latter), while going one step too far into hard-edged decadence—that is, if you chose to see that. The whole point was that you could take Blondie either way. — *William Ruhlmann*

Plastic Letters / Oct. 1977 / Chrysalis ✦✦✦✦
Blondie's second album was a less distinctive version of its first, matching the first record's bright, sharp production (courtesy of Richard Gottehrer), but marking a fall-off in songwriting. The two best tracks—both UK hits—were "Denis," a remake of an oldie, and "(I'm Always Touched by Your) Presence, Dear," written by departed bass player Gary Valentine; that didn't bode well. Nevertheless, those songs were enough to assure the album's British success and to make some noise in the US. But Blondie would take a distinctly different approach next time out. — *William Ruhlmann*

☆ **Parallel Lines** / Sep. 1978 / Chrysalis ✦✦✦✦✦
Blondie turned to British pop producer Mike Chapman for their third album, on which they abandoned any pretensions to new wave legitimacy (just in time, given the decline of the new wave) and emerged as a pure pop band. But it wasn't just Chapman that made *Parallel Lines* Blondie's best album; it was the band's own songwriting, including Deborah Harry, Chris Stein, and James Destri's "Picture This"; Harry and Stein's "Heart of Glass"; Harry and new bass player Nigel Harrison's "One Way or Another"; and two contributions from non-band-member Jack Lee, "Will Anything Happen?" and "Hanging on the Telephone." That was enough to give Blondie a No. 1 on both sides of the Atlantic with "Heart of Glass" and three more UK hits. The album's depth and consistency are impressive; album tracks like "Fade Away and Radiate" and "Just Go Away" are as interesting as the songs pulled for singles. The result is state-of-the-art pop-rock circa 1978, with Harry's tough-girl glamour setting the pattern that would be exploited over the next decade by a host of successors led by Madonna. — *William Ruhlmann*

Eat to the Beat / Oct. 1979 / Chrysalis ✦✦✦✦
Just as Blondie's second album, *Plastic Letters*, was a pale imitation of their debut, their fourth album, *Eat to the Beat*, was a secondhand version of their breakthrough third album, *Parallel Lines*: one step forward, half a step back. There was an attempt, on such songs as "The Hardest Part" and "Atomic," to recreate the rock-disco fusion of the group's one major US hit, "Heart of Glass," without similar success. Elsewhere, the band just tried to cover too many stylistic bases. The British, who had long since been converted, made *Eat to the Beat* another chart-topper, but in the US, which still saw Blondie as a slightly comic one-hit wonder, the album was greeted for what it was—slick corporate rock without the tangy flavor that had made *Parallel Lines* such ear candy. — *William Ruhlmann*

Autoamerican / Nov. 1980 / Chrysalis ✦✦✦
The basic Blondie sextet was augmented, or replaced, by a dozen session musicians for the group's fifth album, *Autoamerican*, on which they continued to expand their stylistic range, with greater success, at least on certain tracks, than they had on *Eat to the Beat*. The rap pastiche "Rapture" and the Caribbean-flavored "The Tide Is High" both went to No. 1 on the singles charts, but they are the only memorable tracks on an album that leads off with a string-filled instrumental and finds Deborah Harry crooning ersatz '20s pop on "Here's Looking at You" and tackling Broadway show music in a cover of "Follow Me" from Camelot. What a mess. — *William Ruhlmann*

★ **The Best of Blondie** / 1981 / Chrysalis ✦✦✦✦✦
Although Blondie made several first-rate albums, most of their best songs were released as singles, which makes *The Best of Blondie* an essential collection. *The Best of Blondie* glosses over their punk roots—very little from the first album, apart from the vicious "Rip Her to Shreds" and the seductive "In the Flesh"—but the band's pop hits are among the finest of their era and encapsulate all of the virtues of new wave. Apart from genuine chart hits like "Heart of Glass," "One Way or Another," "Dreaming," "Call Me," "Atomic," "The Tide Is High," and "Rapture," *Best of Blondie* picks up several of the group's best album tracks, like "(I'm Always Touched by Your) Presence, Dear" and "Hanging on the Telephone." *The Best of Blondie* isn't all you need to know, but it is an excellent introduction to one of the best new wave bands. — *Stephen Thomas Erlewine*

The Hunter / Jul. 1982 / Chrysalis ♦♦

Autoamerican was Blondie's last real album, after which the band collapsed in legal problems and solo aspirations. *The Hunter* was made only because they still owed Chrysalis an album, and it sounds like the obligatory record it was. "Island of Lost Souls" (the album's only US singles chart entry) was a try at remaking "The Tide Is High," and "The Beast" tried to recreate at least the rap section of "Rapture." Elsewhere, Deborah Harry and Co. scraped the bottom of their songwriting barrel for an incomprehensible science fiction epic ("Dragonfly") and other second-rate material. — *William Ruhlmann*

Blonde & Beyond / Nov. 16, 1993 / Chrysalis ♦♦♦

Although it is a collection of rarities, outtakes, B-sides, and forgotten singles, *Blonde & Beyond* contains enough great music to make the disc enjoyable even to casual Blondie fans. — *Stephen Thomas Erlewine*

● **Platinum Collection** / Nov. 1, 1994 / EMI ♦♦♦♦

A double-CD, 47-track collection built around Blondie's singles, including every one of their US and UK A-sides and B-sides. Not a definitive best-of, as it excludes album tracks from consideration, but pretty close. Serious fans will be most interested in five 1975 demos, recorded before the band's first LP. Bootlegged in the past, these include "Once I Had a Love," an early version of "Heart of Glass," and a cover of the Shangri-Las' "Out in the Streets." Also of interest to fanatics are the extensive liner notes, including a detailed family tree and lengthy comments from everyone in the band except Harry and Stein. — *Richie Unterberger*

Blood, Sweat & Tears

f. 1967, New York, NY
Pop-Rock, Jazz-Rock

For a brief period at the end of the '60s and the start of the '70s, Blood, Sweat & Tears, which fused a rock 'n' roll rhythm section to a horn section, held out the promise of a jazz-rock fusion that could storm the pop charts. The band was organized in New York in 1967 out of the remnants of the Blues Project by keyboard player/singer Al Kooper (b. Feb. 5, 1944, Brooklyn, NY) and guitarist Steve Katz (b. May 9, 1945, Brooklyn, NY) of that group and saxophonist Fred Lipsius (b. Nov. 19, 1944, New York, NY). The rhythm section consisted of bassist Jim Fielder (b. Oct. 4, 1947, Denton, TX) and drummer Bobby Colomby (b. Dec. 20, 1944, New York, NY), and the horn section was filled out by trumpeters Randy Brecker (b. Nov. 27, 1945, Philadelphia, PA) and Jerry Weiss (b. May 1, 1946, New York) and trombonist Dick Halligan (b. Aug. 29, 1943, Troy, NY).

This eight-piece band signed to Columbia Records and recorded BS&T's debut album, *Child Is Father to the Man*, which was released in February 1968. Co-founder Kooper then departed, and the group was reorganized. Singer David Clayton-Thomas (b. David Thomsett, Sept. 13, 1941, Surrey, England) was added; Halligan moved to the keyboards; and trumpeters Chuck Winfield (b. Feb. 5, 1943, Monessen, PA) and Lew Soloff (b. Feb 20, 1944, Brooklyn, NY) replaced Brecker and Weiss, with Jerry Hyman (b. May 19, 1947, Brooklyn, NY) being added on trombone. This nine-piece unit, working with producer James William Guercio, made BS&T's self-titled second album, released in January 1969. It was a runaway hit, spawning three gold-selling Top Ten singles, "You've Made Me So Very Happy," "Spinning Wheel," and "And When I Die," selling three million copies and winning the Grammy Award for Album of the Year. It was also BS&T's highwater mark. Guercio left to work on a similar concept with Chicago Transit Authority, and BS&T increasingly became a backup group for Clayton-Thomas. Nevertheless, the third album, *Blood, Sweat & Tears 3* (1970), and the fourth, *Blood, Sweat & Tears 4* (1971), were substantial hits.

Clayton-Thomas went solo in early 1972 but returned in 1974. Numerous other personnel changes took place, as the group's commercial fortunes gradually declined. BS&T left Columbia after the release of its ninth album, *More Than Ever*, in 1976 and signed to ABC Records, for which it made *Brand New Day* (1977). From the late '70s on, BS&T existed largely as a group name for the concert activities of Clayton-Thomas and Colomby, who retained rights to the name. — *William Ruhlmann*

Child Is Father to the Man / Feb. 1968 / Columbia ♦♦♦♦

This is keyboard player/singer/arranger Al Kooper's finest work, an album on which he moves the folk-blues-rock amalgamation of the Blues Project into even wider pastures, taking in classical and jazz elements (including strings and horns), all without losing the pop essence that makes the hybrid work. This is one of the great albums of the eclectic post-*Sgt. Pepper* era of the late '60s, a time when you could borrow styles from Greenwich Village contemporary folk to San Francisco acid-rock and mix them into what seemed to have the potential to become a new American musical form. It's Kooper's bluesy songs, such as "I Love You More Than You'll Ever Know" and "I Can't Quit Her," and his singing that are the primary focus, but the album is an aural delight. This is the sound of a group of virtuosos enjoying themselves in the newly open

possibilities of pop music. Maybe it couldn't have lasted; anyway, it didn't. — *William Ruhlmann*

Blood, Sweat & Tears / Jan. 1969 / Columbia ♦♦♦♦

Arguably, the BS&T that made this self-titled second album, consisting of five of the eight original members and four newcomers, including singer David Clayton-Thomas, was really a different group from the one that made the debut album, *Child Is Father to the Man*, largely under the direction of singer-songwriter/keyboard player/arranger Al Kooper. BS&T Mach II had certain similarities to the original: the musical mixture of classical, jazz, and rock elements was still apparent, and the interplay between the horns and the keyboards was still occurring, even if those instruments were being played by different people. Kooper was even still present as an arranger on two tracks, notably the initial hit "You've Made Me So Very Happy." But the second BS&T, under the aegis of producer James William Guercio, was a less adventurous unit, and, as fronted by Clayton-Thomas, a far more commercial one. Not only did the album contain three songs that neared the top of the charts as singles—"Happy," "Spinning Wheel," and "And When I Die"—but the whole album, including an arrangement of "God Bless the Child" and the radical rewrite of Traffic's "Smiling Phases," was wonderfully accessible. It was a repertoire to build a career on, and BS&T did exactly that, although they never came close to equaling this album. — *William Ruhlmann*

Blood, Sweat & Tears 3 / Jun. 1970 / Columbia ♦♦♦

Blood, Sweat & Tears had a hard act to follow in recording their third album. Nevertheless, BS&T constructed a convincing, if not quite as impressive, companion to their previous hit. David Clayton-Thomas remained an enthusiastic blues shouter, and the band still managed to put together lively arrangements, especially on the Top 40 hits "Hi-De-Ho" and "Lucretia Mac Evil." Elsewhere, they recreated the previous album's jazzing up of Laura Nyro ("He's a Runner") and Traffic ("40,000 Headmen"), although their pretentiousness, on the extended "Symphony/Sympathy for the Devil," and their tendency to borrow other artists' better-known material (James Taylor's "Fire and Rain") rather than generating more of their own, were warning signs for the future. In the meantime, *BS&T 3* was another chart-topping gold hit. — *William Ruhlmann*

Blood, Sweat & Tears 4 / Jun. 1971 / Columbia ♦♦

Having relied largely on outside songwriting for its last two wildly successful albums, Blood, Sweat & Tears decided (as many groups had before) to bring some of that song publishing income into the family by writing their own material. Singer David Clayton-Thomas contributed the Top 40 hit "Go Down Gamblin'," and he and keyboard player Dick Halligan collaborated on another chart entry, "Lisa, Listen To Me." Ex-bandleader Al Kooper even contributed a track, "John the Baptist (Holy John)." But Side two was given over largely to songs by guitarist Steve Katz that were substandard, and the band's cohesion seemed to be disintegrating. Although the album scraped the Top Ten briefly and went gold, it marked the end of BS&T's period of wide commercial success on records. By the next outing, Clayton-Thomas had quit and the band's heyday was behind it. — *William Ruhlmann*

● **Blood, Sweat & Tears' Greatest Hits** / Feb. 1972 / Columbia ♦♦♦♦

Sometimes, a greatest-hits set is timed perfectly to gather a group's most successful and familiar performances just at the point when that group has passed the point of maximum exposure to the public, but before the public memory has had a chance to fade. That was the case when Columbia Records assembled this compilation for release in early 1972. At that point, Blood, Sweat & Tears had released four albums and scored six Top 40 hits, each of which is heard here. But lead singer David Clayton-Thomas had just quit the group, so the unit that recorded songs like "You've Made Me So Very Happy" was not working together anymore. And even when Clayton-Thomas returned, the band would continue to decline commercially. As such, BS&T's *Greatest Hits* captures the band's peak in 11 selections—seven singles chart entries, plus two album tracks from the celebrated debut album when Al Kooper helmed the group, and two more from the Grammy-winning multi-platinum second album. Using the short singles edits of songs like "And When I Die" emphasizes their radio-ready punch over the more extended suitelike arrangements on the albums, but this selection gains in focus what it lacks in ambition. For the millions who learned to love BS&T in 1969 when they were all over AM radio, this is the ideal selection of their most accessible material. — *William Ruhlmann*

● **What Goes Up: Best Of . . . .** / Nov. 7, 1995 / Sony ♦♦♦♦

Blood, Sweat & Tears' 11-track *Greatest Hits* album, released in February 1972, contained all of the group's six Top 40 singles, plus notable tracks from its two best albums, *Child Is Father to the Man* and *Blood Sweat & Tears*. Almost 24 years later came this 32-track, 138-minute, double-CD expansion, much of it extraneous. Where *Greatest Hits* contained the single edits of songs like "You've Made Me So Very Happy" and "And When I Die," here "all titles are original album versions," as the back cover noted, which means the jazzy interludes, frequently having nothing to do with the rest of the song, remained. There were a couple of unreleased tracks, and otherwise the bloated running time was filled out by, for example, four tracks from the 1972 stiff *New Blood*, which didn't even feature singer David Clayton-Thomas. Legacy would have better served consumers by either expanding the original 41-minute *Greatest Hits* to proper CD length with a few bonus tracks or reissuing the first two albums in a double-disc set, again with a few bonus tracks to fill up the time. This compilation did not enhance the band's reputation. And the error-filled liner notes are less than worthless. — *William Ruhlmann*

Luka Bloom (Barry Moore)

b. May 23, 1955, Newbridge, Ireland
Guitar, Vocals / Singer-Songwriter, Contemporary Folk
Before making his American debut, Barry Moore recorded three albums in Ireland. Perhaps because his brother is the revered Irish singer Christy Moore, he changed his name to Luka Bloom—Luka is taken from Suzanne Vega's song, Bloom from James Joyce's *Ulysses*. With his literate, melodic, original songs and impassioned live performances, Bloom earned a devoted following in the New York area, which led to his record contract with Reprise. While he can occasionally suffer from overworked lyrics and a cloying cuteness, Bloom is one of the best post-punk folk performers and songwriters. — *Stephen Thomas Erlewine*

● **Riverside** / Feb. 1990 / Reprise ◆◆◆◆
Expatriate Irishman Luka Bloom cloaks his Celtic folk songs in furious strumming on his "electro-acoustic" guitar, added instrumentation, and echo effects on everything, but he is still a folkie, blowing up his feelings to heroic proportions, whether it's the autobiography of "The Man Is Alive" or the romantic fantasy of "An Irishman in Chinatown." But the content is less convincing than the expression, which is more a characteristic of rock than folk. It isn't that Bloom has much to say, it's that he's so passionate about saying i; he's more Bono than Bob Dylan. Maybe it's an Irish thing. — *William Ruhlmann*

The Acoustic Motorbike / Jan. 1992 / Reprise ◆◆◆◆
Having made his mark in America and moved back home to Ireland, Luka Bloom attempted to incorporate into his Irish folk-rock some of the spirit of the country where he spent four years, covering LL Cool J's "I Need Love" and the Elvis Presley hit "Can't Help Falling in Love." But in his own songs, he didn't go much beyond such surface aspects of the US as Elvis and rap, preferring to devote himself to vague, cliched lyrics of love and longing (some of them not so much rapped as recited), once again set for the most part against his aggressive guitar strumming, various acoustic instruments, and a bottom provided by an Irish bodhran, sometimes played by his brother, Christy Moore. While Bloom's second album expanded somewhat on his first record's stylistic range and maintained its urgency, it lacked the debut's exuberance. Bloom was getting more serious when what he needed to do was to get more substantive. — *William Ruhlmann*

Turf / Jun. 14, 1994 / Reprise ◆◆◆
A portrait of the Irishman as an American neo-folkie. Having experimented with extra instrumentation on his first two albums, Luka Bloom made a man-with-guitar record his third time out, the better to emphasize his songs, which combined a strong folk traditionalism. (One was called "Black Is the Colour [of my true love's hair]"; another described an encounter with a mermaid.) "Freedom Song" mixed the stories of political activists from Ireland and the United States, and "Background Noise" was a tale of violence applicable anywhere, even if it referred to the Irish Troubles. All of this made for a more focused record than Bloom's second album, although his debut remained his most satisfying effort. — *William Ruhlmann*

Michael Bloomfield

b. Jul. 28, 1943, Chicago, IL, **d.** Feb. 15, 1981, San Francisco, CA
Guitar / Electric Chicago Blues, Blues-Rock
Michael Bloomfield was born July 28, 1943, in Chicago. An indifferent student and self-described social outcast, Bloomfield immersed himself in the multicultural music world that existed in Chicago in the 1950s.

He got his first guitar at age 13. Initially attracted to the roots-rock sound of Elvis Presley and Scotty Moore, Bloomfield soon discovered the electrified big-city blues music indigenous to Chicago. At the age of 14 the exuberant guitar *wunderkind* began to visit the blues clubs on Chicago's South Side with friend Roy Ruby in search of his new heroes: players such as Muddy Waters, Otis Spann, Howlin' Wolf, and Magic Sam. Not content with viewing the scene from the audience, Bloomfield was known to leap onto the stage, asking if he could sit in as he simultaneously plugged in his guitar and began playing riffs.

Bloomfield was quickly accepted on the South Side, as much for his ability as for the audiences' appreciation of the novelty of seeing a young white player in a part of town where few whites were seen. Bloomfield

soon discovered a group of like-minded outcasts. Young white players such as Paul Butterfield, Nick Gravenites, Charlie Musselwhite, and Elvin Bishop were also establishing themselves as fans who could hold their own with established bluesmen, many of whom were old enough to be their fathers.

In addition to playing with the established stars of the day, Bloomfield began to search out older, forgotten bluesmen, playing and recording with Sleepy John Estes, Yank Rachell, Little Brother Montgomery, and Big Joe Williams, among others. By this time he was managing a Chicago folk music club, the Fickle Pickle, and often hired older acoustic blues players for the Tuesday night blues sessions. Big Joe Williams memorialized those times in the song "Pick a Pickle" with the line "You know Mike Bloomfield . . . will always treat you right . . . come to the Pickle, every Tuesday night." Bloomfield's relationship with Big Joe Williams is documented in "Me and Big Joe," a moving short story detailing Bloomfield's adventures on the road with Williams.

Bloomfield's guitar work as a session player caught the ear of legendary CBS producer and talent scout John Hammond, Sr., who flew to Chicago and immediately signed him to a recording contract. However CBS was unsure of exactly how to promote their new artist, declining to release any of the tracks recorded by Bloomfield's band, which included harp player Charlie Musselwhite.

With a contract but not much else, Bloomfield returned to playing clubs around Chicago until he was approached by Paul Rothchild, the producer of the Paul Butterfield Blues Band albums. Bloomfield was recruited to play slide guitar and piano on early recordings (later released as *The Lost Elektra Sessions*) that were rejected for not fully capturing the sound of the band. Although more competitors than friends ("I knew Paul, was scared of him," remembered Mike), the addition of Bloomfield to the Butterfield Band provided Paul Butterfield with a musician of equal caliber. Paul and Michael inspired and challenged each other as they traded riffs and musical ideas, one establishing a pattern and the other following it, extending it, and handing it back.

In between recording sessions with the Butterfield Band, Bloomfield backed up Bob Dylan on the classic *Highway 61 Revisited* album, and appeared with him at the Newport Folk Festival in 1965 when Dylan stunned the purist "folk" crowd by playing electric rock 'n' roll. Declining an offer from Dylan to join his touring band, Bloomfield and the Butter Band returned to the studio; with the addition of pianist Mark Naftalin they finally captured their live sound on vinyl.

The first two Butterfield Blues Band albums, the Dylan sessions, and the live appearances by the Butterfield Band firmly established Bloomfield as one of the most talented and influential guitar players in America. The second album featured the Bloomfield composition "East-West," which ushered in an era of long instrumental psychedelic improvisations.

Bloomfield left the Butterfield Blues Band in early 1967, ostensibly to give original guitarist Elvin Bishop, in Mike's words, "a little space." Undoubtedly Bloomfield had also become uncomfortable with Paul Butterfield's position as bandleader and was anxious to lead his own band.

That band, The Electric Flag, included Bloomfield's old friends from Chicago, organist Barry Goldberg and singer-songwriter Nick Gravenites, as well as bass player Harvey Brooks and drummer Buddy Miles. The band was well received at its official debut at the Monterey Pop Festival but quickly fell apart because of drugs, egos, and poor management.

Bloomfield, weary of the road, suffering from insomnia, and uncomfortable in the role of guitar superstar, returned to San Francisco to score movies, produce other artists, and play studio sessions. One of those sessions was a day of jamming in the studio with keyboardist Al Kooper, who had previously worked with Bloomfield on the 1965 Dylan sessions.

Super Session, the resultant release, with Bloomfield on side one and guitarist Stephen Stills on side two, once again thrust Bloomfield into the spotlight. Kooper's production and the improvisational nature of the recording session captured the quintessential Bloomfield sound: the fast flurries of notes, the incredible string bending, the precise attack, and his masterful use of tension and release.

Although *Super Session* was the most successful recording of his career, Bloomfield considered it to be a "scam," more of an excuse to sell records than a pursuit of musical goals. After a followup live album, he "retired" to San Francisco and lowered his visibility.

In the '70s, Bloomfield played gigs in the San Francisco area and infrequently toured as Bloomfield and Friends, a group that usually included Mark Naftalin and Nick Gravenites. Bloomfield also occasionally helped out friends by lending his name to recording projects and business propositions such as the ill-fated Electric Flag reunion in 1974 and the KGB album in 1976. In the mid-'70s Bloomfield recorded a number of albums with a more traditional blues focus for smaller record labels. He also recorded an instructional album of various blues styles for *Guitar Player* magazine.

By the late '70s, Bloomfield's continuing drug and health problems caused erratic behavior and missed gigs, alienating a number of his old associates. Bloomfield continued playing with other musicians, including Dave Shorey and Jonathan Cramer. In the summer of 1980 he toured Italy with classical guitarist Woody Harris and cellist Maggie Edmondson. On November 15, 1980, Bloomfield joined Bob Dylan on stage at the Warfield Theater in San Francisco and jammed on "Like a Rolling Stone," the song they had recorded together 15 years earlier.

Michael Bloomfield was found dead in his car of a drug overdose in San Francisco on February 15, 1981.

Nick Gravenites remembers Michael Bloomfield this way: "I thought he was a huge giant of a person. I think the totality of his character is the thing that impressed me most. People forget how charismatic he was. He had a certain charisma about him, people wanted to be around him, touch the hem of his garment, that sort of thing. I think it was the totality of his character I was impressed with, not only his musical ability but also his intellect, his sense of humor, his compassion, his generosity, all those things that make up a human being. And those are my fondest memories, of character.

"He was quite a forceful personality. He was quite a wit. And also had a very deep character—was very generous, very soulful. The effect that he had on me and people around him, people that knew him and loved his music and stuff was profound.

"Michael's friends, the ones that were closest to him, really loved the guy. And they did it for a lot of reasons. He helped them live their lives, make something out of their lives in many ways, very profoundly. I can still think in terms of those major, those big terms, when I think about Michael." —*Jan Mark Wolkin*

● **Super Session** / 1968 / Columbia ✦✦✦✦
Al Kooper was the mastermind behind this appropriately named album, one side of which features his "spontaneous" studio collaboration with Mike Bloomfield and the other a session with Stephen Stills. The recordings have an off-the-cuff energy that displays the inventiveness of the two guitarists to best advantage. The best-selling recording of Bloomfield's career, it inspired the followup *The Live Adventures of Mike Bloomfield and Al Kooper*. —*Jeff Tamarkin*

The Live Adventures of Mike Bloomfield and Al Kooper / 1969 / Columbia ✦✦
Recorded over three nights in 1968 at the Fillmore Auditorium in San Francisco, the follow-up to the acclaimed *Super Session* has its moments, but is mostly long on '60s noodly grooviness and lacking in focus and inspiration. It's notable (sort of) for Bloomfield's singing debut. —*Cary Wolfson*

It's Not Killing Me / 1969 / CBS ✦✦
Let's see. For his first solo album, take a brilliant young guitarist who can barely sing and put the emphasis on . . . his vocals. Well, somebody thought it was a good idea. Too bad they were wrong. There are just a few examples of that B.B. King-inflected guitar style among the rock and country-flavored throwaways. —*Cary Wolfson*

Live at Bill Graham's Fillmore West / 1969 / CBS ✦✦✦✦
This session from early 1969 featured Nick Gravenites, Mark Naftalin, John Kahn, and Snooky Flowers (among others), with cameos from Taj Mahal and Jesse Ed Davis, but it's clear from the opening notes who the real star is. Over the years, Bloomfield's titanic solos on "Blues on a Westside" have dwarfed the rest of the album in my memory, but the truth is his playing just burns across every track. (More of Michael's great guitar work from these shows is on Nick Gravenites' *My Labors* on Columbia.) —*Cary Wolfson*

Triumvirate / 1973 / Columbia ✦✦✦
In 1973 someone at Columbia evidently decide to try and recoup some of the investment the label had made in Bloomfield and John Hammond—they were thrown into a recording studio along with Dr. John, who had recently scored a hit with "Right Place, Wrong Time." It probably sounded like a good idea at the time, but the results were uninspired. Pass by this CD and pick up any one of his solo recordings instead. —*Jan Mark Wolkin*

Try It Before You Buy It / 1975 / One Way ✦✦
Try It Before You Buy It is one of Michael Bloomfield's neglected albums, and there's a reason why. Although there's some very fine playing scattered throughout the album, the performances are uneven and unfocused. Furthermore, the album leans too close to straight rock 'n' roll for blues purists. If you dig hard, there are some rewards on *Try It Before You Buy It*, but on the whole, it's one that should be left on the shelf. —*Thom Owens*

Living in the Fast Lane / 1980 / AJK ✦✦✦
Michael Bloomfield was a pioneer in blues-rock, one of the performers who found a way to maintain his own sound while paying tribute to the blues greats who created the music he idolized. The ten tracks presented on *Living in the Fast Lane* weren't as vital as his earlier material, but they were done with the same intensity and passion that marked all his numbers. They were backed on several cuts by Duke Tito and the Marin Country Playboys, while on "When I Get Home," the Singers of the Church of God in Christ joined lead vocalist Roger Troy for a rousing, spirit-filled performance that was the album's high point. —*Ron Wynn*

Don't Say That I Ain't Your Man / May 10, 1994 / Sony ✦✦✦✦
Fifteen tracks covering the pioneering blues-rock guitarist's '60s work, which was by far his best and most influential. Bloomfield worked with lots of bands during the decade, and the compilation flits rather hurriedly from his contributions to the Paul Butterfield Blues Band and Electric Flag to his collaborations with Al Kooper and some late-'60s solo tracks. (None of his groundbreaking mid-'60s work with Dylan is here.) Collectors will be interested in the first five songs, which date from previously unreleased sessions produced by John Hammond in late 1964 and early 1965. Featuring Charlie Musselwhite on harmonica, this pre-Butterfield Blues Band outfit plays convincingly, but the material is standard-issue, and Bloomfield's vocals are thin and weak. (They didn't improve much over time.) As befits Bloomfield's considerable but erratic talent, this is an interesting but erratic compilation; seek out the first two Paul Butterfield albums for a more cohesive showcase of his skills. —*Richie Unterberger*

Blossom Toes

f. 1965, England, **db.** 1969
Psychedelic
They never had any commercial success in the UK or the US, but Blossom Toes were one of the more interesting British psychedelic groups of the late '60s. Starting as the Ingoes, just another of thousands of British R&B/beat bands of the mid-'60s, the group hooked up with legendary impresario Giorgio Gomelsky (early mentor of the Stones and manager of the Yardbirds and Soft Machine, among others) in 1966. Gomelsky changed their name and put them on his Marmalade label. Their 1967 debut LP was miles away from R&B, reflecting an extremely British whimsy and skilled, idiosyncratic songwriting more in line with Ray Davies. After some personnel changes, the group released their second (and final) album a couple of years later. Another extremely accomplished work, it was markedly different in character than their first effort, showing a far more sober tone and heavier, guitar-oriented approach.

The group broke up at the end of the decade; members Brian Godding and Brian Belshaw formed the equally obscure B.B. Blunder, and Godding is still active on the fringes of the British experimental rock scene. —*Richie Unterberger*

We Are Ever So Clean / 1967 / Marmalade ✦✦✦✦
Imagine the late-'60s Kinks crossed with a touch of the absurdist British wit of the Bonzo Dog Band, and you have an idea of the droll charm of Blossom Toes' debut album. Songwriters Brian Godding and Jim Cregan were the chief architects of the Toes' whimsical and melodic vision, which conjured images of a sun-drenched Summer of Love, London style. With its references to royal parks, tea time, watchmakers, intrepid balloon makers, "Mrs. Murphy's Budgerigar," and the like, it's a distinctly British brand of whimsy. It has since been revealed that sessionmen performed a lot of these orchestral arrangements, which embellished the band's sparkling harmonies and (semi-buried) guitars. But the cello, brass, flute, and tinkling piano have a delicate beauty that serves as an effective counterpoint. The group sings and plays as though they have wide grins on their faces, and the result is one of the happiest, most underappreciated relics of British psychedelia. —*Richie Unterberger*

If Only for a Moment / 1969 / Marmalade ✦✦✦✦
Brian Godding and Jim Cregan were still Blossom Toes' chief songwriters on their second album, but the LP stands in bold contrast to their debut in sound and attitude. Having scuttled the orchestra and developed their chops in the two-year interlude, the record bears the influence of heavy California psychedelia and Captain Beefheart with its intricate, interwoven guitar lines and occasional gruff dissonance. The more serious instrumental approach spills over to the lyrics, which are somber and at times even gloomy, occasionally reflecting the social turbulence of the late '60s, with their uncertain tenor and references to ominous "peace loving men" and "love bombs." Far less uplifting than their debut, the weighty approach is leavened by the close harmonies and sparkling guitar interplay. While not as memorable as the first album, it's above average late-'60s psychedelia that almost acts as the downer flipside to the stoned, happy-face ambience of their early work. —*Richie Unterberger*

The Psychedelic Sound of Blossom Toes / 1987 / [Bootleg] ✦✦
Not only must the Blossom Toes count as one of the most obscure '60s bands ever to merit a bootleg, but this document of a 1967 show at a Swedish club must rank as one of the weirder '60s boots by any criteria. At this point, the Blossom Toes had one album to their credit, a very

good one of veddy British, orchestral psychedelic pop. In harsh contrast, this is a shambling, raucous, discordant, even free-form electric set, in which the group takes their interest in Captain Beefheart (still very much a cult figure) to barely listenable extremes. A great deal of the record's time is occupied by the 11-minute "Electricity" and the 16-minute "Captain Trip," freakout jams that haven't aged well despite strange chanting and virtually no conventional song structure. The relatively disciplined guitar psychedelia of "Listen to the Silence" (which would appear on their second official LP) is actually pretty good, but the sound isn't so hot. What's more, the two (faintly recorded) acoustic numbers that compose the rest of the album are not, in fact, Blossom Toes, it has been revealed, but British singer Gary Farr, a roadie who took the stage occasionally (and also takes some vocals on "Electricity"). This isn't even especially recommended to the small clique of Blossom Toes fans, but if find it you must, this limited edition can still be detected via mail-order collector companies. —*Richie Unterberger*

● **Collection** / 1988 / Decal ✦✦✦✦
The definitive anthology, packaging most of *We Are Ever So Clean* and the entirety of *If Only For a Moment*. Unfortunately, a couple of minor tracks from the first LP were omitted for space reasons, but as compensation it includes the non-LP 1968 single "Postcard"/"Everyone's Leaving Me Now," which is quite similar in mood to the *Ever So Clean* songs. The double album includes an exhaustive history of the group by John Platt. —*Richie Unterberger*

New Day: Blossom Toes '70 / 1989 / Decal ✦✦✦
Originally titled *Workers Playtime*, this album was attributed to B.B. Blunder when it was first released in 1971. It appears under the Blossom Toes discography because it was reissued, confusingly, as *New Day* in 1989 by Decal, who attributed the LP not to B.B. Blunder, but to "Blossom Toes '70 (formerly B.B. Blunder)." Featuring ex-Blossom Toes Brian Godding, Brian Belshaw, and Kevin Westlake, B.B. Blunder's sole outing had some nice, typically thick, circa 1970-British rock guitars, and some bits of promising melodies buried in the mix. Overall, though, one gets the impression that the group went into the studio before getting the songs into shape. There's a lot of meandering, and the songs don't say much or never get to the point. Mick Taylor makes a little-known cameo appearance on bottleneck guitar on "New Day." —*Richie Unterberger*

Kurtis Blow

b. Aug. 9, 1959, New York, NY
Keyboards, Vocals / Hip Hop, Old School Rap
Arguably rap's first crossover star, at least from a chart standpoint, New Yorker Blow began doing both social protest/Afrocentric material and boasting and posturing material, though not to the degree that has since become commonplace. His landmark recording, "The Breaks," was an eye-opener for its time in terms of pace, verbal dexterity, and its rhythm track. Blow was also a big-time producer at one point, using the likes of Bob Dylan and George Clinton in guest stints and incorporating bits from television shows and cartoons in his production. Blow was finally overhauled by New School producers and rappers in the late '80s, and his early work now sounds quite dated by comparison. —*Ron Wynn*

Kurtis Blow / 1980 / Mercury ✦✦✦✦
Kurtis Blow exploded onto the fledgling rap scene with "The Breaks," still one of the rawest, most hypnotic bits of rhythm and oral narrative ever issued. Blow's defiant, posturing rap, punctuated by drums that seemed to signify an invading army, surprised, shocked, and amazed listeners totally unprepared in 1980 for anything so stark. An edited version got only mild pop response, but the complete single was a huge hit among Black and club audiences. The song was so definitive that it rendered everything else on the LP irrelevant, even the good second single "Hard Times." —*Ron Wynn*

Deuce / 1981 / Mercury ✦✦✦✦
Things cooled quickly for Kurtis Blow after "The Breaks" in 1980. He was unable to get any single from this record on the charts, even though "Rockin'" and "It's Gettin' Hot" were well produced and competently delivered. But rap was still far from being a mainstream phenomenon, and this album did very poorly commercially. —*Ron Wynn*

Ego Trip / 1984 / Mercury ✦✦✦
Kurtis Blow briefly returned to the spotlight with the single "Basketball" from this LP. His brand of sparse, electro-funk rap was fading, and it was clear that Blow's skills were in production rather than performance. "Eight Million Stories" was a decent cut inspired by the old "Naked City" television series, and "Fallin' in Love Again" was among his better romantic efforts; but Blow's albums were always erratic propositions, and this one proved no different. —*Ron Wynn*

★ **Best of Kurtis Blow** / Jun. 7, 1994 / Mercury ✦✦✦✦✦
While he made many groundbreaking singles, Kurtis Blow was never a consistent album artist, making this best-of collection his definitive artistic statement. Throughout the early '80s, Blow helped define what

rap could do, and these tracks confirm his status as one of hip-hop's legendary acts. —*Stephen Thomas Erlewine*

Blue Cheer

f. 1967, San Francisco, CA, db. 1972
Hard Rock, Psychedelic, Heavy Metal, Acid Rock
San Francisco-based Blue Cheer was what, in the late '60s, they used to call a "power trio": Dickie Peterson (b. 1948, Grand Forks, ND) (bass, vocals), Paul Whaley (drums), and Leigh Stephens (guitar). They played what later was called heavy metal, and when they debuted in January 1968 with the album *Vincebus Eruptum* and a Top 40 cover of Eddie Cochran's hit "Summertime Blues," they sounded louder and more extreme than anything that had come before them. As it turned out, they were a precursor of much that would come after. Unfortunately, Blue Cheer itself didn't get much chance to profit from its prescience. Shortly after its breakthrough, the group was wracked by personnel changes. Leigh Stephens was replaced by Randy Holden after the release of the second album, *Outsideinside* (August 1968). Holden left during the recording of the third album, and Bruce Stephens (b.1946) (vocals, guitar), and Ralph Burns Kellogg (keyboards) joined to finish *New! Improved! Blue Cheer* (March 1969). Then Whaley quit and was replaced by Norman Mayell (b. 1942, Chicago), leaving Peterson as the only original member. Bruce Stephens quit during the recording of the fourth album, *Blue Cheer* (December 1969), and Gary L. Yoder joined to complete it. Peterson, Kellogg, Mayell, and Yoder then made *The Original Human Being* (September 1970), and *Oh! Pleasant Hope* (April 1971) before Blue Cheer broke up. Dickie Peterson reorganized a new version of the group in 1979; and in 1985 he, Whaley, and guitarist Tony Ranier released a new Blue Cheer album, *The Beast Is Back . . .* —*William Ruhlmann*

Vincebus Eruptum / Jan. 1968 / Philips ✦✦✦✦
Blue Cheer's debut psychedelic sludgefest features their explosive reworking of Eddie Cochran's "Summertime Blues." —*Rick Clark*

Outsideinside / Aug. 1968 / Philips ✦✦✦✦
Outsideinside may not have the Frisco trio's death-blast version of Eddie Cochran's classic "Summertime Blues," but there's more than enough tape-saturated hard psychedelic sludge here ("Just a Little Bit" [No. 92], and "The Hunter"). —*Rick Clark*

Louder Than God: Best of Blue Cheer / 1986 / Rhino ✦✦✦✦
The fact that this collection is available only on vinyl may be a drawback for some folks, but (on one level) Blue Cheer, in all its grungy glory, makes even more sense on 8-track than on CD, so what's the complaint? After all, this one has "Just a Little Bit," and the Mercury disc doesn't. If you can find their first two albums, *Vincebus Eruptum* and *Outsideinside,* then you will have all the Blue Cheer you'll ever need. —*Rick Clark*

● **Good Times Are So Hard to Find** / Oct. 1990 / Mercury ✦✦✦✦
This overview spans Blue Cheer's entire catalog. If only their first two albums of over-the-top psychedelic distorto-blare had been represented a little more. —*Rick Clark*

Blue Nile

f. 1981, Glasgow, Scotland
Pop-Rock, Dream-Pop
Glasgow's Blue Nile was formed in 1981 by vocalist/guitarist/synthesist Paul Buchanan and synthesizer manipulators Robert Bell and Joseph Moore. The independent single "I Love This Life" was picked up for distribution by the RSO label, which shortly went bankrupt. The band's demo tape wound up at Linn Products, a hi-fi company, who used it to test new equipment. The company liked what it heard and decided to venture into the recording business, signing Blue Nile and releasing its debut album, *A Walk Across the Rooftops,* in 1984. The album received high praise for its melancholy, atmospheric, haunting sound, and was eventually picked up by A&M. Blue Nile was not heard from again until 1989, when they finally released a follow-up, *Hats,* and played their first live shows ever. After a long period of inactivity, the band returned in 1996 with *Peace at Last.* —*Steve Huey*

A Walk Across the Rooftops / May 1984 / A&M ✦✦✦✦
This Scottish trio's 1984 debut, originally on Linn Records, is a beautifully atmospheric collection of synth-heavy songscapes. The dichotomy between the cool synthesized musical washes (with periodic percolating drum machine parts) and the yearning, passionate (yet strangely disconnected) vocals is engaging. This album could have been the soundtrack to Jonathan Pryce's lonely, quenchless dreams in the Terry Gilliam movie, *Brazil.* The Linn version sounds superior to the A&M release. —*Rick Clark*

● **Hats** / Oct. 1989 / A&M ✦✦✦✦
The follow-up to *A Walk Across the Rooftops* was five years in the making. The songs aren't as memorable, but the results are still coolly haunting. "The Downtown Lights" and "Headlights on Parade" are among the standout tracks. —*Rick Clark*

Peace at Last / Jul. 1996 / Warner Brothers ✦✦✦
The members of the Blue Nile seem to have taken seriously all those articles and reviews about what audiophiles and technicians they are, and this time around they've spent a half-dozen years concocting an album that sounds as if they made at least some of it in their living rooms rather than in their space-age studio. They achieve the appearance of simplicity and humanity by foregrounding either an acoustic guitar or piano on most tracks, by restraining other instrumentation, by making their synthesizers sound like strings most of the time, and by using real strings on occasion. All of which creates appropriate settings for Paul Buchanan's songs of domestic contentment. "Happiness," "Sentimental Man," "Holy Love"—the titles tell the story, though they don't reveal the underlying fear that it will all go bust. ("Now that I've found peace at last," Buchanan sings to open up the album, "tell me, Jesus, will it last?") Nor do they explain why a guy who keeps insisting that he's happy sounds so mournful. Buchanan belongs to the Bono/Peter Gabriel school of throaty emotiveness, in which sudden, arbitrary ascensions toward the falsetto signal fits of otherwise unacknowledged passion (or maybe just a sneeze coming on). In Buchanan, the singing style and the loose structure of the songs make his protestations of tranquility unconvincing. That may be what he intends, especially since they lend an implied depth to what is the Blue Nile's lightest effort yet. — *William Ruhlmann*

Blue Öyster Cult

f. 1967, Long Island, NY
Hard Rock, Heavy Metal, Arena Rock
Blue Öyster Cult was the thinking man's heavy-metal group. Put together on a college campus by a couple of rock critics, it maintained a close relationship with a series of literary figures (often in the fields of science fiction and horror), including Eric Von Lustbader, Patti Smith, Michael Moorcock, and Stephen King, while turning out some of the more listenable metal music of the early and mid-'70s. The band that became Blue Öyster Cult was organized in 1967 at Stony Brook College on Long Island by students (and later rock critics) Sandy Pearlman and Richard Meltzer as Soft White Underbelly and consisted of Andy Winters (bass), Donald "Buck Dharma" Roeser (guitar), John Wiesenthal—quickly replaced by Allen Lanier—(keyboards), and Albert Bouchard (drums), with Pearlman managing and Pearlman and Meltzer writing songs. Initially without a lead singer, they added Les Bronstein on vocals. This quintet signed to Elektra Records and recorded an album that was never released. They then dropped Bronstein and replaced him with their road manager, Eric Bloom, as the band's name was changed to Oaxaca. A second Elektra album also went unreleased, though a single was issued under the name the Stalk-Forrest Group.
Cut loose by Elektra, they changed their name again, to Blue Öyster Cult, and signed to Columbia Records in late 1971, by which time Winters had been replaced by Albert Bouchard's brother Joe. *Blue Öyster Cult*, their debut album, was released in January 1972 and made the lower reaches of the charts. Columbia sent a promotional EP, *Live Bootleg*, to radio stations in October, and followed with BÖC's second album, *Tyranny and Mutation*, in February 1973. Their third album, *Secret Treaties*, was released in April 1974 and became their first to break into the Top 100. (It eventually went gold.) BÖC released a live double album, *On Your Feet or on Your Knees*, in February 1975. In May 1976 came their fourth studio album, *Agents of Fortune*, including the Top 40 (Top Ten on some charts) hit single "(Don't Fear) the Reaper" (featured in the classic John Carpenter horror film *Halloween*), which became their first gold and then platinum album. (*On Your Feet* went gold shortly after.) BÖC's sixth overall album, *Spectres*, was released in October 1977 and went gold in January 1978. In September 1978 came a second live album, *Some Enchanted Evening*, which eventually would become BÖC's second million-seller, followed by the studio album *Mirrors* in June 1979. A year later, BÖC released its ninth album, *Cultosaurus Erectus*, with the gold *Fire of Unknown Origin*, containing the Top 40 hit "Burnin' for You," following in June 1981.
In the summer of 1981, drummer Albert Bouchard was replaced by the band's tour manager and lighting designer, Rick Downey. BÖC's third live album, *Extraterrestrial Live*, was released in April 1982, followed by the studio album *The Revolution by Night* in October 1983. Downey left in 1984 and was replaced in 1985 by Jimmy Wilcox. The same year, Lanier left and was replaced by Tommy Zvonchek. BÖC released its 13th album, *Club Ninja*, in January 1986. Bassist Joe Bouchard left in 1986 and was replaced by Jon Rogers. In 1987 Lanier returned to the group, and Ron Riddle replaced Wilcox on drums. BÖC's 14th album, the concept recording *Imaginos*, became their final new album on Columbia Records in July 1988. BÖC scored the movie *Bad Channels* in 1992, by which time Chuck Burgi had replaced Ron Riddle on drums. In 1994 Blue Öyster Cult released *Cult Classic*, an album of rerecorded favorites, in connection with the use of their music in the TV miniseries of horror novelist Stephen King's *The Stand*. — *William Ruhlmann*

Blue Öyster Cult / Jan. 1972 / Columbia ✦✦✦✦
Blue Öyster Cult's debut album provided the missing link between the heavy, blues-based rock of the late '60s and the bombastic heavy metal of the '70s and beyond. You could hear major influences like Steppenwolf, with its melodic, aggressive rock; the Rolling Stones (post-1965); and even boogie bands like Canned Heat. But BOC streamlined the approach, picked up the tempo, overlaid the guitars, brought the rhythm section up in the mix, and de-emphasized the blues, giving the music a machine-like propulsion. Manager/co-producer Sandy Pearlman (who co-wrote five songs) and lyricist Richard Meltzer (who co-wrote two) may have seen the group as a vehicle for their "clever" (in fact, pretentious) lyrics, but in fact, lead vocalist Eric Bloom was the weakest element in the band, and you couldn't make out much of what he had to say over guitarist Donald "Buck Dharma" Roeser's furious power chording. What you could seemed to express some sort of mythology—or demonology; future metal bands would fill their songs with just such half-baked philosophies. *Blue Öyster Cult* was not quite full-fledged heavy metal: the production was too compressed, the playing too light and energetic. But it was the sound of something new and different in the world of hard rock. — *William Ruhlmann*

Tyranny and Mutation / Feb. 1973 / Columbia ✦✦✦✦
Co-producers Murray Krugman and Sandy Pearlman achieved a far sharper, more spacious production on Blue Öyster Cult's second album than they had in the cramped sound of its first, twinning, for instance, the high, ringing tone of Donald Roeser's lead guitar to Albert Bouchard's cymbals or Alan Lanier's keyboards and adding echo to give presence to Eric Bloom's still barely (or not quite) discernable vocals. In a sense, it's remarkable that albums like this have been categorized as heavy metal: despite the fullness of the aural attack, the fast tempos and raunchy sound give it much more the feel of old rockabilly or punk-rock-to-come. — *William Ruhlmann*

Secret Treaties / Apr. 1974 / Columbia ✦✦
If Blue Öyster Cult's first two albums had established its particular brand of high-energy hard rock and murky, if melodramatic, lyrical world view, *Secret Treaties* took a generic approach to that persona. The riffs (many recycled) ruled, and the same sort of imagery—titles like "Career of Evil," "Flaming Telepaths," and "Astronomy"—suggested that BÖC was rocking in place rather than moving forward. Maybe all that suggested a consistency of theme, especially in Sandy Pearlman and Richard Meltzer's mythology for the group, but it sounded dangerously like repetition; they'd said and done these things better on their debut. BÖC would take more than two years to make their next studio album. — *William Ruhlmann*

On Your Feet or on Your Knees / Feb. 1975 / Columbia ✦✦
Blue Öyster Cult's first live album was also its first to peak inside the Top 40, which is more of an indication of the audience the group was building up through extensive touring than of its quality. Songs that had a tight, concentrated impact on studio albums got elongated here, and that impact was dissipated. And the song selection left a great deal to be desired if this were to be a fitting summation of the band's career so far. By its 1974 tour, BÖC had dropped some classics from its first album, and the less impressive material from the third album was no substitute. — *William Ruhlmann*

● **Agents of Fortune** / May 1976 / Columbia ✦✦✦✦
Nothing Blue Öyster Cult had produced previously prepared listeners for its infectious mid-tempo hit, "(Don't Fear) the Reaper," which propelled it into a higher commercial orbit and caused (or reflected) a change in the balance of power in the group. The song was written by guitarist Donald "Buck Dharma" Roeser and was an indication that the band was now largely doing its own songwriting; co-producer Sandy Pearlman earned only one co-writing credit on the record, while drummer Albert Bouchard had five. Poetess Patti Smith, meanwhile, not only co-wrote two tracks, but performed on one, "The Revenge of Vera Gemini." The result was a record much more in a pop-rock vein than the vaunted metal of the first three albums, and BÖC's biggest hit ever. — *William Ruhlmann*

Spectres / Oct. 1977 / Columbia ✦✦✦
On the all-important follow-up to its commercial breakthrough with *Agents of Fortune*, Blue Öyster Cult introduced some enjoyable additions to its repertoire in "Godzilla," and "R.U. Ready 2 Rock," but did not come up with a song as memorable as "(Don't Fear) the Reaper," despite trying the same formula with "Fireworks" and "Nosferatu." Instead of consolidating its success, the group seemed to be, as one of the better songs had it, "Goin' Through the Motions," seemingly unable to follow through on the pop aspirations of the previous album and unwilling to retreat to the metal pretensions of its early records. Talk about being caught between a rock and a hard place—just when Blue Öyster Cult should have been conquering, they seemed ready to retreat. — *William Ruhlmann*

Some Enchanted Evening / Sep. 1978 / Columbia ♦♦
Blue Öyster Cult marks time with a second live album on which they turn out good, if redundant, concert versions of recent favorites like "(Don't Fear) the Reaper" and "Godzilla," and add to their repertoire of live covers such oldies as the MC5's "Kick Out the Jams" and the Animals' "We Gotta Get Out of This Place." A perfectly acceptable, completely unnecessary souvenir record from a hard-touring band of the '70s. (It should perhaps be noted that the mid—to late '70s was a period when more live albums than usual were being released, especially in the wake of Peter Frampton's massively successful 1976 LP *Frampton Comes Alive.*) — *William Ruhlmann*

Mirrors / Jun. 1979 / Columbia ♦♦♦
Blue Öyster Cult tried a new producer on *Mirrors*, replacing longtime mentor Sandy Pearlman with Tom Werman, a CBS staffer who had worked with Cheap Trick and Ted Nugent. The result is an album that tried to straddle pop and hard rock just as those acts did, emphasizing choral vocals (plus female backup) and a sharp, trebly sound. But this approach appeared to displease longtime metal-oriented fans without attracting new ones: "In Thee" became a minor singles-chart entry, but the album broke BÖC's string of five gold or platinum albums in a row. The real reason simply may have been that the songs weren't distinctive enough. Much of this was generic hard rock that could have been made by any one of a dozen '70s arena bands. — *William Ruhlmann*

Cultosaurus Erectus / Jun. 1980 / Columbia ♦♦♦
Signing on with Deep Purple/Black Sabbath producer Martin Birch, Blue Öyster Cult made more of a guitar-heavy hard-rock album in *Cultosaurus Erectus*, after flirting with pop ever since the success of *Agents of Fortune.* (They also promoted this album by going out on a co-headlining tour with Sabbath.) Gone are the female backup singers, the pop hooks, the songs based on keyboard structures, and they are replaced by lots of guitar solos and a beefed-up rhythm section. But the band still was not generating strong enough material to compete with their concert repertoire, so they found themselves in the bind of being a strong touring act unable to translate that success into record sales. — *William Ruhlmann*

Fire of Unknown Origin / Jun. 1981 / Columbia ♦♦♦
Just when Blue Öyster Cult had nearly been written off after a series of mediocre albums, the band came roaring back with *Fire of Unknown Origin*, their best record in five years, on which they found the appropriate mixture of metal, rock and pop that had eluded them since "(Don't Fear) the Reaper." With Sandy Pearlman, Richard Meltzer, and Patti Smith, among others, back in the writing credits, the Cult sounded as if they'd been listening hard to their first two albums and *Agents of Fortune* for inspiration. Images of fire, darkness, and war were everywhere; the guitar riffs were inventive; and the melodies compelling. There was a new hit single in the Top 40 "Burnin' for You," but the overall song quality was unusually high. Somehow, BÖC had recaptured the trashy gothic appeal of its best work, and the result was a gold-selling album that seemed to put the band's career back on track. — *William Ruhlmann*

Extraterrestrial Live / Apr. 1982 / Columbia ♦♦♦
Of Blue Öyster Cult's three live albums, this is the one to own. The two-record set, partially recorded on BÖC's home base of Long Island, contains the band's biggest hits, "(Don't Fear) the Reaper" (making its second live appearance) and "Burnin' for You," as well as longtime concert favorites like "Cities on Flame," "The Red and the Black," and "Godzilla." But it isn't just the superior song selection that gives this album the nod over *On Your Feet or on Your Knees* and *Some Enchanted Evening;* BÖC had regained its momentum in 1982 with *Fire of Unknown Origin*, and this album demonstrated their renewed spirit in the forum in which they were most comfortable—live work. In the absence of a good compilation of studio work, *Extraterrestrial Live* is the best overview of BÖC available. — *William Ruhlmann*

The Revolution by Night / Oct. 1983 / Columbia ♦♦
Blue Öyster Cult seemed to regain its direction with *Fire of Unknown Origin*, but simultaneously, the band was starting to fragment, with founding member and notable songwriter Albert Bouchard departing. On *The Revolution by Night*, BÖC brought in various hired guns, such as Aldo Nova and former Alice Cooper band member Neal Smith, and turned to Loverboy's producer, Bruce Fairbairn, who gave them a similar radio-ready rock sound. But though the album brought BÖC its fourth (and final) singles chart entry in "Shooting Shark," it lacked a distinctive identity. You could close your eyes and not know whether you were listening to Loverboy or Foreigner or any one of several other arena rock bands. No wonder it became the band's lowest charting album in a decade. — *William Ruhlmann*

Club Ninja / Jan. 1986 / Columbia ♦♦
Blue Öyster Cult's gradual disintegration continued with *Club-Ninja*, on which original member Allen Lanier was replaced by keyboard player Tommy Zvoncheck. Several compositions from outside the band were featured, notably the Leggatt Brothers' "White Flags" and a couple of

generic metal exercises by Bob Halligan, who had contributed much the same sort of material to Judas Priest. On what should have been the positive side, Sandy Pearlman was back in the producer's chair. But he did nothing to arrest BÖC's decline into musical anonymity. — *William Ruhlmann*

Career of Evil: The Metal Years / 1987 / Columbia ♦♦
Contrary to what some may believe, Blue Öyster Cult was never strictly a heavy metal band. In fact, some of its greatest triumphs—including "Don't Fear the Reaper" and "Burning for You"—weren't in a metal vein. But there's no denying that the band made its share of outstanding contributions to the genre, which are generally well represented by this "best-of" compilation. Because Blue Öyster Cult tended to be heavier live than in the studio, Columbia did the right thing by favoring its live recordings over its studio material. Blistering live versions of "Godzilla," "Cities on Flame," "Hot Rails to Hell" and "The Red and the Black"—'70s metal classics that no headbanger should be without—pack an undeniably ferocious punch. The pedestrian "Beat Em Up" from 1986's *Club Ninja* was recorded when the group was past its prime; but in general, this CD does a fine job of illustrating just how valuable the rockers' contributions to metal were. — *Alex Henderson*

Imaginos / Jul. 1988 / Columbia ♦♦♦
Blue Öyster Cult went out with a bang as a major-label recording act on their 14th and last new Columbia album, *Imaginos*. Sandy Pearlman seems to have had the idea for this concept album as early as *Secret Treaties*, on which some of its music appeared, and the recording took place over a six-year period. (As a result, album credits give the erroneous impression that the original band had re-formed.) The storyline, which is easier to appreciate in the liner notes than on the record, concerns a mysterious, protean 19th-century figure who has a talent for turning up at key moments in history and influencing them for the worse. This is perhaps BÖC's most consistent album, certainly its most uncompromising (none of its usual nods to pop accessibility), and also the closest thing to a real heavy-metal statement from a band that never quite fit that description. Unfortunately, this ambitious work came out as BÖC was dropping out of the frontline of the music business, so the album that comes closest to defining Blue Öyster Cult turned into its creative swan song. — *William Ruhlmann*

● **Workshop of the Telescopes** / Sep. 26, 1995 / Columbia/Legacy ♦♦♦♦
Blue Öyster Cult was long in need of a thorough career retrospective, and this is it. Thirty-two tracks filling up two discs with a total running time of 154:46, *Workshop of the Telescopes* traces BÖC through 14 years as the kings of lite metal, 1972-1986. Actually, as annotator Arthur Levy notes, there are at least two phases in that era. The first, running through 1974, includes the classic first two albums, *Blue Öyster Cult* and *Tyranny and Mutation*, when BÖC was one of the few acts in those pre-punk days bucking the trend toward soft rock without indulging in the more grotesque aspects of heavy metal. This material takes up disc one. Disc two leads off with "(Don't Fear) the Reaper," which launched the second phase of the band's career, when it sought to balance its hard rocking approach (heard especially in concert) with pop accessibility. Since this period was marked by uneven material, it is ripe for compiling, and the selection here is good. (We could have used a bit more from *Agents of Fortune*, but that's a quibble.) On the whole, *Workshop of the Telescopes* lives up to Levy's description of it as "the ultimate BÖC anthology." It's about time. — *William Ruhlmann*

The Blue Ridge Rangers

f. 1973, United States
Roots-Rock
The Blue Ridge Rangers were never a band. In fact, it was never more than one person: Creedence Clearwater Revival heart and soul John Fogerty. With acrimony over the breakup of Creedence (or more to the point, the jettisoning of rhythm players Stu Cook and Doug Clifford) still fresh, Fogerty released what is ostensibly his first solo album, notable for being an all-covers country/gospel record and for Fogerty's impression of Todd Rundgren by playing all the instruments, overdubbing all the vocals, producing—everything but selling it door-to-door. The point(s) of submerging his identity (Fogerty's face is nowhere on the jacket cover) was to put some distance between himself and the Creedence legacy he wore like an albatross, pay homage to the American vernacular music he loved, and, rather inconspicuously (except for that distinctive voice), announce himself as a solo performer. Oddly enough, life as a solo artist (compounded by lengthy litigation against former Fantasy Records chair Saul Zaentz) didn't seem to agree with Fogerty, and his extremely limited production (a total of four records in 22 years), while not helping him in terms of sales, did, ironically, cement his reputation as an American rock icon. — *John Dougan*

The Blue Ridge Rangers / 1973 / Fantasy ♦♦♦
With wonderfully chosen songs like "Hearts of Stone" and George Jones' classic country weeper "She Thinks I Still Care," Fogerty's solo debut has

held up well over the last two decades. It isn't the most supple or technically proficient one-man recording of all time, but it's a wonderfully engaging record—upbeat, unpretentious, and loaded with good songs. Fogerty's rigid, no-frills drumming took a lot of heat for being mechanical, but no one has ever explained to my satisfaction how Fogerty's abilities on the trap kit are significantly different from Creedence's Doug Clifford. In retrospect, this was a tremendously risky record to make; country music in the early '70s was regarded as the domain of rightwing, rock 'n' roll-hating Nashville traditionalists, and it was reasonable to assume that fans (even staunch ones) wouldn't take kindly to this genre switch. While it wasn't a huge success, it was in no way a disaster, and perhaps more importantly, served as a much-needed rock 'n' roll history lesson. —*John Dougan*

Blue Rodeo

f. 1985, Toronto, Ontario
Folk-Rock, Alternative Country-Rock, Americana
Blue Rodeo's style has drawn comparisons to a number of pop and rock icons, including the Beatles, Buffalo Springfield, the Band, and Bob Dylan. Formed in Toronto, the band is led by the songwriting team of vocalists/guitarists Jim Cuddy and Greg Keelor and features bassist Bazil Donovan, drummer Glenn Milchem, and keyboardist Bob Wiseman, who also plays harmonica and accordion. Their debut album, 1987's *Outskirts*, showcased the group's harmonies and musical interplay in a classic, rootsy folk-rock style. The punchier *Diamond Mine* (1989) covered more lyrical ground, bringing a bit of social commentary into Blue Rodeo's tales of loss and heartbreak, but the recording site (an empty hall in Toronto) dulled the songs' impact somewhat. In 1990 Wiseman recorded his own solo album, *Bob Wiseman Sings Wrench Tuttle: In Her Dreams*. Producer Pete Anderson (Michelle Shocked, Dwight Yoakam) accentuated the group's vocal harmonies on the following year's *Casino*, which was well-received. Even higher praise was reserved for *Lost Together*, which synthesized the previous albums' stylistic changes into a cohesive whole. —*Steve Huey*

Outskirts / 1987 / Discovery ✦✦✦
Outskirts is a highly likeable debut featuring mid-tempo country-rockers fleshed out by tasteful use of organ in the arrangements—a subtle touch that, along with the sheer quality of the material, distinguished Blue Rodeo from the hordes of other Gram Parsons devotees in the mid-'80s. —*Chris Woodstra*

Diamond Mine / 1989 / Discovery ✦✦✦
Diamond Mine is a considerably more quiet affair. Beginning with the very Dylanesque "God and Country," a darker, introverted mood is set by their minimalist approach and slow tempos. —*Chris Woodstra*

● **Casino** / 1991 / Discovery ✦✦✦✦
Casino is a more pop-oriented album. They seem to have finally established their blend of harmonies and laidback country-rock à la the Band and Bob Dylan. Produced by Pete Anderson (Dwight Yoakam, Michelle Shocked). —*Chris Woodstra*

Lost Together / Aug. 4, 1992 / Discovery ✦✦✦✦
Lost Together is easily the best Blue Rodeo album to date. Hit the random button on the disc player and no matter where the laser touches down, you're assured a worthwhile listening experience. Blue Rodeo have built a fortress on the foundation of their previous three outings. The straight pop song "Flying" and ballads "Already Gone" and the epic title track offer added depth and maturity without rehashing previous successes. "Willin' Fool" and "Angels" tackle the progressive elements of Blue Rodeo's second album *Diamond Mine* and sharpen them to a manic, cutting edge. "Fools like You" spits out a defense of native rights, with Greg Keelor doing his best outraged-Bob Dylan impression. —*Roch Parisien*

Five Days in July / Sep. 27, 1994 / Discovery ✦✦✦
Each new Blue Rodeo album seems like the best one yet and *Five Days in July* is no exception. Even the one cover (Rodney Crowell's "Til I Gain Control Again") ends up sounding like a Blue Rodeo original. Also, if you've been slow to embrace her as an artist, Sarah McLachlan's vocal contributions to songs like "What Is This Love" will totally captivate you. —*Jim Worbois*

Nowhere to Here / Sep. 5, 1995 / Discovery ✦✦✦
Blue Rodeo continues to experiment on this release. Opening and closing with expansive mood pieces, it takes a little bit of listening to get into this album. But sandwiched in between lies the real meat of this record. Bluesy ballads such as "Sky" and "Train" are balanced by upbeat pop tunes like "What You Want" and "Better Off as We Are." The rockin' Beatlesque "Get Through to You" shows them in top form. Every song here tends to evoke the pictorial majesty of the Canadian countryside, while never sounding hokey. Once you let these tunes seep into your psyche, you'll find there isn't a bum tune in the bunch. Fantastic! —*James Chrispell*

Blue Things

f. 1964, Kansas, **db.** 1967
Folk-Rock, Pop-Rock
Along with the Remains, the Blue Things are serious contenders for the title of the Great Lost Mid-'60s American Band. The Kansas group was extremely popular in the Midwest and Texas but remained unknown on a national level, despite a deal with RCA. Piloted by the excellent songwriting of singer and guitarist Val Stocklein, the group often sounded like a cross between the Byrds and the Beau Brummels, with its melodic, energetic, guitar-oriented folk-rock and haunting harmonies. The group's sole album (*Listen & See*, 1966) and several singles chart a rapid growth from British Invasion-like material with a heavy Searchers and Buddy Holly influence to full-blown psychedelic efforts with careening guitars, organ, and backward effects.

Quite innovative for the time, these 1966 psychedelic singles met with no more than regional success. The group's impetus was derailed by the departure of Stocklein at the end of 1966, although they struggled on for a bit. Stocklein went to California and recorded a disappointing MOR-folk album for Dot in the late '60s that reprised some of his Blue Things songs. —*Richie Unterberger*

Listen & See / 1966 / RCA ✦✦✦✦
One of the most underappreciated albums of the '60s. Composed of Val Stocklein originals and well-chosen covers, the group synthesized the Beatles and Dylanesque folk-rock with a skill similar to the Byrds. Ringing 12-string and acoustic guitars, melodic harmonies, passionate vocals, and strong material abound on this nearly forgotten near-classic. —*Richie Unterberger*

The Blue Things Story, Vol. 1 (1964-65) / 1987 / Cicadelic ✦✦✦
This collection of 1964 and 1965 demos, coupled with some rare early singles, shows the band at its most British Invasion-influenced. It has quite a few fine Beatlesque harmony rockers by Stocklein, along with some nifty covers. There's a marked difference between the 1964 and 1965 demos, which show the band shifting from British Invasion emulation to a more mature and far more folk-rock-influenced direction. —*Richie Unterberger*

● **The Blue Things Story, Vol. 2 (1965-66)** / 1987 / Cicadelic ✦✦✦✦
Basically a repackage of *Listen & See*, with a couple of the less impressive cover songs deleted. In their place are four fine previously unreleased demos, two of which feature the entire band, two of which are performed by Stocklein alone on acoustic guitar. The epic ballad "Desert Wind" is a special standout among the previously unreleased cuts. —*Richie Unterberger*

The Blue Things Story, Vol. 3 (1966) / 1987 / Cicadelic ✦✦✦
Wraps up their legacy with all of their groundbreaking, non-LP 1966 single sides—"The Orange Rooftop of Your Mind," "One Hour Cleaners," and "You Can Live in Our Tree." It also has half a dozen 1966 demos (several acoustic), some of which are early versions of songs that ended up on *Listen & See*. The package is rounded out by a few impressive 1967 cuts from the post-Stocklein lineup, consisting of a couple of unreleased originals by other band members and their astounding psychedelic fuzz-guitar rearrangement of "Twist and Shout." —*Richie Unterberger*

The Bluebells

f. 1981, Scotland, **db.** 1985
New Wave
During their brief time together in the early '80s, the Bluebells (songwriter Robert [Bobby Bluebell] Hodgens [b. June 6, 1959] [guitar]; Kenneth McClusky [b. Feb. 8, 1962] [vocals/harmonica]; Dave McCluskey [b. Jan. 13, 1964] [drums]; Russell Irvin [guitar] [replaced by Craig Gannon (b. July 30, 1966)]; and Lawrence Donegan [bass] [replaced by Neil Baldwin]) made a small amount of music—several singles, most of which showed up on one EP—but that is not proportional to the quality of their music. Like fellow Scots Aztec Camera, the Bluebells crafted impeccable, jangly guitar-pop, only with better melodies and stronger hooks. Two of their singles ("I'm Falling" and "Young at Heart") hovered around the lower reaches of the UK Top Ten in 1984, but they soon broke up, leaving a small, but impressive, body of work.

David McCluskey and his brother Ken formed a folk duo. Robert Hodgens formed Up. Craig Gannon briefly filled in for bassist Andy Rourke in the Smiths on tour, then stayed as a second live guitarist; he joined Adult Net after being fired from the Smiths in 1986. —*Stephen Thomas Erlewine*

Bluebells / 1983 / Sire ✦✦✦
The Bluebells' critically-acclaimed five-song debut EP established their chiming guitar-pop quite effectively. —*Stephen Thomas Erlewine*

● **Sisters** / 1984 / London ✦✦✦✦
Sisters, the Bluebells' first full-length album, shared some songs with their debut EP, but the repetition doesn't matter, since the record is so

carefully constructed. The group's ringing, hook-laden folk-pop is consistently infectious throughout the course of the album. — *Stephen Thomas Erlewine*

Second / 1992 / London ✦✦
Second is a collection of unreleased early Bluebells recordings that is worthwhile for dedicated fans. — *Stephen Thomas Erlewine*

Blues Magoos

f. 1964, Bronx, NY, db. 1969
Psychedelic
A Bronx-based quintet, denizens of the Greenwich Village club scene, and originally known by the *tres*-psychedelic moniker the Bloos Magoos (yikes!), the Blues Magoos made their mark in 1967 with a rousing, full-throttle, sub-literate, psychedelic garage rock single, "(We Ain't Got) Nothin' Yet." It wasn't a spacy, pretentious song, nor did it contain vague attempts at hippie-era mysticism; rather, it was the kind of simple, direct, infectious rock 'n' roll you could imagine five guys from the Bronx making. With a snotty lead vocal from keyboardist Ralph Scala and some wild-eyed guitar playing courtesy of then-16-year-old Emil "Peppy" Theilheim, America made the Magoos' debut single a Top Ten hit, sending it to No. 5 in January 1967. With this impetus, the band used all the trappings of marketable psychedelia to promote their second album, *Psychedelic Lollipop*, which, despite the title's obvious pandering, was a fairly cool chunk of psych-garage rock: trebly, crappy-sounding guitars; a whiny Farfisa organ; yelled vocals; and a rhythm section that shelved nuance for thudding simplicity. But as the psychedelic era gave way to the hippie era's extended raga-rock proclivities, by 1969 the Magoos seemed anachronistic.

Amazingly, they released a third album, with an equally idiotic title, *Electric Comic Book*, that wasn't nearly as bad as it sounds. The original Magoos split up in 1969, but Theilheim couldn't resist beating a dead horse and led a mediocre blues-rock version of the band into 1972. — *John Dougan*

● **Kaleidescopic Compendium: Best of the Blues Magoos** / May 5, 1992 / PolyGram/Mercury ✦✦✦✦
The Blues Magoos were one of the most underrated US bands of the late 60s, known almost exclusively for their one irresistible hit "(We Ain't Got) Nothing Yet," which charted at No. 5 in July 1967. *Kaleidescopic Compendium: The Best of the Blues Magoos* confirms the group's depth. The disc compiles a generous 23 tracks from their first three albums and a brace of single sides. The group's psychedelia holds up better than most from the period. Andy Sandoval's four-page history of the group is concise, complete, and entertaining. — *Roch Parisien*

The Blues Project

f. 1965, New York, NY
Group / Blues-Rock, Folk-Rock
One of the first album-oriented "underground" groups in the United States, the Blues Project offered an electric brew of rock, blues, folk, pop, and even some jazz, classical, and psychedelia during their brief heyday in the mid-'60s. It's not quite accurate to categorize them as a blues-rock group, although they did plenty of that kind of material; they were more like a Jewish-American equivalent of British bands like the Yardbirds, who used a blues and R&B base to explore any music that interested them. Erratic songwriting talent and lack of a truly outstanding vocalist prevented them from rising to the front line of '60s bands, but they recorded plenty of interesting material over the course of their first three albums, before the departure of their most creative members took its toll.

The Blues Project was formed in Greenwich Village in the mid-'60s by guitarist Danny Kalb (who had played sessions for various Elektra folk and folk-rock albums), Steve Katz (a guitarist with Elektra's Even Dozen Jug Band), flutist/bassist Andy Kulberg, drummer Roy Blumenfeld, and singer Tommy Flanders. Al Kooper, in his early 20s a seasoned vet of rock sessions, joined after sitting in on the band's Columbia Records audition, although they ended up signing to Verve, an MGM subsidiary. Early member Artie Traum (guitar) dropped out during early rehearsals; Flanders would leave after their first LP, *Live at the Cafe Au-Go-Go* (1966).

The eclectic resumes of the musicians, who came from folk, jazz, blues, and rock backgrounds, was reflected in their choice of material. Blues by Muddy Waters and Chuck Berry tunes ran alongside covers of contemporary folk-rock songs by Eric Anderson and Patrick Sky, as well as the group's own originals. These were usually penned by Kooper, who had already built songwriting credentials as the co-writer of Gary Lewis' huge smash "This Diamond Ring," and established a reputation as a major folk-rock shaker with his contributions to Dylan's mid-'60s records. Kooper also provided the band's instrumental highlights with his glowing organ riffs.

The live debut sounds rather tame and derivative; the group truly hit

their stride on *Projections* (late 1966), which was, disappointingly, their only full-length studio recording. While they went through straight blues numbers with respectable energy, they really shone on the folk and jazz-influenced tracks like "Fly Away," Katz's lilting "Steve's Song," Kooper's jazz instrumental "Flute Thing" (an underground radio standard that's probably their most famous track), and Kooper's fierce adaptation of an old Blind Willie Johnson number, "I Can't Keep from Crying." A non-LP single from this era, the pop-psychedelic "No Time like the Right Time," was their greatest achievement and one of the best "great hit singles that never were" of the decade.

The band's very eclecticism didn't augur well for their long-term stability, and in 1967 Kooper left in a dispute over musical direction (he has recalled that Kalb opposed his wishes to add a horn section). Then Kalb mysteriously disappeared for months after a bad acid trip, which effectively finished the original incarnation of the band. A third album, *Live at Town Hall*, was a particularly half-assed project given the band's stature, pasted together from live tapes and studio outtakes, some of which were overdubbed with applause to give the impression that they had been recorded in concert.

Kooper got to fulfill his ambitions for soulful horn rock as the leader of the original Blood, Sweat & Tears, although he left that band after their first album; BS&T also included Katz (who stayed on board for a long time). Blumenfeld and Kulberg kept the Blues Project going for a fourth album before forming Seatrain, and the group re-formed in the early '70s with various lineups, Kooper rejoining for a live 1973 album, *Reunion in Central Park*. The first three albums from the Kooper days are the only ones that count, though; the best material from these is on Rhino's best-of compilation. — *Richie Unterberger*

Live at the Cafe Au-Go-Go / May 1966 / Verve/Forecast ✦✦✦
Although Tommy Flanders (who'd already left the band by the time this debut hit the streets) is credited as sole vocalist, four of the then-sextet's members sang; in fact, Danny Kalb handles as many leads as Flanders (four each), Steve Katz takes center stage on Donovan's "Catch the Wind," and Al Kooper is featured on "I Want to Be Your Driver." The band could be lowdown when appropriate (Kalb's reading of "Jelly, Jelly"), high-energy (Muddy Waters' "Goin' Down Louisiana" sounds closer to Chuck Berry or Bo Diddley), and unabashedly eclectic (tossing in Donovan or Eric Anderson with no apologies). Kalb's moody take on "Alberta" is transcendent, and the uptempo arrangement of "Spoonful" is surprisingly effective. — *Dan Forte*

Projections / Nov. 1966 / Verve/Forecast ✦✦✦✦
Produced by Tom Wilson (Dylan, Zappa), the Blues Project's second effort was their finest hour. In less than a year the enthusiastic live band had matured into a seasoned studio ensemble. Steve Katz' features are lightweight folk, but Al Kooper reworks two gospel themes ("Wake Me, Shake Me," "I Can't Keep from Crying") into ambitious blues-rock compositions, and Danny Kalb proves he's no mere folkie on extended versions of "Two Trains Running" and "Caress Me Baby." Bassist Andy Kulberg switches to flute and Kalb gets psychedelic on the jazzy "Flute Thing," penned by Kooper. — *Dan Forte*

Live at Town Hall / Sep. 1967 / Verve/Forecast ✦✦✦
This LP, released just after Al Kooper left the band, probably pleased neither him nor the other members of the group. According to Kooper, it was a pastiche of studio outtakes and a few live performances, and only one of the songs was actually recorded at New York City's Town Hall. Anyway, this has a meandering, ten-minute "Flute Thing" and decent live versions of "Wake Me Shake Me" and "I Can't Keep from Crying" which, despite a somewhat rawer feel, are not necessary supplements to the fine studio takes. "Where There's Smoke, There's Fire" and the great "No Time like the Right Time" had already been released as singles; to hear them without canned applause, you need only turn to Rhino's first-rate *Best of the Blues Project*. That compilation also contains the other cut of note on this album, an outtake-sounding cover of Patrick Sky's "Love Will Endure." — *Richie Unterberger*

Original Blues Project Reunion in Central Park / 1973 / MGM ✦✦✦
Considering that the original lineup had broken up six years earlier, this ranks as one of the most artistically successful reunions in blues or rock. If there were any ego problems, they don't show; typically Kalb and Kooper shine, but all five are playing as a team. Most important, the members seem to respect their own past—and recreate it with spontaneity and energy. — *Dan Forte*

● **The Best Of The Blues Project [Rhino]** / 1989 / Rhino ✦✦✦✦
With the exception of a live version of "Flute Thing" from the Blues Project's 1973 reunion concert included only on the CD version, this compilation is culled entirely from the albums *Live at the Cafe Au-Go-Go*, *Projections*, and *The Blues Project Live at Town Hall*, all recorded and released in the period 1966-1967. Just as those individual albums do, it confirms the acclaim accorded the Blues Project at the time. The group's sophistication and ability to create a hybrid of musical styles keeps the music from sounding dated. In fact, this music not only stands

as among the best of its time, but it continues to appeal where much of the music made simultaneously fails to escape its era. (Not to be confused with *Best of the Blues Project*, Verve Forecast FTS 3077 [July 1969], which is an earlier compilation with a different selection of songs.) — *William Ruhlmann*

Projections from the Past / 1989 / Hablabel ♦♦♦
A double album of dubious legality, but fairly easy availability. This captures the Blues Project's best lineup—Kooper, Katz, Kalb, Kulberg, and Blumenfeld—live at the Matrix club in San Francisco on September 1, 1966. If there's any revelation to be had from these fair-quality tapes, it's that there's not much of a revelation at all. The group performs a lot of the stronger material from their first and second albums in versions very close to the records. They shine brightest on the more adventurous material with jazz and folk tangents, like "Steve's Song," "Flute Thing," "Catch the Wind," and "Cheryl's Going Home." Most of the rest is competent but not especially brilliant white-boy blues renditions of numbers like "Hoochie Coochie Man," "You Can't Catch Me," and "You Can't Judge a Book By the Cover"; the swaggering "Shake That Baby" is about the best of these. Essential only for serious collectors. Be warned that there are a few (not many) clumsy edits, and that the entire fourth side is simply tracks lifted from their *Live at Town Hall* LP. — *Richie Unterberger*

Anthology / Jan. 28, 1997 / Polygram ♦♦♦♦
The most complete Blues Project collection ever assembled, the two-disc *Anthology* compiles 36 tracks taken from their three albums on Verve and their two records on Capitol, as well as rare singles, previously unreleased songs and alternate versions, and material from solo projects. — *Jason Ankeny*

Blues Traveler

f. 1988, New York, NY
Rock 'n' Roll, Pop-Rock, Blues-Rock
A New York-based blues-rock quartet formed in 1988 by singer/harmonica player John Popper, guitarist Chan Kinchla, bassist Bobby Sheehan, and drummer Brendan Hill, Blues Traveler was part of a revival of the extended jamming style of '60s and '70s groups like the Grateful Dead and Led Zeppelin. Signed to A&M, they released their first album, *Blues Traveler*, in May 1990 and followed it with *Travelers & Thieves* in September 1991. Popper was in a serious car accident in 1992, leaving him unable to perform for a number of months. Fortunately, he recovered, but he had to perform in a wheelchair for a period of time. In April 1993 Blues Traveler released its third album, *Save His Soul*, which became its first to make the Top 100. Blues Traveler's aptly named fourth album, *Four*, released in September 1994, at first looked like a sales disappointment, but it rebounded in 1995 when "Run-Around," a single taken from it, became the group's first chart hit. "Run-Around" became one of the biggest singles of 1995, spending nearly a full year on the charts and sending *Four* into quintuple platinum status. As the group prepared the followup to *Four*, Blues Traveler released the live double-album *Live from the Fall* in the summer of 1996.

Blues Traveller returned in the summer of 1997 with its fifth studio album, *Straight On Till Morning*. — *William Ruhlmann*

● **Blues Traveler** / May 1990 / A&M ♦♦♦♦
Blues Traveler's loose jam structures on basic blues riffs mark them as a band in the tradition of such predecessors as the Grateful Dead. Unlike that communal effort, however, this group has a distinct focal point in virtuoso harmonica player and vocalist John Popper, who keeps things from meandering too much. — *William Ruhlmann*

Travelers & Thieves / Sep. 1991 / A&M ♦♦♦
"I have my moments," John Popper declares, and many of them, as harmonica player, singer, and lyricist are here, on an album that finds Blues Traveler stretching out much as they do onstage. Popper is a man with a lot on his mind, but when he reaches "The Best Part," his verbosity approaches a Walt Whitman-like exuberance, and guitarist Chan Kinchla is right with him, contributing sweet fills here, Pete Townshend-style strumming there. And as for the rhythm work of bassist Bobby Sheehan and drummer Brendan Hill, as Popper says, "It's all in the groove." — *William Ruhlmann*

Save His Soul / Apr. 1993 / A&M ♦♦♦
Led by the guttural vocals and incisive harmonica of imposing frontman John Popper, *Save His Soul* is a savory package that dresses obvious influences in a fresh suit of clothes. While six and 12 strings rule, the true inspiration here is Popper's delivery on harmonica and other wind instruments, spitting in machine-gun-rapid fire or carrying a piercing, emotive melody line with equal ease. Having restrained themselves for most of *Save His Soul*, Blues Traveler close with the seven-minute opus "Fledgling," flowing from epic, orchestral ballad to angst-ridden wall-of-noise. — *Roch Parisien*

Four / Sep. 13, 1994 / A&M ♦♦♦♦
Lacking the rootsier edge of *Save His Soul*, *Four* finds Blues Traveler retreating to their standard blues-boogie formula, with mixed results. Of course, there are some fine songs here—including their breakthrough hit single "Run Around"— but too often the band sounds as if they're coasting. *Four* is a solid record, but it shows signs that the band's formula may be wearing thin. — *Stephen Thomas Erlewine*

Live from the Fall / Jul. 1996 / A&M ♦♦♦♦
Like any jam-oriented band, Blues Traveler has a reputation for being better in concert than they are in the studio. Therefore, it would make sense that the double-disc *Live from the Fall* would be the ideal Blues Traveler album, since it allows the band to stretch out and demonstrate their true talents. In a sense, that is true. The two discs—which were recorded in the fall of 1995, as the band was supporting the surprise success of *Four*—do give the band room to improvise, and they exploit the extra space for all of its worth. Initially, Blues Traveler wanted to release without track indexes, so the listener could hear how each song flowed into the next. And the album does sound like that—like a never-ending medley, where melodic themes pop in and out of the long solos. Occasionally, they detour into covers (War's "Low Rider," John Lennon's "Imagine"), but they mainly weave a tapestry of their own material, including rarities like the B-side "Regarding Steven" and the unreleased "Closing Down the Park." For fans of pop hits like "Run Around" and "Hook," this can be a little irritating, but for those who have been with the band since the beginning, *Live from the Fall* is a priceless document. More than any other album, this showcases what Blues Traveler is about. — *Stephen Thomas Erlewine*

The Bluetones

f. 1994, Hounslow, England
Brit-Pop
The Bluetones filled the gap that the Stone Roses left, providing graceful but muscular guitar pop with slightly psychedelic overtones. The band appeared during the waning days of Brit-pop, which guaranteed them a considerable amount of press coverage that helped their debut album rocket to the top of the charts upon its release in early 1996.

Originally called the Bottlegarden, the Bluetones formed in Hounslow, England, in 1994. The group consisted of guitarist Adam Devlin, drummer Ed Chester, vocalist Mark Morris, and his brother Scott, who played bass. All of the members had previously played in local bands before forming the Bluetones. During 1995 the group released two singles, "Are You Blue or Are You Blind?" and "Bluetonic," on their Superior Quality Recordings label, which received positive reviews in the British music weeklies. By the fall of 1995 they were being touted as the next big thing in Brit-pop, since their sound fell halfway between the Stone Roses and Oasis. Early in 1996 the group released "Slight Return," which shot to No. 2 a month before their debut album, *Expecting to Fly*, was released. *Expecting to Fly* was greeted with mixed reviews, but it debuted at No. 1 on the British charts and became a sizable hit. Despite their British success, the group had trouble breaking America. Furthermore, they were the subject of a quick backlash, as many critics believed the group embodied the conservatism of Brit-pop—the non-LP single "Marblehead Johnson" was welcomed cooly upon its fall release, and it only dented the charts. During early 1997 the Bluetones began working on their second album. — *Stephen Thomas Erlewine*

● **Expecting to Fly** / Jan. 31, 1996 / Blue ♦♦♦♦
If anything, the Bluetones' debut album *Expecting to Fly* is too accomplished. Like their idols, the Stone Roses, the band has made a first album that is assured, low-key, and subtly charming. Unlike the Roses, they haven't made a consistently engaging album, but that isn't a major flaw, given the abundant hooks and melodies on *Expecting to Fly*. Lacking the dance inclinations of the Stone Roses, the Bluetones instead concentrate on perfectly-crafted guitar-pop songs, occasionally stretching out into long jams, like the opener "Talking to Clarry," which is too close to "Breaking into Heaven" for comfort. Nevertheless, when the band kicks into a small, hook-laden song like the chiming, infectious "Bluetonic," they are at their peak. Most of the album has gems like "Bluetonic," whether it's the wonderful "Slight Return" or the liquid riffs of "Things Change," but the record could have used more sonic variety. Where their pre-album singles had several lovely acoustic numbers, there is an over-reliance on loud, fuzzy—but certainly not heavy—guitars that gives the album an unfortunate sameness. However, that feeling begins to fade as each of the songs' melodies comes into focus with repeated listens. — *Stephen Thomas Erlewine*

Colin Blunstone

b. Jun. 24, 1945, Hatfield, Hertfordshire, England
Vocals / Pop-Rock
As the lead singer of the Zombies, Blunstone was one of the greatest '60s rock vocalists, pacing the group's minor-key masterpieces with his inimitable choked and breathy vocals. After retiring from the business briefly in the late '60s (to work in the insurance industry, of all things), he went solo in the early '70s with a string of interesting pop-rock albums that were more of an extension of the late Zombies sound than

the more well-known work of Argent, the other Zombies spin-off act. The Zombies connection is hardly incidental; chief Zombie songwriters Rod Argent and Chris White gave Blunstone some songs, as did Argent member Russ Ballard, though Blunstone penned much of his material himself. With their moody melodies and baroque touches of muted keyboards, classical guitars, and inventive string arrangements, his early-'70s albums sometimes sounded like a mellower take on the direction the Zombies pursued with their pop-psychedelic masterwork *Odessey and Oracle*. Blunstone managed some small British hits with "How Could We Dare Be Wrong," "I Don't Believe in Miracles," and the Top 20 single "Say You Don't Mind," a cover of a tune written and recorded by Denny Laine after he left the Moody Blues and before he joined Wings. Blunstone's first album, *One Year* (1971), was his best, though the follow-ups *Ennismore* and *Journey* also had their moments. —*Richie Unterberger*

- **Some Years: It's the Time of Colin Blunstone** / Oct. 1995 / Legacy/ Epic ✦✦✦✦
Well-chosen 17-track retrospective of his early-'70s work, including all the British hit singles and tracks from his first three solo LPs. Although it's not up to the level of the Zombies' classic records, Zombies fans should like this stuff a lot, especially "Say You Don't Mind," "Andorra," "Though You Are Far Away," and his cover of Tim Hardin's "Misty Roses." —*Richie Unterberger*

Blur

f. 1989, Colchester, England
Alternative Pop-Rock, Pop-Rock, Brit-Pop, Alternative Dance
Initially, Blur was one of the multitude of British bands that appeared in the wake of the Stone Roses, mining the same swirling, pseudo-psychedelic guitar-pop, only with louder guitars. Following an image makeover in the mid-'90s, the group emerged as the most popular band in the UK, establishing themselves as the heir to the English guitar-pop tradition of the Kinks, the Small Faces, the Who, the Jam, Madness, and the Smiths. In the process, the group broke down the doors for a new generation of guitar bands that became labelled "Brit-pop." With Damon Albarn's wry lyrics and the group's mastery of British pop tradition, Blur was the leader of Brit-pop, but they quickly became confined by the movement; since they were its biggest band, they nearly died when the movement itself died. Through some reinvention, Blur reclaimed their position as an art-pop band in the late '90s by incorporating indie-rock and lo-fi influences, which finally gave them their elusive American success in 1997. But the band's legacy remained in Britain, where they helped revitalize guitar-pop by skillfully updating the country's pop tradition and bringing it into the '90s.

Originally called Seymour, the group was formed in London in 1989 by vocalist/keyboardist Damon Albarn, guitarist Graham Coxon, and bassist Alex James, with drummer Dave Rowntree joining the lineup shortly afterward. After performing a handful of gigs and recording a demo tape, the band signed to Food Records, a subsidiary of EMI run by journalist Andy Ross and former Teardrop Explodes keyboardist Dave Balfe. Balfe and Ross suggested that the band change its name, submitting a list of alternate names for the group's approval. From that list, the group took the name Blur.

"She's So High," the group's first single, made it into the Top 50; the follow-up, "There's No Other Way," went Top Ten. Both singles were included on their 1991 Stephen Street-produced debut album, *Leisure*. Although it received favorable reviews, the album fit neatly into the dying Manchester pop scene, causing some journalists to dismiss the band as manufactured teen idols. For the next two years Blur struggled to distance themselves from the scene associated with the sound of their first album.

Released in 1992, the snarling "Pop Scene" was Blur's first attempt at changing their musical direction. A brash, spiteful rocker driven by horns, the neo-mod single was punkier than anything the band had previously recorded, and its hooks were more immediate and catchy. Despite Blur's clear artistic growth, "Pop Scene" didn't fit into the climate of British pop and American grunge in 1992 and failed to make an impression on the UK charts. After the single's commercial failure, the group began work on their second album, *Modern Life Is Rubbish*, a process that would take nearly a year and a half.

XTC's Andy Partridge was originally slated to produce *Modern Life Is Rubbish*, but the relationship between Blur and Partridge quickly soured, so Street was again brought in to produce the band. After spending nearly a year in the studio, the band delivered the album to Food. The record company rejected the album, declaring that it needed a hit single. Blur went back into the studio and recorded "For Tomorrow," which would turn out to be a British hit. Food was ready to release the record, but the group's US record company, SBK, believed there was no American hit single on the record and asked them to return to the studio. Blur complied and recorded "Chemical World," which pleased SBK for a short while; the song would become a minor alternative hit in

the US and charted at No. 28 in the UK. *Modern Life Is Rubbish* was set for release in the spring of 1993 when SBK asked Blur to re-record the album with producer Butch Vig (Nirvana, Sonic Youth). The band refused, and the record was released in May in Britain; it appeared in the United States that fall. *Modern Life Is Rubbish* received good reviews in Britain, peaking at No. 15 on the charts, but it failed to make much of an impression in the US.

Modern Life Is Rubbish turned out to be a dry run for Blur's breakthrough album, *Parklife*. Released in April 1994, *Parklife* entered the charts at No. 1 and catapulted the band to stardom in Britain. The stylized new wave dance-pop single "Girls and Boys" entered the charts at No. five; the single managed to spend 15 weeks on the US charts, peaking at No. 52, but the album never cracked the charts. It was a completely different story in England, as Blur had a string of hit singles including the ballad "To the End" and the mod anthem "Parklife," which featured narration by Phil Daniels, the star of the film version of the Who's *Quadrophenia*.

With the success of *Parklife*, Blur opened the door for a flood of British indie-guitar bands that dominated British pop culture in the mid-'90s. Oasis, Elastica, Pulp, the Boo Radleys, Supergrass, Gene, Echobelly, Menswear, and numerous other bands all benefited from the band's success. By the beginning of 1995, *Parklife* had gone triple platinum, and the band had become superstars. The group spent the first half of 1995 recording their fourth album and playing various one-off concerts, including a sold-out stadium show. Blur released "Country House," the first single from their new album, in August admist a flurry of media attention because Albarn had the single's release moved up a week to compete with the release of "Roll with It," a new single from Blur's chief rivals, Oasis. The strategy backfired. Although Blur won the battle, with "Country House" becoming the group's first No. 1 single, they ultimately lost the war, as Oasis became Britain's biggest band with their second album, *(What's the Story) Morning Glory?*, completely overshadowing the follow-up to *Parklife*, *The Great Escape*. While *The Great Escape* entered the UK charts at No. 1 and earned overwhelmingly positive reviews, it sold in smaller numbers and by the beginning of 1996, Blur was seen as a has-been, especially since they once again failed to break the American market, where Oasis had been particularly successful.

In the face of negative press and weak public support, Blur nearly broke up in early 1996, but they instead decided to spend the entire year out of the spotlight. By the end of the year, Albarn was declaring that he was no longer interested in British music and was fascinated with American indie-rock, a genre that Graham Coxon had been supporting for years. These influences manifested themselves on Blur's fifth album, *Blur*, which was released in February 1997 to generally positive reviews. The band's reinvention wasn't greeted warmly in the UK—the album and its first single, "Beetlebum," debuted at No. 1 and quickly fell down the charts, as the group's mass audience didn't completely accept their new incarnation. However, the band's revamped sound earned them an audience in the US, where *Blur* received strong reviews and became a moderate hit. The success in America eventually seeped over to Britain; and by the spring, the album had bounced back up the charts. —*Stephen Thomas Erlewine*

Leisure / Sep. 1991 / Food/SBK ✦✦✦
"She's So High" and "There's No Other Way" were auspicious debut singles—alternately trancy and melodic, suggesting how shoegazing and baggy beats could be incorporated into pop song structures. Both songs suggested that Blur was capable of a striking debut album, but *Leisure* wasn't it. Mired by directionless soundscapes and incomplete songwriting, *Leisure* was nevertheless full of promise. Whenever the group tread close to the warped psychedelia of Syd Barrett, their compositions sprang to life, and "Sing" was an eerie, entrancing minor-key drone reminiscent of the Velvet Underground's "Venus In Furs." Those moments, however, were few and far between on *Leisure*, since much of the record was devoted to either naive pop like "Bang" or washes of feedback and effects. From *Leisure*, it appeared that Blur was capable only of a pair of fine singles, which is what made the complete reinvention of *Modern Life Is Rubbish* such a surprise. [For the American release of *Leisure*, SBK Records lopped off one of the album's best songs, "Sing," and shuffled the running order for no apparent reason other than having "She's So High" and "There's No Other Way" appear first.] —*Stephen Thomas Erlewine*

Modern Life Is Rubbish / Nov. 16, 1993 / SBK ✦✦✦✦
As a response to the dominance of grunge in the UK and their own decreasing profile in their homeland—and as a response to Suede's sudden popularity—Blur reinvented themselves with their second album, *Modern Life Is Rubbish*, abandoning the shoegazing and baggy influences that dominated *Leisure* for traditional pop. On the surface, *Modern Life* may appear to be an homage to the Kinks, David Bowie, the Beatles, and Syd Barrett, but it isn't a restatement, it's a revitalization. Blur uses British guitar-pop from the Beatles to My Bloody Valentine as a foundation, spinning off tales of contemporary despair. If Damon Albarn weren't such a clever songwriter, both lyrically and melodically,

Modern Life could have sunk under its own pretensions, and the latter half does drag slightly. However, the record teems with life, since Blur refuse to treat their classicist songs as museum pieces. Graham Coxon's guitar tears each song open, either with unpredictable melodic lines or layers of translucent, hypnotic effects, and his work creates great tension with Alex James's kinetic bass. And that provides Albarn a vibrant background for his social satires and cutting commentary. But the reason *Modern Life Is Rubbish* is such a dynamic record and ushered in a new era of British pop is that nearly every song is carefully constructed and boasts a killer melody, from the stately "For Tomorrow" and the punky "Advert" to the vaudeville stomp of "Sunday Sunday" and the neo-psychedelic "Chemical World." Even with its flaws, it's a record of considerable vision and excitement. [The American version of *Modern Life Is Rubbish* substitutes the demo version of "Chemical World" for the studio version on the British edition. It also adds the superb single "Pop Scene" before the final song, "Resigned." — *Stephen Thomas Erlewine*

★ **Parklife** / Apr. 1994 / Food/SBK ✦✦✦✦✦
Modern Life Is Rubbish established Blur as the heirs to the archly British pop of the Kinks, Small Faces, and the Jam, but its follow-up, *Parklife*, revealed the depth of that transformation, as well as the band's own identity. Relying more heavily on Ray Davies' seriocomic social commentary, as well as new wave, *Parklife* runs through the entire history of post-British Invasion Brit-pop in the course of 16 songs, touching on psychedelia, synth-pop, disco, punk, and music-hall along the way. Damon Albarn intended these songs to form a sketch of British life in the mid-'90s, and it's startling how close he came to his goal. Not only did the bouncy, discofied "Girls and Boys" and sing-along chant "Parklife" become anthems in the UK, but they inaugurated a new era of Brit-pop and lad culture, where British youth celebrated their country and traditions. The legions of jangly, melodic bands that followed in the wake of *Parklife* revealed how much more complex Blur's vision was. Not only was their music infinitely detailed—sound effects and brilliant guitar lines pop up all over the record—but the songs were tightly written, with the melodies elegantly interweaving with the chords, as in the graceful, heartbreaking "Badhead." Surprisingly, Albarn, for all of his cold, dispassionate wit, demonstrates a compassion that gives these songs three dimensions, as on the pathos-laden "End of a Century," the melancholy Walker Brothers tribute "To the End," and the swirling, epic closer "This Is a Low." And for all of its celebration of tradition, *Parklife* is a thoroughly modern record in that it bends genres and is self-referential (the mod anthem of the title track is voiced by none other than Phil Daniels, the star of *Quadrophenia*). By tying the past and present together, Blur articulated the mid-'90s zeitgeist and produced an era-defining record. — *Stephen Thomas Erlewine*

The Great Escape / Sep. 1995 / Food/Parlophone ✦✦✦✦
In the simplest terms, *The Great Escape* is the flipside of *Parklife*. Where Blur's breakthrough album was a celebration of the working class, drawing on British pop from the '60s and reaching through the '80s, *The Great Escape* concentrates on the suburbs, featuring a cast of characters trying to cope with the numbing pressures of modern life. Consequently, it's darker than *Parklife*, even if the melancholia is hidden underneath crisp production and catchy melodies. Even the bright, infectious numbers on *The Great Escape* have gloomy subtexts, whether it's the disillusioned millionaire of "Country House," the sycophant of "Charmless Man," or the bleak loneliness of "Globe Alone" and "Entertain Me." Naturally, the slower numbers are even more despairing, with the acoustic "Best Days," the lush, sweeping strings of "The Universal," and the stark, moving electronic ballad "Yuko and Hiro" ranking as the most affecting work Blur has ever recorded. However, none of this makes *The Great Escape* a burden or a difficult album. The music bristles with invention throughout, as Blur delves deeper into experimentation with synthesizers, horns, and strings; guitarist Graham Coxon twists out unusual chords and lead lines, and Damon Albarn spits out unexpected lyrical couplets filled with wit and venemous intelligence in each song. But Blur's most remarkable accomplishment is that it can reference the past. The Scott Walker homage of "The Universal," the Terry Hall/Fun Boy Three cop on "Top Man," the skittish, XTC-flavored pop of "It Could Be You," and Albarn's devotion to Ray Davies move forward while creating a vibrant, invigorating record. — *Stephen Thomas Erlewine*

Blur / Feb. 1997 / Virgin ✦✦✦✦
The Great Escape, for all of its many virtues, painted Blur into a corner and there was only one way out—to abandon the Brit-pop that they had instigated by bringing to the surface the weird strands that always floated through their music. *Blur* may superficially appear to be a break from tradition, but it is a logical progression, highlighting the band's rich eclecticism and sense of songcraft. Certainly they are trying for new sonic territory, bringing in shards of white noise, gurgling electronics, raw guitars, and druggy psychedelia, but these are just extensions of previously hidden elements of Blur's music. What makes it exceptional is how hard the band tries to reinvent themselves within their own framework, and the level at which they succeed. "Beetlebum" runs

through the *White Album* in the space of five minutes; "M.O.R." reinterprets Berlin-era Bowie; "You're So Great," despite the corny title, is affecting lo-fi from Graham Coxon; "Country Sad Ballad Man" is bizarrely affecting, strangled lo-fi psychedelia; "Death of a Party" is an affecting resignation; "On Your Own" is an incredible slice of sing-along pop spiked with winding, fluid guitar, and synth eruptions, while "Look Inside America" cleverly subverts the traditional Blur song, complete with strings. And "Essex Dogs" is a six-minute slab of free verse and rattling guitar noise. *Blur* might be self-consciously eclectic, but Blur is at their best when they are trying to live up to their own pretensions, because of Damon Albarn's exceptional sense of songcraft and the band's knack for detailed arrangements that flesh out the song to its fullest. There might be dark overtones to the record, but the band sounds positively joyous, not only in making noise but wreaking havoc with the expectations of their audience and critics. And that's why *Blur*, though darker on the surface, is ultimately a more life-affirming listen than *The Great Escape*. — *Stephen Thomas Erlewine*

The BoDeans

f. 1984, Waukesha, WI
Roots-Rock, Pop-Rock
The BoDeans are a rock 'n' roll band formed in Waukesha, WI, by singer-songwriters/guitarists Sammy Lianas and Kurt Neumann, who had played together since junior high school, along with a rhythm section of bassist Bob Griffin and drummer Guy Hoffman. The quartet signed to Slash Records (manufactured and distributed by Warner Bros.) and released its first album, the critically well-accepted *Love & Hope & Sex & Dreams* (the title comes from a line in the Rolling Stones song "Shattered") in 1986.

Outside Looking In (1987), produced by Talking Head and Wisconsin native Jerry Harrison, saw the band reduced to a trio with the departure of Hoffman. It broke into the Top 100 best-sellers, as the BoDeans toured with U2, appeared on Robbie Robertson's self-titled debut solo album, and were named "Best New Band" in *Rolling Stone* magazine. By the time of the release of the third album, *Home* (1989), Michael Ramos (keyboards) and Danny Gayol (drums) had joined. This lineup stayed intact for the release of *Black and White* (1991), but the BoDeans were drummerless again as of the release of *Go Slow Down* (1993). After the release of the 1995 live double-album *Joe Dirt Car*, the BoDeans returned in 1996 with *Blend*. Around the time of *Blend*'s release, "Closer to Free," a song taken from *Go Slow Down*, became a hit, thanks to its exposure as the theme song for the popular television show, "Party of Five." — *William Ruhlmann*

● **Love & Hope & Sex & Dreams** / May 1986 / Slash ✦✦✦✦
When the BoDeans appeared with their first album, *Love & Hope & Sex & Dreams*, in 1986, they immediately were filed under "roots rock" (a popular term of the day) because of the Western twang in their guitars, their bouncy beat, and their simple, neo-rockabilly approach to songwriting, not to mention the production of T-Bone Burnett. They led off the album with "She's a Runaway," a song of spousal abuse and revenge that indicated a higher social consciousness than much of the rest of the album, which was typified by "Misery," in which the singer laments that his girlfriend sleeps around. At their best, on "She's a Runaway," "Fadeaway," and "Angels," the BoDeans came up with infectious riffs and made maximum use of the sweet-and-sour vocal interaction between the conventional voice of Kurt Neumann and Sammy Llanas' distinctive nasal whine. Much of the album was slight, but there was enough of an individual sound to the better material to think of the BoDeans as a band of considerable promise. — *William Ruhlmann*

Outside Looking In / Sep. 1987 / Slash ✦✦
Having established themselves as contenders with their debut album, the BoDeans looked to move on to the next level in commercial and artistic terms on their second release, bringing in producer Jerry Harrison of Talking Heads and expanding beyond their roots-rock style, to the extent of occasionally singing in falsetto, adding female backup vocals, and recording near-soul pop numbers like "Runaway Love." But the songwriting wasn't as impressive, and the de-emphasis on such signature sounds as Sammy Llanas' nasal voice inclined the album toward anonymity. (Sequencing didn't help either. Why bury the album's best song, the Byrds-like "What It Feels Like," as the eighth track? In fact, the album improved generally in its second half, when it sounded more like the first record.) Although they broke into the Top 100 best-sellers, they failed to break a chart or radio single, which clouded their future. — *William Ruhlmann*

Home / Jul. 27, 1989 / Slash ✦✦✦
The BoDeans toured as opening act to U2 while promoting their second album, and their third album, *Home*, contained at least four songs with guitar work that seemed to have been copied from the fingers of U2's the Edge. Elsewhere, the BoDeans seemed to be seeking to escape their roots-rock tag by turning out one genre exercise after another—country & Western on "Beaujolais," '60s Motown R&B on "When the Love Is

Good," '50s rock 'n' roll on "Good Work" and "Sylvia." The only times the band sounded like itself were when Sammy Llanas got to do one of his story songs, such as "No One" or "Far Far Away from My Heart," but those sounded more like solo efforts than group works. Things had changed for this band over three albums; initially, they sounded so style-bound that you wondered if any growth was possible, but with this album they were charging off in half a dozen directions at once. —*William Ruhlmann*

Black and White / Apr. 26, 1991 / Slash ✦✦✦
After moderate sales on their first three albums threatened to forever classify them as an alternative band, the BoDeans started tackling bigger themes on *Black and White*, produced by Prince-sideman David Z. The band hardly sounds like the roots-oriented band of their previous efforts, and Sam Llanas and Kurt Neumann sound more ambitious as songwriters. So "Black, White and Blood Red" is about more than race, the same way the anthemic "Naked" is about more than sex, the same way the hooky "Good Things" is about more than some guy who can't meet a girl. *Black and White* is about using individual problems as analogies to social ones. It's also about loneliness and hardship. It also didn't sell that much better (if any) than the first albums. —*Brian Mansfield*

Go Slow Down / Oct. 12, 1993 / Slash ✦✦✦✦
The BoDeans made their best album since their debut by returning to the basic folk and rock elements that had always worked best for them. On their most acoustic outing they also rediscovered themselves as songwriters, pursuing subjects unusually close at hand, whether sex, suicide, or the frustrations of the music business. No matter what the topic, they sounded as if they meant it, and for once their eclecticism worked for them, providing them with a bagful of styles to evoke without overdoing it. *Go Slow Down* may have been the statement of a band that had been through a lot and reached a point of emotional exhaustion, but the BoDeans used their experience to craft their most deeply felt and satisfying music. Two and a half years after the album's release, its lead-off track, "Closer to Free," became a hit after being made the theme song of the "Party of Five" TV series. —*William Ruhlmann*

Joe Dirt Car / Aug. 8, 1995 / Slash ✦✦
The BoDeans have always been an exciting live act, so it's not surprising they would do a concert album. What is surprising is its breadth. This is a 24-track, two-disc set running an hour and 56 1/2 minutes, culled from seven different shows played between 1989 and 1994, most of them in Chicago or Milwaukee, where the audiences sound small and enthusiastic. As such, this is less an ordinary live album than a comprehensive live career retrospective. The focus is on the interplay between bandleaders Kurt Neumann and Sammy Llanas, who come off as a neo-Everly Brothers with lots of electric guitars. The sound is sharp and spare, and the mix and sequencing bring out the energy of a good BoDeans set. At very least, *Joe Dirt Car* represents a notable commitment from the group's record label, after five studio albums that have failed to set sales records. —*William Ruhlmann*

Blend / Nov. 5, 1996 / Warner Brothers ✦✦✦
Blend takes advantage of the increased exposure the BoDeans' "Party of Five" theme song "Closer to Free" gave the group. At its core, the duo's roots-rock sound has remained unaltered, but the production is glossy and the hooks are more prominent, making it ready for adult-alternative-radio. If only the album had enough hooks to make them staples on AAA. Apart from "Heart of a Miracle," the songs are simply pleasant, without melodies that make them stick in your head. It's a thoroughly professional affair, but it lacks the spark of *Go Slow Down*, which now seems more like a fluke than a rejuvenation. —*Stephen Thomas Erlewine*

Tommy Bolin

b. 1951, Sioux City, IA, **d.** Dec. 4, 1976, Miami, FL
Guitar, Keyboards, Vocals / Hard Rock, Heavy Metal
A versatile jazz fusions and hard rock guitarist, Tommy Bolin began his musical career as a member of Lonnie Mack's backing band, leaving to form the band Zephyr in 1968. Zephyr's first album reached the Top 50, but when the follow-up stiffed, Bolin left to form the jazz-rock group Energy with flute player Jeremy Steig. Through Steig, Bolin met Billy Cobham and guested on his *Spectrum*. Having achieved a measure of recognition, Bolin was invited to become the lead guitarist of the James Gang, since Joe Walsh's replacement, Domenic Troiano, had recently departed. Bolin stuck around for the *Bang* and *Miami* albums and then took a job in Deep Purple as Ritchie Blackmore's replacement in 1975, playing on *Come Taste the Band*. When Deep Purple showed signs of breaking up later in the year, Bolin went solo, formed a backing band, and recorded the albums *Teaser* and 1976's *Private Eyes*. In December 1976 Bolin was found dead in a Miami hotel room of a drug overdose. —*Steve Huey*

Teaser / 1975 / Columbia ✦✦✦✦
A scattershot collection, but Bolin's forceful slide work on "The Grind" is worth the hunt. —*Rick Clark*

● **Private Eyes** / 1976 / Columbia ✦✦✦✦
It's a solid showcase for Bolin's no-nonsense lead work in a focused package. —*Rick Clark*

The Ultimate: The Best of Tommy Bolin / Sep. 1989 / Geffen ✦✦✦
An overkill box set, it memorializes this late guitarist. Completists will be disappointed that some of *Teaser*'s best moments are not included. —*Rick Clark*

Michael Bolton (Michael Bolotin)

b. Feb. 26, 1954, New Haven, CT
Vocals / Adult Contemporary, Pop-Rock
Singer-songwriter Michael Bolton had an extensive, though not very successful, career under his real name, Michael Bolotin, before emerging in the mid-'80s as a major soft-rock balladeer. He turned up on RCA Records in the mid-'70s singing—in a gruff, Joe Cocker-like voice—both his own blue-eyed soul songs and cover tunes. Neither record buyers nor critics were much interested. He then became the lead singer in Blackjack, a heavy-metal band that made two albums for Polydor at the end of the '70s and the start of the '80s. In 1983 he changed his name to Michael Bolton, signed to Columbia Records as a solo act, and relaunched his career.

Michael Bolton was released in April 1983 and made the Top 100 bestsellers, as did its single, "Fools Game." At the same time, "How Am I Supposed to Live Without You," which Bolton co-written, became a Top 40 hit for Laura Branigan. Nevertheless, Bolton's second Columbia album, *Everybody's Crazy* (1985) was a commercial flop. His breakthrough came with his third album, *The Hunger*, released in September 1987. On this album, Bolton abandoned the more hard-rock aspects of his style to concentrate on blue-eyed soul singing, both on his own songs, such as "That's What Love Is All About," and on covers like Otis Redding's "(Sittin' on) The Dock of the Bay." Those two songs became Top 40 hits.

Soul Provider, released in July 1989, turned Bolton into a superstar, reaching the Top Ten, selling four million copies, and spawning five Top 40 singles, including Bolton's No. 1 version of "How Am I Supposed to Live Without You" and the Top Ten hits "How Can We Be Lovers" and "When I'm Back on My Feet Again." "How Am I Supposed to Live Without You" won Bolton a Grammy Award for Best Pop Vocal Performance, Male. *Time, Love & Tenderness*, released in April 1991, was even more successful, hitting No. 1, selling six million copies, and featuring four Top 40 hits, including the chart-topping cover of Percy Sledge's "When a Man Loves a Woman" and the Top Ten hits "Love Is a Wonderful Thing" (later the subject of a successful plagiarism suit brought against Bolton by the Isley Brothers) and "Time, Love and Tenderness."

Bolton won another Grammy Award for Best Pop Vocal Performance, Male, for "When a Man Loves a Woman," but he had to put up with abuse from two camps of detractors at the February 1992 ceremony. Just after Bolton had sung, pre-rock songwriter Irving Gordon won the Song of the Year award for "Unforgettable" and pointedly attacked songs that "scream, yell, and have a nervous breakdown" and singers who "have a hernia" when they sing. Backstage, Bolton faced a hostile press corps of critics unhappy with his tendency to copy great soul singers like Redding, Ray Charles, and Sledge. Bolton suggested they apply their lips to a certain part of his anatomy. He further responded with *Timeless (The Classics)* in September 1992, an album made up entirely of cover songs. It went to No. 1, sold three million copies, and featured a Top 40 hit in Bolton's version of the Bee Gees' "To Love Somebody." Bolton's next album of original material, *The One Thing*, came in November 1993. It hit the Top Ten, sold three million copies, and featured the Top Ten hit "Said I Loved You . . . But I Lied." Bolton released *Greatest Hits 1985-1995* in the fall of 1995, which debuted in the Top Ten. The next year, *This Is the Time: Christmas Album* appeared. —*William Ruhlmann*

Michael Bolton / Apr. 1983 / Columbia ✦✦✦
The former Michael Bolotin changed his name but not his style on his initial effort for Columbia Records. Bolton had essayed hard-edged arena rock with his band Blackjack, and here he did much the same thing, shout-singing in his emotive whiskey bellow over slashing guitar power chords (frequently courtesy of Blackjack's Bruce Kulick and his brother Bob), icy keyboard fills, angelic backup choirs, and thundering rhythm sections, all intended to fill the hockey auditoriums of America alongside Journey and Foreigner. For all the cliches, Bolton was an undeniably involving singer, and songs like "Fools Game," the lead-off track and chart single, were satisfying pop efforts that suggested he might offer some competition to emerging mainstream rockers like Bryan Adams. As things would turn out, of course, the true key track was the cover of the Supremes' "Back in My Arms Again." —*William Ruhlmann*

Everybody's Crazy / 1985 / Columbia ✦
Michael Bolton's first Columbia album had offered some reason to suspect he had a future in the pop-rock mainstream despite his arena rock tendencies. But on his second album, he endeavored to make a metal-tinged copy of Foreigner, one in which even his distinctive voice was a minor element among the guitar solos and keyboard flourishes. Bolton wrote or co-wrote all the material, but much of the time he seemed to be fighting to be heard, and when he was, all he had to offer was a mouthful of cliches. When this album missed the charts, it looked as if the singer was going down for the third and last time. — *William Ruhlmann*

The Hunger / Sep. 1987 / Columbia ✦✦✦
Given a third chance to resurrect his third career, Bolton made drastic changes. He decided to stop trying to be Lou Gramm of Foreigner and decided that he really wanted to be—Otis Redding? Well, that's what you'd think from his note-for-note copy of Redding's "(Sittin' on) The Dock of the Bay," which brought him close to the Top Ten. Even more notable, though, was "That's What Love Is All About," an original ballad cowritten by Eric ("Love Has No Pride") Kaz that repositioned Bolton from heavy-metal hunk to tough guy with a tender heart. There had been prior hints that Bolton could sell a big ballad, but they were always buried album tracks. This time, the ballad was issued as a single in advance of the album, and it did the trick. For the rest, Bolton employed a new set of collaborators, including members of Journey and pop songwriting queen Diane Warren. The results were platinum sales and a firm place in the middle of the road. — *William Ruhlmann*

Soul Provider / Jul. 1989 / Columbia ✦✦✦✦
Michael Bolton is no fool, and when he broke through to platinum sales with *The Hunger*, nobody had to tell him to record a follow-up devoted to more of the same. Bolton produced most of the record himself, and he teamed with the cream of the era's romantic rock ballad writers, people like Diane Warren (who gets five co-credits here) and Desmond Child, while the R&B copy this time was Ray Charles' version of "Georgia on My Mind." He also reclaimed "How Am I Supposed to Live Without You" from Laura Branigan. The result was five Top 40 hits and millions of albums sold. Maybe Bolton wasn't the king of the hockey rinks, but his voice was now stoking the romantic fires in bedrooms across America, which is nice work if you can get it. — *William Ruhlmann*

Time, Love & Tenderness / Apr. 1991 / Columbia ✦✦✦✦
Michael Bolton cloned his approach from *Soul Provider* on its follow-up, *Time, Love & Tenderness*, and sold as many records for his trouble. (That's six million copies.) His key collaborator once again was Diane Warren, who applied her goldplated gift for writing contemporary love songs to six tunes, among them the hits "Time, Love and Tenderness" and "Missing You Now" (which featured saxmeister Kenny G). The obligatory R&B carbon copy was Percy Sledge's "When a Man Loves a Woman," which hit No. 1. The only unusual songs came at the beginning and the end. The album led off with "Love Is a Wonderful Thing" (a Top Ten hit), a song in standard '60s R&B mode that would be the subject of a plagiarism suit from the Isley Brothers, and it concluded with "Steel Bars," co-written by Bolton and . . . Bob Dylan? That's what it said, and even if the song wasn't one of Dylan's best, it at least indicated that Bolton might have possibilities that had so far gone unnoticed. — *William Ruhlmann*

Timeless (The Classics) / Sep. 1992 / Columbia ✦✦✦
It's hard to resist the notion that Michael Bolton, who took considerable flak in the press for storming the charts with copycat reproductions of '60s soul hits felt "suddenly compelled," as he put it here in a sleeve note, to devote an entire album to cover songs after publicly confronting his critics at the Grammy Awards ceremony in February 1992. There's not much you can do with "Yesterday" or "White Christmas" at this point. On the other hand, as with his previous R&B appropriations, versions of songs like the Four Tops' "Reach Out I'll Be There" and Sam and Dave's "Hold On, I'm Comin'" succeeded only in confirming Bolton's inferiority to his predecessors. — *William Ruhlmann*

The Artistry of Michael Bolotin / 1993 / RCA ✦✦
A ten-track compilation of Michael Bolton's early recordings of such classic rock staples as Joe Walsh's "Rocky Mountain Way" and the Guess Who's "These Eyes." Since Bolton was still trying to find his style, most of these songs fall flat, but it's interesting to hear his emotive vocals develop. — *Stephen Thomas Erlewine*

The One Thing / Nov. 1993 / Columbia ✦✦✦
You could hardly call an album that neared the top of the charts, stayed in them for ten months, and sold three million copies a flop, but when it's following two straight No. 1s, and the artist's last album of new material stayed in the charts twice as long and sold twice as many copies, you can call it a disappointment. Maybe it was just that this was the fourth—or fifth, if you count the covers album *Timeless (The Classics)*—time around for Bolton's successful formula, but *The One Thing* sounded pro forma even for him. That didn't keep "Said I Loved You . . . But I Lied" from becoming a massive hit on soft-rock radio, but

none of the other tunes really connected with his usually adoring public. It would not be wise, however, to count out a pop star as persistent as Michael Bolton. — *William Ruhlmann*

● **Greatest Hits 1985-1995** / Sep. 19, 1995 / Columbia ✦✦✦✦
Michael Bolton's 17-track, 74-minute *Greatest Hits 1985-1995* is a typical compilation of its time, in the sense that its selections do not exactly mirror the artist's list of successful chart singles and that there are several newly recorded songs included. Actually, Bolton comes a little closer than, say, Bruce Springsteen or Bob Seger to including all the hits. The only ones he leaves out are a cover of the Bee Gees' "To Love Somebody" and "Love Is a Wonderful Thing," which was the subject of a successful plagiarism suit brought against him by the Isley Brothers, while "Steel Bars," a non-hit co-written by Bolton and Bob Dylan, is included. On the radio, Bolton is the king of the power ballad, and while on his regular albums he manages to vary the tempo somewhat, here it's one trudging tale of romantic angst after another. Among the five new songs, "Can I Touch You . . . There?," a Top 40 hit, has a sinuous rhythm, over which Bolton plays a Marvin Gaye-style lover man. "I Found Someone" is Bolton's own recording of a song he co-wrote that was Top Ten hit for Cher in 1988. "This River," written by Diane Warren, sounds dangerously close to Carly Simon's "Let the River Run," especially from a man who's already suffered one plagiarism suit. Though it doubtless will be successful as a catalog item, *Greatest Hits* was another relative sales disappointment for Bolton despite its two million-unit initial sale and Top Ten chart peak. — *William Ruhlmann*

Bon Jovi

f. 1983, Sayreville, NJ
Hard Rock, Pop-Rock, Hair Metal
Few bands embodied the era of pop-metal like Bon Jovi. By merging Def Leppard's loud but tuneful metal with Bruce Springsteen's working-class sensibilities, the New Jersey-based quintet developed an ingratiatingly melodic and professional variation of hard-rock—one that appealed as much to teenagers as to housewives. Bon Jovi skillfully employed professional songwriters to give their songs, especially their power ballads, an appropriately commercial sheen, inaugurating a trend that dominated mainstream hard rock and metal for the next decade. They also made simple performance videos that emphasized lead singer Jon Bon Jovi's photogenic good looks, and these clips helped propel 1986's *Slippery When Wet* and 1988's *New Jersey* into multi-platinum status around the world. Both records were criticized for being more pop than metal, as well as being targeted toward teenyboppers, but the group managed to subtly change their image in the early '90s, moving away from metal and concentrating on straightforward arena-rock and big ballads. The shift in style worked, and Bon Jovi was the only American pop-metal band of the '80s to retain a sizable audience in the '90s.

Jon Bongiovi spent most of his adolescence ditching school to play rock 'n' roll, usually in local bands with his friend David Rashbaum. Bongiovi's cousin Tony owned the famous New York recording studio the Power Station, where Jon hung out. He was hired as a janitor, and soon he was recording demos at the Power Station with several famous musicians, including members of the E Street Band and Aldo Nova. One of these demos, "Runaway," became a hit on New Jersey radio, and Bongiovi formed Bon Jovi to support the song, recruiting not only Rashbaum, but guitarist Dave Sabo, bassist Alec John Such, and drummer Tico Torres. Soon Bon Jovi was the subject of a major-label bidding war, and the group—or, according to some reports, just Bongiovi—signed to Polygram/Mercury in 1983. Upon signing, Jon changed his last name to Bon Jovi in order to de-emphasize his ethnic background, and Rashbaum adopted his middle name Bryan as his last name. Before the group entered the studio, Bon Jovi replaced Sabo with Richie Sambora.

Bon Jovi's eponymous debut album was released in 1984, and "Runaway" became a Top 40 hit. After its success, Tony Bongiovi sued the band, claiming he developed their successful sound; the group settled out of court. The following year, *7800 Fahrenheit* was released and went gold. Despite the band's respectable success, Bon Jovi wasn't becoming the superstars they had hoped to be, and they changed their approach for the next album, *Slippery When Wet*. Hiring professional songwriter Desmond Child as a collaborator, the group wrote 30 songs and auditioned them for New Jersey and New York teenagers, basing the album's running order on their opinions. After the original cover of a busty woman in a wet T-shirt was ditched in favor of the title traced in water on a garbage bag, *Slippery When Wet* was released in 1986. Supported by several appealing, straightforward videos that showcased the photogenic Jon, the album eventually sold nine million copies in the US alone, helping usher in the era of pop-metal. Two songs, "You Give Love A Bad Name" and "Livin' on a Prayer," reached No. 1, while "Wanted Dead or Alive" reached the Top Ten.

Bon Jovi replicated the *Slippery When Wet* formula for 1988's *New Jersey*, which shot to No. 1 upon its release. *New Jersey* was only slightly less successful than its predecessor, selling five million copies and generating two No. 1 singles, "Bad Medicine" and "I'll Be There for You," as well as the Top Ten hits "Born to Be My Baby," "Lay Your Hands on Me" and "Living in Sin." In 1989 the band supported Cher, who was then dating Sambora, on her *Heart of Stone* album, which was recorded while the group was in the midst of an 18-month international tour. After the tour, the band went on hiatus. During their time off, Jon Bon Jovi wrote the soundtrack for *Young Guns II*, which was released in 1990 as the *Blaze of Glory* album. The record produced two hit singles, the No. 1 title track and the No. 12 "Miracle," as well as earning Grammy and Oscar nominations. The next year Bon Jovi reunited to record a fifth album, *Keeping the Faith*, which was released in the fall of 1992. While the album didn't match the blockbuster status of its predecessors, largely because musical tastes had shifted in the four years between *New Jersey* and *Keep the Faith*, it was nevertheless a big hit, and its more straightforward, anthemic sound produced the hit single "Bed of Roses." A hits collection, *Cross Road*, followed in 1994; and in the fall of 1995 they released *These Days*, which proved to be a bigger success in Europe than America. After appearing in the 1996 film *Moonlight and Valentino*, Jon Bon Jovi released his first official solo album in the summer of 1997. —*Stephen Thomas Erlewine*

Bon Jovi / Jan. 1984 / Mercury ✦✦✦
The band's debut, while lacking much of the focus found on subsequent releases, sets the blueprint for future greatness. In a superslick package, they offer a fine balance between hard rock and a strong sense of melody. —*David Jehnzen*

7800 Degrees Fahrenheit / Apr. 1985 / Mercury ✦✦✦
The band's 1985 sophomore effort was slammed by critics upon release, but showed considerable growth in songwriting and playing. It was their first gold record and their last album before entering superstardom with the follow-up, *Slippery When Wet*. Highlights include "In and Out of Love" and "Hardest Part of the Night." —*David Jehnzen*

Slippery When Wet / Aug. 1986 / Mercury ✦✦✦✦
It is probably true that Bon Jovi's breakthrough success with *Slippery When Wet*, their third album, had more to do with lead singer Jon Bon Jovi's mop of curls and winning smile than with anything in the grooves of the record. Nevertheless, the album contained competent contemporary pop-rock, from its Eddie Van Halen-inspired guitar solos to the singer's enthusiastic, husky wail (which owed a lot to Bruce Springsteen). Jon Bon Jovi, guitarist Richie Sambora, and songwriter-for-hire Desmond Child had little more on their minds than girls and rock-as-mythology (even the working-class anthem "Livin' on a Prayer" featured a character who was forced to hock his "six string"), but that may only mean they had identified their audience—young white adolescent males—and were targeting it accurately. —*William Ruhlmann*

New Jersey / Sep. 1988 / Mercury ✦✦✦✦
Bon Jovi had perfected a formula for hard pop-rock by the time of this album, concentrating on sing-along choruses sung over and over again, frequently to a rough, extensively overdubbed chorus, producing an effect not unlike what these songs sounded like in the arenas and stadiums where they were most often heard. The lyrics had that typical pop twist—although they nominally expressed romantic commitment, sentiments such as "Lay Your Hands on Me" and "I'll Be There for You" worked equally well as a means for the band and its audience to reaffirm their affection for each other. The only thing that marred the perfection of this communion was Jon Bon Jovi's continuing obsession with a certain predecessor from his home state; at times, he seemed to be trying to recreate *Born to Run* using cheaper materials. —*William Ruhlmann*

Keep the Faith / Nov. 1992 / Mercury ✦✦✦
After being missing in action for nearly four years, Bon Jovi returns with *Keep the Faith*, an update on their trademark pop-metal sound. Because the rules had changed since *New Jersey*, the band knew they had to shake things up a bit. Bon Jovi wants to be taken seriously this time around—hence, epics like the ten-minute "Dry County" and stabs at significance like "Fear" (plus the new short haircuts). Most of these grand statements fall flat, but there are songs here ("Bed of Roses," "Keep the Faith") that nearly match the glory days. —*Stephen Thomas Erlewine*

● **Cross Road** / Oct. 4, 1994 / Mercury ✦✦✦✦
While Bon Jovi always managed to stick a couple of killer album tracks on their records, their main strength has always been singles. *Cross Road* collects all of their biggest hits, adding a couple of new songs and Jon Bon Jovi's solo hit, "Blaze of Glory," for good measure. Even the band's detractors may not be able to resist the constant flow of big guitars, big hooks, and sweet melodies that pour out on *Cross Roads*. After all, this is what state-of-the-art mainstream hard rock was all about in the late '80s. —*Stephen Thomas Erlewine*

These Days / 1995 / Mercury ✦✦✦
With *These Days*, Bon Jovi firmly established themselves as an adult contemporary act. They still have their fair share of rockers, but they seem half-hearted and incomplete. Instead, the band sounds the most

comfortable with love ballads and working class anthems, from hits "This Ain't a Love Song" and "Lie to Me" to the acoustic "Diamond Ring." In fact, as the years go by, Bon Jovi gets musically stronger. Not only are their best songs stronger now, their playing is more accomplished. Keeping these improvements in mind, it's no surprise that the group was one of the few pop-metal bands to sustain a career in the mid-'90s. —*Stephen Thomas Erlewine*

Graham Bond (Graham John Clifton Bond)

b. Oct. 28, 1937, Romford, Essex, England, **d.** May 8, 1974, London, England
Organ, Saxophone / Blues-Rock, British Invasion, British Blues
An important, underappreciated figure of early British R&B, Graham Bond is known in the US, if at all, for heading the group that Jack Bruce and Ginger Baker played in before they joined Cream. Originally an alto sax jazz player, he was voted "Britain's New Jazz Star" in 1961. He met Bruce and Baker in 1962 after joining Alexis Koerner's Blues Incorporated, the finishing school for numerous British rock and blues musicians. By the time he, Bruce, and Baker split to form their own band in 1963, Bond was playing mostly the Hammond organ, as well as handling the lion's share of the vocals. John McLaughlin was a member of the Graham Bond Organization in the early days for a few months, and some live material that he recorded with the group was eventually issued after most of its members had achieved stardom in other contexts. Saxophonist Dick Heckstall-Smith completed Bond's most stable lineup, which cut a couple of decent albums and a few singles in the mid-'60s.

In its prime, the Graham Bond Organization played rhythm and blues with a strong jazzy flavor, emphasizing Bond's demonic organ and gruff vocals. The band arguably would have been better served to feature Bruce as its lead singer; he is featured surprisingly rarely on their recordings. Nevertheless, their best records were admirably tough British R&B-rock-jazz-soul, and though Bond has sometimes been labeled as a pioneer of jazz-rock, in reality it was much closer to rock than jazz. The band performed imaginative covers and fairly strong original material, and Bond was also perhaps the very first rock musician to record with the Mellotron synthesizer. Hit singles, though, were necessary for British bands to thrive in the mid-'60s, and Bond's group began to fall apart in 1966, when Bruce and Baker joined forces with Eric Clapton to form Cream. Bond attempted to carry on with the Organization for a while with Heckstall-Smith and drummer Jon Hiseman, both of whom went on to John Mayall's Bluesbreakers and Colosseum.

Bond never recaptured the heights of his work with the Organization. In the late '60s, he moved to the US, recording albums with musicians including Harvey Brooks, Harvey Mandel, and Hal Blaine. Moving back to Britain, he worked with Ginger Baker's Airforce, the Jack Bruce Band, and Cream lyricist Pete Brown, as well as forming the band Holy Magick, who recorded a couple of albums. Bond's demise was more tragic than most: he developed serious drug and alcohol problems and an obsession with the occult. He committed suicide by throwing himself into the path of a London Underground train in 1974. —*Richie Unterberger*

● **The Sound of 65** / Mar. 1965 / Edsel ✦✦✦✦
Although the Organization's first album was recorded a mere year or two before Cream's debut, it bears little resemblance to Cream's pioneering hard blues-rock. Instead, it's taut British R&B with a considerable jazz influence. That influence comes not so much from the rhythm section as saxophonist Dick Heckstall-Smith and lead singer/organist Bond himself. This LP is not as exciting or rock-oriented as those of contemporaries like the Rolling Stones or John Mayall, but it contains respectably gritty, mostly original material, with an occasionally nasty edge. There are some obscure treasures of the British R&B explosion, including the original version of "Train Time" (later performed by Cream), the thrilling bass runs on "Baby Be Good to Me," and the group's hardboiled rearrangements of such traditional standards as "Wade in the Water" and "Early in the Morning." Even their blatant stab at commerciality (the ballad "Tammy") has its charm. —*Richie Unterberger*

There's a Bond Between Us / Nov. 1965 / Edsel ✦✦✦✦
Bond's second album stakes out territory similar to his debut in a more polished but slightly less exciting fashion. Some of the covers are a bit routine and hackneyed, and the original material isn't quite as strong (or frequent) as on the first effort. On a few tunes, the group expands from raveups to mellower, jazzier ballads that retain an R&B base. Highlights include the early Jack Bruce composition "Hear Me Calling Your Name" (to which he also contributes a fine lead vocal) and the excellent Bond tune "Walkin' in the Park," which holds up to the best early British R&B numbers. The album is also notable for being one of the very first rock LPs to feature the Mellotron, which Bond uses subtly and well. —*Richie Unterberger*

Graham Bond Organization / 1984 / Charly ✦✦
This live 1964 gig is one of Giorgio Gomelsky's innumerable tapes of
British club acts of the period, several of which would be released many
years later in attempts to cash in on some big names who were present.
These historical documents, never intended for release, ranged from
superb to wretched. This LP (which, like most of these Gomelsky
projects, has been reissued under numerous different covers and titles)
falls about in the middle of this scale. Bond led an erratic, interesting
group that incorporated elements of jazz and improvisation in its blend
of blues, R&B, and rock. Future Cream members Jack Bruce and Ginger
Baker were his rhythm section in his prime, and Dick Heckstall-Smith
handled horns; this is the lineup featured on this set. But it's not deathless stuff. The fidelity, for one, is muddy, especially the bottom, Bruce's
bass suffering the most. The better tunes—"Wade in the Water," "Early in
the Morning," "Train Time," and "Spanish Blues"—are available in better performances and much clearer fidelity on the group's first studio
album, *The Sound of 65*. The rest is routine, even below average in
spots, early British R&B. The Organization may have been among the
most accomplished players on the scene, but they couldn't hold a candle
to the Stones or Yardbirds in terms of imagination and excitement. A
better introduction to the sound of this lineup is the fine Edsel reissue of
The Sound of 65 and *There's a Bond Between Us*, which have been combined in one package. —*Richie Unterberger*

Gary "U.S." Bonds (Gary Anderson)

b. Jun. 6, 1939, Jacksonville, FL
Vocals / R&B, Rock 'n' Roll
After moving to the Norfolk, VA, area in the mid-'50s, young Gary
Anderson began plying his vocal wares, first in church, later with a local
group called the Turks. When he was not yet 21, he was approached by
local record producer Frank Guida to join his tiny Legrand label. Guida
changed Anderson's name to U.S. Bonds, hoping the first release would
get extra airplay by disc jockeys mistaking it for a public service
announcement. The result was the classic "New Orleans," combining
rock-combo raunch with impassioned, scorched soul singing that set the
stage for all that would follow. Guida double- and triple-tracked Bonds'
voice, and the resulting murky production gave all the hits (including
"Quarter to Three," "School Is Out," and "Dear Lady Twist") a party/in-
outer-space quality all their own. Though he has kept recording, making
a couple of excellent solo albums in the early '80s with the help of Bruce
Springsteen, Bonds is best seen today dotting the landscape of oldies
shows the world over, singing the songs that made him famous. —*Cub
Koda*

Dedication / Apr. 1981 / Razor & Tie ✦✦✦
Bruce Springsteen played guitar, sang a duet, wrote three songs, and co-
produced and co-arranged four on Gary U.S. Bonds' comeback album,
recorded 20 years after his heyday. Springsteen also lent his backup
group, the E Street Band, while E Street guitarist Miami Steve (Van
Zandt) also contributed a song and produced the bulk of the record. The
result, naturally, sounds like a Bruce Springsteen and the E Street Band
album with lead vocals by Gary U.S. Bonds. Bonds' elastic tenor, heard
in much greater clarity than it ever was in his early years, has just
enough grit to be soulful, and he puts across effectively the pop-soul
tunes Springsteen and Van Zandt have constructed for him. He also
tackles the Beatles' "It's Only Love" and Bob Dylan's "From a Buick 6,"
and sings Jackson Browne's "The Pretender" as if the lyric were devoid
of irony. It's an enjoyable album that does nothing to change the notion
that Bonds as a recording artist essentially conforms to the intentions of
his producer, whether that's Frank Guida, Jerry Williams, Jr., or Bruce
Springsteen. —*William Ruhlmann*

On the Line / Jun. 1982 / Razor & Tie ✦✦✦
On The Line, Gary U.S. Bonds' second comeback album under the sponsorship of Bruce Springsteen, was even more of a Springsteen record
than its predecessor. This time, Springsteen wrote seven of the 11 songs,
co-produced all of them with Miami Steve (Van Zandt) and again lent
the E Street Band for the sessions. While there were no Springsteen
masterpieces here, the rock 'n' roll revival style of the material, similar to
that on *Dedication*, made it, in effect, the follow-up to Springsteen's *The
River* album, albeit with a different vocalist. And that vocalist was, if
anything, more expressive than the author—on a song like "Out of
Work," one of Springsteen's blue-collar anthems, Bonds sang with the
conviction of a journeyman who knows what work is and what it's like
not to have it. —*William Ruhlmann*

● **The School of Rock 'n' Roll: Best of Gary U.S. Bonds** / Apr. 1990 /
Rhino ✦✦✦✦
Gary U.S. Bonds' biggest hits—"New Orleans," "Twist, Twist Senora,"
and especially "Quarter to Three"—were unquestionably among the
best rock 'n' roll of the early '60s. Beyond that, the going runs a bit thin.
This 18-cut compilation includes all of the above hits, as well as others
from his blitz of Top 40 singles in 1961 and 1962—"School Is Out," the
response record "School Is In" (guess which one did worse), "Dear Lady

Twist," and "Seven Day Weekend." The rest of the CD features B-sides,
flop singles, and unissued material from his stay at the Legrand label in
the early '60s. Most of them feature the dense production, party atmosphere, and West Indian-influenced beats that made his hits so instantly
identifiable. It was nonetheless a formula, and it wears thin over the
course of an entire album. Two of the more interesting cuts are the original 1961 version of "Not Me," which would become a big hit for the
Orlons in 1963 in a slightly sanitized version, and both parts of the 1963
single "Perdido," which works up as manic a party atmosphere as Bonds
ever managed. —*Richie Unterberger*

Boney M

f. 1976, Germany, **db.** 1980
Disco, Euro-Dance
Although they never had much success in America, the Euro-disco
group Boney M was a European phenomenon during the '70s. After
German record producer Frank Farian (b. 1942) recorded the single
"Baby Do You Wanna Bump?" (which was successful in Holland and
Belgium), he created Boney M to support the song, bringing in four West
Indian vocalists who had been working as session singers in Ger-
many—Marcia Barrett (b. Oct. 14, 1948, St. Catherines, Jamaica), Liz
Mitchell (b. July 12, 1952, Clarendon, Jamaica), Maizie Williams (b. Mar.
25, 1951, Monserrat, West Indies), and Bobby Farrell (b. Oct. 6, 1949,
Aruba, West Indies). "Daddy Cool" reached the UK Top Ten in February
1977, followed in April by a remake of Bobby Hebb's "Sunny." In July,
"Ma Baker" just missed the UK No. 1 spot, and "Belfast" hit the Top Ten
in December. In 1978 Boney M was at the height of its popularity with
"Rivers of Babylon"/"Brown Girl in the Ring," which became the second-biggest selling single in UK chart history. "Rivers of Babylon" also
was Boney M's only US Top 40 hit. Boney M's album *Nightflight to
Venus* also topped the UK charts. In October 1978, "Rasputin" became
another UK Top Ten hit, followed by the seasonal chart-topper "Mary's
Boy Child"/"Oh My Lord," which became the fifth-biggest selling single
in UK history. In March 1979, "Painter Man" hit the UK Top Ten, followed in May by "Hooray! Hooray! It's a Holi-Holiday." In September, the
album *Oceans of Fantasy* hit No. 1. The group disbanded in 1980; their
music continues to sell well in Europe, with a compilation hitting the
UK Top Ten in 1994. Farian went on to create the late-'80s dance sensation Milli Vanilli. —*Stephen Thomas Erlewine*

● **The Magic of Boney M [20 Hits]** / 1980 / Atlantic/Hansa ✦✦✦✦
Boney M's top Euro-disco creations—songs that ruled the continent for a
while in the mid-'70s—are compiled on this singularly pleasing singles
collection. —*Stephen Thomas Erlewine*

Bongos

f. 1980, Hoboken, NJ
Power Pop, Jangle-Pop
Hoboken's Bongos—founded as a trio consisting of Richard Barone (guitar, vocals), Rob Norris (bass), and Frank Giannini (drums,
vocals)—made no pretense of being anything other than a pop band; fortunately, they were a good pop band, covering guitar pop from the Byrds
to T. Rex, all of it pulled together by Barone's original songs. Although
he was the focal point, the other members were by no means peripheral;
after their first full-length album, *Drums Along the Hudson* (1982),
James Mastro joined and contributed some stellar hooks. After releasing
a series of singles and an EP on tiny Fetish Records in 1980 and 1981,
the Bongos signed to independent PVC Records. *Drums Along the Hudson* compiled all their previously released tracks. They then moved up
to RCA and released the five-song *Numbers with Wings EP* (1983) and
the album *Beat Hotel* (1985), before leaving RCA and splitting up.
(Later, *Drums Along the Hudson* and a two-fer of *Numbers with Wings*
and *Beat Hotel* were reissued on CD by Razor & Tie.) At their best, the
Bongos made some irresistible guitar pop. —*William Ruhlmann*

Drums Along the Hudson / 1982 / Razor & Tie ✦✦✦
Richard Barone's brief lyrics frequently lack clarity, but he sings them
earnestly, and the trio plays irresistibly catchy, guitar-based pop music.
Heard from the perspective of the following decade, both the playing
and the lyrics sound remarkably prescient (this band could clean up in
the alternative market today), although at the time they sounded noticeably retro. (*Drums Along the Hudson* compiles all the tracks on the UK
EP *Time and the River*, along with the Bongos' previously released singles.) —*William Ruhlmann*

Numbers with Wings / 1983 / RCA ✦✦✦✦
This five-song EP (now available, along with *Beat Hotel*, on a single CD)
marks several upgrades in the Bongos' career. They have added second
guitarist James Mastro, moved up to RCA Records, and brought in producer Richard Gottehrer. Gottehrer, who has a sharp sense of rock 'n' roll
dynamics (listen to his work on the Angels' "My Boyfriend's Back"), is a
felicitous choice, and the added instrumentation (and no doubt better-
budgeted recording and mixing) allows the Bongos to better realize

their pop sound. As a result, songs like "Numbers with Wings," with its echoed vocals and full sound, have the kind of epic sweep Richard Barone's compositions have always suggested without achieving before. Not that the band has become overblown—just fulfilled. — *William Ruhlmann*

Beat Hotel / 1985 / RCA ✦✦✦
Beat Hotel is, in a sense, the Bongos' only "real" album; *Drums Along the Hudson*, its predecessor, was a compilation of previously released single and EP tracks. As such, *Beat Hotel* is a more unified effort than the earlier LP, but lacks the urgent immediacy that all those singles tracks gave it. Richard Barone makes extensive use of a guitar synthesizer to fill out the band's sound, although it's still the normal guitar licks that dominate the music. Barone also sings engagingly, filling his songs with catchy hooks, even though on the lyric sheet it's hard to figure out what he's talking about. It's a shame that *Beat Hotel*, which seems like a transitional album, proved to be the Bongos' final effort—they remain a promising group that never had a chance to reach their potential. — *William Ruhlmann*

● **Beat Hotel/Numbers with Wings** / Jul. 24, 1992 / Razor & Tie ✦✦✦✦
This is a two-fer of the Bongos' last EP and albums. "Barbarella" and the title cut from the Richard Gottehrer-produced *Numbers with Wings* (1983) are the highlights on that set. *Beat Hotel* (1985) is their best-sounding effort, though the songwriting quality isn't as consistent. —*Rick Clark*

The Bonzo Dog Band

f. 1965, GoldsmithsCollege,Lewisham, London, **db.** 1970
Comedy, Psychedelic, Pop-Rock
Besides, perhaps, the Mothers of Invention (with whom they were sometimes compared), the Bonzo Dog Band was the most successful group to combine rock music and comedy. Starting off as the Bonzo Dog Dada Band, then becoming the Bonzo Dog Doo-Dah Band, and then finally just the Bonzo Dog Band, the group was started by British art college students in the mid-'60s. Initially they were inclined toward trad-jazz and vaudevillian routines, but by the time of their 1967 debut album, they were leaning further in pop and rock directions. A brief appearance in the Beatles' *Magical Mystery Tour* film bolstered their visibility, and Paul McCartney (under the pseudonym Apollo C. Vermouth) produced their single "I'm the Urban Spaceman," which reached the British Top Five in 1968. The Bonzos really hit their stride with their second and third albums, which found them adding elements of psychedelia to their already absurdist mix of pop, cabaret, and Dada. The Bonzos could be side-splitting, but their records hold up well because they were also capable musicians and songwriters, paced by Neil Innes and Viv Stanshall (both of whom wrote the lion's share of their best material). The group attempted to move into more serious and musical realms with their 1969 LP *Keynsham*, which, unsurprisingly, was acclaimed as their weakest effort. They broke up shortly afterward; Viv Stanshall made some obscure solo recordings (he was also the grandstanding narrator on Mike Oldfield's "Tubular Bells"). Neil Innes collaborated with members of Monty Python, upon whom the Bonzos were a large influence, as well as writing the songs for and performing in the brilliant Beatles documentary spoof, *The Rutles.* —*Richie Unterberger*

Gorilla / Oct. 1967 / One Way ✦✦✦
Gorilla was the 1967 debut album by the Bonzo Dog Doo-Dah Band, who would thereafter drop the Doo-Dah from their name and establish themselves as the greatest satirical British pop band of all time. Their first effort is far more tentative and tame than their second and third albums, when they hit their stride by expanding their musical and topical recklessness. The Bonzos, after all, did not begin as a rock band, or even a pop band, but as a somewhat vaudevillian comedy outfit that owed a great deal to British music hall traditions. This album may be low-key, but that's not to say it doesn't retain a good deal of charm. The humor is extremely dry, subtle, and British, leaning more toward their trad-jazz roots than the churning London pop-rock scene. It nonetheless includes a few great moments: the deadpan jazz vamp "The Intro and the Outro" (wherein a smarmy MC introduces a bevy of historical figures in a show band, including Adolf Hitler on vibes), the film-noir satire "Mickey's Son and Daughter," and their vicious send-up of "The Sound of Music." It's not recommended as a starting point, but those who already appreciate these wonderful British eccentrics will find this an enjoyable document of the band's more restrained roots. —*Richie Unterberger*

Doughnuts in Granny's Greenhouse / Dec. 1968 / Edsel ✦✦✦✦
Taking the "Doo Dah" out of their name for this 1968 LP, the Bonzos' second album was probably their best. Although they were hardly a rock or pop group in the traditional sense, the Bonzos couldn't help absorbing some of the vibes of British psychedelia, and the heady ambience of the era is reflected in the recklessly diverse and outrageous material. Almost all of the songs were penned by the two top Dogs, Viv Stanshall and Neil Innes, who deflate British blues, psychedelia, and

other pop, jazz, and music-hall styles with priceless wit. Star tracks on this saxophone-heavy album include the doo wop ode to a spacegirl ("Beautiful Zelda"), "Trouser Press" (which gave the late American underground rock magazine its name), the droll series of poker-faced spoken sketches on "Rhinocratic Oaths" (certainly an influence on Monty Python), and the boozy "My Pink Half of The Drainpipe," which ranks as one of the most hysterical and hysterical songs released by a pop group of any era. —*Richie Unterberger*

Tadpoles / Aug. 1, 1969 / One Way ✦✦✦
The Bonzos' third album is a bit of a retreat from the cosmic anything-goes atmosphere of their second LP (*Doughnuts in Granny's Greenhouse*), slanted much more heavily toward their vaudevillian trad-jazz roots. Perhaps that's because Viv Stanshall and Neil Innes, who dominated the second album, contribute only three tunes here. Still, it's never less than entertaining and has some stellar moments, like the psychedelic African safari of "Ali Baba's Camel," the skit "Shirt" (another clear forerunner of Monty Python), and the British hit single "I'm the Urban Spaceman," produced by Paul McCartney. —*Richie Unterberger*

Lets Make Up & Be Friendly / Apr. 1972 / One Way ✦✦

History of the Bonzos / May 24, 1974 / United Artists ✦✦✦✦
Necessarily, the pick among Bonzos albums is Rhino's 1990 collection *The Best of the Bonzo Dog Band*, but only because that one's in print. This compilation was released as a double-LP set in 1974 and, although out of print, is the best Bonzos compilation (and there have been quite a few). Running an hour and 42 minutes and containing 35 tracks that span the Bonzos' five albums and some of their solo work, the album effectively presents their offbeat humor and diverse musical styles, from the 1920s music-hall pop and jazz of their early period to the more rock-oriented material they made later on. The humor is absurd and whimsical rather than laugh-out-loud funny—maybe a single compilation would be the best way to appreciate them—but you can definitely hear the makings of British comedy in the Monty Python mold here. —*William Ruhlmann*

● **The Best of the Bonzo Dog Band** / 1991 / Rhino ✦✦✦✦
This is a well-chosen overview of the playful late-'60s British absurdists' work. Fans of Monty Python should check out this precursor. —*Rick Clark*

The Boo Radleys

f. 1988, Liverpool, England
Alternative Pop-Rock, Shoegazing, Brit-Pop, Dream-Pop
Formed in Liverpool in 1988, the English guitar-pop group the Boo Radleys developed a dedicated cult following in the early '90s before crossing over into the mainstream in the middle of the decade. Originally, the group was one of the lesser lights of the loud, noisy My Bloody Valentine-inspired psychedelic trance-pop bands labelled "shoegazers" by the British weekly music press. By the mid-'90s the Boo Radleys had developed into a more straightforward pop band that didn't use noise and extended guitar workouts as a way of fleshing out their songs, instead using it as the basis of their music.

The Boo Radleys originally consisted of guitarist/songwriter Martin Carr, vocalist/guitarist Sice, bassist Timothy Brown, and drummer Steve Hewitt. The band released their first album, *Ichabod and I*, on a local independent record label in 1990; Hewitt was replaced by Rob Cieka after the release of the record. With the support of influential British disc jockey John Peel, the band signed with Rough Trade Records. The group released the EP *Every Heaven* in 1991; the record made it into the lower regions of the UK charts.

Rough Trade folded shortly after the release of *Every Heaven,* and the Boo Radleys moved to Creation Records, releasing *Everything's Alright Forever* in 1992. *Everything's Alright Forever* was released in the US through Creation's association with Columbia Records, but it didn't gain much attention in America. In England, it received favorable reviews, and the group began to build a fan base. Topping several Best-of-the-Year lists, including *Melody Maker's,* 1993's *Giant Steps* was a critical success in England and sold respectably. In America, the record launched the minor alternative-rock hit "Lazarus" and led to a second-stage spot on Lollapalooza '94.

Released in England in the spring of 1995, the more pop-oriented *Wake Up!* was the band's commercial breakthrough, debuting at No. 1. The bright, horn-driven single "Wake Up Boo" entered in the Top Ten and stayed on the charts until the early summer, preventing the follow-up single "Find the Answer Within" from charting higher than the Top 30. *Wake Up!* was released in America in the fall of 1995 with no promotional push from Columbia, who dropped the band early the next year.

The Boo Radleys returned in the fall of 1996 with *C'Mon Kids,* a self-consciously loud and arty album designed to shake off the band's new-found pop fans. It worked—the album debuted in the Top Ten, but it soon fell off the charts, despite overwhelmingly positive reviews. Early in 1997 the band finalized an American contract with Mercury, and

C'Mon Kids was released in March, half a year after its initial British release. *—Stephen Thomas Erlewine*

Everything's Alright Forever / Aug. 1992 / Columbia ✦✦✦
On their second album, the Boo Radleys begin to refine their mix of grinding guitars and pop melodies. Although their songwriting isn't always impressive, the record shows a great deal of promise. *—Stephen Thomas Erlewine*

Giant Steps / Aug. 31, 1993 / Columbia ✦✦✦✦
Giant Steps is a pastiche of every genre of pop-rock from the British Invasion on. It's an incredibly ambitious and pretentious concept, but the Boo Radley's sense of songcraft has improved enough to make the album work. *Giant Steps* has swirling, noisy guitars, Beach Boys harmonies, the arrangements of Love, and Beatlesque melodies, forming a remarkably original record, rich in detail and ultimately very rewarding. *—Stephen Thomas Erlewine*

● **Wake Up!** / Sep. 12, 1995 / Columbia ✦✦✦✦
With their third album, the Boo Radleys abandoned the overt noise that obscured the pop sensibilities of their early work and scaled back the ambitions of *Giant Steps*. The result is *Wake Up!*, a glorious, brightly-colored gem of a pop record. From the Beach Boy harmonies and trumpet fanfares of the opening "Wake Up Boo!" to the closing epic, McCartney-styled ballad "Wilder," the group winds through many styles of British pop. Much of the darkness—both musically and lyrically—of their previous music has been lifted; in its place is a sterling piece of pure pop, with all the big choruses, bright melodies, and simple hooks that word implies. *Giant Steps* had elements of this grand pop, but it tried too hard. *Wake Up!* doesn't try for as much and in doing so, it achieves more, both musically and commercially. Upon the release of the album and "Wake Up Boo!" single, the Boos became genuine Top Ten pop stars in England. The Boo Radleys were always a band with ambitions. The only difference with *Wake Up!* is that they finally fulfilled them. *—Stephen Thomas Erlewine*

C'mon Kids / Sep. 9, 1996 / Polygram ✦✦✦✦
Wake Up! brought the Boo Radleys pop success that they weren't sure what to do with. After embracing the album's No. 1 success, the group eventually recoiled from the spotlight, and Martin Carr wrote *C'mon Kids* as a direct response to the group's celebrity status in the UK. Simply put, *C'mon Kids* is an attempt to scare away any of the fellow travelers who welcomed the sunny-sounding pop of *Wake Up!* It's a gnarled, twisted, and distorted album, as dense as *Giant Steps* and as loud as the Boos' early EPs. If you can make it through the murky guitars, fragments of songs, altered vocals, and tape effects, there are a number of melodies and creatively crafted songs that make the album nearly as rewarding as *Giant Steps* or *Wake Up!* It takes time to get into *C'mon Kids*, though. At first it's disarming to hear Sice scream his vocals and the Boos play heavy riffs. After a while the melodies begin to reveal themselves, as do the clever song structures and inversions of the band's psychedelic hooks and folk tendencies. *C'mon Kids* might not be as accessible as even *Giant Steps*, but it displays a feverish sense of purpose and a perverse willfullness to refashion their sound that makes it an easy album to admire, if not love. *—Stephen Thomas Erlewine*

Boogie Down Productions

f. 1986, Brooklyn, NY, **db.** 1993
Hip Hop, Gangsta Rap, East Coast Rap, Hardcore Rap
Formed in 1986 by Laurence Krisna Parker and Scott Sterling, Boogie Down Productions quickly became one of the most influential and important hip-hop groups. Parker adopted the name KRS-One (an acronym for Knowledge Reigns Supreme Over Almost Every One) and Sterling became DJ Scott LaRock. They released an independent single, "Crack Attack," in 1986. BDP's groundbreaking 1987 debut, *Criminal Minded*, full of blunt, matter-of-fact tales of life on the mean streets, was a prototype for gangsta-rap. As the album was building to a massive underground success, LaRock was shot to death in the South Bronx as he tried to settle an argument. Instead of calling it quits, KRS-One continued BDP with his brother Kenny Parker and D-Nice as DJs and released *By All Means Necessary* the next year. KRS-One began calling himself "the Teacher," promoting self-awareness and education in his rhymes. KRS-One began touring colleges on the lecture circuit around 1989, and some of his writings appeared in the *New York Times*. It became evident that KRS-One had taken his role as the Teacher too far on 1990's *Edutainment*, where most tracks were lectures pasted over lackluster beats.

KRS-One obliterated any concerns that he sold out on 1992's *Sex and Violence*, where he sounds angrier and stronger than he had in years. However, the album wasn't the commercial blockbuster it could have been. The next year, KRS-One released his first solo album, *Return of the Boom Bap*, which was even better; many hip-hop critics equated it with the seminal *By All Means Necessary*. But by early 1994, it had dropped off the R&B and hip-hop charts. *—Stephen Thomas Erlewine*

★ **Criminal Minded** / 1987 / Sugar Hill ✦✦✦✦✦
Classic early "gangsta" rap work. *Criminal Minded* was the only time the contributions of DJ Scott LaRock (Scott Sterling) were featured on a Boogie Down Productions recording, as he was murdered shortly after this was issued. The toughest, hardest-hitting BDP effort. *—Ron Wynn*

☆ **By All Means Necessary** / 1988 / Jive ✦✦✦✦✦
When his partner Scott LaRock was murdered in the Bronx in 1987, KRS-One seriously considered discontinuing Boogie Down Productions. But thankfully, the thought-provoking MC decided to keep the group going, and delivered one of 1988's finest rap albums with *By All Means Necessary*. Social and political commentary, long KRS' forte, abounds here—ranging from the anti-drug song "Illegal Business" to "Stop the Violence," a heartfelt condemnation of violence in hip-hop circles, to the humorous yet hard-hitting call for safe sex, "Jimmy." In fact, "Stop the Violence" became a rallying cry for KRS, who passionately spoke out against Black-on-Black crime when he founded the Stop the Violence Movement. A superb follow-up to BDP's debut album, *Criminal Minded*, *Necessary* made it abundantly clear that as great a loss as LaRock's death was, KRS could be artistically triumphant on his own. Indeed, it turned out to be one of many excellent post-LaRock BDP albums. *—Alex Henderson*

Ghetto Music: The Blueprint of Hip Hop / Jun. 1989 / Jive ✦✦✦✦
With Boogie Down Productions' third album, *Ghetto Music: The Blueprint of Hip Hop*, KRS-One offered additional proof that he had evolved into one of rap's most intelligent voices. When other MCs were content to simply brag about their microphone skills, KRS focused on his strong point: hard-hitting social and political commentary. KRS is angry, but he's also lucid and thoughtful. From police abuse to obsessive materialism, he denounces injustice without becoming an extremist. In the 1990s, fusing rap and reggae isn't out of the ordinary; but such arresting gems as "Bo! Bo! Bo!" and "Jah Rulez" underscore the fact that KRS was among those combining the two before it became so fashionable. *—Alex Henderson*

Edutainment / Jul. 1990 / Jive ✦✦✦
KRS-One's artistic winning streak continued with *Edutainment*, Boogie Down Productions' fourth album. True to form, he focuses on Black history and speaks out on homelessness, racism, police excesses and materialism with clarity and insight. KRS was often compared to Public Enemy leader Chuck D because of his consistently socio-political focus, but there's no mistaking the fact that his unique mixture of Black nationalism, eastern religion (both Hinduism and Buddhism) and Rastafarian philosophy is very much his own. From a commercial standpoint, he had become a little too intellectual—and wasn't selling as many albums as many in rap's gangster school. But from an artistic perspective, *Edutainment* is as commendable as it is riveting. *—Alex Henderson*

Live Hardcore Worldwide / Mar. 12, 1991 / Jive ✦✦✦
Live albums are a rarity in rap—and understandably so. In contrast to funk and soul bands of the 1960s and '70s—many of whom couldn't wait to "take it to the stage" and were thrilling live—hip-hoppers have been so reliant on technology that their live performances usually leave much to be desired. Many rappers have excelled in the studio only to be frightfully awkward and forgettable live. It came as a major surprise when Boogie Down Productions released this live album. While KRS-One's performances of such gems as "Jimmy," "The Bridge Is Over," "My Philosphy" and "South Bronx" are enjoyable, a lot is clearly lost in the transition from the studio to the stage. Like so many rappers—or for that matter, '90s urban contemporary artists—KRS is simply too studio-oriented to generate the kind of excitement that bands like Parliament and the Ohio Players did on stage. *—Alex Henderson*

Sex and Violence / Feb. 25, 1992 / Jive ✦✦✦
KRS-One demolishes any idea he's losing his clout or anger. *Sex and Violence* is his most chilling, slashing, and effective overall statement since *Criminal Minded*. *—Ron Wynn*

Booker T. & the MG's

f. 1962, Memphis, TN, **db.** 1968
Soul, R&B
As the house band at Stax Records in Memphis, Booker T. & the MG's may have been the single greatest factor in the lasting value of that label's soul music—not to mention Southern soul as a whole. Their tight, impeccable grooves can be heard on classic hits by Otis Redding, Wilson Pickett, Carla Thomas, Albert King, and Sam & Dave, just to name the very most prominent examples. For that reason alone, they would deserve their spot in rock 'n' roll's hall of fame. But in addition to their formidable skills as a house band, on their own they were one of the top instrumental outfits of the rock era, cutting classics like "Green Onions," "Time Is Tight," and "Hang 'em High."

The anchors of the Booker T. sound were Steve Cropper, whose slicing, economic riffs influenced tons of other guitar players, and Booker T.

Jones himself, who provided much of the groove with his floating organ lines. In 1960 Jones started working as a session man for Stax, where he met Cropper. Cropper had been in the Mar-Keys, famous for the 1961 instrumental hit "Last Night," which laid out the protoype for much of the MG's' (and indeed Memphis soul's) sound with its organ-sax-guitar combo. With the addition of drummer Al Jackson and bassist Lewis Steinberg, they became Booker T. & the MG's. In a couple of years or so, Steinberg would be replaced permanently by Donald "Duck" Dunn, who, like Cropper, had also played with the Mar-Keys.

The band's first and biggest hit, "Green Onions" (No. 3, 1962), came about by accident. Jamming in the studio while fruitlessly waiting for Billy Lee Riley to show up for a session, they came up with a classic minor-key, bluesy soul instrumental, distinguished by its nervous organ bounce and ferocious bursts of guitar. For the next five years, they'd have trouble recapturing its commercial success, though the standard of their records remained fairly high, and Stax' dependence upon them as the house band ensured a decent living.

In the late '60s, the MG's really hit their stride with "Hip Hug-Her," "Groovin'," "Soul-Limbo," "Hang 'em High," and "Time Is Tight," all of which were Top 40 charters between 1967 and 1969. As a band that featured two Blacks and two whites playing as tightly together as possible, they also set a somewhat underappreciated example of both how integrated, self-contained bands could succeed, and how both Black and white musicians could play funky soul music. As is the case with most instrumental rock bands, their singles contained their best material, and they're best appreciated via anthologies. But their albums were not inconsequential and were occasionally ambitious. (They did an entire instrumental version of the Beatles' *Abbey Road*, which they titled *McLemore Avenue* in honor of the location of Stax' studios.)

Though they'd become established stars by the end of the decade, the group began finding it difficult to work together, not so much because of personnel problems, but because of logistical difficulties. Cropper was often playing sessions in Los Angeles, and Jones was often absent from Memphis while he finished his music studies at Indiana University. The band decided to break up in 1971, but they were working on a reunion album in 1975 when Al Jackson was shot and killed in his Memphis home by a burglar. The remaining members have been active as recording artists and session musicians since, Cropper and Dunn joining the Blues Brothers for a while in the late '70s.

The MG's got back into the spotlight in early 1992 when they were the house band for an extravagant Bob Dylan tribute at Madison Square Garden. More significantly, in 1993 they served as the backup band for a Neil Young tour, one that brought both them and Young high critical marks. The next year, a comeback album, arranged in much the style of their vintage '60s sides, proved that their instrumental skills were still intact. Like most such efforts, though, it ultimately failed to recreate the spark and spontaneity it so obviously wanted to achieve. —*Richie Unterberger*

Green Onions / Oct. 1962 / Atlantic ✦✦✦✦
The title track was the signature song for Booker T. & the MG's, arguably the finest Southern soul rhythm section of all time. This early '60s album now sells in three figures for good condition copies and higher than that for a sealed, mint edition. It established the immediate greatness of the organ/guitar/bass/drums lineup and demonstrated that Booker T. Jones and Steve Cropper in particular were geniuses on organ and guitar, respectively. This has been reissued on CD. —*Ron Wynn*

Soul Dressing / 1965 / Atlantic ✦✦✦
Assembled mostly from (non-hit) 1963-65 singles, this is solid stuff, but a notch below their peak collections. The best tracks ("Soul Dressing," "Tic-Tac-Toe," "Can't Be Still") are usually included on their best-of anthologies, but "Plum Nellie," featuring some ferocious, cutting-edge solos by Cropper and Jones, is an overlooked highlight. —*Richie Unterberger*

☆ **The Best of Booker T. & the MG's** / Nov. 1968 / Atlantic ✦✦✦✦✦
The Stax Records catalog ended up partially in the bands of Atlantic Records and partially with Fantasy Records, and the dividing point is 1968. That's why there are two Booker T. & the MG's hits compilations. This one, *The Best of*, presents the material owned by Atlantic. There are 12 tracks, covering the group's popular instrumental hits from "Green Onions" in the summer of 1962 to "Groovin'" in the summer of 1967. Booker T. and the MG's scored some of their biggest hits, including "Hang 'em High" and "Time Is Tight," in 1968-1969, and for those you will have to look to the Stax/Fantasy *Greatest Hits*, originally released in October 1970. Just to be confusing, in 1991 Fantasy released an album called *The Best of* that again contains only the later material. (Rhino's *Very Best of* finally combined the two eras.) —*William Ruhlmann*

Best of / 1986 / Fantasy ✦✦✦
Somewhat confusingly, this disc is titled identically to a CD on Atlantic that concentrates on their earlier material. This 17-cut disc draws from 1967-1971, and includes three of their four Top 20 pop hits: "Soul Limbo," "Hang 'em High," and "Time Is Tight." This perhaps lacks a bit of the edge of their mid-'60s recordings, concentrating on loping, relaxed grooves more than biting, incisive chops. The standard remains pretty high, though, with the interplay between Steve Cropper's guitar, Booker T. Jones' organ, and the rhythm section never less than telepathic. Most of the material is original, but even on the covers of period pop hits—including unlikely versions of "Something," "Eleanor Rigby," and "Mrs. Robinson"—the group is soulful and tight. This is perhaps better music for background and party listening than anything else, but within those confines it's quite good. —*Richie Unterberger*

★ **Very Best Of** / Jun. 21, 1994 / Rhino ✦✦✦✦✦
Contains 15 of Booker T. & the MG's pop-chart hits, spanning both the 1962-1967 era (now controlled by Atlantic Records) and the 1968-1971 era (now controlled by Fantasy Records). Not to be confused with the Atlantic *Best of* (81281) or the Fantasy *Best of* (60004). —*William Ruhlmann*

The Boomtown Rats

f. 1975, Dun Laoghaire, Ireland, **db.** 1986
New Wave, Pop-Rock
The Boomtown Rats were an Irish rock band that scored a series of British hits between 1977 and 1980 and were led by singer Bob Geldof, who organized the Ethiopian relief efforts Band Aid and Live Aid.

The Rats were formed in Dun Laoghaire, near Dublin, in 1975 by Geldof (born Robert Frederick Zenon Geldof, Oct. 5, 1954, Dun Laoghaire, Ireland); a former journalist, Johnnie Fingers (keyboards); Gerry Cott (guitar); Garry Roberts (guitar); Pete Briquette (bass); and Simon Crowe (drums). They took their name from Woody Guthrie's novel *Bound for Glory*. The group moved to London in October 1976 and became associated with the punk-rock movement. Signing to Ensign Records, they released their debut single, "Lookin' After No. 1," in August 1977. It was the first of nine straight singles to make the UK Top 15.

Their debut album, *The Boomtown Rats*, was released in September 1977, on Ensign in the UK and on Mercury in the US. Their second album, *Tonic for the Troops*, appeared in June 1978 in the UK, along with their first UK Top Ten hit, "Like Clockwork." In the fall, "Rat Trap" from the album hit No. 1. *A Tonic for the Troops* was released in the US on Columbia Records in February 1979, with two tracks from *The Boomtown Rats* substituted for tracks on the UK version.

The Boomtown Rats' second straight UK No. 1 came in the summer of 1979 with "I Don't Like Mondays," a song inspired by a California teenager who had gone on a killing spree and glibly justified her action with the title line. It was contained on the Rats' third album, *The Fine Art of Surfacing*, released in October 1979, and it subsequently became the band's only US singles-chart entry. The album also contained their next UK Top Ten hit, "Someone's Looking at You."

The Boomtown Rats released their final UK Top Ten hit, "Banana Republic," in November 1980, followed by their fourth album, *Mondo Bon*, in January 1981. At this point, guitarist Gerry Cott left the group, and they continued as a quintet. Their fifth album, *V Deep*, was released in the UK in February 1982. In the US, Columbia initially released only a four-song EP drawn from the album *The Boomtown Rats*, finally releasing the full LP in September, when it failed to chart. Also in 1982, Geldof starred in the movie *Pink Floyd: The Wall*.

Columbia released the six-song compilation *Ratrospective* in March 1983, but rejected the band's newly recorded sixth album, *In the Long Grass*, which was released by Ensign in England. In 1984 Geldof and Midge Ure wrote "Do They Know It's Christmas?" and organized the star-studded Band Aid group to record it for Ethiopian relief, resulting in the biggest-selling single in UK history. Geldof then went on to organize the two Live Aid concerts, held on July 13, 1985, in London and Philadelphia. Geldof's increased visibility led to the belated US release of *In the Long Grass*, but when it failed to chart, the Boomtown Rats were left without a record label. The group folded in 1986, and Geldof launched a solo career. —*William Ruhlmann*

The Boomtown Rats / Sep. 1977 / Mercury ✦✦✦
Anyone who heard The Boomtown Rats' debut single, "Lookin' After No. 1," with its rapid drum beat, slashing guitars, and aggressive singing about impatience with the dole queue, would think of the group as a particularly tight, standard punk rock band on the London scene in 1977. The Rats' debut album also featured the leering "Mary of the Fourth Form," their second single, but the rest of the album revealed more traditional rock influences. "Joey's on the Street Again" sounded like the sort of street opera Bruce Springsteen was aiming for on *The Wild, the Innocent & the E Street Shuffle*. "I Can Make It If You Can" was the sort of ballad the Rolling Stones favored in the mid-'70s. Overall, there were enough power chords and snotty sentiments to justify the punk tag, but it was already clear that the Rats aspired to the mainstream. —*William Ruhlmann*

Tonic for the Troops / Jun. 1978 / Columbia ✦✦✦
Bob Geldof had revealed a taste for the seamy side of things in his lyrics for the Boomtown Rats' first album. On their second record, he fantasized about being Hitler in the person of the Leader of the Pack ("I Never Loved Eva Braun"), romanticized tropical suicide ("Living in an Island"), and identified with a certain wealthy recluse ("Me and Howard Hughes"). The band retained a punk energy on the album's UK hit singles, "Like Clockwork," "She's So Modern," and "Rat Trap" (another of Geldof's Springsteen homages), but musical identity was still a song-by-song affair. (In the US, Columbia replaced "Can't Stop" and "[Watch Out for] The Normal People" with "Mary of the Fourth Form" and "Joey's on the Street Again" from the first album.) — *William Ruhlmann*

The Fine Art of Surfacing / Oct. 1979 / Columbia ✦✦✦
The Boomtown Rats had achieved a peak of band interplay by their third album, leading inevitably to such developments as the use of strings, while lyricist/singer Bob Geldof had taken on as his major subject an acerbic social consciousness about the pressures of modern life. But this didn't always add up to strong songwriting. When it did, on the singles "Someone's Looking at You" and especially "I Don't Like Mondays," the Boomtown Rats could be compelling—Geldof's lyrics seemed acute instead of obvious, the band arrangements seemed crisp and clever rather than gimmicky. But that didn't happen often enough to make *The Fine Art of Surfacing* a consistent success. — *William Ruhlmann*

Mondo Bongo / Feb. 1981 / Columbia ✦✦
On their fourth album, the Boomtown Rats submitted to ambitiousness, with singer Bob Geldof attempting to assume the mantle of Bob Dylan, the Beatles, and the Rolling Stones, while the band tried to keep up with musical fashions in Britain. The combination led to such oddities as a ska-beat rewrite of the Stones' "Under My Thumb" and a couple of side-opening mambos. The band was at its best when it returned to the pop music that was its core on such songs as the Buddy Holly-ish "Don't Talk to Me" and especially the danceable "Up All Night," but they were buried on the second side of an uneven collection that made the Rats' sense of direction seem uncertain. — *William Ruhlmann*

V Deep / Apr. 1982 / Columbia ✦✦
On their fifth album and reduced to a quintet, the Boomtown Rats moved closer to Caribbean rhythms, employing a percussionist and upping the bass guitar in the mix. They even had Dennis Bovell do a dub mix of "House on Fire" and included it at the end of the album. Meanwhile, Bob Geldof's lyrics indicated an increasingly embattled sensibility; he noted in a song called "The Bitter End," "It isn't too far." Unfortunately, nothing here matched the catchy, dance work on the Rats' first three albums, and even in England their star was beginning to fade. In America, Columbia Records at first declined to release the album, opting for a four-track EP, then allowed it to escape in September 1982; it failed to chart. — *William Ruhlmann*

Ratrospective [EP] / Mar. 1983 / Columbia ✦✦✦✦
Ratrospective was a six-song "best of" EP containing the Boomtown Rats' only US singles chart entry, "I Don't Like Mondays," "Rat Trap," which had been a UK chart topper, and other favorites. It was intended as a summing up of the group for the US. Columbia Records rejected the Rats' next album, *In the Long Grass*, and released it only in the wake of lead singer Bob Geldof's Live Aid celebrity. In 1987 Columbia added four tracks to *Ratrospective* to produce *Greatest Hits*. — *William Ruhlmann*

In the Long Grass / May 1985 / Columbia ✦✦✦
The Boomtown Rats' sixth album was very much a return to the pop-rock style of their first two albums—4/4 beats, prominent rock guitar lines, urgent vocals. But as the desperate lyrics (titles include "Drag Me Down" and "Hard Times") implied, the record was more a last hurrah than a new beginning. Upon its 1984 release on Mercury Records in the UK, it did spawn a couple of minor British chart singles, but it missed the LP chart, a major decline for a band that had enjoyed Top Ten success at its height. In America, Columbia Records rejected the album, and only released it a year later to try to cash in on Bob Geldof's fame in connection with his organization of *Live Aid*. — *William Ruhlmann*

The Greatest Hits / 1987 / Columbia ✦✦✦✦
Released in the wake of Bob Geldof's post-Live Aid celebrity, *Greatest Hits* contains all six songs that were on *Ratrospective*, the 1983 EP-only compilation of the Boomtown Rats' hit singles, plus four other tracks to flesh the collection out into a full album. It's a good, basic primer on the Rats, containing all of their essential items ("I Don't Like Mondays," "Rat Trap," "Skin on Skin," "Up All Night"), but it pales next to the more comprehensive 1997 collection *Great Songs of Indifference*, which also features solo cuts from Geldof. — *Stephen Thomas Erlewine*

● **Great Songs of Indifference: The Best of Bob Geldof & the Boomtown Rats** / Apr. 22, 1997 / Sony ✦✦✦✦
Great Songs of Indifference: The Best of Bob Geldof & the Boomtown Rats is the first comprehensive collection compiled on not only the

Boomtown Rats, but also Bob Geldof's solo career. All of the group's biggest hits, including "I Don't Like Mondays," "Looking After Number One" and "Banana Republic," are here, as are a handful of solo tracks; while those aren't as strong as the Rats cuts, they nevertheless sum up Geldof's post-Boomtown career quite effectively. In other words, it's a definitive retrospective. — *Stephen Thomas Erlewine*

Pat Boone (Charles Eugene Patrick Boone)

b. Jun. 1, 1934, Jacksonville, FL
Vocals / Pop, Teen Idol
He was clean-cut, polite to his elders, and glorified the nutritional value of milk. To folks who hated everything the new music stood for, Pat Boone was the perfect '50s rock 'n' roller. But no matter how music historians judge the career of Pat Boone, nobody can dispute his enormous sales record. The well-scrubbed crooner in the white buckskin shoes sold many millions of copies of his sanitized R&B covers during the '50s, helping to facilitate acceptance of rock 'n' roll in the pop marketplace.

Boone's family ties are impressive; he's related to frontier legend Daniel Boone through bloodlines and to country great Red Foley through marriage to his daughter. After debuting on the small Republic imprint in 1954, Boone signed with Dot and took the pop world by storm over the next couple of years with covers of R&B items by Fats Domino, Little Richard, the El Dorados, the Flamingos, Ivory Joe Hunter, and too many others to list here.

With his college-boy good looks and an affinity for smooth ballads, Boone crossed over into TV and films, scoring No. 1 hits in 1957 with "Love Letters in the Sand" from the movie *Bernadine*, and the theme from the movie *April Love*, in both of which he starred.

In 1961 "Moody River" marked Boone's last chart-topper, although he gamely tackled everything from novelty rockers ("Speedy Gonzales") to surf songs ("Beach Girl") to sustain his success. These days, you're most likely to encounter Boone and his family (which includes Debby Boone of "You Light Up My Life" fame) on the contemporary Christian circuit or doing work for charitable organizations, the white bucks and crewcut long since retired. —*Bill Dahl*

Jivin' Pat / Feb. 1986 / Bear Family ✦✦✦✦
All of Boone's rockers—cover versions of Fats Domino, Little Richard, et al.—are included with a revealing set of liner notes. You won't find these elsewhere unless you have an enormous singles collection. —*Hank Davis*

● **Greatest Hits** / 1993 / MCA ✦✦✦✦
Including 18 of his highest charting hits for the Dot label in the '50s and early '60s, this is easily the best basic Boone collection. It doesn't include his hit covers of "At My Front Door" and Little Richard's "Long Tall Sally" and "Tutti Frutti," which is perhaps just as well for all concerned. —*Richie Unterberger*

More Greatest Hits / Oct. 25, 1994 / Varese Sarabande ✦✦✦
Contains 17 of Pat Boone's later and lesser chart hits. — *William Ruhlmann*

Earl Bostic

b. Apr. 25, 1913, Tulsa, OK, **d.** Oct. 28, 1965, Rochester, NY
Alto Sax / R&B, Swing, Groove
Earl Bostic's roots and foundation were steeped in jazz and swing, but he later became one of the most prolific R&B bandleaders. His searing, sometimes bluesy, sometimes soft and moving, alto-sax style influenced many players, including John Coltrane. His many King releases, which featured limited soloing and basic melodic and rhythmic movements, might have fooled novices into thinking Bostic possessed minimal skills; but Art Blakey once said, "Nobody knew more about the saxophone than Bostic, I mean technically, and that includes Bird." Bostic worked in several Midwest bands during the early '30s, then studied at Xavier University. He left school to tour with various groups, among them a band co-led by Charlie Creath and Fate Marable. He moved to New York in the late '30s, where he was a soloist in the bands of Don Redman, Edgar Hayes, and Lionel Hampton. Bostic also led his own combos, whose members included Jimmy Cobb, Al Casey, Blue Mitchell, Stanley Turrentine, Benny Golson, and Coltrane. Bostic toured extensively through the '50s, while cutting numerous sessions for King. His recording of "Flamingo" in 1951 was a huge hit, as were the songs "Sleep," "You Go to My Head," "Cherokee," and "Temptation." Bostic recorded for Allegro, Gotham, and King from the late '40s to the mid-'60s. He made more than 400 selections for King; the label would use stereo remakes of songs with different personnel, then use the same album numbers. After a heart attack, Bostic became a part-time player. His mid-'60s albums were more soul-jazz than R&B. Several of his King LPs are available on CD. —*Ron Wynn and Michael Erlewine*

● **The Best of Earl Bostic** / 1956 / Deluxe ✦✦✦✦
A nice cross-section of this fiery alto-saxist's '50s output, it includes his hits "Sleep" and "Flamingo." —*Bill Dahl*

Boston

f. 1971, Boston, MA

Hard Rock, Pop-Rock, Arena Rock

The arena-rock group behind one of the fastest-selling debut albums in history, Boston was essentially the vehicle of studio wizard Tom Scholz, born March 10, 1947, in Toledo, OH. A rock fan throughout his teen years, he began writing songs while earning a master's degree at the Massachusetts Institute of Technology. After graduation, he began work for Polaroid and eventually joined a local band led by guitarist Barry Goudreau. Though Scholz signed on as a keyboardist, he also began learning guitar, and his quick mastery of the instrument soon allowed him to take full control of the band.

At the same time, Scholz set about constructing his own 12-track recording studio in the basement of his home, where the group—now dubbed Boston, and also consisting of bassist Fran Sheehan, vocalist Brad Delp, bassist Fran Sheehan, and drummer John "Sib" Hashian—recorded the demos that earned them a contract with Epic in 1975. Although some recording and overdubs were later done in Los Angeles, the 1976 release of *Boston* consisted largely of Scholz' original basement tapes; spawning three hit singles ("More Than a Feeling," "Long Time," and "Peace of My Mind"), the LP shot immediately to the top of the charts and remained the best-selling pop debut effort in history before it was supplanted by Whitney Houston's first album in 1986.

Despite the record's overwhelming success, Scholz spent over two years working on the follow-up, 1978's No. 1 hit *Don't Look Back;* a perfectionist, he only then released the album because of intense label pressure for product. Unsatisfied with the results, he swore to produce the next album at his own pace; as a result, the chart-topping *Third Stage* did not appear until 1986, at which time only Scholz and Delp remained from the original line-up.

Scholz spent the next several years in the courtroom. First he was sued by Goudreau, who alleged that Scholz had damaged his solo recording career (they settled out-of-court); next, he won a seven-year battle against Epic, who claimed Boston had reneged on their contract by taking so long between releases. When the band resurfaced in 1994 with *Walk On,* Scholz was the lone remaining member; Delp and Goudreau had reunited in 1992 as RTZ, releasing the album *Return to Zero.*

In addition to his fame as a musician, Scholz also found success as an inventor and businessman. In 1981 he formed Scholz Research & Design, Inc., a company founded to create high-tech music equipment. After first developing the Power Soak, a volume-control device, SR&D introduced the Rockman, an inexpensive, small guitar amplifier with headphones. The Rockman proved phenomenally popular with other musicians, and the capital generated from its sales helped fund Scholz' further musical ambitions. —*Jason Ankeny*

● **Boston** / 1976 / Epic ◆◆◆◆
The album that virtually defined '70s FM rock sold over six million copies and featured the smash hits "More Than a Feeling," "Peace of Mind," and "Let Me Take You Home Tonight." —*Donna DiChario*

Don't Look Back / 1978 / Epic ◆◆◆
Continued success with their rock formula is highlighted by the hit title track. —*Donna DiChario*

Third Stage / 1986 / MCA ◆◆◆
This chart-topping comeback appeared after a seven-year hiatus and a lineup reshuffling that left only singer Brad Delp and guitarist/producer Tom Scholz from the original band. The hits include "Amanda" and "We're Ready." —*Donna DiChario*

Walk On / Jun. 7, 1994 / MCA ◆◆
Boston's long-awaited fourth album—this time it took Tom Scholz a full seven years to complete—failed to capture the attention of most AOR fans and became the group's first record not to spawn a hit single. Perhaps the reason was that AOR and classic-rock stations began losing their audiences in 1992; more likely, it was because Scholz' legendary perfectionism didn't yield the same results as in the past. Although the production is certainly state of the art and is overflowing with detail, there aren't any memorable songs or hooks to justify such extravagance. On the surface, the record sounds fine, but there is no substance beneath the layers of gloss. —*Stephen Thomas Erlewine*

Bottle Rockets

f. 1992, Festus, MO

Roots-Rock, Alternative Country-Rock

Missouri's Bottle Rockets ranked as one of the leading lights of the 1990s roots-rock revival, thanks to a sound that bypassed the punk heritage proudly upheld by most of their contemporaries in favor of a redneck fusion of Southern boogie, country-folk, and crunching rock 'n' roll. The group was fronted by singer/guitarist Brian Henneman, a Missouri native who formed his first band, Waylon Van Halen and the Ernest Tubbadours, in 1977 with friends Tom and Bob Parr. After a succession of names and a steady rise in musical competence, the trio began land-ing club dates both locally and in Illinois, where they became friends with the young Jay Farrar and Jeff Tweedy, who would later start Uncle Tupelo.

In 1985 the trio was playing straight-ahead honky-tonk in the guise of Chicken Truck (so named in honor of the John Anderson song) with a new drummer, Mark Ortmann. Instead of giving in to local crowds who wanted to hear covers instead of originals, the group focused solely on performing their own material, which they began roughing up with a Crazy Horse-like edge. Shortly after frequent tour mates Uncle Tupelo signed a 1990 record deal, however, internal problems led Chicken Truck to disband; while the Parrs returned to civilian jobs, Ortmann moved to Nashville to become a session player, and Henneman became a roadie with Uncle Tupelo, even playing on their *March 16-20, 1992* album.

During his roadie days, Henneman recorded a demo tape of new material, which Tupelo manager Tony Margherita began discreetly shopping around. After cutting a solo single backed by Farrar and Tweedy, he re-formed his old band, replaced Bob Parr with bassist Tom Ray, and renamed the outfit the Bottle Rockets. A year after a 1993 self-titled effort, the band issued their second independent LP, *The Brooklyn Side*, named after a bowling term. A portrait of life in rural, blue-collar America, *The Brooklyn Side* was the subject of lavish critical praise and was later re-released on a major label. —*Jason Ankeny*

Bottle Rockets / Sep. 18, 1993 / East Side Digital ◆◆◆◆
If Neil Young had played guitar and written songs with Lynyrd Skynyrd, it might've come out something like the eponymous debut by Festus, Missouri's own Bottle Rockets. Raw and spirited, with a guitar attack that burns furiously, this record was recorded and mixed in a couple of days. And although it contains some strong material, overall it lacks the focus of the band's follow-up *The Brooklyn Side*. That's not to say that this one should be passed over; there's a satisfying mix of rockers and country-tinged numbers. Frontman and principal songwriter Brian Henneman's keen observations on everyday rural-redneck life and characters are explored with insightful detail in songs about convenience store clerks and trailer inhabitants. In the Southern rock-sounding "Wave That Flag," he takes an angry shot at rebel flag wavers, and the escape of a dead-end life in the ragged and breakneck speed country-rocker "Rural Route." Before the Bottle Rockets, Henneman served as guitar technician and sometime instrumentalist for Uncle Tupelo, and both Jeff Tweedy and Jay Farrar make backup vocal appearances, with Farrar giving a particularly strong performance on the highlight ballad "Kerosene." —*Jack Leaver*

● **The Brooklyn Side** / Sep. 19, 1995 / Atlantic ◆◆◆◆
The Bottle Rockets' brand of Skynyrd-esque raunch 'n' roll is considerably more good-timey than that of most of the band's roots-rock brethren, and their incisive, provocative songwriting skills set them squarely among the genre's elite. *The Brooklyn Side*, produced by Eric "Roscoe" Ambel, is fairly bursting with dead-on character studies exploring the realities and quiet desperation of rural Southern life, from the blackly humorous ("Sunday Sports," about a family man who finds that watching TV in his underwear is "the only way to get away from everything else" in his life) to the poignant ("Welfare Music," a depiction of the struggles facing a young single mother). The band also possesses a wickedly comic edge, as evidenced by "Idiot's Revenge" (a diatribe against alt-rock rhetoric), "1000 Dollar Car" (a eulogy for a used automobile), and the flamethrower single "Radar Gun" (the tale of a sadistic, ticket-happy traffic cop). —*Jason Ankeny*

Bow Street Runners

f. 1969, Fayetteville, NC

Psychedelic

Sounding like a blend of Jefferson Airplane and the Doors, Bow Street Runners was a Fayetteville, NC-based psychedelic band that released one eponymous album in limited quantities on B.T. Puppy Records in 1970. While the group was ignored at the time, *Bow Street Runners* became a collectible item among psychedelic aficionados during the '80s and '90s, leading to its 1996 reissue by Sundazed Records. —*Stephen Thomas Erlewine*

● **The Bow Street Runners** / 1970 / Sundaze ◆◆◆
Using the trippy, folky rock of Jefferson Airplane and eerie, organ-driven soundscapes as a foundation, the Bow Street Runners may not have many original ideas in their head, but that's part of their appeal. Their lone, eponymous album is filled with attempts at hippie mysticism and menacing, swirling fuzzy psychedelia, but the group has neither the inclination nor the talent to turn it into something original. Nevertheless, the group is somewhat distinctive in the ways its attempts fail. "Spunky Monkey" is an aimless and slightly ridiculous blues jam; "Eating from a Plastic Hand" has a silly, ominous minor-key melody; and, best of all, "Watch" sounds like Ringo Starr fronting the Doors. It doesn't make for good or provocative music, but as a late-'60s artifact, it's fascinating. —*Stephen Thomas Erlewine*

Bow Wow Wow

f. 1980, London, England, db. 1983
New Wave
Bow Wow Wow was a quartet organized by UK manager Malcolm McLaren (best known as the mastermind behind the Sex Pistols) at the start of the '80s. McLaren matched the trio of musicians who had constituted Adam Ant's Ants—Matthew Ashman (b. 1962) on guitar, Leigh Gorman (b. 1961) on bass, and David Barbarossa (b. 1961) on drums—with teenage singer Annabella Lwin (b. Oct. 31, 1965), retaining the earlier group's African-derived drum sound. In 1983 Lwin quit the group for a solo career, and the remaining three changed their name to the Chiefs of Relief. Both Lwin and the Chiefs issued their own albums. — *William Ruhlmann*

I Want Candy / 1982 / RCA ++++
This album largely recompiles Bow Wow Wow's first album, plus its *Last of the Mohicans* EP. As such, it includes the hits "Go Wild in the Country," "I Want Candy," and "Louis Quatorze" and presents the band's urgent, rhythmic sound at its most consistent. — *William Ruhlmann*

Girl Bites Dog / Sep. 21, 1993 / EMI ++++
A CD reissue of their first cassette-only release. Featuring a 15-year-old Annabella Lwin singing songs with sex-obsessed themes backed by a driving tribal beat, *Girl Bites Dog* gives a representative view of a band with limited scope. Though it sounds a bit dated today, new wave fanatics will find this newly expanded version essential, especially for the unreleased rarities, B-sides, and extensive discography information. — *Chris Woodstra*

● **Best of Bow Wow Wow** / Oct. 29, 1996 / RCA ++++
The Best of Bow Wow Wow is a thorough overview of Malcolm McLaren's manufactured new wave pop group, featuring all the highlights of the group's albums and EPs—including, of course, "I Want Candy," but also "Go Wild in the Country," "W.O.R.K." and "Do You Want to Hold Me"—as well as the previously unreleased "Where's My Snake." Since the group didn't make consistent albums, *The Best of Bow Wow Wow* is the best way to listen to the band, since it features every one of their worthwhile tracks, plus good liner notes. — *Stephen Thomas Erlewine*

David Bowie (David Robert Jones)

b. Jan. 8, 1947, Brixton, England
Guitar, Keyboards, Saxophone, Vocals / Hard Rock, Art-Rock/Progressive-Rock, Glam Rock, Pop-Rock, Experimental, Proto-Punk, Blue-Eyed Soul
The cliche about David Bowie says he's a musical chameleon, adapting to fashion and trends. While such a criticism is too glib, there's no denying that Bowie demonstrated remarkable skill for perceiving musical trends at his peak in the '70s. After spending several years in the late '60s as a mod and as an all-around music-hall entertainer, Bowie reinvented himself as a hippie singer-songwriter. Before his breakthrough in 1972, he recorded a proto-metal record and a pop-rock album, eventually redefining glam-rock with his ambiguously sexy Ziggy Stardust persona. Ziggy made Bowie an international star, but he wasn't content to continue to churn out glitter-rock. By the mid-'70s, he developed an effete, sophisticated version of Philly soul that he dubbed "plastic soul," which eventually morphed into the eerie avant-pop of 1976's *Station to Station*. Shortly afterward, he relocated to Berlin, where he recorded three experimental electronic albums with Brian Eno. At the dawn of the '80s, Bowie was still at the height of his powers, but following his blockbuster dance-pop album *Let's Dance* in 1983, he slowly sank into mediocrity before salvaging his career in the early '90s. Even when he was out of fashion in the '80s and '90s, it was clear that Bowie was one of the most influential musicians in rock, for better and for worse. Each one of his phases in the '70s sparked a number of subgenres, including punk, new wave, goth-rock, the New Romantics, and electronica. Few rockers ever had such lasting impact.

David Jones began performing music when he was 13 years old, learning the saxophone while he was at Bromley Technical High School; another pivotal event happened at the school, when his left pupil became permanently dilated in a schoolyard fight. After his graduation at 16, he worked as a commercial artist while playing saxophone in a number of mod bands, including the King Bees, the Manish Boys, and Davey Jones and the Lower Third. All three of those bands released singles that were generally ignored, but he continued performing, changing his name to David Bowie in 1966 after the Monkees' Davy Jones became an international star. Over the course of 1966, he released three mod singles on Pye Records, which were all ignored. The next year he signed with Deram, releasing the music-hall, Anthony Newley-styled *David Bowie* that year. Upon completing the record, he spent several weeks in a Scottish Buddhist monastery. Once he left the monastery, he studied with Lindsay Kemp's mime troupe, forming his own mime com-

pany, Feathers, in 1969. Feathers was short-lived, and he formed the experimental art group Beckenham Arts Lab in 1969.

Bowie needed to finance the Arts Lab, so he signed with Mercury Records that year and released *Man of Words, Man of Music*, a trippy singer-songwriter album featuring "Space Oddity." The song was released as a single and became a major hit in the UK, convincing Bowie to concentrate on music. Hooking up with his old friend Marc Bolan, he began miming at some of Bolan's T. Rex concerts, eventually touring with Bolan, bassist/producer Tony Visconti, guitarist Mick Ronson, and drummer Cambridge as Hype. The band quickly fell apart, but Bowie and Ronson remained close, working on the material that formed Bowie's next album, *The Man Who Sold the World*, as well as recruiting Michael "Woody" Woodmansey as their drummer. Produced by Tony Visconti, who also played bass, *The Man Who Sold the World* was a heavy guitar rock album that failed to gain much attention. Bowie followed the album in late 1971 with the pop-rock *Hunky Dory*, an album that featured Ronson and keyboardist Rick Wakeman.

After the release of *Hunky Dory*, Bowie began to develop his most famous incarnation, Ziggy Stardust—an androgynous, bisexual rock star from another planet. Before he unveiled Ziggy, Bowie claimed in a January 1972 interview with the *Melody Maker* that he was gay, helping to stir interest in his forthcoming album. Taking cues from Bolan's stylish glam-rock, Bowie dyed his hair orange and began wearing women's clothing. He began calling himself Ziggy Stardust, and his backing band—Ronson, Woodmansey, and bassist Trevor Bolder—were the Spiders from Mars. *The Rise and Fall of Ziggy Stardust and the Spiders from Mars* was released with much fanfare in England in late 1972. The album and its lavish, theatrical concerts became a sensation throughout England, and helped him become the only glam-rocker to carve out a niche in America. *Ziggy* became a word-of-mouth hit in the US, and the re-released "Space Oddity"—which was now also the title of the re-released *Man of Words, Man of Music*—reached the American Top 20. Bowie quickly followed *Ziggy* with *Aladdin Sane* later in 1973. Not only did he record a new album that year, but he produced Lou Reed's *Transformer*, the Stooges' *Raw Power*, and Mott the Hoople's comeback, *All the Young Dudes*, for which he also wrote the title track.

Given the amount of work Bowie packed into 1972 and 1973, it wasn't surprising that his relentless schedule began to catch up with him. After recording the all-covers *Pin-Ups* with the Spiders from Mars, he unexpectedly announced the band's breakup, as well as his retirement from live performances, during the group's final show that year. He retreated from the spotlight to work on a musical adaptation of George Orwell's *1984*, but once he was denied the rights to the novel, he transformed the work into *Diamond Dogs*. The album was released to generally poor reviews in 1974, but it generated the hit single "Rebel Rebel," and he supported the album with an elaborate and expensive American tour. As the tour progressed, Bowie became fascinated with soul music, eventually redesigning the entire show to reflect his new "plastic soul." Hiring guitarist Carlos Alomar as the band's leader, Bowie refashioned his group into a Philly soul band and recostumed himself in sophisticated, stylish fashions. The change took fans by surprise, as did the double album *David Live*, which featured material recorded on the 1974 tour.

Young Americans, released in 1975, was the culmination of Bowie's soul obsession, and it became his first major crossover hit, peaking in the American Top Ten and generating his first US No. 1 hit in "Fame," a song he co-wrote with John Lennon and Alomar. Bowie relocated to Los Angeles, where he earned his first movie role in Nicolas Roeg's *The Man Who Fell to Earth* (1976). While in Los Angeles, he recorded *Station to Station*, which took the plastic soul of *Young Americans* in darker, avant-garde-tinged directions. It was a huge hit, generating the Top Ten single "Golden Years." The album inaugurated Bowie's persona of the elegant "Thin White Duke," and it reflected Bowie's growing cocaine-fueled paranoia. Soon he decided Los Angeles was too boring and returned to England. He greeted a crowd with a Nazi salute, a signal of his growing, drug-addled detachment from reality. The incident caused enormous controversy, and Bowie left the country to settle in Berlin, where he lived and worked with Brian Eno.

Once in Berlin, Bowie sobered up and began painting, as well as studying art. He also became fascinated by German electronic music, which became evident on *Low*, the first album he did with Eno. Released early in 1977, *Low* was a startling mixture of electronics, pop, and avant-garde technique. While it was greeted with mixed reviews at the time, it proved to be one of the most influential albums of the late '70s, as did its follow-up, *Heroes*, which followed that year. Not only did Bowie record two solo albums in 1977, but he helmed Iggy Pop's comeback records *The Idiot* and *Lust for Life*, and toured anonymously as Pop's keyboardist. He resumed his acting career in 1977, appearing in *Just a Gigolo* with Marlene Dietrich and Kim Novak, as well as narrating Eugene Ormandy's version of *Peter and the Wolf*. Bowie returned to the stage in 1978, launching an international tour that was captured on the double album *Stage*. During 1979, Bowie and Eno recorded *Lodger* in New York, Switzerland, and Berlin, releasing the album at the end of the year. *Lodger* was supported with several innovative videos, as was 1980's *Scary Monsters*. These videos—"DJ," "Fashion," "Ashes to Ashes"—became staples on early MTV.

Scary Monsters was Bowie's last album for RCA, and it wrapped up his most innovative, productive period. Later in 1980 he performed the title role in a stage production of *The Elephant Man*, including several shows on Broadway. Over the next two years, he took an extended break from recording, appearing in *Christiane F* (1982) and the vampire movie *The Hunger* (1982), returning to the studio only for his 1981 collaboration with Queen, "Under Pressure," and the theme for Paul Schrader's remake of *Cat People*. In 1983 he signed an expensive contract with EMI Records and released *Let's Dance*. Bowie had recruited Chic guitarist Nile Rodgers to produce the album, giving the record a sleek, funky foundation, and hired the unknown Stevie Ray Vaughan as lead guitarist. *Let's Dance* became his most successful record, thanks to stylish, innovative videos for "Let's Dance" and "China Girl," which turned both songs into Top Ten hits. Bowie supported the record with the sold-out arena tour *Serious Moonlight*.

Greeted with massive success for the first time, Bowie wasn't quite sure how to react, and he eventually decided to replicate *Let's Dance* with 1984's *Tonight*. While the album sold well, producing the Top Ten hit "Blue Jean," it received poor reviews and ultimately was a commercial disappointment. He stalled in 1985, recording a duet of Martha & the Vandellas' "Dancing in the Street" with Mick Jagger for Live Aid. He also spent more time jet-setting, appearing at celebrity events across the globe, and appeared in several movies—*Into the Night* (1985), *Absolute Beginners* (1986), *Labyrinth* (1986)—that turned out to be bombs. Bowie returned to recording in 1987 with the widely panned *Never Let Me Down*, supporting the album with the *Glass Spider* tour, which also received poor reviews. In 1989 he remastered his RCA catalog with Rykodisc for CD release, kicking off the series with the three-disc box *Sound + Vision*. Bowie supported the discs with an accompanying tour of the same name, claming that he was retiring all of his older characters from performance after the tour. *Sound + Vision* was successful, and *Ziggy Stardust* re-charted amidst the hoopla.

Sound + Vision may have been a success, but Bowie's next project was perhaps his most unsuccessful. Picking up on the abrasive, dissonant rock of Sonic Youth and the Pixies, Bowie formed his own guitar rock combo Tin Machine with guitarist Reeves Gabrels, bassist Hunt Sales, and his drummer brother Tony, who had previously worked on Iggy Pop's *Lust for Life* with Bowie. Tin Machine released an eponymous album to poor reviews that summer and supported it with a club tour that was only moderately successful. Despite the poor reviews, Tin Machine released a second album, the appropriately titled *Tin Machine II*, in 1991, and it was completely ignored.

Bowie returned to a solo career in 1993 with the sophisticated, soulful *Black Tie White Noise*, recording the album with Nile Rodgers and his now-permanent collaborator, Reeves Gabrels. The album was released on Savage, a subsidiary of RCA, and received positive reviews, but his new label went bankrupt shortly after its release, and the album disappeared. *Black Tie White Noise* was an indication that Bowie was trying hard to resuscitate his career, as was the largely instrumental 1994 soundtrack *The Buddha of Suburbia*. In 1995 he reunited with Brian Eno for the wildly hyped, industrial-rock-tinged *Outside*. Several critics hailed the album as a comeback, and Bowie supported it with a co-headlining tour with Nine Inch Nails in order to snag a younger, alternative audience, but his gambit failed—audiences left before Bowie's performance and *Outside* disappeared. He quickly returned to the studio in 1996, recording *Earthling*, an album heavily influenced by techno, jungle, and drum'n'bass. Upon its early 1997 release, *Earthling* received generally positive reviews, but the album failed to gain an audience, and many techno purists criticized Bowie for allegedly exploiting their subculture. —*Stephen Thomas Erlewine*

Space Oddity / 1969 / Rykodisc ✦✦✦
Originally released as *Man of Words/Man of Music*, *Space Oddity* was David Bowie's first successful reinvention of himself. Abandoning both the mod and Anthony Newley fascinations that marked his earlier recordings, Bowie delves into a lightly psychedelicized folk-rock, exemplified by the album's soaring title track. Bowie actually attempts a variety of styles on *Space Oddity*, as if he were trying to find the ones that suited him best. As such, the record isn't very cohesive, but it is charming, especially in light of his later records. Nevertheless, only "Wild Eyed Boy from Freecloud" and "Memory of a Free Festival" rank as Bowie classics, and even those lack the hooks or purpose of "Space Oddity." —*Stephen Thomas Erlewine*

The Man Who Sold the World / 1970 / Rykodisc ✦✦✦✦
Even though it contained no hits, *The Man Who Sold the World*, for most intents and purposes, is the beginning of David Bowie's classic period. Working with guitarist Mick Ronson and producer Tony Visconti for the first time, Bowie developed a tight, twisted heavy guitar rock that appears simple on the surface, but sounds more gnarled upon each lis-

ten. The mix is off-center, with the fuzz-bass dominating the compressed, razor-thin guitars and Bowie's strangled, affected voice. The sound of *The Man Who Sold the World* is odd, and the music itself is bizarre, with Bowie's bizarre, paranoid futuristic tales melded to Ronson's riffing and the band's relentless attack. Musically, there isn't much innovation on *The Man Who Sold the World*. It is almost all hard blues-rock or psychedelic folk-rock, but there's an unsettling edge to the band's performance that makes the record one of Bowie's best albums. [Rykodisc's 1990 CD reissue has four bonus tracks, including the previously unreleased "Lightning Frightening," the single "Holy Holy," and both sides of the 1971 Arnold Corns single, "Moonage Daydream" and "Hang On to Yourself," which are early and inferior versions of songs that would later appear on *Ziggy Stardust*.] —*Stephen Thomas Erlewine*

☆ **Hunky Dory** / 1972 / Rykodisc ✦✦✦✦✦
After the freakish hard-rock of *The Man Who Sold the World*, David Bowie returned to singer-songwriter territory on *Hunky Dory*. Not only did the album boast more folky songs ("Song for Bob Dylan," "Bewlay Brothers"), but he again flirted with the Anthony Newley-esque dancehall music ("Kooks," "Fill Your Heart"), seemingly leaving heavy metal behind. As a result, *Hunky Dory* is a kaleidoscopic array of pop styles, tied together only by Bowie's sense of vision—a sweeping, cinematic melange of high and low art, ambiguous sexuality, kitsch, and class. Mick Ronson's guitar is pushed to the back, leaving Rick Wakeman's cabaret piano to dominate the sound of the album. And the subdued support accentuates the depth of Bowie's material, whether it's the revamped Tin Pan Alley of "Changes," the Neil Young homage of "Quicksand," the soaring "Life on Mars?," the rolling, vaguely homosexual anthem "Oh! You Pretty Things," or the dark acoustic rocker "Andy Warhol." On the surface, such a wide range of styles and sounds would make an album incoherent, but Bowie's improved songwriting and determined sense of style instead made *Hunky Dory* a touchstone for reinterpreting pop's traditions into fresh, post-modern pop music. —*Stephen Thomas Erlewine*

☆ **The Rise & Fall of Ziggy Stardust** / 1972 / Rykodisc ✦✦✦✦✦
Borrowing heavily from Marc Bolan's glam-rock and the future-shock of *A Clockwork Orange*, David Bowie reached back to the heavy rock of *The Man Who Sold the World* for *The Rise & Fall of Ziggy Stardust and the Spiders from Mars*. Constructed as a loose concept album about an androgynous alien rock star named Ziggy Stardust, the story falls apart quickly; but Bowie's fractured, paranoid lyrics were evocative of a decadent, decaying future, and the music echoed an apocalyptic, nuclear dread. Fleshing out the off-kilter metallic mix with fatter guitars, genuine pop songs, string sections, keyboards, and a cinematic flourish, *Ziggy Stardust* is a glitzy array of riffs, hooks, melodrama, and style that was the logical culmination of glam. Mick Ronson plays with a maverick flair that invigorates rockers like "Suffragette City," "Moonage Daydream," and "Hang On to Yourself," while "Lady Stardust," "Five Years" and "Rock and Roll Suicide" have a grand sense of staged drama previously unheard of in rock 'n' roll. And that self-conscious sense of theater is part of the reason *Ziggy Stardust* sounds so foreign. Bowie succeeds not in spite of his pretensions, but because of them, and *Ziggy Stardust*—familiar in structure, but alien in performance—is the first time his vision and execution met in such a grand, sweeping fashion. —*Stephen Thomas Erlewine*

Aladdin Sane / 1973 / Rykodisc ✦✦✦✦
Ziggy Stardust wrote the blueprint for Bowie's hard-rocking glam, and *Aladdin Sane* essentially follows the pattern, for both better and worse. A lighter affair than *Ziggy Stardust*, *Aladdin Sane* is actually a stranger album than its predecessor, buoyed by bizarre lounge-jazz flourishes from pianist Mick Garson and a handful of winding, vaguely experimental songs. Bowie abandoned his futuristic obsessions to concentrate on the detached cool of New York and London hipsters, as on the compressed rockers "Watch That Man," "Cracked Actor," and "Jean Genie." Bowie follows the hard stuff with the jazzy, dissonant sprawls of "Lady Grinning Soul," "Aladdin Sane," and "Time," which manage to be both campy and avant-garde simultaneously, while the sweepingly cinematic "Drive-In Saturday" is a soaring fusion of sci-fi doo-wop and melodramatic teenage glam. He also lets his paranoia slip through in the clenched rhythms of "Panic in Detroit," as well as his oddly clueless cover of "Let's Spend the Night Together." For all the pleasures on *Aladdin Sane*, there's no distinctive sound or theme to make the album cohesive; it's Bowie coasting along on Ziggy Stardust, which means there's a wealth of classic material here, but not enough focus to make the album itself a classic. —*Stephen Thomas Erlewine*

Pin-Ups / 1973 / Rykodisc ✦✦✦
Perhaps the covers album *Pin-Ups* was conceived as a breather, a way for Bowie and the Spiders from Mars to regroup amidst the hysteria of the Ziggy Stardust mania, or perhaps it was meant as a genuine tribute to Bowie's influences. Either way, *Pin-Ups* was the first sign that the Ziggy persona was running out of energy. The album isn't bad—in fact, it's an energetic, infectious collection of relatively obscure British rock 'n'

roll, R&B, and mod anthems—but the timing of a covers album was odd, suggesting that Bowie was running out of ideas. On its own, *Pin-Ups* is quite enjoyable, especially since the selections are fairly arcane. Bowie relies primarily on songs that never were hits in America—even the Kinks, the Who, Yardbirds, and Pink Floyd songs were relatively obscure—which makes the record fascinating. Bowie and the Spiders make songs by the Pretty Things ("Rosalyn," "Don't Bring Me Down"), the Merseys ("Sorrow"), and the Easybeats ("Friday on My Mind") tough and nervy, occasionally surpassing the original versions in terms of attitude. So, if *Pin-Ups* isn't a major entry in Bowie's catalog, it is fun, even though it's a rather undistinguished final effort from the Spiders from Mars. —*Stephen Thomas Erlewine*

Images 1966-1967 / 1973 / London ✦✦✦
This double album is becoming hard to find, which is unfortunate, as it's easily the most comprehensive collection of Bowie's 1966-67 work for Deram. The 21 tracks include the entirety of his 1967 debut album, plus seven stray songs from singles and sessions that were unreleased at the time. Possibly because it wasn't heard by many listeners until it was reissued in the early '70s during Bowie's ascent to stardom, this material has been unfairly maligned. Critics and fans of *Ziggy Stardust* were shocked to discover an all-around entertainer seemingly bent upon becoming the new Anthony Newley. Indeed, much of his work from this era was overbearingly cloying and saccharine, both in the West End matinee aspirations of the lyrics and the unabashedly theatrical orchestration, which bore hardly any resemblance to good old rock 'n' roll whatsoever. One of these, "Laughing Gnome" (featuring Chipmunk-like backup vocals), would cause Bowie considerable embarrassment when it was reissued—and became a hit—in Britain in 1973. The less idiotically cheerful efforts, though, show definite signs of an idiosyncratic talent: the odd character sketches, the fleeting references to transvestites and mysticism, even the occasional London swinging pop number ("Let Me Sleep Beside You"). The best track, "London Boys" (a 1966 single), is a neglected classic look at the downer side of the mod experience, and is the best of his many obscure pre-"Space Oddity" recordings. —*Richie Unterberger*

Diamond Dogs / 1974 / Rykodisc ✦✦
David Bowie fired the Spiders of Mars shortly after the release of *Pin-Ups*, but he didn't completely leave the Ziggy Stardust persona behind. *Diamond Dogs* suffers precisely because of this; he doesn't know *how* to move forward. Originally conceived as a concept album based on George Orwell's *1984*, *Diamond Dogs* evolved into another one of Bowie's paranoid future nightmares. Throughout the album, there are hints that he's tired of the Ziggy formula, particularly in the disco underpinning of "Candidate" and his cut-and-paste lyrics. However, it's not enough to make *Diamond Dogs* a step forward, and without Mick Ronson to lead the band, the rockers are too stiff to make an impact. Ironically, the exception is one of Bowie's very best songs—the tight, sexy "Rebel Rebel." The song doesn't have much to do with the theme. *Diamond Dogs* isn't a total waste, with "1984," "Candidate," and "Diamond Dogs" all offering some sort of pleasure, but it is the first record since *Space Oddity* where Bowie's reach exceeds his grasp. —*Stephen Thomas Erlewine*

David Live / 1974 / Rykodisc ✦✦
The supporting tour for *Diamond Dogs* was supposed to be a theatrical extravaganza, but as he headed out on the road, David Bowie became infatuated with Philly soul and changed his entire approach to reflect his new interest, changing his backing band in the process. As a result, the double-album *David Live* captures Bowie in transition, as he moves from glam-rock to plastic soul. The set list draws heavily from *Ziggy Stardust* -era songs, but there are a few surprises, like a stilted cover of "Knock on Wood" and an inspired version of "All the Young Dudes," a song Bowie gave Mott the Hoople. Since Bowie's attempts at soul are a little awkward at this stage, *David Live* is primarily of interest as a historical document, but there's enough good material to make it worthwhile for fanatics. —*Stephen Thomas Erlewine*

Young Americans / 1975 / Rykodisc ✦✦✦
Bowie had dropped hints during the *Diamond Dogs* tour that he was moving toward R&B, but the full-blown blue-eyed soul of *Young Americans* came as a shock. Surrounding himself with first-rate sessionmen, Bowie comes up with a set of songs that approximate the sound of Philly soul and disco, yet remain detached from their inspirations; even at his most passionate, Bowie sounds like a commentator, as if the entire album was a genre exercise. Nevertheless, the distance doesn't hurt the album. It gives the record its own distinctive flavor, and its plastic, robotic soul helped inform generations of synthetic British soul. What does hurt the record is a lack of strong songwriting. "Young Americans" is a masterpiece, and "Fame" had a beat funky enough that James Brown ripped it off, but only a handful of cuts ("Win," "Fascination," "Somebody Up There Likes Me") come close to matching their quality. As a result, *Young Americans* is more enjoyable as a stylistic adventure than as a substantive record. [The 1991 CD has three bonus tracks,

including the terrific outtake "Who Can I Be Now?"] —*Stephen Thomas Erlewine*

Station to Station / 1976 / Rykodisc ✦✦✦✦
Taking the detached plastic-soul of *Young Americans* to an elegant, robotic extreme, *Station to Station* is a transitional album that creates its own distinctive style. Abandoning any pretense of being a soulman, yet keeping rhythmic elements of soul, Bowie positions himself as a cold, clinical crooner and explores a variety of styles. Epic ballads, disco, and synthesized avant-pop are on *Station to Station*, but what ties it together are a cocaine-induced paranoia and a detached musical persona. At its heart, *Station to Station* is an avant-garde, art-rock album, most explicitly on "TVC15" and the epic sprawl of the title track, but also on the cool crooning of "Wild Is the Wind" and "Word on a Wing," as well as the disco stylings of "Golden Years." It's not an easy album to warm to, but its epic structure and clinical sound were an impressive, individualistic achievement, as well as a style that would prove enormously influential on post-punk. —*Stephen Thomas Erlewine*

☆ **Low** / 1977 / Rykodisc ✦✦✦✦✦
Following through with the avant-garde inclinations of *Station to Station*, yet explicitly breaking with Bowie's past, *Low* is a dense, challenging album that confirmed Bowie's place at rock's cutting edge. Driven by dissonant synthesizers and electronics, *Low* is divided between brief, angular songs and atmospheric instrumentals. Throughout the record's first half, the guitars are jagged and the synthesizers drone with a menacing robotic pulse, while Bowie's vocals are unnaturally layered and overdubbed. During the instrumental half, the electronics turn cool, which is a relief after the intensity of the preceding avant-pop. Half of the credit of *Low*'s success is due to Brian Eno, who explored similar ambient territory on his own releases. Eno functions as a conduit for Bowie's ideas and, in turn, Bowie made respectable, if not quite mainstream, the experimentalism of Eno and of the German synth-group Kraftwerk and the post-punk group Wire. Though a handful of the vocal pieces on *Low* are accessible—"Sound and Vision" has a shimmering guitar hook and "Be My Wife" subverts soul structure in a surprisingly catchy fashion—the record is defiantly experimental and dense with detail, providing a new direction for the avant-garde in rock 'n' roll. —*Stephen Thomas Erlewine*

☆ **Heroes** / 1977 / Rykodisc ✦✦✦✦✦
Repeating the formula of *Low*'s half-vocal/half-instrumental structure, *Heroes* develops and strengthens the sonic innovations Bowie and Eno explored on their first collaboration. The vocal songs are fuller, boasting harder rhythms and deeper layers of sounds. Much of the harder-edged sound of *Heroes* is due to Robert Fripp's guitar, which provides a muscular foundation for the electronics, especially on the relatively conventional rock songs. Similarly, the instrumentals on *Heroes* are more detailed, this time showing a more explicit debt to German synth-pop and European experimental rock 'n' roll. Essentially, the difference between *Low* and *Heroes* lies in the details, but the record is equally challenging and groundbreaking. [The CD reissue includes the previously unreleased instrumental "Abdulmajid" and a remix of "Joe the Lion."] —*Stephen Thomas Erlewine*

Stage / 1978 / Rykodisc ✦✦✦
Stage was David Bowie's second live double-album, documenting his supporting tour for *Heroes*. Supported by a band that featured guitarists Adrian Belew and Carlos Alomar, Bowie doesn't recast his earlier work in a new light—the songs from *Ziggy Stardust* essentially remain the same, as do the selections from *Station to Station*—but they are infused with a new avant-garde spirit that comes to the fore during the songs from *Low* and *Heroes*. Though the newer material isn't arranged differently from the studio versions—and it lacks some of the studio trickery that made the originals so thrilling—the live versions do illustrate that much of the innovation of the Bowie-Eno collaborations lay in their subversion of conventional song structure. That said, *Stage* doesn't offer enough revelations to make it necessary for anyone but hardcore Bowie fanatics. —*Stephen Thomas Erlewine*

Lodger / 1979 / Rykodisc ✦✦✦✦
On the surface, *Lodger* is the most accessible of the three Berlin-era records Bowie made with Brian Eno, simply because there are no instrumentals and there are a handful of concise pop songs. Nevertheless, *Lodger* is still gnarled and twisted avant-pop; what makes it different is how it incorporates such experimental tendencies into genuine songs, something that *Low* and *Heroes* purposely avoided. "D.J.," "Look Back in Anger," and "Boys Keep Swinging" have strong melodic hooks that are subverted and strengthened by the layered, dissonant productions, while the remainder of the record is divided between similarly effective avant-pop and ambient instrumentals. *Lodger* has an edgier, minimalistic bent than its two predecessors, which makes it more accessible for rock fans, as well as giving it a more immediate, emotional impact. It might not stretch the boundaries of rock like *Low* and *Heroes*, but it arguably utilizes those ideas in a more effective fashion. —*Stephen Thomas Erlewine*

Scary Monsters (And Super Creeps) / 1980 / Rykodisc ✦✦✦✦
Bowie returns to relatively conventional rock 'n' roll with *Scary Monsters*, an album that effectively acts as an encapsulation of all of his experiments of the '70s. Re-working glam-rock themes with avant-garde synth flourishes, and reversing the process as well, Bowie creates dense but accessible music throughout *Scary Monsters*. Though it doesn't have the vision of his other classic records, it wasn't designed to break new ground—it was created as a culmination of Bowie's experimental genre-shifting of the '70s. As a result, *Scary Monsters* is Bowie's last great album. While the music isn't far removed from the post-punk of the early '80s, it does sound fresh, hip, and contemporary, which is something Bowie lost over the course of the '80s. [Rykodisc's 1992 reissue includes re-recorded versions of "Space Oddity" and "Panic in Detroit," the Japanese single "Crystal Japan," and the British single "Alabama Song."] — *Stephen Thomas Erlewine*

Let's Dance / 1983 / Virgin ✦✦✦
After summing up his maverick tendencies on *Scary Monsters*, David Bowie aimed for the mainstream with *Let's Dance*. Hiring Chic bassist Nile Rodgers as a co-producer, Bowie created stylish, synthesized post-disco dance music that was equally informed by classic soul and the emerging New Romantic subgenre of New Wave, which was, ironically, heavily inspired by Bowie himself. *Let's Dance* comes tearing out of the gate, propelled by the skittering "Modern Love," the seductively menacing "China Girl," and the brittle funk of the title track. All three songs became international hits, and for good reason; they are catchy, accessible pop songs that have just enough of an alien edge to make them distinctive. However, that careful balance is quickly thrown off by a succession of pleasant but unremarkable plastic soul workouts. "Cat People" and a cover of Metro's "Criminal World" are relatively strong songs, but the remainder of the album indicates that Bowie was entering a songwriting slump. However, the three hits were enough to make the album a massive hit, and their power hasn't diminished over the years, even if the rest of the record sounds like an artifact. — *Stephen Thomas Erlewine*

Love You 'til Tuesday / 1984 / PolyGram ✦✦
The bulk of this reissue comes from the soundtrack to Bowie's little-seen short film of the same name. Completed in early 1969, it was shelved until its re-release on video in 1984. While several of the songs had already been released by Bowie in the UK on Deram, this LP has some slightly different versions. The title track and "When I Live My Dream" are represented by their 45 single takes, not the more familiar album versions; "Sell Me a Coat" has added vocals by John Hutchinson and Hermoine Farthingale, who played with Bowie in his short-lived group Feathers. The previously unreleased "Ching-a-Ling" and "When I'm Five" are in keeping with the fey, fairy-tale, childlike ambience of much of his 1967 material. The version of "Space Oddity" also features Hutchinson and Farthingale, and it is faster and less effective than the eventual hit single version. Rounding out the collection are some of the more well-known numbers from his Anthony Newley period (especially the notorious "Laughing Gnome"), and his 1964 debut single "Liza Jane," an out-and-out R&B number in the Stones/Pretty Things style. This is a scattershot anthology that is pretty much for collectors only, focusing on his uncharacteristically showtune-like 1967 period; that era is more definitively documented on the double album *Images*. — *Richie Unterberger*

Tonight / 1984 / Virgin ✦✦
On the basis of *Tonight*, it appears that David Bowie didn't have a clear idea of how to follow the platinum success of *Let's Dance*. Instead of breaking away from the stylized pop of "Let's Dance" and "China Girl," Bowie delivers another record in the same style. Apart from the single "Blue Jean," none of the material equals the songs on *Let's Dance*, but that didn't stop *Tonight* from becoming another platinum success. Nevertheless, the record stands as one of the weakest albums Bowie ever recorded. — *Stephen Thomas Erlewine*

Never Let Me Down / 1987 / Virgin ✦✦
Bowie broke away from the mainstream pop of *Tonight* with 1987's *Never Let Me Down*, turning in a jumbled mix of loud guitar rockers and art-rock experiments like the failed "Glass Spider." While it's not as consistent as *Tonight*, it's far more interesting, with the John Lennon homage of the title track being one of his most underrated songs. — *Stephen Thomas Erlewine*

Sound + Vision / Sep. 1989 / Rykodisc ✦✦✦✦
Sound + Vision is a triple-disc box set designed to introduce Rykodisc's extensive reissue program of David Bowie's RCA albums. As a result, it has a number of idiosyncrasies that prevent it from becoming a definitive box set. Conceptually, the set was intended to showcase Rykodisc's remastering expertise, as well as the rarities lying in the vaults. Consequently, the song selection is targeted toward hardcore Bowie fans, ignoring such hits as "Jean Genie," "Starman," "Golden Years," and "Fame," among many others. However, there is an abundance of terrific rare material, including the demo for "Space Oddity," the *Man Who*

Sold the World outtake "London Bye Ta-Ta," an alternate "John, I'm Only Dancing," the soulful *Young Americans* outtake "After Today," and a single version of "Rebel Rebel" that arguably is better than the more familiar version. However, such rarities and unpredictable selections ("Red Sails" but not "DJ" from *Lodger*, live versions of "Suffragette City," "Station to Station" and "Breaking Glass") mean that the set is neither a good introduction nor a complement to *Changesbowie*. Instead, it's a good, if frustrating, curio piece for collectors. [The initial pressings of *Sound + Vision* included a bonus disc that contained a CD-video of "Ashes to Ashes," as well as three live tracks. It was replaced in 1995 with a CD-ROM of the same material.] — *Stephen Thomas Erlewine*

★ **Changesbowie** / Mar. 1990 / Rykodisc ✦✦✦✦✦
Changesbowie is a CD greatest hits collection that revamps the original *Changesonebowie* by adding selections from Bowie's late '70s and early '80s albums. Consequently, it functions as a definitive single-disc introduction to David Bowie, featuring all of his major hits from "Space Oddity," "Changes," "Ziggy Stardust," "Jean Genie" and "Rebel Rebel" to "Heroes," "Ashes to Ashes," "Let's Dance," "Modern Love" and "Blue Jean." One complaint: it wasn't necessary to substitute the "Fame '90" remix for the original to hook completists, since it is inferior and had already been issued as a separate single. — *Stephen Thomas Erlewine*

Early On (1964-1966) / 1991 / Rhino ✦✦
Before landing his first commercial success with 1969's "Space Oddity," David Bowie released a number of singles in a variety of styles. He first emerged in the mid-1960s as a mod following the paths of the Who, Kinks, and Rolling Stones. The 17-cut CD *Early On (1964-66)* is by far the most comprehensive anthology of his first works, gathering all six of his first singles and adding five previously unreleased demos from 1965. Fans of Bowie's famous work may be nonplussed by this material, in which the singer shifts from sub-Stones R&B to Who/Kinkish power chords to trendy Swinging London pop in search of his own style. He didn't establish his own identity on these fairly derivative recordings, but that's not to say they aren't without enjoyable aspects. The 1965 single "You've Got a Habit of Leaving" has some fierce Who-styled feedback, "Can't Help Thinking About Me" is an uneasily introspective number that foreshadows his later lyrics, and the acoustic demos find him groping toward a more familiar and distinctive vocal style. Several of the tunes on this collection were produced by the legendary Shel Talmy, who also handled sessions for the Who and Kinks in the mid-'60s. — *Richie Unterberger*

Black Tie White Noise / Oct. 1993 / Virgin ✦✦
A fitfully successful comeback effort by Bowie, *Black Tie White Noise* works best when he subtly tries to update his sound. When he duets with Al B. Sure! on the title track and does a tepid remake of Cream's "I Feel Free," the modernization of soul and glam sounds forced, which never happens on the house beats of "Jump They Say" or the moving reworking of Morrissey's "I Know It's Gonna Happen Someday." Unfortunately, the good songs—and the best material here is easily his best since *Scary Monsters*—are obscured by the filler and ill-conceived dance experimentations. Had it been trimmed by five or six songs, the album could indeed have brought him back to the top of the charts. — *Stephen Thomas Erlewine*

★ **Singles 1969-1993** / Nov. 16, 1993 / Rykodisc ✦✦✦✦✦
Taking *Changesbowie* one step further, *Singles 1969-1993* collects all of David Bowie's biggest hits while picking up such overlooked gems as "Drive-In Saturday" and "Loving the Alien." The comprehensiveness and quality of the songs make *Singles* the best Bowie compilation available; fans will be pleased with the inclusion of the complete lyrics to all of the songs on this two-disc set. — *Stephen Thomas Erlewine*

Rarest One Bowie / 1995 / Trident ✦✦
Even after Rykodisc added previously unreleased bonus tracks to their CD reissues of Bowie's RCA catalog, there still were a number of much-sought-after unreleased songs left in the vaults. *Rarest One Bowie* was intended to collect some of those items that remained unreleased, but it wound up far short of its promise. Although it does contain Bowie's original version of "All the Young Dudes," that is the only studio track here. The remaining eight tracks are devoted to live performances, and while a few of them are quite good—the deservedly legendary "Footstompin'" from "The Mike Douglas Show" and a cover of Cream's "I Feel Free" are highlights—it doesn't add anything significant to Bowie's catalog, and only hardcore fans will find this disappointing collection necessary. — *Stephen Thomas Erlewine*

Santa Monica '72 / Mar. 28, 1995 / Golden Years ✦✦✦

Outside / Sep. 26, 1995 / RCA ✦✦✦
David Bowie has seemed like an artist without direction ever since the success of *Let's Dance*, switching styles and genres with a speed that made him appear nervous, not innovative. Recorded with his former collaborator Brian Eno, *Outside* was intended to return some luster to his rapidly tarnishing reputation. Instead of faux-soul or mainstream pop—or even dissonant hard rock, for that matter—Bowie concentrates

on the atmospheric, disturbing electronic soundscapes of his late-'70s "Berlin" trilogy (*Low*, *Heroes*, and *Lodger*), adding slight, but detectable, elements of industrial, grunge, and ambient techno. Bowie also raised the stakes by making *Outside* the first in a series of concept albums about mystery, murder, art, and cyberspace. Everything that would have made *Outside* a triumphant comeback seemed to be in place, but the album is severely flawed. Not only is the story poorly developed and confusing, but the album is simply too long. Throughout the record, good ideas bubble to the surface but are never fully explored, and the sheer bulk of the album means that the good songs—"Hallo Spaceboy," "Strangers When We Meet," "The Heart's Filthy Lesson"—are buried underneath the weight of the mediocre material. Furthermore, nothing on the album is a departure from Bowie's late-'70s records; when he does experiment with newer musical forms or write about futuristic technology, he seems unsure of himself. That said, *Outside* is Bowie's most satisfying and adventurous album since *Let's Dance*. It's clear that he's trying once again, and when he does hit his mark, he remains a brilliant artist. *—Stephen Thomas Erlewine*

Buddha of Suburbia / Oct. 24, 1995 / Virgin ✦✦✦
It was probably David Bowie's record-company affiliation difficulties that kept this 1993 soundtrack to a British TV miniseries from being released in the US until 1995, when it was slipped out in the wake of his new album, *Outside*. That's too bad, because *The Buddah of Suburbia* is an often engaging collection of songs and instrumental passages that recalls many previous Bowie albums, including such disparate efforts as *The Man Who Sold the World*, *Aladdin Sane*, and *Low*. It's not a major effort by any means, but in another context songs like "Strangers When We Meet" easily could become Bowie favorites. *—William Ruhlmann*

Earthling / Feb. 11, 1997 / Virgin ✦✦✦
Jumping on the post-grunge industrial bandwagon with *Outside* didn't successfully rejuvenate David Bowie's credibility or sales, so he switched his allegiance to techno and jungle for the follow-up, *Earthling*. While jungle is a more appropriate fit than industrial, the resulting music is nearly as awkward. Though he often gets the sound of jungle right, the record frequently sounds as if the beats were simply grafted on top of pre-existing songs. Never are the songs broken open by a new form; they are fairly conventional Bowie songs with fancy production. Fortunately, Bowie sounds rejuvenated by this new form, and songs like "Little Wonder" and "Seven Years in Tibet" are far stronger than the bulk of *Outside*. Still, the record falls short of its goals, and it doesn't offer enough intrigue or innovations to make *Earthling* anything more than an admirable effort. *—Stephen Thomas Erlewine*

The Box Tops

f. 1966, Memphis, TN, **db.** 1970
Pop-Rock, Blue-Eyed Soul
If you forget about the Rascals and the Righteous Brothers, the Memphis-based Box Tops are the finest blue-eyed soul group. Lead singer (and former Big Star honcho) Alex Chilton had a tough, swaggering voice that belied his teenage years, sounding at times as if he were in a cutting match with the young Steve Winwood. Producers Chips Moman and Dan Penn surrounded Chilton with a crack American studio band, giving the music more muscle and deep funk than you'll ever find in "Mary Mary."
Instead of knocking off pimply, lightweight teen-fodder, the Box Tops managed to add another link in the Memphis soul chain, mixing blues, Beatlesque pop, and the sound of Stax, Hi, and Goldwax. And unlike the Monkees, the Box Tops benefited from top-notch material: Dan Penn and Spooner Oldham's "Cry like a Baby" and "I Met Her in Church"; Wayne Thompson's "The Letter" and "Soul Deep"; and the occasional Chilton-penned nugget, such as "I Must Be the Devil." The group's heyday was brief—two years, tops—but their music remains a staple on oldies stations and has retained its vitality for over two decades. *—John Floyd*

● **Best of the Box Tops** / Oct. 1, 1996 / Arista ✦✦✦✦
This compilation boasts "20-bit digital mastering from the original master tapes," if that matters to you. Audiophile considerations aside, it's the best anthology of the group, the 18 songs including all of the hits and their best LP-only tracks. Their credentials as the best pop-oriented blue-eyed soul group fly high, with occasional glimpses of something rootsier, especially the bluesy, Chilton-penned "I Must Be the Devil," which has one of his grittiest vocals. Another high-caliber Chilton original, "(The) Happy Song," affords a glimpse of his lighter, poppier aspirations. *—Richie Unterberger*

Boyz II Men

f. 1988, Philadelphia, PA
Urban, Adult Contemporary, Club/Dance, New Jack R&B
Under the guidance of Michael Bivins of Bell Biv Devoe, the five-man vocal group Boyz II Men became a pop sensation in 1992. Although

they call their music "hip-hop doo wop," there's very little traditional doo wop in it. Instead, they bring the sound of '60s and early-'70s R&B vocal groups into the '90s, adding a little new jack swing to that timeless sound. Their 1991 debut, *Cooleyhighharmony*, featured a massive hit single, "Motownphilly," which exemplifies the best of their dance work. Their second single, a ballad called "It's So Hard to Say Goodbye," was an even bigger hit; its success paved the way for "The End of the Road" (taken from the *Boomerang* soundtrack), the group's follow-up single, which broke Elvis Presley's record for the most weeks spent at No. 1. After releasing a Christmas album in 1993, Boyz II Men went to work on their second album, which appeared in the fall of 1994. *II* proved to be even more successful than its predecessor, selling over seven million copies by summer of 1995 and spawning the record-breaking hit "I'll Make Love to You." *—Stephen Thomas Erlewine*

Cooleyhighharmony / Nov. 2, 1993 / Motown ✦✦✦✦
Boyz II Men's retro sound dominated the 1991 pop and R&B marketplaces, with their singles "It's So Hard to Say Goodbye to Yesterday" and "Motownphilly" hitting the Top Ten on both charts. The album eventually sold over five million copies and put Boyz II Men at the forefront of a movement returning the emphasis in Black popular music to vocal harmonies and a cappella interaction. *—Ron Wynn*

● **II** / Aug. 30, 1994 / Motown ✦✦✦✦
With their second album, Boyz II Men assured their place at the top of the charts, as well as history. "I'll Make Love to You," the album's first single, stayed on top of the charts for over two months, only to be unseated by "On Bended Knee," the album's second single. Not surprisingly, *II* is a carefully constructed crowd pleaser, accentuating all of the finest moments from their hit debut. While there are some high-energy dance tracks, the album's main strength is its slower numbers, where the group's vocals soar. *—Stephen Thomas Erlewine*

Billy Bragg

b. Dec. 20, 1957, Barking, Essex, England
Guitar, Vocals / Urban-Folk, Singer-Songwriter, Alternative Pop-Rock, Folk-Rock, British Folk
Finding inspiration in the righteous anger of punk rock and the socially conscious folk tradition of Woody Guthrie and Bob Dylan, Billy Bragg was the leading figure of the anti-folk movement of the '80s. For most of the decade, Bragg bashed out songs alone on his electric guitar, singing about politics and love. While his lyrics were bitingly intelligent and clever, they were also warm and humane, filled with detail and wit. Even though his lyrics were carefully considered, Bragg never neglected to write melodies that were strong and memorable. Throughout the '80s, he managed to chart consistently in Britain, but he gathered only a cult following in America, which could be due to the fact that he sang about distinctly British subject matter, both politically and socially.
Bragg began performing in the late '70s with the punk group Riff Raff, which lasted only a matter of months. He then joined the British Army, but he quickly bought himself out of his sojourn with £175. After leaving the Army, he began working at a record store; while he was working, he was writing songs that were firmly in the folk and punk protest tradition. Bragg began a British tour, playing whenever he had the chance to perform. Frequently he would open for bands with only a moment's notice; soon, he had built a sizable following, as evidenced by his first EP, *Life's a Riot with Spy vs. Spy* (1983), hitting No. 30 on the UK independent charts. *Brewing Up with Billy Bragg* (1984), his first full-length album, climbed to No. 16 in the charts.
During 1984 Bragg became a minor celebrity in Britain, as he appeared at leftist political rallies, strikes, and benefits across the country; he also helped form the "Red Wedge," a socialist musicians collective that also featured Paul Weller. In 1985 Kirsty MacColl took one of his songs, "New England," to No. seven on the British singles chart. Featuring some subtle instrumental additions of piano and horns, 1986's *Talking to the Taxman About Poetry* reached the UK Top Ten.
Bragg's version of the Beatles' "She's Leaving Home," taken from the *Sgt. Pepper Knew My Father* tribute album, became his only No. 1 single in 1988—as the double-A side with Wet Wet Wet's "With a Little Help from My Friends." That year he also released the EP *Help Save the Youth of America* and the full-length *Workers Playtime*, which was produced by Joe Boyd (Fairport Convention, Nick Drake, R.E.M.). Boyd helped expand Bragg's sound, as the singer recorded with a full band for the first time. The following year, Bragg restarted the Utility record label as a way of featuring noncommercial new artists. *The Internationale*, released in 1990, was a collection of left-wing anthems, including a handful of Bragg originals. On 1991's *Don't Try This at Home*, he again worked with a full band, recording his most pop-oriented and accessible set of songs; the album featured the hit single, "Sexuality." Bragg took several years off after *Don't Try This at Home*, choosing to concentrate on fatherhood. He returned in 1996 with *William Bloke*. *—Stephen Thomas Erlewine*

Life's a Riot with Spy vs Spy / 1983 / Utility/Go!Discs ✦✦✦

Brewing Up / 1984 / Go! Discs ✦✦✦✦
Bragg's second album delivers another clutch of memorable, clever songs. Here the rudimentary voice and electric guitar arrangements prevalent in *Life's a Riot with Spy vs. Spy* are refined and sweetened by occasional use of overdubbed vocals ("Love Gets Dangerous"), organ ("A Lover Sings"), and trumpet ("The Saturday Boy"); this last selection is a jaunty mid-tempo number about unrequited love that makes reference to the Delfonics' "La-La Means I Love You." Occasional 1950s influences surface on this album, most notably Bo Diddley in the jittery "This Guitar Says Sorry" and Chuck Berry in the bouncy "From a Vauxhall Velox" (which has the classic couplet "Some people say love is blind/But I just think that it's a bit short-sighted"). In addition to songs about relationships, there are pointedly critical numbers that deal with social/political issues; examples include "It Says Here" (a ringingly gruff tune that lampoons the press) and "Island of No Return" (a gripping and angry antiwar song). This excellent release has now been supplanted by *Back to Basics*, which combines this album with *Life's a Riot* and *Between the Wars*. —*David Cleary*

Between the Wars [EP / 1985 / Go! Discs ✦✦✦✦
Billy Bragg's earliest releases suggest a no-frills Cockney version of Bob Dylan, with electric guitar substituted for acoustic. This particular platter combines his first and third albums into one release, side one repeating *Life's a Riot with Spy vs. Spy* and the flip side reprising the EP *Between the Wars*. While there are some topically critical songs on the opening side such as "To Have and to Have Not," most of the tracks here deal with personal relationships. "A New England" borrows the racing guitar strum from "Little Honda" and weds it to unsentimental lyrics about love. "The Man in the Iron Mask" is a spare, slow ballad describing a masochist's acceptance of a bad marriage. "The Milkman of Human Kindness" has unusually warm lyrics and a surprisingly expressive melodic line atypical of Bragg's output. Side two is unabashedly left-wing political. The title track is a midtempo folk-song-like number telling the story of a worker willing to look the other way for a government that will take care of him "from cradle to grave" and then finds that his faith is misplaced. There are also two covers, a forthright and sonorous song about an unsuccessful 1649 squatters' rebellion entitled "The World Turned Upside Down" and "Which Side Are You On," a union rallying song given in clipped, angry fashion. This raw, wonderfully effective record has now been superseded by *Back to Basics*, which combines this release with *Brewing Up* into one essential album. —*David Cleary*

Talking with the Taxman About Poetry / 1986 / Go! Discs/Elektra ✦✦✦✦
Bragg's one-man approach is fleshed out on *Talking with the Taxman About Poetry*, his second long-player. "Levi Stubb's Tears" and "The Marriage" include subtle percussion and horn flourishes; "Greetings to the New Brunette" is cushioned in layers of overdubbed acoustic guitars. That makes it Bragg's most satisfying album musically, but the witty, plaintive songs listed above—in addition to "Ideology" and "The Warmest Room"—make it a stirring and evocative lyrical statement as well. —*John Floyd*

● **Back to Basics** / 1987 / Go! Discs/Elektra ✦✦✦✦
This disc brings together Bragg's first three releases (*Life's a Riot with Spy vs. Spy*, *Brewing Up with Billy Bragg*, and the *Between the Wars* EP) and offers the best introduction to his confessional songwriting and uncompromising politics. Highlights include "A New England," "The Busy Girl Buys Beauty," and "A Lover Sings." —*John Floyd*

Help Save the Youth of America E.P.: Live & Dubious / 1988 / Go! Discs/Elektra ✦✦✦
An exceptional album. —*Chip Renner*

Workers Playtime / 1988 / Go! Discs/Elektra ✦✦✦
Bragg's first attempt at working with a full band could be better—most of the songs are mopey and depressing, and some of his socialist manifestos are tiresome and dogmatic. Still, cuts like "She's Got a New Spell," "Must I Paint You a Picture," and "Little Time Bomb" are excellent, and "Waiting for the Great Leap Forward" is a humble and humorous explanation of Bragg's motives and intentions, both political and emotional. —*John Floyd*

The Internationale / Jun. 1990 / Utility/Elektra ✦✦
Billy Bragg's albums have always contained material with the strong political slant of classic folksingers in the Woody Guthrie/Bob Dylan mold. This release shows him at his most muckrakingly fervent and angry. Only "The Marching Song of the Covert Battalions" has music actually composed by Bragg—and that selection contains a lengthy quote of the tune "When Johnny Come Marching Home." The rest are covers of songs (some of them pre-20th century) that either overtly or covertly deal with revolution, radical politics, or pacifist sentiments. The arrangements are a real departure for Bragg, and are most unusual and effective. "I Dreamed I Saw Phil Ochs Last Night" and "Nicaragua Nicaraguita" are for unaccompanied voice. "Marching Song of the Covert Battalions" features prominent clarinet and recorder passages sup-

ported by organ, accordion, and revival-meeting bass drum/cymbals combination. "Red Flag" is an energetic reel set sparsely for voice, whistles, percussion, and minimal guitar. The title track is given a grand, traditional, all-stops-out treatment, arranged for chorus, large brass ensemble, and percussion. The album's best selection, "My Youngest Son Came Home Today," is a dirgelike antiwar number that is very moving and effective. This album is a committed, deeply felt manifesto well worth a listen. Original pressings of this record came with a wide-ranging and enjoyable promotional 45 containing selections by Bragg, Clea & McLeod, Caroline Trettine, and the Young Fresh Fellows. —*David Cleary*

Don't Try This at Home / Sep. 17, 1991 / Go! Discs/Elektra ✦✦✦✦
With full-blown production by the likes of Johnny Marr, and with musical assistance from R.E.M., this would seem like a blatant stab at the post-modern marketplace. Maybe so, but the thrust of his band turns "Accident Waiting to Happen" and "North Sea Bubble" into throttling rockers and makes "Sexuality" his best single. There are also several gorgeous ballads, "Tank Park Salute" and "Wish You Were Here" among them. —*John Floyd*

The Peel Sessions / May 1992 / Strange Fruit ✦✦✦
Because Bragg started his career as a solo act, these live-in-the-studio radio transcriptions don't offer anything you can't find on *Back to Basics*. But fanatics will enjoy the occasional lyric deviations, and "A13 Trunk Road to the Sea" (a rewrite of "Route 66" with British directions) is a keeper. —*John Floyd*

William Bloke / Sep. 9, 1996 / Elektra ✦✦✦
After the release of *Don't Try This at Home*, Billy Bragg went into seclusion for five years, as he raised his child. *William Bloke* reflects a newfound maturity for Bragg, as he tones down his attack and returns to simple, acoustic-based arrangements. Though there are a few songs that are infused with his trademark leftist politics, most of *William Bloke* is comprised of songs about fatherhood and maturity, which are warm, compassionate, and melodic. In short, it's the sound of urban folk settling into adulthood without dreading its responsibilities. —*Stephen Thomas Erlewine*

Brand New Heavies

f. 1985, London, England
Hip Hop, Urban, Club/Dance
As one of the leading "acid-jazz" groups who emerged during the '90s, the Brand New Heavies attracted substantial attention on both sides of the Atlantic for their sometimes clever, sometimes cool mix of quasi-sophisticated vocals, jazz backing, and samples. The London band began in the mid-'80s with drummer/keyboardist Jan Kincaid, percussionist/guitarist Lascelles, guitarist Simon Bartholomew, bassist/keyboardist Andrew Levy, saxophonist Mike Smith, trumpeter Paul Dias, saxophonist/keyboardist Jim Wellman, and vocalist Jay Ella Ruth. They were active on what was then called the "rare groove" circuit, playing funk and soul. They became the Brand New Heavies in the late '80s, cutting the single "Got to Give" for the Cooltempo label. They switched to the Acid Jazz label and style in 1990. Their 1991 debut for Delicious Vinyl/Island did moderately well, but they gained even more exposure (despite generating lackluster sales) with *Heavy Rhyme Experience: Vol 1*, a 1992 record that paired them with several hip-hop groups and big-name rappers. The guest list included Main Source, Gang Starr, Grand Puba, Master Ace, Kool G. Rap, Black Sheep, Ed O.G., Tiger, the Pharcyde, and Jamalski. Vocalist N'Dea Davenport was a contributor to *Jazzmatazz*, a similar all-star jazz/hip-hop set produced by Gang Starr's Guru. Brand New Heavies released their third album, *Brother Sister*, in 1994. —*Ron Wynn*

● **The Brand New Heavies** / 1991 / Delicious Vinyl ✦✦✦✦
Many of the artists who were part of Britain's soul scene of the late-'80s/early-'90s—including Soul II Soul, Lisa Stansfield and Caron Wheeler—took a high-tech neo-soul approach combining '70s-influenced R&B and disco with elements of hip-hop. The equally impressive Brand New Heavies, however, used technology sparingly, stressed the use of "real instruments" and were unapologetically retro and '70s-sounding through and through. Drawing on such influences as the Average White Band and Tower of Power, the Heavies triumph by sticking with the classic R&B approach they clearly love the most. The band has a jewel of a singer in N'Dea Davenport, who is characteristically expressive on "Dream Come True" and "Stay This Way." Real horns—not synthesizers made to sound like horns—enrich those gems as well as the sweaty vocal funk of "People Get Ready" and "Put the Funk Back in It" and the jazz-influenced instrumental "BNH." While this fine album enjoyed cult hit status, it was pretty much ignored by American "urban contemporary" radio. —*Alex Henderson*

Heavy Rhyme Experience, Vol. 1 / Aug. 3, 1992 / Delicious Vinyl ✦✦✦✦
Between their debut and full-fledged second album, Brand New Heavies released an album of collaborations with some of the brightest stars in

hip-hop, such as Gang Starr, Grand Puba, and Main Source. *Heavy Rhyme Experience: Vol. 1* actually works better than their debut, since the rappers bring a gritty street credibility to the group's lush R&B; at its best, the album stands as a splendid fusion of jazz, soul, and hip-hop. —*Stephen Thomas Erlewine*

Brother Sister / Mar. 22, 1994 / Delicious Vinyl ✦✦✦
This album finds the BNH heading back to the groove-driven, horn-splashed, hand-clapping funk of their debut album, with N'Dea Davenport stepping back into her role as diva/lead vocalist. Following the string of distinguished rappers who made BNH's sophomore album a brave if not wholly successful attempt to infuse rap with the energy of live instruments, Davenport delivers the consistency that was missing from that effort. Repeated listens show this album to be catchier than it initially seems (as long as one avoids "Fake," one of the most irritating songs in a long time), and when the BNH really lock into a groove, as they do on "Keep Together," the title track and the instrumental "Snake Hips," they surely do put the funk back in it. —*Peter Stepek*

Excursions...Remixes and Rare Grooves / 1995 / Delicious Vinyl/ Capitol ✦✦

Shelter / May 13, 1997 / Delicious Vinyl ✦✦✦
By the time the Brand New Heavies released *Shelter* in 1997, urban R&B was shifting toward the more organic grooves that they helped pioneer in the early '90s. Although the Heavies were into acid-jazz as well, they smoothed over many of the experimental elements of their music in the mid-'90s, leaving behind a seductive, earthy, and jazzy variation of urban soul. That provided the foundation for *Shelter*, their first album featuring Siedah Garrett as lead singer. Garrett's smooth voice helps push the band toward more conventional territory, but their songwriting is stronger than that of most of their contemporaries, and their sound is funkier and more convincing. While there are no standout singles on *Shelter*, it's a uniformly engaging listen, illustrating that the Brand New Heavies are one of the great underrated urban R&B bands of the '90s. —*Leo Stanley*

Brand Nubian

f. 1989, New Rochelle, NY
Jazz-Rap
Picking up on the so-called "daisy age" sound of De La Soul, Brand Nubian's cool, funky sound serves as a platform for the group's declarations of Islamic faith and for the teachings of the Five Percent Nation. The group's original lineup was composed of lead rapper Maxwell "Grand Puba" Dixon (formerly of the Masters of Ceremony), Lorenzo "Lord Jamar" Dechelaus, Derrick "Sadat X" Murphy, and his cousin DJ Alamo. Following the group's acclaimed 1990 debut, *One for All*, Grand Puba departed for a solo career, taking DJ Alamo with him. The remaining members added DJ Sincere and have continued to record albums detailing their religious beliefs and promoting self-reliance and peace. —*Steve Huey*

● **One for All** / 1990 / Elektra ✦✦✦✦
These post-De La Soul, daisy-age rappers are here to wrap their Islamic-slanted lyrics around challenging, clever, and hard-hitting beats and samples. —*John Floyd*

In God We Trust / Feb. 1993 / Elektra ✦✦✦✦

Toni Braxton

b. Severn, MD
Vocals / Urban, Adult Contemporary, Club/Dance
Toni Braxton made her vocal debut with the single "Love Shoulda Brought You Home" from the *Boomerang* soundtrack. She issued her first full album in 1993, and it soared to the top of both the pop and R&B charts. Braxton eventually earned two Grammy and two Soul Train awards, saw her self-titled release go platinum, and reaped both critical and commercial plaudits for such singles as "Love Shoulda Brought You Home" and "Just Another Sad Love Song." In the summer of 1996 Braxton released her second album, *Secrets*, which entered the charts at No. 2 and produced the No. 1 single, "You're Makin' Me High." —*Ron Wynn*

● **Toni Braxton** / Jul. 1993 / La Face ✦✦✦✦
Toni Braxton is an elegant and earthy songstress, nicely balancing those seemingly divergent traits on her self-titled debut disc. Braxton's husky, enticing voice sounds hypnotic on "Breathe Again," dismayed on "Another Sad Love Song," and disillusioned on "Love Shoulda Brought You Home." But she's never out of control, indignant, or so anguished and hurt that she fails to retain her dignity. It's a sign of how great the Babyface/L.A. Reid production team was that they didn't settle for a defining mood; they presented Braxton with enough diverse emotional settings to hold the interest of urban contemporary males and females. —*Ron Wynn*

Secrets / Jun. 18, 1996 / LaFace ✦✦✦✦
Toni Braxton's second album, *Secrets*, follows through on the promise of her eponymous debut. Like her first album, the majority of *Secrets* was co-produced by Babyface and his partner L.A. Reid, while the material is divided between songs written by songwriters like R. Kelly, Tony Rich, and Diane Warren and originals by Braxton and Babyface. Braxton and Babyface's collaborations are the highlights of the album, combining rich melodies and gorgeous choruses with subtle, clever lyrics that are never laced with clichés. Nearly equalling the original numbers are contributions by Tony Rich ("Come On over Here") and R. Kelly ("I Don't Want To"); with these tracks, both musicians demonstrate why they are considered two of the top songwriters in '90s R&B and soul. *Secrets* does have a couple of weak moments. The numbers produced by David Foster are too predictable in their slick commercial appeal, but Braxton manages to infuse the songs with life and passion that elevate them beyond their generic confines. And her vocal talent is what unites *Secrets* and makes it into a first-rate contemporary R&B collection. Braxton is a singer who can cross over into adult contemporary radio without losing or betraying the soul that lies at the foundation of her music, and her talent burns at its brightest on *Secrets*. —*Stephen Thomas Erlewine*

Bread

f. 1968, Los Angeles, CA, **db.** 1976
Soft Rock, Pop-Rock
Bread was one of the most popular pop groups of the early '70s, earning a string of well-crafted, melodic soft-rock singles, all of which were written by keyboardist/vocalist David Gates. A session musician and producer, Gates met guitarist/vocalist James Griffin in 1968; Griffin had already released a solo album called *Summer Holiday*. Griffin hired Gates to produce a new album, and the pair soon became a group, adding guitarist/vocalist Robb Royer from the band Pleasure Faire, whom Gates had produced early in their career. The trio soon signed with Elektra Records, becoming one of the label's first pop bands. Naming themselves Bread, the group released their self-titled debut album in late 1968. Although it was filled with accessible, melodic, soft rock that became the band's signature sound, the record had no hit singles.

With their second album, *On the Waters*, Bread established themselves as hit-makers. "Make It with You," the first single released from the album, became a No. 1 hit, which led to "It Don't Matter to Me," a song taken from *Bread*, becoming a Top Ten hit. With *On the Waters* becoming a gold record, the group embarked on a tour, adding a full-time drummer, Mike Botts, to the lineup. *Manna*, released in the spring of 1971, wasn't as big a hit as the previous record, but it launched another Top Ten hit with "If." Royer left the group after the album and was replaced by Larry Knechtel, a Los Angeles session musician who played on records by the Byrds, the Beach Boys, and the Monkees, among others. The new lineup released their first single, "Mother Freedom," in the summer of 1971; the single scraped the Top 40 at No. 37. Bread's next single, "Baby I'm-A Want You," became a No. 3 hit at the end of the year. After "Everything I Own" reached No. 5 in January 1972, an album called *Baby I'm-A Want You* was released. Peaking at No. 3, the record became the group's most successful album. A fifth album, *Guitar Man*, followed in the fall of 1972.

At the beginning of 1973, Bread disbanded after a dispute between Gates and Griffin. Griffin claimed that when the group was conceived, the pair agreed that the singles would be divided equally between the two songwriters; Gates wrote most of Bread's hits and wanted to continue to compose the singles. The two parted ways, with each of the musicians pursuing a solo career. Bread reunited in 1976, releasing *Lost Without Your Love* in early 1977. The title track became their last Top Ten hit, peaking at No. 9. The success could not keep the group together, as tensions between Gates and Griffin began to escalate again. After Griffin split from the group, Gates assembled a new version of the band and toured under the name Bread. Griffin sued Gates for using the name Bread, which the duo co-owned. A judge ordered the group not to perform, record, or collect royalty payments until the case was resolved; it wasn't resolved until 1984. In the meantime, Gates and and Griffin pursued solo careers. Of the two, Gates was more successful, scoring a No. 15 hit in 1978 with the title theme to *Goodbye Girl*. However, his career declined in the '80s; by the '90s, he was running a California ranch. Griffin relocated to Nashville, forming Dreamer with Randy Meisner in the early '90s. —*Stephen Thomas Erlewine*

● **Anthology** / 1985 / Elektra ✦✦✦✦
This album includes "Make It with You," "If," "Baby I'm-a Want You," and many other fine-tuned pop gems. —*Dan Heilman*

Retrospective / Jul. 1996 / Rhino ✦✦✦✦
Retrospective is the definitive compilation of Bread, perhaps the definitive soft-rock group of the '70s. If anything, it may be too comprehensive for most listeners. Covering the entire course of Bread's career, plus selected highlights from David Gates in the late '70s and early '80s, the

compilation spans two very full compact discs. For those who want more than the hits but are unwilling to delve into individual albums, the collection is ideal. Listeners who want the hits might find the album tracks a little tedious. Then again, the presence of Gates' solo hits like "The Goodbye Girl" is enticing for even casual fans, since he lacks a solo compilation and there are no sets that cover both his solo career and Bread. Since *Retrospective* does cover all the Bread hits plus solid obscurities and Gates' solo highlights, it does qualify as the definitive collection. In fact, it's hard to imagine how another set could be more thorough. —*Stephen Thomas Erlewine*

The Breeders

f. 1990, Dayton, OH
Alternative Pop-Rock
Initially, the Breeders were conceived as a way for Pixies' bassist Kim Deal and Throwing Muses' guitarist Tanya Donelly to let out some suppressed creative energy. Deal and Donelly both played guitar, leaving bass for Josephine Wiggs of Perfect Disaster. Taking their name from the group Deal led with her twin sister, Kelly, in their teens, the Breeders combined the spareness of Throwing Muses with the shifting dynamics and warped pop sensibilities of the Pixies. *Pod,* their critically acclaimed debut album, was released in 1990. Two years later the group delivered *Safari,* a four-song EP that found the band getting more muscular and melodic. Soon after its recording, Donelly left the Breeders to form her own group, Belly. Kim Deal brought in her sister, Kelly, as her replacement. By this time, their permanent drummer was Jim MacPherson, who was billed as "Mike Hunt" on *Safari.*

As the Breeders were working on their new album in the beginning of 1993, the Pixies split, leaving Kim Deal able to pursue the Breeders full-time. Released late in the summer of 1993, *Last Splash* was a hazier, more disjointed continuation of the hard pop of *Safari.* With the sonic collage of "Cannonball," the Breeders had a crossover hit that catapulted the group into stardom; within a year, the album had gone platinum, and the band had a prime spot on 1994's Lollapalooza tour. —*Stephen Thomas Erlewine*

● **Pod** / 1990 / 4AD/Elektra ✦✦✦✦
At the time *Pod* was released, the Breeders were just a side project for Kim Deal and Tanya Donelly, but the album was much richer than most one-shot records. Taking a little from both the Pixies and Throwing Muses, the Breeders invent an indie-rock style of their own—a sparse, dreamy, elliptical take on guitar pop. While *Pod* may rely on the sheer uniqueness of the band's spare, raw sound, the album wouldn't as nearly as successful if it weren't for the band's exceptional songwriting. From the wonderful, slow guitar grind of "Glorious" and "Iris" to the stripped-down pop of "Doe" and "Iris," *Pod* is full of original guitar-pop pleasures. —*Stephen Thomas Erlewine*

Safari / 1992 / 4AD/Elektra ✦✦✦
There are only four songs, but the Breeders continue to improve, growing more muscular and melodic. All of the songs here, especially "Do You Love Me Now" and a cover of the Who's "So Sad About Us," rival the best on *Pod.* —*Stephen Thomas Erlewine*

Last Splash / Aug. 31, 1993 / 4AD/Elektra ✦✦✦✦
Falling halfway between the adventurous *Pod* and the magnificent heavy guitar-pop of *Safari, Last Splash* is ultimately a disappointing album from the Breeders. Nearly half of *Last Splash* is filled with fragments and songs that sound unfinished. However, there's no denying that when *Last Splash* is good, it's splendid. From the thrilling sonic collage of "Cannonball" to the more traditional pop melodies of "Invisible Man," "I Just Wanna Get Along," "Divine Hammer," and "Drivin' on 9," the best moments on the album are truly terrific, making the underdeveloped "No Aloha," "Hag," "Mad Lucas," "Roi," and the inferior re-recording of "Do You Love Me Now?" all the more infuriating. —*Stephen Thomas Erlewine*

Brick

f. 1972, Atlanta, GA, **db.** 1981
Funk, Disco
Brick was an Atlanta band that created a successful merger of funk and jazz that was called "dazz" in the '70s. Brick's roster included lead vocalist/saxophonist/flutist Jimmy Brown, guitarist/bassist/vocalist Regi Hargis Hickman, lead singer Ray Ransom (who doubled as a bassist/keyboardist/percussionist), and Eddie Irons (who did lead vocals and played drums and keyboards). They recorded "Music Matic" for Main Street in 1976, before signing to the CBS-distributed label Bang. Their first Bang single, "Dazz," topped the R&B charts and was No. 3 pop in 1976, and they continued on Bang until 1982. Brick scored two more huge hits in 1977, "Dusic" and "Ain't Gonna Hurt Nobody," each with a chunky, propulsive beat and catchy, light pop-jazz refrain. Their last Top Ten R&B hit was "Sweat ('Til You Get Wet)" in 1981. —*Ron Wynn*

● **The Best of Brick** / Jun. 13, 1995 / Sony Legacy ✦✦✦
The Best of Brick is a fine compilation featuring all of the funk band's biggest hits, including the Top Ten R&B hits "Dazz," "Dusic," "Ain't Gonna' Hurt Nobody," and "Sweat ('til You Get Wet)." —*Stephen Thomas Erlewine*

Edie Brickell

b. Mar. 10, 1966, Oak Cliff, TX
Vocals / Folk-Rock, Pop-Rock
Edie Brickell was born in 1966 in the Oak Cliff section of Dallas. She attended Southern Methodist University for a year and a half before drinking up enough courage in a bar one night in 1985 to get up on stage with a local band, the New Bohemians. She joined the band and wrote songs over the next year as the band changed and evolved. They finally settled on the personnel of Brad Houser (bass), Kenny Withrow (guitar), and Matt Chamberlain (drums), before taking off for Rockfield Studios in Wales to record their debut album.

That album, *Shooting Rubberbands at the Stars,* revealed Brickell to be a songwriter with a unique perspective and a singer with an intimate, conversational style. The album was hailed by critics and became a massive hit, selling over a million copies and producing the Top Ten hit "What I Am."

After the disappointing performance of their follow-up album, *Ghost of a Dog,* the New Bohemians disbanded. Brickell married Paul Simon, and the couple had a child. After several years of remaining artistically quiet, Brickell released her first solo album in late summer 1994. —*William Ruhlmann*

● **Shooting Rubberbands at the Stars** / 1989 / Geffen ✦✦✦✦
Lead singer Brickell is charmingly unique on this album of light pop with thoughtful lyrics. It features the hit "What I Am." —*Donna DiChario*

Ghost of a Dog / 1990 / Geffen ✦✦✦
An overlooked followup, it found Brickell expanding on her offbeat vocals. —*Donna DiChario*

Picture Perfect Morning / Aug. 16, 1994 / Geffen ✦✦
Edie Brickell's comeback album *Picture Perfect Morning* is a pleasant record of adult contemporary pop, with hints of folk-rock buried underneath the glossy production. Brickell sounds good and the production is impeccable, but the record never creates a consistent mood. More importantly, none of the songs is memorable, lacking distinctive, catchy melodies or memorable lyrics. As a result, the album is fine as background music but it doesn't leave a lasting impact. —*Stephen Thomas Erlewine*

Brinsley Schwarz

f. Oct. 1969, England, **db.** 1975
Rock 'n' Roll, Country-Rock, Pub Rock
Pub rock, the English roots-rock movement of the early '70s, would never have earned a cult following if it weren't for Brinsley Schwarz. Initially, Brinsley Schwarz was a rambling, neo-psychedelic folk-rock band that borrowed heavily from Crosby, Stills & Nash and the Grateful Dead. After a disastrous publicity stunt to promote their debut album, the band went into seclusion outside of London and developed a laid-back, rootsy sound inspired by Eggs Over Easy, an American band that had been playing a mixture of originals and covers in English pubs. After their conversion to pub rock, the Brinsleys ditched their pretensions of stardom and became a down-to-earth, self-effacing rock 'n' roll band. Between 1971 and 1974, Brinsley Schwarz toured England innumerable times, playing pubs across the country. Along the way, they established a circuit for similar bands, like Dr. Feelgood and Ducks Deluxe, to follow. Though the group was nominally guitarist Brinsley Schwarz' band, bassist/lead vocalist Nick Lowe provided the bulk of the group's songs. Lowe developed a distinctive songwriting voice—conversational, melodic, off-beat, and funny—and the band was infused with his skewed sense of humor. Despite strong reviews and a dedicated fan base, the Brinsleys never managed to escape cult status, but they influenced a legion of other artists, creating an underground, back-to-basics movement that laid the foundation for punk rock.

Brinsley Schwarz didn't plan to start a grass-roots movement—they wanted to be stars. Nick Lowe and Brinsley Schwarz had already spent several years in Kippington Lodge, a Tunbridge Wells-based guitar-pop group that released five singles on Parlophone during the mid-'60s, to no success. By 1968 the band was beginning to feel restless with their straightahead pop-rock and was eager to explore psychedelia. Keyboardist Bob Andrews joined the band later that year, and drummer Billy Rankin came aboard in the fall of 1969. By that time, Kippington Lodge had completely revamped their musical style, evolving into a folk-rock band with psychedelic pretensions; they appropriately changed their name, calling themselves Brinsley Schwarz after their lead guitarist.

Ironically, it was around this time that Lowe became the group's lead singer and primary songwriter.

Within a few months Brinsley Schwarz had come to the attention of Dave Robinson, a fledging rock 'n' roll manager who had founded the Famepushers Agency. Robinson developed a complex scheme to elevate Brinsley Schwarz to stardom. According to his plan, the Brinsleys would play an opening set for Van Morrison at the Fillmore East in New York in the spring of 1970, and he would fly all of the leading rock journalists to America to review the show. Late in 1969 Brinsley Schwarz signed a record contract with United Artists, and the band financed the publicity stunt with their advance. The group planned to leave a few days before the show in order to rehearse, but they were denied visas on a technicality. They were finally given visas on the morning of the show; they arrived in New York only hours before the concert. Back in Britain, the journalists ran into trouble, as their plane developed a mechanical fault, delaying the flight for four hours. When the journalists arrived at the Fillmore 18 hours later, they were either drunk or hung-over. When Brinsley Schwarz finally hit the stage, they gave a competent but underwhelming performance, setting the stage for a flood of scathing reviews for both the concert and the eponymously titled debut album, which appeared weeks after the showcase.

Reeling from the Fillmore fiasco, Brinsley Schwarz rented a house outside London and spent their days and nights playing music. By the end of 1970, the group released a second album, *Despite It All*, which indicated that they were evolving into a country-rock outfit; guitarist/ vocalist Ian Gomm joined the band at the end of the sessions for the record. For much of 1971 the Brinsleys rehearsed, developing a blend of country, folk, R&B, and rock 'n' roll that was largely inspired by the Byrds, Van Morrison, and the Band, as well as Eggs Over Easy, whom the group met at the Tally Ho pub in Kentish Town. *Silver Pistol*, released early in 1972, demonstrated their new versatility, but the group truly flexed their muscles in concert, particularly during their regular concerts at the Tally Ho. Soon they had built a small but loyal following, and a number of like-minded bands began playing the same circuit. Eventually, this grassroots phenomenon came to the attention of the UK press, who dubbed the groups "pub rock" and proclaimed Brinsley Schwarz as the genre's leaders.

Nervous on the Road, released in the fall of 1972, was Brinsley Schwarz's best-reviewed album to date, and while it didn't chart, it helped the group land an opening slot for Paul McCartney. Throughout 1973 the Brinsleys toured constantly, playing colleges as well as pubs. As a result, they weren't able to record frequently, which hurt their already weak recording career. In an attempt to land a hit, the band released a series of non-album singles, none of which charted; they were compiled for the *Please Don't Ever Change* album, released in late 1973. Early the next year, the group cut their fifth album with producer Dave Edmunds. Released in the summer of 1974, *New Favourites of Brinsley Schwarz* was more polished than their previous albums, but the record failed to generate sales. The group continued for nearly another year, turning out a handful of singles under other names, before deciding to call it a day in the spring of 1975. After the band's demise Brinsley Schwarz and Bob Andrews became members of Graham Parker's backing band, the Rumour. Ian Gomm pursued a solo career; Rankin played with Terraplane and Big Jim Sullivan's Tiger before retiring from music. Nick Lowe became a successful solo artist and producer, scoring his biggest hit in 1980 with "Cruel to Be Kind," a Brinsley leftover that the band never recorded. — *Stephen Thomas Erlewine*

Brinsley Schwarz / 1970 / One Way ✦✦✦
Brinsley Schwarz's eponymous first album is a classic example of a debut being recorded before the group had fully developed musically. Throughout the record, the band alternates between half-baked hippie sentiments, sub-Crosby, Stills & Nash harmonies, botched progressive-rock, and aimless folk-rock. Melodies and hooks float in and out of the mix, and nothing ever really takes hold. There's a certain charm to the group's haplessness, especially in light of their later work, but it doesn't prevent the album from being a difficult listen. More than anything, *Brinsley Schwarz* functions as an artifact, since the music hardly points the way toward their future. — *Stephen Thomas Erlewine*

Despite It All / 1970 / BGO ✦✦✦
Brinsley Schwarz sounds considerably more focused on their second album, *Despite It All*. Although they haven't completely abandoned their prog and psychedelic pretensions, the group has developed their folk and country fixations, resulting in a handful of strong songs ("The Slow One," "Funk Angel"), and one terrific one in "Country Girl," a fiddle-driven country-rocker that equals the Band at their best. — *Stephen Thomas Erlewine*

Silver Pistol / 1972 / Edsel ✦✦✦✦
With *Silver Pistol*, Brinsley Schwarz came into their own, completing their evolution from a prog-inflected folk-rock band to a pub rock band. The addition of Ian Gomm has strengthened the band's sound, giving them a loose but rocking attack. Gomm also contributed a handful of

fine songs, but Nick Lowe establishes himself as the group's key songwriter with "Silver Pistol," "Nightingale," "The Last Time I Was Fooled," "Egypt," and "Unknown Number," songs that blend country, folk, and rock in an inventive way. They stay within the traditions of country-rock and folk-rock, but they sound fresh through Lowe's melodies and the group's lean sound. Even with two strong songwriters in the band, the album's definitive song is a cover of Jim Ford's "Ju Ju Man," which captures the aesthetic of pub-rock with its laid-back, tongue-in-cheek tale of lovers on the run with rock 'n' roll. — *Stephen Thomas Erlewine*

Nervous on the Road / 1972 / United Artists ✦✦✦✦
Silver Pistol wrote the blueprint for Brinsley Schwarz' pub rock, but *Nervous on the Road* perfected their sound, becoming the definitive pub rock band in the process. *Nervous on the Road* has a fuller, more detailed production than its predecessor, as well as a looser feeling. Even with the smooth production, it sounds as if the band was captured on a good night at the Tally Ho. But what really makes the record is its excellent selection of songs, almost all of which are written by Nick Lowe. "Happy Doing What We're Doing," "Surrender to the Rhythm," and "Nervous on the Road" are all great rock 'n' roll songs about rock 'n' roll, spiked with an off-kilter sense of humor. "Don't Lose Your Grip on Love" is Lowe's first great ballad, while Ian Gomm's "It's Been So Long" is one of his best songs. And the covers of "I Like It like That" and "Home in My Hand" are wonderful pub-rockers and help give the album the feeling of an excellent concert. Nevertheless, what makes *Nervous on the Road* such a fine record is the combination of empathetic performances, unpredictable songwriting, and a charming unpretentiousness, all of which help make the album one of the great forgotten rock &'n'roll records. — *Stephen Thomas Erlewine*

Please Don't Ever Change / 1973 / Edsel ✦✦✦✦
Released in 1973 as Brinsley Schwarz was busy touring and recording the followup to *Nervous on the Road, Please Don't Ever Change* is a collection of singles, live cuts, and radio sessions from the early '70s. The odds-and-sods nature of the record actually works in its favor, since it accentuates the group's ramshackle nature. Sure, there's a fair amount of filler on the record — their ill-advised reggae excursion "The Version (Hypocrite)" is simply mystifying — but unevenness was part of the Brinsleys' charm, and the simply enjoyable cuts make the best tracks feel like classics. And some of them are definitive Brinsley cuts. "I Worry ('bout You Baby)" is a revamped R&B number, the live "Home in My Hand" speeds along with relentless energy, the cover of Goffin/King's "Don't Ever Change" indicates Nick Lowe's latent pop roots, "Down in Mexico" is a hysterical travelogue, and "Play That Fast Thing (One More Time)" is among the classic pub rock singles, distilling the essence of pub rock into one pile-driving song. — *Stephen Thomas Erlewine*

New Favourites / 1974 / United Artists ✦✦✦✦
With their final album, Brinsley Schwarz turns in their most pop-oriented record, filled with infectious gems like "The Ugly Things," "Trying to Live My Life Without You," and "(What's So Funny 'bout) Peace, Love and Understanding." Lowe's songs were the best he had ever written and show that his ambitions were beginning to conflict with those of the rest of the band. Nevertheless, there isn't a weak song or uninspired performance on *New Favourites*, making it an excellent farewell album. — *Stephen Thomas Erlewine*

Nervous on the Road/The New Favourites of Brinsley Schwarz / 1975 / Beat Goes On ✦✦✦✦
Two of Brinsley Schwarz' finest albums, *Nervous on the Road* and *The New Favorites of Brinsley Schwarz*, have been combined on one compact disc. *Nervous on the Road* is the definitive pub rock album, featuring such defining songs as "Happy Doing What We're Doing," "Play That Fast Thing One More Time," and "Home in My Hand." *The New Favorites* is a more polished, commercial collection that points toward Nick Lowe's solo career, but it also has such classic cuts as "(What's So Funny 'bout) Peace, Love and Understanding," "The Ugly Things," and "Down in the Dive." — *Stephen Thomas Erlewine*

★ **Surrender to the Rhythm** / 1991 / EMI ✦✦✦✦✦
The 20-track compilation *Surrender to the Rhythm* is an excellent retrospective of Brinsley Schwarz' career. The compilation is culled from each of the group's albums, touching lightly on their earlier records and drawing heavily from *Silver Pistol, Nervous on the Road*, and *The New Favourites*, which is appropriate, since they were the stronger records. Although *Nervous on the Road* remains a necessary album, *Surrender to the Rhythm* compiles nearly every one of the Brinsleys' greatest tracks, including "Country Girl," "Ju Ju Man," "Down in Mexico," "Play That Fast Thing (One More Time)," "Happy Doing What We're Doing," "Don't Lose Your Grip on Love," "The Ugly Things," a ripping live version of "Home in My Hand," and the original version of Nick Lowe's classic "(What's So Funny 'bout) Peace, Love and Understanding." *Surrender to the Rhythm* offers convincing evidence that Brinsley Schwarz is one of the great underrated bands of the early '70s, while essentially summing up the spirit of pub rock. — *Stephen Thomas Erlewine*

Bronski Beat

f. 1984, London, England, db. 1987
New Wave

A synth-pop trio from London, everything that made Bronski Beat interesting, and at times compelling, came primarily from the larynx of Glasgow-born vocalist Jimmy Somerville. Possessing a soaring tenor voice that frequently exploded into falsetto, Somerville was a rare singer, capable of imbuing even the most rote dance songs with near-palpable heartache and layers of emotional turmoil. Openly gay, Somerville and the Bronskis, despite the rock world's implicit homophobia, became cover darlings of the British music press in 1984 after the UK success of their first two singles, "Why" and "Smalltown Boy" (the latter producing one of the best music videos of all time). From that point on, Bronski Beat seemed poised to rule the pop world (at least in England), releasing a superb cover of the Donna Summer disco hit "I Feel Love" and a remarkable debut album, 1984's *The Age of Consent*. It was only a year later that Somerville announced he was leaving Bronski Beat to form the more explicitly left-wing Communards (with pianist Richard Coles). Bronski Beat took his departure in stride, and the lead vocal slot went to a fairly anonymous singer named John Jon. There were more Bronski Beat recordings, but even fanatics would agree that the band lost everything when it lost Somerville. Ironically, the Communards got off to a fast start with a great cover of Thelma Houston's "Don't Leave Me This Way," but all in all, Somerville's work with them was far less interesting than anything he did in Bronski Beat. By 1989 Somerville was a solo act, his magnificent tenor voice still intact and the quality of the material still in question. —*John Dougan*

● **The Age of Consent** / 1984 / London ✦✦✦✦

To say this is a great album of dance-oriented synth-pop music is to sell it extremely short; this is simply a great album, period. Somerville's soaring tenor may take some getting used to, but the songs, many of them dealing with homophobia and alienation (none more eloquently than "Smalltown Boy"), are compelling vignettes about the vagaries of life as a gay man. Cynics predisposed to dismissing entire genres of music based on trendiness or a limited appeal ("dance music is for dancing, not listening") miss the point in lumping this in with more mindless forays into techno or neo-disco. As the Pet Shop Boys (the world's greatest disco band) proved a few years later, you can have substantive content and wrap it up in a compelling, visceral, dance-oriented package. Few bands understood this better, or earlier, than Bronski Beat. —*John Dougan*

Truthdare Doubledare / 1986 / London ✦✦✦

The Brothers Johnson

f. 1975, Los Angeles, CA
Soul, Funk, Pop-Rock

Guitarist/vocalist George Johnson and bassist/vocalist Louis Johnson formed the band Johnson Three Plus One with older brother Tommy and their cousin Alex Weir while attending school in Los Angeles. When they became professionals, the band backed such touring R&B acts as Bobby Womack and the Supremes. George and Louis Johnson later joined Billy Preston's band, and wrote "Music in My Life" and "The Kids and Me" for him before leaving his group in 1973.

Quincy Jones hired them to play on his LP *Mellow Madness*, and recorded four of them there, including "Is It Love That We're Missing?" and "Just a Taste of Me." Jones took them on a Japanese tour, then produced their debut LP, *Look Out for Number 1*, after they signed with A&M, which was also his label at the time (1976). They scored a No. 1 R&B and No. 3 pop hit with "I'll Be Good to You," and enjoyed R&B chart toppers in 1977 and 1980, respectively, with "Strawberry Letter 23" and "Stomp!," while sustaining a consistent hit presence via such songs as "Get the Funk Out Ma Face" and "Runnin' for Your Lovin'." Jones remade "I'll Be Good to You" in 1989 with Ray Charles and Chaka Khan on his *Back on the Block* release.

The Brothers earned platinum records for *Look Out for Number 1* and *Right on Time*. Jones produced both of these, along with their third and fourth LPs, *Blam* and *Light Up the Night*. The group produced the single "The Real Thing" in 1981. It reached No. 11 on the R&B charts, and the Brothers had another hit with "Welcome to the Club" in 1982. They started doing separate ventures; Louis Johnson played bass on Michael Jackson's *Thriller* LP and recorded a gospel album, while George Johnson worked with Steve Arrington. Leon Sylvers produced their mid-'80s return LP *Out of Control;* it didn't equal their past success, but it got them another R&B hit with "You Keep Coming Back" in 1984. They recorded *Kickin'* in 1988, and co-wrote "Tomorrow" with Siedah Garrett for Jones' *Back on the Block* in 1989. —*Ron Wynn*

● **Greatest Hits** / Jun. 18, 1996 / A&M ✦✦✦✦

Greatest Hits contains all of the Brothers Johnson's biggest singles, including the gold singles "I'll Be Good to You" and "Strawberry Letter 23." In addition to all the familiar hits, there are some lesser-known singles that are nearly as good, making this single-disc compilation the definitive retrospective. —*Stephen Thomas Erlewine*

Arthur Brown

b. Jun. 24, 1944, Whitby, Yorkshire, England
Psychedelic

One of the most electrifying one-shot artists of the '60s, British singer Brown briefly set the charts alight in 1968, as well as thrilling audiences with his theatrical performances, which saw him wearing helmets of fire and outlandish costumes. His debut album was surely one of the most left-field commercial successes of the late '60s, if not of rock history. Besides topping the British charts (and reaching No. 2 in the US) with his brilliantly demonic single "Fire," the self-proclaimed god of hellfire actually scored a Top Ten LP with his 1968 debut. Unveiling Arthur's demented, fire-obsessed lyrical visions and swooping, theatrical vocals, it showcased his band's manic, agitated, psychedelic sound, which was anchored by incendiary drumming, Pete Townshend's production, and an organist who could be best described as Jimmy Smith on acid. Brown's original band broke up in early 1969; in the early '70s, he released several albums with Kingdom Come, which saw him pursuing a maddeningly obscure, and less exciting, brand of arty rock. He's recorded off and on since, but his last flash of fame was his role as a priest in the film version of *Tommy*. —*Richie Unterberger*

● **Crazy World of Arthur Brown** / 1968 / Polydor ✦✦✦✦

Though a bit over-the-top, this album was still powerful and surprisingly melodic, and managed to be quite bluesy and soulful even as the band overhauled chestnuts by James Brown and Screamin' Jay Hawkins. "Spontaneous Apple Creation" is a willfully histrionic, atonal song that gives Captain Beefheart a run for his money. Though this one-shot was not (and perhaps could not ever) be repeated, it remains an exhilaratingly reckless slice of psychedelia. The CD reissue includes both mono and stereo versions of five of the songs. Although the mono mixes lack the full-bodied power of the stereo ones, they're marked by some interesting differences, especially in the brief spoken and instrumental links between tracks. —*Richie Unterberger*

Bobby Brown

b. Feb. 5, 1969, Boston, MA
Vocals / Dance-Pop, Urban, Club/Dance, New Jack R&B

At the end of the '80s, former New Edition member Bobby Brown made the album that made new jack swing a dominant force, not only on the urban charts, but on the pop charts as well. Brown's first album, *King of the Stage*, wasn't that remarkable, but 1988's *Don't Be Cruel* is the definitive new jack album, thanks to L.A. Reid's and Babyface's massive production and songs, including the hits "Don't Be Cruel," "Every Little Step," and "Roni." While recording the follow-up album, Brown married pop star Whitney Houston and they had a child; their marriage has been plagued with tabloid-fueled rumors. In 1992 Brown released *Bobby*, a follow-up record that didn't have the commercial success of *Don't Be Cruel*, mainly because it lacked the focused songs and production that made that album such a huge success. —*Stephen Thomas Erlewine*

King of Stage / 1987 / MCA ✦✦✦

Bobby Brown's style was still fairly close to that of his comrades in New Edition when he recorded his first solo effort, *King of Stage*—an album giving little indication of the hard-edged, aggressive "new jack swing" that was only two years away on *Don't Be Cruel*. While comparisons to his subsequent work are inevitable, *Stage* is a generally decent, though not breathtaking, album that stands on its own merit—and one proving that there was indeed life outside of New Edition for the singer/rapper. Although Cameo leader Larry Blackmon serves as producer on "Girl Next Door," "Spending Time," and "Baby I Wanna Tell You Something" and brings an undeniably Cameo-ish element to these high-tech funk smokers, Brown's individuality comes through loud and clear. But as enjoyable as the Blackmon-produced tracks are, top honors must go to "Seventeen"—a riveting account of a teenage mother who turns to drugs and prostitution—and the unapologetically sentimental, '70s-like soul ballad "Girlfriend." Brown sounds as if he's going through the motions on the Rick James-ish "Your Tender Romance" and the lackluster ballad "Spending Time," but thankfully, *Stage* has more strengths than weaknesses. —*Alex Henderson*

● **Don't Be Cruel** / 1988 / MCA ✦✦✦✦

Don't Be Cruel was to Bobby Brown what *Control* was to Janet Jackson—a tougher, more aggressive project that shed his "bubble gum" image altogether and brought him to a new artistic and commercial plateau. With "My Prerogative" and the title song, Brown became a leader of "new-jack swing"—a forceful, high-tech blend of traditional soul singing and rap/hip-hop that's also associated with Guy and Brown's colleagues from New Edition, Bell Biv DeVoe. Brown had been a strong advocate of rap since his days with New Edition, and on *Cruel*, he did even more rapping than before. But for all the tough-mindedness he exhibited on his "new-jack" hits, the charismatic Bostonian hadn't lost his love of sentimental, old-fashioned R&B romanticism—and he definitely excels in that area on his hits "Every Little Step," "Roni" and "Rock Wit' Cha." Much of *Cruel* was produced by the ubiquitous production/songwriting duo L.A. & Babyface, who've often been accused (and rightly so) of taking a formulaic, cookie-cutter approach to R&B. But here, their work is never less than inspired. —*Alex Henderson*

Dance!...Ya Know It! / 1990 / MCA ✦✦

Cynics tend to dismiss remix albums as cheap exploitation and opportunism on the part of labels. But when the remixing is handled by inventive DJs, they definitely have their pleasures. *Dance... Ya Know It!,* obviously fueled by MCA Records' desire to cash in on the enormous success of Bobby Brown's *Don't Be Cruel,* is neither one of the better nor one of the worst remix albums available. While the primary focus is material from *Cruel*—including the hard and rugged "new jack swing" of "My Prerogative" and "Don't Be Cruel" and the vulnerable romanticism of "Roni," "Every Little Step," and "Rock Wit' Cha"—Brown's debut solo album, *King of Stage,* is represented by remixes of "Seventeen," "Girl Next Door," and "Baby, I Wanna Tell You Something." Much of the remixing is done by hit R&B producers L.A. & Babyface, who are far from adventurous and fail to add anything really new, interesting, or significant to the songs. Though an enjoyable release and one that works well enough as a "best of," *Dance... Ya Know It!* is hardly essential listening for those who already own *Stage* and *Cruel.* —*Alex Henderson*

Bobby / 1992 / MCA ✦✦✦

Brown's follow-up to the groundbreaking *Don't Be Cruel* isn't as innovative or consistent as his previous album, but that doesn't mean it's without any charms; the singles "Humpin' Around," "Good Enough," and "Get Away" are strong and memorable, which almost makes the abundance of filler forgivable. —*Stephen Thomas Erlewine*

Foxy Brown

b. 1979, Brooklyn, NY
Hip Hop

Before she had released any material at all, Foxy Brown appeared on several 1995-96 platinum singles, including her first credit, LL Cool J's "I Shot Ya," as well as Total's "No One Else" remix of Jay-Z's "Ain't No . . . ," Toni Braxton's "You're Makin' Me High" remix and Case's "Touch Me, Tease Me." The incredible success led to a major-label bidding war at the beginning of 1996, and by March, Brown had signed with the Def Jam label as another in the rank of young and hard female rappers.

The Brooklyn native—separate from a similarly named reggae artist—was born in 1979; in 1994, while still a teenager, she won a talent contest in Brooklyn, and was invited to freestyle on stage. At that time, Trackmasters were working on LL Cool J's *Mr. Smith* album, and they decided to let her rap over "I Shot Ya." The single became a hit, prompting Brown's work with Total, Braxton, and Case, as well as her induction into the Firm posse (led by Nas and also including AZ and Cormega). Brown's debut album *Ill Na Na* was produced by Trackmasters and featured appearances from Blackstreet, Method Man, and Kid Capri. It hit No. 7 its first week on the album charts. —*John Bush*

● **Ill Na Na** / Nov. 19, 1996 / Violator/Def Jam ✦✦✦✦

After appearing as a guest on a number of albums, most notably LL Cool J, Foxy Brown finally delivered her debut album *Ill Na Na* in late 1996. On her cameos, the teenage rapper rhapsodized about her three obsessions—fashion, sex, and the mafia—and all three dominate the discourse on *Ill Na Na.* Taken on their own terms, any of those lyrics could get rather tedious, but Foxy Brown has a sexy, assured delivery that makes her superficial preoccupations seductive. Furthermore, the album benefits greatly from the production efforts of the TrackMasterz, who give the music a sleek, contemporary edge that makes even the weaker tracks quite listenable. Foxy Brown is also assisted by cameos from Mobb Deep's Prodigy, Nas, Snoop Doggy Dog, and Az, among others, which gives the album star power; but it doesn't necessarily need it—she has enough charisma to steal the show. —*Stephen Thomas Erlewine*

James Brown

b. May 3, 1928, Macon, GA
Organ, Piano, Drums, Keyboards, Vocals / Soul, Funk, R&B

Soul Brother Number One, the Godfather of Soul, the Hardest Working Man in Show Business, Mr. Dynamite—those are mighty titles, but no one can question that James Brown has earned them more than any other performer. Other singers were more popular, others were equally skilled, but no other African-American musician has been so influential on the course of popular music in the past several decades. And no other musician, pop or otherwise, put on a more exciting, exhilarating stage show. Brown's performances were marvels of athletic stamina and split-second timing. Through the gospel-impassioned fury of his vocals and the complex polyrhythms of his beats, Brown was a crucial midwife in

not just one, but two revolutions in American Black music. He was one of the figures most responsible for turning R&B into soul; he was, most would agree, *the* figure most responsible for turning soul music into the funk of the late '60s and early '70s. Since the mid-'70s, he's done little more than tread water artistically; his financial and drug problems eventually got him a controversial prison sentence. Yet in a sense his music is now more influential than ever, as his voice and rhythms are sampled on innumerable rap and hip-hop recordings, and critics have belatedly hailed his innovations as among the most important in all of rock or soul.

Brown's rags-to-riches-to-rags story has heroic and tragic dimensions of mythic resonance. Born into poverty in the South, he ran afoul of the law by the late '40s on an armed robbery conviction. With the help of singer Bobby Byrd's family, Brown gained parole and started a gospel group with Byrd, changing their focus to R&B as the rock revolution gained steam. The Flames, as the Georgian group were known in the mid-'50s, were signed by Federal/King, and had a huge R&B hit right off the bat with the wrenching, churchy ballad "Please, Please, Please." By now the Flames had become James Brown and the Famous Flames, the charisma, energy, and talent of Brown making him the natural star attraction.

All of Brown's singles over the next two years flopped, as he sought to establish his own style, recording material that was obviously derivative of heroes like Roy Brown, Hank Ballard, Little Richard, and Ray Charles. In retrospect, it can be seen that Brown was in the same position as dozens of other R&B one-shots—talented singers in need of better songs, or not fully on the road to a truly original sound. What made Brown succeed where hundreds of others failed was his superhuman determination, working the chitlin circuit to death, sharpening his band, and keeping an eye on new trends. He was on the verge of being dropped from King in late 1958 when his perseverance finally paid off, as "Try Me" became a No. 1 R&B (and small pop) hit, and several follow-ups established him as a regular visitor to the R&B charts.

Brown's style of R&B got harder as the '60s began, as he added more complex, Latin- and jazz-influenced rhythms on hits like "Good Good Lovin'," "I'll Go Crazy," "Think," and "Night Train," alternating these with torturous ballads that featured some of the most frayed screaming to be heard outside of the church. Black audiences already knew that Brown had the most exciting live act around, but he truly started to become a phenomenon with the release of *Live at the Apollo* in 1963. Capturing a James Brown concert in all its whirling-dervish energy and calculated spontaneity, it reached No. 2 in the album charts, an unprecedented feat for a hardcore R&B LP.

Live at the Apollo was recorded and released against the wishes of the King label. It was these kinds of artistic standoffs that led Brown to seek better opportunities elsewhere. In 1964 he ignored his King contract to record "Out of Sight" for Smash, igniting a lengthy legal battle that prevented him from issuing vocal recordings for about a year. When he finally resumed recording for King in 1965, he had a new contract that granted him far more artistic control over his releases.

Brown's new era had truly begun, however, with "Out of Sight," which topped the R&B charts and made the pop Top 30. For some time, Brown had been moving toward more elemental lyrics that threw in as many chants and screams as words, and more intricate beats and horn charts that took some of their cues from the ensemble work of jazz outfits. "Out of Sight" wasn't called funk when it came out, but it had most of the essential ingredients. These were amplified and perfected on 1965's "Papa's Got a Brand New Bag," a monster that finally broke Brown to the white audience, reaching the Top Ten. The even more adventurous follow-up, "I Got You (I Feel Good)," did even better, making No. 3.

These hits kicked off Brown's period of greatest commercial success and public visibility. From 1965 to the end of the decade, he was rarely off the R&B charts, often on the pop listings, and all over the concert circuit and national television, even meeting with Vice President Hubert Humphrey and other important politicians as a representative of the Black community. His music became even bolder and funkier, as melody was dispensed with almost altogether in favor of chunky rhythms and magnetic interplay between his vocals, horns, drums, and scratching electric guitar (heard to best advantage on hits like "Cold Sweat," "I Got the Feelin'," and "There Was a Time"). The lyrics were now not so much words as chanted, stream-of-consciousness slogans, often aligning themselves with Black pride as well as good old-fashioned (or new-fashioned) sex. Much of the credit for the sound he developed belonged to (and has now been belatedly attributed to) his top-notch supporting musicians, such as saxophonists Maceo Parker, St. Clair Pinckney, and Pee Wee Ellis; guitarist Jimmy Nolen; backup singer and longtime loyal associate Bobby Byrd; and drummer Clyde Stubblefield.

Brown was both a brilliant bandleader and a stern taskmaster, leading his band to walk out on him in late 1969. Amazingly, he turned the crisis to his advantage by recruiting a young Cincinnati outfit called the Pacemakers, featuring guitarist Catfish Collins and bassist Bootsy Collins. Although they stayed with him only about a year, they were crucial to Brown's evolution into even harder funk, emphasizing the rhythm and the bottom even more. The Collins brothers, for their part, put their apprenticeship to good use, helping define '70s funk as members of the Parliament/Funkadelic axis.

In the early '70s, many of the most important members of Brown's late-'60s band returned to the fold, to be billed as the J.B.s (They also made records on their own.) Brown continued to score heavily on the R&B charts throughout the first half of the 1970s, the music becoming even more and more elemental and beat-driven. At the same time, he was retreating from the white audience he had cultivated during the mid- to late '60s; records like "Make It Funky," "Hot Pants," "Get on the Good Foot," and "The Payback" were huge soul sellers, but only modest pop ones. Critics charged, with some justification, that the Godfather was starting to repeat and recycle himself too many times. It must be remembered, though, that these songs were made for the singles-radio-jukebox market and not meant to be played one after the other on CD compilations (as they are today).

By the mid-'70s, Brown was beginning to burn out artistically. He seemed shorn of new ideas, was being outgunned on the charts by disco, and was running into problems with the IRS and his financial empire. There were sporadic hits, and he could always count on enthusiastic live audiences, but by the 1980s he didn't have a label. With the explosion of rap, however, which frequently sampled vintage JB records, Brown was now hipper than ever. He collaborated with Afrika Bambaataa on the critical smash single "Unity," and re-entered the Top Ten in 1986 with "Living in America." Rock critics, who had always ranked Brown considerably below Otis Redding and Aretha Franklin in the soul canon, began to reevaluate his output, particularly his funk years, sometimes anointing him not just as Soul Brother Number One, but as *the* most important Black musician of the rock era.

In 1988 Brown's personal life came crashing down in a well-publicized incident in which he was accused by his wife of assault and battery. After a year skirting hazy legal and personal troubles, he led the police on an interstate car chase after allegedly threatening people with a handgun. The episode ended in a six-year prison sentence that many felt excessive; he was paroled after serving two years.

It's probably safe to assume that Brown, now well into his 60s, will not make any more important recordings, although he continues to perform. Yet his music is probably more popular in the American mainstream today than it's been in over 20 years, not just among young rappers and samplers. For a long time his cumbersome, byzantine discography was mostly out of print, with pieces available only on skimpy greatest-hits collections. A series of exceptionally well-packaged reissues on PolyGram has changed the situation; the *Star Time* box set is the best overview, with other superb compilations devoted to specific phases of his lengthy career, from '50s R&B to '70s funk. —*Richie Unterberger*

Please, Please, Please / 1959 / King ✦✦✦
Though James Brown and His Famous Flames had scored an R&B Top Ten hit in 1956 with "Please, Please, Please," Brown's next nine singles for Federal Records flopped until "Try Me," his third single of 1958, scored. That was when King Records (Federal's parent label) assembled this, Brown's debut album, out of some of those singles sessions. You can hear the sound of a group and its enthusiastic singer looking for a hit, sometimes in the rock 'n' roll of "Chonnie-on-Chon" (1957) or the 1956 B-side "I Feel That Old Feeling Coming On"; sometimes by remaking "Please, Please, Please" under another name, such as "I Don't Know" (1956); sometimes by tackling Coasters-like novelty material such as "That Dood It" (1958); sometimes by aping the smooth Sam Cooke, as on the 1958 B-side "That's When I Lost My Heart"; and once by rewriting "My Bonnie (Lies over the Ocean)" as the 1958 B-side "Baby Cries over the Ocean." Only the two hits were really memorable, but the album presented the sound of a major star-to-be in search of his sound. —*William Ruhlmann*

Try Me! / 1959 / King ✦✦✦
When James Brown and His Famous Flames finally scored a second hit with their 11th single, "Try Me," King Records constructed this 16-track LP, including the hit along with both sides of three of its follow-ups, "I Want You So Bad"/"There Must Be a Reason," "I've Got to Change"/"It Hurts to Tell You," and "Got to Cry"/"It Was You," the B-side of a fourth follow-up, "Don't Let It Happen to Me," the 1957 single "Can't Be the Same"/"Gonna Try," the 1957 B-sides "I Won't Plead No More" and "Messing with the Blues," the B-side of Brown's first hit ("Please Please Please"), "Why Do You Do Me," and three other stray tracks. The earliest work, especially, sounded more like that of a doo wop group than that of a gritty R&B solo singer. None of it measured up to "Try Me," but you could see what Brown had been aiming at, and if the set list comprised what were, in effect, James Brown's greatest flops as fervor. (*Try Me!* was reissued in 1964 under the title *The Unbeatable James Brown—16 Hits.*) —*William Ruhlmann*

Shout & Shimmy / 1962 / King ✦✦✦
On an album named after the R&B Top 40 title hit and featuring the 1961 Top Ten R&B hit "I Don't Mind," James Brown and His Famous Flames can be heard making music in the variety of styles—blues, Little Richard-style rock, doo wop—out of which they eventually would develop the James Brown funk sound of the mid-'60s. (Actually, the music is older than the copyright date, since King cobbled the LP together from non-charting singles and B-sides dating back to 1958.) It's a more primitive sound than they would later achieve, but it remains infectious. (*Shout and Shimmy* was reissued in 1963 under the title *Excitement—Mr. Dynamite.*) —*William Ruhlmann*

★ **Live at the Apollo** / Jan. 1963 / Polydor ✦✦✦✦✦
An astonishing record of James and the Flames tearing the roof off the sucker at the mecca of R&B theatres, New York's Apollo. When King Records owner Syd Nathan refused to fund the recording, thinking it commercial folly, Brown single-mindedly proceeded anyway, paying for it out of his own pocket. He had been out on the road night after night for a while, and he knew that the magic that was part and parcel of a James Brown show was something no record had ever caught. Hit follows hit without a pause—"I'll Go Crazy," "Try Me," "Think," "Please Please Please," "I Don't Mind," "Night Train," and more. The affirmative screams and cries of the audience are something you've never experienced unless you've seen the Brown Revue in a Black theater. If you have, I need not say more; if you haven't, suffice to say that this should be one of the very first records you ever own. —*Rob Bowman*

Prisoner of Love / Sep. 1963 / King ✦✦✦
In the wake of James Brown's first substantial pop hit, "Prisoner of Love," King rushed out this LP, as usual drawing upon old singles ("Try Me," "Lost Someone," "Bewildered"), B-sides ("Waiting in Vain," the organ instrumental "[Can You] Feel It [Part 1]"), and Brown's then-current single, "Signed, Sealed, and Delivered" (not the Stevie Wonder song). The idea seemed to be to put together a collection in the medium-tempo, string-filled, lovelorn style of the hit, so there was a lot of pleading on this record. Brown would always be more interested in the dance floor than the bedroom, but he was a convincing romantic beggar, so the album's loose concept held together. —*William Ruhlmann*

Pure Dynamite! Live at the Royal / Feb. 1964 / King ✦✦✦
It has only eight songs, it's less than half an hour long, and two of the songs are studio tracks with overdubbed audience noise. It's not nearly as well known as his live '60s albums recorded at the Apollo, but *Pure Dynamite!*, recorded live at Baltimore's Royal Theater in 1963, is nearly as good. This is decidedly more raucous than his 1962 *Live at the Apollo*, with the balance leaning toward uptempo ravers like "Shout and Shimmy," "Signed, Sealed, and Delivered," and the set-closing "Good Good Lovin'," all of which are positively kinetic. To break up the pace, there are some R&B torch ballads, including the song without which no J.B. show was complete, "Please, Please, Please." It's also fair to say that the recording quality is primitive, even more so than on his 1962 Apollo gig; the vocals are a bit hollow, and the audience occasionally overwhelms the music with its noisy enthusiasm. Somehow, it doesn't matter much. The performances are so energetic that you can't help getting caught up in the excitement. —*Richie Unterberger*

Papa's Got a Brand New Bag / Aug. 1965 / King ✦✦✦
Papa may have had a brand new bag, but when King Records wanted an LP to go with James Brown's first pop Top Ten hit, he didn't have a brand new set of songs to go with it. So this record leads off with both sides of the single, "Pt. 1" and "Pt. 2," and then fills up the remaining 25 minutes with previously released tracks, many with a dance theme in keeping with the hit, such as "Mashed Potatoes, USA." and "Doin' the Limbo." The result is a miscellaneous compilation, much of which is set at quick tempos. —*William Ruhlmann*

I Got You (I Feel Good) / Jan. 1966 / King ✦✦✦
At the start of 1966, James Brown was at his peak as a crossover star, having hit the pop Top Ten twice in a row in the last six months, first with "Papa's Got a Brand New Bag," and then with his biggest ever pop success, "I Got You (I Feel Good)." But Brown was a singles artist almost exclusively; for him, LPs simply constituted a different configuration in which to re-sell his singles. So his '60s LPs consisted of his current hit plus previously released singles tracks. The *I Got You (I Feel Good)* LP was no exception. Leading off with the title track, it included songs that dated back to 1959's "Good, Good Loving." Of course some of these tracks, such as "Lost Someone," "Night Train," and "Think," were among Brown's classics, so the collection on the whole is appealing, even if arbitrary. —*William Ruhlmann*

It's a Man's Man's Man's World / Aug. 1966 / King ✦✦✦
In the early '60s, James Brown tended to release two vocal albums a year, one in the summer and one in the winter. Each album was keyed to Brown's latest hit single, with the remainder of the record made up of previous Brown recordings; Brown did not record LPs as such. As late as mid-1966, this was still the case, and this album differed only in that it featured not only the title track, an R&B No.1/pop Top Ten hit, and its B-

side, "Is It Yes or Is It No?," but also an earlier 1966 single, "Ain't That a Groove (Part 1 and Part 2)," along with eight oldies such as "Bewildered" and "I Don't Mind" (two 1961 singles). As such, there was slightly more contemporary material here than usual, but at the same time, Brown's evolution into his funk period was beginning to make the juxtapositions of new and old material more jarring. — *William Ruhlmann*

Cold Sweat / Aug. 1967 / King ++++
If "Cold Sweat" was a revolutionary single in 1967, clearly pointing the way to funk music, the *Cold Sweat* LP at least promised to be something new in James Brown's catalog as well. Where Brown's albums had been collections of his current single and miscellaneous older tracks, this one proclaimed on its cover, "All New," "Great Songs," "Never in an Album." This was not quite true. While half of the tracks had been recorded during the first half of 1967, the other half (though previously unreleased) dated from 1964. That wasn't the main problem with the album, though. Having taken a giant step forward with "Cold Sweat," Brown spent the rest of the album stepping back, covering standards such as "Nature Boy" and "Mona Lisa" (associated with Nat "King" Cole), "Fever" (Little Willie John), "Stagger Lee" (Lloyd Price), and other oddities, including "I Loves You Porgy" from *Porgy and Bess*. Brown was never anybody's idea of a smooth ballad singer, and this material was all the more incongruous when packaged with his most remarkable slab of funk yet. — *William Ruhlmann*

Live at the Apollo, Vol. 2 / Aug. 1968 / Rhino ++++
As a whole, this double album is pretty erratic—there are a bunch of torchy R&B ballads that were somewhat anachronistic in light of the explosive funk innovations Brown was unleashing in the studio during this time, and some of those funk hits are reprised here in superbrief versions that seem to cut off before they have a chance to get started. On the other hand, some of it is as essential as anything else Brown ever recorded. In particular, the 20-minute medley of "Let Yourself Go/There Was a Time/I Feel All Right/Cold Sweat" is a magnificent, seamless ball of energy, a landmark performance in the evolution of soul and funk. Other highlights are "Bring It Up" and an 11-minute "It's a Man's, Man's, Man's World." — *Richie Unterberger*

Hot Pants / Aug. 1971 / Polydor +++

There It Is / Jun. 1972 / Polydor ++++

Get on the Good Foot / Nov. 1972 / Polydor +++

Black Caesar / Feb. 1973 / Polydor ++
A classic early '70s soundtrack by James Brown. The film *Black Caesar* was prototype "blaxploitation" fodder, but Brown's soundtrack both defined the urban nightmare the film was trying to depict and garnered him a hit single in "Down and Out in New York City." — *Ron Wynn*

Slaughter's Big Rip-Off / Jul. 1973 / Polydor ++

The Payback / Dec. 1973 / Polydor ++++
A superb funk album by James Brown, one of his '70s masterpieces. The title cut, with its jutting horn charts, lyric hooks, repeated phrases, and striding bass line, was extremely influential, while Brown's trademark screams on the breaks, and the breaks themselves, were later sampled ad infinitum by various hip-hop groups. — *Ron Wynn*

Hell / Jul. 1974 / Polydor ++++

Roots of a Revolution / 1984 / Polydor ++++
A double-CD retrospective of 1956-1964 recordings that charts Brown's progress from doo wop and Little Richard-influenced R&B to the verge of his groundbreaking mid-'60s funk. It doesn't include his biggest hits of the era (which are found on *Star Time*), but these are by and large equally exciting. Many fine overlooked R&B hits and B-sides like "Shout and Shimmy," "I've Got Money," the gospel-influenced "Oh Baby Don't You Weep," and "Maybe the Last Time," which inspired the Rolling Stones' "The Last Time." — *Richie Unterberger*

In the Jungle Groove / 1986 / Polydor ++++
An interesting anthology of leftover funk selections and items from the vast James Brown catalog. Several of these packages have been supplanted by recent Brown CD anthologies. But this one includes some good extended instrumental and vocal funk numbers that aren't on any of the boxed sets. — *Ron Wynn*

Messing with the Blues / 1991 / Polydor +++
Although he is most famous for his innovations in soul and funk music, James Brown never lost sight of his blues and R&B roots. His albums often placed surprisingly rootsy covers of old chestnuts alongside his groundbreaking polyrhythmic workouts. This double CD compiles 30 of the bluesiest items from his vast recorded legacy. Cut between 1957 and 1985, most of the tracks actually date from the '60s; many of these, in turn, were laid down in the early part of the decade, when J.B. was gradually evolving from his more conventional beginnings. The artists whose songs are covered here read like a *Who's Who* of R&B pioneers: Louis Jordan, Roy Brown, Memphis Slim, Ivory Joe Hunter, Fats Domino, Chuck Willis, Little Willie John, Billy Ward, Guitar Slim, and Bobby Bland. It's quite an instructive insight into Brown's not-always-visible

roots. It would be fair to say that this does not rank among his most exciting material, finding him in a smoother and more conventional style than his most innovative work. It is nonetheless always entertaining and accomplished, with Brown's love for this material shining through strongly in his committed interpretations. Especially intriguing are an 11-minute cover of Chuck Willis' "Don't Deceive Me" and a two-part, blues-based rap vamp from the early '70s, "Like It Is, Like It Was (The Blues)." The disc includes several unreleased cuts, alternate takes, and unedited versions of previously released songs. — *Richie Unterberger*

☆ Star Time / Jun. 1991 / Polydor +++++
One of the great box sets of all time. Over four CDs, Brown's recorded legacy is traced from "Please Please Please" in 1956 through his 1984 duet with Afrika Bambaataa, "Unity Pt. 1." With 71 tracks in all, the set places the No. 1 R&B artist ever in his proper perspective as the prime progenitor of funk, one of the architects of soul, and the Godfather of Rap. To have done any one of these things would have been a bid for immortality; having done all three makes him a god. Four CDs at once is virtually too rich for one sitting. The well-written liner notes provide three different perspectives on Brown's career. A cornerstone of any great collection. — *Rob Bowman*

★ 20 All-Time Greatest Hits! / Oct. 1991 / Polydor +++++
A first-rate greatest-hits package that covers the essential soul singles and some of the funk-period material as well. While the finest James Brown package is the boxed set, if you're not going to get that, you wouldn't be far wrong getting this one instead. — *Ron Wynn*

The Greatest Hits of the Fourth Decade / Apr. 14, 1992 / Scotti Bros. +++
Collecting Brown's 1980s hits that didn't make it onto *Star Time*, *Greatest Hits of the Fourth Decade* shows that the period was not among his most creatively fertile, even with the monster hit "Living in America." Still, the disc does pick the best tracks from a dry spell, making it a nice supplement to the box set. — *Stephen Thomas Erlewine*

Love Power Peace / Jun. 23, 1992 / Polydor ++++
James Brown with the then newly-formed JB's—the maestro's second great band, including Bootsy Collins, Phelps Collins, Jabo Starks, Bobby Byrd, and Fred Wesley. *Live at the Apollo* had caught James Brown, the '50s gospel/rhythm and blues singer; *Love Power Peace* captures James the funkster. In the early '70s Brown turned up the funk, recording such litanies for Black America as "Ain't It Funky Now," "Sex Machine," "Give It Up or Turn It Loose," "Super Bad," "Get Up, Get into It, Get Involved," and "Soul Power." They're all here, along with revved-up, white-hot versions of the early and middle-period classics. Brown had planned to release this as a triple album in 1971. When several band members left shortly after it was recorded, Brown switched from King to Polydor Records, leading him to scrap it and record a new studio album instead. In 1992 Polygram decided to make the recording available for the first time. — *Rob Bowman*

Soul Pride: The Instrumentals (1960-69) / Mar. 23, 1993 / PolyGram ++++
Everyone knows how hot James Brown's bands were, but not everyone's aware that he and his sidemen recorded lots of instrumental sides in the '60s. Originally scattered haphazardly over many out-of-print singles and albums, *Soul Pride* brings together the best of this work in one cohesive and chronological package. These cuts are nearly equal in power to J.B.'s vocal performances. Not only does the band cook on most of these insinuating vamps, but you can hear the evolution of the man's sound from gritty R&B to tight-as-a-drum soul to free-form funk. Soul Brother No. 1 himself plays organ and adds unpredictable shouts and screams on most of these tracks. But the chief stars are sidemen like Maceo Parker, Fred Wesley, and Pee Wee Ellis, who broke new ground with their compulsive counterpoint riffs. This fiery two-disc, 36-track box set contains over two hours of music, as well as a few non-LP B-sides and previously unreleased tracks. — *Richie Unterberger*

☆ Foundations of Funk: a Brand New Bag: 1964-1969 / Mar. 19, 1996 / Polydor +++++
There are several worthy James Brown compilations. But this is the one, more than any other, that presents his most fertile and innovative soul and funk material. From 1964's "Out of Sight" through 1969's "Mother Popcorn," this was Brown at the apex of his creativity, turning soul into funk in the mid-'60s, then pushing the rhythm even more to the forefront. Most of his hit singles from this five-year explosion of white heat are on this 27-track, two-CD set, including "Out of Sight," "Papa's Got a Brand New Bag," "I Got You (I Feel Good)," "Say It Loud—I'm Black and I'm Proud," and "Cold Sweat." There are some minor omissions that could be questioned (the absence of the studio version of "Bring It Up," for instance), and big James Brown fans will already have the lion's share of tracks, on the *Star Time* box and other releases. It does, however, contain minor but significant bonuses: an alternate take of "Cold Sweat," a previously unreleased live medley of "Out of Sight" and "Bring It Up," and a previously unreleased live version of "Licking Stick—Lick-

ing Stick." There are also longer versions of "I Don't Want Nobody to Give Me Nothing" (ten minutes!), "I Got the Feelin'," "The Popcorn," and "Brother Rapp" that were edited when they were prepared for official release. —*Richie Unterberger*

Funk Power—1970: A Brand New Thang / Jun. 4, 1996 / Polydor ♦♦♦♦
The period during which Brown was backed by the original JBs (with Bootsy and Catfish Collins) was extremely brief, lasting only a year. But it was an extremely important and influential phase of Brown's career, when he moved from soul-funk to hard funk, stretching out the grooves and putting more stress on the bottom than ever before. This 78-minute disc is the cream of his recordings from the Bootsy Collins era. The nine tracks (the tenth is a brief public-service annoncement) include some of his core funk workouts—"Get Up I Feel like Being a Sex Machine" (two versions), "Super Bad," "Give It Up or Turn It Loose," "Talkin' Loud and Sayin' Nothing," "Get Up, Get into It, Get Involved," and "Soul Power." It's not for those who find Brown's funk phase too monotonous, and indeed the grooves do get a bit similar when experienced all at once. But it's unquestionably the best of Brown's '70s recordings, and indeed some of the hardest funk ever waxed by anyone at any time. As a bonus, the CD has previously unreleased complete versions of "Soul Power" (12 minutes) and "Talkin' Loud and Sayin' Nothing" (14 minutes), as well as a previously unreleased version of "There Was a Time." —*Richie Unterberger*

Make It Funky—The Big Payback: 1971-1975 / Jul. 23, 1996 / Polydor ♦♦♦♦
While the first half of the 1970s saw Brown's sales and art start to slowly decline, at their best he and the JBs remained capable of generating a lot of heat. Record-wise it was a very erratic period, especially on his albums, which makes this two-and-a-half-hour double-disc compilation of his best material from the era especially welcome. Besides his biggest hits from the time ("Make It Funky," "Get on the Good Foot," "The Payback," "Funky President"), it has a number of high-charting R&B 45s that didn't make it onto the *Star Time* box. Familiar hits are sometimes presented in their full unedited mega-versions (12 minutes of "Make It Funky," 14 of "Papa Don't Take No Mess"), and there are also a few previously unreleased outtakes and alternate versions. It's a disappointment only relative to the towering accomplishments of his 1960s and early-'70s classics. On its own terms, it's excellent funk, if rather homogenous taken all at once; there are occasional departures from the formula, like "Down and Out in New York City," with its poppy woodwinds. —*Richie Unterberger*

★ **JB40: 40th Anniversary Collection** / Oct. 8, 1996 / Polygram ♦♦♦♦♦
Brown's catalog was in a shambles for years, but the CD age has reversed the situation to such an extent that you now have a wide variety of greatest-hits options to choose from. On the whole, this might be the best buy, cramming 40 of his biggest hit singles from 1956-1979 onto two discs. It's perhaps a little too weighted toward the '70s (which comprise all of disc two); and some decent moderate-size hits are omitted, like "Oh Baby Don't You Weep," "Bring It Up," and "Get It Together." But it does have the core classics. If you don't want to spring for the *Star Time* box but want more than a single-disc collection, this is the one to have. —*Richie Unterberger*

Maxine Brown

b. Apr. 27, 1932, Kingstree, SC
Vocals / Soul, R&B
Although she never had many hits, Maxine Brown was one of the most underrated soul and R&B vocalists of the '60s. During the '60s she released a series of singles for Nomar and Wand, with only a couple of songs—"All in My Mind," "Funny," "Something You Got," "Oh No Not My Baby"—managing to become either pop or R&B hits. Despite her lack of hits, Brown is acknowledged as one of the finest R&B vocalists of her time, capable of delivering soul, jazz, and pop with equal aplomb.

Born in Kingstree, SC, Brown began performing as child, singing with two New York-based gospel groups when she was a teenager. In 1960 she signed with the small Normar label, which released the smooth ballad "All in My Mind" late in the year. The single became a hit, climbing to No. 2 on the R&B charts (No. 19 pop), and it was quickly followed by "Funny," which peaked at No. 3. Brown was poised to become a star, and she moved to ABC-Paramount in 1962, but she left the label within a year, without scoring any hits. She signed to the New York-based, uptown soul label Wand in 1963.

Brown recorded her best work at Wand, having a string of moderate hits for the label over the next three years. Among these were the Carole King/David Goffin song "Oh No Not My Baby," which reached No. 24 on the pop charts, "It's Gonna Be Alright," and the Chuck Jackson duets "Something You Got," "Hold On I'm Coming," and "Daddy's Home." Part of the reason Brown didn't receive much exposure is that the label focused much of their attention on Dionne Warwick, leaving Maxine to toil in semi-obscurity. In 1969 she left Wand and signed with Common-

wealth United, where she had the minor hits "We'll Cry Together" and "I Can't Get Along Without You." In 1971 she moved to Avco Records, but all of her recordings for the label went ignored, and she faded away over the course of the decade. —*Stephen Thomas Erlewine*

Maxine Brown's Greatest Hits / 1964 / Wand ♦♦♦♦
Maxine Brown had a handful of hits, most of them either laments or teary-eyed ballads, in the early '60s. They're all included on this release. Brown's timing at Scepter/Wand was unfortunate; the label was allocating most of its resources and promotional muscle to breaking Dionne Warwick in the pop market. Neither she nor Chuck Jackson got the push they needed and deserved. —*Ron Wynn*

● **Oh No Not My Baby: The Best of Maxine Brown** / 1990 / Kent ♦♦♦♦
This 28-song CD is undoubtedly the best compilation of this underrated soul singer's work, featuring many of her '60s singles and several tunes from the era that were unreleased until the '80s. This disc draws from her recordings for the Wand label between 1963 and 1967, when Brown was at her artistic peak. Of course the hit title track is a highlight, but there are no clunkers in this excellent collection of overlooked '60s pop-soul, featuring the New York "uptown" production that also graced the records of fellow Wand/Scepter artists like Dionne Warwick and Chuck Jackson. Brown was one of the most versatile soul divas of the '60s, showing the influence of Brill Building pop, girl groups, Motown, and even Stax soul and supper-club ballads. As with a similar artist like Betty Everett, this versatility has worked against her in some ways. Neither full-fledged pop nor unabashedly soul, her work cannot be easily pigeonholed into a certain soul genre, and has cost her the respect that some purists reserve for "deep" soul singers. But her work holds up well. Collectors should be aware that this disc doesn't include any of the records she cut in the early '60s before joining Wand; the version of her 1961 Top 20 hit "All in My Mind" here is from a live 1964 release, not the original single. —*Richie Unterberger*

● **Greatest Hits** / 1995 / Tomato ♦♦♦♦
This 23-track best-of has a lot of overlap with the British import *Oh No Not My Baby;* both cover her mid-'60s period with Wand, and each has some songs not on the other. There's not a crucial difference between the pair, but the nod probably goes to the import, which has more songs and better sound. In its favor, this compilation includes five of her duets with Chuck Jackson, none of which is on the other CD (although the duets don't rank among her best material). It also has a studio version of "All in My Mind," rather than the live one on the British anthology. —*Richie Unterberger*

Something You Got / 1996 / Soul Classics/Ichiban ♦♦♦
All 20 of the duet tracks that Brown and Chuck Jackson recorded for the Wand label between 1965 and 1967, comprising the entirety of their two albums for the company. It's reasonable pop/soul, but not nearly as memorable as the best male-female soul duets of the era (like the ones by Marvin Gaye and various Motown partners, or by Otis Redding and Carla Thomas). Highlights are the early compositions by the Jo Armstead-Nick Ashford-Valerie Simpson team, including a version of "Let's Go Get Stoned" that was recorded (though not released) before Ray Charles' more famous hit rendition. —*Richie Unterberger*

Roy Brown

b. Sep. 10, 1925, New Orleans, LA, **d.** May 25, 1981, San Fernando, CA
Piano, Vocals / R&B, Rock 'n' Roll, West Coast Blues, Jump Blues
When you draw up a short list of the R&B pioneers who exerted a primary influence on the development of rock 'n' roll, respectfully place singer Roy Brown's name near its very top. His seminal 1947 DeLuxe Records waxing of "Good Rockin' Tonight" was immediately ridden to the peak of the R&B charts by shouter Wynonie Harris and subsequently covered by Elvis Presley, Ricky Nelson, Jerry Lee Lewis, and many more early rock icons (even Pat Boone!). In addition, Brown's melismatically pleading, gospel-steeped delivery impacted the vocal styles of B.B. King, Bobby Bland, and Little Richard (among a plethora of important singers). Clearly, Roy Brown was an innovator—and from 1948-1951, an R&B star whose wild output directly presaged rock's rise.

Born in the Crescent City, Brown grew up all over the place: Eunice, LA (where he sang in church and worked in the sugarcane fields), Houston, TX, and finally Los Angeles by age 17. Back then, Bing Crosby was Roy's favorite singer, but a nine-month stint at a Shreveport, LA, night-club exposed him to the blues for the first time. He conjured up "Good Rockin' Tonight" while fronting a band in Galveston, TX. Ironically, Harris wanted no part of the song when Brown first tried to hand it to him. When pianist Cecil Gant heard Brown's knockout rendition of the tune in New Orleans, he had Roy sing it over the phone to a sleepy DeLuxe boss, Jules Braun, in the wee hours of the morning! Though Brown's original waxing (with Bob Ogden's band in support) was a solid hit, Harris' cover beat him out for top chart honors.

Roy didn't have to wait long to dominate the R&B lists himself. He scored 15 hits from mid-1948 to late 1951 for DeLuxe, ranging from the emotionally wracked crying blues "Hard Luck Blues" (his biggest seller of all in 1950) to the party-time rockers "Rockin' at Midnight," "Boogie at Midnight," "Miss Fanny Brown," and "Cadillac Baby." Strangely, his sales slumped badly from 1952 on, even though his frantic "Hurry Hurry Baby," "Ain't No Rockin' No More," "Black Diamond," and "Gal from Kokomo" for Cincinnati's King Records rate among his hottest houserockers.

Brown was unable to cash in on the rock 'n' roll idiom he helped to invent, though he briefly rejuvenated his commercial fortunes at Imperial Records in 1957. Working with New Orleans producer Dave Bartholomew, then riding high with Fats Domino, Brown returned to the charts with the original version of "Let the Four Winds Blow" (later a hit for Fats) and cut the sizzling sax-powered rockers "Diddy-Y-Diddy-O," "Saturday Night," and "Ain't Gonna Do It." Not everything was an artistic triumph; Brown's utterly lifeless cover of Buddy Knox's "Party Doll"—amazingly, a chart entry for Brown—may well be the worst thing he ever committed to wax (rivaled only by a puerile "School Bell Rock" cut during a momentary return to King in 1959).

After a long dry spell, Brown's acclaimed performance as part of Johnny Otis' troupe at the 1970 Monterey Jazz Festival and a 1973 LP for ABC-BluesWay began to rebuild his long-lost momentum. But it came too late—Brown died of a heart attack in 1981 at age 56, his role as a crucial link between postwar R&B and rock's initial rise still underappreciated by the masses. —Bill Dahl

☆ **Blues Deluxe** / 1991 / Charly ✦✦✦✦✦
More tracks (two dozen in all) from Brown's voluminous DeLuxe and King catalogs make this British import well worth searching around for. Hellacious jumps—"Cadillac Baby," "Good Rockin' Man"—and plenty of rarities distinguish this collection by one of the true pioneers of R&B. —Bill Dahl

Mighty Mighty Man! / 1993 / Ace ✦✦✦✦
Another British import that really delivers the rocking goods! This time zeroing in on Brown's 1953-59 King sides exclusively, the 22-cut CD shows that Brown actually picked up his tempos to meet rock's rise head on. The clever sequel "Ain't No Rocking No More," "Black Diamond," "Gal from Kokomo," and "Shake 'Em Up Baby" rate with his hottest rockers, with great support from a crew of Crescent City stalwarts. —Bill Dahl

★ **Good Rocking Tonight: The Best of Roy Brown** / 1994 / Rhino ✦✦✦✦✦
An unassailable 18-cut cross-section of the monstrously popular and influential New Orleans jump blues shouter's sides for DeLuxe, King, and Imperial labels that spans 1947-57 and takes in his seminal "Good Rocking Tonight" (where it all began!), "Rockin' at Midnight," "Boogie at Midnight," and "Love Don't Love Nobody"; the almost unbearably tortured "Hard Luck Blues"; and the unbelievably raunchy two-parter "Butcher Pete." Looking for the origins of rock? Here they are! —Bill Dahl

The Complete Imperial Recordings / Oct. 1995 / Capitol ✦✦✦
In the mid-'50s Brown, like many other early R&B pioneers, was a bit lost amid the rock 'n' roll explosion. From 1956 to 1958, he recorded these 20 tracks for Imperial under the direction of legendary New Orleans R&B producer Dave Bartholomew. Brown and Bartholomew were attempting to update Brown's jump blues/R&B hybrid with a lot of Fats Domino-type Crescent City influence on these sides. The results weren't bad, but with Bartholomew co-writing most of the tunes and using local musicians like saxophonist Lee Allen, Brown sounded more like a journeyman New Orleans R&B singer than an innovative, bluesy forefather of rock 'n' roll. There were a couple of commercial successes; his cover of Buddy Knox' "Party Doll" made the R&B Top 20, and "Let the Four Winds Blow" actually made the pop Top 40, although Fats Domino would have much greater success with the same song when he covered it a few years later. Diluted by occasional pop and rock influences, as well as a substandard variation of "Good Rockin' Tonight," this compilation shouldn't be the first Brown on your shelf. But for those who want to go a little further, it's packaged very well, with thorough liner notes and seven previously unissued cuts. —Richie Unterberger

Ruth Brown

b. Jan. 30, 1928, Portsmouth, VA
Vocals / R&B, Jump Blues
They called Atlantic Records "the house that Ruth built" during the 1950s, and they weren't referring to the Sultan of Swat. Ruth Brown's regal hitmaking reign from 1949 to the close of the '50s helped tremendously to establish the New York label's predominance in the R&B field. Later, the business all but forgot her—she was forced to toil as domestic help for a time—but she's back on top now, her status as a postwar R&B pioneer (and tireless advocate for the rights and royalties of her peers) recognized worldwide.

Young Ruth Weston was inspired initially by jazz chanteuses Sarah Vaughan, Billie Holiday, and Dinah Washington. She ran away from her Portsmouth home in 1945 to hit the road with trumpeter Jimmy Brown,

whom she soon married. A month with bandleader Lucky Millinder's orchestra in 1947 ended abruptly in Washington, DC, when she was canned for delivering a round of drinks to members of the band. Cab Calloway's sister Blanche gave Ruth a gig at her Crystal Caverns nightclub and assumed a managerial role in the young singer's life. DJ Willis Conover dug Brown's act and recommended her to Ahmet Ertegun and Herb Abramson, bosses of a fledgling imprint named Atlantic.

Unfortunately, Brown's debut session for the firm was delayed by a nine-month hospital stay caused by a serious auto accident en route to New York that badly injured her leg. When she finally made it to her first date in May 1949, she made up for lost time by waxing the torch ballad "So Long" (backed by guitarist Eddie Condon's band), which proved to be her first hit.

Brown's seductive vocal delivery was incandescent on her Atlantic smashes "Teardrops in My Eyes" (an R&B chart-topper for 11 weeks in 1950), "I'll Wait for You," and "I Know" in 1951; 1952's "5-10-15 Hours" (another No. 1 rocker); the seminal "(Mama) He Treats Your Daughter Mean" in 1953; and a tender Chuck Willis-penned "Oh What a Dream" and the timely "Mambo Baby" the next year. Along the way, Frankie Laine tagged her "Miss Rhythm" during an engagement in Philly. Brown belted a series of her hits on the groundbreaking TV program "Showtime at the Apollo" in 1955, exhibiting delicious comic timing while trading sly one-liners with emcee Willie Bryant (ironically, ex-husband Jimmy Brown was a member of the show's house band!).

After an even two dozen R&B chart appearances for Atlantic that ended in 1960 with "Don't Deceive Me" (many of them featuring hell-raising tenor sax solos by then-hubby Willis "Gator" Jackson), Brown faded from view. After raising her two sons and working a nine-to-five job, Brown began to rebuild her musical career in the mid-'70s. Her comedic sense served her well during a TV sitcom stint co-starring with McLean Stevenson in "Hello, Larry"; in a meaty role in director John Waters' 1985 sock-hop satire film *Hairspray*, and during her 1989 Broadway starring turn in *Black and Blue* (which won her a Tony Award).

There have been more records for Fantasy in recent years (notably 1991's jumping *Fine and Mellow*), and a lengthy tenure as host of National Public Radio's "Harlem Hit Parade" and "BluesStage." Brown's nine-year ordeal to recoup her share of royalties from all those Atlantic platters led to the formation of the nonprofit Rhythm & Blues Foundation, an organization dedicated to helping others in the same frustrating situation.

Factor in all those time-consuming activities, and it's a wonder Ruth Brown has time to sing anymore. But she does (quite royally, too), her pipes mellowed but not frayed by the decades that have seen her rise to stardom not once, but twice. —Bill Dahl

☆ **Miss Rhythm (Greatest Hits and More)** / Jan. 1989 / Rhino ✦✦✦✦✦
They used to refer to Atlantic Records in its early years as "the house that Ruth built," and the 40 tracks inhabiting these two discs offer unassailable insight as to why. As one of the premier R&B divas of the early '50s, Brown's seductive, earthy style found her belting the rockers (the R&B chart-toppers "Teardrops from My Eyes," "Mama He Treats Your Daughter Mean," "5-10-15 Hours") and caressing the ballads ("So Long," "Have a Good Time," "Oh What a Dream"), backed by some of New York's finest session players (including then-hubby Willis "Gator" Jackson on scorching tenor sax). Covers 1949-1960 and takes Brown from the beginnings of R&B to the heyday of rock ("Wild Wild Young Men" is positively frantic, while the Bobby Darin-penned "This Little Girl's Gone Rockin'" is lightweight but utterly charming). Essential stuff! —Bill Dahl

★ **Best of Ruth Brown** / Jun. 18, 1996 / Rhino ✦✦✦✦
For those who want a cheaper and more concise collection of her best Atlantic cuts than the two-CD *Miss Rhythm*, this superb 23-track CD has the cream of her '50s work, including no less than 19 Top Ten R&B singles. Charting her evolution from her jazzy debut, "So Long," through jump blues and early rock 'n' roll, it also adds a bonus of two previously unissued live cuts from 1959. —Richie Unterberger

Jackson Browne

b. Oct. 9, 1948, Heidelberg, Germany
Guitar, Piano, Keyboards, Vocals / Singer-Songwriter, Soft Rock, Pop-Rock
In many ways, Jackson Browne was the quintessential sensitive Californian singer-songwriter of the early '70s. Only Joni Mitchell and James Taylor ranked alongside him in terms of influence, but neither artist tapped into the post-'60s zeitgeist like Browne. While the majority of his classic '70s work was unflinchingly personal, it nevertheless provided a touchstone for a generation of maturing baby boomers coming to terms with adulthood. Not only did his introspective, literate lyrics strike a nerve, but his laidback folk-rock set the template for much of the music to come out of California during the '70s. With his first four albums, Browne built a loyal following that helped him break into the main-

stream with 1976's *The Pretender*. During the late '70s and early '80s, he was at the height of his popularity, as each of his albums charted in the Top Ten. Midway through the '80s, Browne made a series of political protest records that caused his audience to gradually shrink, but when he returned to introspective songwriting with 1993's *I'm Alive*, he made a modest comeback.

Born in Heidelberg, West Germany, Jackson Browne and his family moved to Los Angeles when he was three years old, and by the time he was a teenager, Browne had developed an interest in folk music. He began playing guitar and writing songs, which he sang at local folk clubs. Early in 1966 he was invited to join the Nitty Gritty Dirt Band, whom he had met through the Los Angeles folk circuit. Although he was with the band for only a few months, the group recorded a handful of his songs on their first two records. By the beginning of 1967 he had signed a publishing deal with Nina Music, a division of Elektra Records; Nina helped Browne secure songs on albums by Tom Rush and Steve Noonan in 1968. During 1967 and 1968, he lived in New York's Greenwich Village, where he played in Tim Buckley's backing band. Browne also began working with Nico, who recorded three of his songs on her *Chelsea Girl* album. When their relationship disintegrated in 1968, he returned to Los Angeles, where he unsuccessfully tried to record a solo album and form a folk group with Ned Doheny and Jack Wilce. Browne continued to play local clubs, and his reputation as a songwriter continued to grow, with Linda Ronstadt and the Byrds recording his songs. By the end of 1971, he had signed with David Geffen's fledgling Asylum Records on the strength of his widely circulated demo tape.

Jackson Browne was released in the spring of 1972, spawning the Top Ten hit single "Doctor My Eyes." Shortly after "Doctor My Eyes" reached its peak position, "Take It Easy," a song Browne co-wrote with Glenn Frey, became the Eagles' breakthrough hit. Many songs from his debut, including "Rock Me on the Water" and "Jamaica Say You Will," became singer-songwriter standards, but the album itself didn't establish Browne as a pop star, despite its hit single. On his second album, *For Everyman* (1973), he began a long-term collaboration with instrumentalist David Lindley. *For Everyman* was a commercial disappointment, but it consolidated his cult following.

Released in the fall of 1974, *Late for the Sky* expanded Browne's audience significantly, peaking at No. 14 on the charts and going gold by the beginning of the next year. Browne's first wife, Phyllis, committed suicide in the spring of 1976, but in the wake of the tragedy he recorded his commercial breakthrough album, *The Pretender*. The record climbed into the Top Ten upon its fall 1976 release, going platinum in the spring of 1977. In the summer, Browne launched an extensive tour, recording a new album while he was on the road. The resulting record, *Running on Empty* (1977), was a bigger success than its predecessor, peaking at No. 3 and launching the hit singles "Running on Empty" and "Stay / The Load-Out." With his career riding high, Browne began to pursue political and social causes, most notably protesting the use of nuclear energy.

The success of *Hold On*, the 1980 follow-up to *Running on Empty*, is evidence of Jackson Browne's popularity. Though the album wasn't as well-crafted as its predecessors, it became his only No. 1 album upon its summer release. In the summer of 1982 "Somebody's Baby," from the soundtrack of *Fast Times at Ridgemont High*, became Browne's biggest hit, climbing to No. 7 on the US charts. Divided between love songs and political protests, *Lawyers in Love* was another hit, due to success of the hit singles "Lawyers in Love," "Tender Is the Night," and "For A Rocker." Nevertheless, the album also showcased a newly found social consciousness, which dominated 1986's *Lives in the Balance*. The album lacked any hit singles, but its fiery condemnation of the Reagan era won an audience; the album stayed on the charts for over six months and went gold.

Jackson Browne continued to write primarily political songs on 1989's *World in Motion*, but the record became his first album not to go gold. Browne was quiet for the next four years, working on a variety of social causes and suffering a painful public breakup with his girlfriend, actress Daryl Hannah. He finally returned with a comeback effort in the fall of 1993 entitled *I'm Alive*. Comprised of personal songs, *I'm Alive* received his best reviews since the late '70s, and the record went gold without producing any major hits. In the spring of 1996, Browne released *Looking East*, which failed to gain the same attention as *I'm Alive*. — *Stephen Thomas Erlewine*

☆ **Jackson Browne** / Jan. 1972 / Asylum ✦✦✦✦✦

An auspicious debut that doesn't sound like a debut. Although only 23, Browne had kicked around the music business for several years and developed an unusual use of language, studiedly casual yet full of striking imagery, and a post-apocalyptic viewpoint to go with it. He sang with a calm certainty over spare, discreetly placed backup that highlighted the songs and always seemed about to disappear. In song after song, Browne described the world as a desert in need of moisture. In "Doctor My Eyes," the album's most propulsive song and a Top Ten hit, he sang, "Doctor, my eyes/Cannot see the sky/Is this the prize/For having learned how not to cry?" If Browne's outlook was cautious, its

expression was original. His conditional optimism seemed to reflect hard experience, and in the early 1970s, a lot of his listeners shared that perspective. Like any great artist, Browne articulated the tenor of his times. But the album has long since come to seem a timeless collection of reflective ballads touching on still-difficult subjects—suicide (explicitly), depression and drug use (probably), spiritual uncertainty and desperate hope—all in calm, reasoned tones, and all with an amazingly eloquent sense of language. *Jackson Browne's* greater triumph is that, having perfectly expressed its times, it transcended them as well. — *William Ruhlmann*

For Everyman / Oct. 1973 / Asylum ✦✦✦✦

Jackson Browne faced the nearly insurmountable task of following a masterpiece in making his second album. Having cherry-picked years of songwriting the first time around, he turned to some of his secondary older material, which was still better than most people's best and, ironically, more accessible—notably such songs as "These Days," which had been covered six times already, dating back to Nico's *Chelsea Girl* album in 1967, and "Take It Easy," a co-composition with the Eagles' Glenn Frey, which had been a Top 40 hit for the group in 1972. Browne unsuccessfully looked for another hit single with the uptempo "Red Neck Friend," reminisced about meeting his wife and starting a family in the coy "Ready or Not," and, at the end, finally came up with a new song to rank with those on the first album in the philosophical title track, which reportedly was his more positive reply to Crosby, Stills, Nash & Young's "Wooden Ships." (David Crosby sang harmony.) Musically, the album was still restrained, but not as austere as *Jackson Browne*. The singer had hooked up with multi-instrumentalist David Lindley, who would introduce interesting textures to his music on a variety of stringed instruments for the next several years. All of which is to say that *For Everyman* was a less consistent collection than Browne's debut album. But Browne's songwriting ability remained impressive. — *William Ruhlmann*

★ **Late for the Sky** / Sep. 1974 / Asylum ✦✦✦✦✦

On his third album, Jackson Browne returned to the themes of his debut record (love, loss, identity, apocalypse), and, amazingly, delved even deeper into them. "For a Dancer," a meditation on death like the first album's "Song for Adam," is a more eloquent eulogy; "Farther On" extends the "moving on" point of "Looking into You"; "Before the Deluge" is a glimpse beyond the apocalypse evoked on "My Opening Farewell" and the second album's "For Everyman." If Browne had seemed to question everything in his first records, here he questioned even himself. "For me some words come easy, but I know that they don't mean that much," he sang on the opening track, "Late for the Sky," and added in "Farther On," "I'm not sure what I'm trying to say." Yet his seeming uncertainty and self-doubt reflected the size and complexity of the problems he was addressing in these songs, and few had ever explored such territory, much less mapped it so well. "The Late Show," the album's thematic center, doubted but ultimately affirmed the nature of relationships, while by the end, "After the Deluge," if "only a few survived," the human race continued nonetheless. It was a lot to put into a pop music album, but Browne stretched the limits of what could be found in what he called "the beauty in songs," just as Bob Dylan had a decade before. — *William Ruhlmann*

The Pretender / Nov. 1976 / Asylum ✦✦✦

On *The Pretender*, Jackson Browne took a step back from the precipice so well defined on his first three albums, but doing so didn't seem to make him feel any better. Employing a real producer, Jon Landau, for the first time, Browne made what sounded like a contemporary rock record, but this made his songs less effective; the ersatz Mexican arrangement of "Linda Paloma" and the bouncy second half of "Daddy's Tune," with its horn charts and guitar solo, undercut the lyrics. The man who had delved so deeply into life's abyss on his earlier albums was in search of escape this time around, whether by crying ("Here Come Those Tears Again"), sleeping ("Sleep's Dark and Silent Gate"), or making peace with estranged love ones ("The Only Child," "Daddy's Tune"). None of it worked, however, and when Browne came to the final track—traditionally the place on his albums where he summed up his current philosophical stance—he delivered "The Pretender," a cynical, sarcastic treatise on moneygrubbing and the shallow life of the suburbs. Primarily inner-directed, the song's defeatist tone demands rejection, but it is also a quintessential statement of its time, the post-Watergate '70s; dire as it might be, you had to admire that kind of honesty, even as it made you wince. — *William Ruhlmann*

Running on Empty / 1977 / Asylum ✦✦✦

Having acknowledged a certain creative desperation on *The Pretender*, Jackson Browne lowered his sights (and raised his commercial appeal) considerably with *Running on Empty*, which was more a concept album about the road than an actual live album, even though its songs were sometimes recorded on stage (and sometimes on the bus or in the hotel). Although unlike most live albums, it consisted of previously unrecorded songs, Browne had less creative participation on this album than on any other he ever made, solely composing only two songs, co-writing four others, and covering another four. And he had less to say; the title song and leadoff track neatly conjoined his artistic and escapist themes. Figuratively and creatively, he was out of gas, but like "the pretender," he still had to make a living. The songs covered all aspects of touring, from Danny O'Keefe's "The Road," which detailed romantic encounters, and "Rosie" (co-written by Browne and his manager Donald Miller), in which a soundman pays tribute to auto-eroticism, to, well, "Cocaine," to the travails of being a roadie ("The Load-Out"). Audience noises, humorous asides, loose playing—they were all part of a rough-around-the-edges musical evocation of the rock 'n' roll touring life. It was not what fans had come to expect from Browne, of course, but the disaffected were more than outnumbered by the newly converted. (It didn't hurt that "Running on Empty" and "The Load-Out"/"Stay" both became Top 40 hits.) As a result, Jackson Browne's least ambitious, but perhaps most accessible, album ironically became his biggest seller. But it is not characteristic of his other work. For many, it will be the only Browne album they will want to own, just as others always will regard it disdainfully as *Jackson Browne Lite.* —*William Ruhlmann*

Hold Out / 1980 / Asylum ♦♦
If Jackson Browne had convincingly lowered the bar set by his first three albums on his fourth and fifth ones, his sixth, *Hold Out,* found him once again seeking some measure of satisfaction, albeit in reduced circumstances. His songs were less philosophical, but they were also more personal. In "Of Missing Persons," he once again took on a eulogy as his subject, but unlike "Song to Adam" or "For a Dancer," here the song was directed to his late friend's daughter and encouraged her recovery; it was more a song for the living than for the dead. Newly aware of the world around him ("Boulevard"), he was also newly sensitive to others, notably on the mutual dependency song "Call It a Loan." But the personal tone sometimes made him less sure-footed as a performer; "Hold On Hold Out," the traditional big, long, last song on the album, was awkwardly, not winningly, intimate, just as the attention-grabbing lead-off track, "Disco Apocalypse," was merely foolish instead of whatever it may have been intended to be (satire? drama?). If Browne was still trying to write himself out of the cul-de-sac he had created for himself early on, *Hold Out* represented an earnest attempt that nevertheless fell short. —*William Ruhlmann*

Lawyers in Love / 1983 / Asylum ♦♦
Jackson Browne's messages had always seemed so important that one tended to overlook the sheer songwriting craft that went into his work, craft that was apparent, for example, on his 1982 single "Somebody's Baby," which became his biggest hit ever (and which appears on none of his albums, being available only on the soundtrack to *Fast Times at Ridgemont High*), and on songs like "Downtown," a street-life portrait on his seventh album, *Lawyers in Love*. The craft seemed all the more important because Browne was so intent on turning his back on the conundrums that had obsessed him in the past. On "Cut It Away," he sang of his desire to remove his "desperate heart" (a phrase he had used before), to rid himself of "this crazy longing for something more/This question that I don't have the answer for." In place of such ambitions, Browne substituted the beginnings of social concern ("Say It Isn't True") and, most imaginatively, a humorous look at contemporary trash culture in the title track, one of the more exhilaratingly silly moments in Browne's generally dour catalog. But the craft, and the familiar tightness of Browne's veteran studio/live band, couldn't hide the essentially retread nature of much of this material. —*William Ruhlmann*

Lives in the Balance / 1986 / Asylum ♦♦♦
Usually among the most introspective of songwriters, Jackson Browne cast his gaze on the world outside on *Lives in the Balance* and did not like what he saw. Beginning with "For America," he lamented his previous indifference to social issues—"I went on speaking of the future/While other people fought and bled"—but immediately tried to make up for lost time. The album's context, of course, was five years of Ronald Reagan's presidency, with what the Left saw as indifference to the plight of the poor at home and a dangerously aggressive policy against insurgent movements in the Central American countries of El Salvador and Nicaragua that they feared would lead to a Vietnam-like war. Without naming those places, Browne wrote and sang passionately against poverty in the songs "Soldier of Plenty" and "Lawless Avenues" and against war in "For America," "Lives in the Balance," and "'Til I Go Down." Elsewhere, his more familiar themes of romantic ("In the Shape of a Heart") and philosophical ("Black and White") disillusionment also made appearances. But, from its hard rock sound and forceful singing to its frankly agitprop lyrics, *For America* remained primarily a political statement, and if Browne sounded more involved in his music than he had in some time, the specificity of its approach inevitably limited its appeal and its long-term significance. —*William Ruhlmann*

World In Motion / Jun. 1989 / Elektra ♦♦
Jackson Browne continued amassing a repertoire best suited to an Amnesty International benefit on his second highly politicized album,

World In Motion. War, homelessness, and Oliver North (though not by name) were condemned; freedom, truth, and Nelson Mandela were praised. Now and then Browne drew parallels between the personal and the political, notably in the double-edged "Anything Can Happen," but for the most part he sermonized, frequently adopting the generalized terms and reasoning that sermons usually employ. Except for the gloomy viewpoint, it was hard to recognize the Jackson Browne of his first few albums amid all the commentary, and even if you agreed with his overall political stance, that was disappointing. —*William Ruhlmann*

I'm Alive / Oct. 1993 / Elektra ♦♦♦
Jackson Browne abandoned politics for the war between the sexes on *I'm Alive*. "I have no problem with this crooked world," he sang. " . . . My problem is you." The album detailed the ups and downs of a relationship, starting with the defiant post-breakup title track and then doubling back to describe irritation ("My Problem Is You"), devotion ("Everywhere I Go," "I'll Do Anything"), increasing tension ("Miles Away," "Too Many Angels"), separation ("Take This Rain," "Two of Me, Two of You"), forgiveness ("Sky Blue and Black"), and finally acceptance ("All Good Things"). Longtime fans welcomed the album as a return in style to the days of *Late for the Sky,* but a closer model might have been *Hold Out,* a complementary album concerned with the flowering of an affair rather than the withering of one, since Browne eschewed the greater philosophical implications of romance and, falling back on stock imagery (angels, rain), failed to achieve an originality of expression. Just as, in *Hold Out,* one wasn't so much inspired as informed that Browne had found love, on *I'm Alive,* one wasn't so much moved as told that he'd lost it. While it was good news that he wasn't tilting at windmills anymore, Browne did not make a full comeback with the album, despite a couple of well-constructed songs. —*William Ruhlmann*

Looking East / Feb. 1996 / Elektra ♦♦♦
Jackson Browne begins his most Los Angeles-oriented album standing in the Pacific Ocean "Looking East" across the country and, as usual, doing so without much approval, but with a persistent hope. After reflecting on his youth in "The Barricades of Heaven," he compares the rich and poor in "Some Bridges" and takes time out to watch a little television in "Information Wars," before considering romance in "I'm the Cat," "Culver Moon," and "Baby How Long" and childhood in "Nino." He then decides he would like to be "Alive in the World," as opposed to inside his head or "behind some wall," and declares of that world, "It Is One." Thus, we are taken on another of Jackson Browne's tours, which manages to travel to outer and inner space without leaving the county of Los Angeles. After 24 years of record-making, he remains puzzled by the same personal and philosophical issues, and he approaches them in the same way, alternately hopeful and pessimistic, but more often than not ending up determined to persevere. He now uses fewer words, so that the songs sometimes seem no more than sketches, and he continues to set them to loping rock rhythms played against slabs of ringing guitar with traces of world music. Here, he co-credits eight of the ten songs to his backup musicians, but the haunting, long-line melodies remain familiar from his earlier work. But then, *Looking East* is a highly referential work from an artist who started where most end and has been earnestly seeking the right direction ever since. *Looking East* finds him in his own backyard, still searching. —*William Ruhlmann*

Brownsville Station

f. 1969, Ann Arbor, MI, **db.** 1979
Rock 'n' Roll, Hard Rock, Boogie Rock
A Detroit-area rock 'n' roll band formed in 1969 by guitarist Cub Koda. Original members included Mike Lutz (guitar), T.J. Cronley (drums), and Tony Driggins (bass). Initially influenced by Chuck Berry, Bo Diddley, Jerry Lee Lewis, and other '50s rockers, their early albums included inspired covers and genre-faithful originals, all presented in Marshall stack, double-bass-drum bigness. Far more effective as a live act (with Koda's onstage banter influencing everyone from J. Geils' Peter Wolf to Alice Cooper), the group finally hit paydirt in late 1973 with their No. 3 hit, the Koda-penned "Smokin' in the Boys' Room." After disbanding the group in 1979, Koda went on to a career as a solo recording artist (see separate entry) and as a journalist for several music magazines. —*Stephen Thomas Erlewine*

No B.S. / 1970 / Warner Brothers ♦♦♦♦
Their debut album, featuring pedal-to-the-metal renditions of "Road Runner," "Rumble," and "Be Bop Confidential." —*Stephen Thomas Erlewine*

Brownsville Station / 1977 / Private Stock ♦♦♦
Their next-to-last album, featuring the cult favorite "The Martian Boogie." —*Stephen Thomas Erlewine*

● **Smoking in the Boys' Room: The Best of Brownsville Station** / Dec. 14, 1993 / Rhino ♦♦♦♦
A roaring romp through the Brownsville Station's back pages, compiled

by Cub Koda himself, *Smokin' in the Boys' Room* makes a convincing case that these Ann Arbor, MI, garage punks were one of the most underrated rock 'n' roll bands of the 1970s. —*Stephen Thomas Erlewine*

Jack Bruce (John Symon Asher Bruce)

b. May 14, 1943, Glasgow, Scotland
Bass, Vocals / Electric British Blues, Art-Rock/Progressive-Rock
Although some may be tempted to call multi-instrumentalist, songwriter, and composer Jack Bruce a rock 'n' roll musician, blues and jazz are what this innovative musician really loves. As a result, these two genres are at the base of most of the recorded output from a career that goes back to the beginning of London's blues scene in 1962. In that year, he joined Alexis Korner's Blues Incorporated.

Bruce's most famous songs are, in essence, blues tunes: "Sunshine of Your Love," "Strange Brew," "Politician," and "White Room." Bruce's best-known songs remain those he penned for Cream, the legendary blues-rock trio he formed with drummer Ginger Baker and guitarist Eric Clapton in July, 1966. Baker and Bruce played together for five years before Clapton came along, and although their trio lasted only until November 1968, the group is credited with changing the face of rock 'n' roll and bringing blues to a worldwide audience. Through their creative arrangements of classic blues tunes like Robert Johnson's "Crossroads," Skip James' "I'm So Glad," Willie Dixon's "Spoonful," and Albert King's "Born Under a Bad Sign," the group helped popularize blues-rock and led the way for similar groups that came about later on, like Led Zeppelin.

Bruce was born May 14, 1943, in Lanarkshire, near Glasgow, Scotland. His father was a big jazz fan, and he credits people like Louis Armstrong and Fats Waller among his earliest influences. He grew up listening to jazz and took up bass and cello as a teen. After three months at the Royal Scottish Academy of Music, he left, disgusted with the politics of music school. After traveling around Europe for a while, he settled into the early blues scene in 1962 in London, where he eventually met drummer Ginger Baker. He played with British blues pioneers Alexis Korner and Graham Bond before leaving in 1965 to join John Mayall's Bluesbreakers, whose guitarist was Eric Clapton. But in the time he spent with Graham Bond, he recalls performing upwards of 300 shows. This gave him time to get his chops together without having to practice. With Manfred Mann, with whom he also played before forming Cream, Bruce learned about the business of making hit songs. The group's reputation for long, extended blues jams began at the Fillmore in San Francisco at a concert organized by impresario Bill Graham. Bruce later realized that Cream gave him a chance to succeed as a musician, and admitted that if it weren't for that group, he might never have escaped London. After Cream split up in November 1968, Bruce formed Jack Bruce and Friends with drummer Mitch Mitchell and guitarist Larry Coryell. Recording-wise, Bruce took a tack away from blues and blues-rock, leaning more in a folk-rock direction with his solo albums *Songs for a Tailor* (1969), *Harmony Row* (1971), and *Out of the Storm* (1974).

In 1970 and 1971 he worked with Tony Williams Lifetime before putting together another power trio with guitarist Leslie West and drummer Corky Laing in 1972, simply called West, Bruce and Laing. After working with Frank Zappa on his album *Apostrophe* in 1974, Bruce was at it again in '75 with the Jack Bruce Band, where members included keyboardist Carla Bley and guitarist Mick Taylor. Again on the road in 1980 with Jack Bruce and Friends, the latter version of the group included drummer Billy Cobham, keyboardist David Sancious, and guitarist Clem Clempson, formerly of Humble Pie. In the early '80s, he formed another trio, B.L.T., this time with guitarist Robin Trower, before working with Kip Hanrahan on his three solo albums.

Through three and a half decades, Bruce has always been a supreme innovator, pushing himself into uncharted waters with his jazz and folk-rock compositions. Bruce's bluesiest albums would have to include all of his work with Cream, the albums *B.L.T.* and *Truce* with Robin Trower, some of his West, Bruce and Laing recordings, and several of his albums from the 1980s and early '90s. These include *Willpower* (PolyGram, 1988); *A Question of Time* (Epic Records, 1989), which includes guest performances by Albert Collins, Nicky Hopkins and Baker; and his CMP Records live career retrospective album, recorded in Cologne, France, *Cities of the Heart* (1993). Bruce's most recent release is 1995's *Monkjack*, an album of his jazz piano compositions, which he performs with organist Bernie Worrell, issued on the CMP Record label. —*Richard Skelly*

Songs for a Tailor / 1969 / Atco ✦✦✦✦
There's not a weak song on this first and most accessible solo album. "Theme for an Imaginary Western" (also made popular by Mountain) is one of the finest songs Bruce has ever recorded. Musically, this is more subdued and keyboard-oriented than Bruce's work with Cream. —*Rick Clark*

Harmony Row / 1971 / Atco ✦✦✦
Bruce's third effort is a much more challenging listen, possessing more complicated arrangements and impenetrable lyrics than *Songs for a Tailor*. Among the album's many highlights are the aggressive multi-time-signature rock of "You Burned the Tables on Me" and the haunting "Victoria Sage." —*Rick Clark*

● **Willpower: A Twenty-Year Retrospective** / 1989 / Atco ✦✦✦✦
Willpower is a well-compiled overview of Bruce's entire solo output, with choice unreleased tracks. This is the place to start if you are budgeting one disc of his music for your collection. Otherwise, get *Songs for a Tailor*. —*Rick Clark*

Peabo Bryson

b. Apr. 13, 1951, Greenville, SC
Vocals / Urban, Adult Contemporary
Vocalist Peabo Bryson was among the premier silky-voiced soul artists who emerged as the softer, more sophisticated urban-contemporary sound became dominant in the '70s and '80s. Bryson, who was born in Greenville, SC, sang with Al Freeman & the Upsetters in 1965, and was in the group Moses Dillard & the Tex-Town Display from 1968 to 1973. He was a producer and composer for Atlanta's Bang Records in the early '70s, and sang in Michael Zager's Moon Band. His self-titled debut LP and several singles were recorded for Bang's subsidiary company Bullet, among them "Do It with Feeling," "Underground Music," "It's Just a Matter of Time," "Just Another Day," and "I Can Make It Better." All were moderate R&B hits. Bryson moved to Capitol in 1978, where his first album, *Reaching for the Sky*, went gold, and the title track was a No. 6 R&B hit. He remained in the Moon Band until 1979, departing after "I'm So Into You" spent two weeks as the nation's No. 2 R&B hit in 1978. Bryson has continued a prolific career as both lead act and duet participant. He has made hit duets with Natalie Cole, Roberta Flack, Melissa Manchester, and Regina Belle. Bryson recorded for Capitol until 1984, when he switched to Elektra, and enjoyed more success with "If Ever You're in My Arms Again." He moved to Columbia in 1991, issuing *Can You Stop the Rain*. He's also enjoyed more acclaim making duets with Belle. —*Ron Wynn*

● **Collection** / Jun. 1984 / Capitol ✦✦✦✦
A best-of covering Bryson's Capitol years, 1978-1983, much of it given over to his collaboration with Roberta Flack, including the hits "Tonight, I Celebrate My Love" and "You're Lookin' like Love to Me." —*William Ruhlmann*

B.T. Express

f. 1973, Brooklyn, NY, **db.** 1981
Funk, Disco
This funk-disco group was formed by Jeff Lane in Brooklyn during the '70s. They started in 1972 as the King Davis House Rockers and later were called the Brooklyn Trucking Express. The roster consisted of saxophonist/vocalist Bill Risbrook; percussionist Dennis Rowe; guitarist Rick Thompson; saxophonist/flutist Carlos Ward; keyboardist Michael Jones (Kashif); lead guitarist/vocalist Wesley Hall; drummer Leslie Ming; bassist, organist, and vocalist Louis Risbrook; and vocalist Barbara Joyce Lomas. Their debut LP *Do It 'til You're Satisfied* had two No. 1 R&B and Top Ten pop hits in the title cut and "Express." Subsequent LPs yielded two more R&B Top Ten singles, "Give It What You Got/ Peace Pipe" in 1975 and "Can't Stop Groovin' Now, Wanna Do It Some More" in 1976. After 1977's "Shout It Out," which cracked the R&B Top 20 (No. 12), the group slumped with the album *Shout!* They were off the charts until 1980. They made a slight comeback that year with *B.T. Express 1980*, though only the single "Give Up the Funk (Let's Dance)" made it into the Top 30 (No. 24). They later recorded for Record Shack, Earthtone, and King Davis, but couldn't duplicate their earlier success. Kashif scored hits as a producer, performer, and composer in the '80s. —*Ron Wynn*

● **The Best of B.T. Express** / May 27, 1997 / Rhino ✦✦✦✦
Best of the B.T. Express is a comprehensive overview of the group's best disco and soul singles, featuring all of their biggest hits from Roadshow and Columbia, including "Express," "Give It What You Got," "Can't Stop Groovin' Now, Wanna Do It Some More," "Shout It Out," "Give Up the Funk (Let's Dance)" and "Do It ('Til You're Satisfied)." —*Stephen Thomas Erlewine*

Roy Buchanan

b. Sep. 23, 1939, Ozark, AL, d. Aug. 14, 1988, Fairfax, VA
Guitar / Blues-Rock
Buchanan's reputation as a hot-shot guitarist extends back to the beginnings of rock 'n' roll itself. On the road and recording with Dale Hawkins by his teens, Buchanan became the law of the land around Washington, DC, by the mid- to late '60s. His use of the Fender Telecaster, using high harmonic squeals in place of feedback and distortion, was part and par-

cel of rock guitar's vocabulary by the early '70s. A reluctant superstar, Buchanan later became more unfocused as his career waned, but his unique stylings remain etched into his best records.

Sadly, when Buchanan seemed on the verge of a comeback in 1986, he hung himself in a police cell after he was arrested on a drunk-driving charge. He left behind a number of records that testify that he was a consummate guitarist, capable of tones and techniques that other guitarists only dream of. —*Cub Koda*

Roy Buchanan / Aug. 1972 / Polydor ✦✦✦✦
His debut album, with a skunk-hot stage band. Buchanan's guitar sizzles on tracks like "Haunted House," "Sweet Dreams," and "The Messiah Will Come Again." —*Cub Koda*

Second Album / 1973 / Polydor ✦✦✦
More blues-based than his debut, with great stretched-out jams showcasing some of his best playing. —*Cub Koda*

That's What I Am Here For / Feb. 1974 / Polydor ✦✦✦
Excellent blues-rock guitar, it includes the riveting Hendrix tribute "Hey Joe." —*David Szatmary*

Live Stock / Aug. 1975 / Polydor ✦✦✦✦
Brilliant live blues-rock guitar by the legend who turned down a spot in the Rolling Stones. A must for guitar-hero fans. —*David Szatmary*

You're Not Alone / Apr. 1978 / Atlantic ✦✦✦
Piercing guitar solos explode in a spacey atmosphere. —*David Szatmary*

When a Guitar Plays the Blues / Jul. 1985 / Alligator ✦✦✦
This is an excellent example of the blues-rock guitar virtuoso's recent work. —*David Szatmary*

● **Sweet Dreams: The Anthology** / Sep. 22, 1992 / Polydor ✦✦✦✦
Over two CDs, *Sweet Dreams* collects the finest moments from Buchanan's '70s albums, including nine unreleased tracks; as a career retrospective, it's the finest collection available. —*Stephen Thomas Erlewine*

Guitar on Fire: Atlantic Sessions / Apr. 20, 1993 / Rhino ✦✦✦

Lindsey Buckingham

b. Oct. 3, 1948, Palo Alto, CA
Guitar, Vocals / Pop-Rock
Before he joined Fleetwood Mac, Lindsey Buckingham was sketching out his brand of Brian Wilson-influenced pop with Stevie Nicks in the folkie duo Buckingham/Nicks. Mick Fleetwood invited the duo to join his band in late 1974. The band's pop tendencies flowered under Buckingham's direction. Not only did he provide the group with some brilliant, surprisingly dark pop songs, he sharpened the other members' songs with his production, arrangements, and breathtaking guitar-playing. Buckingham left the band after their 1987 album *Tango in the Night*, to concentrate on his solo work.

While Buckingham's solo albums are deceptively simple and calm on the surface, there are complex arrangements and emotions beneath the smooth production. None of them has sold anything approaching the level of *Rumours*, or even *Tango in the Night*. But they are rich, layered pop albums. His first solo record, *Law & Order*, had a hit single with "Trouble." —*Stephen Thomas Erlewine*

Buckingham Nicks / 1973 / Polydor ✦✦✦
Buckingham Nicks, the duo album made by Lindsey Buckingham and Stevie Nicks in 1973, which served in effect as an audition tape for their entry into Fleetwood Mac in 1974, is hard not to hear as a dry run for works like *Fleetwood Mac* and *Rumours*. Many of the musical characteristics associated with those albums are here, from Nicks' torn voice and mysterious, romantic lyrics to Buckingham's fluid acoustic and electric guitar playing and his inventive arranging. One song, "Crystal," even turned up re-recorded on *Fleetwood Mac*, and the rest are consistent with the style of the later hits. *Buckingham Nicks* lacks some of the polish of the Fleetwood Mac records, and its songwriting is not as consistent overall, but it is of a piece with some of the most popular music of the 1970s. —*William Ruhlmann*

Law and Order / Oct. 1981 / Asylum ✦✦✦✦
Lindsey Buckingham's talents as guitarist, arranger, and producer were particularly well suited to Fleetwood Mac, a band in which he was only one among three songwriters whose material complemented each other's. As a solo artist, Buckingham retains his strengths, but he encounters a form-over-substance problem. The seven songs he wrote for his debut album come across as sketches, musical pieces for which he has constructed interesting guitar riffs and the occasional sonic effect, plus a lyric tag—"Trouble," "That's How We Do It in L.A." But they have not been fleshed out into full-fledged songs, perhaps because Buckingham hasn't much interest in lyrics, or because he declines to use more than one or two of his ideas per tune. On the eclectic choice of covers ("September Song," "A Satisfied Mind"), Buckingham at least has fully composed and written pieces to work with, but he embalms them in his production techniques. As such, *Law and Order* comes off as a high-

quality demo of largely unfinished material. (Nevertheless, "Trouble" became a Top Ten single.) —*William Ruhlmann*

Go Insane / Jul. 1984 / Asylum ✦✦✦
Lindsey Buckingham's second album, like his first, *Law and Order*, was a triumph of studio wizardry over songwriting craft. Buckingham's work was ear-catching, but once he'd gotten your attention with some gimmicky sound effect or busy arrangement, he had very little to tell you. The exception was the album's most ambitious piece, the closing track, "D.W. Suite," on which Buckingham, always strongly influenced by the Beach Boys, took on what sounded like an elaborate tribute to Beach Boy Dennis Wilson, who died while the album was being made. The title track, which also had massed choral sounds (all made by Buckingham) reminiscent of a Fleetwood Mac track, became a Top 40 hit, but the album lacked the accessibility to make it more than a moderate seller, and at least at this point it appeared that Buckingham's solo albums were going to serve as laboratory experiments in which he tried out new musical ideas before bringing them to greater popular attention through Fleetwood Mac. —*William Ruhlmann*

● **Out of the Cradle** / Jun. 16, 1992 / Reprise ✦✦✦✦
Lindsey Buckingham quit Fleetwood Mac after the release of their *Tango in the Night* album in 1987 and the subsequent five years working on his first post-Mac solo album, *Out of the Cradle*. Perhaps because he was now focused on his solo career, Buckingham reined in the experimental style of his first two albums, producing more conventional, accessible material, much of it similar to his later work with Fleetwood Mac. The inventiveness this time was heard largely in Buckingham's electro-acoustic guitar style, which combined the power of a rock guitarist with the delicacy and precision of a classical nylon-string player. Perhaps the biggest difference from his previous solo work, however, was that Buckingham actually wrote a group of songs that were about something, not just riffs full of aural tricks. Unfortunately, Buckingham had never fully established himself in the public mind as an entity apart from Fleetwood Mac, so taking eight years between solo albums made *Out of the Cradle* a tough sell. Which means that, although this is his most listenable solo album, not many people heard it. —*William Ruhlmann*

The Buckinghams

f. 1966, Chicago, IL, **db.** 1970
Pop-Rock
If everyone on the northwest side of Chicago who claims to have hung out with the Buckinghams during their heyday had faithfully bought all their releases, the rock group might have sold more records than the Beatles.

Popular attractions while still in high school, the quintet changed its name from the Pulsations to the Buckinghams to reflect the British Invasion craze and signed with Chicago's USA Records in 1966. Backing Dennis Tufano's buoyant lead vocals with prominent harmonies and punchy soul-styled brass, the group came across the wistful "Kind of a Drag," and in short order, the Buckinghams had a million-selling pop chart-topper on their hands. They quickly graduated to recording for Columbia.

As long as songwriter Jim Holvay supplied more material of the same high quality as "Kind of a Drag," the Buckinghams were sitting pretty. Holvay co-wrote "Don't You Care," "Hey Baby (They're Playing Our Song)," and the pseudo-psychedelic "Susan," and they all proved to be major hits for the band. The group's R&B roots surfaced on a vocal adaptation of Cannonball Adderley's jazz standard "Mercy, Mercy, Mercy," their second-biggest hit.

But the Buckinghams' fortunes soon changed drastically. One of the top-selling rock groups of 1967, they managed only one hit after early 1968, and by 1970 the group was kaput. Two original members, guitarist Carl Giammarese and bassist Nick Fortuna, have since revived the Buckinghams for oldies tours. —*Bill Dahl*

● **Mercy Mercy Mercy (A Collection)** / Aug. 27, 1991 / Columbia ✦✦✦✦
These mid-'60s hitmakers from Chicago hold up well with their neat blend of pop and soul. All of their hits and more can be found on this 18-song anthology. —*Jeff Tamarkin*

Jeff Buckley

b. Nov. 17, 1966, Los Angeles, CA, **d.** May 29, 1997, Memphis, TN
Organ, Guitar, Vocals / Singer-Songwriter, Alternative Pop-Rock, Folk-Rock, Adult Alternative Pop-Rock
Because he was the son of cult songwriter Tim Buckley, Jeff Buckley faced more expectations and pre-conceived notions than most singer-songwriters. Perhaps it wasn't surprising that Jeff Buckley's music was related to his father's by only the thinnest of margins. Buckley's voice was grand and sweeping, which fit with the mock-operatic grandeur of his Van Morrison-meets-Led Zeppelin music. Buckley began playing as a high school student in New York. Eventually he moved to Los Angeles

to study music; while he was there, he performed with several jazz and funk bands, as well as playing with Shinehead, a leader in the dancehall reggae movement. A few years later, he moved back to New York, forming Gods & Monsters with the experimental guitarist Gary Lucas. The band became a hip name, but their life-span was short. Buckley began a solo career playing clubs and coffeehouses, building up a considerable following. Soon he signed a record deal with Columbia, releasing the *Live at Sin-E* EP in November 1993. It received good reviews, but they didn't compare to the raves Buckley's full-length debut, 1994's *Grace*, received. Unlike the EP, the album was recorded with a full band, which gave the record textures that surprised some of his long-time New York followers. Nevertheless, it made several year-end "Best of 1994" lists and earned him a belated alternative hit, "Last Goodbye," in the spring of 1995.

A long hiatus followed as Buckley worked on material for his follow-up effort, provisionally titled *My Sweetheart, the Drunk*. Originally slated to be produced by Tom Verlaine, who later dropped out of the project, Buckley finally began work on the record in Memphis in late spring of 1997. On the night of May 29, he and a friend traveled to the local Mud Island Harbor, where Buckley spontaneously decided to go swimming in the Mississippi River and leaped into the water fully-clothed. A few minutes later, he disappeared under the waves; authorities were quickly contacted, but to no avail. On June 4, his body was found floating near the city's famed Beale Street Area. Buckley was 30 years old. —*Stephen Thomas Erlewine*

Live at Sin-E / 1993 / Columbia ✦✦✦
Jeff Buckley resented being called a folk singer, but he made his name playing solo acoustic sets like this one on the New York coffee circuit. Sony released this live EP before his first fully produced rock album, *Grace*, perhaps to attract attention to the raw power of Buckley's greatest gift, his voice. These four songs certainly accomplished that end. Buckley hurdled seemingly unreachable octaves, suspended notes for what seems like minutes, and belted out his falsetto without a scintilla of restraint. That's a positive inasmuch as it allowed him to show off his considerable talent; it's a negative when it *sounded* like he was showing off. But his ten-minute cover of Van Morrison's "The Way Young Lovers Do" is a tour de force of strumming and scatting, and his acoustic "Eternal Life" has an electricity that is paradoxically lacking on the plugged-in album version. —*Darryl Cater*

● **Grace** / Aug. 23, 1994 / Columbia ✦✦✦✦
Jeff Buckley was many things, but humble wasn't one of them. *Grace* is an audacious debut album, filled with sweeping choruses, bombastic arrangements, searching lyrics and, above all, the richly textured voice of Buckley himself, which resembled a cross between Robert Plant, Van Morrison, and his father Tim. And that's a fair starting point for his musi. *Grace* sounds like a Led Zeppelin album written by an ambitious folkie with a fondness for lounge jazz. At his best—the soaring title track, "Last Goodbye," and the mournful "Lover, You Should've Come Over"—Buckley's grasp met his reach with startling results; at its worst, *Grace* is merely promising. —*Stephen Thomas Erlewine*

Tim Buckley

b. Feb. 14, 1947, Washington, D.C., d. Jun. 29, 1975, Santa Monica, CA
Guitar, Vocals / Singer-Songwriter, Folk-Rock, Jazz-Rock
One of the great rock vocalists of the 1960s, Tim Buckley drew from folk, psychedelic rock, and progressive jazz to create a considerable body of adventurous work in his brief lifetime. His multi-octave range was capable of not just astonishing power, but great emotional expressiveness, swooping from sorrowful tenderness to anguished wailing. His restless quest for new territory worked against him commercially. By the time his fans had hooked into his latest album, he was onto something else entirely, both live and in the studio. In this sense he recalled artists such as Miles Davis and David Bowie, who were so eager to look forward and change that they confused and even angered listeners who wanted more stylistic consistency. However, his eclecticism has also ensured a durable fascination with his work that has engendered a growing cult, often with listeners who were too young (or not around) to appreciate his music when he was active.

Buckley emerged from the same 1960s Orange County, CA, folk scene that spawned Jackson Browne and the Nitty Gritty Dirt Band. Mothers of Invention drummer Jimmy Carl Black introduced Buckley and a couple of musicians Buckley was playing with to the Mothers' manager, Herbie Cohen. Although Cohen may have first been interested in Buckley as a songwriter, he realized after hearing some demos that Buckley was also a diamond in the rough as a singer. Cohen became Buckley's manager and helped the singer get a deal with Elektra.

Before Buckley had reached his 20th birthday, he'd released his debut album. The slightly fey but enormously promising effort highlighted his soaring melodies and romantic, opaque lyrics. Baroque psychedelia was the order of the day for many Elektra releases of the time, and Buckley's early folk-rock albums were embellished with contributions from musi-

cians Lee Underwood (guitar), Van Dyke Parks (keyboards), Jim Fielder (bass), and Jerry Yester. Larry Beckett was also an overlooked contributor to Buckley's first two albums, co-writing many of the songs.

The fragile, melancholic, orchestrated beauty of the material had an innocent quality that was dampened only slightly on the second LP, *Goodbye and Hello* (1967). Buckley's songs and arrangements became more ambitious and psychedelic, particularly on the lengthy title track. This was also his only album to reach the Top 200, where it peaked at number 171. Buckley was always an artist who found his primary constituency among the underground, even for his most accessible efforts. His third album, *Happy Sad*, found him going in a decidedly jazzier direction in both his vocalizing and his instrumentation, introducing congas and vibes. Though it seemed a retreat from commercial considerations at the time, *Happy Sad* actually concluded the triumvirate of recordings that are judged to be his most accessible.

The truth was, by the late '60s Buckley was hardly interested in folk-rock at all. He was more intrigued by jazz; not only sounding modern jazz (as heard on the posthumous release of acoustic 1968 live material, *Dream Letter*), but also its most avant-garde strains. His songs became much more oblique in structure and skeletal in lyrics, especially when the partnership with Larry Beckett was ruptured after the latter's induction into the army. Some of his songs abandoned lyrics almost entirely, treating his voice itself as an instrument, wordlessly contorting, screaming, and moaning, sometimes quite cacophonous. In this context, *Lorca* was viewed by most fans and critics not just as a shocking departure, but a downright bummer. No longer was Buckley a romantic, melodic poet; he was an experimental *artiste* who sometimes seemed bent on punishing both himself and his listeners with his wordless shrieks and jarringly dissonant music.

Almost as if to prove that he was still capable of gentle, uplifting, jazzy pop-folk, Buckley issued *Blue Afternoon* around the same time. *Blue Afternoon* and *Lorca* were issued almost simultaneously, on different labels. While an admirable demonstration of his versatility, it was commercial near-suicide, each album canceling the impact of the other, as well as confusing his remaining fans. Buckley found his best middle ground between accessibility and jazzy improvisation on 1970's *Starsailor*, which is probably the best showcase of his sheer vocal abilities, although many prefer the more cogent material of his earliest albums.

By this point, though, Buckley's approach was jeopardizing his commercial survival. And not just on record; he was equally uncompromising as a live act, as the posthumously issued *Live at the Troubadour 1969* demonstrates, with its stretched-to-the-limit jams and searing improv vocals. For a time, he was said to have earned his living as a taxi driver and chauffeur; he also flirted with films for a while. When he returned to the studio, it was as a much more commercial singer-songwriter; some have suggested that various management and label pressures were behind this shift.

As much of a schism as Buckley's experimental-jazz period created among fans and critics, his final recordings have proved even more divisive, even among big Buckley fans. Some view these efforts—which mix funk, sex-driven lyrical concerns, and laid-back L.A. session musicians—as proof of his mastery of the blue-eyed soul idiom. Others find them a sad waste of talent, or relics of a prodigy who was burning out rather than conquering new realms. Neophytes should be aware of the difference of critical opinion regarding this era, but on the whole his final three albums are his least impressive. Those who feel otherwise usually cite the earliest of those LPs, *Greetings from L.A.* (1972), as his best work from his final phase.

Buckley's life came to a sudden end in the middle of 1975, when he died of a heroin overdose just after completing a tour. Those close to him insist that he had been clean for some time and lament the loss of an artist who, despite some recent failures, still had much to offer. Buckley's stock began to rise among the rock underground after the Cocteau Twins covered his "Song for the Siren" in the 1980s. The posthumous releases of two late-'60s live sets (*Dream Letter* and *Live at the Troubadour 1969*) in the early '90s also boosted his profile, as well as unveiling some interesting previously unreleased compositions. His son Jeff Buckley went on to mount a musical career as well before his own death in 1997. —*Richie Unterberger*

● **Tim Buckley** / 1966 / Asylum ✦✦✦✦
Buckley's 1966 debut was the most straightforward and folk-rock-oriented of his albums. The material has a lyrical and melodic sophistication that was astounding for a 19-year-old. The pretty, almost precious songs are complemented by appropriately baroque, psychedelic-tinged production. If there was a record that exemplified the '60s Elektra folk-rock sound, this may have been it, featuring production by Elektra owner Jac Holzman and Doors producer Paul Rothchild, Love and Doors engineer Bruce Botnick, and string arrangements by Jack Nitzsche. That's not to diminish the contributions of the band, which included his longtime lead guitarist Lee Underwood and Van Dyke Parks on keyboards. Buckley was still firmly in the singer-songwriter

camp on this album, showing only brief flashes of the experimental vocal flights, angst-ridden lyrics, and soul influences that would characterize much of his later work. It's not his most adventurous outing, but it's one of his most accessible, and retains a fragile beauty. —*Richie Unterberger*

Goodbye & Hello / 1967 / Asylum ✦✦✦✦
With his second album, Buckley began exploring different sonic territory, adding exotic instruments and a distinct, winding jazz influence to his increasingly complex lyrics. —*Stephen Thomas Erlewine*

Dream Letter: Live in London / Jul. 1968 / Rhino/Bizarre ✦✦✦✦
This live double-disc set captures Buckley's jazzy folk and passionate mega-octave vocal in fine form. Lee Underwood (guitar), David Friedman (vibes), and Danny Thompson (bass) provide empathetic support. —*Rick Clark*

Happy Sad / 1969 / Asylum ✦✦✦✦
Buckley began to turn toward softer, more introspective, and slightly jazzy tunes on his third record. This album of six lengthy compositions features some of his loveliest songs, including "Strange Feelin'," "Sing a Song for You," and the exuberant, 12-minute "Gypsy Woman." —*Richie Unterberger*

Blue Afternoon / 1969 / Rhino/Bizarre ✦✦✦✦
Buckley's atmospheric melancholy folk-jazz shines on the first four tracks, "Happy Time," "Chase the Blues Away," "I Must Have Been Blind," and "The River." Those tracks alone make this worth having. —*Rick Clark*

Lorca / 1970 / Asylum ✦✦✦
Buckley stunned and, to a rare degree, alienated fans with the dissonant, at times wearying, avant-garde exercises in vocal gymnastics that took up the entire first side of this LP. Side two was far more accessible, though Buckley's fusion of folk instrumentation with jazzy improvisation on extended compositions continued to take him further away from his folk-rock roots. —*Richie Unterberger*

Starsailor / 1970 / Rhino/Bizarre ✦✦✦✦
After his beginnings as a gentle, melodic baroque folk-rocker, Buckley gradually evolved into a downright experimental singer-songwriter who explored both jazz and avant-garde territory. *Starsailor* is the culmination of his experimentation, and alienated far more listeners than it exhilarated upon its release in 1970. Buckley had already begun to delve into jazz fusion on late-'60s records like *Happy Sad*, and explored some fairly "out" acrobatic, quasi-operatic vocals on his final Elektra LP, *Lorca*. With former Mother of Invention Bunk Gardner augmenting Buckley's group on sax and alto flute, Buckley applies vocal gymnastics to a set of material that's as avant-garde in its songwriting as its execution. At his most anguished (which is often on this album), he sounds as if his liver is being torn out—slowly. Almost as if to prove he can still deliver a mellow buzz, he throws in a couple of pleasant jazz-pop cuts, including the odd, jaunty French tune "Moulin Rouge." Surrealistic lyrics, heavy on landscape imagery like rivers, skies, suns, and jungle fires, top off a record that isn't for everybody, or even for every Buckley fan, but endures as one of the most uncompromising statements ever made by a singer-songwriter. —*Richie Unterberger*

Greetings from L.A. / 1972 / Rhino/Bizarre ✦✦✦
A grittier rock approach supports Buckley's plunge into eroticism. Buckley's uncaged wailing and lyrical urgency convey a great deal of sexual tension and an absence of inner peace. Intense stuff, it's considered by many to be his best. —*Rick Clark*

Sefronia / 1973 / Manifesto ✦✦
Buckley went deeper into white funk, despite two problems: white funk was not the forte of these L.A. session musicians and female backup vocalists, and not the style with which Buckley himself had the greatest empathy. His voice isn't as stunning as usual on his next-to-last album, but the bigger problem is the material, which is usually forced and pedestrian. Glimmers of quality can be heard on his cover of Fred Neil's "The Dolphins," and the strange two-part title track, which is a throwback to his more ambitious vocal workouts of times past. —*Richie Unterberger*

Look at the Fool / 1974 / Manifesto ✦✦
Buckley's final album was a sad, burned-out affair, suffering from weak, poorly conceived material and washed-out soul-rock arrangements. Most troublingly, Buckley's voice—the one asset he could always count on—had itself begun to deteriorate. Here his vocals were distressingly thin, like torn socks that have gone through the laundry cycle one too many time. —*Richie Unterberger*

Peel Sessions / Jul. 1, 1991 / Strange Fruit ✦✦
Recorded in April 1968 for the BBC, these five songs—a short album, or long EP's, worth—show Buckley at his most melodic and intimate. As on his posthumously issued 1968 concert recording *Dream Letter*, the instrumentation is sparser than on his Elektra albums. On these sessions, he was backed only by longtime guitarist Lee Underwood and

Carter Collins on percussion. This set features songs from his second and third albums, as well as a couple of cuts that didn't make it onto record in the '60s. Highlighted by a ten-minute medley of "Hallucinations" and "Troubadour," it's a worthwhile addition to the Buckley canon. —*Richie Unterberger*

Live at the Troubadour 1969 / Mar. 22, 1994 / Rhino/Bizarre ✦✦✦
A previously unreleased, recently unearthed recording that catches Buckley at the time he began to incorporate jazz-influenced vocal improvisation and dense, impressionistic lyrics into his recordings. Backed by a small combo, it features loose numbers with bloodcurdling vocal scatting and instrumental jamming. The nine tracks on this 78-minute disc are drawn mostly from his *Lorca* and *Blue Afternoon* albums and include two previously unavailable songs. —*Richie Unterberger*

Honeyman / Nov. 1995 / Manifesto ✦✦✦
A previously unreleased live 1973 radio broadcast, in excellent sound, that offers a valuable supplement to Buckley's often disappointing final albums. Buckley's last LPs were marred by unsympathetic L.A. production, and this presents the material with much sparser, focused, and appropriate arrangements. As the songs originate mostly from the *Sefronia* and *Greetings from L.A.* records (although a couple of songs from the '60s do appear), this couldn't be placed among his best work, or even among his best live albums (*Dream Letter* and *Troubadour 1969* are both considerably better). Buckley's vocals are great, though, and if the tunes are sometimes too funky for their own good, this is generally good stuff, especially his riveting interpretation of Fred Neil's "Dolphins," which alone is probably worth the price of admission for Buckley fans. —*Richie Unterberger*

Buffalo Springfield

f. 1966, Los Angeles, CA, **db.** 1968
Rock 'n' Roll, Country-Rock, Folk-Rock
Few American groups have produced the wealth of talent of Buffalo Springfield. The group's formation is the stuff of legend: driving on Sunset Boulevard in Los Angeles, Stephen Stills and Richie Furay spotted a hearse that Stills was sure belonged to Neil Young, a Canadian he had crossed paths with earlier. Indeed it did, and with the addition of fellow hearse passenger and Canadian Bruce Palmer on bass and ex-Dillard Dewey Martin on drums, the cluster of ex-folkies determined, as the Byrds had just done, to become a rock 'n' roll band.

Over a 19-month period during 1967 and 1968, Buffalo Springfield released three impressive albums. Their debut, including their sole big hit (Stills' "For What It's Worth"), established them as the best folk-rock band in the land barring the Byrds, though the Springfield were a bit more folk- and country-oriented. The second, *Again*, is their masterpiece, as the group expanded their folk-rock base into tough hard rock and psychedelic orchestration. Possessing three strong songwriters with distinctly different, yet complementary, styles—Stills, Young, and Furay (the last of whom didn't begin writing until the second LP)—they also had strong and often conflicting egos, particularly Stills and Young. The group, which held almost infinite promise, rearranged their lineup several times, Young leaving the group for periods and Palmer fighting deportation, until disbanding in 1968. Their final album, although it contained some excellent material, clearly shows the group's fragmenting into solo directions.

Even more than the Byrds, Buffalo Springfield's sound was undeniably American, drawing from rock, folk, and country. The intense clash of creative energies, however, finally caused the demise of the band in May 1968. Stephen Stills went on to Crosby, Stills & Nash. Neil Young joined that group briefly for *Deja Vu*, then went on to pursue an erratic solo career with periods of great success and brilliant music. After Springfield, Jim Messina and Richie Furay founded the country-rock group Poco. After Poco, Messina recorded a string of hits during the '70s with Kenny Loggins, as Loggins & Messina. —*Rick Clark & Richie Unterberger*

Buffalo Springfield / 1967 / Atco ✦✦✦
Their strong debut contains the Stephen Stills classic "For What It's Worth" and Neil Young's "Nowadays Clancy Can't Even Sing." "Sit Down I Think I Love You" and "Go and Say Goodbye" are also highlights. —*Rick Clark*

★ **Buffalo Springfield Again** / 1967 / Atco ✦✦✦✦✦
On what is by far their best effort, Stills, Furay, and Young each contribute some great songs: the hits "Bluebird," "Mr. Soul," and "Rock & Roll Woman," plus standouts like "A Child's Claim to Fame," "Hung Upside Down," "Broken Arrow," "Everydays," and "Expecting to Fly." —*Rick Clark*

Last Time Around / 1968 / Atco ✦✦✦
Their last album showcases a couple of gems in Furay's "Kind Woman" and Young's "On the Way Home." —*Rick Clark*

Best of Buffalo Springfield . . . Retrospective / 1969 / Atco ✦✦✦
This is a decent sampler for the uninitiated. It contains all their hits and some key album tracks but isn't comprehensive enough to be essential. —*Rick Clark*

● **Buffalo Springfield [Collection]** / 1973 / Atco ✦✦✦✦
Not to be confused with their self-titled studio debut album, this double LP, which can still be found without too much hassle, is clearly the best Springfield compilation, at least until the overdue day when a box set appears that includes everything recorded by this superb band. It does miss some good songs, especially from the first album, but zeroes in on their very best work, and includes a nine-minute version of "Bluebird" available nowhere else, as well as excellent liner notes. —*Richie Unterberger*

Stampede / [Bootleg] ✦✦✦
The group was nearly set to release a record of this name as their second LP, going so far as to take a cover photo. Despite rumors to the contrary, it seems as though the album was never finished, and that some of the material originally intended for it did actually appear on their later LPs. But the myth of an entire lost Springfield record inspired several bootlegs of the same name, containing outtakes from their early sessions. These outtakes, written mostly by Stills, may not constitute an actual lost album, but they're by and large superb nonetheless. "Neighbor, Don't You Worry," "We'll See," "My Kind of Love," and "Baby Don't Scold Me" (which appeared briefly on early pressings of the first Springfield LP) are all first-rate, charging folk-rock that would have fit in well on the group's debut album. There are also considerably different alternate takes of Young's "Do I Have to Come Right Out and Say It" and "Down to the Wire"; one version of the latter did appear on Neil's *Decade* collection. This studio material is usually packaged with interesting acoustic, solo Stills and Young demos from the early Springfield era, as well as live material from an early 1967 high school show—marginal fidelity, excellent performances. Not a lost grail, the *Stampede* collection is nonetheless necessary for Springfield fans and highly enjoyable on its own merits. —*Richie Unterberger*

Buffalo Tom

f. 1986, Boston, MA
Rock 'n' Roll, Alternative Pop-Rock
When they released their first album in 1989, the Boston-based trio Buffalo Tom was written off as Dinosaur Jr. junior. Admittedly, their debut was in debt to J Mascis's thundering guitar and folk-tinged songs, and it didn't help that Mascis produced the record. Over time, Buffalo Tom stripped away their grungier influences and developed into a straightahead rock group of the early '90s, capable of throttling rockers and beautiful ballads.

Comprised of guitarist/vocalist Bill Janovitz, bassist/vocalist Chris Colbourn, and drummer Tom Maginnis, Buffalo Tom began to develop their own style with their second album, 1990's *Birdbrain*, which featured a noticeable improvement in songwriting. In 1992 Buffalo Tom released *Let Me Come Over*, a gritty set of driving rock and achingly melancholy ballads; several of its tracks became alternative-radio staples, including the gorgeous ballad "Taillights Fade." Despite increased critical praise and some radio airplay, the album didn't sell. The follow-up, 1993's *Big Red Letter Day*, featured a more polished, radio-ready production, but the album received only a small push from radio and MTV. "Soda Jerk," the first single from the album, became a minor alternative-radio and MTV hit. After a year-long tour, the group returned in the summer of 1995 with *Sleepy Eyed*, a return to the more direct sound of *Let Me Come Over*. —*Stephen Thomas Erlewine*

Buffalo Tom / 1989 / SST ✦✦✦

Birdbrain / Nov. 1990 / Beggars Banquet ✦✦✦
Birdbrain is a transitional record that marks the beginnings of Buffalo Tom's move away from the guitar-drenched sound that earned them the perjorative nickname Dinosaur Jr. Junior into leaner, more acoustically-driven pop-rock. While Dinosaur Jr.'s J. Mascis is still on as producer, his influence is measurably diminished this time out, as evidenced on the tense, delicate "Enemy" and an acoustic cover of the Psychedelic Furs' "Heaven." And speaking of psychedelia, *Birdbrain* draws on elements of '60s acid-rock too, as well as the feedback that defined the Buffalo Tom of yore. —*Jason Ankeny*

● **Let Me Come Over** / Mar. 10, 1992 / Beggars Banquet ✦✦✦✦
With *Let Me Come Over*, Buffalo Tom comes into its own, producing a remarkably strong album filled with exceptional songwriting. The Dinosaur Jr. comparisons are no longer accurate; now, the band sounds slightly like R.E.M. crossed with the Replacements, but that's just a starting point—the band has carved out its own brand of guitar-heavy rock 'n' roll, somewhere between college-rock and traditional, classic rock. Buffalo Tom proves equally adept at pulling off the driving "Staples" and "Mountains of Your Head," the majestic folk-rock of "Mineral," the ballads "Larry," "Frozen Lake," and the gorgeous "Taillights Fade," which

is a masterpiece. *Let Me Come Over* is the breakthrough album from one of America's best rock 'n' roll bands of the 1990s. —*Stephen Thomas Erlewine*

Big Red Letter Day / Nov. 2, 1993 / Beggars Banquet ✦✦✦✦
Following the excellent *Let Me Come Over*, *Big Red Letter Day* features a slightly more polished production, but it doesn't diminish the band's increasingly powerful songwriting and forceful rock 'n' roll. Buffalo Tom is America's best mainstream rock band, but is still undeservedly stuck on its fringes, as *Big Red Letter Day* proves. —*Stephen Thomas Erlewine*

Sleepy Eyed / Jul. 11, 1995 / East West ✦✦✦
Retreating from the slick studio production of *Big Red Letter Day*, Buffalo Tom's last shot at the big-time is a stripped-down, driving folk-rock record. By now, the group has removed most of its noisier tendencies, preferring to rock with the beat instead of against it. The simplicity of the sonics makes a good background for the lyrics, which are some of the group's best to date. "Summer" and "Tangerine" prove that the group not only has more graceful lyrics than Soul Asylum, their hooks are stronger and their playing is tighter—in short, it rocks harder. —*Stephen Thomas Erlewine*

Jimmy Buffett

b. Dec. 25, 1946, Pascogoula, MS
Guitar, Vocals / Country-Rock, Singer-Songwriter, Pop-Rock
Singer-songwriter Jimmy Buffett has translated his easy-going Gulf Coast persona into more than just a successful recording career—he has expanded into clothing, nightclubs, and literature. But the basis of the business empire that keeps him on the *Fortune* magazine list of highest-earning entertainers is his music.

Buffett moved to Nashville to try to make it in country music in the late '60s. Signed to Barnaby, he released one album, *Down to Earth* (1970), the single from which, a socially conscious song called, "The Christian?," suggested he might be more at home protesting in Greenwich Village. (Barnaby "lost" his second album, *High Cumberland Jubilee*, though they would find it and release it after he became successful.) Instead, he moved to Key West, FL, where he gradually evolved the beach bum character and tropical folk-rock style that would endear him to millions.

Signing to ABC-Dunhill Records (later absorbed by MCA), Buffett achieved notoriety but not much else with his second (released) album, *White Sport Coat & a Pink Crustacean* (1973), which featured a song called, "Why Don't We Get Drunk" (". . . and screw?," goes the chorus). Buffett revealed a more thoughtful side on *Living & Dying in 3/4 Time* (1974), with its song of marital separation "Come Monday," his first singles-chart entry. But it took the Top Ten song "Margaritaville" and the album in which it was featured, *Changes in Latitudes, Changes in Attitudes* (1977), to capture Buffett's tropical worldview and, for a while, turn him into a pop star.

By the start of the '80s, Buffett's yearly albums had stopped going gold, and he briefly tried the country market again. But by the middle of the decade, it was his yearly summer tours that were filling his bank account. As a steadily growing core of Sun Belt fans he dubbed "Parrotheads" made his concerts into Mardi Gras-like affairs. Buffett launched his Margaritaville line of clothes and opened the first of his Margaritaville clubs in Key West. He also turned to fiction writing, landing on the bestseller lists.

His recording career, meanwhile, languished, though a hits compilation sold millions; a 1990 live album, *Feeding Frenzy*, went gold; and a 1992 box-set retrospective, *Boats, Beaches, Bars & Ballads*, became one of the bestselling box sets ever. Buffett finally got around to making a new album in 1994, when *Fruitcakes* became one of his fastest-selling records. It was followed in 1995 by *Barometer Soup* and *Banana Wind* in 1996. —*William Ruhlmann*

Down to Earth / 1970 / Barnaby ✦✦
On his debut album, Buffett lands squarely in the Kris Kristofferson school of thoughtful Nashville singer-songwriters, notably challenging religious zealots and right-wingers in "The Christian?" One of his earliest story songs, "The Captain and the Kid," is also included. —*William Ruhlmann*

A White Sport Coat and a Pink Crustacean / Jun. 1973 / MCA ✦✦✦
Buffett was beginning to put in place his folk/rock/country sound and his laidback, humorous, hedonistic persona with this album, which features later concert favorites like "Why Don't We Get Drunk (and Screw)" and "Grapefruit—Juicy Fruit." —*William Ruhlmann*

Living and Dying in 3/4 Time / Feb. 1974 / MCA ✦✦✦
Jimmy Buffett was already on the second edition of his Coral Reefer Band by the time his third album rolled around. He had also firmly established his Gulf Coast beach-bum/poet persona, but he hadn't written a classic song until "Come Monday," which put him, and the album, on the map. —*William Ruhlmann*

A-1-A / Dec. 1974 / MCA ✦✦✦
A little hardworking for a beachcomber, Buffett released a second album in 1974. It was his most perfect evocation of noncareerist hedonism yet, even if its most telling song, "A Pirate Looks at Forty," was unusually thoughtful for a party animal. —*William Ruhlmann*

Rancho Deluxe / 1975 / United Artists ✦✦✦
This is the soundtrack to a movie written by Buffett's brother-in-law, novelist Thomas McGuane. Buffett appeared in the movie and sang "Livingston Saturday Night" with slightly more risqué lyrics than he would later in his career. —*William Ruhlmann*

High Cumberland Jubilee (1972) / 1976 / Barnaby ✦✦
When Buffett's first album, *Down To Earth*, stiffed, Barnaby let him record this follow-up, then "lost" it. It was finally released after his career started to take off in 1976, but is still a minor effort. —*William Ruhlmann*

Havana Daydreamin' / Jan. 1976 / MCA ✦✦✦✦
Buffett's best overall collection of songs yet bears the influence of Steve Goodman, who wrote "This Hotel Room" and cowrote "Woman Goin' Crazy on Caroline Street." But a personal favorite is Buffett's own "My Head Hurts, My Feet Stink, and I Don't Love Jesus." —*William Ruhlmann*

Changes in Latitudes, Changes in Attitudes / Jan. 1977 / MCA ✦✦✦✦
Buffett's biggest-selling regular release contains his biggest hit single, "Margaritaville." It's also a peak in terms of songwriting, both for the artist himself and in his covers of the work of Steve Goodman and Jesse Winchester, among others. Funny, wistful, and celebratory, the album is the definitive statement of Buffett's worldview. —*William Ruhlmann*

Son of a Son of a Sailor / Mar. 1978 / MCA ✦✦✦✦
If this album was a slight step down from its predecessor, it was almost equally successful commercially, and it contained its share of terrific material, notably the uptempo hit "Cheeseburger in Paradise" and one of Buffett's older songs, "Livingston Saturday Night." —*William Ruhlmann*

You Had to Be There / Oct. 1978 / MCA ✦✦
Buffett has made most of his considerable fortune out of the following he's developed through his concerts, and this double-record live set recorded before an enthusiastic crowd at the Fox in Atlanta serves notice of what's to come. It also serves as a consistent best-of for the artist, most of whose albums are uneven. —*William Ruhlmann*

Volcano / Aug. 1979 / MCA ✦✦
The album that should have consolidated Buffett's status as a major star after his last two hits instead started him down the road to cult status, largely because songs like "Fins" and the title track, which are entertaining enough in concert, aren't really strong material, and they're the best things here. —*William Ruhlmann*

Coconut Telegraph / Feb. 1981 / MCA ✦✦
More Caribbean rhythms and weak jokes—"The Weather Is Here, Wish You Were Beautiful"—plus, in Mac McAnally's "It's My Job," a whiff of the elitism always implied in Buffett's stance. —*William Ruhlmann*

Somewhere over China / Jan. 1982 / MCA ✦✦
Perhaps inevitably, Buffett begins to descend from self-satisfaction to self-pity on tracks like "Where's the Party" and "I Heard I Was in Town." Here and on such tracks as "If I Could Just Get It on Paper," it's apparent that the fast life is losing its charm for the singer. —*William Ruhlmann*

One Particular Harbour / Sep. 1983 / MCA ✦✦
Another collection for the cult, including the humorous "We Are the People Our Parents Warned Us About" and a cover of Van Morrison's "Brown Eyed Girl." —*William Ruhlmann*

Riddles in the Sand / Sep. 1984 / MCA ✦✦
Buffett, who never cared for country music, hires Nashville insider Jimmy Bowen as his producer, goes to Fan Fair, puts on a cowboy hat on his album cover, and scores country hits with cheating songs like "Who's the Blonde Stranger?" Actually, things haven't changed that much; it's just a marketing move. —*William Ruhlmann*

Last Mango in Paris / Jun. 1985 / MCA ✦✦✦
Buffett's rapid recording schedule tended to outrun his muse in the late '70s and early '80s, resulting in some uneven albums with occasional good songs. This time he came up with a far more consistent collection, including three entries on the country charts: "Gypsies in the Palace," "If the Phone Doesn't Ring, It's Me," and "Please Bypass This Heart." —*William Ruhlmann*

● **Songs You Know by Heart** / Oct. 1985 / MCA ✦✦✦✦
If anybody ever needed a compilation, it was Jimmy Buffett, who by this time had put out 14 new studio albums in 15 years but managed to accumulate only a handful of memorable songs among them. And just about all of them are here. Unless you're a Parrothead, this will be all you'll need of Jimmy Buffett. —*William Ruhlmann*

Floridays / Jun. 1986 / MCA ✦✦
If *Mango* suggested a new interest in recording and a new care in songwriting, *Floridays* marked a scuttling of such efforts. The lead-off track, "I Love the Now," was co-written by Buffett and Carrie Fisher, which just goes to show that good novelists don't necessarily write good songs together. —*William Ruhlmann*

Hot Water / Jun. 1988 / MCA ✦✦
The best song is Jesse Winchester's oldie "L'Air de la Louisiane." "Smart Woman (In a Real Short Skirt)" did not restore Buffett to the favor of feminists. And you don't get on the radio by complaining that they don't play your "Homemade Music" because there's something wrong with them. —*William Ruhlmann*

Off to See the Lizard / Jun. 1989 / MCA ✦✦
By this point, record making was starting to become just a small part of Jimmy Buffett, Inc., and this is a piece of musical product, efficiently produced and highly consumable, but not very nourishing. Not surprisingly, Buffett didn't bother to make another studio album for five years. —*William Ruhlmann*

Feeding Frenzy / Oct. 1990 / MCA ✦✦
Buffett's real business is summer touring, and this second live outing was overdue. It also makes a good sampler of his work since his last one, but unfortunately even carefully selected, the later work is inferior to the early work. —*William Ruhlmann*

Boats, Beaches, Bars & Ballads / May 1992 / MCA ✦✦✦✦
This four-disc, 72-track anthology is essential for Parrotheads (Buffett fans) who don't miss his concerts but aren't so hardcore that they have to own every single thing Buffett ever released. Each disc revolves around a theme (Boats, Beaches, Bars, Ballads). All of his hits and popular album tracks are here, as well as some previously unreleased material. The box includes the Parrothead Handbook, a 64-page booklet that provides a well-assembled collection of photos, reflections from Buffett, and explanations of his songs. The sound on this set is first-rate. —*Rick Clark*

Before the Beach / May 25, 1993 / MCA ✦✦
Yet another reissue of Buffett's first two Barnaby albums, this time released on his own record label, on one CD, and minus the controversial "The Christian?" —*William Ruhlmann*

Fruitcakes / May 24, 1994 / MCA ✦✦
On his first new studio album in five years, Buffett starts out talking about an investment banker, an appropriate concern for this sun-bleached entrepreneur. Soon enough, the sprung calypso rhythms kick in, and you can imagine the Parrotheads swaying and chuckling along, especially when Buffett indulges in the kind of comic raps common to his stage shows. He also covers the Grateful Dead's "Uncle John's Band," one more appropriation in his careful observation of that band's marketing plan. There's also a cover of the Kinks' "Sunny Afternoon," a wealthy man's lament, which is uncomfortably on target. But even with half a decade to come up with original material, Buffett hasn't gotten much to add to his usual sun-and-sand philosophy, and for all his millions he remains a pleasant, but distinctly minor, singer-songwriter. —*William Ruhlmann*

Barometer Soup / Aug. 1, 1995 / Margaritaville ✦✦
Having gotten back the record-making habit with *Fruitcakes*, Jimmy Buffett repaired to the Monroe County Library in Key West during the winter of 1994-95 with cohorts Russ Kunkel, Jay Oliver, Roger Guth, and Peter Mayer, where they read fiction and came up with most of the songs on this album. Hence, we have "Remittance Man," drawn from Mark Twain's *Following the Equator*, and "Diamond as Big as the Ritz," loosely adapted from F. Scott Fitzgerald's short story. Typically, there are also the comedy numbers "Bank of Bad Habits" and "Don't Chu-Know" and an appropriation consistent with Buffett's philosophy, James Taylor's "Mexico." Much of the music is low-key, though there are a couple of uptempo tunes to add to the concert repertoire. As Jimmy Buffett albums go, this is another one. —*William Ruhlmann*

Banana Wind / Jun. 1996 / Margaritaville ✦✦✦
Banana Wind is typical latter-day Jimmy Buffett. Over laidback, Caribbean-inflected folk-rock, Buffett waxes eloquent about boats, booze, sun, and women. Although the sound of the album certainly is pleasant, there's not a single distinctive song on the record, which means it's good for Parrotheads, but casual fans should let this *Banana Wind* sail on by. —*Stephen Thomas Erlewine*

The Buggles

f. 1979, England, db. 1980
New Wave
As the answer to the trivia question "What was the first act ever played on MTV?," the Buggles assured their place in pop music history. Vocalist and bassist Trevor Horn and keyboardist Geoff Downes formed the electro-pop duo in England in 1979 after having met two years earlier as session musicians. Their first single, "Video Killed the Radio Star," hit

No. 1 in the UK in late 1979; when MTV went on the air in 1981, the prophetically titled record's video was the first ever broadcast on the fledgling cable network.

Although the Buggles enjoyed three more British hits—"The Plastic Age," "Clean Clean," and "Elstree"—both Horn and Downes were more interested in production than performing. In 1980 they helmed Yes' *Tormato*, and later joined the group as replacements for Rick Wakeman and Jon Anderson. After Yes' break-up, Downes signed on with Asia, while Horn formed ZTT Records and produced hits for the likes of Frankie Goes to Hollywood and ABC. —*Jason Ankeny*

● **The Age of Plastic** / 1980 / Island ✦✦✦✦
A debut techno-pop effort for *Drama* -era Yes members Trevor Horn and Geoff Downes, it includes "Video Killed the Radio Star," which MTV appropriately used to christen its channel. —*Rick Clark*

Adventures In Modern Recording / Feb. 1982 / EMI ✦✦

L.T.J. Bukem

b. 1967, London, England
Jungle/Drum 'N Bass
One of the prime innovators in the jungle/drum 'n' bass movement, L.T.J Bukem gained fame as an auteur in all fields of the genre: as a top-flight breakbeat DJ, producer, owner of his own Good Looking/Looking Good Records and, of course, for his recordings—inspired by elegiac Chicago house and moody Detroit techno, but with his own personally developed rhythms instead of the sampled beats prevalent in jungle. As the style gained momentum and eventually fragmented in the mid-'90s, Bukem became a figurehead for the so-called "intelligent" movement of jungle. Instead of focusing on solo LPs, though, his several full-length releases are DJ mix albums or compilations featuring artists from his label.

Born in London in 1967, Danny Williamson was adopted and raised in Watford by strict Baptist parents, earning his nickname from TV's *Hawaii Five-O* ("Book 'em, Danno"). He left school (and home) at age 16, and spent most of his time listening to rare-groove jazz and soul, Detroit techno, and Chicago house. Bukem made the natural move to DJ status later in the '80s, taking primary inspiration from the dub and hip-hop sets by London sound-system selector Alistair. In 1991 he opened the West End club Speed with fellow DJ Fabio, spinning breakbeat records while MC Conrad added verbal gymnastics over the top. Bukem's debut single "Logical Progression" had appeared the year before, but "Demon's Theme" (1991)—a soulful alternative to the prevalent hardcore darkstep style—marked the debut of his own Good Looking Records. After several releases on the label, the 1993 single "Music" introduced L.T.J Bukem to the general dancefloor public and led to his work during 1993-94 as a producer for Grooverider, Goldie, and a host of Good Looking/Looking Good artists—PFM, ILS & Solo, Seba & Lo-Tec, Tayla, and Funky Technicians.

The jungle phenomenon began to peak as a commercial force in 1995, led by the appearance of Goldie's *Timeless* album. L.T.J Bukem provided the alternative to Goldie's darkstep with his ascendence to the throne of intelligent jungle and an accompanying major-label deal. During early 1996, Bukem released the GL/LG compilation *Higher Limits, Vol. 1* and an excellent contribution to the *Mixmag Live!* series of DJ albums. His first release as part of the major-label deal—with London Records in the UK, FFRR in America—was the July 1996 label retrospective *Logical Progression*. After a subsequent DJ tour of America (his first), Bukem moved in a new direction with the album *Earth, Vol. 1*. A compilation of his catch-all Earth label, it included several drum 'n' bass tracks, but was also inspired by hip-hop (courtesy of Poets of Thought), jazz, and soul. —*John Bush*

● **L.T.J Bukem Presents Logical Progression** / 1996 / Good Looking/London ✦✦✦✦
The best overview of L.T.J Bukem's accomplishments, *Logical Progression* functions three ways: as a Bukem basic-trainer, a retrospective of his Good Looking and Looking Good labels, and as a DJ mix album (though the latter occurs only on disc two). Bukem's most famous recordings ("Demon's Theme," "Music," "Horizons") appear here, as well as the Looking Good anthem "Links" by Chameleon and contributions from PFM, Peshay, Photek and Funky Technicians. Bukem himself mixes disc two, though the relative constraints inherent in the album's nature make the mixing a bit of a disappointment—at least compared to his volume in the *Mixmag Live!* series. Still, the house influences and steady rhythms make *Logical Progression* perhaps the best introduction to jungle for those not used to hyper-speed breakbeats. —*John Bush*

Mixmag Live!, Vol. 3 / 1996 / Moonshine ✦✦✦✦
Unlike his *Logical Progression* compilation, Bukem's volume in the *Mixmag Live!* series enables him to choose tracks apart from his Good Looking/Looking Good stable, and he ends up using only PFM and his own "Music" single from his roster (though GL/LG artists Funky Technicians do appear, recording for another label). To compensate, Bukem mixes in tracks from the mid-'90s new school, including Source Direct's

"Exit 9" and the Photek single "We Can Change the Future" (recorded as Code of Practice). The mixing is a bit more freestyle than on the restricting *Logical Progression*, so enthusiasts who want a true sampling of L.T.J Bukem's DJ skills—rather than an overview of his label's output—should spring for this first. —*John Bush*

Earth, Vol. 1 / 1996 / Earth ✦✦✦✦
LTJ Bukem's second compilation of material from Good Looking and Looking Good Records includes outings from two additional labels, Cookin' and Nexus. Accordingly, *Earth, Vol. 1* features a broad range of material. Paul Hunter's Poets of Thought project contributes much of the variety, including two hip-hop tracks and the Latin soul-jazz flavor of "Samba with JC." Other highlights include the debut of Pablo ("Do What You Gotta Do"), Doc Scott's "Tokyo Dawn," and Bukem's "Moodswings." The only drawback is Bukem's sense of conscious artistic vision; each track is described, analyzed, and given purpose, subverting the impact of the album as a whole. —*John Bush*

Sandy Bull

b. 1941, New York, NY
Guitar / Folk, Folk-Rock
Long before Ry Cooder, Leo Kottke, Richard Thompson, and others were impressing us with their ability to hop from genre to genre, Sandy Bull was gliding from classical and jazz to ethnic music and rock 'n' roll with grace and verve. Accompanied on his first two albums by renowned jazz drummer Billy Higgins, Bull produced some of the first extended instrumental compositions for guitar that incorporated elements of folk, jazz, and Indian and Arabic-influenced dronish modes. Not "rock" by any stretch of the imagination, it's nevertheless easy to see that it could have had an influence on the rock musicians who began incorporating eclectic and Middle Eastern sensibilities into their music a few years later. After his debut, Bull expanded his arsenal from the acoustic guitar and banjo to include oud, bass, and electric guitar. After his second album, however, his recordings were less focused and less impressive. In the 1970s he dropped out of music altogether due to drug problems, although he began recording again in the late '80s. —*Richie Unterberger*

Fantasias for Guitar & Banjo / Aug. 1963 / Vanguard ✦✦✦
Bull's debut is most notable for the side-long cut "Blend," a 22-minute track on a folk (more or less) album in the days when that just wasn't done outside of classical and jazz records. The second side features imaginative interpretations of traditional gospel and Southern mountain tunes, as well as a work by German composer Carl Orff. —*Richie Unterberger*

● **Inventions for Guitar & Banjo** / 1965 / Vanguard ✦✦✦✦
On his second and best album, Bull added more instruments and a bit of electricity. The centerpiece of the record is "Blend II"; like "Blend" from his first album, it is a melange (somewhat more electric in tone) of folk, jazz, and the Middle East, this time 24 minutes' worth. Also included on this 54-minute LP are two versions (electric and acoustic) of a Bach passage, a composition from the 14th century (Guillaume de Machaut's "Triple Ballade"), and Luiz Bonfa's "Manha de Carnival." A heavily reverbed (with drums), extended version of Chuck Berry's "Memphis, Tennessee" closes the set with an unexpected blast of rock 'n' roll. —*Richie Unterberger*

Sonny Burgess

b. 1931, Newport, AR
Guitar / Rockabilly
Sonny Burgess is one of the wildest rockers to record for the legendary Sun label in Memphis. He and his band the Pacers came out of Newport, AR, with a hard-rocking style that, unlike that of most rockabillies, owed little or nothing to country music. With his red-dyed hair, matching stage suit and guitar, and wild stage performances, Burgess and the Pacers made mincemeat of the competition on many of the early-'50s rock 'n' roll package tours. Though his Sun releases never brought him much in the way of commercial success, his recordings nonetheless remain landmarks of the early rockabilly style. Currently touring and recording with other Memphis alumni in the Sun Rhythm Section, the rockin' flame that is Sonny Burgess refuses to be snuffed. —*Cub Koda*

● **We Wanna Boogie** / 1990 / Rounder ✦✦✦✦
If you want a fairly definitive compilation of the Sun material by this minor rockabilly figure, but don't want to go the whole nine yards for the expensive import double CD on Bear Family, this domestic anthology is a recommended alternative. The 13 tracks contain six sides from his '50s singles (including the most noted, "Red Headed Woman" and "My Bucket's Got a Hole in It"), and seven other cuts from the '50s that were unissued at the time. —*Richie Unterberger*

The Classic Recordings 1956-1959 / Jul. 1991 / Bear Family ✦✦✦✦
Sonny's complete output for Sun spread over two CDs. Wild and crazed, featuring Burgess' spitfire guitar and booming vocals and the relentless drive of the Pacers in support. —*Cub Koda*

Sonny Burgess / Jun. 18, 1996 / Rounder ✦✦✦✦
Trying to bring back an old artist from the '50s seldom works, but here is an album that proves it *can* be done and done right. Producer Gary Tallent keeps Burgess focused with the lead vocal and blistering lead guitar duties squarely on his shoulders, gives him a pile of great songs from the likes of Radney Foster, Fred James, Dave Alvin, Steve Forbert, and Springsteen to interpret, then frames it all with a backing band that's the essence of drive and simplicity. The spotlight stays on Burgess throughout, just letting him do what he does best. While it all sounds simple enough, it seldom if ever happens on these kinds of affairs, making the achievement of this record all that more astounding. A modern rockabilly classic, this also features a wonderful guest appearance turn by Scotty Moore and the Jordanaires on Henry Gross' "Bigger than Elvis." The tray card on this reads, "Sonny Burgess has still got it." Believe it. *—Cub Koda*

Solomon Burke

b. 1936, Philadelphia, PA
Vocals / Soul
While Solomon Burke never made a major impact upon the pop audience—he never, in fact, had a Top 20 hit—he was an important early soul pioneer. On his 1960s singles for Atlantic, he brought a country influence into R&B with emotional phrasing and intricately constructed, melodic ballads and mid-tempo songs. At the same time, he was surrounded by sophisticated "uptown" arrangements, and provided with much of his material, by his producers, particularly Bert Berns. The combination of gospel, pop, country, and production polish was basic to the recipe of early soul. While Burke wasn't the only one pursuing this path, not many others did so as successfully. And he, like Otis Redding and Wilson Pickett, was an important influence upon the Rolling Stones, who covered Burke's "Cry to Me" and "Everybody Needs Somebody to Love" on their early albums.

Burke's gospel roots were deeper than those of most soul stars. He was preaching at his family's Philadelphia church and hosting his own gospel radio show even before he'd reached his teens. He began recording gospel and R&B sides for Apollo in the mid- to late '50s. Like several former gospel singers (Aretha Franklin, Wilson Pickett), he was steered in a more secular direction when he signed with Atlantic in the 1960s.

Burke had a wealth of high-charting R&B hits in the early half of the '60s, some of which crossed over to the pop listings. "Just out of Reach," "Cry to Me," "If You Need Me," "Got to Get You off My Mind," "Tonight's the Night," and "Goodbye Baby (Baby Goodbye)" were the most successful of these, although unlike Franklin or Pickett, he wasn't able to expand his R&B base into a huge pop following. He left Atlantic in the late '60s, and spent the next decade hopping between various labels, getting his biggest hit with a cover of Creedence Clearwater Revival's "Proud Mary" in 1969, and recording an album in the late '70s with cult soulster Swamp Dogg as producer.

In the 1980s and 1990s, Burke became one of the most visible living exponents of classic soul music, continuing to tour and record albums in a rootsy, at times gospelish, style. Although these were critically well received, their stylistic purity also ensured that their market was primarily confined to roots music enthusiasts, rather than a pop audience. His live and later recorded work, however, is a favorite of those who want to experience a soul legend with talent and stylistic purity relatively intact. *—Richie Unterberger*

Solomon Burke / 1962 / Kenwood ✦✦✦
The early hits that made Solomon Burke a new force on the soul scene. His quavering delivery, robust sound, and huge presence had both the emphatic earnestness of gospel and the celebratory spirit of soul. Burke strained, roared, sighed, and exploded on his early hits, telling masterful stories and making each song a total experience. *—Ron Wynn*

Lord We Need a Miracle / 1979 / Savoy ✦✦✦
One-time boy preacher Solomon Burke returned to his gospel roots on this earth-shaking date. There's nothing secular about anything here, from the lyrics to Burke's impassioned, heartfelt cries, shouts, and roars. The only problem was that he'd been away from gospel so long that many in the church community didn't take this album seriously. *—Ron Wynn*

Let Your Love Flow / 197 / Shanachie ✦✦✦✦
Jerry Williams (Swamp Dogg) produced an excellent late-'70s soul session for the legendary Solomon Burke on the tiny Infinity records label. Williams mixed upbeat numbers with a pronounced Afro-Latin beat and confessional country/soul tunes emphasizing Burke's trademark song sermons. The music was much too raw and rural for the pseudo-sophisticated big city radio set, but Southern soul loyalists treasured it. Shanachie's CD reissue includes two bonus cuts, and its digital sound displays the strength, clarity, and power of Burke's voice. Shanachie gets high praise for reissuing the album but low marks for the horrendous misspelling of Burke's name all over the CD. *—Ron Wynn*

A Change Is Gonna Come / 1986 / Rounder ✦✦✦✦
While he wasn't scoring chart hits anymore, Burke hadn't lost any of his prowess by the mid-'80s. He cut one of the decade's great soul statements for Rounder in 1985. It's available on CD and should be a revelation for anyone unaware of Burke's singing and performing zeal. His oral narratives were as smashing and memorable as his vocals, and the assembled band included a super three-piece horn section led by alto, tenor, and baritone saxophonist Foots Samuel. This was no nostalgia trip, but a contemporary soul journey that retains its appeal years after its initial release. *—Ron Wynn*

You Can Run But You Can't Hide / 1987 / Mr. R&B ✦✦✦✦
You Can Run But You Can't Hide collects 20 tracks from Burke's formative years at Apollo, recorded between 1955-1959. The material tends to be more pop-oriented than his classic Atlantic sides, but his singing is nearly as impressive as it is on his hits. *—Stephen Thomas Erlewine*

The Bishop Rides South / 1988 / Charly ✦✦✦✦
When Burke left Atlantic, he signed with New York City's Bell Records. Bell wisely sent Solomon down to Muscle Shoals. Two 1969 hits, covers of "Uptight Good Woman" and "Proud Mary," resulted, along with a slew of classic Southern soul covers. *—Rob Bowman*

● **Home in Your Heart** / Apr. 21, 1992 / Rhino ✦✦✦✦
Home in Your Heart—The Best of Solomon Burke is a 41-track two-disc set that covers Burke's Atlantic recordings from 1961 to 1968. Seventeen of those tracks charted. All are superior examples of country-soul and gospel-soul. *—Rob Bowman*

T-Bone Burnett

b. Jan. 18, 1945, St. Louis, MO
Vocals / Singer-Songwriter, Roots-Rock, Folk-Rock
Despite critical acclaim as a performer, the rootsy singer-songwriter T-Bone Burnett earned his greatest renown as a producer, helming recording sessions for acts ranging from Roy Orbison and Elvis Costello to Counting Crows and Sam Phillips. Born John Henry Burnett on January 18, 1945, in St. Louis, MO, he grew up in Fort Worth, TX, soaking up the area's indigenous blend of blues, R&B, and Tex-Mex sounds. Instead of attending college, he opted to open his own Fort Worth recording studio, while also performing in a series of blues bands. In the early 1970s he relocated to Los Angeles, producing sessions for Gene Clark and Delbert McClinton.

After recording his own 1972 debut *The B-52 Band and the Fabulous Skylarks*, Burnett toured with Delaney and Bonnie before helming Bob Neuwirth, a singer-songwriter known for his ties to Bob Dylan. Three years later, Dylan invited Burnett to play guitar on his Rolling Thunder Revue tour, and Burnett's beliefs reportedly influenced Dylan's later conversion to Christianity. After the Revue concluded, Burnett and fellow Rolling Thunder alumni Dave Mansfield and Steve Soles founded the Alpha Band, releasing their eponymous debut in 1977. *Spark in the Dark* followed later that year, and, like its predecessor, failed to find commercial favor. When 1978's *Statue Makers of Hollywood* met a similar fate, the Alpha Band split, and Burnett returned to his solo career.

He resurfaced in 1980 with the acclaimed *Truth Decay*, which, like all of his solo work, found its lyrical center in his spiritual concerns. A move to Warner Bros. followed for 1982's *Trap Door* EP, and 1983's full-length *Proof Through the Night* featured guests Pete Townshend, Ry Cooder, and Richard Thompson. Still, commercial success eluded him, and so he continued working as a producer, overseeing highly regarded records like Los Lobos' *How Will the Wolf Survive?*, Marshall Crenshaw's *Downtown*, and the BoDeans' *Love & Hope & Sex & Dreams*.

After recording a self-titled 1986 solo effort, Burnett agreed to produce *The Turning*, an album for the successful Christian pop singer Leslie Phillips. The album won wide acclaim even from secular outposts, but it was to be Phillips' last overtly religious release. Instead, she began performing under her nickname Sam, and with Burnett's aid landed a deal with the Virgin label for 1987's acclaimed *The Indescribable Wow*. Before recording her 1991 LP *Cruel Inventions*, Phillips and Burnett wed, and he remained in the producer's seat for her later efforts, including 1994's *Martinis and Bikinis* and 1996's *Omnipop*.

Despite his additional success manning albums like Elvis Costello's masterful 1986 effort *King of America*, as well as producing the star-studded 1987 Roy Orbison tribute *A Black and White Night*, Burnett continued his solo career. Like earlier efforts, 1988's *The Talking Animals* won raves from the press but failed to find an audience outside of his devoted cult following. His output dwindled as his production work increased, and only in 1992 did he release a follow-up, the spartan *Criminal in My Own Hat*. Instead, Burnett remained one of the most prolific and distinctive producers of his day, crafting successes like Costello's *Spike*, Counting Crows' *August and Everything After*, the Wallflowers' *Bringing Down the Horse*, and Gillian Welch's *Revival*. The solo *Tooth of Crime* followed in 1997. *—Jason Ankeny*

Truth Decay / 1980 / Takoma ✦✦✦✦
The first album after his stint with the Alpha Band was a great mix of Texas roadhouse R&B/blues-based rock, with hard-folk acoustic instrumental augmentation. Thematically, *Truth Decay* was a refreshing departure from some of the Alpha Band's relentless moralizing. Burnette still took some heavy-handed shots on songs like "Madison Ave" and "House of Mirrors," but the presence of tracks like the gritty rocker "Boomerang," "Talk Talk Talk Talk Talk," and "Love at First Sight" makes this a must-own for lovers of Dylanish rock. —*Rick Clark*

Trap Door [EP] / 1982 / Warner Brothers ✦✦✦
From his clever reading of the Marilyn Monroe standard "Diamonds Are a Girl's Best Friend," to stunning folk-rock originals like "Hold On Tight" and "I Wish You Could Have Seen Her Dance," to the thoughtful closer "Trap Door," this EP is Burnette's most consistently satisfying release. Too bad it wasn't a full-length album. Too bad it's not out yet on CD. —*Rick Clark*

Proof Through the Night / 1983 / Warner Brothers ✦✦✦
Truth Decay and *Trap Door* had earned Burnette loads of critical praise, but this follow-up featured strong performances (by an all-star lineup) and impressive production, although tracks like "Hefner and Disney" and "The Sixties" were smug, overreaching concept pieces (recalling the Alpha Band's later work) that undermined the overall strength of this release. —*Rick Clark*

T-Bone Burnette / 1986 / Dot ✦✦✦
Recorded digitally, straight to two-track, Burnette's self-titled Dot Records release is a heartfelt, low-key affair, featuring flawless country-folk musicianship and a strong collection of originals and covers. Among the highlights are "River of Love," "Shake Yourself Loose," and a version of Tom Waits' "Time." —*Rick Clark*

Talking Animals / 1988 / Columbia ✦✦
● **The Criminal Under My Own Hat** / Jul. 14, 1992 / Columbia ✦✦✦✦
On his first album in four years, Burnette adopts a spare instrumentation dominated by Marc Ribot's angular guitar work to complement a set of close-to-the-bone lyrics that strip love of sentimentality, castigate politicians and evangelists, and, as the album title (echoed in the song "Criminals") attests, do not spare the songwriter himself. The result is a gripping record in the best tradition of Burnette's mentor, Bob Dylan. —*William Ruhlmann*

Johnny Burnette

b. Mar. 28, 1934, Memphis, TN, d. Aug. 1, 1964, Clear Lake, CA
Guitar, Vocals / Rockabilly, Pop-Rock
A contemporary of Elvis Presley in the Memphis scene of the mid-'50s, Burnette played a similar brand of fiery, spare wildman rockabilly. With his brother Dorsey (on bass) and guitarist Paul Burlison forming his Rock 'N Roll Trio, he recorded a clutch of singles for Decca in 1956 and 1957 that achieved nothing more than regional success. Featuring the groundbreaking fuzzy tone of Burlison's guitar, Johnny's energetic vocals, and Dorsey's slapping bass, these recordings—highlighted by the first rock 'n' roll version of "Train Kept a-Rollin'"—compare well to the classic Sun rockabilly of the same era. The trio disbanded in 1957, and Johnny found pop success as a teen idol in the early '60s with hits like "You're Sixteen" and "Dreamin'." Burnette died in a boating accident in 1964. His brother Dorsey achieved modest success as a solo act in the early '60s, and Burlison recently resurfaced as a member of the Sun Rhythm Section. —*Richie Unterberger*

Tear It Up / 1978 / Solid Smoke ✦✦✦✦
Seventeen of their purest rockabilly cuts from their 1956-57 prime. Highlights include "Train Kept a-Rollin'," "Rock Therapy," and "Honey Hush." —*Richie Unterberger*

● **Rockabilly Boogie** / 1989 / Bear Family ✦✦✦✦
All of the Johnny Burnette Trio's primal rockabilly records, including the blazing "Train Kept a-Rollin," are collected on this single-disc compilation. The alternate takes might border on overkill, but the original takes remain powerful years after they were recorded. —*Stephen Thomas Erlewine*

The Best of Johnny Burnette: You're Sixteen / 1992 / Capitol ✦✦✦✦
Burnette's best pop-oriented recordings are featured on this collection, including the classic "You're Sixteen." —*Stephen Thomas Erlewine*

Tony Burrows

Vocals / Pop-Rock, Bubblegum
Though Burrows never had a hit under his own name, he holds the unusual honor (you can look it up in the *Guiness Book of Records*) of having four records in the British Top Ten at once—all under different names. The British session vocalist sang Edison Lighthouse's "Love Grows (Where My Rosemary Goes)," White Plains' "My Baby Loves Lovin'," the Pipkins' ridiculous "Gimme Dat Ding," and the Brotherhood of Man's "United We Stand," all of which were big hits in both the US

and UK in 1970. With his high range and pleasantly anonymous-yet-versatile pipes, Burrows was an ideal tool for songwriters looking to craft bubblegum or light pop-rock for the AM airwaves. They were looking for hit songs, not for hit artists, and what did it matter to most consumers that the "groups" didn't really exist? Burrows continued to lend his voice for hire throughout the '70s, entering the Top Ten again in 1974 with his lead on First Class' Beach Boys tribute, "Beach Baby." —*Richie Unterberger*

● **Love Grows (Where My Rosemary Goes)** / Aug. 27, 1996 / Varese ✦✦✦✦
Not a Tony Burrows album proper, but an 18-song compilation of records that he sang lead on from 1969 through 1985 (mostly from the first half of the 1970s), for Edison Lighthouse, First Class, White Plains, the Brotherhood of Man, the Pipkins, the Flowerpot Men, and others. All the big hits are here ("Love Grows," "Gimme Dat Ding," "My Baby Loves Lovin'," "United We Stand," "Beach Baby"), as well as quite a few misses. It's candy-floss early '70s pop of the most disposable variety, many of the flops being pale Beach Boys imitations. —*Richie Unterberger*

Bush

f. 1992, London, England
Alternative Pop-Rock, Post-Grunge
Led by guitarist/vocalist Gavin Rossdale, Bush became the first post-Nirvana British band to hit it big in America. Of course, they became a hit by playing by the grunge rules; they had loud guitars, guttural vocals, stop-start rhythms, and extreme dynamics. Formed in late 1992 by Rossdale, Bush landed an American record deal before they had a British label. *Sixteen Stone*, their debut album produced by Clive Langer and Alan Winstanley (producers of early-'80s hits by Madness and Elvis Costello, among others), was released in late 1993 by Interscope Records. By the end of December, Bush's "Everything Zen" video had landed in MTV's Buzz Bin, and the album began to take off; by spring of 1995, the record had gone gold, despite a stack of bad reviews. By that time, the band was successful enough in the US to land a British record deal, although they weren't able to match their American success in the UK.

Over the course of 1995, *Sixteen Stone* became a major hit in the US, with "Little Things" reaching No. 4 on the modern rock charts in the spring; later that year "Comedown" and "Glycerine" both reached No. 1 on the modern rock charts, as well as crossing over into the pop Top 40. Despite their success, Bush received scathing reviews from the press and many alternative-rock insiders, who believed the group was manufactured. To counter such charges, the band asked Steve Albini—notorious for his abrasive productions for not only Pixies, Nirvana, and PJ Harvey, but also countless indie bands—to helm their second album. The resulting *Razorblade Suitcase* was released in time for the Christmas season of 1996. It was greeted with mixed reviews that were, nevertheless, more positive than those surrounding *Sixteen Stone*, and the album entered the US charts at No. 1, as well as making inroads headway in the UK. However, by the spring of 1997, the album had stalled somewhat, producing only one major hit in "Swallowed," and reaching only double-platinum status. —*Stephen Thomas Erlewine*

● **Sixteen Stone** / Dec. 5, 1994 / Trauma/Interscope ✦✦✦✦
Bush's grunge-by-the-numbers is certainly well produced. Under the guidance of Clive Langer and Alan Winstanley—the kings of early-'80s British pop—Bush turns in an album that follows all the rules and sounds of American hard rock, specifically Nirvana and Pearl Jam. Their songwriting isn't original, nor is it particularly catchy. What makes "Everything Zen" and "Little Things" memorable is the exact reproduction of all of Nirvana's trademarks, only with a more professional execution; in other words, all the guitars keep rhythm perfectly, and Gavin doesn't shred his throat when he sings, he projects from his diaphragm. As far as pop craftmanship goes, it's actually quite impressive. It would be even more so if they had songs to accompany their sounds. —*Stephen Thomas Erlewine*

Razorblade Suitcase / Nov. 19, 1996 / Trauma/Interscope ✦✦✦
Bush was criticized from most quarters of the music press for sounding too much like Nirvana on their debut album, *Sixteen Stone*, so in order to shed all of the comparisons . . . well, they hired producer Steve Albini (Nirvana, Pixies, PJ Harvey) and proceeded to record their own version of Nirvana's dark, difficult *In Utero*. Actually, *Razorblade Suitcase*, Bush's second album, cribs heavily from two of Albini's best productions, *In Utero* and Pixies' *Surfer Rosa*—they even hired Vaughn Oliver, the designer behind *Surfer Rosa*, to do the artwork. Of course, relying so much on their idols only brings out Bush's weakness. Granted, Albini has helped make the band sound tougher, simply by stripping away the layers of effects and concentrating on a hard, driving rhythm and stopstart dynamics. The problem is Gavin Rossdale has not come up with any hooks, which means while *Razorblade Suitcase* is more pleasing and visceral on the surface, it offers nothing to make it memorable. —*Thomas Erlewine*

Kate Bush

b. Jul. 30, 1958, Bexleyheath, Kent, England
Piano, Keyboards, Vocals / Art-Rock/Progressive-Rock, Pop-Rock
One of the most successful and popular solo female acts to come out of England in the past 20 years, Kate Bush is also one of the most unusual, with her keening vocals and unusually literate and complex body of songs. As a girl, Catherine Bush amused herself playing an organ in the barn behind her parents' house. By the time she was a teenager, Bush was writing songs of her own. A family friend, Ricky Hopper, heard her music and arranged for a demo to be recorded, which brought Bush to the attention of Pink Floyd lead guitarist David Gilmour. By the time Bush was 16, she had signed to EMI Records, though the company made the decision to bring her along slowly. She studied dance, mime, and voice, and continued writing. By 1977 she was ready to enter the recording studio and begin her formal career, which she did with an original song, "Wuthering Heights," based on material from Emily Brontë's novel.

"Wuthering Heights" rose to No. 1 on the British charts. Bush became an overnight sensation and was obligated to turn in an accompanying album in short order. This she did with *The Kick Inside*, a collection of material she had written over the previous three years; the album reached No. 3 and sold over a million copies in the UK.

Bush's second album, *Lionheart*, reached No. 6 but didn't achieve anything like the sales totals or critical acclaim of its predecessor. In England during the spring of 1979, Bush embarked on what proved to be the only concert tour of her career to date, playing a series of shows highlighted by 17 costume changes, lots of dancing, and complex lighting. The tour proved both exhausting and financially disastrous, and Bush has avoided any but the most limited live concert appearances since, primarily in support of certain charitable causes.

By this time Bush was established as one of the most challenging and eccentric artists ever to have achieved success in rock music, with a range of sounds and interests that constantly challenged listeners. "Babooshka" (1980) became her first Top Five single since "Wuthering Heights," and her subsequent album *Never for Ever* entered the British charts at No. 1 in September 1980. During this period, Bush began co-producing her own work, a decisive step toward refining her sound and establishing her independence from her record company. Although 1982's *The Dreaming* reached No. 3, the single "There Goes a Tenner" failed to reach the charts, and most observers felt that Bush had lost her audience. Bush was unfazed by the criticism, and began taking steps to make herself even more independent of her record company by establishing a home studio.

After two years' absence, Bush re-emerged in August 1985 with "Running Up That Hill," which reached No. 3 on the English charts and became her second biggest-selling single. The accompanying album, *Hounds of Love*, the first record made in her 48-track home studio, debuted on the British charts at No. 1 in September 1985 and remained there for a full month. Soon after, "Running Up That Hill" gave Bush her long-awaited American breakthrough, reaching No. 30 on *Billboard's* charts. The changes in her sound and her development as a writer/performer were showcased in the January 1987 best-of collection *The Whole Story*. That same year, Bush won the Best British Female Artist award at the sixth annual BRIT Awards in London. In October 1989, Bush's first new album in almost four years, *The Sensual World*, reached the British No. 2 spot. Bush's next album, *The Red Shoes* (1993), debuted in the American Top 30, the first time one of her albums had ever charted that high. *—Bruce Eder*

The Kick Inside / 1978 / EMI America ✦✦✦✦
Bush's first album is her most unabashedly romantic, the sound of an impressionable and highly precocious teenage singer-songwriter spreading her wings for the first time. "Wuthering Heights" was a monster hit everywhere in the world except America, and it's still an impressive debut nearly 20 years later, but Bush would do better work than this. *—Bruce Eder*

Lionheart / 1978 / EMI America ✦✦✦
Bush's second album was something of a disappointment, lacking the depth and certainty of direction of her debut. The title track is an enigmatic paean to her mother country, and "Wow" is a strong vocal workout but somewhat on the obscure side, and the rest is enjoyable and teasing but nowhere near what Bush is capable of. *—Bruce Eder*

Never for Ever / 1980 / EMI America ✦✦✦
Kate Bush returned to form on her third album, which is steeped in images of violence and anger ("Babooshka," "The Wedding List") but also includes fascinating references to classical music ("Delius"). Very finely produced as well. *—Bruce Eder*

The Dreaming / 1982 / EMI America ✦✦
Bush's most daring album is regarded as a failure by most fans, steeped as it is in mystical imagery. On a production level, the album is beauti-

fully made, but the songwriting is accessible to only a relatively small circle of listeners. *—Bruce Eder*

Hounds of Love / 1985 / EMI America ✦✦✦✦
Bush's strongest album to date marked her breakthrough into the American charts and yielded a set of dazzling videos. The material ranges from the sensual ("Hounds of Love," "Running up That Hill"—the latter one of the most sensual recordings ever made) to the mystical ("Hello Earth," "The Morning Fog"). This was also the first album produced by Bush entirely at her own home studio, and the results are spellbinding, the layered instruments recalling the Beatles at the most ornate, but also displaying an exquisite timbral range, bringing out the richness of the individual instruments. Note: The British edition of this and Bush's earlier albums all have significantly better sound than their American editions and are worth finding as imports. [In 1997, as a part of EMI's 100th Anniversary, *Hounds of Love* was reissued, augmented with rare singles, B-sides, outtakes etc. from the same period.] *—Bruce Eder*

● The Whole Story / 1986 / EMI America ✦✦✦✦
Bush's first best-of is an excellent compilation/overview, encompassing all her best-known songs (including "Wuthering Heights" with an improved, re-recorded vocal track) up through the major tracks off *Hounds of Love* and her follow-up single, the haunting and dramatic "Experiment IV." *—Bruce Eder*

The Sensual World / Oct. 1989 / Columbia ✦✦✦✦
The follow-up to *Hounds of Love* is almost its match, a collection of material devoted to Bush's perceptions of love and sensuality. The best track, however, is "This Woman's Work," from a now-forgotten feature film, a beautiful and poignant look at the female psyche at its most gentle and giving. *—Bruce Eder*

This Woman's Work (1978-1990) / 1990 / EMI ✦✦✦✦
Excellent box collecting all of Bush's work, including obscure B-sides, odd mixes, and other rarities in one place. The notes are skimpy, and some people who already own some of her individual CDs will be unhappy having to duplicate their purchases, but the rarities are fascinating, and because this set is from England, it uses the superior British masters on the 1978-1985 albums. (British import) *—Bruce Eder*

The Red Shoes / Nov. 2, 1993 / Columbia ✦✦
Something of a step backward for Bush, with not much new ground covered. The beat throughout is pretty strong and catchy, her voice is in excellent form, and if one can ignore an obvious lift from the Spinners ("Rubberband Girl"), the record is enjoyable, although the title song is a little obscure. *—Bruce Eder*

Billy Butler

b. Jun. 7, 1945, Philadelphia, PA
Vocals / Soul
The younger brother of Jerry Butler, Billy Butler wasn't nearly as well known as his sibling, but he recorded some fine Chicago soul in the 1960s. Recording for OKeh under producer Carl Davis, Butler's mid-'60s singles were quite similar to labelmates Major Lance's and (less obviously) Curtis Mayfield's as stellar examples of the finest features of the Chicago soul sound. Similar to Motown in its full, brassy production, the Chicago brand was earthier, with stronger tinges of gospel, doo wop, and Latin influences. Nor was Butler terribly similar to his brother Jerry, with a punchier, more uptempo sound. With the backing group the Enchanters, Billy recorded consistently fine singles for OKeh from 1963 to 1966, scoring R&B hits with "I Can't Work No Longer" (1965) and "Right Track" (1966). Butler left OKeh after 1966 and recorded for a variety of labels, denting the R&B charts with the singles "Get on the Chase" (1969) and "Free Yourself" (1971). A songwriter of note, he contributed material to fellow Chi-town soul greats Major Lance, Gene Chandler, and his brother Jerry. *—Richie Unterberger*

● Right Track / 1985 / Edsel ✦✦✦✦
Sixteen of the sides Butler cut for the OKeh label from 1963 to 1966; most of them were written by himself or Curtis Mayfield. While not quite in the same league as Mayfield, this is near-classic soul: strong material, production, and backup harmonies on this mix of uptempo numbers and ballads, paced by Butler's fluid vocals. *—Richie Unterberger*

Jerry Butler

b. Dec. 8, 1939, Sunflower, MS
Vocals / Soul, R&B
It would be safer to talk about Jerry Butler's careers than about his career. Up from Mississippi, he joined Curtis Mayfield in the Impressions around 1957. They began recording the following year and broke through with *For Your Precious Love*, touted by some as the first soul record. Inevitably, he went solo and fell—or was pushed—into the pop mainstream. Reunited with Mayfield (the latter as a writer), Butler announced his return with *He Will Break Your Heart* in 1960. His subse-

quent recordings for Vee-Jay trod the turf where pop and R&B meet; the best are excellent.

After Vee-Jay went broke in 1966, Butler signed with Mercury and was soon placed with the team of Gamble and Huff, who produced him in Philadelphia. Jerry Butler's mellow baritone and the sweet Philly sound were a winning combination, as attested by pop and R&B hits like "Only the Strong Survive" and "Hey, Western Union Man." After the Gamble and Huff deal dissolved in 1970, Butler's career went slowly downhill. Deals with Motown and even Gamble and Huff's Philadelphia International label couldn't deliver the goods. There's something for everyone in Butler's prolificacy, but unfortunately little of it is available to sample.

Jerry Butler has made musical and political noise during the '80s and '90s. He won election to Cook County's board of supervisors in the late '80s. Butler also issued recordings on his own Fountain label, but they were hampered by poor distribution. He recorded *Time & Faith* for Urgent, a label distributed by Ichiban, in 1992. Butler has retained his soothing, dynamic sound and ability to sound simultaneously cool and soulful, even if his voice has lost some range and sheen. Mercury released *Iceman: The Mercury Years Anthology* in 1992, the definitive collection of his Polygram tracks, and his earlier work for Vee Jay has also been reissued. Rhino released *The Best of Jerry Butler, 1958-1969* in 1987. —*Colin Escott*

★ **The Best of Jerry Butler [Rhino]** / 1987 / Rhino ✦✦✦✦✦
The primary value of this 14-song collection is that it includes material from both the Vee-Jay and Mercury eras. Butler fans are much better advised to get the compilations that cover his output for each label in much greater depth (*The Ice Man* for Vee-Jay, *Iceman: The Mercury Years* for Mercury). For the casual fan, though, it might be the best buy, as it's the only best-of spanning both labels, and includes all of his biggest hits. —*Richie Unterberger*

Ice Man / 1992 / Vee-Jay ✦✦✦✦
Featuring 25 of his Vee-Jay singles, including three hits with the Impressions, *The Ice Man* is the best retrospective of Butler's early years available. —*Stephen Thomas Erlewine*

☆ **Iceman: The Mercury Years** / Feb. 4, 1992 / PolyGram ✦✦✦✦✦
A glorious 44-song double-disc set, it collects Butler's best Mercury sides, with several previously unreleased songs and alternate mixes. The liner notes are crummy, though. —*John Floyd*

Paul Butterfield

b. Dec. 17, 1942, Chicago, IL, **d.** May 4, 1987, Hollywood, CA
Flute, Guitar, Harmonica, Vocals / Electric Chicago Blues, Blues-Rock
Butterfield grew up in Chicago's Hyde Park, and according to his brother Peter, "There was a lot of music around Hyde Park, a place unique in Chicago because it was an island in the Southside ghetto, and a bastion of liberal politics. When we grew up there was a crime problem—mostly due to scattered groups of Puerto Ricans and poor white trash—but no one made a connection to the Black community as a source of crime. We grew up about half a block from something called the International Houses, and you would see people from all over the world in the immediate area. "

Butterfield was culturally sophisticated. His father was a well known attorney in the Hyde Park area, and his mother was a painter. Butterfield took flute lessons from an early age, and by the time he reached high school, was studying with the first-chair flautist of the Chicago Symphony. He was exposed to both classical music and jazz from an early age. Butterfield ran track in high school and was offered a running scholarship to Brown University, which he had to refuse after a serious knee injury. From that point onward, he turned toward the music scene around him. He began learning the guitar and harmonica.

He met singer Nick Gravenites and started hanging around outside Chicago blues clubs, listening. He and Gravenites began to play together at various campuses—Ann Arbor, University of Wisconsin, and the University of Chicago. His parents sent him off to the University of Illinois, but he would put in a short academic week, return home early (but not check in), and play and hang out at the blues clubs. Soon, he was doing this six or seven days a week, with no school at all. When this was discovered by his parents, he dropped out of college and turned to music full time.

Butterfield practiced long hours by himself—just playing all the time. His brother Peter writes, "He listened to records, and he went places, but he also spent an awful lot of time, by himself, playing. He'd play outdoors. There's a place called The Point in Hyde Park, a promontory of land that sticks out into Lake Michigan, and I can remember him out there for hours playing. He was just playing all the time. . . . It was a very solitary effort. It was all internal, like he had a particular sound he wanted to get and he just worked to get it. "

In the meantime, Elvin Bishop had come from Oklahoma to the University of Illinois on a scholarship and had discovered the various blues venues for himself. Elvin remembers, "One day I was walking around

the neighborhood and I saw a guy sitting on a porch drinking a quart of beer—white people that were interested in blues were very few and far between at that time. But this guy was singing some blues and singing it good. It was Butterfield. We gravitated together real quick and started playing parties around the neighborhood, you know, just acoustic. He was playing more guitar than harp when I first met him. But in about six months, he became serious about the harp. And he seemed to get about as good as he ever got in that six months. He was just a natural genius. And this was in 1960 or 1961."

Butterfield and Bishop began going down to the clubs, sitting in, and playing with all the great Black blues players—then in their prime. Players like Otis Rush, Magic Sam, Howlin' Wolf, Junior Wells, Little Walter, and especially Muddy Waters. They often were the only whites there, but they were soon accepted because of their sincerity, their sheer ability, and the protection of players like Muddy Waters, who befriended them.

An important event in the history of introducing blues to white America came in 1963 when Big John's, a club located on Chicago's White North Side, invited Butterfield to bring his band there and play on a regular basis. He said "Sure," and Butterfield and Bishop set about putting such a band together. They pulled Jerome Arnold (bass) and Sam Lay (drums) from Howlin' Wolf's band (with whom they had worked for the past six years!), by offering them more money. Butterfield and Bishop (the core team), Arnold, and Lay were all about the same age, and these four became the Butterfield Blues Band. They had been around for a long time and knew the Chicago blues scene and its repertoire cold. This new racially mixed band opened at Big John's, was very successful, and made a first great step to opening up the blues scene to white America.

When the new group thought about making an album, they looked around for a lead guitarist. Michael Bloomfield, who was known to Butterfield from his appearances at Big John's, joined the band early in 1965. Bloomfield, somewhat cool at first to Butterfield's commanding manner, warmed to the group as Butterfield warmed to his guitar playing. It took a while for Bloomfield to fit in, but by the summer of that year, the band was cookin'. Mark Naftalin, another music student, joined the band while they were actually in the studio creating that first album on Elektra. He sat in (playing the Hammond organ for the first time!), and Butterfield liked the sound. Naftalin recorded eight of the 11 tracks on the first album during that first session. After the session, Butterfield invited Naftalin to join the band and go on the road with them. These six, then, became the Paul Butterfield Blues Band.

The first two Butterfield Blues albums are essential from a historical perspective. While *East-West*, the second album, with its Eastern influence and extended solos (See: Michael Bloomfield) set the tone for psychedelic rockers, it was that incredible first album that alerted the music scene to what was coming.

Although it has been perhaps over-emphasized in recent years, it is important to point out that the release of *The Paul Butterfield Blues Band* on Elektra in 1965 had a huge effect on the white music culture of the time. that first album had an enormous impact on young (and primarily white) rock players, who were used to hearing blues covered by groups like the Rolling Stones. Here is no deferential imitation of Black music by whites, but a racially mixed, hard-driving blues album that, in a word, rocked. It was a signal to white players to stop making respectful tributes to Black music, and just play it. In a flash the image of blues as old-time music was gone. Modern Chicago style urban blues was out of the closet and introduced to mainstream white audiences, who loved it. The Butterfield band appeared at the Newport Folk Festival late in 1965 to rave reviews.

Perhaps the next major event in the Butterfield band came when drummer Sam Lay became ill late in 1965. Jazz drummer Billy Davenport was called in and soon became a permanent member of the group. Davenport was to become a key element in the development of the second Butterfield Blues Band album, *East-West* (See: Mark Naftalin.)

Fueled by Bloomfield's infatuation with Eastern music and Indian ragas at the time and aided by Davenport's jazz-driven sophistication on drums, there arose in the group a new music form that was to greatly affect rock music—the extended solo. There is little question that here is the root of psychedelic (acid) rock—a genuine fusion between East and West.

Those first two albums served as a wakeup call to an entire generation of white would-be blues musicians. Speaking as one who was on the scene, that first Butterfield album stopped us in our tracks, and we were never the same afterward. It changed our lives.

The third album (released in 1967), *The Butterfield Blues Band: The Resurrection of Pigboy Crabshaw* is the last album that preserves any of the pure blues direction of the original group. By this time, Bloomfield had left to create his own group, the Electric Flag, and, with the addition of a horn section (including a young David Sandborn), the band was drifting more toward an R&B sound. Mark Naftalin left the group soon after this album, and the Butterfield band took other forms.

Later Butterfield material somehow misses the mark. He never lost his ferocity or integrity, but the synergy of that first group was special. There has been some discussion in the literature about the personal transformation of Butterfield as his various bands developed. It is said that he went from being a self-centered bandleader (shouting orders to his crew à la Howlin' Wolf) to a more democratic style of leadership, providing his group with musical freedom (like Muddy Waters). For what it's worth, it is clear that the best music is in those first two (maybe three) albums. Subsequent albums, although also interesting, have not gotten as much attention from reviewers.

When I knew Butterfield (during the first three albums), he was always intense, somewhat remote, and even, on occasion, downright unfriendly. Although not much interested in other people, he was a compelling musician and a great harp player. Bloomfield and Naftalin, also great players, were just the opposite—always interested in the other guy. They went out of their way to inquire about you, even if you were a nobody. Naftalin, well known around the San Francisco Bay Area, continues to this day to support blues projects and festivals (Marin County Blues Festival, etc.) in the San Francisco Bay area.

After Bloomfield and Naftalin left the group, Butterfield spun off on his own more and more. The next two albums, *In My Own Dream* (1968) and *Keep On Moving* (1969) moved still farther away from the blues roots until in 1972, Butterfield dissolved the group, forming the group Better Days. This new group recorded two albums, *Paul Butterfield's Better Days* and *It All Comes Back*. After that, Butterfield faded into the general rock scene, with an occasional appearance here and there, as in the documentary *The Last Waltz* (1976)—a farewell concert from the Band. The albums *Put It in Your Ear* (1976) and *North South* (1981) were attempts to make a comeback, but both failed. Paul Butterfield died of drug-related heart failure in 1987.

Even to this day, Butterfield remains one of the only white harmonica players to develop his own style (another is William Clarke)—one respected by Black players. Butterfield has no real imitators. Like most Chicago-style amplified harmonica players, Butterfield played the instrument like a horn—a trumpet. Although he sometimes used a chromatic harmonica, Butterfield mostly played the standard Hohner Marine Band in the standard cross position. Remember, he was left-handed and held the harp in his left hand, but in the standard position with the low notes facing to the left. He tended to play single notes rather than bursts of chords. His harp playing is always intense, understated, concise, and serious; only Big Walter Horton has a better sense of note selection.

The effect of the Butterfield Blues Band on aspiring white blues musicians was enormous, and the impact of the band on live audiences was stunning. Butterfield the performer was always intense, serious, and definitive—no doubt about this guy. Blues purists sometimes like to quibble about Butterfield's voice and singing style, but the moment he picked up a harmonica, that was it. He is one of the finest harp players (period).

Butterfield and the six members of the original Paul Butterfield Blues Band made a huge contribution to modern music, turning a whole generation of white music lovers onto the blues as something other than a quaint piece of music history. The musical repercussions of the second Butterfield album, *East-West*, continue to echo through the music scene even today! (See: Michael Bloomfield, Mark Naftalin.)

We would like to thank *Blues Access* magazine for permission to use the quotes by Peter Butterfield and Elvin Bishop from the excellent article by Tom Ellis. —*Michael Erlewine*

☆ **Paul Butterfield Blues Band** / 1965 / Elektra ◆◆◆◆◆
Butterfield's unique amplified harmonica style is already present on this classic first album—a wakeup call for a generation of young white players used to hearing blues filtered through covers by groups like the Rolling Stones or as a part of music history. Here was a racially mixed group of brilliant young players that rocked—an historic album. Great guitar from Michael Bloomfield and Elvin Bishop. With Mark Naftalin (organ), Jerome Arnold (bass), and Sam Lay (drums). —*Michael Erlewine*

★ **East-West** / 1966 / Elektra ◆◆◆◆◆
The second Butterfield album had an even greater effect on music history, paving the way for experimentation that is still being explored today. This came in the form of an extended blues-rock solo (some 13 minutes)—a real fusion of jazz and blues inspired by the Indian raga. This ground-breaking instrumental was the first of its kind and marks the root from which the acid rock tradition emerged. —*Jeff Tarmarkin and Michael Erlewine*

The Resurrection of Pigboy Crabshaw / 1968 / Elektra ◆◆◆◆
In his third album, Butterfield adds a horn section and the direction of the group has started to veer away from straight Chicago-style blues toward a sound more influenced by R&B. By this time, Bloomfield has left the group and Elvin Bishop (aka Pigboy Crabshaw) takes over on

lead guitar. A lot of great tunes here, like "Driftin' and Driftin'." —*Michael Erlewine*

Offer You Can't Refuse / 1972 / Red Lightnin' ◆◆◆
An album released on the Red Lightnin' label in 1972 consisting of one side of Big Walter Horton and the other side with very early Paul Butterfield (1963) (See: Big Walter Horton). Contains six tracks with Butterfield, Smokey Smothers on guitar, Jerome Arnold on bass, and Sam Lay on drums. This was recorded at Big John's, the North Side Chicago club where the Butterfield Band first played in 1963—some two years before the material on the first Paul Butterfield Blues Band album, which was released in 1965. The six tracks include two instrumentals, "Got My Mojo Working" and the Butterfield-authored tune "Loaded." Although this is very early Butterfield, the harp playing is excellent and already in his own unique style. The singing is a little rough and heavy sounding. Butterfield fans will want to find this rare vinyl for musical and historical reasons. —*Michael Erlewine*

The Original Lost Elektra Sessions / Jul. 18, 1995 / Rhino ◆◆◆◆
All but one of these 19 tracks were recorded in December 1964 as Butterfield's projected first LP; the results were scrapped and replaced by their official self-titled debut, cut a few months later. With both Bloomfield and Bishop already in tow, these sessions rank among the earliest blues-rock ever laid down. Extremely similar in feel to the first album, it's perhaps a bit rawer in production and performance, but not appreciably worse or different than what ended up on the actual debut LP. Dedicated primarily to electric Chicago blues standards, this is well worth acquiring for Butterfield fans, as most of the selections were never officially recorded by the first lineup (although different renditions of five tracks showed up on the first album and the *What's Shakin'* compilation). —*Richie Unterberger*

Strawberry Jam / 1996 / Winner ◆◆◆
These nine cuts are from various live performances of the Paul Butterfield Blues Band during their heyday in the middle-to-late '60s. This album was put together by Mark Naftalin, who played keyboards on those first few incredible Butterfield albums. Don't look for the clearest sound (it's adequate) because these are live tunes recorded at clubs, often with minimal equipment. It is the music that is in focus here—a window into that incredible band at a time when they were hot. Those of us who were on the scene at the time know that, although the original Butterfield albums are great, the band was a total knockout when heard live. Featuring Butterfield's harmonica, here are glimpses into that time and music. Most of the tunes have appeared elsewhere, but the extended instrumental "Strawberry Jam" (written by Naftalin) is unique to this album—worth hearing. It features great guitar by Elvin Bishop. —*Michael Erlewine*

East-West Live / Sep. 1996 / Winner ◆◆◆◆
The tune "East-West" from the second Butterfield Blues Band album of the same name made music history. It is arguably the first extended rock solo, a fusing of blues-rock with Eastern scales and tone. Here is the root of psychedelic acid rock. Now, thanks to Mark Naftalin (the original Butterfield keyboardist), we have three live recordings of "East-West" recorded in 1966-1967 that capture the origin and development of this classic tune. The first example (some 12 minutes) was taped prior to the edited studio version; the second (16 minutes) and third (28 minutes) were recorded after the album was cut. There is some great music (and music history) here. —*Michael Erlewine*

The Butthole Surfers

f. 1982, San Antonio, TX
Alternative Pop-Rock, Experimental, Indie-Rock
Arguably the most infamously named band in the annals of popular music—for years, radio found their moniker unspeakable, and the press deemed it unprintable—the Butthole Surfers long reigned among the most twisted and depraved acts ever to bubble up from the American underground. Masters of calculated outrage, the group fused the sicko antics of shock-rock with a distinct and chaotic mishmash of avant-garde, hardcore, and Texas psychedelia. Sleazy, confrontational, and spiteful songs like "The Revenge of Anus Presley," "Bar-B-Q Pope," and "The Shah Sleeps in Lee Harvey Oswald's Grave" seemed destined to guarantee the Buttholes little more than a lifetime of cultdom. Yet by the mid-1990s, they were left-field Top 40 hitmakers, success perhaps their ultimate subversion of mainstream ideals.

The seeds of their formation dated to 1977, when future frontman Gibby Haynes, the son of the Dallas-based children's TV host known as "Mr. Peppermint," met guitarist Paul Leary while attending college in San Antonio. Four years later, Haynes—then completing his graduate work in accounting—and Leary formed the Ashtray Baby Heads, later dubbed Nine Foot Worm Makes Home Food. They became the Butthole Surfers only after a radio announcer mistakenly took the title of an early song to be the group's name. In 1981 they signed to Dead Kennedys frontman Jello Biafra's label Alternative Tentacles, and two years later issued their hallucinatory eponymous debut, also issued on colored vinyl under the name *Brown Reason to Live.*

After a succession of bassists and drummers, the Surfers' lineup stabilized with the 1983 addition of drummers King Coffey (formerly of the Hugh Beaumont Experience) and Theresa Nervosa; at the same time, their bizarre live gigs—a traveling freak show combining nude dancers, film clips of sex-change operations, and Haynes' pyromaniacal behavior—began to win a devout cult following. In 1984 they issued the concert set *Live PCPPEP.* A move to the Chicago-based indie Touch and Go precipitated a turn toward even greater thematic offensiveness, as evidenced by tracks like "Concubine" and "Lady Sniff" from 1985's *Psychic... Powerless... Another Man's Sac.*

After the EP *Cream Corn from the Socket of Davis,* the Buttholes resurfaced in 1986 with *Rembrandt Pussyhorse,* a twisted trip into neopsychedelia featuring a brutal deconstruction of the Guess Who's "American Woman," as well as new bassist Jeff "Tooter" Pinkus. The introduction of Haynes' "Gibbytronix" vocal effects unit increased the level of dementia for 1987's *Locust Abortion Technician,* an extremist fusion of punk, metal, art-rock, and worldbeat rhythms. Following 1988's faux-Zeppelin rant *Hairway to Steven,* the group issued *Double Live,* a mock bootleg released through their own Latino Bugger Veil imprint. After a pair of EPs, 1989's *Widowermaker!* and 1990's *The Hurdy-Gurdy Man,* they remained uncharacteristically silent until 1991's uneven *Pioughd,* recorded for the Rough Trade label.

For many observers, the biggest shock in a career built on outrageous behavior arrived in 1992, when the Buttholes signed with major label Capitol, which promptly reissued *Pioughd,* after the demise of Rough Trade. After entering the studio with producer and former Led Zep bassist John Paul Jones, they emerged in 1993 with the LP *Independent Worm Saloon;* the first single and video "Who Was in My Room Last Night?" both garnered a surprising amount of airplay, much to the chagrin of the many media outlets that begrudgingly referred to the group as the "BH Surfers." After a series of side projects—most notoriously Haynes' group P, which also featured movie star Johnny Depp—the band (now a trio consisting of Haynes, Leary, and Coffey) returned in 1996 with *Electriclarryland,* scoring a major chart hit with the trip-hop-flavored "Pepper." —*Jason Ankeny*

Butthole Surfers / 1983 / Alternative Tentacles ✦✦✦✦
The Buttholes' punks-on-acid debut mini-LP owes as much to Captain Beefheart and rockabilly as it does to hardcore punk and thrash, setting Gibby Haynes' processed vocals against a backdrop of skewed, sludgy noise-riffing. Yet at the same time, the songs display a surprisingly melodic, structured sensibility, which draws the listener into the band's decidedly not fake dementia. Contains such necessary items as "The Shah Sleeps in Lee Harvey's Grave," "The Revenge of Anus Presley," and "Bar-B-Q Pope." —*Steve Huey*

Live PCPPEP / 1984 / Alternative Tentacles ✦✦✦
This EP offers grungy live versions of material from the group's debut. A loud, frightening assault on the ears highlighted by Paul Leary's guitar work, even if these songs don't quite duplicate the insanity of the originals. —*Steve Huey*

Psychic... Powerless... Another Man's Sac / 1985 / Touch & Go ✦✦✦✦
On their first full-length album, the Butthole Surfers begin to fuse their art-punk, heavy metal, and rockabilly influences into their own twisted, often disgusting vision. The metal-meets-Texas boogie of "Lady Sniff," for example, is enlivened by various bodily-function sound effects (vomiting, belching, coughing up phlegm, etc.). Possibly the Buttholes' most vulgar album (and that says something), the CD version also contains the follow-up EP, *Cream Corn from the Socket of Davis.* —*Steve Huey*

Cream Corn from the Socket of Davis / 1985 / Touch & Go ✦✦✦
This EP follows in much the same vein as *Another Man's Sac,* so it's only fitting that the two were combined on one CD reissue. *Cream Corn* sees Paul Leary beginning to use electronic effects to shape his noisy guitar racket. "Moving to Florida" is the immediately obvious highlight. —*Steve Huey*

Rembrandt Pussyhorse / 1986 / Touch & Go ✦✦✦✦
The Butthole Surfers begin to experiment with psychedelia and expanded instrumentation, adding piano, organ, and violin, plus a variety of guitar effects and tape manipulation techniques. *Rembrandt Pussyhorse* illustrates their arty side better than their previous releases, and contains a bizarre, deconstructed version of the Guess Who's "American Woman." Psychedelia never sounded quite like this. —*Steve Huey*

● **Locust Abortion Technician** / 1987 / Touch & Go ✦✦✦✦
The aural equivalent of a nightmarish acid trip and arguably the band's best album (or worst, depending on your point of view), *Locust Abortion Technician* tops the psychedelic, artsy sonic experimentation of *Rembrandt Pussyhorse* while keeping one foot planted firmly in the gutter. The record veers from heavy Sabbath sludge (even parodying that band on "Sweat Loaf") to grungy noise-rock to progressive guitar and tape effects to almost folky numbers in one big, gloriously schizo-

phrenic mess. Gibby Haynes debuts his "Gibbytronix" vocal effects unit here as well. —*Steve Huey*

Hairway to Steven / 1988 / Touch & Go ✦✦✦✦
One of the band's more accessible recordings, relatively speaking, *Hairway to Steven* is inspired by the sounds of the 1960s while simultaneously subverting and twisting them into a vision uniquely the band's own, utilizing acoustic guitars and Jimi Hendrix-influenced guitar psychedelia, as well as the Buttholes' now-trademark vocal and tape effects, featuring found sounds like tweeting birds and dubbed-in crowd noises. *Hairway* also contains a surprising amount of melody and songcraft, as well as some of Paul Leary's best guitar playing. Note: the album's all-untitled songs are identified only by pictures on the jacket. —*Steve Huey*

Double Live / 1989 / Touch & Go ✦✦
Essentially a self-released bootleg, *Double Live* is a mammoth collection of 29 songs (on the CD version) featuring a cover of R.E.M.'s "The One I Love." Unfortunately, the band can't quite duplicate its manic studio sound onstage, given their reliance on tape manipulation and effects, but the album still gets crazy in places. —*Steve Huey*

Widowermaker! [EP] / 1989 / Touch & Go ✦✦✦
A four-song EP of typical Butthole sound effects, gross humor, and insanity. —*Steve Huey*

Pioughd / 1991 / Capitol ✦✦
Pioughd was the Buttholes' first album of original material in three years, and considering the time it took to make the record, it's a bit of a disappointment. Not that it's bad; in fact, some of it is their best. But it's rather uninspired and restates many of their old ideas in a more streamlined, accessible fashion. —*Stephen Thomas Erlewine*

Independent Worm Saloon / Mar. 23, 1993 / Capitol ✦✦✦
Something has definitely changed in the music industry when the Butthole Surfers are recording for a major label, with none other than Led Zeppelin's John Paul Jones producing. And they still haven't sold out. *Independent Worm Saloon* follows the course of their past few albums—a hard '70s punk-metal bottom with lots of avant-noise noodlings and wacked-out vocals on top. The safest it gets is the heavy riff-rocker "Who Was in My Room Last Night?" (which MTV aired during the daytime); the Buttholes still include gross-outs like the heaves that begin "Clean It Up" or "The Annoying Song," which is exactly what it says it is. *Independent Worm Saloon* may run a bit long, but the times that the Butthole Surfers' shock-rock hits the mark excuse most of the indulgences. —*Stephen Thomas Erlewine*

Hole Truth... And Nothing Butt / Mar. 27, 1995 / Trance Syndicate ✦✦✦
A neo-bootleg collection of live performances, singles and rare tracks, *The Hole Truth... And Nothing Butt* isn't quite aimed at neophytes, since most of this material would appeal to collectors. Nevertheless, the album offers a fairly effective overview of the shock-punks and isn't a bad way to get acquainted with their catalog. —*Stephen Thomas Erlewine*

Electriclarryland / May 1996 / Capitol ✦✦✦
On *Electriclarryland,* their second major-label album, the Butthole Surfers continue the streamlined direction they began with *Independent Worm Saloon,* which basically means it's a loud guitar rock album. Even though there's potential for the record to become unnecessarily generic, it's to the Buttholes' credit that they still have the desire to throw enough bizarre wrenches into the machinery to keep most of their diehard audience satiated. Certainly, *Electriclarryland* will sound way too tame for fans of *Locust Abortion Technican* and *Hairway to Steven,* and they're right, to a certain extent. There is nothing on this guitar-heavy record to please listeners accustomed to their unhinged, perverse '80s recordings. But *Electriclarryland* is a logical maturation for the band. It's odd to think of the Buttholes maturing, but that is the case with this album. They have a couple of jangly pop numbers that appear to be played relatively straight, and the heavier numbers have a pile-driving inevitability that makes them memorable. In short, *Electriclarryland* rocks, and it rocks hard, with enough energy for bands half the Buttholes' age. And underneath the seemingly normal surface, the Buttholes have thrown in enough jokes and have twisted around enough clichés to prove that the band may mature, but they'll never really grow up. —*Stephen Thomas Erlewine*

The Buzzcocks

f. 1975, Manchester, England
Punk
Formed in Manchester, England, in 1975, the Buzzcocks were one of the most influential bands to emerge in the initial wave of punk rock. With their crisp melodies, driving guitars, and guitarist Pete Shelley's biting lyrics, the Buzzcocks were one of the best, most influential punk bands. The Buzzcocks were inspired by the Sex Pistols' energy, but they didn't copy the Pistols' angry political stance. Instead, they brought that intense, brilliant energy to the three-minute pop song. Shelly's alter-

nately funny and anguished lyrics about adolescence and love were some of the best and smartest of his era; similarly, the Buzzcocks' melodies and hooks were concise and memorable. Over the years, their powerful punk-pop has proven enormously influential, with echoes of their music being apparent in everyone from Hüsker Dü to Nirvana.

Before the Buzzcocks, the teenaged Pete Shelley had played guitar in various heavy metal bands. In 1975 he enrolled in the Bolton Institute of Technology. While he was at school, Shelley joined an electronic music society, which is where he met Howard Devoto, who had enrolled at BIT in 1972. Both Shelley and Devoto shared an affection for the Velvet Underground, while Devoto was also fascinated by the Stooges. While they were still in school, Shelley and Devoto began rehearsing with a drummer, covering everything from the Stooges to Brian Eno. The trio never performed live and soon fell apart. Shelley and Devoto remained friends, and several months after their initial musical venture dissolved, the pair read the first live review of the Sex Pistols in the *NME* and decided to see the band in London. After witnessing the band twice in February 1976, the pair decided to form their own band, with the intent of replicating the Pistols' London impact in Manchester.

Both musicians decided to change their last names—Peter McNeish became Pete Shelley and Howard Traford became Howard Devoto—and took their group's name from a review of *Rock Follies* that ended with the quotation "Get a buzz, cock." The Buzzcocks began rehearsing, picking up local drummer and bassist Garth Smith. Shortly after their formation, Shelley and Devoto booked a local club, the Lesser Free Trade Hall, with the intent of persuading the Sex Pistols to play in Manchester. They succeeded in bringing the Pistols to Manchester, but the Buzzcocks had to pull out of their own gig when both the bassist and drummer left the group before the concert. At the Pistols show, Shelley and Devoto met Steve Diggle, who joined the Buzzcocks as their bassist, and the group found their drummer John Maher through an advertisement in the *Melody Maker*. Within a few months, the band played their first concert, opening for the second Sex Pistols show at the Lesser Free Trade Hall in July 1976. By the end of the year, the Buzzcocks had played a handful of gigs and helped establish Manchester as the second biggest punk rock city in England, ranking just behind London.

In October 1976 the Buzzcocks recorded their first demo tape, which remained unreleased. At the end of 1976 the group joined the Sex Pistols on their "Anarchy Tour." After the tour, Shelley borrowed a couple hundred pounds from his father, and the band used the money to record their debut EP, *Spiral Scratch*. The record was the first do-it-yourself, independently released record of the punk era. *Spiral Scratch* appeared on the band's New Hormones record label in January 1977; initially only 1,000 copies were pressed. Shortly after the release of the EP, Devoto quit the group and returned to college; later in the year, he formed Magazine. After Devoto's departure, Pete Shelley assumed the role of lead vocalist, Steve Diggle moved to guitar, and Garth Smith became the band's bassist. By June 1977, the Buzzcocks were attracting the attention of major record labels. By September they had signed with United Artists Records, who gave the band complete artistic control.

The Buzzcocks certainly tested the limits of that artistic control with their debut single, "Orgasm Addict." Released in October 1977, the single didn't become a hit because its subject matter was too explicit for BBC radio, but it generated good word of mouth. After its release, Garth Smith was kicked out of the group and was replaced by Steve Garvey. The Buzzcocks' second single, "What Do I Get?," became their first charting single, scraping the bottom of the Top 40. In March the band released their first album, *Another Music in a Different Kitchen*. In September 1978 the Buzzcocks released their second full-length record, *Love Bites*.

The rapid pace of the band's recording and performing schedules quickly had its effects on the group. Not only were the concerts and recordings wearing the band down, the members were consuming alcohol and drugs in great amounts. Early in 1979 they recorded their third album, *A Different Kind of Tension*, which displayed some signs of wear and tear. After the album's release in August, they embarked on their first American tour, which wasn't successful. Nevertheless, the band was enjoying the peak of their popularity at home in Britain. Later in 1979 the singles collection *Singles Going Steady* was released in America.

The inner and outer tensions culminated in 1980, when they drastically cut back their performance schedule, but they persevered with recording, cutting the EP *Parts 1-3*, which was released as three separate singles over the course of the year. During 1980, United Artists was bought out by EMI, who cut back support of the Buzzcocks. The group began working on their fourth album in early 1981, but were prevented from recording by EMI. The label wanted to release *Singles Going Steady* in the UK before the band delivered their fourth album. The Buzzcocks refused. Consequently, EMI didn't give the band an advance to cover the recording costs of the fourth album. Pete Shelley decided to break up the band instead of fight the label. The Buzzcocks broke up in 1981. Immediately after the split, Shelley pursued a solo career that produced the hit single "Homosapien" but soon went dry. Steve Diggle

formed Flag of Convenience with John Maher, who quit the band shortly after its formation. Steve Garvey moved to New York, where he played with Motivation for a few years. In 1989 the group re-formed and toured the United States. The following year, Maher left the band, and former Smiths drummer Mike Joyce joined the band on tour. By 1990 the reunion had become permanent; after Joyce's brief tenure with the band, the lineup of the reunited Buzzcocks featured Shelley, Diggle, bassist Tony Barber, and drummer Phil Barker. The new version of the band released their first album, *Trade Test Transmission*, in 1993. After its release, the band toured frequently. In spring of 1996 the Buzzcocks released their fifth studio album, *All Set*. —*Stephen Thomas Erlewine*

Spiral Scratch / Jan. 29, 1977 / New Hormones ✦✦✦

★ **Singles Going Steady** / 1979 / IRS ✦✦✦✦✦
This single LP should convert those of you unwilling to jump right in and buy three CDs of Buzzcocks bliss—16 tracks, and not a dud among them, including everything from the hilarious sex-junkie tale "Orgasm Addict" to the frustration of "Oh Shit" and "Something's Gone Wrong Again." This could be, track for track, one of the greatest rock albums ever made. Fast and furious, with Pete Shelley sounding wonderfully snotty, this is a piece of heaven pressed into 12 inches of vinyl. —*John Dougan*

Peel Sessions / 1988 / Dutch East India ✦✦✦
If you crave another fix, these 14 tracks recorded for John Peel's *BBC 1* radio show are just the medicine you need. Recording quality is good and grubby, and the band is in fine fettle, especially on the great song about existential angst, "I Don't Know What to Do with My Life." —*John Dougan*

Product / 1989 / Restless ✦✦✦✦
Product is a triple-disc box set that contains all of the Buzzcocks' studio recordings—totalling three LPs and 12 singles—following the departure of Howard Devoto, as well as one outtake and eight live songs taken from a 1978 concert. Collecting all of the Buzzcocks' major music in one place confirms the influence and depth of the band's tense, nervy music and Pete Shelley's terse, melodic songwriting. Though the bulk of this material is available individually, the set is essential for hardcore Buzzcocks fans, especially since it contains a detailed, definitive band history. —*Stephen Thomas Erlewine*

Time's Up / 1991 / Document ✦✦✦
A fascinating semi-legitimate release of all the studio work the Howard Devoto-fronted band recorded in Manchester in October 1976. This is an expensive disc that clocks in at only 24 minutes, but it's 24 pretty great minutes. Some of the material (e.g., the cover of Captain Beefheart's "I Love You, You Big Dummy") Devoto took with him to Magazine, but the rest is prime Buzzcocks: "Orgasm Addict," "Breakdown," and "Boredom" to name but a few. With Devoto singing lead, the band sounds a bit more Sex Pistols-ish (something that would change when Shelley took over singing lead), and therefore a tad more ominous. Difficult to find but well worth the effort. —*John Dougan*

Operator's Manual: The Buzzcocks Best / Nov. 12, 1991 / IRS ✦✦✦✦
A 25-song set, it duplicates 11 songs from the *Singles* album. It also contains the best of their three albums, only one of which was released in the US, and showcases a different side of the band. —*John Floyd*

Entertaining Friends / Nov. 3, 1992 / IRS ✦✦✦
Entertaining Friends is from a Hammersmith Odeon show in London in 1979 and is mostly good, but not transcendent. Although, to be fair, the band gets better as the set progresses. —*John Dougan*

Different Kind of Tension / Buzzcocks, Pts. 1-3 / 1993 / IRS ✦✦✦✦
Even at the end of their career, the Buzzcocks were recording an amazing array of ferocious pop songs. Their last album, *A Different Kind of Tension*, featured some of Pete Shelley's best songs, including some of the most personal material he has ever written. *Parts One, Two, Three* collect the band's last three singles, which are all quite impressive. —*Stephen Thomas Erlewine*

Trade Test Transmission / Jun. 2, 1993 / Caroline ✦✦✦
While it doesn't have the tight, repressed energy of their earliest records, *Trade Test Transmission* is a surprisingly effective comeback album from the Buzzcocks, showing that the band can still turn out some terrific pop-rock. —*Stephen Thomas Erlewine*

Love Bites/Another Music in a Different Kitchen / Feb. 22, 1994 / IRS ✦✦✦✦
While the Buzzcocks' singles captured the band's energetic, tightly wound pop style perfectly, the band experimented a bit more with song structures on their full-length albums. Many of the album tracks were in the vein of their classic singles, but the band also played some twisted, draining instrumental sections that were almost as impressive as their concise pop songs. Of their first two albums, the debut *Another Music in a Different Kitchen* is the stronger record, but *Love Bites* is only a shade weaker. —*Stephen Thomas Erlewine*

French / Jan. 23, 1996 / IRS ♦♦

The re-formed Buzzcocks (Pete Shelley and Steve Diggle with a new rhythm section) play a 23-song set at L'Arapaho Club in Paris on April 12, 1995. Combining '70s material with songs from *Trade Test Transmission*, it's a thorough outing that must have been a workout for the audience, though on record it seems to pull back from the brink on which the old band used to play. Part of the fascination of the initial wave of punk was its dangerous unpredictability, which is by definition a hard thing to recapture. Still, the Buzzcocks haven't mellowed, and Shelley and Diggle still make a driving guitar team. — *William Ruhlmann*

All Set / Apr. 1996 / IRS ♦♦♦

The Buzzcocks have been the most consistently entertaining of all of the punk/post-punk reunions simply because Pete Shelley has never forgotten how to write a hook. Though the band might not sound as tense and dynamic as they did in their glory days, *All Set* is by no means a disgrace. The group is energetic and forceful throughout the album, giving just enough of a boost to Shelley's spiky melodies and hooks. After all these years, he has mellowed somewhat but he still knows how to write a concise, catchy pop song. *All Set* is a minor entry in the Buzzcocks' rich catalog, but it is nevertheless an enjoyable one. — *Stephen Thomas Erlewine*

Bobby Byrd

b. South Carolina
Organ, Piano, Vocals / Acid Jazz

As a long-running right-hand man, Bobby Byrd performed an invaluable function in the James Brown Show, warming up the crowds as a solo singer, then retreating to the sidelines as a member of the Famous Flames, Brown's backup vocal group. Indeed, without Byrd, James Brown might never have made it out of Georgia; in the early '50s, Byrd and his family sponsored Brown's parole from prison, and Byrd gave Brown a spot in his vocal group, the Flames (which, of course, Brown eventually took over and relegated to the background). Like many of Brown's close associates and support musicians, Byrd got a chance to record his own records under Brown's direction, releasing numerous Brown-produced singles between the early '60s and early '70s. Some of these were even modest R&B hits—"We're in Love" (1965) and "I Need Help (I Can't Do It Alone)" (1970) were the biggest, making the R&B Top 20. Brown's backing musicians (and sometimes Brown himself) often figured heavily in the arrangements, and unsurprisingly the tracks often sounded like James Brown records featuring a different vocalist. The unfortunate problem was that Byrd was an average, even nondescript, soul singer, sounding much more like a poor person's Sam & Dave than a facsimile of Soul Brother Number One. The records were often fine, and the early '70s hard funk singles in particular (which usually featured the JB's) cook, but you can't help wondering if they might sound a lot better with J.B. himself on the front line. Still, fans of the James Brown groove will find a lot to like in Byrd's best recordings, in much the same way as they'll enjoy the *James Brown's Funky People* series of recordings that J.B. oversaw (but did not sing lead on). Certainly Eric B. & Rakim thought so, reworking one of Byrd's best singles (1971's "I Know You Got Soul") so faithfully that legal action ensued. After splitting from Brown in 1973, Byrd has recorded sporadically and performed often (particularly in Europe), releasing his most recent album, *On the Move*, in 1994. — *Richie Unterberger*

● **Bobby Byrd Got Soul: The Best of Bobby Byrd** / Aug. 22, 1995 / Polydor ♦♦♦♦

As is the case with the JBs and other James Brown protégés, Bobby Byrd's legacy is spread over numerous out-of-print, difficult-to-find vinyl records. So this 22-song retrospective, which gathers numerous singles and a couple of previously unreleased tracks spanning 1964 to 1973, is a welcome consolidation of his most significant work into one package. Solid stuff, covering both standard soul from the '60s and hard funk (usually featuring the JBs) from the early '70s, though it sounds a lot more like a James Brown record with a different vocalist than a Bobby Byrd record that happens to benefit from James Brown's backing crew. Brown produced (and occasionally contributed to) all of the recordings here, and duets with Bobby on the 1968 single "You've Got to Change Your Mind." — *Richie Unterberger*

The Byrds

f. 1964, Los Angeles, CA, **db.** 1973
Country-Rock, Psychedelic, Folk-Rock

Although they attained the huge success of the Beatles, Rolling Stones, and the Beach Boys for only a short time in the mid-'60s, time has judged the Byrds to be nearly as influential as those groups in the long run. They were not solely responsible for devising folk-rock, but they were certainly more responsible than any other single act (Dylan included) for melding the innovations and energy of the British Invasion with the best lyrical and musical elements of contemporary folk music.

The jangling, 12-string guitar sound of leader Roger McGuinn's Rickenbacker was permanently absorbed into the vocabulary of rock. They also played a vital role in pioneering psychedelic rock and country-rock, the unifying element being their angelic harmonies and restless eclecticism.

Often described in their early days as a hybrid of Dylan and the Beatles, the Byrds in turn influenced Dylan and the Beatles almost as much. The Byrds' innovations have echoed nearly as strongly through subsequent generations, in the work of Tom Petty, R.E.M., and innumerable alternative bands of the post-punk era that feature those jangling guitars and dense harmonies.

Although the Byrds had perfected their blend of folk and rock when their debut single, "Mr. Tambourine Man," topped the charts in mid-1965, it was something of a miracle that the group had managed to coalesce in the first place. Not a single member of the original quintet had extensive experience on electric instruments. Jim McGuinn (he'd change his first name to Roger a few years later), David Crosby, and Gene Clark were all young veterans of both commercial folk-pop troupes and the acoustic coffeehouse scene. They were inspired by the success of the Beatles to mix folk and rock. McGuinn had already been playing Beatles songs acoustically in Los Angeles folk clubs when Clark approached him to form an act, according to subsequent recollections, in the Peter & Gordon style. David Crosby soon joined to make them a trio, and they made a primitive demo as the Jet Set that was bursting with promise. With the help of session musicians, they released a single on Elektra as the Beefeaters that, while a flop, showed them getting quite close to the folk-rock sound that would electrify the pop scene in a few months.

The Beefeaters, soon renamed the Byrds, were fleshed out to a quintet with the addition of drummer Michael Clarke and bluegrass mandolinist Chris Hillman, who was enlisted to play electric bass, although he had never played the instrument before. The band was so lacking in equipment in their early stages that Clarke played on cardboard boxes during their first rehearsals, but they determined to master their instruments and become a full-fledged rock band. (Many demos from this period would later surface for official release.) They managed to procure a demo of a new Dylan song, "Mr. Tambourine Man"; by eliminating some verses and adding instantly memorable 12-string guitar leads and Beatlesque harmonies, they came up with the first big folk-rock smash (though the Beau Brummels and others had begun exploring similar territory). For the "Mr. Tambourine Man" single, the band's vocals and McGuinn's inimitable Rickenbacker were backed by session musicians, although the band themselves (contrary to some widely circulated rumors) performed on their subsequent recordings.

The first long-haired American group to compete with the British Invasion bands visually as well as musically, the Byrds were soon anointed as the American counterpart to the Beatles by the press, legions of fans, and George Harrison himself. Their 1965 debut LP, *Mr. Tambourine Man*, was a fabulous album that mixed stellar interpretations of Dylan and Pete Seeger tunes with strong, more romantic and pop-based originals, usually written by Gene Clark in the band's early days. A few months later, their version of Seeger's "Turn! Turn! Turn!" became another No. 1 hit and instant classic, featuring more great chiming guitar lines and ethereal, interweaving harmonies. While their second LP (*Turn! Turn! Turn!*) wasn't as strong as their debut full-length, the band continued to move forward at a dizzying pace. In early 1966, the "Eight Miles High" single heralded the birth of psychedelia, with its druglike (intentionally or otherwise) lyrical imagery, rumbling bass line, and a frenzied McGuinn guitar solo that took its inspiration from John Coltrane and Indian music.

The Byrds suffered a major loss right after "Eight Miles High" with the departure of Gene Clark, their primary songwriter and, along with McGuinn, chief lead vocalist. The reason for his resignation, ironically, was fear of flying, although other pressures were at work as well. "Eight Miles High," amazingly, would be their last Top 20 single. Many radio stations banned the record for its alleged drug references, halting its progress at No. 14. This ended the Byrds' brief period as commercial challengers to the Beatles, but they regrouped impressively in the face of the setbacks. Continuing as a quartet, McGuinn, Crosby, and Hillman would assume songwriting responsibilities. The third album, *Fifth Dimension*, contained more groundbreaking folk-rock and psychedelia on tracks like "Fifth Dimension," "I See You," and "John Riley," although it (like several of their classic early albums) mixed sheer brilliance with tracks that were oddly half-baked or carelessly executed.

Younger Than Yesterday, (1967) which included the small hits "So You Want to Be a Rock 'n' Roll Star" and "My Back Pages" (another Dylan cover), was another high point, Hillman and Crosby in particular taking their writing to a new level. In 1967 Crosby would assert a much more prominent role in the band, singing and writing some of his best material. He wasn't getting along so well with McGuinn and Hillman, though, and was jettisoned from the Byrds partway into the recording of *The Notorious Byrd Brothers*. Gene Clark, drafted into the band as a replacement, left after only a few weeks, and by the end of 1967, Michael

Clarke was also gone. Remarkably, in the midst of this chaos (not to mention diminishing record sales), they continued to sound as good as ever on *Notorious*. This was another effort that mixed electronic experimentation and folk-rock mastery with aplomb, with hints of a growing interest in country music.

As McGuinn and Hillman rebuilt the group one more time in early 1968, McGuinn mused upon the exciting possibility of a double album that would play as nothing less than a history of contemporary music, evolving from traditional folk and country to jazz and electronic music. Toward this end, he hired Gram Parsons, he has since said, to play keyboards. Under Parsons' influence, however, the Byrds were soon going full blast into country music, with Parsons taking a large share of the guitar and vocal chores. In 1968 McGuinn, Hillman, Parsons, and drummer Kevin Kelly recorded *Sweetheart of the Rodeo*, which was probably the first album to be widely labeled as country-rock.

Opinions as to the merits of *Rodeo* remain sharply divided among Byrds fans. Some see it as a natural continuation of the group's innovations; other bewail the loss of the band's trademark crystalline guitar jangle, and the short-circuited potential of McGuinn's most ambitious experiments. There's no doubt that it marked the end, or at least a drastic revamping, of the "classic" Byrds sound of the 1965-68 period (bookended by the *Tambourine Man* and *Notorious* albums). Parsons, the main catalyst for the metamorphosis, left the band after about six months, partially in objection to a 1968 Byrds tour of South Africa. It couldn't have helped, though, that McGuinn replaced several of Parsons' lead vocals on *Rodeo* with his own at the last minute, ostensibly due to contractual obstacles that prevented Parsons from singing on Columbia releases. (Some tracks with Parsons' lead vocals snuck on anyway, and a few others surfaced in the 1990s on the Byrds box set).

Chris Hillman left the Byrds by the end of 1968 to form the Flying Burrito Brothers with Parsons. Although McGuinn kept the Byrds going for about another five years with other musicians (most notably former country picker Clarence White), essentially the Byrds name was a front for Roger McGuinn and backing band. Opinions, again, remain sharply divided about the merits of latter-day Byrds albums. McGuinn was (and is) such an idiosyncratic and pleasurable talent that fans and critics are inclined to give him some slack; no one else plays the 12-string as well, he's a fine arranger, and his Lennon-meets-Dylan vocals are immediately distinctive. Yet aside from some good echoes of vintage Byrds like "Chestnut Mare," "Jesus Is Just Alright," and "Drug Store Truck Drivin' Man," nothing from the post-1968 Byrds albums resonates with nearly the same effervescent quality and authority of their classic 1965-68 period. This is partly because McGuinn is an erratic (though occasionally fine) songwriter; it's also because the Byrds at their peak were very much a unit of diverse and considerable talents, not just a front for their leader's ideas.

The Byrds' diminishing importance must have stung McGuinn doubly in light of the rising profiles of several Byrds alumni as the '60s turned into the '70s. David Crosby was a superstar with Crosby, Stills, Nash & Young; Hillman, Parsons, and (for a while) Michael Clarke were taking country-rock further with the Flying Burrito Brothers; even Gene Clark, though he'd dropped out of sight commercially, was recording some respected country-rock albums on his own. The original quintet actually got back together for a one-off reunion album in 1973; though it made the Top 20, it was one of the most flagrant examples of the futility of a great band's reuniting in an attempt to recapture the lightning one last time.

The original Byrds continued to pursue solo careers and outside projects throughout the 1970s and 1980s. McGuinn, Clark, and Hillman had some success at the end of the 1970s with an adult contemporary variation on the Byrds' sound; in the 1980s, Crosby battled drug problems while Hillman enjoyed mainstream country success with the Desert Rose Band. The Byrds' legend was tarnished by squabbles over which members of the original lineup had the rights to use the Byrds name; for quite a while, drummer Michael Clarke even toured with a "Byrds" that featured no other original members. The Byrds were inducted into the Rock & Roll Hall of Fame in 1991. Gene Clark died several months later, and Michael Clarke died in 1993. —*Richie Unterberger*

☆ **Mr. Tambourine Man** / 1965 / Columbia ◆◆◆◆◆
One of the greatest debuts in the history of rock, *Mr. Tambourine Man* was nothing less than a significant step in the evolution of rock 'n' roll itself, demonstrating that intelligent lyrical content could be wedded to compelling electric guitar riffs and a solid backbeat. It was also the album that was most responsible for establishing folk-rock as a popular phenomenon, its most alluring traits being McGuinn's immediately distinctive 12-string Rickenbacker jangle and the band's beautiful harmonies. The material was uniformly strong, whether they were interpreting Dylan (on the title cut and three other songs, including the hit single "All I Really Want to Do"), Pete Seeger ("The Bells of Rhymney"), or Jackie De Shannon ("Don't Doubt Yourself, Babe"). The originals were lyrically less challenging, but equally powerful musically, especially Gene Clark's

"I Knew I'd Want You," "I'll Feel a Whole Lot Better," and "Here Without You"; "It's No Use" showed a tougher, harder-rocking side and a guitar solo with hints of psychedelia. The CD reissue adds six less impressive (but still satisfying) bonus tracks and alternate takes from the same era. —*Richie Unterberger*

Turn! Turn! Turn! / 1966 / Columbia ◆◆◆◆
The group's second album was a disappointment only in comparison with *Mr. Tambourine Man*. They couldn't maintain such a level of consistent magnificence, and the follow-up was not quite as powerful or impressive. It was still quite good, however, particularly the ringing No. 1 title cut, a classic on par with the "Mr. Tambourine Man" single. Elsewhere they concentrated more on original material, Gene Clark in particular offering some strong compositions with "Set You Free This Time," "The World Turns All Around Her," and "If You're Gone." A couple more Dylan covers were included as well, and "Satisfied Mind" was their first foray into country-rock, a direction they would explore in much greater depth throughout the rest of the '60s. The CD adds seven decent alternate takes and bonus tracks, the most interesting being a version of Dylan's "It's All Over Now, Baby Blue," and an enigmatic Gene Clark song, "The Day Walk (Never Before)." —*Richie Unterberger*

Fifth Dimension / Jul. 1966 / Columbia ◆◆◆◆
Although *Fifth Dimension* was wildly uneven, its high points were as innovative as any rock music being recorded in 1966. Immaculate folk-rock was still present in their superb arrangements of the traditional songs "Wild Mountain Thyme" and "John Riley." For the originals, they devised some of the first and best psychedelic rock, often drawing from the influence of Indian raga in the guitar arrangements. "Eight Miles High," with its astral lyrics, pumping bass line, and fractured guitar solo, was a Top 20 hit, and one of the greatest singles of the '60s. The minor hit title track and the country-rock-tinged "Mr. Spaceman" are among their best songs; "I See You" has great 12-string psychedelic guitar solos; and "I Come and Stand at Every Door" is an unusual and moving update of a traditional rock tune, with new lyrics pleading for peace in the nuclear age. At the same time, the R&B instrumental "Captain Soul" was a throwaway, "Hey Joe" not nearly as good as the versions by the Leaves or Jimi Hendrix, and "What's Happening?!?!" the earliest example of David Crosby's disagreeably vapid hippie ethos. These weak spots keep *Fifth Dimension* from attaining truly classic status. The CD reissue has six notable bonus tracks, including the single version of the early psychedelic cut "Why" (the B-side to "Eight Miles High"), a significantly different alternate take of "Eight Miles High," "I Know My Rider" (with some fine McGuinn 12-string workouts), and a much jazzier, faster instrumental version of "John Riley." —*Richie Unterberger*

☆ **Younger Than Yesterday** / 1967 / Columbia ◆◆◆◆◆
Younger Than Yesterday was somewhat overlooked at the time of its release during an intensely competitive era that found the Byrds on a commercial downslide. However, time has shown it to be the most durable of the Byrds' albums, with the exception of *Mr. Tambourine Man*. Crosby, McGuinn, and especially Hillman come into their own as songwriters on an eclectic but focused set blending folk-rock, psychedelia, and early country-rock. The sardonic "So You Want to Be a Rock 'n' Roll Star" was a terrific single; "My Back Pages," also a small hit, was the last of their classic Dylan covers; "Thoughts and Words," the flower-power anthem "Renaissance Fair," "Have You Seen Her Face," and the bluegrass-tinged "Time Between" are all among their best songs. The jazzy "Everybody's Been Burned" may be David Crosby's best composition, although his "Mind Gardens" is one of his most excessive. The CD reissue has six bonus tracks, including the fine Crosby-penned single "Lady Friend" and notably different alternate versions of "Mind Gardens" and "My Back Pages." —*Richie Unterberger*

★ **The Byrds' Greatest Hits** / 1967 / Columbia ◆◆◆◆◆
Even though this collection covers only the first half of their career, it contains more primo stuff than *20 Essential Tracks* (see below). The mastering here isn't quite as good as that on the box set. —*Rick Clark*

The Notorious Byrd Brothers / Jan. 1968 / Columbia ◆◆◆◆
A classic psychedelic opus, it draws from the space-rock of *Younger...* and *Fifth...* while hinting at the country-rock to come with cuts like "Change Is Now" and "Old John Robertson." The 12-string electrics are downplayed. Production techniques like phasing, vari-speeded vocals, sound effects, and baroque string and horn arrangements play a bigger role, while the melodies and vocal execution are much spacier. Highlights include Carole King's yearning "Goin' Back," "Draft Morning," "Dolphins Smile," and "Wasn't Born to Follow" (featured in the movie *Easy Rider*). —*Rick Clark*

☆ **Sweetheart of the Rodeo** / Aug. 1968 / Columbia ◆◆◆◆◆
The Byrds made this groundbreaking country-rock classic with the songwriting aid of new member Gram Parsons. "One Hundred Years from Now" features some incredibly fine guitar and pedal-steel work from Clarence White and Lloyd Green, respectively. Versions of Dylan's "Nothing Was Delivered" and "You Ain't Going Nowhere" are pure magic, and renditions of the Louvin Brothers' "The Christian Life" and

William Bell's "You Don't Miss Your Water" are standouts too. —*Rick Clark*

Preflyte / 1969 / Columbia ✦✦✦
A blip in the Byrds' discography that could easily be missed, as all of the songs from these pre-*Mr. Tambourine Man* sessions are also found on the much more widely available *In the Beginning*. Byrds fans really need to track this down, though, because six of the 11 cuts are actually entirely different versions than the ones that appear on *In the Beginning*, and in some cases the differences are substantial. "You Showed Me," in particular, appears here in a bare-bones, almost acoustic version with a heart-wrenching Gene Clark vocal; this is the sound of the Byrds at their very birth in the nest. It's a matter of taste, but to my ears the takes of "She Has a Way" and "Here Without You" on *Preflyte* are clearly superior to the ones used on *In the Beginning*, though the arrangements are very similar. Originally released on the small Together label, this was reissued on Columbia a few years later; the Columbia pressing is much easier to find, can still be easily (and affordably) found in used stores, and has enough otherwise unavailable quality material to make the search worth the effort. —*Richie Unterberger*

Dr. Byrd & Mr. Hyde / 1969 / Columbia ✦✦
Not one of their best, this still contains two notable tracks, "This Wheel's on Fire" and "King Apathy III." There is a continued country influence, but rock still predominates. —*Rick Clark*

The Ballad of Easy Rider / Feb. 1969 / Columbia ✦✦✦
This is another beautiful gem with hardly a weak cut. "Gunga Din," with its delicate arpeggios, is one of the finest moments by a later incarnation of the Byrds. By this time, their characteristic 12-string sound was all but gone. —*Rick Clark*

Untitled / 1970 / Columbia ✦✦✦
Originally a double-record set (one live LP/one studio) and now on a single CD, this contains their last hit of any substance, "Chestnut Mare." The studio tracks are uneven, but tracks like the reflective "Just a Season," "Truck Stop Girl," "All the Things" and much of the live stuff make this set worth having, if only for Clarence White's remarkable guitar playing. —*Rick Clark*

Byrdmaniax / 1971 / Columbia ✦✦
What could have been known as an above average Byrds album became a flawed near-disaster when their producer overdubbed keyboards, string, and heavenly choirs while the band was on tour. So what could have been, wasn't and fairly good tunes were awash with a syrupy glop. True, there are some things here that weren't messed with. Clarence White's "Green Apple Quick Step" is a fresh breath of bluegrass breeze, as is Roger McGuinn's re-write of "Chestnut Mare," this time titled "Pale Blue." And while there is nothing terrible here, one wonders how the album would've sounded before all the overdubs. A Byrds version of what happened to the Beatles with *Let It Be*. —*James Chrispell*

The Byrds [1973] / 1973 / Asylum ✦✦
With news of the original five members of the Byrds recording a new album together, speculation ran high long before this record was released. Therefore, it wasn't much of a surprise when people were disappointed at what they heard. But what no one realized was that this was a record made by *five* individuals that had once been collectively known as "The Byrds." Taken in that context, *Byrds* is a fine album indeed. Original songs as well as covers stand up today as a very strong effort that, although flawed, does not disappoint. —*James Chrispell*

In the Beginning / 1988 / Rhino ✦✦✦
Before signing to Columbia Records, the Byrds made hours of rehearsal and demo tapes as they perfected their blend of folk and rock. The *Preflyte* album, released in the late '60s, presented nearly a dozen of those cuts. This CD takes the bulk of that LP and embellishes it with alternate takes and previously unreleased tracks. Discography-wise, this 17-song disc is a real tongue-twister. Five of the 11 *Preflyte* tracks reappear in the exact same version, along with six alternate takes of *Preflyte* cuts. There are also alternate takes of both sides of their 1964 Elektra single (released as the Beefeaters), the primitive acoustic demo "The Only Girl I Adore" (previously available only on an obscure Elektra compilation), a previously unissued early version of "It's No Use" (later on their first LP), and the previously totally unreleased original "Tomorrow Is a Long Ways Away," in both electric and acoustic versions. Amidst the collector details, one shouldn't lose sight of the fact that the music is excellent, though more tentative and less polished than their "official" Columbia work. The harmonies are angelic and the melodies beautiful. Though this is more derivative of the early Beatles than their later Dylan-influenced folk-rock, one can hear the group's unsurpassed crystalline blend of guitars and voices approaching full bloom. With the exception of an early version of "Mr. Tambourine Man," all the cuts are originals, most of which are fine and never appeared on their later albums; there are many good, otherwise unavailable Gene Clark songs in particular. Minor complaint: Some of the alternate takes here are inferior to those on the original *Preflyte* album. —*Richie Unterberger*

Never Before / 1989 / Murray Hill ✦✦✦
This 17-song compilation of alternate takes, unreleased songs, and assorted oddities from the Byrds' mid-'60s prime is a necessary purchase for their many fanatics, but a bit choppy and insubstantial in places. The highlights are many: a rough but endearing previously unreleased cover of Dylan's "It's All Over Now, Baby Blue"; an alternate take of "Eight Miles High" that is quite different from (though not as good as) the hit version; a couple of pretty David Crosby ballads (including "Triad," later covered by the Jefferson Airplane); a cover of the traditional folk tune "I Know You Rider" with scintillating 12-string guitar solos from Roger McGuinn; "Why," the raga-rock B-side of "Eight Miles High" (both the original 45 version and an alternate take are included); and the non-LP B-side of "Turn, Turn, Turn," "She Don't Care About Time" (written by Gene Clark). A couple of instrumental jams show McGuinn at his most recklessly experimental. "Flight 713" is a taut, almost jazzy piece, while the synthesizer burps of "Moog Raga" give an insight into the electronic direction the group might have pursued if Gram Parsons hadn't joined the band. On the down side, some of the outtakes were clearly throwaways, and the stereo version of their first single was hardly a coveted item. The 1968 B-side "Lady Friend," one of Crosby's best compositions, is ruined by a ham-fisted drum track overdubbed in the 1980s (it was restored to its original version on the box set). A ragtag collection, yes, but there are plenty of stellar moments, and this CD (together with *In the Beginning*) rounds up virtually everything from the group's classic period that didn't appear on their first five albums. —*Richie Unterberger*

☆ **The Byrds [Box Set]** / Oct. 1990 / Columbia ✦✦✦✦✦
This thoughtfully compiled four-disc box set features great sound from remastered and remixed tracks. The remixes generally manage to maintain the essential integrity of the original tracks, but there are some that entirely miss the spirit, like "Just a Season" and a toothless "Why" (which, by the way, is *not* the sought-after version found on the B-side of "Eight Miles High.") Regardless, it's a must-own for anyone interested in finding out about one of America's greatest groups. —*Rick Clark*

20 Essential Tracks from the Boxed Set: 1965-90 / 1991 / Columbia ✦✦✦
That may have been the case for the first 16 cuts, but why include the four 1990 reunion tracks, when there's better material left on the box? An okay choice for the budget-minded, but that's about it. —*Rick Clark*

In the Studio / [Bootleg] ✦✦✦
Comprised of alternate versions, false starts, and backing tracks of songs from the Byrds' first three LPs, you're not going to turn to this for casual listening. But as academic documents of major groups go, this is first-rate, with 70 minutes of music, sparkling sound, and a chance to hear the group polishing their material in the studio. No radically different takes or arrangements surface, but aficionados will be especially interested in the appearance of the backing track to "Stranger in a Strange Land," a long-rumored Byrds original that had never even appeared on bootleg before. —*Richie Unterberger*

David Byrne

b. May 14, 1952, Dumbarton, Scotland
Guitar, Vocals / Alternative Pop-Rock, Experimental, Pop-Rock
Best known for his groundbreaking tenure fronting the New Wave group Talking Heads, David Byrne's solo work, while not as successful, was no less adventurous, encroaching upon such diverse media as world music, filmmaking, and performance art. Born May 14, 1952, in Dumbarton, Scotland, Byrne was raised in Baltimore, MD. The son of an electronics engineer, he played guitar in a series of teenage bands before attending the prestigious Rhode Island School of Design, where, feeling alienated from the largely upper-class student population, he dropped out after one year. However, he remained in the Providence area, performing solo on a ukulele before forming the Artistics (also known as the Autistics) with fellow students Chris Frantz and Tina Weymouth.

After changing the name of the band to Talking Heads and enlisting onetime Modern Lover Jerry Harrison, the group signed to Sire Records. A series of LPs, including the debut *Talking Heads '77*, 1978's *More Songs About Buildings and Food*, and 1980's *Remain in Light* followed, establishing the quartet as one of contemporary music's most visionary talents. During a band sabbatical in 1981, Byrne teamed with Brian Eno, the producer of much of the Heads' work, for the collaborative effort *My Life in the Bush of Ghosts*, a complex, evocative album that fused electronic music with Third World percussion and hypnotic vocal effects. That same year, Byrne began exploring theatre, composing *The Complete Score from the Broadway Production of "The Catherine Wheel,"* a dance piece choreographed by Twyla Tharp.

Byrne's next solo work appeared in 1985 with *Music for "The Knee Plays,"* a New Orleans brass band-influenced project composed for a portion of Robert Wilson's theatrical epic *CIVIL warS*. In 1986 Byrne wrote, starred in, and directed the feature film *True Stories,* a series of comic vignettes based on press clippings culled from tabloid publications like the *Weekly World News*. He also wrote and produced the majority of music for the film's score, in addition to performing his usual duties for that year's Talking Heads LP, also named *True Stories*. In 1988 he wrote the score to the Jonathan Demme comedy *Married to the Mob* and, in tandem with Ryuichi Sakamoto and Cong Su, won an Academy Award for his musical work on Bernardo Bertolucci's historical epic *The Last Emperor*.

Also in 1988, Byrne's fascination with world music, a longtime influence on his herky-jerky performance style as well as the Talking Heads' complex polyrhythms, inspired him to form his own record label, Luaka Bop, to give widespread American release to global music. That same year, the Heads released *Naked*, their final proper LP, leaving Byrne to give future solo work his full attention. In 1989 he resurfaced with *Rei Momo*, a collection inspired by Latin rhythms, and directed the documentary *Ile Aiye (The House of Life)*, which focused on the rituals of Yoruban dance music. In 1991 he again collaborated with Robert Wilson on *The Forest*, writing music for a full orchestra. 1992's *Uh-Oh* marked Byrne's return to more conventional rock performance, a direction continued on a self-titled effort issued in 1994. *Feelings*, recorded with members of Morcheeba and Devo, followed in 1997. *—Jason Ankeny*

My Life in the Bush of Ghosts / Feb. 1981 / Sire ✦✦✦✦
An experimental album combining complex, African-influenced rhythm tracks with a variety of found voices taken from radio broadcasts. Eerie and appealing. *— William Ruhlmann*

The Catherine Wheel / Dec. 1981 / Luaka Bop ✦✦✦
This is Byrne's score for a Broadway dance production choreographed and directed by Twyla Tharp. Its sound—with herky-jerky rhythms and unusual sounds, along with Byrne's own vocals and odd lyrics on many songs—will be familiar to Talking Heads fans. As originally released, only the cassette version contained the full 73-minute score, although an abridged songs-from LP was also issued. *— William Ruhlmann*

Music for the Knee Plays / May 1985 / ECM ✦✦✦
This music was composed for use in segments of Robert Wilson's opera *Civil Wars*. Byrne uses a variety of stately horn charts and recites impressionistic lyrics between and over them. The album concludes with the hilariously absurd "In the Future." *— William Ruhlmann*

Sounds from "True Stories" / 1986 / Luaka Bop ✦✦✦
Stylistically all over the map, this set of songs for Byrne's film (not to be confused with the Talking Heads album *True Stories*) ranges from the cowboy hoedown of "Cocktail Desperado" to a short piece for reeds written by Meredith Monk. Members of the Heads turn up, as does the Kronos Quartet. *— William Ruhlmann*

● **Rei Momo** / Oct. 1989 / Luaka Bop ✦✦✦✦
On his first full-fledged solo album, Byrne indulges his fascination with Latin and South American musical styles, employing a variety of native

musicians but mixing up the sounds to suit his own distinctly non-purist vision and singing over the tracks the same kind of witty, oddball lyrics found on Talking Heads albums. (When released, the cassette version contained three more tracks than the LP.) *— William Ruhlmann*

The Forest / Jun. 1991 / Luaka Bop ✦✦
In 1988 David Byrne collaborated with Robert Wilson on a "theatre piece" called *The Forest* that premiered in Berlin. (Byrne previously had worked with Wilson on *Civil Wars*, resulting in his album *Music for the Knee Plays*.) Byrne's orchestral score served as the basis for this more extended version, released three years later on his Luaka Bop label. The music is stately, near-classical, and like none of his other recordings except his Academy Award-winning music for *The Last Emperor*. Byrne always was an eclectic, and in a purely musical environment (there are a few stray lyrics, but nothing to speak of), he is free to move from the European classical tradition to traditions of Japan and the Middle East, among others. Depending upon your point of view, the result is either a pleasant travelogue or a mess. Or maybe both. *— William Ruhlmann*

Uh-Oh / Mar. 1992 / Luaka Bop ✦✦✦
Uh-Oh was only David Byrne's second pop-oriented solo album and his first to be released after the formal end of Talking Heads. Though informed by his various investigations into world music, the album was a natural successor to the Talking Heads records, relying on involved percussion tracks topped by Byrne's quirky singing and lyrics. By this point, disaffected fans may have grown accustomed to the idea that a David Byrne solo album could contain anything from an extended flirtation with Latin styles (*Rei Momo*) to an eclectic instrumental score (*The Forest*), to name only his most recent solo projects. Maybe Byrne and his record label failed to get out the message that he was back to making Heads-style pop-rock (he didn't organize a tour until the album had come and gone on the charts), but *Uh-Oh* never reached its potential audience. Talking Heads fans should give it a listen. *— William Ruhlmann*

David Byrne / May 24, 1994 / Luaka Bop ✦✦
David Byrne took a spare, direct approach on his third song-based solo album, which lent his work intimacy but did little to restore his commercial prospects, despite a first single, "Angels," that was a ringer for the Talking Heads song "Once in a Lifetime." In fact, the limited instrumentation and focus on Byrne's voice tended to create difficulties with his typically quirky lyrics; with the words in close-up, one wanted them to make some kind of sense. In a denser musical structure, such as the mbaqanga-flavored "You and Eye," one might share his enjoyment, but on other tracks with less to offer aurally, the disturbing question "What is he talking about?" became inescapable. *— William Ruhlmann*

C

The C.A. Quintet

f. Minneapolis, MN
Psychedelic
Virtually no one outside Minneapolis heard of the C.A. Quintet during their late '60s heyday. It was their fortune, or curse, to actually reach a considerably bigger international audience when their album was reissued in the 1980s. Starting as a rather conventional pop/soul/garage band, their one and only album, *Trip Thru Hell* (1968), was a worthy slice of dark psychedelia. With spooky organ and the occasional trumpet of singer and songwriter Ken Erwin, the group's murky and macabre vision—dotted with trips through hell, cold spiders, Sleepy Hollow lanes, Colorado mornings, and the like—was genuinely original and chilling. *Trip Thru Hell* sold only 700-800 copies when it was first issued, but after gaining status among hardcore '60s psychedelic collectors, it was reissued in 1983. The group also released a few non-LP singles in 1967 and 1968, most in a much poppier vein. —*Richie Unterberger*

● **Trip Thru Hell** / 1968 / Sundazed ✦✦✦✦
There's not much to compare this album to, even in the weird musical climate of 1968. There are echoes of Country Joe & the Fish and the Doors, perhaps, in the mysterioso organ and morbid imagery. Not that Ken Erwin was in the same league as Jim Morrison, or even Country Joe, as a songwriter. But with the exception of the brassy good-time cut "Underground Music," this album is more demented gloomy than most psychedelia. Occasional pealing bells and curdling screams (to say nothing of the Boschlike cover art) add to the foggy underworld menace. The 1995 domestic CD is a first-class job; the 12 bonus cuts gather some rare non-LP singles, alternate takes, and previously unreleased songs, and the liner notes feature extensive interviews with Ken Erwin and engineer Steve Longman. —*Richie Unterberger*

Cabaret Voltaire

f. 1973, Sheffield, England
Electronic, Ambient, Experimental, Post-Punk
Cabaret Voltaire's story is that of a common cult band. They never sold many records, and they were never critics' darlings, but their influence was great. Their effect on techno, industrial, and electronic music is immense. Taking the electronic experiments of Brian Eno and the avant-garde bent of Can, Cabaret Voltaire added a hypnotic, almost trance-like beat, along with television and record sound bites. All of these techniques became popular during the early '90s, when groups like the techno conglomeration Front 242 and the hard, industrial Ministry expanded on these ideas. What sounded avant-garde in the late '70s and early '80s has become the standard in clubs and raves around the world.

Since 1979, Cabaret Voltaire has recorded a staggering number of albums. Some are impressive; others are almost inaccessible. As they've grown older, their electronics have become more danceable; in 1991, they fit comfortably into the acid house, although their music was darker than most of that style. For much of their music, sound is the primary concern, not songs or compositions. Consequently, their albums can be dense, difficult listening that require patience. Even so, it is impossible to deny the importance of Cabaret Voltaire, no matter how inaccessible their music may be at times. —*Stephen Thomas Erlewine*

Mix-Up / 1979 / Mute ✦✦

The Voice of America / 1981 / Mute ✦✦

Red Mecca / 1981 / Mute ✦✦✦✦
Cabaret Voltaire's first consistent record, *Red Mecca* offers a highly stylized revision of Mancini's score for *Touch of Evil*, set to a dark, dense, electronic landscape. —*Stephen Thomas Erlewine*

2 X 45 / 1982 / Mute ✦✦✦✦

Johnny YesNo / 1983 / Mute ✦✦

The Crackdown / 1983 / Some Bizarre ✦✦✦✦
One of Cabaret Voltaire's strongest albums, *The Crackdown* features the band working a number of menacing electronic textures into a basic dance/funk rhythm; the result is one of their most distinctive, challenging records. —*Stephen Thomas Erlewine*

Micro-Phonies / 1984 / Virgin ✦✦✦

Drinking Gasoline / 1985 / Caroline ✦✦✦

The Covenant, the Sword & The Arm / 1985 / Some Bizarre ✦✦✦

Code / 1987 / Manhattan ✦✦✦

The Golden Moments of Cabaret Voltaire / 1987 / Rough Trade ✦✦✦✦
A solid collection of Cabaret Voltaire's earliest recordings, featuring some of the noisiest and bleakest music they have ever recorded. —*Stephen Thomas Erlewine*

Eight Crepscule Tracks / 1988 / Positive ✦✦✦

Groovy, Laidback & Nasty / 1990 / Capitol ✦✦✦

● **The Living Legends** / Jul. 1990 / Mute ✦✦✦✦
Collecting both sides of a number of singles the band made for Rough Trade, *The Living Legends* offers the best introduction to Cabaret Voltaire's influential electronic soundscapes. —*Stephen Thomas Erlewine*

Listen up with Cabaret Voltaire / Sep. 1990 / Mute ✦✦✦✦
It may be a collection of rarities and outtakes, but *Listen Up With Cabaret Voltaire* is one of their strongest albums, giving listeners a good sense of the band's accomplishments. —*Stephen Thomas Erlewine*

Colours / 1991 / Mute ✦✦✦

Plasticity / Oct. 20, 1993 / Instinct ✦✦✦

The Cadets

f. 1954, Los Angeles, CA
R&B, Doo WopDoo Wop
This West Coast group used two names for recording sessions. They called themselves "the Jacks" when doing dates for Modern and "the Cadets" on RPM. They began as a gospel group during the late '40s in Los Angeles. Ted Taylor, Aaron Collins, Lloyd McCraw, and Will Jones were the original lineup, and the Cadets were among the more popular bands doing R&B covers. The Cadets' lone hit was "Stranded in the Jungle," which they recorded for Modern as the Jacks in 1956. It peaked at No. 8 R&B and No. 15 pop. Davis and Collins would join the Flares in 1961, while Taylor would enjoy solo success as a blues, soul, and gospel vocalist. Jones joined the Coasters in 1958 and remained there for over a decade. Collins' sisters, Betty and Rose, also recorded for Modern/RPM as "the Teen Queens." —*Ron Wynn*

● **The Cadets Greatest Hits** / Relic ✦✦✦✦

The Cadillacs

f. 1953, Harlem, NY
Doo Wop
Equally adept at polished ballads and torrid rockers, the Cadillacs were one of New York's top doo wop groups. The Harlem quintet signed with Josie in 1954 and debuted with the beautiful "Gloria," but with Earl Carroll's (b. Nov. 2, 1937) prominent, energetic lead vocals, the Cadillacs became known for humorous jump material and hot choreography after "Speedoo" hit big for them in 1956. Tapping into the novelty R&B market pioneered by the Coasters, the Cadillacs cut a load of great rockers during the late '50s, such as "Peek-a-Boo" and "Please, Mr. Johnson,"

and performed in the quickie flick *Go, Johnny, Go!* in 1959. Carroll left to join the Coasters in 1958, but the group persevered, eventually signing with Mercury. Carroll has re-formed the Cadillacs in recent years. —*Bill Dahl*

★ **The Best of the Cadillacs** / 1990 / Rhino ✦✦✦✦✦

Although completists will have to have the multi-disc set on Collectables, for the rest of us this seldom-championed but nonetheless superlative single-disc compilation will more than fill the bill. At 18 tracks, a few collectors' favorites are understandably absent ("Wishing Well," "Jaywalkin'"), but *all* of the major and minor hits are aboard, clearly showcasing the group's ability to tackle everything from beautiful ballads ("Gloria," "The Girl I Love") to jump numbers ("Speedo," "My Girl Friend") to Coaster-style novelties ("Peek-a-Boo," "Please, Mr. Johnson") and do it all with style and grace. Covering their stint with Josie Records from 1954 to 1960 in straight chronological fashion, with excellent liner notes from John Neilson, this particular comp offers great value for the bread and should be one of your very first stops in assembling a definitive doo wop collection. The Cadillacs were one of the first and one of the very best, and here's where you go to dig their basic message. —*Cub Koda*

John Cafferty

b. Narrangansett, RI
Rock 'n' Roll

Arguably the quintessential one-shot band of all time, Cafferty and Co. (who, back in the early '70s, were simply a hack New England bar band) had their 15 minutes of fame courtesy of a ridiculously overwrought 1983 film called *Eddie and the Cruisers* (starring the ridiculously overwrought Michael Pare), which dealt with the suspicious death of a fictional singer-songwriter, modeled on a conflation of Bob Dylan and Bruce Springsteen, who had made the transition from smart rock 'n' roller to serious artist. Seems as though Eddie had recorded a "brilliant" but unreleased album that fused Chuck Berry-style rock 'n' roll with French Symbolist poetry (all this in 1963!). A record way ahead of its time, the master tapes of *The Dark Side* (ooh, now that's a heavy title) went missing, right around the time of Eddie's "death." Needing a band to supply music for the film, the producers used the Springsteenish-sounding Cafferty and his clock-punching backup band. With the Springsteenish single "On the Dark Side" leading the way, Cafferty led, arguably, the most anonymous band with a hit record in the history of rock 'n' roll. With the movie doing reasonably well in theaters and extremely well on video, sales of Cafferty's album (which, ironically, had been out for months before the band's involvement with the film and barely caused a murmur) skyrocketed. But as the movie faded from the public consciousness, so did Cafferty's lousy, cynical imitation of Springsteen. —*John Dougan*

Eddie & The Cruisers [O.S.T.] / 1983 / RCA ✦✦✦✦

There was a year's delay before this film, which concerns the mysterious death of a fictional 60s rock star, took off via video and cable TV; but when it did, the soundtrack album, featuring such songs as "On the Dark Side" and "Tender Years," by John Cafferty And The Beaver Brown Band, took off with it. To most, the music sounded like Bruce Springsteen clones, but it was appealing nonetheless. —*William Ruhlmann*

Tough All Over / 1985 / Scotti Brothers ✦✦✦

On the strength of the double platinum soundtrack to *Eddie and the Cruisers*, John Cafferty and the Beaver Brown Band were able to record *Tough All Over*, an album of their original songs, and release it under their own name. Released in the summer of 1985 at the tail-end of Eddie-mania, the record managed to spawn hard-rocking Top 40 hits, "C-I-T-Y" and "Tough All Over," which strongly recalled Springsteen, much like the rest of Cafferty's songs. Besides the two hits, *Tough All Over* lacked material that ranked with the best of the *Eddie and the Cruisers* soundtrack. Nevertheless, the album stayed on the charts for an impressive 32 weeks. —*Stephen Thomas Erlewine*

Roadhouse / 1988 / Scotti Brothers ✦✦

Released in 1988, after *Eddie and the Cruisers* had faded from public consciousness, *Roadhouse* repeated the formula John Cafferty and the Beaver Brown Band established on the *Eddie* soundtrack—simple, three-chord rock 'n' roll in the vein of Bruce Springsteen. In terms of quality, *Roadhouse* wasn't much worse than *Tough All Over*, but the band's moment had passed and the album failed to chart. After its release the group returned to recording under the name Eddie and the Cruisers. —*Stephen Thomas Erlewine*

Eddie & The Cruisers 2: Eddie Lives / 1989 / RCA ✦✦

The soundtrack to the sequel for *Eddie & the Cruisers* follows the basic blueprint of John Cafferty's songs for the first film—they're all high energy, pounding three-chord rock 'n' roll. However, Cafferty wasn't able to come up with a batch of songs as good as "The Dark Side," which leaves the soundtrack as bland and predictable as the movie it was supporting. —*Stephen Thomas Erlewine*

Eddie & The Cruisers: The Unreleased Tapes / Oct. 22, 1991 / Scotti Brothers ✦

Eddie & The Cruisers: Live and in Concert / May 22, 1992 / RCA ✦

Cake

f. 1994, Sacramento, CA
Alternative Pop-Rock

Cake's all-purpose eclectic rock appeared nationwide in 1995, when Capricorn released *Motorcade of Generosity*. The Sacramento-based band includes guitarist Greg Brown, bassist Victor Damiani, trumpeter Vince Di Fiore, vocalist and guitarist John McCrea, and drummer Todd Roper. —*John Bush*

Motorcade of Generosity / 1994 / Capricorn ✦✦

A new and welcome addition to the ever-growing quirk-rock genre, Cake's funky guitar rock recalls the absurdity of Phish's genre-hopping jams (and vocalist John McCrea's nasal levity is a dead ringer for Phish's Trey Anastasio). There are some very entertaining songs here: "Rock 'n' Roll Lifestyle" is a hilarious and thoroughly laudable sendup of the excesses of rock fans; "Jolene" begins as their most tightly crafted song and then dissolves into a deliciously messy jam session. Quirky music does demand a high standard of consistency, because its triviality can easily become tiresome. Cake's minimalist jams occasionally get repetitive; their sparing arrangements use two guitars, bass, drums, and a horn. But there are enough standouts here to easily qualify *Motorcade* as a keeper. —*Darryl Cater*

● **Fashion Nugget** / Sep. 17, 1996 / Capricorn ✦✦✦

Sounding like a suburban, melodic white-funk-injected version of King Missile's performance art/standup comedy, "The Distance" became a novelty hit in the fall of 1996, sending Cake's second album, *Fashion Nugget*, to gold status. Certainly "The Distance" was the only reason *Fashion Nugget* went gold, because the remainder of the album is too collegiate and arcane for mainstream music tastes. It isn't because it is obscure or intellectual—it's because the band's smirking. An "ironic" cover of Gloria Gaynor's "I Will Survive" is the key to the album, sending the signal that Cake considers themselves above *everyone* else, and nothing is too insignificant to make fun of. And that wouldn't necessarily have been a problem if they had either wit or musical skills that would make their music either funny or listenable. Instead, they wallow in sophomoric jokes that rely on self-consciously elaborate wordplay. Occasionally their blend of collegiate musical styles—funk, hip-hop alternative rock—makes the music easy to digest in small doses, such as "The Distance," but it isn't varied enough to prevent the album from becoming tedious. —*Stephen Thomas Erlewine*

J.J. Cale

b. Dec. 5, 1938, Oklahoma City, OK
Guitar, Vocals / Blues-Rock, Singer-Songwriter, Pop-Rock

Notorious for his laidback, rootsy style, J.J. Cale (b. Jean Jacques Cale) is best known for writing "After Midnight" and "Cocaine," songs that Eric Clapton later made into hits. But Cale's influence wasn't only through songwriting; his distinctly loping sense of rhythm and shuffling boogie became the blueprint for the adult-oriented roots-rock of Clapton and Mark Knopfler, among others. Cale's refusal to vary the sound of his music over the course of his career caused some critics to label him a one-trick pony, but he managed to build a dedicated cult following with his sporadically released recordings.

Born in Oklahoma City but raised in Tulsa, OK, Cale played in a variety of rock 'n' roll bands and Western swing groups as a teenager, including one outfit that also featured Leon Russell. In 1959, at the age of 21, he moved to Nashville, where he was hired by the Grand Ole Opry's touring company. After a few years he returned to Tulsa, where he reunited with Russell and began playing local clubs. In 1964 Cale and Russell moved to Los Angeles with another local Oklahoma musician, Carl Radle.

Shortly after he arrived in Los Angeles, Cale began playing with Delaney and Bonnie. He played with the duo for only a brief time, beginning a solo career in 1965. That year he cut the first version of "After Midnight," which would become his most famous song. Around 1966 Cale formed the Leathercoated Minds with songwriter Roger Tillison. The group released a psychedelic album called *A Trip down Sunset Strip* the same year.

Deciding that he wouldn't be able to forge a career in Los Angeles, Cale returned to Tulsa in 1967. Upon his return, he set about playing local clubs. Within a year, he had recorded a set of demos. Radle obtained a copy of the demos and forwarded it to Denny Cordell, who was founding a record label called Shelter with Leon Russell. Shelter signed Cale in 1969. The following year, Eric Clapton recorded "After Midnight," taking it to the American Top 20 and thereby providing Cale with exposure and royalties. In 1972 Cale released his debut album, *Naturally*, on Shelter Records; the album featured the Top 40 hit "Crazy

Mama," as well as a re-recorded version of "After Midnight" that nearly reached the Top 40, and "Call Me the Breeze," which Lynyrd Skynyrd later covered. Cale followed *Naturally* with *Really*, which featured the minor hit "Lies," later that same year.

After the release of *Really*, J.J. Cale adopted a slow work schedule, releasing an album every other year or so. *Okie*, his third album, appeared in 1974. Two years later he released *Troubadour*, which yielded "Hey Baby," his last minor hit, as well as the original version of "Cocaine," a song that Clapton would later cover. By this point Cale had settled into a comfortable career as a cult artist, and he rarely made any attempt to break into the mainstream. One more album on Shelter Records, *Number Five*, appeared in 1979 and then he switched labels, signing with MCA in 1981. MCA released only one album (1981's *Shades*), and Cale moved to Mercury Records the next year, releasing *Grasshopper*.

In 1983 Cale released his eighth album, *No.8*. The album became his first not to chart. After its release, Cale left Mercury and entered a long period of seclusion, reappearing in late 1989 with *Travelog*, which was released on the British independent label Silvertone; the album appeared in America the next year. *Number 10* was released in 1992. The album failed to chart, but it re-established his power as a cult artist. He moved to the major label Virgin in 1994, releasing *Close to You* the same year. It was followed by *Guitar Man* in 1996. — *Stephen Thomas Erlewine*

Naturally / Dec. 1971 / Mercury ✦✦✦
J.J. Cale's debut allbum, *Naturally*, was recorded after Eric Clapton made "After Midnight" a huge success. Instead of following Slowhand's cue and constructing a slick blues-rock album, Cale recruited a number of his Oklahoma friends and made a laidback country-rock record that firmly established his distinctive, relaxed style. Cale included a new version of "After Midnight" on the album, but the true meat of the record lay in songs like "Crazy Mama," which became a hit single," and "Call Me the Breeze," which Lynyrd Skynyrd later covered. On these songs and many others Cale effortlessly captured a lazy, rolling boogie that contradicted all the commerical styles of boogie, blues, and country-rock. Where his contemporaries concentrated on solos, Cale worked the song and its rhythm, and the result was a pleasant, engaging album that was in no danger of raising anybody's temperature. — *Thom Owens*

Really / Dec. 1972 / Mercury ✦✦✦
Cale's guitar work manages to be both understated and intense here. The same is true of his seemingly offhand singing, which finds him drawling lines like "You get your gun, I'll get mine" with disarming casualness. But he has trouble coming up with original material as strong as that on his debut, and for some, his approach will be too casual; there are many times, when the band is percolating along and Cale is muttering into the microphone, that the music seems to be all background and no foreground. You may find yourself waiting for a payoff that never comes. — *William Ruhlmann*

Okie / May 1974 / Mercury ✦✦✦
Cale moves toward country and gospel on some songs here, but since those are two of his primary influences, the movement is slight. And longtime producer Audie Ashworth attempts to place more emphasis on Cale's vocals on some songs by double-tracking them and pushing them up in the mix. But much of this is still low-key and bluesy in what was becoming Cale's patented style. — *William Ruhlmann*

Troubadour / Sep. 1976 / Mercury ✦✦✦✦
Producer Audie Ashworth introduced some different instruments, notably vibes and what sound like horns (although none are credited), for a slightly altered sound here. But Cale's albums are so steeped in his introspective style that they become interchangeable. If you like one of them, chances are you'll want to have them all. This one is notable for introducing "Cocaine," which Eric Clapton covered on his *Slowhand* album a year later. — *William Ruhlmann*

5 / Aug. 1979 / Mercury ✦✦
As Cale's influence on others expanded, he just continued to turn out the occasional album of bluesy, minor-key tunes. This one was even sparer than usual, with the artist handling bass as well as guitar on many tracks. Listened to today, it sounds so much like a Dire Straits album, it's scary. (Mark Knopfler & Co. had appeared in 1978, seven years after Cale.) — *William Ruhlmann*

Shades / Feb. 1981 / Mercury ✦✦

Grasshopper / Mar. 1982 / Mercury ✦✦
J.J. Cale drifts toward a more pop approach on this album, starting with the lead-off track, "City Girls," which could almost but not quite be a hit single. The usual blues and country shuffle approach is in effect, but Audie Ashworth's production is unusually sharp, the playing has more bite than usual, and Cale, whose vocals are for the most part up in the mix, sounds more engaged. It's not clear, however, that this is an improvement over his usual laidback approach, and, in any case, it

shouldn't be over-emphasized—this is still a J.J. Cale album, with its cantering tempos and single-note guitar runs. It's just that, when you have a style as defined as Cale's, little movements in style loom larger. — *William Ruhlmann*

8 / 1983 / Mercury ✦✦
Twelve years and eight albums into his recording career, Cale's approach has changed little, and here is another collection of groove tunes that act as platforms for the artist's intricate guitar playing. He is sometimes accompanied by a female vocalist, co-writer Christine Lakeland. — *William Ruhlmann*

● **Special Edition** / 1984 / Mercury ✦✦✦✦
Sinuous rhythms, conversational singing, and, most of all, intricate, bluesy guitar playing characterize Cale's performances of his own songs. This compilation, covering 11 years of recording, includes the songs Eric Clapton, who borrowed heavily from Cale's style in his 1970s solo work, made famous: "After Midnight" and "Cocaine." — *William Ruhlmann*

Travel Log / Feb. 1990 / Silvertone ✦✦✦✦
Cale's first album in six years finds him taking a more aggressive stance in terms of tempos and playing, although he remains a man with a profound sense of the groove and, especially as a singer, a minimalist. But as he says, "Shuffle or die." — *William Ruhlmann*

10 / Nov. 10, 1992 / Silvertone ✦✦✦
There are no major surprises on Cale's tenth outing; fans get the same dependable, unassuming, comfy results, like a well worn but form-fitting pair of slippers. Subtle licks percolate and resonate from the front-porch jam session on "Jailer" and "Low Rider." "Lonesome Train" and "Shady Grove" choogle along, as amiable as they are hypnotic. The closest thing to a twist comes with the phased vocals and spiralling guitar runs of "Digital Blues."It would be easy to imagine *Number 10* getting completely buried behind a wash of '90s white noise, but for those prepared to kick off their boots and sit a spell, Cale's latest offers up some seductive rewards. — *Roch Parisien*

Closer to You / Aug. 23, 1994 / Virgin ✦✦

Guitar Man / Jun. 25, 1996 / Virgin ✦✦✦
J.J. Cale's albums usually sound interchangeable, and his twelfth release, *Guitar Man*, is no exception. Although he has recorded *Guitar Man* as a one-man band effort, it sounds remarkably relaxed and laidback, like it was made with a seasoned bar band. That doesn't mean there's much excitement on the album, but Cale's music has never been about excitement—it's more about laying back and letting the music flow. Of course, that approach results in remarkably uneven records, and *Guitar Man* is no exception. There's a handful of very good songs, but there's nothing on the level of his previous classics. It's just another pleasant J.J. Cale album, nothing more but nothing less, either. — *Thom Owens*

John Cale

b. Mar. 9, 1942, Garnant, South Wales
Organ, Bass, Guitar, Piano, Harpsichord, Keyboards, Viola, Vocals / Art-Rock/Progressive-Rock, Experimental, Proto-Punk
While John Cale is one of the most famous and, in his own way, influential underground rock musicians, he is also one of the hardest to pin down stylistically. Much has been made of his schooling in classical and avant-garde music, but much of what he's recorded has been decidedly song-oriented and close to the mainstream at times. Terming him a forefather of punk and new wave isn't exactly accurate, either. Those investigating his work for the first time under that premise may be surprised at how consciously accessible much of his output is, at times approaching (but not quite attaining) a fairly "normal" rock sound. There is always tension between the experimental and the accessible in Cale's solo recordings, meaning that he usually finds himself (not unwillingly) caught between the cracks: too weird for commercial success, and yet not really weird or daring enough to place him among the top rank of rock's innovators.

Any assessment of Cale's solo contributions also tends to be overshadowed by his other considerable achievements. Before launching his solo career, he was, with Lou Reed, a primary creative force behind the Velvet Underground, as bassist, viola player, keyboardist, and occasional co-songwriter (the exact nature of his compositional contributions is still a matter of heated debate among the group). He was without question one of the most influential producers of pre-punk, punk, and new wave, overseeing important recordings by the Stooges, Nico, Patti Smith, the Modern Lovers, and Squeeze. Ultimately he may be better remembered for his work in the Velvets, and as a producer, than for his own large discography.

The son of a Welsh coal miner (his father) and schoolteacher (his mother), Cale was a child prodigy of sorts, performing an original composition on the BBC before he entered his teens. In the early '60s, he drifted toward the avant-garde, gaining a scholarship (with help from Aaron Copland and Leonard Bernstein) to study music in the United

States. Moving to New York in 1963, he participated in an 18-hour piano recital with John Cage. (Pictures of Cale performing at the event made the *New York Times*.) More important, he became a member of LaMonte Young's minimalist ensemble the Dream Syndicate, whose use of repetitious drones would influence the arrangements of his next group, the Velvet Underground.

Cale founded the Velvets with Reed and guitarist Sterling Morrison in the mid-'60s. Cale met Reed when the latter was a struggling songwriter for the rock 'n' roll exploitation label Pickwick Records. He tested the rock waters as part of the Primitives (with Reed and fellow Dream Syndicate member Tony Conrad), who did a few live shows to promote a silly novelty, "The Ostrich," that Reed had written and recorded at Pickwick. What Cale and Reed shared was an ambition to bring the sensibilities of the avant-garde to rock music.

They succeeded in doing so over the next three years with the Velvet Underground. While Reed was the most important member of the band as the lead singer and primary songwriter, Cale was just as crucial in devising the band's *sound*. Cale was responsible for the most experimental elements of their first two albums, *The Velvet Underground & Nico* and *White Light/White Heat* (1967), especially with his droning viola parts on "Venus in Furs," "Heroin," and "Black Angel's Death Song"; his pounding piano on "I'm Waiting for the Man" and "All Tomorrow's Parties"; his deadpan narration of "The Gift"; and the white-noise organ of "Sister Ray."

Yet Cale was ousted from the band in an apparent power play by Lou Reed in the summer of 1968. Accounts still vary as to whether he was fired or quit, but it's been suggested that Reed's ego found Cale's talents threatening to his leadership of the band. Sterling Morrison has said that Reed told him and Velvets drummer Maureen Tucker that if Cale didn't leave, he would leave instead; the pair reluctantly opted to side with Reed. The Velvets would continue to make great music for a couple of years, but their experimental edge was considerably blunted by Cale's absence.

Cale was soon busy producing ex-Velvets singer Nico's baroque-gothic *The Marble Index* (1969) and the Stooges' self-titled debut album (also 1969). Though about as different as two projects could be, both were extremely influential (though initially extremely low-selling) cult items that helped lay the ground for punk and new wave about five years later.

In 1970 Cale began his proper solo career with one of his best albums, *Vintage Violence*. Those expecting a slab of radicalism were in for a surprise: the material was the work of a low-key, accessible singer-songwriter working in the mold of the Band rather than the Velvets. Listeners wouldn't have to wait long for something a bit more radical; his next album, *Church of Anthrax*, was a collaboration with minimalist composer Terry Riley that was almost entirely instrumental.

In some respects, these two records defined the poles of Cale's solo career. Even at his most accessible, his music had a moody, even morbid, edge that precluded much radio airplay. Even at its most experimental, it was never as avant-garde as, say, LaMonte Young. Cale would reserve his most experimental outings for collaborations with Riley, Brian Eno, and, much further down the road, Lou Reed.

On his own, he was more concerned with crafting songs, delivered in his lilting if thin Welsh burr, and inventively arranged. It was in his arrangements that his musical training and avant-garde background were most evident, in its eclecticism (even drawing from country-rock and guest shots from Lowell George at times) and touches of classical music. Sometimes he'd take out his viola, but generally he focused on the more traditional instruments of guitar and keyboards.

Cale has covered a wide territory on his solo albums without ever quite making his mark as a major artist. His songs and concepts are interesting, but ultimately he does not have the striking traditional rock talents of someone like, say, his old rival Lou Reed. The hooks aren't that sharp, the lyrics—often dealing with the psychological and social dilemmas of late 20th-century life, in somewhat arty terms—not as gripping.

Toward the end of the late '70s especially, his approach became harder-rocking and a bit vicious, especially in concert, where he would adopt a number of flamboyant costumes and theatrical poses that verged on the confrontational (especially in a notorious incident in which he killed a chicken onstage). Generally he was most successful in a more subdued and brooding mode, as on *Vintage Violence* or, much later, *Music for a New Society* (1982). His discography is so large and variable that the two-CD career retrospective, *Seducing Down the Door*, might be the best place to start for those with enough interest to buy more than one or two Cale records.

Cale never abandoned his production activities, and indeed a few of the albums with his credits are destined to endure as more important statements than anything he's done on his own. His sessions with Jonathan Richman and the Modern Lovers (from the early '70s, but not released until a few years later) anticipated punk and new wave. Patti Smith's *Horses* (1975) was one of the best and most influential recordings of the 1970s. There were albums with Nico, and records with

Squeeze, Sham 69, and others; for a couple of years in the early '70s, he was even a staff producer at Warner, handling unlikely clients like Jennifer Warnes.

After the mid-'80s, Cale slowed (but did not curtail) work on his own releases. His most high-profile outings since then have been collaborations. *Wrong Way Up* (1990) matched him with Brian Eno. *Songs for Drella* (1990), which got a lot more media ink, reunited him at long last with Reed, with whom he had feuded on and off for a couple of decades; the album was a song-cycle tribute to their recently deceased mentor and ex-Velvet Underground manager, Andy Warhol. Well received both on record and in performance, it may have been one of the factors that finally caused the pair to bury the hatchet and reform the Velvet Underground for a 1993 live European tour (and live album). These events were not as successful with the critics; more disturbingly, Reed and Cale were on the outs yet again by the end of the tour, with feuds over direction, leadership, and songwriting credits apparently resurfacing with a vengeance.

Prospects for an American Velvet Underground tour never came to realization, Cale and Reed vowing never to work with each other again. The death of Sterling Morrison in 1995 ended any reunion hopes, although it did apparently serve to reconcile Reed and Cale, who played together when the Velvet Underground were inducted into the Rock & Roll Hall of Fame in 1996. Cale doesn't need Reed to keep busy (or vice versa). In the 1990s, he's continued to record as a soloist and a soundtrack composer. His latest and most ambitious collaboration is *The Last Day on Earth* (1994), a song cycle and theatrical production written and performed with cult singer-songwriter Bobby Neuwirth. —*Richie Unterberger*

Vintage Violence / Mar. 25, 1970 / Columbia ✦✦✦
Given that Cale supposedly wielded the strongest avant-garde/dissonant sensibilities on the first Velvet Underground albums, it's surprising that his first solo LP has a light, playful, cheerful feel. With its rollicking piano, acoustic guitars, and occasional pedal steel and mournful violin, as well as the obtuse, narrative/reflective lyrics, there's a comfortable, meditative lilt to these tunes, as well as a nonchalant charm not far removed from the early work of former cohort Lou Reed. Cale lets his darker undertones come to the fore on the stark ballad "Amsterdam" and the swirling, truly ominous "Ghost Story." —*Richie Unterberger*

Church of Anthrax / Feb. 10, 1971 / Columbia ✦✦✦
Cale and Terry Riley produce a dense instrumental sound that is equal parts jazz, rock, and contemporary classical on this album. (There is also one vocal track, sung by Adam Miller.) A bit too busy to be called "minimalist," a bit too intense to be called "ambient," it is sometimes reminiscent of the fusion style later pioneered by the likes of Miles Davis and Frank Zappa. Not easy listening by any means, but rewarding. —*William Ruhlmann*

The Academy in Peril / Jul. 19, 1972 / Reprise ✦✦✦
Cale moved to Warner Bros.' Reprise label in 1972 for his second solo album, an all-instrumental collection on which he made greater use of his classical and avant-garde training, employing the Royal Philharmonic Orchestra for two cuts and naming tunes after Brahms and John Milton. The result is an imaginative, though unfocused, album that expanded Cale's musical horizons, if not his audience. —*William Ruhlmann*

Paris 1919 / Mar. 1973 / Reprise ✦✦✦✦
John Cale's third solo album possessed a rare beauty, demonstrating that the classically trained avant-garde rock 'n' roll viola player could, when he wished, make melodic pop music with a lush elegance. —*William Ruhlmann*

Fear / Oct. 1, 1974 / Island ✦✦✦✦
Moving to Island Records for his fourth solo album (and third try at a pop vocal approach), Cale brought in Roxy Music guitarist Phil Manzanera and turned to a harder rocking style on the title track and "Gun." But "You Know More than I Know" and other songs showed he retained the melodic qualities and talent for thoughtful ballads displayed on *Paris 1919*. —*William Ruhlmann*

Slow Dazzle / Mar. 25, 1975 / Island ✦✦✦
On the second installment of a trilogy made for Island in the mid-'70s, Cale played (as one song title had it) "Dirtyass Rock 'N' Roll," anticipating the coming punk movement. *Slow Dazzle* includes Cale's drastic reconstruction of "Heartbreak Hotel." —*William Ruhlmann*

Helen of Troy / Nov. 14, 1975 / Island ✦✦✦
Island Records declined to release this, the third of its John Cale albums, in the US, which meant fans had to scramble for the import copy of a record that featured guitarist Chris Spedding and a song selection highlighted by the Cale classic "I Keep a Close Watch" and his version of Jonathan Richman's "Pablo Picasso," which he had produced earlier for the Modern Lovers. —*William Ruhlmann*

Guts / 1977 / Island ✦✦✦✦
Guts is a compilation album selecting the best from Cale's three Island releases of 1974-1975: *Fear, Slow Dazzle,* and *Helen Of Troy.* —*William Ruhlmann*

Animal Justice / Sep. 1977 / Illegal ✦✦
This is a three-song, 45 rpm, 12-inch import EP featuring the hard rock track "Chicken Shit," a cover of Chuck Berry's "Memphis," and another of Cale's literary musicalizations, "Hedda Gabler." It has some of the same extreme rock venom of the second Velvet Underground album. —*William Ruhlmann*

Sabotage/Live / Dec. 1979 / Spy ✦✦✦
By 1979 Cale was leading a hard rock band (and wearing a hardhat onstage), and this live album, recorded at New York's CBGB, finds him angrily churning out songs like "Mercenaries (Ready for War)" and the title track, in which be declares, "Military intelligence isn't what it used to be." Was it ever? —*William Ruhlmann*

Honi Soit / Mar. 10, 1981 / A&M ✦✦✦
Cale's first "new" studio album in six years was an excellent pop-rock collection paced by its leadoff track, "Dead or Alive." —*William Ruhlmann*

Music for a New Society / Aug. 1982 / Island ✦✦✦✦
Cale's calmest collection of music since *Paris 1919* contains an excellent version of "Close Watch," as well as the haunting "Chinese Envoy." —*William Ruhlmann*

Caribbean Sunset / Jan. 1984 / ZE ✦✦
With a rock band backing him up and Brian Eno on A.M.S. pitch changer, Cale makes another straightforward pop-rock collection. Talk about first takes—on "Experimental Number I," Cale calls out chord changes to the band as it plays the song! —*William Ruhlmann*

Comes Alive / Sep. 1984 / Mango ✦✦
Employing the same trio that backed him on *Caribbean Sunset,* Cale turns in a set of familiar favorites on this album, culled from a show at the London Lyceum in February 1984. Some of his best later songs, such as "Dead or Alive" and "Chinese Envoy," are included. Also contains Cale's cover of the Velvet Underground favorite "Waiting for the Man." —*William Ruhlmann*

Artificial Intelligence / Sep. 6, 1985 / Beggars Banquet ✦✦
Guitarist David Young is the only holdover on this album of run-of-the-mill songs co-written with rock journalist Larry Sloman, the best of which is the ballad "Dying on the Vine." But Cale's and James Young's keyboards form the basis of the sound. —*William Ruhlmann*

Words for the Dying / Sep. 1989 / Opal ✦✦✦

Songs for Drella / 1990 / Sire ✦✦✦✦
Lou Reed and John Cale's tribute to Andy Warhol brings out the best in both of them. It's a spare collection, the only instruments being Reed's guitar and Cale's keyboards and viola. The songs trace Warhol's life in a witty, conversational way that evokes his spirit far better than any biographical work of the artist yet attempted. —*William Ruhlmann*

Wrong Way Up / Oct. 16, 1990 / Opal ✦✦✦✦
Both Eno and John Cale have always flirted with conventional pop music throughout their careers, while reserving the right to go off on less accessible experiments, which means they've always held out the promise that they would make something as attractive as this collection, on which Eno comes as close to the mainstream as he has since *Another Green World,* and Cale is as catchy as he's been since *Honi Soit.* The result is one of the best albums either one has ever made. —*William Ruhlmann*

Even Cowgirls Get the Blues / Sep. 10, 1991 / ROIR ✦✦
An archival release of live performances at CBGB in December 1978 and December 1979 finds Cale in a caustic hard rock mode, not unlike the *Sabotage/Live* album recorded in between. Patti Smith's rhythm section, Ivan Kral and Jay Dee Dougherty, accompany Cale, and Judy Nylon, sounding a lot like Smith, takes occasional vocals. —*William Ruhlmann*

Fragments of a Rainy Season / Sep. 25, 1992 / Hannibal ✦✦✦✦
It's hard to imagine John Cale on MTV, but if he appeared on *Unplugged,* the result probably would sound like this. Alone, Cale accompanies himself on acoustic piano and guitar, playing a retrospective set of some of his best and most accessible music. The emphasis is on his more contemplative material, such as the early *Paris 1919* album, his later *Words for the Dying,* which features the poetry of Dylan Thomas set to music, and other notable Cale ballads. He does throw in some rock 'n' roll fervor and some of his noisy *avant-garde* effects on numbers like "Guts," but for the most part this is a John Cale who, while intense, is quiet and dignified. —*William Ruhlmann*

● **Seducing Down the Door** / Jul. 5, 1994 / Rhino ✦✦✦✦
The range of John Cale's work can be shocking. It's hard to believe that

the piano duets with minimalist composer Terry Riley on *Church of Anthrax,* the lush orchestral pop of *Paris 1919,* and the raucous, dissonant guitar rock of "Gun" and the rest of *Fear* are all the work of the same man. This well chosen 38-track, two-hour double-CD/cassette anthology does nothing to reconcile the apparent musical contradictions in Cale's classical-to-punk sensibility, but it does bring coherence and consolidation to a recording career that, spread across a multitude of labels and plagued by popular indifference, has been difficult to grasp as a whole. —*William Ruhlmannn*

Island Years / Jul. 1996 / Island ✦✦✦✦
This double CD combines all three of his mid-'70s Island albums (*Fear, Slow Dazzle,* and *Helen of Troy*) in one package, with the addition of some interesting bonus tracks: outtakes from *Slow Dazzle* and *Helen of Troy,* the B-side "Sylvia Said," "Leaving It up to You" (which appeared only on early copies of *Helen of Troy,* before "Coral Moon" took its place), and "Mary Lou" (from the 1977 *Guts* compilation). This was undeniably one of Cale's most fertile periods. There is also no other body of work from the mid-'70s with such a confluence of listenable FM radio-ready tunes and sneaky, at times subversive, experimentation, its eclecticism encompassing art rock, macabre recitations, and Beach Boy pastiches. —*Richie Unterberger*

Walking on Locusts / Sep. 24, 1996 / Hannibal ✦✦
One of Cale's more determinedly normal-sounding efforts. Indeed, at times it almost appears as if Cale is targeting the "Triple-A" (album-oriented adult alternative) market. It also sometimes seems as if the songs have been run through the shiny, slightly quirky production machine of a label such as ECM. (The guitars, especially, have a post-modern slickness.) Cale's never going to sound anonymous, but there's little to catch one's attention here. —*Richie Unterberger*

The Call

f. 1980, California, **db.** 1990
Rock 'n' Roll, Alternative Pop-Rock
Led by vocalist and songwriter Michael Been, California's the Call mixed the fire and social awareness of the Clash with the passion and big, anthemic sound of early U2, plus a healthy dose of Christian mysticism. The band included guitarist Tom Ferrier, bassist Greg Freeman (replaced by keyboardist Jim Goodwin in 1984), and drummer Scott Musick. The group broke through in 1983 with the minor hit "The Walls Came Down" from *Modern Romans;* later LPs *Reconciled* and *Let the Day Begin* were also moderately successful. However, the Call never quite achieved the transcendence they were aiming for and broke up; Been compiled the band's best tracks on *The Walls Came Down: Best of the Mercury Years.* —*Steve Huey*

The Call / 1982 / Mercury ✦✦

Modern Romans / 1983 / Mercury ✦✦✦

Scene Beyond Dreams / 1984 / Mercury ✦✦✦

Reconciled / 1986 / Elektra ✦✦✦✦
One of their best efforts, It features the hit "Everywhere I Go"—Christian mysticism with a nervy edge. —*Rick Clark*

Into the Woods / 1987 / Elektra ✦✦✦

Let the Day Begin / May 1989 / MCA ✦✦✦✦
The title cut was a major rock hit in spite of poor retail distribution. Other highlights include the rude rough-and-tumble rock of "Same Ol' Story." —*Rick Clark*

Red Moon / Aug. 1990 / MCA ✦✦✦✦
Pressured for new product, Been rose to the occasion, creating some of his most affectingly passionate music, particularly the stirring title cut, as well as "What's Happened to You?" (reminiscent of the Band), "Like You've Never Been Loved," "This Is Your Life," and "Floating Back." The organic style of production works beautifully with the music. —*Rick Clark*

● **The Walls Came Down: The Best of the Mercury Years** / Jun. 11, 1991 / Mercury ✦✦✦✦
This great collection of the band's early career contains the fiery debut single "The Walls Came Down." It was compiled by Been. —*Rick Clark*

Camel

f. 1972, Surrey, England
Art-Rock/Progressive-Rock
Camel never achieved the mass popularity of fellow British progressive-rock bands like the Alan Parsons Project, but they cultivated a dedicated cult following. Over the course of their career, Camel experienced numerous changes, but throughout the years, Andrew Latimer remained the leader of the band.

Formed in 1972 in Surrey, Camel originally consisted of Latimer (guitar, flute, vocals), Andy Ward (drums), Doug Ferguson (bass), and keyboardist Peter Bardens, previously of Them. By the end of 1973, the group signed with MCA and released their eponymous debut. In 1974 the band switched record labels, signing with Decca's Gama subsidiary, and released *Mirage*. In 1975 Camel released their breakthrough album *The Snow Goose*, which climbed into the British Top 30. The band's English audience declined with 1976's *Moonmadness*, but the album was more successful in America, reaching No. 118—the highest chart position the band ever attained in the US. After the release of *Moonmadness*, Ferguson left the band and was replaced by Richard Sinclair (ex-Caravan); at the same time, the group added saxophonist Mel Collins. Latimer and Bardens argued during the recording of 1977's *Rain Dances*, and those tensions would come to a head during the making of 1978's *Breathless*. After *Breathless* was completed, Bardens left the band. Before recording their next album, Camel replaced Bardens with two keyboardists—Kit Watkins (Happy the Man) and Jim Schelhaas (Caravan)—and replaced Sinclair with Colin Bass.

By the time Camel released their 1979 album, *I Can See Your House from Here*, rock 'n' roll had been changed by the emergence of punk rock, which resulted in less press coverage for progressive rock, as well as decreased record sales. Camel suffered from this shift in popular taste—*I Can See Your House from Here* received less attention than any of the band's other releases since their debut. Latimer returned to writing concept albums with 1981's *Nude*. In 1982 drummer Andy Ward was forced to leave the band after suffering a severe hand injury. Camel's 1982 album, *The Single Factor*, was a slicker, more accessible affair than previous Camel records, but it failed to chart. *Stationary Traveller* (1984) was another concept album.

After the release of the 1984 live album *Pressure Points*, Camel entered a hibernation that lasted until the early '90s. In 1985 Decca dropped Camel from its roster. Latimer wasn't able to find a new label, because he was embroiled in a difficult legal battle with Camel's former manager Geoff Jukes; Camel eventually won the lawsuit in the late '80s. Throughout this period, Camel produced no new music. In 1988 Latimer sold his home in England and moved to California, where he founded the independent label Camel Productions. By the time Camel recorded their follow-up to *Stationary Traveller* in the early '90s, the band was, for most intents and purposes, simply Andrew Latimer and a handful of session musicians. *Dust and Dreams* (1991) was the first release on Camel Productions. In 1993, PolyGram released a double-disc Camel retrospective, *Echoes*. In early 1996, Camel released *Harbour of Tears*. —*Stephen Thomas Erlewine*

Camel / 1973 / MCA ♦♦
Camel was still finding its signature sound on its eponymous debut album. At this point, Peter Bardens and his grand, sweeping organ dominate, and Andrew Latimer sounds tentative on occasion. Furthermore, the music fluctuates uncertainly between arty improvisations, jazz-inflected rhythms, and uninspired rock numbers. There are hints of promise scattered throughout the album, but the record never gels into something special. —*Daevid Jehnzen*

Mirage / 1974 / Janus ♦♦♦
With their second album, *Mirage*, Camel begins to develop its own distinctive sound, highlighted by the group's liquid, intricate rhythms and the wonderful, unpredictable instrumental exchanges by keyboardist Peter Bardens and guitarist Andy Latimer. Camel also distinguishes itself from prog-rock peers with the multi-part suite "Lady Fantasy," which suggests the more complex directions they would take a few albums down the line. Also, Latimer's graceful flute playing distinguishes several songs on the record, including "Supertwister," and it's clear that he has a more supple technique than such contemporaries as Ian Anderson. Camel is still ironing out some quirks in the sound on *Mirage*, but it's evident that they are coming into their own. —*Daevid Jehnzen*

The Snow Goose / 1975 / Janus ♦♦♦
Camel's classic period started with *The Snow Goose*, an instrumental concept album based on a novella by Paul Gallico. Although there are no lyrics on the album—two songs feature wordless vocals—the music follows the emotional arc of the novella's story, which is about a lonely man named Rhayader who helps nurse a wounded snow goose back to health with the help of a girl called Fritha whom he recently befriended. Once the goose is healed, it is set free, but Fritha no longer visits the man because the goose is gone. Later, Rhayader is killed during a battle as he defends his village from intruders. The goose returns during the battle, and it is then named La Princesse Perdue, symbolizing the hopes that can still survive even during the evils of war. With such a complex fable to tell, it is no surprise that Camel keeps its improvisational tendencies reigned in, deciding to concentrate on surging, intricate soundscapes that telegraph the emotion of the piece without a single word. And even though *The Snow Goose* is an instrumental album, it is far more accessible than some of Camel's later work, since it relies on beautiful sonic textures instead of musical experimentation. —*Stephen Thomas Erlewine*

Moonmadness / 1976 / Janus ♦♦♦
Abandoning the lovely soundscapes of *Snow Goose*, Camel delved into layered guitar and synthesizers similar to those of Pink Floyd's *Wish You Were Here* on the impressive *Moonmadness*. Part of the reason behind the shift in musical direction was the label's insistence that Camel venture into more commercial territory after the experimental *Snow Goose*, and it is true that the music on *Moonmadness* is more akin to traditional English progressive rock, even though it does occasionally dip into jazz-fusion territory with syncopated rhythms and shimmering keyboards. Furthermore, the songs are a little more concise and accessible than those of its predecessor. That doesn't mean Camel has abandoned art. *Moonmadness* is indeed a concept album, based loosely on the personalities of each member; "Chord Change" is Peter Bardens, "Air Born" is Andy Latimer, "Lunar Sea" is Andy Ward, and "Another Night" is Doug Ferguson. Certainly it's a concept that is considerably less defined than that of *The Snow Goose*, and the music isn't quite as challenging, but that doesn't mean that *Moonmadness* is devoid of pleasure. In fact, with its long stretches of atmospheric instrumentals and spacey solos, it's quite rewarding. —*Daevid Jehnzen*

Rain Dances / 1977 / Deram ♦♦♦♦
Rain Dances, Camel's fifth release, offers the most consistent and representative package in their saga. This is the band at its best. The addition of Caravan-cofounder Richard Sinclair proves profitable, as do a few colorist touches by Brian Eno on "Elke." Mel Collins' woodwinds are among the highlights, especially on *Tell Me* and the title track. From beginning to end, this project flows gracefully. —*Matthew Plichta*

Breathless / 1978 / Arista ♦♦♦♦
With *Rain Dances*, Camel began exploring shorter, more concise songs, but it wasn't until the followup, *Breathless*, that they truly made a stab at writing pop songs. Although they didn't completely abandon improvistory prog-rock—there are several fine, jazzy interludes—most of the record is comprised of shorter songs, designed for radio play. While the group didn't quite achieve that goal, *Breathless* is nevertheless a more accessible record than Camel's other albums, which tend to focus on instrumentals. Here, they try to be a straightforward prog-rock band, and while the results are occasionally a little muddled, it is on the whole suprisingly successful. —*Daevid Jehnzen*

● **I Can See Your House from Here** / 1979 / Deram ♦♦♦♦
Although not an honest representation of the band's character, this is undoubtedly their most popular work. The one-time addition of American Kit Watkins produces some fine keyboard lead work. Rupert Hines' resourceful production and appearances by Phil Collins and Mel Collins round out this strong import release. "Survival" and "Who We Are" feature some fine orchestrations, and guitarist Latimer delivers exceptional lead work on the album's closer, "Ice." —*Matthew Plichta*

Nude / 1981 / Decca ♦♦♦♦
A new, larger version of Camel debuted on *Nude*, a concept album about a Japanese soldier who was stranded on a deserted island during World War II and stayed there, oblivious to the outside world, for 29 years. More ambitious than *I Can See Your House from Here*, *Nude* is in many ways just as impressive. Although it's a less accessible effort, it has a number of quite intriguing passages, particularly since it boasts heavier improvisation, orchestration, and even some worldbeat influences. It's not as spacey as Camel's earlier progressive rock records, but it is quite atmospheric, creating its own entrancing world. —*Daevid Jehnzen*

The Single Factor / 1982 / Passport ♦♦
Following the ambitious song cycle *Nude*, Camel attempted their version of an Alan Parsons Project album with *The Single Factor*. Considering that Parsons was having hits that year with songs like "Eye in the Sky," it's not surprising that Camel tried to capture the same audience, but their talent didn't lie with pop music—it lay with atmospheric instrumentals and creating detailed soundscapes. Consequently, *The Single Factor* sounds a little forced and often fails to capture the group's magic, even though there are a few strong moments on the record. —*Daevid Jehnzen*

Stationary Traveller / 1984 / Decca ♦♦♦
Although *Stationary Traveller* is a concept album, musically it falls into line with its predecessor *The Single Factor*, which found Camel trying to refashion themselves as the Alan Parsons Project. Where *The Single Factor* suffered from Camel's trying to write pop hooks, *Stationary Traveller* finds the band breaking down the barriers, opening up their relatively concise songs with long, atmospheric instrumental passages. The album's lyrics, which were written by Susan Hoover, are about divided Berlin and its political, emotional, and physical divisions. Often, the lyrics and music—which work as individual entities—don't quite work together, since they follow different emotional directions, but the

record remains a worthwhile listen, especially since it features Andy Latimer on pan flute. —*Daevid Jehnzen*

Compact Compilation / 1986 / Rhino ✦✦✦✦
Rhino's *A Compact Compilation* is a surprisingly thorough collection of highlights from Camel's '70s albums, hitting most of the group's highlights, including "Lady Fantasy," "Rhayader Goes to Town," "Lunar Sea," "Metrognome," and "Rain Dances." Although Camel's music makes more sense on their original concept albums, and the sound quality of *A Compact Compilation* could have been better, it remains a good introduction for neophytes. —*Daevid Jehnzen*

The Collection / 1986 / Castle ✦✦✦
Castle's Camel *Collection* is a reasonably thorough overview of highlights from the group's '70s albums, but it leaves out too many highlights and representative tracks to make it a good introduction for novices. —*Daevid Jehnzen*

Dust and Dreams / 1991 / Camel ✦✦✦✦
As with *Nude* and *The Snow Goose*, Camel continues refining their concept album approach, here based on Steinbeck's *The Grapes of Wrath*. Latimer maintains a symphony-like coherence throughout, with subtle character-based themes. Guest vocalist Mae McKenna has a hand in "Rose of Sharon," a gem of lyrical and musical depth. This album was produced and packaged by Latimer himself and may be harder to find than their others. [Available from Camel Productions, PO Box 4876, Mt. View, CA 94040.] —*Matthew Plichta*

● **Echoes: The Retrospective** / Jul. 20, 1993 / PolyGram ✦✦✦✦
There might be a song or two that die-hard fans will miss, but this double-disc set is the place to go for anyone looking for that one essential CD purchase of Camel's music. Featured are solid remastering and great liner notes and track annotation. —*Rick Clark*

Harbour of Tears / Jan. 20, 1996 / Camel ✦✦
Harbour of Tears explores the origins of Camel guitarist (and, by this time, only founding member) Andrew Latimer's family, tracing the Latimers as they emigrate from Ireland. Latimer sets the stage with a handful of descriptive, narrative songs at the beginning; by the end of the record, he's telling his story with his music. Though the album is a little rich for casual listeners, those willing to delve into Latimer's sweeping saga will find *Harbour of Tears* enthralling. —*Stephen Thomas Erlewine*

Cameo

f. 1974, New York, NY
Funk, Urban, Quiet Storm
Over the years, Cameo has reflected the numerous changes in the world of funk. When they started in 1974, they frequently toured with Parliament and Funkadelic, which is a clue to how their sound was styled. Even though they were in the hard funk vein of George Clinton's classic outfits, they were not copycats. As the '70s became the '80s, they started to play around with their sound slightly. In 1984 they found a successful style—the synth-powered title track to their album *She's Strange*. But that only hinted at what was to come. With 1986's *Word Up*, Cameo recorded a funk classic; bass-driven and synth heavy, the album was the sound of the mid-'80s. "Word Up" was also the song that broke them into the mainstream, reaching the Top Ten on the pop charts; thankfully, the album had a whole album's worth of good songs. *Word Up* proved to be the pinnacle of Cameo's career. Although the group kept recording and touring into the '90s, their style became a bit formulaic, as synthesizers and robotic funk took precedence over songs in their later records. By the mid-'90s, Cameo was finished as recording artists, but they still could tour successfully. —*Stephen Thomas Erlewine*

Cardiac Arrest / 1977 / Chocolate City ✦✦✦
The first major album for Cameo, who were then doing straight funk. The album scored three hits, among them the definitive "We All Know Who We Are" and the infectious "Rigor Mortis." They were still using horns and had 13 members in the group. —*Ron Wynn*

Ugly Ego / 1978 / Casablanca ✦✦✦
Another great funk treatise, with the first-rate uptempo tune "Insane" and a decent romantic song, "Give Love a Chance." They were slowly moving towards a new sound, although the influence of classic horn-driven funk bands like the Ohio Players and Bar-Kays is still prominent. —*Ron Wynn*

Secret Omen / 1979 / Casablanca ✦✦✦✦
Cameo leaped over their rivals with this 1979 release. "I Just Want To Be" was their finest single to that point, and "Sparkle" made a good album cut and counter-tune. It was the band's biggest hit album as well, starting them on a string of five gold records. —*Ron Wynn*

Cameosis / 1980 / Casablanca ✦✦✦
When Cameo released this 1980 LP, Larry Blackmon was still heading a large band that relied on horn-driven funk, reflecting the influence of

second-generation Bar-Kays. There were signs of stagnation throughout *Cameosis*, but including the neglected single "Why Have I Lost You" from the *We Know Who We Are* album was a stroke of genius. They landed a Top Ten R&B hit with "Shake Your Pants," but this wasn't among their best funk LPs. —*Ron Wynn*

Feel Me / 1980 / Casablanca ✦✦✦✦
One of two great funk albums Cameo issued in 1980. This one had another tremendous single, "Your Love Takes Me Out," a good second uptempo tune, "Keep It Hot," and was among the few '70s-style productions still viable at that point. The group hadn't yet streamlined its roster or changed its sound. —*Ron Wynn*

Knights of the Sound Table / 1981 / Casablanca ✦✦✦✦
Things were still rolling for Cameo with this '81 date. It was their first album to also be issued in England, and it scored more hits for them, with "Freaky Dancin'" reaching the No. 3 spot on the R&B charts. Changes were coming soon, but they still retained the familiar horn-dominated sound. —*Ron Wynn*

Alligator Woman / 1982 / Casablanca ✦✦✦
The final '70s-oriented funk release by Cameo was another smash in 1982. They got three hits from this album, with "Flirt" making the Top Ten and "Just Be Yourself" and the title cut also doing well. The surging horn charts would soon be a memory, but *Alligator Woman* provided a fitting conclusion to Cameo's first phase. —*Ron Wynn*

Style / 1983 / Atlanta Artists ✦✦✦
A key transitional album for Cameo. The group had pared its lineup to four core members, revamped its instrumental and production focus, and was now incorporating more electronics and sophisticated studio techniques. They also established their own label and relocated to Atlanta. This album laid the groundwork for the highly successful albums of the late '80s, and was their declaration of independence from the Ohio Players/Bar-Kays sound they had used to build their reputation. —*Ron Wynn*

She's Strange / 1984 / Casablanca ✦✦✦✦
This was the final large-group Cameo album. Blackmon realized that horn-driven funk was finished as a commercial entity in R&B production, and he stripped the group to a core trio the next year. However, the title track was the group's biggest R&B hit ever; it stayed atop the charts for four weeks, longer than the superior tunes "Word Up" or "Candy." "Talkin' out the Side of Your Neck" was a good message track. Blackmon showed his savvy by making the change in direction even as he was still reaping commercial dividends from the old style. —*Ron Wynn*

Single Life / 1985 / Casablanca ✦✦✦
This was a transitional album for Cameo, the first with a core trio and a refocused production and creative emphasis. They were now a synth-dominated band with a snaking bass sound, rather than a horn-oriented group playing elaborate arrangements and using multiple vocalists. Blackmon's through-the-nose Sly Stone imitation and a tighter style yielded immediate results; both the title track and "Attack Me with Your Love" were Top Ten R&B hits. Cameo was now right in the urban contemporary flow. —*Ron Wynn*

Word Up / 1985 / Casablanca ✦✦✦✦
Cameo's definitive album came as a surprise to those who classed them a good journeyman band. The title track became a national catch phrase in the African-American community, and "Word" remains a linguistic staple in hip-hop circles. It was also a first-rate song, with a hypnotic rhythm track and arrangement and Blackmon's best lead vocal. The follow-up singles "Candy" and "Back and Forth" were also excellent. Cameo eventually scored its only platinum album, and "Word Up" was their lone Top Ten pop hit. —*Ron Wynn*

● **The Best of Cameo** / May 18, 1993 / Casablanca ✦✦✦✦
Larry Blackmon and his Cameo mates ruled funk's domain for over a decade. Cameo evolved from its origins as a horn-based and dominated ensemble into a synthesizer-oriented group that still featured sturdy bass lines and exuberant vocals, but was in tune with urban and Black America's new sensibility. These 14 selections range from the formative cuts "Rigor Mortis," "Shake Your Pants," and "It's Over" to the definitive "Word Up," "Candy," and "Back and Forth." Blackmon's alternately sneering, defiant, and aggressive vocals were the constant from Cameo's beginnings in the 1970s to their emergence as funk's reigning champions in the 1980s. —*Ron Wynn*

Best of Cameo, Vol. 2 / May 21, 1996 / Mercury ✦✦✦✦
Fifteen songs and 78 minutes for those who want a little more than what's on sale on *The Best of Cameo*. It spans their whole career, and includes R&B hits like "Freaky Dancin'," "Keep It Hot," "Be Yourself," "Insane," "We're Going Out Tonight," "Feel Me," and "Alligator Woman" (the definite highlight, even if it wasn't one of their highest charters). Nona Hendryx guests on "Don't Be So Cool," and Miles Davis does the same for "In the Night." —*Richie Unterberger*

Tevin Campbell

b. 1978, Texas
Vocals / Urban, New Jack R&B

There's some dispute over who actually discovered Texas child sensation Tevin Campbell. Some accounts credit flutist Bobbi Humphrey, while much of the publicity material credits Quincy Jones. Campbell was in the 1988 television show "Wally & the Valentines" and appeared in Prince's film *Graffiti Bridge*. He made a splashy impression on Jones' *Back on the Block* LP, singing lead on "Tomorrow." He was 14 at the time. Campbell made such an impact that he earned a solo deal with Jones' Qwest label. His 1991 LP *T.E.V.I.N.* included two big R&B and pop hits, "Round and Round" and "Tell Me What You Want Me to Do." His second release, *I'm Ready*, was issued in 1993. In June 1996 he released his third album *Back to the World.* —*Ron Wynn*

● **T.E.V.I.N.** / Nov. 19, 1991 / Warner Brothers ◆◆◆◆
If *T.E.V.I.N.* had been recorded by an adult instead of a teenager, the album would still be impressive, but the fact that Tevin Campbell was only 14 years old when this was made makes it all the more amazing. Campbell's voice is remarkably expressive, able to handle both ballads and uptempo dance tracks without losing confidence. When he has the right material—like the hit single, Prince's "Round and Round"—the results are flawless; if the material is weak, he's merely enjoyable. —*Stephen Thomas Erlewine*

I'm Ready / Oct. 26, 1993 / Warner Brothers ◆◆◆
Teen star Tevin Campbell's *I'm Ready* signaled a compositional and performance maturity reminiscent of Stevie Wonder's coming-of-age material in the late '60s. His voice, though still youthful, was stronger, warmer, and more distinctive, and he made the romantic lyrics of such tunes as "Don't Say Goodbye Girl," "The Halls of Desire," and the title track plausible, if somewhat overdone. He also demonstrated a willingness to tackle social concerns, although "Uncle Sam" seemed a bit dated, with references to Vietnam and Birmingham. He was most effective on ballads, notably "Always in My Heart." Those who expected Campbell to have fallen by the wayside or thought he was just another prodigy whose career wouldn't evolve have already been proven wrong. —*Ron Wynn*

Back to the World / Jun. 25, 1996 / Qwest ◆◆◆◆
Back to the World is where Tevin Campbell returns as a man, ready to prove that he is no longer the child prodigy of yesteryear. For the most part, he succeeds in establishing himself as a vocalist of prodigious talents and significant worth. Of course, it was clear even in his earliest recordings that he was something special—a vocalist who could sing with a sweet, easy grace but remain soulful and not cloying in the slightest. No matter how Campbell tries to phase out that sweetness on *Back to the World*—after all, one of the first steps of maturity is to shed your childhood affectations—he retains that appealing quality, which makes the album all the more endearing. That's not to say that the uptempo cuts don't work. On the contrary—they are state-of-the-art pieces, thanks to the talents of producers like Puffy Combs, whose "I Need You" is a highlight. But the key to the record's success is how Campbell grows and matures without sacrificing his gift for pure, sweet, contemporary soul. *Back to the World* is proof positive that the teen idol is now a man. —*Leo Stanley*

Camper Van Beethoven

f. 1983, Santa Cruz, CA, db. 1990
Vocals, Group / Alternative Pop-Rock, Indie Rock, Jangle-Pop

At the time of their 1985 debut, Camper Van Beethoven's merging of punk, folk, ska, and world musics was truly a revelation. Self-described as "surrealist absurdist folk," the band formed in Santa Cruz, CA, after singer-songwriter David Lowery of Redlands, CA, with his dry humor and valley-boy voice (sometimes confused with a faux English accent), and boyhood friends Chris Molla and Chris Pedersen disbanded Box of Laffs. Victor Krummenacher was added on bass, and soon they were joined by Greg Lisher (guitar) and Jonathan Segel (violins, keyboards, mandolin). It was Segel's violin that would prove to be the band's hallmark at a time when alternative rock had yet to be invented, and indie-rock was still shy of roots music or traditional instruments. The 1985 re-release of their debut *Telephone Free Landslide Victory* made the Top Ten in the 1986 *Village Voice* annual Pazz and Jop Poll, as did their second album, *II & III*, and *Camper Van Beethoven*, both released in 1986. On *II & III*, they went for a purer indie-rock sound with touches of country, as evidenced in their "Sad Lovers Waltz" and their cover of Sonic Youth's "I Love Her All the Time." The band deftly switched modes from punk to ska to rock on alternate takes, but by this time Molla had left the fold. The third album, confusingly titled *Camper Van Beethoven*, continued the thread, but the outstanding tracks, like "Joe Stalin's Cadillac," were all in the more straight-ahead indie-rock vein. However, the band would consistently blow people's minds by tossing around things like a reverent version of Pink Floyd's "Interstellar Overdrive." For their

Virgin Records debut, subsequent to the label's US re-launch in 1988, the band took a more serious tack for *Our Beloved Revolutionary Sweetheart*, and the band that had once been confined to low budgets and small studio facilities stretched out, perhaps a little too aggressively. For *Key Lime Pie*, the band's final release in 1989, they took it as far as it could go. Morgan Fichter had replaced Segel by this time. Krummenacher, Pedersen, and Lisher continued to play together in what began as a side project in 1985, Monks of Doom, and turned into full-time jobs for them, with four albums and an EP to their credit. Though no longer working as the Monks, the trio, as well as Segel and Camper touring guitarist David Immergluck, continue to play together in various formations. Jonathan Segel released three albums as Hieronymous Firebrain from 1990-94 and two with Jack and Jill for the Magnetic label. Krummenacher released a solo record *A Great Laugh*, also for Magnetic, and continues to work with members of Tarnation in Lava. Immergluck and Fichter continue to tour and play sessions with bands of considerable renown (Counting Crows and Natalie Merchant, respectively, among others); Lowery took some time off before forming Cracker, and doesn't co-mingle with his former bandmates. —*Denise Sullivan*

● **Telephone Free Landslide Victory** / 1985 / IRS ◆◆◆◆
This is the stunning debut by a group of kids from Santa Cruz who merged clever lyrics and a keen sense of humor with international folk music, punk rock, country, and ska. The distinguishing instrument, violin, is what gave the band their unique sound on the straight-ahead college radio classic "Take the Skin Heads Bowling," as well as their cover of Black Flag's "Wasted," the absurdist "The Day That Lassie Went to the Moon," and the unabashedly cute "Where the Hell is Bill?" —*Denise Sullivan*

II & III / Jan. 1986 / IRS ◆◆◆
The band takes its country and hillbilly leanings and runs with them on tunes like "Abundance," "Sad Lovers Waltz," and Sonic Youth's "I Love Her All the Time," but their engaging and quirky ode to punk and psychedelia, "(We're a) Bad Trip," was beloved by college radio. —*Denise Sullivan*

Camper Van Beethoven / Aug. 1986 / IRS ◆◆◆
Not a bad record, for it includes a faithful rendition of Pink Floyd's "Interstellar Overdrive" and the brilliant "Joe Stalin's Cadillac," but by this time the Balkan folk-punk form had grown a little tired, and it became evident that it was time for CVB to tone down the ever-expanding parameters leading them all over the musical map. Taken as a trilogy, the first three records make perfect sense. —*Denise Sullivan*

Our Beloved Revolutionary Sweetheart / 1988 / Virgin ◆◆◆◆
All of Camper's hard work paid off by the time they released their major-label debut, a record that combines their humor, matured skills as musicians, and all-around ability to incorporate all kinds of music into something their own. "Eye of Fatima" swings, "One of These Days" lilts, "Turquoise Jewelry" is a romp, and "Life Is Grand" is joyous. They'd dropped the ska and polkas, but retained their folk roots. In actual fact, though, there's a dark side to almost every song and an overall melancholy that portends things to come. The processed drum sound is the only drawback. —*Denise Sullivan*

Key Lime Pie / Sep. 1989 / Virgin ◆◆◆◆
Even darker than the band's previous efforts. This is a band at the height of its powers, though some hear a band falling apart on its final release. Classic, reigned-in production and David Lowery's songwriting are both in the A+ category, though at the time, the band was suffering from some kind of alterna-backlash. The album is well worth reassessing and might even serve as a nice introduction, as "Sweethearts," "When I Win the Lottery," and "I Was Born in a Laundromat" are all outstanding slices of alterna-folk-psych-rock. —*Denise Sullivan*

Camper Vantiquities / Mar. 23, 1993 / Virgin ◆◆◆
A collection of B-sides, rarities, and the entire EP *Vampire Can Mating Oven* (an anagram of the band's moniker), the disc is essential for the Camper completist. The songs "Never Go Back" and "Seven Languages" are beauties in their own right, and the covers of the Kinks' "I'm Not Like Everybody Else" and Ringo Starr's "Photograph" are a perfect fit for the band who excelled at everything odd and unexpected during their too-brief stay in the late '80s. —*Denise Sullivan*

Can

f. 1968, Cologne, West Germany, db. 1978
Electronic, Art-Rock/Progressive-Rock, Experimental, Kraut-Rock

Always at least three steps ahead of contemporary popular music, Can was the leading avant-garde rock group of the '70s. From their very beginning, their music didn't conform to any commonly held notions about rock 'n' roll—not even those of the countercultures. Inspired more by 20th century classical music than Chuck Berry, their closest contemporaries were Frank Zappa or possibly the Velvet Underground. Yet their music was more serious and inaccessible than that of either of those artists. Instead of recording tight pop songs or satire, Can experimented with noise, synthesizers, nontraditional music, cut-and-paste techniques, and, most importantly, electronic music; each album marked a significant step forward from the previous album, investigating new territories that other rock bands weren't interested in exploring.

Throughout their career, Can's lineup was fluid, featuring several different vocalists over the years; the core band members remained keyboardist Irmin Schmidt, drummer Jaki Leibezeit, guitarist Michael Karoli, and bassist Holger Czukay. During the '70s they were extremely prolific, recording as many as three albums a year at the height of their career. Apart from a surprise UK Top 30 hit in 1978—"I Want More"—they were never much more than a cult band; even critics had a hard time appreciating their music.

Can debuted in 1969 with the primitive, bracing *Monster Movie*, the only full-length effort to feature American-born vocalist Malcolm Mooney. In 1970, *Soundtracks*, a collection of film music, introduced Japanese singer Kenji "Damo" Suzuki, and featured "Mother Sky," one of the group's best-known compositions. With 1971's two-record set *Tago Mago*, Can hit its visionary stride, shedding the constraints of pop forms and structures to explore long improvisations, angular rhythms, and experimental textures.

In 1972, *Ege Bamyasi* refined the approach and incorporated an increasingly jazz-like sensibility into the mix; *Future Days*, recorded the next year as Suzuki's swan song, traveled even further afield into minimalist, almost ambient, territory. With 1974's *Soon Over Babaluma*, Can returned to more complicated and abrasive ground, introducing dub rhythms as well as Karoli's shrieking violin. *Unlimited Edition* in 1976 and 1977's *Saw Delight* proved equally restless and drew on a wide range of ethnic musics.

When the band split in 1978 after the success of the album *Flow Motion* and the hit "I Want More," they left a body of work that has proven surprisingly groundbreaking. Echoes of Can's music can be heard in Public Image Limited, the Fall, and Einsturzende Neubauten, among others. As with much aggressive and challenging experimental music, Can's music can be difficult to appreciate, but their albums offer some of the best experimental rock ever recorded. —*Stephen Thomas Erlewine*

Monster Movie / 1969 / Mute ✦✦✦✦
Can's debut is the only full-length, proper release to feature original vocalist Malcolm Mooney, whose free-form ranting is matched by a raw, aggressive dynamic unlike anything else in the group's canon. Driving, dissonant songs like the extraordinary "Father Cannot Yell" and "Outside My Door" even owe a rather surprising debt to psychedelia and garage rock. More indicative of things to come is the closer, "Yoo Doo Right," a 20-minute epic built on the kinds of hypnotic motifs and minimal rhythms that quickly became Can trademarks. —*Jason Ankeny*

Soundtracks / 1970 / Mute ✦✦✦
Malcolm Mooney passes the baton to Damo Suzuki for *Soundtracks*, a collection of film music featuring contributions from both vocalists. The dichotomy between the two singers is readily apparent; Suzuki's odd, strangulated vocals fit far more comfortably into the group's increasingly intricate and subtle sound, allowing for greater variation than that allowed by Mooney's stream-of-consciousness discourse. —*Jason Ankeny*

Tago Mago / 1971 / Mute ✦✦✦✦
The double LP *Tago Mago* is Can's breakthrough record, a triumph over form and structure. Comprised largely of epic, side-long compositions like "Halleluhwah" and "Aumgn," the album sheds the constraints of accepted songcraft to tackle Stockhausen-influenced avant-garde concepts, improvisational pieces, tape manipulations, even free-floating ambient structures. Even the most "traditional" songs, like "Paperhouse" and "Mushroom," sound otherworldly. —*Jason Ankeny*

Ege Bamyasi / 1972 / Mute ✦✦✦✦
The excellent *Ege Bamyasi* capitalizes on the lessons of the experimental *Tago Mago* while shoehorning the group's more outre leanings into tighter song structures. Songs like "One More Night" and "Sing Swan Song" benefit from oddly gleaming textures, while "Pinch" and "Spoon" flirt with, respectively, funk and Middle Eastern rhythms. —*Jason Ankeny*

Future Days / 1973 / Mute ✦✦✦✦
Damo Suzuki's final effort is Can's most atmospheric and beautiful record, a spartan collection of lengthy, jazz-like compositions recorded with minimal vocal contributions. Employing keyboard washes to create a breezy, almost oceanic feel (indeed, two of the tracks are titled "Spray" and "Bel Air"), the mix buries Suzuki's voice to bring drummer Jaki Liebezeit's complex rhythms to the foreground. Despite the deceptive tranquility of its surface, *Future Days* is an intense work, bubbling with radical ideas and concepts. —*Jason Ankeny*

Soon Over Babaluma / 1974 / Mute ✦✦✦
Michael Karoli and Irmin Schmidt assume vocal duties for *Soon over Babaluma*, which also introduces a fascination with dub-influenced rhythms and Karoli's dissonant violin work into the group's increasingly

heady brew. While returning to the more difficult, abrasive textures of Can's earlier work, the album continues the group's more recent trend toward lengthy, fluid song structures. Another complex, impressive record. —*Jason Ankeny*

Landed / 1975 / Mute ✦✦
Another erratic waxing features some great guitar and Babaluma-style grooves, but on the whole it is unfocused. —*Myles Boisen*

Flow Motion / 1976 / Mute ✦✦
More pop aspirations and overt use of ethnic textures yield mixed results, as was typical of the band's later years. —*Myles Boisen*

Unlimited Edition / 1976 / Mute ✦✦✦
These studio outtakes, from Can's history up to 1975, are fascinating electronic and ethnic musical excursions. —*Myles Boisen*

Saw Delight / 1977 / Mute ✦✦✦
This effort is a nice mix of trance/groove instrumentals, ethnic sampling, and silly vocals in English. —*Myles Boisen*

Can / 1979 / Mute ✦✦
This one suffers without bassist Holger Czukay, and from overblown pop keyboards. —*Myles Boisen*

● **Cannibalism 1** / 1980 / Mute ✦✦✦✦
Given the cohesion of the group's studio albums, Can's songs work surprisingly well in compilation form, as evidenced by *Cannibalism 1*, a collection of tracks taken from the first six years of the group's existence. Covering ground from 1969's *Monster Movie* to 1974's *Soon Over Babaluma* (although nothing from 1973's superb *Future Days* makes the cut), the sampler compiles many of the group's high points (including "Father Cannot Yell," "She Brings the Rain," "Mushroom" and "Soup"), and offers a thorough overview of Can's eclectic musical history to date, even if the abridged versions of cuts like "Mother Sky," "Aumgn," and "Halleluhwah" don't measure up to the full-length renditions featured on the original albums. —*Jason Ankeny*

Delay . . . 1968 / 1981 / Mute ✦✦✦
Although recorded in the late 1960s, the material included on *Delay 1968* did not appear commercially until 1981. A collection of cuts featuring early vocalist Malcolm Mooney, these seven songs are among the very first Can ever recorded. While nowhere near as intricate or assured as the group's later work, the visceral energy of tracks like the deranged "Uphill" and "Butterfly" is undeniable. —*Jason Ankeny*

Cannibalism 2 / 1990 / Mute ✦✦✦✦

Cannibalism 3 / 1990 / Mute ✦✦✦
A compilation drawn from the solo releases of various Can members (though it would seem that percussionist Jaki Leibezeit has made his way onto the majority of them) between 1979 and 1991. The curious musical moments include band works as well as departing for musical territory far divergent from anything known to fans of the band. Many will find these fascinating selections tempt them to acquire full albums. —*Steven McDonald*

Anthology 1968-1993 / 1995 / Mute ✦✦✦✦

Canned Heat

f. 1966, Los Angeles, CA, **db.** 1981
Group / Blues-Rock, Boogie Rock
A hard-luck blues band of the '60s, Canned Heat was founded by blues historians and record collectors Al Wilson and Bob Hite. They seemed to be on the right track and played all the right festivals (including Monterey and Woodstock, making it very prominently into the documentaries about both) but somehow never found a lasting audience.

Certainly their hearts were in the right place. Their debut album—released shortly after their appearance at Monterey—was every bit as deep into the roots of the blues as any other combo of the time mining similar turf, with the exception of the original Paul Butterfield band. Hite was nicknamed "The Bear" and stalked the stage in the time-honored tradition of Howlin' Wolf and other large-proportioned bluesmen. Wilson was an extraordinary harmonica player, with a fat tone and great vibrato. His work on guitar, especially in open tunings (he played on Son House's rediscovery recordings of the mid-'60s, incidentally) gave the band a depth and texture to which most other rhythm players could only aspire. Henry Vestine—another dyed-in-the-wool record collector—was the West Coast's answer to Michael Bloomfield and capable of fretboard fireworks at a moment's notice. Their breakthrough moment occurred with the release of their second album, establishing them with hippie ballroom audiences as the "kings of the boogie." As a way of paying homage to the musician from whom they got the idea in the first place, they later collaborated on an album with John Lee Hooker that was one of the elder bluesman's most successful outings with a young white (or Black, for that matter) combo backing him up. After two big chart hits with "Goin' up the Country" and an explosive version of Wilbert Harrison's "Let's Work Together," Wilson died under mysterious (probably drug-related) circumstances in 1970, and Hite carried on with various reconstituted versions of the band until his death from a heart seizure just before a show in 1981. —*Cub Koda & Bruce Eder*

● **The Best of Canned Heat** / 1972 / EMI America ✦✦✦✦
All of Canned Heat's best tracks and biggest hits ("Goin' up the Country," "On the Road Again") are included on this single-disc collection. —*Stephen Thomas Erlewine*

On the Road / 1989 / EMI ✦✦✦✦
On the Road is a compilation concentrating entirely on Canned Heat's earliest recordings, hitting all the highlights ("On the Road Again," "Goin' up the Country") from their biggest albums and offering most casual fans a definitive—if not a little too comprehensive—overview. —*Stephen Thomas Erlewine*

Uncanned! The Best of Canned Heat / May 17, 1994 / EMI America ✦✦✦✦
Uncanned! The Best of Canned Heat is exactly what it claims to be—the definitive portrait of the blues-soaked hippie boogie band. Spreading 41 tracks (including numerous rarities, alternate takes, and Levi commercials) over two CDs, the set is perfect for the hardcore Canned Heat collector. For casual fans, the collection simply contains too much music; they would be better served by the single-disc collection, *The Best of Canned Heat. —Stephen Thomas Erlewine*

Freddy Cannon

b. Dec. 4, 1940, Lynn, MA
Vocals / Rock 'n' Roll
No one would claim that Freddy Cannon was one of the great early rock 'n' roll singers. His throaty rasp rated much higher for enthusiasm than impressive chops, and his 17 hit singles were often repetitious variations of his most successful tunes. Yet he did his own small part to keep the rock 'n' roll spirit burning in the late '50s and early '60s, a time at which it sometimes seemed in danger of being extinguished. He was an unabashed rock 'n' roller, for one thing, even when he was fed ancient Tin Pan Alley standards to retool for teenagers. And he was not one to let the lack of top-notch skills stand in the way of putting his heart into his vocals. His enthusiasm is infectious, though much of his material cannot be rescued by enthusiasm alone. Sometimes categorized as a teen idol, he was in fact too raw to fit comfortably into that mold (not to mention not quite good-looking enough). As ludicrous as it sounds, he was something of an early prototype of rock 'n' roller as Everyman, where spirit and fun counted more than conventional skill.

Cannon made his first record as part of the Spindrifts, a Boston group that went nowhere. In 1959 he hit the Top Ten with his first solo outing, "Tallahassee Lassie," a downright raw number with pounding piano, handclaps, and a raunchy guitar solo that was his best single. The Little Richard-esque shouts of "Woo" that punctuated the song would become his most familiar vocal trademark, and in fact was recycled a little too often for comfort over the next few years. "Way Down Yonder in New Orleans" (1959) made No. 3, and Cannon recorded other ancient pop tunes like "Chattanooga Shoe Shine Boy" and "Muskrat Ramble" with much more middling success; on these, he can sound something like Bobby Darin's evil doppelganger. For in-house material, he relied on Swan Records producers Bob Crewe (who would later oversee the 4 Seasons) and Frank Slay, and these were usually formulaic, if executed with spirit. His biggest hit, "Palisades Park" (which reached No. 3 in 1962), was not written by Crewe/Slay but by, of all people, future "Gong Show" host Chuck Barris.

Cannon left Swan for Warner Brothers in 1963. While the British Invasion should have spelled near-instant death, Cannon in fact managed to land a couple of his biggest hits, "Abigail Beecher" and "Action," in the mid-'60s. The latter was cut with top Los Angeles session men Hal Blaine, Leon Russell, James Burton, Glen Campbell, and David Gates—a far cry from the simpler fare of his Swan days. An artistic rebirth was not in the making, though, and Cannon never hit the charts again after "The Dedication Song" in early 1966. —*Richie Unterberger*

● **The Best of Freddy "Boom Boom" Cannon** / Nov. 21, 1995 / Rhino ✦✦✦✦
The definitive collection. Twenty tracks, 17 of them Top 100 singles, including "Tallahassee Lassie," "Way Down Yonder in New Orleans," "Palisades Park," "Abigail Beecher," and "Action," as well as a rare 1958 single by the Spindrifts. The other selections really aren't up to the level of the best hits, despite occasional raw detours like "Buzz Buzz A-Diddle-It" and the odd novelty "If You Were a Rock and Roll Record," with the immortal line, "If you were a rock and roll record, I know they'd sell a million of you." —*Richie Unterberger*

The Capitols

f. Jan. 1966, Detroit, MI
Soul
The energetic Detroit-based Capitols capitalized on mid-'60s R&B dance

fever with one of the most memorable entries of the genre, "Cool Jerk." Successful local producer Ollie McLaughlin signed the trio—lead singer Sam George, Donald Norman (who wrote most of the group's material under his real surname of Storball), and Richard Mitchell—to his Karen logo, and the irresistible "Cool Jerk" made them an overnight sensation. After a couple more chart entries later that year, the trio faded quickly. George was murdered on March 17, 1982. —*Bill Dahl*

● **Golden Classics** / Apr. 1990 / Collectables ✦✦✦✦
Dance-oriented mid-'60s Detroit soul, this features the notable classic "Cool Jerk." —*Bill Dahl*

The Capris

f. 1957, Ozone Park, NY
Doo Wop
The only major Capris hit, the romantic "There's a Moon Out Tonight," is a New York street-corner harmony classic. Doo wop was back in fashion by 1961, and it was no longer limited to R&B aggregations. Led by Nick Santo (born Nick Santamaria in 1941), the Capris named themselves after the Isle of Capri in Italy. The Queens, NY, natives originally cut "There's a Moon Out Tonight" for the obscure Planet imprint in 1958, but when the song was reissued on Lost Nite (and eventually on Old Town) it became a national smash its second time around in early 1961. After many moons out of the spotlight, the Capris came back triumphantly in 1981 with an album on Ambient Sound and an appearance on the PBS-TV series "Soundstage." —*Bill Dahl*

● **There's a Moon Out Tonight** / 1982 / Collectables ✦✦✦✦
Nick Santo's anguished, innocent-sounding lead on "There's a Moon Out Tonight" became a hit some three years after the song was originally issued. By this time they had disbanded, but regrouped in a hurry trying to milk the hit. This album collects ten tunes they cut for Planet, most of them superior to "There's a Moon Out Tonight," but none of them able to duplicate that song's success. —*Ron Wynn*

There's a Moon Out Again! / 1982 / Ambient Sound ✦✦✦
Recorded in 1982, live two-track, here's a perfect example of what a great modern-day doo wop album should be. —*Cub Koda*

Captain & Tennille

f. 1973, Los Angeles, CA
Soft Rock
Vibrant, relentlessly upbeat harmonies made Captain (born Daryl Dragon, Aug 27, 1942) & Tennille (born Toni Tennille, May 8, 1943) stars during the latter half of the '70s. Dragon, dubbed the "Captain" because of his distinctive headgear, had played keyboards with the Beach Boys before teaming with his wife. Their first hit on A&M, the buoyant "Love Will Keep Us Together," was a million-selling chart-topper in 1975, and a reissue of their 1974 single "The Way I Want to Touch You" also went gold. The couple hung three more gold records in their den in 1976—"Lonely Night (Angel Face)," "Shop Around," and Willis Alan Ramsey's "Muskrat Love"—and that was enough for ABC-TV to install them as hosts of their own variety program. "Do That to Me One More Time" was the last No.1 item for the pair in 1979. —*Bill Dahl*

● **Captain & Tennille's Greatest Hits** / 1977 / A&M ✦✦✦✦
A solid collection of all of their mid-'70s hits. —*Stephen Thomas Erlewine*

Captain Beefheart

b. Jan. 15, 1941, Glendale, CA
Guitar, Harmonica, Keyboards, Vocals / Art-Rock/Progressive-Rock, Psychedelic, Experimental, Proto-Punk
Born Don Van Vliet, Captain Beefheart was one of modern music's true innovators. The owner of a remarkable four-and-one-half octave vocal range, he employed idiosyncratic rhythms, absurdist lyrics, and an unholy alliance of free jazz, Delta blues, latter-day classical music and rock 'n' roll to create a singular body of work virtually unrivalled in its daring and fluid creativity. While he never came even remotely close to mainstream success, Beefheart's impact was incalculable, and his fingerprints were all over punk, New Wave, and post-rock.

Van Vliet was born January 15, 1941, in Glendale, CA. When he was four, his artwork brought him to the attention of Portuguese sculptor Augustinio Rodriguez, and Van Vliet was declared a child prodigy. In 1954 he was offered a scholarship to study in Europe; his parents declined the proposal, however, and the family instead moved to the Mojave Desert, where the teen was befriended by a young Frank Zappa. In time Van Vliet taught himself saxophone and harmonica, and joined a pair of local R&B groups, the Omens and the Blackouts.

After a semester at college, he and Zappa moved to Cucamonga, CA, where they planned to shoot a film, *Captain Beefheart Meets the Grunt People*. As the project remained in limbo, Zappa finally moved to Los Angeles, where he founded the Mothers of Invention; Van Vliet later returned to the Mojave area, adopted the Beefheart name, and formed the first lineup of his backing group, the Magic Band, with guitarists Alex St. Clair and Doug Moon, bassist Jerry Handley, and drummer Paul Blakely in 1964.

In their original incarnation, the Magic Band was a blues-rock outfit that became staples of the teen-dance circuit. They quickly signed to A&M Records, where the success of the single "Diddy Wah Diddy" earned them the opportunity to record a full-length album. Comprised of Van Vliet compositions like "Frying Pan," "Electricity," and "Zig Zag Wanderer," the record was rejected by label president Jerry Moss as "too negative," and a crushed Beefheart went into seclusion. After replacing Moon and Blakely with guitarist Antennae Jimmy Semens (born Jeff Cotton) and drummer John "Drumbo" French (fleshed out by guitarist Ry Cooder) recut the songs in 1967 as *Safe as Milk*.

After producer Bob Krasnow radically remixed 1968's hallucinatory *Strictly Personal* without Beefheart's approval, he again retired. At the same time, however, Zappa formed his own Straight Records, and soon approached Van Vliet with the promise of complete creative control. A deal was struck, and after writing 28 songs in a nine-hour frenzy, Beefheart formed the definitive line-up of the Magic Band—made up of Semens, Drumbo, guitarist Zoot Horn Rollo (born Bill Harkleroad), bassist Rockette Morton (Mark Boston), and bass clarinetist the Mascara Snake (Victor Fleming)—to record the seminal 1969 double album *Trout Mask Replica*.

Following 1970's similarly outre *Lick My Decals Off, Baby*, Beefheart adopted an almost commercial sound for the 1972 releases *The Spotlight Kid* and *Clear Spot*. Shortly thereafter, the Magic Band broke off to form Mallard, and Beefheart was dropped by his label, Reprise. After a two-year layoff, he released a pair of pop-blues albums, *Unconditionally Guaranteed* and *Bluejeans and Moonbeams*, with a new, short-lived Magic Band; after another fallow period, 1978's *Shiny Beast (Bat Chain Puller)* marked a return to the eccentricities of his finest work.

After 1982's *Ice Cream for Crow*, Van Vliet again retired from music, this time for good. He returned to the desert, took up residence in a trailer, and focused on painting. In 1985 he mounted the first major exhibit of his work, done in an abstract, primitive style reminiscent of Francis Bacon. Like his music, his art won wide acclaim, and some of his paintings sold for as much as $25,000. In the 1990s Van Vliet dropped completely from sight when he fell prey to multiple sclerosis. —*Jason Ankeny*

Safe as Milk / 1967 / Buddah ✦✦✦✦
Beefheart's first proper studio album is a much more accessible, pop-inflected brand of blues-rock than the efforts that followed in the late '60s—which isn't to say that it's exactly normal and straightforward. Featuring Ry Cooder on guitar, this is blues-rock gone slightly askew, with jagged, fractured rhythms; soulful, twisting vocals from Van Vliet; and more doo wop, soul, straight blues, and folk-rock influences than he would employ on his more avant-garde outings. "Zig Zag Wanderer," "Call on Me," and "Yellow Brick Road" are some of his most enduring and riff-driven songs, although there's plenty of weirdness on tracks like "Electricity" and "Abba Zaba." —*Richie Unterberger*

★ **Trout Mask Replica** / 1969 / Reprise ✦✦✦✦✦
Originally released and produced by Frank Zappa as a double album on his Bizarre/Straight label, *Trout Mask Replica* is the definitive Captain Beefheart album. To some, it is just plain weird, perhaps even anti-music. To others, it is blues with a warp or rock 'n' roll at the absolute cutting edge. Deeply rooted in blues and jazz, the Captain taught each member of the Magic Band their extremely complex individual parts over the course of a year. Playful and challenging at the same time, rhythmically kinetic, poetically beautiful, it is an absolute masterpiece. —*Rob Bowman*

Lick My Decals Off, Baby / 1970 / Bizarre ✦✦✦✦
The bookend release to *Trout Mask Replica*, this time produced by the Captain himself. Sample title "The Smithsonian Institute Blues (The Big Dig)" should give you a sense that this is not an ordinary rock 'n' roll record. Just a shade less essential than *Trout Mask Replica*. —*Rob Bowman*

Mirror Man / 1970 / One Way ✦✦✦
An early version of the Captain's Magic Band, recorded live in Los Angeles, probably in 1968. (The cover says 1965, but that is undoubtedly erroneous.) Stunning extended versions of four Beefheart originals, including his Robert Johnson-inspired "Tarotplane." —*Rob Bowman*

The Spotlight Kid / Clear Spot / 1972 / Reprise ✦✦✦✦
The Spotlight Kid (1972) and *Clear Spot* (1973) have been released on one CD. The Captain became slightly more accessible on these two early-'70s releases, accenting the rock 'n' roll ingredients. Slide guitar abounds on some of the most asymmetrical riffs imaginable throughout *The Spotlight Kid*. The lyrics are just as playful. *Clear Spot* is the Captain at his most balanced—accessible without deserting the avant-garde. "Big-Eyed Beans from Venus" became one of his all-time classics. —*Rob Bowman*

Shiny Beast (Bat Chain Puller) / Jan. 1978 / Bizarre ✦✦✦✦
The Captain's comeback album, with the second edition of the Magic Band. As good as *Clear Spot* or *The Spotlight Kid*, with a slightly different temperament and a touch of synthesizer. —*Rob Bowman*

Doc at the Radar Station / 1980 / Blue Plate ✦✦✦✦
The masterpiece of the Captain's late-'70s/early-'80s resurrection. This time, the new Magic Band had coalesced into an ensemble of frightening power. Cross-rhythms abut each other in some of the most hyperkinetic settings imaginable. There's not a weak song or performance to be found. Buy this. —*Rob Bowman*

Ice Cream for Crow / 1982 / Blue Plate ✦✦✦✦
The Captain's last album as of this writing, with no sign that he'll ever return. A couple of changes in the Magic Band and the Captain, perhaps losing a bit of steam, make this album undistinguished. There is nothing poor here; if you are into the Captain, you will want to own this. However, everything else listed is recommended first. —*Rob Bowman*

Legendary A&M Sessions / 1984 / A&M ✦✦✦
Before gaining a cult with his avant-garde excursions in the late '60s, Captain Beefheart wielded a much more traditional sort of blues-rock. That's not to say that these two obscure mid-'60s A&M singles (packaged together on this five-song EP, which adds a previously unreleased track from the same era) aren't well worth hearing. The Captain's Howlin' Wolf-like growl led a tough outfit that ranked among the best early American blues-rock groups, and among the few that could reasonably emulate the Rolling Stones' toughness. Produced, unbelievably enough, by future Bread leader David Gates, this reissue includes their regional hit cover of Bo Diddley's "Diddy Wah Diddy." The best track, though, is "Moonchild," their shameless derivation of Howlin' Wolf's "Smokestack Lightning." Featuring wailing harmonica, stomping riffs, and adventurous, quasi-psychedelic production, it was actually written by Gates himself. To think that the same man was also responsible for "If" and "Baby I'm A-Want You" blows the mind. —*Richie Unterberger*

The Best Beefheart / 1989 / Pair ✦✦✦
This is basically a combination of *Safe as Milk* and *Mirror Man* on one CD, minus *Mirror Man*'s "Tarotplane." For those who care enough about the Captain to want all or most of his material, that's a significant omission. If you're basically looking for *Safe as Milk* and not the far more avant-garde and challenging *Mirror Man*, though, this isn't a bad acquisition, maintaining the original running order of the *Safe as Milk* tracks. The *Mirror Man* songs can be viewed as bonus cuts (and, in Pair's defense, it would have been impossible to fit the lengthy *Tarotplane* onto the disc). —*Richie Unterberger*

Caravan

f. 1968, England, db. 1983
Art-Rock/Progressive-Rock
Along with the Soft Machine, Caravan was one of two eccentric, distinctively British art-rock bands to grow out of Canterbury's Wilde Flowers. Caravan itself was founded in 1968 by guitarist/vocalist Pye Hastings, keyboardist David Sinclair, bassist/vocalist Richard Sinclair, and drummer Richard Coughlan. The band immediately set itself off from the rest of the art-rock pack with its gentle melodies, complicated improvisational passages, and British folk-influenced arrangements, sometimes featuring strings and woodwinds. Caravan received a fair amount of critical acclaim for its early work, particularly 1971's *In the Land of the Grey and Pink*. The first of many personnel changes followed that album when David Sinclair joined Matching Mole and was replaced by former Delivery member Steve Miller for *Waterloo Lily*. Richard Sinclair left after that album, and David returned for *For Girls Who Grow Plump in the Night* and *Caravan and the New Symphonia*. *Cunning Stunts* (1975) came out of left field to become Caravan's only charting album in the US, but critics and fans found that the group's charm had evaporated into an obsession with technical perfection. Hastings fronted the group into the '80s, and their last album, 1983's *Back to Front*, featured all the original members. The group has performed occasionally since then and played several London club dates in 1991 with several former members of Camel. —*Steve Huey*

Caravan / 1968 / Verve ✦✦

If I Could Do It All over Again I'd Do It All Over You / 1970 / London ✦✦✦

In the Land of the Grey and Pink / 1971 / London ✦✦✦✦

Waterloo Lily / 1972 / London ✦✦✦
Waterloo Lily follows Caravan's first personnel changes, resulting in a spotty and unfocused album, though not without merits. Keyboardist Steve Miller plays electric piano in a bluesier style than his predecessor, Dave Sinclair, an organist. The band competently executes the jazzier, extended material that comprises about half the disc; the sloppy fade in/ fade out of the extended suites "Nothing at All" and "It's Coming Soon" make the music seem almost inconsequential. Pye Hastings' shorter

songs carry the album, especially the marvellous "The World Is Yours." —*Jim Powers*

For Girls Who Grow Plump in the Night / 1973 / London ✦✦✦✦

Cunning Stunts / 1975 / Repertoire ✦✦✦

Blind Dog at St Dunstans / 1976 / Arista ✦✦

Best of Caravan / 1987 / London ✦✦✦
A fine single-disc collection of some of their best moments, but the double-disc *Canterbury Tales* offers a better portrait of the group. —*Stephen Thomas Erlewine*

● **Canterbury Tales: The Best of Caravan** / Feb. 22, 1994 / Decca ✦✦✦✦
Canterbury Tales is a generous two-disc helping of this great progressive-rock band's first seven albums. The compilation draws most heavily from the albums *If I Could Do It All Over Again . . .*, *In the Land of the Grey and Pink*, *For Girls Who Grow Plump in the Night*, and *Caravan and the New Symphonia*. There are also selections from *Cunning Stunts*, *Waterloo Lily*, and *Caravan*. A good balance is struck between Caravan's shorter single-length pop songs and its more extended suites. The liner notes feature an informative biographical and discographical essay and lots of photographs and credits. The remastering is excellent. —*Jim Powers*

The Cardigans

f. 1992, Jonkoping, Sweden
Alternative Pop-Rock, Indie Rock, Dream-Pop
One of the most pleasing pop groups of the '90s, the Cardigans' sugary confections would grow annoying very quickly if they weren't backed by great musicianship and clever arrangements. The band's 1995 breakout album *Life* reflected the Cardigans at their most saccharine—the sunny disposition of vocalist Nina Persson being the major argument in favor—and critics inserted the group into the space-age pop revivalist camp. The Cardigans later proved that they were more difficult to pigeonhole, however.

Even the band's origins show that their later appearance was quite misleading; two heavy metal fanatics formed the group in October 1992 in Jonkoping, Sweden. Guitarist Peter Svensson met bassist Magnus Sveningsson in a hardcore group, though he had previously trained in music theory and jazz arranging. The two later grew tired of metal and decided to form a pop band with Nina Persson—an art-school friend who had never sung professionally—plus keyboard player Lars-Olof Johansson and drummer Bengt Lagerberg.

All five Cardigans moved into a small apartment in 1993 and began recording a demo tape, which entered the possession of producer Tore Johansson later that year. He liked what he heard and invited the group to record at his Malmo studio. Signed to the dance-oriented Stockholm label, the Cardigans released *Emmerdale* in May 1994. The single "Rise & Shine" became a hit on Swedish radio soon after the release of the LP, and a readers poll in Sweden's *Slitz* magazine voted *Emmerdale* the best album of 1994.

The Cardigans spent the last half of 1994 touring Europe and recording their second album. A satirical response to their moody debut, *Life* showed the band at their most upbeat, including an angelic picture of Nina in an ice-skating outfit for the cover. Released in March 1995—with several re-recordings of songs from *Emmerdale*—the album eventually sold one and a half million copies worldwide and became especially popular in Japan, where it achieved platinum status.

A deal with Minty Fresh gave the Cardigans an American release of *Life* in spring 1996, and the group played eight sold-out shows in the US that summer. The American major labels began to notice, and Mercury signed them soon after. *First Band on the Moon*, released in September 1996, de-emphasized the pure pop in favor of abstract arrangements and some rather violent themes. The album fared okay in America despite good reviews, but it became the Cardigans' second platinum record in Japan only three weeks after its release. —*John Bush*

Emmerdale / 1994 / Trampolene [Canada] ✦✦✦
Though the sky is sunny on the cover, *Emmerdale* is quite a melancholy affair. The first song, "Sick & Tired" (the single), hints that all is not well in the Cardigans' camp, and later songs ("Black Letter Day," "After All . . .," "Cloudy Sky") also capture a depressed mood that conflicts with the mostly upbeat and positive arrangements. Of course, all but two of the original songs were written by a converted metal fan, bassist Magnus Sveningsson. In keeping with that fact, the cover of "Sabbath Bloody Sabbath" shouldn't surprise anyone, though its clever arrangement and the touching vocals of Nina Persson—even though she's throwing around Ozzy Osbourne lyrics—render the song practically unrecognizable. In the end, the battle between positive arrangements and melancholy lyrics creates a wistful mood that suits the Cardigans well. —*John Bush*

● **Life** / 1995 / Minty Fresh ✦✦✦✦
With tongue firmly in cheek, the Cardigans decided to play up the candyfloss arrangements of their debut for the second album, *Life*. Where

Emmerdale studied an introverted melancholy, *Life* is undiminished in both its independent-minded exuberance ("Hey! Get Out of My Way") and zest to enjoy life with others ("Daddy's Car," "Gordon's Gardenparty"). The incredible production and quality of arrangement from the debut are here also, even more strikingly crisp and spot-on. (More than 50 instruments were used on the 14 songs included on the Minty Fresh American release.) Though the Cardigans planned *Life* as something of a joke, it became one of the finest pop albums of the '90s. —*John Bush*

First Band on the Moon / Sep. 17, 1996 / Mercury ✦✦✦
For listeners who had caught up with the Cardigans on their breakout album *Life*, the group's third album was a confusing pastiche that included several conventional pop songs, but added tracks with left-field arrangements and some (comparatively) disturbing lyrics. In reality, however, the group had simply returned to the mood and feel of their debut album. On *Emmerdale*, the melancholy was personal and solitary in nature, but here depression is focused on unfaithful lovers—in songs for which vocalist Nina Persson helped out with lyrics, and those written by the rest of the band ("Choke," "Step on Me," "The Great Divide"). Even the single "Lovefool" is a depressing lament of unrequited affection, and the presence of another Black Sabbath cover ("Iron Man") certainly isn't an immediate upper. Still, *First Band on the Moon* is saved by the Cardigans' core strengths: Persson's vocals and Svensson's arrangements. —*John Bush*

Cardinal

f. 1994, Boston, MA, db. 1995
Alternative Pop-Rock
Cardinal was a one-off project from singers/songwriters Richard Davies and Eric Matthews. The duo came together in 1994 when ex-Moles frontman Davies' relocated from his native Australia to the US; he wrote and sang all but one of the songs that comprised Cardinal's self-titled debut, while the Oregon-born Matthews arranged the compositions, layering them with ornate strings, horns, and pianos inspired by the lush, baroque sounds of late-'60s pop. While *Cardinal* was released to great acclaim, internal strife quickly split the duo, and both Davies and Matthews embarked on solo careers. —*Jason Ankeny*

● **Cardinal** / 1994 / Flydaddy ✦✦✦✦
The lone LP from the pairing of Richard Davies and Eric Matthews is majestic chamber-pop of the highest order: lush and ornate, *Cardinal* recalls the heyday of the Left Banke, Love and *Smile* -era Beach Boys with unerring accuracy. Whatever the creative tensions underscoring the album, the duo are remarkably sympathetic collaborators; never before or since have Davies' sophisticated compositions been so elegantly and sublimely arranged, nor have Matthews' own solo symphonic efforts been constructed around such ace songs—"If You Believe in Christmas Trees," "You've Lost Me There" and "Dream Figure" are perfectly balanced and finely nuanced orchestral masterpieces in miniature. —*Jason Ankeny*

Mariah Carey

b. Mar. 22, 1970, New York, NY
Vocals / Dance-Pop, Urban, Adult Contemporary, Pop-Rock, Club/ Dance
Mariah Carey has a remarkable multi-octave voice, an astonishing instrument that can reach heights rivaled only by Whitney Houston. Like Houston, Carey works the pop-soul ballad territory, occasionally spiked by some catchy dance-oriented pop. Fortunately, Carey hasn't had a shortage of good material; all of her three albums feature impeccably crafted singles designed for continuous radio play. While she was an overnight sensation with her first single, 1990's "Vision of Love," it wasn't until 1992 that she won over many skeptical critics with her unadorned *MTV Unplugged* performance; 1995's *Daydream* also won acclaim. Her records have all sold several million copies, and she has dominated the singles chart since her first album. It's a track record that very few artists can match. —*Stephen Thomas Erlewine*

Mariah Carey / May 1990 / Columbia ✦✦✦
This extremely impressive debut is replete with smooth-sounding ballads and uplifting dance/R&B cuts. Carey convincingly seizes many opportunities to display her incredible vocal range on such memorable tracks as the popular "Vision of Love" (featured during her television debut on "The Arsenio Hall Show," an appearance noted by many as her formal introduction to stardom), the energetic "Someday," and the moody sounds of the hidden treasure "Vanishing." With this collection of songs acting as a springboard for future successes, Carey establishes a strong standard of comparison for other breakthrough artists of this genre. —*Ashley S. Battel*

Emotions / Sep. 1991 / Columbia ✦✦✦
A strong follow-up to Carey's self-titled debut album, *Emotions* puts to rest any concern about a "sophomore jinx." The same mix of dance/ R&B/ballads that gave Carey's debut such tremendous appeal can be

found with equal strength on this release. Most notably, the gospel influences of "If It's Over" (with music co-written by Carole King), the yearning cries for a lost love in "Can't Let Go," and the catchy, upbeat title track all serve to send the listener on a musical journey filled with varying emotions. However, the one emotion that prevails upon completion of the album is definitely a positive one—satisfaction! —*Ashley S. Battel*

MTV Unplugged EP / Mar. 1992 / Columbia ✦✦✦
Although Mariah Carey doesn't come close to following the traditional *Unplugged* format of only a voice and a guitar (she brought in strings and backup vocalists), her *MTV Unplugged EP* (which includes her hit version of the Jackson 5's "I'll Be There") is her best record to date, proving that her talents as a vocalist are considerable. —*Stephen Thomas Erlewine*

Music Box / Sep. 1993 / Columbia ✦✦✦✦
Mariah Carey has been stung by critical charges that she's all vocal bombast and no subtlety, soul, or shading. Her response was to make an album in which her celebrated octave-leaping voice would be downplayed and she could demonstrate her ability to sing softly and coolly. Well, she was partly successful; she trimmed the volume on *Music Box*. Unfortunately, she also cut the energy level. Carey sounds detached on several selections. She scored a couple of huge hits, "Hero" and "Dreamlover," where she did inject some personality and intensity into the leads. Most other times, Carey blended into the background and let the tracks guide her, instead of pushing and exploding through them. It was wise to display other elements of her approach, but sometimes excessive spirit is preferable to an absence of passion. —*Ron Wynn*

● **Daydream** / Oct. 3, 1995 / Columbia ✦✦✦✦
Mariah Carey certainly knows how to construct an album. Positioning herself directly between urban R&B (with tracks like "Fantasy") and adult contemporary (with songs like "One Sweet Day," a duet with Boyz II Men), Carey appeals to both audiences equally because of the sheer amount of craft and hard work she puts into her albums. *Daydream* is her best record to date, featuring a consistently strong selection of songs and a remarkably impassioned performance by Carey. A few of the songs are second-rate—particularly the cover of Journey's "Open Arms"—but *Daydream* demonstrates that Carey continues to perfect her craft and that she has earned her status as an R&B/pop diva. —*Stephen Thomas Erlewine*

Eric Carmen

b. Aug. 11, 1949, Cleveland, OH
Vocals / Pop-Rock
Eric Carmen was the lead vocalist and songwriter of the Raspberries, an early-'70s band heavily influenced by mid-'60s pop, especially the Beatles. For his 1975 self-titled debut album, Carmen looked even farther into the past, to the early 20th century. His two hit singles, the heavily produced ballads "All by Myself" and "Never Gonna Fall in Love Again," were based on pieces by Russian classical composer Serge Rachmaninoff. The rest of the album and Carmen's subsequent, less commercially successful albums were a pastiche of classic pop styles. Carmen didn't enjoy a big commercial success again until 1987's "Hungry Eyes," from the *Dirty Dancing* concert tour. —*Kenneth M. Cassidy*

Eric Carmen / 1975 / Rhino ✦✦✦
Carmen achieved far greater success with his debut solo album than he ever had with his old group, the Raspberries. In part this was because, freed from the restrictions of leading a rock band, he could indulge his taste in big, lush ballads. That's what he did here, especially on the album's three Top 40 hits, one of which, "All by Myself," was a gold-selling No. 2 hit. —*William Ruhlmann*

● **The Best of Eric Carmen** / 1988 / Arista ✦✦✦✦
This album lacks Carmen's 1988 hit "Make Me Lose Control," but it does sample six of the eight singles-chart entries he enjoyed from 1975 to 1980, plus interesting album cuts such as "Hey Deanie," the Shaun Cassidy hit written by Carmen, and, of course, his comeback hit, "Hungry Eyes," from the *Dirty Dancing* soundtrack. —*William Ruhlmann*

The Carpenters

f. 1968, New Haven, CT, db. 1983
Pop, Soft Rock, Pop-Rock
With their light, airy melodies and meticulously crafted, clean arrangements, the Carpenters stood in direct contrast to the excessive, gaudy pop-rock of the '70s; yet they were among the most popular artists of the decade, scoring 12 Top Ten hits, including three No. 1 singles.

Karen Carpenter's calm, pretty voice was the most distinctive element of their music, settling in perfectly amidst the precise, lush arrangements provided by her brother Richard. The duo's sound drew more from pre-rock pop than rock 'n' roll, but that didn't prevent the Carpenters from appealing to a variety of audiences, particularly Top 40, easy

listening and adult contemporary. While their popularity declined during the latter half of the '70s, they remained one of the most distinctive and recognizable acts of the decade.

The Carpenters formed in the late '60s in Downey, CA, after their family moved from their native New Haven, CT. Richard had played piano with a cocktail jazz trio in a handful of local Connecticut nightclubs. Once the family had moved to California, he began to study piano and support Karen in a trio that featured Wes Jacobs (tuba/bass). With Jacobs and Richard forming her backup band, Karen was signed to the local label Magic Lamp, which released two unsuccessful singles by the singer. The trio won a Battle of the Bands contest at the Hollywood Bowl in 1967, which led to a record contract with RCA. Signing under the name the Richard Carpenter Trio, the group cut four songs that were never released. Jacobs left the band at the beginning of 1968.

After Jacobs' departure, the siblings formed Spectrum with Richard's college friend John Bettis. Spectrum fell apart by the end of the year, but the Carpenters continued performing as a duo. The pair recorded some demos at the house of Los Angeles session musician Joe Osborn; the tape was directed to Herb Alpert, the head of A&M Records, who signed the duo to his label in early 1969.

Offering, the Carpenters' first album, was released in November 1969. Neither *Offering* nor the accompanying single, a cover of the Beatles' "Ticket to Ride," made a big impression. However, the Carpenters' fortunes changed with their second single, a version of Burt Bacharach and Hal David's "(They Long to Be) Close to You." Taken from the album *Close to You*, the single became the group's first No. 1, spending four weeks on the top of the US charts. "Close to You" became an international hit, beginning a five-year period when the duo was one of the most popular recording acts in the world. During that period the Carpenters won two Grammy Awards, including Best New Artist of 1970, and had an impressive string of Top Ten hits, including "Rainy Days and Mondays," "Superstar," "Hurting Each Other," "Goodbye to Love," "Yesterday Once More," and "Top of the World."

After 1975's No. 4 hit "Only Yesterday," the group's popularity began to decline. For the latter half of the '70s, the duo was plagued by personal problems. Richard had become addicted to prescription drugs; in 1978 he entered a recovery clinic, kicking his habit. Karen, meanwhile, became afflicted with anorexia nervosa, a disease she suffered from for the rest of her life. On top of their health problems, the group's singles had stopped reaching the Top Ten; by 1978 they weren't even reaching the Top 40. Consequently, Karen decided to pursue a solo career, recording a solo album in 1979 with Phil Ramone; the record was never completed, and she returned to the Carpenters later that year. The reunited duo released their last album of new material, *Made in America*, in 1981. The album marked a commercial comeback, as "Touch Me When We're Dancing" made it to No. 16 on the charts. However, Karen's health continued to decline, forcing the duo out of the spotlight. On February 4, 1983, Karen was found unconscious at her parents' home in New Haven; she died in the hospital that morning from cardiac arrest caused by her anorexia.

After Karen's death, Richard Carpenter concentrated on production work and assembling various compilations of the Carpenters' recorded work. In 1987 he released a solo album called *Time*, which featured guest appearances by Dusty Springfield and Dionne Warwick. —*Stephen Thomas Erlewine*

● **The Singles (1969-1973)** / Nov. 1973 / A&M ✦✦✦✦
Exactly what it claims to be, this compilation contains ten of the Carpenters' 12 Top Ten hits, from "Close to You" to "Top of the World." They continued to make the charts until 1982, but the bulk of their memorable pop hits, the songs that reintroduced soft, melodic music to the masses and rolled back the rock revolution, are here. —*William Ruhlmann*

Yesterday Once More / May 1985 / A&M ✦✦✦✦
A two-CD set with 27 songs, this includes mostly their big hits, like "We've Only Just Begun" and "Mr. Postman," but there are a few sleeper cuts, too. —*Bil Carpenter*

James Carr

b. Jun. 13, 1942, Memphis, TN
Sax (Tenor), Vocals / Soul
Considered to be among the very greatest of "deep" Southern male soul singers, James Carr had a succession of R&B hits on the Memphis Goldwax label that were gems of "country" soul, the wonderful '60s marriage of Southern Black R&B vocalists with songs written in a country format and played mostly by white musicians. Carr's dark, gospel-inflected style, marked by a subtle, rich voice that is almost frightening in its intensity and range, has been compared to that of Otis Redding and Percy Sledge; many reviewers would class him even above these formidable peers. "At the Dark End of the Street," the first songwriting collaboration between Dan Penn and Chips Moman, is Carr's undisputed masterpiece. Also recorded by Aretha Franklin, Clarence Carter, Linda

Ronstadt, and Ry Cooder, it is the quintessential country-soul take on adulterous love.

Carr's career initially was short; Goldwax ceased operation in 1969, and Carr cut only one other single for Atlantic in 1971; however, he has recently emerged from retirement with a new album on Goldwax. His work stands at the apex of '60s soul—with Aretha, Otis, Percy, and Wilson—essential stuff! —*Christine Ohlman*

● **The Essential James Carr** / Feb. 21, 1995 / Razor & Tie ++++
When the soul era of the mid-'60s was in full bloom, for a period of three years James Carr was the maker of some of its mightiest music. His warm, soulful voice could make the reading of virtually anything he touched (even his version here of the Bee Gees' "To Love Somebody") a transcendent event. He is also the mystery man of the genre, unlettered and imbued with an almost childlike innocence, disappearing for a decade after these recordings were made, with charges of mental instability cropping up whenever his name is mentioned. But music this special doesn't come without a price, and certainly Carr paid that price, not unlike the gospel singers who influenced him who sometimes sang themselves to death right on stage. But the music will always win out, because personal problems aside, the music James Carr made is as deep as Southern soul music gets, on a par with the best of a Sam Cooke or an Otis Redding. Tracks like "You've Got My Mind Messed Up," "Pouring Water on a Drowning Man" and his masterpiece, "The Dark End of the Street," are classics of the genre, and this 20-track collection is where you go to get the big picture on an artist who deserves a much wider hearing. —*Cub Koda*

Paul Carrack

b. Apr. 22, 1951, Sheffield, England
Keyboards, Vocals / Pop-Rock, Blue-Eyed Soul
Despite his distinctive, soulful singing style, British keyboardist Paul Carrack's most popular work has not been done under his own name. He is the voice on Ace's "How Long," Squeeze's "Tempted," and Mike & The Mechanics' "The Living Years." Carrack finally began to score his own hits in the late '80s. —*William Ruhlmann*

The Nightbird / 1980 / Vertigo +++

Suburban Voodoo / Aug. 1982 / Epic +++
With Suburban Voodoo, Paul Carrack re-launched his solo career after a successful stint with Squeeze that produced a hit with his lead vocal on "Tempted." By this point, Carrack was playing with Nick Lowe, who produced *Suburban Voodoo*, and the album sounds very much like a Lowe album with Carrack singing. That's all to the good, though, since Carrack's supple voice is well suited to Lowe's updated '60s rock 'n' roll style. Carrack scored his first solo Top 40 hit with "I Need You," but that was one of the slighter tracks on an unusually tuneful album. —*William Ruhlmann*

When You Walk in the Room / 1987 / Chrysalis ++

One Good Reason / Nov. 1987 / Chrysalis ++++
The third of Carrack's four solo albums of the '80s is the best-realized showcase for his soulful vocals. It produced four singles-chart entries, the most successful of which was the Top Ten hit "Don't Shed a Tear," Carrack's first big hit under his own name. —*William Ruhlmann*

Groove Approved / Oct. 1989 / Chrysalis +++
After pulling four singles off 1987's *One Good Reason*, Paul Carrack looked to be on the verge of finally establishing himself as a solo star. Instead, he stumbled with the follow-up, *Groove Approved*, a solid, workman-like collection that featured only one Top 40 number in "I Live by the Groove." One suspects that this had less to do with the album's real commercial potential than with upheavals in the record company, which was being sold by its founders to EMI during this period. Yet afterward, Carrack went back to working with Squeeze and Mike and the Mechanics, putting his solo career on hold. —*William Ruhlmann*

● **Collection: Twenty-One Good Reasons** / Jan. 25, 1994 / Chrysalis ++++
Containing not only his solo hits but the ones that he sang for Ace ("How Long"), Squeeze ("Tempted"), and Mike and the Mechanics ("Silent Running" and "The Living Years"), as well as two songs with Carlene Carter, *Twenty-One Good Reasons: The Paul Carrack Collection* is the one Carrack disc to own. —*Stephen Thomas Erlewine*

Carrackter Reference / May 24, 1995 / Demon ++++

Blue Views / Jan. 1996 / IRS/EMI +++
After spending eight years working with Mike and the Mechanics, among other bands and side projects, Paul Carrack returned in 1997 with *Blue Views*. Carrack's side projects since the mid-'80s have all been variations on slick but soulful pop-rock, so it's not a surprise that *Blue Views* sounds as if it could have followed *Groove Approved* in 1991. That's not necessarily a bad thing, since Carrack's vocals are terrific and the sound is appealingly polished. The material is a bit too spotty to

make it a triumphant comeback, but the best moments, including a version of the Eagles' "Love Will Keep Us Alive," are solid adult contemporary pop. —*Stephen Thomas Erlewine*

Joe "King" Carrasco (Joseph Teutsch)

b. Dumas, Texas
Guitar, Vocals / Tex-Mex, New Wave
Texas native Joe "King" Carrasco has devoted his career to re-creating the Tex-Mex, Farfisa organ rock 'n' roll sound of such '60s groups as the Sir Douglas Quintet and Sam the Sham & the Pharoahs. After playing in a succession of bands around Texas in the late '60s and early '70s, Carrasco founded El Molino in 1976 and recorded *Tex-Mex Rock-Roll* in 1978. (The album was reissued by ROIR in 1989.) By 1979 he had formed the Crowns and was calling his music "nuevo wavo," playing especially in New York, where he appeared on stage in a cape and crown. He was signed to the UK Stiff label and Joe Boyd's Hannibal label in the US, and released *Joe "King" Carrasco and the Crowns* in 1980. By 1982 he had moved up to major label MCA for *Synapse Gap*, followed by *Party Weekend* (1983). These missed the charts, however, and although Carrasco has recorded since, turning increasingly political meanwhile, his work has been harder to find. *Bandido Rock* (1987) on Rounder was credited to Joe King Carrasco y Las Coronas. —*William Ruhlmann*

Joe "King" Carrasco and El Molino / 1978 / Big Beat +++
This UK release is a reissue of *Joe "King" Carrasco and El Molino*, originally released in a limited edition by Texas label Lisa Records in 1978. The album was reissued in the US under the title *Tex-Mex Rock-Roll* by ROIR in 1989. —*William Ruhlmann*

Joe "King" Carrasco and the Crowns / Nov. 1980 / Hannibal +++
At a time when the New York club scene was dominated by the remnants of punk and quirky power pop of Devo and the B-52s, Joe "King" Carrasco, whose music complemented those styles, constituted comic relief. He would sweep on in his crown and cape and play Farfisa organ-based mid-'60s-style Tex-Mex rock 'n' roll. Carrasco was a delightful club act, but inevitably that didn't translate adequately to vinyl. Nevertheless, this, his first national release, made a brave attempt, and even if you couldn't have Joe jumping on your table at home, a song like "Caca de Vaca" was bound to raise a smile. (This album was released originally by Stiff Records in the UK with a slightly different track listing.) —*William Ruhlmann*

Synapse Gap / 1982 / MCA ++++
Joe "King" Carrasco's Crowns boasted a beefed-up sound on their major label debut, which leaned more toward guitar rock with a loud rhythm section than earlier, cheesier Tex-Mex efforts. That did not constitute an improvement necessarily, though it probably was intended to broaden Carrasco's appeal. For the most part, this didn't lessen the band's effervescence, though the reggae tune was a bit trendy (it even featured harmonies by Michael Jackson!) and the overall impression was of an artist closer to the mainstream than the border. —*William Ruhlmann*

● **Anthology** / Mar. 21, 1995 / One Way ++++
This is an 18-track compilation drawn from Joe "King" Carrasco's two MCA albums *Synapse Gap (Mundo Total)* (1982) and *Party Weekend* (1983). —*William Ruhlmann*

The Cars

f. 1976, Boston, MA, db. 1988
New Wave, Pop-Rock
Blondie may have had a string of No. 1 hits, and Talking Heads may have won the hearts of the critics—but the Cars were the most successful American New Wave band to emerge in the late '70s. With their sleek, mechanical pop-rock, the band racked up a string of platinum albums and Top 40 singles that made them one of the most popular American rock 'n' roll bands of the late '70s and early '80s. While they were more commercially oriented than their New York peers, the Cars were nevertheless inspired by proto-punk, garage rock, and bubblegum pop. The difference was in packaging. Where their peers were as inspired by art as music, the Cars were strictly a rock 'n' roll band, and while their music occasionally sounded clipped and distant, they had enough attitude to cross over to album rock radio, which is where they made their name. Nevertheless, the Cars remained a New Wave band, picking up cues from the Velvet Underground, David Bowie, and Roxy Music. Ric Ocasek and Ben Orr's vocals uncannily recalled Lou Reed's dead-pan delivery, while the band's insistent, rhythmic pulse was reminiscent of Berlin-era Iggy Pop. Furthermore, the group followed Roxy Music's lead and had artist Alberto Vargas design sexy illustrations of pinups for their record sleeves. These airbrushed drawings were the group's primary visual attraction until 1984, when they made a series of striking videos to accompany the singles from *Heartbeat City*. The videos for "You Might Think," "Magic," and "Drive" became MTV staples, sending the Cars to near-superstar status. Instead of following through with their

success, the Cars slowly faded away, quietly breaking up after releasing one final album in 1987.

Ric Ocasek (guitar, vocals) and Ben Orr (bass, vocals) had been collaborators for several years before forming the Cars in 1976. Ocasek began playing guitar and writing songs when he was 10. After briefly attending Antioch College and Bowling Green State University, he dropped out of school and moved to Cleveland, where he met Orr, who had led the house band on the TV show "Upbeat" as a teenager. The two began writing songs and led bands in Cleveland, New York City, Woodstock, and Ann Arbor before settling in Cambridge, MA, in the early '70s. In 1972 they were the core of a folk trio named Milkwood. The band released an album on Paramount Records in late 1972 that was ignored; the record featured keyboards by a session musician named Greg Hawkes. By 1974 Ocasek and Orr had formed Cap'n Swing, which featured Elliot Easton on lead guitar. Cap'n Swing became a popular concert attraction in Boston, but the group broke up in 1975. Ocasek, Orr, and Easton formed a new band called the Cars in 1976 with former Modern Lovers drummer Dave Robinson and keyboardist Hawkes.

Early in 1977, the Cars sent a demo tape of "Just What I Needed" to the influential Boston radio station WBCN, and it quickly became the station's most-requested song. For the remainder of 1977 the group played Boston clubs, and by the end of the year, they signed with Elektra Records. The group's eponymous debut album appeared in the summer of 1978, and it slowly built a following, thanks to the hit singles "Just What I Needed" (No. 27), "My Best Friend's Girl" (No. 35), and "Good Times Roll" (No. 41). The Cars stayed on the charts for over two and a half years, delaying the release of the group's second album, Candy-O. It would eventually sell over six million copies.

Recorded early in 1979, Candy-O wasn't released until later that summer. The album was an instant hit, quickly climbing to No. 3 on the charts and going platinum two months after its release. The record launched the Top Ten hit "Let's Go" and sent the band to the arena rock circuit. Perhaps as a reaction to their quick success, the group explored more ambitious territory on 1980's Panorama. Though the album wasn't as big a hit as its predecessors, it nevertheless peaked at No. 5 and went platinum. Before recording their fourth album, several band members pursued extracurricular interests, with Ocasek earning a reputation as a successful New Wave producer for his work with Suicide and Romeo Void. The Cars released their fourth album, Shake It Up, in the fall of 1981, and it quickly went platinum, with its title track becoming the group's first Top Ten single.

After the success of Shake It Up, the Cars recorded the soundtrack to the short film Chapter-X and then took an extended leave, with Ocasek, Orr, and Hawkes all recording solo albums in 1982; Ocasek also produced the debut album from the hardcore punk band, Bad Brains. The Cars reconvened in 1983 to record their fifth album, Heartbeat City, which was released in early 1984. Supported by a groundbreaking, computer-animated video, the album's first single "You Might Think" became a Top Ten hit, sending Heartbeat City to No. 3 on the album charts. Three other Top 40 singles—"Magic" (No. 12), "Drive" (No. 3), and "Hello Again" (No. 20)—followed later that year, and the record went triple platinum in the summer of 1985. At the end of the year, the group released The Cars' Greatest Hits, which featured two new hit singles, "Tonight She Comes" and "I'm Not the One."

The Cars were on hiatus for much of 1985 and 1986, during which time Ocasek, Easton, and Orr recorded solo albums. During 1987 the group completed their seventh album, Door to Door. The album was a moderate hit upon its summer release in 1987, launching the single "You Are the Girl," which peaked at No. 17. Door to Door had seemed half-hearted, sparking speculation that the group was on the verge of splitting up. The Cars announced in February 1988 that they had, indeed, broken up. All of the members pursued solo careers, but only Ocasek released albums with regularity. —Stephen Thomas Erlewine

The Cars / May 1978 / Elektra ✦✦✦✦
On the heels of the new wave, the Cars' debut album was a mechanized rock delight, its music spare and precise, yet undeniably catchy, with sly references to the Beatles and Tommy James and the Shondells. Vocalists Rick Ocasek and Ben Orr sounded oddly dispassionate, as if they were singing in a foreign language. But that didn't stop "Just What I Needed," "My Best Friend's Girl," and "Good Times Roll" from becoming modest hits. —William Ruhlmann

Candy-O / Jun. 1979 / Elektra ✦✦✦
The Cars' debut album was still charting more than a year after its release when its carbon-copy follow-up, Candy-O, appeared sporting a cover drawing by Vargas, noted for his Playboy illustrations of voluptuous women. Candy-O duplicated its predecessor's success, outpacing the first album as the single "Let's Go" (the Cars' biggest hit so far) became one of the summer songs of the year. "It's All I Can Do" hit, as well. —William Ruhlmann

Panorama / Aug. 1980 / Elektra ✦✦
Although it sprinted up the charts and sold the expected million copies, the Cars' third album was a disappointment, with only the single "Touch and Go" scraping into the Top 40 and the rest unmemorable. —William Ruhlmann

Shake It Up / Nov. 1981 / Elektra ✦✦✦
Making extensive use of video promotion, the Cars rebounded sharply with their fourth album, whose title track was actually their first Top Ten single. The album also featured the underrated "Since You're Gone." —William Ruhlmann

Heartbeat City / Mar. 1984 / Elektra ✦✦✦✦
A break of three years gave the Cars plenty of time to write strong material. At the same time, Michael Jackson's Thriller had expanded the number of singles that could be pulled from one album, good news for the radio-friendly Cars, who scored five hits off this album, including the Top Tens "You Might Think" and "Drive." As a result, the album became the Cars' all-time best-seller. —William Ruhlmann

● **Greatest Hits** / Oct. 1985 / Elektra ✦✦✦✦
Ultimately, the Cars were a singles band. Here are those singles, including the biggest ones, "Drive," "Shake It Up," "You Might Think," and "Tonight She Comes." —William Ruhlmann

Door to Door / Aug. 1987 / Elektra ✦✦
A major disappointment, presaging the band's 1988 split, Door to Door still managed to feature the hit "You Are the Girl." But guitarist/singer Rick Ocasek, who produced, was more interested in his solo career by this time. —William Ruhlmann

Just What I Needed: The Cars Anthology / Nov. 7, 1995 / Rhino ✦✦✦✦
Over the course of two CDs and 40 tracks, Just What I Needed: The Cars Anthology runs through all of the Cars' greatest hits and strongest album tracks, adding exciting rarities like demos and covers of "The Little Black Egg" and "Funtime" for good measure. Even though the collection is quite comprehensive, it is never tedious, nor is it too much for the casual fan; in fact, the set works better as an album than the single-disc greatest hits collection. By including nearly all of the band's worthwhile material, Just What I Needed is the definitive Cars compilation. —Stephen Thomas Erlewine

Clarence Carter

b. Jan. 14, 1936, Montgomery, AL
Guitar, Keyboards, Vocals / Soul, R&B
A blind soul singer whose numerous hits of the late '60s and early '70s epitomized the Muscle Shoals rhythm & blues sound, Carter hit the big time with his Atlantic single "Patches" (1970) and won a lasting place in the annals of Southern soul with others like "Slip Away" and "Too Weak to Fight." In 1981 Carter broke out of a dry spell with the Venture album Let's Burn, featuring a track called "Workin' (On a Love Building)," which set the theme for much of what was to follow: robust, lascivious, lovemaking boasts. More recent tracks, such as his salacious reworking of Tampa Red's "Love Me with a Feeling" and the jukebox favorite "Strokin'" (too risque for some radio stations), further solidified the carnal Carter image. Still primarily a soul/R&B singer, Carter has incorporated more hard blues elements in his music recently than in the Muscle Shoals days, despite his new and unblues-minded penchant for playing and programming all the instruments on his albums. —Jim O'Neal

This Is Clarence Carter / 1968 / Atlantic ✦✦✦✦
Fine country-soul, blues, and humorous/novelty tracks by Clarence Carter, then at his peak both artistically and musically. He didn't score any big hits from this album, but played with the exuberance and earthy charisma that marked his biggest Atlantic hits. —Ron Wynn

The Dynamic Clarence Carter / 1969 / Atlantic ✦✦✦✦
Clarence Carter was churning out classic Southern soul in the late '60s. Everything clicked, from soap opera-ish tale of deprivation to sexually suggestive boasts, country/soul ballads, and uptempo wailers. This isn't so much an album as a string of great singles, all of them sung with fire, conviction, and passion. —Ron Wynn

Let's Burn / 1977 / Venture ✦✦✦
Fine Southern soul, light blues, and humorous, bawdy cuts from Clarence Carter. The single "Working on a Love Building" got some national attention, as did the title cut. The production was minimal, but Carter's gritty, earnest vocals were consistently effective. —Ron Wynn

Touch of Blues / 1989 / Ichiban ✦✦✦✦
Not as blues-oriented as some might think, Touch of Blues focuses primarily on the thing Clarence Carter had been known for since the mid-1960s: earthy, unpretentious Southern-style soul music. To be sure, the CD does contain more 12-bar blues material than Carter usually embraced, including "It's a Man Down There" and heartfelt versions of T-Bone Walker's "Stormy Monday" and B.B. King's "Rock Me Baby." But R&B is dominant, and Carter's followers (a great many of them in the

South) were quite receptive to such good-humored, lighthearted soul as "Why Do I Stay Here (And Take This Shit from You)" and the risque "Kiss You All Over." One medium that wasn't at all receptive to *Touch of Blues* was urban contemporary radio, which has pretty much ignored Carter's Ichiban recordings. But thankfully, Carter has enough of a following to do okay without urban radio's support. —*Alex Henderson*

Between a Rock and A Hard Place / 1990 / Ichiban ✦✦✦
Clarence Carter entered the 1990s sounding very much as he had in the 1960s. While the O'Jays, Gladys Knight, and other soul survivors had turned to urban contemporary songs in the '80s, Carter refused to change his style. Though *Between a Rock and a Hard Place* and other albums he's done for Ichiban Records have their share of keyboards and synthesizers, there's no mistaking the fact that the Montgomery, AL. native's forte was still Southern-style soul music. Though the album isn't quite on a par with *Touch of Blues*, a 54-year-old Carter demonstrates that his powers hadn't decreased on down-home offerings like "Pickin' Em Up, Layin' Em Down," "If You See My Baby," and the humorous "Things Ain't like They Used to Be." A remake of Carter's '60s hit "Too Weak to Fight" pales in comparison to the original version, but this CD has more strengths than weaknesses. —*Alex Henderson*

The Dr.'s Greatest Prescriptions: The Best of Clarence Carter / 1992 / Ichiban ✦✦✦
As long as Clarence Carter has been recording first-class soul music, it isn't surprising that more than one compilation is titled *The Best of Clarence Carter*. This particular compilation spotlights his work for Ichiban Records, a small Atlanta-based label that has also recorded Curtis Mayfield, the Chi-Lites, Eddie Floyd, and quite a few other soul veterans. One of Ichiban's best selling artists, Carter has pretty much rejected high-tech urban contemporary sounds and stuck with the type of earthy Southern music that's been his forte since the 1960s. In fact, this CD underscores the fact that his Ichiban output is almost as strong as his classic Atlantic recordings. The best known track here is Carter's risque hit "Strokin'," but he's equally adept at everything from the smooth "I Was in the Neighborhood" to the good-natured "Kiss You All Over" to the blues smoker "Love Me with a Feeling." Most of Carter's Ichiban discs are well worth hearing, but for those unfamiliar with his work for that label, this collection can serve as an engaging introduction. —*Alex Henderson*

● **Snatchin' It Back** / 1992 / Rhino ✦✦✦✦
Snatchin' It Back—The Best of Clarence Carter is a great compilation, spotlighting Carter's stellar guitar work and trademark vocals on classics like "Slip Away," "Too Weak to Fight," and "Lookin' for a Fox." His great "Tell Daddy" (covered by Etta James as "Tell Mama") is included. Dave Marsh contributes the liner notes. Soul music at its funky best, and *the* compilation to own if you're a Carter fan. —*Christine Ohlman*

Peter Case

b. Apr. 5, 1954, Buffalo, NY
Guitar, Vocals / Singer-Songwriter, Folk-Rock, Contemporary Folk
After disbanding the Los Angeles new wave/power-pop group the Plimsouls, Peter Case launched a career as a singer-songwriter, specializing in the flat-pick guitar style and semi-autobiographical stories of drifters, delivered in narrative style.

Born in the '50s and growing up in upstate New York, Case was inspired, like any number of young men of his generation, by Elvis Presley and the Beatles. He was also a fan of the folk and blues of Mississippi John Hurt, Leadbelly, and Woody Guthrie; as a teenager he took to the troubadour's life, playing coffeehouses and busking. He was discovered on the streets of San Francisco in 1976 by songwriter Jack Lee, with whom he collaborated in the Nerves, a short-lived but influential power-pop act. The meeting led to a move to L.A. and the formation of the Plimsouls in 1980. After the group found success with the power-pop standard "A Million Miles Away," they called it quits, and Case debuted with *Peter Case* for Geffen in 1986. It was a collection of hard folk songs produced by T-Bone Burnett, and included co-writes with Burnett and Case's first wife, Victoria Williams, along with performances by John Hiatt and Roger McGuinn. Case was among a handful of rockers who had been honing his acoustic songs in clubs, helping to launch the so-called "unplugged" movement. In 1989 he released *The Man with the Blue Post-Modern Fragmented Neo-Traditionalist Guitar*, again with the help of choice musicians like David Hidalgo, Ry Cooder, and Benmont Tench. In a *Rolling Stone* interview that year, Bruce Springsteen cited Case as the songwriter he was listening to most at the time. For 1992's *Six-Pack of Love*, Case chucked the folk aesthetic for something more rock-oriented, but the collection flopped, as did his liaison with Geffen. He regrouped and self-released *Peter Case Sings like Hell*, recorded with Marvin Etzioni in a Los Angeles living room, in 1993. The strength of that release earned him a new recording contract with Vanguard in 1995, and Case came on strong for *Torn Again*, his best set of spare songs about lonesome losers since *Blue Guitar*. In 1996 the Plimsouls re-formed for some reunion shows and recording. Case continues to tour as a solo act. In 1997 he was hosting a weekly evening for song-

writers at Santa Monica's revived Ash Grove folk club. —*Denise Sullivan*

Peter Case / 1986 / Geffen ✦✦✦✦
The solo debut by the former new wave and power-popper came as a surprise in 1986, a time when few rock musicians had yet conceived the idea of "unplugged." Case shines on his "Steel Strings," "I Shook His Hand," "Old Blue Car," and "Walk in the Woods"—all songs that hearken back to a simpler time, delivered by top-drawer musicians like Jim Keltner, Van Dyke Parks, and John Hiatt—and in Case's own, incredibly strong vocal style. —*Denise Sullivan*

The Man with the Blue Post Modern Fragmented Neo-Traditionalist Guitar / Apr. 11, 1989 / Geffen ✦✦✦✦
As more musicians started to catch the wave of the return to roots and acoustic music, Case had already delivered one gem, and this follow-up was the crowning jewel on his king-of-neo-folk crown. Again, a host of name musicians like David Hidalgo, Ry Cooder, and Benmont Tench were pulled in to work out Case's songs. The story of "Poor Old Tom," the love song "Two Angels," and the semi-autobiographical "Entella Hotel" are timeless pieces by a songwriter experiencing an artistic peak. —*Denise Sullivan*

Six-Pack of Love / Mar. 1992 / Geffen ✦✦✦
A failed attempt at expanding his folk roots and augmenting it with the tricky production of Mitchell Froom, Case's simple songs were lost in the morass. A number of songs were co-written with legendary artists whom Case admires (Billy Swan, John Prine), but they don't stand up against the sheer force of Case's voice and Froom's inexplicable arrangements. Nonetheless, "Beyond the Blues" by Case, Tom Russell, and Bob Neuwirth and the jaunty tragedy (!) "Never Coming Home" make the record worth owning. —*Denise Sullivan*

Sings Like Hell / Apr. 5, 1994 / Vanguard ✦✦✦✦
After a tumultuous tenure with a giant label, Case took time to regroup and reassess his roots on *Sings Like Hell*, a set of unaccompanied traditional and modern folk songs delivered in Case's forthright manner, completely in step with the trend toward mainstream rock's reclaiming roots music. The perfect introduction to traditional American music for rock fans; folk and blues fans will also appreciate the richness in Case's delivery. His reading of "Lakes of Pontchartrain" is one for the books. —*Denise Sullivan*

● **Torn Again** / Apr. 25, 1995 / Vanguard ✦✦✦✦
Case returns to the form he perfected on his second album and again turns to producers Larry Hirsch and J. Steven Soles for a collection of rock and folk songs—and his first album of original material in three years. The tone of the pop song "Baltimore" recalls his Plimsouls sound, while "Anything" and "Breaking the Chain" are gentler, metaphorical songs with a folk-rock base. More heartfelt and less hardened, Case sings for the grown-ups. —*Denise Sullivan*

Shaun Cassidy

b. Sep. 27, 1958, Los Angeles, CA
Vocals / Pop-Rock, Bubblegum, Teen Idol
A major teen idol of the late 1970s, actor/singer Shaun Cassidy rocketed to fame both on the pop charts and on television, much as his half-brother David Cassidy had done earlier in the decade. The son of actors Jack Cassidy and Shirley Jones, he was born in Hollywood on September 27, 1959, and formed his first band at the age of 11. After signing with Mike Curb's division of Warner Bros. in 1975, Cassidy issued his 1976 debut single "Morning Girl," which became a major European hit and made the singer the subject of considerable fan adulation and teen-magazine scrutiny. The follow-up, a cover of Eric Carmen's "That's Rock 'n' Roll," was also a success abroad, especially in Australia.

Cassidy's first American release followed in early 1977: a cover of the Crystals' 1963 classic "Da Do Ron Ron," it immediately hit No. 1, and overnight he became a heartthrob in his native land as well as internationally. Cassidy's fame increased with the 1977 premiere of "The Hardy Boys Mysteries," a weekly TV series based on the popular teen detective novels, and his self-titled debut LP went platinum. "That's Rock 'n' Roll" was also reissued for American audiences, and went gold. The 1977 follow-up *Born Late* was another success, spawning the Top Ten hit "Hey Deanie."

Cassidy's fame proved short-lived, however; 1978's *Under Wraps* struggled to crack the Top 40, and 1979's *Room Service* failed even to chart. With 1980's *Wasp*, he recruited producer Todd Rundgren in an attempt to make a serious rock album, performing material from the likes of David Bowie, Pete Townshend, and David Byrne; however, the LP stiffed, and Cassidy's recording career was essentially finished. Television became his primary focus, and he starred in the 1980 series "Breaking Away," followed several years later by a stint on the soap opera "General Hospital." After starring with David Cassidy and Petula Clark in Broadway's *Blood Brothers* in 1993, he returned to television as the creator and producer of the 1995 program "American Gothic." —*Jason Ankeny*

● **Greatest Hits** / May 1993 / Curb ✦✦✦✦
Curb's 12-track *Greatest Hits* contains all of Shaun Cassidy's biggest hits, including "Da Doo Ron Ron," "That's Rock 'n' Roll," "Hey Deanie," and "Do You Believe in Magic." While the minor hit "Our Night" is omitted, the remainder of the collection is devoted to entertainingly lightweight originals from Cassidy ("Hard Love," "Teen Dream," "Break for the Street") and covers of the Who's "So Sad About Us" and Ian Hunter's "Once Bitten, Twice Shy," making it a representative and enjoyable overview of Cassidy's brief run as a teen idol. —*Stephen Thomas Erlewine*

Cast

f. 1993, Liverpool, England
Brit-Pop
As one of the most traditional guitar bands to emerge during the Britpop era of the mid-'90s, Cast has weathered negative criticism from certain quarters of the media, who labelled them mere revivalists. But the criticism didn't prevent Cast from becoming a very, very popular band within Britain after the success of Oasis and Blur. Led by vocalist/guitarist John Power, Cast carved out a sound that was heavily indebted to the British Invasion of the early '60s, but it was infused with a mystical, pseudo-hippie lyrical sensibility, upon which Power expounded in all of his interviews. What really made Cast into a success was Power's gift of simple, classic pop hooks, as demonstrated on the hit singles "Fine Time," "Alright," and "Walkaway."

The roots of Cast lay in the La's, the seminal late '80s British guitarpop combo led by Lee Mavers. John Power was the bassist in the La's from their inception in the mid-'80s to the early '90s, when the band had a major British hit with their eponymous debut album. Following the supporting tour for the record, the La's were scheduled to record a second album, but it soon became clear that not only was Mavers not going to write a batch of new songs any time soon, but he wasn't going to allow Power to contribute his own material. Power left the band, forming Cast with guitarist Liam Tyson, bassist Peter Wilkinson, and drummer Keith O'Neill early in 1994.

Cast received its first big break when Elvis Costello had the group open for him on his summer 1994 UK tour. By the end of 1994 Cast had signed a record contract with Polydor Records and began recording with John Leckie (XTC, Stone Roses). "Fintime," Cast's debut single, reached No. 17 on the pop charts in the spring, followed by another hit single, "Alright," in the summer. *All Change*, the band's debut, was released in October 1995, debuting in the British Top Ten.

Over the course of 1996, Cast's audience continued to grow, as *All Change* worked its way toward platinum status, and the band toured America several times, gaining a cult audience. In the fall the band released the single "Flying," their first new recording since their debut. The single entered the British charts at No. 4. Cast's second album, *Mother Nature Calls*, was released in the spring of 1997. —*Stephen Thomas Erlewine*

● **All Change** / Oct. 1995 / Polydor ✦✦✦✦
Cast's *All Change* serves as the perfect antidote to the inner rage fueling much American alternative rock; it would be hard to imagine a more gloriously upbeat backbeat of a guitar pop record, one that appeals to the eternal adolescent in each of us. The group's pedigree derives from good stock, founder John Power having served time with another fine Mersey combo, the La's. But Cast transcends the hackneyed expectations of its environment, structure, and genetics through sheer, relentless quality of songcraft and performance. No sooner has one wide-eyed, hook-infested injection stormed the synapses demanding total capitulation than another of equal potency lines up to take its place. Cast vocals recall Small Faces-era Steve Marriott fused, in places, to Suede's Brett Anderson. There's a soft-psych feel to several tracks (try "Sandstorm") that calls to mind "Pictures of Matchstick Men"-era Status Quo; Cast has clearly assimilated several volumes of Bam Caruso's *Rubble* and A.I.P.'s *Electric Sugarcube Flashbacks* series, without sacrificing its power-Mod backbone. Production is brittle and uncluttered. On the lyrics front, all is positively cheery, anthemic stuff about truth, honour, living well, having fun, and getting the girl, delivered exuberantly enough to strip away several coats of accumulated cynicism and almost make you believe it's possible. Two favorites are the shifting falsetto angst anthem "Tell It like It Is" and the ballad "Walk Away"—a clue to how Mott the Hoople's "Roll Away the Stone" would have come out recorded in 1967. —*Roch Parisien*

Mother Nature Calls / Apr. 14, 1997 / Polydor ✦✦✦
If Cast's debut album *All Change* was trad-rock at its most joyous, the second album, *Mother Nature Calls*, is considerably more problematic. Electing to expand their sound slightly instead of replicating *All Change*, Cast paints itself into a corner. They haven't abandoned the traditional Brit-pop stylings of their debut, but they've strengthened them with a tougher sound and neo-hippie mysticism that manifests itself not

only in John Power's dippy lyrics, but in trippy instrumental sections. In theory, this is a way out of the trad-rock straitjacket, but in practice it falls flat. The main problem is that Power's melodies aren't nearly as sharp or memorable as they were on the debut; this immediately brings attention to his lyrics, which are naive and often embarrassingly simplistic. Nor does Cast have enough charisma to save the songs with energetic, distinctive performances when they're flailing. These problems become all the more evident when they do get it right, such as on the shimmering "Guiding Star," the punchy "She Sun Shines" and the hearttugging "I'm So Lonely (Calling You Back)," and they have the same sparkling joy that made *All Change* a delight. But that's a rarity on *Mother Nature Calls*. When the tunes and attitude are there, such weaknesses are easy to overlook, but since Cast comes up deficient on both counts, *Mother Nature Calls* is simply a dull listen. —*Stephen Thomas Erlewine*

Jimmy Castor

b. Jun. 22, 1943, New York, NY
Saxophone, Vocals / Funk
A master of novelty/disco funk, saxophonist Jimmy Castor started as a doo wop singer in New York. He wrote and recorded "I Promise to Remember" for Wing wth the Juniors in 1956, a group whose roster included Al Casey, Jr., Orton Graves, and Johnny Williams. Castor replaced Frankie Lymon in the Teenagers in 1957 before switching to sax in 1960. He appeared on several soul-jazz and Afro-Latin sessions and had a solo hit with "Hey Leroy, Your Mama's Callin' You" on Smash in 1966. Castor also played sax on Dave "Baby" Cortez' hit "Rinky Dink." He formed the Jimmy Castor Bunch in 1972 and signed with RCA. Their first release, *It's Just Begun*, launched Castor's next phase with the song "Troglodyte (Cave Man)." It was a Top Ten R&B and pop smash. Castor continued the trend in 1975 with "The Bertha Butt Boogie" and later recorded "E-Man Boogie," "King Kong," "Bom Bom," and "Amazon." The Castor band included keyboardist/trumpeter Gerry Thomas, bassist Doug Gibson, guitarist Harry Jensen, conga player Lenny Fridle, Jr., and drummer Bobby Manigault. Thomas left the band to join the Fatback band. Castor recorded as a solo performer from 1976 until 1988. He had one of his bigger hits in many years with a 1988 revival of "Love Makes a Woman," which paired him with disco diva Joyce Sims. Castor had his own label, Long Distance, in the '80s. —*Ron Wynn*

● **Everything Man: Best of the Jimmy Castor Bunch** / Nov. 21, 1995 / Rhino ✦✦✦✦
Castor was pegged as a novelty artist, and rightly so, considering that his biggest hits were "Troglodyte," "Bertha Butt Boogie," and "King Kong." Still, even the novelty cuts featured some primordial funk, particularly in the percolating guitars of the early '70s cuts. With 17 songs that include all of his chart hits and some notable album cuts, this is the definitive collection, and probably all that any listener needs. Aside from the '70s funk material (which became less impressive and more discofied as the decade progressed), it also has his 1966 Latin-soul hit "Hey, Leroy, Your Mama's Callin' You," and a Frankie Lymon soundalike single he cut in 1956 as leader of Jimmy Castor & the Juniors. —*Richie Unterberger*

Cat Heads

f. 1985, San Francisco, CA, db. 1988
Group / Alternative Pop-Rock, Indie Rock
A San Francisco supergroup of underground musicians, the Cat Heads formed in 1985. Singer and guitarist Mark Zanandrea was from the Leaches and Love Circus, guitarist Sam Babbit from the Ophelias, drummer Melanie Clarin played with just about everyone in town, and bassist Alan Korn hailed from X-Tal. The band traded vocal and songwriting chores to create a chaotic mix of folk-rock, indie-rock, joke-rock, and country. Its 1987 debut, *Hubba*, was produced by the Rain Parade's Matt Piucci, and its follow-up, 1988's *Submarine*, was produced by Camper Van Beethoven's David Lowery. With so much insider support, it's a small wonder that the Cat Heads didn't survive the late-'80s post-R.E.M. groundswell of alternative bands, but instead disbanded after touring behind their second album. All former members continue to work in Bay Area bands too numerous to list here. Babbit and Korn immediately formed the (ex) Cat Heads after the group's demise. Zanandrea and Clarin remained collaborators in It Thing. Zanandrea and Babbit regrouped in 1996 under the name Androgynauts, and Babbitt and Korn reunited with the (ex) Cat Heads to form the Mudsills. —*Denise Sullivan*

Hubba / 1987 / Restless ✦✦✦
A band with three songwriters and four singers, *Hubba* plies punk, postpunk, folk-rock, and country. The band excelled at it all: "Hangin' Around" perfectly captures the indie-rock spirit of the times; "New White Wings" is psychedelic, "Need to Know" has that back-porch Stones sound, and "Lullaby" is just plain Velvety. "Golden Gate Park," a punk rock song mocking hippies, went down well in San Francisco circa 1987,

but the appeal of the Cat Heads' strange humor and multi-genre aesthetic was lost on the rest of the world. —*Denise Sullivan*

● **Submarine** / 1988 / Restless ✦✦✦✦
The Cat Heads' extreme stylistic waverings coalesced on *Submarine*, with the focus mostly on the band's melodic psychedelic/country leanings. "Postcard," "Sister Tabitha," and "Upside Down" are wonderful originals. Co-producer David Lowery (at that time of Camper Van Beethoven, later of Cracker) seems to favor singer Clarin's contributions. The album was the band's swan song and remains listenable and unmired in the '80s production that marred so many of the era's recordings. —*Denise Sullivan*

Our Frisco / 1989 / Twitch City ✦✦✦
Bassist Alan Korn and guitarist Sam Babbit stayed together and enlisted multi-instrumentalist Barry Hall and drummer John Stuart (Flying Color) to record one final record of Cat Heads-related material, and even invited drummer Melanie Clarin to sing along on the great protest number "Anti-Song." Sadly, it lacks the spunk of the original Cat Heads, as everything comes out a little tentative. —*Denise Sullivan*

Cat Power

b. United States
Vocals, Guitar / Singer-Songwriter, Indie Rock
Cat Power was the alias of Chan Marshall, a Southern-bred singer-songwriter whose father Charlie was an itinerant pianist. After dropping out of high school, Marshall found herself in New York. Performing under the name Cat Power, she was booked as the opening act for Liz Phair, where she met Sonic Youth drummer Steve Shelley and Two Dollar Guitar's Tim Foljahn, who agreed to become her backing band. After the release of 1995's *Dear Sir* and 1996's *Myra Lee*—both recorded on the same day—Cat Power signed to Matador for 1996's *What Would the Community Think?*, which won acclaim for Marshall's unsettling, emotional songs and cathartic vocals. —*Jason Ankeny*

Dear Sir / Oct. 1995 / Runt ✦✦✦
Myra Lee / Mar. 1996 / Smells Like Records ✦✦✦✦
● **What Would the Community Think** / Sep. 10, 1996 / Matador ✦✦✦✦

Catatonia

f. 1991, Wales
The most traditional pop band of all the Welsh bands to emerge in the post-Brit-pop days of the mid-'90s, Catatonia reworked the sound of jangling late-'80s alternative rock with the punchy, amateurish indie-rock attack. Comprised of vocalist Cerys Matthews, guitarist/vocalist Mark Roberts, guitarist Owen, bassist Paul Jones, and drummer Aled Richards, Catatonia formed in Cardiff, Wales, in the early '90s. Matthews and Roberts used to busk together in Cardiff before officially forming the band.

Catatonia released its first EP, *For Tinkerbell*, in 1993. At the time, the band featured Matthews, Roberts, Jones, drummer Dafydd Ieuan, and keyboardist C. Pegg. The same lineup recorded *Hooked*, which was released the next year. After the release of *Hooked*, both Pegg and Ieuan left the band; Dafydd went on to join Super Furry Animals. Replacing Ieuan with Aled Richards, the group released "Sweet Catatonia" in late 1995 and then added Owen as a second guitarist. Early in 1996 "You've Got a Lot to Answer For" became the band's first charting single, appearing at No. 35 on the British charts. A full-length album, *Way Beyond Blue*, followed in September, and it was greeted with positive reviews, peaking at No. 40 on the charts. —*Stephen Thomas Erlewine*

The Sumblime Magic of Catatonia / Feb. 1996 / Nursery ✦✦✦✦
The Sublime Magic of Catatonia is the group's first, independent album, and while it's a little rough around the edges, it is a ragged collection of terrific pop, highlighted by "Bleed," "Whale," "Hooked," and "Fall Beside Her." —*Stephen Thomas Erlewine*

● **Way Beyond Blue** / Sep. 30, 1996 / Blanco Y Negro ✦✦✦✦
Catatonia's major-label debut *Way Beyond Blue* is an infectious set of jangle-pop, injected with the punkish attitude of indie-rock. The guitars ring as if they were recorded in the late '80s, but it has a muscular backbone, and vocalist Cerys Matthews has a tough edge to her voice, so the music never sounds weak. A good majority of the songs—from "Sweet Catatonia" and "You've Got a Lot to Answer For" to "Painful" and "Way Beyond Blue"—are excellent, shimmering pop gems, making it an impressive debut. —*Stephen Thomas Erlewine*

Catherine Wheel

f. Apr. 1990, Great Yarmouth, England
Hard Rock, Alternative Pop-Rock, Shoegazing
Like many other British guitar bands of the early '90s, Catherine Wheel relied heavily on distortion as a way of creating texture and using airy vocals as atmosphere. While their melodies are actually quite straightforward, they are submerged in layers of guitar effects and droning chords. Like Lush and Ride, Catherine Wheel's blend of hooks and white noise forms pop songs, not free-form explorations with a floating melody. It is that quality that created a buzz in Britain around their first EP, *She's My Friend*, in 1991. Their subsequent two albums, 1992's *Ferment* and 1993's *Chrome*, earned them a solid fan base in England. The heavy rock attack of 1995's *Happy Days* increased their following in America. *Like Cats and Dogs*, a collection of B-sides and unreleased tracks, followed in 1996. —*Stephen Thomas Erlewine*

Ferment / Jun. 9, 1992 / Fontana ✦✦✦
Chrome / Jul. 20, 1993 / PolyGram ✦✦✦✦
Despite his obvious inflection toward The Teardrop Explode's Julian Cope, Rob Dickinson's lead vocals serve well; breathy and wistful on numbers like "Crank," but capable of stronger angst when called upon. His palette is restricted to a certain quality of expression however—there is little place on *Chrome* for such colorful concepts as joy or playfulness. Ultimately, this somewhat claustrophobic musical and emotional range boxes in Catherine Wheel and restricts *Chrome* to being a very good (rather than great) listening experience despite its loftier ambitions.—*Roch Parisien*

● **Happy Days** / May 1995 / Fontana/Mercury ✦✦✦✦
After releasing two records that faithfully followed the noisy, swirling trance-like psychedelia of My Bloody Valentine, Catherine Wheel trims all of their excesses on *Happy Days*. What is left is a throttling, pounding heavy metal band that accentuates the rhythm, not the texture. The change in direction is surprisingly effective and accessible; none of their previous work has been as immediate as "Way Down" or as bracing as "God Inside My Head," nor has it been as melodic as "Judy's Staring at the Sky," a duet with Tanya Donelly. Perhaps the switch to a heavier attack shouldn't be surprising— *Chrome* was filled with harder guitars—but the fact it has produced the band's best music is a pleasant shock. —*Stephen Thomas Erlewine*

Like Cats and Dogs / Sep. 9, 1996 / Polygram ✦✦✦
Like Cats and Dogs is an odds-and-ends collection that compiles B-sides, rarities, and live tracks Catherine Wheel released during the early '90s. While this should have been just been a batch of also-rans and half-baked ideas, the record is actually is a cohesive set, demonstrating the band's versatility. There's a harder edge to the live cuts than the original studio versions, while the B-sides are fine covers or successful forays into new musical territory, including psychedelia and wistful acoustic pop. *Like Cats and Dogs* remains an album for the converted, but it has something to offer even casual fans. —*Stephen Thomas Erlewine*

Nick Cave

b. Sep. 22, 1957, Warracknabeal, Australia
Organ, Piano, Vocals / Alternative Pop-Rock, Post-Punk
After goth pioneers the Birthday Party called it quits in 1983, singer-songwriter Nick Cave assembled the Bad Seeds, a post-punk supergroup featuring former Birthday Party guitarist Mick Harvey on drums, ex-Magazine bassist Barry Adamson, and Einsturzende Neubauten guitarist Blixa Bargeld. With the Bad Seeds, Cave continued to explore his obsessions with religion, death, love, America, and violence with a bizarre, sometimes self-consciously eclectic hybrid of blues, gospel, rock, and arty post-punk, although in a more subdued fashion than his work with the Birthday Party. Cave also allowed his literary aspirations to come to the fore; the lyrics are narrative prose, heavy on literary allusions and myth-making, and take some inspiration from Leonard Cohen. Cave's gloomy lyrics, dark musical arrangements, and deep baritone voice recall the albums of Scott Walker, who also obsessed over death and love with a frightening passion. However, Cave brings a hefty amount of post-punk experimentalism to Walker's epic dark pop.

Cave released his first album with the Bad Seeds, *From Her to Eternity*, in 1984. It contained a noteworthy cover of Elvis Presley's "In the Ghetto," foreshadowing much of Cave's style and subject matter on the follow-up, *The Firstborn Is Dead. Kicking Against the Pricks*, an all-covers album, broke the band in England with the help of "The Singer," which hit No. 1 on the UK Independent charts. The album also strengthened Cave's reputation as an original interpreter and a vocal stylist of note.

After 1986's *Your Funeral . . . My Trial*, Cave took a two-year hiatus from recording, partially to appear in Wim Wenders' 1987 film *Wings of Desire*, and then returned with *Tender Prey*, which featured Cramps guitarist Kid Congo Powers and Cave's strongest vocal performance up to that point. Cave's productivity picked up immensely over the next two years after he kicked a heroin habit. He had two books (1988's *King Ink*, a collection of lyrics, plays, and prose, and 1989's *And the Ass Saw the Angel*, a novel) published, appeared in the 1989 Australian film *Ghosts . . . of the Civil Dead* as a prisoner, recorded a soundtrack to the film with Harvey and Bargeld, and released 1990's *The Good Son*, his most relaxed, quiet album. Cave received his due as one of the leading figures in alternative rock when he was invited to perform on the 1994 edition of the Lollapalooza tour to promote his *Let Love In* album. Early in 1996 he released *Murder Ballads,* a collection of songs about murder. *Murder Ballads* became Cave's most commercially successful album to date, and, with typical perversity, he followed it with the introspective and personal *The Boatman's Call* in early 1997. —*Stephen Thomas Erlewine & Steve Huey*

● **From Her to Eternity** / 1984 / Mute ✦✦✦✦
Desperate and ominous, this is a chilling love letter. —*John Dougan*

The Firstborn Is Dead / 1985 / Mute ✦✦✦✦
Recorded with the Bad Seeds, this album contains angst directly influenced by early American folk-blues. —*John Dougan*

Kicking Against the Pricks / 1986 / Mute ✦✦✦✦
All covers, all unique, all recorded with the Bad Seeds. More rock from your worst nightmare. —*John Dougan*

Your Funeral . . . My Trial / 1986 / Mute ✦✦✦
A double EP, less focused but still good. —*John Dougan*

The Good Son / Oct. 1990 / Mute/Elektra ✦✦
Slightly Brazilian-influenced, still worthwhile, but his least essential. —*John Dougan*

Henry's Dream / May 12, 1992 / Mute/Elektra ✦✦✦
Henry's Dream, Nick Cave's apocalyptic, post-modern reading of gospel and the blues, is one of Cave's strongest albums. —*AMG*

Live Seeds / Sep. 28, 1993 / Mute/Elektra ✦✦✦
Although it won't appeal to anyone but hardcore Nick Cave fans, *Live Seeds* is a terrific live recording, capturing the essence of Cave's intense concerts. Recorded during the course of the band's 1992/1993 Euopean and Australian tour, *Live Seeds* is divided between older material and songs from the recent *Henry's Dream.* While the newer songs aren't quite as strong as the older items, the band plays with conviction, making the record an excellent souvenir for dedicated fans. —*Stephen Thomas Erlewine*

Let Love In / Apr. 19, 1994 / Mute/Elektra ✦✦✦
Let Love In is a darker, more brooding album than *Henry's Dream,* making it one of Nick Cave's most harrowing records. —*David Jehnzen*

Murder Ballads / Feb. 1996 / Mute/Reprise ✦✦✦
In some ways, *Murder Ballads* is the record Nick Cave has been waiting to make for his entire career. Death and violence have always haunted his music, even when he wasn't explicitly singing about the subject. On *Murder Ballads,* he sings about nothing but death in the most gruesome, shocking fashion. Divided between originals and covers, the record is awash in both morbid humor and sobering horror, as the Bad Seeds provide an appropriate backdrop for the carnage, alternating between blues, country, and lounge-jazz. Opening the affair is "Song for Joy," a tale from a father who has witnessed his family's death at the hands of a serial killer. It is the most disturbing number on the record, lacking any of the gallows humor that balances the other songs. Cave's duets with Kylie Minogue ("Where the Wild Roses Grow") and PJ Harvey ("Henry Lee") are intriguing, but the true *tours de force* of the album are "Stagger Lee" and "O'Malley's Bar." Working from an obscure, vulgar variation on "Stagger Lee," Cave increases the sordidness of the song, making Stagger an utterly unredeemable character. The original "O'Malley's Bar" is even stronger, as he spins a bizarrely funny epic of one man's slaughter of an entire bar. During "O'Malley's Bar," Cave and the Bad Seeds are at the height of their powers, and the performance ranks among the best they have ever recorded. —*Stephen Thomas Erlewine*

The Boatman's Call / Mar. 4, 1997 / Mute/Reprise ✦✦✦✦
Murder Ballads brought Nick Cave's morbidity to near-parodic levels, which makes the disarmingly frank and introspective songs of *The Boatman's Call* all the more startling. A song cycle equally inspired by Cave's failed romantic affairs and religious doubts, *The Boatman's Call* captures him at his most honest and despairing. While he retains a fascination with Gothic, Biblical imagery, it has little of the grand theatricality and self-conscious poetics that made his albums emotionally distant in the past. This time, there's no posturing, either from Cave or the Bad Seeds. The music is direct, but it has many textures, from blues to jazz, which offer a revealing and sympathetic bed for Cave's best, most affecting songs. *The Boatman's Call* is one of his finest albums and arguably the masterpiece he has been promising throughout his career. —*Stephen Thomas Erlewine*

Celibate Rifles

f. 1982, Sydney, Australia
Alternative Pop-Rock

Quick, who's Australia's best rock band? If you guessed Midnight Oil, you probably have the most supporters. But for my money, there's never been an Australian rock 'n' roll band better (or more consistent) than Sydney's Celibate Rifles. Playing stripped-down, loud, and fast Ramones-inspired guitar rock, the Celibate Rifles were one of the earliest punk bands to emerge during the post-Radio Birdman/Saints era.

Taking their cues from these Aussie bands, along with American hard rock of the Stooges, MC5, and Blue Oyster Cult, the Rifles, led by the twin guitar attack of Kent Steedman and Dave Morris and the deadpan baritone of vocalist Damien Lovelock, exploded out of the gate in 1982 with a series of records (released in Australia only) fueled by high-speed guitars, wah-wah-strangulated solos, and cartoonish, tongue-in-cheek lyrics.

Playing initially for crowds of hard-rock-loving surfers, it didn't take long for the Rifles to develop a following. Outside Australia, however, they were virtually unknown. That changed in 1985 with the release of *Quintessentially Yours,* a lengthy EP that was a collection of tracks from earlier albums. Although the Rifles didn't receive the attention of many lesser American and English bands, the releases kept coming, and they were all excellent. What didn't help was the band's seeming disinterest in touring America. [The Rifles last toured America in 1987, which is too bad, because their great live album *(Kiss, Kiss, Bang, Bang),* recorded at CBGB's on that tour, proves them to be a white-hot live band.

As they continued recording and maturing, the Rifles were unafraid to take risks with their tried and true loud-and-fast sound. Soon, acoustic guitars entered the mix, tempos slowed, pianos tinkled in the background, and vocal harmonies were added. None of this increased technical skill and studio experimentation diluted the band's strengths (i.e., feral power); in fact, it may well have made them a better and more interesting band. Another development was the increased politicization and social consciousness of their material. No longer were they simply sarcastic, funny boys; rather, they were addressing serious political, environmental, and social issues, thanks to Lovelock's sharp, insightful lyrics, all without any condescension or simplistic rhetoric.

In 1989 Rifles albums were suddenly no longer available in domestic release, a fact that didn't help the band in their quest to develop an American following. As a result, their great album *Blind Ear* was available (when you could find it) only as a high-priced Aussie import. Also, there were signs that the Rifles were nearing the end: Steedman and Morris were playing around Sydney with other musicians and producing new bands, Lovelock released a solo album *(It's a Wig, Wig, Wig, World)* with members of the Church, and the time between Rifles releases seemed to grow longer. Another dispiriting sign was the 1992 release of *Heaven on a Stick,* which, despite a wonderful title, sounded tired and tossed off. Fortunately, all this speculation turned out to be wrong, and in late 1994, the Rifles stormed back with *Spaceman in a Satin Suit,* an exhilarating return to form. A nonstop barrage of power, volume, and sharp songwriting, it shreds virtually every effort by the current generation of guitar-based alternarock careerists, and is easily the band's best record since *Blind Ear.* They may be a grizzled bunch of punk rockers, but there's nothing the Celibate Rifles couldn't teach young rock bands. Precious few of the soon-to-be-trivia-question groups currently glutting alternative rock will have careers this impressive 15 years down the road. —*John Dougan*

The Turgid Miasma of Existence / 1986 / Hot ✦✦✦✦
The first recording of new Celibate Rifles material to be released in America. Now fully incorporating acoustic guitars, cellos, zithers, and bass clarinets (!) into the mix, this record is more eclectic than your average Rifles release, but amazingly, there are no false moments, bad songs, or failed experiments. From the opening salvo of "Bill Bonney Regrets" through the hair-raising "Conflict of Instinct" to the sarcastically funny closing track "New Mistakes," this is a simply wonderful record that will sound refreshingly direct and engaging another 15 years from now. Lovelock's lyrics are especially wonderful, running the gamut from terse imagism to comedic tomfoolery to polemical broadsides. The album is dedicated to James Darroch, the original Rifles bass player who left in 1984 to form the great, little-known Eastern Dark (one very good EP, *Long Live the New Flesh*). Darroch died in a car accident while *Miasma* was being recorded. —*John Dougan*

Mina Mina Mina / 1986 / What Goes On ✦✦✦
Much of the earliest material recorded by the Rifles (covering the years 1982-84) is difficult to find in its original form, but these two records do an excellent job of anthologizing those heady post-Birdman/Saints days. Mostly speedy (guitars, guitars, and more guitars!!) and poppy, there are some hilarious songs ("Let's Get Married"), some that show a strong '70s influence ("God Squad"), and some that indicate the band's growing maturity ("Back in the Red"). Although they would make better records, the exuberance and excitement of this music, as well as its power, haven't diminished a bit since the day it was recorded. —*John Dougan*

Kiss Kiss Bang Bang / 1987 / What Goes On ✦✦✦
Live, loud, and fast. Turn it up to 11. Added bonus: the definitive version of Radio Birdman's supercharged Aussie punk anthem "Burn My Eye." —*John Dougan*

● **Roman Beach Party** / 1987 / What Goes On ✦✦✦✦
Around the time of this record's release I was proclaiming to anyone within the sound of my very loud voice that this was going to be the LP that broke the Rifles with the college radio crowd (pre-alternative rock)

in America. It was more direct and hard-hitting than *Miasma*, but it didn't sacrifice smarts, nor did it pander to a punk-rock crowd that was evolving into a neo-heavy-metal crowd. It was around the time of this LP that MTV's early alternative-rock show "The Cutting Edge" (hosted by Fleshtones lead singer Peter Zaremba) had the Rifles play live. Of course they were last, and that meant staying up until the wee hours of the morning, but if you did, you saw a ripsnorting version of *Roman Beach Party*'s opening track, the anti-televangelism ode "Jesus on T.V." Unfortunately, this appearance didn't translate into huge record sales, and those who missed out on *Roman Beach Party* ignored one of the classiest hard-rock records of the '80s. —*John Dougan*

Blind Ear / 1989 / True Tone-EMI ✦✦✦✦
The best Celibate Rifles recording? Yes, but only on the days I don't think it's *Roman Beach Party*, or maybe *Mina Mina Mina*. Along with being the only album in Australian rock history to contain two songs about the troubles in Northern Ireland ("Sean O'Farrell" and "Belfast"), *Blind Ear* continues the Rifles' maturation process from snarling young punks to snarling adult punks. Sounding at times like the Stones (and I mean that as a compliment), the Rifles—now nearly a decade into their career—were recording some of their best songs. For proof, listen to the two aforementioned, along with their critique of yuppiedom ("Wonderful Life") and the closing track, "O Salvation." Another record that should have been huge. —*John Dougan*

Spaceman in a Satin Suit / 1994 / Hot ✦✦✦✦
Starting off with one of the hardest, fastest, ecstatic bursts of rock they've ever recorded ("Spirits"), *Spaceman* is a resounding assertion that this band's career is far from over. In fact, this record wipes the floor with nearly every note issued by the endless succession of post-Nirvana, MTV-approved alternative rock bands. Like the Ramones (and perhaps Motorhead), the Rifles seem to get better with age, and for all of us punks way past 30, that's life-affirming news. —*John Dougan*

Chad & Jeremy

f. 1964, London, England, db. 1967
British Invasion, Pop-Rock
The American success of the folkish duo of Chad Stuart (b. Dec. 10, 1943, Durham, England) and Jeremy Clyde (b. Mar. 22, 1944, Buckinghamshire, England) pointed up the impact of the British Invasion led by the Beatles in February 1964. Chad & Jeremy charted only once in their native country, but their single "Yesterday's Gone," released in May 1964, was the first of 11 US chart hits they achieved through 1966. The biggest of these, and their only Top Ten, was "A Summer Song" (July 1964). Adopting a lighter approach than many of their Merseybeat contemporaries, Chad & Jeremy focused on pop revivals such as "Willow, Weep for Me" and songs from Broadway shows, such as "I Have Dreamed" from *Carousel*, both Top 40 hits for them. Having moved to Hollywood, they were frequent television guests, both on music shows such as "Hullabaloo" and series like "Batman." Their commercial progress was complicated after 1965, when they signed to Columbia Records, while Capitol Records continued to issue their earlier recordings (previously issued on the World Artists label), so that they were forced to compete with themselves.

They recorded the musically ambitious *Of Cabbages and Kings* (September 1967) in the wake of the Beatles' *Sgt. Pepper's Lonely Hearts Club Band*. They broke up after the commercial failure of its equally ambitious follow-up, *The Ark* (September 1968). Jeremy Clyde established himself as a British stage actor. The duo reunited for a new album in 1983. —*William Ruhlmann*

Painted Dayglow Smile / Jul. 14, 1992 / Columbia/Legacy ✦✦✦✦
Chad & Jeremy signed to Columbia Records in March 1965, after spending a year on composer John Barry's Ember Records. During their three and a half years on Columbia, the duo made five albums and a couple of stray singles, as their music became increasingly ambitious and their sales declined to practically nothing. Hence, this compilation contains their last few Top 40 hits, "Before and After," "I Don't Wanna Lose You Baby," and "Distant Shores," plus a selection of album tracks, flop singles, and rarities. The album is part of Sony's "Rock Artifacts" series, and that's a fitting subtitle. These are certainly interesting curiosities; just don't mistake this for a Chad & Jeremy greatest hits album. —*William Ruhlmann*

Yesterdays Gone [Greatest Hits] / 1994 / Drive Archive ✦✦✦
This discount-priced compilation contains 14 of the 29 tracks Chad & Jeremy recorded for Ember Records (UK)/World Artists Records (US) in 1964-1965. All seven of the duo's World Artists singles are included, among them the hits "A Summer Song," "Willow, Weep for Me," "Yesterday's Gone," and "If I Loved You." An attempt to clean up the sound has been made, and there are brief, informative liner notes by Mark Humphrey. Thus, at a reduced price, this is a reasonable bare-bones presentation of Chad & Jeremy's best-known early hits. —*William Ruhlmann*

● **Best Of** / Feb. 27, 1996 / One Way ✦✦✦✦
Twenty songs from the 1964-65 World Artists era, including the hits "Yesterday's Gone," "A Summer Song," "Willow, Weep for Me," and "If I Loved You." It doesn't have any of their Columbia material, but it's the most thorough overview on CD of their early career. At its best, the folk-pop is reminiscent of a softer Peter & Gordon. However, rock-oriented listeners will find the easy listening-oriented covers, like "The Girl from Ipanema" and "September in the Rain," hard to swallow. The total absence of original dates, songwriting credits, and historical liner notes is inexcusable. —*Richie Unterberger*

The Chairmen of the Board

f. 1969, Detroit, MI, **db.** 1976
Soul
Best-known for the stuttering No. 3 single "Give Me Just a Little More Time," the Chairmen of the Board was one of the smoothest and most popular soul acts to emerge from Detroit in the early '70s. Although their time at the top of the R&B charts was brief—their first Top Ten arrived in 1970, their last in 1973—they recorded a handful of '70s soul classics, all distinguished by the high, trembling vocals of General Norman Johnson, who also wrote the bulk of the group's material.

Born and raised in Norfolk, VA, Johnson began singing in the church choir when he was a child, eventually forming his first vocal group, the Humdingers, when he was 12. During high school, he formed the Showmen, and in his senior year, the group recorded the rock 'n' roll tribute, "It Will Stand." The single scraped the pop and R&B charts in 1961, and Johnson stayed with the Showmen for the next seven years, releasing a series of singles on Minit and Swan Records that became regional hits. By the end of the group's career, they had become staples on the Beach Music circuit on the East Coast. Johnson decided to leave the group for a solo career in 1968, eventually working his way to Detroit, where he signed with former Motown producers and songwriters Holland-Dozier-Holland's fledgling Invictus record label. Johnson formed a group with former Showman Danny Woods; ex-Stone Soul Children Harrison Kennedy; and Eddie Curtis, who had sung with Lee Andrews & the Hearts and Huey Smith & the Clowns. Originally, the group was called the Gentlemen, but they quickly changed their name to the Chairmen of the Board.

The Chairmen of the Board's first single, "Give Me Just a Little More Time," was an instant hit, reaching No. 3 on the pop charts and No. 8 R&B in early 1970, putting Invictus on the map. Two other singles, "(You've Got Me) Dangling on a String" and "Everything's Tuesday," followed, establishing them as R&B chart contenders, but they failed to climb past 38 on the pop charts. Although the subsequent "Pay to the Piper" reached No. 13 on pop, it was their last Top 40 hit. Between 1971 and 1974, the Chairmen of the Board received more support from the R&B audience, with songs like "Chairman of the Board" (1971) and "Finder's Keepers" (1973) reaching the Top Ten. Despite this constant stream of singles, the band stopped recording in 1971, which led to a temporary breakup. The following year they re-formed and toured throughout the Southeast Beach Music circuit, where their singles were continually regional hits. Although the Chairmen were having trouble reaching the charts, Johnson's songs became hits for the likes of Clarence Carter ("Patches"), Freda Payne ("Bring the Boys Home"), and Honey Cone, who had no less than three hits—"Want Ads," "Stick Up," "One Monkey Don't Stop No Show"—with his compositions.

The Chairmen of the Board continued touring and releasing albums until 1976, when they disbanded, with each memeber releasing solo albums. Johnson and Woods continued performing under the Chairmen name for a short time before Johnson moved to Arista in the late '70s. He had a handful of hits for the label, all of which demonstrated contemporary disco influences, before reuniting with Woods as the Chairmen in the early '80s. Over the next two decades the duo regularly toured the Southeast to much success. —*Stephen Thomas Erlewine*

● **Greatest Hits** / Jan. 9, 1992 / Fantasy ✦✦✦✦
When hit songwriters/producers Holland/Dozier/Holland left Motown Records and founded Hot Wax/Invictus, there was plenty of cause for optimism. And, to be sure, the labels had their share of Motown-ish "uptown soul" hits, courtesy of the Honey Cone, 100 Proof (Aged in Soul), Freda Payne, and Laura Lee. Another of the company's strong points was the Chairmen of the Board, a vocal harmony group that, like the Four Tops at Motown, could be gritty and sweet at the same time. Leader/singer General Norman Johnson, in fact, had a Levi Stubbs-like quality. Though not quite on a par with HDH's work with the Tops, enjoyably Detroit-sounding hits like "Dangling on a String," "Give Me Just a Little More Time," and "Pay to the Piper" showed that the team's knack for finding memorable, hook-laden soul/pop hadn't gone away. The group gets away from its Four Tops-influenced approach on the arresting "Try My Love On for Size" and the surprisingly bluesy "Chairman of the Board," a moderate hit. Unfortunately, the Chairmen's success—like that of Hot Wax/Invictus—was short-lived. —*Alex Henderson*

The Challengers

f. 1963, Los Angeles, CA
Surf

One of the most popular of the early Southern Californian surf bands, the Challengers were formed by drummer Richard Belvy after he left the Belairs, who had recorded one of the very first surf singles, "Mr. Moto." The Challengers' debut LP, *Surfbeat* (early 1963), was one of the very first all-instrumental surf albums and sold 200,000 copies, an astronomical number for a regional act. Recording several albums over the next couple of years, most of their repertoire consisted of covers of popular rock and surf tunes. They were exciting at the time, but their lack of originality can make their work seem generic several decades later. The moody "K-39," also available on surf compilations, is their best and most famous cut. —*Richie Unterberger*

Surfbeat / 1963 / Sundazed ✦✦✦✦
Certainly their most popular and influential LP, devoted mostly to competent and elegantly executed covers of early rock and surf standards, with a couple original tunes. Like all of the Challengers' Sundazed reissues, it adds a few bonus cuts. —*Richie Unterberger*

Surfing with the Challengers / 1963 / Sundazed ✦✦✦
Their second album stuck to the same formula as the first, with a bit more routine results, though "Tidal Wave" is a standout. —*Richie Unterberger*

● **K-39** / 1964 / Sundazed ✦✦✦✦
Their first four LPs are quite similar overall, but if you have to choose one, the nod would go to the last of the quartet. Featuring the title track (their most famous performance), it also has hot versions of "Telstar" and "Mark of Zorro," and three bonus cuts of their competent forays into vocal hot rod music. —*Richie Unterberger*

Challengers on the Move / 196? / Sundazed ✦✦✦
Perhaps the most pop-oriented and calmest of the early Challengers LPs (though not by much) in terms of material selection. Collectors will be interested in one of the four CD bonus cuts, "Lead Foot," an early version of "K-39." —*Richie Unterberger*

Tidal Wave! / Sep. 29, 1995 / Sundazed ✦✦✦
It's rare that a minor band such as the Challengers rates a package of the sort of alternate takes and rarities that you'll find on a Rolling Stones bootleg. That's what this 18-track compilation is, though. Half are alternate takes, five songs were previously unissued in any form, and three come from their rare 1965 LP *Surf's Up*. This doesn't offer any radical redefinition of the Challengers' oeuvre, but it certainly doesn't suffer in comparison with their official vintage albums. In fact, you're about as well off with this compilation as with any of their proper full-length recordings, and some tracks do burn, such as "Satan's Theme" and "Moovin' & Groovin." Sound quality is excellent. —*Richie Unterberger*

The Chameleons

f. 1981, Middleton, Manchester, England, db. 1986
Alternative Pop-Rock

The atmospheric pop band the Chameleons formed in Manchester, England, in 1981 from the ashes of a number of local groups: vocalist/bassist Mark Burgess began with the Cliches, guitarists Reg Smithies and Dave Fielding arrived from the Years, and drummer John Lever (who quickly replaced founding member Brian Schofield) originated with the Politicians. After establishing themselves with a series of high-profile BBC sessions, the Chameleons signed to Epic and debuted with the EP *Nostalgia*, a tense, moody set produced by Steve Lillywhite that featured the single "In Shreds."

When sales did not live up to expectations, the quartet was released from their contract. After signing to Statik, they returned in 1983 with their first full-length effort, *Script of the Bridge*. *What Does Anything Mean? Basically* followed in 1985, and with it came a new reliance on stylish production. After its release, the Chameleons signed to Geffen and emerged two years later with *Strange Times*. The dark, complex record proved to be the group's finale, however. They split after the sudden death of manager Tony Fletcher. Burgess and Lever continued in the Sun and the Moon; Smithies and Fielding later reunited in the Reegs. —*Jason Ankeny*

Script of the Bridge / 1983 / Statik ✦✦✦✦
A neglected classic of the early '80s, the Chameleons' first LP recalls the brooding grandeur of the Church and the Psychedelic Furs, but with a sound based more on conventional rock than the prevalent punk sounds of the '80s. Alternating moody paranoia with majestic drive, vocalist Mark Burgess shines on "Monkeyland," and comes up with a grooving bass line on "As High as You Can Go." Guitarist Reg Smithies frames the songs with intricate texture, especially on the album's best songs, "Up the Down Escalator" and "Thursday's Child." —*John Bush*

What Does Anything Mean? Basically / 1985 / Statik ✦✦✦
Owing a greater debt to keyboards and strings, the Chameleons' second album proved much more atmospheric than the debut. Pushed to the background, however, are Burgess' songwriting and the guitar lines of Smithies, two commodities which had made the Chameleons sparkle. In fact, "Looking Inwardly" and "Singing Rule Britannia" (on which Burgess reprises a few lines from the Beatles' "She Said She Said") are the only tracks where the two best elements in the Chameleons' sound are finally given full effect, and they prove to be the only highlights. The Statik CD release adds the early 1981 tracks "In Shreds" and "Nostalgia" to the original LP program. —*John Bush*

● **Strange Times** / 1986 / Geffen ✦✦✦✦
At the peak of their powers, the Chameleons combined the strong songwriting and driving guitars of their debut with atmospherics and production techniques gained from *What Does Everything Mean? Basically* to create their best album. Roaring out of the gate with "Mad Jack," *Strange Times* slows down for a tender acoustic ballad ("Tears") but then builds energy on "Soul in Isolation"—highlighted by the cascading drum workout of John Lever—and "Swamp Thing." The rest of the album alternates mood and energy as well, with atmospheric synth lines that later come crashing down in a hail of guitars. Out of print for several years, *Strange Times* was reissued in 1995 with five additional tracks (originally available in limited copies with the LP), including an airy cover of the Beatles' "Tomorrow Never Knows" and a more straight-ahead reworking of David Bowie's "John, I'm Only Dancing." —*John Bush*

The Fan and the Bellows / 1989 / Caroline ✦✦✦
The Fan and the Bellows collects 11 of the band's early recordings from 1981 to 1983, including the classic title track. —*Chris Woodstra*

Tripping Dogs / 1990 / Glass Pyramid ✦✦✦
Recorded during rehearsals in 1985. —*Steve Aldrich*

Peel Sessions / 1990 / Dutch East India ✦✦✦✦
Lacking an American best-of compilation, *Peel Sessions* serves as the best domestic overview of the band's total career, though the three sessions were recorded before the classic *Strange Times*. Most of the tracks appear on the first two albums in different form, though "The Fan and the Bellows" is a classic never issued on LP. The Chameleons shine on this disc, which is more energetic than their sometimes lethargic studio dates. —*John Bush*

Live Shreds / Cleopatra ✦✦✦
Live Shreds draws from two different shows—the first half from the Hacienda Club in 1983 and the second half from the Gallery Club in 1982. Though the live versions do not differ drastically from the studio recordings, fans of the band will nevertheless find this an essential purchase. —*Chris Woodstra*

Gene Chandler

b. Jul. 6, 1937, Chicago, IL
Vocals / Soul, R&B

Chandler is remembered by the rock 'n' roll audience almost solely for the classic novelty and doo wop-tinged soul ballad "Duke of Earl"; with the unforgettable opening chant of the title leading the way, the song was a No. 1 hit in 1962. He's esteemed by soul fans as one of the leading exponents of the '60s Chicago soul scene, along with Curtis Mayfield and Jerry Butler. Born Eugene Dixon, he was a member of the doo wop group the Dukays, and "Duke of Earl" was actually a Dukays recording; Dixon was renamed Gene Chandler, and the single credited him as a solo singer.

Chandler never again approached the massive pop success of that chart-topper (although he occasionally entered the Top 20), but he was a big star with the R&B audience in the mid-'60s with straightforward mid-tempo and ballad soul numbers, many of which were written by Curtis Mayfield and produced by Carl Davis. Chandler's success became more fitful after Mayfield stopped penning material for him, although he enjoyed some late '60s hits, and had a monster pop and soul smash in 1970 with "Groovy Situation." His last successes were the disco and dance-influenced R&B hits "Get Down" (1978) and "Does She Have a Friend?" (1980). —*Richie Unterberger*

The Duke of Earl / 1993 / Vee-Jay ✦✦✦✦
Gene Chandler exploded on the '60s soul scene with "Duke of Earl," a brilliant piece of novelty/love song material. His hit singles could be formulaic, but Chandler's expressive, haunting voice never failed to lift a trite lyric or punctuate a great one. This 23-cut set contains many songs previously available only as singles, and mixes the requisite hits with nicely done obscurities like "London Town," "Day to Day," and "Baby, That's Love." This isn't the complete Gene Chandler output, but it's certainly got most of his prime early numbers and lots of smashes. —*Ron Wynn*

● **Nothing Can Stop Me: Gene Chandler's Greatest Hits** / Aug. 30, 1994 / Varese Sarabande ✦✦✦✦
This 20-track CD is the only collection that has all of his most popular recordings, from "Duke of Earl" through his soul hits for Constellation, Vee Jay, Checker, Mercury, and Chi-Sound, spanning 1962 to 1980.(All but three tracks were released before 1968.) Some fans might prefer *The Duke of Earl*, which focuses on his Vee Jay years, but this has a much wider breadth and includes "Groovy Situation." Curtis Mayfield wrote eight of the songs, although they don't fully measure up to the Chicago soul he was writing for his own group, the Impressions, at the time. —*Richie Unterberger*

Bruce Channel

b. Nov. 28, 1940, Jacksonville, TX
Vocals / Rock 'n' Roll
Bruce Channel's "Hey Baby"—a classic one-shot, No. 1 hit from 1962—is one of the many records proving that, during a period in which rock has sometimes been characterized as near death, the form was continuing to evolve in unexpected and delightful ways. An irresistible mid-tempo shuffle from the first few bars of homespun harmonica (played by Delbert McClinton), it was a seemingly effortless blend of rock, blues, country, and Cajun beats, featuring Channel's lazy, drawling vocals and an instantly catchy tune. It was perhaps too much of a natural—Channel could never recapture the organic spontaneity of the track, failing to re-enter the Top 40 despite many attempts.
The Texan had written "Hey Baby" around 1959 with his friend Margaret Cobb, and had already been performing the tune for a couple of years before recording it amidst a series of demos for Fort Worth producer Major Bill Smith. First released locally on Smith's label, it was picked up for national distribution by Smash. Channel would continue to write most of his own material (sometimes in collaboration with Cobb) for a series of moderately enjoyable follow-ups that echoed the riffs of "Hey Baby" too closely.
McClinton played his immediately identifiable harmonica on several of these and made his own contribution to rock history in 1962, when he was touring as a member of Channel's band in Britain. On one of their shows, they were supported by a then-unknown Liverpool group, the Beatles, who had yet to cut their first record. John Lennon was smitten by McClinton's style of playing and picked up some pointers that he put to use on the Beatles' very first single, "Love Me Do"; in fact, McClinton's influence can be easily detected in Lennon's harmonica playing on many early Beatles tracks from 1962 and 1963.
Channel did get another Top 20 hit in Britain in 1968, "Keep On," which was written by Wayne Carson Thompson (famous for penning the Box Tops' "The Letter"). Nothing else clicked in a big way on either side of the ocean, and by the late '70s he was working in Nashville as a songwriter. —*Richie Unterberger*

● **Hey Baby!** / 1990 / Teenager ✦✦✦✦
Nineteen of his vintage sides, many mining the same Cajun-Tex-Mex-shuffle groove as "Hey Baby," sometimes simply rewriting the song sideways by inserting or mildly modifying its key riffs. It's still highly enjoyable stuff, just too derivative of his one great hit to qualify him as a true original. McClinton plays harmonica on several of the tracks, and also wrote one of them, "My Baby." The LP includes the 1968 British hit "Keep On." The sound and liner notes aren't that great; this interesting early exponent of Southern swamp rock deserves a more carefully packaged retrospective on CD. —*Richie Unterberger*

The Chantays

f. 1962, Santa Ana, CA
Surf
In 1963 this teenage group from Santa Ana, CA, had one of the biggest and best instrumental surf hits, "Pipeline." Competent players who went heavy on the rumbling bass, ghostly reverb, and electric keyboards, they were very much a one-shot act; their repertoire was crowded with rock 'n' roll covers and "Pipeline" soundalikes, and none of their follow-up singles charted. —*Richie Unterberger*

● **Pipeline** / 1963 / Varese Sarabande ✦✦✦✦
A CD reissue of their 1963 debut album, with the addition of "Pipeline"'s B-side and both sides of the non-LP flop follow-up single. Mostly it's lesser variations of the "Pipeline" formula, including one instrumental penned by Tony Asher, Brian Wilson's writing partner for much of the *Pet Sounds* album. It doesn't include the single "Beyond," which can be found on the surf volume of Rhino/*Guitar Player*'s *Legends of Guitar* series. —*Richie Unterberger*

The Chantels

f. 1956, Bronx, NY, **db.** 1970
R&B, Doo Wop, Girl-Group
One of the very first girl groups, the Chantels are best known for their

1957 hit "Maybe." Between 1957 and 1963, the trio racked up a number of hit singles, but none of them was ever as popular as "Maybe," which came to be regarded as one of the definitive singles of the genre.
All five members of the Chantels—Arlene Smith, Lois Harris, Sonia Goring, Jackie Landry, and Rene Minus—met as children, when they sang in the choir of Saint Anthony of Padua, a Bronx-area school. Arlene Smith was the leader of the quintet. Smith wrote all of the group's early material, and she was the one who convinced the other girls—whose ages ranged between 14 and 17 at the time—to audition for Richard Barrett, a record producer and a member of the doo wop group the Valentines. Barrett signed the band to End Records and produced the Chantels' first single, a Smith song called "He's Gone." Released in the summer of 1957, the single peaked at No. 71. However, the group's second single—another Smith composition called "Maybe"—was a smash hit, peaking at No. 2 on the R&B charts and No. 15 on the pop charts in early 1958. "Maybe" sold more copies than its chart position suggests; the single was pirated by several other small record labels, and those sales were not tallied for the final chart position.
For the next year the Chantels tried in vain to deliver a follow-up as successful as "Maybe." Two hit singles—"Every Night (I Pray)" and "I Love You So"—followed on End Records, but the label dropped them after a handful of other records failed to make an impact. Around that time, Smith left the group to pursue a solo career, and Harris had left the group. The Chantels didn't replace either singer and continued as a trio.
In the summer of 1959 the group supported Richard Barrett on his single "Summer's Love," which peaked at No. 29 on the R&B charts. In 1961 the Chantels signed with Carlton Records, where they had two minor pop hits: "Look in My Eyes" and "Well, I Told You." Carlton dropped the group the next year, and the group moved to Ludix, where they had a minor hit with "Eternally" in the spring of 1963.
The Chantels continued performing until the end of the decade; they officially disbanded in 1970. A few years later Arlene Smith re-formed the Chantels, recruiting four new members; the other original members all retired from the entertainment business. Smith continued to lead various incarnations of the Chantels into the '90s. When she wasn't touring the oldies circuit with the Chantels, Smith worked as a schoolteacher. —*Stephen Thomas Erlewine*

● **The Best of the Chantels** / May 1990 / Rhino ✦✦✦✦
One of the leading girl groups of the late '50s, they were distinguished by Arlene Smith's impassioned leads. —*Bill Dahl*

Harry Chapin

b. Dec. 7, 1942, Greenwich Village, NY, **d.** Jul. 16, 1981, Jericho, NY
Guitar, Vocals / Singer-Songwriter, Contemporary Folk
Harry Chapin's career as a popular singer-songwriter was cut short by an auto accident in 1981, but he left behind a series of recordings that his fans continue to treasure more than a decade after his death. Chapin was never a critically acclaimed singer-songwriter. Critics accused him of over-sentimentalizing his subjects and attaching heavy-handed morals to his socially aware story-songs; the heavily orchestrated arrangements that accompanied many of his songs didn't help his case with the critics, either. Nevertheless, Chapin earned a devoted audience during the '70s, through his music and his charity work as a social activist.
Chapin began performing while he was in high school, singing in the Brooklyn Heights Boys' Choir and forming a band with his brothers Tom and Stephen. During college he decided to pursue a career as a documentary filmmaker; in 1968 he directed the Oscar-nominated *Legendary Champions*. In 1971 he switched careers, concentrating on music. Chapin recruited a backing band through an ad in the *Village Voice;* the respondents included bassist John Wallace, guitarist Ron Palmer, and cellist Tim Scott. The group began performing in various clubs around New York, and the singer/sognwriter was soon signed to Elektra records.
Heads and Tails, Chapin's first album, was released in the summer of 1972 and became a success thanks to the hit single "Taxi," which soon became the songwriter's signature tune. Later that year he released his second album, *Sniper and Other Love Songs*, which didn't fare quite as well as his debut. *Short Stories*, Chapin's third album, appeared in the spring of 1973; it spent 23 weeks on the chart due to the success of the single "W.O.L.D.," a story about the life of a disc jockey. After recording his fourth album, *Verities and Balderdash*, Chapin disbanded his backing band and began work on his musical *The Night That Made America Famous*; both Wallace and Masters worked on the show, along with guitarist Doug Walker, drummer Howie Fields, and Chapin's brothers Tom, Steve, and Jim. While he was working on the musical, *Verities and Balderdash* became his biggest hit, peaking at No. 4 on the US charts and becoming a gold record. The album's success was benefited by the No. 1 single "Cat's in the Cradle," a song about an inconsiderate, career-oriented father that was based on a poem written by Chapin's wife.
The Night That Made America Famous opened February 26, 1975. It closed April 6, after 75 performances; the show would earn two Tony

nominations. Chapin won an Emmy that spring for his contributions to ABC television's children's series "Make a Wish," which was hosted by his brother Tom. That spring the singer-songwriter co-founded World Hunger Year, a charity designed to raise money to fight international famine; the organization earned over $350,000 in its first year. In the fall of 1975 Chapin delivered *Portrait Gallery*, his follow-up to *Verities and Balderdash*. While the album performed respectably, peaking at No. 53, it failed to recapture the mass audience of his previous album.

Greatest Stories—Live, a double album released in the spring of 1976, became the singer-songwriter's second gold album, peaking at No. 48. Chapin was becoming more politically active throughout 1976, as evidenced by his role as a delegate at that summer's Democratic Convention. Late in 1976 he released *On the Road to Kingdom Come*, which spent six weeks on the charts. The 1977 double album *Dance Band on the Titanic* was on the charts for a few more weeks, but it didn't spawn a hit single. The next year Chapin met with President Jimmy Carter, discussing the need for a Presidential Commission on Hunger; he also released *Living Room Suite* that summer, which peaked at No. 133.

Chapin released a second live album, *Legends of the Lost and Found—New Greatest Stories Live*, in the fall of 1979; it was his least successful album, spending only three weeks on the charts. In 1980 he signed with Boardwalk records, releasing *Sequel* that fall; the title track of the album was a sequel to his first hit single, "Taxi," and became his last Top 40 hit.

On July 16, 1981, Chapin was driving to a business meeting when his car was rear-ended by a tractor-trailer on the Long Island Expressway near Jericho, NY. The accident caused his gas tank to explode, killing the singer-songwriter. A memorial fund was established in his name, with Elektra Records providing the initial donation of $10,000. Over the years, the fund has raised an estimated $5 million for a variety of social causes that were close to Chapin's heart. —*Stephen Thomas Erlewine*

Heads & Tales / Mar. 1972 / Elektra ✦✦✦✦
Chapin's breakthrough album included "Taxi." —*Dan Heilman*

Verities & Balderdash / 1974 / Elektra ✦✦✦✦

● **Anthology of Harry Chapin** / 1985 / Elektra ✦✦✦✦
Anthology of Harry Chapin is a fine 11-track collection that contains the cream of the inconsistent singer-songwriter's career, including "Taxi," "Sunday Morning Sunshine," "She Is Always Seventeen," "WOLD," "I Wanna Learn a Love Song," "Better Place to Be," and "Cat's in the Cradle." —*Stephen Thomas Erlewine*

Tracy Chapman

b. Mar. 20, 1964, Cleveland, OH
Guitar, Vocals / Singer-Songwriter, Adult Alternative Pop-Rock
Tracy Chapman helped restore singer-songwriters to the spotlight in the '80s. The multi-platinum success of Chapman's eponymous 1988 debut was unexpected, and it had lasting impact. Although Chapman was working from the same confessional singer-songwriter foundation that had been popularized in the '70s, her songs were fresh and powerful, driven by simple melodies and affecting lyrics. At the time of her first album, only a handful of artists were performing such a style successfully, and her success ushered in a new era of singer-songwriters that lasted well into the '90s. Furthermore, her album helped usher in the era of political correctness—along with 10,000 Maniacs and R.E.M., Chapman's liberal politics proved enormously influential on American college campuses in the late '80s. Of course, that meant that Chapman's subsequent recordings got mixed reactions; but after several years out of the spotlight, she managed to make a very successful comeback in 1996 with her fourth album, *New Beginning*, thanks to the Top Ten single "Give Me One Reason."

Raised in a working class neighborhood in Cleveland, Tracy Chapman learned how to play guitar as a child and began to write her own songs shortly afterward. After high school, she won a minority placement scholarship and decided to attend Tufts University, where she studied anthropology and African studies. While at Tufts she became fascinated with folk-rock and singer-songwriters, and began performing her own songs at coffeehouses. Eventually she recorded a set of demos at the college radio station. One of her fellow students, Brian Koppelman, heard Chapman play and recommended her to his father, Charles Koppelman, who ran SBK Publishing. In 1986 she signed with SBK, and Koppelman secured a management contract with Elliot Roberts, who had worked with Neil Young and Joni Mitchell. Roberts and Koppelman helped Chapman sign to Elektra in 1987.

Chapman recorded her debut album with David Kershenbaum, and it was released in the spring of 1988. *Tracy Chapman* was greeted with enthusiastic reviews, and she set out on the road supporting 10,000 Maniacs. Within a few months she played at the internationally televised concert for Nelson Mandela's 70th birthday party, where her performance was greeted with thunderous applause. Soon, the single "Fast Car" began climbing the charts, eventually peaking at No.6. The album's sales soared with the single, and by the end of the year the record had

gone multi-platinum. Early the next year the record won four Grammys, including Best New Artist.

It was an auspicious beginning to Chapman's career, and it was perhaps inevitable that her second album, 1989's darker, more political *Crossroads*, wasn't as successful. Although it was well-reviewed, the album peaked at No. 9 and quickly fell down the charts. After *Crossroads*, Chapman spent a few years in seclusion, returning in 1992 with *Matters of the Heart*. The album was greeted with mixed reviews and weak sales. Three years later she returned with *New Beginnings*, which received stronger reviews than its predecessor. The bluesy "Give Me One Reason" was pulled as the first single, and it slowly became a hit, sending the album into the US Top Ten in early 1996. It was a quiet, successful comeback from an artist most observers had already consigned to cult status. —*Stephen Thomas Erlewine*

★ **Tracy Chapman** / 1988 / Elektra ✦✦✦✦✦
With her choked voice and acoustic guitar, Tracy Chapman reawakened social awareness and demonstrated the power of folk music on her debut album, singing of homelessness and desperation and "Talkin' 'bout a Revolution." Contains the Top Ten hit "Fast Car." —*William Ruhlmann*

Crossroads / Sep. 1989 / Elektra ✦✦✦
Tracy Chapman's self-titled debut album of 1988 was an incredibly tough act to follow, but the folk-rocker delivered an inspired sophomore effort with *Crossroads*. While it falls short of the excellence of her stunning debut, *Crossroads* is a heartfelt, honest offering that's well worth obtaining. Dedicated to South African freedom fighter Nelson Mandela, the anthemic "Freedom Now" is one of Chapman's best protest songs. Equally compelling is "Subcity," a lament for the poor, disenfranchised underclass that stands on the outside of the American Dream, looking in. Much of the time, however, Chapman isn't going for immediacy; introspective and subtle songs like "Bridges," "Be Careful of My Heart," and "All That You Have Is Your Soul" require at least several listenings in order to be fully appreciated. —*Alex Henderson*

Matters of the Heart / Apr. 28, 1992 / Elektra ✦✦
Less bold and angry than her previous work, *Matters of the Heart* covers an acoustic course that touches equally on personal vignettes and social commentary. With her fluid, rapid-fire delivery, Chapman takes aim at society and lands several direct hits, devoid of self-righteousness: songs about the downtrodden ("Bang Bang Bang"), feminism ("Woman's Work"), and freedom ("I Used to Be a Sailor"). The album's centerpiece is "If These Are the Things," a subtle, passionate masterpiece about coming to grips with innocence lost. A couple of songs suffer from too much sweetening in the studio, diluting the impact of Chapman's potent lyrics. The extraneous bells and whistles dressing up "Dreaming on a World" provide the most obvious example of a trend Chapman would do well to avoid in the future. —*Roch Parisien*

New Beginning / Nov. 14, 1995 / Elektra ✦✦✦
One might assume that the difference between Tracy Chapman's third album, which spent less than three months in the charts and failed to go gold after her first two albums had sold in the millions, and her fourth, which restored her to substantial commercial success, was the album's hit single, "Give Me One Reason." In fact, after a disappointing start, *New Beginning* turned around and started selling a few months after its release and before the single took off. It went gold the week that "Give Me One Reason" hit the charts. Of course, having a hit single helps, too, but since "Give Me One Reason" is a nearly generic blues song that isn't particularly characteristic of Chapman or of the album, it may have brought in an audience that didn't get what it expected. Though she has added a backup band, Chapman continues to take a simple musical approach that focuses attention on her voice and to sing lyrics that alternate between intimate emotional portraits and broad political generalizations that seem more felt than deeply thought out. Three songs here—"Heaven's Here on Earth," "The Rape of the World," and the title cut—are about the state of the whole world, which is viewed in either excessively sunny or gloomy terms. As such, Chapman's relationship songs, though they too can be a little vague, register more powerfully because they are so personal. As the title suggests, Chapman is adopting a more open and hopeful posture in both her feelings and her politics on *New Beginning*, and while the surprise success of "Give Me One Reason" is heartening from a career perspective, that's the real news here. —*William Ruhlmann*

The Charlatans

f. 1966, San Francisco, CA, **db.** 1970
Psychedelic, Folk-Rock
No relation to the British alternative rock band the Charlatans, this San Francisco group has been widely credited as starting the Haight/Ashbury psychedelic scene. In retrospect, their contribution was more of a social one, planting seeds of a rock counterculture with their unconventional, at times outrageous, dress and attitudes. While they occasionally delved into guitar distortion and fractured, stoned songwriting, the

Charlatans' music was rooted in good-time jug-band blues, not psychedelic freakouts. That's not to say their records didn't have a low-key, easygoing charm, although they didn't match the innovations of the Jefferson Airplane and other peers. They cut demos for a couple of labels in 1966, but most of the material they recorded at this time was unissued, and the commercial explosion of San Francisco rock passed them by. The band eventually did release a nationally distributed album in the late '60s, by which time personnel changes had diluted some of the crazy energy of the original lineup, but the LP has its engaging moments. —*Richie Unterberger*

The Charlatans / 1969 / Groucho ♦♦♦
The word is that this album failed to capture the group's essence, but it has its share of good stuff. Their good-timey sound is balanced by an engaging sincerity and folky, melodic compositions reminiscent of very early Jefferson Airplane, although there are a couple of ho-hum jug-band tunes. But the production and performances are too complacent and tame, lacking the spaced-out recklessness of the San Francisco scene that groups like the Airplane captured so well on record. —*Richie Unterberger*

Alabama Bound / 198? / Eva ♦♦♦♦
Mid-1966 demos, recorded by Lovin' Spoonful producer Erik Jacobsen. Featuring blues, good-time music, and tentative psychedelia, it doesn't sound as crazy as one might have thought, but it remains the only glimpse into the band at their most original during their early days. Also includes a live, ten-minute 1969 recording of the title track. —*Richie Unterberger*

● **First Album/Alabama Bound** / Feb. 1996 / ROIR ♦♦♦♦
Eva Records' 24-song CD reissue of its two former LPs has far better sound than either of the vinyl discs. The material is enhanced, and the best of it (like the live "Alabama Bound") is indispensable. The notes are still rather sketchy, but this is a worthwhile acquisition. —*Bruce Eder*

● **The Amazing Charlatans** / Sep. 17, 1996 / Big Beat ♦♦♦♦
After almost 30 years, there's finally a definitive document of one of the first San Francisco psychedelic groups—or at least as definitive a document as surviving tapes allow. This compilation assembles 23 tracks from their demos for the Kama Sutra and Autumn labels, as well as a couple of later sessions recorded at San Francisco area studios. Much of this material has been bootlegged on both vinyl and tape, but here it appears in by far its best fidelity to date. Those expecting psychedelic fireworks will be surprised. There's some acid-soaked folk-rock here (most notably "We're Not on the Same Trip" and "I Saw Her," the two best cuts), but on the whole it's much more of a travelog of roots music, with white blues, jugband, folk, country, and music hall influences much more to the fore. Sure the Charlatans never really got the opportunity to flex their muscles in the studio, but it's also true that they didn't possess either the songwriting or instrumental chops to rival the Jefferson Airplane or Moby Grape. If you gear your expectations to the appropriate level, there's plenty of good-time mid-to-late-'60s Bay Area rock to savor here. Big Beat's meticulous packaging and programming also ensure that an important chapter in psychedelic/San Francisco music has been properly packaged for the first time. —*Richie Unterberger*

The Ones Who Started It All . . . / Shark ♦♦
Beware of this bootleg-type collection of mid-'60s material; almost all of it shows up, in much better fidelity, on the official *Amazing Charlatans* compilation on Ace, which also has about twice as many tracks. The sleeve doesn't tell you so, but the one song that is not included on the Ace retrospective, "Styrofoam," is not even a Charlatans song, but an early '70s cut by Loose Gravel (which included Charlatans member Mike Wilhelm). —*Richie Unterberger*

Charlatans UK

f. 1989, Manchester, England
Alternative Pop-Rock, Brit-Pop, Neo-Psychedelia
For many years, the Charlatans [UK] were perceived as the also-rans of Madchester, the group that didn't capture the zeitgeist like the Stone Roses or the band that failed to match the mad genre-bending of the Happy Mondays. Of course they were more traditional than either of their peers. Working from a Stonesy foundation, the Charlatans added dance-oriented rhythms and layers of swirling organs straight out of '60s psychedelia. At first the Charlatans had great promise, and their initial singles—including "The Only One I Know"—were hits, but as Madchester and "baggy" faded away, the group began to look like relics. It was commonly assumed that their third album, 1994's *Up to Our Hips*, was the end of the line. However, the Charlatans made a remarkable comeback in 1995 with their eponymous fourth album, which found them embracing not only the flourishing Brit-pop movement, but underground dance and techno, as well as their mainstay classic rock. *The Charlatans* debuted at No. 1, and the group was hailed as survivors. As the band was recording its follow-up album in 1996, organist Rob Collins, who had defined the band's sound, died in a car crash. The Char-

latans decided to continue as a quartet, and their subsequent album, *Tellin' Stories*, debuted at No. 1 upon its 1997 release, suggesting that they had become one of the great British journeyman bands of the '90s.

At the time of their formation in 1989, it appeared that the Charlatans were all about transience. Inspired by the emergence of the Stone Roses, Rob Collins (keyboards), Jon Baker (guitar), Martin Blunt (bass), and Jon Brookes (drums) formed the Charlatans, rehearsing with a variety of vocalists before Tim Burgess joined as their singer. The group attempted to land a record contract with no success, so they formed Dead Dead Good Records and released their debut 12-inch single "Indian Rope" in January 1990. Collins' dynamic, sweeping Hammond organ distinguished the group from their Madchester peers, and the single became a No. 1 hit on the indie charts. By the spring, they had signed with Beggars Banquet, releasing "The Only One I Know" a few months later. Borrowing heavily from the Stones, jangle-pop, and funk, "The Only One I Know" became a monster hit, climbing into the pop Top Ten and becoming the group's signature single. After another hit single, "Then," the band's debut album *Some Friendly* was released in the fall, debuting at No. 1.

It was a remarkable beginning to their career, so perhaps it was inevitable that bad luck hit early in 1991. As they launched their first American tour, the Charlatans were forced to add "UK" to their name, since a San Francisco garage rock band from the '60s already had claims on the name. The group returned to Britain, where they played a concert at the Royal Albert Hall. After the gig, Baker announced he was leaving the group. He was replaced by Mark Collins (no relation). The group was sidetracked further by Blunt's bout with severe depression. By the time the band finally released their second album, *Between 10th & 11th*, Madchester had become passe, and the album was ignored by the public and earned mixed reviews.

Despite their declining popularity, the Charlatans soldiered on. They hit another setback in late 1992, when Rob Collins was arrested as an accessory to armed robbery. The situation had been entirely accidental—Collins had been drinking with an old friend and wound up following him into a liquor store—but he was sentenced to eight months imprisonment. Before he went to jail, he laid down the tracks for the band's third album, which was released in early 1994, after he had left prison. *Up to Our Hips* received stronger reviews than its predecessor, and its single, "Can't Get Out of Bed," was a bigger hit than anything on *Between 10th & 11th*. It was the beginning of a comeback that culminated in the summer of 1995.

Before release of the group's eponymous third album, Tim Burgess sang on the Chemical Brothers' "Life Is Sweet," which re-established his hip indie credentials and gave him, and the Charlatans, credibility in techno circles. Appropriately, *The Charlatans* demonstrated a deeper dance sensibility, as well as more concise tunes, and it unexpectedly entered the British charts at No. 1. After release of the album, the Charlatans re-entered the front rank of British rock bands and were at the peak of their popularity, as well as critical acclaim. The group was still unable to crack the American market—initially, they were barred from touring the country due to Rob Collins' arrest—but they remained popular throughout Europe and Asia.

As the group was recording their follow-up to *The Charlatans*, Rob Collins was killed in a drunk driving accident as he headed to the studio. Although Collins was pivotal to the band's signature sound, they carried on without him, completing their fifth album, *Tellin' Stories*, with the assistance of Primal Scream's keyboardist, Martin Duffy. *Tellin' Stories* was released in the UK in the spring of 1997 to generally strong reviews and entered the charts at No. 1. —*Stephen Thomas Erlewine*

Some Friendly / 1990 / Beggars Banquet ♦♦♦
The Charlatans' debut album, *Some Friendly*, may lack a consistently compelling set of songs, but the group's trancey blend of swirling organs, Stonesy guitars, and Madchester rhythms makes it an impressive first effort, especially since "The Only One I Know" has the resonance of a classic single. —*Stephen Thomas Erlewine*

Between 10th & 11th / Apr. 14, 1992 / Beggars Banquet ♦♦♦
The Charlatans' sophomore effort is surprisingly more successful than the group's debut. While lacking the knockout punch of anything as strong as "The Only One I Know," this set steers clear of the underdeveloped material that marred much of the previous album, without deviating from the basic formula. It's proof positive that the Charlatans can succeed without the hype that surrounded their arrival. —*Steve Aldrich*

Up to Our Hips / Mar. 22, 1994 / Beggars Banquet ♦♦♦
As the Manchester craze fades further into the past, the Charlatans continue to streamline their vaguely psychedelic pop approach. On *Up to Our Hips*, the band refashions '60s British Invasion pop for the 1990s, removing most of the dance tendencies lying beneath the surface of their previous albums. As "Can't Get out of Bed" shows, their songwriting skills have continued to improve, ranking the album alongside their earlier, more popular releases. —*Stephen Thomas Erlewine*

● **Charlatans [UK]** / Sep. 12, 1995 / Beggars Banquet ✦✦✦✦
The Charlatans demonstrated signs of a revival on *Up to Our Hips*, but
that record in no way suggested the full-fledged return to form of *The
Charlatans [UK]*, the group's most ambitious, focused, and successful
album. The group hasn't changed its sonic approach, but their music has
deepened, incorporating heavy dance elements without losing their core
sound. Occasionally the album relies too heavily on trippy dance instrumentals, but those are funkier and wilder than ever before, and they fit
neatly next to the group's Stonesy pop, which is consistently catchy this
time around. *The Charlatans [UK]* illustrates how a working rock 'n' roll
band can balance traditional rock and modern, post-acid house music.
The results are frequently glorious. —*Stephen Thomas Erlewine*

Tellin' Stories / Apr. 21, 1997 / Beggars Banquet ✦✦✦✦
The Charlatans made a surprising comeback in 1995, turning in an
eponymous album that earned them their best reviews and sales. *Tellin'
Stories*, the follow-up to *The Charlatans*, should have been triumphant,
but tragedy struck midway through its recording, when keyboardist Rob
Collins was killed in a car accident. Collins was an integral part of the
band's lineup, creating a distinctive, swirling, neo-psychedelic sound,
and it seemed unlikely that the band could carry on without him, much
less record a record as earthy and warm as *Tellin' Stories*. Primal
Scream's Martin Duffy volunteered to help the band complete the
album, which was basically written before Collins' death; that might
explain why there are no overt references to his absence anywhere on
the album. Instead, *Tellin' Stories* is another collection of classicist rock
'n' roll spiked with dance beats, much like any other Charlatans album.
Where its predecessor was more informed by mechanicized beats, the
rhythms are more organic, which perfectly suits the rolling "North
Country Boy," the sweeping "One to Another," and the heart-tugging
"How Can You Leave Us?" And, like any other Charlatans album, it
doesn't quite hold together, falling apart with instrumentals and ill-conceived songs toward the end. On the whole, however, *Tellin' Stories* is
more consistent than their earlier records, and the best songs showcase
the band at their strongest, which is quite an achievement, considering
the traumas the Charlatans underwent during its recording. More than
anything, that's a fitting salute to Rob Collins. —*Stephen Thomas
Erlewine*

Ray Charles (Ray Charles Robinson)

b. Sep. 23, 1930, Albany, GA
*Piano, Vocals / Soul, R&B, Blues, Piano Blues, Urban Blues, Pop, Soul
Jazz, Jazz Blues, Country-Soul*
Ray Charles was the musician most responsible for developing soul
music. Singers like Sam Cooke and Jackie Wilson also did a great deal
to pioneer the form, but Charles did even more to devise a new form of
Black pop by merging '50s R&B with gospel-powered vocals, adding
plenty of flavor from contemporary jazz, blues, and (in the '60s) country.
Then there is his singing—his style is among the most emotional and
easily identifiable of any 20th-century performer, up there with the likes
of Elvis and Billie Holiday. He's also a superb keyboard player, arranger,
and bandleader. The brilliance of his 1950s and 1960s work, however,
can't obscure the fact that he's made few dead vocal tracks since the mid-
'60s, though he's recorded often and tours to this day.
    Blind since the age of six (from glaucoma), Charles studied composi-
tion and learned many instruments at the St. Augustine School for the
Deaf and the Blind. His parents had died by his early teens, and he
worked as a musician in Florida for a while before using his savings to
move to Seattle in 1947. By the late '40s, he was recording in a smooth
pop/R&B style derivative of Nat "King" Cole and Charles Brown. He got
his first Top Ten R&B hit with "Baby, Let Me Hold Your Hand" in 1951.
Charles' first recordings have come in for their fair share of criticism, as
they are much milder and less original than the classics that would follow, although they're actually fairly enjoyable, showing strong hints of
the skills that were to flower in a few years.
    In the early '50s Charles' sound started to toughen as he toured with
Lowell Fulson, went to New Orleans to work with Guitar Slim (playing
piano on and arranging Slim's huge R&B hit, "The Things That I Used to
Do"), and got a band together for R&B star Ruth Brown. It was at Atlantic Records that Ray truly found his voice, consolidating the gains of
recent years and then some with "I Got a Woman," a No. 2 R&B hit in
1955. This is the song most frequently singled out as his pivotal performance, on which Charles first truly let go with his unmistakable gospelish moan, backed by a tight, bouncy, horn-driven arrangement.
    Throughout the '50s, Charles ran off a series of R&B hits that,
although they weren't called "soul" at the time, did a lot to pave the way
for soul by presenting a form of R&B that was sophisticated without sacrificing any emotional grit. "This Little Girl of Mine," "Drown in My
Own Tears," "Hallelujah I Love Her So," "Lonely Avenue," and "The
Right Time" were all big hits. But Charles didn't really capture the pop
audience until "What'd I Say," which caught the fervor of the church
with its pleading vocals and the spirit of rock 'n' roll with its classic elec-

tric piano line. It was his first Top Ten pop hit and one of his final Atlantic singles, as he left the label at the end of the '50s for ABC.
    One of the chief attractions of the ABC deal for Charles was a much
greater degree of artistic control of his recordings. He put it to good use
on early-'60s hits like "Unchain My Heart" and "Hit the Road Jack,"
which solidified his pop stardom with only a modicum of polish
attached to the R&B he had perfected at Atlantic. In 1962 he surprised
the pop world by turning his attention to country and Western music,
topping the charts with the "I Can't Stop Loving You" single, and making
a hugely popular album (in an era in which R&B/soul LPs rarely scored
high on the charts) with *Modern Sounds in Country and Western
Music*. Perhaps it shouldn't have been so surprising; Charles had always
been eclectic, recording quite a bit of straight jazz at Atlantic, with noted
jazz musicians like David "Fathead" Newman and Milt Jackson.
    Charles remained extremely popular through the mid-'60s, scoring
big hits like "Busted," "You Are My Sunshine," "Take These Chains from
My Heart," and "Crying Time," although his momentum was slowed by
a 1965 bust for heroin. This led to a year-long absence from performing,
but he picked up where he left off with "Let's Go Get Stoned" in 1966.
Yet by this time Charles was focusing less on rock and soul, in favor of
pop tunes, often with string arrangements, that seemed aimed more at
the easy-listening audience than anyone else. Charles' influence on the
rock mainstream was as apparent as ever; Joe Cocker and Steve Winwood, in particular, owe a great deal of their style to him, and echoes of
his phrasing can be heard more subtly in the work of greats like Van
Morrison.
    One approaches sweeping criticism of Charles with hesitation; he's
an American institution, after all, and his vocal powers have barely
diminished over the years. The fact remains, though, that his work on
record since the late '60s has been very disappointing. Millions of listeners yearned for a return to the all-out soul of his 1955-1965 classics, but
Charles had actually never been committed to soul above all else. Like
Aretha Franklin and Elvis Presley, his focus is more upon all-around pop
than many realize; his love of jazz, country, and pop standards is evident, even if his more earthy offerings are the ones that truly broke
ground and will stand the test of time. He's dented the charts (even the
country ones) occasionally, and can command devoted international
concert audiences whenever he feels like it. For good or ill, he's ensured
his imprint upon the American mass consciousness in the 1990s by
singing several ads for Diet Pepsi. The CD era has seen several excellent
packages that focus on various chronological/thematic phases of the
legend's career. —*Richie Unterberger*

The Great Ray Charles / 1956 / Atlantic ✦✦✦
A superb late '50s instrumental album showcasing the jazz side of Ray
Charles. Quincy Jones provided the arrangements, and the Charles band
included Fathead Newman and Hank Crawford. The CD version
includes six marvelous bonus cuts, among them a remarkable cover of
Fats Waller's "Ain't Misbehavin'." —*Ron Wynn*

Ray Charles / Jul. 1957 / Atlantic ✦✦✦
These are animated soul and R&B recordings, although the rock 'n' roll
links are pretty obvious as well. The songs, vocals, arrangements, and
production are great; only the sound quality falters. But they can also be
obtained on many other anthologies with far superior sound. —*Ron
Wynn*

Ray Charles at Newport / Oct. 1958 / Atlantic ✦✦✦✦
For his appearance at the Newport Jazz Festival on July 5, 1958, Charles
pulled out all the stops, performing raucous versions of "The Right
Time," "I Got a Woman," and "Talkin' 'bout You." (This album was reissued in 1973 as a two-record set, packaged with *Ray Charles in Person*
under the title *Ray Charles Live* [Atlantic SD 2-503].) —*William Ruhlmann*

The Genius of Ray Charles / 1959 / Atlantic ✦✦✦✦
Half lushly orchestrated (by Ralph Burns) blues ballads that spotlight
the sophisticated (dare we say tender?) side of the man, the other half
big band-backed gems (including Charles' glorious remake of Louis Jordan's "Let the Good Times Roll" and the jauntiest version of "Alexander's
Ragtime Band" you'll ever hear), this 1959 album marked his ascension
to genuine Genius status and remains a benchmark of his lengthy
career. —*Bill Dahl*

What'd I Say / Sep. 1959 / Atlantic ✦✦✦
At a concert held at Herndon Stadium in Atlanta on May 28, 1959, Ray
Charles turns in a blistering version of "What'd I Say" and takes on the
big band era with versions of Tommy Dorsey's "Yes Indeed!" and Artie
Shaw's "Frenesi," not to mention performances of "The Right Time" and
"Tell the Truth." (This album was reissued in 1960 under the title *Ray
Charles in Person* and again in 1973 as a part of a two-record set, pack-
aged with *Ray Charles at Newport* under the title *Ray Charles Live*
[Atlantic 503].) —*William Ruhlmann*

The Genius Hits the Road / Jul. 1960 / ABC/Paramount ✦✦✦
Great blues, soul, and jazzy pop from Ray Charles, then in the midst of
perhaps his most creative streak as a performer. Charles' vocals were

animated, urgent, and spectacular, while the arrangements, production, material, and instrumental backing were equally splendid. —*Ron Wynn*

The Genius After Hours / 1961 / Rhino ✦✦✦✦
A great all-instrumental album, with Charles playing straight jazz, pop tunes, blues, and combinations of all those forms and more. Some equally fine solos from Fathead Newman, Hank Crawford, and Charles on keyboards and alto sax. —*Ron Wynn*

Genius + Soul " Jazz / Mar. 1961 / DCC ✦✦✦
A memorable big band session, it produced the instrumental hit "One Mint Julep." —*Hank Davis*

Ray Charles & Betty Carter / Jul. 1961 / DCC ✦✦✦
This pairing of two totally idiosyncratic vocalists acquired legendary status over the decades in which it had been out of print. But the proof is in the listening; it doesn't represent either artist's best work. There is certainly a powerful, often sexy rapport between the two—Charles in his sweet balladeering mode, Carter with her uniquely keening, drifting high register—and they definitely create sparks in the justly famous rendition of "Baby, It's Cold Outside." The main problem is in Marty Paich's string/choir arrangements, which too often cross the line into treacle, whereas his charts for big band are far more listenable. Charles' sweetness can get a bit cloying, too, although some of the old grit emerges on "Takes Two to Tango." On the CD reissue—remixed by Charles himself—Dunhill adds the great, rare B-side to the "Unchain My Heart" single, "But On The Other Hand Baby," and two excellent if unrelated album cuts,"I Never See Maggie Alone" (1964) and "I Like to Hear It Sometime" (1966). —*Richard S. Ginell*

The Genius Sings the Blues / Oct. 1961 / Atlantic ✦✦✦✦
Down-home, anguished laments and moody ballads were turned into triumphs by Ray Charles. He sang these songs with the same conviction, passion, and energy that made his country and soul vocals so majestic. This has not as of yet turned up in the reissue bins, but it is probably headed in that direction. —*Ron Wynn*

☆ **Modern Sounds in Country & Western Music** / Jan. 1962 / Rhino ✦✦✦✦✦
Modern Sounds in Country & Western Music is historically important and considered by most critics to be a classic, but some have mixed feelings about it. Charles' interpretations of songs recorded by Hank Williams, Eddy Arnold, Floyd Tillman, and Don Gibson are superb, but so often the arrangements by Marty Paich, Gerald Wilson, and Gil Fuller threaten to drown him in a sea of lachrymose bric-a-brac. "I Can't Stop Loving You" and "You Don't Know Me" were Top Ten pop and R&B. —*Rob Bowman*

☆ **Modern Sounds in Country & Western, Vol. 2** / Oct. 1962 / Rhino ✦✦✦✦✦
Charles' second installment of *Modern Sounds in Country and Western Music* is every bit as essential as the first, containing stellar interpretations of "Your Cheatin' Heart" and "You Are My Sunshine." —*Stephen Thomas Erlewine*

Ingredients in a Recipe for Soul / Jul. 1963 / DCC ✦✦✦✦
Ray Charles' 1963 ABC-Paramount album digitally verbatim, followed by four bonus tracks, notably the rare 1959 single "My Baby (I Love Her, Yes I Do)," an obscure Percy Mayfield goodie from 1964 ("Something's Wrong"), and Charles' 1960 version of Big Maceo's "Worried Life Blues." Charles tapped a host of disparate songwriters for this solid LP—everyone from Mel Tormé to Leroy Carr to Oscar Hammerstein—but the most memorable item is probably his irresistibly brassy remake of Harlan Howard's C&W classic "Busted." —*Bill Dahl*

Country & Western Meets Rhythm & Blues / Aug. 1965 / ABC/Paramount ✦✦✦
A partially successful revisiting by Charles of his country sessions of the early '60s. These songs weren't quite as transcendent as those on the prior dates, but he showed once again that the lines between country, R&B, and soul weren't as rigid as many in the various camps thought. —*Ron Wynn*

Ain't It So / Sep. 1979 / Atlantic ✦✦✦
One of the better albums from Charles' second sojourn at Atlantic in the '70s. Here, he gives us an uptempo version of Irving Berlin's "What'll I Do," and similarly revamps such standards as "Some Enchanted Evening" and "Blues in the Night." —*William Ruhlmann*

Greatest Hits, Vol. 1 / 1987 / DCC ✦✦✦✦
The first of two DCC compilations to collect the best of Brother Ray's 1960s' stint at ABC-Paramount Records, when he flew off in a dozen different stylistic directions. Included on this 20-track disc are Charles' immortal rendering of "Georgia on My Mind"; the sinuously bluesy "Unchain My Heart"; the Latin-beat instrumental "One Mint Julep"; personalized remakes of the country standards "Born to Lose," "Your Cheating Heart," and "Crying Time"; and his exultant rendition of the soulful "Let's Go Get Stoned." —*Bill Dahl*

Greatest Hits, Vol. 2 / 1987 / DCC ✦✦✦✦
More seminal performances from the '60s ABC catalog of the Genius (DCC split the classics evenly between the two discs, making both of them indispensable). His beloved "Hit the Road Jack" (one of several Percy Mayfield copyrights dotting Charles' repertoire), the daring country crossover "I Can't Stop Loving You," an electric-piano powered "Sticks and Stones," a wise "Them That Got," and a wonderfully mellow "At the Club" rank with the 20-song disc's standouts (though versions of the Beatles' "Yesterday" and the corny "Look What They Done to My Song, Ma" end the set on a bummer note). —*Bill Dahl*

☆ **Greatest Country Western Hits** / 1988 / DCC ✦✦✦✦✦
Collecting the highlights from Charles' two *Modern Sounds in Country and Western Music* albums, *Greatest Country Western Hits* features some of the most essential country-soul material ever recorded. —*Stephen Thomas Erlewine*

Soul Brothers/Soul Meeting / 1989 / Atlantic ✦✦✦✦
A great two-disc package that combined the pivotal Ray Charles sessions with Milt Jackson. The special release even had some bonus tracks, and the remastering and annotation were marvelous. There was no question about the quality of the tracks; Charles and Jackson were instantly compatible, with Jackson getting to display blues elements he normally suppressed when playing with the Modern Jazz Quartet, and Charles getting space to present his jazz and improvising skills. —*Ron Wynn*

☆ **The Birth of Soul** / Oct. 1, 1991 / Rhino ✦✦✦✦✦
The title isn't just hype. This absolutely essential three-disc box is where soul music first took shape and soared, courtesy of Ray Charles' church-soaked pipes and bedrock piano work. Brother Ray's formula for inventing the genre was disarmingly simple: he brought gospel intensity to the R&B world with his seminal "I Got a Woman," "Hallelujah I Love Her So," "Leave My Woman Alone," "You Be My Baby," and the primal 1959 call-and-response classic "What'd I Say." There's plenty of brilliant blues content within these 53 historic sides: Charles' mournful "Losing Hand," "Feelin' Sad," "Hard Times," and "Blackjack" ooze after-hours desperation. No blues collection should be without this box set, which comes with well-researched notes by Robert Palmer, a nicely illustrated accompanying booklet, and discographical info aplenty. —*Bill Dahl*

The Birth of a Legend / 1992 / Ebony ✦✦✦✦
Of all the countless compilations that have been stitched together of Ray Charles' early sides for Jack Lauderdale's Swing Time Records, this two-disc box is the only CD package that treats these enormously important works with the respect they deserve (meaning decent mono sound quality instead of murky electronic reprocessed stereo dubbed from vinyl, cogent liner notes, and full discographical annotation). This is where the Genius began, imitating Charles Brown at the very start (1949) and sounding like nobody but Brother Ray by 1952 (when he defected to Atlantic and hit the real big time). Forty-one tracks in all. —*Bill Dahl*

Blues & Jazz / 1993 / Rhino/Atlantic ✦✦✦✦
Another easy access point for Charles' seminal Atlantic catalog. This two-disc set is evenly split between his bluesiest sides on the first disc and a selection of his greatest jazz sides on disc two (gorgeously showcasing the sax work of David "Fathead" Newman on several pieces). Charles was a masterful blues purveyor; his "I Believe to My Soul" is simultaneously invested with heartbreak and humor, while the earlier "Sinner's Prayer," "The Sun's Gonna Shine Again," and the gospel-based "A Fool for You" emanate both hope and deep pain. —*Bill Dahl*

The Early Years / 1994 / Tomato ✦✦✦
In the late '40s and early '50s, Charles recorded several dozen sides for the Swingtime/Downbeat label, 30 of which are presented here. As has been noted many times by critics, these usually found Charles in a Nat "King" Cole swing-blues groove that was much smoother than the gritty R&B/soul he'd record for Atlantic in the later '50s; the influence of urban blues balladeer Charles Brown is also evident. Some critical essays, in fact, may lead you to believe that this work is trivial, but while it's undeniably derivative, it's enjoyable on its own terms, and not without strong hints of the searing soulfulness that was to come. Some of the selections are delivered with such polish that it doesn't even sound like Charles. But on the more anguished and fast-tempoed cuts in particular, you can hear him starting to arrive at the phrasing and emotion that would flower in the mid-'50s. Unfortunately, like most Tomato reissues, the sound is substandard; even assuming that the master tapes can't be located, a better job was probably possible, and a couple of cuts even duplicate skips from the vinyl. Exact dates and songwriting credits are also missing, although Pete Welding's essay does at least discuss the material on the discs in some detail, unlike many of Tomato's liner notes. —*Richie Unterberger*

★ **Best of Atlantic** / Jul. 19, 1994 / Rhino ✦✦✦✦✦
The 20-track compilation (only 12 tracks on cassette) *The Best of Atlantic* compiles all of Ray Charles' Top Ten R&B hits for Atlantic Records, from "I've Got a Woman" and "This Little Girl of Mine" to "Drown in My

Own Tears," "Hallelujah I Love Her So," "Lonely Avenue," "(Night Time Is) The Right Time," and "What'd I Say (Part 1)." In addition to the big hits, there are minor hits that nevertheless showcase Charles at his peak, like "Swanee River Rock" and "Just for a Thrill." For fans who want only the hits and don't want to invest in the splendid three-disc set *The Birth of Soul, The Best of Atlantic* is an essential purchase. — *Stephen Thomas Erlewine*

Chavez

f. 1993, New York, NY
Indie Rock
The angular indie rock unit Chavez was led by singer/guitarist Matt Sweeney, the former frontman of New Jersey's Skunk. After the group's demise, Sweeney joined the New York band Wider, which included one-time Live Skull drummer James Lo; when Wider dissolved in 1992, Sweeney began playing with ex-Bullet Lavolta guitarist Clay Tarver. Lo joined not long after, and with bassist Davey Hoskins, Chavez cut its first demo recordings in late 1993. After Hoskins' exit and the recruitment of bassist Scott Masciarelli, the band made its live debut; soon, the anthemic 1994 debut single "Repeat the Ending" and a reputation for stunning live sets made Chavez a hot commodity on the New York club scene. Their acclaimed debut *Gone Glimmering* and the follow-up EP *Pentagram Ring* appeared in 1995; the full-length *Ride the Fader* followed a year later. — *Jason Ankeny*

Gone Glimmering / May 18, 1995 / Matador ◆◆◆◆
Despite the group's tendency to meander, Chavez's *Gone Glimmering* is an impressive debut, finding the group marrying complex, grinding riffs to cerebral melodies and hooks. — *Stephen Thomas Erlewine*

● **Ride the Fader** / Nov. 5, 1996 / Matador ◆◆◆◆
Working from the basic foundation they established on *Gone Glimmering*, Chavez spins off into new territories on their second album, *Ride the Fader*. Equal parts post-hardcore punk and prog-metal, Chavez's music is intellectual guitar rock—riffs are fractured and self-consciously asymmetrical, winding in on themselves and then turning inside out. What prevents *Ride the Fader* from becoming a tedious, pompous exercise in experimental rock is visceral directness, combined with detail. Chavez is a powerful, muscular band, capable of giving their densely packed songs a startling immediacy. — *Stephen Thomas Erlewine*

Cheap Trick

f. 1973, Rockford, IL
Hard Rock, New Wave, Power Pop, Pop-Rock
Combining a love for British guitar-pop songcraft with crunching power chords and a flair for the absurd, Cheap Trick provided the necessary links between '60s pop, heavy metal, and punk. Led by guitarist Rick Nielsen, the band's early albums were filled with highly melodic, well written songs that drew equally from the crafted pop of the Beatles, the sonic assault of the Who, and the tongue-in-cheek musical eclecticism and humor of the Move. Their sound provided a blueprint for both power-pop and arena rock; it also had a surprisingly long-lived effect on both alternative and heavy-metal bands of the '80s and '90s, who also relied on the combination of loud riffs and catchy melodies.

Cheap Trick's roots lie in Fuse, a late-'60s Rockford, IL, band formed by Rick Nielsen and bassist Tom Petersson, which released an unsuccessful album on Epic in 1969. After the record failed to gain any attention, the band relocated to Philadelphia and changed their name to Sick Man of Europe. The group toured Europe unsuccessfully in 1972, returning to Illinois in 1973. Upon their return to Rockford, Nielsen and Petersson changed their band's name to Cheap Trick, adding drummer Bun E. Carlos and vocalist Randy "Xeno" Hogan. Hogan was fired the next year, and ex-folk singer Robin Zander joined the group. Between 1974 and the band's first album in 1977, Cheap Trick toured constantly, playing over 200 concerts a year, including opening slots for the Kinks, Kiss, Santana, Journey, and Boston. During this time, the band built up a solid catalog of original songs that would eventually comprise their first three albums; they also perfected their kinetic live show.

Cheap Trick signed with Epic Records in 1976, releasing their self-titled debut in early 1977. The record sold well in America, but it failed to chart. However, it became a massive success in Japan, going gold upon release. Later that year the band released their second album, *In Color*. *In Color* backed away from the harder-rocking *Cheap Trick*, featuring a slicker production and quieter arrangements that spotlighted the band's melodic skills. Because of their constant touring, the record made it into the US charts, peaking at No. 73; in Japan it became another gold-seller.

The band realized when they toured the country in early 1978 that they were virtual superstars in Japan. Their concerts were selling out within two hours, and they packed Budokan Arena. Cheap Trick's concerts at Budokan Arena were recorded for release; the record appeared after their third album, 1978's *Heaven Tonight*. *Heaven Tonight* captured both the loud, raucous energy of their debut and the hook-laden songcraft of *In Color*, leading to their first Top 100 single, "Surrender,"

which peaked at No. 62. However, it was the performances on *At Budokan* (1979) that captured the band's energetic, infectious live show, resulting in their commercial breakthrough in the US. The album stayed on the charts for over a year, peaking at No. 4 and eventually selling over three million copies. A live version of "I Want You to Want Me" pulled from the album became their first Top Ten hit. Later that year the group released their fourth studio album, *Dream Police*, which followed the same stylistic approach of *Heaven Tonight*. It also followed *At Budokan* into the Top Ten, selling over a million copies and launching the Top 40 hit singles "Voices" and "Dream Police." In the summer of 1980 the group released an EP of tracks recorded between 1976-79 called *Found All the Parts*.

Petersson left the group in the summer of 1980 to form a group with his wife Dagmar; he was replaced by Jon Brant. The first album recorded with Brant was the George Martin-produced *All Shook Up*, released toward the end of 1980. The album performed respectably, peaking at No. 24 and going gold, but the single "Stop This Game" failed to crack the Top 40. Epic rejected an album the group recorded in early 1981, forcing the band back into the studio to record an entirely new record. *One on One*, the group's seventh album, appeared in 1982. Although it peaked at No. 39, the record was more successful than *All Shook Up*, eventually going platinum. Nevertheless, the group was entering a downhill commercial slide, despite the fact that their music was becoming increasingly polished. *Next Position Please*, released in 1983, failed to launch a hit single and spent only 11 weeks on the charts. *Standing on the Edge* (1985) and *The Doctor* (1986) suffered similar fates, as the group was slowly losing its creative spark.

Petersson rejoined the band in 1988, and the group began working on a new record with the help of several professional songwriters. The resulting record, *Lap of Luxury*, was a platinum Top 20 hit, featuring the No. 1 power ballad "The Flame" and a Top Ten version of Elvis Presley's "Don't Be Cruel." *Busted*, released in 1990, wasn't as successful as *Lap of Luxury*, peaking at No. 48 and effectively putting an end to the group's comeback. Cheap Trick signed with Warner Brothers in 1994, releasing *Woke Up with a Monster*; the record spent two weeks on the chart, peaking at 123. That same year, Epic Records released a sequel to *At Budokan, Budokan II*. Compiled from the same shows as *At Budokan*, the record provided an effective reminder of why the group was so popular in the late '70s, not only for the public, but for the band as well. Following the poor performance of *Woke Up with a Monster*, Cheap Trick decided to go back to the basics. They were dropped from Warner, but several alternative rockers who were influenced by Cheap Trick gave the band opportunites to restore their reputation. Smashing Pumpkins had the band open their tour in 1995, and the group played several dates on the 1996 Lollapalooza tour. That same year, the box set *Sex America Cheap Trick* appeared to good reviews, and the band signed with the fledgling indie Red Ant. Early in 1997 the group released a Steve Albini-produced single on Sub Pop, which was followed by *Cheap Trick*, their acclaimed debut for Red Ant, in the spring. — *Stephen Thomas Erlewine*

☆ **Cheap Trick** / 1977 / Epic ◆◆◆◆◆
Cheap Trick's eponymous debut is an explosive fusion of Beatlesque melodic hooks, Who-styled power, and a twisted sense of humor partially borrowed from the Move. But that only begins to scratch the surface of what makes *Cheap Trick* a dynamic record. Guitarist Rick Nielsen has a powerful sense of dynamics and arrangments, which gives the music an extra kick, but he also can write exceptionally melodic and subversive songs. Nothing on *Cheap Trick* is quite what it seems. While the songs have hooks and attitude that arena-rock was sorely lacking in the late '70s, they are also informed by a bizarre sensibility, whether it's the driving "He's a Whore," the dreamy "Mandocello," or the thumping Gary Glitter perversion "ELO Kiddies." "The Ballad of TV Violence" is about mass murder, while "Daddy Should Have Stayed in High School" concerns pedophiles. All of it is told with a sense of humor, but it doesn't come off as cheap or smirking because of the group's hard-rocking drive and Robin Zander's pop-idol vocals. Even "Oh, Candy," apparently a love song on first listen, is an affecting tribute to a friend who committed suicide. In short, Cheap Trick revels in taboo subjects with abandon, devoting themselves to the power of the hook, as well as sheer volume and gut-wrenching rock 'n' roll. Though the record was more musically accomplished than punk rock, it shared the same aesthetic. The combination of off-kilter humor, bizarre subjects, and blissful power-pop made *Cheap Trick* one of the defining albums of its era, as well as one of the most influential. — *Stephen Thomas Erlewine*

In Color / 1977 / Epic ◆◆◆◆
Though Cheap Trick's second album *In Color (And in Black and White)* draws from the same stockpile of Midwestern barroom favorites as their debut album, it was produced by Tom Werman, who had the band strip away their raw attack and replace it with a shiny, radio-ready sound. Consequently, *In Color* doesn't have the visceral attack of its predecessor, but it has the same sensibility and a similar set of spectacular songs. From the druggy psychedelia of "Downed" and the bubblegum sing-

along "I Want You to Want Me" to the "California Girls" homage of "Southern Girls," the album has the same encyclopedic knowledge of rock 'n' roll, as well as the good sense to subvert it with a perverse sense of humor. Portions of the album haven't dated well, simply due to the glossy production, but the songs and music on *In Color* are as splendid as the debut. —*Stephen Thomas Erlewine*

☆ **Heaven Tonight** / 1978 / Epic ✦✦✦✦✦
Heaven Tonight, like *In Color*, was produced by Tom Werman, but the difference between the two records is substantial. Where *In Color* often sounded emasculated, *Heaven Tonight* regains the powerful, arena-ready punch of *Cheap Trick*, but crosses it with a clever radio-friendly production that relies both on synthesizers and studio effects. Even with the fairly slick production, Cheap Trick sounds ferocious throughout the album, slamming heavy metal, power-pop, and hard rock together in a humongous sound. "Surrender," the definitive Cheap Trick song, opens the album with a tale about a kid whose parents are hipper than he, and the remainder of the record is rollercoaster ride, peaking with the sneering "Auf Wiedersehen," the dreamily psychedelic title track, the roaring rocker "On Top of the World," the high-stepping, tongue-in-cheek "How Are You," and the pulverizing cover of the Move's "California Man." *Heaven Tonight* is the culmination of the group's dizzying early career, summing up the strengths of their first two albums, their live show, and their talent for inverting pop conventions. They were never again quite as consistently thrilling on record. —*Stephen Thomas Erlewine*

★ **Live at Budokan** / Feb. 1979 / Epic ✦✦✦✦✦
While their records were entertaining and full of skillful pop, it wasn't until *Live at Budokan* that Cheap Trick's vision truly gelled. Many of these songs, like "I Want You to Want Me" and "Big Eyes," were pleasant in their original form, but they seemed like sketches compared to the roaring versions on this album. With their ear-shatteringly loud guitars and sweet melodies, Cheap Trick unwittingly paved the way for much of the hard rock of the next decade, as well as a surprising amount of alternative rock of the 1990s, and it was *Live at Budokan* that captured the band in all of its power. —*Stephen Thomas Erlewine*

Dream Police / Oct. 1979 / Epic ✦✦✦✦
At the Budokan unexpectedly made Cheap Trick stars, largely because "I Want You to Want Me" had a tougher sound than its original studio inclination. Perversely—and most things Cheap Trick have done are somehow perverse—the band decided *not* to continue with the direct, stripped-down sound of *Live at Budokan*, which would have been a return to their debut. Instead, the group went for their biggest, most elaborate production to date, taking the synthesized flourishes of *Heaven Tonight* to extremes. While it kept the group in the charts, it lessened the impact of the music. Underneath the gloss, there are a number of songs that rank among Cheap Trick's finest, particularly the paranoid title track, the epic rocker "Gonna Raise Hell," the tough "I Know What I Want," the simpy pop of "Voices," and the closer "Need Your Love." Still, *Dream Police* feels like a let-down in comparison to its predecessors, even though it would later feel like one of the group's last high-water marks. —*Stephen Thomas Erlewine*

All Shook Up / 1980 / Epic ✦✦
With the legendary George Martin sitting in the producer's chair for this one, you'd think that Cheap Trick would have had it made. Unfortunately, that wasn't the case, for with *All Shook Up*, the hits stopped coming and the near constant touring was beginning to take its toll. Well worth seeking out, but it's not the best in Cheap Trick's notable history. —*James Chrispell*

Found All the Parts / 1980 / Epic ✦✦✦
This EP consists of four cuts that hadn't yet found their way onto Cheap Trick's releases. Of note is their version of the Beatles' "Day Tripper." A nostalgic bit of history. —*James Chrispell*

One on One / 1982 / Epic ✦✦✦
Tom Petersson left the group after the muddled *All Shook Up*, which was another sign that Cheap Trick was entering a confused period, and *One on One*, the first record the group recorded with his replacement Jon Brant, confirms that suspicion. Though it has two fine singles with the power ballad "If You Want My Love" and the lewd rocker "She's Tight," both songs fall short compared to their old standards. Still, they sound like gems compared to the remaining album. Though *One on One* is nowhere near as ambitious as *All Shook Up*, the songwriting is forced and stilted, lacking not only imagination, but hooks. A couple of cuts—"Lookin' Out for Number One," "Love's Got a Hold On Me"—work as standard-issue arena-rockers, but by and large, *One on One* is another disappointment. —*Stephen Thomas Erlewine*

Next Position Please / 1983 / Epic ✦✦✦
Perhaps sensing something was going wrong, Cheap Trick hired superstar producer Todd Rundgren for *Next Position Please*. Rundgren helped the band return to the appealing pop-rock of their *In Color* days, albeit stamping it with his heavy-handed production. However, Cheap Trick does benefit from Rundgren's control, since it gives them a sense

of focus lacking on *All Shook Up* and *One on One*. Though the record was hampered somewhat by Epic's insistence on adding a bad cover of the Motors' terrific "Dancin' the Night Away" and the lightweight "You Say Jump," *Next Position Please* is effectively a return to form for Cheap Trick, boasting their most consistent set of songs since *Heaven Tonight*. "I Can't Take It," "Borderline," "Younger Girls," "Heaven's Falling," and "Invaders of the Heart" may not quite reach the heights of the first three albums, but they come within shooting distance, making *Next Position Please* Cheap Trick's last satisfying record. —*Stephen Thomas Erlewine*

Standing on the Edge / 1985 / Epic ✦✦
Sounding more assured with *Standing On the Edge*, Cheap Trick shows once again that they always had a way with a great pop tune. "Tonight It's You" is pure pop and was a glimpse of what the band would sound like in the very near future. It's flawed, but okay. —*James Chrispell*

The Doctor / 1986 / Epic ✦

Lap of Luxury / 1988 / Epic ✦✦✦
Cheap Trick's comeback album is by no means a return to the creativity and vitality of their glory days. But even though *Lap of Luxury* is largely formulaic, the band's strongest collection of material in some time fills that late-'80s pop/metal formula quite well. Combining grandly romantic power ballads ("Ghost Town") with catchy hard rockers ("Never Had a Lot to Lose"), *Lap of Luxury* consistently delivers strong hooks and well-crafted songs, proving that Cheap Trick was still capable of outdoing many of the bands they helped inspire. The album produced two Top Five singles in a cover of Elvis Presley's "Don't Be Cruel" and the band's first No. 1 hit, "The Flame." —*Steve Huey*

Busted / Jun. 1990 / Epic ✦✦
Busted stalled Cheap Trick's commercial comeback, and it's easy to hear why. The songs are underdeveloped, as the band repeats the same mostly lackluster chorus hooks *ad infinitum* and fails even to approach the best material on *Lap of Luxury*. *Busted* sadly sounds as though the band didn't even have any formulaic ideas left. —*Steve Huey*

Greatest Hits / 1992 / Epic ✦✦✦✦
The greatest failing of *Greatest Hits* is the fact that much of Cheap Trick's best material didn't come near the charts. "I Want You to Want Me," "Surrender," and "Dream Police" either climbed the charts or scraped them, as did the fine singles "Ain't That a Shame," "Voices," "If You Want My Love," and "She's Tight," but many of their stone-cold classics—including "He's a Whore," "Oh, Candy," "Downed," "Southern Girls," "Auf Wiedersehen"—weren't successes. What were successes were pleasant arena-rockers and power ballads like "Tonight It's You," "The Flame," and "Don't Be Cruel," and that's what forms the basis of *Greatest Hits*, along with an extraneous new rendition of the Beatles' "Magical Mystery Tour." Casual fans who want only the hits will be satiated by this collection, but the album misses the point of Cheap Trick, and thereby doesn't work as either introduction or retrospective. —*Stephen Thomas Erlewine*

Budokan II / Feb. 1994 / Epic ✦✦✦✦
Budokan II is exactly what it says it is—the sequel to Cheap Trick's career-making *Live at Budokan*. Picking up where its predecessor left off (the tracks even begin at number 11), the record contains all of the band's classics—"ELO Kiddies," "Southern Girls," "California Man," "Downed," "How Are You," "On Top of the World," "Oh Caroline," "Auf Wiedersehen," "Speak Now or Forever Hold Your Piece"—that didn't make the first records. While the performances aren't quite as tight as *At Budokan*—possibly because they weren't doctored as heavily in the studio—the record is nevertheless a muscular, energetic set of definitive power-pop and will please not only diehard fans of Cheap Trick, but casual fans attracted by *Live at Budokan*. —*Stephen Thomas Erlewine*

Woke Up with a Monster / Mar. 22, 1994 / Warner Brothers ✦✦✦
Cheap Trick's Warners debut, produced by Ted Templeman (Van Halen, Little Feat) is their best album in years, certainly since 1983's *Next Position Please;* it's easily an equal to *Dream Police*. In spite of some uneven spots, there is more fire in their sound here and, when they go for the kind of big rock ballads that became their metier in recent years, there is enough attitude to counteract most of the tendency towards sappiness. Highlights are "You're All I Wanna Do," "Let Her Go," "My Gang," and the title cut. —*Rick Clark*

Sex America Cheap Trick / Aug. 1996 / Sony ✦✦✦
Sex America Cheap Trick is a classic example of a botched box set. Spanning four discs and 64 songs, the box contains nearly all of the group's hit singles and an amazing number of rarities—a grand total of 30 outtakes, live tracks, demos, single versions, soundtrack songs, and B-sides. Despite the abundance of material, a lot of essential items are missing, and there are several odd inclusions. Many of the group's biggest hits and concert staples are present, but Cheap Trick classics like "He's a Whore," "Downed," "Come On, Come On," "Taxman, Mr. Thief," "California Man," and several others are inexplicably absent. Furthermore, the final two discs bog down in slick radio-ready pop, even though they rescue all the highlights from the band's decidedly uneven

'80s recordings. Still, the rarities—particularly single versions of early tracks like "Oh, Candy" and "Southern Girls," demos like "Fan Club," and a ripping live set—are usually worthy, even if they might have been better showcased on a double-disc rarities set. —*Stephen Thomas Erlewine*

Cheap Trick [1997] / Apr. 29, 1997 / Red Ant ✦✦✦
Titled *Cheap Trick* like the group's debut album, presumably because the record represents a new beginning, *Cheap Trick* is indeed their most powerful, direct, and melodic album in years, and certainly their heaviest since their late-'70s heyday. Stripping away all of the glossy, big-budget excesses of their late-'80s and early-'90s major-label releases, Cheap Trick keep their sound to the basics—loud guitars, crunching chords, and sweet melodies. Certainly the unvarnished sound helps the record sound immediate, but the real key to the success of *Cheap Trick* is the reinvigorated songwriting. Most of the songs are written by the band themselves, with only a couple of cuts featuring outside songwriters, and the result is a tight, melodic set of hard rockers and ballads. Not everything on the album is first-rate—the forced opener "Anytime" is almost a fatal misstep—and a couple of songs are simply pleasant, but there are more terrific moments—"Hard to Tell," "You Let a Lotta People Down," "Say Good Bye," "It All Comes Back to You"—than there have been on any Cheap Trick record in years. It's a fine, distinguished comeback, and one that suggests that the group could continue making records just as good for several more years. —*Stephen Thomas Erlewine*

Chubby Checker

b. Oct. 3, 1941, Philadelphia, PA
Vocals / R&B, Rock 'n' Roll
He taught America how to twist. Not just the kids, who always learned the latest steps, but everyone—from society matrons and jetsetters to the proverbial man in the street.
Rock 'n' roll was becoming complacent when Chubby Checker came along in 1960 with his note-for-note remake of Hank Ballard and the Midnighters' "The Twist" and got it moving again. The husky Philadelphia lad, known as Ernest Evans until Dick Clark's wife decided he resembled Fats Domino, had already waxed a few 45s for the local Parkway label, including a novelty called "The Class" that found him imitating Fats, Elvis, and even the Chipmunks. But it was "The Twist," a No. 1 hit not once but twice (in 1960 and 1961), that made him an international celebrity.
Checker quickly became the nation's leading dance specialist, introducing "The Hucklebuck," "The Fly," "Pony Time," and "Limbo Rock" to the gyrating masses and successfully recycling his initial routine into "Let's Twist Again" and "Slow Twistin'." While racking up monster sales figures for Parkway, Checker starred in a couple of quickie exploitation films, *Twist Around the Clock* and *Don't Knock the Twist*, later trying his hand at folk songs when the twist fad finally began to fade.
The British Invasion led to some lean years for Checker, although he got a little revenge by charting with a cover of the Beatles tune "Back in the U.S.S.R." in 1969. But he continued to put on a high-energy show that inevitably led to that classic million-seller—and Chubby Checker proved every time out that he was still the king of the Twist. —*Bill Dahl*

● **Chubby Checker's Greatest Hits** / Nov. 1972 / ABKCO ✦✦✦✦
In 1972, when nostalgia for late-'50s and early-'60s rock 'n' roll was bringing Chuck Berry and others back into the charts, Allen Klein's ABKCO Records obtained the rights to reissue Chubby Checker's Cameo-Parkway singles on this 15-track hits LP. Checker actually had many more hits than just "The Twist" and "Let's Twist Again," and this LP presents his other dance tunes—"Pony Time," "The Fly," "Limbo Rock"—and several of his later, less successful singles when he was trying to branch out into a sort of Harry Belafonte-style folk approach. But the heart of the collection is still the early-'60s dance tunes, which demonstrate that while Checker was not a great rocker, he still, like Freddy Cannon and Gary US Bonds, was one of the people keeping the flame of rock 'n' roll flickering between the time Buddy Holly's plane went down in Iowa and the day the Beatles flew in from London. (Released on LP, this album is long out of print, and it is listed as Checker's "pick" album because, as of 1995, there is no in-print album containing his original hits.) —*William Ruhlmann*

The Chemical Brothers

f. 1989, Manchester, England
Acid House, Techno, Club/Dance, Trip-Hop, Electronica
Manchester post-techno duo Tom Rowlands and Ed Simons, aka the Chemical Brothers, have often been described as making "techno for headbangers," referring to the somewhat lo-calorie, big-dumb-sex appeal of their music. Sample-heavy and big on dance-floor dramatics, the Brothers got their start tag-teaming the back room at London's famous Heavenly Sunday Social Club after making the acquaintance of influential DJ Andrew Weatherall. The pair released a few EPs on the house-dominated Junior Boys' Own label in the early '90s under the

name the Dust Brothers, and switched to their current moniker when rights were found to be owned by a US production duo of the same name (famous for their work on the Beastie Boys' *Paul's Boutique*). The Brothers found quick hype after a series of highly regarded remix projects for the Prodigy, Saint Etienne, Leftfield, Weatherall's Sabres of Paradise, and Manic Street Preachers, and released a full-length album to critical acclaim in 1995.
The Chemical Brothers spent most of 1996 working on their second album, occasionally playing concerts and doing a handful of remixes. In the fall the duo returned with "Setting Sun," a song they co-wrote with Oasis' Noel Gallagher, who also provided vocals. "Setting Sun" became the group's first No. 1 single in the UK, and it also made significant inroads in America, becoming a buzz clip on MTV and earning airplay in influential radio markets. It set the foundation for *Dig Your Own Hole*, the Chemicals' hotly anticipated second album. After the release of the "Block Rockin' Beats" single, which also reached No. 1 in the UK, *Dig Your Own Hole* was released in April 1997 to enthusiastic reviews. The album debuted at No. 1 on the British charts and No. 14 on the American charts—a shockingly high debut, since America had previously been resistant to techno. —*Sean Cooper*

Exit Planet Dust / Aug. 15, 1995 / Astralwerks ✦✦✦✦
The former Dust Brothers make oblique reference to litigation averted on their debut full-length. The Brothers' sound is big on bombast, replete with screeching guitar samples and lots of sirens and screaming divas. A breakthrough album of sorts, *Exit* was, upon its release, one of the few European post-techno albums to make any sort of headway into the stateside market. —*Sean Cooper*

● **Dig Your Own Hole** / Apr. 8, 1997 / Astralwerks ✦✦✦✦
Taking the swirling eclecticism of their post-techno debut *Exit Planet Dust* to the extreme, the Chemical Brothers blow all stylistic boundaries down with their second album, *Dig Your Own Hole*. Bigger, bolder, and more adventurous than *Exit Planet Dust*, *Dig Your Own Hole* opens with the slamming cacophony of "Block Rockin' Beats," where hip-hop meets hardcore techno, complete with a Schoolly D sample and an elastic bass riff. Everything is going on at once in "Block Rockin' Beats," and it sets the pace for the rest of the record, where songs and styles blur in a continuous kaleidoscope of sound. It rocks hard enough for the pop audience, but it doesn't compromise either the Chemicals' sound or the adventurous, futuristic spirit of electronica. Not even "Setting Sun," with its sly homages to the Beatles' "Tomorrow Never Knows" and Noel Gallagher's twisting, catchy melody, sounds like retro psychedelia; it sounds vibrant, unexpected, and utterly contemporary. There are no distinctions between different styles, and the Chemicals sound as if they're having fun, building *Dig Your Own Hole* from fragments of the past, distorting the rhythms and samples, and pushing it forward with an intoxicating rush of synthesizers, electronics, and layered drum machines. The Chemical Brothers might not push forward into self-consciously arty territories like some of their electronic peers, but they have more style and focus, constructing a blindingly innovative and relentlessly propulsive album that's an exhilarating listen—one that sounds positively new and utterly inviting at the same time. —*Stephen Thomas Erlewine*

Cher

b. May 20, 1946, El Centro, CA
Vocals / Adult Contemporary, Soft Rock, Pop-Rock
After untying the knot with Sonny Bono in 1974, Cher developed into a pop icon of a magnitude many times brighter than during her '60s duet days with her husband. Even while married to Sonny, Cher was hitting the charts as a solo act with "Bang Bang (My Baby Shot Me Down)" in 1966 and "You Better Sit Down Kids" in 1967, both on Imperial, and her output on Kapp included the 1971 No. 1 hit "Gypsys, Tramps & Thieves." The gold records continued with "Half-Breed" in 1973 and "Dark Lady" in 1974, both chart-toppers on MCA. In 1979 "Take Me Home" was Cher's last smash for eight years, but she wasn't idle, starring in the acclaimed motion pictures *Silkwood* and *The Witches of Eastwick* and winning the 1987 Best Actress Oscar for her role in *Moonstruck*. Cher roared back in 1989 with "After All," a duet with Peter Cetera, and the anthemic solo outing "If I Could Turn Back Time," both on Geffen. Whether she's hawking memberships for a health-club chain or tearing up a concert stage, Cher endures as one of the nation's premier celebrities. —*Bill Dahl*

● **Greatest Hits** / 1974 / MCA ✦✦✦✦
Cher's early-'70s hits, including "Gypsys, Tramps and Thieves," "Half-Breed," and "Dark Lady," are compiled on this collection. —*Stephen Thomas Erlewine*

Cher [Geffen] / 1987 / Geffen ✦✦✦✦
Cher's late-'80s musical comeback was fueled by her success as an actress, not her songs, but her first album of the 1980s was a surprisingly consistent set of slick contemporary pop, including the hit "We All Sleep Alone." —*Stephen Thomas Erlewine*

Heart of Stone / Jun. 1989 / Geffen ✦✦✦
One of the most mature albums of Cher's career, this focuses on relationships from a 40-year-old's perspective rather than a teenager's. Cuts include "If I Could Turn Back Time," "Just Like Jesse James," and a duet with Peter Cetera, "After All." —*Bil Carpenter*

Bang Bang, My Baby Shot Me Down: The Best of Cher / Sep. 17, 1990 / EMI America ✦✦✦✦
Bang Bang, My Baby Shot Me Down—The Best of Cher collects more than 20 of Cher's '60s solo cuts on the Imperial label. There is the Motown-styled "Dream Baby," but it's mostly folk-pop including little-known gems like the pensive "She's Not Better Than Me." —*Bil Carpenter*

Best of the Casablanca Years / Jun. 1996 / Chronicles ✦✦
Cher's *The Best of the Casablanca Years* collects all of her hit singles from the late '70s, and there weren't that many. Only three singles charted in the Top 100 and only one—the No. 8 "Take Me Home"—cracked the Top 40. So the rest of the collection is padded with album tracks, making the disc into a mammoth, 17-track compilation. Nearly everything she released on the label is included, and it all sounds similar; it's all insistent, mildly catchy, disco. During this era, Cher didn't work with particularly gifted producers or songwriters, which meant her disco tracks were undistinguished. Occasionally she had a strong song like "Take Me Home," but she was more likely to cut a wealth of mediocre material, throwing in a few genuinely embarassing tracks along the way. And that means *The Best of the Casablanca Years* is an artifact of the late '70s that is of use only for dedicated Cher fans. It's a well produced and thorough collection, but no one but the most devoted fan needs to own this music. —*Stephen Thomas Erlewine*

Neneh Cherry

b. Mar. 10, 1964, Stockholm, Sweden
Vocals / Dance-Pop, Alternative Dance, Urban, Alternative Rap
The stepdaughter of jazz trailblazer Don Cherry, vocalist Neneh Cherry forged her own groundbreaking blend of pop, dance, and hip-hop, which presaged the emergence of both alternative rap and trip-hop. She was born Neneh Mariann Karlssson on March 10, 1964, in Stockholm, Sweden, the daughter of West African percussionist Amadu Jah and artist Moki Cherry. Raised by her mother and her trumpeter stepfather in both Stockholm and New York City, Cherry dropped out of school at age 14, and in 1980 she relocated to London to sing with the punk group the Cherries.
    After brief flings with the Slits and the Nails, she joined the experimental funk outfit Rip Rig + Panic, and appeared on the group's albums *God* (1981), *I Am Cold* (1982), and *Attitude* (1983). When the band broke up, Cherry remained with one of the spin-off groups, Float Up CP, and led them through one album, 1986's *Kill Me in the Morning*. The band proved short-lived, however, and Cherry began rapping in a London club, where she earned the attention of a talent scout who signed her to a solo contract. Her first single, "Stop the War," railed against the invasion of the Falkland Islands.
    After attracting some notice singing backup on The The's "Slow Train to Dawn" single, she became romantically and professionally involved with composer and musician Cameron McVey, who, under the alias Booga Bear, wrote much of the material that would comprise Cherry's 1989 debut LP *Raw Like Sushi*. One song McVey did not write was "Buffalo Stance," the album's breakthrough single; originally tossed off as a B-side by the mid-'80s pop group Morgan McVey, Cherry's cover was an international smash that neatly summarized the album's eclectic fusion of pop smarts and hip-hop energy.
    A pair of hits—the eerie "Manchild" and "Kisses on the Wind"—followed, but shortly after the record's release Cherry was sidelined with Lyme disease. Apart from a cover of Cole Porter's "I've Got You Under My Skin" for the 1990 *Red Hot + Blue* benefit album, she remained silent until 1992's *Homebrew*. A more subdued collection than *Raw Like Sushi*, it featured cameos from Gang Starr and R.E.M.'s Michael Stipe, as well as writing and production assistance from Geoff Barrow, who layered the track "Somedays" with the same distinct trip-hop glaze he later perfected as half of the duo Portishead. While the album was not as commercially successful as its predecessor, Cherry returned to the charts in 1994 duetting with Youssou N'Dour on the global hit "Seven Seconds." After another lengthy layoff spent with her children, she resurfaced with the atmospheric *Man* in 1996. —*Jason Ankeny*

● **Raw Like Sushi** / May 1989 / Virgin ✦✦✦✦
Those arguing that the most individualistic R&B and dance music of the late '80s and early to mid-'90s came out of Britain could point to Neneh Cherry's unconventional *Raw like Sushi* as a shining example. An unorthodox and brilliantly daring blend of R&B, rap, pop, and dance music, *Sushi* enjoyed little exposure on America's conservative urban contemporary radio formats, but was a definite underground hit. Full of personality, the singer/rapper is as thought-provoking as she is witty and humorous when addressing relationships and taking aim at less-than-

kosher behavior of males and females alike. Macho "homeboys" and casanovas take a pounding on "So Here I Come" and the hit "Buffalo Stance," while women who are shallow, cold-hearted, or materialistic get lambasted on "Phoney Ladies," "Heart," and "Inna City Mamma." Cherry's idealism comes through loud and clear on "The Next Generation," a plea to take responsibility for one's sexual actions and give children the respect and attention they deserve. —*Alex Henderson*

Homebrew / Oct. 27, 1992 / Virgin ✦✦✦✦
Despite the absence of a knockout single like "Buffalo Stance," *Homebrew* is a stronger album than *Raw Like Sushi*. On *Homebrew*, Cherry's melding of hip-hop and R&B is so complete that no seams show; it doesn't belong to either genre, but stands on its own. It takes a couple of plays before it starts to sink in, but after some time, even Michael Stipe's rap on "Trout" seems completely natural. —*Stephen Thomas Erlewine*

Man / 1996 / Hut ✦✦✦

Vic Chesnutt

b. 1965, Georgia
Vocals, Guitar / Urban-Folk, Singer-Songwriter, Alternative Pop-Rock
Though Michael Stipe had been a fan of Vic Chesnutt since the late '80s, producing his first two full-lengths, it took the *Sweet Relief Two* tribute album to make Chesnutt a star in mid-1996. The album featured artists such as Madonna, Hootie & the Blowfish, Smashing Pumpkins, and R.E.M. covering the songs of Chesnutt, a paraplegic who was injured in a car accident when he was 18.
    The singer-songwriter began playing contemporary acoustic folk around Athens, GA, soon after his injury. A show at the 40 Watt Club brought him to the attention of Stipe, who helped with production on 1989's *Little* and 1991's *West of Rome*, both on Texas Hotel Records. Chesnutt's third album, *Drunk*, followed in late 1993, but the release of his fourth album was delayed by Chesnutt's membership in Brute, a project with members of Widespread Panic, including David A. Schools, Michael Houser, Todd Nance, John Hermann, Johnny Hickman, David Lowery, and John Keane. After *Sweet Relief Two* was released in July 1996, Capitol signed Chesnutt and released *About to Choke*, his major-label debut, in the fall of that year. A documentary video of Chesnutt's life called *Speed Racer* was produced and directed by Peter Sillen, and has aired on PBS. —*John Bush*

● **Drunk** / Jan. 17, 1994 / Caroline ✦✦✦✦

West of Rome / Feb. 9, 1994 / Texas Hotel ✦✦✦

Little / Jul. 15, 1994 / Texas Hotel ✦✦

Is the Actor Happy / May 23, 1995 / Caroline ✦✦✦

About to Choke / Nov. 12, 1996 / Capitol ✦✦✦✦
About to Choke appeared only a few months after the Vic Chestnutt tribute album *Sweet Relief II*, which meant that it received more attention in the media than most of his other records. However, it's likely that it would have been put into the spotlight anyway, since it is another exceptional set of songs, delivered with the gritty vulnerability that makes his music so affecting. Chesnutt's music is a little more textured and full-bodied on *About to Choke* than his previous albums, but that adds depth and maturity to his music, which also means it's one of his most accessible efforts. —*Thom Owens*

The Chi-Lites

f. 1960, Chicago, IL, db. 1983
Soul
One of the most popular smooth soul groups of the early '70s didn't hail from Philadelphia or Memphis, the two cities known for sweet, string-laden soul. Instead, the Chi-Lites were from Chicago, a town better-known for its gritty urban blues and driving R&B. Led by vocalist Eugene Record, the Chi-Lites had a lush, creamy sound distinguished by their four-part harmonies and layered productions. During the early '70s, they racked up 11 Top Ten R&B singles, ranging from the romantic ballads "Have You Sween Her" and "Oh Girl" to protest songs like "(For God's Sake) Give More Power to the People" and "There Will Never Be Any Peace (Until God Is Seated at the Conference Table)." All the songs featured Record's warm, pleading tenor and falsetto, and the majority of the group's hits were written by Record, often in collaboration with other songwriters, including his wife, Barbara Acklin.
    The Chi-Lites had been around for nearly a decade before they finally had a hit in the late '60s. Eugene Record, Robert Lester, and Clarence Johnson formed the doo wop group the Chanteurs in the late '50s, and they released one single on Renee Records in 1959. Shortly afterward Creadel "Red" Jones and Marshall Thompson, who had sung with the Desideros, teamed with the trio to form the Hi-Lites. Over the next four years, the Hi-Lites released a number of singles on local labels. In 1964 they changed their name to Marshall & the Chi-Lites, adding the "C" as tribute to their hometown Chicago. By the end of the year, Johnson left the group, and the remaining quartet truncated their name to the Chi-

Lites. Over the next four years, the group continued to perform and release independent singles, with Record slowly emerging as the group's lead singer, songwriter, and producer.

In 1968 the Chi-Lites signed with the large Chicago indie label Brunswick Records, and early the next year "Give It Away" became their first national hit single, reaching No. 10 on the R&B charts. Despite the moderate success of "Let Me Be the Man My Daddy Was," the group wasn't able to deliver another big hit until "Are You My Woman? (Tell Me So)" climbed into the R&B Top Ten in early 1971, beginning a string of ten Top 10 hits that ran intermittently over the next four years. The followup to "Are You My Woman?," "(For God's Sake) Give More Power to the People," was their first pop hit, setting the stage for a pair of slow, soulful ballads, "Have You Seen Her" and "Oh Girl," which both reached No. 1 on the R&B charts; the latter was a No. 1 pop hit as well, in the spring of 1972.

Shortly after the release of the hit "Stoned Out of My Mind," the Chi-Lites began to splinter in 1973, when Jones left the group and was replaced by Stanley Anderson, who was quickly replaced by Willie Kensey. The revamped lineup had three Top Ten R&B hits—"Homely Girl," "There Will Never Be Any Peace (Until God Is Seated at the Conference Table)," and "Toby"—before they replaced Kensey with Doc Roberson. Shortly afterward, Brunswick became involved in serious financial problems, which prevented the label from promoting the group's record. Frustrated, Record left the band to become a solo recording artist for Warner Bros. The remaining trio, augmented by David Scott and Danny Johnson (who was replaced by Vandy Hampton in 1977), signed with Mercury, but none of their singles was a hit.

The original lineup of the Chi-Lites re-formed in 1980, and the group began recording for Eugene Record's label, Chi-Sound. Although their first singles were more successful than their Mercury Records, they didn't have a genuine hit until 1982, when "Hot on a Thing (Called Love)" reached No. 15. The next year they moved to Larc Records, where they had their final Top Ten hit with "Bottoms Up." Late that year Creadel Jones retired, and the group continued to tour as a trio throughout the remainder of the decade. Record left the group again in 1990 to record as a solo artist. He was replaced by Anthony Watson. By the early '90s, Jones had re-joined the group, and this version of the Chi-Lites became a regular on the oldies and soul circuit during the '90s. —*Stephen Thomas Erlewine*

★ **Greatest Hits** / 1992 / Rhino ♦♦♦♦♦
All of the Chi-Lites' best songs and biggest hits—including "Oh Girl," "(For God's Sake) Give More Power to the People," and "Stoned Out of My Mind"—are collected on the definitive single-disc retrospective *Greatest Hits*. —*Stephen Thomas Erlewine*

Greatest Hits, Vol. 2 / Oct. 15, 1996 / Rhino ♦♦♦
Greatest Hits, Vol. 2 picks up where Rhino's first volume of Chi-Lites' *Greatest Hits* left off, compiling all of the group's lesser-known R&B hit singles. The compilation contains recordings that the group made between 1968 and 1981 for the record labels Dakar, Brunswick, Mercury, and Chi-Sound. Though there are a few gems on the record—including "I Like Your Lovin' (Do You Like Mine)," "A Lonely Man," and "You Got to Be the One"—the material on *Greatest Hits, Vol. 2* by and large pales in comparison to the songs on the first collection. Still, fans of the group's smooth soul sound will find several cuts to treasure on this album. —*Stephen Thomas Erlewine*

Chic

f. 1977, New York, NY, **db.** 1985
Funk, Disco
Chic was the best and most influential disco band of the latter half of the '70s, earning hits with both their own records and the outside productions of co-leaders Nile Rodgers and Bernard Edwards. Beginning their career as the Big Apple Band, the group changed their name to Chic in 1977 after Walter Murphy & the Big Apple Band had a No. 1 hit with "A Fifth of Beethoven." Along with the change in name came a change in music, from fusion to disco. Edwards (bass), Rodgers (guitar), and Tony Thompson (drums) hired Norma Jean Wright and Alfa Anderson to sing, and they recorded a demo of "Dance Dance Dance." Atlantic picked it up in late 1977 after a series of rejections from other record labels; the single sold a million copies in one month, catapulting Chic into the forefront of the disco scene. After Wright left for a solo career, Luci Martin joined the band. Chic's biggest hits—"Le Freak" (No. 1), "I Want Your Love" (No. 7), and the "Good Times" (No. 1)—came in 1978-1979, and as disco started to fade, so did the group's popularity. Still, Chic's influence was apparent throughout the '80s; "Good Times" alone spawned Queen's hit "Another One Bites the Dust" (a complete rip-off), and Sugarhill Gang used the record as the foundation for "Rapper's Delight," arguably the first rap single. Nile Rodgers was one of the most successful producers of the early '80s, scoring hits with David Bowie's *Let's Dance*, Madonna's *Like a Virgin*, and Mick Jagger's solo debut, *She's the Boss*. Edwards' solo productions weren't as consistent as Rodgers', but

the Power Station's album (which featured Tony Thompson on drums) was a hit. Chic re-formed in 1992, but failed to recapture the fire of its glory days. —*Stephen Thomas Erlewine*

★ **Dance Dance Dance: Best of Chic** / Nov. 5, 1991 / Atlantic ♦♦♦♦♦
You think disco was nothing more than assembly-line funk and freeze-dried beats? Then step into the crisp grooves and walloping boogie on this stunning collection of Chic's '70s recordings. Such hits as "Good Times," "Dance Dance Dance," and "Le Freak" show the stylistic innovations of James Brown and Sly Stone as a blueprint for a new era of funk. Bernard Edwards' basslines are so provocative they seem to talk, while Nile Rodgers' skeletal guitar runs back to Steve Cropper's slashing style. Sure, the songs don't say much. Sure, the dance mixes collected here ramble on after about six minutes. But once you step into these grooves—grooves that influenced an entire generation of artists from David Byrne to Prince—you will realize that these were indeed good times. —*John Floyd*

The Best of Chic, Vol. 2 / Nov. 10, 1992 / Rhino ♦♦♦♦
Filling the gaps left by the first volume, *Best of Chic—Vol. 2* proves with its collection of album tracks and singles that Chic was not merely a great disco band, but was a great band, period. —*Stephen Thomas Erlewine*

Chicago (Chicago Transit Authority)

f. Feb. 15, 1967, Chicago, IL
Adult Contemporary, Soft Rock, Pop-Rock
Chicago is second only to the Beach Boys as the most successful American rock band of all time. The group formed officially on February 15, 1967, in the city from which it eventually would take its name. The band members intended to launch a rock group with a fully integrated horn section (a novel idea at the time), so the original lineup was a sextet consisting of Walter Parazaider (b. Mar. 14, 1945) on saxophone and woodwinds, Lee Loughnane (b. Oct. 21, 1946) on trumpet, Terry Kath (b. Jan. 31, 1946–d. Jan. 23, 1978) on guitar and vocals, Danny Seraphine (b. Aug. 28, 1948) on drums, James Pankow (b.Aug 20, 1947) on trombone, and Robert Lamm (b. Oct 13, 1944) on organ and vocals. Initially, the group did without a bass player. But in December 1967, bassist/vocalist Peter Cetera (b. Sep. 13, 1944) joined from rival band the Exceptions. Under the guidance of manager/producer James William Guercio, who initially named them Chicago Transit Authority (the name was shortened after the real C.T.A. objected), the group moved to Los Angeles and signed to Columbia Records, recording its debut album, *Chicago Transit Authority*, in January 1969. It sold over two million copies and spawned four chart singles, beginning a string of massive hits that lasted to the end of the decade, with each album cover sporting a variation on the Chicago logo and a sequential title with a roman numeral: *Chicago II*, *Chicago III*, etc. (Later, ordinary numbers were used.) Chicago's music was a mixture of styles, from hard rock to light pop, incorporating elements of jazz and classical, but after Cetera's "If You Leave Me Now" became a gold-selling No. 1 hit in 1976, the group became more identified with romantic ballads than anything else. Chicago went into decline after a split with Guercio in 1977 and the accidental death of Kath in 1978. But it rebounded in 1982 with "Hard to Say I'm Sorry" and the million-selling *Chicago 16*, and was able to sustain its renewed popularity despite Cetera's departure for a solo career in 1985. After several years of hits, Chicago's popularity began to decline in the early '90s, as the group retired to the oldies circuit. —*William Ruhlmann*

Chicago Transit Authority / Apr. 1969 / Chicago ♦♦♦♦
The first rock 'n' roll band to successfully integrate a horn section, Chicago Transit Authority (later Chicago), fresh from years on the Midwest bar circuit, demonstrated a wide versatility on its debut album. The band seemed capable of playing everything from lounge music to hard rock, and here it mixed ballad material with gritty funk and psychedelic guitar, often on the same song. This time capsule of the varying strands of popular music in the late '60s features the hits "Does Anybody Really Know What Time It Is?," "Beginnings," and "Questions 67 and 68." —*William Ruhlmann*

Chicago II / Jan. 1970 / Chicago ♦♦♦♦
With its second double album (now on one CD), Chicago became even more ambitious and even more successful, mounting the extended "Suite for a Girl in Buchannon," from which were excerpted the hit singles "Make Me Smile" and "Colour My World." Also featured is "25 or 6 to 4." —*William Ruhlmann*

Chicago III / Jan. 1971 / Chicago ♦♦
With this album, Chicago had released three double-record sets within two years, which glutted the market and drained the band members' creativity. The result was a fall-off in quality and in sales, although *Chicago III* did manage to stay on the charts over a year, selling a million copies. There were only two Top 40 hits, "Free" and "Lowdown," neither of which is among the group's best. —*William Ruhlmann*

At Carnegie Hall, Vols. 1-4 / Oct. 1971 / Chicago ✦
Carnegie Hall may be prestigious, but it has never been a good rock venue, and Chicago seems intimidated on this four-LP (three-CD) set, recreating material from its first three albums. Completists should note the inclusion of the anti-Nixon "A Song for Richard and His Friends," not previously available. — *William Ruhlmann*

Chicago V / Jul. 1972 / Chicago ✦✦✦
The group's avant-garde roots are explored on the set-opening "A Hit by Varese," while the album also includes the autobiographical "Alma Mater" and the hits "Saturday in the Park" and "Dialogue." — *William Ruhlmann*

Chicago VI / Jun. 1973 / Chicago ✦✦✦
Chicago demonstrates all its strength here, turning in one of its great ballads in "Just You 'n' Me" and one of its great rockers in "Feelin' Stronger Every Day." Elsewhere, the group takes on its negative reviews in "Critics' Choice" and acknowledges the impact of Los Angeles stardom on Midwestern kids in "Something in This City Changes People." — *William Ruhlmann*

Chicago VII / Mar. 1974 / Chicago ✦✦
Originally intended as a jazz-oriented record, Chicago's first double studio album since *Chicago III* (now on one CD) is an ambitious but ultimately uneven affair, buttressed by the hit singles "(I've Been) Searchin' So Long," "Call on Me," and "Wishing You Were Here." — *William Ruhlmann*

Live in Japan 1972 / 1975 / Chicago ✦✦✦
It's unfortunate that this album is available only in Japan, because it's a tremendous improvement over *Carnegie Hall*. But with a four-LP live set already in release, Columbia wasn't about to put out another one, and nobody has thought to release it domestically since. — *William Ruhlmann*

Chicago VIII / Mar. 1975 / Chicago ✦✦
Chicago keyboardist Robert Lamm had been the band's main songwriter to this point, and although he contributed four of the ten songs here, only his "Harry Truman" was memorable. The album's biggest hit was James Pankow's "Old Days," but little else stands out. — *William Ruhlmann*

● **Greatest Hits** / Nov. 1975 / Chicago ✦✦✦✦
The biggest hits of Chicago's first five years of recording, including "Just You 'n' Me," "Feelin' Stronger Every Day," "Wishing You Were Here," "Call on Me," and "(I've Been) Searchin' So Long." — *William Ruhlmann*

Chicago X / Jun. 1976 / Chicago ✦✦
It was here that Chicago began to turn toward "power" ballads, but only because it was scoring only modest hits with more eclectic material such as Robert Lamm's "Another Rainy Day in New York City" and John Pankow's "You Are on My Mind," while Peter Cetera's "If You Leave Me Now" topped the charts, went gold, and won Grammy Awards for arrangement and vocal performance. — *William Ruhlmann*

Chicago XI / Sep. 1977 / Chicago ✦✦
On its last album to be produced by James William Guercio and to feature guitarist Terry Kath, Chicago turns in another competent but unremarkable effort. Peter Cetera's "Baby, What a Big Surprise" is his follow-up to "If You Leave Me Now," Robert Lamm continues to wax political on "Policeman" and "Vote for Me," and "Take Me Back to Chicago" accurately expresses an exhausted band's sentiments at this point. — *William Ruhlmann*

Hot Streets / Sep. 1978 / Columbia ✦✦
Chicago had a new producer in Phil Ramone, a new guitarist in Donnie Dacus, a real album title, and their picture on the cover here, all of which seemed to spell a new beginning for the group. But despite two Top 15 hits with "Alive Again" and "No Tell Lover," this was Chicago's first album to miss the Top Ten; it did not mark the rejuvenation Chicago and its fans hoped it would. The album remains the black sheep in Chicago's catalog. When CDs came in, the group declined to have it issued in the new medium, so it went out of print. When Chicago acquired the rights to its Columbia Records albums in 1995 and reissued them on its own Chicago Records imprint, it again skipped *Hot Streets*, though it did leave a catalog number (12) available, in case it changed its mind. — *William Ruhlmann*

Chicago 13 / Aug. 1979 / Chicago ✦
Disaster strikes. Chicago tries to go disco with "Street Player"; new guitarist Donnie Dacus gets his own single with "Must Have Been Crazy" (it flopped); there are no big ballads. In fact, there's nothing more worth mentioning. — *William Ruhlmann*

Chicago XIV / Jul. 1980 / Chicago ✦
Peter Cetera's "Song for You" has charm, and Robert Lamm's "Manipulation" has a certain punk edge. At another time, on another album, either might have worked, if redone properly. The rest is dross, and the best you can say is that at least Chicago had touched bottom. — *William Ruhlmann*

Chicago's Greatest Hits, Vol. 2 / 1981 / Chicago ✦✦✦
This album chronicles Chicago's gradual transformation in the second half of the '70s into a group that produced big ballads, usually sung by Peter Cetera. And here they are, starting with "If You Leave Me Now" and continuing with "Baby, What a Big Surprise" and the nostalgic "Old Days." — *William Ruhlmann*

If You Leave Me Now / 1982 / Columbia ✦✦
This is how the music business works: You drop an act that was once successful and has hit the skids. Then the act has a comeback with another company. What do you do? Release a compilation of previously released tracks that are still available on various other albums. At least a few people will mistake it for new product and take it home. — *William Ruhlmann*

Chicago 16 / Jun. 1982 / Full Moon ✦✦
With its back to the wall, Chicago switched record labels, dropped Donnie Dacus in favor of Bill Champlin (of the Sons of Champlin), brought in producer David Foster as new Svengali, and went back to power ballads. And it all worked, at least commercially. "Hard to Say I'm Sorry" was the summer ballad of 1982, the album went Top Ten, and Chicago was back in business, albeit with far more limited musical goals than it had had at the beginning. — *William Ruhlmann*

Chicago 17 / May 1984 / Full Moon ✦✦
With sales of four million, this is the biggest-selling regular studio album Chicago has made. That's what happens when you really go for the ballads: "Stay the Night," "Hard Habit to Break," "You're the Inspiration," and "Along Comes a Woman" all fit into that category; all featured Peter Cetera, and all made the Top 40. Not surprisingly, Cetera decamped soon after. — *William Ruhlmann*

Chicago 18 / Sep. 1986 / Full Moon ✦✦
It is an article of faith in corporate lore that everyone is expendable, and Chicago Music, Inc., responded to the departure of Peter Cetera by hiring another blonde, bass-playing tenor with sex appeal in the person of Jason Scheff. Some people were fooled, especially by the power ballad "Will You Still Love Me?," but others weren't (the album stopped at gold), and longtime fans were dismayed at the re-recording of "25 or 6 To 4." — *William Ruhlmann*

Chicago 19 / Jun. 1988 / Full Moon ✦✦
This album contained four Top Ten hits—"I Don't Wanna Live Without Your Love," "Look Away" (which hit No. 1), "You're Not Alone," and "What Kind of Man Would I Be?,"—yet did not reach the Top Ten on the album list, definite proof that Chicago was reaching an easy-listening (or "Adult Contemporary") radio audience but missing the rock audience. It paid the bills, though. — *William Ruhlmann*

● **Greatest Hits: 1982-1989** / Nov. 1989 / Full Moon ✦✦✦
Chicago returned from a career dip in 1982 with "Hard to Say I'm Sorry" and continued to hit with power ballads, among them "Hard Habit to Break" and "You're the Inspiration," all sung by Peter Cetera. But the streak continued after Cetera departed in 1985, as Jason Scheff stepped in and Chicago went on to score hits like "Will You Still Love Me?," "I Don't Wanna Live Without Your Love," and "Look Away," which are all heard here. — *William Ruhlmann*

Group Portrait / 1991 / Columbia ✦✦✦✦
If the two *Greatest Hits* collections don't look like adequate places to go, but you want to have some Chicago in your collection, then *Group Portrait* is an extremely comprehensive box set that chronicles all the hits and important album tracks. You'll probably never find a more complete history on the band than that provided in the set's booklet. — *Rick Clark*

Twenty 1 / Jan. 1991 / Full Moon ✦✦
The '90s found Chicago's lineup minus drummer Danny Seraphine, but with guitarist DeWayne Bailey, who had been a sideman, a full-fledged member. It also found the group at the closest thing to a career crisis in a decade. This album sold poorly and spun off only one Top 40 hit, "Chasin' the Wind," despite containing some typical, if not outstanding, material in tunes like "You Come to My Senses" (which belatedly scaled the AC chart) and "Explain It to My Heart." Clearly, a new approach was in order. — *William Ruhlmann*

Night & Day: Big-Band / May 23, 1995 / Giant ✦✦
Generally, when contemporary performers have taken on retro projects like this one, they have tended to emphasize their fidelity to the sources—consider Linda Ronstadt hiring arranger/conductor Nelson Riddle to recreate his string backgrounds for albums like *What's New*. Chicago takes a different approach to the swing band classics it tackles here—it Chicago-izes them. The arrangements are by trombonist James Pankow, who manages to make everything from Duke Ellington's "Caravan" to Glenn Miller's theme "Moonlight Serenade" sound like a lost Chicago track. Those familiar with the originals, many of which were instrumental hits, may be surprised to hear the lyrics to songs like "Sing, Sing, Sing." Clearly, the group is aiming more at pleasing contemporary fans than evoking nostalgia, and it succeeds in re-inventing some well-

established standards, even if older fans may find some of these versions radically altered. *— William Ruhlmann*

Heart of Chicago 1967-97 / Apr. 22, 1997 / Warner Brothers ✦✦✦
Heart of Chicago 1967-97 is a cheap way to celebrate Chicago's 30th anniversary. Featuring 13 arbitrarily picked hits from throughout the band's career—from "Saturday in the Park" and "Does Anybody Really Know What Time It Is" to "If You Leave Me Now," "You're the Inspiration," "Hard to Say I'm Sorry," and "Look Away"—it adds two new tracks, the Lenny Kravitz-produced "The Only One" and "Here in My Heart," which was co-written by Glen Ballard and James Newton Howard. Although Chicago has enlisted heavy hitters for the new tracks, both fall flat. And as a thorough hits collection, *Heart of Chicago 1967-97* is unsuccessful as well, since it omits such hits as "25 or 6 to 4" and "Baby, What a Big Surprise," but it works well as a sampler for casual fans, since it has only the biggest hits. *— Stephen Thomas Erlewine*

The Chiffons

f. 1960, Bronx, NY
Girl-Group, Brill Building Pop
One of the best early-'60s New York girl groups, combining sassiness and innocence on several of the style's greatest classics. The Chiffons had some singles under their belt when they reached No. 1 with "He's So Fine," whose classic "doo-lang, doo-lang" riff was appropriated by George Harrison in 1970 for his own chart-topper, "My Sweet Lord." (Harrison was subsequently ordered to pay substantial damages to the original publishers, though he always claimed the resemblance was unintentional.) Their follow-up, Goffin-King's "One Fine Day," was just as good, featuring killer piano riffs from King herself. Actually cut as a Little Eva track, the Chiffons' vocal was substituted, resulting in a Top Five hit. There were a couple other memorable hits ("I Have a Boyfriend" and the Motown-influenced "Sweet Talkin' Guy") and interesting misfires like the Martha & the Vandellas-inspired "The Real Thing," as well as some singles issued as the Four Pennies. The group recorded quite a bit of material during the '60s, much of it derivative; the hits are their best tracks by far. *— Richie Unterberger*

● **Greatest Recordings** / 1990 / Ace ✦✦✦✦
A generous collection that features not only their greatest hits, but many forgotten songs that are surprisingly good. *— Stephen Thomas Erlewine*

Billy Childish

b. 1958, Chatham, England
Guitar, Vocals / Alternative Pop-Rock, Indie Rock
Few performers in rock history have been as ferociously prolific as Billy Childish. In fact, a complete discography of his work as a solo performer and with his various bands would take up quite a few pages. A singer, songwriter, artist, poet, critic, fanzine editor, and guitarist who suffers from severe dyslexia, he's a punk-inspired Renaissance man. However, you may have never heard of him or of any of the more than 50 recordings he's made either solo or with one of his many bands (Pop Rivets, the Milkshakes, Thee Mighty Caesars, the Delmonas, Thee Headcoats, and the Natural Born Lovers), *or* have read any of his more than 40 books of poetry and assorted scribblings. Childish has been recording since 1979, playing a rough-and-tumble, punk-inspired approximation of what is normally called garage rock. Not one for elaborate production techniques, the consistent element of Childish's music is that all of it sounds as though it was recorded and mixed in about an hour. He values immediacy and intensity and frequently seems itching to move on to the next song, or, more specifically, the next band. A truly primitive talent (due to his learning disability, he has had little formal education) who, a la Jad and David Fair of Half Japanese, eschews technical ability for pure emotion, Childish occupies an artistic role somewhere between mad genius and bratty goofball. Unfailingly sure of himself and his vision, his music is as honest and emotionally direct as one is likely to hear. Unfortunately, he also lacks the discipline of self-editing, and as a result, some of his lesser work rambles incoherently or simply sounds so similar as to be uninteresting. Fifteen years after his first single, "Fun in the UK" (a tongue-in-cheek send-up of the Sex Pistols' "Anarchy in the UK"), Childish is still producing material at an amazing rate, epitomizing the endurance and drive of an artist who in many ways is the archetypal rock outsider. *— John Dougan*

● **I Am the Billy Childish** / 1991 / Sub Pop ✦✦✦✦
There is simply too much Billy Childish music available (good, bad and indifferent) to examine here in great detail. Fortunately, America's super-hip indie label Sub Pop released this superb Two-CD anthology that gets to the heart of Childish's aesthetic, offering an extremely strong selection of material that covers a nearly 14-year period. Subtitled *50 songs from 50 Records,* you will get a taste of nearly all of Childish's bands and hear "Fun in the UK," which he recorded with his short-lived Pop Rivets. Fans of idiosyncratic singer-songwriters like Kevin Coyne and Jonathan Richman may find themselves immediately enamored of

Childish's defiantly different approach to rock 'n' roll. If that's the case, the liner information in this set provides a solid discographical overview of Childish's work from the late '70s up to the early '90s. Buyer alert: this set was originally limited to 1,500 copies; it's a mystery as to how many are still for sale. *—John Dougan*

Chilli Willi & the Red Hot Peppers

f. 1971, London, England, **db**. Feb. 1975
Rock 'n' Roll, Pub Rock
Chilli Willi and the Red Hot Peppers were one of the main British pub rock groups of the early '70s, playing a laid-back, yet rocking, mixture of rock 'n' roll, R&B, country, and folk. The band had its origins in a folk-rock duo formed by ex-Junior's Blues Band members Martin Stone (vocals, guitar, mandolin) and Phil "Snakefinger" Lithman (vocals, guitar, piano, lap steel, fiddle). Lithman moved to San Francisco in the late '60s, leaving Stone to play with Savoy Brown and Mighty Baby. The duo reunited in the early '70s, recording *Kings of Robot Rhythm* with vocalist Jo-Ann Kelly and various members of Brinsley Schwarz. *Kings* was released in 1972; that same year, the duo expanded to a band, adding Paul "Dice Man" Bailey (guitar, banjo, saxophone), Paul Riley (bass), and drummer Pete Thomas. During the next two years, Chilli Willi and the Red Hot Peppers became a popular live act in Britain. The full band released *Bongos over Balham* in 1974, but the record sold poorly and the band split in February 1975. Thomas became the drummer for Elvis Costello's backing band, the Attractions; Riley played with Graham Parker; Bailey formed Bontemps Roulez; and Stone played with the Pink Fairies before quitting the music business. Lithman moved back to San Francisco, where he began to work with his former associates, the Residents, under the name Snakefinger. *— Stephen Thomas Erlewine*

● **Kings of the Robot Rhythm** / 1972 / Revelations ✦✦✦✦
Bongos over Balham / 1974 / Mooncrest ✦✦✦

The Chills

f. Oct. 1980, Dunedin, New Zealand
Alternative Pop-Rock
The Chills were one of New Zealand's best and most popular bands of the '80s, making a small but consistent series of chiming, hook-laden guitar pop. Both the songs and the arrangements were constructed with interweaving guitar hooks and vocal harmonies, creating a pretty, almost lush, sound that never falls into cloying sentimentality. Throughout their existence, the band's personnel changed frequently—there were more than ten different lineups—with the only constant member being guitarist Martin Phillips, the band's founder.

Phillips began playing with the New Zealand punk band the Same in 1978. Following in the footsteps of the Clean and the Enemy, the Same played mostly covers, creating a raw fusion of British Invasion and garage rock. However, the group never recorded. Phillips applied the same approach for the Chills, the band he formed in 1980 with his sister Rachel and Jane Dodd (bass) after the Same fell apart.

In 1982 the Chills signed with Flying Nun, the influential New Zealand independent record label, and released several singles that never were widely distributed in America and Europe. During this time, the group went through an enormous number of members. Future Great Unwashed member Peter Gutteridge was a member, as was the Clean's David Kilgour, keyboardist Faser Batts, bassist Terry Moore, guitarist Martin Kean, keyboardist Peter Allison, drummer Martyn Bull, and drummer Alan Haig. While these incarnations of the Chills recorded plenty of singles, they never made an album. Released on the UK record label Creation, the group's first album, *Kaleidoscope World* (1986), was a collection of their early singles; it was later released in the US on Homestead.

With the lineup of Phillips, bassist Justin Harwood, keyboardist Andrew Todd, and drummer Caroline Easther—the group's tenth lineup—the Chills recorded their first proper album, *Brave Worlds,* in 1987. Produced by Mayo Thompson, the leading figure of the cult band the Red Crayola and a former member of Pere Ubu, the record did not satisfy the band, which claimed it was too loose and underproduced. The group, particularly Phillips, was more satisfied with their second full-length album, 1990's *Submarine Bells,* their first record released on an American major label. *Submarine Bells* was recorded with yet another version of the band, with Jimmy Stephenson replacing Easther, who was suffering from tinnitus. The album was well received by critics and college radio, but it failed to break the band into the mainstream in either America or Britain. Two years later they released *Soft Bomb,* which suffered the same fate as *Submarine Bells.* The next year Martin Phillips broke up the Chills again, but the group reconvened in 1996 to release *Sunburnt. — Stephen Thomas Erlewine*

Brave Worlds / 1987 / Homestead ✦✦✦
The band's first proper album (years after making their recording debut) was something of a disappointment, both in terms of production and

material. The sound is too blurry and homogenous, and the songs aren't distinctive enough to surmount that obstacle, although they strive to attain the group's typically foggy, vaguely psychedelic atmosphere. —*Richie Unterberger*

● **Kaleidoscope World** / 1989 / Homestead ✦✦✦✦
Kaleidoscope World is the Chills' essential document, although it's not an album, but a collection of tracks from early and mid-'80s EPs, singles, and compilation cuts. Perhaps that's not surprising: the Chills are more skilled at crafting interesting odds and sods than sustaining interest over the course of an album, where their somewhat monochrome approach tends to drag things down. The influence of Syd Barrett/early Pink Floyd is stronger on these early tracks than it would be on subsequent releases, both on the easygoing singalong numbers and the more experimental outings. The highlight (of both the album and the Chills' career) is their New Zealand hit single, the haunting "Pink Frost." —*Richie Unterberger*

Submarine Bells / Feb. 1990 / Slash ✦✦✦✦
For *Submarine Bells*, the Chills achieved a far more satisfactory balance between oddball pop and modern studio technology than they had on *Brave Words*. While the ambition still outstrips the actual results, Martin Phillipps refines his melodic gifts in more baroque and harmonic directions, at times showing the influence of the Beach Boys' more sophisticated recordings. —*Richie Unterberger*

Soft Bomb / Jun. 30, 1992 / Slash ✦✦✦
New Zealand's the Chills turn in their hard-as-diamond pop style for something a little more whimsical and relaxed on *Soft Bomb*. The group is as efficient and generous as usual, however, delivering a filling 17 slices of jangly guitar confectionary. —*Roch Parisien*

Heavenly Pop Hits / 1995 / Flying Nun ✦✦✦✦
This Australian-only collection gives a 16-track summary of the band from the beginning to 1992's *Soft Bomb*. There is some predictable overlap with *Kaleidoscope World*, the still-essential early years collection, but *Heavenly Pop Hits* is more comprehensive, adding the more polished but just as pleasing singles from the later uneven albums. [Initially, *Heavenly Pop Hits* was packaged with a 6-track rarities disc.] —*Chris Woodstra*

Sunburnt / Oct. 8, 1996 / Flying Nun ✦✦✦

Alex Chilton

b. Dec. 28, 1950, Memphis, TN
Guitar, Vocals / Rock 'n' Roll
In a business that reinvents itself at every turn, Alex Chilton has managed to survive for three decades with a three-fold career as well—his early recordings with the Box Tops, the three albums he did with Big Star in the mid-'70s, and the spate of cool, but chaotic, solo albums he's recorded since then. To some he's a classic hit-maker from the '60s. To others he's a genius British-style pop musician and songwriter. To yet another audience, he's a doomed and despairing artist who spent several years battling the bottle, delivering anarchistic records and performances while thumbing his nose at all pretenses of stardom, a quirky iconoclast whose influence has spawned the likes of the Replacements and Teenage Fanclub.

Even though he grew up in and around Memphis, there isn't anything remotely Southern about Alex Chilton. Chilton is fully aware of his surroundings and in tune spiritually with its most lunatic fringe aspects, but his South has more to do with genteel Southern intellectualism than rednecks.

Chilton started playing music in local Memphis high school combos, alternating between bass and rhythm guitar with a stray vocal thrown in, finally working himself up to professional status with a group called the DeVilles. After acquiring a manager with recording connections tied to Memphis hitmakers Chips Moman and Dan Penn, Alex and the group—newly renamed Box Tops—recorded "The Letter," a record that sounded white enough to go No. 1 on the pop charts and yet Black enough to track on R&B stations, too. Chilton was still in his teens, but armed with a strong conception of how pop and R&B vocals should be handled. With the hand of vocal coach Dan Penn firmly in place, the hits kept coming, with "Cry like a Baby," "Soul Deep," and "Sweet Cream Ladies" all showing visible chart action. The Box Tops were stars by AM radio singles standards, but tours opened Chilton's eyes to the world and what it had to offer. And what that world seemed to offer to Alex was a lot more artistic freedom than he had as nominal leader of the Box Tops.

After a few errant solo sessions, Chilton found himself in Big Star with singer/guitarist Chris Bell. Their blend of ethereal harmonies, quirky lyrics, and Beatlesque song structure appeared to be radio-friendly, but distribution for their label, Ardent Records, spelled disaster. With Bell gone and the label hanging on by a thread, Chilton went into the studio with producer Jim Dickinson and attempted to put together the third Big Star album. These sessions, now known as *Sister Lovers*, are legendary in some quarters. So much has been read into this record-

ing, primarily the myth that Chilton became a pop artist who, in the face of critical success but commercial apathy, suddenly rebelled against the system and became a "doomed artist on a collision course to Hell." Chilton himself dismisses all such romantic notions: "I think that to say that it's a fairly druggy sort of album that is the work of a confused person trying to find himself or find his creative direction is a fair statement about the thing."

Around 1976 Chilton started producing a wild cross-section of solo outings for various foreign and American independent labels, all featuring his love for obscure material, barbed-wire guitar playing, howling feedback, and bands who sounded barely familiar with the material. Plugging into the bohemian punk rock scene of New York City, Chilton's anarchic approach and attitude fit the scene like a glove. In addition to his gigging and performing schedule, Alex produced the debut session by the Cramps, helping to land their deal with I.R.S. Records. Chilton was getting legendary enough to end up having a song by the Replacements named after him. Through the late '80s into the early '90s, Alex split his time between recording, gigging overseas plugging his latest release, and playing oldies shows in the US, reprising his old Box Tops hits. In the early '90s Chilton—relocated to New Orleans, his demons behind him—began releasing a series of excellent solo albums on the newly revived Ardent label and even participated in a couple of Big Star "reunions." —*Cub Koda*

Bach's Bottom / 1975 / Razor & Tie ✦✦✦
Recorded during one of Chilton's more chaotic periods, *Bach's Bottom* is an interesting document of misguided talent. It's not so much the music as it is the sense of what is going on around the music that makes this 1975 outing fascinating. Chilton's dismemberment of "Free Again," "Take Me Home and Make Me Like It," the Beatles' "I'm So Tired," and "Jesus Christ" are pretty funny, while his great self-productions of "Bangkok" and the Seeds' "Can't Seem to Make You Mine" reveal his penchant for making something special happen at times when everything seems to be falling apart. —*AMG*

Like Flies on Sherbert / 1979 / Cooking Vinyl ✦
On the strength of his Big Star releases from the early 1970s and a host of live performances he gave during the latter half of the 1970s, Alex Chilton had rightly become a rock connoisseur's darling and an inspiration to independent-label bands throughout the United States. Despite all this favorable attention, he would not return to the studio until 1980. Sadly, this release is a dreadful disappointment. Production values are among the worst this reviewer has ever heard: sound quality is terrible, instrumental balances are careless and haphazard, and some selections even begin with recording start-up sound. Chilton's false-start vocal on "Boogie Shoes" is simply left in without correction. Many of the songs here stop dead or fall apart rather than ending properly. Instrumental playing is universally slipshod and boorish, and vocals are sloppy and lackluster. A cover of the Lonnie Mack hit "I've Had It" contains vocals that, without exaggeration, sound like a group of tavern inebriates trying to sing. An attempt to burlesque Elvis Presley's vocal excesses in "Girl after Girl" misfires badly. A few of Chilton's songs here, such as "My Rival" and "Hook or Crook," aren't bad in their own right and would have been listenable had they been performed and produced better. Regrettably, this album cannot be recomended under any circumstances. —*David Cleary*

Feudalist Tarts / 1985 / Big Time ✦✦✦
Alex Chilton disappeared from view after the debacle of *Like Flies on Sherbert*. This comeback EP, released after a five-year album silence, is a fine and rootsy delight worthy of its artist's reputation. Many of the songs on this platter contain prominent brass and saxophone backing textures; the horn section gets a chance to shine in its own right on the jazzy shuffle number "Stuff" and takes full advantage of it. "Lost My Job" is a raw blues selection featuring enjoyable Dylanesque harmonica touches. "Paradise" is an appealing, forthright 1950s-style crooning number. There are three successful covers here as well, including a a smooth version of the Carla Thomas hit "B-A-B-Y" and a solidly funky rendition of Slim Harpo's blues selection "Tee Ni Nee Ni Noo." The latter affords Chilton some excellent solo opportunities for harmonica and guitar, all of which are executed in attractively gritty fashion; at the end of this number, there is an especially nice interplay section between the trumpet, saxophone, and harmonica. Chilton's singing is reserved at times, but always eloquent. Production and sound quality are fine here. This release is well worth hearing. —*David Cleary*

No Sex / 1986 / Big Time ✦✦✦✦
This brief EP keeps Alex Chilton's winning streak alive and well. The title track is a chunky, no-nonsense rocker with half-serious, half-waggish doomsaying lyrics about the AIDS epidemic. "Underclass" is a rambunctious blues song with ironic lyrics about being a "have not." Mid-tempo funk is explored on "Wild Kingdom"; the selection provides excellent solo chances for guitarist Chilton and saxophonist Jim Spake, both of whom prove equal to the opportunity presented. Slightly dis-

torted sound quality tarnishes this last song a bit. This release is excellent and well worth a listen. —*David Cleary*

Black List / 1990 / New Rose ✦✦
This attempts to successfully mine the retro-music lodestone found in *High Priest*, *Feudalist Tarts*, and similar releases of this period. Half the songs here are blues numbers of differing stripes: "Jailbait" is an irresistibly rocking song featuring prominent organ and baritone saxophone that has humorous, worldly lyrics in praise of the speaker's underaged sweetie; "Baby Baby Baby" is a fine down-and-dirty slow-tempo selection with rudimentary verses; Furry Lewis' "I Will Turn Your Money Green" is an enjoyably lazy, loping number. Other styles are showcased as well. The Chilton original "Guantanamerika" is a smooth, almost jazz-lounge-oriented ditty with ironic lyrics. A cover of "Nice and Easy Does It" reveals a fine song given as a sophisticated crooner's tune. There's also a bouncy, faithful cover of the 1960s surf-style car classic "Little GTO," on which Chilton plays all the instruments and sings all the vocals. Sound quality is top-notch. Performances are first-rate, with as always excellent solo work from guitarist Chilton and saxophonist Jim Spake; Chilton's singing is a bit strained on the high notes on "Little GTO," but is otherwise fine. This excellent release is strongly recommended. —*David Cleary*

● **19 Years: A Collection** / Feb. 1991 / Rhino ✦✦✦✦
While it draws heavily on Big Star's disturbing third album (five tracks), *19 Years* offers a surprisingly coherent and listenable overview of Chilton's wildly inconsistent solo career, collecting some of the finest songs he has written since Big Star, as well as several exuberant covers ("Can't Seem to Make You Mine," "With a Girl like You," and "Volare"). —*AMG*

Cliches / Feb. 11, 1994 / Ardent ✦✦✦
With just an acoustic guitar and voice, Alex Chilton delivers a low-key not-too-perfectly-performed collection of standards, like "All of You," "Save Your Love for Me," "Let's Get Lost," and even Mel Torme's "The Christmas Song." It's Chilton's subtlest work yet, and one of his best albums. —*Rick Clark*

Feudalist Tarts/No Sex / May 1, 1994 / Razor & Tie ✦✦✦✦
By the mid-'80s, Chilton had located to New Orleans and recorded *Feudalist Tarts*, his first album in six years. Unlike its predecessor, *Like Flies on Sherbert*, *Feudalist Tarts* marked a return to a more ordered sound that reflected Chilton's love for R&B and blues. Among the highlights are versions of Slim Harpo's "Tee Ni Nee Ni Noo," Carla Thomas' "B-A-B-Y," and his own "Lost My Job." *Feudalist Tarts* was followed by the *No Sex* EP, which is included on this disc. "Underclass" and the title track are among Chilton's finer compositions—rich in rude rootsy sounds and sarcastic deadpan humor. —*Rick Clark*

High Priest/Black List / May 1, 1994 / Razor & Tie ✦✦✦
High Priest displays a more playful Chilton with versions of Dean Martin's "Volare," Bill Black's "Raunchy," and Charlie Rich's Sun classic "Lonely Weekends." His originals "Dalai Lama" and "Thing for You" are equally fine. *Black List*, which followed *High Priest*, opens with a great send-up of the hot rod anthem "Little GTO" and Walter Lewis' bluesy "I Will Turn Your Money Green" is the high point. Chilton plays all the instruments on both of those cuts. "Magnetic Field" and "Jailbait" are solid originals. —*Rick Clark*

A Man Called Destruction / Sep. 12, 1995 / Ardent ✦✦
Since the mid-'80s, all Alex Chilton albums are basically interchangeable. Chilton and his bar band get together, knock off a handful of mediocre new songs and several (mostly obscure) R&B and rock 'n' roll oldies. Now that Chilton is more or less sober, his pitch is a bit better, yet there isn't anything particularly special about *A Man Called Destruction*, other than the delightfully corny "What's Your Sign?" where Alex sings the horoscope in an attempt to pick up a girl. It's the best thing here and he didn't write it. —*Stephen Thomas Erlewine*

1970 / Apr. 1996 / Ardent ✦✦✦
1970 comprises the sessions that would have formed Alex Chilton's first solo album. As the title suggests, Chilton recorded these songs after he left the Box Tops but right before he joined Big Star—appropriately, the music sounds caught between the Box Tops' blue-eyed soul and Big Star's jangly power-pop. In that respect, it has more in common with his numerous solo recordings than either of his bands. And like his solo records, *1970* is wildly uneven and lacks focus. It careens between charming tributes to R&B and pop (a medley of the Archies' "Sugar, Sugar" and James Brown's "There Was a Time"), and his originals, which only hint at the heights he would reach with Big Star. If *1970* does anything, it illustrates that Chilton needs a strong collaborative force like Chris Bell to bring out the best in his music. —*Stephen Thomas Erlewine*

The Chocolate Watchband

f. 1965, Los Altos, California, **db.** 1968
Psychedelic, Garage Rock
The Chocolate Watchband never charted a record nationally. Indeed, ask

most casual 1960s rock fans about them and you'll probably get little more than a blank stare. Most will probably remember their AVI Records labelmates the Standells more clearly, because they actually managed to chart a few singles. Alas, the Watchband had the disadvantage of being a punkier band than the Standells, and also being essentially two bands as a recording unit.

The group had its start in Los Altos, CA, in 1965, where guitarist Mark Loomis joined Ned Torney (guitar) in a fledgling band that later included Danny Phay (vocals), Rich Young (bass), Jo Kemling (organ), and Gary Andrijasevich (drums). This early incarnation of the Watchband found great, albeit short-lived, popularity on the local band scene, but never recorded. Phay, Torney, and Kemling were later inducted into a rival band, the Otherside, which was formed out of a band called the Topsiders; Young was drafted into the US Army. Loomis recruited Andrijasevich, Topsider guitarist Sean Tolby, bassist Bill Flores, and vocalist David Aguilar; this unit, also named the Chocolate Watchband, made its debut in San Francisco and the surrounding area in the spring of 1966.

The quintet was a mod-outfitted garage punk unit par excellence, their sound founded on English-style R&B with a special fixation on the Rolling Stones at their most sneering. They eventually got a recording/management contract with Ed Cobb, a former member of the 1950s vocal ensemble the Four Preps. The group's first single was a cover of Davie Allan's "Blues Theme"; the single was a great showcase for the band, except for the fact that it was released under the alias of "The Hogs." The band's first album, *No Way Out*, featured much tampering by the producers. By the time the record came out in June 1967, the group had already begun breaking up. A new incarnation of the Watchband was born in the guise of Flores and Tolby, with Tim Abbott on lead guitar, Mark Whittaker on drums, and Chris Finders on lead vocals. This lineup lasted only through the end of 1967, when Abbott and Flinders exited. Tolby moved over to lead guitar, and Aguilar returned for a few shows; but essentially the Watchband's existence as a viable performing unit was over.

The group's producers had other ideas, however. Another album, *The Inner Mystique*, was released in February 1968, sporting the band's name but not too much else associated with the group. Cobb would have one more go at keeping the Watchband alive with *One Step Beyond*. By the time the record was made in the summer of 1968, all of the band had moved on to other projects, but Flores was persuaded to rejoin Tolby, Andrijasevich, Loomis (later replaced by Phil Scoma), and Phay for one more chance in the studio.

That would probably have been the end of the group's story, but in the early '80s, a curious thing happened—record buyers and, more particularly, young musicians in America and Europe, discovered the Watchband. Their albums had always been collectors' items, but now the prices began escalating; a set of Australian reissues of the group's albums quickly found a market in America and Europe. More people heard the Chocolate Watchband's music and saw their movie appearances in the 1980s than in the 1960s. Thus, it was no surprise when, in 1994, Sundazed Records reissued the complete Watchband catalog on compact disc. —*Bruce Eder*

No Way Out / 1967 / Sundazed ✦✦✦
Possibly the best garage-punk album ever to make it out the door from a major label in the '60s, despite the presence of some non-Watchband tracks. "Are You Gonna Be There (At the Love-In)" is worth the price of admission, and "Let's Talk About Girls" makes an unforgettable opening track. Reissued on Sundazed for CD, and worth owning in that form, as an original on vinyl might set you back $100 or more. —*Bruce Eder*

The Inner Mystique / 1968 / Sundazed ✦✦✦
The group's second album, like its first, features too many tracks that really aren't the Watchband, but this time some of it even works. Side One of the original long-player consisted mostly of a bunch of psychedelic studio noodling courtesy of musicians hired by the producer, but even among these, "In the Past" is a bejeweled psychedelic treasure that ought to be in any collection. The rest is pure garage-punk, raw and undiluted, including savage covers of the Kinks' "I'm Not Like Everybody Else" and Bob Dylan's "It's All Over Now, Baby Blue," and "Medication," rendered here in a version superior in its lustful decadence to the original by their labelmates the Standells. Reissued in unbelievably good sound, with bonus tracks, on Sundazed Records in the '90s. —*Bruce Eder*

One Step Beyond / 1969 / Sundazed ✦✦✦
A last-gasp effort at milking some money out of the band's name is a fairly weak album, seldom above fair-to-mediocre musically, except for lead singer David Aguilar's "Don't Need Your Lovin'," rounded out by some killer bonus tracks ("Sitting There Standing," etc.). The notes are a brilliant finish to the Watchband saga, tying up a pile of loose ends. —*Bruce Eder*

● **The Best of the Chocolate Watchband** / 1983 / Rhino ✦✦✦✦
The first CD-era collection of this hard-luck band's work was also the best compilation of the band's work, but it was a good idea done a little

too early. The sound is deficient compared with Rhino's usual standard, and the notes were later outdone by Sundazed Records' reissue of the band's complete catalog. It's still a good starter, however, if one can find it. —*Bruce Eder*

The Choir

f. 1965, Cleveland, OH
Power Pop, Garage Rock
Stars in their Cleveland hometown, unknown elsewhere (except for the minor national hit "It's Cold Outside"), the Choir played an accomplished, if a bit anachronistic, British Invasion-influenced pop-rock in the late '60s. The Mersey-mod hybrid "It's Cold Outside" went to No. 1 in Cleveland in 1967. The group was then picked up by Roulette, but a couple of subsequent singles were subject to inappropriate material and over-production, and stiffed. Obscure and unissued material by the Choir is beginning to appear on CD and reveals their branching out from power-pop to encompass progressive sounds as they changed personnel in the late '60s. Members of the group later played in the Raspberries, and the Choir is still fondly remembered in Cleveland for their strong and melodic original material. —*Richie Unterberger*

● **Choir Practice** / 1994 / Sundazed ✦✦✦✦
This 18-song CD is the first official compilation that covers their entire career, from 1966 to 1969. As the group cut only a few singles during their lifetime, most of this is previously unissued, culled from their generous vault of demos. Much anticipated by 1960s collectors, it's a bit of a disappointment, despite a fair number of highlights. The Americanized mod-Merseybeat of "It's Cold Outside" is delightful; other originals like "I'd Rather You Leave Me" and "Don't Change Your Mind" show similarly irresistible harmony vocals, crafting a catchy '60s pop-rock sound that avoids sappiness. The final tracks, cut in 1969 after several personnel changes, have slightly updated progressive rock influences, but retain a core of smart pop-rock hooks. Some of the demos, though, are a bit weak, particularly the soul-rockish ones from 1968. Most crucially, though, it fails to include a number of fine previously available tracks, like the version of the beautiful ballad "Treeberry" that was briefly available on a Bomp EP (the sketchy acoustic demo here pales by comparison), and several moody numbers from the 1969 lineup (also available for a time on a cassette-only reissue in the 1980s). The crunchy Stonesish B-side of "It's Cold Outside," "I'm Going Home," is also inexplicably missing. Perhaps this is because the compilers made every effort to include material from the original master tapes and couldn't locate the masters for those tracks. It's still not a bad compilation for '60s collectors, but it could have been better. —*Richie Unterberger*

Lou Christie (Lugee Alfredo Giovanni Sacco)

b. Feb. 19, 1943, Glen Willard, PA
Vocals / Pop-Rock, Bubblegum
Lou Christie's shrieking, falsetto-soaked vocals led to prolonged pop stardom through the '60s. Born Lugee Sacco, Christie began recording in 1960 in Pittsburgh. "The Gypsy Cried," cut in 1962, was released on the local C&C logo and leased to Roulette, where it proved to be Christie's first sizable hit. After encoring for Roulette the next year with "Two Faces Have I," Christie moved to MGM and scored a million-seller in 1966 with the ambitious chart-topper "Lightnin' Strikes." The daring "Rhapsody in the Rain" was another major hit the same year. Christie returned to the Top Ten for the last time in 1969, with "I'm Gonna Make You Mine," on the bubblegum-oriented Buddah label. He remains a dynamic attraction on the oldies circuit. —*Bill Dahl*

● **Enlightnin'ment: The Best of Lou Christie** / 1991 / Rhino ✦✦✦✦
This solid collection contains "Lightnin' Strikes," "Two Faces Have I," and others. —*Dan Heilman*

The Church

f. 1980, Sydney, Australia
Alternative Pop-Rock, Neo-Psychedelia
Best known for the shimmering "Under the Milky Way," their lone Top 40 hit, the Australian band the Church combined the jangling guitar-pop of '60s icons like the Byrds with the opaque wordplay of frontman Steve Kilbey to create a lush, melancholy brand of neo-psychedelia rich in texture and melody. Formed in Sydney in 1980 by vocalist/bassist Kilbey with guitarist Peter Koppes and drummer Nick Ward, the Church recruited second guitarist Marty Willson-Piper before debuting the next year with *Of Skin and Heart*, an evocative collection highlighted by the ringing "The Unguarded Moment," a major success down under.
After replacing Ward with drummer Richard Ploog, the group resurfaced in 1982 with *The Blurred Crusade*, a stunning effort featuring mature standouts like "Almost with You" and "When You Were Mine." In 1983 *Seance* continued to refine the Church's atmospheric sound, and

the subsequent success of the EPs *Persia* and *Remote Luxury* helped earn the band an American deal with Warner Bros., which issued the excellent *Heyday* in 1986. After moving to Arista, the Church teamed with famed session guitarists Danny Kortchmar and Waddy Wachtel to record 1988's *Starfish*, their most artistically and commercially successful effort to date. Highlighted by "Under the Milky Way," the album also featured the minor hits "Reptile" and "Spark," a marvelous pop blast penned by Willson-Piper.
The follow-up, 1988's *Gold Afternoon Fix*, failed to repeat the success of its predecessor, as the single "Metropolis" garnered only minor airplay. Ploog left the Church before the release of 1992's *Priest Aura*, which featured former Patti Smith Group drummer Jay Dee Daugherty. By 1994's *Sometime Anywhere*, only Kilbey and Willson-Piper remained, recording with the aid of a drum machine. When the album failed to crack the charts, Arista dropped the group. With new drummer Tim Powles, the Church issued 1996's *Magician Among the Spirits* on the tiny white label; a subsequent tour marked Koppes' return to the fold. —*Jason Ankeny*

Of Skin and Heart / 1981 / Arista ✦✦✦✦
On their debut, *Of Skin and Heart*, the Church play a straightforward pop-rock firmly rooted in new wave, though owing no small debt to '60s pop. Edgier and more direct than their later work, it ranks among their finest for that very reason. None of the excesses and ambitions that would sometimes get out of hand on later releases is present, though much of the band's basic formula was laid down—Steve Kilbey's cool, detached vocals and slightly surrealistic lyrics combined with some outstanding pop hooks, nice harmonies, and layers of ringing guitar. The classic "Unguarded Moment" (arguably one of the greatest singles of the '80s) overshadows much of the material on the album, but there is really no shortage of great songs here. [The album was originally released in the US as *The Church* with some tracks dropped in favor of three tracks from singles released around the same time. In 1988 Arista released *Of Skin and Heart* on CD in its original form with the added tracks from *The Church* tacked on to the end.] —*Chris Woodstra*

The Blurred Crusade / 1982 / Arista ✦✦✦
Of Skin and Heart was clearly a new wave album, but *Blurred Crusade* was very much akin to the emerging jangle-pop movement in the US, the band taking a cue from the Byrds. With shimmering 12-string work from Marty Willson-Piper, combined with Kilbey's obscure lyrics and otherworldly delivery, the band creates a dreamy soundscape that is quite evocative. While it seems that the lush sound and decidedly melancholy mood are the most important aspects of the album, they still manage some outstanding, catchy songs like "When You Were Mine." —*Chris Woodstra*

Seance / 1983 / Arista ✦✦✦
Seance can be viewed either as their most excessive work or the culmination of the band's neo-psychedelic (and Kilbey's especially) mystical obsessions. A very textural album with full arrangements that incorporate lush strings alongside the jangling guitars of *Blurred Crusade*, there are some better-than-average atmospheric pop songs (such as "Fly" and "Electric Lash," one of their finest songs). Ultimately, though, the album is bogged down by an attitude emphasizing concept and sound over songs. —*Chris Woodstra*

Remote Luxury / 1984 / Arista ✦✦✦✦
Remote Luxuries isn't a proper album, but rather a combination of two EPs—*Remote Luxuries* and *Persia*—recorded around the same time. And though it wasn't conceived as an album per se, the two EPs work well together, forming a coherent album of more meditative pieces that dabble in psychedelia and folk-rock while still retaining some great hooks and melodies. There is a certain sameness to the sound, but there are some clear highlights, like "A Month of Sundays" and "Shadow Cabinet." —*Chris Woodstra*

Heyday / 1986 / Arista ✦✦✦✦
Less overtly psychedelic than previous Church releases, the Peter Walsh-produced *Heyday* is a shimmering leap into more straightforward territory. Steve Kilbey's melodies are catchy and concise; "Tristesse" recalls fellow Aussies the Go-Betweens, "Columbus" is majestic jangle-pop, and "Tantalized" is more propulsive than anything the group's done since *The Blurred Crusade*'s stellar "When You Were Mine." —*Jason Ankeny*

● **Starfish** / 1988 / Arista ✦✦✦✦
The Church reached their creative and commercial pinnacle with *Starfish*, a lush, sparkling set which launched their lone Top 40 hit, the chiming "Under the Milky Way." Opening with the luxuriously dreamy "Destination," the record is the group's most cohesive and assured; not only are Steve Kilbey's songs his most consistently strong—the single "Reptile" sports a snakelike hook perfectly evocative of its title, and "Hotel Womb" is intoxicating—but Marty Willson-Piper and Peter Koppes' contributions ("Spark" and "A New Season," respectively) are gems as well. —*Jason Ankeny*

Hindsight / 1988 / EMI ✦✦✦
This Australian-only double CD collects rare B-sides and EPs. Though this is obviously targeted for completists and collectors, it actually gives a good picture of the band's diversity. —*Chris Woodstra*

Gold Afternoon Fix / Feb. 1990 / Arista ✦✦✦
Expectations were high after *Starfish*'s success, and the band was set to make further inroads with the alternative rock crowd. With their follow-up, *Gold Afternoon Fix*, the Church stripped their sound, producing their most heavy-hitting and direct album since the debut. (It's also their most polished.) Though they haven't completely left behind the subtle mysticism and atmospheric grooves (as evident in the dreamy "Disappointment"), *Gold Afternoon Fix* rocks harder than any of their previous work and contains some of their most engaging songs, like "Metropolis," "Russian Autumn Heart," and "You're Still Beautiful." —*Chris Woodstra*

Priest " Aura / Mar. 10, 1992 / Arista ✦✦
The emergence of grunge pretty much left old-school "college rock" acts out in the cold, but the Church stubbornly carried on with business as usual anyway, with an album that makes no pretense of an audience. Aside from a couple of really good songs ("Ripple" and "Feel"), the band returned to the more expansive sound of their pre-hit days, creating an interesting (though mostly indulgent and overly long) atmospheric soundscape. And though Kilbey is earnest in his word-heavy statements, very little of it sticks. —*Chris Woodstra*

Sometime Anywhere / May 24, 1994 / Arista ✦✦✦
By the time of *Sometime Anywhere* (possibly a play on Todd Rundgren's *Something/Anything*), the Church had been reduced to a studio-bound duo of Marty Willson-Piper and Steve Kilbey. The two obviously had no concerns about being able to recreate the album in a live setting, instead producing an album densely packed with layers of sounds, building on their previous ethereal pop with ethnic instrumentation and even dabbling in techno in places. None of the songs has the catchiness of their best singles, but that doesn't seem to be the point of this project anyway. Instead, most of the songs are near-epic in length, completely creating the atmospheric, hypnotic soundscape they had incorporated on previous albums. However, with *Sometime Anywhere*, they do it more successfully than ever before, with more impressive results. [*Sometime Anywhere* was originally packaged with a second disc of worthwhile outtakes from the sessions.] —*Chris Woodstra*

Quick Smoke at Spots / 1996 / Mushroom ✦✦✦✦
A Quick Smoke at Spots is a 16-track rarities collection that spans the band's mid-period from 1986 to 1990, picking up where *Hindsight* left off. The rarities aren't nearly as interesting as those found on *Hindsight*, but for fans, this is a nice addition. —*Chris Woodstra*

Cibo Matto

f. 1994, New York, NY
Alternative Pop-Rock, Trip-Hop, Indie Rock, Alternative Dance
A Japanese-born duo relocated to New York and christened with an Italian band name, Cibo Matto's music mirrored the melting-pot aesthetics of their origins, resulting in a heady brew of funk samples, hip-hop rhythms, tape loops, and fractured pop melodies topped off by surreal narratives sung in a combination of French and broken English.

The group comprised vocalist Miho Hatori and keyboardist/sampler Yuka Honda, a pair of expatriate Japanese women who arrived in the US independently. Honda, a onetime member of Brooklyn Funk Essentials, settled in New York in 1987, and Hatori, an alum of the Tokyo rap unit Kimidori and a former club DJ, followed six years later. After meeting in 1994, they first teamed in the Boredoms-inspired noise outfit Leitoh Lychee (translated as "frozen lychee nut"); after the group's breakup, the duo formed Cibo Matto, Italian for "food madness." (Their love of culinary delights quickly became the stuff of legend.)

The group soon emerged as a sensation among the Lower Manhattan hipster elite, gaining fame for their incendiary live shows backed by guests including the Lounge Lizards' Dougie Bowne (Honda's ex-husband), Bernie Worrell, Masada's Dave Douglas, and Skeleton Key's Rick Lee. After a pair of acclaimed 1995 independent singles, "Birthday Cake" and "Know Your Chicken," Cibo Matto signed to Warner Bros., surfacing in 1996 with the Mitchell Froom/Tchad Blake-produced *Viva! La Woman*, a delirious, stunningly inventive record celebrating love, food, and love of food. The duo toured with guest bassist Sean Lennon and Jon Spencer Blues Explosion drummer Russell Simins, and the EP *Super Relax* followed in 1997. —*Jason Ankeny*

Viva! La Woman / Jan. 16, 1996 / Warner Brothers ✦✦✦✦
Fresh and funky, female and Japanese, the trip-hop/rap duo Cibo Matto have been the recipients of a lot of hype. Fortunately, it's well founded; all trendiness aside, *!Viva! La Woman* is an innovative and catchy mix of eclectic samples and stream-of-consciousness lyrics. The likes of Paul Weller, Ennio Morricone, and Duke Ellington combine with observations like "My weight is three hundred pounds . . . my favorite is beef jerky" (from "Beef Jerky") and "Shut up and eat! You know my love is

sweet!" from ("Birthday Cake") in a fun and refreshing way. The tone of the album varies with each song: on tracks like "Sugar Water" and "Artichoke" Cibo Matto plays it spooky and ethereal, while "Birthday Cake" and the single "Know Your Chicken" find them as a couple of cryptic Beastie Girls, tossing off wacky non sequiturs over found soundscapes. Cibo Matto cook up a tasty appetizer of their talent with *!Viva! La Woman*. Like their tongue-in-cheek cover of "The Candy Man," Cibo Matto makes everything they bake satisfying and delicious. A diverse and entertaining album, *Viva! La Woman* leaves the listener hungry for more of their crazy food for thought. —*Heather Phares*

Super Relax / Jan. 28, 1997 / Warner Brothers ✦✦✦✦
Granted, the four separate versions of *Viva! La Woman's* sublime "Sugar Water" are unnecessary, but the rest of the material on Cibo Matto's follow-up EP *Super Relax* is superb. No longer relying solely on Yuka Honda's slice-and-dice samples, the duo's sound is considerably more organic this time out; "Spoon" locks into an infectious groove worthy of Luscious Jackson, while the live "BBQ" is breathlessly manic. The highlights, however, are the two covers: the first, a rendition of Antonio Carlos Jobim's "Aguas de Marco" (also found on the benefit LP *Red Hot and Latin*), opens up a vast new global playground of exotic textures and rhythms for the group to romp around in, while their exemplary take on the Stones' "Sing This All Together" proves Honda and vocalist Miho Hatori are equally capable of tackling straightforward rock 'n' roll. —*Jason Ankeny*

The Circle Jerks

f. 1979, Los Angeles, CA
Hardcore Punk, Heavy Metal
One of the leading lights on the Los Angeles hardcore scene of the early '80s, the Circle Jerks were formed when Black Flag vocalist Keith Morris left that group after their *Nervous Breakdown* EP and hooked up with former Redd Kross guitarist Greg Hetson. The band's early lineup was rounded out by bassist Roger (Dowding) Rogerson and drummer Lucky Lehrer. The Jerks developed a stellar live reputation among the skateboarding and slam dancing crowds and released their debut album, *Group Sex*, in 1980. A year later, they were featured in the L.A. punk documentary *The Decline of Western Civilization* and appeared on the soundtrack. The albums *Wild in the Streets* and *Golden Shower of Hits* continued in much the same loud, fast, tastelessly funny vein, and the latter included a medley of AM radio hits like "Along Comes Mary," "Afternoon Delight," "Having My Baby," and "Love Will Keep Us Together" done Circle Jerks style.

The Circle Jerks' later albums pursued more of a heavy metal direction and featured the rhythm section of Zander Schloss and Keith Clark. In spite of attracting little attention outside their core following, they continued to perform live, releasing an anthology of concert performances titled *Gig* in 1992. The Circle Jerks pulled off one of 1995's more memorable publicity stunts when they recorded a version of the Soft Boys' "I Wanna Destroy You" on their major-label debut, *Oddities, Abnormalities and Curiosities*, with a lead vocal by former teen queen Debbie Gibson; Gibson later made crowd-surfing cameo appearances to perform the song live at several Jerks gigs. —*Steve Huey*

Group Sex / Mar. 1981 / Epitaph ✦✦✦✦
This fast and loud debut by the early California thrash combo offers the best intro to their pungent social commentary and bad jokes. —*John Floyd*

Wild in the Streets / 1982 / Epitaph ✦✦✦
Wild in the Streets doesn't have the wild, appealingly offensive mixture of crude lyrics and frenetic riffs that made the Circle Jerks' debut *Group Sex* a minor hardcore classic, but there are enough tracks that nearly make the mark—including a tongue-in-cheek cover of "Put a Little Love in Your Heart" and the title track, which is a version of the theme song to the '60s teen exploitation flick of the same name—to make it worthwhile for Orange County punk fanatics. —*Stephen Thomas Erlewine*

● **Golden Shower of Hits** / 1983 / Rhino ✦✦✦✦
Another batch of gleeful vulgarity, *Golden Shower of Hits* features the notorious "Jerks on 45," along with their trademark wise-assed punk. The band tempers their attack just slightly throughout, making it their most listenable album. —*Stephen Thomas Erlewine*

Wonderful / 1985 / Combat ✦

VI / 1987 / Combat ✦✦✦
This strong album is one of the band's best. Tempos here are slowed down from that of standard hardcore; as a result, the songs here inhabit the uneasy netherworld between punk and heavy metal traversed most successfully by the Stooges and the Dictators. Only Keith Morris' raspy, growling vocals retain the band's tie with classic hardcore. Songwriting is still inconsistent, but there are a surprisingly large number of strong selections here—and all are performed with fiery energy. Highlights include "Casualty Vampire," "I Don't," and the top-notch "Beat Me Senseless." There's also a rushed and raw cover of the Creedence Clear-

water Revival chestnut "Fortunate Son." This platter is well worth hearing. —*David Cleary*

Oddities, Abnormalities and Curiosities / Jun. 1995 / Mercury ✦✦✦

Eric Clapton (Eric Patrick Clapp)

b. Mar. 30, 1945, Ripley, England
Guitar, Vocals / Rock 'n' Roll, Electric British Blues, Blues-Rock, Adult Contemporary, Pop-Rock, British Blues
By the time Eric Clapton launched his solo career with the release of his self-titled debut album in August 1970, he was long established as one of the world's major rock stars because of his group affiliations—the Yardbirds, John Mayall's Bluesbreakers, Cream, and Blind Faith—affiliations that had demonstrated his claim to being the best rock guitarist of his generation. That it took Clapton so long to go out on his own, however, was evidence of a degree of reticence unusual for one of his stature. And his debut album, though it spawned the Top 40 hit "After Midnight," was typical of his self-effacing approach; Ii was, in effect, an album by the group in which he had lately been featured, Delaney & Bonnie & Friends.

Not surprisingly, before his solo debut had even been released, Clapton had retreated from his solo stance, assembling from the D&B&F ranks the personnel for a group, Derek and the Dominos, with which he played for most of 1970. Clapton was largely inactive in 1971 and 1972, due to heroin addiction, but he performed a comeback concert at the Rainbow Theatre in London on January 13, 1973, resulting in the album *Eric Clapton's Rainbow Concert* (September 1973).

But Clapton did not launch a sustained solo career until July 1974, when he released *461 Ocean Boulevard*, which topped the charts and spawned the No. 1 single "I Shot the Sheriff."

The persona Clapton established over the next decade was less that of guitar hero than arena rock star with a weakness for ballads. The follow-ups to *461 Ocean Boulevard*, *There's One in Every Crowd* (April 1975), the live *E.C. Was Here* (August 1975), and *No Reason to Cry* (August 1976), were less successful. But *Slowhand* (November 1977), which featured both the powerful "Cocaine" (written by J.J. Cale, who had also written "After Midnight") and the hit singles "Lay Down Sally" and "Wonderful Tonight," was a million-seller, and its follow-ups, *Backless* (November 1978), featuring the Top Ten hit "Promises," the live *Just One Night* (May 1980), and *Another Ticket* (April 1981), featuring the Top Ten hit "I Can't Stand It," were all big sellers.

Clapton's popularity waned somewhat in the first half of the '80s, as the albums *Money and Cigarettes* (February 1983), *Behind the Sun* (March 1985), and *August* (November 1986) indicated a certain career stasis. But he was buoyed up by the release of the box set retrospective *Crossroads* (April 1988), which seemed to remind his fans how great he was. *Journeyman* (November 1989) was a return to form.

It would be his last new studio album for nearly five years, though in the interim he would suffer greatly and enjoy surprising triumph. On March 20, 1991, Clapton's four-year-old son was killed in a fall. While he mourned, he released a live album, *24 Nights* (October 1991), culled from his annual concert series at the Royal Albert Hall in London, and prepared a movie soundtrack, *Rush* (January 1992). The soundtrack featured a song written for his son, "Tears in Heaven," that became a massive hit single.

In March 1992 Clapton recorded a concert for *MTV Unplugged* that, when released on an album in August, became his biggest-selling record ever. Two years later, Clapton returned with a blues album, *From the Cradle*, which became one of his most successful albums, both commercially and critically. *Crossroads 2: Live in the '70s*, a box set chronicling his live work from the '70s, was released to mixed reviews. In early 1997, Clapton, billing himself by the pseudonym "x-sample," collaborated with keyboardist/producer Simon Climie as the ambient new-age and trip-hop duo T.D.F. The duo released *Retail Therapy* to mixed reviews in early 1997. —*William Ruhlmann*

Eric Clapton / Jul. 1970 / Polydor ✦✦✦✦
Eric Clapton's eponymous solo debut was recorded after he completed a tour with Delaney & Bonnie. Clapton used the core of the duo's backing band and co-wrote the majority of the songs with Delaney Bramlett—accordingly, *Eric Clapton* sounds more laidback and straightforward than any of the guitarist's previous recordings. There are still elements of blues and rock 'n' roll, but they're hidden beneath layers of gospel, R&B, country, and pop flourishes. And the pop element of the record is the strongest of the album's many elements—"Blues Power" isn't a blues song and only "Let It Rain," the album's closer, features extended solos. Throughout the album, Clapton turns out concise solos that de-emphasize his status as guitar god, even when they display astonishing musicality and technique. That is both a good and a bad thing—it's encouraging to hear him grow and become a more fully rounded musician, but too often the album needs the spark that some long guitar solos would have given it. In short, it needs a little more of Clapton's personality. —*Stephen Thomas Erlewine*

461 Ocean Boulevard / Jul. 1974 / Polydor ✦✦✦✦
461 Ocean Boulevard is Eric Clapton's second studio solo album, arriving after his side project of Derek & the Dominos and a long struggle with heroin addiction. Although there are some new reggae influences, the album doesn't sound all that different from the rock, pop, blues, country, and R&B amalgam of *Eric Clapton*. However, *461 Ocean Boulevard* is a tighter, more focused outing that enables Clapton to stretch out instrumentally. Furthermore, the pop concessions on the album—the sleek production, the concise running times—don't detract from the rootsy origins of the material, whether it's Johnny Otis' "Willie and the Hand Jive," the traditional blues "Motherless Children," Bob Marley's "I Shot the Sheriff," or Clapton's emotional originals, "Better Make It Through Today" and "Let It Grow." With its relaxed, friendly atmosphere and strong bluesy roots, *461 Ocean Boulevard* set the template for Clapton's '70s albums. Though he tried hard to make an album exactly like it, he never quite managed to replicate its charms. —*Stephen Thomas Erlewine*

There's One in Every Crowd / Mar. 1975 / Polydor ✦✦
Having stayed out of the recording studio for four years prior to making his comeback album, *461 Ocean Boulevard*, Eric Clapton returned to recording only a few months later to make its follow-up, *There's One in Every Crowd*. Perhaps he hadn't had time to write or gather sufficient material to make a similarly effective album, since the result is a scattershot mixture of styles, leading off with two gospel tunes, one a reggae version of "Swing Low, Sweet Chariot." One member of his band, George Terry, had written a sequel to "I Shot the Sheriff," "Don't Blame Me," which Clapton sang in his best impersonation of Bob Marley's voice. The album's best track, naturally, was the blues cover, Clapton's take on Elmore James' "The Sky Is Crying." But *There's One in Every Crowd* was a disappointing follow-up to *461 Ocean Boulevard*, and fans let Clapton know it. While the former album had topped the charts and gone gold, the latter didn't even make the Top Ten. —*William Ruhlmann*

E.C. Was Here / Aug. 1975 / Polydor ✦✦✦
Since Eric Clapton and his longtime fans have always thought of him primarily as a bluesman, it is curious that this live album, which is devoted to extended guitar solos on blues standards like "Have You Ever Loved a Woman," "Rambling on My Mind," and "Further On up the Road," didn't become a massive hit. Maybe it was that the once reclusive Clapton was now spitting out new albums every six months, but *E.C. Was Here* did not achieve the renown it deserved upon release, and Clapton, who had been reluctant to put out a straight blues album to begin with, didn't try anything similar again for almost 20 years, instead making sure to keep his records within a pop framework that usually diluted their effectiveness. In its CD reissue, with "Drifting Blues" extended to its full 11 minutes, the album is even more impressive. —*William Ruhlmann*

No Reason to Cry / Aug. 1976 / Polydor ✦✦✦
When he gave a speech inducting the Band into the Rock & Roll Hall of Fame, Eric Clapton said that after he heard their debut album, *Music from Big Pink*, he wanted to join the group, notwithstanding the fact that they already had a guitarist in Robbie Robertson. In the winter of 1975-1976, when he cut *No Reason to Cry* at the Band's Shangri-la Studio in Malibu, CA, he came as close as he ever would to realizing that desire. Clapton is a musical chameleon; though some of *No Reason to Cry* is identifiable as the kind of pop-rock Clapton had been making since the start of his solo career (the best of it being "Hello Old Friend," which became his first Top 40 single in two years), the most memorable music on the album occurs when Clapton is collaborating with members of the Band and other guests. He duets with Band bassist Rick Danko on Danko's "All Our Past Times," and with Bob Dylan on Dylan's "Sign Language," as Robertson's distinctive lead guitar is heard rather than Clapton's. As a result, the album is a good purchase for fans of Bob Dylan and the Band, but not necessarily for those of Eric Clapton. (The CD reissue adds a bonus track, "Last Night," which is a traditional 12-bar blues song credited to Clapton.) —*William Ruhlmann*

Slowhand / Nov. 1977 / Polydor ✦✦✦✦
After the all-star *No Reason to Cry* failed to make much of an impact commerically, Eric Clapton returned to using his own band for *Slowhand*. The difference is substantial—where *No Reason to Cry* struggled hard to find the right tone, *Slowhand* opens with the relaxed, bluesy shuffle of J.J. Cale's "Cocaine" and sustains it throughout the course of the album. Alternating between straight blues ("Mean Old Frisco"), country ("Lay Down Sally"), mainstream rock ("Cocaine," "The Core") and pop ("Wonderful Tonight"), *Slowhand* doesn't sound schizophrenic, because of the band's grasp of the material. This is laidback virtuosity—although Clapton and his band are never flashy, their playing is masterful and assured. That assurance and the album's eclectic material make *Slowhand* rank with *461 Ocean Boulevard* as Eric Clapton's best album. —*Stephen Thomas Erlewine*

Backless / Nov. 1978 / Polydor ✦✦✦
Having made his best album since *461 Ocean Boulevard* with *Slowhand*, Eric Clapton followed with *Backless*, which took the same authoritative, no-nonsense approach. If it wasn't quite the masterpiece, or the sales monster, that *Slowhand* had been, this probably was because of that usual Clapton problem—material. Once again, he returned to the Oklahoma hills for a song from J.J. Cale, but "I'll Make Love to You Anytime" wasn't quite up to "Cocaine" or "After Midnight." Bob Dylan contributed two songs, but you could see why he hadn't saved them for his own album, and Clapton's own writing contributions were mediocre. Clapton did earn a Top Ten hit with Richard Feldman and Roger Linn's understated pop shuffle "Promises," but it was not one of his more memorable recordings. Of course, Clapton's blues playing on the lone obligatory blues cut, "Early in the Morning" (presented in its full eight-minute version on the CD reissue), was stellar. (*Backless* was his last album to feature the backup group that had been with him since 1974.) — *William Ruhlmann*

Just One Night / Apr. 1980 / Polydor ✦✦✦✦
Although Eric Clapton has released a bevy of live albums, none of them has ever quite captured the guitarist's raw energy and dazzling virtuosity. The double-live album *Just One Night* may have gotten closer to that elusive goal than most of its predecessors, but it is still lacking in many ways. The most notable difference between *Just One Night* and Clapton's other live albums is his backing band. Led by guitarist Albert Lee, the group is a collective of accomplished professionals who have managed to keep some grit in their playing. They help push Clapton along, forcing him to spit out crackling solos throughout the album. However, the performances aren't consistent on *Just One Night*. There are plenty of dynamic moments like "Double Trouble" and "Rambling on My Mind," but they are weighed down by pedestrian renditions of songs like "All Our Past Times." Nevertheless, more than any other Clapton live album, *Just One Night* suggests the guitarist's in-concert potential. It's just too bad that the recording didn't occur on a night when he *did* fulfill all of that potential. — *Stephen Thomas Erlewine*

Another Ticket / Feb. 1981 / Polydor ✦✦✦
Now, here's a star-crossed album. Polydor rejected the first version of it, produced by Glyn Johns, and Eric Clapton was forced to cut it all over again with Tom Dowd. Then, a few dates into a US promotional tour coinciding with its release, Clapton collapsed and was found to be near death from ulcers due to his alcoholism. Finally, it turned out to be the final record of his 15-year association with Polydor, which therefore had no reason to promote it. Nevertheless, the album made the Top Ten, went gold, and spawned a Top Ten single in "I Can't Stand It." And the rest of it wasn't too shabby, either. The first and last Clapton studio album to feature his all-British band of the early '80s, it gave considerable prominence to second guitarist Albert Lee and especially to keyboard player/singer Gary Brooker (formerly leader of Procol Harum), and they gave it more of a blues-rock feel than the country-funk brewed up by the Tulsa shuffle crew Clapton had used throughout the 1970s. Best of all, Clapton had taken the time to write some songs—he's credited on six of the nine selections—and tunes such as the title track and "I Can't Stand It" held up well. This wasn't great Clapton, but it was good, and it deserved more recognition than conditions allowed it at the time. — *William Ruhlmann*

Time Pieces: Best of Eric Clapton / May 1982 / Polydor ✦✦✦✦
Time Pieces is a good single-disc collection of Eric Clapton's solo hits—including "I Shot the Sheriff," "After Midnight," "Wonderful Tonight," Derek & the Domino's "Layla," and "Cocaine"—that has since been supplanted by the more thorough *The Cream of Eric Clapton*, which combines his solo work with selections of his Cream and Blind Faith work. Nevertheless, the compilation still provides a good introduction for neophyte Clapton fans, especially those who just want copies of his '70s hits. — *Stephen Thomas Erlewine*

Money and Cigarettes / Feb. 1983 / Reprise ✦✦✦✦
Recorded with some old friends—including Ry Cooder, Duck Dunn, and Albert Lee—*Money and Cigarettes* is one of Clapton's finest albums. Instead of being an empty exercise in studio professionalism, the record is an appealing, low-key effort featuring some of the smoothest blues Clapton has ever played. — *Stephen Thomas Erlewine*

Time Pieces II/Live in the '70s / 1985 / Polydor ✦✦✦
Neither a career retrospective nor a rarities collection, *Time Pieces II: Live in the '70s* is an odd record. Featuring a selection of material recorded in concert at various points in the '70s, the album never gives an accurate impression of Clapton's progression as a guitarist—it's sequenced haphazardly, with tracks falling outside of strict chronological order. Nevertheless, there are a number of fine performances here, especially on album tracks like "Tulsa Time" and "If I Don't Be There by Morning," as well as the extended solos of "Rambling on My Mind." Diehard fans will find things of interest on *Time Pieces II*, but the album can be safely ignored by most listeners. — *Stephen Thomas Erlewine*

Behind the Sun / Mar. 1985 / Reprise ✦✦✦
Clapton's career was in decline in the early '80s when he switched from Polydor to Warner Bros., and his debut Warner album, *Money and Cigarettes*, became his first to fall below gold-record status in more than six years. As a result, Warner looked critically at his follow-up, the Phil Collins-produced *Behind the Sun*, in the fall of 1984 and rejected the first version submitted, insisting that he record several new songs written by Jerry Williams, backed by Los Angeles session players under the auspices of company producers Lenny Waronker and Ted Templeman. Warner then emphasized the new tracks, releasing two of them, "Forever Man" (which reached the Top 40) and "See What Love Can Do," as singles. The resulting album, not surprisingly, was somewhat schizophrenic, though the company may have been correct in thinking that the album as a whole was competent without being very exciting. The added tracks were not bad, but they were not the surefire hits they were supposed to be. As usual, there was some effective guitar soloing (notably on "Same Old Blues"), but despite the tinkering, *Behind the Sun* was not one of Clapton's better albums. (It went gold after nearly two years in release.) — *William Ruhlmann*

August / Nov. 1986 / Reprise ✦✦
Eric Clapton adopted a new, tougher, hard R&B approach on *August*, employing a stripped-down band featuring keyboard player Greg Phillinganes, bassist Nathan East, and drummer/producer Phil Collins, plus, on several tracks, a horn section and, on a couple of tracks, backup vocals by Tina Turner, and performing songs written by old Motown hand Lamont Dozier, among others. The excellent, but incongruous, leadoff track, however, was "It's in the Way That You Use It," which Clapton and Robbie Robertson had written for Robertson's score to the film *The Color of Money*. Elsewhere, Clapton sang and played fiercely on songs like "Tearing Us Apart," "Run," and "Miss You," all of which earned AOR radio play. That radio support may have helped the album to achieve gold status in less than six months, Clapton's best commercial showing since 1981's *Another Ticket*, despite the album's failure to generate a hit single. The title commemorates the birth in August 1986 of Clapton's son Conor. (The CD version of the album contains the bonus track "Grand Illusion.") — *William Ruhlmann*

☆ **Crossroads** / Apr. 1988 / Polydor ✦✦✦✦✦
A four-disc box set spanning Eric Clapton's entire career—running from the Yardbirds to his '80s solo recordings—*Crossroads* not only revitalized Clapton's commerical standing, but it established the rock 'n' roll multi-disc box set retrospective as a commercially viable proposition. Bob Dylan's *Biograph* was successful two years before the release of *Crossroads*, but Clapton's set was a bonafide blockbuster. And it's easy to see why. *Crossroads* manages to sum up Clapton's career succinctly and thoroughly, touching upon all of his hits and adding a bevy of first-rate unreleased material (most notably selections from the scrapped second Derek & the Dominos album). Although not all of his greatest performances are included on the set—none of his work as a session musician or guest artist is included, for instance—every truly essential item he recorded is present on these four discs. No other Clapton album accurately explains why the guitarist was so influential, or demonstrates exactly what he accomplished. — *Stephen Thomas Erlewine*

Journeyman / Nov. 1989 / Reprise ✦✦✦✦
For most of the '80s, Eric Clapton seemed rather lost, uncertain of whether he should return to his blues roots or pander to AOR radio. By the mid-'80s, he appeared to have made the decision to revamp himself as a glossy mainstream rocker, working with synthesizers and drum machines. Instead of expanding his audience, it only reduced it. Then came the career retrospective *Crossroads*, which helped revitalize his career, not only commercially, but also creatively, as *Journeyman*—the first album he recorded after the success of *Crossroads*—proved. Although *Journeyman* still suffers from an overly slick production, Clapton sounds more convincing than he has since the early '70s. Not only is his guitar playing muscular and forceful, his singing is soulful and gritty. Furthermore, the songwriting is consistently strong, alternating between fine mainstream rock originals ("Pretending") and covers ("Before You Accuse Me," "Hound Dog"). Like any of Clapton's best albums, there is no grandstanding to be found on *Journeyman*—it's simply a laidback and thoroughly engaging display of Clapton's virtuosity. On the whole, it's the best studio album he's released since *Slowhand*. — *Stephen Thomas Erlewine*

24 Nights / Oct. 8, 1991 / Reprise ✦✦
Eric Clapton, who had not released a live album since 1980, had several good reasons to release one in the early '90s. For one thing, his spare backup band of keyboardist Greg Phillinganes, bassist Nathan East, and drummer Steve Ferrone was his best live unit ever, and its powerful live versions of Cream classics like "White Room" and "Sunshine of Your Love" deserved to be documented. For another, since 1987 Clapton had been playing an annual series of concerts at the Royal Albert Hall in London, putting together various special shows—blues nights, orchestral nights, etc. The double album *24 Nights* was culled from two years

of such shows, 1990 and 1991, and it demonstrated the breadth of Clapton's work, from his hot regular band to assemblages of bluesmen like Buddy Guy and Robert Cray to examples of his soundtrack work with an orchestra led by Michael Kamen. The result was an album that came across as a lavishly constructed retrospective and a testament to Clapton's musical stature. But it made little impact upon release (though it quickly went gold), perhaps because events overcame it. Three months later, Clapton's elegy for his baby son, "Tears in Heaven," was all over the radio, and a few months after that he was redefining himself on *MTV Unplugged*—a live show as austere as *24 Nights* was grand. Still, it would be hard to find a more thorough demonstration of Clapton's abilities than the one presented here. — *William Ruhlmann*

Unplugged / Aug. 18, 1992 / Reprise ✦✦✦✦
Clapton's *Unplugged* was responsible for making acoustic-based music, and *Unplugged* albums in particular, a hot trend in the early '90s. Clapton's concert was not only one of the finest *Unplugged* episodes, but was some of the finest music he had recorded in years. Instead of the slick productions that tainted his '80s albums, the music was straightforward and direct, alternating between his pop numbers and traditional blues songs. The result was some of the most genuine, heartfelt music the guitarist has ever committed to tape. It was also some of his most popular; the album sold over seven million copies in the US and won several Grammies. — *Stephen Thomas Erlewine*

From the Cradle / Sep. 13, 1994 / Reprise ✦✦✦✦
For years, fans craved an all-blues album from Clapton; he waited until 1994 to deliver *From the Cradle*. The album manages to recreate the ambience of postwar electric blues, right down to the bottomless thump of the rhythm section. If it wasn't for Clapton's labored vocals, everything would be perfect. As long as he plays his guitar, he can't fail—his solos are white-hot and evocative, original and captivating. When he sings, Clapton loses that sense of originality, choosing to mimic the vocals of the original recordings. At times, his overemotive singing is painful; he doesn't have the strength to pull off Howlin' Wolf's growl or the confidence to replicate Muddy Waters' assured phrasing. Yet, whenever he plays, it's easier to forget his vocal shortcomings. Even with its faults, *From the Cradle* is one of Clapton's finest moments. — *Stephen Thomas Erlewine*

● **The Cream of Clapton** / Mar. 7, 1995 / Polydor ✦✦✦✦
Eric Clapton was contracted to Polydor Records from 1966 to 1981, first as a member of Cream, then Blind Faith, and later as a solo artist and as the leader of Derek and the Dominos. This 19-track, 79-minute disc surveys his career, presenting an excellent selection from the period, including the Cream hits "Sunshine of Your Love," "White Room," and "Crossroads"; "Presence of the Lord," Clapton's finest moment with Blind Faith; "Bell Bottom Blues" and "Layla" from Derek and the Dominos; and 11 songs from Clapton's solo work, among them the hits "I Shot the Sheriff," "Promises," and "I Can't Stand It." The selection is thus broader and better than that found on 1982's *Time Pieces* collection, and with excellent sound and liner notes by Clapton biographer Ray Coleman, *The Cream of Clapton* stands as the single-disc best-of to own for Clapton's greatest recordings. (Not to be confused with the popular 1987 Polydor [UK] compilation *The Cream of Eric Clapton*, which has since been retitled *The Best of Eric Clapton*.) — *William Ruhlmann*

Eric Clapton's Rainbow Concert [expanded] / Jul. 25, 1995 / Polydor ✦✦✦
In these days of CD expansion, it is not unusual for a record company to reissue an old album with a bonus track or two. This reconstruction of the January 13, 1973, comeback concert by Eric Clapton is something else again, however. The original six-track LP ran less than 27 minutes; the new 14-track CD runs almost 74 minutes. The eight additions—"Layla," "Blues Power," "Bottle of Red Wine," "Bell Bottom Blues," "Tell the Truth," "Key to the Highway," "Let It Rain," and "Crossroads"—make the disc an effective recapitulation of Clapton's career over the previous seven years, including his solo work and his appearances with John Mayall's Bluesbreakers, Cream, and Derek and the Dominos. Despite the addiction that had kept him largely homebound for almost two years, Clapton played well, though the all-star backup band was as ragged as it was spirited. The loose feel of the evening was brought out in the stage announcements, many by Pete Townshend, who even mentioned a social disease just before introducing "Presence of the Lord." This still isn't a great Eric Clapton show, but it has been transformed from a historical curiosity to a historical document. — *William Ruhlmann*

Crossroads 2: Live in the '70s / Apr. 2, 1996 / Polydor/Chronicles ✦✦✦
Crossroads was a box set that appealed to both beginners and fanatics. *Crossroads 2 (Live in the Seventies)* appeals only to fanatics. Spanning four discs and consisting almost entirely of live material (there are a handful of studio outtakes), this is music that will enthrall only completists and archivists. For those listeners, there is a wealth of fascinating, compelling performances here, as well as a fair share of mediocre,

uninspired tracks. The key word for the entire album is detail—it is an album for studying the intricacies of Clapton's playing and how it evolved. For example, it's easy to hear the differences and progressions between the four versions of Robert Johnson's "Rambling on My Mind." And it is Clapton who evolves, not his supporting band; although they are proficient, they are hardly exciting. However, their static, professional support provides a nice bed over which to chart Slowhand's growth over the course of the decade, simply because he is *always* the focal point. *Crossroads 2* may be only for collectors, but for those collectors, it is a treasure, even if some of the tracks are fool's gold. — *Stephen Thomas Erlewine*

The Dave Clark Five

f. 1961, Tottenham, London, England, **db.** 1970
British Invasion
For a very brief time in 1964, it seemed that the biggest challenger to the Beatles phenomenon was the Dave Clark Five. From the Tottenham area of London, the quintet had the fortune to knock "I Want to Hold Your Hand" off the top of the British charts with "Glad All Over," and was championed (for about 15 minutes) by the British press as the Beatles' most serious threat. They were the first British Invasion band to break in a big way in the States after the Beatles, though the Rolling Stones and others quickly supplanted the DC5 as the Fab Four's most serious rivals. The Dave Clark Five reached the Top 40 17 times between 1964 and 1967 with memorable hits like "Glad All Over," "Bits and Pieces," "Because," and a remake of Bobby Day's "Over and Over," as well as making more appearances on "The Ed Sullivan Show" than any other English act. The DC5 were distinguished from their British contemporaries by their larger-than-life production, Clark's loud stomping drum sound, and Mike Smith's leathery vocals. Though accused by detractors of lacking finesse and hipness, they had a solid ear for melodies and harmonies and wrote much of their early material, the best of which has endured quite well, although their albums were fairly weak. Interestingly, and unusually for that era, bandleader Dave Clark managed and produced the band himself, negotiating a much higher royalty rate than artists of that period usually received. After a couple of years of superstardom, the group proved unable to either keep up with the changing times or maintain a high standard of original compositions, and called it quits in 1970. — *Rick Clark & Richie Unterberger*

Dave Clark Five/The Washington D.C.'s / 1993 / Repertoire ✦✦✦
A rather strange reissue, this compiles both sides of all three of the rare singles that the DC5 put out in the UK in 1961-1963 on the small Ember label before joining Columbia. Much less impressive than their British Invasion hits, they display the group as a run-of-the-mill band without an identity, casting about with weak pop, country, and instrumental material, although one of the songs ("I Knew It All the Time") was actually a small hit in America in early 1967. "Chaquita" was a cool instrumental ripoff of "Tequila" on the first DC5 album, but the early version here isn't nearly as good. On this CD, these tracks are combined with 17 songs by the unknown British band the Washington D.C.'s, who happened to share an album with the Dave Clark Five on an exploitative Ember reissue after "Glad All Over" became a hit. — *Richie Unterberger*

● **History of the Dave Clark Five** / Aug. 3, 1993 / Hollywood ✦✦✦✦
For many years, the Dave Clark Five was one of the few major groups of the 1960s whose work was unavailable on compact disc. This two-disc, 50-track reissue not only rectifies that situation but arguably includes more than all but devoted fans will want to hear. All of the band's mammoth mid-'60s hits —"Glad All Over," "Bits and Pieces," "Because," "Catch Us if You Can," "Any Way You Want It," and others—are included, and while they don't rival the work of British Invasion heavyweights like the Beatles, Stones, and Kinks, they still burst with exuberant melodies and harmonies and dense production. This compilation also features worthy lesser-known hits like "Try Too Hard" and "Everybody Knows," as well as obscure but commendable beat ballads and raveups from their B-sides and albums. Nonetheless, there is a fair amount of filler, and their post-1966 work is undistinguished by either artistic growth or the hooks and heavy beat of their early material. But at their peak, the DC5 captured the *joie de vivre* of the British Invasion with a lasting power that cannot be dismissed. This reissue includes a comprehensive booklet featuring recollections from Dave Clark himself. — *Richie Unterberger*

Dee Clark (Delecta Clark)

b. Nov. 7, 1938, Blytheville, AR, d. Dec. 7, 1990
Vocals / Soul, R&B
Dee Clark was a solid R&B vocalist who had some huge hits in the late '50s and early '60s. The Arkansas-born singer moved to Chicago as a child and was in the Hambone Kids with Sammy McGrier and Ronny Strong. They recorded for Okeh in 1952; the next year Clark sang with the Goldentones. This group later became the Kool Gents, then recorded as the Delegates for Vee-Jay in 1956. Clark went solo in 1957 and in

1958 enjoyed his first smash with "Nobody for You," an Abner release that reached No. 3 R&B and just missed the Top 20 on the pop charts. He continued a string of R&B winners with "Just Keep It Up," "Hey Little Girl," and "How About That" for Abner in 1959 and 1960. Clark teamed with guitarist Phil Upchurch to write "Raindrops" in 1961, his signature tune. The song peaked at No. 3 R&B and No. 2 pop, and was his last major hit. Clark continued performing through the '60s, '70s, and '80s, but never again was a factor, though "Raindrops" remains a staple on oldies radio. —*Ron Wynn*

● **Rain Drops [Vee-Jay]** / 1994 / Vee-Jay ✦✦✦✦
Dee Clark was one of the most adaptable R&B vocalists of the '50s and early '60s, as this 25-song reissue shows. He did songs in a Little Richard mode, an Afro-Latin setting, and also performed ballads, novelty tunes ("Kangaroo Hop"), and covers ("Cupid"). Clark's gem was "Raindrops," a song with enough drama, hooks, and appeal to nearly top both the pop and R&B charts. It was his biggest hit, but not his only fine number. Many cuts such as "Nobody But You," "What Kind of Fool," and the newly issued "Bring Back My Heart" equal or even top the tune that made him famous. —*Ron Wynn*

Gene Clark

b. Nov. 17, 1946, Tipton, MO, d. May 24, 1991, Sherman Oaks, CA
Guitar, Vocals / Progressive Bluegrass, Country-Rock, Folk-Rock
Very few musicians had as much influence in creating new styles of music as Gene Clark. As co-founder of the Byrds, he helped pioneer what was to become known as folk-rock. Clark and Bob Dylan were the most prolific songwriters of the genre. After leaving the group, he and banjoist Doug Dillard invented newgrass, a progressive blend of traditional bluegrass instrumentation augmented by electronics, drums, piano, and even harpsichord. Clark's first solo album, *Gene Clark with the Gosdin Brothers*, contained country-rock, preceding the Byrds' *Sweetheart of the Rodeo* by nearly two years and the first Flying Burrito Brothers album by three years.

Harold Eugene Clark was the oldest of 12 children. He left college to join the New Christy Minstrels in 1962. Upon hearing the Beatles' "She Loves You," he left the group and moved to California, where he met Roger (then known as Jim) McGuinn and David Crosby. Mandolin player Chris Hillman was given his first electric bass lesson by Clark, and Michael Clarke was recruited from a beach party to play drums. The five became the Jet Set, the Beefeaters, and finally, the Byrds, where their cover of Dylan's "Mr. Tambourine Man" shot to the top of the charts worldwide in May 1965. Clark left the Byrds in early 1966 to pursue a solo career, releasing *Gene Clark with the Gosdin Brothers* in 1967. The next year *The Fantastic Expedition of Dillard and Clark* heralded the dawning of newgrass. After two years, the ever-restless Clark left the band and recorded the Dylan-esque *White Light*, voted album of the year in Holland in 1971 and praised by *Rolling Stone* as the album he was born to make. The next year *Roadmaster* was released, an 11-song masterpiece that featured the five original Byrds on two tracks, foreshadowing the re-forming of the group in 1973 for *Byrds*, produced by David Crosby. Despite the fact the record sold millions and went gold, the group quickly disbanded.

No Other in 1974 and *Two Sides to Every Story* in 1977 reconfirmed Clark as one of the great songwriters of his era. He joined Roger McGuinn and Chris Hillman for two albums, *McGuinn, Clark and Hillman* in 1978 and *City* in 1979. The group toured extensively until Clark departed once again, and it would be five years before he would release *Firebyrd*, which includes remakes of "Mr. Tambourine Man" and "Feel a Whole Lot Better." Clark continued to play solo both at home and in Europe before joining up with Carla Olson (Textones) for *So Rebellious a Lover* in 1987. Clark also performed in A Tribute to the Byrds for several years starting in 1985; it included former Byrd Michael Clarke on drums and, at various times, Rick Danko, Blondie Chaplin, John York, Rick Roberts, Billy Darnell, and Michael Curtis. In addition to his solo efforts, Clark appeared on albums by the Flying Burrito Brothers, Roger McGuinn, Bob Lind, Cooker, the Textones, and Primitive Future. Gene Clark died a few months after he and the Byrds were inducted into the Rock and Roll Hall of Fame. He left behind hundreds of songs; an indelible mark in folk-rock, bluegrass, and country music; and millions of fans who mourned the loss of one of the greatest songwriters and musical innovators of all time. —*Dan Pavlides*

Gene Clark with the Gosdin Brothers / 1967 / Columbia ✦✦✦
Byrds Michael Clarke and Chris Hillman provide the rhythm section, and future Byrd Clarence White, banjoist Doug Dillard, Glen Campbell and even Leon Russell help create country-rock and newgrass overtones in addition to Clark's familiar folk-rock stylings. —*Dan Pavlides*

● **Echoes** / 1967 / Columbia ✦✦✦✦
Basically this is a CD reissue of his 1967 debut album, *Gene Clark & The Gosdin Brothers*. The Byrds comparison is really unavoidable: it's both Clark's best solo work and, not coincidentally, the one that resembles the Byrds most strongly. Indeed, this could easily pass for a some-

what less-than-average vintage Byrds album, with actual Byrds Chris Hillman and Michael Clarke forming the rhythm section, and Vern and Rex Gosdin on guitar (hence the LP title). To be brutal, it doesn't measure up to Clark's best songs from his Byrds days, but it's fairly strong, melodic, '60s folk-rock nonetheless, perhaps with a bit of a more countrified, laidback, generic feel. "So You Say You Lost Your Baby," "Echoes," and especially "Tried So Hard" are standouts. The CD adds three interesting previously unreleased outtakes from the era, as well as six of the best early Byrds songs graced by Clark's songwriting and vocals. —*Richie Unterberger*

American Flyer / 1971 / MediaArts ✦✦
White Light / 1971 / A&M ✦✦✦
Clark's most Dylanesque album. —*Dan Pavlides*
Roadmaster / 1972 / Edsel ✦✦✦✦
Reunited five Byrds play on two tracks. One of Gene Clark's best ever. —*Dan Pavlides*
No Other / 1974 / Line ✦✦✦
Gene Clark called this album "overdub city" in a 1986 interview, laughing at the glam-rock photo taken of him on the poster insert. Nevertheless, it remains a worthwhile outing. —*Dan Pavlides*
Kansas City Southern / 1975 / Ariola ✦✦
Two Sides to Every Story / 1977 / RSO ✦✦
Byron Berline, Al Perkins, John Hartford, and Emmylou Harris join Gene Clark for this country/folk-rock effort. —*Dan Pavlides*
Firebyrd / 1987 / Takoma ✦✦
Gene Clark's post-Byrds solo career was as frought with false starts, and unmet promises as his two years with the Byrds were filled with fame, fulfillment, and recognition. *Firebyrd* was an artistic triumph and a commercial disaster; released to rave reviews and an enthusiastic response, as one of the finest solo projects ever to come from an ex-Byrd, it was killed by poor distribution. (Demand in Europe, especially Germany and Italy, where fan interest in Clark and the Byrds was very high, resulted in high premiums being paid for used copies.) "Rain Song," "Rodeo Rider," and "Something About You" were some of Clark's best songs in years, and his covers of two old Byrds numbers, "Mr. Tambourine Man" and "Feel a Whole Lot Better," are perfectly credible reinterpretations, and he even does justice to Gordon Lightfoot's "If You Could Read My Mind." Not a "lost Byrds album" by any means, but a must-own for any serious Byrds fan. (see *This Byrd Has Flown*) —*Bruce Eder*
So Rebellious a Lover / 1987 / Razor & Tie ✦✦✦
Country—and folk-flavored duets include John Fogerty's "Almost Saturday Night" and Clark's haunting motorcycle mantra "Gypsy Rider." —*Dan Pavlides*
Silhouetted in Light / 1992 / Edsel ✦✦✦
A very good 15-track live CD featuring Gene Clark and Carla Olson at their best. The sound is good and the song selection impressive. Pick up this import—highly recommended. —*Chip Renner*
This Byrd Has Flown / Oct. 1995 / Edsel ✦✦✦✦
This Byrd Has Flown is an expanded British import CD of *Firebyrd*, with extra tracks added from later recording sessions. The songs add a considerable amount to the original album. "C'est La Bonne Rue" is a hot little rocker, and "All I Want" is one of Clark's most poignant and impassioned love songs; by itself it's worth the price of the album. The notes by drummer/singer/composer Andy Kandanes add considerable information about the circumstances behind the recording of *Firebyrd* and Clark's later career, up until his death in May 1991. —*Bruce Eder*
American Dreamer / Feb. 11, 1997 / Raven ✦✦✦✦
Kudos to Australia's Raven for assembling this fine 24-track overview of Clark's most fertile period. Included are three Clark-penned Byrds stunners, two of the best from his first solo album, six from the Dillard and Clark albums (the Velvet Crush-covered "Why Not Your Baby" is unfortunately overlooked), a Flying Burritos-backed gem, two ersatz Byrds-reunion cuts from *Road Master*, a whopping six from *White Light*, "Full Circle" from the otherwise tepid 1973 reunion, and two selections from *No Other* (though not the This Mortal Coil-covered "Strength of Strings"). An interesting early mix of "Full Circle" is included as a bonus. For the uninitiated, this is a great place to start, but even a fanatic will be pleased by the inclusion of the hard-to-find *White Light* cuts and Sid Griffin's fannish liner notes. —*Michael Ribas*

Petula Clark

b. Nov. 15, 1932, Epsom, England
Vocals / Pop-Rock
The most commercially successful female singer in British chart history, Petula Clark was born November 15, 1932, in Epsom, England. Trained to sing by her soprano mother, Clark embarked on a stage career at the age of seven; soon she was a fixture on British radio programs, and she began hosting her own regular show "Pet's Parlour"—a series spotlight-

ing patriotic songs designed to boost the morale of wartime audiences—at the age of 11.

After entertaining British troops alongside fellow child stars Julie Andrews and Anthony Newley, Clark made her film debut with *A Medal for the General* in 1944. By the dawn of the 1950s she was a superstar throughout the UK, with a resume of close to two dozen films. In 1954 "The Little Shoemaker" was her first Top 20 single, while 1960's "Sailor" was her first chart-topper. Still, Clark struggled with her inability to shed her adolescent image. After selling over a million copies of 1961's "Romeo," she married and relocated to France, establishing a strong fan base there on the strength of hits including "Ya-Ya Twist," "Chariot," and "Monsieur," which spotlighted a new, more sophisticated pop sound anchored by her crystalline vocals.

Riding the wave of the British Invasion, Clark was finally able to penetrate the US market in 1964 with the Grammy-winning "Downtown," the first single by a British woman ever to reach No. 1 on the American pop charts. It was also the first in a series of American Top Ten hits (most written and arranged by Tony Hatch) which included 1965's "I Know a Place" and 1966's "I Couldn't Live Without Your Love" and the No. 1 smash "My Love." At the same time, she remained a huge star throughout Europe, topping the British charts in 1967 with "This Is My Song," taken from the film *A Countess from Hong Kong*. In addition to hosting her own BBC series, she starred in the 1968 NBC television special "Petula," which triggered controversy when sponsors requested that a segment with guest Harry Belafonte be cut in deference to Southern affiliates; ultimately, the show aired in its intended form.

As the 1960s drew to a close, Clark's commercial stature slipped, although singles like "Don't Sleep on the Subway," "The Other Man's Grass Is Always Greener," and "Kiss Me Goodbye" still charted on both sides of the Atlantic. In 1968 she revived her film career by starring in *Finian's Rainbow*, followed a year later by *Goodbye, Mr. Chips*. In later years Clark focused primarily on international touring, headlining the 1981 London revival of Rodgers and Hammerstein's *The Sound of Music*. After starring in the 1990 musical *Someone Like You*, which she co-wrote, she made her Broadway debut in *Blood Brothers* in 1993. In 1988 an acid-house remix of "Downtown" reached the UK Top Ten, another honor for the female singer awarded the most gold records in British pop history. —*Jason Ankeny*

● **The Greatest Hits of Petula Clark** / 1986 / GNP ✦✦✦✦
This import collection is much crisper and more vibrant-sounding than the domestic releases. All the major US hits are here, plus some British and European chart successes never heard in the US. —*Bruce Eder*

The Pye Years / 1995 / RPM ✦✦✦
Two of Clark's mid-'60s British albums, *Petula Clark Sings the International Hits* (1965) and *This Is My Song* (1967), combined on one CD, with three B-sides added as bonus tracks. *International Hits*, as the title implies, is devoted to covers of standards and then-popular hit songs. Often that spells snoozefest, but it's more interesting than you might think, mainly because of the MOR-meets-Swinging London ear candy of Tony Hatch's production. A few of these songs, like "I (Who Have Nothing)," are actually pretty dynamic interpretations, and "You Can't Keep Me From Loving You" in particular is a performance on par with her mid-'60s hits. *This Is My Song*, although it includes the hits "Don't Sleep in the Subway" and "This Is My Song," is considerably duller, with less imaginative arrangements. The highlights are actually Clark's own compositions, like "Resist" (another obscurity with hit potential) and the anti-war "On the Path of Glory." The three B-sides include a couple of self-penned items and a brassy number, "High," co-written by Lee Hazlewood and Billy Strange. —*Richie Unterberger*

The Clash
....
f. 1976, London, England, db. 1986
Rock 'n' Roll, Punk
The Sex Pistols may have been the first British punk rock band, but the Clash were the definitive British punk rockers. Where the Pistols were nihilistic, the Clash were fiery and idealistic, charged with righteousness and a leftist political ideology. From the outset, the band was more musically adventurous, expanding their hard rock 'n' roll with reggae, dub, and rap rockabilly, among other roots music. Furthermore, they were blessed with two exceptional songwriters in Joe Strummer and Mick Jones, each with a distinctive voice and style. The Clash copped heavily from classic outlaw imagery, positioning themselves as rebels with a cause. As a result, they won a passionately devoted following on both sides of the Atlantic. While they became rock 'n' roll heroes in the UK, second only to the Jam in terms of popularity, it took the Clash several years to break into the American market, and when they finally did in 1982, they imploded several months later. Though the Clash never became the superstars they always threatened to be, they restored passion and protest to rock 'n' roll. For a while they really did seem like "the only band that mattered." For a band that constantly sang about

revolution and the working class, the Clash had surprisingly traditional roots. Joe Strummer (b. John Graham Mellor, August 21, 1952) was the son of a British diplomat and had spent most of his childhood in boarding school. By the time he was in his early 20s, he had busked on the streets of London and had formed a pub-rock band called the 101'ers. Around the same time, Mick Jones (b. June 26, 1955) was leading a hard rock group called the London SS. Unlike Strummer, Jones came from a working class background in Brixton. Throughout his teens, he was fascinated with rock 'n' roll, and he had formed the London SS with the intent of replicating the hard-driving sound of Mott the Hoople and Faces. Jones' childhood friend Paul Simonon (b. December 15, 1956) joined the group as a bassist in 1976 after hearing the Sex Pistols; he replaced Tony James, who would later join Generation X and Sigue Sigue Sputnik. At the time, the band also featured drummer Tory Crimes (b. Terry Chimes), who had recently replaced Topper Headon (b. Nicky Headon, May 30, 1955). After witnessing the Sex Pistols in concert, Joe Strummer decided to break up the 101'ers in early 1976 in order to pursue a new, harder-edged musical direction. He left the band just before their first single, "Keys to Your Heart," was released. Along with fellow 101'er guitarist Keith Levene, Strummer joined the revamped London SS, now renamed the Clash.

The Clash performed its first concert in the summer of 1976, supporting the Sex Pistols in London. Levene left the band shortly afterward. Hiring Bernard Rhodes, a former business associate of the Sex Pistols' manager Malcolm McLaren, as their manager, the Clash set out on the Pistols' notorious "Anarchy Tour" late in 1976. Though only three concerts were performed on the tour, it nevertheless raised the Clash's profile, and the band secured a record contract in February 1977 with British CBS. Over the course of three weekends, the group recorded their debut album. Once the sessions were completed, Terry Chimes left the group, and Headon came aboard as the band's drummer. In the spring, the Clash's first single, "White Riot," and eponymous debut album were released to great critical acclaim and sales in the UK, peaking at No. 12 on the charts. The American division of US decided *The Clash* wasn't fit for radio play, so it decided not to release the albu; but the import of the record became the largest-selling import of all time. Shortly after the UK release of *The Clash*, the band set out on the whirlwind "White Riot" tour supported by the Jam and the Buzzcocks. The tour was highlighted by a date at London's Rainbow Theatre, when the audience tore the seats out of the venue. During the "White Riot" tour, CBS pulled "Complete Control" off the album as a single, and as a response, the Clash recorded "Complete Control" with reggae icon Lee "Scratch" Perry.

Throughout 1977 Strummer and Jones were in and out of jail for a myriad of minor indiscretions, ranging from vandalism to stealing a pillowcase, while Simonon and Headon were arrested for shooting racing pigeons with an air gun. The Clash's outlaw image was bolstered considerably by such events, but the band also began to branch out into social activism, such as headlining a Rock Against Racism concert. Released in the summer of 1978, the single "(White Man) In Hammersmith Palais" demonstrated the band's growing social consciousness. Shortly after the single peaked at No. 32, the Clash began working on their second album with producer Sandy Pearlman, a former member of Blue Öyster Cult. Pearlman gave *Give 'em Enough Rope*, a clean but powerful sound designed to break the American market. Although that didn't happen—the album peaked at 128 on the US charts in the spring of 1979—the record became an enormous hit in Britain, debuting at No. two on the charts.

Early in 1979 the Clash began their first American tour, called "Pearl Harbor '79." That summer the band released the UK-only EP *The Cost of Living*, which featured a cover of the Bobby Fuller Four's "I Fought the Law." After the late summer release of *The Clash* in America, the group set out on their second US tour, hiring Mickey Gallagher of Ian Dury's Blockheads as a keyboardist. On both of their US tours, the Clash had R&B acts like Bo Diddley, Sam & Dave, Lee Dorsey, and Screamin' Jay Hawkins support them, as well as neo-traditionalist country-rocker Joe Ely and the punk rockabilly band the Cramps. The choice of supporting acts indicated that the Clash was becoming fascinated with older rock 'n' roll and all of its legends. That fascination became the driving force behind the breakthrough double-album *London Calling*. Produced by Guy Stevens, who formerly worked with Mott the Hoople, *London Calling* boasted an array of styles ranging from rockabilly and New Orleans R&B to anthemic hard rock and reggae. Retailing at the price of a single album, the record debuted at No. 9 on the UK charts in late 1979 and climbed to No. 27 on the US charts in the spring of 1980.

The Clash successfully toured the US, the UK, and Europe in early 1980, during which time the pseudo-documentary *Rude Boy* was released in England. During the summer the band released the Dutch-only, dub-inflected single "Bankrobber," which they recorded with DJ Mikey Dread; by the fall, the British branch of CBS was forced by popular demand to release the single. Shortly afterward, the band went to New York to begin the tension-filled, self-produced sessions for their follow-up to *London Calling*. In November, a US-only EP of odds and ends entitled *Black Market Clash* was released. The following month, the triple-record set *Sandanista!* appeared in the UK and the US. The crictical reaction to the album was decidedly mixed, with American critics reacting more favorably than their British counterparts. Furthermore, the band's audience in the UK was shrinking slightly; *Sandanista!* was the first record the group released that sold more copies in the US than the UK.

After spending much of 1981 touring and resting, the Clash reconvened late in the year to record their fifth album with producer Glyn Johns, a former engineer/producer for the Rolling Stones, Who, and Led Zeppelin. Headon left the band shortly after the sessions finished; the press statement said he parted with the group due to political differences, but it was later revealed that the split was due to his heavy drug use. The band replaced Headon with their old drummer, Terry Chimes, around the spring release of *Combat Rock*. The album was the Clash's most commercially successful effort, entering the UK charts at No. 2 and climbing into the American Top Ten in early 1983, thanks to the Top Ten hit single "Rock the Casbah." In the fall of 1982 the Clash opened for the Who on their farewell tour. Though the tour helped *Combat Rock* scale the US charts, the Clash were routinely booed off the stage on every date of the tour.

Although the Clash were at the height of their commercial powers in 1983, the band was beginning fall apart. Chimes was fired in the spring and was replaced by Pete Howard, formerly of Cold Fish. During the summer, the band headlined the US Festival in California; it would be their last major appearance. In September Joe Strummer and Paul Simonon fired Mick Jones becuase he "drifted apart from the original idea of the Clash." Jones formed Big Audio Dynamite the next year, while the Clash hired guitarists Vince White and Nick Sheppard to fill his vacancy. Throughout 1984 the band toured America and Europe, testing the new lineup. The revamped Clash finally released their first album, *Cut the Crap*, in November. The album was greeted with overwhelmingly poor reviews and sales; it would later be disowned by Strummer and Simonon.

Early in 1986 Strummer and Simonon decided to permanently disband the Clash. Several years later Simonon formed the roots-rock band Havana 3 A.M., which released only one album, in 1991; after the record's release, he concentrated on painting. After reuniting with Jones to write songs for Big Audio Dynamite's second album, 1986's *No. 10 Upping Street*, Strummer drifted between musical and film careers, appearing in Alex Cox's *Straight to Hell* (1986) and Jim Jarmusch's *Mystery Train* (1989). He also scored *Permanent Record* (1988) and Cox's *Walker* (1987). Strummer released a solo album, *Earthquake Weather*, in 1989. Shortly afterward he joined the Pogues as a touring rhythm guitarist and vocalist. By 1991 he had quietly drifted away from the spotlight. For the remainder of the decade, Strummer was quiet, appearing on only one other recording—Black Grape's 1996 Top Ten hit, "England's Irie."

Though Strummer and Simonon were both quiet, and Jones was busy with various incarnations of Big Audio Dynamite, rumors of a Clash reunion continued to circulate throughout the '90s. When "Should I Stay or Should I Go?" appeared in a Levi's television commercial in 1992, the song was re-released in the UK by CBS, and it shot to No. 1, fueling reunion speculation. The rumors appeared again in 1995 and 1996, when the Sex Pistols decided to reunite, but the Clash remained quiet. —*Stephen Thomas Erlewine*

☆ **The Clash** / 1977 / Epic ✦✦✦✦✦
Never Mind the Bollocks may have appeared revolutionary, but the Clash's eponymous debut album was pure, unadultarated rage and fury, fueled by passion for both rock 'n' roll and revolution. Though the cliche about punk rock was that the bands couldn't play, the key to the Clash is that they give that illusion, but they really could play *hard*. The charging, relentless rhythms, primitive three-chord rockers, and the poor sound quality give the album a nervy, vital energy. Joe Strummer's slurred wails perfectly compliment the edgy rock, while Mick Jones' clearer singing and his charged guitar breaks make his numbers righteously anthemic. Even at this early stage, the Clash was experimenting with reggae, most notably on the Junior Murvin cover "Police and Thieves" and the extraordinary "White Man in Hammersmith Palais," which was one of five tracks added to the American edition of *The Clash*. "Deny," "Protex Blue" "Cheat," and "48 Hours" were removed from the British edition and replaced for the US release with the British-only singles "Complete Control," "White Man in Hammersmith Palais," "Clash City Rockers," "I Fought the Law," and "Jail Guitar Doors," all of which were stronger than the items they replaced. Though the sequencing and selection were slightly different, the core of the album remained the same, and each of the songs retains its power individually. Few punk songs expressed anger quite as bracingly as "White Riot," "I'm So Bored with the USA.," "Career Opportunities," and "London's Burning," and their power is all the more incredible several decades later. Rock 'n' roll is rarely as edgy, invigorating, and sonically revolutionary as *The Clash*. —*Stephen Thomas Erlewine*

Give 'em Enough Rope / Dec. 1978 / Epic ✦✦✦✦
For their second album, the Clash worked with the American hard-rock producer Sandy Pearlman, best known for his work with Blue Öyster Cult and the Dictators. The teaming was quite controversial within the punk community, and the sound of *Give 'em Enough Rope* is considerably cleaner, but the more direct sound hardly tamed the Clash. While the record doesn't burn with the same intense, amateurish energy of *The Clash*, it does have a big, forceful sound that is nearly as powerful. What keeps *Give 'em Enough Rope* from being a classic is its slightly inconsistent material. Many of the songs are outright classics, particularly the first half of the record ("Safe European Home," "English Civil War," "Tommy Gun," "Julie's in the Drug Squad") and "Stay Free," but the group loses some momentum toward the end. Even with such flaws, *Give 'em Enough Rope* ranks as one of the strongest albums of punk era. —*Stephen Thomas Erlewine*

★ **London Calling** / Dec. 1979 / Epic ✦✦✦✦✦
Give 'em Enough Rope, for all its many attributes, was essentially a holding pattern for the Clash, but the double-album *London Calling* is a remarkable leap forward, incorporating the punk aesthetic into rock 'n' roll mythology and roots music. Before, the Clash had experimented with reggae, but that was no preparation for the dizzying array of styles on *London Calling*. There's punk and reggae, but there's also rockabilly, ska, New Orleans R&B, pop, lounge-jazz, and hard-rock; and while the record isn't tied together by a specific theme, its eclecticism and anthemic punk function as a rallying call. While many of the songs—particulary "London Calling," "Spanish Bombs," and "The Guns of Brixton"—are explicitly political, by acknowledging no boundaries the music itself is political and revolutionary. But it is also invigorating, rocking harder and with more purpose than most albums, let alone double-albums. Over the course of the record, Strummer and Jones (and Paul Simonon, who wrote "The Guns of Brixton") explore their familiar themes of working-class rebellion and anti-establishment rants, but they also tie them in to the old rock 'n' roll traditions and myths, whether it's rockabilly greasers or Stagger Lee, as well as mavericks like doomed actor Montgomery Clift. The result is a stunning statement of purpose and one of the greatest rock 'n' roll albums ever recorded. —*Stephen Thomas Erlewine*

Sandinista! / Dec. 1980 / Epic ✦✦
The Clash sounded as if they could do anything on *London Calling*. For its triple-album followup, *Sandinista!*, they tried do *everything*, adding dub, rap, gospel, and even children's choruses to the punk, reggae, R&B, and roots-rock they already were playing. Instead of presenting a band with a far-reaching vision, as *London Calling* did, *Sandinista!* plays as a messy, confused jumble, which means that its numerous virtues are easy to ignore. Amid all the dub experiments, backward tracks, unfinished songs, and instrumentals, there are a number of classic Clash songs that rank among their best, including "Police on My Back," "The Call-Up," "Somebody Got Murdered," "Charlie Don't Surf," "Hitsville UK," and "Lightning Strikes (Not Once, But Twice)," but it's difficult for anyone but the most dedicated listeners to find them. A few of the failed ideas were worth exploring, but even more—like the children's choir version of "Career Opportunities" or the Terry Doggs song "Lose This Skin"—were not. As the cliche says, there's a great single album within these three records, and those songs make *Sandinista!* worthwhile. Nevertheless, its sloppy attack is disheartening after the tour-de-force of *London Calling* and the focused aggression of *The Clash*. —*Stephen Thomas Erlewine*

Combat Rock / Jun. 1982 / Epic ✦✦✦
On the surface of things, *Combat Rock* appears to be a retreat from the sprawling stylistic explorations of *London Calling* and *Sandinista!* The pounding arena-rock of "Should I Stay or Should I Go?" makes the Clash sound like an arena rock band, and much of the album boasts a muscular, heavy sound, courtesy of producer Glyn Johns. But things aren't quite that simple. *Combat Rock* contains heavy flirtations with rap, funk, and reggae, and it even has a cameo by poet Allen Ginsberg. If this album is, as has often been claimed, the Clash's sell-out effort, it's a very strange way to sell out. Even with the infectious, dance-inflected New Wave pop of "Rock the Casbah" leading the way, there aren't many overt attempts at crossover success, mainly because the group is tearing in two separate directions. Mick Jones wants the Clash to inherit the Who's righteous arena rock stance, and Joe Strummer wants to forge ahead into Black music. The result is an album that is nearly as inconsistent as *Sandinista!*, even though its finest moments—"Should I Stay or Should I Go," "Rock the Casbah," "Straight to Hell"—illustrate why the Clash was able to reach a larger audience than ever before with the record. —*Stephen Thomas Erlewine*

Cut the Crap / 1985 / Epic ✦✦
Hoping to keep the Clash a raw punk phenomenon, Joe Strummer and Paul Simonon kicked Mick Jones out of the band after the success of *Combat Rock*, hiring three unknowns to replace him for *Cut the Crap*. As the title suggests, the group attempts to get back to its roots by stick-

ing to short, fast, hard punk songs. Unfortunately, they sound like a parody of a classic punk band. With the exception of the surprisingly nervy "This Is England," this is all formulaic, tired punk rock that doesn't have the aggression or purpose of early Clash records, let alone the hardcore punk with which the band was now competing. It's a sad end to one of the greatest rock 'n' roll bands, not even offering much of interest for the dedicated fans. —*Stephen Thomas Erlewine*

Story of the Clash, Vol. 1 / 1988 / Epic ✦✦✦✦
The Story of the Clash, Vol. 1 is a severely flawed but useful double-disc retrospective of the Clash's career. Over 28 tracks, most of the Clash's best-known songs are featured, but they're presented out of chronological order, which robs the music of much of its impact. Still, most of the major numbers—"White Riot," "White Man in Hammersmith Palais," "Tommy Gun," "London Calling," "Train In Vain," "Bankrobber," "Rock the Casbah," "Should I Stay or Should I Go"—are included, making it a useful collection for casual fans. —*Stephen Thomas Erlewine*

Clash on Broadway / Nov. 19, 1991 / Epic ✦✦✦✦
Clash on Broadway is a fine triple-disc, 63-song box set covering the Clash's entire career. Although there are very few rarities, it does include all of the band's important songs, including cuts that were available only on EPs, singles, and B-sides. As a result, it's a useful box set even for dedicated fans, presenting their evolution in a logical fashion. Nevertheless, compilations don't always suit the Clash well, because *The Clash* and *London Calling* were powerful individual works in their own right, and hearing them cut up in this fashion alters their impact. Even so, for anyone looking for one set illustrating why the Clash were a great, important and, influential band, *Clash On Broadway* explains exactly why. —*Stephen Thomas Erlewine*

Super Black Market Clash / 1994 / Epic ✦✦✦✦
An expanded version of the *Black Market Clash* EP, *Super Black Market Clash* adds assorted singles and remixes to the original recording. A couple of tracks aren't that interesting, but the majority of the disc is splendid, featuring some of the band's best, but unfortunately overlooked tracks, including "Armagideon Time," "The Prisoner," "Gates of the West," and "Capital Radio One." —*Stephen Thomas Erlewine*

Otis Clay

b. Feb. 11, 1942, Waxhaw, MS
Vocals / Soul, R&B, Soul Blues
Otis Clay made most of his best-known records in Memphis during the early '70s, but he's still universally hailed as Chicago's deep-soul king. In a city filled to overflowing with legendary blues artists, Clay has become the proud standard bearer for Chicago's enduring soul tradition.

Like so many of his contemporaries, Clay's intense vocal style reflects a gospel background. He made the secular jump in 1965, signing with Chicago's One-derful Records and issuing a series of gospel-tinged soul records that were a lot grittier than the customary Windy City soul sound. Clay inaugurated Atlantic's Cotillion subsidiary in 1968 with a supercharged cover of the Sir Douglas Quintet's "She's About a Mover," produced by Rick Hall in Muscle Shoals shortly before the singer joined forces with Hi Records boss Willie Mitchell. With the relentlessly driving Hi Rhythm Section in tow, Clay waxed his biggest seller in 1972, "Trying to Live My Life Without You," later covered very successfully by Bob Seger. Although Clay's tenure on Hi may have been his most commercially potent, he's steadily recorded and gigged ever since. He is a genuine hero in Japan, where he's recorded two live albums filled with the churning grooves, punchy horns, and searing vocals that characterize the best deep soul—no matter where it's recorded. —*Bill Dahl*

Live In Japan / Oct. 22, 1983 / Bullseye Blues ✦✦✦
Otis Clay has long been one of the top R&B/soul singers, and this CD, with its backing horn riffs, repetitive vamps, and gospel influences, is a strong example of his music. Fans of 1960's R&B will want Clay's spirited concert performance. —*Scott Yanow*

That's How It Is / 1991 / Hi ✦✦✦✦
Twenty-one of the finest tracks Clay recorded for Hi during the 1970s are collected on this outstanding compilation. —*Stephen Thomas Erlewine*

● **The Best of the Hi Records Years** / Jul. 23, 1996 / Capitol ✦✦✦✦
Best of the Hi Records Years is an excellent collection of Otis Clay's early-'70s heyday, featuring such songs as "If I Could Reach Out" and the classic "Trying to Live My Life Without You." Although these recordings aren't quite as gritty as his singles for One-derful! and Cotillion Records, since the tight Hi rhythm sections keeps things at a steady, sexy groove, they are nevertheless excellent and deeply soulful, and are arguably his best work, making this compilation an essential addition to any comprehensive '70s soul collection. —*Stephen Thomas Erlewine*

The Clean

f. 1978, Dunedin, New Zealand
Alternative Pop-Rock
The Clean was one of the most influential New Zealand bands of the

post-punk era. The band formed in Dunedin in 1978, when Hamish Kilgour (drums) and his brother David (guitar) recruited David's school friend, guitarist Peter Gutteridge. Soon afterward, they opened for New Zealand punk rockers Enemy.

The Clean was one of the first bands in the country to play original material. They carved out a distinctive noisy, but melodic, sound, distinguished by David's screeching, distorted guitar. When the Kilgour brothers decided in 1979 to relocate the band to Auckland, Gutteridge had already left the lineup. The Clean played with a rotating bassist before David quit the band and moved back to Dunedin, where he was introduced to bassist Robert Scott, and the two started playing together. News of his brother's new musical relationship prompted Hamish to move back to Dunedin and begin the Clean again.

In early 1980 the group began playing around town in earnest. In early 1981 a fan named Roger Shepherd began Flying Nun Records to release a single by the Clean, "Tally Ho!" With its jagged guitar, sweet melody, and persistent organ, "Tally Ho!" reached No. 19 on the charts.

As they prepared to record their first album, they discovered that the few New Zealand engineers didn't care for the band's material. The Clean didn't fight, they backed down, deciding to record on a four-track under the guidance of Chris Knox and Doug Hood. In November, the *Boodle Boodle Boodle* EP was released; it surprised every observer by climbing to No. 4 on the New Zealand charts.

Boodle and the 1982 EP *Great Sounds Great* captured the quirky sides of the Clean's sound, since they did not have the technology to replicate the band's roaring live sound. Later in 1982 the group released their loudest single yet, "Getting Older." Soon after its release, David Kilgour exited the band. Robert Scott left after David's departure, forming a band of his own, the Bats. Hamish Kilgour moved to Christchurch—where Flying Nun Records was located—and bought his own four-track. After Hamish had begun writing and recording, David came up to Christchurch to help finish up the solo tracks, as well as to record some Clean songs. The resulting music, released under the name the Great Unwashed, was collected on the album *Clean Out of Our Minds*. The music was a departure from the Clean's punk-injected sound; it was folkier and more acoustic.

To promote the record, the Kilgours reunited with Peter Gutteridge while still using the name the Great Unwashed. On the ensuing tour, the band concentrated on Gutteridge's backlog of material; at the beginning of 1984, they recorded an EP called *Singles*. *Singles* earned quite a bit of airplay and sales. Bassist Ross Humphries was added so David Kilgour and Gutteridge could both play guitar. But the Great Unwashed broke up within a year. Hamish Kilgour formed Bailter Space with guitarist Alister Parker, Gutteridge began developing a new band called Snapper, and David stopped playing for a few years.

The Clean—the lineup featuring Robert Scott—reunited in 1988 for two concerts in London; a five-song EP culled from the shows was released a year later. The members of the band were encouraged by the results and decided to embark on a world tour. After the tour ended, the band recorded an album that was more straightforward and pop-oriented than their previous material. The record, *Vehicle*, was released in the spring of 1990, and the band supported its release with a world tour. After the tour's completion, the band split again. David Kilgour formed Stephen, Scott returned to the Bats, and Hamish Kilgour was inactive. The group reunited in 1994 to record *Modern Rock*, released in late 1995, followed by *Unknown Country* in 1996. —*Stephen Thomas Erlewine*

Oddities / 1983 / Flying Nun ✦✦✦
Oddities collects a disc's worth of rarities that, despite the extreme lo-fi recording quality, display the band's knack for creating sloppy pop gems. Originally released on cassette only in 1983, *Oddities* was later reissued on CD in 1994 with additional tracks. A nice companion to *Compilation*. —*Chris Woodstra*

● **Compilation** / 1986 / Homestead ✦✦✦✦
Compilation offers a nearly complete overview of the Clean's legendary early recordings, including the classic "Tally Ho" single, highlights from their two EPs (*Boodle Boodle* from 1981 and 1982's *Great Sounds*) and six live bonus tracks (on the CD version only). —*Chris Woodstra*

Oddities 2 / 1988 / Flying Nun ✦✦✦
Oddities 2 is a cassette-only release of rarities, B-sides, and live tracks from their first pre-break-up period (1979-1984), along with some live recordings from their alter-ego project, the Great Unwashed. Though the recording quality is predictably spotty, the songs are surprisingly strong. —*Chris Woodstra*

Vehicle / 1990 / Rough Trade ✦✦✦
The Clean reunited in 1988 for a couple of concerts and followed with *Vehicle* in 1990, their first proper LP. Their pre-breakup material stands as their greatest achievement, but this slightly more polished effort still shines with their trademark fractured pop songs that combine a punky attitude and a classic pop sensibility. —*Chris Woodstra*

Modern Rock / Oct. 10, 1995 / Summershine ✦✦✦

Unknown Country / Nov. 5, 1996 / Flying Nun ✦✦✦

Cleaners from Venus

f. 1980, England
Alternative Pop-Rock, Pop-Rock
The most extensive of singer-songwriter Martin Newell's various projects, Cleaners from Venus recorded some of the finest—and most neglected—British pop-rock of the 1980s. Its failure to find a wider audience is due at least in part to its unconventional method of distribution. After a short, bitter experience in the music business recording for a large label, Newell retreated to his home studio in the beginning of the 1980s, determined not to have to play by the usual compromising music business rules. As the chief of Cleaners from Venus, he and cohorts recorded several albums on their own and distributed them via self-produced cassettes that were available chiefly by mail. Thousands of such acts work in this manner in the cassette underground, but most of them are either off-puttingly amateurish, or forebodingly avant-garde and experimental. Cleaners from Venus were distinguished from the usual lot because they specialized in extremely witty, cheery, and compact pop songs.

But their choice to use underground distribution networks made sense. The musicians were too eccentric and, at times, experimental to withstand the homogenizing influence of record companies. What they lacked in technique—the early tapes often have a hissy sound and thumpy percussion—they more than made up for in pure heart. Newell, who wrote and sang virtually all the material, is a tuneful British eccentric in the mold of Ray Davies or Andy Partridge of the XTC, with a humor akin to Monty Python or the Bonzo Dog Band. Cleaners from Venus couldn't be pigeonholed as revivalists, however, due to the '80s jangle of the guitars, and the expressively yearning qualities of Newell's vocals; the melodies were almost always infectious and bursting with harmonies.

Newell's main partner in the early days of Cleaners from Venus was drummer Lol Elliott. By the mid-'80s Martin had hooked up with the more conventionally skilled pianist Giles Smith, and the Cleaners' recording techniques had improved to the level of "real" records. One result was the glorious *Living with Victoria Grey* tape, with uniformly strong songs that usually reflected pastoral English life with affectionate irony. Another result of their (by cassette underground standards) increasing success and popularity were deals to produce bona fide vinyl LPs for record labels; they even got a deal with RCA in Germany. Almost predictably, the records, with bigger budgets and increased attention to audiophile concerns, sounded a bit mechanical and white-washed compared to the cassettes, even when Cleaners were re-recording material that had originally been released on tape.

By the end of the 1980s, Newell had discontinued the Cleaners from Venus and founded a new, very similar project called Brotherhood of Lizards, which lasted for a while before bassist Nelson (no last name) joined New Model Army. In the 1990s, Newell has established a solo career on indie labels (see separate entry) that finds him carrying on the Cleaners' tradition of thinking pure pop in an undiluted manner. Giles Smith has written a book about his obsessive rock fandom, *Lost in Music*, which draws to some degree upon his experiences in Cleaners from Venus. There have been a couple of Cleaners compilations, but unfortunately much of the group's best work is heard on their privately produced cassettes, which can be hard to find. —*Richie Unterberger*

Blow Away Your Troubles / 1981 / (no label) ✦✦
The only Cleaners project where the home production values are a serious impediment to pleasurable listening. There's lots of muffle, and too much bottom, on these 1980-81 efforts, "recorded on a hand-cranked, mud-cooled, reel-to-reel, sound-on-sound tape recorder" (from the sleeve note). As a *songwriter*, however, Newell was already a talent of some distinction. It's too bad these weren't recorded better, but Newell fans will appreciate the melodic strength of much of the material. "Marilyn on a Train," in particular, is about as achingly tuneful as anything he's come up with in his whole career. —*Richie Unterberger*

On Any Normal Monday / 1982 / (no label) ✦✦✦
Because the fidelity here is rather primitive compared to his later tapes and records, it's likely that only serious Newell/Cleaners fans will want to get this deep into his discography. If (only slightly) funky production values don't bother you (or actually please you), you shouldn't be disappointed with this. The songs are there, and that's the important thing. Nicely catchy, interesting compositions, sung with a sense of humor, especially "Be an Idiot Popstar" (a David Byrne satire, perhaps?) and the lounge-pop satire "A Fool like You." —*Richie Unterberger*

In the Golden Autumn / 1983 / (no label) ✦✦✦✦
Martin Newell—working on this particular project with Martin Chapman and Paul Ripley-Thomas—really began to hit his stride on this tape, which was filled to the gills with fetching melodies and odd, evocative lyrics, like Syd Barrett with a far stronger hold on reality. The limitations of home recording technology are sometimes a drawback, particularly

in the boxy quality of the percussion. Yet it's also a good illustration of how imaginative home recording auteurs can be, especially in the tinkly pianos, hauntingly echoing guitar jangles, and the mysterious ways the guitars and voices are often altered via various effects. It's tied together with his unique mix of cheery optimism and longing regret/nostalgia. Aside from *Living with Victoria Grey*, it's the Cleaners cassette that is most deserving of CD reissue. —*Richie Unterberger*

Under Wartime Conditions / 1984 / Acid Tapes ✦✦✦
Actually this was first issued as a tape in 1984, and then on vinyl in 1986. It's not the most outstanding of their efforts, but it's a reasonably solid survey of their combination of savvy pop melodies with idiosyncratically English weirdness. "Song for Syd Barrett" isn't the only thing here reminiscent of Television Personalities, but Newell crafts a more diverse sound, using touches of glockenspiel, drum machine, sleighbells, and even a saucepan to embellish the guitar-rock core. —*Richie Unterberger*

● Living with Victoria Grey / 1986 / (no label) ✦✦✦✦
One of the lost treasures of '80s rock, this is a rousingly melodic set of jangly guitar tunes reflecting the charms and foibles of modern-day England, with zany sound bites a la Monty Python linking the tracks. "Ilya Kuryakin Looked at Me" and the gorgeous, acoustic "Clara Bow" illustrate Newell's knack for paying homage to past heroes with a curious sense of loss and ambiguity. "Victoria Grey," on the other hand, is anthemic guitar power-pop at its best; "Pearl" (written by XTC's Andy Partridge) is an a cappella meeting of the Turtles and the Beach Boys. The best album that Cleaners from Venus ever did, it was made available only on cassette, and would be worthy of CD reissue. —*Richie Unterberger*

Going to England / 1987 / Ammunition ✦✦
A major disappointment, even though this contains some of Newell's strongest songwriting. Many of these songs were first released on the superb *Living with Victoria Grey* cassette; subjected to antiseptic production in studios with bigger budgets, the impact of the songs is neutered. There are few other clearer examples of the heart of a group's vision being torn out by over-professionalism. The material's heard to much better effect on the *Living with Victoria Grey* tape, which will unfortunately be hard to locate (though hardly any more so than this import LP). —*Richie Unterberger*

Town and Country / 1988 / RCA ✦✦✦✦
A big improvement on *Going to England*. The sound is still somewhat cleaned-up from what you'll hear on Cleaners cassettes, but not so much so that it gets in the way of the songs. Some of Newell's most jubilant ("Let's Get Married") and gleefully silly ("I Was a Teenage Idiot Dancer") writing is here; "The Beat Generation and Me" is one of the best examples of his ability to write about the icons of the past with bittersweet nostalgia that steers clear of revivalism. Giles Smith proves to be a songwriter of merit as well on his two compositions, particularly the dainty "Felicity." —*Richie Unterberger*

Number 13 / Jun. 1990 / Man At The Off License ✦✦✦✦
No surprises here, just the well-constructed, deviously quirky pop-rock that one came to expect from Cleaners from Venus. Everything here was written and played in a bedroom on an eight-track machine by "the Psychedelic Gardener" (i.e. Martin Newell). It's probably one of Cleaners' most straightforward releases, but also one of the most accomplished, with a few songs that would be re-recorded for Newell's solo album, *The Greatest Living Englishman*. —*Richie Unterberger*

The Cleftones

f. 1955, Jamaica, Queens, NY, db. 1964
Doo Wop
Formed in Queens, NY, in 1955, the Cleftones consisted of five friends from Jamaica High School—Herb Cox (lead), Warren Corbin (bass), Charlie James (first tenor), William McClain (baritone), and Berman Patterson (second tenor). Originally signed to Gee, the group released its first single, "You Baby You," late in 1955; an up-tempo doo wop song, the record became a regional hit. "Little Girl of Mine," the Cleftones' second single, broke nationally, charting at No. 8 R&B and No. 57 pop in 1956; two other similar singles, "Can't We Be Sweethearts" and "String Around My Heart," were released the same year, but they failed to attract national attention. "See You Next Year," a ballad the group recorded in 1957, did not earn an audience outside of New York. Two years later McClain left the group and was replaced by Gene Pearson from the Rivileers. Patricia Spann was added to the Cleftones' lineup that year, which helped nudge the band away from traditional group-oriented doo wop harmonies and toward a vocal sound dominated by the lead vocals. In 1961 the Cleftones realized the potential of the sound with their smash hit version of the standard "Heart and Soul"; it became the group's biggest hit, reaching No. 18 on both pop and R&B charts. Later that year the group had another hit with "For Sentimental Reasons," but the band had reached a peak with "Heart and Soul" and was

never able to reach those heights again. The Cleftones broke up in 1964, three years after their greatest success. —*Stephen Thomas Erlewine*

● **The Best of the Cleftones** / 1991 / Rhino ✦✦✦✦
The careening "Heart and Soul" was their only hit (1961), but doo wop nuts will love this entire set. —*John Floyd*

George Clinton
....

b. Jul. 22, 1940, Kannapolis, NC
Synthesizer, Keyboards, Vocals / Funk, Urban
The mastermind of the Parliament/Funkadelic collective during the 1970s, George Clinton broke up both bands by 1981 and began recording solo albums, occasionally performing live with his former bandmates as the P-Funk All-Stars. Born in Kannapolis, NC, on July 22, 1940, Clinton became interested in doo wop while living in New Jersey during the early '50s. He formed the Parliaments in 1955, based out of a barbershop back room where he straightened hair. The group had a small R&B hit during 1967, but Clinton began to mastermind the Parliaments' activities two years later. Recording as both Parliament and Funkadelic, the group revolutionized R&B during the '70s, twisting soul music into funk by adding influences from several late-'60s acid heroes: Jimi Hendrix, Frank Zappa, and Sly Stone. The Parliament/Funkadelic machine ruled Black music during the '70s, capturing over 40 R&B hit singles (including three No. 1s) and recording three platinum albums.

By 1980 George Clinton began to be weighed down by legal difficulties arising from Polygram's acquisition of Parliament's label, Casablanca. Jettisoning both the Parliament and Funkadelic names (but not the musicians), Clinton signed to Capitol in 1982 both as a solo act and as the P-Funk All-Stars. His first solo album, 1982's *Computer Games*, contained the Top 20 R&B hit "Loopzilla." Several months later, the title track from Clinton's *Atomic Dog* EP hit No. 1 on the R&B charts; it stayed at the top spot for four weeks, but it managed only No. 101 on the pop charts. Clinton stayed on Capitol for three more years, releasing three studio albums and frequently charting singles—"Nubian Nut," "Last Dance," "Do Fries Go with That Shake"—in the R&B Top 30. During much of the three-year period from 1986 to 1989, Clinton was embroiled in legal difficulties (resulting from the myriad royalty problems latent during the '70s recordings of over 40 musicians for four labels under three names). Also problematic during the latter half of the '80s was Clinton's disintegrating reputation as a true forefather of rock; by the end of the decade, however, a generation of rappers reared on P-Funk were beginning to name-check him.

In 1989 Clinton signed a contract with Prince's Paisley Park label and released his fifth solo studio album, *The Cinderella Theory*. After one more LP for Paisley Park (*Hey Man, Smell My Finger*), Clinton signed with Sony 550. His first release, 1996's *T.A.P.O.A.F.O.M.* ("the awesome power of a fully operational mothership), reunited the funk pioneer with several of his Parliament/Funkadelic comrades from the '70s. Clinton's *Greatest Funkin' Hits* (1996) teamed old P-Funk hits with new-school rappers such as Digital Underground, Ice Cube, and Q-Tip. —*John Bush*

● **Computer Games** / Nov. 5, 1982 / Capitol ✦✦✦✦
Former Parliament and Funkadelic leader George Clinton made a major comeback under his own name with this album, whose irresistible grooves, vocal choruses, and absurd humor were essentially identical to the music of Funkadelic's salad days. Were you wondering where that "woof-woof" cheer heard on Arsenio Hall and at Black concerts came from? Check out "Atomic Dog." —*William Ruhlmann*

You Shouldn't-Nuf Bit Fish / Dec. 1983 / Capitol ✦✦✦
While it kept the funk percolating, George Clinton's follow-up to his post-Parliament-Funkadelic solo debut *Computer Games* didn't boast any tracks as compelling (or as nutty) as "Atomic Dog," though "Nubian Nut" and "Last Dance," which made the R&B Top 40, were fun. Most of the second side was funk without form, a common failing of Clinton's approach. —*William Ruhlmann*

Some of My Best Jokes Are Friends / Jul. 1985 / Capitol ✦✦✦
With technology having taken over R&B in a major way by the mid-'80s, George Clinton made a point of "updating" his P-Funk by being much more high-tech and using keyboards, drum machines, and sequencers extensively. On his third "solo album," *Some of My Best Jokes Are Friends*, Clinton even recruits Britain's very technology-oriented new waver Thomas Dolby to help with the production on a few cuts. *Jokes* is far from his best effort, and sometimes comes across as forced and unnatural. But the CD definitely has its strong points, including the addictive "Bodyguard," the eerie "Bangladesh," and anti-war protest songs "Bullet Proof" and "Thrashin'." With Parliament and Funkadelic, Clinton often had fun making strong social and political statements in a subliminal fashion; this time, however, he's much more direct. Despite its strengths, *Jokes* is an album that only Clinton's most devoted followers should invest in; those exploring his innovations for the first time would do much better to purchase one of his classic Parliament or

Funkadelic albums of the '70s (or, for that matter, his first "solo album" *Computer Games*.) —*Alex Henderson*

Best of George Clinton / 1986 / Capitol ✦✦✦
This focuses on the best early Clinton material outside of the Parliament/Funkadelic arena. Most of the tracks aren't as humorously spectacular as "Atomic Dog," but there are a couple of clever ones from other albums, such as "Loopzilla." —*Ron Wynn*

Mothership Connection (Live from the Summit, Houston, Texas) / 1986 / Capitol ✦✦
Credited to George Clinton Parliament Funkadelic, *The Mothership Connection (Live from the Summit, Houston, Texas)* is a discount-priced, six-track mini-LP consisting of one side devoted to the 24-minute soundtrack for a video of the same name, backed with three previously released Clinton studio tracks. A sprawling, often impressive concert recording featuring the immense Mothership Connection organization under George Clinton's reign. This set was perhaps the only time any album conveyed the sense of spectacle, chaos, wild humor, and musical mayhem that were routinely on display during their live shows. —*Ron Wynn*

R&B Skeletons in the Closet / Apr. 1986 / Capitol ✦✦✦✦
A definite improvement over the uneven *Some of My Best Jokes Are Friends*, the considerably more focused and confident *R&B Skeletons in the Closet* is one of George Clinton's strongest solo efforts. The P-Funkster continues using technology extensively, but this time, his blend of technology and "real instruments" sounds much more natural. Though not quite in a class with Parliament classics like *Mothership Connection* or *Funkentelechy vs. the Placebo Syndrome* or Funkadelic treasures ranging from *Cosmic Slop* to *Uncle Jam Wants You, Skeletons* is a superb collection that's well worth acquiring. The CD kicks into high gear with the wildly infectious "Hey Good Lookin'" and maintains that high level of excitement on such driving, sweaty, funk treasures as "Do Fries Go with That Shake?," the appropriately titled "Intense," and the title song. Clinton's eccentricity and outrageous sense of humor serve him well on "Electric Pygmies" and "Mix-Master Suite," an unorthodox, quirky, and cinematic ode to hip-hop drawing on everything from jazz to classical music to Western movies. Many of Clinton's long-time associates are on hand to help make this album the artistic success it is, including saxman Maceo Parker, trombonist Fred Wesley, and the ever-amusing Bootsy Collins. —*Alex Henderson*

The Cinderella Theory / Aug. 1989 / Paisley Park ✦✦✦
On his first album for Prince's Paisley Park record label, George Clinton's willingness to experiment with samplers and hip-hop (including guest appearances by such artists as Chuck D and Flavor Flav of Public Enemy) resulted in a slightly inconsistent record, but it has more than enough truly fine songs to make *The Cinderella Theory* rank among his best solo albums. —*Stephen Thomas Erlewine*

Hey Man, Smell My Finger / Oct. 1993 / Paisley Park ✦✦✦✦
Hey Man, Smell My Finger is everything a great George Clinton album should be—conceptually disjointed, overlong, silly, sloppy, and funky as hell. Thankfully, the music here is his best since *Computer Games*, and the album proves just how responsible he is for much of the music of the 1990s, as the irresistible single "Paint the White House Black" illustrates with its numerous cameos. —*Stephen Thomas Erlewine*

T.A.P.O.A.F.O.M. [The Awesome Power of a Fully-Operational Mothership] / Jun. 1996 / 550 Music/Epic ✦✦
The Awesome Power of a Fully-Operational Mothership is the first George Clinton album to show signs of a Dr. Dre G-funk influence. Where his previous album, *Hey Man, Smell My Finger*, was pretty much nothing but standard P-funk, *Awesome Power* slows the beat down just as Dre does on *The Chronic*. The difference is, Dre actually works those grooves into songs, where Clinton just lets the funk meander. He doesn't even try to write songs—he operates under the belief that ceaseless jamming and randomly interjected vocals constitute a good groove. And they do, when given the right source material and musicians. On *Awesome Power*, Clinton has neither. The musicians may have all played with various incarnations of Parliament, but they sound tired and bored on the album; there isn't a single instant when they latch on to a good groove. On *Awesome Power*, George Clinton sounds more out of touch with contemporary funk and R&B than he ever has. —*Stephen Thomas Erlewine*

Greatest Funkin' Hits / Oct. 29, 1996 / Capitol ✦✦✦
Greatest Funkin' Hits has something of a misleading title. It implies that all of George Clinton's biggest solo hits, in their original forms, are featured on this compilation. Instead, *Greatest Funkin' Hits* takes Clinton's best-known songs—not just solo hits like "Atomic Dog" and "Do Fries Go with That Shake," but also Parliament/Funkadelic songs like "Flashlight," "Mothership Connection," "Knee Deep," and "Bop Gun"—and presents them in remixed forms. Sometimes the remixes are good—Coolio's take on "Atomic Dog" is fun, and Ice Cube's appear-

ance on "Bop Gun (One Nation)" is terrific—but often, the remixes are perfunctory and uninspired, making the album a tedious listening experience. Most importantly, it should not be considered in any way as a greatest-hits album; it's simply another in a long line of pointless Clinton-associated remix albums. —*Leo Stanley*

Clover

f. Jul. 1967, Mill Valley, CA, **db.** 1978
Rock 'n' Roll, Country-Rock, Pub Rock
Clover is one of those bands that is remembered for its illustrious associations rather than its actual accomplishments. It was a country-rock band formed in Mill Valley, CA, in July 1967 by Johnny Ciambotti (bass), John McFee (guitar, vocals), Alex Call (guitar, vocals), and Mitch Howie (drums). This lineup made two albums for nearby Fantasy Records in the early '70s, after which Howie left and the group was expanded to a sextet with the addition of Huey Lewis (harmonica, vocals), Sean Hopper (keyboards, vocals), and Mickey Shine (drums). Clover moved to England in 1976 at the behest of Nick Lowe, where they made two more albums and served as the backup group on Elvis Costello's debut album, *My Aim Is True*. They returned to the US in 1978 and broke up, with McFee going on to the Doobie Brothers and Lewis and Hopper forming the nucleus of Huey Lewis & the News. —*William Ruhlmann*

Love on the Wire / 1977 / Mercury ✦✦✦
Not surprisingly, Clover's fourth and final album, the second of its British sojourn, had a harder rock edge than its predecessors. Clover had come to England as a California country-rock outfit, only to land in the middle of the punk-rock revolt. Its first British album, *Clover* (or *Unavailable*, as it was called in the UK), retained the country sound, but by the end of 1977, the band was all uptempo rock and twin guitar leads, courtesy of Alex Call and John McFee. The music wasn't punk, exactly, but it was more aggressive. Still, Clover remained an essentially good-natured musicians' band, as the loose a cappella version of Leiber and Stoller's "Keep on Rolling" demonstrated. In another time and place, maybe that would have mattered. —*William Ruhlmann*

● **Clover [Mercury]** / 1977 / Mercury ✦✦✦✦
In 1976 Clover relocated from Mill Valley, CA, to London, where the group hooked up with managers/record company executives Jake Riviera and Dave Robinson and signed to PolyGram Records, which, in early 1977, released this, their third album. In the UK, the LP appeared on PolyGram's Vertigo label and was called *Unavailable;* in the US, PolyGram's Mercury label felt that title was a bit uncommercial and opted for the generic *Clover*, which, as it happened, had already been used for their Fantasy Records debut album in 1970. In any case, it was apparent that Riviera and Robinson felt that they'd hit upon a more authentic, American version of Brinsley Schwartz—country-rock with an edge. In fact, the band was all over the map stylistically. There were two lead singers, the smooth-voiced Alex Call and the gruffer Huey Lewis, and they sounded too different to be in the same band, much less on the same song. Multi-instrumentalist John McPhee kept introducing touches of steel guitar and violin into what otherwise were rock tracks, while Lewis' harmonica was full of blues. It might have made for an interesting mixture if the result were a distinct musical identity, but either because of the songwriting or the arranging, it wasn't. And while the move across the Atlantic had earned the group a Dew recording contract, it also landed them in an emerging punk-rock scene with which they had nothing in common. "I come so far from San Francisco to walk these streets alone," sang Call, and despite the group's talent, it was easy to see why. —*William Ruhlmann*

Chronicle / 1979 / Fantasy ✦✦✦✦

The Clovers

f. 1948, Washington, D.C.
R&B, Doo Wop
One of the earliest doo wop vocal groups, formed in the late '40s in Washington, DC. Original members were Buddy Bailey, Matthew McQuater, Hal Lucas, Jr., and Harold Winley. Bobby Mitchell had replaced Bailey by the time the group was signed to the fledgling Atlantic label in 1950. The Clovers racked up 13 Top Ten R&B hits between 1951 and 1954, all showcasing their solid harmonies and unerring rhythmic verve.

Before the early '50s, most non-gospel Black vocal groups were in the smooth pop vein of the Inkspots and Mills Brothers. Then the Clovers burst on the scene in 1951 with "Don't You Know I Love You," and things would never be the same.

Under the influence of Atlantic Records' Ahmet Ertegun (who wrote and produced most of their early songs), the Clovers combined quartet harmony, the big dance beat of the R&B jump bands, and the rawer sounds of urban blues into an exciting new blend that caught on with

the young Black audience and put them consistently at the top of the R&B charts in the early '50s.

Going beyond this, just as their contemporary B.B. King was doing for blues, lead singers Buddy Bailey and later Charlie White brought a gospel influence to Ertegun's bluesy R&B songs—helping to lay the foundation for the soul music to come. —*George Bedard & Cub Koda*

★ **Down in the Alley: The Best of the Clovers** / Oct. 1, 1991 / Rhino ✦✦✦✦✦
Down in the Alley—Best of the Clovers is an excellent compilation of their best and earliest sides, including "Nip Sip," "Don't You Know I Love You," and "One Mint Julep." —*Cub Koda*

Love Potion No. 9 / The Best of the Clovers / 1991 / EMI America ✦✦✦✦
Love Potion No. 9 / The Best of the Clovers features their later sides for United Artists, including the classic title track. —*Cub Koda*

The Coasters

f. Feb. 1956, Los Angeles, CA, **db.** 1972
R&B, Rock 'n' Roll, Doo Wop
Possibly the most popular doo wop group of the '50s, the Coasters started on the West Coast as the Robins, scoring hits under the writing-and-production helm of Jerry Leiber and Mike Stoller. When Atlantic signed Leiber and Stoller as a production team, the group split into two factions; the core of the group became the Coasters and moved to New York to record, while the Robins continued on the West Coast, to diminishing acclaim. The Coasters' hits, some of the most finely crafted, well written, and hilarious in the genre, continued throughout the decade. Carl Gardner's sly leads and Bobby Nunn's bass singing defined their sound through numerous personnel changes. When their time on the charts came to an end, a number of "Coasters" groups suddenly proliferated (much like the Drifters), many of them still dotting the landscape of a million oldies shows and still singing those classic songs. —*Cub Koda*

☆ **50 Coastin' Classics: Anthology** / Nov. 24, 1992 / Rhino ✦✦✦✦
Although it may well be too much for the casual fan, this double CD is easily the best Coasters retrospective ever assembled. Besides featuring every one of their hits, it contains nine strong tunes cut in the mid-'50s by the Robins, who evolved into the Coasters after some personnel changes. As for the enticing obscurities, "Three Cool Cats" and "Besame Mucho" were cut by the Beatles on unreleased recordings in the early '60s, and "Ain't That Just Like Me" would be a small hit for the Searchers. "Down in Mexico" and "Brazil" are cool R&B/Latin melodramas, and "Shoppin' for Clothes," "What About Us," and "That Is Rock & Roll" are half-forgotten vignettes of youthful independence that stack up against the best songs of Jerry Leiber and Mike Stoller, who wrote most of the group's material. Indeed, there's little difference in quality between the hits and the B-sides on this comp, either in the group's matchless ensemble R&B/comedy vocals or Leiber/Stoller's witty songwriting. The accompanying booklet features comments on most of the tracks by Leiber and Stoller themselves. —*Richie Unterberger*

★ **The Very Best of the Coasters** / 1993 / Rhino ✦✦✦✦
The Coasters were the 1950s' (and early rock's) dominant novelty/comic R&B ensemble, benefiting from Jerry Leiber and Mike Stoller's lyrical wit and inspired production. They weren't simply proficient clowns; the Coasters were a skilled vocal unit whose talents were used on slice-of-life narratives, prophetic youth manifestos, and even an occasional teen anthem, as well as the prototype humorous vehicles "Yakety Yak" and "Poison Ivy." Although Rhino has already given them the deluxe two-disc treatment, consumers who either don't want that much Coasters material or prefer only the hits are nicely served by this 18-track anthology. It contains every major release, plus valuable lesser-known selections such as "Shoppin' for Clothes" and "What About Us." —*Ron Wynn*

Eddie Cochran

b. Oct. 3, 1938, Oklahoma City, OK, **d.** Apr. 17, 1960, Wiltshire, England
Guitar, Vocals / Rock 'n' Roll, Rockabilly
Somehow, time has not accorded Eddie Cochran quite the same respect as other early rockabilly pioneers like Buddy Holly, or even Ricky Nelson or Gene Vincent. This is partially attributable to his very brief lifespan as a star; he had only a couple of big hits before dying in a car crash during a British tour in 1960. He was in the same league as the best rockabilly stars, though, with a brash, fat guitar sound that helped lay the groundwork for the power chord. He was also a good songwriter and singer, celebrating the joys of teenage life—the parties, the music, the adolescent rebellion—with an economic wit that bore some similarities to Chuck Berry. Cochran was more lighthearted and less ironic than Berry, though, and if his work was less consistent and not as penetrating, it was almost always exuberant.

Cochran's mid-'50s beginnings in the record industry are a bit confusing. His family had moved to Southern California around 1950, and in 1955 he made his first recordings as half of the Cochran Brothers. Here's the confusing part: although the other half of the act was really named Hank Cochran, he was *not* Eddie's brother. (Hank Cochran would become a noted country songwriter in the 1960s.) Eddie was already an accomplished rockabilly guitarist and singer on these early sides, and he started picking up some session work as well, also finding time to make demos and write songs with Jerry Capehart, who became his manager.

Cochran's big break came about in novel fashion. In mid-1956, while Cochran and Capehart were recording music for low-budget films, Boris Petroff asked Eddie if he'd be interested in appearing in a movie that a friend was directing. The film was *The Girl Can't Help It*, and the song he would sing in it was "Twenty-Flight Rock." This is the same song that Paul McCartney would use to impress John Lennon upon their first meeting in 1957. (Paul could not only play it, but knew all of the lyrics.)

Cochran had his first Top 20 hit in early 1957, "Sittin' in the Balcony," with an echo-chambered vocal reminiscent of Elvis. That single was written by John D. Loudermilk, but Eddie would write much of his material, including his only Top Ten hit, "Summertime Blues." A definitive teenage anthem with hints of the overt protest that would seep into rock music in the 1960s, it was also a technical tour de force for the time: Cochran overdubbed himself on guitar to create an especially thick sound. One of the classic early rock singles, "Summertime Blues" was revived a decade later by proto-metal group Blue Cheer, and was a concert staple for the Who, who had a small American hit with a cover version. (Let's not mention Alan Jackson's country rendition in the 1990s.)

That, disappointingly, was the extent of Cochran's major commercial success in the US. "C'mon Everybody," a chugging rocker that was almost as good as "Summertime Blues," made the Top 40 in 1959 and gave Eddie his first British Top Tenner. As is the case with his buddy Gene Vincent, though, you can't judge his importance by mere chart statistics. Cochran was very active in the studio, and while his output wasn't as consistent as Buddy Holly's (another good friend of Eddie's), he laid down a few classic or near-classic cuts that are just as worthy as his hits. "Somethin' Else," "My Way" (which the Who played in concert at the peak of psychedelia), "Weekend" (covered by the Move), and "Nervous Breakdown" are some of the best of these, and belong in the collection of every rockabilly fan. He was also (like Holly) an innovator in the studio, using overdubbing at a time when that practice was barely known on rock recordings.

Cochran is more revered today in Britain than the United States, due in part to the tragic circumstances of his death. In the spring of 1960 he toured the UK with Vincent, to a wild reception, in a country that had rarely had the opportunity to see American rock 'n' roll stars in the flesh. En route to London to fly back to the States for a break, the car Cochran was riding in, with his girlfriend (and songwriter) Sharon Sheeley and Gene Vincent, was in a serious accident. Vincent and Sheeley survived, but Cochran died less than a day later, at the age of 21. —*Richie Unterberger*

Portrait of a Legend / 1985 / Rockstar ✦✦✦
Fine-looking and fine-sounding collection of unreleased stereo versions and alternate takes, this is nonetheless unnecessary for all but Cochran completists. In the spirit of numerous Beatles bootlegs (though this LP is quite official), these are, in the main, studio recordings with small (sometimes minute) differences in the mixing, or stereo versions that are not easy to come by on official releases, although mono versions of the exact same takes are plentiful. There are plenty of fine songs here ("Weekend," "Summertime Blues," "C'mon Everybody," "Three Steps to Heaven"), but they're better heard both in their more common versions and in the context of a coherent anthology. And if you need to settle for just one version of "Summertime Blues" or "C'mon Everybody," why spring for the "Summertime Blues" *without* the echoed vocal, or "C'mon Everybody" *missing* a guitar overdub? —*Richie Unterberger*

The Early Years / 1988 / Ace ✦✦✦
Compilation of 16 tracks from the mid-'50s, most or all dating from before Cochran's breakthrough to national recognition with "Twenty-Flight Rock." Some were recorded when Eddie was half of the Cochran Brothers, with (the unrelated) Hank Cochran; there are also tracks credited to Jerry Capehart and Albert Stone, on which Eddie most likely had a prominent role, as session man or producer (the liner notes are resolutely unhelpful in providing exact details). Most of this is pretty solid rockabilly, not much below the standards of Cochran's best releases. There are also a couple of hot instrumentals and ballad-type numbers on which Eddie employs a husky, echoed Elvisoid delivery. A decent release, but assembled in a scattershot fashion. If you're interested enough in Cochran to want to track this down, you may well also be interested enough in him to spring for a box set, and most or all of these are contained on whatever box set you manage to locate. —*Richie Unterberger*

Box Set / 1988 / Liberty ✦✦✦
This six-LP import—which still, somehow, manages not to include every track Cochran recorded—is excessive for the non-fanatic. Nevertheless, it does include quite a few obscure, interesting, pre-fame performances from the mid-'50s (some as part of the Cochran Brothers). Other bonuses include a live 1960 British TV broadcast, an album's worth of sessions and his work as a producer, and entire sides of instrumentals and stereo versions, as well as a 32-page booklet. —*Richie Unterberger*

★ **Legendary Masters** / Mar. 1990 / EMI America ✦✦✦✦✦
The definitive single-disc collection of Cochran's best: "Summertime Blues," "Cut Across Shorty," "Something Else," "Come on Everybody," and "Twenty-Flight Rock." All the hits; all the feeling. —*Cub Koda*

Singin' to My Baby/Never To Be / Feb. 23, 1993 / Capitol ✦✦✦✦
Two original albums on one compact disc, with only two hits between the two—"Sittin' in the Balcony" and "Twenty Flight Rock." But for devoted fans of Eddie Cochran, this lovingly packaged CD is worth their time, even if some of the material is slightly weak. *Singin' to My Baby* concentrates on ballad material; the posthumously released *Never To Be Forgotten* has more rockers. —*Stephen Thomas Erlewine*

Bruce Cockburn

b. May 27, 1945, Pembroke, Ontario, Canada
Dulcimer, Guitar, Vocals / Singer-Songwriter, Contemporary Folk
Immensely popular in his native Canada, singer-songwriter Bruce Cockburn has found only cult success south of the border, in spite of a rich, varied body of work and considerable critical nods. He has won numerous Juno Awards and has kept the quality control on most of his albums at a high level. Cockburn began his musical career traveling through Europe and performing in the streets; he later enrolled at Boston's Berklee School of Music. Before recording his self-titled solo debut in 1970, Cockburn played organ in a Top 40 cover band and then harmonica in a blues group. Cockburn's first decade of work (1970-1979) is largely literate, singer-songwriter folk-rock, often with a strong Christian tone and mystical, devotional lyrics. In 1979 Cockburn had his only major US single, "Wondering Where the Lions Are," which peaked at No. 21. The accompanying album, *Dancing in the Dragon's Jaw*, saw Cockburn augmenting his music with worldbeat rhythms, an approach he would continue over his next few albums. Cockburn toned down his Christian viewpoint for much of the 1980s, partially as a way of disconnecting himself from the American religious right, which he found antithetical to his own spiritual beliefs, and partially to concentrate on more humanitarian, political subject matter. Cockburn had traveled extensively across several continents, which provided him with a wide musical palette and plenty of injustice to address in his songs. In 1984 Cockburn produced an AOR hit, "If I Had a Rocket Launcher," whose accompanying video depicted conditions in war-torn Central America and gained a fair amount of MTV play. Cockburn's later 1980s work took on a more streamlined rock sound, and his political agenda was weighted towards environmental concerns, as well as oppression. In the 1990s, Cockburn's work has returned to a more introspective feel. —*Steve Huey*

Bruce Cockburn / 1971 / Epic ✦✦
Bruce Cockburn's self-titled debut's blend of diversity, enthusiasm, and innocence never quite resurfaced in Cockburn's work, especially in his more clinical, politically inclined tracts of later decades. The opening number "Going to the Country" still evokes that hippie-esque, back-to-the-earth movement as well as any song ever recorded, complete with a sly wink that keeps it fresh to this day. And since this *was* 1970, the album also comes equipped with some of those quaint excesses of the period; try the nasal tone poem gracing "The Bicycle Trip." "Musical Friends" remains a lively, happy-go-lucky classic with piano signature lifted from Paul McCartney's playbook; it's difficult to picture the dour Cockburn of more recent years ever having this much fun. In contrast, "Thoughts on a Rainy Afternoon" offers a trance-like, introspective atmosphere reminiscent of British folkie legend Nick Drake. —*Roch Parisien*

High Winds White Sky / 1971 / Columbia ✦✦
Cockburn's second release is a much more mature effort. This time around, he not only accompanies himself on guitar, but uses piano and backup musicians to flesh out the arrangements to great effect. Highlights here include "Golden Serpent Blues" and "One Day I Walk," which was to be covered by Tom Rush. Another fine effort. —*James Chrispell*

Sunwheel Dance / 1972 / Columbia ✦✦
Showing a decidedly English traditional feel in spots, *Sunwheel Dance* is a surprise for those who were looking for more of the same. It takes on different textures and hues depending on the song, from simple folk ("Feet Fall on the Road") to jazz-influenced instrumentals ("Sunwheel Dance") to a country-folk blues in "Dialogue with the Devil." Cockburn has begun to show that he couldn't be categorized, and while that made listening to his music so enjoyable, he had a hard time at the retail level. But if you're willing to take a little time and listen with an open ear, you'll find much here to celebrate. —*James Chrispell*

Night Vision / 1973 / Columbia ✦✦
A little darker this time out (hence the title), Bruce Cockburn's fourth album holds even greater rewards. Backed by a complete band, many of the songs hold up better through time. Sure, there are still the light-hearted folksy bits like "The Blues Got the World . . . ," but there's also a gutsier sound exemplified in "You Don't Have to Play the Horses" and even a trick out of the Tom Waits song-style on "Mama Just Wants to Barrelhouse All Night Long." No matter what type of music you're looking for, there's something here that will tickle your fancy. —*James Chrispell*

Salt, Sun and Time / 1974 / True North ✦✦✦
After coming across with a band, Bruce Cockburn pulled back and came up with an album that recalls his first release. That's not to say that the sound is folky, it's not. There's a much more complex feel to what's here, especially the instrumental title track, which shows a strong John Martyn influence. And while the songs are complex in texture and feel, they aren't hard to get into. In fact, this album grows on you the more you play it. Truly something that has endured. —*James Chrispell*

Joy Will Find a Way / 1975 / Columbia ✦✦✦
Each of his early efforts hold up well to repeated plays, but this is one of the best from that period. Cockburn's wonderfully delicate acoustic guitar sounds great here, tastefully aided with spare sympathetic accompaniment. "Burn" and the title cut were popular tracks in Canada, but "A Long-Time Love Story" and "A Life Story" project a quiet strength that's entrancing. —*Rick Clark*

In the Falling Dark / 1976 / Columbia ✦✦✦✦
The follow-up to *Joy Will Find a Way* possesses some Cockburn standards in "Festival of Friends," the propulsive folk-jazz of "Silver Wheels," the meditative "Lord of the Starfields," and the title cut. The lyrics involve increasingly complex mystical Christian metaphors. Cockburn's exceptional guitar technique is showcased on the instrumental "Water into Wine." —*Rick Clark*

Circles in the Stream / 1977 / Island ✦✦✦
Recorded live at Massey Hall in Toronto, Ontario, all of Bruce Cockburn's fine standout songs are here. Fronting a band of sympathetic musicians, Cockburn runs through the favorites as well as such new tunes as "Deer Dancing Round a Broken Mirror" and his salute to the Canadian Indian "Red Brother, Red Sister." As live albums go, this one does the trick just fine. —*James Chrispell*

Further Adventures of Bruce Cockburn / 1978 / East Side Digital ✦✦✦
Included is more electric guitar and diverse instrumental backup. Some of the material tends to drag, but "Prenons La Mer" and "Can I Go with You?" sparkle with Cockburn's stunning guitar interplay and strong melodies. "Laughter" and "Rainfall" are standouts, too. —*Rick Clark*

Dancing in the Dragon's Jaws / 1979 / Columbia ✦✦✦✦
Cockburn's first stateside success produced a No. 21 pop hit with "Wondering Where the Lions Are," but there is much better material to be found here on one of his best albums. The lyrics tend to be spacier, and, musically, Cockburn begins to aggressively synthesize Third World rhythms with his singer-songwriter-style folk. —*Rick Clark*

Humans / Nov. 1980 / Columbia ✦✦✦✦
This follow-up isn't as accessible as *Dancing in the Dragon's Jaws*, but it's possibly Cockburn's most brilliant artistic statement, where the general human condition and (more personally) a divorce cause this Christian mystic to dig deep and grapple with down-to-earth issues. With some of his most powerfully poetic lyrics he maintains a fine balance between lofty intentions and grave disappointments. Musically, it is a heady dose of worldbeat folk. —*Rick Clark*

Inner City Front / 1981 / Columbia ✦✦✦
This transitional self-produced effort featured more musical diversity, from the techno-dirge of "The Strong One" to the reggae-like "Justice." "Loner" provides a dramatic highlight. Cockburn's human rights concerns and his left-of-center politics dominate more mystical fascinations. —*Rick Clark*

The Trouble with Normal / 1983 / Columbia ✦✦✦✦
On this, another consistently strong effort, Cockburn's brainy lyrics occasionally border on the didactic, but the imagery is usually brilliant. "Waiting for the Moon" is one of his most beautiful songs. The title cut is released in two totally different versions; the True North rendition is preferable. —*Rick Clark*

Stealing Fire / 1984 / Columbia ✦✦✦
It features a more streamlined, sophisticated rock sound. "If I Had a Rocket Launcher" became a powerful left-field AOR hit in 1984. "Lovers in a Dangerous Time" and "Nicaragua" are highlights. "Maybe the Poet" is a low point, being the highbrow artistic equivalent to Barry Mann's hideous, self-congratulatory ode to the value of pop-song craftsmen, "Who Put the Bomp (In the Bomp, Bomp, Bomp)." But it's a fine album overall. —*Rick Clark*

World of Wonders / 1986 / Columbia ✦✦✦
Cockburn's noble agenda to enlighten the planet about human oppression (with numerous on-the-money observations) sometimes makes the listener feel a little bludgeoned in the process. Nevertheless, it has more than enough highlights to make this well worth seeking out, particularly "Berlin Tonight," "Call It Democracy," "Lily of the Midnight Sky," and the title cut. —*Rick Clark*

Rumours of Glory / 1986 / Plane ✦✦✦
This well-compiled 1985 anthology is heavy on Cockburn's middle period. In spite of some duplication, it's a nice complement to the *Waiting for a Miracle* double-disc. (Import) —*Rick Clark*

● **Waiting for a Miracle** / Jan. 1987 / Gold Castle ✦✦✦✦
This double-disc best-of collection is geared around Cockburn's Canadian singles—an odd approach, considering that much of his strongest material never enjoyed radio airplay. Because of that, *Waiting for a Miracle (Singles 1970-1987)* isn't definitive, but it is a very good collection (mainly because Cockburn is practically incapable of writing a bad song). Nevertheless, Cockburn has yet to receive the kind of treatment he deserves for a collection. *Waiting for a Miracle* is the best overview of Cockburn's music, by default. (Canadian Import) —*Rick Clark*

Big Circumstance / 1989 / Columbia ✦✦✦
Cockburn tries to balance the edge-rock approach of recent work with more reflective earlier sounds. He's most successful at illuminating big issues when he's focusing on his personal backyard (on "Understanding Nothing," "Don't Feel Your Touch") rather than the "Tibetan Side of Town." Surprise element: Cockburn displays rare flashes of humor. —*Rick Clark*

Live / Jun. 1990 / Gold Castle ✦✦✦
Stripped-down-combo reworkings of favorite Cockburn tracks are included, plus "Always Look on the Bright Side of Life," a death-humor ode from the crucifixion scene in Monty Python's *Life of Brian*. —*Rick Clark*

Nothing But a Burning Light / Nov. 5, 1991 / Columbia ✦✦✦
This T-Bone Burnett-produced effort finds Cockburn returning to the more introspective, quiet spirit of his earlier work, including his most open Christian expressions in years, particularly "Cry of a Tiny Babe," a Cockburn-style Christmas story, and "Somebody Touched Me." "One of the Best Ones" is classic reflective Cockburn. Although not one of his best albums, it's a nice breather from the relentless heaviness of his last few efforts. —*Rick Clark*

Dart to the Heart / Mar. 1, 1994 / Columbia ✦✦✦
With the exception of a few revved-up numbers (some with slide guitar and horns), this is a fairly subdued affair, featuring Cockburn's exquisite guitar work and insightful lyricism that is simultaneously grounded and mystical. It's a typically fine album for this consummate artist. —*Rick Clark*

Clarity of Night / Feb. 4, 1997 / Rykodisc ✦✦
Clarity of Night is something of a comeback effort for Bruce Cockburn, since *Dart to the Heart* was largely ignored, but it's a strange comeback record. Instead of returning to his singer-songwriter roots, Cockburn decided to experiment with jazz and varying sonic textures. Despite his ambitions, he doesn't quite have the skills to execute his new, vaguely experimental music convincingly. Bassist Rob Wasserman and vibraphonist Gary Burton play their hearts out, but the music falls flat, even with the presence of guest artists like Bob Weir, Bonnie Raitt, Ani DiFranco, Patty Larkin, Maria Muldaur and Jonatha Brooke. A few songs are worthwhile for aficionados, but even dedicated Cockburn fans will be disappointed by the aimless quality of *Clarity of Night*. —*Thom Owen*

Joe Cocker (John Robert Cocker)

b. May 20, 1944, Sheffield, England
Vocals / Blues-Rock, Adult Contemporary, Soft Rock, Pop-Rock
After starting out as an unsuccessful pop singer (working under the name Vance Arnold), Joe Cocker found his niche singing rock and soul in the pubs of England with his superb backing group, the Grease Band. He hit No. 1 in the UK in November 1968 with his version of the Beatles' "A Little Help from My Friends." His career really took off after he sang that song at Woodstock in August 1969. A second British hit came with a version of Leon Russell's "Delta Lady" in the fall of 1969. (By then Russell was Cocker's musical director.) The albums *With a Little Help from My Friends* (April 1969) and *Joe Cocker!* (November 1969) went gold in America. In 1970 Cocker's cover of the Box Tops' hit "The Letter" became his first US Top Ten. His first peak of success came when Russell organized the "Mad Dogs & Englishmen" tour of 1970, featuring Cocker and over 40 others, and resulting in a third gold album and a concert film. Subsequent efforts were less popular, and problems with alcohol (both on stage and off) reduced Cocker's once-powerful voice to a croaking rasp. But he returned to the US Top Ten with the romantic ballad "You Are So Beautiful" in 1975 and topped the charts in a duet with Jennifer

Warnes on "Up Where We Belong," the theme from the 1982 film *An Officer and a Gentleman.* He has survived, still charting into the '90s, albeit with less frequency than he did in the '70s and '80s. —*Cub Koda & William Ruhlmann*

With a Little Help from My Friends / Apr. 1969 / A&M ✦✦✦✦
The album that foisted Joe Cocker on an unsuspecting public is full of tasteful, raucous covers, Cocker's trademark hysterical vocals, and outstanding studio backing by pros like Jimmy Page and Steve Winwood. —*Tom Graves*

Joe Cocker! / Oct. 1969 / A&M ✦✦✦✦
The rare sophomore effort that is an improvement over the first, it features great tracks (and vocals) like "Delta Lady" and "She Came In Through the Bathroom Window." Arguably, it's Cocker's most soulful album. —*Tom Graves*

Mad Dogs & Englishmen / Aug. 1970 / A&M ✦✦✦✦
A superb document of Cocker's high-energy 1970 tour, it includes about a zillion musicians and hangers-on. All the goods are here, and many consider this Cocker's last great moment. —*Tom Graves*

I Can Stand a Little Rain / Aug. 1974 / A&M ✦✦✦
With *I Can Stand a Little Rain,* Joe Cocker returned to interpreting songs instead of essaying his original songs. As usual, there are a couple of highlights, but a couple of awkward choices prevent the album from being as effective as *Joe Cocker!* or *Mad Dogs and Englishmen.* —*Stephen Thomas Erlewine*

Jamaica Say You Will / Aug. 1975 / A&M ✦✦
The comeback that Joe Cocker had achieved with 1974's *I Can Stand A Little Rain* and its hit single, "You Are So Beautiful," was not sustained by the follow-up, *Jamaica Say You Will.* The reason was simple: that bane of the interpretive singer, a lack of strong material. When there were exceptions, they tended not to be handled well. Randy Newman's "I Think It's Going to Rain Today" was sped up and overarranged, and although the Jackson Browne title track was a strong piece of material, it worked because of its restraint, not in the overwrought way Cocker treated it. —*William Ruhlmann*

Stingray / Apr. 1976 / A&M ✦✦✦
Recorded in Jamaica, *Stingray* was an attempt to meld Joe's raspy vocals with reggae music. It was an experiment that had mixed results. Using crack New York session men instead of Jamaicans somewhat defeated the purpose, but did work well in offsetting the reggaefied tunes. Joe turns in a fine vocal performance throughout and shines on such covers as "A Song for You" and Bob Dylan's "The Man in Me." *Stingray* is full of gems worth seeking out. —*James Chrispell*

Joe Cocker's Greatest Hits / Nov. 1977 / A&M ✦✦✦
Greatest Hits features most, but not all (no "She Came In Through the Bathroom Window" or "It's a Sin When You Love Somebody"), of his biggest hits from the early '70s. Nevertheless, there's plenty of fine music here, making the record a solid compilation. —*Stephen Thomas Erlewine*

Luxury You Can Afford / Aug. 1978 / A&M ✦✦✦

Space Captain / 1982 / Cube ✦✦✦

Sheffield Steel / Jun. 1982 / Island ✦✦✦
Joe Cocker's sole Island album found him backed by some of Jamaica's finest. Again, balancing reggae with rockin' soul, Joe found many good tunes to cover, among them Jimmy Cliff's "Many Rivers to Cross," Steve Winwood's "Talking Back to the Night," Jimmy Webb's "Just like Always," and Bob Dylan's "Seven Days." But while these and the rest of the record make for fine listening, there were no hits. —*James Chrispell*

Civilized Man / May 1984 / Capitol ✦✦
Joe Cocker has always been a good interpreter of other writers' material and on *Civilized Man* he continues to find new avenues to travel. Be it the old '50s tune "There Goes My Baby" or Squeeze's "Tempted," Cocker takes a song and makes it his own. But, while nothing here isn't worth listening to, one feels that Cocker is trying to find a new grip on what he's been doing for so long. Transitional. —*James Chrispell*

● **Classics, Vol. 4** / 1987 / A&M ✦✦✦✦
A solid collection from his 1967-1976 peak, it includes "Feeling Alright," "You Are So Beautiful," and "With a Little Help from My Friends." —*Dan Heilman*

Unchain My Heart / Oct. 1987 / Capitol ✦✦
Unchain My Heart was the release Joe Cocker had been rebuilding for. The title cut returned him to the Top 40, and the song "A Woman Loves a Man" followed it there and was in the *Bull Durham* film soundtrack. A solid effort from a veteran. —*James Chrispell*

One Night of Sin / Aug. 1989 / Capitol ✦✦
With *One Night of Sin,* Joe and his cohorts decided not to mess with the hit formula they'd found with *Unchain My Heart.* Therefore, *One Night . . .* suffers a bit in comparison. However, that is not to say that this isn't great '80s Joe Cocker, because everything here has something

to recommend it. Includes the hit "When the Night Comes" and Joe's updated version of Peggy Lee's "Fever." —*James Chrispell*

Live! / May 1990 / Capitol ✦✦✦
This is a solid, R&B-heavy live concert. —*Dan Heilman*

Night Calls / Jul. 6, 1992 / Capitol ✦✦✦
Cocker's rep has always been as a superb interpreter of other people's material. For *Night Calls,* the Sheffield native peaks with the opening track—a memory-engraving rendition of the Brian Adams/Diane Warren-penned "Feels Like Forever." It's the higher profile songs that ultimately disappoint on *Night Calls.* Cocker eventually works up a lather towards the end of "You've Got to Hide Your Love Away," but it never reaches the standard of other Beatles classics in his repertoire ("With a Little Help from My Friends," "She Came In Through the Bathroom Window"). The biggest let-down is the lack of commitment projected on Elton John's "Don't Let the Sun Go Down On Me." Still, even slumming Cocker sounds more real and soulful than, say, Michael Bolton in his wildest dreams. —*Roch Parisien*

The Best of Joe Cocker / Mar. 16, 1993 / Capitol ✦✦✦✦
Although Cocker's Capitol material wasn't as consistent as his A&M work, this compilation successfully distills the highlights, including the splendid "When the Night Comes," onto a single CD. —*Stephen Thomas Erlewine*

Have a Little Faith / Sep. 8, 1994 / 550 Music/Epic ✦✦✦
After eight years and five studio albums (plus a live album and a best-of album) with Capitol Records, Joe Cocker moved to 550 Music, a new Sony Music imprint, for *Have a Little Faith.* Produced by Chris Lord-Alge and his manager, Roger Davies, Cocker turned in a label debut full of well-chosen songs sung with authority. The title track, John Hiatt's "Have a Little Faith in Me," was a good choice for Cocker, as it contained that mixture of tenderness and toughness the singer has always brought out so well. Unfortunately, the new label affiliation did nothing for Cocker; *Have a Little Faith* flopped. —*William Ruhlmann*

Long Voyage Home / Nov. 21, 1995 / A&M ✦✦✦✦
Long Voyage Home: The Silver Anniversary Collection is nearly the definitive Joe Cocker anthology, covering his recording career from the late '60s to the mid-'90s, featuring material from all the labels he recorded for—A&M, Elektra, Island, and Capitol. After an early single from 1965 (a version of the Beatles' "I'll Cry Instead"), the set skips ahead to his late-'60s recordings with his Mad Dogs & Englishmen troupe. From there, the collection doesn't miss many of Cocker's greatest hits or favorite album tracks. In addition to the familiar tracks, there are a handful of unreleased cuts that are tantalizing for the collector; casual fans will find them of marginal interest. —*Stephen Thomas Erlewine*

Cocteau Twins

f. 1979, Grangemouth, Scotland
Alternative Pop-Rock, Dream-Pop
A group whose distinctly ethereal and gossamer sound virtually defined the enigmatic image of their record label 4AD, the Cocteau Twins were founded in Grangemouth, Scotland, in 1979. Taking their name from an obscure song from fellow Scots Simple Minds, the Cocteaus were originally formed by guitarist Robin Guthrie and bassist Will Heggie and later rounded out by Guthrie's girlfriend Elizabeth Fraser, a unique performer whose swooping, operatic vocals relied less on any recognizable language than on the subjective sounds and textures of verbalized emotions.

In 1982 the trio signed to 4AD, the arty British label then best known as the home of the Birthday Party, whose members helped the Cocteaus win a contract. The group debuted with *Garlands,* which offered an embryonic taste of their rapidly developing, atmospheric sound, crafted around Guthrie's creative use of distorted guitars, tape loops, and echo boxes and anchored in Heggie's rhythmic bass as well as an omnipresent Roland 808 drum machine. Shortly after the release of the *Peppermint Pig* EP, Heggie left the group, and Guthrie and Fraser cut 1983's *Head over Heels* as a duo; nonetheless, the album largely perfected the Cocteaus' gauzy formula and established the foundation from which the group would continue to work for the duration of its career.

In late 1983, ex-Drowning Craze bassist Simon Raymonde joined the band to record the EP *The Spangle Maker;* as time wore on, Raymonde became an increasingly essential component of the Cocteau Twins, gradually assuming an active role as a writer, arranger, and producer. With their lineup firmly solidified, they issued the 1984 EP *Pearly-Dewdrops' Drop,* followed by the LP *Treasure,* their most mature and consistent work yet. A burst of creativity followed, as the Twins issued three separate EPs—*Aikea-Guinea, Tiny Dynamite,* and *Echoes in a Shallow Bay*—in 1985, trailed a year later by the acoustic *Victorialand* album, the *Love's Easy Tears* EP and *The Moon and the Melodies,* a collaborative effort with minimalist composer Harold Budd.

With 1988's sophisticated *Blue Bell Knoll,* the trio signed an international contract with Capitol Records that greatly elevated their commercial visibility. After 1990's *Heaven or Las Vegas,* the Cocteaus severed their long-standing relationship with 4AD; notably, the album also found Fraser's vocals offering the occasional comprehensible turn of phrase, a trend continued on 1993's *Four-Calendar Cafe.* In 1995 they explored a pair of differing musical approaches on simultaneously released EPs. While *Twinlights* offered subtle acoustic sounds, *Otherness* tackled ambient grooves, remixed by Seefeel's Mark Clifford. In 1996 the *Milk and Kisses* LP, on the other hand, marked a return to the band's archetypal style. —*Jason Ankeny*

Garlands / 1982 / 4AD ◆◆

The lone full-length effort recorded with original bassist Will Heggie, *Garlands* represents the Cocteau Twins' sound at its earliest stages of development; although tracks like "Wax and Wane" and "Blind Dumb Deaf" lack the refinement of later work, all of the pieces—inscrutable vocals, textured guitars, and luminous sonic sheen—are clearly in place. —*Jason Ankeny*

Head over Heels / 1983 / 4AD ◆◆◆◆

Recorded simply with the duo of Elizabeth Fraser and Robin Guthrie, *Head over Heels* nevertheless represents a major leap over the Cocteau Twins' earliest work. Fraser's vocals are more assured, and the songs begin to strive as much for substance as atmosphere; Sugar Hiccup" and "Musette and Drums" mark a move towards more concrete melodies, while "In Our Angelhood" breaks the album's gently hypnotic mood with an agreeably uptempo rhythm. —*Jason Ankeny*

Treasure / 1984 / 4AD ◆◆◆◆

A triumph of texture and melody, *Treasure* is the Cocteau Twins' first truly stellar record. The full-length debut of Simon Raymonde, it reveals him to be the final component necessary to make the group's ambitions a reality; songs like "Ivo" and "Pandora (for Cindy)" shimmer with new clarity and focus, while Elizabeth Fraser's vocals grow significantly in resonance and emotional scope, conveying hope, fear, joy, and sorrow in a language more powerful than words. —*Jason Ankeny*

Tiny Dynamine / 1985 / 4AD ◆◆

Moon and the Melodies / 1986 / 4AD ◆◆◆

The Moon and the Melodies is a collaboration between the Cocteau Twins and keyboardist/composer Harold Budd that fits soundly between the stylistic signatures of the two, both of whom make organic music that relies heavily on electronics. Budd's use of spacious treated piano and keyboard sounds (influenced by a previous collaborator, Brian Eno) combine with the Cocteau Twins' shimmering waves of guitars and Elizabeth Fraser's layered wordless vocals to create what amounts to a soundtrack to a dream about sleeping, with saxophones courtesy of Richard Thomas (of the now defunct Dif Juz) breathing further life into the music. Too bland to be the best introduction to the music of either, but a welcome addition to the collection of fans of both. —*Peter Stepek*

Love's Easy Tears / 1986 / 4AD ◆◆◆

Victorialand / 1986 / 4AD ◆◆◆

Recorded without the M.I.A. Simon Raymonde, *Victorialand* reduces the group's sound to little more than Elizabeth Fraser's voice and Robin Guthrie's treated acoustic guitar. The result is one of the most austere and psychedelic releases in the Cocteau Twins' oeuvre; still, while tracks like "Fluffy Tufts," "Oomingmak," and "How to Bring a Blush to the Snow" showcase Fraser's vocals with minimal accompaniment, the mysteries of her impressionistic lyrics remain as complex as ever. —*Jason Ankeny*

Pink Opaque / 1986 / 4AD ◆◆◆◆

A strong introduction to the Cocteau Twins' early work, *The Pink Opaque* compiles career highlights spanning from the group's debut *Garlands* through to the *Alkea-Guinea* EP. Among the selections: "Pearly Dewdrops' Drop," "The Spangle Maker," "Millemillenary," and "Lorelei." —*Jason Ankeny*

● Blue Bell Knoll / 1988 / 4AD ◆◆◆◆

The group's major-label debut, *Blue Bell Knoll* doesn't alter their identity to make their music any more mainstream or any less enigmatic; to their credit, tracks like "Carolyn's Fingers," "The Itchy Glowbo Blow," and "A Kissed Out Red Floatboat" are archetypal Cocteaus efforts, although at times the formula is beginning to grow a bit wearisome. —*Jason Ankeny*

Heaven or Las Vegas / 1990 / 4AD ◆◆◆

Heaven or Las Vegas is like a beacon in the fog; more than any other release in the Cocteaus' catalog, it makes a sincere attempt to cut through the group's impregnable atmospherics to convey a message communicable by more earthly means. While the intent of tracks like "Iceblink Luck," "Cherry-Coloured Funk," and the title cut remains anyone's guess, they're performed with a renewed sense of focus and urgency; at the same time, fragments of Elizabeth Fraser's lyrics even float by in English, further balancing the songs between thought and impression. —*Jason Ankeny*

Four-Calendar Cafe / Sep. 27, 1993 / Capitol ◆◆◆

The Cocteau Twins' first release after their exodus from the 4AD stable, *Four-Calendar Cafe* is also, tellingly, their most earthbound effort; as with *Heaven or Las Vegas,* the emphasis here is on substance as much as style. "Evangeline," "Bluebeard," and "Know Who You Are at Every Age" continue the trio's advance into more accessible melodic and lyrical ground without sacrificing even an ounce of their trademark ethereality. —*Jason Ankeny*

Milk and Kisses / Apr. 1996 / Capitol ◆◆◆

Throughout the '80s, the Cocteau Twins created some of the most beautiful and innovative music of the decade. Liz Fraser's uncanny, gossamer voice and Robin Guthrie's shimmery guitar work both garnered acclaim and inspired bands. *Milk and Kisses* finds the band in a comfortable rut; they've created, and now perfected, a style of music so distinctive that there seems to be little recent creative growth. The result is a beautiful, lush, but somewhat dated and unengaging album that tends to wash over the listener without making any real impact. It is, however, everything that a Cocteau Twins album promises; hypnotic, dreamy, awash in ethereal voices and delicate, liquid guitars. "Tishbite" in particular delivers an accessible dream-pop sound that sounds nice while it's playing but fails to have anything really memorable about it, a problem that plagues most of *Milk and Kisses.* "Half-Gifts," "Rilkean Heart," and "Treasure Hiding" have an airy, otherwordly prettiness to them—but that's about it. Necessary for Cocteau Twins diehards and potentially interesting to those who have never heard the band before, *Milk and Kisses* says nothing, but says it beautifully. —*Heather Phares*

Leonard Cohen

b. Sep. 21, 1934, Montreal, Quebec, Canada
Guitar, Vocals / Singer-Songwriter
One of the most interesting and enduring, if not the most successful, singer-songwriters of the late 1960s, Leonard Cohen has retained a substantial following for more than 30 years, along with the attention of critics who long since ceased worrying about new works by most of his contemporaries.

Cohen was born nearly a decade earlier than the Beatles or the Rolling Stones, and a year before Elvis Presley, but his personal, social, and intellectual background couldn't be more different from *any* rock stars of any generation, nor can he be easily compared even to any members of the generation of folksingers that came of age in the 1960s. He didn't start performing or recording until he was in his mid-30s, after he had already written several books. As an established novelist and poet, his literary accomplishments far exceed those of Bob Dylan, though as a performer, his rather monotone voice is less appealing than Dylan's.

Leonard Cohen was born into a middle-class Jewish family in the Montreal suburb of Westmount. His father, a clothing merchant, died when Cohen was nine years old. Cohen was raised in a progressive environment and was encouraged to express himself at an early age. He took up the guitar at age 13, initially as a way to impress a girl, but within a year or two was singing his own songs at local cafes. He majored in English at McGill University, and despite average grades, won the McNaughton Prize in creative writing before graduating in 1955. His first book of poetry, *Let Us Compare Mythologies,* was published the next year and became a critical success. Two more books of his poetry followed, along with an attempt to join the family business and a stint at Columbia University, but primarily Cohen wrote. His work was popular enough to pay him a modest royalty which, when coupled with government-sponsored literary grants and a family legacy, allowed him to live comfortably. He also lived a very free lifestyle, involving many women, experiments with LSD when it was still legal, and travels around the world. Cohen became almost as well known in Canada for his iconoclastic behavior as his writing, and seemed to benefit from these extra-literary activities, in terms of recognition, especially in America.

Two novels, *The Favorite Game* (1963) and *Beautiful Losers* (1966), solidified his reputation in mid-decade. He had written songs ever since his mid-teens, and even these began attracting attention. Judy Collins, one of the top folk talents to emerge during the mid-1960s, cut a version of Cohen's "Suzanne" that proved extremely popular, garnering considerable radio airplay and becoming one of her most popular numbers, and she persuaded Cohen to join her on the folksong circuit. He made his debut during the summer of 1967 at the Newport Folk Festival, followed by a pair of sold-out concerts in New York City and an appearance singing his songs and reciting his poems on the CBS network television show "Camera Three." At around the same time, actor/singer Noel Harrison brought "Suzanne" onto the pop charts with a recording of his own.

Cohen was signed to Columbia Records, and in early 1968 his first album, *The Songs of Leonard Cohen,* was released. Despite its spare production and melancholy subject matter—or, very possibly, because of it—the album was an immediate hit by the standards of the folk music world and the budding singer-songwriter community. College students by the thousands bought it—in its *second* year of release, the record sold over 100,000 copies. *The Songs of Leonard Cohen* was as close as Cohen ever got to mass audience success. His next album, *Songs from a Room* (1969), was characterized by a similar spirit of melancholy but was less well received commercially and critically. The album did have a pair of tracks, "Bird on a Wire" and "The Story of Isaac," that became standards rivaling "Suzanne." Cohen's third album, *Songs of Love and Hate* (1971), showed a slackening of interest in his work, as his following retreated to well-established cult status, despite the presence of the acclaimed songs "Joan of Arc" and "Famous Blue Raincoat." *Leonard Cohen: Live Songs* was released in 1973.

Despite critical misgivings about his vocal abilities, Cohen always had enough of a following to justify another long-player every other year or so. Meanwhile, in 1973 his music became the basis for a theatrical production called *Sisters of Mercy*, conceived by Gene Lesser and loosely based on Cohen's life, or at least a fantasy version of his life. A three-year lag ensued between *Songs of Love and Hate* and Cohen's next album, and most critics and fans just assumed he'd hit a dry spell. His 1974 release *New Skin for Old Ceremony* seemed to justify his fans' continued faith in his work. The new songs were still depressing and bleak, but also surprising in the language and their revelations. Columbia Records released *The Best of Leonard Cohen* in 1975. In 1977 Cohen reappeared with *Death of a Ladies' Man*. Cohen's most controversial album, *Death of a Ladies' Man* was produced by the reclusive and enigmatic producer Phil Spector and suffered from the worst attributes of Cohen's and Spector's work; it was overly dense and self-consciously imposing in its sound, and it virtually bathed the listener in Cohen's depressive persona, still limited in presentation to a monotone delivery.

Cohen's next two albums, *Recent Songs* (1979) and *Various Positions* (1985, Passport Records), attracted relatively little attention despite their strong song lineups. *I'm Your Man* (1988, Columbia), however, benefitted from the release a year earlier of Jennifer Warnes' *Famous Blue Raincoat*, a collection of Cohen's best work presented by a singer with a very attractive voice. It sold very well and served to remind the public of the worth of Cohen's music. Cohen rose to the occasion with *I'm Your Man*, introducing largely new albeit rather black humor) to his mix of pessimism and poetic conceits, with the result that the album was his bestselling record in more than a decade. Four years later, Cohen released *The Future*, an album that dwelt on the many threats facing mankind in the coming years and decades. Not the stuff of pop charts or MTV heavy rotation, it attracted Cohen's usual coterie of fans, and enough press interest and sales to justify the release in 1994 of his second concert album, *Live*. —*Bruce Eder*

★ **The Songs of Leonard Cohen** / 1968 / Columbia ✦✦✦✦✦
A breathtaking and perfect debut, *Songs of Leonard Cohen* marked the emergence of one of the most enduring, unique, and brilliant voices in popular music. Led off by the gorgeous "Suzanne," previously a hit for both Judy Collins and Noel Harrison, the album is an exposed nerve, a Fellini-esque parade of losers, victims, and fallen angels. Brittle and unforgiving, tracks like "So Long, Marianne," "Winter Lady," and "Sisters of Mercy" are unflinchingly honest and desolate; the subdued beauty of the songs' spartan backdrop only adds to their force. Cohen takes acoustic folk, for so long a musical expression of empowerment and hope, and bleeds it dry of all its redemptive qualities. A masterpiece of perversity and pain. —*Jason Ankeny*

Songs from a Room / 1969 / Columbia ✦✦✦✦
Somehow even darker and more melancholy than *Songs of Leonard Cohen*, *Songs From a Room* is an emotionally claustrophobic set produced with austere beauty by Bob Johnston. The arrangements are eerily spare, heightening the impact of Cohen's weary vocals; the intermittent and idiosyncratic appearance of a Jew's harp only adds to the record's overwhelming sense of disorientation. While not as uniformly strong as its predecessor, *Songs From a Room* does contain a number of Cohen's finest compositions, including "Bird on the Wire," "Lady Midnight," and "Story of Isaac." —*Jason Ankeny*

Songs of Love and Hate / 1971 / Columbia ✦✦✦✦
"Famous Blue Raincoat," "Joan of Arc," and more great Cohen songs. —*William Ruhlmann*

Leonard Cohen: Live Songs / 1973 / Columbia ✦✦
New Skin for the Old Ceremony / 1974 / Columbia ✦✦✦
Containing some mighty fine tunes, *New Skin For the Old Ceremony* continues the well-crafted songwriting Leonard Cohen is noted for. It includes such Cohen standards as "Chelsea Hotel No.2," a song he wrote about his relationship with Janis Joplin; "Lover Lover Lover"; and "There Is a War." Well-arranged, well-crafted, good Leonard Cohen. —*James Chrispell*

The Best of Leonard Cohen / 1975 / Columbia ✦✦✦✦
The Best of Leonard Cohen samples 12 of the many highlights from the singer's first four studio LPs. With a heavy emphasis on the debut *Songs of Leonard Cohen* and its follow-up *Songs From a Room*, the set

includes such masterpieces as "Suzanne," "So Long, Marianne," and "Bird on the Wire," as well as later efforts including "Chelsea Hotel" and "Famous Blue Raincoat." —*Jason Ankeny*

Death of a Ladies' Man / 1977 / Columbia ✦✦
While not the unmitigated disaster conventional wisdom holds it to be, *Death of a Ladies' Man* remains one of Leonard Cohen's least successful efforts. In a 180-degree turn from the spare, muted settings of most of Cohen's work, the record is produced by Phil Spector, whose trademark Wall of Sound swallows the singer whole; Cohen's songs are up to snuff, and Spector's vision remains as awe-striking as ever, but the two artists are simply incompatible. Apart from a few bright spots ("True Love Leaves No Traces," "Paper Thin Hotel"), *Death of a Ladies' Man* is an ambitious failure. —*Jason Ankeny*

Recent Songs / 1979 / Columbia ✦✦✦
Dark, smokey, a return to the old, could all be descriptions of *Recent Songs*. This came as a relief for those Cohen fans who were put off by his work with Phil Spector. And, although the songs here haven't become hits or standards like so many other Cohen songs, they are well worth the listening experience. —*James Chrispell*

Various Positions / 1985 / Passport ✦✦✦
Recorded with vocalist Jennifer Warnes (who later cut the LP *Famous Blue Raincoat*, a collection of Cohen compositions), *Various Positions* is a stunning return to form—Cohen's strongest work since *New Skin for the Old Ceremony*. Cryptic and spartan, the set continues in the eclectic vein of recent efforts, but with greater clarity and focus, resulting in an intriguingly diffuse collection ranging from the Serge Gainsbourgesque pop of "Dance Me to the End of Love" to the boozy, country-inflected "The Captain." —*Jason Ankeny*

I'm Your Man / 1988 / Columbia ✦✦✦✦
A stunningly sophisticated leap into modern musical textures, *I'm Your Man* re-establishes Leonard Cohen's mastery. Against a backdrop of keyboards and propulsive rhythms, Cohen surveys the global landscape with a precise, unflinching eye: the opening "First We Take Manhattan" is an ominous fantasy of commercial success bundled in crypto-fascist imagery, while the remarkable "Everybody Knows" is a cynical catalog of the landmines littering the surface of love in the age of AIDS. —*Jason Ankeny*

The Future / Nov. 10, 1992 / Columbia ✦✦✦✦
On his latest recording, Canada's poet-musician laureate has glimpsed *The Future*, and it's not a pretty sight. Cohen's apocalyptic vision takes us through a morbid roll-call that includes torture, environmental destruction, drug abuse, abortion, sexual abuse, murder, Stalin, Charles Manson, Hiroshima, and (shudder) lousy poets. And that's just the title track. Instrumental backings focus mostly on unobtrusive textures—synths, strings, female backing vocals, and the occasional flavor of pedal steel guitar, mandolin, fiddle, and horns. —*Roch Parisien*

Live / Jun. 28, 1994 / Columbia ✦✦

Coldcut

f. 1986, London, England
House, Techno, Club/Dance, Trip-Hop, Electronica
DJs Jonathon More and Matt Black, aka Coldcut, rose to acclaim in the mid-'80s through production and remix work for a number of modern rock, hip-hop, and dance outfits, including Yaz, Lisa Stansfield, Junior Reid, Blondie, Eric B. & Rakim, and Queen Latifah. While that connection has pegged them as a product of the UK acid house and rave scenes, the pair's larger commitment has been to urban breakbeat styles such as hip-hop, ambient dub, and jungle, the three of which have constituted the bulk of their recorded output since their first mid-'80s white-label EP, *Hey Kids, What Time Is It?* Comprising project titles like Hedfunk, Hex, DJ Food, and Coldcut, More and Black have assembled an empire of UK breakbeat and experimental hip-hop through their Ninja Tune/Ntone labels and been a unifying force in underground experimental electronic music through their eclectic radio show, "Solid Steel," and club and tour dates.

More and Black got their start, not surprisingly, as radio DJs, working at the pirate station Network 21 during the first half of the '80s, and latching onto the snowballing club scene mid- to late-decade. Their claim to early fame, *Hey Kids, What Time Is It?* was modeled on the cut'n'scratch turntable aesthetic of underground deck heroes like Grandmaster Flash and Double D & Steinski. Widely regarded as the UK's first breaks record and an influential force in bringing identity to London's nascent club culture, the record—released as a US import billed to DJ Coldcut to avoid sample litigation—opened as many doors for More and Black as it did for DJs, bringing scads of production and remix work their way. The attention (and sales royalties) allowed them to launch their Ninja Tune and Ntone labels, which together have been home to some of the most acclaimed and influential artists of London's post-rave underground scene, including DJ Food, Drome, Journeyman, 9 Lazy 9, Up, Bustle & Out, and the Herbaliser.

Although Coldcut was their earliest nom de plume, after a befuddled contract with Arista, the name has languored in legal channels for the past few years. The intervening period found the pair no less active, releasing a flood of material under different names and continuing to work with young groups. In 1995 the Coldcut name came back to More and Black, and the pair celebrated with a mix-CD on the Journeys by DJ label dubbed *70 Minutes of Madness*. The release is credited with bringing to wider attention the sort of freestyle mixing the pair has always been known for through their radio show and their steady club dates, a style that has since taken off through clubs like Blech and the Heavenly Sunday Social. New material as Coldcut is currently in production. —*Sean Cooper*

● **What's That Noise?** / Sep. 1989 / Big Life/Tommy Boy ✦✦✦✦
More and Black give breaks the full-length treatment. At times more song-oriented than that implies, the pair move from syrupy house and dancefloor fare to hardcore funk and breakbeat to soupy sonic weirdness. A clear indicator of things to come, the album was reissued stateside by Reprise. —*Sean Cooper*

Philosophy / 1994 / Arista ✦✦✦✦
The duo's disastrous major-label debut was worry-free acid jazz made even more palatable by vocalists Ade and China's canned, predictable delivery. The album did produce a minor legend in Mixmaster Morris' remix of "Autumn Leaves," but aside from that it's a dry, muddy beaker with little of interest. —*Sean Cooper*

Journeys by DJ—70 Minutes of Madness / 1996 / Music Unites/Sony ✦✦✦✦
Although this mixed CD is a compilation of material by numerous artists (from Harold Budd to Dillinja, Joanna Law to the Jedi Knights), only some of which is the pair's own, it's an ample illustration of the sort of freestyle approach to composition the pair helped popularize. The group jumps from style to style at will, drawing out the connections between hip-hop, jungle, techno, electro, ambient, and beyond, with first-rate mixing and turntable work. —*Sean Cooper*

Coldcut & DJ Food Fight / Jan. 1997 / Ninja Tune [Canada] ✦✦✦
The second mix album released by the preeminent DJing team in trip-hop, *Coldcut & DJ Food Fight* is limited by the inclusion of only Ninja Tune artists (including Luke Vibert, Funki Porcini, Up Bustle & Out, DJ Vadim, the Herbaliser and Drome, plus Coldcut and DJ Food themselves). As such, it suffers from a lack of variety, with only several breakbeat tracks to leaven the decidedly trip-hoppish affair. Though Coldcut's mixing and scratching skills are stellar, and the various samples provide sustained interest, the album just doesn't measure up to 1995's classic *Journey by DJ*. While the previous album moved from Boogie Down Productions to Jhelisa Anderson and Mantronix to Photek with grace, the inherent limitations of a Ninja Tunes-only mix LP sinks the whole affair before it begins. (*Coldcut & DJ Food Fight* was released as half of a double-disc compilation called *Cold Krush Cuts*, which also includes DJ Krush's *Back in the Base* mix LP.) —*John Bush*

Jude Cole

b. East Moline, IL
Guitar, Vocals / Adult Contemporary, Pop-Rock
Jude Cole joined the British power-pop band the Records in 1980, after their first album was released; he stayed with them for one album. After a few years Cole re-emerged with his own solo record, 1987's *Jude Cole*, which was a much slicker, mainstream-oriented affair than any of the Records' records. It did have its charm, but it was ignored. That was not the case with his second album, 1990's *A View from 3rd Street*, which had a bonafide hit single with the sweet, yearning "Baby, It's Tonight." Another single from the album went Top 40, as Cole enjoyed a surprise success. Although he wasn't able to repeat his success with the follow-up, it was another solid album of mainstream pop-rock, full of shiny hooks and sleek, memorable melodies. —*Stephen Thomas Erlewine*

Jude Cole / 1987 / Reprise ✦✦✦✦
● **A View from 3rd Street** / Mar. 27, 1990 / Reprise ✦✦✦✦
Start the Car / Aug. 25, 1992 / Reprise ✦✦✦
I Don't Know Why I Act This Way / Oct. 1995 / Island ✦✦

Lloyd Cole

b. Jan. 31, 1956, Buxton, England
Vocals / Singer-Songwriter, Alternative Pop-Rock
Through both his lauded work fronting the Commotions and his more eclectic solo efforts, Lloyd Cole established himself as one of the most articulate and acute songwriters of the postpunk era. Born January 31, 1961, in Buxton, England, Cole formed the Commotions in 1982 while studying philosophy at the University of Glasgow. Originally a large soul band, the group eventually trimmed itself to a quintet that included

keyboardist Blair Cowan, guitarist Neil Clark, bassist Lawrence Donegan, and drummer Stephen Irvine.

The uncommon quality of Cole's songwriting earned the Commotions a contract with British Polydor, and in 1984 they debuted with *Rattlesnakes*, a wry, heartfelt record of jangling guitar pop stuffed with references to the likes of *Jules and Jim*, Simone de Beauvoir, Norman Mailer and *On the Waterfront*. "Perfect Skin," the shimmering first single, reached the UK Top 30. Produced by the hit-making team of Alan Winstanley and Clive Langer, 1985's *Easy Pieces* was a slicker effort that included the singles "Lost Weekend" and "Brand New Friend," both of which earned significant airplay on alternative radio outlets.

After the release of 1987's *Mainstream*, Cole disbanded the Commotions and moved to New York City to establish himself as a solo performer. There he joined forces with noted session drummer Fred Maher, who enlisted ex-Voidoid Robert Quine on guitar and an up-and-coming singer-songwriter named Matthew Sweet to play bass for Cole's eponymously titled 1990 solo debut, which continued much in the vein of his work with the Commotions. *Don't Get Weird on Me, Babe*, however, marked a major artistic shift in 1991, as the entire second half of the album explored lush, string-sweetened cabaret music, arranged by Paul Buckmaster (known for his work with Elton John and the Rolling Stones).

Commercial success continued to elude Cole, however, and it took 1993's *Bad Vibes*—a diverse effort touching upon psychedelia and electronics—a year to find US distribution. By the time of 1995's *Love Story*, his sound had come full circle; a return to the more minimalist, folk-rock inspired work with the Commotions, the LP not coincidentally marked Cole's reunion with the band's guitarist, Neil Clark. —*Jason Ankeny*

Rattlesnakes / Oct. 1984 / Capitol ✦✦✦✦
The Commotions' debut is also their peak moment; while Cole's ambitions and pretentions would occasionally overwhelm his later work, the fresh-scrubbed *Rattlesnakes* easily skirts such pitfalls. Couched in a sparkling folk-rock setting, Cole's songs drop all the right names (Norman Mailer, Arthur Lee, Simone de Beauvoir), reference all the right films (*Jules and Jim*, *On the Waterfront*), and touch all the right emotional bases (wounded heartbreak, unrequited love, arch flippancy). Similarly, his vocals strike the perfect balance between clinical distance and complete romantic submission; for all of the literate polish *Rattlesnakes* possesses, it never loses touch with its humanity. —*Jason Ankeny*

Easy Pieces / Nov. 1985 / Capitol ✦✦✦
Producers Clive Langer and Alan Winstanley, as is their wont, created a shimmering pop surface for Lloyd Cole & the Commotions' second album, sweetening the tracks with string and brass counter-melodies and emphasizing the chiming highs of the guitar and keyboards for an attractive sound that echoed the earnestness of British bands like the Hollies and Herman's Hermits, circa 1966. It was, of course, like sugar-coating cyanide capsules, given Lloyd Cole's pleasantly sung lyrics, which detailed philosophical disillusionment, romantic discord, and, yes, at least attempted suicide. In the UK, *Easy Pieces* was a Top Ten hit. But although the album saw something like a proper release in the US and the Commotions toured extensively, no American breakthrough materialized. —*William Ruhlmann*

Mainstream / Sep. 1987 / Capitol ✦✦
If Lloyd Cole was less worried about depressing his listeners on his third album, he also seemed determined to stir them up, adopting various personae in his songs, from the lover who loses interest shortly after the wedding ceremony in "Jennifer She Said" (a UK Top 40 hit) to Sean Penn. There were a few song narrators who seemed close to the singer himself, and they sounded just as discontented. There was little to alleviate the vitriol in the music, which was unusually muted, and long before the end Cole had begun to sound like a crank. The album's saving grace was "Hey Rusty," a song with a Springsteen-like theme and a U2-like musical track. If there were more songs this coherent, specific, and moving, *Mainstream* might have ranked with Cole's first two albums. —*William Ruhlmann*

● **1984-1989** / Jun. 1989 / Capitol ✦✦✦✦
The compilation *1984-1989* features nearly all of the best moments from Lloyd Cole & the Commotions' three albums, making it the perfect introduction to his music. —*Stephen Thomas Erlewine*

Lloyd Cole / Feb. 1990 / Capitol ✦✦✦
In the two and a half years after the release of *Mainstream*, Lloyd Cole signed to Capitol Records for the US, split from the Commotions, and moved to New York. For his first solo album, he assembled a team consisting of two New York band veterans—drummer/co-producer Fred Maher and guitarist Robert Quine, both of whom had played in Richard Hell's Voidoids and Lou Reed's backup group, plus bassist Matthew Sweet and Commotions keyboard player Blair Cowan. As a result, *Lloyd Cole* boasts a tougher, harder sound than the Commotions records. Cole's vocals, meanwhile, have become more direct and less stylized.

Cole's lyrics are also less adorned, and he has lightened up somewhat. Much of *Lloyd Cole* is musically astringent in a way Cole hasn't managed previously, even if the album is far less ambitious than his first two records. — *William Ruhlmann*

Don't Get Weird on Me Babe / Sep. 16, 1991 / Capitol ✦✦✦
While it's not exactly sunny, *Don't Get Weird on Me Babe* is Cole's most accessible and pop-oriented album to date, filled with fine understated pop-rockers like "She's a Girl and I'm a Man." — *Stephen Thomas Erlewine*

Bad Vibes / Oct. 1993 / Rykodisc ✦✦✦
Bad Vibes, Lloyd Cole's sixth new studio album, marks a big change in terms of sound. Producer Adam Peters and mixer Bob Clearmountain have tried to recreate the experimental days of the mid-'60s, employing a wide variety of studio gimmicks. But if *Bad Vibes* is Lloyd Cole's most produced record, it also is his earliest. The singer's voice is recorded (sometimes with echo or double-tracking) especially high in the mix, and his singing is as stylized as it was on his first two albums, though in a different way. Here, he affects a sardonic, disengaged tone. All of this makes *Bad Vibes* Cole's most varied and most ambitious album, but far from his best. The odd sound stage and attitude are anything but accessible, and Cole himself has rarely been as vitriolic. (The US Rykodisc version contains two bonus tracks, "For the Pleasure of Your Company" and "4 M.B.," not contained on the Fantana version.) — *William Ruhlmann*

Love Story / Oct. 3, 1995 / Rykodisc ✦✦✦
It stands to reason that a Lloyd Cole album called *Love Story* would not have a happy beginning or middle, much less ending. Actually, though, it does start out happy, "Trigger Happy," that is, and later on, Cole is "Happy for You," in which he sings, "If you love him, you should leave me." In between, things get no sunnier, as Cole and his characters drink and despair, but carry on. That determination is very much part of Cole's negative world view: "Everybody knows this is nowhere," he says, to coin a phrase, "but you've gotta be there." (Except, one supposes, for Lucy, who jumps from the 39th floor in the rollicking "Let's Get Lost.") Typically, Cole couches these sentiments in melodic folk-rock, so that, with the volume low and just following the attractive lilt of his voice, a listener might find this a a far more soothing piece of music than it turns out to be on closer examination. — *William Ruhlmann*

Natalie Cole

b. Feb. 6, 1950, Los Angeles, CA
Piano, Vocals / Soul, Urban, Adult Contemporary, Quiet Storm
The daughter of jazz and pop legend Nat "King" Cole, Natalie Cole has forged a successful career in two phases, doing R&B/urban contemporary and then jazz-based pop. She made her stage debut at age 11 and sang in college. Cole met the writing and producing team of Chuck Jackson and Marvin Yancey in 1973. The next year they collaborated on some sessions that were recorded at Curtis Mayfield's Curtom studios in Chicago. These helped her land a deal with Capitol, and she teamed with Jackson/Yancey for a string of hit albums and singles from 1975 until 1983. Such LPs as *Inseparable, Natalie, Thankful, Unpredictable*, and *I Love You So* yielded five No. 1 R&B hits between 1975 and 1977. These included "This Will Be, "Inseparable," "Our Love," and "I've Got Love on My Mind." She stayed with Capitol until 1983, then switched to Epic for her final album with the Jackson/Yancey tandem. Cole made duets with Peabo Bryson in 1979 and 1980 and Ray Parker, Jr., in 1987. She scored more hits with "Jump Start," "I Live for Your Love," and "Over You" in 1987, and "Pink Cadillac," a cover of a Bruce Springsteen tune, in 1988, and then made her stylistic shift. Cole eased into the transition with "When I Fall in Love," a number her father recorded in 1957. It was included on her 1987 LP, *Everlasting*. She fully embraced the move with the 1991 LP *Unforgettable with Love*, earning Grammy awards and landing a No. 1 pop album that eventually sold over five million copies. The title track featured her doing a duet with her father via electronic elaboration. She continued the jazzy trend with *Take a Look* in 1993, and has toured and done television specials working with a large orchestra conducted by Nelson Riddle. *Holly & Ivy* (1994) and *Stardust* (1996) continued Cole's exploration of American pop standards. — *Ron Wynn*

Inseparable / 1975 / Capitol ✦✦✦
Natalie Cole scored her initial fame as a soul singer with a pronounced Aretha Franklin influence. This was her first hit album, and Cole soared to the top of the R&B charts as both "This Will Be" and "Inseparable" were No. 1 R&B singles ("This Will Be" also was a Top Ten pop song). Nineteen years later, this album still stands as arguably her finest; it contains more earnest, aggressive, and honest material than most of her other albums. — *Ron Wynn*

Natalie / 1976 / One Way ✦✦✦
Her second early '70s album, when people were actually comparing Cole with Aretha Franklin. Those comparisons were later shown to be both premature and inaccurate, as she was never really a soul vocalist. But this album did quite well, with "Mr. Melody" becoming her fourth straight R&B Top Ten hit, and the only one of her first five singles that didn't top the R&B charts. Cole returned in the '90s to the style she perfected on these early albums. — *Ron Wynn*

Unpredictable / 1977 / Capitol ✦✦✦
Natalie Cole continued a strong run of hit albums and singles with her third '70s release. This was her second album in 1977 and earned her another hit with "Be Mine Tonight." Cole's career and personal life were going smoothly at this point, and Marvin Yancey, her husband at the time, was co-producing her material. — *Ron Wynn*

Natalie Live! / 1978 / One Way ✦✦✦
Natalie Cole's first live record had some pleasant and a few boisterous versions of previous studio hits. It followed two consecutive platinum releases and was released during her peak period as a straight soul singer. Such singles as "Mr. Melody," "I've Got Love on My Mind" and "Sophisticated Lady (She's a Different Lady)" were an early clue that Cole was not only capable of cutting jazz-based pop, but that she was quite good at it. — *Ron Wynn*

The Collection / 1988 / Capitol ✦✦✦✦
This contains the finest soul and sophisticated pre-rock pop tracks from Cole's days at Capitol (1975-1981). Cole made some superb singles in her early days, especially "This Will Be" and "Inseparable." At the same time, she laid the foundation for the early-'90s change that would surprise those who slept on "Mr. Melody" or "I've Got Love on My Mind." Her voice was actually more suited for these songs than the soul numbers, which were as much production and arranging triumphs as vocal victories. — *Ron Wynn*

● **Unforgettable** / Sep. 10, 1991 / Elektra ✦✦✦✦
A major change of direction for Natalie Cole, *Unforgettable* found the singer abandoning the type of R&B/pop she'd been recording since 1975 in favor of jazz-influenced pre-rock pop along the lines of Nat "King" Cole's music. It was a surprising risk that paid off handsomely—both commercially and artistically. Nay-sayers who thought that so radical a change would be commercial suicide were proven wrong when the outstanding *Unforgettable* sold a shocking five million units. Quite clearly, this was an album Cole was dying to make. Paying tribute to her late father on "Mona Lisa," "Nature Boy," "Route 66" and other gems that had been major hits for him in the 1940s and early '50s, a 41-year-old Cole sounds more inspired than she had in well over a decade. On the title song, overdubbing was used to make it sound as though she were singing a duet with her father—dishonest perhaps, but certainly enjoyable. Thankfully, standards and pre-rock pop turned out to be a primary direction for Cole, who was a baby when the title song became a hit for her father in 1951. — *Alex Henderson*

Take a Look / 1993 / Elektra ✦✦✦✦
Those who questioned whether Natalie Cole had either the will or skill to succeed with another session of pre-rock popular music need wonder no more. There are another 18 jazz-tinged and early pop numbers, with some unexpected pleasures ("Calypso Blues," "It's Sand Man") and spectacular triumphs ("Cry Me a River," "Fiesta in Blue," "I'm Beginning to See the Light"). Cole is now completely comfortable with the pacing, flow and sensibility of pre-rock material; she has no problems with articulation or delivery, either. — *Ron Wynn*

Stardust / Sep. 24, 1996 / Elektra ✦✦✦
Continuing her successful foray into the American songbook, Cole served as executive producer on her third album of pop standards. Eighteen selections, including works by Hoagy Carmichael and songs associated with Nat, Ella, Sarah, and Dinah. Big band orchestration and a trumpet solo by Wynton Marsalis on "He Was Too Good to Me." Guest players include FourPlay, Everette Harp, George Duke, and John Pizzarelli. Cole originally recorded Nat's "When I Fall in Love" ballad on her *Everlasting* album. Here she does a duet with dad a la "Unforgettable." She also closes the album with a solo version sung in Spanish. — *Bill Carpenter*

Collective Soul

f. 1992, Stockbridge, GA
Pop-Rock, Post-Grunge, Hard Rock
With their catchy, melodic pop-rock and mildly distorted but warm guitar tone, Collective Soul leapt out of Stockbridge, GA, to the top of the 1990s AOR world. Vocalist/guitarist/songwriter Ed Roland, whose parents prohibited listening to music, originally founded the band in the mid-'80s after dropping out of the Berklee School of Music due to lack of funds and getting a job in a 24-track recording studio. The band drew no interest whatsoever from any label, and a disheartened Roland called it quits in 1992 to put together a songwriter's demo in hopes of finding work. A demo of "Shine" caught the attention of several radio stations and eventually Atlantic Records, and Roland hastily put together a new version of Collective Soul with his brother Dean on guitar, Ross Chil-

dress on lead guitar, Will Turpin on bass, and original drummer Shane Evans. "Shine" became an AOR smash and was an inescapable hit on MTV and radio during the spring and summer of 1994; it helped the band's debut album, *Hints, Allegations and Things Left Unsaid*, sell over a million copies by the end of the year. Their self-titled follow-up was released in 1995 and spawned the radio hits "Gel," "December," and "The World I Know." *Disciplined Breakdown*, Collective Soul's third album, was released in March 1997. — *Steve Huey*

Hints Allegations and Things Left Unsaid / Mar. 22, 1994 / Atlantic ✦✦✦

The big hit "Shine" was the necessary bridge between modern rock radio and mainstream classic rock. The sound is fashionably grungy during the verses, but the choruses are pure late-'70s rock. The production on this album is rather uneven. — *Rick Clark*

● **Collective Soul** / Mar. 14, 1995 / Atlantic ✦✦✦✦
Recorded with a full band, Collective Soul's self-titled second album betters their debut both in songwriting and sound, since they can actually make a track like "Gel" rock. — *Stephen Thomas Erlewine*

Disciplined Breakdown / Mar. 11, 1997 / Atlantic ✦✦✦✦
Disciplined Breakdown has to be one of only a handful of records inspired by a songwriter's breakup with his manager, but despite its origins, the album is another smartly assembled arena-rock collection from Collective Soul. Ed Roland knows how to co-opt contemporary alternative-rock trends and re-fashion them into hard-rocking anthems, as evidenced by the first single, "Precious Declaration." He still has a problem coming up with a consistent set of songs, but *Disciplined Breakdown* is nearly as slickly entertaining as Collective Soul's eponymous second album, and its best moments indicate that Roland is beginning to develop a distinctive hard-rock style of his own. — *Stephen Thomas Erlewine*

The Collins Kids

f. 1954, California
Rockabilly
By the time Lawrence (b. 1944) and Lawrencine (b. 1942) Collins were 11 and 13, respectively, they were already tearing it up on country package shows, recording for Columbia Records, and performing on national TV almost weekly. Older sister Lorrie held up the cowgirl fringe-rustling-against-nylons teenage-sensuality department; kid brother Larry was a bundle of hyperkinetic energy, bopping all over the place while laying down exciting, twangy guitar breaks learned firsthand from the "King of Doublenecked Mosrite," Joe Maphis. As time went on, The Collins' recordings veered from mawkish brother/sister country-style duets to white-hot rockabilly, and they were just reaching their peak when Lorrie eloped, effectively breaking up the act. Revered by rockabilly collectors the world over, their filmed television appearances and recordings are testimony to the fact that the Collins Kids weren't just "good for their age," they were just plain good. — *Cub Koda*

● **Introducing Larry and Lorrie** / 1958 / Columbia ✦✦✦✦
For those who don't want to spring for the lengthy and expensive Bear Family box, this is an excellent distillation of 12 of their best late-'50s rockabilly sides. "Hoy Hoy," "Whistle Bait," "Mercy," "Just Because," and "Party" rank among the most smokin' rockabilly sides ever waxed. — *Richie Unterberger*

Hop, Skip And Jump / Aug. 1991 / Bear Family ✦✦✦✦
The Collins Kids were a brother-and-sister act that got real good real young and made it out of their native Oklahoma, settling in California, where they landed a radio/TV hookup with Tex Ritter's Town Hall Party out of Compton. What we have here is another excellent CD box set from Bear Family, two discs with booklet in an album-size format. Everything's here, from the great early sides like "Beetle Bug Bop," "The Cuckoo Rock," "I'm in My Teens," and "The Rockaway Rock" to the rockabilly classics "Just Because," "Hoy Hoy," "Mercy," "Sweet Talk," and "Party," through the Maphis/Collins guitar instrumentals to Larry and Lorrie's solo sides from the end of the trail. Joe Maphis' great guitar is sprayed all over the place, and the master tape transfer is as clear as you expect stuff out of the Columbia vaults produced by Don Law to be. A booklet crammed full of great live photos and excellent liners by Colin Escott round out the package. — *Cub Koda*

Rockin' on T.V. / 1993 / Krazy Kat ✦✦✦✦
Larry and Lorrie, the Collins Kids, were a live act to be savored. In their early days, they were cute without being cloying, highly energetic without being annoying. As they moved into their teens by the late '50s, Larry had developed into a phenomenal guitarist while Lorrie had bloomed into a beautiful teenager with a voice that could belt out both rock 'n' roll and sensual ballads. The recordings contained on this CD stem from live television appearances on the *Town Hall Party* television show, culled mostly from shows in February and May of 1959 and January 1960. Tex Ritter and Jay Stewart were the hosts of this West Coast version of the *Grand Ole Opry*, and some of their introductions and

interview chat has been left on between numbers. Larry and Lorrie were the nominal rock 'n' roll act on the show; their appearances would always give a show a quick shot of much-needed energy between the staid and traditional country acts, and that energy and youthful passion literally leaps off this disc. The Kids clock in with aces-up versions of "Kokomo," "Hoy Hoy," "Hot Rod," "Chantilly Lace," a blistering "Way Down Yonder in New Orleans," and "Dance to the Bop," while Larry and Joe Maphis' duets on "Feisty," "Under the Double Eagle," "Wildcat," and "Hurricane" are guitar showcases with the accent on show. Lorrie's sultry voice is heard to great effect on "Waiting Just for You," an original they never got around to recording. Perhaps the most intriguing tunes here are a trio of Buddy Holly numbers ("That'll Be the Day," "Peggy Sue," and "Oh Boy!") rearranged to fit Larry and Lorrie, in completely different keys and with completely different guitar breaks than the original versions. There's not a lot of Collins Kids material available and this collection makes a wonderful addition to their small but rocking discography. — *Cub Koda*

Television Party / TV ✦✦✦
Fourteen lo-fi songs from vintage television broadcasts, on a label of questionable legitimacy. There's a 31-song compilation of this stuff on a 1993 Krazy Kat album; hold out for that one instead. — *Richie Unterberger*

Bootsy Collins

b. Oct. 26, 1951, Cincinnati, OH
Bass / Funk, Disco
Bootsy (born William Collins, Oct. 26, 1951, Cincinnati) is a funk/R&B bassist/singer/bandleader. He formed his first group, the Pacesetters, in 1968, featuring his brother Phelps "Catfish" Collins (guitar), Frankie "Kash" Waddy (drums), and Philippe Wynne. From 1969 to 1971, the group functioned as James Brown's backup band and was dubbed the JB's. In 1972 Bootsy joined George Clinton's Parliament/Funkadelic. He launched Bootsy's Rubber Band as a spin-off of P-Funk in 1976, the band including his brother Phelps, Waddy, Joel "Razor Sharp" Johnson (keyboards), Gary "Mudd-Bone" Cooper (drums), and Robert "P-Nut" Johnson (vocals), along with "the Horny Horns." (He was sometimes billed alone as Bootsy, and sometimes as William "Bootsy" Collins.)

Signing to Warner Bros. Records, he enjoyed the first of his 15 R&B singles chart entries in 1976 with "Stretchin' Out (In a Rubber Band)." His most successful singles were "The Pinocchio Theory" (1977) and the chart-topping "Bootzilla" (1978). He also released six albums on Warner through 1982, including the gold-sellers *Ahh . . . The Name Is Bootsy Baby!* (1977) and *Bootsy? Player of the Year* (1978), then took a six-year recording hiatus and returned on Columbia in 1988 with the appropriately named *What's Bootsy Doin'?* In 1989 Bootsy was a member of the Bootzilla Orchestra on Malcolm McLaren's album *Waltz Dancing*. In 1990 Bootsy was a featured guitarist and bassist with the dance music trio Deee-Lite. Bootsy's New Rubber Band released *Blasters of the Universe* on August 2, 1994. — *William Ruhlmann*

Stretchin' out in Bootsy's Rubber Band / 1976 / Warner Brothers ✦✦✦✦
The debut album that launched the solo career of bassist Bootsy Collins, after years of playing with everyone from James Brown to George Clinton (with whom he continued working and recording for years). The title cut and several others established Collins' viability outside the Parliament/Funkadelic empire and contained some excellent uptempo jams. — *Ron Wynn*

Ahh . . . The Name Is Bootsy, Baby! / 1977 / Warner Brothers ✦✦✦✦
His second album is a fine introduction into Bootsy's bizarre and throbbing funky fairy-tale world. — *John Floyd*

Bootsy? Player of the Year / Feb. 1978 / Warner Brothers ✦✦✦
"I've got a cartoon mind," Bootsy declares, and his goofy outlook colors this funk excursion, which maintains his phat bass lines while incorporating everything from "America the Beautiful" to "Buffalo Gals." If Bootsy is not above using a TV commercial theme as the basis for a song ("Roto-Rooter"), he is as influential as he is inclusive—betcha Ray Parker, Jr. heard that cut before he wrote "Ghostbusters," with its similar "Who ya gonna call?" tag line. But best of all is Bootsy's No. 1 R&B hit "Bootzilla," an engaging cacophony of beat, chant, and bluster. Bootsy was always the cartoon face of the P-Funk mob, and *Player of the Year* was his bootsiest album yet. — *William Ruhlmann*

This Boot Is Made for Fonk-N / Jul. 1979 / Warner Brothers ✦✦✦
Good, but frequently repetitive funk and comic material from bassist Bootsy Collins. His snappy, looping bass lines and presence were beginning to sag a bit, and the material wasn't consistently creative or clever enough to overcome some severe weaknesses. But when it was good, Collins and company still made some memorable funk. — *Ron Wynn*

Ultra Wave / Nov. 1980 / Warner Brothers ✦✦
The Rubber Band doesn't seem to have been functioning at this point, so *Ultra Wave* is a "solo" Bootsy album, not that the sound is distinguish-

able. In fact, the problem here is not that there's too much Bootsy, it's that there's not enough. All albums that emerge from the P-Funk Mothership deliver the funk by definition, but what separates the good and great ones from the merely okay ones is an individual vision, whether it's P-Funk leader George Clinton's or Bootsy's. On *Ultra Wave*, there are tracks that could fit easily not only on any other P-Funk album, but also on those of P-Funk's more diluted competitors, the Ohio Players, say, or even Earth, Wind and Fire. "Is That My Song?" asks one title, and it's a fair question. — *William Ruhlmann*

The One Giveth, the Court Taketh Away / May 1982 / Warner Brothers ✦✦✦
One of the final albums before Bootsy Collins took a break from bandleading and returned to doing mostly session work. There were more entertaining numbers than dreary ones, and Collins and company had their final chart singles during 1982. — *Ron Wynn*

What's Bootsy Doin'? / 1988 / Columbia ✦✦✦✦
This pounding set is Collins' best work, with plenty of grooves for the brain and the booty. — *John Floyd*

Jungle Bass / Apr. 1990 / 4th & Broadway ✦✦✦
A comeback/return album for outstanding funk bassist Bootsy Collins. He signed with 4th and Broadway in 1990 and issued his first album as a leader in nearly ten years, although he had played with Trouble Funk, L.J. Reynolds, and a number of other artists. Although it didn't have the inspired comic masterpieces or first-rate funk jams of his past albums, it was at least a decent vehicle for Collins' bass lines and rhythms. — *Ron Wynn*

● **Back in the Day: The Best of Bootsy** / Aug. 9, 1994 / Warner Brothers ✦✦✦✦
Most of Bootsy's albums are dense with funk, spending a great deal of time concentrating on the all-mighty groove. With such a reliance on extended runs, it might seem that a compilation wouldn't make sense, but *Back in the Day* cuts away the excesses of his albums and offers a concise distillation of what Collins is about. — *Stephen Thomas Erlewine*

Edwyn Collins

b. Aug. 23, 1959, Edinburgh, Scotland
Vocals, Guitar / Alternative Pop-Rock
Best known for his tenure fronting the Scottish pop revivalists Orange Juice as well as his international solo hit "A Girl like You," singer Edwyn Collins was born in Edinburgh, Scotland, in 1959. In 1976 he formed the Nu-Sonics, which resurfaced three years later as Orange Juice; the leading proponent of the Glasgow neo-pop scene, the band earned a devoted cult following but little commercial success, and by the early 1980s Collins was the only remaining founding member. After a self-titled 1984 release failed to chart, Orange Juice disbanded, and Collins was freed from his contract with the group's label, Polydor.

A solo career seemed imminent, but the singer struggled; dogged by a reputation as a stubborn, difficult perfectionist unmoved by prevailing commercial attitudes, Collins found no one willing to offer him a contract, and only after a pair of sold-out London performances did Creation's Alan McGee sign him to the label's Elevation subsidiary in 1986. The singles "Don't Shilly Shally" (produced by Cocteau Twin Robin Guthrie) and "My Beloved Girl" followed, but both failed to chart; in 1987, Elevation folded, and after Collins and McGee had a falling out, the singer was again left without a contract.

Some months later, Collins accepted the opportunity to record at a small German studio run by a group of devoted Orange Juice fans; cut with the aid of producer Dennis Bovell as well as Aztec Camera frontman Roddy Frame, the resulting LP *Hope and Despair*—a brooding, ambitious collection spotlighting Collins' smooth, soulful baritone—was eventually picked up by the Demon label and issued in 1989. The album proved quite successful on the independent charts, and soon Collins returned to the studio to record 1990's spartan *Hellbent on Compromise;* when the LP failed to repeat its predecessor's good fortune, Demon dropped him, and another long sabbatical followed.

After spending much of the decade's first half in the producer's seat, overseeing sessions from artists including longtime pal Paul Quinn, the Rockingbirds, A House, and Frank & Walters, Collins finally earned another shot as a performer; after signing with the tiny UK indie Setanta, he recorded 1994's *Gorgeous George*, a scathing, shimmering set of retro-pop highlighted by the single "A Girl like You." Slowly, the song became a massive hit throughout Europe as well as the US and returned Collins to the charts for the first time since the 1983 Orange Juice smash "Rip It Up," finally establishing the long-standing cult hero as something of a household name. — *Jason Ankeny*

Hope and Despair / 1989 / Demon ✦✦✦

Hellbent on Compromise / 1990 / Demon ✦✦✦

● **Gorgeous George** / 1994 / Bar/None ✦✦✦✦
Edwyn Collins made a remarkable and unexpected comeback with *Gorgeous George*, and it's not hard to see why. The album represents a consolidation of Collins' skills as a songwriter, demonstrating both his vicious wit and his effortless melodicism. Working with former Sex Pistols drummer Paul Cook and bassist Claire Kenny, he develops the hardest-hitting musical attack of his career, but it's also surprisingly versatile, capable not only of glam-rock, but also jangle-pop, folk-rock, and blue-eyed soul. And while Collins can occasionally be accused of lyrical sniping—the attack on Guns N' Roses in "North of Heaven" is simply silly—there's no denying that when his words and music hit the same target, such as on the darkly catchy Iggy Pop tribute "A Girl like You," the results are wonderfully cerebral pop music. — *Stephen Thomas Erlewine*

Judy Collins

b. May 1, 1939, Seattle, WA
Guitar, Keyboards, Vocals / Folk, Singer-Songwriter, Folk-Rock
Judy Collins was one of the major interpretive folksingers of the '60s. A child prodigy at classical piano, she turned to folk music at the age of 15 and released her first album, *A Maid of Constant Sorrow,* in 1961 when she was 22. That album and its follow-up, *The Golden Apples of the Sun,* consisted of traditional folk material, with Collins' pure, sweet soprano accompanied by her acoustic guitar playing. By the time of *Judy Collins No.3,* she had begun to turn to contemporary material and to add other musicians. (Jim, later Roger, McGuinn tried out his first arrangements of "The Bells of Rhymney" and "Turn, Turn, Turn" on this album, before using them with the Byrds.)

Collins' musical horizons were expanded further by 1966 and the release of *In My Life,* which added theater music to her repertoire and introduced her audience to the writing of Leonard Cohen; it was one of her six albums to go gold. Her first gold-seller, however, was 1967's *Wildflowers,* which contained her hit version of "Both Sides Now" by the then-little-known songwriter Joni Mitchell.

By the '70s, Collins had come to be identified as much as an art song singer as a folksinger and had also begun to make a mark with her original compositions. Her best known performances cover a wide stylistic range: the traditional gospel song "Amazing Grace," the Stephen Sondheim Broadway ballad "Send in the Clowns," and such songs of her own as "My Father" and "Born to the Breed."

Collins recorded less frequently after the end of her 23-year association with Elektra Records in 1984, though she made two albums for Gold Castle. In 1990 she signed to Columbia Records and released *Fires of Eden,* her 23rd album. — *William Ruhlmann*

Maid of Constant Sorrow / 1961 / Elektra ✦✦✦
Collins' talent is to sing these traditional chestnuts without the prissiness of so many female folk singers. Her phrasing has enough strength to stand up to the "Prickile Bush" and give in to "Wild Mountain Thyme." — *Richard Meyer*

Golden Apples of the Sun / 1962 / Elektra ✦✦✦
Collins takes on such diverse repertoire as Gary Davis' "Twelve Gates to the City," "Crow on the Cradle" and her setting of "Golden Apples of the Sun." — *Richard Meyer*

3rd Album / 1963 / Elektra ✦✦✦
Having established herself as one of the foremost interpreters of traditional material, Collins did the same for contemporary folk songwriters on this album, which mixed standards with pristine covers of compositions by Dylan, Bob Gibson, Pete Seeger, Ewan MacColl, and Shel Silverstein. With Jim McGuinn arranging and playing second guitar and banjo, this album, which included a fine version of Seeger's "Turn! Turn! Turn!," had a clear (if overlooked) influence on the folk-rock he pioneered with the Byrds a couple of years later. — *Richie Unterberger*

Judy Collins' Concert / 1964 / Elektra ✦✦✦
On this live set recorded at Town Hall in New York in 1964, Collins stirs up the audience with a rich mixture of traditional and contemporary covers, including Billy Ed Wheeler's "Coal Tattoo" and Paxton's "Ramblin' Boy." — *Richard Meyer*

5th Album / 1965 / Elektra ✦✦✦✦
Collins took a major stride forward with this fine, consistent album, tailoring both her material and arrangements to reflect contemporary changes shaking folk and folk-rock. Features stellar interpretations of songs by several major '60s songwriters (Dylan, Eric Andersen, Phil Ochs, Gordon Lightfoot, Malvina Reynolds, Richard Farina), and first-rate accompaniment by some of the day's finest folk and folk-rock musicians, including Eric Weissberg, Bill Lee, Danny Kalb, John Sebastian, and Richard Farina (although no drums are present). — *Richie Unterberger*

In My Life / 1966 / Elektra ✦✦✦✦
Collins, who by this point had moved from the acoustic renderings of traditional folk ballads to more extensive instrumentation and the work

of contemporary folk writers, takes another step here, turning to tasteful string arrangements by Joshua Rifkin and adding theater music from *Threepenny Opera* and *Marat/Sade* to the Bob Dylan covers. She also starts covering Leonard Cohen ("Suzanne," "Dress Rehearsal Rag"). —*William Ruhlmann*

Wildflowers / 1967 / Elektra ✦✦✦
Passionate and filled with memorable passages. Includes her hit "Both Sides Now" and her first major original composition "Since You Asked." Leonard Cohen's "Priests" has not appeared elsewhere. —*Bruce Eder and William Ruhlmann*

Who Knows Where the Time Goes / 1968 / Elektra ✦✦✦
Rock and country leanings are found on this album featuring guitarists James Burton and Stephen Stills. Includes the hit "Someday Soon" and Collins' own brilliant "My Father." —*William Ruhlmann*

Recollections / 1969 / Elektra ✦✦✦✦
Collins sings "Tomorrow Is a Long Time," "Early Mornin' Rain," and "Winter Sky." This is a best-of compilation. —*Richard Meyer*

Whales & Nightingales / 1970 / Elektra ✦✦✦
Judy Collins found herself in the Top 40 with her adaptation of "Amazing Grace." *Whales & Nightingales* is full of good songs ranging from Bob Dylan's "Time Passes Slowly" to songs by Jacques Brel and Pete Seeger. Collins also had a hit with her adaptation of the song "Farewell to Tarwathie," which she sang over the accompaniments of humpback whales. It opened new doors for her and folk music in general. —*James Chrispell*

Living / 1971 / Elektra ✦✦✦
A much more contemporary record than her previous releases, *Living* shows Judy Collins stretching out, although sometimes this could be said to show her stretching a little too far. Contains her versions of Ian Tyson's "Four Strong Winds," Leonard Cohen's "Famous Blue Raincoat," and Joni Mitchell's "Chelsea Morning." However, it also shows that while she interprets songs well, her version of Bob Dylan's "Just like Tom Thumb's Blues" lets one see that not all songs fit well into the Collins style. —*James Chrispell*

● **Colors of the Day: Best of Judy Collins** / 1972 / Elektra ✦✦✦✦
Colors of the Day: Best of Judy Collins is a fine 12-track collection containing most of her best-known songs from the late '60s, including "Both Sides Now," "Who Knows Where the Time Goes," "Albatross," "Amazing Grace," "Since You Asked," and "Someday Soon." —*Stephen Thomas Erlewine*

True Stories and Other Dreams / 1973 / Elektra ✦✦✦
Collins at her most political, saluting Che Guevara, among others. Elaborately produced and well sung. —*Bruce Eder*

Judith / 1975 / Elektra ✦✦✦
A soaring collection of songs from the Depression, '70s Broadway ("Send in the Clowns"), and modern C&W. —*Bruce Eder & William Ruhlmann*

Bread and Roses / 1976 / Elektra ✦✦
A mixture of contemporary tunes and political statements, *Bread and Roses* was Judy Collins' attempt to put her personal politics before the public. What results is a mixed bag, with songs such as Elton John's "Come Down in Time" alongside Victor Jara's "Prayer for the Laborer." Coming after her lushly produced *Judith*, it only confused her fans. —*James Chrispell*

☆ **So Early in the Spring . . .** / 1977 / Elektra ✦✦✦✦✦
So Early in the Spring, the First 15 Years. Double-album best-of covering the years 1961 to 1976; the place to start and also some of the best singing in contemporary folk music. —*William Ruhlmann*

Hard Times for Lovers / 1979 / Elektra ✦✦
Hard Times For Lovers is full of tunes from contemporary writers and great standards, including two theme songs from two different movies. Collins sings like a woman who's had a hard time with love. For the hard-core Judy Collins fans. —*James Chrispell*

Fires of Eden / Sep. 1990 / CBS ✦✦✦✦
A graceful, personal, and finely crafted work that crosses between art song and folk music. —*Bruce Eder*

Live at Newport / Oct. 25, 1994 / Vanguard ✦✦✦
A 13-song compilation of material recorded at the 1959, 1963, 1964, and 1966 Newport Folk Festivals; it would have been nice if they'd been able to document what year each song was recorded. In any case, it does reflect Collins' artistic growth during this period, from an interpreter of strictly traditional fare to more contemporary material by Bob Dylan, Richard Farina, and others. Highlights include her versions of "Turn, Turn, Turn," "Blowin' In The Wind," "Hey, Nelly Nelly," "Get Together," "Hard Lovin' Loser," and "The Great Silkie," which has the same melody the Byrds used for "I Come and Stand at Every Door" on their *Fifth Dimension* album. All of the songs are previously unreleased, except "The Greenland Whale Fisheries," a duet with Theodore Bikel. On some tracks Collins is accompanied on upright bass by Bill Lee, and on second

guitar by Steve Mandell or Eric Weissberg. With good sound, a nice if not essential, addition to the Collins catalog. —*Richie Unterberger*

Phil Collins

b. Jan. 31, 1951, Chiswick, London, England
Drums, Vocals, Keyboards / Adult Contemporary, Soft Rock, Pop-Rock
Phil Collins' ascent to the status of one of the most successful pop and adult-contemporary singers of the '80s and beyond was probably as much of a surprise to him as it was to many others. Balding and diminutive, Collins was almost 30 years old when his first solo single, "In the Air Tonight," became a No. 2 hit in his native UK. (The song was a Top 20 hit in the US.) Between 1984 and 1990, Collins had a string of 13 straight US Top Ten hits.

Long before any of that happened, however, Collins was a child actor/singer who appeared as "the Artful Dodger" in the London production of *Oliver!* in 1964. (He also has a cameo in *A Hard Day's Night*, among other films.) He got his first break in music at the end of his teens, when he was chosen to be a replacement drummer in the British art-rock band Genesis in 1970. (Collins maintained a separate jazz career with the band Brand X, as well.) Genesis was fronted by singer Peter Gabriel. They had achieved a moderate level of success in the UK and the US with elaborate concept albums before Gabriel abruptly left in 1974. Genesis auditioned 400 singers without success, and then decided to let Collins have a go.

The result was a gradual simplifying of Genesis' sound and an increasing focus on Collins' expressive, throaty voice. *And Then There Were Three . . .* went gold in 1978, and *Duke* was even more successful. Collins made his debut solo album *Face Value* in 1981, which turned out to be a bigger hit than any Genesis album. It concentrated on Collins' voice, often in stark, haunting contexts such as the piano-and-drum dirge "In the Air Tonight," which sounded like something from John Lennon's debut solo album, *John Lennon/Plastic Ono Band*.

During the '80s, Collins balanced his continuing solo work with Genesis with enormous success. In 1992 Genesis released *We Can't Dance* and began an extensive tour. Upon its completion, Collins released *Both Sides* in 1993, and the record became his first album not to produce a major hit single or go multi-platinum. In 1995 he announced that he was leaving Genesis permanently. The next year, he released *Dance into the Light*. Although the album was a flop, its subsequent supporting tour was a success. —*William Ruhlmann*

Face Value / 1981 / Atlantic ✦✦✦✦
Collins proves himself a passionate singer (and distinctive drummer) with a gift for both deeply felt ballads and snarling rockers. His debut album transformed him from the frontman of Genesis to a solo star who happened to be in Genesis, too. Contains "In the Air Tonight" and "I Missed Again." —*William Ruhlmann*

Hello, I Must Be Going / 1982 / Atlantic ✦✦✦
As his hit cover of "You Can't Hurry Love" demonstrates, Collins began to inject his highly melodic pop songwriting with more soul and R&B influences on his second solo album. While some of the material was successful, much of it showed that he was still coming to grips with how to incorporate R&B techniques into his style; in retrospect, *Hello, I Must Be Going* laid the groundwork for his breakthrough album, *No Jacket Required*. —*Stephen Thomas Erlewine*

● **No Jacket Required** / 1985 / Atlantic ✦✦✦✦
From ballads like the No. 1 "One More Night" to uptempo funk like the No. 1 "Sussudio," another tour de force in what was by now one of the most identifiable styles in pop music. The 1985 Grammy winner for Album of the Year. —*William Ruhlmann*

But Seriously / Nov. 1989 / Atlantic ✦✦✦
This chart-topping fourth album contains "Another Day in Paradise," "I Wish It Would Rain Down," "Do You Remember?," and "Something Happened on the Way to Heaven," all Top Five hits. —*William Ruhlmann*

Serious Hits . . . Live! / 1990 / Atlantic ✦✦
Phil Collins runs through his hits with surprising energy on *Serious Hits . . . Live!*, but the record remains an artifact for dedicated fans, not casual listeners. —*Stephen Thomas Erlewine*

Both Sides / Nov. 9, 1993 / Atlantic ✦✦✦
Returning to the stark, melancholy sounds of *Face Value*, Phil Collins delivers a personal album with *Both Sides* in more than one sense of the word. Collins played all of the instruments on *Both Sides*, and the songs are troubled, haunting tales of regret, romance, and society. Although Collins has not lost his flair for melody, the songs are edgier than most of his recent work. Some fans might not go along with Collins on this dark ride, but *Both Sides* is one of his most artistically satisfying albums. —*Stephen Thomas Erlewine*

Dance into the Light / Oct. 22, 1996 / Atlantic ✦✦✦
After the bleak *Both Sides*, Phil Collins delivered the considerably lighter *Dance into the Light*, his first upbeat pop album since 1985's *No*

Jacket Required. Not only was it a return to the musical style that brought him to the top of the charts during the '80s, but *Dance into the Light* was the first record Collins released since leaving Genesis, which made it all the more crucial to his career. For the most part, the album treads familiar territory—R&B-influenced dance-pop, sensitive ballads, and brooding mid-tempo ruminations—but there are several occasions where he stretches out, incorporating worldbeat influences into his style. And that's where the problem with *Dance into the Light* lies—ten years after the breakthroughs of Paul Simon's *Graceland,* Collins' idea of adventurous music remains worldbeat, which has already passed out of public consciousness. Furthermore, his polyrhythms are surprisingly stiff for a drummer, which sinks all of the more experimental tracks. The remainder of the album is pleasant, but offers no distinctive melodies, which means that the albums sounds fine while it's on, but leaves nothing behind once it's finished. —*Stephen Thomas Erlewine*

The Colourfield

f. 1983, Manchester, England, db. 1987
New Wave
By the summer of 1983, the Fun Boy Three were peaking in popularity and Terry Hall disbanded the group. Hooking up with ex-Swinging Cats members Toby Lyons and Karl Shale, Hall moved to Manchester and formed the Colourfield, a more lush and melodic outfit than the Fun Boy Three. In January 1984, the band released their first single, "The Colourfield," which just missed the Top 40. It was followed later that summer with "Take," which didn't even come close to the Top 40. The Colourfield had its first hit in January 1985, when "Thinking of You" reached No. 12. It was followed by "Castles in the Air," another failed single that preceded the release of their debut album, *Virgins and Philistines,* by just a few weeks. Like the band's singles, *Virgins and Philistines* failed to gain a large audience for the Colourfield. The band released a second album, *Deception,* in the spring of 1987. During the sessions, Lyons left the band, leaving Hall to finish the album by himself; to complete the album, Hall hired Raquel Welch's band. —*Stephen Thomas Erlewine*

● **Virgins & Philistines** / Jan. 1985 / Chrysalis ◆◆◆◆
A good mix of folk and rock comes from this band led by Terry Hall (ex-Specials, Fun Boy Three). Hall is an interesting if somewhat gloomy writer. —*Kenneth M. Cassidy*

Deception / Apr. 1987 / Chrysalis ◆◆

Ray Columbus & the Invaders

f. 1964, New Zealand, db. 1966
Pop-Rock
One of the best New Zealand groups of the '60s, and the first to successfully react to the changes wrought by the British Invasion. Starting out as a fairly accomplished outfit in the mold of Cliff Richard & the Shadows, though rawer, the group hit the top of the charts in both New Zealand and Australia with "She's a Mod" in 1964. A cover of an obscure British beat single by the equally obscure Senators, it took obvious inspiration from "She Loves You" with its yeah-yeah chorus, but it was a strong harmony rocker than most of the biggest singles of the '60s in Australia. Although their biggest hit was quite Beatlesque, most of the group's repertoire (much of it self-penned) was in a decidedly more pronounced R&B direction. The Invaders would have most likely ground ashore had they actually made a determined effort to invade the US or UK markets, but they were a decent outfit that stood way above most other Kiwi acts in 1964. The group managed a few more New Zealand hits but couldn't crack Australia in as big a way again, before splitting in 1966. Ray Columbus actually tried to crack the States as a solo artist for a year or two, recording the collectible psychedelic "Kick Me" single with a California group, the Art Collection. —*Richie Unterberger*

● **Anthology** / 1981 / Epic ◆◆◆◆◆
This 16-track compilation includes all of their key singles: "She's A Mod" and the N.Z. hits "C'Mon And Swim," "Now You Shake," "Till We Kissed," and "Yo Yo." According to the liner notes, the Yardbirds' management considered having the band cover the moody, bluesy "Now You Shake" as a single in early 1966. Also includes a live version of "She's A Mod" and their 1963 take on "I Wanna Be Your Man," which was one of the first overseas Beatle covers. —*Richie Unterberger*

Shawn Colvin

b. Jan. 10, 1958, Vermillion, SD
Guitar, Vocals / Singer-Songwriter, Adult Alternative Pop-Rock, Contemporary Folk
Shawn Colvin is one of the bright spots of the so-called "new folk movement" that began in the late '80s. And though she grew out of the somewhat limited "woman with a guitar" school, she has managed to keep the form fresh with a diverse approach, avoiding the clichéd sentiments and all-too-often formulaic arrangements that have plagued the genre.

In less than a decade of recording, Colvin has emerged as a songcrafter with plenty of pop smarts, which has earned her a broad and loyal following.

Shawn Colvin was born in Vermillion, SD, on January 10, 1958. By age ten, she found a passion for music, teaching herself guitar. After moving to London, Ontario, and then Carbondale, IL, Colvin formed the Shawn Colvin Band, a hard rock outfit whose high-energy demands soon strained her voice. She moved to Austin, TX, and joined the Western swing band the Dixie Diesels, singing with the band until nodes forced a temporary retirement at age 24. In 1983 she moved to New York, where she found a home in the city's singer-songwriter scene, building a following in New York and Boston through constant gigs. Through the '80s she worked her way up the folk circuit, also appearing in off-Broadway shows such as *Pump Boys and Dinettes, Diamond Studs,* and *Lie of the Mind.* Her work appeared in *Fast Folk Magazine,* and she got her first break in 1987 singing backup on Suzanne Vega's hit "Luka."

By 1988 she found a songwriting partner in John Leventhal, Colvin providing the lyrics to his melodies. A live tape sold at gigs (*Live '88*) attracted the attention of Columbia Records, who signed her the same year in the wake of success from like-minded performers Tracy Chapman, Suzanne Vega, and the Indigo Girls. *Steady On,* released in 1989, won the Grammy for Best Contemporary Folk Recording. Colvin's 1992 follow-up, the more pop-oriented *Fat City,* earned her two more nominations—Best Contemporary Folk Recording and Best Female Pop Vocal for the single "I Don't Know Why"—as well as considerable critical praise and a growing crossover audience. "I Don't Know Why" became a big adult contemporary hit. *Cover Girl,* an album of cover songs, met with mixed reviews and modest sales in 1994, but she again earned a nomination for Best Contemporary Folk Recording. In late 1996 Colvin released *A Few Small Repairs.* In addition to her normal recording activities, Colvin has dueted with Tony Bennett for the film *It Could Happen to You* and made a cameo appearance in the film *Grace of My Heart,* singing one song for the soundtrack. —*Chris Woodstra*

Steady On / Oct. 1989 / Columbia ◆◆◆
Sharp production, surprising arrangements, and Shawn Colvin's alternately breathy and ringing vocals give the best possible forum for her astute reflections on life and love. The album's roots go into rock and country as well as folk. —*William Ruhlmann*

Fat City / Oct. 1992 / Columbia ◆◆◆◆
For her second album, Shawn Colvin took a temporary break from long-time collaborator and producer John Leventhal, teaming up instead with Larry Klein. And while the strongest songs—"Tennessee," "Climb On (A Back That's Strong)" and "Object of My Desire"—are Colvin/Leventhal collaborations, credit should be given to Klein, who incorporated a glossy, more dynamic production and top-notch session players for a stronger and more accessible album. In addition to turning in a strong batch of songs, Colvin shows much more diversity, tackling everything from rootsy rockers to more sensitive folk ballads with equally passionate delivery. "I Don't Know Why" (the first song she wrote) and "Round of Blues" both found considerable success in adult contemporary radio formats, adding to her growing fan base. —*Chris Woodstra*

Cover Girl / Aug. 23, 1994 / Columbia ◆◆
When Shawn Colvin first turned up playing Greenwich Village folk clubs in the early 1980s, she used to perform a variety of cover songs, often taking rock recordings and re-imagining them for her girl-with-guitar format. When Colvin began recording in the late '80s, however, she concentrated on her own original material. *Cover Girl* brings her interpretive abilities back into focus. Songs like the Police's "Every Little Thing [He] Does Is Magic" and Talking Heads' "This Must Be the Place (Naive Melody)" are the most radical reworkings here, but not the best, perhaps because they depend on their original productions. Colvin is more successful in choosing classic but not well-known songs already in the folk idiom—Greg Brown's "One Cool Remove," Willis Alan Ramsey's "Satin Sheets," and Rolly Solley's "Killing the Blues." A fan from the old Village days can only lament that she didn't choose to include her version of Dire Straits' "Romeo and Juliet." —*William Ruhlmann*

Live '88 / Oct. 1995 / Plump ◆◆◆
It's a folkie tradition and an economic boon to carry with you tapes to sell at your gigs, and before Shawn Colvin released her first Columbia Records album, *Steady On,* she used to sell a tape made at an April 1988 show in Somerville, MA, containing acoustic versions of songs that later turned up on her Columbia releases—"Diamond in the Rough," "Shotgun Down the Avalanche," "I Don't Know Why," and "Knowing What I Know Now," among others. In the studio, such songs acquired arrangements and other instrumentation, which may have made them more commercial but didn't improve them. Now Colvin's management has launched Plump Records and released her live tape (with a couple of additions), though her contract with Columbia is still in effect. And guess what? It's still her best recording. —*William Ruhlmann*

● **A Few Small Repairs** / Oct. 1, 1996 / Sony ✦✦✦✦
A Few Small Repairs, the proper follow-up to *Fat City*, was recorded on the heels of Colvin's divorce. And while the album is certainly a response, she avoids the obvious clichés in dealing with the aftermath, revealing instead the complex thought processes and complete range of human emotion, from anger, sadness, confusion, yearning, and disillusionment to resolve and recovery. Colvin has always been a songwriter of note, but with *A Few Small Repairs*, she reaches new heights, painting hauntingly vivid images that address not only relationships but also life in general with great insight. The subject matter predictably gives a generally dark mood to the album, but musically, it is both diverse and irresistibly catchy. The album marks a reunion with former collaborator/producer John Leventhal, and the two have found a perfect blend between words, music, and tasteful, organic arrangements for Colvin's finest effort to date. — *Chris Woodstra*

Combustible Edison

f. 1994, Providence, RI
Alternative Pop-Rock, Cocktail
What to do if you've been slogging away in the rock underground for a decade to slight critical acclaim without making any appreciable artistic or commercial headway? In the mold of David Johansen/Buster Poindexter, the band Christmas decided to retool themselves as lounge lizards. On their debut album, the Providence, RI, group plays cocktail jazz, exotica, torch ballads, and B-movie spy/guitar themes. To complete their transformation, the band has adopted ice cream-colored tuxedoes in their live performances; one member of the group has adopted the pseudonym "The Millionaire," and former Christmas singer Liz Cox calls herself "Miss Lily Banquette" as she croons languid jazz-pop tunes. After debuting in 1994 with *I, Swinger*, Combustible Edison issued *Schizophonic* in 1996. — *Richie Unterberger*

● **I, Swinger** / Mar. 1994 / Sub Pop ✦✦✦✦
Combustible Edison's goofy and irreverent mix owes a lot more to the music of the 1950s and early '60s than to new wave; they sound as if they've stumbled on a treasure trove of dime-store albums in their aunt's attic and can't quite get over the experience. Their immaculate re-creation of late-'50s/early-'60s cheese is fun . . . to a point. Treading the line between self-conscious irony and the ridiculous, it probably won't prove to be more durable than those old Christmas (the band, not the season) albums. But then, nobody could have predicted the Martin Denny revival, either. — *Richie Unterberger*

Schizophonic / Feb. 27, 1996 / Sub Pop ✦✦✦

Come

f. 1990, Boston, MA
Alternative Pop-Rock, Indie Rock
The dark and dissonant blues-rock band Come formed in Boston in 1990. The group was led by singer/guitarist Thalia Zedek—a recovering heroin addict and veteran of the indie-rock scene whose career included tenures fronting Live Skull, Uzi, the Dangerous Birds, and White Women—and guitarist Chris Brokaw, also the drummer for Codeine. Fleshed out by a pair of Athens, GA, refugees—former Kilkenny Cats bassist Sean O'Brien and onetime Bar-B-Q Killers drummer Arthur Johnson—Come spent its first year of existence improvising and jamming before recording "Car," a single for the Sub Pop label that made them one of the most highly touted new acts on the underground scene.
After signing to Matador, Come recorded their superbly atmospheric 1992 debut *Eleven: Eleven* in less than eight days; in 1994, they resurfaced with both an EP, *The Wrong Side*, and a full-length album, *Don't Ask Don't Tell*. After the band backed Steve Wynn on his solo album *Melting in the Dark*, both O'Brien and Johnson exited in 1995, leaving Zedek and Brokaw to record 1996's *Near Life Experience* with two different rhythm batteries; while Tortoise's Bundy K. Brown and the Jesus Lizard's Mac McNeilly backed the duo on half of the tracks, Rodan alumni Tara Jane O'Neil and Kevin Coultas provided support on the rest. — *Jason Ankeny*

Eleven: Eleven / 1992 / Matador ✦✦✦
Come's debut album, *Eleven: Eleven* is a thoroughly impressive fusion of punk, Stones-style rock 'n' roll, and blues. All the songs are slow and churning, ground out by post-punk/blues guitars with weary, scarred vocals that grab your attention. *Eleven: Eleven* is genuinely harrowing and disturbing, easy to admire but not necessarily easy to listen to; for those who make an attempt to meet Come halfway, *Eleven: Eleven* rewards their effort in full. (The CD includes a superb version of the Rolling Stones' "I Got the Blues.") — *Stephen Thomas Erlewine*

● **Don't Ask Don't Tell** / Oct. 1994 / Matador ✦✦✦✦
Come opens up the dense, heavy psycho-blues of their debut album *Eleven: Eleven* without losing their harrowing intensity on their impressive follow-up *Don't Ask Don't Tell*. Even with the more expansive production, Thalia Zedek's wrenching vocals and bruising guitar aren't any

easier to take; there's no way her brutal songs could be casual listening. However, that doesn't mean it isn't rewarding listening. — *Stephen Thomas Erlewine*

Near Life Experience / May 21, 1996 / Matador ✦✦✦✦
Come's *Near Life Experience* covers old territory for the band and heads in new, exciting directions. Singers/guitarists Thalia Zedek and Chris Brokaw weathered the departure of the band's original rhythm section a year ago, (replaced by 11 different musicians for this album, including bassists and drummers from groups like the Jesus Lizard, Retsin, Tortoise, and Rachel's.) Whoever's playing on the tracks, it's clear from the opening of "Hurricane" that Come is a re-energized, even more powerful band than they used to be, and that *Near Life Experience* is their most concise and affecting release yet. Come's trademark bluesy-punk sound is still apparent on songs like "Hurricane" and "Bitten," but the group stretches in different directions with gentle ballads like "Weak as the Moon" and "Slow Eyed." Zedek's voice is as gravelly and emotive as ever, and with the different song styles on *Near Life Experience*, has even more room to express itself. Brokaw also sings lead (a first) on two of the album's more accessible tracks, the single "Secret Number" and "Shoot Me First." Though it's only eight tracks long, Come pack more musical experiences into *Near Life Experience* than most groups do in an entire discography. — *Heather Phares*

Commander Cody

f. Jul. 19, 1944, Ann Arbor, MI
Rock 'n' Roll, Country-Rock, Western Swing Revival
Commander Cody and the Lost Planet Airmen were equally adept at stripped-down basic rock 'n' roll, R&B, and gritty country-rock. Commander Cody's country-rock rocked harder than the Eagles or Poco; essentially, the group was a bar band. Much like English pub rock bands such as Brinsley Schwarz and Ducks Deluxe, Commander Cody resisted the overblown and bombastic trends of early-'70s rock, preferring a basic, no-frills approach. Commander Cody and the Lost Planet Airmen never had the impact of the British pub rockers, but their straightforward energy gave their records a distinguishing drive; they could play country, Western swing, rockabilly, and R&B, and it all sounded convincing.
The group originally formed in 1967 in Ann Arbor, MI. Commander Cody (born George Frayne, IV; piano), John Tichy (lead guitar), Steve Schwartz (guitar), Don Davis (bass), Don Bolton (aka the West Virginia Creeper pedal steel guitar), and Ralph Mallory (drums) formed the original lineup. When the group relocated to San Francisco the next year, only Frayne, Bolton, and Tichy made the move; the group's membership included Billy C. Farlowe (vocals, harp), Andy Stein (fiddle, saxophone), guitarist Billy Kirchen, bassist "Buffalo" Bruce Barlow, and drummer Lance Dickerson at the time of their 1971 debut album, *Lost in the Ozone*. The next year the group scored a fluke Top Ten hit with "Hot Rod Lincoln," taken from their second album, *Hot Licks, Cold Steel and Trucker's Favourites*. Commander Cody was never able to capitalize on the single's success, partly because their albums never completely captured their live energy. They continued to release albums until Tichy left the band in 1976. Commander Cody released his first solo album, *Midnight Man*, in 1977, and then he re-formed the group as the Commander Cody Band. The group recorded three albums between 1977 and 1980. — *Stephen Thomas Erlewine*

Lost in the Ozone / 1971 / MCA ✦✦✦✦
This is the monumental debut by one of country music's insurgent pioneer bands. Along with the New Riders of the Purple Sage, the Outlaws, and .38 Special, the Commander and his boys saved the '70s from the doldrums. Formed in Michigan in 1965 while the members were attending college, the group based their music on a theory of Western swing. Playing with electric instruments, including the all-important steel and fiddle, and a good dose of irreverence allowed the band to adhere to their own agenda. Moving to San Francisco, they began to build a following and soon signed with Paramount. This first release, a combination of original tunes and some dusty covers, was only a taste of the things to come. Cody & His Airmen were at the head of a parade that continues through the '90s. Songs by Billy C. Farlow like "Daddy's Gonna Treat You Right" and the ever popular "Lost in the Ozone" were instant hits with the country-rock and hippy crowds. But the rednecks loved them, too, and this was an amazing social phenomenon. Cody, whose real name is George Frayne, partnered with Farlow on a number of songs from this first collection that still pack a wallop. "Wine Do Yer Stuff" and the tearful "Seeds and Stems (Again)" left no doubt where these boys were coming from. A strong honky tonk album that swings, *Lost in the Ozone* is a viable recording. Cover tunes performed with energy and humor won over crowds everywhere. "Hot Rod Lincoln" is still played on outlaw country radio stations, as is "20 Flight Rock," a boogie number that lets everything hang out. With not a single cut wasted, this is one of the buried gems of modern country music, displaying guitarman Bill Kirchen at his wildest and Bruce Barlow, Lance Dick-

erson, Andy Stein, John Tichy, Bobby Black, West Virginia Creeper, Farlow, and Commander Cody comin' out of the chute ready to change the world for the better. —*Jana Pendragon*

Hot Licks, Cold Steel & Truckers' Favorites / 1972 / MCA ✦✦✦
Again, a groundbreaking release from the wildest band in country music (during the '70s). This time around they are honoring the American trucker. With their own trucker tunes, "Truck Stop Rock" and "Semi Truck" leading the way, this LP includes some classics like "Looking at the World Through a Windshield," "Mama Hated Diesels," and the grandaddy of the bunch, "Truck Drivin' Man," a performance hit for Rick Nelson and the New Riders of the Purple Sage as well. Other high-powered covers include Little Richard's "Tutti Frutti" done up in a way no one will forget. The Cajun "Diggy Liggy Lo" is given a workout, as is "Rip It Up," and the Commander's class-A performance of "It Should've Been Me" leaves no doubt as to the punch this outfit gives to everything they do. From the band comes "Cravin' Your Love," "Watch My .38," and "Kentucky Hills of Tennessee." As with *Lost in the Ozone*, this is top-flight music in every regard and shows another side to this great band. —*Jana Pendragon*

Country Casanova / 1973 / MCA ✦✦✦
A studio effort, this didn't reflect their live prowess but was still a good time. —*Jeff Tamarkin*

Live Deep in the Heart of Texas / 1974 / Paramount ✦✦✦✦

Commander Cody & His Lost Planet Airmen / 1975 / Warner Brothers ✦✦✦
This was their first recording for Warner Brothers after leaving Paramount. With songs by Hoyt Axton and Lowell George, as well as plenty of contributions from Farlow, Tichy, Barlow, and all the rest, this is another good outing for the wild boys. The Tower of Power horn section lends a hand, making their big sound even bigger. Their cover of "Don't Let Go" is outstanding, and "House of Blue Lights" never rocked or shuffled and twanged the way the Airmen do it. With plenty of hillbilly stuff to go around, "California Okie" stands proud. A tip of the hat to the South is found on "That's What I Like About the South." "Keep On Lovin' Her," "Hawaii Blues," and "Four or Five Times" are also wonders to behold. "Willin'," done up right here, fits the band perfectly. This Lowell George tune is a standard now, and when the Airmen did it their way, they gave a whole new meaning to the song. —*Jana Pendragon*

We've Got a Live One Here / 1976 / Warner Brothers ✦✦✦✦
This is really the final hurrah for the band, in spite of the fact that there were more recordings to follow. This is a two-record set from their 1976 tour of Europe, with most of the original members still on board. After this tour, George Frayne, aka Commander Cody, broke up the band, which included Norton Buffalo. While this live recording is just as powerful as the preceding *Live Deep in the Heart of Texas*, it is obvious that some of their fire is burning mighty low. Still, this bunch always did their best work on stage, and they never failed to satisfy. Full of old standards, some new favorites, and plenty of wattage to make it all work just right, the standout tunes are the Commander Cody classics like "Seeds and Stems," "Too Much Fun," and "Lost in the Ozone." Other numbers that bring back the good old days include the Airmen's version of "Milkcow Blues" and "San Antonio Rose." Trucker songs, big with the continental crowd, are "Semi Truck," "Lookin' at the World Through a Windshield," and "18 Wheels." Other numbers of note are "One of Those Nights," written by Farlow, Frayne, and Kirchen, as well as the Commander's sendups of "Smoke! Smoke! Smoke!," and "Riot in Cell Block No.9," and "Hot Rod Lincoln." The era of Commander Cody & His Lost Planet Airmen was a special moment in time that created a place for hipsters, cosmic cowboys, rednecks, and the working class to come together and enjoy some real American music. Never will there be another band like this one or recordings like the ones they made between 1971 and 1976. They ended this project with "Lost in the Ozone," bringing the band and its audience full circle. —*Jana Pendragon*

Very Best of...Plus / 1986 / See For Miles ✦✦✦✦
Containing 22 tracks, all pulled from the group's first three albums, *The Very Best of...Plus* condenses the best of Commander Cody & His Lost Planet Airmen to a single disc, making it an excellent introduction to one of the finest American country-rock bands of the early '70s. —*Stephen Thomas Erlewine*

Sleazy Roadside Stories / 1988 / Relix ✦✦✦
The Cody septet cooks on this Texas jam, cut live in 1973. —*Jeff Tamarkin*

Aces High / 1990 / Relix ✦✦✦
The Commander and his current band in various late-'80s recordings. Not as sharp as the original stuff, but still fairly deranged. —*Jeff Tamarkin*

● **Too Much Fun: Best of Commander Cody** / Oct. 1990 / MCA ✦✦✦✦
Not only could they play the hell out of their instruments, but C.C. and his Lost Planet Airmen were a virtual melting pot of American

music—country, R&B, rockabilly, Western swing. And always too much fun. —*Jeff Tamarkin*

Live from Deep in the Heart of Texas / 1991 / MCA ✦✦✦✦
This is Commander Cody & His Lost Planet Airmen at their best, live on stage and out on the road with the New Riders of the Purple Sage. What a bill and what a grand time for a live album. This is how it really was—wild, loud, and fun. Again, they intersperse their own songs with old favorites. "Armadillo Stomp" was penned for this event, and a woolly version of "Down to Seeds and Stems Again Blues" has the crowd on its feet. Their "Oh Momma Momma" and "Too Much Fun" became legendary during this performance. But it is their reworking of Buck Owens' "Crying Time" that makes them such a wonderful country band. Johnny Horton's "I'm Comin' Home" is also masterful, as is their take on a favorite cowboy tune, "Sunset on the Sage." "Mean Woman Blues" is another highlight. As for the Commander, his wanton style is evident in the Leiber-Stoller tune "Riot in Cell Block No.9," and he makes it his own vehicle for a theatrical performance. Every cut is perfection; every cut is substantial. This 1973 performance is evidence that Commander Cody & His Lost Planet Airmen was one fine honky tonk band, perhaps one of the finest. —*Jana Pendragon*

The Commodores

f. 1967, Tuskegee, AL, **db.** 1985
Soul, Funk, Urban, Pop-Rock
The Commodores got their start by being the opening act for the Jackson 5. Largely through the lyrics of Lionel Richie, the band broke out nationally in the mid-'70s. Their initial success was mainly with dance tunes, but in the late '70s Richie began turning out love ballads such as "Easy," "Still," and "Three Times a Lady." His departure for solo stardom crippled the band, but not before they had one more huge success with "Nightshift" in 1985. Today the group plays state fairs and oldies venues. Members included Lionel Richie (replaced in 1984 by J.D. Nicholas), Thomas McClary (who left in 1984), Ronald LaPread, William King, Walter Orange, and Milan Williams. —*Rick A. Bueche*

Machine Gun / Jul. 1974 / Motown ✦✦✦✦
The album that introduced the Alabama-based Commodores. It's still in the Southern funk genre, with slithering beats, exploding synthesizer lines, and great arrangements and riffs. The title tune was played at parties all over the country, and the followup single "The Zoo (Human Zoo)" was great as well. —*Ron Wynn*

Caught in the Act / Feb. 1975 / Motown ✦✦✦✦
A spectacular second album by the Southern funksters, arguably their best overall. It had both powerhouse uptempo tunes and hit ballads, and the group's energy, spontaneity, and drive were still building. It's also the studio album that comes closest to duplicating the quality of their live performances during that era. —*Ron Wynn*

Movin' On / Oct. 1975 / Motown ✦✦
The second great album the Commodores released in 1975. They hadn't yet made the crossover connection but were among the top R&B, funk, and disco draws of the mid—and late '70s, churning out both excellent uptempo party tunes and good, if sometimes maudlin, ballads. —*Ron Wynn*

Hot on the Tracks / Jun. 1976 / Motown ✦✦✦
Another great mid-'70s album, although it had more punch with the slower cuts than the uptempo ones. The Commodores were now established stars, and they continued to dominate both the R&B charts and the touring circuit. They were also close to making the move to pop, which came with their next album. "Just to Be Close to You" and "Sweet Love" are two of their best ballads, and they've held up much better than some songs that sold far more copies. —*Ron Wynn*

Commodores / Mar. 1977 / Motown ✦✦✦
The Commodores' early years were spent on the Southern funk circuit, where their energetic, catchy tunes and keyboard-oriented funk made them edgy and radio staples. They scored seminal hits with "Brick House" and "Slippery When Wet," although it became apparent quite early that lead vocalist Lionel Richie also had a bright future as a solo balladeer, with such tunes as "Easy" signaling his future on adult contemporary and Quiet Storm/urban contemporary radio. This collection highlights early uptempo and ballad hits. —*Ron Wynn*

Natural High / May 1978 / Motown ✦✦✦
Another huge hit album for the Commodores, still riding the crest of both R&B and pop waves in the late '70s. "Three Times a Lady" was the group and Lionel Richie's first No. 1 pop hit and their fifth R&B chart topper. It began an unfortunate obsession with sappy themes that eventually would redirect both his and the group's focus from the great funk and uptempo dance tunes that had initially made them famous. —*Ron Wynn*

Greatest Hits / Oct. 1978 / Motown ✦✦✦✦
A very representative anthology gathering the Commodores' prime uptempo and ballad material. It shows that they were quite versatile in

their heyday, capable of being humorous or romantic with equal ease. They never topped "Brick House" for explosiveness, and "Easy" was arguably their finest slow song. The Commodores dominated the R&B charts in the late '70s and early '80s, earning four No. 1 and three other Top Ten R&B singles, plus two No. 1s and three other Top Ten pop hits. —*Ron Wynn*

Midnight Magic / Jul. 1979 / Motown ✦✦✦
The Commodores closed out the '70s in great style, dominating the pop and R&B charts with this album. It reached the No. 3 spot, and the song "Still" was their second No. 1 pop hit, and yet another R&B winner, one of three smash songs they had on those charts in 1979. Richie was then balancing things between being their lead singer, penning sappy love songs, and doing songwriting for others. —*Ron Wynn*

Heroes / Jun. 1980 / Motown ✦✦✦
The Commodores opened the '80s in great shape. This album once more put them in the pop and R&B top Ten, and they scored more big hits with the title track, "Old Fashion Love," and even some quasi-gospel, "Jesus Is Love." This was one of their last powerhouse albums, but no one suspected at the time that they wouldn't dominate the '80s as they had the '70s. —*Ron Wynn*

In the Pocket / Jun. 1981 / Motown ✦✦✦
The last album with both Lionel Richie and Thomas McClary, and their final statement as the group that had been the South's most commercially potent since the early '70s. Neither "Oh No" nor "Lady, You Bring Me Up" topped either chart, though both were huge R&B and pop hits. Richie had been making noises about leaving and would be gone within a year, followed by McClary a year later. —*Ron Wynn*

● **All the Greatest Hits** / Nov. 1982 / Motown ✦✦✦✦
While there are many Commodores greatest hits packages available, *All the Great Hits* offers most of their biggest hits, making it ideal for the casual fan. —*Stephen Thomas Erlewine*

Commodores Anthology / Apr. 1983 / Motown ✦✦✦✦
The anthology series was Motown's best greatest hits line until they issued the two box set *Hitsville* packages in '93. They compiled not just the hits but the important singles on the Commodores anthology, and the sound quality was better than on either *Command Performances* or the two-in-one line. —*Ron Wynn*

Nightshift / Jan. 1985 / Motown ✦✦✦
The Commodores made one final stab at regaining R&B glory when Lionel Richie and producer/arranger James Anthony Carmichael both left in the mid-'80s. J.D. Nicholas became their lead singer, and Dennis Lambert assumed production duties. They rebounded temporarily when "Nightshift" leaped out of an otherwise ordinary album to become a Grammy-winning R&B and pop smash. It stayed atop the R&B charts for a month and peaked at No. 3 pop. Unfortunately, it was also the end for Thomas McClary, who left the group when the album had run its course. It was their next-to-last hit and basically the end for the band, although they continued for a couple more years. —*Ron Wynn*

Anthology: The Best of the Commodores / Feb. 7, 1995 / Motown ✦✦✦✦
The revamped 1995 edition of *Anthology* includes all of the group's hit singles, as well as significant album tracks and singles that didn't chart, making it the definitive portrait of the popular, groundbreaking urban contemporary group. —*Sara Sytsma*

● **Ultimate Collection** / Mar. 25, 1997 / Motown ✦✦✦✦
The various stages of the Commodores' tenure on Motown are summarized on the excellent *Ultimate Collection*, which features 13 Top Ten hits including the monumental "Brick House," "Machine Gun," "Slippery When Wet," "Sweet Love," "Just to Be Close to You," "Fancy Dancer," "Easy," "Too Hot Ta Trot," "Three Times a Lady," "Still," "Lady (You Bring Me Up)" and "Nightshift." —*Jason Ankeny*

Con Funk Shun

f. 1972, Memphis, TN, **db.** 1988
Funk, Quiet Storm
This Memphis-based group was among the premier funk and soul ensembles of the '70s and '80s. Lead vocalist and guitarist Michael Cooper and drummer Louis McCall formed Project Soul as California high school students. They became Con Funk Shun in 1972, when Cooper and McCall moved to Memphis. They added bassist/keyboardist Cedric Martin, keyboardist Danny Thomas, saxophonist Karl Fuller, keyboardist/vocalist Melvin Carter, and saxophonist/percussionist Zebulon Paulle Harrel. Con Funk Shun began as an in-house band at Stax, backing various acts, while recording their own material. Some of this was later issued on Fretone, a Memphis label. They signed with Mercury in 1976, and had a long run with them until the mid-'80s. "Ffun" topped the R&B charts in 1977, and through 1986, Con Funk Shun had eight Top Ten R&B hits on Mercury, although they never scored a single Top Ten or Top 20 pop hit. Their sound and appeal were completely tailored to funk, soul, and later urban contemporary audiences. They did danceable

ditties, comic pieces, and competent love songs and ballads, especially "Baby, I'm Hooked (Right into Your Love)." Deodato and Leon Ware were two of their producers at various times. Cooper became a star in his own right after Con Funk Shun disbanded in the late '80s. —*Ron Wynn*

● **The Best of Con Funk Shun** / 1992 / PolyGram ✦✦✦✦
This is a solid compilation of Con Funk Shun's influential late '70s and early '80s funk. —*AMG*

Best of Con Funk Shun, Vol. 2 / May 21, 1996 / Mercury ✦✦✦
A mix of LP cuts and moderate-to-big R&B hits, the most famous of those being the novelty "Electric Lady," and "Too Tight" (presented here in an extended version). —*Richie Unterberger*

Concrete Blonde

f. 1982, Los Angeles, CA, **db.** 1995
Alternative Pop-Rock
Concrete Blonde grew out of the Los Angeles post-punk club circuit that produced bands like X, Wall of Voodoo, and the Go-Go's, but it wasn't until 1987 that the band even recorded its first album. The group was founded by singer-songwriter/bassist Johnette Napolitano and guitarist Jim Mankey, who played bass in Sparks with his brother Earle during the '70s. The two met while working at a studio owned by Leon Russell and were soon recording collaborations at Earle's studio. The two called themselves Dream 6 and released an EP through a French independent label, which was later reissued by Capitol. Their insistence on complete artistic control was offputting to the major labels who took notice, however, and it wasn't until 1987 that the group signed to I.R.S. and changed its name to Concrete Blonde at the suggestion of labelmate Michael Stipe.

Concrete Blonde recorded its self-titled debut album with Harry Rushakoff on drums, which betrayed the influence of the Pretenders. In 1989 *Free* was a tighter showcase for Napolitano's developing songwriting and produced a college radio hit with "God Is a Bullet." The morose, textured *Bloodletting*, a more accomplished record than either of its predecessors, broke the band to a wider audience with the left-field Top 20 hit "Joey," the tale of a love affair ended by alcoholism. Former Roxy Music drummer Paul Thompson played on both *Bloodletting* and its 1992 follow-up, *Walking in London*. The next year's *Mexican Moon* reflected Napolitano's interest in Hispanic music and culture, but Concrete Blonde's commercial fortunes had declined since *Bloodletting*, and Napolitano broke up the band. In 1995 Napolitano resurfaced in the band Pretty Twisted with partner Holly Vincent. Two years later, Napolitano and Mankey reunited for an album with the Los Angeles band Los Illegals. —*Steve Huey*

Concrete Blonde / 1987 / IRS ✦✦
With the addition of a new drummer, Jim Mankey and Johnette Napolitano's Dream 6 became Concrete Blonde, but the changes did nothing to bring musical focus to the partnership. When this debut album was released, IRS Records emphasized the track "Still in Hollywood," financing a video and promoting it to radio. The song borders on punk rock, as Mankey repeats the same riff over and over and Napolitano spits out the angry lyric like Exene Cervenka (except, of course, she is careful to stay on key). But the song's message is confused: Most aspiring stars try to *get to* Hollywood, no? Even more confused is the multiplicity of musical styles that demonstrated that Concrete Blonde's main characteristic was ambition, not talent. Napolitano didn't much care if she became the next Chrissie Hynde or the next Pat Benatar, as long as she became the next *something*. —*William Ruhlmann*

Free / Apr. 1989 / IRS ✦✦
This sophomore effort is an improvement over their slapdash-sounding debut, with punchier arrangements supporting Johnette Napolitano's throaty dramatics. Highlights include the forceful "God Is a Bullet" and the poppish "Happy Birthday." —*Rick Clark*

Bloodletting / May 1990 / IRS ✦✦✦✦
With their third album, *Bloodletting*, Concrete Blonde refashioned themselves as a mainstream modern-rock band, adding layers of effects on the guitars and pushing Johnette Napolitano's dramatic vocals to the forefront. The band benefits from the cleaner sound, which gives them a more forceful, engaging presence. Even with the stronger production, the group still can sink into Napolitano's pseudo-goth pretentions and they occasionally suffer from a lack of strong melodies — after all, their breakthrough hit "Joey" doesn't have a real hook, it became a hit because it sounds like a mock power-ballad. Nevertheless, *Bloodletting* is substantially more focused than their earlier albums, in terms of both songwriting and performance, and Concrete Blonde rarely matched its overall consistency again. —*Stephen Thomas Erlewine*

Walking in London / Mar. 1992 / IRS ✦✦✦
Continuing in a vein similar to that on *Bloodletting*, it contains "Ghost of a Texas Ladies' Man." —*Rick Clark*

Mexican Moon / Oct. 19, 1993 / IRS ✦✦✦
Intended as the band's farewell album, *Mexican Moon* finds Johnette
Napolitano exploring her fascination with Mexican and Hispanic culture, resulting in an album that can be varied and fascinating and, at
times, ponderous and tedious. Even with the slight indulgences, the
album is among Concrete Blonde's best and is a fine, elegant way to
wrap up their career. — *Stephen Thomas Erlewine*

Still in Hollywood / Nov. 1, 1994 / IRS ✦✦

● **Recollection: Best Of** / Feb. 20, 1996 / IRS ✦✦✦✦
Despite their obvious ambition, Concrete Blonde rarely made consistent
albums, which is why the 18-track *Recollection: The Best Of* is welcome.
Collecting all of the group's high points, not just singles like "Joey," "Still
in Hollywood," "Ghost of a Texas Ladies Man," "Walking in London,"
and "Heal It Up," but album tracks like "Tomorrow, Wendy," "Scene of a
Perfect Crime," "Bloodletting," and "Mexican Moon." Although it would
have been nice if *Recollection* had been presented in chronological
order instead of in the jumbled mess that constitutes its final sequencing, it remains an excellent overview of Concrete Blonde's career.
— *Stephen Thomas Erlewine*

Concrete Blonde y Los Illegals / May 5, 1997 / Ark 21 ✦✦✦
Just three years after their "retirement," Concrete Blonde's Johnette
Napolitano and Jim Mankey reunited to record an album with the Los
Angeles-based Mexican band Los Illegals. The resulting album, appropriately titled *Concrete Blonde y Los Illegals*, was a fusion of hard rock
and Latin music, leaning heavily on the latter. It's a stylistic departure
that reads better than it plays, since the two groups aren't able to write a
convincing batch of songs that would make their ideas more persuasive.
— *Thom Owens*

The Connells
f. 1984, Raleigh, NC
Alternative Pop-Rock, Jangle-Pop
The Raleigh, NC-based jangle-pop outfit the Connells formed in the
spring of 1984. Fronted by guitarist Mike Connell and his bassist
brother David, the first incarnation of the group featured vocalist Doug
McMillan and drummer John Schultz and were soon replaced by former
Johnny Quest percussionist Peele Wimberley. In late 1984 the quartet
recorded a four-song demo; after one of the tracks, "Darker Days," was
selected to appear on the North Carolina compilation *More Mondo*, the
Connells' ranks expanded with the addition of singer/guitarist George
Huntley, who made his debut on a March 1985 session co-produced by
Don Dixon.
  With the help of the band's friend Ed Morgan, the resulting demo
made its way to the offices of the British label Demon, which agreed to
fund the recording of enough additional tracks to complete a full-length
LP. *Darker Days* was released in Europe by Demon in 1985, and when
Morgan returned to the US, he formed his own label, Black Park, to
issue the album domestically. After the low-budget videos for the tracks
"Seven" and "Hats Off" garnered MTV airplay, the Connells won a contract with the TVT label before entering producer Mitch Easter's Drive-
In Studios to record 1987's brooding, more assured *Boylan Heights*,
which featured the superb single "Scotty's Lament."
  The edgier *Fun and Games* followed in 1989, and a year later the
group resurfaced with *One Simple Word*, scoring an alternative radio
hit with the single "Stone Cold Yesterday." After a three-year tour that
saw the Connells add keyboardist Steve Potak to their lineup in 1991,
they finally returned to the studio to begin work on 1993's *Ring*, highlighted by the single "Slackjawed," as well as "74-75," a major hit
throughout Europe. After another three-year hiatus, the Connells issued
1996's *Weird Food and Devastation*, released concurrently with Huntley's solo debut *brain junk. — Jason Ankeny*

Darker Days / 1986 / TVT ✦✦✦
The band's first album suffers from lack of direction and inexperience.
They show a great deal of promise but fail to distinguish themselves
much from the hordes of other southern folk-pop bands. — *Chris Woodstra*

● **Boylan Heights** / 1987 / TVT ✦✦✦✦
Their second album shows a great improvement over its predecessor.
With help from producer Mitch Easter, the band effectively combines
Southern jangly guitars with Celtic influences. One of the more distinc-
tive, though generally overlooked college rock albums of the late-'80s.
— *Chris Woodstra*

Fun & Games / 1989 / TVT ✦✦
Fun & Games marks a slight dip in quality. The songwriting is still top
notch but, at times covered by their new heavier sound. — *Chris Woodstra*

One Simple Word / 1990 / TVT ✦✦✦✦
In the course of four albums, The Connells have evolved their own style
within the jangling guitar-rock sound so prevalent in alternative bands
of the 80s. Mainly it's been a matter of writing more distinctive songs

and having them sung by guitarist George Huntley so they sink in. This
is their first album to cross over from the category of "promising" to the
beginnings of a fulfillment of that promise. — *William Ruhlmann*

Ring / 1994 / TVT ✦✦✦✦

Weird Food & Devastation / Aug. 20, 1996 / TVT ✦✦✦
Weird Food & Devastation follows the pattern of the Connells' previous album, *Ring*, by adding harder-edged guitars to their ringing guitar pop. The Connells aren't able to come up with a set of memorable
songs for *Weird Food*, but the album nevertheless remains a pleasurable listen, especially for fans of Southern jangle-pop (R.E.M., Let's
Active) or melodic alternative rock in the vein of Buffalo Tom.
— *Thom Owens*

The Contours
f. 1959, Detroit, MI
Soul, R&B, Motown
One of Berry Gordy's earliest discoveries at Motown, the hard-rocking
Contours cultivated a new generation of fans when their "Do You Love
Me" was featured in the 1987 hit movie *Dirty Dancing*. Led by gravelly-
voiced Billy Gordon, the quintet scored an R&B chart-topper in 1962
with the rollicking "Do You Love Me" on Gordy's label, then smoothed
out their sound just a bit for the mid-'60s soul classics "First I Look at the
Purse" and "Just a Little Misunderstanding." Dennis Edwards, who
joined the group well after "Do You Love Me," was recruited to replace
David Ruffin as lead of the Temptations in 1968. — *Bill Dahl*

● **Do You Love Me** / 1962 / Motown ✦✦✦✦
This rough-edged, early-'60s Motown group deserves more than its
enduring one-hit status for "Do You Love Me?" — *Bill Dahl*

Ry Cooder
b. Mar. 15, 1947, Los Angeles, CA
*Guitar, Vocals / Modern Electric Blues, Modern Acoustic Blues, Blues-
Rock, Country-Rock, Ethnic Fusion, Roots-Rock*
Whether serving as a session musician, solo artist, or soundtrack composer, Ry Cooder's chameleon-like fretted instrument virtuosity, songwriting, and choices of material encompass an incredibly eclectic
range of North American musical styles, including rock 'n' roll, blues,
reggae, Tex-Mex, Hawaiian, Dixieland jazz, country, folk, R&B, gospel,
and vaudeville. The 16-year-old Cooder began his career in 1963 in a
blues band with Jackie DeShannon and then formed the short-lived
Rising Sons in 1965 with Taj Mahal and Spirit drummer Ed Cassidy.
Cooder met producer Terry Melcher through the Rising Sons and was
invited to perform at several sessions with Paul Revere and the Raiders. During his subsequent career as a session musician, Cooder's
trademark slide guitar work graced the recordings of such artists as
Captain Beefheart (*Safe as Milk*), Randy Newman, Little Feat, Van
Dyke Parks, the Rolling Stones (*Let It Bleed, Sticky Fingers*), Taj
Mahal, and Gordon Lightfoot. He also appeared on the soundtracks of
Candy and *Performance*.
  Cooder made his debut as a solo artist in 1970 with a self-titled album
featuring songs by Leadbelly, Blind Willie Johnson, Sleepy John Estes,
and Woody Guthrie. The follow-up, *Into the Purple Valley*, introduced
longtime cohorts Jim Keltner on drums and Jim Dickinson on bass, and
it and *Boomer's Story* largely repeated and refined the syncopated style
and mood of the first. In 1974 Cooder produced what is generally
regarded as his best album, *Paradise and Lunch*. Its follow-up, *Chicken
Skin Music*, showcased a potent blend of Tex-Mex, Hawaiian, gospel,
and soul music, and featured contributions from Flaco Jimenez and
Gabby Pahuini. In 1979 *Bop 'til You Drop* was the first major-label
album to be recorded digitally. In the early '80s, Cooder began to augment his output with soundtrack work on such titles as *Blue Collar, The Long Riders*, and *The Border;* he has gone on to compose music
for *Southern Comfort, Goin' South, Paris, Texas, Streets of Fire, Bay,
Blue City, Crossroads, Cocktail, Johnny Handsome, Steel Magnolias,*
and *Geronimo. Music by Ry Cooder* (1995) compiled two discs' worth of
highlights from Cooder's film work.
  In 1992 Cooder joined Keltner, John Hiatt, and renowned British
tunesmith Nick Lowe, all of whom had played on Hiatt's *Bring the Family*, to form Little Village, which toured and recorded one album. Cooder
next turned his attention to world music, recording the album *A Meeting by the River* with Indian musician V.M. Bhatt. Cooder's next project,
a duet album with renowned African guitarist Ali Farka Toure titled
Talking Timbuktu, won the 1994 Grammy for Best World Music
Recording. — *Steve Huey*

Ry Cooder / 1970 / Reprise ✦✦✦
His debut serves as a neat prototype, with its Sleepy John Estes and
Woody Guthrie covers. It also introduces a most talented musician in its
leader. But it's still a prototype; the best was yet to come. — *Jeff Tamarkin*

Into the Purple Valley / Jan. 1971 / Reprise ✦✦✦✦
First there are no other credits for musicians; because of his reputa-

tion for honesty in music, I will assume that he plays all the instruments, including the ones with no strings. He is known as a virtuoso on almost every stringed instrument and on this CD he demonstrates this ability on a wide variety of instruments. The main focus of the music here is on the era of the Dust Bowl, and what was happening in America at the time, socially and musically. Songs by Woody Guthrie, Leadbelly, and a variety of other people show Ry's encyclopedic knowledge of the music of this time, combined with an instinctive feel for the songs. "Phenomenal" is the descriptive word to describe his playing, whether it is on guitar, Hawaiian "slack key" guitar, mandolin, or more arcane instruments he has found. This is a must for those who love instrumental virtuosity, authentic reworkings of an era, or just plain good music. —Bob Gottlieb

Boomer's Story / Feb. 1972 / Reprise ✦✦✦✦
Largely laidback and bluesy, this album features a number of paeans to an America long lost. —Jeff Tamarkin

● **Paradise & Lunch** / 1974 / Reprise ✦✦✦✦
Working with an intriguing collection of veteran musicians, the master musician and archivist turns in a stunning set of timeless remakes and new compositions. —Jeff Tamarkin

Chicken Skin Music / 1976 / Reprise ✦✦✦✦
Hawaiian traditional music meets Leadbelly and Ben E. King on Cooder's gospelization of rock and soul. —Jeff Tamarkin

Showtime / 1976 / Warner Brothers ✦✦✦
Recorded live in 1976, Cooder cooks and struts his stuff on this grand tour of his abilities. The great Flaco Jimenez is on accordion. —Jeff Tamarkin

Jazz / 1978 / Warner Brothers ✦✦✦
A tribute to Dixieland, with a stopover at the blues hotel. Joseph Byrd's arrangements on tunes by Bix Beiderbecke, Joseph Spence, et al., are inspired. —Jeff Tamarkin

Bop 'til You Drop / 1979 / Warner Brothers ✦✦
Cooder has disowned this early digital recording, and he's right; not only is the sound dry, but the music is rather lifeless. Although it has some bright moments, it's not his best. —Jeff Tamarkin

Long Riders / 1980 / Reprise ✦✦
Borderline / 1980 / Warner Brothers ✦
Ry is off track here on covers of old rock 'n' roll songs. The warmth of the earlier recordings is missing, and his already indistinguished vocals are hopeless here. —Jeff Tamarkin

The Slide Area / 1982 / Warner Brothers ✦✦
Cooder is forgetting what he does best; his forays into soul and old rock 'n' roll are interesting but not mouth-watering. Over-produced. —Jeff Tamarkin

Ry Cooder Live / 1982 / Warner Brothers ✦✦✦
Get Rhythm / 1987 / Warner Brothers ✦✦✦
Self-producing this time, Cooder gets the old rock 'n' roll right. Johnny Cash and Chuck Berry are pretty darn funky. Cooder can still play slide guitar like no one else. —Jeff Tamarkin

Music by Ry Cooder / Jul. 11, 1995 / Warner Brothers ✦✦✦✦
Since he's a limited vocalist with erratic songwriting skills, one could justifiably argue that the soundtrack medium is the best vehicle for Cooder's talents, allowing him to construct eclectic, chiefly instrumental pieces drawing upon all sorts of roots music and ethnic flavors (often, but not always, employing his excellent blues and slide guitar). This two-CD, 34-song compilation gathers excerpts from 11 of the soundtracks he worked on between 1980 and 1993. (Three of the cuts, from the 1981 film *Southern Comfort*, are previously unreleased.) As few listeners (even Cooder fans) are dedicated enough to go to the trouble of finding all of his individual soundtracks, this is a good distillation of many of his more notable contributions to this idiom, although it inevitably leaves out some fine moments. Still, it's well programmed and evocative, often conjuring visions of ghostly landscapes and funky border towns. —Richie Unterberger

Sam Cooke (Sam Cook)

b. Jan. 22, 1931, Clarksdale, MS, d. Dec. 11, 1964, Los Angeles, CA
Vocals / Soul, R&B, Pop-Rock, Rock 'n' Roll
A performer whose sophisticated, crystalline vocal delivery and alchemical fusion of pop and gospel laid the foundations for the rise of modern soul music, Sam Cooke was a singer of remarkable spiritual resonance, a supreme talent whose vision transcended all barriers of race and faith. A champion of creative rights who wrote much of his own material and even established his own business empire to better realize his far-reaching musical ambitions, Cooke was also a champion of civil rights who used his stature as a performer to break down the color lines separating blacks from whites. A major crossover success, his brilliant career was

tragically brief, but his shadow looms large over the generations of artists who emerged in his wake.

Born Sam Cook on January 22, 1931, in Clarksdale, MS, he was one of eight sons of a Baptist minister. He was a featured vocalist in the church choir throughout his childhood, and teamed with three of his siblings in a quartet dubbed the Soul Children. As a teen, Cooke became a member of the gospel group the Highway QCs, performing in churches and auditoriums across the nation. In 1950 he joined the Soul Stirrers, recording and touring with the group for nearly six years and achieving a significant level of success within the gospel community on the strength of lead turns on efforts including "Nearer to Thee" and "Touch the Hem of His Garment."

In 1956 he made his secular pop debut with the single "Lovable," recorded under the alias Dale Cooke in an attempt not to alienate his gospel fan base; however, when Art Rupe, the owner of Soul Stirrers' label, Specialty, objected to producer "Bumps" Blackwell's plans for a follow-up effort, Cooke was released from his contract. Upon signing to the tiny Keen label, he resurfaced in 1957 under his own name with the self-penned "You Send Me," a majestic soul confection that sold some two million copies and made him a star. A series of hits—most of them light romantic ballads and novelty tunes—followed over the next two years, most notably the Top 40 hits "Wonderful World," "Only Sixteen," and "Everybody Likes to Cha Cha."

As the 1960s dawned, Cooke began taking an active interest in the music business, founding his own independent label, SAR, producing hits for the Simms Twins and the Valentinos, and releasing early efforts from Bobby Womack and fellow Soul Stirrers alum Johnnie Taylor; additionally, he established his own publishing imprint, Kags Music, and even created his own management firm. At the same time, he left Keen to sign with RCA. Upon his arrival at the label, Cooke's music adopted a grittier, more gospel-influenced feel; his RCA debut, a reworking of "Chain Gang," became his biggest hit in some time, peaking at No. 2 in 1960.

At RCA Cooke's gifts reached their full potential as he reeled off a string of early 1960s hits ranging from the bluesy "Sad Mood" to the gospel-pop of "Bring It On Home to Me," to the smooth soul of "Another Saturday Night" and the buoyant R&B of "Twisting the Night Away." While remaining primarily a singles artist, in 1963 he issued the superb *Night Beat*, a moody, intimate collection steeped heavily in the blues; unlike most pop albums of the era, which fleshed out a couple of hits with an abundance of filler, *Night Beat* was a complete and ambitious artistic statement, comprised purely of prime material. As his reputation as a performer grew, Cooke established fervent fan bases in both the pop and R&B markets, and eventually he graduated from the 'chitlin' circuit" of Black-owned venues to Las Vegas casino stages and white nightclubs, emerging as a crossover superstar.

And then, at the peak of his career, Sam Cooke died. The circumstances surrounding his murder on December 11, 1964, remain hazy. According to initial reports, he was shot three times by Bertha Franklin, the manager of Los Angeles' Hacienda Motel, who claimed she acted in self-defense after Cooke raped a 22-year-old woman and then turned to Franklin herself after the young woman escaped, taking his clothes with her. The shooting was ruled a justifiable homicide, but in subsequent years it has been rumored that a number of crucial details surrounding the case were buried in deference to Cooke's wife and children, who wished to avoid any further publicity and scrutiny. Decades later, a satisfactory resolution to the matter has yet to be reached.

Even given the scandalous circumstances of his death, Cooke remained a major presence. *At the Copa*, a triumphant live set recorded at the elite New York club, was released in the month of his passing, and the single "Shake" reached the Top Ten a few weeks later. "A Change Is Gonna Come," another posthumous 1965 smash, was his true epitaph—a thoughtful, spiritually charged assessment of the then-current state of American race relations, it presaged the ascendent civil rights movement with remarkable clarity. In the years after his murder, Cooke's stature continued to grow. Disciples including Otis Redding and Al Green carried on his legacy with dignity and grace, and reissues and unreleased material—most notably 1985's *Live at the Harlem Square Club, 1963*, an incendiary concert recorded in Miami—appeared regularly. In 1986 he was named a charter inductee of the Rock & Roll Hall of Fame. —Jason Ankeny

Night Beat / Aug. 1963 / ABKCO ✦✦✦✦
Intense, spiraling uptempo numbers, gripping ballads, and simply marvelous performances by a legend who sadly wouldn't be around much longer. Originally released in August 1963, *Night Beat* [RCA 2709] was reissued on CD on June 6, 1995 [ABKCO 1124]. —Ron Wynn

Sam Cooke at the Copa / Oct. 1964 / ABKCO ✦✦✦
Cooke's classic live album is a mixed bag—he was playing to a White supper-club audience and altered his sound accordingly, favoring ballads and folk songs over most of his celebrated classic soul numbers.

The voice is there, and the style, but he never does cut loose completely, and the backing band is too clean. —*Bruce Eder*

The Legendary Sam Cooke / 1974 / Candlelite Music/RCA Special Products ✦✦✦✦
Usually it's best to steer way clear of these sorts of budget packages, but this is an exception, primarily because Cooke's catalog has been handled so poorly. This triple album has 30 songs from Cooke's RCA peak, including all the big smashes, and quite a few big and small hits ("Little Red Rooster," "Good News," "Sugar Dumplin'," "Sad Mood," "That's It, I Quit, I'm Movin' On") that don't appear on the only decent Cooke anthology currently in print (*The Man and His Music*). That makes it a decent pickup if you find a cheap used copy, but the real solution would be to have RCA finally get its act together and give the man the multi-disc retrospective he deserves. —*Richie Unterberger*

☆ **Live at the Harlem Square Club** / Jun. 1985 / RCA ✦✦✦✦✦
Long believed lost, this live album—rejected for release in 1963 by Cooke's managers, who wanted to broaden his appeal to white listeners—captures Cooke playing to a largely Black crowd, and it couldn't be more different from his *At the Copa* live album. A hot, sweaty performance, with Cooke and a proper band luxuriating in his most soulful material in its most wrenching and impassioned form. —*Bruce Eder*

★ **The Man & His Music** / Feb. 1986 / RCA ✦✦✦✦✦
The ultimate Sam Cooke collection, and really the only one worth owning, covering his post-1957 career from his pop music breakthrough ("You Send Me") to his final impassioned social statement, "A Change Is Gonna Come" (which is included in its seldom-heard uncut version). Few stones are left unturned, the sound is clean and sharp, and the tragedy of Cooke's early death is recalled with each play of this collection. —*Bruce Eder*

His Earliest Recordings / 1991 / Specialty ✦✦✦✦
A superb collection of 25 of the earliest recordings made by Sam Cooke, including "Touch the Hem of His Garment." —*Stephen Thomas Erlewine*

Rhythm and the Blues / Oct. 24, 1995 / RCA ✦✦✦✦
From the title, you might infer that this 20-track compilation—taken from early-'60s sessions, and principally composed of LP-only cuts—aims to showcase Cooke's most soulful side. That's true to some degree, but this isn't his funkiest stuff; for that, look to *Live at the Harlem Square Club 1963*, or even his most uptempo singles. Most of this is in fact suave pop/R&B, the emphasis sometimes falling on the pop, with lightly swinging, jazzy arrangements and some orchestration. Cooke didn't write most of the material here, and while "Little Red Rooster" (a hit single) represents the earthiest extreme that the CD touches upon, there are also quite a few songs that were originally performed by jazz/popsters from the '20s, '30s, and '40s. Certainly these are decent offerings; Cooke's a great singer and interpreter, and the arrangements are smooth without being overdone. But it's neither Cooke at his very best (the hits compilation *Man and His Music* is much better) or his grittiest (that honor belongs to *Harlem Square*). It does restore much of his better obscure material to wide availability and is recommended to those who have the above-mentioned albums and want more Cooke, although the 1963 LP *Night Beat* (reissued on CD in 1995) is a bluesier and better one to check out first. —*Richie Unterberger*

The Cookies

f. 1953, Brooklyn, NY, **db.** 1963
Girl-Group, Brill Building Pop
The forerunner of Ray Charles' Raelettes, the original Cookies were Margie Hendrix, Ethel "Earl-Jean" McCrea, and Pat Lyles. They recorded for Lamp (Aladdin) in 1954, and Jesse Stone brought them to Atlantic in 1955. They recorded three sessions under the Cookies banner and scored a Top Ten R&B hit with "In Paradise" in 1956. The group also backed Joe Turner and Chuck Willis on their hit recordings in 1956 before being absorbed into the Charles empire and becoming the Raelettes. Almost six years later, a new trio emerged as the Cookies on Dimension, with only McRea from the first group in its lineup. They did backup vocals for Neil Sedaka, Little Eva, and Carole King, while scoring two Top Ten R&B, and one Top Ten and one Top 20 pop hit in 1962 and 1963. "Don't Say Nothin' Bad (About My Baby)" was their biggest, peaking at No. 3 R&B (No. 7 pop) in 1963. "Girls Grow Up Faster than Boys" was their final chart outing in November 1963. —*Ron Wynn*

● **Don't Say Nothin' Bad About the Cookies** / 1991 / Teenager ✦✦✦✦
This import compilation includes the hits "Chains" and "Don't Say Nothin' Bad About My Baby," and is jammed with obscure Goffin-King tunes. The problem is, most of them aren't anywhere nearly as good as the hits the team penned for the Cookies or other girl groups. It does include the obscure gem "Girls Grow Up Faster Than Boys," a sassy cut that's as good as the two hits. —*Richie Unterberger*

Coolio

b. Compton, CA
Vocals / Hip Hop, West Coast Rap
Coolio (born Artis Ivey) is a native of Compton, CA. His variation of the P-Funk-inspired rap of Dr. Dre is calmer, less violent, and funnier. Recorded with his DJ Bryan "Wino" Dobbs, Coolio's 1994 debut album, *It Takes a Thief*, was a smash hit, selling over a million records and featuring the No. 3 single "Fantastic Voyage." His second record, 1995's *Gangsta's Paradise*, was an even bigger hit, thanks to the title track, which was the biggest rap single of the year. —*Stephen Thomas Erlewine*

It Takes a Thief / Jul. 19, 1994 / Tommy Boy ✦✦✦✦
Just when it looked like rap would completely succumb to the violent hyperbole and mean-spirited "realness" of gangsta rap, new blood entered the scene in 1994 to nudge the genre back toward friendlier turf. That new blood included Nas, Craig Mack, and Coolio, whose *It Takes a Thief* starts with the easy-rolling funk of Lakeside's "Fantastic Voyage" and goes from there, infusing rap with a much-needed sense of humor and the promise of good times. While Coolio is no simp—"County Line" playfully explores the hassles of welfare, while some tracks dip into gangsta territory—he manages to make rap a cool, inclusive journey. —*Eddie Huffman*

● **Gangsta's Paradise** / Nov. 21, 1995 / Tommy Boy ✦✦✦✦
Most of Coolio's hit debut *It Takes a Thief* was fairly upbeat material, but the appearance of the stark single "Gangsta's Paradise" in the summer of 1995 signaled a change in the rapper's music. Driven by an ominously deep bass line and slashing strings, the creeping, threatening funk of "Gangsta's Paradise" was the most chilling thing Coolio had recorded to date, but the menace didn't come at the expense of his considerable talent for immediate, catchy hooks. Consequently, the single shot to the top of the charts and hovered in the Top Ten for many weeks. The album followed shortly afterwards, and it didn't fail to deliver on the promise of the single. Not only did Coolio expand his sound, but his songwriting skills improved, as *Gangsta's Paradise* has very few weak moments. Alternating between slow, funky grooves and elastic, party-ready anthems, *Gangsta's Paradise* is proof that Coolio is one of the most exciting and interesting hip-hop artists of the mid-'90s. —*Stephen Thomas Erlewine*

Alice Cooper

b. Feb. 4, 1948, Detroit, MI
Vocals / Hard Rock, Heavy Metal, Pop-Rock
Originally, there was a band called Alice Cooper led by a singer named Vincent Damon Furnier. Under his direction, Alice Cooper pioneered a grandly theatrical and violent brand of heavy metal that was designed to shock. Drawing equally from horror movies, vaudeville, and Black Sabbath, Led Zeppelin, and the Stooges, the group created a stage show that featured electric chairs, guillotines, fake blood, and huge boa constrictors, all coordinated by the heavily made-up Furnier. In time Furnier adopted the name for his androgynous onstage personality. While the visuals were extremely important to the group's impact, the band's music was nearly as distinctive. Driven by raw, simple riffs and melodies that derived from '60s guitar pop as well as showtunes, it was rock 'n' roll at its most basic and catchy, even when the band ventured into psychedelia and art rock. After the original group broke up and Furnier began a solo career as Alice Cooper, his music lost most of its theatrical flourishes, becoming straightforward heavy metal, but his stage show retained all of the trademark props that made him the king of shock rock.

Furnier formed his first group, the Earwigs, as an Arizona teenager in the early '60s. Changing the band's name to the Spiders in 1965, the group was eventually called the Nazz (not to be confused with Todd Rundgren's band of the same name). The Spiders and the Nazz both released local singles that were moderately popular. After discovering there was another band called the Nazz in 1968, the group changed its name to Alice Cooper. According to band legend, the name came to Furnier during a ouija board session, where he was told he was the reincarnation of a 17th-century witch of the same name. Comprised of vocalist Furnier, who would soon begin calling himself Alice Cooper; guitarist Mike Bruce; guitarist Glen Buxton; bassist Dennis Dunaway; and drummer Neal Smith, the group moved to California in 1968. There the group met Frank Zappa and his manager, Shep Gordon, who signed Alice Cooper to their new label Straight Records.

Alice Cooper released their first album, *Pretties for You*, in 1969. *Easy Action* followed early in 1970, but it failed to chart. The group's reputation in Los Angeles was slowly shrinking, so the band moved to Furnier's hometown of Detroit. For the next year the group refined their bizarre stage show. Late in 1970 the group signed with Warner Brothers and began recording their third album with producer Bob Ezrin. With Ezrin's assistance, Alice Cooper developed their classic heavy-metal crunch on 1971's *Love It to Death,* which featured the No. 21 hit single "Eighteen"; the album peaked at No. 35 and went gold. The success enabled the group to develop a more impressive, elaborate live show, which made them highly popular concert attractions across the US and eventually the UK. *Killer,* released late in 1971, was another gold album. Released in the summer of 1972, *School's Out* was Alice Cooper's break-through record, peaking at No. 2 and selling over a million copies. The title song became a Top Ten hit in the US and a No. 1 single in the UK. *Billion Dollar Babies,* released the next year, was the group's biggest hit, reaching No. 1 in both America and Britain; the album's first single, "No More Mr. Nice Guy," became a Top Ten hit in Britain, peaking at No. 25 in the US. *Muscle of Love* appeared late in 1973, but it failed to capitalize on the success of *Billion Dollar Babies.* After *Muscle of Love* Furnier fired the rest of Alice Cooper, retaining the name for a solo career; the rest of the band released one unsuccessful album under the name Billion Dollar Babies. In the fall of 1974, a compilation of Alice Cooper's five Warner albums, entitled *Alice Cooper's Greatest Hits,* became a Top Ten hit.

For his first solo album, Cooper hired Lou Reed's backing band from *Rock 'n' Roll Animal*—guitarists Dick Wagner and Steve Hunter, bassist Prakash John, keyboardist Joseph Chrowski, and drummer Penti Glan—as his supporting group. *Welcome to My Nightmare,* Alice Cooper's first solo album, was released in the spring of 1975. The record wasn't a great departure from his previous work, and it became a Top Ten hit in America, launching the hit acoustic ballad "Only Women Bleed." Its follow-up, 1976's *Alice Cooper Goes to Hell,* was another hit, going gold in the US. After *Alice Cooper Goes to Hell,* Cooper's career began to slip, partially due to changing trends and partially due to his alcoholism. Cooper entered rehabilitation in 1978, writing an album about his treatment called *From the Inside* (1978) with Bernie Taupin, Elton John's lyricist. During the early '80s, Cooper continued to release albums and tour, but he was no longer as popular as during his early-'70s heyday.

Cooper made a successful comeback in the late '80s, sparked by his appearances in horror films and a series of pop/metal bands that paid musical homage to his classic early records and concerts. *Constrictor,* released in 1986, began his comeback, but it was 1989's *Trash* that returned Cooper to the spotlight. Produced by the proven hit maker Desmond Child, *Trash* featured guest appearances by Jon Bon Jovi, Richie Sambora, and most of Aerosmith; the record became a Top Ten hit in Britain and peaked at No. 20 in the US, going platinum. "Poison," a ballad featured on the album, became Cooper's first Top Ten since 1977. Since the release of *Trash,* he has continued to star in the occasional film, tour, and record, although he wasn't able to retain the audience recaptured with the album. —*Stephen Thomas Erlewine*

Pretties for You / 1969 / Bizarre ✦✦✦
Alice Cooper's debut album had none of his legendary grotesque hard rock; instead, *Pretties for You* was an earnest, but flawed, stab at psychedelia which occasionally catches fire. —*Stephen Thomas Erlewine*

Love It to Death / Jan. 1971 / Warner Brothers ✦✦✦✦
The best studio album by Cooper features the classic "Eighteen." Other standouts: "Caught in a Dream," "Long Way to Go," and "Black Juju." —*Rick Clark*

Killer / Feb. 1971 / Warner Brothers ✦✦✦✦
Some of the more theatrical pieces undermine the album's strengths. It contains the hits "Under My Wheels" and "Be My Lover." —*Rick Clark*

School's Out / 1972 / Warner Brothers ✦✦✦✦
The title cut of one of Cooper's best albums was a Top Ten hit. —*Rick Clark*

Billion Dollar Babies / 1973 / Warner Brothers ✦✦✦✦
It's not as mindbendingly outrageous or hard-rocking as *School's Out, Killer,* or *Love It to Death,* but with its conscious attempt at pop cross-over ("No More Mr. Nice Guy" and "Elected"), *Billion Dollar Babies* is just as perverse as the earlier records, as well as being more consistent than any of his other proper albums. Sometimes selling out just a little bit might not be such a bad thing. —*Stephen Thomas Erlewine*

★ **Greatest Hits** / 1974 / Warner Brothers ✦✦✦✦✦
While he made many classic hard-rock singles, Alice Cooper never made a consistently enjoyable album, making *Greatest Hits* a necessity. It might not cover *all* of his best tracks, but everything you need to know is here. —*Stephen Thomas Erlewine*

Welcome to My Nightmare / 1975 / Atlantic ✦✦✦✦
Although it contained the hit ballad "Only Women Bleed," what made this release a classic album for Alice Cooper was probably its excellent variety of music. Dance fans will appreciate the disco-oriented title track, mellowed fans will enjoy "Only Women Bleed," and fans of Cooper's classic rock will love catchy songs such as "The Black Widow" and "Cold Ethyl." And for those who are entertained by Cooper's bizarre melodies, take note—this album contains what is probably his creepiest song ever, the extremely disturbing "Steven." *Welcome to My Nightmare*

is by far the finest album Alice Cooper has yet released in his solo career. —*Barry Weber*

Alice Cooper Goes to Hell / 1976 / Warner Brothers ✦✦
Conceived as a concept surrounding Alice Cooper's dark side, *Goes To Hell* worked in some ways and not in others. He did get a hit single from the song "I Never Cry," another in a series of sensitive ballads, but much of the rest sounds like bad Broadway tunes set to a rock beat. Alice had come a long way from shocking rock audiences with his early antics. It wasn't always for the better. —*James Chrispell*

Alice Cooper Show / Dec. 1977 / Warner Brothers ✦✦
This live album unquestionably fails to capture the essence of Alice Cooper performing live. While listeners may hear the sound of a guillotine or the roar of a beast in the background, *The Alice Cooper Show* is surprisingly lifeless and lacks many of Cooper's biggest hits. Those that made it to the album, such as "I'm Eighteen" and "School's Out," run short, as significant verses are absent. All in all, there is definitely something missing. —*Barry Weber*

From the Inside / 1978 / Metal Blade ✦✦
From the Inside was hardly Alice Cooper's best-selling or most accessible album. An intensely personal account of his recovery from substance abuse, it tends to be one of his most abstract efforts and lacks the immediacy of *Billion Dollar Babies, Welcome to My Nightmare* or *Alice Cooper Goes to Hell.* There are no rock anthems here a la "School's Out" or "18," no hit pop ballads a la "Only Women Bleed" or "I Never Cry" and no celebrations of shock value like "I Love the Dead" or "The Black Widow." Instead, the singer honestly documents the way he confronted his demons and emerged victorious. Sometimes this introspective effort is too self-indulgent and intellectual for its own good, but at its best, *From the Inside* is as riveting as it is inspiring. —*Alex Henderson*

Constrictor / 1986 / MCA ✦✦✦
Although *Constrictor* still fails to retain the musical quality that was on his earlier albums, it was Alice Cooper's best release at the time since 1976's *Goes to Hell.* The album opens with the catchy "Teenage Frankenstein" and continues with pop-oriented music that is not excellent but is far from poor. The dance composition "He's Back (The Man Behind the Mask)" was used in the sixth *Friday the 13th* installment and is a nice variation from the music he usually puts out. While it may not be for all his fans, *Constrictor* marks the beginning of Alice Cooper's inevitable '80s comeback. —*Barry Weber*

Raise Your Fist and Yell / 1987 / MCA ✦✦✦
As the predecessor to the popular *Trash, Raise Your First and Yell* continues the attempt to revive Alice Cooper's immensely popular career. The release contains music similar to *Constrictor,* but with much more wild guitar and in-your-face attitude to keep it interesting. In a daring move by Cooper, *Raise Your Fist and Yell* also returns to shocking lyrics and songs, such as the eerie ballad "Gail," that characterize his popular villainous role. But as dark as the content is, the album is still very entertaining and, as we have come to expect from Cooper, very fun. —*Barry Weber*

Trash / Jul. 1989 / Epic ✦✦✦✦
Alice Cooper hadn't had a hugely successful album in over a decade when, in 1989, he teamed up with Bon Jovi producer Desmond Child for *Trash*—a highly slick and commercial, yet edgy, pop/metal effort that temporarily restored him to the charts in a big way. Fueled by the irresistible hit single "Poison," the album temporarily gave back to Cooper the type of visibility he deserved. There's nothing shocking here, and Cooper's ability to generate controversy had long since faded. But while the escapist *Trash*—which was clearly aimed at the Motley Crue/Guns 'N Roses crowd—may not be the most challenging album of Cooper's career and isn't in a class with *School's Out* or *Billion Dollar Babies,* it's fun and quite enjoyable. And it was great to see the long-neglected Cooper on MTV next to so many of the '80s rockers he had influenced. —*Alex Henderson*

Hey Stoopid / Jul. 2, 1991 / Epic ✦✦✦✦
Unfortunately, the return to the high end of the charts that Alice Cooper enjoyed with 1989's *Trash* was short-lived. On his similar follow-up—another slick pop/metal effort—Cooper no longer had the input of hit producer/songwriter Desmond Child and worked with Peter Collins instead. The result is an album that, although generally enjoyable and far from bad, isn't essential. The CD's more memorable offerings include the clever and amusing "Feed My Frankenstein," the dramatic "Love's a Loading Gun" and the inspired title song—which admonishes rockers not to self-destruct. But despite its strong points, *Hey Stoopid* is for only Cooper's more devoted followers. —*Alex Henderson*

Last Temptation / Jul. 1994 / Sony ✦✦✦✦
This bizarre but entertaining album marks the first time in a long while that Alice Cooper's powerful lyrics and singing relate to his shocking onstage theatrics. From the acoustic opening of "Sideshow" to the dramatic and gripping "Cleansed by Fire," *The Last Temptation* proves that

Cooper retains the ability to out-shock bands that have attempted to imitate him. Like many of his earlier albums, each of the ten tracks unfolds like chapters in one exciting storyline about a boy losing his sanity. While there are some ballads such as the saddened tune "It's Me," the disc consists of controversial lyrics and hair-raising metal that might even be confused with the music of Ozzy Osbourne. The classic composing and outstanding vocals make this one of his best albums. —*Barry Weber*

Classiks / Aug. 22, 1995 / Epic ✦✦✦
Released in 1995, *Classiks* is a greatest-hits compilation of Alice Cooper's Epic releases up through *The Last Temptation*. The problem is, however, that some of those hits are missing. Although it contains songs such as "Poison," classics like "Bed of Nails" and "Might as Well Be on Mars" are surprisingly absent. Instead of those studio tracks, listeners are given mediocre live excerpts from his 1990 video release *Trashes the World. Classiks'* last song, an unnecessary remake of Jimi Hendrix' "Fire," was originally intended to be released on *Hey Stoopid* but was instead put on this album as a previously unreleased track. It may be a good pick for new and/or dedicated fans of Alice Cooper, but longtime fans of Alice Cooper would be better off with his studio releases, because many songs that failed to achieve the popularity of "Lost in America" or "Poison" are still just as interesting. —*Barry Weber*

Cop Shoot Cop

f. 1987, New York, NY
Alternative Pop-Rock, Indie-Rock, Experimental
Starting with their intentionally confrontational (and controversial) name, New York City's Cop Shoot Cop are descended from the darker impulses of the early-'80s "no-wave" movement that produced noisy, disagreeable, anti-social—but often very intriguing—bands such as Mars, DNA, and Teenage Jesus & the Jerks. As with those combos, the Cops eschew the impulse of pop altogether, preferring a rumbling, clattering, deafening, metallic sound that focuses on the band's two-bass, no-guitar attack. The song narratives tend towards simplistic doom-and-gloom observations that "life sucks, man"—a point they often belabor. But when this bummer-rock clicks, it's oddly compelling, if slightly intimidating stuff, crammed to the gills with the standard litany of contemporary urban angst: anomie, alienation, and boredom. Add to this the odd meters, the yelling (he never describes it as singing) by low-end bassist Natz, and forays into pure noise, and what you end up with is an anti-rock style that, despite its repetitive tendencies, is furious, frightening, and powerful. Oddly, despite the inherent anti-commerciality of their music, as well as the band's disdain for corporate-controlled major labels, they did land a contract with Interscope Records (home of Helmet), part of the Atlantic family. Despite the more accessible sound of their recent records, Cop Shoot Cop remains an acquired taste, even for those who like their rock edgy and uncompromising. —*John Dougan*

Consumer Revolt / 1990 / Big Cat ✦✦

Suck City / Nov. 19, 1992 / Interscope ✦✦✦

● **Ask Questions Later** / Mar. 30, 1993 / Interscope ✦✦✦✦
Opening with the relentlessly stomping "Surprise, Surprise," this is Cop Shoot Cop at their harsh, semi-tuneful best. (How is "Everybody Loves You When You're Dead" for a title?) Natz' monotone yelling could use a little variation, but all in all, this is a rampaging record that is undone only by its misanthropic singlemindedness. What makes *Ask Questions Later* the most successful Cop Shoot Cop record is that it takes more chances and is, as a result, more rewarding. Not for the fainthearted, this record, despite its minor concessions to accessibility, is still a snarling, feral chunk of postmodern rock noise. —*John Dougan*

Release / Sep. 13, 1994 / Interscope ✦✦✦
It's certainly not the case that each Cop Shoot Cop record gets more accessible; perhaps it's more the case that they grow on you with each release. *Release* doesn't have the highs of *Ask Questions Later*, but the rolling, tumbling sonic assault is still confrontational and better understood by those predisposed to their sound. Never ones to be accused of selling out, the Cops are in fine form here and have proven to the cynics that despite their antipathy towards the rock marketplace, they can peacefully coexist with the major-label powers and produce a consistently interesting body of work. —*John Dougan*

Julian Cope

b. Oct. 21, 1957, Deri, Mid Glamorgan, Wales
Organ, Guitar, Vocals / Alternative Pop-Rock, Post-Punk, Neo-Psychedelia
Midway through the recording of the Teardrop Explodes' third album, leader Julian Cope decided to go solo and dissolved the band. Cope's reputation as a rock eccentric was already well established, and after his solo debut, *World Shut Your Mouth*, many believed he was downright deranged. The music strongly echoed the garage rock of Roky Erickson and the psychedelia of Syd Barrett, two of rock's most notorious LSD addicts, while Cope himself intentionally slashed his stomach with a broken microphone and gave interviews advocating the use of hallucinogens during his supporting tour. Cope strengthened his image of mental imbalance on the cover of his second album, *Fried*, by picturing himself cowering naked under a giant tortoise shell.

In 1986 Cope scored a surprise UK Top 20 hit with a re-recorded version of "World Shut Your Mouth," and Island attempted to introduce the singer to US audiences with the *Julian Cope* EP. Cope followed his success with *Saint Julian* in 1987, his first album since recovering from his earlier mental difficulties. However, he was forced to cancel a supporting tour for the follow-up LP *My Nation Underground* due to illness. While Cope took a break from the public eye, he released *Skellington*, a follow-up to *Fried* rejected by Mercury, and *Droolian*, a series of demos and experiments, in 1989 and 1990, respectively, through his fan club. He served notice of his return in 1990 by showing up at an anti-poll tax demonstration in London dressed as an alien named Mr. Sqwubbsy. The next year he scored a UK hit with "Beautiful Love" and released the critically acclaimed double album *Peggy Suicide*. *Peggy Suicide* set a tone for much of Cope's subsequent work; it was an ambitious concept album addressing political, environmental, and spiritual issues in Cope's own idiosyncratic, sometimes confusing way. *Jehovahkill* and *Autogeddon*, the latter of which examined social evils through the metaphor of an automobile, followed but were less successful artistically and attracted less critical attention. —*Steve Huey*

World Shut Your Mouth / 1984 / Mercury ✦✦✦
Julian Cope's solo debut *World Shut Your Mouth* (which, rather confusingly, does not include the track of the same name) salvages the songs intended for the Teardrop Explodes' aborted third album, continuing in the same neo-psychedelic direction. Tracks like "Sunshine Playroom," "Elegant Chaos," "Metranil Vavin," and "Kolly Kibber's Birthday" are as fanciful and delirious as their titles, filtering period organ riffs, oddball sound effects, and drug-addled wordplay into bright, engaging pop melodies. —*Jason Ankeny*

Fried / 1984 / Mercury ✦✦✦
The aptly-titled *Fried* (complete with a cover featuring a naked Julian Cope on all fours beneath a giant tortoise shell) is a portrait of utter dementia. "Bill Drummond Said," "O King of Chaos," and "The Bloody Assizes" aren't so much songs as hallucinations, free-associative ramblings tethered by a remarkably intuitive backing band. The diary of a madman. —*Jason Ankeny*

Julian Cope / 1986 / Island ✦✦✦
This solo "mini-LP" contained five tracks and ran nearly 16 minutes. The first track was called "World Shut Your Mouth," but actually there had been no such song on the album of the same name, and this was an all-new recording. It revealed the solo Cope to be a straight-ahead rocker for the most part. "World" (which became Cope's first US singles chart entry) was a guitar-driven anthem set to a martial beat, and Cope's cover of Pere Ubu's "Non Alignment Pact" fell just short of punk. Cope retained his punk anger in the lyrics, which included "Umpteenth Unnatural Blues," in which he expressed the desire for a violent death. Still, until that occurred, *Julian Cope* gave notice that its namesake had a claim to rock prominence. —*William Ruhlmann*

Saint Julian / Mar. 1987 / Island ✦✦✦
Julian Cope returns from the brink of madness with *Saint Julian*, a surprisingly slick and bombastic effort produced by Ed Stasium and Warne Livesey. Led off by the singles "World Shut Your Mouth" and "Trampolene," the LP marks Cope's movement into mainstream rock territory. The results are mixed; while he hasn't been this coherent in years, many of the songs lack the personality and energy of his most imaginative and crazed work. —*Jason Ankeny*

My Nation Underground / Oct. 1988 / Island ✦✦✦✦
Julian Cope's follow-up to *Saint Julian* is another hard-edged pop-rock collection, paced by its lead-off track, a medley of two 1965 hits, the Vogues' "Five O'Clock World" and Petula Clark's "I Know a Place," with Cope's apocalyptically altered lyrics. In his version, it's the missiles that blow, not the whistle. Cope follows this pessimistic vision throughout the album, but that doesn't keep him from making accessible music that drives home his message. —*William Ruhlmann*

Skellington / 1989 / CopeCo/Zippo ✦✦✦✦
Originally believed to have been recorded at about the same time as *Fried*, the stark, raving *Skellington* actually dates to the late-'80s gray area between *My Nation Underground* and *Peggy Suicide*, and represents one of the most bizarre and demented chapters in the Julian Cope story. A spare, mostly acoustic effort, *Skellington* is hilariously surreal. There's an ode to "Robert Mitchum" (complete, inexplicably enough, with a verse in French), a love song for an "Incredibly Ugly Girl," and even a braying salute to a "Little Donkey." The record's centerpiece, "Out of My Mind on Dope and Speed," best sums it up. Once again, Cope's loss of brain cells is our gain. —*Jason Ankeny*

Droolian / 1990 / MoFoCo-Zippo ✦✦✦✦
Like its companion piece *Skellington*, *Droolian* compiles some of Julian Cope's more bizarre acoustic home recordings; a kind of prelude to *Peggy Suicide*, it includes a rough early take of "Safe Surfer" as well as "Sqwubbsy," a paean to the big-headed freak depicted throughout *Peggy*'s sleeve art. Among the other highlights: "Look After Your Leathers," "Unisex Cathedral" and "Jellypop Perky Jean." —*Jason Ankeny*

Peggy Suicide / Mar. 1991 / Island ✦✦✦✦
Discovering a common ground between sheer dementia and melodic cohesion, *Peggy Suicide* emerges as the strongest album of Julian Cope's career. A sprawling concept record exploring the trials and tribulations of the title character—Cope's vision of Mother Earth—it features a uniformly strong collection of songs and consistently inventive arrangements and textures; "East Easy Rider" adopts a loping hip-hop rhythm, "Head" is shimmering funk, "Hanging Out & Hung Up on the Line" is a jet-powered rave-up and "Beautiful Love" achieves a kind of chamber-pop grandeur. Cope's thematic aims are just as ambitious—*Peggy Suicide* is an impassioned environmental warning which avoids easy platitudes, instead creating its own language and mythology to drive its message home. —*Jason Ankeny*

● **Floored Genius: The Best of Julian Cope & the Teardrop Explodes 1979-1991** / Oct. 20, 1992 / Island ✦✦✦✦
An impressive career overview spanning Julian Cope's origins as the frontman of the Teardrop Expodes to his emergence as the crackpot prophet of *Peggy Suicide*, *Floored Genius* is a strong introduction to one of the most eclectic and erratically brilliant artists of the post-punk era. A warts-and-all collection juxtaposing would-be stadium pop ("World Shut Your Mouth," "Charlotte Anne"), chemical freak-outs ("Out of My Mind on Dope and Speed," "Jellypop Perky Jean") and twisted shamanic passion ("Beautiful Love," "East Easy Rider"), the set brings Cope's warped history into new focus. Even at his most excessive, he remains a one-of-a-kind talent. —*Jason Ankeny*

Jehovahkill / Dec. 8, 1992 / Island ✦✦
Idiot savant or fool on the hill? Eight albums on, *Jehovahkill* does little to clarify the enigma. On first listen, you get the impression that Cope really has gone off the deep end this time. But patience with this 70-minute epic pays off. There is method to Cope's madness. Divided into three "phases," the disc makes an intriguing argument for looking to pre-Christian spirituality for a signpost out of our modern moral conundrums, even if music and lyrics deal with the theme rather more abstractly than the enclosed liner notes, photographs, and poetry. While this disc is a fave of several music critics and Cope-ophiles, *Jehovahkill* may be a bit of sensory overload for many. The uninitiated might consider starting off with *Floored Genius*, a compilation of Cope's previous Teardrop and solo work. —*Roch Parisien*

Head On / 1994 / Ma-Gog ✦✦✦✦

Floored Genius, Vol. 2 (1983-91) / Feb. 21, 1994 / Dutch East ✦✦✦✦
Like its predecessor, *Floored Genius 2* assesses the many twists and turns of Julian Cope's career; instead of spotlighting singles and album tracks, however, the focus here is on the singer's myriad BBC radio performances. Among the highlights: "The Greatness and Perfection of Love," "O King of Chaos," "Crazy Farm Animal" and "Double Vegetation." —*Jason Ankeny*

Autogeddon / Aug. 9, 1994 / American ✦✦
On *Autogeddon*, Julian Cope uses the automobile as a metaphor for his view of civilization in general, which he finds deplorable and inescapable. Listeners may be reminded of the solo albums of Syd Barrett, since Cope begins with his voice and acoustic guitar and adds electric instruments and percussion, often with the same uncertain tempos of Barrett's falling-apart arrangements. Jim Morrison also comes to mind, especially on "Don't Call Me Mark Chapman," on which Cope eventually leaves music behind and just recites his lyrics as poetry. That poetry can be both obscure and threatening; it's not clear what he's talking about in the song, but maybe we don't really want to know. Few people work as hard at being self-indulgent as Julian Cope, and while he will part company with many fellow travelers on *Autogeddon*, it's hard to say whether that's because he's picked up speed or run out of gas. —*William Ruhlmann*

20 Mothers / Oct. 31, 1995 / Echo ✦✦✦✦
Another lengthy grabbag of contrasting musical styles and left-wing world politics mixed with eccentric personal concerns, *20 Mothers* is a more produced effort than its ramshackle predecessor, *Autogeddon*, though at times it descends to the near-demo offhandedness characteristic of that effort. Just as often, however, Cope turns out blistering rock (the ironically titled "By the Light of the Silvery Moon") or Depeche Mode/Erasure-style synth-dance pop ("Just like Pooh Bear"). Generally speaking, as one song ends, it's anybody's guess what may come next. But whether playing acoustic folk or psychedelic rock, whether commenting on crop circles or Kurt Cobain, Julian Cope retains a nervy confidence. He may be a gadfly with a thousand offbeat opinions, but he

isn't tentative about them. Still, the tone combined with the viewpoint tends to mean he is more likely to amuse you than to involve you. The downside of being a gadfly is that you can be easily dismissed as a harmless nut. —*William Ruhlmann*

Elvis Costello

b. Aug. 25, 1955, Liverpool, England
Guitar, Keyboards, Vocals / Rock 'n' Roll, Singer-Songwriter, New Wave, Pop-Rock, Pub Rock
When Elvis Costello's first record was released in 1977, his bristling cynicism and anger linked him with the punk and new wave explosion. A cursory listen to *My Aim Is True* proves that the main connection that Costello had with the punks was his unbridled passion. He tore through rock's back pages taking whatever he wanted, as well borrowing from country, Tin Pan Alley pop, reggae, and many other musical genres. Over his career, that musical eclecticism has distinguished Costello's records, as have his fiercely literate lyrics. Because he supports his lyrics with richly diverse music, Costello is one of the most innovative, influential, and best songwriters since Bob Dylan.

The son of British bandleader Ross McManus, Costello (born Declan McManus) worked as a computer programmer during the early '70s and performed under the name D.P. Costello in various folk clubs. In 1976 he became the leader of country-rock group Flip City. During this time, he recorded several demo tapes of his original material with the intention of landing a record contract. A copy of these tapes made its way to Jake Riviera, one of the heads of the fledgling independent record label Stiff. Riviera signed Costello to Stiff as a solo artist in 1977; the singer-songwriter adopted the name Elvis Costello at this time, taking his first name from Elvis Presley and his last name from his mother's maiden name.

With former Brinsley Schwarz bassist Nick Lowe producing, Costello began recording his debut album with the American band Clover providing support. "Less Than Zero," the first single released from these sessions, appeared in April 1977. The single failed to chart, as did its follow-up, "Alison," which was released the next month. By the summer of 1977 Costello's permanent backing band had been assembled. Featuring bassist Bruce Thomas, keyboardist Steve Nieve, and drummer Pete Thomas (no relation to Bruce), the group was named the Attractions; they made their live debut in July 1977.

My Aim Is True, his debut album, was released in the summer of 1977 to positive reviews; the album climbed to No. 14 on the British charts but wasn't released on his American label, Columbia Records, until later in the year. Along with Nick Lowe, Ian Dury, and Wreckless Eric, Costello participated in the *Stiffs Live* package tour in the fall. At the end of the year, Jake Riviera split from Stiff Records to form Radar Records, taking Costello and Lowe with him. Costello's last single for Stiff, the reggae-inflected "Watching the Detectives," became his first hit, climbing to No. 15 at the end of the year.

This Year's Model, Costello's first album recorded with the Attractions, was released in the spring of 1978. A rawer, harder-rocking record than *My Aim Is True*, *This Year's Model* was also a bigger hit, reaching No. 4 in Britain and No. 30 in America. Released the next year, *Armed Forces* was a more ambitious and musically diverse album than either of his previous records. It was another hit, reaching No. 2 in the UK and cracking the Top Ten in the US "Oliver's Army," the first single from the album, also peaked at No. 2 in Britain; none of the singles from *Armed Forces* charted in America. In the summer of 1979, he produced the self-titled debut album by the Specials, the leaders of the ska-revival movement.

In February 1980 the soul-influenced *Get Happy!!* was released; it was the first record on Riviera's new record label, F-Beat. *Get Happy!!* was another hit, peaking at No. 2 in Britain and No. 11 in America. Later that year, two collections of B-sides, singles, and outtakes called *Taking Liberties* were released in America; in Britain, a similar album called *Ten Bloody Marys and Ten How's Your Fathers* appeared as a cassette-only release, complete with different tracks than the American version.

Costello and the Attractions released *Trust* in early 1981; it was his fifth album in a row produced by Nick Lowe. *Trust* debuted at No. 9 in the British charts and worked its way into the Top 30 in the US. During the spring of 1981, Costello and the Attractions began recording an album of country covers with famed Nashville producer Billy Sherrill, who recorded hit records for George Jones and Charlie Rich, among others. The resulting album, *Almost Blue*, was released at the end of the year to mixed reviews, although the single "A Good Year for the Roses" was a British Top Ten hit.

Costello's next album, *Imperial Bedroom* (1982), was an ambitious set of lushly arranged pop produced by Geoff Emerick, who engineered several of the Beatles' most acclaimed albums. *Imperial Bedroom* received some of his best reviews, but it failed to yield a Top 40 hit in either England or America; the album did debut at No. 6 in the UK For 1983's *Punch the Clock*, Costello worked with Clive Langer and Alan

Winstanley, who were responsible for several of the biggest British hits in the early '80s. The collaboration proved commercially successful, as the album peaked at No. 3 in the UK (No. 24 in the US) and the single "Everyday I Write the Book" cracked the Top 40 in both Britain and America. Costello tried to replicate the success of *Punch the Clock* with his next record, 1984's *Goodbye Cruel World*, but the album was a commercial and critical failure.

After the release of *Goodbye Cruel World*, Costello embarked on his first solo tour in the summer of 1984. Costello was relatively inactive during 1985, releasing only one new single, "The People's Limousine," a collaboration with singer-songwriter T-Bone Burnett released under the name the Coward Brothers. He also produced *Rum, Sodomy and the Lash*, the second album by the punk-folk band the Pogues. Both projects were indications that he was moving toward a stripped-down, folky approach, and 1986's *King of America* confirmed that suspicion. Recorded without the Attractions and released under the name the Costello Show, *King of America* was essentially a country/folk album, and it received the best reviews of any album he had recorded since *Imperial Bedroom*. It was followed at the end of the year by the edgy *Blood and Chocolate*, a reunion with the Attractions and producer Nick Lowe. Costello would not record another album with the Attractions until 1994.

During 1987 Costello negotiated a new worldwide record contract with Warner Brothers Records and began a songwriting collaboration with Paul McCartney. Two years later he released *Spike*, the most musically diverse collection he had ever recorded. *Spike* featured the first appearance of songs written by Costello and McCartney, including the single "Veronica." "Veronica" became his biggest American hit, peaking at No. 19. Two years later, he released *Mighty Like a Rose*, which echoed *Spike* in its diversity but was a darker, more challenging record. In 1993 Costello collaborated with the Brodsky Quartet on *The Juliet Letters*, a song cycle that was the songwriter's first attempt at classical music. He also wrote an entire album for former Transvision Vamp singer Wendy James called *Now Ain't the Time for Your Tears*. That same year Costello licensed the rights to his pre-1987 catalog (*My Aim Is True* to *Blood and Chocolate*) to Rykodisc in America.

Costello re-united with the Attractions to record the majority of 1994's *Brutal Youth*, the most straightforward and pop-oriented album he had recorded since *Goodbye Cruel World*. The Attractions backed Costello on a worldwide tour in 1994 and played concerts with him throughout 1995. In 1995 he released his long-shelved collection of covers, *Kojak Variety*. In the spring of 1996, Costello released *All This Useless Beauty*, which featured a number of original songs he had given to other artists but never recorded himself. — *Stephen Thomas Erlewine*

☆ **My Aim Is True** / Aug. 1977 / Rykodisc ✦✦✦✦✦
Elvis Costello's debut album is a pop landmark that indicates the future that may exist for the spirit of punk in the wider genre of rock music. Backed by the American group Clover (featuring then-future Doobie Brother John McFee but not harmonica player Huey Lewis), Costello displays all the characteristics that would serve him throughout his career: a caustic wit he uses to savage himself and others, a broad imagination—"(The Angels Wanna Wear My) Red Shoes" is one of the best pieces of rock whimsy ever written—an unsentimental but compelling sense of romance ("Alison"), and an astonishing verbal facility, all enmeshed with a pop encyclopedist's musical knowledge. One of the greatest first albums in pop history. — *William Ruhlmann*

☆ **This Year's Model** / Jul. 1978 / Rykodisc ✦✦✦✦✦
Where *My Aim Is True* implied punk rock with its lyrics and stripped-down production, *This Year's Model* sounds like punk. Not that Costello's songwriting has changed; *This Year's Model* is comprised largely of leftovers from *My Aim Is True* and songs written on the road. It's the music that changed. After releasing *My Aim Is True*, Costello assembled a backing band called the Attractions, which were considerably tougher and wilder than Clover, who played on his debut. The Attractions were a rock 'n' roll band, which gives *This Year's Model* a reckless, careening feel. It's nervous, amphetamine-fueled, nearly paranoid music. The group sounds as if they're spinning out of control as soon as they crash in on the brief opener, "No Action," and they never get completely back on track, even on the slower numbers. Costello and the Attractions speed through *This Year's Model* at a blinding pace, which gives his songs—which were already meaner than the set on *My Aim Is True*—a nastier edge. "Lipstick Vogue," "Pump It Up," and "(I Don't Want to Go to) Chelsea" are all underscored with sexual menace, while "Night Rally" touches on a bizarre fascination with fascism that would blossom on his next album, *Armed Forces*. Even the songs that sound relatively lighthearted—"Hand in Hand," "Little Triggers," "Lip Service," "Living in Paradise"—are all edgy, thanks to Costello's breathless vocals, Steve Nieve's carnivalesque organ riffs, and Nick Lowe's bare-bones production. Of course, the songs on *This Year's Model* are typically catchy and help the vicious sentiments sink into your skin, but the most remarkable thing about the album is the sound; Costello and the Attractions never rocked this hard, or this vengefully, ever again. (The 1993 compact disc reissue standardized the sequencing of *This Year's Model* on both

sides of the Atlantic, restoring the album to its original British running order and adding six bonus tracks. The first three tracks are singles and B-sides, including the classic rant "Radio, Radio," the organ-driven '60s pop of "Big Tears," and the frenetic "Crawling to the USA." The remaining three tracks—"Running Out of Angels," "Greenshirt," and "Big Boys"—are all demos.) — *Stephen Thomas Erlewine*

☆ **Armed Forces** / 1979 / Rykodisc ✦✦✦✦✦
After releasing and touring the intense *This Year's Model*, Elvis Costello quickly returned to the studio with the Attractions to record his third album, *Armed Forces*. In contrast to the stripped-down pop and rock of his first two albums, *Armed Forces* boasted a detailed and textured pop production, but it was hardly lavish. However, the more spacious arrangements—complete with ringing pianos, echoing reverb, layered guitars and harmonies—accent Costello's melodies, making the record more accessible than his first two albums. Perversely, while the sound of Costello's music was becoming more open and welcoming, his songs became more insular and paranoid, even though he cloaked his emotions well. Many of the songs on *Armed Forces* use politics as a metaphor for personal relationships, particularly fascism, which explains its working title, *Emotional Fascism*. Occasionally, the lyrics are forced, but the music never is; the album demonstrates the depth of Costello's compositional talents and how he can move with ease from the hook-laden pop of "Accidents Will Happen" to the paranoid "Goon Squad." Some of the songs, like the light reggae of "Two Little Hitlers" and the impassioned "Party Girl," build on his strengths, while others, like the layered "Oliver's Army," take Costello into new territories. It's a dense but accessible pop record and ranks as his third masterpiece in a row. (The Rykodisc/Demon 1993 CD reissue of *Armed Forces* restored the album to its original British running order, adding the B-side cover of Nick Lowe's "(What's So Funny 'Bout) Peace, Love and Understanding"—which had been subsituted for "Sunday's Best" on the American version of *Armed Forces*—as one of the disc's bonus tracks. The CD also includes the B-sides "My Funny Valentine," "Tiny Steps," "Clean Money," the free single "Talking in the Dark" / "Wednesday Week" which was included with the intial Radar pressings of *Armed Forces*, and the *Live at Hollywood High* EP, also on the first Radar edition.) — *Stephen Thomas Erlewine*

☆ **Get Happy!!** / 1980 / Rykodisc ✦✦✦✦✦
Featuring 20 tracks of energetic, amphetamine-driven soul, *Get Happy!!* captures Costello at his most vicious and clever. While his words and puns are pithy, it's the constant barrage of songs that makes the album work. Not all of the songs are first-rate, but the great majority are. — *Stephen Thomas Erlewine*

☆ **Trust** / Feb. 1981 / Rykodisc ✦✦✦✦✦
Following the frenzied pop-soul of *Get Happy*, Elvis Costello & the Attractions quickly returned to the studio and recorded *Trust*, their most ambitious and eclectic album to date. As if proving his stylistic diversity and his sophistication after the concentrated genre experiment of *Get Happy*, Costello assembled *Trust* as a stylistic tour-de-force, packing the record with a wild array of material. "Clubland" has jazzy flourishes, "Lovers' Walk" rolls to a Bo Diddley beat, "Luxembourg" is rockabilly-redux, "Watch Your Step" is soul-pop, "From a Whisper to a Scream" rocks as hard as anything since *This Year's Model*, "Shot with His Own Gun" is Tin Pan Alley pop, "Different Finger" is the first country song he put on an official album. And that's not even counting highlights like "New Lace Sleeves" and "White Knuckles," which essentially stick to Costello's signature pop but offer more complex arrangements and musicianship than before. In fact, both "complexity" and "sophistication" are keywords to the success of *Trust*. Without delving into the minutely textured arrangements that would dominate his next pop album, *Imperial Bedroom*, Costello & the Attractions demonstrate their musical skill and savvy by essentially sticking to their direct sound of their four-piece band. In the process, they recorded arguably their most impressive album, one that demonstrates all sides of Costello's songwriting and performing personality without succumbing to pretentiousness. — *Stephen Thomas Erlewine*

Almost Blue / Nov. 1981 / Rykodisc ✦✦✦
Costello's "country record" is usually written off as a vanity project, but *Almost Blue* is quite a bit more than that. It's one of the most entertaining cover records in rock 'n' roll, simply because of its enthusiasm. The album begins with a roaring version of Hank Williams' "Why Don't You Love Me" and doesn't stop. Costello sings with conviction on the tear-jerking ballads, as well as barn burners like "Tonight the Bottle Let Me Down." It's clear that Costello knows this music, and it's also clear who he learned it from—Gram Parsons. Costello covers Parsons' "Hot Burrito No. 1" and "How Much I Lied," and all of the music on *Almost Blue* recalls Parsons' taste for hardcore honky-tonk and weepy ballads. It's to Costello's credit that he made a record relying on emotion to pay tribute. — *Stephen Thomas Erlewine*

☆ **Imperial Bedroom** / Jul. 1982 / Rykodisc ♦♦♦♦♦
Having gotten his country album out of his system with *Almost Blue*, Elvis Costello returned to pop music with *Imperial Bedroom*. And it wasn't just pop-rock—it was *pop* in the classic, Tin Pan Alley sense. In order to accurately convey the advances in songwriting, as well as his desire to experiment with studio sonics, Costello didn't return to his longtime producer Nick Lowe. Instead, he chose to hire Geoff Emerick, who produced all of the Beatles' most ambitious records. And that gives a good idea of what *Imperial Bedroom* sounds like; it's traditional pop songs given a post-*Sgt. Pepper* production. Essentially, the songs on *Imperial Bedroom* are an extension of Costello's jazz and pop infatuations on *Trust*. All of Costello's writing is more complex and intricate, with the verses and choruses seamlessly flowing together. Conversely, the lyrics are quite bitter and brutal, but you wouldn't know that from the shiny surface of the production. The interweaving layers of "Beyond Belief" and the whirlwind intro are the most overtly dark sounds on the record, with most of the album given over to the orchestrated, melancholy torch songs and pop singles. Never once do Costello and the Attractions deliver a rock 'n' roll song. The album is all about sonic detail, from the accordion on "The Long Honeymoon" to the lilting strings on "Town Cryer." Of course, the detail and the ornate arrangements immediately peg *Imperial Bedroom* as Costello's most ambitious album, but that doesn't mean it's his absolute masterpiece. *Imperial Bedroom* remains one of Costello's essential records because it is the culmination of his ambitions and desires; it's where he proves that he can play with the big boys, as both songwriter and record-maker. It may not have been a commercial blockbuster, but it certainly earned the respect of legions of musicians and critics who would have previously disdained such a punk rocker. And perhaps that's also the reason that he abandoned this immaculately crafted style of work on his next album, *Punch the Clock*. —*Stephen Thomas Erlewine*

Punch the Clock / 1983 / Rykodisc ♦♦♦
Perhaps frustrated by the lack of commercial success *Imperial Bedroom* encountered, Elvis Costello enlisted British hitmakers Clive Langer and Alan Winstanley to produce its follow-up, *Punch the Clock*. The difference between the two records is immediately noticeable. *Punch the Clock* has a slick, glossy surface, complete with layered synthesizers, horns, studio effects, and the backup vocals of Afrodisiac. The approach isn't necessarily misguided, since Costello is as much a pop musician as he is a singer-songwriter, and many of the best moments on the record—"Everyday I Write the Book," "Let Them All Talk"—work well as shiny pop singles. However, the problem with *Punch the Clock* is that Costello is entering a fallow songwriting period. The best moments, the anti-war ballad "Shipbuilding" and the eerie pseudo-rap "Pills and Soap," are as articulate and effective as any of his past work, but frequently Costello falls short of meeting his standards, particularly when he's trying to write a song in the style of his older songs. Nevertheless, the sheen of the Langer & Winstanley production makes *Punch the Clock* a pleasurable listen. Costello's uneven writing means that only portions of the album are memorable. —*Stephen Thomas Erlewine*

Goodbye Cruel World / 1984 / Rykodisc ♦♦
During the making of *Goodbye Cruel World*, Costello was undergoing a multitude of personal problems, including a divorce, that resulted in a number of poor production decisions and ill-conceived, unformed songs. Like *Punch the Clock*, *Goodbye Cruel World* was produced by Clive Langer and Alan Winstanley, the top British hit makers of the '80s. Consequently, most of the record suffers from a stiff, synthesized production that instantly dates the record. In some cases—like the duet with Daryl Hall, "The Only Flame in Town," and the cover of the lost Hi R&B gem "I Wanna Be Loved"—the songs benefit from the shiny, streamlined production but it obscures the merits of the finest songs on the album. "Room with No Number," "The Comedians," "Sour Milk-Cow Blues," and "Peace in Our Time" all cry out for a simple, stripped-down presentation, but they're weighted down with stylized sounds and trendy synthesizers; however, once the sound of the album settles in, the strength of these songs is apparent. The remainder of *Goodbye Cruel World* isn't as memorable, primarily because Costello's uninspired vocals and the Attractions' muted performances fail to make the weaker songs musically compelling. —*Stephen Thomas Erlewine*

King of America / Jan. 1986 / Rykodisc ♦♦♦♦
Stripping away much of the excess that cluttered *Punch the Clock* and *Goodbye Cruel World*, Elvis Costello returned to his folk-rock and pub-rock roots with *King of America*, creating one of his most affecting and personal records. Costello literally took the album as a return to roots, billing himself by his given name, Declan MacManus, and replacing the Attractions with Los Angeles session men (although his old band appears on one cut), who give the album a rootsy but sleek veneer that sounds remarkably charged after the polished affectations of his Langer/Winstanley productions. And not only does the music sound alive, but so do his songs, arguably his best overall set since *Trust*. Work-ing inside the limits of country, folk, and blues, Costello writes literate, introspective tales of loss, heartbreak, and America that are surprisingly moving; he rarely got better than "Brilliant Mistake," "Glitter Gulch," "American Without Tears," "Big Light," and "Indoor Fireworks." What separates *King of America* from the underrated *Almost Blue* is that Costello's country now sounds lived-in and worn, bringing a new emotional depth to the music, and that helps make it one of his masterpieces. —*Stephen Thomas Erlewine*

Blood & Chocolate / Feb. 1986 / Rykodisc ♦♦♦♦
Costello returned to the Attractions as quickly as he had abandoned them, hiring the band and old producer Nick Lowe to record *Blood & Chocolate*, his second record in one year. Where *King of America* was a stripped-down, roots-rock affair, *Blood & Chocolate* is a return to the harder rock of *This Year's Model*. Occasionally there are hints of country and folk, but the majority of the album is straightahead rock 'n' roll; the opener, "Uncomplicated," has only two chords. The main difference between the reunion and the Attractions' earlier work is the tone. *This Year's Model* was tense and out-of-control, where *Blood & Chocolate* is controlled viciousness. "Tokyo Storm Warning," "I Hope You're Happy Now," and "I Want You" are the nastiest songs he has ever recorded, both lyrically and musically; Costello snarls the lyrics and the Attractions bash out the chords. *Blood & Chocolate* doesn't retain that high level of energy throughout the record, and loses momentum toward the end of the album. Still, it's a lively and frequently compelling reunion, even if it is rather mean-spirited. —*Stephen Thomas Erlewine*

Out of Our Idiot / 1987 / Demon ♦♦♦
Following in the tradition of *Taking Liberties* and *Ten Bloody Marys & Ten How's Your Fathers*, *Out of Our Idiot* compiles 21 rarities Elvis Costello released during the early and mid-'80s, usually under pseudonyms. Many of these songs are collaborations—"Seven Day Weekend" is a rollicking duet with Jimmy Cliff; Elvis sings "Baby It's You" with Nick Lowe; Costello and T-Bone Burnett form the Coward Brothers—hence the album's billing as a "various artists" record, which is indicative of its freewheeling, goofy humor. Even with a cover of Richard Thompson's harrowing "Withered and Died," *Out of Our Idiot* is pure fun, and it's not just for collectors. Costello's throwaways are frequently excellent, whether it's covers (Yoko Ono's "Walking on Thin Ice," Smokey Robinson's "From Head to Toe," "So Young"), genre exercises, jokes or full-fledged songs. Most of the songs on *Out of Our Idiot* were later included as bonus tracks in the Demon/Rykodisc reissue series, but this remains the only place "Little Goody Two Shoes" (a working version of "Inch By Inch") is available. Besides, it's a great listen in its own right. —*Stephen Thomas Erlewine*

Spike / 1989 / Warner Brothers ♦♦
Throughout his career Elvis Costello has always been prolific; thus it was surprising, even given the change in record labels for the US, when he took a whole 20 months between *Blood & Chocolate* and this follow-up. But the musical growth he exhibits makes the wait worthwhile. The musical settings range from the stark folk of "Tramp the Dirt Down" to the pop sprightliness of "Veronica" (a collaboration with Paul McCartney that became Costello's first American Top 20 hit) and the New Orleans jazz sound of "Deep Dark Truthful Mirror," featuring the Dirty Dozen Brass Band. The lyrics are among his best. —*William Ruhlmann*

Mighty Like a Rose / May 14, 1991 / Warner Brothers ♦♦
Teaming up with producer Mitchell Froom, Costello created his densest, most difficult album with *Mighty Like a Rose*. Although the songwriting is patchy, it is the production—filled with clattering percussion, off-kilter arrangements, and angular dissonant guitar—that makes the record impenetrable to all but the most devoted fans. There are still pop hooks, particularly on the sunny Beach Boys-style "The Other Side of Summer," "Playboy to a Man" and the sighing ballads "All Grown Up" and "So Like Candy," but Costello spends most of the album exploring, which means that the melodies are winding and the lyrics are pompous and cryptic. Froom's self-consciously "challenging" production amplifies the weaknesses of the music, turning the record into a claustrophobic and tedious mess. —*Stephen Thomas Erlewine*

The Juliet Letters / Jan. 19, 1993 / Warner Brothers ♦♦♦
Costello's collaboration with the Brodsky Quartet is an intriguing, if flawed, attempt at crossing pop with chamber music. Some songs rely too much on clever arrangements, but most of the tracks are surprisingly successful and accessible. —*Stephen Thomas Erlewine*

2 1/2 Years / Oct. 12, 1993 / Rykodisc ♦♦♦♦
Rykodisc launched its Elvis Costello reissue series with *2 1/2 Years*, a box set featuring his first three albums with the previously promotional-only *Live at the El Mocambo*, which is only available in the box. Costello fans know the studio albums by heart and will be pleased by the remastering and bonus tracks, while the highly sought-after *Live at the El Mocambo* proves that in addition to being an extremely talented songwriter, Costello was a hell of a rocker. —*Stephen Thomas Erlewine*

Brutal Youth / Mar. 8, 1994 / Warner Brothers ✦✦✦

Costello's first album with the Attractions since *Blood and Chocolate*, *Brutal Youth* suffers from soft, mushy production and the inclusion of too many songs. Apart from these two flaws, the record is highly enjoyable, recalling the stripped-down eclecticism of *Trust* and the force of *This Year's Model*. Costello's songs are strong and lean; it's his least affected and pretentious writing since *Blood and Chocolate*. —*Stephen Thomas Erlewine*

● **The Very Best of Elvis Costello and the Attractions** / Oct. 25, 1994 / Rykodisc ✦✦✦✦

A solid complement to Ryko's Costello reissue series if you don't want to pick up each individual album. Of course, the 22 tracks (drawn from his first 11 albums and, according to the liner notes, "hand-picked by Elvis himself") also sport the crisply remastered sound featured on the rest of the series. "The Very Best Of" halts abruptly at 1986's *Blood and Chocolate*, his last release for Columbia. —*Roch Parisien*

Kojak Variety / May 9, 1995 / Warner Brothers ✦✦

With *Almost Blue*, Elvis Costello wanted to be a honkytonker. With *Kojak Variety*, he's a crooner, picking forgotten tunes by both minor and major artists (anyone from Screamin' Jay Hawkins to Bob Dylan). From his song selections to the pseudo-avant-rock/R&B band, Costello doesn't make any obvious moves. Yet that doesn't mean that the record is difficult; it just shows the depths of Costello's affection for music and record collecting (which is also clear from his loving, detailed liner notes). Costello and his band (featuring guitarists James Burton and Marc Ribot, drummer Jim Keltner and Attraction Pete Thomas) play with gusto, tearing through the songs with the vigor of a bar band on a Friday night. Some of the rockers sound slightly forced, although there's no denying the power of Costello's passionate vocals, even if he stretches his range a little too much (Little Richard's "Bama Lama Bama Loo"). What matters here are the performances, and the majority of *Kojak Variety* is filled with fine interpretations. *Kojak Variety* does what any good covers album should do—it makes you want to seek out the originals. —*Stephen Thomas Erlewine*

Deep Dead Blue, Live at Meltdown / Nov. 1995 / Nonesuch ✦✦

All This Useless Beauty / May 14, 1996 / Warner Brothers ✦✦✦

After his second covers album, *Kojak Variety*, Elvis Costello set out to assemble a collection of songs he had written for other artists but never recorded himself—sort of a reverse covers album. As it turned out, that idea used only as a launching pad; the resulting album, *All This Useless Beauty*, is a mixture of nine old and three new songs. Given its origins, it's surprising that the record holds together as well as it does. The main strength of *All This Useless Beauty* is the quality of the individual songs. Each song can stand on its own as an individual entity, as the music is as sharp as the lyrics. Although the music is certainly eclectic, it's accessible, which wasn't the case with *Mighty Like a Rose*. Furthermore, the production is more textured and punchier than Mitchell Froom's botched job on *Brutal Youth*. *All This Useless Beauty* doesn't quite add up to a major statement, but the simple pleasures it offers make it one of the more rewarding records of the latter part of Costello's career. —*Stephen Thomas Erlewine*

Costello & Nieve / Dec. 3, 1996 / Warner Brothers ✦✦✦

Elvis Costello embarked on a small, intimate tour with his longtime pianist Steve Nieve in the spring of 1996 to promote *All This Useless Beauty*. All of the shows from the five-date tour were recorded, and highlights from each show were issued on a series of promotional EPs that were later released commercially as the box set *Costello & Nieve*. Stripped down to their basics, the songs from *All This Useless Beauty* sit elegantly next to Costello classics, as well as several lesser-known gems from his rich back catalog. The performances are all understatedly passionate, and rank among the best that Costello has given, making *Costello & Nieve* five discs that any hardcore fan will treasure. —*Stephen Thomas Erlewine*

The Count Bishops

f. 1974, England, db. 1979

Garage Rock

Although amounting to little more than a footnote in the early days of English punk rock, the Count Bishops were a fine, energetic, R&B-based band capable of kicking out a fierce racket of noise that sounded like a grimier version of seminal British R&B revivalists Dr. Feelgood. Originally fronted by journeyman American singer Mike Spencer, the Count Bishops' 1975 debut EP, *Speedball*, released on Ted Carroll's wonderful Chiswick Records, was a straightahead slice of R&B that featured the spooky, exhilarating "Train, Train." Surprisingly, the band unceremoniously dumped Spencer and recorded their self-titled debut with fellow Englishman Dave Tice, who had a voice so gruff it sounded as though he gargled with ground glass. A ripsnorting live record followed (by this time they had dropped "Count" from their name), but it was clear that the band was simply treading water. By 1979 the thoroughly mediocre

Cross Cuts was released to public apathy, guitarist Zenon de Fleur was killed in a car wreck, and lead guitarist Johnny Guitar hooked up with Dr. Feelgood. The Bishops called it a career. —*John Dougan*

● **Count Bishops** / 1977 / Dynamite ✦✦✦✦

Kicking off with a great cover of the Kinks' "I Need You," this solid, unpretentious debut album should belong in the home of every fan of English R&B from the Yardbirds to the Pretty Things to Dr. Feelgood. Guitarists Johnny Guitar and Zenon de Fleur keep it tight and simple, never wasting a note, and vocalist Dave Tice is so macho, it's enough to make you laugh. The originals are OK, if somewhat predictable blues-based rave-ups, but the energy and good cheer more than make up for the album's derivative nature. Not a deep album by any stretch of the imagination, just good dirty fun. —*John Dougan*

Live [12 Inch] / 1978 / Chiswick ✦✦✦

A hunk of greasy rock and R&B that's not the most original record you're likely to hear; it is fun, loud, sloppy, and endearing. Vocalist Dave Tice's growl is a hoot, as are the Chuck Berry pyrotechnics of Johnny Guitar. Two great covers: Fleetwood Mac's barroom anthem "Somebody's Gonna Get Their Head Kicked in Tonight" and the Standells' "Good Guys Don't Wear White." As the old saying goes: made loud to be played loud! —*John Dougan*

The Best of the Count Bishops / Oct. 1995 / Chiswick ✦✦✦✦

Count Five

f. 1965, San Jose, CA, **db.** 1967

Psychedelic, Garage Rock

This San Jose quintet scored one of the biggest garage-psychedelic hits of the '60s with "Psychotic Reaction," a derivative but riveting American adaptation of the Yardbirds' guitar rave-ups. The single reached No. 5 in late 1966, but the group was unable to come anywhere close to duplicating its success. Their sole album and collectible follow-up flop singles, like "Psychotic Reaction," emulate the Yardbirds, Rolling Stones, and Who with less memorable results, although they have their moments. —*Richie Unterberger*

● **Psychotic Reaction: The Complete Psychotic Reaction** / Jul. 22, 1994 / Performance ✦✦✦✦

Replaces previous Count Five collections as the most thorough retrospective of the group, with 18 of their tracks from the 1960s. —*Richie Unterberger*

Counting Crows

f. Aug. 1991, San Francisco, CA

Adult Alternative Pop-Rock, Folk-Rock

With their angst-filled hybrid of Van Morrison, the Band, and R.E.M., Counting Crows became an overnight sensation in 1994. Only a year earlier, the band was a group of unknown musicians, filling in for the absent Van Morrison at the Rock & Roll Hall of Fame ceremony; they were introduced by an enthusiastic Robbie Robertson. Early in 1993 the band recorded their debut album, *August & Everything After*, with T-Bone Burnett; it was released in the fall. It was a dark, somber record, driven by the morose lyrics and expressive vocals of Adam Duritz; the only up-tempo song, "Mr. Jones," became their ticket to stardom. What made Counting Crows was how they were able to balance Duritz' tortured lyrics with the sound of the late '60s and early '70s; it made them one of the few alternative bands to appeal to listeners who thought that rock 'n' roll died in 1972. *Recovering the Satellites* followed in 1996. —*Stephen Thomas Erlewine*

● **August & Everything After** / Sep. 14, 1993 / DGC ✦✦✦✦

Counting Crows became the surprise success story of 1994 with *August & Everything After*, which skillfully filters the classic rock of Van Morrison and the Band through the post-punk sensibilities of R.E.M. and the Cure. With his verbose lyrics and twisting melodies, lead singer and songwriter Adam Duritz resembles a cross between Morrison and Rick Danko, and his songs are more weathered than one might expect on a debut. Apart from the single "Mr. Jones," the album is rather gloomy, with melancholy, jangling guitars and a somber, solemn mood. Counting Crows crossed over because they were able to keep that gloom from resembling Joy Division or the Cure (or even *Automatic for the People*), instead sounding like something straight out of the classic years of 1968 to 1972. It's modern music for people who don't like modern music. —*Stephen Thomas Erlewine*

Recovering the Satellites / Oct. 15, 1996 / Geffen ✦✦✦✦

For their second album, *Recovering the Satellites*, Counting Crows crafted a self-consciously challenging response to their unexpected success. Throughout the record, Adam Duritz contemplates his loss of privacy and sudden change of fortunes, among other angst-ridden subjects. In one sense, it's no difference from the subjects that dominated *August & Everything After*, but his outlook is lacking the muted joy that made "Mr. Jones" into a hit. Similarly, the music is slightly more somber, but the approach is harder and more direct, which gives even the ballads a more affecting, visceral feel. *Recovering the Satellites* occasionally bogs down in its own pretention—for a roots-rock band, the group certainly has a lot of artsy goals—but when they scale back their ambitions to simple folk-rock, such as on the single "A Long December," they are at their most articulate. —*Stephen Thomas Erlewine*

Country Joe & the Fish

f. 1965, Berkeley, CA
Psychedelic, Folk-Rock
One of the original and most popular San Francisco Bay Area psychedelic bands, Country Joe & the Fish was formed by lead singer Country Joe McDonald (b. Jan. 1, 1942). The Berkeley group still had one foot in the jugband sound on their first EP, released in 1965 (featuring a folk version of their anthem "I-Feel-like-I'm-Fixin'-to-Die Rag"). By the time of their second EP in 1966, though, they had plunged full-tilt into the burgeoning psychedelic sound, with raga-ish, heavily distorted guitars and farfisa organ, displayed to its full glory on the instrumental "Section 43." Versions of songs from those limited edition EPs were combined with other material for their first and best album, *Electric Music for the Mind and Body*. McDonald and his group combined protest politics, free love, and psychedelic drugs with a good-time humor on this 1967 release. After a similar, less impressive follow-up, the band began to disintegrate, and they never recaptured the highs of the early days. McDonald went on to an intermittently successful, more folk-rock oriented solo career, achieving his greatest moment of notoriety with his version of "Fixin'-to-Die" (complete with the obscene "Fish Cheer") at the Woodstock festival. —*Richie Unterberger*

● **Electric Music for the Mind and Body** / 1967 / Vanguard ✦✦✦✦✦
Their full-length debut is their most joyous and cohesive statement, and finds the band's psychedelic swirl of distorted guitar and organ at its most inventive. Ranging in mood from good-timey to downright apocalyptic, it includes most of their best tunes. —*Richie Unterberger*

I Feel Like I'm Fixing to Die / 1967 / Vanguard ✦✦✦✦
The Fish's second album is quite similar to their first in its organ-heavy psychedelia with Eastern-influenced melodic lines, but markedly inferior to the debut, and much more of a period piece. There's more spaciness and less comic energy here, and while the band were undoubtedly serious in their explorations, some of these songs are simply silly in their cosmic naivete. To be crueler, there is no other album that exemplifies so strongly the kind of San Francisco psychedelia that Frank Zappa skewered on his classic *We're Only in It for the Money*. The weeping, minor-key melodies, liquid guitar lines, and earnestly self-absorbed quests to explore the inner psyche— it's almost as if they put themselves up as a dartboard for The Mothers to savage. For all that, the best songs are good; "Who Am I" and "Thursday" are touching psychedelic ballads. But more notably, the title cut—whose brash energy is atypical of the album —was a classic anti-war satire that became one of the decade's most famous protest songs, and the group's most famous track. —*Richie Unterberger*

Together / 1968 / Vanguard ✦✦✦✦
Together Country Joe & the Fish's third album, was the group's most consistent, most democratic, and best-selling record. Unlike their first two albums, which were dominated by Country Joe McDonald's voice and compositions, *Together* featured the rest of the band—guitarists Barry Melton and David Cohen, bassist Bruce Barthol and drummer Chicken Hirsh—almost as prominently as McDonald. That's usually a formula for disaster, but in this case it gave the album more variety and depth: McDonald tended to favor droning mantras like the album-closing "An Untitled Protest," which worked better when contrasted with the likes of Melton's catchy anti-New York diatribe, "The Streets of Your Town," and the group-written "Rock and Soul Music." Songs like the latter cast the group as a soul revue, true, and they couldn't quite pull that off, but *Together* had the charming quality of unpredictability; you never knew what was coming next. Unfortunately, what came next in the band's career was a split. Barthol was out by September 1968, Cohen and Hirsh following in January 1969. Thereafter, McDonald and Melton fronted various Fish aggregations, but it was never the same, even when this lineup regrouped for *Reunion* in 1977. —*William Ruhlmann*

Here We Are Again / 1969 / Vanguard ✦✦
By the time of Country Joe & the Fish's fourth album, the group seemed to consist of only Joe McDonald and Barry Melton, who had started the band in the beginning. *Here We Are Again* continued CJ&F's move toward pop (especially on "Here I Go Again") and bluesy rock and away from their folk and jug-music beginnings. But there were no songs to match some of the idiosyncratic winners on earlier albums, and the anonymous studio backing lacked the spontaneity of the original Fish. Though there would be one more new album in 1970 (*C.J. Fish*), Country Joe & the Fish no longer existed as anything other than a name, a fact that would be underlined in December 1969 by the simultaneous releases of *Greatest Hits* and McDonald's solo album, *Thinking of Woody Guthrie*. —*William Ruhlmann*

Greatest Hits /1969 / Vanguard ✦✦✦
Technically speaking, Country Joe & the Fish didn't have any hits; they only released five singles between 1967 and 1969, and none of them achieved anything in the way of mass popularity. They did, however, achieve notoriety with several songs, notably "Fish Cheer" and "I-Feel-Like-I'm-Fixin'-to-Die Rag," and some of those are included among the nine selections and less-than-33-minute running time of this *Greatest Hits* set. Some, such as "Janis" and "Rock and Soul Music," aren't, however, and this compilation has long-since been superseded by such successors as *The Life and Times of Country Joe & the Fish from Haight-Ashbury to Woodstock* (1971) and *The Collected Country Joe & the Fish* (1987). —*William Ruhlmann*

The Collected Country Joe & the Fish /1987 / Vanguard ✦✦✦✦
CJ & the F are well represented on *Collected Country Joe & the Fish (1965-1970)*, a 19-track compilation that traces their development from a politically-oriented folk/jug band ensemble to a politically oriented rock and soul band. Most of the material comes from 1967, the band's high-water mark, and the centerpiece is the still-cutting "I-Feel-like-I'm-Fixin'-to-Die Rag." —*William Ruhlmann*

The First Three EPs / 1987 / Decal ✦✦✦
The first recordings by Country Joe & the Fish (1965-1966) and his early solo material (1971). It includes "I-Feel-like-I'm-Fixin'-to-Die Rag," "Superbird," and "Tricky Dicky." —*William Ruhlmann*

Live at the Fillmore West / Mar. 12, 1996 / Vanguard ✦✦
Seventy-seven-minute disc of music recorded in January 1969, at the farewell performances of the Fish's most famous lineup, with Jack Casady of the Jefferson Airplane taking the place of the recently departed Bruce Barthol. The sound is good, but it's only for diehards, as the songs aren't among their best compositions, and the arrangements are way too prone to the uninteresting jamming that eventually gave San Francisco psychedelia a bad name. Jerry Garcia, Jorma Kaukonen, Steve Miller, and Mickey Hart all guest on the final cut, "Donovan's Reef Jam," which at 38 minutes is something of an endurance test. —*Richie Unterberger*

Don Covay

b. Mar. 1938, Orangeburg, SC
Vocals / Soul
An R&B and soul songwriting great, Don Covay compositions have been recorded by everyone from the Rolling Stones to Jimi Hendrix, from Gladys Knight to Wilson Pickett, and many others. Covay was the son of a Baptist preacher. He sang in his family's gospel group, the Cherry-Keys, as a youngster. Covay was born in Orangeburg, SC, but grew up in Washington, DC, and joined the Rainbows alongside Marvin Gaye, John Berry, and Billy Stewart in the '50s. Covay also performed as a solo singer with Little Richard, who recorded Covay as "Pretty Boy" on the Atlantic release "Bip Bop Bip." Covay had moderate success with the single "Pony Time," which he co-wrote with Berry, for the Arnold label in 1960. He began to hit his stride in 1964. Besides fronting Don Covay and the Goodtimers, he wrote "Mercy Mercy," "Sookie Sookie," and "See Saw," and had tunes recorded by Gene Chandler and Aretha Franklin. Covay did both blues and soul numbers for Janus and Mercury labels in the '70s. His biggest hit as a performer was "See Saw," which made it to No. 5 on the R&B charts in 1965. But his most electrifying number was 1973's "I Was Checkin' Out While She Was Checkin' In," which made it to No. 6. Covay was also part of the short-lived Soul Clan, with Solomon Burke, Arthur Conley, Ben E. King, and Joe Tex in 1968. Their "Soul Meeting," made it to No. 34, but wasn't quite the elaborate or explosive number everyone had envisioned. Covay made one LP for Gamble and Huff's Philadelphia International label in 1976, but *Travelin' in Heavy Traffic* proved a disappointment. Covay recorded for Newman in 1980, and got his last chart single with "Badd Boy." Some of his singles were reissued on a 1992 Mercury release, *Checkin' In with Don Covay*. An all-star gathering that included Ron Wood, Robert Cray, Bobby Womack, Iggy Pop, Peter Wolf, King, Todd Rundgren, Billy Squier, and Jimmy Witherspoon recorded a tribute album to Covay in 1993. —*Ron Wynn*

● **Mercy Mercy: The Definitive Don Covay** / Oct. 19, 1994 / Razor & Tie ✦✦✦✦
Mercy Mercy: The Definitive Don Covay compiles 23 tracks from throughout the soul singer's career. Encompassing everything from the R&B stomp of "Bip Bop Bip" and "Pony Time" to the seductive soul of "I Was Checkin' Out While She Was Checkin' In" and "No Tell Motel," the disc makes a convincing argument that Covay was one of the great overlooked R&B/soul artists of the '60s. —*Stephen Thomas Erlewine*

Cowboy Junkies

f. 1985, Toronto, Ontario
Alternative Pop-Rock, Adult Alternative Pop-Rock, Americana, Alternative Country-Rock
Although it was solely a way to gain attention, the Cowboy Junkies'

name goes a long way in describing the Canadian band's sound. At its core, the group's music is based in country and folk traditions, except their tempos are slow and lethargic, their guitars are languid, and Margo Timmins' vocals are lovely, yet hauntingly detached.

The Cowboy Junkies have their roots in the Hunger Project, an unsuccessful Toronto-based group formed by guitarist/songwriter Michael Timmins and bassist Alan Anton in 1979. After the band failed, the duo moved to the United Kingdom and formed an experimental instrumental group called Germinal. It was also unsuccessful, so the two musicians moved back to Toronto, where they began working with Timmins' sister Margo and his drummer brother, Peter. Under the name Cowboy Junkies, the group recorded their first album, *Whites off Earth Now!!*, in 1986, releasing it on a Canadian independent label. Two years later they recorded *The Trinity Sessions* in an abandoned church, using only one microphone. The album may have cost only $250 to record, but it sparked a small sensation, with the band's reworkings of "Blue Moon," "I'm So Lonesome I Could Cry," "Walking After Midnight," and "Sweet Jane" earning them a diverse and dedicated cult following.

The success of *The Trinity Sessions* allowed the band to record on a bigger budget. The result was 1990's *The Caution Horses*, which featured more of Michael Timmins' original songs. *The Caution Horses* didn't earn as much press as their previous album, but they maintained a sizable cult, which stuck by the band through their next two records, *Black-Eyed Man* (1992) and *Pale Sun, Crescent Moon* (1993). After the stop-gap live album in late 1995, *200 More Miles, Live Performances 1985-1994*, the Cowboy Junkies returned with *Lay It Down* in 1996. —*Stephen Thomas Erlewine*

Whites Off Earth Now!! / 1986 / RCA ◆◆◆
Featuring only one original song, the Cowboy Junkies' debut *Whites Off Earth Now!!* captures the band forming their own sound through covers, including songs by Robert Johnson and Bruce Springsteen. It's not as captivating as their later releases, but it's fascinating to hear their signature country-on-valium sound develop. Margo Timmins sings beautifully. —*Stephen Thomas Erlewine*

● **The Trinity Sessions** / 1988 / RCA ◆◆◆◆
Recorded with one microphone in an abandoned church, their second album achieves a haunting ambience. —*John Floyd*

The Caution Horses / Feb. 1990 / RCA ◆◆
The country influences are clearer and more energetic here, but most of the original material (with the exception of "Sun Comes Up, It's Tuesday Morning") is boring. —*John Floyd*

Black-Eyed Man / Feb. 11, 1992 / RCA ◆◆◆
The Cowboy Junkies stick with their style of low-key songs steeped in country blues. Songwriter and guitarist Michael Timmins writes storysongs full of rain and street life and regret, and they are movingly sung by Margo Timmins. Two Townes Van Zandt songs, including his classic "To Live Is to Fly," fit right in. —*William Ruhlmann*

Pale Sun, Crescent Moon / Nov. 23, 1993 / RCA ◆◆◆◆
A refreshed, revitalized sound that doesn't sacrifice the delicate touches that first made them unique; rugged, but still pristine. Much of the new spark emanates from the strings of honorary Junkie Ken Myhr, who peals out intense, biting lead guitar throughout. Especially prominent is his incendiary slide work on "Seven Years" and a spectacular cover of Dinosaur Jr.'s "The Post." Still, it's hard to imagine a ballad instrument more haunting and ethereal than Margo Timmins' voice. —*Roch Parisien*

200 More Miles, Live Performances 1985-1994 / Oct. 10, 1995 / RCA ◆◆◆
Subtitled "Live Performances 1985-1994" (though the earliest track comes from Halloween 1986), *200 More Miles*, which concluded the Cowboy Junkies' contract with RCA, was a 17-track compilation of concert recordings. Its five and a half cover songs spanned the group's influences: "Blue Moon Revisited (A Song for Elvis)" drew upon the Rodgers & Hart song (that's the half) as interpreted by the king of rock 'n' roll; "Me and the Devil Blues" from the king of the Delta blues singers, Robert Johnson; "I'm So Lonesome I Could Cry" by the king of country music, Hank Williams; "Walking After Midnight" by the queen, Patsy Cline; and "State Trooper" and "Sweet Jane" from a couple of rock's crown princes, Bruce Springsteen and Lou Reed. Of course, this was for the most part downbeat material, and the Cowboy Junkies rendered it in their usual transfixing, if soporific style. They did the same on a set of Michael Timmins originals, such as "Sun Comes Up, It's Tuesday Morning" and "Murder, Tonight, in the Trailer Park." (John Prine guests on "If You Were the Woman and I Was the Man.") "Before I do some rock 'n' roll, I always like to sit down," Margo Timmins noted at the outset, and she wasn't kidding. —*William Ruhlmann*

Lay It Down / Feb. 27, 1996 / Geffen ◆◆◆

Studio: Selected Studio Recordings 1986-95 / Nov. 12, 1996 / RCA ◆◆◆◆
Studio: Selected Studio Recordings is a fine compilation of highlights from the Cowboy Junkies' albums, including such songs as "Sweet Jane" and "Misguided Angel," as well as the previously unreleased "Lost My Driving Wheel." While this is a thoughtfully compiled retrospective, *The Trinity Sessions* remains the definitive Cowboy Junkies album, although this isn't a bad way to collect much of the best material from their frequently uneven records. —*Stephen Thomas Erlewine*

The Cowsills

f. 1966, Newport, RI, db. 1971
Power Pop, Pop-Rock, Bubblegum
The real-life antecedent to the Partridge Family, but an actual family and a better group, the Cowsills consisted of five teen and pre-teen siblings plus Mom. After some flop singles, producer Artie Kornfeld helped take the Newport, RI, group to No. 2 in 1967 with "The Rain, the Park, the Other Things." The well-produced, well-harmonized single was actually a good slice of flower-power-pop, even if the group had nothing to do with psychedelia in real life, projecting an almost unbearably wholesome image. Mining the territory between the Mamas & the Papas and the Partridge Family, they had a few other hits in the late '60s, the biggest of which was their cringingly embarrassing version of the theme song to the Broadway hit *Hair*, which went to No 2 in 1969. Group member Susan Cowsill, surprisingly enough, resurfaced in the mid-'90s as a member of the alternative rock group Continental Drifters. —*Richie Unterberger*

The Cowsills / 1967 / Razor & Tie ◆◆
Featuring "The Rain, the Park, and Other Things," this really isn't half-bad mainstream late-'60s pop, with a heavy Mamas & Papas fixation. It's not nearly as good as the Mamas & the Papas, of course, and doesn't stand up to in-depth listening. The CD reissue adds bonus tracks of their themes for the movie *The Impossible Years* and the TV series "Love American Style." —*Richie Unterberger*

● **The Best of the Cowsills** / 1968 / Polydor ◆◆◆◆
Here's everything you wanted to hear from this family group ("The Rain, the Park and Other Things," "Indian Lake," "Hair" from the musical *Hair*, among others) which was the real-life basis for the Partridge Family TV series. —*Larry Lapka*

The Cowsills in Concert / 1969 / Razor & Tie ◆
Put most charitably, this 1969 set of covers of huge '60s hits like "Good Vibrations," "Please Mr. Postman," "Paperback Writer," and (we kid you not) "Sunshine of Your Love" leaves itself open to all sorts of cruel jokes. Such as noting that all things considered, you're much better off with the original versions. Engineered by Val Valentin, who also worked on the Velvet Underground's *White Light/White Heat*—such are the ups and downs of the record business. The CD reissue includes a rare EP that (again, we kid you not) was originally recorded for the American Dairy Association. — *Richie Unterberger*

Kevin Coyne

b. Jan. 27, 1944, Derby, England
Vocals / Singer-Songwriter
There are plenty of more heralded singer-songwriters, but few have produced more good work or have done so for longer than Kevin Coyne. Virtually unknown in America, Coyne has over 30 records, most of them very good, that deal primarily with outsiders: men, women, and children arbitrarily shunted to the fringes of society, or worse, locked away and left alone. He can be extraordinarily compassionate and, in the blink of an eye, angry, anguished, and accusatory. Perhaps the most durable and telling image of Kevin Coyne is the cover photo of his album *In Living Black and White*. On the front, Coyne is smiling and politely bowing to an unseen audience; the back of the album jacket is the same photo taken from the rear, with Coyne clutching an open straight razor.

Born in Derby, England, in 1944, Coyne, like many rock 'n' roll performers who came of age in early post-war Britain, was an art-school student who fell in love with American R&B. Living a bohemian life in late-'60s London, Coyne was employed for a while as a socio-therapist for alcoholics and the emotionally disturbed, jobs that would profoundly affect his approach to music. In 1969 his first band, Siren, signed to influential BBC DJ John Peel's specialty label Dandelion. Two years and two excellent records later, Peel dissolved his label, and Coyne embarked on a solo career. Married with two children, Coyne supported both his family and musical career by returning to social work. In many ways, his solo debut, *Case History*, set the tone for his career. Based on his social work experiences, it was a riveting examination of the desperate search for love by those forcibly shunted to the fringes of society. With his bluesy voice wailing almost inconsolably, *Case History* is a naked examination of people (Coyne included) whose lives are in constant turmoil—betrayed, institutionalized, unwanted, and mostly unloved. The characters in these songs cry out for attention, and Coyne, never one to buy into England's bureaucratic social work system, howls right along with them.

Case History was very nearly Coyne's swan song, but after a self-imposed exile from music, an opportunity to continue recording as a solo act with almost complete artistic freedom proved too powerful an incentive. In 1973, Coyne began a relationship with the then-fledgling Virgin Records, who seemed willing to embrace the decidedly non-commercial, difficult performer. For the next eight years he recorded some of his best music and, somewhat surprisingly, attained a modicum of commercial success, albeit in Europe only. These were mostly edgy, folk-rock records tinged with an avant-garde feel for performance art (Coyne is a published poet too), clearly not easy listening by any stretch of the imagination; neither were these records overly pretentious or unapproachable.

By the early '80s, Coyne was recording for independent labels, making frustrating, semi-successful records that were erratically released and difficult to find. Exacerbating this bad situation were his worsening mental and physical states: chronic depression culminating in a nervous breakdown and alcoholism that, along with ending his marriage, nearly ended his life. By the end of the decade, he had relocated to Germany, formed a new band, fallen in love, and seemed to be sharpening his songwriting skills.

One can only guess at what the rest of the '90s will be like for Kevin Coyne, but chances are good that whatever he does, the music he records will always be interesting. Still, that assessment remains an educated guess. His recent recordings are nearly impossible to find, and most inquiries into his current activities, at least in this country, will doubtlessly yield the response, "Who's Kevin Coyne?" In late 1994 there was a major CD reissue series (only in England, of course) of Coyne's work, including two late-'80s/early-'90s records (*Legless in Manila* and *Wild Tiger Love*) that went mostly unheard, even by fans. —*John Dougan*

Case History / 1971 / Dandelion ✦✦✦✦
Coyne's first solo recording is a triumphant, if occasionally bleak, look at life's outsiders. Using his time as social worker in a government-run mental hospital as a basis for his narratives, Coyne deals with issues of intense alienation, indifference, substance abuse (to which he was no stranger), and mental instability in a world that would rather forget these people existed, and a labyrinthine governmental bureaucracy that often denies their humanity. This is not a happy record and is only infrequently hopeful, but it's never cynical; nor does Coyne indulge in glib condescension. He acts as a subjective documentarian, an advocate for a group of people who desperately need one. Reissued on CD with extra tracks by the import label Dandelion/See For Miles in 1994. —*John Dougan*

● **Marjory Razorblade** / 1973 / Virgin ✦✦✦✦
Marjory Razor Blade was Coyne's return to rock 'n' roll after a two-year "retirement" to go back to social work. A two-LP set in England, edited to a single disc in America, it contains some of his most stunning material and, arguably, his single greatest song, "House on the Hill." A harrowing tale of institutional life, as told by an overmedicated patient, it's as emotionally complex and well-written a song as one is likely to hear. Still, tracks like "Eastbourne Ladies," which pokes fun at stylish women at English seaside resorts, proves that Coyne the satirist is capable of making people laugh as well as cry. With so many albums available, it's difficult (close to impossible) to find one Coyne recording that's vastly superior to the others. However, if you bought this or *Case History*, you'd be listening to Coyne in his prime. —*John Dougan*

Blame It on the Night / 1974 / Virgin ✦✦✦
At times it sounds as if Coyne is attempting to make his music more commercial here, with the full, generic mid-'70s arrangements and occasional horns. That's a proposition as fruitless as selling snow to the Eskimos. Coyne is never going to be a mainstream artist; it seems more sensible to let him rip and be eccentric, playing in acoustic, stripped-down, bluesy contexts. Fortunately, that's what he does on about half the album, sounding his borderline lunatic self on "Don't Delude Me," and opting for an eerie, cryptic mood on "Blame It on the Night," and "Witch," with its flamenco guitars and undercurrent of suspicious paranoia. How not to gain commercial airplay, lesson 14: write lyrics such as "I cannot stand her friends anymore, I will wipe them across the floor" (from "Witch").——*Richie Unterberger*

Matching Head & Feet / 1975 / Virgin ✦✦✦
By the mid-'70s, Coyne was becoming very much a "cult" artist, one who would be appreciated by a small but significant segment of fans, who would buy new releases not so much because they wanted the particular record, but because they liked the particular artist. This is the kind of collection that is going to be sought mostly by that cult, as it's not one of his stronger efforts, and not likely to be adopted by anyone who hasn't previously been exposed to Coyne. The arrangements are more conventional than most of his previous work (a pre-Police Andy Summers han-

dles guitar), and much of the results are routine. Not lifeless, though; anything sung by Coyne will have roughness around the edges (and his voice here sometimes sounds not just raw, but downright worn). And songs about folks who carry guns and knives and smash the faces of their wives (in "Turpentine") are not your usual rock fare. The words *are* unconventional, but the settings are average in a mid-'70s way, which dilutes the lyrics' impact, and makes this an unmemorable effort on the whole. —*Richie Unterberger*

In Living Black & White / 1976 / Virgin ✦✦✦
As with *Marjory Razor Blade*, this live recording was edited to one disc for American consumption. My advice is to find the two-LP import and get the whole Kevin Coyne experience. Backed by a great band (perhaps his best), with dazzling guitar playing from soon-to-be Police guitarist Andy Summers, Coyne is in great form here, bellowing and braying the songs with inexhaustible energy. Excellent versions of "House on the Hill," the searing "Turpentine," and "Fat Girl" (about a depressed, overweight woman's suicide). A great record from start to finish. —*John Dougan*

Dynamite Daze / 1978 / Virgin ✦✦✦
Coming at the height of Punk, Kevin Coyne, nevertheless, had modest success with *Dynamite Daze*. Here he continues with his confessional rockers and folk-inflected English tunes on a record only slightly less appealing than previous efforts. —*James Chrispell*

Babble / 1979 / Virgin ✦✦✦
A match made in heaven: Coyne singing a series of songs about the successes and failures of communication between lovers, with the female perspective provided by German chanteuse (ex-Henry Cow/Slapp Happy/Art Bears) Dagmar Krause. Rather than sing duets, Coyne and Krause trade songs in a series of statements and responses. Occasionally the songwriting is thin, but the powerful singing and intense emotions more than make up for any lapses. This is a richly rewarding and frequently compelling record about love, communication, and commitment that is never sanctimonious, obvious, or cloying. Difficult to find (damn near impossible), but well worth the effort. —*John Dougan*

Boxed Set: Dandelion Years / 1980 / Butt ✦✦✦✦
This three-disc box set includes both *Siren* and *Case History*, making it an essential release. The *Siren* material holds up extremely well, thankfully eschewing art-rock (which was becoming all the rage in late-'60s London) for a grubby, blues-based pub-rock sound. Coyne is in particularly good form (and good spirits), making this a wonderful glimpse into his early years. Unfortunately, in America this box set seemed to disappear almost immediately after its release. Good luck finding a copy. —*John Dougan*

Peel Sessions / 1990 / Dutch East India ✦✦
Until a multi-disc anthology comes out covering Coyne's 20-year-plus career, this single CD is a valuable entry for the benighted into Coyne's world. Although it doesn't pack the wallop of *Case History* or *Marjory Razor Blade*, it doesn't quit its punches or serve up filler and pass it off as inspiration (well, it does once on the silly "Eye Up Me Duck"). There is material recorded as late as 1990, for those wondering as to his recent whereabouts, and while this collection isn't dazzling, it's illuminating. —*John Dougan*

Wild Tiger Love / 1991 / Golden Hind/Rockport ✦✦✦
Since his 1970s peak, Coyne's voice has deepened and lost some of its rough edge. As a poet, his powers are pretty much undimmed; even a nominally romantic song like "The Bungalow Song" has a bit of paranoid madness creeping in at the edges. When Coyne sticks primarily to acoustic guitar, the results are pretty good. Problems arise when the arrangements are filled out with a more generic rock band sound. Coyne, like so many artists, is a case of "less is more"; the more "produced" cuts, with their lazily mainstream tonal qualities, sit uneasily beside stark oddities like "Fish Brain" and "Open Up the Gates." The better, more passionate cuts may make this worth tracking down for serious Coyne fans, but it's a patchy recording overall. —*Richie Unterberger*

Tough and Sweet / 1993 / Rockport ✦✦
Albums such as these can make one wish that Coyne would choose to define himself as a folk singer, rather than a rock one. When he or other parties involved in the recording go for a full-band sound, the results are usualy misfires. Coyne's idiosyncratic narratives aren't well-suited for heavy modern rock tracks or fusionoid touches. He's not the Virgin Prunes, and at any rate shouldn't trying to be to lower himself to Gavin Friday's standards. As a songwriter, he remains as honest a cat as they come, but the incongruous qualities of the arrangements make these 21 songs a tough proposition. —*Richie Unterberger*

Elvira: Songs from the Archive / 1994 / Golden Hind/Rockport ✦✦✦
A combination of two separate sessions, one from 1979, one from 1983. The 1979 tracks were originally conceived as a one-woman show about Elvira Barney, an English debutante who shot her boyfriend. The show never went into production. Almost all of the tracks feature no instrumentation save Coyne's acoustic guitar. It's suitably harrowing

stuff, typical of Coyne's fine walk between sanity and instability, though here he is taking on the persona of another character. (The fact that it's a female character adds another level of strangeness.) The 1983 sessions, by contrast, have abrasive, sometimes chaotic backing that skirts free jazz, though Coyne's lyrics remain chillingly sardonic and neurotic. It's worth searching for if you liked Coyne's early, sparse recordings. —*Richie Unterberger*

● **Sign Of The Times** / 1994 / Virgin Records (UK) ◆◆◆◆
Uneasy listening for the psychotic set—if the often splintered music doesn't put you off, the tortured, lonely lyrics may, and if that doesn't do it, Coyne's hurt, angry, forceful vocals ought to do the trick. Coyne's songs come out of his experience working with psychiatric patients, people living on the edge. One of the songs in this compilation, "Witch," provides quite a graphic view of his history, with the accompanying wordless vocal turning into helpless shrieking as the main vocal sneers and snaps through a narrative that becomes gradually more psychotic as it goes on. Coyne, alas, is both brilliant and *painful*, an artist who is difficult to take in anything but small doses. This compilation touches on the highlights of the records Coyne made for Virgin and should serve as an excellent introduction to his work. —*Steven McDonald*

The Adventures of Crazy Frank / 1995 / Rockport ◆◆◆
A bit of an upturn for Coyne, this is a song cycle of sorts about a troubled, alcoholic comedian whose life bears some similarity to Coyne's own experiences. It's a more low-key, unforced affair than some of his previous '90s albums. Sometimes the rough, weathered quality of his voice makes him sound like a male counterpart to post-*Broken English* Marianne Faithfull; at his mellowest moments, he sounds a bit like a very debauched Van Morrison. On the whole it's one of his gentlest, most compassionate works, though not one of his more impressive. —*Richie Unterberger*

Cracker

f. 1991, California
Alternative Pop-Rock
While he was the frontman for Camper Van Beethoven, it seemed that it would take nothing short of a miracle to make guitarist/singer David Lowery a favorite of mainstream rockers, but that's what he and his second band, Cracker, have become. Led by Lowery and guitarist Johnny Hickman, Cracker is much more straightforward than Camper; Cracker concentrates on rock and country, creating a twisted, rootsy rock 'n' roll that sounds like a post-punk Rolling Stones or Little Feat. While their self-titled 1992 debut had moments of raw brilliance, Cracker's second album, 1993's *Kerosene Hat*, fulfilled their promise. Powered by the hit single "Low," the album was a hard-rocking meeting of traditional rock and post-punk sensibilities. Like Camper Van Beethoven's albums, it deserved to be heard by a wide audience; this time Lowery found a larger audience. *Kerosene Hat* eventually went gold.

Cracker released a third album, *The Golden Age*, in the spring of 1996. The album didn't repeat the success of its predecessor, falling off the charts within three months of its release.—*Stephen Thomas Erlewine*

Cracker / Mar. 10, 1992 / Virgin ◆◆◆◆
Apart from David Lowery's tendency to slip in some smug, self-serving lyrics, Cracker's debut is a terrific rock 'n' roll record, full of energetic three-chord bashers and surprisingly moving ballads. —*Stephen Thomas Erlewine*

● **Kerosene Hat** / Aug. 24, 1993 / Virgin ◆◆◆◆
With their second album, Cracker has lost the smarmy self-righteousness that plagued their otherwise fine debut, replacing it with a surprisingly solid rocking core. *Kerosene Hat* is David Lowery's least affected album yet; its humor is no stranger than the Stones' "Dead Flowers" or Little Feat's "Fat Man in a Bathtub," two groups that Cracker strongly recalls throughout the album. *Kerosene Hat* is more blues—and country-based than their debut, but it sounds natural, since their songwriting has improved and the band has grown tighter. —*Stephen Thomas Erlewine*

The Golden Age / Apr. 2, 1996 / Virgin ◆◆◆
Kerosene Hat, Cracker's second album, was an unexpected hit because of its off-kilter charm. Though Cracker rocked hard throughout the record, they also threw in fractured pop and country tunes that gave the album a broader appeal. The band's follow-up album, *The Golden Age*, tries to expand on that appeal by burying the weirdness inherent in David Lowery's songwriting with loud, grungy guitars and a more streamlined production. The change is evident from the record's lead-off track, "I Hate My Generation." With its pounding rhythms and grunge-drenched guitars, it may have been intended as a parody of '90s Generation-X angst, but the riffs and melodies are so slight that it fails embarassingly. In fact, most of the louder numbers on *The Golden Age* are forced and underdeveloped. What saves the record is when Cracker

turns the volume down, whether it's the country-rock of the title track, the goofy pop of "How Can I Live Without You," or the dusty psychedelia of "Bicycle Spaniard." Once you dig past the surface of the loud guitars, it becomes apparent that quiet gems are scattered throughout *The Golden Age*, and that is what makes the album worthwhile listening. —*Stephen Thomas Erlewine*

Carl Craig

b. Detroit, MI
Techno, Club/Dance, Electronica
Noted second-wave Detroit techno artist Carl Craig is a bridge of sorts between the old school of Motor City innovators and the newer school of underground deck-wreckers like Underground Resistance, AUX 88, and Drexciya. A contemporary of techno originators such as Derrick May and Juan Atkins, Craig engineered a number of crucial tracks during techno's early years, even co-writing the Rhythim Is Rhythim classic "Stringz of Life," before embarking on his own career as a composer. His credits include a flurry of different pseudonyms (Paperclip People, Yennek, Psyche, and 69 among them) and a long list of groundbreaking releases, including "Bug in the Bassbin," "Crackdown," "4 Jazz Funk Classics," and "Jam the Box." Although his music, like that of his predecessors Atkins and May, is rooted in a strongly political aesthetic futurism, Craig's compositional ideas often derive from a decidedly different origin—that of academic electronic composition. As a student of electronic music theory in the mid-'80s, Craig studied the work of Kraftwerk, YMO, and Yello side by side with highbrow artists such as Wendy Carlos, Morton Subotnick, and Pauline Oliveros, coming up with wide-ranging fusions of dance-based and avant-garde music that had his instructors scratching their heads. Craig released his first tracks in 1990 on Transmat and his own Retroactive label (which would later morph into the influential Detroit institution Planet E Communications). He's since released more than a dozen EPs and 12-inches for a number of different labels, finally releasing his debut album-length work (on a major label, no less), *Landcruising*, in 1995. Craig has also been widely hailed as a remixer, reworking tracks for everyone from house staples like Brian Transeau and Inner City to international pop sensations like Yello, the Orb, and Tori Amos. —*Sean Cooper*

Landcruising / 1995 / Blanco Y Negro ◆◆◆◆

● **More Songs About Food and Revolutionary Art** / Mar. 24, 1997 / SSR ◆◆◆◆

The Cramps

f. 1976, New York, NY
Alternative Pop-Rock, Post-Punk, Rockabilly Revival
The Cramps' unique sound synthesizes classic rockabilly, touches of psychedelia, and lyrical fare devoted mostly to monster movies and sleazy sex into an infectious, gloriously tasteless conglomeration of American trash culture. While their subject matter may verge on offensive to some, their obvious sense of humor and the fun, disposable feel of their best work prevent the listener from ever taking things too seriously. The group was formed by vocalist Erick "Lux Interior" Purkhiser and guitarist Kirsty "Poison Ivy Rorschach" Wallace, who met in Sacramento and found they shared an affinity for obscure '50s rockabilly and trash records and junk culture. The two moved back to Interior's native Ohio and then to New York in 1975, where, as a vehicle for indulging their obsessions, they formed the Cramps with guitarist Bryan Gregory and his sister Pam "Balam" Gregory on drums. Miriam Linna replaced Pam Balam after a few months, and the Cramps became favorites at the renowned punk club CBGB's. Linna left in 1977 to join Nervus Rex; she later cofounded *Kicks* magazine and the '50s rock 'n' roll-oriented Norton Records label.

After drummer Nick Knox joined the fold, the Cramps went to the legendary Sun studio, with cult icon Alex Chilton producing, to record several singles, later released on the *Gravest Hits* EP. Chilton also produced their minimalistic 1980 debut album, *Songs the Lord Taught Us*. Gregory left the band very suddenly afterwards without explanation; he reportedly tried his hand at being a warlock, sex-shop owner, and tattoo artist afterwards. He was replaced by ex-Gun Club guitarist "Kid Congo" Powers for *Psychedelic Jungle*. After the 1983 live EP *Smell of Female*, the Cramps sued I.R.S. for lack of support; the case was settled out of court and resulted in the Cramps' being released from the label. Nothing more was heard from the band in the way of new material for years; their only new album prior to 1990, 1986's *A Date with Elvis*, was not released in the US until four years later. In the meantime, they toured extensively with a succession of female guitarists and new bassist Candy Del Mar, who was on board for their 1990 Poison Ivy-produced album *Stay Sick!* Lux Interior and Poison Ivy continue to tour with a Cramps lineup featuring bassist Slim Chance and drummer Jim Sclavunos. —*Steve Huey*

Songs the Lord Taught Us / May 1980 / IRS ✦✦✦✦
An inspired collection that ranks as the Cramps' strongest studio album, *Songs the Lord Taught Us* mixes energetic covers of rockabilly classics ("Tear It Up," "Strychnine") with demented originals displaying an obsession with grade-B horror movies and American trash culture ("TV Set," "Zombie Dance," "I Was a Teenage Werewolf"). The minimalist approach enhances the weird, almost psychedelic atmosphere, with no bass and purely skeletal drumming, plus Lux Interior's somewhat amateurish vocals; wild, raw, and entertaining, *Songs the Lord Taught Us* is essential Cramps psychobilly. —*Steve Huey*

Psychedelic Jungle / May 1981 / A&M ✦✦✦✦
Psychedelic Jungle doesn't barrel along at the breakneck pace of *Songs the Lord Taught Us*, but even at the slower tempos, songs like "The Crusher" and "Voodoo Idol" are still entertainingly trashy slices of junk-culture weirdness. It may be just a cut below their debut, but it's still one of the group's best efforts. *Psychedelic Jungle* was later reissued on CD with the addition of the group's early *Gravest Hits* EP. —*Steve Huey*

Smell of Female / 1983 / Enigma ✦✦✦
This six-song live EP was recorded at New York City's Peppermint Lounge and captures the Cramps' in-concert mania with pretty good sound quality. While it doesn't quite live up to the group's previous standards of inspired insanity, there are some great moments, such as "Thee Most Exalted Potentate of Love," while "I Ain't Nothin' But a Gorehound" is perhaps the ultimate Cramps anthem. The CD reissue contains three non-LP bonus tracks. —*Steve Huey*

● **Bad Music for Bad People** / 1984 / IRS ✦✦✦✦
Legal hassles with their label prompted the Cramps to leave IRS, which issued this 11-track overview of the band's tenure there following their departure. The compilation features both LP and non-LP single sides, including the gems "New Kind of Kick" and "Drug Train," as well as a few prime album tracks and obscurities like the outlandishly offensive "She Said." It serves as a good introduction to the band, but those interested in pursuing this period further will find more great material on the albums. —*Steve Huey*

Creature from the Black Leather Lagoon / 1984 / Enigma ✦✦✦
The only Cramps release of new material between 1983 and 1986, this five-song EP contains the demented sleaze of the title track and tunes like "Jackyard Backoff" and "Beat Out My Love," plus covers of "Jailhouse Rock" and a live version of Carl Perkins' "Her Love Rubbed Off." —*Steve Huey*

Date with Elvis / 1986 / Big Beat ✦✦✦
After *Psychedelic Jungle*, the Cramps experienced personnel and record label difficulties; they would not release another studio album until this one, five years later. Gone here are the tinny sound quality and horror-flick-based lyrics of prior releases, replaced by clearer sonics and an often hilarious obsession with sex (examples of the latter can be found on "What's Inside a Girl?," "The Hot Pearl Snatch," "Cornfed Dames," "(Hot Pool of) Womanneed," "How Far Can Too Far Go?," and the uproarious single "Can Your Pussy Do the Dog?"). There are numerous sly references in the verses to high and low culture icons, including "Shake it one time for me" (a line from Jerry Lee Lewis' "Whole Lotta Shakin' Goin' On"), "I'll be dancing through the flames/Like a devil in disguise" (a nod to the Elvis Presley hit), and "Now there's more things in Tennessee/Than is dreamed of in your philosophy" (a paraphrase of a line from Shakespeare's *Hamlet*). Most of the songs here are in various rockabilly-derived styles featuring either garage-band fuzz or Duane Eddy twanging guitar from Poison Ivy. Vocalist Lux Interior is in excellent form here, exhibiting a fair bit of variety within his usual 1950s-derived approach. "Kizmiaz" is unique in the band's oeuvre, being a smarmy parody of 1960s hippie feel-good music; Ivy joins Interior on vocals here. Intonation is off in a few numbers (notably on "Kizmiaz," "The Hot Pearl Snatch," and "Can Your Pussy Do the Dog?"), but this is not enough to detract from the overall excellence here. This rollicking and energetic platter in particular is the equal of any in their canon and an essential listen. —*David Cleary*

Rockin' 'n Reelin' in Auckland New Zealand / 1987 / Vengeance ✦✦✦
From 1986 to 1990, the Cramps eschewed studio work in favor of extensive touring; this album documents a live show from August 1986. The sound quality is crude at best, but the Cramps' music and attitude are just as crude, so the already wild performances are actually somewhat enhanced. The repertoire relies heavily on *A Date With Elvis* and also features covers of "Heartbreak Hotel" and "Do the Clam." —*Steve Huey*

Stay Sick! / Jan. 1990 / Capitol/Enigma ✦✦
The Cramps waited four years after their top-notch *A Date with Elvis* before releasing their next studio album. The result is, unfortunately, one of the weakest platters in their canon. Most all the songs here follow the same rockabilly-based formula of previous releases; unfortunately, much of the group's usual fire is missing. Too many of the selections (such as "Daisys Up Your Butterfly," "Everything Goes," "All Women Are

Bad," and a cover of "Muleskinner Blues") are cast in a moderate jogging tempo, and instrumental playing shows minimal song-to-song contrast, lacking the manic craziness of their best work. Lux Interior's vocals are comparatively reserved (though there are some exceptions, such as the snarling cover of "Shortnin' Bread") and are often somewhat submerged in the sound mix. Lyrics, too, are a bit tame by Cramps standards, the major exception being "Mama Oo Pow Pow," which has gleefully tacky verses about spanking and discipline that rival their most tasteless. "God Damned Rock 'n' Roll" is for all practical purposes a middling parody of Bob Seger's "Old Time Rock and Roll." The biggest surprise is the atypically soaring vocal on the better-than-average song "Journey to the Center of a Girl." This album is not terrible by any means, but it's not an essential listen, either; in a nutshell, the biggest problem with *Stay Sick* is that it's not sick enough. —*David Cleary*

Look Mom No Head! / Nov. 1991 / Restless ✦✦✦
The Cramps' humor has always relied on trashy tastelessness, but even at its most offensive, it is usually delivered with a wink, preventing it from degenerating into mindless vulgarity. Unfortunately, *Look Mom No Head* doesn't do a good job of retaining this balance, as the flat performances and lack of intensity and energy fail to supply the irony necessary for the Cramps' music to work well. Sleaze without fun is simply embarrassing. —*Steve Huey*

Collection / Oct. 19, 1993 / Castle ✦✦✦

FlameJob / Oct. 11, 1994 / Warner Brothers ✦✦✦
Something of a return to form, *FlameJob* features the band's most committed, energetic performances in quite some time, with wild, crazed vocals from Lux Interior and sizzling guitar work from Poison Ivy enlivening some of the band's most entertainingly stupid and crude offerings in recent memory, including "Let's Get Fucked Up" and "Inside Out and Upside Down (With You)." The failed stylistic experiments of some recent work are gone, replaced by simple, straightahead vintage Cramps psychobilly. Also featured is a cover of "Route 66." —*Steve Huey*

The Cranberries

f. 1990, Limerick, Ireland
Alternative Pop-Rock, Adult Alternative Pop-Rock
Combining the melodic jangle of post-Smiths indie-guitar-pop with the lilting, trance-inducing sonic textures of late '80s dream-pop and adding a slight Celtic tint, the Cranberries became one of the more successful groups to emerge from the pre-Britpop UK indie scene of the early '90s. Led by vocalist Dolores O'Riordan, whose keening, powerful voice is the most distinctive element of the group's sound, the band initially made little impact in the United Kingdom. It wasn't until the lush ballad "Linger" became an American hit in 1993 that the band also achieved mass success in the UK. After the success of "Linger," the Cranberries quickly became international stars, as both their 1993 debut album, *Everybody Else Is Doing It, So Why Can't We* and its 1994 follow-up, *No Need to Argue*, sold millions of copies and produced a string of hit singles. By the time of their third album, 1996's *To the Faithful Departed*, the group had added distorted guitars to its sonic palette and attempted to make more socially significant music, which resulted in a downturn in the band's commercial fortunes.

Originally, the Cranberries were a band called the Cranberry Saw Us. Brothers Noel and Mike Hogan (guitar and bass, respectively) formed the band in Limerick, Ireland, with drummer Fergal Lawler in 1990. After the departure of the group's original singer Niall, the trio placed an advertisement for a female singer. Dolores O'Riordan responded and auditioned by writing lyrics and melodies to some of the band's existing demos. When she returned with a rough version of "Linger," the group hired her on the spot. Shortly after she joined, the band recorded a demo tape that they sold in record stores throughout Ireland. After the original run of 300 copies sold out, the group truncated their name to the Cranberries and sent another demo tape, which featured early version of both "Linger" and "Dreams," to record companies throughout the UK. The tape was made at Xeric studios, which was run by Pearse Gilmore, who would later become their manager. At the time the tape was made, all of the members were still in their late teens.

The demo tape earned the attention of both the UK press and record industry, and there soon was a bidding war between major British record labels. Eventually, the group signed with Island Records. The Cranberries headed into the studio with Gilmore as their producer to record their first single, "Uncertain." The title proved to be prophetic, as the band did indeed sound ill at ease on the single, leading to poor reviews in the press, in addition to tensions between the group and Gilmore. Before they were scheduled to record their debut in 1992, the Cranberries discovered that Gilmore had signed a secret deal with Island to improve his studios. The tensions within the band became so great that they nearly broke up. Instead, the band severed all relations with Gilmore, hired Geoff Travis of Rough Trade as their new manager, and hired Stephen Street, who had previously worked with the Smiths, as their new producer.

The Cranberries' debut album, *Everybody Else Is Doing It, So Why Can't We?*, was released in the spring of 1993, followed by a single of "Dreams." Neither the album or the single gained much attention, nor did a second single, "Linger." In the summer and fall of 1993, the band toured the United States, opening for The The and Suede, respectively; frequently the Cranberries were given a friendlier reception than either of the headliners. The strong live shows led to MTV's putting "Linger" into heavy rotation. By the end of the year, the single was on its way to becoming a crossover hit. Eventually, the single reached No. 8 on the US charts, while the album went double platinum. *Everybody Else* and "Linger" began to take off in Britain in early 1994; the album eventually peaked at No. 1 during the summer.

O'Riordan married the band's tour manager, Don Burton, in a much-publicized ceremony in July 1994. The marriage, as well as the group's videos, emphasized the singer as the focal point of the band. O'Riordan's position in the group continued to rise with the autumn release of the group's second album, *No Need to Argue*. Boasting a slightly harder, more streamlined sound, yet still produced by Stephen Street, the record debuted at No. 6 on the US charts and eventually outsold its predecessor; within a year it went triple platinum, spawning the No. 1 modern rock hit "Zombie" and the No. 11 "Ode to My Family."

During the tour for *No Need to Argue*, rumors began to circulate that O'Riordan was going to leave the band to pursue a solo career, which the band vehemently denied. Nevertheless, the rumors persisted until the band began recording their third album with producer Bruce Fairburn, who had previously worked with Aerosmith. The resulting album, *To the Faithful Departed*, was a tougher, more rock-oriented album. Upon its spring 1996 release, the album entered the charts at No. 6, but its first single, "Salvation," failed to become a hit on par with "Zombie," "Linger" or "Ode to My Family." Consequently, the album slipped down the charts relatively quickly and only went platinum, which was slightly disappointing in light of its two predecessors' multi-platinum status. During the fall of 1996, the group cancelled their Australian and European tour, sparking another round of rumors about whether O'Riordan was about to lauch a solo career. —*Stephen Thomas Erlewine*

● **Everybody Else Is Doing It, So Why Can't We** / Apr. 20, 1993 / Island ✦✦✦✦

Dolores O'Riordan possesses one of those gorgeous, elastic voices that you can fall in love with on first listen and not tire of on the 20th. She yelps exotically to a vibrato guitar backing on "Dreams;" emotes seductively on "Pretty;" thickly breathes the lyrics to "Not Sorry;" and soars through the urgent pop roller-coaster of "How." The group paints a seamless, unobtrusive, almost orchestral backdrop that shatters into sonic shards at all the right moments of emphasis. —*Roch Parisien*

No Need to Argue / 1994 / Island ✦✦✦✦

With their second album, *No Need to Argue*, the Cranberries have managed to avoid a sophomore slump by turning in a set of songs that builds on their debut's finest moments. With the exception of the distorted march of "Zombie," there aren't that many great departures from the band's atmospheric, melodic guitar-pop. Most of the credit goes to the gutsy, beautiful singing of Dolores O'Riordan, who manages to squeeze emotion out of even the most mundane lyrics ("Ode to My Family"). —*Stephen Thomas Erlewine*

To the Faithful Departed / Apr. 30, 1996 / Island ✦✦

The Cranberries' second album, *No Need to Argue*, elevated them to the ranks of multimillion selling stars. Evidently that gave them the confidence to jettison producer Stephen Street and work with Aerosmith/Van Halen producer Bruce Fairbairn for their third album, *To the Faithful Departed*. Ironically, this doesn't quite give the band the muscular kick that propelled songs like "Zombie" on *No Need to Argue*. Although Fairbairn has helped the Cranberries abandon their more atmospheric, trance qualities, the band has buried the guitars throughout *To the Faithful Departed*, probably in an attempt to accentuate Dolores O'Riordan's lyrics. That wasn't a particularly wise move. O'Riordan has taken the band's success as a vindication of her naive philosophies, which propel nearly every song on *To the Faithful Departed*. O'Riordan's preaching would be forgivable if the band had come up with catchy hooks, but the album lacks the crackling melodies that formed the core of their first two albums. The Cranberries still shine on their ballads, but the new songs aren't quite as affecting as their older work. —*Stephen Thomas Erlewine*

Cranes

f. 1988, Portsmouth, England
Alternative Pop-Rock, Dream-Pop
Cranes was one of the major trance-pop/shoegazing groups of the early '90s, combining ethereal vocals and melodies with loud, droning guitars. Cranes was formed by brother and sister Jim (drums) and Alison Shaw (vocals) in 1988 in Portsmouth, England; guitarist Mark Francombe and

bassist Matt Cope joined the band two years later. The group independently released their first album, *Fuse*, on cassette in 1990; a small local label released *Self Non Self* the same year to good reviews. That led to a record contract with Dedicated, an English label. Later that year Cranes released their first EP for the label, *Inescapable*, which earned them a lot of attention, including a *Melody Maker* cover story; a second EP, *Espero*, also earned positive reviews, including a *Melody Maker* Single of the Week. The next year, the band released their first album, *Wings of Joy*, which received favorable reviews on both sides of the Atlantic, as well as earning a sizable cult following, including the Cure's Robert Smith. Smith picked Cranes to open for the Cure on their 1992 world tour. *Forever*, the group's second album, was released in 1993. It expanded their cult slightly, but 1994's *Loved* found the band in a holding pattern commercially. After releasing the limited edition *Tragedy of Orestes and Electra* in late 1996, the Cranes returned with *Population 4*, which was greeted with mixed reviews. —*Stephen Thomas Erlewine*

Wings of Joy / Nov. 1991 / Dedicated ✦✦✦

● **Forever** / May 1993 / Dedicated ✦✦✦✦

Loved / Oct. 11, 1994 / Arista ✦✦✦

Tragedy of Orestes and Electra / Oct. 29, 1996 / Dedicated ✦✦✦
Tragedy of Orestes and Electra is a limited-edition adaptation of Sartre's *Les Mouches*. The Cranes have written a chamber music backdrop for Alison Shaw's narration, which floats over cellos and harpsichords. It's more of an interesting side project than an actual album, and its ambitions often outstrip its achievements, but it is fascinating for hardcore Cranes fans. [Only 4000 copies of *Tragedy of Orestes and Electra* were pressed.] —*Stephen Thomas Erlewine*

Population 4 / Feb. 11, 1997 / Dedicated ✦✦
Population 4 marks a step backward for the Cranes, as the band gets more involved in soundscapes and less interested in songs. While their shimmering waves of distorted guitars and airy vocals still sound good, the group's sound is no longer fresh, and they have chosen not to develop it any further; the Cranes sound nearly identical to their second album. Furthermore, their songwriting has stalled. Not only do they have no new styles or structures, but they have failed to come up with the trancy hooks that propelled their first three albums, making *Population 4* an outright failure. —*Stephen Thomas Erlewine*

Cream

f. 1966, England, db. 1968
Electric British Blues, Blues-Rock, Hard Rock, Psychedelic
Although Cream was only together for a little more than two years, its influence was immense, both during the late-'60s peak and in the years after the breakup. Cream was the first top group to truly exploit the power-trio format, in the process laying the foundation for much blues-rock and hard rock of the 1960s and 1970s. It was with Cream, too, that guitarist Eric Clapton truly became an international superstar. Critical revisionists have tagged the band as overrated, citing the musicians' emphasis upon flash, virtuosity, and showmanship at the expense of taste and focus. This was sometimes true of their live shows in particular, but in reality the best of their studio recordings were excellent fusions of blues, pop, and psychedelia, with concise original material outnumbering the bloated blues jams and overlong solos.

Cream could be viewed as the first rock supergroup to become superstars, although none of the three members was that well known when the band formed in mid-1966. Eric Clapton had the biggest reputation, having established himself as a guitar hero first with the Yardbirds, and then in a more blues-intensive environment with John Mayall's Bluesbreakers. (In the States, however, he was all but unknown, having left the Yardbirds before "For Your Love" made the American Top Ten.) Bassist/singer Jack Bruce and drummer Ginger Baker had both been in the Graham Bond Organisation, an underrated British R&B combo that drew extensively upon the jazz backgrounds of the musicians. Bruce had also been, very briefly, a member of the Bluesbreakers with Clapton, and also briefly a member of Manfred Mann when he became especially eager to pay the rent.

All three musicians yearned to break free of the confines of the standard rock/R&B/blues group, in a unit that would allow them greater instrumental and improvisational freedom, somewhat in the mold of a jazz outfit. Eric Clapton's stunning guitar solos would get much of the adulation, but Bruce was at least as responsible for shaping the group's sound, singing most of the material in his rich voice. He also wrote their best original compositions, sometimes in collaboration with outside lyricist Pete Brown.

At first Cream's focus was electrified and amped-up traditional blues, which dominated their first album, *Fresh Cream*; it made the British Top Ten in early 1967. Originals like "N.S.U." and "I Feel Free" gave notice that the band was capable of moving beyond the blues, and they truly found their voice on *Disraeli Gears* in late 1967; it consisted mostly of group-penned songs. Here they fashioned invigorating, sometimes beguiling, hard-driving psychedelic pop, which included plenty of memorable melodies and effective harmonies along with the expected crunching riffs. "Strange Brew," "Dance the Night Away," "Tales of Brave Ulysses," and "S.W.L.A.B.R." are among their best tracks, and the album broke the band bigtime in the States, reaching the Top Five. It also generated their first big US hit single, "Sunshine of Your Love," which was based on one of the most popular hard-rock riffs of the '60s.

With the double album *Wheels of Fire*, Cream topped the American charts in 1968, establishing themselves alongside the Beatles and Hendrix as one of the biggest rock acts in the world. The record itself was a more erratic affair than *Disraeli Gears*, perhaps dogged by the decision to present separate discs of studio and live material; the concert tracks in particular did much to establish their reputation, for good or ill, for stretching songs way past the ten-minute mark on stage. The majestically doomy "White Room" gave Cream another huge American single, and the group was firmly established as one of the biggest live draws of any kind. Their decision to disband in late 1968—at a time when they were seemingly on top of the world—came as a shock to most of the rock audience.

Cream's short lifespan, however, was, in hindsight, unsurprising given the considerable talents, ambitions, and egos of its members. Clapton in particular was tired of blowing away listeners with sheer power, and wanted to explore more subtle directions. After a farewell tour of the States, the band broke up in November 1968. In 1969, however, they were in a sense bigger than ever; a posthumous album featuring both studio and live material, *Goodbye*, made No. 2, highlighted by the haunting Eric Clapton-George Harrison composition "Badge," which remains one of Cream's most beloved tracks.

Clapton and Baker would quickly resurface in 1969 as half of another short-lived supergroup, Blind Faith, and Clapton, of course, went on to one of the longest and most successful careers of anyone in the rock business. Bruce and Baker never attained nearly as high a profile after leaving Cream, but both have kept busy in the ensuing decades with various interesting projects in rock, jazz, and experimental music. *—Richie Unterberger*

Fresh Cream / Dec. 1966 / Polydor ✦✦✦
Cream's debut album was largely rooted in the blues, and included here are highly charged versions of such standards as Willie Dixon's "Spoonful," Muddy Waters' "Rollin' and Tumblin'," and bassist Jack Bruce's "N.S.U."—which took on a whole new life on stage. On this record they sound somewhat flat and uninspired. *—Rob Bowman*

Disraeli Gears / Nov. 1967 / Polydor ✦✦✦✦
Cream's sophomore effort was a substantial step forward. Interestingly, part of the reason seems to be that they stopped covering American blues musicians and started writing their own psychedelic blues-based hybrids. "Sunshine of Your Love" was the big AM radio hit and "Tales of Brave Ulysses," "Strange Brew," and "S.W.L.A.B.R." received substantial FM play. *—Rob Bowman*

Wheels of Fire / Jun. 1968 / Polydor ✦✦✦✦
Wheels of Fire was a two-album set, one disc recorded in the studio, the second on stage in San Francisco. Side Three contains the definitive live version of what became Clapton's signature piece, Robert Johnson's "Crossroads," plus a version of "Spoonful" that clocks in just short of 17 minutes. On such pieces, Cream approached blues-based rock with a jazz aesthetic, using the song as a framework to begin and end a performance. The strength of the performance is in the improvisation. When it worked, as it does on "Spoonful," they were brilliant. When it didn't, as on "Traintime" and "Toad," the band became excess incarnate. The studio disc contained their second Top Ten single, Jack Bruce's "White Room," as well as a stunning cover of Albert King's "Born Under a Bad Sign." Other tracks, particularly those written by Ginger Baker, do not hold up. *—Rob Bowman*

Goodbye / Jan. 1969 / Polydor ✦✦✦
As the title implies, this is Cream's farewell. By the time it was issued, the band had broken up. Three studio recordings that were left were coupled with extended live versions of "I'm So Glad," "Politician," and "I'm Sitting on Top of the World." The live tracks burn. Clapton, Bruce, and Baker each take credit for one of the studio tracks. Clapton's cut, "Badge," was co-written by George Harrison and remains what was surely the prettiest melody to ever grace a Cream recording. *—Rob Bowman*

Live Cream, Vol. 1 / Apr. 1970 / Polydor ✦✦✦
Cream was a band born to the stage. This is their most consistently brilliant album. Four of the five cuts appeared on *Fresh Cream*. The fifth, "Lawdy Mama," is a traditional blues piece that makes its first appearance here. All but "Lawdy Mama" are given extended jazz-based treatment. The dialog among the three musicians as the jams develop is fascinating. Foreground and background seem to dissolve as all three musicians take charge, using the full range of their instruments. Perfor-

mances like this single-handedly raised the stakes of musicianship in rock. *—Rob Bowman*

Live Cream, Vol. 2 / Mar. 1972 / Polydor ✦✦✦
More live Cream concentrating on material from their *Disraeli Gears* and *Wheels of Fire* albums plus an extended workout on Freddie King's "Hideaway." *—Rob Bowman*

Klook's Kleet '66 / 1995 / (no label) ✦✦✦✦
A significant addition to the pool of unreleased Cream material, this has eight alternate versions/outtakes from their earliest sessions in the summer of '66, as well a different version of "Lawdy Mama" from '67, a Falstaff Beer commercial, and seven songs recorded live at the Klook's Kleet club in 1966. It's the studio outtakes that you'd want this for; the fidelity is phenomenal, at the same level of an official release. Contains alternate versions of many of the songs from their first album, with differences ranging from minor to major. "Sweet Wine," with a long extended feedback solo from Clapton, is particularly noteworthy, and "You Make Me Feel," an odd and frankly none-too-impressive bit of English pop, is an original that would never be released by the group. The liner notes say that the Kloots Kleet acetates were recorded for consideration as a live album, but it's hard to see how that would have happened, as the fidelity is tinny and the vocals muffled. More in line with the standards of typical live bootlegs of the era, it does offer serious fans the chance to hear (approximately) how they sounded onstage at their inception, with a few staples of their early repertoire ("N.S.U.," "Crossroads") and a couple of less-done-to-death numbers ("Meet Me in the Bottom," "Steppin' Out"). *—Richie Unterberger*

★ **The Very Best of Cream** / May 9, 1995 / Chronicles ✦✦✦✦✦
There have been many compilations drawn from the four albums Cream originally released between 1966 and 1969. But the one most commonly available since the early 1980s was the ten-track *Strange Brew: The Very Best of Cream* (1983) (Polydor 811 639), a bare-bones collection focusing on the group's hit singles. Note, then, that this album, despite the similar title, is a newly compiled 1995 CD/cassette containing all of the recordings on *Strange Brew*, plus ten more. It is thus the most comprehensive Cream anthology on the market, including all the group's essential tracks on a single disc with superior sound in a package containing good annotations. *— William Ruhlmann*

Steppin' Out [bootleg] / Invasion Unlimited ✦✦✦
The best unreleased Cream to circulate widely, this collects 18 performances for the BBC between 1966 and 1968. These fine straightahead renditions, with mostly very good sound, include the best tracks from their early albums, with the notable absence of their two biggest hits, "White Room" and "Sunshine of Your Love." The two versions of the instrumental title track, one of Clapton's prime showcases in his Bluesbreakers days, are special highlights. These BBC sessions are available under a number of different guises; this particular package is the most thorough. *—Richie Unterberger*

The Creation

f. 1966, Middlesex, England, **db.** 1968
Rock 'n' Roll, British Invasion, Psychedelic, Mod
No other band came closer to emulating the feedback-ridden autodestruction of the early Who than the Creation, who had a couple of minor British hit singles in 1966 with "Making Time" and "Painter Man." The sonic resemblance is hardly surprising; the Creation was produced by Shel Talmy, who also produced the Who's earliest records, and lead guitarist Eddie Phillips was even asked by Pete Townshend to join the Who as second guitarist. Phillips' feedback freakouts were grounded by solid mod power chords and British Invasion harmonies. The Creation produced several interesting singles between 1966 and 1968, and although they achieved brief stardom in Germany, they never made it big in the UK. Ronnie Wood was briefly a member before the group disbanded in 1968. *—Richie Unterberger*

● **How Does It Feel to Feel** / 1982 / Edsel ✦✦✦✦
Unquestionably the best of the several Creation repackages floating around. Includes virtually all of their 1966-68 singles and a few other stray tracks of interest from the same period. *—Richie Unterberger*

Creedence Clearwater Revival

f. 1967, El Cerrito, CA, **db.** Oct. 1972
Rock 'n' Roll
At a time when rock was evolving further and further away from the forces that had made the music possible in the first place, Creedence Clearwater Revival brought things back to their roots with their concise synthesis of rockabilly, swamp pop, R&B, and country. Though CCR was very a much a group in their tight, punchy arrangements, their vision was singer, songwriter, guitarist, and leader John Fogerty's. Fogerty's classic compositions for Creedence evoked enduring images of Americana and reflected burning social issues of the day. The band's genius

was their ability to accomplish this with the economic, primal power of a classic rockabilly ensemble.

The key elements of Creedence had been woodshedding in bar bands for about a decade before their breakthrough to national success in the late '60s. John's older brother Tom formed the Blue Velvets in the late '50s in El Cerrito, CA, a tiny suburb across the bay from San Francisco. By the mid-'60s, with a few hopelessly obscure recordings under their belt, they'd signed to Fantasy, releasing several singles as the Golliwogs that went nowhere. In fact, there's little promise to be found on those early efforts, primarily because Tom, not John, was doing most of the singing. The group found themselves only when John took the reins, singing and writing virtually all of their material.

On their first album as Creedence Clearwater Revival in 1968, the group played it both ways, offering extended, quasi-psychedelic work-outs of the '50s classics "I Put a Spell on You" and "Suzy Q." The latter became their first big hit, but the band didn't really bloom until "Proud Mary," a No. 2 single in early 1969 that demonstrated John's talent at tapping into Southern roots music and imagery. It was the start of a torrent of classic hits from the gritty, Little Richard-inspired singer over the next two years, including "Bad Moon Rising," "Green River," "Down on the Corner," "Travelin' Band," "Who'll Stop the Rain," "Up Around the Bend," and "Lookin' out My Back Door."

Creedence also made good albums, but their true forte was as a singles band. Their LPs contained some filler, both in the forms of average original material and straightforward covers of rock 'n' roll chestnuts. When the Beatles broke up in early 1970, CCR was the only other act that provided any competition in the fine art of crafting bold, super-catchy artistic statements that soared to the upper reaches of the charts every three or four months. Although they hailed from the San Francisco area, they rarely succumbed to the psychedelic indulgences of the era. John Fogerty also proved adept at voicing the concerns of the working class in songs like "Fortunate Son," as well as partying with as much funk as any white rock band would muster on "Travelin' Band" and "Down on the Corner."

With John Fogerty holding such a strong upper hand, Creedence couldn't be said to have been a democratic unit, and Fogerty's dominance was to sow the seeds of the group's quick dissolution. Tom Fogerty left in 1971 (recording a few unremarkable solo albums of his own), reducing the band to a trio. John allowed drummer Doug Clifford and bassist Stu Cook equal shares of songwriting and vocal time on the group's final album, *Mardi Gras* (1972), which proved conclusively that Fogerty's songs and singing were necessary to raise CCR above journeyman status.

It was John Fogerty, of course, who produced the only notable work after the quartet broke up. Even his solo outings, though, were erratic and, for nearly ten years, nonexistent as he became embroiled in a web of business disputes with Fantasy Records. His 1984 album *Centerfield* proved he could still rock in the vintage Creedence mode when the spirit moved him, but Tom Fogerty's death in 1990 ended any hope of a CCR reunion. — *Richie Unterberger*

Creedence Clearwater Revival / 1968 / Fantasy ✦✦✦
The band's unique swampy crunch was already well developed on this fine debut. It opens with a riveting version of Screamin' Jay Hawkins' hit "I Put a Spell on You." A gritty psychedelic version of Dale Hawkins's creation "Suzy Q" was Creedence's first hit. — *Rick Clark*

Bayou Country / 1969 / Fantasy ✦✦✦
John Fogerty's songwriting voice gains new focus, particularly in "Proud Mary," the band's most popular song, and "Penthouse Pauper." "Bootleg" features a powerfully spare groove, and "Born on the Bayou," with its rock-solid pulse and economical lead-guitar work, is one of the band's better attempts at stretching out. Nevertheless, the long jams found here cause the album to lose some steam. — *Rick Clark*

☆ **Willy & the Poor Boys** / 1969 / Fantasy ✦✦✦✦✦
There's not a weak cut here, just more hits like "Down on the Corner" and the relentless wrong-side-of-the-tracks railing of "Fortunate Son." By the time of *Willy*, this California band had captured the spirit of the South more believably than most bands from that region. Versions of "The Midnight Special" and "Cotton Fields," and instrumentals like the down-home "Poorboy Shuffle" and "Side o' the Road," with its Booker T. groove, helped underscore that perception. — *Rick Clark*

☆ **Green River** / 1969 / Fantasy ✦✦✦✦✦
Fogerty tightens things up with this great collection of songs. It contains the truly great hits "Green River," "Lodi," and "Bad Moon Rising." "Wrote a Song for Everyone," "Cross-tie Walker," and "Tombstone Shadow" are classic hits. There's a super version of "The Night Time Is the Right Time." — *Rick Clark*

Cosmo's Factory / 1970 / Fantasy ✦✦✦✦
"Ramble Tamble" and a masterful version of "I Heard It Through the Grapevine" may run a little too long, but the remainder of the album is letter-perfect. Pointing out highlights here is useless. Most of these tracks were hits as well. — *Rick Clark*

Pendulum / 1970 / Fantasy ✦✦✦
Creedence loses some steam here by wasting too much time on lengthy groove numbers like "Pagan Baby," "Born to Move," and "Rude Awakening," a horrible attempt at creating something serious-sounding, and an irritating waste of time. In spite of those miscalculations, most bands could only hope for as many good songs as "Have You Ever Seen the Rain?," "Hey Tonight," "It's Just a Thought," "Molina," and "(Wish I Could) Hide Away." — *Rick Clark*

Creedence Gold / 1972 / Fantasy ✦✦✦✦
Creedence Gold is a good collection of Creedence Clearwater Revival's hit singles that was supplanted by the thorough *Chronicle*. — *Stephen Thomas Erlewine*

Mardi Gras / 1972 / Fantasy ✦✦✦
Maybe Fogerty was running out of steam, but in the name of democratization, each of the other band members got to toss in their creative licks on this album. After so many great albums, this one sounds half-hearted. Only "Sweet Hitch-Hiker," "Someday Never Comes," and a cover of the Ricky Nelson tune "Hello Mary Lou" recall the band's earlier magic. — *Rick Clark*

★ **Chronicle, Vol. 1** / 1976 / Fantasy ✦✦✦✦✦
Chronicle, Vol. 1 contains every one of Creedence Clearwater Revival's original 19 hit singles—including "Proud Mary," "Bad Moon Rising," "Green River," "Down on the Corner," "Travelin' Band," "Up Around the Band," and "Have You Ever Seen the Rain"—plus "I Heard It Through the Grapevine," which became a hit at the same time this double-record compilation was released. It's a lean, concise collection that tells you everything you need to know about Creedence. Several of the band's individual albums are essential, but *Chronicle* is not only an excellent introduction to the group, it offers proof that group was one of the definitive singles bands of the late '60s. Rarely has a greatest hits collection been so well-assembled. (The compact disc edition is hampered by the inclusion of the full-length, 11-minute album version of "I Heard It Through the Grapevine"; its presence slows down the momentum of the collection considerably). — *Stephen Thomas Erlewine*

The Royal Albert Hall Concert / 1980 / Fantasy ✦✦✦
This solid no-frills live concert covers many of the band's hits, plus time for some meat-and-potatoes groove-jammin' with ten minutes of "Keep On Chooglin'." — *Rick Clark*

☆ **Chronicle, Vol. 2** / 1986 / Fantasy ✦✦✦✦✦
Chronicle, Vol. 2 effectively compiles all of the highlights from Creedence Clearwater Revival's career that weren't on the first volume. All of the singles were included on *Chronicle*, so *Chronicle, Vol. 2* is comprised solely of album tracks. That doesn't mean these are lesser items. On the contrary, the majority of these songs—"Born on the Bayou," "Tombstone Shadow," "Wrote a Song for Everyone," "It Came out of the Sky," "Midnight Special"—rank among their best performances. Of course, a couple of great tracks remain on CCR's individual albums, notably "Bootleg," but *Chronicle, Vol. 2* is an ideal choice for listeners who want a little more than the hits but are unwilling to delve into the proper albums. — *Stephen Thomas Erlewine*

Marshall Crenshaw

b. Nov. 11, 1953, Detroit, MI
Guitar, Vocals / Rock 'n' Roll, New Wave, Power Pop, Pop-Rock
Singer-songwriter Marshall Crenshaw has built up an impressive body of work, showing a fine craft for everything he approaches, while stubbornly following his own creative muse to reach that end. To say that Crenshaw has had an interesting career so far would be putting it mildly. He's been in the movies and he's been in the road show version of *Beatlemania*. His songs have been plastered all over the soundtracks to several hit movies and covered by artists as diverse as Robert Gordon, Bette Midler, Kelly Willis, Marti Jones, and the Gin Blossoms. He got a group of like-minded show business acquaintances together and put out a book, *Hollywood Rock & Roll*, on all the great and lousy rock 'n' roll movies in existence. He's put together comps of his own for record companies (most notably *Hillbilly Music, Thank God!* for the short-lived Bug Music label) and has contributed chapters to books on vintage guitar collecting. Crenshaw is a true rock 'n' roll renaissance man while remaining the everyman.

Born in Detroit and raised in the surrounding area, Crenshaw played in a number of different bands in high school, eventually landing in his first professional combo, ASTIGAFA (an acronym for "A Splendid Time Is Guaranteed for All," cribbed from the back of *Sgt. Pepper*). Although nothing releasable came of this venture, it surely cemented the basic ingredients of his style that would surface full bloom at the dawn of his solo career. According to Crenshaw, "That band really didn't have a high profile in Detroit, but I was using that time, working alone, woodshedding, gathering information. Around '73, I just stopped listening to the radio and just became immersed listening to old 45s from the '50s and early '60s. It seemed to me that there was more immediacy in those records than the stuff that was on the radio at that time." But just as his ears learned to love echoey mono '50s records, his songwriting influences went in an opposite direction. "One batch of stuff that I really feel that I was strongly influenced by was a lot of the R&B-pop kind of stuff that was around in the early '70s. I just love that romantic kind of R&B kind of sound, all those chord changes in those tunes."

But Detroit was not a musical hotbed in the late '70s, so Crenshaw responded to an ad in *Rolling Stone* and auditioned for the Broadway musical *Beatlemania*. Hired as a John Lennon understudy, Crenshaw moved to New York City and quickly found himself in a heady, competitive situation. After serving a six-month "Beatle boot camp" training, he appeared with the show for six months in Hollywood and San Francisco, then finished up his last six months with the production on the road. Though he found the show creatively stifling, it made him sit down and figure out what kind of music he wanted to do and eventually—after buying a four-track recorder—he started making demos whenever he was home.

Soon Crenshaw was armed with demos galore—dropping them off to any show business connection that might listen—and his younger brother was playing drums in his trio, which was starting to plug into New York City's burgeoning new wave club scene. About that time Crenshaw hooked up with local scenester Alan Betrock, who had recently started his own label, Shake Records. It was Crenshaw's debut single "Something's Gonna Happen" on Betrock's label that kicked up enough noise to bring major label interest. Signing with Warner Brothers in 1982, Marshall recorded five superbly crafted studio albums before leaving seven years later to sign with MCA for one album, *Life's Too Short*. During this flurry of activity, Crenshaw also flexed his acting muscles, portraying a high school bandleader in *Peggy Sue Got Married* and Buddy Holly in *La Bamba*. He also made a guest appearance on the Nickelodeon series "Pete and Pete." Emerging from a three-year hiatus, Marshall signed with the independent label Razor & Tie label, released a live album (*Live: My Truck Is My Home*) in 1994, and in 1996 released a new studio effort, *Miracle of Science*. —*Cub Koda*

● **Marshall Crenshaw** / 1982 / Warner Brothers ✦✦✦✦
His incredible debut revealed Crenshaw to be a fully formed songwriter in the Beatles and Buddy Holly super-melodic pop tradition. Like the work of those influences, the best material here seems timeless. "Someday, Someway" was a moderate hit, even though it (and others like "Cynical Girl," "Girls," "The Usual Thing," and "Mary Anne") seemed written in stone. Crenshaw does include one fine cover of "Soldier of Love," recorded originally by Arthur Alexander and later by the Beatles. Criticism: Why has Warner chosen not to include Crenshaw's fine B-sides as bonus tracks from this period on this or his other CDs? —*Rick Clark*

Field Day / 1983 / Warner Brothers ✦✦✦✦
For those expecting a repeat of his fine debut effort, Crenshaw made an unexpected left turn and sought out in-demand producer Steve Lillywhite, whose credits (Psychedelic Furs, XTC, U2, Ultravox) read like an alternative rock Who's Who. The heavily treated drum sounds and walls of guitar may have initially put off some fans, but *Field Day* demonstrated that Crenshaw was making impressive strides as a songwriter and musician. "Whenever You're on My Mind" (a great single that should've been a hit), "Our Town," "All I Know Right Now," and "Monday Morning Rock" are highlights. —*Rick Clark*

Downtown / 1985 / Warner Brothers ✦✦✦✦
With the help of producer T-Bone Burnett and a handful of session sidemen, Crenshaw delivered a strong collection of originals and covers. Highlights include a version of Ben Vaughn's "I'm Sorry (But So Is Brenda Lee)" and Crenshaw's own "The Distance Between." This is one of Crenshaw's best efforts. —*Rick Clark*

Mary Jean & 9 Others / 1987 / Warner Brothers ✦✦✦
Not quite as strong as his first three full-length albums, *Mary Jean* does possess some standout tracks in "Calling Out for Love (at Crying Time)," a version of Peter Case's "Steel Strings," and the title cut. It was produced by Don Dixon, whose credits include the Smithereens. —*Rick Clark*

Good Evening / Jun. 1989 / Warner Brothers ✦✦✦
This effort drew heavily on outside material, with songs by Richard Thompson, Dianne Warren, John Hiatt, the Isley Brothers, and Bobby Fuller. David Kershenbaum's production is typically classy but is unable to keep this from being Crenshaw's weakest release. —*Rick Clark*

Life's Too Short / May 14, 1991 / MCA ✦✦✦
Crenshaw changes labels and brings on producer Ed Stasium (Living Colour, Smithereens). The result is a more vibrant, harder-rocking sound. Highlights include "Better Back Off," "Don't Disappear Now," "Face of Fashion," and "Fantastic Planet of Love." This is his strongest release since *Downtown*. —*Rick Clark*

Live: My Truck Is My Home / Sep. 20, 1994 / Razor & Tie ✦✦✦
Fourteen tracks taken from various sources (soundboard tapes, etc.) from performances plucked from 1982, 1987, 1990, 1991, 1992, and

1994. Loads of great Crenshaw material ("You're My Favorite Waste of Time," "Cynical Girl"), explosive guitar that seldom surfaces on his studio efforts the way it does here, and plenty of deadpan humor (the picture of Bo "Billy, Don't Be a Hero" Donaldson on the disc itself says it all) make this a great live album with quirks that keep it ahead of the pack. —*Cub Koda*

Miracle of Science / Jul. 23, 1996 / Razor & Tie ✦✦✦
Crenshaw's first studio effort for the indie Razor & Tie imprint also marks a return to his earlier, stripped-down approach of his debut album. Playing most of the instruments himself (including drums), there's a far more organic feel to the tunes presented here than his last major-label efforts. In addition to solid Crenshaw pop originals like "What Do You Dream Of?," "Laughter," and "Starless Summer Sky," his takes on Dobie Gray's "The 'In' Crowd" and the countryish "Who Stole That Train" also show him as always to be a prime interpreter of other folks' great songs as well. —*Cub Koda*

The Crests

f. 1956, New York, NY
Doo Wop
One of the most successful integrated doo wop groups, the Crests waxed the classic ballad "16 Candles" in 1959. Formed in 1956, they began recording the next year for Joyce, where they inched onto the pop lists with "Sweetest One." Moving to the brand-new Coed logo, Johnny Maestro's (b. May 7, 1930) warm tenor made "16 Candles" a national smash, and pop/R&B hybrids like "The Angels Listened In" and "Step by Step" also did well. Maestro went solo in 1960, scoring the next year with "Model Girl" on Coed, while the Crests attempted to survive on their own. Maestro eventually reclaimed stardom as leader of Brooklyn Bridge, an 11-piece aggregation that hit with "Worst That Could Happen" in 1968. —*Bill Dahl*

● **The Best of the Crests** / 1990 / Rhino ✦✦✦✦
All of the Crests' hits, including the classic "16 Candles" and "Trouble in Paradise," are collected on this splendid 18-track disc. —*Stephen Thomas Erlewine*

The Crew-Cuts

f. 1952, Toronto, Ontario, **db.** 1964
Pop-Rock, Pop
On most informed lists of rock 'n' roll villains, the Crew Cuts would rank near the top. They weren't rock 'n' rollers in the first plac; their clean-cut white harmony glee-club approach was really in the style of early and mid-'50s groups such as the Four Aces, the Four Lads, and the Four Freshmen. The Canadian quartet differed from those acts, however, in their concentration on covers of songs originally recorded by R&B/doo wop vocal groups. Their cover of the Chords' "Sh-Boom" set the pattern, going to number one in 1954 and setting the stage for their other commercially successful pop treatments of R&B hits by the Penguins, Gene & Eunice, Otis Williams & the Charms, the Robins, the Spaniels, the Nutmegs, and others.

The Toronto foursome already had a Top Ten hit under their belts with their first major label single, "Crazy 'bout Ya Baby," before tackling "Sh-Boom"; what's more, their first hit had been a group original, not an R&B cover. When the Crew Cuts got hold of "Sh-Boom," they gave the song a far more standard and white pop treatment than the Chords had, complete with big-band type orchestration. Although the original Chords version still became one of the first Top Ten rock 'n' roll hits, the Crew Cuts' cover outsold it by a wide margin, finding far easier entrance into established radio formats and mainstream white audiences.

The Crew Cuts were regular visitors to the Top 20 over the next couple of years, repeating the "Sh-Boom" syndrome with songs like "Earth Angel," their second-biggest hit at No. 3 (though nobody remembers the Crew Cuts' version today, the Penguins' original having long established supremacy with audiences and on oldies stations). Their strategy of foraging for sources among Black R&B vocal singles was widely imitated throughout the industry, by Pat Boone, the McGuire Sisters, Georgia Gibbs, and numerous others. Many rock historians point out—with a great deal of justification—that this amounted to an attempt by the music establishment to buck the oncoming threatening storm of the rock era by watering it down into a more palatable and conventional form that in reality had little to do with rock at all. For a while, it worked—the white covers frequently outsold the Black R&B originals throughout 1954-56. But after Elvis, Chuck Berry, and others had staked their own claim on superstardom, it became increasingly obvious that teenagers preferred the real article, and that the entrenchment of authentic rock 'n' roll was inevitable.

Some revisionists have claimed, dubiously, that the Crew Cuts actually helped pave the way for the acceptance of rock in the mainstream by giving all those doo wop songs a far greater audience than they could have found if they were ghettoized in the R&B community. After a while, however, the Crew Cuts themselves were being widely outsold by their sources; "Young Love" (a cover, of course, although this time of the country classic by Sonny James) was their last Top 20 hit in early 1957. Their Mercury hits are far more properly classified as pop vocal outings than rock 'n' roll, owing much more to pre-rock harmony and band arrangements. By 1958 they'd left Mercury for stints with RCA and other labels; they broke up in 1964. —*Richie Unterberger*

● **The Best of the Crew Cuts: The Mercury Years** / Jul. 16, 1996 / Mercury ✦✦✦✦
Twenty-two tracks from their 1954-57 prime, with over a dozen hits, including "Sh-Boom," "Earth Angel," "Crazy 'bout Ya Baby," and "Ko Ko Mo." Now that the original R&B/doo wop versions of most of the material are available for easy comparison, you'd have to be nuts to prefer these whitewashed covers, which sound incredibly quaint and lightweight. The Crew Cuts were never a bona fide rock 'n' roll group, however. Judged solely within the context of other young white male harmony pop quartets of the time, such as the Four Freshmen and the Four Aces, they acquit themselves well with their accomplished vocal arrangements. —*Richie Unterberger*

Jim Croce

b. Jan. 10, 1943, Philadelphia, PA, **d.** Sep. 20, 1973, Natchitoches, LA
Guitar, Vocals / Singer-Songwriter, Soft Rock
A singer-songwriter whose enormous pop success in the early '70s was cut short by his death in a plane crash. A Philadelphia native who had worked the coffeehouse circuit for almost ten years when he was signed to ABC Records in 1971, Croce had a warm singing voice that served him well on his comic uptempo hits ("You Don't Mess Around with Jim," "Bad, Bad Leroy Brown") as well as his sincere ballads ("Operator"). "I Got a Name," "Time in a Bottle," and "I'll Have to Say I Love You in a Song" were posthumous Top Ten hits. —*William Ruhlmann*

You Don't Mess Around with Jim / 1972 / ABC ✦✦✦
Croce's debut ABC album was also his commercial breakthrough, topping the charts for five weeks, largely due to the comic, uptempo title tune, a story song about competing pool hustlers. Croce also reached the Top 20 with the change-of-pace ballad "Operator (That's Not the Way It Feels)." Just after his death, ABC issued the LP track "Time in a Bottle," and a newly ironic message propelled it to No. 1. William Ruhlmann

I Got a Name / 1973 / ABC ✦✦✦
In his third album in just two years, Jim Croce continued to mine the success of his previous efforts. *I Got a Name* includes the title track and "I'll Have to Say I Love You in a Song," which sailed into the Top 20 alongside nine other songs rich in the singer-songwriter tradition. —*James Chrispell*

● **Photographs & Memories: His Greatest Hits** / 1974 / Atlantic ✦✦✦✦
Photographs & Memories: His Greatest Hits is a compilation containing Croce's best songs and biggest hits, including the No. 1 hits "Bad, Bad Leroy Brown" and "Time in a Bottle." —*William Ruhlmann*

Time in a Bottle/Greatest Love Songs / 1977 / Atlantic ✦✦✦✦
Since it contains only his love ballads, fans who prefer his sweetly sentimental songs like "Operator" and "Time in a Bottle" to story-songs like "Bad, Bad Leroy Brown" and "You Don't Mess Around with Jim" will find *Time in a Bottle* the essential compilation; despite the amount of good material here, *Photographs and Memories* remains a better collection, because it presents both sides of the popular singer-songwriter. —*Stephen Thomas Erlewine*

The 50th Anniversary Collection / Sep. 22, 1992 / Saja ✦✦✦✦
While it has too much material for the casual listener, the two-disc *50th Anniversary Collection* is the definitive package for the hardcore Jim Croce fan, covering all of his hits, as well as many forgotten album tracks. —*Stephen Thomas Erlewine*

David Crosby

b. Aug. 14, 1941, Los Angeles, CA
Vocals / Singer-Songwriter, Folk-Rock, Pop-Rock
Crosby was an original member of the groundbreaking '60s Los Angeles band the Byrds. During his time with them, Crosby's smooth harmonic capabilities and airy lead-vocal style provided a major ingredient in their distinctive sound. He also wrote or co-wrote some wonderfully trippy songs during his stint with them, including "Lady Friend," "Everybody's Been Burned," "Draft Morning," "Dolphins Smile," "Why," "Eight Miles High," "What's Happening?" and "I See You," a song Yes recorded on their debut album. Crosby left the Byrds and helped found the richly harmonic, mellow acoustic-rock trio Crosby, Stills & Nash in 1968. They enjoyed enormous success in their first few years, but solo projects and Crosby's drug problems (and subsequent late-'80s cleanup) resulted in the band's sporadic output. In 1989 Crosby released *Oh Yes I Can,* his first solo album since 1971, along with a best-selling autobiography called *Long Time Gone.* Four years later, he returned with *Thousand Roads. It's All Coming Back Now* followed in 1995. —*Rick Clark*

● **If I Could Only Remember My Name** / Feb. 22, 1971 / Atlantic ✦✦✦✦
On his first solo album, the velvet-voiced hippie crooner invited half of Northern California to join him. It's vintage Crosby, ranking with the best of CSNY group efforts. —*Jeff Tamarkin*

Oh Yes I Can / Jan. 23, 1989 / A&M ✦✦✦
His post-rehab reintroduction to the world of creativity finds a reflective Crosby still in fine voice and trying a few new things with his music. —*Jeff Tamarkin*

Thousand Roads / May 4, 1993 / Atlantic ✦✦✦
For his third solo album, *Thousand Roads,* Crosby increased the participation of his guests and attempted to redefine himself as an artist. Crosby acted primarily as an interpretive singer, penning only one of the ten songs and contributing to two others. The result certainly was a craftsmanlike set of songs written by pop professionals—Phil Collins, Jimmy Webb, Marc Cohn, John Hiatt, Paul Brady, Stephen Bishop—and produced by the cream of pop producers—Don Was, Glyn Johns, and Phil Ramone. The failings were, first, that Crosby's individuality was lost and second, that, as the list suggests, his choices were more calculated than inspired. The problem with David Crosby as a solo artist was not how to make him sound more conventional, it was how to make his unconventionality work. *Thousand Roads* solved the wrong problem; the album was Crosby's least successful in the record stores. —*William Ruhlmann*

It's All Coming Back Now / Jan. 24, 1995 / Atlantic ✦✦
Recorded December 7, 1993, at the Whisky-A-Go-Go in Hollywood, this is a David Crosby live album and a good representation of his solo concert performance. In fact, it's a little better than usual, since Crosby is joined by singers Chris Robinson of the Black Crowes and his old partner Graham Nash. Crosby splits the 71-minute set just about evenly between more recent solo efforts—including two newly written songs—and faithful renditions of favorites from his Crosby, Stills, Nash & Young days. Inadvertently, the set list confirms that the latter represent his best work, while at the same time we've heard songs like "Long Time Gone" and "Wooden Ships" so often in studio and live performances that there isn't much reason to have additional recordings of them. The album's chief virtue is in the expression of Crosby's personality, but there isn't enough of that. So, while these are often spirited performances, they don't add to our understanding of the artist the way a live album should. —*William Ruhlmann*

Crosby Stills & Nash (and Young)

f. 1968, Laurel Canyon, CA
Singer-Songwriter, Folk-Rock, Pop-Rock
The musical partnership of David Crosby (b. Aug. 14, 1941), Stephen Stills (b. Jan. 3, 1945), and Graham Nash (b. Feb. 2, 1942), with and without Neil Young (b. Nov. 12, 1945), was not only one of the most successful touring and recording acts of the late '60s, '70s, and early '80s—with the colorful, contrasting nature of the members' characters and their connection to the political and cultural upheavals of the time—it was the only American-based band to approach the overall societal impact of the Beatles. The group was a second marriage for all the participants when it came together in 1968. Crosby had been a member of the Byrds, Nash was in the Hollies, and Stills had been part of Buffalo Springfield. The resulting trio, however, sounded like none of its predecessors and was characterized by a unique vocal blend and a musical approach that ranged from acoustic folk to melodic pop to hard rock. CSN's debut album, released in 1969, was perfectly in tune with the times, and the group was an instant hit. By the time of their first tour (which included the Woodstock festival), they had added Young, also a veteran of Buffalo Springfield, who maintained a solo career. The first CSN&Y album, *Deja-vu,* was a chart-topping hit in 1970, but the group split acrimoniously after a summer tour. *Four Way Street,* a live double album issued after the breakup, was another No. 1 hit. (When it finally was released on CD in 1992, it was lengthened with more live material.) In 1974 CSN&Y re-formed for a summer stadium tour without releasing a new record. Nevertheless, the compilation *So Far* became their third straight No. 1. Crosby, Stills and Nash re-formed without Young in 1977 for the album *CSN,* another giant hit. They followed with *Daylight Again* in 1982, but by then Crosby was in the throes of drug addiction and increasing legal problems. He was in jail in 1985-86, but cleaned up and returned to action, with the result that CSN&Y reunited for their second studio album, *American Dream,* in 1988. CSN followed with *Live It Up* in 1990, and though that album was a commercial disappointment, the trio remains a popular live act. I embarked on a 25th anniversary tour in the summer of 1994 and released a new album, *After the Storm.* —*William Ruhlmann*

Crosby, Stills & Nash / May 29, 1969 / Atlantic ✦✦✦✦
The group's debut album is a scintillating blend of personal poetry, topical politics, and splendid, spare production. "Suite: Judy Blue Eyes" caught everybody's ear, but every track here is worthwhile, and the success of the album can be measured by the fact that every song here

could have been a single or a B-side. "Marrakesh Express," "Pre-Road Downs," and "Lady of the Island" stand out. —*Bruce Eder*

☆ **Deja-vu** / Mar. 11, 1970 / Atlantic ✦✦✦✦✦
This was the group's triumph, displaying a broader musical scope than that found on the CSN debut record. Each of the four members contributed high-quality material, with Stills turning in the leadoff track, "Carry On," Nash contributing such standards as "Teach Your Children" and "Our House," Crosby presenting the title track, and Young adding the characteristic "Helpless." There was also the hit version of Joni Mitchell's "Woodstock." Flawless harmonies, thoughtful lyrics, accomplished playing: this is state-of-the-art '70s rock music and continues to be the best explanation of CSN&Y's enormous stature and enduring legacy. —*William Ruhlmann*

Four Way Street / Apr. 7, 1971 / Atlantic ✦✦✦✦
This 1992 expanded version of the original double live album (originally released on April 7, 1971) by CSN&Y is now an indispensable part of any collection, with additional Neil Young and Graham Nash material (and even a version of "King Midas in Reverse," the old Hollies tune) that any serious listener will want. Some of the extended guitar jams between Stills and Young ("Southern Man") go on longer than strict musical sense would dictate, but it seemed right at the time, and they capture a form that was far more abused in other hands after this group broke up. —*Bruce Eder*

● **So Far** / Aug. 1974 / Atlantic ✦✦✦✦
Released to coincide with CSN&Y's 1974 reunion tour, this compilation remains the best representation of the group's early work, featuring such hits as "Teach Your Children" and "Suite: Judy Blue Eyes." It also put the one-off single "Ohio/Find the Cost of Freedom" (CSN&Y's response to the shooting of four anti-war student protestors at Kent State University) on an album for the first time. —*William Ruhlmann*

CSN / Jun. 17, 1977 / Atlantic ✦✦✦
A fair and somewhat slick reprise, highlighted by "Dark Star." A valiant attempt to re-create the good spirits of the first album amid the malaise of the '70s. —*Bruce Eder*

Replay / Dec. 1980 / Atlantic ✦✦
Although this is a decent anthology of their hits and most well-known album tracks, with a few remixes, it's no substitute for the first album. —*Bruce Eder*

Daylight Again / Jun. 21, 1982 / Atlantic ✦✦✦
Originally a Stills and Nash project, but with the drug-addled Crosby added virtually in name only for commercial reasons (Timothy Schmit and Art Garfunkel provide many of the harmonies), this turned out better than expected, featuring Nash's reflective "Wasted on the Way" and Stills' "Southern Cross," both hits and respectable additions to the CSN repertoire. —*William Ruhlmann*

Allies / Jun. 6, 1983 / Atlantic ✦✦
A mediocre live album cobbled together from shows dating back six years, apparently released as a souvenir for people attending the group's '83 summer tour. —*William Ruhlmann*

American Dream / Nov. 3, 1988 / Atlantic ✦✦
There are some excellent songs here, notably Young's "This Old House" and Crosby's "Compass," but the quartet didn't really jell on its first new studio album in 14 years. Certainly, expectations were so high that the album seemed much worse than it really was, and in retrospect it seems a workmanlike effort simply lacking the spark that made this group so much more than the sum of its parts. —*William Ruhlmann*

Live It Up / Jun. 11, 1990 / Atlantic ✦✦
More than the harmonies or the scandals, what made CSN a major force was that they wrote great songs. That's what is missing on their first full-fledged trio album since *CSN* in 1977. They sing earnestly and well, and they are augmented, as ever, by the small, efficient army of players, such as Craig Doerge and Joe Vitale, who have made a career supporting them, but they just don't come up with the big songs they've led listeners to expect. (In fact, there are quite a few songs by others.) As a result, this is the least satisfying of CSN's studio albums. Not surprisingly, it flopped badly in record stores. —*William Ruhlmann*

Crosby, Stills & Nash Box Set / Oct. 1991 / Atlantic ✦✦✦✦
Seventy-seven tracks make up this four-CD box retrospective the various permutations of Crosby, Stills and Nash (and Young) from 1968 to 1990. The set is dotted with unreleased tracks from abortive album sessions (CSN&Y may have recorded only two studio albums, but they sure tried a lot of other times), and there are also good choices from both solo work and the well-known material. For a neophyte, it may be on the long side, but seasoned fans can welcome this lavish tribute. —*William Ruhlmann*

After the Storm / Aug. 16, 1994 / Atlantic ✦✦

Christopher Cross (Christopher Geppert)

b. May 3, 1951, San Antonio, TX
Vocals / Adult Contemporary, Pop, Soft-Rock
Cross (born Christopher Geppert) came out of the blue in 1980 with his self-titled debut of slight, soft pop. He managed to clean up at the following year's Grammys, beating out previous record-holder Frank Sinatra with a total of five awards. That album generated several substantial hits with "Ride like the Wind," "Never Be the Same," "Say You'll Be Mine," and the transcendent "Sailing," which went No. 1 and won Song of the Year. Cross briefly continued his success with several more hits like "Think of Laura," "All Right," and the No. 1 "Arthur's Theme (The Best That You Can Do)," from the movie *Arthur*, before sinking from sight. Cross' last album, the 1988 release *Back of My Mind*, failed to chart, indicating that what fan base he had enjoyed no longer existed. —*Rick Clark*

● **Christopher Cross** / Jan. 1980 / Warner Brothers ✦✦✦✦
This Michael Omartian-produced collection of light pop, which featured the atmospheric "Sailing," cleaned up at the 1980 Grammy presentations. Cross' rather thin tenor is given ample support from Michael McDonald, Don Henley, guitarist Eric Johnson, and other Los Angeles "A"-list session pros. —*Rick Clark*

Another Page / Jan. 1983 / Warner Brothers ✦✦✦
Christopher Cross had a lot to live up to in following his self-titled debut album, which had sold a million copies (now up to four million), spawned four Top 40 hits, including the No. 1 "Sailing," and won him five Grammy Awards, including Album of the Year, Song of the Year, Record of the Year (the last two for "Sailing"), and Best New Artist. So, he took three years to make *Another Page*, which, unsurprisingly, sounded a lot like its predecessor. Cross concentrated on smooth pop arrangements, over which he sang greeting-card romantic sentiments in an innocent, Brian Wilson-like tenor. No one would confuse the result with anything truly heartfelt or with real rock 'n' roll, but Cross' soothing approach was still good enough to put two of his songs, "All Right" and "No Time for Talk," into the Top 40 and earn a gold record certification. Then, nearly a year after the album's release, TV soap opera "General Hospital" began featuring the maudlin ballad "Think of Laura," and *Another Page* suddenly had a third single, this one a Top Ten hit. —*William Ruhlmann*

Every Turn of the World / Nov. 1985 / Warner Brothers ✦✦
Having suffered a commercial decline with the ballad-filled *Another Page*, Christopher Cross took a harder rocking approach with his third album, *Every Turn of the World*. Gone were the Los Angeles session aces and the SoCal chorus of famous fellow pop singers, as Cross wielded his SynthAxe and producer/co-writer Michael Omartian his keyboards, along with a rhythm section, on a selection of uptempo songs, many of which had save-the-world themes. It didn't work. "Charm the Snake," the typically energetic lead-off single, sputtered on the charts, while Cross' core audience of "adult contemporary" ballad fans deserted him, and the album was a sales disaster. If anybody had tried turning over the LP and sampling tunes like the Beach Boys tribute "Love Found a Home," they would have discovered a couple of more characteristic Cross songs, but it was too little, too late. —*William Ruhlmann*

Back of My Mind / 1988 / Warner Brothers ✦✦
Since the spectacular success of his first album, Christopher Cross had suffered a steady commercial decline in its successors, and the slide continued with *Back of My Mind*. Having taken a more uptempo approach on *Every Turn of the World*, Cross returned to pop balladeering here, and though tracks like "I Will (Take You Forever)" certainly matched the work of such gutless peers as Peter Cetera and Richard Marx, who were eating up the charts in 1988, Cross was treated as a has-been, bleating out his songs of generalized romantic and filial devotion over synth-strings and drum programming. —*William Ruhlmann*

Window / Mar. 21, 1995 / Priority ✦✦
Christopher Cross made a belated comeback in 1995 with *Window*. Cross hadn't made any great changes to his adult contemporary ballad stylings, although the record certainly bears the stamp of mid-'90s production techniques. Perhaps he would have been able to re-enter the charts if he had been able to come up with a selection of material that was melodically engaging, but most of the record is devoid of anything resembling hooks; instead, it relies on its production to make an impact. As a result, *Window* is a bland collection of faceless, mellow pop that works only as background music. —*Stephen Thomas Erlewine*

Sheryl Crow

b. Feb. 11, 1962, Kennett, MO
Vocals / Singer-Songwriter, Pop-Rock, Adult Alternative Pop-Rock
After many years of paying her dues as a backup singer for Don Henley, Eric Clapton, Rod Stewart, and Michael Jackson, Sheryl Crow finally got a chance to make her own album in 1993. Growing out of a series of

informal jam sessions with Los Angeles studio veterans, the relaxed but gritty blues-rock of *Tuesday Night Music Club* became a hit in the spring of 1994, thanks to the single "Leaving Las Vegas," a slightly surreal travelog that shows only the beginning of her talent. Later that summer the laidback "All I Want to Do" was released, and it became an across-the-boards success, pushing *Tuesday Night Music Club* into the Top Ten and into multi-platinum status. Her 1996 self-titled follow-up was also hugely successful. —*Stephen Thomas Erlewine*

● **Tuesday Night Music Club** / Aug. 3, 1993 / A&M ✦✦✦✦
Sheryl Crow's debut album *Tuesday Night Music Club* is a loose, melodic, gritty record with subtle country underpinnings. Throughout the album, she shows that not only does she have an impressive, bluesy voice, but she is a considerably talented songwriter, as "Leaving Las Vegas" and "Run Baby Run" prove. —*Stephen Thomas Erlewine*

Sheryl Crow / Sep. 24, 1996 / A&M ✦✦✦✦
On the surface, *Sheryl Crow* isn't that different from her debut album, *Tuesday Night Music Club*. Crow still favors early '70s rock 'n' roll, complete with Stonesy guitars, folky ballads, and bluesy singing. The music may be a little darker in tone, but it sounds essentially the same as the loose, friendly roots-rock of *Tuesday Night Music Club*. What is different is Crow's attitude. It's clear from the start of *Sheryl Crow* that, although she still works with collaborators, she is the leader; there is none of the ramshackle, anything-goes ambience of her debut. Since she is in control, she doesn't let the music slip into the hippie-ish concerns of her debut. Most of the songs on *Sheryl Crow* are either edgy relationship songs or social commentary, often infused with feminism. Crow's concepts are sometimes better than the result, but the music is tough and varied, filled with hooks and fairly gritty melodies, and that makes the lyrical weaknesses easy to ignore. On the whole, *Sheryl Crow* is a stronger, more diverse collection than its predecessor, even if it lacks a standout single on the level of "All I Wanna Do" or "Strong Enough." —*Stephen Thomas Erlewine*

Crowded House

f. Jul. 1985, Melbourne, Australia, db. Jun. 1996
Pop-Rock
An institution in their homeland, a two-hit wonder in the US and, during the last half of their ten-year career, bona fide stars in the UK and most of Europe, Crowded House recorded some of the best pop music of the late '80s and early '90s. Leader Neil Finn's carefully crafted songs, meticulous eye for lyrical detail, and gift for melody are matched by few other songwriters.

Crowded House formed in 1985 when Neil Finn dissolved Split Enz rather than carry on after his brother Tim, the group's founding member, left to pursue a solo career. Instead of carrying through with the new wave direction of latter-day Split Enz, Neil moved in favor of a stripped down, back-to-basics combo featuring ex-Enz drummer Paul Hester, bassist Nick Seymour, and guitarist Craig Hooper. Initially, the group dubbed themselves after Finn's middle name, touring Australia and recording demos as the Mullanes. Hooper was dropped shortly after this formative period. In June 1985 the group headed to Los Angeles to shop for a record label, eventually signing with Capitol Records. Capitol requested that the band change their name, and they settled on Crowded House, a reflection of their living conditions in L.A. They began work on their debut, enlisting the help of then-unknown producer Mitchell Froom. A partnership between the band and the producer formed, making Froom nearly a fourth member. The partnership benefited both the band and the producer—the band was helped by Froom's direct approach and more "American" sound as well as his input as a musician, and Froom was able to build a career as a high-profile producer.

Crowded House's self-titled debut didn't gain much attention upon its release in the summer of 1986, due to insufficient promotion from Capitol Records. In wake of the weak support from Capitol, the band took matters into their own hands. Rather than setting out on an expensive large-scale tour, the band took a more low-profile route, playing acoustic sets for industry insiders and for small crowds at ethnic restaurants and in record stores. This unorthodox approach began a buzz within the industry. On the talk-show circuit, they won over American and Canadian audiences with their charm and wit as well as their wacky antics. By February 1987, the album broke into the American Top 40, eventually peaking at No. 12. The album spawned the No. 2 hit single "Don't Dream It's Over" and "Something So Strong," which reached No. 7. In Australia and New Zealand, multi-platinum success followed.

Released in 1988, *Temple of Low Men* was anything but a sophomore slump; Neil Finn's new songs were among his finest, showcasing a notable progression in his songcraft. The album's slightly darker material, however, made for a more difficult listen and, although the material was stronger, the record lacked the immediate appeal of the debut. This, coupled with Capitol's lack of promotional support, led to

disappointing sales—the album barely broke the US.Top 40, and the single "Better Be Home Soon" stalled at No. 42. Since hope had basically run out for the album, they abandoned plans for a major US tour. A three-month break in touring revitalized the band for a well received Australian and Canadian tour, but by mid-1989 the band had effectively broken up.

Late in 1989 Neil reunited with his brother Tim, and the duo began writing songs together for the first time, with the intention of releasing the material on a proposed Finn Brothers album. The collaboration was successful and the duo was prolific, writing 14 songs in a very short time. After the initial sessions with Tim, Neil began working on a new set of songs designed for the next Crowded House album, but he soon found the new material unsatisfactory. Neil decided to combine the better moments of the Finn Brothers project and the scrapped third album, adding his brother as a fourth member of Crowded House.

Crowded House's third album, *Woodface*, released in the summer of 1991, proved the decision to combine the material from the two scrapped records was sound; the album certainly represents their finest recorded moments. Although the choice of "Chocolate Cake" as a leadoff single was both misleading and off-putting to American audiences, effectively sinking the album's chances of success in the US, England and Europe embraced the band for the first time. After about six months of dormancy, they began charting in the UK and Europe with several singles, including the smash "Weather with You." The British success of "Weather with You" helped *Woodface* achieve platinum status in the UK and led the group to several headlining concerts at Wembley Arena.

Tim, for all of his invaluable contributions in the writing and recording of *Woodface*, proved extraneous to the band's live show. He left in November 1991, as the band was in the middle of their tour and just before their breakthrough success in England. After the success of *Woodface*, both Neil and Tim Finn were awarded OBEs from the Queen of England in 1993; the honor was bestowed for their contribution to the arts.

In early 1993 Crowded House regrouped to record their fourth album, adding American guitarist Mark Hart (who had briefly toured with the band around the time of *Temple of Low Men*) and dropping Mitchell Froom as their producer, opting instead for ex-Killing Joke member Youth. *Together Alone* was released in October 1993 (January 1994 in North America) to unanimously positive reviews and solid sales in every country except the United States. Upon its release, *Together Alone* entered the English charts at No. 4; at the time, *Woodface* was still in the UK charts. After the album was released, Crowded House embarked on a successful European tour. They were beginning an American tour when Paul Hester decided to leave the band to spend more time with his new family. Hiring a session drummer, the band rounded out the tour, eventually returning to Australia.

By the end of 1994 Neil Finn decided to cut back on the touring to work on side projects, which included some production work for Dave Dobbyn and a second try at a Finn Brothers album with Tim. The Finn Brothers finally released their long-awaited duet album in the fall of 1995. In June 1996, Neil officially broke up Crowded House. That same month, *Recurring Dream: The Very Best of Crowded House* was released, entering the UK and Australian charts at No. 1. After a handful of "final shows" in various locations, Crowded House played their official farewell show at the Sydney Opera House on Sunday, November 24, 1996, to 100,000 fans as a benefit for the Sydney Children's Hospital Fund. —*Chris Woodstra*

Crowded House / Jun. 1986 / Capitol ✦✦✦
Their Top 40 debut is loaded with highly melodic, pop gems. Strong, upbeat songwriting and vocal harmonies from this talented trio, featuring the hits "Don't Dream It's Over" and "Something So Strong." —*Scott Bultman*

Temple of Low Men / Jul. 1988 / Capitol ✦✦✦✦
After the success of Crowded House's debut and the band's gruelling promotion schedule, Neil Finn was clearly showing signs that he was no longer happy being New Zealand's zany ambassador to the US. While the material on *Temple of Low Men* demonstrates great leaps in quality over its predecessor, it is a darkly difficult album, especially for those expecting *Crowded House, Pt. 2*. In short, there are no immediately accessible singles. Instead, Finn digs into the depths of his emotional psyche with obsessive detail, crafting a set of intense, personal songs that range from the all-too-intimate look at infidelity of "Into Temptation" to the raucous exorcism of "Kill Eye." Through all of this introspective soul-searching, Finn reveals most of all his true mastery of melody. —*Chris Woodstra*

Woodface / Jul. 2, 1991 / Capitol ✦✦✦✦
Where Crowded House's previous album, *Temple of Low Men*, showcased the often dark side of a man alone with his thoughts, *Woodface* represents the joy of reunion and the freedom of a collaborative

effort—more than half of the album was originally conceived as a Finn Brothers project, which was Tim and Neil's first crack at writing together. The songs are easily their finest to date, combining flawless melodies and the outstanding harmonies of the brothers' perfectly matched voices. —*Chris Woodstra*

Together Alone / Oct. 18, 1993 / Capitol ✦✦✦
More experimental and musically varied than any of their previous releases, *Together Alone* finds Crowded House branching out into traditional Maori music and heavy guitars, as well as the shining pop songcraft that is Neil Finn's trademark. Picking up a new guitarist and adding the production skills of ex-Killing Joke member Youth, Crowded House energizes their sound without losing sight of Neil Finn's classic pop songwriting, as "Locked Out" and "Distant Sun" prove. —*Stephen Thomas Erlewine*

● **Recurring Dream: The Very Best of Crowded House** / Jun. 24, 1996 / Capitol ✦✦✦✦
Recurring Dream is a 19-track collection that assembles most of the band's singles and adds three new studio tracks to entice fans—"Not the Girl You Think You Are," "Instinct," and "Everything Is Good for You." As a career summary, the collection works fairly well, though the nonchronological sequencing makes for a slightly confusing listen. Nevertheless, for a band with no shortage of great material (there's not a bad album in the bunch), *Recurring Dream* is a good place to get acquainted with them. Initial pressings also came with a second disc that compiles highlights from the band's always entertaining live shows. Maybe a disc of non-album rarities and B-sides would have been a better choice, but for fans this is an essential addition. —*Chris Woodstra*

The Crows

f. 1951, New York, NY, **db.** 1954
Doo Wop
One of the first doo wop groups, one of the first so-called "bird" groups, and one of the first acts of any kind to score a bona fide rock 'n' roll hit record, the Crows were among the more important one-shot artists in rock 'n' roll history. Discovered at New York's Apollo Theater in 1952, the Crows were one of the many groups pioneering doo wop with their infectious, cheerful vocals and harmonies, use of nonsense syllables, and modified jump blues instrumental backing. Cut in 1953, "Gee," with its irresistible melody, naively enthusiastic street-corner singing, and Charlie Christian-like guitar solo, was far and away their best single. It was also their only successful one, although it needed almost a year to take off, reaching No. 14 in the pop charts (and No. 2 in the R&B charts) in early 1954. After recording about a half-dozen other 45s between 1952 and 1954, the group broke up with little fanfare only months after "Gee" fell off the hit parade. —*Richie Unterberger*

● **Gee, It's the Crows** / 1988 / Murray Hill ✦✦✦✦
Sixteen sides covering their complete output for the Jubilee and Rama labels between 1952 and 1954, including all their singles, as well as 45s on which they backed Fatman Humphries (as the 4 Notes) and Lorraine Ellis. It's a respectable mix of uptempo numbers and ballads that will appeal to few listeners besides doo wop aficionados. By far the best of the batch besides "Gee" is their final single, "Sweet Sue," a snazzy, uptempo cut with a thumping beat. "I Love You So," the flipside of "Gee," is also well remembered by doo wop fans, and was covered a few years later by the Chantels. Includes detailed liner notes and discography. —*Richie Unterberger*

The Cryan' Shames

f. 1964, Chicago, IL, **db.** 1970
Pop-Rock
The Cryan' Shames were a big deal in Chicago in the mid- and late '60s, when a bunch of their singles hit the local Top Ten; some of them were small national hits, as well. The biggest of these was "Sugar and Spice," a cover of a Searchers' song (itself a cover of a Drifters' hit) that made the Top 50 in 1966 and was later featured in the *Nuggets* anthology of '60s garage bands. In their original incarnation, the Shames leaned toward the pop end of the garage. Borrowing heavily from the Beatles, Byrds, and Yardbirds, guitarist Jim Fair wrote a clutch of energetic guitar pop-rockers with sparkling harmonies. After 1966, unfortunately, the group pursued an increasingly mainstream pop direction featuring saccharine arrangements and material. In this respect they uncannily mirrored the devolution of local rivals the New Colony Six, who also shifted from tough pop-rock to MOR in their bid for national success. —*Richie Unterberger*

● **Sugar & Spice (A Collection)** / Jul. 14, 1992 / Columbia ✦✦✦✦
This 18-song compilation spans 1966 to 1969, and features their singles and key album cuts. Despite its good intentions, this well-packaged ret-

rospective runs out of octane after the first half dozen songs. —*Richie Unterberger*

The Crystals

f. 1961, Brooklyn, NY, **db.** 1966
Girl-Group, Pop-Rock
This Brooklyn female vocal group had R&B roots, but the Crystals were really a pop ensemble whose best songs perfectly expressed the romantic innocence of the early '60s. Barbara Alston, Lala Brooks, Dee Dee Kennibrew, Mary Thomas, and Patricia Wright were the original lineup formed by Benny Wells while still in high school. Wells served as their first manager. The remarkable producer Phil Spector heard them rehearsing and signed them to his Philles label, where they had several classic songs. "There's No Other like My Baby" got things started in 1961, making it to No. 5 on the R&B charts and to No. 20 on the pop charts. "Uptown" cracked the R&B and pop Top 20; then came "He's a Rebel," arguably their finest song and one of the era's landmarks. Darlene Love was lead vocalist, and both "Rebel" and the successful follow-up "He's Sure the Boy I Love" featured Love and the Blossoms but were credited to the Crystals. The actual Crystals returned in 1963 minus Mary Thomas, who left to get married. They had two more huge hits, "Da Doo Ron Ron (When He Walked Me Home)" and "Then He Kissed Me" in 1963, each one making the Top Ten on both the R&B and pop lists. But the party ended in 1964, as their final two singles for Philles both flopped, and relations with Spector degenerated. Wright left and was replaced by Frances Collins. They bought themselves out of their Philles contract in 1965 and signed with United Artists, only to get dropped a year later. They disbanded, then re-formed in 1971. Since then, various editions of the Crystals have been plentiful on the oldies circuit, but of the originals, only Kennibrew was still involved. —*Ron Wynn*

● **The Best of the Crystals** / Sep. 22, 1992 / ABKCO ✦✦✦✦
All of the Crystals' biggest hits are included on this comprehensive collection, which also features many forgotten singles and album tracks; while some of the lesser-known material might not match the standards of the classic singles, many songs do come close. —*Stephen Thomas Erlewine*

The Cult

f. 1982, Bradford, W. Yorks, England, **db.** 1995
Hard Rock, Alternative Pop-Rock
After a succession of name and stylistic changes, the Cult emerged in 1984 as one of England's leading heavy metal revivalists. Picking up the pseudo-mysticism and native American obsessions of the Doors, the guitar-orchestrations of Led Zeppelin, and the three-chord crunch of AC/DC, while adding touches of post-punk goth-rock, the Cult gained a dedicated following in their native Britain with mid-'80s singles like "She Sells Sanctuary" before breaking into the American metal market in the late '80s with "Love Removal Machine." Though the group managed one Top Ten American record with 1989's *Sonic Temple*, the band was plagued with offstage tensions and problems that prevented them retaining their popularity. After a pair of unsuccessful records, the Cult split in 1995.

The origins of the Cult lie in the Southern Death Cult, a goth-rock outfit formed by vocalist Ian Astbury (b. May 14, 1962) in 1981. Astbury was the son of a merchant navy man, which meant he moved frequently during his youth; at one point in his childhood, his family lived in Canada, where the young Ian became fascinated with native Americans, which would become a recurring theme in his songwriting. Astbury eventually settled in Bradford, Yorkshire, where he met a group comprised of David Burrows (guitar), Barry Jepson (bass), and Haq Quereshi (drums). Ian joined as lead vocalist (performing with the last name of "Lindsay," which was his mother's maiden name) and had the group renamed the Southern Death Cult. At only their fifth concert, the band was attracting audiences of 2,000. In December 1982, the Southern Death Cult released their first single—the double A-side "Moya"/"Fatman"—and the next month, they supported Bauhaus on tour. Though the group's future was looking bright, Astbury pulled the plug on the band because he was frustrated with the positive articles he was receiving in the press. The remaining three members joined Getting the Fear, which eventually became Into a Circle; in the late '80s, Quereshi became a member of Fun-Da-Mental. All of the Southern Death Cult recordings were eventually released in 1986.

After the disbandment of the Southern Death Cult, Astbury shortened the name of the group to Death Cult and recruited guitarist Billy Duffy—who had previously played with Morrissey in the pre-Smiths band the Nosebleeds, as well as Theatre of Hate—drummer Ray Mondo, and bassist Jamie Stewart, who had previously played with Ritual. Death Cult released an eponymous EP in the summer of 1983; on the EP, Astbury reverted to his given name. Later in the year, Mondo was replaced by Nigel Preston, who had played with Duffy in Theatre of

Hate; coincidentally, Mondo became the drummer for Preston's previous band, Sex Gang Children.

In early 1984, the band shed "Death" from the title, fearing that the word gave them the misleading appearance of being a goth band. Where both Southern Death Cult and Death Cult had been overtly influenced by post-punk, the Cult was a heavy hard-rock band, with slight psychedelic flourishes. *Dreamtime*, the group's first album, was released in the fall of 1984, accompanied by the single "Spiritwalker," which reached No. 1 in the UK in the spring. *Dreamtime* reached No. 21 on the UK charts. In the spring of 1985, Preston left the group. For the group's summer single, "She Sells Sanctuary," the band was joined by Big Country's drummer, Mark Brzezicki. "She Sells Sanctuary" became a major UK hit, peaking at No. 15. During the recording of the second album, *Love*, drummer Les Warner joined the group. *Love*, released in the fall of 1985, continued the hard-rock direction of its teaser single and became a No. 4 hit in Britain.

For their third album, the Cult shuffled its lineup—Stewart moved to rhythm guitar, while former Zodiac Mindwarp bassist Kid Chaos joined the lineup—and hired Rick Rubin as producer. The result, *Electric*, was their hardest, heaviest record to date. The first single from the album, "Love Removal Machine," became a No. 18 hit in the spring of 1987, and the album itself reached No. 4 in the UK upon its April release. Later that year *Electric* gained the Cult a fan base within America, and the album cracked the US Top 40.

In 1988 the group fired Chaos and Warner, replacing the latter with Matt Sorum; the band failed to hire another bassist. The new lineup released *Sonic Temple*, which would prove to be its most successful album. The hit single "Fire Woman" helped propel the album into the American Top Ten, and within no time, the Cult were hanging out with Motley Crue and Aerosmith, as well as supporting Metallica on the Damaged Justice tour. Though the group was experiencing its best sales, it was fraying behind the scenes, due to in-fighting and substance abuse. By the time they recorded their follow-up to *Sonic Temple*, Sorum had left to join Guns 'N Roses and Stewart had quit; they were replaced by drummer Mickey Curry and bassist Charlie Drayton. The resulting album, *Ceremony*, was released in the fall of 1991 to weak reviews and disappointing sales.

After the release of *Ceremony*, the group took a break for the next three years. In 1993 the band released the UK-only hits compilation *Pure Cult*, which debuted at No. 1. By the summer of 1993, the Cult had a new rhythm section, featuring former Mission bassist Craig Adams and drummer Scott Garrett. This lineup recorded *The Cult*, which was released in late 1994 to poor reviews and sales. In the spring of 1995, the Cult disbanded, with Ian Astbury forming the Holy Barbarians later in the year. Billy Duffy played briefly with Miles Hunt's Vent 414 before leaving to pursue a solo project. —*Stephen Thomas Erlewine*

Dreamtime / 1984 / Beggars Banquet ♦♦

Love / 1985 / Sire ♦♦♦
Apart from the monolithic rock 'n' roll masterpiece "She Sells Sanctuary," *Love* is devoid of memorable riffs and melodies. —*Stephen Thomas Erlewine*

Electric / 1987 / Beggars Banquet/Sire ♦♦♦♦
After four years of evolving from a goth-rock band with two longer names (Southern Death Cult, Death Cult), the Cult emerged on this Rick Rubin production as a full-fledged heavy metal band. Billy Duffy pulls out monstrous guitar riffs, and lead singer Ian Astbury declaims like a latter-day Jim Morrison. It also contains "Love Removal Machine." —*William Ruhlmann*

Sonic Temple / 1989 / Beggars Banquet/Sire/Reprise ♦♦♦
A change of producer and drummers has no discernible impact on the Cult's driving metal assault. —*William Ruhlmann*

Ceremony / Sep. 24, 1991 / Beggars Banquet/Sire/RepriseSire ♦♦♦
Ceremony continued the straightforward attack of *Sonic Temple*, and while the songs weren't quite as strong as those on the previous record, it delivered a bracing heavy-metal roar. —*David Jehnzen*

Cult / 1994 / Beggars Banquet/Sire/Reprise ♦♦
As the years go by, the Cult becomes more traditional, which is a mixed blessing. At its best, the Cult can sound as powerful as any other hard-rock outfit, but they have trouble coming up with enough decent riffs and songs to fill an album. The band *sounds* good on *The Cult*—they've just neglected to write songs worthy of their skills. —*Stephen Thomas Erlewine*

● **High Octane Cult** / Nov. 5, 1996 / Warner Brothers ♦♦♦♦
A few hardcore fans might find favorite tracks missing, but the single-disc *High Octane Cult* distills the essence of the band by featuring all of their best-known tracks—"Love Removal Machine," "She Sells Sanctuary," "Fire Woman," "Edie (Ciao Baby)"—as well as a selection of strong album cuts and two good, but unremarkable, new songs ("In the Clouds," "Beauty's on the Street"). —*Stephen Thomas Erlewine*

Culture Club

f. 1981, London, England, **db.** 1986
New Wave, Pop-Rock, Blue-Eyed Soul

Few New Wave groups were as popular as Culture Club. During the early '80s, the group racked up seven straight Top Ten hits in the UK and six Top Ten singles in the US with their light, infectious pop-soul. Though their music was radio-ready, what brought the band stardom was Boy George, the group's charismatic, cross-dressing lead singer. George wore flamboyant dresses and heavy makeup, creating a disarmingly androgynous appearanceance that was a sensation on early MTV. George also had a biting wit and frequently came up with cutting quips that won Culture Club heavy media exposure in both America and Britain. Although closely aligned with the New Romantics—they were both inspired by Northern soul and fashion—Culture Club had sharper pop sense than their peers, and they consequently had a broader appeal. However, their time in the spotlight was brief. Not only could they not withstand the changing fashions of MTV, but the group was fraught with personal tensions, including Boy George's drug addiction. By 1986 the group had broken up, leaving behind several singles that rank as classics of the New Wave era.

The son of a boxing club manager, Boy George (b. George O'Dowd, June 14, 1961), found himself attracted to the glam-rock of T. Rex and David Bowie as a teenager. During the post-punk era of the late '70s, he became a regular at London new romantic clubs. Along with his cross-dressing friends Marilyn and Martin Degville (a future member of Sigue Sigue Sputnik), George became well known around the London underground for his extravagant sense of style, and Malcolm McLaren invited him to join an early version of Bow Wow Wow. George appeared briefly with the band as Lieutenant Lush before leaving to form In Praise Of Lemmings with bassist Mikey Craig (b. February 15, 1960). When guitarist Jon Suede joined the group, they changed their name to Sex Gang Children. Within a few months, the band met Jon Moss (b. September 11, 1957), a professional drummer who had previously played with Adam & the Ants and the Damned.

By 1981 Boy George had renamed the group Culture Club, and Suede had been replaced by Roy Hay (b. August 12, 1961), a former member of Russian Bouquet. Toward the end of the year they recorded a set of demos for EMI, but the label turned them down. Early in 1982 the band signed a contract with Virgin Records, releasing "White Boy" in the spring. Neither "White Boy" nor its followup, "I'm Afraid of Me," made the charts, but the British music and fashion press began running articles about Boy George. In the fall, Culture Club released their breakthrough single, "Do You Really Want to Hurt Me," which rocketed to the top of the charts. Shortly afterward, the band's debut, *Kissing to Be Clever*, climbed to No. 5 on the UK charts, and the non-LP single "Time (Clock of the Heart)" reached No. 3. Early in 1983 *Kissing to Be Clever* and "Do You Really Want To Hurt Me" began climbing the US charts, with the single peaking at No. 2. "Time" reached No. 2 in the US shortly after the non-LP British single "Church of the Poison Mind" attained the same position in the UK. "I'll Tumble 4 Ya" became a Top Ten hit in America that summer.

By the time Culture Club's second album, *Colour By Numbers*, was released in the fall of 1983, the band was the most popular pop-rock group in America and England. "Karma Chameleon" became a No. 1 hit on both sides of the Atlantic, while the album reached No. 1 in the UK and No. 2 in the US. Throughout 1984 the group racked up hits, with "It's a Miracle" and "Miss Me Blind" reaching the Top Ten. The group returned in the fall with its third album, *Waking Up With the House On Fire*. While "The War Song" reached No. 2 in the UK, the album was a disappointment in America, stalling at platinum; its predecessor went quadruple platinum.

After a brief tour in February, Culture Club went on hiatus for 1985, with Craig, Moss, and Hay pursuing extracurricular musical projects in the interim. During the year, Boy George—who had previously denounced drugs in public—became addicted to heroin. Furthermore, his romance with Moss, which had always been rocky, began to disintegrate. All of these problems were kept hidden, but it became evident that something was wrong when Culture Club returned to action in the spring of 1986. Though their comeback single, "Move Away," became a hit on *From Luxury to Heartache* stayed on the charts for only a few months. Rumors of George's heroin addiction began to circulate, and by the summer, he announced that he was indeed addicted to the drug. In July he was arrested by the British police for possession of cannabis. Several days later, keyboardist Michael Rudetski, who played on *From Luxury to Heartache*, was found dead of a heroin overdose in George's home. Rudetski's parents tried unsuccessfully to press wrongful death charges on Boy George.

While Boy George was battling heroin addiction, and his subsequent dependence on prescription narcotics, Culture Club broke up. George confirmed the group's disbandment in the spring of 1987, and he began a solo career later that year. While his solo career produced several dance hits in Europe, George didn't land an American hit until 1992, when his cover of Dave Berry's "The Crying Game" was featured in the Academy Award-nominated film of the same name. In 1995 George published his autobiography, *Take It Like a Man*. —*Stephen Thomas Erlewine*

Kissing to Be Clever / 1982 / Virgin ✦✦✦✦
Appealing lightly synthesized '80s pop music, featuring the infectious ballad hit "Do You Really Want to Hurt Me." —*William Ruhlmann*

Colour by Numbers / 1983 / Virgin ✦✦✦✦
More melodic bouncy pop led by Boy George's engaging singing on "Karma Chameleon" and other songs. —*William Ruhlmann*

Waking up with the House on Fire / 1984 / Virgin ✦✦
The career of Boy George and Culture Club was on a steady upward climb for two years by the fall of 1984, so the group had every reason to expect that their third album, *Waking Up with the House on Fire*, would enjoy similar success, but it was not to be. The lead-off single, "The War Song," put off many fans, but the problem may have been less the music on *Waking Up*, which was typically frothy and propulsive, than the passing of a fad. By late 1984 Boy George had been sideswiped in the image department by Michael Jackson, Prince, and Madonna. So, while it's true that *Waking Up* didn't contain any song as catchy as "Karma Chameleon," the album's real failure was one of timing. —*William Ruhlmann*

From Luxury to Heartache / 1986 / Virgin ✦✦
For their fourth album, *From Luxury to Heartache*, Culture Club jettisoned producer Steve Levine in favor of pop/R&B veteran Arif Mardin, seeking to reverse the commercial decline they had suffered with their third album. When the danceable leadoff track, "Move Away," rose into the singles chart, that seemed like a good decision, and the rest of the album followed through with a pronounced drum sound and a relentless beat. The group's flamboyance was played down in an attempt to redefine Culture Club as dance floor favorites. But previously the group had enjoyed a broad-based pop appeal, and by focusing on one part of their constituency, they ultimately sacrificed the rest. What's more, to make this kind of music, you didn't need a group; all you needed was a lead singer and some synthesizers. No wonder Boy George went solo before the year was out. —*William Ruhlmann*

● **At Worst . . . The Best of Boy George and Culture Club** / Nov. 2, 1993 / Virgin ✦✦✦✦
The success of "The Crying Game" marked a comeback for Boy George, especially in the US, where his solo career had never taken hold beyond the dance clubs. SBK (distributor of his label, Virgin) took advantage of his resurgence by compiling this 75-minute, 19-track album, which combines his former group Culture Club's biggest hits with selections from his solo work. The ten Culture Club tracks are of a piece, from 1982's "Do You Really Want to Hurt Me" (which here leads off with an ominous voice intoning, "Popularity breeds contempt") to "Love Is Love," which wasn't a hit, but is a better choice than the missing "The War Song," which was. The solo tracks are a more mixed batch, and not only because Top 40 UK hits like "Keep Me in Mind," "Sold," and "To Be Reborn" are missing. They often rely on loud percussion tracks that strand Boy George's tender tenor somewhere in the distance. He remains most effective on rhythmic ballads, whether "Do You Really Want to Hurt Me," "Everything I Own" (his chart-topping first UK solo hit), or "The Crying Game." —*William Ruhlmann*

The Cure

f. 1976, Crawley, England
Alternative Pop-Rock, Goth-Rock, Post-Punk

Out of all the bands that emerged in the immediate aftermath of punk rock in the late '70s, the Cure was one of the most enduring and popular. Led through numerous incarnations by guitarist/vocalist Robert Smith (b. April 21, 1959), the band became notorious for their slow, gloomy dirges and Smith's ghoulish appearance. But the public image often hid the diversity of the Cure's music. At the outset, they played jagged, edgy pop songs; they slowly evolved into a more textured outfit. As one of the bands that planted the seeds for goth-rock, the group created towering layers of guitars and synthesizers, but by the time goth caught on in the mid-'80s, the Cure had moved away from the genre. By the end of the '80s, the Cure had crossed over into the mainstream, not only in their native England, but in the United States and in various parts of Europe.

Originally called the Easy Cure, the band was formed in 1976 by schoolmates Robert Smith (vocals, guitar), Michael Dempsey (bass), and Laurence "Lol" Tolhurst (drums). Initially, the group was played dark, nervy guitar-pop with pseudo-literary lyrics, as evidenced by the Albert Camus-inspired "Killing an Arab." A demo tape featuring "Killing an Arab" reached Chris Parry, an A&R representative at Polydor Records; by the time he received the tape, the band's name had been truncated to the Cure. Parry was impressed with the song and arranged for its release on the independent label Small Wonder in December 1978. Early in

1979 Parry left Polydor to form his own record label, Fiction, and the Cure was one of the first bands he signed. "Killing an Arab" was re-released in February 1979, and the Cure set out on their first tour of England. The Cures' debut album, *Three Imaginary Boys*, was released in May 1979 to good reviews in the British music press. Later that year the group released the non-LP singles "Boys Don't Cry" and "Jumping Someone Else's Train." That same year the Cure embarked on a major tour with Siouxsie and the Banshees. During the tour, the Banshees' guitarist John McKay left and Robert Smith stepped in; for the next decade or so, Smith would frequently collaborate with members of the Banshees.

At the end of 1979 the Cure released a single, "I'm a Cult Hero," under the name the Cult Heroes. After the release of the single, Dempsey left the band to join the Associates. Dempsey was replaced by Simon Gallup at the beginning of 1980. At the same time, the Cure added a keyboardist, Matthieu Hartley, to their lineup. The band's second album, *Seventeen Seconds*, was released in the spring of 1980. The addition of a keyboardist expanded the group's sound—it was now more experimental—and frequently they would immerse themselves in slow, gloomy dirges. Nevertheless, the band still wrote pop hooks, as demonstrated by their first UK hit single, "A Forest," which peaked at No. 31. After the release of *Seventeen Seconds*, the Cure began their first world tour. After the Australian leg of the tour, Matthieu Hartley left the band. In 1981 they released their third album, *Faith*, which peaked at No. 14 and spawned the minor hit single "Primary." The Cure's fourth album, the doom-laden, introspective *Pornography*, was released in 1982. *Pornography* expanded their cult audience even further and cracked the UK Top Ten. After the *Pornography* tour was completed, Simon Gallup quit the band, and Lol Tolhurst moved from drums to keyboards. At the end of 1982 the Cure released a new single, the dance-tinged "Let's Go to Bed."

Robert Smith devoted most of the beginning of 1983 to Siouxsie and the Banshees, recording the *Hyaena* album with the group and appearing as the band's guitarist on the album's accompanying tour. Smith also formed a band with Banshees bassist Steve Severin called the Glove that same year. The Glove released their only album, *Blue Sunshine*, later in 1983. By the late summer of 1983, a new version of the Cure—featuring Smith, Tolhurst, drummer Andy Anderson, and bassist Phil Thornalley—was assembled and they recorded a new single, the jaunty "The Lovecats." The song was released in the fall of 1983 and became the group's biggest hit to date, peaking at No. 7 on the UK charts. In 1984 the new lineup of the Cure released *The Top*. Despite the pop leanings of the No. 14 hit "The Caterpillar," *The Top* was a return to the bleak soundscapes of *Pornography*. During the world tour supporting *The Top*, Anderson was fired. In early 1985, after completion of the tour, Thornalley left. The Cure revamped its lineup after his departure, adding drummer Boris Williams, guitarist Porl Thompson, and bassist Simon Gallup. Later in 1985, the Cure released their sixth album, *The Head on the Door*. The album was the most concise and pop-oriented record the group had ever released, which helped send it into the UK Top Ten and to No. 59 in the US—the first time the band had broken the American Hot 100. "In Between Days" and "Close to Me"—both pulled from *The Head on the Door*—became sizable UK hits, as well as popular underground and college-radio hits in the US.

The Cure followed the breakthrough success of *The Head on the Door* in 1986 with the compilation *Standing on a Beach: The Singles*. *Standing on a Beach* reached No. 4 in the UK, but more importantly it established the band as a major cult act in the US; the album peaked at No. 48 and went gold within a year. In short, *Standing on a Beach* set the stage for 1987's double album *Kiss Me, Kiss Me, Kiss Me*. The album was eclectic, but it was a hit, spawning four hit singles in the UK ("Why Can't I Be You," "Catch," "Just like Heaven," "Hot Hot Hot!!!") and the group's first American Top 40 hit, "Just like Heaven." After the supporting tour for *Kiss Me, Kiss Me, Kiss Me*, the Cure's activity came to a halt. Before the Cure began working on their new album in early 1988, the band fired Lol Tolhurst, claiming that relations between him and the rest of the band had been irrevocably damaged. Tolhurst would soon file a lawsuit, claiming that his role in the band was greater than stated in his contract and, consequently, he deserved more money.

In the meantime, the Cure replaced Tolhurst with former Psychedelic Furs keyboardist Roger O'Donnell and recorded their eighth album, *Disintegration*. Released in the spring of 1989, the album was more melancholy than its predecessor, but it was an immediate hit, reaching No. 3 in the UK and No. 14 in the US, and spawning a series of hit singles. "Lullaby" became the group's biggest British hit in the spring of 1989, peaking at No. 5. In the late summer, the band had their biggest American hit with "Lovesong," which climbed to No. 2. On the *Disintegration* tour, the Cure began playing stadiums across the US and the UK. In the fall of 1990, the Cure released *Mixed Up*, a collection of remixes featuring a new single, "Never Enough."

After the *Disintegration* tour, Roger O'Donnell left the band, and the Cure replaced him with their roadie, Perry Bamonte. In the spring of

1992, the band released *Wish*. Like *Disintegration*, *Wish* was an immediate hit, entering the British charts at No. 1 and the American charts at No. 2, as well as launching the hit singles "High" and "Friday I'm in Love." The Cure embarked on another international tour after the release of *Wish*. One concert, performed in Detroit, was documented on a film called *Show* and on two albums, *Show* and *Paris*. The movie and the albums were released in 1993.

Porl Thompson left the band in 1993 to join Jimmy Page and Robert Plant's band. After his departure, Roger O'Donnell re-joined the band as a keyboardist and Perry Bamonte switched from synthesizers to guitars. During most of 1993 and early 1994, the Cure were sidelined by the lawsuit from Lol Tolhurst. After the settlement in the band's favor in the fall of 1994, the group was set to record a follow-up album to *Wish*, but drummer Boris Williams quit just as they were about to begin the record. The Cure recruited a new drummer through advertisements in the British music papers. By the spring of 1995, Jason Cooper had replaced Williams. Throughout 1995, the Cure recorded their tenth proper studio album, pausing to perform a handful of European musical festivals in the summer. The album, titled *Wild Mood Swings*, was finally released in the spring of 1996. —*Stephen Thomas Erlewine*

Three Imaginary Boys / Jun. 1979 / Fiction ✦✦✦✦
Bursting with high-energy playing and bare-bones production, the band's first album showcases Robert Smith's most concise songwriting. Smith's now common themes of isolation, alienation and despair are present, this time presented in perfect three-minute form with a more aggressive stance. *Three Imaginary Boys* ends up sounding like a slightly more tuneful version of Wire's *Pink Flag* and quite unlike anything else they would record later on. —*Chris Woodstra*

Boys Don't Cry / Jan. 1980 / Elektra ✦✦✦✦
Boys Don't Cry combines the finer moments of *Three Imaginary Boys* with the singles released around the same time—the title track, "Jumping Someone Else's Train," and the often misinterpreted "Killing an Arab," as well as "Plastic Passion." The adding of the singles makes this the perfect encapsulation of the band's early days. —*Chris Woodstra*

Seventeen Seconds / May 1980 / Elektra ✦✦✦
Still capturing the more accessible pop elements and angular post-punk leanings of *Three Imaginary Boys*, *Seventeen Seconds* marks a move toward the despair for which the band would become best known. The tempos are slowed down considerably, and the addition of subtle synthesizers to minimalist arrangements builds a darkly evocative atmosphere of depression. —*Chris Woodstra*

Faith / Sep. 1981 / Elektra ✦✦✦
Continuing the trend set by *Seventeen Seconds*, *Faith* is an even darker affair. Smith sings with suicidal resignation through eight somber epics of gloom typified by the title track and "The Funeral Party," raising the funeral march tempo only for the single "Primary." The atmosphere created is chilling, though very few of the songs stand out. That's probably not the point anyway—as a mood-setting piece, *Faith* is quite effective. —*Chris Woodstra*

Pornography / 1982 / Elektra ✦✦✦
Pornography is the culmination of the band's gloom-and-doom period. It's not that they've changed their mood much since *Faith*—this is still pretty bleak stuff—but this album marks a more aggressive stance, incorporating faster, near-tribal rhythms and layers of heavy, distorted guitars that serve to bring out Smith's echoed vocals and doom-laden lyrics like "It doesn't matter if we all die." *Pornography* isn't their most interesting album—much of it suffers from same-sounding monotony—but it did manage to crack the UK Top Ten and was undoubtedly influential in the emerging goth-rock movement. —*Chris Woodstra*

Japanese Whispers / 1984 / Sire ✦✦✦
After reaching the depths of gloom, Smith recast himself as something of a British pop eccentric, releasing three singles—"The Walk," "Let's Go to Bed," and "The Lovecats"—that revealed an accessible and upbeat, nearly bubbly, side. *Japanese Whispers* collects those singles, along with their slightly less interesting B-sides. The singles were compiled on the more comprehensive *Standing on a Beach* collection, but as a collection of Smith's brief period of whimsy, there is no better collection than *Japanese Whispers*. —*Chris Woodstra*

The Top / 1984 / Sire ✦✦
Where their previous albums were gloomy and depressing, *The Top* is downright scary in places. The opener, "Shake Dog Shake," doesn't sound too dissimilar to the songs found on *Pornography*, but the album quickly shifts gears from that point on, with rapid style and mood changes that go from manic to nightmarish near-psychedelia with disturbing themes and a swirl of odd sounds. Ultimately, *The Top* is the band's least consistent album and their most difficult listen, but it is an interesting study in paranoid chaos, and it provides a fascinating look at a band (and more specifically, leader Robert Smith) spinning out of control. —*Chris Woodstra*

Concert: Live / 1984 / Fiction ✦✦
A solid collection of the band's 1984 tour promoting *The Top*. Although the songs differ only slightly in their live form, this album works well as a "best of the early years" collection. —*Chris Woodstra*

The Head on the Door / 1985 / Elektra ✦✦✦✦
The Cure refocused and ultimately hit their stride with *Head on the Door*, producing an album that not only more effectively depicted gloom, but showed enough pop smarts to make it memorable (and even danceable). The band scored a hit with the infectious, New Order-ish "In Between Days" (which managed to beat New Order at their own game) and the highly memorable "Close to Me," but the album's outstanding trait is its diversity. They managed to combine a wide variety of influences, but incorporating rhythms from the Far East and South America to fine effect. The Cure made more accomplished albums later on and had bigger hits, but none combined artistic ambition with really catchy songs as well as *Head on the Door*. —*Chris Woodstra*

★ **Standing on a Beach: The Singles** / 1986 / Elektra ✦✦✦✦✦
Standing on a Beach: The Singles collects all of the Cure's biggest UK hits and best-known songs from the late '70s and early '80s. Spanning "Killing an Arab" and "Boys Don't Cry" to "The Lovecats," "In Between Days," and "Close to Me," *Standing on a Beach* captures some of the finest—and most influential—post-punk music. At their best, the Cure was nervy, intellectual, catchy, and foreboding, all at once. No matter how carefully crafted the Cure's individual albums were, their finest moments occurred on singles like these, when they distilled their essence into surprisingly catchy, but decidedly left-of-center, pop singles. *Standing on a Beach* not only selects highlights from their uneven early albums, it collects many of the group's terrific non-LP singles. It's a definitive retrospective of the Cure and is one of the finest albums of the '80s. (The compact disc version of *Standing on a Beach* was entitled *Staring at the Sea* and featured four songs that were not on the vinyl editon. The cassette version of *Standing on a Beach* included several B-sides.) —*Stephen Thomas Erlewine*

Kiss Me, Kiss Me, Kiss Me / 1987 / Elektra ✦✦✦
Simultaneously more accessible and ambitious than any of the Cure's previous albums, the double-album *Kiss Me, Kiss Me, Kiss Me* finds Robert Smith expanding his pop vocabulary by tentatively adding bigger guitars, the occasional horn section, lite-funk rhythms and string sections. It's eclectic, to be sure, but it's also a mess, bouncing from idea to idea and refusing to develop some of the most intriguing detours. Even if *Kiss Me* doesn't quite gel, its best moments—including the deceptively bouncy "Why Can't I Be You?" and the stately "Just Like Heaven"—are remarkable and help make the album one of the group's very best. —*Stephen Thomas Erlewine*

Disintegration / May 1989 / Elektra ✦✦✦✦
Expanding the latent arena-rock sensibilities that peppered *Kiss Me, Kiss Me, Kiss Me* by slowing them down and stretching them to the breaking point, the Cure reached the peak of their popularity with the crawling, darkly seductive *Disintegration*. It's a hypnotic, mesmerizing record, comprised nearly entirely of epics like the soaring, icy "Pictures of You. The handful of pop songs, like the concise and utterly charming "Love Song," don't alleviate the doomy atmosphere. The Cure's gloomy soundscapes have rarely sounded so alluring, however, and the songs—from the pulsating, ominous "Fascination Street" to the eerie, string-laced "Lullaby"—have rarely been so well-constructed and memorable. It's fitting that *Disintegration* was their commercial breakthrough, since, in many ways, the album is the culmination of all the musical directions the Cure was pursuing over the course of the '80s. —*Stephen Thomas Erlewine*

Mixed Up / Oct. 19, 1990 / Elektra ✦✦
An assortment of remixes, re-recordings, old singles, and one new song ("Never Enough"). Most of the remixes are quite radical, leaving only the bare bones of the original song. There are enough oddities and rare tracks on *Mixed Up* to make it necessary for Cure fans, but it's too specialized for casual listeners. —*Stephen Thomas Erlewine*

Wish / Apr. 21, 1992 / Elektra ✦✦✦
On the surface, *Wish* sounds happier than *Disintegration*, and the sunny British Invasion hooks of the hit single "Friday I'm in Love" certainly seem to indicate that the record is a brighter affair than its predecessor. Dig a little deeper, and the album reveals itself to be just as tortured, and perhaps more despairing than its predecessor. Granted, the sound of the record, with its jangling guitars and simple arrangements, is more immediately accessible than the epic gloom of *Disintergration*, but nearly every song finds Robert Smith wracked with depression. Unfortunately, the even-handed production makes the record sound very similar, so it is less compelling than it might have been, but there are a handful of gems ("High," "A Letter to Elise," "Wendy Time," "Friday I'm in Love") that make the record worthwhile. —*Stephen Thomas Erlewine*

Paris / Oct. 26, 1993 / Elektra ✦✦
Show featured mostly hit singles; *Paris* features the songs that built their cult, including "Close to Me" and "Letter to Elise." Consequently, most fans will find this the more interesting of the two live albums, and, out of the two records, it is the more consistent and satisfying. —*Stephen Thomas Erlewine*

Show / Nov. 23, 1993 / Elektra ✦✦
Concentrating on their recent, pop-oriented material, *Show* is a good, if unspectacular, representation of the Cure in concert. Only devoted fans need to own this album. —*Stephen Thomas Erlewine*

Wild Mood Swings / May 21, 1996 / Fiction/Elektra ✦✦✦
After the relatively straightforward pop of *Wish*, the Cure moved back toward stranger, edgier territory with *Wild Mood Swings*. Actually, that's only part of the truth. As the title suggests, there's a vast array of textures and emotions on *Wild Mood Swings*, from the woozy mariachi lounge horns of "The 13th" to the perfect pop of "Mint Car" and the monolithic dirge of "Want." In between the extremes, Robert Smith and the Cure—which now features a radically reworked lineup, with several key players from *Wish* now missing—explore some simpler territory, from contemplative acoustic numbers tinged with strings to swooning neo-psychedelia. But what ties it all together is conviction. Smith sounds more content than he ever has, but he sings with more passion than he has for a number of years. Of course, the Cure hasn't significantly changed the sound—tinny synthesizers and guitar effects that haven't appeared on an album since 1988 are in abundance throughout the record—but the variety of sounds and strength of performance offer enough surprises to make *Wild Mood Swings* more than just another Cure record. —*Stephen Thomas Erlewine*

Curve

f. 1991, London, England, **db.** Jul. 1994
Alternative Pop-Rock, Shoegazing, Dream-Pop
Considering Curve's towering monolith of guitar noise, dance tracks, dark goth, and airy melodies, it's strange that the two core members—guitarist Dean Garcia and vocalist Toni Halliday—met through David Stewart of Eurythmics. Halliday met Stewart while she was a teenager, and they remained friends for years; Garcia played on Eurythmics' *Touch* and *Be Yourself Tonight*. Garcia and Halliday played together in State of Play, which released one album and two singles in the late '80s to little notice.

After the failure of that band, they parted ways, only to reunite in the beginning of the '90s. Renaming themselves Curve, Halliday and Garcia released three EPs that became independent hits in 1991. Although they were critically acclaimed as well, some members of the UK press attacked Halliday for not being a genuine member of the indie scene. Despite the negative press, their next EP and first album, 1992's *Doppelganger*, hit No. 1 on the UK's indie charts. By the time of the following year's *Cuckoo*, Curve had added two guitarists and a drummer, with Garcia moving to the bass. *Cuckoo* was noisier and more experimental than their previous releases, although it did have a couple of pop songs that were tighter than their usual singles. However, the album didn't make as big a splash in the UK as previous releases had; Curve split several months after the album's release. —*Stephen Thomas Erlewine*

Pubic Fruit / 1992 / Anxious/Charisma ✦✦✦
Pubic Fruit collects Curve's early EPs, which were as ambitious as *Doppelganger* but not quite as well-constructed. Nevertheless, it's an engaging listen for fans of the group. —*Stephen Thomas Erlewine*

Doppelganger / Mar. 10, 1992 / Anxious/Charisma ✦✦✦✦
Doppelganger established Curve's thick, neo-psychedelic sound, complete with swirling distorted guitars and trance-like melodies from Toni Halliday. While some of the songs were slightly weak, their vision is strong throughout. —*Stephen Thomas Erlewine*

● **Cuckoo** / Sep. 21, 1993 / Anxious/Charisma ✦✦✦✦
On its second album, Curve expands its adventurous soundscapes, which are often unfairly pigeonholed as dream-pop. Curve has larger ambitions than shoegazing, as *Cuckoo* proves. With more varied textures and better songs than *Doppelganger*, *Cuckoo* shows that Curve is only beginning to hit its stride. —*Stephen Thomas Erlewine*

Cypress Hill

f. 1988, Los Angeles, CA
Hip Hop, West Coast Rap
Members of Cypress Hill were notable for being the first Latino hip-hop superstars, but they became notorious for their endorsement of marijuana, which actually isn't a trivial thing. Not only did the group campaign for its legalization, but its slow, rolling bass-and-drum loops pioneered a new, stoned funk that became extraordinarily influential in '90s hip-hop—it could be heard in everything from Dr. Dre's G-Funk to

the chilly layers of English trip-hop. DJ Muggs was responsible for the sound and B-Real, with his pinched nasal voice, was responsible for the rhetoric that made them famous. The pro-pot position became a little ridiculous toward the end of the band's career, but there was no denying that the actual music had a strange, eerie power, particularly on the band's first two albums. Although B-Real remained an effective lyricist, and Muggs' musical skills did not diminish, the group's last album, *Temples of Boom*, was perceived by many critics as self-parodic; the group disintegrated shortly afterward.

DVX, the original incarnation of Cypress Hill, formed in 1986 when Cuban-born brothers Sen Dog (b. Senen Reyes, November 20, 1965) and his brother Mellow Man Ace hooked up with fellow Los Angeles natives DJ Muggs (b. Lawrence Muggerud, January 28, 1968) and B-Real (b. Louis Freese, June 2, 1970). The group began pioneering a fusion of Latin and hip-hop slang, developing their own style by the time Mellow Man Ace left the group in 1988. Renaming themselves Cypress Hill after a local street, the group continued to perform around Los Angeles, eventually signing with Ruffhouse/Columbia in 1991.

With its stoned beats, B-Real's exaggerated nasal whine, and cartoonish violence, the group's eponymous debut became a sensation in early 1992, several months after its initial release. The singles "How I Could Just Kill a Man" and "The Phuncky Feel One" became underground hits, and the group's publicly pro-marijuana stance earned them many fans in the alternative rock community. Cypress Hill followed the album with *Black Sunday* in the summer of 1993, and while it sounded remarkably similar to the debut, it nevertheless became a hit, entering the album charts at No. 1 and spawning the crossover hit "Insane in the Brain." With *Black Sunday*, Cypress Hill's audience became predominately white, collegiate suburbanites, which caused them to lose some support in the hip-hop community. The group didn't help matters much in 1995 when they toured with the fifth Lollapalooza before the release of their third album, *Temples of Boom*. A darker, gloomier affair than their first two records, *Temples of Boom* was greeted with mixed reviews, and while it initially sold well, it failed to generate a genuine hit single. However, it did perform better on the R&B charts than on the pop charts.

Instead of capitalizing on their regained hip-hop credibility, Cypress Hill slowly fell apart. Sen Dog left in early 1996, and Muggs spent most of the year working on his solo album. *DJ Muggs Presents the Soul Assassins* was released to overwhelmingly positive reviews in early 1997, leaving Cypress Hill's future in much doubt. —*Stephen Thomas Erlewine*

★ **Cypress Hill** / Aug. 13, 1991 / Ruffhouse ✦✦✦✦✦
Asked what the main differences between East Coast and West Coast rap are, many MCs will generalize that while Eastern rappers are primarily concerned with rhyming technique, the West's strength is its beats and lyrics. With this self-titled debut album, Los Angeles' Cypress Hill successfully combined West Coast gangster-rap themes with the type of complex, abstract rapping associated with New York and Philadelphia. While "How I Could Just Kill a Man," "Hole in the Head" and other disturbing accounts of urban crime and gang violence were lyrically inspired by L.A.'s pervasive problems, it's quite clear that the Angelinos were paying close attention to the abstract rapping of the East. As captivating as this CD's East-meets-West flavor is, it's hard to defend the type of drug use promoted and glamorized on such odes to marijuana abuse as "Something for the Blunted" and "Stoned Is the Way of the Walk." Before 1991, numerous rappers had gone out of their way to discourage drug use, but with Cypress' ascension, it became fashionable in rap circles to promote drugs. —*Alex Henderson*

Black Sunday / Jul. 27, 1993 / Columbia ✦✦✦✦
It doesn't matter that *Black Sunday* follows the same formula as *Cypress Hill*, because it does so in such an intoxicating, convincing manner. Bolstered by the splendid singles "We Ain't Goin' Out Like That," "When the Sh— Goes Down," and "Insane in the Brain," *Black Sunday* is a surreal, stoned vision of contemporary hip-hop culture that is as funny as it is frightening. —*Stephen Thomas Erlewine*

Cypress Hill III (Temple of Boom) / Oct. 31, 1995 / Ruffhouse/Columbia ✦✦✦
A dark, paranoid album that wallows in its own bottomless grooves, *Temples of Boom* is filled with interesting sonic textures, but very few compelling songs. Occasionally, Muggs tries to limit his soundscapes to the traditional Cypress Hill sound, but his contributions at least show imagination, which isn't the case with B-Real and Sen Dog's predictable rhymes about pot, crime and parties. The sonic textures make it worthwhile for hardcore fans, but it's hard to sustain attention over the course of the record. —*Stephen Thomas Erlewine*

Unreleased & Revamped / Aug. 1996 / Sony ✦✦
On *Cypress Hill III: Temple of Boom*, Cypress Hill sounded a little tired, clinging to their slow, druggy beat a bit too much. The *Unreleased & Revamped* EP was released a few months after the album,

which signals that the EP is an attempt to salvage their reputation. That suspicion is confirmed by the list of remixers and collaborators. None of the guests—from the Fugees and A Tribe Called Quest to Redman, MC Eiht and Erick Sermon—is a traditional West Coast rapper; they are musicians who are pushing the boundaries of hip-hop in 1996. In another attempt to restore their street credibility, Cypress Hill has distanced themselves from the alternative rock audience they cultivated through an appearance at Lollapalooza and with *Temples of Boom*. So, the group has clearly tried to make a break from its trademark sound, and the attempt is marginally successful. "Boom Biddy Bye Bye," which features a remix from the Fugees, is particularly successful, but most of the EP contains the germs of an idea, not the fruition of one. Still, the EP is encouraging to long-term fans who may have thought that Cypress Hill had lost the plot with *Temples of Boom*. *Unreleased & Revamped* suggests they are about to get back on track. —*Stephen Thomas Erlewine*

Cyrkle

f. 1966, Easton, PA, **db.** 1967
Pop-Rock

The Cyrkle's biggest hit, 1966's "Red Rubber Ball," was co-written by Bruce Woodley, a member of the Seekers, and Paul Simon. With Tom Dawes and Don Dannemann as lead vocalists, the folk-tinged group managed by Beatles manager Brian Epstein came together at a Pennsylvania college and signed with Columbia. After "Red Rubber Ball" bounced up the charts, the group encored with "Turn-Down Day." They made their last pop-chart appearance in late 1967. —*Bill Dahl*

● **Red Rubber Ball (A Collection)** / 1966 / Columbia ✦✦✦✦
Basically a two-hit wonder of the mid-'60s ("Red Rubber Ball," "Turn-Down Day"), the Cyrkle had Beatles and Paul Simon connections and were themselves fine examples of lightweight folkie pop. Everything of note they ever did is on this album. —*Jeff Tamarkin*

D

Terence Trent D'Arby

b. Mar. 15, 1962, New York, NY
Guitar, Drums, Keyboards, Saxophone, Vocals / Soul, Urban, Pop-Rock
Terence Trent D'Arby emerged in 1987 amid a storm of publicity. Claiming his debut record was the best since *Sgt. Pepper*, his brash arrogance captured headlines throughout the UK, eventually winding their way back to America—which, ironically, is the exact opposite of how D'Arby conducted his career.

During the early '80s, Terence Trent D'Arby was a soldier for the United States Army. While posted in Germany, he joined a funk band called Touch, that marked the beginning of his musical career. After leaving the Army, he moved to London, where he recorded the demo tape that led to his record contract with CBS. D'Arby's first single, "If You Let Me Stay," rocketed into the UK Top Ten upon its release. Its accompanying album, *Introducing the Hardline According to Terence Trent D'Arby*, was also a massive success, hitting No. 1 and spending over a year in the top half of the chart.

D'Arby didn't have a major hit in the US until 1988, when the sparse funk of "Wishing Well" hit No. 1. The ballad "Sign Your Name" followed it into the Top Five, and *Introducing* ended up selling over two million copies.

All of the success—both commercial and critical—had D'Arby poised as a major act, artistically and popularly. D'Arby's mix of soul, rock, pop, and R&B recalled Prince in its scope and sound, but his sensibility was grittier and earthier. At least they were at first. By the time of his second album, 1989's *Neither Fish nor Flesh*, his ambitions were more nakedly pretentious. The record carried the weighty subtitle "A Soundtrack of Love, Faith, Hope & Destruction" and attacked many self-consciously important themes, including homosexuality and environmental destruction. In addition to the self-import of the lyrics, the music added a variety of new textures, from Indian drones to straightahead '50s R&B.

All of the added baggage was too much for his audience, and *Neither Fish nor Flesh* dropped off the charts quickly, without so much as one hit single. It took D'Arby a full four years to record a new album. When *Terence Trent D'Arby's Symphony or Damn*—an album containing many of the same ideas as *Neither Fish nor Flesh*, only better executed—was released in 1993, it received favorable reviews, as well as some airplay on modern rock radio stations and MTV. It was enough for D'Arby to regain some credibility, but it wasn't enough to make the album a hit. Two years later, he released *TTD's Vibrator*, which met the same fate as *Symphony or Damn*. —*Stephen Thomas Erlewine*

Introducing the Hardline According to Terence Trent D'Arby / 1987 / Columbia ◆◆◆◆
Introducing the Hardline According to Terence Trent D'Arby is a strong debut by this young, cocky Black British singer, who wrote virtually every note, played a multitude of instruments, and claimed that his was the most important album since the Beatles' *Sgt. Pepper*. Hits included "If You Let Me Stay," "Dance Little Sister," "Sign Your Name," and the No. 1 "Wishing Well." His first album is a curious mixture of old and new styles. Although the production is quite modern, D'Arby shows his roots in the work of older artists, borrowing a page or two from Michael Jackson and Stevie Wonder, while James Brown appears to have had the strongest influence on D'Arby's stage presence. —*Rob Bowman*

Neither Fish nor Flesh / Oct. 1989 / Columbia ◆◆◆
D'Arby's sophomore effort was considered a disappointment by most. More experimental than the first, it was also less focused. If possible, his ego seemed to have grown even larger with D'Arby taking up to ten playing credits on any given track. —*Rob Bowman*

● **Terence Trent D'Arby's Symphony or Damn** / May 11, 1993 / Columbia ◆◆◆◆
Falling halfway between the modern R&B of *Introducing the Hardline* and the extravagant *Neither Fish nor Flesh*, *Symphony or Damn* is Terence Trent D'Arby's most ambitious album yet. It's also his best, because it takes the fine songwriting of his debut and melds it to the sonic excesses of *Fish*. Sure, some of it is embarrassing (it's hard not to cringe during the "Welcome to My Monasteryo" declaration at the beginning of the album), but more often than not, D'Arby's experimentations succeed, and succeed grandly, at that. —*Stephen Thomas Erlewine*

TTD's Vibrator / Jun. 1, 1995 / Work ◆◆◆
Symphony or Damn was an impressive comeback for Terence Trent D'arby, pulling together the melodic songcraft of his debut and the conceptual ambitions of *Neither Fish nor Flesh*. *TTD's Vibrator* follows the same pattern of *Symphony or Damn*, only without the songs to support the ambitions. —*Stephen Thomas Erlewine*

Daft Punk

f. 1992, Paris, France
House, Club/Dance, Electronica
In similar company with new-school French progressive dance artists such as Motorbass, Air, and DJ Dmitri, the Parisian duo Daft Punk (DJs Guy-Manuel De Homem-Christo and Thomas Bangalter) has quickly risen to acclaim by adapting a love for first-wave acid house and techno to their younger roots in pop, indie rock, and hip-hop. The pair's first projects together included Darling, a voiceless indie cover band; their current recording name derives from a review in UK music weekly *Melody Maker* of a compilation tape on which Darling was featured, released by krautrock revivalists Stereolab. (Their lo-fi DIY cover of a Beach Boys song was derided as "daft punk.") Subsequently ditching the almost inevitable creative cul-de-sac of rock for the more appealing rush of the dance floor, the pair released their debut single, "The New Wave," in 1993 on the celebrated Soma label. Instantly hailed by the dance music press as the work of a new breed of house innovators, the single was followed by "Da Funk," the band's first true hit; the record has sold 30,000 copies worldwide and seen thorough rinsings by everyone from Kris Needs to the Chemical Brothers.

Although the group had released only a trio of singles ("The New Wave" and "Da Funk," as well as the 1996 limited pressing of "Musique"), in early 1996 Daft Punk was the subject of a minor bidding war. The group eventually signed with Virgin, with their first long-player, *Home Work*, appearing early the following year. A brief preview of the album, "Musique," was also featured on the Virgin compilation *Wipeout 2097* next to tracks from Photek, Future Sound of London, the Chemical Brothers, and Source Direct. As with the earlier singles, the group's sound is a brazen, dance floor-oriented blend of progressive house, funk, electro, and techno, with sprinklings of hip-hop-styled breakbeats and excessive, crowd-firing samples, similar to other anthemic dance-fusion acts such as the Chemical Brothers and Monkey Mafia. In addition to his role in Daft Punk, Thomas Bangalter operates the Roule label and records under his own name. (His Touche single "Trax on Da Rocks" was an underground smash). —*Sean Cooper*

● **Homework** / Mar. 25, 1997 / Virgin ◆◆◆◆
Daft Punk's full-length debut is a funk-house hailstorm, giving real form to a style of straightahead dance music not attempted since the early fusion days of on-the-one funk and dance-party disco. Thick, rumbling bass, vocoders, choppy breaks and beats, and a certain brash naivete permeate the record from start to finish, giving it the edge of an almost certain classic. While a few fall flat, the best tracks make this one essential. —*Sean Cooper*

The Daily Flash

f. 1967, Seattle, WA, **db.** 1968

Psychedelic, Folk-Rock

More than any other Seattle group of the '60s, the Daily Flash assimilated the folk-rock and psychedelic sounds of the day into a sound that was both forward-looking and commercial. Specializing in electric rearrangements of contemporary folk songs that emphasized their harmonies and 12-string guitar, the Flash was also capable of psychedelic rock, as on "Jack of Diamonds," which featured blistering feedback guitar. They cut a couple of regional singles and appeared with many of the leading psychedelic groups of the day in California, but never managed to launch their own career, or even record an album. They broke up in early 1968; guitarist Doug Hastings played briefly with Buffalo Springfield and was a member of Rhinoceros. — *Richie Unterberger*

I Flash Daily / 1985 / Psycho ✦✦✦

An archival reissue that patches together an entire album by presenting both sides of their two singles with three previously unreleased studio recordings and a couple of lengthy live songs. As interpreters, the Flash showed a great deal of skill, adapting compositions by Eric Andersen, Dylan, Ian Tyson, and Fred Neil to full-blown folk-rock arrangements with a touch of baroque pop. As songwriters, their capabilities were undemonstrated; only one of the seven studio recordings on side one is a group original. ("Jack of Diamonds" and Fred Neil's "Green Rocky Road" are erroneously credited to the band.) Side two is a bit of a waste, with a live 1967 cover of Herbie Hancock's "Canteloupe Island" and an okay live 1966 rendition of Dylan's "Queen Jane Approximately" (which they had covered on their first single). — *Richie Unterberger*

Dick Dale

b. May 4, 1937, Boston, MA

Surf

The father of surf music, guitarist Dick Dale to a great degree invented and defined the form in the early '60s with his pioneering use of Fender reverb, dazzling staccato playing, and thundering instrumentals that incorporated Middle Eastern and Latin melodic influences. Playing guitars strung for right-handers with his left hand (as Hendrix would years later), he had an agreement with Fender instruments to "road test" new amplification equipment before it was manufactured for the general public, and found that its hollow, sustained tones evoked the mood of surfing, then catching on in a big way in his Southern California stomping grounds. Dale's impact was largely limited to Southern California, but his influence was vast, helping ignite surf music and contributing several of the genre's most enduring classics, especially "Let's Go Trippin'" and "Miserlou" (both of which were covered by the Beach Boys on their early albums). In the 1990s, Dale made an unexpectedly successful comeback with newly recorded material that closely echoed his vintage sides. — *Richie Unterberger*

★ **King of the Surf Guitar: The Best of Dick Dale** / Aug. 4, 1989 / Rhino ✦✦✦✦✦

King of the Surf Guitar: Best of Dick Dale is the definitive compilation of the father of surf-rock, containing 18 of his best-known songs, including all of his biggest hits ("Miserlou," "Let's Go Trippin'," "The Scavenger"), all presented in their original versions and in excellent audio. In addition to showcasing the roots of surf, *King of the Surf Guitar* demonstrates what a skilled and eclectic guitarist Dale was. Dale was one of the first guitarists in rock 'n' roll to rely on studio and guitar effects and fuse elements of world musics to his sound, and every one of his experiments is captured on this disc. It's a definitive retrospective. — *Stephen Thomas Erlewine*

The Damned

f. 1976, England, **db.** 1989

Punk, Goth-Rock

The Damned usurped the Sex Pistols, working behind their backs to become the first British punk band to release a record, and the first to have a hit single (the epochal "New Rose") and the first to tour America. That, in a nut shell, is the appeal of the Damned. They weren't revolutionaries; they were drunken louts who would do anything for a prank. Like many of their first-generation punk peers, the band was rooted in pub-rock, playing simple three-chord pounders, but the group played fast, loose, and sloppy, often sounding as if everything was about to fall apart. Their 1977 debut *Damned Damned Damned* epitomized this sound, and they never quite captured it again, partially because of their limited talent and partially because of their defiant, boundless stupidity. After the debut, the Damned released a pair of similar records that weren't quite as successful, before delving into a bizarre affair with goth-rock for several years in the early '80s. By the time that was worked out of their system, several key members had left the band; and the group had nothing more than a cult following, but they still managed the odd hit single in the UK until the late '80s, when the Damned decided to call it a day. But

that wasn't the end of the story. During the '90s, the band continually reunited in various incarnations, playing concerts across England and functioning as a sort of bizarre punk nostalgia act.

Of course at the beginning of their career, it would have been unthinkable to consider the Damned a band with a long future. Like many British punks, the group's members had played in a variety of pub-rock and fledgling punk bands, most notably Brian James (b. Brian Robertson, guitar), who had played in London S.S. with Mick Jones, Paul Simonon, and Terry Chimes, all of whom would later form the Clash. In its last days, London S.S. also featured Rat Scabies (b. Chrill Miller, drums), and once the group disbanded, he and James went on to join *NME* journalist Nick Kent's Subterraneans, which also featured Captain Sensible (b. Ray Burns, bass). After the Subterraneans fell apart, James, Scabies, and the Captain formed the Masters of the Backside with vocalist Chrissie Hynde. The group was managed by Malcolm McLaren, and it quickly imploded, with Hynde going on to form the Pretenders and McLaren leaving to manage the Sex Pistols. The remaining trio carried on, hiring vocalist Dave Vanian, a former gravedigger Scabies met at his sister's funeral, and becoming the Damned.

The Damned's rise to notoriety was quick and ridiculous. Performing their first concert in London in July 1976, the group quickly became a sensation due to its drunken, riotous performances which featured Scabies attacking the audience and Vanian dressed as a vampire. Within two months, the band signed with the fledgling Stiff Records and its accompanying management, and the match couldn't have been more perfect. The Damned and Stiff were both pranksters, determined to take a bad joke as far as it could go, and that sensibility made the group the first British punk band to release a record. By the fall of 1976, the Sex Pistols had captured the attention of Britain's rock audience, but they had yet to release a record due to various problems with labels. Stiff decided to steal the Pistols' thunder by rushing the Damned into the studio to record their debut single, "New Rose," with producer Nick Lowe as quickly as possible. "New Rose" appeared in October, a full month before "Anarchy in the UK," and while it didn't chart, it was a huge underground hit, leading Stiff towards a distribution deal with Island. The single also began a rivalry with the Sex Pistols that peaked when the Damned were thrown off the supporting slot for the Pistols' ill-fated "Anarchy in the UK" tour in December of 1976 after the first gig. Undaunted, Stiff booked the band for several concerts in New York, Los Angeles, and San Francisco in early 1977, making the Damned the first UK punk band to play the US. In the spring of 1977, the band's Lowe-produced debut, *Damned Damned Damned*, was released, again beating all other British punks to the punch.

Damned Damned Damned was well received and the pulled single, "Neat Neat Neat"/"Stab Your Back," reached the Top 40. The Damned was riding at the crest of popularity when things began to go wrong in the summer of 1977. James insisted that the band add a second guitarist, so Lu (b. Robert Edmunds) joined just before the band entered the studios with the legendary British Invasion producer Shel Talmy to record their second album. Talmy didn't work out, so the group hired Pink Floyd's Nick Mason to helm *Music for Pleasure*. Upon its release in November, the album was received quite poorly, and Scabies left the band to work with guitarist Keith Levene and keyboardist Richard Sohl. John Moss replaced him for the subsequent British tour, but by the spring the Damned had broken up. Captain Sensible formed King and James formed Tanz Der Youth, while Moss and Lu joined a group called the Edge; Moss would later join Culture Club. By the end of 1978, Scabies, Sensible, and Vanian had reunited, adding King bassist Henry Badowski, initially playing under the name Les Punks and then the Doomed because James retained the rights to the Damned name. Early in 1979 they regained their original name and added former Saint Alistair Ward as bassist, signing to Chiswick Records. "Love Song" and "Smash It Up" became Top 40 hits later that year, and the accompanying album, *Machine Gun Etiquette*, was greeted warmly.

In 1980 Ward was replaced by Paul Gray, the former bassist for Eddie & the Hot Rods, and the group recorded the goth-tinged *The Black Album*, which became their first album released in America. As the Damned attempted to expand their sound, they added keyboardist Roman Jugg, who was featured on 1982's *Strawberries*, an unsuccessful record for Bronze Records. That same year Captain Sensible released a solo album, *Women and Captains First*, which featured the new wave novelty "Wot," a Top 40 hit. Gray left in 1983, and the next year the Captain had a Top Ten solo hit with "Glad It's All Over," leading him to leave the group that summer for a solo career. Replacing Grey with Bryn Merrick, the Damned signed to MCA and released the full-fledged goth album *Phantasmagoria*, which entered the UK charts at No. 11. The next year, the non-LP single "Eloise," a cover of Barry Ryan's 1968 hit, became the biggest single of the group's career, and the band released *Anything* at the end of the year. In 1987 the double-disc compilation *The Light at the End of the Tunnel* appeared.

Although the Damned had a surprising number of Top 40 hits between 1985 and 1987, their audience steadily declined, and in 1989 they decided to split after a farewell tour of the UK. Two years later the group reunited for a British tour, the first of several reunion tours occurring sporadically over the course of the '90s. — *Stephen Thomas Erlewine*

★ **Damned Damned Damned** / Apr. 16, 1977 / Frontier ✦✦✦✦✦
With its raw, stripped-down production and primal three-chord bashing, the Damned's debut was a landmark punk album. It never deviated from the sound of "New Rose," but that didn't matter—with its simplistic approach and relentless energy, *Damned Damned Damned* defined an era. — *Stephen Thomas Erlewine*

Music for Pleasure / Nov. 1977 / Demon ✦✦
Quickly dismissed by critics at the time as a shocking misstep, *Music for Pleasure* is not quite as bad as the Nick Mason (Pink Floyd) production would indicate—though close. Its failure led to Stiff Records' dropping them and to the first of many temporary breakups. — *Chris Woodstra*

Machine Gun Etiquette / Dec. 1979 / Roadrunner ✦✦✦✦
A newly re-formed version of the Damned (with a new lineup) makes a surprising return to form with 1979's *Machine Gun Etiquette*, a psychedelic-tinged punk masterpiece. With the punk anthem "Smash It Up" and the UK hits "Love Song" and "I Just Can't Be Happy Today," the band proves that it hasn't given up the fight yet. — *Chris Woodstra*

Black Album / Dec. 1980 / Chiswick ✦✦✦
The band's most accomplished and mainstream effort (at least attempt) to date, this sprawling double album obviously takes its inspiration from the Beatles' *White Album* for its title and attempts at stylistic diversity—ranging from power-pop to a bloated quasi-concept side to raw rock 'n' roll. Unfortunately, despite several gems, the end result is a fairly inaccessible album. It was released as an edited single LP in America but was virtually overlooked. — *Chris Woodstra*

The Best of the Damned / 1981 / Roadrunner ✦✦✦✦
Rock 'n' roll doesn't get much more recklessly fun than the early recordings of the Damned, one of the bands that (along with the Sex Pistols, the Clash, and Sham 69) helped to define early British punk rock. While the late-'70s gems *Damned Damned Damned*, *Music for Pleasure*, and *Machine Gun Etiquette* are all well worth acquiring, *The Best of the Damned* can serve as a fine introduction to the band's early years. In fact, such hard-hitting, freewheeling classics as "New Rose," "Smash It Up," "I Just Can't Be Happy Today," "Love Song," and the outrageous "Jet Boy, Jet Girl" are essential listening for anyone with even a casual interest in the punk movement. Characterized by their rawness, these classics are considerably different from the more polished and produced gothic material the Damned would record in the 1980s—which ranged from inspired to forgettable. If listeners can own only one Damned CD, this is it. — *Alex Henderson*

Live at Shepperton / 1982 / Ace ✦✦
While unnecessary, this live show from 1980 does an adequate job of capturing the band, flaws and all. Most of the favorites from the period are covered, though (not surprisingly) no new light is shed on them. — *Chris Woodstra*

Strawberries / 1982 / Bronze ✦✦✦
A more cohesive album, *Strawberries* finally achieves the pop sound and diversity they were looking for on *The Black Album*. Easily their finest moment since leaving punk behind. The band seems comfortable (and unexpectedly competent) stretching out, with strings and horns embellishing the arrangements. — *Chris Woodstra*

Phantasmagoria / 1985 / Off Beat ✦✦✦
Now essentially Dave Vanian's vehicle, the Damned make an attempt to jump on the goth-rock bandwagon. Unfortunately for the band, they end up sounding like a poorly executed parody of the genre more than anything else. Only on "Grimly Fiendish," which is pleasantly reminiscent of Madness, and "Is It a Dream" does the band make a lasting impression with better-than-average Brit-pop. — *Chris Woodstra*

Anything / 1986 / MCA ✦
They didn't learn their lesson on *Phantasmagoria*, and made another, even less successful try at the goth-rock arena. A cover of Love's "Alone Again Or" is the album's sole saving grace. — *Chris Woodstra*

The Light at the End of the Tunnel / 1987 / MCA ✦✦✦✦
While it would have been much more effective if sequenced chronologically, *The Light at the End of the Tunnel* is a fine compilation of the Damned's long and surprisingly varied career. — *Stephen Thomas Erlewine*

Final Damnation / 1989 / Restless ✦✦
The Damned was almost eight years past its prime by the time *Final Damnation* was recorded live in London in 1988. The once-great band had been highly erratic during the '80s, and one had no idea whether a Damned offering would be exciting or miss the mark entirely. Thankfully, the Damned was in decent form at the reunion concert documented here. Tearing into such punk classics as "New Rose," "Love Song," "Smash It Up" and "I Just Can't Be Happy Today," the rockers

sound fairly inspired and keep the audience on its toes. These versions aren't in a class with the originals, but even so, hearing them revisited with this much spirit and enthusiasm is nothing to complain about. — *Alex Henderson*

Chaos Years / Mar. 18, 1997 / Cleopatra ✦✦
The Chaos Years is a 12-track compilation of rarities and unreleased cuts the Damned recorded between 1977 and 1982, designed to appeal to hardcore Damned collectors. However, even diehard fans may find the preponderance of live cuts dismaying, and demos of songs like "I Just Can't Be Happy Today" and "Love Song" offer no significant insight. *The Chaos Years* appeals only to completists, and not even to archivists. — *Stephen Thomas Erlewine*

Dantalian's Chariot

f. 1967, London, England, db. 1968
Psychedelic
One of the most brilliant, obscure, psychedelic singles of the late '60s—indeed, one of the most brilliant, obscure, rock singles of any kind from the era—was Dantalian's Chariot's "Madman Running Through the Fields." This 1967 effort was British pop-psych at its zenith, strongly reminiscent of (and as good as) the classic early sides by Syd Barrett's Pink Floyd. What made it all the stranger was that it was the debut single by a group of veteran musicians who, just a few months earlier, had been playing jazz/R&B fusion as Zoot Money's Big Roll Band. Money, a journeyman keyboard player and singer, had made a few records without getting anything close to a hit; his band featured a young Andy Somers, more than a decade before the guitarist would reach stardom with the Police (as Andy Summers).

Such was the impact of psychedelic music in 1967, however, that by the middle of the year, Money had decided to totally revamp his sound. R&B/jazz/soul had become passe; now it was important to write your own material, and reflect the mind-expanding experience. With Somers still in tow, Zoot Money's Big Roll Band became Dantalian's Chariot. The music, written primarily by Money and Somers, changed as radically as the name, with airy melodies, spacey lyrics, and guitar/organ-driven arrangements. The band hit the London underground circuit inhabited by such acts as Pink Floyd and Soft Machine, and made their debut recording as Dantalian's Chariot ("Madman") in the summer of 1967.

The single, innovative as it was, didn't make any commercial waves. Although they were a respected live act, their new direction wasn't supported by EMI, which dropped the band. A psychedelic-minded LP was worked on, but not released. Some of the material appeared on an early 1968 record, which the Direction label assembled from various tunes cut over the past year. The fact that the album was credited to Zoot Money and the Big Roll Band, rather than Dantalian's Chariot, was an indication that their psychedelic direction, again, would not find support on the industry level.

All of this was not as great a tragedy as it might appear. A collection of psychedelic-oriented Dantalian's Chariot tracks (several previously unreleased) did emerge in 1996, and while it shows them to be an interesting outfit, nothing comes close to the magnificence of "Madman Running Through the Fields." Dantalian's Chariot came to an end in the spring of 1968, with Somers joining the Soft Machine (and subsequently Eric Burdon's Animals); Money would also join Eric Burdon's Animals around the same time. Drummer Colin Allen went on to chalk up stints in John Mayall's band. — *Richie Unterberger*

Chariot Rising / 1996 / Wooden Hill ✦✦✦
A close facsimile of what Dantalian's Chariot's unreleased album would have sounded like, taken from ten tracks recorded in 1967, several of which were previously unissued. "Madman Running Through the Fields" is essential listening for anyone who likes Pink Floyd, with its happy-go-mad lyrics, astral organ, Syd Barrett-esque guitar, and sudden quiet breaks into pastoral flute passages. Nothing else here is nearly as striking, but it's decent, somewhat prototypical early underground British psychedelia, though the songwriting can be kind of forced. The wistfully ebullient "Sun Came Bursting Through My Clouds" (the B-side of "Madman") is probably their best secondary effort; instrumentally-oriented explorations like "Soma" and "This Island" get freakier. — *Richie Unterberger*

Danzig

f. 1987, Los Angeles, CA
Hard Rock, Heavy Metal
During his time in the seminal hardcore band the Misfits, vocalist Glenn Danzig displayed a fascination with outlandish, graphic, often gory imagery. In forming the more heavy metal-oriented band Samhain, Danzig's lyrics delved into typical metal subject matter, but took the concept of darkness to an extreme. After the demise of Samhain, Danzig formed his own eponymous band with Samhain guitarist John Christ, ex-Misfits drummer Eerie Von on bass, and longtime hardcore drummer Chuck Biscuits (D.O.A., Black Flag, Circle Jerks); this band would prove a

more effective vehicle for Danzig's obsession with the dark side. While that obsession can seem cartoonish at times, there is more to the band than meets the eye . Danzig obviously relishes casting himself as the menacing, evil heavy metal frontman, and his theatricality often seems to indicate that his posturing is not meant to be taken very seriously. At the same time, the darkness of Danzig's vision has increasingly expressed itself over the band's career in a heavily romanticized, brooding, gothic sensibility, more quietly sinister and darkly seductive than obviously threatening or Satanic, and the group's music has progressed from simple, blues-based heavy metal riffs to more atmospheric, coldly haunting song textures that attempt to sonically replicate the feel of the lyrics.

Glenn Danzig cofounded the Misfits in Lodi, NJ, in 1977. When the hardcore band broke up in 1983, Danzig formed the metallic, brooding Samhain in order to experiment with different sounds, but that project imploded as well. The band Danzig was put together in 1987 and quickly inked a deal with Rick Rubin's Def American label. Their self-titled debut found Danzig playing the Satanic metal singer role to the hilt, even if the band's songs sounded much the same. *Danzig II Lucifuge* followed in 1990, and it broadened the band's musical palette, expanding on the simple blues riffs of the debut with more extensive forays into that style. *Danzig III How the Gods Kill* marked a full-fledged entry into the realm of gothic romanticism, working to create moods rather than pounding heavy-metal aggression; "Dirty Black Summer" and "How the Gods Kill" became staples on MTV's "Headbanger's Ball." Glenn Danzig next released a solo project, *Black Aria*, a quasi-operatic attempt at depicting the fall of Satan from heaven. The band broke through into the mainstream in 1993, when a live video for "Mother," a song originally released on *Danzig*, became an inescapable smash on MTV and even charted as a single, nearly cracking the *Billboard* Top 40. Meanwhile, Danzig contributed a track entitled "Thirteen" to Johnny Cash's acclaimed 1994 effort *American Recordings*. The more experimental *Danzig 4* was released in 1994 and entered the charts at No. 29, but its quiet, moody, atmospheric subtlety didn't find as much favor with the band's new audience as the anthemic "Mother"; some longtime fans dismissed it as mellow and therefore commercial. During the supporting tour, Chuck Biscuits left the band and was replaced by Joey Castillo. After the tour, Danzig broke up the band and formed a new version featuring ex-Prong guitarist/vocalist Tommy Victor, drummer Castillo, and bassist Josh Lazie; this lineup released *Danzig 5: Blackacidevil* on Halloween 1996. *Blackacidevil* was ignored by both the press and the public, falling out of the charts after a mere three weeks. — *Steve Huey*

Danzig / 1988 / Def American ✦✦✦
Danzig debuts with a record of simple, pounding, bluesy metal featuring lead singer Glenn Danzig's trademark Elvis-meets-Jim Morrison bellow and outlandishly dark, evil lyrics. There isn't a great deal of musical variety or complexity here, but the band powers its way through such signature tunes as "Twist of Cain," "Am I Demon," and the (future) hit "Mother" with a primal energy. Plus, Danzig's tongue-in-cheek posturing as the ultimate unholier-than-thou heavy metal frontman gives the record a definite appeal, even if one is not inclined to view his theatrics as dangerous or threatening. — *Steve Huey*

Danzig II: Lucifuge / Jun. 1990 / Def American ✦✦✦✦
Danzig's second release is also their most diversified. They explore their blues roots with a couple of boogies, a slow shuffle, and a slide number, throwing in a '50s-reminiscent ballad in waltz time for good measure. Glenn Danzig's theatrical vocals don't prevent these numbers from working surprisingly well (except when he attempts a Mississippi-delta accent on "Killer Wolf"), demonstrating his talents and range of expression as a vocalist. The simple, somewhat standard blues-metal riffs of their debut are here ("Snakes of Christ" is a flat-out rewrite of *Danzig's* "Twist of Cain"), but not as plentiful, making the record more interesting and listenable. "Her Black Wings" ranks with the band's best songs. — *Steve Huey*

● **Danzig III: How the Gods Kill** / Jul. 14, 1992 / Def American ✦✦✦✦
Featuring disturbing cover art from H.R. Giger, Danzig's third album continues to expand the band's musical range; rather than pounding away at simple blues riffs, the atmospheric title track (yet another rewrite of "Twist of Cain," this time at a slower tempo) and the haunting ballad "Sistinas" attempt to match their music with the darkness of Glenn Danzig's lyrics, resulting in two of the album's high points. Danzig's vocals are more subtle in places, and John Christ's guitar work continues to improve. Arguably the definitive Danzig album. — *Steve Huey*

Black Aria / 1993 / Plan 9/Caroline ✦✦
In an attempt to expand on the more atmospheric excursions of *How the Gods Kill*, Glenn Danzig composed this mostly instrumental work, which was heavily influenced by opera and classical music. While Danzig's willingness to experiment for a potentially rigid heavy metal audience is admirable, and while *Black Aria* does do a good job of evoking a

mood of melancholy darkness, it also doesn't make much of an impression, as Danzig largely neglected to compose melodies. — *Steve Huey*

Thrall: Demonsweatlive / May 25, 1993 / Def American ✦✦✦
Danzig's breakthrough EP features three new studio tracks (*Thrall*) and live performances of four of the band's most popular songs (*Demonsweatlive*). The live version of "Mother" was the hit, of course, but there are other worthwhile moments—the new tracks include "It's Coming Down," a threatening rocker, and a cover of Elvis Presley's "Trouble," and the live material is also highlighted by "Sistinas," one of the band's best songs. — *Steve Huey*

Danzig 4 / Dec. 1994 / American ✦✦✦
Danzig's experiments with using texture and atmosphere to evoke their trademark mood of darkness and evil come to the forefront on their fourth full-length album, with John Christ contributing more effects and fuller chord voicings. The band has also started to craft their songs, using different instruments and a few industrial sounds in the background of some tracks. Not all of the experiments are successful or interesting, partially due to inconsistent songwriting, but out of all their releases, the music here comes the closest to reflecting the darkness of Glenn Danzig's lyrics. Some, however, may miss their more energetic earlier albums. — *Steve Huey*

Blackacidevil / Oct. 29, 1996 / Hollywood ✦✦✦
Even though it was more metal-oriented than *4*, *Blackaciddevil* fell through the cracks upon its late 1996 release. Producer Bill Kennedy gives Danzig a harder, edgier sound than before, but the group has trouble coming up with hooks, which makes Glenn Danzig's standard demonic lyrics a little tedious to anyone but hardcore fans. — *Stephen Thomas Erlewine*

Bobby Darin

b. May 14, 1936, Bronx, NY, **d.** Dec. 20, 1973, Los Angeles, CA
Vocals / Pop, Folk-Rock, Pop-Rock, Brill Building Pop, Traditional Pop
There's been considerable discussion about whether Darin should be classified as a rock 'n' roll singer, a Vegas hipster cat, an interpreter of popular standards, or even a folk-rocker. He was all of these and none of these. Throughout his career he made a point of not becoming committed to any one style to the exclusion of others; at the height of his nightclub fame he incorporated a folk set into his act. When it appeared he could have gone on indefinitely as a sort of junior version of Frank Sinatra, he would periodically record pop-rock and folk-rock singles whose principal appeal lay outside of the adult pop market. At one point he started calling himself Bob Darin and recorded songs with vague anti-establishment overtones that could be said to be biting the largely bourgeois hands that fed his highest-paying gigs. It may be most accurate to say that Darin was, above all, a *singer* who wanted to do a lot of things, rather than make his mark as a particular stylist. That may have cost him some points as far as making it to the very top of certain genres, but it also makes his work more versatile than almost any other vocalist of his era.

When Darin had his first hits in the late '50s, he was a teen idol of sorts, albeit a teen idol with much more talent and mature command than the typical singer in that style. The novelty-tinged "Splish Splash" was his breakthrough smash, followed by "Queen of the Hop" and the ballad "Dream Lover." There was a slight R&B feel to Darin's delivery that may well have influenced R&B-pop-rock singers such as Dion, though it would be an exaggeration to call Darin a blue-eyed soul man. In late 1959 he found a new direction when the swinging "Mack the Knife," a tune from Brecht-Weill's *Threepenny Opera*, made No. 1. The song came from an album of pop standards, heralding his move toward light big band jazz, which was consolidated by the Top Ten success of "Beyond the Sea" in 1960.

In the early '60s, Darin had mostly abandoned rock for the adult pop market, becoming a huge success on the Vegas-nightclub circuit, and moving into the all-around entertainer mode with starring roles in movies (including one as a non-singing jazz musician in John Cassavetes' *Too Young Blues*). He also continued to score regular hits with the likes of "You Must Have Been a Beautiful Baby," "Things," and "Lazy River." To keep people guessing, there was also a hit cover of "What'd I Say" and some country tunes (one of which, "You're the Reason I'm Living," made No. 3 on the pop charts). Around 1963 he put a folk section into his nightclub act that employed guitarist Roger McGuinn, then a couple of years away from fame as the leader of the Byrds.

Darin didn't make the expected retreat into Rat Pack land when his records stopped making the upper reaches of the charts in the mid-'60s. In 1965 there was a rather nice self-penned jangly folk-rocker, "When I Get Home," that become a British hit for the Searchers. Another 1965 flop, "We Didn't Ask to Be Brought Here," was an unexpected anti-war tune. When he made his return to the Top Ten in late 1966, it was with a cover of a gentle Tim Hardin folk-rock song, "If I Were a Carpenter." His final Top 40 hit the next year, "Lovin' You," opted for material by another major folk-rock composer, John Sebastian.

Darin may indeed have been far more hip and politically aware than the average nightclub act, covering tunes by Dylan and the Rolling Stones, participating in a 1965 civil rights march to Alabama, and penning some Dylan-influenced songs of his own in the late '60s. It doesn't seem accurate to say that this was the true Bobby Darin, shedding his show-biz skin for something that came to him more naturally; in 1967, the same year he covered Jagger-Richards' "Back Street Girl," he also recorded material for an album entitled *Bobby Darin Sings Doctor Dolittle*. By the early '70s he was working Vegas and similar joints again, exchanging his blue jeans for a tuxedo, and hosting a TV variety series. In a much odder turn of events, he was now recording for Motown, although these efforts met little success.

Born with a rheumatic heart, Darin was always aware that his time might be limited, and he died near the end of 1973 during open-heart surgery. He left behind a considerable quantity (and diversity) of recorded work, and underwent a critical reevaluation of sorts, especially among rock critics, which might have aided his election to the Rock and Roll Hall of Fame in 1990. A 1996 four-CD box set, divided into thematic discs, attempted to put his wide-ranging efforts into perspective. —*Richie Unterberger*

● **The Ultimate Bobby Darin** / Jun. 1988 / Warner Brothers ✦✦✦✦
It offers a thorough look at Darin's rock and pop hits, including "Mack the Knife," "Dream Lover," "Splish Splash," and the breathtaking "Beyond the Sea." —*John Floyd*

Capitol Collectors Series / 1989 / Capitol ✦✦✦✦
A compilation of Darin's mid-'60s singles, which showcase Darin's diversity even if the majority of the set leans heavily on his pop material. Comprehensive liner notes, intelligent track selection, and great fidelity make this worth picking up. —*Stephen Thomas Erlewine*

Splish Splash / Nov. 12, 1991 / Atco ✦✦✦✦
The first installment of a definitive two-volume Bobby Darin retrospective, *Splish Splash* concentrates on his earlier hits, including "Dream Lover," "Baby Face," "You Must Have Been a Beautiful Baby," "Multiplication," and the title track. —*Stephen Thomas Erlewine*

Mack the Knife / 1991 / Atco ✦✦✦✦
Darin's later hits, including "Mack the Knife," "Beyond the Sea," "Guys and Dolls," "Black Coffee," and "Artificial Flowers," are collected on this second volume of Atco's fine two-part retrospective. —*Stephen Thomas Erlewine*

Spotlight On . . . Bobby Darin / 1995 / Capitol ✦✦✦
If you've a yen for the most pop-oriented area of Darin's repertoire, head for this disc, which presents 20 of his most mainstream Capitol outings from 1962 to 1965. Devoted to pop standards, over half of the tracks feature orchestras working under conductor Billy May. It also has a bit more collector appeal than the typical volume of Capitol's *Spotlight* series in that it contains six previously unreleased tracks, including versions of "Alabamy Bound," "I Got Rhythm," "I'm Sitting on Top of the World," and "All of You." —*Richie Unterberger*

As Long as I'm Singing: The Bobby Darin Collection / Nov. 21, 1995 / Rhino ✦✦✦✦
A four-CD box set spanning several styles, labels, and eras, this will stand as the most thorough retrospective of Darin's eclectic career. Thorough, however, doesn't necessarily mean the best. There's a lot of material here—96 songs, including not only the hits, but obscure flops, B-sides, album cuts, and 11 previously unreleased tracks. Too much material, really, if you're not a committed fan. Because Darin covered a lot of different genres, it's not programmed chronologically, but by style—one disc for "The Rock 'n' Roll Years" (which, truth be told, were often closer to pop than rock), two to his pop sides, and one to his folk and country outings. In hindsight (and in the enclosed 64-page book), much has been made of Darin's versatility. But while it's true he could handle a range of genres competently, versatility does not automatically equate with quality. Just as a baseball player who can play all the positions is not necessarily a great player, Darin's unusual eclecticism did not mean that he was as great a singer as some who concentrated only on rock, or only on pop, or only on folk. There are some neat surprises here—the mid-'60s protest folk-rock of "We Didn't Ask to Be Brought Here," the full-bodied pop of "When I Get Home" (covered by the Searchers for a British hit), the fine rendition of "Nature Boy," and the reasonably cogent and sincere late '60s folk-rock (when he briefly billed himself as "Bob" Darin). But a lot of it is no more than competent, and some of it (especially the slighter rock efforts) are less than that. That almost diametrically opposed range of sounds (it's a long way from "Splish Splash" to "Mame" and "If I Were a Carpenter," after all) means that not many listeners except Darin fanatics will be able to get through the whole set without skipping over a lot of the tracks; the pop sides may hold little appeal for the rock/folk fans, and vice versa. —*Richie Unterberger*

James Darren

b. 1936, Philadelphia, PA
Vocals / Pop-Rock, Teen Idol, Brill Building Pop
Even more than the typical teen idol's, James Darren's roots in authentic rock 'n' roll were tenuous. Darren began recording for Colpix in the late '50s at the beginning of a screen career that saw him star in numerous films, most notably *Gidget*. More at home with standard middle-of-the-road, show tune material than rock, and not much of a singer in any case, Darren was nonetheless marketed as a pop-rock performer to his predominantly young female constituency. He ran off quite a few novelty-tinged hit singles in the early '60s, of which "Goodbye Cruel World," which made No. 3, was the biggest and best. Top Brill Building songwriters—including the Goffin-King, Mann-Weil, and Pomus-Shuman teams, as well as Bob Crewe, Gloria Shayne, and Howard Greenfield—gave Darren material, albeit material that was well below their usual standards. He recorded quite a bit after his early '60s heyday, reaching the Top 40 in 1967 with "All" and charting as late as 1977 with "You Take My Heart Away." —*Richie Unterberger*

● **The Best of James Darren** / Nov. 15, 1994 / Rhino ✦✦✦✦
Eighteen songs, mostly from the early '60s, that rank among the least impressive teen idol recordings, although they were far from the least popular. Includes all his Colpix hits, highlighted by "Goodbye Cruel World" and the uncharacteristically hard-driving late-'64 effort "Just Think of Tonight," as well as his later chart entries "All" and "You Take My Heart Away." —*Richie Unterberger*

Das EFX

f. 1991, Petersburg, VA
Hip Hop, East Coast Rap
With their first album, DAS EFX caused a minor revolution based on their speedy, quick-tongued stuttering; it helped that they backed their rhymes with thick, funky tracks. The album was a major success, scoring a Top 40 pop single and going gold. On their second LP, *Straight Up Sewaside*, the duo of Drayz and Skoob Effect slightly altered their approach. They downplayed the high speed stuttering, though they continued with the intense rhyming and confrontational themes that made their debut so memorable. —*AMG*

● **Dead Serious** / Apr. 7, 1992 / East West ✦✦✦✦
Their raps are often lightweight, but this album has made an immediate and substantial impact in the hip-hop community. —*Ron Wynn*

Straight Up Sewaside / Nov. 16, 1993 / East West ✦✦✦
It may not be as revolutionary or immediately memorable as the twisting rhymes of *Dead Serious*, but the harder-edged styles of *Straight Up Sewaside* have enough slamming rhythms and rhymes to satisfy most fans. —*Stephen Thomas Erlewine*

Hold It Down / Oct. 1995 / East West ✦✦
Although the duo tries very hard, there isn't much on *Hold It Down*, Das EFX's third album, that makes it different from their previous records. The production is a bit leaner, and their delivery is a bit harder; but that doesn't disguise the fact that the beats aren't as strong as on their earlier albums, nor are their raps as exciting and inventive. Nevertheless, there are some strong moments on *Hold It Down*, and it should please fans of the duo, even if it doesn't appeal to the same large audience that embraced their debut. —*Stephen Thomas Erlewine*

David & David

f. Los Angeles, CA
Pop-Rock
Although they only recorded one album, the Californian duo of David Baerwald and David Ricketts made some of the finest mainstream pop of the '80s. With its slick surfaces and memorable melodies, 1986's *Boomtown* was deceptively smooth; beneath the production, the songs were tales of despair and broken dreams in the Reagan era. David & David scored a surprise hit in 1986 with "Welcome to the Boomtown"; it was their only single that charted. Baerwald began a critically acclaimed solo career in 1990; Ricketts has not released anything since *Boomtown*. —*Stephen Thomas Erlewine*

● **Boomtown** / 1986 / A&M ✦✦✦✦
Los Angeles musicians David Baerwald and David Ricketts joined forces to create subtle, moody, and darkly atmospheric rock, culminating in their Top 40 hit "Welcome to the Boomtown." —*Donna DiChario*

Dave Davies

b. Feb. 3, 1947, Muswell Hill, London, England
Guitar / Rock 'n' Roll, Arena Rock
Although he took a largely subordinate role to his brother Ray in the Kinks, Dave Davies' fierce guitar work and hoarse, but effective, background (and occasional lead) vocals were key elements of the band's appeal. Dave also occasionally wrote songs for the Kinks that showed

him to be a writer of considerable skill and wit, if not up to the same level as Ray. In the late '60s, Dave made some solo singles that met with critical success in Britain, although they were unknown in the US. "Death of a Clown" (included on the Kinks' *Something Else* LP) made No. 3 on the British charts in 1967, and the follow-up "Susannah's Still Alive" also did fairly well. Dave began to consider making a solo album, but after a couple of other solo singles flopped, he seemed to lose heart and abandoned his plans. (Some unreleased solo tracks from this period turned up on the obscure Kinks bootleg *Good Luck Charm.*) In the 1980s Dave finally began a solo career in earnest, releasing a series of mainstream rock albums that found little critical or commercial acclaim. —*Richie Unterberger*

Afl 1: 3603 / 1980 / RCA ◆◆◆

Dave Davies / 1980 / RCA ◆◆

Glamour / 1981 / RCA ◆◆

Chosen People / 1983 / Warner Brothers ◆◆

● **The Album That Never Was** / 1987 / PRT ◆◆◆◆
When Dave Davies racked up a couple British hits in 1967, rumors were rife that the Kinks' lead guitarist would cut a solo album of his own. He never did—not in the '60s, anyway—and this album is a facsimile of what might have been, packaging some ultra-rare solo singles of the time with tracks that Davies wrote and sang on some of the Kinks' late-'60s records. They show him to be a fine, underappreciated singer and songwriter in a Dylanesque folk-rock mode. —*Richie Unterberger*

The Spencer Davis Group

f. 1963, Birmingham, England
Guitar / British Invasion
His ferocious soul-drenched vocals belying his tender teenage years, Stevie Winwood powered the Spencer Davis Group's three biggest US hits during their brief lifespan as one of the British Invasion's most convincing R&B-based combos.

Guitarist Davis formed the band with Winwood on organ, his brother Muff Winwood on bass, and drummer Peter York. Signing on with producer Chris Blackwell, the quartet got their first hit (the blistering "Keep On Running") from another of Blackwell's acts, West Indian performer Jackie Edwards. After topping the British charts in 1965, the song struggled on the lower reaches of the US Hot 100.

The group's two hottest sellers were self-penned projects. "Gimme Some Lovin'" and "I'm a Man" were searing showcases for the adolescent Winwood's gritty vocals and blazing keyboards and the band's pounding rhythms. Although they burned up the charts even on this side of the ocean in 1967, the quartet never capitalized on their fame with an American tour. At the height of their power, Winwood left to form Traffic, leaving Davis without his dynamic front man. The bandleader focused on producing other acts, including a Canadian ensemble called the Downchild Blues Band during the early '80s. —*Bill Dahl*

Their First LP / 1965 / Fontana ◆◆◆
The group's first album is basically a reflection of their early repertoire and very heavy on the R&B/soul standards. It is dominated by covers of Ike & Tina Turner, the Coasters, John Lee Hooker, Little Walter, Brenda Holloway, and others; only three of the tunes are original. Two of these are written by Stevie Winwood, the other by Spencer Davis; Winwood's midtempo soul number "It Hurts Me So" is easily the best of them. Winwood is in fine voice and the group is energetic, but this is neither as good as their best work nor nearly as good as the best British R&B albums of the era by competitors like Them and the Rolling Stones. Includes their first two British singles, "Dimples" and "I Can't Stand It." —*Richie Unterberger*

Autumn 66 / 1966 / Fontana ◆◆◆
At the peak of their popularity, the Spencer Davis Group's albums were considerably less impressive than their hits and a bit thin on imagination, although they were never less than competent. This, their third LP, relies heavily on soul covers, as well as a few oft-covered blues standards ("Midnight Special," "Mean Woman Blues," "Dust My Blues"). Highlights were their second British No.1 hit, "Somebody Help Me," the decent group original "High Time Baby," Winwood's organ-based instrumental "On the Green Light," and "When I Get Home," which (like "Somebody Help Me") was a hit in Britain, but not the US. —*Richie Unterberger*

Heavies / 1969 / United Artists ◆◆◆
A hodgepodge of some of the group's lesser-known tracks, this actually contains some of their better performances. The instrumental jam "Waltz for Lumumba" sounds like a prototype for some of the ideas Winwood would employ in Traffic. The group original, "Hey Darling," is a smoldering, moody blues; "Mean Woman Blues" and "Watch Your Step" are a couple of their best uptempo, and most guitar-oriented, R&B covers; "Please Do Something" is a good cover of a Don Covay tune; and "Back into My Life Again" was co-written by Jackie Edwards, who was responsible for their first few British hits. Put together by United Artists

after the group had broken up to capitalize on Winwood's ascent to superstardom in Traffic, it's nonetheless a decent compilation of some of their more interesting odds and ends. —*Richie Unterberger*

● **Golden Archive Series** / 1984 / Rhino ◆◆◆◆
The best compilation of their best moments. Fourteen songs, including both of their US hits, "I'm a Man" and "Gimme Some Lovin'"; the UK chart-toppers "Keep On Running" and "Somebody Help Me"; the smaller UK hit "When I Come Home"; and several fine R&B covers, all from 1964-66. —*Richie Unterberger*

● **Best of the Spencer Davis Group** / 1985 / EMI America ◆◆◆◆
While it isn't as consistent or effective as Rhino's *Golden Archive Series,* EMI's *Best of the Spencer Davis Group* contains all the hits that a casual fan could want ("Gimmie Some Lovin'," "I'm a Man," "Keep On Running," "Somebody Help Me"), and several of the band's better lesser-known songs. —*Stephen Thomas Erlewine*

Taking out Time 1967-1969 / 1994 / RPM ◆◆
With the loss of Stevie Winwood, the Spencer Davis Group was just another rock band. But that didn't keep them from marching onward until the end of the decade, with a few more personnel changes. This compilation of 20 previously unreleased tracks is taken from radio/TV broadcasts and studio outtakes, as well as their near-complete unreleased 1969 album *Letters from Edith.* The '67-68 cuts are middling pop-flavored psychedelia that's heavy on the organ-guitar combination, with the odd slice of above-average material ("With Their New Face On") and strange stylistic detours (a couple of Jimmy Webb songs). Guitarist Ray Fenwick comes to the fore as songwriter on the *Letters from Edith* sessions. This finds them groping for a style—some country-rock here, a bit of jazzy funk there, and some lowest-common-denominator psych-prog as well—without much success, though the jazz-soul instrumental organ showcase "Firefly" isn't bad. —*Richie Unterberger*

Eight Gigs a Week: The Steve Winwood Years / Apr. 22, 1996 / Island/Chronicles ◆◆◆◆
Unfortunately, this two-CD, 51-song set—which covers virtually everything the group recorded with Steve Winwood from 1964-67—was available only as a British import as of mid-1996. The gap between the band's best and worst material was considerable. Quite a few of their R&B covers are surprisingly routine, and the occasional cuts that don't have Winwood on lead vocals are downright pedestrian. Because of this inconsistency, the general fan's better off with the Rhino best-of, if it can be found. If you want to get more, though, this is the first and last place to go, with all the hit singles, everything from their three albums, an early EP, some B-sides, and a couple of previously unissued tracks. And some of the obscure material is really good, whether in a straight R&B/blues or more soulful vein. Be aware that the version of "Gimme Some Lovin'" here is the less dynamic, original British mix, minus some backup vocals and percussion. —*Richie Unterberger*

Tyrone Davis

b. May 4, 1938, Greenville, MS
Vocals / Soul
Perennially a ladies' choice, Tyrone Davis just seems to naturally appeal to women. That's not to say that gents haven't bought his churning Chicago soul records too—his impressive hit-making career reaches back to 1968, and there's no end in sight. His mentor, noted singer Harold Burrage, coached his charge well, and Davis debuted on wax in 1965 as "Tyrone the Wonder Boy" on the local Four Brothers logo. Far more wondrous were Davis' classy efforts for Chicago's Dakar label, commencing with the remorseful R&B chart-topper "Can I Change My Mind" in 1968, continuing with "Is It Something You've Got" in 1969, and the million-selling classic "Turn Back the Hands of Time" in 1970. With Willie Henderson producing, the cats at Dakar were forging a fresh, vital new Chicago soul sound, and Tyrone Davis was right there at its forefront. Davis remained with Dakar until 1976, his warm, assured vocals powering the likes of "I Had It All the Time" and "Turning Point," before moving over to Columbia without missing a beat. These days, Tyrone hops from one label to the next, seemingly with each new release—but he's still no stranger to the urban contemporary charts, and the women still love him. What more could he possibly ask for? —*Bill Dahl*

● **Greatest Hits [Rhino]** / Mar. 24, 1992 / Rhino ◆◆◆◆
Tyrone Davis combined influences from hard-edged, country-tinged urban blues and more tightly arranged, horn-dominated soul. He sang surging uptempo tunes, churning ballads, heartache songs, and tribute numbers, and moved from material dominated by brassy arrangements to numbers reliant on his narratives and persona. This 17-track CD begins with his earliest hits, such as "Can I Change My Mind" and "Is It Something You've Got," and continues into smoother but no less urgent tunes such as "Turning Point," "There It Is," and "One Way Ticket." Because this collection covers only his Dakar material, things end at

1976, after which he left for Columbia. But for soul fans, Tyrone Davis' greatest music came on Dakar. —*Ron Wynn*

In the Mood: Best of Tyrone Davis / Jun. 4, 1996 / Sony ✦✦✦✦

Ronnie Dawson

b. 1939, Dallas, TX
Guitar, Vocals / Rockabilly

Dawson is a Dallas rockabilly guitarist and singer noted in the late '50s for his shocking white brush cut and high-pitched, boyish vocals that made him sound even younger than his teenage years. His rare singles on regional labels are highly valued by rockabilly collectors. Dawson sounded like a raw, upper-register Gene Vincent, and the connection is not entirely coincidental. He shared Vincent's manager, and his greatest song, the manic "Action Packed" (with its insistent "Hear me!" shouted refrain), was written by Jack Rhodes, who also wrote a couple of Vincent's best tunes ("Woman Love" and "B-I-Bickey-Bi-Bo-Bo-Go"). Dawson could also sing convincingly on more grinding and bluesy numbers.

After a few singles, Dawson was briefly picked up by Swan Records, which tried unsuccessfully to mold him into a teen idol. After a fine single for Columbia under the name Commonwealth Jones, Dawson retreated to smaller labels for a time. He worked as a session drummer for the semi-legendary Texas producer Major Bill Smith, playing on Bruce Channel's "Hey Baby" and Paul & Paula's "Hey Paula"; like most first-generation rockabilly singers, he tried his hand at country music as well. His rediscovery was hastened by the inclusion of "Action Packed" in Rhino's *Rock This Town* anthology of rockabilly classics, and he has resumed active performing and recording. —*Richie Unterberger*

Still a Lot of Rhythm / 1988 / No Hit ✦✦✦

Dawson's first comeback effort was impressive in that it found him in good (if noticeably lower) voice, though the material was average and the performances a bit restrained. No need to look for the hard-to-find British import; it's been reissued domestically, in its entirety, as bonus material on Crystal Clear's *Monkey Beat!!* CD. —*Richie Unterberger*

Rockinitis / 1989 / Crystal Clear ✦✦✦

Dawson's second LP since his mid-'80s rediscovery is an above-average latter-day rockabilly effort, sensibly avoiding temptations to modernize the sound with too much clutter. Dawson's voice has lowered considerably since his early days, meaning that instead of sounding like a little kid, he sounds like a young man (although he was about 50 when this was recorded). The American CD reissue adds a bonus cut, "Sloppy Drunk," not on the original British release. —*Richie Unterberger*

● **Rockin' Bones** / 1990 / No Hit ✦✦✦✦

This 20-track CD has all his essential early recordings, with both sides of five singles. (The Swan teen idol efforts aren't included.) Besides "Action Packed," highlights are the subsequent A-sides "Do Do Do" and "Rockin' Bones," as well as a spooky rendering of "Riders in the Sky." The unreleased tracks include several raw demos he cut prior to his first single, as well as a few outtakes from his Columbia session that feature some harmonica work by Delbert McClinton. —*Richie Unterberger*

Monkey Beat!! / Oct. 1994 / Crystal Clear ✦✦✦✦

Monkey Beat!! confirms Dawson's status as the most vital of the middle-aged rockabilly singers still performing and recording in the 1990s. It's actually rawer (in the positive sense of the term) than the two previous comeback albums he recorded for No Hit in the late '80s. He's in fine, spontaneous voice, and the material (including a few originals), as always, avoids overdone standards. As a significant bonus, the CD tacks on the entirety of his 1988 album, *Still a Lot of Rhythm*, originally released on the British No Hit label; it's a respectable but tamer effort than the first half of the program. —*Richie Unterberger*

Just Rockin' & Rollin' / Jun. 1996 / Upstart ✦✦✦

A more easygoing effort than *Monkey Beat!!*, with a decidedly more countrified influence. Echoes of Tex-Mex creep in here and there as well, and a few tracks have a horn section. A lot of Dawson fans will prefer Ronnie's wilder latter-day releases, where he lets go more, and where singing and playing skirt a more reckless, dangerous edge. Rockabilly's a limited form, though, and he should get some credit for playing around with the format mildly, instead of just serving up more of the same. It's a solid, fine track record of reasonably strong material, though Dawson himself wrote little of it. —*Richie Unterberger*

● **Rockin' Bones: the Legendary Masters** / Sep. 17, 1996 / Crystal Clear ✦✦✦✦

Two-CD, 34-song overview of Dawson's early recordings, spanning 1957 to 1962. Includes most of his singles from the era, and a tall heap of acetates, demos, and alternate takes; in fact, over half of the material was unreleased at the time. The stylistic variety is a little manic, moving from raw home demo rockabilly-blues to straight studio rockabilly (including the classic "Action Packed") to teen idol pop to country arrangements that prominently feature banjo. It's the definitive compilation, though, of the early work of this one-of-a-kind rockabilly singer. It has almost all of the tracks of the previous collection of his early sides

(on No Hit), and replaces that disc as the anthology of choice. —*Richie Unterberger*

Bobby Day

b. Jul. 1, 1932, Fort Worth, TX, **d.** Jul. 15, 1990
Vocals / Rock 'n' Roll, Doo Wop

An important cog in Los Angeles' doo wop community during the '50s, Day wrote three often-covered early rock classics in 1957-1958. Day was part of the Hollywood Flames, one of the area's top R&B vocal groups, and briefly part of Bob & Earl, later to hit without Day on "Harlem Shuffle." Day formed his own group, the Satellites, in 1957, cutting the original "Little Bitty Pretty One" for Class Records. A nearly identical cover by Thurston Harris beat the original out, so Day countered with the driving "Rockin' Robin" in 1958, an R&B chart-topper. Its flip, "Over and Over," was a hit in its own right, although the Dave Clark Five's 1965 revival is better remembered today. Day waxed a few more hits for Class in 1959, including "That's All I Want" and a derivative "The Bluebird, the Buzzard & the Oriole," flitting from label to label during the '60s. —*Bill Dahl*

● **The Original Rockin' Robin** / 1991 / Ace ✦✦✦✦

Bobby Day's "Rockin' Robin" remains a classic. That and 25 other original recordings show up on this solid British import. —*Jeff Tamarkin*

Dazz Band

f. 1977, Cleveland, OH
Funk

The Cleveland-based Dazz Band was one of the more popular funk groups of the early '80s. Bobby Harris formed the group in the late '70s, taking members from two Cleveland funk bands, Bell Telefunk and the Kinsman Grills house band. The end result was an eight-piece band featuring Harris, Skip Martin III, Pierre DeMudd on horns and vocals, guitarist Eric Fearman, bassist Michael Wiley, drummer Isaac Wiley, keyboardist Kevin Frederick, and percussionist Kenny Pettus. Harris' concept for the group was "danceable jazz"; he shortened the description to "dazz" and called the group Kinsman Dazz. Under that name, the group had two small hits in the US during 1978 and 1979. In 1980 they changed their name to the Dazz Band and signed to Motown.

Let the Music Play, the band's first release for the record label, was released in 1981. Once the group veered away from the more melodic, pop-oriented dance music that dominated their debut and started playing a tougher, more groove-oriented funk, the Dazz Band began racking up the hits. "Let It Whip," taken from their second album, *Keep It Live* (1982), reached No. 5 and won a Grammy Award for Best Performance by an R&B Vocal Duo or Group. While they never reached those heights again, the Dazz Band had a string of six consecutive Top 100 albums that ran until 1986; during that time, they scored two other Top 100 singles, "Joystick" and "Let It All Blow." In 1985 Fearman and Frederick left the band; they were replaced by Marlon McClain and Keith Harrison, respectively. The Dazz Band switched labels to Geffen in 1986. That year they had their final charting album, *Wild and Free*. Soon after its release, the band switched to RCA. The group failed to have another hit and quietly faded away. —*Stephen Thomas Erlewine*

● **Funkology: the Definitive Dazz Band** / Nov. 15, 1994 / Motown ✦✦✦✦

Funkology: The Definitive Dazz Band is a comprehensive overview of the early-'80s funk band, featuring all of their major hits, including "Let It Whip," "One for the Fun," "Joystick" and "Let It All Blow." —*Stephen Thomas Erlewine*

The dB's

f. 1978, Winston-Salem, NC
Alternative Pop-Rock, Power Pop, Jangle-Pop

Along with Let's Active, the dB's defined the Southern power-pop/jangle-pop movement of the early-to-mid-'80s. The band's music was a quirky blend of smart pop and psychedelia crossed with the more experimental side of new wave. Though they never received widespread recognition outside of critical acclaim, they provided a key link between Big Star and '80s alternative guitar acts such as R.E.M.

Formed in 1978 in Winston-Salem, NC, the original lineup of the band featured Chris Stamey (guitar, vocals, keyboards), Gene Holder (bass), and Will Rigby (drums). All three members had spent time in Stamey's legendary group the Sneakers, a group he cofounded with Mitch Easter. After relocating to New York, the dBs released their debut single, "(I Thought) You Wanted to Know," for Stamey's Car label. Guitarist/vocalist/keyboardist Peter Holsapple, who had worked with Stamey in the band Rittenhouse Square in the early '70s, joined the band by the end of 1978. Holsapple and Stamey shared the songwriting chores during the band's early years.

The dB's were unable to secure a US recording contract, so they signed to the British Albion label. They released two albums on Albion:

Stands for Decibels (1981) and *Repercussions* (1982). Both records received rave reviews but little sales. Stamey left in 1983 to resume a solo career. Rick Wagner was added on bass but was replaced shortly by Jeff Beninato. With Holsapple fronting the group, they signed to Bearsville in 1984 and released *Like This*, a more conventional jangle-pop album with strong country leanings. Bearsville's internal problems doomed the album despite its obvious hit potential. They eventually left to sign with I.R.S. Records in 1987, where they released *The Sound of Music*. The album managed to break the Top 200, and college radio support was strong. The dB's received some crucial exposure when they opened for R.E.M. on their *Document* tour in the end of 1987, but by the end of 1988, the band decided to break up.

Holsapple and Stamey reunited in 1991 for a duo project, releasing *Mavericks* later that year. *Mavericks* was the only album the duo ever released. After its release, Stamey continued with solo projects; he also continued to contribute to the Golden Palominos. Holder went on to join the Wygals and more recently has worked as a producer and guest musician for other artists. Will Rigby released one solo album, *Sick Phenomenon* in 1985. Holsapple joined R.E.M. as an occasional touring member in 1991 and formed his own band, the Continental Drifters, with wife Susan Cowsill. In 1994 Holsapple, Rigby, Beninato, and new member Eric Peterson (guitar) re-formed the dBs and recorded *Paris Avenue*, which was released on the Monkey Hill label. —*Chris Woodstra*

● **Stands for Decibels** / 1981 / IRS ◆◆◆◆
On their debut, the dB's combined a reverence for British pop and arty, post-punk leanings that alternate between minimalism and a love of quirky embellishment, odd sounds, and unexpected twists; *Stands for Decibels* is clearly a collegiate pop experiment, but rarely is experimentation so enjoyable and irresistibly catchy. Singing and songwriting duties are shared equally by Chris Stamey and Peter Holsapple—Stamey, more quirky and psychedelic-leaning with a winsome, pure-pop whine, is nicely balanced by Holsapple's more earthy drawl and straightforward approach. The album stands not only as a landmark power-pop album but also as a prototype for much of the Southern jangle that would follow. [*Stands for Decibels* remained criminally unavailable in the US for years. When IRS reissued it on CD in 1989, Holsapple's "Judy" was added as a bonus track.] —*Chris Woodstra*

Repercussion / 1982 / IRS ◆◆◆◆
Repercussion is very much of a piece with the debut, repeating much of the same formula that made *Stands for Decibels* great—terrific harmonies, winning melodies and catchy hooks with subtle quirks thrown into the mix. This time, they feature a fuller, more polished sound, but the impact of the songs isn't diminished. Stamey left shortly after *Repercussion* to pursue a solo career. ["pH Factor" was added as a bonus track to the IRS CD reissue in 1989.] —*Chris Woodstra*

Like This / 1984 / Rhino ◆◆◆
From the opening notes of "Love Is for Lovers," this is obviously no ordinary dB's record. The group, now pared down to a trio fronted by Peter Holsapple, have stripped away the arty quirks of the first two albums, opting instead for straight-ahead, rootsy rockers and country-rock romps. Amid the more muscular, guitar-based sound, Holsapple turns in his same instantly endearing melodies, especially on the album highlight, "Lonely Is as Lonely Does," his most beautiful song to date. [Rhino's CD reissue adds an unnecessary extended remix of "A Spy in the House of Love."] —*Chris Woodstra*

The Sound of Music / 1987 / IRS ◆◆◆
What Peter Holsapple calls "the band's most blatant attempt to make a commercial album" sounds like it—but it's also very enjoyable. There's some tremendous merges of melody and lyrics here, from the satiny pop of "I Lie," the funny kick of "Working for Somebody Else," and the folky Holsapple-Syd Straw duet, "Never Before and Never Again." —*Kit Kiefer*

Ride the Wild Tom Tom / Aug. 17, 1993 / Rhino ◆◆
A wonderful collection of early demos—mostly pre-*Stands for Decibels*. Even though this isn't the place to start with the dB's, it is a must-own for fans of the band who already have the first two albums. —*Rick Clark*

Paris Avenue / Oct. 4, 1994 / Monkey Hill ◆◆◆
With *Paris Avenue*, the dB's—featuring only Peter Holsapple and Will Rigby from the band's original lineup—effectively pick up right where they left off with seven years with *The Sound of Music*. While they're certainly past their groundbreaking days, *Paris Avenue* is a welcome return and serves as a good example of what good pop music is all about—fortunately some things never change. —*Chris Woodstra*

De La Soul

f. 1987, Amityville, Long Island, NY
Hip Hop, Alternative Rap
At the time of its 1989 release, De La Soul's debut album *3 Feet High and Rising* was hailed as the future of hip-hop. With its colorful, neo-psychedelic collage of samples and styles, and the Long Island trio's low-

key, clever rhymes and goofy humor, the album sounded like nothing else in hip-hop. Where most of their contemporaries drew directly from old school rap, funk, or Public Enemy's dense sonic barrage, De La Soul was gentler and more eclectic, taking in not only funk and soul, but pop, jazz, reggae, and psychedelia. Though their style earned them critical raves and strong sales intially, De La Soul found it hard to sustain the momentum of their career in the '90s, as their alternative rap was sidetracked by the popularity of the considerably harder-edged gangsta rap.

De La Soul formed while the trio—Posdnous (born Kelvin Mercer, August 17, 1969), Trugoy the Dove (b. David Jude Joliceur, September 21, 1968), and Pasemaster Mase (b. Vincent Mason, March 27, 1970)—were attending high school in the late '80s. The stage names of all of the members derived from in-jokes: Posdnous was an inversion of Mercer's DJ name, Sound-Sop; Trugoy was an inversion of Joliceur's favorite food, yogurt. De La Soul's demo tape, "Plug Tunin'," came to the attention of Prince Paul, the leader and producer of the New York rap outfit Stetsasonic. Prince Paul played the tape to several colleagues and helped the trio land a contract with Tommy Boy Records.

Prince Paul produced De La Soul's debut album, *3 Feet High and Rising*, which was released in the spring of 1989. Several critics and observers labeled the group a neo-hippie band, because the record praised peace and love, as well as proclaiming that this was the dawning of "the D.A.I.S.Y. age" (Da Inner Sound, Y'all). Though the trio was uncomfortable with the hippie label, there was no denying that the humor and eclecticism presented an alternative to the hardcore rap that dominated hip-hop. De La Soul quickly were perceived as the leaders of a contigent of New York-based alternative rappers which included A Tribe Called Quest, Queen Latifah, the Jungle Brothers and Monie Love; all of these artists dubbed themselves the Native Tongues Posse.

For a while it looked as if De La Soul and the Native Tongues Posse would eclipse hardcore hip-hop in popularity. "Me Myself and I" became a Top 40 pop hit in the US (No. 1 R&B), while the album reached No. 24 (No. 1 R&B) and went gold. At the end of the year, *3 Feet High and Rising* topped many best-of-the-year lists, including *The Village Voice*. With all of the acclaim came some unwanted attention, most notably in the form of a lawsuit by the Turtles. De La Soul had sampled the Turtles' "You Showed Me" and layered it with a French lesson on a track on *3 Feet High* called "Transmitting Live from Mars," without getting the permission of the '60s pop group. The Turtles won the case, and the decision had substantial impact not only on De La Soul, but on rap in general. After the suit, all samples had to be legally cleared before an album could be released. Not only did this result in rap's reverting to instrumentation, thereby altering how the artists worked, it also meant that several albums in the pipeline had to be delayed for samples to clear. One of those albums was De La Soul's second album, *De La Soul Is Dead*.

When *De La Soul Is Dead* was finally released in the spring of 1991, it received decidedly mixed reviews, and its darker, more introspective tone didn't attract as big an audience as its lighter predecessor. The album peaked at No. 26 pop on the US charts, No. 24 R&B, and spawned only one minor hit, the No. 22 R&B single "Ring Ring Ring (Ha Ha Hey)." De La Soul worked hard on their third album, finally releasing the record in late 1993. The result, entitled *Buhloone Mindstate*, was harder and funkier than either of its predecessors, but it didn't succumb to gangsta rap. Though it received strong reviews, the album quickly fell off the charts after peaking at No. 40, and only "Breakadawn" broke the R&B Top 40. The same fate greeted the trio's fourth album, *Stakes Is High*. Released in the summer of 1996, the record was well-reviewed, but it didn't find a large audience and quickly disappeared from the charts. —*Stephen Thomas Erlewine*

★ **Three Feet High and Rising** / 1989 / Tommy Boy ◆◆◆◆◆
One of rap's seminal and groundbreaking releases, De La Soul's *Three Feet High and Rising* proved to have as great an influence on alternative rap as Ice-T and N.W.A's recordings did on gangster rap. With this innovative and highly experimental debut album, the Long Island visionaries presented a cerebral alternative to hardcore rap's aggression and macho boasting. This softer approach to rap—both musically and lyrically—would have a tremendous influence on A Tribe Called Quest, Digable Planets, the Pharcyde and other alternative rappers. Drawing on influences ranging from jazz to psychedelic rock and soul to '70s P-funk, De La doesn't hesitate to be abstract and complex. In fact, the album's lyrics aren't always very accessible. Like a lot of jazz, *Three Feet High and Rising* is a challenging CD that reveals more and more of its richness with repeated listening. —*Alex Henderson*

De La Soul Is Dead / May 13, 1991 / Tommy Boy ◆◆◆◆
De La Soul threw a curveball at listeners with its second album, *De La Soul Is Dead*—taking a slightly harder and tougher approach, but remaining highly musical, distinctive and recognizable. Though not quite as consistently appealing as the debut, De La Soul was still one of rap's most inviting acts, and remained quite experimental and unpredictable. *Dead* is less lighthearted than *Rising*, but offerings like "Oodles of O's" and "Pease Porridge" made it clear that the group could

still be enjoyably quirky and eccentric. One song that definitely isn't amusing is "Millie Pulled a Pistol on Santa," an unsettling commentary on child molestation that cuts like a knife without preaching. Like the first album, *De La Soul Is Dead* is a very abstract and cerebral effort that needs several listenings to be fully appreciated. *—Alex Henderson*

Buhloone Mindstate / Sep. 21, 1993 / Tommy Boy ✦✦✦
Continually trying to turn up the revolution that was their debut, *Buhloone Mindstate* is a return to Daisy Age positive vibes. The beats are big, the samples are fresh, and the melodies are enticing. While the first two albums featured intros and sidelights along the way, *Buhloone Mindstate* has only 15 tracks (11 songs). With help from friends Guru, Maceo Parker, and Biz Markie, De La Soul approaches the perfection of *Three Feet High and Rising*, if not the initial effect. *—John Bush*

Stakes is High / Jul. 2, 1996 / Tommy Boy ✦✦✦
Seven years after its debut album, De La Soul was still one of the most unpredictable and risk-taking groups in rap. On the excellent *Stakes Is High*, the Long Island natives continue to thrive on the abstract and the cerebral. Instead of the lightheartedness that characterized *Three Feet High and Rising*, De La favors a harder, tougher approach that's closer to second album *De La Soul Is Dead*. Jazz remains a strong influence for the group, which samples the improvised works of Milt Jackson, Lou Donaldson, and Chico Hamilton as well as classic soul by the likes of the Commodores and Sly & the Family Stone. This eclectic approach certainly didn't hurt the group's popularity in alternative rock and acid jazz circles, but in 1996, rap's hardcore seemed much more interested in gangster rap. *—Alex Henderson*

Dead Boys

f. 1976, Cleveland, OH
Punk
Forming from the ashes of Cleveland's semi-legendary Rocket from the Tombs, the Dead Boys were one of the first punk bands to escalate the level of violence, nihilism, and pure ugliness of punk rock to extreme new levels. After they relocated to New York, ex-Rocket members guitarist Cheetah Chrome and drummer Johnny Blitz hooked up with guitarist Jimmy Zero, bassist Jeff Magnum, and vocalist Stiv Bators to form the Dead Boys. Their music wasn't very special; even by the relaxed standards of punk, it was loose and incompetent, bordering on the stupidity of heavy metal. "Sonic Reducer" and "Ain't It Fun," the band's two best songs, were holdovers from former Rocket from the Tombs members David Thomas and Peter Laughner, who went on to form Pere Ubu. What distinguished the Dead Boys, and what makes them notorious to this day, is their pure nastiness, much of it coming from Bators. Their two albums—*Young, Loud and Snotty* and *We Have Come for Your Children*—are brutal, wallowing in their own self-serving nihilism; they embodied the punk stereotypes held by the mainstream. After two albums, the band split. Bators formed Lords of the New Church, and the rest of the members slid into obscurity. In 1990, Bators died of injuries sustained from being hit by a bus in Paris. *—Stephen Thomas Erlewine*

● **Young Loud & Snotty** / Oct. 1977 / Sire ✦✦✦✦
A truly vulgar and tasteless slab of nihilistic punk rock, the Dead Boys' first album included the classic "Sonic Reducer," which was buried in a mess of relentless, sub-heavy metal pounding. *—Stephen Thomas Erlewine*

We Have Come for Your Children / Jun. 1978 / Sire ✦✦✦
Highlighted by the snarling "Ain't It Fun," the Dead Boys' second album was as nasty and raw as the first. *—Stephen Thomas Erlewine*

Dead Can Dance

f. 1981, Melbourne, Australia
Alternative Pop-Rock, Dream-Pop
Dead Can Dance combines elements of European folk music—particularly music from the Middle Ages and the Renaissance—with ambient pop and worldbeat flourishes. Their songs are of lost beauty, regret and sorrow, inspiration and nobility, and of the everlasting human goal of attaining a meaningful existence.

Over the course of their career, Dead Can Dance has featured a multitude of members, but two musicians have remained at the core of the band—guitarist Brendan Perry and vocalist Lisa Gerrard. Perry had previously been the lead vocalist and bassist for the Australian-based punk band the Scavengers, a group that was never able to land a recording contract. In 1979 the band changed their name to the Marching Girls, but they still weren't able to sign a contract. The next year, Perry left the group and began experimenting with electronic music, particularly tape loops and rhythms. In 1981 Perry formed Dead Can Dance with Lisa Gerrard, Paul Erikson, and Simon Monroe. By 1982 Perry and Gerrard decided to relocate to London; Erikson and Monroe decided to stay in Australia.

Within a year, Dead Can Dance had signed a record deal with 4AD. In the spring of 1984 they released their eponymous debut album, com-

prised of songs the pair had written in the previous four years. By the end of the year, the group had contributed two tracks to *It'll End in Tears*, the first album by This Mortal Coil, and had released an EP called *Garden of the Arcane Delights*. In 1985 Dead Can Dance released their second album, *Spleen and Ideal*. The album helped build their European cult following, peaking at No. 2 on the UK indie charts.

For the next two years, Dead Can Dance was relatively quiet, releasing only two new songs in 1986, both of which appeared on the 4AD compilation *Lonely Is an Eyesore*. *Within the Realm of a Dying Sun*, the group's third album, appeared in 1986. In 1988 the band released their fourth album, *The Serpent's Egg*, and wrote the score for the Agustin Villarongas film *El Nino de La Luna*, which also featured Lisa Gerrard's acting debut.

Aion, Dead Can Dance's fifth album, was released in 1990. Also in 1990 the group toured America for the first time, earning rave reviews. The next year the group was involved in various festivals and theatrical productions. In 1992 the compilation *A Passage in Time* was released on Rykodisc, making it the first American release of Dead Can Dance music. Early in 1993 the group provided the score to *Baraka* and contributed songs to *Sahara Blue*. In the fall of 1993, the group released *Into the Labyrinth*, which became their first proper studio album to receive an American release. *Into the Labyrinth* was a cult success throughout the US and Europe. It was followed by another American and European tour, which was documented on the 1994 album and film *Toward the Within*. In 1995 Lisa Gerrard released her debut solo album, *The Mirror Pool*. In the summer of 1996 Dead Can Dance released *Spiritchaser* and embarked on an international tour. *—Stephen Thomas Erlewine & Vladimir Bogdanov*

Dead Can Dance / 1984 / 4AD ✦✦✦
Anyone who's discovered Dead Can Dance with the later albums will get a major surprise on listening to this debut album. It's not that it's a bad album—it's just *very* odd to hear a more industrial kind of sound coming from them. The tone is much harsher and more mechanical than later outings, with Lisa Gerrard and Brendan Perry having their voices pushed much further back in the mix than might be expected—neither of them recorded all that well, when it comes down to it. For all that, the Dead Can Dance mix of contemporary and ancient music still manages to come through—it just happens to have a lot of rough, grating edges. *—Steven McDonald*

Spleen and Ideal / 1985 / 4AD ✦✦✦
Well balanced in terms of both mood and style, this album brings you the whole new world of hopeless hope and aimless urge and search. *—Vladimir Bogdanov*

Within the Realm of a Dying Sun / 1987 / 4AD ✦✦✦✦
Probably their most subtle and intelligent album, it touches the deepest levels of our identity. *—Vladimir Bogdanov*

Serpent's Egg / 1988 / 4AD ✦✦✦
This is an interesting combination of Slavonic and European medieval music. *—Vladimir Bogdanov*

Aion / Sep. 1990 / 4AD ✦✦✦✦
True medieval sound is combined with all the variety of modern studio techniques. Not an imitation at all, it's just enriched with an old musical tradition. *—Vladimir Bogdanov*

● **A Passage in Time** / Oct. 1991 / Rykodisc ✦✦✦✦
Dead Can Dance has long been known for their hauntingly beautiful weaving of traditional and modern music, stunningly presented on their compilation *A Passage in Time*. The tracks represent a healthy serving from their previous albums and include two new pieces unavailable elsewhere. Using an eclectic mixture of gothic, descant, Middle Eastern, medieval and early Renaissance music, as well as sacred music of the 18th and 19th centuries, Dead Can Dance is truly unique. Vocals by Brendan Perry and Lisa Gerrard are featured, less than half of which are sung in English; Gerrard's gorgeously chilling vocals are consistent high points. Instruments like the Turkish saz, Chinese yang ch'in and the hurdy-gurdy blend with synth and strings. For their many fans, *A Passage in Time* is a valued addition; for those new to the territory, this release will leave no doubt as to why people rave about this group. *—Backroads Music/Heartbeats*

Into the Labyrinth / Sep. 14, 1993 / 4AD ✦✦✦
Into the Labyrinth explores world beat territory more heavily than Dead Can Dance's previous releases and the results are impressive, if not altogether perfect. *Into the Labyrinth* also marks the inclusion of more vocal tracks, some of which could even be labeled pop songs, and not bad ones at that. *—AMG*

Toward the Within / Oct. 25, 1994 / 4AD ✦✦✦
Dead Can Dance's albums are so meticulously constructed that the mere thought of a live album seems ridiculous. However, Dead Can Dance are more clever than the average band. When it came time for them to record a live album, they came upon an ingenious solution: instead of capturing their classics live, they decided to record an album of all-new

material. Naturally, the result still appeals to the hardcore fan as much as the standard live formula, yet *Toward the Within* shows that Dead Can Dance's mesmerizing music continues to evolve, incorporating different strands of world music all the while. —*Stephen Thomas Erlewine*

Spiritchaser / Jun. 25, 1996 / 4AD ✦✦✦

Dead Kennedys

f. 1978, San Francisco, CA, db. 1987
Hardcore Punk

The Dead Kennedys merged revolutionary politics with hardcore punk music and, in the process, became one of the defining hardcore bands. Often they were more notable for their politics than their music, but that was part of their impact. The Kennedys were more inspired by British punk and the fiery, revolutionary-implied politics of the Sex Pistols than the artier tendencies of New York punk rockers. Under the direction of lead vocalist Jello Biafra, the Dead Kennedys became the most political and—to the eyes of many observers, including Christians and right-wing politicians—the most dangerous band in hardcore. By the mid-'80s, the band had become notorious enough to open themselves up to prosecution for obscenity (concerning a poster in their 1985 *Frankenchrist* album), and the court battle sped the band toward a breakup, but they left a legacy that influenced countless punk bands that followed.

Biafra (vocals; born Eric Boucher) formed the Dead Kennedys in 1978 in San Francisco; the other members included guitarist East Bay Ray, bassist Klaus Flouride, and drummer Ted (born Bruce Slesinger). The band played locally for the first two years of their career, occasionally venturing outside the Bay Area. Within a year the band released its first independent single, "California Uber Alles," an attack on (then) Governor Jerry Brown. It was followed shortly afterward by their second single, "Holiday in Cambodia." In 1979 Biafra ran for mayor of San Francisco; he finished fourth. By this time the band had become quite popular in both the American and British underground. In 1980 the band released their debut album, *Fresh Fruit for Rotting Vegetables*, on IRS Records. After its release, Ted left the band; he was replaced by drummer Darren H. Peligro.

After the release of *Fresh Fruit for Rotting Vegetables*, the Dead Kennedys formed their own independent record label, Alternative Tentacles, in 1981. The first release on the label was the Kennedys' EP, *In God We Trust*. That same year, the single "Too Drunk to Fuck" scraped the bottom of Britain's pop Top 40, despite being banned from airplay. In 1982 the Kennedys released their second full-length album, *Plastic Surgery Disasters*. After its release, the band took a hiatus, during which band members—most notably Klaus Flouride—performed with various side projects. During that time, Alternative Tentacles began to establish itself as a major force in the American underground.

The Dead Kennedys returned in 1985 with *Frankenchrist*, which earned the band its greatest notoriety. Included with the album was a poster of the Swiss artist H.R. Giger's *Landscape No.XX*, a garish illustration of penises and anuses. A year after the release of the album, the Kennedys and Alternative Tentacles were prosecuted under revised California anti-obscenity laws for distributing pornography to minors, because of the poster. For the next two years the band was embroiled in a bitter legal battle, during which Biafra emerged as one of the most articulate advocates of free speech. In the summer of 1987 the case ended with a hung jury and was dismissed.

Although the Dead Kennedys emerged victorious from the court battle, they didn't remain a band much longer. Just before the prosecution began in 1986, the band released *Bedtime for Democracy*, which turned out to be their last official album. After the case was settled, the Kennedys split, releasing the posthumous compilation *Give Me Convenience or Give Me Death* in 1987. Biafra embarked on a solo career, releasing musical and spoken word recordings sporadically over the next decade and a half. Flouride returned to his fledgling solo career, releasing two albums in the late '80s and early '90s. —*Stephen Thomas Erlewine*

★ **Fresh Fruit for Rotting Vegetables** / 1980 / Alternative Tentacles ✦✦✦✦✦

The DK's 1980 debut was as important to the West Coast hardcore scene as the Sex Pistols' *Bollocks* was to disenfranchised British punks. Despite a few clunkers, *Fresh Fruit* is an explosive and scalding blast of political and social fury, underpinned by Jello Biafra's wise-ass vocals and Klaus Flouride's pseudo-surf guitar wailing. Most of the band's best songs are here. —*John Floyd*

In God We Trust, Inc. / Feb. 1981 / Alternative Tentacles ✦✦✦

DK's anti-religion seven-song EP varies from all other material in thrashy-metallic nature. Each song is a speedy, essentially unintelligible gem of punk lore with super-dominating guitars and heavier drums. It includes "Religious Vomit" and "Dog Bite" and culminates in a cover of the classic "California Uber Alles" entitled "We've Got a Bigger Problem Now," dealing with Ronald Reagan instead of Jerry Brown. —*Julian Katz*

Plastic Surgery Disasters/In God We Trust, Inc. / 1982 / Alternative Tentacles ✦✦✦✦

Their second effort captures their frenetic live set, full of mayhem and confusion, but with an underlying feeling of greatness. Nonconformist, anti-establishment sentiment is eloquently made sensible by talented frontman Jello Biafra. Punk at its best, musically and lyrically, it includes "Terminal Preppie," "Government Flu," and "Winnebago Warrior." —*Julian Katz*

Frankenchrist / 1985 / Alternative Tentacles ✦✦✦

Released after a three-year studio hiatus, this album picks up right where *Plastic Surgery Disasters* left off. As always, the lyrics are among the most literate and angry in all of rock 'n' roll. "Goons of Hazard" scores the culture of guns and the rednecks who love them, utilizing full-textured hard rock to set the verses. "Soup Is Good Food" lacerates the concept of disposable people in disposable jobs, pairing this idea with repeated guitar-riff-based music that suggests a nightmare version of 1960s songs. "Jock-O-Rama" excoriates organized sports and macho attitudes; musically, the outer sections wed rockabilly and hardcore influences, sandwiching a slow middle section that spoofs martial numbers like Barry Sadler's "Ballad of the Green Berets." "This Could Be Anywhere" has critical lyrics about racism and classism set to music highly reminiscent of the Sex Pistols. "Hellnation" has garbled, wide-range, muckracking verses set to stun-speed punk that recalls numbers from *In God We Trust Inc.* The excellent "MTV—Get off the Air" lambasts the corporate influences on rock 'n' roll; musically, the song exhibits a tripartite structure, using a vacuously poppy opening, a speed hardcore central section, and a mid-tempo rocking finale that prominently features trumpet (a very brief coda reprise of hardcore ends the number). The finest selection on this album (and perhaps in the whole Dead Kennedys' canon) is the anthemic "Stars and Stripes of Corruption." This number also utilizes a three-part construct, consisting here of a hard-rocking midsection flanked by faster, punk-oriented material. The verses here are stunningly detailed, describing what the band believes is wrong with the United States and what the solutions should be. If there is a song that spells out the group's philosophy in a nutshell, this is it. Original pressings of this album contained a poster of a painting by H.R. Giger entitled "Penis Landscape," which got the band in serious legal trouble; the resulting court case ended in a mistrial and charges were later dropped, but the group did not survive the ordeal, recording a final album, *Bedtime for Democracy*, around the time of the trial and breaking up not long afterward. This wonderful and challenging album is very highly recommended. —*David Cleary*

Bedtime for Democracy / 1986 / Alternative Tentacles ✦✦

The Dead Kennedys go out in a blaze of snarling, walloping, defiant glory in their final studio release. A bushel basket's worth of entrenched interests get drubbed here, including scientists, the military, the power hungry, macho attitudes, classism, lie detectors, Ronald Reagan and his economic policies, the press, the entertainment industry, and the commercialization of rock and revolutionary attitudes. Most of the songs here are in a manic speed-punk style reminiscent of the album *In God We Trust Inc.*, including a frenetic cover of the Johnny Paycheck chart hit "Take This Job and Shove It." A few songs slow the tempo a bit and resemble frantic rockabilly; of these, "Hop with the Jetset" lampoons the privileged classes and "I Spy" savages government agents, while "Where Do Ya Draw the Line" is a plea in favor of anarchy. "D.M.S.O." is a highly atypical number, a quiet, furtive selection that strongly resembles the movie theme to *The Pink Panther*. There are two lengthy anthemic selections as well—"Cesspools in Eden," a hard rock number with unusual chord changes and lyrics that rail against toxic waste, and "Chickenshit Conformist," which alternates slow and hyperfast sections and sports wide-ranging verses that constitute a scathing indictment of the rock music industry. As in earlier releases, the rushed hardcore numbers often garble or swallow up the well-written lyrics (if you want people to follow you into revolution, your ideas need to be intelligible). The album cover sports witheringly disparaging artwork; also included in this release are two muckraking newspapers, one containing clip-art and the other written articles about the obscenity trial embroiling the band at that point. This album is not a total success, but the Dead Kennedys surely had the satisfaction of knowing they went out on their own terms. It's all well worth hearing. —*David Cleary*

Give Me Convenience or Give Me Death / 1987 / Alternative Tentacles ✦✦✦✦

A useful compilation, it not only collects many essential nona-album cuts but rounds up the best material from the otherwise desultory follow-ups to *Fresh Fruit*. —*John Floyd*

The Dead Milkmen

f. 1983, Philadelphia, PA
Alternative Pop-Rock

Philadelphia pop-punk quartet featuring vocalist Rodney Anonymous (who sometimes adds "Amadeus" or "Mellencamp" to his name), guitarist Joe Jack Talcum, bassist Dave Blood, and drummer Dean Clean. The Milkmen are renowned for their dumb, obnoxious sense of humor, which they frequently focus on pop culture. Some critics love them, some critics hate them, but all agree that the Milkmen are sophomoric and snotty. "Bitchin' Camaro," from their debut *Big Lizard In My Backyard*, was a minor alternative-radio hit. The band got a small measure of publicity when Detroit Tiger infielder Jim Walewander praised them in interviews, and had a minor MTV hit with *Beelzebubba*'s "Punk Rock Girl." Unfortunately, they were never as consistently funny as they tried to be, and were dropped from Enigma after *Metaphysical Graffiti*. Their subsequent releases found them trying to learn how to be serious, and their popularity had almost disappeared by the time they broke up in 1994. *—Steve Huey*

● **Big Lizard in My Backyard** / 1985 / Enigma ✦✦✦✦
You can hardly refer to any Dead Milkmen album as a classic, but *Big Lizard* comes close. Stupid, sophomoric, and quite tuneful, this is when the jokes were still funny or, at the very least, still worth listening to. Features "Bitchin' Camaro" and the tastelessly funny "Takin' Retards to the Zoo." *—John Dougan*

Eat Your Paisley / 1986 / Enigma ✦✦✦
After *Big Lizard*, Milkmen albums are mostly inconsistent, hit-or-miss affairs. This one is more of a showcase for the dippy side of their sense of humor; only a couple of tracks reproduce the snottiness of their debut. It's for real diehards only. *—Steve Huey*

Bucky Fellini / 1987 / Enigma ✦✦✦✦
Another inconsistent outing, but this one is helped out by the dead-on "Instant Club Hit (You'll Dance to Anything)," a satire of pretentious alternative European dance artists, and a few cover tunes, including a parody of "Watching Scotty Grow" ("Watching Scotty Die"). *—Steve Huey*

Beelzebubba / 1988 / Fever ✦✦✦
Probably their best post-*Big Lizard* album, this contains some of the most memorable Milkmen tracks, including songs about wife-beating and drinking bleach, the anthemic "Life Is Shit," and the MTV semi-hit "Punk Rock Girl." There still are a few clunkers, but those are outweighed (for the most part). Anonymous proves on "Stuart" that perhaps he would be funnier if he just forgot about trying to sing and instead delivered ranting monologues. *—Steve Huey*

Metaphysical Grafitti / Apr. 1990 / Enigma ✦✦
Too bad the songs on this one revert to inconsistency, because Anonymous throws in a few more ranting monologues, which provide most of the album's best moments. Fans of the Milkmen's sense of humor may find this one worthwhile, as there are a few good songs, and the album-closing monologue about Cousin Earl's maggot farm is easily the most disgusting thing the Milkmen have ever done, period. *—Steve Huey*

Soul Rotation / Apr. 14, 1992 / Hollywood ✦
The Milkmen switch to Hollywood Records, a label owned by Disney, and it shows. The juvenile gross-out humor and snotty attitude that made the Milkmen great are gone. *—Steve Huey*

Not Richard But Dick / Oct. 12, 1993 / Hollywood ✦✦
While *Not Richard, But Dick* shows signs of the Milkmen's former sophomoric outlandishness ("Let's Get the Baby High"), the length (under half an hour) shows that the band was running desperately short on ideas, as evidenced by most of the album's failure to hold the listener's interest—there isn't even much of the stylistic experimentation that marked *Soul Rotation*. Without their trademark sense of humor, the Milkmen are an average-at-best punk-pop band without much to say. "I Dream of Jesus" is a tribute to/ripoff of John S. Hall's monologues with King Missile. *—Steve Huey*

Chaos Rules—Live at the Trocadero / Nov. 8, 1994 / Restless ✦✦
As they prepared to wind up their career, the Milkmen returned to their old label for this extended live set, which features material from their first five Restless albums. The original gigs from which this album was culled (two shows in Philadelphia performed two years apart) also contained material from the group's Hollywood albums, but due to legal restrictions, those songs were excised from this release. The album is probably better for it, as these songs document the group's prime period, even if these versions don't quite compare to the originals. *—Steve Huey*

Stoney's Extra Stout (Pig) / Nov. 7, 1995 / Restless ✦✦
A studio album recorded upon their return to Restless, *Stoney's Extra Stout (Pig)* continues in the vein of their output for Hollywood Records—attempts at being serious coupled with self-consciously wacky imagery that doesn't even sound like an *attempt* to be funny. Thankfully, the Milkmen called it a career with this one. *—Steve Huey*

Bill Deal & the Rhondels

b. Virginia Beach, VA
Vocals / R&B, Rock 'n' Roll
Combining soul-inflected vocals with brassy, uptempo R&B-inspired

grooves, Bill Deal & the Rhondels remain favorites on the Carolina "beach music" circuit to this day. The group was part of the Norfolk, VA, scene during the early '60s, and Deal played organ on Jimmy Soul's 1963 smash "If You Wanna Be Happy" on Legrand Records. The Rhondels apparently preferred reviving R&B obscurities to writing their own material, and it paid off; in 1969 their supercharged remake of the Maurice Williams hit "May I" gave the group their first hit, and they followed it up with a pair of blasting Tams covers, "I've Been Hurt" and "What Kind of Fool Do You Think I Am," all on the Heritage logo. The Rhondels charted for the final time in early 1970 with "Nothing Succeeds like Success." *—Bill Dahl*

● **Vintage Rock** / 1969 / Heritage ✦✦✦✦✦
In the beach music scene of Virginia in the late 1960s, nobody could shake a dance floor like Bill Deal & the Rhondels. A horn-powered band like Blood, Sweat & Tears or Chicago, but with an eye firmly scoping out the club floor at all times, Deal and his octet knew their audience cold. And that audience liked to dance, dance, dance to their favorites, and Bill and the band responded with hoof shaking rearrangements of Tams singles and other shag-worthy material. While seldom remembered today, Deal and the band racked up five chart singles in a year's time, and those well-crafted 45s ("What Kind of Fool (Do You Think I Am)," "May I," "Swingin' Tight," "I've Been Hurt," and "Nothing Succeeds Like Success") form the core of this 15-track collection's appeal. Not even remotely hip, creative, or innovative, but as grade-A floor-moving music of the time period, this compilation is a delightful invitation to the dance. *—Cub Koda*

The Best of Bill Deal & The Rhondels / May 16, 1994 / Sequel ✦✦✦✦

Chris Deburgh

b. Oct. 15, 1948, Argentina
Guitar, Vocals / Adult Contemporary, Art-Rock/Progressive-Rock, Soft Rock, Pop-Rock
An art-rocker who occasionally writes pop-oriented material, Chris Deburgh has never been as popular in his native Britain or the United States as he was in other areas of the world. In America, he's managed only two Top 40 hits—1983's "Don't Pay the Ferryman" (No. 34) and the No. 3 ballad "The Lady in Red" (1987). In Britain, he's had the same number of Top 40 singles—"The Lady in Red" was a No. 1 hit and "Missing You" peaked at No. 3 —but he's had a number of minor hits. Nevertheless, he has gained an astounding popularity in other countries, particularly Norway and Brazil.

Deburgh signed with A&M Records in 1974, releasing his debut album the next year. Before its release, he supported Supertramp on their *Crime of the Century* tour, building himself a small fan base. His debut, *Far Beyond These Castle Walls*, was a folk-tinged stab at fantasy in the tradition of the Moody Blues that failed to chart upon its release in February 1975. That July he released a single from the album called "Flying." It didn't make an impression in the UK, but it stayed on top of the Brazilian charts for 17 weeks. This became a familiar pattern for the singer-songwriter, as every one of his '70s albums failed to chart in the UK or US, while they racked up big sales in Europe and South America. In 1981 he had his first UK chart entry with *Best Moves*, a collection culled from his early albums. It set the stage for 1982's Rupert Hine-produced *The Getaway*, which reached No. 30 on the UK charts and No. 43 in the US, thanks to the eerie single "Don't Pay the Ferryman." Deburgh's follow-up album, *Man on the Line*, also performed well, charting at 69 in the US and 11 in the UK.

Deburgh had an across-the-board success with the languid ballad "The Lady in Red" in late 1986; the single became a No. 1 hit in England (No. 3 in America) and its accompanying album, *Into the Light*, reached No. 2 in the UK (No. 25 in the US). That Christmas season, a re-release of Deburgh's 1976 holiday song "A Spaceman Came Travelling" became a Top 40 hit in the UK. *Flying Colours*, his follow-up to *Into the Light*, entered the British charts at No. 1 upon its 1988 release, but it failed to make the American charts. Deburgh never hit the US charts again, and his commercial fortunes began to slide slightly in Britain in the early '90s; yet he retained a devoted following around the world. *—Stephen Thomas Erlewine*

Far Beyond These Castle Walls / 1975 / A&M ✦✦
Chris Deburgh's debut album clearly stated his musical roots in classic melodic rock and folk ballads; sometimes his songwriting developed into complete fantasy tales. *—Vladimir Bogdanov*

Spanish Train and Other Stories / 1976 / A&M ✦✦
Spanish Train and Other Stories is a sincere and daring attempt by the young songwriter, showing a great deal of intelligence and inherent musical culture. This album established Deburgh's presence in Canada and northern European countries. The irresistible "A Spaceman Came Travelling" became a British radio hit. *—Vladimir Bogdanov*

At the End of a Perfect Day / 1977 / A&M ✦✦

This album has a slightly transitional, transitory feel. There are fewer "stories" than on *Spanish Train*, and there is a far-away, travelling flavor to many of the songs. While the majority are gentle, almost wistful ballads, "Brazil" stands out with its uptempo Latin rhythm. "Broken Wings" is the highlight, with its heartfelt tale of shattered dreams and fragile hope. —*Ali Sinclair*

Crusader / 1979 / A&M ✦✦✦

Although it features ambitious and sometimes overweighted compositions, *Crusader* still has Deburgh's usual melodic beauty and straightforward rhythmic arrangments. —*Vladimir Bogdanov*

Eastern Wind / 1980 / A&M ✦✦

This transitional album was no doubt a step forward from *Spanish Train*, but it never was a major success, except in Scandinavia, where it outsold the Beatles' *Let It Be*. —*Vladimir Bogdanov*

The Getaway / 1982 / A&M ✦✦✦

A powerful, strong collection of well-produced, well-balanced songs that show his vocal and writing skills at their best. "Don't Pay the Ferryman" is one of the best known of all of his recordings, but there is something on *The Getaway* for every mood and temperament. "Borderline," a wartorn ballad, soars with pain and hope from its quiet piano backing with just-the-right touch of plaintive lead guitar; "I'm Counting on You" portrays a father's hopes and doubts; and "The Getaway" is fun, cheerful, and strong. A good album and one of Deburgh's best. —*Ali Sinclair*

Man on the Line / May 1984 / A&M ✦✦✦

Man on the Line was the Chris Deburgh album that came between the modest breakthrough success of *The Getaway* and its Top 40 hit "Don't Pay the Ferryman" and the major career-making success of the goldselling *Into the Light* and its Top Ten hit "Lady in Red." To anyone who had liked "Don't Pay the Ferryman," it suggested that the song's virtues, especially Deburgh's emotion-filled voice and the widescreen, melodramatic production style, were not unique to one performance. Whether treating the conflicting intimate emotions of "Much More than This" and "The Head and the Heart" or taking on political issues in "The Sound of a Gun" and the title track, Deburgh gave all his vocals a theatrical urgency that was augmented by Rupert Hine's synthesized keyboard textures and a constant dance beat. The appropriately titled "High on Emotion" got halfway up the singles chart, but it wouldn't be until Deburgh eased off with the elegant "Lady in Red" that he'd become a real household name in the US, as he had long been around the world. —*William Ruhlmann*

Into the Light / 1986 / A&M ✦✦✦✦

Chris Deburgh's eighth album, *Into the Light*, released in his 11th year as a recording artist, finally broke him through to the two major record markets he had not conquered previously, the UK and the US. The reason was simple: The album contained a romantic ballad, "The Lady in Red," which topped the British charts and came close to doing the same thing in America. Heard within the context of *Into the Light*, however, Deburgh's big Anglo-American hit sounds like a slight tune, buried as the fourth track on the first side. On the rest of the album, it's easy to hear why Deburgh was such a success in South America and Europe before his breakthrough. *Into the Light* is an album full of simple melodic songs set to two kinds of Eurodisco beats—medium tempo and slow tempo. Deburgh delivers hooks as reliably as any pop performer; if a phrase, usually the song title, is worth singing once, it's worth singing 15 or 20 times more. In fact, these are songs for people for whom English is a second language. The imagery is all primary—sun, moon, fire, water—and the statements are all easily translatable into any European language (though they'd sound more complicated in German, of course). And the sentiments have a European tinge. In addition to the idealized love songs (including "The Lady in Red," which is part of that limited genre, of "Gee, honey, you really dolled yourself up" songs, along with Eric Clapton's "Wonderful Tonight"), Deburgh has politics on his mind, though he expresses it in terms just as simple as those in the love songs. "Last Night" tells us war is bad, "Say Goodbye to It All" tell us war is bad, "The Spirit of Man" tells us to hang on anyway, and the album-closing trilogy, "The Leader/The Vision/What About Me?," introduces that perennial European favorite, fascist dictatorship. Which is bad, too, though Deburgh gets close to the end before he gets around to saying so. —*William Ruhlmann*

Flying Colours / 1988 / A&M ✦✦✦✦

A No. 1 album in Great Britain, *Flying Colours* is by far Deburgh's most pop-oriented album. Crisp and clear arrangments, catchy melodies, and simple lyrics make it a favorite of fans. —*Vladimir Bogdanov*

● **Lady in Red: Very Best of Chris Deburgh** / 1991 / A&M ✦✦✦✦

Lady in Red: The Very Best of Chris DeBurgh is a fine overview of his biggest hits, featuring his two American hits ("The Lady in Red," "Don't Pay the Ferryman"), plus his other British hit ("Missing You") and several European singles that illustrate why he's an international favorite. —*Rodney Batdorf*

Joey Dee

b. Jun. 11, 1940, Passaic, NJ
Rock 'n' Roll

Joey Dee led the house band at New York's Peppermint Lounge, immortalizing the joint in his 1961 chart-topper "Peppermint Twist." Born Joseph DiNicola in Passaic, NJ, Dee teamed with veteran producer Henry Glover to cut "Peppermint Twist" for Roulette, and the huge hit led to a starring role in the film *Hey, Let's Twist*. Most of Dee's hits, including a supercharged revival of the Isley Brothers' hit "Shout" in 1962, were firmly in the Twist mode, although he took a successful stab at a softer sound that year with a Johnny Nash tune, "What Kind of Love Is This." Dee gave several future stars early breaks with the Starliters, notably the Ronettes, three-quarters of the Young Rascals, and Jimi Hendrix. Dee is still active on the oldies circuit. —*Bill Dahl*

● **Best of Joey Dee & Starliters: Hey Let's Twist** / Jun. 1990 / Rhino ✦✦✦✦

Best of Joey Dee & Starliters: Hey Let's Twist is a representative early-'60s compilation by the man who made the "Peppermint Twist" a national craze. —*Bill Dahl*

Deee-Lite

f. 1986, New York, NY, **db.** 1996
Dance-Pop, House, Club/Dance

With the massive popularity of their hit single "Groove Is in the Heart," Deee-Lite brought the colorful sights and sounds of New York's club culture into the mainstream. Formed in 1986, the trio was led by vocalist Lady Miss Kier (born Kieren Kirby in Youngstown, OH) and fleshed out by a pair of deejays, Super DJ Dmitry (a classically-trained guitarist and Russian emigre born Dmitry Brill) and Jungle DJ Towa Towa (born Doug Wa-Chung in Tokyo, Japan).

Fusing house, techno, rap, ambient, and funk music with an outrageous visual flair largely influenced by the drag-queen community (Kier's fondness for Fluevog platform shoes helped the 1970s fashion revival gather steam), Deee-Lite became hugely popular among New York club denizens, and the trio's own unique cultural make-up earned them a following that ignored racial and sexual boundaries. In 1990 they debuted with the album *World Clique*, a crossover smash thanks to hits like the loping classic "Groove Is in the Heart" (featuring the fluid bass of Bootsy Collins and the saxophone of Maceo Parker) and "Power of Love."

With their 1992 follow-up *Infinity Within*, Deee-Lite's music turned overtly political, as songs touched hot topics like the environment, safe sex, and democracy. Towa Towa left the group soon after; rechristened Towa Tei, he released his solo debut *Future Listening* in 1995. Kier and Dmitry, meanwhile, enlisted DJ Ani for 1994's *Dewdrops in the Garden*, a sensual outing influenced by the growing rave culture. After the release of 1996's remix album Sampadelic Relics and Dancefloor Oddities, Deee-Lite disbanded. —*Jason Ankeny*

● **World Clique** / Aug. 1990 / Elektra ✦✦✦✦

Deee-Lite's first and most consistent album, *World Clique* blends DJ Dmitry's and DJ Towa Tei's groovy, neo-retro house beats with Lady Miss Kier's sultry voice. The result is a nonstop dance album with as much artistic integrity as booty-shakin' power. Even though "Groove Is in the Heart" was the breakout hit from this album, tracks like "Smile On," "What Is Love?" and "World Clique" make this one of the best dance albums of the '90s. —*Heather Phares*

Infinity Within / Jun. 23, 1992 / Elektra ✦✦✦

Infinity Within is Deee-Lite's difficult second album. The group's social activism overtakes their instinctive infectiousness, producing well-intentioned but not especially memorable tracks like "I Had a Dream I Was Falling Through a Hole in the Ozone Layer" and "Rubber Lover." —*Heather Phares*

Dewdrops in the Garden / Aug. 2, 1994 / Elektra ✦✦✦✦

Dewdrops in the Garden sees DJ Towa Tei take a vacation from the band, replaced with DJ On-E—just one of the album's not-so-subtle rave references. The tracks on *Dewdrops in the Garden* are either pseudo-rave instrumentals or witty, funky showcases for Lady Kier's rich vocals. While it's somewhat inconsistent, songs like "Apple Juice Kissin'," "Picnic in the Summertime" and "Call Me " radiate with the group's innate charisma. —*Heather Phares*

Dancefloor Oddities & Sampladelic Relics / Oct. 29, 1996 / Elektra ✦✦✦

Dancefloor Oddities & Sampladelic Relics is a collection of remixes of classic Dee-Lite tracks, including "Groove Is in the Heart" and "Power of Love." The bulk of the compilation consists of new mixes, and while they do help update Dee-Lite's music for late-'90s dance-clubs, they don't have the visionary power of the original versions—or the remixes from the early '90s, for that matter—making it of interest only to dedicated fans of the group. —*Stephen Thomas Erlewine*

Deep Purple

f. 1968, Hertford, England
Hard Rock, Heavy Metal, Arena Rock
Formed in 1968, Deep Purple found success on Bill Cosby's Tetragrammaton label with remakes of Joe South's "Hush" (No. 4) and Neil Diamond's "Kentucky Woman" (No. 38). When Tetragrammaton went under shortly afterward, Deep Purple switched to Warner, with a change in lineup, including the addition of dramatic lead singer Ian Gillan.

Their first effort on Warner, Jon Lord's *Concerto for Group and Orchestra*, was a ponderously overblown affair that died a quick death in the marketplace. From there on out, the band pursued a hard-rock direction, generating their greatest successes on *Machine Head*, *Burn*, and the live double record set *Made in Japan*. In 1975 Deep Purple earned the dubious distinction of being named the "world's loudest band" in the *Guinness Book of World Records*. Much of Deep Purple's appeal during their heyday (from 1970's *In Rock* to 1973's *Made in Japan*) came from the lightning-fast duels between keyboardist Jon Lord and lead guitarist Ritchie Blackmore.

Deep Purple successfully carried on after Blackmore, Gillan, and bassist Roger Glover departed (at different times), with a lineup featuring ex-Trapeze member Glen Hughes (bass, vocals), Tommy Bolin (lead guitar, vocals), and David Coverdale (lead vocals). Coverdale would later front the popular MTV/AOR band Whitesnake. *—Rick Clark*

Shades of Deep Purple / 1968 / Tetragrammaton ✦✦✦✦
This is worthwhile mainly for their psychezilla cover of Joe South's "Hush," which pits Ritchie Blackmore's flame-throwing guitar bursts against Jon Lord's chugging organ. *—Tom Graves*

Deep Purple in Rock / 1970 / Warner Brothers ✦✦✦✦
The album on which Deep Purple decided they were rockers after all; they turned up the amps to prove it. Ian Gillan on vocals (added at this time) became the archetype for heavy metal screamers thereafter. Check out "Speed King," "Bloodsucker," and "Flight of the Rat" for your daily dose of high voltage. *—Tom Graves*

Fireball / 1971 / Warner Brothers ✦✦✦✦
Fireball solidified the band's reputation as purveyors of maximum-dosage heavy metal. Ritchie Blackmore steals the show with a wall of grinding chords and greased-lightning lead flourishes. At this juncture the band began to challenge Led Zeppelin's position as hard rock's most successful act. *—Tom Graves*

★ **Machine Head** / 1972 / Warner Brothers ✦✦✦✦✦
The definitive '70s heavy-metal album, each locomotive song ("Highway Star," "Space Truckin'") blasts off like World War III. The highlight is the AOR staple "Smoke on the Water," which has a mandatory riff for anyone owning a guitar. It still fries ears 20 years after the fact. *—Tom Graves*

Purple Passages / 1972 / Warner Brothers ✦✦
A compilation of Deep Purple's early work released to cash in on the group's *Machine Head* inspired success, *Purple Passages* contains the highlights from their late-'60s records, including "Hush" and "Kentucky Woman." *—Stephen Thomas Erlewine*

Who Do We Think We Are / Jan. 1973 / Warner Brothers ✦✦✦
The last gasp for the classic Deep Purple lineup, *Who Do We Think We Are* isn't as rock-solid as their previous records, but its best moments, including the deliriously stupid "Woman from Tokyo," are bludgeoning hard rock of the highest order. *—Stephen Thomas Erlewine*

Made in Japan / Apr. 1973 / Warner Brothers ✦✦✦✦
Not only could they kick ass in the studio, they could stir up a hornet's nest on stage, too. This double-album (one CD) set recorded in Japan includes most of their best material ("Highway Star," "Smoke on the Water") and pushes the metal envelope even further. Ritchie Blackmore is in peak form throughout. *—Tom Graves*

Burn / 1974 / Warner Brothers ✦✦✦
Burn is Deep Purple's first album with lead singer David Coverdale. While it's not quite up to the standards of *Machine Head* and *Made in Japan*, it featured enough hot riffs and well-constructed heavy rockers to make it a Top Ten success and an album rock favorite. *—Stephen Thomas Erlewine*

Stormbringer / 1974 / Metal Blade ✦✦
Stormbringer, Ritchie Blackmore's last album with Deep Purple, falls short of the excellence of *Machine Head* and *Who Do We Think We Are*, but nonetheless boasts some definite classics—including the fiery "Lady Double Dealer," the ominous title song (a Gothic-metal treasure), the sweaty "High Ball Shooter" and the melancholy ballad "Soldier of Fortune." Most of the other songs on the decent, if uneven, *Stormbringer* (which Metal Blade reissued on CD in the early '90s) are not essential. Like *Come Taste the Band*, *Stormbringer* will be of interest to Purple's more enthusiastic fans rather than casual listeners, who would be much better off starting out with either of the above-mentioned studio projects or the live *Made In Japan*. *—Alex Henderson*

Come Taste the Band / 1975 / Metal Blade ✦✦✦
When Ritchie Blackmore departed Deep Purple in the mid-1970s and formed Elf (which evolved into Blackmore's Rainbow and featured Ronnie James Dio), his replacement was Tommy Bolin. To be sure, Blackmore was a darn tough act to follow, but Bolin proved himself to be a fine guitarist in his own right on *Come Taste The Band*, his first album with Purple. But unfortunately, Bolin didn't have exceptional material to work with—decent and likable, but hardly exceptional. While sweaty, yet melodic, cuts like "Dealer," "Lady Luck" and "You Keep On Moving" are far from bad, nothing here is in a class with "Smoke on the Water" or "Highway Star." Purple's more hardcore devotees will want this album (reissued on CD in the early 1990s), though it's far from the best representation of their '70s work. *—Alex Henderson*

Made in Europe / 1976 / Metal Blade ✦✦
When We Rock, We Rock & When We Roll, We Roll / 1978 / Warner Brothers ✦✦✦✦
When We Rock, We Rock & When We Roll, We Roll is a solid, if incomplete collection from their 1968-1974 peak years. *—Dan Heilman*

The Best of Deep Purple in the '80's / 1994 / Mercury ✦✦✦
The Best of Deep Purple in the '80's may be inconsistent and unsatisfying, but that's an accurate reflection of the group's career during the decade. Even though it's fitfully entertaining, *Best Of* features all of the highlights the group recorded during the '80s and is preferable to the albums they released during the era. *—Stephen Thomas Erlewine*

Archive Alive / May 20, 1997 / Archive/Navarre ✦✦✦
Archive Alive is a double-disc set of previously unreleased live material from Deep Purple, including a complete concert from the group's peak period in the mid-'70s. In addition to the full concert, there's a selection of bonus tracks, and taken together, the set offers a good portrait of Deep Purple live on stage, making it a nice addition to the serious collector's library. *—Stephen Thomas Erlewine*

Def Leppard

f. 1977, Sheffield, England
Hard Rock, Pop-Rock, Heavy Metal
Def Leppard in many ways was the definitive hard rock band of the '80s. Many bands rocked harder and were more dangerous than the Sheffield quintet, but few others captured the spirit of the times quite as well. Emerging in the late '70s as part of the New Wave of British Heavy Metal, the group actually owed more to the glam-rock and metal of the early '70s; their sound was equal parts T. Rex, Mott the Hoople, Queen, and Led Zeppelin. By toning down their heavy riffs and emphasizing the melody, Def Leppard was poised for crossover success by 1983's *Pyromania*, and they skillfully used the fledgling MTV to their advantage. The group was blessed with photogenic good looks, but they also crafted a series of innovative, exciting videos that made them into stars. They intended to follow *Pyromania* quickly, but were derailed when their drummer lost an arm in a car accident, the first of many problems that plagued the group. Def Leppard managed to pull through such tragedies, and they even expanded their large audience with 1987's blockbuster *Hysteria*. As the '90s began, mainstream hard rock shifted from Leppard's signature pop-metal toward edgier, louder bands, but the group maintained a sizable audience into the late '90s and was one of only a handful of '80s metal groups to survive the decade more or less intact.

Def Leppard had its origins in a Sheffield-based group that Rick Savage (bass) and Pete Willis (guitar) formed in their late teens in 1977. A few months later, vocalist Joe Elliott, a fanatic follower of Mott the Hoople and T. Rex, joined the band, bringing the name Deaf Leopard. After a spelling change, the trio, augmented by a now-forgotten drummer, began playing local Sheffield pubs, and within a year they had added guitarist Steve Clark and a new drummer. Later in 1978 they recorded their debut EP *Getcha Rocks Off* and released it on their own label, Bludgeon Riffola. The EP became a word-of-mouth success, earning play on the BBC. The group members were still in their teens.

After the release of *Getcha Rocks Off*, Rick Allen was added as the band's permanent drummer, and Def Leppard quickly became the subject of the British music weeklies. Soon they signed with AC/DC's manager Petter Mensch, who helped them secure a contract with Mercury. *On Through the Night*, the band's full-length debut, was released in 1980 and instantly became a hit in the UK, also earning significant airplay in the US, where it reached No. 51 on the charts. Over the course of the year, Def Leppard relentlessly toured Britain and America, including opening slots for Ozzy Osbourne, Sammy Hagar, and Judas Priest. *High 'n' Dry* followed in 1981, and it became the group's first platinum album in the US, thanks to MTV's strong rotation of "Bringin' on the Heartbreak." MTV would be vital to the band's success in the '80s.

As the band recorded the follow-up to *High 'n' Dry* with producer Mutt Lange, Pete Willis was fired from the band for alcoholism, and Phil Collen, a former guitarist for Girl, was hired to replace him. The resulting album, 1983's *Pyromania*, became an unexpected blockbuster, due not only to Def Leppard's skillful, melodic metal, but also to MTV's relentless airing of "Photograph" and "Rock of Ages." *Pyromania* went on to sell 10 million copies, establishing Def Leppard as one of the most popular bands in the world. Despite its success, the band was about to enter a trying time. After an extensive international tour, the group re-entered the studio to record the follow-up, but producer Lange was unavailable, so they began sessions with Jim Steinman, the man responsible for Meat Loaf's *Bat Out of Hell*. The pairing turned out to be ill-advised, so the group turned to its former engineer, Nigel Green. One month into recording, Rick Allen lost his left arm in a New Year's Eve car accident. The arm was reattached, but it had to be amputated when an infection set in.

Without a drummer, Def Leppard's future looked cloudy, but by the spring of 1985—just a few months after his accident—Allen began learning to play a custom-made electronic kit assembled for him by Simmons. Soon the band resumed recording, and within a few months Lange was back on board, but once he joined the team, he judged the existing tapes inferior and had the band begin work all over again. The recording continued throughout 1986, and that summer, the group returned to the stage for the European Monsters of Rock tour. Def Leppard finally completed its fourth album, now titled *Hysteria*, early in 1987, releasing it that spring to lukewarm reviews; many critics felt that the album compromised Leppard's metal roots for sweet pop flourishes. The record was slow out of the starting gates—"Women," the first single, failed to really take hold. But with the second single, "Animal," *Hysteria* began to take off. It became the group's first Top 40 hit in the UK, but more importantly, it began a string of six straight Top 20 hits in the US, which included "Hysteria," "Pour Some Sugar on Me," "Love Bites," "Armageddon It," and "Rocket," the latter in 1989, a full two years after the release of *Hysteria*. During those two years, Def Leppard was unavoidable. They were the kings of high school metal, ruling the pop charts and MTV, and teenagers and bands alike replicated their teased hair and ripped jeans, even when the grimy hard rock of Guns N' Roses took hold in 1988.

Hysteria proved to be the peak of Leppard's popularity, but their follow-up remained eagerly awaited in the early '90s. During the recording, Steve Clark died from an overdose of alcohol and drugs. Clark had long had a problem with alcohol, and after the *Hysteria* heyday, the band forced him to take a sabbatical; he did enter rehab, but to no apparent effect. In fact, his abuse was so crippling that Collen had to play the majority of the guitar leads on *Hysteria*. After Clark's death, Def Leppard resolved to finish its forthcoming album as a quartet, releasing *Adrenalize* in the spring of 1992. *Adrenalize* was greeted with mixed reviews, and even though the album debuted at No. 1 and contained several hit singles, including "Let's Get Rocked," "Have You Ever Needed Someone So Bad," and "Make Love like a Man," the record was a commercial disappointment in the wake of *Pyromania* and *Hysteria*. After the release of *Adrenalize*, the group added former Whitesnake guitarist Vivian Campbell.

In 1993 Def Leppard released the rarities collection *Retro Active*, featuring a new single, "Miss You in a Heartbeat," which scraped the lower reaches of the Top 40. Two years later the group released the greatest hits collection *Vault* while preparing their sixth album. *Slang* arrived in the spring of 1996, and while it was more adventurous than its predecessor, it was greeted with indifference, proving that Leppard's heyday had passed; it was now simply a very popular cult band. — *Stephen Thomas Erlewine*

On Through the Night / 1980 / Mercury ✦✦✦
Their US debut includes "Rock Brigade." — *AMG*

High 'n' Dry / 1981 / Mercury ✦✦✦
This includes "Bringing On the Heartache." — *AMG*

☆ **Pyromania** / 1983 / Mercury ✦✦✦✦✦
Although Def Leppard's first two workmanlike metal albums, *On Through the Night* and *High 'n' Dry*, had already established the band in both England and the US, it was *Pyromania* that broke the sound (and sales) barrier for them. *Pyromania*'s acute emphasis on pop sensibilities in songs like "Photograph" and "Rock Rock ('til You Drop)" over numbing thonk made the album a huge crossover success with the more conservative AOR market. MTV video saturation with key *Pyromania* songs didn't hurt either. — *Tom Graves*

☆ **Hysteria** / 1987 / Mercury ✦✦✦✦✦
If *Pyromania* was great pop-metal, *Hysteria* upped the ante a few more notches. With dense, elaborate instrumental layering and meticulous engineering, the album became known almost as much for its production values as for its terrific music. Drummer Rick Allen, who lost an arm in an automobile accident, adds an even harder core of bottom end with his specially rigged drum kit. As hardhitting as it is slick sounding, *Hysteria* became the standard-bearer for pop metal with anthemic tracks like "Rocket" and "Pour Some Sugar on Me." This is one of the masterpieces of the '80s that renewed the faith, for many, in sensible hard rock. — *Tom Graves*

Adrenalize / Dec. 24, 1992 / Mercury ✦✦✦
The jury may still be out on *Adrenalize*, but with the band's misfortunes (guitarist Steve Clark died of a drug overdose), they can be forgiven for slipping a bit after the mega-success of *Hysteria*. That's not to dismiss *Adrenalize*, however, which still has a heaping helping of Leppard's patented Brit-pop crash-and-burn fusion. — *Tom Graves*

Retro Active / Oct. 5, 1993 / Mercury ✦✦✦
It may be just a collection of B-sides and lost tracks, but *Retro Active* rocks harder and more convincingly than *Adrenalize*. It also has twice the hooks, making it of interest to more than just hardcore Def Leppard fans. — *Stephen Thomas Erlewine*

● **Vault: Def Leppard's Greatest Hits** / Oct. 31, 1995 / Mercury ✦✦✦✦
Def Leppard was untouchable in the '80s. Over the course of four albums, the band established itself as one of the best and most popular hard-rock/heavy-metal groups of the decade, scoring a long list of hit singles. *Vault: Def Leppard's Greatest Hits—1980-1995* compiles the biggest of those hits, as well as selections from their first album of the '90s, *Adrenalize*, and the outtakes collection *Retro Active*. Essentially, Def Leppard's legacy rests on two albums, 1983's *Pyromania* and 1987's *Hysteria*. On both records, the group created a sleek, shiny brand of hard rock powered by huge, catchy melodies and guitar hooks that owed more to Mott the Hoople and T. Rex than Deep Purple and Black Sabbath. It was a polished but potent sound, whether the band turned out rockers ("Photograph," "Rocket") or ballads ("Bringin' On the Heartbreak," "Love Bites"). *Vault* has all of the necessary items, from "Pour Some Sugar on Me" to "Rock of Ages." It's not a perfect collection—it's not sequenced chronologically, it includes too much material from *Adrenalize*, and the new "When Love and Hate Collide" is simply average—but that doesn't stop *Vault* from being a great greatest hits collection. — *Stephen Thomas Erlewine*

Slang / May 14, 1996 / Mercury ✦✦✦
After the lackluster performance of *Adrenalize*, Def Leppard realized it was time to abandon their trademark wall-of-guitars sound. Jettisoning producer Mutt Lange—who, admittedly, was busy producing his wife, country singer Shania Twain—the group stripped their sound to the basics for *Slang*. There are very few layers-of-guitar effects on the album, just straight, crunching chords. Most notably, Rick Allen has returned to playing acoustic drums after playing an electronic kit for nearly a decade. The change in approach is apparent and welcome—Def Leppard hasn't sounded so immediate since *Pyromania*. Furthermore, they decided to expand their musical vocabulary slightly, working elements of R&B and funk into the rhythms. Not all of the experiments work, but Def Leppard sounds revitalized, particularly when they attack a straightforward rocker. *Slang* would have been even better if they had come up with a set of hooks that sounded as alive as their performance, but the album is a much-needed return to form for the group. — *Stephen Thomas Erlewine*

Del Amitri

f. 1982, Glasgow, Scotland
Folk-Rock, Pop-Rock, Adult Alternative Pop-Rock
Glasgow's Del Amitri has gained a strong cult following for their country- and folk-inflected rock 'n' roll and the quality songwriting of bassist/ vocalist Justin Currie and guitarist Iain Harvie, plus the frequently ironic lyrics of the former. Currie and Harvie formed the band in 1982, releasing the independent single "Sense Sickness" in 1983 with guitarist Bryan Tolland and drummer Paul Tyagi. In 1984 the band was invited to record for BBC DJ John Peel, and tours with acts like the Fall and the Smiths helped the group build a fan base and get a deal with Chrysalis. Del Amitri's self-titled debut album was released in 1985 and featured a country- and new wave-influenced brand of pop-rock, but unfortunately, the group had appeared on the cover of *Melody Maker* two months before its release; critics slammed the album in the wake of excessive hype, while potential fans perceived the lack of product in record stores as a sign of the album's quality. However, a network of fans helped organize a low-budget Del Amitri tour of the US. Encouraged, the band returned to England and hammered out new material, which helped get them signed to A&M in 1987. Tolland was replaced by guitarist David Cummings, and Tyagi by drummer David Cummings; the group added keyboardist Andy Alston. In 1990 *Waking Hours* accentuated Del Amitri's roots-rock feel and produced the British singles "Kiss This Thing Goodbye," "Nothing Ever Happens," and "Spit in the Rain"; the former scraped the lower reaches of the US Top 40. The 1992 follow-up, *Change Everything*, solidified their popularity in the UK and produced another minor American chart single, "Always the Last to Know." Drummer Brian McDermott left the band in 1994 and was replaced by Ashley Soan. *Twisted* was released early in 1996. — *Steve Huey*

Del Amitri / 1985 / Chrysalis ✦✦✦
Sounding like a gang of snotty pop antagonists, Del Amitri came out swinging on this quirky and often brilliant debut. Vocalist Justin Currie's lyrics were intelligent and witty, laced with sarcasm and venom. With

jaunty rhythms and quirky melodies, calling them the bastard sons of XTC and Elvis Costello would not have been too far off the mark. Highlights include "Sticks and Stones Girl" and "Hammering Heart." —*Spaz Schnee*

● **Waking Hours** / 1989 / A&M ✦✦✦✦
After four years in hibernation, Del Amitri emerged as a gang of mature pop stars. Dropping their edgy quirkiness, Justin and the boys explored their Scottish folk roots, refashioned their sound, and quickly established themselves as a rock band with heart. Still retaining a bit of the Elvis Costello musical heritage, the Dels added a dose of Elvis Presley (check out Currie's sideburns!) and a healthy chunk of Van Morrison. This time, the critics came in droves and the public started to take notice. Highlights include "Nothing Ever Happens," "Stone Cold Sober" and "Kiss This Thing Goodbye." —*Spaz Schnee*

Change Everything / Jun. 9, 1992 / A&M ✦✦✦✦
Contrary to the album's title, the Dels kept on doing what they were doing and released an even better album than *Waking Hours*. Although the songs here were not as good as any individual song from their past, the album as a whole was their best yet. —*Spaz Schnee*

Twisted / Feb. 28, 1995 / A&M ✦✦✦✦
Taking a tiny step backwards, Del Amitri did not top their previous outing this time, but they remained true to their musical cause. The fact that they sound a bit tired may mean that it is time to re-evaluate their journey. —*Spaz Schnee*

Del Fuegos

f. 1983, Boston, MA, **db.** 1990
Roots-Rock
Part of the roots-rock movement of the 1980s, the Del Fuegos hailed from Boston and released several acclaimed albums during the mid-'80s before falling into critical disfavor. The band was formed and led by brothers Dan (vocals) and Warren Zanes (guitar) and featured a rhythm section of bassist Tom Lloyd and former Embarrassment drummer B. Woody Giessmann. Their energetic debut, *The Longest Day*, was released on the Slash label in 1984 to wide acclaim for its simple '60s-influenced rock 'n' roll energy, high-quality songwriting, and wide emotional range. Released in 1985, *Boston, Mass.* was a homage to the group's working-class roots *a la* Bob Seger, but 1987's *Stand Up* was a major misstep, panned by critics as bland, boring, and indulgent. Giessmann left the band, which recorded one more album, 1989's *Smoking in the Fields*, which reflected a newfound maturity and love of R&B. In spite of their return to critical favor, the band quietly disappeared shortly after the release of *Smoking in the Fields*. —*Steve Huey*

The Longest Day / 1984 / Slash ✦✦✦✦
An explosive garage-meets-roots-rock debut from the Boston rockers. —*David Szatmary*

● **Boston, Mass.** / 1985 / Slash ✦✦✦✦
Building from the blue-collar foundation of *The Longest Day*, the Del Fuegos crafted another winning record of straightahead rock 'n' roll with their second album, *Boston, Mass.* While the record isn't as bracing as the debut, it features a better, more consistent selection of songs, and the group's sound is clean, professional, and hard-rocking, making the album an infectious and entertaining, if unassuming, collection of roots-rock. —*Stephen Thomas Erlewine*

Stand Up / 1987 / Slash ✦✦✦
A tone-downed, more bluesy effort, it includes guests James Burton and Tom Petty. —*David Szatmary*

Delaney & Bonnie

f. 1966, Los Angeles, CA, **db.** 1972
Blues-Rock, Pop-Rock
Delaney Bramlett (b Jul 1, 1939) and his wife Bonnie (b Nov 8, 1944) recorded a series of blues and country-influenced albums in the late '60s and early '70s. A variety of musicians played in Delaney & Bonnie's band, including Eric Clapton, Dave Mason, Duane Allman, Leon Russell, Rita Coolidge, Jim Gordon, Bobby Whitlock, and Carl Radle. Clapton, Gordon, Whitlock, and Radle formed Derek & the Dominoes after performing together on Delaney & Bonnie's 1969-70 tour. Delaney & Bonnie's records were a strong influence on Eric Clapton's style in the '70s. The group broke up after the Bramletts' marriage collapsed in 1972. —*Kenneth M. Cassidy*

● **Delaney & Bonnie & Friends on Tour with Eric Clapton** / Jun. 1970 / Atco ✦✦✦✦
Recorded with Eric Clapton, *On Tour* features Delaney & Bonnie's blend of country, rock, blues, and gospel. It includes "I'm Coming Home." —*Kenneth M. Cassidy*

The Best of Delaney & Bonnie / Nov. 1990 / Rhino ✦✦✦
This is a good overview of their brief career. —*Kenneth M. Cassidy*

The Delfonics

f. 1965, Philadelphia, PA, **db.** 1974
Soul, Quiet Storm
A sweet ballad-oriented Philadelphia vocal trio, the Delfonics proved highly popular in the late '60s and early '70s. Lead singer William Hart's high-pitched tenor effortlessly sailed into falsetto range on their first hit in 1968, "La-La—Means I Love You," a typically smooth ballad filled with swirling strings. Hart and co-producer Thom Bell wrote most of the group's early smashes, including the majestic "Didn't I (Blow Your Mind This Time)" in 1970. The group's hit-making reign ended in 1974. —*Bill Dahl*

● **The Best of the Delfonics** / 1990 / Arista ✦✦✦✦
The Delfonics were arguably the premier sweet soul band of the late '60s and early '70s; their shimmering harmonies and William Hart's agonizing falsetto, coupled with Stan Watson's production and Thom Bell's arranging and writing touches, created many unforgettable love songs. While their hits have been frequently collected and reissued, this CD set, while short (37 minutes), includes among its 12 tracks every major hit except "Over and Over." Engineering guru Bill Inglot used original masters, fully capturing the trio's marvelous interaction, the songs' sweeping arrangements, and the great mix of vulnerability, hurt, and poignance that characterized their finest hits. —*Ron Wynn*

The Dell-Vikings

f. 1955, Pittsburgh, PA
R&B, Doo Wop
One of the first integrated acts during rock 'n' roll's infancy, the Dell-Vikings recorded a beloved classic in 1956, "Come Go with Me." The quintet was formed at Pittsburgh's Air Force Serviceman's Club in 1955 while the members were stationed there. They recorded their immortal "Come Go with Me," written by bass singer Clarence Quick, in the basement of a local deejay and sold the master to tiny FeeBee Records. When given national distribution on Dot, the upbeat tune proved a monster hit. Upon their discharge, four members split to form a new "Del Vikings" on Mercury, hitting in 1957 with "Cool Shake." Kripp Johnson, meanwhile, stayed with Dot, assembling a new lineup of "Dell-Vikings" that included a young Chuck Jackson, and hitting at precisely the same time with "Whispering Bells." All the confusion about the two groups may have ultimately sunk both, since those were the last hits for either lineup. —*Bill Dahl*

● **Dell Vikings** / 1988 / Collectables ✦✦✦✦
Solid hits by one of doo wop's first integrated groups. —*Bill Dahl*

The Best of the Del Vikings: The Mercury Years / Jul. 16, 1996 / Mercury ✦✦✦
Read the title carefully, because the Dell-Vikings' two great doo wop hits—"Come Go with Me" and "Whispering Bells"—were *not* recorded for Mercury, and so are not contained on this compilation. This disc has 22 sides they recorded for Mercury in 1957-58, with a lineup that had some but not all of the members that recorded "Come Go with Me" and "Whispering Bells." (To make matters more confusing, a different Dell-Vikings, led by Kripp Johnson, who had sung lead on "Whispering Bells," kept recording for a different label.) The Mercury Dell-Vikings did have a Top 20 hit right out of the box, "Cool Shake" (included here), but never had a big single again. Most of this is routine doo wop that's below the standards of their Dot sides, sometimes clouded by inadvisable attempts at pop-oriented material and production. It's of value only to hard-core doo wop bugs, who will appreciate the inclusion of many tracks available only on rare EPs, singles, and compilations, as well as one previously unissued in the US. The intro to "The Bells," by the way, bears a close similarity to the famous wordless scats that kicked off the Marcels' classic "Blue Moon" several years later. —*Richie Unterberger*

The Dells

f. 1952, Chicago, IL, **db.** 1986
Soul, Doo Wop
After nearly four decades of recording an incredible legacy of hits, the Dells have made only one personnel change in their entire professional career. Perhaps that's why the venerable R&B vocal group can boast such a remarkably consistent track record. The quintet from Chicago's south suburbs has weathered stylistic shifts from doo wop and soul to disco and urban contemporary, and every permutation in between. Their harmony remains as striking as ever, with Marvin Junior's earths-haking lead enduring as the group's focal point.

Signing with Vee-Jay in 1955, their creamy vocal blend on "Oh, What a Night" gave the Dells their first major R&B hit the next year, but it would be nearly a decade before they returned to the winner's circle with another dreamy classic, "Stay in My Corner." By then Chicago's R&B sound had changed drastically—doo wop was dead and soul was king—but the Dells adapted effortlessly, regularly scaling the charts for the Chess subsidiary Cadet with "There Is," "Always Together," "Give

Your Baby a Standing Ovation," and a marathon remake of "Stay in My Corner" that afforded Junior's booming baritone room to roam.

Seemingly an indestructible force (turning up on the R&B charts as recently as 1984), the succinct harmonies of the Dells span entire generations of R&B history. —*Bill Dahl*

There Is / 1968 / Chess ✦✦✦✦
This rich 1966-1968 Chicago soul has little of the overproduction that marred the powerful R&B quintet's later Chess output. —*Bill Dahl*

The Dells / 1969 / Chess ✦✦✦✦
Tremendous vocals and production, coupled with superb ballads and good uptempo cuts. The Dells were never better than during the late '60s, when they moved to Cadet and Charles Stepney's vision was fulfilled. Although he was never fully credited, lead singer Marvin Jr. stands as one of soul's great vocalists, and he showed it repeatedly on this set. Johnny Carter's floating falsetto was another major weapon expertly utilized in the Dells' soul success. —*Ron Wynn*

Love Is Blue / 1969 / Cadet ✦✦✦✦
A fine album that included their excellent version of the title cut, some other stirring ballads, and some good uptempo tunes. The Dells were now in peak form, with Marvin Jr.'s booming voice and Charles Stepney's productions and good arrangements turning them into the hitmakers they never were in the doo-wop days. —*Ron Wynn*

Oh, What a Night / 1970 / Collectables ✦✦✦✦
Earlier doo-wop classics by the venerable Windy City R&B vocal group, this showcases their impeccable harmony on the gorgeous title track and similar fare. —*Bill Dahl*

Freedom Means / 1971 / Cadet ✦✦✦
A fine early-'70s date, with the title track one of the more socio-political songs the Dells ever recorded. Both Marvin Jr. and Johnny Carter were in fine form, and while this was pretty basic material, they sang it with passion and exuberance. —*Ron Wynn*

Sweet As Funk Can Be / 1972 / Cadet ✦✦✦
Although not as striking as some other Dells albums, this was still good enough. There were some first-rate ballads, a few decent uptempo tracks, and plenty of fine lead vocals, as always, by Marvin Jr., with Johnny Carter's angelic answering falsetto coming in right on time. —*Ron Wynn*

I Touched a Dream / 1980 / 20th Century ✦✦✦✦
The last great Dells album, and one of the year's big surprises. The Dells were on another new label, and now were working with Carl Davis and Eugene Record (also of the Chi-Lites). The pair simply restored the Dells' strengths; each production made sure Marvin Jr.'s roaring leads and Johnny Carter's wavery falsetto were at the forefront. They also got them a superb ballad in the title track, a good message song in "It's All About the Paper," and other fine cuts. —*Ron Wynn*

★ **On Their Corner** / Mar. 10, 1992 / Chess ✦✦✦✦✦
Excellent compilation of their late-'60s sides, like "Oh What a Night," "Stay in My Corner," "The Love We Had Stays on My Mind," and "Give Your Baby a Standing Ovation." —*Stephen Thomas Erlewine*

Dreams of Contentment / Nov. 17, 1993 / Vee-Jay ✦✦✦✦
The Dells never made it over the hump while at Vee-Jay, despite making impressive singles. They were a top-flight doo wop group, but they couldn't find a way to advance beyond the R&B margins. Only when they moved to Chess, changed style, and made Marvin Junior the lead singer did they enjoy success they deserved. Still, as this 24-track reissue shows, there wasn't anything wrong with their Vee-Jay output. They experimented on such numbers as "Lil Darlin'," "It's Not for Me to Say," and "It's Not Unusual" with jazz/pop harmonies and covers. In addition, songs like "Now I Pray" and "Pain in My Heart" are wonderfully sung and harmonized, even if they weren't huge sellers. —*Ron Wynn*

Passionate Breezes: The Best of 1975-1991 / Oct. 1995 / Mercury ✦✦✦
By the last half of the '70s, the Dells had already gone through two phases in their career, transforming themselves from an R&B vocal group into a smooth soul outfit and scoring hits in both incarnations. During the late '70s and '80s, the group continued to perform, usually in the same vein as their early-'70s hits. Even if the strength of their voices hadn't diminished, their audience had. Nevertheless, much of the material they recorded during this era was fine, as *Passionate Breezes: Best of 1975-1991* proves. It's not as compulsively listenable as the group's doo wop hits or their early-'70s material, but there is still enough first-rate music here to satisfy fans. —*Stephen Thomas Erlewine*

Bring Back the Love: Classic Dells Soul / Feb. 27, 1996 / Chess ✦✦✦✦

Sandy Denny

b. Jan. 6, 1948, Wimbledon, England, d. Apr. 21, 1978, London, England
Guitar, Piano, Vocals / Folk-Rock, British Folk
Maddy Prior, Jacqui McShee, and June Tabor all give her a run for her

money, but the late Sandy Denny remains the pre-eminent British folk-rock singer. In addition to recording several albums of her own, Denny was an integral force behind the best work of the most respected British folk-rock band of all, Fairport Convention, and contributed mightily to recordings by the Strawbs and Fotheringay. It's impossible for words to fully evoke the haunting, spectral presence of her powerful and penetrating alto voice, which seemed to bring the mythology of English moors and folktales to life in contemporary, 20th-century settings.

Denny was studying to be a nurse when she began to pursue music seriously in the mid-'60s, partially at the encouragement of the then-struggling Simon & Garfunkel, whom she met when they were still unknown. She was also friendly with the American folk singer Jackson Frank, and recorded a couple of his songs on her first album (now available as *The Original Sandy Denny*). While this solo acoustic recording was her most traditional folk effort, it showed considerable potential, which she came closer to realizing on the 1967 album she recorded as a member of the Strawbs. This found her singing with fuller folk-rock arrangements, and included her first recorded composition, "Who Knows Where the Time Goes." The song gave Sandy her first international recognition when Judy Collins recorded it in 1968.

Denny was tapped to replace Judy Dyble in Fairport Convention in 1968, and is prominently featured on their late-'60s albums *What We Did on Our Holidays*, *Unhalfbricking*, and *Liege and Lief*. These are recognized not only as Fairport's best work, but as some of the finest British folk-rock records of all time. Although Denny shared the lead vocal chores with other members of the group, it was her singing that highlighted the best tracks, such as "Tam Lin," "Fotheringay," and "Autopsy" (the last two of which she wrote).

Denny left Fairport Convention in 1970, and while both she and Fairport would produce some worthwhile work in the future, it's fair to say that neither band nor singer would reach the same peaks again. She formed the short-lived Fotheringay, which included her future husband Trevor Lucas on guitar, but which disbanded after one decent album (a planned second LP was never completed). She recorded a few solo albums for Island in the 1970s that sometimes suffered from unsympathetic over-production and weak material, though the highlights were worth hearing. There was also an unremarkable album of oldies covers that she helped out with as a member of the Bunch, a British folk supersession of sorts that included Richard Thompson. When mainstream rock listeners heard her voice in the 1970s, however, it was usually not on her own records, but as a guest vocalist on Led Zeppelin's "The Battle of Evermore."

Much of the best of Denny's later solo work, oddly, is found on live and BBC recordings, some of which surfaced on the box set *Who Knows Where the Time Goes?* (Others appear on the bootleg *Dark the Night*.) While Denny was a first-rate folk-rock singer, she usually didn't mesh well with mainstream rock or hard rock arrangements, and the live work usually framed her vocals in more appropriately sparse settings. She joined Fairport again for a while in the mid-'70s, appearing on the 1975 album *Rising for the Moon*, but the reunion didn't really excite the participants or the audiences, and she left for good in 1976. Her final LP, *Rendezvous*, came out in 1977; the next year, she died from injuries sustained in a fall down a flight of stairs. —*Richie Unterberger*

Sandy Denny / 1970 / Saga ✦✦✦

North Star Grassman and the Ravens / 1971 / Hannibal ✦✦✦
Some second thoughts and reapproaches to older work. —*Bruce Eder*

Sandy / 1972 / A&M ✦✦✦✦
Those seeking initiation into the ranks of Denny fans may consult listings for Fairport Convention and Fotheringay. Also, try this solo album, which features many of the same players (Richard Thompson, Dave Swarbrick, etc.) and contains a good collection of Denny originals, along with her rendition of Dylan's "Tomorrow Is a Long Time." —*William Ruhlmann*

The / 1972 / A&M ✦✦

Like an Old Fashioned Waltz / 1973 / Hannibal ✦✦

Rendezvous / 1977 / Hannibal ✦✦✦
Stylistically varied, if not so fresh as her album *Sandy*. —*Bruce Eder*

Sandy Denny & The Strawbs / 1985 / Hannibal ✦✦✦
Pre-Fairport Denny with a British bluegrass band that later moved into progressive rock (without her). Her voice and a moody rendition of her classic "Who Knows Where the Time Goes" make it worthwhile. —*Bruce Eder*

Who Knows Where the Time Goes [Box Set] / 1986 / Hannibal ✦✦✦✦
This magnificently produced multi-disc box set presents a complete portrait of Sandy Denny, the haunting singer; the melodic, mournful songwriter; and the mesmerizing bandleader of Fairport Convention and Fotheringay. Much of the material is previously unheard, but it's all of a piece with Denny's accomplished work on her solo albums and in her

groups. The album makes the case for Denny as a major folk artist. *—William Ruhlmann*

● **The Best of Sandy Denny [Best of Box]** / 1989 / Hannibal ✦✦✦✦
A concise collection of key tracks and an excellent introduction. *—Bruce Eder*

Original Sandy Denny / 1991 / Trojan ✦✦✦
Denny's first recording, originally released in 1967, is her most traditional effort. Backed only by her own acoustic guitar, Denny's voice is assured, pure, and powerful on her debut. The album features traditional folk staples like "This Train," "Make Me a Pallet on Your Floor," and "Pretty Polly," as well as covers of Tom Paxton's "Ramblin' Boy" and "Milk and Honey." There are also a couple of songs by the obscure American songwriter Jackson Frank, one of which she would soon perform with Fairport Convention ("You Never Wanted Me"). Although this has little of the folk-rock cross-pollination that Denny would soon master with Fairport and others, it is still an impressive LP that shows her voice in as haunting and commanding form as her more renowned recordings. *—Richie Unterberger*

Dark the Night [bootleg] / 1995 / Nixed ✦✦✦✦
Excellent not just by bootleg standards, but by any standards, this 73-minute disc assembles unreleased demos and BBC sessions from 1966, 1972, and 1973. Two BBC performances from 1966, and seven demos from the same year, show Denny at her purest and most traditional, her voice accompanied only by acoustic guitar. These early cuts are similar to the obscure *Original Sandy Denny* album (also recorded around 1966) in showcasing her amazing high, soaring vocals on a mixture of traditional material and contemporary folk songs. What's more, the sound quality is excellent, at least as good as the official *Original Sandy Denny;* only one song from that album is also performed on this disc, which includes Dennis covering unexpected tunes like Dylan's "It Ain't Me Babe" and cult folkie Jackson Frank's "Blues Run the Game." The 1972-73 BBC sessions, in stellar quality, feature Denny originals from the period and a couple of jazz/pop covers with basic, straightforward arrangements. As Denny's solo albums often suffered from over-production, these performances actually benefit from the sparseness. Closing the CD are two odd but atmospheric pieces from the obscure 1972 soundtrack *Pass of Arms.* It might not be that easy for everyone to find, but Sandy Denny fans need this disc; it not only fills in important gaps, but stands up well against her best solo releases. *—Richie Unterberger*

Attic Tracks 1972-1984 / 1995 / Raven ✦✦✦✦
The perfect—and we do mean *perfect*—complement to Hannibal Records' *Who Knows Where the Time Goes* box. *Attic Tracks* (so named to distinguish it from Dylan's *Basement Tapes*) is an 18-song collection from Australia's Raven Records consisting of unreleased songs, outtakes, and extreme rarities, recorded by Sandy Denny and her former husband, the late Trevor Lucas. Included are tracks from Fairport's 1974 tour ("The Ballad of Ned Kelly"); Denny's beautiful, passionate French version of "Listen, Listen," entitled "Ecoute, Ecoute"; a pair of Denny demos ("One More Chance," "Rising for the Moon") given to Fairport Convention for their recording of the *Rising for the Moon* album; the lost 1975 Lucas/Fairport track "Tears"; "Losing Game," a Flying Burrito Bros. track recorded by Denny and Lucas, in a broad, brassy, hard-rocking version in 1972 and finished in 1976, but never released; the forgotten 1977 Denny B-side "Still Waters Run Deep"; Lucas' version of Bob Dylan's "Forever Young"; three songs from the last concert that Denny ever gave, including one of her longest, liveliest versions of "Who Knows Where the Time Goes" on record; and Denny's fiery reading of the Little Feat song "Easy to Slip," recorded during the making of her *Rendezvous* album. The big surprise, however, is Lucas' gently soulful cover of the Australian hit "Girls on the Avenue," on which his voice has an extraordinary "haunt count" and the accompaniment is nothing less than ravishing, in a mid-'70s pop vein—Paul McCartney should only make such records! A unique collection, and a necessary addition to the possessions of any fan of Fairport Convention or Sandy Denny. *—Bruce Eder*

One Last Sad Refrain: the Final Concert 11/27/77 [bootleg] / Nixed ✦✦✦
Less than six months after this performance, Sandy Denny would be dead. Her last concert, however, found her voice in pretty good shape, with accomplished backup, although the band is kind of prototypically bland in a mid-'70s rock sort of way. One of these tracks ("The Lady") actually shows up on the *Who Knows Where the Time Goes?* set; the rest is in very good fidelity, superb for a bootleg, and just below the standards you would expect on an official release. A mournful country-rock guitar is heard through much of the program, highlighted by "The Sea," a reading of Dylan's "Tomorrow Is a Long Time," and "Who Knows Where the Time Goes." As a significant bonus, the CD also has four songs from the very obscure 1972 *Swedish Fly Girls* soundtrack; these selections are curious but nice folk-rock, given an odd orchestral pop sort of production. *—Richie Unterberger*

John Denver (John Henry Deutchendorf)
b. Dec. 31, 1943, Roswell, NM
Guitar, Vocals / Singer-Songwriter, Soft Rock, Folk-Rock
In the '70s, John Denver's simple, melodic, light folk-pop made him one of the decade's biggest stars. In the '60s, he played with his idols the Chad Mitchell Trio, turning into a talented songwriter while he was with the group. Denver left for a solo career in 1969; later in the year, his "Leaving on a Jet Plane" became a big hit for Peter, Paul and Mary. In no time, Denver established himself as a star in his own right, with songs like "Take Me Home, Country Roads," "Rocky Mountain High," "Sunshine on My Shoulders," "Annie's Song," and "Thank God I'm a Country Boy" becoming pop standards of the decade. After the '70s were over, Denver's career began to lose its commercial momentum and he turned to social work, while recording the occasional album. Denver continues to record and perform in the '90s, consistently pleasing his fans. *—Stephen Thomas Erlewine*

● **Greatest Hits** / 1973 / RCA ✦✦✦✦
A good collection of his early (and best) era, 1969-1973. Note that John Denver re-recorded some of his hits for this collection. *—Dan Heilman*

Greatest Hits, Vol. 2 / 1977 / RCA ✦✦✦✦
More pop, less folk, and more hits. *—Dan Heilman*

Greatest Hits, Vol. 3 / 1985 / RCA ✦✦✦✦
Not many hits, but it still features notable '80s tracks. *—Dan Heilman*

Reflections: Songs of Love & Life / Oct. 29, 1996 / RCA ✦✦✦✦
Reflections: Songs of Love & Life is a collection of John Denver's most sentimental soft-rock hits from the '70s, including "Annie's Song," "Sunshine on My Shoulders," "I'm Sorry," and "How Can I Leave You Again." Though it isn't a thorough retrospective, it is useful for casual fans who just want Denver's famous ballads. *—Stephen Thomas Erlewine*

Depeche Mode

f. 1980, Basildon, England
Synth-pop, Alternative Pop-Rock, Post-Punk
Originally a product of Britain's new romantic movement, Depeche Mode went on to become the quintessential electro-pop band of the 1980s. One of the first acts to establish a musical identity based completely around the use of synthesizers, the group began their existence as a bouncy dance-pop outfit but gradually developed a darker, more dramatic sound that ultimately positioned them as one of the most successful alternative bands of their era.

The roots of Depeche Mode (French for "fast fashion") dated to 1976, when Basildon, England-based keyboardists Vince Clarke and Andrew Fletcher first teamed to form the group No Romance in China. The band proved short-lived, and by 1979 Clarke had formed French Look, another duo featuring guitarist/keyboardist Martin Gore. Fletcher soon signed on, and the group rechristened itself Composition of Sound. Initially, Clarke handled vocal chores, but in 1980 singer David Gahan was brought in to complete the lineup. After one final name change to Depeche Mode, the quartet jettisoned all instruments except their synthesizers, honing a slick, techno-based sound to showcase Clarke's catchy melodies.

After building a following on the London club scene, Depeche Mode debuted in 1980 with "Photographic," a track included on the *Some Bizzare Album* label compilation. After signing to Mute Records, they issued "Dreaming of Me" in early 1981; while neither the single nor its follow-up "New Life" caused much of a stir, their third effort, "Just Can't Get Enough," became a Top Ten UK hit, and their 1981 debut LP *Speak and Spell* was also a success. Just as Depeche Mode appeared poised for a major commercial breakthrough, however, principal songwriter Clarke abruptly exited to form Yazoo with singer Alison Moyet, leaving the group's future in doubt.

As Gore grabbed the band's songwriting reins, the remaining trio recruited keyboardist Alan Wilder to fill the void created by Clarke's departure; while 1982's *A Broken Frame* deviated only slightly from Depeche Mode's earlier work, Gore's ominous songs grew more assured and sophisticated by the time of 1983's *Construction Time Again. Some Great Reward*, issued the next year, was their artistic and commercial breakthrough, as Gore's dark, kinky preoccupations with spiritual doubt ("Blasphemous Rumours") and psychosexual manipulation ("Master and Servant") came to the fore; the egalitarian single "People Are People" was a major hit on both sides of the Atlantic, and typified the music's turn towards more industrial textures.

In 1986 the atmospheric *Black Celebration* continued the trend toward grim melancholy and further established the group as a major commercial force. After the superb single "Strangelove," Depeche Mode issued 1987's *Music for the Masses;* a subsequent sold-out tour yielded the 1989 double live set *101*, as well as a concert film directed by the legendary D.A. Pennebaker. Still, despite an enormous fan base, the group was considered very much an underground cult phenomenon before release of 1990's *Violator,* a Top Ten smash that spawned the hits "Enjoy the Silence," "Policy of Truth," and "Personal Jesus."

With the alternative music boom of the early 1990s, Depeche Mode emerged as one of the world's most successful acts, and their 1993 LP *Songs of Faith and Devotion* entered the charts at No. 1. However, at the peak of their success, the group began to unravel; first Wilder exited in 1995, and then Gahan was the subject of a failed suicide attempt. (He later entered a drug rehabilitation clinic to battle an addiction to heroin.) After a four-year layoff, Depeche Mode—continuing as a trio—released 1997's *Ultra,* which featured the hits "Barrel of a Gun" and "It's No Good." *—Jason Ankeny*

Speak & Spell / 1981 / Sire ✦✦✦
Primarily the work of Vince Clarke, *Speak & Spell* is Depeche Mode's most easily accessible, albeit least representative, effort. Under Clarke's influence, the group focuses on bright, catchy dance-pop relatively free of the gloom that characterizes their later records. The highlights—"Just Can't Get Enough," "New Life," and "Dreaming of Me"—were also the record's hits, emphasizing the band's stature as a singles act. *—Jason Ankeny*

A Broken Frame / 1982 / Sire ✦✦✦
Recorded by the remaining trio in the wake of Vince Clarke's exit, *A Broken Frame* marks the emergence of Martin Gore as Depeche Mode's primary songwriter. While there's little thematic deviation from *Speak & Spell,* the record does begin to expand the group's stylistic range—"My Secret Garden" adopts a funk rhythm, "Satellite" sports a ska beat, and "Monument" even bears a vague Eastern influence. While slightly darker than its predecessor, *A Broken Frame* is a transitional record only in the loosest sense; instead of bridging the gap to the group's future, it more accurately serves as the conclusion to the first phase of their career. *—Jason Ankeny*

Construction Time Again / 1983 / Sire ✦✦✦
With *Construction Time Again* Depeche Mode came into their own. Recorded with the newly-added Alan Wilder, the album jettisons the group's bubbly dance-pop in favor of a more complex and mature approach. While retaining their synth-based identity, the band introduces a more ominous and textured sound better suited to Martin Gore's increasingly dark lyrical concerns. The hit "Everything Counts" is a corrosive swipe at the music industry, while "Shame" is a similarly bitter attack on personal responsibility. *—Jason Ankeny*

People Are People / 1984 / Sire ✦✦✦
The US-only compilation *People Are People* collects material from the Depeche Mode LPs *A Broken Frame* and *Construction Time Again,* along with a number of single sides. In addition to the hit title track, the set features "Everything Counts" and "Pipeline." *—Jason Ankeny*

Some Great Reward / 1984 / Sire ✦✦✦✦
Depeche Mode hit an early peak with *Some Great Reward,* a grim, biting record that fuses the group's trademark synths with a menacing industrial clamor. Martin Gore's increasingly ominous thematic fetishes turn even more dramatic here; "Blasphemous Rumours" is a scathing attack on organized religion, while "Master and Servant" explores sexual submissiveness at its kinkiest. Only "People Are People," a heartfelt call for equality and the group's first major US hit, lightens the mood. *—Jason Ankeny*

● **Catching Up with Depeche Mode** / 1985 / Sire ✦✦✦✦
Like its predecessor *People Are People, Catching Up With Depeche Mode* attempts to fill in gaps in the group's extensive discography by compiling singles and album tracks taken from their four previous studio LPs. Dating back to the band's Vince Clarke-penned hits ("Just Can't Get Enough," "Dreaming of Me"), the set culminates with tracks like "Master and Servant" and "Blasphemous Rumours," which bear the full fruit of Martin Gore's dark obsessions; a preview of *Black Celebration* is even offered via "Fly on the Windshield." *—Jason Ankeny*

Black Celebration / 1986 / Sire ✦✦✦✦
A work of relentlessly grim solemnity, *Black Celebration* is Depeche Mode's most extreme album, a nihilistic catalog of doubt, fear, and loathing. A collection of dense electronic pieces that resemble nothing so much as funeral dirges, the record is immersed in its own despair. Martin Gore's songs are all variations on the same bleakly unforgiving theme, resulting in a kind of inescapable claustrophobia; the central melody line which repeatedly reappears through the record enhances its suffocating, maze-like grip, although all lines of distinction between tracks like "Fly on the Windscreen," "Stripped," and "World Full of Nothing" are lost in the process. *—Jason Ankeny*

Music for the Masses / 1987 / Sire ✦✦✦✦
Music for the Masses backs away from the dark brooding *Black Celebration,* but only slightly. Though the sound of *Music for the Masses* is slightly brighter, Depeche Mode's synths still create a gloomy, atmospheric mood. The real step forward on the record is in terms of pop sensibility—Martin Gore is beginning to show a melodic flair that the band

has largely lacked since Vince Clarke's departure, as "Never Let Me Down Again" proves. *—Stephen Thomas Erlewine*

101 / 1989 / Sire ✦✦✦
Essentially a double-live greatest hits album, *101* is arguably the most enjoyable record Depeche Mode ever released. Cutting away the excesses of their albums and leaving only their hits and most popular album tracks, the record demonstrates why the band earned such a devoted following. It also demonstrates how devoted that following was; although the songs sound nearly identical to the studio versions, the audience frequently goes into hysterics, singing along with the songs and enthusiastically cheering. That reaction makes *101* not only Depeche Mode's most listenable album, but also their most human, emotional record. *—Stephen Thomas Erlewine*

Violator / Feb. 1990 / Sire ✦✦✦
Depeche Mode's commercial breakthrough album is a mixed bag. Unlike their previous album, *Violator* truly is music for the masses. Throughout the album, occasional spells of catchy hooks emerge from beneath the thudding machines (most notably on the excellent "Personal Jesus" and the hit single "Enjoy the Silence). On the strength of these flashes of melody, the album crossed over into the mainstream, but for the most part *Violator* is a dull, tedious drag. *—Stephen Thomas Erlewine*

Songs of Faith & Devotion / Mar. 23, 1993 / Sire ✦✦✦
Depeche Mode attempted to reinvent themselves with *Songs of Faith & Devotion,* much as U2 did with *Achtung Baby.* In addition to their signature synthesizers, the group adds more guitar and strings to the music, frequently with rock and gospel flourishes that previously would have been unthinkable on a Depeche disc. Often these moments of departure are the most exciting on the album, like the terrific one-chord stomp of "I Feel You" or the nearly-soulful "Walking in My Shoes," which both feature animated vocals by Dave Gahan. Despite the new musical directions, there's nothing here that will alienate old fans; in fact, it might gain Depeche Mode a few new listeners. *—Stephen Thomas Erlewine*

Songs of Faith & Devotion Live / May 1993 / Sire ✦
Songs of Faith & Devotion Live is a song-for-song reprise of Depeche Mode's previous album, *Songs of Faith & Devotion.* Since most of the group's music is constructed on machines and synthesizers, there is virtually no distinction between this record and the one crafted in the studio, other than the occassional cheer from the audience and grunt from David Gahan. In short, it's music as commerce in the most blatant, unapologetic fashion possible. Even diehard fans can consider skipping this collection. *—Stephen Thomas Erlewine*

ULTRA / Apr. 15, 1997 / Warner Brothers ✦✦✦
After two albums of stadium-oriented modern rock, Depeche Mode returned to the core of their sound for *ULTRA,* namely, electronic dance music. The return coincided with an explosion of exposure for electronica, but the group doesn't sound as if they're entirely jumping on the trip-hop/techno bandwagon, even though they have borrowed many of the same production techniques. And those gloomy, foreboding sounds enhance the songs, especially since most of the tunes indirectly refer to David Gahan's near-fatal drug overdose, Alan Wilder's departure, and Andy Fletcher's nervous breakdown. With producer Tim Simenon (Bomb the Bass), Depeche Mode constructs soundscapes that borrow equally from trip-hop and industrial, adding drum loops and samples along the way. Sonically, it's an impressive effort, but Martin Gore's songwriting is surprisingly deficient this time around. Try as he may, Gore has written no hooks to draw listeners into the soundscapes, and that leaves *ULTRA* seeming distant instead of cathartic. *—Stephen Thomas Erlewine*

Derek & the Dominos

f. 1970, Los Angeles, CA, **db.** 1972
Group / Rock 'n' Roll, Blues-Rock
Derek & the Dominos was formed by guitarist/singer Eric Clapton (born Eric Patrick Clapp, Mar. 30, 1945, Ripley, Surrey, England) with other former members of Delaney & Bonnie & Friends, in the spring of 1970. The rest of the lineup was Bobby Whitlock (b. 1948, Memphis, TN) (keyboards, vocals), Carl Radle (b. 1942, Oklahoma City, OK,–d. May 30, 1980) (bass), and Jim Gordon (b. 1945, Los Angeles) (drums). The group debuted at the Lyceum Ballroom in London on June 14 and undertook a summer tour of England. From late August to early October they recorded the celebrated double album *Layla and Other Assorted Love Songs* (November 1970) with guitarist Duane Allman sitting in. They then returned to touring in England and the US, playing their final date on December 6.

The *Layla* album was successful in the US, where "Bell Bottom Blues" and the title song charted as singles in abbreviated versions, but it did not chart in the UK. The Dominos reconvened to record a second album in May 1971, but split up without completing it. Clapton then retired temporarily from the music business, nursing a heroin addiction.

In his absence, and in the wake of Allman's death in a motorcycle accident on October 29, 1971, the Dominos and *Layla* gained stature. Re-released as a single at its full, seven-minute length in connection with the compilation album *History of Eric Clapton* (Atco 803) (March 1972), "Layla" hit the Top Ten in the US and the UK in the summer of 1972. (It would return to the UK Top Ten in 1982.) A live album, *Derek and the Dominos in Concert* (January 1973), taken from the 1970 US tour, was also a strong seller.

Time has only added to the renown for the group, which is now rated among Eric Clapton's most outstanding achievements. The 1988 Eric Clapton box set retrospective *Crossroads* featured material from the abortive second album sessions. *The Layla Sessions* was a 1991 box set expanding that album across three CDs/cassettes. *Live at the Fillmore* (1994) offered an expanded version of the *In Concert* album. — *William Ruhlmann*

★ **Layla & Other Assorted Love Songs** / Nov. 1970 / Polydor ✦✦✦✦✦
Wishing to escape the superstar expectations that sank Blind Faith before it was launched, Eric Clapton retreated with several sidemen from Delaney & Bonnie to record the material that formed *Layla & Other Assorted Love Songs.* From these meager beginnings grew his greatest album. Duane Allman joined the band shortly after recording began, and his spectacular slide guitar pushed Clapton to new heights. Then again, Clapton might have gotten there without him, considering the emotional turmoil he was in during the recording. He was in hopeless, unrequited love with Patti Boyd, the wife of his best friend, George Harrison, and that pain surges throughout *Layla*, especially on its epic title track. But what really makes *Layla* such a powerful record is that Clapton, ignoring the traditions that occasionally painted him into a corner, simply tears through these songs with burning, intense emotion. He makes standards like "Have You Ever Loved a Woman" and "Nobody Knows You (When You're Down and Out)" into his own, while his collaborations with Bobby Whitlock, including "Anyday" and "Why Does Love Got to Be So Sad?," teem with passion. And, considering what a personal album *Layla* is, it's somewhat ironic that the lovely coda "Thorn Tree in the Garden" is a solo performance by Whitlock, and that the song sums up the entire album as well as "Layla" itself. — *Stephen Thomas Erlewine*

Derek & The Dominos in Concert / Jan. 1973 / Polydor ✦✦✦
While it isn't nearly as intense as *Layla*, *Derek & the Dominos in Concert* offers some fine playing by Clapton and his band and easily ranks among his best live albums. — *Stephen Thomas Erlewine*

The Layla Sessions / Sep. 1990 / Polydor ✦✦✦
Featuring two discs of outtakes and jams, the three-CD box *The Layla Sessions* manages to detract from the original by surrounding it with endless, dull instrumentals. Then again, all the unreleased material proves what a well-constructed album *Layla* is. — *Stephen Thomas Erlewine*

Live at the Fillmore / Feb. 22, 1994 / Polydor ✦✦✦
In his liner notes, Anthony DeCurtis calls *Live at the Fillmore* "a digitally remixed and remastered version of the 1973 Derek and the Dominos double album *In Concert*, with five previously unreleased performances and two tracks that had only appeared on the four-CD Clapton retrospective, *Crossroads.*" But this does not adequately describe the album. *Live at the Fillmore* is not exactly an expanded version of *In Concert*; it is a different album culled from the same concerts that were used to compile the earlier album. *Live at the Fillmore* contains six of the nine recordings originally released on *In Concert*, and three of its five previously unreleased performances are different recordings of songs also featured on *In Concert*—"Why Does Love Got to Be So Sad?," "Tell the Truth," and "Let It Rain." The other two, "Nobody Knows You When You're Down and Out" and "Little Wing," have not been heard before in any concert version. Even when the same recordings are used on *Live at the Fillmore* as on *In Concert*, they have, as noted, been remixed and, as not noted, re-edited. In either form, Derek and the Dominos' October 1970 stand at the Fillmore East, a part of the group's only US tour, finds them a looser aggregation than they seemed to be in the studio making their only album, *Layla and Other Assorted Love Songs.* A trio backing Eric Clapton, the Dominos leave the guitarist considerable room to solo on extended numbers, five of which run over ten minutes each. Clapton doesn't show consistent invention, but his playing is always directed, and he plays more blues than you can hear on any other Clapton live recording. — *William Ruhlmann*

Descendents
f. 1979, Los Angeles, CA
Hardcore Punk, Punk-Pop
Fueled by "rejection, food, coffee, girls, fishing and food," the Descendents sprang up during the halcyon days of the Los Angeles punk scene. Fusing the blind rage of hardcore with an unexpectedly wry, self-depre-

cating wit and a strong melodic sensibility that set them distinctly apart from their West Coast brethren, they gradually emerged as one of the most enduring and adored bands of their time. Formed in 1979, the Descendents' first lineup consisted of vocalist/guitarist Frank Navetta, vocalist/bassist Tony Lombardo, and drummer Bill Stevenson; initially sporting an edgy power-pop sound inspired by the Buzzcocks, the group issued a debut single, "Ride the Wild," and then vanished.

When the Descendents resurfaced in 1981, they were a four-piece fronted by vocalist Milo Auckerman, a beloved figure within the hardcore community, who infused the group's identity with both unmitigated teen angst and a healthy dose of goofball humor. Amid a relentless, caffeine-powered touring schedule, the Descendents found time to record the 1981 EP *Fat*, a collection spotlighting both Auckerman's affection for fast food ("Weinerschnitzel," "I Like Food") and distaste for parental guidance ("My Dad Sucks"). A year later the group issued their debut LP, *Milo Goes to College;* despite the considerable levity of tracks like "Bikeage" and "Suburban Home," the title was no joke—Auckerman was indeed headed off to study biochemistry, and when Stevenson joined the ranks of Black Flag, the Descendents went on sabbatical.

In 1985 the group re-formed, with SWA alum Ray Cooper replacing Navetta on guitar; after the release of the more pop-flavored album *I Don't Want to Grow Up*, ex-Anti bassist Doug Carrion assumed Lombardo's duties. A sunnier perspective informed 1986's *Enjoy!*, as evidenced by the inclusion of a cover of the Beach Boys' "Wendy," but after 1987's lackluster *All*, the group split again. After Stevenson formed a new group, also dubbed All, the only Descendents products to appear for a number of years were a pair of live releases, 1987's *Liveage!* and 1989's *Hallraker*. Somewhat surprisingly, Auckerman and Stevenson re-formed the Descendents in 1996 with All bassist Karl Alvarez and guitarist Stephen Egerton; in addition to mounting a tour, the group recorded a new album, *Everything Sucks.* — *Jason Ankeny*

Fat / 1981 / SST ✦✦✦

Milo Goes to College / 1982 / SST ✦✦✦✦
Indisputably their best. Fast, furious, and funny, the Descendents never sounded this unabashedly joyous again. Essentially a farewell record (lead singer Milo was actually going to college), its songs are great slice-of-life tales of bored middle-class life in the perpetually sunny environs of L.A. — *John Dougan*

Bonus Fat / 1985 / SST ✦✦✦
A compilation of their superb first EP, plus assorted tracks. You'll never find a better culinary tune than "I Like Food." — *John Dougan*

I Don't Want to Grow up / 1985 / SST ✦✦✦
O.K., so don't. Good but not great. — *John Dougan*

Enjoy / 1986 / SST ✦✦

All / 1987 / SST ✦✦✦
Although they were slowing down, this is primal stuff. — *John Dougan*

Liveage / 1987 / SST ✦✦✦
Great gig live in Minneapolis. — *John Dougan*

Hallraker: Live! / 1989 / SST ✦✦

● **Somery** / Jul. 16, 1991 / SST ✦✦✦✦
Somery is an overview of the Descendents' SST records, drawing equally from each record. Although this means a handful of great songs from their best albums are missing, *Somery* nevertheless selects the highlights from their occasionally uneven records, making it a useful and comprehensive retrospective. — *Stephen Thomas Erlewine*

Everything Sucks / Sep. 24, 1996 / Epitaph ✦✦✦

Jackie DeShannon
b. Aug. 21, 1944, Hazel, KY
Guitar, Vocals / Singer-Songwriter, Folk-Rock, Pop-Rock, Brill Building Pop
Few performers have enjoyed as versatile a career as Jackie DeShannon, and although she made a couple of well-remembered Top Ten pop hits in the '60s, she's never achieved the level of success or artistic recognition she deserves. Starting as a pop-rockabilly singer as a teenager in the late '50s, she quickly developed into one of the Los Angeles pop scene's hottest songwriters, penning hits for Brenda Lee, the Fleetwoods, and Irma Thomas, and often collaborating with noted songwriter Shari Sheeley. One of the first established rock figures to see the potential for crossbreeding rock and folk, she was a midwife to the birth of folk-rock, with the wonderful singles "Needles and Pins" and "When You Walk in the Room." Using the circular, jangling guitar lines that would become a prime feature of early folk-rock, both of those songs were covered by the Searchers for much bigger hits. She also wrote "Don't Doubt Yourself Babe," covered by the Byrds on their first album, and penned a couple of Marianne Faithfull's early hits. In the mid-'60s, she also found time to write some songs with then-sessionman Jimmy Page and perform as an opening act for the Beatles on the group's first big American tour. DeShannon's famous affiliations and success as a songwriter have sometimes

obscured her own enormous talents. She's a superb singer, capable of both sweet ballads and (more satisfyingly) a gutsy, soulfully husky delivery. She performed her own material with an honest, vulnerable, intelligent intensity that pre-figured the singer-songwriter movement by several years, and demonstrated command of pop, soul, hard rock, girl group, and country styles. Her greatest success, however, came not with her own material, but with Bacharach-David's "What the World Needs Now Is Love," which made the Top Ten in 1965. Perhaps as a result, she gravitated toward more middle-of-the-road pop sounds in the last half of the '60s, though she cut a good deal of strong material, both her own and that of and emerging writers like Randy Newman, Tim Hardin, and Warren Zevon. The soft-rock "Put a Little Love in Your Heart" gave her another Top Ten hit in 1969, and she made some well-received singer-songwriter albums in the 1970s. One of the songs from her '70s LPs, "Bette Davis Eyes," became a No. 1 hit for Kim Carnes in 1981. —*Richie Unterberger*

This Is Jackie Deshannon / 1965 / Imperial ✦✦✦
Issued in the wake of her mammoth hit "What the World Needs Now Is Love" (included here), this album saw Jackie moving in an orchestrated ballad direction. If her work in that field doesn't hold up as well as her more rock-oriented material, she still did quite a good job of it, handling big production numbers like "Summertime," "Don't Let the Sun Catch You Crying," "I'm Gonna Be Strong," and "Take Me Tonight" with soulful, full-throated gusto. Her best effort in this style, actually, was Bacharach-David's "A Lifetime of Loneliness," which was a small hit (and is featured on this LP). As was their wont with Jackie, Imperial/Liberty didn't help matters by pasting on a few odd tracks from her early-'60s girl group days; they're good, but out of place in the context of this album. A fairly strong but spotty recording by a great artist who was never afforded the opportunities to fulfill her potential. —*Richie Unterberger*

You Won't Forget Me / 1965 / Imperial ✦✦✦
This was also issued, with very minor track alterations, in 1964 on Liberty as *Breakin' It Up on the Beatles Tour!*; this version, issued after her Top Ten hit "What the World Needs Now Is Love," is much easier to find. It was probably the strongest album by this mercurial artist, who never seemed to corral enough top-rank material to produce a first-rate LP, despite recording dozens of fine songs throughout the '60s. Arranged by Jack Nitzsche, it's also her most girl group and rock-oriented, featuring mostly original material, written alone or in collaboration with Nitzsche, Sharon Sheeley, and a young, unknown Randy Newman. DeShannon also acquits herself well on a couple of Buddy Holly covers, "Oh, Boy" and "Maybe Baby." —*Richie Unterberger*

Put a Little Love in Your Heart / 1969 / Imperial ✦✦✦
DeShannon co-wrote her second Top Ten hit, the title track, with Jimmy Holiday and Randy Myers, and this album contains more of the fruit of their collaboration, including the follow-up, a Top 40 hit called "Love Will Find a Way." —*William Ruhlmann*

New Arrangement / 1975 / Columbia ✦✦✦
Excellent updating of DeShannon's sound. Includes her co-composition "Bette Davis Eyes," which Kim Carnes took to the top of the charts six years later. —*William Ruhlmann*

● **Pop Princess** / 1981 / EMI Australia ✦✦✦✦
Rhino and EMI have come out with fairly extensive CD compilations of DeShannon's work, but this 23-song Australian album—if it can be found—is probably the best. It concentrates almost solely on her '60s recordings (one 1959 track is included), which remains her most fertile era. It also has a few excellent singles that didn't make it onto either compilation. These include the early-'60s girl group-type efforts "It's Love Baby," "Baby (When Ya Kiss Me)," "I Won't Turn You Down," and "Should I Cry?"— most written by DeShannon, all flops, and all worth hearing. Even more mainstream efforts like "A Proper Girl" and Jim Webb's "The Girls' Song" are not on other reissues, either, and are worth a listen. The gatefold package contains informative liner notes, photos, and an exhaustive discography that includes dozens of songs she wrote for other performers. —*Richie Unterberger*

Trouble with Jackie Dee / 1991 / Teenager ✦✦
At first glance, this compilation of many rare DeShannon sides from the early and mid-'60s—most of which have not been reissued elsewhere—looks enticing. What it ends up proving, however, is that the prolific singer-songwriter wrote quite a few puffy tunes in addition to her classics. Most of the tracks on side one came out as flop Liberty singles in the early '60s (the first of which she issued under the name Jackie Dee, hence the title of this compilation). Her 1959 debut "Buddy" is decent rockabilly, and her version of Leiber and Stoller's "Trouble" is okay, but the rest is surprisingly shallow teen idol fodder, including a duet with Bobby Vee. Side two, from a slightly later vintage, is far gutsier and better, though several of these cuts have been reissued, like the dramatic "You Won't Forget Me" and the gospel-influenced "Glory Wave." The Buddy Holly covers are all right, and "Try to Forget Him" is good girl group-type material, as is the obscure early Randy Newman compo-

sition "Did He Call Today Mama." "After Last Night" (not a DeShannon original), on the other hand, was done much better by the obscure girl group the Rev-Lons. You get the idea; these are the kind of artifacts that will matter only to hard-bitten fans, though some of them aren't bad at all. —*Richie Unterberger*

The Best of Jackie DeShannon / Feb. 1, 1991 / Rhino ✦✦✦✦
This set contains all of DeShannon's best-known singles, as well as other notable original songs like "Bette Davis Eyes." —*Rick Clark*

● **What the World Needs Now . . . : The Definitive Collection** / Jul. 26, 1994 / EMI ✦✦✦✦
DeShannon's work is actually too diverse to be satisfactorily captured on an anthology, even one that includes 28 tracks, as this one does. Still, considering how hard the one DeShannon anthology that might be better than this one is to find (the Australian import *Pop Princess*), this has to be cited as the recommended first purchase. Focusing on her output for Liberty between 1959 and 1970, it has all the essentials: her two Top Ten hits, the minor hits like "A Lifetime of Loneliness," the original versions of "Needles and Pins" and "When You Walk in the Room," and a host of fine girl-group, ballad, folk-rock, and singer-songwriter flop singles. From the collector's viewpoint, the most interesting songs are the rarities. The six previously unreleased tracks include the exuberant "Breakaway," a hit for Irma Thomas; the rocker "Dream Boy," cut in 1964 in Britain with Jimmy Page on guitar; and a cover of Tim Hardin's "Reason to Believe." A couple of interesting rarities are "For Granted" (from the little-seen movie *C'mon, Let's Live a Little*) and the 45 version of "Splendor in the Grass," a somewhat sloppy folk-rock performance on which Jackie was backed by the Byrds. —*Richie Unterberger*

Devo

f. Sep. 1976, Akron, OH
New Wave, Post-Punk
One of New Wave's most innovative and (for a time) successful bands, Devo was also perhaps one of its most misunderstood. Formed in Akron, OH, in 1972 by Kent State art students Jerry Casale (bass) and Mark Mothersbaugh (vocals), along with Bob Casale (guitar), Bob Mothersbaugh (lead guitar), and Alan Myers (drums), Devo took its name from the concept of "de-evolution," the idea that instead of evolving, mankind has actually regressed, as evidenced by the problems and herd mentality of American society. Their music echoed this view of society as rigid, repressive, and mechanical with jerky, robotic rhythms, an obsession with technology and electronics (the group was among the first non-art-rock bands to make the synthesizer a core element), and often atonal melodies and chord progressions, all filtered through the perspectives of social misfits, outcasts, and flat-out weirdos. After attracting the attention of luminaries like David Bowie and Iggy Pop through their soundtrack work for the short film *The Truth About De-Evolution*, Devo recorded its 1978 debut, *Q: Are We Not Men? A: We Are Devo!* under the auspices of pioneering producer Brian Eno. The record was a cult sensation, helped in part by the band's concurrent emphasis on its highly stylized visuals—videos, costumes that made the band members look alike, etc. Their third album, *Freedom of Choice*, featured the smash single "Whip It," and the fledgling MTV network made the accompanying video into a staple. However, after those first three albums, the group began to run out of ideas, both musical and conceptual. Besides, their simple, basic electronic sound had proven very influential, and other bands were already expanding on some of Devo's ideas. After a series of largely uninteresting albums, the band called it quits early in the '90s. Casale and Mothersbaugh concentrated on other projects until a brief reunion for several dates on 1996's Lollapalooza tour.

Gerald Casale and Mark Mothersbaugh both attended art school at Kent State University at the outset of the 1970s. With friend Bob Lewis, who joined an early version of Devo and later became their manager, the theory of de-evolution was developed with the aid of a book entitled *The Beginning Was the End: Knowledge Can Be Eaten*, which held that mankind had evolved from mutant, brain-eating apes who are currently going insane. The theory was adapted to fit a view of American society as a rigid, dichotomized instrument of repression that ensured that its members behaved like clones, marching through life with mechanical, assembly-line precision and no tolerance for ambiguity.

The whole concept was treated as an elaborate joke until Casale witnessed the infamous National Guard killings of student protestors at the university; suddenly there seemed to be a legitimate point to be made. The first incarnation of Devo was formed in earnest in 1972, with Casale, Mark Mothersbaugh, and Mark's brothers Bob and Jim, the latter of whom played homemade electronic drums. Jerry's brother Bob joined as an additional guitarist, and Jim left the band to be replaced by Alan Myers. The group honed its sound and approach for several years (a period chronicled on Rykodisc's *Hardcore* compilations of home recordings), releasing a few singles on its own Booji Boy label and inventing more bizarre concepts: Mothersbaugh dressed in a baby-faced mask as Booji (pronounced "boogie") Boy, a symbol of infantile regression; there were recurrent uses of the image of the potato as a lowly vegetable without individuality; the band's costumes presented them all as identical clones with processed hair; and all sorts of sonic experiments were performed on records, using real and homemade synthesizers as well as toys, space heaters, toasters, and other objects to create bizarre textures. Devo's big break came with its score for the short film *The Truth About De-Evolution*, which won a prize at the 1976 Ann Arbor Film Festival; when the film was seen by David Bowie and Iggy Pop, they were impressed enough to secure the group a contract with Warner Brothers. The Brian Eno-produced *Q: Are We Not Men? A: We Are Devo!* was seen as a call to arms by som. Others found Devo's sound, imagery, and material threatening—*Rolling Stone*, for example, called the group fascists. But such criticism missed the point. Devo dramatized conformity, emotional repression, and dehumanization in order to attack them, not to pay tribute to them.

While *Duty Now for the Future* was another strong effort, the band broke through to the mainstream with 1980's *Freedom of Choice*, which contained the gold-selling single "Whip It" and represents a peak in their sometimes erratic songwriting. However, their peak proved to be short-lived: 1981's *New Traditionalists* was darker, more serious, and less interesting, and Devo somehow seemed to be running out of new ideas, an assessment only confirmed by *Oh, No! It's Devo* and later releases. Problems plagued the band as well. Bob Lewis successfully sued for theft of intellectual property after a tape of Mothersbaugh was found acknowledging Lewis' role in creating de-evolution philosophy, and the sessions for *Oh, No!* were marred by an ill-considered attempt to use poetry written by would-be Reagan assassin John Hinckley as lyrical material.

As the '80s wore on, Devo found itself relegated to cult status and critical indifference, not at all helped by the lower quality of their albums, and the members became involved in other projects. Alan Myers, sensing a shift toward electronic drums, left in 1986 and was replaced by ex-Sparks and Gleaming Spires drummer David Kendrick. Mark Mothersbaugh moved into composing for commercials and soundtracks, writing theme music for MTV's "Liquid Television," Nickelodeon's "Rugrats," "Pee-Wee's Playhouse," and the Jonathan Winters sitcom "Davis Rules." He also played keyboards with the Rolling Stones, programmed synthesizers for Sheena Easton, and sang backup with Debbie Harry. Buoyed by success, Mothersbaugh opened a production company called Mutato Muzika. Jerry Casale, meanwhile, who directed most of the band's videos, directed a video clip for the Foo Fighters' "I'll Stick Around." No reunions were expected, but as Devo's legend grew and other bands acknowledged their influence (Nirvana covered "Turnaround," while "Girl U Want" has been recorded by Soundgarden, Superchunk, and even Robert Palmer), their minimalistic electro-pop was finally given new exposure on six dates of the 1996 Lollapalooza tour, to enthusiastic fan response. The next year, Devo released a CD-Rom and again played selected dates on the Lollapalooza tour. —*Steve Huey*

Q: Are We Not Men? A: We Are Devo! / Jul. 1978 / Warner Brothers ✦✦✦✦

Devo's debut shows why the band still has a small but rabidly dedicated following well after their artistic peak. Their sound here is mostly guitar-based, with odd melodies and crazily jerky rhythms. With songs about masturbation ("Uncontrollable Urge"), freaks ("Mongoloid"), and technology ("Space Junk"), plus their patented de-evolution philosophy (the anthem "Jocko Homo," about the regression of mankind) and a wickedly deranged deconstruction of "(I Can't Get No) Satisfaction," Devo took punk's anti-mainstream, D.I.Y. spirit and filtered it through the sensibilities of weirdoes, nerds, and outcasts, relentlessly (and bizarrely) satirizing American culture and briefly picking up, attitude-wise, where the Mothers of Invention left off. —*Steve Huey*

Duty Now for the Future / Jul. 1979 / Warner Brothers ✦✦✦✦

Most of the aural weirdness on Devo's second album comes from the band's experiments with homemade synthesizer technology. As a result, both the guitars and jerky rhythms play a lesser role in their sound. Although it isn't quite as interesting, it's still appropriately strange, and Devo still doesn't sound quite like anyone else. *Duty* is loosely structured around the theme of everyday corporate drudgery and its effects on individuals. —*Steve Huey*

Freedom of Choice / Jul. 1980 / Warner Brothers ✦✦✦✦

Freedom of Choice, arguably Devo's strongest musical effort, revolves around relationships, insecurity, and the lack of flexibility in the American psyche. Their arrangements achieve an effective balance between guitars and synths, and the band's highly stylized visual component, this time featuring flowerpot-shaped "energy dome" hats, paid off in the video for "Whip It." The single went gold and helped the album sell over a million copies. Just barely less essential than *Q: Are We Not Men?* —*Steve Huey*

New Traditionalists / 1981 / Warner Brothers ✦✦✦

Pegged as a novelty act after the mainstream success of "Whip It" and *Freedom of Choice*, Devo apparently decided to emphasize its underlying ideas about American culture as an antidote. From the opening statement of purpose "Through Being Cool," *New Traditionalists* presents those views in a more straightforward way, with the unfortunate result that Devo is not nearly as absurdly amusing or interesting. The band often comes off as heavy-handed (pointing out on the otherwise terrific "Beautiful World" that the lyrics are intended to be ironic, just in case you didn't get the rather obvious point), as though it wants to make Serious Artistic Statements—but this isn't how Devo's best music works. Furthermore, the band's tendencies towards minimalistic, synth-centered arrangements and melodic deficiencies are much more pronounced here, making the music itself less interesting. *New Traditionalists* does have some very worthwhile moments, but it is disappointing, and it marks the beginning of the band's decline. —*Steve Huey*

Oh, No! It's Devo / 1982 / Warner Brothers ✦✦✦

By this point, much of the band's endearing quirkiness had evaporated. Their sound here was not all that distinguishable from other new wave groups, and apart from a few songs, such as "That's Good" and "Peek-a-Boo," they simply weren't as musically or lyrically interesting as before. Incredibly, it seemed that Devo had not only lost its focus, but was out of ideas as well. Subsequent releases would only confirm this assessment. —*Steve Huey*

Shout / 1984 / Warner Brothers ✦✦

The creative decline begun on *New Traditionalists* and continued through *Oh, No! It's Devo* becomes complete. The original music on *Shout* lacks the pointed, absurd satire of classic Devo, while the music itself is generally dull; the record's only highlight is a typically Devo-ized version of Jimi Hendrix' "Are You Experienced?" Not surprisingly, the band went on hiatus to concentrate on other projects shortly afterwards. —*Steve Huey*

E-Z Listening Disc / 1987 / Rykodisc ✦✦

The first Rykodisc collection of unreleased and/or forgotten Devo material consists of the band's re-recordings of 19 favorite songs in an intentionally schmaltzy instrumental style reminiscent of Muzak. These were previously available only on mail-order cassettes sold by the band itself, and this accurately reflects the nature of the material: it's a not-quite-hilarious novelty for diehard fans only. —*Steve Huey*

Total Devo / 1988 / Enigma ✦✦

No longer innovative or obviously intelligent and barely even entertaining, Devo returns on a new label (sans longtime drummer Alan Myers) for another go-round. Diehards may want this album for the "Disco Dancer" single, but even that doesn't quite measure up to past Devo successes. —*Steve Huey*

Now It Can Be Told (Devo at the Palace 12/9/88) / 1989 / Enigma ✦✦

Released as a three-sided album, Devo continued to flounder with *Now It Can Be Told*, a live performance as undistinguished as their recent studio efforts. Again, diehards may find items such as a slowed-down, mostly acoustic rearrangement of "Jocko Homo" necessary, but few others will. —*Steve Huey*

Smooth Noodle Maps / Jun. 1990 / Enigma ✦✦

Even if Devo is no longer capable of compelling, ironic observations on American culture, they are still able to make their music somewhat interesting, as this dance-intensive, electronic-oriented album proves. While still inconsistent, especially in terms of subject matter, the band does try some new ideas in its arrangements. "Post Post-Modern Man" is a decent single, too. —*Steve Huey*

Hardcore Devo, Vol. 1 / Aug. 1990 / Rykodisc ✦✦✦

While it is inconsistent, the first of Rykodisc's compilations of early four-track recordings made in Devo's basement is a necessary item for devoted fans. In addition to the original Booji Boy releases of "Satisfaction," "Jocko Homo," and "Mongoloid," *Hardcore Vol. 1* contains the full-length version of "Mechanical Man," the sarcastic satire of "Social Fools," and the flat-out weirdness of songs like "Golden Energy," "I'm a Potato," and "Uglatto." Most of these songs had never been previously available in an authorized format; many are reminiscent of the minimalist weirdness of the Residents. While some tracks are a bit short on melody, and the sound quality is mostly (and understandably) crude, they amply illustrate Devo's D.I.Y. garage-band origins and their seemingly inexhaustible (at that point) supply of satirically humorous ideas, as well as the fact that the band's patented sound was present right from the start of their long gestational period. —*Steve Huey*

The Rest: Greatest Misses / Dec. 1990 / Warner Brothers ✦✦✦

This compilation, released concurrently with *Greatest Hits*, collects some of the band's stranger experiments, early album tracks, and a few rarities, such as the Booji Boy releases of "Be Stiff" and "Mechanical Man" (both available on the *Hardcore* compilations) and a UK B-side, "Penetration in the Centerfold." It does serve as a good supplement to the *Greatest Hits* collection, even if it is a bit haphazard, but listeners who want more than one Devo disc are advised to go ahead and purchase the first three albums rather than these two compilations—it's a better way to appreciate their achievements, and it's more entertaining. —*Steve Huey*

● **The Greatest Hits** / Dec. 1990 / Warner Brothers ✦✦✦✦
While *Greatest Hits* contains all of the truly necessary items, it also tends to overlook some of the better album tracks from Devo's early period (easily their best work) in favor of a more balanced overview, which means that later albums receive more exposure than they really deserve. The import collection *Hot Potatoes: The Best of Devo* has stronger selections and is the preferred single-disc overview of Devo's career, but if you can't find it and only want one Devo disc, this will do. —*Steve Huey*

Hardcore, Vol. 2 / Aug. 23, 1991 / Rykodisc ✦✦✦
Like its predecessor and true to its title, *Hardcore Vol. 2* is an indispensable item for any hardcore Devo fan. Featuring over an hour's worth of raw, four-track basement recordings from the years 1974-1977, the disc contains such necessities as the atmospheric instrumental "Booji Boy's Funeral," the mechanized blues shuffle of "37," the mock sports anthem "Let's Go," the gleeful bubblegum-pop parody "Goo Goo Itch" (revealing a surprisingly strong sense of melody), and the sheer aural dementia of "U Got Me Bugged," as well as "Be Stiff," which later became the theme song for the pioneering British indie label Stiff Records. Also featured are early versions of "Clockout" and their cover of Lee Dorsey's "Working in a Coalmine." While there are a number of misses as well—some tracks are all robotic rhythms with no melody, and others come off as the mildly misogynistic rantings of sexually frustrated misfits—the compilation again proves the depth of development and detail in Devo's satirical vision far prior to their 1978 debut album. —*Steve Huey*

Devo Live: The Mongoloid Years / Oct. 1992 / Rykodisc ✦✦
This live EP was issued by Warner in order to get some Devo product on the shelves following the success of "Whip It." While not bad, the performances here aren't markedly different from the studio versions of these songs, which, with the exception of "Be Stiff," are all drawn from *Freedom of Choice*. —*Steve Huey*

Adventures of the Smart Patrol / Aug. 27, 1996 / Discovery ✦✦
The music on *Adventures of the Smart Patrol* was used as a soundtrack to Devo's interactive CD-ROM video game of the same title. There are two brand new songs, "Theme from the Smart Patrol" and "That's What He Said," plus a number of Devo standards and alternate versions of "U Got Me Bugged" and "Jocko Homo" drawn from the Devo archives. As a repackaging, the music works better in the context of the game. —*Steve Huey*

Dexys Midnight Runners

f. Jul. 1978, Birmingham, England
Rock 'n' Roll, New Wave, Pop-Rock
When Dexys Midnight Runners were at their peak in the early '80s, UK critics hailed their lead singer-songwriter Kevin Rowland as a genius capable of fusing soul, pop, Irish folk, new wave, and rock into one seamless, unique mix. Although the band wasn't able to fulfill its promise, the best of the music was remarkable. On their first album, *Searching for the Young Soul Rebels*, the group featured scores of horns along with accomplished songwriting from Rowland. It became a sensation in England, although it didn't dent the charts in America. After the album's release, three members of the band formed the Bureau, leaving Rowland to refashion Dexy's Midnight Runners. What he came up with was a departure from the debut, although it shared the same spirit. Instead of soul, the band was rooted in folk and celtic music on their second album, *Too-Rye-Ay*, which produced the enormous international hit, "Come On Eileen." Rowland seemed lost in the wake of his success, lacking a new idea for his music; the last Dexy's album was bland and directionless, as was his solo album, 1988's *The Wanderer*. After the album's release, Rowland entered a period of seclusion. In early 1997, he signed with Creation Records and was scheduled to deliver an album by the end of the year. —*Stephen Thomas Erlewine*

Searching for the Young Soul Rebels / Jul. 1980 / EMI America ✦✦✦✦
While it's a fascinating fusion of punk and soul, Dexy's Midnight Runners' debut album isn't quite as wonderful as the band's cult claims it is, but it does offer a number of genuinely impressive and impassioned songs. —*Stephen Thomas Erlewine*

● **Too-Rye-Ay** / Aug. 1982 / Mercury ✦✦✦✦
For the second Dexy's Midnight Runners album, Kevin Rowland refashioned the band as country/folk/punk rockers. Much like *Searching for the Young Soul Rebels*, *Too-Rye-Ay* is more interesting in theory than in practice, but it's the stronger of the two records, thanks to the irresistible hit single "Come On Eileen." —*Stephen Thomas Erlewine*

Don't Stand Me Down / Sep. 1985 / Mercury ✦✦
In the three years between the release of *Too-Rye-Aye* and *Don't Stand Me Down*, bandleader Kevin Rowland once again revamped Dexy's Midnight Runners. Musically, Rowland had evolved a combination of the soul sound of the first album and the folkie approach of the second, retaining both the horns of the former and the strings of the latter. But long passages of *Don't Stand Me Down* were spoken, not sung, by Rowland in conversation with Adams. "Listen to This" proved that Rowland was still capable of turning out a catchy, Motown-derived pop song when he chose, but the bulk of *Don't Stand Me Down*, which sold disappointingly, must have sounded idiosyncratic to British listeners and nearly incomprehensible to Americans. —*William Ruhlmann*

Very Best Of / 1991 / Mercury ✦✦✦✦
Very Best of Dexy's Midnight Runners, a 19-track collection, gives a comprehensive look at the band. Though the import price tag may be prohibitive, it is notable for the inclusion of the rare "Because of You"—the charming theme to the British television show "Brush Strokes"—unavailable elsewhere. —*Chris Woodstra*

It Was Like This / 1996 / EMI ✦✦✦✦
It Was like This collects the entirety of *Searching for the Young Soul Rebels* and adds all the B-sides from the album, plus alternate mixes of "Geno" and "Dance Stance," plus a version of "Respect" recorded for the BBC. The reissue is packaged with care and attention to detail, highlighted by Kevin Rowland's liner notes, making the compact disc the definitive version of Dexy's debut album. —*Stephen Thomas Erlewine*

Neil Diamond

b. Jan. 24, 1941, Brooklyn, NY
Guitar, Vocals / Adult Contemporary, Pop, Soft Rock, Pop-Rock
Neil Diamond built a career, first as a pop songwriter, and then as a pop singer, that has withstood the changing fashions of music, especially rock, over more than 25 years. Born in Brooklyn, Diamond was writing and recording in New York in his teens, though he graduated from Erasmus High School and attended New York University for a time. In 1965 he signed to Bang Records as an artist while also working as a songwriter. In 1966 he reached the Top Ten with his "Cherry, Cherry," while the Monkees took his "I'm a Believer" to No. 1. "Cherry, Cherry" was the first of five straight Top 20 hits, among them "Girl, You'll Be a Woman Soon."

Diamond began to develop into more of an individual writer in the mold of Bob Dylan and Paul Simon in the late '60s, and this led to his move to Uni Records in 1968, where he continued to score hits like "Sweet Caroline," "Holly Holy," and "Cracklin' Rosie," in a pop-rock style laced with gospel and country influences. His albums also began to go gold consistently beginning with 1969's *Touching You, Touching Me*.

Diamond signed a lucrative contract with Columbia Records in 1973 that began with his soundtrack to the film *Jonathan Livingston Seagull*. His 1976 album, *Beautiful Noise*, was produced by Robbie Robertson of the Band; it was his first album to go platinum. In 1980, Diamond starred in a remake of the film *The Jazz Singer*. Its soundtrack was another million-seller for him.

Diamond had developed into a dynamic live performer over the years, and his concert recordings were among his most successful. In the late '80s and early '90s, while updating his sound, he faded from the singles charts, though his albums continued to sell consistently and his shows continued to sell out. According to *Amusement Business*, he was the top concert draw in the US for the first six months of 1992.

In early 1996 Diamond released *Tennessee Moon*, a country music album that was his first set of newly recorded material in five years. *Tennessee Moon* became a hit on the country charts, peaking at No. 3 and going gold within six months of its release. —*William Ruhlmann*

Velvet Gloves & Spit / 1968 / MCA ✦✦✦
Most of Neil Diamond's albums are cluttered with filler, but few of his records were as flat-out strange as *Velvet Gloves & Spit*. Apart from "Two Bit Manchild," the album is comprised of lesser-known material, some of it good ("Modern Day Version of Love," "Honey-Drippin' Times"), and some of it just weird. The unintelligible "Knackelflerg" is one thing, but "The Pot Smoker's Song" is something else entirely. With its trippy, spoken-word testimonials about the dangers of drugs (including one addict that claims to shoot heroin into his spine) punctuated by Neil's ridiculous, sing-song chorus ("Pot, pot / Gimmie some pot/ Forget who you are / You can be who you're not"), it's anti-drug pontificating at its worst, but it's a strangely fascinating artifact and it helps distinguish *Velvet Gloves & Spit* from Diamond's catalog of uneven albums. —*Stephen Thomas Erlewine*

Touching You, Touching Me / 1969 / MCA ✦✦✦✦
Diamond's first regular album release to sell in substantial numbers, *Touching You, Touching Me* contains the gold Top Ten single "Holly Holy," a Diamond composition, but is mostly notable for its covers of standards by other songwriters: "Everybody's Talkin'," "Mr. Bojangles," "Both Sides Now," and the chart entry "Until It's Time for You to Go."

These helped signal that Diamond was thinking of himself less as a Brill Building hack than as a peer of Fred Neil, Jerry Jeff Walker, Joni Mitchell, and Buffy Sainte-Marie. — *William Ruhlmann*

Tap Root Manuscript / 1970 / MCA ✦✦✦✦
The follow-up to *Touching You, Touching Me* was an ambitious set of songs, all originals except for a Top 20 cover of "He Ain't Heavy . . . He's My Brother," including the side-long suite "The African Trilogy" (which featured the hit "Soolaimon"), the No. 1 hit "Cracklin' Rosie," and "Done Too Soon." Going gold within two months, this album confirmed Diamond's breakthrough as a recording star. — *William Ruhlmann*

Stones / 1971 / MCA ✦✦
Driven by the hit singles "I Am . . . I Said" and "Crunchy Granola Suite," *Stones* is a stronger album than most of Neil Diamond's late-'60s records. Instead of padding the album with mediocre originals, Neil picked several fine covers to fill out the remainder of the album, including Roger Miller's "Husbands and Wives," Joni Mitchell's "Chelsea Morning," Leonard Cohen's "Suzanne," Randy Newman's "I Think It's Gonna Rain," Jacques Brel's "If You Go Away," and Tom Paxton's "The Last Thing on My Mind." There are still a few weak patches on *Stones*, but the record remains an engaging collection of mainstream pop. — *Stephen Thomas Erlewine*

Moods / 1972 / MCA ✦✦✦
Moods finds Neil Diamond attempting to craft a more ambitious and substantial album than his usual pop record through heavy orchestration, but the results only work when he sticks to catchy pop-rock, as on "Song Sung Blue," "High Rolling Man" and "Play Me." — *Stephen Thomas Erlewine*

Hot August Night / 1972 / MCA ✦✦✦✦
This double-record set is the album that established Diamond's reputation as a live performer. Containing passionately performed versions of his biggest hits up to this time, it sold the best of any album he'd had so far, going gold the month of its release. — *William Ruhlmann*

Rainbow / 1973 / MCA ✦✦✦
Rainbow is a compilation that relies solely on compositions by folk-rock singer-songwriters and modern day pop craftsmen, which means that the record is more consistent than the average Neil Diamond album, even if it lacks the distinctive spark that one of his originals would have lent the album. Still, there are fine performances here, and Diamond does justice to "Everybody's Talkin'," "Both Sides Now," "Chelsea Morning," and "He Ain't Heavy, He's My Brother." — *Stephen Thomas Erlewine*

Jonathan Livingston Seagull / Oct. 1973 / Columbia ✦✦✦
Columbia Records' multi-million-dollar signing of Diamond was questioned by industry-ites who felt president Clive Davis had paid too high a price. Davis had left the company by the time this, Diamond's first Columbia album, was released in October 1973, but it was posthumous vindication. The soundtrack to a forgettable film based on a trivial best-seller, *Jonathan Livingston Seagull*, sold two million copies, spinning off the singles "Be" and "Skybird," even if, in retrospect, it is not one of Diamond's more consistent efforts. — *William Ruhlmann*

★ **His Twelve Greatest Hits** / 1974 / MCA ✦✦✦✦✦
Actually, this is 12 songs that were hits for Diamond on Uni between 1969 and 1972. "Cracklin' Rosie" is here, along with Diamond's other chart-topper of the period, "Song Sung Blue," and the Top Ten hits "Sweet Caroline" and "Holly Holy." — *William Ruhlmann*

Serenade / Oct. 1974 / Columbia ✦✦
Neil Diamond's first regular album release for Columbia Records, following the success of the movie soundtrack *Jonathan Livingston Seagull*, *Serenade* is a slight effort characterized by Diamond's attempts to make pop sentiments seem more profound by grafting more auspicious art references onto them. But whether he's name-dropping Picasso or Longfellow, Diamond still has greeting card sentiments on his mind. Nevertheless, the catchiest of these autodidactic exercises, "Longfellow Serenade," which combines comments about "winged flight" with the exhortation, "Come on, baby, ride," was a Top Ten hit. — *William Ruhlmann*

Beautiful Noise / 1976 / Columbia ✦✦✦
A beautifully recorded concept album about Diamond's own emergence from the Brooklyn streets and from the Brill Building's Tin Pan Alley. Produced by Robbie Robertson. — *William Ruhlmann*

Love at the Greek / Jan. 1977 / Columbia ✦✦
Love at the Greek captures Neil Diamond at the height of his late-'70s excess. Considerably less kinetic and exciting than the previous double-live album *Hot August Night*, *Love at the Greek* finds Diamond at the peak of his powers as a schmaltzy showman, hamming up each of his songs for the audience. It's the kind of performance that will please both dedicated fans, who will love Neil's no-holds-barred showmanship, as well as listeners with an ear for kitsch, who will no doubt treasure Dia-

mond's immortal introduction "Ladies and Gentlemen . . . the Fonz! Henry Winkler!" on "Song Sung Blue." — *Stephen Thomas Erlewine*

I'm Glad You're Here with Me Tonight / Feb. 1977 / Columbia ✦✦
I'm Glad You're Here with Me Tonight suffers from stilted, polished production and a poor selection of songs; "Free Man in Paris" and "God Only Knows" may be great songs, but they're not suited to Diamond's easy-listening arrangements. Only "You Don't Bring Me Flowers" stands out among the bland filler, and that is better heard on his subsequent album, also titled *You Don't Bring Me Flowers*. — *Stephen Thomas Erlewine*

You Don't Bring Me Flowers / 1978 / Columbia ✦✦✦
Reprising "You Don't Bring Me Flowers" from *I'm Glad You're Here With Me Tonight*, Neil Diamond constructed his finest late '70s record with *You Don't Bring Me Flowers*. Although the glossy production will be a little too sterile for some listeners, the shiny, radio-ready sound is appealing, and the songs—including the title track and "Forever in Blue Jeans"—are consistently entertaining, even if they are a little similar. — *Stephen Thomas Erlewine*

September Morn / 1979 / Columbia ✦✦
On *September Morn*, Neil Diamond began to push the borders of easy listening, concentrating more on immaculately polished studio craft than songcraft. The songs are quite inconsistent, and even the best songs—"Dancing in the Street," "The Sun Ain't Gonna Shine Anymore," "Stagger Lee"—are given inappropriately stiff and colorless arrangements. The title track nearly reaches the adult contemporary heights of "You Don't Bring Me Flowers," but overall the record demonstrates little personality. — *Stephen Thomas Erlewine*

The Jazz Singer / 1980 / Capitol ✦✦✦✦
Diamond's only notable screen appearance was his starring role in this remake of the 1927 movie that was Hollywood's first real talkie and originally featured Al Jolson. Diamond wrote a new score, featuring his biggest latter-day hits, "Love on the Rocks," "Hello Again," and "America," and as a result this soundtrack album became his biggest seller ever—five million copies and counting. — *William Ruhlmann*

Heartlight / 1982 / Columbia ✦✦
Although Diamond has continued to sell healthy quantities of his albums and to fill arenas for his concerts, *Heartlight* and its title song, which was a Top Ten hit, were his last record releases as what might be called a frontline artist, one who makes contemporary music for a contemporary audience and sells a million copies on release. It's a typical album for Diamond at this point, full of romantic sentiments rendered in highly-produced settings and employing the cream of L.A. studio musicians, but lacking the excitement of his early work and the ambition of his middle period. — *William Ruhlmann*

Twelve Greatest Hits, Vol. 2 / May 1982 / Columbia ✦✦✦✦
Keying off the title of an earlier hits collection on another label, Columbia's *12 Greatest Hits Volume II* summed up Neil Diamond's first eight years with the label, 1973-1981, as well as his successful 1980 soundtrack for *The Jazz Singer* on Capitol Records. Five of the 12, "Longfellow Serenade," "You Don't Bring Me Flowers" (with Barbra Streisand), "Love on the Rocks," "Hello Again," and "America," were Top Ten hits. Another six, "Be," "If You Know What I Mean," "Desiree," "Forever in Blue Jeans," "September Morn," and "Yesterday's Songs," made the Top 40, and the last, "Beautiful Noise," was the title track of Diamond's best album of the period. The songs shared a catchiness that belied Diamond's shallow philosophizing and thinly veiled lust, and they made a consistent collection out of what had been a series of uneven albums. And, since Diamond made the Top Ten only one more time, the album capped his hit-making days. This is the record to buy instead of investing in the Columbia catalog. — *William Ruhlmann*

★ **Classics: The Early Years** / 1983 / Columbia ✦✦✦✦✦
A terrific collection featuring his earliest and best songs, like "Kentucky Woman," "Girl, You'll Be a Woman Soon," "Cherry, Cherry," "Thank the Lord for the Night Time," "Solitary Man," "I'm a Believer," and "Red Red Wine." — *Stephen Thomas Erlewine*

Primitive / 1984 / Columbia ✦✦
Primitive attempts to capitalize on the easy-listening success of *Heartlight* by replicating its sound and structure. In other words, it's another collection of lightweight romantic ballads that are stifled by the immaculate production. Diamond's collaborations with Burt Bacharach ("Turn Around," "Sleep with Me Tonight," "Crazy") show some signs of life, particularly the graceful "Turn Around," but they're not enough to save the album from being a generally uninvolving affair. — *Stephen Thomas Erlewine*

Headed for the Future / 1986 / Columbia ✦✦
Having stumbled with *Primitive*, Diamond attempted, with *Headed for the Future*, to re-establish himself as a contemporary artist, co-writing with Stevie Wonder, recording songs by Bryan Adams and Maurice White of Earth, Wind and Fire, employing nine producers and nine recording studios. The result was a slight upturn in sales and Diamond's

last singles chart entry with the title track. But the album was also overblown and unfocused, record-making by committee, and Neil Diamond as an individual artist was getting lost in the process. — *William Ruhlmann*

Hot August Night 2 / 1987 / Columbia ♦♦
Hot August Night 2 might not capture Neil Diamond at the peak of his career as its predecessor did, but it makes a convincing case for Diamond's skills as a showman. Running through his biggest hits, Diamond turns in a flashy, showy performance. His vocal ability may have eroded a bit in the '80s, but he still knew how to get a live crowd excited. For the most part, that excitement translates to record, making *Hot August Night 2* an enjoyable listen, but not an essential one. — *Stephen Thomas Erlewine*

The Best Years of Our Lives / 1988 / Columbia ♦♦♦
Turning to David Foster as producer, Diamond made a more focused, if still somewhat overdone record that, with such songs as the title track and "This Time," was targeted at his adult audience, although he still made a play for the kids by covering Tracy Chapman's "Baby, Can I Hold You." — *William Ruhlmann*

Lovescape / Aug. 27, 1991 / Columbia ♦♦
Diamond's first album in 22 years that didn't go gold, *Lovescape* was a major, if not very distinguished, effort in which Diamond covered "One Hand, One Heart" from *West Side Story* and duetted with Kim Carnes on his own "Hooked on the Memory of You." Six producers are credited on the 15 tracks, but all that money and effort once again resulted in an album in which the artist nearly gets lost. — *William Ruhlmann*

The Greatest Hits (1966-1992) / May 19, 1992 / Columbia ♦♦♦
Columbia has been Diamond's label since 1973, and it acquired the rights to his Bang material of 1966-1968. But MCA still controls the recordings from 1968-1973. That's why (although you won't find out by reading the album cover) this two-disc, 37-track retrospective consists of the original versions of such hits as "Cherry, Cherry" (1966) and "You Don't Bring Me Flowers" (1978) but covers the middle period with re-recordings and live renditions of 13 of Diamond's biggest hits. As such, this collection gets only a qualified recommendation. — *William Ruhlmann*

Glory Road: 1968 to 1972 / Jun. 30, 1992 / MCA ♦♦♦♦
A fine two-disc retrospective of Diamond's late-'60s and early-'70s tracks, it includes some of his biggest hits—"Cracklin' Rosie," "Sweet Caroline," and "Song Sung Blue," among others. If *His Twelve Greatest Hits* doesn't offer enough material, *Glory Road* is the definitive retrospective of his years with Uni/MCA. — *AMG*

Up on the Roof: Songs from The Brill Building / Sep. 28, 1993 / Columbia ♦♦♦
This is Diamond's equivalent of, say, one of Barbra Streisand's *Broadway* albums. It's Broadway that Diamond is returning to as well; specifically, the corner of 49th Street, where he and many others turned out songs for music publishers. Some of these songs were written there; most were only in the spirit of that modern Tin Pan Alley. Handling the work of his then-rivals, such as "Spanish Harlem," "A Groovy Kind of Love," and "River Deep, Mountain High," Diamond adopts his usual hammy style. Peter Asher patented a neo-'60s production style in crafting oldies for Linda Ronstadt in the '70s, and he does the same thing here. Actually, this record sounds exactly like you would expect: just call to mind a familiar song like "Will You Love Me Tomorrow" and imagine what it would sound like if Neil Diamond sang it. Fans can decide for themselves whether it's valid and, perhaps more problematic, necessary. — *William Ruhlmann*

Live in America / 1995 / Columbia ♦♦♦
Much like its predecessor *Hot August Night 2*, *Live in America* captures Neil Diamond at the height of his powers as a showman. By the time *Live in America* was recorded, it had been several years since he had a hit; in fact, the closest he had come to the top of the charts was when UB40 took a reggae remake of "Red Red Wine" to No. 1. That doesn't mean the album is a wash-out. Diamond hauls out his old hits—including an approximation of UB40's interpretation of "Red Red Wine"—and gives one hell of a show. — *Stephen Thomas Erlewine*

Tennessee Moon / Feb. 1996 / Columbia ♦♦♦
Neil Diamond mounted a major comeback with *Tennessee Moon*, his first collection of new material in nearly five years. Instead of capitalizing on the pseudo-hipster status he had acquired with the early '90s alternative rockers, particularly Urge Overkill, Diamond headed to Nashville to write and record *Tennessee Moon*. Appropriately, the album is rooted in contemporary country, spiked with hints of the pop craftsmanship that made him popular in the '60s. Not all of the songs were written by Diamond or his collaborators, who included Raul Malo of the Mavericks; the combination of originals and professionally written made-to-order songs works well, leaving the overall quality of the material rather high. *Tennessee Moon* suffers from an overabundance of songs, as well as a slightly sterile production, but it remains one of

Neil Diamond's most successful records of the '80s and '90s. — *Stephen Thomas Erlewine*

In My Lifetime / Oct. 29, 1996 / Sony ♦♦♦♦
In My Lifetime is a triple-disc, 71-track box set spanning Neil Diamond's entire career, from his early Bang hits, through his heyday at MCA to his latter-day adult contemporary hits for Columbia. Demos, alternate takes, and live cuts are interspersed throughout the box. Not all of Diamond's greatest songs are here— obscurities like "Two-Bit Manchild" would have been welcome—but all of the classics are present. Aside from the flimsy book-style packaging, the only real problem with the set is the rarities. While the songwriting demos from the beginning of his career are of interest to both dedicated and casual fans, latter-day demos and alternate takes are of interest only to hardcore collectors and break the rhythm of the album. Nevertheless, if anyone wants just one Neil Diamond album, *In My Lifetime* is the one to get. It has all the songs you know, plus several great lesser-known gems, presented in crisp, clear sound and with an excellent biography and discography. — *Stephen Thomas Erlewine*

Dick & Dee Dee

f. 1961, Santa Monica, CA
Pop-Rock
A difficult-to-categorize male-female duo from Los Angeles, Dick and Dee Dee had pretty fair success with material that drew from doo wop, teen idol fare, pop, and even soul/R&B in the first half of the 1960s. The pair's biggest and best hit was their first, the moody, minor-key mid-tempo ballad "The Mountain's High," which reached No. 2 in 1961. Much of their material (including "The Mountain's High") was written by Dick (full name Dick St. John), and the high, screechy (in a positive sense) vocals of Dee Dee in particular led some listeners to incorrectly assume they were Black. They reached the Top 30 with a few more pop-oriented follow-ups—"Young and in Love," "Turn Around," and "Tell Me"—in the next couple of years, but got their second biggest smash with their toughest number, the blue-eyed soulish "Thou Shalt Not Steal," in 1964. A popular touring act in their day (appearing with the Beach Boys and Rolling Stones among others), they faded from view after the mid-'60s. — *Richie Unterberger*

● **The Best of Dick & Dee Dee** / Jun. 6, 1995 / Varese Vintage ♦♦♦♦
Well-chosen 12-song best-of includes all their chart hits. "The Mountain's High" and "Thou Shalt Not Steal" remain the clear highlights, though some of the rest is interesting early-'60s pop fare. Includes the rare 1965 single "Blue Turns to Grey," a Jagger/Richard cover produced by Andrew Loog Oldham that has the Stones themselves on backing instruments and vocals. — *Richie Unterberger*

The Dickies

f. 1977, Los Angeles, CA
Punk
For the Dickies, punk rock wasn't a way to vent anger, it was a way to make fun of things. More than anything, the Los Angeles quartet was distinguished by their simplistic, nearly moronic sense of humor. Basing their musical attack as well as their lyrical obsessions on early Ramones records, the Dickies played a speedy, hooky variation on standard three-chord rock, singing ludicrous, campy songs about the "Attack of the Mole Men." In addition to their wacky originals, the group recorded zany, jokey covers of rock 'n' roll classics like "Paranoid," "Eve of Destruction," and "Communication Breakdown," as well as oddities like "Eep Opp Ork (Uh, Uh)," a pseudo-rockabilly number from a "Jetsons" episode.

The Dickies formed after the initial punk explosion of 1977. The band comprised vocalist Leonard Graves Phillips, guitarist Stan Lee, bassist Billy Club, keyboardist Chuck Wagon, and drummer Karlos Kaballero; all of the names were assumed, of course. Two years later, the group released their debut album, *The Incredible Shrinking Dickies*, on A&M Records. Throughout their career, the Dickies deviated only slightly from the fast and catchy punk of their debut. Their earlier records leaned toward the California hardcore punk that was popular at the time, while the later records slow down a little, approaching heavy metal territory. Over the course of six albums between 1979 and 1989, the group's audience never grew beyond a cult following. They stopped recording in the early '90s, but echoes of their music could be heard in Green Day's multi-platinum 1994 hit album *Dookie*. — *Stephen Thomas Erlewine*

The Incredible Shrinking Dickies / 1979 / A&M ♦♦♦♦
This first release by the California-based Dickies contains songs best described as percolating, hyperactive cartoon hardcore, colored with a noticeable bit of Ramones influence. All the songs on this album are frantically fast and very short; over half the selections here have durations under two minutes, and only the instrumental number "Rondo" is longer than three minutes. Most of the tunes here have agreeably goof-

ball lyrics that are often only semi-intelligible. Chucklesome touches such as dog-barking vocals in "Poodle Party," a quote from the Champs' instrumental "Tequila" in "Shadow Man," cuckoo clock noises in "Mental Ward," and a rubber ducky solo in "Curb Job" help keep the songs firmly tongue-in-cheek. Black Sabbath's "Paranoid," the Monkees' "She," and Barry McGuire's "Eve of Destruction" are given the same dizzy treatment as everything else here. This album is good, crazy fun and worth a listen. —*David Cleary*

Dawn of the Dickies / 1979 / A&M ♦♦♦♦
The Dickies march boldly past the three-minute song duration mark on their second release. Tempos for the most part here are a little less frantic, allowing the inherent tunefulness of these songs to come through more clearly. A few selections, particularly those with monster movie lyrics, are set to noticeably slower music; one of these numbers, "Attack of the Mole Men," sports highly unusual chord progressions and comes as close to being a big production number as the group ever gets. Comparisons to the Ramones are more obvious here as well, particularly on the singable could-have-been-an-avant-garde-Pep-Boys-commercial "Manny, Moe & Jack," and the frenetic "I'm a Chollo"; the latter song eventually turns into something approximating a funhouse version of a Yardbirds rave-up. The maudlin Moody Blues tune "Nights in White Satin" gets an uproariously funny trampling here; not only is the song given at breakneck speed, but the original version's expressive flute solo is played nearly note-for-note on grinding guitar and is further adorned with faux heavy-metal embellishments. This surprisingly strong platter is well worth hearing. —*David Cleary*

Stukas Over Disneyland / 1983 / Restless ♦♦♦
This album, released after a four-year silence, shows the band training their popcorn wiseguy sights somewhat away from the hardcore and Ramones influences of earlier platters to that of power-pop and 1960s songs. The former of the two new influences is showcased in the tunefully memorable "Pretty Please Me" and "If Stuart Could Talk"; the latter is evident in "Rosemary" (with its Beatles-on-caffeine bridge), "Wagon Train" (which sports a broad tune that evokes comparisons to old television Western show theme songs), "Out of Sight, Out of Mind" (featuring a chorus that echoes the one in Ricky Nelson's "Garden Party"), and especially the title track (which exhibits noticeable surf music and Chuck Berry influences and sets ironic, humorous lyrics detailing a Disney-based world takeover). Bows to their earlier punk influences can be seen in the uproariously funny "She's a Hunchback" (complete with smart-aleck references to the Victor Hugo novel) and a giddy cover of the Led Zeppelin classic "Communication Breakdown." The 1988 re-release appends three songs ("Gigantor," "I'm Okay, You're Okay," and "Bedrock Barney") cast in their old cartoon hardcore manner; while all are likable and welcome, the addition of these numbers makes this release seem more stylistically schizophrenic than it originally was. Regardless of the version obtained, this excellent album is an enjoyable and recommended listen. —*David Cleary*

We Aren't the World! / 1986 / Combat ♦♦♦
Originally released only on cassette, *We Aren't the World* is an exhaustive collection of 21 (mostly) live tracks from 1978-1985 that prove that the band hasn't changed that much over the years. The most interesting thing about the album is the presence of their four-song 1977 demo, which is the crudest and most scintillating rock 'n' roll they ever captured on tape. —*Stephen Thomas Erlewine*

Killer Klowns from Outer Space / 1988 / Enigma ♦♦♦
After paying tribute to a number of trashy B-movies and writing a number of original songs that sounded as though they were based on similar junk culture, the Dickies got to indulge their obsession in reality by contributing the theme song to the low-grade comedy/horror film *Killer Klowns From Outer Space*. The remainder of the EP is not quite as inspired, but fans will want the album for that track, as well as a cover of Jet Screamer's "Eep Opp Ork (Uh, Uh)," a rockabilly tune featured in an episode of "The Jetsons." —*Steve Huey*

Second Coming / 1989 / Enigma ♦♦
The Dickies' first full-length album of new material since *Dawn of the Dickies, Second Coming* finds the band straining somewhat to find the magic of its early releases. The remake of Gene Pitney's "Town Without Pity" isn't as wacky as previous efforts in that vein, while "Goin' Homo" makes the band's trademark stupid humor sound rather ugly and mean-spirited as well. However, there is some worthwhile material for fans, including punk-pop originals like "Cross-Eyed Tammy" and an effectively nutty version of "Hair." Two tracks from the *Killer Klowns* EP are repeated here as well. —*Steve Huey*

● Great Dictations (The Definitive Dickies Collection) / 1989 / A&M ♦♦♦♦
An overview of the Dickies' tenure at A&M (the peak of their career) released in conjunction with *Second Coming, Great Dictations* collects rare non-LP singles and compiles some of the best tracks from *The Incredible Shrinking Dickies* and *Dawn of the Dickies*. Dedicated fans will still want to get the original albums, but the rarities make this one

necessary as well, and the casual fan will find the disc a perfect introduction. —*Steve Huey*

Idjit Savant / Jan. 17, 1995 / Relativity ♦♦♦
Six years after their first comeback, the Dickies return with another effort showing little deviation from their past work, but the band's songwriting is surprisingly consistent and melodic, and the production is more streamlined than *Second Coming*. Few would have predicted that the Dickies' tenure as active recording artists would last this long, and *Idjit Savant* is a testament to their endurance and continued ability to rock out with a healthy sense of humor. —*Steve Huey*

The Dictators
....

f. 1974, Bronx, NY, **db.** 1978
Hard Rock, Proto-Punk

Formed in 1974, NYC's Dictators were one of the finest and most influential proto-punk bands to walk the earth. Alternately reveling in and satirizing the wanton excesses of a rock 'n' roll lifestyle and lowbrow culture (e.g., wrestling, TV, fast food), the Dictators, whose worldview was defined by bassist/keyboardist and former fanzine publisher (*Teenage Wasteland Gazette*) Andy (occasionally Adny) Shernoff and renegade rock critic/theorist Richard Meltzer, played loud, fast rock 'n' roll fueled by a love of '60s American garage rock, British Invasion pop, and the sonic onslaught of the Who. Driven by the guitar barrage of Scott "Top Ten" Kempner and Ross "the Boss" Funichello and fronted by indefatigable ex-roadie and wrestler Handsome Dick Manitoba (aka Richard Blum), it seemed that nothing stood in the way of the Dictators and mega-popularity. But that's not what happened. There were complications with record companies, personnel changes (one-time bassist Mark Mendoza left for Twisted Sister; original drummer Stu Boy King was replaced by Richie Teeter), radio hated them, critical response was lukewarm, and lots of audiences didn't get the jokes. Supporters remained loyal and vociferous (especially Meltzer), but it didn't turn into anything tangible. Ironically, what didn't help at all was the rise of the New York punk scene, which only diverted attention from them and onto bands they influenced (e.g., the Ramones). They did manage to release three fine albums, but by 1978, it was over, and the Dictators broke up in the face of the public apathy and overstated accusations of sellout that greeted what was to be their final album, *Bloodbrothers*. Since then, individual members have kept busy. Kempner put together the Del-Lords and now records as a solo act; Ross the Boss spent a few years in the goofy, macho heavy-metal band Manowar and later joined Shernoff and Manitoba in the punk/metal combo Manitoba's Wild Kingdom; Shernoff also works as a producer. In 1991, there was a brief reunion tour (with Top Ten) that proved they hadn't lost a step after all these years. —*John Dougan*

● Go Girl Crazy / 1975 / Epic ♦♦♦♦
A great debut release that went almost totally ignored in its day. Although Manitoba appears on the LP cover, it's Shernoff who does the bulk of the lead singing. Many of the songs—"The Next Big Thing," "Master Race Rock," "Teengenerate," and "(I Live For) Cars and Girls"—became live staples and are accurate examples of the Dictators' style and abundant sense of humor. —*John Dougan*

Manifest Destiny / 1977 / Asylum ♦♦♦
By this time, Manitoba was considered the full-time lead singer (although Shernoff and Kempner sing plenty) and the band was hitting its stride. Despite a longish dud track that closes side one ("Disease"), *Manifest Destiny* shows off the Dictators' strong (and often tender) pop smarts, especially on Shernoff's "Sleepin' with the Television On" and Kempner's "Hey Boys." Also, there's a fast and furious cover of the Stooges' "Search and Destroy." —*John Dougan*

Bloodbrothers / 1978 / Asylum ♦♦♦
Unjustly maligned at the time as an attempt to sell out to a more mainstream hard-rock/heavy-metal audience, *Bloodbrothers* (named after the novel by Richard Price) may, ironically, turn out to be the Dictators' best record (it's certainly the most consistent). It's nonstop, ragin' full-on from the moment Shernoff counts down the opening track "Faster and Louder" (which is) to the ferocious cover of the Flamin' Groovies classic "Slow Death" that closes the record. Sandwiched in between are a tribute to Richard Meltzer ("Borneo Jimmy"), a dark song about teenage prostitutes ("The Minnesota Strip") and a million-miles-per-hour love song, "Stay with Me." Critical history has dictated (pun intended) that the two earlier records are better, but when I need a 'Tators fix this is the one I play, over and over and over. —*John Dougan*

Live, Fuck 'em If They Can't Take a Joke / 1981 / ROIR ♦♦♦
Originally a cassette-only release of a reunion gig in New York in 1981 (since re-released on CD), this is a fine document of the Dictators' feral power and endless charm as a live act. The sound is only so-so, but it never interferes with the reckless abandon or fun the guys are having. Great guitar playing by Ross the Boss; Manitoba is in fine fettle, too. —*John Dougan*

Bo Diddley (Ellas Otha Bates McDaniels)

b. Dec. 30, 1928, McComb, MS

Guitar, Violin, Vocals / R&B, Rock 'n' Roll

He only had a few hits in the 1950s and early '60s, but as Bo Diddley sang, "You Can't Judge a Book by Its Cover." You can't judge an artist by his chart success, either, and Diddley produced greater and more influential music than all but a handful of the best early rockers. The Bo Diddley beat—bomp, ba-bomp-bomp, bomp-bomp—is one of rock 'n' roll's bedrock rhythms, showing up in the work of Buddy Holly, the Rolling Stones, and even pop-garage knockoffs like the Strangeloves' 1965 hit "I Want Candy." Diddley's hypnotic rhythmic attack and declamatory, boasting vocals stretched back as far as Africa for their roots, and looked as far into the future as rap. His trademark otherworldly vibrating, fuzzy guitar style did much to expand the instrument's power and range. But even more important, Bo's bounce was fun and irresistibly rocking, with a wisecracking, jiving tone that epitomized rock 'n' roll at its most humorously outlandish and freewheeling.

Before taking up blues and R&B, Diddley had actually studied classical violin, but he shifted gears after hearing John Lee Hooker. In the early '50s he began playing with his longtime partner, maraca player Jerome Green, to get what Bo's called "that freight train sound." Billy Boy Arnold, a fine blues harmonica player and singer in his own right, was also playing with Diddley when the guitarist got a deal with Chess in the mid-1950s (after being turned down by rival Chicago label Vee-Jay). His very first single, "Bo Diddley"/"I'm a Man" (1955), was a double-sided monster. The A-side was soaked with futuristic waves of tremolo guitar, set to an ageless nursery rhyme; the flip was a bump-and-grind, harmonica-driven shuffle, based around a devastating blues riff. The result was not exactly blues, or even straight R&B, but a new kind of guitar-based rock 'n' roll, soaked in the blues and R&B, but owing allegiance to neither.

Diddley was never a top seller on the order of his Chess rival Chuck Berry, but over the next half-dozen or so years, he'd produce a catalog of classics that rival Berry's in quality. "You Don't Love Me," "Diddley Daddy," "Pretty Thing," "Diddy Wah Diddy," "Who Do You Love?," "Mona," "Road Runner," "You Can't Judge a Book by Its Cover"—all are stone-cold standards of early, riff-driven rock 'n' roll at its funkiest. Oddly enough, his only Top 20 pop hit was an atypical, absurd back-and-forth rap between him and Jerome, "Say Man," that came about almost by accident as the pair were fooling around in the studio.

As a live performer, Diddley was galvanizing, using his trademark square guitars and distorted amplification to produce new sounds that anticipated the innovations of '60s guitarists like Jimi Hendrix. In Great Britain, he was revered as a giant on the order of Chuck Berry and Muddy Waters. The Rolling Stones in particular borrowed a lot from Bo's rhythms and attitude in their early days, although they officially covered only a couple of his tunes, "Mona" and "I'm Alright." Other British R&B groups like the Yardbirds, Animals, and Pretty Things also covered Diddley standards in their early days. Buddy Holly covered "Bo Diddley" and used a modified Bo Diddley beat on "Not Fade Away"; when the Stones gave the song the full-on Bo treatment (complete with shaking maracas), the result was their first big British hit.

The British Invasion helped increase the public's awareness of Diddley's importance, and ever since then he's been a popular live act. Sadly, though, his career as a recording artist—in commercial and artistic terms—was over by the time the Beatles and Stones hit America. He'd record with ongoing and declining frequency, but after 1963 he'd never write or record any original material on par with his early classics. Whether he'd spent his muse, or just felt he could coast on his laurels, is hard to say. But he remains a vital part of the collective rock 'n' roll consciousness, occasionally reaching wider visibility via a 1979 tour with the Clash, a cameo role in the film *Trading Places*, a late '80s tour with Ronnie Wood, and a 1989 television commercial for sports shoes with star athlete Bo Jackson. —*Richie Unterberger*

Bo Diddley in the Spotlight / 1960 / Chess ✦✦✦✦
As with all of Bo Diddley's first five albums (except *Have Guitar Will Travel*), the most important cuts (but not all the good ones) off this album have been included on *The Chess Box* from MCA, which doesn't mean that this isn't a good separate issue, just somewhat redundant if you have the box. There are surprises from these 1960-vintage recordings, including the languid, Caribbean-sounding "Limber"; the soft, romantic "Love Me"; the do-wop style "Deed and Deed I Do"; the loping "Walkin' and Talkin'"; and upbeat, gospel-tinged rockers such as "Let Me In," interspersed with the hot and raunchy "Road Runner," "The Story of Bo Diddley," "Craw-Dad" (a genuine diamond-in-the-rough), and "Signifying Blues," and solid instrumentals like "Scuttle Bug" (really "Live My Life" with the vocals removed and Otis Spann over-dubbed on piano), that make this record more than worthwhile. —*Bruce Eder*

Bo Diddley Is a Lover . . . Plus / 1961 / See For Miles ✦✦✦✦
Very welcome digital British import reissue of Bo's 1961 Checker album, bolstered by a handful of bonus tracks (including his rendering of Willie Dixon's "My Babe"). On second guitar for many of these sides is Peggy Jones, one of Diddley's prize pupils. Some of the better-known titles include "Not Guilty," "Hong Kong, Mississippi," and the bragadocious title cut. —*Bill Dahl*

Bo Diddley / Jul. 1962 / Checker ✦✦✦
Bo's music was beginning to slip in sales—though he remained a popular concert act—when Chess released this album in the summer of 1962. "I Can Tell," written by Samuel Smith, showed Bo trying out a slower, more seductively soulful sound, a whole four-and-half-minutes long. It is different, though not very distinguished. "Bo's Twist" isn't much more impressive, a fairly standard instrumental with an unusually grungy (like you were expecting Julian Bream) guitar sound, with the first prominent appearance of an organ in the backing of a Bo Diddley record; "Sad Sack" is a somewhat more successful instrumental. "Mr. Kruschev" is one of the funniest, most delightfully nonsensical pieces of topical songwriting Bo ever engaged in, writing about wanting to go into the army and go over to see the Soviet leader and get him to stop nuclear testing, to a background of "Hut, two—three four!" "You All Green" is first-rate Bo, and deserved to be anthologized somewhere. "You Can't Judge a Book by the Cover" was the one standard from the album, but other tracks deserving of better exposure include "Bo's Bounce" and "Who May Your Lover Be," which takes off from Howlin' Wolf's "Moaning at Midnight," recasting it in a Bo Diddley beat, with Bo sounding a lot like Wolf here, and "Give Me a Break (Man)," a very animated, impromptu guitar jam. The filler tracks include "Mama Don't Allow No Twistin'," Bo's take on "Mama Don't Like Music," a song that was old when country-and-Western/novelty singer Smiley Burnette covered it successfully in the 1930's; "Babes in the Woods," featuring a backing chorus mimicking the doo wop parody "Get a Job"; and "Diddling," a routine Bo instrumental. —*Bruce Eder*

Bo Diddley Is a Gunslinger / 1963 / Chess ✦✦✦✦
Not only does it sport one of the most striking album covers of its era (Diddley decked out in cowboy finery, about to get the drop on some unfortunate varmint with one of his hottest guitars lying at his feet), this 1963 album contains some fine music. The title track continues the legend of you-know-who, while "Ride On Josephine" and "Cadillac" rock like hell (and Ed Sullivan must have been glad to see that Diddley finally learned "Sixteen Tons"). Two bonus cuts, "Working Man" and "Do What I Say," make this one a must. —*Bill Dahl*

Bo Diddley's Beach Party / 1963 / Checker ✦✦✦✦
A blistering live album, especially in geniune mono (the rechanneled stereo is barely passable)—and quite simply the finest live rock 'n' roll album of its era, cut live by Bo and band at Myrtle Beach, SC, on July 5 and 6, 1963. From the opening track (erroneously listed as "Memphis" and credited to Chuck Berry as composer) to the final note, this is some of the loudest, raunchiest guitar-based rock 'n' roll ever preserved. It also bears an uncanny resemblence to the sound that the Rolling Stones achieved on their own *Got Live If You Want It*, which only shows how much the Stones learned from Bo. Highlights include "Gunslinger," "Hey Bo Diddley," "Road Runner," and "I'm All Right." The sound doesn't necessarily translate ideally to compact disc, but that shouldn't dissuade anyone. Currently out of print, but well worth the search. —*Bruce Eder & Cub Koda*

Two Great Guitars / 1964 / Chess ✦✦
Diddley shared this 1964 Chess album with his labelmate Chuck Berry. They duel it out on a pair of incredibly lengthy instrumentals (brilliantly titled "Chuck's Beat" and "Bo's Beat") that get tiresome long before they run their full course. Better (and briefer) are two numbers where they don't cross paths—Diddley's rendering of "When the Saints Go Marching In" and Berry's amazing country breakdown "Liverpool Drive." A couple of bonus Bo Diddley sides ("Stay Sharp" and "Stinkey") also make this digital re-incarnation worth acquiring. —*Bill Dahl*

Hey, Good Lookin' / Apr. 1965 / Checker ✦✦✦
One of Bo's least known albums, mostly recorded in April 1964 and released a year later, at the point when his records weren't selling in America. With an edgy, raunchy sound and modern record techniques (it's in stereo), Bo and band come up with a solid '60s version of his original sound. The title track is a real jewel, featuring Jerome Green on the maracas and Lafayette Leake on the piano. "Mama Keep Your Big Mouth Shut" isn't a bad soul-styled number, with Bo abandoning his standard beat in favor of a smoother, more Motown-like sound. He tries for a similar sound on "I Wonder Why (People Don't Like Me)" and "Brother Bear." In addition to the title track (which is NOT the Hank Williams tune), the Bo Diddley beat gets a workout on "La La La," "Rain Man," and "Bo Diddley's Hoot'nanny." Bo gets to have some real fun on "London Stomp," his commentary on the sudden fashionability of British rock 'n' roll, parodying the accents and attitudes of bands he encountered on his visit to England in October 1963. Other tracks sound as if

they'd have worked well as part of extended jams of the kind that Bo did on stage; "Yeah Yeah Yeah," in particular, could've come from the middle of one of Bo's 15-minute shuffle-and-chant workouts and would've been great in such as setting, although here, as a free-standing 2:25 track, it's a little weak. There is some filler here, most notably "Let's Walk a While" and "Rooster Stew," but that can be forgiven in view of the strength of the rest of the material. —*Bruce Eder*

☆ **Bo Diddley/Go Bo Diddley** / 1986 / Chess ✦✦✦✦✦
There are precious few weak tracks on this combination of Bo Diddley's first two late-'50s albums for Chess/Checker, which boasts a plethora of classics ("Bo Diddley," "I'm a Man," "Before You Accuse Me," "Crackin' Up," "Little Girl," even his electric violin workout "The Clock Struck Twelve"). The only drawback: someone failed to notice that "Dearest Darling" was on both LPs, so . . . it's on here twice! —*Bill Dahl*

☆ **The Chess Box [Chess]** / Jul. 1990 / MCA ✦✦✦✦✦
Not every single track you'll ever want or need by the legendary shave-and-a-haircut rhythm R&B/rock pioneer, but a great place to begin. Two discs (45 songs) in a great big box with a nice accompanying booklet contain the groundbreaking introduction "Bo Diddley" (never again would he be referred to as Ellas McDaniel); its swaggering flipside,"I'm a Man"; the killer follow-ups "Diddley Daddy," "I'm Looking for a Woman," "Who Do You Love?," and "Hey Bo Diddley"; signifying street-corner humor ("Say Man"); piledriving rockers ("Road Runner," "She's Alright," "You Can't Judge a Book by Its Cover"); and numerous stunning examples of his daringly innovative guitar style. —*Bill Dahl*

Rare & Well Done / Sep. 10, 1991 / Chess ✦✦✦✦
Sixteen extreme rarities from the deepest recesses of the Chess vaults that date from 1955-1968. The grinding "She's Fine, She's Mine" and snarling "I'm Bad" are comparatively well known, at least to collectors; far more obscure are the previously unissued "Heart-O-Matic Love," "Cookie-Headed Diddley," and "Moon Baby." —*Bill Dahl*

Bo's Blues / 1993 / Ace ✦✦✦✦
Twenty-two of Bo Diddley's best blues-oriented sides from the Chess catalog, including some rare stuff—the rip-roaring 1959 outing "Run Diddley Daddy," a jive-loaded "Cops and Robbers" from 1956 that features maraca shaker Jerome Green more than Diddley, and a surging "Down Home Special." If you think that everything Bo Diddley ever made has that same shave-and-a-haircut beat, this collection will set you straight! —*Bill Dahl*

The Chess Box [Charly] / 1993 / Charly ✦✦✦✦
Bringing this box set home on the train, it started gyrating to a shave-and-a-haircut-two-bits beat on my lap . . . no, not really, but that would be a great TV ad for this release. Charly Records' *The Chess Years* has assembled most—though not quite all—of the music that the Originator recorded for Chess Records, which, unfortunately, means a lot of his lesser work as well—282 recordings, made between 1955 and 1974, on 12 CDs; looking at it is like staring across the Grand Canyon, except you *want* to jump into this if you have any sense. If the collection seems like overkill, that's because it is, and there's some poor material here from the late 1960s/early 1970s, when Bo was searching for a new commercial sound. His covers of Al Kooper's "I Love You More Than You'll Ever Know" or the Band's "The Shape I'm In" from *Another Dimension* are soulful and moving, but just not what one buys a Bo Diddley album to hear (and we could've done without the girlie chorus on "Bad Moon Rising"). There are more than enough jewels—and jewels that are likely *never* to appear otherwise on compact disc—to attract serious rock 'n' roll listeners, *if* you can swing the price, which is around $120. The highlights (which would be far more costly on vinyl today) include "Bo Meets the Monster," his catchy (and very funny) answer to "Purple People Eater"; "Here 'Tis," which became famous when covered by the Yardbirds, but only really comes to life in the hands of the originator; the comical "Bucket," "Lazy Woman," and "Run Diddley Daddy"; the rousing, slashing "Puttentang"; the side-splittingly funny biographical song "All Together," a sort of sequel to "The Story of Bo Diddley"; the complete *Bo Diddley's Beach Party* album, and a handful of demos from the late 1960 sessions that yielded tracks for the *Bo Diddley Is a Twister* album. Additionally, the collection gives the listener a chance to see how Bo explored different variations on his sound, adapting it to doo wop, folk music, and even Calypso, all of which worked better than one would have expected, and soul and funk, which didn't. The sessionography is very detailed and pretty cool, and the notes are among the better biographical accounts of Bo's life and career—oh, and there are lots of pictures of Bo and the Duchess re-created throughout the set. There are problems with the master, however; momentary gaps exist in one or two songs, and the sound quality on certain material, such as the live *Beach Party*, leaves something to be desired. But at its best, and that is often, at least through the mid-1960s, this set presents one of the primal forces in rock 'n' roll. —*Bruce Eder*

Let Me Pass Plus / 1994 / See For Miles ✦✦✦
Another British import version of a vintage Checker album, with a few highly desirable bonus cuts at the end to further recommend it. Most of

the CD mirrors Diddley's 1965 *500% More Man* LP (the title track obviously being a sequel to his "I'm a Man"), but the extra items include the amusing "Mama, Keep Your Big Mouth Shut" and a danceable "We're Gonna Get Married." —*Bill Dahl*

A Man Amongst Men / May 21, 1996 / Code Blue ✦✦✦
Bo Diddley's major-label '90s comeback effort *A Man Amongst Men* is overflowing with guest stars, but it rarely gels into something distinctive. The presence of such heavyweights as Keith Richards, Ron Wood, and Jimmie Vaughan actually weighs down the set, preventing Diddley from digging deep into the grooves. The band never quite rocks hard enough, and no one tears off an inspired solo . *A Man Amongst Men* is pleasant, but it never approaches compelling listening. —*Stephen Thomas Erlewine*

★ **His Best (Chess 50th Anniversary Collection)** / Apr. 8, 1997 / MCA ✦✦✦✦✦
With his various hits and anthology packages all out of print and the multi-disc deluxe box set out of pocketbook reach for most casual consumers, MCA finally comes up with a 20-track compilation that hits the bullseye and makes this rock pioneer's best and most influential work available to everyone. The song list reads like a primer for '60s British rhythm and blues and '90s blues bands: "Bo Diddley," "I'm a Man," "Diddley Daddy," "Pretty Thing," "Before You Accuse Me," "Hey! Bo Diddley," "Who Do You Love," "Mona," and "Roadrunner" are the tracks that made the legend and put his sound on the map world wide. The transfers used on this set are exemplary, the majority of them utilizing masters that have a few extra seconds (or more) appended to the fades, which will cause even hardliners to hear these old standards with fresh ears. Especially revelatory are the long versions of "I Can Tell" and "You Can't Judge a Book by Its Cover." If the box set is too big a trigger to pull and you want all of Bo's influential sides in one package, this one should be first-stop shopping of the highest priority. —*Cub Koda*

Ani DiFranco

b. Sep. 23, 1970, Buffalo, NY
Guitar, Vocals / Urban-Folk, Singer-Songwriter
A folkie in punk's clothing, Ani DiFranco battled successfully against the Goliath of corporate rock to emerge as one of the most influential and inspirational cult heroines of the 1990s. DiFranco released her records through her own indie label, Righteous Babe, slowly but steadily building a devout grass-roots following on the strength of a relentless tour schedule. An ardent feminist and an open bisexual, her songs tackled issues like rape, abortion, and anger tempered by the poignant candor of singer-songwriter confessionalism.

Born in Buffalo, NY, on September 23, 1970, DiFranco began her career at the age of nine, when her guitar teacher helped her land her first gig—performing a set of Beatles covers—at an area coffeehouse. Befriended by the likes of Suzanne Vega and Michelle Shocked, she later gave up music to study ballet, but at the age of 14 returned to the guitar and began composing her first songs. A year later, alienated from her crumbling family structure, she left home, living with friends while making the rounds of the Buffalo folk clubs.

By the age of 19 DiFranco had written over 100 original songs, and after briefly studying art she relocated to New York City to further her musical aspirations. Besieged by requests from fans for tapes of her performances, she recorded a demo and pressed 500 copies of a self-titled cassette to sell at shows. The tape—a spartan acoustic folk collection of intensely personal essays on failed relationships and gender inequities—quickly sold out, and in 1990 DiFranco founded Righteous Babe to better distribute her recordings, which were slowly spreading across the country on the strength of a substantial word-of-mouth following.

In 1991, after issuing the assured *Not So Soft*, DiFranco hit the road alone, touring the nation in her Volkswagen and playing gigs wherever she could find them. Her cult blossomed, and her distinct image—shaved head, tattoos, and body piercings—soon became the de rigueur look for her fans as well. As albums like 1992's *Imperfectly* and 1993's *Puddle Dive* expanded her musical ambitions as well as her following, DiFranco became the subject of considerable major-label interest, but she steadfastly rejected all offers as Righteous Babe grew to become a highly viable business venture.

DiFranco continued playing over 200 dates a year, and soon even the mainstream media took notice of her cottage-industry music; after 1994's masterful *Out of Range*, she exploded with the following year's *Not a Pretty Girl*, which garnered notice from outlets ranging from CNN to the *New York Times*. In 1996 *Dilate*, a sprawling, eclectic work detailing a heated love affair with a man—much to the chagrin of her lesbian followers—even debuted in the Top 100 of the *Billboard* charts, a stunning achievement for an independent release. The live set *Living in Clip* followed in 1997. —*Jason Ankeny*

Ani Difranco / 1989 / Righteous ✦✦
Not So Soft / 1991 / Righteous Babe ✦✦✦

Imperfectly / 1992 / Righteous Babe ✦✦✦✦
Puddle Dive / 1993 / Righteous Babe ✦✦✦✦
Out of Range / Jul. 26, 1994 / Righteous Babe ✦✦✦✦
DiFranco spruces up her sparse folk arrangements with the odd brass band, accordion, and even an electric guitar or two, but the meat of these songs is still her distinctively funky acoustic guitar style. (She borrowed her rhythmic plucking technique from R&B, but unplugged, it bears no resemblance to its genre of origin.) Meanwhile, DiFranco's spunky activist lyrics are tempered here by a bigger dose of vulnerability than in previous albums, which allows for a unique mix of anger, humor, and poignancy. The best songs this time around are not bitter but quietly reflective ("You Had Time, "Buildings and Bridges," "If He Tries Anything"). — *Darryl Cater*

Like I Said / Jul. 26, 1994 / Righteous Babe ✦✦✦
● **Not a Pretty Girl** / Jul. 18, 1995 / Righteous Babe ✦✦✦✦
On *Not a Pretty Girl*, Ani DiFranco stakes out the same territory she has in her previous albums, but she still turns in a number of biting, funny songs. — *Sara Sytsma*

More Joy Less Shame / 1996 / Righteous Babe ✦✦
The unusual prospect of remixes by a folk artist is promising, and the songs Ani DiFranco has chosen ("Joyful Girl" and "Shameless" from *Dilate*) seem well suited to the format. Unfortunately, DiFranco merely finds a few interesting sounds and repeats them until they're no longer interesting. The live recordings ("Joyful Girl" with Doc Severinsen's orchestra, "Both Hands" solo) are more engaging. — *Darryl Cater*

Dilate / May 21, 1996 / Righteous Babe ✦✦✦✦
Ani Di Franco doesn't really expand her sonic palette on *Dilate*, but she doesn't need to. Di Franco racked up a dedicated cult audience on the basis of her conviction. There's not much melody on any of her songs, but there are messages and, thankfully, a fair share of humor. *Dilate* suffers from a bit too much repetition, but when Di Franco lands on a good hook—such as "Superhero" or "Done Wrong"—the results suggest that she could reach a wider audience. — *Thom Owens*

Living in Clip / Apr. 22, 1997 / Righteous Babe ✦✦✦✦
For all of their cult popularity, Ani DiFranco's studio albums were frequently hampered by mannered performances, which is precisely what her live shows were not. In concert, DiFranco plays her songs with infectious energy, frequently twisting the melody lines and digressing into rambling, entertaining stories and jokes. That side of Ani DiFranco is finally captured in the double-disc live album, *Living in Clip*. Supported by bassist Sara Lee and drummer Andy Stochansky, she runs through 32 songs, including the previously unreleased "Gravel," plus all of her best-known songs, occasionally spinning off stories and humorous anecdotes and illustrating exactly why a rabid cult following developed around her appealingly edgy persona and songs. — *Thom Owens*

Digable Planets

f. 1991, New York, NY
Urban, Alternative Rap, Jazz-Rap
Though they were not the first to synthesize jazz and hip-hop, Digable Planets epitomized the laidback charm of jazz hipsters better than any group before or since. The trio's 1993 debut album *Reachin' (A New Refutation of Time and Space)* was a mellow ride packed with samples from Art Blakey, Sonny Rollins, and Curtis Mayfield, and the single "Rebirth of Slick (Cool like Dat)" became a Top 20 pop hit. After embarking on an ambitious tour that included several live musicians, the Planets returned in late 1994 with their best album yet. *Blowout Comb* continued the group's jazz-rap fusion, but also saw them branching out to embrace the old-school sound of the street as well. Digable Planets formed in the early '90s, when Butterfly (b. Ishmael Butler, Brooklyn, NY) met Ladybug (b. Mary Ann Vierra, Silver Springs, MD) while attending college in Massachusetts. The two later hooked up with Doodlebug (b. Craig Irving, Philadelphia, PA) in Washington, DC, and began recording. Their first single, "Rebirth of Slick (Cool like Dat)," released on the Pendulum subsidiary of Warner, hit the R&B Top 10 while their debut *Reachin' (A New Refutation of Time and Space)* was a critical and commercial success. Digable Planets' tour had a laidback vibe more in keeping with a jazz show than a hip-hop concert, though the live musicians were criticized for doing little more than re-creating samples. The trio solved that problem with the release of their second album, *Blowout Comb*, in late 1994. Much stronger than its predecessor, it used fewer samples and even included several solos; with no strong single to carry it, however, *Blowout Comb* sold less well than *Reachin'.* — *John Bush*

● **Reachin' (A New Refutation of Time and Space)** / Sep. 27, 1993 / Pendulum ✦✦✦✦
Digable Planets' debut album was one of the more successful fusions of jazz and rap, blending the two genres into a funky, seamless, stylish sound, without losing the integrity of jazz or hip-hop street credibility. — *Stephen Thomas Erlewine*

Blowout Comb / Oct. 18, 1994 / Pendulum ✦✦✦✦
Digable Planets set the hip-hop world on its ear with their jazz-inflected debut, *Reachin'. Blowout Comb*, not only offers a deeper exploration of their jazz roots, but also more politicized and harder-edged lyrics than their debut, even if it lacks a single song as impressive as "Rebirth of Slick (Cool Like Dat)." — *Stephen Thomas Erlewine*

Digital Underground

f. 1987, Oakland, CA, **db.** 1996
Hip Hop, Club/Dance, West Coast Rap
While hip-hop was consumed by the hardcore, noisy political rap of Public Enemy and the gangsta rap of N.W.A., Digital Underground sneaked out of Oakland with its bizarre, funky homage to Parliament-Funkadelic. Building most of their music from samples P-Funk records and developing a similarly weird sense of style and humor, highlighted by Shock-G outrageous costumes and the whole band's parade of alter egoes. Of all these alter egoes, Shock-G's Humpty Hump—a ridiculous comical figure with a Groucho Marx nose and glasses, and a goofy, stuttering voice—was the most famous, especially since he was immortalized on their breakthrough single, "The Humpty Dance." Over the course of their career, Digital Underground has featured numerous members, but throughout it all, Shock-G has remained at its core, developing the band's sound and style, which they had from the outset, as their 1990 debut *Sex Packets* proved. *Sex Packets* was an instant hit, thanks to the loopy single "The Humpty Dance," and while they never scaled such commercial heights ever again, their role in popularizing George Clinton's elastic funk made them one of the most important hip-hop groups of their era.

Shock-G (b. Gregory E. Jacobs, August 25, 1963) had spent most of his childhood moving around the East Coast with his family, eventually settling in the Bay Area of California. He dropped out of high school in the late '70s and spent several years pursuing a life of crime before eventually going to college to study music. Along with Chopmaster J, Shock G formed Digital Underground in 1987, and the duo released a single, "Underwater Rimes," that year that went to No. 1 in the Netherlands. In 1989 the group signed with Tommy Boy, and that summer "Doowutchyalike" became an underground hit. By that time, Digital Underground had expanded significantly, featuring DJ Fuze, Money-B (b. Ron Brooks), and Schmoovy-Schmoov (b. Earl Cook). *Sex Packets*, the group's debut album, was released in the spring of 1990, and "The Humpty Dance," which was rapped by Shock G's alter ego Humpty Hump, climbed all the way to No. 11 on the pop charts, peaking at N. 7 on the R&B charts. With its P-Funk samples, jazzy interludes, and innovative amaglam of samples and live instrumentation, *Sex Packets* received positive reviews and went platinum by the end of the year.

Digital Underground followed *Sex Packets* in early 1991 with *This Is an EP Release*, their first recording to feature rapper Tupac Shakur. The EP went gold and set the stage for their second album, *Sons of the P*, which was released that fall. On the strength of the gold single "Kiss You Back," *Sons of the P* also went gold, but it received criticism for its similarity to *Sex Packets*. By the time Digital Underground delivered its third album, *The Body Hat Syndrome*, in late 1993, hip-hop had become dominated by gangsta rap, particularly the drawling G-funk of Dr. Dre, which, ironically, was heavily indebted to George Clinton. Consequently, their fan base diminished significantly, and *The Body Hat Syndrome* disappeared shortly after its release. Nearly three years later, Digital Underground returned with *Future Rhythm*, which spent a mere three weeks on the charts. — *Stephen Thomas Erlewine*

★ **Sex Packets** / Jan. 1990 / Tommy Boy ✦✦✦✦✦
With their debut album *Sex Packets*, Digital Underground kick-started the Parliament/Funkadelic obsessions that dominated the hip-hop world of the early '90s. Digital Underground essentially creates a full-length tribute to George Clinton's warped fantasy world, taking both the elastic bass lines and the goofy, surreal sense of humor and adopting it to their own purposes. With their ridiculous sense of humor and endless, loping synth-laced grooves, the two hit singles, "The Humpty Dance" and "Doowutchyalike," seem to tell the whole story, but that's not the case. Within the album tracks of *Sex Packets* are jazzy experiments, hardcore funk, and loads of innovative rhymes and grooves that set the pace for much of the music that followed. Furthermore, the Underground has a good-natured, welcoming sense of humor that infuses everything on *Sex Packets*, particularly the tongue-in-cheek sci-fi mini-opera that comprises the title track. Although they made some musical innovations on their two subsequent albums, Digital Underground never made an album as consistently engaging as their debut. — *Stephen Thomas Erlewine*

This Is an EP Release / Feb. 1990 / Tommy Boy ✦✦✦
Two decent remixes from their debut pad this half-hour mini-opus. The new stuff ("Same Song," "Nuttin' Nis Funky") attests to the Underground's staying power and to their devotion to the funk. — *John Floyd*

Sons of the P / Oct. 15, 1991 / Tommy Boy ✦✦✦✦
Digital Underground's love of George Clinton and Parliament/
Funkadelic was still more than obvious on its second full-length album.
Sons of the P, which falls short of the overall excellence of *Sex Packets*,
nonetheless has much to admire. This time, the Oakland group isn't as
consistently lighthearted as before, and doesn't shy away from insightful
social commentary on "Heartbeat Props" (which pays tribute to accomplished Black Americans in both politics and the arts), "The Higher
Heights of Spirituality," and "No Nose Job." But even so, the album is a
danceable, fun, and delightfully quirky effort reminding us how influential Clinton's P-Funk remained. Indeed, the fact that artists as different-
sounding as Digital Underground and the Red Hot Chili Peppers owe so
great an artistic debt to Clinton makes it obvious just how far-reaching
his influence is. —*Alex Henderson*

The Body Hat Syndrome / Oct. 5, 1993 / Tommy Boy ✦✦✦
With their third album, Digital Underground doesn't change its style
much at all, but that isn't bad. Instead, *The Body-Hat Syndrome* is a
goofily endearing mess of P-Funk-inspired hip-hop, with enough good
humor and beats to satisfy their fans. —*Stephen Thomas Erlewine*

Future Rhythm / Jun. 1996 / Radikal ✦✦
With each new album, Digital Underground develops and deepens its
homage to George Clinton's P-Funk, coming up with new, inventive
ways to carry on the tradition. Unlike the G-Funk-inspired crews in
Southern California, the Underground plays fast and loose with their
inspiration, keeping true to the wild-ass eclecticism of Parliament/
Funkadelic's best moments. On *Future Rhythm*, DU has added a concept of their own: moving the funk and hip-hop into the next century.
Unfortunately, the music never sounds any different than the group's
previous releases, with the notable exception of the exclusion of the
good-time party raps that always ranked among the crew's finer
moments. So the concept never quite takes hold, and the music is similar to the group's other recordings, but so what? Digital Underground
has found a way to infuse hip-hop with not only the sound but the spirit
of George Clinton in a way no other rapper (with the exception of Dr.
Dre, who took the sound but ignored the spirit) has ever done. And that
means that even their lesser efforts, such as *Future Rhythm*, have some
fine cuts to offer. —*Leo Stanley*

Dino, Desi & Billy

f. 1964, Los Angeles, CA
Pop-Rock
A Hollywood trio barely into their teens when they hit the charts in
1965, Dino, Desi & Billy anticipated the bubblegum fad with records
that usually featured none of their own contributions, except their characterless vocals. That may be phrasing matters too kindly. The best bubblegum is far more distinctive and catchy than the lowest-common-
denominator Los Angeles session pop-rock that they recorded. But they
knew the right people, as they say in the business, which made them
stars for a brief time, although they never had an ounce of credibility.

This mid-'60s trio was kind of a cross between the Monkees and Gary
Lewis in a few key respects. Like Gary Lewis, their very opportunities to
record came about primarily because of their distinguished Hollywood
fathers. In the case of these guys, however, the nepotism was rather
extreme. Dino was Dino Martin, son of singer/comedian Dean Martin,
and Desi was the son of Lucille Ball and Desi Arnaz. Along with classmate Billy Hinsche, they began playing for fun. They'd barely gotten
their equipment together when they auditioned for Dean Martin's
buddy, Frank Sinatra—who just happened to record for and run Martin's
label, Reprise. By the end of 1964 they'd released their first single for the
label, although it was made clear to them that session musicians would
handle the instruments.

Top producers and arrangers Lee Hazlewood, Billy Strange, and
Jimmy Bowen would oversee the trio's recording dates over the next
couple of years. "I'm a Fool" made the Top 20 in 1965; "Not the Lovin'
Kind" got into the Top 30 a few months later. None of the group had
reached the age of 15 yet, but there they were, playing to screaming
crowds as a support act to a Beach Boys tour in 1965, and (for a few
months) outselling Sinatra on his own label. This despite (or because
of?) the fact that their music was innocuously bland in the extreme,
making the Monkees (who also used a pool of Los Angeles session players) sound positively innovative and hard-nosed in comparison.

Dino, Desi & Billy never got into the Top 40 after 1965, but they
recorded singles and albums for years to come. They were the recipients
of compositions by top pop-rock songwriters like Lee Hazlewood, David
Gates, Boyce-Hart, Clint Ballard, Jr., and Bonner-Gordon. But it seemed
these songsmiths took care not to give them anything *too* good, in the
manner of Goffin-King's substandard leftovers for early '60s teen idols.

Billy Hinsche's sister married Carl Wilson, which probably helped the
band secure a Brian Wilson composition (which Hinsche helped finish
off) for one of their final Reprise singles in 1970, "Lady Love." The group
did start to get involved in their recording sessions, as players and com-

posers, toward the end of the '60s. But the talent wasn't there, and in any
case the results were much more pop than rock.

Perhaps it's being unduly touchy to come down on the band so hard;
they had no aspirations toward anything but wholesome fun, apparently, and 98% of other kids their age would have taken advantage of
the same connections given the same silver spoons. Keep in mind,
though, that bands like Dino, Desi & Billy took away valuable airtime
and sales from much better groups that really needed it, in an era in
which chart considerations were much more vital to ensure an ongoing
career. And if you don't believe that, look at the nosedive experienced
after the mid-'60s by the Kinks—who, as it happened, were on Dino,
Desi & Billy's US label, and may have been competing for the same promotional budget. —*Richie Unterberger*

● **Rebel Kind: Best Of** / Feb. 27, 1996 / Sundazed ✦✦✦✦
Twenty songs from their 1964-70 Reprise recordings, wisely concentrating on their singles (as their albums were overpopulated with covers of
familiar hits). Includes "The Rebel Kind," "I'm a Fool," and several
smaller hits and non-hits, some of which were never released on album.
Extensive liner notes by the Smithereens' Dennis Diken. Beach Boys
fans may want to note the presence of the 1970 non-LP single "Lady
Love," written by Brian Wilson and Billy Hinsche. —*Richie Unterberger*

Dinosaur Jr.

f. 1983, Amherst, MA
Alternative Pop-Rock, Grunge, Indie-Rock, Hard Rock
Dinosaur Jr. was largely responsible for returning lead guitar to indie-
rock and, along with their peers the Pixies, injected late-'80s alternative rock with monumental levels of pure guitar noise. As the group's
career progressed, it turned into a vehicle for J. Mascis' songwriting and
playing, which had the result of turning Dinosaur's albums into largely
similar affairs. Over time, Mascis shed his hardcore punk roots and
revealed himself to be a disciple of Neil Young, crafting simple songs
that were delivered at a crushing volume and spiked with shards of
feedback. Consequently, Dinosaur Jr's '90s albums—when the group
was essentially a front for Mascis—don't sound particularly revolutionary, even with their subtle sonic innovations, but their original '80s
records for SST were a different matter. On their early records, Dinosaur
lurched forward, taking weird detours into free-form noise and melodic
soloing before the songs are brought back into relief by Mascis' laconic
whine. Dinosaur's SST Records laid the foundation for alternative rock's
commercial breakthrough in the early '90s, and while the band's profile
was raised substantially in the wake of Nirvana's success, they never
really became much bigger than highly respected cult figures.

J. Mascis (b. Joseph D. Mascis; guitar, vocal) formed Dinosaur Jr. in
Amherst, MA, after his hardcore punk band Deep Wound broke up in
1983. Hooking up with fellow high school student Lou Barlow (bass),
Mascis initially played drums in Dinosaur, but shortly afterward, former
All White Jury drummer Murph (b. Emmett "Patrick" Murphy), joined
the group, and J. moved to guitar. Over the next year, the group developed a local following, and in 1985 the trio released their debut album,
Dinosaur, on the Homestead label. The record and the group's crushingly loud concerts developed a cult following over the next year. By the
end of 1986, a hippie-rock group called Dinosaur—featuring former
members of Jefferson Airplane and Country Joe & the Fish—sued the
band, which changed its name to Dinosaur Jr.

In 1987 Dinosaur Jr. signed to Black Flag's indie label SST and
released *You're Living All Over Me*, which became an underground sensation, with groups like Sonic Youth championing Mascis' wild, feedback-drenched guitar. Early in 1988 they released the seminal single
"Freak Scene," a song that captured the feeling and tone of the emerging
American post-punk underground. "Freak Scene" became a college
radio hit, and it led the way for their acclaimed 1988 album *Bug*.
Although the band's popularity continued to grow, tensions were developing between Mascis and Barlow, who rarely talked to each other. In
1989 Mascis told Barlow that the group was breaking up; the following
day, he "re-formed" Dinosaur Jr., this time without Barlow, who went on
to form Sebadoh.

Without Barlow, Dinosaur Jr. relied on a rotating array of guest bassists, including Don Fleming and the Screaming Trees' Van Conner. In
1989 the group had an underground hit with their non-LP cover of the
Cure's "Just like Heaven." The next year they signed with Sire Records.
After "Just like Heaven," Mascis remained quiet for several years, as he
produced acts like Buffalo Tom and collaborated with friends like Sonic
Youth and Fleming's Velvet Monkeys. *Green Mind*, Dinosaur's 1991
major-label debut, was recorded almost entirely alone by Mascis, and its
varied, eclectic sound was received poorly in many alternative rock circles. Before the *Green Mind* tour, former Snakepit member Mike
Johnson became the group's full-time bassist. On the subsequent tour,
Dinosaur Jr. was supported by Nirvana, whose success with *Nevermind*
soon overshadowed Dinosaur's. Instead of capitalizing on the commercial breakthrough of alternative rock, Dinosaur released an EP, *What-*

ever's Cool with Me, in early 1992 and disappeared to record their next album.

Released early in 1993, *Where You Been* benefited greatly from the commercial breakthrough of alternative rock, and many of the articles surrounding the album's release hailed Mascis as an alternative godfather. It became the first Dinosaur album to chart, peaking at No. 50, and it generated the modern rock hit "Start Choppin." That summer the group played on the third Lollapalooza tour. Mascis recorded the band's next album without Murph, who unceremoniously left the band; he later joined the Lemonheads. Dinosaur Jr. released *Without a Sound* in 1994 to mixed reviews, but the album was a moderate hit, thanks to the MTV and modern rock hit "Feel the Pain." In the fall of 1995 Mascis launched his first solo acoustic tour, which was captured on his first official solo album, *Martin & Me*, released in the spring of 1996. After contributing several Brian Wilson-styled songs to Alison Anders' 1996 film *Grace of My Heart*—he also made an appearance in the movie—Mascis completed Dinosaur's next album on his own, leaving Johnson to his solo career. Upon its spring 1997 release, *Hand It Over* was hailed as Mascis' best album in years, although it failed to generate a significant hit. *—Stephen Thomas Erlewine*

Dinosaur / 1985 / Homestead ✦✦✦

Released before the group was forced to change their name to Dinosaur Jr. by an obscure psychedelic group, the band's debut *Dinosaur* is a noisy, impressive, but uneven array of pseudo-hardcore numbers, sonic experiments, and sprawling hard rock. Although the band doesn't land on any distinctive style, their ambition of marrying Neil Young and Sonic Youth sounds intriguing, and it has enough outstanding moments to indicate that the group was capable of the stylistic breakthrough they achieved on *You're Living All Over Me. —Stephen Thomas Erlewine*

★ You're Living All Over Me / 1987 / SST ✦✦✦✦

A blitzkrieg fusion of hardcore punk, Sonic Youth-style noise freak-outs, heavy metal, and melodic hard rock in the vein of Neil Young, *You're Living All Over Me* was a turning point in American underground rock 'n' roll. With its thin, unbalanced mix, the album sounds positively menacing and edgy. Lou Barlow's bass barrels forward over Murph's clanking drums, with J. Mascis' guitar twisting pummeling riffs and careening, occasionally atonal, solos. It established guitar heroics as a part of indie-rock, bringing the noise of Sonic Youth into more conventional song structures. Mascis' laconic, self-absorbed whine was a distinct departure from the furious post-hardcore rants and the mumbling Michael Stipe imitations that dominated indie-rock. While the songwriting is uneven, the best moments of *You're Living All Over Me*—"Little Fury Things," "Raisans," "In a Jar" and Barlow's proto-Sebadoh "Poledo"—retain their power, and it's possible to hear the record's influence throughout alternative rock. *—Stephen Thomas Erlewine*

Bug / 1988 / SST ✦✦✦✦

Bug is more cleanly produced and more accessible than *You're Living All Over Me*. It expands on the strengths of its predecessor and establishes Dinosaur Jr. as a major band in the American underground. Although the majority of the album is firmly situated in the sprawling, noisy metallic fusion of hard rock and avant-noise, *Bug* also demonstrates that J. Mascis has a talent for winding folk-rock, particularly on "The Post" and "Pond Song." As on its predecessor, the songs on *Bug* are quite uneven, but the album does represent a major step forward for Mascis, particularly on the masterpiece of the record, "Freak Scene," a surprisingly catchy song encapsulating within three minutes the appeal and pitfalls of indie-rock. *—Stephen Thomas Erlewine*

Green Mind / Feb. 1991 / Blanco y Negro/Sire/Warner Brothers ✦✦✦✦

Many consider *Green Mind* to be a weak, uninspired effort, but Dinosaur Jr.'s major-label debut is a strong, varied album, featuring some of J. Mascis' best songwriting, as well as some of his best, most fluid guitar work. Essentially a solo effort by Mascis (Murph only appears on three tracks), *Green Mind* finds him stretching and expanding his traditional sonic assault with more acoustic guitars and tighter melodies. With its gentle Mellotron and lovely, sighing melody, "Thumb" stands as one of Mascis' finest songs; "Muck" is a surprisingly enjoyable stab at funk, "How'd You Pin That One on Me" is a great guitar workout, "Puke & Cry" and "I Live for That Look" are impressive folk-punk, and "The Wagon" rivals "Freak Scene" in its depiction of the underground scene. *—Stephen Thomas Erlewine*

Fossils / Aug. 1991 / SST ✦✦✦✦

A brief, eight-song compilation of the group's SST singles, *Fossils* effectively sums up the power and vision of Dinosaur Jr.'s early work. Not only does it contain the two masterpieces from *You're Living All Over Me* and *Bug*—"Little Fury Things" and "Freak Scene," respectively—but it gathers several excellent B-sides, including sardonic covers of Peter Frampton's "Show Me the Way" and the Cure's "Just Like Heaven," making it an excellent retrospective of Dinosaur's influential and erratic indie recordings. *—Stephen Thomas Erlewine*

Whatever's Cool with Me / Oct. 22, 1991 / Blanco y Negro/Sire/ Warner Brothers ✦✦✦

"Whatever's Cool with Me" is definitive Dinosaur Jr.—roaring rhythm guitars, legato solos, weary lyrics and a winding, penetrating melody. The other five B-sides on the EP are solid, but unremarkable, highlighted by a tongue-in-cheek rewrite of David Bowie's "Quicksand." *—Stephen Thomas Erlewine*

Where You Been / Feb. 9, 1993 / Blanco y Negro/Sire/Warner Brothers ✦✦✦✦

Dinosaur Jr.'s full-throttle punk roar keeps diminishing as time goes by, but that doesn't mean the music is any less powerful; if anything, it's getting stronger. *Where You Been* sounds similar to most other Dinosaur Jr. albums—there's no mistaking J Mascis' trademark wrenching guitar and vocals—but the album is filled with terrific songs like "Get Me" and "Start Choppin," even if the guitar meanders a bit too much. *—Stephen Thomas Erlewine*

Without a Sound / Aug. 23, 1994 / Blanco y Negro/Sire/Warner Brothers ✦✦

J Mascis fired long-time drummer Murph before the recording of *Without a Sound*, which came as a surprise to Murph. The change in personnel hasn't changed Dinosaur Jr.'s sound much; the only difference between *Without a Sound* and *Where You Been* is a more pronounced country leaning (particularly on the album's high point, the rollicking "I Don't Think So") and shorter, more concise performances. The overpowering fuzz tones of Mascis' guitar, which tend to hide his more expressive vocals, make digging out the gems on this album a little more difficult than necessary. *—Stephen Thomas Erlewine*

Hand It Over / Mar. 25, 1997 / Blanco y Negro/Sire/Warner Brothers ✦✦✦✦

Bouncing back from the staid *Without A Sound*, J. Mascis turns in his most eclectic album since *Green Mind* with Dinosaur Jr.'s *Hand It Over*. Dinosaur's bedrock sound hasn't changed—it's still a sprawling, electric mess of hard rock filtered through folk-rock song structures—but Mascis plays with the arrangements, adding strings, trumpets and, on a handful of tracks, My Bloody Valentine's slippery guitar orchestrations and vocals (Kevin Shields and Belinda Butcher both sing on the album). These additions make the music sound fresh, but they would only be window-dressing if Mascis' songs weren't as strong as they are. Again, his progressions are subtle, but songs like "I Don't Think," "Nothin's Goin' On," "Can't We Move This" and "Sure Not Over You" are fine additions to his catalog, and help make *Hand It Over* one of Dinosaur Jr.'s most consistent and best records. *—Stephen Thomas Erlewine*

Dion and the Belmonts

f. Jul. 18, 1939, Bronx, NY
Rock 'n' Roll, Doo Wop, Teen Idol

Bridging the era between late-'50s rock and the British Invasion, Dion DiMucci (b. Jul. 18, 1939) was one of the top white rock singers of his time, blending the best elements of doo wop, teen idol, and R&B styles. Some revisionists have tried to cast him as a sort of early blue-eyed soul figure, although he was probably more aligned with pop-rock, at first as the lead singer of the Belmonts, and then as a solo star. Drug problems slowed him down in the mid-'60s, but he made some surprisingly interesting progressions into blues-rock and folk-rock as the decade wore on, culminating in a successful comeback in the late 1960s, although he was unable to sustain its commercial and artistic momentum for long.

When Dion began recording in the late 1950s, it was as the lead singer of a group of friends who sang on Bronx street corners. Billing themselves as Dion and the Belmonts (Dion had released a previous single with the Timberlanes), their first few records were prime Italian-American doo wop; "I Wonder Why" was their biggest hit in this style. His biggest single with the Belmonts was "A Teenager in Love," which pointed the way for the slightly self-pitying, pained odes to adolescence and early adulthood that would characterize much of his solo work.

Dion went solo in 1960 (the Belmonts did some more doo wop recordings on their own), moving from doo wop to more R&B/pop-oriented tunes with great success. He handled himself with a suave, cocky ease on hits like "The Wanderer," "Runaround Sue," "Lovers Who Wander," "Ruby Baby," and "Donna the Prima Donna" that cast him as either the jilted, misunderstood youngster or the macho lover, capable of handling anything that came his way (on "The Wanderer" especially).

In 1963 Dion moved from Laurie to the larger Columbia label, an association that started promisingly with a couple of big hits right off the bat, "Ruby Baby" and "Donna the Prima Donna." By the mid-'60s, his heroin habit (which he'd developed as a teenager) was getting the best of him, and he did little recording and performing for about five years. When he did make it into the studio, he was moving in some surprisingly bluesy directions; although much of it was overlooked or unissued at the time, it can be heard on the *Bronx Blues* reissue CD.

In 1968 he kicked heroin and re-emerged as a gentle folk-rocker with a No. 4 hit single, "Abraham, Martin and John." Dion would focus upon mature, contemporary material on his late '60s and early '70s albums, which were released to positive critical feedback, if only moderate sales. The folk phase didn't last long; in 1972 he reunited with the Belmonts, and in the mid-'70s cut a disappointing record with Phil Spector as producer. He's been recording and performing fairly often over the last two decades (sometimes singing Christian music) to indifferent commercial results. But his critical rep has risen steadily since the early '60s, with many noted contemporary musicians showering him with praise and citing his influence, including Dave Edmunds (who produced one of his periodic comeback albums) and Lou Reed (who guested on that record). —*Richie Unterberger*

Runaround Sue / 1961 / The Right Stuff ✦✦✦
Includes the title track; "The Wanderer"; the minor hit "The Majestic"; covers of "Little Star," "In the Still of the Night," "Kansas City," "Dream Lover," and "Take Care of My Baby"; and a few other songs that follow the blueprint of his early-'60s hits. The singing is good, but the best tracks are the hits, and they're on all the Dion compilations of note. —*Richie Unterberger*

Lovers Who Wander / 1962 / The Right Stuff ✦✦✦
A better-than-average early-'60s effort. Besides the oft-anthologized singles "Lovers Who Wander," "Little Diane," "Sandy," and "(I Was) Born to Cry," it has some hot covers "The Twist," "Stagger Lee," and "Shout") that Dion makes his own. The haunting "Lost for Sure," which Dion co-wrote, is one of his best obscure Laurie-era tracks. —*Richie Unterberger*

Dion / 1968 / The Right Stuff ✦✦✦✦
Featuring his Top Five comeback single "Abraham, Martin and John," this folk-rock and blues-flavored effort remains his most fully realized album. In addition to the impressive anti-war original "He Looks a Lot like Me," it contains mature interpretations, arranged both acoustically and with strings, of songs by Fred Neil, Joni Mitchell, Leonard Cohen, Bob Dylan, and Lightnin' Hopkins (though the florid version of Jimi Hendrix' "Purple Haze" is embarrassing). The CD reissue adds the highly sought-after non-LP B-side "Daddy Rollin'," a Dion original that ranks as his most country-blues-influenced performance. —*Richie Unterberger*

★ **24 Golden Greats** / 1983 / Arista ✦✦✦✦✦
24 Golden Greats contains all of Dion & the Belmonts' biggest hits, plus all of Dion's solo hits from the late '60s and early '70s, making it the definitive compilation of the vocalist's long, successful career. —*Stephen Thomas Erlewine*

Greatest Hits / 1987 / Columbia ✦✦✦✦
A solid compilation of Dion's solo sides, including "Donna the Prima Donna," "Ruby Baby," and others. —*Cub Koda*

Bronx Blues: The Columbia Recordings / Feb. 2, 1991 / Columbia ✦✦✦✦
In the mid-'60s, Dion turned away from teen-idol doo wop material and cut several sides in a solid R&B/blues/folk vein. The best of those sides are collected here. —*Cub Koda*

Road I'm On: Retrospective / Feb. 18, 1997 / Sony ✦✦✦✦
Dion's mid-'60s Columbia period was a strange and rather mysterious one. After notching up some solid hits that were more or less in his early-'60s rock style ("Ruby Baby," "Donna the Prima Donna"), he dove into blues, folk, and folk-rock with varying degrees of success. Although the results were usually pretty interesting, commercially he seemed to have disappeared (a situation not helped by either his heroin problems or the failure of some of the material to get released). This is a good, if imperfect, two-CD overview of the Columbia years, moving from the expected early hits to quite a few tasty surprises, including covers of Woody Guthrie, Chuck Berry, Willie Dixon, "Work Song" (penned by Nat Adderley and Oscar Brown), Tom Paxton, and Bob Dylan's "It's All Over Now, Baby Blue." There are also a number of pretty fair self-penned originals in a folk-rock, slightly Dylanish style, unsurprising considering that Dion was recording with one-time Dylan producer Tom Wilson in late '65. It doesn't make a 100% convincing argument that Dion would have matured into a top-rank blues-folk-rocker if not for his drug problems, but it has integrity, and the material is usually well sung, whether pop or not. About half a dozen of the tracks were previously unreleased; there are also a couple of new recordings from 1996. This does not, by the way, make the 1991 *Bronx Blues* CD (much of it drawn from the same era) redundant. Almost half of the tracks from that disc don't appear, the most serious omission being the cover of Dylan's "Baby, I'm in the Mood for You," which was probably Dion's best mid-'60s recording. —*Richie Unterberger*

Celine Dion

b. Mar. 30, 1968, Charlemagne, Quebec, Canada
Vocals / Adult Contemporary, Pop-Rock
In her native Canada and France, Celine Dion's popularity as a singer began when she was a teenager. Her polished, yet soulful, adult contemporary pop didn't break in the United States until 1991 (when she

released a record recorded in English), but when it did there was no stopping the hits. From "Where Does My Heart Beat Now" to the theme to *Beauty and the Beast*, Dion has been a fixture on the American pop charts since 1992. In 1996 Celine Dion enjoyed her biggest hit to date with "Because You Loved Me," the theme from the film *Up Close and Personal*. The song became the biggest adult contemporary hit of all time and propelled her own album, *Falling into You*, into the pop Top Ten and multi-platinum status. —*Stephen Thomas Erlewine*

Unison / Aug. 21, 1990 / Epic ✦✦✦
A fine, sophisticated American debut from this popular Canadian singer, featuring the hit singles "(If There Was) Any Other Way" and "Where Does My Heart Beat Now." —*Stephen Thomas Erlewine*

Celine Dion / Mar. 31, 1992 / Epic ✦✦✦✦
Featuring the hit singles "Beauty and the Beast," "Love Can Move Mountains," and "If You Asked Me To," Celine Dion's follow-up to her successful American debut is an even stronger and more accomplished record than her previous album. —*Stephen Thomas Erlewine*

The Colour of My Love / Nov. 9, 1993 / 550 Music/Epic ✦✦✦

● **Falling into You** / Mar. 12, 1996 / 550 Music/Epic ✦✦✦✦
Celine Dion's *Falling into You* returned the Canadian vocalist to the top of the American charts, and for good reason. Although the album is formulaic, it is a well-executed, stylish, and catchy formula, accentuating her natural vocal charm. Dion shines on ballads like "Because You Love Me" and mock-epics like Jim Steinman's "It's All Coming Back to Me Now." Between those two peaks, she tackles dance-pop and love songs with grace; that effortless elegance saves the mediocre material on the album from being tedious. Though there are a couple of weak tracks, *Falling into You* is a remarkably well-crafted set of adult contemporary pop, and Dion's best album. —*Stephen Thomas Erlewine*

Dire Straits

f. 1977, London, England, db. 1993
Rock 'n' Roll, Pop-Rock
Dire Straits emerged during the post-punk era of the late '70s, and while their sound was minimalistic and stripped-down, they owed little to punk. If anything, the band was a direct outgrowth of the roots-revivalism of pub rock, but where pub rock celebrated good times, Dire Straits was melancholy. Led by guitarist/vocalist Mark Knopfler, the group built their sound upon the laidback blues-rock of J.J. Cale, but they also had jazz and country inflections, occasionally dipping into the epic song structures of progressive rock. The band's music was offset by Knopfler's lyrics, which approximated the winding, stream-of-consciousness narratives of Bob Dylan. As their career progressed, Dire Straits became more refined, and their new maturity happened to coincide with the rise of MTV and the compact disc. These two musical revolutions from the mid-'80s helped make Dire Straits' sixth album, *Brothers in Arms*, an international blockbuster. The band joined Eric Clapton, Phil Collins, Steve Winwood and other self-consciously mature veteran rock 'n' rollers in the late '80s who designed their music to appeal to aging baby boomers. Despite the band's international success, they couldn't sustain their stardom, waiting a full six years to deliver a followup to *Brothers in Arms*, by which time their audience had shrunk significantly.

Mark Knopfler (b. August 12, 1949) was always the main force behind Dire Straits. The son of an architect, Knopfler studied English literature at Leeds University, and worked briefly as a rock critic for the *Yorkshire Evening Post* while at college. He began teaching English after his graduation, leading a pub-rock band called Brewer's Droop at night. By 1977 Mark was playing with his brother David (guitar) and his roommate, John Illsley (bass). During the summer of 1977 the trio cut a demo with drummer Pick Withers. A London DJ named Charlie Gillett heard the demo and began playing "Sultans of Swing" on his BBC show "Honky Tonkin'." After a tour opening for Talking Heads, the band began recording their debut for Vertigo Records with producer Muff Winwood in early 1978. By the summer, they had signed with Warner in America, releasing their eponymous debut in the fall. Thanks to the Top Ten hit "Sultans of Swing," *Dire Straits* was a major success in both Britain and America, with the single and album climbing into the Top Ten on both sides of the Atlantic.

Dire Straits established the band as a major force on album-oriented radio in America, and their second album, *Communiqué* (1979), consolidated their audience, selling three million copies worldwide. As the group was recording its third album, Dave Knopfler left the band to pursue a solo career; he was replaced by former Darling member Hal Lindes. Like its predecessor, *Making Movies* was a sizable hit in America and Britain, even though the band was criticized for musically treading water. Nevertheless, the record went gold on the strength of the radio and MTV hits "Romeo and Juliet" and "Skateaway." Dire Straits followed the album two years later with *Love Over Gold*, an album filled with long, experimental passages, plus the single "Private Investigations" which became a No. 2 hit in the UK. The album went gold in America and spent four weeks at No. 1 in Britain. Shortly after the release of *Love Over Gold,* former Rockpile drummer Terry Williams replaced Withers.

During 1982, Mark Knopfler began exploring musical avenues outside of Dire Straits, scoring the Bill Forsyth film *Local Hero* and playing on Van Morrison's *Beautiful Vision.* Apart from releasing the *Twisting By the Pool* EP early in 1983, Dire Straits was quiet for the majority of 1983 and 1984, as Knopfler produced Bob Dylan's *Infidels,* as well as Aztec Camera and Willy De Ville; he also wrote "Private Dancer" for Tina Turner's comeback album. In the spring of 1984, the band released the double-album *Dire Straits Live—Alchemy* and by the end of the year, they had begun recording their fifth studio album with their new keyboardist, Guy Fletcher. Released in the summer of 1985, *Brothers in Arms* was Dire Straits' breakthrough album, making the band international stars. Supported by the ground-breaking computer-animated video for "Money for Nothing," a song that mocked music videos, the album became a blockbuster, spending nine weeks at the top of the American charts and selling over nine million copies; in England, the album became the biggest-selling album of the '80s. "Walk of Life" and "So Far Away" kept *Brothers in Arms* in the charts through 1986, and Dire Straits played over 200 dates in support of the album. Once the tour was completed, Dire Straits went on hiatus for several years, as Knopfler produced records by Randy Newman and Joan Armatrading, scored films, toured with Eric Clapton, and recorded a duet album with Chet Atkins (*Neck and Neck,* 1990). In 1989 he formed the country-rock group Notting Hillbillies, whose sole album *Missing . . . Presumed Having a Good Time* became a British hit upon its spring 1990 release. During the extended time off, John Illsley recorded his second album; first appeared in 1984.

In 1990 Knopfler reconvened Dire Straits, which now featured Illsley, Clark, Fletcher, and various session musicians. The band released *On Every Street* in the fall of 1991 to great anticipation. However, the album failed to meet expectations—it only went platinum in America and it didn't crack the UK Top 40—and failed to generate a hit single. Similarly, the tour was a disappointment, with many tickets going unsold in both the US and Europe. Once the tour was completed, the live album *On the Night* was released in the spring of 1993 and the band again went on hiatus. In 1996 Mark Knopfler launched his solo career with *Golden Heart.* *—Stephen Thomas Erlewine*

Dire Straits / Oct. 1978 / Warner Brothers ✦✦✦✦
Dire Straits' minimalistic interpretation of pub-rock had already crystallized by the time they released their eponymous debut. Driven by Mark Knopfler's spare, tasteful guitar lines and his husky warbling, the album is a set of bluesy rockers. And while the bar-band mentality of pub-rock is at the core of Dire Straits—even the group's breakthrough single, "Sultans of Swing," offered a lament for a neglected pub-rock band—their music is already beyond the simple boogies and shuffles of their forefathers, occasionally dipping into jazz and country. Knopfler also shows an inclination towards Dylanesque imagery, which enhances the smoky, low-key atmosphere of the album. While a few of the songs fall flat, the album is remarkably accomplished for a debut, and Dire Straits had difficulty surpassing it throughout their career. *—Stephen Thomas Erlewine*

Communiqué / Jun. 1979 / Warner Brothers ✦✦
Rushed out less than nine months after the surprise success of Dire Straits' self-titled debut album, the group's sophomore effort, *Communiqué* seemed little more than a carbon copy of its predecessor, with less compelling material. Mark Knopfler and Co. had established a sound (derived largely from J.J. Cale) of laidback shuffles and intricate, bluesy guitar-playing, and *Communiqué* provided more examples of it. But there was no track as focused as "Sultans of Swing," even if "Lady Writer" (a lesser singles chart entry on both sides of the Atlantic) nearly duplicated its sound. As a result, *Communiqué* sold immediately to Dire Straits' established audience, but no more, and it did not fare as well critically as its predecessor or its follow-up. *—William Ruhlmann*

Making Movies / Oct. 17, 1980 / Warner Brothers ✦✦✦✦
Without second guitarist David Knopfler, Dire Straits began to move away from its roots-rock origins into a jazzier variation of country-rock and singer-songwriter folk-rock. Naturally, this means that Mark Knopfler's ambitions as a songwriter are growing, as the storytelling pretensions of *Making Movies* indicate. Fortunately, his skills are increasing, as the lovely "Romeo and Juliet," "Tunnel of Love" and "Skateaway" indicate. And *Making Movies* is helped by a new wave-tinged pop production, which actually helps Knopfler's jazzy inclinations take hold. The record runs out of steam toward the end, closing with the borderline offensive "Les Boys," but the remainder of *Making Movies* ranks among the band's finest work. *—Stephen Thomas Erlewine*

Love over Gold / Sep. 1982 / Warner Brothers ✦✦✦✦
Adding a new rhythm guitarist, Dire Straits expands its sounds and ambitions on the sprawling *Love over Gold.* In a sense, the album is their prog-rock effort, containing only five songs, including the 14-minute opener "Telegraph Road." Since Mark Knopfler is a skilled, taste-

ful guitarist, he can sustain interest even through the languid stretches, but the long atmospheric instrumental passages aren't as effective as the group's tight blues-rock, leaving *Love over Gold* only a fitfully engaging listen. *—Stephen Thomas Erlewine*

Twisting by the Pool [EP] / Feb. 1983 / Warner Brothers ✦✦✦
Dire Straits followed the ponderous *Love over Gold* five months later with a three-song EP paced by its title track, which lived up to its name by adopting a twist beat, making it the closest thing to exuberant rock 'n' roll this seemingly humorless band had ever attempted. "Two Young Lovers" had the same early rock feel, and even "If I Had You" was taken at a quicker tempo than had become common on Dire Straits albums. *Twisting by the Pool* didn't quite turn Dire Straits into a dance band, but it went a long way toward lightening up the group's image and repertoire. *—William Ruhlmann*

Alchemy: Dire Straits Live / Mar. 1984 / Warner Brothers ✦✦✦
There is an interesting contrast on this 94-minute double-disc live album (recorded at London's Hammersmith Odeon in July 1983) between the music, much of which is slow and moody, with Mark Knopfler's muttered vocals and large helpings of his fingerpicking on what sounds like an amplified Spanish guitar, and the audience response. The arena-size crowd cheers wildly and claps and sings along, when given half a chance, as though each song were an uptempo rocker. When they do have a song of even medium speed, such as "Sultans of Swing" or "Solid Rock," they are in ecstasy. That Dire Straits' introspective music loses much of its detail in a live setting matters less than that it gains presence and a sense of anticipation. Alan Clark's keyboards help to fill out the sound and give Knopfler's spare melodies a certain majesty, but Dire Straits remains an overgrown pub band with a Bob Dylan fixation, and that's exactly how the crowd likes it. (The CD version of the album contains one extra track, "Expresso Love," which adds a needed change of pace to the otherwise slow-moving first disc.) *—William Ruhlmann*

Brothers in Arms / May 1985 / Warner Brothers ✦✦✦✦
Brothers in Arms brought the atmospheric, jazz-rock inclinations of *Love over Gold* into a pop setting, resulting in a surprise international best-seller. Of course, the success of *Brothers in Arms* was helped considerably by the clever computer-animated video for "Money for Nothing," a sardonic atttack on MTV. But what kept the record selling was Knopfler's increased sense of pop songcraft—"Money for Nothing" had an indelible guitar riff, "Walk of Life" is a catchy uptempo boogie variation on "Sultans of Swing," and the melodies of the bluesy "So Far Away" and downtempo Everly Brothers-style "Why Worry" were wistful and lovely. Dire Straits had never been so concise or pop-oriented, and it wore well on them. Though they couldn't maintain that consistency through the rest of the album—only the jazzy "Your Latest Trick" and the flinty "Ride Across the River" make an impact—*Brothers in Arms* remains one of their most focused and accomplished albums and, in its succinct pop sense, it is distinctive within their catalog. *—Stephen Thomas Erlewine*

● **Money for Nothing** / Oct. 1988 / Warner Brothers ✦✦✦✦
This best-of collection contains Dire Straits' biggest hits as well as some key album tracks. "Sultans of Swing," "Walk of Life," "Money for Nothing," plus a live version of "Telegraph Road" from *Love over Gold,* are among the highlights. Even though this may be a fairly representative sampler, listening to the better albums in their entirety is the best way to hear this band. *—Rick Clark*

On Every Street / Sep. 1991 / Warner Brothers ✦✦
It took Mark Knopfler more than six years to craft a follow-up to Dire Straits' international chart-topper *Brothers in Arms,* but although *On Every Street* sold in the expected multimillions worldwide on the back of the band's renown and a year-long tour, it was a disappointment. Knopfler remained a gifted guitar player with tastes in folk ("Iron Hand"), blues ("Fade to Black"), and rockabilly ("The Bug"), among other styles, but much of the album was low-key to the point of being background music. The group had long since dwindled to original members Knopfler and bassist John Illsley, plus a collection of semi-permanent sidemen who provided support but no real musical chemistry. This was not the comeback it should have been. *—William Ruhlmann*

On the Night / May 11, 1993 / Warner Brothers ✦✦
A live document of Dire Straits' 1991-92 world tour supporting the *On Every Street* album, *On the Night* works sporadically, offering enough good material to interest fans but not enough to win back the commercial audience earned by *Brothers in Arms.* *—Stephen Thomas Erlewine*

Live at the BBC / Jun. 26, 1995 / Winsong ✦✦✦
Always a quiet act, Dire Straits dissolved quietly in 1995 as Mark Knopfler prepared his first full-fledged solo album. Meanwhile, this documentary effort, the group's third live recording, appeared to chronicle their early days. Most of it was recorded in July 1978, so it is in effect a concert version of the self-titled debut album. Tacked on at the end is a 12-minute version of "Tunnel of Love" from 1981, bringing the total time to 46 minutes. It's a modest effort from a modest band and, in that sense, a

better representation of them than *Alchemy* or *On the Night*, both of which reflected their worldwide popularity. — *William Ruhlmann*

Dirty Looks

f. 1979, Staten Island, NY, **db.** 1981
Rock 'n' Roll, Power Pop
Dirty Looks (not to be confused with the late-'80s metal band of the same name) was formed in the late '70s on Staten Island, NY. Composed of Patrick Barnes (guitar/vocals), Peter Parker (drums/vocals), and Marco Sin (bass/vocals), the trio began playing their hard-rocking power-pop at Max's Kansas City and CBGB's, where they were discovered by Stiff Records' Dave Robinson. Robinson signed them, anticipating they were "the next big thing." After releasing one brilliant single ("Let Go"), a good but unfortunately overlooked debut LP for Stiff, and a mediocre follow-up, the band faded into obscurity. — *Chris Woodstra*

Dirty Looks / 1980 / Stiff ✦✦✦✦
The band's self-titled debut showed a lot of promise with its lean, hard-driving power-pop and near-perfect single "Let Go." Just barely out of touch with the times, they drifted a little too close to bar-band territory to fit in with the new wave of the time. — *Chris Woodstra*

● **Turn It Up** / 1981 / Stiff ✦✦✦
After failing with the edgy approach, the band enlisted Nick Garvey (ex-Ducks Deluxe/Motors) for production and moved toward a slicker, more mainstream sound—a poor choice, considering that Garvey was probably better suited to bring out the rock 'n' roll side of the band. None of the songs even approaches the last batch. A sad end to a band that could have been. — *Chris Woodstra*

The Divine Comedy

f. 1989, London, England
Alternative Pop-Rock, Brit-Pop
The Divine Comedy is the alias for Neil Hannon, an English pop singer-songwriter with aspirations of becoming a New Wave fusion of Scott Walker, Morrissey, and Electric Light Orchestra. During the early '90s, he built up a strong cult following with a pair of idiosyncratic, critically-acclaimed records before his third album, *Casanova*, became a mainstream success in the wake of Brit-pop and Pulp's popularity. "Becoming More Like Alfie" and "Something for the Weekend," both pulled from *Casanova*, became hits after receiving significant airplay from Radio One DJ Chris Evans, and the Divine Comedy moved from British indie-rock favorites to a minor mainstream cult in their own right.

Originally the Divine Comedy was an R.E.M.-influenced guitar-driven trio, formed in Londonderry, Ireland, by Neil Hannon (vocals, guitar; born in Londonderry November 7, 1970), George McCullagh (bass), and Kevin Traynor (drums). Inspired by R.E.M., the trio released an EP, *Fanfare for the Comic Muse*, in the spring of 1990 and supported the record with a few concerts, including a supporting slot for My Bloody Valentine. In 1991 John Allen joined the band as lead vocalist, and the group released the EP *Timewatch*, which was recorded that fall when Hannon was still vocalist. The next year, they relocated to London, where they regularly supported Suede on club gigs. Produced by Edwyn Collins, the *Europop* EP was released later in 1992. It was the last recording the original lineup would release.

After *Europop*, the Divine Comedy fell apart, and Hannon went back to Londonderry, where he began to write songs again. In 1993 he was signed to Setanta as the Divine Comedy and released *Liberation* to positive reviews. *Promenade* followed in 1994, again to positive reviews throughout the UK music press; it appeared on year-end lists from *NME*, *Melody Maker*, and *Q*, among others. After the release of *Promenade*, Blur, Oasis, and Pulp made British indie-rock acceptable for the pop mainstream, and the Divine Comedy benefitted from their progress. Released early in 1996, *Casanova* was greeted with enthusiastic reviews, and it slowly began to build an audience. "Something for the Weekend" became a staple on Chris Evans' radio show, and he had the Divine Comedy on his "TFI Friday" television show, making it the first TV appearance for Hannon. When it was released as a single a month later, "Something for the Weekend" entered the charts at 14. Soon, Hannon was appearing not only on the cover of *Melody Maker*, but there were articles about him throughout the mainstream press, from *The Guardian* to *Just Seventeen*. "Becoming More Like Alfie" was released in August, and while it peaked at No. 27, it nevertheless expanded the band's audience, as did "The Frog Princess," which reached No. 15 in November. The Divine Comedy supported the final single with a tour with a 30-piece orchestra, culminating with a concert at Lord Shepherds Bush Empire, which provided the basis for the band's next album, *A Short Album About Love*. Released to coincide with Valentine's Day 1997, *A Short Album About Love* was greeted with positive reviews and the strongest initial sales of any Divine Comedy record to date. — *Stephen Thomas Erlewine*

Liberation / Aug. 1993 / Setanta ✦✦✦
Despite Neil Hannon's tendency to reach much further than he can grasp, *Liberation* is a lovely debut, demonstrating a gift for graceful melodies, detailed orchestrations, and a deft wit. Occasionally, Hannon gets too clever for his own good, but his deep baritone croon and melodic skills make such lapses in taste forgivable. — *Stephen Thomas Erlewine*

Promenade / Mar. 1994 / Setanta ✦✦✦✦
The Divine Comedy's second album, *Promenade*, is more complex and rewarding than their debut. A concept album about two lovers spending the final day of the 20th century together, *Promenade* follows the couple throughout the day, with each song representing another hour and a half. Neil Hannon's melodic skills have only deepened, which means the album is a sweet, graceful listen, even when its concept bogs down and his wit becomes overbearing. — *Stephen Thomas Erlewine*

● **Casanova** / 1996 / Setanta ✦✦✦✦
Casanova is the Divine Comedy's masterpiece, an elegant record that balances urbane wit with detailed, flamboyant pop arrangements. Sounding like a cross between Jarvis Cocker and Damon Albarn, Neil Hannon is occasionally too smug and clever for his own good—witness the mock cockney accent on "Becoming More Like Alfie"—but his musical virtues outweigh his witty inclinations, making epics like "Something for the Weekend," "Middle-Class Heroes" and "The Frog Princess" positively soar. — *Stephen Thomas Erlewine*

A Short Album About Love / Feb. 1997 / Setanta ✦✦✦✦
Following the success of *Casanova*, Neil Hannon decided to indulge his Scott Walker fetish by recording a lush, symphonic mini-album with a 30-piece orchestra. Released to coincide with Valentine's Day, *A Short Album About Love* is, if anything, an even better record than *Casanova*, simply because Hannon holds nothing back. These are grandiose, extravagant songs that work because of their very pretensions. His deep, baritone croon has never sounded more affecting, and his songs are easily among his best, making *A Short Album About Love* much more than a record for hardcore fans. — *Stephen Thomas Erlewine*

The Divinyls

f. 1981, Sydney, Australia
Pop-Rock, Hard Rock, Arena Rock, New Wave
The Divinyls combined the raw, simple hard rock of AC/DC with a new wave pop sensibility. Formed in 1981 in Sydney, Australia, by vocalist Christina Amphlett and guitarist Mark McEntee, the band's first release was a soundtrack for the 1982 Australian film *Monkey Grip*, which featured an appearance by Amphlett. Taken from the EP *Monkey Grip*, the single "Boys in Town" became an Top Ten hit in Australia, leading to a contract with Chrysalis Records. The band released their first full-length album, *Desperate*, in 1983. The record became a hit in Australia, but it didn't make much of an impression in the US or the UK. *What a Life*, their second album, appeared in 1985 and managed to chart in the US, but its Australian sales did not equal *Desperate*. After the release of 1988's *Temperamental*, the Divinyls officially became a duo, with original bassist Rick Grossman leaving the band to join the Hoodoo Gurus. Three years later the group released *Divinyls*. The album became their first big hit album in America and Britain, thanks to the single "I Touch Myself," a catchy, tongue-in-cheek song about masturbation. In both countries, the song was treated as a novelty, and subsequent singles failed to chart. — *Stephen Thomas Erlewine*

Desperate / 1983 / Chrysalis ✦✦✦
This Australian band, built around Christina Amphlett's hiccuping vocals and Mark McEntee's rude grunge-guitar work, made an impressive debut with *Desperate*, a record that blends the thick chorusy guitar sound of the Pretenders with a punkish hard rock recklessness. Raw, ugly noises abound on this, their best studio album. Highlights include "Take a Chance," "Only Lonely," and "Boys in Town." — *Rick Clark*

What a Life! / 1985 / Chrysalis ✦✦
● **Essential** / 1987 / Chrysalis ✦✦✦✦
Essential Divinyls is a terrific 12-track compilation of the Australian duo's early— and mid-'80s singles, including such songs as "Pleasure and Pain," "Temperamental," "Back to the Wall," and "Boys in Town," offering a good overview of their pre-"I Touch Myself" records. — *Stephen Thomas Erlewine*

Temperamental / 1988 / Chrysalis ✦✦
Divinyls / Jan. 29, 1991 / Virgin ✦✦✦
In 1991, Australia's Divinyls generated some controversy in the US when lead singer Chrissie Amphlett sang about female masturbation on "I Touch Myself." Far from explicit, the PG-rated hit shouldn't have come as such a shock to American ears. At any rate, this self-titled CD offers exactly what one generally expects from the Divinyls: rockin' intensity combined with new wave-ish quirks and a strong melodic sense. Though not mind-blowing, it's respectable and generally appealing. Hardcore Divinyls enthusiasts will find the eerie "Love School" and

infectious offerings like "Make Out Alright," "Bless My Soul (It's Rock-n-Roll)" and "I Touch Myself" to be well worth acquiring. *Desperate* would be a better introduction to the Divinyls, but this is a release with many more strengths than weaknesses. —*Alex Henderson*

The Dixie Dregs

f. 1975, Miami, FL
Fusion, Southern Rock
One of the top jazz-rock fusion ensembles ever, the Dixie Dregs combined virtuoso technique with eclecticism and a sense of humor and spirit too frequently lacking in similar projects. Guitarist Steve Morse and bassist Andy West played together as high school students in Augusta, GA, in a conventional rock band called Dixie Grit. When Morse was expelled from school for refusing to cut his hair, he enrolled at the University of Miami School of Music, where he met violinist Allen Sloan, who had played with the Miami Philharmonic, and drummer Rod Morgenstein. The three decided to form a band, and Morse convinced West to come to Miami. The Dixie Dregs completed their lineup with keyboardist Steve Davidowski. Their first album, *The Great Spectacular*, was recorded for a class project in 1975 and later released by the band (it is long out of print). After graduation, the quintet began playing live around the South and got their break after opening for Sea Level in 1976, when a representative from Capricorn Records was impressed enough to sign them. Mark Parrish, a former member of Dixie Grit, replaced Davidowski for their official debut, 1977's *Free Fall*. Their follow-up, *What If*, proved to be one of their most artistically successful albums, and the Dregs played at the 1978 Montreux Jazz Festival with T. Lavitz replacing Parrish. Half of *Night of the Living Dregs* contains excerpts from that concert. The group shortened their name to the Dregs for 1981's *Unsung Heroes*, and added both vocalists and three-time national fiddling champ Mark O'Connor, whose old-timey playing style added another dimension to the group's sound, for *Industry Standard*. The Dregs then disbanded; the highly respected Morse formed his own band and recorded several albums, later joining Kansas from 1986 to 1988, while Morgenstein hooked up with pop-metallists Winger.

The Dregs reunited briefly in 1988 for a series of live dates, but a full-fledged reunion didn't take place until 1992, with Morse, Lavitz, Morgenstein, and Dave LaRue of the Steve Morse Band in West's place. Allen Sloan rejoined only briefly, with his position then filled by ex-Mahavishnu Orchestra member Jerry Goodman. *Bring 'em Back Alive* was culled from the group's tour, and 1994's *Full Circle* was also well-received. —*Steve Huey*

The Great Spectacular / 1975 / (no label) ✦✦
Free Fall / 1977 / Polydor ✦✦✦
A potent debut, it presents the Dregs' melodic instrumental fusion to fine effect. —*Jas Obrecht*

What If / 1978 / Polydor ✦✦✦✦
Of all the albums by the Dregs, this is the one to get. Steve Morse's melodies have an otherwordly elegance on songs like "Night Meets Light." The band plays with just the right amount of restraint. Ken Scott's production is, at turns, atmospheric and immediate. "Take It off the Top" is a fine rocker. —*Rick Clark*

Night of the Living Dregs / 1979 / Polydor ✦✦✦✦
This is a good half-live, half-studio set. —*Jas Obrecht*

Dregs of the Earth / 1980 / Arista ✦✦✦
Unsung Heroes / 1981 / Arista ✦✦✦
Industry Standard / 1982 / Arista ✦✦✦
● **Divided We Stand: Best of the Dixie Dregs** / Jul. 1989 / Arista ✦✦✦✦
A decent selection of their best work while signed to Capricorn, it includes "Cruise Control," a live version of "Refried Funky Chicken," and a healthy sampling from *What If.* —*Rick Clark*

Bring 'em Back Alive / Feb. 1992 / Capricorn ✦✦✦
Full Circle / Jun. 7, 1994 / Capricorn ✦✦

Don Dixon

b. North Carolina
Bass, Guitar, Keyboards, Vocals / Singer-Songwriter, Pop-Rock, Jangle-Pop
While his own records never reached a mass audience, Don Dixon was one of the major figures in the post-punk Southern guitar pop of the '80s. Dixon produced R.E.M., Let's Active, the Smithereens, and Marti Jones, bringing his sharp pop sensibilities to their already highly melodic songs. But his true talents shine in his solo albums. Dixon is able to recall everything from Beatlesque pop and Southern soul to gritty country and R&B with his lean, muscular pop; he adds an engagingly twisted lyrical view to his effortlessly eclectic music, making him one of the best subversive pop singer-songwriters since Nick Lowe. —*Stephen Thomas Erlewine*

Most of the Girls Like to Dance but Only Some of the Boys Do / 1985 / Enigma ✦✦✦✦
Dixon put together *Most of the Girls Like to Dance but Only Some of the Boys Do* out of demos cut from 1981-1984. It's a kind of best-of from a man with a pure pop sensibility and a wicked sense of humor when it comes to matters romantic. (The 1986 CD version adds two songs to make a total of 16.) —*William Ruhlmann*

Romeo at Juilliard / Sep. 1987 / Enigma ✦✦✦✦
Dixon's domestic debut featured more of his skewed songs, and here he was aided and abetted by such compatriots as Mitch Easter and Marti Jones (who is his wife). —*William Ruhlmann*

Chi-Town Budget Show / 1988 / Enigma ✦✦✦
An intimate live album featuring many of the best songs from the two previous albums. —*William Ruhlmann*

Eee / Sep. 20, 1989 / Enigma ✦✦✦
● **If I'm a Ham, Well You're a Sausage** / Mar. 3, 1992 / Restless ✦✦✦✦
While he is known mainly through his production work, this extensive best-of collection shows Dixon to be an equally sharp songwriter and performer, collecting the highlights of his albums as well as a handful of rare tracks. —*Chris Woodstra*

Romantic Depressive / Mar. 28, 1995 / Sugar Hill ✦✦✦
Don Dixon produces another set of well-crafted mid-'60s-style pop-rock songs on his Sugar Hill Records debut, playing most of the instruments and singing in his husky voice. The album title catches the tone of many of the lyrics, which turn on romantic reversals. Though Dixon continues to sound like a man who never got over the British Invasion of 1964, he does locate one song several years later, reminiscing in "Lottery of Lives" about a point in the Vietnam Era when his student deferment was in doubt. —*William Ruhlmann*

DJ Cam

b. Paris, France
DJ / Hip Hop, Electronica
Parisian hip-hop devotee Laurence Cam is one of a few but growing number of French artists updating hip-hop for the chill-out crowd, drawing on the beats'n'samples groundwork of producers such as Rakim, DJ Premier, and Prince Paul and combining it with broad, impressionistic strokes of dub, jazz, and soundtrack-y ambience. Like countrymen the Mighty Bop and La Funk Mob, Cam is stylistically closest to Mo'Wax artists such as DJ Shadow and DJ Krush; minimalist, downbeat instrumental hip-hop built from obscure samples and stomp-box turntable accompaniment, bent and twisted into new, artfully arranged compositions. His debut, 1994's *Underground Vibes*, was released on the tiny French label Street Jazz, and was followed by a live recording for the Inflammable imprint (one of only a few "live" recordings in a genre so reliant on the temporal concessions of the recording studio). Dubbed *Underground Live*, the album featured performed extrapolations of many of the tracks from his debut, as well as a few new and improvised tracks. Now nearly impossible to find, those first two albums were reissued in America by Shadow Records, packaged together as the single-CD priced *Mad Blunted Jazz* (particularly useful since acquiring both on import could run more than $50!).

Although Cam's music has found little acceptance in his home country, where racial tension has stratified the hip-hop community into rigid definitions of what the music is—and who should be making it (Cam himself is white)—audiences in the UK, Japan, and America have begun picking up on his style. In 1996 Cam was featured on, among many others, the sprawling Mo'Wax compilation *Headz 2*, remixed tracks for such artists as Tek 9 and La Funk Mob, and most recently collaborated on live and in-studio projects with Snooze and DJ Krush. (Hhe co-wrote a few tracks on the latter's 1997 Mo'Wax release, *Mi Sound*.) Cam's most recent LP, *Substances*, was released by Inflammable in 1997. —*Sean Cooper*

Underground Vibes / 1994 / Street Jazz ✦✦✦✦
Cam's debut collection of "abstract hip-hop" finds similar company in artists such as DJ Krush, Howie B., and the Solid Doctor, with pitched down, echo-chamber beats, sparse jazz and funk quotes, and turntable atmospherics combining in a smooth, impressionistic affair. The album was reissued by Shadow records—with his live Inflammable follow-up, *Underground Live*—as *Mad Blunted Jazz* in 1996. —*Sean Cooper*

Underground Live / Jun. 11, 1996 / Inflammable ✦✦✦✦
Live hip-hop albums are hardly common, but then neither is Cam's approach here, seamlessly blending loping, downtempo breaks with thick, dubby basslines; deft, heavily treated scratching; and instrumental samples and vocal drop-ins that make for a solid, tight flow. Cam presents live, tricked-up improvisations of tracks from his debut album, *Underground Vibes*, as well as a few new ones. The album was reissued as disc two of the domestic Shadow label's double Cam release *Mad Blunted Jazz*. —*Sean Cooper*

● **Mad Blunted Jazz** / Nov. 12, 1996 / Shadow ✦✦✦✦
This handy double-pack combines Cam's first two full-length releases, *Underground Vibes* and *Underground Live*, released on Street Jazz and Inflammable, respectively. Hazy, downtempo instrumental hip-hop with shades of jazz, funk, and soul. —*Sean Cooper*

Substances / 1997 / Inflammable ✦✦✦
A far more diverse set of relaxed (and occasionally not so) deviations from clubland, with bits of jungle, electro, and even house creeping into the mix. Cam has broadened the scope of his sound here; where previous releases tended to focus on sonic depth rather than breadth, atmosphere occupying first chair, *Substances'* sample arrangements are in places almost epic, and the beatwork is far more complex and inventive. —*Sean Cooper*

DJ Jazzy Jeff & the Fresh Prince

f. Philadephia, PA
Pop-Rap, Hip Hop
If you're looking for bubblegum rap, these guys are your best bet. The Prince spins his teen-suburban tales in a pleasant, if facile fashion, and Jeff isn't bad on the turntable. Don't look for anything gritty or street-smart; when Jeff boasts that he can beat Mike Tyson, that's about as menacing as it gets. The Fresh Prince starred in the early-'90s TV sitcom "The Fresh Prince of Bel Air." Will Smith, the "Fresh Prince" part of the team, has greatly expanded his horizons in the '90s. He appeared in the films *Six Degrees of Separation* and *Bad Boys*, and tried to expand his hip-hop horizons enough to offset the talk that his raps had become hopelessy whitebread and irrelevant. *Homebase* in 1991 included "Dog Is a Dog" and the Top Ten pop hit "Summertime," with Smith's rap done in a leaner, harder fashion even if the lyrics were pretty much family hour. But by *Code Red* in 1993 it seemed Smith had made peace with his image and was back to laidback, pop-oriented material such as "Boom! Shake the Room," "I Wanna Rock," and "Can't Wait to Be with You," which had a guest stint from Christopher Williams. —*John Floyd*

Rock the House / 1987 / Jive ✦✦✦
A ten-song work originally issued on Pop Art Records and later picked up by Jive. Containing the hit "Girls Ain't Nothing But Trouble," which launched them as the kings of teen/clean rap, it had maximum crossover appeal but retained a large following among the core hip-hop audience. —*Ron Wynn*

● **He's the D.J. I'm the Rapper** / 1988 / Jive ✦✦✦✦
Their commercial breakthrough contains their No. 12 hit "Parents Just Don't Understand," and other good-time raps. —*Dan Heilman*

And in This Corner . . . / Oct. 1989 / Jive ✦✦✦
More wit and whim from Jeff and the Prince, this time with assistance from saxes, flutes, and trumpets. Though not as commercially successful as its predecessors, it's actually a more faithful rap work. —*Ron Wynn*

Homebase / Jul. 23, 1991 / Jive ✦✦✦✦
After enduring a temporary sales slump, DJ Jazzy Jeff and the Fresh Prince roared back with *Homebase*. They scored a huge pop and R&B hit with "Summertime," using Kool & the Gang's "Summer Madness" single for the music base while Will Smith rapped about romantic hopes and community barbeques. He landed another Top 20 single with "Ring My Bell," this time reworking Anita Ward's oldie while offering his own double-entendre take. Undoubtedly helped by the success of his television show, this album returned the duo to platinum status, even as Smith showed once more (protests to the contrary notwithstanding) that he was an accomplished pop rapper. —*Ron Wynn*

Code Red / Oct. 12, 1993 / Jive ✦✦✦
After years of proclaiming that he wouldn't do gangsta rap, the Fresh Prince finally succumbs to a harder-edged style on *Code Red*. And surprisingly, he pulls it off well, thanks to sharp production and his endearing personality. —*Stephen Thomas Erlewine*

DJ Krush

b. Japan
DJ, Producer / Club/Dance, Trip-Hop, Electronica
Japanese turntablist and producer DJ Krush is one of the few island-nation throw-ups to be embraced by the global hip-hop world. Releasing material through Sony in Japan, Mo'Wax and Virgin in the UK, and Axiom, Shadow, and A&M in America, Krush's heady brand of experimental, (largely) instrumental hip-hop has been praised by everyone from hardcore underground hip-hop 'zines like *The Bomb* to the speckless offices of *Rolling Stone* and *Spin*.

Beginning as a bedroom DJ in the mid-'80s after the Japanese leg of the Wildstyle tour, Krush moved into mobile DJing, backing up rappers, and eventually solo production. Although his Japan-only debut freely mixed elements of R&B and acid jazz with the beefy breakbeat backbone of mid-tempo hip-hop, Krush's work has since tended more toward the abstract, applying heavy effects and sample manipulation to thick, smart breaks; layered, almost ambient textures; and subtle, inventive

scratching. Krush came to larger acclaim in the mid-'90s through his association with the London-based Mo'Wax label, which released his *Strictly Turntablized* in 1994 and *Meiso* in 1996, both reissued stateside by A&M. While *Turntablized* is closer to a collection of DJ tools, *Meiso* is a return of sorts to his earlier work, including rappers such as Guru and CL Smooth on a few tracks and incorporating a wider variety of instrumental sounds and atmospheres. Krush is also featured on a number of various artist collections, including Mo'Wax's celebrated *Headz*, as well as *Altered Beats* and *Axiom Dub* (both out on Bill Laswell's Axiom label). —*Sean Cooper*

● **Strictly Turntablized** / 1994 / Mo' Wax ✦✦✦
Basically a DJ tools-type breaks record, *Strictly Turntablized* stands up to repeat listenings thanks to atmospheric production and some interesting needle work. Although horns, piano, and other sampled instruments work their way into the mix, Krush is at his best when he focuses on the beats, evoking mood and emotion through loping percussion and thick bass kicks. —*Sean Cooper*

Back in the Base / Jan. 1997 / Ninja Tune [Canada] ✦✦✦
DJ Krush's full-length works have always been a bit hard to swallow given the predominance of mid-tempo trip-hop beats, and his contribution to *Cold Krush Cuts*, the double-disc Ninja Tunes mix compilation (one disc of Krush, one of Coldcut) is no different. Restricted to using only Ninja Tune artists (DJ Vadim makes eight appearances!), the material is similar-sounding and repetitious—even more so than Krush's albums. Aside from the chosen records, Krush's mixing skills are okay but overshadowed by Coldcut & DJ Food on the other disc. —*John Bush*

DJ Shadow

b. 1973, Hayward, CA
DJ / Trip-Hop, Electronica
DJ Shadow's Josh Davis is widely credited as a key figure in developing the experimental instrumental hip-hop style associated with the London-based Mo'Wax label. His early singles for the label, including "In/Flux" and "Lost and Found (S.F.L.)," were all-over-the-map mini-masterpieces combining elements of funk, rock, hip-hop, ambient, jazz, soul, and used-bin incidentalia. Although he'd already done a scattering of original and production work by the time Mo'Wax's James Lavelle contacted him about releasing "In/Flux" on the fledgling imprint, it wasn't until his association with Mo'Wax that his sound began to mature and cohere. Mo'Wax released his longest single to date in 1995—the 40-minute single in four movements "What Does Your Soul Look Like," which topped the British indie charts—and Davis has gone on to co-write, remix, and produce tracks for labelmates DJ Krush and Doctor Octagon.

Josh Davis grew up in Hayward, CA, a predominantly lower-middle class suburb of San Francisco. The odd white suburban hip-hop fan in the hard rock-dominated early '80s, Davis gravitated toward the turntable/mixer setup of the hip-hop DJ over the guitars, bass, and drums of his peers. He worked his way through hip-hop's early years into the heyday of crews like Eric B. & Rakim, Ultramagnetic, and Public Enemy—groups that prominently featured DJs in their ranks. Davis had already been fiddling around with making beats and breaks on a four-track while he was in high school, but it was his move to the NorCal cow-town of Davis to attend university that led to the establishment of his label as an outlet for his original tracks. Hooking up with Davis' few b-boys (including eventual Sole Sides artists Blackalicious and Lyrics Born) through the college radio station, Shadow began releasing the "Reconstructed from the Ground Up" mixtapes in 1991 and pressed his 17-minute hip-hop symphony "Entropy" in 1993. His tracks spread widely through the DJ-strong hip-hop underground, eventually catching the attention of Mo'Wax. Shadow's first full-length, *Entdroducing*, was released in late 1996. —*Sean Cooper*

Entropy / 1993 / Sole Sides ✦✦✦
Shadow's first full-blown blast of heady, groove-heavy instrumental experiments, released on his own Sole Sides label. One continuous track moving from upbeat deck-work and bin-shuddering beats through thick, downtempo head music. The flip is a forgettable vehicle for rapper and labelmate Asia Born (now Lyrics Born). —*Sean Cooper*

In/Flux / 1993 / Mo' Wax ✦✦✦✦
Somewhat sloppy, it almost doesn't matter, given the scope and originality of the result. Moving from a kinetic, signature Shadow opening through uptempo funky breakbeats and stony, textured, downbeat hip-hop, it's easy to see how influential "In/Flux" was on a generation of musicians looking for somewhere to take hip-hop. —*Sean Cooper*

Lost and Found (S.F.L.) / 1994 / Mo' Wax ✦✦✦
A split with DJ Krush, Shadow's side kipes the opening drum break from U2's "Sunday Bloody Sunday," cutting and layering it over chilling guitar and organ samples. The vocal break was lifted, according to Davis, from a late-'60s prison record. —*Sean Cooper*

What Does Your Soul Look Like? / 1995 / Mo' Wax ✦✦✦✦
"Soul"'s four parts are united in name only, with Shadow moving from solemn breakbeat-noir through alternately light, uptempo and slower, more questioning moods. Like past releases, his needlework is inspired, with textured, musical scratches that do more than simply accentuate. Shadow's best, most unified work. *—Sean Cooper*

Hardcore (Instrumental) Hip-Hop / 1996 / Mo' Wax /Excursions ✦✦✦
Shadow on the nepotism tip with his Sole Sides crew Chief X-Cel and Gift of Gab on the flip. Shadow steals the show with another extended meditation on outbound hip-hop, this time with stronger beatwork than past releases. A throwaway "Scratchapella" and a nice mid-tempo instrumental break run out the side. *—Sean Cooper*

● **Entroducing…** / Nov. 1996 / Mo' Wax /ffrr ✦✦✦✦
As a suburban Californian kid, DJ Shadow tended to treat hip-hop as a musical innovation, not as explicit social protest, which goes a long way toward explaining why his debut album *Entroducing…* sounded like nothing else at the time of its release. Using hip-hop, not only its rhythms but its cut-and-paste techniques, as a foundation, Shadow created a deep, endlessly intriguing world on *Entroducing*, one where there are no musical genres, only shifting sonic textures and styles. Shadow created the entire album from samples, almost all pulled from obscure, forgotten vinyl, and the effect is that of a hazy, half-familiar dream—parts of the record sound familiar, but it's clear that it only suggests music you've heard before, and that the multi-layered samples and genres create something new. And that's one of the keys to the success of *Entroducing*—it's innovative, but it builds on a solid historical foundation, giving it a rich, multi-faceted sound. It's not only a major breakthrough for hip-hop and electronica, but for pop music. *—Stephen Thomas Erlewine*

The D.O.C.

f. Texas
G-Funk, West Coast Rap
After the release of his debut album, the career of Texas-born rapper the D.O.C. was shattered by a car crash that almost took his life. Although he could no longer rap as he used to, his former producer Dr. Dre featured the rapper on his groundbreaking album *The Chronic*, which built on the foundation laid by the D.O.C.'s *No One Can Do It Better*; he was also featured on Snoop Doggy Dogg's *Doggystyle*. The D.O.C. returned in early 1996 with *Helter Skelter*, his first album in nearly seven years. The album received mixed reviews and failed to earn a large audience, leaving the charts a few months after its release. *—Stephen Thomas Erlewine*

★ **No One Can Do It Better** / 1989 / Ruthless ✦✦✦✦✦
Despite the D.O.C.'s connection to the members of N.W.A.—including its producer, Dr. Dre and Ruthless Records' founder, the late Eazy-E—not a trace of gangster rap is to be found on the Dallas rapper's debut album, *No One Can Do It Better*. N.W.A's influence on this enjoyable, though not remarkable, disc is musical rather than lyrical. Avoiding social or political commentary, the D.O.C. devotes himself almost entirely to rap's time-honored tradition of boasting. What makes this album come alive is his strong technique and Dre's imaginative production. At a time when so many East Coast rappers were content to sample James Brown over and over—often sounding tired and clichéd in the process—Dre took a much more musical, though equally aggressive, approach emphasizing melody and harmony as well as beats. On *No One*, everything from reggae to heavy metal is fair game for Dre and the D.O.C. This album was still burning up the charts when a car crash almost killed the D.O.C. and greatly decreased his ability to rap. *—Alex Henderson*

Helter Skelter / Jan. 23, 1996 / Giant ✦✦✦
After releasing his debut album *No One Can Do It Better*, the D.O.C. suffered a severe car accident which did irreparable damage to his vocal chords. It left him with a thin, raspy voice that was simply unusable for several years. In 1996 he made a comeback with *Helter Skelter*, an album that illustrated how ragged his voice was. While the backing tracks to *Helter Skelter* are solid, if generic, gangsta rap recorded by a live band, the D.O.C. simply doesn't have enough power to make the songs interesting. Sometimes the harsh growl of his voice sounds threatening, giving the tracks a menacing power. Too often, the D.O.C. simply sounds tired and worn. It's admirable that he attempted the comeback, but the musical results don't justify the effort. *—Stephen Thomas Erlewine*

Dr. Dre

b. Feb. 18, 1965, Los Angeles, CA
Keyboards, Vocals / Hip Hop, Gangsta Rap, G-Funk, West Coast Rap
More than any other rapper, Dr. Dre was responsible for moving away from the avant-noise and political stance of Public Enemy and Boogie Down Productions, as well as the party vibes of old-school rap. Dre pioneered gangsta rap and his own variation of the sound, G-Funk. BDP's early albums were hardcore but cautionary tales of the criminal mind, but Dre's records with NWA celebrated the hedonistic, amoralistic side of gang life. Dre was never much of a rapper—his rhymes were simple and his delivery was slow and clumsy—but as a producer, he was extraordinary. With NWA he melded the noise collages of the Bomb Squad with funky rhythms. On his own, he reworked George Clinton's elastic funk into the self-styled G-Funk, a slow-rolling variation that relied more on sound than content. When he left NWA in 1992 he founded Death Row Records with Suge Knight, and the label quickly became the dominant force in mid-'90s hip-hop, thanks to his debut, *The Chronic*. Soon, most rap records imitated its sound, and his productions for Snoop Doggy Dogg, Warren G, and Blackstreet were massive hits. For nearly four years, G-funk dominated hip-hop, and Dre had enough sense to abandon it and Death Row just before the whole empire collapsed in late 1996. Dre retaliated by forming a new company, Aftermath, and while it was initially slow getting started, his bold moves forward earned critical respect.

Dr. Dre (b. Andre Young, February 18, 1965) became involved in hip-hop during the early '80s, performing at house parties and clubs with the World Class Wreckin' Cru around South Central Los Angeles, and making a handful of recordings along the way. In 1986 he met Ice Cube, and the two rappers began writing songs for Ruthless Records, a label started by former drug pusher Eazy-E. Eazy tried to give one of the duo's songs, "Boyz N The Hood," to HBO, a group signed to Ruthless. When the group refused, Eazy formed NWA—an acronym for Niggaz With Attitude—with Dre and Cube, releasing their first album in 1987. A year later, N.W.A. delivered *Straight Outta Compton*, a vicious hardcore record that became an underground hit with virtually no support from radio, the press, or MTV. N.W.A. became notorious for their hardcore lyrics, especially those of "Fuck tha Police," which resulted in the FBI's sending a warning letter to Ruthless and its parent company Priority, suggesting that the group should watch their step.

Most of the group's political threat left with Ice Cube when he departed in late 1989 amidst many financial disagreements. While Eazy-E appeared to be the undisputed leader after Cube's departure—and he was certainly responsible for the group approaching near-parodic levels with their final pair of records—the music was in Dre's hands. On both the 1990 EP *100 Miles and Runnin'* and the 1991 album *Efil4zaggin* ("Niggaz 4 Life" spelled backward), he created dense, funky sonic landscapes that were as responsible for keeping NWA at the top of the charts as Eazy's comic-book lyrics. While the group was at the peak of their popularity in 1991, Dre began to make efforts to leave the crew, especially after he was charged with assaulting the host of a televised rap show in 1991. The next year, Dre left the group to form Death Row Records with Suge Knight. According to legend, Knight held NWA's manager at gun point, threatening to kill him if he refused to let Dre out of his contract.

Dr. Dre released his first solo single, "Deep Cover," in the spring of 1992. Not only was the record the debut of his elastic G-funk sound, it also was the beginning of his collaboration with rapper Snoop Doggy Dogg. Dre discovered Snoop through his stepbrother, Warren G, and he immediately began working with the rapper; Snoop was on Dre's 1992 debut *The Chronic* as much as Dre himself. Thanks to the singles "Nuthin' But a 'G' Thang," "Dre Day," and "Let Me Ride," *The Chronic* was a multi-platinum, Top Ten smash, and the entire world of hip-hop changed with it. For the next four years, it was virtually impossible to hear mainstream hip-hop that wasn't affected in some way by Dr. Dre and his patented G-Funk. Not only did he produce Snoop Dogg's 1993 debut *Doggystyle*, but he orchestrated several soundtracks, including *Above the Rim* and *Murder Was the Case* (both 1994), which functioned as samplers for his new artists and production techniques, and he helmed hit records by Warren G ("Regulate") and Blackstreet, among others, including a hit reunion with Ice Cube, "Natural Born Killaz." During this entire time, Dre released no new records, but he didn't need to—all of Death Row was under his control and most of his peers mimicked his techniques.

The Death Row dynasty held strong until the spring of 1996, when Dre grew frustrated with Knight's strong-arm techniques. At the time, Death Row was devoting itself to 2-Pac's label debut *All Eyez On Me* (which featured Dre on the breakthrough hit, "California Love"), and Snoop was busy recovering from his draining murder trial. Dre left the label in the summer of 1996 to form Aftermath, declaring gangsta rap was dead. While he was subjected to endless taunts from his former Death Row colleagues, their sales slipped by 1997 and Knight was imprisoned on racketeering charges by the end of the year. Dre's first album for Aftermath, the various artists collection *Dr. Dre Presents… The Aftermath* received considerable media attention, but the record didn't become a hit, despite the presence of his hit single "Been There Done That." Even though the album wasn't a success, the implosion of Death Row in 1997 proved that Dre's inclinations were correct at the time. —*Stephen Thomas Erlewine*

★ **The Chronic** / 1993 / Death Row ✦✦✦✦✦
With its deeply funky George Clinton-inspired grooves, whining synthesizers, female backing vocals, and romantic gangsta tales, *The Chronic* redefined hip-hop for the 1990s. Dr. Dre's genius lies in keeping the funk loose but concise, creating perfect singles like "Down Wit Dre Day," "Let Me Ride," and "Nuthin' But A 'G' Thang." For all his musical genius, Dr. Dre remains an unspectacular rapper, which makes Snoop Doggy Dogg all the more remarkable. Snoop raps as much as Dre throughout *The Chronic*, and his surreally menacing drawl shows the reality behind the stylized portraits of sex and violence. —*Stephen Thomas Erlewine*

First Round Knockout / May 21, 1996 / Triple X ✦✦
Back N Tha Day / Sep. 24, 1996 / Blue Dolphin ✦
Back N Tha Day is one of many budget-priced compilations of Dr. Dre's early, pre-NWA material but it *is* different from the rest. Instead of relying on Dre's occasionally awkward old-school material, the compilation consists entirely of mid-'90s *remixes* of his old-school recordings, adding two previously unreleased tracks as enticement for hardcore fans, who probably gave up following these scatter-shot releases long ago. Since Dre's old-school, early-'80s recordings are of only historical interest anyway, *Back N Tha Day* qualifies as the most exploitive release among legions of exploitive records. —*Stephen Thomas Erlewine*

Dr. Dre Presents the Aftermath / Nov. 26, 1996 / Aftermath/Interscope ✦✦✦✦
Dr. Dre shifted directions drastically half way through 1996, leaving Death Row Records and abandoning gangsta rap, claiming that he had "Been There, Done That." So Dre founded a new record label, Aftermath, and built an artist roster consisting entirely of new, unproven talent. He also decided not to concentrate on rap, signing urban R&B acts as well as hip-hop. Aftermath's intial release was the various artists compilation *Dr. Dre Presents... The Aftermath* and one listen proves that Dre wasn't kidding when he said he wasn't interested in gangsta anymore. There are a number of rappers on *The Aftermath*, even a handful of hardcore rappers, but nothing fits into the standard G-funk template. The true revelation of the album is Dre's skill for urban R&B and soul, all of which sounds fresh and exciting compared to several of the fairly pedestrian hip-hop productions. Despite the success of these urban productions, none of the performers makes much of an impact—the tracks are impressive only because they demonstrate Dre's musical versatilty and skill. In fact, the two tracks that really stand out—Dre's stately, sexy "Been There, Done That" and the powerful "East Coast / West Coast Killas," which features cameos by B-Real, KRS-1, Nas, and RBX—are a combination of terrific production and personality, which is usually what results in great singles. But that doesn't mean that *The Aftermath* is a wash-out. Instead, it's a promising fresh start for Dr. Dre that is full of potential and enough great music to make it a vital listen. —*Stephen Thomas Erlewine*

Dr. Feelgood

f. 1971, Canvey Island, England, **db.** 1994
Rock 'n' Roll, Pub Rock
Dr. Feelgood was the ultimate working band. From their formation in 1971 to lead vocalist Lee Brilleaux's untimely death in 1994, the band never left the road, playing hundreds of gigs every year. Throughout their entire career, Dr. Feelgood never left simple, hard-driving rock 'n' roll behind, and their devotion to the blues and R&B earned them a devoted fan base. That following first emerged in the mid-'70s, when Dr. Feelgood became the leader of the second wave of pub-rockers. Unlike Brinsley Schwarz, the laidback leaders of the pub-rock scene, Dr. Feelgood was devoted to edgy, Stonesy rock 'n' roll, and their sweaty live shows—powered by Brilleaux's intense singing and guitarist Wilko Johnson's muscular leads—became legendary. While the group's stripped-down, energetic sound paved the way for English punk rock in the late '70s, their back-to-basics style was overshadowed by the dominance of punk and new wave, and the group had retreated to cult status by the early '80s.

Brilleaux (vocals, harmonica), Johnson (guitar), and John B. Sparks (bass) all played in several blues-based bar bands around Canvey Island, England, before forming Dr. Feelgood in 1971. Taking their name from a Johnny Kidd & the Pirates song, the group was dedicated to playing old-fashioned R&B and rock 'n' roll, including both covers and originals by Johnson. John Martin (drums), a former member of Finian's Rainbow, was added to the lineup, and the group began playing the pub-rock circuit. By the end of 1973, Dr. Feelgood's dynamic live act had made them the most popular group on the pub-rock circuit, and several labels were interested in signing them. They settled for United Artists, and they released their debut album, *Down by the Jetty*, in 1974.

According to legend, *Down By the Jetty* was recorded in mono and consisted almost entirely of first takes. While it was, in fact, recorded in stereo, the rumor added significantly to Dr. Feelgood's purist image, and the album became a cult hit. The next year, the group released *Malpractice*—also their first US release—which climbed into the UK Top 20 on the strength of the band's live performances and positive reviews. In 1976 the band released the live album *Stupidity*, which became a smash hit in Britain, topping the album charts. Despite its thriving British success, Dr. Feelgood was unable to find an audience in the States. One other American album, *Sneakin' Suspicion*, followed in 1977 before the band gave up on the States; they never released another record in the US.

Sneakin' Suspicion didn't replicate the success of *Stupidity*, partially because of its slick production, but mainly because the flourishing punk rock movement overshadowed Dr. Feelgood's edgy roots-rock. Wilko Johnson left the band at the end of 1977 to form the Solid Senders; he later joined Ian Dury's Blockheads. Henry McCullough played on Feelgood's '77 tour before John "Gypie" Mayo became the group's full-time lead guitarist. Nick Lowe produced 1978's *Be Seeing You*, Mayo's full-length debut with Dr. Feelgood. The album generated the 1979 Top Ten hit "Milk and Alcohol," as well as the Top 40 hit "As Long as the Price Is Right." Two albums, *As It Happens* and *Let It Roll*, followed in 1979, and Mayo left the band in 1980. He was replaced by Johnny Guitar in 1980, who debuted on *A Case of the Shakes*, which was also produced by Nick Lowe.

During their first decade together, Dr. Feelgood never left the road, which was part of the reason founding members John Martin and John Sparks left the band in 1982. Lee Brilleaux replaced them with Buzz Barwell and Pat McMullen, and continued touring. Throughout the '80s, Brilleaux continued to lead various incarnations of Dr. Feelgood, settling on the rhythm section of bassist Phil Mitchell and drummer Kevin Morris in the mid-'80s. The band occasionally made records—including *Brilleaux*, one of the last albums on Stiff Records, in 1976—but concentrated primarily on live performances. Dr. Feelgood continued to perform to large audiences into the early '90s, when Brilleaux was struck by cancer. He died in April 1994, three months after he recorded the band's final album, *Down at the Doctor's*. The remaining members of Dr. Feelgood hired vocalist Pete Gage and continued to tour under the band's name. Former Feelgoods Gypie Mayo, John Sparks, and John Martin formed the Practice in the mid-'80s, and they occasionally performed under the name Dr. Feelgood's Practice. —*Stephen Thomas Erlewine*

Down by the Jetty / Jan. 1975 / United Artists ✦✦✦✦
Dr. Feelgood's debut album is on a par with the early Rolling Stones albums as a demonstration of R&B fervor. Every track burns. —*Bruce Eder*

● **Malpractice** / Feb. 1975 / Columbia ✦✦✦✦
Guitarist Wilko Johnson's songs shine against such inspired covers as "Riot in Cell Block No. 9." And his Stonesy playing takes no prisoners. —*Bruce Eder*

Stupidity / 1976 / United Artists ✦✦✦✦
Comprised of recordings taken from 1975 tours, the live *Stupidity* finally captures the relentless, hard-driving energy of Dr. Feelgood at its peak. All the music on *Stupidity* is presented raw and without overdubs, making it clear that the dynamic friction between guitarist Wilko Johnson and vocalist Lee Brilleaux could propel the band toward greatness. While many of the versions here don't differ in form from the original studio versions, these unvarnished performances are considerably more exciting, revealing the Johnson originals "She Does It Right" and "All Through the City" as minor rock 'n' roll classics. —*Stephen Thomas Erlewine*

Sneakin' Suspicion / 1977 / Columbia ✦✦✦✦
Wilko Johnson's last album with Dr. Feelgood continues to be dominated by his tough guitar playing, although fewer of his songs are heard. —*Bruce Eder*

Be Seeing You / 1977 / United Artists ✦✦✦✦
The Nick Lowe-produced *Be Seeing You*, Dr. Feelgood's first album with guitarist John Mayo, was only slightly weaker than the group's previous records. Although Mayo was still working his way into the band's sound, Dr. Feelgood retained their tough, hard-rocking appeal. —*Stephen Thomas Erlewine*

Private Practice / 1978 / United Artists ✦✦
Although producer Richard Gottehrer gives *Private Practice* a sound that's just a little too clean and restrained, the album nevertheless is a fine set of professional R&B and rock 'n' roll. The material on the album is a little uneven, but with the assistance of Nick Lowe, the Feelgoods wrote a pair of tight, catchy rockers in "Milk and Alcohol" and "It Wasn't Me," which stood out among the entertaining, yet generally generic, songs. —*Stephen Thomas Erlewine*

As It Happens / 1979 / United Artists ✦✦
The live *As It Happens* captures Dr. Feelgood at one of its weakest stages, as John Mayo was still finding his place in the group. Further-

more, the band relies on second-rate material throughout the record, making *As It Happens* a minor addition to the group's catalog. —*Stephen Thomas Erlewine*

Let It Roll / 1979 / United Artists ✦✦

Let It Roll was an improvement on the band's two previous records, yet it still wasn't up to the standards of *Sneakin' Suspicion* and *Malpractice*. —*Stephen Thomas Erlewine*

A Case of the Shakes / 1980 / United Artists ✦✦✦

A Case of the Shakes, the group's second album recorded with Nick Lowe, proved that Dr. Feelgood's last three records simply captured the band in a transitional phase. On *Shakes*, the band returns to form, ripping through a set of catchy three-chord rockers that are invigorated by Lowe's new wave-tinged production. —*Stephen Thomas Erlewine*

On the Job / 1981 / Liberty ✦✦

On the Job, recorded live at Manchester University, was the end of several eras for Dr. Feelgood. It was their last record for EMI, meaning it was their last major-label album, and it was their last recording with Gypie Mayo. As a result, it sounds rather tired. The group never sounds particularly bad, but it's clear that their spirits were slightly broken, and neither the material, which is entirely from *Let It Roll* and *A Case of the Shakes*, nor the performances are noteworthy. Unfortunately, *On the Job* sounds like the contractual obligation it was. —*Stephen Thomas Erlewine*

Casebook / 1981 / Liberty ✦✦✦✦

Although it's far from perfect—"I Can Tell" and "Keep It Out of Sight" are both missing, for instance—*Casebook* is an adequate overview of the group's early records, featuring enough classic material ("Roxette," "She Does It Right," "She's a Wind Up," "Milk and Alcohol") to make it an effective, if flawed, retrospecitve and introduction. —*Stephen Thomas Erlewine*

Fast Women & Slow Horses / 1982 / Chiswick ✦✦

Fast Women & Slow Horses is the sound of Dr. Feelgood in a crisis—there's a reason why it's the last album to feature the original rhythm section of John Martin and John Sparks. The group is uncertain whether it wants to pursue a pop crossover or stick to R&B, and the whole record suffers as a result. The production is clean and stiff, the performances bland, and the material, with the exception of Difford and Tillbrook's passable "Monkey," largely undistinguished. Even though it meant that the original group had to effectively disband, *Fast Women & Slow Horses* signaled it was time for a change within the group itself. —*Stephen Thomas Erlewine*

Doctor's Orders / 1984 / Demon ✦✦✦

Lee Brilleaux returned with a completely new lineup of Dr. Feelgood for *Doctor's Orders*, a record that returned the band to its pile-driving R&B and rock 'n' roll roots. The band sounds more accomplished and professional than ever before. There's little of the wild energy that distinguished their first records, but that's actually not a bad thing, because they have enough sensibility to be skilled, not slick. Supported by the new band, Brilleaux manages to turn in the grittiest Dr. Feelgood record in years, making *Doctor's Orders* a fine comeback from a band that seemed to have lost the plot. —*Stephen Thomas Erlewine*

Mad Man Blues / 1986 / ID ✦✦✦✦

Lee Brilleaux and Dr. Feelgood sound positively revitalized on *Mad Man Blues*, a collection of raw versions of blues standards that is their best album since 1977's *Be Seeing You*. —*Stephen Thomas Erlewine*

Brilleaux / 1986 / Grand ✦✦✦

Lee Brilleaux invested in the groundbreaking British independent label Stiff when it was being launched in the mid-'70s, so it is sort of appropriate that Dr. Feelgood eventually recorded for the label. The only trouble is, it wasn't in 1976, when Stiff and Feelgood were at their peak, it was in 1986, as Stiff was sliding towards bankruptcy and the Doctors were far from their popular heyday. Dave Robinson, in his infinite wisdom, decided that the way to restore both his label and the Feelgoods to their proper glories was by refashioning the band as radio-ready, R&B-tinged popsters. Of course, that ran contrary to the group's entire career, but they decided to follow his advice, and with producer Will Birch, the group assembled their most eclectic batch of songs ever. Although the smoother sound strips much of Feelgood's gritty essence, *Brilleaux* remains a varied, entertaining record—it's a welcome change of pace from the driving rockers, even if it wasn't welcomed by radio as originally planned. —*Stephen Thomas Erlewine*

Classic / 1987 / Stiff ✦✦✦

Case History / 1987 / EMI ✦✦✦✦

Case History—The Best of Dr. Feelgood is a fine, basic primer of the group's best moments, featuring such Feelgood staples as "She Does It Right," "Roxette," "As Long as the Price Is Right," "She's a Wind Up," "Down at the Doctors" and "Milk and Alcohol." It does shortchange the group's early records somewhat, but it remains a fine single-disc introduction. —*Stephen Thomas Erlewine*

Singles—The UA Years / 1989 / Liberty ✦✦✦✦

Singles—The UA Years is a terrific double-album set that chronicles all of Dr. Feelgood's major singles, from 1976's "Roxette" to 1986's "See You Later Alligator." Although the hits-only approach leaves out some major Feelgood songs, *Singles* remains a first-rate retrospective; for many years, it was the best Dr. Feelgood collection available. The 1997 double-disc *Twenty-Five Years of Dr. Feelgood* later replaced *Singles* as the definitive retrospective, but there are enough songs on this collection to make it worthwhile for serious fans who don't want to spring for either the box set *Lookin' Back* or the entire catalog. —*Stephen Thomas Erlewine*

Live in London / 1990 / Grand ✦✦

Down at the Doctors / 1995 / Grand ✦✦✦

Down at the Doctors captures Lee Brilleaux's last concert before his death in the spring of 1994. Culled from concerts performed on January 24 and 25, 1994, the set features many of Feelgood's classic songs, including "Milk and Alcohol" and "Down at the Doctors," plus unexpected, delightful covers of Nick Lowe's "Heart of the City" and "Road Runner." It's a surprisingly energetic and thoroughly enjoyable record that serves as an excellent epitaph for Brilleaux, who remained one of the hardest-working performers in rock 'n' roll until the very end. —*Stephen Thomas Erlewine*

Looking Back / Nov. 1995 / EMI ✦✦✦

Theoretically, Dr. Feelgood could have produced a fine multi-disc box set, but the four-disc *Looking Back* isn't it. Although it contains the group's very best songs, including large portions of *Down by the Jetty* and *Malpractice*, it is cluttered with mediocre latter-day material, and the entire final disc is devoted to Lee Brilleaux discussing his cancer. Although his testimonial is moving, it would have been better heard on a separate disc, not as part of a comprehensive retrospective. Then again, *Looking Back* is filled with so many songs that only serious fans, the kind who would want an interview disc, will find it necessary. For most fans, even those with a fairly deep interest in the band, the comprehensive double-disc *Twenty-Five Years of Dr. Feelgood* is a more logical choice. —*Stephen Thomas Erlewine*

Dr. John

b. Nov. 21, 1940, New Orleans, LA
Piano, Vocals / R&B, Rock 'n' Roll, Piano Blues, New Orleans R&B

Although he didn't become widely known until the 1970s, Dr. John had been active in the music industry since the late '50s, when the teenager was still known as Mac Rebennack. A formidable boogie and blues pianist with a lovable growl of a voice, his most enduring achievements have fused New Orleans R&B, rock, and Mardi Gras craziness to come up with his own brand of "voodoo" music. He's also quite accomplished and enjoyable when sticking to purely traditional forms of blues and R&B. On record, he veers between the two approaches, making for an inconsistent and frequently frustrating legacy that often makes the listener feel as if the Night Tripper (as he's nicknamed himself) has been underachieving.

In the late '50s, Rebennack gained prominence in the New Orleans R&B scene as a session keyboardist and guitarist, contributing to records by Professor Longhair, Frankie Ford, and Joe Tex. He also did some overlooked singles of his own, and by the 1960s had expanded into production and arranging. After a gun accident damaged his hand in the early '60s, he gave up the guitar to concentrate on keyboards exclusively. Skirting trouble with the law and drugs, he left New Orleans in the mid-'60s for Los Angeles, where he found session work with the help of fellow New Orleans expatriate Harold Battiste.

Rebennack renamed himself Dr. John the Night Tripper when he recorded his first album, *Gris-Gris*. According to legend, this was hurriedly cut with leftover studio time from a Sonny & Cher session, but it never sounded hastily conceived. In fact, its mix of New Orleans R&B with voodoo sounds and a tinge of psychedelia was downright enthralling, and may have resulted in his greatest album. He began building an underground following with both his music and his eccentric stage presence, which found him conducting ceremonial-type events in full Mardi Gras costume.

Dr. John was nothing if not eclectic, and his next few albums were granted mixed critical receptions because of their unevenness and occasional excess. They certainly had their share of admirable moments, though, and Eric Clapton and Mick Jagger helped out on *The Sun Moon and Herbs* in 1971. The next year's *Gumbo*, produced by Jerry Wexler, proved Dr. John was a master of traditional New Orleans R&B styles, in the mold of one of his heroes, Professor Longhair. In 1973 he got his sole big hit, "In the Right Place," which was produced by Allen Toussaint, with backing by the Meters. In the same year, he also recorded with Mike Bloomfield and John Hammond, Jr. for the *Triumvirate* album.

The rest of the decade, unfortunately, was pretty much a waste musically. Dr. John could always count on returning to traditional styles for a good critical reception, and he did so constantly in the 1980s. There were solo piano albums, sessions with Chris Barber and Jimmy Witherspoon, and *In a Sentimental Mood* (1989), a record of pop standards. These didn't sell all that well, though. A more important problem was that he's capable of much more than recastings of old styles and material. In fact, by this time he was usually bringing in the bacon not through his own music, but via vocals for numerous commercial jingles.

It's continued pretty much in the same vein throughout the 1990s: New Orleans supersessions for the *Bluesiana* albums, another outing with Chris Barber, an album of New Orleans standards, and *another* album of pop standards. In 1994 *Television* did at least offer some original material. However, at this point it seems that he will usually rely upon cover versions for the bulk of his recorded work, though his interpretive skills will always ensure that these are more interesting than most such efforts. His autobiography, *Under a Hoodoo Moon*, was published by St. Martin's Press in 1994. — *Richie Unterberger*

Gris Gris / 1968 / Repertoire ✦✦✦✦
The most exploratory and psychedelic outing of Dr. John's career, a one-of-a-kind fusion of New Orleans Mardi Gras R&B and voodoo mysticism. Great rasping, bluesy vocals, soulful backup singers, and eerie melodies on flute, sax, and clarinet, as well as odd Middle Eastern-like chanting and mandolin runs. It's got the setting of a strange religious ritual, but the mood is far more joyous than solemn. — *Richie Unterberger*

Babylon / 1969 / Atco ✦✦✦
Dr. John's ambition remained undiminished on his second solo album, *Babylon*, released shortly after the groundbreaking voodoo-psychedelia-New Orleans R&B fusion of his debut, *Gris-Gris*. The results, however, were not nearly as consistent or impressive. Coolly received by critics, the album nonetheless is deserving of attention, though it pales a bit in comparison with *Gris-Gris*. The production is sparser and more reliant on female backup vocals than his debut. Dr. John remains intent on fusing voodoo and R&B, but the mood is oddly bleak and despairing, in comparison with the wild Mardi Gras-gone-amok tone of his first LP. The hushed, damned atmosphere and afterhours R&B sound a bit like Van Morrison on a bummer trip at times, as peculiar as that might seem. "The Patriotic Flag-Waiver" (sic), in keeping with the mood of the late '60s, damns social ills and hypocrisy of all sorts. An FM underground radio favorite at the time, its ambitious structure remains admirable, though its musical imperfections haven't worn well. To a degree, you could say the same about the album as a whole. But it has enough of an eerie fascination to merit investigation. — *Richie Unterberger*

Remedies / 1970 / Atco ✦✦

Sun Moon & Herbs / Sep. 1971 / Atco ✦✦✦

Dr. John's Gumbo / Apr. 1972 / Atco ✦✦✦✦
Gumbo bridged the gap between post-hippie rock and early rock 'n' roll, blues, and R&B, offering a selection of classic New Orleans R&B, including "Tipitina" and "Junko Partner," updated with a gritty, funky beat. There are not as many psychedelic flourishes as on his first two albums, but the ones that are present enhance his sweeping vision of American roots music. And that sly fusion of styles makes *Gumbo* one of Dr. John's finest albums. — *Stephen Thomas Erlewine*

In the Right Place / Mar. 1973 / Atco ✦✦✦

Desitively Bonaroo / Apr. 1974 / Atco ✦✦✦

Hollywood Be Thy Name / 1975 / Beat Goes On ✦✦

City Lights / Feb. 1978 / Horizon ✦✦✦

Tango Palace / 1979 / Horizon ✦✦
Dr. John's second and final album for the Horizon jazz subsidiary of A&M Records finds him working with producers Tommy LiPuma and Hugh McCracken on a rollicking set that emphasizes his New Orleans roots while attempting to update his sound with '70s effects such as deep, plucked bass notes and occasional disco rhythms. The album leads off with "Keep That Music Simple," a somewhat caustic admonition to musicians and the music business whose message is disregarded elsewhere on the record, as LiPuma and McCracken seek to cover all stylistic bases from funk to fusion to second line. Dr. John emerges from the production intact, but he is not quite as swampy as when heard at his best. — *William Ruhlmann*

Dr. John Plays Mac Rebennack / 1981 / Clean Cuts ✦✦✦✦

Brightest Smile in Town / 1983 / Clean Cuts ✦✦✦
Doctor John's second solo piano album finds him combining country, blues, and New Orleans standards with originals, half of them instrumentals and half of them containing vocals that sound like they were recorded off the piano microphone. This is not a high-tech recording, by any means, but in its unadorned way it does capture the flavor of Doctor John as directly as any record he's made. — *William Ruhlmann*

In a Sentimental Mood / Apr. 1989 / Warner Brothers ✦✦✦
On Dr. John's first major-label effort and first vocal studio album in ten years, he performs a set of pop standards including Cole Porter's "Love for Sale" and Johnny Mercer's "Accentuate the Positive." After starting

out with a wild stage act and unusual costumes, Dr. John has evolved into a vocal stylist and piano virtuoso, which makes the idea of doing this sort of material appealing. And he does it well, turning out a leisurely duet with Rickie Lee Jones on "Makin' Whoopee" that won a Grammy (Best Jazz Vocal Performance, Duo or Group) and giving sad feeling to "My Buddy." Maybe he has changed since the *Gris Gris* days, but even a mellowed Dr. John is a tasty one. — *William Ruhlmann*

Bluesiana II / 1991 / Windham Hill ✦✦✦
Previously, Windham Hill Records released *Bluesiana Triangle*, a jazz trio album by drummer Art Blakey, pianist Dr. John, and reed man David "Fathead" Newman. Blakey passed away in 1990, but in the spring of 1991, Dr. John and Newman organized this second Bluesiana session, featuring trombonist Ray Anderson, drummer Will Calhoun, bassists Essiet Okon Essiet and Jay Leonhart (on different tracks), and percussionist Joe Bonadio. The resulting music again justifies the name, blues played in a funky Louisiana style with plenty of room for extended jazzy soloing. Though much of the material was written by Dr. John and he does sing occasionally, this is not a conventional Dr. John vocal album. It does contain some excellent playing, however. — *William Ruhlmann*

Goin' Back to New Orleans / Jun. 23, 1992 / Warner Brothers ✦✦✦
Having cut an album of standards on his first Warner Brothers album, *In a Sentimental Mood* (1989), Dr. John turned its follow-up to a collection of New Orleans standards. On an album he described in the liner notes as "a little history of New Orleans music," Dr. John returned to his hometown and set up shop at local Ultrasonic Studios, inviting in such local musicians as Pete Fountain, Al Hirt, and the Neville Brothers and addressing the music and styles of such local legends as Jelly Roll Morton, Huey "Piano" Smith, Fats Domino, James Booker, and Professor Longhair. The geography may have been circumscribed, but the stylistic range was extensive, from jazz and blues to folk and rock. And it was all played with festive conviction—Dr. John is the perfect archivist for the music, being one of its primary popularizers, yet he had never addressed it quite as directly as he did here. — *William Ruhlmann*

Anthology / Oct. 19, 1993 / Rhino ✦✦✦✦
Over his 35 years of recording, Mac "Dr. John" Rebennack has worn many hats, from '50s greasy rock 'n' roller to psychedelic '70s weirdo to keeper of the New Orleans music flame. All of these modes, plus more, are excellently served up on this two-disc anthology. From the early New Orleans sides featuring Rebennack's blistering guitar work ("Storm Warning" and "Morgus the Magnificent") to the fabled '70s sides as the Night Tripper, to his present-day status as repository of the Crescent City's noble musical tradition, this is the one you want to have for the collection. — *Cub Koda*

Television / Mar. 29, 1994 / GRP ✦✦
Dr. John's debut for GRP doesn't deviate from any release he's made for several other labels. It's still his chunky, humorous take on New Orleans funk; these are his songs, visions and performances, and there's none of the elevator material or laidback, detached fare that's a customary GRP byproduct. Such songs as "Witchy Red," "Spaceship Relationship," and the title selection are a delicate mix of seemingly outrageous but actually quite sharp commentary and excellent musical performances from Dr. John on keyboards, Hugh McCracken on guitar, and several other veterans, among them the great Red Tyler on tenor sax. While not quite as fiery as his classic sessions for Atlantic, if anyone can bring the funk to a company that's famous for avoiding it, it's Dr. John. — *Ron Wynn*

Afterglow / Feb. 7, 1995-Feb. 9, 1995 / Blue Thumb ✦✦✦
Producer and GRP Records president Tommy LiPuma, a longtime associate of Dr. John's, revived his old Blue Thumb label as an imprint of GRP/MCA with this album, which served as something of a sequel to the last Dr. John/Tommy LiPuma collaboration, *In A Sentimental Mood*. On that earlier album, the two had covered pop standards. Here, they again turned to evergreens by the likes of Irving Berlin and Duke Ellington. But if *Sentimental Mood* was stylistically linked to the '20s and '30s, *Afterglow* was more a recreation of the late '40s and early '50s, with its big-band arrangements and the inclusion of jump blues numbers like Louis Jordan's "I Know What I've Got." Such songs allowed Dr. John plenty of room to play his trademark New Orleans piano solos, and, in the second half of the record, some of the Doctor's own compositions were snuck in among the classics without disturbing the mood. Of course, the dominant sound remained Dr. John's gravel-and-honey voice, an even more appropriate instrument for these bluesier standards than it was for the *Sentimental* ones. — *William Ruhlmann*

● **The Very Best of Dr. John** / Apr. 25, 1995 / Rhino ✦✦✦✦
The Very Best of Dr. John compiles the best moments from the comprehensive double-disc *Anthology*, making it a more effective, and cheaper, introduction for casual fans. — *Stephen Thomas Erlewine*

Crawfish Soiree / Feb. 11, 1997 / Aim ✦✦✦

Dr. Octagon

f. 1995, Los Angeles, CA
Rap, Hip Hop, Trip-Hop, Electronica
After single-handedly redefining "warped" as the mind and mouth behind the Bronx-based Ultramagnetic MCs, "Kool" Keith Thornton—aka Rhythm X, aka Dr. Octagon—headed for the outer reaches of the stratosphere with this solo project. A one-time psychiatric patient at Bellevue, Thornton's lyrical thematics are as free-flowing here as they ever were with the NY trio, connecting complex meters with fierce, layers-deep metaphors and veiled criticisms of those who "water down the sound that comes from the ghetto." The debut Octagon single, "Earth People," was quietly released in late 1995 on the San Francisco-based Bulk Recordings, and the track spread like wildfire through the hip-hop underground, as did the subsequent self-titled full-length released the following year. Featuring internationally renowned DJ Q-Bert (also of the Invisible Skratch Picklz) on turntables, as well as the Automator and DJ Shadow behind the boards, *Dr. Octagon's* leftfield fusion of sound collage, fierce turntable work, and bizarre, impressionistic rapping found audiences in the most unlikely of places, from hardcore hip-hop heads to jaded rock critics. Although a somewhat sophomoric preoccupation with body parts and scatology tends to dominate the album, Thornton's complex weave of associations and shifting references is quite often amazing in its intricacy. The record found its way to the UK-based abstract hip-hop imprint Mo'Wax (for whom Shadow also records) in mid-'96, and was licensed by the label for European release. (Mo'Wax also released a DJ-friendly instrumental version of the album titled, appropriately, *Instrumentalyst.*) The widespread popularity of the group eventually landed Thornton at Geffen subsidiary Dreamworks in 1997; the label gave *Dr. Octagon* its third release mid-year, adding a number of bonus cuts. —*Sean Cooper*

● **Dr. Octagonecologyst [Dr. Octagon]** / 1996 / DreamWorks ✦✦✦✦
With his 1996 debut release (reissued in 1997 on DreamWorks with a handful of new tracks), Dr. Octagon—a.k.a. Kool Keith—upped the ante and pushed the limits of what was considered hip-hop. Released on the innovative British label Mo' Wax, it caused shockwaves throughout the music community that heard it. Unfortunately, few people actually heard the dizzying and claustrophobic production created by the Automator, the turntable wizardry of DJ Q-bert, and the insane rhymes of Kool Keith. Without a doubt, this is destined to become not just a hip-hop classic, but a classic album more generally. Released in 1996 during a year that saw an increased amount of sonic experimentation, this release rose to the top for the risks it took. —*Kembrew McLeod*

Instrumentalyst: Octagon Beats / 1996 / Mo Wax ✦✦✦
This is essentially the entire *Dr. Octagon* album sans vocals and slightly remixed. If any other artist released an album such as this it would be considered throwaway trash . . . something for the hardcore fans. But *Dr. Octagon's* backing tracks are so fresh and original, it's actually nice to just hear the beats minus the rhymes. —*Kembrew McLeod*

Thomas Dolby

b. Oct. 14, 1958, Cairo, Egypt
Guitar, Keyboards / Synth-Pop, New Wave
Though he never had many hits, Thomas Dolby became one of the most recognizable figures of the synth-pop movement of early-'80s new wave, due largely to his skillful marketing. Dolby promoted himself as a kind of mad scientist, an egghead who had successfully harnassed the power of synthesizers and samplers, using them to make catchy pop and light electro-funk. Before he launched a solo career, Dolby had worked as a studio musician, technician, and songwriter; his most notable work as a songwriter was "New Toy," which he wrote for Lene Lovich, and Whodini's "Magic's Wand." In 1981 he launched a solo career, which resulted in a number of minor hits and two big hits—"She Blinded Me with Science" (1982) and "Hyperactive" (1984). After "Hyperactive," his career faded, as he began producing more frequently, as well as exploring new synthesizer and computer technology. Dolby continued to record into the '90s, but by that time, he was strictly a cult act.

Dolby's interest in music arose through his interest in computers, electronics, and synthesizers. The son of a British archeologist, Thomas Dolby (b. Thomas Morgan Robertson, October 14, 1958) originally attended college to study meteorology, but he was soon side-tracked by electronics, specifically musical equipment. He began building his own synthesizers when he was 18 years old. Around the same time, he began to learn how to play guitar and piano, as well as how to program computers. Eventually, his schoolmates gave him the nickname of "Dolby," which was the name for a noise-reduction technology for audiotapes; he would eventually take the nickname as a stage name.

In his late teens, Dolby was hired as a touring sound engineer for a variety of post-punk bands, including the Fall, the Passions, and the Members; on these dates, he would use a PA system he had built himself. In 1979 he formed the arty post-punk band Camera Club with

Bruce Wooley, Trevor Horn, Geoff Downes, and Matthew Seligman. Within a year, he had left the group and joined Lene Lovich's backing band. Dolby gave Lovich his song "New Toy," which became a British hit in 1981. That same year, he released his first solo single, "Urges," on the English independent label Armageddon. By the fall, he had signed with Parlophone and released "Europa and the Pirate Twins," which nearly cracked the UK Top 40.

Dolby started playing synthesizer on sessions for other artists in 1982. That year he appeared on Foreigner's *4*, Def Leppard's *Pyromania*, and Joan Armatrading's *Walk Under Ladders*. Also in 1982 he wrote and produced "Magic's Wand" for Whodini; the single became one of the first million-selling rap singles. Even with all of these achievements, 1982 was most noteworthy for the release of Dolby's first solo album, *The Golden Age of Wireless*, in the summer of 1982; the record reached No. 13 in England, while it was virtually forgotten in America. "Windpower," the first single from the record, became his first Top 40 UK hit in the late summer.

In January 1983, Dolby released an EP, *Blinded by Science*, which included a catchy number called "She Blinded Me with Science" that featured a cameo vocal appearance by the notorious British eccentric Magnus Pike, who also appeared in the song's promotional video. *Blinded by Science* was a minor hit in England, but the EP and the single became major American hits in 1983, thanks to MTV's heavy airplay of the "She Blinded Me with Science" video. Eventually the song reached No. 5 on the US charts, and it was included on a resequenced and reissued version of *The Golden Age of Wireless*, which peaked at No. 13 in America.

The Flat Earth, Dolby's second album, appeared in early 1984 and was supported by the single "Hyperactive." The single became his biggest UK hit, peaking at No. 17. Though *The Flat Earth* reached No. 35 on the US charts, Dolby's momentum was already beginning to slow; none of the singles released from the album cracked the American Top 40. Nevertheless, Dolby was in demand as a collaborator, and he worked with Herbie Hancock, Howard Jones, Stevie Wonder, George Clinton, and Dusty Springfield. During 1985 he produced Clinton's *Some of My Best Jokes are Friends*, Prefab Sprout's *Steve McQueen* (*Two Wheels Good* in the US), and Joni Mitchell's *Dog Eat Dog*, as well as supporting David Bowie at Live Aid. Also in 1985 he began composing film scores, starting with *Fever Pitch*. In 1986 he composed the scores for *Gothic* and *Howard the Duck*, on which he was credited as Dolby's Cube. That credit led to a lawsuit from the Dolby Labs, who eventually prohibited the musician from using the name "Dolby" in conjunction with any other name than "Thomas."

Aliens Ate My Buick, Dolby's long-delayed third album, appeared in 1988 to poor reviews and weak sales, even though the single "Airhead" became a minor British hit. That same year Dolby married actress Kathleen Beller. For the rest of the late '80s and early '90s, Dolby continued to score films and produce, and he began building his own computer equipment. His fourth album, *Astronauts & Heretics*, was released in 1992 on his new label, Giant. Despite the presence of guest stars like Eddie Van Halen, Jerry Garcia, Bob Weir, and Ofra Haza, the album was a flop. The next year Dolby founded the computer software company Headspace, which released *The Virtual String Quartet* as its first program. For the rest of the '90s, Headspace occupied most of Dolby's time and energy. In 1994 he released *The Gate to the Mind's Eye*, a soundtrack to the videogame *Mind's Eye*. Also that year Capitol released the greatest-hits collection, *Retrospectacle*. —*Stephen Thomas Erlewine*

The Golden Age of Wireless / Mar. 1983 / Capitol ✦✦✦✦
This contains Dolby's biggest hit, the humorously quirky "She Blinded Me with Science." Highlights include "Radio Silence," "Europa and the Pirate Twins," "Windpower," "One of Our Submarines," and "Airwaves"—a track that should've been a single. All in all, this is a very solid collection of early-'80s synth-pop. (*The Golden Age of Wireless* originally was released in May 1982 as Harvest/Capitol 12203. In the wake of the success of "She Blinded Me with Science," it was reissued in March 1983 with that track and another added (and two others dropped) as Harvest/Capitol 12271, later reissued on CD as Capitol 46009.) —*Rick Clark*

The Flat Earth / Feb. 1984 / Capitol ✦✦✦
A departure from the style of his debut, this moody and atmospheric album adds jazz and Joni Mitchell-esque elements to warm his synth textures. Only "White City" and the single, "Hyperactive!," feature the hard dance beats of his early hits. —*Scott Bultman*

Aliens Ate My Buick / Apr. 1988 / EMI/Manhattan ✦✦
Thomas Dolby didn't do his career much good by waiting four years between album releases. Pop music trends shifted away from the quirky synth-pop Dolby had pioneered in 1983-84, and though he employed a heavy funk beat aimed at the discos and even covered a George Clinton song, Dolby seemed less a true dance floor king than a commentator on the same, especially in such songs as the (non-charting) single "Airhead," "Pop Culture," and "The Ability to Swing." Dolby's flirtation with film

had also added an eclecticism to his style that embraced '40s jazz vocalese ("The Key to Her Ferrari") and European balladeering ("Budapest by Blimp"). As ever, Dolby was a man of many ideas, but on *Aliens Ate My Buick* they failed to add up to a coherent statement. *—William Ruhlmann*

Astronauts & Heretics / Jul. 1992 / Giant ✦✦✦

Gate to the Mind's Eye / Oct. 18, 1994 / Giant ✦✦✦
Soundtrack work suits Thomas Dolby, who here turns in a variety of musical settings for a computer animation video that include everything from moody electronic instrumentals and dance tracks to a '30s pop pastiche complete with horn section ("Nuvague"). Five of the nine tracks have vocals, two of which are contributed by Dr. Fiorella Terenzi. Dolby himself sings, raps, and even murmurs Napoleon's words of love to Josephine. As a nonvisual listening experience, it all seems scattered, but *The Gate to the Mind's Eye* demonstrates Dolby's continuing inventiveness. *—William Ruhlmann*

● **Best of Thomas Dolby: Retrospectacle** / Apr. 4, 1995 / Capitol ✦✦✦✦
After what had seemed like a promising start with "She Blinded Me with Science" in 1983, Thomas Dolby charted with only two other singles in the US (though he had nine chart singles in his native UK, 1981-1992). This 16-track compilation, embracing both his Capitol/EMI and Warner Brothers recordings, demonstrates that Dolby deserved better. His synthesizer-based songs are consistently catchy and clever; especially notable are early songs like "Urges" and "Leipzig" that have not previously appeared on a US album. "One of Our Submarines," Dolby's cover of Dan Hicks' "I Scare Myself," and "Hyperactive!" all hold up well. Some of the later (non-hit) material from the albums *Aliens Ate My Buick* and *Astronauts & Heretics* is less impressive; a better choice could have been made from those records. But for the most part, this is an efficient collection that justifies its name. *—William Ruhlmann*

Fats Domino

b. Feb. 28, 1928, New Orleans, LA
Piano, Vocals / R&B, Rock 'n' Roll, Piano Blues, New Orleans R&B
The most popular exponent of the classic New Orleans R&B sound, Fats Domino sold more records than any other Black rock 'n' roll star of the 1950s. His relaxed, lolling boogie-woogie piano style and easygoing, warm vocals anchored a long series of national hits from the mid-'50s to the early '60s. Through it all, his basic approach rarely changed. He may not have been one of early rock's most charismatic, innovative, or threatening figures, but he was certainly one of its most consistent.

Domino's first single, "The Fat Man" (1950), is one of the dozens of tracks that have been consistently singled out as a candidate for the first rock 'n' roll record. As far as Fats was concerned, he was just playing what he'd already been doing in New Orleans for years, and would continue to play and sing in pretty much the same fashion even after his music was dubbed "rock 'n' roll."

The record made No. 2 on the R&B charts and sold a million copies. Just as important, it established a vital partnership between Fats and Imperial A&R man Dave Bartholomew. Bartholomew, himself a trumpeter, would produce Domino's big hits, co-writing many of them with Fats. He would also usually employ New Orleans session greats like Alvin Tyler on sax and Earl Palmer on drums—musicians who were vital in establishing New Orleans R&B as a distinct entity, playing on many other local recordings as well (including hits made in New Orleans by Georgia native Little Richard).

Domino didn't cross over into the pop charts in a big way until 1955, when "Ain't That a Shame" made the Top Ten. Pat Boone's cover of the song stole some of Fats' thunder, going all the way to No. 1. (Boone was also bowdlerizing Little Richard's early singles for pop hits during this time.) Domino's long-range prospects weren't damaged, however; between 1955 and 1963, he racked up an astonishing 35 Top 40 singles. "Blueberry Hill" (1956) was probably his best (and best-remembered) single; "Walking to New Orleans," "Whole Lotta Loving," "I'm Walking," "Blue Monday," and "I'm in Love Again" were also huge successes.

After Fats left Imperial for ABC-Paramount in 1963, he would enter the Top 40 only one more time. The surprise was not that Fats fell out of fashion, but that he'd maintained his popularity so long while the essentials of his style remained unchanged. This was during an era, remember, when most of rock's biggest stars had their careers derailed by death or scandal, or were made to soften up their sound for mainstream consumption. Although an active performer in the ensuing decades, his career as an important artist was essentially over in the mid-'60s. He did stir up a bit of attention in 1968 when he covered the Beatles' "Lady Madonna" single, which had been an obvious homage to Fats' style. *—Richie Unterberger*

★ **My Blue Heaven: The Best of Fats Domino** / Jul. 30, 1990 / EMI America ✦✦✦✦✦
For the budget-minded fan, this 20-track single disc compilation of Fats Domino's Imperial smashes will serve nicely. Not much of his early prerock stuff—"The Fat Man" and "Please Don't Leave Me" are all that's

here—but there's plenty of his hit-laden output from 1955 on—"Ain't It a Shame," "Blue Monday," "I'm in Love Again," "Blueberry Hill," "I'm Ready," etc. One small but substantial difference between this set and the larger packages: it uses non-sped-up masters of his mid-'50s material (some of his hits from this era were mastered slightly faster than true pitch). Even if they're not historically correct, these versions actually sound better! *—Bill Dahl*

☆ **They Call Me the Fat Man: The Legendary Imperial Recordings** / Oct. 22, 1991 / EMI America ✦✦✦✦✦
If you can't quite finance the Bear Family box, this four-disc compilation is the next best thing; an even 100 of the best Imperial sides, including a great many from 1958 on, that turn up in crystal-clear stereo (as they also do on the Bear Family package). All the hits are aboard, along with a nice cross-section of the important non-hits. The saxes (usually including Herb Hardesty and sometimes Lee Allen) roar with typical Crescent City power, Fats rolls the ivories, and magic happens—over and over again! Another nice booklet with plenty of photos (but a less detailed discography without sideman credits). *—Bill Dahl*

Out of New Orleans / 1993 / Bear Family ✦✦✦✦
An amazing piece of work—a massive eight-disc box set that contains every one of Fats Domino's 1949-1962 Imperial waxings. That's a tremendous load of one artist, but the legacy of Domino and his partner Dave Bartholomew is so consistently innovative and infectious that it never grows tiresome. From the clarion call of "The Fat Man," Domino's debut, to the storming "Dance with Mr. Domino" in 1962, he typified everything charming about Crescent City R&B, his Creole patois, and boogie-based piano, a non-threatening vehicle for the rise of rock 'n' roll. A thick, photo-filled book accompanies the disc, and there's an exhaustive discography that makes sense of Domino's many visits to Cosimo Matassa's studios. If you care about Fats Domino, this is the package to purchase! *—Bill Dahl*

Fat Man: 25 Classic Performances / Aug. 20, 1996 / Capitol ✦✦✦✦
Ostensibly replacing the compact disc *My Blue Heaven* as the definitive single-disc collection of Fats Domino's biggest hits singles, *Fat Man: 25 Classic Performances* features most of Fats Domino's biggest hits, but it inexplicably neglects such hits as "Walking to New Orleans," "Be My Guest," and "I'm Gonna Be a Wheel Someday." The only justification for the omission of so many hits is that the intent of the collection is to portray Fats Domino as the R&B heavyweight that he undoubtedly is, but seldom receives credit for being. Nevertheless, *Fat Man* masquerades as a greatest hits collection, billing itself as "25 Classic Performances," which leads you to believe that it is simply another hits collection. As an R&B compilation, *Fat Man* is strong—and, like any proper R&B collection, it presents the singles at the speed at which they were recorded, not the sped-up versions that became hits—but *My Blue Heaven* remains a preferable collection and introduction to Fats. *—Stephen Thomas Erlewine*

Don & Dewey

f. 1966, Pasadena, CA
R&B
Wailing in tandem like twin Little Richards, Don & Dewey cut numerous blistering rockers for Specialty from 1957 to 1959 without registering a single hit, only to see other acts revive their songs to much greater acclaim. Don Harris (b. 1938) and Dewey Terry (b. 1938) were born and raised in Pasadena, CA, joining a group called the Squires and recording for Vita before branching off on their own. Their Specialty output included the savage rockers "Jungle Hop," "Koko Joe" (written by Sonny Bono), and "Justine," the latter pair later covered by the Righteous Brothers. Don & Dewey's Specialty discography also includes the original "I'm Leavin' It up to You," a hit for Dale & Grace; "Big Boy Pete," ditto for the Olympics; and "Farmer John," the Premiers' only smash. Don laid down his guitar for a violin during the '60s and, billed as "Sugarcane" Harris, sawed his rocked-out fiddle beside John Mayall and Frank Zappa. *—Bill Dahl*

● **Jungle Hop** / 1991 / Specialty ✦✦✦✦
Wild '50s rock 'n' roll duets from Don "Sugarcane" Harris and Dewey Terry, backed by the same Specialty house band that recorded with Little Richard and others. A lot of these songs were covered by other people, but NOBODY cut these guy's versions. *—George Bedard*

Lonnie Donegan (Anthony James Donegan)

b. Apr. 29, 1931, Glasgow, Scotland
Banjo, Guitar, Vocals / Country, Blues, Folk, Skiffle, Rockabilly, Pop-Rock
To look at Lonnie Donegan today, in pictures taken decades ago when he was topping the British charts—dressed in a suit, his hair cut short and strumming an acoustic guitar—he looks like a musical non-entity. But in 1954, before anyone knew what rock 'n' roll was, Donegan was cool, and his music was hot. Relatively little remembered outside of

England, Donegan invented a style of music, skiffle, that completely altered the pop culture landscape and the youth around him, and for a time ruled popular music through that new form. What's more, his music was vital to the early musical careers and future histories of the Beatles, the Stones, and hundreds of other groups—and he did it before Elvis was known anywhere outside of Memphis and before Bill Haley was perceived as anything but a western swing novelty act.

Anthony James Donegan was born in Glasgow, Scotland on April 29, 1931, the son of a classical violinist who had played with the Scottish National Orchestra. Donegan received no encouragement to play an instrument or choose music as a profession, for his father, like many talented musicians during the economic slump of the 1930's, was continually out of work. He first became interested in the guitar at age nine, but it was to be another five years before he took matters into his own hands and bought his first guitar. He mostly listened to swing and vocal acts during the early 1940's, although he also heard some Indian music on the BBC, and African songs as transliterated for movies. But it was country-and-western and blues records, especially those by Frank Crumit and Josh White, that really attracted Donegan's interests, and he began learning to play songs like "Frankie and Johnny," "Putting on the Style," and "House of the Rising Sun." Before long he was working backwards from Josh White to Blind Lemon Jefferson, Bessie Smith, and Leadbelly, among others, and by the end of the 1940's, Donegan was as literate in American blues as anyone born in England.

He began playing guitar around London, and was coaxed into his first band one night when someone approached him on the train and invited him to audition to play banjo for a new group. The man extending the invitation was Chris Barber, himself a young aspiring jazzman. Donegan had never even held a banjo before but agreed to come to the audition, then bought a banjo and tried to fake his way through the tryout. His bluff didn't work but the mix of personalities did, and he was in Barber's first band. The only way Donegan had of mastering his instrument was by listening to old records and painstakingly working out the music and a technique. After serving in the British Army for several years, absorbing American blues and folk music over the American Forces radio network, he formed his own group, the Tony Donegan Jazz Band, in 1952. During a live performance, the master of ceremonies made a mistake in his announcement, accidentally introducing him as "Lonnie Donegan." The name stuck.

Donegan and his band hooked back up with Barber, who'd kept his band going throughout the previous two years, and eventually Barber and Donegan linked up with fellow jazzman Ken Colyer. The Ken Colyer Jazzmen, as they were called, specialized in Dixieland jazz, and built a formidable reputation. It was during these shows, between sets by the full band, that Donegan would come on stage with two other players and perform his own version of American blues, country, and folk standards, punched up with his own rhythms and accents, on acoustic guitar or banjo, backed by upright bass and drums. The name "skiffle" was hung on this music as a way of referring to it on the group's posters; the word, according to Donegan, was suggested by Ken Colyer's brother Bill, who remembered an outfit called the Dan Burley Skiffle Group, based in Chicago in the 1930's. It seemed to fit, and it caught on; the Ken Colyer Jazzmen became almost as popular for Donegan's between-set skiffle songs as they were for their Dixieland music.

Colyer quit the group early in 1954, and Barber took over the leadership. The Chris Barber Jazz Band, as they became known, were popular enough to justify the recording of an album for Decca, *New Orleans Joy*, which featured songs representative of the group's live set, including a selection from Donegan's skiffle repertoire. The album sold 60,000 copies in its first month of release, prompting the label to begin lifting individual songs off the album as singles. Each of those was a success, and eventually "Rock Island Line," a Donegan skiffle number, came up for release. The single had a 22 week run on the English charts, peaking at No. 8. As "Rock Island Line" took the country by storm, Decca suddenly had one of the bigger—and most wholly unexpected—hits in its history up to that time. Before the smoke cleared, "Rock Island Line" also managed to reach the top 20 in America, a major feat for a British artist at that time. In six months, "Rock Island Line" sold three million copies, 50 times the initial sales of the album it came from; it was exceptionally popular among England's teenagers, who accounted for most of its sales.

Donegan was suddenly a star, with a public that wanted more music from him. His next single for Decca, "Diggin' My Potatoes," cut at London's Royal Festival Hall, was banned by the BBC for its suggestive lyrics—this hurt sales but also gave Donegan a slight veneer of daring and rebelliousness that didn't hurt his credibility with the kids. Decca gave up on Donegan soon after, believing that skiffle was a flash-in-the-pan fad. The next month he was cutting a song for EMI's Columbia label, and by the spring of 1955 was signed to Pye Records, where his single "Lost John" hit No. 2 in England. (Donegan also proved to be a popular performer in America, playing on bills with Chuck Berry, among others.) He cut his first solo album, *Showcase*, in 1956; he also appeared in

the 1957 British juke-box movie *The Six-Five Special*, ripping through a killer live rendition of "Jack 'O Diamonds" as well as a fine cover of Woody Guthrie's "The Grand Coulee Dam."

While Donegan was racking up hits—"Bring a Little Water, Sylvie," "Don't You Rock Me, Daddy-O," "Cumberland Gap" and "Does Your Chewing Gum Lose Its Flavor on the Bedpost Overnight?" all in less than three years—thousands of skiffle groups were springing up all over England. New artists, most notably Tommy Steele and, later, Cliff Richard, started out playing skiffle music and put their own stamp on the material before moving on to other sounds. Among the many tens of thousands of British teens he inspired were members of the Beatles, Gerry & The Pacemakers, and the Searchers. By mid-1958, however, skiffle was waning rapidly as a commercial sound, but Donegan continued to appear on the charts right into 1962. Only when the next wave of young rockers came along, who like Donegan had their own ideas about music and what they wanted to do with it, did he finally fade from the charts.

He continued to record sporadically during the 1960's, but after 1964 was primarily occupied as a producer for most of the decade at Pye Records. Donegan's attempt at a recording comeback late in the 1960's was unsuccessful, but in 1974, a new boomlet for skiffle music in Germany brought him on tour and into the studio anew, and the following year he and Chris Barber toured together and recorded a new long-player, *The Great Re-Union Album*. In 1976, however, after another series of shows and recordings in Germany, Donegan suffered a heart attack that left him sidelined, and he moved to California to recuperate. In 1978, however, he was back in the studio, recording the album that was his first chart entry in 15 years, *Putting on the Style*, an all-star skiffle-style album recorded with Ringo Starr, Elton John, Brian May, Peter Banks and others. A follow-up album featuring Albert Lee presented Donegan working in a somewhat less familiar country & western vein. By 1980, he was making regular concert appearances again, and a new album with Barber followed, and he continued performing and recording sporadically throughout the 1990s. *—Bruce Eder*

Showcase / 1956 / Pye ✦✦✦✦

The first great blues album to come out of England. Donegan's debut album is absolutely first-rate acoustic folk-blues, featuring some of the songs he'd been playing for close to ten years, including "Frankie and Johnny," and stuff he learned from Leadbelly records, like "I'm Alabammy Bound," among other folk and blues standards. The sound is raw and crisp, featuring Denny Wright's crisp lead guitar licks behind Donegan's emphatic strumming and superb vocals. He didn't have Elvis' rich baritone, but he could wail the blues better than anyone else in England at the time (including Alexis Korner and Cyril Davies), and he knew how to make the tension in a song rise across five minutes like no one else around. Leroy Carr's "How Long How Long Blues" gets a good workout, but the highlight of this forgotten jewel of an album is Donegan's moody rendition of "I'm a Ramblin' Man," a dark blues standard that shows off the guitar interplay between Donegan and Wright to great effect and features what may be Donegan's best blues vocal ever. Leadbelly's "I'm Alabammy Bound" gives Donegan and Wright a chance to share vocals; Wright had a coarse bass/baritone that went well with Donegan's blues tenor. Note: The contents of *Showcase* are available on Bear Family's eight-CD set *More Than "Pye in the Sky." —Bruce Eder*

Lonnie / 1958 / Pye ✦✦✦

Donegan's second album, recorded in March 1958, shows some greater sophistication. In place of sheer volume on the singing, he uses more subtle inflections throughout this mix of blues, gospel, and folk, which includes covers of traditional gospel songs like "Ain't You Glad You Got Religion" and two Lee Hays songs ("Lonesome Traveller," "Times Are Getting Hard Boys"), Blind Willie Johnson's "Light From the Lighthouse," and Lonnie Johnson's "I've Got Rocks in My Bed" (which is good, but exists in an even better outtake issued by Bear Family in 1993). Jimmy Currie had taken over on lead guitar by this time, and proved more flexible than Denny Wright, with more complex lead guitar passages, although Wright evidently could play harder when the need arose, but otherwise the band is unchanged. Not as strong as the first album, with more of a folk music orientation, but not bad either. Note: The material from *Lonnie* is available on Bear Family's eight-CD collection *More Than "Pye in the Sky." —Bruce Eder*

Rides Again / 1959 / Pye ✦✦✦✦

Donegan's third full-length album, cut in October 1959, is another jewel and features a largely new band, apart from drummer Nicholls. Donegan never compromised on his sound, and the opening track, a rippling version of Furry Lewis' "Fancy Talkin' Tinker," shows him with as strong a commitment to the blues as ever. Leadbelly's "Take This Hammer" and "John Hardy" are also featured, along with Ernest Tubb's "Talking Guitar Blues" and traditional numbers like "Mr. Froggy" (aka "Froggy Went A-Courting"). Lead guitarist Les Bennetts is probably the strongest player Donegan ever had to work with, as exhibited by his smooth, fluid style on the diversity of material here, from Lewis' blues to gospel numbers like "Gloryland." Donegan shines on banjo on "The Goldrush Is Over." The real gem, however, is the cover of "House of the Rising Sun," a song that Donegan learned from Josh White, which gets a somber, moodily dramatic performance, with lots of guitar flourishes from Bennetts. And just for contrast, the album includes a bluesy cover of Cole Porter's "Miss Otis Regrets." —*Bruce Eder*

Sing Hallelujah / 1962 / Pye ✦✦✦✦

Donegan's most Elvis-like album, with mostly gospel and devotional music. Recorded in early 1962, this album features Donegan in the best vocal performance of his career. Denny Wright is back on guitar, but most of the material is more opulent in its arrangements, featuring piano and a backing chorus (the Kestrels, including Roger Greenaway, sounding like the Jordanaires). Songs include "Nobody Knows the Trouble I've Seen," "Born in Bethlehem," "Steal Away," Leadbelly's "Pick a Bale of Cotton," Sister Rosetta Tharpe's "This Train," and A. P. Carter's "Keep On the Sunny Side." "Steal Away" may be the best performance Donegan ever commited to record, and the rest is above average. Note: All of the material on *Sing Hallelujah* is available on the eight-CD collection *More Than "Pye in the Sky.* —*Bruce Eder*

Folk Album / 1965 / Pye ✦✦✦

Pye was about two years late jumping on the folk music bandwagon, but despite the bad timing, Donegan himself is in good form on what proved to be his last new album for the label. The band isn't as tight as his '50s group (although Denny Wright is present on guitar), and the sound is fairly elaborate, complete with a female backing chorus that is recorded with surprising taste and restraint. Songs by Billy Ed Wheeler ("Blistered," "The Reverend Mr. Black") and Mike Settle ("Bound for Zion," "Where in This World Are We Going"), are covered, along with Bob Dylan's "Fare Thee Well." Donegan has a good voice and sings with a lot of passion, and had he done an album like this two years earlier he might've had a hit. As it was, he was competing with more rough-hewn, authentic sounding singers (including Dylan himself), and he just doesn't sound "folkie" enough for 1965, even if he comes off as completely rural on "The Doctor's Daughter." Note: All of the tracks on *Folk Album* are available on the eight-CD collection *More Than "Pye in the Sky.*" —*Bruce Eder*

Puttin' on the Style / 1977 / United Artists ✦✦✦

After an absence of 15 years or more as a major name in British rock, Donegan re-emerged with this '70s version of his old skiffle sound. (Why nobody tried this with Donegan seven years earlier, when Mungo Jerry hit with their updated skiffle number "In the Summertime," is anyone's guess.) Chances are that UA in America was lured into distributing this album by the presence on the record of such rock-star skiffle fans as Ringo Starr, Elton John, Nicky Hopkins, Mick Ralphs, Albert Lee, Rory Gallagher, Brian May, Ron Wood, Peter Banks, Michelle Phillips, and (like, unreal) the Rev. James Cleveland. Unfortunately, audiences at least in America were rather oblivious to it all, and it was ignored, rapidly becoming a collector's item. The record isn't bad, but overall it seems overproduced, a sort of skiffle supersession, a treatment to which the music doesn't lend itself. It was more fun to listen to than almost any other recording that Ringo *et al* participated in during the late 1970s, however, a real labor of love for all concerned. —*Bruce Eder*

Sundown / 1978 / Chrysalis ✦✦✦

Donegan cut a second '70s comeback album backed by guitarists Albert Lee and Doug Kershaw, playing country-and-western songs. —*Bruce Eder*

● The EP Collection / 1992 / See For Miles ✦✦✦✦

In England, before the Beatles and the Rolling Stones came along, EPs (four-song extended play singles) outsold albums. This compilation of the best of Donegan's EPs is the definitive Lonnie Donegan collection, eclipsing any album or CD that existed previously on his work. It is certainly the best hits compilation there ever has been on him, containing the 1956 hit "Rock Island Line" and its B-side, "Digging My Potatoes," plus 23 more fairly hard-rocking tracks dating up through 1962, all very crisply remastered, with original artwork represented and a very detailed biography. —*Bruce Eder*

More Than "Pie in the Sky" / 1993 / Bear Family ✦✦✦✦

Eight CDs, and nearly ten hours of music may seem like overkill to most onlookers, but this is a box set that truly justifies itself, once you've listened to it. What is here is amazing. This set presents Lonnie Donegan as the prodigious musical talent he actually was, a white bluesman extraordinaire and a country, rockabilly, and gospel singer of no small merit as well. No, he didn't have Elvis Presley's voice, or his way with the girls, but Donegan had musical talent by the ton. His blues stylings on songs like the previously unreleased alternate take of Lonnie Johnson's "I've Got Rocks in My Bed" or Leroy Carr's "Hoe Long How Long Blues" will astonish anyone who thinks that British blues began with the Rolling Stones or even with Alexis Korner (who had never been anywhere near a recording studio when Donegan cut some of this stuff). His covers of numbers by Cole Porter (in a blues style, no less) and Bob Dylan (from Donegan's final

Pye album) will amaze anyone who never got past "Rock Island Line." And the unedited live set from Conway Hall in 1957 will delight anyone who likes great, exciting concert recordings. And most of the rest is of as high quality as these rarities. The only drawback is the $180 price-tag, but that's the cost of quality. The profusely annotated and illustrated booklet is a bonus. —*Bruce Eder*

The EP Collection, Vol. 2 / 1994 / See For Miles ✦✦✦

Surprisingly strong (and nearly as important as Volume One) collection of the rest of Donegan's classic skiffle material, including the complete contents of his live EP *Donegan on Stage.* The novelty tunes share space with some surprisingly solid early rock 'n' roll, and all of it is fast-paced and entertaining. —*Bruce Eder*

Donner Party

f. 1986, San Francisco, CA
Group / Alternative Pop-Rock, Indie Rock
San Francisco's Donner Party released one self-titled album in 1987 before they were brought to the attention of then-Camper Van Beethoven's David Lowery, who signed them to his Pitch A Tent label for their second and final recording in 1988. The power trio played shrewd pop, executed naively, mainly because singer Sam Coomes delivered his whimsical lyrics in a strained, nonchalant vocal style. The purposefully childlike approach by the rest of the band (drummer and vocalist Melanie Clarin and Reinhold Johnson) veered from a primitive folk-rock sound to full-tilt, noisy indie-rock. Clarin played with the group while simultaneously recording and touring with another San Francisco guitar-based band, the Cat Heads. Clarin continues to record with an array of Bay Area bands, while Coomes relocated to Portland and formed Motorgoat and Quasi. —*Denise Sullivan*

● The Donner Party / 1987 / Cryptovision ✦✦✦✦

The first album by San Francisco's Donner Party is a joyous tribute to folk and pre-alternative rock delivered in a naive style recalling Jonathan Richman and Daniel Johnston. Chief songwriter, guitarist, and vocalist Sam Coomes had a stunning flair for capturing the most bizarre subjects and turning them into finely crafted pop without drowning in his own eccentricities. But the band plays in a somewhat primitive style; though not accomplished, they are completely endearing, particularly on the tracks "Godlike Porpoise Head of Blue-Eyed Mary" and "The Owl of Minerva." —*Denise Sullivan*

Donner Party / 1988 / Pitch A Tent ✦✦

The second eponymously titled album by the Donner Party is a completely different recording than the first, in spite of the shared titles. By this time the band had become more proficient and attempted more complex song structures, but their humor and naivete were never lost, particularly in evidence on "When I Was a Baby" and "Lost in Hoboken." —*Denise Sullivan*

Food for Thought / Jan. 1, 1995 / Infamous ✦✦✦

Donovan (Donovan Leitch)

b. Feb. 10, 1946, Glasgow, Scotland
Guitar, Harmonica, Vocals / Singer-Songwriter, British Invasion, Psychedelic, Folk-Rock, British Folk
When Donovan first appeared on the British pop scene in the mid-'60s, he was touted as the British Invasion's answer to Bob Dylan. The unfortunate comparison led to a battle of the bands of sorts, immortalized in the Dylan documentary *Don't Look Back,* where Dylan shot down one of Donovan's pretty acoustic ditties with "It's All Over Now, Baby Blue." All of which has cast a harsher light on Donovan's early work than it merits. Certainly he wasn't as deep as Dylan, but the acoustic tracks he recorded in the mid-'60s, including the British hits "Catch the Wind" and "Colours," were affecting, thoughtful, and tuneful, especially considering he was still in his teens at the time.

In late 1965 Donovan hooked up with manager Allen Klein and a new producer, Mickie Most (who also worked with the Animals, Herman's Hermits, and Lulu), who steered the young singer away from acoustic folk and into psychedelic pop. His more excessively cosmic lyrics haven't worn well, but in general the combination was quite successful, with seductive and ornate arrangements backing Donovan's gentle musings, which could be more humorous and biting than he's been given credit for. Between 1965 and 1969, he scored a series of memorable hits, including "Sunshine Superman," "Mellow Yellow" (containing a Paul McCartney cameo), "Hurdy Gurdy Man" (with Jeff Beck), and "Atlantis." His initial pair of psychedelic albums, *Sunshine Superman* and *Mellow Yellow,* were quite strong, but after a while his full-length efforts began to sound unduly repetitive and overly florid. By the early '70s Donovan had begun to fade and struggle for relevancy, although he's been an active performer since, and has periodically mounted comebacks, most recently with the Rick Rubin-produced 1996 album *Sutras.* —*Rick Clark & Richie Unterberger*

Catch the Wind / Jun. 1965 / Hickory ♦♦
Donovan's first album found the 19-year-old following in the footsteps of Bob Dylan, that is, the whimsical folkie Dylan of 1963. Even the hit "Catch the Wind" echoed Dylan's "Blowin' in the Wind," in form if not in content. Nevertheless, Donovan has his own charm and was already beginning to establish his own sound here. — *William Ruhlmann*

Fairytale / Nov. 1965 / Hickory ♦♦
Although it contains his hits "Colours" and "Universal Soldier," on which he moves to the more poetic and political styles of '64 Dylan, Donovan's second album still finds him aping his hero and falling dangerously behind the quickly moving musical trends of the '60s. By the time this album was released, folk had become folk-rock, and Donovan was in danger of being left behind the times. — *William Ruhlmann*

Sunshine Superman / Sep. 1966 / Epic ♦♦♦♦
Probably the singer-songwriter's best album, embracing folk, blues, and a druggy psychedelia, and driven by crisp rhythm guitars (especially on the title track). It starts to sound the same after a bit, but at its release, even this was a point of recommendation—it set a hazy, drugged-out mood. The use of the mono master helps, because it's punchier. — *Bruce Eder*

Mellow Yellow / Jan. 1967 / Epic ♦♦♦
Despite the psychedelic pop nature of hit singles like the notorious title track, Donovan still retained some of his folkie charm on songs like "Writer in the Sun" (which he wrote when a contractual dispute led him to think his recording career was over). And "Sunny South Kensington" found him at his name-dropping, trendy best. — *William Ruhlmann*

For Little Ones / Dec. 1967 / Epic ♦♦
This children's album made up the second of the two-disc *A Gift from a Flower to a Garden*, and was released simultaneously as a separate album. With his whimsical style, Donovan is a natural children's artist, and this was the first of several recordings in this vein. — *William Ruhlmann*

Wear Your Love Like Heaven / Dec. 1967 / Epic ♦♦♦
Donovan's double album *A Gift from a Flower to a Garden* was simultaneously released as two single albums as well. This is the first, a psychedelic pop album containing the title track single and other like selections. — *William Ruhlmann*

A Gift from a Flower to a Garden / Dec. 1967 / Beat Goes On ♦♦♦
A blast from hippie past—a flower-decorated double album made up of precious trippy music spiced with a haunting melody or two ("Wear Your Love like Heaven"). — *Bruce Eder*

Donovan in Concert / Jul. 1968 / Epic ♦♦
Donovan mostly eschewed his hits on this live album, which found him at the height of his Flower Power period, gently intoning folkish songs over a soft accompaniment of acoustic instruments. He's charming, but you can't help wondering whether his teenage fans (who scream when his father introduces him) weren't a little let down by the set list. It takes "Mellow Yellow" to bring them to life. — *William Ruhlmann*

Hurdy Gurdy Man / Oct. 1968 / Epic ♦♦♦
For this performer, this is a hard-rocking album, driven by some loud electric guitar subbing for sitar, which dresses up the plainer folk melodies and turns the title tune into a near-classic. — *Bruce Eder*

● **Donovan's Greatest Hits** / Jan. 1969 / Epic ♦♦♦♦
Entertaining but flawed collection of Donovan's psychedelic-era hits, fleshed out with too-languid re-recordings of his pre-CBS folk successes, including "Colours." It's unfortunate that the producers used the stereo versions, which don't sound nearly as good as the mono. — *Bruce Eder*

Barabajagal / Aug. 11, 1969 / Epic ♦♦♦♦
Donovan was moving beyond his hippie-dippie phase by this point, collaborating with the Jeff Beck Group on the title track, protesting the Vietnam War with "Susan on the West Coast Waiting," adapting the epic style of Beatles songs like "Hey Jude" on the hit "Atlantis" (which features Paul McCartney) and turning in two of his most charming, child-like songs in "Happiness Runs" and "I Love My Shirt." Overall, this may be Donovan's strongest collection of original songs, other than his compilations. — *William Ruhlmann*

Open Road / 1970 / Epic ♦♦♦
Although it was a disappointing seller and signaled the start of Donovan's commercial decline, *Open Road* could have been a new beginning for the singer. Stripping down to a "Celtic rock" format that managed to be hard and direct, yet still folkish, Donovan turned out a series of excellent songs, notably the minor hit "Riki Tiki Tavi," that seemed to show him moving toward a roots-oriented sound of considerable appeal. Unfortunately, he was derailed by record company hassles and perhaps his own burnout, and *Open Road* turned out to be a sidestep rather than a step forward. — *William Ruhlmann*

Cosmic Wheels / Mar. 1973 / Epic ♦♦
Donovan came back after a three-year absence with this disappointing collection, which failed to recreate past triumphs and, in "The Intergalactic Laxative," proved embarrassing. — *William Ruhlmann*

Essence to Essence / Dec. 1973 / Epic ♦♦
Donovan had the best of L.A. session help here, but his writing remained cosmic ("Operating Manual for Spaceship Earth" was the title of the lead-off track), and he seemed to have lost the knack for appealing whimsy that had floated his career thus far. — *William Ruhlmann*

7-Tease / Nov. 1974 / Epic ♦♦
Donovan rocked a little harder, on this Norbert Putnam-produced, Nashville-recorded album, but to little greater effect than on his other comeback efforts. — *William Ruhlmann*

Slow Down World / May 1976 / Epic ♦♦
Donovan had become distinctly bitter about his status by this time, as indicated by the song "A Well Known Has-Been," but he gamely gave record-making another shot, although "Liberation Rag" found him trying a little too hard to keep up with the times and "Children of the World" found him much too preachy. — *William Ruhlmann*

Donovan / 1977 / Castle ♦♦
Donovan was reunited with his old producer, Mickie Most, and his old record company head, Clive Davis, for this label debut, which has a tight, sharp, punkish edge to it, notably on the lead-off track, "Local Boy Chops Wood." Unfortunately, no one paid attention. — *William Ruhlmann*

Spotlight / 1981 / PRT ♦♦♦♦
Donovan's acoustic, pre-psychedelic work was shoddily packaged in the United States, spread out over several albums in a haphazard fashion. This 24-track double LP reissue covers most of his work from this period (basically, 1965), including the hits "Catch the Wind" and "Colours," as well his cover of Buffy St. Marie's "Universal Soldier" and the memorable originals "Josie" and "Hey Gyp." This early phase is often unfairly dismissed by critics as sub-Dylan musings. Donovan was indeed the closest counterpart to Dylan in the mid-'60s, but he was distinctly more pop-oriented, and had a gentle, wistful songwriting voice all his own, even if it wasn't as complex as Dylan's. While this material lacks the punch of his best psychedelic work, it is of a consistently high standard and lacks the occasional overly cosmic vision that has dated some of his later '60s recordings. While this reissue captures all the essential highlights of Donovan's pre-electric career, it's missing a few cuts and is packaged rather tackily; a comprehensive double-CD compilation of the 30 or so tracks he recorded for the British Pye label during this time would be welcome. — *Richie Unterberger*

Lady of the Stars / 1983 / Allegiance ♦♦
Donovan rerecorded some old hits—"Season of the Witch" and "Sunshine Superman"—and cut some new songs for this independent label release. The result is a pleasant but inconsequential effort. — *William Ruhlmann*

The Classics Live / 1991 / Great Northern Arts ♦♦♦
Fresh stage recordings of Donovan's '60s hits, well produced and arranged, and laced with a certain amount of humor from the passage of time and the druggy sensibilities behind them. "Sunshine Superman" is an intrinsically good song, although the infectious beat of the original Mickie Most production is missed in spite of the good playing. — *Bruce Eder*

Live In Concert / 1992 / QED ♦♦♦♦
Like a lot of 1960s folk-rock veterans, Donovan has found his biggest modern audience in new recordings of his classic hits. This British release is one of them, a 1990s all-acoustic show running an hour and covering such material as "Sunshine Superman," "Jennifer Juniper," "Catch the Wind," "The Hurdy Gurdy Man," "Universal Soldier," "Atlantis," "Colours," "Cosmic Wheels," "Young Girl Blues," and "Wear Your Love Like Heaven," among others. His voice is better here than it was for many '60s performances, and the recording quality is excellent. The old Columbia *Live in Concert* still has a certain dopey (in more ways than one) charm, having been recorded in the midst of flower power, but these performances are more engaging and include a bigger cross-section of his repertory. "Hurdy Gurdy Man," for example, works amazingly well without the psychedelic guitar of the studio original, complete with Donovan's wry recollections of his time with the Maharishi, the Beatles, Mia Farrow *et al*, and an extra verse associated with George Harrison. "Sunshine Superman" (which includes Donovan's harmonica playing), "Cosmic Wheels," and "Atlantis" are better songs here than their originals. A couple of numbers that should be here aren't ("Hey Gyp" would be welcome, and one is surprised that Donovan doesn't do more with "There Is a Mountain," given how famous the song is courtesy of the Allman Brothers), but this is still a pleasure. — *Bruce Eder*

● **Troubadour: The Definitive Collection 1964-1976** / Aug. 4, 1992 / Epic ✦✦✦✦
This two-disc, 44-track retrospective album (initially released as a box set) chronicles Donovan's decade-long career at Epic Records, with the few folk hits he recorded before joining the label and a couple of early demos added. All the hippie hits of the '60s are included, plus a judicious selection of the less successful '70s recordings. Good liner notes by Brian Hogg and Derek Taylor. — *William Ruhlmann*

Early Years / Oct. 1994 / Griffin ✦✦✦
In the absence of a more comprehensive package, *The Early Years* does an adequate job of presenting Donovan's "Britain's answer to Bob Dylan" period, focussing mainly on his folky singles and B-sides from 1965. — *Chris Woodstra*

Sutras / Oct. 15, 1996 / Warner Brothers ✦✦✦
Like Johnny Cash before him, Donovan was selected by producer Rick Rubin as a childhood hero he would like to restore to glory. With Rubin's encouragement and production, Donovan does make an impressive comeback with *Sutras*, which is reminiscent of his earliest records. *Sutras* abandons the colorful psychedelic pop of his best-known songs for the spare acoustic folk of his first records, and while Donovan's songwriting is a little uneven, the warmth of the performances is charming and welcoming, especially for long-time fans. — *Stephen Thomas Erlewine*

The Doobie Brothers

f. Mar. 1970, San Jose, CA, **db.** 1982
Pop-Rock, Arena Rock, Boogie Rock
As one of the most popular Californian pop-rock bands of the '70s, the Doobie Brothers evolved from a mellow, post-hippie boogie band to a slick, soul-inflected pop band by the end of the decade. Along the way, the group racked up a string of gold and platinum albums in the US, along with a number of radio hits like "Listen to the Music," "Black Water," and "China Grove."

The roots of the Doobie Brothers lay in Pud, a short-lived California country-rock band in the vein of Moby Grape featuring guitarist/vocalist Tom Johnston and drummer John Hartman. After Pud collapsed in 1969, the pair began jamming with bassist John Shogren and guitarist Patrick Simmons. Eventually the quartet decided to form a group, naming themselves the Doobie Brothers after a slang term for marijuana. Soon the Doobies had earned a strong following throughout Southern California, especially among Hell's Angels, and they were signed to Warner Bros. in 1970. The band's eponymous debut was ignored upon its 1971 release. Shogren was replaced by Tiran Porter, and the group added a second drummer, Michael Hossack, for 1972's *Toulouse Street*. Driven by the singles "Listen to the Music" and "Jesus Is Just Alright," *Toulouse Street* became the group's breakthrough. *The Captain and Me* (1973) was even more successful, spawning the Top Ten hit "Long Train Runnin'" and "China Grove." Keith Knudsen replaced Hossack as the group's second drummer for 1974's *What Once Were Vices Are Now Habits*, which launched their first No. 1 single, "Black Water," and featured heavy contributions from former Steely Dan member Jeff "Skunk" Baxter.

Baxter officially joined the Doobie Brothers for 1975's *Stampede*. Before the album's spring release, Johnston was hospitilized with a stomach ailment and was replaced for the supporting tour by keyboardist/vocalist Michael McDonald, who had also worked with Steely Dan. Although it peaked at No. 4, *Stampede* wasn't as commercially successful as its three predecessors, and the group decided to let McDonald and Baxter, who were now official Doobies, revamp the band's light country-rock and boogie. The new sound was showcased on 1976's *Takin' It to the Streets*, a collection of light funk and jazzy pop that resulted in a platinum album. Later that year the group released the hits compilation, *The Best of the Doobies*. In 1977 the group released *Livin' on the Fault Line*, which was successful without producing any big hits. Johnston left the band after the album's release to pursue an unsuccessful solo career. After his departure, the Doobies released their most successful album, *Minute by Minute* (1979), which spent five weeks at No. 1 on the strength of the No. 1 single "What a Fool Believes." Hartman and Baxter left the group after the album's supporting tour, leaving the Doobie Brothers as McDonald's backing band.

After a year of auditions, the Doobies hired ex-Clover guitarist John McFee, session drummer Chet McCracken, and former Moby Grape saxophonist Cornelius Bumpus and released *One Step Closer* (1980), a platinum album that produced the Top Ten hit "Real Love." During the tour for *One Step Closer*, McCracken was replaced by Newmark. Early in 1982 the Doobie Brothers announced they were breaking up after a farewell tour, which was documented on the 1983 live album, *The Doobie Brothers' Farewell Tour*. After the band's split, McDonald pursued a successful solo career, while Simmons released one unsuccessful solo record. In 1987 the Doobies reunited for a concert at the Hollywood Bowl, which quickly became a brief reunion tour; McDonald declined to

particpate in the tour. By 1989 the early '70s lineup of Johnston, Simmons, Hartman, Porter, and Hossack, augmented by percussionist and former Doobies roadie Bobby La Kind, had signed a contract with Capitol Records. Their reunion album, *Cycles*, went gold upon its summer release in 1989, spawning the Top Ten single "The Doctor." *Brotherhood* followed two years later, but it failed to generate much interest. For the remainder of the '90s, the group toured the US, playing the oldies circuit and '70s revival concerts. By 1995 Michael McDonald had joined the group again. — *Stephen Thomas Erlewine*

The Doobie Brothers / 1971 / Warner Brothers ✦✦✦

Toulouse Street / 1972 / Warner Brothers ✦✦✦✦
After a promising but ill-formed debut, the Doobie Brothers returned with *Toulouse Street*, a better-written and more energetically performed effort that became a platinum record on the strength of its catchy single, "Listen to the Music." — *Stephen Thomas Erlewine*

The Captain & Me / 1973 / Warner Brothers ✦✦✦✦
Their best early album features "China Grove." — *Dan Heilman*

What Were Once Vices Are Now Habits / 1974 / Warner Brothers ✦✦✦
Apart the tight "Black Water," the Doobie Brothers' follow-up to their breakthrough *The Captain and Me* was a tepid affair, lacking the strong material of the previous album. — *Stephen Thomas Erlewine*

Stampede / 1975 / Warner Brothers ✦✦
With the addition of ex-Steely Dan guitarist Jeff "Skunk" Baxter, the Doobie Brothers became a more musically ambitious and accomplished band, without sacrificing their capability to rock 'n' roll. However, *Stampede* suffers from the same flaw as *What Were Once Vices*—a lack of consistent material. — *Stephen Thomas Erlewine*

● **Best of the Doobies** / 1976 / Warner Brothers ✦✦✦✦
Featuring 11 of the group's best-known songs from their first five albums (from 1971's *The Doobie Brothers* to 1976's *Takin' It to the Streets*), *The Best of the Doobie Brothers* contains the boogie-rock band's very best songs, including the big hits "Listen to the Music," "Jesus Is Just Alright," "Long Train Runnin'," "China Grove," "Black Water," "Takin' It to the Streets." For most casual fans, *The Best of the Doobie Brothers* is the perfect summation of the group's early career, before they turned into a slick, jazzy blue-eyed soul band in the late '70s. — *Stephen Thomas Erlewine*

Takin' It to the Streets / 1976 / Warner Brothers ✦✦✦✦
Jeff "Skunk" Baxter left after *Stampede* and keyboardist/vocalist Michael McDonald—who also recorded with Steely Dan—joined the band. Under McDonald's direction, the group departed from their trademark bluesy country-rock on *Takin' It to the Streets*, taking a laidback pop-soul approach that touched on jazz and white funk. The result was a commercial and artistic success, providing a blueprint for the band's next two records. — *Stephen Thomas Erlewine*

Livin' on the Fault Line / 1977 / Warner Brothers ✦✦✦
Livin' on the Fault Line follows the same pattern as *Takin' It to the Streets*, yet it lacks the fine songwriting of its predecessor. — *Stephen Thomas Erlewine*

Minute by Minute / 1978 / Warner Brothers ✦✦✦✦
Due to health problems, founding member Tom Johnson departed after *Livin' on the Fault Line*, leaving Michael McDonald as the leader of the Doobie Brothers. McDonald, in turn, wrote his finest set of songs for *Minute by Minute*, highlighted by the No. 1 single "What a Fool Believes." — *Stephen Thomas Erlewine*

One Step Closer / 1981 / Warner Brothers ✦✦
One Step Closer was less impressive than *Minute by Minute* not only because it lacked the strong songwriting of the previous album, but because the band sounded tired and uninspired. Unsurprisingly, it was the final studio album the Doobie Brothers made before breaking up. — *Stephen Thomas Erlewine*

The Best of the Doobies, Vol. 2 / 1981 / Warner Brothers ✦✦✦✦
This is the best of the Michael McDonald era. — *Dan Heilman*

Cycles / 1989 / Capitol ✦
The original lineup of the Doobie Brothers reunited in 1989, releasing *Cycles*. Thanks to a successful tour and single ("The Doctor"), the album went gold, but the music was just a rehashed version of the bluesy boogie of their early albums, only stiffer and less inspired. — *Stephen Thomas Erlewine*

Brotherhood / Apr. 15, 1991 / Capitol ✦✦

Rockin' Down the Highway / Jul. 1996 / Sony ✦✦
In the spring of 1996, the Doobie Brothers performed a benefit concert for the Wildlife Conservation Society, which was captured on the double-disc live album, *Rockin' Down the Highway*. During the show, all three of the group's lead vocalists—Tom Johnston, Michael McDonald, and Patrick Simmons—performed with the group, which was a first in the band's history. Fittingly, the Doobies used the concert to celebrate

their past, playing hits like "Black Water," "China Grove," and "What a Fool Believes," but they also decided to showcase two new songs, which had never been released. Unsurprisingly, these songs pale in comparison to the hits, which the band play with affection, if not overwhelming energy. And since the group is laidback and nostalgic throughout *Rocking' Down the Highway*, the album is best-suited for fans who are also nostalgic for the band's glory days. In other words, it's pleasant, but entirely unnecessary. —*Stephen Thomas Erlewine*

The Doors

f. Jul. 1965, Los Angeles, CA, db. 1973
Rock 'n' Roll, Psychedelic

The Doors, one of the most influential and controversial rock bands of the 1960s, were formed in Los Angeles in 1965 by UCLA film students Ray Manzarek, keyboards, and Jim Morrison, vocals, with drummer John Densmore, and guitarist Robby Krieger. The group never added a bass player, and their sound was dominated by Manzarek's electric organ work and Morrison's deep, sonorous voice, with which he sang and intoned his highly poetic lyrics. The group signed to Elektra Records in 1966 and released its first album, *The Doors*, featuring the hit "Light My Fire," in 1967.

Like "Light My Fire," the debut album was a massive hit, and it endures as one of the most exciting, groundbreaking recordings of the psychedelic era. Blending blues, classical, Eastern music, and pop into sinister but beguiling melodies, the band sounded like no other. With his rich, chilling vocals and somber poetic visions, Morrison explored the depths of the darkest and most thrilling aspects of the psychedelic experience. Their first effort was so stellar, in fact, that the Doors were hardpressed to match it, and although their next few albums contained a wealth of first-rate material, the group also began running up against the limitations of their recklessly disturbing visions. By their third album, they had exhausted their initial reservoir of compositions, and some of the tracks they hurriedly devised to meet public demand were clearly inferior to, and imitative of, their best early work.

On *The Soft Parade*, the group experimented with brass sections, with mixed results. Accused (without much merit) by much of the rock underground of being pop sellouts, the group charged back hard with the final two albums they recorded with Morrison, on which they drew upon stone-cold blues for much of their inspiration, especially on 1971's *L.A. Woman*.

From the start, the Doors' focus was the charismatic Morrison, who proved increasingly unstable over the group's brief career. In 1969 Morrison was arrested for indecent exposure during a concert in Miami, an incident that nearly derailed the band. Nevertheless, the Doors managed to turn out a series of successful albums and singles through 1971, when, upon the completion of *L.A. Woman*, Morrison decamped for Paris. He died there, apparently of a drug overdose. The three surviving Doors tried to carry on without him, but ultimately disbanded. Yet the Doors' music and Morrison's legend continued to fascinate succeeding generations of rock fans. In the mid-'80s, Morrison was as big a star as he'd been in the mid-'60s, and Elektra has sold quantities of the Doors' original albums plus reissues and releases of live material over the years, while publishers have flooded bookstores with Doors and Morrison biographies. In 1991 director Oliver Stone made *The Doors*, a feature film about the group starring Val Kilmer as Morrison. —*William Ruhlmann & Richie Unterberger*

☆ **The Doors** / Jan. 1967 / Elektra ✦✦✦✦✦
One of the most remarkable debut albums in rock history introduced the powerful singing of Jim Morrison, his provocative lyrics, and the group's spare, direct guitar/organ sound. "Light My Fire" became an instant standard but the album also contained such Doors classics as "Break on Through (to the Other Side)," "Twentieth Century Fox," and, of course, that Oedipal odyssey "The End." —*William Ruhlmann*

Strange Days / Oct. 1967 / Elektra ✦✦✦
The band's second effort isn't as consistently stunning as their debut, but is overall a very successful continuation of the themes of their classic first album. Besides the hit "People Are Strange," it includes "You're Lost Little Girl," "Love Me Two Times," and "Moonlight Drive," which remain among the group's finest songs. —*Richie Unterberger*

Waiting for the Sun / Jul. 1968 / Elektra ✦✦✦
Singles like "Hello, I Love You" and "The Unknown Soldier" are on *The Best of the Doors*, but many of the standouts on this album are gentle songs like "Summer's Almost Gone," "Yes, the River Knows," and "Wintertime Love," which demonstrate that Morrison & Co. can be lyrical without losing their power. —*William Ruhlmann*

The Soft Parade / Jul. 1969 / Elektra ✦✦✦
Probably the most underrated Doors collection because the addition of horns and strings ("Wishful Sinful") turns it into a more exploratory album than their more basic music usually attempted. But "Tell All the People" is the group at its most revolutionary, and the long title track is

among its most ambitious. This included the hit "Touch Me" as well as "Wild Child," one of their best rockers. —*William Ruhlmann*

Morrison Hotel/Hard Rock Cafe / 1970 / Elektra ✦✦✦✦
A bluesy, hard-rock album that nevertheless contains some of Morrison's most visionary poetry. —*William Ruhlmann*

13 / Feb. 1970 / Elektra ✦✦✦✦
A one-disc hits compilation issued before the Doors' final album and thus lacking "Riders on the Storm," but nevertheless a good sampler of the singles that maintained the Doors' enormous popularity in the late '60s and remain rock standards today. —*William Ruhlmann*

Absolutely Live / Sep. 1970 / Elektra ✦✦
This sprawling collection demonstrated that, in concert, the Doors could be an enervating as well as an elevating experience. There are no hits, but there's a lot of Morrison—improvising, reciting poetry, sometimes singing. Not a record for the uninitiated. (Combined with *Alive, She Cried* and *Live at the Hollywood Bowl* for CD release under the title *In Concert*.) —*William Ruhlmann*

L.A. Woman / Apr. 1971 / Elektra ✦✦✦✦
Morrison's final testament shows him at the height of his ability to bring striking images to the lyrics of rock music, and the group produces some of its most trancelike music. —*William Ruhlmann*

Other Voices / Oct. 1971 / Elektra ✦✦
The Doors seem to have been planning to make this trio album even before Jim Morrison's death, since it was released shortly afterward. It has the Doors' characteristic instrumental sound and some effective songs, notably "Ships W/Sails," but there's no replacing Morrison's voice. —*William Ruhlmann*

Weird Scenes Inside the Gold Mine / Jan. 1972 / Elektra ✦✦✦
A two-LP compilation that fills in the Doors' hits not included on *13* and concentrates on some of their longer album tracks. —*William Ruhlmann*

Full Circle / Jul. 1972 / Elektra ✦✦
Ray Manzarek sometimes echoes Morrison's authoritative vocal style, and the band tries out a variety of different approaches on this second trio album, but the songs just aren't up to snuff, and Manzarek just isn't Morrison. When he tries "Good Rocking Tonight," you can't help thinking what Morrison could have done with the same material. —*William Ruhlmann*

Alive, She Cried / Oct. 1983 / Elektra ✦✦
A more conventional concert album than *Absolutely Live*, containing an interesting reading of Them's "Gloria" and hits like "Light My Fire." (Combined with *Absolutely Live* and *Live at the Hollywood Bowl* for CD release under the title *In Concert*.) —*William Ruhlmann*

★ **The Best of the Doors** / 1985 / Elektra ✦✦✦✦✦
A well-chosen, 18-track compilation balancing the radio hits with the longer, more complex song poems. It's a good sampler, but this is one group for whom you need to hear the whole story. Reissued on CD in 1991 with one bonus track. —*William Ruhlmann*

Live at the Hollywood Bowl / Jun. 1987 / Elektra ✦✦✦
The Doors' most focused concert recording, from a show held on July 5, 1968, that also was filmed. There is also a home video of the show. (This album was combined with *Absolutely Live* and *Alive, She Cried* for release on CD under the title *In Concert*.) —*William Ruhlmann*

In Concert / May 21, 1991 / Elektra ✦✦✦
The Doors could be erratic live, as this double CD shows. Still, it's a fair example of their in-concert charms. —*Jeff Tamarkin*

● **Greatest Hits** / Oct. 15, 1996 / Elektra ✦✦✦✦
Although the version of "The End" included on *Greatest Hits* is taken from the *Apocalypse Now* soundtrack and filled with sound effects, this single-disc collection remains a terrific overview of the Doors' career, featuring all of their biggest hits and best-known songs, and thereby functioning as a fine introduction for neophytes. —*Stephen Thomas Erlewine*

Live at the Matrix, San Francisco, March 10, 1967 / [Bootleg] ✦✦✦✦
Far and away the best unreleased Doors material out there, this is one of the highest fidelity live tapes of the era of any rock act, capturing the Doors just before "Light My Fire" made them superstars. More than any of their officially sanctioned live recordings, this showcases the Doors as a hard-working club unit, with a slightly raw feel not present on any other document. Morrison and the band are in top form on a selection of off-the-beaten tracks from their first albums, including "My Eyes Have Seen You," "Summer's Almost Gone," "Break on Through," and "People Are Strange." The blues/R&B covers are less compelling, but interesting in that several were never officially released by the group, including "Money," "I'm a King Bee," and "Summertime." —*Richie Unterberger*

Live in Seattle, June 5, 1970 / [Bootleg] ✦✦✦
An hour-plus, fairly good fidelity recording that ranks as the best live boot of their final days. Although much has been written about what a

shambles Morrison was in at this time, the performances here are quite tight, and the extended renditions of warhorses like "Roadhouse Blues," "Five to One," "The End," and "When the Music's Over" are pretty interesting. Also has a version of "Mystery Train" and the unreleased original "Someday Soon." —*Richie Unterberger*

Rock Is Dead / [Bootleg] ♦♦♦
Around 1969, the group cut a semi-legendary 40 minutes or so of the rambling opus "Rock Is Dead," a tongue-in-cheek obituary that combines Morrison's poetry with offhand musical quotes from rock and blues oldies that simultaneously parody and pay homage to the band's inspirations. Not a vital piece of art by any means, but fascinating insight for Morrison/Doors aficionados, reflecting the group's mystical vision and the burnout they were feeling as the pressure of commercial expectations, Morrison's dissolution, and legal hassles mounted. Available under a variety of different titles; *Love Me Tender*, if you can find it, adds some interesting late-'60s studio outtakes. —*Richie Unterberger*

1965 Demos / (no label) ♦♦♦
In September 1965, the Doors recorded a crude five-song demo in three hours, intended for getting a contract (which they actually got with Columbia, although nothing was recorded before it was annulled). Robby Krieger had yet to join the band at this point; present at the session were Morrison, Manzarek, and Densmore, with Manzarek's brothers Rick (guitar) and Jim (harmonica), and a forgotten female bass player. The results have been bootlegged so frequently (usually in the company of other Doors rarities) that it's useless to list a specific compilation. It won't be too hard to find one of them, though, identifiable by the inclusion of primitive versions of "Moonlight Drive," "Hello, I Love You," "Summer's Almost Gone," "My Eyes Have Seen You," and "End of the Night." Both Morrison and the band sound quite a ways from developing their sound: Morrison's vocals are far more tentative, Manzarek plays bluesy piano instead of organ, and there are hardly any guitars. Most surprisingly, "Hello, I Love You" and "My Eyes Have Seen You" are arranged in a manner that strongly recalls the early Kinks, much more so than the versions that ended up on the early Doors albums. Not a strong recording on its own merits, but a fascinating glimpse into the birth of the band. —*Richie Unterberger*

Lee Dorsey

b. Dec. 24, 1924, New Orleans, LA, d. Dec. 1, 1986, New Orleans, LA
Vocals / Soul, R&B, New Orleans R&B
The effervescent approach of Lee Dorsey perfectly summarizes the infectious charm of early-'60s New Orleans R&B. Dorsey specialized in good-humored music with a touch of second-line funk thrown in to make it all the more irresistible. Although he had already waxed a couple of singles, Dorsey caught the country by total surprise in 1961 with his deceptively simple nursery-rhyme-style "Ya Ya" on Bobby Robinson's Fury label. Arranged by prolific New Orleans pianist Allen Toussaint, the track proved an R&B chart-topper and a major pop hit to boot.

Dorsey's laconic vocal charms served him well on "Ya Ya" and the Earl King-penned follow-up "Do Re Mi," and the mid-'60s found him working with Toussaint on the funky smashes "Ride Your Pony" and "Working in the Coal Mine," this time for Amy Records. It's little remembered that Dorsey was responsible for the original 1970 version of Toussaint's "Yes We Can," revived to much greater acclaim by the Pointer Sisters (who tacked on an extra "Can"). From all accounts, Dorsey remained an exceedingly humble R&B star who preferred tinkering with cars to touring the country. He died of emphysema in 1986. —*Bill Dahl*

Ya Ya / 1962 / Relic ♦♦♦♦
This terrific overview of the good-humored New Orleans singer's early-'60s classics (for Bobby Robinson's Fury label) features direct-from-masters sound quality. —*Bill Dahl*

● **Holy Cow!: Best of Lee Dorsey** / 1985 / Arista ♦♦♦♦
A nice single-disc anthology featuring the best-known cuts and biggest pop hits of New Orleans R&B and soul singer Lee Dorsey, one of the Crescent City's best comic/novelty artists and a fine traditional R&B vocalist as well. The title track, "Working in a Coal Mine," and "Ride Your Pony" are superb songs that use the second line rhythm and boast outstanding arrangements, clever lyrics, and great vocals. —*Ron Wynn*

The Downliners Sect

f. Great Britain
British Invasion, British Blues
Of all the British R&B bands to follow in the Rolling Stones' footsteps, the Downliners Sect was arguably the rawest. The Sect didn't as much interpret the sound of Chess Records as attack it, in a way that made the Pretty Things seem positively suave by comparison. Long on crude energy and hoarse vocals, but short on originality and songwriting talent, the band never had a British hit, although they had some sizable singles in other European countries. Despite their lack of commercial success or appeal, the band managed to record three albums and various EPs and singles between 1963 and 1966, with detours into country-rock and an EP of death-rock tunes. The Sect's early work continues to attract connoisseurs of '60s garage and punk. —*Richie Unterberger*

● **The Sect** / 1964 / Columbia ♦♦♦♦
Their rawest and most R&B-oriented, firmly rooted in the same influences as the Stones and Pretty Things. Includes punk covers of Chuck Berry, Bo Diddley, Muddy Waters, Jimmy Reed, et al., and a few originals in the same vein. —*Richie Unterberger*

Nite at Gt. Newport Street / 1964 / RBC ♦♦
Live demo disc, featuring the Sect at its rawest and most satisfying, complete with the zaniest, most satisfying cover of Bo Diddley's "Cadillac" ever recorded. Included complete on *The Definitive Downliners Sect.* —*Bruce Eder*

The Country Sect / 1965 / Columbia ♦♦
The funniest band on the British blues scene tries its hand at American country-blues, with surprisingly good results—sort of the Rolling Stones with a comically looser approach. —*Bruce Eder*

Sect Sing Sick Songs / 1965 / Columbia ♦♦
In 1965 the Downliners Sect managed to release not one, but two records that counted as among the least commercial rock efforts of the period. One was their album of country songs, and the other was this, a four-song EP of death rock. On side one they cover Jimmy Cross' gross "I Want My Baby Back" (now a Dr. Demento standard) and "Leader of the Pack," changing the title to "Leader of the Sect." Side two has the lyrically indecipherable "Midnight Hour" and a cornball teen lament entitled "Now She's Dead." Unusual concept and pedestrian execution, although they beat the Cramps to it by a good dozen years or so. —*Richie Unterberger*

The Rock Sect's In / 1966 / Columbia ♦♦♦
Their wildly erratic third album includes some tepid material but also some of their best tracks, especially their vicious run-through of the early British rock 'n' roll standard "Brand New Cadillac." It's most notable for the appearance—through God-knows-what channels—of "Why Don't You Smile Now," which was written by Lou Reed, John Cale, and two unknowns before the Velvet Underground formed. —*Richie Unterberger*

I Want My Baby Back / 1978 / Charly ♦♦♦
A collection of 1960s tracks that is now supplanted in value, content, and sound by the See For Miles Records *Definitive Downliners Sect.* —*Bruce Eder*

Be a Sect Maniac / 1983 / Out Line ♦♦
Dubious sound mars this collection, which is as close to a hits compilation as existed. Now irrelevant in the wake of the *Definitive Downliners Sect.* —*Bruce Eder*

Definitive Downliners Sect: Singles A's & B's / Dec. 1994 / See For Miles ♦♦
Definitive, yes—both sides of all eight of their Columbia singles, both sides of their one EP single, their 1965 *The Sect Sing Sick Songs* EP, their ultra-rare self-released *Gt. Newport Street* EP from early 1964, and demos of "Cadillac" and "Roll Over Beethoven" from '63 and '64 respectively. Twenty-nine songs in all, spanning 1963-67, many of which didn't make it onto the three albums they released during this period. Good? No, not really. As performers the Sect didn't only verge on inept, they were at times downright careless, as if they couldn't be bothered to polish things a bit in the studio. As (infrequent) songwriters, their talent was nearly nonexistent. It's hard to believe anyone thought most of these sides had any commercial potential, either in the band or at the record label; the material is largely lackluster, and not even especially well chosen (a few of the songs on their first and third LPs would have been much better bets). Highlights are the *Newport* EP, which at least finds them playing things a bit straight and passionate, with a ramshackle version of "Green Onions" and a good cut of Bo Diddley's "Nursery Rhymes"; the 1965 single "Bad Storm Coming" is a fairly moody number. That's a pretty low return on a band that enjoys a vociferous following among some collectors, although they were really a pedestrian British R&B band with a propensity toward parched humor and odd novelty tunes that hasn't aged well. —*Richie Unterberger*

Nick Drake

b. Jun. 19, 1948, Burma, d. Nov. 25, 1974, Birmingham, England
Guitar, Vocals / Singer-Songwriter, Folk-Rock, Folk, British Folk
A singular talent who passed almost unnoticed during his brief lifetime, Nick Drake produced several albums of chilling, somber beauty. With hindsight, these have been come to be recognized as peak achievements of both the British folk-rock scene and the entire rock singer-songwriter genre. Sometimes compared to Van Morrison, Drake in fact resembled Donovan much more in his breathy vocals, strong melodies, and the acoustic-based orchestral sweep of his arrangements. His was a much darker vision than Donovan's, however, with disturbing themes of mel-

ancholy, failed romance, mortality, and depression lurking just beneath, or even well above, the surface. Ironically, Drake has achieved a far greater stature in the decades after his death, with an avid cult following that grows by the year.

Part of Drake's failure to attract a mass audience was attributable to his almost pathological reluctance to perform live. It was at a live show in Cambridge, however, that a member of Fairport Convention saw Drake perform, and recommended the singer to producer Joe Boyd. Boyd, already a linchpin of the British folk-rock scene as the producer for Fairport and the Incredible String Band, asked Drake for a tape, and was impressed enough to give the 20-year-old a contract in 1968.

Drake's debut, *Five Leaves Left* (1969), was the first in a series of three equally impressive, and quite disparate, albums. With understated folk-rock backing (Pentangle bassist Danny Thompson plays bass on most of the cuts), Drake created a vaguely mysterious, haunting atmosphere, occasionally embellished by tasteful baroque strings. His economic, even pithy, lyrics hinted at melancholy, but any thoughts of despair were alleviated by the gorgeous, uplifting melodies and Drake's calm, measured vocals. *Bryter Later* (1970) was perhaps his most upbeat effort, featuring support from members of Fairport Convention and traces of jazz in the arrangements. On some cuts, the singer-songwriter dispensed with lyrics altogether, offering only gorgeous, orchestrated instrumental miniatures that stood well on their own.

Neither album sold well, and Drake, already a brooding loner, plunged into serious depression that often found him unable to make music, work, or even walk and talk. He managed to produce one final full-length work, *Pink Moon* (1972), a desolate solo acoustic album that ranks as one of the most naked and bleak statements in all of rock. He did record a few more songs before his death, but no more albums were completed, although the final sessions (along with some other fine unreleased material) surfaced on the posthumous compilation *Time of No Reply*.

Drake's final couple of years were marked by increasing psychiatric difficulties, which found him hospitalized at one point for several weeks. He had rarely played live during his days as a recording artist, and at one point declared his intention never to record again, although he wished to continue to write songs for others. (It's been reported that French chanteuse Francoise Hardy recorded some of Drake's songs, but she hasn't released any.) On November 26, 1974, he died in his parents' home from an overdose of antidepressant medication; suicide has been speculated, although some of his family and friends dispute this.

In the manner of the young romantic poets of the 19th century who died before their time, Drake is revered by many listeners today, with a following that spans generations. Baby boomers who missed him the first time around found much to revisit once they discovered him, and his excessive loneliness speaks directly to contemporary alternative rockers who share his sense of morose alienation. *—Richie Unterberger*

Five Leaves Left / 1969 / Hannibal ✦✦✦✦
Nick Drake's debut album skillfully augments his haunting folk-based songs with tasteful strings that accentuate the gorgeous melancholy of his music. *—Stephen Thomas Erlewine*

Bryter Layter / 1970 / Hannibal ✦✦✦✦
While the strings on Nick Drake's second album are more prominent, they rarely take away from the impact of his music, which is significantly less sad on this record. However, *Bryter Layter* isn't lighthearted—it's a reflective piece of music that gains power from its own introspection. *—Stephen Thomas Erlewine*

Pink Moon / 1972 / Hannibal ✦✦✦✦
On his last album, Nick Drake strips away all of the excess instrumentation of his first two albums, keeping only the bare essentials. The result is a stark, brilliant album of despair, loneliness, and alienation that is startling in its emotional power. *—Stephen Thomas Erlewine*

★ **Fruit Tree** / 1986 / Hannibal ✦✦✦✦✦
Fruit Tree is a four-disc box set that features all three of Nick Drake's studio albums (*Five Leaves Left, Bryter Layter, Pink Moon*) and the rarities collection *Time of No Reply*. In other words, it contains every known recording that Drake made during his brief lifetime, and listening to the set, the depth of his talent becomes abundantly clear. And the four discs are not overkill. The quality of Drake's songs are startlingly high, and anyone who purchases one disc will eventually need the other three, making *Fruit Tree* a logical way to acquire all of the records at once. *—Stephen Thomas Erlewine*

Time of No Reply / 1986 / Hannibal ✦✦✦
A collection of ten previously unreleased tracks recorded between 1968 and 1974, the songs on *Time of No Reply* rank with Nick Drake's finest work. *—Stephen Thomas Erlewine*

Way to Blue: An Introduction to Nick Drake / Oct. 4, 1994 / Hannibal ✦✦✦
A selection of 16 tracks from all three of his studio albums and the *Time Of No Reply* collection, compiled by Drake's producer, Joe Boyd. Of course the music is excellent, but Drake's albums stand so well on their

own that this collection of piecemeal offerings hardly works as the best way to experience his distinctively haunting brand of folk-rock. *—Richie Unterberger*

Tanworth-in-Arden 1967/68 / [Bootleg] ✦✦✦
Long circulated as a tape among hardcore fans, these 18 solo acoustic songs were recorded by Drake at home; most or all of them were probably laid down before he had ever entered a studio. The sound quality is fuzzy, but given how little Drake recorded before his death, and how absolutely no unreleased material exists other than the four CDs included on his *Fruit Tree* box set, this is a Holy Grail (or at least a silver goblet) of sorts for Drake fanatics. Most of the material is in a far more traditional acoustic folk and blues vein than his official releases, which show a big leap in both songwriting maturity and instrumental sophistication. Here Nick sounds much like very early (acoustic) Donovan, covering traditional folk songs, "Summertime," "Get Together," and early Dylan; his originals are often quite derivative of these influences (and several compositions credited to Drake on the liner notes are in fact covers, or extremely derivative of existing standards). The best cuts—"Winter Is Gone," "The Reason of the Seasons," "To the Garden"—show the emergence of a more idiosyncratic talent. Minor complaints: four songs from the original tape are missing (two do appear on *Fruit Tree*), some entertaining between-song banter has been eliminated, and there's a major typo in the CD title (this was in fact recorded in *Tamworth-in-Arden*). *—Richie Unterberger*

The Dramatics

f. 1962, Detroit, MI
Soul, Quiet Storm
Popular Detroit R&B vocal aggregation that scored numerous hits for Volt and maintained their momentum through the disco era. The early Dramatics hits for Volt lived up to their billing with the emphatic vocals of Ron Banks (b. May 10, 1951) powering the funky "Whatcha See Is Whatcha Get," their first big-seller in 1971, and the R&B chart-topping ballad "In the Rain" the next year. The quintet was just as successful later in the decade, signing with ABC in 1975 and scoring repeatedly throughout disco-fever days. *—Bill Dahl*

● **The Best of the Dramatics** / 1976 / Stax ✦✦✦✦
In the 1960s, Stax Records was best known for raw Southern soul that rejected the type of sleekness and pop sensibilities favored by the Northern soulsters at Motown. But by the early '70s, Memphis soul was losing its popularity, and Stax' A&R department started to emphasize Northern and so-called "uptown" soul in order to stay competitive. One of Stax/Volt's biggest sellers was the Dramatics, a Detroit group that, like the Temptations at Motown and the O'Jays in the Gamble & Huff camp, effectively combined gritty soul belting with a sleek production style. Thanks to major hits ranging from the delightfully funky "Whatcha See Is Whatcha Get" to slow jams and ballads like "Hey You! Get off My Mountain," "Toast to the Fool," and the melancholy "In the Rain," the Dramatics were on quite a roll in the early-to-mid-'70s. All of those gems are included on the hour-long CD *The Best of the Dramatics*, which offers a fine overview of the quintet's Stax/Volt years. Many Dramatics albums are worth owning, but if a listener were allowed to own only one Dramatics CD, this would be it. *—Alex Henderson*

ABC Years 1974-1980 / Nov. 21, 1995 / SCL ✦✦✦
The Dramatics were one of the best soul groups of the early '70s, scoring a series of hits for Volt Records. After leaving Volt, they went to ABC Records in 1974 and stayed there until the end of the decade. The hits began to become a little bit smaller, and that's partially because they were either covering other people's hits ("Me and Mrs. Jones") or lacked solid material. *ABC Years 1974-1980* collects their biggest hits from this period. While the music on the collection isn't as consistently thrilling as their early '70s hits, there are a couple of gems buried in these 11 tracks that make the album worthwhile for dedicated fans. *—Stephen Thomas Erlewine*

Best of Volt / Stax ✦✦✦✦
The Dramatics were one of Stax' finest soul vocal groups, using Ron Banks' rising soprano, L.J. Reynolds' booming baritone, and Willie Ford's emphatic bass to create enticing love songs with excellent harmonizing at the top, in the middle, and at the bottom of the scale. Their albums tended to be erratic affairs, with outstanding love songs and sometimes dismal, formulaic dance tunes. This is one of many collections that spotlight their hits on the Stax/Volt label. *—Ron Wynn*

Dream Syndicate

f. 1981, Los Angeles, CA, db. 1989
Group / Alternative Pop-Rock, Paisley Underground, Jangle-Pop
Dream Syndicate is at the foundation (alongside the Velvet Underground, the Stooges, and R.E.M.) of contemporary alternative music sheerly because at the time when most bands were experimenting with

new technology, the Syndicate deigned to bring back the guitar. Fronted by Steve Wynn (b. Feb. 21, 1960) and including Karl Precoda (guitar), Dennis Duck (drums), and Kendra Smith (bass), the band formed in Los Angeles after Smith and Wynn had relocated there from Davis, CA. They debuted with a self-titled, unbelievably Velvet Underground-like EP on Wynn's own Down There label. It was shortly off to Ruby/Slash for *Days of Wine and Roses*, the most lauded record on the college charts that year. The record has been cited as influential by artists as diverse as Kurt Cobain and the Black Crowes' Chris Robinson. Live, they had developed into an assaultive guitar band prone to jamming, which helped tag them as leaders of Los Angeles' Paisley Underground movement.

In 1984 *Medicine Show* was met with mixed response by the college crowd. By this time, Smith had left the band and was replaced by Dave Provost on bass and Tom Zvoncheck on keyboards. Wynn took his cues from Neil Young and Crazy Horse on the record rather than Lou Reed (who was considered a preferable source at the time), and the rootsier sound caused a backlash with the fan base. A new lineup and falling morale, as the band label-hopped, spawned *Out of the Grey* (Big Time) in 1986 and the Elliot Mazer-produced *Ghost Stories* (Enigma) in 1989. The band had realigned to include Mark Walton on bass and Paul B. Cutler on guitar. They recorded *Live at Raji's* in 1989 as their swan song. Wynn has since recorded four solo albums, two with Gutterball (featuring the House of Freaks and Silo Bob Rupe), and is continuously collaborating with other musicians. Wynn's 1996 solo record had him backed by the Boston band Come. Smith went on to work in Opal with David Roback, a prototype version of his Mazzy Star, and has released two solo albums. Duck continues to work with Wynn as a touring drummer, and Precoda is M.I.A. Bassist Mark Walton plays with the Continental Drifters. A documentary of the band's last tour, *Weathered and Torn*, is available on video. *—Denise Sullivan*

The Days of Wine and Roses / 1982 / Slash ✦✦✦✦
A watershed record, since it heralded the return of the noisy guitar to rock music after punk began new wave and left us awash in synthesizers. Critical accolades helped earn the L.A. Paisley Underground scene that spawned the band some national attention. Steve Wynn and his crew mine Velvets—and Stooges-based guitar rock, but merge it with a California sensibility and his young man's version of dark, poetic confusion. The title track clocks in at over seven minutes, a time that for years had been relegated to tracks by outmoded '70s bands. But the Syndicate never cared—they just rocked on. *—Denise Sullivan*

Dream Syndicate [EP] / 1982 / Down There ✦✦✦
Dream Syndicate shows with this EP that there was a dark side to L.A.'s paisley underground. Here they come across as part Velvet Underground, part Dylanesque rockers, and all-around punk revolutionaries who rocked as if they meant it. *—James Chrispell*

● **Medicine Show** / 1984 / A&M ✦✦✦✦
More Neil Young and Crazy Horse than the previous Lou Reed and the Velvet Underground-inspired album, the Syndicate rips through eight fairly traditional rock songs, save for the feedback. The CD reissue includes *This Is Not the Dream Syndicate Album... Live!*, five songs performed from the album. "The Medicine Show" and the similar "John Coltrane Stereo Blues" are the keepers, and check the guitar on "Bullet with My Name on It." The record wrestles with American roots music in a way college rockers probably weren't familiar with, and thus it was almost universally hated at the time. Wynn admits in the liner notes to the CD reissue that this is his favorite release with the band. *—Denise Sullivan*

This Is Not the New Dream Syndicate / 1984 / A&M ✦✦

Dream Syndicate / 1985 / Demon ✦✦✦

Out of the Grey / 1986 / Big Time ✦✦✦
Like nearly everything released that year, *Out of the Grey* suffered from a touch of the post-new wave flu. But "50 in a 25 Zone" has that old, bluesy Syndicate spirit, as does "Now I Ride Alone," and Steve Wynn is still an exceptional vocal stylist, bringing heart and meaning to every word he writes. *—Denise Sullivan*

50 in a 25 Zone / 1987 / Big Time ✦✦

Ghost Stories / 1988 / Restless ✦✦✦
Opening with the self-referential "The Side I'll Never Show," and produced by Neil Young and Crazy Horse vet Elliot Mazer, Wynn and Co. mine the dark and rusty terrain of folk and blues-rock that they ultimately made work to their advantage on this very straightahead rock album. Wynn's vocal style and forthright lyrics never really connected with the masses at the time, but years later, it's clear he was making music for the ages. *—Denise Sullivan*

Live at Raji's / 1989 / Enigma ✦✦✦✦
A fond farewell from the preeminent '80s distorto-rock band. All the classics are here: "Days of Wine and Roses," "The Medicine Show," "That's What You Always Say." Even the previously uninspired "Forest for the Trees" sounds good on this night. *—Denise Sullivan*

● **Tell Me When It's Over: The Best of Dream Syndicate** / Jun. 23, 1992 / Rhino ✦✦✦✦
These 15 tracks contain the cream of the crop of this Los Angeles band's independent and major label work. Among the highlights are "When You Smile," "Tell Me When It's Over," and "Halloween" from their 1982 Ruby/Slash EP *Days of Wine and Roses*. The collection captures their dense Velvet Underground-style rock in all its fiery glory. The booklet is loaded with a detailed history, many photos, lyrics, and track and personnel listings. *—Rick Clark*

Lost Tapes 1985-88 / 1995 / Normal ✦✦

The Drifters

f. May 1953, New York, NY
R&B, Doo Wop

Originally a backup group formed around the soaring vocal talents of Clyde McPhatter, the Drifters—like their '50s counterparts, the Platters and the Coasters—have turned out to be one of the most enduring "franchises" in rock 'n' roll. Though it's been years since any of the original members have been involved (almost all of them being long deceased), chances are if there's an "oldies but goodies" stage show somewhere tonight, some form of the Drifters will be on stage, singing the hits that made the original group a legend. Unlike other groups who lost key members along the way and never regained their artistic or commercial footing, the various incarnations of the Drifters produced distinctly memorable material every step of the way. Depending on what time frame you come in on during their 40-plus years as a group, you'll discover that they turned from a hard rhythm and gospel doo wop aggregation to one of the smoothest and most romantic ever to grace an AM radio. One of the first Black R&B groups to use a string section on their records ("There Goes My Baby," 1959), their middle period sound defined universal love and the good life as seen through the eyes of the ghetto, an arresting combination that won them crossover appeal. That they not only moved, but prospered, with the times is testimony to their rightly deserved longevity.

In 1953 Clyde McPhatter already held a reputation in the R&B community as one of its finest tenor lead voices. He had been plucked from a gospel group to become a member of Billy Ward and the Dominoes, a doo wop aggregation that combined classic "blow harmony" sounds with Clyde's agonized, fervent vocals. Originally McPhatter was so concerned about the backlash from the gospel community over the way he sang secular material that he claimed to be related to the group's leader, appearing in magazine articles and such as "Clyde Ward." But with the back-to-back success of "Have Mercy Baby," "The Bells," and others, McPhatter soon grew restless to be out on his own. The promise of an Atlantic recording contract prompted him to leave the group and come to New York to form the original version of the Drifters with Bill Pinkey (aka Pinkney) and Andrew and Gerhard Thrasher from the gospel quartet the Wonderland Thrashers.

The sound of the new group combined with Atlantic's production expertise to form an ideal marriage, both aesthetically and commercially, and almost immediately the hits started coming, one after another. "Money Honey," "Let the Boogie Woogie Roll," "Such a Night," "Honey Love," and a bizarre arrangement of Irving Berlin's "White Christmas" all made the Top Ten on the R&B charts. But this run would soon be interrupted as Clyde was drafted for military service, a move that had far-reaching effects on the rest of his career.

The group quickly replaced McPhatter with Johnny Moore and scored three more hits, "Ruby Baby," "Adorable," and "Your Promise to Be Mine." In 1958 manager George Treadwell disbanded the group but, realizing that they still had a few years to go on their Atlantic contract and a yearly commitment to perform at the Apollo Theater, tapped an unknown group called the Five Crowns—with lead singer Ben E. King—to become the new Drifters. This incarnation of the group is the one most fans readily remember, as King's lead vocals, combined with Lieber and Stoller's excellent songwriting, produced groundbreaking hits such as "Save the Last Dance for Me," "There Goes My Baby," "Dance with Me," "Lonely Winds," and "This Magic Moment." King went solo in 1960 and Rudy Lewis stepped in as the new lead singer, producing seven Top 40 hits, including the classics "On Broadway" (featuring a young Phil Spector on lead guitar) and "Up on the Roof." After Lewis' drug-related death in 1964, Johnny Moore once again stepped in as lead singer, producing their final hits, "Under the Boardwalk" and "Saturday Night at the Movies." When the group's Atlantic contract finally ran out in 1972 (!), Moore took the group to England and signed with Bell Records, producing three more UK Top Ten hits before leaving in 1980. Since that time, various versions of the group—some legal, most not—have dotted the landscape of the oldies circuit, and any lineup could feature any combination of the 50-odd members who passed through their ranks over the years. *—Cub Koda*

☆ **Let the Boogie Woogie Roll: Greatest Hits** / 1988 / Rhino ✦✦✦✦✦
Let the Boogie Woogie Roll: Greatest Hits is the definitive account of the

early group (1953-1958) and Clyde McPhatter's greatest sides. The double-disc set features classic singles like "Money Honey," "Such a Night," "Honey Love," "What'cha Gonna Do," "Ruby Baby," and "Drip Drop" among its 40 tracks. —*Bruce Eder*

☆ **All-Time Greatest Hits & More: 1959-1965** / 1988 / Rhino ✦✦✦✦✦
All Time Greatest Hits & More: 1959-1965 is a towering and magnificent collection of some of the best popular R&B ever done this side of Sam Cooke. This double-disc collection contains the biggest hits Ben E. King, Rudy Lewis, and Johnny Moore sang for the group, including "There Goes My Baby," "This Magic Moment," "Save the Last Dance for Me," "Sweets for My Sweet," "I Count the Tears," "Some Kind of Wonderful," "Up on the Roof," "On Broadway," and "Under the Boardwalk." —*Bruce Eder*

★ **The Very Best of the Drifters** / Apr. 20, 1993 / Rhino ✦✦✦✦✦
Combining all the greatest hits from both the Clyde McPhatter and Ben E. King eras, the single-disc *The Very Best of the Drifters* serves as the perfect introduction to the seminal R&B vocal group. —*Stephen Thomas Erlewine*

Rockin' & Driftin': The Drifters Box / 1996 / Rhino ✦✦✦✦
A three-CD, 79-song box spanning all incarnations of the group, from 1953 to 1976 (although only six of the tracks date from after 1966). Sure, there's a lot of classic music here—all of the big hits, and many interesting flops and B-sides. Assuming, however, that the audience for this set is mostly limited to serious Drifters fans, it's likely that many or most already have the *Let the Boogie Woogie Roll* and *All-Time Greatest Hits & More* compilations, which cover just about all of the essential cuts from the box. If you already own those CDs, you may well want to pass this up, but if you have yet to build a serious Drifters collection, this will supply virtually everything you need. And then some. Some of this is pretty extraneous, particularly the '70s cuts. A significant bonus is their previously unreleased 1963 version of "Only in America," a song that was ultimately given to Jay & the Americans (who had a hit with it) because it was deemed too controversial for a Black group to release. —*Richie Unterberger*

Drivin' 'n' Cryin'

f. 1986, Atlanta, GA
Group / Rock 'n' Roll, Folk-Rock, Roots-Rock, Alternative Pop-Rock
Formed in Atlanta in 1986, the hard-rocking, Southern roots-music-steeped Drivin' 'n' Cryin' was never embraced on a national level, but it reigned supreme in the region. Originally made up of singer-songwriter Kevn Kinney on guitar and vocals, Tim Nielsen on bass, and Paul Lenz on drums, the band's debut was the timeless hard rock/bluegrass fusion *Scarred But Smarter* (1986) on 688 Records, the label that grew out of the punk-era Atlanta club of the same name. The band followed with *Whisper Tames the Lion* in 1988 for Island and replaced Lenz with Jeff Sullivan on drums. There were high hopes for the band at the time, because of the success of R.E.M.; all things Southern were tipped to become the next big thing. But Drivin' 'n' Cryin's uniquely Southern spin on rock was lost on the rest of the world. Persevering with *Mystery Road*, with the addition of R.E.M. guitar roadie Buren Fowler on lead guitar, the band didn't alter style all that much. For *Fly Me Courageous* (1990), the band finally took on the heavy metal mantle and ended up with a good hard rock record, with the odd folk track thrown in. The result was perhaps shocking and less than fashionable in the years when alternative music was just coming into its own. Drivin' 'n' Cryin's greatest strength was as a live band; they toured tirelessly around the South, drawing an enthusiastic, college-age audience. A Drivin' 'n' Cryin' show in Atlanta had to be seen to be believed—the sound of the crowd singing along would actually drown out Kinney's own unusually strong voice. That same year, Kinney recorded the beautiful acoustic folk LP *MacDougal Blues* for Island. Drivin' 'n' Cryin's *Smoke* was released for Island in 1993 and finished the band's liaison with the label. It was followed by another, even sparer solo album by Kinney, *Down Out Law* (Mammoth) in 1994. He accompanied his solo releases by touring with R.E.M. guitarist Peter Buck, who produced the first album, while he and the band also filled the gap between its fifth and sixth records performing acoustic dates throughout the South. By the time the more gentle *Wrapped in Sky*, the band's Geffen debut in 1996, hit the shelves, they were nearly forgotten—lost in the void in which many bands of their generation would find themselves in the wake of grunge. Kinney, Nielsen, and Sullivan have held strong with the addition of Joey Huffman on keyboards for *Wrapped in Sky*. Fowler has since left the fold. The band continues to record, and during 1997 was working on an album to be self-released. —*Denise Sullivan*

Scarred But Smarter / 1986 / Island ✦✦✦✦
A strong debut from the Atlanta rock band that is by no means mired in the dodgy, processed production sounds that marred so many records released in this period. A cross between punky hard rock and bluegrass, the band would later refine their direction, but the title track and "Another Scarlet Butterfly" are great showcases for songwriter Kinney's

budding career as the voice for a new generation of Southern rockers. —*Denise Sullivan*

Whisper Tames the Lion / 1987 / Island ✦✦✦✦
Still inflected with hillbilly/bluegrass roots and edging ever closer toward the hard rock sound they would ultimately embrace, this album was produced by New York No Wave drummer Anton Fier. It offers a good mix of both styles, as on the steady title cut, the hard-rocking boogie "Powerhouse," and gentle "The Friend Song," an anthem of sorts for the band's college-age fans throughout the South. —*Denise Sullivan*

Mystery Road / 1989 / Island ✦✦✦
Though not as strong as *Whisper Tames the Lion, Mystery Road* keeps Drivin' 'n' Cryin' in search of the best way to fuse their harder rock leanings with their traditional Southern roots, as they vacillate from the crunch of "You Don't Know Me" to the wistful "Peacemaker." Peter Buck guests on electric dulcimer throughout. However, in the end, this is the least memorable record in the Drivin' 'n' Cryin' canon. —*Denise Sullivan*

Fly Me Courageous / 1991 / Island ✦✦✦
Still rolling along, Drivin' 'n' Cryin' were suspected of selling out entirely on this mostly heavy, Geoff Workman-produced project. But songs like "Let's Go Dancing" are right in step with the band's roots—it's just that they sound increasingly odd next to tracks like the title song or the straightahead metal rocker "The Innocent." —*Denise Sullivan*

Smoke / 1993 / Island ✦✦✦
As time goes by, Drivin' 'n' Cryin' keep evolving into the heirs to the Southern rock throne. *Smoke*, while not as impressive or original as previous efforts, offers some crunching rock, but it really shines during the country-tinged acoustic numbers "What Difference Does It Make" and "When You Come Back." —*Stephen Thomas Erlewine*

Wrapped in Sky / Aug. 29, 1995 / Geffen ✦✦✦✦
The most overlooked and underrated of the Southern rock band's albums, this release came out in the gap following two solo records by lead singer Kevn Kinney, when the band was thought to have packed it in. Taking the Dylanesque folk style Kinney used on his solo recordings with D&C's penchant for old-fashioned rock 'n' roll, the use of keyboards throughout is a tasteful addition to their ever-evolving sound. "Saving Grace" is an untraditional gem of a power ballad. —*Denise Sullivan*

Drugstore

f. 1993, London, England
Dream-Pop, Alternative Pop-Rock
Named in honor of filmmaker Gus Van Sant's indie classic *Drugstore Cowboy*, the dark, atmospheric British-based trio Drugstore formed in London in 1993. The group was led by vocalist/bassist Isabel Monteiro, an expatriate Brazilian who relocated to the UK in 1990. After singing in a number of short-lived groups, she eventually teamed with drummer and Los Angeles native Mike Chylinski, and soon Drugstore began to take shape. Claiming to hate her haunting, smoky voice, Monteiro insisted that the fledgling group test other singers, but when none of the auditions proved suitable, she grudgingly agreed to handle vocal chores.

After originating as a thrash outfit, Drugstore's sound gradually grew slower and more dreamy, hotwiring their music's languid psychedelic beauty with crashing waves of distortion and white noise. Instead of recording a demo, the group issued their debut single, "Alive," on their own Honey label in the spring of 1993. After a flurry of critical acclaim, the follow-up, "Modern Pleasure," appeared as an installment in the Rough Trade Singles Club series. Inviting guitarist Daron Robinson to join the group full-time, Drugstore soon signed to the Go-Discs! label; after issuing the *Starcrossed* EP at the beginning of 1995, their stunning self-titled debut album followed later in the year. —*Jason Ankeny*

Drugstore / 1995 / Go! Discs/London ✦✦✦
Drugstore is a bit more experimental and uptempo than Mazzy Star, but the musical style and Isabel Monteiro's vocals are so similar to Mazzy Star that one can't help but pigeonhole the band. This self-titled debut is a good album nevertheless. —*John Bush*

Ducks Deluxe

f. 1972, London, England
Rock 'n' Roll, Pub Rock
If the old scientific adage is true—that for every action there is an equal and opposite reaction—than British pub-rockers Ducks Deluxe were purely and simply a reaction. With the mid-'70s English pop scene dominated by glitter/glam-rockers like Gary Glitter and Sweet or blustery, chops-heavy art-rockers like Yes, Tull, Genesis, etc., Ducks Deluxe represented none of the above. One of the first pub-rock bands, the Ducks played basic American-style blues and boogie with remarkable panache and thorough disregard for the whims of the zeitgeist. They never were hugely popular, but the unpretentious, do-it-yourself, working-class attitude they and their contemporaries (most notably seminal pub-rockers Dr. Feelgood) exuded influenced the English punk scene that was right

around the corner. With friends like Dave Edmunds producing their records, the Ducks (guitarist/vocalist Sean Tyla, guitarist Martin Belmont, bassist Nick Garvey, and keyboardist Andy McMasters) came up with engaging, though not life-changing, records that celebrated the simple joys of rock 'n' roll. Sure, much of it sounds like recycled Chuck Berry, but there's an infectious enthusiasm that the fan in you, who simply wants to hoist a pint of lager and hear some Little Richard, will love. Ironically, to get the biggest promotional boost in America, the Ducks Deluxe LP was released three years after they'd split up. This little bit of shift marketing came as a result of ex-Ducks going on to more prominent bands like the Motors, the Rumour, and the Tyla Gang. —*John Dougan*

● **Ducks Deluxe/Taxi to the Terminal Zone** / 1974 / Edsel ✦✦✦✦
Both of the group's albums, *Ducks Deluxe* and *Taxi to the Terminal Zone*, compiled on one CD with one song from each removed to fit the format's time restriction—really a best-of, and worth any three Led Zeppelin albums. —*Bruce Eder*

Jumpin' / 1975 / Skydog ✦✦✦

All Too Much / 1975 / Skydog ✦✦✦✦
The final studio work by the band—Sean Tyla (vocals, guitar), Martin Belmont (guitar), Mick Groom (bass), and Tim Roper (drums)—is as good as anything the group ever did on RCA. This album, an expanded version of their *Jumpin'* EP from Skydog, opens up with a high-energy version of "I Fought the Law" that makes Bobby Fuller's original sound like the work of a high-school band. Two very different versions of "Something's Going On," a killer version of "Here Comes the Night," the romantic rocker "Amsterdam Dog" (highlighted by some great electric slide), the funky "Cannons of the Boogie Night," and the anthem-like "Rock and Roll for Every Boy and Girl" (which opens almost like a burlesque of the finale of the Who's "Won't Get Fooled Again") are some of the remaining highlights. The nine Ducks Deluxe tracks are rounded out with two lesser Sean Tyla-produced songs from Left Hand Drive, and all of it is played with a drive, passion, and precision that make *All Too Much* all-too-difficult to resist, especially as a standard price release. (Japanese import)—*Bruce Eder*

Don't Mind Rockin' Tonite / 1978 / RCA ✦✦✦
After RCA failed to do much for the band when the label released their self-titled debut record in 1974, the powers that be decided that this collection of material from their two previous LPs, along with some outtakes and B-sides, would engender more interest in the band now that they had some punk/new wave credibility. Well, it was a good thought, but it didn't work. Marketing avarice notwithstanding, this is a fine, loose-limbed, fast and funky record chock full of guitar bombs from Martin Belmont and some macho growling from Sean Tyla. The pure pop of "Love's Melody" (written by McMasters) is jarring in juxtaposition to all the blues-based grunting, but nothing detracts from the good vibe this record and the Ducks produced in their short existence. —*John Dougan*

Last Night of a Pub Rock Band / 1981 / Blue Moon ✦✦

Living on the Front Line / 1994 / Magnum ✦✦✦✦
This compilation (credited to "The Heroes of Pub Rock") opens with five tracks by Ducks Deluxe, two studio recordings (one the original version of "Somethin's Goin' On") and three decent sounding, intense live tracks (including renditions of "Little Queenie" and "Route 66") recorded at the band's farewell gig at the 100 Club in London, where they're joined by Nick Lowe, Lee Brilleaux, and Martin Stone. Also contains tracks by Nick Lowe, Mick Green, the Pirates, Wilko Johnson and the Lew Lewis Band, and Das Luftwaffegeschaft, all of whom are worthwhile in their own right. (British import) —*Bruce Eder*

The Dukes of Stratosphear

f. 1985, Swindon, England
Alternative Pop-Rock, Psychedelic, Neo-Psychedelia, Pop-Rock
In 1985 the British pop band XTC recorded an EP of affectionate parodies of '60s psychedelia and guitar-pop called *25 O'Clock*. Instead of releasing the EP under their own name, they released the record under the name the Dukes of Stratosphear. Working with producer John Leckie, all three members of the group adopted pseudonyms—Andy Partridge was Sir John Johns, Colin Moulding was the Red Curtain, and David Gregory was Lord Cornelius Plum. For this one project Gregory's brother Ian joined the band under the name Ian E.I.E.I. Owen. The EP was released without mention of XTC's name anywhere on the record, and the group claimed they had nothing to do with the project.
   Two years after the appearance of *25 O'Clock*, the Dukes of Stratosphear released a full album, *Psonic Psunspot*. By the time *Psonic Psunspot* appeared in 1987, XTC was beginning to admit in interviews that they were indeed the Dukes of Stratosphear. Later in 1987 both the EP and album were released on a single compact disc, *Chips from the Chocolate Fireball*. —*Stephen Thomas Erlewine*

● **Chips from the Chocolate Fireball** / 1987 / Geffen ✦✦✦✦
During the mid-'80s, XTC developed a deep fascination with '60s psychedelia that manifested itself on their late 1986 masterpiece *Skylarking*. While *Skylarking* was filled with lush pop reminiscent of the Beatles and the Beach Boys, it was generally a sober affair, since they decided to leave many of the lighter songs off the album for B-sides and future albums. During this time, they decided to develop their alter-egos of the Dukes of Stratosphear, which was a way to let all of their infatuation with psychedelia flourish. Both the EP *25 O'Clock* and the full-length *Psonic Psunspot*, collected on the single-disc *Chips from the Chocolate Fireball*, capture the sound of '60s psychedelia remarkably well. All of the sonic details, from the fuzz guitars to the cavernous echoes and sound effects, are in place, as are the self-consciously trippy lyrics. But what makes the Dukes of Stratosphear far more than a comedy band are the songs, which happen to be some of the best pure pop tunes that XTC ever wrote. "My Love Explodes" has a tense, spiraling guitar line and melody, "Little Lighthouse" and "You're My Drug" are wonderful pastiches, "The Mole from the Ministry" is a devilish homage to "I Am the Walrus" and Bowie, and the group rarely wrote a song as infectious as the bright, jangling "Vanishing Girl." Despite the clever craftsmanship, XTC has never sounded so carefree or effortless, and they've rarely been quite as immediately catchy or consistent. *Chips from the Chocolate Fireball* is too good to be overlooked as a side-project folly, because it truly is some of the best music XTC ever made. And, coincidentally, it's some of the best psychedelic pop ever recorded, as well. —*Stephen Thomas Erlewine*

The Duprees

f. 1962, Jersey City, NJ
Doo Wop
One of the final Italian doo wop groups to make a wave in the early '60s, the Duprees were in some senses not a rock 'n' roll act at all. They relied on updates of pre-rock pop standards for most of their material, dressed up in classy big-band arrangements. Their New Jersey street-corner roots were still audible in their doo wop harmonies, giving their treatments of moldy oldies enough of a contemporary flavor to compete in the rock and pop marketplace. They were very good at what they did, and in 1962-63, they were very successful. "You Belong to Me" (previously recorded by Jo Stafford, Patti Page, Dean Martin, *and* Joni James) made the Top Ten, and "My Own True Love" (from the soundtrack of *Gone with the Wind*), "Have You Heard," and "Why Don't You Believe Me" were also Top 40 hits. The Duprees were already retro when they were at their peak, and were washed out by the British Invasion, although they continued to record throughout the late '60s, sometimes in a Jay & the Americans/Vogues style. —*Richie Unterberger*

You Belong to Me / 1962 / Collectables ✦✦✦✦
Debut album, featuring the title track hit and 11 other doo wop classics done in typical early-'60s NYC production style. —*Cub Koda*

Have You Heard / 1963 / Sundazed ✦✦✦✦
Second album, companion piece to *You Belong to Me*. —*Cub Koda*

● **The Best of the Duprees [Rhino]** / Aug. 1990 / Rhino ✦✦✦✦
Eighteen songs from their 1962-64 recordings for the Coed label. Has all the hits, several flops and B-sides, a previously unreleased song, and a few album tracks, including one of the most stirring versions of "Exodus" ever committed to vinyl. —*Richie Unterberger*

The Best of the Duprees: Heritage Years / May 31, 1994 / Sequel ✦✦✦✦

● **Their Complete Coed Masters** / Mar. 19, 1996 / Ace ✦✦✦✦
If you're interested enough in the Duprees to invest in an album, you may as well cough up a few extra bucks for this import 31-song single-disc collection, which offers 13 more tracks than the domestic best-of on Rhino. It has everything they cut for Coed between 1962 and 1964, as well as a single that lead singer Joey Vann released in 1965 (rumored to have used the Duprees as backing vocalists). Their Coed output was very consistent, so fans of the group will find the additional material not present on the Rhino CD well worth acquiring. —*Richie Unterberger*

Duran Duran

f. 1978, Birmingham, England
Dance-Pop, Synth-Pop, New Wave, Pop-Rock, Club/Dance, New Romantic
Duran Duran personified New Wave for much of the mainstream audience. And for good reason, too. Duran Duran's reputation was built through music videos, which accentuated their fashion-model looks and glamourous sense of style. Without music videos, it is likely that the band's pop-funk—described by the group as the Sex Pistols meets Chic—would never have made the group international pop stars. While Duran Duran did have sharper pop sensibilities than their New Romantic contemporaries like Spandau Ballet and Ultravox, none of their peers exploited MTV and music video like the Birmingham-based quintet.

Each video the group made was distinctive, incorporating a number of cinematic styles to showcase the band as either part of the jet-setting elite ("Rio") or as worldly adventurers ("Hungry Like the Wolf"). While early videos like "Girls on Film" and "The Chauffeur" sparked controversy in England over their sexual content, their best-known clips were often based on hit contemporary movies. "Hungry Like the Wolf" uncannily recalled *Raiders of the Lost Ark*, while "Union of the Snake" and "The Wild Boys" brought to mind *The Road Warrior*. The clever videos helped make Duran Duran's rise to popularity remarkably swift. Between 1982 and 1984, they rocketed from underground British post-punk sensations to teen idols. But their fall from grace was equally fast. By the late '80s, the group's lineup had fragmented, and the remaining members had trouble landing hit singles. Nevertheless, the group pulled off a surprising, if short-lived, comeback in the early '90s as a sophisticated soft-rock trio.

Inspired by David Bowie and Roxy Music, as well as post-punk and disco, schoolmates Nick Rhodes (keyboards) and John Taylor (guitar) formed Duran Duran in 1978 with their friends Simon Colley (bass, clarinet) and Stephen Duffy (vocals). Taking their name from a character in Roger Vadim's psychedelic sci-fi film *Barbarella*, the group began playing gigs in the Birmingham club Barbarella, supported by a drum machine. Within a year, Duffy and Colley both left the group—Duffy would later form the Lilac Time—and were replaced by former TV Eye vocalist Andy Wickett and drummer Roger Taylor. After recording a demo, John Taylor switched to bass, and guitarist John Curtis joined the band, only to leave within a matter of months. The group placed an ad in *Melody Maker* that drew the attention of Andy Taylor, who became their guitarist, but Duran Duran was still having trouble finding a vocalist. After Wickett's departure in 1979, a pair of singers passed through the group before Simon LeBon, a former member of the punk band Dog Days and a drama student at Birmingham University, joined in early 1980.

By the end of 1980, Duran Duran had become popular within the burgeoning New Romantic circuit in England and had secured a record contract with EMI. "Planet Earth," the band's first single, quickly rose to No. 12 upon its spring 1981 release. Immediately Duran Duran became the leaders of the New Romantic movement, becoming a sensation in the British music and mainstream press. The group's popularity increased through their cutting-edge music videos, especially the bizarre, racy clip for "Girls on Film." Although the BBC banned the Godley & Creme-directed video, the single became the group's first Top Ten hit, setting the stage for the fall release of their eponymous debut album. *Duran Duran* reached No. 3 upon its release and stayed in the charts for 118 weeks. The band quickly followed the album with *Rio* in the spring of 1982. *Rio* entered the charts at No. 2, and its singles—"Hungry Like the Wolf" and "Save a Prayer"—became Top Ten hits. By the November release of the US-only remix EP *Carnival*, the band were superstars in Europe, but only just beginning to make headway in America. Their exposure in the US was helped greatly by the emergence of MTV, which put the group's stylish videos into heavy rotation. MTV's constant playing of the videos paid off, and "Hungry Like the Wolf" became a Top Ten hit early in 1983. *Rio* followed the single into the Top Ten, eventually selling over two million copies.

Duran Duran-mania was in full-swing across America, with "Is There Something I Should Know" reaching the Top Ten—it became the group's first English No. 1 that summer—and the group's first album climbing its way to No. 10. Duran Duran capitalized on their popularity by releasing *Seven and the Ragged Tiger* in time for 1983's holiday season. The record hit No. 1 in the UK and No. 8 in the US, spawning the hit singles "Union of the Snake" and "The Reflex," their first No. 1 US hit and their second British chart-topper. The band took an extended break after completing their year-and-a-half long international tour in the spring of 1984. In November they released the non-LP single "Wild Boys," which reached No. 2 in the UK and the US, where it was added to the live album *Arena*.

By 1985 Duran Duran fever was beginning to cool off, and after the band completed the title track for the James Bond film *A View to a Kill*, the group went on hiatus. Andy and John Taylor formed the supergroup the Power Station with vocalist Robert Palmer and former Chic drummer Tony Thompson in January, releasing their eponymous debut album in the spring; it spawned the Top Ten singles "Some Like It Hot" and "Get It On (Bang a Gong)." The remaining members of Duran Duran—Nick Rhodes, Simon LeBon, and Roger Taylor—responded with their own side project, Arcadia, which released an album called *So Red the Rose* in the fall of 1985; the album launched the Top Ten hit "Election Day." Early in 1986 Roger Taylor announced he was taking a year-long sabbatical from the group. He never returned. Several months later Andy Taylor also left, reducing Duran Duran to a trio. Late in 1986 the band released *Notorious*, their first album in nearly three years. While it was relatively successful, going platinum in the US and generating a Top Ten hit with the title track, it was noticeably less popular than their earlier records. For the remainder of the decade, Duran Duran's popular-

ity continually declined, with 1988's *Big Thing* producing "I Don't Want Your Love," their last Top Ten single for five years.

The greatest hits album *Decade* was released late in 1989, followed several months later by *Liberty*, the first Duran Duran album to fail to go gold. By that point, former Missing Persons guitarist Warren Cuccurullo had become a permanent member of the group. In 1993 the band returned from a prolonged hiatus with *Duran Duran*, a mature, layered record of lite funk and soulful adult contemporary pop that became a surprise hit. "Ordinary World" and "Come Undone" became Top Ten hits in America, with the former reaching the Top Ten in the UK as well; the album itself climbed into the Top Ten in both continents and went platinum in America. Not only did the record restore their commercial status, but it earned them some of the best reviews of their career. The group followed the album with one of their poorest-received efforts, the all-covers *Thank You*, that managed to go gold in America despite its negative reviews. While Duran Duran was recording the follow-up to *Thank You* in 1996, John Taylor left the band to pursue a solo career. *—Stephen Thomas Erlewine*

Duran Duran [First] / 1981 / Capitol ✦✦✦✦
Duran Duran's self-titled debut effectively established their slick, catchy synth-pop sound. Featuring the decadent "Girls on Film" and "Planet Earth," the album set the pace for scores of new wave bands in the early '80s, which were subsequently dubbed the new romantics. *—Stephen Thomas Erlewine*

Rio / 1982 / Capitol ✦✦✦✦
Rio was Duran Duran's breakthrough album, selling over two million copies in the United States. The album's success was helped immeasurably by a series of slick, big-budget videos that featured the band cavorting in various exotic locations. However, the music on the album was as noteworthy as the accompanying videos. *Rio* featured more ambitious arrangements, with the group pursuing a more dance-oriented direction without losing its sense of pop songcraft. With the hit singles "Hungry like the Wolf," "Rio" and "Save a Prayer" forming the core of the record, *Rio* stands as their best, most accomplished record. *—Stephen Thomas Erlewine*

Seven and the Ragged Tiger / 1983 / Capitol ✦✦✦
Seven and the Ragged Tiger was released at the height of Duran Duran-mania and it shows. Throughout the album, the group replicates the sound of *Rio*, yet they have failed to write strong material. Although they are catchy, the singles "Union of the Snake" and "The Reflex" aren't on par with "Hungry like the Wolf" and "Rio." Only the brooding "New Moon on Monday" matches the inspired pop-craft of *Rio*. *—Stephen Thomas Erlewine*

Arena / 1984 / Capitol ✦✦
Seeing Duran Duran in concert in 1984 was like seeing a video come to life. The group put on a spectacular show, filled with impressive light shows and videos. Since the concerts featured so many visuals, the band could not vary the tempos greatly, resulting in music that nearly replicated the studio versions of the songs. *Arena* accurately reproduces the sound and feeling of these concerts. Duran Duran sounds tight and professional (probably due to studio overdubbing), but Simon Le Bon sounds a little winded, maybe because of all the dancing he had to do during the course of the show. The new Nile Rodgers-produced single "The Wild Boys" was added to the album as bait and the strategy worked—peaking at No. 4, *Arena* was Duran Duran's highest-charting album and sold over two million copies. Nevertheless, it's the most inconsequential album in their entire catalog, even if it's fun. *—Stephen Thomas Erlewine*

Notorious / 1986 / Capitol ✦✦✦
After a brief hiatus, Duran Duran returned as a trio in 1986 with *Notorious*. The spare groove of the title track made it clear that the band was trying to shed its teeny-bopper image and refashion themselves as a pop band for yuppies. Thanks to Nile Rodgers' polished, radio-friendly production, *Notorious* was a success, as the band found a middle ground between synth-pop and white funk. *—Stephen Thomas Erlewine*

Big Thing / 1988 / Capitol ✦✦
Big Thing replicated the clean, mechanized funk of *Notorious*, yet the band failed to come up with a batch of strong songs. The naggingly catchy "I Don't Want Your Love" made it into the Top Ten, but the remainder of the album was bland and undistinguished. *—Stephen Thomas Erlewine*

● Decade: Greatest Hits / Nov. 15, 1989 / Capitol ✦✦✦✦
Decade is an excellent singles compilation, featuring all of the highlights from Duran Duran's heyday—"Planet of Earth," "Girls on Film," "Rio," "Is There Something I Should Know," "Union of the Snake," "The Reflex," "The Wild Boys," "Save a Prayer," "A View to a Kill"—plus late-'80s hits like "Notorious," "Skin Trade," "I Don't Want Your Love" and "All She Wants Is." By juxtaposing their stylish new wave pop against their latter-day lite-funk experiments, the group's decline becomes shockingly evident, but no other Duran Duran album sums up their

appeal like *Decade*, and it's hard to imagine another compilation working the same ground as effectively. —*Stephen Thomas Erlewine*

Liberty / Aug. 13, 1990 / Capitol ✦
Apart from the greatest-hits collection *Decade*, *Big Thing* was the lowest-charting Duran Duran album to date, prompting the band to rework their sound for 1990's *Liberty*. Unfortunately, the group had no idea what direction they wanted to pursue. *Liberty* features everything from disco to guitar rock, adding elements of Motown, Philly soul, and new wave along the way. The stylistic diversity might have worked if the band had material to support it, but nothing on the record matched their best work; it didn't even match the finest moments of *Big Thing*. —*Stephen Thomas Erlewine*

Duran Duran [1993] / 1993 / Capitol ✦✦✦✦
Duran Duran came back out of nowhere in early 1993 with a new album and a huge hit, "Ordinary World." The group sounds more relaxed and mature than it did during their glory days, but not all that much has changed; instead of personifying the days of early-'80s synthesized dance-pop, the music is smooth dance-pop for the '90s. Taken on its own terms, *Duran Duran* works every bit as well as *Duran Duran*, *Rio* or *Seven and the Ragged Tiger*. "Ordinary World" and "Come Undone" are wonderful pop singles that sit between some passable album tracks and the occasional embarrassment, namely the wretched cover of the Velvet Underground's "Femme Fatale." In other words, Duran Duran is back and as good as ever. —*Stephen Thomas Erlewine*

Thank You / Apr. 1995 / Parlophone/EMI ✦
An album of Duran Duran covering their "influences" was never something even the most dedicated fan wanted to hear, but the band had the audacity to record *Thank You*, a collection of the group's favorite songs. Featuring songwriters as diverse as Bob Dylan and Sly Stone, *Thank You* works best when the band realizes the monumental silliness of their cover, as on "White Lines," which is performed with Grandmaster Flash himself, and the acoustic blues rendition of Public Enemy's "911 Is a Joke." Or, it works when they can reinvent material like Lou Reed's "Perfect Day" into a slick MOR ballad. When *Thank You* doesn't work, it's because the band doesn't quite get what made the original version special ("Lay Lady Lay" and "Watching the Detectives"). Too many plain, mediocre songs (the Doors' "Crystal Ship") prevent the album from being either unintentionally funny or genuinely successful. The record is solely a curiosity and not a very interesting one at that. —*Stephen Thomas Erlewine*

Ian Dury

b. May 12, 1942, Upminster, Essex, England
Vocals / Disco, Rock 'n' Roll, New Wave, Pub Rock
Rock 'n' roll has always been populated by fringe figures, cult artists who managed to develop a fanatical following because of their outsized quirks, but few cult rockers have ever been quite as weird, or beloved, as Ian Dury. As the leader of the underappreciated and ill-fated pub-rockers Kilburn & the High Roads, Dury cut a striking figure; he remained handicapped from a childhood bout with polio, but stalked the stage with dynamic charisma, spitting out music-hall numbers and rockers in his thick Cockney accent. Dury was 28 at the time he formed Kilburn, and once they disbanded, conventional wisdom would have suggested that he was far too old to become a pop star, but conventional wisdom never played much of a role in Dury's career. Signing with the fledgling indie label Stiff in 1978, Dury developed a strange fusion of music-hall, punk rock, and disco that brought him to stardom in his native England. Driven by a warped sense of humor and a pulsating beat, singles like "Hit Me with Your Rhythm Stick," "Sex & Drugs & Rock & Roll," and "Reasons to Be Cheerful (Part 3)" became Top Ten hits in the UK, but Dury's most distinctive qualities—his dry wit and wordplay, thick Cockney brogue, and fascination with music hall—kept him from gaining popularity outside England. After his second album, Dury's style became formulaic, and he faded away in the early '80s, turning to an acting career instead.

At the age of seven, Ian Dury was stricken with polio. After spending two years in hospital, he attended a school for the physically handicapped. He attended the Royal College of Art, and after graduation he taught painting at the Canterbury Art College. In 1970, when he was 28 years old, Dury formed his first band, Kilburn & the High Roads. The Kilburns played simple, '50s rock 'n' roll, occasionally making a detour into jazz. Over the next three years, they became a fixture on England's pub-rock circuit. By 1973 their following was large enough that Dury could quit his teaching job. Several British critics became dedicated fans, and one of them, Charlie Gillett, became their manager. Gillett helped the band sign to the Warner subsidiary Raft, and the group recorded an album for the label in 1974. Warner refused to release the album, and after some struggling, the Kilburns broke away from Raft and signed with the Pye subsidiary Dawn in 1975. Dawn released *Handsome* in 1975, but by that point, the pub-rock scene was in decline, and

the album was ignored. Kilburn & the High Roads disbanded by the end of the year.

After the dissolution of the Kilburns, Dury continued to work with the band's pianist/guitarist, Chaz Jankel. By 1977 Dury had secured a contract with Stiff Records, and he recorded his debut with Jankel and a variety of pub-rock veterans—including former Kilburn Davey Payne—and session musicians. Stiff had Dury play the 1977 package tour *Live Stiffs* in order to support his debut album *New Boots and Panties!!*, so he and Jankel assembled the Blockheads, recruiting guitarist John Turnbull, pianist Mickey Gallagher, bassist Norman Watt Roy, and drummer Charley Charles. Dury and the Blockheads became a very popular act shortly after the *Live Stiffs* tour, and *New Boots and Panties!!* became a major hit, staying on the UK charts for nearly two years; it would eventually sell over a million copies worldwide. The album's first single, "What a Waste," reached the British Top Ten, while the subsequent non-LP single "Hit Me with Your Rhythm Stick" climbed all the way to No. 1.

Ian Dury had unexpectedly become a superstar in Britain, and American record companies were suddenly very interested in him. Arista won the rights to distribute Dury's Stiff recordings in the US, but despite overwhelmingly positive reviews, *New Boots and Panties!!* stiffed in America, and the label instantly dropped him. Despite his poor US sales, Dury was still riding high in his homeland, with his second album, *Do It Yourself*, entering the UK charts upon its summer release in 1979. Dury supported the acclaimed album, which saw him delving deeply into disco, with an extensive tour capped off by the release of the single "Reasons to Be Cheerful (Part 3)," which climbed to No. 3. Once the tour was completed, Jankel left the band and Dury replaced him with Wilko Johnson, former lead guitarist for Dr. Feelgood. With Johnson, Dury released his last Stiff album, *Laughter*, which received mixed reviews but respectable sales upon its 1980 release. The next year he signed with Polydor Records and reunited with Jankel. The pair flew to the Bahamas to record his Polydor debut with reggae superstars Sly Dunbar and Robbie Shakespeare. The resulting album, *Lord Upminster*, received mixed reviews and poor sales upon its 1981 release; the album was notable for the inclusion of the single "Spasticus Autisticus," a song that Dury wrote for the United Nations Year of the Disabled, but it was rejected.

After the failure of *Lord Upminster*, Dury quietly backed away from a recording career and began to concentrate on acting. 1984's *4000 Weeks Holiday*, an album recorded with his new band, the Music Students, was his last major record of the '80s. He appeared in several plays and television shows, as well as the Peter Greenaway film *The Cook, the Thief, His Wife and Her Lover* and Roman Polanski's movie *Pirates*. He also began to write jingles for British commercials. In 1989 he wrote the musical *Apples* with Mickey Gallagher, and he appeared in the stage production of the play. Dury returned to recording in 1992 with *The Bus Driver's Prayer and Other Stories*. —*Stephen Thomas Erlewine*

New Boots and Panties!! / 1977 / Edsel ✦✦✦✦
Ian Dury's primary appeal lies in his lyrics, which are remarkably clever sketches of British life delivered with a wry wit. Since Dury's accent is thick and his language dense with local slang, much of these pleasures aren't discernable to casual listeners, leaving the music to stand on its own merits. On his debut album, *New Boots and Panties!*, Dury's music is at its best, and even that is a bizarrely uneven fusion of pub-rock, punk rock and disco. Still, Dury's off-kilter charm and irrepressible energy make the album gel, with the disco pulse of "Wake Up and Make Love With Me" making perfect sense next to the gentle tribute "Sweet Gene Vincent," the roaring punk of "Blockheads" and the revamped music-hall of "Billericay Dickie" and "My Old Man." [Repertoire's 1996 CD reissue adds five essential singles—"Sex and Drugs and Rock and Roll," "Razzle in My Pocket," "You're More Than Fair," "England's Glory," "What a Waste"—that nearly make the disc a Dury best-of.] —*Stephen Thomas Erlewine*

Do It Yourself / 1979 / Edsel ✦✦✦✦
Ian Dury's music always bordered on the functional, since it was used as a backdrop for his wry vignettes and stories, but on his second album *Do It Yourself*, that aspect came to the fore. Largely abandoning the punk inflections that were scattered throughout *New Boots and Panties!*, *Do It Yourself* is a record of midtempo pub-rock disco—competently played, but rarely engaging. Dury's stories are all wonderful, filled with humor and penetrating detail, but only a handful of tracks, such as the terrific "Inbetweenies," are married to actual hooks, and by the end of the record, the steady disco throb has become a little numbing. Even with these faults, *Do It Yourself* remains one of Dury's very best records, since his lyrical facility throughout the album is simply amazing. [Repertoire's 1996 CD reissue of *Do It Yourself* improves the album considerably by adding several singles—"Hit Me with Your Rhythm Stick," "There Ain't Half Been Some Clever Bastards," "Reasons to Be Cheerful, Part 3," "Common as Muck," "I Want to Be Straight"—that are far more successful disco/pub-rock fusions than anything on the album.] —*Stephen Thomas Erlewine*

Laughter / 1980 / Stiff ✦✦✦

Working with lead guitarist Wilko Johnson (Dr. Feelgood), Ian Dury gradually moves away from disco with his third album, *Laughter*. The steady dance pulse is still apparent, but it's balanced by rockers and pub singalongs that give the album more depth. That doesn't necessarily make it a better album, however. Dury's humor is at its most basic, as the titles of "Uncoolohol," "Take Your Elbow Out of the Soup You're Sitting on the Chicken," "Oh Mr. Peanut" and "Fucking Ada" indicate, and his lyrics aren't quite as stunningly fluid as before. Still, the record is fun, and "Superman's Big Sister," "Yes & No (Paula)" and "Over the Points" are pretty infectious, but the record can't help but illustrate that Dury's peak period is over. —*Stephen Thomas Erlewine*

● **Jukebox Dury** / 1981 / Stiff ✦✦✦✦

Although Ian Dury's albums all had their share of highpoints, he functioned best as a singles artist, and *Jukebox Dury* is the definitive single collection. Not only are his four Top 40 hits all featured ("What a Waste," "Hit Me with Your Rhythm Stick," "Reasons to Be Cheerful (Pt. 3)," "I Want to Be Straight"), but so are Stiff singles and album tracks like "Wake Up and Make Love to Me," "Razzle in My Pocket," "Common as Muck," "Inbetweenies," "Sweet Gene Vincent" and "Sex & Drugs & Rock & Roll"—in other words, it has every essential song Dury ever recorded. Rhino's *Sex & Drugs & Rock & Roll* compilation used this as its foundation, but it eliminated two of its best songs, "Wake Up" and "Sweet Gene Vincent," and added several other tracks to give it a more comprehensive overview, but *Juke Box Dury*, with its concise 12 tracks, remains the one defintive compilation. —*Stephen Thomas Erlewine*

Lord Upminster / Nov. 1981 / Polydor ✦✦✦

When Ian Dury left Stiff Records, he also left the Blockheads behind, recording *Lord Upminster* with reggae superstars Robbie Shakespeare and Sly Dunbar as producers. *Lord Upminster* turned out to be a set of uninspired funk that lacks the joyful energy of his three previous records. —*Stephen Thomas Erlewine*

4000 Weeks Holiday / 1984 / Polydor ✦✦

4000 Weeks Holiday suffers from a polished, radio-ready production that is entirely devoted to Ian Dury's fascination with disco and lite-funk. Over these slick backing tracks, Dury runs through a familiar litany of working-class anthems, love songs, social commentaries, and bad jokes, all delivered with noticeably less inspiration than before. Despite a couple of bright moments, *4000 Weeks Holiday* represents Dury at a creative nadir. —*Stephen Thomas Erlewine*

Apples / 1989 / WEA ✦✦✦

Rebounding after the tepid *4000 Weeks Holiday*, Ian Dury delivers the low-key and thoroughly charming *Apples*. Although the music is considerably more relaxed than any other Dury album, it's the perfect backdrop for Dury's clever, literate stories, which resonate with great humor and detail. *Apples* may lack a stand-out song or melody, but the whole of the record is quite engaging, and it represents a respectable and modest comeback for Dury. —*Stephen Thomas Erlewine*

The Bus Driver's Prayer and Other Stories / 1992 / Edsel ✦✦✦

Picking up where *Apples* left off—it even includes that record's "The Bus Driver's Prayer," a clever Cockney rewrite of the Lord's Prayer, as the title track—*The Bus Driver's Prayer and Other Stories* is an engaging collection of character sketches and stories from Ian Dury. The album may lack strong hooks and melodies, yet Dury diehards will find that his wry observations are just as subtle and humorous as ever. —*Stephen Thomas Erlewine*

● **Sex & Drugs & Rock & Roll: Best of Ian Dury and the Blockheads** / Apr. 28, 1992 / Rhino ✦✦✦✦

Everything you'd ever want in one package. This does an excellent job of combining Dury's rock with his slippery funk/disco and does so in such a way that it sounds perfectly natural. Every home should have a copy of the song "Sex & Drugs & Rock & Roll," but a big plus is having the salacious and horny "Wake Up and Make Love with Me." Durable, funny, and energetic to the core, this is indispensable. —*John Dougan*

Bob Dylan

b. May 24, 1941, Duluth, MN

Guitar, Harmonica, Piano, Keyboards, Vocals / Rock 'n' Roll, Country-Rock, Singer-Songwriter, Folk-Rock, Folk

Bob Dylan's influence on popular music is incalculable. As a songwriter, he pioneered several different schools of pop songwriting, from confessional singer-songwriter to winding, hallucinatory, stream-of-consciousness narratives. As a vocalist, he broke down the notions that in order to perform, a singer had to have a conventionally good voice, thereby redefining the role of vocalist in popular music. As a musician, he sparked several genres of pop music, including electricfied folk-rock and country-rock. And that just touches on the tip of his achievements. Dylan's force was evident during the height of his popularity in the '60s—the Beatles' shift toward introspective songwriting in the mid-'60s never would have happened without him—but his influence echoed through-

out several subsequent generations. Many of his songs became popular standards, and his best albums were undisputed classics of the rock 'n' roll canon. Dylan's influence on folk music was equally powerful, and he marks a turning point in its 20th century evolution, as the genre moved away from traditional songs and toward personal songwriting. Even when his sales declined in the '80s and '90s, Dylan's presence was calculable.

For a figure of such substantial influence, Dylan came from humble beginnings. Born in Duluth, MN, Bob Dylan (b. Robert Allen Zimmerman, May 24, 1941) was raised in Hibbing, MN, from the age of six. As a child he learned to play guitar and harmonica, forming a rock 'n' roll band called the Golden Chords when he was in high school. After graduation in 1959, he began studying art at the University of Minnesota in Minneapolis. While at college, he began performing folk songs at coffeehouses under the name Bob Dylan, taking his last name from the poet Dylan Thomas. Already inspired by Hank Williams and Woody Guthrie, Dylan began listening to blues while at college, and the genre wove its way into his music. Dylan spent the summer of 1960 in Denver, where he met bluesman Jesse Fuller, the inspiration behind the songwriter's signature harmonica rock and guitar. By the time he returned to Minneapolis in the fall, he had grown substantially as a performer and was determined to become a professional musician.

Dylan made his way to New York City in January 1961, immediately making a substantial impression on the folk community of Greenwich Village. He began visiting his idol Guthrie in the hospital, where he was slowly dying from Huntington's chorea. Dylan also began performing in coffeehouses, and his rough charisma won him a significant following. In April he opened for John Lee Hooker at Gerde's Folk City. Five months later, Dylan performed another concert at the venue, which was reviewed positively by Robert Shelton in the *New York Times*. Columbia A&R man John Hammond sought out Dylan on the strength of the review and signed the songwriter in the fall of 1961. Hammond produced Dylan's eponymous debut album (released in March 1962), a collection of folk and blues standards that boasted only two original songs. Over the course of 1962, Dylan began to write a large batch of original songs, many of which were political protest songs in the vein of his Greenwich contemporaries. These songs were showcased on his second album, *The Freewheelin' Bob Dylan*. Before its release, *Freewheelin'* went through several incarnations. Dylan had recorded a rock 'n' roll single, "Mixed Up Confusion," at the end of 1962, but his manager Albert Grossman made sure the record was deleted because he wanted to present Dylan as an acoustic folkie. Similarly, several tracks with a full backing band that were recorded for *Freewheelin'* were scrapped before the album's release. Furthermore, several tracks recorded for the album—including "Talking John Birch Society Blues"—were eliminated from the album before its release.

Comprised entirely of original songs, *The Freewheelin' Bob Dylan* made a huge impact in the US folk community, and many performers began covering songs from the album. Of these, the most significant were Peter, Paul & Mary, who made "Blowin' in the Wind" into a huge pop hit in the summer of 1963 and thereby made Bob Dylan into a recognizable household name. On the strength of Peter, Paul & Mary's cover and his opening gigs for popular folkie Joan Baez, *Freewheelin'* became a hit in the fall of 1963, climbing to No. 22 on the charts. By that point, Baez and Dylan had become romantically involved, and she was beginning to record his songs frequently. Dylan was writing just as fast, and was performing hundreds of concerts a year.

By the time *The Times They Are A-Changin'* was released in early 1964, Dylan's songwriting had developed far beyond that of his New York peers. Heavily inspired by poets like Arthur Rimbaud and John Keats, his writing took on a more literate and evocative quality. Around the same time, he began to expand his musical boundaries, adding more blues and R&B influences to his songs. Released in the fall of 1964, *Another Side of Bob Dylan* made these changes evident. However, Dylan was moving faster than his records could indicate. By the end of 1964, he had ended his romantic relationship with Baez and had begun dating a former model named Sara Lowndes. Simultaneously, he gave the Byrds "Mr. Tambourine Man" to record for their debut album. The Byrds gave the song a ringing, electric arrangement, but by the time the single became a hit, Dylan was already exploring his own brand of folk-rock. Inspired by the British Invasion, particularly the Animals' version of "House of the Rising Sun," Dylan recorded a set of original songs backed by a loud rock 'n' roll band for his next album. While *Bringing It All Back Home* (spring, 1965) still had a side of acoustic material, it made clear that Dylan had turned his back on folk music. For the folk audience, the true breaking point arrived a few months after the album's release, when he played the Newport Folk Festival supported by the Paul Butterfield Blues Band. The audience greeted him with vicious derision, but he had already been accepted by the growing rock 'n' roll community, as well as the mainstream press, who were fascinated by his witty, surreal, and caustic press confences. Dylan's spring tour of Britain was the basis for D.A. Pennebaker's documentary *Don't Look Back*, a film that captures the songwriter's edgy charisma and charm.

Dylan made his breakthrough to the pop audience in the summer of 1965, when "Like a Rolling Stone" became a No. 2 hit. Driven by a circular organ riff and a steady beat, the six-minute single broke the barrier of the three-minute pop single. Dylan became the subject of innumerable articles, and his lyrics became the subject of literary analysis across the US and UK. Well over 100 artists covered his songs between 1964 and 1966; the Byrds and the Turtles, in particular, had big hits with his compositions. *Highway 61 Revisited*, his first full-fledged rock 'n' roll album, became a Top Ten hit upon its fall 1965 release. "Positively 4th Street" and "Rainy Day Women No.12 & 35" became Top Ten hits in the fall of 1965 and spring of 1966, respectively. After the spring 1966 release of the double-album *Blonde On Blonde*, he had sold over 10 million records around the world.

During the fall of 1965, Dylan hired the Hawks, formerly Ronnie Hawkins' backing group, as his touring band. The Hawks, who would change their name to the Band in 1968, would become Dylan's most famous backing band, primarily because of their intuitive chemistry and "wild, thin mercury sound," but also because of their British tour in the spring of 1966. The tour was the first time Britain had heard the electric Dylan, and their reaction was disagreeable and violent. At the tour's penultimate date—usually referred as the Royal Albert Hall concert, but generally acknowledged to have occured in Manchester—an audience member called Dylan "Judas," inspiring a positively vicious version of "Like a Rolling Stone" from the Band. The performance was immortalized on bootleg albums, and it indicates the intensity of Dylan in the middle of 1966. He had assumed control of Pennebaker's second Dylan documentary, *Eat the Document*, and was under deadline to complete his book *Tarantula*, as well as record a new record. After the British tour, he returned to America.

On July 29, 1966, he was injured in a motorcycle accident outside of his hometown, Woodstock, NY, suffering injuries to his neck vertebrae and a concussion. Details of the accident remain elusive; although he was reportedly in critical condition for a week and had amnesia, some biographers have questioned its severity. The event was a turning point in his career. After the accident, Dylan became a recluse, disappearing into his home in Woodstock and raising his family with his wife, Sara. After a few months, he retreated with the Band to a rented house, subsequently dubbed Big Pink, in Bearsville to record a number of demos. For several months, Dylan and the Band recorded an enormous amount of material, ranging from old folk, country, and blues songs to newly-written originals. The songs indicated that Dylan's songwriting had undergone a metamorphosis, becoming streamlined and more direct. Similarly, his music had changed, owing less to traditional rock 'n' roll, and demonstrating heavy country, blues, and traditional folk influences. None of the Big Pink recordings were intended to be released, but tapes from the sessions were circulated by Dylan's music publisher with the intent of generating cover versions. Copies of these tapes, as well as other songs, were available on illegal bootleg albums by the end of the '60s; it was the first time that bootleg copies of unreleased recordings had been widely circulated. Portions of the tapes were officially released in 1975 as the double-album *The Basement Tapes*.

While Dylan was in seclusion, rock 'n' roll had become heavier and artier in the wake of the psychedelic revolution. When Dylan returned with *John Wesley Harding* in December 1967, its quiet, country ambience was a surprise to the general public, but it was a significant hit, peaking at No. 2 in the US and No. 1 in the UK. Furthermore, the record arguably became the first significant country-rock record to be released, setting the stage for efforts by the Byrds and the Flying Burrito Brothers later that year. Dylan followed his country inclinations on his next album, 1969's *Nashville Skyline*, which was recorded in Nashville with several of the country industry's top session men. While the album was a hit, spawning the Top Ten single "Lay Lady Lay," it was criticized in some quarters for uneven material. The mixed reception was the beginning of a full-blown backlash that arrived with the double album *Self Portrait*. Released early in 1970, the album was a hodge-podge of covers, live tracks, reinterpretations, and new songs that was greeted with vicious reviews from all quarters of the press. Dylan followed the album quickly with *New Morning*, which was hailed as a comeback.

After release of *New Morning*, Dylan began to wander restlessly. In 1971, he moved back to Greenwich Village, published *Tarantula* for the first time, and performed at the Concert for Bangladesh; it would be his only live performance in the first half of the decade. During 1972 he began an acting career by playing Alias in Sam Peckinpah's *Pat Garrett and Billy the Kid*, which was released in 1973. He also wrote the soundtrack for the film, which featured "Knockin' on Heaven's Door," his biggest hit since "Lay Lady Lay." The *Pat Garrett* soundtrack was the final record released under his Columbia contract before he moved to David Geffen's fledgling Asylum Records. As retaliation, Columbia assembled *Dylan*, a collection of *Self Portrait* outtakes, for release at the

end of 1973. Dylan recorded only one album, 1974's *Planet Waves*—coincidentally his first No. 1 album—before he moved back to Columbia. The Band supported Dylan on *Planet Waves* and its accompanying tour, which became the most successful tour in rock 'n' roll history; it was captured on 1974's double-live album, *Before the Flood*.

Dylan's 1974 tour was the beginning of a comeback culminated by 1975's *Blood on the Tracks*. Largely inspired by the disintegration of his marriage, *Blood on the Tracks* was hailed as a return to form and it became his second No. 1 album. After jamming with folkies in Greenwich Village, Dylan decided to launch a gigantic tour, loosely based on traveling medicine shows. Lining up an extensive list of supporting musicians—including Joan Baez, Joni Mitchell, Ramblin' Jack Elliott, Arlo Guthrie, Mick Ronson, Roger McGuinn, and poet Allen Ginsberg—Dylan dubbed the tour the Rolling Thunder Revue and set out on the road in the fall of 1975. For the next year the Rolling Thunder Revue toured on and off, with Dylan filming many of the concerts. During the tour, *Desire* was released to considerable acclaim and success, spending five weeks on the top of the charts. Throughout the Rolling Thunder Revue, Dylan showcased "Hurricane," a protest song he had written about boxer Rubin Carter, who had been imprisoned for murder. The live album *Hard Rain* was released at the end of the tour. Dylan released *Renaldo and Clara*, a four-hour film based on the Rolling Thunder tour, to poor reviews in early 1978.

Early in 1978, Dylan set out on another extensive tour, this time backed by a band that resembled a Las Vegas lounge band. The group was featured on the 1978 album *Street Legal* and the 1979 live album *At Budokan*. At the conclusion of the tour in 1979, Dylan announced that he was a born-again Christian, and he launched a series of Christian albums that fall with *Slow Train Coming*. Though the reviews were mixed, the album was a success, peaking at No. 3 and going platinum. His supporting tour for *Slow Train Coming* featured only his new religious material, much to the bafflement of his long-term fans. Two other religious albums—*Saved* (1980) and *Shot of Love* (1981)—followed, both to poor reviews. In 1982 Dylan traveled to Israel, sparking rumors that his conversion to Christianity was short-lived. He returned to secular recording with 1983's *Infidels*, which was greeted with favorable reviews.

Dylan returned to performing in 1984, releasing the live album *Real Live* at the end of the year. *Empire Burlesque* in 1985, but its odd mix of dance tracks and rock 'n' roll won few fans. However, the five-album/triple-disc retrospective box set *Biograph* appeared that same year to great acclaim. In 1986 Dylan hit the road with Tom Petty & the Heartbreakers for a successful and acclaimed tour, but his album that year, *Knocked Out Loaded*, was received poorly. The next year he toured with the Grateful Dead as his backing band; two years later, the souvenir album *Dylan & the Dead* appeared.

In 1988 Dylan embarked on what became known as "The Never-Ending Tour"—a constant stream of shows that ran on and off into the late '90s. That same year he released *Down in the Groove*, an album largely comprised of covers. The Never-Ending Tour received far stronger reviews than *Down in the Groove*, but 1989's *Oh Mercy* was his most-acclaimed album since 1974's *Blood on the Tracks*. However, his 1990 followup, *Under the Red Sky*, was received poorly, especially when compared to the enthusiastic reception for the 1991 box set *The Bootleg Series, Vol. 1-3 (Rare & Unreleased)*.

For the remainder of the '90s, Dylan divided his time between live concerts and painting. In 1992 he returned to recording with *Good As I Been to You*, an acoustic collection of traditional folk songs. It was followed in 1993 by another folk album, *World Gone Wrong*, which won the Grammy for Best Traditional Folk Album. After the release of *World Gone Wrong*, Dylan released a greatest hits album and a live record. —*Stephen Thomas Erlewine*

Bob Dylan / Mar. 19, 1962 / Columbia ✦✦✦
For the most part, Bob Dylan's debut album positions him as an interpretive singer of rural folk songs, and already influential at that. Led Zeppelin borrowed "In My Time of Dyin'," but the most striking track is the Dylan original "Song to Woody," his tribute to Woody Guthrie, which leaves no doubt he intends to carry on in his mentor's footsteps. —*William Ruhlmann*

☆ **The Freewheelin' Bob Dylan** / May 27, 1963 / Columbia ✦✦✦✦✦
The most important collection of original songs issued in the '60s. "Don't Think Twice, It's All Right," "Girl from the North Country," "A Hard Rain's A-Gonna Fall," "Masters of War," and, especially, "Blowin' in the Wind" have long since become standards, and their sheer range, from bitter protest to wry romantic regret, is astonishing, not to mention the absurd apocalyptic humor of some of the album's other tracks. The songs were so strong that they put across Dylan's limited, rough vocal style at a time when such a voice normally would have seemed completely unacceptable in a professional singer. This album transformed the notion of what "good" singing was. —*William Ruhlmann*

The Times They Are A-Changin' / Jan. 13, 1964 / Columbia ✦✦✦✦
Dylan devoted most of his third album to hard, uncompromising topical or "protest" songs, starting with the anthemic title track and continuing through "The Lonesome Death of Hattie Carroll," "Ballad of Hollis Brown," "Only a Pawn in Their Game," and "With God on Our Side."
— *William Ruhlmann*

☆ **Another Side of Bob Dylan** / Aug. 8, 1964 / Columbia ✦✦✦✦✦
The first of two transitional albums in which Dylan moved beyond protest, and then beyond folk music. Here, in songs like "Chimes of Freedom" and "My Back Pages," he suggested that social issues were much more complicated than the increasingly polarized times made them seem. His lyrics, meanwhile, also became more complicated and poetic. Other singers would mine this album for hits with "All I Really Want to Do" and "It Ain't Me, Babe." — *William Ruhlmann*

☆ **Bringing It All Back Home** / Mar. 22, 1965 / Columbia ✦✦✦✦✦
Dylan added a bluesy rock-band backing for the first half of this album, and the lyrics of the new songs are compendiums of allusions and witticisms—"Subterranean Homesick Blues," "Maggie's Farm," "Mr. Tambourine Man," "It's All Right, Ma (I'm Only Bleeding)." Even the love songs achieve a new poetic height—"She Belongs to Me," "Love Minus Zero/No Limit," "It's All Over Now, Baby Blue." — *William Ruhlmann*

☆ **Highway 61 Revisited** / Aug. 30, 1965 / Columbia ✦✦✦✦✦
Taking the first, electric side of *Bringing It All Back Home* to its logical conclusion, Bob Dylan hired a full rock 'n' roll band, featuring guitarist Michael Bloomfield, for *Highway 61 Revisited*. Opening with the epic "Like a Rolling Stone," *Highway 61 Revisited* careens through nine songs that range from reflective folk-rock ("Desolation Row") and blues ("It Takes a Lot to Laugh, It Takes a Train to Cry") to flat-out garage rock ("Tombstone Blues," "From a Buick 6," "Highway 61 Revisited"). Dylan had not only changed his sound, but his persona, trading the folk troubadour for a streetwise, cynical hipster. Throughout the album, he alternates between druggy, surreal imagery, which can have a sense of either menace or beauty, and the music reflects that, jumping between soothing melodies and hard, bluesy rock. And that is the most revolutionary thing about *Highway 61 Revisited*—it proved that rock 'n' roll needn't be collegiate and learned in order to be literate, poetic, and complex. — *Stephen Thomas Erlewine*

☆ **Blonde on Blonde** / May 16, 1966 / Columbia ✦✦✦✦✦
If *Highway 61 Revisited* played as a garage rock record, the double album *Blonde on Blonde* inverted that sound, blending blues, country, rock, and folk into a wild, careening, and dense sound. Replacing the fiery Michael Bloomfield with the intense, weaving guitar of Robbie Robertson, Dylan led a group comprised of his touring band the Hawks and session musicians through his richest set of songs. *Blonde on Blonde* is an album of enormous depth, providing endless lyrical and musical revelations on each play. Leavening the edginess of *Highway 61* with a sense of the absurd, *Blonde on Blonde* is comprised entirely of songs driven by inventive, surreal, and witty wordplay, not only on the rockers but on winding, moving ballads like "Visions of Johanna," "Just like a Woman," and "Sad Eyed Lady of the Lowlands." Throughout the record, the music matches the inventiveness of the songs, filled with cutting guitar riffs, liquid organ riffs, crisp pianos, and even woozy brass bands ("Rainy Day Women No.12 & 35"). It's the culmination of Dylan's electric rock 'n' roll period; he would never again release a studio record that rocked this hard, or had such bizarre imagery. — *Stephen Thomas Erlewine*

★ **Bob Dylan's Greatest Hits** / Mar. 27, 1967 / Columbia ✦✦✦✦✦
A ten-song retrospective of the work of the most impressive—and most protean—singer-songwriter of the period 1963 to 1966. Please note that, while this album is listed as the "pick" of this period of Dylan's career due to its general accessibility, a full understanding of the popular music of the '60s is impossible unless the listener is familiar with its three predecessors. *Greatest Hits* combines folk-protest standards like "Blowin' in the Wind" and "The Times They Are A-Changin'" with his folk-rock hits "Like a Rolling Stone" and "Rainy Day Women No.12 & 35." — *William Ruhlmann*

☆ **John Wesley Harding** / Dec. 27, 1967 / Columbia ✦✦✦✦✦
Bob Dylan returned from exile with *John Wesley Harding*, a quiet, country-tinged album that split dramatically from his previous three albums. A calm, reflective album, *John Wesley Harding* strips away all of the wilder tendencies of Dylan's rock albums—even the then-unreleased *Basement Tapes* he made the previous year—but it isn't a return to his folk roots. If anything, the album is his first serious foray into country, but only a handful of songs, such as "I'll Be Your Baby Tonight," are straight country songs. Instead, *John Wesley Harding* is informed by the rustic sound of country, as well as many rural myths, with seemingly simple songs like "All Along the Watchtower," "I Dreamed I Saw St. Augustine" and "The Wicked Messenger" revealing several layers of meanings with repeated plays. Although the lyrics are somewhat enigmatic, the music is simple, direct and melodic, providing a touchstone

for the country-rock revolution that swept through rock in the late '60s. — *Stephen Thomas Erlewine*

☆ **Nashville Skyline** / Apr. 9, 1969 / Columbia ✦✦✦✦✦
John Wesley Harding suggested country with its textures and structures, but *Nashville Skyline* was a full-fledged country album, complete with steel guitars and brief, direct songs. It's a warm, friendly album, particularly since Dylan is singing in a previously unheard gentle croon; the sound of his voice is so different it may be disarming upon first listen, but it suits the songs. While there are a handful of lightweight numbers on the record, at its core are several excellent songs—"Lay Lady Lay," "To Be Alone with You," "I Threw It All Away," "Tonight I'll Be Staying Here with You," as well as a duet with Johnny Cash on "Girl from the North Country"—that have become country-rock standards. And there's no discounting that *Nashville Skyline*, arriving in the spring of 1969, established country-rock as a vital force in pop music, as well as a commercially viable genre. — *Stephen Thomas Erlewine*

Self-Portrait / Jun. 8, 1970 / Columbia ✦✦
That Dylan was suffering writer's block should have been apparent from the skimpy *Nashville Skyline*, but he shocked his following by turning out this two-record set devoted mostly to covers of songs by the Everly Brothers and Simon and Garfunkel. A few tracks were drawn from Dylan's concert performance at the Isle of Wight on Aug. 31, 1969, and they proved ragged. For an audience accustomed to Dylan's classic '60s albums, this first album of the '70s was a crushing disappointment. — *William Ruhlmann*

New Morning / Oct. 21, 1970 / Columbia ✦✦✦✦
Dylan rushed out *New Morning* in the wake of the commercial and critical disaster *Self Portrait*, and the difference between the two albums suggests that its legendary failed predecessor was intentionally flawed. *New Morning* expands on the laidback country-rock of *John Wesley Harding* and *Nashville Skyline* by adding a more pronounced rock 'n' roll edge. While there are only a couple of genuine classics on the record ("If Not for You," "One More Weekend"), the overall quality is quite high, and many of the songs explore idiosyncratic routes Dylan had previously left untouched, whether it's the jazzy experiments of "Sign on the Window" and "Winterlude," the rambling spoken-word piece "If Dogs Run Free," or the Elvis parable "Went to See the Gypsy." Such offbeat songs make *New Morning* a charming, endearing record. — *Stephen Thomas Erlewine*

★ **Bob Dylan's Greatest Hits, Vol. 2** / Nov. 17, 1971 / Columbia ✦✦✦✦✦
Where Dylan's first *Greatest Hits* took its title literally, *Greatest Hits, Vol. 2* is a greatest hits album only in the loosest sense of the term. While the double album does contain several genuine hits—"Lay Lady Lay," "Tonight I'll Be Staying Here with You," the non-LP "Watching the River Flow"—it is largely comprised of album tracks that became classics, either through Dylan's own version or through covers. These include "Don't Think Twice, It's All Right," "All I Really Want to Do," "My Back Pages," "Maggie's Farm," "She Belongs to Me," "If Not for You," "Just like Tom Thumb's Blues," among many others. There are also a number of rarities scattered throughout the 21 songs, including a live version of "Tomorrow Is a Long Time" from 1963, a live take of "The Mighty Quinn (Quinn, the Eskimo)" and the *Basement Tapes* songs "I Shall Be Released," "Down in the Flood," and "You Ain't Goin' Nowhere." While some of the cuts may not be immediately familiar to some listeners, *Greatest Hits, Vol. 2* in many ways is a more accurate picture of the depth and breadth of Dylan's talents, making it an excellent introduction. And it's not just for casual fans, because the rarities and sequencing are revealing for even devoted Dylan fans. — *Stephen Thomas Erlewine*

Pat Garrett & Billy the Kid [soundtrack] / Jul. 13, 1973 / Columbia ✦✦
Dylan's soundtrack for this Sam Peckinpah-directed Western in which he co-starred consists of some folkish instrumentals, several takes of a ballad called "Billy," and "Knockin' on Heaven's Door," a simple song that has become one of his best-remembered compositions. — *William Ruhlmann*

Dylan / Nov. 16, 1973 / Columbia ✦
Commonly regarded as the worst album in Bob Dylan's catalog, *Dylan* is a collection of nine outtakes from the *Self Portrait* album Columbia assembled after the singer briefly jumped ship for David Geffen's fledgling Asylum Records. Dylan didn't want the record to be released, and it's easy to see why; it is a collection of covers that are poorly performed on purpose. Tackling both contemporary writers (Joni Mitchell's "Big Yellow Taxi," Jerry Jeff Walker's "Mr. Bojangles"), pop songs ("Can't Help Falling in Love," "A Fool Such as I"), and traditional numbers ("The Ballad of Ira Hayes," "Spanish Is the Loving Tongue"), Dylan attempts to sabotage each number, but none of the results is quite so shocking, or funny, as the deconstructions on *Self Portrait*. While *Dylan* is indeed a negligible album, it isn't unlistenable; it has a pleasant pop-rock sheen, and Dylan sings in his *Nashville Skyline* croon. Nevertheless, it adds nothing to his canon, and only diehard fans with a perverse sense of humor will find the record worth a listen. — *Stephen Thomas Erlewine*

Planet Waves / Jan. 17, 1974 / Columbia ✦✦✦
A companion work to its predecessor, *New Morning*, this first album to be recorded with Dylan's backup group, the Band, mixes pronouncements of marital and familial contentment with severe criticisms of the singer himself and others. Contains "Forever Young." — *William Ruhlmann*

Before the Flood / Jun. 20, 1974 / Columbia ✦✦✦
This double album chronicles Bob Dylan and the Band's US tour of January and February 1974. It features souped-up performances of many of Dylan's hits and best songs as well as a good selection of work by the Band. — *William Ruhlmann*

★ **Blood on the Tracks** / Jan. 17, 1975 / Columbia ✦✦✦✦✦
A stunning, mature statement in which the songwriter faced the conflicting elements of his life, the uncertainties of life in general, and the virtues of kindness and generosity. Incidentally, he also invented new songwriting structures and composed some of the most appealing music of his career. Still perhaps Dylan's most listenable and compelling album, this best represents his post-'60s work. — *William Ruhlmann*

☆ **The Basement Tapes** / Jun. 26, 1975 / Columbia ✦✦✦✦✦
A two-disc set of ad hoc performances from 1967, albeit refurbished slightly for this release, *The Basement Tapes* provides the missing link between Dylan's long, poetic songs of the mid-'60s and the shorter, more direct songs of the late '60s. Some of the songs had already become well known: "Too Much of Nothing," "Tears of Rage," "This Wheel's on Fire," and "You Ain't Goin' Nowhere." — *William Ruhlmann*

Desire / Jan. 16, 1976 / Columbia ✦✦✦✦
A rough-and-tumble collection cut with a band Dylan was assembling for the *Rolling Thunder* tour. "Hurricane" recounts the tale of an unjustly imprisoned boxer, "Romance in Durango" and "Black Diamond Bay" are short stories in song, and "Sara" is a last plaintive plea from the singer to his wife. — *William Ruhlmann*

Hard Rain / Sep. 10, 1976 / Columbia ✦✦
A live album recorded on the second leg of the Rolling Thunder Revue tour in the spring of 1976 and similar to a TV special shown the month of its release. This was not the Revue at its best. Nevertheless, the album is notable for the radical reworkings of "Lay Lady Lay" and "I Threw It All Away." — *William Ruhlmann*

Street Legal / Jun. 15, 1978 / Columbia ✦✦✦
Using a big band assembled for a world tour, Dylan presents a group of songs, some of which are as imagistic—and as bitter—as his mid-'60s material. Particularly notable are the tone poem "Changing of the Guards" and the desperate but moving "Señor." — *William Ruhlmann*

At Budokan / 1979 / Columbia ✦✦
A two-disc accounting of Bob Dylan's 1978 world tour during one of its early stops. The songs have again been rearranged in a style many found too grandiose, but the band is frequently effective. — *William Ruhlmann*

Slow Train Coming / Aug. 18, 1979 / Columbia ✦✦✦
Among Dylan's best-played (members of Dire Straits participate) and best-produced recordings, this album reflects Dylan's religious conversion. At its best, on "Gotta Serve Somebody" and "When You Gonna Wake Up," the album presents cautionary messages similar to those Dylan had served up throughout his career. — *William Ruhlmann*

Saved / Jun. 20, 1980 / Columbia ✦✦
Just as fervent as he was on *Slow Train Coming*, Dylan is less inspired (sorry) as a songwriter here, and his preachiness is likely to be a bit much even for believers. — *William Ruhlmann*

Shot of Love / Aug. 12, 1981 / Columbia ✦✦
Dylan's need to sing only about his faith recedes, and his muse returns, notably on "Every Grain of Sand," one of his finest '80s songs. In 1985, this album was re-released with the non-LP B-side "The Groom's Still Waiting at the Altar," another of Dylan's better later songs, added. — *William Ruhlmann*

Infidels / Nov. 1, 1983 / Columbia ✦✦✦
Dylan emerged from his overt references to Christianity with his sense of moral outrage reawakened. He expressed it in songs defending Israel and attacking unions on this impassioned collection, which also includes "Jokerman," as impressive a piece of socially conscious poetry as he'd ever produced, and the love songs "Sweetheart like You" and "Don't Fall Apart on Me Tonight." — *William Ruhlmann*

Real Live / Dec. 3, 1984 / Columbia ✦✦✦
A souvenir of Dylan's 1984 European tour that is notable for the revised lyrics to "Tangled Up in Blue." — *William Ruhlmann*

Empire Burlesque / Jun. 8, 1985 / Columbia ✦✦✦✦
Dylan's strongest song collection since *Blood on the Tracks*, this album also benefits from excellent backup work by members of Tom Petty's Heartbreakers, among others, and a remix by dance expert Arthur Baker. Dylan himself sounds unusually engaged as well, especially on such songs as "Emotionally Yours" (later an R&B hit for the O'Jays) and

the moving autobiographical folk ballad "Dark Eyes." — *William Ruhlmann*

☆ **Biograph** / Oct. 28, 1985 / Columbia ✦✦✦✦✦
A five-LP, three-CD retrospective of Dylan's first 20 years of recording, with an emphasis on presenting some of the mountain of unreleased songs that began leaking out unofficially in the late '60s. The only reason this massive, brilliantly executed album is not listed as an essential pick is its cost. It's not a bad place to start trying to appreciate the whole of Dylan's achievement. — *William Ruhlmann*

Knocked out Loaded / Aug. 8, 1986 / Columbia ✦✦
A hodgepodge of tracks recorded between 1984 and 1986, some written by others, some in collaboration. Mostly dispensable, it is saved from a "Poor" rating by the rambling "Brownsville Girl," co-written with playwright Sam Shepard. — *William Ruhlmann*

Down in the Groove / May 31, 1988 / Columbia ✦✦
Lacking the ambitious undercurrent of *Knocked Out Loaded*, *Down in the Groove* is a modest, occasionally careless, collection of blues, rock, and folk numbers, split evenly between originals and covers. Dylan didn't expend much energy during the sessions that comprise *Down in the Groove*, and it shows. Many of the performances sound unfinished or like afterthoughts. Still, there's a certain ragged charm to the best cuts on the record, whether it's his sober "Death Is Not the End" or the lighthearted throwaway collaborations with Grateful Dead lyricist Robert Hunter, "Ugliest Girl in the World" and "Silvio." The album is quite entertaining, despite its numerous faults. — *Stephen Thomas Erlewine*

Royal Albert Hall / 1989 / [Bootleg] ✦✦✦✦
Recorded in May 1966 during Dylan's British tour with the Hawks (soon to become the Band), this documents a landmark in the history of Dylan, folk-rock, and rock itself. Although Dylan had been recording electric rock 'n' roll for a year at this point, his appearances with a full band continued to arouse tremendous controversy and even hostility, as much of the folk audience that formed his original constituency viewed him as a sellout. He divided his sets between acoustic and rock formats; this bootleg comes from the electric half, in which he performed eight of his mid-'60s tunes, including "Like a Rolling Stone," "Just like Tom Thumb's Blues," "Ballad of a Thin Man," the unreleased "Tell Me Mama," and radically reworked arrangements of "I Don't Believe You" and "One Too Many Mornings," which had appeared in plaintive acoustic versions on his albums. The songs are delivered with a fierceness and tight ensemble backing that exceed the energy of his mid-'60s albums, and must have been quite a revelation for the more open-minded members of the audience. Some of the less open-minded customers are heard heckling Dylan on this recording, to which he responds by heckling right back and charging into a stormy version of "Like a Rolling Stone" that holds nothing in reserve. It's been said that this isn't actually from Albert Hall, (it is certainly from the 1966 British tour), but regardless, it's way, WAY overdue for official release. Most Dylan fans and many serious rock scholars have a copy already. — *Richie Unterberger*

Dylan & the Dead / Feb. 6, 1989 / Columbia ✦
Quite possibly the worst album by either Bob Dylan or the Grateful Dead, the live *Dylan and the Dead* completely squanders its promise. Working from an intriguing selection of songs—it includes staples like "Knockin' on Heaven's Door" and more obscure gems like "Joey"—the Dead and Dylan contribute listless, meandering versions that are simply boring. Both artists have done much better—reportedly they have done better together, according to various bootleg fans—but *Dylan and the Dead* is a sad, disheartening document. — *Stephen Thomas Erlewine*

Oh Mercy / Sep. 22, 1989 / Columbia ✦✦✦
This stunning album demonstrated that, after more than 25 years, Dylan was perfectly capable of writing songs of topical concern, high poetry, and unflinching self-examination to match any of his best work of the '60s and '70s. — *William Ruhlmann*

Under the Red Sky / Sep. 11, 1990 / Columbia ✦✦
Oh Mercy was widely praised as Dylan's best album since *Blood on the Tracks*, so hopes were high for his follow-up, *Under the Red Sky*, which was to be produced by Don Was, the man who revitalized the careers of Bonnie Raitt and Iggy Pop. In a typical stroke of perversity, Dylan turned in his most inane set of material ever—*Self Portrait* may have been weak, but it had nothing on "Wiggle Wiggle," "Handy Dandy," and "2 X 2." In all likelihood, he was trying to return to a direct, blues-based form of songwriting, but nearly every song falls flat, lacking hooks or cleverness. Was did give the record a professional gloss, which makes the entire thing listenable, but the songs themselves drift into the air. After releasing *Under the Red Sky*, Dylan didn't release an original song for a full seven years, suggesting that the record was just the beginning of a dry spell. — *Stephen Thomas Erlewine*

Bootleg Series / Mar. 26, 1991 / Columbia ✦✦✦✦
The floodgates opened with the release of this 58-song collection of outtakes and unreleased songs from throughout Dylan's career, an outpouring that demonstrated what all the bootleggers and their customers had

known all along: that Dylan's throwaways were better than everyone else's keepers. It's amazing to think that, while turning out some of the most impressive albums of his time, Dylan was holding back material often equally good. — *William Ruhlmann*

Good As I Been to You / Oct. 27, 1992 / Columbia ✦✦✦
After a scattered decade's worth of albums ranging from terrific to terrible, Bob Dylan's second release of the '90s is a return to the acoustic folk that established his career. Naturally, it's not as breathtaking as *The Freewheelin' Bob Dylan* or his debut album, but it is an expert collection of standards by an expert folksinger. *Good as I Been to You* also proves he's a great guitarist. — *Stephen Thomas Erlewine*

World Gone Wrong / Oct. 28, 1993 / Columbia ✦✦✦
Although it follows the same formula as *Good as I Been to You*, *World Gone Wrong* cuts deeper. Dylan's collection of (mainly) obscure blues and folk songs is genuinely moving, one of his best albums of the past decade. On *World Gone Wrong*, Dylan says more with other people's songs than most do with their own, creating a vicious, worried commentary about modern society with a collection of traditional songs. — *Stephen Thomas Erlewine*

Thin Wild Mercury Music [bootleg] / 1994 / Spank ✦✦✦
A very interesting compilation of Dylan's best rare/unreleased material from the mid-'60s. In most cases you can hear why these were rejected for inclusion on his '65-66 albums; the song is unfinished, or the arrangement too unpolished. But there are very good, substantially different alternate takes here: a beautiful acoustic "Love Minus Zero/No Limit," a "Visions of Johanna" with ghostly organ, a more melodic, gentle version of "It's All Over Now, Baby Blue," a scarifying solo piano rendition of "She's Your Lover Now." The fragments and instrumentals (including a really nice wordless arrangement of "I'll Keep It With Mine") are always interesting at the least. Also includes some fine cuts that were technically officially released, but may be missing from the archives of some collectors, like the great European single "If You Gotta Go, Go Now," and the slow version of "Can You Please Crawl Out Your Window" that briefly appeared on a single by mistake. For a laugh, the CD ends with a bungled '65 promotional message from Bob himself, followed by a chaotic attempt at "If You Gotta Go, Go Now" (probably recorded with the drummer from John Mayall's band in England in 1965). — *Richie Unterberger*

Greatest Hits, Vol. 3 / Nov. 15, 1994 / Columbia ✦✦✦
Dylan's first greatest hits album was released in 1967, and his second in 1971. Twenty-three years later comes his third, and it's a reasonable compilation of the better-known songs he has produced over the period, notably standards like "Knockin' on Heaven's Door" and "Forever Young," Dylan chart hits like "Tangled Up in Blue" and "Hurricane," songs that have been covered extensively by other singers, such as "Ring Them Bells," and some of the better album tracks, such as "Changing of the Guard" and "Brownsville Girl." In an effort to span the period, a few lesser, later songs, such as "Silvio" and "Under the Red Sky," are included, while some stronger, earlier songs are not ("Simple Twist of Fate," "Senor," "Emotionally Yours," and "Everything Is Broken"). But on the whole, the selection is excellent, and this is the album to get for that Dylan fan who stopped listening to him at the end of the '60s. (Includes the previously unreleased 1989 track "Dignity.") — *William Ruhlmann*

MTV Unplugged / Apr. 25, 1995 / Columbia ✦✦
This show, taped for MTV, finds Dylan turning in an 11-song set, with eight of the songs dating from his 1963-67 heyday, including such standards as "The Times They Are A-Changin'" and "Like A Rolling Stone." ("John Brown," a powerful anti-war song from 1963, had not been released on a Dylan album previously.) The '70s are represented by "Knockin' on Heaven's Door," and the '80s by "Shooting Star" and "Dignity" (a trunk song, the studio version of which had emerged only the previous November on *Bob Dylan's Greatest Hits, Volume 3*). Dylan, accompanied by a competent five-piece band, approaches his material in a gentler fashion than on some of the originals—"The Times They Are A-Changin" and "With God on Our Side," for example, seem sadder and less defiant than they did back in 1964. Otherwise, unlike some other

Unplugged performances, this one doesn't offer a noticeably different view of the artist's work. But then, Dylan has been unplugged for much of his career, anyway. — *William Ruhlmann*

Guitars Kissing & The Contemporary Fix [Bootleg] / 1996 / [Bootleg] ✦✦✦✦
Here is one of the most famous Dylan live performances, his concert on May 17, 1966, at the Manchester Free Trade Hall in England. Finally preserved intact on two discs—one for the seldom-heard acoustic set, the other for the tumultuous electric turn with the Hawks—the fidelity is absolutely astounding. The acoustic set finds Dylan totally changing his folkie set list, eschewing "The Times They Are A-Changin'" and better-known protest songs for material no further back than "She Belongs to Me" and "Mr. Tambourine Man," with acoustic versions of tunes like "Fourth Time Around," "Visions of Johanna," "It's All Over Now, Baby Blue," "Desolation Row," and "Just like a Woman" that would later surface on record in full-band versions. But it is the second disc—the electric stuff with a newly-recruited Hawks—that's the big ticket here. Everything from the furor surrounding Dylan's so called defection from folk to the sinful sellout of wedding his music to rock 'n' roll is on open-wound display in the eight-song set. Opening with the unreleased "Tell Me Mama," the Hawks are brash, confident, brutal, and unrelenting as Dylan asserts his position as only he can, storming through ominous versions of "Baby, Let Me Follow You Down," "Just Like Tom Thumb's Blues" (an even more drugged-out version of which would be recorded on this same tour and deposited on the B-side of "I Want You") and "Leopard Skin Pill Box Hat." The show reaches its apogee with "Like a Rolling Stone," a version chock full of all the venom inherent in the song, splashed all over the crowd. A landmark document of Dylan at the absolute height of his powers, bootleg or no, this is one album no true fan can afford to be without. — *Cub Koda*

Carnegie Hall / [Bootleg] ✦✦✦✦
Recorded by Columbia in 1964 as a possible live release, but shelved, not for reasons of artistic merit or sonic deficiencies. Bootlegged under a variety of titles, this is probably the best pre-electric-period unreleased Dylan concert to own, from the perspectives of fidelity, performance, and breadth of material. Besides featuring the core of his early repertoire, from "Times They Are A-Changin'" and "Mr. Tambourine Man" down to less celebrated numbers like "Spanish Harlem Incident" and "To Ramona," there are also a few unreleased or barely released tunes, the best of which is an acoustic version of "If You Gotta Go, Go Now." There are also a few duets with Joan Baez, which actually don't count among the highlights of this 95-minute program. — *Richie Unterberger*

The Dylan/Cash Sessions / [Bootleg] ✦✦✦
During the *Nashville Skyline* sessions in February 1969, Dylan teamed up with Johnny Cash to record over a dozen songs. Only one of these made it onto *Nashville Skyline* ("Girl from the North Country"). Most of the rest are here, in perfect fidelity. If you were to judge this as a proper studio album, the notices wouldn't be too positive, due to the ragged and tentative performances. Judged as a loose, informal meeting of two giants, it's very pleasurable listening, though more for Cash's contributions than Dylan's. With full band backing (including Carl Perkins on electric guitar), the pair run through easygoing, rockabilly-tinged versions of Dylan songs, Cash songs, old Sun rockabilly chestnuts ("That's All Right Mama" and "Matchbox"), and a bit of country gospel. Cash, in fact, dominates the proceedings: he sings lead more often, and the mere two Dylan tunes ("Girl from the North Country" and "One Too Many Mornings" are outweighed by a larger heaping of Cash classics ("Big River," "I Walk the Line," "I Still Miss Someone," "Ring of Fire," "Guess Things Happen That Way"). The CD might even appeal more to Cash fans than Dylan ones, especially as Dylan's singing is not up to scratch; his timing is off, he often sings on one note, and he even needs to be occasionally cued by Cash for the words. The disc includes three interesting Dylan performances from a TV broadcast on "The Johnny Cash Show" in May 1969, as well as five less essential quadrophonic mixes of *Nashville Skyline* tracks. — *Richie Unterberger*

E

(E)

b. Virginia
Vocals / Pop-Rock

Virginia singer-songwriter and multi-instrumentalist (E) projects a humorously idiosyncratic loser (Woody Allen-meets-Brian Wilson in the sandbox) mentality. In fact, (E)'s wistful melancholy and tainted hopefulness, as well as his delicately quirky melodicism and dense production smarts, recall the reclusive Beach Boy's better moments. After two albums, 1992's *Hello Cruel World* and 1993's *Broken Toy Shop*, E formed the Eels, a three piece combo that combined E's quirky pop smarts with a decidedly edgier alterna-sound. The band signed to the new Dream Works label and released their first album, *Beautiful Freak*, in 1996. Both the album and the single "Novacaine for the Soul" saw considerable promotional push that resulted in heavy airplay on radio and MTV, but sales failed to reflect the exposure. —*Chris Woodstra and Rick Clark*

● **A Man Called (E)** / Feb. 4, 1992 / Polydor ✦✦✦✦
A Man Called (E) is a wonderful collection of pop gems, tapped from the soul of Beach Boys' *Pet Sounds*, *Tumbleweed Connection* -era Elton John, *White Album* Beatles, and early Todd Rundgren. (E) performed practically every instrument in this keyboard-rich production. Highlights from this impressive debut are "Hello Cruel World," "Fitting in with the Misfits," and "Are You and Me Gonna Happen?" —*Rick Clark*

Broken Toy Shop / Dec. 7, 1993 / Polydor ✦✦✦
On his second album, (E) offers more of the same highly crafted pop-rock that graced his debut; although the overall quality of songs is just a notch lower than his first album, *Broken Toy Shop* nevertheless features many delightful pop gems. —*Stephen Thomas Erlewine*

The E-Types

f. Salinas, CA, db. 1967
Garage Rock, Pop-Rock

In the mid-'60s, this group from Salinas, CA, played a pleasant blend of British Invasion-inspired pop-rock and a touch of garage. With prominent keyboards, three-part harmonies, and original material with minor-keyed shifts, they sounded something like a mix between the Zombies and the Turtles. Very popular within their (pretty limited) stomping grounds, they made no impact whatsoever on a national level, issuing four singles on small labels (most of them with producer Ed Cobb, who also handled the Standells and the Chocolate Watch Band). Certainly they were a promising outfit, capable of offering strong original material (most of which, oddly, was penned by a friend who wasn't in the band, Larry Hosford). They didn't have enough time to convert that promise into truly significant work, however. They disbanded in 1967, when their carefully executed pop-rock was falling out of fashion in California, in favor of psychedelia. —*Richie Unterberger*

● **Introducing . . . The E-Types** / 1995 / Sundazed ✦✦✦✦
Twenty-two tracks, including both sides of their four singles and previously unissued demos, outtakes, and live performances. The four singles are legitimately fine finds if you collect obscure '60s pop-garage. "Long Before," "I Can't Do It," and "Put the Clock Back on the Wall" are outstanding, and the cover of Lennon-McCartney's "Love of the Loved" (which the Beatles never officially released themselves) rates as one of the best unknown Beatle covers of the '60s. Most of the rest of this archival compilation is padding, though, consisting largely of faithful British Invasion covers and some outtakes that are markedly inferior to their singles. It's an enjoyable listen for collectors of mid-

'60s rock, boasting considerably more pop-oriented material and accomplished production than the garage norm. But it couldn't be considered in the top drawer of this sort of thing. —*Richie Unterberger*

The Eagles

f. 1971, Los Angeles, CA, db. 1982
Country-Rock, Soft Rock, Pop-Rock

The Eagles were among the most successful rock groups of the '70s, and their blend of country, folk, and rock continues to sell well in catalog. The group's four original members were Los Angeles session and group veterans assembled by producer John Boylan in 1970 as backup musicians for Linda Ronstadt on her *Silk Purse* album. They then served as her backup band for two years. The four were Glenn Frey (b. Nov. 6, 1948), guitarist; Bernie Leadon (b. Jul. 19, 1947), banjo and mandolin; Randy Meisner (b. Mar. 8, 1948) bass; and Don Henley (b. Jul. 22, 1947) drums. All four sang, though Henley and Frey took most leads. Signed to Ronstadt's label, Asylum, they issued their first album, *The Eagles*, in June 1972. It was a moderate hit (going gold a year and a half later) and produced the Top 40 hits "Take It Easy" (written by Frey and Jackson Browne), "Witchy Woman," and "Peaceful Easy Feeling."

The second Eagles LP, a semi-concept album called *Desperado* (1973) that emphasized an "outlaw" image, was somewhat less successful. For their third album, *On the Border* (1974), the group added guitarist Don Felder. This was a breakthrough record, going gold in three months and producing the No. 1 hit "Best of My Love," which didn't top the charts until almost a year after the album's release, just in time to set up their fourth album. *One of These Nights* (1975), the first of four straight albums to top the charts, featured the title track, "Lyin' Eyes," and "Take It to the Limit," both Top Ten hits.

The Eagles released a greatest-hits album in 1976 (it now stands at 14 million sales, the best-selling hits record of all time) and suffered the loss of Leadon, who was replaced by former James Gang leader Joe Walsh (b. Nov. 20, 1947). At the end of the year, they released *Hotel California*, which has now sold nine million copies. Its hits included the ominous title track, "New Kid in Town," and "Life in the Fast Lane."

In 1977 Meisner left the band and was replaced by former Poco member Timothy B. Schmit (b. Oct. 30, 1947). It took the Eagles until the fall of 1979 to complete *The Long Run*, another million-seller, featuring the chart-topper "Heartache Tonight" and Top Ten successes with the title track and "I Can't Tell You Why." The next year saw the release of a live album, but by 1981 the Eagles had split up. All five members have since released solo albums, the most successful of which have been by Henley and Frey.

In 1994 the Eagles reunited for a summer stadium tour and recorded an album as part of an appearance on the TV show "MTV Unplugged" that featured several new songs. The resulting album, *Hell Freezes Over*, was released in November 1994; it debuted at number one and sold over five million copies by June 1995. —*William Ruhlmann*

The Eagles / Jun. 1972 / Asylum ✦✦✦
The Eagles' tentative debut album is notable for its single hits, "Take It Easy," "Witchy Woman," and "Peaceful Easy Feeling." (It also contains a rare Jackson Browne composition, "Nightingale.") The album has more of a bluegrass tone (courtesy of Bernie Leadon) than the band would later pursue. —*William Ruhlmann*

Desperado / Apr. 1973 / Asylum ✦✦✦
A concept album equating rock 'n' roll musicians with Old West outlaws, the Eagles' second album contains the hit "Tequila Sunrise," the

THE EAGLES

song "Desperado," which has become a standard, and the recurring "Doolin-Dalton," co-written with J.D. Souther and Jackson Browne. — *William Ruhlmann*

On the Border / Mar. 1974 / Asylum ✦✦✦
A transitional Eagles album (and their commercial breakthrough), this contained songs like "Already Gone" and "James Dean" (co-written by Jackson Browne) that hark back to their earlier uptempo rock style, but also "Best of My Love" and Tom Waits' "Ol' 55," ballads that showed off their harmonies and won them a whole new audience. — *William Ruhlmann*

One of These Nights / Jun. 1975 / Asylum ✦✦✦
The Eagles' breakthrough album, a convincing mix of heady rockers and lush ballads, featuring the Top Ten hits "One of These Nights," "Lyin' Eyes," and "Take It to the Limit." — *William Ruhlmann*

★ Their Greatest Hits (1971-1975) / Feb. 1976 / Asylum ✦✦✦✦✦
The reason this is such a great greatest-hits album is that it includes almost all the best tracks from the Eagles' first four albums, eight Top 40 hits including the No. 1 hits "Best of My Love" and "One of These Nights," plus the favorites "Tequila Sunrise" and "Desperado." This is the essential Eagles for the period. (As of mid-1995, *Their Greatest Hits (1971-1975)* was the second-best-selling album of all time in the US, with certified sales of 22 million copies.) — *William Ruhlmann*

☆ Hotel California / Dec. 1976 / Asylum ✦✦✦✦✦
A concept album about the dissipated life of Southern California rock stars, from being the "New Kid in Town" to living "Life in the Fast Lane" to holing up in the "Hotel California" fearing it's all been "Wasted Time" and turning to "The Last Resort." This album and Pink Floyd's *The Wall* are aural versions of *A Star is Born* for the rock generation. — *William Ruhlmann*

The Long Run / Sep. 1979 / Asylum ✦✦✦
The long-awaited follow-up to *Hotel California* and the Eagles' last studio album proved a considerable disappointment, although it sold in the expected multimillions and included the hits "Heartache Tonight," "The Long Run," and "I Can't Tell You Why." — *William Ruhlmann*

Eagles Live / Nov. 1980 / Asylum ✦✦
The Eagles were always a yawn in concert, and this profit-taking re-creation of their hits demonstrates the lifelessness they brought to live work. Today's fans should listen before forking over all those bucks to sit in the stadiums and experience it themselves. — *William Ruhlmann*

Eagles Greatest Hits, Vol. 2 / Oct. 1982 / Asylum ✦✦✦
This will save you from having to buy *The Long Run*, an inconsistent album best remembered for its hit songs, all of which are here, along with the ones from *Hotel California*. — *William Ruhlmann*

Hell Freezes Over / Nov. 8, 1994 / Geffen ✦✦
The Eagles were never a great live band, which makes the process of reinventing their hits slightly harder. But they are smart businessmen, so they realized that they didn't need to reinvent themselves; if they reunited, the public would care only about seeing the band again and just hearing the hits. When the Eagles finally reunited in 1994 for a mammoth tour, they began their tour with an MTV "Unplugged" set. The result is *Hell Freezes Over*. The band accentuates their country leanings, but everything winds up sounding much duller than their original recordings because they accentuate their relaxed vibe, not their rootsiness. Although the album sold well, it's not nearly as captivating as the original versions. — *Stephen Thomas Erlewine*

Earth, Wind & Fire

f. 1969, Chicago, IL
Soul, Funk, Disco, Urban, Quiet Storm
Earth, Wind & Fire was the most successful R&B group of the second half of the '70s. EW&F was founded by Maurice White (b.Dec 19, 1942) and his brother Verdine (b.Jul 25, 1951) in Chicago in 1969, and they released their self-titled debut album on Warner Brothers in 1970. After the 1971 release of the second album, *The Need of Love*, White reorganized the group, bringing in Philip Bailey (b.May 8, 1951) as co-lead singer for the recording of the third album, *Last Days and Time* on Columbia.

EW&F encapsulated many strains of Black pop from before their time. Their high-pitched harmony vocals called to mind groups such as the Temptations, while their funkiness was reminiscent of Sly and the Family Stone, and their horn section sometimes evoked the work of James Brown and others. Over this, Maurice White laid his own brand of African-inspired kalimba music for a thorough synthesis that nonetheless bore a particular musical stamp unique to Earth, Wind & Fire.

The band began to break through with its fourth album, *Head to the Sky*, in 1973. EW&F's first R&B Top Ten hit was "Mighty Mighty," from their first gold album, *Open Our Eyes*, which went to No. 15 in

the pop charts and contained the R&B hit "Kalimba Story." EW&F's breakthrough to a mass audience, however, came in 1975 with the release of *That's the Way of the World*, the soundtrack to a film in which the group appeared. Led by its gold-selling No. 1 single, "Shining Star," the album topped the pop charts.

Equally successful were the partially live *Gratitude* (1975), *Spirit* (1976), *All 'n All* (1977), *The Best of Earth, Wind & Fire—Vol. 1* (1978), and *I Am* (1979). Several albums in the early '80s did almost as well, but after the relative failure of *Electric Universe* in 1983, EW&F disbanded. It re-formed for the 1987 release *Touch the World*.

Earth, Wind & Fire returned to the R&B/urban universe in 1990 with the LP *Heritage*, an attempt to update their sound with hip-hop and new jack ingredients. Hammer and the Boys, as well as old school veteran Sly Stone, made guest appearances but couldn't rekindle the old magic. They tried again in '93 with *Millennium*, switching labels to Reprise and ending a relationship with Columbia dating back to 1972. Columbia issued a deluxe box set of their greatest hits in 1992, *The Eternal Dance*. — *William Ruhlmann and Ron Wynn*

Earth, Wind & Fire / 1971 / Warner Brothers ✦✦✦
Earth, Wind & Fire is the debut album from the band of the same name; originally released in 1971, it contains all of the trademarks of the best soul music from the early part of that decade, as well as some of the distinguishing characteristics that have made Earth, Wind & Fire such a consistently successful soul/R&B aggregate ever since. *Earth, Wind & Fire* approximates the sound of the Isley Brothers from this same period, both in style—the rhythms beat with the strong pulse of soul, R&B, funk *and* rock 'n' roll, with a freewheeling sense of improvisation that feels like jazz, in hard-rocking tempos, with plenty of sing-along chanted vocals and screaming (if not psychedelic) electric guitar—and in substance, with most songs addressing social issues under titles such as "Help Somebody," "Love Is Life," "C'Mon Children" and "This World Today." "Bad Tune" features the kalimbas of Maurice White, along with the soaring vocal harmonies and spiritual air of the lyrics among the primary trademarks of this band. White & Co. went on to further distill and then elaborate on their sound, most notably with the later assimilation of Philip Bailey as lead vocalist, but *Earth, Wind & Fire* presents them at the point from which it all began. — *Chris Slawecki*

The Need of Love / 1971 / Warner Brothers ✦✦✦
The Need of Love is R&B "head music," with Earth, Wind & Fire mixing all the psychedelia and experimentation going on in rock and jazz in 1971 into their R&B/soul repertoire. So *The Need of Love* begins with a free-form, ten-minute opus titled "Energy," with wind and brass solos squirming around and above rumbling, percussion rhythm beds of varying time signatures (sort of like a Pharoah Sanders take on R&B), while other titles include "Beauty" and "Everything Is Everything" (which suggests jazz-R&B fusioneers from this same period such as Roy Ayers). The ballad "I Think About Lovin' You" provides some much-needed grounding, with composer Sherry Scott's soft and tender lead vocal couched in vocal harmonies straight from a starlit, warm doo wop summer's night. — *Chris Slawecki*

Last Days and Time / 1972 / Columbia ✦✦✦
Earth, Wind & Fire were nothing if not ambitious, and by the time of their third album, they had forged an individual sound by absorbing nearly everything that had gone before them in the previous ten years. It was as if they were trying to encapsulate every eclectic foray pursued by Motown, from catchy, rhythmic pop to churning funk, and even from Stevie Wonder singing borrowed folk songs like "Blowin' in the Wind" (here, Bailey did "Where Have All the Flowers Gone") to the schmaltzy, string-filled pop that spelled legitimacy to Motown. Not only that, they wanted to incorporate Sly and the Family Stone's horn-filled, gutbucket R&B and some of the fusion style of Weather Report. On *Last Days and Time*, they succeeded in pulling all that into their orbit, but they hadn't yet managed one crucial thing: they hadn't learned to write hits. That would come next. — *William Ruhlmann*

Head to the Sky / May 1973 / Columbia ✦✦✦
The album that made them the 1970s' top pop/funk and crossover R&B act. Their previous album had been better produced than anything on Warner Bros., and this one had excellent message songs, their finest playing, outstanding arrangements, and soaring vocals by Philip Bailey and Jessica Cleaves. The uptempo tracks were some of the best the group ever made. — *Ron Wynn*

Another Time / 1974 / Warner Brothers ✦✦✦
Once Earth, Wind & Fire became the top Black music band in the world, Warner Bros. realized the mistake they had made in not giving Maurice White complete creative freedom. They rushed out this anthology featuring the group's early music, hoping to piggyback off their huge Columbia hits. These songs are certainly worth hearing again, but few people who hadn't originally purchased the Warner Bros. tracks were enticed to get them. — *Ron Wynn*

ALL MUSIC GUIDE TO ROCK

William Ruhlmann

Open Your Eyes / Mar. 1974 / Columbia ✦✦✦
Earth, Wind & Fire were in peak form during the mid-'70s. Their fast songs had driving beats and excellent arrangements and were sung with the perfect mix of energy and conviction. The slow songs, particularly those featuring Philip Bailey, were moving and often anthemic. This album got them two Top Ten R&B hits and three songs on the charts, and kept their momentum going. —*Ron Wynn*

That's the Way of the World / Mar. 1975 / Columbia ✦✦✦✦
Sleekly produced '70s pop/R&B, highlighted by the stirring "Shining Star" and the atmospheric title track. —*William Ruhlmann*

Gratitude / Dec. 1975 / Columbia ✦✦✦✦
A two-record set that blended live and studio cuts and was a testimony to the band's immense popularity at the time. It was a huge success and even topped the charts for a time, something that live sets never did, especially live albums by Black funk bands. Saxophonist Donald Myrick's blistering solos on the live cuts immediately put him in the spotlight, even though he'd been an active session musician for years, while Philip Bailey's spiraling, wondrous vocals were in the forefront throughout the record. —*Ron Wynn*

Spirit / Sep. 1976 / Columbia ✦✦✦✦
Another huge '70s album for Earth, Wind & Fire. The title track was among their biggest singles ever and represented another triumph for Philip Bailey. They had three other huge hits in 1976 and were without question the reigning kings of crossover Black music. —*Ron Wynn*

All 'n All / Nov. 1977 / Columbia ✦✦✦
The Earth, Wind & Fire juggernaut kept rolling with this late-'70s album. While they had turned more and more to the pop side, they had three more smash singles during this time, and their stage shows became even more varied, entertaining, and ambitious. Although this album doesn't have the same passion or emphatic vocals as some of its predecessors, it was a worthy addition to their '70s legacy. —*Ron Wynn*

★ **The Best of Earth, Wind & Fire, Vol. 1** / Nov. 1978 / Columbia ✦✦✦✦✦
Best of Earth, Wind & Fire, Vol. 1 contains the bulk of their hits from the mid-'70s, including "Shining Star," "September," "Got to Get You into My Life," "Sing a Song," "Getaway," and several other hits. —*Stephen Thomas Erlewine*

I Am / Jun. 1979 / Columbia ✦✦✦
The gorgeous ballad "After the Love Has Gone" and the bouncy "Boogie Wonderland" (featuring the Emotions) lead this consistent collection. —*William Ruhlmann*

Faces / Oct. 1980 / Columbia ✦✦✦
Although the band was catching more flak from critics for an alleged obsession with socio-political commentary and quasi-mystical references, R&B audiences hadn't yet tired of Earth, Wind & Fire. While this album admittedly had less memorable material and was more dependent on what had become production cliches and stock devices, it still landed plenty of hits on the charts. But it was becoming clear to even the most devoted fans that singles like "In the Stone" and "Let Me Talk" weren't their finest hour. —*Ron Wynn*

Raise! / Oct. 1981 / Columbia ✦✦
The end was near for Earth, Wind & Fire. This wasn't quite the disaster it was made out to be at the time, but it was their least distinguished overall album since the early days on Warner Bros., with the exception of their participation in the disastrous *Sgt. Pepper's Lonely Hearts Club Band* film soundtrack in 1978. "Let's Groove" was just a recycled mid-tempo tune from the mid-'70s, and everything else sounded desultory and uninspired. It was no surprise that after two more albums White and company decided to take some time away from the scene. —*William Ruhlmann*

Powerlight / Feb. 1983 / Columbia ✦✦✦
Even though *Raise!* was an artistic disappointment, it was a commercial success. *Powerlight*, EW&F's first album in nine years to miss the Top Ten, showed that fans were catching on to the group's decline. There were still hits, at least on the R&B chart, in "Fall in Love with Me" and "Side by Side," but the formula was growing stale. —*William Ruhlmann*

Electric Universe / Nov. 1983 / Columbia ✦✦
Creatively exhausted, EW&F turned to L.A. studio hacks like David Foster (Chicago) and Martin Page (Starship) for their characteristically bland material. Typical was Page's lead-off track, "Magnetic," which, although a Top Ten R&B hit, could have been by anyone. There were no substantial pop hits, the album sold poorly, and EW&F split up. —*William Ruhlmann*

Touch the World / Oct. 1987 / Columbia ✦✦✦
Earth, Wind & Fire came close to recapturing their '70s glory on this late '80s vehicle, missing more because of stylistic changes on the Black music scene than any failings on their part. Indeed, the song

"System of Survival" did actually top the R&B charts for a week, and the overall album got favorable reviews and good support. It just wasn't the blockbuster effort that the group had routinely enjoyed in the past. —*Ron Wynn*

The Best of Earth, Wind & Fire, Vol. 2 / 1988 / Columbia ✦✦✦✦
The second collection covering hit singles from the '70s' top funk and soul band, Earth, Wind & Fire. This anthology has recently been supplanted by a box set covering virtually all of their big Columbia singles and some early Warners material. If you enjoyed their disco and late '70s cuts more than the early tracks, this anthology is worth getting. —*Ron Wynn*

Heritage / Jan. 1990 / Columbia ✦✦
A disappointing comeback vehicle for Earth, Wind & Fire. They still had the seamless funk production and exuberant collective vocals, but there was no standout single, and the attempt at generating attention through Afrocentric commentary didn't raise any eyebrows or score any hits. —*Ron Wynn*

The Eternal Dance / Sep. 8, 1992 / Columbia ✦✦✦✦
Covering three discs and including all the hits, as well as a healthy selection of rarities, *The Eternal Dance* is not designed for the casual listener; only hardcore fans will remain enthralled through the numerous rarities. Most listeners will be content with the two greatest hits collections, but this comprehensive box set remains essential for hardcore Earth, Wind & Fire fans. —*Stephen Thomas Erlewine*

Millennium / Sep. 14, 1993 / Reprise ✦✦
Since the mid-1980s, Earth, Wind & Fire's output had been erratic and quite uneven. One never knew whether the veteran soul/funk band would come out with something as impressive as *Touch the World* or something as embarrassing as *Heritage*. After many years with Columbia, EWF switched to Warner Bros.—ironically, a label that gave Maurice White and friends the boot back in 1972—with *Millennium*. While *Heritage* found EWF bending over backwards to appeal to urban contemporary tastes, sounding unnatural and even silly in the process, *Millennium* is a more honest and organic recording. Though hardly in a class with *That's The Way of the World* or *Spirit*—or for that matter, *Touch the World*—*Millennium* is a decent offering that finds the crew being true to itself. Much of the material, especially "Sunday Morning," "Chicago (Chi-Town) Blues" and "Honor the Magic," is fairly memorable. Unfortunately, the urban contemporary audience wasn't receptive to EWF's honesty. As influential as EWF had been, and as often as it had been sampled in hip-hop, the group was treated as if it was expendable. —*Alex Henderson*

Elements of Love: Ballads / Jun. 1996 / Columbia ✦✦✦✦

The Easybeats

f. 1963, Sydney, Australia, **db.** 1970
Pop-Rock
The most successful Australian rock group of the 1960s, the Easybeats were nearly as popular as the Beatles in their homeland in the mid-'60s. In 1965 and 1966 they ran off a rapid string of seven Top Ten singles in Australia with peppy variations on the early Beatle and Merseybeat sound. With a nervous energy that featured staccato guitar lines, unexpected tempo changes, and strong original material, they also betrayed strong debts to the Kinks, Who, and Small Faces, although their songs were generally cheerier and more lightweight. Like all of the aforementioned bands, the Easybeats stand as one of the earliest and foremost exponents of pure power-pop. In late 1966 the Easybeats moved to London and hooked up with legendary producer Shel Talmy (Who, Kinks) in an attempt to crack the international pop market. Against all the odds, they did so the first time out with the classic "Friday on My Mind," which hit the British Top Ten and the American Top 20. Some ill-chosen follow-ups, however, deflated their momentum, although the group—led by the increasingly adventurous combination songwriting/production team of guitarists George Young and Harry Vanda—were keeping up with the tenor of the times by expanding the scope of their lyrics and arrangements. Cuts like "Falling off the Edge of the World," "Come In You'll Get Pneumonia," and "Good Times" drew raves from peers like Lou Reed and Paul McCartney, although few listeners actually heard them at the time. After a few generally dispiriting years in London (during which they were nonetheless quite active in the studio), the group disbanded in late 1969 after a homecoming tour of Australia, where they had been superstars throughout the decade. Vanda and Young remained international cult figures with their extensive production work, and they recaptured pop success for a time as masterminds of Flash & the Pan. —*Richie Unterberger*

Easy / 1965 / Repertoire ✦✦✦
Their first album, not available outside Australia until the 1990s. The Vanda-Young songwriting partnership had yet to dominate the band in their early days, and most of the (entirely original) material here

comes from the pens of George Young and singer Stevie Wright. It's more Merseybeatish and less oriented toward power-pop and staccato guitar attacks than their subsequent releases, which isn't really detrimental; it doesn't scale the peaks the band would shortly climb, but neither does it have the overdone good-time mania that made some of their efforts hard to take in more than limited doses. A fairly consistent, if not incredibly remarkable, relic from the Beat era, including their first big Australian hit, "She's So Fine." —*Richie Unterberger*

It's 2 Easy / 1966 / Repertoire ✦✦✦
Until this CD reissue, the Easybeats' second album, *It's 2 Easy*, had only been issued in Australia. Originally released in 1966, the LP features four Australian hit singles ("Women," "Come and See Her," "Wedding Ring," and "Sad and Lonely and Blue") and ten other original tunes in a peppy style reminiscent of the early Beatles. It doesn't come close to matching the actual quality of the early Beatles tunes, but it's also considerably higher in quality than the average British Invasion album in that it features entirely original material. Most of it was penned by guitarist George Young and singer Stevie Wright; guitarist Harry Vanda would not team up with Young to form the famous Vanda-Young partnership until "Friday on My Mind" later that year. This CD features a generous 13 bonus tracks that will be of considerable interest to specialist collectors, including various B-sides, EP tracks, mono versions, and outtakes from the mid-'60s, some of which have never been available outside Australia. The best of these are two tracks from a 1966 EP: the hard-hitting power-pop tune "I'll Make You Happy" and "Too Much," which recalls the best of the Kinks' similar midtempo numbers from the same era. —*Richie Unterberger*

Volume 3 / 1966 / Albert ✦✦✦
The hardest Easybeats album to find (now available on CD) contains some of their rarest material, never issued outside of Australia. It's actually not worth making a special effort for unless you're a big fan of the group. Like their first two, Australia-only LPs, it's accomplished guitar pop-rock with a heavy British Invasion influence, but not outstanding. The best songs ("Sorry," "Funny Feelin'") have been reissued on Easybeats anthologies. —*Richie Unterberger*

Friends / 1969 / Repertoire ✦✦
Originally released in 1969, *Friends*, the Easybeats' last album, was a curiously half-baked and deflated affair, despite some interesting moments. The Australian group's trademark peppiness gave way to a world-weary tone, perhaps as a result of their roller-coaster ride through near-Beatles-like fame in their native land and limited success elsewhere. Apparently much of this collection was actually half-finished demos, which accounts for the fairly sparse feel on several tracks. The least successful songs are the forced rock 'n' roll boogies, with overwrought vocals from lead singer Stevie Wright. The more pensive tracks, like the title tune, have an oddly compelling, hollow feel of resignation bordering on gloom that starkly contrasts with their more well known mid-'60s material. The Harry Vanda/George Young songwriting team wrote all of the album's songs, including the group's final single, "St. Louis." This CD reissue adds 11 songs to the original LP from various late '60s singles, obscure Australian compilations, and alternate mixes. All are reasonably enjoyable; none is essential. —*Richie Unterberger*

The Shame Just Drained / 1977 / Albert ✦✦✦
For a group that really only scored one major international hit, the Easybeats' songwriting team—Harry Vanda and George Young—were very busy bees indeed in the studio in the late '60s. All but one of the songs on this 15-track compilation are taken from sessions between late 1966 and late 1968 that were unreleased at the time; five come from an album that was canned at the last minute. Apparently there were about 20 more outtakes where that came from. Don't pay any mind to the ridiculous claim in the sleeve note that "had all the material been released in the sequence (and quantity) it was created, then the Easybeats' impact might have been far more notable and we might today be comparing their albums alongside *Rubber Soul*, *Aftermath*, and other rock milestones." This is cheery late-'60s pop with mild psychedelic influences, echoing the Small Faces, the Turtles, and especially the Kinks. The cheeriness, in fact, verges on childish and sickly sweet in places. It's not bad. In fact, it's occasionally pretty good; it's just not incredibly significant. By far the best track is "Mr. Riley of Higginbottom & Clive," a bit of dry class satire that compares well with Ray Davies' vignettes from the same era. —*Richie Unterberger*

Absolute Anthology / 1980 / EMI ✦✦✦✦
A two-CD package from Australia, with ear-stunning sound and two hours of golden classics. The collection of choice. —*Bruce Eder*

Raven EP LP, Vol. 2 / 1982 / Raven ✦✦✦
A compilation of three EPs originally released on the Australian reissue label Raven, hence the strange title. The Easybeats recorded extremely prolifically during their five-year career, and this gathers about a dozen unreleased tracks, a few stray cuts that ended up on

fairly rare LPs or EPs, and three (yes, three) Coke jingles. The best of these offerings are six demos from early 1965; all originals, they show the band at their most British Invasion-influenced and have a mawkish, innocent charm, though they're hardly classic. The rest of the material is typical mid– to late-period Easybeats: extremely clever insofar as quirky songwriting and guitar playing, cheerful almost to the point of being grating, and not nearly as lasting or important as their obvious reference points (the Beatles, Kinks, Who, and Small Faces). Includes a couple of unimpressive covers (of "Hound Dog" and the Nashville Teens' "Find My Way Back Home"). —*Richie Unterberger*

● **The Best of the Easybeats** / 1985 / Rhino ✦✦✦✦
A well-devised collection that pales in sound and content next to its Australian competitor. —*Bruce Eder*

Eazy-E

b. Sep. 7, 1964, Compton, CA, **d.** Mar. 26, 1995, Los Angeles, CA
Vocals / *West Coast Rap, Gangsta Rap, Hardcore Rap, Hip Hop*
After leaving N.W.A., rapper Eazy-E led a career that was filled with controversy and was considerably successful commercially, even if it never matched the creativity of his previous band. Eazy-E began his solo career in 1988 with *Eazy-Duz-It;* it was his only full-length album.

Eazy-E left N.W.A. after the 1991's *Niggaz4Life* hit the top of the charts. The break-up of N.W.A. was extremely bitter, and Eazy in particular earned the wrath of Dr. Dre, and Eazy and Dre carried out their feud on record throughout the early '90s.

Even though he released several hit EPs, Eazy's career was in decline when he announced he was suffering from AIDS in early March 1995; he only learned that he had the disease in the previous month. Three weeks later, the rapper died on March 26, 1995; he was 31 years old. —*Stephen Thomas Erlewine*

● **Eazy-Duz-It** / 1988 / Ruthless ✦✦✦✦
N.W.A. was a few months away from releasing the seminal *Straight Outta Compton* when Priority put out the late Eazy-E's debut solo album, *Eazy-Duz-It*, in late 1988. Though it falls short of *Compton's* consistent excellence, this landmark album boasts some veritable gangster rap classics, including "Ruthless Villain," "Nobody Move," and "Boyz-N-the-Hood." Though the influence of Ice-T and Schoolly D is evident, Eazy's lyrics are even more graphic. Because he rapped in the first person about the harsh realities of L.A.'s Compton ghetto, the former drug dealer (who died of AIDS-related causes in 1995) was accused of glamorizing inner-city violence—Eazy maintained that he simply set out to educate and tell it like it is. Interestingly, much of album isn't gangster rap, and in fact, songs ranging from "Radio" to the Bootsy Collins-inspired "We Want Eazy" is essentially raucous party music. —*Alex Henderson*

5150 Home 4 Tha Sick / Dec. 28, 1992 / Priority ✦✦
Eazy-E issued this ill-conceived, stiffly rapped EP, which generated some quick response and then disappeared. —*Ron Wynn*

It's On (Dr. Dre 187um) Killa / Nov. 5, 1993 / Ruthless ✦✦✦
Eazy-E fired back in the unending war of words with former N.W.A. comrade Dr. Dre on the EP *It's On (Dr. Dre 187um) Killa*. At the time of the EP's release, Eazy-E had already lost credibility in hip-hop circles for appearing at Republican fund-raisers and supporting one of the officers involved in the Rodney King incident. Thus, his charges that Dre is a fraud lack consistency and weight; in addition, his raps sound tired and lame throughout the disc. Where Eazy-E was once cocky, funny, and often intriguing, he now sounds merely bitter. Besides the usual sexist and sexual posturing, he even reprises N.W.A.'s debut single "Boyz in tha Hood" again. The song was once an entertaining manifesto, but now it's just dated, "G" mix and all. —*Ron Wynn*

Str8 off Tha Streetz / 1995 / Ruthless ✦✦
At the time of his death, Eazy-E was completing a comeback album that was intended to restore his street credibility, which had taken a savage beating in the early '90s. *Str8 off the Streetz of Muthaphukkin Compton*, the album he left unfinished, does show more ambition than his previous *It's On*, but it's unlikely that it would have made him a star again. Collaborating with his former NWA partners Ren and Yella, Eazy-E sounds revitalized, but the music simply isn't imaginative. Instead of pushing forward and creating a distinctive style, it treads familiar gangsta territory, complete with bottomless bass, whining synthesizers, and meaningless boasts. The occasional track, like the surrealistic "The Muthaphukkin Real" and the menacing "Ole School Shit," illustrate what Eazy-E could have done if not tied to pedestrian production, but the majority of *Str8 off the Streez* is depressingly by-the-books. Sadly, the album is the farthest thing from a graceful departure. —*Stephen Thomas Erlewine*

Eternal E / Dec. 1995 / Ruthless/Priority ✦✦✦✦

Echo & the Bunnymen

f. Sep. 1978, Liverpool, England
Alternative Pop-Rock, Post-Punk, Neo-Psychedelia

Echo & the Bunnymen's dark, swirling fusion of gloomy post-punk and Doors-inspired psychedelia brought the group a handful of British hits in the early '80s, while attracting a cult following in the United States.

The Bunnymen grew out of the Crucial Three, a late '70s trio featuring vocalist Ian McCulloch, Pete Wylie, and Julian Cope. Cope and Wylie left the group by the end of 1977, forming the Teardrop Explodes and Wah!, respectively. McCulloch met guitarist Will Seargent in the summer of 1978, and the pair began recording demos with a drum machine, which the duo called "Echo." Adding bassist Les Pattinson, the band made its live debut at the Liverpool club Eric's at the end of 1978, calling themselves Echo & the Bunnymen.

In March 1979 the group released their first single, "Pictures on My Wall"/"Read It in Books," on the local Zoo record label. The single and their popular live performances led to a contract with Korova. After signing the contract, the group discarded the drum machine, adding drummer Pete de Freitas.

Released in the summer of 1980, their debut album *Crocodiles* reached No. 17 on the UK charts. *Shine So Hard*, an EP released in the fall, became their first record to crack the UK Top 40. With the more ambitious and atmospheric *Heaven Up Here* (1981), the group began to gain momentum, thanks to positive reviews; it became their first UK Top Ten album. Two years later, *Porcupine* appeared, becoming the band's biggest hit (peaking at No. 2 on the UK charts) and launching the Top Ten single "The Cutter."

"The Killing Moon" became the group's second Top Ten hit at the beginning of 1984, but its follow-up, "Silver," didn't make it past No. 30 when it was released in May. *Ocean Rain* was released that same month to great critical acclaim; peaking at No. four in Britain, the record became the Bunnymen's first album to chart in the US Top 100. The next year was a quiet one for the band, as they released only one new song, "Bring On the Dancing Horses," which was included on the compilation *Songs to Learn and Sing*. De Freitas left the band at the start of 1986 and was replaced by former Haircut 100 drummer Mark Fox; by September, de Freitas rejoined the group.

Echo & the Bunnymen returned with new material in the summer of 1987, releasing the single "The Game" and self-titled album. *Echo & the Bunnymen* became their biggest American hit, peaking at No. 51. It was a success in England as well, reaching No. 4. However, the album indicated that the group was in a musical holding pattern. At the end of 1988, McCulloch left to pursue a solo career; the rest of the band decided to continue without the singer. Tragedy hit the band in the summer of 1989, when de Freitas was killed in an auto accident. McCulloch released his first solo album, *Candleland*, in the fall of 1989; it peaked at No. 18 in the UK and No. 159 in the US. Echo & the Bunnymen released *Reverberation*, their first album recorded without McCulloch, in 1990; it failed to make the charts. McCulloch released his second solo album, *Mysterio*, in 1992. Two years later Ian McCulloch and Will Sergeant formed Electrafixion, releasing their first album in 1995. In 1997 the duo reteamed with Pattinson to re-form Echo & the Bunnymen, issuing the LP *Evergreen*. *—Stephen Thomas Erlewine*

Crocodiles / 1980 / Sire ♦♦♦♦
Echo and the Bunnymen's first album is also one of their best. The music here most resembles that of full-textured 1960s garage rock featuring vibrant guitars and earnest singing, a cross perhaps between the 13th Floor Elevators, the Byrds, and the Doors. Other oblique stylistic references can be seen in the songs "Pride" (the Police) and "Monkeys" (Joy Division). Guitar textures are ringingly full and energetic, in a few cases (most notably "Villiers Terrace") hinting at the sound later used by 1980s New Sound-style bands like R.E.M. and the Windbreakers. Vocalist Ian McCulloch sings in a soaring, emotional, all-stops-out manner free from tasteless excess, delivering lyrics that are attractive enough, if often obscure. The music exhibits an undercurrent of desperation, made palatable by a pervadingly edgy, energetic drive. Highlights include the fast and hard-rocking title track, the intriguing production number "Happy Death Men," and "Do It Clean," which adds organ to the mix and has a memorable, yearning chorus. This fine release is well worth hearing and strongly recommended. *—David Cleary*

A Promise / 1981 / Korova ♦♦
Heaven Up Here / Jul. 1981 / Sire ♦♦♦
While darker and more intense than *Crocodiles*, Echo and the Bunnymen's sophomore effort lacks the immediacy of their debut; the songs are subpar, relying too much on atmosphere and texture instead of substance. Although a few of the tracks, including "A Promise" and "All I Want," are keepers, the vast majoirity of *Heaven Up Here* is too

self-indulgent and ridiculously gloomy to warrant serious consideration among the group's most enduring work. *—Jason Ankeny*

Porcupine / 1983 / Sire ♦♦♦
The group's third album is a solid outing, a noticeably better listen than its predecessor, *Heaven Up Here*. Songs are intriguing and elaborate, often featuring swooping, howling melodic lines. Arrangements here owe a lot to 1960s psychedelia and feature lots of reverb, washed textures, intricate production touches, and altered guitar sounds. Ian McCulloch's vocals are yearning, soaring, and hyper-expressive here, almost to the point of being histrionic, most notably on "Clay," "Ripeness," and the title track. Driving bass and drums lend the songs urgency and keep the music from collapsing into self-indulgence. Parallels between the group's US contemporaries such as Translator, Wire Train, and R.E.M. can be drawn, though all seem to have developed aspects of this style at about the same time—and none utilize it as flamboyantly as the Bunnymen do. Highlights here include "Back of Love" (with its galloping drumbeat and fragmented, yet ardent vocal line) and "Gods Will Be Gods" (which gradually speeds up from beginning to end, working itself into a swirling frenzy). This album is well worth hearing. *—David Cleary*

Ocean Rain / 1984 / Sire ♦♦♦♦
Ocean Rain more or less continues the basic yearning 1960s-oriented approach of prior Bunnymen releases, though there are some important differences. In general, the arrangements here are cleaner, less swirlingly cluttered, though production values are still interesting and imaginative. The songs are a bit more focused and straightforward than on immediately preceding albums; some selections, such as "Silver," "Seven Seas," and "My Kingdom" contain memorable melodic hooks. Under such circumstances, Ian McCulloch's vocals often sound overwrought and forced, most noticeably on "My Kingdom" and "Thorn of Crowns." The latter song is unusual, based on a Bo Diddley-influenced rhythmic pattern. "Crystal Days" and "Silver" show more R.E.M.-oriented guitar work than before. And the curious "Nocturnal Me," with its gypsy-like tremolo guitar, jittery strings, oboe-and-piano-colored texture, and darkly affected vocals, has a distinct Roxy Music flavor. While not one of the group's better releases, this platter is not a bad listen. *—David Cleary*

● **Songs to Learn & Sing** / 1985 / Sire ♦♦♦♦
A fine anthology collecting all of the singles from their golden period of 1980 to 1985. In the end, Echo & the Bunnymen were a great singles band, so this is the ideal way to either get acquainted with the group or revisit them. *—Chris Woodstra*

Echo & the Bunnymen / 1987 / Sire ♦♦♦♦
This fine release (not to be confused with the self-titled 1983 EP) is the Bunnymen's best since their debut, *Crocodiles*. The album catches the group at a fortuitous career juncture; the clutch of songs here is among the hookiest and most memorable the band would ever write, while the arrangements are noticeably clean and punchy, mostly eliminating strings and similar clutter to focus almost exclusively on guitars, keyboards, drums, and occasional percussion touches. The warmly expressive "All My Life," which might perhaps have received an overheated arrangement on prior albums, benefits especially from this approach. The band rocks out convincingly on other selections, such as "Satellite" and "All in Your Mind." Pete DeFreitas' solid drumming at times veers towards the danceable on tracks like "Lost and Found," "Lips Like Sugar," and the overtly Doors-influenced "Bedbugs and Ballyhoo." Surprisingly, vocalist Ian McCulloch appears to have rediscovered the maxim "less is more"; his singing is comparatively restrained and tasteful here, resulting in a more natural, unforced emotiveness that is extremely effective. Production values are excellent, with many subtle touches that do not detract from the album's overall directness. In short, doing it clean really pays off here; this energetic, top-notch album is highly recommended. *—David Cleary*

Reverberation / Dec. 1990 / Sire ♦♦
A Bunnymen album in name only, *Reverberation* features neither Ian McCulloch nor drummer Pete DeFreitas, the victim of a fatal 1989 motorcycle accident. A derivative effort inspired by the Manchester rave scene, the album pales in comparison to even the original quartet's weakest work, and is recommended to completists only. *— Jason Ankeny*

Echobelly

f. 1992, London, England
Alternative Pop-Rock, Brit-Pop

Led by vocalist Sonya Aurora Madan, Echobelly fused the ironic, self-absorbed viewpoint of the Smiths with stylish Blondie posturing and a solid guitar crunch. Defiantly politically correct, the group cultivated a fair amount of praise within the British press at the beginning of their career, but as the Brit-pop craze of the mid-'90s wore on, the group was slowly eclipsed by such contemporaries as Elastica and

Sleeper. Nevertheless, Echobelly earned a dedicated cult following in the US and UK, as well as a devoted fan base within Japan.

Madan formed Echobelly circa 1992 with Glenn Johansson (guitar), Debbie Smith (guitar), Alex Keyser (bass), and Andy Henderson (drums). The group's first single, "Bellyache," was released in late 1993 to positive reviews from the UK weekly music press and managed to debut at No. 15 on the indie charts. By early 1994 they broke the Top 40 with "I Can't Imagine the World Without Me." *Everybody's Got One*, the band's debut album, was released in the fall of 1994 to positive reviews and strong sales within the UK; it was released in the US in the spring of 1995 to little attention.

By the summer of 1995, British indie-guitar music had overtaken the pop consciousness, and Echobelly was poised to break into the mainstream. Though the band was plagued by some behind-the-scenes problems—bassist Alex Keyser was replaced by James Harris after the recording of their second album, *On*,—they didn't quite manage to make the leap. "Great Things," the first single from *On*, entered the charts at No. 13, but subsequent singles and the album itself didn't fare as well. Nevertheless, the group retained a strong following within Japan over the course of 1995, where they were considered superstars. — *Stephen Thomas Erlewine*

● **Everybody's Got One** / Oct. 25, 1994 / Epic ✦✦✦✦
Echobelly's debut album is a dynamite mix of brash ambition, undeniable energy, and smart pop songwriting. Lead singer Sonya Aurora Madan's swooping voice occasionally recalls the highly emotional phrasing of Morrissey, but her lyrics never reach his grand self-pity. Instead, she is supremely confident ("I Can't Imagine the World Without Me"), which makes the melodic roar of the band all the more satisfying. Filled with soaring guitar hooks, propulsive energy, and wonderfully elliptical melodies, *Everyone's Got One* showcases a band that sounds as personal as the Smiths, yet as confident as Blondie. — *Stephen Thomas Erlewine*

On / Oct. 17, 1995 / Work ✦✦✦
Beginning with the ferocious secondhand Blondie raver "Car Fiction," Echobelly's second album gets off to a great start, speeding through three terrific slices of guitar-pop that equal anything on *Everybody's Got One*. After that, the quality of the album begins to dip slightly, with the melodies and hooks getting progressively weaker with each track. Nevertheless, the band's sound is more aggressive and muscular than before, and the charm and style of vocalist Sonia Aurora Madan never wear thin. — *Stephen Thomas Erlewine*

Eddie & the Hot Rods

f. 1975, Canvey Island, England
Rock 'n' Roll, New Wave, Power Pop, Pub Rock
Arriving during the waning days of pub rock, Eddie & the Hot Rods helped usher in punk rock in the United Kingdom. Working from the same bluesy, Stonesy three-chord foundation as contemporaries like Dr. Feelgood, the Hot Rods were faster, tougher, wilder, and louder than any other pub-rock band. They also celebrated adolescent abandon, unlike their peers, who usually concentrated on working-class subjects. Developing a substantial cult following by touring the pub circuit relentlessly, Eddie & the Hot Rods, with their fast, tough rock 'n' roll, made the pub-rock taverns more willing to book wilder acts like the Damned and the Sex Pistols, thereby firing the first shot in the UK punk revolution. They also made some inroads on the pop charts with their 1976 debut EP *Live at the Marquee* and the singles "Teenage Depression" and "Do Anything You Wanna Do," but by the time the latter reached the Top Ten in the summer of 1977, Eddie & the Hot Rods and their bar-band demeanor had already begun to appear outdated. The group's following declined sharply over the next two years, and they disbanded in 1980. Although they never wound up as stars, the band undeniably made an impact in the birth of punk rock.

Barrie Masters (vocals), Dave Higgs (guitar), Pete Wall (guitar), Rob Steel (bass), and Steve Nichols (a.k.a. Steve Nicol, drums) formed Eddie & the Hot Rods in Southend, Essex, London, in the spring of 1975. The "Eddie" in their name derived from a dummy the group would beat up during the course of their early concerts. Wall and Steel left the group by the end of the year; the band replaced only Steel, hiring 15-year-old schoolboy Paul Gray as their bassist. Around this time, Lew Lewis was added as a harmonica player. Shortly afterward, the Hot Rods continued as a quartet, earning a reputation as an explosively energetic live band, thanks in no small part to their manager Ed Hollis, who turned the band on to the driving rock 'n' roll of Detroit bands like the Stooges. Early in 1976 the group released their first single, "Writing on the Wall," on Island Records. Not long afterward, Lewis was asked to leave the band because of his out-of-control behavior; he would later form the Lew Lewis Reformer. By spring 1976, they had become the most popular band on the dying pub-rock circuit, breaking house records at the Marquee Club during the summer. A live EP was recorded during these concerts and released in the fall.

Live at the Marquee nearly made the British Top 40, and the group's following continued to grow. By the end of the year, "Teenage Depression" became the band's first hit single, reaching No. 35 on the charts, and an album by the same name became a moderate success.

Early in 1976 former Kursaal Flyers guitarist Graeme Douglas joined the Hot Rods, and with his addition, the group became slightly more radio-friendly and a little less raw. "Do Anything You Wanna Do," a powerful pop single that was credited to the Rods, illustrated their new sound and became their first genuine hit, reaching the Top Ten in the summer of 1977. Although the success of "Do Anything You Wanna Do" was encouraging, the slicker record and its accompanying album, *Life on the Line*, arrived at the dawn of the punk era, which was perceived as considerably rawer and more dangerous than the Hot Rods. The band continued to perform, but their crowds were beginning to shrink dramatically. *Thriller* was ignored upon its 1979 release, and Island dropped them shortly afterward; the group moved to EMI. Early in 1980, Douglas left the band, followed shortly afterward by Gray, who joined the Damned; he was replaced by Tony Cranney. In the wake of these departures, the Hot Rods released a final album, *Fish 'n' Chips*, in April of 1981, but after it was ignored, the band broke up. Barrie Masters joined the Inmates, and Steve Nichol joined One the Juggler.

After the Inmates and One the Juggler failed to make an impact, Masters and Nichol re-formed the Hot Rods with guitarist Warren Kennedy and bassist Tony Cranney. The new lineup recorded a live album for the independent Waterfront Records, but the group broke up shortly afterward. In 1985, the group re-formed with Masters, Nichol, Kennedy, and bassist Russell Strutter.

In 1992 the original, classic lineup of the Hot Rods—Masters, Nichol, Higgs, Gray—reunited for a European tour. Upon its completion, Higgs left the group, and the remaining trio continued with guitarist Steve Walwyn, who was on leave from Dr. Feelgood because of Lee Brilleaux' illness. Shortly afterwards, former Feelgood Gordon Russell joined. He, too, was only briefly a member of the band, and was replaced by Mick Rodgers, a former member of Manfred Mann's Earthband. In 1994 the Hot Rods were offered a one-shot contract with the Japanese label Creative Man Records, and the group made its first album in 16 years—*Gasoline Days*. The album was released in the UK in the spring of 1996 and in Japan. The next year Rodgers returned to the Earthband, and he was replaced by Madman Keyo. That year Nichol suffered a car accident, and while he recovered, Jess Phillips was the group's drummer. — *Stephen Thomas Erlewine*

Live at the Marquee / Aug. 1976 / Island ✦✦✦✦
Eddie & the Hot Rods were first and foremost a great live band, so it makes perfect sense for their debut EP to show the band in their natural setting. *Live at the Marquee*, though only four songs (all covers), clearly shows how the band's wild and raw energy helped to inspire the punk explosion. — *Chris Woodstra*

Teenage Depression / Dec. 1976 / Island ✦✦✦
The band's first studio album is a fine effort in the spirit of Dr. Feelgood, bridging the gap between pub rock and punk rock. Wild, raw, and rebellious—everything a rock 'n' roll album should be. — *Chris Woodstra*

Life on the Line / 1977 / Island ✦✦✦✦
Life on the Line adds guitarist Graeme Douglas (ex-Kursaal Flyers), helping to bring out the band's pure pop sensibility. This is their finest moment and also their last really great album. Includes the brilliant "Do Anything You Want to Do," a British hit. — *Chris Woodstra*

Thriller / 1977 / Island ✦✦
Thriller reveals a band that has quickly slipped out of touch. They're unable to keep up with "the kids" anymore and they end up sounding like grumpy old rock 'n' roll purists. As an added bonus, Linda McCartney makes a rare guest vocal appearance. — *Chris Woodstra*

● **End of the Beginning: Best of** / 1994 / Island ✦✦✦✦
A nearly flawless collection, *End of the Beginning* documents the band's golden period of 1976-1979 with the infectious singles, inspired live workouts, album tracks, and a rarity or two for the collectors. This is an important, though unfortunately overlooked, part of British punk rock's roots that shouldn't be missed. — *Chris Woodstra*

Duane Eddy

b. Apr. 26, 1938, Corning, NY
Guitar / Rock 'n' Roll, Instrumental Rock
Although Duane Eddy's instrumental hits from the late '50s can sound unduly basic and repetitive (especially when taken all at once), he was vastly influential. Perhaps the most successful instrumental rocker of his time, he may also have been the man most responsible (along with Chuck Berry) for popularizing the electric rock guitar. His distinctively low, twangy riffs could be heard on no less than 15 Top 40 hits

between 1958 and 1963. He was also one of the first rock stars to crack the LP market.

That low, twangy sound was devised in collaboration with producer Lee Hazlewood, an Arizona disc jockey whom Eddy had met while hanging out at a radio station as a teenager. By the late '50s, Hazlewood had branched out into production. Before Duane began recording, his principal influence had been Chet Atkins, but at Hazlewood's suggestion, he started concentrating on guitar lines at the lower end of the strings. His opening riff of his debut single, "Movin' and Groovin'," would be lifted for the Beach Boys five years later to open "Surfin' USA." It was the next 45, "Rebel Rouser," that would really break him as a national star, reaching the Top Ten in 1958. Opening with a down-and-dirty, heavily echoed guitar riff, it remains the tune with which he's most often identified.

Eddy's phenomenally successful run of hits over the next few years was to some extent a variation on the "Rebel Rouser" theme. With cowboy whoops from the backup band helping driving things along, they weren't nearly as innovative as work of Link Wray during the same era, but they were much more popular. The singles—"Peter Gunn," "Cannonball," "Shazam," and "Forty Miles of Bad Road" were probably the best—also did their part to help keep the raunchy spirit of rock 'n' roll alive, during a time in which it was in danger of being watered down. Much of that raunch was not due solely to Eddy himself, but to the honking sax solos of Steve Douglas, who would go on to become one of the top session players in the industry. Eddy would have his biggest hit, however, in 1960, when he sweetened the twang with strings for the movie theme "Because They're Young."

Eddy's records were also huge influences on legions of budding guitar players. In England, the Shadows no doubt took Eddy as one of the chief inspirations for their spare, moody sound, as one listen to their most famous hit, "Apache," makes obvious. More subtly, his influence can also be heard in the work of George Harrison. For evidence, listen to the growling riffs that decorate the verse of "I Want to Hold Your Hand."

Eddy started to lose momentum in the early '60s, and left the Jamie label in 1962 for the much bigger RCA. "(Dance with the) Guitar Man," which featured an atypical chorus of female vocals, would be his last Top 20 hit that same year. His albums—often based on loose themes, like *A Million Dollars Worth of Twang, Twisting with Duane Eddy*, and *Surfing with Duane Eddy*—kept him afloat to some degree. But his style doggedly refused evolution, although scattered cuts indicate he was capable of abandoning the twang for more bluesy or straight-out rock sounds. The British Invasion wiped him out commercially, although he recorded intermittently over the next couple of decades. In 1986 he enjoyed a brief comeback when the Art of Noise built their "Peter Gunn" hit around his guest contributions; Paul McCartney, George Harrison, Ry Cooder, and Jeff Lynne all helped produce a 1987 album. It's that run of late-'50s and early-'60s hits, though, for which he'll principally be remembered. —*Richie Unterberger*

★ **Twang Thang: Anthology** / May 18, 1993 / Rhino ✦✦✦✦✦
Duane Eddy was America's first bona fide rock 'n' roll guitar hero, playing minimalistic riffs that any kid with a pawnshop guitar could aspire to with a little determination and elbow grease. This two-CD anthology offers the finest retrospective of his career available, with all facets of his career being well documented, from the early hits to later collaborations with the famous rockers he initially inspired. Featuring just enough rarities to keep it from being merely a greatest-hits package, this truly showcases Eddy at his best. —*Cub Koda*

Twangin' from Phoenix to L.A. / Nov. 29, 1994 / Bear Family ✦✦✦✦

That Classic Twang / Apr. 4, 1995 / Bear Family ✦✦✦✦

Dave Edmunds

b. Apr. 15, 1944, Cardiff, Wales
Bass, Guitar, Keyboards, Vocals / Rock 'n' Roll, Roots-Rock, New Wave, Pub Rock

Roots-rockers are seldom as purist as Dave Edmunds. Throughout his career, he stayed true to '50s and '60s rock 'n' roll. For Edmunds, rock 'n' roll history stopped somewhere in 1963, after the Beach Boys' first singles but before the Beatles' hits. After establishing himself as a hot-shot lead guitarist in the blues-rockers Love Sculpture, he launched his solo career by painstakingly re-creating oldies in his own studio, usually recording every track by himself. Through all of his efforts, he learned how to uncannily replicate the sound of Sun, Chess, and Phil Spector records, which not only helped him garner several UK hits in the early '70s, but led to successful production work with artists like the Flamin' Groovies and Brinsley Schwarz. In the late '70s, he hit the peak of his career when he teamed up with former Schwarz bassist Nick Lowe to form Rockpile. For several years, Edmunds recorded albums with Rockpile and toured relentlessly with the band, which resulted in a string of hit UK singles. After the group imploded in the early '80s, he slowly disappeared from the mainstream, even as he

made his most commercial music with producer Jeff Lynne; Edmunds eventually retreated to cult status in the '90s.

Dave Edmunds never abandoned the music he discovered as a teenager in Cardiff, Wales. He learned to play guitar by playing with Everly Brothers and Elvis Presley records, picking out leads by James Burton, Chet Atkins, and Scotty Moore. He was also fascinated by Phil Spector's records, as well as American blues and country. Edmunds began playing in various British blues bands in the early '60s, eventually forming Love Sculpture with bassist John Williams and drummer Bob Jones, who was later replaced by Terry Williams. Love Sculpture's gimmick was playing bluesy, psychedelicized versions of classical songs, and their interpretation of Khachaturian's "Sabre Dance" became a British Top Five hit in 1968. Within a year, the group rode out their success and broke up.

Edmunds returned to his home in Wales and constructed the eight-track studio, Rockfield, in Monmouthshire, where he holed up and taught himself how to meticulously recreate the sounds of his favorite records. Many of these recordings were made almost entirely by Edmunds, usually with Williams assisting on bass. One of the first records released from the Rockfield sessions was actually one of the least indicative of his style, since it interpreted the source material instead of replicating it. Featuring his vocal piped in through a telephone line, Edmunds' revamped version of Smiley Lewis' "I Hear You Knockin'" became a fluke hit, reaching the Top Ten in both America and England, and he quickly followed it with the *Rockpile* LP, a collection of straightforward oldies covers that became a modest success. Over the next few years he recorded the material that became his second album, *Subtle as a Flying Mallet*, as well as producing records by similar-minded rockers like Ducks Deluxe, the Flamin' Groovies, and Brinsley Schwarz.

During 1974 Edmunds made a brief appearance in the film *Stardust* and helped assemble the soundtrack. Also that year, he produced the Brinsleys' last record, *New Favourites*. During the recording, he struck up a friendship with bassist Nick Lowe, who over the next few years became his key collaborator. Lowe helped Edmunds move away from covers and into performing new songs, largely written by Lowe, that recreated the spirit of old rock 'n' roll. After the 1975 release of *Subtle as a Flying Mallet*—it produced two Top Ten UK hits with "Baby I Love You" and "Born to Be with You"—Edmunds began to rely on Lowe's original material and sought out newer songs in the same vein, as well as more obscure oldies. In return, Lowe joined Edmunds' touring band, Rockpile, which also featured drummer Terry Williams and guitarist Billy Bremner. The first record the pair worked on heavily together was 1977's *Get It*, which also was Edmunds' first record for Led Zeppelin's label, Swan Song.

Get It was well received, as was 1978's *Tracks on Wax 4*, the first album Edmunds recorded with Rockpile as his backing band. By that point, Rockpile was touring constantly, earning terrific reviews in the UK press, who grouped the band with the burgeoning new wave movement largely because of their drunken, reckless energy. In 1979 the band entered the studio to simultaneously cut Edmunds' *Repeat when Necessary* and Lowe's *Labour of Lust*, and the sessions were captured on the BBC documentary *Born Fighter*. Both records were hits, with *Repeat when Necessary* generating the major British hit "Girls Talk," as well as the Top 20 "Queen of Hearts," which Juice Newton later replicated for her breakthrough success. Rockpile entered the studio in 1980 to record the group's first full-fledged album, *Seconds of Pleasure*. During the recording, tensions between Edmunds and Lowe began to surface, resulting in an album that failed to capture the band's live sound. *Seconds of Pleasure* was a moderate success, but the group disbanded after its supporting tour.

Twangin', Edmunds' first post-Rockpile album, appeared in 1981 and featured contributions from Williams and Bremner. The album was a minor hit, generating a hit cover of John Fogerty's "Almost Saturday Night." Edmunds signed with Columbia the next year, releasing *D.E. 7th*, another moderately successful record. With 1983's *Information*, Edmunds began working with producer Jeff Lynne, a former member of Electric Light Orchestra. Not surprisingly for a prog-rock veteran, Lynne brought Edmunds a more measured sound, encouraging him to work with synthesizers and drum machines. While greeted with mixed reviews, *Information* was successful in the US, resulting in the hit "Slipping Away." The pair followed the same formula for 1984's *Riff Raff*, which was an unqualified bomb.

During the early '80s Edmunds had produced records for rockabilly revivalists the Stray Cats and, in 1984, he produced the Everly Brothers' comeback record, *EB84*. As his solo career stalled in the wake of *Riff Raff*, Edmunds concentrated on production, working on several acclaimed records, including k.d. lang's debut *Angel with a Lariat* and the Fabulous Thunderbirds' breakthrough *Tuff Enuff*. He returned to his own career in 1987 with the live *I Hear You Rockin',* which went ignored. Three years later, he released *Closer to the Flame,* his first studio record in six years, to mixed reviews. That same year, he reunited with Nick Lowe to produce Lowe's *Party of One.* Rhino Records released the double-disc compilation *Anthology* in 1993, and the next year, Edmunds returned with *Plugged In,* his first set of one-man-band material since *Subtle as a Flying Mallet. Plugged In* was received with good reviews, and Edmunds supported the album with his first tour in several years. —*Stephen Thomas Erlewine*

Rockpile / 1972 / Mamou ✦✦✦
Dave Edmunds' debut album *Rockpile* established his sound—not only his revivalist tendencies, but also his method of meticulously recreating the sound and style of classic early rock 'n' roll, R&B, and country records. Edmunds plays nearly every instrument on the album, with bassist John Williams being the only full-time collaborator. As a result, the record doesn't sound "live"; it has a pinched, precise quality that may contradict the spontaneity that was at the core of the original singles, but it does offer an other-worldly quality that makes the record distinctive. Take the hit "I Hear You Knocking," which has a mechanical rhythm and a weird, out-of-phase vocal that qualifies as an original interpretation, unlike his by-the-book take on Chuck Berry's "The Promised Land," which suffers from the stiff rhythms. Still, the best moments on *Rockpile* come from songs like "Down, Down, Down," an obscure gem that manages to recreate not only the sound, but the feeling of classic rock 'n' roll, perhaps because Edmunds wasn't concerned with recreating one of his beloved singles. —*Stephen Thomas Erlewine*

Subtle as a Flying Mallet / 1975 / RCA ✦✦✦
Taking the one-man band aesthetic to an extreme, Dave Edmunds recorded nearly all of his second album *Subtle as a Flying Mallet* on his own, hiring a bassist and a drummer for only a pair of tracks. Edmunds took several years to complete the record, probably because it took a considerable amount of effort to recreate these songs so throughly; he spends so much attention on detail that he refuses to change the sex on "Da Doo Ron Ron." Alternating between Spector classics, the Everly Brothers, Chuck Berry, and a variety of R&B, country, and pop numbers, Edmunds hits on all the styles of the late '50s and early '60s, but he spends so much time on duplicating the sound that he sucks the joy out of the music; it is positively eerie to hear these songs performed by one man, who spent weeks overdubbing himself to sound like his own wall of sound. And the main problem with *Subtle as a Flying Mallet* is that these are not reinterpretations, they are recreations, and there's little point in hearing a one-man version of rock classics unless he offers new ideas. When Edmunds works with obscure material, like the Chordettes' "Born to Be with You," or with newer items like Nick Lowe's "She's My Baby," the results are better, because the songs are less familiar, which makes his painstaking production exciting; but his isolation makes *Subtle as a Flying Mallet* sound less like a revival and more like a creepy science experiment. —*Stephen Thomas Erlewine*

Get It / 1977 / Swan Song ✦✦✦✦
Get It marks a significant departure from Dave Edmunds' early records, as it is the first time he's backed by a full band. Most of *Get It* was recorded with a fledgling version of Rockpile, with other session men filling in when necessary, and the live band gives the album a lively feel that he had previously ignored. Just as importantly, the song selection is more carefully considered than before, containing only a handful of classics and obscure rock 'n' roll, and concentrating on pub rock staples ("Get Out of Denver," "Back to School Days," "JuJu Man") and songs written or co-written by Nick Lowe, which gives the album a freshness lacking on his early records. Lowe's homages to the Everly Brothers ("Here Comes the Weekend," "I Knew the Bride"), and Phil Spector ("Little Darlin'") are more appealing than Edmunds' recreations of the originals, because Lowe's songs are lyrically and musically clever, and he knows how to make them sound like forgotten classics. That's why *Get It* is one of Dave Edmunds' very best albums. —*Stephen Thomas Erlewine*

Tracks on Wax 4 / 1978 / Swan Song ✦✦✦✦
Tracks on Wax 4 is the first official Rockpile collaboration, and its hard-driving, unified sound makes it one of Dave Edmunds' very best records. Like *Get It, Tracks on Wax 4* relies primarily on originals and contemporary pub-rock songs, leaving behind the classic oldies. The older songs on the record are obscurities like Chuck Berry's "It's My Own Business" and Jan & Dean's "Thread Your Needle." Built on such fine songs as the rockabilly-tinged "Trouble Boys," the Everly-esque "Never Been in Love," "Television," "Readers Wives," and "Deborah," *Tracks on Wax 4* is a tight, snappy, rock 'n' roll record that is derailed only by a version of Nick Lowe's classic "Heart of the City," where Lowe's original vocal is stripped away and replaced by a new take by Edmunds. Only then does the record recall Edmunds' perfectionist nature. —*Stephen Thomas Erlewine*

Repeat When Necessary / 1979 / Swan Song ✦✦✦✦
Recorded simultaneously with Nick Lowe's *Labour of Lust, Repeat when Necessary* continues the winning streak of *Get It* and *Tracks on*

Wax 4 simply by sticking to the formula. Though Rockpile's sound is a little cleaner here than before, nothing's changed but the songs, which are uniformly excellent. Culled primarily from pub-rock contemporaries (and containing no Lowe songs whatsoever), the record contains four classics: Elvis Costello's galloping "Girls Talk," Graham Parker's relentless "Crawling from the Wreckage," the funny (a rarity of Edmunds) "Creature from the Black Lagoon," and the country-rocker "Queen of Hearts," which would later become a hit for Juice Newton in exactly the same arrangement. A few songs come close to meeting this high standard, but they are occasionally hampered by a tightness similar to the pinched rhythms of *Subtle as a Flying Mallet.* The early Huey Lewis song "Bad Is Bad" and the old Brinsley Schwarz number "Home in My Hand" in particular are hurt by this. But these are minor flaws; *Repeat when Necessary* is an energetic, old-fashioned rock 'n' roll record that ranks as Edmunds' last great album. —*Stephen Thomas Erlewine*

Single's A's & B's / 1980 / Harvest ✦✦✦
With 20 tracks Edmunds issued with Love Sculpture and Rockpile in the late '60s and early '70s, this import collection is certainly the best retrospective of his early years, if you can find it. Edmunds' image is that of a roots-rocker, and you'll find a lot of that here, ranging from the huge 1970 hit "I Hear You Knocking" to pedestrian oldies covers. Actually, though, he wasn't at all settled on this identity at the time, also cutting some psychedelia, folk-rock, and primitive art-rock. The magnificent Love Sculpture version of Khachaturian's "Sabre Dance," featuring faster-than-light riffs by Edmunds, was a British Top Ten hit; "Farandole" was an unsuccessful attempt to do the same for Bizet. Cuts like "Seagull," Tim Rose's oft-covered "Morning Dew," "In the Land of the Few," and the Moody Blues-like "River to Another Day" are uncharacteristically wistful reflections of late-'60s hippie rock. The album includes the rare 1967 single by Edmunds' pre-Love Sculpture band, the Human Beans. —*Richie Unterberger*

Twangin' / 1981 / Swan Song ✦✦✦
Twangin' was recorded as Rockpile was in the process of breaking up, and the record suffered as a result. Where the previous Rockpile collaborations were loose and rocking, *Twangin'* is tight and precise, as if Edmunds recorded it on his own. Only on "The Race Is On" does the record truly cut loose, and he's backed by the Stray Cats on that one. Still, there's a number of fine moments on the record, particularly in the pseudo-New Wave pulse of John Hiatt's "Something Happens," the pub-rock of Mickey Jupp's "You'll Never Get Me Up (In One of Those)," and the gorgeous Everlyesque "(I'm Gonna Start) Living Again if It Kills Me." The rest of the record is pleasant filler that could have used some of the old Rockpile spark. —*Stephen Thomas Erlewine*

● The Best of Dave Edmunds / 1981 / Swan Song ✦✦✦✦
The Best of Dave Edmunds is a terrific single-disc retrospective picking highlights from Edmunds' best albums, which were all recorded with Rockpile. While Edmunds' tight-assed covers of "Singin' the Blues" and John Fogerty's "Almost Saturday Night" should never have been included, the rest of the album captures the rock revivalist at his best, containing nearly all of his finest moments ("Deborah," "Girls Talk," "I Knew the Bride," "Here Comes the Weekend," "Trouble Boys," "Crawling from the Wreckage," "JuJu Man," "Queen of Hearts"). —*Stephen Thomas Erlewine*

D.E. 7th / 1982 / Columbia ✦✦✦
Dave Edmunds assembled a self-consciously eclectic roots-rock album for *D.E. 7th,* his first post-Rockpile effort. Instead of returning to one-man band status, Edmunds hired a new band, which prevented him from returning to the studied perfectionism of his early work. Nevertheless, *D.E. 7th* lacks the pop sensibilities that made early Edmunds a guilty pleasure, concentrating instead on roots music. While that occasionally means missteps like "Deep in the Heart of Texas," it also means the wonderful bluegrass-stomp "Warmed Over Kisses (Left Over Love)," the country-rocker "Bail You Out," the Cajun-tinged "Louisiana Man," and the excellent Springsteen cover "From Small Things (Big Things One Day Come)." The rest of *D.E. 7th* is uneven, but there a few enjoyable cuts, and compared to what came later, it's certainly more fun. —*Stephen Thomas Erlewine*

Information / 1983 / Columbia ✦✦
For some inexplicable reason, Dave Edmunds decided to shoot for mass success with *Information,* enlisting Jeff Lynne of the Electric Light Orchestra to give him a contemporary, synthesized sheen. Since Edmunds always sounded reluctant when Rockpile strayed too close to new wave, the sudden change of heart is puzzling, especially considering the weakness of the material. Lynne steers the guitarist towards generally undistinguished material, with the exception of his own "Slipping Away," which pulsates with a surprisingly infectious synthetic beat and an undeniably catchy hook which manages to be both contemporary and rootsy. If the rest of *Information* had the same vibe, it would have been a success, but the synthesizers dominate the record, making it a lifeless album. —*Stephen Thomas Erlewine*

Riff Raff / 1984 / Columbia ✦✦
Since "Slipping Away" was a minor hit, Edmunds brought Jeff Lynne back to produce *Riff Raff*, a record that essentially replicates the sound and style of *Information*. Lynne has a tighter hold on the album than before, and Edmunds rarely sounds as energetic as he does on his best records, mainly because the processed rhythms are at odds with his roots-rock sensibilities. Like *Information*, there are a few good moments on the record, particularly in the giddy "Rules of the Game," but overall, *Riff Raff* is Edmunds' weakest record. —*Stephen Thomas Erlewine*

Dave Edmunds Band Live: I Hear You Rockin' / 1987 / Columbia ✦✦✦
Dave Edmunds was always notorious for his perfectionist approach to studio recordings, so his skills as a live performer were often overlooked. Although it has been doctored slightly in the studio, *Dave Edmunds Band Live: I Hear You Rockin'* is an energetic, enjoyable record that demonstrates that the roots-rocker can be a fun, charismatic performer when he chooses. The album's set-list draws heavily from his classic late-'70s records ("Girls Talk," "Here Comes the Weekend," "Queen of Hearts," "Crawling from the Wreckage," "I Knew the Bride," "Ju Ju Man"), adding the hits "I Hear You Knockin'" and "Slipping Away," plus "Information," for good measure. It's a basic primer, delivered with passion, making it a fine record for diehard fans. —*Stephen Thomas Erlewine*

Closer to the Flame / 1990 / Capitol ✦✦
The wait between *Riff Raff* and its follow-up was a full six years, so it isn't surprising that *Closer to the Flame* finds Dave Edmunds abandoning the new wave flourishes of his Jeff Lynne productions for a straightforward roots-rock sensibility. The record still suffers from stiff production. The rhythms are extremely mannered and the sound of the record is slightly sterile, but Edmunds manages to tear into a handful of driving rockers, including Mickey Jupp's "Don't Talk to Me" and "Stockholm," and his version of Al Anderson's "Never Take the Place of You" is his most affecting performance in years. —*Stephen Thomas Erlewine*

The Anthology (1968-1990) / Apr. 20, 1993 / Rhino ✦✦✦✦
A double-disc set covering Dave Edmunds' entire career, the 41-song *Anthology (1968-1990)* does a fine job of capturing his musical evolution, even if it is not without its faults. To a certain extent, *Anthology* is a definitive compilation, since it begins with Love Sculpture's infamous "Sabre Dance" and runs through his early solo recordings ("I Hear You Knockin'"), before hitting Rockpile ("Trouble Boys," "Deborah," "Girls Talk," "Crawling from the Wreckage," "Queen of Hearts") and Edmunds' overly-synthesized recordings with Jeff Lynne, adding a couple of rarities like the excellent Carlene Carter duet "Baby Ride Easy" along the way. However, the track selection is uneven, including far too many Love Sculpture songs and Lynne collaborations, which tends to dilute the spirit of Edmunds' best music. Still, *Anthology* is the best overview of Edmunds' entire career, even if the single-disc *The Best of Dave Edmunds* may be a better, more consistent introduction for many listeners. —*Stephen Thomas Erlewine*

Plugged In / Jul. 19, 1994 / Forward ✦✦
Returning to the one-man band approach of his early records, Dave Edmunds crafted a fine comeback with *Plugged In*. Though his method is similar in execution to *Subtle as a Flying Mallet*, the impact is different, primarily because he has stripped away much of his Spectorian pop influences and sticks to a menu of ready-made roots-rockers. Alternating between covers and originals, the song selection is solid, even if only a handful of songs stand out. Among the highlights is an exciting version of Jerry Reed's instrumental "The Claw," a sweet cover of Al Anderson's "Better Word for Love," and the sunny pop of "Beach Boy Blood (In My Veins)." While the studied, solitary performance on *Plugged In* can be a little stiff, it's songs like these that make the album his best record in years. Still, "Sabre Dance '94" was entirely unnecessary. —*Stephen Thomas Erlewine*

The Edsels

f. 1959, Youngstown, OH, db. 1961
Doo Wop
A brief encounter with fame came for the Edsels when they recorded the doo wop masterpiece "Rama Lama Ding Dong." Originally released in 1959, the single became a hit some three years later, thanks to the efforts of diligent record collectors and disc jockeys.
Taking their name from Ford's legendary failed automobile, the Edsels formed in the tiny mill town of Campbell, OH, in the late '50s. The group consisted of lead vocalist George Jones Jr., James Reynolds, Marshall Sewell, Harry Greene, and Larry Greene. The group auditioned for a local Ohio music publisher in 1958. Through the publisher, the group landed a record deal with the small Dub Records. The Edsels' first single was a song Jones had written, "Rama Lama

Ding Dong." (The first pressings on Dub Records were mislabeled "Lama Rama Ding Dong.")
"Rama Lama Ding Dong" became a local hit but made no impact nationally. In 1961, disc jockeys began playing the song again because it sounded similar to the Marcels' current hit, "Blue Moon." Within a few months, the single was re-released on Twin Records—this time with the correct song title—and it quickly scaled the pop charts, peaking at No. 21. Ironically, the group had broken up by the time "Rama Lama Ding Dong" became a hit in 1961. —*Stephen Thomas Erlewine & Cub Koda*

● **Rama Lama Ding Dong** / 1992 / Relic ✦✦✦✦
A complete 16-track collection of the group's best sides, including the title track, one of the great nonsense doo wop sides of all time. —*Cub Koda*

Jonathan Edwards

b. Jul. 28, 1946, Aitkin, MN
Guitar, Harmonica, Vocals / Progressive Bluegrass, Singer-Songwriter, Folk-Rock
Best remembered for his crossover hit "Sunshine," country and folk singer-songwriter Jonathan Edwards was born July 28, 1946, in Aitkin, MN, and grew up in Virginia. While attending military school, he began playing guitar and composing his own songs. After moving to Ohio to study art, he became a fixture on local club stages, playing with a variety of rock, folk, and blues outfits, often in tandem with fellow students Malcolm McKinney and Joe Dolce.
In 1967 Edwards and his bandmates relocated to Boston, where they permanently changed their name to Sugar Creek and became a full-time blues act, issuing the 1969 LP *Please Tell a Friend*. Wanting to return to acoustic performing, he left the group to record a solo album. Near the end of the 1970 sessions, one of the finished tracks, "Please Find Me," was accidentally erased, forcing Edwards to instead record a brand new composition. The song was "Sunshine," and when it was released as a single the next year, it quickly became a Top Five pop hit.
With the release of 1972's *Honky-Tonk Stardust Cowboy*, Edwards' music began gravitating towards straightahead country; his label was at a loss as to how to market the record, however, and over the course of two more albums, 1973's *Have a Good Time for Me* and the following year's live *Lucky Day*, his sales sharply declined. Soon Edwards dropped out of music, buying a farm in Nova Scotia.
In 1976 Edwards' friend Emmylou Harris enlisted him to sing backup on her sophomore record *Elite Hotel;* the cameo resulted in a new record deal and the LP *Rockin' Chair*, recorded with Harris' Hot Band. *Sail Boat*, cut with most of the same personnel, appeared a year later. Another layoff followed, however, and when Edwards resurfaced—with an eponymous 1982 live record—it was on his own label, Chronic.
After touring the nation with a production of the musical *Pump Boys and Dinettes*, Edwards joined the bluegrass group the Seldom Scene, issuing the 1983 LP *Blue Ridge*. After a 1987 solo children's record, *Little Hands*, Edwards moved to Nashville; his 1989 album *The Natural Thing* generated his biggest country hit, "We Need to Be Locked Away." A follow-up, *One Day Closer*, appeared in 1994. —*Jason Ankeny*

● **Jonathan Edwards** / 1971 / Atco ✦✦✦✦
This album is best known for Edwards' hit, "Sunshine" and the song "Shanty," which radio stations around the country call "The Friday Song." If either of these songs is as far as you've gotten with this album, you are missing a great deal. Edwards has a great sense of melody, which means there is not a weak track on this record. Aside from the previously mentioned numbers, one or two of the songs on the record have taken on a life of their own. "Don't Cry Blue," for instance, has been knocking around bluegrass circles for some years. One listen and you'll know why this album has never gone out of print. —*Jim Worbois*

Honky-Tonk Stardust Cowboy / 1972 / Atco ✦✦✦✦
Edwards continues where the first record left off and continues to grow as an artist. In addition to his own fine songs, Edwards chose to include a few covers like Jesse Colin Young's "Sugar Babe," the Mills Brothers' "Paper Doll" (complete with faux "trombone" solo), and the title track. The title track did receive some airplay on country radio in 1972 but was never the hit it should have been. If you find a copy of this one, grab it. —*Jim Worbois*

Have a Good Time for Me / 1973 / Atco ✦✦✦
While this album has no Edwards originals, there is no shortage of tasty tunes. Edwards has mainly covered songs by three writers—Joe Dolce, Malcom McKinney, and Orphans' Eric Lillyequist (who has appeared on each of Edwards' records to this point)—each of whom has captured the style and essence of Jonathan Edwards. Highly enjoyable. —*Jim Worbois*

Lucky Day / 1974 / Atco ✦✦✦
Unlike many live albums where you get to hear the artists rehash their hits and not much else, Edwards not only gives us a look at his musical roots (Merle Haggard, Jimmy Martin, and Gov. Jimmy Davis) but some surprises as well. One of the most surprising is a highly irreverent version of the Chi-Lites' hit, "Have You Seen Her?" with Edwards' seemingly improvised recitation. This is also the first of Edwards' records on which his band Orphan is credited by name. (Their records are also well worth checking out.) Recommended. —*Jim Worbois*

Rockin' Chair / 1976 / Reprise ✦✦
In 1976 Edwards had a new label, new backing musicians, and a new producer, the then *very* hot Brian Ahern. Unfortunately, change is not always a good thing. The songs and the band are both very good, but the intimate feel of the early albums is missing here, and that was one of the things that always made Edwards' records so appealing. That lack of intimacy seems to fall on the producer's shoulders and should not be held against the artist. Despite the flaws in production, this is still a fine collection of songs and performances from a regrettably overlooked artist. —*Jim Worbois*

Sailboat / 1977 / Reprise ✦✦
This just doesn't have the feel of a Jonathan Edwards album. It could be blamed on the relatively few Edwards originals, which leave the feeling that the creation of this record was more or less removed from the artist's hands. It's a pleasant enough collection, especially if you ever wondered what Jonathan Edwards would sound like singing other songwriters' songs. (His version of "Never Together" predates Carlene Carter's near-hit by a year.) Still, if this is your first exposure to this artist, you might be tempted to skip the rest of his work, and that would be a major mistake. —*Jim Worbois*

Live / 1980 / Chronic ✦✦✦

Blue Ridge / 1985 / Sugar Hill ✦✦✦

One Day Closer / Nov. 21, 1994 / Rising ✦✦

Natural Thing / Feb. 4, 1997 / Rising ✦✦✦

Eels

f. 1995, Los Angeles, CA
Alternative Pop-Rock, Post-Grunge
Several years before he formed the Eels in 1995, vocalist/guitarist (E) released two underrated solo albums for Polydor. Taking the same idiocratic pop sensibility but with an increased use of trip-hop technology, the Eels—(E) plus Tommy Walter and Butch Norton—signed to the Dreamworks label and released *Beautiful Freak* in mid-1996. The single "Novocaine for the Soul" became a No. 1 hit on alternative radio. —*John Bush*

Beautiful Freak / Aug. 13, 1996 / Dreamworks ✦✦✦✦
Eccentric and quirky are the best ways to describe the Eels' debut effort, *Beautiful Freak*. Concise pop tunes form the backbone of the album, but tinges of despair and downright meanness surface just when you've been lulled into thinking this is another pop group, as titles like "My Beloved Monster," "Your Lucky Day in Hell," and "Novocaine for the Soul" indicate. All in all, *Beautiful Freak* is a satisfying first record. —*James Chrispell*

808 State

f. 1988, Manchester, England
House, Techno, Club/Dance
A pioneer of the acid house sound, 808 State formed in Manchester, England, in 1988 when Martin Price, the owner of the city's legendary record store Eastern Bloc and the founder of the independent label Creed, first joined forces with local musician and producer Graham Massey. After teaming with collaborator Gerald Simpson, 808 State recorded its debut EP *Newbuild* in 1988, and began remixing tracks for groups like the Inspiral Carpets.

After Simpson exited to form his solo project A Guy Called Gerald, Price and Massey enlisted DJs Andrew Barker and Darren Partington (known together as the Spinmasters) for the recording of 1989's *Quadrastate* EP, which earned the group a huge club hit with the track "Pacific." After signing with ZTT, they released the album *808:90*, which was embraced by the burgeoning rave culture. 808 State's next single, "The Only Rhyme That Bites," recorded with hip-hopper MC Tunes, marked a dramatic shift into hardcore rap, but was another huge hit.

A series of diverse singles followed, culminating in the 1991 album *Ex: el*, which featured guest vocals from New Order's Bernard Sumner and Bjork; the same year, 808 State also wrote, produced, and performed the music for the MC Tunes LP *The North at Its Heights*. In 1992 Price left to work as a solo producer, later forming his own label, Sun Text. The remaining trio continued in 1993 with *Gorgeous*, and

handled remix work for the likes of David Bowie, Soundgarden, and Bomb the Bass before returning with the experimental *Don Solaris* in 1996. —*Jason Ankeny*

Newbuild / 1988 / Creed State ✦✦✦✦
The group's 1988 album debut is firmly acid-house, without the genre experimentations that characterize later albums such as *90*. Nevertheless, the mid-'90s generation of techno progressives (including Aphex Twin) saluted this album's raw edge as a major influence. —*John Bush*

● **808 Utd. State 90** / Jun. 1990 / Tommy Boy ✦✦✦✦
One of the best house albums ever recorded, *Utd. State 90* is a hypnotic, trance-inducing collection of colorful samples and endlessly inventive rhythm tracks. —*Stephen Thomas Erlewine*

Ex:el / May 9, 1991 / Tommy Boy ✦✦✦✦
Vocal contributions from Bernard Sumner (of New Order) and Bjork spice the house collective's growing electro-pop style with experiments in jazzy house and other genres. —*John Bush*

Gorgeous / Jan. 19, 1993 / Tommy Boy ✦✦✦
Gorgeous is 808 State's most vocal-oriented effort, and features a number of fairly anonymous and forgettable guest singers. The record is most successful when it sticks to the group's trademark atmospheric dance instrumentals, although even those are fairly run-of-the-mill. —*Jason Ankeny*

Don Solaris / 1996 / ZTT ✦✦

Einstürzende Neubauten

f. Apr. 1, 1980, Berlin, Germany
Industrial, Alternative Pop-Rock
Along with Cabaret Voltaire and Throbbing Gristle, Germany's Einsturzende Neubauten ("collapsing new buildings") helped pioneer industrial music with an avant-garde mix of white-noise guitar drones, vocals verging on unlistenable at times, and a clanging, rhythmic din produced by a percussion section consisting of construction materials, hand and power tools, and various metal objects. Neubauten was founded by vocalist/guitarist Blixa Bargeld and percussionist and American expatriate N.U. Unruh in Berlin as a performance art collective; their early activities included a seemingly inexplicable half-naked appearance on the Berlin Autobahn, where the duo spent some time beating on the sides of a hole in an overpass. The group's early lineup also included percussionists Beate Bartel and Gudrun Gut, plus contributor and sound engineer Alexander Van Borsig; their earliest recordings are mostly unstructured, free-form noise issued on various cassettes and singles, including their first single, "Fuer den Untergang," 1981 EP *Schwarz*, and 1982 album *Kollaps*. Some of these recordings are compiled on the *80-83 Strategies Against Architecture* collection, with live shows on the cassette-only *2 X 4*. Bartel and Gut were replaced by ex-Abwarts member F.M. Einheit (who served as Neubauten's chief machinery operator) in 1983, when guitarist and electronics expert Alexander Hacke and Abwarts bassist Marc Chung also joined. A tour of England opening for the Birthday Party resulted in a contract with Some Bizarre Records, which released the slightly more structured *Portrait of Patient O.T.*, as well as consternation from club owners and journalists over Neubauten's stage demolitions and frequent ensuing violence.

When Nick Cave left the Birthday Party and formed his backing band the Bad Seeds, Bargeld became the guitarist and toured and recorded with Cave over most of the decade. He remained with Neubauten, however, which released *1/2 Mensch* in 1986, showcasing its wider range of expression. The group disbanded briefly but soon reformed, and have released albums off and on since then (currently for Elektra). While Bargeld remains a Bad Seed, Van Borsig and Hacke contributed to the remainder of the Birthday Party's recordings as Crime and the City Solution. Elektra has reissued both *Strategies Against Architecture* compilations, while most of the group's '80s albums remain available on the independent Thirsty Ear label. —*Steve Huey*

Portrait of Patient O T / 1983 / Some Bizarre ✦✦✦

● **Strategies Against Architecture** / 1984 / Positive ✦✦✦✦
Radical noisy primitivism. Occasionally stunning. —*John Dougan*

2 X 4 / 1984 / ROIR ✦✦✦
Live noise with power tools. Fun! —*John Dougan*

Haus der Luege / 1989 / Rough Trade ✦✦
Like its predecessor *Fuenf auf der Nach Oben Offenen Richterskala*, *Haus der Luege* ("House of Lies") represents a detour from the trademark Neubauten noise into low-key, subtle textures. While the group hasn't forgone found industrial sounds, they've instead integrated them more thoroughly into the songs; while the volume is restrained, the music is still taut, relying on the unpredictability of the new approach for its intensity. —*Jason Ankeny*

Strategies Against Architecture, Vol. 2 / May 21, 1991 / Elektra
✦✦✦✦

Radical, noisy primitivism, part two. —*John Dougan*

Tabula Rasa / Feb. 16, 1993 / Elektra ✦✦✦✦

A surprisingly restrained Neubauten outing, *Tabula Rasa* favors mood and atmosphere over noise and fury. —*Jason Ankeny*

Mark Eitzel

b. Jan. 30, 1959, Walnut Creek, CA
Singer-Songwriter, Alternative Pop-Rock

Formerly the lead singer-songwriter of the critically acclaimed alternative rock band American Music Club, Mark Eitzel made his solo debut in 1991 when, during a hiatus from the group, he recorded the acoustic LP *Songs of Love: Live in London*. When AMC disbanded after the release of 1995's *San Francisco*, Eitzel continued as a solo performer, issuing his proper debut *60 Watt Silver Lining* in 1996. The superb *West*, co-written and recorded with R.E.M. guitarist Peter Buck, followed a year later. —*Stephen Thomas Erlewine*

Songs of Love: Live at the Borderline—1/19/91 / 1991 / Demon ✦✦✦

60 Watt Silver Lining / Mar. 19, 1996 / Warner Bros. ✦✦✦

Mark Eitzel's *60 Watt Silver Lining* is the first step in a new direction for the former leader of American Music Club. With its trimmed-down percussion and bass, the clear, calm lines of Bruce Kaphan's piano, and the unhurried rhythms and atmospheric moods of the songs, you could almost call *60 Watt Silver Lining* a jazz album. But on the whole, the record is not a radical departure from his previous work; Eitzel is and always has been a sincere and deeply introspective songwriter, and many of the album's best songs share a grounding in real-life people and places. He takes his newfound freedom as a solo artist to the furthest extreme with "Wild Sea"—a free-form, stream-of-consciousness ramble through visions of "old ghosts," "drowned words" and "frozen prayers"—but never completely abandons rock 'n' roll or his sense of humor: "Cleopatra Jones," as much of a rocker as anything here, follows directly behind "Saved," a love song Eitzel says he wrote for Barbra Streisand. It's clear that this is a songwriter who will continue to surprise us for a long, long time. —*Kurt Wolff*

● **West** / May 5, 1997 / Warner Brothers ✦✦✦✦

The El Dorados

f. 1954, Chicago, IL, db. 1957
R&B

One of the leading R&B vocal groups on Vee Jay Records, the Chicago-based El Dorados scored a large crossover hit in 1955 with the infectious, jumping "At My Front Door." The group had only one other charting record—1956's "I'll Be Forever Loving You." The group made several other fine records before their breakup in 1959. —*Stephen Thomas Erlewine*

● **Bim Bam Boom** / Nov. 17, 1993 / Vee-Jay ✦✦✦✦

The El Dorados didn't enjoy sustained success or notoriety and really weren't a top-echelon doo wop group. They did make one superb song in 1955: "At My Front Door" is a landmark of the genre; it had every ingredient, from a simple, catchy theme to first-rate harmonizing and Pirkle Moses' finest lead. The El Dorados made many other good tunes, and an occasionally inspired one like "I'll Be Forever Loving You" or "A Fallen Tear," before quitting Vee-Jay in a money dispute and subsequently disbanding. Almost their entire output is available on this 25-song reissue. It's a chance for fans to revisit triumphs and for newcomers to hear why they did have a brief time in the spotlight. —*Ron Wynn*

Elastica

f. Oct. 1992, London, England
Alternative Pop-Rock, Brit-Pop

Elastica's brief, angular, and catchy punk rock became a hit on both sides of the Atlantic in 1995. While the group reworks both the sound and the image of new wave and punk rockers like Adam & the Ants, Wire, the Buzzcocks, and Blondie, the band's songs are more pop-oriented and hook-driven than most of their influences, and Justine Frischmann's cool sexuality is earthier, yet more detached, than Debbie Harry's.

Guitarist/vocalist Justine Frischmann began performing professionally in the early '90s, forming Suede with her boyfriend, Brett Anderson. In addition to naming the band, Frischmann was the group's original guitarist and continued to perform with them when lead guitarist Bernard Butler joined. However, she left the group soon after her relationship with Anderson ended. Frischmann formed Elastica after leaving Suede in 1991. Recruiting guitarist Donna Matthews, drummer Justin, and bassist Annie Holland through advertisements, the final

lineup of the band was set in 1993. Elastica released their first single, the roaring three-chord, two-minute punk rocker "Stutter," at the end of 1993. The single was a limited edition run and it quickly sold out, thanks to radio airplay and rave reviews. "Line Up" followed a few months later. It also sold very well, but some critics claimed the band appropriated the melody from Wire's "I Am the Fly." For most of 1994 the group was relatively quiet, playing the occasional concert and recording; nevertheless, the band's name stayed in the British press, largely due to Frischmann's romance with Damon Albarn, the lead singer for Blur, England's most popular band of 1994. Released in the fall of that year, "Connection," their biggest hit yet, suffered the same criticism, this time for taking the keyboard riff from Wire's "Three Girl Rhumba." On the eve of the March 1995 release of their debut album, the group was taken to court by Wire's publishers, as well as the publishers of the Stranglers (who claimed Elastica's new single, "Waking Up," took the riff from the punk band's "No More Heroes"); both cases were settled out of court before the album was released.

Entering the charts at No. 1, Elastica's self-titled first album became the fastest-selling debut in the UK, beating the record Oasis' *Definitely Maybe* set only seven months earlier. As well as being a popular success, the record received overwhelmingly positive reviews. Like Oasis, Elastica managed to have a hit single in America with "Connection"; the single was a major modern rock radio hit, as well as reaching the Top 40 on the singles chart. Elastica continued to make headway in America by replacing Sinead O'Connor on the 1995 Lollapalooza tour. —*Stephen Thomas Erlewine*

● **Elastica** / Mar. 14, 1995 / DGC ✦✦✦✦

Elastica's debut album may cop a riff here and there from Wire or the Stranglers, yet no more than Led Zeppelin did with Willie Dixon or the Beach Boys with Chuck Berry. The key is context. Elastica can make the rigid artiness of Wire into a rocking, sexy single with more hooks than anything on *Pink Flag* ("Connection") or rework tThe Stranglers' "No More Heroes" into a more universal anthem that loses none of its punkiness ("Waking Up"). But what makes *Elastica* such an intoxicating record is not only how the 16 songs speed by in 40 minutes, but that the songs are nearly all classics. The riffs are angular like early Adam & the Ants, the melodies tease like Blondie, and the entire band is as tough as the Clash, but they never seem anything less than contemporary. Justine Frischmann's detached sexuality adds an extra edge to her brief, spiky songs; "Stutter" roars about a boyfriend's impotence, "Car Song" makes sex in a car actually sound sexy, "Line Up" slags off groupies, and "Vaseline" speaks for itself. Even if the occasional riff sounds like an old wave group, the simple fact is that hardly any new wave band made records this consistently rocking and melodic. —*Stephen Thomas Erlewine*

Electric Flag

f. Apr. 1967, San Francisco, CA, db. 1974
Blues-Rock, Psychedelia

When guitarist Mike Bloomfield left the Paul Butterfield Blues Band in 1967, he wanted to form a band that combined blues, rock, soul, psychedelia, and jazz into something new. The ambitious concept didn't come off, despite some interesting moments; maybe it was *too* ambitious to hold all that weight. Bloomfield knew for sure that he wanted a horn section in the band, which he began forming with a couple of friends, keyboardist Barry Goldberg and singer Nick Gravenites Although the trio were all veterans of the Chicago music scene, the group based themselves in the San Francisco area. They were bolstered by a rhythm section of bassist Harvey Brooks (who had played on some of Bob Dylan's mid-'60s records) and drummer Buddy Miles; on top of that came a horn section.

Oddly, before even playing any live concerts, the group recorded the soundtrack for the 1967 psychedelic exploitation movie *The Trip*, which afforded them the opportunity to experiment with some of their ideas without much pressure. Their live debut was at the 1967 Monterey Pop Festival (although they didn't make it into the documentary film of the event), but their first proper studio album didn't come out until the spring of 1968.

A Long Time Comin' was an erratic affair, predating Blood, Sweat & Tears and Chicago as a sort of attempt at a big band rock sound. Calling it an early jazz-rock outing is not exactly accurate; it was more like late '60s soul-rock-psychedelia that sometimes (but not always) employed prominent horns. Indeed, it sometimes didn't always sound like the work of the same band—or, at least, you could say that it seemed torn between blues-rock, soul-rock, and California psychedelic influences. The album's success is even harder to judge in light of the facts that Gravenites really wasn't a top-notch vocalist, and that the band's instrumental skills outshone their songwriting ones.

There was enough promise on the album to merit further exploration, but it had hardly been released before the Flag began to droop. Goldberg left, followed shortly by Bloomfield, the most important component of the group's vision. A fragmented band recorded an infe-rior follow-up, but by 1969 they had split up. They did reunite (with Bloomfield) in 1974 for a Jerry Wexler-produced album that got little notice. —*Richie Unterberger*

Trip [O.S.T.] / 1967 / Edsel ✦✦✦
Before the Electric Flag had recorded their first album or even played live, they composed and performed the soundtrack to *The Trip*, the 1967 psychedelic exploitation film starring Peter Fonda, directed by Roger Corman, and written by Jack Nicholson. This odd but worth-while relic is entirely instrumental, and as befits the subject matter, wildly eclectic, veering from ragtime and hurdy-gurdy music to basic soul-rock and sweeping, spacey psychedelia and harsh electronics. One of the funkiest snippets, "Flash, Bam, Pow," was later used by Fonda in *Easy Rider*. —*Richie Unterberger*

A Long Time Comin' / 1968 / Columbia ✦✦✦✦
Ex-Butterfield Band guitarist/drummer Miles and others put this soul-rock band together in 1967. This debut is a testament to their ability to catch fire and keep on burnin'. —*Jeff Tamarkin*

An American Music Band / 1968 / One Way ✦✦✦

Electric Flag / 1969 / Columbia ✦✦

Band Kept On Playing / 1974 / Atlantic ✦✦

Groovin' Is Easy / 1983 / Thunderbolt ✦✦✦

● **Old Glory: the Best of Electric Flag** / Oct. 1995 / Columbia/Legacy ✦✦✦✦
A near-definitive anthology, including almost all of the debut LP (but not every last item), key songs from the second album, and some pre-viously unissued demos, alternate takes, and performances from the 1967 Monterey Pop Festival. —*Richie Unterberger*

Electric Light Orchestra

f. 1971, Birmingham, England
Art-Rock/Progressive-Rock, Pop-Rock
Formed in 1971 from the ashes of one of Britain's greatest eccentric rock bands, the Move, the Electric Light Orchestra drew heavily from the ornately lumbering "I Am the Walrus"-period Beatles. This is shown to extreme effect on their oddly engaging debut, *No Answer*. Of particular note is the track "10538 Overture."

Move expatriates Roy Wood, Jeff Lynne, and Bev Bevan formed the initial nucleus of ELO, but multi-instrumentalist Wood split after *No Answer* to form the bizarrely '50s-influenced Wizzard. Their sopho-more release, *ELO II*, retained some of the off-key crunch of the debut, but it is clearly a transition to what became a very slick, highly orches-trated pop-hit factory. Between 1975 and 1981, ELO managed 17 Top 40 hits, among which were "Evil Woman" (No. 10), "Telephone Line" (No. 7), "Don't Bring Me Down" (No. 4), "Hold On Tight" (No. 10), "Shine a Little Love" (No. 8) and the wonderful "Can't Get It Out of My Head" (No. 9). ELO also scored a No.24 hit with "Do Ya," which was the Move's only stateside chart hit. ELO increasingly became a side project to leader Jeff Lynne's successful outside artist productions, which included Brian Wilson, Dave Edmunds, Tom Petty, the Travel-ing Wilburys, Randy Newman, and George Harrison. —*Rick Clark*

No Answer / 1972 / Jet ✦✦✦✦
Their most lively album, this debut is driven by Roy Wood's manic musical sensibilities. An energetic offshoot of the Move's final album. —*Bruce Eder*

On the Third Day / 1973 / Jet ✦✦✦✦
ELO's sound came togther here, hooked around rocked-up classics and Jeff Lynne's guitar. —*Bruce Eder*

Electric Light Orchestra 2 / 1973 / Jet ✦✦
A middling second album with dull stretches that are almost balanced by the rip-roaring "Roll Over Beethoven." —*Bruce Eder*

Eldorado / 1975 / Jet ✦✦✦✦
Pretentious pseudo-concept rock with some hot old-style rock 'n' roll grace notes. —*Bruce Eder*

Face the Music / 1975 / Jet ✦✦✦✦
Superb production and a good song lineup featuring "Evil Woman" and "Strange Magic." —*Bruce Eder*

Ole' ELO / 1976 / Jet ✦✦✦✦
The early hits, marred only by the unnecessary cutting of "Roll Over Beethoven." —*Bruce Eder*

A New World Record / 1976 / Jet ✦✦✦
A superbly crafted and dark-hued body of songs, all melodic and delectable. —*Bruce Eder*

Out of the Blue / 1977 / Jet ✦✦✦
An over-produced, overwrought piece of pop fluff masquerading as something important. —*Bruce Eder*

● **ELO's Greatest Hits** / 1979 / Jet ✦✦✦✦
Most of ELO's biggest and best hits—"Evil Woman," "Rockaria," "Tele-phone Line"—are included on this solid but slightly skimpy collection. —*Stephen Thomas Erlewine*

Discovery / 1979 / Jet ✦✦

Time / 1981 / Jet ✦✦

Secret Messages / 1983 / Jet ✦✦

Balance of Power / 1986 / Epic ✦✦

Afterglow / Jun. 1990 / Epic ✦✦✦✦
Although it contains all the hits and the remastering sounds superb, the three-disc box set *Afterglow* is likely to be more ELO than anyone but the most devoted fans would want from an anthology. —*Stephen Thomas Erlewine*

ELO's Greatest Hits, Vol. 2 / 1995 / Epic ✦✦

Strange Music: the Best of Electric Light Orchestra / Apr. 11, 1995 / Epic/Legacy ✦✦✦✦
Strange Music concentrates more on ELO's pop hits than *Afterglow*, which makes for a better, more listenable collection. All of the hits are accounted for, along with the group's '70s AOR staples, making it the one definitive collection. ELO may have been an album rock band but their best moments were individual songs; consequently, *Strange Music* doesn't ignore their best attributes, it accentuates them. —*Stephen Thomas Erlewine*

The Electric Prunes

f. 1965, Woodland Hills, CA, **db.** 1969
Psychedelic
The Electric Prunes were not so much a self-contained group as a front for some talented L.A. songwriters and producers; they by and large played the music on their records, but the vision and inspiration came from elsewhere. Nonetheless, they produced a few great psyche-delic garage songs, especially the scintillating "I Had Too Much to Dream Last Night," which mixed distorted guitars and pop hooks with inventive, oscillating reverb. Songwriters Annette Tucker and Nancie Mantz wrote much of the Prunes' material, much of which was crafted in the studio by Dave Hassinger, who had engineered some classic Rolling Stones sessions in the mid-'60s. "Too Much to Dream" was a big hit in 1967, and the psychedelicized Bo Diddley follow-up "Get Me to the World on Time" was just as good, and also a hit. Nothing else by the group made it big, and their initial pair of albums were quite erratic, although a few scattered tracks were nearly as good as those singles. Although they began to write more of their own material on their second album, their subsequent releases were apparently the products of personnel that had little to do with the original lineup. Their third LP, *Mass in F Minor*, was a quasi-religious concept album of psychedelic versions of prayers; a definitively excessive period piece, its best song ("Kyrie Eleison") was lifted for the *Easy Rider* soundtrack. None of the original Prunes was still in the lineup when the band dissolved, unnoticed, at the end of the '60s. —*Richie Unter-berger*

● **Long Day's Flight** / 1986 / Edsel ✦✦✦✦
This 18-track compilation includes the best cuts from their first two albums, as well as a couple of non-LP singles. Pruned to the best six or seven cuts, it would have made a ferocious EP. Some of the mate-rial is simply unmemorable, as the band pounds away in a sub-Stones bluesy fuzz style in the mode of the Standells or Chocolate Watch Band. Besides the two hits, there are a few first-rate cuts that meld garage pop to inspired psychedelic production, like "Train for Tomor-row," "Hideaway," "Long Day's Flight," "You Never Had It Better," "Sold to the Highest Bidder" (featuring a guitar made to sound like a balalaika), and their cover of Goffin/King's "I Happen to Love You." —*Richie Unterberger*

Electronic

f. 1989, Manchester, England
Synthesizer / Alternative Pop-Rock, Alternative Dance
One of the first supergroups from post-punk Great Britain, Electronic is the on-off project formed by New Order's Bernard Sumner and Johnny Marr, former guitarist of the Smiths. The duo released "Get-ting Away with It" in December 1989, with both Sumner and Neil Ten-nant of the Pet Shop Boys on vocals. The single just missed the Top Ten in England, but that was the end of Electronic for over two years; Sumner and Tennant returned to their respective groups, while Marr played on albums by The The and Billy Bragg.

Electronic's sophomore single "Get the Message" finally appeared in April 1991, and an eponymous debut album followed in June. The non-album single "Disappointed" was released just over a year later. Sumner then returned to New Order to record their sixth album, *Republic*, while Marr returned to his sideman role with The The and the Pretenders. The duo reunited to record again—this time with help from former Kraftwerk member Karl Bartos—and released *Raise the Pressure* in July 1996. *—John Bush*

● **Electronic** / May 28, 1991 / Warner Brothers ✦✦✦✦

Raise the Pressure / Jul. 9, 1996 / Warner Brothers ✦✦✦

Eleventh Dream Day

f. 1981, Chicago, IL

Alternative Pop-Rock, Indie Rock

One of the most resilient and criminally underappreciated bands to rise from the Midwestern underground community, the career of the noisy guitar unit Eleventh Dream Day was a textbook study in alt-rock endurance; despite a nightmarish major-label tenure, ill-timed roster changes, and commercial indifference, the group persevered, ultimately emerging as elder statesmen of the flourishing Chicago independent scene of the mid-'90s.

Eleventh Dream Day's origins dated to 1981, when singer/guitarist Rick Rizzo met vocalist/drummer Janet Beveridge Bean at the University of Kentucky. Inspired by punk, Rizzo taught himself to play guitar with the aid of Neil Young's *Zuma* songbook; Young remained the group's major inspiration throughout their career, his incendiary aesthetic informing much of Rizzo's own raw, rootsy style. The couple soon relocated to Chicago, where they teamed with bassist Douglas McCombs and guitarist Baird Figi. After several years of honing their explosive live set, Eleventh Dream Day finally recorded their eponymous debut EP for the Amoeba label in 1987.

The full-length *Prairie School Freakout*, recorded in one six-hour span with a buzzing, dilapidated amplifier, followed in 1988, and brought Eleventh Dream Day to the attention of Atlantic Records, which signed the group for 1991's assured *Beet*. Despite critical acclaim, the record failed to find an audience; *Lived to Tell* followed in 1992 and suffered the same fate as its predecessor. In the middle of a tour to promote the album, Figi abruptly quit, and was replaced by Bodeco's Matthew "Wink" O'Bannon before 1993's superb *El Moodio*.

After three commercial strikes, Atlantic unceremoniously dropped the group. After a hiatus that allowed Rizzo and Bean to concentrate on raising their newborn child, Eleventh Dream Day enlisted co-producers Brad Wood and John McEntire (McCombs' partner in the post-rock supergroup Tortoise) for 1994's *Ursa Major*, released on City Slang. After another break—during which time Rizzo returned to college, Bean focused on her country side project Freakwater, and O'Bannon exited to return to Bodeco—Eleventh Dream Day signed to the Chicago-based indie Thrill Jockey to record 1997's *Eighth*. *—Jason Ankeny*

Prairie School Freakout / 1988 / Amoeba ✦✦✦

Beet / Nov. 1989 / Atlantic ✦✦✦

Beet only hints at what was to come, but in retrospect it holds up pretty well. The songs are strong, and the playing is energetic, but this is not the place where the epiphanies are. *—John Dougan*

● **Lived to Tell** / Jan. 16, 1991 / Atlantic ✦✦✦✦

The underrated album of 1991. *Lived to Tell* is a resounding triumph exhibiting all of Eleventh Dream Day's strengths without ever sounding like generic alternative rock. Sad, combative, and raging, this is a record that reveals more with each play. *—John Dougan*

El Moodio / Apr. 6, 1993 / Atlantic ✦✦✦✦

EDD got the big heave-ho from Atlantic when *El Moodio* stiffed. But I can't come up with a single reason as to why this album didn't make them the toast of MTV's Buzz Bin. Perhaps not as galvanizing as *Lived to Tell*, but there's no dross here, just lots and lots of guitars, passion, and energy. *—John Dougan*

Ursa Major / 1994 / Atavistic ✦✦✦

Now recording for an indie label, guitarist Wink O'Bannon quit before the recording of *Ursa Major*, and Janet Bean was also consumed with her excellent side band Freakwater, but this record was winner number three. A tad more experimental (and some would argue less accessible, though not me) than earlier records, *Ursa Major* is still loaded with supple, pretty melodies and intense, rampaging guitars. *—John Dougan*

Eighth / Feb. 11, 1997 / Thrill Jockey ✦✦✦✦

The Elvis Brothers

f. 1980, Chicago, IL

Power Pop

The Elvis Brothers were a power pop trio (with a hint of rockabilly and roots rock) comprised of Rob Elvis (guitar, vocals), Graham Elvis (bass, vocals), and Brad Elvis (drums). Formed in the early '80s in Chicago, the band released a pair of albums for Portrait (*Movin' Up* in 1983 and *Adventure Time* in 1985) that, while not groundbreaking, were well-crafted pop, highly regarded in power pop circles. The Broth-

ers were dropped from Portrait when their sound fell from favor in the mid-'80s. The original lineup returned in 1992 with the limited edition *Now Dig This* for the independent Recession label. Recession has also reissued the first two albums on one compact disc. *—Chris Woodstra*

Movin' Up / 1983 / Portrait ✦✦✦✦

The cover says it all as the Elvis Brothers are dressed in the standard power-pop regalia of the late '70s and early '80s. On the front cover, the group is standing in a Beatlesque pose and caught in mid-jump, ala *A Hard Day's Night* on the back. What you get inside is a nice LP of light, enjoyable, pop songs. Once you've picked up most of the artists represented on *D.I.Y.*, this may be a good record to search out. *—Jim Worbois*

Adventure Time / 1985 / Portrait ✦✦✦

Now Dig This / 1993 / Recession ✦✦✦

Seven years after their unfortunate breakup, the Brothers returned in 1992, picking up right where they left off with a rootsy take on power pop. While this may not quite measure up to their first two albums, it's a welcome return and quite a lot of fun, especially for the band's cult following who are, after all, probably the only ones who sought out the album. Only a small, limited pressing was done—all of them signed by the band. *—Chris Woodstra*

● **Movin Up/Adventure Time** / Oct. 3, 1995 / RCS ✦✦✦✦

A two-fer that combines the Elvis Brothers' first two releases—1983's *Movin Up* and 1985's *Adventure Time*—two long-lost gems that are an essential addition to any power pop collection. *—Chris Woodstra*

Joe Ely

b. Feb. 9, 1947, Amarillo, TX

Guitar, Vocals / Progressive Country, Country-Rock, Outlaw Country, Americana

In the '70s, C&W was full of artists referred to as "outlaws," mavericks who bucked the stodgy Nashville music establishment by writing their own songs, recording with their road bands, and producing their own records. The genre produced a slew of acts, but Lubbock, TX, native Joe Ely epitomized the form. Unlike most of that era's big names, Ely remains a viable artist. He got his start in the early '70s, working with Butch Hancock and Jimmie Dale Gilmore in a group called the Flatlanders. Their only album didn't go far, and the group broke up. (Rounder reissued the album in 1990.) Around the mid-'70s, Ely formed an eclectic group that was able to swing from Cajun and Western to honky-tonk stomps and rockabilly; it was signed to MCA in 1977. Ely released an eponymous debut that year, using songs written by ex-Flatlanders Gilmore and Butch Hancock and throwing in some of his own road-worn, oddly poetic originals. The next year brought *Honky Tonk Masquerade*, the cornerstone of Ely's legacy and one of modern country's most ambitious albums. Further albums (especially *Live Shots*, recorded during his European tour with The Clash) brought Ely to the attention of rock fans and netted ecstatic reviews in country and pop magazines (but, mysteriously, produced no hits). MCA dropped Ely in 1983, and he woodshedded until 1987, when the independent Hightone label signed him and released *Lord of the Highway*. Another Hightone album followed before Ely (whose influence was being felt by the new breed of country neo-traditionalists) re-signed with MCA, releasing another live set and *Love and Danger*. He's yet to top his late-'70s achievements, but Ely remains an energetic and passionate live performer and an occasionally inspired songwriter. *—John Floyd*

Joe Ely / 1977 / MCA ✦✦✦✦

Ely's first album came out while country's outlaw movement was in full swing, but *Joe Ely* took it one better. This is a roots-rocking country album with tunes by Jimmie Dale Gilmore ("Treat Me Like a Saturday Night") and Butch Hancock ("She Never Spoke Spanish to Me," "If You Were a Bluebird") that deserve the near-classic status their cult of fans has bestowed on them. *—Brian Mansfield*

● **Honky Tonk Masquerade** / 1978 / MCA ✦✦✦✦

Ely's best album, *Honky Tonk Masquerade* contains everything from Texas weepers ("Because of the Wind") to roadhouse rockers ("Fingernails"). Among the best tunes are Jimmie Dale Gilmore's "Tonight I Think I'm Gonna Go Downtown" and Butch Hancock's "West Texas Waltz." Nobody made country records like this in 1978. Come to think of it, they still don't. *—Brian Mansfield*

Down in the Drag / 1979 / MCA ✦✦✦

Simply another set of decent country songs. Ely's momentum was gone: His band, for the first time, sounded like tired and bored pros. *—John Floyd*

Live Shots / 1980 / MCA ✦✦✦✦

Ely partakes of the musical diversity of his hometown, Lubbock, TX, freely mixing country, rock, Tex-Mex, and hard honky-tonk music in excellent songs he writes himself or borrows from his friend Butch

Hancock. This is a live best-of covering his first three albums, recorded on tour in England. —*William Ruhlmann*

Musta Notta Gotta Lotta / 1981 / MCA ✦✦✦

Hi-Res / 1984 / MCA ✦✦
The only one of Ely's MCA albums the label hasn't issued on CD, *Hi-Res* is a synthesizer-heavy record that came after Ely learned about Apple computers. Preferable versions of "Cool Rockin' Loretta" and "She Gotta Get the Gettin'" appear on *Live at Liberty Lunch.* —*Brian Mansfield*

Lord of the Highway / 1987 / Hightone ✦✦✦
After a long recording layoff, Ely picked up where he'd left off in 1984 with this typical collection, whose best songs—"Me and Billy the Kid" and "Are You Listenin' Lucky?"—were Ely originals. —*William Ruhlmann*

Dig All Night / 1988 / Hightone ✦✦✦

Milkshakes & Malts / 1988 / Sunstorm ✦✦✦

Live at Liberty Lunch / Sep. 1990 / MCA ✦✦✦
This live album was recorded over two days at Liberty Lunch in Austin, TX. Ely's band has evolved from a country band with Tejano roots to a hard-rocking Texas ensemble highlighted by guitarist David Grissom, who later defected to John Cougar Mellencamp. —*Brian Mansfield*

Love & Danger / Sep. 29, 1992 / MCA ✦✦✦✦
Ely is stark and restless . . . His muse still roams the highways in search of whatever, his romance doomed by a twist of fate. He's a more objective observer, a storyteller who captures the tragic side of the well-defined characters of "The Road Goes On Forever" and "Every Night About This Time." Ely conveys much—if not most—of a song's emotion through his inspired electric guitar playing. The string-bending is at high-pressure intensity for "Love Is the Beating of Hearts," then drops deep, sonorous, and echoed for "Slow You Down." —*Roch Parisien*

No Bad Talk or Loud Talk 1977–'81 / Apr. 25, 1995 / Edsel ✦✦✦✦

Letter to Laredo / Aug. 29, 1995 / MCA ✦✦✦✦
Flamenco guitarist Teye is the dominant instrumentalist on a Joe Ely album that fits the "unplugged" tag—drums, electric bass, and various, mostly acoustic guitars and occasional accordion and harmonica—and that could be played without complaint in any cantina along the Rio Grande. Ely is joined in his story songs about Southwest life and romantic devotion by Raul Malo, Jimmie Dale Gilmore, and Bruce Springsteen, while Butch Hancock and Tom Russell contribute the strongest material; Hancock's is a sequel, "She Finally Spoke Spanish to Me," and Russell's is the tragic story of a man who bets his future on a cock fight. *Letter to Laredo* is a mood piece with less of the raw energy of many of Ely's albums, but the singer is in his element, and his mastery of the form is obvious. —*William Ruhlmann*

Time for Travellin' / Aug. 6, 1996 / Edsel ✦✦✦

The Embarrassment

f. 1979, Wichita, KS, **db.** 1990
Alternative Pop-Rock, Post-Punk
The Embarrassment emerged from Wichita, KS, in 1979; although influenced by punk and new wave, their relative isolation from the thriving musical environments of New York or Los Angeles allowed them to create a distinctly self-styled and original sound built on complex guitar dynamics and tense rhythms. Inspired by the Ramones, the Stooges, and the Sex Pistols, vocalist John Nichols, guitarist Bill Goffrier, and drummer Brent Giessmann formed their first band, the Mainliners, in high school. At college, they recruited bassist Ron Klaus, and before making their debut on a local university station, the quartet adopted their new name from a line in Kurt Vonnegut's novel *Bluebeard* in which a character notes that there is one word that sums up the human experience—embarrassment.

The group bowed in 1979 with the taut, ferocious single "Sex Drive," which won the Embarrassment acclaim from the New York music press as well as comparison to the Feelies, another nerdy and bespectacled group carving out a similarly angular style. After reappearing in 1981 with an assured, eponymous-titled EP featuring the scathing "Celebrity Art Party" and the wry "Wellsville," the group recorded 1983's dark, ambitious *Death Travels West*, a thematic examination of voyage and discovery. After returning to the studio to cut another handful of superb songs (released in 1984 as *The Embarrassment LP*, which included the 1981 EP), the group disbanded; while Giessmann joined the Del Fuegos, Goffrier formed Big Dipper. In 1988 the Embarrassment re-formed as a side project of sorts; in 1990 they issued a new album, *God Help Us*, and mounted a tour before again calling it quits. An exhaustive retrospective titled *Heyday: 1979-83* appeared in 1995. —*Jason Ankeny*

● **Heyday 1979-1983** / Oct. 17, 1995 / Bar/None ✦✦✦✦
The complete recorded sum of the Embarrassment's pre-reunion career is collected on the godsend two-disc set *Heyday: 1979-83.* In addition to both sides of their debut single "Sex Drive"/"Patio Set," the first disc—dubbed "The Standards"—also collects the entirety of their self-titled 1981 EP, *Death Travels West*, the *Retrospective* cassette and their posthumously released 1987 eponymous LP. Among the many highlights are "(I'm a) Don Juan," "Wellsville," "Rhythm Line," and "Woods of Love." The second disc—"The Scarcities"—reins in live tracks and assorted sampler contributions, including a herky-jerky cover of Michael Jackson's "Don't Stop 'til You Get Enough." Essential stuff for devotees of early-1980s American post-punk. —*Jason Ankeny*

Emerson, Lake & Palmer

f. 1970, Bournemouth, England, **db.** Dec. 1978
Group / Art-Rock/Progressive-Rock
Emerson, Lake & Palmer were progressive rock's first supergroup. Greeted by the rock press and the public as something akin to conquering heroes, they succeeded in broadening the audience for progressive rock from hundreds of thousands into tens of millions of listeners, creating a major radio phenomenon as well. Their flamboyance on record and in the studio echoed the best work of the heavy metal bands of the era, proving that classical rockers could compete for that arena-scale audience. Over and above their own commercial success, the trio paved the way for the success of such bands as Yes, who would become their chief rivals for much of the 1970s.

Keyboardist Keith Emerson planted the seeds of the group in late 1969 when his band the Nice shared a bill at the Fillmore West with King Crimson, an up-and-coming band that featured lead singer and bassist Greg Lake. Emerson and Lake first discussed the possibility of collaborating at that point, but only after the Crimson lineup began disintegrating during their first US tour did Lake finally opt to leave the group (after agreeing to sing on the forthcoming Crimson album). Upon officially teaming in 1970, Emerson and Lake auditioned several drummers, including Mitch Mitchell, before they approached Carl Palmer, a former member of the Crazy World of Arthur Brown, who later hooked up with bandmates Vincent Crane in an experimental band called Atomic Rooster.

The trio's first rehearsals mostly picked up from the Nice's and King Crimson's repertoires, including such well known numbers as "Rondo" and "21st Century Schizoid Man." In August 1970, even as they were working on the songs that would ultimately comprise their first album, ELP played its first show at Plymouth, just ahead of the Isle of Wight Festival in August 1970. The group's self-titled debut album was finished the next month and released in November; an instant success, it rose to the Top Five in England and the Top 20 in America. The single "Lucky Man" also was a hit, and their stage act rapidly became the stuff of legend.

The recording of their second album, 1971's *Tarkus*, tested the group's cohesiveness while stretching their sound in new directions. Emerson was interested in further exploiting the range of the Moog synthesizer, and had conceived of an extended suite built around an opening eruption of sound, while Palmer had come up with an unusual drum pattern that he was eager to use. When they tried to present their ideas to Lake, who had assumed the mantle of producer with the first album, however, he couldn't really grasp the piece. He balked, arguments ensued, and for a time it looked as though there might be no second album.

The group eventually agreed to disagree about the proposed track: "Tarkus" became the title of the new album, and ultimately defined the ELP sound as most people understood it; the song was loud and bombastic, somewhat gloomy in its lyrical tone, and exultant in its instrumental power. A descendant of "The Three Fates" and "Tank" from the first album, "Tarkus" was a much denser piece of music, featuring not only multiple overdubs of instruments but textures that ultimately proved very difficult to recreate on stage. After *Tarkus* hit the No. 1 spot on the English charts and reached the Top Ten in America, their March 21, 1971 concert at Newcastle City Hall—featuring the group's adaptation of Mussorgsky's *Pictures at an Exhibition*—was recorded for release, and became another major hit.

It was eight months before ELP's next record, *Trilogy*, was released in July 1972. In the interim, the group toured extensively, and they made it their business to cultivate the college audience that took most naturally to their work. With *Trilogy*, the partnership was back fully in balance, with each member taking an equal share of musical responsibility. Moreover, Lake never sang better, nor did the group ever sound more comfortable and laid back; among the eight very solid numbers in a classical-rock vein, there was tucked a track that became virtually the band's signature tune, their version of Aaron Copland's "Hoedown."

Such was the group's credibility that when it came time to record a version of the first movement of Alberto Ginastera's *Piano Concerto No. 1* and the publisher denied them permission, they approached the composer himself, who fully approved and applauded the track that became "Toccata" on *Brain Salad Surgery*, released in 1973 on their own record label, Manticore (named for one of the mythological creatures portrayed in "Tarkus"). Through Manticore ELP also released material by Pete Sinfield and the Italian progressive-rock band PFM. Sinfield's presence as a composer with Lake on *Brain Salad Surgery* helped strengthen one of the group's lingering weaknesses, their lyrics; where Lake's use of language had always tended toward the pleasant but simplistic, Sinfield, a veteran of King Crimson, provided lyrical complexity nearly as daunting as the best of their music.

In the wake of this string of successes, ELP released a triple live album, *Welcome Back My Friends to the Show That Never Ends*, in August 1974, but their streak came to a halt with *Works*, an album that also marked the dissolution of the group sound. At the time, each member was feeling constrained by the presence of the others, and their inclination was to release a trio of solo albums; cooler heads prevailed, however, and they reasoned that none of their solo works would sell remotely as well as an ELP album. The result was *Works*, a double album released in March 1977. The album consisted of three solo sides and a fourth side on which the group did two extended collaborative efforts, "Pirates" and "Fanfare for the Common Man."

The record fared poorly, and the group was never the same. *Works* destroyed ELP's unity, and their main motivation for recording seemed only to be their contractual obligations. Worse still, they'd squandered valuable time with work on the double album, time during which the public's taste was changing. The progressive bands were coming in for special criticism, and the notion of extended suites, conceptual rock albums, and classical-rock fusion now seemed hopelessly ponderous and pretentious, as the rise of punk rock and disco seemed to undermine any notion of intellectualism in rock. *Works Vol. 2*, released in November 1977, was nothing more than a collection of obscure B-sides and odd tracks dating back four years, while their next album of new material, *Love Beach*, was later described by the band members themselves as nothing more than a matter of going through the motions.

ELP split up in 1979. Lake embarked on a moderately successful solo career, Emerson took to composing film scores and recorded the occasional solo project, and after a stint with the band PM, Palmer joined the pop supergroup Asia. In the mid-1980s Emerson and Lake got together with drummer Cozy Powell as the short-lived Emerson, Lake & Powell, complete with a self-titled 1985 album. In 1991, Emerson, Lake & Palmer reunited for an album called *Black Moon*, followed by a fairly successful tour. In 1993 they released *Live at Royal Albert Hall*. Their attempt at another new album, *In the Hot Seat*, was doomed to failure by Emerson's developing of a repetitive stress disorder in one hand which required surgery and restricted the group's ability to record or perform. *—Bruce Eder*

Emerson, Lake & Palmer / 1970 / Atlantic ✦✦✦✦
Lively, ambitious, almost entirely successful debut album, made up of keyboard-dominated instrumentals ("The Barbarian," "Three Fates") and romantic ballads ("Lucky Man") showcasing all three members' very daunting talents. This album, which reached the Top 20 in America and got to No. 4 in England, showcased the group at its least pretentious and most musicianly. With the exception of a few moments on "Three Fates" and perhaps "Take a Pebble," there's not much excess, and there is a lot of impressive musicianship here. "Take a Pebble" might've passed for a Moody Blues track of the era, but for the fact that none of the Moodies' keyboardmen could solo like Keith Emerson. Even here, in a relatively balanced collection of material, the album shows the beginnings of a dark, savage, imposingly Gothic edge that had scarcely been seen before in so-called "art rock," mostly courtesy of Emerson's larger-than-life organ and synthesizer attacks. Greg Lake's beautifully sung, deliberately archaic "Lucky Man" had a brush with success on FM radio, and Carl Palmer became the idol of many thousands of would-be drummers based on this one album (especially for "Three Fates" and "Tank"), but Emerson emerged as the overpowering talent here for much of the public. The reissues of this album on either the Victory or Rhino labels are much superior in sound and graphics to the older Atlantic compact disc. *—Bruce Eder*

Tarkus / 1971 / Atlantic ✦✦✦
This album nearly broke the trio up, but instead its title track delivered the first definitive ELP composition, an apocalyptic piece that gave most listeners their first experience of the full range of the Moog synthesizer. The rest is pretty forgettable, and since the title track also appears on the group's box set, owners of the latter may skip this release. The Mobile Fidelity, Victory, or Rhino versions are all worth owning, however, over the Atlantic version. *—Bruce Eder*

Pictures at an Exhibition / 1971 / Atlantic ✦✦✦
One of the seminal documents of the progressive rock era, a record that made its way into the collections of millions of high school kids who never heard of Mussorgsky and knew nothing of Russia's Nation-

alist "Five." It does some violence to Mussorgsky, but it is also the most energetic and well realized live release in the trio's catalog, and it makes a fairly compelling case for adapting classical pieces in this way. At the time, it introduced "classical-rock" to millions of listeners, including the classical community, most of whose members regarded this record as something akin to an armed assault. The early-'70s live sound is a little crude by today's standards, but the tightness of the playing (Palmer is especially good) makes up for any sonic inadequacies. Emerson is the dominant musical personality here, but Lake and Palmer get the spotlight enough to prevent it from being a pure keyboard showcase. *—Bruce Eder*

Trilogy / 1972 / Atlantic ✦✦✦✦
The first real group effort once ELP was established, a very romantic sounding album, with a very restrained use of the synthesizer, which stands in for an orchestra here, rather than setting new boundaries in electronic sound. Mobile Fidelity, Victory, and Rhino each has out an excellent version of this disc. *—Bruce Eder*

Brain Salad Surgery / 1973 / Atlantic ✦✦✦✦
The trio's most representative and fully realized album, and their most decidedly electronic sounding. ELP move into space-rock and sci-fi rock in a fierce way, with a huge array of electronic sounds, all very dramatic. In addition to the "Karn Evil Nine" suite, the worthwhile songs include "Jerusalem" and "Still You Turn Me On." The album design was impressive enough to justify several premium-priced reissues that recreate it on CD. The Victory or Rhino versions are preferred. *—Bruce Eder*

Ladies & Gentlemen (Welcome Back My Friends to the Show That Never Ends) / 1974 / Manticore ✦✦
For serious fans only. Not quite an adequate sounding document of their stage act. Others should stick with *Pictures at an Exhibition*. *—Bruce Eder*

Welcome Back My Friends to the Show That Never Ends / 1974 / Victory Music ✦✦
A triple live LP becomes a double CD, not terribly impressive except as a document of the band's sound. Unlike Yes, whose *Yessongs* this set resembles, they just weren't as good at doing their songs on stage as they were in the studio, although it's all pretty energetic. The remastering doesn't help much. *—Bruce Eder*

Works, Vol. 1 / Oct. 1977 / Atlantic ✦✦✦
This double-disc set helped break up the trio's unity, but it still contains some great music. Emerson's "Piano Concerto," although really a sophomore music-school effort, has some good moments, Lake's side has three good songs, and Palmer is always worth hearing. The group's side is relatively weak for all of the bombast, although "Fanfare for the Common Man" has some bracing moments. The Rhino and Victory versions are far superior to the Altantic release. *—Bruce Eder*

Works, Vol. 2 / Oct. 1977 / Atlantic ✦✦
Musical leftovers, and pretty dispensable. *—Bruce Eder*

Love Beach / 1978 / Atlantic ✦✦
A record that the group released only because they owed it to their original label, and that's all one needs to know. *—Bruce Eder*

In Concert / 1979 / Atlantic ✦✦
A half-hearted release, intended to fulfill contracts and not much else. Their third live album, and their least interesting, although it was later expanded and improved in reissue form as *Works Live*. *—Bruce Eder*

The Best of ELP / 1980 / Atlantic ✦✦
A pure cash-in effort by their original label, barely adequate as a single LP compilation. *—Bruce Eder*

Black Moon / 1992 / Victory Music ✦✦
The original trio's first studio album in a dozen years suffers from the inevitable aging and darkening of Lake's voice, and a lack of real impetus, although it does contain one first-rate classical adaptation, "The Dance of the Knights" from Prokofiev's *Romeo and Juliet*. *—Bruce Eder*

● **The Atlantic Years** / Jul. 14, 1992 / Atlantic ✦✦✦✦
This double-disc set is a solid two-and-a-half hours' overview of ELP's career highlights, including "The Endless Enigma (Parts 1 & 2)," "Fugue," "Knife-Edge," "Take a Pebble," "Lucky Man," "From the Beginning," "Fanfare for the Common Man," "Still . . . You Turn Me On," Greg Lake's "Father Christmas," and excerpts from *Pictures at an Exhibition*. *—AMG*

Live at Royal Albert Hall / 1993 / Victory Music ✦✦

Works Live / Nov. 2, 1993 / Victory Music ✦✦
Improved and expanded 1990s reissue version of *In Concert*, from the trio's last tour of the 1970s, showcasing their latter day repertory. Not a definitive presentation of the trio, but a nice historical footnote. *—Bruce Eder*

The Return of the Manticore / Nov. 16, 1993 / Victory Music ✦✦✦✦
This four-CD box set draws on music from across ELP's history, although the emphasis is, naturally, on the pre-1979 breakup material. The remasterings were welcomed at the time, although their whole catalog was later upgraded, and as a bonus, the band has included a handful of unreleased tracks, including a live version of the Nice's "Rondo" from 1970 and their first studio recording of *Pictures at an Exhibition.* The booklet isn't much more than adequate, if that, without a lot of detail and more photos than text. *—Bruce Eder*

The Emotions

f. 1968, Chicago, IL, db. 1979
Soul, Quiet Storm
A trio of sisters with a strong gospel base, the Emotions (based in Chicago) were one of the leading female R&B acts of the '70s. Lead singer Sheila Hutchinson and her sisters Wanda and Jeanette were only teenagers when they crashed the soul charts in 1969 with the engaging "So I Can Love You," but they sang gospel as children and enjoyed secular fame locally before signing with Memphis-based Volt and working with producers Isaac Hayes and David Porter. When Stax folded in 1975, the group hooked up with Maurice White of Earth, Wind & Fire, an association that led to the No. 1 pop/R&B hit "Best of My Love" in 1977.

Two years after *Best of My Love,* Maurice White and the Emotions collaborated on "Boogie Wonderland," which was both a No. 2 R&B and No. 6 pop hit. They issued three more albums on White's ARC label from 1979 to 1981, but were unable to duplicate their earlier success. They moved to the Red label for the 1984 LP *Sincerely,* which included the single "All Things Come in Time." They issued three other singles from the album, but none made much impact, though each one charted. They then signed with Motown, but issued only one album, *If I Only Knew.* Sheila Hutchinson was a featured vocalist on Garry Glenn's "Feels Good to Feel Good" in 1987. Pam and Jeanette Hutchinson did background vocals on Helen Baylor's gospel song "There's No Greater Love" in 1990. Wanda Hutchinson and Jeanette sang on Earth, Wind & Fire's *Heritage* in 1990. *—Bill Dahl and Ron Wynn*

● **Best of My Love: The Best of the Emotions** / Mar. 12, 1996 / Columbia/Legacy ✦✦✦✦
This 16-track, 69-minute disc surveys the Emotions' five-year, five-album stay on Columbia Records (and the custom label ARC), which was the group's most successful period, featuring the gold No. 1 hit "Best of My Love" and the gold Top Ten hit "Boogie Wonderland" (on which the Emotions backed their mentors, Earth, Wind & Fire), both of which are heard here, along with four other songs that saw action on the pop charts. Surprisingly, the Emotions' five singles that made only the R&B charts are excluded in favor of album tracks. Unlike their earlier period at Stax, at Columbia the Emotions essentially were an adjunct to EW&F and its leader, Maurice White, and since EW&F featured tenor and falsetto vocals, the similarity was often heightened, especially on "Boogie Wonderland." Nevertheless, the sisters sang well over the horns and disco rhythms that characterized the pop/R&B music of the period. *— William Ruhlmann*

So I Can Love You/Untouched / Mar. 19, 1996 / Stax ✦✦✦✦
Combining their first two albums onto one CD, this is the best compilation of the group's Stax material, offering polished sweet soul with a gospel tinge. *—Richie Unterberger*

Alec Empire

b. May 2, 1972, Berlin, Germany
Ambient, Hardcore Techno, Post-Rock/Experimental, Electronica
The founder of Berlin's Digital Hardcore Recordings label, Alec Empire created some of the most abrasive musical works of the '90s, recording both as himself and with the trio Atari Teenage Riot. Empire's music—lo-fi industrial breakbeats played at the speed of thrash—embraced the energy of punk, the uncompromising ferocity of industrial music, and the futurism of techno. As such, he gained converts in several fields, while recording for the Belgian ambient/techno label Force Inc./Mille Plateaux as well as the Beastie Boys' Grand Royal Records, on which his American releases appeared.

Born on May 2, 1972, in West Berlin, Alec Empire was influenced by rap and the breakdancing scene. Later he began listening to early punk, and played in several bands during the late '80s. By the turn of the decade, Empire became fascinated by the sound of acid and techno, though he detested the drug culture inherent at raves. He began recording EPs for Force Inc.—as well as its subsidiary Mille Plateaux—and formed Atari Teenage Riot in 1992 with Carl Crack and Hanin Elias. A slightly more rock-oriented project, ATR nevertheless focused on the extreme; their political themes and screamed vocals were inspired by punk, but the music concentrated on acid synth and distorted breakbeats. After an Atari Teenage Riot deal with British

Phonogram collapsed, Empire used the cash in hand from the Phonogram contract to found Digital Hardcore Recordings in 1994, releasing EPs that year for himself as well as EC80R, DJ Bleed and Sonic Subjunkies.

In 1995 Mille Plateax released three Alec Empire albums: the compilation *Limited Editions 90-94,* his proper debut album *Generation Star Wars,* and *Low on Ice (The Iceland Sesssions).* That same year, Atari Teenage Riot recorded *1995,* the first album to be released on Digital Hardcore. After 1996's *Hypermodern Jazz 2000.5,* his fourth LP for Mille Plateax, Empire issued his first album for Digital Hardcore, *The Destroyer.* Soon after, the collective—including ATR and EC80R—toured the States at the invitation of Grand Royal Records, the label operated by the Beastie Boys. Grand Royal began releasing seven-inch singles by Empire, ATR, and EC80R at the end of 1996. Early the next year, many of Empire's albums were given US releases, and Atari Teenage Riot released its American debut, *Burn Berlin Burn. —John Bush*

Limited Editions 90-94 / 1994 / Mille Plateaux ✦✦✦✦
● **Generation Star Wars** / 1995 / Mille Plateaux ✦✦✦✦

En Vogue

f. Jul. 18, 1988, Oakland, CA
Urban, Club/Dance, New Jack R&B
The female vocal quartet En Vogue was conceived and put together by the production team of Denzil Foster and Thomas McElroy, both former members of Club Nouveau. Foster and McElroy wanted a vocal group who could exude sultriness and intelligence in addition to vocal proficiency, and as producers, they wanted material that would fuse R&B and girl-group traditions with hip-hop and new jack swing rhythms. The two held auditions and settled on a membership of former Miss Black California Cindy Herron, Maxine Jones, Dawn Robinson, and Terry Ellis. The new group performed two songs on Foster and McElroy's *FM2* album, and the producers crafted an image of them as stylish, sophisticated, and sexy. Originally called For You, the women switched to the more elegant Vogue, and then En Vogue after learning of another group with a very similar name.

En Vogue's debut album, *Born to Sing,* appeared in 1990 and launched the pop crossover smash "Hold On," which peaked at No. 2 and helped the album go platinum. The group attracted comparisons to the Supremes, even though group members shared lead vocals and intentionally designated no particular singer the "star." In between albums, Herron appeared in the film *Juice.* When En Vogue returned in 1992 with *Funky Divas,* critical and commercial response was overwhelming. The album's wide array of styles, from pop, rock, and R&B to rap, rock, and reggae, was lauded in print. The first three singles—"My Lovin' (You're Never Gonna Get It)," "Giving Him Something He Can Feel" (both covers of songs written by Curtis Mayfield), and "Free Your Mind" (which borrowed a chorus line from George Clinton)—reached the Top Ten, and the album went multiplatinum. En Vogue was in the Top Ten again in 1993, backing Salt-N-Pepa on their hit "Whatta Man." *—Steve Huey*

Born to Sing / 1990 / Atlantic ✦✦✦
A youthful unit with classic girl-group chops. *—Ron Wynn*

● **Funky Divas** / Sep. 1, 1992 / East West ✦✦✦✦
En Vogue are incredible singers, which is what makes *Funky Divas* a delight. Naturally, the singles are the high points on the album, but the rest of the album is hardly filler—it proves that En Vogue possess great talent. *—Stephen Thomas Erlewine*

Runaway Love / Sep. 21, 1993 / East West ✦✦
Runaway Love was a stopgap EP released after the major success of *Funky Divas.* Apart from the great title track, there is little in this collection of filler and remixes of interest to anyone but dedicated fans. *—Stephen Thomas Erlewine*

England Dan & John Ford Coley

f. 1970, Austin, TX, db. 1981
Pop, Soft Rock
Successful mid- to late-'70s soft-pop duo. England Dan was Dan Seals, brother of Seals & Croft's Jim Seals. *—Rick Clark*

The Best of England Dan & John Ford Coley / 1979 / Big Tree ✦✦✦✦
It contains "I'd Really Like to See You Tonight" (No. 2), "Nights Are Forever Without You" (No. 10), "We'll Never Have to Say Goodbye Again" (No. 9), and "Love Is the Answer" (No. 10). *—Dan Heilman*

● **The Very Best of England Dan & John Ford Coley** / Nov. 19, 1996 / Rhino ✦✦✦✦
A definitive compilation of the duo's 1970s soft-rock hits, featuring the Top Ten hits "I'd Really Love to See You Tonight," "Nights Are Forever Without You," "We'll Never Have to Say Goodbye Again," and "Love Is the Answer." *—Jason Ankeny*

The English Beat

f. 1978, Birmingham, England, **db.** 1983
New Wave, Ska-Revival

One of the earliest and most important ska-revivalist groups, Birmingham's the Beat formed in 1978 (the band had to change its name to the English Beat in the US to avoid confusion with Paul Collins' band of the same name). The multiracial band carved a distinct sound through the use of alternating lead vocals by guitarist Dave Wakeling and punk-toaster/rapper Ranking Roger, supported by a tight band consisting of Andy Cox (guitar), Dave Steel (bass), and Everett Moreton (drums).

The addition of 50-year-old saxophonist Saxa, who originally played with Prince Buster and Desmond Dekker, gave the band credibility and fleshed out its sound. An opening spot for the Selecter led to the band's signing to 2-Tone, where they released the hit single "Tears of a Clown," a wonderful version of the Smokey Robinson classic.

In 1980 the band decided to form their own 2-Tone inspired label, Go-Feet (distributed by Arista). A string of hit singles followed in the UK, including "Mirror in the Bathroom." Their debut LP, *I Just Can't Stop It*, combined the early hits with other pop/ska-oriented material. "Stand Down Margaret," with its anti-Thatcher stance, found the band moving in a more political direction, leading to several benefit gigs for "radical" causes. Musically, the Beat slowed down the tempo for a more traditional reggae sound showcased on 1981's *Wha'ppen*. This direction failed to bring the chart success of its predecessor.

Featuring a more pop-oriented approach, 1982's *Special Beat Service* helped the band increase its US fan base through MTV exposure of "Save It for Later" and "I Confess," but the band members decided to call it quits later that same year. Wakeling and Ranking Roger went on to form General Public, and Cox and Steel formed Fine Young Cannibals. —*Chris Woodstra*

☆ **I Just Can't Stop It** / Oct. 1980 / IRS ♦♦♦♦♦
The Beat's debut is a true landmark of the period, perfectly blending intense politics with a playful, yet driving dance beat. While the sound could be mimicked by other revivalists, the top-notch songwriting represented on this album is what set them apart. *I Just Can't Stop It* plays like a *Greatest Hits* album (most of their hits are found here) and still holds up today. —*Chris Woodstra*

Wha'ppen? / Jun. 1981 / IRS ♦♦♦
After the nearly perfect debut, the Beat seem somewhat directionless on *Wha'ppen?* No longer instantly danceable, the tunes have slowed to sub-reggae tempo with more political content (though less focused this time around). The two unmemorable singles, "Drowning" and "Doors of Your Heart," failed to make an impact in the charts, and only "Dreamhome in N.Z." leaves any lasting impression. —*Chris Woodstra*

Special Beat Service / 1982 / IRS ♦♦♦♦
The final Beat album focuses less on politics and more on the subject of personal relationships. Their most polished effort, the band leaves behind their early ska influences in favor of jangly pop that, at times, delves into African and Latin rhythms. Includes the flawless singles "Save It for Later" and "I Confess." —*Chris Woodstra*

● **What Is Beat?** / 1983 / IRS ♦♦♦♦
While the best introduction to Beat is still the first album, *What Is Beat* does a good job of collecting the hits from each of the three albums. The live tracks and remixes are a nice addition for completists but are generally unnecessary for anyone else. —*Chris Woodstra*

b.p.m: The Very Best of the Beat / Nov. 1995 / Arista ♦♦♦♦
b.p.m: The Very Best of the Beat nearly duplicates the original *What is Beat?* collection, covering all of the band's hit singles. Initial runs of the album came with an additional disc of remixes and dub versions, making it a nice, though not necessary, addition for fans and completists. —*Chris Woodstra*

Enigma

f. 1990, Germany
New Age, Ethnic Fusion, Club/Dance

With their 1991 hit, "Sadeness," Enigma brought the new age fascination with Gregorian chants and old-world culture to the clubs; the resulting single was both unique and irresistible. The rest of the album followed that pattern successfully, although without quite matching the stunning success of the hit single.

On their second album, 1994's *Cross of Changes*, some of the old-world elements remained, but the new age angle came to the forefront in a set of slick, radio-friendly dance-pop. *Enigma 3: Le Roi Est Mort, Vive le Roi* followed in 1996. —*Stephen Thomas Erlewine*

● **MCMXC A.D.** / 1990 / Charisma ♦♦♦♦
Driven by the Gregorian chants of the hit single "Sadeness Part I," Enigma's debut album is an interesting fusion of new age sensibilities and dancefloor rhythms. —*Stephen Thomas Erlewine*

The Cross of Changes / Feb. 8, 1994 / Charisma ♦♦♦
On Enigma's second album, their latent new age tendencies come to the forefront and occasionally obscure their usually captivating dance tracks. —*Stephen Thomas Erlewine*

Enigma 3: Le Roi Est Mort, Vive Le Roi / Nov. 26, 1996 / Virgin ♦♦♦
With *Enigma 3: Le Roi Est Mort, Vive Le Roi*, the group continues to phase out the dance elements of their music, moving toward lush sonic landscapes, informed by both electronics and worldbeat. The result is a fascinating, intriguing listen, especially for listeners already attuned to Enigma's idiosyncratic take on new age. —*Rodney Batdorf*

Brian Eno

b. May 15, 1948, Woodbridge, England
Synthesizer / Electronic, Ambient, Art-Rock/Progressive-Rock, Experimental

Ambient pioneer, glam-rocker, hit producer, multimedia artist, technological innovator, worldbeat proponent, and self-described non-musician—over the course of his long, prolific, and immensely influential career, Brian Eno was all of these things and much, much more. Determining his creative pathways with the aid of a deck of instructional, tarot-like cards called Oblique Strategies, Eno championed theory over practice, serendipity over forethought, and texture over craft; in the process, he forever altered the ways in which music is approached, composed, performed, and perceived, and everything from punk to techno to new age bears his unmistakable influence.

Brian Peter George St. John le Baptiste de la Salle Eno was born in Woodbridge, England, on May 15, 1948. Raised in rural Suffolk, an area neighboring a US Air Force base, as a child he grew enamored of the "Martian music" of doo wop and early rock 'n' roll broadcast on American Armed Forces radio. A tenure at art school introduced him to the work of contemporary composers John Tilbury and Cornelius Cardew, as well as minimalists John Cage, LaMonte Young, and Terry Riley. Instructed in the principles of conceptual painting and sound sculpture, Eno began experimenting with tape recorders, which he dubbed his first musical instrument, finding great inspiration in Steve Reich's tape orchestration "It's Gonna Rain."

After joining the avant-garde performance art troupe Merchant Taylor's Simultaneous Cabinet, as well as assuming vocal and "signals generator" duties with the improvisational rock unit Maxwell Demon, Eno joined Cardew's Scratch Orchestra in 1969, later enlisting as a clarinetist with the Portsmouth Sinfonia. In 1971 he rose to prominence as a member of the seminal glam band Roxy Music, playing the synthesizer and electronically treating the band's sound. A flamboyant enigma decked out in garish makeup, pastel feather boas, and velvet corsets, his presence threatened the focal dominance of frontman Bryan Ferry, and relations between the two became strained. Finally, after just two LPs—1972's self-titled debut and 1973's brilliant *For Your Pleasure*—Eno exited Roxy's ranks to embark on a series of ambitious side projects.

The first, 1973's *No Pussyfooting*, was recorded with Robert Fripp; for the sessions Eno began developing a tape-delay system, dubbed "Frippertronics," which treated Fripp's guitar with looped delays in order to ultimately employ studio technology as a means of musical composition, thereby setting the stage for the later dominance of sampling in hip-hop and electronica. Eno soon turned to his first solo project, the frenzied and wildly experimental *Here Come the Warm Jets*, which reached the UK Top 30 on the strength of the proto-punk hit "Seven Deadly Finns." During a brief tenure fronting the Winkies, he mounted a series of British live performances despite ill health; less than a week into the tour, Eno's lung collapsed, and he spent the early part of 1974 hospitalized.

Upon recovering, he traveled to San Francisco, where he stumbled upon a set of postcards depicting a Chinese revolutionary opera, which inspired 1974's *Taking Tiger Mountain (By Strategy)*, another spawling, free-form collection of abstract pop. A 1975 car accident which left Eno bedridden for several months resulted in perhaps his most significant innovation, the creation of ambient music: unable to move to turn up his stereo to hear above the din of a rainstorm, he realized that music could assume the same properties as light or color, and blend thoroughly into its given atmosphere without upsetting the environmental balance. Heralded by the release of 1975's minimalist *Another Green World*, Eno plunged completely into ambient with his next instrumental effort, *Discreet Music*, the first chapter in a ten-volume series of experimental works issued on his own Obscure label.

After returning to pop structures for 1977's *Before and After Science*, Eno continued his ambient experimentation with *Music for Films*, a collection of fragmentary pieces created as soundtracks for imaginary motion pictures. Concurrently, he became a much-sought-after collaborator and producer, teaming with the German group Cluster as well as David Bowie, for whom he produced the landmark trilogy *Low, Heroes,* and *Lodger.* Additionally, Eno produced the seminal No Wave compilation *No New York* and in 1978 began a long, fruitful union with Talking Heads, his involvement expanding over the course of the albums *More Songs About Buildings and Food* and 1979's *Fear of Music* to the point that by the time of 1980's world music-inspired *Remain in Light,* Eno and frontman David Byrne shared co-writing credits on all but one track. Friction with Byrne's bandmates hastened Eno's departure from the group's sphere, but in 1982 he and Byrne reunited for *My Life in the Bush of Ghosts,* a landmark effort that fused electronic music with a pioneering use of Third World percussion.

In the interim, Eno continued to perfect the concept of ambient sound with 1979's *Music for Airports,* a record designed to calm air passengers against fears of flying and the threat of crashes. In 1980 he embarked on collaborations with minimalist composer Harold Budd (*The Plateau of Mirror*) and avant-trumpeter Jon Hassell (*Possible Musics*) as well as Quebecois producer Daniel Lanois, with whom Eno would emerge as one of the most commercially successful production teams of the 1980s, helming a series of records for the Irish band U2 (most notably *The Joshua Tree* and *Achtung Baby*) that positioned the group as one of the world's most respected and popular acts. Amidst this flurry of activity, Eno remained dedicated to his solo work, moving from the earthbound ambience of 1982's *On Land* to other worlds for 1983's *Apollo Atmospheres and Soundtracks,* a collection of space-themed work created in tandem with Lanois and Eno's brother Roger. In 1985 Eno resurfaced with *Thursday Afternoon,* the soundtrack to a VHS cassette of "video paintings" by artist Christine Alicino.

After producer John Cale's 1989 solo effort *Words for the Dying,* the duo collaborated on 1990's *Wrong Way Up,* the first record in many years to feature Eno vocals. Two years later he returned with the solo projects *The Shutov Assembly* and *Nerve Net,* followed in 1993 by *Neroli; Glitterbug,* a 1994 soundtrack to a posthumously-released film by Derek Jarman, was subsequently reworked by Jah Wobble and issued in 1995 as *Spinner.* In addition to his musical endeavors, Eno frequently ventured into other realms of media, beginning in 1980 with the vertical-format video *Mistaken Memories of Medieval Manhattan;* along with designing a 1989 art installation to help inaugurate a Shinto shrine in Japan and 1995's *Self-Storage,* a multimedia work created with Laurie Anderson, he published a diary, 1996's *A Year with Swollen Appendices,* and formulated *Generative Music I,* a series of audio screen-savers for home computer software. —*Jason Ankeny*

No Pussyfooting / Nov. 1973 / EG ✦✦✦✦
Robert Fripp's collaboration with Brian Eno. A musical landscape made up of sedate guitar feedback echoed, repeated, and otherwise treated by tape recorder. Today this would be classified under "new age." The follow-up, *Evening Star,* is similar. —*William Ruhlmann*

Here Come the Warm Jets / Jan. 1974 / EG ✦✦✦✦
Eno's solo debut features complex but tight pop songs with bizarre and often hilarious lyrics, which puncture the treated guitar and keyboard textures. —*John Floyd*

Taking Tiger Mountain (By Strategy) / Nov. 1974 / EG ✦✦✦✦
They lack the vibrant and energetic rock-laced enthusiasm of *Here Come the Warm Jets,* but these experimentations within the pop format give art-rock a good name. —*John Floyd*

Evening Star / 1975 / Antilles ✦✦✦
Robert Fripp and Brian Eno's second collaboration is similar to their first, *No Pussyfooting,* in that it combines Fripp's interest in droning tape loops with Eno's taste in sound landscapes. Electronic instrumental music with a meditative air. —*William Ruhlmann*

★ **Another Green World** / Nov. 1975 / EG ✦✦✦✦✦
Eno's masterpiece contains a sumptuous aural melange of dense ambient instrumental snippets and rich, often beautiful pop melodies. This is one of those albums that should be enjoyed in one concentrated sitting. —*John Floyd*

Discreet Music / Dec. 1975 / EG ✦✦✦✦
Taking a cue from Satie's idea of "musique d'ameublement" (furniture music, that just exists like furnishings in an apartment, played so as not to draw attention to itself (not really Muzak, a company which seeks to produce a more intentional work-product effect), Eno created several albums of what he termed "ambient music" which combined a softer style of pattern music (influenced by Bryars, Nyman, Harold Budd) with environmental noises. *Discreet Music* is probably the best of these, using an Oliveros-style tape delay arrangement to slowly change patterns of repeating sounds. —*Blue Gene Tyranny*

After the Heat / 1978 / Sky ✦✦✦
After The Heat is Eno's collaboration with Dieter Moebius and Hans-Joachim Roedelius of the German avant-garde group Cluster. It consists of slow-moving instrumentals full of repeated synthesizer sound patterns and sustained guitar notes in the "ambient" style familiar from Eno's collaborations with Robert Fripp and albums of his own, such as *Discreet Music.* (One song, "Broken Head," features recited vocals by Eno, and on another, "The Belldog," he sings. On "Tzima N'arki," he sings backwards.) —*William Ruhlmann*

☆ **Before & After Science** / May 1978 / EG ✦✦✦✦✦
This thrashing partial return to more basic song structures is punctuated by the exhilarating "King's Lead Hat." —*John Floyd*

Music for Films / Oct. 1978 / EG ✦✦✦
Recorded intermittently between 1975 and 1978, *Music for Films* compiles moody, instrumental electronic pieces intended as soundtrack material for imaginary motion pictures; the songs are brief and fragmentary, ranging from the haunting "Sparrowfall" to the luminous, densely-layered "Quartz." —*Jason Ankeny*

Ambient 1: Music for Airports / Mar. 1979 / EG ✦✦✦✦
Four subtle, slowly evolving pieces grace Eno's first conscious effort at creating ambient music. The composer was in part striving to create music that approximated the effect of visual art. Like a fine painting, these evolving soundscapes don't require constant involvement on the part of the listener. They can hang in the background and add to the atmosphere of the room, yet the music also rewards close attention with a sonic richness absent in standard types of background or easy-listening music. —*Linda Kohanov*

Ambient 2: The Plateaux of Mirror / 1980 / EG ✦✦✦

Fourth World Vol. 1: Possible Musics / 1980 / EG ✦✦✦

Ambient 3: Day of Radiance / 1981 / EG ✦✦✦

Ambient 4: On Land / Apr. 1982 / EG ✦✦✦✦
Eno's most masterful ambient effort to date was created as a musical antidote to the confusion of life in New York City. An earthy sense of repose underlies intricate sonic essays. —*Linda Kohanov*

Working Backwards 1983-1973 / 1983 / EG ✦✦✦
The soundtrack to a VHS cassette of Christine Alicino's "video paintings" (which can be viewed properly only when the monitor is stood on its side), *Thursday Afternoon* is an hour-long, uninterrupted ambient piece created in Eno's "holographic" compositional style, in which even the most brief snippet of music is representative of the performance as a whole. —*Jason Ankeny*

Music for Films, Vol. 2 / 1983 / EG ✦✦✦
Like its predecessor, *Music for Films Volume 2* collects more of Eno's scores for non-existent motion pictures. —*Jason Ankeny*

More Blank Than Frank / 1986 / EG ✦✦
More Blank Than Frank compiles highlights from Eno's legendary albums *Here Come the Warm Jets, Taking Tiger Mountain (By Strategy), Another Green World,* and *Before and After Science.* —*Jason Ankeny*

Desert Island Selection / 1986 / EG ✦✦✦✦
A CD-only survey of Eno's first four albums, with songs hand-picked and annotations written by Eno himself. —*John Floyd*

Music for Films 3 / 1988 / Opal ✦✦✦

Wrong Way Up / Oct. 1990 / Opal ✦✦✦✦
Both Eno and Cale have always flirted with conventional pop music throughout their careers, while reserving the right to go off on less accessible experiments, which means they've always held out the promise that they would make something as attractive as this synthesizer-dominated collection, on which Eno comes as close to the mainstream as he has since *Another Green World* and Cale is as catchy as he's been since *Honi Soit.* The result is one of the best albums either one has ever made. —*William Ruhlmann*

Nerve Net / Sep. 1992 / Opal ✦✦
Nerve Net appears to be Eno's attempt to turn the page on his ambient work and strike out in a more cluttered, noisy, quasi-industrial direction for the '90s. While the liner notes would have us believe that his polyrhythmic dabbling is all very forward looking, this kind of stuff has all been done before. —*Roch Parisien*

The Shutov Assembly / Oct. 1992 / Opal ✦✦✦
If *The Shutov Assembly* is reminiscent of Brian Eno's earlier "ambient" music projects dating back to *Discreet Music* (1975), it shouldn't be surprising. Recorded between 1985 and 1990, the atmospheric, slow-moving sound patterns are more, the artist contends, like paintings than music. *The Shutov Assembly,* dedicated to Russian painter Sergei Shutov is, like the similar works in his catalog (he cites *Music for Films, On Land, Music for Airports, Thursday Afternoon,* and *Nerve Net,* as well as *Discreet Music*), as much a concept as a record. —*William Ruhlmann*

Neroli / Aug. 3, 1993 / Caroline ✦✦✦
Named after an oil derived from orange blossoms intended as an aid for clear thoughts, *Neroli* is subtitled "Thinking Music Part IV"; an hour-long electronic piece, it represents Eno at his most ambient, with no rhythmic pulse and only scattered hints of melody. —*Jason Ankeny*

Eno Box II / Nov. 16, 1993 / Virgin ✦✦✦✦
The first of two retrospective box sets devoted to the groundbreaking work of Brian Eno, *II* concentrates on his pop and vocal material, including some selections from the unreleased *My Squelchy Life*. Although his music still makes the most sense in the context of his albums, *II* is solid crash-course introduction to his work, which remains as revolutionary today as it was when it was released. —*Stephen Thomas Erlewine*

Eno Box I / Mar. 22, 1994 / Virgin ✦✦✦✦
Box I features a cross-section of Eno's influential ambient music; while this music often works better in its original context, the box offers a good introduction to Eno's innovative instrumental work. —*Stephen Thomas Erlewine*

Enya

b. May 17, 1961, Donegal, Ireland
Keyboards, Vocals / New Age, Alternative Pop-Rock, Contemporary Instrumental
With her blend of folk melodies, synthesized backdrops and classical motifs, Enya created a distinctive style of music that more closely resembled new age music than the folk and Celtic music that provided her initial influences. Enya is from Gweedore, County Donegal, Ireland, which she left in 1980 to join the Irish band Clannad, the group that already featured her older brothers and sisters. She stayed with Clannad for two years, before hooking up with producer Nicky Ryan and lyricist Roma Ryan, with whom she recorded film and television scores. The result was a successful album of TV music for the BBC. Enya then recorded *Watermark* (1988), which featured her distinctive, flowing music and multi-overdubbed trancelike singing; the album sold four million copies worldwide. *Watermark* established Enya as an international star and launched a successful career that lasted well into the '90s.

Enya (born Eithne Ni Bhraonain) was born into a musical family. Her father, Leo Brennan, was the leader of the Slieve Foy Band, a popular Irish show band; her mother was an amateur musician. Most important to Enya's career were her siblings, who formed Clannad in 1976 with several of their uncles. Enya joined the band as a keyboardist in 1979, and contributed to several of the group's popular television soundtracks. In 1982 she left Clannad, claiming that she was uninterested in following the pop direction the group had begun to pursue. Within a few years, she was commissioned, along with producer/arranger Nicky Ryan and lyricist Roma Ryan, to provide the score for a BBC-TV series called "The Celts." The soundtrack was released in 1986 as her eponymous solo album.

Enya didn't receive much notice, but Enya and the Ryans' second effort, *Watermark*, became a surprise hit upon its release in 1988. "Orinoco Flow," the first single pulled from the album, became a No. 1 hit in Britain, helping the album eventually sell four million albums worldwide. Enya spent the years after the success of *Watermark* rather quietly; her most notable appearance was a cameo on Sinead O'Connor's *I Do Not Want What I Haven't Got*. She finally released *Shepherd Moons*, her follow-up to *Watermark*, in 1991. *Shepherd Moons* was more successful than its predecessor, entering the US charts at No. 17 and eventually selling over ten million copies worldwide.

Again, Enya was slow to follow up on the success of *Shepherd Moons*, spending nearly four years working on her fourth album. The record, entitled *Memory of Trees*, was released in December 1995. *Memory of Trees* entered the US charts at No. 9 and sold over two million copies within its first year of release. —*Stephen Thomas Erlewine & William Ruhlmann*

Enya / 1987 / Atlantic ✦✦✦

● **Watermark** / 1988 / Reprise ✦✦✦✦
The US was a little slower than the rest of the world to admire Enya's blend of ethereal multi-tracked vocals and subtly flowing music, but this album's single, "Orinoco Flow (Sail Away)," which topped the charts elsewhere, was a Top 25 hit, and the album went gold. —*William Ruhlmann*

Shepherd Moons / Nov. 1991 / Reprise ✦✦✦✦
While it follows the same basic formula as the multi-million-seller *Watermark*, *Shepherd Moons* isn't quite as captivating, but that's only a relative term. Most of the album captures the same mystical, trance-inducing mood that made *Watermark* a success and Enya was rewarded accordingly—it sold as much as her previous album. —*Stephen Thomas Erlewine*

Celts / Nov. 1992 / Reprise ✦✦✦
The history of this album is as follows: In the mid-1980s, Enya recorded the soundtrack for a BBC television documentary called "The Celts." The music was released on BBC Records in the UK in December 1986 under the title *Enya*. It was released initially in the US on Atlantic Records (81842) in 1987. In November 1992, WEA Records in the UK issued a revised version of the album under the title *The Celts*, containing a newly re-recorded track, "Portrait (Out of the Blue)." This version of the album was released in the US on Reprise Records in June 1995. In any of its forms, the album is characteristic of the airy style of Enya's later big bits, *Watermark* and *Shepherd Moons*, though in a slightly less ornate setting. —*William Ruhlmann*

Memory of Trees / Dec. 5, 1995 / Reprise ✦✦✦
Memory of Trees took Enya four years to complete, but most fans will find the wait worthwhile. Enya doesn't depart from her trademark sound—there are still layers of atmospheric synthesizers and ethereal vocals—yet it doesn't repeat *Watermark* and *Shepherd Moons*, it builds on them. *Memory of Trees* may lack the original spark that made its predecessors so fascinating, but it remains an endlessly intriguing listen. —*Sara Sytsma*

Episode Six

f. 1965, England, db. 1969
British Invasion
Most famous for including bassist Roger Glover and singer Ian Gillan before they joined Deep Purple, Episode Six managed to release no less than nine British singles between 1966 and 1969 without coming close to a hit record or establishing a solid identity. Also prominently featuring organist/singer Sheila Carter-Dimmock, the group's 1966-67 singles were rather light pop-rock harmony numbers, with an occasional ballad and a bit of a soul influence. Light years removed from Deep Purple, Episode Six was nothing if not eclectic in their choice of material, trying numbers by the Hollies, the Beatles, the Tokens, and Charles Aznavour, as well as a British hot-rod tune (written by Glover). While their repertoire lacked focus, their singles were pleasant, and their fine cover of Tim Rose's "Morning Dew" would have been a deserving hit.

In 1967 they began to fuse pop and psychedelia with reasonably impressive results, especially the single "I Can See Through You" (written by Glover), one of the finest British psychedelic obscurities. Their final two singles showed the band going in a much more progressive direction and anticipating some of the most indulgent art-rock of the '70s with "Mozart Versus the Rest," which assaulted one of the composer's most famous riffs with manic electric guitars. Episode Six folded in 1969, after Gillan and Glover had joined Deep Purple. —*Richie Unterberger*

● **Roots of Deep Purple: the Complete Episode Six** / 1994 / Collectables ✦✦✦✦
This definitive 28-track anthology includes everything recorded by the group—all of their singles, solo efforts by a couple of group members, and six previously unreleased songs. Although it's more a reflection of the pop trends of the day than an original vision, it's enjoyable listening, with some fine harmonies and reasonably strong material. —*Richie Unterberger*

EPMD

f. 1987, Brentwood, NY
East Coast Rap, Hip Hop
Erick Sermon and Parrish Smith didn't have much to recommend themselves—minimalistic, sample-reliant production and a monotone rapping style—but their recordings as EPMD were tremendously successful in hip-hop's underground during the late '80s and early '90s. Over the course of four albums (from the 1988 classic *Strictly Business* to 1992's *Business Never Personal*), they rarely varied from two themes, the dissing of sucker MCs and recounting sexual exploits.

Though EPMD's hardcore style influenced the urban-oriented gangsta '90s, Erick Sermon (b. Nov. 25, 1968) and Parrish Smith (b. May 13, 1968) were both raised in Long Island's suburb of Brentwood. They moved into rap separately, with Smith DJing for Rock Squad on a single for Tommy Boy. After coming together in 1987—naming themselves EPMD, short for "Erick and Parrish Making Dollars"—the duo recorded "It's My Thing" in three hours. The single was later licensed to Chrysalis, and EPMD signed to Sleeping Bag/Fresh Records for debut album *Strictly Business*. Propelled by several strong singles ("You Gots to Chill," the title track), the album eventually went gold, as did 1989's follow-up, *Unfinished Business*. Signed to Def Jam by the beginning of the '90s, EPMD returned in 1990 with *Business as Usual* and *Business Never Personal* two years later. The duo split later in 1992, though, prompting solo careers for each; Sermon debuted in 1993 with *No Pressure*, and Smith made his statement on 1994's *Shade Business*. —*John Bush*

★ **Strictly Business** / 1988 / Priority ✦✦✦✦✦
Erick Sermon is a classic example of using a disadvantage to one's advantage. Having a lisp and a slight speech impediment didn't prevent Sermon from pursuing a career as a rapper—and in fact, his lisp caught on in a big way and was a key element of EPMD's distinctive sound. In contrast to the hyper, forceful tendencies of many rappers, Erick and partner Parrish Smith's style of rapping is relaxed and deadpan. On *Strictly Business*, their gold debut album, the Long Islanders aren't very substantial lyrically—all they talk about is how strong their rapping skills are and how pathetic sucker MCs are. But their sound was so unique, fresh, and distinctive that such classics as "You Gots to Chill," "Strictly Business," and "The Steve Martin" proved impossible to resist. —*Alex Henderson*

Unfinished Business / 1989 / Priority ✦✦✦✦
EPMD avoided the dreaded sophomore curse and kept its artistic momentum on its second album, *Unfinished Business*. Once again, the duo triumphed by going against the flow. When MCs ranging from Public Enemy to Sir Mix-a-Lot to N.W.A. weren't hesitating to be abrasive and hyper, EPMD still had a sound that was decidedly relaxed by rap standards. For the most part, EPMD's lyrics aren't exactly profound—boasting and attacking sucker MCs is still their favorite activity. However, Erick and Parrish do challenge themselves a bit lyrically on "You Had Too Much to Drink" (a warning against drunk driving) and "Please Listen to My Demo," which recalls the days when they were struggling. But regardless of subject matter, they keep things exciting by having such an appealing, captivating sound. —*Alex Henderson*

Business as Usual / 1990 / Def Jam ✦✦✦
Business as Usual is an ironic title for EPMD's third album—for in terms of production, it was anything but business as usual for the Strong Island rappers. While *Strictly Business* and *Unfinished Business* favored a very simple and basic approach to production consisting primarily of samples (many of them clever) and drum machines, the production is busier and more involved this time—and even suggests Marley Marl. Unfortunately, the sampling isn't as clever as before. What didn't change was EPMD's relatively laidback approach to rapping and a preoccupation with sucker MCs. Though not as inspired as its two predecessors, the album does have its moments—including "Rampage" (which unites EPMD with LL Cool J), "Give the People" and "Gold Digger," a candid denunciation of "material girls" who exploit and victimize men financially after a divorce. —*Alex Henderson*

Business Never Personal / Jul. 28, 1992 / Ral ✦✦✦✦
EPMD's terse, thick-tongued rapping style was back on point with their fourth album. Although behind the scenes turmoil finally split Erick Sermon and Parrish Smith, they were together and cooking on this 1992 record. They scored their final signature single with "Crossover," a dead-on commentary directed at rappers putting pop hopes ahead of hip-hop values. "Headbanger" and "Can't Hear Nothing But the Music" were other sterling tracks from their last great album. —*Ron Wynn*

Erasure

f. 1985, London, England
Dance-Pop, Alternative Pop-Rock, Club/Dance
After disbandment of the short-lived synth-pop group Yaz, former Depeche Mode member Vince Clarke formed Erasure in 1985 with singer Andy Bell. Like Yaz and Depeche Mode, Erasure was a synth-based group, but it had stronger dance inclinations, as well as a sharper, more accessible sense of pop songcraft, than either of Clarke's previous bands. Furthermore, Erasure had the flamboyantly eccentric Andy Bell—one of the first openly gay performers in pop music—as its focal point. Bell's keening, high voice and exaggerated sense of theatrically became the band's defining image. In their native Britain, Erasure was successful from their inception. After a few years, the duo achieved commercial success in America with 1988's "Chains of Love," but they remained, in essence, a cult band on both sides of the Atlantic, cultivating a dedicated fan base over the course of their career.

Before forming Erasure, Clarke was one of the founding members of the groundbreaking synth-pop outfit Depeche Mode. He left after recording only one album with the group, choosing to form Yaz with Alison Moyet instead. After Yaz released two albums, Moyet left to pursue a solo career. Clarke participated in a short-lived alliance with vocalist Feargal Sharkey and producer Eric Radcliffe called the Assembly in 1984. After a single with vocalist Paul Quinn, he decided to form Erasure. Clarke placed an advertisement for vocalists in a British

music newspaper and received over 40 demo tapes, from which Andy Bell was selected as his partner.

Released in 1986, Erasure's first album, *Wonderland*, received poor reviews and weak sales. The duo quickly followed the album with "Sometimes," a preview from their forthcoming second album. "Sometimes" reached No. 2 on the UK charts, beginning a string of successful singles that would run into the '90s. *The Circus*, the group's second album, was released in the spring of 1987 and peaked at No. 6 on the UK charts. *The Innocents*, Erasure's third album, became their first No. 1 album in Britain upon its release in 1988. The album featured the group's first American hit, "Chains of Love," which reached No. 12 in the US; its follow-up, "A Little Respect," peaked at No. 14 in America. At the end of 1988 Erasure released the *Crackers International* EP, which reached No. 2 in Britain.

Erasure's fourth album, *Wild!*, appeared in 1989 and like its predecessor, it reached No. 1 in the UK, as did its successor, 1991's *Chorus*. Erasure released the *Abba-Esque* EP, a tribute to the Swedish pop group ABBA, in 1992; it became their first No. 1 single in the UK. Later that year Erasure released a compilation of their British singles, *Pop—The First Twenty Hits*. Two years later the duo released its fifth album, *I Say, I Say, I Say*, which featured the hit single "Always," their first American hit since 1988. Erasure's eponymous sixth album was released in the fall of 1995. It was followed in the spring of 1997 by *Cowboy*. —*Stephen Thomas Erlewine*

Wonderland / May 1986 / Sire ✦✦✦✦
Vince Clarke's inventive synthesizer music is immediately identifiable, no matter who the singer is. Here the former Depeche Mode/Yaz leader does his electronic wonders behind emotive singer Andy Bell (who bears a certain vocal resemblance to Yaz' Alison Moyet). Clarke's irresistible music is the best argument there is for synthesizers, and Bell is an appealing front man. —*William Ruhlmann*

The Circus / Mar. 1987 / Sire ✦✦✦
Erasure broke through to mass acceptance in their native UK with their second album, *The Circus*, which contained four chart singles, three of which made the Top Ten. The album stayed in the charts more than two years. In America, the group's relentless synthesizer-based music, heavy beat, and emotive, romantically tinged vocals marked them as a dance music phenomenon. "Victim of Love" became a major club hit, and *The Circus* was Erasure's first album to reach the charts, however briefly. Vince Clarke and Andy Bell were simply continuing to turn out inventive pop tracks, the best (which is to say, the catchiest) being "Sometimes" and "Victim of Love." —*William Ruhlmann*

Two Ring Circus / Dec. 1987 / Sire ✦✦
Originally released on two 45 rpm LPs, *The Two Ring Circus* was a remix version of songs from Erasure's second regular album release, *The Circus*. The first six tracks were extended, beat-heavy takes on such songs as "Sometimes" and "Victim of Love." The last three tracks were re-recordings with orchestra (and without synthesizer). *The Two Ring Circus* played to Erasure's core audience of dance music fans, though it would take their next regular album release to expand that following significantly. —*William Ruhlmann*

The Innocents / Apr. 1988 / Sire ✦✦✦✦
Erasure emerged from the dance clubs with this million-selling US breakthrough album, which contains the Top 15 hits "A Little Respect" and "Chains of Love." —*William Ruhlmann*

Crackers International / Apr. 1989 / Sire ✦✦✦
This six-track EP helped bridge the gap between the April 1988 release of *The Innocents* and the October 1989 release of *Wild!* "Stop!" and "Knocking on Your Door" (both heard in original and 12-inch remix versions) were typical hi-NRG Erasure tracks, with driving dance beats and forceful tenor vocals by Andy Bell, but they did not embrace the broader pop audience the group had reached with the 1988 singles "Chains of Love" and "A Little Respect." "She Won't Be Home" was a Christmas song, reflecting the seasonal release of the EP in November 1988 in the UK. —*William Ruhlmann*

Wild! / Oct. 1989 / Sire ✦✦
In the UK, *Wild!*, Erasure's fourth album, topped the charts, just as its predecessor, *The Innocents*, had done, spinning off four hit singles in the process. But in America, where *The Innocents* had been Erasure's commercial breakthrough, it was a different story. Maybe it was the lead-off single, "Drama!," a hard-core dance track with ponderous lyrics about "the infinite complexities of love," but *Wild!* saw Erasure falling back on its disco audience rather than continuing to expand into the mainstream. The group tried different sounds, beginning with a piano instrumental and including the Spanish-flavored "La Gloria," but much of the material was just more of the synthesized dance tracks familiar from previous records. Despite their continuing appeal at home, Erasure seemed to be stagnating creatively. —*William Ruhlmann*

Chorus / Oct. 1991 / Sire ✦✦

Chorus, Erasure's fifth album, was a look back at its earliest synth-pop style, after the relatively eclectic approach taken on its predecessor, *Wild!* Vince Clarke's instrumental tracks employed familiar electronic keyboard sounds, rather like the synth-dance music of the early '80s that he pioneered with Depeche Mode and Yaz. That was good enough to give Erasure its third straight UK No. 1 and four more hit singles, but in the US, where the title track just stumbled into the lower reaches of the singles charts, the group had fallen back on a dance-oriented cult following, its music sounding dangerously old-fashioned. — *William Ruhlmann*

Abba-Esque / Jun. 30, 1992 / Mute ✦✦✦

A fun EP of ABBA covers, it's worthwhile for any Erasure fan. — *AMG*

● **Erasure Pop!: the First 20 Hits** / Nov. 24, 1992 / Sire ✦✦✦✦

Pop!—The First 20 Hits is exactly what it claims to be—a collection of Erasure's biggest singles, which makes it the best place to get acquainted with this synth-pop band. — *Stephen Thomas Erlewine*

I Say I Say I Say / May 17, 1994 / Mute/Elektra ✦✦✦

I Say I Say I Say, Erasure's sixth full-length album, was something of a new start for the group after its successful EP of ABBA covers and greatest hits compilation. And it earned them their long-awaited third US Top 40 hit with "Always." But while the group maintained a mass following in Britain and a dance following in America, Erasure still seemed like proponents of a style that had long since peaked and passed into decline, which may have accounted for the wistful, vaguely spiritual tone of Andy Bell's lyrics. Early on, Erasure had seemed to represent a radical change in the sound of pop music, but nine years, six albums, and several EPs later, they seemed like just another weightless British pop band who happened to use synthesizers a lot. — *William Ruhlmann*

Erasure / Oct. 24, 1995 / Elektra ✦✦✦

It's been a long way from the bouncy dance hits of Erasure's early days to this thoughtful, expansive collection whose eponymous title suggests a new beginning. The 11 tracks run 71 1/2 minutes, leaving room for extended instrumental passages. (The lack of breaks between the songs contributes to the sense of a single long musical piece.) But it isn't so much the length as the slower tempos and reflective lyrics, which often conflate romance with religion, that make *Erasure* the group's most ponderous album. "Fingers & Thumbs (Cold Summer's Day)" is the obvious uptempo dancefloor hit, but that's an atypical track on an album that finds Andy Bell singing about fear and grace and sanctuary. Maybe AIDS is the subtextual subject in all this, or maybe Bell and Clarke are just getting philosophical after seven albums. Whatever the reasons, they are becoming the Pink Floyd of the synth pop set. — *William Ruhlmann*

Cowboy / Apr. 22, 1997 / Warner Brothers ✦✦✦

For *Cowboy*, Erasure hooked up with Orbital producer Gareth Jones, and the record appropriately has some light trip-hop and ambient flourishes. Nevertheless, Erasure can't change their modus operandi no matter how hard they try, and the result is a new sound that never sounds new. Furthermore, Andy Bell and Vince Clarke have hit a songwriting rut, and all of the songs blend, with very few individual tunes standing out, suggesting that the group is beginning to run out of ideas. — *Stephen Thomas Erlewine*

Eric B. & Rakim

f. 1985, New York, NY, db. 1992

Hip Hop, East Coast Rap

One of rap's most influential acts during the 1980s, Eric B & Rakim made the sampling of James Brown records the main source for hiphop's sound during the late '80s and early '90s, beginning with their stellar debut, *Paid in Full*. While Eric B dazzled listeners with his turntable techniques, Rakim pointed the way toward the easy-rollin' style of the '90s with his laidback raps, though forceful in content. Each of the duo's first three albums achieved gold status, and they even managed the Top Five R&B hit "Friends" in 1989.

While working as a mobile DJ for New York's WBLS during 1985, Eric Barrier met William Griffin, a top MC who had grown up on Long Island. The two began recording together and emerged with "Eric B Is President." The single appeared in 1986 on Harlem's Zakia label, and became a street sensation.

Signed to 4th & Broadway the following year, Eric B & Rakim released their debut album, *Paid in Full*. The LP's success led to a contract with Uni/MCA in 1988, and their second album, *Follow the Leader*, was released that year. Two more albums followed, *Let the Rhythm Hit 'Em* (1990) and *Don't Sweat the Technique* (1992), after which the duo broke up. By the mid-'90s, Eric B. had emerged as a solo act on his own 95th Street label. — *John Bush*

★ **Paid in Full** / 1987 / 4th & Broadway ✦✦✦✦✦

Their debut contains new mixes of early singles ("I Ain't No Joke," "Eric B. Is President") and adds some prime stuff, including the monumental "Paid in Full," which became a heavily sampled item in the late '80s. — *John Floyd*

☆ **Follow the Leader** / 1988 / UNI ✦✦✦✦✦

On their second album, Eric B. & Rakim deliver an album that expands on the power of their debut. Taking a cue from the Coldcut remix of "Paid In Full" that became a hit after the release of *Paid in Full*, *Follow the Leader* has a looser, wilder beat than its predecessor. Eric B. uses the spare, James Brown-influenced grooves that dominated *Paid in Full* as a starting point, adding all kinds of production flourishes that flesh out the funk without watering it down. Not only are Eric B.'s musical accomplishments impressive, but so are Rakim's rhymes, which are more detailed and complex than before, even if his subject matter didn't change much. In short, *Follow the Leader* is the second hip-hop classic Eric B. & Rakim delivered in a row; it captures the duo at the top of their game. — *Leo Stanley*

Don't Sweat the Technique / 1990 / MCA ✦✦✦✦

While it doesn't match their trailblazing work of the late '80s, *Don't Sweat the Technique* is a solid effort from this influential duo. — *Stephen Thomas Erlewine*

Let the Rhythm Hit 'Em / May 1990 / MCA ✦✦✦

This subdued set works its magic more subtly, but the title is no joke. — *John Floyd*

Eric's Trip

f. 1990, Moncton, New Brunswick, Canada, db. 1996

Alternative Pop-Rock, Indie Rock

A product of the same Eastern Canada indie-rock community that also gave rise to the superb Jale and Sloan, the noise-pop quartet Eric's Trip formed in Moncton, New Brunswick, in 1990. The group, which took their name from a Sonic Youth song, brought together a number of longtime veterans of the Moncton scene. Drummer Mark Gaudet first surfaced in the mid-1970s as a member of Purple Knight and later performed with the Whoremoans and No Explanation, while vocalist/guitarist Rick White and guitarist Chris Thompson debuted in 1984 as members of, respectively, Bloodstain and Dang. In 1989 White and Thompson teamed in the Forest, which recruited vocalist/bassist Julie Doiron-Claytor the next year; when Gaudet joined some months later, Eric's Trip was born.

The band debuted with a self-titled 1990 cassette; a massive amount of material followed, stretching across the 1991 tapes *Caterpillars* and *Drowning*, the 1992 EPs *Warm Girl* and *Belong*, and 1993's *Peter*. After becoming the first Canadian artist signed to Sub Pop, Eric's Trip issued the EP *Songs About Chris*, followed by *Julie and the Porthole to Dimentia* (recorded for the tiny Sappy label) before closing out 1993 with their full-length Sub Pop debut *Love Tara*. After 1994's *Gordon Street Haunting* EP and the *Forever Again* LP, Doiron-Claytor's pregnancy forced the group into a hiatus; after 1996's *Purple Blue*, Eric's Trip announced their breakup. White soon resurfaced in Elevator to Hell, while Doiron-Claytor continued performing under the name Broken Girl; Gaudet joined the re-formed Purple Knight, and Thompson appeared in Moonsocket. — *Jason Ankeny*

Love Tara / Jun. 1993 / Sub Pop ✦✦✦

Their full-length debut, *Love Tara*, introduced this lo-fi pop band to the world with beautiful and noisy tracks like "Smother." This record was also one of the first to mark Sub Pop's journey from the Seattle grunge scene to a lighter, more melodic form of music. — *Heather Phares*

● **Forever Again** / 1995 / Sub Pop ✦✦✦✦

At 17 tracks, the group's expansive follow-up could be considered too long to hold attention, but Eric's Trip's power to soothe nd seethe at the same time is captivating. Tracks like "New Love" confirm that the band's sound is a study in contradictions. It's instantly catchy, but it sounds as if it was recorded on an answering machine; it's punk rock, but it's dreamy, too. The sound effects on the album (rainy day and a busy street) heighten the entrancing mood on "Forever Again." — *Heather Phares*

Purple Blue / Jan. 16, 1996 / Sub Pop ✦✦

Roky Erickson

b. Jul. 15, 1947, Dallas, TX

Guitar, Vocals / Rock 'n' Roll, Psychedelic

Like Syd Barrett, a common point of reference, Roky Erickson rose to cult-hero status as much for his tragic personal life as for his music; in light of his legendary bouts with madness and his mythic drug abuse, the influence exerted by his garage-bred psychedelia was often lost in the shuffle.

Born Roger Kynard Erickson on July 15, 1947, in Dallas, TX, he began playing the piano at age five; by age 12, he had also taken up the guitar. The child of an architect and would-be opera singer, Erickson dropped out of high school to become a professional musician. In 1965 he penned his most famous composition, "You're Gonna Miss Me," which he first recorded with a group called the Spades. The song and his high, swooping tenor brought him to the attention of another area band, the psychedelia-influenced 13th Floor Elevators, whose lyricist and jug player Tommy Hall invited Erickson to join; the Elevators soon cut their own version of "You're Gonna Miss Me," and took the single to No. 56 on the pop charts in 1966.

The record's success earned the band a deal with International Artists, but as their fame grew, so did their notoriety with local law enforcement officials, who took exception to the group's heavy experimentation with (and public support of) marijuana and LSD. The Elevators became the subject of considerable police harassment, and after Erickson was arrested for the possession of one joint in 1969, he pleaded insanity to avoid a prison term. A three-and-a-half year stint in the state's Hospital for the Criminally Insane followed; Erickson was diagnosed as a schizophrenic and subjected to extensive electroshock therapy, Thorazine, and other psychoactive treatments.

Though released from the hospital in 1973, Erickson was never the same person. He returned to performing with a new band, Bleib Alien, but his songs—a series of horror-film influenced numbers including "Red Temple Prayer (Two-Headed Dog)," "Don't Shake Me Lucifer," and "I Walked with a Zombie"—found little success. He did retain a devoted cult following, but his popularity was fully exploited by managers who took advantage of his instability to draw the singer into a series of unfair publishing contracts that resulted in a steady stream of unauthorized releases from which Erickson earned not a cent. In 1982 he signed a legal affadavit declaring that a Martian had taken residence in his body, and gradually disappeared from music as the decade wore on.

By the 1990s Erickson was struggling to survive on a $200 monthly Social Security stipend; after an arrest on mail theft charges (later dropped), he was re-institutionalized. In 1990, however, artists like R.E.M., ZZ Top, John Wesley Harding, and the Jesus & Mary Chain recorded his songs for the album *Where the Pyramid Meets the Eye: A Tribute to Roky Erickson*, which brought his work to a wider audience than ever before. In 1993 Erickson performed publicly for the first time in many years at the Austin Music Awards; a few months later, he returned to the studio with guitarists Charlie Sexton and Butthole Surfers' Paul Leary to record a number of new songs. In 1995 Leary's bandmate King Coffey released Erickson's *All That May Do My Rhyme* on his Trance Syndicate label. —*Jason Ankeny*

Holiday Inn Tapes / 1987 / Fan Club ◆◆◆
Listeners familiar with Erickson primarily via his deranged vocals and compositions with the 13th Floor Elevators and as a solo act may be shocked by the low-key, acoustic intimacy of this album. Recorded on December 1, 1986, at the Holiday Inn Red River in Austin, TX, Roky's acoustic guitar and vocals are the whole show on this ten-song performance. Going easy on the horror/monster/mystical imagery, Erickson reprises a couple of Buddy Holly classics, traditional folk tunes, and the Elevators' "May the Circle Remain Unbroken." Just to remind you that this is Roky Erickson, "The Singing Grandfather" (different versions of which open and close this album) begins with the line, "The singing grandfather will saw off your head." Sound (played into a portable recorder) is fair but quite listenable, and Roky's plaintive, yearning vocals are touching. His acoustic picking isn't bad either, although he stumbles or loses the beat once in a while (and for Roky, once in a while is an acceptable margin of error). This doesn't deliver the outrage that many have come to expect from Erickson, but it shows a glimpse of the man behind the madness. —*Richie Unterberger*

● **You're Gonna Miss Me** / Sep. 27, 1991 / Restless ◆◆◆◆
Erickson's peculiar rock vision has been too schizophrenic to produce one essential album. *You're Gonna Miss Me—The Best of Roky Erickson* rounds up the finest cuts from Erickson's solo career, from a remake of "Bermuda" up to the slashing "Don't Slander Me" and "Don't Shake Me Lucifer." An alternately rocking and frightening compilation, it has fine liner notes by John Morthland. —*John Floyd*

All That May Do My Rhyme / Feb. 13, 1995 / Trance Syndicate ◆◆◆
His mind may be fried, but Roky's vocal talents are relatively intact on this mid-1990s effort, which turns out to be one of his more subdued, folkier outings. (About half of the tracks, however, are actually remixes of sessions from the mid-'80s.) Roky's most excessive traits are mostly absent; he sounds sort of like an eccentric, updated Buddy Holly. It's the kind of roots rock that may well please the more open-minded fans of, for instance, John Fogerty or Van Morrison, although

the compositions are more pleasant than inspired. Charlie Sexton and Butthole Surfer Paul Leary make low-key session appearances; Texas singer Lou Ann Barton duets with Roky on "Starry Eyes" (reprised at the end with a version on which Roky handles all the vocals). A significant bonus, not listed on the sleeve, is "We Got Soul," the rare and fine mid-'60s single cut by Roky's first group, the Spades, before Erickson joined the 13th Floor Elevators. —*Richie Unterberger*

Esquerita (Eskew Reeder)

b. New Orleans, LA, **d.** 1986, New York City, NY
Piano, Vocals / Rock 'n' Roll
With a six-inch pompadour, brocaded shirts, rhinestone shades, and a rhythmic, belligerent style of piano playing, Esquerita was the original Little Richard, years before Mr. Penniman tutti-frutti'd his way to stardom. Working around the Dallas-New Orleans circuit in the early '50s, Esquerita's shot at the big time came when Capitol Records decided they needed their own version of Little Richard, after signing their answer to Elvis, Gene Vincent. The resulting recordings, though smartly produced, stand as some of the most untamed and unabashed sides ever issued by a major label. Long revered by rock 'n' roll fans the world over, they make Little Richard's Specialty sides look highly disciplined by comparison. Though Esquerita continued to record in a tamer style through the '60s, his Capitol sides stand as a monument to the potential of rock 'n' roll's lunatic power and the off-kilter genius of Esquerita. —*Cub Koda*

● **Capitol Collectors Series** / 1990 / Capitol ◆◆◆◆
One of the great lost rock 'n' roll wildmen, Esquerita was as crazed as Little Richard (to whom he was an inspiration musically and visually). All of his key Capitol tracks can be found on this 28-song CD. —*Jeff Tamarkin*

Gloria Estefan

b. Jan. 9, 1957, Havana, Cuba
Dance-Pop, Latin Pop, Adult Contemporary, Pop-Rock, Club/Dance
More than any other pop group, Miami Sound Machine and lead singer Gloria Estefan (b. Jan 9, 1957) have brought Latin-American (particularly Cuban) music into the mainstream. They originated in the Miami Cuban community, and many of their early recordings were sung in Spanish. Their hits have included "Conga" (No. 10), "Bad Boy" (No. 8), "Words Get in the Way" (No. 5), "Anything for You" (No. 1), "1-2-3" (No. 9) and "Rhythm Is Gonna Get You" (No. 5).

In 1987 the group officially changed its name to Gloria Estefan & Miami Sound Machine. Not surprisingly, the next two years saw the direction of the group's music shift toward her vocals. In 1989 Estefan released her first solo album, *Cuts Both Ways*, which spawned the No. 1 hit "Don't Wanna Lose You."

The next year the group's tour bus was in a serious accident when traveling in New York. Estefan's suffered several broken vertebrae and underwent successful surgery. Estefan and the group's career was postponed for nearly a year by the accident. She released *Into the Light* in 1991, which showed her inching toward adult-contemporary territory. She followed *Into the Light* with a Latin album, *Mi Tierra*, in 1993. The next year she released a collection of covers called *Hold Me Thrill Me Kiss Me*. In 1995 Estefan released her second Latin album, *Abriendo Puertas*. The next year, she released *Destiny*. —*Rick Clark*

Eyes of Innocence / 1984 / Epic ◆◆
Gloria Estefan has a nice voice and does an interesting live show, but her albums are about as rigidly produced and routinely performed as anyone's this side of Julio Iglesias. This has some light Afro-Latin influences, but otherwise is generic pop. —*Ron Wynn*

Primitive Love / 1986 / Epic ◆◆◆
Gloria Estefan occasionally gets an above-average song, and her live show sometimes includes an Afro-Latin spot where she returns to her roots. Neither was the case on this mid-'80s set, which is certainly well produced, engineered, and arranged. If you're a fan, you enjoyed it. Otherwise, it was tough sledding. —*Ron Wynn*

Let It Loose / 1988 / Epic ◆◆◆◆
The group was still billed as "Gloria Estefan & Miami Sound Machine" on this album, which showed the singer and her bandleader husband, Emilio, retaining the jazzy, Latino flavor of their earlier music while moving determinedly into the pop mainstream and incidentally positioning Gloria as a superstar. Such goals were reached by a record that sold two million copies, went Top Ten, and produced the hits "Rhythm Is Gonna Get You," "Betcha Say That," "Can't Stay Away from You," "Anything for You," and "1-2-3." —*William Ruhlmann*

Cuts Both Ways / Jul. 1989 / Epic ◆◆◆
Dispensing with the "Miami Sound Machine" name, Estefan continued to successfully mix Latin-tinged dance numbers with strong ballads on this million-selling Top Ten solo album, which included

"Don't Wanna Lose You," "Get on Your Feet," and "Here We Are."
— *William Ruhlmann*

Into the Light / Dec. 2, 1991 / Epic ✦✦✦
With this successful album, Estefan demonstrated that she had recovered from her serious accident of 1990. The album contains the telling hit "Coming Out of the Dark" but showed her moving even farther toward the middle of the road and sacrificing her younger fans in the process; most of the singles from this album performed better on the adult contemporary charts than on the Hot 100. — *William Ruhlmann*

● **Greatest Hits** / Oct. 6, 1992 / Epic ✦✦✦✦
All of Gloria Estefan's hits, with and without the Miami Sound Machine, are here, making *Greatest Hits* the best Estefan CD available. — *AMG*

Mi Tierra / Jun. 22, 1993 / Sony ✦✦✦✦
Estefan's all-Spanish album will cut down the amount of Top 40 radio play she receives, but her fans will be pleased with *Mi Tierra*, one of her more consistent albums. — *AMG*

Hold Me Thrill Me Kiss Me / Oct. 18, 1994 / Epic ✦✦✦
A stretch for Estefan, it's a genuinely worthy one, even if it sometimes strays too far from her Latin roots. This album of classic covers includes brilliant pop hits ("How Can I Be Sure," "Turn the Beat Around"), moments of genuine pathos ("Traces," "It's Too Late"), and some pure dreck ("You've Made Me So Very Happy"). While the record enhances Estefan's reputation as a savvy, sophisticated pop singer, it also lays bare her limitations, confirming that she's more stylist than soulstress. — *Eddie Huffman*

Abriendo Puertas / Sep. 26, 1995 / Epic ✦✦✦

Destiny / Jun. 1996 / Epic ✦✦✦
With *Destiny*, Gloria Estefan ties together the Cuban and Latinbeat influences she had been exploring on her Spanish albums with the adult contemporary pop that dominated her early-'90s records. It's a stylish concept, and, for the most part, Estefan pulls it off. Like most of her albums, *Destiny* suffers from uneven material and a creeping sense of sameness between the songs, but Estefan's voice keeps getting stronger with age, which helps her rescue the weaker material on the record. And the best moments of *Destiny*—including the Olympic anthem "Reach," "I'm Not Giving You Up," and "Higher," among others—rank with her finest work. — *Stephen Thomas Erlewine*

Melissa Etheridge

b. May 29, 1961, Leavenworth, KS
Guitar, Vocals / Rock 'n' Roll, Blues-Rock, Singer-Songwriter, Adult Alternative Pop-Rock
Melissa Etheridge's gutsy electric blues-rock has earned her favorable comparisons to Rod Stewart and Janis Joplin, as well as a considerable fan base across America. Not only is she a solid live performer, but she has written several songs that have become AOR favorites since the late '80s, including "Bring Me Some Water" and "Similar Features." Although she earned some fans with her debut in 1988, her audience has increased with each new album. When she revealed in 1992 that she is a lesbian, her commercial fortunes were not hurt at all; in fact, her audience continued to grow. Because it is rooted in the heartbreak and turmoils of everyday life, Etheridge's music has a widespread appeal that makes her one of the top concert draws and AOR acts of the '90s. — *Stephen Thomas Erlewine*

● **Melissa Etheridge** / 1988 / Island ✦✦✦✦
A powerful debut with occasionally strident performances, it includes "Bring Me Some Water," a fine acoustic rocker. "Similar Features," a scathing indictment of a former lover, is a standout. — *Rick Clark*

Brave and Crazy / Sep. 1989 / Island ✦✦✦
Not a trace of the dreaded sophomore curse was to be found on Melissa Etheridge's second album. On *Brave and Crazy*, the throaty singer/guitarist/composer is slightly more reflective than on her first release, but no less confident. Nor is she is any less rootsy. Etheridge's earthiness is a large part of her appeal, and she uses it most advantageously on the gutsy rockers "Skin Deep" and "Let Me Go," as well as more reflective pieces such as "Testify," "You Used to Love to Dance" and "You Can Sleep While I Drive" (which, like a lot of Bruce Springsteen's songs, equates long drives with freedom and liberation). As introspective as things get on this CD, Etheridge never becomes wimpy or self-pitying. For all its vulnerability, *Brave and Crazy* is the work of someone who comes across as a survivor. — *Alex Henderson*

Never Enough / Mar. 17, 1992 / Island ✦✦✦
Nothing here matches the raw power of "Bring Me Some Water," but this outing blends the thoughtful virtues of *Brave and Crazy* with the more rocking elements of her debut. Etheridge also synthesizes urban-dub rhythms and rap on tracks like "2001" (a single) and "Must Be Crazy for Me." It also includes the single "Ain't It Heavy." — *Rick Clark*

Yes I Am / Sep. 21, 1993 / Island ✦✦✦✦
Etheridge's gutsy acoustic guitar-based rock is given a slightly more atmospheric treatment on this outing. Her voice is front and center in the mix and the instrumentation conveys power, but there is an evenness to the dynamics here that keep her natural theatrical delivery from totally getting across. Nevertheless, "All American Girl" is a highlight, as is "I'm the Only One." A good album, it's not her best. — *Rick Clark*

Your Little Secret / Nov. 14, 1995 / Island ✦✦
Your Little Secret was positioned as the album that would establish Melissa Etheridge as a genuine superstar, following through on the success of *Yes I Am*. *Your Little Secret* may deliver the sound that made Etheridge popular, only without any of the style and finesse. Throughout the record, she relies on bombast instead of passion to get her point across, which becomes draining by the overlong, over-dramatic conclusion, "This War Is Over." Etheridge also comes up with a few memorable hooks and melodies, relying on her powerful, bluesy wail to carry the songs. However, since there is no melodic foundation to the music, it all collapses under its own weight, leaving *Your Little Secret* the weakest album she has released. — *Stephen Thomas Erlewine*

Eurythmics

f. 1980, London, England, **db.** 1990
Synth-Pop, New Wave, Pop-Rock
Eurythmics were one of the most successful duos to emerge in the early '80s. Where most of their British synth-pop contemporaries disappeared from the charts as soon as new wave faded away in 1984, Eurythmics continued to have hits until the end of the decade, making vocalist Annie Lennox a star in her own right, as well as establishing intstrumentalist Dave Stewart as a successful, savvy producer and songwriter. Originally, the duo channeled the eerily detached sound of electronic synthesizer music into pop songs driven by robotic beats. By the mid-'80s, singles like "Sweet Dreams (Are Made of This)" and "Here Comes the Rain Again" had made the group into international stars; and they had begun to experiment with their sound, delving into soul and R&B. As the decade wore on, the duo's popularity eroded somewhat. By the late '80s they were having trouble cracking the Top 40 in America, although they stayed successful in the UK. During the early '90s, Eurythmics took an extended hiatus, as both Lennox and Stewart pursued solo careers.

The origins of Eurythmics lay in the Tourists, a British post-punk band of the late '70s formed by Lennox and Stewart. The pair met in London while she was studying at the Royal Academy of Music. Stewart had recently broken up his folk-rock group Longdancer and was writing songs with guitarist Pete Coombes. Stewart and Lennox became lovers and musical partners, forming a group called Catch with Coombes, which quickly evolved into the Tourists in 1979. Though the band was together for only two years, the Tourists released three albums—*The Tourists, Reality Effect*, and *Luminous Basement*—which all were moderate hits in England; two of their singles, "I Only Want to Be with You" and "So Good to Be Back Home Again," became Top Ten hits.

During 1980 Lennox and Stewart's romantic relationship dissolved and, along with it, the Tourists. Though they were no longer lovers, Lennox and Stewart decided to continue performing together under the name Eurythmics and headed to Germany to record their debut album. Featuring support from various members of Can and Blondie's drummer Clem Burke, among others, the duo's debut *In the Garden* was released in 1981 to positive reviews, but weak sales. After the failure of *In the Garden*, Stewart set up a home studio and Eurythmics recorded a second album, *Sweet Dreams (Are Made of This)*, that was released in 1983.

"Love Is a Stranger" was the first British single pulled from the album, and it became a minor hit in the fall of 1982, a few months before the LP appeared. The title track was released as a single in the spring, and it rocketed to No. 2 on the UK charts; shortly afterward, it climbed to No. 1 on the American charts. "Sweet Dreams (Are Made of This)" was helped enormously by its stylish, androgynous video, which received heavy airplay from MTV, who had only recently become a major influence within the music industry. After "Sweet Dreams," Eurythmics' re-released "Love Is a Stranger" reached the UK Top Ten (No. 23 US), beginning a string of hit singles that ran for a year. *Touch*, the duo's third album, was released toward the end of 1983 and continued their success throughout 1984, spawning the hits "Who's That Girl?" (No. 3, UK; No. 21, US), "Right by Your Side" (No. 10, UK; No. 29, US) and "Here Comes the Rain Again" (No. 8, UK; No. 4 US). During the course of 1984, Annie Lennox's theatrical gender-bending was becoming increasingly notorious, which helped record sales. At the end of the year they released the soundtrack for the film adaption of *1984*, which received poor reviews and sales, despite the Top Ten UK placing of its single, "Sexcrime (Nineteen Eighty-Four)."

Released in the spring of 1985, Eurythmics' fourth album, *Be Yourself Tonight* boasted a tougher, R&B-influenced sound and featured a duet with Aretha Franklin, "Sisters Are Doin' It for Themselves." The duet became one of three hit singles from the album, in addition to "Would I Lie to You?" (No. 17, UK; No. 5, US) and "There Must Be an Angel (Playing with My Heart)" (No. 1, UK; No. 22, US). *Revenge*, released the next year, followed the R&B and soul inclinations of *Be Yourself Tonight* to a harder-rocking conclusion. Though the album peaked at No. 12 in the US and spawned the No. 14 hit "Missionary Man," its sales were noticebly weaker than its precessor. In the UK the group was slightly more popular—"Thorn in My Side" reached the Top Ten—but it was evident that the group was past their peak popularity.

Eurythmics began branching out into other areas. During 1985 and 1986, Dave Stewart produced a number of superstars, including Bob Dylan, Daryl Hall, Tom Petty, and Mick Jagger. Annie Lennox began a short-lived acting career, appearing in *Revolution*. Eurythmics reconvened in 1987 to release *Savage*, which was greeted with mixed reviews and weak sales. That same year, Stewart married Siobhan Fahey, a former member of Bananarama who had also appeared in the "Love Is a Stranger" video; she would later be a member of Shakespear's Sister, which was prodcued by Stewart. In 1988 Lennox had a hit duet with Al Green with "Put a Little Love in Your Heart," taken from the *Scrooged* soundtrack. The following year, Eurythmics released *We Too Are One*, which sold well in Britain, reaching No. 1, but poorly in America, despite "Don't Ask Me Why"'s becoming their first Top 40 hit since "Missonary Man." Reviews were decidedly mixed on the album.

Eurythmics quietly went on hiatus as of 1990, releasing *Greatest Hits* the next year. Lennox began a solo career in 1992, releasing *Diva*, an album that would eventually sell over two million copies. Stewart continued producing records and writing film soundtracks, as well as forming a band called Spiritual Cowboys. In 1995 he officially launched a solo career with the release of *Greetings from the Gutter*. — *Stephen Thomas Erlewine*

In the Garden / 1981 / RCA ♦♦
Eurythmics' debut album, *In the Garden*, is the missing link between the work of the Tourists, who included both Dave Stewart and Annie Lennox, and 1983's commercial breakthrough, *Sweet Dreams (Are Made of This)*. Co-produced by Kraftwerk producer Conny Plank at his studio in Cologne, Germany, it has some of the distant, mechanistic feel of the European electronic music movement, but less of the pop sensibility of later Eurythmics. The chief difference is in Lennox's singing: even when the musical bed is appealing, Lennox floats ethereally over it, and the listener doesn't focus on her. As a result, *In the Garden* wasn't much of a success, though when Eurythmics streamlined their sound and emphasized Lennox's dominating voice on subsequent releases, they found mass popularity. — *William Ruhlmann*

Sweet Dreams (Are Made of This) / Jan. 1983 / RCA ♦♦♦♦
Much commotion was caused by the MTV video clip for the hit title track from Eurythmics' breakthrough second album, which played up vocalist Annie Lennox's androgynous image. — *Donna DiChario*

Touch / Nov. 1983 / RCA ♦♦♦♦
The follow-up to the success of *Sweet Dreams* showed a more confident Lennox and Stewart, ready to expand their stylistic range. It contains the Top 40 hits "Here Comes the Rain Again," "Who's That Girl," and "Right by Your Side." — *Scott Bultman*

1984 (For the Love of Big Brother) / Nov. 1984 / RCA ♦♦
While it is not billed as an original motion picture soundtrack, this album does contain, as a jacket note indicates, "music derived from Eurythmics' original score of the motion picture *1984*," and it was treated as a side project for marketing purposes, not as Eurythmics' full-fledged fourth new studio album. Fair enough. Much of the album is instrumental, and the closest thing to a pop song, "Sexcrime (Nineteen Eighty-Four)" (which was a Top Ten hit in the UK), like the other vocal numbers, relates to the movie's future fiction theme. As such, the album is substandard if judged as an independent Eurythmics album, adequate if judged as a soundtrack. — *William Ruhlmann*

Be Yourself Tonight / May 1985 / RCA ♦♦♦♦
Showing sparks of Motown influence with the hit "Would I Lie to You?" and others, Stevie Wonder adds a harmonica solo to "There Must Be an Angel." — *Donna DiChario*

Revenge / Jul. 1986 / RCA ♦♦♦
On their fifth album, Eurythmics moved away from the austere synth-pop of their previous work and toward more of a neo-'60s pop-rock stance. "Missionary Man" (which went Top 40 as a single in the US and charted in the UK) featured a prominent harmonica solo, while "Thorn in My Side" had a chiming guitar riff reminiscent of the

Searchers and a fat sax solo. Of course, the primary element in the group's sound remained Annie Lennox' distinctive alto voice, which was still impressive, even if the material was slightly less so. *Revenge* was a successful album, reaching the Top Ten in the UK and going gold in the US, but it was a disappointment compared to their last three albums. And creatively, it was a step down as well—there was nothing here that they hadn't done a little better before. — *William Ruhlmann*

Savage / Nov. 1987 / RCA ♦♦
If *Revenge*, Eurythmics' fifth album, marked a slight fall-off in the group's commercial and artistic accomplishments, *Savage*, their sixth collection, confirmed that decline. In the US, the album failed to generate a substantial hit single and sold poorly compared to previous efforts. In the more faithful UK, the album hit the Top Ten and spun off four chart singles, but none that matched earlier hits. Musically, Eurythmics, for the most part, abandoned the more conventional pop-rock they recently had been pursuing, returning to the synthesized dance music and arch tone of their early hit "Sweet Dreams (Are Made of This)." But they still seemed less inspired than before. — *William Ruhlmann*

We Too Are One / Sep. 1989 / Arista ♦♦♦
Switching to Arista Records in the US, Eurythmics made their last album together with *We Too Are One*, and they went out in style. Calling upon a broad pop range, their seventh album was their best since *Be Yourself Tonight* in 1985. The sound was varied, the melodies were strong, and the lyrics were unusually well crafted. In retrospect, the album can be seen as a dry run for Annie Lennox' debut solo album, *Diva* (1992); songs like "Don't Ask Me Why" (which grazed the US Top 40) serve as precursors to the dramatic ballads to come. There is, however, an air of romantic resignation throughout *We Too Are One*, appropriate to its valedictory nature. The disc spawned four chart singles in the UK and returned Eurythmics to No. 1 in the album charts, but it did not substantially improve Eurythmics' reduced commercial standing in the US, confirming that it was time for Lennox and Dave Stewart to pursue other opportunities. — *William Ruhlmann*

● **Greatest Hits** / May 1991 / Arista ♦♦♦♦
Whether cool and sophisticated or impassioned and soulful, this duo of singer Annie Lennox and guitarist Dave Stewart creates stylish and compelling rock. — *Donna DiChario*

Live 1983-1989 / Nov. 15, 1993 / Arista ♦♦
The Eurythmics ruled the studio, not the stage, making this two-CD collection an interesting but not absorbing listen. — *Stephen Thomas Erlewine*

Betty Everett

b. Nov. 23, 1939, Greenwood, MS
Piano, Vocals / Soul, R&B, Pop-Rock
Betty Everett sang gospel growing up in Greenwood, MS, before relocating to Chicago and moving into secular music. She began recording for Cobra in 1958, then joined Vee-Jay in the early '60s and started to land hit records. Her original version of "You're No Good," though sung with fire and verve, didn't make much impact until it was turned into a No. 1 pop hit by Linda Ronstadt in 1975. Her next single, "The Shoop Shoop Song (It's in His Kiss)," was her first major release, peaking at No. 6 pop in 1964. Her next success was the duet "Let It Be Me" with Jerry Butler, a soul version of the Everly Brothers tune that reached No. 5 R&B that same year. Everett's finest song as a solo act was 1969's "There Comes a Time," which reached No. 2 on the R&B charts and cracked the pop Top 30 at No. 26. Everett was now on Uni, where she remained until 1970. She continued recording for Fantasy until 1974 and made one other record for United Artists in 1978. — *Ron Wynn*

There'll Come a Time / 1969 / Varese Sarabande ♦♦♦♦
Everett made her best records for Vee-Jay in the mid-'60s, but this album, originally released on Uni in 1969, isn't far behind in merit. Featuring her No. 2 R&B single (and Top 40 pop hit) "There'll Come a Time," this has much more of a sweet soul flavor than her Vee-Jay sides, at times blending the trademarks of her brassy native Chicago scene with a Philadelphia influence. It's far from *too* sweet, though, with strong material, punchy arrangements, and Everett's always dependably energetic and warm vocals. Also contains the R&B hit "I Can't Say No to You"; the CD reissue adds three valuable 1969-70 singles that were previously unavailable on album, including the Top 20 R&B hit "It's Been a Long Time," arranged by Donny Hathaway and written by Kenny Gamble, Leon Huff, and Jerry Butler. — *Richie Unterberger*

● **The Shoop Shoop Song** / Nov. 22, 1993 / Vee-Jay ♦♦♦♦
Though sometimes classified as a "girl group" singer because of the Top Ten success of "The Shoop Shoop Song," Betty Everett's main thrust was much more in the R&B/soul vein. This excellent 25-track

anthology of her 1963-65 material shows her facility with various soul, R&B, and pop styles. She had three other minor hits—the original hit version of "You're No Good," the energetic Goffin/King pop-rocker "I Can't Hear You," and Van McCoy's soulful "Gettin' Mighty Crowded"—all of which are featured here. But most of the other material is equally enjoyable, including other early efforts by McCoy, Valerie Simpson and Nick Ashford, and even P.F. Sloan (whose "Can I Get to Know You" is presented in a much earthier, slower version than the Turtles' rendition several years later). This CD doesn't include her hit duets with fellow Chicago soulster Jerry Butler, but is a consistently enjoyable retrospective of an underrated singer who straddled the soul and pop worlds. —*Richie Unterberger*

The Fantasy Years / Oct. 3, 1995 / Fantasy ✦✦✦
For the first half of the 1970s, Everett recorded updated soul-pop for the Fantasy label with mixed but generally positive results. This 18-track compilation features cuts from two mid-'70s LPs, as well as various singles from the early '70s, including the R&B hits "I Got to Tell You," "Ain't Nothing Gonna Change Me," and "Sweet Dan." Not nearly as pop-oriented as her more famous mid-'60s recordings, this finds Everett in fine, expressive voice, but somewhat at the mercy of the quality of the material, which is variable. The selections from the 1975 *Happy Endings* album are kind of anonymous, but much of the rest is good, gutsy '70s soul. Johnny "Guitar" Watson helps out on a few numbers, as co-producer, guitarist, and occasional songwriter, and a couple were cut in Memphis with the Hi Rhythm Section. —*Richie Unterberger*

The Everly Brothers

f. 1954, Brownie, KY, db. 1973
Rock 'n' Roll, Country-Rock, Pop-Rock, Close Harmony
The Everly Brothers were not only among the most important and best early rock 'n' roll stars, but among the most influential rockers of any era. They set unmatched standards for close, two-part harmonies, and infused early rock 'n' roll with some of the best elements of country and pop music. Their legacy was and is felt enormously in all rock acts that employ harmonies as prime features, from the Beatles, Simon & Garfunkel, and legions of country-rockers to modern-day roots rockers like Dave Edmunds and Nick Lowe (who once recorded an EP of Everlys songs together).

Don (born February 1, 1937) and Phil (born January 19, 1939) were professionals way before their teens, schooled by their accomplished guitarist father Ike, and singing with their family on radio broadcasts in Iowa. In the mid-'50s they made a brief stab at conventional Nashville country with Columbia. When their single flopped, they were cast adrift for quite a while until they latched onto Cadence. Don invested their first single for the label, "Bye Bye Love," with a Bo Diddley beat that helped lift the song to No. 2 in 1957.

"Bye Bye Love" began a phenomenal three-year string of classic hit singles for Cadence, including "Wake Up Little Susie," "All I Have to Do Is Dream," "Bird Dog," "('Til) I Kissed You," and "When Will I Be Loved." The Everlys sang of young love with a heart-rending yearning and compelling melodies. The harmonies owed audible debts to Appalachian country music, but were imbued with a keen modern pop sensibility that made them more accessible without sacrificing any power or beauty. They were not as raw as the wild rockabilly men from Sun Records, but they could rock hard when they wanted. Even their mid-tempo numbers and ballads were executed with a force missing in the straight country and pop tunes of the era. The duo enjoyed a top-notch support team of producer Archie Bleyer, great Nashville session players like Chet Atkins, and the brilliant songwriting team of Boudleaux and Felice Bryant. Don, and occasionally Phil, wrote excellent songs of their own, as well.

In 1960 the Everlys left Cadence for a lucrative contract with the then-young Warner Brothers label. (Though it's not often noted, the Everlys would do a lot to establish Warners as a major force in the record business.) It's sometimes been written that the duo never recaptured the magic of their Cadence recordings, but actually Phil and Don peaked both commercially and artistically with their first Warners releases. "Cathy's Clown," their first Warners single, was one of their greatest songs and a No. 1 hit. Their first two Warners LPs, employing a fuller and brasher production than their Cadence work, were not just among their best work, but two of the best rock albums of the early '60s. The hits kept coming for a couple of years, some great ("Walk Right Back," "Temptation"), some displaying a distressing, increasing tendency toward soft pop and maudlin sentiments ("Ebony Eyes," "That's Old Fashioned").

Don and Phil's personal lives came under a lot of stress in the early '60s: They were drafted into the Army (together), and studied acting for six months, but never made a motion picture. More seriously, Don developed an addiction to speed and almost died of an overdose in late 1962. By that time, their career as chart titans in the US had

ended; "That's Old Fashioned" (1962) was their last Top Ten hit. Their albums became careless, erratic affairs, which was all the more frustrating because many of their flop singles of the time were fine, even near-classic efforts that demonstrated they could still deliver the goods.

Virtually alone among first-generation rock 'n' roll superstars, the Everlys stuck with no-nonsense rock 'n' roll and remained determined to keep their sound contemporary, rather than drifting toward soft pop or country like so many others. Although their mid-'60s recordings were largely ignored in America, they contained some of their finest work, including a ferocious Top 40 single in 1964 ("Gone, Gone, Gone"). They remained big stars overseas. In 1965 "Price of Love" went to No. 2 in the UK at the height of the British Invasion. They incorporated jangling Beatle/Byrdesque guitars into some of their songs, and recorded a fine album with the Hollies (who were probably more blatantly influenced by the Everlys than any other British band of the time). In the late '60s, they helped pioneer country-rock with the 1968 album *Roots*, their most sophisticated and unified full-length statement. None of this revived their career as hit-makers, though they could always command huge audiences on international tours, and hosted a network TV variety show in 1970.

The decades of enforced professional togetherness finally took their toll on the pair in the early '70s, which saw a few dispirited albums and, finally, an acrimonious breakup in 1973. They spent the next decade performing solo, which only proved—as is so often the case in close-knit artistic partnerships—how much each brother needed the other to sound his best. In 1983, enough water had flowed under the bridge for the two to resume performing and recording together. The tours, with a backup band led by guitarist Albert Lee, proved they could still sing well. The records (both live and studio) were fair efforts that, in the final estimation, were not in nearly the same league as their '50s and '60s classics, although Paul McCartney penned a small hit single for them ("On the Wings of a Nightingale"). Although it was one of the most successful and dignified reunions in rock annals, this, too, could not last; as of this writing, the Everlys have not performed or recorded together since the early '90s. —*Richie Unterberger*

The Everly Brothers [Cadence] / 1958 / Cadence ✦✦✦✦
Although the Everlys hadn't quite fully matured as artists, their debut is a fine, consistent effort divided between original material and respectably energetic covers of early rockers by Little Richard, Gene Vincent, and Ray Charles. Besides their first few hits, it includes some superb, underappreciated tracks that are nearly as good, like "Should We Tell Him" and "I Wonder If I Cared as Much." —*Richie Unterberger*

Songs Our Daddy Taught Us / 1959 / Rhino ✦✦✦
The Everlys had reached their commercial peak when they made this album of sparsely arranged traditional songs, a concept that was quite a surprise from a top rock 'n' roll act, and considerably ahead of its time. It's actually not as enduring as their early rockers and pop ballads, but the singing is superb on their interpretations of standards like "Barbara Allen" and "Kentucky." —*Richie Unterberger*

The Fabulous Style of the Everly Brothers / 1960 / Rhino ✦✦✦✦
The best of their original Cadence albums, packed with hits ("Bird Dog," "All I Have To Do Is Dream," "When Will I Be Loved," "'Til I Kissed You") and other classic tracks ("Devoted to You," "Let It Be Me," "Since You Broke My Heart," "Like Strangers"). Almost all of the songs show up on their greatest hits collections, so it might be a superfluous purchase for all but serious fans, despite its top-drawer quality. —*Richie Unterberger*

It's Everly Time / 1960 / Warner Brothers ✦✦✦✦
While the Everlys' sound was diluted by more elaborate production in the '60s, that's not at all true on this LP, which is one of their very best. Not a stiff among the 12 tracks, most of which are barely known outside of serious Everly fans. Includes six stellar contributions by Boudleaux and Felice Bryant, one of Don Everly's best compositions ("So Sad"), and incredible harmony singing throughout. —*Richie Unterberger*

A Date with the Everly Brothers / 1961 / Warner Brothers ✦✦✦✦
Although the material is not on the killer level of *Everly Time*, there are some very fine songs on their second Warner LP. Includes "Cathy's Clown," their raucous cover of Little Richard's "Lucille," "Love Hurts" (which preceded Roy Orbison's hit version), and "So How Come" (covered by the Beatles in 1963 on the BBC). —*Richie Unterberger*

The Very Best of the Everly Brothers [Warner Bros.] / Aug. 1964 / Warner Brothers ✦
The operative word here is: beware. This does indeed have 12 of their biggest hits, but half of them are re-recorded versions of Cadence-era material. It's not that they're bad or radically different (after all, they were recorded only a few years later). But why settle for these when only the originals will do? —*Richie Unterberger*

Gone, Gone, Gone / 1965 / Warner Brothers ✦✦

A jumble of tracks from varying sessions that, despite some excellent moments, was indicative of the general directionlessness of the Everlys' career at this point. The title song was their final Top 40 single of the '60s, and indeed one of their greatest performances. "The Ferris Wheel," also a 1964 single, was a decent, moody ballad that was a minor hit in both America and the UK; for some reason, it was excluded from the double-CD compilation of their best '60s work, *Walk Right Back*. Otherwise, the album contains a few other songs cut in 1964, and some odds and ends from sessions in the early '60s. The Everlys, John D. Loudermilk, and the great Boudleaux/Felice Bryant songwriting team wrote almost all of the material on this album, but unfortunately it was not up to the standards of either the writers or the performers. —*Richie Unterberger*

Two Yanks in England / 1966 / Demon ✦✦✦

At first glance, this seems like a cash-in on the British Invasion. Recorded in London in 1966, no less than eight of the 12 songs were written by the Hollies (who released their own versions of many of the tunes). There are also covers of hits by the Spencer Davis Group and Manfred Mann. With a harder rock guitar sound (though not overdone or inappropriate) than previous Everlys discs, the duo's interpretations are actually worth hearing in their own right. The harmonies are fabulous, and indeed, the Everlys improve a few of the Hollies' songs substantially. "So Lonely" and "Hard Hard Year," in particular, have a lot more force, transforming the tunes from decent Hollies album tracks to excellence. Because so much of the material is non-original, this couldn't be placed in the top rank of Everly Brothers recordings. But it is a good effort that shows them, almost ten years after "Bye Bye Love," still at the top of their game and still heavily committed to a rock 'n' roll sound. This was a bold contrast to other '50s white rock 'n' rollers with roots in country, most of whom had retreated to tamer country-oriented sounds by the mid-'60s. —*Richie Unterberger*

Roots / 1968 / Warner Brothers ✦✦✦✦

Considered one of the finest early country-rock albums, this showed the Everlys, unlike virtually every other top rock 'n' roll act of the '50s, keeping abreast of contemporary rock and pop trends. In the manner of their 1958 LP *Songs Our Daddy Taught Us*, the concept was to cover songs by performers and composers who had been influential on the duo, including Jimmie Rodgers, Merle Haggard, traditional standards, and a couple of numbers by Ron Elliott of the Beau Brummels. Although this laidback, tasteful, acoustic-oriented recording isn't as outstanding as their classic early hits, the vocals are superb, conveying qualities of innocence tempered by experience. —*Richie Unterberger*

Nashville Tennessee Nov 1955 / 1981 / Bear Family ✦✦

Before beginning their rock 'n' roll career with Cadence Records in 1957, the Everlys recorded one straight country single for Columbia in late 1955. Backed by the guitars, steel, bass, and fiddle of Carl Smith's Tunesmiths, this standard mid-'50s Nashville country offered few hints of the duo's further greatness, other than their shining harmonies. This four-song, 12-inch EP includes both sides of the single and two previously unreleased cuts from the same sessions. All four of the tunes were written by the Everlys themselves and are of mostly historical interest. —*Richie Unterberger*

The Reunion Concert / 1984 / Mercury ✦✦✦

Lively, if ultimately too slick, this concert recording ties up a few loose ends. —*Bruce Eder*

Eb 84 / 1984 / Mercury ✦✦✦

All They Had to Do Was Dream / 1985 / Rhino ✦✦✦

Alternate takes of much of their strongest material from the Cadence era, cut between 1957 and 1960. A bit more tentative than the familiar renditions, these aren't as good as the versions that ended up on official releases, but are enjoyable and fascinating glimpses of works in progress, and the singing is excellent throughout. Includes different versions of hits like "Wake Up Little Susie," "All I Have to Do Is Dream," "Til I Kissed You," and "When Will I Be Loved." —*Richie Unterberger*

★ **Cadence Classics: Their 20 Greatest Hits** / 1986 / Rhino ✦✦✦✦✦

The single-disc collection *Cadence Classics: Their 20 Greatest Hits* compiles all of the Everly Brothers' hits, plus many terrific album tracks, from the duo's recordings for Cadence Records in the late '50s. Most of the Everlys' biggest hits, including "Bye Bye Love," "I Wonder If I Care As Much, "Wake Up, Little Susie," "This Little Girl of Mine," "All I Have to Do Is Dream," "Claudette," "Bird Dog," "Devoted to You," "Problems," "Message to Mary," "('Til) I Kissed You," "Let It Be Me," and "When Will I Be Loved." *Cadence Classics* misses no essential track, making it a definitive collection and the perfect introduction to the duo's sound. —*Stephen Thomas Erlewine*

Hidden Gems from the Warner Years / 1989 / Ace ✦✦✦✦

This collects 14 songs that originally appeared on non-hit singles between 1962 and 1965; many of them had never been on LP. This material strongly counters the view that the Everlys faded artistically after "Cathy's Clown." The writing credits for these strong compositions read a bit like a who's who of early-'60s pop-rock, with contributions from Gerry Goffin, Mann/Weill, Doc Pomus & Mort Shuman, Sonny Curtis, Boudleaux and Felice Bryant, and the Everlys themselves. The singing is fabulous, and the arrangements still strong, rock-oriented, and tastefully produced. Tracks like "Nancy's Minuet" (1963), a great Don Everly original and one of their best paeans to lovelorn melancholia, and "You're the One I Love" (1964), a fine, brooding midtempo rocker, stand with their very best work. Only three of these appear on the '60s Everlys anthology *Walk Right Back*, making this a necessary purchase for Everlys fans. —*Richie Unterberger*

Classic Everly Brothers / 1992 / Bear Family ✦✦✦✦

The three-disc box set *Classic Everly Brothers* collects all of their Cadence recordings, including alternate takes, as well as several early radio shows and the four tracks the duo recorded for Columbia in 1955. While this music is the most essential the brothers ever made, the disc of rarities is only of interest to devoted fans. Nevertheless, the sound on the box is stellar, the liner notes are excellent, and the whole package is wonderful; for hardcore fans, the set is worth the money. —*Stephen Thomas Erlewine*

The Mercury Years / Jul. 20, 1993 / Mercury ✦✦✦✦

Mercury Years collects all of the finest moments from their two 1980s albums; its best moments, like "On the Wings of a Nightingale," are surprisingly strong. —*Stephen Thomas Erlewine*

☆ **Walk Right Back: The Everly Brothers on Warner Bros.** / Sep. 14, 1993 / Warner Archive ✦✦✦✦✦

This two-CD, 50-track compilation assembles the Everly Brothers' most memorable recordings of the 1960s. Although their work from this period has sometimes been criticized as inferior to their classic '50s recordings for Cadence, the best of these songs are a match for anything the duo recorded. As it happens, the strongest of these tunes are drawn from their first two albums for Warners in the 1960s, including the hits "Cathy's Clown" and "So Sad." In the following years, their material suffered from increasing inconsistency and ill-suited production. Yet the Brothers continued to intermittently hit the mark squarely—not only with early-'60s hits like "Crying in the Rain" and "Temptation," but neglected flop singles like "Nancy's Minuet" and "You're the One I Love," as well as the hard-rocking minor 1964 hit "Gone Gone Gone" (their last Top 40 single). They also showed a willingness to incorporate the hard-rocking beat of the British Invasion into their work that was not shared by any of the other major stars of the '50s. This compilation misses a number of fine B-sides and non-hit singles from the early and mid-'60s (check the Ace import collection *Hidden Gems* for those), and perhaps leans too heavily on their tepid late-'60s country-rock. But it's a good overview of a body of work that is often unfairly overlooked. —*Richie Unterberger*

☆ **Heartaches & Harmonies [Box Set]** / Oct. 18, 1994 / Rhino ✦✦✦✦✦

This four-CD, 102-song set includes all of their key performances, as well as many overlooked ones, dating from a previously unreleased 1951 radio performance of "Don't Let Our Love Die" to a 1990 live rendition of the very same tune. Opening with a disc's worth of classic Cadence performances, most of the next three CDs are given over to their largely overlooked Warner Bros. '60s output, including many interesting flop singles and album tracks, as well as top-notch rarities like an alternate version of the supremely moody "Nancy's Minuet" and the mid-'60s outtake "And I'll Go." Fine liner notes with detailed comments from the Everlys themselves, but it still manages to miss some great tunes (like the 1964 single "You're the One I Love" and various tracks from their late-'50s and early-'60s LPs, and shouldn't be considered a definitive collection of all their great performances. And the hard fact is, a lot of their post-1966 material (which comprises some of disc three and all of disc four) is kind of boring. —*Richie Unterberger*

Like Strangers / Encore ✦✦

While inessential for all but serious Everly Brothers fanatics, this collection of studio outtakes and alternate versions, most from the early half of the '60s, is not a bad thing to have if you want to get your hands on as much as possible. The sound, while not state-of-the-art, is certainly okay; some of these may have shown up on various quasi-legal reissues in Europe, although it's really difficult to ascertain unless you have a mammoth Everlys library. Some of the songs are awful ("The Sheik of Araby"), but a significantly different version of "Temptation," with stop-and-go bursts of guitar, is a highlight, as is the 1964 outtake "I Think of Me." Scholars will appreciate the February 1960 rehearsal tapes of "Like Strangers" (nine takes) and "When Will I Be Loved" (five takes), which aren't wonderful as pure listening, but do yield some insight into how the songs were crafted and changed before their final versions. The LP also has a couple of live recordings from the 1980s. —*Richie Unterberger*

Everything But the Girl

f. 1982, Hull, England
Alternative Pop-Rock, Pop-Rock, Club/Dance, Alternative Dance, Electronica

Originating at the turn of the 1980s as a leader of the lite-jazz movement, Everything But the Girl became an unlikely success story more than a decade later, emerging at the vanguard of the fusion between pop and electronica. Founded in 1982 by Hull University students Tracey Thorn and Ben Watt, the duo took their name from a sign placed in the window of a local furniture shop, which claimed "for your bedroom needs, we sell everything but the girl." At the time of their formation, both vocalist Thorn and songwriter/multi-instrumentalist Watt were already signed independently to the Cherry Red label; Thorn was a member of the sublime Marine Girls, while Watt had issued several solo singles and collaborated with Robert Wyatt.

Everything But the Girl debuted in 1982 with a samba interpretation of Cole Porter's "Night and Day"; the single was a success on the UK independent charts, but the duo nonetheless went on hiatus as Thorn recorded a solo EP, *A Distant Shore*, while Watt checked in with the full-length *North Marine Drive* in 1983. EBTG soon reunited to record a cover of the Jam's "English Rose" for an *NME* sampler; the track so impressed former Jam frontman Paul Weller that he invited the duo to contribute to the 1984 LP *Cafe Bleu*, the debut from his new project, the Style Council.

Everything But the Girl's own beguiling 1984 debut, *Eden*, followed on the heels of the single "Each and Every One," a UK Top 40 hit. The jazz-pop confections of the group's early work gave way to shimmering jangle-rock by the time of 1985's *Love Not Money*, while a subtle country influence crept into the mix for 1986's lush, orchestral *Baby, the Stars Shine Bright*. The beautifully spare *Idlewild* followed in 1988, spawning the single "I Don't Want to Talk About It," a poignant cover of a song by the late Crazy Horse guitarist Danny Whitten that became EBTG's biggest hit to date, landing at the No. 3 spot on the British charts.

Watt and Thorn traveled to Los Angeles to record 1990's slick, commercial *The Language of Life*, produced by Tommy LiPuma and featuring a guest appearance by jazz great Stan Getz. After a return to pop textures with 1991's *Worldwide*, Everything But the Girl mounted a series of club performances that resulted in 1992's *Acoustic*, a spartan set of covers (including Elvis Costello's "Alison," Bruce Springsteen's "Tougher Than the Rest" and Mickey and Sylvia's "Love Is Strange") which presaged the coming ascendancy of the "Unplugged" concept. In the wake of the record's release, Watt fell prey to Churg-Strauss Syndrome, a rare auto-immune system disease which brought him to the brink of death; after a year in recovery, he wrote several new songs that the duo recorded for inclusion on *Home Movies*, a 1993 hits collection.

In 1994 EBTG collaborated with dub-trance innovators Massive Attack on their LP *Protection;* Thorn's vocal turn highlighted the hit title track, and the cinematic Massive Attack sound clearly informed Everything But the Girl's own 1994 effort *Amplified Heart*, another strong and eclectic outing featuring an appearance by guitar great Richard Thompson. In 1995 the soulful single "Missing" was innovatively remixed by DJ Todd Terry, and after first becoming a club sensation the track blossomed as a major international hit, reaching the No. 2 position on the US pop charts. More importantly, Terry's remix, combined with the lessons of the Massive Attack sessions, launched the duo into an entirely new—and equally satisfying—musical direction. With 1996's brilliant *Walking Wounded*, Everything But the Girl dove headfirst into electronica, crafting sophisticated, assured excursions into trip-hop, drum 'n' bass, and jungle. —*Jason Ankeny*

Everything But the Girl / 1984 / Blanco y Negro/Sire ✦✦✦
The music fad of the moment in 1984 in England was a revival of the early-'60s Brazilian pop sound of Antonio Carlos Jobim, Astrud Gilberto, and Stan Getz, updated to current sensibilities, and the two main practitioners were Sade and Everything But the Girl. On this revised version of their UK debut album, *Eden*, altered for US consumption, the duo of Tracey Thorn and Ben Watt performed their three UK chart singles, "Each and Every One," "Mine," and "Native Land," in a calm, unruffled style keyed to Thorn's warm, if slightly unfocused, vocal style. If the music had a flaw, it was that the sound, with its light sambas and steady ballads, spare instrumentation and careful sax solos, impressed more than individual songs did, perhaps because Thorn's way of phrasing meant you could listen to "Mine," for example, several times before catching on to its feminist theme. Still, Everything But the Girl was more direct and had less of the exotic affectation of Sade (which, however, may help explain why it was she, and not they, who succeeded in America). —*William Ruhlmann*

Love Not Money / Apr. 1985 / Blanco y Negro/Sire ✦✦✦
On their second album, Everything But the Girl took a more contemporary pop approach while retaining the spareness of their debut. They also upped the ante in their songwriting, tackling a range of issues from the Irish Troubles to the troubles of movie star Frances Farmer, with lots of criticism of the stratification and sexism of the current social and economic system thrown in. Tracey Thorn's careworn voice proved an excellent vehicle for such essentially pessimistic sentiments, and even if *Love Not Money* made for a dour listening experience, it was nevertheless compelling. (The "special US edition" of the album, released by Sire Records, differed from the Blanco Y Negro version from the UK in that it featured the pop-sounding "Heaven Help Me" and a cover of the Pretenders' "Kid." Neither enhanced the album's commercial appeal; it made the Top Ten back home, but did not chart stateside.) —*William Ruhlmann*

Baby, the Stars Shine Bright / Aug. 1986 / Blanco y Negro/Sire ✦✦✦
On their third album, Everything But the Girl tries another departure on their craftsmanlike ballad style, hiring a full orchestra to give a lush backing to songs usually concerned more with sexual than national politics. Their last album, *Love Not Money*, may have boasted a considerable social agenda, but here Tracey Thorn sings of romantic disappointment and illicit liaisons, only occasionally bowing to such favorite themes as the lure of fame ("Country Mile"), fantasies about American movie stars ("Sugar Finney," which is "for Marilyn Monroe," and has the chorus, "America is free, cheap and easy"), and fears of fascism ("Little Hitler"). Thorn's throbbing voice is well-suited to the emotional concerns of the lyrics, and Ben Watt creates attractive, string—and horn-filled backings for them. So, Everything But the Girl has found yet another way effectively to vary what would have seemed to be a limited musical style. —*William Ruhlmann*

Idlewild / Feb. 1988 / Blanco y Negro/Sire ✦✦✦✦
Thorn and Watt made a couple of albums with a cocktail-jazz backup and one with strings before trying a small unit for the intimate songs of their most accessible recording. The setting is perfect for such moving compositions as "Love Is Here Where I Live" and "Apron Strings." Start here, then go on to the rest of this remarkable group's catalog. —*William Ruhlmann*

The Language of Life / Jan. 1990 / Atlantic ✦✦
It may have been the logical extension of Everything But the Girl's ersatz cool-jazz approach to finally go all the way by hiring veteran producer Tommy LiPuma and a studio full of fusion stars like Joe Sample (the Crusaders), Russell Ferrante (the Yellowjackets), Michael Brecker, and, finally, Stan Getz, whose early-'60s albums of Brazilian jazz are a main touchstone for the group. With such firepower, *The Language of Life*, at least musically, may be the album that Ben Watt and Tracey Thorn have been trying to make from the beginning. But it falls down in its songwriting, largely because of the near-disappearance of Thorn and her edgy lyrics; Watt takes over for a series of so-so love songs. And the bottom of the barrel is hit with a cover of Womack and Womack's "Take Me," intended as an erotic come-on and sounding more like a lullaby. —*William Ruhlmann*

Worldwide / Sep. 1991 / Atlantic ✦✦✦
Ben Watt and Tracey Thorn returned to the direct record-making style of their first two albums on *Worldwide*. Here, the music was carried largely by Watt's bank of keyboards. But the duo's lyrical concerns reflected their recent frenetic lifestyle. Sooner or later, every group that lasts makes a road album, and this was the one for Everything But the Girl, its songs nostalgically reminiscing about childhood back in England, along with reflections on the big-time touring life in America. Happily, there was still room for a few of Everything But the Girl's complicated adult love songs, notably Thorn's "Understanding," though even that one talked about how love "depends on geography." The breezy subject matter contrasted with the more contemplative music. —*William Ruhlmann*

Acoustic / Jun. 1992 / Atlantic ✦✦
Acoustic presents two side projects in one. The first half of it consists of Everything But the Girl's covers of six songs by other contemporary performers. The second half contains two live recordings and four re-recordings of songs from Everything But the Girl's repertoire. All of the songs are performed with spare, acoustic instrumentation. The group's favorites are predictable—Bruce Springsteen, Elvis Costello, and Tom Waits at their quietest—and while the choices are indisputably good ones—"Alison," "Downtown Train," Cyndi Lauper's "Time After Time"—they are also familiar, and Ben Watt and Tracey Thorn don't bring anything new to them. Their own material is calm and contemplative anyway, so stripping away the synthesizers doesn't affect the arrangements much. *Acoustic* is a pleasant-sounding, inessential Everything But the Girl album. —*William Ruhlmann*

● **Amplified Heart** / Jul. 19, 1994 / Atlantic ✦✦✦✦
Despite its title, *Amplified Heart* is one of Everything But the Girl's more acoustic works. A simple instrumentation of guitars and key-

boards, augmented here and there by British folk-rock veterans like Richard Thompson, Danny Thompson, and Dave Mattacks, serves to set up a series of songs of romantic disillusionment. Declaring "My life is just an image of a roller coaster, anyway" and "I don't understand anything," among other things, over and over the songs speak of confusion and disappointment deriving from failed love affairs. The approach is much more introspective than that taken on the group's last new original album, *Worldwide*, but Tracey Thorn and Ben Watt's musical restraint supports it well. This is an album to listen to when you've just broken up with your lover, or even when you're just in the mood to think about lost lovers from long ago—self-pity set to music. —*William Ruhlmann*

The Best of Everything But the Girl / 1996 / Blanco Y Negro ◆◆◆◆
The Best of Everything But the Girl is divided between selections from their early records and remixes of '90s hits, such as "Missing." Consequently, the album draws a slightly misleading portrait of their career, but it still functions as an excellent introduction to the band, since it features many of their best songs, including "Apron Strings." —*Stephen Thomas Erlewine*

Walking Wounded / May 21, 1996 / Atlantic ◆◆◆◆
With *Walking Wounded*, Everything But the Girl put an acceptable face on trip-hop, jungle and techno, opening up the world of experimental dance music to a new audience. At its core, Everything But the Girl is a pop group, which means they automatically abandon the free-form song structures that characterize most of trip-hop and techno. In a sense, that dilutes the impact of the music, but the duo found a way around that by seamlessly incorporating the rhythms into carefully crafted songs. They work the same ground as Massive Attack, but their songwriting is more accessible and less adventerous than the groundbreaking Bristol group. Furthermore, Everything But the Girl never approach the tarnished glamour of Portishead, the kineticism of Bjork, or the brilliantly evocative soundscapes of Tricky. Essentially, the beats are used as window-dressing—the group's music hasn't changed that much. —*Stephen Thomas Erlewine*

Everything But the Girl Vs. Drum & Bass / Oct. 22, 1996 / Atlantic ◆◆◆
The *Everything... Drums & Bass* EP is comprised of remixes of several tracks from Everything But the Girl's first full-fledged dance album, *Walking Wounded*. Most of the EP consists of fine remixes of the album's title track, but the best cut is a version of "Single" remixed by Photek. —*Stephen Thomas Erlewine*

The Exciters

f. 1961, Jamaica, NY
Girl-Group
Despite the presence of lone male Herb Rooney, the Exciters made some of the best girl-group records of the early '60s. Led by vibrant-voiced Brenda Reid, the originally all-female quartet came from Jamaica, NY, as the Masterettes. After signing with saxist Al Sears as their manager, they switched their name to the Exciters and cut "Tell Him" in 1962 for United Artists. Produced by Jerry Leiber and Mike Stoller, the brilliant uptown soul effort proved a major smash. Reid's roaring pipes were expertly spotlighted on the follow-ups "He's Got the Power," "Get Him," and their original reading of "Do-Wah-Diddy," immortalized later that year by Manfred Mann. The group later appeared on Roulette, Band, Shout, and RCA. Reid and Rooney were married for a time, and Reid now performs with her children backing her. —*Bill Dahl*

The Hit Power of the Exciters / 1986 / Raven ◆◆◆
For a few years this was the only Exciters compilation available, rendering it invaluable to girl group collectors. The early '90s *Tell Him* CD on EMI, however, outdoes it decisively, with considerably more tracks. —*Richie Unterberger*

● **Tell Him /EMI Legends of Rock 'n' Roll Series** / 1991 / EMI America ◆◆◆◆
This girl-group R&B has full-fledged, violin-laden productions backing Brenda Reid's soul-drenched lead vocals. —*Bill Dahl*

F

Fabian

b. Feb. 6, 1943, Philadelphia, PA
Vocals / Pop, Teen Idol, Brill Building Pop

Thanks to a series of performances on Dick Clark's *American Bandstand,* Fabian rocketed to stardom in the late '60s. With his stylish good looks and mild rock 'n' roll, he became one of the top teen idols of the era; luckily, he had the support of the legendary songwriting team of Doc Pomus and Mort Shuman, who provided him with "Turn Me Loose," "Hound Dog Man," and "I'm a Man," among other songs. Fabian's fame peaked in 1959 with the million-selling "Tiger" single; after that, he valiantly tried to become a movie star. When Congress fingered him as one of the performers who benefited from payola, his already ailing career was given a nearly fatal blow; under questioning, Fabian explained that his records featured a substantial amount of electronic doctoring in order to improve his voice. After the hearings, he starred in some more movies in the '60s, without regaining the audience of his peak years. — *Stephen Thomas Erlewine*

● **The Best of Fabian** / Jun. 6, 1995 / Varese Vintage ✦✦✦✦
Compared to some import collections that are available, this ten-song CD is on the skimpy side. But it does include all of his late-'50s and early-'60s chart hits, which should satisfy all but obsessively rabid collectors, and as a domestic release, it's considerably cheaper and more readily available than the other comps. — *Richie Unterberger*

The Fabulous Thunderbirds

f. 1974, Austin, TX
Group / Rock 'n' Roll, Modern Electric Blues, Blues-Rock, Electric Texas Blues

With their fusion of blues, rock 'n' roll, and R&B, the Fabulous Thunderbirds helped popularize roadhouse Texas blues with a mass audience in the '80s and, in the process, they helped kick-start a blues revival during the mid-'80s. During their heyday in the early '80s, they were the most popular attraction on the blues bar circuit, which eventually led to a breakthrough to the pop audience in 1986 with their fifth album, *Tuff Enuff.* The mass success didn't last too long, and founding member Jimmie Vaughan left in 1990, but the Fabulous Thunderbirds remained one of the most popular blues concert acts in America during the '90s.

Guitarist Jimmie Vaughan formed the Fabulous Thunderbirds with vocalist/harpist Kim Wilson in 1974; in addition to Vaughan and Wilson, the band's original lineup included bassist Keith Ferguson and drummer Mike Buck. Initially, the group also featured vocalist Lou Ann Barton, but she left the band shortly after its formation. Within a few years, the Thunderbirds became the house band for the Austin club Antone's, where they would play regular sets and support touring blues musicians. By the end of the decade, they had built a strong fan base, which led to a record contract with the local Takoma Records.

In 1979 the Fabulous Thunderbirds released their eponymous debut on Takoma. The record was successful enough to attract the attention of major labels, and Chrysalis signed the band the next year. *What's the Word,* the group's second album, was released in 1980 and was followed in 1981 by *Butt Rockin'.* By the time the Thunderbirds recorded their 1982 album *T-Bird Rhythm,* drummer Mike Buck was replaced by Fran Christina, a former member of Roomful of Blues.

Although the Fabulous Thunderbirds had become favorites of fellow musicians—they opened shows for the Rolling Stones and Eric Clapton—and had been critically well-received, their records didn't sell particularly well. Chrysalis dropped the band after the release of *T-Bird Rhythm,* leaving the band without a record contract for four years. While they were in limbo, they continued to play concerts across the country. During this time, bassist Keith Ferguson left the band and was replaced by Preston Hubbard, another former member of Roomful of Blues. In 1985 they finally landed another record contract, signing with Epic/Associated.

After the deal was complete, the T-Birds entered a London studio and recorded their fifth album with producer Dave Edmunds. *Tuff Enuff* was released in the spring of 1986 and, unexpectedly, became a major crossover success. The title track was released as a single, and its accompanying video received heavy play on MTV, which helped the song reach the American Top Ten. The success of the single sent the album to No. 13 on the charts; *Tuff Enuff* would eventually receive a platinum record. "Wrap It Up," a cover of an old Sam & Dave song, was the album's second single, and it became a Top Ten album rock track. Later in 1986 the T-Birds won the W.C. Handy Award for best blues band.

The Fabulous Thunderbirds' follow-up to *Tuff Enuff, Hot Number,* arrived in the summer of 1987. Initially, the album did fairly well—peaking at No. 49 on the charts and spawning the Top Ten album rock hit "Stand Back"—but it quickly fell off the charts. Furthermore, its slick, radio-ready sound alienated their hardcore following of blues fans. "Powerful Stuff," a single from the soundtrack of the Tom Cruise film *Cocktail,* became a No. 3 album rock hit in the summer of 1988. It was included on the next year's *Powerful Stuff* album, which proved to be a major commercial disappointment; it spent only seven weeks on the charts.

After the two poorly received follow-ups to *Tuff Enuff,* Jimmie Vaughan left the band to play in a duo with his brother, Stevie Ray Vaughan; after Stevie Ray's death in the summer of 1990, Jimmie pursued a full-time solo career. The Fabulous Thunderbirds replaced Vaughan with two guitarists, Duke Robillard and Kid Bangham. The first album from the new lineup, *Walk That Walk, Talk That Talk,* appeared in 1991. After the release of *Walk That Walk, Talk That Talk,* Epic/Associated dropped the Fabulous Thunderbirds.

During the early '90s, the Fabulous Thunderbirds were in limbo, as Kim Wilson recorded a pair of solo albums—*Tigerman* (1993) and *That's Life* (1994). Wilson re-assembled the band in late 1994, and they recorded their ninth album, *Roll of the Dice,* which was released on Private Music in 1995. After its release, the band returned to actively touring the United States. — *Stephen Thomas Erlewine*

The Fabulous Thunderbirds / 1979 / Chrysalis ✦✦✦✦
Their debut album, with the original lineup of Wilson, Vaughn, Buck, and Ferguson stompin' through a roadhouse set of covers and genreworthy originals. One of the few White blues albums that works. — *Cub Koda*

What's the Word / 1980 / Chrysalis ✦✦✦✦
Second album, equally powerful. Some of their best, including the offkilter "Los Fabulosos Thunderbirds" and "Running Shoes." — *Cub Koda*

Butt Rockin' / 1981 / Chrysalis ✦✦✦

T Bird Rhythm / 1982 / Chrysalis ✦✦✦

Tuff Enuff / 1986 / Epic ✦✦✦
Their breakthrough success. The title track and soul covers point the band in a new, more mainstream direction. — *Cub Koda*

Hot Number / 1987 / Epic ✦✦

Powerful Stuff / 1989 / Epic ✦✦
Like the previous *Hot Number, Powerful Stuff* is a weak collection of watered-down blues-rock that makes too many concessions to the commerical constraints of AOR radio stations. Occasionally, the band works up some energy or Jimmie Vaughan or Kim Wilson turns out a good solo, but for the most part, *Powerful Stuff* is bland, faceless mainstream rock 'n' roll. — *Thom Owens*

The Essential / Jun. 18, 1991 / Chrysalis ✦✦✦✦
Nice compilation of the early Chrysalis albums on one CD. —*Cub Koda*

Walk That Walk, Talk That Talk / Dec. 1991 / Epic ✦✦✦
Walk That Walk, Talk That Talk is the first album the Fabulous Thunderbirds recorded without Jimmie Vaughan. It takes two guitarists—two good guitarists, by the way—to fill his place, and even with Duke Robillard and Kid Bangham on board, there is something missing. Though the T-birds have returned to straightahead blues-rock, abandoning the overly commercial production of their previous three albums, they don't sound as distinctive as they did with Vaughan. Kim Wilson blows some good harp, Robillard throws out a few stellar solos, and Bangham can almost keep up with him, but on the whole, the album is a disappointment. —*Thom Owens*

● **Hot Stuff: The Greatest Hits** / Aug. 25, 1992 / Epic ✦✦✦✦
The best tracks from the Fabulous Thunderbirds' more rock-oriented years at CBS Associated Records are collected on this single-disc compilation. —*Stephen Thomas Erlewine*

Roll of the Dice / Aug. 1, 1995 / Private Music ✦✦✦
The Fabulous T-Birds' second album without Jimmie Vaughan is an improvement over *Walk That Walk, Talk That Talk,* featuring a tighter, more focused band and hotter playing. Nevertheless, the band takes a couple of missteps, particularly with a limp version of "Zip-a-Dee-Doo-Dah." —*Stephen Thomas Erlewine*

Best Of / 1997 / EMI ✦✦✦✦
The Best of the Fabulous Thunderbirds is a terrific 22-track UK collection hitting all the highlights of the group's first four albums and offering a nearly flawless overview of the band's bluesiest period. —*Stephen Thomas Erlewine*

Faces

f. Mar. 1969, London, England, db. Sep. 1975
Rock 'n' Roll, Hard Rock
When Steve Marriott left the Small Faces in 1969, the three remaining members brought in guitarist Ron Wood and lead singer Rod Stewart to complete the lineup and changed their name to the Faces, which was only appropriate since the group now only slightly resembled the mod-pop group of the past. Instead, the Faces were a rough, sloppy rock 'n' roll band, able to pound out a rocker like "Had Me a Real Good Time," a blues ballad like "Tell Everyone," or a folk number like "Richmond," all in one album. Stewart, already becoming a star in his own right, let himself go wild with the Faces, tearing through covers and originals with abandon. While his voice didn't have the power of Stewart's, bassist Ronnie Lane's songs were equally impressive and eclectic. Wood's rhythm guitar had a warm, fat tone that was as influential and driving as Keith Richards' style.

Notorious for their hard-partying, boozy tours, and ragged concerts, the Faces lived the rock 'n' roll lifestyle to the extreme. When Stewart's solo career became more successful than the Faces', the band slowly became subservient to his personality; after their final studio album, *Ooh La La,* in 1973, Lane left the band. After a tour in 1974, the band called it quits. Wood joined the Rolling Stones, drummer Kenny Jones eventually became part of the Who, and keyboardist Ian McLagan became a sought-after supporting musician; Stewart became a superstar, although he never matched the simple charms of the Faces.

While they were together, the Faces never sold that many records and were never considered as important as the Stones, but their music has proven extremely influential. Many punk rockers in the late '70s learned how to play their instruments by listening to Faces records; in the '80s and '90s, guitar-rock bands from the Replacements to the Black Crowes took their cue from the Faces as much as the Stones. Their reckless, loose, and joyous spirit has stayed alive in much of the best rock 'n' roll of the past two decades. —*Stephen Thomas Erlewine*

First Step / 1970 / Warner Brothers ✦✦✦✦
On their first album, the Faces established the pattern they would follow throughout their four albums—a ragged mix of breakneck rockers ("Shake, Shudder"), sensitive yet gritty ballads ("Devotion"), folk songs ("Stone"), revelatory covers (Bob Dylan's "Wicked Messenger"), and relaxed, friendly rockers ("Three Button Hand Me Down"). Although two instrumentals on the second side are one too many (Ron Wood's "Pineapple and the Monkey" is pretty great), the Faces seldom got better than the first half of *First Step.* —*Stephen Thomas Erlewine*

☆ **Long Player** / 1971 / Warner Brothers ✦✦✦✦✦
With their second effort, the Faces grew more muscular and loose, rocking with loose abandon on "Bad N' Ruin" and "Had Me a Real Good Time," two of their best songs. At the same time, their ballads improved, with Stewart's "Tell Everyone" and Lane's "Richmond" rivaling each other for the most touching number on the album. Out of the two live tracks, "I Feel So Good" goes on a little too long, but "Maybe I'm Amazed" is tremendous—the Faces tear into the song, transforming it from a McCartney ballad to a heartfelt cry of devotion. *Long Player* is a

sloppy, terrific record; although it may have a couple of weak moments, it has the heart and soul of the band. —*Stephen Thomas Erlewine*

★ **A Nod Is As Good As a Wink...To a Blind Horse** / 1971 / Warner Brothers ✦✦✦✦✦
Boasting "Stay with Me," the only hit the Faces ever had, *A Nod is As Good As a Wink* is their most consistent record, and arguably their best. "Stay with Me" and "Miss Judy's Farm" showcase the band at their best; they're all over the place, threatening to fall apart altogether before they snap it all back into place. Nobody rocked better than this, and the album is full of such terrific moments, including a rollicking cover of Chuck Berry's "Memphis." As with all of the Faces' albums, it's a little messy, but it is a classic rock 'n' roll band at the top of their form. —*Stephen Thomas Erlewine*

Ooh La La / 1973 / Warner Brothers ✦✦✦
Although it's routinely lambasted as an uninspired effort or a sell-out, *Ooh La La* is a tight rock 'n' roll album, with its best moments—"Cindy Incidentally" and "Borstal Boy"—ranking among the Faces' best songs. —*Stephen Thomas Erlewine*

Snakes & Ladders / 1976 / Warner Brothers ✦✦✦
Snakes & Ladders is a fine 12-song overview of the Faces, containing some of the group's best songs ("Had Me a Real Good Time," "Stay with Me," "Miss Judy's Farm," "Sweet Lady Mary," "Ooh La La," "Cindy Incidentally"), along with a couple of mediocre cuts ("Pineapple and the Monkey," "Flying") and the unremarkable, single-only "Pool Hall Richard." Though it gives a sense of what made the Faces a great rock 'n' roll band, it falls far short of being a definitive retrospective or introduction. —*Stephen Thomas Erlewine*

Donald Fagen

b. Jan. 10, 1948, Passaic, NJ
Keyboards / Soft Rock, Pop-Rock, Jazz-Rock
Donald Fagen was one of the two masterminds behind Steely Dan, the seminal jazz-pop band of the '70s. Fagen's solo work has been a continuation of the band's work of the early '80s—carefully constructed and arranged, intricately detailed pop songs that are more substantial than their stylish surface may indicate. His 1982 solo debut, *The Nightfly,* was the best album he had made in years; it covered the same ground as the last two Steely Dan albums, but surpassed it in terms of ambition and achievement.

After the success of *The Nightfly,* Fagen suffered a case of writer's block; for the rest of the decade he contributed music to the occasional film and briefly wrote a column for *Premiere* magazine in the mid-'80s. In the early '90s, he toured with the New York Rock and Soul Revue as he finished the material for his second album. With his former Steely Dan partner Walter Becker producing, 1993's *Kamakiriad* sounded like *Aja* recorded with '90s technology. It had some success on the adult-contemporary charts, but it was overshadowed by the duo's decision to reform Steely Dan and tour for the first time in nearly 20 years; the tour was a massive success. —*Stephen Thomas Erlewine*

● **The Nightfly** / Oct. 1982 / Warner Brothers ✦✦✦✦
For his debut solo album after leaving Steely Dan, Fagen turned in a typically sophisticated jazz-pop collection tied to a lyrical theme concerning the late '50s and early '60s. One song takes the Kennedy administration's slogan, "The New Frontier," as a title, while another, "The Goodbye Look," is set in Cuba around the time of Castro's takeover. Steely Dan lovers will feel right at home. —*William Ruhlmann*

Kamakiriad / May 25, 1993 / Reprise ✦✦✦✦
After eleven years, Donald Fagen delivered his second album, *Kamakiriad,* in the summer of 1993. Where the sophisticated eclecticism of *The Nightfly* was warm and welcoming, *Kamakiriad* is insular; it takes several listens before all of the pieces fall into place. While all of the album *sounds* terrific, the melodies are subtler and tend to get buried under the meticulous arrangements. However, the hooks and melodies emerge after a couple of plays, as do Fagen's wry, witty lyrics. —*Stephen Thomas Erlewine*

Jad Fair

b. San Francisco, CA
Alternative Pop-Rock, Post-Punk, Experimental
There are plenty of performers rock critics compliment by using the label "primitive," but few, if any, can hold a candle to the greatest American rock primitive, Jad Fair. With his fantastic and increasingly influential band Half Japanese or as a solo performer, Fair has constructed a prolific and extremely interesting career, writing and recording songs that display an uncomplicated emotional directness, unselfconscious (almost hokey) charm and warmth, and a genial simplicity. Although Fair's recent recordings are certainly more accessible—in some ways resembling those of another great American primitive, Jonathan Richman—his stock-in-trade is still the ability to compose and play music without any discernable (i.e., traditional) musical talent. Although he

has "played" guitar since the mid-'70s, Fair, according to past and present members of Half Japanese, still can't name a chord, plays riffs almost by accident, and wouldn't have it any other way.

Fair's career as a solo artist began in 1980. It wasn't that he was particularly upset or unhappy with the direction he and brother David were leading Half Japanese, but rather that he needed another outlet with which to satisfy his obsessive desire to make music. The first efforts were tentative, and in terms of the noise vs. music factor (more noise than music), akin to early Half Japanese records. But by the mid- to late '80s, Fair's solo records were becoming more accessible, due to the contributions of celebrities and Half Japanese fans such as Dinosaur Jr.'s J Mascis, NRBQ's Terry Adams, Yo La Tengo's Ira Kaplan, and Gumball mastermind Don Fleming. And while the records got a little more polished, they certainly never lost a bit of Fair's childlike view of the world, nor his explosive, giddy belief in rock's liberating potential and endless possibilities. In Fair's world, love is the key to solving the world's problems, but his naivete-as-philosophy is never rank or manipulative (you always believe that he believes); although he can sound cloying at times, the honesty and joy of this music will let you forgive his occasional excesses. By not being your typical singer-songwriter, Jad Fair has made the world a safe place for those who care passionately about rock 'n' roll, but who don't feel the need to achieve any degree of virtuosity. —*John Dougan*

Everybody Knew . . . But Me / 1982 / Press ✦✦✦
Early, more extreme Jad. His singing is surrounded by metallic clattering and only the barest concessions to traditional pop song forms. The songs tend to be about love and, uh, love, but the rather limited narratives in no way detract from what is a mostly wonderful listening experience. Although this is an accurate portrait of what Jad was up to at the time, it's recommended for adventure seekers, noise-pop fans, and those who unequivocally loved the first two Half Japanese records. —*John Dougan*

● **Jad Fair and Daniel Johnston** / 1989 / Homestead ✦✦✦✦
Those not familiar with Daniel Johnston's work should know that his approach to pop songwriting is similar to Fair's, with the exception that he suffers from serious bouts with manic depression and severe delusional behavior. That said, this pairing of these two musical savants is a successful foray into pop music as therapy. Neither one is blessed with a great voice (or technically, a good voice), the songs tend to be about simple pleasures, and the instrumentation is sparse. Despite flashes of happiness, this is by and large not a happy record; it's more of a soul-baring exercise. —*John Dougan*

I Like It When You Smile / 1992 / Psycho ✦✦✦
This is the Fair release with the largest number of heavy hitters providing musical support (Terry Adams, J. Mascis, Don Fleming) and some of it rocks in a radio-friendly (for Jad anyway) fashion that's downright jarring. But there is enough of the trademark Fair mania and out-of-tune playing (a downright messy, atonal cover of "On the Sunny Side of the Street") to keep diehards happy, while expanding the minds of newcomers to Jad Fair's warm and wonderful world. —*John Dougan*

Fairport Convention

f. 1967, London, England
Folk-Rock, British Folk
The best British folk-rock band of the late '60s, Fairport Convention did more than any other act to develop a truly British variation on the folk-rock prototype by drawing upon traditional material and styles indigenous to the British Isles. While the revved-up renditions of traditional British folk tunes drew the most critical attention, the group were also (at least at the outset) talented songwriters as well as interpreters. They were comfortable with conventional harmony-based folk-rock as well as tunes that drew upon more explicitly traditional sources, and boasted some of the best singers and instrumentalists of the day. A revolving door of personnel, however, saw the exit of their most distinguished talents, and basically changed the band into a living museum piece after the early '70s, albeit an enjoyable one, with integrity.

When Fairport formed around 1967, their goal was not to revive British folk numbers, but to play harmony- and guitar-based folk-rock in a style strongly influenced by California groups of the day (especially the Byrds). The lineup that recorded their self-titled debut album in 1968 featured Richard Thompson, Ian Matthews, and Simon Nicol on guitars; Ashley Hutchings on bass; Judy Dyble on vocals; and Martin Lamble on drums. Most of the members sang, though Matthews and Dyble were the strongest vocalists in this early incarnation; all of their early work, in fact, was characterized by blends of male and female vocals, influenced by such American acts as the Mamas and the Papas and Ian & Sylvia. While their first album was derivative, it had some fine material, and the band was already showing a knack for eclecticism, excavating overlooked songs by Joni Mitchell (then virtually unknown) and Emitt Rhodes.

Fairport didn't reach their peak until Dyble was replaced after the

first album in 1968 by Sandy Denny, who had previously recorded both as a solo act and with the Strawbs. Denny's penetrating, resonant style qualified her as the best British folk-rock singer of all time, and provided the band with the best vocalist they would ever have. *What We Did on Our Holidays* (1968) and *Unhalfbricking* (1969) are their best albums, mixing strong originals, excellent covers of contemporary folk-rock songs by the likes of Mitchell and Dylan, and imaginative revivals of traditional folk songs that mixed electric and acoustic instruments with a beguiling ease.

Matthews had left the band in early 1969, and Lamble (still in his teens) died in an accident involving the group's equipment van in mid-1969. That forced Fairport to regroup, replacing Lamble with Dave Mattacks, and adding Dave Swarbrick on fiddle. Their repertoire, too, became much more traditional in focus, and electrified traditional folk numbers would dominate their next album, *Liege and Lief* (1969). Here critical thought diverges; some insist that this is unequivocally their peak, marking a final escape from their '60s folk-rock influences into a much more original style; this school of thought severely underestimates their songwriting talents. Others feel that they were at their best when mixing original and outside material, and contemporary and traditional styles, in fact becoming more predictable and derivative when they opted to concentrate on British folk chestnuts.

The *Liege and Lief* lineup didn't last long; by the end of the '60s, Ashley Hutchings had left to join Steeleye Span, replaced by Dave Pegg. More crucially, Denny was also gone, helping to form Fotheringay. Thompson was still on board for *Full House* (1970), but by the beginning of 1971 he, too, had departed, leaving Nicol as the only original member.

Fairport have kept going, on and off (mostly on), for the last 25 years, touring and performing frequently. It may be too harsh to dismiss all of their post-Thompson records out of hand; *Angel Delight* (1971), the first recorded without the guitarist on board, was actually their highest-charting LP in the UK, reaching the Top Ten. Nicol's exit in late 1971 erased all vestiges of connections to their salad days. Fairport was now not so much a continuous entity as a concept, carried on by musicians dedicated to the electrified British folk style that had been mapped out on *Liege and Lief.*

So it continues to this day, supported by a devoted fan base (*Dirty Linen,* the top American roots music magazine, originally began as a Fairport Convention fanzine). Denny would actually return to the group for about a year and a half in the 1970s, before her death in 1978; Nicol rejoined in 1976. Keeping track of Fairport's multitudinous lineup changes is a daunting task, and the group has coexisted on an erratic basis with the various other projects of the most frequent members (Nicol, Mattacks, and Pegg, the last of whom has played with Jethro Tull since the late '70s). They have played annual reunion concerts during the 1980s and '90s (sometimes joined onstage by Fairport alumni like Thompson), events that have turned into one of the most popular folk festivals in Europe. They've also released some albums of new material intermittently throughout the last couple of decades, mostly pleasant, unexceptional traditional-oriented outings that appeal primarily to diehards.

The most distinguished graduates of Fairport, however, have continued to shape the British folk and folk-rock scene with notable solo and group projects. Richard Thompson is one of the most critically acclaimed singer-songwriters in the world; Ian Matthews made some interesting recordings as a solo act and with Plainsong and Matthews Southern Comfort; Denny sang with Fotheringay and released several solo albums, before her death; and Hutchings carried on the most traditional face of British folk-rock with Steeleye Span, the Albion Band, and the Etchingham Steam Band. —*Richie Unterberger*

Fairport Convention [1st] / Jun. 1968 / Polydor ✦✦✦✦
By far the most rock-oriented of Fairport's early albums, this was recorded before Denny joined the band (Judy Dyble handles the female vocals). Unjustly overlooked by listeners who consider the band's pre-Denny output insignificant, this is a fine folk-rock effort that takes far more inspiration from West Coast '60s sounds than traditional British folk. Good originals and excellent covers of a variety of obscure tunes by Joni Mitchell, Dylan, Emmitt Rhodes, and Jim & Jean. —*Richie Unterberger*

What We Did on Our Holidays / Jan. 1969 / Hannibal ✦✦✦✦
Sandy Denny's haunting, ethereal vocals give Fairport a big boost on her debut with the group. A more folk-based album than their initial effort, divided between original material and a few well-chosen covers. This contains several of their greatest moments: Sandy Denny's "Fotheringay," Richard Thompson's "Meet on the Ledge," the obscure Joni Mitchell composition "Eastern Rain," the traditional "She Moves Through the Fair," and their version of Dylan's "I'll Keep It with Mine." —*Richie Unterberger*

★ **Unhalfbricking** / Jul. 1969 / Hannibal ✦✦✦✦✦
Richard Thompson and Sandy Denny shine throughout this record,

which is considered by some to be their Fairport peak together. The second album by a tragically short-lived Fairport Convention lineup seems top-heavy with Dylan tunes, three of them included, but they're done with such verve and freshness that they seem perfectly appropriate. As for the rest, Denny's performance on "Autopsy" is outshone only by her work in the apocalyptic nine-minute "A Sailor's Life," which is one of the great English folk-rock showcases, a rival to such works as Phil Ochs' "Crucifixion" and Bob Dylan's "Desolation Row," as a song that just makes the listener "white out" inside, mouth open, when it's over. Also highlighted by the definitive Denny recording of "Who Knows Where the Time Goes." Take in the powerhouse drumming, and realize what the band lost when Martin Lamble died. — *William Ruhlmann & Bruce Eder*

☆ **Liege and Lief** / Dec. 1969 / A&M ✦✦✦✦✦
This album, regarded by many as the best record that Fairport Convention ever issued, was also Sandy Denny's and Ashley Hutchings' exit album, highlighted by the scintillating "Tam Lin" and "Matty Groves," the haunting "Raynardine" and "Crazy Man Michael," and the soaring "Come All Ye." Voted the best folk album of all time by the readers of Britain's *Folk Roots* magazine. Features Thompson and Denny along with fiddler Dave Swarbrick. — *Stephen Winnick, William Ruhlmann & Bruce Eder*

Full House / Jul. 1970 / Hannibal ✦✦✦✦
Sandy Denny and bassist Ashley Hutchings are gone. Thompson and Swarbrick take over as singers, Dave Pegg (more recently of Jethro Tull) plays bass, and the result, strangely enough, is an album that may be more viscerally exciting than *Liege and Lief*, if not quite as important as that record, since it came first. Not only does the singing here retain the high standard of the earlier incarnation of the group (check out the harmony singing on "Sir Patrick Spens" and "Flowers of the Forest"), but the playing throughout has greater urgency and punch, from the rousing Thompson-Swarbrick opener "Walk Awhile" to the haunting, moody, dazzling nine-minute "Sloth," which remained part of the group's live set for years. An indispensable recording, and one that anybody who wants to truly know this band, or, especially, to take in some of the best work of Richard Thompson's career must own. (His playing on "Sloth" alone makes it worthwhile.) Swarbrick's fiddle and viola playing is also some of the best of his career. Ironically, Thompson would make this his last full-time studio venture with Fairport, but what a way to go! — *Stephen Winnick & Bruce Eder*

Angel Delight / Jun. 1971 / Island ✦✦✦
Richard Thompson exits the Fairport lineup, leaving the band reduced to a quartet of Simon Nicol, Dave Swarbrick, Dave Pegg, and Dave Mattacks. The loss of big guns Thompson and Denny was felt, but amazingly, although it isn't nearly as well known as *Liege and Lief* or *Full House*, this record reached the highest chart position of any Fairport LP, making No. 8 in England. Swarbrick led the group in even more of a traditional British folk vein. By now everybody involved was singing (with Nicol and Swarbrick usually alternating on lead), and they managed to pull it off, mostly by virtue of the honesty of their voices and instrumental work almost as vital and animated as any in their history. From the beautifully sung and exciting opener "Lord Marlborough," the album should strike a responsive chord with any folk or folk-rock enthusiast. Especially enjoyable are the singing on the buoyantly humorous title track, and the viola/violin duet between Swarbrick and Nicol on "Bridge over the River Ash." — *Bruce Eder & William Ruhlmann*

Babbacombe Lee / Nov. 1971 / Island ✦✦✦
The group's only concept album (similar in some ways to the Pretty Things' *S.F. Sorrow*), built around the life story of John "Babbacombe" Lee, a Victorian-era condemned murderer. Lee's story, from his boyhood poverty to his time in the Royal Navy, his being invalided out and forced to work in the service of Miss Keyes, to his murder and his sentence of death, and the failure of the gallows three times, is told in song, and all but one of those songs are originals. The all-male Fairport seldom sang better, nor did the post-Thompson band ever play with more panache, and some of the songs are beautiful—but a few are lugubrious, and as with most other concept albums, the fit between the songs and the larger subject ultimately isn't entirely comfortable for the listener. All of the material was confusing because the group, for some reason, never put titles on the individual songs, instead stringing them together in longer sections. The critics loved it, but the listeners stayed away in droves for the first time since the band's debut album. — *Bruce Eder*

Rosie / Mar. 1973 / Island ✦✦✦
After the departure of Simon Nicol, the group was reconstituted with the addition of Sandy Denny's husband, Trevor Lucas, and Jerry Donahue, both formerly of Fotheringay. Their first album was a miscalculation, a failed attempt to crack the pop music market. There was lots of original songs done in a modern folk-rock sound, many written by Lucas, although the best was the title track by Swarbrick (which featured Denny, Thompson, and Thompson's future wife, Linda Peters, as guest artists). The Lucas compositions were all pleasant (especially "Knights of

the Road," and the haunting "The Plainsman"), but tend to make one think more of Gordon Lightfoot sounding archaic than of previous incarnations of Fairport. The only exceptions are "Peggy's Pub" and "The Hens March Through the Midden," instrumentals that recall the group's old sound. — *Bruce Eder & William Ruhlmann*

Nine / Oct. 1973 / A&M ✦✦
Fairport Convention's ninth album is their most uneven. The group shows extraordinary virtuosity and musical instincts on folk-based tracks such as "The Hexamshire Lass" and "The Brilliancy Medley & Cherokee Shuffle" (which features some of the best mandolin playing you're ever likely to hear from an English band), but on numbers like "Polly on the Shore" and "To Althea from Prison," where the band supplies the music to traditional lyrics, they simply fall flat. It isn't even that the playing is bad, so much as that the failed numbers are uniformly lugubrious in the way they're treated. Part of the problem lies with the fact that while Lucas and Donahue were good guitarists, they weren't terribly interesting; where Richard Thompson always came up with something surprising, unexpected on Fairport's songs, Lucas and Donahue stick with fairly routine pop music sounds, more in keeping with the Eagles than the group that recorded *Liege and Lief*, *Full House*, and *House Full*. Lucas' "Bring 'em Down" is a decent song, with some strong singing and playing by the composer and a lovely and powerful fiddle solo by Swarbrick, but it overstays its welcome and loses its cohesion; "Sloth" it is not. Too much of the album is taken up by easily forgotten contemporary-style rockers like "Big William" and throwaways such as the countrified "Pleasure and Pain." Not even the upbeat, riff-heavy "Possibly Parsons Green" makes up for this problem. And the rather plain cover art didn't help matters any when it came to selling this record. — *Bruce Eder*

A Fairport Live Convention / Jul. 1974 / Island ✦✦✦
The presence of Sandy Denny raises expectations for the group's first released live album. Recorded on the band's 1973 world tour, it features songs such as "Matty Groves" and "Sloth," as well as the Swarbrick instrumental "Fiddlestix," their then current single "Rosie," and a nod to the group's origins as interpreters of American rock 'n' roll and folk-rock, in the form of Dylan's "Down in the Flood" and Chris Kenner's "Something You Got." Denny's solo abilities are showcased on "John the Gun." The problem is the uneven quality of the recording, from three different venues, each seemingly lacking intimacy and warmth. This may explain why it was never released in America, and why Island released the superior *Live at the L.A. Troubadour/House Full* just two years later. As the only live document of Denny with the band, however, this record is vital to Fairport completists. — *Bruce Eder & William Ruhlmann*

Rising for the Moon / Jun. 1975 / Island ✦✦✦
Although there's nothing here as overpowering as "Sailor's Life" or "Sloth," this record is still a choice release, as Sandy Denny's official return to Fairport. She wrote or co-wrote seven of its 11 songs, and dominates most of the others with her voice. This lineup (Denny, Dave Swarbrick, Dave Pegg, Jerry Donahue, Trevor Lucas, and Bruce Rowland, with Dave Mattacks—who quit part way through—drumming on some of the tracks) went for the gold with rock veteran Glyn Johns in the producer's spot. The result was the only Fairport album done after the departure of Richard Thompson that doesn't sound anemic in the electric guitar department. Some of the songs, especially the title track and "Restless," have the feel of compact, breezy pop/country-rock, reminiscent of the Eagles or Firefall, although it's hard to imagine either of those groups turning in anything with the ethereal beauty of Denny's performance on "White Dress" or "Dawn." Those songs and "Stranger to Himself" could easily have been on one of her solo albums. Others, like Trevor Lucas' "Iron Lion," sound almost like Fairport's version of the Rolling Stones' "Dead Flowers." Only the Swarbrick/Pegg "Night-time Girl" resembles Fairport's established work from their earlier history. This was the last album and the last incarnation of Fairport Convention to present itself to the public as a contemporary rock group, and their last (apart from 1987's *In Real Time*) release on a major label. Beyond this point, they became part of the folk revival circuit, albeit with a huge audience. (British import) — *Bruce Eder*

● **Fairport Chronicles** / 1976 / A&M ✦✦✦✦
A well-chosen early best-of collection. — *William Ruhlmann*

Gottle O'Geer / May 1976 / Island ✦✦
Fairport Convention split in half in December 1975, with Sandy Denny, Trevor Lucas, and Jerry Donahue leaving; the remaining trio of Dave Swarbrick, Dave Pegg, and Bruce Rowland then made this contractual obligation album, which was credited to "Fairport Featuring Dave Swarbrick." As you might expect, it's fairly listless. — *William Ruhlmann*

Live at L. A. Troubadour / 1977 / Island ✦✦✦
With Fairport off the label, Island Records reached back and released this live recording from 1970, featuring the last Richard Thompson lineup of the band. It was a forceful album, but it has since been super-

seded by *House Full*, a revised version of the same material. —*William Ruhlmann*

Bonny Bunch of Roses / Feb. 1977 / Vertigo ✦✦

Tipplers Tales / May 1978 / Vertigo ✦✦✦
Some of Fairport's finest traditional song performances are here, from yet another lineup. Singer/guitarist Simon Nicol, the only original Fairporter left, begins to take a more active role. —*Stephen Winick*

Farewell, Farewell / 1979 / Simon's ✦✦✦
This fine live album documents their farewell tour. —*Stephen Winick*

Moat on the Ledge / 1982 / Stony Plain ✦✦✦
Fairport Convention officially disbanded in 1979, only to become the hosts of a yearly folk festival/reunion concert every August in England. This album is taken from the 1981 show. It features original Fairport members Simon Nicol, Judy Dyble, and Richard Thompson, plus later members Dave Swarbrick, Dave Pegg, Dave Mattacks, and Bruce Rowland, and it's a good recapitulation of the band's style, with such numbers new to the repertoire as Bob Dylan's "Country Pie" and Thompson's "Woman or a Man." —*William Ruhlmann*

Gladys' Leap / 1985 / Varrick ✦✦✦
After six years, Fairport re-formed and released this fine record featuring mostly newly composed material. —*Stephen Winick*

Expletive Delighted! / 1986 / Varrick ✦✦✦
The group's only all-instrumental album is alternately enjoyable and maddening. On the down side, there was no earthly reason why Dave Mattacks' drums had to be recorded as loud as they are on certain tracks. But "Portmeirion" and "Expletive Delighted" are as delicate and beautiful as any work that this version of the band has done. Richard Thompson and Jerry Donahue turn up on electric guitar for the rippling finale "Hanks for the Memories," a reconsideration of instrumentals ranging from "Apache" and "Pipeline" to "Peter Gunn." —*Bruce Eder*

House Full / 1986 / Hannibal ✦✦✦✦
Although its release date is 16 years later, this 1970 live recording is of a piece with *Full House* and should be discovered in tandem with the studio album. A revised version of *Live at the L.A. Troubadour* (originally released on vinyl in 1976), with different takes and/or songs, taken from a group of September 1970 concert performances by the Richard Thompson-led 1970 lineup of Fairport, one of its strongest incarnations. A 12-minute version of "Sloth" dominates the proceedings, but even better is the fact that, at 48 minutes, this is one of Fairport's longer albums, so there is lots of room for other material, including a shattering Thompson-sung rendition of "Matty Groves," and a pair of numbers, "Staines Morris" and "Banks of the Sweet Primroses," scheduled for this group's never-realized second studio album (though the latter made it into the studio history of the four-man Fairport that followed). —*Bruce Eder & William Ruhlmann*

Heyday / 1987 / Hannibal ✦✦✦✦
This collection of 14 BBC performances from 1968 and 1969 is just as outstanding as their late-'60s studio albums, and shows their mastery of an astonishing range of material. Most of these songs were not recorded on the group's official releases, and include covers of gems by Joni Mitchell, Eric Andersen, Johnny Cash, Leonard Cohen, Gene Clark, Richard Farina, the Everlys, and Bob Dylan. —*Richie Unterberger*

In Real Time: Live '87 / 1987 / Island ✦✦
All that's right and wrong with the surviving band. An electric and eclectic live album that's over-loud and over-done. —*Bruce Eder*

Red & Gold / 1989 / Rough Trade ✦✦

Five Seasons / Dec. 1990 / Rough Trade ✦✦✦
Fairport Convention's 17th studio album in 22 years finds them a competent, craftsmanlike unit led by Simon Nicol, who has developed into a strong singer. If they never aspire to the heights achieved with more impressive lineups, they nevertheless continue to find traditional and new material that suits them, sometimes by turning to newest members Ric Saunders and Martin Allcock, who are accomplished instrumentalists. —*William Ruhlmann*

25th Anniversary / Oct. 10, 1994 / Import ✦✦✦
Recorded live to DAT at a performance that had fiddler Chris Leslie filling in for Ric Sanders, who had injured himself in an accident involving a plate glass window. (Sanders was able to provide keyboards, however.) A festive outing, with numerous guests (including Fairport founders Richard Thompson and Ashley Hutchings), the two-disc set ranges from the sublime (a ferocious, Boiled in Lead-style take of "Matty Groves") to the slightly surreal ("John Barleycorn" with the lyrics screwed up). The sound is unfortunately too bright and metallic, and the mix, taken from the soundboard, is sometimes atrocious, but trimming the highs helps with the former, while the latter, in the spirit of live shows, can simply be ignored. Not the best example of Fairport, but *highly* entertaining. —*Steven McDonald*

A Chronicle of Sorts 1967-1969 [bootleg] / 1995 / Nixed ✦✦✦✦
A major find for Fairport fanatics, this collects 23 unreleased performances from the late '60s in acceptable-to-excellent fidelity, mostly from the BBC (with a few tracks from TV clips and one 1968 studio outtake). Running 77 minutes, it's divided roughly equally between the Judy Dyble and the Sandy Denny eras. Only one of these songs ("Reno, Nevada") shows up on the official comp of early Fairport BBC cuts, *Heyday*. And even then, this is a much different version than the *Heyday* take of "Reno, Nevada," running seven minutes and featuring some dazzling psychedelic guitar riffs. Otherwise, there's a wealth of material that's not officially available in either live or studio versions, including covers of several early Joni Mitchell songs, Bob Dylan's "Dear Landlord," Tim Buckley's "Morning Glory," Eric Andersen's "Violets of Dawn," and a send-up of "Light My Fire." Plus it has good live run-throughs of songs from their early albums like "Chelsea Morning," "Fotheringay," "Autopsy," "Si Tu Doi Partis," and others. It's just as effective as *Heyday* in demonstrating the band's interpretive skills and eclecticism in their early folk-rock days, though the sound quality isn't as stellar. —*Richie Unterberger*

Jewel in the Crown / Jun. 6, 1995 / Green Linnet ✦✦✦
On their third album in five years, Fairport Convention, which now boasts a steady lineup (nearly a decade together!) for the first time in its history, carries on two traditions. The shorter-term one is the tradition of Fairport itself, a band intended to blend contemporary rock with folk, often in the form of work by current singer-songwriters, here including Clive Gregson and Leonard Cohen. The longer term one is the tradition of Scots-Irish music, with its jigs and reels and story songs that date back to the Middle Ages. Sometimes, the band combines the two traditions, recording songs like Steve Tilston's "The Naked Highwayman" and Ralph McTell and band member Maartin Allcock's "The Islands," which update traditional themes in interesting ways. (Allcock, by the way, has added an extra "A" to his first name since we last heard from him.) Simon Nicol, the only original member of Fairport Convention dating back to 1967, has developed into a sturdy baritone singer, and multi-instrumentalist Allcock carries the bulk of the musical burden. *Jewel in the Crown* is a well-balanced collection of songs that is true to the spirit of Fairport Convention and its antecedents. —*William Ruhlmann*

Old-New-Borrowed-Blue / Jul. 16, 1996 / Green Linnet ✦✦✦✦
This is Fairport Convention's first all-acoustic album in their 29-year history. The material, recorded variously in the studio and at a December 30, 1995, concert, displays the eclectic nature of the 1990s version of the band, folk-styled originals such as "There Once Was Love/Innstruck" juxtaposed with covers of James Taylor and Loudon Wainwright III songs, reprises of vintage Fairport numbers like Richard Thompson's "Genesis Hall," "Crazy Man Michael," and the epic "Matty Groves," and even some vintage swing elements. The playing is exquisite, and the vocalizing by Simon Nicol and Dave Pegg is extraordinary, particularly on "There Once Was Love," "Frozen Man," "The Hiring Fair," and "Lalla Rookh." —*Bruce Eder*

Faith No More

f. 1982, San Francisco, CA
Alternative Pop-Rock, Heavy Metal, Funk Metal
With their fusion of heavy metal, funk, hip-hop, and progressive rock, Faith No More has earned a substantial cult following. By the time they recorded their first album in 1985, the band had already had a string of lead vocalists, including Courtney Love; their debut, *We Care a Lot*, featured Chuck Mosley's abrasive vocals, but it was driven by Jim Martin's metallic guitar. Faith No More's next album, 1987's *Introduce Yourself*, was a more cohesive and impressive effort; for the first time, the rap and metal elements didn't sound as if they were fighting each other.

In 1988 the rest of the band fired Mosley; he was replaced by Bay Area vocalist Mike Patton during the recording of their next album, *The Real Thing*. Patton was a more accomplished vocalist, able to change effortlessly between rapping and singing, as well as adding a considerably more bizarre slant to the lyrics. Besides adding a new vocalist, the band had tightened their attack, and the result was the genre-bending hit single "Epic," which established them as a major hard-rock act.

Following up the hit wasn't as easy, however. Faith No More followed their breakthrough success with 1992's *Angel Dust*, one of the more complex and simply confounding records ever released by a major label. Although it sold respectably, it didn't have the crossover potential of the first album. When the band toured in support of the album, tensions between the band and Martin began to escalate; rumors began to circulate that his guitar had been stripped from some of the final mixes of *Angel Dust*. As the band was recording its fifth album in early 1994, it was confirmed that Martin had been fired. Faith No More recorded *King for a Day, Fool for a Lifetime* with Mr. Bungle guitarist Trey Spruance. During tour preparations he was replaced by Dean Mentia. —*Stephen Thomas Erlewine*

Introduce Yourself / 1987 / Slash ✦✦✦

● **The Real Thing** / Jun. 1989 / Slash ✦✦✦✦
An unusual combination of heavy metal, rap, and hard rock, appealing to head bangers and popsters alike. —*Donna DiChario*

Angel Dust / 1992 / Slash ✦✦✦✦
It's quite diverse and eclectic, with its range of styles going from lounge jazz to power-pop and all-out industrial grindcore. The songwriting shows a lot of talent, especially from Mike Patton, whose vocal range is used to its full potential on this album, the band's fourth. —*John Book*

King for a Day, Fool for a Lifetime / Mar. 28, 1995 / Slash ✦✦
Faith No More's first album since the departure of guitarist Jim Martin is surprisingly direct and metallic, lacking even the keyboard flourishes that invigorated *Angel Dust* and *The Real Thing*. The sporadic ventures into '70s soul, skewed funk, and vaguely experimental pop are present, but they seem as if they were dusted off for the occasion, repeating everything they said before. Without successful diversions, Faith No More is a standard metal band. They're competent, to be sure, but they offer nothing out of the ordinary, except that odd song about enemas. —*Stephen Thomas Erlewine*

Marianne Faithfull

b. Dec. 29, 1946, Hampstead, London, England
Vocals / Pop-Rock, Girl-Group
Few stars of the 1960s have reinvented themselves as successfully as Marianne Faithfull. Coaxed into a singing career by Rolling Stones manager Andrew Loog Oldham in 1964, she had a big hit in both Britain and the US with her debut single, the Jagger/Richards composition "As Tears Go By" (which prefaced the Stones' own version by a full year). Considerably more successful in her native land than the States, she had a series of hits in the mid-'60s that set her high, fragile voice against delicate orchestral pop arrangements—"Summer Night," "This Little Bird," Jackie De Shannon's "Come and Stay with Me." Not a songwriter at the outset of her career, she owes more of her fame as a '60s icon to her extraordinary beauty and her long-running romance with Mick Jagger, although she offered a taste of things to come with her compelling 1969 single "Sister Morphine," which she co-wrote (and which the Stones later released themselves on *Sticky Fingers*).
In the 1970s Faithfull split up with Jagger, developed a serious drug habit, and recorded rarely, with generally dismal results. In late 1979 she pulled off an astonishing comeback with *Broken English*. Displaying a croaking, cutting voice that had lowered a good octave since the mid-'60s, Faithfull had also begun to write much of her own material, and addressed sex and despair with wrenching realism. After allowing herself to be framed as a demure chanteuse by songwriters and arrangers throughout most of her career, Faithfull had found her own voice and suddenly sounded more relevant and contemporary than most of the stars she had rubbed shoulders with in the '60s. Faithfull's recordings in the 1980s and 1990s have been sporadic and erratic, but generally quite interesting; *Strange Weather*, a Hal Willner-produced 1987 collection of standards and contemporary compositions that spanned several decades for its sources, was her greatest triumph of the decade. In 1994 she published her self-titled autobiography; the recent biography *As Tears Go By*, by Mark Hodkinson, is a more objective and thorough account of her life and times. One continues to look forward to unexpected twists on forthcoming recordings, a statement one can apply to few other performers who emerged during the 1960s. —*Richie Unterberger*

Marianne Faithfull / May 1965 / London ✦✦✦
Her erratic, self-titled debut features lovely baroque arrangements by Mike Leander and decent tunes like "As Tears Go By," Jackie DeShannon's "Come and Stay with Me" and "In My Time of Sorrow," and Bacharach-David's "If I Never Get to Love You," as well as fairly crummy covers of hits by the Beatles, Herman's Hermits, and Petula Clark. Look for the Japanese CD reissue; it adds six non-LP bonus tracks from mid-'60s singles, including a couple (the girl-groupish "The Sha La La Song," the melancholy "The Morning Sun") that rank among her best '60s recordings. —*Richie Unterberger*

Dreaming My Dreams / Jan. 1977 / Nems ✦✦✦
Marianne Faithfull's first new album in a decade revealed the weathered voice she later would put to good, if harrowing, use in a series of albums for Island Records starting with *Broken English* in 1979. Here, that voice was smoothed out and used for pop and country material including such songs as "I'll Be Your Baby Tonight," "I'm Not Lisa," and "It Wasn't God Who Made Honky Tonk Angels." Faithfull had loosened up considerably since the chaste schoolgirl days of "As Tears Go By," and *Dreaming My Dreams* suggested that her hard life could be analogous to that of a country music star. Faithfull didn't have the accent to match that assertion, but she did have the attitude. (Re-released in slightly altered form as *Faithless* in March 1978.) —*William Ruhlmann*

Faithless / Mar. 1978 / Sony ✦✦✦
Marianne Faithfull's first new album in a decade revealed the weathered voice she later would put to good, if harrowing, use in a series of albums for Island Records starting with *Broken English* in 1979. Here, that voice was smoothed out and used for pop and country material including such songs as "I'll Be Your Baby Tonight," "I'm Not Lisa," and "It Wasn't God Who Made Honky Tonk Angels." Faithfull had loosened up considerably since the chaste schoolgirl days of "As Tears Go By," and Faithless suggested that her hard life could be analogous to that of a country music star. Faithfull didn't have the accent to match that assertion, but she did have the attitude. (Faithless was a slightly altered version of the January 1977 album *Dreaming My Dreams*. It was reissued on CD in 1991 with four bonus tracks.) —*William Ruhlmann*

● **Broken English** / Nov. 1979 / Island ✦✦✦✦
After a lengthy absence, Faithfull resurfaced on this 1979 album, which took the edgy and brittle sound of punk rock and gave it a shot of studio-smooth dance rock. Faithfull's whiskey-worn vocals perfectly match the bitter and biting "Why'd Ya Do It" and revitalize John Lennon's "Working Class Hero." —*John Floyd*

Dangerous Acquaintances / Sept. 1981 / Island ✦✦✦
A rather lukewarm, disappointing follow-up to *Broken English*, on which Faithfull seemed to be retreating from that album's sonic and lyrical risks. Although *Broken English* had found most of its audience with the new wave/alternative crowd (songs like "Why'd Ya Do It," after all, were too shocking to get commercial airplay), *Dangerous Acquaintances* seemed to be moving back to more mainstream rock territory, particularly in the arrangements. It's always a possible sign of trouble when there are over a dozen session musicians in the credits, and much of the record's music has a sort of anonymous feel. The songs, too, are less striking (and less angrily risqué) than those of *Broken English*, although Faithfull was still carving her own identity with lyrics about romantic duplicity. The most commercially accessible track, "For Beauties Sake," was co-written by Faithfull and Steve Winwood. —*Richie Unterberger*

A Child's Adventure / Mar. 1983 / Island ✦✦
Faithfull pegged her comeback to a brutal survivalist persona, but by this fourth album of her second career, she had mellowed at least to the extent of constructing flowing song structures with her collaborators, Barry Reynolds and Wally Badarou, that eased the bitterness still found in many of her lyrics. *A Child's Adventure* is thus more listenable, but less compelling, than her other albums of the period. —*William Ruhlmann*

Marianne Faithfull's Greatest Hits / 1987 / ABKCO ✦✦✦✦
While missing a few fine album tracks, this is an excellent 16-song distillation of her '60s recordings. Includes all of her British and American hits—"As Tears Go By," "This Little Bird," "Summer Nights," and "Come and Stay with Me." Bonuses include "In My Time of Sorrow," an obscure mid-'60s folk-rocker co-written by Jackie DeShannon and Jimmy Page, and her 1969 single "Sister Morphine" (co-written with the Rolling Stones), predating the *Sticky Fingers* version; it's easily her most powerful performance of the decade. —*Richie Unterberger*

Strange Weather / Jul. 1987 / Island ✦✦✦✦
Faithfull's 1987 release recast her as a nicotine-stained chanteuse, approaching such standards as "Boulevard of Broken Dreams" and "Penthouse Serenade" with a ravaged, world-weary demeanor that recalls the latter-day recordings of Billie Holiday. She also tackles some blues and jazz material and turns "As Tears Go By" into the gut-wrenching torch ballad neither the Stones nor Faithfull could ever have done in the '60s. A dark, challenging masterpiece. —*John Floyd*

Blazing Away / Mar. 1990 / Island ✦✦✦
This live disc was recorded at the Brooklyn St. Anne's Cathedral. With a song list that stretches back to her '60s singles, this is something of a career overview. But the wisdom and maturity she applies to the material—both old and new—make this a document that attests to Faithfull's continued vitality and brave artistic commitment. —*John Floyd*

Faithfull: A Collection of Her Best Recordings / Aug. 23, 1994 / Island ✦✦✦
This best-of basically covers the years 1979 to 1994, though it reaches back to 1964 for Marianne Faithfull's first recording and first hit, "As Tears Go By," and includes "She," slated for the upcoming 1995 album *A Secret Life*. Five of the 11 songs are drawn from Faithfull's strongest album, 1979's *Broken English*, including the bitter title track and "Why'd Ya Do It." Otherwise, compiler Chris Blackwell makes little attempt to present a balance among Faithfull's recordings—there is nothing at all from *Dangerous Acquaintances* or *A Child's Adventure*, and only one track each from *Strange Weather* and *Blazing Away*. But there is a good newly recorded cover of Patti Smith's "Ghost Dance" co-produced by Keith Richards and featuring other members of the Rolling Stones, and Blackwell rescues Faithfull's rendition of the title theme for the movie *Trouble in Mind* from the soundtrack album. It adds up to an excellent

compilation that highlights Faithfull's strengths as a singer. —*William Ruhlmann*

A Secret Life / Mar. 21, 1995 / Island ✦✦✦
For her first studio album comprised of mostly original material in over a decade, Faithfull enlisted noted composer Angelo Badalamenti (who collaborated with David Lynch for the *Twin Peaks* TV soundtrack) to write music for her lyrics and produce. Faithfull is still in rippingly fine voice, and her words still penetrate. But while Badalamenti's densely orchestral arrangements can be effectively noirish, they can also create an inappropriately cold and detached ambience, despite standout tracks like "Flaming September" and "She." —*Richie Unterberger*

The Falcons

f. 1959, Detroit, MI, **db.** 1962
Soul
The Falcons are often credited with having cut the first true soul record in 1959 with "You're So Fine," and a host of '60s soul stars called themselves Falcons at one time or another, including founder Eddie Floyd, Wilson Pickett, Sir Mack Rice, and 100 Proof Aged in Soul's Joe Stubbs. Originally an integrated R&B group headed by Floyd, the Falcons debuted on Mercury in 1955. Under the production aegis of Robert West, the Falcons' sound became more gospel-based as time passed, and with Stubbs as lead, the seminal "You're So Fine" was a major hit in 1959. Pickett screamed the gospel-fired ballad "I Found a Love" to national prominence on West's LuPine label in 1962, backed by guitarist Robert Ward's Ohio Untouchables. When Pickett went solo shortly thereafter, the members went their separate ways. West recruited another group, the Fabulous Playboys, who took over the Falcons name, but with little success. —*Bill Dahl*

● **I Found a Love** / 1986 / Relic ✦✦✦✦
A more incendiary collection, thanks to the addition of Wilson Pickett as the Falcons' front man. —*Bill Dahl*

You're So Fine / 1986 / Relic ✦✦✦✦
Prototypical early Detroit soul from this rough-edged vocal group that featured Eddie Floyd and Joe Stubbs. —*Bill Dahl*

The Fall

f. 1977, Manchester, England
Post-Punk
Out of all the late-'70s punk and post-punk bands, none was longer-lived or more prolific than the Fall. Throughout their career, the band underwent a myriad of lineup changes, but at the center of it all was vocalist Mark E. Smith. With his snarling, nearly incomprehensible vocals and consuming, bitter cynicism, Smith became a cult legend in indie and alternative rock. Over the course of their career, the Fall went through a number of shifts in musical style, but the foundation of their sound was a near-cacophonic, amelodic jagged jumble of guitars, sing-speak vocals, and keyboards. During the late '70s and early '80s, the band was at their most abrasive and atonal. In 1984 Smith's American wife Brix joined the band as a guitarist, bringing a stronger sense of pop melody to the group. By the mid-'80s, the band's British following was large enough to result in two UK Top 40 hits, but in essence, the group has always been a cult band—their music was always too abrasive and dense for the mainstream. Only hardcore fans can differentiate between the Fall's many albums, but the Fall, like many cult bands, inspired a new generation of underground bands, ranging from waves of sounda-like indie-rockers in the UK to acts in America and New Zealand, which is only one indication of the size and dedication of their small, devoted fan base.

Before forming the Fall in 1977, Mark E. Smith worked on the docks in Manchester, where he had auditioned and failed with a number of local heavy metal groups. Smith wasn't inspired by metal in the first place; his tastes ran more toward the experimental rock 'n' roll of the Velvet Underground, as well as the avant-garde art-rock of Can. Eventually he found several similarly inclined musicians—guitarist Martin Bramah, bassist Tony Friel, keyboardist Una Baines, and drummer Karl Burns—and formed the Fall, taking the group's name from the Albert Camus novel. The band cut an EP, *Bingo Master's Breakout*, that was funded by the Buzzcocks' label New Hormones, but it sat unreleased for nearly a year, because the band couldn't find anyone who wanted to sign them. The Fall were outsiders, not fitting in with either the slick new wave or the amateurish, simple chord-bashing of punk rock. Consequently, they had a difficult time landing a record contract. After a while, the group had gained some fans, including Danny Baker, the head of the *Adrenaline* fanzine, who persuaded Miles Copeland to release the EP on his Step Forward independent label.

During 1978 Smith replaced bassist Friel with Marc Riley (bass, guitar, keyboards) and keyboardist Baines with Yvonne Pawlett, to make the Fall more accessible. The new lineup recorded the band's first full-length album, *Live at the Witch Trials*, released in 1979. The Fall contin-

ued to tour, playing bars and cabaret clubs and, in the process, began to slowly build a fan base. Radio 1 DJ John Peel had become a fervent fan of the band, letting them record a number of sessions for his show, which provided the group with a great deal of exposure.

Before recording the Fall's second album, Smith changed the band's lineup, firing Pawlett, Bramah, and Burns, and hiring guitarist Craig Scanlon, bassist Steve Hanley, and drummer Mike Leigh; Riley moved to lead guitar from bass during this lineup shift. Scanlon and Hanley would become integral members of the Fall, staying with the band for the duration of their career. The new lineup recorded and released *Dragnet* late in 1979. The next year, the Fall parted with Step Forward and signed with Rough Trade, where they released the live album *Totale's Turns (It's Now or Never)*, the studio *Grotesque (After the Gramme)* and several acclaimed singles, including "Totally Wired" and "How I Wrote Elastic Man," in the course of 1980. Paul Hanley joined the group as a second drummer before the *Grotesque* album. Though several Fall recordings appeared in 1981, they were all archival releases with the exception of the *Slates* EP. After the release of *Slates*, drummer Karl Burns rejoined the group. In early 1982 the band released the full-length *Hex Enduction Hour*, which received some of the group's strongest reviews to date. Since the group was having trouble with Rough Trade, the album was released on Kamera Records, as was its follow-up, *Room to Live*, which also appeared in 1982. After its release, Riley left the band.

The major turning point in the Fall's career arrived in 1983, when Mark E. Smith met Brix Smith (born Laura Elise Smith) in Chicago while the Fall were on tour. The pair married within a few months and Brix, who originally played bass, joined the group as their second guitarist, replacing Riley; her first record with the group was 1983's *Perverted by Language*. Brix brought a more melodic pop sense to the band, as demonstrated by 1984's *The Wonderful and Frightening World of the Fall*, their first album for Beggars Banquet. After the *Call for Escape Route* EP, the Fall struck up an alliance with ballet choreographer Michael Clark, who eventually collaborated on a ballet called *I Am Kurious Oranj* with Mark E. Smith. The Fall wrote the music and libretto for the ballet and performed the work several times during late 1984 and early 1985; an album of the music eventually appeared in 1988. By 1985 the Smiths were collaborating, resulting in more structured, melodic songs like the singles "No Bulbs" and "Cruiser's Creek." Midway through 1985, Steve Hanley had to take a leave of absence and classically-trained Simon Rogers joined as the temporary bassist. Once Hanley returned, Rogers moved over to keyboards. The new lineup with Rogers recorded *This Nation's Saving Grace*, which was released in the fall of 1985 to terrific reviews. Rogers stayed for one more album, 1986's *Bend Sinister*, but he remained involved with the Fall for several years. *Bend Sinister* was recorded with Burns' replacement Simon Wolstencroft and after its release, Rogers was replaced by keyboardist Marcia Schofield, who had previously played in Khymer Rouge.

In 1986, the Fall unexpectedly began to have charting singles, as their cover of the Other Half's "Mr. Pharmacist" became a minor hit in the fall. Over the next few years, the group appeared in the lower reaches of the charts consistently, breaking into the Top 40 with 1987's "Hit the North" and 1988's cover of the Kinks' "Victoria," which signalled how much more accessible the band had become with the addition of Brix' arrangements. After the 1988 release of the Simon Rogers-produced *The Frenz Experiment*, Brix divorced Smith, and she left the Fall in 1989; original guitarist Martin Bramah replaced her. The musical result of the separation was a shift back to the darker, more chaotic sound of their early albums, as shown on the first post-Brix album, 1990's *Extricate*. Though *Extricate* was well-received, Smith decided to alter the lineup that recorded the album. He fired both Schofield and Bramah while the Fall was touring Australia. Featuring new keyboardist Dave Bush, *Shift-Work* was released in 1991, followed by *Code: Selfish* the next year.

In 1993, the Fall signed with Matador Records, which provided them with their first American record label in several years. Their first release for the label, *The Infotainment Scam*, was recorded with the returning Karl Burns, who provided drums. Neither *The Infotainment Scam* nor its 1994 follow-up *Middle-Class Revolt* sold many records in the US, despite good reviews, and the Fall were again left without an American label as of 1995. Not that it mattered—they retained their devoted following in Britain, where both albums performed respectably. Brix rejoined the Fall during the supporting tour for *Middle-Class Revolt* and appeared on 1995's *Cerebral Caustic*. By the summer of 1996, Brix had departed the band again, and Mark E. Smith was developing a new lineup of the Fall. —*Stephen Thomas Erlewine*

Live at the Witch Trials / Jan. 1979 / A&M ✦✦✦✦
Perhaps of the early material, the best place to start is *Live at the Witch Trials*. Under the guidance of producer Bob Sargeant, this album harnesses the essence of the Fall's early sound: jagged, colliding guitars, stiff, repetitive percussion, and Mark E. Smith's nasal, singsong ranting. It's dissonant, but not so harsh as to be totally unapproachable. In fact, Sargeant (who later went on to produce records by far poppier bands

like the English Beat) accents the rhythmic bottom, so that even when the music lurches like a drunken Frankenstein's monster, it does swing enough to be captivating. Of course, this is assuming that Smith's vocals haven't prevented you from enjoying this (and really, they shouldn't). Tunes like "Rebellious Jukebox" and "Music Scene" will win you over with their caustic appeal. —*John Dougan*

Dragnet / Oct. 1979 / Step Forward ✦✦✦✦

Totale's Turns (It's Now or Never) / May 1980 / Rough Trade ✦✦✦

Grotesque (After the Gramme) / Nov. 1980 / Rough Trade ✦✦✦
Grotesque is more extreme than its predecessor, *Live at the Witch Trials*. Extreme in the sense that traditional song form is almost totally dispensed with for cacophony built around thuddingly simple guitar riffs. It's not totally alienating, but it's not where potential Fall fans (unless you have a jones for barely structured rock noise) should start. Oddly, despite being anti-rock to the point of being almost anti-music, some great songs emerge through the trebly crashing and bashing. —*John Dougan*

Early Years 77-79 / 1981 / Step Forward ✦✦✦
Like its predecessor, *Grotesque, Early Years 77-79* is more extreme than *Live at the Witch Trials*. Extreme in the sense that traditional song form is almost totally dispensed with for a din of cacophony built around thuddingly simple guitar riffs. It's not totally alienating, but it's not where potential Fall fans (unless you have a jones for barely structured rock noise) should start. Oddly, despite being anti-rock to the point of almost being anti-music, there are some great songs that emerge through the trebly crashing and bashing. —*John Dougan*

Hex Enduction Hour / Mar. 1982 / Kamera ✦✦✦

Perverted by Language / Dec. 1983 / Rough Trade ✦✦✦✦
Closing the early Fall period is *Perverted by Language*, which also starts the (what I call) "Brix Period." It was during this time that Smith married American guitarist Brix Smith, who brought a stronger pop sense to the band. Suddenly, Fall albums, although still essentially abrasive, were more tuneful, and loaded with fuzztone garage-raunch guitar playing. Brix' first effort as a full-time Fall member is a winner, with tracks like "I Feel Voxish" and the parody of the excessively health-conscious "Eat Y'self Fitter" pushing the Fall into a new terrain that would bring them (surprise!) chart success in England. —*John Dougan*

The Wonderful and Frightening World of the Fall / Sep. 1984 / Beggars Banquet ✦✦✦✦
The high point of the "Brix Period" may well have been the release of *Wonderful and Frightening World of the Fall*. Where before the music was tense, jumpy, and anarchic, here it was focused, harder-hitting, and rocked more. To some, it signaled the end of the Fall, but that was an unfair assessment. Granted, the music changed slightly, but it didn't diminish the band's potency. And for all the time that Mark Smith had dominated the band, it was becoming clear that Brix' talents as a writer and musician were formidable and were deservedly taking some of the spotlight. —*John Dougan*

Hip Priests & Kamerads / Mar. 1985 / Situation 2 ✦✦✦

This Nation's Saving Grace / Sep. 1985 / Beggars Banquet ✦✦✦✦
This Nation's Saving Grace could almost qualify as a dance record if it were a little smoother, but the songs are catchy, and for the Fall, almost upbeat. As far as solid groove goes, this is their toughest, funkiest record. —*John Dougan*

Bend Sinister / Oct. 1986 / Beggars Banquet ✦✦✦✦
Not entirely surprisingly for an album named after a Vladimir Nabokov novel, *Bend Sinister* is dark and haunting, comprised nearly entirely of tense, jagged guitar dirges that give the record a claustrophobic power. There are the occasional glimpses of hooks, such as on the catchy "Shoulder Pads," but for the most part, *Bend Sinister* finds the Fall at a doomy peak. —*Stephen Thomas Erlewine*

Domesday Pay-Off (Triad Plus) / 1987 / Big Time ✦✦✦✦

The Fall In: Palace of Swords Reversed / Nov. 1987 / Rough Trade ✦✦✦✦
The anomalous release during this period was *A Palace of Swords Reversed*, a collection of non-LP tracks and assorted odds and sods from 1980-83. Despite its patchwork arrangement, it's a remarkably cohesive document and one of the Fall's best efforts. —*John Dougan*

The Frenz Experiment / Mar. 1988 / Beggars Banquet ✦✦
The Frenz Experiment and *I Am Kurious Oranj* sound as if they were recorded on the same day, although the latter was a score commissioned for an experimental ballet. *Frenz* has a great cover of the Kinks' "Victoria," as well as production values never before heard on Fall records (high quality). —*John Dougan*

I Am Curious Oranj / Oct. 1988 / Beggars Banquet ✦✦✦
Both *The Frenz Experiment* and *I Am Kurious Oranj* sound as if they were recorded on the same day, although the latter was a score commis-

sioned for an experimental ballet. *Oranj* isn't as completely satisfying as *Frenz*, but was (so I am told) much better than the ballet. —*John Dougan*

Seminal Live / Jun. 1989 / Beggars Banquet ✦✦
Seminal Live is a live recording made during the Brix period, but it's thoroughly mediocre and not worth the bother. —*John Dougan*

Extricate / Feb. 1990 / Fontana ✦✦✦✦
The Smiths had divorced around the time of *Extricate*, but Brix' presence could still be felt on Fall records. Some thought the mid-'80s signaled an end to the ragged, jagged Fall of old; the '90s must have made them apoplectic. Working with producers Rex Sergeant, Craig Leon, and Adrian Sherwood, the post-apocalyptic sound of the '70s had been smoothed to a sheen. There were still moments of anarchy and dissonance, but generally they were swaddled in synth-driven beats and high-tech production that smoothed out any remaining rough edges. Again, this was not a bad thing; after all Mark E. Smith was still upfront and still ranting, but even he was singing more, and shocking as that was, it made for even better music. For this period, the place to start is *Extricate*, which proved beyond a doubt that the Fall were not too old to still be a part of this punk rock thang. Since this record follows on the heels of the Smiths' divorce, it's tempting to assume that Mark E. Smith's ranting has a more conspicuous target, but enigmatic as he tends to be, this is mere speculation. Still, "Sing! Harpy" and the title track will give you pause as to the source of Smith's considerable consternation. The band sounds great, especially longtime members Stephen Hanley and Craig Scanlon. Extra kudos to the solid backbeat provided by Simon Wolstencroft. —*John Dougan*

★ **458489 A-Sides** / Sep. 1990 / Beggars Banquet ✦✦✦✦✦
Bypassing their edgy, early singles and concentrating on their artier, more eclectic work of the mid—and late '80s, *458489 A-Sides* encapsulates nearly all of the Fall's many attributes. All of the singles on *A-Sides* are culled from the era when Brix Smith was in the band, arguably the band's most cohesive and rewarding years. Drawing from their strongest albums—*The Wonderful and Frightening World of the Fall, This Nation's Saving Grace, Bend Sinister, The Frenz Experiment*—*A-Sides* offers an excellent introduction to the Fall. It is both a useful retrospective and a kind of road map, pointing out the differences between albums. For neophytes and the uninitiated, there is no better sampler, and for longtime fans, the collection reiterates what a fine singles band the Fall were in their heyday. —*Stephen Thomas Erlewine*

458489 B-Sides / Dec. 1990 / Beggars Banquet ✦✦✦✦

Peel Sessions / 1991 / Peerless ✦✦✦

Shift-Work / Apr. 1991 / Fontana ✦✦✦
Although *Shiftwork* and *Code: Selfish* are very good, they are almost indistinguishable from one another and the sameness works against them. That being said, let me contradict myself and suggest you buy *Code: Selfish*, which is notable for "Birmingham School of Business School" and a cover of Hank Williams' "Just Waiting." —*John Dougan*

Code: Selfish / Mar. 1992 / Fontana ✦✦✦
Although *Shiftwork* and *Code: Selfish* are very good, they are almost indistinguishable from one another and the sameness works against them. —*John Dougan*

The Infotainment Scam / May 18, 1993 / Matador ✦✦✦✦

The Collection / Oct. 19, 1993 / Castle ✦✦✦

Middle Class Revolt / May 1994 / Matador ✦✦✦✦
During the Brix era, Fall recordings were less likely to automatically be released in America. Still, hip American indie label Matador decided that these seminal punksters deserved better, and their last two records were made available in America. *Infotainment Scam* is the better of the two, if only because *Middle Class Revolt* sounds carelessly conceived, but the sound that has defined the Fall in the '90s remains intact. —*John Dougan*

Cerebral Caustic / May 18, 1995 / Permanent ✦✦✦

27 Points / Sep. 5, 1995 / Permanent ✦✦✦

Merrell Fankhauser

b. Dec. 23, 1943, Louisville, KY
Singer-Songwriter, Art-Rock/Progressive-Rock, Psychedelic
One of the most interesting cult figures in rock history, Fankhauser's best work came as the leader of several interesting groups during the '60s and early '70s: the Impacts (instrumental surf), Merrell & the Exiles (solid British Invasion-style rock), Fapardokly (great Byrdsish folk-rock), the H.M.S. Bounty (fine late-'60s folk-rock), and Mu (spaced-out progressive blues/psychedelia). When Mu broke up in the mid-'70s, Fankhauser began working as a solo artist, issuing a series of independent albums that continue to this day. These usually show him in a considerably mellower and more mainstream folk-rock mood than his best, earlier work, sometimes recalling Crosby, Stills & Nash, and often featuring violinist Mary Lee. —*Richie Unterberger*

● **The Maui Album** / 1988 / Reckless ✦✦✦✦
Fankhauser's first solo outing, originally titled *Merrell Fankhauser* and
released in 1976, remains his best post-Mu work. Very light and serene
folk-rock that owes little to trends of its era, predominantly acoustic in
feel, often featuring Mary Lee on violin and harmony vocals. The 1988
reissue is enhanced by four previously unreleased Mu tracks, dating
from 1974. —*Richie Unterberger*

Early Years 1964-1967 / 1994 / Legend Music ✦✦
Credited to Merrell & the Exiles, this is a selection of rarities and unreleased material by Fankhauser's mid-'60s band, essentially the one that
cut the great rare psych-folk-rock album that was credited to Fapardokly. It's pretty much a collection of outtakes with a few rare non-LP
singles thrown in, and as such doesn't measure up to the best of
Fankhauser's '60s material. Often derivative of the British Invasion, folk-
rock, and early '60s teen pop, it's not bad, just not terribly memorable.
The fake British Invasion of cuts like "Send Me Your Love" rank as the
highlights. It also has his late-'60s non-LP single cover of Fred Neil's
"Everybody's Talkin'," although for some reason it's missing one of his
mid-'60s non-LP 45s, "Can't We Get Along"/"That's All I Want From
You"; it was reissued on a rarities tape that Merrell himself released, if
you can find it. Future Mu and Captain Beefheart guitarist Jeff Cotton
appears on most of the tracks; future Beefheart drummer John French
also appears on a few. —*Richie Unterberger*

Merrell Fankhauser & H.M.S. Bounty

f. 1967, Los Angeles, CA
Singer-Songwriter, Art-Rock/Progressive-Rock, Psychedelic
After cutting some fine folk-rock and psychedelia on ultra-rare records
with his group the Exiles, guitarist, singer, and songwriter Merrell
Fankhauser moved to Los Angeles, retitled his backing group H.M.S.
Bounty, and recorded a fine, if obscure, slice of pop-psychedelia in 1968,
Things. The diverse offerings on the group's sole LP recalled such fellow
Californian heavyweights as the Byrds, Buffalo Springfield, Moby
Grape, and even Captain Beefheart. They weren't quite in the same
league as those legends, but the album has a light and enigmatic air all
its own, and is well worth investigation by fans of late-'60s West Coast
psychedelia. The group evolved into the interesting mystical avant-
garde/blues/progressive rock group Mu in the early '70s. —*Richie
Unterberger*

● **Things** / 1968 / Sundazed ✦✦✦✦
Fine, tuneful '60s psychedelia with a pop edge, featuring Fankhauser's
first-rate songwriting and warm vocals. About half of the tunes are
excellent, especially the country-rocker "Your Painted Lives," the folk-
rock ballad "Ice Cube Island," and "A Visit with Ashiya," one of the best
raga-rock songs ever cut. The reissue adds a bluesy non-LP B-side, "Flying Home," that looks forward to the innovations of Mu; it also has a
poppier non-LP single from the late '60s. —*Richie Unterberger*

Fapardokly

f. 1965, Los Angeles, CA, **db.** 1966
Psychedelic, Folk-Rock
An enigma in the world of '60s rock collectibles that would be barely
worth explaining if the music weren't so fine. There was never a group
called Fapardokly; the 12 songs on their self-titled album were recorded
by Merrell & the Exiles, a Southern California group headed by legendary cult folk-rocker Merrell Fankhauser. That group cut several singles
for the tiny Glenn label, some of which are collected here, before heading off in a psychedelic direction and mutating into H.M.S. Bounty. The
equally tiny UIP label decided to gather a few of the Glenn singles, add
a few more psychedelically oriented tracks that Merrill and his group
had recorded, and release the package as the work of a group called
Fapardokly. Although it was not recorded or intended as a unified work,
it stands as one of the great lost folk-rock classics of the 1960s.
Fankhauser went on to make more excellent obscure recordings with
H.M.S. Bounty in the late '60s and Mu in the early '70s. —*Richie Unterberger*

● **Fapardokly** / 1966 / Sundazed ✦✦✦✦
One of the most sought-after rock rarities of the '60s, this album was
stylistically uneven, as can be expected from an LP cobbled together
from recordings spanning a few years. About half, however, is sparkling psychedelic folk-rock, recalling *Fifth Dimension* Byrds with its
shimmering 12-string guitars, multipart harmonies, and occasional
trippy lyrics. Although the early material is more pop-oriented and
doesn't fit in as well, it's pretty solid, recalling the Zombies and (in
the very earliest tracks) Ricky Nelson. "Lila," "Tomorrow's Girl," and
"Super Market" are genuine lost '60s treasures, and much of the rest
of the album isn't far behind. After a couple of European LP reissues,
it was finally reissued on CD, with three bonus tracks, in 1995.
—*Richie Unterberger*

Richard and Mimi Farina

f. 1964, Los Angeles, CA
Folk-Rock
Richard Farina was a noted counterculture author and folksinger in the
early '60s. Married for a time to folksinger Carolyn Hester, he was an
early intimate of Bob Dylan, and in fact recorded a collectible album
with Dylan (playing under the pseudonym "Blind Boy Grunt") and Ric
Von Schmidt in 1963. After marrying Joan Baez' sister Mimi, he formed
a folk-rock duo that released two acclaimed albums in the mid-60s.
Unlike folk-rock figureheads such as the Byrds, the Farinas were far
more firmly rooted in folk than rock.

Their recordings effectively flavored their material (mostly written by
Richard) with jangling electric guitars and a rhythm section, ably
assisted by such session players as guitarist Bruce Langhorne (who also
played on Dylan's first electric recordings), bassist Felix Pappalardi, and
harmonica player John Hammond. The Farinas themselves also played
guitar, autoharp, and dulcimer. Least successful with blues, they
recorded some effective Appalachian-flavored material and several
excellent, bona fide midtempo folk-rockers and ballads. Their best
songs effectively balanced world-wise, sardonic observations with good-
natured, melodic optimism.

The Farinas' promising career ended with the death of Richard in a
motorcycle accident on his birthday in 1966. His novel of the same year,
Been Down So Long It Looks Like Up To Me, became a cult favorite.
Since Richard's death, Mimi Farina has sporadically recorded and performed as a solo act. —*Richie Unterberger*

Celebrations for a Grey Day / 1965 / Vanguard ✦✦✦
The duo's debut effectively laid out their approach: Appalachian-like
instrumentals that put the dulcimer to the fore alternate with strong
contemporary folk compositions, which are by turns mournful and
high-spirited. The world-weary "Reno Nevada" (a part of Fairport Convention's repertoire in their early days) is the duo's best song. —*Richie
Unterberger*

Reflections in a Crystal Wind / 1965 / Fontana ✦✦✦
Basically a continuation of the first album with a slightly more electric
feel, finding Richard developing deeper insight and a subtler touch.
—*Richie Unterberger*

Memories / 1968 / Vanguard ✦✦✦
A posthumous collection of odds and ends, this actually holds considerable appeal for anyone who likes their pair of fully realized albums. The
12 songs include a few studio outtakes, a few solo turns by Mimi on
compositions written by Richard but incompletely recorded at the time
of his death, a couple of performances from the 1965 Newport Folk Festival, and a couple of Joan Baez tracks from sessions for an aborted
album Richard was producing with her. These leftovers are generally up
to the standard of the two "real" albums, especially "The Quiet Joys of
Brotherhood" (covered by Fairport Convention) and "Morgan the Pirate"
(a farewell to Bob Dylan, according to the sketchy liner notes). The two
cuts by Baez (which Richard wrote or co-wrote), especially the compel-
lingly melancholy "All the World Has Gone By," are excellent, leading
one to wonder if the projected album they came from would have been
one of Baez' best if it had been completed. These may be leftovers, but
it's a worthwhile collection nonetheless. —*Richie Unterberger*

● **Best of** / 1971 / Vanguard ✦✦✦✦
While a 26-song double album is not ordinarily recommended as the
best introduction to such a short-lived act, the Farinas' work was so con-
sistent that it makes sense to pick up this compilation, which combines
Celebrations for a Grey Day and *Reflections in a Crystal Wind*.
—*Richie Unterberger*

The Farm

f. 1983, Liverpool, England, **db.** 1994
Alternative Pop-Rock, Club/Dance
One of the stranger overnight success stories in pop history, the chameleon-like Farm was formed in Liverpool, England, in 1983 by singer
Peter Hooton, a onetime youth worker searching for a musical outlet to
voice his political concerns. Rounded out by guitarist Stevie Grimes,
bassist Phil Strongman, and drummer Andy McVann, the first incarnation of the Farm recalled both the leftist identity and horn-powered
sound of the Redskins; dubbed "the Soul of Socialism," the group promoted its music not only through live appearances but also via *The End*,
a soccer fanzine published by Hooton.

Despite a handful of independent singles and the addition of a full-
time brass section comprised of Anthony Evans, Steve Levy, George
Maher, and John Melvin, the Farm found little interest in their pop-flavored Northern soul. Still, they soldiered on, even weathering the 1986
death of McVann, who perished in a car crash after attempting to outrun
the police. With drummer Roy Boulter installed as McVann's replacement and bassist Carl Hunter substituting for the newly exited Strongman, the Farm dropped their horn section and added keyboardist Ben-

jamin Leach and second guitarist Keith Mullen, resulting in a move towards synth-pop; 1988's "Body and Soul," their fourth overall single and the first from their new lineup, became a minor club hit.

Still, the Farm struggled; finally, in 1990 they approached dance producer Terry Farley, who agreed to produce a sample-heavy cover of the Monkees' "Stepping Stone." The single fell just shy of the Top 40, and suddenly the group found themselves aligned with the baggy-pants club culture movement promoted by the likes of Happy Mondays and the Soup Dragons. The Farm's next single, "Groovy Train," hit the UK Top Ten, while the anthemic follow-up "All Together Now"—based on the melody of Pachelbel's *Canon*—landed in the Top Five and sold over 500,000 copies.

Eight years after their inception, the Farm finally issued their debut LP *Spartacus* in 1991; the album entered the British charts at No. 1, and international deals with Sony and Sire quickly followed. The band's moment in the limelight was brief, however; their next two singles, "Don't Let Me Down" and "Mind," both failed to penetrate the Top 30, and 1991's quickly produced follow-up LP, *Love See No Colour*, sank without a trace. Aside from a Top 20 cover of the Human League's "Don't You Want Me?" in 1992, the Farm essentially vanished from sight, releasing 1994's *Hullabaloo* to minimal notice. —*Jason Ankeny*

● **Spartacus** / Apr. 17, 1991 / Sire ✦✦✦✦
The Farm's debut album *Spartacus* is one of the more ridiculous by-products of baggy, containing all of its rolling, neo-psychedelic grooves and blissfully colorful pop hooks, but very little of its charm, character, or substance. Since baggy was never about substance, this is particularly damning. Still, the Farm manages to turn out a couple of goofily endearing singles with "Groovy Train" and "All Together Now," but the group shows no real feeling for dance-club rhythms, or even pop hooks. As an artifact, *Spartacus* is fascinating, since it demonstrates how far over the top the entire Madchester phenomenon went, even if the record itself isn't necessarily good listening. —*Stephen Thomas Erlewine*

Love See No Colour / Nov. 3, 1992 / Sire ✦✦✦
Love See No Colour is essentially a retread of *Spartacus* without the benefit of a single as catchy as "Groovy Train" or "All Together Now," which means that it's characterless baggy without hooks or distinctive rhythms. It demonstrates that the Farm have run out of what few ideas they had and are recycling them with diminishing returns. Again, it's interesting as a period piece, but little else. —*Stephen Thomas Erlewine*

Hullabaloo / May 10, 1994 / Sire ✦✦
The Farm had hit the end of the road with 1992's *Love See No Colour*, which means 1994's *Hullabaloo* was unnecessary. Indeed, the album is comprised entirely of bland, colorless material that recycles baggy for no apparent reason. It sounds purposeless on the originals, but when the group covers the Flamin' Groovies' "Shake Some Action," the results are simply ridiculous. *Hullabaloo* wasn't a particularly graceful way to end the band's career, but then again, the Farm never handled their career gracefully. —*Stephen Thomas Erlewine*

Mylene Farmer

b. Quebec, Canada
Vocals / Art-Rock/Progressive-Rock, Europop, Club/Dance
Since 1985, Mylene Farmer (born in Quebec, but raised in France) and her musical collaborator, Laurent Boutonnat, have expanded the Birkin-Gainsbourg bedroom fantasy song into an entire cosmology of sighing songs, pensive and melancholy and fitfully melodic dances in which *fin de siecle libertinism* is the motive principle and intoxicated hallucination the saving grace. It's popular throughout Euro-land and not unknown even in the US. —*Michael Freedberg*

Ainsi Soit Je . . . / 1988 / Polydor ✦✦✦✦
Ambitiously stylish, this thick mix of powerful dance rhythms and sensual melodies is both accessible and subtle. Sometimes uneven in its overall composition, it offers superb sound quality. —*Vladimir Bogdanov*

En Consert / 1989 / Polydor ✦✦✦

● **L'antre . . .** / 1991 / Alex ✦✦✦✦
Marked with the same stylistic integrity as her previous albums, this is without a doubt Mylene Farmer's masterpiece. Compositions are still elaborate and carefully designed but they now have a more refined and transparent feel. The deep, dark reflections about life that are so typical of the artist are enriched by the sparkling energy of her powerful, sometimes hysterical irony and the calm confidence of her velvet-soft voice. —*Vladimir Bogdanov*

Anamorphosee / Dec. 12, 1995 / Polydor ✦✦✦

Fastbacks

f. 1981, Seattle, WA
Alternative Pop-Rock, Indie Rock
This Seattle quartet generates a sound alternating between punkish pop

and poppish punk. Recording sporadically between 1982 and the present, the band benefits from sometime Young Fresh Fellows guitarist Kurt Bloch and the sneering vocals of Kim Warnick, who also doubles as bassist. They are an extremely underrated group. —*David Szatmary*

. . . And His Orchestra / 1987 / Pop Llama ✦✦✦✦
Recorded between 1981 and 1985, this album features 20 songs from a driving Seattle band that alternates between pop-ish punk and punk-ish pop. Fueled by Kurt Block's guitar. —*David Szatmary*

Very Very Powerful Motor / 1990 / Pop Llama ✦✦✦
Thanks to some tougher guitars and rawer vocals, *Very, Very Powerful Motor* is the most punkish album the Fastbacks have released, but the songs never lack strong melodies. —*Stephen Thomas Erlewine*

● **Zucker** / Jan. 29, 1993 / Sub Pop ✦✦✦✦
With its speedy, energetic riffs and bright melodies, *Zucker* is one of the Fastbacks' best albums. —*Stephen Thomas Erlewine*

Bike-Toy-Clock-Gift / 1994 / Lucky ✦✦✦

Answer the Phone Dummy / Oct. 25, 1994 / Sub Pop ✦✦✦

New Mansions in Sound / Jun. 18, 1996 / Sub Pop ✦✦✦✦

The Fat Boys

f. 1982, Brooklyn, NY
Hip Hop, Old School Rap
One of early rap's most successful acts, the Fat Boys parlayed a combined weight of over 750 pounds into a comic novelty act that sustained them through several albums and hit singles. Originally known as the Disco 3, Brooklynites Mark "Prince Markie Dee" Morales, Damon "Kool Rockski" Wimbley, and Darren "Buff the Human Beat Box" Robinson won a talent contest at Radio City Music Hall in 1983, thanks in part to Robinson's talent for using his mouth to improvise hip-hop rhythms and a variety of sound effects. The trio changed their name and recorded a series of good-time party anthems and songs humorously exploiting their weight; their first few records were produced by Kurtis Blow and feature fusions of hip-hop with reggae and rock. The Fat Boys hit commercial peak with 1987's platinum LP *Crushin'*, a collection of entertaining party tunes that included a hit collaboration with the Beach Boys, "Wipeout." The group took the opportunity to star in the comedy film *Disorderlies* that year. *Coming Back Hard Again* essentially repeated the formula of *Crushin'*; the cover this time was "The Twist (Yo' Twist)," which featured backing from Chubby Checker. However, audience tastes were changing, and the Fat Boys' gimmicky novelty act was quickly becoming passe. The group tried to expand its artistic and street credibility with the ill-advised "rap opera" *On and On*, which promptly stiffed and prefaced the group's breakup. Prince Markie Dee recorded a solo album in 1992 and has gone on to a successful R&B songwriting/producing career. Darren Robinson died of a heart attack in December 1995. —*Steve Huey*

● **All Meat No Filler: Best of Fat Boys** / Mar. 18, 1997 / Rhino ✦✦✦✦
All Meat No Filler: The Best of the Fat Boys is an excellent 18-track compilation of all of the Fat Boys' biggest hits, including "Fat Boys," "Human Beat Box," "Jail House Rap," "Can You Feel It," "The Fat Boys Are Back," "Hard Core Reggae," "Falling in Love," "Wipeout" (with the Beach Boys) and "The Twist (Yo, Twist!)" (with Chubby Checker). Although some of the latter-day cuts have aged poorly, the Fat Boys' earliest singles are ground-breaking and timeless records, proving that they weren't merely a novelty act. —*Stephen Thomas Erlewine*

The Fatback Band

f. 1970, United States, **db.** 1985
Funk
A seminal funk ensemble, the Fatback Band made many great singles through the '70s and early '80s, ranging from humorous novelty tunes to energetic dance vehicles and even occasional political/message tracks. The original lineup featured drummer Bill Curtis, trumpeter George Williams, guitarist Johnny King, bassist Johnny Flippin, saxophonist Earl Shelton, and flutist George Adam. Synthesizer player Gerry Thomas, saxophonist Fred Demerey, and guitarist George Victory were integral parts of the group during their peak years. They began recording for Perception in the early '70s, and had moderate luck with "Street Dance" in 1973. They moved to Event in 1974, and while funk audiences loved such songs as "Wicki-Wacky" and "(Are You Ready) Do the Bus Stop," they didn't generate much sales action. Their first sizable hit was "Spanish Hustle" in 1976, which reached No. 12 on the R&B charts. They shortened their name to Fatback in 1977 and landed their first Top Ten R&B hit with "I Like Girls" in 1978. In many circles their 1979 single "King Time III (Personality Jock)" is considered the first rap single. But their biggest year was 1980. They scored two Top Ten R&B hits with "Gotta Get My Hands on Some (Money)" and "Backstrokin'," their finest tune. Fatback kept going through the mid-'80s, landing one more Top 20 hit with "Take It Any Way You Can Want It" in 1981. They were backed by

the female vocal trio Wild Sugar in 1981-82, and Evelyn Thomas provided the lead vocal for "Spread Love" in 1985, their last song for Spring. Fatback also recorded a pair of LPs for Cotillion in 1984 and 1985. —*Ron Wynn*

● **21 Karat Fatback (The Best Of)** / 1995 / Southbound ✦✦✦✦
21 Karat Fatback (The Best Of) is an excellent collection of the group's hit singles, featuring such R&B hits as "I Like Girls," "Gotta Get My Hands on Some (Money)" and "Backstrokin'." —*Leo Stanley*

Faust

f. 1971, Wumme, Germany
Art-Rock/Progressive-Rock, Experimental, Kraut-Rock
"There is no group more mythical than Faust," wrote Julian Cope in his book *Krautrocksampler*, which detailed the pivotal influence the German band exerted over the development of ambient and industrial textures. Producer/overseer Uwe Nettelbeck, a onetime music journalist, formed Faust in Wumme, Germany, in 1971 with founding members Hans Joachim Irmler, Jean Herve Peron, Werner "Zappi" Diermaier, Rudolf Sosna, Gunther Wustoff, and Armulf Meifert. Upon receiving advance money from their label, Nettelbeck converted an old schoolhouse into a recording studio, where the group spent the first several months of its existence in almost total isolation, honing their unique, cacophonic sound with the aid of occasional guests like minimalist composer Tony Conrad and members of Slapp Happy.

Issued on clear vinyl in a transparent sleeve, Faust's eponymously titled debut LP surfaced in 1971; although sales were notoriously bad, the album—a noisy sound collage of cut-and-paste musical fragments—did earn the group a solid cult following. Another lavishly packaged work, *Faust So Far*, followed in 1972, and earned the group a contract with Virgin, who issued 1973's *The Faust Tapes*—a fan-assembled collection of home recordings—for about the price of a single, a marketing ploy that earned considerable media interest. After *Outside the Dream Syndicate*, a collaboration with Tony Conrad, the band released 1973's *Faust IV*, a commercial failure that resulted in the loss of their contract with Virgin, who refused to release the planned *Faust 5*.

When Nettelbeck turned his focus away from the group, Faust disbanded in 1975, and the members scattered throughout Germany; however, after more than a decade of playing together in various incarnations, Faust officially reunited around the nucleus of Irmler, Peron, and Dermaier for a handful of European performances at the outset of the 1990s. In 1993 they made their first-ever US live appearance backing Conrad, followed by a series of other stateside performances; after several live releases, a pair of new studio albums, *Rien* and *You Know fAUst*, followed in 1996. —*Jason Ankeny*

Faust / 1971 / Recommended ✦✦✦✦
The impact of Faust cannot be overstated; their debut album was truly a revolutionary step forward in the progress of "rock music." It was pressed on clear vinyl, packaged in a clear sleeve, with a clear plastic lyric insert. The black X-ray of a fist on the cover graphically illustrates the hardcore music contained in the grooves, an amalgamation of electronics, rock, tape edits, acoustic guitars, musique concrete, and industrial angst. The level of imagination is staggering, the concept is totally unique, and it's fun to listen to as well. —*Archie Patterson*

● **Faust So Far** / 1972 / Recommended ✦✦✦✦

Faust Tapes / 1973 / Cuneiform ✦✦✦✦

Faust IV / 1973 / Virgin ✦✦✦

Munich & Elsewhere / 1986 / Recommended ✦✦✦

● **71 Minutes of Faust** / 1996 / Recommended ✦✦✦✦

You Know fAUst / Feb. 25, 1997 / Recommended ✦✦✦
Faust's comeback album *You Know fAUSt* is a surprisingly vital return, finding the group at the wild, recklessly experimental peak of *The Faust Tapes* and *Faust IV*. Largely shedding the blistering *musique concrete* of their reunion concerts, the band concentrates on creating mainly instrumental soundscapes of synthesizers, organs, horns, droning guitars, and pulsating rhythms. While the sound isn't as revolutionary as it once was, it is undeniably more accomplished—and frequently just as exciting—as their earlier recordings. —*Stephen Thomas Erlewine*

Charlie Feathers

b. Jun. 12, 1932, Hollow Springs, MS
Guitar, Vocals / Traditional Country, Rockabilly
Charlie Feathers is many things to many fans of rock and country music. To some, he's a superb country stylist who can take almost any piece of material and stamp it with the full force of his personality. To others, he's one of rockabilly's great pioneers, there at the dawn of Sun Records and still a fully functioning practitioner. And Feathers' stubborn insistence on combining elements of country, raw blues, and bluegrass to make his own version of the rockabilly experience has shown him to be one of the genre's most original and enduring artists.

Feathers was born in Holly Springs, MS, with music all around the sharecropping community he grew up in. After day jobs in Illinois and Texas, Feathers moved to Memphis in 1950, working for a box manufacturer until a bout with spinal meningitis left him hospitalized. Listening to the radio there on a daily basis, he emerged from his stay determined to become a professional singer. By 1954 Feathers was working his way into the confines of Sam Phillips' Memphis Recording Service, with an eye toward getting something released on Sun Records. He filled in whenever and wherever he could, helping with arrangement ideas, even playing spoons on a Miller Sisters session. Demoing songs for steel guitarist Stan Kesler found him getting half credit on the Elvis Sun side, "I Forgot to Remember to Forget." Phillips decided to start a local nonunion label called Flip to test out new artists and, after pairing Feathers with country session songwriter-musicians Bill Cantrell and Quinton Claunch, released the first Feathers single on that label, the classic "Peepin' Eyes" coupled with "I've Been Deceived." The record kicked enough noise locally to get Feathers transferred to Sun for a second single, but the artist had bigger visions. Although Phillips saw him as "a superb country stylist," Feathers wanted to rock, and cut many Sun demo sessions in that style. When Phillips turned a deaf ear to it all, Feathers' impatience led him to Memphis rival Meteor Records, where he waxed the two-sided rockabilly classic "Tongue-Tied Jill" and "Get with It." This single garnered enough Memphis airplay to cement a deal with King Records, and it is here that the "Charlie Feathers as rockabilly legend" story begins in earnest. The dozen or so sides he cut as singles for King are the greatest '50s rockabilly tracks to escape the hegemony of the Sun studios, with "One Hand Loose," "Bottle to the Baby," "Everybody's Lovin' My Baby," and "I Can't Hardly Stand It" all becoming classics of the genre. Their territorial success got Feathers on numerous package tours and multiple appearances on Dallas' "Big D Jamboree." When the King contract ran out, Feathers continued to record one-off singles of very high musical quality, for a variety of Memphis labels, while stubbornly playing his music for whatever local audience cared to listen.

When the rockabilly revival started up in Europe in the early '70s, Charlie Feathers became the first living artist up for deification by collectors. His old 45s suddenly became worth hundreds of dollars, and every interviewer wanted to know why Charlie never really made it big and what his true involvement with Sun consisted of. Feathers embroidered the story with a skewed view of rock 'n' roll history with each retelling, to be sure, but once he picked up his guitar and sang to reinforce his point, the truth came out in his music. Never mind why he didn't make it back in the '50s; he could still deliver the goods *now*.

With health problems plaguing him from his diabetes and a surgically removed lung, Feathers continues on his own irascible course, recording his first album for a major label in 1991 (Elektra's American Masters series) and continuing to perform and record for his wide European fan base. Charlie Feathers is truly an American music original. —*Cub Koda*

Live in Memphis / 1979 / Barrelhouse ✦✦✦
Loose early-'70s recordings. Great, but unfortunately out of print. —*Cub Koda*

● **Jungle Fever** / 1987 / Kay ✦✦✦✦
Boasting a generous 20 tracks, *Jungle Fever* is the best available compilation of Charlie Feathers' original rockabilly recordings; all of his best-known songs are collected here, including "Get with It" and "Tongue-Tied Jill." —*Stephen Thomas Erlewine*

Rock-a-Billy / May 1991 / Zu-Zazz ✦✦✦✦
Superb collection of rare and unissued sides, 1954-1973, showcasing Feathers' mastery of rockabilly and country material. —*Cub Koda*

Tip Top Daddy / 1995 / Norton ✦✦✦
Call this one "Charlie Feathers Unplugged" if you want to, but what we have here is a bushelbasket of unissued acoustic demos from 1958 to 1973 from the King of Rockabilly. It doesn't much matter *when* Feathers cut something as long as he was into it when the tape was rollin' and here are 23 tracks that bear that simple fact out. It also doesn't seem to matter much if Feathers wrote the tune or not, because everything he puts his pipes to—along with his consummate arranging talents—bears the crazed redneck mark of hizzown personality. Electric guitar fleshes out a couple of tracks here and there, but in the main it's pure, unvarnished Charlie Feathers, and that's worth more than the next dozen hat hunk albums that come down the pike. —*Cub Koda*

The Feelies

f. 1977, Hoboken, NJ, **db.** 1992
Alternative Pop-Rock, Jangle-Pop
The Feelies, consisting of Glenn Mercer (guitar/vocals), Bill Million (guitar/vocals), Keith DeNunzio (bass), Vinny DeNunzio (drums), and part-time member Anton Fier (drums), formed in New Jersey in 1977. In 1980

they released their debut avant-pop masterpiece *Crazy Rhythms* to critical acclaim, but to no commercial response. Mercer and Million left the band dormant while working on outside projects such as the Trypes, Willies, and Yung Wu; Fier left to work on his own Golden Palominos projects. Revived interest in the band, thanks in part to R.E.M.'s Peter Buck's citing the band as an influence, led to a reactivated version of the Feelies in 1986, featuring Brenda Sauter on bass and Dave Weckerman on percussion. Produced by Peter Buck, *The Good Earth* was released in 1986 by Coyote to an enthusiastic college radio audience. They continued to be college radio mainstays for the rest of the decade, though mainstream success has eluded them. —*Chris Woodstra*

● **Crazy Rhythms** / Apr. 1980 / A&M ✦✦✦✦
The Feelies' debut picks up where the Velvet Underground and Television left off, using unconventional structures to create an album that is stark, nervous and detached. While it was virtually ignored at the time, *Crazy Rhythms* would prove to be a blueprint for much of the mid-'80s' guitar-based alternative rock. —*Chris Woodstra*

No One Knows / 1986 / Coyote ✦✦✦
This brief EP takes two excellent songs from the album *The Good Earth* and pairs them with two covers. "The High Road" and "Slipping (Into Something)" both utilize strummed acoustic guitar textures, submerged Lou Reed-style vocals, and a vibrant New South sound. The former is a midtempo loping number, while the latter is faster and more jittery; the final section of "Slipping (Into Something)" also layers on nervous electric guitar lines and speeds up the tempo. The Beatles' "She Said, She Said" gets a faithful, if understated reading, while Neil Young's "Sedan Delivery" alternates between sections that are by turns punky fast and grandiosely slow. This is an attractive release worth hearing. —*David Cleary*

The Good Earth / 1986 / Coyote ✦✦✦
After a six-year break, the Feelies return with R.E.M.'s Peter Buck producing. The result, not so surprisingly, is a fine alternative folk-pop album in the spirit of early R.E.M. Though not matching the debut's brilliance, *The Good Earth* creates a pleasant enough atmosphere and is a welcome return. —*Chris Woodstra*

Only Life / 1988 / A&M ✦✦✦✦
Only Life moves from the light acoustic strumming of 1986's *The Good Earth* into a slightly harder electric sound while still retaining much of the textured and atmospheric qualities that made its predecessor so charming. There is more of a return to the driving rhythms of the first album, and the entire album has a feeling of the Velvet Underground revisited. —*Chris Woodstra*

Time for a Witness / Mar. 5, 1991 / A&M ✦✦
By this time, the band is trapped by the formula. They *have* matured and found a slightly more relaxed sound, but the progress is minimal. The result is a close approximation of a Feelies album but, unfortunately, not much else. —*Chris Woodstra*

Bryan Ferry

b. Sep. 26, 1945, Washington, England
Harmonica, Piano, Keyboards, Vocals / Pop-Rock
While his tenure as the frontman for the legendary Roxy Music remained his towering achievement, singer Bryan Ferry also carved out a successful solo career which continued in the lush, sophisticated manner perfected on the group's final records. Born September 26, 1945, in Washington, England, Ferry, the son of a coal miner, began his musical career as a singer with the rock outfit the Banshees while studying art at the University of Newcastle Upon Tyne under pop-conceptualist Richard Hamilton. He later joined the Gas Board, a soul group featuring bassist Graham Simpson; in 1970 Ferry and Simpson formed Roxy Music.

Within a few years Roxy Music had become phenomenally successful, affording Ferry the opportunity to cut his first solo LP in 1973. Far removed from the group's arty glam-rock, *These Foolish Things* established the path that all of Ferry's solo work—as well as the final Roxy Music records—would take, focusing on elegant synth-pop interpretations of '60s hits like Bob Dylan's "A Hard Rain's a-Gonna Fall," the Rolling Stones' "Sympathy for the Devil," and the Beatles' "You Won't See Me," all rendered in the singer's distinct, coolly dramatic manner.

Roxy Music remained Ferry's primary focus, but in 1974 he returned with a second solo effort, *Another Time, Another Place*, another collection of covers ranging from "You Are My Sunshine" to "It Ain't Me, Babe" to "Smoke Gets in Your Eyes." His third venture, 1976's *Let's Stick Together*, featured remixed, remade, and remodeled versions of Roxy Music hits as well as the usual assortment of covers. In 1977 *In Your Mind* was Ferry's first collection of completely original material; the next year's *The Bride Stripped Bare*, a work inspired by his broken romance with model Jerry Hall, split evenly between new songs and covers.

Ferry did not record another solo album until 1985's *Boys and Girls*, a sleek, seamless effort that was his first "official" solo release after the

Roxy break-up. For 1987's *Bete Noire*, he was joined by former Smiths guitarist Johnny Marr on the shimmering "The Right Stuff," and notched his only US Top 40 hit with "Kiss and Tell." Another covers collection, *Taxi* followed in 1993; *Mamouna*, an LP of originals, appeared a year later. —*Jason Ankeny*

These Foolish Things / Oct. 1973 / Reprise ✦✦✦✦
As a side project during his Roxy Music tenure, Ferry recorded this album of drastic rearrangements of a variety of standards, most of them from the '60s. The Beatles, the Rolling Stones, and especially Bob Dylan never sounded like this before. —*William Ruhlmann*

Another Time, Another Place / Jul. 1974 / Reprise ✦✦✦
Same concept, different songs, as the suave Ferry recasts "Smoke Gets in Your Eyes," Sam Cooke, and several country standards. —*William Ruhlmann*

Let's Stick Together / Sep. 1976 / Reprise ✦✦✦
When Roxy Music broke up in 1976, Bryan Ferry's solo career moved from being a sideline to his main occupation. His initial post-Roxy single, "Let's Stick Together," was a UK hit, prompting the release of this cobbled-together album, which consists of outtakes from his two albums of pop covers and some alternate versions of Roxy songs, recorded from 1973 to 1976. It is thus more a marketing item than a real artistic statement, but it has some interesting moments. —*William Ruhlmann*

In Your Mind / Feb. 1977 / Reprise ✦✦
Although it is his fourth solo album overall, this is really Bryan Ferry's debut as a full-fledged solo artist, the follow-up to Roxy Music's 1975 album *Siren*. As such, however, it is a serious disappointment. Although its driving lead-off track, "This Is Tomorrow" (a UK Top Ten hit), is a good introduction, the album lacks the flair of Ferry's work with Roxy Music, and it signals that he will be less of a success without the group. —*William Ruhlmann*

The Bride Stripped Bare / Sep. 1978 / Reprise ✦✦
Ferry tried to recapture the feel of his first two solo albums with R&B covers like "Hold On (I'm Coming)" and "Take Me to the River" while carrying on the Roxy tradition with a few originals, but it didn't work. The commercial failure of this album sent Ferry back into the arms of his Roxy Music compatriots for a reunion of the more successful group. —*William Ruhlmann*

Boys and Girls / May 1985 / Reprise ✦✦✦✦
With the second (and presumably final) disbanding of Roxy Music, Ferry turned full time to his solo career, so this album is more of a follow-up to 1982's *Avalon*, the last Roxy album, than to 1978's *The Bride Stripped Bare*, the previous Ferry solo release. It brilliantly continues the ethereal dance-floor charm of *Avalon*. —*William Ruhlmann*

● **Street Life: 20 Greatest Hits** / Apr. 1986 / EG ✦✦✦✦
Covering both Ferry and Roxy Music's best-known songs, *Street Life* is the best introduction to the stylish art-rocker's career. —*Stephen Thomas Erlewine*

Bête Noire / Oct. 1987 / Reprise ✦✦✦✦
Enlisting Madonna producer Patrick Leonard to assist, Ferry matches his studiedly languorous vocals to densely percussive dance tracks. —*William Ruhlmann*

Taxi / Mar. 1993 / Reprise ✦✦
For Ferry, cover albums have become both artistic statements and a way to buy time. *Taxi*, delivered some six years after *Bete Noire*, is filled with the kind of contradictions inherent in such a dual purpose. Nothing on the album is particularly revelatory; it's his third album entirely composed of covers, so Ferry's slick, stylish approach is familiar. However, Ferry is such a singular singer that *Taxi* escapes being a worthless exercise. Although there are some songs that don't hit the mark, there are several moments (particularly "Will You Love Me Tomorrow" and "Amazing Grace") that make up for such missteps. —*Stephen Thomas Erlewine*

Mamouna / Sep. 20, 1994 / Capitol ✦✦✦✦
Ferry's first album of original material since *Bete Noire* finds the ex-Roxy Music singer in a familiar seductive mood. While working within his standard dance-oriented darkness, Ferry incorporates several new touches—namely, several pseudo-world music touches. None of it would have worked if Ferry hadn't blended them in so seamlessly with his stylish pop, which hasn't dated in the seven years that he's been away. —*Stephen Thomas Erlewine*

Fever Tree

f. 1966, Houston, TX, **db.** 1970
Psychedelic
A minor, if reasonably interesting, late '60s psychedelic group, Houston's Fever Tree are most famous for their single "San Francisco Girls," with its dramatic melody, utopian lyrics, and searing fuzz guitar. Most of their best material, ironically, was written by their over-30 husband-wife pro-

duction team, Scott & Vivian Holtzman, who had previously written material for Tex Ritter and the *Mary Poppins* soundtrack. These odd bedfellows produced some fairly distinctive material with more classical/baroque influences and orchestral string arrangements than were usually found in psychedelic groups. Their pretty, wistful ballads (enhanced on their first album by arranger David Angel, who had also worked on Love's classic *Forever Changes*) endure better than their dirge-like fuzz grinders, which epitomize some of the more generic aspects of heavy psychedelia. Releasing four albums (the third of which, *Creation*, included guest guitar by future ZZ Top axeman Billy Gibbons), their records grew weaker and more meandering with time, and the group disbanded in 1970. —*Richie Unterberger*

● **San Francisco Girls: The Best of Fever Tree** / 1986 / Era ✦✦✦✦
Well-chosen 16-song anthology featuring songs from their first three albums, leaning most heavily on their self-titled 1968 debut. Also has a couple of early singles and a thorough history of the band. —*Richie Unterberger*

The 5th Dimension

f. 1966, Los Angeles, CA
Pop-Rock, Pop
They didn't sound anything like an R&B group, and their soaring, lighter-than-air harmonic blend frequently proved more palatable to pop audiences than to Black record buyers. But do not suggest, even for a second, that the 5th Dimension was in any way lacking in soul.

Formed as the Versatiles in 1965, the slick quintet changed its name at the request of Johnny Rivers, who had just signed them to his brand new label, Soul City. Up-and-coming songwriter Jimmy Webb supplied the group with their first pop smash, "Up, Up and Away," in 1967, and the group's monumental rise mirrored the song's high-flying imagery. Another prolific composer, Laura Nyro, handed the 5th Dimension several megahits, notably "Stoned Soul Picnic" and "Wedding Bell Blues," but their biggest seller hailed from the groundbreaking musical *Hair*. The Grammy-winning "Aquarius/Let the Sunshine In" held down the No. 1 slot on the pop lists for six weeks in 1969.

After several more hits, Marilyn McCoo and Billy Davis, Jr., who had married while part of the group, successfully branched off as a duo, while Lamonte McLemore, Ron Townson, and Florence LaRue kept the 5th Dimension on the soul charts, losing a head-to-head battle with Diana Ross for hit status on "Love Hangover" in 1976. —*Bill Dahl*

● **Greatest Hits on Earth** / Sep. 1972 / Arista ✦✦✦✦
Until Rhino issued this anthology, this was the best hits package for the 5th Dimension, a group that in its peak was among the best at doing lighthearted pop with a soulful foundation. Certainly they weren't a hardcore R&B or earthy singing group, but they did put some punch into songs that were really kind of silly otherwise, like "Wedding Bell Blues." —*Ron Wynn*

Anthology 1967-1973 / 1986 / Rhino ✦✦✦✦
Anthology 1967-1973 contains all of the 5th Dimension's biggest hits, including "Up Up and Away," "Stoned Soul Picnic," "Wedding Bell Blues," and "Aquarius/Let the Sunshine In," making it an excellent introduction to the group's easy-listening soul. *Anthology* is more comprehensive than *Greatest Hits on Earth*, but it was never released on compact disc for various licensing reasons, so the previous compilation remains the easiest way to acquire the group's hits. —*Stephen Thomas Erlewine*

54-40

f. 1981, Vancouver, British Columbia
Alternative Pop-Rock, Roots-Rock, Jangle-Pop
Vancouver's 54-40 take their name from James K. Polk's presidential campaign slogan "Fifty-Four Forty or Fight," which sought to expand the US border northward. 54-40 formed in 1981 as a trio consisting of Brad Merritt (bass), Darryl Neudorf (drums), and Neil Osborne (vocals); they began touring the Western Canadian club circuit, without gaining much attention. In 1984 Phil Comarelli was added on guitar and vocals; Neudorf left shortly thereafter and was replaced by Matt Johnson (not The The's frontman). By the time of the band's self-titled album in 1986, their folk/roots approach had earned them favorable comparisons to R.E.M. Subsequent albums have found the band moving into harder-edged territory. A lack of US interest led to 1992's exclusive Canadian release *Dear Dear*, but by 1994 continued success in their homeland helped to make a US release possible for *Smilin' Buddah Cabaret* in 1995. —*Chris Woodstra*

Set the Fire / 1984 / Mo-Da-Mu ✦✦
● **54-40** / 1986 / Reprise ✦✦✦✦
54-40 are a typical college rock outfit from the '80s. They play smart, snappy music with just enough angst so as to catch your attention. They had solid production, good hooks, just about everything it takes to make

it. So, why didn't they? This album is great. It includes "I Go Blind" which Hootie & the Blowfish have covered, although 54-40's version is better. An impressive debut and one of the band's finest moments. —*James Chrispell*

Show Me / 1987 / Warner Brothers ✦✦✦
Show Me sometimes shows its influences a little too plainly. Not that this is bad, but playing the "Name the influence" game can take away some of the enjoyment. "One Day in Your Life," for example, is a good song, patterned after Midnight Oil. The same goes for "Walk in Line." That doesn't mean that they aren't enjoyable to listen to. It's like the band is trying to "show" you where they're coming from. It's not bad, but a little more of themselves would have been better. Call this one transitional, but entertaining, nonetheless. —*James Chrispell*

Fight for Love / Mar. 1989 / Reprise ✦✦✦
Dear Dear / 1992 / Columbia ✦✦
Vancouver's answer to R.E.M.'s thoughtful, hook-filled pop has consolidated all of its strongest elements for this, its fifth disc. As befits a Canadian perspective, Neil Osborne's lyrics are more rooted to earth than Michael Stipe's fanciful flights, but the songs have the same quality of stimulating both intellect and hips. Osborne makes the best of a limited vocal range by weaving a groove with his fellow musicians, as if his voice were just another instrument. There's a lean, sinewy quality to the playing: focused energy with no excess fat. "Lovers and Losers" begins with Petty-like sing-speak and smooth Southern shuffle before erupting to a ferocious conclusion. The most notable of several highpoints on *Dear Dear* are "You Don't Get Away (That Easy)," with its unsettling, echoed chorus, and the mystical, Latin-tinged pop of "Book." —*Roch Parisien*

Smilin' Buddha Cabaret / 1994 / TriStar/Sony ✦✦✦
After going through a period where the band had no American label, Canada's 54-40 came crashing back into this country with a vengeance. Absorbing the Seattle grunge influences and adapting them to their own pop-rock sensibilities, *Smilin' Buddah Cabaret* delivers a wide variety of music. From the metallic "Radio Luv Song" to the rock steady "Assoholic" to the acoustically introspective "Friends End," 54-40 prove time and again that they know what they're doing. —*James Chrispell*

Fine Young Cannibals

f. 1984, Birmingham, England
Pop-Rock, Dance-Pop
When the English Beat splintered, bassist David Steele and guitarist Andy Cox formed the Fine Young Cannibals with Roland Gift. Although the band's fusion of early rock, Motown-style R&B, pop, and modern dance is tight and loaded with hooks, the real attraction is Gift's soaring falsetto; he sounds like a classic soul singer. Their 1985 debut album was critically acclaimed, but it was the 1989 follow-up, *The Raw & the Cooked*—with the No. 1 singles "She Drives Me Crazy" and "Good Thing"—that made the band major hit makers. Apart from a remix album in 1990 and Gift's occasional film role, the group has been quiet since their breakthrough success. —*Stephen Thomas Erlewine*

Fine Young Cannibals / Dec. 1985 / IRS ✦✦✦
Roland Gift's vocals are the find here, backed by the R&B/pop music provided by ex-Beat members Andy Cox and David Steele. —*William Ruhlmann*

● **The Raw & The Cooked** / Feb. 20, 1989 / IRS ✦✦✦✦
FYC rode to massive success on the tender-and-terrified singing of Roland Gift and the neo-Motown sheen of the No. 1 hits "She Drives Me Crazy" and "Good Thing." —*William Ruhlmann*

The Raw & the Remix / Dec. 1990 / IRS ✦✦
Coming up on two years since the release of *The Raw & The Cooked*, and with no new album in sight, IRS Records put together various 12-inch remix versions of songs from the 1989 album and released this 59-minute collection. There are extended, alternate versions of such hits as "She Drives Me Crazy," "Good Thing," and "Don't Look Back." Off the dance floor, none of this improves on the originals. —*William Ruhlmann*

Fine Young Cannibals' Finest / Nov. 26, 1996 / MCA ✦✦✦✦
Fine Young Cannibals released only two albums, so it's slightly unusual that they even have a greatest hits collection like *Fine Young Cannibals' Finest*. After all, a dedicated fan will have both records, and casual fans will want only the singles on *The Raw and the Cooked*, thereby eliminating the audience for the collection. Despite these misgivings, *Finest* does its job well, featuring 12 of their biggest hits and best-known songs ("She Drives Me Crazy," "Johnny Come Home," "Good Thing," "Suspicious Minds," "Don't Look Back"), plus two unreleased cuts ("The Flame" and "Since You've Been Gone") to entice collectors. If you want the highlights, *Finest* is fine, but most fans will want to stick with the two original albums. —*Stephen Thomas Erlewine*

Fingerprintz

f. 1978, England, **db.** 1981
New Wave
Now sadly relegated to footnote status, England's Fingerprintz were one of the few bands that lent credibility to the marketing-inspired expression "new wave." Formed by Scottish-born singer/guitarist Jimmie O'Neill in 1978, the 'Printz slowed down punk's careening guitar rock, adding clever, rhythmic twists and turns and offering up deftly written stories about lust, angst, and urban desolation. The problem was finding an audience; the music was certainly spot-on, but one can only guess as to what kept hordes of people away. Certainly it wasn't the quality of their recorded work, which, despite occasional concessions to slick production, is mostly smart, insightful songs. Perhaps it was simply a matter of being out of step with the zeitgeist or just not getting a break. O'Neill decided to call it a day after the third and final 'Printz record, *Beat Noir*, in 1981. However, the story has a sort of happy ending: O'Neill and fellow 'Printz guitarist Cha Burns formed the Silencers in 1987, a band that reaped much greater commercial success than did the 'Printz. Ironically, the Silencers' records weren't nearly as good as those of Fingerprintz. As of this writing, all three Fingerprintz records were long out of print, which is a thinly veiled recommendation for someone to compile a CD anthology. —*John Dougan*

• **The Very Dab** / 1979 / Virgin ✦✦✦✦
This is the most "punk"-like recording the 'Printz ever made, and its rough-hewn charm is immediately engaging. The songs, however, are not all light and happy pop songs, and that gives the record an extra edge. O'Neill and Burns' guitars are aggressive and intrusive (that's a compliment), and this record was one of the great left-field (and now long-forgotten) surprises of the late '70s. —*John Dougan*

Dancing with Myself / 1979 / Virgin ✦✦✦

Distinguishing Marks / 1980 / Virgin ✦✦✦
With producer Nick Garvey (ex-Ducks Deluxe and Motors) leading the way, *Distinguishing Marks* has all the rough edges smoothed away, but not so much as to have a negative impact on the music. O'Neill's songs are still loaded with dark emotional undercurrents and melodramatic narratives, but they aren't self-pitying, narcissistic exercises. In fact, this LP marked a maturational process that continued with their third and last record. Still, no record better sums up the excellence of Fingerprintz than this one. —*John Dougan*

Beat Noir / 1981 / Virgin ✦✦✦
After being dropped by Virgin due to lack of interest in the American market, hipper-than-thou English indie label Stiff signed the 'Printz and released their oddest record. The songs didn't depart from O'Neill's usual concerns (angst, urban anomie), the rock/pop influences of the preceding records gave way to a funkier, near reggae, backbeat. More than any of their other recordings, *Beat Noir* is rhythmically dense, a little intimidating at first, but a joy once you get to know it. —*John Dougan*

Finn Brothers

f. 1994
Pop-Rock, Adult Alternative Pop-Rock
Brothers Tim and Neil Finn have been making music together since their childhood in Te Awamutu, New Zealand, continuing to international success in Split Enz and Crowded House. However, it wasn't until late 1989 that they actually started writing together—a reunion that yielded more than a dozen songs for a proposed Finn Brothers side project. That album was scrapped, and most of the material was absorbed by Crowded House's *Woodface* (1991) and *Together Alone* (1993), as well as Tim's 1993 solo album, *Before and After*. The brothers' project resumed in late 1994, and in four weeks they completed an album called simply *Finn*. The album, released in the fall of 1995 (the summer of 1996 in the US), showed a much more casual side of the Finns and was less pop-oriented than their previous musical collaborations. The brothers play nearly all of the instruments themselves, ranging from the primitive to the exotic. After initial pressings of *Finn*, the duo changed their name to the Finn Brothers to avoid confusion with a band with a similar name. —*Chris Woodstra*

• **Finn** / Oct. 1995 / Discovery ✦✦✦✦
Finn is the long rumored and awaited collaboration between brothers Tim and Neil Finn. The first reports of the project in 1990 promised an album of "just acoustic guitars and lots of harmonies," and when that material was absorbed by Crowded House for *Woodface*, it was proven that the team was capable of making near-perfect pop. Those expecting *Woodface Part 2*, however, are in for a surprise—*Finn* is a moody, atmospheric album that shows a more spontaneous and experimental side with the brothers playing all of the instruments, including ukuleles, Chamberlain keyboards, Mellotron, and tea chest bass. Though most projects of this nature get hung up on the "concept," this one succeeds because the Finns' pop songwriting sense allows the songs to come first.

Despite the lack of polish and the odd setting, the material on this album is among the pair's finest, together or apart. —*Chris Woodstra*

Tim Finn

b. Jun. 25, 1952, Te Awamutu, New Zealand
Keyboards, Vocals / Pop-Rock
Singer-songwriter keyboardist/guitarist Tim Finn was born in Te Awamutu, New Zealand. Influenced by not only British Invasion acts like the Beatles, the Move, and the Kinks, but also his Catholic upbringing and the communal sing-alongs of the native Maori people, Finn founded the '70s art-rock-turned-New-Wave band Split Enz, leading the band through several albums to moderate international success. The success of the between-albums solo project *Escapade* led to his leaving the band in 1983. He followed with the more ambitious second album *Big Canoe* (1985), which went virtually ignored (it was unreleased in the US until the success of his brother's band, Crowded House, stirred up enough interest by 1988). Finn returned in 1989 with a self-titled album for Capitol Records. Despite good reviews, this, too, failed to make much impact. He joined his brother Neil Finn's band, Crowded House, for their *Woodface* album but left mid-tour and released his fourth solo album, *Before and After* in 1993. In 1994 he joined Hothouse Flowers' Liam O Maonlai and Andy White, releasing an album under the group name ALT. A long-rumored collaboration between the Finn brothers was finally released in late 1995 under the name Finn Brothers. (It was released in the spring of 1996 in the US.) Finn returned to his solo career by the fall of 1996. —*Scott Bultman and Chris Woodstra*

Escapade / 1983 / A&M ✦✦✦
After Split Enz's *Time & Tide*, Tim Finn took his first break from the band with *Escapade*, a collection of light pop songs, some of which dated back to the late '70s but never seemed to quite fit in the Enz format. A flawed, though fun, album, *Escapade* managed several hits in Australasia and Europe and revealed a considerably brighter, more mainstream aspect of Finn's writing. And while the album was successful and a satisfying diversion, it unquestionably served to derail the forward momentum of Split Enz and led to Finn's leaving the band the next year. —*Chris Woodstra*

Big Canoe / 1985 / Virgin ✦✦✦
Tim Finn teamed up with playwright Jeremy Brock for his second solo outing, *Big Canoe*. Although the collaboration is predictably ambitious—probably Finn's most ambitious since the early days of Split Enz—beneath all the overblown arrangements and slightly dated production lie some terrific songs. Material like "No Thunder No Fire No Rain," "Hyacinth," and "Carve You in Marble" deserves a better setting, but the album is still able to shine, and some minor flaws are forgivable, especially to diehard fans. *Big Canoe* also marks a welcome reunion between Finn and ex-Enz collaborator Phil Judd, who contributes sitar and rhythm guitar to a couple of tracks. —*Chris Woodstra*

• **Tim Finn** / 1989 / Capitol ✦✦✦✦
Perhaps in response to the failed big production of *Big Canoe* and the success of brother Neil's back-to-basics outfit, Crowded House, Finn simplified his approach for his self-titled album, joining forces with Crowded House producer Mitchell Froom. In this touching and intensely personal album, Finn bares all, revealing self-doubts, regrets, and a failed relationship in intricate detail. Despite the subject matter, the album has an optimistic, uplifting overall tone, with tasteful adult-pop arrangements perfectly complementing his strongest melodies and finest songwriting to date. Though the sound and sentiments could have (and should have) easily found an audience in the emerging "adult alternative pop" format, the album went virtually ignored. —*Chris Woodstra*

Before & After / Aug. 10, 1993 / Capitol ✦✦✦✦
On his fourth solo album, Finn dabbles in dance-pop, pseudo-reggae, and folky ballads, with a different set of producers on nearly every track. While this leads to a certain lack of consistency, Finn's songwriting has never been stronger. He has the most success on the self-produced, stripped-down tracks where his strong sense of melody and knack for catchy pop hooks are allowed to be in the forefront. "Persuasion," co-written by Richard Thompson, and "In Love with It All," written with his brother, Neil Finn (Crowded House), are highlights. —*Chris Woodstra*

Firefall

f. 1975, Boulder, CO, **db.** 1983
Country-Rock, Adult Contemporary, Soft Rock, Pop-Rock
The mellow, easy, country-rock sounds of Firefall, coupled with the group's penchant for pop melodies and high-pitched harmonies, produced a series of successful LPs in the late '70s and a series of chart singles, including the Top Ten hit "You Are the Woman." The group was formed by former Flying Burrito Brother Rick Roberts, who handled vocals, guitar, and most of the songwriting duties; he was joined by fellow ex-Burrito and Byrd Michael Clarke on drums, ex-Spirit and Jo Jo Gunne bassist Mark Andes, guitarist/vocalist Jock Bartley, guitarist/

vocalist/songwriter Larry Burnett, and keyboardist/woodwind player David Muse, who joined in 1977. The group recorded its self-titled debut in 1976; it and its follow-up, *Luna Sea*, both went gold, and their third album, *Elan*, went platinum. However, the group's commercial fortunes began to decline, and even though Muse experimented with adding different instruments to the overall sound, Firefall's relaxed, toned-down approach simply wore out its welcome as pop trends moved elsewhere. Jock Bartley reformed the group in 1994 for the album *Messenger*. —*Steve Huey*

Firefall / 1976 / Atlantic ✦✦✦✦
This debut effort, their best album, includes the hits "You Are the Woman" and "Cinderella." —*Rick Clark*

● **Greatest Hits** / Sep. 1, 1992 / Rhino ✦✦✦✦
Rhino's *Greatest Hits* is by far the most comprehensive collection ever assembled on Firefall, featuring a full 18 tracks, including all 11 of the group's charting singles, as well as smartly selected highlights from their albums. It's hard to imagine a more thorough collection than this, and for most fans, it will be all the Firefall they'll ever need. —*Stephen Thomas Erlewine*

fIREHOSE

f. 1985, San Pedro, CA, **db.** 1994
Alternative Pop-Rock
In 1985, after D. Boon's death at age 28 signalled the end of the Minutemen, bassist Mike Watt and drummer George Hurley threw in their lot with then-22-year-old former Ohio State University student, guitar player, and Minutemen fanatic Ed Crawford to form fIREHOSE. Taking their group name from a line in Bob Dylan's "Subterranean Homesick Blues," fIREHOSE continued in the Minutemen tradition of breathtaking musicianship combined with caustic lyrical fusillades inspired by the writing of the Beat Generation and the erect-middle-finger indignation of the Blank Generation. However, with Crawford's decidedly folkie bent insinuating itself into the mix, fIREHOSE's songs began to expand into more traditional verse-chorus-verse songwriting symmetry. And although fIREHOSE never equaled the Minutemen's output in terms of sheer audacity and emotional depth, Crawford, Watt, and Hurley recorded rock that was muscular, dense, and daring, along with being tremendously heartfelt. They never patronized audiences or comported themselves as "rock stars"; they were, instead, the quintessential post-punk "people's band." Although they achieved wider notoriety than did the Minutemen (eventually recording for a major label), fIREHOSE called it quits in early 1994 after a desultory, dispirited final LP (*Mr. Machinery Operator*). Still, nearly all of their recorded work stands as some of the best late-'80s/early-'90s indie rock. —*John Dougan*

Ragin', Full-On / 1986 / SST ✦✦✦
The title is a bit of a misnomer, since this record seethes more than it rages, but all and all, it was a fine debut. Crawford's (here he was referred to as Ed Fromohio) singing is tentative and a bit wan, but the songs are strong, and Watt and Hurley are one of rock's great rhythm sections. —*John Dougan*

● **If'n** / 1987 / SST ✦✦✦✦
On release number two, Crawford's guitar is assertive and drives the band more. Just as important, however, is that the songwriting has grown sharper and more compelling (especially on the romping "Sometimes"), and Crawford sings with more reckless abandon here. No sophomore slump, not by a long shot. —*John Dougan*

Sometimes / 1988 / SST ✦✦
Fromohio / 1989 / SST ✦✦✦✦
A bit of a retrenchment and perhaps not a wholly successful record. Here, fIREHOSE sounds like a band reevaluating its place in the world and only occasionally coming up with compelling answers. An easy record to slough off as more of the same. But while it may not be an essential record, it isn't bad either. —*John Dougan*

Flyin' the Flannel / Apr. 23, 1991 / Columbia ✦✦✦
If indie-rock purists were ready to scream "sellout" when fIREHOSE signed with Columbia, they were sorely disappointed when Crawford, Watt, and Hurley released this louder-than-usual, revved-up hunk of clang and strum that in no way repudiated fIREHOSE's reputation as a fiercely independent band. Less controlled and more traditionally "rock" than previous records, *Flyin' the Flannel* really is ragin' full-on and may well be their best. —*John Dougan*

Live Totem Pole / 1992 / Columbia ✦✦✦
A fun, mostly covers, seven-song EP that proves what a great live band fIREHOSE was. Ferocious and fast, the highlight is a rousing (and perhaps definitive) version of Superchunk's anti-slacker theme song "Slack Motherfucker." —*John Dougan*

Mr. Machinery Operator / Feb. 16, 1993 / Columbia ✦✦
fIREHOSE's final album was a pile-driving slab of post-punk rock, tamed by J. Mascis' production; occasionally, the guitars are too thick for

the band's style of music, but overall, this was a fine way to close the book on their career. —*Stephen Thomas Erlewine*

Fishbone

f. 1979, Los Angeles
Alternative Pop-Rock, Funk Metal, Ska-Metal
Combining equal parts of deep funk, high energy punk, and frantic ska, the Los Angeles-based Fishbone were one of the most distinctive and eclectic alternative rock bands of the late '80s. With their hyperactive, self-conscious diversity, goofy sense of humor, and sharp social commentary, the group gained a sizable cult following during the late '80s, but they were never able to earn a mainstream audience.

Led by vocalist/saxophonist Angelo Moore, the group formed in 1979 while the band was still in junior high; the original lineup comprised Moore, Chris Dowd, Kendall Jones, Walter Kibby, II, John Norwood Fisher, Fish, and Charlie Down. After performing in local clubs during the early '80s, the group signed with Columbia Records in the mid-'80s, releasing a self-titled EP in 1985. The next year, Fishbone released their first full-length album, *In Your Face*. While it was marred by a somewhat slick production, the sheer energy of their performances burned through the slightly polished surface. In 1987 the band released the Christmas EP *It's a Wonderful Life (Gonna Have a Good Time)*.

Truth and Soul (1988), Fishbone's second album, captured the band at their most ambitious, as they slammed back and forth between heavy metal and funk, throwing in an acoustic number and a cover of Curtis Mayfield's "Freddie's Dead" for balance. The album expanded their audience and charted at No. 153. But the band didn't record a new album for another three years. In the meantime, they made two EPs—*Ma and Pa* (1989) and *Bonin' in the Boneyard* (1990)—which basically comprised several B-sides. Before 1991's *The Reality of My Surroundings*, Charlie Down left the band and was replaced by John Bigham. *The Reality of My Surroundings* didn't depart from the band's wreckless eclecticism; it refined it. The album was a hit, peaking at No. 49 and receiving positive reviews. However, the record didn't establish the band as a mainstream success, nor did 1993's *Give a Monkey a Brain and He'll Swear He's the Center of the Universe* despite their appearance at the third Lollapalooza. Even when the third wave of ska revival began to rise to popularity in 1996, Fishbone were left behind, as their '96 record *Chim Chim's Bad Ass Revenge*—their first album for Arista—was ignored, as was the double-disc compilation *Fishbone 101: Nuttasaurusmeg Fossil Fuelin*. Despite their poor sales, the group remained a popular concert attraction. —*Stephen Thomas Erlewine*

Fishbone / 1985 / Columbia ✦✦✦
What a debut! Fierce, funny, and ferocious. —*John Dougan*

Truth & Soul / 1988 / Columbia ✦✦✦✦
A perfect mix of their anarchic, chaotic debut with their more recent, thrashier sound still mixes uppity ska beats and licks with Sly and the Family Stone-style funk (good-feeling, choral, beautifully coordinated upbeat soul) and harder, Living Colour-style guitar-driven chops, but this time it comes together better than ever. It prances all over the musical spectrum but never loses its pace or identity. "Ma and Pa," "Freddie's Dead," and funk-punk anthem "Bonin' in the Boneyard." —*Julian Katz*

● **The Reality of My Surroundings** / Apr. 23, 1991 / Columbia ✦✦✦✦
Needs editing, but contains some inspiring moments. —*John Dougan*

Give a Monkey a Brain and He'll Swear He's the Center of the Universe / May 25, 1993 / Columbia ✦✦
Fishbone's standard careening eclecticism is refined on *Give a Monkey a Brain*. Instead of freely flowing between different styles, as they did on *The Reality of My Surroundings*, the band's sound is reined in (presumably in an attempt to make Fishbone palatable for the mainstream), making the album impressively diverse but frustrating; they never cut loose as they do in almost all of their concerts. Nevertheless, there's enough good material here to make it worthwhile for dedicated fans. —*Stephen Thomas Erlewine*

Chim Chim's Bad Ass Revenge / Apr. 1996 / Arista/Rowdy ✦✦
Fishbone 101: Nuttasaurusmeg Fossil Fuelin / Sep. 24, 1996 / Sony ✦✦✦✦
Comprised of one disc of hits and one disc of rarities, the double-disc retrospective *Fishbone 101: Nuttasaurusmeg Fossil Fuelin* attempts to fulfill the needs of both the collector and the casual fan and seems to only partly satisfy neither. The first disc, featuring hits and cult classics "Freddie's Dead" and "Everyday Sunshine," is a fine overview of their career, hitting nearly all of the band's best moments. On its own, it would be the album to own for casual fans. However, the second disc, while of utmost interest to dedicated followers, is filled with B-sides, demos, alternate takes, and rarities that will simply bore neophytes. Of course, all of this material is necessary for collectors, but they will probably be frustrated by the extraneous hits collection on the set. If *Fishbone 101* had been separated into two individual collections, both albums would have fulfilled their goals perfectly. As it stands, it's a set that is bound to frustrate

both casual and hardcore fans, and thereby can be recommended only with reservations. —*Stephen Thomas Erlewine*

The Five Americans

f. 1965, Dallas, TX, **db.** 1969
Garage Rock, Pop-Rock, Bubblegum
In 1966-67 this Dallas group enjoyed some modest national success with the No. 5 hit "Western Union," as well as a few other Top 40 entries, "I See the Light," "Zip Code," and "Sound of Love." Dominated by high, bubbling organ lines and clean harmony vocals, the group favored high-energy pop-rock far more than British Invasion or R&B-inspired sounds, although a bit of garage/frat rock raunch could be detected in their stomping rhythms. Recording prolifically throughout the last half of the '60s (often with ex-rockabilly star Dale Hawkins as producer), and writing much of their own material, they were ultimately too lightweight and bubblegumish to measure up to either the era's better pop-rock or garage bands. Their 1966 hit "I See the Light" is their toughest and best performance. —*Richie Unterberger*

● **Western Union** / 1989 / Sundazed ✦✦✦✦
Twenty-song best-of includes all their big and small hits, as well as quite a few rarities and an extensive group history. —*Richie Unterberger*

The "5" Royales

f. 1952, Winston-Salem, NC, **db.** 1965
R&B
The "5" Royales were a relatively unheralded, but significant, link between early R&B and early soul in their combination of doo wop, jump blues, and gospel styles. Their commercial success was relatively modest—they had seven Top Ten R&B hits in the 1950s, most recorded in the span of little over a year between late 1952 and late 1953. A few of their singles would prove extremely popular in cover versions by other artists, though—James Brown and Aretha Franklin tore it up with "Think," Ray Charles covered "Tell the Truth," and the Shirelles (and later the Mamas & the Papas) had pop success with "Dedicated to the One I Love." Almost all of their material was written by guitarist Lowman Pauling, who influenced Steve Cropper with his biting and bluesy guitar lines, which at their most ferocious almost sound like a precursor to blues-rock.

Pauling's guitar is pretty muted on their early sides, which sometimes walk the line between gospel and R&B. The gospel elements aren't surprising, given that the Royales were originally known as the Royal Sons Quintet when they formed in Winston-Salem, N.C. In fact, they were still known as the Royal Sons Quintet when they began recording for Apollo in the early '50s, although they had six members. They would change their name to the "5" Royales in 1952, although they would, confusingly, remain a six-man outfit for a while; the quotes around the 5 in their billing were designed to alleviate some of the confusion. The Apollo singles "Baby Don't Do It" and "Help Me Somebody" made No. 1 on the R&B charts in 1953, and they had a few other hits for Apollo before being lured to King Records in 1954.

Although the group would remain on King for the rest of the 1950s, they would enter the R&B Top Ten only two more times, with "Think" and "Tears of Joy" (both in 1957). Their later sides, however, are their best, as Pauling became much more assertive on the guitar, dashing off some piercing and fluid solos. Some of these solos are among the heaviest and wildest in '50s rock, on both relatively well known cuts like "Think," and virtually unknown numbers like "The Slummer the Slum." Greil Marcus once wrote something to the effect that a young Eric Clapton would once have paid to hold Pauling's coat. They remained primarily a harmony vocal group, though, and if their late-'50s sides are considerably more modernized than their early Apollo hits, they're still a lot closer to doo wop than soul.

Even when their records weren't selling, the "5" Royales were a popular touring band. Their constant activity at King Records in all likelihood had some influence on the young James Brown, then starting his career on the same label; one of Brown's first big R&B hits was a frenetic cover of "Think." They couldn't sustain themselves without more hits, though. After leaving King and recording some more sides in the early '60s, they finally broke up by 1965. —*Richie Unterberger*

★ **Monkey Hips and Rice: the "5" Royales Anthology** / Mar. 8, 1994 / Rhino ✦✦✦✦✦
The "5" Royales certainly did their share of forgettable period-piece tunes, but they also had transcendent songs like "Think," "Just as I Am," and "Dedicated to the One I Love." They enjoyed a lengthy run, creating many hits and a few gems, which are all available on this sparkling two-disc set. The opening disc sets the stage, showing their gospel origins and the rather routine cuts the band did in its formative period. They began to evolve into a more substantial unit in the mid-'50s, and by the late '50s were a sterling unit cutting emphatic, appealing numbers. Most of these appear on the second disc. By the early '60s, they had run their course, but their legacy and impact were secure. This offers the most

complete picture of the "5" Royales and their superb music. —*Ron Wynn*

The Five Satins

f. 1956, New Haven, CT, **db.** 1961
Doo Wop
The Five Satins are best known for the doo wop classic "In the Still of the Night," a song that was popular enough to make the group one of the most famous doo wop outfits, although they never had another hit of the same magnitude.

The origins of the Five Satins lie in the Scarlets, a New Haven, CT, doo wop group led by Fred Parris. The Scarlets formed in 1953, while Parris was still in high school. The group had a local hit with "Dear One" the next year. In 1954 Parris formed the Five Satins with vocalists Al Denby, Ed Martin, and Jim Freeman. Within the next year, Parris had the group record "In the Still of the Night," a song he had recently written, in the basement of a local church. The first single the group released was "In the Still of the Night." The single was released on Standard Records in the spring of 1956. By the end of the year, it had been leased to Ember and it became a huge hit, peaking at No. 3 on the R&B charts and No. 25 on the pop charts.

By the time "In the Still of the Night" scaled the charts, Parris had been drafted into the army. He was stationed in Japan when the song became a hit, and he was still in Japan when the group recorded the follow-up single, "To the Aisle." For that single, Bill Baker handled the lead vocals. "To the Aisle" became a Top Ten R&B hit in the summer of 1957. Parris returned from the army in 1958. Upon his return, he re-organized the group, adding Richie Freeman, Sylvester Hopkins, West Forbes, and Lou Peeples. This incarnation of the group had a minor hit in the fall of 1959 with "Shadows."

In 1960 "In Still of the Night" re-entered the pop charts, thanks to its exposure on Art Laboe's first *Oldies but Goodies* compilation. The repeated success of the single sparked another minor hit for the band in 1960, a cover of the standard "I'll Be Seeing You." During the remainder of the '60s and early '70s, Parris led various incarnations of the Five Satins through oldies revues in America and Europe; they also recorded occasionally during this time.

In 1974, the group signed a contract with Kirsner Records and released a single, "Two Different Worlds." Two years later they briefly changed their name to Black Satin and released a single called "Everybody Stand Up and Clap Your Hands (For the Entertainer)," which became a Top 50 R&B hit.

Shortly afterward, the group reverted to the Five Satins name. In 1982 the Five Satins had their last hit with a doo wop medley entitled "Memories of Days Gone By." The single, which was released on Elektra Records, peaked at No. 71 on the pop charts. For the remainder of the '80s and '90s, Fred Parris led various lineups of the Five Satins, and the group performed regularly at oldies shows in America and Europe. —*Stephen Thomas Erlewine*

● **In the Still of the Night** / 1990 / Relic ✦✦✦✦
Everything you need from this sumptuous and smoochy late-night doo wop quintet is here. The title cut is a work of art worth listening to over and over. —*John Floyd*

The Five Stairsteps

f. 1965, Chicago, IL, **db.** 1976
Soul
The Five Stairsteps were a Windy City family affair initially consisting of four brothers and a sister; later on, five-year-old Cubie Burke toddled aboard, and even mom and pop got into the act. Curtis Mayfield discovered the group at a talent contest, and they debuted in 1966 on his Windy C logo with the tender "You Waited Too Long," their first hit. Lead singer Clarence Burke, Jr. was only 15 years old in 1966, but his attractive leads on "World of Fantasy" and "Come Back" displayed a wealth of emotion. The group enjoyed its biggest pop hit in 1970 with the classic "O-o-h Child" for Buddah. After a few years apart, the group re-formed and notched a final hit, "From Us to You," on George Harrison's Dark Horse label in 1976. Four of the Burkes recorded as the Invisible Man's Band, scoring a sizable seller in 1980 with "All Night Thing," and bassist Keni Burke has recorded as a solo artist. —*Bill Dahl*

● **Greatest Hits** / Apr. 18, 1990 / Collectables ✦✦✦✦
This hits package examines the adolescent Chicago soul group from their mid-'60s beginnings with their 1970 bubblegum soul hit "O-o-h Child." —*Bill Dahl*

Comeback: Best of the Five Stairsteps / Aug. 19, 1996 / Sequel ✦✦✦✦
Comeback: The Best of the Five Stairsteps contains all of the group's major R&B hits, from "You Waited Too Long" and "World of Fantasy" to "O-o-h Child." For some listeners, there may be a little bit too much material here, especially since their lesser-known singles weren't quite

as good as the hits, but this remains the definitive overview of the group's career. —*Stephen Thomas Erlewine*

The Fixx

f. 1980, London, England, **db.** 1991
New Wave, Pop-Rock
A London-based new wave group that managed to sustain a successful career in America for several years in the mid-'80s, the Fixx always flirted with mainstream pop with their catchy, keyboard-driven music. College friends vocalist/keyboardist Cy Curnin and drummer Adam Woods advertised in the music press in the early '80s for additional members; guitarist Jamie West-Oram, keyboardist Rupert Greenall, and bassist Charlie Barret responded to the ad. Taking the name the Portraits, the band recorded a single for Ariola Records, "Hazards in the Home," which failed to gather much attention. Within a year the band had changed the name to the Fixx and recorded "Lost Planes," the single that led to a record contract with MCA.

The Fixx released their debut album, the Rupert Hine-produced *Shuttered Room,* in 1982. The record spawned two minor UK hits, "Stand or Fall" and "Red Skies," and spent a short time in the charts. In America, none of the singles was a hit, but the album stayed on the charts for nearly a year. After *Shuttered Room,* Barret left the group and was replaced by Dan K. Brown. *Reach the Beach,* released in 1983, established them as a hit-making force in the US. The terse, pulsating "One Thing Leads to Another" became a No. 4 hit, sending the album into the Top Ten. *Reach the Beach* would go platinum by the end of the year, launching two more Top 40 singles—"Saved by Zero" and "Sign of Fire." Despite all of their American success, the Fixx failed to break back into the British charts with *Reach the Beach;* in fact, they never had another British hit. The Fixx returned in 1984 with *Phantoms.* While it performed well—it peaked at No. 19 and went gold—it didn't match the success of *Reach the Beach;* after it launched the No. 15 single "Are We Ourselves?" the record fell off the charts. Although their audience was shrinking, the band kept their basic, synth-driven sound intact for 1986's *Walkabout,* which featured the hit "Secret Separation." After *Walkabout,* the Fixx stopped working with producer Rupert Hineand developed a harder, more guitar-oriented sound for 1988's *Calm Animals.* The album charted at No. 72, but it spawned no hit singles. *Ink* (1991), the group's last album, didn't reverse their declining fortunes, even though they tried to update their sound with an emphasis on guitars and slick, dance-ready beats. After the record failed to recapture their mainstream audience, the Fixx quietly faded away. —*Stephen Thomas Erlewine*

Shuttered Room / 1982 / MCA ✦✦✦
The Fixx' debut album *Shuttered Room* suffers from inconsistent and unmelodic songwriting, but producer Rupert Hine helps turn the group's generic new wave into engaging synth-pop. Even with Hine's support, only a couple of tracks ("Red Skies," "Stand or Fall," "Shuttered Room") stand out, but the band's clean, mechanical attack makes the record enjoyable. —*Stephen Thomas Erlewine*

Reach the Beach / 1983 / MCA ✦✦✦✦
Reach the Beach is a significant step forward from the Fixx' debut album *Shuttered Room,* simply because the band can now craft immediately accessible, incessantly catchy pop-rock melodies. "One Thing Leads to Another" has a big, ringing guitar hook that's hammered home by the dance-beat, while "Saved by Zero" and "The Sign of Fire" are cool, robotic slices of synth-pop. Although the rest of the album isn't quite as catchy as those three hits, *Reach the Beach* remains a pleasant collection of immaculately produced and stylishly danceable new wave. —*Stephen Thomas Erlewine*

Phantoms / 1984 / MCA ✦✦✦
Phantoms repeats the formula of *Reach the Beach* with somewhat diminishing returns, but "Are We Ourselves?" is a first-rate single from a band that, by now, has proven that singles, not albums, are their strong point. —*Stephen Thomas Erlewine*

Walkabout / 1986 / MCA ✦✦✦
With its layered synthesized textures and ponderous songs, *Walkabout* displays a bit more ambition than the average Fixx album, but its best moments arrive when the group concentrates on pop songs, such as the trancy "Secret Separation." Unfortunately, only a handful of songs on *Walkabout* come close to matching the hooks of "Secret Separation," suggesting that the Fixx have begun to run out of ideas. —*Stephen Thomas Erlewine*

React / 1987 / MCA ✦✦
Since they had begun to recycle ideas within the studio, the Fixx decided to release a live album for the followup to 1986's *Walkabout.* Comprised of recordings made at two Canadian concerts from 1986, *React* is a competent but uninvolving document of the Fixx in concert, turning out all of their major hits in a professional manner. In other words, only diehard fans will find this of much interest, and even they will fail to be

impressed by the three new songs added to the album as an enticement to collectors. —*Stephen Thomas Erlewine*

Calm Animals / 1988 / RCA ✦✦
The Fixx attempted to redefine themselves as a guitar-driven mainstream rock band for 1988's *Calm Animals,* their first album for RCA Records. Although their stylistic revamping isn't embarrassing, it isn't executed well, particularly because the group has failed to write any memorable songs. Consequently, *Calm Animals* produced no hits, and the group left RCA after releasing this lone album. —*Stephen Thomas Erlewine*

● **One Thing Leads to Another: Greatest Hits** / Oct. 1989 / MCA ✦✦✦✦
One Thing Leads to Another: Greatest Hits is a terrific 12-track collection that features all of the Fixx' biggest singles ("One Thing Leads to Another," "Red Skies," "The Sign of Fire," "Saved by Zero," "Are We Ourselves?"), plus a live version of "Stand or Fall." Although the album isn't presented in chronological order, it remains an excellent, comprehensive overview of the band's best moments. —*Stephen Thomas Erlewine*

Ink / Feb. 19, 1991 / Impact ✦✦
Returning to MCA after a brief detour on RCA, the Fixx resumed recording after a three-year hiatus following the release of *Calm Animals* with 1991's *Ink.* Essentially, *Ink* is *Calm Animals* with a stronger dance-rock backbeat and even fewer memorable songs. Unsurprisingly, the effort bombed, and the Fixx drew to a close shortly afterward. *Ink* may not have been a graceful way to bow out, but it does offer ample evidence that the group had run out of ideas. —*Stephen Thomas Erlewine*

Roberta Flack

b. Feb. 10, 1939, Ashville, NC
Piano, Vocals / Soul, Urban, Soft Rock, Pop-Rock
Classy, urbane, reserved, smooth, and sophisticated—all of these terms have been used to describe the music of Roberta Flack, particularly her string of romantic, light-jazz ballad hits in the 1970s, which continue to enjoy popularity on MOR-oriented adult contemporary stations. Flack was the daughter of a church organist and started playing piano early enough to get a music scholarship and eventual degree from Howard University. After a period of student teaching, Flack was discovered singing at a club by jazz musician Les McCann and signed to Atlantic. Her first two albums were well received but produced no hit singles; however, that all changed when a version of Ewan MacColl's "The First Time Ever I Saw Your Face," from her first LP, was included in the soundtrack of *Play Misty for Me.* The single zoomed to No. 1 in 1972 and remained there for six weeks, becoming that year's biggest hit. Flack followed it with the first of several duets with Howard classmate Donny Hathaway, "Where Is the Love." "Killing Me Softly with His Song" became Flack's second No. 1 hit (five weeks) in 1973, and after topping the charts again in 1974 with "Feel Like Makin' Love," Flack took a break from performing to concentrate on recording and charitable causes. She charted several more times over the next few years, but a major blow struck in 1979 when Hathaway committed suicide. Devastated, Flack eventually found another partner in Peabo Bryson, with whom she toured in 1980. The two recorded together in 1983, scoring a hit duet with "Tonight, I Celebrate My Love." Flack spent the remainder of the '80s touring and performing, often with orchestras, and also several times with Miles Davis. She returned to the Top Ten once more in 1991 with "Set the Night to Music," a duet with Maxi Priest. —*Steve Huey*

First Take / 1969 / Atlantic ✦✦✦✦
The album that launched Roberta Flack's career. She had been doing background vocals and also recording with Les McCann, who helped her land at Atlantic. The single "The First Time Ever I Saw Your Face" zoomed into the pop stratosphere after it was included in Clint Eastwood's film *Play Misty For Me.* —*Ron Wynn*

Chapter Two / Aug. 1970 / Atlantic ✦✦✦✦
A great album and the release that made Roberta Flack a major soul and R&B artist in the early '70s. She had a soft, compelling, alluring voice, and was able to convincingly switch gears and also convey anger, regret, hurt, or despair. Those who thought Flack was a one-hit wonder, or didn't think she could make the transition from doing mostly jazz to other styles, were convinced otherwise. —*Ron Wynn*

Quiet Fire / Nov. 1971 / Atlantic ✦✦✦
Another super Roberta Flack album. She had now become one of the masters of what some described as "middle-class soul," restrained, elegant ballads sung in an exuberant but non-gospel fashion. It continued her string of Top 20 albums on both the R&B and pop side, and remains a staple on urban contemporary and adult contemporary outlets. —*Ron Wynn*

Roberta Flack Featuring Donny Hathaway / Apr. 1972 / Atlantic ✦✦✦✦
A duet classic, and perhaps the most popular album Roberta Flack made. Their single "Where Is the Love" dominated urban contemporary radio for almost the entire year, while "You've Got a Friend" was just as

influential and was later covered by numerous artists (of course they didn't write it, but a lot of folks thought they did). It did so well that Flack eventually did other duet material and also became very close to Hathaway. —*Ron Wynn*

Killing Me Softly / Aug. 1973 / Atlantic ✦✦✦✦
The title track was another smash for Roberta Flack, and the album continued in the same tradition as *Chapter Two* and *A Quiet Fire*. She made simmering ballads, declarative message songs, and better-than-average uptempo numbers, and at the time was among the top-selling female vocalists in any style. —*Ron Wynn*

The Best of Roberta Flack / 1980 / Atlantic ✦✦✦✦
Showcases her biggest ballads, including "First Time Ever I Saw Your Face," "Feel Like Making Love" and "Killing Me Softly with His Song," as well as her duets with Donny Hathaway, "Where Is the Love" and "The Closer I Get to You." —*Bil Carpenter*

Born to Love / Jul. 1983 / Capitol ✦✦✦
A duet set with Peabo Bryson on which they sing mood songs like "Tonight, I Celebrate My Love" and "You're Lookin' Like Love to Me." —*Bil Carpenter*

● **Softly with These Songs: The Best of Roberta Flack** / Jun. 22, 1993 / Atlantic ✦✦✦✦
While it includes almost everything on *Best of Roberta Flack*, *Softly With These Songs* covers material after 1980, including the hits "Tonight, I Celebrate My Love" and "Making Love," which makes it the preferable compilation. —*Stephen Thomas Erlewine*

The Flamin' Groovies

f. 1965, San Francisco, CA, db. 1979
Rock 'n' Roll, Power Pop
One of America's greatest, most influential, and legendary cult bands, the Flamin' Groovies came out of the San Francisco area in 1965 playing greasy, bluesy, rock 'n' roll with a liberal sprinkling of British Invasion panache in an era soon to be dominated by hippie culture and hyperextended raga-rock freakouts. Caught in a double bind of playing the wrong kind of music at the wrong time (as well as not looking the part), the Groovies were almost completely forgotten as the Fillmore/Avalon Ballroom scenes, dominated by the Dead, the Jefferson Airplane, et al., rendered them anachronistic. The plain truth, however, was that despite not being in tune with the zeitgeist, the Groovies made great music, and they managed to sustain a career that lasted for over two decades.

What made the Groovies such a formidable band was the double dynamite supplied by guitarist Cyril Jordan and singer/wildman Roy A. Loney. Together they formed an uneasy partnership that guided the band through its most fertile period, from 1968-1971. In 1968, for next to nothing, the band recorded a seven-song EP entitled *Sneakers*. This little bit of ingenuity resulted in a contract with Epic and the huge sum of $80,000 (1968 dollars, mind you) to be spent on their debut recording, *Supersnazz*. It was a great album that didn't sell but did get them dropped from Epic. Quickly singing with Kama Sutra, the Groovies closed the '60s and started the '70s with two terrific records (*Flamingo* and *Teenage Head*), but public apathy and the increasingly tempestuous relationship between Jordan and Loney led to the latter's departure for a solo career in 1971. Jordan, now free to run the band as a "benevolent" dictator and indulge his passion for a more folk-rock (read: Byrds) focus, hired guitarist/vocalist Chris Wilson, curiously added the apostrophe to their first name, and in 1972 moved the band to England.

Oddly enough, the Groovies had a larger, more enthusiastic following in Europe (especially in England and Germany) than they did in the States, and it seemed perfectly reasonable to assume that if great rewards were to be reaped, it would happen in Europe first. Hooking up with Dave Edmunds, who was keen to produce them, Jordan and company recorded a handful of songs as early as 1972. However, this seemingly natural collaboration yielded little until 1976, when the Groovies released their finest post-Loney effort, *Shake Some Action*. Loaded with ringing guitars, great covers, and Edmunds' spongy, bass-heavy production, *Shake Some Action* became a well-received album in punk-era Britain, as did the fine follow-up, *Flamin' Groovies Now*. This new notoriety brought renewed interest in the Groovies in America, but the string of good albums ended abruptly with the mostly covers and mostly forgettable *Jumpin' in the Night* in 1979. Clearly, the band had run out of gas. That fact, however, did little to convince Cyril Jordan that the Flamin' Groovies were no longer viable.

So, after five or six years of no new music—there were instead countless repackagings, anthologies, and lousy bootlegs—the band ended up in Australia, now reduced to Jordan and a bunch of unknowns (with the exception of longtime bassist George Alexander), shamelessly covering '60s material and living off the band's legend. Apparently Jordan, 20-plus years since the Groovies' first record, still flogs a version of the band to anyone willing to listen. Expectations for quality new music by the Groovies are at an all-time low. It should be noted that after his

departure in 1971, Roy Loney, after a couple of music industry jobs, made (and still makes) some wonderful records with his band the Phantom Movers (with ex-Groovies drummer Danny Mihm). Loney still occasionally works behind the counter at Jack's Record Cellar in San Francisco (stop in and say hello), and has most recently been recording with the Young Fresh Fellows. —*John Dougan*

Sneakers [10 Inch] / 1968 / Snazz ✦✦✦
The group's earliest release, recorded in early 1968, was originally issued as a seven-song ten-inch. Featuring mostly Roy Loney originals, the band mashed together garage rock, San Francisco psychedelia, the Lovin' Spoonful, and blues for this derivative set. Nonetheless, there was a good deal of charm in the over-amped, hyper-speedy execution—less finesse than their more renowned Bay Area peers, but less pretension than most of them. The easygoing blues-rock of "The Slide," the tunefully moody "Lovetime," and the insanely fast fusion of '20s pop and '60s rock on "My Yada" were standouts. The entire record has been reissued on CD as part of Sundazed's *Supersneakers*, which also includes ten live tracks recorded in 1968. —*Richie Unterberger*

Supersnazz / 1968 / Epic ✦✦✦
For an unknown band, Epic sank a lot of money into this record, and wasn't happy when it didn't sell. But that's hardly the fault of the band, who sound great despite the intrusive overproduction of novice knob-twiddler Steve Goldman. Loney's yelping lead vocals are in fine form, and the rest of the band rocks with a reckless abandon and stunning succinctness that was totally out-of-step with the times. —*John Dougan*

Flamingo / 1970 / Kama Sutra ✦✦✦✦
Licking their wounds after the Epic fiasco, the Groovies resurfaced on the much smaller Kama Sutra label and tore off this chunk of delirium that marked their best early-'70s work. Jordan and second guitarist Tim Lynch fire off salvo after salvo of James Burton-tinged riffing, while Loney is, well, himself; his twitchy, rockabilly-styled vocalizing never wears thin. There's a great cover of Little Richard's "Keep a-Knockin'," and even better is Loney's hip and hilarious "Second Cousin." —*John Dougan*

Teenage Head / 1971 / Big Beat ✦✦✦✦
The last and best Flamin' Groovies record made with Roy Loney, *Teenage Head* is probably the most influential record they ever made. A favorite of the hip New York rock crowd (many of whom are thanked on the album jacket), this is a rip-snorter from the Loney/Jordan-penned "High Flyin' Baby" to the cover of Randy Newman's "Have You Seen My Baby?" The title track is a classic bit of teenage angst that sounds as fresh today as it did 24 years ago. —*John Dougan*

☆ **Shake Some Action** / 1976 / AIM ✦✦✦✦✦
The Groovies disappeared into the wilds of Europe after *Teenage Head*, which barely earned them a cult following over here. They went through a few personnel changes, honed their sound to an even finer point, and developed a few more musical smarts. Then came *Shake Some Action*, the debut of the Flamin' Groovies' Mark II, where they rocked out British-style for most of it (while still acknowledging their American roots), only louder and more passionately than any British Invasion band had played since 1964. The sound was a complete anachronism in the mid-'70s, but it got them noticed and earned them a cult following. The guitar sound is straight 1964 Beatles (a la "Not a Second Time") alternating with Kinks material of the same era, the vocals are the plaintive wailing of lovesick young rock gods, and the effect is stunning even 20 years after. Maybe the greatest British Invasion album since 1964. Reissued by Australia's AIM Records on CD, and well worth tracking down as an import. —*Bruce Eder*

Still Shakin' / 1976 / Buddah ✦✦✦✦
Buddah Records, the successor to Kama Sutra, seeing that the boys were finally getting their due in the rock press, put together this cool little cash-in effort, which combined the best tracks from *Flamingo* and *Teenage Head* with a bunch of outtakes into a sort of "best-of" the Mark I Groovies. The leftover tracks are even rawer and better than the released material, and this record only added to the passion that fans old and new felt for the band. —*Bruce Eder*

The Flamin' Groovies Now! / 1978 / Sire ✦✦✦✦
So the group is getting all kinds of great press, and even some radio play from their comeback album on Sire, and embarks on a national tour, playing clubs like the Bottom Line in New York before every rock V.I.P. who could wangle a ticket. And to accompany the tour, they put out an album of yet more British invasion-style (and pre-British Invasion—they covered Cliff Richard & the Shadows' 1958 hit "Move It" alongside Beatles and Stones material) tracks. The sound on this record was a notable improvement over *Shake Some Action*, and the group had lost none of its flair for the period or the style, but there was also precious little new ground covered, which cost them some credibility with the press, even if it didn't bother the fans at all. Their cover of the Gene Clark/Byrds classic rocker "Feel a Whole Lot Better" was one of the best remakes of a '60s classic ever recorded, outdoing the original at every turn (a few fans

suggested that the Byrds might reunite to cover the Groovies' "Shake Some Action" in return). —*Bruce Eder*

Jumpin' in the Night / 1979 / Sire ✦✦✦
The Groovies' third British Invasion-revival style album was actually even better than the second, but Sire by this time was hedging its bets, replacing a cover of the Rolling Stones' "19th Nervous Breakdown" with Warren Zevon's "Werewolves of London" on the US version. It didn't gain the band any added sales, and alienated hardcore fans, who had to buy the import to get the Stones cover. By this time, the record company was losing interest and the band was going through major personnel changes as well; it would be a while before the Groovies turned up on another full-length album. —*Bruce Eder*

Flamin' Groovies Studio '68 / 1984 / Eva ✦✦✦
The very earliest Flamin' Groovies material ever to be issued, taken from studio tapes cut on January 10, 1968. Lead singer Roy Loney's songs dominate this session, which includes a couple of Lovin' Spoonful numbers and a version of the blues "Sportin' Life"; a couple of the tunes would later show up on their *Sneakers* EP. Most of this material is good-timey, blues/R&B-influenced rock, in the spirit of the earliest recordings of the Charlatans, Dead, and Big Brother. The jugband influence of the Lovin' Spoonful also pervades a few tracks, in an unimpressive fashion. This hardly stacks up with the best San Francisco rock of the time; its appeal will largely lie with Groovies fanatics (a not inconsiderable audience) looking for a glimpse of the group's roots. By far the most impressive track is "Good Morning, Mr. Stone," a seven-minute psychedelic workout with guitar work inspired by Jeff Beck, Pete Townshend, and Jorma Kaukonen, as well as a brief lift of a snatch of the Who's "A Quick One." —*Richie Unterberger*

The Gold Star Tapes / 1984 / Skydog ✦✦✦
The Flamin' Groovies were off Sire Records, and without a major label contract, when this mysterious four-song EP turned up as an import in US shops. The sound is ragged, as the material was taken from acetates rather than master tapes, and the work on this material was never really finished. But oh the covers of Byrds material like "She Don't Care About Time," and the Phil Spector '60s classic "River Deep, Mountain High," which makes every other rock band version of that song (even the one by the Easybeats) look anemic by comparison. —*Bruce Eder*

• **Groovies' Greatest Grooves** / Jul. 1989 / Sire ✦✦✦✦
More or less what it says, a 24-song best-of including much of their finest Sire Records material, including a few rarities and outtakes (including "River Deep, Mountain High," and most of their best Beatles and Dylan covers—but why no real Stones covers?), rounded out with a few of the better tracks from the pre-Sire Kama Sutra period. The notes are voluminous and enjoyable, and the music holds up even two decades later. An essential part of any serious rock record collection. —*Bruce Eder*

Supersneakers / Nov. 19, 1996 / Sundazed ✦✦✦
A combination of the *Sneakers* indie ten-inch from 1968 and ten tracks from a 1968 gig at a San Francisco club. (The live material had previously been issued on the French import *Flamin Groovies '68* in the mid-'80s.) The studio tracks from *Sneakers* decidedly outshine the looser, more indulgent live takes, several of which duplicate *Sneakers* material. It's the definitive document of their pre-major label days, though, when they fused garage rock with blues, psychedelia, and the Lovin' Spoonful, complete with historical liner notes. —*Richie Unterberger*

In Person! / May 6, 1997 / Norton ✦✦✦
While the bins of collector shops have long been glutted with hapless bootlegs and semi-legal compilations of Flamin' Groovies outtakes and demo tapes (reducing a once collectible cult band to "so what?" status with each new release), this live radio broadcast recorded at the Fillmore West does much to enhance their reputation as San Francisco's only "real" rock 'n' roll band during those halcyon days of peace, love and bad sitar music. Recorded during the Fillmore's closing week on June 30, 1971, the band was bottom billed, fourth on the slate under Santana and a host of other hippie bands. It's obvious from this tape that the band took the stage with attitude aplenty, as the opening clarion call of "I Can't Explain" (with its intro and first half inadvertently lopped off by KSAN engineers doing the remote broadcast) and Chuck Berry's "Sweet Little Rock and Roller" quickly attest. But as wonderful as the Groovies were as a cover band supreme (and there *are* some great takes of set staples like "Shakin' All Over," "Have You Seen My Baby," "Walkin' the Dog," and "Louie Louie"), the versions of "Slow Death," "Road House," "Doctor Boogie"—itself a rewrite of Doctor Ross' "Boogie Disease"—and "Teenage Head" show that the band was much more than just enthusiastic revivalists. The disc concludes with an interesting slow non-Yardbirds-like cover of Bo Diddley's "I'm a Man" and the original "Headin' for the Texas Border," taken from a live show at the Matrix in 1970. If you've been put off by the plethora of slipshod packages abounding on this group, take heart, because this one delivers the goods in a loud, proud, and big way. —*Cub Koda*

The Flaming Lips
....
f. 1983, Oklahoma City, OK
Alternative Pop-Rock, Neo-Psychedelia, Dream-Pop
Of the innumerable one-hit wonders littering the cultural landscape, few, if any, were so brave, so frequently brilliant, and so deliciously weird as the Flaming Lips. To even classify the Lips as merely a one-hit wonder is to do the group a grave injustice. Although their standing as a commercial entity proved little more than a blip on the radar screen, their moment of Top 40 success was simply another pit-stop on one of the more surreal and haphazard career trajectories in pop music—an acid-bubblegum band with as much affinity for sweet melodies as blistering noise assaults, their off-kilter sound, uncommon emotional depth and bizarre history (packed with tales of self-immolating fans and the like) firmly established them as one of the true originals of the post-punk era.

The Flaming Lips formed in Oklahoma City in 1983, when founder and guitarist Wayne Coyne allegedly stole a collection of musical instruments from an area church hall and enlisted his vocalist brother Mark and bassist Michael Ivins to start a band. Giving themselves the nonsensical name the Flaming Lips (its origin variously attributed to a porn film, an obscure drug reference, or a dream in which a fiery Virgin Mary plants a kiss on Wayne in the backseat of his car), the band made their live debut at a local transvestite club. After progressing through an endless string of drummers, they recruited percussionist Richard English before recording their self-titled debut, issued on green vinyl on their own Lovely Sorts of Death label in 1985.

When Mark Coyne soon departed to get married, Wayne assumed full control of the group; in addition to remaining its lead guitarist, he also became their primary singer and songwriter. Continuing as a trio, the Lips released 1986's *Hear It Is*, followed a year later by *Oh My Gawd!!* While touring in support of the Butthole Surfers, they played Buffalo, NY, where they were befriended by concert promoter Jonathan Donahue; after a jam session with Donahue's nascent band Mercury Rev, he and Coyne became close friends, and Donahue eventually signed on as the group's sound technician.

After recording 1988's difficult *Telepathic Surgery*, English exited, reducing the Lips to the core duo of Coyne and Ivins; after adding drummer Nathan Roberts, Donahue adopted the name Dingus and became a full-time member in time to cut 1990's stellar *In a Priest Driven Ambulance* while simultaneously recording the brilliant Mercury Rev debut *Yerself Is Steam*. After the band made a series of hopeful phone calls to Warner Bros., the company signed them in 1991, and in 1992 their oft-delayed major-label debut *Hit to Death in the Future Head* appeared to little commercial notice; Donahue soon exited to focus his full energies on Mercury Rev, followed by the departure of Roberts.

With new guitarist Ronald Jones and drummer Steven Drozd, they cut 1993's sublime *Transmissions from the Satellite Heart*, which they supported by playing the second stage at Lollapalooza and touring the nation in a Ryder truck. Initially, the album stiffed; however, nearly a year after its initial release, the single "She Don't Use Jelly" became a grass-roots hit, and against all odds the Flaming Lips found themselves on the Top 40 charts. They took full advantage of their requisite 15 minutes of fame, appearing everywhere from MTV's annual Spring Break broadcast to an arena tour in support of Candlebox to a memorably surreal lip-synched performance on the teen soap opera "Beverly Hills 90210," where supporting character Steve Sanders (portrayed by actor Ian Ziering) uttered the immortal words "You know, I've never been a big fan of alternative music, but these guys rocked the house!"

After the 1994 release of a limited-editon sampler of odds-and-ends titled *Providing Needles for Your Balloons*, the Lips returned in 1995 with *Clouds Taste Metallic*, a strikingly mature and diverse collection highlighted by the singles "Bad Days" (also heard in the film *Batman Forever*), "This Here Giraffe," and "Brainville." Despite the inclusion of the remarkably melodic "Psychiatric Explorations of the Fetus with Needles," "Christmas at the Zoo" (rumored to be under consideration for inclusion on an upcoming John Tesh holiday record), and the epic "Guy Who Got a Headache and Accidentally Saves the World," the album nonetheless failed to live up to the commercial success of *Transmissions*, and the band was once again relegated to cult status.

In 1996 the Lips' world went haywire. First, Jones disappeared to undertake a spiritual odyssey from which he did not return. Then Drozd's hand was almost amputated needlessly after he was bitten by a spider. At about the same time, Ivins was the victim of a bizarre hit-and-run accident when a wheel came off another vehicle and slammed into his car, trapping him inside. Ironically, Coyne was having car problems of his own when rumors of his latest sonic foray—conducting an orchestra of 40 automobiles, all with their tape decks playing spectally composed music at the same time—prompted fan discussion of his possible psychological collapse. "I would try to tell people what I was doing and found that I couldn't explain it very well," Coyne later remarked about the project, dubbed the Parking Lot Experiment. "Plus, I had a sore on the side of my tongue for a week and it made me talk kind of weird. I'm sure they thought I was retarded."

By the next year, the Flaming Lips (who continued as a trio, opting not to attempt to replace Jones) were back in the studio, recording an album that, according to Coyne, would be "so different and exciting it will either make us millionaires or break us"—in short, a set of four discs designed to be played simultaneously. A previously-unreleased track, "Hot Day," also appeared in early 1997 on the soundtrack to Richard Linklater's film *SubUrbia*. —*Jason Ankeny*

The Flaming Lips / 1985 / Restless ✦✦✦
An erratic, underdeveloped debut, the five-track *The Flaming Lips* nonetheless succeeds on the strength of its ingenuity, wit, and bracing dementia. Even from the outset, the group sounds like no one else. "My Own Planet" is a rallying cry of alienation and independence, while "Bag Full of Thoughts" and "Garden of Eyes/Forever Is a Long Time" are idiot-savant gems. —*Jason Ankeny*

Hear It Is / 1986 / Restless ✦✦✦✦
Wayne Coyne assumes full control of the Lips with *Hear It Is*, an aggressively noisy effort that builds significantly upon the promise of their eponymous debut. The opening "With You" is the group's first truly great moment, a heartfelt love song that builds from beautiful simplicity to climax in a tidal wave of sonic mayhem before crashing back to earth. No less impressive are the grungy "Jesus Shootin' Heroin," the luminous "She Is Death," and the childlike "Godzilla Flick." —*Jason Ankeny*

Oh My Gawd!!!... The Flaming Lips / 1987 / Restless ✦✦✦✦
The galvanizing *Oh My Gawd!!!* is a considerable improvement over previous efforts, crystallizing the group's sonic and narrative identity in its embryonic stages. The centerpiece "One Millionth Billionth of a Millisecond on a Sunday Morning" is a ten-minute psychedelic epic of impressively noisy grandeur, while "Love Yer Brain" is a sensitive ode to a troubled companion (albeit one that recommends heavy drug use over suicide). Paranoia runs rampant on the opening "Everything's Explodin'," while "Ode to C.C. Part 2" details a scary brush with a Jesus freak; finally, the title of "Maximum Dream of Evil Knievel" is alone worth the price of admission. —*Jason Ankeny*

Telepathic Surgery / 1989 / Restless ✦✦
The album was designed as showcase for the mind-blowing 23-minute sonic collage "Hell's Angel Cracker Factory," but the Lips realized at the last minute that they probably needed to include some actual songs as well. A disjointed and often difficult record, it's the only true disappointment in the group's oeuvre; by and large, songs like "Shaved Gorilla" and "Chrome Plated Suicide" lack personality, although the monologue "UFO Story" is dandy. —*Jason Ankeny*

In a Priest Driven Ambulance / Sep. 1990 / Restless ✦✦✦
In a Priest Driven Ambulance ranks as the first truly brilliant Flaming Lips album; the first effort to feature guitarist Jonathan "Dingus" Donahue, it's a loose concept record that brings Wayne Coyne's longstanding obsessions with religion bubbling to the surface. The thematic glue creates a structural framework unlike anything found on previous albums, resulting in a newfound sense of cohesion and depth. Songs like "Rainin' Babies" and "Five-Stop Mother Superior Rain" offer unforeseen levels of poignancy, while guitar freak-outs such as "Unconsciously Screamin'" and "Mountain Side" slash and burn with remarkable potency. For the Lips, the future begins here. —*Jason Ankeny*

Hit to Death in the Future Head / Aug. 11, 1992 / Warner Brothers ✦✦✦
With *Hit to Death in the Future Head*, the Lips make the leap to major-label status as though it were the moment they've been waiting for all their lives. Though not as conceptually tight as *In a Priest Driven Ambulance*, the LP is no less cohesive or imaginative, and in its way serves as the bridge between the band's noisier, more hallucinatory indie work and the acid-bubblegum aesthetic perfected on their later Warner Bros. albums. Nowhere are the band's pop smarts more evident than on "The Sun," which freely quotes Carole King's "So Far Away," or on the undeniably catchy "Gingerale Afternoon (The Astrology of a Saturday)" and "Frogs"; tracks like "Felt Good to Burn" and "Halloween on the Barbary Coast," meanwhile, indulge fully in the trademark weirdness that got the group this far. (And speaking of indulgence, check out the unlisted bonus track, which offers some 29 minutes of speaker-hopping static assault.) —*Jason Ankeny*

● **Transmissions from the Satellite Heart** / Jan. 1993 / Warner Brothers ✦✦✦✦
The addition of guitarist Ronald Jones and drummer Steven Drozd recharges the Lips' batteries for the superb *Transmissions from the Satellite Heart*, another prismatic delicacy that continues the group's drift towards pop nirvana. In typical fashion, the record's left-field hit, the freakshow sing-along "She Don't Use Jelly," bears little resemblance to the album as a whole; the remainder of *Transmissions* is much more sonically and structurally ambitious. The towering "Moth in the Incubator" keeps generating new layers of noise before erupting into an

amphetamine waltz; "Pilot Can at the Queer of God" divebombs with kamikaze recklessness; and the slow-burning "Oh My Pregnant Head" is as mind-expanding as its title. —*Jason Ankeny*

Clouds Taste Metallic / Sep. 19, 1995 / Warner Brothers ✦✦✦✦
The same extraordinary madness that infected the best work of Brian Wilson rears its head on the shimmering and melodic *Clouds Taste Metallic*, a masterful collection that completes the Flaming Lips' odyssey into the pop stratosphere. The *Pet Sounds* comparisons are obvious—two of the highlights are titled "This Here Giraffe" and "Christmas at the Zoo"—but not unfair; like Brian Wilson, Wayne Coyne has refined his unique vision into something both highly personal and powerfully universal. Similarly, while Coyne's lyrics remain as acid-damaged and inscrutable as ever, his densely constructed songs convey emotional complexities far beyond the scope of their head-case titles ("Psychiatric Explorations of the Fetus with Needles," "Guy Who Got a Headache and Accidentally Saves the World"); galvanized by equal parts newfound maturity and childlike wonderment, *Clouds Taste Metallic* is both the Flaming Lips' most intricate and most irresistible work. —*Jason Ankeny*

The Flamingos

f. 1952, Chicago, IL
Doo Wop
Both prolific and seminal in their influence and impact, the Flamingos may have been the greatest harmonizing vocal ensemble ever, and were certainly among the premier units of the doo wop/R&B era. Cousins Jake and Zeke Carey moved to Chicago from Baltimore in 1950. They met Paul Wilson and Johnny Carter at the Church of God and Saints of Christ Congregation, a Black Jewish church. They began singing in the choir, and the foursome met Earl Lewis (not the Channels' lead vocalist) through one of the members' sisters, who was Lewis' girlfriend at the time. They originally called themselves the Swallows but had to change names when they found out that a Baltimore group already had the name. Carter suggested El Flamingos, which was changed to the Five Flamingos, and later the Flamingos. Ralph Leon of the King Booking Agency eventually became their manager. Sollie McElroy replaced Lewis as their lead singer in the early '50s, with Lewis joining the Five Echoes. They recorded with Chance in 1953, and "If I Can't Have You" attracted some attention and did well in the Midwest and on the East Coast. "That's My Desire" and "Golden Teardrops" were marvelously sung numbers, particularly "Golden Teardrops," with its sweeping harmonies on top and bottom framing McElroy's wondrous lead. But none of their great Chance recordings generated enough national attention to make the R&B charts, nor did the three numbers they recorded for Parrot. McElroy departed and was replaced by Nate Nelson. They enjoyed their first chart success with Checker in the late '50s, scoring a Top Ten R&B hit with "I'll Be Home" in 1956. They temporarily disbanded in 1956 and regrouped in 1957 with Nelson, Jake Carey, Paul Wilson, and Tommy Hunt as the lineup, and the group now a quartet. Zeke Carey returned in 1958, and they signed with End late that year. "I Only Have Eyes for You" in 1959 was their biggest hit, peaking at No 3 R&B and No. 11 pop. It was a cover of a song that had been a huge hit for Eddy Duchin in 1934, and was the start of a productive period that saw the Flamingos issue four albums for End and get two more R&B Top 30 singles, one the Sam Cooke composition "Nobody Loves Me Like You" in 1960. Hunt left in 1961, and the group returned briefly to Checker in 1964. They later recorded for Phillips, Julman, and Polydor, but couldn't regain their former standing. They remained among the genre's most beloved groups, and anthologies of their material on Chance and Checker have been reissued. In 1993, *The Flamingos Meet the Moonglows* was reissued by Vee-Jay. —*Ron Wynn*

★ **The Doo Bop She Bop: The Best of the Flamingos** / May 1990 / Rhino ✦✦✦✦✦
The Doo Bop She Bop: Best of the Flamingos is an 18-track collection that compiles all of the Flamingos' biggest hits and best songs. *The Doo Bop She Bop* ignores the group's latter-day soul hits and concentrates solely on their doo wop material, which makes for a stronger, more cohesive collection. "I Only Have Eyes for You" is the acknowledged classic, while "I'll Be Home" and "A Kiss from Your Lips" were hits in their own right, but the compilation proves that the Flamingos were one of the greatest doo wop groups with its lesser-known numbers like "The Vow" and "The Ladder of Love." —*Stephen Thomas Erlewine*

Complete Chess Masters Plus / May 20, 1997 / MCA ✦✦✦✦
The Flamingos didn't have many hits while they were at Checker, but those two singles—"I'll Be Home" and "A Kiss from Your Lips"—were terrific, sketching out the lush sound that would later blossom on "I Only Have Eyes for You." *Complete Chess Masters Plus* contains all 18 songs, including two previously unreleased tracks, the group recorded for Checker and Chess, and although it's not a definitive career overview, it's an essential item for collectors of doo wop and vocal R&B, since it's lovingly packaged and contains numerous gems, including "The Vow" and "Dream of a Lifetime." —*Stephen Thomas Erlewine*

Flash and the Pan

f. 1976, Australia
New Wave
The best-known alter-ego of the Vanda/Young songwriting team (the creative force behind the Easybeats), Flash and the Pan began simply as a between-production project in 1976. By 1979, the project had turned out a novelty hit with the single "Hey St. Peter." A second single, "Down Among the Dead," also became a hit throughout Australia and Europe, inspiring the release of the album *Flash and the Pan*. American radio began playing import copies, which led to a deal with Epic Records. The album would soon reach the Top 100 in the US, despite the lack of a supporting tour. They released two more albums with some minor success in the UK but failed to make much impact, due to the part-time nature of the project. —*Chris Woodstra*

● **Collection** / Oct. 4, 1994 / Epic ◆◆◆◆
This 15-track collection provides the best picture of the band. All of the singles, including the classic "Hey St. Peter" and "Down Among the Dead," can be found here, so this should satisfy most listeners. —*Chris Woodstra*

Flash & The Pan/Lights in the Night / Jan. 14, 1997 / Renaissance ◆◆◆

Fleetwood Mac

f. 1967, London, England
Group / Electric British Blues, Blues-Rock, Pop-Rock, British Blues
While most bands undergo a number of changes over the course of their career, few groups experienced such radical stylistic changes as Fleetwood Mac. Initially conceived as a hard-edged British blues combo in the late '60s, the band gradually evolved into a polished pop-rock act over the course of a decade. Throughout all of their incarnations, the only consistent members of Fleetwood Mac were drummer Mick Fleetwood and bassist John McVie, the rhythm section who provided the band with its name. Ironically, they had the least influence over the musical direction of the band. Originally, guitarists Peter Green and Jeremy Spencer provided the band with its gutsy, neo-psychedelic blues-rock sound, but as both guitarists descended into mental illness, the group began moving toward pop-rock with the songwriting of pianist Christine McVie. By the mid-'70s, Fleetwood Mac had relocated to California, where they added the soft-rock duo of Lindsey Buckingham and Stevie Nicks to their lineup. Obsessed with the meticulously arranged pop of the Beach Boys and the Beatles, Buckingham helped the band become one of the most popular groups of the late '70s. Combining soft rock with the confessional introspection of singer-songwriters, Fleetwood Mac created a slick but emotional sound that helped 1977's *Rumours* become one of the biggest-selling albums of all-time. The band retained their popularity into the early '80s, when Buckingham, Nicks, and Christine McVie all began pursuing solo careers. The band reunited for one album, 1987's *Tango in the Night*, before splintering in the late '80s. Buckingham left the group initially, but the band decided to soldier on, releasing one more album before Nicks and McVie left the band in the early '90s, hastening the group's commercial decline.

The roots of Fleetwood Mac lie in John Mayall's legendary British blues outfit the Bluesbreakers. John McVie (bass) was one of the charter members of the Bluesbreakers, joining the group in 1963. Peter Green replaced Eric Clapton in 1966, and Mick Fleetwood (drums) was in the band briefly in 1967. Inspired by the success of Cream, the Yardbirds, and Jimi Hendrix, the trio decided to break away from Mayall in 1967, making their debut at the British Jazz and Blues Festival in August; by that time, slide guitarist Jeremy Spencer had joined the band. Fleetwood Mac soon signed with Blue Horizon, releasing their eponymous debut the next year. *Fleetwood Mac* was an enormous hit in the UK, spending over a year in the Top Ten. Despite its British success, the album was virtually ignored in America. During 1968 the band added guitarist Danny Kirwan. The next year they recorded *Fleetwood Mac in Chicago* with a variety of bluesmen, including Willie Dixon and Otis Spann. The set was released later that year, after the band had left Blue Horizon for a one-album deal with Immediate Records; in the US, they signed with Reprise/Warner Bros., and by 1970, Warner began releasing the band's British records as well.

Fleetwood Mac released *English Rose* and *Then Play On* during 1969, which both indicated that the band were expanding their music, moving away from their blues-purists roots. That year, Green's "Man of the World" and "Oh Well" were No. 2 hits. Though his music was providing the backbone of the group, Peter Green was growing increasingly disturbed, due to his large ingestion of hallucinogenic drugs. After announcing that he was planning to give away all of his earnings away, Green suddenly left the band in the spring of 1970; he released two solo albums over the course of the '70s, but he rarely performed after leaving Fleetwood Mac. The band replaced him with Christine Perfect, a vocalist/pianist who had earned a small but loyal following in the UK by

singing with Spencer Davis and the Chicken Shack. She had already performed uncredited on *Then Play On*. Contractual difficulties prevented her becoming a full-fledged member of Fleetwood Mac until 1971; by that time she had married John McVie.

Christine McVie didn't appear on 1970's *Kiln House*, the first album the band recorded without Peter Green. For that album, Jeremy Spencer dominated the band's musical direction, but he had also been experiencing mental problems because of heavy drug use. During the band's American tour in early 1971, Spencer disappeared; it was later discovered that he left the band to join the religious cult the Children of God. Fleetwood Mac had already been trying to determine the direction of their music, but Spencer's departure sent the band into disarray. Christine McVie and Danny Kirwan began to move the band towards mainstream rock on 1971's *Future Games*, but new guitarist Bob Welch exerted a heavy influence on 1972's *Bare Trees*. Kirwan was fired after *Bare Trees* and was replaced by guitarists Bob Weston and Dave Walker, who appeared on 1973's *Penguin*. Walker left after that album, and Weston departed after making its follow-up, *Mystery to Me* (1973). In 1974, the group's manager Clifford Davis formed a bogus Fleetwood Mac and had the band tour the US. The real Fleetwood Mac won a lawsuit against the imposters, (who began performing under the name Stretch), but the lawsuit kept the band off the road for most of the year. In the interim, they released *Heroes Are Hard to Find*. Late in 1974 Fleetwood Mac moved to California, with hopes of re-starting their career. Welch left the band shortly after the move to form Paris.

Early in 1975 Fleetwood and McVie were auditioning engineers for the band's new album when they heard *Buckingham-Nicks*, an album recorded by the soft-rock duo Lindsey Buckingham and Stevie Nicks. The duo was asked to join the group, and their addition revived the band's musical and commercial fortunes. Not only did the pair write songs, but they brought distinctive talents the band had been lacking. Buckingham was a skilled pop craftsman, capable of arranging a commercial song while keeping it musically adventurous. Nicks had a husky voice and a sexy, hippie, gypsy stage persona that gave the band a charismatic frontwoman. The new lineup of Fleetwood Mac released their eponymous debut in 1975, and it slowly became a huge hit, reaching No. 1 in 1976 on the strength of the singles "Over My Head," "Rhiannon," and "Say You Love Me." The album would eventually sell over five million copies in the US alone.

While Fleetwood Mac had finally attained their long-desired commercial success, the band was fraying behind the scenes. The McVies divorced in 1976, and Buckingham and Nicks' romance ended shortly afterward. The internal tensions formed the basis for the songs on their next album, *Rumours*. Released in the spring of 1977, *Rumours* became a blockbuster success, topping the American and British charts and generating the Top Ten singles "Go Your Own Way," "Dreams," "Don't Stop," and "You Make Loving Fun." It would eventually sell over 17 million copies in the US alone, making it the second biggest-selling album of all time. Fleetwood Mac supported the album with an exhaustive, lucrative tour and then retired to the studio to record the follow-up. A wildly experimental double album conceived largely by Buckingham, *Tusk* (1979) didn't duplicate the enormous success of *Rumours*, but it did go multi-platinum and featured the Top Ten singles "Sara" and "Tusk." In 1980 they released the double-album *Live*.

After the *Tusk* tour, Fleetwood, Buckingham, and Nicks all recorded solo albums. Of the solo projects, Stevie Nicks' *Bella Donna* (1981) was the most successful, peaking at No. 1 and featuring the hit singles "Stop Draggin' My Heart Around," "Leather and Lace," and "Edge of Seventeen." Buckingham's *Law and Order* (1981) was a moderate success, spawning the Top Ten *Trouble*. Fleetwood, for his part, made a world music album called *The Visitor*. Fleetwood Mac reconvened in 1982 for *Mirage*. More conventional and accessible than *Tusk*, *Mirage* reached No. 1 and featured the hit singles "Hold Me" and "Gypsy."

After *Mirage*, Buckingham, Nicks, and Christine McVie all worked on solo albums. There were a number of reasons for the hiatus. Each member had his/her own manager, Nicks was becoming the group's breakaway star, Buckingham was obsessive in the studio, and each member was suffering from various substance addictions. Nicks was able to maintain her popularity, with *The Wild Heart* (1983) and *Rock a Little* (1985) both reaching the Top 15. Christine McVie also had a Top Ten hit with "Got a Hold on Me" in 1984. Buckingham received the strongest reviews of all, but his 1984 album *Go Insane* failed to generate a hit. Fleetwood Mac reunited to record a new album in 1985. Buckingham, who had grown increasingly frustrated with the musical limitations of the band, decided to make it his last project with the group. When the resulting album, *Tango in the Night*, was finally released in 1987 it was greeted with mixed reviews but strong sales, reaching the Top Ten and generating the Top 20 hits "Little Lies," "Seven Wonders," and "Everywhere."

Buckingham left Fleetwood Mac, and the group replaced him with guitarists Billy Burnette and Rick Vito. The new lineup of the band recorded their first album, *Behind the Mask*, in 1990. It became the band's first album since 1975 not to go gold. After its supporting tour, Nicks and Christine McVie announced they would continue to record with the group, but not tour. Vito left in 1991, and the group released the box set *25 Years—The Chain* the next year. The classic Fleetwood Mac lineup of Fleetwood, the McVies, Buckingham, and Nicks reunited to play President Bill Clinton's inauguration in early 1993, but the concert did not lead to a full-fledged reunion. Later that year Nicks was replaced by Bekka Bramlett and Dave Mason; Christine McVie left shortly afterward. The new lineup of Fleetwood Mac began touring in 1994, releasing *Time* the next year to little attention. While the new version of Fleetwood Mac wasn't commercially successful, neither were the solo careers of Buckingham, Nicks, and McVie, prompting speculation about a full-fledged reunion in 1997. —*Stephen Thomas Erlewine*

Peter Green's Fleetwood Mac / Feb. 1968 / Blue Horizon ✦✦✦✦
Fleetwood Mac's debut LP was a highlight of the late '60s British blues boom. Green's always inspired playing, the capable (if erratic) songwriting, and the general panache of the band as a whole placed them leagues above the overcrowded field. Elmore James is a big influence on this set, particularly on the tunes fronted by Jeremy Spencer ("Shake Your Moneymaker," "Got to Move"). Spencer's bluster, however, was outshone by the budding singing and songwriting skills of Green. The guitarist balanced humor and vulnerability on cuts like "Looking for Somebody" and "Long Grey Mare," and with "If I Loved Another Woman," he offered a glimpse of the Latin-blues fusion that he would perfect with "Black Magic Woman." The album was an unexpected smash in the UK, reaching No. 4 on the British charts. —*Richie Unterberger*

English Rose / Jan. 1969 / Epic ✦✦✦✦
Under the direction of Peter Green, Fleetwood Mac is heard as a British blues group, although its most notable performances are on Green's original tunes "Black Magic Woman" and "Albatross," both British hits. —*William Ruhlmann*

Pious Bird of Good Omen [Comp] / Aug. 1969 / Blue Horizon ✦✦✦✦
This is a compilation of Fleetwood Mac's early period, 1967-1968, featuring both sides of its debut single, "I Believe My Time Ain't Long"/"Rambling Pony" and many blues covers, as well as the hits "Albatross" and "Black Magic Woman." —*William Ruhlmann*

Then Play On / Oct. 1969 / Reprise ✦✦✦
The most diverse and accomplished album by the Peter Green-led lineup. Features some wrenching, introspective originals that draw from both blues and progressive rock, highlighted by the doomy British hit single "Oh Well." —*Richie Unterberger*

Kiln House / Sep. 1970 / Reprise ✦✦✦
Fleetwood Mac's first album after the departure of their nominal leader, Peter Green, finds the remaining members, Mick Fleetwood, John McVie, Jeremy Spencer, and Danny Kirwan (plus McVie's wife, Christine) trying to maintain the band's guitar-rave, blues-rock approach, with the burden falling on Spencer and Kirwan. They don't embarrass themselves, but none of this is of the caliber of Green's work. —*William Ruhlmann*

Future Games / Nov. 1971 / Reprise ✦✦✦
By the time of this album's release, Jeremy Spencer had been replaced by Bob Welch and Christine McVie had begun to assert herself more as a singer and songwriter. The result is a distinct move toward folk-rock and pop; this album sounds almost nothing like Peter Green's Fleetwood Mac. Welch's eight-minute title track has one of his characteristic haunting melodies, and with pruning and better editing it could have been a hit. Christine McVie's "Show Me a Smile" is one of her loveliest ballads. Initial popular reaction was mixed; the album didn't sell as well as *Kiln House*, but it sold better than any of the band's first three albums in the US. In the UK, where the original lineup had been more successful, *Future Games* didn't chart at all, the same fate that would befall the rest of its albums until the Lindsey Buckingham-Stevie Nicks era. —*William Ruhlmann*

Bare Trees / Mar. 1972 / Reprise ✦✦✦✦
On *Bare Trees*, Fleetwood Mac married the gritty electric blues-rock of their earlier incarnations to the classic pop sensibilities that would later become fully realized in 1975's *Fleetwood Mac*. Bob Welch's "Sentimental Lady" and Christine McVie's soulful "Spare Me a Little of Your Love" are highlights. Danny Kirwan revealed an ability to compose highly melodic material that didn't constrain the band's legendary musical chemistry. —*Rick Clark*

Penguin / Mar. 1973 / Reprise ✦✦
Fleetwood Mac's first album made after the departure of Danny Kirwan features the additions of guitarist Bob Weston and singer Dave Walker. By now Bob Welch and Christine McVie were the dominant forces in the band, and all traces of blues-rock were gone, replaced by Welch's hypnotic melodies and McVie's romantic sentiments married to uptempo pop tunes. This album gave Fleetwood Mac its best US chart showing yet, but the wonder is that this phase in the band's career wasn't even more popular. —*William Ruhlmann*

Mystery to Me / Oct. 1973 / Reprise ✦✦✦
At this point, Fleetwood Mac is a mainstream rock band whose songs alternate between guitarist/singer Robert Welch and keyboard player/singer Christine McVie. —*William Ruhlmann*

Heroes Are Hard to Find / Sep. 1974 / Reprise ✦✦✦
Welch's peak as a songwriter (with new highs by Christine McVie) is also his swan song with the group. —*William Ruhlmann*

Fleetwood Mac in Chicago / 1975 / Sire ✦✦
A two-record set culled from sessions the Peter Green/Danny Kirwan/Mick Fleetwood/John McVie edition of the band held at Chess Studios in Chicago in January 1969 with such blues legends as Otis Spann and Willie Dixon. Despite their awe, the Brits hold their own on a set of standards. (Reissued on CD under the title *In Chicago 1969* on April 26, 1994.) —*William Ruhlmann*

☆ **Fleetwood Mac** / Jul. 1975 / Reprise ✦✦✦✦✦
"Monday Morning," a sunny slice of folk-rock with Beach Boys harmonies, opens *Fleetwood Mac* and makes it clear that the band is no longer a blues-rock outfit. Lindsey Buckingham and Stevie Nicks were the catalysts for Fleetwood Mac's successful re-emergence as a mainstream pop-rock band. While Buckingham contributed only three songs, he helped the band develop a coherent vision, providing crystal clear backings for Nicks' hippie anthems and Christine McVie's remarkably improved pop-soul. McVie dominates the album, contributing some of her finest songs, including the sighing "Over My Head" and the bouncy "Say You Love Me." Nicks' songs function as folky counterpoints to McVie's sweet pop, and she rarely wrote songs as memorably affecting as "Rhiannon (Will You Ever Win)" or "Landslide." Remarkably, *Fleetwood Mac* is a blockbuster album that isn't dominated by its hit singles, and its album tracks ("World Turning," "Sugar Daddy," "Crystal") demonstrate a depth of both songwriting and musicality that blossomed on *Rumours*. —*Stephen Thomas Erlewine*

Original Fleetwood Mac / 1977 / Sire ✦✦
This collection of outtakes from the group's early days probably dates from 1967-68, and finds the band at their most reverently bluesy. Peter Green wrote most of the material on this set, which is quite similar to the band's first couple of albums in its purist British take on traditional electric blues forms. The material, however, isn't nearly as strong as the best early Fleetwood Mac; not that the band should be faulted for that, as this is an outtake collection, after all. A couple of the tunes featuring Jeremy Spencer are actually taken from an audition that Spencer's pre-Fleetwood Mac outfit, the Levi Set, recorded for the Blue Horizon label in England. The best track is the driving instrumental "Fleetwood Mac," and has been rumored to be an outtake from Green's days with John Mayall's Bluesbreakers. —*Richie Unterberger*

★ **Rumours** / Feb. 4, 1977 / Reprise ✦✦✦✦✦
The new lineup that Fleetwood Mac successfully unveiled with their eponymous 1975 album became even more successful with the multi-platinum *Rumours*, which was the band's most celebrated album and one of the best-selling albums of all time. To be sure, this was a very different-sounding Fleetwood Mac than the blues-rock outfit of the late '60s—and this edition of the band generally wasn't well received by rock critics, who tend to be critical of all things commercial. But as commercial and slick as *Rumours* is, the music has a lot of heart, and never comes across as insincere. From Christine McVie's optimistic "Don't Stop" (which President Bill Clinton used as his campaign theme song in 1992) to Lindsey Buckingham's remorseful "Go Your Own Way," *Rumours* is consistently memorable. In fact, the folk-ish "Gold Dust Woman" (covered by Courtney Love and Hole in 1996) and the melancholy hit "Dreams" made it quite clear just how much depth and substance Stevie Nicks was capable of. —*Alex Henderson*

Tusk / Oct. 1979 / Reprise ✦✦✦✦
Where *Rumours* achieved greatness through turmoil, its double album followup *Tusk* is the sound of a band imploding. Lindsey Buckingham began to assume control of Fleetwood Mac during the *Rumours* sessions, but he dominates *Tusk*, turning the album into a paranoid roller-coaster ride where sweet soft-rock is offset by feverish cocaine fantasies. Christine McVie and Stevie Nicks don't deviate from their established balladry, soft-rock, and folk-rock templates, and all their songs are first-rate, whether it's McVie's "Over and Over" or Nicks' "Sara." Buckingham gives these mainstream-oriented songs off-kilter arrangements, so they can fit neatly with his nervy, insular, yet catchy songs. Alternating bracing pop-rockers like "The Ledge" and "What Makes You Think You're the One" with melancholic, Beach Boys-style ballads like "Save Me a Place" and "That's All Forever," Buckingham subverts pop-rock with weird arrangements and unpredictable melodies, which are nevertheless given accessible productions. This is as weird as mainstream pop can get, pushing on the borders of the avant-garde. Even its hit title track is a strange, menacing threat punctuated by a marching band. Because of its ambitions, *Tusk* failed to replicate the success of its two predecessors (it still went double platinum), but it earned a dedicated cult audience for fans of twisted, melodic pop. —*Stephen Thomas Erlewine*

Fleetwood Mac Live / Dec. 1980 / Reprise ✦✦✦
Fleetwood Mac's first live album finds it at its popular height, pumping out hit after hit. To its credit, the group nevertheless puts out: Fleetwood drums like a demon and Buckingham plays fiercely. All the hits you'd expect are here, spread across two discs, and there's also a charming backstage rendition of the Beach Boys' "Farmer's Daughter." — *William Ruhlmann*

Mirage / Jun. 1982 / Reprise ✦✦✦
Fleetwood Mac retreated from the insular strangeness of *Tusk* and returned to straightforward pop songcraft for *Mirage*. Boasting a glossy, friendly production that makes even the lesser numbers pleasant and ingratiating, *Mirage* suffers from a lack of substance. *Rumours* had raw emotion to give it a core, and *Tusk* had Lindsey Buckingham's runaway ambition. For its part, *Mirage* sounds as if its sole goal is to sustain Fleetwood Mac's popularity, and while there may be a handful of terrific songs—notably the hit singles "Gypsy," "Love in Store" and "Hold Me"—it simply isn't as compelling as the group's previous three albums. —*Stephen Thomas Erlewine*

Jumping at Shadows / 1985 / Varrick ✦✦✦
Recorded live in Boston in 1969, this finds the Peter Green-era Mac at their best on seven lengthy but focused cuts. Includes versions of "Black Magic Woman" and "Oh Well," as well as a couple of straight blues covers and some Danny Kirwan material. —*Richie Unterberger*

Cerulean / 1985 / Shanghai ✦✦✦
From the same 1969 Boston gigs that produced *Jumping at Shadows*, this double album's appeal is more limited, with a heavier emphasis on straight blues boogie and eccentric '50s rock 'n' roll parodies that featured Jeremy Spencer. Highlights are the 16-minute version of the British hit "Green Manalishi" and the 24-minute version of "Rattlesnake Shake." —*Richie Unterberger*

Tango in the Night / 1987 / Reprise ✦✦✦
Artistically and commercially, the Stevie Nicks/Lindsey Buckingham/Mick Fleetwood/Christine and John McVie edition of Fleetwood Mac had been on a roll for over a decade when *Tango in the Night* was released in early 1987. This would, unfortunately, be Buckingham's last album with the pop-rock supergroup; he definitely ended his association with the band on a creative high note. Serving as the album's main producer, Buckingham gives an edgy quality to everything from the haunting "Isn't It Midnight" to the poetic "Seven Wonders" to the dreamy "Everywhere." Though Buckingham doesn't overproduce, his thoughtful use of synthesizers is a major asset. Without question, "Family Man" and "Caroline" are among the best songs ever written by Buckingham, who consistently brings out the best in his colleagues on this superb album. —*Alex Henderson*

● **Greatest Hits [Reprise]** / Nov. 1988 / Reprise ✦✦✦✦
Greatest Hits is a fine overview of Fleetwood Mac's hit-making years, containing the bulk of the group's Top 40 hits of the late '70s and '80s, including "Over My Head," "Rhiannon," "Say You Love Me," "Go Your Own Way," "Dreams," "Don't Stop," "Tusk," "Sara," "Hold Me," "Gypsy," and "Little Lies." Minor hits like "Think About Me," "Love in Store" and "Seven Wonders" are missing, making room for the new songs "As Long As You Follow" (which actually became a hit) and "No Questions Asked." Overall, *Greatest Hits* is an excellent choice for casual listeners. —*Stephen Thomas Erlewine*

Behind the Mask / Apr. 10, 1990 / Reprise ✦✦
Lindsey Buckingham's departure proved to be a severe blow when Fleetwood Mac unveiled a new lineup with the disappointing *Behind the Mask*. Stevie Nicks' last album with the band. Nicks, Christine and John McVie, and Mick Fleetwood are joined by new members Rick Vito (vocals, lead guitar) and Billy Burnette (vocals, guitar) on this generally weak effort. The production (courtesy of Greg Ladanyi and Fleetwood Mac) is often bland and faceless, and most of the songs are among the least inspired the band ever recorded. The album has a few strong points, including "Save Me" and "Freedom," a haunting number featuring Nicks. But most of the material is quite forgettable. And there would be even less reason for optimism in 1993, when Nicks left as well. —*Alex Henderson*

25 Years: The Chain / Nov. 24, 1992 / Reprise ✦✦✦
Overall, Fleetwood Mac's four-CD box set, *25 Years—The Chain*, contains a lot of great music, with plenty of the 1970s hits that made them one of the biggest bands in the world. It fails as a complete chronicle; not enough weight is given to the early, blues-based Mac with Peter Green, and there are too many songs (nearly a whole disc's worth) from the lightweight 1980s albums. Also, the haphazard song sequencing doesn't help matters—it doesn't make the case for Fleetwood Mac's music as a body of work, and it doesn't trace the evolution, which should be apparent from the diversity of the music. If nothing else, *25 Years—The Chain* offers evidence that Lindsey Buckingham was a brilliant pop composer and that the band's '70s success was well-deserved. —*Stephen Thomas Erlewine*

Peter Green's Fleetwood Mac Live at the BBC / Oct. 1995 / Castle ✦✦
A substantial (and official) supplement to the band's recorded legacy with Peter Green, this double CD features 36 songs broadcast between 1967 and 1971, in mostly superlative sound. (The few numbers that aren't 100% clean are certainly of listenable fidelity.) The title, though, isn't 100% accurate; half a dozen tracks were recorded shortly after Green left the band, and since Green is still listed as part of the lineup for all but one of these in the liner notes, Castle Communications either has the dates or personnel wrong. Anyway, the music gives a good idea of the range of the band in their earliest, and by many accounts, best incarnation. It is not, however, all blues-rock by any means; quite a few of these are given over to Jeremy Spencer-dominated parodies of '50s rock, and while these are entertaining in a modest fashion, the best moments, unsurprisingly, are when guitarists Danny Kirwan and (more particularly) Green play their own material. Some of Green's most well-known compositions from the era are here ("Man of the World," "Albatross," "Rattlesnake Shake," and "Oh Well"), and in the usual BBC tradition these have a sparer and rougher feel than the studio versions, though they don't neither match nor redefine them. Of most interest to early Mac fans will be the inclusion of several numbers they never recorded in the studio (although some, like "Sandy Mary" and "Only You," did appear on live albums that weren't issued until the 1980s). "Preachin'," "Preachin' Blues," and "Early Morning Come" are otherwise unavailable showcases for Spencer, Green, and Kirwan, respectively, that demonstrate their facility with no-nonsense, down-home blues when they got in a serious mood. While this isn't as essential a collection as *Then Play On* or the numerous best-of anthologies covering the Peter Green era, it presents more solid evidence of the band's skills in both blues-rock and surprisingly straight rock (a cover of Tim Hardin's "Hang On to a Dream" is the surprise find of the set), though some may find the detours into comedy and '50s rock irksome. —*Richie Unterberger*

Time / Oct. 10, 1995 / Warner Brothers ✦✦
Fleetwood Mac suffered more personnel changes after the release of *Behind the Mask* in 1990, with Stevie Nicks and Rick Vito leaving, to be replaced by newcomer Bekka Bramlett (daughter of Delaney and Bonnie) and veteran Dave Mason. As a result, the group slipped down another notch in terms of quality and attention. Christine McVie could always be relied on to turn in her quotient of four or five perky songs of romantic devotion; Mason checked in with "Blow by Blow," a statement of renewed purpose that was braver than it was accurate; and Bramlett was an appealing, emotive singer. But despite the familiar rhythm section, this simply was not the group that made the great blues-rock of the 1960s or the group that made the great pop-rock of the '70s. And nobody was fooled. *Time* didn't even make the charts. —*William Ruhlmann*

The Fleetwoods

f. 1958, Olympia, WA, **db.** 1963
Pop, Doo Wop, Pop-Rock

Although the Fleetwoods' sound was smooth, without many of the rougher edges of doo wop groups, they were one of the few White vocal groups of the late '50s and early '60s to enjoy success not only on the pop charts, but also on the R&B charts. The Fleetwoods' forte was ballads. Beginning with their 1959 debut single "Come Softly to Me," the group racked up a number of hits over the next three years, and nearly all of them were ballads. The group broke up in 1963, but their songs—particularly "Come Softly to Me"—became pop-rock classics of the pre-British Invasion era.

Gretchen Christopher, Barbara Ellis, and Gary Troxell formed the Fleetwoods while attending high school in Olympia, WA. Originally the group consisted only of Christopher and Ellis, but the duo soon asked Troxell to accompany them on trumpet. Shortly after his arrival in the group, Troxell abandoned the trumpet and concentrated on singing, after the other two members heard a portion of a song he had written. After some contributions from Christopher and Ellis, the group had written "Come Softly to Me." They began performing the song at various events around Olympia, eventually gaining the attention of Bob Reisdorff, who ran the Seattle-based Dolphin Records.

Dolphin released "Come Softly to Me" early in 1959 and the song became an instant hit, climbing to No. 1 on the pop charts and No. 5 on the R&B charts; it also reached the Top Ten in UK. The Fleetwoods weren't able to immediately produce a follow-up single as successful as their debut, but their third single, "Mr. Blue," was a No. 1 pop and Top Five R&B hit in the US in late 1959. By the time of its release, Dolphin had changed its name to Dolton. For the next three years the Fleetwoods had a string of minor pop hits. The group wasn't able to consistently place singles in the upper regions of the charts, partially because Troxell was drafted at the height of the group's popularity at the end of 1959. Troxell was replaced by Vic Dana, who would later have a string of his own hit singles in the early '60s. The Fleetwoods' last Top Ten single arrived in the spring of 1961, when "Tragedy" climbed the US charts. The group disbanded two years later, after releasing their final single, a cover of Jesse Belvin's "Goodnight My Love." Over the next three decades the Fleetwoods reunited occasionally to perform concerts and oldies revues. In 1973 the group recorded an album with producer Jerry Dennon, but it was unsuccessful. In 1990 the Fleetwoods—featuring Christopher, Troxel, and instead of Ellis a singer named Cheryl Huggins—played a tour on the American oldies circuit after Rhino released the *Best of the Fleetwoods*. —*Stephen Thomas Erlewine*

● **The Best of the Fleetwoods** / May 1990 / Rhino ◆◆◆◆
Rhino's *Best of the Fleetwoods* contains all of their hits ("Come Softly to Me," "Mr. Blue," and 16 other songs) on a smartly assembled collection. —*Stephen Thomas Erlewine*

Come Softly to Me: the Very Best of The Fleetwoods / Aug. 10, 1993 / EMI ◆◆◆◆
The single-disc collection *Come Softly to Me—The Very Best of the Fleetwoods* is a treasure for devoted fans, featuring alternate takes, radio commercials, a comprehensive discography, fine liner notes, and unreleased tracks. Casual listeners will find all of this material extraneous; they will find everything they need on Rhino's collection. —*Stephen Thomas Erlewine*

Flipper

f. 1978, San Francisco, CA
Alternative Pop-Rock, Hardcore Punk
They came, they saw, and they conquered—sort of. Never topping the charts or possessing a huge following, San Francisco's Flipper, even in today's alternarock sweepstakes, would still be considered a fringe act. But in 1982 they were the toast of rock critics across the country with their post-hardcore punk masterpiece "Sex Bomb." Clocking in at over seven minutes, possessing one riff played over and over (and sloppier and sloppier), with vocalist Will Shatter screaming rather than singing (total lyrics: "She's a sex bomb/My baby/yeah"), it was a remarkable record: loud, proud, defiantly obnoxious, and relentlessly dumb. But in its own gleeful and intentionally moronic way it was (and remains) a perfect record.

With "Sex Bomb" providing the impetus, Shatter and fellow Flippers vocalist/bassist Bruce Loose, drummer Steve DePace, and guitarist Ted Falconi emerged from the fractious muck of the California hardcore punk scene (Shatter and DePace played in the Bay area hardcore band Negative Trend in the late '70s) with a crushingly loud, slowed-down sound that resembled the Stooges at their most drug-addled (cf. "We Will Fall" from the first Stooges LP). Flipper didn't care if you loved or loathed them (most everyone I knew loathed them), they simply played until you couldn't stand it anymore. There was something wonderfully uncomplicated about this attitude, which is probably the reason that Flipper, despite being seen as a one-shot band, had a career that lasted longer than 15 minutes.

Their debut album, *Album—Generic Flipper*, included "Sex Bomb" along with a handful of good-to-great songs about anonymity and desperation that were not all bleak or without moments of humor. In fact, Flipper may have been the first hardcore/post-hardcore band to essay life-affirming messages on its album (no matter how tongue-in-cheek it might sound). So, although there's a track called "Life Is Cheap" there is also "Life" which offers the sentiment: "I too have sung death's praises/ But I'm not gonna sing that song anymore." Adding the oft-stated sentiment, "Life is the only thing worth living for." Hmmm. How, uh, unpunk.

With much of the rock press singing their praises (and deservedly so), Flipper went on to demi-celebrity status as the reigning kings of American underground rock, for a few years. They never released anything as mind-blowingly good as *Album*, but until they split up in 1987, the music was usually very good. Precipitating their breakup was Shatter's death from a heroin overdose, with the remaining members spending the next half dozen years stepping in and out of music. In 1992, Flipper fan and American Recordings label honcho Rick Rubin encouraged the remaining members to record a new album. The subsequent effort, *American Grayfishy*, only hinted at their greatness. —*John Dougan*

● **Album—Generic Flipper** / 1982 / Def American ◆◆◆◆
It's an exercise in futility to write hundreds of words about a record so gloriously simple and direct. Thudding, loud, and liberating, this is a classic piece of American underground rock. As the old expression goes, made loud to be played loud. —*John Dougan*

Gone Fishin' / 1984 / Subterranean ◆◆◆
After the glow of *Album*, *Gone Fishin'* may sound like a bit of a disappointment, primarily due to the cleaned up (for Flipper anyway) sound, but that shouldn't stop you from enjoying this record. Not as confrontational or as gloriously unhinged, *Gone Fishin'* still has moments that will poleaxe you with their power. —*John Dougan*

Blow'n' Chunks: Live / 1984 / Combat ◆◆
Recorded live in 1983, this includes tracks from *Album* and some that would show up on their next LP. Recorded with all the subtlety of trains colliding at high speed, this is a ferocious, intimidating chunk of noise

that gets to the heart of Flipper's caustic and confrontational live shows. —*John Dougan*

Public Flipper Limited / 1986 / Subterranean ◆◆◆
A two-record set of live material recorded between 1980-82, this is as good as *Blow'n' Chunks* and essential for born-again Flipperphiles. The sound is messy and grimy, but that enhances the experience. It's easy to see that *Album* was without a doubt their benchmark record and that even the good material released after it (like this LP) couldn't equal its high (low?) standards. —*John Dougan*

Sex Bomb Baby / 1988 / Subterranean ◆◆◆
In terms of quality, this is nearly as good as *Album*. A collection of singles with some odds and ends thrown in, *Sex Bomb Baby* reveals more of Flipper's intoxicating anarchy. Includes the great "The Woman Who Swallowed a Fly," a children's story perverted in a way you've never heard before. This is an important addition to any Flipper collection. —*John Dougan*

American Grafishy / Jan. 12, 1993 / Warner Brothers ◆◆
Flipper's 1993 comeback album *American Grafishy* was the band's tightest record. Consequently, it was also their heaviest and most predictable album. Remove the loose clatter and amateurish recklessness that always distinguished the band, and nothing distinctive is left. And that's what happened on *American Grafishy*. —*Stephen Thomas Erlewine*

A Flock of Seagulls

f. 1980, Liverpool, England, **db.** 1989
New Wave, New Romantic
As well-known for their bizarrely teased hair as their hit single "I Ran (So Far Away)," A Flock of Seagulls were one of the most infamous one-hit wonders of the New Wave era. Growing out the synth-heavy and ruthlessly stylish New Romantic movement, A Flock of Seagulls were a little too robotic and arrived a little too late to be true New Romantics, but their sleek dance-pop was in debt to the short-lived movement. The group benefitted considerably from MTV's heavy rotation of the "I Ran" video in the summer of 1982, but they were unable to capitalize on their sudden success and disappeared nearly as quickly as they rocketed up the charts.

Hairdresser Mike Score (lead vocals, keyboards) formed A Flock of Seagulls with his brother Ali (drums) and fellow hairdresser Frank Maudsley (bass) in 1980, adding guitarist Paul Reynolds several months later. The group released their debut EP on Cocteau Records early in 1981, and while the record failed to chart, its lead track "Telecommunication" became an underground hit in Eurodisco and New Wave clubs. The band signed a contract with Jive by the end of the year, and their eponymous debut album appeared in the spring of 1982. "I Ran (So Far Away)" was released as the first single from the album, and MTV quickly picked up on its icily attractive video, which featured long shots of Mike Score and his distinctive, cascading hair. The single climbed into the American Top Ten, taking the album with it. In the UK, "I Ran" didn't make the Top 40, but "Wishing (If I Had a Photograph of You)" reached No. Ten later that year; in America, that single became a Top 40 hit in 1983, after "Space Age Love Song" peaked at No. 30. "Wishing" was taken from the group's second album, *Listen* (1983), which was moderately successful.

However, the band's fortunes crashed shortly after the release of *Listen*, as 1984's *The Story of a Young Heart* failed to produce any hit singles. Reynolds left after the album and was replaced by Gary Steadnin; the band also added keyboardist Chris Chryssaphis. The new lineup was showcased on 1986's *Dream Come True*, which failed to chart. Shortly after its release, the band broke up. Mike Score assembled a new lineup in 1989, releasing the single "Magic" and touring the USA. The band failed to make any impact and split by the end of the year. —*Stephen Thomas Erlewine*

A Flock of Seagulls / 1982 / Jive ◆◆◆◆
A Flock of Seagulls scored one big hit, "I Ran," in the driving, quick-tempo dance style that characterized most of their work. It's here, along with several similar tracks. —*William Ruhlmann*

The Story of a Young Heart / Aug. 1984 / Jive/Arista ◆◆
The fortunes of A Flock of Seagulls, which had diminished when *Listen*, the follow-up to the self-titled debut album, had failed to match its success, fell further with this third album. The group's beat-happy synthesized sound remained in place, as it had since the Top Ten success of "I Ran (So Far Away)." But this time the best showing they could manage was the singles chart entry "The More You Live, the More You Love," and *The Story of a Young Heart* became their last album to enjoy even modest sales. —*William Ruhlmann*

● **The Best of A Flock of Seagulls** / 1987 / Jive ◆◆◆◆
Every good song A Flock of Seagulls ever recorded is available on this fine collection, including the new wave classic "I Ran (So Far Away)." —*Stephen Thomas Erlewine*

Eddie Floyd

b. Jun. 25, 1935, Montgomery, AL
Vocals / Soul
Eddie Floyd came aboard the good ship Stax at the behest of his friend Al Bell and immediately made himself useful as a composer for label-mates Carla Thomas, William Bell, Otis Redding (originally intended to be the recipient of "Knock on Wood"), and Atlantic's Wilson Pickett.

Floyd's own mid-'60s output included "Raise Your Hand," which used the same Booker T. & the MGs-powered thrust as "Knock on Wood," and "Big Bird," written partially in shocked response to the tragic death of Redding. Floyd remained loyal to Stax right up to its bitter demise, his engaging vocals resulting in major hits with the gentle "I've Never Found a Girl" and a lively remake of Sam Cooke's "Bring It On Home to Me."

Whenever Floyd re-teams with his old Stax pals—guitarist Steve Cropper, bassist Duck Dunn, and sometimes Booker T. Jones on organ—the long-ago Memphis magic instantly returns. With Floyd happily leading the throngs through "Raise Your Hand" and "Knock on Wood," it's 1966 all over again. —*Bill Dahl*

Knock on Wood / 1967 / Stax ✦✦✦✦
In contrast to the 1970s—when artists ranging from Curtis Mayfield to Parliament/Funkadelic were praised for their albums—singles defined soul music in the 1960s. It has often been pointed out that many Stax and Motown albums of the '60s had their share of filler; nonetheless, others were full of gems that should have been released as singles. Reissued on CD in 1991, *Knock on Wood* is one of Eddie Floyd's best albums. The soul shouter successfully embraced sleeker Northern soul on other projects, but here, he sticks to the type of raw, hard-edged Memphis soul that Stax was first known for. From the unforgettable title song (a No. 1 R&B hit) to covers of J.J. Jackson's "But It's Alright," Jerry Butler's "I Stand Accused," and Wilson Pickett's "634-5789," this CD beautifully illustrates the splendor of down-home Southern R&B. —*Alex Henderson*

I've Never Found a Girl / 1968 / Stax ✦✦✦
The title track was one of Floyd's biggest hits, while the other songs were fairly standard Southern soul, not particularly outstanding by Stax standards but well sung and performed. —*Ron Wynn*

You've Got to Have Eddie / 1969 / Stax ✦✦✦
Although he wasn't getting massive hits, Eddie Floyd continued to make solid Southern soul material in the late '60s. This album did have three moderately successful singles, but more importantly, every track features effective wailing leads and country/blues arrangements. An excellent example of the Stax sound. —*Ron Wynn*

California Girl / 1970 / Stax ✦✦✦
Eddie Floyd got the '70s underway in fine form with this release. The title track and two other singles, including a good version of "My Girl," made their way into the charts, and Floyd got good mileage out of the album, even though there were danger signs ahead for the Stax label. —*Ron Wynn*

Down to Earth / 1971 / Stax ✦✦
Another consistent release for Eddie Floyd, although it met with less success than most of his other releases. Only one single charted, and it didn't stay there long. But Floyd still sang with hard-edged drive and conviction, and he had the reliable Stax studio pros and producers giving it the necessary support. —*Ron Wynn*

Baby Lay Your Head Down / 1973 / Stax ✦✦
Eddie Floyd got one of his last chart hits with the title track, a song that initially was being circulated as "Baby, Let Me Take You in My Arms." The rest of the album was formula soul, well produced, earnestly sung, and expertly played, but still formula material. —*Ron Wynn*

● **Chronicle** / 1979 / Stax ✦✦✦✦
Singer-songwriter/producer Eddie Floyd, a former member of the Falcons, shines on originals such as "Soul Street" and "I've Got to Have Your Love" as well as covers such as Sam Cooke's "Bring It On Home to Me" and Smokey Robinson's "My Girl." This 1979 collection includes all of Floyd's singles between 1968 and 1974.

Rare Stamps / Mar. 21, 1993 / Stax ✦✦✦✦
A pair of remarkable soul hits, "Knock on Wood" and "I've Never Found a Girl," enabled Eddie Floyd to attain national success in 1968. But the longtime singer and composer, whose roots dated back to the Detroit group the Falcons in the late '50s, was a steady, if not spectacular, performer for many years before and after those two songs. Several of Floyd's finest pieces are compiled on the 25-track CD *Rare Stamps*, including a wonderful testimonial to Otis Redding, "Big Bird." There are also two super duets with Mavis Staples, "Never Let You Go" and "Ain't That Good," which rank with anything that the label issued. —*Ron Wynn*

The Flying Burrito Brothers

f. 1969, Nashville, TN
Country-Rock
The Flying Burrito Brothers helped forge the connection between rock and country, and with their 1969 debut album, *The Gilded Palace of Sin*, they virtually invented country-rock. Though the band's glory days were brief, they left behind a small body of work that proved vastly influential, both in rock and country. The Flying Burrito Brothers reunited in the '70s, albeit without their founding members Gram Parsons and Chris Hillman, and continued performing and recording in a variety of incarnations into the '80s.

Originally, the Flying Burrito Brothers were a group of Los Angeles musicians who gathered to jam. Gram Parsons and Chris Hillman took the band's name when they were forming a band after leaving the Byrds. Parsons had helped steer the Byrds toward country during his brief stint with the band, as captured on the 1968 album *Sweetheart of the Rodeo*. After the release of *Sweetheart*, he left the Byrds, followed shortly afterward by Hillman. The duo added pedal steel guitarist "Sneaky" Pete Kleinow and bassist Chris Ethridge to the band and set about recording their debut album with a variety of session drummers.

The Gilded Palace of Sin, the Flying Burrito Brothers' debut album, was released in the spring of 1969. Although the album sold only 40,000 copies, the band developed a devoted following, which happened to include many prominent musicians in Los Angeles, as well as Bob Dylan and the Rolling Stones. Around this time, Parsons and Stones guitarist Keith Richards became good friends, which led to Parsons' losing interest in the Burritos. Before the band recorded their second album, Ethridge left and was replaced by Bernie Leadon, and the group hired ex-Byrd Michael Clarke as their permanent drummer.

Burrito Deluxe, the group's second album, was released in the spring of 1970. After its release, Gram Parsons left the group and was replaced by Rick Roberts, a California songwriter. Roberts' first album with the band, *The Flying Burrito Brothers*, was released in 1971. After its release, Kleinow left to become a session musician, and Leadon departed to join the Eagles. The Burritos hired pedal steel guitarist Al Perkins and bassist Roger Bush to replace them, as well as adding guitarist Kenny Wertz and fiddler Byron Berline to the lineup. This new version of the group recorded the live album *The Last of the Red Hot Burritos*, which was released in 1972. Before its release, the band splintered. Berline, Bush, and Wertz left to form Country Gazette, while Hillman and Perkins joined Manassas. Roberts assembled a new band to tour Europe in 1973 and then dissolved the group, choosing to pursue a solo career. Roberts would later form Firefall with Michael Clarke.

Close Up the Honky Tonks, a double-album Flying Burrito Brothers compilation, was released in 1974 because of the burgeoning interest in Gram Parsons. Capitalizing on the collection and the cult forming around Parsons, Kleinow and Ethridge formed a new version of the Flying Burrito Brothers in 1975. The duo recruited Floyd "Gib" Gilbeau (vocals, guitar, fiddle), bassist Joel Scott Hill, and drummer Gene Parsons and recorded *Flying Again*, which was released on Columbia Records in 1975.

Ethridge left the band after the release of *Flying Again;* he was replaced by Skip Battin, who appeared on the 1976 album *Airborne.* Also in 1976, a collection of Gram Parsons-era outtakes entitled *Sleepless Nights* was released on A&M Records.

For the two decades after their 1975 reunion, the Flying Burrito Brothers performed and recorded sporadically, undergoing the occasional lineup change. In 1979 the group released *Live from Tokyo* on Regency Records; the album spawned their first country hit, a cover of Merle Haggard's "White Line Fever," which hit the charts in 1980. Also in 1980 the group abbreviated its name to the Burrito Brothers when they signed a contract with Curb Records. The Burrito Brothers' *Hearts on the Line* spawned three minor country chart hits in 1981. *Sunset Sundown*, the Brothers' second Curb album, appeared in 1982 and, like its predecessor, produced three minor hits. After the release of *Sunset Sundown*, Kleinow left the band to become an animator and special-effects creator in Hollywood. The group carried on without him, led by Gib Gilbeau and John Beland. That incarnation of the band fell apart in 1985, the same year that Kleinow assembled yet another version of the band. For the next three years, this incarnation of the Flying Burrito Brothers toured America and Europe. In 1988 the group split again, although it did occasionally reunite for further tours and recordings in the '90s. —*Stephen Thomas Erlewine*

☆ **The Gilded Palace of Sin** / Feb. 1969 / A&M ✦✦✦✦✦
The birth of country-rock. Gram Parsons and Chris Hillman, aided by Sneaky Pete Kleinow and Chris Ethridge, create a hybrid by combining rock attitude with country sentiments and change the course of popular music. Really. —*William Ruhlmann*

Burrito Deluxe / Apr. 1970 / A&M ✦✦✦✦
The follow-up to the brilliant *Guilded Palace of Sin* finds the band somewhat directionless ,with Gram Parsons losing interest and playing

a less active role. While the Parsons/Hillman-penned "Cody Cody" and a touching rendition of the Rolling Stones' "Wild Horses" capture some of the previous album's magic, *Burrito Deluxe* is somewhat of a letdown. Parsons left for a solo career shortly after. —*Chris Woodstra*

The Flying Burrito Brothers / May 1971 / A&M ✦✦✦
On their first post-Parsons album, the Burritos (now led by Hillman and Rick Roberts, and with future Eagle Bernie Leadon replacing Ethridge) make an honest step forward in country-rock. Includes the Roberts song "Colorado." —*William Ruhlmann*

The Last of the Red Hot Burritos / Apr. 1972 / A&M ✦✦
Last of the Red Hot Burritos, the fourth Flying Burrito Brothers album, was a live recording by the current lineup, led by sole original member Chris Hillman, billed as the group's swan song and released after their breakup. By now, the Burritos had evolved into a competent country-rock band with a repertoire of country standards such as "Orange Blossom Special" (featuring Byron Berline on fiddle), but few of the originals by Gram Parsons and Hillman. *Last of the Red Hot Burritos* would have been a respectable, if unexceptional, way to go out, if in fact this had been the end of the group. But three years later, Kleinow and original bass player Chris Ethridge would resurrect the name, and there would be editions of the Burritos performing and recording, with legal, if not moral, legitimacy, long into the future. —*William Ruhlmann*

Close Up the Honky-Tonks / Jun. 1974 / A&M ✦✦✦✦
A&M Records seemed to close the book on the Flying Burrito Brothers with *Close Up the Honky-Tonks*, a 23-track, double-LP compilation. A combination best-of and odds-and-sods career wrap-up, the album contained one LP given over to tracks from the Burritos' first two records, *The Gilded Palace of Sin* and *Burrito Deluxe*, plus the non-LP single "The Train Song." The second disc presented 11 previously unreleased tracks, most of them cover songs, ranging from the Bee Gees' "To Love Somebody" to the Everly Brothers' "Wake Up, Little Susie." Co-founder Gram Parsons was featured on the five songs on side three, while side four came from the Rick Roberts era of the band. The Burritos would lack a one-disc best-of until A&M came up with the CD/cassette release *Farther Along* in 1988. So for more than a decade, *Close Up the Honky-Tonks* was the definitive Burritos compilation, and even now, when it is out of print, it contains some excellent performances available nowhere else. —*William Ruhlmann*

Flying Again / Sep. 1975 / Columbia ✦✦
The last that had been heard of the Flying Burrito Brothers was a 1973 European tour organized by Rick Roberts, replacement for founding member Gram Parsons, with a few hired guns. But with Parsons' growing posthumous legend, the band's name retained currency, and former bassist Chris Ethridge and former pedal steel guitarist "Sneaky" Pete Kleinow retained legal rights to that name. They brought in guitarist/fiddle player Floyd "Gib" Gilbeau, guitarist Joel Scott Hill, and former Byrds drummer Gene Parsons, and relaunched the Burritos with this album of competently played country-rock. Words like "travesty" and "insult" have been used to describe it, on the grounds that Ethridge and Kleinow were trading on Parsons' reputation, but on its own, the album is an adequate, if unremarkable set. Just don't pick it up looking for the old glory. (Out of print.) —*William Ruhlmann*

Sleepless Nights / Apr. 1976 / A&M ✦✦✦
A&M Records seemed to have exhausted its stock of Flying Burrito Brothers outtakes on *Close Up the Honky-Tonks* in 1974, but the continuing posthumous regard for Gram Parsons caused the company to unearth another seven tracks, six covers of country classics like "Tonight the Bottle Let Me Down" and "Green, Green Grass of Home," plus a version of the Rolling Stones' "Honky Tonk Women," all originally intended for what annotator Bud Scoppa called "a pure, honest country album" that the Burritos apparently never finished. To this half-of-an-album, A&M added two tracks from *Close Up the Honky-Tonks* and three Parsons solo outtakes (with Emmylou Harris on backup vocals) licensed from Reprise Records. The result, credited to "Gram Parsons/The Flying Burrito Brothers," is a tribute to Parsons' heartbreaking tenor, especially because the tracks are little more than underproduced demos. It's not on par with *The Gilded Palace of Sin*, *Burrito Deluxe*, or *G.P.*, but it should be of interest to fans. —*William Ruhlmann*

Live from Tokyo / 1978 / Regency ✦✦
The second edition of the Flying Burrito Brothers, launched by "Sneaky" Pete Kleinow in 1975, turned out to have as many personnel shifts as the first edition put together by Gram Parsons in 1968. This lineup played familiar Burrito songs such as "Hot Burrito No.2" and "Colorado," as well as a selection of honky-tonk country standards. Far from the greatest of Burrito Brothers bands, this one nevertheless was superior to later versions, and the music was efficiently played before an enthusiastic audience. As the group's live albums go, however, the one to get is still *Last of the Red Hot Burritos*. (*Live from Tokyo* was reissued by Relix Records in 1991 under the title *Close Encounters to the West Coast*.) —*William Ruhlmann*

Cabin Fever / 1985 / Relix ✦
This 1985 live album chronicles a Burritos lineup anchored by original member "Sneaky" Pete Kleinow and singer/guitarist Skip Battin, who first joined the band in 1976. It is in essence a Gram Parsons/Burritos/Byrds tribute album on which the band tries unsuccessfully to address Parsons classics like "Wheels" and "Hickory Wind" as well as the Byrds' "Mr. Spaceman." The sound quality is low and the performances substandard. Skimpy packaging fails to tell you where it was recorded or even who the other members of the band are. —*William Ruhlmann*

Live from Europe / 1986 / Relix ✦✦
Relix Records, which has curious ideas about marketing, released a second Flying Burrito Brothers live album in 1986, the year after it released the live *Cabin Fever*. The same lineup of original member "Sneaky" Pete Kleinow, guitarist Skip Battin, and the previously uncredited rhythm section of bassist Greg Harris and Jim Goodall once again came off as a Burritos/Gram Parsons/Byrds tribute band, with a few of its own new songs thrown in. It was a reasonable enough concept for a live show, but back home on the record player versions of songs like "Christine's Tune (Devil in Disguise)" and "Citizen Kane" didn't hold a candle to the original recordings. Maybe to Relix and its Dead Head fans, who hew to the notion that all live shows should be taped and disseminated, this sort of release made sense, but not to average fans. —*William Ruhlmann*

Dim Lights, Thick Smoke and Loud, Loud Music / Mar. 1987 / Edsel ✦✦✦
The British Edsel label's *Dim Lights, Thick Smoke and Loud, Loud Music*, the first try at a Flying Burrito Brothers compilation in a decade, is not a best-of. Because the label had recently reissued the Burritos' first two albums, *The Gilded Palace of Sin* and *Burrito Deluxe*, this 13-song collection is drawn from the rarities and outtakes first released on the A&M albums *Close Up the Honky-Tonks* and *Sleepless Nights* after the original group's (and Gram Parsons') demise. Specifically, as the album notes report, " . . . [I]t brings together for the first time on one record all the Burritos' material that features Gram Parsons and that wasn't on those first two LPs." The songs are for the most part covers of country music standards presented as demos or working versions that probably never would have been released if it were not for Parsons' death. Parsons, of course, is the reason the Burritos continue to interest fans, and he sings well here, but this half-finished material does not compare to the first two albums. —*William Ruhlmann*

★ Farther Along: Best of / 1988 / A&M ✦✦✦✦✦
Farther Along: The Best of the Flying Burrito Brothers is a nearly flawless compilation, containing a full 21 tracks of the pioneering group's best material. All but two of the songs from *The Gilded Palace of Sin* are included on the collection, as are all of the highlights from *Burrito Deluxe* and a handful of rarities and outtakes. In short, it's a definitive collection containing all of the Burrito Brothers' finest moments. It's indispensable to any rock or country collection. —*Stephen Thomas Erlewine*

Back to Sweethearts of the Rodeo / 1990 / Disky ✦✦✦
This 28 song double-CD set, intended as a farewell album to the Burritos' legions of European fans, consists of songs recorded in Sheffield, AL, in 1986 and 1987 by the final incarnation of the Burrito Bros., John Beland and Gib Gilbeau (vocals, guitars), James Hooker (piano), Alan Jones (bass), Roger Clark (drums), Wayne Bridge (steel guitar), Steve Nathan (synthesizer), and Butch Johnson (harmonies). Most of the tunes are originals by Beland and Gilbeau, which are above average mid-tempo country-rock with some pleasant hooks and catchy choruses and harmonies; most are fairly romantic, and some are very beautiful, especially tracks like "Shoot for the Moon" and "Baby Won't You Let Me Be the One." Interspersed are a few more ambitious story-songs, such as "Moonlight Rider," a few rockers like "Gold Guitar," and covers of stuff by Buck Owens and Felice and Boudleaux Bryant ("Take a Message to Mary"). Ironically, to most listeners the group here will sound very similar to the Eagles, one of the bands formed in the wake of the original Burrito Bros.—but they also sound a lot like Swampwater, Beland and Gilbeau's first band, circa 1970, who were near contemporaries of the original Burritos. Whatever one's reference point, they're worth checking out. —*Bruce Eder*

Close Encounters to the West Coast / Jul. 1, 1991 / Relix ✦✦
The second edition of the Flying Burrito Brothers, launched by "Sneaky" Pete Kleinow in 1975, turned out to have as many personnel shifts as the first edition put together by Gram Parsons in 1968. This lineup played familiar Burrito songs such as "Hot Burrito No.2" and "Colorado," as well as a selection of honky-tonk country standards. Far from the greatest of Burrito Brothers bands, this one nevertheless was superior to later versions, and the music is efficiently played before an enthusiastic audience. As the group's live albums go, however, the one to get is still *Last of the Red Hot Burritos*. (*Close Encounters to the West Coast* is a 1991 reissue of the 1978 Regency Records album *Live from Tokyo*.) —*William Ruhlmann*

Flying Color

f. 1984, San Francisco, CA, **db.** 1990
Group / Rock 'n' Roll, Alternative Pop-Rock, Power Pop
In the wake of the Rickenbacker revolution started by R.E.M., Flying Color formed in San Francisco in 1984 when bassist Hector Penalosa, from the Southern California cult band the Zeros, hooked up with guitarist Dale Duncan from the San Francisco underground band Love Circus and guitarist Richard Chase and drummer John Stuart. The band released one single in 1985, "Dear Friend," followed by the album *Flying Color* in 1987. Upon the album's release, Chase left the fold and guitarist Chris von Sneidern joined the band. There was no mistaking Flying Color's jangle and harmonies as Beatles-influenced. They even wore the requisite mod clothes, but at a time when the college charts were dominated by English synthesizer bands, Flying Color's clean, harmonious pop sounded amazingly fresh (and years after its release, it still does). The band broke up in 1990; all members continued to perform solo or with other groups, to varying degrees of success. In 1996 Duncan, Stuart, and von Sneidern re-formed and began recording again, just around the time *Flying Color* was issued on CD for the first time. *—Denise Sullivan*

Flying Color / 1987 / Frontier ✦✦✦✦
In the tradition of John, Paul, and George, Flying Color's three mop-topped songwriters traded lead vocals and writing chores on their one and only album, a timeless tribute to ringing guitars. Probably even more derivative of the Byrds or Buffalo Springfield than the Beatles, Flying Color's perfect, guitar-based pop and harmonies marked a movement in rock that would take another ten years to take hold in the mainstream, but the album—in particular the standout tracks "Dear Friend" and "Through Different Eyes"—sounds just as vital as when it was released. *—Denise Sullivan*

Dan Fogelberg

b. Aug. 13, 1951, Peoria, IL
Guitar, Keyboards, Vocals / Singer-Songwriter, Soft Rock
Peoria, IL, native Dan Fogelberg has built a devoted following over the years with his laidback, folky singer-songwriter style. A pianist since 14, Fogelberg switched to guitar and played local coffeehouses while majoring in art at the University of Illinois, where he met ex-student and REO Speedwagon manager Irving Azoff. Fogelberg relocated to Los Angeles and played the folk circuit while doing session work, landing a tour spot with Van Morrison at one point. Fogelberg's 1972 debut, *Home Free,* didn't make much of an impact, and he was dropped from Columbia. However, Fogelberg's connection with Azoff led to a deal with Epic. Fogelberg's Epic debut, *Souvenirs,* became his first in a string of seven consecutive platinum albums. He increased his visibility by touring with the Eagles in 1975. Fogelberg's popularity peaked in 1980 with the release of *Phoenix,* which contained the No. 2 hit single "Longer." His follow-up, *The Innocent Age,* was a double concept album, and four Top 20 singles were pulled from it. After the release of a greatest hits package, Fogelberg's commercial appeal began to evaporate; none of his subsequent albums has gone platinum, but they continue to sell well to a core of fans. In 1993 *River of Souls* saw Fogelberg experimenting with worldbeat sounds as a backdrop for his lyrical musings. *—Steve Huey*

Home Free / 1973 / Columbia ✦✦✦✦
This debut, recorded in Nashville and produced by Norbert Putnam, is a nice blend of haunting acoustic-guitar-based numbers ("Stars," "Be on Your Way"), some supported by tasteful string-section work ("To the Morning," "Wysteria," "Hickory Grove"). There are also a few country/light-rock items in "Anyway I Love You," "Long Way Home (Live in the Country)," and "More Than Ever." *—Rick Clark*

Souvenirs / 1975 / Epic ✦✦✦
This Joe Walsh-produced effort includes Fogelberg's first hit, "Part of the Plan." Overall, this isn't as strong as the debut. *—Rick Clark*

Netherlands / 1977 / Epic ✦✦✦✦
Fogelberg returns to Norbert Putnam for this effort, which ranges from the heavily orchestrated, highly dramatic title cut to light CSN-style folk-rock like "Once Upon a Time." It's one of Fogelberg's better albums, in spite of his tendency for grandiose statement. *—Rick Clark*

Twin Sons of Different Mothers / 1978 / Epic ✦✦✦
This album contains duets with flutist Tim Weisberg. It's a nice diversion, featuring a good remake of the Hollies hit "Tell Me to My Face." There are some pleasant instrumental numbers here. Fogelberg scored a hit with "The Power of Gold." *—Rick Clark*

Phoenix / 1980 / Full Moon ✦✦✦✦
Fogelberg's highest-charting album features his widest stylistic stretches, from the ultra-sentimental acoustic hit "Longer" to extended rockish numbers like "Face the Fire," "Wishing on the Moon," and the title cut. *—Rick Clark*

The Innocent Age / 1981 / Full Moon ✦✦✦✦
An ambitious song cycle, it details the experience of coming of age. Several of Fogelberg's biggest hits ("Leader of the Band," "Same Old Lang Syne," "Hard to Say," and "Run for the Roses") are on this set. *—Rick Clark*

● **Greatest Hits** / 1985 / Full Moon ✦✦✦✦
Even though this collection fails to address much of his best non-single material, most of his obvious hits are here (heavy on the sentimental), making this a fairly safe starting place for someone wanting to get into Fogelberg. *—Rick Clark*

High Country Snows / 1985 / Full Moon ✦✦✦
It's a well-recorded foray into more traditional acoustic country music. *—Rick Clark*

John Fogerty

b. May 28, 1945, Berkeley, CA
Guitar, Vocals / Rock 'n' Roll, Roots-Rock
John Cameron Fogerty achieved fame as the lead singer-songwriter and guitarist in Creedence Clearwater Revival and has since gone on to a chart-topping solo career. Born in Berkeley, CA, Fogerty and his brother Tom organized the group that would become Creedence as the Golliwogs in the late '50s. As Creedence, they released nine Top Ten singles, all written by Fogerty, between 1969 and 1971, starting with the standard "Proud Mary." They also scored eight gold albums between 1968 and 1972, all fueled by Fogerty's simple, driving rock songs and his burly baritone, intoning deceptively poetic ("Bad Moon Rising") and even political ("Fortunate Son") lyrics.

Creedence split up in 1972. Fogerty at first confused his considerable following by releasing an album of covers, on which he played all the instruments, under the name the Blue Ridge Rangers in 1973. This was followed by a formal solo album, *John Fogerty,* in 1975, and then silence for more than nine years while the artist worked out business problems with Creedence's old label. But Fogerty returned at the end of 1984 with a Top Ten single, "The Old Man Down the Road," and a No. 1 album, *Centerfield.* *Eye of the Zombie* was a less successful follow-up in 1986. After the failure of *Eye of the Zombie,* Fogerty went into seclusion. For the next 11 years he remained quiet but finally released a new album in 1997. *—William Ruhlmann*

John Fogerty / 1975 / Asylum ✦✦
Forgettable post-Creedence exercise. *—Jeff Tamarkin*

● **Centerfield** / Apr. 1985 / Warner Brothers ✦✦✦✦
The comeback album that proved the ex-Creedence firebrand still knew how to rock and make it count. Includes "The Old Man down the Road," "Rock and Roll Girls," and "Centerfield." *—Jeff Tamarkin*

Eye of the Zombie / 1986 / Warner Brothers ✦✦
The disappointing follow-up to *Centerfield,* too high-tech and low-profile. *—Jeff Tamarkin*

Blue Moon Swamp / May 20, 1997 / Warner Brothers ✦✦✦✦
Listening to the easy roots-rock shuffle of *Blue Moon Swamp,* it's hard to believe that it took John Fogerty a full decade to write and record the album. It's not just because the album isn't a great stylistic departure from his past work, it's because *Blue Moon Swamp* sounds so natural and unforced. Nothing on the album sounds fussy, nor does it sound like a meticulous reconstruction of the past. Instead, Fogerty's songs and performances are richly evocative of tradition, but they're vibrant and living for the present, which makes the rockabilly, blues, country, and swampy rock 'n' roll sound fresh. It's not as raw or as hooky as Creedence Clearwater Revival, nor is it as pop-oriented as *Centerfield,* but it's a warm, laidback and mature record that is roots-rock at its very best. *—Stephen Thomas Erlewine*

Foghat

f. 1971, London, England, **db.** 1984
Hard Rock, Heavy Metal, Boogie Rock
Foghat specialized in simple, hard-rocking blues-rock, releasing a series of best-selling albums in the mid-'70s. While the group never deviated from their basic boogie, they retained a large audience until 1978, selling out concerts across America and earning five gold and two platinum albums. Once punk and disco came along, the band's audience dipped dramatically, but the group continued performing until 1980.

With its straightahead, three-chord romps, the band's sound was American in origin, but the members were all natives of England. Guitarist/vocalist "Lonesome" Dave Peverett and drummer Roger Earl were members of the British blues band Savoy Brown, who left that group in the early '70s. Upon their departure, they formed Foghat with guitarist Rod Price and bassist Tony Stevens. Foghat moved to the United States, signing a record contract with Bearsville Records, a new label run by Albert Grossman. Their first album, *Foghat,* was released in the summer of 1972 and became a hit on album rock radio; a cover of Willie Dixon's "I Just Want to Make Love to You" even made it to the lower regions of the singles charts. For their next album, the group didn't change their formula at all. In fact, they didn't even change the *title* of the album. Like the first record, the second was called *Foghat;* it was distinguished by a picture of a rock and a roll on the front cover. Foghat's second album was their first gold record, and it established them as a popular arena rock act. Their next five albums—*Energized* (1974), *Rock and Roll Outlaws* (1974), *Fool for the City* (1975), *Night Shift* (1976), *Foghat Live* (1977), and *Stone Blue* (1978)—all were best-sellers and went at least gold. "Slow Ride," taken from *Fool for the City*, was their biggest single, peaking at No. 20. *Foghat Live* was their biggest album, selling over two million copies. After 1975 the band went through a series of bass players; Price left the band in 1981 and was replaced by Erik Cartwright.

In the early '80s, Foghat's commercial fortunes declined rapidly, with their last album, 1983's *Zig-Zag Walk*, barely making the album charts. The group broke up shortly afterward, although they have reunited for various tours in the late '80s and early '90s. —*Stephen Thomas Erlewine*

● **The Best of Foghat** / Oct. 1990 / Rhino ◆◆◆◆
Rhino's *Best of Foghat* is an excellent 16-track collection featuring every one of the hard-rocking boogie band's best-known songs, from "Slow Ride" and "I Just Want to Make Love to You" to "Fool for the City," "Drivin' Wheel" and "Ride, Ride, Ride." In short, it's all the Foghat most fans will ever need. —*Stephen Thomas Erlewine*

The Best of Foghat, Vol. 2 / Jan. 24, 1992 / Rhino ◆◆◆◆
If *Best of Foghat* made you hungry for more, *Best of Foghat, Vol. 2,* with no hit singles, only album tracks, and including two live cuts and an outtake, should satiate your desire. —*Stephen Thomas Erlewine*

Ben Folds Five

b. 1994, Chapel Hill, NC
Alternative Pop-Rock, Adult Alternative Pop-Rock
Ben Folds Five is actually a trio, composed of singer/pianist/composer Ben Folds, bassist Robert Sledge, and drummer Darren Jessee. Unabashedly pop, Folds draws his songwriting style from influences such as Randy Newman, while his rhythm section takes its cue from the Jimi Hendrix Experience. Folds formed the trio in his hometown of Chapel Hill, NC, as a way to avoid musical professionalism; he had previously worked as a session drummer in Nashville and had a role in an off-Broadway production of *The Buddy Holly Story*. Citing burnout, Folds returned home in 1994, put together Ben Folds Five with two of his friends, and recorded a self-titled debut album, which was released a year later. After signing to Sony, the trio issued *Whatever and Ever Amen* in 1997. —*Steve Huey*

● **Ben Folds Five** / Aug. 8, 1995 / Passenger ◆◆◆◆

Whatever and Ever Amen / Mar. 18, 1997 / Sony ◆◆◆◆
Expanding on the hook-laden songcraft of their eponymous debut, the Ben Folds Five turn in another glitzy array of Todd Rundgren-esque, piano-driven pop on their second album, *Whatever and Ever Amen*. Though it isn't as consistently tuneful and clever as their first record, *Whatever and Ever Amen* has a snazzy sense of popcraft. The hooks of "The Battle of Who Could Care Less," "Brick," and "Fair" sink in nearly as effortlessly as Billy Joel, Elton John, or Joe Jackson—which makes the record enjoyable ear candy. Occasionally, Folds' smug humor—whether it's the alternative-rock skewering of "The Battle" or the borderline misogynist humor of "Song for the Dumped"—can undercut his melodic gifts, but *Whatever and Ever Amen* is confirmation that the showy pop pleasures of his first record were no fluke. —*Thom Owens*

Wayne Fontana & the Mindbenders

f. 1963, Manchester, England, db. 1968
Vocals / British Invasion
Lester Bangs said it best, in his essay on the British Invasion in *The Rolling Stone Illustrated History of Rock & Roll:* "Wayne Fontana & the Mindbenders may have been a one-shot group, but what a shot. 'The Game of Love,' with its heavy bass, 'Louie Louie' chording, Bo Diddley break and Fontana's rich, wailing vocals, was an instant classic, a perfect example of the rock 'n' roll band of no apparent distinction but with a masterpiece in them anyway." Make that two masterpieces, although Fontana had split for a solo career before the group topped the charts again with "A Groovy Kind of Love." The Manchester, England, group were competent and energetic performers, but suffered the bane of many early British Invasion acts in the ultra-competitive days of 1966—they didn't write strong material. After some low-charting followups to "Game of Love," Fontana left for a solo career that saw him gaining only a couple of British hits, "Come on Home" and Graham Gouldman's "Pamela, Pamela." After "Groovy Kind of Love," the Mindbenders had another British Top 20 hit with "Ashes to Ashes," then cut a string of flop singles, and made a memorable appearance in the *To Sir with Love* film. Graham Gouldman was briefly a member before the group called

it a day in 1968, though he and Mindbenders singer/guitarist Eric Stewart would work together again in 10CC. —*Richie Unterberger*

Hit Single Anthology / 1991 / Fontana ◆◆
In 1965, Wayne Fontana & the Mindbenders struck with one of the British Invasion's greatest one-shots, the No. 1 hit "Game of Love." When Fontana split for a solo career shortly afterwards, the Mindbenders scored another mammoth hit that was nearly as memorable, "A Groovy Kind of Love." This 23-song anthology—featuring the most successful singles by Fontana & the Mindbenders, both together and as separate entities—does not, unfortunately, offer anything in the same league as those two smashes. They did manage a couple of other UK hits, "Um Um Um Um Um Um" and "Just a Little Bit Too Late" (both included here), in their original incarnation, but neither is especially memorable. Dependent upon outside writers for virtually all of their material, Fontana & Co. had little to distinguish them from literally hundreds of other middling British Invasion-era groups except their extraordinary luck in latching on to a couple of pieces of great material. Upon splitting from the Mindbenders, Fontana pursued a Tom Jones-like balladeering direction that has worn badly. The Mindbenders, while remaining rock-oriented, offered nearly as little. Stick with the two hit singles, on which they miraculously secured masterful pieces of tuneful and dynamic British Invasion pop. —*Richie Unterberger*

● **Best Of Wayne Fontana & The Mindbenders** / 1994 / Fontana ◆◆◆◆
Well-chosen 20-track anthology covering the hits and the best of their rare 1964-68 singles, as well as a couple of rare cuts from UK LPs and EPs. It's actually a distinct improvement upon its UK counterpart *Hit Single Anthology*, as it includes the fine "It's Getting Harder All of the Time/"Off and Running" single from the *To Sir with Love* soundtrack, and eliminates some of the weak covers and Wayne Fontana solo singles. —*Richie Unterberger*

Foo Fighters

f. 1995, Seattle, WA
Alternative Pop-Rock, Grunge
While he was drumming with Nirvana, Dave Grohl was recording original songs at home that never received public release. Those tapes would become the foundation of the Foo Fighters, the band he formed in 1995, after the death of Kurt Cobain. Like Nirvana, the Foo Fighters melded loud, heavy guitars with pretty melodies and mixed punk sensibilities with a sharp sense of pop songwriting.

Dave Grohl began playing guitar and writing songs in his early teens, as well as performing with a variety of hardcore punk bands. In the late '80s, when he was still in his teens, he joined the Washington, DC-area hardcore band Scream as their drummer. During the final days of Scream, Grohl began recording his own material in the basement studio of his friend Barrett Jones. Some of Grohl's songs appeared on Scream's final album, *Fumble*. After Scream's 1990 summer tour, Grohl joined Nirvana and moved to Seattle.

After Nirvana recorded *Nevermind*, Grohl went back to the DC-area and recorded a handful of tracks that would appear on *Pocketwatch*, a cassette released by Simple Machines. For most of 1992 he was busy with Nirvana, but when the band stayed off the road, he recorded solo material with Jones, who had moved to Seattle. The pair kept recording throughout early 1993, when Grohl returned to Nirvana to record *In Utero*. Grohl had toyed with the idea of releasing another independent cassette in the summer of 1993, but the plans never reached fruition. After Kurt Cobain's suicide in 1994, the drummer kept quiet for several months. In the fall of 1994, booking time in a professional studio, Grohl and Jones recorded in a week the album that became the Foo Fighters' debut. Boiling down his backlog of songs to about 15 tracks, Grohl played all of the instruments. He made 100 copies of the tape, passing it out to friends and associates. In no time, Dave Grohl's solo project became the object of a fierce record-company bidding war.

Instead of embarking on a full-fledged solo career, Grohl decided to form a band. Through his wife he met Nate Mendel, the bassist for Sunny Day Real Estate. Shortly before the pair met, Jeremy Enigk, the leader of Sunny Day Real Estate, had converted to Christianity and quit the band, effectively ending the group's career. Not only did Mendel join Grohl's band, but so did Sunny Day's drummer, William Goldsmith; former Germs and Nirvana guitarist Pat Smear rounded out the lineup. The band, named the Foo Fighters after a World War II secret force that allegedly researched UFOs, signed a contract with Capitol Records. The band's self-titled debut, consisting solely of Dave Grohl's solo recordings, was released on July 4, 1995. It was an instant success in America, as "This Is a Call" garnered heavy alternative and album rock airplay. By early 1996, the album was certified platinum in the US.

Throughout 1996, the Foo Fighters supported the album with an extensive tour, enjoying a crossover hit with "Big Me" that spring. Late in the year, the group began recording their second album with producer Gil Norton. During the sessions, William Goldsmith left the band due to creative tensions, leaving Grohl to drum on the majority of the album. Before the record's release in the spring of 1997, Goldsmith was replaced by Taylor Hawkins, who had previously drummed with Alanis Morissette. *The Colour and the Shape*, the Foo Fighters' second album and the first they recorded as a band, was released in May 1997. —*Stephen Thomas Erlewine*

● **Foo Fighters** / Jul. 4, 1995 / Roswell/Capitol ◆◆◆◆
Essentially a collection of solo home recordings by Dave Grohl, the Foo Fighters' eponymous debut is a modest triumph. Driven by big pop melodies and distorted guitars, Foo Fighters does strongly recall Nirvana, only with a decidedly lighter approach. If Kurt Cobain's writing occasionally recalled John Lennon, Dave Grohl's songs are reminiscent of Paul McCartney; they're driven by large, instantly memorable melodies, whether it's the joyous outburst of "This Is a Call" or the gentle pop of "Big Me." That doesn't mean Grohl shies away from noise; toward the end of the record, he piles on several thrashers that make more sense as pure aggressive sound than songs. Since he recorded the album by himself, they aren't as powerful as most band's primal sound workouts, but the results are impressive for a solo musician. Nevertheless, they aren't as strong as his fully formed pop songs, and that's where the true heart of the album lies. *Foo Fighters* has a handful of punk-pop gems that show, given the right musicians and songwriters, the genre had not entirely become a cliche by the middle of the '90s. —*Stephen Thomas Erlewine*

The Colour and the Shape / May 20, 1997 / Capitol ◆◆◆
Since the first Foo Fighters album was a collection of Dave Grohl solo recordings, their second album *The Colour and the Shape* is in many ways their official debut, and it certainly does sound different than its predecessor. Producer Gil Norton has tightened up the sound considerably—his control was so tight that drummer William Goldsmith left the band during the recording, leaving Grohl to record the rhythm tracks for the bulk of the album. Certainly, Norton's big, shiny sound makes *The Colour and the Shape* sound more professional than the debut, but the presence of a full band makes a difference, too. The full Foo Fighters make Grohl's songs heavier, not punkier, which may be a little unsettling to fans of the debut's ragged, amateurish edge. It's also strange that the album has such a glossy, arena-ready sound, since Grohl's songs are introspective, quite different than the endearing punk-pop of its predecessor. They're also not quite as catchy as before, but the band compensates by delivering them with a brutal energy. Still, the lack of immediate hooks prevents *The Colour and the Shape* from truly catching fire. —*Stephen Thomas Erlewine*

Steve Forbert

b. 1955, Meridian, MS
Guitar, Harmonica, Vocals / Singer-Songwriter, Pop-Rock, Contemporary Folk
Anointed "the new Dylan" upon his recording debut, folk-rock singer-songwriter Steve Forbert was born in Meridian, MS, in 1955. After learning guitar at age 11, he spent his high school years playing in a variety of local bands before quitting his job as a truck driver and moving to New York City at the age of 21. There he performed for spare change in Grand Central Station before working his way up to the Manhattan club circuit.

After signing to Nemperor, Forbert debuted in 1978 with *Alive on Arrival*, which earned critical acclaim for its taut, poetic lyrics. The follow-up, 1979's *Jackrabbit Slim*, was his most successful outing, reaching the Top 20 on the strength of the hit single "Romeo's Tune" (allegedly inspired by the late Supreme Florence Ballard). However, both 1980's *Little Stevie Orbit* and a self-titled 1982 effort fared poorly, and Forbert was dropped by his label.

He spent much of the decade in Nashville, where he continued honing his songwriting skills and performed regularly throughout the South. In 1988 he signed to Geffen, where the E Street Band's Garry Tallent produced his comeback album, *Streets of This Town*. Pete Anderson took over the production reins for 1992's *The American in Me*, but Forbert's continued lack of chart success prompted the label to cut him loose. After 1994's live effort *Be Here Now*, he recorded *Mission of the Crossroad Palms* for Giant the next year. *Rocking Horse Head* followed in 1996. —*Jason Ankeny*

Alive on Arrival / 1978 / Nemperor ◆◆◆◆
Forbert takes the folk-rock singer-songwriter format, already 13 years old at this point, and gives it a fresh, exuberant, almost punkish appeal. —*William Ruhlmann*

Jackrabbit Slim / Oct. 1979 / Nemperor ◆◆◆◆
Although *Jackrabbit Slim* was Steve Forbert's best-selling album, containing his only Top 40 hit, "Romeo's Tune," and his only other chart single, "Say Goodbye to Little Jo," it took Nemperor (formerly part of CBS, now part of Sony) 17 years to put it out on CD (on Sept. 3, 1996). It sounds as good as it did before, thanks both to Forbert's excellent songwriting (also included: "January 23-30, 1978," one of his best diary songs) and to John Simon's production. In a newly added note, Forbert

says Simon was a late addition, after his producer was stolen by Barbra Streisand. If he means Gary Klein, who handled Streisand's 1979 *Wet* album, one can only conclude that he traded up. Simon, whose previous credits included the Band, understood Forbert's folk-rock-pop style perfectly, making this the best marriage of artist and producer on what is also the artist's best material. —*William Ruhlmann*

Little Stevie Orbit / Sep. 1980 / Nemperor ◆◆◆
Little Stevie Orbit was seen as a disappointment at the time of its release because it did not generate a hit single on the order of "Romeo's Tune," and thus failed to consolidate the commercial success Steve Forbert had achieved with his second album, *Jackrabbit Slim*. In retrospect, however, it is a spirited, rollicking collection on which Forbert sounds increasingly comfortable fronting a rock band on a series of lighthearted songs such as "I'm an Automobile" and "If You've Gotta Ask You'll Never Know." It may not have made him a superstar, but *Little Stevie Orbit* provided some strong additions to Steve Forbert's concert repertoire for years to come. —*William Ruhlmann*

Steve Forbert / Jul. 1982 / Nemperor ◆◆
Steve Forbert hit quite a few stylistic bases on his fourth, self-titled album, maybe too many. From the horn-filled, Motown-tinged "Ya Ya (Next to Me)" to a faithful cover of Jackie DeShannon's mid-'60s classic "When You Walk in the Room" to the lush, string-heavy "Oh So Close (And Yet So Far Away)" to the uptempo country two-step "You're Darn Right," Forbert couldn't be pinned down to a genre (certainly not folk-rock). But there was too little of the spunky tone of songs like "It Takes a Whole Lotta Help (To Make It on Your Own)" that had sparked Forbert's previous albums. (Unfortunately, Forbert's proposed fifth album was rejected by his record company in 1984, and it took him six years to follow this album.) —*William Ruhlmann*

Streets of This Town / Apr. 1988 / Geffen ◆◆◆
Coming back after a six-year layoff, Forbert displays a previously unheard edge of bitterness that only deepens his thoughtful lyrics. And he rocks harder than ever. —*William Ruhlmann*

The American in Me / Jan. 1992 / Geffen ◆◆◆
Steve Forbert never had a chance of living up to the "new Dylan" kiss of death that critics smeared on his collar with his first releases in the late '70s. Four albums of wit and optimism gave way to a six-year drought without a record contract. With *The American in Me*, Forbert has found a healthier, more balanced perspective. The pressures and uncertainties of growing up, taking on responsibilities, and looking back on missed opportunity make up the central theme linking the disc's ten songs. This isn't a disc for the kids. It's for the parents out there who can still touch the rebel spirit within themselves and who have no desire to age gracefully. —*Roch Parisien*

● **Best of: What Kinda Guy?** / Apr. 13, 1993 / Columbia/Legacy ◆◆◆◆
Excellent compilation featuring a generous 19 tracks, including his hit "Romeo's Tune." A great place to get acquainted with this underrated singer-songwriter. —*Stephen Thomas Erlewine*

Mission of the Crossroad Palms / Mar. 28, 1995 / Giant ◆◆◆
Steve Forbert turns in an album of craftsmanlike tunes on his seventh album, including story songs such as "It Sure Was Better Back Then" (a working man's reminiscence) and "The Trouble with Angels" (in which an ex-beauty queen robs the till to pay for her infertility treatments). There is also one of Forbert's philosophical treatises ("It Is What It Is [And That's All]") and the humorously multi-referential "Lay Down Your Weary Tune Again" (risky territory for a former New Dylan). But the best song may be Forbert's ode to infidelity, "Don't Talk to Me." The point, though, is that Forbert has flowered into a distinctive, broad-based songwriter and that, in E Street Band bassist Garry Tallent, he has found a sympathetic producer able to showcase his voice and lyrics properly. Now, if he could just reconnect with his audience. —*William Ruhlmann*

Rocking Horse Head / Sep. 24, 1996 / Warner Brothers ◆◆◆
While *Mission of the Crossroad Palms* marked a revuse juvenation of Steve Forbert's talents, *Rocking Horse Head* captures the songwriter at a bit of a standstill. Though producer Brad Jones has assembled an excellent alternative-country backing band, featuring three core members of Wilco, Forbert's songwriting is a bit inconsistent, which makes the record frustrating. Sonically, it's a tough, committed affair, but there isn't as much substance behind the sound as there should be. —*Stephen Thomas Erlewine*

Force MDs

f. 1983, Staten Island, NY
Rap, Urban, Quiet Storm, Hip-Hop
Although not as well-known as other New York hip-hop acts of the early '80s, Staten Island's Force MDs were one of the first vocal groups to fuse doo wop-influenced harmonies with hip-hop beats. Originally a street troupe known as the LDs, the group sang and danced on Greenwich Village street corners and the Staten Island ferry. Its members included brothers "Stevie D." and Antoine "TCD" Lundy, their uncle Jesse Lee

Daniels, and friends Trisco Pearson and Charles "Mercury" Nelson. The group hooked up with DJ Dr. Rock, and billing themselves as Dr. Rock and the MCs, began playing in local hip-hop venues. However, by the time the group signed to Tommy Boy in 1984 as the Force MDs (MD standing for "musical diversity"), they had evolved into a more straightforward R&B vocal group, distinguished mostly by their street attitude. The MDs had a string of R&B hits through the '80s, but their only pop hit was the Top Ten Jimmy Jam/Terry Lewis-penned ballad "Tender Love," which was featured in the movie *Krush Groove*. The group's first R&B number one, "Love Is a House," came out in 1987, but their popular appeal began to ebb the next year. Mercury and Trisco left in 1990 and were replaced by Rodney "Khalil" Lundy and Shaun Waters. The group released the album *Get Ready* in 1994 as several members worked with other artists as producers. —*Steve Huey*

Love Letters / 1984 / Tommy Boy ✦✦✦
The Force MDs were rolling along when they issued this album in the mid-'80s. Their hip-hop/doo wop fusion yielded two sizable hits, among them the Top Ten smash "Tears." The album did well among both R&B/soul fans and hip-hop/rap and urban contemporary audiences. —*Ron Wynn*

Chillin' / 1986 / Tommy Boy ✦✦✦✦
A mid-'80s album featuring the Long Island hip-hop/doo wop group the Force MDs. They predated the current hot trend featuring singing groups blending classic R&B and soul harmonies with hip-hop productions. While their sound now seems dated, it was revolutionary in its time. This album had three chart hits, and the group was then at its peak. —*Ron Wynn*

Touch and Go / 1987 / Tommy Boy ✦✦✦
The title track was a Top Ten R&B hit, and the Force MDs were at their best on this album. The leads, harmonies, songs, production, and arrangements never sounded better, and they certainly paved the way for the many new jack vocal groups of the '90s. —*Ron Wynn*

Step to Me / Sep. 4, 1990 / Tommy Boy ✦✦✦
The Force MDs were a dominant ensemble in the mid—and late '80s. They struck just the right chord between classicism and modernism with their hip-hop/doo wop blend, and although this wasn't their biggest album, it still did quite well among both old and young Black music fans. —*Ron Wynn*

● **For Lovers and Others: Greatest Hits** / Feb. 18, 1992 / Tommy Boy ✦✦✦✦

Frankie Ford

b. Aug. 4, 1939, Gretna, LA
Vocals / Rock 'n' Roll, New Orleans R&B, R&B
It's ironic that some of the greatest New Orleans R&B of the 1950s was sung by a White man. Although he could have passed for a teen idol, Frankie Ford sang with as much grit as anyone of any color in the Crescent City. He recorded some fine singles for the Ace label in the late '50s, particularly the pounding "Sea Cruise," which made the Top 20 in 1959, and remains one of the hits most identified with the classic New Orleans R&B sound. "Sea Cruise" actually began life as a Huey "Piano" Smith song with Bobby Marchan on vocals, but producer Johnny Vincent had the inspired idea of dubbing Ford's singing on top of Smith's backing track. "Sea Cruise," with its bleating foghorn and irresistible piano groove, was an impossible act to follow, and Ford never approached the Top 20 again. But he cut several more gutsy sides for Ace that featured top New Orleans players like Huey Smith and saxophonist Red Tyler; one of the best, "Roberta," was covered by the Animals in the mid-'60s. A few of his singles found him following ill-advised swing jazz and teen idol directions, and he faded from view in the 1960s, although he made a cameo appearance in the film version of Alan Freed's life. —*Richie Unterberger*

● **Let's Take a Sea Cruise** / 1990 / Ace ✦✦✦✦
Fine collection of 18 vintage sides, including "Sea Cruise" and "Roberta," establishes Ford's claim as one of the first of the great White R&B singers. Most of this is first-rate New Orleans R&B with a swinging bounce, enhanced by Ford's cool and cocky vocals, although a few tracks are lame excursions into trad jazz or teen idol fare. For now it's the definitive Ford anthology, but there's room for improvement: documentation for when the tracks were originally released is nonexistent, and much of the music was obviously dubbed from vinyl records, not from master tapes. —*Richie Unterberger*

Foreigner

f. 1976, New York, NY
Hard Rock, Pop-Rock, Arena Rock
Foreigner was formed in 1976 by Mick Jones (ex-Spooky Tooth) and Ian McDonald (ex-King Crimson). The band was an instant success with the release of their debut album in 1977, which showcased the talents of guitarist Jones and lead singer Lou Gramm. Jones and Gramm also wrote

most of the band's material. The songs, mainly hard rock, boasted strong melodies and memorable guitar riffs. The band never strayed far from this formula but, to keep things fresh, added some interesting touches. For example, Junior Walker's sax on "Urgent" and the gospel vocals of Jennifer Holliday and the New Jersey Mass Choir on "I Want to Know What Love Is" helped elevate these songs above the ordinary. Gramm left the band in the late '80s for a solo career. Foreigner recruited a new lead singer, but Gramm's writing and distinctive vocals are sorely missed. —*Kenneth M. Cassidy*

Foreigner / 1977 / Atlantic ✦✦✦
No-nonsense rock 'n' roll catapulted the band's debut all the way to the top of the charts with the hits "Cold as Ice" and "Feels like the First Time." —*Donna DiChario*

Double Vision / 1978 / Atlantic ✦✦✦
Building on the success of the first album, this follow-up yielded the Top 20 hits "Hot Blooded," "Double Vision," and "Blue Morning, Blue Day." —*Donna DiChario*

Head Games / 1979 / Atlantic ✦✦✦

4 / 1981 / Atlantic ✦✦✦✦
The strength of Lou Gramm's powerhouse vocals and the band's synth-pop texturing carried this album to No. 1. It produced several major hits, including "Urgent," which featured a sax solo by Junior Walker, and "Waiting for a Girl like You." —*Donna DiChario*

Records / 1982 / Atlantic ✦✦✦✦
All the band's early (including those from *4*) radio-friendly hits are here in this collection of straight-ahead rock 'n' rollers. It includes "Waiting for a Girl like You," "Hot Blooded," and more. —*Donna DiChario*

Agent Provocateur / 1984 / Atlantic ✦✦✦

Inside Information / 1987 / Atlantic ✦✦✦

Unusual Heat / Jun. 17, 1991 / Atlantic ✦✦✦

● **The Very Best . . . and Beyond** / Sep. 22, 1992 / Atlantic ✦✦✦✦
Very Best . . . and Beyond collects not only all the major hits from Foreigner's early years ("Feels like the First Time," "Head Games," "Hot Blooded"), but also features their hits from the late '80s ("I Want to Know What Love Is," "Say You Will"), making the set preferable to *Records*. —*Stephen Thomas Erlewine*

Mr. Moonlight / 1995 / Atlantic ✦✦
Foreigner extracts the same recipe of old from the cryogenics lab, punctuated by that oh-so-'80s studio keyboard sound. Never mind the juvenile grunts and sighs punctuating the truly excruciating "Big Dog." Pull up for a helping of freeze-dried power ballads before playing spot-the-cliche with the likes of "All I Need to Know," "I Keep Hoping," "Hand on My Heart," and "Until the End of Time" (the group partially redeeming itself on this last track with the hiring of Duane Eddy for some tastefully moody guitar). To be fair, Lou Gramm is still in relatively fine, grainy voice, which only serves to render this whole simulation exercise more scary. —*Roch Parisien*

Fotheringay

f. 1970, London, England
Folk-Rock, British Folk
A short-lived offshoot of Fairport Convention, featuring key member and leader Sandy Denny. A second album was planned but never completed; tracks from it turn up on the triple-CD Denny anthology *Who Knows Where the Time Goes*. This is far more interesting and beguiling than their work with Fairport Convention, especially the Bob Dylan songs, but it lacks Fairport's precision and focus. —*Bruce Eder & William Ruhlmann*

● **Fotheringay** / 1970 / Hannibal ✦✦✦✦
Also featured are Trevor Lucas and Jerry Donahue, both of whom eventually joined Fairport when Denny rejoined. The album is a close relative of Denny's other solo and group work and features several of her flowing ballads, showcasing her lovely voice. A footnote, but a pleasing one. —*Bruce Eder & William Ruhlmann*

The Four Seasons

f. 1961, Newark, NJ
Pop-Rock
Although they were one of the very biggest rock 'n' roll groups of the 1960s, the Four Seasons—unlike, say, the Beatles, Rolling Stones, or the Byrds—don't excite virtually automatic respect from listeners and critics. A big factor is their most distinguishing trademark, the shrill falsetto vocals of their lead singer, Frankie Valli. Many also find their material—gently moralistic, romantic tunes with tightly arranged group harmonies that updated doo wop ethos into the 1960s—too cornball and clean-cut.

Whatever your feelings about the group, though, there's no denying their considerable importance. No other White American group of the time, save the Beach Boys, boasted such intricate harmonies, though the Four Seasons were much more firmly in the Italian-American doo wop tradition. Their uptown production values were contemporary and, in certain respects, innovative. The R&B influence in their music was large, and some of their early singles enjoyed success with the R&B audience; in fact, some listeners thought that the Four Seasons were Black when the group landed their first hits. And they were immensely successful, making the Top Ten 13 times between 1962 and 1967 with hits like "Sherry," "Big Girls Don't Cry," "Dawn," "Rag Doll," and "Let's Hang On."

The Four Seasons had been around for a long time before they got their first hit in 1962. Frankie Valli had made his first record in 1953, and in 1956 made a little noise with the Four Lovers' "Apple of My Eye." The Newark, NJ, group included future Four Season Tommy DeVito on guitar, and in subsequent years Valli would record flops for RCA, Decca, Cindy, and Gone, sometimes as a soloist, sometimes with groups. In the early '60s, the group, now known as the Four Seasons, were doing backup vocals for other artists.

Philadelphia producer Bob Crewe started working with the Seasons in 1962, and his contributions would be inestimable in the following years. Not only did he produce all of their big '60s hits, but he would write much of their material in collaboration with group member Bob Gaudio. It was Valli's near-soprano, though, that dominated their No. 1 hit "Sherry," as it would on the rest of their hits. "Big Girls Don't Cry," "Walk like a Man," and "Candy Girl" all followed within the next year—big smashes all, the first two (like "Sherry") featuring stomping, almost martial handclaps. "Candy Girl" offered evidence of versatility, with its samba-like rhythms and glissando flourishes.

The British Invasion did little to diminish the Seasons' fortunes, at least initially. In 1964 they moved from Vee-Jay (which also, for a brief time, had rights to the Beatles) to Philips. Their production became more sophisticated and dramatic while remaining unabashedly pop, and in 1964 they had several of their biggest hits: "Dawn," "Ronnie," "Rag Doll," "Save It for Me," and "Big Man in Town" (as well as a gem-like B-side, "Silence Is Golden," which would be a hit in 1967 for the Tremeloes). The Four Seasons' influence, oddly, was also felt on a couple of tracks by the biggest British Invasion bands: the Beatles' "Tell Me Why" and the Rolling Stones' "The Singer Not the Song" both launched into ear-straining falsettos at points, whether as a satire, tribute, or both.

The winning streak basically continued through 1967, although they would never again be as huge. "Let's Hang On," "Working My Way Back to You," "Opus 17," "I've Got You Under My Skin," "Beggin'," and "Marianne" were all big hits, working in some mild soul influences. They also, just for kicks, released a couple of silly singles under a pseudonym, the Wonder Who?, that even pre-teens quickly identified as the Seasons under disguise. The Wonder Who?'s 1965 Top 20 hit, "Don't Think Twice," easily qualifies as the most ridiculous Dylan cover ever to hit the Top 40.

Guitar-oriented, more socially conscious rock and soul had been making inroads into the Four Seasons' audience for a while, but the times really caught up with them by the end of 1967. The group would make the Top 40 only one more time before their mid-'70s reunion. In the late '60s Valli, while maintaining his position in the Seasons, had kicked off a solo career that went straight for the heart of showbizzy pop on his biggest single, the No. 2 hit "Can't Take My Eyes off You." The Four Seasons did attempt to address social concerns of the day on the late-'60s album *Genuine Imitation Life Gazette*, which usually met with derisive snickers from the few that heard it.

The Four Seasons struggled on into the 1970s; by the time they signed with a Motown subsidiary in 1971, Valli and Gaudio were the only original members left. They briefly returned to the top of the charts in the mid-'70s with "Who Loves You" and the nostalgic "December, 1963 (Oh, What a Night)"; at the same time, Valli had a resurgence as a soloist, reaching No. 1 with "My Eyes Adored You" and making the Top Ten with "Swearin' to God." It couldn't last, any more than the group could turn back the clock to December 1963, that last moment when they reigned as the most successful White rock group in the world, unaware of the oncoming invasion by the Beatles. They've remained active off and on during the last two decades on the nostalgia circuit, without gaining any notable successes on record. —*Richie Unterberger*

25th Anniversary / 1987 / Rhino ✦✦✦✦

Frankie Valli and the Four Seasons scored hits from 1962 to 1978 under a variety of guises. Lead singer Valli started making solo records in 1965, and he had his own hits. They are all included in this long-overdue four-disc set, which runs from the Seasons' "Sherry" to Valli's "Grease." —*William Ruhlmann*

★ Anthology / 1988 / Rhino ✦✦✦✦✦

Over the course of 20 tracks, *Anthology* covers all of the Four Seasons' essential hits, as well as Valli's solo "Can't Take My Eyes off You"; it's the definitive collection. —*Stephen Thomas Erlewine*

Rarities, Vol. 1 / Sep. 1990 / Rhino ✦✦✦

The Four Seasons did manage to hold their own for a while during the initial onslaught of the British Invasion, but it would be foolish to pretend that their albums and B-sides were as strong as those by the best British Invasion groups. Nevertheless, they did issue some decent tracks aside from their hits during their prime that have been overlooked by all but die-hard fans. *Rarities, Vol. 1* collects 20 songs from the group's 1964-66 heyday, drawing heavily from their 1964 albums *Rag Doll* and *Dawn*. Several of the tunes were composed by the team of Bob Gaudio and Bob Crewe that wrote most of their biggest hits. They are indeed respectable, but simply not as memorable as their million-sellers, sometimes sounding like competent but lesser versions of smashes like "Dawn" and "Ronnie." One highlight is the odd death-on-the-surf ballad "No Surfin' Today," which shows a pronounced Southern California influence. As for rarities, you get a 1963 bowling commercial and a 1965 radio promo, and the second single by the notorious Wonder Who? This group, a thinly veiled pseudonym for the Seasons, scored the most unlikely Top 20 cover of a Dylan song ever with their castrato version of "Don't Think Twice, It's Alright." For their follow-up, the "group" tackled Shirley Temple's "On the Good Ship Lollipop"; both it and the flipside are included here, though they are less overlooked gems than historical novelties. —*Richie Unterberger*

The Four Tops

f. 1956, Detroit, MI
Soul, R&B, Motown

The Four Tops are the most stable, consistent, and dependable of the successful R&B/pop vocal acts to emerge from Motown Records in the 1960s. Unlike the Temptations, they have had no personnel changes; unlike the Supremes and the Miracles, their lead singer never felt the need to step out on his own. At the same time, the Four Tops personified the musical hybrid Motown sought; they had the grittiness of gospel and R&B, but they were smooth enough to appeal to pop audiences.

The group was formed in Detroit in 1953 by lead singer Levi Stubbs, Jr., Renaldo "Obie" Benson, Lawrence Payton, and Abdul "Duke" Fakir when they were still in high school. They recorded for several labels before signing to Motown in 1963. "Baby, I Need Your Loving" (July 1964), written and produced by the team of Brian Holland, Lamont Dozier, and Eddie Holland, was their first substantial hit, setting the pattern for a series of songs showcasing Stubbs' emotive wail set against the Benson-Payton-Fakir harmony line. Need and longing would be the hallmarks of Stubbs' singing on such songs as "Ask the Lonely" (January 1965), which launched a string of R&B Top Ten/pop Top 40 hits over the next two years. Its follow-up, "I Can't Help Myself" (April 1965), hit No. 1 and was itself followed by "It's the Same Old Song" (July 1965); "Something About You" (October 1965); "Shake Me, Wake Me (When It's Over)" (February 1966); "Loving You Is Sweeter than Ever" (May 1966); a second No. 1, "Reach Out, I'll Be There" (August 1966); "Standing in the Shadows of Love" (November 1966); "Bernadette" (February 1967); "7 Rooms of Gloom" (May 1967); and "You Keep Running Away" (August 1967).

At that point, the Holland-Dozier-Holland team left Motown, depriving the Four Tops of their writing and producing talent. The label at first had some trouble finding material for them, having them cover songs like "Walk Away Renee" and "If I Were a Carpenter." In 1970, however, they rebounded with "It's All in the Game," "Still Water (Love)," a duet with the Supremes on "River Deep—Mountain High," and "Just Seven Numbers (Can Straighten Out My Life)," all of which made the R&B Top Ten and the pop Top 40. They scored one more R&B Top Ten on Motown with "(It's the Way) Nature Planned It" before moving to Dunhill (later acquired by ABC, then by MCA) Records, where they enjoyed another string of hits, including "Keeper of the Castle" (October 1972), the gold-selling "Ain't No Woman (Like the One I Got)" (January 1973), "Are You Man Enough" (June 1973), "Sweet Understanding Love" (September 1973), "One Chain Don't Make No Prison" (April 1974), and "Midnight Flower" (July 1974). They returned to the R&B Top Ten with "Catfish" (August 1976), and moved to Casablanca (since acquired by PolyGram) for the R&B No. 1 "When She Was My Girl" (September 1981).

The Four Tops returned to Motown in 1983, and by 1988 were signed to Arista. Their hit-making days presumably behind them, they remain a solid concert act with a repertoire of favorites and a catalog that continues to be repackaged successfully. —*William Ruhlmann*

● The Greatest Hits / Aug. 1967 / Motown ✦✦✦✦

The first of what would be many greatest hits and anthology packages featuring the Four Tops. At this point, they had had enough chart hits for a good single album set, which is what this is. It has long since lost its value with the release of numerous superior packages. —*Ron Wynn*

★ Anthology / Jul. 1974 / Motown ✦✦✦✦✦

Until they get the deluxe box set CD treatment, this three-record/two-CD set qualifies as the ultimate Four Tops Motown statement. It includes all the landmark hits, plus good numbers from their final days at Motown in the 1970s (they did return in the mid-'80s), such as "Still Water" and "Just Seven Numbers." —*Ron Wynn*

The Best of the Four Tops (1972—1976) / Oct. 25, 1990 / MCA ✦✦✦✦
This collection covers their best Dunhill tracks from the 1970s, which did include two big hits in "Ain't No Woman (Like the One I Got)" and "Are You Man Enough." "Keeper of the Castle" was also a Top Ten R&B single, and it seemed as if the Four Tops were in stride again. The Dunhill period yielded two more Top Ten R&B smashes with "One Chain Don't Make No Prison" and "Midnight Flower," and is a much better period than some fans consider. —*Ron Wynn*

Until You Love Someone: More of the Best (1965-1970) / Feb. 16, 1993 / Rhino ✦✦✦
This compilation gathers 18 non-hit album tracks from eight LPs that the Four Tops cut for Motown between 1965 and 1970 (some of which appeared on B-sides). A major soul group they might have been, but the Tops' pinnacle was actually quite brief, and that's reflected in this collection. No less than two-thirds of the songs date from 1965 and 1966, six from 1965's *Second Album* alone. Not so coincidentally, all but one of those cuts were written by the legendary Holland/Dozier/Holland songwriting team. The production is faultless, the songs very characteristically HDH, and Levi Stubbs' lead vocals are unfailingly gritty and pleasurable. Yet none of these has the unforgettable hooks of their hit singles of the period like "Reach Out, I'll Be There" and "I Can't Help Myself." As enjoyable as the formula is, the uniformity of the sound limits this disc's appeal to serious Motown and soul collectors. Curiosities among the non-HDH cuts include little-known tunes by Smokey Robinson and Stevie Wonder, and a non-hit single from 1969, "What Is a Man." —*Richie Unterberger*

Peter Frampton

b. Apr. 22, 1950, Beckenham, Kent, England
Guitar, Vocals / Pop-Rock, Arena Rock
Before he shot to solo superstardom in the mid-'70s, guitarist Peter Frampton was a British teen idol in the late '60s thanks to his work with the Herd and looks worthy of being named "Face of 1968" in several British magazines. The next year, Frampton joined ex-Small Faces front man Steve Marriott in Humble Pie, remaining for two years before departing for a solo career. After performing on Nilsson's *Son of Schmilsson*, Frampton recorded his solo debut *Wind of Change* in 1972 and formed a backing band, Frampton's Camel, to support him on tour. Members included ex-Spooky Tooth drummer Mick Kellie, ex-Cochise keyboardist Mickey Gallagher, and former Bell and Arc bassist Rick Wills. Frampton toured extensively for the next few years but broke up Frampton's Camel in 1974, a year before his *Frampton* LP went gold. Recorded at San Francisco's Winterland, 1976's double album *Frampton Comes Alive* was a staggering success, selling over six million copies and becoming the biggest-selling live rock album ever at that time. It showcased Frampton's mastery of the talk-box guitar effect and his penchant for in-concert theatrics. It produced three hit singles ("Show Me the Way," "Baby, I Love Your Way," and "Do You Feel Like We Do"). The follow-up LP, *I'm in You*, produced Frampton's biggest hit in the title track, but his career was temporarily put on hold by a near-fatal car crash in the Bahamas in 1978. Frampton had made his acting debut as Billy Shears in that year's ill-received film version of *Sgt. Pepper's Lonely Hearts Club Band*, directed by Robert Stigwood. Personal problems halted a full-scale comeback after Frampton's recovery; he recorded sporadically throughout the '80s, but none of these efforts caught fire with the public. He had been planning a Humble Pie reunion with Steve Marriott in 1991 when Marriott's home burned down, killing him. Nevertheless, Frampton released a self-titled album for Relativity in 1994, followed by *Frampton Comes Alive II* in 1995. —*Steve Huey*

Frampton Comes Alive / 1976 / A&M ✦✦✦✦
In the 1980s and '90s, many artists (especially in R&B and urban contemporary) have been so reliant on technology that their live shows pale in comparison to their studio recordings. But in the '70s, the opposite was sometimes true. Compared to *Frampton Comes Alive*—the best-selling live album ever—Peter Frampton's studio efforts sound downright tame. The Humble Pie graduate packed one hell of a punch onstage—where he was most comfortable—and in fact, the live versions of "Show Me the Way," "Do You Feel like I Do," "Something's Happening," "Shine On," and other album-rock staples are much more inspired, confident, and hard-hitting than the studio versions. Commercially as well as artistically, this package (a two-LP set that later became a two-CD set) was undeniably Frampton's crowning achievement. Period. —*Alex Henderson*

Shine On: A Collection / Oct. 20, 1992 / A&M ✦✦✦✦
Shine On: A Collection is a double-disc, 30-song set featuring all of Peter Frampton's best-known songs and biggest hits, plus a couple of rarities and unreleased cuts for hardcore fans. While the collection is far too thorough for casual listeners, any fan who wants to dig deeper than *Frampton Comes Alive!* should start with *Shine On*, particularly since

most of Frampton's individual older albums have been out of print for years. —*Stephen Thomas Erlewine*

● **Greatest Hits** / Jun. 18, 1996 / A&M ✦✦✦✦
By compiling all of Peter Frampton's biggest hits—in their hit versions, so "Show Me the Way" and "Baby, I Love Your Way" are from *Frampton Comes Alive*, not the studio albums—on one disc, *Greatest Hits* functions as the definitive retrospective on the guitarist. It has a better selection than the single disc *Classics, Vol. 12*, and it is more concise and listenable than the double-disc box *Shine On: A Collection*, which means it's the only collection that provides an effective, manageable overview of Frampton. —*Stephen Thomas Erlewine*

Connie Francis

b. Dec. 12, 1938, Newark, NJ
Vocals / Pop, Brill Building Pop
Considered the leading pop female singer of her era, Connie Francis usually sang of her latest broken heart with a teardrop in her voice. The Newark, NJ, native started performing as a child, signing with MGM Records in 1955, but she suffered two years of bombs before the torch ballad "Who's Sorry Now" shot up the charts in 1958. Although she specialized in sobbing tales of woe, Francis proved she could rock with Neil Sedaka's "Stupid Cupid" in 1958 and "Lipstick on Your Collar" the next year. Francis scored two nNo. 1 hits in 1960—the twangy "Everybody's Somebody's Fool" and "My Heart Has a Mind of Its Own," and she branched into acting with a starring role in *Where the Boys Are*, the archetypal spring-break movie. "Don't Break the Heart That Loves You" was Francis' last pop chart-topper in 1962, but she continued to rank high in the pop pantheon throughout the decade, with forays into ethnic and country idioms. —*Bill Dahl*

● **The Very Best of Connie Francis** / Oct. 1963 / Polydor ✦✦✦✦
Though many best-of's exist on the market, this one leans more heavily toward her earlier rock 'n' roll hits. (Originally released in October 1963 as a 15-track LP by MGM Records, *The Very Best of Connie Francis* was reissued in 1986 on CD with six bonus tracks by Polydor Records.) —*Cub Koda*

White Sox, Pink Lipstick . . . & Stupid Cupid / Jul. 1993 / Bear Family ✦✦✦✦
Subtitled "Connie Francis in the 1950s," this massive five-CD, six-and-a-quarter-hour, 134-track box set traces Connie Francis' recording career from before the beginning, containing five performances from early television appearances prior to Francis' teens, to the end of the decade, when the 21-year-old was the biggest female star in pop music. Both sides of the ten flop singles she made between 1955 and 1957 are included (reissued for the first time since the original MGM 45s); then, starting with "Who's Sorry Now," come all of Francis' early hits and B-sides, along with alternate takes and outtakes. It becomes clear that the singer followed two different tracks, recording rock 'n' roll-oriented singles for the teenage market and more traditional pop albums for the grown-ups. So, in addition to the hits, we have all the material from the adult-oriented LPs *The Exciting Connie Francis* and *My Thanks to You*, plus the genre exercises *Connie Francis Sings Rock 'N' Roll Million Sellers* and *Country and Western Golden Hits*, all released in 1959. —*William Ruhlmann*

Kissin', Twistin ', Goin' Where the Boys Are / Apr. 16, 1996 / Bear Family ✦✦✦✦

Frankie Goes to Hollywood

f. 1980, Liverpool, England, **db.** 1987
Dance-Pop, New Wave
On the back of an enormous publicity campaign, Frankie Goes to Hollywood dominated British music in 1984. Frankie's dance-pop borrowed heavily from the then-current hi-NRG movement, adding a slick pop sensibility and production. What really distinguished the group was not their music, but their marketing campaign. With a series of slogans, T-shirts, and homoerotic videos, the band caused enormous controversy in England and managed to create some sensation in the United States. But by the time their second album, *Liverpool*, was released in 1986, the group's audience had virtually disappeared.

Based in Liverpool, Frankie Goes to Hollywood formed in 1980, comprising ex-Big in Japan vocalist Holly Johnson, vocalist Paul Rutherford, guitarist Nasher Nash, bassist Mark O'Toole, and drummer Peter Gill. Originally the group was called Hollycaust, but they changed their name to Frankie Goes to Hollywood—taken from an old headline about Frank Sinatra's acting career—by the end of the year. The band didn't make anything of note until 1982, when they appeared on the British television program "The Tube" with a rough version of the video for "Relax." The appearance attracted attention from several record labels and from record producer Trevor Horn. Horn signed them to his label, ZTT. Late in 1983, Frankie's first single, the Horn-produced "Relax"/"Ferry Cross the Mersey," was released. A driving dance number,

"Relax" featured sexually suggestive lyrics that would soon lead to great controversy.

Around the time of the release of "Relax," Frankie's promotional director Paul Morley, a former music journalist, orchestrated a massive, intricate marketing campaign that soon paid off in spades. Morley designed T-shirts that read "Relax" and "Frankie Says . . . ," which eventually appeared across the country. The group began playing up their stylish, campy homosexual imagery, especially in the first video for "Relax." The video was banned by British TV, and a new version was shot. Similarly, Radio 1 banned the single, and the rest of the BBC radio and television networks quickly banned the record as well. Consequently, "Relax" shot to No. 1 in January 1984 and soon sold over a million copies. Frankie's second single, the political "Two Tribes," was released in June 1984. The single, which was also produced by Trevor Horn, entered the charts at No. 1; it went gold in seven days. "Two Tribes" stayed at No. 1 for nine weeks and eventually sold over a million copies. Then "Relax" went back up the charts, peaking at No. 2.

Frankie-mania had taken England by storm, but it took a while to catch on in America. "Relax" peaked at No. 67 in the spring of 1984, while "Two Tribes" just missed the Top 40 in the fall. *Welcome to the Pleasuredome*, the band's Trevor Horn-produced debut double album, entered the UK charts at No. 1, and their third single, the ballad "The Power of Love," also reached No. 1. *Welcome to the Pleasuredome* reached No. 33 in early 1985 in the US, prompting the re-release of "Relax"; this time around, it made it into the American Top Ten.

"Rage Hard," the first single from their second album, peaked at No. 4 in the UK during the summer of 1986. It was followed by the release of *Liverpool*, which reached No. 5 on the British charts. Frankie Goes to Hollywood began their final tour in early 1987; by April, the band had broken up. Holly Johnson went on to pursue a solo career, which began in earnest in 1989 after a long legal battle with ZTT. Paul Rutherford also began a solo career, but neither his nor Johnson's was particularly successful. Johnson was diagnosed with AIDS in the early '90s and retired from music. —*Stephen Thomas Erlewine*

Welcome to the Pleasuredome / 1984 / ZTT/Island ✦✦✦✦
Upbeat British dance music with melodramatic vocals and lyrics that are sexually and politically provocative. The sound of Frankie Goes to Hollywood swept Britain in the years 1983-1985. Here is the widescreen debut double album, containing the hits "Relax," "Two Tribes," "The Power of Love," and the title track. —*William Ruhlmann*

Liverpool / 1986 / ZTT/Island ✦✦

● **Bang! Greatest Hits** / Mar. 22, 1994 / ZTT/Island ✦✦✦✦
This good collection includes all the worthwhile songs Frankie Goes to Hollywood ever recorded. —*AMG*

Aretha Franklin

b. Mar. 25, 1942, Memphis, TN
Piano, Vocals / Soul, Dance-Pop, R&B, Gospel, Urban, Quiet Storm
Aretha Franklin is one of the giants of soul music, and indeed of American pop as a whole. More than any other performer, she epitomized soul at its most gospel-charged. Her astonishing run of late-'60s hits with Atlantic Records—"Respect," "I Never Loved a Man," "Chain of Fools," "Baby I Love You," "I Say a Little Prayer," "Think," "The House That Jack Built," and several others—earned her the title "Lady Soul," which she has worn uncontested ever since. Yet as much of an international institution as she's become, much of her work—outside of her recordings for Atlantic in the late '60s and early '70s—is erratic and only fitfully inspired, making discretion a necessity when collecting her records.

Franklin's roots in gospel run extremely deep. With her sisters Carolyn and Erma (both of whom would also have recording careers), she sang at the Detroit church of her father, Reverend C.L. Franklin, while growing up in the 1950s. In fact, she made her first recordings as a gospel artist at the age of 14. It has also been reported that Motown was interested in signing her when it was a tiny start-up. Ultimately, however, Franklin ended up with Columbia, to which she was signed by the renowned talent scout John Hammond.

Franklin recorded for Columbia constantly throughout the first half of the '60s, notching occasional R&B hits (and one Top 40 single, "Rock-a-bye Your Baby with a Dixie Melody"), but never truly breaking out as a star. The Columbia period continues to generate considerable controversy among critics, many of whom feel that Franklin's true aspirations were being blunted by pop-oriented material and production. In fact there's a reasonable number of fine items to be found on the Columbia sides, including the occasional song ("Lee Cross," "Soulville") where she belts out soul with real gusto. It's undeniably true, though, that her work at Columbia was considerably tamer than what was to follow, and suffered in general from a lack of direction and an apparent emphasis on trying to develop her as an all-around entertainer, rather than as an R&B/soul singer.

When Franklin left Columbia for Atlantic, producer Jerry Wexler was determined to bring out her most soulful, fiery traits. As part of that plan, he had her record her first single, "I Never Loved a Man (The Way I Love You)," at Muscle Shoals in Alabama with esteemed Southern R&B musicians. In fact, that was to be her only session actually at Muscle Shoals, but much of the remainder of her '60s work would be recorded with the Muscle Shoals Sound Rhythm Section, although the sessions would actually take place in New York City. The combination was one of those magic instances of musical alchemy; the backup musicians provided a much grittier, and more soulful and R&B-based accompaniment for Franklin's voice, which soared with a passion and intensity suggesting a spirit that had been allowed to fly for the first time.

In the late '60s Franklin became one of the biggest international recording stars in all of pop. Many also saw Franklin as a symbol of Black America itself, reflecting the increased confidence and pride of African-Americans in the decade of the civil rights movements and other triumphs for the Black community. The chart statistics are impressive: ten Top Ten hits in a roughly 18-month span between early 1967 and late 1968, for instance, and a steady stream of solid mid-to-large-size hits for the next five years. Her Atlantic albums were also huge sellers, and far more consistent artistically than those of most soul stars of the era. Franklin was able to maintain creative momentum, in part, because of her eclectic choice of material, which encompassed first-class originals and gospel, blues, pop, and rock covers, from the Beatles and Simon & Garfunkel to Sam Cooke and the Drifters. She was also a fine, forceful, and somewhat underrated keyboardist.

Franklin's commercial and artistic success was unabated in the early '70s, during which she landed more huge hits with "Spanish Harlem," "Bridge over Troubled Water," and "Day Dreaming." She also produced two of her most respected, and earthiest, album releases with *Live at Fillmore West* and *Amazing Grace*. The latter, a 1972 double LP, was a reinvestigation of her gospel roots, recorded with James Cleveland and the Southern California Community Choir. Remarkably, it made the Top Ten, counting as one of the greatest gospel-pop crossover smashes of all time.

Franklin had a few more hits over the next few years—"Angel" and the Stevie Wonder cover "Until You Come Back to Me" being the most notable—but generally her artistic inspiration seemed to be tapering off, and her focus drifting toward more pop-oriented material. Her Atlantic contract ended at the end of the 1970s, and since then she's managed to get intermittent hits—"Who's Zooming Who" and "Jump to It" are among the most famous—without remaining anything like the superstar she was at her peak. Many of her successes were duets, or crafted with the assistance of newer, glossier-minded contemporaries such as Luther Vandross. There was also another return to gospel in 1987 with *One Lord, One Faith, One Baptism*.

Critically, as is the case with many '60s rock legends, there have been mixed responses to her later work. Some view it as little more than a magnificent voice wasted on mediocre material and production. Others seem to grasp any excuse they can to praise her whenever there seems to be some kind of resurgence of her soul leanings. Most would agree that her recordings after the mid-'70s are fairly inconsequential when judged against her prime Atlantic era. The blame is often laid at the hands of unsuitable material, but it should also be remembered that—like Elvis Presley and Ray Charles—Franklin never thought of herself as confined to one genre. She always loved to sing straight pop songs, even if her early Atlantic records gave one the impression that her true home was earthy soul music. If for some reason she returned to straight soul shouting in the future, it's doubtful that the phase would last for more than an album or two. In the meantime, despite her lukewarm recent sales record, she's an institution, assured of the ability to draw live audiences and immense respect for the rest of her lifetime, regardless of whether there are any more triumphs on record in store. —*Richie Unterberger*

Aretha Arrives / 1967 / Atlantic ✦✦✦
Her second Atlantic album features hip "Aretha-fied" covers from Sinatra's "That's Life" to Question Mark & the Mysterians' "96 Tears." A great record utilizing King Curtis and the Muscle Shoals musicians heard on most of Aretha's classic Atlantic work, it includes "Baby I Love You." —*George Bedard*

☆ **I Never Loved a Man (The Way I Love You)** / 1967 / Atlantic ✦✦✦✦✦
I Never Loved a Man The Way I Love You is Franklin's first Atlantic album—an electrifying breakthrough in her somewhat stymied (Columbia) career. The Muscle Shoals sound featured here became legendary. —*George Bedard*

☆ **Lady Soul** / 1968 / Atlantic ✦✦✦✦✦
Great personnel again—King Curtis, Bobby Womack, Frank Wess, and others, including a guest spot by Eric Clapton. Several classic songs, including the lesser-known "Ain't No Way" by Carolyn Franklin and the hits "Chain of Fools" and "Natural Woman." —*George Bedard*

Aretha Now / 1968 / Atlantic ✦✦✦✦
Though a bit short on running time at ten songs, this still caught Franklin at the peak of her early form. "Think," "I Say a Little Prayer," "See

Saw," and "I Can't See Myself Leaving You" were all big hits. Her choice of cover material included some of her most R&B-drenched early Atlantic cuts, like "Night Time Is the Right Time," "You Send Me," and "I Take What I Want." —*Richie Unterberger*

Aretha in Paris / 1968 / Atlantic ✦✦✦
Atlantic's Jerry Wexler once said that this concert album was an embarrassment to him, criticizing the inferior band (actually, the musicians that usually accompanied her live in the late '60s). Composed of her first few big singles and cuts from her first three albums, it doesn't match the classic studio versions, and could be considered her least essential '60s Atlantic LP. That's not to say, though, that it doesn't sound pretty good, with fine if basic readings of a lot of her most popular late-'60s material, although the horns fall distressingly out of tune at a key point in the instrumental break of "Chain of Fools." —*Richie Unterberger*

Soul '69 / 1969 / Atlantic ✦✦✦✦
One of her most overlooked '60s albums, on which she presented some of her jazziest material, despite the title. None of these cuts was a significant hit, and none was an Aretha original. She displayed her characteristically eclectic taste in the choice of cover material, handling compositions by Percy Mayfield, Sam Cooke, Smokey Robinson, and, at the most pop-oriented end of her spectrum, John Hartford's "Gentle on My Mind" and Bob Lind's "Elusive Butterfly." Her vocals are consistently passionate and first-rate, as is the musicianship; besides contributions from the Muscle Shoals rhythm section, session players include respected jazzmen Kenny Burrell, Ron Carter, Grady Tate, David Newman, and Joe Zawinul. —*Richie Unterberger*

This Girl's in Love with You / 1970 / Atlantic ✦✦✦
The title song (a cover of Herb Alpert's "This Guy's In Love with You") might lead you to believe this is one of Aretha's more pop-oriented albums, but in fact, this is the only song of the sort on this solid and fairly earthy effort. Besides the hit singles "Call Me" and "Share Your Love with Me," it includes her most well-known Beatle covers ("Eleanor Rigby" and "Let It Be"), and her interesting version of "The Weight," a Top 20 single featuring slide guitar by Duane Allman. —*Richie Unterberger*

Sweet Bitter Love / 1970 / Columbia ✦✦
Some uneven, but superbly sung, light pop, overproduced R&B, and soul from Aretha Franklin's days on Columbia. The label has been steadily recycling Franklin material, and while much of it deserves a second listen, there are some better anthologies than this one. The title track, however, is an excellent number, and there are some others that are equally solid. —*Ron Wynn*

Spirit in the Dark / 1970 / Atlantic ✦✦✦✦
Spirit in the Dark was one of Aretha Franklin's more overlooked albums from her Atlantic prime, despite the inclusion of a couple of hit singles (the title track and "Don't Play That Song"). The disc includes five of her own compositions (the most she ever recorded for a single album) and her usual eclectic choice of cover material. On this record, the covers ranged from B.B. King and Dr. John to Jimmy Reed and Goffin/King's "Oh Not My Baby." The album also benefits from great backup players; both the Muscle Shoals rhythm section and the Dixie Flyers contributed to the sessions, and Duane Allman lends his guitar to a couple of tracks. Though it doesn't rank with her very best Atlantic LPs, it's an exuberant and remarkably consistent effort. The 1993 CD reissue has detailed liner notes on the songs and sessions by David Nathan. —*Richie Unterberger*

Live at Fillmore West / 1971 / Atlantic ✦✦✦
Aretha Franklin's 1971 LP *Live at Fillmore West* was as seminal a soul breakthrough as Albert King's visit had been for blues. It finally cemented her status beyond soul audiences as both a recording and live attraction, and it matched her with a phenomenal rhythm section in King Curtis and the Kingpins. Franklin adroitly mixed pop, rock, and soul material throughout the three nights, including Stephen Stills' "Love the One You're With," Bread's "Make It with You," and the Beatles' "Eleanor Rigby," as well as tried and true favorites "Respect," "Don't Play That Song" and "Spirit in the Dark," which brought Ray Charles out of the audience for a spirited duet. There's more than enough here to make this absolutely essential, regardless of whether you have the original vinyl. —*Ron Wynn*

Amazing Grace / 1972 / Atlantic ✦✦✦✦
Aretha Franklin disproved the notion that once you leave the church, you can't go back. She returned in triumph on this 1972 double album, making what might be her greatest release ever in any style. Her voice was chilling, making it seem as if God and the angels were conducting a service alongside Franklin, Rev. James Cleveland, the Southern California Community Choir, and everyone else in attendance. Her versions of "How I Got Over" and "You've Got a Friend" are legendary. —*Ron Wynn*

Hey Now Hey / 1973 / Atlantic ✦✦✦
Hey Now Hey (The Other Side of the Sky) was just about Franklin's last gasp before succumbing to disco. This odd album, with its cheesy, junky artwork, contains some gems; notable are a poignant cover of Bern-

stein's "Somewhere," a sparkling "Moody's Mood," and the beautiful Carolyn Franklin composition "Angel." —*George Bedard*

With Everything I Feel in Me / 1974 / Atlantic ✦✦✦
This respectable but not-earth-shattering release was part of the gradual decline of Franklin's artistic and commercial achievements at Atlantic. The lead-off track, "Without Love," was a Top Ten R&B hit, and the title track, written by Franklin, was Top 20 R&B. There were a couple of familiar but completely rearranged Burt Bacharach tunes and a contribution from Stevie Wonder. Franklin was in good voice, and the studio band was accomplished, but this was all a far cry from the standard Franklin had set in the late '60s. It was also a far cry from the sales she enjoyed then; this was her first new album since her 1967 breakthrough to peak below the Top 30. —*William Ruhlmann*

Let Me in Your Life / 1974 / Atlantic ✦✦✦
A nice, if at times overbearing, mid-'70s Franklin set. She was still singing with the stunning delivery, amazing timing, and majestic soul that highlighted her late-'60s releases. Her version of "Until You Come Back to Me (That's What I'm Gonna Do)" is the only one that might be superior to Stevie Wonder's great original, while "I'm in Love" and the title cut are prime Franklin. —*Ron Wynn*

You / 1975 / Atlantic ✦✦
The first album that represented signs of stagnation. Aretha Franklin had issued two excellent albums in 1974, but in 1975 she just didn't get enough quality songs to flesh out *You.* While she still put everything into them, often salvaging dismal lyrics and awkward production, Franklin equaled past glories only on the song "It Only Happens (When I Look at You)." Otherwise, it was a case of wonderful vocals but little else. —*Ron Wynn*

Sparkle / 1976 / Rhino ✦✦✦✦
Aretha Franklin's career was in a down period in the mid-'70s when she collaborated with Curtis Mayfield to sing his compositions for the film *Sparkle.* The film proved a non-event, but for Franklin it marked a return to glory. Once again she was the Queen of Soul, doing the chilling, spectacular leaps, cries, whoops, and shouts that defined secularized gospel in the late '60s. The title cut was a sizable hit, while "Giving Him Something He Can Feel" became an anthem. Mayfield's lyrics and production shouldn't be overlooked; he added just the right amount of background trappings, and the Kitty Haywood Singers provided Franklin's best continuing backgrounds since the Sweet Inspirations. —*Ron Wynn*

Love All the Hurt Away / 1981 / Arista ✦✦
Aretha Franklin's post-Atlantic material has the same problems as the Columbia cuts. There are too many songs in which the wondrous Franklin voice was simply inserted into otherwise routine situations, with singles issued to take advantage of her hard-earned credibility and reputation. The title cut was a nice duet between Franklin and George Benson, and there were some other decent songs, but this was overall a disappointment. —*Ron Wynn*

Jump to It / 1982 / Arista ✦✦✦
Aretha Franklin scored some hits with this early '80s album and managed to make concessions to urban contemporary tastes without totally distoring her classic soul sound. While it's certainly not in the class of past recordings, the title cut gave Franklin her first No. 1 of the '80s, and "Love Me Right" was a decent followup. —*Ron Wynn*

Get It Right / 1983 / Arista ✦✦✦
Luther Vandross scored a popular success with *Jump to It,* but this followup is less impressive and proved less successful. Vandross wrote most of the material, including the No. 1 R&B title track and the R&B Top Ten hit "Every Girl (Wants My Guy)," although he also has Franklin tackle the Temptations hit "I Wish It Would Rain," in a painfully overwrought production. With this record, what had seemed to be an artist/producer marriage made in heaven hit the rocks. —*William Ruhlmann*

Never Grow Old / 1984 / Chess ✦✦✦
Actually credited to "Reverend C.L. Franklin and Aretha Franklin," this album was recorded live—very live—in church. The Reverend Franklin takes most of the leads on traditional gospel songs, with keyboard accompaniment, shouting and singing, although his daughter also has a couple of spotlights. The music is moving, and the audience is moved: one or two of them scream uncontrollably. —*William Ruhlmann*

Who's Zoomin' Who? / 1985 / Arista ✦✦✦
Franklin continued finding ways to accommodate the urban contemporary production style and retain her soulfulness. The single "Freeway of Love" was a monster hit in both clubs and on radio, while the title track and "Another Night" also did well across the board. The cut with the Eurythmics even got a little attention at rock stations. —*Ron Wynn*

Aretha / 1986 / Arista ✦✦
Don't be confused by the generic title; this is a new Aretha Franklin album from 1986 and a moderately succesful one, notable for containing five R&B hits, four of which also made the pop charts: "Jumpin' Jack

Flash" (produced by Keith Richards and featured in the Whoopi Goldberg movie of the same title), "Jimmy Lee" (No. 2 R&B), "I Knew You Were Waiting (For Me)" (a duet with George Michael that went No. 1 pop), "Rock-a-Lott," and "If You Need My Love Tonight" (a duet with Larry Graham). *—William Ruhlmann*

★ **30 Greatest Hits** / 1986 / Atlantic ✦✦✦✦✦
The double-disc set *30 Greatest Hits* contains all of Aretha Franklin's greatest hits from the '60s and early '70s, from 1967's "I've Never Loved a Man (The Way I Love You)" and "Respect" to 1973's "Until You Come Back to Me (That's What I'm Gonna Do)." It's an essential, comprehensive collection—the ideal purchase for fans who want more than just the biggest hits, but don't want to invest in the box set. *—Stephen Thomas Erlewine*

One Lord, One Faith, One Baptism / 1987 / Arista ✦✦✦
Although nowhere as anthemic as *Amazing Grace* (what could be?), this was still much better than most contemporary gospel. There were sociopolitical speeches by Jesse Jackson and Carl Franklin for those who wanted earthly concerns addressed alongside spiritual ones, but the real impact came from Franklin's rousing voice and the contributions of such guest stars as Mavis Staples and Aretha's sisters Erma and Carolyn. If she hadn't issued *Amazing Grace* or *Aretha Gospel* as a teen, this set might have gotten better notices and more critical respect. Instead, it was virtually dismissed, and it deserves better than that. *—Ron Wynn*

Through the Storm / 1989 / Arista ✦✦✦
Having scored in the recent past with producer Narada Michael Walden and some star duets, Franklin and Arista turned out another album with the same approach but less successful results. The title duet with Elton John went Top 20, but its followup, "It Isn't, It Wasn't, It Ain't Never Gonna Be" was an embarrassing failure for both Franklin and the previously pop-perfect Whitney Houston. The rest was even less distinguished, including a song with the Four Tops and Kenny G and a remake of the old hit "Think." *—William Ruhlmann*

Jazz to Soul / Jul. 14, 1992 / Columbia ✦✦✦
She's Billie Holiday. No, she's Ella Fitzgerald. No, wait, she's Dinah Washington. The conventional wisdom on Aretha Franklin's tenure at Columbia Records is that the label didn't know what to do with her, and that may be true, but you can't say they didn't try. On these 39 recordings, spread across two discs and cut between 1960 and 1965, Franklin and her producers look for ways to frame her obvious vocal talents, but always in terms of uptown jazz and non-rock-pop formats. Much of the result is appealing, and it's only in light of the transcendent soul music Franklin made from her first day at Atlantic Records in 1967 that this work comes across as merely exploratory. "Show me the way to get to Soulville," she demands in 1964. She finally found the way, and that was that. *—William Ruhlmann*

☆ **Queen of Soul: The Atlantic Recordings** / 1993 / Rhino ✦✦✦✦✦
The Queen of Soul: The Atlantic Recordings is an 86-track, four-disc box set that covers Aretha Franklin's Atlantic career, from 1967's "I Never Loved a Man (The Way I Love You)" to 1976's "Something He Can Feel." Over the course of the set, all of Aretha's best-known songs, including all of her Top Ten pop and R&B singles, are included. For fans who know only the singles, the set is primarily notable for the wealth of album tracks and forgotten singles that are included, which nearly equal the hits in terms of quality. Stopping just short of her move to disco, *The Queen of Soul* just misses being a totally comprehensive collection, but it remains definitive. It may miss some of her later hits, but every one of her greatest tracks is on the box. *The Queen of Soul* is one of the cornerstones of any soul collection. *—Stephen Thomas Erlewine*

Greatest Hits (1980-1994) / Feb. 22, 1994 / Arista ✦✦✦
Greatest Hits (1980-1994) rounds up the biggest hits from the latter part of Aretha Franklin's career, including "Jump to It," "Freeway of Love," "Who's Zoomin' Who," and "I Knew You Were Waiting (For Me)," a duet with George Michael. The album does a good job of selecting the highlights from a slightly uneven era for Aretha. *—Stephen Thomas Erlewine*

The Very Best of Aretha Franklin, Vol. 1 / Mar. 22, 1994 / Rhino ✦✦✦✦
30 Greatest Hits is still the essential document for the Atlantic years, but this is certainly an excellent 16-track primer of her most popular late-'60s tracks. Most of them are also on *30 Greatest Hits*. But if you've got a particular yen for Aretha's early Atlantic period (which was also her very best), you'll find all the biggest smashes from that era here, including "Respect," "Chain of Fools," "Think," "The House That Jack Built," "Baby I Love You," "I Never Loved a Man," and so forth. *—Richie Unterberger*

The Very Best of Aretha Franklin, Vol. 2 / Mar. 22, 1994 / Rhino ✦✦✦✦
Covering 1970-76, this isn't quite as top-notch as *The Very Best of, Vol. 1*. And, like *Very Best of, Vol. 1*, much of this is also found on the more comprehensive *30 Greatest Hits* (although some of it is not). Still, it contains the prime stuff from the first half of the '70s, including "Spanish

Harlem," "Don't Play That Song," "Bridge over Troubled Water," and "Until You Come Back to Me," along with less-traveled items like "Oh Me Oh My" and "Brand New Me." *—Richie Unterberger*

Love Songs / Jan. 14, 1997 / Rhino ✦✦✦✦
Musically, this collection's hard to fault—16 romantic tunes from the 1967-76 Atlantic years, including such hits as "Baby I Love You," "I Say a Little Prayer," "A Natural Woman," and "Call Me." Whether you want to add this to your collection depends very much on the way you assemble records. If you want to get these tunes, many of them are heard in better contexts on a number of greatest-hits anthologies. Its appeal is principally to the casual Aretha fan who prefers her softer side. *—Richie Unterberger*

Early Years / Feb. 11, 1997 / Sony ✦✦✦
When Aretha was recording for Columbia in the 1960s, the label didn't seem to know what to do with her. Now that they're reissuing material from that time on CD, they *still* don't know what to do with her. It's hard to determine why someone would pick this over the far more extensive double-disc, *Jazz to Soul*, that covers the some era. Nevertheless, about half of this doesn't show up on that collection, which means short value overall, but some value at least. It's generally considered that Aretha's Columbia output has been somewhat undervalued, and this is a good cross-section of ballads and grittier R&B-influenced items. It's usually overproduced, but not in as unlistenable fashion as some old-school critics might have you believe. But it's hard to determine what focus (if any) this collection has, especially as it's missing her most soulful (and therefore best) Columbia cuts, "Lee Cross" and "Soulville." *—Richie Unterberger*

Freakwater

f. 1987, Louisville, KY
Alternative Country-Rock
Freakwater is an acoustic side project of the Eleventh Day family tree, featuring Dream Day drummer/singer Janet Bean (who plays guitar in Freakwater) and her friend Catherine Ann Irwin, with contributions from various other musicians. This is only "alternative rock" in the marketing sense; the Kentucky-bred singers largely stick to acoustic folk/country with close harmonies and strong Appalachian overtones, sometimes employing fiddle, pedal steel, mandolin, and dobro. Mixing strong original material (mostly written by Irwin) with traditional numbers and songs by the likes of Bill Monroe, Freakwater's albums stand as some of the finest maverick, progressive acoustic records of recent years. *—Richie Unterberger*

Freakwater / 1989 / Amoeba ✦✦✦
Their debut, a short LP, or a long EP, depending on how you look at it, presents plaintive, raw country-folk in a modern context without sounding forced. *—Richie Unterberger*

● **Dancing Under Water** / 1991 / Thrill Jockey ✦✦✦✦
A bit more polished than their debut, but hardly slick, with harmonies and the sobbing lead vocals of Irwin at the fore. This is recommended above the debut for a simple reason: The CD includes all of the songs from *Freakwater* as bonus tracks, eliminating the need to look for the first album. *—Richie Unterberger*

Feels Like the Third Time / May 23, 1995 / Thrill Jockey ✦✦✦

Old Paint / Oct. 10, 1995 / Thrill Jockey ✦✦✦✦
After a four-year gap since their second album, Freakwater returned with another solid effort that's not as bare-bones as their debut, but a little earlier than *Dancing Under Water*. Not a lot of new ground is broken, but it somehow doesn't sound at all tiresome. All of their strengths remain in place: fine, mournful harmonies, good original songs, some well-chosen covers (Loudon Wainwright's "Out of This World" is a particular highlight), and nice unobtrusive touches of pedal steel and fiddle embellishing the acoustic guitars. This is modern country-folk at its best, and in fact would really be more suitable for the roots-country audience, except that the execution is too direct, the production too basic, and the songwriting too heartfelt for the contemporary country marketplace. Thus it is that the group's primary listenership is the alternative rock community, which is country's loss. Few performers today are performing roots music so convincingly, without sounding forced or dated. *—Richie Unterberger*

John Fred

b. May 8, 1941, Baton Rouge, LA
Vocals / Pop-Rock, Blue-Eyed Soul
Remembered only for his fluke 1968 No. 1 hit "Judy in Disguise," John Fred actually made quite a few records in the '60s. Though he was from Louisiana, Fred's vocals strongly recall Eric Burdon at times, and Georgie Fame's at others. A capable songwriter ("Judy in Disguise" was an original), he also cut several fine, deep Southern soul ballads that distinguish him as one of the best American White R&B singers. *—Richie Unterberger*

● **History of John Fred & the Playboys** / 1991 / Paula ✦✦✦
Eclectic 26-song assortment of pop-rock/soul/R&B. Highlights are his 1964 cover of John Lee Hooker's "Boogie Chillen," which stands up to the best early British R&B; the odd, moody "Agnes English" and "Sun City," which shows a strong Animals influence, and of course "Judy in Disguise." A 1958 track that he cut as a teenager recalls a frat-rock Frankie Ford with its low-wattage emulation of the New Orleans sound. Unfortunately there is little in the way of liner notes here, but the grooves prove Fred to be a versatile stylist with much greater depth than the usual one-shot. —*Richie Unterberger*

Freddie & the Dreamers

f. 1961, Manchester, England, **db.** 1968
British Invasion, Pop-Rock
Freddie & the Dreamers were the clowns of the British Invasion, playing their pop music for laughs while the other groups of the time were dead serious. Lead singer Freddie Garrity (b. Nov 14, 1940) began playing in skiffle groups in the late '50s, switching to rock 'n' roll in the early '60s. After the Beatles broke the American market wide open, Freddie & the Dreamers followed in the flood of acts that tried to duplicate the overwhelming success of the Beatles. The group's hits were more numerous in the UK than in America, where they had only one Top Ten hit, the No. 1 "I'm Telling You Now." As 1965 turned into 1966, the group stopped charting in the US, and the hits began to dwindle in the UK; by 1968 the original group disbanded. Garrity continues to tour with a new version of the Dreamers. —*Stephen Thomas Erlewine*

The Best of Freddie & The Dreamers / Jun. 2, 1992 / EMI America ✦✦✦✦
Yes, "I'm Telling You Now" is here, and so is "Do the Freddie," an absurd attempt at fashioning a dance craze, but so are "How About Trying Your Luck with Me," "When I'm Home with You," and "Brown and Porters (Meat Exporters) Lorry." In other words, it's more than a definitive collection, with 25 tracks (many previously unreleased in the US) and a comprehensive discography. —*Stephen Thomas Erlewine*

The Fredric

f. 1967, Grand Rapids, MI, **db.** 1970
Psychedelic, Pop-Rock
From Grand Rapids, MI, the Fredric issued a rare, limited-run album in the late '60s, *Phases and Faces*, that's highly valued in some collector quarters. It would be ultimately inaccurate to call this garage psychedelia; it's too clean-cut and poppy, with conscientious harmonies, guitar-organ interplay, and light lovelorn lyrics. They were a very young group, and it shows in the callow songwriting, despite the well executed arrangements. The single "Red Pier" made some modest local noise, and by 1970 they were signed to Capitol, who changed their name to the Rock Garden. They disbanded shortly after beginning their relationship with Capitol; drummer-vocalist David Idema eventually had a hit, "Run Joey Run," as David Geddes. —*Richie Unterberger*

Phases and Faces / 1968 / Arf! Arf! ✦✦✦
A reissue of the 1968 album, with four bonus tracks from a non-LP single and a few songs that were cut for a never-completed second album. It's innocent, even naive, teen pop-rock with a mild psychedelic touch, particularly in the organ riffs. But it's not strong or distinct enough to rank anywhere near the best of either the garage or psychedelic genres. —*Richie Unterberger*

Free

f. 1968, London, England, **db.** 1973
Blues-Rock, Hard Rock
Famed for their perennial "All Right Now," Free helped lay the foundations for the rise of hard rock, stripping the earthy sound of British blues down to its raw, minimalist core to pioneer a brand of proto-metal later popularized by 1970s superstars like Foreigner, Foghat, and Bad Company. Free formed in London in 1968 when guitarist Paul Kossoff and drummer Simon Kirke, then members of the blues unit Black Cat Bones, first spotted vocalist Paul Rodgers performing with his group Brown Sugar. After deciding to form their own band, the trio recruited 16-year-old bass phenom Andy Fraser from the ranks of John Mayall's Bluesbreakers; with the aid of Alexis Korner, who suggested the name Free, the fledgling band signed to the Island label, issuing their bluesy debut *Tons of Sobs* in 1968.
Free's eponymous 1969 follow-up expanded on their roots-based sound, incorporating rockers like Albert King's "The Hunter" as well as muscular ballads like "Lying in the Sunshine." Although both of the first two albums fared poorly on the charts, 1970's *Fire and Water* became a tremendous hit on the strength of the primal "All Right Now," a Top Five smash powered by Rodgers' gritty, visceral vocals. After headlining 1970's Isle of Wight festival, the group appeared destined for superstardom, but the LP *Highway* did not fare nearly as well as anticipated, and

after a grueling tour that yielded 1971's *Free Live*, the band dissolved amidst ego clashes and recriminations.
While Rodgers went on to form Peace and Fraser founded Toby, Kossoff and Kirke teamed with bassist Tetsu Yamauchi and keyboardist John "Rabbit" Bundrick to record the album *Kossoff, Kirke, Tetsu and Rabbit*. When none of these new projects proved successful, the original lineup of Free re-formed to record 1972's *Free at Last*, which launched the hit "Little Bit of Love." However, drug problems nagged the group, as Kossoff's longtime battle with heroin continued to worsen; soon Fraser exited to form Sharks with Chris Spedding, leaving Rodgers and Kirke to record the majority of 1973's *Heartbreaker* while a drug-addled Kossoff watched from the sidelines. Soon the group disbanded again, this time for good. While Rodgers and Kirke went on to found Bad Company, Kossoff formed Back Street Crawler before dying of a drug-induced heart attack on March 19, 1976. —*Jason Ankeny*

Tons of Sobs / 1968 / A&M ✦✦
Free's first long player landed them heavily in the midst of the British blues-rock genre. Solid orginals were complimented by a standard blues tune and a Motown R&B workout. This hard rocking start is highlighted by the heavy guitar of Paul Kossoff and the deep-throated vocals of Paul Rodgers. An impressive debut. —*James Chrispell*

Free / 1969 / A&M ✦✦✦
Free's second outing contained all original material and was less blues-based. The loping bass and snakey guitar figures appear to be a blueprint of things to come. Paul Rodger's dynamic vocal range is pushed steadily to the fore, and cuts such as "Songs of Yesterday" and "Woman" fit well alongside introspective selections like "Mouthful of Grass" or "Mourning, Sad Mourning." A solid set from a band just beginning to hit its stride. —*James Chrispell*

Fire and Water / 1970 / A&M ✦✦✦✦
This classic Free album features their biggest hit, "All Right Now," as well as key Free tracks, "Heavy Load," "Mr. Big," and the title track. —*Rick Clark*

Highway / Feb. 1971 / A&M ✦✦✦
After the blockbuster success of their previous disc, Free appeared to fumble the ball in mid-court. Although containing such fine tunes as "The Stealer" and "The Hiway Song," this album was a much mellower follow-up than one would imagine. Best when you're in a more laidback mood, it is a fine effort, nonetheless. —*James Chrispell*

Free Live / Sep. 1971 / A&M ✦✦
Recorded before, but put out after, the group's first break-up, *Free Live!* is often a very spirited effort. Including such concert hits as "Fire and Water," "Mr. Big," and "All Right Now," it shows Free in top form. *Free Live* also contains the moody studio track "Get Where I Belong," which was a staple of FM radio. —*James Chrispell*

Free at Last / 1972 / A&M ✦✦✦
Free re-formed and brought back much of the old fire while integrating the mellowness, so things weren't as the patchwork that often marred previous efforts. Both "Catch a Train" and "Little Bit of Love" burned with magic fire while "Travelin' Man" and "Sail On" proved to be first-rate ballads. Not perfect, but closer than before. —*James Chrispell*

● **The Best of Free** / 1973 / A&M ✦✦✦✦
A solid compilation showcasing "All Right Now" and other semi-hits, this is a worthwhile sampler for the uninitiated. —*Dan Heilman*

Heartbreaker / 1973 / PolyGram ✦✦
What should have been the first peak in a solid rise to stardom proved to be an epitaph from a band not without its share of problems. But *Heartbreaker* is an amazing album, chock-full of good tunes and a togetherness lacking in past efforts. It includes the Top 40 hit "Wishing Well" as well as "Easy on My Soul" which Paul Rodgers covered again when he and Simon Kirke formed Bad Company. An impressive album that appears to be the swan song for Free. —*James Chrispell*

Molten Gold: The Anthology / Oct. 5, 1993 / A&M ✦✦✦✦
With their big riffs and bluesy melodies, Free virtually defined hard rock in the early '70s, and *Molten Gold: The Anthology* shows that this wasn't such a meager achievement. Throughout the two discs, it becomes clear that the key to Free's rock 'n' roll was their rhythm section, which powered their riffs to perfection. This is the definitive Free, two discs of pure hard rock. —*Stephen Thomas Erlewine*

Bobby Freeman

b. Jun. 13, 1940, San Francisco, CA
Vocals / R&B
Bobby Freeman's energetic vocals punctuated two R&B dance hits in the late '50s and mid-'60s. The San Francisco performer started the Romancers as a 14-year-old and later formed the West Coast Vocaleers, whose sound was much more pop-oriented than the Harlem group of the same name. Freeman's single "Do You Want to Dance" just missed topping the R&B charts in 1958, staying at No. 2 for two weeks (No. 5 pop). It was

one of three hits he enjoyed that year on Josie, although "Betty Lou Got a New Pair of Shoes" and "Need Your Love" reached only No. 20 and No. 29, respectively. "C'Mon and Swim" parlayed the 1964 dance craze into his second Top Ten R&B hit, reaching No. 5. But the follow-up went to the water once too often, as "S-W-I-M" fizzled at No. 56. Both were for Autumn. It was also Freeman's final visit to the R&B charts. —*Ron Wynn*

● **Best of** / 1992 / Sequel ♦♦♦♦

Doug E. Fresh

b. Sep. 17, 1966, New York, NY
Hip Hop, Old School Rap
New Yorker Doug E. Fresh (born Doug E. Davis) got his initial notoriety for being the "human beatbox," able to approximate and imitate a rhythm machine. He had a string of hit singles with his then-partner Ricky Dee in the early and mid-'80s, notably "The Show (Oh, My God)" in 1985, which included guest stints from jazz veteran trumpeter Jimmy Owens and synthesizer player Bernard Wright. Fresh had a long absence from the scene after 1988's *The World's Greatest Entertainer* and has just resurfaced with a new release on a small independent label. —*Ron Wynn*

Oh, My God! / 1986 / Reality ♦♦♦♦
Zany rhymes, slashing beats, with bits and pieces of everything from reggae to gospel to funk. —*Ron Wynn*

● **The World's Greatest Entertainer** / 1988 / Reality ♦♦♦♦
With the exception of the monster hit "Keep Risin' to the Top," Fresh trimmed the religious zealotry and increased the lyrical and rhythmic potency. —*Ron Wynn*

Doin' What I Gotta Do / Apr. 27, 1992 / Bust It ♦♦♦

Play / Nov. 1995 / Gee Street ♦♦

Greatest Hits, Vol. 1 / Aug. 1996 / Bust It ♦♦♦♦
Greatest Hits, Vol. 1 collects all of Doug E. Fresh's biggest singles—including "La Di Da Di," "Keep Risin' to the Top," and "The Show," adding a couple of new tracks produced by Sean "Puffy" Combs for good measure. It's a concise and entertaining retrospective that sums up his career very well. —*Stephen Thomas Erlewine*

Friends of Dean Martinez

f. 1995, Tucson, AZ
Alternative Pop-Rock, Cocktail
A Southwestern alternative rock supergroup of sorts, Arizona's Friends of Dean Martinez features past and present members of Giant Sand and Naked Prey. Giant Sand leader Howe Gelb, though not a member of the group, plays guest keyboards on their debut album, *The Shadow of Your Smile*, a surprisingly retro set of guitar-based instrumentals inspired by instrumental and surf rock of the late '50s and early '60s. With plenty of lounge music and desert country guitar twang thrown in, it's certainly retro in feel, but not revivalist; with Bill Elm's keening steel guitar at the forefront and occasional insertions of found sound and experimental bits, they evoke open dusty landscapes, with wit and, one suspects, a bit of tongue-in-cheek irony. At any rate, it's a refreshing change from the often too-serious alternative rock paths that the musicians pursue in their full-time bands. —*Richie Unterberger*

The Shadow of Your Smile / Aug. 22, 1995 / Sub Pop ♦♦♦
A post-modern fusion of Santo & Johnny, Dick Dale and the Ventures, with a heaping side order of Tex-Mex border music. Whether the musicians are playing this straight or not, they're playing it very well, and the result is good fun, even if it's totally uncharacteristic of the material offered by the Giant Sand/Naked Prey axis in the past. —*Richie Unterberger*

The Friends of Distinction

f. 1969, Los Angeles, CA, **db.** 1970
Soul, R&B, Pop-Rock
A Los Angeles pop-influenced R&B group modeled after the 5th Dimension, the Friends of Distinction briefly carved out their own pop/R&B niche in 1969-70. Two members (Floyd Butler and Harry Elston) had been in the Hi-Fi's (a group that spawned a pair of 5th Dimension members), and the Friends' breezy vocal blend was quite similar, although weighted toward the ladies (three women, two men). Their first RCA hit in 1969 was a vocal treatment of Hugh Masekela's hit instrumental "Grazing in the Grass," and they encored with "Going in Circles," a mellow number that was a minor hit, and the dazzling "Love or Let Me Be Lonely." —*Bill Dahl*

● **Best of Friends of Distinction** / Nov. 26, 1996 / RCA ♦♦♦♦
The Best of Friends of Distinction is a 20-track compilation that contains every R&B hit the late '60s/early '70s soul group had during their chart run ("Grazing in the Grass," "Going in Circles," "Love or Let Me Be Lonely," "Time Waits for No One," "I Need You"), plus 15 other songs that

highlight the best of their album tracks and failed singles. Most casual fans will be satisfied by having the Friends' classic singles on various artist soul hits collections, but for anyone who wants to dig deeper, this definitive compilation is unquestionably the finest ever assembled for the band. —*Stephen Thomas Erlewine*

Front 242

f. 1982, Brussels, Belgium
Industrial, Alternative Pop-Rock
When the Belgian synth-dance group began recording in 1982, their style followed the cold, clinical work of Kraftwerk and Cabaret Voltaire, but their music had none of the dark mystery or threat of those early electronic bands. As the decade progressed, they captured that mystery; by the end of the decade, Front 242 were on the cutting edge of the experimental industrial dance groups, combining political sound bites with their dance samples and beats. Their 1988 club hit, "Headhunter," cemented their reputation and provided a good example of their aggressive style. After their 1988 album, *Front by Front*, the group left the seminal industrial record label Wax Trax for Epic. Front 242's first major label release, 1991's *Tyranny for You*, showed no concessions and was another strong statement. However, their subsequent albums in the '90s showed that the group was beginning to slip from the cutting edge. By the mid-'90s, their cult had declined significantly, and the group lost their contract with Epic. *Mut@ge.Mix@ge*, released in 1996, was their first independent release since their recordings for Wax Trax in the '80s. —*Stephen Thomas Erlewine*

Official Version (1986-1987) / 1987 / Epic ♦♦♦♦
With its dense, claustrophobic mix of samples and relentless, hard beats, *Official Version* was the first consistently impressive Front 242 record. —*Stephen Thomas Erlewine*

Back Catalogue / 1987 / Wax Trax! ♦♦♦
A collection of early 12-inch singles, *Back Catalogue* is the best way to get acquainted with Front 242's early days. —*Stephen Thomas Erlewine*

● **Front by Front** / 1988 / Epic ♦♦♦♦
While it reiterates the music of *Official Version*, *Front by Front* features a stronger political message, as well as their signature single, "Headhunter." —*Stephen Thomas Erlewine*

Tyranny (for You) / Jan. 24, 1991 / Epic ♦♦♦♦
More aggressive and militant than its predecessors, *Tyranny (for You)* is an impressionistic, angry album that captured the underlying chaos of the early '90s with its dark, brutal rhythm tracks alone. —*Stephen Thomas Erlewine*

06:21:03:11 up Evil / May 25, 1993 / Epic ♦♦♦
Although it isn't a bad album by any means, Front 242 seems at a loss for ideas on *06:21:03:11 up Evil*, which lacks the sonic power and conceptual force of their three previous albums. —*Stephen Thomas Erlewine*

05:22:09:12 Off / Nov. 2, 1993 / Epic ♦♦

Mut@ge.Mix@ge / Dec. 17, 1996 / RRE ♦♦

Fugazi

f. 1988, Washington, D.C.
Alternative Pop-Rock, Hardcore Punk, Indie Rock
Fugazi is as famous for its strident anti-corporate stance as for their music. Fugazi's leader, singer/guitarist Ian MacKaye, refuses to charge over $5 for a concert and keeps the prices of recordings low by releasing them through his own record label, Dischord. Their vehement political stance can overshadow their musical accomplishments; they are one of the few bands that prove it's possible for hardcore punk to expand beyond its rigid structures. With the seminal DC hardcore band Minor Threat, MacKaye defined straight-edge hardcore; with Fugazi, he breaks and rewrites the very rules he established.
Since their 1988 debut EP, Fugazi has gained a substantial fan base without the help of mainstream press or MTV airplay; the band would rather talk to fanzines than to the mainstream press. By the time of their 1993 album, they charted on *Billboard*'s Top 200 without any commercial push. Through their anti-rock star stance, Fugazi have become rock stars. —*Stephen Thomas Erlewine*

● **13 Songs** / Apr. 1990 / Dischord ♦♦♦♦
Fugazi's first album, actually a compilation of a self-titled 1988 EP and 1989's *Margin Walker* EP, set a course for the rest of the band's career, distanced from Ian MacKaye's thrash beginnings and more reliant on dissonance and noise, without deserting the power of Minor Threat's punch. Including the punk anthem "Waiting Room" as well as other highlights like "Margin Walker" and "Bulldog Front," *13 Songs* is the most confrontational album Fugazi ever released. —*John Bush*

Repeater + 3 Songs / Apr. 1990 / Dischord ♦♦♦♦
Even more energetic than the band's first two EPs (collected on *13 Songs*), Fugazi's proper debut album also shows a growing maturity and

lyrical depth, with a crisper production job. Though lacking the classic riffs of the early anthem "Waiting Room," several songs (the title track, "Merchandise," "Styrofoam") are just as propulsive and hard-hitting. Balancing out the thrash are midtempo shots such as "Shut the Door" and "Two Beats Off." The CD issue combines the original album with the *3 Songs* EP. — *John Bush*

Steady Diet of Nothing / Jul. 1, 1991 / Dischord ✦✦✦✦
Repeater showed a more mature Fugazi, and its follow-up *Steady Diet of Nothing* continued that direction. Just as on Fugazi's earlier works, the lyrics on "Dear Justice Letter" and "KYEO" (Keep Your Eyes Open) are hard-hitting and almost paranoid in their disgust for politics and capitalism of any kind, but throughout *Steady Diet of Nothing*, the group focuses more on mood and, surprisingly, musicianship. The balance between Fugazi's hardcore roots and atmospheric future created their most consistently listenable album, if not the most energetic. — *John Bush*

In on the Kill Taker / Jun. 30, 1993 / Dischord ✦✦✦
The band's farthest departure from hardcore punk yet, *In on the Kill Taker* does include a few great paranoid punk songs—such as "Public Witness Program," "Great Cop," and "Smallpox Champion"—but the straightahead themes are overshadowed by experimental and atmospheric textures. Case in point: the moody "Rend It" and the almost four minutes of feedback that close "23 Beats Off." — *John Bush*

Red Medicine / Jun. 1995 / Dischord ✦✦✦
On Fugazi's fifth LP, the band continue to move farther from their hardcore past. It's not that they've mellowed out; the aggression and fury at everything commercial and political is still there, but, as on 1993's *In on the Kill Taker*, Fugazi intersperse their uptempo rants with guitar-effects experimentation and slower tracks. The song forms are more complex than on previous releases and, while the album is not immediately captivating, repeated listenings reveal the music's depth and maturity—a more fulfilling form of appreciation, anyway. — *John Bush*

Fugees

f. 1992, New York, NY
Hip Hop, Alternative Rap
Wyclef Jean ("Clef") and Prakazrel Michel ("Pras") are producers/MCs of Haitian descent who joined with rapper/singer Lauryn Hill to form the Fugees. Their 1994 debut, *Blunted on Reality*, combined reggae, rock, and funk with their ragga-tinged delivery and was released on Columbia Records.
The Fugees released their second album, *The Score*, in early 1996. *The Score* became the surprise hip-hop hit of the year, reaching No. 1 on the pop charts and selling over four million copies within its first four months of release. — *John Bush*

Blunted on Reality / Feb. 1, 1994 / Ruffhouse ✦✦✦
● **The Score** / Feb. 1996 / RuffHouse ✦✦✦✦
An open, yet funky, collage of hip-hop, soul, blues, jazz, and reggae, the Fugees' second album, *The Score*, is a great step forward for the New York trio. On their debut, the group sketched out a pattern similar to the multi-ethnic, edgy music on *The Score*, but they didn't deliver it with the authority that they do here. The Fugees cover Bob Marley's "No Woman, No Cry" and Roberta Flack's "Killing Me Softly," which gives an idea of their range, as well as their intent to carry on the soul/R&B tradition. They pull it off with a surprisingly amount of style and innovation. With its intelligent, gritty lyrics and brave eclecticism, *The Score* simply sounds like few rap records of the mid-'90s. — *Stephen Thomas Erlewine*

The Score: Bootleg Versions [EP] / Nov. 26, 1996 / Sony ✦✦✦
Released several months after the Fugees became stars, *Bootleg Versions* is an EP of remixes from the Fugees' two albums, *Blunted on Reality* and *The Score*. None of the new mixes has the spark or fire of the originals, but some of the reworking will be of interest to hardcore fans. By and large, however, it doesn't add any new dimension to the Fugees' music. — *Leo Stanley*

The Fugs

f. 1964, New York, NY, **db.** 1970
Rock 'n' Roll, Folk-Rock
Arguably the first "underground" rock group of all time, the Fugs formed at the Peace Eye bookstore in New York's East Village in late 1964. The nucleus of the band throughout its many personnel changes was Peace Eye owner Ed Sanders, and fellow poet Tuli Kupferberg. Sanders and Kupferberg had strong ties to the beat literary scene, but charged, in the manner of their friend Allen Ginsberg, full steam ahead into the maelstrom of '60s political involvement and psychedelia. Surrounded by an assortment of motley refugees from the New York folk and jugband scene (including Steve Weber and Peter Stampfel of the Holy Modal Rounders), some of whom could barely play their instruments, the group nonetheless was determined to play rock 'n' roll their

way—which meant rife with political and social satire, as well as explicit profanity and sexual references that were downright unheard of in 1965. Starting on the legendary avant-garde ESP label, the Fugs' debut was full of equal amounts of chaos and charm, but their songwriting and instrumental chops improved surprisingly quickly, resulting in a great second album that was undoubtedly the most shocking and satirical recording ever to grace the Top 100 when it was released. After cutting an unreleased album for Atlantic, they moved on to Frank Sinatra's Reprise label, unleashing a few more albums of equally satirical material that was more instrumentally polished, but equally scathing lyrically. Breaking up around 1970, Sanders and Kupferberg have continued to write prose and poetry, and sometimes write and perform music, both on their own and as part of Fugs reunions. By breaking lyrical taboos of popular music, they helped pave the way for the even more innovative outrage of the Mothers of Invention, the Velvet Underground, and others. — *Richie Unterberger*

The Fugs' First Album / 1965 / Fantasy ✦✦✦
Engagingly sloppy, even raw performances on their debut, which draws on leftist politics, the poetry of William Blake, and the joys of sex. Some of this is wearily cacophonous, but "Slum Goddess," "Supergirl," "I Couldn't Get High," and "Nothing" are among their funniest songs. The CD reissue adds 11 bonus tracks: seven studio cuts from the same era (the sarcastic "CIA Man" is a highlight), three live songs from 1965, and an eight-minute spoken word piece. — *Richie Unterberger*

● **The Fugs** / 1966 / Fantasy ✦✦✦✦
At the time of its release, the Fugs' second (self-titled) album contained the most outrageous lyrics ever heard on a Top 100 rock 'n' roll LP. The group, with roots in New York's underground folk and poetry scenes, flung themselves wholeheartedly into all-out rock 'n' roll on this 1966 record, which addresses concerns like free love, the madness of war, and government repression. The CD reissue of this classic includes two previously unreleased live performances and three tracks from the unreleased album they recorded for Atlantic in 1967. — *Richie Unterberger*

Tenderness Junction / 1967 / Reprise ✦✦✦
The band opted for a considerably more conventional rock sound more in keeping with the era's psychedelic tenor on their first major-label release. The material isn't as strong and the satirical humor not as biting as their earlier efforts, though it's characteristically witty stuff. Highlights include "Turn On/Tune In/Drop Out" and "War Song"; "Aphrodite Mass" is an ambitious if not terribly memorable five-part suite. — *Richie Unterberger*

Live from the '60s / 1994 / Ace ✦✦✦✦
For anyone who thinks the Velvet Underground was as outré as successful cult 1960s bands got, this is the *real* stuff. Taken from the personal tape collection of Ed Sanders, it's 50 minutes of unadulterated live Fugs, from their first concert in Greenwich Village to dates from Sweden, Wisconsin, and Texas played between 1967 and 1969. All of it is pretty raw, but that's good, because it's real. The material represents the different sides of the group's sound very well; "The Swedish Nada" has them sounding like the punk equivalents of the Doors, while "The Garden Is Open" ventures into VU territory, with Dan Kooch's violin creating a positively demonic sound, and "The Exorcism of the Grave of Senator Joseph McCarthy" (conducted at the senator's grave with Allen Ginsberg present) is like little else ever recorded by an alleged rock group. There's a lot of history here, and some fascinating music captured in generally fair fidelity. The perfect gift for anyone who already has all of the Velvets' material, or thinks the Doors were poet poseurs. — *Bruce Eder*

Fuller & Kaz

f. 1978, United States
Folk-Rock, Pop-Rock
Craig Fuller and Eric Kaz teamed up for this one-off project after the break-up of their previous band, American Flyer. The band split after two pleasant, but commercially disappointing, efforts for United Artists in the mid-'70s. As a member of Pure Prairie League for two albums, Fuller scored a hit with "Amie," while Kaz was a successful songwriter, with tunes covered by the likes of Linda Ronstadt, Bonnie Raitt, and the Nitty Gritty Dirt Band, as well as being a member of the Children of Paradise and the Blues Magoos. — *Brett Hartenbach*

● **Craig Fuller & Eric Kaz** / 1978 / Columbia ✦✦✦✦
With producer/engineer Val Garay (Eric Carmen, Pablo Cruise, Linda Ronstadt), Craig Fuller & Eric Kaz found a sympathetic ear for their romantic, acoustic-based pop-rock. Garay's production, for the most part, stays out of the way of the material, which with Fuller's throaty tenor, carries the record. A handful of ordinary songs and Kaz' less than commanding vocals occasionally drag the album down, but cuts such as Fuller's "Feel That Way Again," the Kaz standard "Cry like a Rainstorm," and their collaboration "Annabella" make *Fuller/Kaz* worthwhile for anyone interested in the genre. — *Brett Hartenbach*

Bobby Fuller Four

f. Oct. 22, 1942, El Paso, TX, **db.** Jul. 18, 1966
Vocals / Rock 'n' Roll, Pop-Rock

With his blatant reverence for Buddy Holly, fellow Texan Bobby Fuller was a bit of an anomaly in the mid-'60s. With his Stratocaster guitar and brash, full sound, at his best Fuller sounded like Holly might have, had he survived into the '60s. Cracking the Top 30 in 1966 with a cover of Holly's "Love's Made a Fool of You," and then the Top Ten with "I Fought the Law" (written by one-time Cricket Sonny Curtis), Fuller had just become a star when he died in mysterious circumstances in a parked car in Hollywood. (The police thought it was a suicide; just about everyone who knew him disagreed.) Fuller's relatively short period of national stardom actually crowned a good half dozen years of recording, during which he released many outstanding tracks. After a few singles in his hometown of El Paso in the early '60s, he moved to California with his combo in 1964, and briefly had aspirations of playing surf music before hooking up with producer Bob Keene. In the short time he recorded for Mustang in 1965 and 1966, he waxed quite a few fine tracks (most self-penned) besides his hits, including "Let Her Dance," "Another Sad and Lonely Night," "My True Love," "Never to Be Forgotten," "Fool of Love," and "The Magic Touch." Rocking, tuneful, and infectiously joyous, they showed Fuller to be a worthy inheritor of early rock 'n' roll and rockabilly traditions without sounding self-consciously revivalist. While it's hard to imagine Fuller maintaining his success in the era of psychedelia, he no doubt would have gone on to produce interesting work. A talented and prolific songwriter and a studio wiz who drew from Eddie Cochran and (though only slightly) the full guitar sound of the British Invasion as well as Buddy Holly, he recorded a great deal of unreleased studio and live material that was issued in the 1980s, when the depth of his loss began to be appreciated. —*Richie Unterberger*

● **The Best of Bobby Fuller Four** / 1981 / Rhino ◆◆◆◆
A great 18-track compilation of his best work that is truly all killer, no filler. While there's some other good Fuller to be found, this is definitely the prime stuff from his mid-'60s recordings for Mustang: "I Fought the Law," "Let Her Dance," "The Magic Touch," "Love's Made a Fool of You," "Fool of Love," "My True Love," and other equally fine if lesser-known sides. —*Richie Unterberger*

Bobby Fuller Tapes, Vol. 1 / 1983 / Rhino ◆◆◆
Not released until nearly 20 years after his death, this rare material—recorded in El Paso between 1960 and 1964—is less polished and even more overtly Buddy Holly-influenced than his mid-'60s tracks. But they're nearly as affecting and tuneful, and feature many strong Fuller originals. —*Richie Unterberger*

Live Again / 1984 / Eva ◆◆◆
According to legend, the Bobby Fuller Four were one hell of a live band. These previously unreleased live recordings from 1964 are indeed accomplished, but keep in mind that in those days, unestablished acts stuck mostly to well-known cover versions, and Fuller was no exception. Most of this set was composed of R&B/rock chestnuts along the lines of "Whole Lotta Shakin' Goin' On," "Night Train," "Peggy Sue," and "Little Bitty Pretty One"; there's a slight nod to the raging British Invasion with "From Me to You" and "House of the Rising Sun." Good though not imperfect fidelity on these cleanly executed but hardly revelatory interpretations. Fuller showed the true scope of his talents on his studio recordings of 1965 and 1966, and though this album demonstrates the band were first-class live players, it shows nothing of their originality. As such, it is recommended only to serious fans. —*Richie Unterberger*

Bobby Fuller Tapes, Vol. 2 / 1984 / Voxx ◆◆◆
The second major excursion into the vaults for previously unreleased Fuller material isn't nearly as interesting as Vol. 1, primarily because this collection of rare singles, alternate versions, live recordings, and outtakes from 1960-64 is composed mostly of cover versions. Still, Fuller's brash vocals and guitars are worth hearing, though they don't redefine Little Richard, Jerry Lee Lewis, and Buddy Holly's originals. The best of the lot are the versions of "Pretty Girls Everywhere," "Baby I Don't Care," and the sizzling five-minute instrumental version of "Miserlou." Also includes the original 1964 version of "I Fought the Law," the first-class Fuller rockabilly original "Bodine," and a haunting instrumental version of "My True Love." "Shakedown" is as raw and dirty as he ever got, but unfortunately, the version on this LP was mastered from a scratchy rare single (though the fidelity on the rest of the album is excellent). —*Richie Unterberger*

Bobby Fuller Instrumental Album / 1985 / Rockhouse ◆◆◆
In between his rockabilly roots in El Paso and hitting it big as a modern-day reincarnation of Buddy Holly in the mid-'60s, Bobby Fuller briefly entertained aspirations of playing surf music. Updated Holly and Cochranisms were his true forte, so this album—composed mostly of surf and R&B instrumentals from 1964—doesn't measure up to his best work in the least. That's not to say it's bad. If nothing else, it's further evidence of how disciplined and versatile his band was. Much of the mate-

rial was unreleased before this compilation. (Collectors should know that, although the liner notes claim that the 1961 single by the Venturas on this LP features guitarist Jim Reese, Reese himself denies any knowledge of the group.) —*Richie Unterberger*

Live at PJ's Plus! / Jul. 1991 / Ace ◆◆◆
Long rumored to have been "lost," these tapes resurfaced more than 25 years after the Bobby Fuller Four recorded at PJ's in December 1965. The final results are a perfect rock 'n' roll time capsule. These live recordings give the listener an excellent sample of the band's performance, complete with the requisite medley and popular cover songs that even bands with hit records were obligated to do at the request of club owners. Highlights include "Anytime at All" by the Beatles and Larry William's classic "Slow Down," along with the band's familiar hits like "Let Her Dance" and "I Fought the Law." A definite "must" for every Fuller fan and anyone who fondly remembers live rock 'n' roll from the mid-'60s. —*Dan Pavlides*

Shakedown! The Texas Tapes Revisited / Oct. 1996 / Del-Fi ◆◆◆◆
Although a lot of this has previously appeared on various out-of-the-way reissues, this is the best compilation to date of the material Fuller recorded between 1961 and 1964 before signing with the Mustang label. The two-disc, 52-track package has both sides of the seven singles he made for the Yucca, Eastwood, Exeter, and Todd labels, as well as a wealth of unreleased cuts and alternate versions. It's not as polished as his more renowned mid-'60s records, and it's more derivative of his '50s heroes, particularly Buddy Holly. But it's almost as good as Fuller's most celebrated work, marked by a combination of incessant brash energy and infectious Hollyesque melodies. Fuller's confident vocals and guitar playing, even at this early stage, were equally capable of delivering raucous rockabilly and sensitive, emotional performances. Completists should note that although some of this hasn't seen the light of day before, this reissue doesn't gather *everything* he did during these years; other cuts are scattered on other compilations. Many of the previously released tracks, though, appear here in much better fidelity, and the discs are carefully sequenced to spread the alternate takes far apart from each other, icing the cake of an excellent reissue. —*Richie Unterberger*

Fun Boy Three

f. 1981, Coventry, England, **db.** 1983
New Wave

The Specials were one of the most popular and influential bands in the UK, scoring a streak of seven straight Top Ten singles. Their popularity culminated with the prophetic "Ghost Town," which spent three weeks at No. 1 in the summer of 1981. The "Ghost Town" single was the last to feature Terry Hall and the original lineup; after its release Hall split with the group's other two vocalists, Lynval Golding and Neville Staples, to form the Fun Boy Three.

Where the Specials were a ska-revival band, the Fun Boy Three was a new wave pop group with distinctly weird, skeletal, and experimental overtones. The band released their first single, "The Lunatics (Have Taken Over the Asylum)," shortly after they departed from the Specials. The single peaked at No. 20 late in 1981. Early in 1982 the group charted again with "It Ain't What You Do (It's the Way That You Do It)," a duet with Bananarama on an old Jimmie Lunceford song. The Fun Boy Three finally released their eponymous debut in the spring of 1982. That summer they had a hit with a cover of George Gershwin's "Summertime." The group recorded a second album with Talking Heads leader David Byrne late in 1982. The resulting album, *Waiting*, appeared in the spring of 1983, concurrently with the Top Ten singles "The Tunnel of Love" and "Our Lips Are Sealed," a song Hall wrote with Jane Wiedlin, who had made it into a hit the previous year with her group, the Go-Go's.

By the summer of 1983, the Fun Boy Three were peaking in popularity and Hall disbanded the group. —*Stephen Thomas Erlewine*

The Fun Boy Three / Mar. 1982 / Chrysalis ◆◆◆
Hall sings lead and Staples and Golding chant behind him on the group's beat-heavy ballads on such hits as "It Ain't What You Do . . . ," on which they are joined by Bananarama. —*William Ruhlmann*

Waiting / Feb. 1983 / Chrysalis ◆◆
David Byrne-produced second album contains the Boys' own version of their song "Our Lips Are Sealed," a hit for the Go-Go's. —*William Ruhlmann*

● **The Best of the Fun Boy Three** / 1984 / Chrysalis ◆◆◆◆
This collects all of the essential moments of the short-lived band. Two non-LP tracks are an added bonus: a cover of Gershwin's "Summertime" and their collaboration with Bananarama, "Really Saying Something." —*Chris Woodstra*

The Best of the Fun Boy Three: Really Saying Something / 1997 / Chrysalis ◆◆◆
Instead of concentrating on the single versions of hits like "Our Lips Are

Sealed," *The Best of the Fun Boy Three—Really Saying Something* includes remixed versions of nearly all of the group's best-known songs. While this is a selling point for some collectors—after all, many of these 12-inch mixes have not been on CD before—for most fans, it makes the compilation an ultimately frustrating listen, since the extended mixes and alternate versions aren't nearly as infectious as the originals. *—Stephen Thomas Erlewine*

Funkadelic

f. 1968, Detroit, MI, **db.** 1981
Soul, Funk, Rock 'n' Roll, Psychedelic

Though it often took a back chair to its sister group Parliament, Funkadelic furthered the notions of Black rock begun by Jimi Hendrix and Sly Stone, blending elements of '60s psychedelia and blues with the deep groove of soul and funk. The band pursued album statements of social/political commentary while Parliament stayed in the funk singles format, but Funkadelic nevertheless paralleled the more commercial artists' success, especially in the late '70s when the interplay between bands moved the Funkadelic sound closer to a unified P-Funk style.

Funkadelic began life supporting George Clinton's doo wop group, the Parliaments. After having performed for almost ten years, the Parliaments had added a rhythm section in 1964—for tours and background work—consisting of guitarist Frankie Boyce, his brother Richard on bass, and drummer Langston Booth; two years later, the trio enlisted in the Army. By mid-1967 Clinton had recruited a new backing band, including his old friend Billy "Bass" Nelson (b. Jan. 28, 1951, Plainfield, NJ) and guitarist Eddie Hazel (b. April 10, 1950, Brooklyn, NY). After several temporary replacements on drums and keyboards, the addition of rhythm guitarist Lucius "Tawl" Ross (b. Oct. 5, 1948, Wagram, NC) and drummer Ramon "Tiki" Fulwood (b. May 23, 1944, Philadelphia, PA) completed the lineup.

The Parliaments recorded several hits during 1967, but trouble with the Revilot label backed Clinton into a corner. He hit upon the idea of deserting the Parliaments' name and instead recording their backing group, with the added vocal "contributions" of the former Parliaments—same band, different name. Billy Nelson suggested the title Funkadelic, to reflect the members' increased inspiration from LSD and psychedelic culture. Clinton formed the Funkadelic label in mid-1968 but then signed the group to Detroit's Westbound label several months later.

Released in 1970, Funkadelic's self-titled debut album listed only producer Clinton and the five members of Funkadelic—Hazel, Nelson, Fulwood, and Ross, plus organist Mickey Atkins—but included all the former Parliaments plus several Motown sessionmen and Rare Earth's Ray Monette. Keyboard player Bernie Worrell also appeared on the album uncredited, even though his picture was included on the inner sleeve with the rest of the band.

Worrell (b. April 19, 1944, Long Beach, NJ) was finally credited on the second Funkadelic album (1970's *Free Your Mind . . . And Your Ass Will Follow*). He and Clinton had known each other since the early '60s, and Worrell soon became the most crucial cog in the P-Funk machine, working on arrangements and production for most later Parliament/Funkadelic releases. His strict upbringing and classical training (at the New England Conservatory and Juilliard), as well as the boom in synthesizer technology during the early '70s, gave him the tools to create the horn arrangements and jazz fusion-inspired synth runs that later trademarked the P-Funk sound. Just after the release of their third album, *Maggot Brain*, P-Funk added yet another big contributor, Bootsy Collins. The throbbing bassline of Collins (b. Oct. 26, 1951, Cincinnati, OH) had previously been featured in James Brown's backing band, the JBs (along with his brother, guitarist Catfish Collins). Bootsy and Catfish were playing in a Detroit band in 1972 when George Clinton saw and hired them.

The Clinton/Worrell/Collins lineup premiered on 1972's *America Eats Its Young*, but soon after its release several original members left the camp. Eddie Hazel spent a year in jail after a combination drug possession/assault conviction, Tawl Ross left the band for medical reasons relating to an overdose of LSD and speed, and Bill Nelson quit after more financial quarrels with Clinton. Funkadelic hired teenaged guitar sensation Michael Hampton as a replacement, but both Hazel and Nelson would return for several later P-Funk releases.

Funkadelic moved to Warner Bros. in 1975 and delivered its major-label debut *Hardcore Jollies* one year later to lackluster sales and reviews. The same year, Westbound raided its vaults and countered with *Tales of Kidd Funkadelic.* Ironically, the album did better than *Hardcore Jollies* and included an R&B Top 30 single, "Undisco Kidd." In 1977 Westbound released *The Best of the Early Years*, while Funkadelic recorded what became its masterpiece (and arguably the best P-Funk release ever), 1978's *One Nation Under a Groove.*

During the most successful year in Parliament/Funkadelic history, Parliament hit the charts first with "Flash Light," P-Funk's first R&B No. 1. "Aqua Boogie" would hit No. 1 as well late in the year, but Funkadelic's

title track to *One Nation Under a Groove* spent six weeks at the top spot on the R&B charts during the summer. The album, which reflected a growing consistency in styles between Parliament and Funkadelic, became the first Funkadelic LP to reach platinum (the same year that Parliament's *Funkentelechy vs. the Placebo Syndrome* did the same). In 1979 Funkadelic's "(Not Just) Knee Deep" hit No. 1 as well, and its album (*Uncle Jam Wants You*) reached gold status.

At just the point that Funkadelic appeared to be at the top of its powers, the band began to unravel. As is sometimes the case, commercial success began to dissolve several old friendships. In 1977 original Parliaments members Fuzzy Haskins, Calvin Simon, and Grady Thomas had left the P-Funk organization to record on their own. In early 1981 they hit the R&B charts with a single called "Connections and Disconnections," recorded as Funkadelic. To confuse matters more, the original Funkadelic appeared on the charts at the same time, with the title track to *The Electric Spanking of War Babies.*

During 1980 Clinton began to be weighed down by legal difficulties arising from Polygram's acquisition of Parliament's label, Casablanca. Jettisoning both the Parliament and Funkadelic names (but not the musicians), Clinton began his solo career with 1982's *Computer Games.* He and many former Parliament/Funkadelic members continued to tour and record throughout the '80s as the P.Funk All Stars, but the decade's disdain of everything to do with the '70s resulted in critical and commercial neglect for the world's biggest funk band, especially one that had in part spawned the sound of disco. During the early '90s, the rise of funk-inspired rap (courtesy of Digital Underground, Dr. Dre and Warren G.) and funk-rock (Primus and Red Hot Chili Peppers) re-established the status of Clinton & Co., one of the most important forces in the recent history of Black music. *—John Bush*

Funkadelic / 1970 / Westbound ✦✦✦
The music is serious, but George Clinton is as tongue-in-cheek as ever. The album opens up with his voice, proposing "If you will suck my soul, I will lick your funky emotions," and proceeds in and out of that vein for 40 minutes. This album is raw and pure funk, with often twangy guitars and deep, low, yet prominent, bass lines. It takes the quirky, basic groove of the Meters and renders it heavy and grungy, while maintaining the straight-faced humor that Clinton has made famous. *—Julian Katz*

Free Your Mind . . . and Your Ass Will Follow / 1970 / Westbound ✦✦✦
Not quite as promising as its title and classic cover would indicate, *Free Your Mind and Your Ass Will Follow* is full of faux religious rambling and spacey studio overdubs and effects, but still manages to pull it off in the endearing Clinton style of blending soul, heavy metal, gospel, and bad sci-fi movies, coming up with gems such as "Friday Night, August the Fourteenth" and "Funky Dollar Bill." *—Julian Katz*

☆ **Maggot Brain** / 1971 / Westbound ✦✦✦✦✦
Perhaps the best early Funkadelic album, *Maggot Brain* showed guitarist Eddie Hazel's increased contribution to the band on the ten-minute title track, which epitomizes the P-Funk machine by working a Hendrix-fronting-the-Family Stone vibe. The album also increased the group's commercial status (with the No. 27 R&B single "I Wanna Know If It's Good for You"), but its abstract thematic content discouraged less adventurous listeners. One exception to the abstractions was "You and Your Folks, Me and My Folks," which spoke of the beauty of an interracial romance. "Can You Get to That," the third single culled from the album, proved that Funkadelic remembered the sweet soul music on which most of its members had been reared. *—John Bush*

America Eats Its Young / 1972 / Westbound ✦✦✦
An ambitious double-LP, *America Eats Its Young* featured Funkadelic's first attempt at overt political criticism. The cover made the title explicit by depicting the Statue of Liberty gorging on infants. Besides the political commentary and the ecology bender of "If You Don't Like the Effects, Don't Produce the Cause," the band still manages to groove on several tracks, such as "Loose Booty" and "Biological Speculation." A bit bloated and definitely worthy of an editing job, *America Eats Its Young* comes packed with great songs. *—John Bush*

Cosmic Slop / 1973 / Westbound ✦✦✦✦
Funkadelic's fifth LP backs away from the political commentary of *America Eats Its Young*, making it more of an inheritor to the unrestrained funk of *Maggot Brain* than anything else. Instead, the band is ready to get on the good foot, with classic tracks like "No Compute" and the title song, another long instrumental jam in the same league as *Maggot Brain's* title song. *—John Bush*

Standing on the Verge of Getting It On / 1974 / Westbound ✦✦✦
Funkadelic returned to the charts with *Standing on the Verge of Getting It On;* both the title track and "Red Hot Mama" fared well with R&B listeners, and the band's sixth album proved to be the smoothest, most flowing LP the band had produced up to that point. Unlike previous albums, which used the Parliaments' doo wop past occasionally, *Standing on the Verge of Getting It On* is consistently based in rock. Though highlights are not especially frequent, the album was a solid stab at cre-

ating the kind of brilliance later found on *One Nation Under a Groove.*
—John Bush

Let's Take It to the Stage / Apr. 1975 / Westbound ✦✦✦✦
A confusingly titled studio album, *Let's Take It to the Stage* precipitated the massive P-Funk tour of 1976 and showed the band moving closer to the radio-ready sound of Parliament. The songs are tighter and shorter, less prone to lengthy jamming; also, the ever-prevalent guitars are pushed down in the mix, emphasizing vocals and Bernie Worrell's keyboard vamps. Worrell especially shines on "Atmosphere," the last track. *—John Bush*

Funkadelic's Greatest Hits / Aug. 1975 / Westbound ✦✦✦
Just before Clinton and Funkadelic jumped ship for Warner Bros., Westbound compiled the best tracks from their first seven albums. Other than the exclusion of "Me and My Folks, You and Your Folks," the selections are good for the most part, but since Westbound updated their catalogue just two years later—with *The Best of the Early Years, Vol. 1*—this package is unnecessary (and out of print, at that). *—John Bush*

Hardcore Jollies / 1976 / Warner Brothers ✦✦✦✦
A transitional album and the first Funkadelic recorded for the major label Warner Bros., *Hardcore Jollies* lacks highlights but shows Clinton & Co. working toward the continuous, flowing groove that marks his later material. Guitarist Eddie Hazel—who provided some great moments on earlier albums—is absent, but replacement Michael Hampton proved himself equal to the task on the instrumental title track. *—John Bush*

Tales of Kidd Funkadelic / 1976 / Westbound ✦✦✦
Some leftover jams, songs, and funk pieces from the Funkadelic era. George Clinton was in the midst of moving Funkadelic to another label, and the Westbound folk released a bunch of vault material to get another Funkadelic album on the market. There were still some fine cuts, but the random element prevented it from being a great album because it lacked the thematic organization and vision Clinton provided for the concept LPs. *—Ron Wynn*

The Best of the Early Years, Vol. 1 / 1977 / Westbound ✦✦✦✦
Better than the previous Westbound compilation, *The Best of the Early Years, Vol. 1* takes one track from each of the first two Funkadelic albums, two from *Maggot Brain* and *America Eats Its Young*, three from *Cosmic Slop* and one selection from *Let's Take It to the Stage*. By properly focusing on the best tracks from the best albums, Westbound chronicled Funkadelic's early career quite well; still, the best place to hear these tracks is on their original albums. *—John Bush*

★ **One Nation Under a Groove** / 1978 / Warner Brothers ✦✦✦✦✦
Early on *One Nation Under a Groove* George Clinton asks the rhetorical question "Who Says a Funk Band Can't Play Rock?" Only a fool needs to ask, since the answer is the album itself. *One Nation Under a Groove* is the most fully realized slice of P-Funk. Parliament put out albums as funky as this, but they got bogged down in their concepts, while Funkadelic always traded too heavily in psychedelic cliches and art-rock trappings to really let loose. But that's not the case with *One Nation.* On this record, the concept is underplayed, letting the funk come to the forefront. Some died-in-the-wool Funkadelic fans might lament the lack of electric guitar freak-outs, but no matter—this is music of a supreme vision. Besides, the guitars are there, pushing along the funk in an effortless fashion, which helps draw attention to the vocals, which are alternately sexy and downright hilarious. Don't think of *One Nation Under a Groove* as a collection of songs. Think of it as one sustained funk symphony, and you'll be on the right track. Clinton never got this consistently funky again. *—Leo Stanley*

Uncle Jam Wants You / 1979 / Warner Brothers ✦✦✦✦
Perhaps overly influenced by the popularization of the disco movement, Funkadelic created in *Uncle Jam Wants You,* an album that succumbs to the dance floor but, in marked contrast to earlier triumphs, doesn't work as simple listening music. "(Not Just) Knee Deep" was the band's second No. 1 single, and one of their best ever, but the album begins to wear on side two, with several questionable filler tracks. *—John Bush*

The Electric Spanking of War Babies / 1981 / Warner Brothers ✦✦✦✦
On the final Funkadelic album—excepting of course *Connections & Disconnections,* released that same year by a splinter lineup also billed as Funkadelic—Clinton bows out in style with a solid album. He gets help from both past legends of funk (Sly Stone, on "Funk Gets Stronger II") and future names (Roger Troutman of Zapp on "Funk Gets Stronger I"). Guitarist Michael Hampton once again shines with a guitar solo on the lengthy title track. *—John Bush*

Who's a Funkadelic / 1981 / Rhino ✦
Who's a Funkadelic? is a 1992 CD re-release of the 1981 album recorded by original Parliament members Fuzzy Haskins, Calvin Simon, and Grady Thomas, who left the P-Funk fold in the late '70s and later recorded *Connections & Disconnections* with no help from

George Clinton. Though the trio spend most of the album criticizing Clinton's shifty business practices (which may be quite valid), the only thing that comes through is how much they need his production expertise. Never quite terrible, *Connections & Disconnections* makes small claims at mediocrity on scattered tracks. *—John Bush*

Connections & Disconnections / 1981 / LAX ✦
Original Parliament members Fuzzy Haskins, Calvin Simon and Grady Thomas left the fold for 1981's *Connections & Disconnections,* also billed as Funkadelic but in fact containing no contributions by George Clinton. Though the trio spend most of the album criticizing Clinton's shifty business practices (which may be quite valid), the only thing that comes through is how much they need his production expertise. Never quite terrible, *Connections & Disconnections* makes small claims at mediocrity on scattered tracks. Eleven years later, the album was re-released on CD as *Who's a Funkadelic?—John Bush*

★ **Music for Your Mother** / Mar. 31, 1993 / Westbound ✦✦✦✦✦
This two-disc set collects all the great Funkadelic singles and B-sides and presents them in remastered glory. The list includes such gems as "Funky Dollar Bill," "Cosmic Slop," "Let's Take It to the Stage," and "I'll Bet You." Unfortunately, some of Funkadelic's finest efforts were album-length and/or suite pieces, so some brilliant material not issued on singles was omitted. But it's as comprehensive a collection as possible under the circumstances (lacking the later material owned by Priority), and Rob Bowman's notes are extensive and nicely done. *—Ron Wynn*

Live: Meadowbrook, Rochester, Michigan 12th September 1971 / 1996 / Westbound ✦✦✦
Not released until 1996, this was an unusual gig for the band, who were breaking in a new rhythm section (this may have been their first show) without much or any rehearsal. You can't tell from this 77-minute disc, which offers a typically amorphous, freefloating set of Black rock—which is to say, judged by most standards, it's not typical music at all. Seguing from spaced-out jams to occasional numbers with vocals by George Clinton, and throwing in imaginative improvisations by guitarist Eddie Hazel and keyboardist Bernie Worrell, it sounds something like a combination of Jimi Hendrix, James Brown, and Sun Ra. The 14-minute "Maggot Brain" verges on prog rock/psychedelia (in the good sense), with its almost mystical guitar lines; earthier pleasures are offered with cuts like "I Call My Baby Pussycat" (two versions). The fidelity is pretty good, though the vocals lack the presence of the instruments. Funkadelic is still shown to their best advantage on their studio recordings of the era, but this is certainly a fascinating find for fans, augmented by detailed liner notes about the gig by Rob Bowman. *—Richie Unterberger*

Funky Kings

f. 1976, Los Angeles, CA, **db.** 1977
Group / Country-Rock, Pop-Rock
Formed in 1976 for Clive Davis' Arista Records, Funky Kings was an interesting teaming of three singer-songwriters, Jack Tempchin (*Peaceful Easy Feeling, Already Gone*), Jules Shear, and Richard Stekol, with a funk rhythm section of bassist Bill Bodine and drummer Frank Cotinola, and a steel guitarist, Greg Leisz. With the California country-rock, singer-songwriter sound a hot commodity in the mid-'70s, Davis had high hopes that the Kings would become the next Eagles. The group received little notice, though, aside from some minor airplay for the first single, Tempchin's "Slow Dancing"; when Arista passed on a second recording, they disbanded after one album. Tempchin did find success the next year with "Slow Dancing" when it reached the Top Ten for Johnny Rivers.

Tempchin went on to record one LP for Arista, as well as collaborating with former Eagle Glenn Frey on material for Frey's solo efforts. Shear formed the critically acclaimed Jules and the Polar Bears before releasing a number of highly lauded, if not commercially successful, albums on his own. His songs have been recorded by a number of artists and reached the charts thanks to renditions by the Bangles and Cyndi Lauper. Stekol, who has had his songs covered by singers including Kim Carnes and Iain Matthews, has done session work with Shear, Kenny Loggins, and Katy Moffatt, as well as releasing a solo effort in 1991. *—Brett Hartenbach*

Funky Kings / 1976 / Arista ✦✦✦✦
Because Funky Kings were based around three fine songwriters, song for song their one and only release holds up much better than most country-rock records of the time. Jules Shear, Jack Tempchin, and Richard Stekol turn in a fine batch of tunes ranging from the Eagle-like country-rock of Tempchin's "Singing in the Streets" to Shear's rocking "Let Me Go" and Stekol's bittersweet "My Old Pals." The backing by rhythm section Bill Bodine and Frank Cotinola, and Greg Leisz on steel, dobro, and guitar, is first-rate throughout. *Funky Kings* remains quite listenable and stands as one of the better efforts to come out of the mid-'70s L.A. sound. *—Brett Hartenbach*

Billy Fury

b. Apr. 17, 1941, Liverpool, England, d. Jan. 28, 1983
Vocals / Rock 'n' Roll, British Invasion
England's best rock singer of the pre-Beatles era, Fury, born in Liverpool, was the most talented of England's Elvis clones and near-clones of the very early '60s; he also wrote some of his own songs. A strong singer with a very suggestive stage presence, Fury also had the benefit of a fine backing band, including rockabilly guitarist Joe Brown. His recordings from 1963 onward, backed by the Tornados (of "Telstar" fame), lack this power, but Fury still made the charts through the mid-'60s, and, before his death in the mid-'80s, retained the respect and admiration of the British rock establishment he helped to form. — *Bruce Eder*

Billy Fury / 1963 / BGO ✦✦
This was Fury's biggest-selling album of the '60s, reaching the British Top Ten. But it wasn't very good, typifying the kind of teen idol fare that rode high on the British charts before Merseybeat. He could rock half-decently when given the chance, but most of the numbers are pop ballads, replete with light orchestration and crooning female backup vocals. Fury will always have his champions in England; just read the wildly enthusiastic historical liner notes to this reissue for starters. But to Yankee ears, this record sounds suspiciously like the kind of British pop fluff that the Beatles and their minions were specifically reacting against. The CD reissue on BGO combines this and the 1963 live album *We Want Billy!* on one CD. — *Richie Unterberger*

We Want Billy / 1963 / BGO ✦✦
Recorded live in Decca's studio No. 3, in front of several hundred screaming girls, with the Tornados (yes, the "Telstar" guys) backing him up. This is an energetic set, but one that, viewed in the cold light of history, is not enduring. Fury may have been one of the best of the pre-Beatle rockers, but that doesn't make him great. About half of this "concert" date consists of rock 'n' roll oldies like "Sweet Little Sixteen" and "Unchain My Heart," sung in a competent sub-Elvis mold (though the Tornados aren't about to make anyone forget Scotty Moore or James Burton). There's also a lengthy medley of many of his early-'60s pop hits, which are better heard in their studio versions. The Tornados' arrangements have a certain dated charm, with a rinky-dink organ and tinny reverb guitar. But this has little more than nostalgic value, and not even that for American listeners, who were never aware of Fury in the first place. The CD reissue on BGO combines this and the 1963 studio album *Billy* on one CD. — *Richie Unterberger*

The Billy Fury Story / 1977 / Decca ✦✦✦
Fury has been repackaged ad infinitum in the UK. This double LP is one of the better sets to pick up if you still prefer vinyl, including the entirety of his 1960 album *The Sound of Fury* and various singles from 1958 to 1965. *The Sound of Fury* is respectable rockabilly-inspired material; the singles are largely faithful, forgettable covers of American rock and pop hits, the moody 1960 ballad "Wondrous Place" and the brassy pop of 1965's "In Thoughts of You" (his final British Top Ten hit) being standouts. — *Richie Unterberger*

● Sound of Fury Plus 10 / 1988 / PolyGram ✦✦✦✦
The best rock album recorded in England before the rise of the Beatles (Andy White, the guest drummer on "Love Me Do," plays the skins on this, too). A hard-rocking gem driven by Fury's powerful voice and Joe Brown's superb guitar. This reissue has ten bonus tracks. — *Bruce Eder*

The Future Sound of London

f. 1989, London, England
Ambient Techno, Club/Dance, Trip-Hop, Electronica
First recognized as the dance duo behind such club hits as "Stakker" (as Humanoid) and "Papua New Guinea," FSOL have since become one of the most acclaimed and respected international experimental ambient groups, incorporating elements of techno, classical, jazz, hip-hop, electro, industrial, and dub into expansive, sample-heavy tracks, often exquisitely produced. Notoriously enigmatic and often disdainful of the press, the group's Gary Cobain and Brian Dougans have worked their future-is-now aesthetic into a variety of different fields, including film and video, 2- and 3-D computer graphics and animation, the Internet, radio broadcast, and, of course, recorded music. Although they usually disdain their earlier work as play-for-pay club fare not representative of their contemporary musical vision, many of the thematic concerns of their earlier 12-inches and their first, heavily dance-oriented LP, *Accelerator,* have followed them into their more recent work. Usually filed under "ambient," the work is often much more than that, drawing from the history of experimental electronic music with a relentlessness that has helped to push the calmer elements of that genre's reputation into decidedly more difficult directions. The pair have also grown in repute as remixers, obliterating tracks by Curve, Jon Anderson, David Sylvian and Robert Fripp, and Apollo 440 and rebuilding pieces of almost majestic complexity with the remnants. The duo's most recent works, *Lifeforms* and *ISDN,* are both important stopping points on the road of rabid hybridization characteristic of post-rave European experimental electronica (ambient, jungle, trip-hop, ambient dub, etc.), and the pair's somewhat punk rock attitude despite their success has done much to underscore the scene's underground roots. — *Sean Cooper*

Accelerator / 1991 / Virgin ✦✦✦✦
Still quite rooted in a dance music aesthetic, *Accelerator* shows shades of things to come in its dense, effusive orchestration and experimental beats. A satisfying first effort. — *Sean Cooper*

ISDN / 1994 / Astralwerks ✦✦✦✦
A masterful, nearly seamless fusion of ambient, trip-hop, soul-jazz, electro, industrial-leaning techno, and styles yet unclassified, reportedly recorded live for ISDN uplink to various radio stations around the world (hence the name). The Astralwerks reissue plays havoc with the track listing, subtracting three cuts, substituting a pair from the *Farout EP,* and adding a new track, "Kai," but the decision to issue a double-vinyl version was a good one. — *Sean Cooper*

The Far-Out Son of Lung and the Ramblings of a Madman [EP] / 1994 / Virgin ✦✦✦
Originally released on white-label, this four-track collection of highlights from the group's ISDN concerts hit like a genrecidal bomb, working jazz, hip-hop, funk, and ambient simultaneously, and forcing eventual release of the full-length collection, *ISDN.* — *Sean Cooper*

● Lifeforms / May 27, 1994 / Astralwerks ✦✦✦✦
A groundbreaking double-CD collection of shimmering, detailed ambient techno, self-indulgent at times, but breathtakingly so. Dougans and Cobain approach sound like sculpture here, fashioning commonplace sounds like birds' wings, waves, and dopplering machinery into impressive, multilayered, three-dimensional objects, at once digital and oddly human. — *Sean Cooper*

Dead Cities / Oct. 29, 1996 / Astralwerks/Virgin ✦✦✦✦
FSOL's penchant for sustained thematics registers here in an extended narrative of decay, with *Blade Runner*-esque themes (and even a *Blade Runner* sample!) running through over an hour of stunning aural collage. As usual, the music is impossible to pin down, moving from beatless ambient through downbeat breaks, fast jungly rhythms, and dense, noisy passages reminiscent of *ISDN*'s more formless segments. Perhaps not as experimental as previous efforts, *Dead Cities* is also more mature, relying more on smart arrangements than production gimmickry. A limited pressing of the CD also included a nearly 200-page book of stories, graphics, and video stills. — *Sean Cooper*

G

Warren G.

b. 1971, Long Beach, CA

Vocals / Club/Dance, G-Funk, West Coast Rap

Born Warren Griffin III, Warren G. exploded out of the burgeoning Long Beach rap scene in 1994 with the smash single "Regulate," a duet with longtime friend Nate Dogg, and its accompanying album, *Regulate... G Funk Era.* G. grew up in Long Beach listening to his parents' extensive collection of jazz, soul, and funk records, also frequently hanging out at the local V.I.P. record store. As a teenager, he and his friends Nate Dogg and future superstar Snoop Dogg formed a rap group called 213, after their area code. Unfortunately, all three had brushes with the law and spent time in jail, which motivated them to get jobs, working on their music as a side note. Eventually, the V.I.P. record store allowed the trio to practice and record in a back room. It was here that Snoop cut the demo "Super Duper Snooper," which G. played for his half-brother, Dr. Dre, at a party. Dre invited all three to his studio and wound up collaborating with Snoop on *The Chronic;* while G. also made several contributions, he opted to develop his talents mostly outside of Dre's shadow. He honed his musical skills while producing such artists as MC Breed and 2Pac. A break came when his vocal collaboration with Mista Grimm, "Indo Smoke," appeared on the *Poetic Justice* soundtrack. Soon after that, G. recorded his debut album for Death Row. "Regulate" appeared on the *Above the Rim* soundtrack and was released as a single. It quickly became a massive hit, peaking at No. 2 on the *Billboard* charts and pushing the album to the same position. The album eventually went triple platinum, with "This D.J." becoming his second Top Ten hit.

Warren G took nearly three years to complete his second album, returning in the spring of 1997 with *Take a Look over Your Shoulder,* which was greeted with decidedly mixed reviews and weak sales. *—Steve Huey*

● **Regulate... G Funk Era** / Jun. 7, 1994 / Def Jam ✦✦✦✦
Dr. Dre's little brother Warren G proved that he was a talent in his own right with his debut record, *Regulate... G Funk Era.* With his music's slow, bass-heavy grooves and layers of synthesizers, Warren G does sound slightly similar to his older brother, but his album is more relaxed. But that doesn't mean he's soft. In fact, his casual mix of singing and speaking is often more evocative than Dre's standard thundering beats and whining keyboards. Plus, Warren G's sly, direct lyrics manage to convey the tragedy of the ghetto. *—Stephen Thomas Erlewine*

Take a Look over Your Shoulder / Mar. 25, 1997 / Def Jam ✦✦
Warren G's debut album was a refreshing, soulful variation on G-funk, but his second album, *Take a Look over Your Shoulder,* is one of the most predictable and tired entries in the G-funk canon. As always, the record is impeccably produced, filled with deep grooves and slow, funky beats, but the music never does anything adventurous. Even if the music is predictable, it can be fitfully enjoyable, which can't be said about Warren G's lazy rhyming. None of his lyrics rise above the perfunctory level, and occasionally, they sink so low as to be embarrassing, as on the completely misguided cover of Bob Marley's "I Shot the Sheriff." From an artist who once seemed so promising, it's a disheartening turn of events. *—Leo Stanley*

Peter Gabriel

b. Feb. 13, 1950, London, England

Synthesizer, Percussion, Keyboards, Vocals / Art-Rock/Progressive-Rock, Pop-Rock

As the leader of Genesis in the early '70s, Peter Gabriel helped move progressive rock to new levels of theatricality. In his solo career, Gabriel was no less ambitious, but he was more subtle in his methods. With his first eponymous solo album in 1977, he began exploring darker, more cerebral territory, incorporating avant-garde, electronic, and worldbeat influences in his music. The record, as well as its two similarly titled successors, established Gabriel as a critically acclaimed cult artist, and with 1982's *Security,* he began to move into the mainstream. "Shock the Monkey" became his first Top 40 hit, paving the way for his multi-platinum breakthrough *So* in 1986. Accompanied by a series of groundbreaking videos and the No. 1 single "Sledgehammer," *So* became a multi-platinum hit, and Gabriel became an international star. Instead of capitalizing on his sudden success, he began to explore other interests, including recording soundtracks and running his company, Real World. By the time he returned to pop with 1992's *Us,* his mass audience had faded away, and he spent the remainder of the '90s working on multimedia projects for Real World.

After his departure from Genesis in 1976, Peter Gabriel began work on the first of three consecutive eponymously titled albums; each record was named *Peter Gabriel,* as if they were editions of the same magazine, he said. In 1977 his first solo album appeared and became a moderate success, due to the single "Solsbury Hill." Another self-titled record followed in 1978 and received weaker reviews. Gabriel's third eponymous album was his artistic breakthrough. Produced by Steve Lillywhite and released in 1980, the album established Gabriel as one of rock's most ambitious, innovative musicians, as well as one of its most political; "Biko," a song about the murdered anti-apartheid activist, became one of the biggest protest anthems of the '80s. "Games Without Frontiers," with its eerie chorus, nearly reached the Top 40.

In 1982 Gabriel released *Security,* which was an even bigger success, earning positive reviews and going gold on the strength of the startling video for "Shock the Monkey." Just as his solo career was taking off, Gabriel participated in a one-shot Genesis reunion to finance his WOMAD—World of Music, Arts and Dance—Festival. WOMAD was designed to bring various world musics and customs to a Western audience, and it soon turned into an annual event; a live double album was released that year to commemorate the event. As Gabriel worked on his fifth album, he contributed the soundtrack to Alan Parker's 1984 film *Birdy.* His score was highly praised and won the Grand Jury Prize at Cannes that year. After founding Real World, Inc.—a corporation devoted to developing bridges between technology and multi-ethnic arts—in 1985, he completed his fifth album, *So.*

Released in 1986, *So* became Gabriel's commercial breakthrough, largely because his Stax homage "Sledgehammer" was blessed with an innovative video that combined stop-action animation with live action. *So* climbed to No. 2 as "Sledgehammer" hit No. 1, with "Big Time"—featuring a video very similar to "Sledgehammer"—reaching the Top Ten and "In Your Eyes" hitting the Top 30. As *So* was riding high on the American and British charts, Gabriel co-headlined the first benefit tour for Amnesty International in 1986 with Sting and U2. Another Amnesty International Tour followed in 1988, and the next year, Gabriel released *Passion: Music for "The Last Temptation of Christ,"* a collection of instrumentals used in Martin Scorsese's film. *Passion* was the furthest Gabriel delved into worldbeat, and the album was widely acclaimed, winning the Grammy Award in 1989 for Best New Age Performance. In 1990 he released the hits compilation *Shaking the Tree.*

Gabriel labored long on the pop-music follow-up to *So,* finally releasing *Us* in the spring of 1992. During the recording of *Us,* Gabriel went through a number of personal upheavals, including a painful divorce, and those tensions manifested themselves on *Us,* a much darker record than *So.* For various reasons, not the least of which was the fact that it was released six years after its predecessor, *Us* wasn't as commercially successful as *So,* despite positive reviews. Only one single, the "Sledgehammer" knock-off "Steam," reached the Top 40, and the album stalled at platinum sales. In 1993, Gabriel embarked on the most ambitious

WOMAD tour to date, touring the United States with a roster including Crowded House, James, and Sinead O'Connor, with whom he had an on-off romantic relationship. The next year, he released the double-disc *Secret World Live*, which went gold. Later in 1994 he released the CD-ROM *Xplora*, one of many projects he developed with Real World. For the next three years, Gabriel concentrated on developing more multimedia projects for the company. —*Stephen Thomas Erlewine*

Peter Gabriel [1] / 1977 / Atco ♦♦♦♦
His strong debut, produced by Bob Ezrin (Pink Floyd, Alice Cooper), features the hit "Solsbury Hill," which addressed Gabriel's breakup with Genesis. The sound reflects some of Genesis' art-rock sensibilities ("Moribund the Burgermeister"), while charting some more accessible styles (in Gabriel's eccentric fashion) like the fairly straightahead rock of "Modern Love." Other highlights include the portentous "Here Comes the Flood" and "Humdrum." —*Rick Clark*

Peter Gabriel [2] / 1978 / Atco ♦♦♦
King Crimson's Robert Fripp produced this follow-up. Overall, this effort is more uneven, but there are some real highlights in the form of "D.I.Y." and the aggressively dissonant rocker "On the Air." —*Rick Clark*

★ **Peter Gabriel [3]** / 1980 / Geffen ♦♦♦♦♦
On this, the third of three self-titled efforts, Gabriel teams up with producer Steve Lillywhite (XTC, Psychedelic Furs, U2) and produces a masterpiece. From the chilling opener, "Intruder," to "Biko," an impassioned tribute to murdered South African poet and activist Steven Biko, Lillywhite's experimental (and very left-of-center) approach to sound is a perfect match for Gabriel's convoluted tales from the dark side of human nature. Arguably, it is Gabriel's best work thus far. —*Rick Clark*

Security / 1982 / Geffen ♦♦♦
Produced by David Lord and Gabriel, this is really a transitional album, borrowing from the heavily treated approach to sound found on the Lillywhite work while embracing more worldbeat rhythms. The music is less dissonant. Thematically, Gabriel picks up the human-rights thread he started with "Biko" on "Wallflower." "Kiss of Life" suggests a hopefulness emerging in his work. It includes the hit "Shock the Monkey." —*Rick Clark*

Plays Live / 1983 / Geffen ♦♦♦
Gabriel has always been an excellent performer. This live set is proof, in spite of some slight post-gig doctoring. Nevertheless, most of these songs work best in the arid confines of the studio atmosphere. —*Rick Clark*

Music from the Film "Birdy" / 1985 / Geffen ♦♦♦
This instrumental work was Gabriel's first major soundtrack undertaking. Fans of Gabriel's texturous arrangements and melodies (some here are drawn from earlier material) should check out this fine work. —*Rick Clark*

So / 1986 / Geffen ♦♦♦♦
After a four-year layoff from his last studio album (*Security*), Gabriel returned with his most upbeat record, infusing funk, worldbeat, and gospel. The more accessible production, by Daniel Lanois (U2) and Gabriel, helped make this album a worldwide commercial success. It includes the hits "In Your Eyes," "Sledgehammer," "Big Time." —*Rick Clark*

Passion / Jun. 1989 / Geffen ♦♦♦
For the soundtrack for Martin Scorsese's film *The Last Temptation of Christ*, Gabriel drew inspiration from field recordings of musicians in the Middle East, fusing those recordings with his own atmospheric sound tapestries for a powerful collection of music. —*Rick Clark*

Shaking the Tree: Sixteen Golden Greats / Dec. 1990 / Geffen ♦♦♦♦
This is an odd best-of collection. True, it includes his hits, but Gabriel isn't merely a singles artist. As a result, there are many important album tracks that are glaring omissions from a more well-rounded picture of Gabriel's artistry. The title, no doubt, is an indicator of the tossed-off nature of this set. —*Rick Clark*

Us / Sep. 29, 1992 / Geffen ♦♦♦
Us marks Peter Gabriel's first (nonsoundtrack) studio effort since 1986's *So* and, more importantly, his most introspective and self-analytical work since leaving Genesis in 1975. Gabriel has done much to promote international music in recent years through his Real World record label, and he calls in a fistful of I.O.U.s for *Us*. The most distinctive imports are exotic percussion sounds that percolate subtly throughout the recording. Intensely personal portrayals of love, longing, loss, and the dark emotions they can generate permeate atmospheric pieces such as "Blood of Eden," "Only Us," "Washing in the Water," and "Secret World." Gabriel makes group therapy a fascinating place to spend an hour and, thankfully, never loses sight of those rays of hope that pierce through from the other side. —*Roch Parisien*

Revisited / Nov. 10, 1992 / Atlantic ♦♦♦
A good but useless compilation of Peter Gabriel's first two solo albums. *Revisited* contains some wonderful music, but fans would be better

served by the individual albums, and casual fans will prefer *Shaking the Tree*, which has all of his big hits, including material featured here. —*Stephen Thomas Erlewine*

Secret World Live / Sep. 13, 1994 / Geffen ♦♦
Peter Gabriel's second double-disc live album doesn't have the energy of *Plays Live*, which isn't surprising; his newer material is more subtle and doesn't easily lend itself to live performances. That's part of the reason why the *Secret World* tour was filled with cutting-edge visuals and stage effects. Unfortunately, it's very hard to record a light show, and the result is a thoroughly bland album. —*Stephen Thomas Erlewine*

Serge Gainsbourg

b. Apr. 2, 1928, Paris, France, d. Mar. 2, 1991, Paris, France
Guitar, Piano, Vocals / Pop-Rock, Cabaret
Serge Gainsbourg was the dirty old man of popular music; a French singer-songwriter and provocateur notorious for his voracious appetite for alcohol, cigarettes, and women, his scandalous, taboo-shattering output made him a legend in Europe but only a cult figure in America, where his lone hit "Je T'Aime . . . Moi non Plus" stalled on the pop charts—fittingly enough—at number 69.

He was born Lucien Ginzberg in Paris on April 2, 1928. His parents were Russian Jews who fled to France after the 1917 Bolshevik uprising. After studying art and teaching, he turned to painting before working as a bar pianist on the local cabaret circuit. Soon he was tapped to join the cast of the musical *Milord L'Arsoille*, where he reluctantly assumed a singing role; self-conscious about his rather homely appearance, Gainsbourg initially wanted only to carve out a niche as a composer and producer, not as a performer.

Still, he made his recording debut in 1958 with the album *Du Chant a la Une!*; while strong efforts like 1961's *L'Etonnant Serge Gainsbourg* and 1964's *Gainsbourg Confidentiel* followed, his jazz-inflected solo work performed poorly on the charts, although compositions for vocalists ranging from Petula Clark to Juliette Greco to Dionne Warwick proved much more successful. In the late 1960s, he befriended the actress Brigitte Bardot, and later became her lover; with Bardot as his muse, Gainsbourg's lushly arranged music suddenly became erotic and delirious, and together, they performed a series of duets—including "Bonnie and Clyde," "Harley Davidson" and "Comic Strip"—celebrating pop culture icons.

After he become involved with Jane Birkin, they recorded the 1969 duet "Je T'Aime . . . Moi non Plus," a song with steamy lyrics and explicit heavy breathing that he originally penned for Bardot. Although banned in many corners of the globe, it reached the top of the charts throughout Europe and became an underground classic later covered by performers ranging from Donna Summer to Ray Conniff.

Gainsbourg returned in 1971 with *Histoire de Melody Nelson*, a dark, complex song cycle that signalled his increasing alienation from modern culture: drugs, disease, suicide, and misanthropy became thematic fixtures of his work, which grew more esoteric, inflammatory, and outrageous with each release. Although Gainsbourg never again reached the commercial success of his late-1960s peak, he remained an imposing and controversial figure throughout Europe, where he was both vilified and celebrated for his shocking behavior, which included burning 500 francs on a live television broadcast and recording a reggae version of the sacred "La Marseillaise."

Gainsbourg also created a furor with the single "Lemon Incest," a duet with his daughter, the actress Charlotte Gainsbourg. He posed in drag for the cover of 1984's *Love on the Beat*, a collection of songs about male hustlers, and made sexual advances towards Whitney Houston on a live TV broadcast. Along with his pop music oeuvre, Gainsbourg scored a number of films and directed and appeared in a handful of features, most notably 1976's *Je T'Aime . . . Moi non Plus*, which starred Birkin and Andy Warhol mainstay Joe Dallesandro. He died March 2, 1991. —*Jason Ankeny*

● **Comic Strip** / Feb. 11, 1997 / Polygram ♦♦♦♦
Serge Gainsbourg's remarkable pop hits are best represented on *Comic Strip*, an indispensable set collecting 20 tracks recorded between 1966 and 1969. In addition to the lushly erotic "Je T'Aime . . . Moi Non Plus"—Gainsbourg's best-known record—*Comic Strip* includes the title track and "Bonnie and Clyde," his collaborations with Brigitte Bardot, as well as "Initials B.B.," a sweeping paean to his duet partner, "the most beautiful woman on earth." Other highlights include "Chatterton" (a bouncy celebration of suicide), "Torrey Canyon" (a prescient warning against threats to the environment), and the self-explanatory "Soixante Neuf Annee Erotique" ("69 Erotic Year"). —*Jason Ankeny*

Couleur Cafe / Feb. 11, 1997 / Polygram ♦♦♦♦
A French craze for exotic rhythms and dances like the cha-cha and the mambo inspired Serge Gainsbourg to explore Latin and Caribbean rhythms at the outset of his career; *Couleur Cafe* collects 20 of these beat-driven recordings, which span 1959 to 1974. More than his jazz performances of the same period, the earliest songs on the set presage the

direction taken on his pop records; in addition to the distinctly snotty attitude that pervades cuts like "Laissez-Moi Tranquille" and "L'Anthracite," the nine tracks taken from the 1964 LP *Gainsbourg Percussions* innovatively embrace African rhythms while focusing on the thematic concerns (specifically cigarettes, American culture, and young girls) of his seminal later work. —*Jason Ankeny*

Du Jazz Dans Le Ravin / Feb. 11, 1997 / Polygram ✦✦✦✦
While Serge Gainsbourg rose to infamy as a pop star, he actually got his start playing jazz; the 20-track collection *Du Jazz Dans le Ravin* samples his early work from between 1958 and 1964, at which point he chose to "go commercial." While neither as imaginative nor as distinctive as his pop material, Gainsbourg's jazz sides clearly presage his future work; bright and colorful, cuts like "Requiem Pour un Twisteur" and "Ce Mortel Ennui" offer much of the same attitude and outlook that defined his later, more provocative music. —*Jason Ankeny*

Galaxie 500

f. 1986, Boston, MA, **db.** 1991
Alternative Pop-Rock, Dream-Pop
Though criminally overlooked in their own lifetime, Galaxie 500 later emerged as one of the pivotal underground groups of the post-punk era. Dreamy and enigmatic, their minimalist dirges presaged the rise of both the shoegazer and slowcore movements of the 1990s. The group formed in Boston in 1986 and comprised vocalist/guitarist Dean Wareham (a transplanted New Zealand native), bassist Naomi Yang, and drummer Damon Krukowski, longtime friends who first met in high school in New York City before all three attended Harvard University. Wareham and Krukowski initially teamed in the short-lived Speedy and the Castenets, which split after their bass player experienced a religious conversion; upon re-forming, the duo recruited Yang to play bass, although she had no prior musical experience.

Named after a friend's car, Galaxie 500 began performing live throughout Boston and New York before recording a three-song demo tape which they sent to Shimmy Disc honcho Kramer, who agreed to become the trio's producer. After bowing in early 1988 with the singles "Tugboat" and "Oblivious" (the latter track featured on a flexi-disc included in an issue of *Chemtcal Imbalance* magazine), they issued their full-length debut, *Today*, which highlighted the group's distinct, evolving sound pitting Wareham's eerie, plaintive tenor, elliptical songs, and slow-motion guitar textures against Yang's warm, fluid bass lines and Krukowski's lean drumming.

After signing to the US branch of Rough Trade, Galaxie 500 issued its defining moment, 1989's evocative *On Fire*, a remarkably assured and rich record including the superb singles "Blue Thunder" and "When Will You Come Home." After a limited-edition seven-inch release featuring live renditions of the Beatles' "Rain" and Jonathan Richman's "Don't Let Our Youth Go to Waste," the group returned in 1990 with *This Is Our Music*, a diffuse collection spotlighting the wry, sunny single "Fourth of July" and a haunting cover of Yoko Ono's "Listen, the Snow Is Falling." Following a subsequent tour, Galaxie 500 disbanded after Wareham phoned Yang and Krukowski to say he was quitting the group.

A few months later, after Wareham formed his new band, Luna, Rough Trade went bankrupt, and with the label's demise went the trio's three albums, as well as their royalties. In 1991, at an auction of Rough Trade's assets, Krukowski purchased the master tapes for the group's music, and five years later the Rykodisc label issued a box set containing Galaxie 500's complete recorded output; a previously unreleased 1990 live set, dubbed *Copenhagen*, followed in 1997. In the meantime, after first resurfacing under the name Pierre Etoile, Krukowski and Yang recorded as Damon and Naomi; additionally, the duo served as the rhythm section for the Wayne Rogers-led Magic Hour. —*Jason Ankeny*

● **Today** / 1987 / Rykodisc ✦✦✦✦
Galaxie 500's bow lacks the pea-soup atmosphere of the trio's later work; their early sound, though already unique and beautiful, is simply too skeletal to equal the all-enveloping intoxication of *On Fire*. The songs, however, are confident and assured, carefully balancing the gauzy torpor of Dean Wareham's guitar with the insistent rhythms of bassist Naomi Yang and drummer Damon Krukowski. An auspicious debut. —*Jason Ankeny*

On Fire / 1989 / Rykodisc ✦✦✦
On Fire is Galaxie 500's crowning achievement; striking a perfect balance between the comparatively thin sound of *Today* and the overly-slick production of *This Is Our Music*, the album manufactures a thick, enveloping atmosphere all its own. Markedly more assured than *Today*, the interplay between Dean Wareham's gauzy guitar and Naomi Yang's warm, liquid bass immerses Wareham's minimalist songs in slow-motion waves of fragile noise; much of the appeal of such superb cuts as "Blue Thunder," "When Will You Come Home" and their cover of George Harrison's "Isn't It a Pity" derives from their seeming temporality—the songs threaten to evaporate at any given moment. —*Jason Ankeny*

This Is Our Music / 1990 / Rykodisc ✦✦✦✦
Having perfected their brand of atmospheric drone-pop with *On Fire*, Galaxie 500 smartly expand into more dynamic and structured ground with *This Is Our Music*, a brighter, more colorful collection that occasionally falls prey to uninspired songwriting; the lifeless melodies of "Hearing Voices" and "Summertime" pale in comparison to such standouts as the single "Fourth of July" (a shimmering example of the band's often-neglected sense of humor), "Way Up High," and an evocative cover of Yoko Ono's "Listen, the Snow Is Falling," sung by bassist Naomi Yang. —*Jason Ankeny*

Galaxie 500 / Sep. 24, 1996 / Rykodisc ✦✦✦✦
Rykodisc's *Galaxie 500* box set contains all three of the group's original albums—*Today, On Fire,* and *This Is Our Music*—plus an additional disc of rarities and singles, making it a definitive retrospective, designed with collectors in mind. The packaging is gorgeous and the sound is a considerable improvement from the original Rough Trade releases; the only drawback of the box set is the fact that it is the only place any Galaxie 500 albums are currently available, and it was issued in an extremely limited run. However, the box could not have been done any better. It's essential for all the band's fans. —*Stephen Thomas Erlewine*

Copenhagen / Apr. 29, 1997 / Rykodisc ✦✦✦
Released in 1997, seven years after Galaxie 500 disbanded, *Copenhagen* captures the group's final concert on their final European tour. The concert was recorded for Danish National Radio on December 1, 1990. To listeners who thought of Galaxie 500's music as so light that it would float away, the quiet force of the music will come as a revelation. —*Stephen Thomas Erlewine*

Rory Gallagher

b. Mar. 2, 1949, Ballyshannon, Ireland, **d.** Jun. 14, 1995
Guitar, Vocals / Blues-Rock, British Blues
For a career that was cut short by illness and a premature death, guitarist, singer, and songwriter Rory Gallagher accomplished a lot in the blues music world. Although Gallagher didn't tour the US nearly enough, spending most of his time in Europe, he was known for his no-holds-barred, marathon live shows at clubs and theaters around the United States. Gallagher was born in Ballyshannon, County Donegal, Irish Republic, on March 2, 1949. He passed away from complications of liver transplant surgery on June 14, 1995, at age 46. Shortly after his birth, his family moved to Cork City, and at age nine he became fascinated with American blues and folk singers he heard on the radio. An avid record collector, he had a wide range of influences including Leadbelly, Buddy Guy, Freddie King, Albert King, Muddy Waters, and John Lee Hooker. Gallagher would always try to mix some simple country blues songs onto his recordings.

Gallagher began his recording career after moving to London, when he formed a trio called Taste. The group's self-titled debut album was released in 1969 in England and later picked up for US distribution by Atco/Atlantic. Between 1969 and 1971, with producer Tony Colton behind the board, Gallagher recorded three albums with the group before they split. Gallagher began performing under his own name in 1971, after recording his 1970 debut, *Rory Gallagher* for Polydor Records in the UK. The album was picked up for US distribution by Atlantic Records, and later that year he recorded *Deuce*, also released by Atlantic in the US.

His prolific output continued, as he followed up *Deuce* with *Live in Europe* (1972) and *Blueprint* and *Tattoo*, both in 1973. *Irish Tour 1974*, like *Live in Europe*, did a good job of capturing the excitement of his live shows on tape, and he followed that with *Calling Card* for Chrysalis in 1976 and *Photo Finish* and *Jinx* for the same label in 1978 and 1982. By this point Gallagher had made several world tours, and he took a few years' rest from the road. He got back into recording and performing live again with the 1987 release (in the UK) of *Defender*. His last album, *Fresh Evidence*, was released in 1991 on the Capo/I.R.S. label. Capo was his own record and publishing company that he set up in the hopes of eventually exposing other great blues talents.

Some of Gallagher's best work on record was recorded with Muddy Waters on *The London Sessions* (Chess, 1972) and with Albert King on *Live* (RCA/Utopia). Gallagher made his last US tours in 1985 and 1991, and he admitted in interviews that he wasa guitarist who fed off the instant reaction and feedback a live audience could provide. In a 1991 interview, he told this writer: "I try to sit down and write a Rory Gallagher song, which generally happens to be quite bluesy. I try to find different issues, different themes, and different topics that haven't been covered before . . . I've done songs in all the different styles . . . train blues, drinking blues, economic blues. But I try to find a slightly different angle on all these things. The music can be very traditional, but you can sort of creep into the future with the lyrics."

For a good introduction to Gallagher's unparalleled prowess as a guitarist, singer, and songwriter, pick up *Irish Tour 1974, Calling Card*, or *Fresh Evidence*, all available on compact disc. —*Richard Skelly*

Deuce / 1971 / Atlantic ✦✦
On *Deuce*, Rory Gallagher was just beginning to develop a distinctive style. He doesn't quite have all of the elements mastered yet—his concentration seems to slip on certain tracks, while other cuts aren't particularly strong songs—but it's fascinating to hear him forge something new out of his Chicago blues roots. — *Thom Owens*

Rory Gallagher / 1971 / Atlantic ✦✦✦
Rory Gallagher's eponymous debut is an entertaining but relatively undistinguished collection of blues-rock, highlighted by his flash slide guitar. — *Thom Owens*

Live in Europe/Stage Struck / 1972 / IRS ✦✦✦
The live album *Live in Europe/Stage Struck* captures Rory Gallagher at his finest, as he tears his way through many of his very best songs. Though the performance quality is a little uneven, there are gems scattered throughout the record, including smoking versions of "Messin' with the Kid" and "Laundromat." — *Thom Owens*

Tattoo / 1973 / Castle ✦✦✦
Rory Gallagher forges a distinctive style on *Tattoo*, one of his strongest albums. Working with a tight quartet, he's given a solid foundation for his terrific solos. It's especially exciting to hear him supported by a piano. All of the players deliver with conviction and studied passion, which makes the record an exciting listen. — *Thom Owens*

Irish Tour '74 / 1974 / IRS ✦✦✦✦
With *Irish Tour '74*, Rory Gallagher hit his highwater mark. Recorded live on tour, Gallagher displays a remarkable empathy with his band, as they churn out crunching riffs and fluid, soulful solos. Many of his best songs are on the set, and they far eclipse the studio versions. — *Thom Owens*

Calling Card / 1976 / IRS ✦✦✦✦
After the excellent live set *Irish Tour '74*, Rory Gallagher delivered his best studio album, *Calling Card*. The record captures the dynamic interplay between the guitarist and his band; they burn with a roaring intensity. It doesn't hurt that the songs are the best batch that Gallagher ever came up with for a record. The combination of top-notch performances and first-rate songs equals the hardest-edged and most rewarding studio set the guitarist ever cut. — *Thom Owens*

● **Edged in Blue** / 1992 / Edsel ✦✦✦✦
Edged in Blue is a solid, if not exactly definitive, retrospective of Rory Gallagher's career that offers a fine introduction to the British blues star. — *Thom Owens*

Game Theory

f. 1982, Sacramento, CA, db. 1990
Alternative Pop-Rock, Power Pop, Paisley Underground, Jangle-Pop
Game Theory was loosely associated with the Paisley Underground movement of the early '80s, and though they certainly had a retro-'60 sound with psychedelic leanings, the band owed its greatest debt to the proto-power pop of Big Star.

Leader Scott Miller's song craft, distinctive voice (self-described as a "miserable whine") and intelligent lyrics (often obscure but rarely pretentious) carved a sound that, while firmly rooted in traditional pop, was truly original and defined an era of college rock.

Formed in Sacramento in 1982, the first incarnation included ex-Alternative Learning member Scott Miller (singer-songwriter, guitarist), Fred Juhos (bass), Nancy Becker (keyboards), and Michael Erwin (drums). Within four months of forming and before ever playing a live gig, the band recorded their first album, *Blaze of Glory*, in Miller's bedroom. Only 500 copies were pressed and sent out to college radio (according to the legend, wrapped in trash bags). The album, while a pleasant amalgam of '60s pure pop and the quirkier elements of new wave, only hinted at the band's potential. They began playing live in the same circles as Dream Syndicate and Thin White Rope; rumblings of the Paisley Underground scene were just beginning. The *Pointed Accounts of People You Know* EP in 1983 and the *Distortion* EP (produced by Michael Quercio of paisley-peers the Three O'Clock) the next year quickly earned the band a following and drew favorable comparisons to Big Star.

In 1985, with the help of producer Mitch Easter, they recorded their first proper album, *Real Nighttime*, for Enigma Records. Internal tensions broke the band up before its release, leaving Miller to carry on with a new lineup consisting of Shelley LaFrenier (keyboard), Gil Ray (drums), and Suzie Ziegler (bass); Easter would continue as the band's producer and essentially a fifth member in the studio throughout the rest of their career. The new group immediately began recording *Big Shot Chronicles* by late 1985, the album once again showing great leaps in quality. By this time, they had become staples of college radio, though mainstream recognition eluded them. Miller seemed to accept the destiny of the band (obscurity) when he created his most excessive, and ultimately most enjoyable, album, 1987's *Lolita Nation*, a sprawling double album packed with obscure pop-culture references and riddled with

experimental sounds and song fragments. *Lolita Nation* also marked the addition of guitarist/vocalist Donnette Thayer.

They took one more stab at the mainstream with the more accessible *Two Steps from the Middle Ages* in 1988, but its commercial failure took its toll on the band, leading to several more personnel changes, including the temporary exit of Miller himself. Miller finally dissolved the band in 1990 to form the similar-sounding, though more eclectic, Loud Family. — *Chris Woodstra*

Blaze of Glory / 1982 / Rational ✦✦
Recorded in Scott Miller's bedroom, a mere four months after forming and before the band had ever played live, *Blaze of Glory* is a predictably unfocused and undistinguished debut. While they would later be lumped in with the Paisley Underground movement, this album owes a greater debt to new wave and power-pop than to the Velvet Underground or psychedelia. Only 500 copies were pressed for college radio consumption, but the tracks were later compiled on the *Distortion of Glory* CD. — *Chris Woodstra*

Real Nighttime / 1985 / Alias ✦✦✦
This is the band's first effort with Mitch Easter (R.E.M., Let's Active) producing. Miller's Alex Chilton fixation comes to the fore here, and it generally works nicely. The single "24" was a breezy alternative college hit. Other highlights include "Curse of the Frontierland," with its Big Star-influenced guitar figure, and the delicately reflective "If and When It All Falls Apart." — *Rick Clark*

Big Shot Chronicles / 1986 / Alias ✦✦✦✦
The band's sound and Miller's songwriting are more aggressive here, delivering an appealingly punchy power-pop sound. It's a fine album with many tracks to recommend; "I've Tried Subtlety" is a strong, over-amped T-Rex rocker, while "Like a Girl Jesus" shines with Easter's mildly psychedelic production touches. "Erica's World" is a wonderfully quirky rocker, and "Regenisraen" showcases the band's harmonic capabilities. — *Rick Clark*

Lolita Nation / 1987 / Enigma ✦✦✦✦
Many fans of the band claim that this is a creative peak for Game Theory. *Lolita Nation* is loaded with odd juxtapositions of experimental sounds and spoken passages. The material, while dazzling in places, is rather inconsistent. "The Real Sheila" and "We Love You, Carol and Alison" are highlights, and both of them are found on *Tinker*. — *Rick Clark*

Two Steps from the Middle Ages / 1988 / Enigma ✦✦
With *Two Steps from the Middle Ages*, it seems Scott Miller was having second thoughts about the band's direction. Where *Lolita Nation* jumped wildly through experimental territory, this time out, they opted for a more radio-ready approach—unfortunately though, not college radio where their real support was. And while there is no shortage of good pop music here, overall the results are somewhat bland compared to previous efforts. — *Chris Woodstra*

● **Tinker to Evers to Chance (Selected Highlights 1982-1989)** / Mar. 1990 / Enigma ✦✦✦✦
For the uninitiated, this collection of highlights from 1982 to 1989 is the best place to start, containing a healthy selection from their later Mitch Easter-produced albums. — *Rick Clark*

Distortion of Glory / 1994 / Alias ✦✦
Distortion of Glory collects the band's early (and long out-of-print) EPs. An interesting look at their formative years, but only fans need to bother. — *Chris Woodstra*

Gang of Four

f. 1977, Leeds, England, db. 1984
Alternative Pop-Rock, New Wave, Post-Punk
Formed in 1977 by Leeds University students Jon King (vocals), Andy Gill (guitar), Dave Allen (bass), and Hugo Burnham (drums), Gang of Four (along with the Fall, Mekons, and Liliput) produced some of the most exhilarating and lasting music of the early English post-punk era of 1978-1983. Fueled by the fury of punk rock and radical political theory, Gang of Four successfully welded the two in an inspired display of polemics and music that addressed the vagaries of life in the modern world (including love and romance) as matters of political inquiry. Despite the fact that this sounds rife with the potential for being long on rhetoric and short on groove, such was not the case. What made Gang of Four's polemical clang 'n' roll so compelling was that it worked as harsh, bracing, and ultimately liberating rock 'n' roll. With Allen and Burnham combining as a formidable and frequently very funky rhythm section, Gill didn't play guitar as much as emit thick wads of semi-tuneful distortion, while King "sang" in a dry, declamatory fashion similar to that of the Fall's Mark E. Smith. The rhythms were stripped down and jagged; at times Gill would dispense with guitar solos entirely and "play" non-solos, which were (surprise!) silence. Song titles sounded like the titles of radical political essays: "At Home He's a Tourist," "Damaged Goods," "It's Her Factory," "Love like Anthrax," "To Hell with Poverty," all of it openly challenging the audience's preconceived notions about rock music, per-

formance, the cult of celebrity, and the nature of politics. And in doing so, GOF conveyed rage, confusion, and loss of identity as well as any band of its time.

After three consecutive sensational albums, as well as a handful of EPs and singles, Allen left in 1982 to form the more danceable and less overtly political Shriekback, while Gill, King, and Burnham recorded the misguided "radical soul/R&B" record *Hard* with veteran American producers Ron and Howard Albert (who'd previously worked with Stephen Stills' Manassas and Firefall). A near-total disaster, *Hard* signalled that the end was nigh. Gill and King, who by this point had final say-so on the band's musical and political direction, sacked Burnham, and the now Gang of Two released a so-so live album (*At the Palace*) and called it quits in 1984. But legends die hard, and Gang of Four experienced a mini-renaissance in the early '90s with the release of two excellent collections (*A Brief History of the Twentieth Century* and *The Peel Sessions Album*). King and Gill put together a new Gang of Four and released the tepid but not disgraceful *Mall* in 1991. Despite the clumsy and haphazard finish, Gang of Four remains, to ears opened wide by punk rock, an extremely important band. —*John Dougan*

★ **Entertainment!** / 1979 / Infinite Zero ✦✦✦✦✦
With songs like "Love Like Anthrax" and "Damaged Goods," you soon realize that the title of this release is heavy on sarcasm. Still, a decade and a half after its debut, *Entertainment!* still sounds direct, exciting, and uncompromising. And, in spite of GOF's anti-pop tendencies, songs like "I Found That Essence Rare" explode into a sing-along chorus that is delightfully shocking. True to their collectivist spirit, Gill, King, Burnham, and Allen are a forceful musical unit, and the strength in this unity makes for a great fusion of punk, pop, and politics. Easily one of the best records of the post-punk era. Issued on CD by Infinite Zero in 1995. —*John Dougan*

Solid Gold / May 1981 / Warner Brothers ✦✦✦✦
Another tongue-in-cheek title, another great record. A little more abstract and anti-pop than *Entertainment!*, *Solid Gold* is, arguably, the most abrasive record GOF ever made. Burnham and Allen play dance-defiant, choppy grooves, while King and Gill explore more contentious political terrain. Some of *Solid Gold*'s best songs are the most challenging and confrontational ("Why Theory?" and "Paralysed"). Clearly hitting its stride as a band, by this time GOF was a force to be reckoned with, and without a doubt post-punk's best band. —*John Dougan*

Songs of the Free / 1982 / Warner Brothers ✦✦✦✦
Recorded under the influence of Chic records and a burgeoning post-punk dance culture, *Songs of the Free* is the most accessible of GOF's first three records, but that in no way indicates a compromise of principles or an egregious attempt to sell out. The more polished arrangements, backup vocalists, and slight studio sweetening do little to mask the sarcasm and ironic intent of songs like "I Love a Man in a Uniform" (a dance club "hit" in the early '80s) or the bitter "We Live As We Dream, Alone." A record that appeals to the aficionado as well as the benighted, *Songs of the Free* indicated that the GOF could simultaneously embrace and attack pop music without sounding disingenuous. Music for the mind and body. —*John Dougan*

Hard / 1983 / Warner Brothers ✦✦✦
The final studio LP released before the group's 1984 dissolution, *Hard* continues Gang of Four's long-standing tradition of ironic LP titles; this time, however, the joke's on them. Produced by Ron and Howard Albert, best known for their work with Crosby, Stills & Nash and Firefall, *Hard* is anything but. The taut, bracing energy of past glories has fallen by the wayside, replaced by morose, uninspired dirges. On this strangely apolitical album, even Jon King's lyrics lack bite, and his vocals lack any sense of urgency. —*Jason Ankeny*

At the Palace / 1984 / Mercury ✦✦
Recorded in Hollywood, *At the Palace* documents a live performance during Gang of Four's 1984 farewell tour, with only Jon King and Andy Gill remaining from the group's original lineup. Among the tracks: "At Home He's a Tourist," "History Is Not Made by Great Men," "Paralysed," and "We Live As We Dream, Alone." —*Jason Ankeny*

Peel Sessions / 1990 / Dutch East India ✦✦✦
One of the best *Peel Sessions* releases available, these 11 tracks were recorded for John Peel's BBC radio show in 1979 and 1981. Thrilling from start to finish, this features the Gang raw and live. —*John Dougan*

● **Brief History of the Twentieth Century** / Dec. 1990 / Warner Brothers ✦✦✦✦
A great starting point. This 20-track anthology covers all of GOF's best album material (even the one good song from the execrable *Hard*) and includes a wonderful liner essay by longtime GOF fan and fellow theorist Greil Marcus. Although *Entertainment!* is perhaps the most striking Gang release available, this compilation, due to its length, breadth and quality, is the best place to become acquainted with this formidable band. —*John Dougan*

Mall / May 7, 1991 / Polydor ✦✦
Seven years after the band's breakup, founding members Jon King and Andy Gill reteamed for *Mall*, a minor return to form that improves on 1983's abysmal *Hard* but fails to recapture the ferocity of Gang of Four's most stunning work. Slickly produced, with a heavy emphasis on synthesizers and ersatz funk rhythms, the lyrical focus returns the group to the political arena. As suggested by the title, *Mall* is laced with the usual examinations of consumerism and the economy, while the sample-heavy "F.M.USA." is an essay on the Vietnam War. An odd cover of Bob Marley's "Soul Rebel" rounds out the set. —*Jason Ankeny*

Shrinkwrapped / Sep. 19, 1995 / Castle ✦✦✦
Bleak and unforgiving, *Shrinkwrapped* picks up where the preceding *Mall* (and, for that matter, *Entertainment!*) left off, exploring life in a consumer culture under the specter of capitalism on tracks like "The Dark Ride," "Unburden," and its companion piece, "Unburden Unbound." Less glossy and overproduced than other recent efforts, cuts including "Better Him Than Me" and "I Parade Myself" restore the group to their noisy roots. —*Jason Ankeny*

Gang Starr

f. 1988, Brooklyn, NY
Jazz-Rap, Hip Hop
These Brooklyn rappers are near the top among hip-hop artists influenced by and interested in jazz. In 1989, longtime jazz and Black-pop publicist Elliot Horne placed a poem he wrote with them, and the group used it as the foundation for the song "Jazz Music" on their debut *No More Mr. Nice Guy*. That track was later included on the soundtrack for Spike Lee's *Mo Better Blues*. The group has also used saxophonist and *Tonight Show* bandleader Branford Marsalis and included acoustic as well as electric instruments on their follow-up release *Step in the Arena*. They've also discussed the jazz/rap connection in such magazines as *The Source* and *The Wire*. (They did make a big gaffe on one cut though, crediting Dizzy Gillespie with playing the saxophone rather than the trumpet.)

Both Gang Starr and their main man Guru have been in the limelight in 1993 and 1994. Guru teamed with old and new jazz types Donald Byrd, Roy Ayers, and Ronnie Foster, as well as vocalist N'Dea Davenport and other guest stars, for the session *Jazzmatazz*. He later did some New York club dates with some of the same musicians. Gang Starr issued *Hard to Earn* in March of 1994; it debuted on the *Billboard* R&B charts at No. 2. —*Ron Wynn*

No More Mr. Nice Guy / 1989 / EMI America ✦✦✦
Plenty of attitude, although not so strong otherwise. —*Ron Wynn*

Step in the Arena / 1991 / Chrysalis ✦✦✦
It has its moments. —*Ron Wynn*

● **Daily Operation** / 1992 / Chrysalis ✦✦✦✦
Arguably the best example of the hip-hop/jazz coalition, Gang Starr's latest continues the trailblazing path. —*Ron Wynn*

Hard to Earn / Mar. 8, 1994 / Chrysalis ✦✦✦✦
Although they were pioneers in the hip-hop/jazz movement, Gang Starr is still primarily a rap group. They reaffirm that on their newest venture, a 17-track set that's much more on the hard-hitting hip-hop tip than a restating of their jazz connections. The disc also offers more evidence that Guru is among rap's finest wordsmiths and verbal improvisers; whether moving over a midtempo groove, doing autobiographical sketches, criticizing other rappers, or just describing his environment and feelings, Guru's tone and voice are an effective mix of striking and reflective. *Hard To Earn* ranks as one of 1994's outstanding rap albums. —*Ron Wynn*

The Gap Band

f. 1967, Tulsa, OK
Soul, Funk, Quiet Storm
A funk septet led by brothers Ronnie (vocals, trumpet, keyboards), Charles (lead vocals, keyboards), and Robert Wilson (vocals, bass), all cousins of Bootsy Collins, the Gap Band enjoyed a successful run on the R&B charts during the '80s with its Sly Stone-influenced boogie. The group took their name from the initials of three streets—Greenwood, Archer, and Pine—in their Tulsa, OK, neighborhood. The brothers met Leon Russell in 1974, who signed them to his Shelter label; this led to a recording session with A&M, a self-titled debut on Tattoo/RCA, and a deal with Mercury. A string of R&B Top Ten hits followed, including "I Don't Believe You Want to Get Up and Dance (Oops, Up Side Your Head)." By the time of *Gap Band III*, the group was established as hit-makers, and the album and its follow-up went platinum on the strength of hits like "Burn Rubber (Why You Wanna Hurt Me)," "Early in the Morning," and "Outstanding." The group recorded the title song to Keenen Ivory Wayans' blaxploitation parody *I'm Gonna Git You Sucka* in 1988 as their chart success continued. Charles Wilson and Eurythmic Dave Stewart co-wrote the soundtrack to the 1990 film *Rooftops;* Wil-

son then joined the Eurythmics' backing band in 1990 and guested on their *We Too Are One.* He remained with the Gap Band, though, which continued to tour and resumed recording after a six-year hiatus in 1995 with *Ain't Nothin' But a Party,* which was followed in 1996 by *V Jammin.* —*Steve Huey*

● **Best Of** / 1995 / Mercury ◆◆◆◆
The Best of the Gap Band collects nearly every hit and key album track by the seminal funk group, making it the perfect introduction and arguably their only essential record. —*David Jehnzen*

Garbage

f. 1993, Wisconsin
Alternative Pop-Rock
Garbage built on the sonic landscapes of My Bloody Valentine, Curve, and Sonic Youth, adding a distinct sense of accessible pop songcraft. Garbage was the brainchild of producers Butch Vig, Duke Erikson, and Steve Marker. Inttially, Garbage was an informal jam session between the three producers held in Marker's basement, but they eventually recruited vocalist Shirley Manson, who had previously sung with Angelfish and Goodbye Mr. MacKenzie.

Vig is a native of Viroqua, WI, who learned to play piano as a child and drums as a teenager. He attended the University of Wisconsin briefly before pursuing a career in music. The first band he joined after leaving college was Spooner, with whom he played drums. Also in Spooner was Erikson, who sang and played guitar. Marker was a native of New York who moved to Wisconsin to attend college. He became a fan of Spooner and began recording their songs. Vig left Spooner shortly afterwards, but he kept in touch with the band. After a few years, Spooner became Firetown and Vig played drums in the new outfit.

Firetown broke up in the late '80s without having achieved much success. Before the formation of Firetown, Vig and Marker bought an eight-track cassette recorder and set up a makeshift studio in a local warehouse. This studio was dubbed Smart Studios, and Vig recorded numerous local punk and alternative bands at the warehouse. By the late '80s, Smart had become one of the hippest recording studios in America. Many records released on Touch & Go, Sub Pop, and Twin/Tone, among other indie labels, were made at Smart. Vig and Smart broke into the big time in 1991 after he produced Nirvana's *Nevermind. Nevermind* elevated Butch Vig to the status of a superstar producer, and for the next two years he produced numerous American alternative superstars, including Sonic Youth, Smashing Pumpkins, and L7.

Shortly after Vig became a star, he and Marker began playing together, eventually asking Erikson to join them. Hence, Garbage was officially formed in 1993, after Erikson joined the duo. After a year of playing, they hired Shirley Manson after seeing Angelfish on MTV. Manson began her musical career at an early age, joining Goodbye Mr. MacKenzie as a teenager; she played keyboards and sang backing vocals in the band. For the next few years she toured with the band before leaving to form Angelfish, whom she led through an eponymous 1994 album.

Garbage recorded their debut album in late 1994 and early 1995. Their eponymous first album appeared in the fall of 1995 on Almo Sounds. After receiving support from radio and MTV, the album began to climb the charts toward the end of 1995. When the second single, "Queer," received heavy airplay. By the summer of 1996, *Garbage* had gone gold in the United States. —*Stephen Thomas Erlewine*

Garbage / Aug. 15, 1995 / Almo Sounds/Geffen ◆◆◆◆
Garbage's self-titled debut has all the trappings of alternative rock—offkilter arrangements, occasional bursts of noise, a female singer with a thin, airy voice—but it comes off as pop, thanks to the glossy production courtesy of bassist Butch Vlg. Not only is the sound of the record slick and professional, but all the songs are well-crafted pop songs. Unfortunately, only a handful of the songs are memorable, but those that are—"Vow" and "Queer," in particular—are small, trashy alternative pop gems. —*Stephen Thomas Erlewine*

Jerry Garcia

b. Aug. 1, 1942, San Francisco, CA, **d.** Aug. 9, 1995, San Francisco, CA
Guitar, Vocals / Rock 'n' Roll, Country-Rock, Folk-Rock
Jerry Garcia was the lead guitarist, vocalist, and spokesman for the seminal '60s rock 'n' roll band the Grateful Dead. Throughout his career, he led the Dead through numerous changes, becoming one of the most famous figures in the history of rock 'n' roll. Simultaneously, Garcia pursued an eclectic array of side projects, ranging from the bluegrass group Old and In the Way to his folky solo recordings. Garcia stayed active as a member of the Grateful Dead and as a solo performer until his death in 1995.

Garcia learned to play guitar when he was 15 years old, originally playing folk and rock 'n' roll. In 1959, when he was 17 years old, he spent a brief time in the army. When he left the military after a matter of months, he moved to Palo Alto, CA, where he met and became friends

with Robert Hunter, who would later become his lyricist. Garcia bought a banjo in 1962 and began playing in local bluegrass bands. Within a few years, he was a member of Mother McCree's Uptown Jug Champions, a popular local bluegrass and folk band whose membership included Bob Weir and Pigpen. In 1965 this group evolved into the Warlocks, which would in turn become the Grateful Dead in 1966.

Over the course of the next five years, the Grateful Dead began building a reputation as a mesmerizing live act. During this time, Garcia guested with a number of bands, both in concert and in the studio; among the artists he appeared with are the New Riders of the Purple Sage (a band which he helped form), Jefferson Starship, and Crosby, Stills, Nash and Young. In 1970, the Dead began to shift their music back toward their folk, country, and bluegrass roots with the albums *Workingman's Dead* and *American Beauty.* The next year, Garcia began a solo career with *Hooteroll?,* which was released on Douglas Records. For the next few years, Garcia recorded solo albums frequently, often with keyboardist Merl Saunders. In 1973, he was one of the founding members of the bluegrass supergroup Old and In the Way, which also featured David Grisman, Vassar Clements, and John Kahn.

Garcia's solo efforts slowed in the early '80s, as he battled heroin addiction and diabetes. After the Grateful Dead scored their first hit album in 1987 with *In the Dark,* Garcia pursued a number of solo projects, including several acoustic duet records with David Grisman and a handful of live tours and albums with the Jerry Garcia Acoustic Band. For the first half of the '90s, Garcia concentrated on Grateful Dead tours and albums, as the band confirmed their status as one of the most popular concert acts in America. However, the guitarist slowly sank back into heroin addiction. Late in the summer of 1995, he entered Serenity Knolls, a drug rehabilitation facility in Forest Knolls, CA. While he was attempting to recover, Garcia died in his sleep of a heart attack on August 9, 1995. Several months after his death, the Grateful Dead announced their disbandment. —*Stephen Thomas Erlewine*

Hooteroll? / 1971 / Grateful Dead ◆◆◆
Howard Wales, who is co-credited on this album, is a keyboard player, and Jerry Garcia's first non-Grateful Dead album release finds the two, along with such Garcia band stalwarts as drummer Bill Vitt and bassist John Kahn, playing exploratory instrumental music that touches on jazz and rock. Originally released in 1971 on Douglas Records, the album was reissued on CD on Grateful Dead Records in 1987 with two added tracks. —*William Ruhlmann*

● **Garcia** / Jan. 1972 / Grateful Dead ◆◆◆◆
In essence, this is a Grateful Dead record, featuring as it does the band's leader/singer/guitarist, its drummer, and its lyricist. Except for the few instrumental/experimental cuts, the material has been incorporated into the Dead's concert repertoire. In fact, this is a perfect follow-up to the folk-rock song albums the Dead produced in 1970, *Workingman's Dead* and *American Beauty*—albums the band itself has never really followed up. —*William Ruhlmann*

Live at the Keystone / 1973 / Fantasy ◆◆
A live double album recorded in July 1973 by a band featuring Garcia with keyboardist Merl Saunders, bassist John Kahn, and drummer Bill Vitt. The set indicates Garcia's eclectic taste; the band covers Bob Dylan, Jimmy Cliff, Rodgers and Hart, and Arthur Crudup, among others. Somehow, though, it all has the same loosely structured, unhurried style familiar from Garcia's work with the Grateful Dead and dominated by his dense, considered, single-note guitar solos and calmly trembling tenor voice. —*William Ruhlmann*

Reflections / Jan. 1976 / Grateful Dead ◆◆◆
Again, a Dead album in everything but name, with several tracks featuring the entire band, perhaps most memorably on "It Must Have Been the Roses." —*William Ruhlmann*

Cats Under the Stars / 1978 / Arista ◆◆◆
The first real "Garcia Band" album is paced by songs that would not sound out of place at a Dead concert. As a matter of fact, the album has garnered increased interest in the '90s as the Dead added the leadoff track "Rubin and Cherise" to its repertoire. —*William Ruhlmann*

Run for the Roses / 1982 / Arista ◆◆◆
One of the last Dead-related albums released before the band's hiatus from recording in the mid-'80s, this is a typical effort, with covers of the Beatles and Bob Dylan, plus a couple of minor Garcia-Hunter compositions. —*William Ruhlmann*

Almost Acoustic / Dec. 1988 / Grateful Dead ◆◆◆
Garcia got his start in bluegrass, and here he assembles the Jerry Garcia Acoustic Band (some of whom he started playing with) to handle a live set full of Jimmie Rodgers, Mississippi John Hurt, and traditional mountain music. —*William Ruhlmann*

Compliments of Garcia / 1989 / Grateful Dead ◆◆
On his second solo album, Garcia adopts an approach more typical of his solo live shows than the Grateful Dead, writing none of the material himself and tackling everything from Irving Berlin's "Russian Lullaby"

to Smokey Robinson's "The Hunter Gets Captured by the Game." The songs are taken at slightly sluggish tempos compared to the originals, especially ones that used to be frantic rockers. Most of this material is beyond Garcia's limited vocal range, but he gets points for trying. (Since Garcia unimaginatively gave this album the same title as his first solo album, Deadheads differentiated between the two by referring to the *Compliments of Garcia* legend written on promotional copies of this album. In reissuing the album on CD in 1989, Grateful Dead Records adopted their title.) — *William Ruhlmann*

Jerry Garcia & David Grisman / 1991 / Acoustic Disc ✦✦✦✦
A guitar-and-mandolin duet album, exquisitely produced, with this pair trying a variety of styles from Garcia's "Friend of the Devil" to the ambitious instrumental "Arabia." — *William Ruhlmann*

Jerry Garcia Band / Aug. 27, 1991 / Arista ✦✦✦
A double live album recorded in 1990 and featuring extended versions of songs by Bruce Cockburn, Bob Dylan, Smokey Robinson, the Beatles, the Band, Los Lobos, and others. The Garcia Band serves a kind of songbook function for its listeners (as, indeed, does the Dead), which may mean that its chief virtue is as instruction: if you're familiar with the originals, you don't really need to hear Garcia's covers, but if, like many Deadheads, you don't have much music outside the band's orbit, this may help lead you to other good music. — *William Ruhlmann*

Not for Kids Only / Oct. 1993 / Acoustic Disc ✦✦✦
On their second duo album, Jerry Garcia and David Grisman play songs either written for or applicable to children, among them Elizabeth Cotten's "Freight Train" and "Teddy Bears' Picnic." It's a delightful record that lives up to its title, and also marks the development of Garcia/Grisman as a full partnership, with Grisman contributing as many vocals as Garcia and the two trading off on guitar and mandolin. — *William Ruhlmann*

How Sweet It Is / Apr. 15, 1997 / Arista ✦✦✦
Recorded at San Francisco's Warfield Theatre during 1990, *How Sweet It Is* captures the Jerry Garcia Band running through a selection of originals and covers. While it isn't as fluid or surprising as the double-disc 1991 set *Jerry Garcia Band*, which was culled from the same shows, it's nevertheless an entertaining set, especially for devoted fans, who will cherish previously unheard Garcia covers of songs like "Think" and the title track. — *Stephen Thomas Erlewine*

Art Garfunkel

b. Oct. 13, 1941, Queens, NY
Vocals / Adult Contemporary, Soft Rock, Pop-Rock
After Simon & Garfunkel, one of the most successful duos in pop history, split up in 1970, Art Garfunkel became a solo artist, as well as pursuing an acting career. Garfunkel's pure, high tenor had been one of the most distinctive elements of the duo's music, but Simon wrote all of the group's hits. Not surprisingly, Garfunkel relied on other songwriters, from Jimmy Webb and Randy Newman to rock 'n' roll standards like "I Only Have Eyes for You," throughout his solo career. As a solo performer, he was never quite as successful as he was with Simon & Garfunkel, but he did have a number of Top 40 hits in the mid-'70s.

Garfunkel didn't begin a solo career until 1973. Between 1970 and 1973, he acted, appearing in two Mike Nichols films, *Catch 22* and *Carnal Knowledge*. *Angel Clare*, his first solo record, was co-produced with Simon & Garfunkel producer Roy Halee and released in the fall of 1973. It established the style—a light, carefully arranged and constructed melodic soft-rock—he would follow throughout his solo career. The album became a Top Ten hit on the strength of the single "All I Know," which peaked at No. 9. Two years later he returned with the Richard Perry-produced *Breakaway*, the most successful album of his solo career. The record peaked at No. 7, with a version of the Flamingos' "I Only Have Eyes for You" reaching No. 18 on the US charts; in Britain, the single topped the charts. That same fall, he reunited with Paul Simon for the first time, performing on *Saturday Night Live*. In December, Simon's "My Little Town," featuring Garfunkel on backing vocals, became a Top Ten hit.

In the fall of 1977 Garfunkel released his third album, *Watermark*, which consisted primarily of Jimmy Webb covers. However, when the first single from the album failed to chart, the album was reissued in early 1978 with a cover of Sam Cooke's "Wonderful World" that featured supporting vocals from Simon and James Taylor. Released as a single, "Wonderful World" peaked at No. 17. The next year, *Fate for Breakfast* appeared. Although it performed well in Britain, reaching No. 2, the album signalled that his American audience was beginning to shrink; none of the singles made the Top 40, and the album reached only No. 67. In the fall of 1979 he filmed two movies, *Bad Timing* and *Illusions*. *Scissors Cut*, a reunion with producer Roy Halee released in 1981, did nothing to reverse his sliding commercial potential; it didn't even break into the Top 100 albums.

After the release of *Scissors Cut*, Simon & Garfunkel reunited for a concert in New York's Central Park. The concert was so successful that

the duo decided to embark on a year-long world tour. During the tour, tensions mounted between the pair and they split again after it was completed. After a lengthy quiet period, Garfunkel re-emerged in 1988 with *Lefty*, which spent a mere eight weeks in the American charts and failed to make the British charts. He did not release another album until 1993's rarities compilation *Up 'til Now*. After its release, Garfunkel took another extended break, returning in 1997 with the live album *Across America*. — *Stephen Thomas Erlewine*

Angel Clare / Sep. 1973 / Columbia ✦✦✦✦
Garfunkel (he was billed without his first name here) had a lot riding on his debut solo album, and *Angel Clare*, named after a character in Thomas Hardy's novel *Tess of the D'Urbervilles*, lived up to the heightened expectations for the man who had sung "Bridge over Troubled Water" and other Simon & Garfunkel favorites. Garfunkel took no chances, issuing as the first single Jimmy Webb's "All I Know," which was arranged in a similar style to "Bridge" and made the Top Ten. Elsewhere on the record, Garfunkel took a more spirited approach, notably on a version of Van Morrison's "I Shall Sing" that was reminiscent of Simon & Garfunkel's "Cecilia" and made the Top 40. Certainly there was enough firepower on the record, which featured guitarists Jerry Garcia and J.J. Cale. But much of it was filled with stately, orchestra-laden ballads, sung by Garfunkel in his naive, breathy tenor. If Simon & Garfunkel had been the thinking man's Everly Brothers, Garfunkel alone turned out to be the thinking man's Johnny Mathis. — *William Ruhlmann*

Breakaway / Oct. 1975 / Columbia ✦✦✦
The second time around, Art Garfunkel turned to pop producer Richard Perry, who liked to record in studios rather than cathedrals and who replaced the angelic style of the first album with a lush pop approach. The result was Garfunkel's best-selling album. The title track and a cover of "I Only Have Eyes for You" reached the Top 40 (the latter topped the UK charts), though the most prominent song was the Simon & Garfunkel reunion single "My Little Town." But the album was full of wise pop choices, among them Bruce Johnston's "Disney Girls," Stevie Wonder's "I Believe (When I Fall in Love It Will Be Forever)," and Hal David and Albert Hammond's "1199 Miles from L.A." Perry proved that, given the right material and production, the problem of the relative sameness of Garfunkel's vocal approach could be overcome. — *William Ruhlmann*

Watermark / Oct. 1977 / Columbia ✦✦✦
The original idea was for Art Garfunkel to record an album of songs written by Jimmy Webb. But when the lead-off single, "Crying in My Sleep," failed to make the charts, Columbia Records withdrew the album and induced Garfunkel to put together a cover of Sam Cooke's "(What A) Wonderful World" with Paul Simon and James Taylor harmonizing. The single and a revised version of the LP then made the Top 40. But it's still a Garfunkel-sings-Webb album, except for one song. And the initial idea was a good one: Garfunkel handles Webb's wistful pop songs well, and he has made good choices from Webb's songbook, dating back to the 1960s, though avoiding his big hits. The result is Garfunkel's most cohesive solo album. (The original version of *Watermark*, on test pressings and only a very few commercial copies, was available briefly in October 1977. The revised version, containing "[What A] Wonderful World," was released in January 1978.) — *William Ruhlmann*

Fate for Breakfast / Mar. 1979 / Columbia ✦✦
For his fourth solo album, Art Garfunkel opted to make a light contemporary pop record on the order of Breakaway, but for the most part the material was mediocre and the backup slick and unfeeling. "Since I Don't Have You" was an obvious choice for a singer who had scored with a similar '50s oldie, "I Only Have Eyes for You," but it was the album's only chart single, and *Fate for Breakfast* was as disappointing at the cash register as it was on the turntable. — *William Ruhlmann*

Scissors Cut / Aug. 1981 / Columbia ✦✦
After the disappointment of *Fate for Breakfast*, Art Garfunkel returned to old friends for his fifth solo album, co-producing with Roy Halee, who had worked with Simon & Garfunkel and on Garfunkel's debut album, *Angel Clare*, and singing several songs written by Jimmy Webb, who had written nearly all the songs on Garfunkel's third album, *Watermark*. But though *Scissors Cut* came closer to the sound of a good Garfunkel album, material remained a problem. "A Heart in New York," the LP's sole American chart single, was second-rate, as were many of the other compositions. Garfunkel scored a surprise No. 1 hit in Great Britain with the Mike Batt-written and produced "Bright Eyes," the theme from the movie *Watership Down*, but that wasn't enough to make the album on the whole a success. Garfunkel then re-teamed with Paul Simon for a world concert tour, and it was five years before he was back in record stores with the seasonal release *The Animals' Christmas* and nearly seven years before his next regular solo album, *Lefty*. — *William Ruhlmann*

Lefty / Mar. 1988 / Columbia ✦✦
Art Garfunkel's first regular studio album in nearly seven years was a pleasant enough exercise that did nothing to arrest his commercial or artistic decline. The idea of covering "I Have a Love" from *West Side Story* was a good one; the obligatory '50s cover, "So Much in Love," was well performed; and "Love Is the Only Chain" was a good piece of material, even if better performed by authors Pam Rose and Mary Ann Kennedy (who joined Garfunkel on this recording). The version of "When a Man Loves a Woman," so far away from Percy Sledge's emotional original, served to illustrate Garfunkel's detached approach to his material. But much of the album consisted of second-rate songs, frequently written by Stephen Bishop. — *William Ruhlmann*

● **Garfunkel: Best of** / Oct. 1990 / Columbia ✦✦✦✦
This is a good overview of Garfunkel's solo work. Most of his airplay tracks are included here. — *Rick Clark*

Up 'til Now / Oct. 28, 1993 / Columbia ✦✦
Art Garfunkel gives his "deepest thanks to Mitchell Cohen at Columbia for the concept of this album." But what is the concept? It contains everything from the original Simon & Garfunkel recording of "The Sound of Silence" (from their *Wednesday Morning 3 A.M.* album) to tracks from previous Garfunkel solo albums, stray songs apparently intended for albums never made, movie and TV themes, a live performance, and even a comedy routine with Paul Simon called "The Breakup"—you name it. So, perhaps the concept is what the Who called "odds and sods." In any case, it's marginal. — *William Ruhlmann*

Across America / May 27, 1997 / Virgin ✦✦
Art Garfunkel returned to recording in 1997 with *Across America*, a live album intended to commemorate his walk across America. Comprised largely of oldies, the record is a pleasant enough nostalgia trip, but it doesn't have enough distinguished performances (a version of "52nd Street Bridge Song" sung with his six-year old son is notable, but it certainly isn't accomplished) to make the record a worthy addition to the collections of even devoted fans. — *Stephen Thomas Erlewine*

Marvin Gaye (Marvin Pentz Gay, Jr.)

b. Apr. 2, 1939, Washington, D.C., **d.** Apr. 1, 1984, Los Angeles, CA
Keyboards, Vocals / Soul, R&B, Urban, Motown, Quiet Storm
One of the most gifted, visionary and enduring talents ever launched into orbit by the Motown hit machine, Marvin Gaye blazed the trail for the continued evolution of popular Black music. Moving from lean, powerful R&B to stylish, sophisticated soul to finally arrive at an intensely political and personal form of artistic self-expression, his work not only redefined soul music as a creative force but expanded its impact as an agent for social change.

Marvin Pentz Gay, Jr. (in the style of his hero Sam Cooke, he added the "e" to his surname as an adult) was born April 2, 1939, in Washington, DC. The oldest of three children born to Marvin Sr., an ordained minister in the House of God—a conservative Christian sect fusing elements of orthodox Judaism and Pentecostalism that imposes strict codes of conduct and observes no holidays—he began singing in church at the age of three, quickly becoming a soloist in the choir. He later took up piano and drums, and music became Gaye's escape from the nightmarish realities of his home life; throughout his childhood, his father beat him on an almost daily basis.

After graduating high school, Gaye enlisted in the US Air Force. Upon his discharge, he returned to Washington and began singing in a number of street-corner doo wop groups, eventually joining the Rainbows, a top local attraction. With the help of mentor Bo Diddley, the Rainbows cut "Wyatt Earp," a single for the Okeh label that brought them to the attention of singer Harvey Fuqua, who in 1958 recruited the group to become the latest edition of his backing ensemble, the Moonglows. After relocating to Chicago, the Moonglows recorded a series of singles for Chess including 1959's "Mama Loocie." While touring the Midwest, the group performed in Detroit, where Gaye's graceful tenor and three-octave vocal range won the interest of fledgling impresario Berry Gordy Jr., who signed him to the Motown label in 1961.

While first working at Motown as a session drummer and playing on early hits by Smokey Robinson and the Miracles, he met Gordy's sister Anna and married her in late 1961. Upon mounting a solo career, Gaye struggled to find his voice, and early singles failed; finally, his fourth effort, "Stubborn Kind of Fellow," became a minor hit in 1962, and his next two singles—the 1963 dance efforts "Hitch Hike" and "Can I Get a Witness"—both reached the Top 30. With 1963's "Pride and Joy," Gaye scored his first Top Ten smash, but he often found his role as a hitmaker stifling. His desire to become a crooner of lush romantic ballads ran in direct opposition to Motown's all-important emphasis on chart success, and the ongoing battle between his artistic ambitions and the label's demands for commercial product continued throughout Gaye's long tenure with the company. With 1964's *Together*, a collection of duets with Mary Wells, Gaye scored his first charting album; the duo also notched a number of hit singles together, including "Once Upon a Time"

and "What's the Matter with You, Baby?" As a solo performer, Gaye continued to enjoy great success, scoring three superb Top Ten hits—"Ain't That Peculiar," "I'll Be Doggone," and "How Sweet It Is (To Be Loved by You)"—in 1965. In total, he scored some 39 Top 40 singles for Motown, many of which he also wrote and arranged. With Kim Weston, the second of his crucial vocal partners, he also established himself as one of the era's dominant duet singers with the stunning "It Takes Two."

Gaye's greatest duets, however, were with Tammi Terrell, with whom he scored a series of massive hits penned by the team of Nickolas Ashford and Valerie Simpson, including 1967's "Ain't No Mountain High Enough" and "Your Precious Love," followed by 1968's "Ain't Nothing like the Real Thing" and "You're All I Need to Get By." The team's success was tragically cut short in 1967 when, during a concert appearance in Virginia, Terrell collapsed into Gaye's arms onstage, the first evidence of a brain tumor that abruptly ended her performing career and finally killed her on March 16, 1970. Her illness and eventual loss left Gaye deeply shaken, marring the chart-topping 1968 success of "I Heard It Through the Grapevine," his biggest hit and arguably the pinnacle of the Motown Sound.

At the same time, Gaye was forced to cope with a number of other personal problems, not the least of which was his crumbling marriage. He also found the material he recorded for Motown to be increasingly irrelevant in the face of the tremendous social changes sweeping the nation, and after scoring a pair of 1969 Top Ten hits with "Too Busy Thinking About My Baby" and "That's the Way Love Is," he spent the majority of 1970 in seclusion, resurfacing early the next year with the self-produced *What's Going On,* a landmark effort marking a dramatic shift in both content and style that forever altered the face of Black music. A highly percussive album that incorporated jazz and classical elements to forge a remarkably sophisticated and fluid soul sound, *What's Going On* was a conceptual masterpiece that brought Gaye's deeply held spiritual beliefs to the fore to explore issues ranging from poverty and discrimination to the environment, drug abuse, and political corruption; chief among the record's concerns was the conflict in Vietnam, as Gaye structured the songs around the point of view of his brother Frankie, himself a soldier recently returned from combat.

The ambitions and complexity of *What's Going On* baffled Berry Gordy, who initially refused to release the LP; he finally relented, although he maintained that he never understood the record's full scope. Gaye was vindicated when the majestic title track reached the No. 2 spot in 1971, and both of the follow-ups, "Mercy Mercy Me (The Ecology)" and "Inner City Blues (Make Me Wanna Holler)," also reached the Top Ten. The album's success guaranteed Gaye continued artistic control over his work and helped loosen the reins for other Motown artists, most notably Stevie Wonder, to also take command of their own destinies. Consequently, in 1972, Gaye changed directions again, agreeing to score the blaxploitation thriller *Trouble Man;* the resulting soundtrack was a primarily instrumental effort showcasing his increasing interest in jazz, although a vocal turn on the moody, minimalist title track scored another Top Ten smash.

The long-simmering eroticism implicit in much of Gaye's work reached its boiling point with 1973's *Let's Get It On,* one of the most sexually charged albums ever recorded; a work of intense lust and longing, it became the most commercially successful effort of his career, and the title cut became his second No. 1 hit. *Let's Get It On* also marked another significant shift in Gaye's lyrical outlook, moving him from the political arena to a deeply personal, even insular stance that continued to define his subsequent work. After teaming with Diana Ross for the 1973 duet collection *Marvin and Diana,* he returned to work on his next solo effort, *I Want You;* however, the record's completion was delayed by his 1975 divorce from Anna Gordy. The dissolution of his marriage threw Gaye into a tailspin, and he spent much of the mid-1970s in divorce court; to combat Gaye's absence from the studio, Motown released the 1977 stopgap *Live at the London Palladium,* which spawned the single "Got to Give It Up (Pt. 1)," his final No. 1 hit.

As a result of a 1976 court settlement, Gaye was ordered to make good on missed alimony payments by recording a new album, with the intention that all royalties earned from its sales would then be awarded to his ex-wife. The 1978 record, a two-LP set sardonically titled *Here, My Dear,* bitterly explored the couple's relationship in such intimate detail that Anna Gordy briefly considered suing Gaye for invasion of privacy. In the interim, he had remarried and begun work on another album, *Lover Man,* but scrapped the project when the lead single "Ego Tripping Out"—a telling personal commentary presented as a duet between the spiritual and sexual halves of his identity, which biographer David Ritz later dubbed the singer's "divided soul"—failed to chart. As his drug problems increased and his marriage to new wife Janis also began to fail, he relocated to Hawaii in an attempt to sort out his personal affairs.

In 1981, long-standing tax difficulties and renewed pressures from the I.R.S. forced Gaye to flee to Europe, where he began work on the ambitious *In Our Lifetime,* a deeply philosophical record which ultimately severed his long-standing relationship with Motown after he claimed the label had remixed and edited the album without his consent; additionally, Gaye stated that the finished artwork parodied his original intent, and that even the title had been changed to drop an all-important question mark. Upon signing with Columbia in 1982, he battled stories of erratic behavior and a consuming addiction to cocaine to emerge triumphant with *Midnight Love*, an assured comeback highlighted by the luminous Top Three hit "Sexual Healing." The record made Gaye a star yet again, and in 1983 he made peace with Berry Gordy by appearing on a television special celebrating Motown's silver anniversary. That same year, he also sang a soulful and idiosyncratic rendition of "The Star-Spangled Banner" at the NBA All-Star Game that instantly became one of the most controversial and legendary interpretations of the anthem ever performed; it was to be his final public appearance.

Gaye's career resurgence brought with it an increased reliance on cocaine; finally, his personal demons forced him back to the US, where he moved in with his parents in an attempt to regain control of his life. Tragically, the return home only exacerbated his spiral into depression; he and his father quarreled bitterly, and Gaye threatened suicide on a number of occasions. Finally, on the afternoon of April 1, 1984—one day before his 45th birthday—Gaye was shot and killed by the Reverend Marvin Gay, Sr. in the aftermath of a heated argument. In the wake of his death, Motown and Columbia teamed to issue two 1985 collections of outtakes, *Dream of a Lifetime*—a compilation of erotic funk workouts teamed with spiritual ballads—and the big-band-inspired *Romantically Yours*. (*Vulnerable*, a collection of ballads that took over 12 years to complete, finally saw release in 1996.) With Gaye's death also came a critical re-evaluation of his work, which deemed *What's Going On* to be one of the landmark albums in pop history, and his 1987 induction into the Rock and Roll Hall of Fame permanently enshrined him among the pantheon of musical greats. —*Jason Ankeny*

That Stubborn Kinda Fellow / Jan. 31, 1963 / Motown ✦✦✦
Vintage Gaye and Motown, following all the formulas that made the label the '60s' finest record company. The title track was an instant classic and is still among his finest '60s uptempo tunes. The other cuts are just as fantastic, and any doubts anyone might have had about Gaye were immediately and forever quashed with this album. —*Ron Wynn*

When I'm Alone I Cry / Apr. 1, 1964 / Motown ✦✦
Hard as it may be to believe today, at the beginning of his career, Gaye was far more interested in crooning jazz standards than singing soul music, and took every opportunity to vent his jazz pipes in the studio. However much he may have wished otherwise, just about every listener agrees that he was a great soul singer, but a mediocre jazz vocalist. This album, cut at a time when he was already a rising soul star, consists of ten pop-jazz standards and is really of interest only to collectors. Certainly it's competently done, but it's supper-club fare, in which Gaye comes off as a sub-Nat King Cole rather than his own man. The CD reissue, interestingly, presents the entire album in both mono and stereo versions. —*Richie Unterberger*

Marvin Gaye and Kim Weston / 1966 / Motown ✦✦✦
Although they weren't as great a team as Gaye and Tammi Terrell, the Gaye/Weston duo turned out a few solid numbers. The finest was "It Takes Two," a steamy bit of uptempo soul that came close to equaling any fast duet number Gaye ever made at Motown. The rest was well done, but not quite on the same level. —*Ron Wynn*

☆ **Marvin Gaye's Greatest Hits, Vol. 2** / 1967 / Motown ✦✦✦✦✦
Other than the *Anthology* line, this was for quite a while the best single album set featuring Gaye's early and mid-'60s hits. There isn't a dud in the bunch, but both the *Super Hits* and *Anthology* line give you more cuts, while the boxed set has more variety. But this isn't by any stretch a bad release. —*Ron Wynn*

M.P.G. / Apr. 30, 1969 / Motown ✦✦✦
An underrated late '60s album, this one has sometimes been overlooked because it seemed like a generic throwaway. But it included some outstanding songs. Motown wisely has included it on their list of Gaye albums that got reissued on CD. —*Ron Wynn*

Super Hits / 1970 / Motown ✦✦✦✦
A fabulous anthology, one of the best Motown ever released. Both *Super Hits* packages were crammed full, and the sound and selections were first rate. Motown has issued the first volume on CD, but thus far not the second—a major mistake. —*Ron Wynn*

That's the Way Love Is / Jan. 8, 1970 / Motown ✦✦✦
The title cut was another Gaye classic, while much of the other material was equally impressive. Gaye was beginning to become disillusioned with Motown, but that hadn't affected his album output or his singing. Anyone hearing this wouldn't have suspected that Gaye was about to unleash *What's Going On*. —*Ron Wynn*

☆ **What's Going On** / May 20, 1971 / Motown ✦✦✦✦✦
Shortly after Marvin Gaye turned 30, he became the first Motown artist with a measure of creative control. *What's Going On* was the result,

surely Marvin's finest moment and, along with a number of Stevie Wonder's early-'70s releases, one of a handful of *great* Motown albums. A concept album, *What's Going On* chronicled a multitude of societal ills. Ironically, Motown owner Berry Gordy did not want to release it. He was convinced it held no commercial potential. Gordy couldn't have been more wrong. *What's Going On* catapulted Marvin Gaye into superstardom. Three No. 1 singles were pulled from the album: the title song, "Mercy Mercy Me (The Ecology)," and "Inner City Blues (Make Me Wanna Holler)." This was the first album where Gaye's voice was overdubbed multiple times, creating a one-man vocal group. The result was a level of timbral integration in the harmonies that became a Gaye trademark. —*Rob Bowman*

Trouble Man / Dec. 8, 1972 / Motown ✦✦✦
Marvin Gaye turned to soundtracks in the early '70s, and came out with one that ranked right alongside the epic scores done by Curtis Mayfield and Isaac Hayes. The film itself was a typical '70s "blaxploitation" effort, but Gaye's vocals, seamless production, and a nice mix of uptempo funk, light ballads, and pseudo-macho camp were brilliant. —*Ron Wynn*

☆ **Let's Get It On** / Aug. 28, 1973 / Motown ✦✦✦✦
Let's Get It On is one of the most erotic recordings known to mankind. Inspired by Gaye's obsession with a teenage girl, Janis Hunter, who would later become his second wife, side one is a self-contained suite. Side two, including "You Sure Love to Ball," is nearly pornographic. Over time, five songs would chart from the album, including one of his concert standards, "Distant Lover." —*Rob Bowman*

★ **Anthology** / 1974 / Motown ✦✦✦✦✦
With *Anthology* you can get an overview of Gaye's Motown work without having to plunk down the money for *The Marvin Gaye Collection* box set. The two-disc set contains most of his major hits (although not his No. 1 hit "Let's Get It On"), including "Inner City Blues (Make Me Wanna Holler)," "Mercy Mercy Me (The Ecology)," "I Heard It Through the Grapevine," "Trouble Man," "I'll Be Doggone," "What's Going On," "Hitch Hike," "Can I Get a Witness," and "Pride and Joy," as well as his numerous duets with Kim Weston and Tammi Terrell, like "Ain't No Mountain High Enough," "Ain't Nothing like the Real Thing," "It Takes Two," and "Your Precious Love." —*AMG*

I Want You / Mar. 16, 1976 / Motown ✦✦✦
Featured are dynamic vocal and rhythmic arrangements. —*Rick A. Bueche*

Here My Dear / Dec. 15, 1978 / Motown ✦✦✦✦
On one of the stranger releases in popular music, *Here, My Dear,* Gaye stands emotionally naked. Over the course of this two-album set, Marvin chronicles the dissolution of his marriage (to company president Berry Gordy's sister Anna). The level of detail is nearly painful as Marvin accuses Anna of keeping him from seeing his son, having a restraining order issued against him, and holding their separation up for ransom. Marvin also tells us of his cocaine habit and his obsession with prostitutes. In a trace of irony not lost on the singer, Anna received all royalties from the album as per their divorce agreement. Upon hearing it, she reportedly contemplated suing for invasion of privacy. —*Rob Bowman*

In Our Lifetime / Jan. 15, 1981 / Motown ✦✦✦
Another of Gaye's uneven, yet appealing releases. He was searching for the right songs and didn't always find them. He was also hurting again, suffering personal and professional problems that he ultimately failed to solve. This made his songs both poignant and painful, and that's what makes this album worth hearing, despite its problems. —*Ron Wynn*

Midnight Love / Oct. 1982 / Columbia ✦✦✦✦
Gaye's comeback album contains its share of fluff but "Sexual Healing" is one of the greatest R&B singles of all time. Black radio felt that way as well; the song stayed No. 1 for ten weeks, remaining on the charts for a total of 27 weeks. —*Rob Bowman*

The Marvin Gaye Collection / Sep. 1990 / Motown ✦✦✦
Marvin Gaye has more than enough great music to make a superb box set, but the haphazard *Marvin Gaye Collection* isn't it. The four discs within the set are arranged thematically—one terrific disc of hits, one good disc of duets, one largely uninteresting disc of rarities, and one wildly uneven disc of ballads. By spreading out the material this way, Motown shortchanges Gaye's musical accomplishments; there is no sense of growth or innovation. Although many of the songs are wonderful, some of the selections are puzzling—they seem to be chosen because they're arcane, not because they're significant. This very quality makes *The Marvin Gaye Collection* essential for his most devoted fans; however, most fans will find this box set disappointing. —*Stephen Thomas Erlewine*

Norman Whitfield Sessions / Aug. 23, 1994 / Motown ✦✦✦
All of Gaye's recordings with producer Norman Whitfield are collected on the appropriately titled *The Norman Whitfield Sessions*. The sessions proved beneficial to both Gaye and Whitfield, as they produced the classic "I Heard It Through the Grapevine." While nothing on the set

matches that seminal single, most of the music is captivating. Nevertheless, the disc will appeal mainly to the devoted Marvin Gaye collector, since most of the material is either alternate takes or outtakes. —*Stephen Thomas Erlewine*

The Master 1961-1984 / Apr. 25, 1995 / Motown ✦✦✦✦
The average fan is better off with *Anthology*, which covers almost all of Gaye's true classics. But for those who want the hits and then some, and have the budget and interest to go further, this four-CD box set is an excellent retrospective of his career. The 89 tracks include all the chart hits (both on his own and with Mary Wells, Kim Weston, Tammi Terrell, and Diana Ross) and many interesting B-sides, album tracks, and misses. There are also over a dozen previously unreleased cuts, most dating from the early part of his career; they don't rank among his best work, but they're almost all good and interesting. With a long essay by his biographer, David Ritz, this is the best overview of Gaye's evolution and versatility, and a much-recommended alternative to the previous Gaye box, *The Marvin Gaye Collection*. —*Richie Unterberger*

★ **Anthology [1995]** / Aug. 22, 1995 / Motown ✦✦✦✦✦
The Marvin Gaye Anthology released in 1995 is an entirely different compilation from the three-LP *Anthology* originally released in 1974 and reissued as a double-CD in 1986. The earlier version contained 40 tracks, starting with "Stubborn Kind of Fellow" and running through "Trouble Man." The new one, on two CDs or cassettes, contains 47 tracks, also starting with "Stubborn Kind of Fellow," but running through "Heavy Love Affair." As such, it is more comprehensive, containing such later hits as "Let's Get It On," "I Want You," and "Got to Give It Up—Pt. 1" that were not featured on the earlier edition (but not "Sexual Healing," which Gaye recorded after leaving Motown). Only a couple of Gaye's Top Ten R&B/Top 40 pop hits are missing, and there is a smattering of rarities. The 1995 *Anthology* falls neatly between the single-disc *Every Great Motown Hit* and the four-disc box set *The Master 1961-1984* as a thorough hits collection at a reasonable price. —*William Ruhlmann*

Vulnerable / Mar. 25, 1997 / Motown ✦✦✦
Vulnerable is the end result of a project entitled *The Ballads* that Marvin Gaye began in 1966. Gaye intended the project as a showcase for his crooning, as well as a way to pay tribute to the pop and jazz standards he loved. It was a labor of love that took him 12 years to complete, and even after it was finished, the record wasn't released until 1997. Was it worth the wait? For dedicated fans, it certainly was, since Gaye's voice is as beautiful and soulful as ever. However, anyone who is not a dedicated fan will find *Vulnerable* intriguing but significantly flawed, especially since several of the songs seem ill-suited for Gaye's seductive vocals. Which means that even though *Vulnerable* is a nice addendum to his catalog, it's little more than a curiosity. —*Stephen Thomas Erlewine*

Gloria Gaynor

b. Sep. 7, 1949, Newark, NJ
Vocals / Disco
Gaynor sang with the Soul Satisfiers before being discovered at the Wagon Wheel in New York in the early '70s. Probably the first "disco queen," Gaynor helped popularize, through her music, the "segue" or "extended mix" that came to represent disco music. Her 1979 cut, "I Will Survive," became a woman's anthem in the vein of Helen Reddy's "I Am Woman." She continued to thrive in Europe during the '80s and continued recording throughout the following decade. —*Bil Carpenter*

● **Greatest Hits** / 1982 / Polydor ✦✦✦✦
Greatest Hits is a 12-track collection that features all of Gloria Gaynor's biggest, including "Never Can Say Goodbye," "I Will Survive," "Reach Out (I'll Be There)," "Walk On By" and "(If You Want It) Do It Yourself," making it a definitive retrospective. —*Stephen Thomas Erlewine*

J. Geils Band

f. 1967, Boston, MA, **db.** 1985
Rock'n'Roll, Blues-Rock, Pop-Rock
The J. Geils Band was one of the most popular touring rock 'n' roll bands in America during the '70s. Where their contemporaries were influenced by the heavy boogie of British blues-rock and the ear-splitting sonic adventures of psychedelia, the J. Geils Band was a bar band pure and simple, churning out greasy covers of obscure R&B, doo wop, and soul tunes, cutting them with a healthy dose of Stonesy swagger. While their muscular sound and the hyper jive of frontman Peter Wolf packed arenas across America, it only rarely earned them hit singles. Seth Justman, the group's main songwriter, could turn out catchy R&B-based rockers like "Give It to Me" or "Must of Got Lost," but these hits never led to stardom, primarily because the group had trouble capturing the energy of their live sound in the studio. In the early '80s, the group tempered their driving rock with some pop, and the makeover paid off with the massive hit single "Centerfold," which stayed at No. 1 for six weeks. By the time the band prepared to record a follow-up, tensions between

Justman and Wolf had grown considerably, resulting in Wolf's departure, which quickly led to the band's demise.

Guitarist Jerome Geils, bassist Danny Klein, and harpist Magic Dick (b. Richard Salwitz) began performing as an acoustic blues trio sometime in the mid-'60s. In 1967 drummer Stephen Jo Bladd and vocalist Peter Wolf joined the group, and the band went electric. Before joining the J. Geils Band, Bladd and Wolf played together in the Boston-based rock revivalist band the Hallucinations. Both musicians shared a love of arcane doo wop, blues, R&B, and rock 'n' roll; Wolf had become well known by spinning obscure singles as a jive-talking WBCN DJ called Woofuh Goofuh. Wolf and Bladd's specialized tastes became a central force in the newly revamped J. Geils Band, who positioned themselves as tough, '50s greasers in opposition to the colorful psychedelic rockers that dominated the East Coast in the late '60s. Soon the band had earned a sizable local following, including Seth Justman, an organist who was studying at Boston University. Justman joined the band in 1968, and the group continued to tour for the next few years, landing a record contract with Atlantic in 1970.

The J. Geils Band was a regional hit upon its early 1970 release, and it earned favorable reviews, especially from *Rolling Stone*. The group's second album, *The Morning After*, appeared later that year, and the Top 40 hit "Looking for a Love" expanded their following. However, the band continued to win new fans primarily through their concerts, so it was no surprise that their third album, 1972's *Full House*, was a live set. It was followed by *Bloodshot*, which climbed into the Top Ten on the strength of the Top 40 hit, "Give It to Me." After the relative failure of 1973's *Ladies Invited*, the band had another hit with 1974's *Nightmares*, which featured the No. 12 single "Must of Got Lost." While their live shows remained popular throughout the mid-'70s, both *Hot Line* (1975) and the live *Blow Your Face Out* (1976) were significant commercial disappointments. The band revamped their sound and shortened their name to "Geils" for 1977's *Monkey Island*. While the album received good reviews, it failed to bring increased sales.

In 1978 the J. Geils Band left Atlantic Records for EMI, releasing *Sanctuary* later that year. *Sanctuary* slowly gained a following, becoming their first gold album since *Bloodshot*. *Love Stinks* (1980) expanded the group's following even more, peaking at No. 18 and setting the stage for 1981's *Freeze-Frame*, the band's highwater mark. Supported by the infectious single "Centerfold"—which featured a memorable video that received heavy MTV airplay—and boasting a sleek, radio-ready sound, *Freeze-Frame* climbed to No. 1. "Centerfold" shot to the top of the charts late in 1981, spending six weeks at No. 1; its follow-up, "Freeze-Frame," was nearly as successful, reaching No. 4 in the spring of 1982. The live album *Showtime!* became a gold album shortly after its late 1982 release. While the band was experiencing the greatest commercial success of its career, relationships between the members, particularly writing partners Justman and Wolf, were volatile. When the band refused to record material Wolf had written with Don Covay and Michael Jonzun, he left the band in the middle of 1983 recording session. Justman assumed lead vocals, and the group released *You're Gettin' Even While I'm Gettin' Odd* in late 1984, several months after Wolf's successful solo debut, *Lights Out*. The J. Geils Band's record was a failure, and the band broke up in 1985. Magic Dick and Geils, calling himself Jay instead of Jerome, reunited in 1993 to form the contemporary blues band Bluestime. —*Stephen Thomas Erlewine*

The J. Geils Band / 1970 / Atlantic ✦✦✦✦
Their debut paid homage to the likes of Otis Rush, John Lee Hooker, and Motown through blistering covers, but originals such as "Wait" and "What's Your Hurry" more than hold their own. Magic Dick steals the show on this one. —*John Floyd*

The Morning After / 1971 / Atlantic ✦✦✦
It's rare when a group's sophomore effort is as good as their debut. *The Morning After* by the J. Geils Band is that, and in some ways, even better. Tighter and more focused than their debut, the band found success on the singles charts with "Looking for a Love." Again, they laid original material alongside blues covers, but the sound was always their own—exciting, enjoyable rocking blues. —*James Chrispell*

Full House Live / 1972 / Atlantic ✦✦✦
Live is the way the J. Geils Band should be experienced; they put on a show like few others, and *Full House* is the proof. From start to finish, there is not one bad cut. From the opener, "First I Look at the Purse" right on through "Looking for a Love," these guys don't give up an inch. —*James Chrispell*

Bloodshot / 1973 / Atlantic ✦✦
More hot, rockin' rhythm and blues from these guys out of Boston. *Bloodshot* includes their Top 40 hit "Give It to Me," as well as the great opener, "(Ain't Nothin' But a) House Party," plus soulful struts and bluesy shuffles in between. It's a wonder these guys could tour almost constantly and still turn out great albums one after another. On *Bloodshot*, the J. Geils Band make it appear easy. —*James Chrispell*

Ladies Invited / 1973 / Atlantic ✦✦✦
On this, their first album of all original material, something appeared to be amiss. Perhaps it was road fatigue—only the band knows for sure, but *Ladies Invited* didn't burn up the charts like their previous efforts, nor did it have that all-important hit single. It's well done and worthwhile, but lacks spark. —*James Chrispell*

Nightmares . . . and Other Tales from the Vinyl Jungle / 1974 / Atlantic ✦✦✦
After a brief sidestep, the J. Geils Band came roaring back with a very urban-jungle sort of album that percolates with beat and rocks with enthusiastic excitement. Here lies the reggae-ish "Give It to Me," as well as the concert staple "Detroit Breakdown." A fertile release from some of the hardest rockers of the '70s. —*James Chrispell*

Hotline / 1975 / Atlantic ✦✦
It appears that with *Hotline* the J. Geils Band backtracked a bit by including a few new originals alongside proven R&B workouts in what one is tempted to call a formula. But *Hotline* is still well worth listening to; it includes "Love-itis," which is entirely worth the price of the rest. —*James Chrispell*

Blow Your Face Out / 1976 / Atlantic ✦✦✦
If you're looking to put on a party record from the mid-'70s, grab hold of *Blow Your Face Out* and crank up the volume. Known as a great live band, J. Geils and Co. stomp through one of the most exciting live sets put on vinyl (and tape and CD). The title says it all. —*James Chrispell*

Monkey Island / 1977 / Atlantic ✦✦✦✦
One of the great lost albums, *Monkey Island* is where the Geils Band make the blues their own. It's an elaborately produced, adventurous set that analyzes their commerical failure and looks for answers to hard-to-ask questions. Unlike their 1972 live album *Full House*, *Monkey Island* refuses to pander to blues conservatists or boogie-rock hammerheads; the album is steeped in the kind of pathos and bitterness that infuse the Stones' *Sticky Fingers*. The album flopped, but it remains the group's most personal statement. —*John Floyd*

Sanctuary / 1978 / EMI America ✦✦✦
The Geils sound is retooled into a streamlined shuffle that owes much to the production and songwriting floriation of keyboardist Seth Justman. Their soul and blues chops are still apparent, but they've worked them into a sound that manages to elaborate on the experiments of *Monkey Island* while still paying homage to their early days. —*John Floyd*

The Best of the J. Geils Band / 1979 / Atlantic ✦✦✦✦
Pulling the decent material from these otherwise unspectacular mid-'70s albums makes this an adequate overview of the band's achievements. It's the best place to sample such minor hits as "Must of Got Lost" and "Give It to Me." —*John Floyd*

Love Stinks / 1980 / EMI America ✦✦✦
The title cut brought the band an across-the-board hit, and the near new wave production touches don't get in the way of the crack rhythm section or Geils' tasty leads. A new sound for a new decade. —*John Floyd*

Freeze Frame / 1981 / EMI America ✦✦✦✦
Tempering their bar-band R&B with a touch of new wave pop production, the J. Geils Band finally broke through into the big leagues with *Freeze Frame*. Fans of the hard-driving rock of the group's '70s albums will find the sleek sound of *Freeze Frame* slightly disorienting, but the production gives the album cohesion. Good-time rock 'n' roll remains at the core of the group's music, but the sound of the record is glossier, shining with synthesizers and big pop hooks. With its sing-along chorus, "Centerfold" exemplifies this trend, but it's merely the tip of the iceberg. "Freeze Frame" has a great stop-start chorus; "Flamethrower" and "Piss on the Wall" rush along on hard-boogie riffs; and "Angel in Blue" is terrific neo-doo wop. There's still a handful of throwaways, but even the filler has a stylized, synthesized flair that makes it enjoyable, and the keepers are among the band's best. —*Stephen Thomas Erlewine*

Showtime! / 1984 / EMI America ✦✦

You're Gettin' Even While I'm Gettin' Odd / 1984 / EMI ✦✦

Flashback / 1988 / EMI America ✦✦✦
Flashback is a brief but entertaining overview of the J. Geils Band's early-'80s hits, featuring the hit singles "Centerfold," "Freeze-Frame," "Flamethrower," "Love Stinks," "I Do," and "Just Can't Wait." —*Stephen Thomas Erlewine*

● **Houseparty: Anthology** / 1992 / Rhino ✦✦✦✦
The superb two-disc anthology *Houseparty* concentrates on the rousing, full-throttle blues-boogie of their heyday, including a full album's worth of live material (ten songs from their three live albums). The pop success of *Love Stinks* and *Freeze Frame* makes sense in the context of the set, but the songs that cut the deepest are the blues-rock numbers on the first disc and the live songs. Thankfully, the compilers (*Trouser Press* editor Ira Robbins and band members Peter Wolf and Seth Justman) end *Houseparty* with three songs from *Sanctuary*, helping secure the image

of the J. Geils Band as one of America's top rock 'n' roll groups. —*Stephen Thomas Erlewine*

Gene
f. 1993, Watford, England
Alternative Pop-Rock, Brit-Pop
Gene will forever be haunted by comparisons to the Smiths, especially since lead singer Martin Rossiter favors the same strangled croon and tortured loneliness of Morrissey. Nevertheless, under the direction of guitarist Steve Mason, Gene developed a tougher sound than the Smiths, drawing not only from the fey tradition of British indie-pop, but from the three-chord chunk of the Faces, the working-class punk of the Jam, and the soulful stomp of Motown. Most critics didn't hear such subtle differences, and opinions on the group's worth were fiercely divided upon the release of the first single in 1994. Gene developed a devoted following that helped them become one of the leading artists of the Brit-pop second tier in 1995, even if the band had trouble breaking into the States.

The roots of Gene lay in a band called Spin, which featured guitarist Steve Mason and drummer Matt James. Spin disbanded after their career was sidetracked by their bassist's injury in a car crash, but Mason and James continued playing together, recruiting bassist Kevin Miles through a mutual friend. The trio eventually met Welsh native Martin Rossiter, and the quartet formed Gene in 1993. Over the course of the next few months, the band wrote a batch of songs and had performed a number of concerts by the end of the year. A pair of music journalists, Keith Cameron and Roy Wilkinson, formed the Costermonger label in order to release Gene's debut single, "For the Dead," in April 1994. Nearly every copy of the limited-edition release sold out within the first week, and Gene soon became favorites of the British music weeklies. That July, "Be My Light, Be My Guide" became a No. 1 hit on the indie charts, and Gene emerged as one of the leading new bands of the burgeoning Brit-pop movement. Major-label interest beckoned, and the group signed with Polydor, who subsidized Costermonger in the UK. An acclaimed third single, "Sleep Well Tonight," followed in September, and in January 1995, Gene was named Best New Act at *NME*'s Brat Awards.

Until the release of the group's debut album, *Olympian*, in the spring of 1995, Gene had continued to build momentum, partially because Martin Rossiter had adopted Morrissey's technique of giving articulate, outrageous, and witty interviews. *Olympian*, however, was greeted with mixed reviews, and although the group had a sizable fan base—the album debuted in the Top Ten—they were soon overshadowed by the legions of groups that popped up in the wake of Blur and Oasis' success. Even so, "Haunted by You" and "Olympian" both became Top 20 hits. Early in 1996 *To See the Lights*, a collection of B-sides and BBC sessions, was released in England. For the remainder of the year, Gene was quiet, preparing a second album, *Drawn to the Deep End*. "Fighting Fit" was released as a teaser in the fall and became a Top Ten hit, but *Drawn to the Deep End* didn't follow through on its success. Although it debuted in the Top Ten in early 1997, it was greeted with decidedly mixed reviews and quickly fell down the charts, although the group's core audience remained loyal. —*Stephen Thomas Erlewine*

● **Olympian** / Jun. 6, 1995 / Polydor ✦✦✦✦
Kicking off with the sprightly "Haunted by You," *Olympian* immediately conjures images of the Smiths, particularly "This Charming Man." Martin Rossiter's voice also sways like Morrissey, but his band plays their songs as if they were hard rockers, bringing a desperate edge to their best material. Most of *Olympian*'s finest moments were singles. Aside from "Haunted by You," the epic sweep of "Sleep Well Tonight" and the gentle urgency of the title track form the heart of the album; two other singles were added to the American version, including the stellar "Be My Light, Be My Guide." While Gene manages to carve out an identity indebted to the Smiths but not dominated by them, they also fail to produce an album of consistently compelling material; considering that it's a debut album, that's not a fatal flaw. And Gene's best material shows they are capable of transcending their influences. —*Stephen Thomas Erlewine*

To See the Lights / Jan. 1996 / Costermager ✦✦✦✦
The easy joke is, *To See the Lights* is Gene's *Hatful of Hollow*. True, the album is a collection of B-sides, nonalbum singles, radio sessions, and live tracks, but, like the Smiths' *Hatful of Hollow* before it, the album illustrates the band's strengths more effectively than their debut album, *Olympian*. Several of Gene's greatest songs, including the roaring title track, the anthemic "Be My Light, Be My Guide," and the gorgeous "I Can't Decide If She Really Loves Me," are rounded up on the album. Also, the live versions of the *Olympian* singles are better, illustrating that the band can rock with a vengeance. It might appear to be an album designed solely for fans, but *To See the Lights* is a better, more compulsively listenable album than *Olympian*. —*Stephen Thomas Erlewine*

Drawn to the Deep End / Mar. 1997 / A&M ✦✦✦
Gene thrashes all over the place on their second album, *Drawn to the Deep End*, as if they were anxious to shake off any comparison to the

Smiths. Opening with the textured, near-art-rock of "New Amusements" and moving into the revamped pop-soul stomp of "Fighting Fit," the record initially doesn't sound like the tragically doomed bed-sit pop of *Olympian*, and it seems like *Drawn to the Deep End* might be a great leap forward. Unfortunately, Gene doesn't quite have the vision to carry through with the promise. Quite a few cuts kick with either a self-determined drive ("Speak to Me Someone") or a sense of tragic grace ("Where Are They Now?") or, at best, both, like "We Could Be Kings." But the band quickly become victims of their own ambition and botched execution. The record becomes bogged down with turgid ballads or failed experiments that come off as weak art-rock. Still, the Queen-styled chorus of "I Love You, What Are You?" is charming, and it is endearing to hear the band try so hard to move forward; but the lack of focus makes the album less affecting than the hero-worship of *Olympian.* — *Stephen Thomas Erlewine*

General Public

f. 1983, Birmingham, England, **db.** 1987
New Wave, Ska-Revival, Pop-Rock, Club/Dance
This UK duo of vocalist Dave Wakeling (b.Feb. 19, 1956) and "toaster" Ranking Roger (b.Feb. 21, 1961) was formed from the split of the English Beat in 1983. General Public released two albums before they split. In 1994 General Public reunited and had a surprise hit single with their UB40-style interpretation of the Staple Singers' "I'll Take You There," taken from the *Threesome* soundtrack. This led to the release of a new album, *Rub It Better*, in 1995. — *William Ruhlmann*

● **All the Rage** / 1984 / IRS ✦✦✦✦
The vocal duo from the English Beat turn in an album of passionate pop-rock, little of which bears the ska style of the parent group. Most effective are the uptempo, Motown-style songs, especially the Top 30 hit "Tenderness." — *William Ruhlmann*

Hand to Mouth / 1986 / IRS ✦✦✦
Although it still has some of the pop smarts that informed *All the Rage*, General Public has toned down their ska and reggae roots, making *Hand to Mouth* a more professional, but less exciting, album. — *Stephen Thomas Erlewine*

Rub It Better / Apr. 4, 1995 / Epic ✦✦✦
General Public earned a second shot with its Top 40 cover of "I'll Take You There" in 1994. But the group took a year to complete this reunion album, which did not include the hit. Instead, Dave Wakeling and Ranking Roger alternated tracks, with Wakeling's employing the dense, multi-rhythmic sound found on producer Jerry Harrison's solo albums and Roger's in a more conventional reggae-with-toasting style. Only occasionally (for example, on "Handgun") did Wakeling display the talent for catchy pop he had previously shown on songs like "Save It for Later" and "Tenderness." *Rub It Better* suggested that General Public had re-formed without a clear idea of what kind of music it wanted to make or who its audience was. Wakeling and Roger remained a talented twosome, but one in need of direction. — *William Ruhlmann*

Generation X

f. 1976, London, England, **db.** 1981
Punk
An early London punk band (1978-1981), Generation X featured Billy Idol and Tony James (later to form Sigue Sigue Sputnik). Often criticized as being too commercially minded, Gen X was definitely the smoothest and most pop-oriented of their rebellious crowd. Their first album is considered the best, with the US version offering a slightly improved song set. Their third and last, *Kiss Me Deadly*, was more an Idol/James project than a band effort and was produced by Keith Forsey, who shaped Idol's solo sound. This album contained an early version of "Dancing with Myself," which was eventually Idol's first big solo pop success. As to whether they were a band of crass opportunists or true champions of the punk spirit, Billy Idol's career and Sigue Sigue Sputnik's dubious distinction of having the first advertisement on a pop record speak volumes. — *Scott Bultman*

Generation X / 1979 / Chrysalis ✦✦✦✦
Generation X had punk attitude and subject matter on their debut album, which includes their answer song to the Who, "Your Generation," and the generic "One Hundred Punks." But the group's music already had more of a melodic mainstream rock sound than punk's raw assault, and frontman Billy Idol's snarl was straight out of Elvis Presley. — *William Ruhlmann*

Valley of the Dolls / 1979 / Chrysalis ✦✦✦

Kiss Me Deadly / 1981 / Chrysalis ✦✦✦
Idol and bassist Brian James rehearse for their post-Gen X careers, as a solo artist and as the leader of Sigue Sigue Sputnik, respectively. This album contains the dance hit "Dancing with Myself." — *William Ruhlmann*

● **Best of Generation X** / 1985 / Chrysalis ✦✦✦✦
Collecting the highlights from their three uneven albums as well as their EP, *Best of Generation X* features nearly everything of value the band recorded. — *Stephen Thomas Erlewine*

Genesis

f. 1966, Godalming, England
Group / Art-Rock/Progressive-Rock, Pop-Rock
One of the most successful rock acts of the 1970s, 1980s, and 1990s, Genesis enjoyed a longevity exceeded only by the likes of the Rolling Stones and the Kinks, in the process providing a launching pad for the superstardom of members Peter Gabriel and Phil Collins. The group had its roots in the Garden Wall, a band founded by 15-year-olds Peter Gabriel and Tony Banks in 1965 at Charterhouse School in Godalming, Surrey, where fellow students Michael Rutherford and Anthony Phillips were members of another group called Anon. The two groups initially merged out of expediency, as the older members of each graduated. Gabriel, Banks, Rutherford, Phillips, and drummer Chris Stewart soon formed the New Anon and recorded a six-song demo featuring songs primarily written by Rutherford and Phillips.

The Charterhouse connection worked in their favor when an ex-student, recording artist and producer Jonathan King, heard the tape and arranged for the group to continue working in the studio, developing their sound. It was also King who renamed the band Genesis. In December 1967 the group had their first formal recording sessions. Their debut single, "The Silent Sun," was released in February 1968 without attracting much notice from the public. A second single, "A Winter's Tale," followed just about the time that Dave Stewart quit; his replacement, John Silver, joined just in time to participate in the group's first LP sessions that summer. King later added orchestral accompaniment to the band's tracks, in order to make them sound even more like the Moody Blues, and the resulting album, entitled *From Genesis to Revelation*, was released in March 1969.

Music seemed to be shaping up as a brief digression in the lives of the members as they graduated from Charterhouse that summer. The group felt strongly enough about their work, however, that they decided to try it as a professional band; it was around this time that Silver exited, replaced by John Mayhew. They got their first paying gig in September 1969 and spent the next several months working out new material. Genesis soon became one of the first groups signed to the fledgling Charisma label, and they recorded their second album, *Trespass*, that spring. After its completion, the unit went through major personnel changes. Phillips, who had developed crippling stage fright, was forced to leave the lineup in July 1970, followed by Mayhew.

Enter Phil Collins, a onetime child actor turned drummer, and former member of Hickory and Flaming Youth.

The group's lineup was completed with the addition of guitarist Steve Hackett, a former member of Quiet World. His presence and that of Collins toughened up the group's sound, which became apparent immediately upon the release of their next album, *Nursery Cryme*. The theatrical attributes of Gabriel's singing fit in well with he group's live performances during this period, as he began to make ever more extensive use of masks, make-up, and props in concert, telling framing stories in order to set up their increasingly complicated songs. When presented amid the group's very strong playing, this aspect of Gabriel's work turned Genesis' performances into multi-media events.

Foxtrot, issued in the fall of 1972, was the flashpoint in Genesis' history, and not just on commercial terms. The writing, especially on "Supper's Ready," was as sophisticated as anything in progressive rock, and the lyrics were complex, serious, and clever, a far cry from the usual overblown words attached to most prog-rock. Genesis' live performances by now were practically legend, and in response to the demand, in August 1973 Charisma released *Genesis Live*, an album assembled from shows in Leicester and Manchester originally taped for an American radio broadcast. In 1973 *Selling England by the Pound*, the group's most sophisticated album to date, was also released.

Release of the ambitious double LP *The Lamb Lies Down on Broadway* in late 1974 marked the culmination of the group's early history; in May 1975, after a show in France, Gabriel announced that he was leaving Genesis for personal reasons. The group tried auditioning potential replacements, but it became clear that the remaining members all preferred that drummer Collins take over the role of lead singer. The band returned to the studio as an official quartet in October 1975 to begin work on their new album; the resulting *Trick of the Tail* made No. 3 in England and No. 31 in America, the best chart showing up to that time for a Genesis album. Its success completely confounded critics and fans, who'd been unable to conceive of Genesis without Peter Gabriel.

The group seemed to be on its way to even bigger success as 1977's *Wind and Wuthering* became another smash. But then Hackett announced that he was leaving, on the eve of the release of a new double live album, *Seconds Out;* he was replaced on the subsequent American and European tours by Daryl Steurmer, but there was no permanent replacement in the studio. In 1978 Genesis released *And Then There Were Three*, which abandoned any efforts at progressive rock in favor of a softer, much more accessible and less ambitious pop sound. After a flurry of solo projects, the group reconvened for 1980's *Duke*, which became their first chart-topper in England and hit No. 11 in America.

The continued changes in their sound helped turn Genesis into an arena-scale act. *Abacab*, released in late 1981, was another smash, and 1983's self-titled *Genesis* furthered the group's record of British chart-toppers and American top Ten hits, becoming their second million-selling US album while also yielding their first American Top Ten single, "That's All." Two years later the group outdid themselves with the release of their most commercially successful album to date, *Invisible Touch*, which went platinum several times over in America. Its release coincided with the biggest tour in their history, a string of sold-out arena shows that cast the group in the same league as concert stalwarts like the Rolling Stones and the Grateful Dead. Their 1991 album *We Can't Dance* debuted at No. 1 in England and got to No. 4 in America. *—Bruce Eder*

From Genesis to Revelation / Mar. 1969 / Decca ✦✦
This collection of music, which has appeared under license to various labels in addition to Decca and London, in different configurations, is largely of historical interest. The group was still in its formative stages, the members barely past their 18th birthdays and still working out what they wanted to sound like. Mostly they sound like the Bee Gees trying to be the Moody Blues. (Picture something similar to the sound of the former group's *Odessa* album.) "The Silent Sun" and "Where the Sour Turns to Sweet" are pleasant enough, but scarcely indicate the potential of the group or its members. A pleasant enough piece of pop-psychedelia/art-rock, but not a critically important release, except to the truly dedicated. *—Bruce Eder*

Trespass / Oct. 1970 / Atco ✦✦
The group's first truly progressive album, and their first record for the Charisma label (although *Trespass* was released in America by ABC, which is how MCA comes to have it today), is important mostly as a formative effort. Peter Gabriel, Tony Banks, and Michael Rutherford are here, but the guitarist is Anthony Phillips, and the drummer is John Mayhew. Gabriel, Banks, Phillips, and Rutherford are responsible for the compositions, which are far more ambitious than the group's earlier efforts ("Silent Sun" etc.). Unfortunately, much of what is here is more interesting for what it points toward than what it actually *does*. The group reflects a peculiarly dramatic brand of progressive rock, very theatrical as music, but not very successful. The lyrics are complex enough, but lack the unity and clarity that would make Genesis' subsequent albums among the most interesting of prog-rock efforts to analyze. Gabriel's voice is very expressive but generally lacks power and confidence, while the conventional backup vocalizing by the others is wimpy; and Phillips' playing is muted. Tony Banks' keyboards are dominant, which isn't that bad, but it isn't the Genesis that everyone came to know. The soft, lyrical "Visions of Angels" and "Stagnation" are typical, gentle works by a band that later learned how to rock much harder. Only one of the songs here, "The Knife"—which rocks harder than anything else on *Trespass* and is easily the best track on the album—lasted in the group's concert repertory past the next album. The MCA CD sounds good enough, though it was not remastered at the time the Charisma/Atlantic output by the band was redone. *—Bruce Eder*

Nursery Cryme / Nov. 1971 / Atco ✦✦✦
The group's first fully realized, mature album is still somewhat uneven, but the stuff that does work well works so well that it carries the record. This includes "The Musical Box," which became a highlight of the group's live shows, presenting Gabriel's extraordinary abilities as a singer/actor as well as hinting at a level of lyrical sophistication that dazzled many fans and onlookers. "Return of the Giant Hogweed" was an even better showcase for the group's playing. The "Definitive Edition Remaster" version runs circles around the sound on all previous versions, although a certain weakness in the engineering (obviously in the original recording, and beyond repair) remains, especially where the presence of Collins' drums in relation to the rest of the band (particularly on the acoustic passages) is concerned. *—Bruce Eder*

Foxtrot / Oct. 1972 / Atco ✦✦✦
This was the point where all of the talent simmering and occasionally boiling up out of Genesis blew the lid off the pot. There isn't a weak song here, and the two showpieces, "Watcher of the Skies" and "Supper's Ready," presented the group at its strongest in medium-length and extended-length songs. The lyrical complexities of the latter were not easily sorted out, but they were clever enough and inviting enough not to put off any potential fans, and as handled by Gabriel, they demanded attention. And not only is the band playing loud on a lot of this album, but the engineer captured them perfectly. The Definitive Remastered Edition released in 1995 supplants all prior versions of the compact disc. *—Bruce Eder*

★ **Selling England by the Pound** / Jan. 1973 / Atco ✦✦✦✦✦
By the Ezra Pound, no doubt—seriously, the influence of T.S. Eliot and other early 20th-century literary figures crops up throughout the opening and closing portions of this album, with the rest of the songs given over to more conventional subject matter. The original group's strongest single album and, for those not predisposed to enjoy the double-disc *Lamb Lies Down on Broadway*, the peak of their output. The production is note-perfect, and not an instrument is out of place. The Definitive Remastered Edition from 1996 is a significant improvement, in sound and packaging, over the earlier version from Atlantic. *—Bruce Eder*

Genesis: Live / Jun. 1973 / Atco ✦✦✦
Essentially a live best-of with one glaring omission, *Live* was issued in America nearly a year after it reached the Top Ten in England. A well-recorded showcase of the early group's concert sound, much of what is here actually works better than the studio versions of the same songs. "The Musical Box," "The Knife," "Return of the Giant Hogweed," and "Watcher of the Skies" are heard in livelier, tighter versions than their excellent originals. The only drawback is that in preparing to CD, nobody thought to try to retrieve the performance of "Supper's Ready" from the same set of tapes that yielded the original LP; it would've been a nice CD bonus. The Definitive Remastered Edition is not only superior to earlier versions of this disc, but is easier to find as well. *—Bruce Eder*

★ **The Lamb Lies Down on Broadway** / Nov. 1974 / Atco ✦✦✦✦✦
The group's only double studio album was the culmination of their early period, featuring Peter Gabriel in a bravura performance in the role of Rael, a New York street hustler, in this musical drama. The singing and playing are all strong, and the remastered edition from 1995 is the first CD edition that sounds as good as (or better than) the superb original Atco pressing from 1975. The piece's length makes it something of an acquired taste, but most serious fans regard this as the best record the group ever cut. *—Bruce Eder*

Trick of the Tail / Mar. 1976 / Atco ✦✦✦✦
The quality of the group's first post-Peter Gabriel album astonished everyone, especially coming out after an 18-month gap following *The Lamb Lies Down on Broadway*. The opening number, "Dance on a Volcano," almost deliberately recalls "At the Cinema" from *Selling England by the Pound* in melody and structure, and Phil Collins sounds more like Peter Gabriel than Gabriel himself did. Tony Banks' and Steve Hackett's "Entangled" was the prettiest song the group had recorded up to that time, a gossamer textured piece about sleep and dreaming in which a strummed acoustic guitar makes its most prominent appearance ever on a Genesis song, supported by the sweetest singing of Collins' career. Not all of the material is in league with these two songs, but all of it has some moments of tremendous beauty, and Tony Banks' "Robbery, Assault and Battery," with its bold, hard-rocking choruses and extended song structure, would have been worthy of inclusion on any of the group's earlier records. Even "Los Endos," an instrumental finale that ought to be considered a cop-out in the absence of a good song, provides the quartet with an opportunity to showcase its still considerable collective skills to which few fans could object. The 1995 "Definitive Edition Remaster" is a vast improvement in sound and packaging over the earlier CD version, and is the one worth picking up. *—Bruce Eder*

Wind and Wuthering / Jan. 1977 / Atlantic ✦✦✦✦
For many veteran fans, *Wind & Wuthering* was the last near-great Genesis album, as well as their last album to feature a progressive rock sound. The group's second (and last) album as a quartet, it features the requisite long-form songs, complete with slashing guitars, rippling synthesizers, sweeping Mellotron passages, and elegant piano parts, along with some beautifully complex and poetic lyrics. Songs like "Eleventh Earl of Mar," "One for the Vine," and "All in a Mouse's Night" are the equals of the better (but not the best) work from the band's Peter Gabriel era, but the most important song on this album was Michael Rutherford's "Your Own Special Way," an edited version of which became their first single to make the American charts (and only their second British chart hit). Although most of the songs are more complex and challenging, they also present a sense of marking time, while "Your Own Special Way" pointed the way toward the simpler, more accessible sound that the group was moving toward. The 1995 reissue, part of Atco's "Definitive Edition Remaster" series, from the original master tapes is considerably more impressive than the original late-'80s CD and includes full lyrics and production credits as well. *—Bruce Eder*

Seconds Out / Nov. 1977 / Atlantic ✦✦
On its second live album (a double), recorded in 1976 and 1977, Genesis tried to make the case that its two manifestations, Genesis-with-Peter Gabriel and Genesis-without-Peter Gabriel, were actually one entity. They didn't succeed, sounding instead like, on the one hand, the new post-Gabriel Genesis on side one and most of side four, and on the other hand, a Gabriel/Genesis soundalike band on sides two and three, on which Phil Collins handled Gabriel's vocals on such favorites as "Supper's Ready." *—William Ruhlmann*

And Then There Were Three / Mar. 1978 / Atlantic ✦✦✦
The birth of the modern Genesis, a pop-rock trio led by singer/drummer Phil Collins, playing tightly constructed, short, catchy songs. The best of the bunch here is "Follow You, Follow Me," a hit on both sides of the Atlantic. (It was the first Genesis gold album in the US.) — *William Ruhlmann*

Duke / Apr. 1980 / Atlantic ✦✦✦
Released in April 1980, *Duke* found Genesis completely geared up as a maker of concise, appealing pop singles, and it was an immediate, across-the-board hit, topping the UK chart and almost making the US Top Ten, while the singles "Misunderstanding" and "Turn It On Again" became radio favorites on both sides of the Atlantic. — *William Ruhlmann*

● **Abacab** / Sep. 1981 / Atlantic ✦✦✦✦
Genesis had perfected its rhythmic, densely chorded, passionate trio music with this, their first US million-seller and Top Ten hit, which includes the Top 40 singles "Abacab," "No Reply at All," and "Man on the Corner." — *William Ruhlmann*

Three Sides Live / Jun. 1982 / Atlantic ✦✦✦
On its third live album (another double), Genesis brought listeners up-to-date on the trio version of the group and its recent hit singles from *Abacab* and *Duke*. The UK version of the album (Charisma GE 2002), despite the title, was an all-live album, while the American version (Atlantic SD 2-2000), had three live sides and a fourth side of studio material, including the Top 40 hit "Paperlate" (which appeared in the UK as part of an EP called *3 By 3*). — *William Ruhlmann*

Genesis / Oct. 1983 / Atlantic ✦✦✦✦
Genesis' third straight No. 1 studio album in the UK was also its biggest seller yet in the US, making the Top Ten and selling three million copies. Its big US hit was "That's All," while Britain preferred "Mama." "Illegal Alien" and "Taking It All Too Hard" also charted. — *William Ruhlmann*

Invisible Touch / Jun. 1986 / Atlantic ✦✦✦
The biggest Genesis hit to date, this multi-million-selling release features five Top Five hits, including the No. 1 title track, "Throwing It All Away," "Land of Confusion," "Tonight, Tonight, Tonight," and "In Too Deep." — *William Ruhlmann*

We Can't Dance / Oct. 28, 1991 / Atlantic ✦✦✦
Genesis' first album in five years was another enormous hit, even if it failed to match the sales of 1986's *Invisible Touch*. In the UK, it was the group's fifth straight studio album to hit No. 1; in the US, it was their fifth straight Top Ten and sold four million copies. "No Son of Mine" (something of an answer to "The Living Years," by Mike Rutherford's splinter group, Mike and the Mechanics) broke the group's string of Top Five singles by getting only to No. 12, but it was followed by the No. 7 "I Can't Dance," as well as three more Top 25 hits: "Hold On My Heart," "Jesus He Knows Me" (a satire of evangelist preachers), and "Never a Time." — *William Ruhlmann*

Genesis Live: The Way We Walk, Vol. 1 (The Shorts) / Nov. 17, 1992 / Atlantic ✦✦
Live: The Way We Walk—Vol. 1: The Shorts is the first part of a two-disc live document of Genesis, supporting their 1991 album *We Can't Dance*. It concentrates on the shorter hit singles and will appeal to their mainstream fans. — *AMG*

Genesis Live: The Way We Walk, Vol. 2 (The Longs) / Feb. 9, 1993 / Atlantic ✦✦
Live: The Way We Walk—Vol. 2: The Longs features the extended compositions that made Genesis a trailblazer in the progressive rock field during the '70s. Fans of those albums will prefer this volume to the first installment. — *AMG*

Gentle Giant

f. 1969, England, **db.** 1980
Group / Art-Rock/Progressive-Rock
Formed at the dawn of the progressive rock era in 1969, Gentle Giant seemed poised for a time in the mid-1970's to break out of its cult band status, but somehow it never made the jump. Somewhat closer in spirit to Yes and King Crimson than to Emerson, Lake & Palmer or the Nice, their unique sound melded hard rock and classical music, with an almost medieval approach to singing.

Gentle Giant was born out of the ruins of Simon Dupree & the Big Sound, an R&B-based outfit led by brothers Derek, Ray, and Phil Shulman. After switching to psychedelia in 1967 and scoring their only major hit that year with "Kites," as Gentle Giant the group abandoned both the R&B and psychedelic orientations of the previous band; Derek sang and played guitar and bass, Ray played sang and played bass and violin, and Phil handled the saxophone, augmented by Kerry Minnear on keyboards and Gary Green on guitar. Their original lineup also featured Martin Smith on drums, but they went through several percussionists in the first three years of their existence. In 1970 Gentle Giant signed to the Vertigo label, and their self-titled first album—a shockingly

daring work mixing hard rock and full electric playing with classical elements—came out later that year. Their second effort, 1971's *Acquiring the Taste*, was slightly more accessible, and their third, *Three Friends*, featuring Malcolm Mortimore on drums, was their first record to be released in the US (on Columbia). Their fourth album, 1973's *Octopus*, looked poised for a breakthrough; it seemed as though they had found the mix of hard rock and classical sounds that the critics and the public could accept, and they finally had a permanent drummer in the person of John Weathers, an ex-member of the Graham Bond Organisation.

In 1974, however, Gentle Giant began coming apart. Phil Shulman decided to give up music after the *Octopus* tour, and became a teacher. Then the group recorded the album *In a Glass House*, their hardest rocking record yet, which Columbia's US arm rejected as too uncommercial. The two-year gap in their American release schedule hurt their momentum, and they weren't heard from again until the Capitol release of *The Power and the Glory* in 1975.

Gentle Giant released *Free Hand*, their most commercial album, in 1976, but then followed it up with the jarringly experimental *Interview*. After the 1978 double album *Playing the Fool*, the group went through a seeming change of heart and issued a series of albums aimed at mainstream audiences, even approaching disco, but by the end of the 1970s their popularity was in free-fall. Minnear, who had been playing an ever-more central role since the mid-1970s, had already left the group when Gentle Giant called it quits in 1980. Ray Shulman later became a producer and had considerable success in England working with bands like the Sundays and the Sugarcubes, while Derek Shulman became a New York-based record company executive. — *Bruce Eder*

Gentle Giant / 1970 / Polydor ✦✦✦✦
Astonishingly daring debut album, not as focused or overpowering as King Crimson's first, but still crashing down barriers and steamrolling expectations. The mix of medieval harmonies and electric rock got stronger on subsequent albums, but the music here is still pretty jarring. Kerry Minear was probably the only prog-rock keyboard player of the era who allowed his synthesizers to sound like themselves and not mimic orchestras; Gary Green's guitars are alternately loud and brittle or soft and lyrical, and always surprising; and the presence of saxes and trumpets (courtesy of Phil Shulman) was unusual in any rock band of the era—all of which explains how Gentle Giant managed to attract a cult following but hadn't a prayer of moving up from that level of recognition. "Funny Ways" was the softest prog-rock song this side of Crimson's "I Talk to the Wind," but a lot of the rest is pretty intense in volume and tempo changes. "Nothing at All" by itself is worth the price of the CD, the release of which marked the first appearance of this album in the US catalog, 20 years after it was recorded. — *Bruce Eder*

Acquiring the Taste / 1971 / Polydor ✦✦✦✦
The band's second album is a major advance on its first, featuring superior singing, playing, and songwriting, as well as a more unified sound, without sacrificing the element of surprise in their first record. Many of the melodies and even the riffs here (check out Gary Green's first guitar flourish on "Pantagruel's Nativity") have a pretty high haunt count, and all of the musicianship displays an elegance seldom heard even in progressive circles. The record also rocks really hard. Elements of hard rock and Gregorian chants mix freely and, amazingly enough, *well* throughout this album. — *Bruce Eder*

Three Friends / 1972 / Columbia ✦✦✦✦
The band's third album (and their first self-produced effort, Tony Visconti having run the sessions on the two previous records) was another advance, this time in the direction of a harder rock sound. Everything sounds turned up here, especially the guitars, the bass, and the electronic keyboards. *Three Friends* hardly sacrificed any of the group's progressive intentions, however, and there are some softer moments here, such as the playful, sprightly first half of "Schooldays"; the harmonies and arrangements still had a distinctly medieval feel, and the melodies, though a little harder to discern (which made them even more appealing when they did become obvious) were quite engaging. This is supposed to be a concept album, about the relationship between three friends across a lifetime, and the original notes and lyrics have been reprinted, but none of that is necessary in order to enjoy the songs. — *Bruce Eder*

● **Octopus** / 1972 / Columbia ✦✦✦✦
Octopus is Gentle Giant's *magnum opus*, where all the disparate elements of *Acquiring the Taste* come together with bizarre, intertwining vocals. Though it is slightly less extreme than its predecessor, it is actually more accomplished, demonstrating new levels of near-mathematical complexity. — *Daevid Jehnzen*

In a Glass House / 1973 / Columbia ✦✦✦✦
Precisely why this album, recorded in 1973, has never been released in the United States is one of those minor mysteries of the pop music business. The group was reduced to a quintet with the departure of elder brother Phil Shulman, but its sound is unchanged, and the group may actually be tighter without the presence of his saxophones. The time sig-

natures are still really strange, and the tempo changes are sometimes jarring, as is the wide range of dynamics, but this is also one of the group's most pleasing records. They rock out in various places, and elsewhere perform all kinds of little experiments with percussion instruments ("An Inmate's Lullaby"), or create a strange, otherworldly sort of modern medieval-style music ("Way of Life"). None of it except possibly "A Reunion" is light listening, but the challenge does yield some rewarding sounds. — *Bruce Eder*

Free Hand / 1975 / One Way ✦✦✦✦
In spite of the band's continuing fascination with rhythmic complication, *Free Hand* contains a more rockish feel. "On Reflection" and "His Last Voyage" are nice showcases for the band's vocal arrangements and considerable dynamic performance skills. — *Rick Clark*

Collection / Oct. 19, 1993 / Castle ✦✦✦
Live: Playing the Fool / Mar. 19, 1996 / One Way ✦✦✦✦
This live album (originally a double LP but put onto one CD) was released in the wake of a single-disc bootleg of the same name taken off an FM radio concert. The repertory includes lots of stuff from their early albums, including the never-released-in-the-US *In a Glass House*. The sound is very vivid and close, whether the band is rocking to "Just the Same" or re-creating the medieval-style a cappella vocals to "On Reflection." One Way has done an unusually good job with the sound on this album, and the original art has also been nicely re-created. This disc will obviously appeal to serious fans most of all, but even neophytes might consider this as an early acquisition. — *Bruce Eder*

● **Edge of Twilight** / 1997 / Vertigo ✦✦✦✦
Edge of Twilight is a thorough overview of Gentle Giant's years at Vertigo Records, containing nearly every highlight from each of their early records. As a result, it's not only a perfect introduction to the strange, provocative world of Gentle Giant, it could be all the Gentle Giant most prog-rock fans need. — *Daevid Jehnzen*

Barbara George

b. Aug. 16, 1942, New Orleans, LA
Vocals / Soul, New Orleans R&B, R&B
George's "I Know (You Don't Love Me No More)" topped the R&B charts in 1961 and has proven a popular cover item ever since. The New Orleans native had never been in the studio before she brought her extremely catchy melody to Harold Battiste's fledgling A.F.O. label. Benefiting from her pleasing, unpolished vocal and a melodic cornet solo by Melvin Lastie, the tune caught fire, vaulting high on pop playlists. Amazingly, nothing else George did ever dented the charts, although she waxed some listenable follow-ups for A.F.O. and Sue. — *Bill Dahl*

● **I Know (You Don't Love Me Anymore)** / 1962 / Collectables ✦✦✦✦
This catchy New Orleans R&B from the early '60s features coy and charming vocals by George. — *Bill Dahl*

Lowell George

b. Apr. 13, 1945, Hollywood, CA, **d.** Jun. 29, 1979, Arlington, VA
Guitar, Vocals / Rock 'n' Roll, Singer-Songwriter, Blues-Rock
As Little Feat was disbanding in late 1978, their lead guitarist/songwriter Lowell George recorded a solo album, *Thanks I'll Eat It Here*, that sounded as loose and funky as the band in their prime. After its release the next year, he set out on tour to support the album. Sadly, George died of a heart attack while on the road; he left behind a body of gritty, eclectic, and funky rock 'n' roll. On the first five Little Feat albums, his songwriting and instrumental talents are more apparent than on his solo effort, but that doesn't detract from the record's pleasures. — *Stephen Thomas Erlewine*

● **Thanks I'll Eat It Here** / 1979 / Warner Brothers ✦✦✦✦
While it's surprisingly short on original songs, Lowell George's solo album *Thanks I'll It Eat Here* is as relaxed and funky as any Little Feat album from the last half of the 1970s. — *Stephen Thomas Erlewine*

Lightning-Rod Man / Nov. 2, 1993 / Bizarre ✦✦✦
Before emerging as a cult star in the 1970s, Lowell George was a presence on the L.A. folk-rock/psychedelic scene in the 1960s. With his group the Factory, he only managed to release one single during this time. *Lightning-Rod Man* rescues 15 tunes cut by this unit, including the single and over a dozen outtakes and demos. Almost exclusively original material, most of these tracks were recorded in 1966 and 1967. They show the group pursuing a slightly eccentric folk-rock vision that neither bears much similarity to George's more famous work nor matches the best work done in this genre by their L.A. peers. At times they echo Kaleidoscope in their vaguely spacey, good-natured folkish rock; just as often, they take cues from Captain Beefheart and Frank Zappa in their skewed blues-rock and obtuse songwriting. In fact Zappa himself produced and played on a couple of the demos, and one-time Mothers of Invention members Elliot Ingber and Roy Estrada show up on a few others. A few songs cut toward the end of the decade feature a

heavier, bluesier sound that shows George edging in a different direction. An enjoyable vault find, but not a major revelation. — *Richie Unterberger*

The Georgia Satellites

f. 1980, Atlanta, GA
Rock 'n' Roll
At a time when rock 'n' roll didn't care about its roots, the Georgia Satellites came crashing into the charts with a surprise hit single to remind everybody where the music had come from. The hit single, 1986's "Keep Your Hands to Yourself," rocked as hard as an old Chuck Berry song, as well as being almost as clever. The Satellites weren't a back-to-basic roots band, either—their straightforward sound borrowed equally from Berry, the Rolling Stones, the Faces, Little Feat, and AC/DC, with a Southern backwoods bent. At their best, the Satellites were just a damn good rock 'n' roll band, driven by the classic, yet fresh, songwriting of lead singer/guitarist Dan Baird. On the strength of "Keep Your Hands to Yourself," their first major-label album sold well, but the follow-up, *Open All Night*, did not; radio and MTV had treated the band as a kind of novelty—a bunch of hicks kicking out rock 'n' roll offered a break between the slick pop-metal of Bon Jovi and Peter Gabriel's introspective pop. By the time they released *Open All Night* in 1988, no one was interested, even if the album was only slightly weaker than the debut. After one more album, 1989's *In the Land of Salvation and Sin*, the band called it quits. Guitarist Rick Richards joined Izzy Stradlin's Ju Ju Hounds three years later; Baird pursued a solo career and had a small hit in late 1992 with "I Love You Period."
During the mid-'90s, the Georgia Satellites reunited without Baird. They released *Shaken not Stirred* in 1997. — *Stephen Thomas Erlewine*

Georgia Satellites / 1986 / Elektra ✦✦✦✦
Dirty Rolling Stones-like guitar grunge played by Rick Richards and topped by the adenoidal singing of Dan Baird. Especially enjoyable on the hits "Keep Your Hands to Yourself" and "Battleship Chains." — *William Ruhlmann*

Open All Night / 1988 / Elektra ✦✦✦
The Georgia Satellites' follow-up to their surprise hit is as loose and rocking as their previous album, but wasn't as successful. The few who did buy the album were treated to some of the rawest and funniest pure rock 'n' roll of the 1980s, highlighted by the sleazy humor of "Mon Cheri" and the title track, as well as the stomping cover of the Beatles' "Don't Pass Me By." — *Stephen Thomas Erlewine*

In the Land of Salvation and Sin / Oct. 1989 / Elektra ✦✦✦
On the Georgia Satellites' final album, Dan Baird decides that he's a songwriter like Lowell George—a traditionalist who adds a healthy dose of ironic humor without losing respect for the music's roots. While his ambitions are ripe with pretensions, his band keeps him in check, and *In the Land of Salvation and Sin* is a terrific record, full of intelligent songs that are never pompous and never fail to rock like hell. — *Stephen Thomas Erlewine*

● **Let It Rock: The Best of the Georgia Satellites** / Jan. 19, 1993 / Elektra ✦✦✦✦
Most of the band's best tracks are on this generous compilation, which features not only their hits ("Keep Your Hands to Yourself" and "Battleship Chains"), but rarities like their sublime John Fogerty medley "Almost Saturday Night/Rockin' All Over the World" from the out-of-print *Rubaiyat* collection. — *Stephen Thomas Erlewine*

Shaken Not Stirred / 1997 / 3NM ✦✦
It made sense that the Georgia Satellites reunited without Dan Baird, especially since Rick Richards' career as a Ju Ju Hound disappeared along with leader Izzy Stradlin. However, their comeback needn't have been as dispiriting as *Shaken Not Stirred*. The band can still rock out, but they lack the wild, careening energy of their late-'80s heyday. More importantly, they not only choose to re-cover their version of Joe South's "Games People Play," as well as the Beatles' "Rain" and the Faces' "My Fault," but "Battleship Chains" and "Can't Stand the Pain," songs *they* made popular with their debut album. It's a weird move, and it's all the more uncomfortable considering the blandness of the new, original songs. *Shaken Not Stirred* occasionally shows signs of life, but it should have been tougher and looser to be a truly triumphant comeback. — *Stephen Thomas Erlewine*

Lisa Germano

b. 1958, Mishawaka, IN
Fiddle, Violin, Vocals / Alternative Pop-Rock, Dream-Pop
Violinist Lisa Germano became known for her fluid, gutsy style through her work with John Mellencamp, which is captured on the *Big Daddy* and *Lonesome Jubilee* albums. Germano's solo work is much darker and more atmospheric than Mellencamp's albums; her 1991 solo debut, *On the Way Down from Moon Palace*, displayed some promising songwriting along with her acclaimed instrumental prowess. Germano's sec-

ond album, 1993's *Happiness*, was even better, but the record didn't sell very well when it was first released on Capitol, prompting her to change record labels in 1994. She signed with 4AD, who released a resequenced and remixed *Happiness* in the spring of 1994; the new version of the album emphasized her music's underlying dark melancholy, which the original version only hinted at. Later in 1994 she released *Geek the Girl*, her first album for 4AD, to very positive reviews. Two years later, Germano released *Excerpts from a Love Circus*. —*Stephen Thomas Erlewine*

On the Way Down from Moon Palace / 1991 / Major Bill ✦✦✦
Words that come to mind on Germano's debut album—haunting, delicate, disturbing, abrasive, sparse, intimate, beautiful. The instrumentals, like the title track, "Dark Irie," and "Simply Tony," have a marvelous fragile beauty, while "Dig My Own Grave" is a herky-jerky, rude, acoustic rocker. Other highlights include "The Other One," "Guessing Game (Or the Music Business)," and "Hangin' with a Demon." —*Rick Clark*

● **Happiness** / Jul. 27, 1993 / Capitol/EMI ✦✦✦✦
Germano's sophomore effort is a harrowing descent into black humor, anger, and general misery. With her deadpan little girl voice, Germano makes "You Make Me Want to Wear Dresses" sound as if that is the last thing she wants to do, while she drives the point home on the transcendent dissonance of "Puppet." —*Rick Clark*

Geek the Girl / Oct. 25, 1994 / 4AD ✦✦✦✦
Geek the Girl manages to eclipse both of Germano's previous albums by accentuating both the folkiness in her music and its awkward, dreamy qualities. The album is a song cycle about a girl trying to come of age, both emotionally and sexually, but the story never overwhelms the tensely charming songs. It's musically richer than the average alternative angst-fest, incorporating traditional Italian melodies into Germano's folky songwriting, which touches on everything from unstructured stream-of-consciousness melodies to tight pop songs. But what makes *Geek the Girl* even more satisfying is that Germano doesn't take the easy way out and wallow in self-pity. Instead, she offers a glimmer of hope with the last two songs, making *Geek the Girl* a richly rewarding and moving record. —*Stephen Thomas Erlewine*

Excerpts from a Love Circus / Sep. 9, 1996 / 4AD ✦✦✦✦

The Germs

f. 1977, Los Angeles, CA, **db.** 1980
Punk
Living fast and dying young is one of rock's great cliches, but no phrase better describes the reasons for the demise of L.A. punkers the Germs. Capable of creating a firestorm of noisy, confrontational music, they were ultimately undone by their perversely charismatic lead singer, a madman named Paul Beahm, better known to the world at large first as Bobby Pyn, later and more famously as Darby Crash, who died Sid Vicious-style out on the mainline at age 22.

Taking musical cues from the Sex Pistols (and English punk in general), as well as the CBGB's scene, adding the theatricality of Bowie, Iggy, and Lou Reed, Crash was the perfect frontman for the Germs. Backed by guitarist Pat Smear (most recently of Nirvana and the Foo Fighters), bassist Lorna Doom, and drummer Don Bolles, the Germs kicked up a hellacious racket that strayed from fast/loud punk into art-damage and garage grunge. On stage, their gigs bordered on performance art, with Crash in full Iggy frenzy, diving into the crowd, adorning himself with whatever foodstuffs the audience provided, wearing less and less clothing, all done with the band cranking out noisy spasms of simple, but effective, rock noise.

Never capturing this mania on record (how could you?) the Germs' recording career is based on the sole record made during Crash's short life. Produced by Germs fan Joan Jett, *(GI)* was a fine hunk of early L.A. punk rock that was more literate and compelling than what was being offered by lesser local luminaries such as the Zeroes and the Weirdos. Smear's guitar playing is especially volatile, matching the mewling vocals of Crash note for note. It may not be life-changing music, but the white-hot, adrenal rush is a little bit of heaven.

By the time Crash filled his veins with heroin in 1980, the Germs were pretty much over. Crash's behavior had become increasingly unpredictable; he was spending time in England, and began performing as a solo act upon returning to L.A. Consequently, the valuable recorded work in this final period is spotty, but, thankfully much of it shows up on the definitive Germs release *Germs (MIA)— The Complete Anthology*. —*John Dougan*

(GI) / 1979 / Slash ✦✦✦✦
It captures the black, foreboding explosiveness of West Coast punk during the late '70s and highlights the sandpaper cries of Darby Crash (who died of a drug overdose shortly after the album was recorded). —*David Szatmary*

What We Do is Secret / 1981 / Slash ✦✦✦

● **Germs (M.I.A.)—The Complete Anthology** / Aug. 3, 1993 / Slash ✦✦✦✦
The essential Germs anthology contains all of *(GI)* as well as some of the best tracks from *What We Do Is Secret*, and a handful of recordings made for the William Friedkin film *Cruising*. (The filmmaker best known for *The Exorcist* reportedly saw the Germs live and was knocked out by their extreme performance.) Some of the early stuff, especially "Forming" and the live "Sex Boy" wander into avant-garde noise rock, all meandering atonality and screeching hysteria. But the material from *(GI)* still sounds great and proves conclusively that the Germs had, in spite of themselves, turned into a tight, explosive rock band. Generous at 30 tracks, this is seminal late-'70s L.A. punk that set the stage for a generation of hardcore bands. —*John Dougan*

Lisa Gerrard

b. Melbourne, Australia
Vocals / Alternative Pop-Rock, Dream-Pop
In collaboration with Brendan Perry, Lisa Gerrard is half of the duo Dead Can Dance, which has been releasing arty goth-rock on the 4AD label since the mid-'80s. Gerrard began her solo career with the 1995 release *The Mirror Pool*, which contained a lot of work that wouldn't fit comfortably into the DCD oeuvre. Combining these fragments with music that she composed and arranged digitally before reconfiguring them into scores that could be performed, it also draws on a composition by Handel and traditional Iranian music. Recorded and produced largely at her home in rural Australia, it extends the world music inclinations of recent Dead Can Dance albums by featuring bouzouki, tablas, and camel drums, though the somber, orchestrated pomp of Dead Can Dance is also present in her operatic, often wordless vocals, and string/woodwind passages (some of which were performed by Australia's Victorian Philharmonic Orchestra). —*Richie Unterberger*

The Mirror Pool / Aug. 22, 1995 / 4AD ✦✦✦
If this is rock, it's rock of the artiest and most ambitious sort, focusing on both the gloomy orchestration that has graced much of Dead Can Dance's output, and melismatic vocal workouts that owe much to Indian and Middle Eastern music. It's sometimes a wearyingly downbeat affair, the most orchestrated sections sounding much like highly accomplished soundtrack music for very serious art house films. But these are outweighed by lengthy movements of dignified beauty, most often when Gerrard sings in her Persian cantorial style (although the purely instrumental pieces have their highlights as well). It's a challenging work, but like Dead Can Dance's most recent albums, it may actually find a wider audience than the goth-rock with which Gerrard first made her mark, due both to its wider palette of sounds and its greater emotional range. —*Richie Unterberger*

Gerry & the Pacemakers

f. 1959, Liverpool, England, **db.** Oct. 1966
British Invasion, Pop-Rock
As unfathomable as it seems from the distance of over 30 years, for a few months Gerry & the Pacemakers were the Beatles' nearest competitors in Britain. Managed (like the Beatles) by Brian Epstein, Gerry Marsden and his band burst out of the gate with three consecutive No. 1 UK hits in 1963, "How Do You Do It," "I Like It," and "You'll Never Walk Alone." If the Beatles defined Merseybeat at its best in early 1963, Gerry & the Pacemakers defined the form at its most innocuous, performing bouncy, catchy, and utterly lightweight tunes driven by rhythm guitar and Marsden's chipper vocals. Compared to the Beatles and other British Invasion heavies, their sound seem quaint indeed. That's not to say they were trivial; their hits were certainly likable and energetic and are fondly remembered today, even if the musicians lacked the acumen (or earthy image) to develop their style from its relentlessly upbeat and poppy base.

Marsden formed the group in the late '50s, featuring himself on guitar and lead vocals, his brother Fred on drums, Les Chadwick on bass, and Arthur Mack on piano (to be replaced in 1961 by Les McGuire). They worked the same Liverpool/Hamburg circuit as the Beatles, and ran neck and neck with their rivals in local popularity. They were signed by Epstein in mid-1962 (the first band to do so besides the Beatles), and began recording for the EMI/Columbia label in early 1963, under the direction of producer George Martin. Their first single was a Mitch Murray tune that Martin had wanted the Beatles to record for *their* debut, "How Do You Do It?" The Beatles did record a version (found on the *Anthology 1* release), but objected to its release, finding it too sappy, and in any case they were more interested in recording their own, gutsier original compositions. It suited Marsden's grinning, peppy style well, though, and went to No. 1 before it was displaced from the top spot by the Beatles' third 45, "From Me to You."

The Pacemakers would never vary much from the clattering guitar-dominated pop of their first singles, turning again to Mitch Murray for the follow-up, "I Like It," and remaking an old pop standard for their next effort, "You'll Never Walk Alone." It's not universally known that Gerry Marsden actually wrote much of the band's material, and he penned most of their subsequent hits, including "It's All Right" (their gutsiest and best performance) and "I'm the One." He also wrote "Don't Let the Sun Catch You Cryin' " (sharing credits with the rest of the group) and "Ferry Cross the Mersey," ballads that Martin embellished with light string arrangements, which may (or may not) have helped prepare the producer for deploying strings on Beatle tracks starting in 1965.

Like the Beatles, Gerry & the Pacemakers got to star in their own film, *Ferry Cross the Mersey*, although this wasn't nearly as successful as *A Hard Day's Night*. By 1965, in fact, the group's popularity in Britain was seriously declining, although they held on a bit longer in the States, where (in common with several other groups) some of their back catalog belatedly made the hit parade many months after it was first issued in the UK. Like virtually all of the other Liverpool groups, the Pacemakers proved unable to evolve on the same plane as the Beatles or the best other British bands. Never the hippest of acts image-wise, with their conservative suits and short hair, they were rapidly becoming outdated, sticking to the same basic feel-good formula that had seemed fresh in 1963, but was utterly passé by 1966. That's the year they had their last American Top 40 hit, "Girl on a Swing"; they disbanded in October. Gerry Marsden became a popular cabaret and children's TV entertainer, sometimes performing with the Pacemakers on the oldies circuit. He also contributed vocals to British chart-topping revivals (not with the Pacemakers) of "You'll Never Walk Alone" and "Ferry Cross the Mersey" in the 1980s. —*Richie Unterberger*

The EP Collection / 1987 / See For Miles ◆◆◆◆
A truly definitive collection, with all the hits and the most interesting nonhits. Includes the ultra-rare live *Gerry in California* concert recording from 1966. —*Bruce Eder*

● **Best of Gerry & the Pacemakers: The Definitive Collection** / Oct. 15, 1991 / EMI America ◆◆◆◆
The title promises more than it really delivers in content, if not sound. It'll do for the casual listener. —*Bruce Eder*

The Gerry Cross the Mersey: Best Of / Oct. 1995 / Razor & Tie ◆◆◆◆
Sixteen-track best-of includes all of their British and American hits, as well as some of their best B-sides. The more extensive EMI America best-of has all of these songs and more, and so is still recommended as the first purchase. But for just about everybody, this has all the Gerry you need, and all but two of the songs are in stereo, if that's an important consideration. —*Richie Unterberger*

Geto Boys

f. 1986, Houston, Texas
Gangsta Rap, Hardcore Rap, Southern Rap, Hip Hop
Though the controversial subject matter of gangsta rap wasn't much of a barrier to popular success during the '90s, the Geto Boys' recordings proved almost too extreme for widespread exposure. Blocked from distributing their 1990 major-label debut by Geffen—who insisted that a track dealing with necrophilia as well as murder was a step too far—the group was saved by producer Rick Rubin, who arranged another distributor for the album, released on his own Def American label. The controversy, which occurred two years earlier than similar censorship incidents involving Ice-T and 2 Live Crew, gave the Geto Boys a large amount of publicity. Their follow-up *We Can't Be Stopped* eventually hit platinum, though the trio of Scarface, Willie D., and Bushwick Bill began to fracture by 1993. After releasing solo albums during the mid-'90s, the Geto Boys reunited in 1996 for their most praised album yet, *The Resurrection*.

When the Geto Boys came together in 1986, though, it was with a completely different lineup. Formed as the Ghetto Boys in Houston by rap entrepreneur James "Lil' J" Smith (and signed to his Rap-A-Lot label), the group originally consisted of Prince Johnny C., the Slim Jukebox, and DJ Reddy Red. During 1987-88, both Johnny C. and the Jukebox quit, forcing Smith to add a dwarf dancer-turned-rapper named Bushwick Bill (b. Richard Shaw, Jamaica) and two Rap-A-Lot solo acts: Ackshen (aka Scarface [b. Brad Jordan, Houston]) and Willie 'D' Dennis (b. Houston).

After the Geto Boys' 1990 self-titled album caught the ear of hip-hop impresario Rick Rubin (LL Cool J, Beastie Boys), Rubin re-mixed and re-recorded tracks from the album. He was ready to release it on his Def American label in 1990 when distributor Geffen balked at "Mind of a Lunatic," a track that described necrophilia with a murder victim. By late 1990 Rubin had found another distributor, Giant Records, and the album was released as *Grip It! On That Other Level* that same year.

The Geto Boys' association with controversy was far from over, though; rap groups were a hot topic for moral-minded politicians during the early '90s, and several leaders used the Geto Boys as an example of the state of modern music. The fires were fanned in 1991 before the release of the group's second proper LP, *We Can't Be Stopped*. Before the

release of the album, Bushwick Bill had lost an eye in a shooting incident with his girlfriend, and the cover featured Willie D. and Scarface wheeling Bill into an emergency room, with a prominent shot of the damaged eye. Inside the album, proceedings were among the most extreme in the history of recorded music. Obviously, radio airplay was non-existent, but *We Can't Be Stopped* still went platinum in early 1992, thanks to the underground hit "Mind Playing Tricks on Me," one of the most effective inner-city vignettes in hip-hop history.

By 1993 all three members had begun solo careers, though Willie D. was the only one completely separated from the band, citing artistic differences. Scarface and Bill continued with new member Big Mike, releasing *Uncut Dope* in 1993 and *Makin' Trouble* the next year, but split late in 1994. Just one year later, Willie D. returned to the fold for another Geto Boys release, *The Resurrection*, which showed the group in fine form. —*John Bush*

Grip It! On That Other Level / 1990 / Rap-a-Lot ◆◆◆
The Geto Boys hit the national spotlight with this debut, which disgusted many, frightened a few others, and won them a niche in hip-hop's growing "gangsta" constituency. From the sheer repulsiveness of "Let a Ho Be a Ho" and "Do It Like a G.O." to the frightening nihilism of "Mind of a Lunatic" and "Life in the Fast Lane," this was one group definitely uninterested in pop/mainstream approval. The rapping ranged from surly to sleazy; the beats were sometimes popping, sometimes slashing; and even the most loyal fan would have a tough time finding something good to say about "Trigga Happy Nigga" or "Scarface." —*Ron Wynn*

Geto Boys / 1990 / Rap-a-Lot/Def American ◆◆◆◆
This disturbing CD inspired quite a bit of controversy when Geffen Records refused to distribute it unless the Geto Boys agreed to tone down their violent and profane lyrics. American Records founder Rick Rubin (who had produced everyone from L.L. Cool J to Slayer to the Beastie Boys) countered that the Houston gangster rappers shouldn't have to compromise their artistic vision, and sought distribution elsewhere. When the Geto Boys was finally released, it hadn't been toned down a bit. Adding a horror-movie element to their accounts of inner-city crime and violence, the Geto Boys paint a brutally honest and sobering picture of urban life. The members of this group grew up in the tough Houston ghetto known as the Fifth Ward, and don't hesitate to inform listeners just how ugly things can get in so oppressive an environment. From "Assassins" (originally released in 1988) to "Mind of a Lunatic" (a shocking depiction of a mental patient's psychopathic terror spree), this album proves that Rubin did the right thing by holding his ground. —*Alex Henderson*

We Can't Be Stopped / Jul. 1, 1991 / Rap-a-Lot/Priority ◆◆◆◆
The cover of the Geto Boys' *We Can't Be Stopped* shows a member with his eye poked out. It's grotesque, but realistic—a realistic cover for an album whose violent, profane lyrics paint a vivid and accurate picture of life as the Geto Boys knew it growing up in Houston's tough ghetto known as the Fifth Ward. This CD isn't as thought-provoking as Ice-T, N.W.A or Ice Cube can be—nor is it the Geto Boys' best offering. But it's an engaging, disturbing effort that comes across as much more heartfelt than the numerous gangster rap albums by the N.W.A and Cube clone and wannabes who jumped on the gangster bandwagon in the early '90s. *We Can't Be Stopped* serves as an unsettling reminder of the ugly social conditions allowed to fester in poor inner-city neighborhoods. —*Alex Henderson*

● **Uncut Dope: Geto Boys' Best** / 1992 / Rap-a-Lot ◆◆◆◆
With various members opting for solo projects and the group disintegrating, Rap-A-Lot Records primed the pump one last time with what was essentially a greatest hits CD. It wasn't totally a retrospective because it included "Damn It Feels Good to Be a Gangsta," the ultimate genre definition piece and the last significant Geto Boys composition. "And My Word," "Actions Speak Louder Than Words" and "The Unseen" were other fresh jams that joined the Geto Boys anthems "Mind Playing Tricks on Me," "Assassins," "Scarface" and "Mind of a Lunatic," among others. The old/new menu made this the one to grab if one Geto Boys CD is all you need. —*Ron Wynn*

Till Death Do Us Part / Mar. 19, 1993 / Rap-a-Lot ◆◆◆
The Geto Boys' last album finds them expanding on the success of "Mind Playing Tricks on Me" with "Six Feet Deep," but more frequently, it keeps to their standard, grotesque gangsta rap with "Murder Ave." and "This Dick's for You." On these tracks, the whole shock formula seems like a worn-out trick and points the way to their eventual disbanding. —*Stephen Thomas Erlewine*

The Resurrection / Apr. 2, 1996 / Rap-a-Lot/Noo Trybe ◆◆◆◆
After spending nearly five years apart, the Geto Boys reunited in 1996 and released *The Resurrection*. Since they were more notorious for their lyrical violence than their music—only 1991's "We Can't Be Stopped," with its stunning single "Mind Playing Tricks on Me," showed the band experimenting musically—it comes as a surprise that *The Resurrection* is such a strong album. Although the band never deviates from their

standard blood-guts-sex lyrical routine, they have a greater sense of humor throughout the album. More importantly, they perform with energy, and their backing tracks are vigorous and funky. As a result, *The Resurrection* outstrips every other Geto Boys record. It is the leanest, meanest, and funkiest thing they've recorded. —*Stephen Thomas Erlewine*

Gigolo Aunts

f. 1986, Potsdam, NY
Alternative Pop-Rock, Power Pop
Taking their name from the Syd Barrett song, the effervescent power-pop unit Gigolo Aunts first came together in 1981 in Potsdam, NY, as Sniper. The group—comprised of vocalist/guitarist Dave Gibbs, brothers Phil and Steve Hurley (on lead guitar and bass, respectively) and drummer Phil Brouwer—went through a series of names like Marauder and Rosetta Stone before settling on Gigolo Aunts (a suggestion from Gibbs' father) and moving to Boston in 1986.

In 1988 the band issued its debut *Everybody Happy* to little notice, and receded from view until Gibbs began playing guitar with fellow East Coast popsters Velvet Crush, whom he joined for a UK tour. While overseas Gibbs made a number of crucial contacts with the likes of Creation Records' Alan McGee and the members of Teenage Fanclub, and interest in the Gigolo Aunts began to build. A series of assured EPs—*Gigolo Aunts, Gun*, and *Full-On Bloom*—appeared to strong reviews, as did 1994's full-length *Flippin' Out*. After Gibbs and Phil Hurley turned down offers to join the reunited Big Star, they issued the 1995 EP *Where I Find My Heaven;* shortly after its release, Brouwer was replaced by drummer Fred Eltringham. —*Jason Ankeny*

Everybody Happy / 1988 / Coyote ✦✦✦
● **Flippin' Out** / Apr. 12, 1994 / RCA ✦✦✦✦
This Boston foursome has a varied approach to power-pop; lead guitarist Phil Hurley appears to have mastered hard rock (the catchy "Bloom"), moving ballads (the title track), and pop songs ("Mrs. Washington," a close parody of "Mrs. Robinson") with an ease that gives this album its consistency. Dave Gibbs' sugar-sweet vocals and backing harmonization are the perfect accompaniment. —*John Bush*

Learn to Play Guitar / Feb. 26, 1997 / Wicked Disc ✦✦✦

Gin Blossoms

f. 1987, Tempe, Arizona
Pop-Rock, Adult Alternative Pop-Rock
After an impressive debut EP, the Gin Blossoms rocketed out of the college pop charts and into the mainstream with their 1993 hit single, "Hey Jealousy." Combining the ringing guitar hooks of the Byrds and R.E.M. with a solid, rootsy drive, the band's breakthrough full-length album, *New Miserable Experience*, was filled with songs as strong as "Hey Jealousy," including the second hit single, "Found Out About You." *New Miserable Experience* and its singles dominated radio and MTV for the next year—both "Hey Jealousy" and "Found Out About You" were in heavy radio rotation nearly a year after their initial release—pushing the sales of their debut album over a million copies.

During 1995 the Gin Blossoms recorded their second album. In the summer of that year, the group contributed "'Til I Hear It from You," a song they co-wrote with Marshall Crenshaw, to the soundtrack of *Empire Records*. "'Til I Hear It from You" became a major radio hit, but it was never released as an official single until it was the B-side of "Follow You Down," the first single from the group's second album, *Congratulations... I'm Sorry*. Upon its release in February 1996, *Congratulations... I'm Sorry* charted well, but within six months of its release, it had disappeared from the charts. —*Stephen Thomas Erlewine*

Up & Crumbling / 1992 / A&M ✦✦✦
The Gin Blossoms' debut EP *Up & Crumbling* is an appealing five-song slice of jangly power-pop, filled with ringing hooks and sweet melodies. Since two of the songs (including "Alison Road") wound up on their full-length debut *New Miserable Experience* and a couple of others became B-sides, its value has decreased somewhat, but it remains an engaging listen. —*Stephen Thomas Erlewine*

● **New Miserable Experience** / Aug. 4, 1992 / A&M ✦✦✦✦
With their rootsy, melodic fusion of R.E.M. and the Byrds, the Gin Blossoms carry jangle into the '90s with their breakthrough album. Powered by the hit singles "Hey Jealousy" and "Found Out About You," *New Miserable Experience* is a solid, consistent album that offers an exciting vision of contemporary heartland rock. —*AMG*

Congratulations... I'm Sorry / Feb. 13, 1996 / A&M ✦✦✦
Most observers wondered if the Gin Blossoms would be able to deliver a consistent second album after the departure (and subsequent suicide) of Doug Hopkins, their former guitarist, who wrote "Hey Jealousy" and "Found Out About You," the two big hits from the band's debut. *Congratulations... I'm Sorry* proves that they can. The Gin Blossoms haven't backed away from the sound that made *New Miserable Experience* a

hit. It's filled with chiming guitars, sweet melodies, and simple, catchy hooks, as well as a sturdy grasp of traditional pop-rock songwriting that results in a number of gems. The only fault of *Congratulations... I'm Sorry* is that it sounds a bit *too* close to the debut; there's virtually no difference in terms of style and production. As such, it builds a case for their craftsmanship. The Gin Blossoms may not have much new to say, but they say it well throughout *Congratulations... I'm Sorry*. —*Stephen Thomas Erlewine*

Ginger

f. 1992, Kelowna, British Columbia, Canada
Pop-Rock
When vocalist/guitarist and founding member Kevin Kane left Canada's acclaimed Grapes of Wrath due to the cliched musical and personal differences, the remaining members—Chris Hooper (drums), Tom Hooper (vocals, bass, guitars), and Vincent Jones (keyboards)—carried on with the like-sounding and equally enjoyable Ginger. The band returned to Nettwerk Records (Grapes of Wrath's original label), releasing a self-titled, Canadian-only EP in 1993 and the full-length *Far Out* in 1994. *Far Out* was eventually released in the US in 1995. The band followed with *Suddenly I Came to My Senses* in late 1996 for EMI Canada. —*Chris Woodstra*

Ginger / 1993 / Nettwerk ✦✦✦
The combo's first release picks up effectively where Grapes of Wrath left off with five songs of pleasantly jangly folk-pop that occasionally flirt with pseudo-psychedelia. Only "The Earth Revolves Around You" appears on *Far Out*, so fans are advised to seek this out. —*Chris Woodstra*

● **Far Out** / 1994 / Nettwerk ✦✦✦✦
Far Out is a well-paced album that clearly stands alongside the finer moments of Grapes of Wrath, alternating quieter, introspective moments with upbeat rockers and pure Beatle-esque pop. —*Chris Woodstra*

Gary Glitter (Paul Gadd)

b. May 8, 1940, Banbury, Oxfordshire, England
Vocals / Rock 'n' Roll, Glam Rock
After many years of trying to become a star, Paul Gadd finally hit the winning formula in 1972—the glam rock king, Gary Glitter. Complete with extravagant makeup, silver outfits, and high boots, Glitter looked as trashy as his music sounded. Glitter and producer Michael Leander created pop records that weren't intended to be serious music—infectious singles that sounded perfect for the three minutes that they were playing; after they were finished, they seemed slightly embarrassing. With its mammoth drum beat, growling guitar, dumb instrumental hook, and incessant chorus of "Hey!," his debut single, "Rock and Roll, Part Two," was a huge hit in both the UK and the US. Although he never had another hit in America, Glitter was a superstar in Britain throughout the mid-'70s, scoring three No. 1 singles. Surprisingly, Glitter's cheerfully idiotic, catchy glam rock became somewhat influential over the next decade; Joan Jett covered several of his songs, as did the Human League, Generation X, Planet Control, and Brownsville Station. —*Stephen Thomas Erlewine*

● **Rock 'n' Roll: The Best of Gary Glitter** / 1990 / Rhino ✦✦✦✦
Although he's best known for the knuckle-headed sports anthem "Rock 'n' Roll Part Two," Glitter had plenty of other glam-rock delights that were equally good, if not better. *Rock 'n' Roll—The Best of Gary Glitter* lovingly collects his best singles, from "Rock 'n' Roll Part Two" to such unsung riff-rockers as "Do You Wanna Touch Me (Oh Yeah!)" and "I'm the Leader of the Gang (I Am!)." It's dumb, it's catchy, it's loud—everything good rock 'n' roll should be. A nice guilty pleasure. —*Stephen Thomas Erlewine*

The Go-Betweens

f. 1978, Brisbane, Australia, db. Dec. 31, 1989
Alternative Pop-Rock, New Wave
The Go-Betweens were perhaps the quintessential cult band of the '80s. They came from an exotic locale (Brisbane, Australia), moved to a major recording center (in their case, London) in a sustained bid to make a career out of music, released album after album of music seemingly tailor-made for the radio in spite of their having little use for contemporary Top 40 musical/lyrical formulas, and earned considerable critical praise and a small but fervent international fan base. Though they split up at the end of the decade, both songwriters have moved on to respectable solo careers that, while rarely reaching the heights the Go-Betweens scaled, continue to uphold their legacy. Robert Forster and Grant McLennan began as teenagers obsessed with the earthy rock of Dylan, CCR, and the Velvet Underground and encouraged by the Australian punk of the Saints. As collected on *The Able Label Singles*, their first two singles show a fondness for scruffy, British Invasion/New Wave-

influenced pop rock. Picking up permanent drummer Lindy Morrisson, they recorded their debut LP, moved to England, and signed a short-lived deal with Rough Trade. Going for a lush, tuneful sound crammed with nonstandard rock instrumentation, they went on to record five more excellent LPs. Though their pre-Beggars Banquet albums were traditionally hard to find in the States, that label finally reissued all six albums on CD in 1996. —*Michael Ribas*

Send Me a Lullabye / 1981 / Beggars Banquet ✦✦✦
On their first LP, the Go-Betweens largely abandoned the "wild mercury sound" of their first singles and opted for a more up-tempo/downcast approach similar to that of Josef K, 77 -era Talking Heads, the Fire Engines, and other new wave heroes. Still, they made it work by writing personal, poetic lyrics and by rarely forgetting to mate their angst to a sturdy pop framework. —*Michael Ribas*

Very Quick on the Eye-Brisbane, 1981 / 1982 / Man Made ✦✦
Though now included in the band's official discography, this little-heard (and hard to find) bootleg of outtakes from the *Send Me a Lullabye* sessions is hardly essential, except of course for completists. —*Michael Ribas*

Before Hollywood / 1983 / Beggars Banquet ✦✦✦✦
Australia's Go-Betweens are a curious anomaly, an intellectual's pop band. The songs on this album show touches of R.E.M., the Cure, Television, and 1960s organ-dominated bands such as the Zombies—but these tunes are for the most part unlike those of any other group. Unusual chord progressions, frequent use of meter changes and uneven phrase lengths, inventive production touches, wide varieties of texture, and intelligent if sometimes obscure lyrics occur throughout this worthy album. Within their style, the band rocks in songs like "Ask" and "By Chance" or croons more sedately in selections such as "As Long as That" and "Dusty in Here." And "Two Steps Step Out" is a fine, memorable tune, perhaps the album's best. This release is highly recommended, especially for those who listen with their brains as well as their feet. —*David Cleary*

Spring Hill Fair / 1984 / Beggars Banquet ✦✦✦✦
Their most overlooked album (probably because it never saw US release), the Go-Betweens' third works best when it doesn't try to come on too clever. Thus, while the spoken-sung "River of Money" falls flat on its face, the poppier "Bachelor Kisses," "Draining the Pool for You," and "Man o' Sand to Girl o' Sea" are resounding successes, on par with the best music that the '80s had to offer. In all, one of their lushest, most affecting records. —*Michael Ribas*

Metal & Shells / 1985 / PVC ✦✦✦
This vinyl-only compilation was useful in acquainting at least a few Americans with the Go-Betweens' early (and in the US, otherwise unissued) recordings. Though fans are best served by the complete albums, it's worth picking up used for the curious non-fan since it contains among its treasures one of the best tracks from *Spring Hill Fair* not included on *1978-1990*, "Unkind & Unwise." —*Michael Ribas*

Liberty Belle & the Black Diamond Express / 1986 / Beggars Banquet ✦✦✦✦
Here the Go-Bees (as their Japanese fans nicknamed them) continued the superb blend of ambitious lyrics and string—and horn-embellished rock music that they initiated in *Spring Hill Fair*. In a smart musical (and commercial) maneuver, they had Tracey Thorn of Everything but the Girl help sing on "Head Full of Steam," the album's highlight. That it also contains such gems as the graceful "Bow Down" and the rollicking "Spring Rain" makes it a strong contender for their best album. —*Michael Ribas*

The Able Label Singles [EP] / 1986 / Situation Two ✦✦✦
Snatch up this UK/Australian-only EP if you see it; it reissues Forster and McLennen's fascinating earliest recordings, revealing an endearingly goofy bubblegum streak that's most effective when they subvert it on the Modern Lovers-ish "Karen." —*Michael Ribas*

Tallulah / 1987 / Beggars Banquet ✦✦✦✦
Though the they had moved from strength to strength until this point, *Tallulah* sounds half-hearted. There are a few good songs, but in general the music isn't as catchy as before and some of the lyrics are too self-consciously poetic to be enjoyable. However, the planets did align for the majestic "Bye Bye Pride," which is as close to an anthem as they ever came. —*Michael Ribas*

/ 1987 / Beggars Banquet ✦✦✦

16 Lovers Lane / 1988 / Beggars Banquet ✦✦✦✦
Finally, after years of critical acclaim, a Go-Betweens album was released in the US by a major label and given a reasonable promotional push. Though it's unusual for final albums by long-standing bands to be much good, *Sixteen Lovers Lane* was an improvement over *Tallulah*. The sound was more radio-friendly than ever (and the "big" single, "Streets of Your Town," even got a little airplay) but it was all for naught. —*Michael Ribas*

● **1978-1990** / Aug. 27, 1990 / Capitol ✦✦✦✦
Until they get their own box set (yeah, right) this will have to do as a summation of the Go-Betweens' rewarding body of work. To their fans' frustration, several of their best numbers were left off in favor of some so-so ones. Even so, this collection is invaluable because besides a complete discography, personnel history, and liner notes courtesy of Forster and McLennan, it contains a few interesting unreleased tracks, two good early non-LP singles ("People Say" and "I Need Two Heads"), as well as some of the best of the Go-Betweens' frequently amazing B-sides, including the shimmering "Rock and Roll Friend." From that perspective, it's a worthy epitaph for one of the best Australian bands ever. (Collectors/world travelers: look for the double CD/record Japanese/UK versions; they include all the tracks mentioned above. The US release is a single CD that eliminates six of the rarities.) —*Michael Ribas*

The Go-Go's

f. 1978, Los Angeles, CA, **db.** May 1985
New Wave, Pop-Rock
The Go-Go's were the most popular all-female band to emerge from the punk/new wave explosion of the late '70s and early '80s, becoming one of the first commercially successful female groups that wasn't controlled by male producers or managers. While their hit singles—"We Got the Beat," "Our Lips Are Sealed," "Vacation," "Head over Heels"—were bright, energetic new wave pop, the group was an integral part of the California punk scene. And they did play punk rock, even if many of their rougher edges were ironed out by the time they recorded their first album, 1981's *Beauty and the Beat*. Even as they became America's darlings, the Go-Go's lived the wild life of rockers, swallowing as many pills and taking as much cocaine as possible, trashing hotel rooms, and just generally being bad. More importantly, their earliest music—now collected on *Return to the Valley of the Go-Go's*—was raw and rocking; it may not have directly inspired the female alternative rockers and riot grrrls of the '90s, but it certainly foreshadowed it.

Originally formed in 1978 as the Misfits, the group featured Belinda Carlisle (vocals), Jane Wiedlin (guitar, vocals), Charlotte Caffey (lead guitar, keyboards), Margot Olaverra (bass), and Elissa Bello (drums); the group soon changed their name to the Go-Go's and began playing local parties and small clubs in California. In 1979 Gina Schock became the group's drummer. During that year the band recorded a demo and supported the British ska revival group Madness in both Los Angeles and England. The Go-Go's spent half of 1980 touring England, earning a sizable following and releasing "We Got the Beat" on Stiff Records. An import copy of "We Got the Beat" became an underground club hit in the US, which meant the band was popular enough to sell out concerts, but they had a difficult time landing a record contract.

At the end of 1980, bassist Olaverra became ill and had to stop performing; she was replaced by Kathy Valentine, a guitarist who had never played bass before. Early in 1981 the Go-Go's signed with IRS Records. Released in the summer of 1981, their debut album, *Beauty and the Beat*, became one of the surprise hits of the year, staying at No. 1 for six weeks and selling over two million copies; "Our Lips Are Sealed" hit No. 20 and a re-recorded version of "We Got the Beat" spent three weeks at No. 2.

The next year the group released *Vacation*. Although it sold well—the album made the Top Ten and went gold, spawning the Top Ten hit single "Vacation"—it failed to keep the momentum of the first record. During the next year the band was unable to perform, as Caffey recovered from a broken wrist. In 1984 the Go-Go's returned with *Talk Show*, their most musically ambitious album. While it had two Top 40 hits—the No. 11 "Head over Heels" and "Turn to You"—it failed to go gold. By the end of the year, Wiedlin had left the band; the Go-Go's broke up in May 1985. Belinda Carlisle became the most successful solo artist, scoring a string of mainstream pop singles in the late '80s, including the No. 1 single "Heaven Is a Place on Earth." For a while, Charlotte Caffey was in Carlisle's backing group; she eventually formed the Graces, who released *Perfect View* in 1990. Jane Wiedlin recorded two solo albums and acted in a few films. Wiedlin also organized the group's brief 1990 reunion, where they performed at a benefit for People for the Ethical Treatment of Animals; they also recorded a version of "Cool Jerk" for their 1990 *Greatest Hits* album. The Go-Go's reunited once more in 1994, recording three new songs for the double-disc compilation *Return of the Valley of the Go-Go's;* after recording the songs, the group decided to continue as a full-time unit. —*Stephen Thomas Erlewine*

Beauty & the Beat / Jul. 1981 / IRS ✦✦✦✦
Although the relatively polished production belies the Go-Go's punk roots, *Beauty & the Beat* remains one of the cornerstone albums of new wave, bristling with energy, revamped surf-rock and girl-group hooks, and an intoxicating sense of fun. The infectious, bouncy "We Got the Beat" and the pulsating "Our Lips Are Sealed," which Jane Wiedlin co-wrote with Terry Hall, sent *Beauty & the Beat* to unexpected hit status,

but they only scratch the surface of the wonderful pop songs that comprise the record. Nearly every song on the record is a delight, propelled by big, catchy hooks and an exuberant sense of fun. "Lust to Love," "Skidmarks on My Heart," "Tonite" and "Fading Fast" could have been hits in their own right, but as it stands, they help make *Beauty & the Beat* into a terrifically exiciting pop album. —*Stephen Thomas Erlewine*

Vacation / Aug. 1982 / IRS ✦✦✦
The surprise success of *Beauty & the Beat* meant that the Go-Go's were expected to remain hitmakers, so perhaps it shouldn't have come as a surprise that their second album, *Vacation*, was a considerably slicker affair than their debut. Sporting a glossy yet alluring finish, the album had an appealing, radio-ready sound, but it was at the expense of the giddy sense of fun that made *Beauty & the Beat* such a vibrant record. However, *Vacation* is far from a washout. Although half the album is padded with filler, the very best moments are terrific pop songs, highlighted by the bouncy "This Old Feeling" and the classic title track. —*Stephen Thomas Erlewine*

Talk Show / 1984 / IRS ✦✦✦
For their third album, the Go-Go's abandoned all pretense of being punk, or even new wave, and went for an unabashed mainstream pop masterpiece. They nearly achieved their goal with *Talk Show*, an album filled with great pop songs but undermined by its own ambition. *Talk Show* has a sharper sound than its predecessors, with bigger guitars and drums, which helps drive home the accomplished pop hooks of "Turn to You," "I'm the Only One," and "Yes or No." However, the record is cluttered with half-realized songs and an overly detailed production that occasionally prevents the songs from reaching their full potential. But when the production and song are teamed well, the results are incredible, such as the surging "Head over Heels," another classic single from the group. Unfortunately, those moments don't arrive frequently enough to make *Talk Show* the new wave classic that it wants to be. —*Stephen Thomas Erlewine*

● **Greatest** / Oct. 1990 / IRS ✦✦✦✦
The hits collection *Greatest* tries to reduce the Go-Go's' career to that of a mainstream pop-rock band, downplaying their punk and new wave roots. Of course those can't be entirely erased, especially since the hits "Our Lips Are Sealed" and "We Got the Beat" form the core of the collection, but the song selection on the 14-track compilation leans a little too heavily on latter-day material and lesser songs, including an extraneous, previously unreleased cover of "Cool Jerk" that was added as bait for collectors. As a brief overview, *Greatest* is adequate since it does contain all the hit singles, but it's also misleading, since it doesn't capture the group's punky spirit. Nevertheless, it's a cheaper, more manageable introduction than the double-disc set *Return to the Valley of the Go-Go's*, even though serious fans should choose that collection instead. —*Stephen Thomas Erlewine*

Return to the Valley of the Go-Go's / Oct. 18, 1994 / IRS ✦✦✦✦
Because it doesn't ignore the group's punk and new wave roots, the double-disc set *Return to the Valley of the Go-Go's* is far more entertaining than the single-disc collection *Greatest Hits*. All of the hits are included, as well as many rarities as good as anything they officially released. Not only is the music intoxicating, but the liner notes are filled with priceless photos and memorabilia, which makes the set the one definitive Go-Go's album. —*Stephen Thomas Erlewine*

The Godfathers

f. 1985, London, England
Alternative Pop-Rock
The Godfathers were founded by brothers Peter and Chris Coyne in London in 1985. Vocalist Peter and bassist Chris were joined by guitarists Kris Dollimore and Mike Gibson and drummer George Mazur. Coming ten years after Britain's punk explosion, they nevertheless built on that music's rage and force. Their debut album, *Hit by Hit*, was released in the US on the indie label Link in 1986 and was followed by *Birth, School, Work, Death* on Epic in 1988, which made the Top 100 bestsellers, as the title song was played on album rock radio. Their third album, *More Songs About Love and Hate* (1989), featured the popular college radio track "She Gives Me Love," but was less commercially successful. They released a fourth album, *Unreal World*, on Epic in 1991. —*William Ruhlmann*

● **Birth, School, Work, Death: Best of the Godfathers** / Mar. 26, 1996 / Epic/Legacy ✦✦✦✦
Assembled by bandleaders Peter and Chris Coyne, this 18-track, 65-minute compilation contains more than just selections from the Godfathers' three Epic Records albums of 1988-1991, going back to their debut single, "Lonely Man," from 1985. As much pre-metal hard rock as late-blooming punk, the music is angry, driving, and derivative. ("Just Because You're Not Paranoid Doesn't Mean to Say They're Not Going to Get You!," making its first appearance on an album, is the MC5's "Kick Out the Jams" under another name.) It is also energetic and ambitious.

("We wanted to make a record that would last forever," the Coynes write of the title track in the liner notes, "and boy, did we do it.") Of course, conviction does not equal distinction, and the Godfathers never quite became a Dr. Feelgood, much less a Clash, for the late '80s. But this album represents some brave attempts to do so. (The album's title, unfortunately, is identical to that of the group's Epic Records debut, so note that it is not to be confused with Epic 40946, also called *Birth, School, Work, Death*.) —*William Ruhlmann*

The Godz

f. 1966, New York, NY, **db.** 1973
Psychedelic, Experimental, Hard Rock
Few bands in the annals of rock 'n' roll were stranger than the New York City-based Godz. Recording for the wonderfully idiosyncratic ESP-DISK label from the mid-'60s until the early '70s (although nothing they recorded after 1968 is worth hearing), the Godz coughed up some of the strangest, most dissonant, purposely incompetent rock noise ever produced. Part of the Lower East Side scene that produced post-Beat avant-hippie rockers/performance artists the Fugs and the Holy Modal Rounders, as well as honest-to-God beat performers like Allen Ginsberg, the Godz recorded the most extreme music, while being secretive about themselves. As the late critic Lester Bangs noted in his essay (the only one I'm aware of concerning the Godz in a major rock publication—*Creem* 1971), the Godz " . . . are a pure test of one of the supreme traditions of rock 'n' roll: the process by which a musical band can evolve from beginnings of almost insulting illiteracy to wind up several albums later romping and stomping deft as champs."

Despite Bangs' essay, there are few, if any, detailed histories of this enigmatic band. What is known is that the Godz consisted of guitarist Jim McCarthy, bassist Larry Kessler, autoharpist Jay Dillon, and drummer Paul Thornton. McCarthy, the ostensible leader of the group, went solo in 1973, but the Godz were pretty much over by that point. As to what happened after they split, McCarthy became a photographer, Kessler is a record dealer, Thornton is an actor, and Dillon is living in the wilds of New Jersey. But none of that is as interesting as the three squalling bits of avant-garde noise/junk they recorded from 1966-68. Sounding like a prototype for Half Japanese or the Shaggs, the Godz play as if they discovered their instruments ten minutes before the tape started rolling. The singing is intentionally off-key, almost parodic, and the songs . . . well, they sound more like improvised snippets than actual compositions. And while that may not be your idea of pop music, this works, in large part due to the absolute glee and unself-consciousness with which these clowns approached their peculiar brand of aural nonsense. You may not want to play this every day, but if your tastes run to the fringes of popular music, missing out on the Godz would be unforgivable.

Normally, there is a caveat with a listing such as this one indicating that the records are impossible to find—not true here! Although ESP-DISK recordings were never easy to find in the first place, Bernhard Mikulski, who runs the German label ZYX, is planning to reissue (assuming he hasn't already) the entire ESP-DISK catalog at very affordable prices. This means that the majesty of the Godz can be yours, and you won't need a second mortgage to buy expensive imports.

A final note: in the late '70s, there was a terrible Midwestern heavy metal band, also called the Godz, who made two execrable albums for Casablanca. There is absolutely no relation between the two bands, and music by the heavy-metal Godz should be avoided at all costs. —*John Dougan*

● **Contact High** / 1966 / ESP ✦✦✦✦
Clocking in at a hair over 25 minutes, *Contact High* is an unholy mess of a record. Opening with the track "White Cat Heat," which consists of clumsily strummed acoustic guitars, arrhythmic percussion, and Jim McCarthy and Larry Kessler screeching like a couple of, uh, cats in heat, it gets weirder. Best tracks are "1+1 Equals?" and the hilarious "Lay in the Sun" (total lyrics: "All I want to do is lay in the sun"). For those who like their pop on the cutting edge, begin here and don't turn back. —*John Dougan*

Godz Two / 1967 / ESP ✦✦✦✦
Only a label as adventurous as ESP would allow a band like the Godz to make second record, and *2* is as extreme as *Contact High*, and as good. A little more psychedelic sound here, but nothing that detracts from the Godz' relentless amateurish spirit and abilities. If you were sold on *Contact High*, having this is important. —*John Dougan*

Third Testament / 1968 / ESP ✦✦✦
Although they went on to record into the 1970s, this is the last decent Godz record, primarily because it's the last one that incorporates their distinctive meandering and lack of technical merit with their growing interest in psychedelic rock. True Godz fanatics will tell you that *Third Testament* is a significant dropoff from *2*, but not to these ears. And while it doesn't pack the visceral wallop of *Contact High*, there's enough dementia here for a lifetime of fun. —*John Dougan*

Golden Earring

f. 1964, The Hague, Netherlands, **db.** 1991
Hard Rock, Pop-Rock

Best known in the US for its hard rock material, Golden Earring has been the most popular homegrown band in the Netherlands since the mid-'60s, when they were primarily a pop group. The group was founded by guitarist/vocalist George Kooymans and bassist/vocalist Rinus Gerritsen, then schoolboys, in 1961; several years and personnel shifts later, they had their first Dutch hit, "Please Don't Go," and in 1968 hit the top of the Dutch charts first of many times with "Dong-Dong-Di-Ki-Di-Gi-Dong," a song that broadened their European appeal. By 1969 the rest of the lineup had stabilized, with lead vocalist and multi-instrumentalist Barry Hay and drummer Cesar Zuiderwijk. They experimented with their style for several years before settling on straightforward hard rock, initially much like that of the Who, who invited them to open their 1972 European tour. Golden Earring signed to the Who's Track label, which released a compilation of Dutch singles, *Hearing Earring,* helping the group break through in England. In 1974 the *Moontan* LP spawned the single "Radar Love," a Dutch No. 1, UK Top Ten, and US No. 13 hit. The group toured America opening for the Doobie Brothers and Santana, but the lack of a follow-up ensured that their popularity remained short-lived in America, even though they remained a top draw in Europe over the rest of the 1970s. In 1982 they made a brief American comeback with the album *Cut* and the Top Ten single "Twilight Zone," but as before, Golden Earring could not sustain its momentum and faded away in the US marketplace. All of Golden Earring's basic lineup has recorded as solo artists in Europe. "Radar Love" enjoyed a second round of popularity when pop-metal band White Lion covered the song in 1989. *—Steve Huey*

Just Earring / 1965 / Polydor ◆◆◆
Long before Golden Earring were an international act, they were a typical Continental beat group, billing themselves initially as "the Golden Earrings." Their 1965 debut was a lightweight but enjoyable effort, highly derivative of British beat circa 1964-65, especially the Beatles, Kinks, and Zombies; all but one of the tunes were original compositions. *—Richie Unterberger*

● **The Continuing Story of Radar Love** / Oct. 1989 / MCA ◆◆◆◆
The Continuing Story of Radar Love collects all of the hits and highlights from Golden Earring's career, ranging from the hard rock of "Radar Love" to the new wave-tinged "Twilight Zone." It's the only collection that contains both songs, and it is the only album most fans will need. *—Stephen Thomas Erlewine*

The Golden Palominos

f. 1982, New York, NY
Alternative Pop-Rock

The Golden Palominos were not a group per se, but rather the revolving-door project of drummer, programmer and bandleader Anton Fier. Born June 20, 1956, in Cleveland, OH, Fier first made his mark as the drummer on the Feelies' seminal 1980 debut *Crazy Rhythms.* After leaving the group, he joined the punk-jazz unit the Lounge Lizards before returning to Cleveland, where he was recruited by the legendary New Wave band Pere Ubu for the album *Song of the Bailing Man.*

After exiting Ubu, Fier relocated to downtown New York City, where he founded the first Golden Palominos line-up in 1981. In its primary live incarnation, the band was an avant-funk supergroup comprised of Fier and another drummer, David Moss, saxophonist John Zorn, guitarist Arto Lindsay, and a pair of bassists, Bill Laswell and Jamaaladeen Tacuma; on their self-titled 1983 debut, the Palominos were augmented by Fred Frith, Nicky Skopelitis, and Mark Miller.

Over the next few years, Fier moved away from the first record's experimental noise into far more traditional pop territory; simultaneously, he largely jettisoned the first album's lineup in favor of an ever-changing collection of punk legends, post-punk superstars, up-and-comers, and NYC-scene vets. After enlisting ex-Raybeat Jody Harris to help him co-write much of the music, Fier recruited vocalists ranging from R.E.M.'s Michael Stipe and Cream's Jack Bruce to PIL's John Lydon and newcomer Syd Straw; rounded out by musicians like former dB Chris Stamey, guitar greats Richard Thompson and Henry Kaiser, and P-Funk alumni Bernie Worrell and Mike Hampton, the revamped Golden Palominos reached an early peak with 1985's *Visons of Excess,* a diverse, yet cogent, collection highlighted by a cover of Moby Grape's "Omaha" and the original "Boy (Go)."

With 1986's *Blast of Silence,* the group flirted with elements of country and folk; while Stipe and Lydon were noticeably absent, many of the other players featured on *Visions of Excess* remained, along with additions including guitarist T-Bone Burnett, ex-Numbers Band singer Robert Kidney, artist/producer Don Dixon, singer-songwriter Peter Blegvad, Matthew Sweet, and Flying Burrito Brothers alum Sneaky Pete Kleinow. On 1989's moody *A Dead Horse,* Fier again shifted gears, settling on a lineup of Laswell, Skopelitis, Kidney, and ex-Information Society vocalist Amanda Kramer, along with a handful of guests, including former Rolling Stone Mick Taylor.

In 1991 *Drunk with Passion* returned to the all-star format; Stipe and Thompson again rejoined the fold, welcoming newcomers like Sugar's Bob Mould. *This Is How It Feels,* a sophisticated concept album inspired by the Graham Greene novel *The End of the Road,* followed in 1993; along with core members like Laswell, Skopelitis, Worrell, and Kramer, the record spotlighted vocalists Lori Carson and Lydia Kavanaugh, as well as bass great Bootsy Collins. In 1994 *Pure* featured many of the same principal players, while 1996's *Dead Inside,* essentially from a trio comprised of Fier, ex-Psychedelic Furs guitarist Knox Chandler, and vocalist/lyricist Nicole Blackman, explored electronic and ambient soundscapes. *—Jason Ankeny*

The Golden Palominos / 1983 / Celluloid ◆◆◆
The first effort from Anton Fier's revolving-door band is the record that most reflects the group's downtown New York origins. Recalling the avant-funk of Material, *The Golden Palominos* spotlights a core roster of Fier, guitarists Arto Lindsay and Fred Frith, bassist Bill Laswell, and multi-instrumentalist John Zorn. The music is wildly experimental, incorporating turntables and other hip-hop staples (a rather adventurous notion back in 1983) as well as other oddball ideas (clarinets played under water and the like) that miss the mark as often as they hit, but make for fascinating listening, nevertheless. *—Jason Ankeny*

Visions of Excess / 1985 / Celluloid ◆◆◆◆
The first in a long series of about-faces and left turns, *Visions of Excess* forgoes the noise-funk of the Golden Palominos' debut in favor of more pop-oriented material and a staggering lineup of underground luminaries. Built around a nucleus of Anton Fier, bassist Bill Laswell, guitarist Jody Harris, and keyboardist Bernie Worrell, the album recruits vocalists from Jack Bruce to John Lydon to, most impressively, Michael Stipe, who turns in striking performances on the opening "Boy (Go)" (featuring guitarist Richard Thompson), the Jefferson Airplane-like "Clustering Train," and a cover of Moby Grape's "Omaha." The real find of the record is singer Syd Straw, who makes her debut on the lovely "(Kind of) True" and "Buenos Aires" and more than holds her own with the big guns. *—Jason Ankeny*

Blast of Silence / 1986 / Celluloid ◆◆◆
Another all-star effort, *Blast of Silence* shifts the Palominos' focus to country, folk and blues, bringing talents like Matthew Sweet, T-Bone Burnett, and Peter Blegvad into the fold. While treating their rootsy influences with care and authenticity, the songs are subtly subversive—Nicky Skopelitis' guitar coda on the folky "Something Becomes Nothing" suddenly spins off into wah-wah land, while the blues structure of "(Something Else Is) Working Harder" allows the occasional ray of acoustic guitar-pop to shine through its cracks. Best of all is a cover of Peter Holsapple's "Diamond," featuring a memorable vocal turn from Syd Straw. *—Jason Ankeny*

A Dead Horse / 1989 / Celluloid ◆◆◆
By and large, *A Dead Horse* tosses out the supersession approach of previous Golden Palominos efforts to concentrate on a steady core roster of Anton Fier, Bill Laswell and Nicky Skopelitis; vocal chores are evenly divided among the Numbers Band's Robert Kidney and Amanda Kramer, formerly of Information Society. A subdued, moody effort, *A Dead Horse* lacks the energy and spark of the group's earlier work; only Kramer's lovely "Darklands" makes much of a lasting impression. *—Jason Ankeny*

Drunk with Passion / Sep. 17, 1991 / Nation/Charisma ◆◆◆◆
Fier and Bill Laswell are joined by Stipe, Thompson, Carla Bley, and former Hüsker Dü singer-songwriter and guitarist Bob Mould on this album. *—William Ruhlmann*

● **A History (1982-1985)** / Jul. 21, 1992 / Metrotone/Restless ◆◆◆◆
This is a fine sampler of the Golden Palominos' first two records. *—AMG*

● **A History (1986-1989)** / Jul. 21, 1992 / Metrotone/Restless ◆◆◆◆
This is a fine sampler of the Golden Palominos' third and fourth records. *—AMG*

This Is How It Feels / Sep. 28, 1993 / Restless ◆◆◆◆
Anton Fier and Bill Laswell use Lori Carson as their regular vocalist here, with three songs sung by Lydia Kavanaugh. Guest musicians include Bootsy Collins, Nicky Skopelitis, and Bernie Worrell. The key figure, however, is Carson, who co-wrote all the songs on which she sings, making this, in effect, a Lori Carson solo album. Carson explores the argumentative, often brutal aspects of romance in songs that have a dreamy effect despite the involved rhythm tracks. Her double-tracked, interweaving vocals, with their repeated phrases and blunt sentiments, have a disorienting, yet compelling force. *—William Ruhlmann*

Pure / Oct. 11, 1994 / Restless ◆◆◆◆
The Golden Palominos manage to convey much of the same darkly seductive atmosphere as on their other shimmering experimental pop records. *—Stephen Thomas Erlewine*

No Thought, No Breath, No Eyes, No Heart / Mar. 14, 1995 / Restless
◆◆◆

Dead Inside / Oct. 8, 1996 / Restless ◆◆◆
Unlike previous Golden Palominos records, which boasted a bevy of
guest stars, Anton Fier worked with only one other musician for *Dead
Inside*—poet Nicole Blackman. With Blackman providing appropriately
bleak poetry, Fier has created one of the most evocative and disturbing
soundscapes to grace any Golden Palominos album. Though that means
Dead Inside is darker than any of the group's other albums, it isn't necessarily more challenging; it's just hard to get inside these detached and
death-obsessed sounds. —*Stephen Thomas Erlewine*

Golden Smog

f. 1989, Minneapolis, MN
Alternative Country-Rock
A boozy, side-project covers band that gradually evolved into a kind of
roots-rock supergroup, Golden Smog was a loosely affiliated unit comprised, at various times, of members of Soul Asylum, the Replacements,
Wilco, the Jayhawks, Run Westy Run, and the Honeydogs. The group
first came together in the Minneapolis area in the late '80s as a country-
rock reaction to the punk and hardcore sounds that dominated the Twin
Cities' musical scene at the time; eventually Golden Smog became
something of a fixture at local clubs, where they played a handful of
shows annually. From the onset, the lineup was mercurial, although
Run Westy Run vocalist Kraig Johnson as well as guitarists Dan Murphy
(Soul Asylum) and Gary Louris (the Jayhawks) were relative constants.
Smog shows were usually thematically based, in keeping with the
tongue-in-cheek nature of the project; one performance was devoted
exclusively to Eagles covers, while another paid homage to the Rolling
Stones, and was billed "Her Satanic Majesty's Paycheck."
    Somewhat unexpectedly, a five-cut covers EP, *On Golden Smog*,
appeared in 1992. While the closing track, a rendition of Thin Lizzy's
"Cowboy Song" sung by Soul Asylum roadie Bill Sullivan, followed in
the project's original devil-may-care spirit, the remainder of the record
was considerably more focused, keeping in line with the primary musical work of the band members who, this time out, were essentially
Johnson, Murphy, Louris, Jayhawks bassist Marc Perlman, and ex-
Replacements drummer Chris Mars, along with Soul Asylum vocalist
Dave Pirner (on a cover of Bad Company's "Shooting Star"). Even more
unexpectedly, the next Golden Smog effort—1996's full-length *Down by
the Old Mainstream*—was made up largely of original material composed strictly for the project. With a lineup that included Johnson, Murphy, Louris, Perlman, Wilco frontman Jeff Tweedy, and Honeydogs
drummer Noah Levy (all of whom recorded under pseudonyms as a
result of contractual obligations), the record bore few reminders of the
Smog's beer-soaked origins, instead revealing a more mature and
thoughtful band breaking free of the restraints of their day jobs and having some serious fun in the process. —*Jason Ankeny*

On Golden Smog / Dec. 11, 1992 / Crackpot ◆◆◆
After a few years of haphazard shows in and about their native Minne-
apolis, the members of Golden Smog were approached by a small local
label to put out a record; many, many beers later, *On Golden Smog*
appeared. Complete with sleeve art by then-drummer Chris Mars, the
five-song EP is comprised entirely of covers, including Hair's "Easy to Be
Hard," the obscure '60s band Michelangelo's "Son," Bad Company's
"Shooting Star" (sung by Soul Asylum's Dave Pirner), and Thin Lizzy's
"Cowboy Song," fronted by Soul Asylum roadie Bill Sullivan. —*Jason
Ankeny*

● **Down by the Old Mainstream** / 1995 / Rykodisc ◆◆◆◆
Like most supergroup projects, Golden Smog's *Down By the Old Mainstream* is a loose, relaxed affair that sounds as if it was a lot of fun to
record. Unlike most supergroups, the members of Golden Smog
improve on their regular bands. Comprised of a number of alternative
country-rock stars—including Wilco's Jeff Tweedy, the Jayhawks' Gary
Louris, and Soul Asylum's Dan Murphy—the musicians are relaxed and
loose, giving the songs a raw, rootsy kick. Since the album wasn't carefully considered, it has an offhand charm that is sometimes lacking from
Jayhawks and Soul Asylum albums. Not all of the songs are first-
rate—"Pecan Pie" and "Red Headed Stepchild" are a bit too cute to be
effective—but the performances are full of grit and fire, which is what
makes *Down By the Old Mainstream* such an engaging listen.
—*Stephen Thomas Erlewine*

Goldie

b. 1965, Wolverhampton, England
DJ / Jungle/Drum 'N Bass
The first superstar that the '90s jungle phenomenon produced, Goldie
popularized the fusion of two dissimilar musical cultures—hip-hop and
rave—that spawned drum 'n' bass (as jungle is also known). Though he
did not invent the genre (give most of the credit to breakbeat DJs such

as Fabio and Grooverider), Goldie pioneered one now-popular jungle
production technique: time-stretching, the process of speeding up or
slowing down a vocal sample to give the illusion of shifting tempo. After
several successful singles on his own Metalheadz label, he engineered
one of jungle's best full-length works of art, *Timeless*.
    The native of Wolverhampton, England, studied art in a predomi-
nantly white school, but became fascinated with hip-hop music and the
graffiti art inspired by it. Goldie also joined several break-dancing crews
around Wolverhampton; after forming one of his own, he joined the
local B-Boys Crew and often journeyed to London for all-day events,
hooking up with Nellee Hooper and 3-D (later of Massive Attack) while
there. Trips to New York to appear in a film documentary on graffiti art
and to his father's home in Miami broadened his experience, but it was
back in London—where, for a time he owned the Try I shop in Walsall
that sold customized gold teeth—that Goldie was introduced to the
breakbeat culture that birthed jungle. At the nightclub Rage, Grooverider and Fabio mixed sped-up breakbeats of the past to distort rave
music, making it even more frenetic than previous attempts. Goldie was
hooked, and gradually switched his allegiance to jungle from the jazz-
and rap-inspired scene that helped generate trip-hop.
    Goldie released his first single, "Terminator," in 1993 on the Synthetic
label using the alias Metalheads; the name was later taken for his influential Metalheadz label, which has released material from a legion of
crucial jungle artists—Photek, Doc Scott, Peshay, Alex Reece, Wax Doctor, Dillinja, Lemon D., J Majik, and Source Direct. Later singles such as
"Angel" and remixes for 4 Hero's Reinforced label spread Goldie's fame,
and in 1995 he signed a contract with London Records. The first major-
label single was "Timeless," and his debut album of the same name followed in late 1995. He gained fame in early 1996 when an American
tour supporting Bjork sparked a relationship between the two; they
were later married. Goldie continues to record as Metalheads and the
Rufige Kru, and has collaborated with A Guy Called Gerald as the Two
Gs. —*John Bush*

● **Timeless** / Oct. 17, 1995 / ffrr ◆◆◆◆
Respected by the underground and lauded by the press, Goldie's album
debut proves he's no fluke. But from the first few minutes of *Timeless*,
listeners might wonder what's so different about jungle and its first
superstar. The sweeping synths and lilting female vocals that form the
intro to the title-track opener could be taken from any above-average
house anthem. All questions are answered, however, once the beat kicks
in. Manic, echoey percussion rolls around and through the song while a
muscular dub bassline pounds additional sonic territory. The beat fades
in and out, appearing and re-appearing with all the stealth of a charging
rhino. The seven other tracks are just as uncompromising, even adopting a hip-hop beat for the R&B flavor of "State of Mind." Though jungle
might be jarring for first-time listeners unused to mid-tempo melodies
functioning as a bed for hyperspeed beats, *Timeless* makes it a much
smoother ride. —*John Bush*

Platinum Breakz / Jul. 1996 / Metalheadz/ffrr ◆◆◆◆
The first compilation of Goldie's Metalheadz label is a roll call of jungle's most crucial artists: Photek, Source Direct, Dillinja, J. Majik, Alex
Reece, Peshay and Lemon D. Released around the same time as L.T.J
Bukem's *Logical Progression*, *Platinum Breakz* proves that Bukem has
no business talking about intelligent jungle; though the styles of Metalheadz and Bukem's Looking Good/Good Looking imprints are quite
similar—that is, somewhat house-influenced breakbeats—most of the
contributions on *Logical Progression* have simple rhythms and are usually drowned out by extra, unneeded effects. The beats and percussion
work on *Platinum Breakz* stand alone, besides spare synth lines and the
occasional diva vocal. The rhythms constantly shift around, stopping
and restarting. While *Logical Progression* begins to sound samey, the
artists on *Platinum Breakz* are easily differentiated. Highlights are difficult to define, though Source Direct, Photek, Dillinja and J Majik's contributions are a very small step above the rest. Goldie's only contribution—recorded as the Rufige Kru—is okay but gets overshadowed.
—*John Bush*

Ian Gomm

b. Mar. 17, 1947, Ealing, England
Guitar, Vocals / Rock 'n' Roll, New Wave, Pub Rock
Former guitar player in England's greatest pub-rock band, Brinsley
Schwarz, Gomm went on to an understated, yet fairly rewarding, solo
career in the late '70s and early '80s. Playing more power-pop than pub-
rock as a solo artist, Gomm was a strong, if derivative, singer-songwriter
whose clear, warm voice made up for the occasional banality of his lyrics. But even at his most obvious and cloying, Gomm was likable and
winning, if only because of his sunny disposition and his way with a guitar riff. Curiously, after three good solo records, he pretty much disappeared. His best album is his first, *Summer Holiday*, which was released
in England only. His American releases for Stiff/Epic (some of which

included material from *Summer Holiday*) are solid, at times inspired, craftsmanship. —*John Dougan*

● **Gomm with the Wind** / 1978 / Stiff ✦✦✦✦
Part of the ill-fated marriage of the great English independent label Stiff and the massive distribution power of the CBS subsidiary label Epic, *Gomm with the Wind* was probably the most ignored of all the records released under this agreement, but, like *Summer Holiday*, it's a sturdy piece of pop with Gomm acquitting himself quite nicely on Johnny Rivers' schmaltz-pop classic "Swaying to the Music (Slow Dancin')." —*John Dougan*

Summer Holiday / 1978 / Albion ✦✦✦
With the "hit" "Hold On" here, *Summer Holiday* is a wonderful record. Loaded with chiming guitars, snappy songs, and Gomm's earnest vocals, only the world's meanest musical Scrooge could hate a record like this. By no means is this a record that will change your life, but few people make records like this anymore, at least not without sounding smug and calculated. —*John Dougan*

What a Blow / 1980 / Stiff ✦✦✦

The Village Choice / 1982 / Albion ✦✦

Images / 1986 / Decal ✦✦

Lesley Gore

b. May 2, 1946, New York, NY
Vocals / Girl-Group, Brill Building Pop
The most commercially successful solo singer to be identified with the girl group sound, Lesley Gore hit the No. 1 spot with her very first release, "It's My Party," in 1963. Produced by Quincy Jones, who fattened the teenager's sound with double-tracked vocals and intricate backup vocals and horns, she reeled off a few more big hits in 1963 and 1964, including "Judy's Turn to Cry," "She's a Fool," "You Don't Own Me," "That's the Way Boys Are," and "Maybe I Know." She wasn't the most soulful girl group singer by a long shot, but she projected an archetype of female adolescent yearning. Her best songs survive as classics, particularly the irresistibly melodic "Maybe I Know" and "Look of Love" (both written by Ellie Greenwich and Jeff Barry) and "You Don't Own Me," an anthem of independence with a feminist theme that was considerably advanced for early 1964.

So what was Quincy Jones doing producing a white suburban teenager who had never recorded before? A couple of demos she recorded with her vocal coach made their way to Mercury's president, who recommended her to Jones, the label's A&R head. For their first session, Gore and Jones picked "It's My Party" out of a pile of about 200 demos. The "It's My Party" single was rush-released when Jones found out that Phil Spector also had plans to record the same song with the Crystals.

"It's My Party" and the weaker sequel, "Judy's Turn to Cry," have given Gore a somewhat unfair bratty image. Those are the hits that are remembered the most, but much of her subsequent material was both more mature (or, perhaps more accurately, less immature) and stronger. The singles were also very well produced, with orchestral arrangements (by Claus Ogermann) that hewed closer to mainstream pop than Phil Spector's Wall of Sound. Retrospectives of Quincy Jones' career usually downplay or omit his work with Gore, although it was among his most commercially successful; he's known now for recordings that are, well, funkier. But his success with Gore did a lot to build his already impressive résumé within the industry.

Gore appeared on the legendary "T.A.M.I. Show" alongside such heavyweights as the Rolling Stones, James Brown, and Smokey Robinson, but after 1964 her star plummeted. Mercury was still investing a lot of care in her sessions throughout the rest of the '60s, and her material and arrangements showed her capable of greater stylistic range than many acknowledged. But after the mid-'60s, Jones no longer worked with the singer on a regular basis. "Sunshine, Lollipops and Rainbows" (1965) and "California Nights" (1967), both of which were co-written by Marvin Hamlisch, would be her only Top 20 entries after 1964. She played the cabarets after her days as an active recording artist, and eventually had some success as a songwriter for other performers. —*Richie Unterberger*

● **Anthology** / 1986 / Rhino ✦✦✦✦
Superlative compilation of Leslie's best sides, including "It's My Party," "Judy's Turn to Cry," and "You Don't Own Me." —*Cub Koda*

● **It's My Party: Mercury Anthology** / Jun. 18, 1996 / Mercury ✦✦✦✦
Fifty-two-track double CD has all the hits and then some. It may seem excessive for those who *only* want the hits, and some of the selections (particularly from the late '60s) are weak. But Gore had more worthy B-sides, album cuts, and low-charting singles than most people assume, and there are a good number of those on this collection: "Wonder Boy" (a white Martha & the Vandellas cop), "Off and Running" (covered by the Mindbenders in the *To Sir with Love* film), "Look of Love" (one of Greenwich-Barry's greatest girl group-style songs), a cover of Laura Nyro's "Wedding Bell Blues" (which lost out on the charts to the Fifth

Dimension's version), and interesting little-known compositions by Goffin-King, Paul Anka, Van McCoy, Marvin Hamlisch, and Gore herself. Gore covered more territory than the teen self-pity anthems for which she's most remembered, and this anthology, while not enough to make you demand her election to the Rock and Roll Hall of Fame, is not nearly as relentlessly lightweight as her detractors would have you imagine. Includes some tracks that were previously unavailable on album, or previously unreleased in the US. —*Richie Unterberger*

Gorky's Zygotic Mynci

f. 1990, Camarthen, Wales
Alternative Pop-Rock, Brit-Pop, Neo-Psychedelia
Sounding like a bizarrely sweet and whimsical cross between progressive rock, psychedelia, and pure pop, Gorky's Zygotic Mynci were one of the most original and distinctive bands to emerge from the vital post-Brit-pop Welsh scene of the mid-'90s. Gorky's music followed unconventional time signatures and structures, as well as instrumentation (boasting everything from droning moog synthesizers to slurring trombones and steel guitars) and melodic patterns. Furthermore, the band's lyrics were rarely about conventional pop-rock subjects, and they frequently sang in Welsh, which made their already odd music sound even more alien to most listeners. Nevertheless, the Gorkys developed a strong cult following in Britian, as well as America, ranking behind Super Furry Animals as the most popular band to emerge from the mid-'90s Welsh scene.

Ironically, Gorky's Zygotic Mynci (which is Welsh for Dimwit Reproductive Monkey; the last word is pronounced as "monkey") formed long before Super Furry Animals. Unlike many Welsh bands of their age, the members of Gorkys did not begin a band after the Manic Street Preachers appeared in the early '90s—they began playing in the mid-'80s, when the band members were barely in their teens. Euros Childs (vocals, keyboards), Megan Childs (violin), John Lawrence (guitar), Richard James (bass), and Euros Rowlands (drums) were all attending school in Carmarthen, Wales, when they formed the group. Lawrence, James, and Euro Childs began making tapes in the bedroom, and they eventually added Euro's sister Megan and Euros Rowlands to the lineup. All of the group members came from upper-middle class families, with Rowlands' father, Dafydd, being a poet who is the archdruid of the Welsh culture celebration Eisteddfod, while Lawrence's mother is a politician. The connections helped Gorky's Zygotic Mynci enter the Welsh culture quite rapidly. Throughout their teens, the band recorded and played festivals, as well as appearing on local television and radio. Eventually, the band signed with the Welsh independent label Ankst.

Gorky's Zygotic Mynci released three albums on Ankst—*Tatay, Bwyd Time, Llanfwrog*—before moving to Mercury Records in 1996. Their last album for Ankst reached No. 1 on the UK independent charts. In 1996 their first American album, *Introducing Gorky's Zygotic Mynci*, was released. A compilation of their early Welsh albums and EPs, the record received positive reviews, but it failed to make significant inroads for the group in America. —*Stephen Thomas Erlewine*

● **Introducing Gorky's Zygotic Mynci** / Aug. 20, 1996 / Polygram ✦✦✦✦
Introducing Gorky's Zygotic Mynci compiles highlights from the Welsh band's first two UK albums, plus their singles and EPs for the Ankst Record label. While it might not be an official album, it is an excellent introduction to Gorky's wild, sunny eclecticism, featuring everything from warped art-pop to homages to the Soft Machine's Kevin Ayers. What stops the music from becoming too precious is the group's surprising facility for pop hooks and their cheerful sense of humor; it might be bizarre music, but it is never alienating. —*Stephen Thomas Erlewine*

Barafundle / Apr. 7, 1997 / Fontana ✦✦✦✦
Like their indie records, Gorky's Zygotic Mynci's major-label debut *Barafundle* sparkles with a lilting, naive, neo-psychedelia and folky reconstituted art-rock. Gorky's do owe quite a lot to the perverse pretensions of early-'70s art-rock, but their approach is entirely different; it is more tuneful and concise, with none of the self-conscious aspirations of classic art-rock, just the willful sense of experimentation. *Barafundle* is the band's best album to date, comprised of equal portions of ridiculously catchy, sing-song melodies and weird, flowery noises. It may occasionally recall the baroqueness of Canterbury art-rock, and it may be a little too precious at times, but *Barafundle* demonstrates that few '90s bands have created a sound as singular and open-minded as Gorky's Zygotic Mynci. —*Stephen Thomas Erlewine*

Graham Gouldman

b. May 10, 1946, Manchester, England
Guitar, Vocals / British Invasion, Pop-Rock
Before forming 10cc with Eric Stewart, Graham Gouldman was a major presence in the British Invasion, writing hits for the Yardbirds, Hollies, Herman's Hermits, and others. "For Your Love," "Bus Stop," "Look Through Any Window," "Heart Full of Soul," and "No Milk Today" are

among his most famous compositions. Gouldman wrote some of the finest tunes of the era, using haunting, shifting minor key melodies as well as similar efforts by the Zombies and Beatles. He also cut a lengthy string of flop singles, as a solo artist and with his group the Mockingbirds, and released a nifty solo album of his own in the late '60s.
—*Richie Unterberger*

● **Graham Gouldman Thing** / 1968 / Edsel ♦♦♦♦
Gouldman issued this solo album in 1968, featuring his own versions of the hits "For Your Love," "Bus Stop," and "No Milk Today" with eight other original tunes. The album blends pensive, acoustic guitar-driven compositions with light orchestral arrangements. It's a pleasant record, but ultimately does not measure up to the monster hit covers of his tunes. He's only an adequate singer, and the slower, more elaborately produced versions of "Bus Stop" and "For Your Love" are not nearly as good as the hard-charging renditions by the Yardbirds and Hollies. A decent curio, though, highlighted by "Pawnbroker" and "Upstairs Downstairs," which would have fit in well on the Hollies' 1966-67 records.
—*Richie Unterberger*

Davey Graham

b. 1940, England
Guitar, Vocals / Folk, British Folk
One of the most eclectic guitarists of the 1960s, Graham's mixture of folk, blues, jazz, Middle Eastern sounds, and Indian ragas was an important catalyst of the British folk scene. Like Sandy Bull and John Fahey—two folk-based guitarists with a similar taste for genre-bending experimentation—Graham could not be said to be a rock musician. But like Bull and Fahey, he shared the eagerness of the '60s psychedelic rockers to stretch out and incorporate unpredictable influences into his music. While he wasn't much of a singer, Graham's taste in material was broad and shrewd, encompassing blues, ragas, Joni Mitchell, Charles Mingus, and the famous instrumental "Anji," which Graham recorded in 1962, way before the more famous versions by Bert Jansch and Simon & Garfunkel. Besides cutting several albums of his own work in the 1960s with sympathetic, low-key rhythm sections, he also recorded with traditional folk singer Shirley Collins and British blues father Alexis Korner. Graham recorded only sporadically after the 1960s, although he performed with the renowned acoustic guitar wizards Stefan Grossman and Duck Baker. —*Richie Unterberger*

The Guitar Player . . . Plus / 1963 / See For Miles ♦♦♦♦
Graham established himself as one of the most innovative players in acoustic music with his 1963 debut, *The Guitar Player*. With this album, Graham became one of the first folk guitarists to fuse traditional virtuosity with cross-currents from contemporary jazz and blues. Accompanied by drummer Bobby Graham (a top British sessionman who played on many British Invasion rock records, including several by the Kinks), Davey invigorates pop and traditional standards, as well as compositions by Sonny Rollins, the Adderleys, and Ray Charles. Neither jazz nor folk, Graham displays eclectic bounce that was quite visionary for its time and remains fresh today; in his subsequent 1960s recordings, he would branch out into Middle Eastern and psychedelic sounds as a natural extension of his experimental bent. As a significant bonus, the 1992 CD reissue of this album includes the three tracks from his rare 1962 EP *3/4 A.D.* One of these is the original version of "Anji," which was reworked by Simon & Garfunkel on one of their early albums; another features British blues-rock godfather Alexis Korner on second guitar.
—*Richie Unterberger*

Midnight Man / 1966 / Decca ♦♦♦♦
Graham went into a somewhat harder-rocking bluesy groove on this record, though a strong jazz feel was always present in the rhythm especially. More than any other Graham LP, this offers proof that the guitarist would have established himself as a major star on the folk circuit in the '60s—if only his singing were better. As a guitarist, he's simply wonderful, combining folk, jazz, and blues styles into an invigorating, idiosyncratic style that can both swing and attain a delicate sadness. As an interpreter, he's relentlessly imaginative, breathing new vigor into overdone R&B standards, or devising fresh folk arrangements for Beatles and Paul Simon tunes. But as a vocalist, he's adequate at best; if he had possessed even the modest expressiveness of a Bert Jansch, the material would be that much more striking. Almost none of these tracks is available on Graham compilations, and this rare LP is definitely worth seeking by those who are familiar with some of his other '60s work. Especially excellent are the jazzy "Hummingbird," and the instrumental cover of Lalo Schifrin's "The Fakir," which blends the rhythmic drive of Charles Mingus with hypnotic ragaesque riffs. —*Richie Unterberger*

Large as Life & Twice as Natural / 1968 / London ♦♦♦♦
With the exception of 1965's *Folk Blues and All Points in Between*, this is Graham's finest non-compilation album. It's also his most fully arranged and rock-influenced effort, with backing by a meaty ensemble featuring Danny Thompson (of Pentangle) on bass and British blues stalwarts Jon Hiseman and Dick Heckstall-Smith (Graham Bond, Colos-

seum) on drums and sax, respectively. Even Graham's singing sounds better than usual. Graham offers some decent white boy blues, but more interesting are his frequent excursions into raga folk-rock of sorts, especially on "Blue Raga" (learned from Ravi Shankar and Ali Akbar Khan). The raga-jazz interpretation of Joni Mitchell's "Both Sides Now," which moves from meditative opening drones into a freewheeling explosion of modal folk-rock, is one of the highlights of Graham's career on record, and one of the best expressions of his ability to make a standard his own. —*Richie Unterberger*

Hat / 1969 / Decca ♦♦♦
There's no such thing as a bad Graham album from the 1960s. While *Hat* isn't necessarily the first one you should dig into, it offers the standard pleasures that you expect from his records: excellent, feverishly imaginative acoustic guitar playing, vibrant jazz-blues arrangements, and covers of the blues, Paul Simon, and Lennon-McCartney. He's just as capable of good-time blues ("I'm Ready") as a folk cover of "Getting Better" from *Sgt. Pepper* as dark, slightly dissonant instrumentals with a modal/Eastern flavor. As is the case with most of his '60s albums, it's very hard to find, especially in the US, where Graham did not have a record deal. —*Richie Unterberger*

Holly Kaleidoscope / 1970 / Decca ♦♦♦
Graham's final Decca LP was co-billed to his wife at the time, Holly Gwyn (credited simply as "Holly"), although she appears only on a few tracks. While it's a characteristic Graham effort, right down to the token Beatles covers (here they're "Blackbird" and "Here, There and Everywhere"), it's somewhat more sparsely arranged than most of his previous records. Given that Graham was never that good a singer, enlisting a female vocalist seemed a sensible enough move. But although Holly is a better singer than Davey, she's nothing special, her presence amounting to neither a plus nor a minus on the whole. It's not one of Graham's more notable albums, but it's respectable, and the guitar work, of course, is nothing less than stellar. —*Richie Unterberger*

Godington Boundary / 1970 / President ♦♦♦
This isn't Graham's most focused or impressive album, but is basically in the same league as most of his early catalog. It's more jazz-oriented than most of his work; he sings rather less than usual, and occasionally goes into lengthy improvisations (as on his cover of "The Work Song"). Graham's wife Holly gets co-billed, as she did on his previous LP *Holly Kaleidoscope*, but actually she contributes to only a few numbers; she's more of a guest artist than a true collaborator. Indian/raga influences come into play once in a while, and on the whole it's somewhat quirkier than his previous string of albums. It would also be the last the public would hear from Graham on record for quite some time, as he found himself without a contract for most of the 1970s. —*Richie Unterberger*

● **Folk, Blues, All Points in Between** / 1985 / See For Miles ♦♦♦♦
Side One includes the entirety of his 1965 album *Folk, Blues And Beyond;* Side Two features seven tracks from three of his late-'60s LPs. The 1965 record was probably his most accomplished, as Graham handled blues, jazz, and Northern African music with aplomb. His other '60s recordings were more erratic, but the highlights gathered here matched his 1965 work, peaking with the original "No Preacher Blues," his folk-jazz cover of Joni Mitchell's "Both Sides Now," and the Indian-influenced "Blue Raga." —*Richie Unterberger*

Grand Funk Railroad

f. 1968, Flint, MI, **db.** 1983
Hard Rock, Arena Rock, Boogie Rock
One of the 1970s' most successful hard rock bands, in spite of critical pans and somewhat reluctant radio airplay (at first), Grand Funk Railroad built a devoted fan base through constant touring; a loud, simple take on the blues-rock power trio sound; and strong working-class appeal. The band was formed by Flint, MI, guitarist/songwriter Mark Farner and drummer Don Brewer, both former members of a local band called Terry Knight and the Pack. They recruited former ? and the Mysterians bassist Mel Schacher in 1968, and Knight retired from performing to become their manager, naming the group after Michigan's well known Grand Trunk Railroad. They performed free at the 1969 Atlanta Pop Festival, and their energetic, if not technically proficient, show led Capitol Records to sign them at once. While radio shied away from Grand Funk Railroad, the group's strong work ethic and commitment to touring produced a series of big-selling albums over the next few years; five of their eight releases from 1969 to 1972 went platinum, and the others all went gold. Meanwhile, Knight promoted the band aggressively, going so far as to rent a Times Square billboard to advertise *Closer to Home*, which turned out to be the band's first multi-platinum album in spite of a backlash from the rock press. However, Grand Funk Railroad fired Knight in March 1972. He promptly sued; the band spent most of the year in a court battle that ended when they bought Knight out.
    Keyboardist Craig Frost joined the group for the *Phoenix* LP at the end of 1972. After that album, the band's name was officially shortened to Grand Funk, and the group finally scored a big hit single (No. 1, in

fact) with the title track of the Todd Rundgren-produced *We're an American Band*. The follow-up, *Shinin' On*, contained another No. 1 hit in a remake of Little Eva's "The Loco-Motion." However, after Grand Funk's next album, *All the Girls in the World Beware!!*, interest in the group began to wane. Reverting to Grand Funk Railroad, they remained together in 1976 solely to work with producer Frank Zappa on *Good Singin', Good Playin'*. Farner left for a solo career, and the remainder of the band released an album as Flint with guitarist Billy Elworthy.

Grand Funk Railroad re-formed in 1981 with Dennis Bellinger on bass and released two albums; only *Grand Funk Lives* managed to scrape the bottom of the charts. The group disbanded again, with Brewer and Frost joining Bob Seger's Silver Bullet Band and Farner embarking on a new career as a contemporary Christian artist; his "Isn't It Amazing" was a No. 2 gospel hit in 1988. *—Steve Huey*

● **Capitol Collectors Series** / Feb. 26, 1991 / Capitol ✦✦✦✦
This is the place to start. All of Grand Funk's hits are here: the classic "We're an American Band," Todd Rundgren's perverse production of "Loco-Motion," their thudding remake of the Animals' "Inside Looking Out," the epic "Closer to Home/I'm Your Captain," "Heartbreaker," and other big favorites. *—Rick Clark*

More of the Best / 1991 / Rhino ✦✦✦✦
This set does a decent job of picking key tracks not found on the *Capitol Collectors Series* album. Included is the fuzz-bass-heavy "Paranoid" and boogie numbers like "Are You Ready?" and "Got This Thing on the Move." Fans may wish for a more incisive selection from their first three albums. *—Rick Clark*

Grandmaster Flash (Joseph Saddler)

f. Jan. 1, 1958, Bronx, NY
Hip Hop, Club/Dance, Electro-Funk, Electric Funk, Old School Rap
Grandmaster Flash (born Joseph Saddler, January 1, 1958) and the Furious Five (Cowboy, Keith Wiggins; Melle Mel, Melvin Glover; Kidd Creole, Danny Glover; Mr. Ness, Eddie Morris; and Rahiem, Guy Williams) were the most important group in the early days of rap music and, in fact, developed certain crucial aspects of the genre. Saddler was the DJ, providing the musical bed by manipulating records on turntables, scratching them, repeating particular instrumental sections, and thus creating new music out of collages of existing recordings. The most important such work was the single "The Adventures of Grandmaster Flash on the Wheels of Steel," released in 1981.

Most of the group's records, however, featured the interlocking raps of the five rappers, and the most significant of these was "The Message" (1982), led primarily by Melle Mel, which turned away from the party subjects of many current rap records to focus on urban social issues.

The group had split by 1984, with Melle Mel going off on his own. It later re-formed in 1987.

Grandmaster Flash resurfaced in the public consciousness in late 1993, thanks to interviews done in *Rolling Stone* and *The Source* and Rhino reissues featuring such legendary tracks as "White Lines" and "Grandmaster Flash on the Wheels of Steel." Grandmaster Flash and Melle Mel attempted a comeback in 1997 with the album *Right Now*, which failed to gain much attention upon its spring release. *—William Ruhlmann*

The Message / 1982 / Sugar Hill ✦✦✦✦
Grandmaster Flash & the Furious Five merged the Afrocentric consciousness expressed by such early rappers as Gil Scott-Heron and the Last Poets with B-boy production to create "The Message," an all-time rap anthem. It was the focal point of this LP, which included "It's Nasty" and "Scorpio," two other strong cuts that might have been winners on their own. Unfortunately, rather than a starting point, this album proved to be their peak. *—Ron Wynn*

The Source / 1986 / Elektra ✦✦✦
Grandmaster Flash's follow-up to *The Message* was his first minus the Furious Five. Things weren't the same from a compositional or performance standpoint, as his raps seemed weaker and his rhymes almost devoid of crispness, humor, or insight. Only "Ms. Thang" and "Street Scene" offered any hint of the incisiveness or vision depicted in "The Message." *—Ron Wynn*

Da Bop Boom Bang / 1987 / Elektra ✦✦
The fire was gone and the imagination and flair diminished on this 1987 album. Grandmaster Flash sounded too tired on such cuts as "Big Black Caddy," "Get Yours" and "U Know What Time It Is" to recapture the spirit and bristling intensity that made "The Message" an anthem. He was sadly more effective doing nonsense like "Them Jeans." *—Ron Wynn*

On the Strength / 1988 / Elektra ✦
Grandmaster Flash and the Furious Five tried to regroup on this 1988 release, but old school hip-hop had been lapped by the charge of the new school. There was little interest in or response to such cuts as "Tear

the Roof Off" and "Boy Is Dope," while "Fly Girl" and "Magic Carpet Ride" sounded dated and weary. *—Ron Wynn*

★ **Message from Beat Street: the Best of Grandmaster Flash** / Apr. 19, 1994 / Rhino ✦✦✦✦✦
Grandmaster Flash was one of the most important, groundbreaking rap artists of the early '80s, and all of his most important records—with and without Melle Mel and the Furious Five—are collected on this essential 11-track disc, which includes the classic tracks "The Message" and "White Lines (Don't Don't Do It)." *—Stephen Thomas Erlewine*

Adventures Of: More of the Best / Jul. 1996 / Rhino ✦✦✦✦
Although many of Grandmaster Flash's best, biggest, and most groundbreaking work was compiled on *Message from Beat Street: The Best of*, *The Adventures of Grandmaster Flash: More of the Best* is necessary for any comprehensive rap collection. The rest of Grandmaster Flash's most important singles, many of which have not appeared on compact disc before, are corralled onto this single disc. On the whole, the album concentrates on the group's latter-day efforts for Elektra Records, but the cream of the album is the handful of singles for Sugarhill, including the pioneering "The Adventures of Grandmaster Flash on the Wheels of Steel," which presents the group at its freshest and most innovative. Some of the Elektra recordings are a little rote and by-the-book, but the Sugarhill songs help make this an essential purchase. *—Stephen Thomas Erlewine*

Grant Lee Buffalo

f. 1992, Los Angeles, CA
Alternative Pop-Rock, Adult Alternative Pop-Rock, Americana
Under the leadership of guitarist/songwriter Grant Lee Phillips, Grant Lee Buffalo became a major buzz band in 1993 with their debut album, *Fuzzy*. The band's searching, often political, folk-rock has shades of everyone from David Bowie and John Lennon to R.E.M. and Bob Mould. Phillips' songwriting received a large amount of critical praise, as did their electrifying live performances. The band captured a larger following in Europe than their native America, earning near-universal critical praise upon the release of *Fuzzy*. During 1993 the band toured constantly, building a solid cult following all over the world. The next year they delivered their second record, *Mighty Joe Moon*. In 1996 they released *Copperopolis*. *—Stephen Thomas Erlewine*

● **Fuzzy** / Feb. 23, 1993 / Slash ✦✦✦✦
While Grant Lee Phillips' songwriting is quite impressive, what makes Grant Lee Buffalo's debut album, *Fuzzy*, memorable is the band's muscular folk-rock. Equally adept at propulsive rock 'n' roll and haunting ballads, the band turns Phillips' best songs into rough gems, as "Jupiter and Teardrop" and "Fuzzy" prove. *—Stephen Thomas Erlewine*

Mighty Joe Moon / Sep. 20, 1994 / Slash/Reprise ✦✦✦✦
With their second album, Grant Lee Buffalo strips back their sound to its bare essentials, which accentuates Grant Lee Phillips' rural myths. Not only does the approach make songs like "Lone Star Song" rock viciously, but it makes the bittersweet beauty of ballads like the gorgeous "Mockingbirds" all the more poignant. *—Stephen Thomas Erlewine*

Copperopolis / Jun. 1996 / Slash/Reprise ✦✦✦
With their third album, *Copperopolis*, Grant Lee Buffalo headed farther into the dense Americana fusions that permeated their first two albums. Although there are hints of Bowie-esque art rock on the fringes of *Copperopolis*, most of the album is informed by rootsy amaglams of Dylan, R.E.M., Pearl Jam, and the Pixies. It's political, anthemic rock that doesn't make any literal sense. Every once in awhile, Grant Lee Phillips pulls out an evocative metaphor or a provocative melody, but too frequently the band's concepts are more admirable than their music. And that is more true of *Copperopolis* than any of their other albums, simply because their fusion is becoming more cerebral and less natural as time passes. *—Stephen Thomas Erlewine*

Grapes of Wrath

f. 1983, Kelowna, British Columbia, Canada, **db.** 1992
Alternative Pop-Rock, Jangle-Pop
Grapes of Wrath was a jangly alternative folk-pop quartet formed in Kelowna, British Columbia, in 1983 by brothers Chris Hooper (drums) and Tom Hooper (bass) along with vocalist/guitarist Kevin Kane and keyboardist Vincent Jones. In 1984 they signed to Nettwerk Records and relocated to Vancouver, where they recorded a four-song self-titled EP that earned the band some initial local exposure. In 1985 the full-length *September Bowl of Green* gave them national recognition and critical acclaim. Ready to make a stab at the US, they enlisted the help of Tom Cochrane (ex-Red Rider) for production of the follow-up *Tree House*. Though it failed to break big, it did yield a hit single in Canada with "Peace of Mind." Subsequent singles and two more albums, *Now and Again* (1989) and *These Days* (1991), did well in their homeland but earned few sales elsewhere. In 1992 Kane left the band, and the remain-

ing members went on to become Ginger. Ginger released *Far Out* on Nettwerk in 1994 (released in the US in 1995) and followed with *Suddenly I Came to My Senses* in late 1996. Kevin Kane released a solo album, *Neighborhood Watch* in 1996 for On/Off Records in Canada. —*Chris Woodstra*

September Bowl of Green / 1986 / Capitol ✦✦✦
Their first LP shows a band unsure whether to follow R.E.M.'s folky lead or post-punk's dreamy abstraction. Fortunately, the jangly guitars and harmonies win out for a pleasing, though unspectacular, debut. Highlights include the single "Misunderstanding," as well as "Love Comes Around" and "A Dream (About You)." The CD version adds two previously unreleased tracks. —*Chris Woodstra*

Treehouse / 1987 / Capitol ✦✦✦✦
Early comparisons to R.E.M. are clearly justified on *Treehouse*, a jangly folk-pop masterpiece. On this, their second album, the band seem considerably more confident and focused. Crisp and bright production, courtesy of Tom Cochrane (ex-Red Rider), compliment the glorious harmonies and melancholy, introverted songs perfectly. A sadly overlooked classic of '80s guitar rock. —*Chris Woodstra*

● **Now and Again** / Sep. 1989 / Capitol ✦✦✦✦
Producer Anton Fier, leader/drummer of the Golden Palominos, imbues this Vancouver quartet's third full-length album with a lush early-'70s sound, at times approaching an Elton John/*Tumbleweed Connection* - style blend of orchestration and occasional pedal-steel augmentation (by Sneaky Pete Kleinow). Chuck Leavell plays keys on this outing as well. Melodically, the band tends to sound samey, partly attributable to the band's rather tight singing tonalities. Highlights include the reflective "All the Things I Wasn't." —*Rick Clark*

These Days / Aug. 27, 1991 / Capitol ✦✦✦
John Leckie (the Posies, Let's Active) produces this follow-up to *Now and Again* by giving the band a slightly heavier, more organic band-like sound. In spite of an improved performance edginess, the band still lacks the proper dynamics for their melodies to stand out in relief. Leckie's production, while loaded with nice touches, fails to help the band in overcoming their limitations. —*Rick Clark*

Seems Like Fate 1984-1992 / 1994 / Nettwerk/EMI ✦✦✦
Seems Like Fate is a 20-track collection that attempts to chronicle the band's career. Unfortunately the disc's emphasis on non-LP material, unnecessary remixes over the original single versions, and nonchronological sequencing creates confusion, ultimately doing a disservice to one of Canada's best bands of the late '80s. As an introduction, it fails miserably, though as a rarities compilation, fans will probably find it an essential addition to their collection. —*Chris Woodstra*

The Grass Roots

f. 1964, Los Angeles, CA, db. 1980
Pop-Rock
The Grass Roots had a series of major hits—most notably "Let's Live for Today," "Midnight Confessions," "Temptation Eyes," and "Two Divided by Love"—that help define the essence of the era's best AM radio. Although the group's members weren't even close to being recognizable, and their in-house songwriting was next to irrelevant, the Grass Roots managed to chart 14 Top 40 hits, including seven gold singles and one platinum single, and two hits collections that effortlessly went gold. The group's history is also fairly complicated, because there were at least three different groups involved in the making of the songs identified as being by "the Grass Roots."

The Grass Roots was originated by the writer/producer team of P.F. Sloan and Steve Barri as a pseudonym under which they would release a body of Byrds/Beau Brummels-style folk-rock. Sloan and Barri were contracted songwriters for Trousdale Music, the publishing arm of Dunhill Records, which wanted to cash in on the folk-rock boom of 1965. Dunhill asked Sloan and Barri to come up with this material, and a group alias under which they would release it. The resulting "Grass Roots" debut song, "Where Were You When I Needed You," sung by Sloan, was sent to a Los Angeles radio station, which began playing it. The problem was, there was no "Grass Roots." The next step was to recruit a band that could become the Grass Roots. Sloan found a San Francisco group called the Bedouins that seemed promising on the basis of their lead singer, Bill Fulton. Fulton recorded a new vocal over the backing tracks laid down for the P.F. Sloan version of the song. The Bedouins were, at first, content to put their future in the hands of Sloan and Barri as producers, despite the fact that the group was more blues-oriented than folk-rock. However, the rest of the group was offended when Fulton was told to record their debut single, a cover of Bob Dylan's "The Ballad of a Thin Man," backed by studio musicians. When that single, released in October 1965, became only a modest hit for the Bedouins—except for their drummer, Joel Larson—departed for San Francisco, to re-form as the Unquenchable Thirst. Sloan and Barri continued to record. "Where Were You When I Needed You" was released in

mid-1966 and peaked at No. 28, but the album of the same name never charted.

Amid the machinations behind *Where Were You When I Needed You*, no "real" Grass Roots band existed in 1966. A possible solution came along when a Los Angeles band called the 13th Floor submitted a demo tape to Dunhill. This group, consisting of Warren Entner (vocals, guitar, keyboards), Creed Bratton (lead guitar), Rob Grill (vocals, bass), and Rick Coonce (drums), was offered the choice of recording under their own name, or taking over the name the Grass Roots, putting themselves in the hands of Sloan and Barri, and taking advantage of the Grass Roots' track record. They chose the latter, with Rob Grill as primary lead vocalist. The first track cut by the new Grass Roots in the spring of 1967 was "Let's Live for Today," a new version of a song that had been an Italian hit, in a lighter, more uptempo version, for a band called the Rokes. "Let's Live for Today" was an achingly beautiful, dramatic, and serious single that shot into the Top Ten upon its release in the summer of 1967. An accompanying album, *Let's Live for Today*, reached only No. 75. The group began spreading its wings in the studio with their next album, *Feelings*, recorded late in 1967, which emphasized the band's material over Sloan and Barri's. This was intended as their own statement of who they were, but it lacked the commercial appeal of anything on *Let's Live for Today*, sold poorly, and never yielded any hit singles. Eleven months went by before the group had another chart entry, and during that period, Sloan and Barri's partnership broke up, with Sloan departing for New York and an attempt at a performing career of his own. The band considered splitting up as all of this was happening. The Grass Roots' return to the charts (with Barri producing), however, was a triumphant one; in the late fall of 1968, "Midnight Confessions" reached No. 5 on the charts and earned a gold record. "Midnight Confessions" showed the strong influence of Motown, and the R&B flavor of the song stuck with Barri and the band.

In April 1969 Creed Bratton left the band, to be replaced by Denny Provisor on keyboards and Terry Furlong on lead guitar. Now a quintet, the Grass Roots went on cutting records without breaking stride, enjoying a string of Top 40 hits that ran into the early '70s, peaking with "Temptation Eyes" at No. 15 in the summer of 1971. Coonce and Provisor left at the end of 1971, to be replaced by Reed Kailing on lead guitar, Virgil Webber on keyboards, and Joel Larson—of the original Bedouins/Grass Roots outfit—on drums. They arrived just in time to take advantage of the No. 16 success of "Two Divided by Love," which was the last of the Grass Roots' big hits. The Grass Roots soldiered on for a few more years, reaching the Top 40 a couple of times in 1972, but their commercial success slowly slipped away during 1973. They kept working for a few more years, but called it quits in 1975. Rob Grill remained in the music business on the organizing side, and by 1980 was persuaded by his friend John McVie to cut a solo album, *Uprooted*, which featured contributions by Mick Fleetwood and Lindsay Buckingham. By 1982, amid the burgeoning oldies concert circuit and the respect beginning to be accorded the Grass Roots, Grill formed a new Grass Roots—sometimes billed as Rob Grill and the Grass Roots—and began performing as many as 100 shows a year. Their presence on various oldies package tours has seen to it that the Grass Roots name remains visible in the '90s. —*Bruce Eder*

Where Were You When I Needed You? / 1966 / Varese Sarabande ✦✦✦✦
Before the Grass Roots reached the peak of their pop-rock popularity, they were a much more folk-rock-oriented outfit. Indeed, this debut album is a matter of much confusion; apparently the original Grass Roots were pretty much a front for the songwriting team of P.F. Sloan and Steve Barri, who ended up performing on much of the album themselves. In any case, this is decent, though not top-of-the-line, early folk-rock, falling about halfway between the Byrds and more pop-oriented peers like the Turtles and the Mamas and the Papas. Highlights include the hit track and other Sloan-Barri originals like "Lollipop Train," "Look Out Girl," "This Is What I Was Made For," and "You Baby," which was a hit for the Turtles. The CD reissue adds six bonus tracks from rare singles, the best of which is the uncharacteristically tough "Tip of My Tongue" (not the obscure Lennon-McCartney composition). —*Richie Unterberger*

● **Anthology: 1965-1975** / Jul. 2, 1991 / Rhino ✦✦✦✦
It may be expensive, and two CDs of their work may seem like overkill, but this double-disc set is the one to get. Not only does it contain every hit and each single, and every B-side, from 1965's "Where Were You When I Needed You" through 1975's glorious "Mamacita," but the sound is extraordinary, far better than on any of the other hits compilations, and provides several revelations about the quality of their work. Highlights, in addition to the expected hits "Let's Live for Today," "Midnight Confessions," "Two Divided by Love" etc., include tracks like "Is It Any Wonder," with a chorus as radiant as anything the Mamas and the Papas ever recorded, and the seldom heard, vibrant "Mamacita." If you could never imagine listening to 120 minutes of Grass Roots material (this

reviewer couldn't, either), this set will make you feel differently. —*Bruce Eder*

All Time Greatest Hits / Jul. 1996 / MCA ✦✦✦✦
All Time Greatest Hits collects the Grass Roots' 16 biggest hits—including "Let's Live for Today," "Midnight Confessions," "Temptation Eyes," "Sooner or Later," and "Two Divided By Love"—on a single-disc. For casual fans who don't want to invest in Rhino's double disc *Anthology*, *All Time Greatest Hits* is a necessary item. —*Stephen Thomas Erlewine*

The Grateful Dead

f. 1965, San Francisco, CA, db. 1995
Rock 'n' Roll, Country-Rock, Psychedelic, Folk-Rock
The Grateful Dead are the longest-lived of the San Francisco "acid rock" groups of the '60s. In the '90s, after more than 25 years in action, the Dead were still playing to enough satisfied customers on the road (most of them "Deadheads") to make them one of the top-grossing concert acts in the music business.

The group was formed in 1965 by bluegrass enthusiast Jerry Garcia (b. Aug. 1, 1942–d. Aug. 9, 1995) on guitar and vocals, Ron "Pigpen" McKernan (b. Sept. 8, 1945–d. Mar. 8, 1973) on vocals and organ, Bob Weir (b. Oct. 16, 1947) on guitar and vocals, classical music student Phil Lesh (b. Mar. 15, 1945) on bass and vocals, and Bill Kreutzmann (b. Apr. 7, 1946) on drums. From the beginning, they brought together a variety of influences, from Garcia's country background to Pigpen's feeling for blues (his father was an R&B radio DJ) and Lesh's education in contemporary "serious" music. Add to that the experimentation encouraged at some of the group's first performances at novelist Ken Kesey's "acid test" parties—multimedia events intended to replicate (or accompany) the experience of taking the then-legal drug LSD—and you had a musical mixture of styles often played with extended improvisational sections that could go off in nearly any direction.

The band signed to Warner Brothers in 1967, experiencing some difficulties early on with the restrictions of standard recording practices and the company's interest in producing a conventionally commercial product. As a result, the group's first few albums were somewhat tentative but showed promise for the future, especially with the key additions of Mickey Hart as a second drummer in 1967 and Garcia's old friend Robert Hunter as the band's lyricist. The Dead finally hit their stride with the release of *Live/Dead*, a double album, in 1969. (They were always more comfortable on stage than in the studio.) Two studio albums in 1970, *Workingman's Dead* and *American Beauty*, found them exploring folk-rock and more tightly constructed song forms and, along with extensive touring, won them a much larger audience.

In the second half of the '70s, the Dead recorded a series of commercially-oriented albums for Arista, then concentrated on road work for the better part of the '80s. *In the Dark*, released in 1987, was their first studio album in seven years. It sold a million copies and produced the band's first Top Ten hit in "Touch of Grey." The Dead continued to tour, notably doing shows with Bob Dylan, and at the start of the '90s, they began to release vintage material on their own Grateful Dead Merchandising label. Garcia died of heart failure on August 9, 1995. A few months after his death, the surviving members of the Grateful Dead disbanded. —*William Ruhlmann*

The Grateful Dead / Mar. 17, 1967 / Warner Brothers ✦✦
The Grateful Dead's debut album finds them uncomfortable in the studio, rushing tempos and otherwise failing to reproduce the feel of their live shows. Nevertheless, the group covers much of its then-current repertoire, including such long-term favorites as "Beat It On Down the Line," "Cold Rain and Snow," and "New, New Minglewood Blues." —*William Ruhlmann*

Anthem of the Sun / Jul. 18, 1968 / Warner Brothers ✦✦✦
The Grateful Dead spent six months recording their second album in studios and at concerts. The result came closer to an accurate portrait of them, highlighted by the four-part, 12-minute "That's It for the Other One." Still, the extensive mixing and editing made the sound dense and uninviting, especially to those not yet converted to the group's approach. —*William Ruhlmann*

Aoxomoxoa / Jun. 20, 1969 / Warner Brothers ✦✦✦
The addition of poet Robert Hunter as lyricist marked the beginning of a consistent set of imagery in the Dead's words to match their musical interplay, especially on songs like "St. Stephen" and "China Cat Sunflower." But the aural experiments were still making for trying listening as the Dead continued to search for a way to capture their concert feel on disc. —*William Ruhlmann*

Live/Dead / Nov. 10, 1969 / Warner Brothers ✦✦✦✦
Long, trancelike songs with allusive lyrics (such as the classic "Dark Star") and R&B workouts featuring Pigpen's bluesy voice characterize this album, which is the basic document in the early Dead catalog—it's what most fans would like them to sound like every night. —*William Ruhlmann*

☆ **Workingman's Dead** / May 1970 / Warner Brothers ✦✦✦✦✦
A folk-rock, tightly arranged Dead, singing (in harmony!) some of their best songs, from "Uncle John's Band" to "Casey Jones." —*William Ruhlmann*

★ **American Beauty** / Nov. 1970 / Warner Brothers ✦✦✦✦✦
Workingman's Dead, part two—more of the songs that have served as the band's basic repertoire ever since these albums were released. Includes "Box of Rain," "Friend of the Devil," "Sugar Magnolia," "Ripple," and, of course, "Truckin'." —*William Ruhlmann*

Grateful Dead / Oct. 1971 / Warner Brothers ✦✦✦
The Dead's second double live album (now on a single CD) introduces a couple of excellent Garcia/Hunter compositions, "Bertha" and "Wharf Rat," and allows Bob Weir to indulge his taste for what Deadheads would come to call "cowboy songs": Merle Haggard's "Mama Tried" and Kris Kristofferson's "Me & Bobby McGee." The album became the Dead's first gold record, probably on the momentum of *Workingman's Dead* and *American Beauty*. It also failed to match *Live/Dead* as a concert album, so that, coming off the band's recent peaks, it seemed less effective than it was. Now, it seems like one of the Dead's better, more coherent records. (Not to be confused with *The Grateful Dead*, the band's debut album. They resorted to *Grateful Dead* as a title when Warner wouldn't let them call the album *Skull Fuck*.) —*William Ruhlmann*

Europe '72 / Nov. 1972 / Warner Brothers ✦✦✦✦
Released as a three-record set, *Europe '72* is now a double CD. But it's still a long album, notable for introducing more Garcia-Hunter songs, especially "Brown-Eyed Woman," and for incorporating onto one album the variety of musical styles to be heard at a Dead concert, as well as the sheer duration necessary to appreciate the experience. Which means that, while this may not be the place a new fan wants to start, it's a Deadhead favorite. —*William Ruhlmann*

History of the Grateful Dead, Vol. 1 (Bear's Choice) / Jul. 13, 1973 / Warner Brothers ✦✦✦
This is a contractual obligation album, a record given to Warner Brothers Records to complete the Dead's commitment to the label. It was recorded in February 1970 and is something of a tribute to the late keyboardist/vocalist Ron "Pigpen" McKernan, who is heard frequently. Pigpen highlights an 18-minute version of Howlin' Wolf's "Smokestack Lightnin'." But this is a nonessential Dead album. "Bear" is the band's friend/soundman/drug manufacturer Owsley Stanley. The album is misnamed; it does not provide a "history," and there was never any Volume 2. —*William Ruhlmann*

Wake of the Flood / Nov. 15, 1973 / Grateful Dead ✦✦✦✦
The Grateful Dead's first studio album in three years was also their first for their own record label. It's a strong collection, featuring such Garcia-Hunter songs as "Mississippi Half-Step Uptown Toodleoo," "Row Jimmy," and "Stella Blue," songs that would become concert staples, as well as Bob Weir's "Weather Report Suite." —*William Ruhlmann*

Skeletons from the Closet: The Best of The Grateful Dead / 1974 / Warner Brothers ✦✦✦
This is an 11-song compilation, five of whose songs come from *Workingman's Dead* or *American Beauty*. It presents a sampling of the Dead's 1967-1972 period, focusing on their more accessible material. In that sense, it is recommended to the uninitiated who want to get a feel for the group; not surprisingly, it is a perennial seller, turning up week after week on *Billboard* magazine's Top Pop Catalog chart. The initiated, however, despise it. In a survey of Deadheads conducted by *DeadBase*, it was rated above only *Dylan and the Dead* as the worst Grateful Dead album. —*William Ruhlmann*

Grateful Dead from the Mars Hotel / Jun. 27, 1974 / Grateful Dead ✦✦✦
The Grateful Dead's second independent album was an uneven one, containing favorites like "Scarlet Begonias," "U.S. Blues," and "China Doll," but also a fair amount of filler. —*William Ruhlmann*

Blues for Allah / Sep. 1, 1975 / Grateful Dead ✦✦✦✦
Opening with the suite that has become a concert favorite, "Help on the Way"/"Slip Knot!"/"Franklin's Tower," and containing the anthemic "The Music Never Stopped," *Blues for Allah* is another Grateful Dead album containing a few band classics and a lot of filler. Note, however, that some fans seem to value the filler. In its survey of Deadheads, *DeadBase* found *Blues for Allah* to be the band's most popular studio album after *Workingman's Dead* and *American Beauty*. —*William Ruhlmann*

Steal Your Face / Jun. 26, 1976 / Grateful Dead ✦✦
A double live album recorded in October 1974 just before the start of a hiatus in performing by the Dead and not released until 20 months later, to coincide with the feature film *The Grateful Dead Movie*, shot at the same shows. It is universally hated by Deadheads, and why would anyone else want to listen to it? Primary evidence that the Dead needed to take a break from touring in 1974. —*William Ruhlmann*

● What a Long Strange Trip It's Been / 1977 / Warner Brothers ✦✦✦✦
This is a two-disc compilation of the Grateful Dead covering its tenure at
Warner Brothers Records, 1967-1972, and as such the most extensive
sampler of their work in existence. Well-chosen, it contains many of
their best songs from the period and is notable for giving album release
to the studio-recorded single version of "Dark Star," the Dead's most
requested song. Relative newcomers to the band (those who bought
Skeletons from the Closet and liked it) can get a stronger dose here, and
then perhaps go on to the individual albums. Of course, Deadheads hate
this record. — *William Ruhlmann*

Terrapin Station / Jul. 27, 1977 / Arista ✦✦✦
The best of the early Arista albums, containing the extended "Terrapin
Station" suite. — *William Ruhlmann*

Shakedown Street / Nov. 15, 1978 / Arista ✦✦
Using Little Feat leader Lowell George as producer should have been a
great idea, but somehow it didn't work out. The Dead have salvaged
"Fire on the Mountain" and "I Need a Miracle" for live work from this
collection, but it's one of their least satisfactory studio ventures. — *William Ruhlmann*

Go to Heaven / Apr. 28, 1980 / Arista ✦
Another misstep. Whatever the Dead were trying to accomplish in the
studio, whether it was to expand their following into the mainstream or
change their style, they failed here. Deadheads rank this as the group's
worst-ever studio album, and it's hard to argue with them. The Dead
stayed out of the studio for seven years after this. — *William Ruhlmann*

Reckoning / Apr. 1, 1981 / Arista ✦✦✦
Having given up on studio work after the disaster of *Go to Heaven*, the
Dead recorded a series of concerts in New York and San Francisco in
October 1980 for two live albums. This is the first, a set of acoustic mate-
rial that will remind many listeners of the rustic feel of the classic *Work-
ingman's Dead* and *American Beauty* albums, although much of it con-
sists of traditional and bluegrass material favored by Jerry Garcia. The
original two-LP set was fit onto one CD in 1987 by eliminating the
Dead's cover of Elizabeth Cotten's "Oh Babe It Ain't No Lie.") — *William
Ruhlmann*

Dead Set / Aug. 1981 / Arista ✦✦✦
The second of the Dead's two live albums recorded at shows in October
1980, this presents an electric set featuring some material previously
heard on Jerry Garcia solo albums and some of the group's less successful '70s material. As such, it is far from the Dead's best live album, but it
is representative of their work at the time. — *William Ruhlmann*

In the Dark / Jul. 6, 1987 / Arista ✦✦✦✦
The comeback, with "Touch of Grey," "West L.A. Fadeaway," and "Black
Muddy River." For anyone who wondered how these old hippies could
have such a following 20 years after the hippies disappeared, here's the
answer. — *William Ruhlmann*

Built to Last / Oct. 31, 1989 / Arista ✦✦
Supposedly, the Dead had broken their studio jinx with *In the Dark* and
finally learned how to make good albums without an audience in front
of them. So why was this followup such a letdown? Perhaps because
they hadn't taken seven years to write and perfect new material as they
had with the previous album. The dominant songwriter here was keyboard player Brent Mydland (who died the following year), while the
crucial songwriting team of Garcia and Hunter contributed only minor
efforts. Chastened, the Dead once again retreated from studio work.
— *William Ruhlmann*

Without a Net / Sep. 1990 / Arista ✦✦✦
A double-CD live album notable for featuring performances by jazz saxophonist Branford Marsalis and the Dead's version of Traffic's "Dear Mr.
Fantasy," a concert favorite. Unintentionally, the album serves as the epitaph to keyboard player Brent Mydland, who died shortly after its completion, bringing about another change in the band's direction. — *William Ruhlmann*

One from the Vault / Apr. 15, 1991 / Grateful Dead ✦✦✦
With this album, issued on the group's own merchandising label, the
Grateful Dead began to address the needs of an audience that had long
since taken to making their own tapes of every Dead performance. Such
an audience, of course, would be interested in record releases containing
vintage live shows, and the Dead began by issuing this 16-year-old concert, which occurred shortly after they completed their 1975 album
Blues for Allah and while they were nominally retired from live work. It
contains all the material featured on that album, plus such recent Dead
songs as "U.S. Blues" and such favorites as "The Other One." It made for
a modest beginning to the Dead's archival investigations, and only
whetted fans' appetites for what might follow. — *William Ruhlmann*

Infrared Roses / Nov. 1, 1991 / Grateful Dead ✦✦
Each Grateful Dead concert includes a long instrumental section, part of
which is devoted to a drum solo and part to group improvisation, the
parts dubbed "Drums" and "Space" by Deadheads. This two-disc set con-

sists of excerpts from such performances, as electronically treated by
Dead soundman Bob Bralove. It is one of the Dead's more esoteric
releases and not to be confused with a regular, song-filled album. For
fans and aficionados of experimental music only. — *William Ruhlmann*

Two from the Vault / 1992 / Grateful Dead ✦✦✦
Two discs' worth of the Dead in all their psychedelic glory, this second
volume of live material from the archives stems from two shows in
August 1968, when their improvisational headiness balanced out with
Pigpen bringing the proceedings solidly back down to earth. For those
who may have wondered what *Anthem of the Sun* might have sounded
like minus the studio collage mix—here's the answer. — *Steve Aldrich*

Dick's Picks, Vol. 1 / Dec. 1993 / Grateful Dead ✦✦✦
This recording of a Grateful Dead concert performed in Tampa, FL, on
December 19, 1973, inaugurates a new series of archival releases that
differs from the band's already established *From the Vaults* series in
that it is to feature somewhat lower fidelity, "what you hear is what you
get" tapes as the liner notes put it, subject to editing problems, incompleteness, etc. Perhaps to make up for that, this double-CD album was
not offered to retail, but distributed only through mail order, and it was
sold at a discount price. For all that, this is a good, if laidback, Dead set,
led off by a 14-minute version of "Here Comes Sunshine." That song
comes from *Wake of the Flood*, which was the band's current album
release at the time, and much of that LP's other material turns up, notably a complete, 16-minute "Weather Report Suite," along with favorites
like "Truckin" and "Playing in the Band," the latter at a running time of
21 minutes. As promised, the recording quality is noticeably unen-
hanced, but Dead Heads won't mind, and casual fans won't bother.
— *William Ruhlmann*

Dick's Picks, Vol. 2 / 1995 / Grateful Dead ✦✦✦
The second of the Grateful Dead's low-fidelity archival series of live concerts on CD finds the group in Columbus, OH, on Halloween 1971. This
was a relatively low-key time for the band, which had been reduced to a
quintet by the temporary departure of second drummer Mickey Hart
and in which original keyboard player/vocalist Ron "Pigpen" McKernan
had been replaced by Keith Godchaux. They open with a 23-minute version of "Dark Star," segue into "Sugar Magnolia" and "St. Stephen," and
conclude with a medley of "Not Fade Away" and "Going down the Road
Feeling Bad," filling one 58-minute disc. The performance is representative of the group and the period, not perhaps as impressive as *The
Grateful Dead* album, a live record released the month this concert
occurred. For non-Deadheads, all this will seem redundant; for Deadheads, it's another show to add to the collection. — *William Ruhlmann*

Hundred Year Hall / Sep. 26, 1995 / Grateful Dead ✦✦✦
Hundred Year Hall was the archival release of an abridged Frankfurt,
Germany, show from the Grateful Dead's famed *Europe '72* tour. The set
represents an interesting transitional point in the band's history. The
1972 Dead was a seven-member outfit that still contained Ron "Pigpen"
McKernan, though his replacement, Keith Godchaux, had already
joined, along with his wife, Donna Jean. The group had only one drummer, Bill Kreutzmann, during this stage, so the extended improvisations
came mostly from the team of Jerry Garcia, Bob Weir, and Phil Lesh. But
if the band was in transition, it was also still riding the performing and
composing high of the early '70s, and both the recent original songs
(including standards like "Truckin"') and the jams were frequently
inspired. An epic medley of "Turn On Your Lovelight" and "Going down
the Road Feelin' Bad," two favorite covers, was a directed, energetic performance with a minimum of noodling. — *William Ruhlmann*

Dick's Picks, Vol. 3 / Nov. 7, 1995 / Grateful Dead ✦✦✦
The third volume of the Grateful Dead's mail-order-only series of unen-
hanced live recordings takes us to Pembroke Pines, FL, on May 22, 1977,
for a two-CD, two-hour-and-20-minute set focusing on material from
the group's most recent album, *Blues for Allah*, and its upcoming one,
Terrapin Station. Typical of the Dead's archival releases, this one contains extended performances (average length of the 16 tracks: 8 3/4 minutes) that normally never would be released on disc, performances that
constitute the essence of the Dead for their fans. A good example is the
nearly 16-minute version of "Sugaree," on which Jerry Garcia turns in
the kind of solo work that defines him as a guitarist—unhurried, lovely
note series that seem directionless and yet, cumulatively, produce the
indefinable transportive effect of the Grateful Dead at its best. The
whole set finds Garcia in top form, and since this album was released
only three months after his death, it made a fitting epitaph, even if there
doubtless was more to come. — *William Ruhlmann*

☆ Dick's Picks, Vol. 4 / Mar. 1, 1996 / Grateful Dead ✦✦✦✦✦
Though this is the third Grateful Dead album to be released since the
death of bandleader Jerry Garcia and the group's subsequent decision to
disband, it is the first one that wasn't already in the pipeline. Its release
offers evidence that the Dead organization, which had begun releasing
selected recordings of live shows as a courtesy to fans while raking in
most of its revenues through roadwork, has changed its priorities. *Dick's
Picks, Volume Four* isn't just another Grateful Dead concert recording,

it's *the* recording: February 13-14, 1970, the Dead's debut at the Fillmore East, and a show consistently ranked by Deadheads as among the five best live tapes ever. This stand, some of which was released in 1973 on the *History of the Grateful Dead, Vol. 1 (Bear's Choice)* (there is no overlap with this album) finds the Dead gearing up to record *Workingman's Dead*, and already songs like "Casey Jones" and "Dire Wolf" have crept into the set. But there is so much more: half-hour versions of "That's It for the Other One," "Turn On Your Lovelight" (a showcase for Pigpen), and, in a near-definitive performance, the Dead's signature song, "Dark Star." Much of the then recently released *Live/Dead* material is heard, not to mention a rare performance of "Mason's Children." But it isn't just the set list that makes this a legendary show, it's the playing—amazing interaction among the players on every song, with Garcia noodling his way to nirvana. While it would be an exaggeration to say that if you own this three-CD, three-hour-and-ten-minute album you have all you need of the Grateful Dead on disc, the overstatement is only slight. As Bob Weir says at the outset, "This ain't a show, it's a party." — *William Ruhlmann*

Dozin' at the Knick / Oct. 29, 1996 / Arista ✦✦✦

Great Buildings

f. 1980, United States
Rock 'n' Roll, New Wave, Power Pop
Great Buildings was a power pop/new wave group formed in the early '80s by Danny Wilde (vocal/guitar), Richard Sanford (drums), Philip Solem (guitar/vocals), and Ian Ainsworth (bass/keyboard/vocals). They recorded one self-titled album for Columbia in 1981 before breaking up a short time later. Wilde went on to release on solo album in 1989 for Geffen before teaming up again with Solem to form the Rembrandts the next year. The Rembrandts released three albums between 1991 and 1995 and found moderate success with "Just the Way It Is, Baby" in 1990 and "I'll Be There for You" (the theme to the television show "Friends") in 1995. —*Chris Woodstra*

Apart from the Crowd / 1981 / Columbia ✦✦✦✦
Before the Rembrandts there was Great Buildings, one of a series of bands that were part of Columbia Records' "Developing Artists" series. Sadly, many people missed the chance to catch this early effort from Wilde and Solem. One listen and you know these two have an ear for a catchy pop tune. Fortunately, the failure of this record didn't signal the end of the duo. Find this one, if you can. —*Jim Worbois*

The Great Society

f. 1964, San Francisco, CA, **db.** 1966
Psychedelic
Before joining the Jefferson Airplane, Grace Slick sang lead and played various instruments for the Great Society, who were nearly as popular as the Airplane in the early days of the San Francisco psychedelic scene. Instrumentally, the Great Society were not as disciplined as the Airplane. But they were at least their equals in imagination, infusing their probing songwriting with Indian influences, nifty minor key melodic shifts, and groundbreaking, reverb-soaked psychedelic guitar by Grace's brother-in-law, Darby Slick. Darby was also responsible for penning "Somebody to Love," which Grace brought with her to the Airplane, who took it into the Top Five in 1967. The Great Society broke up in late 1966 after recording only one locally released single; after the Airplane became stars, Columbia issued a couple of live albums of the Great Society performing at San Francisco's Matrix Club in 1966. — *Richie Unterberger*

● **Collector's Item** / 1966 / Columbia ✦✦✦✦
This CD reissue combines both of the Great Society's live albums on one disc, and features "Somebody to Love" in its original slower, more menacing version. It also includes the Society's extended version of Grace Slick's "White Rabbit," along with several other haunting originals that strike an exhilarating balance between tight songwriting and psychedelic jamming. This is far more than a "Collector's Item"; it's a genuinely exciting glimpse into the birth of psychedelic music. —*Richie Unterberger*

Born to Be Burned / 1995 / Sundazed ✦✦✦
An interesting if marginal collection of previously unreleased material from late 1965. Recorded at a pretty early stage in the band's development, this is largely comprised of demos that the group recorded during their short-lived association with the Autumn label. Both the songwriting and execution are pretty sketchy and tentative, sounding considerably closer to garage rock than their later psychedelic recordings. Certainly there's a fair amount of promise here, particularly in the songs by Grace and Darby Slick, which far outshine the basic Rolling Stonesy derivations by the band's other songwriter, David Miner. Miner, a below-average garage growler, unfortunately shared the lead vocal duties with the immeasurably superior Grace Slick, who already sounds searing and confident. But unlike *Collector's Item*, which contains some of the

finest (and most unjustly overlooked) psychedelic music ever recorded, this is really mostly of interest to scholars and collectors. The material is far weaker here, and the ragaish Indian influences that characterized their most innovative work had yet to surface. It does include some songs that also appear on *Collector's Item* ("Born to Be Burned," "Daydream Nightmare," "That's How It Is," "Father Bruce"), but these versions are far more skeletal and less forceful. The highlight is their lone, rare single, which featured the first (pre-Jefferson Airplane) version of "Somebody to Love" and the flipside "Free Advice," one of the first examples of raga-rock. —*Richie Unterberger*

Green Day

f. 1989, Berkeley, CA
Alternative Pop-Rock, Punk Revival, Punk-Pop
Out of all the post-Nirvana American alternative bands to break into the pop mainstream, Green Day was second only to Pearl Jam in terms of influence. At their core, Green Day were simply punk revivalists, recharging the energy of speedy, catchy three-chord punk-pop songs. Though their music wasn't particularly innovative, they brought the sound of late-'70s punk to a new, younger generation with *Dookie*, their 1994 major-label debut. Green Day wasn't able to sustain their success—*Dookie* sold over eight million, while its follow-up, *Insomniac*, sold only a quarter of its predecessor—but their influence was far-reaching, since they opened the doors for a flood of American neo-punk, punk metal, and third-wave ska-revivalists.

Green Day was part of the southern California underground punk scene. Childhood friends Billie Joe Armstrong (guitar, vocals) and Mike Dirnt (bass; born Mike Pritchard) formed their first band, Sweet Children, in Rodeo, CA, when they were 14 years old. By 1989 the group had added drummer Al Sobrante and changed their name to Green Day. That year the band independently released their first EP, *1,000 Hours*, which was well received in the southern California hardcore punk scene. Soon the group had signed a contract with the local independent label Lookout and replaced Sobrante with John Kiftmeyer. *39/Smooth*, Green Day's first album, was released later that year. Shortly after its release, the band replaced Kiftmeyer with Tre Cool (born Frank Edwin Wright, III); Tre Cool became the band's permanent drummer.

Throughout the early '90s, Green Day continued to cultivate a cult following, which only gained strength with the release of their second album, 1992's *Kerplunk*. The underground success of *Kerplunk* led to a wave of interest from major record labels; the band eventually decided to sign with Reprise. *Dookie*, Green Day's major label debut, was released in the spring of 1994. Thanks to MTV support for the initial single "Longview," *Dookie* became a major hit. The album continued to gain momentum throughout the summer, with the second single, "Basket Case," spending five weeks on top of the American modern rock charts. At the end of the summer, the band stole the show at Woodstock '94, which helped the sales of *Dookie*. By the time the fourth single, "When I Come Around," began its seven-week stay at No. 1 in the modern rock charts in early 1995, *Dookie* had sold over five million copies in the US alone; it would eventually top eight million in America, selling over ten million copies internationally. *Dookie* also won the 1994 Grammy for Best Alternative Music Performance.

Green Day quickly followed *Dookie* with *Insomniac* in the fall of 1995; during the summer, they hit No. 1 again on the modern rock charts with "J.A.R.," their contribution to the *Angus* soundtrack. *Insomniac* performed well initially, entering the US charts at No. 2, and selling over two million copies by the spring of 1996; but none of its singles—including the radio favorite "Brain Stew/Jaded"—was as popular as those from *Dookie*. In the spring of 1996, Green Day abruptly cancelled a European tour, claiming exhaustion. After the cancellation, the band spent the rest of the year resting and writing new material. —*Stephen Thomas Erlewine*

1039/Smoothed Out Slappy Hour / 1991 / Lookout ✦✦
1039/Smoothed Out Slappy Hour compiles Green Day's first album *39/ Smooth* and its first two EPs, *1,000 Hours* and *Slappy*, on one CD. At this point, the trio was trying to find a style, and its speedy punk-pop songs lack strong hooks and their noisy clamor isn't exciting, it's thin and uninvolving. There are a couple of indications of Green Day's potential scattered across the disc, particularly in Billie Joe's sense of humor, but only the last tracks, all culled from the 1990 *Slappy* EP, have any real spark. —*Stephen Thomas Erlewine*

Kerplunk / Jan. 17, 1992 / Lookout ✦✦✦
Green Day's best independent record is fueled more by their attitude and sonic aggression than their riffs. —*Stephen Thomas Erlewine*

● **Dookie** / Feb. 1, 1994 / Reprise ✦✦✦✦
After two albums of indie guitar punk, Green Day made the jump to the majors with *Dookie*. Based on MTV's constant playing of "Longview," the band became a major crossover success; *Time* even hailed the album as the best rock 'n' roll record of 1994. While *Dookie* isn't that good, it is quite good. For once, Green Day has genuine songs and hooks

to go along with their muscular, roaring guitars, making *Dookie* not only their most accessible album, but also their best. —*Stephen Thomas Erlewine*

Insomniac / Oct. 10, 1995 / Reprise ◆◆◆
Dookie gave Green Day success, but it was never really clear whether they wanted it. However, given the incessantly catchy songwriting of Billie Joe, the success made sense. Green Day were traditionalists without realizing it, learning all of their tricks through secondhand records and second-generation California punk bands. They didn't change their sound in the slightest after signing to a major label, which meant that they couldn't revert to a harsher, earlier sound as a way to shed their audience for *Dookie*'s follow-up, *Insomniac*. Instead, they kept their blueprint and made it a shade darker. Throughout *Insomniac*, there are vague references to the band's startling multi-platinum breakthrough, but the album is hardly a stark confessional on the level of Nirvana's *In Utero*. It's a collection of speedy, catchy songs in the spirit of the Buzzcocks, the Jam, the Clash, and the Undertones, but played with more minor chords and less melody and recorded with a bigger, hard rock-oriented production. While nothing on the album is as immediate as "Basket Case" or "Longview," the band has gained a powerful sonic punch, which goes straight for the gut but sacrifices the raw edge they so desperately want to keep and makes the record slightly tame. Billie Joe hasn't lost his talent for simple, tuneful hooks, but after a series of songs that all sound pretty much the same, it becomes clear that he needs to push himself a little bit more if Green Day ever wants to be something more than a good punk-pop band. As it is, they remain a good punk-pop band, and *Insomniac* is a good punk-pop record, but nothing more. —*Stephen Thomas Erlewine*

Green on Red

f. 1981, Los Angeles, CA, db. 1993
Group / Alternative Pop-Rock, Paisley Underground
Always wary of their Paisley Underground tag, it was only Green on Red's debut EP that leaned on the psychedelic sounds of the '60s before they traded it in for a boozy, all-American sound. They have been credited as latter-day forbears of the No Depression sound forged by Wilco and Son Volt.

Singer and songwriter Dan Stuart, Chris Cacavas (keyboards), and Jack Waterson (bass) formed their first group in Tucson, AZ, in 1979. Relocating to L.A., drummer Steve MacNicol joined up and the band released their debut EP on Steve Wynn's Down There label in 1982. By 1983 the band had dumped the trippy psychedelic stuff for *Gravity Talks*, their Slash debut. By the time 1985's *Gas Food Lodging* rolled around and the band had added guitarist Chuck Prophet, they were earning critical accolades, but their greatest success came overseas with the release of 1986's *No Free Lunch* (Polygram). Between albums, Stuart paused to work with Steve Wynn and a smattering of their respective band members from their *Danny and Dusty* album, a record that allowed Stuart his "drunken bum" persona. Prophet and Stuart continued to hone their darkish, down-and-out loser blues on *The Killer Inside Me* (1987, Mercury) and *Here Come the Snakes* (1989, Mercury), but by the time 1989's *This Time Around* (Mercury) came out, interest in their work stateside had ceased. Cacavas had left the fold to begin what had become a consistent, albeit overlooked, solo career. The Prophet/Stuart duo found an audience for their music in Europe for *Scapegoats* (1991, China) and *Too Much Fun* (1992, Off Beat), but ultimately traded in the madness of what had become their collaboration for quieter lives. Stuart relocated to Spain, and Prophet continues the solo career he launched in 1990. His 1997 release *Homemade Blood* (Cooking Vinyl) bears little resemblance to the ramshackle outfit that was Green on Red. As it turns out, Prophet was a sleeper. —*Denise Sullivan*

EP / 1981 / Green on Red ◆◆◆
Chris Cacavas' organ drives the band's sound on this debut recording that pegged Green on Red as part of the Paisley Underground movement of L.A. bands devoted to '60s guitar rock. The swirling sound of "Death and Angels" and "Aspirin" sometimes recalls the riffage of the Seeds and Love, thus the tag. But the band soon would shed its novice skin, so this EP turns out to be a neat curiousity. —*Denise Sullivan*

Green on Red / 1982 / Down There ◆◆◆

Gravity Talks / 1983 / Slash ◆◆
Green on Red's tinge of psychedelia was provided by Chris Cacavas' organ. But already, the band had traded in most psychedelic references for an Americana influence, along the lines of John Fogerty spiked with Roky Erickson. Completists might find they need it, but better work comes on the band's next record, *Gas Food Lodging*. —*Denise Sullivan*

Gas Food Lodging / 1985 / Enigma ◆◆◆
By adding guitarist Chuck Prophet to its lineup, Green on Red began its odyssey into the land of roots-rock. Termed "American music" at the time, *Gas Food Lodging* is a hybrid of styles—a little Neil Young with Crazy Horse, some Dream Syndicate, even a little Pete Seeger (hence

their cover of "We Shall Overcome"). Good music played by boys becoming men. —*James Chrispell*

No Free Lunch / 1985 / One Way ◆◆
Released in Europe nearly a year before seeing the light of day in America, *No Free Lunch* is more of an EP than an album. Containing just seven songs and clocking in at a mere 23 minutes, this is short but sweet listening. Recorded in England, *No Free Lunch* rocks away on such tunes as "Time Ain't Nothing" and includes a cover of Willie Nelson's "Funny How Time Slips Away." —*James Chrispell*

The Killer Inside Me / 1987 / Mercury ◆◆
This was to be Green on Red's breakthrough album, but it wilted on the vine. Very Americanesque in its imagery and song detail, *The Killer Inside Me* was as roots-rock as they come, but the rather shoddy musical inventions didn't grab anyone but staunch fans. Still, it's a good record to listen to on a hot summer evening. —*James Chrispell*

Here Come the Snakes / 1989 / Restless ◆◆◆◆
Produced by Jim Dickinson and Joe Hardy, Dan Stuart and Chuck Prophet finally cracked the Memphis sound by steeping themselves in the environment and surrounding themselves with the musicians who made their name there. From the get-go, Prophet's guitar is the cornerstone to the *Let It Bleed* mood that fires this record from "Keith Can't Read" throughout, though it ends up with the very Neil Young-like "D.T. Blues." —*Denise Sullivan*

Live at the Town & Country / 1989 / Polydor ◆◆

This Time Around / 1989 / Mercury ◆◆◆
The band were reduced to essentially a two-piece, Dan Stuart and Chuck Prophet, and some hired help, including Eagle Bernie Leadon. The album's best tracks are the slow ones; "Good Patient Woman" and the crawling "You Couldn't Get Arrested." Produced by Glyn Johns, it's an OK record; it's just that by this time Stuart's drunken-loser schtick has worn thin. Really thin. —*Denise Sullivan*

Scapegoats / 1991 / China ◆◆◆

● **Best of Green on Red** / 1995 / China ◆◆◆◆

Gas Food Lodging/Green on Red / Jan. 15, 1996 / Mau Mau ◆◆◆◆

Green River

f. 1983, Seattle, WA, db. 1988
Alternative Pop-Rock, Grunge
In the mid-'80s, before "grunge" became a specific musical style, before Sub Pop was considered a training league for major labels, many postpunk rock fans didn't believe Seattle had a worthwhile musical scene. Green River helped change that. With its ugly, loud, sub-Stooges guitar grind, Green River was the first band to make Sub Pop a hip underground label. At their best, the band made a powerful, brutal guitar rock that merged '70s heavy metal and '60s garage punk with '80s post-punk; at their worst, they were a sludgy, depressing mess.

Green River were together for three years before the band splintered. Singer Mark Arm and occasional guitarist Steve Turner formed Mudhoney. Guitarist Stone Gossard and bassist Jeff Ament formed Mother Love Bone, which would eventually turn into Pearl Jam. The roots of Mudhoney's garage grunge and Pearl Jam's revisionist '70s hard rock can be heard on Green River's three EPs. —*Stephen Thomas Erlewine*

● **Rehab Doll/Dry as a Bone** / 1987 / Sub Pop ◆◆◆◆
Green River's only album is a brutal collection of primal Stooges-style guitar grind and punked-up metal riffing. The CD includes the equally powerful *Dry as a Bone* EP. —*Stephen Thomas Erlewine*

Al Green

b. Apr. 13, 1946, Forrest City, AR
Vocals / Soul, R&B, Gospel
Al Green was the first great soul singer of the '70s and arguably the last great Southern soul singer. With his seductive singles for Hi Records in the early '70s, Green bridged the gap between deep soul and smooth Philadelphia soul. He incorporated elements of gospel, interjecting his performances with wild moans and wails, but his records were stylish, boasting immaculate productions that rolled along with a tight beat, sexy backing vocals, and lush strings. The distinctive Hi Records sound that the vocalist and producer Willie Mitchell developed made Al Green the most popular and influential soul singer of the early '70s, influencing not only his contemporaries, but veterans like Marvin Gaye. Green was at the peak of his popularity when he suddenly decided to join the ministry in the mid-'70s. At first he continued to record secular material, but by the '80s, he was concentrating solely on gospel. During the late '80s and '90s, he occasionally returned to R&B, but he remained primarily a religious performer for the rest of his career. Nevertheless, Green's classic early-'70s recordings retained their power and influence throughout the decades, setting the standard for smooth soul.

Green was born in Forest City, AR, where he formed a gospel quartet, the Green Brothers, at the age of nine. The group toured throughout the

South in the mid-'50s, before the family relocated to Grand Rapids, MI. The Green Brothers continued to perform in Grand Rapids, but Al's father kicked the boy out of the group after he caught his son listening to Jackie Wilson. At the age of 16 Al formed an R&B group, Al Green and the Creations, with several of his high school friends. Two Creation members, Curtis Rogers and Palmer James, founded their own independent record company, Hot Line Music Journal, and had the group record for the label. By that time, the Creations had been re-named the Soul Mates. The group's first single, "Back Up Train," became a surprise hit, climbing to No. 5 on the R&B charts early in 1968. The Soul Mates attempted to record another hit, but all of their subsequent singles failed to find an audience.

In 1969 Al Green met bandleader and Hi Records vice president Willie Mitchell while on tour in Midland, TX. Impressed with Green's voice, Mitchell signed the singer to Hi Records and began collaborating with him on his debut album. Released in early 1970, Green's debut album *Green is Blues* showcased the signature sound he and Mitchell devised—a sinewy, sexy groove highlighted by horn punctuations and string beds that let Green showcase his remarkable falsetto. While the album didn't spawn any hit singles, it was well received and set the stage for the breakthrough success of his second album. *Al Green Gets Next to You* (1970) launched his first hit single, "Tired of Being Alone," which began a streak of four straight gold singles. *Let's Stay Together* (1972) was his first genuine hit album, climbing to No. 8 on the pop charts; its title track became his first No. 1 single. *I'm Still in Love with You*, which followed only a few months later, was an even greater success, peaking at No. 4 and launching the hits "Look What You Done for Me" and "I'm Still in Love with You."

By the release of 1973's *Call Me*, Green was known as both a hit-maker and an artist who released consistently engaging, frequently excellent, critically acclaimed albums. His hits continued uninterrupted through the next two years, with "Call Me," "Here I Am," and "Sha-La-La (Make Me Happy)" all becoming Top Ten, gold singles. At the height of his popularity, Green's former girlfriend, Mrs. Mary Woodson, broke into his Memphis home in October 1974 and poured boiling grits on the singer as he was bathing, inflicting second-degree burns on his back, stomach, and arm; after assaulting Green, she killed herself with his gun. Green interpreted the violent incident as a sign from God that he should enter the ministry. By 1976 he had bought a church in Memphis and had become an ordained pastor of the Full Gospel Tabernacle. Though he had begun to seriously pursue religion, he had not given up singing R&B, and he released three other Mitchell-produced albums—*Al Green Is Love* (1975), *Full of Fire* (1976), *Have a Good Time* (1976)—after the incident. However, his albums began to sound formulaic, and his sales started to slip by the end of 1976, with disco cutting heavily into his audience.

In order to break free from his slump, Green stopped working with Willie Mitchell in 1977 and built his own studio, American Music, where he intended to produce his own records. The first album he made at American Music was *The Belle Album*, an intimate record that was critically acclaimed but failed to win a crossover audience. *Truth and Time* (1978) failed even to generate a major R&B hit. During a concert in Cincinnati in 1979, Green fell off the stage. Interpreting the accident as a sign from God, Green retired from performing secular music and devoted himself to preaching. Throughout the '80s, he released a series of gospel albums on Myrrh Records. In 1982 Green appeared in the gospel musical *Your Arms Too Short to Box with God* with Patti LaBelle. In 1985 he reunited with Willie Mitchell for *He Is the Light*, his first album for A&M Records.

Green tentatively returned to R&B in 1988 when he sang "Put a Little Love in Your Heart" with Annie Lennox for the Bill Murray comedy *Scrooged*. Four years later, he recorded his first full-fledged soul album since 1978 with the UK-only *Don't Look Back*. In 1995 he released *Your Heart's in Good Hands*, an adult contemporary record that represented his first secular album to be released in America since *Truth and Time*. Though the album received positive reviews, it failed to become a hit.

Al Green was inducted to the Rock and Roll Hall of Fame in 1995. —*Stephen Thomas Erlewine*

Green Is Blues / 1970 / The Right Stuff ✦✦✦
The first album linking the soul-singing greatness of Al Green with the production brilliance and expertise of Willie Mitchell. The results were mutually beneficial; Green got the great production, arrangements, and backing from the Hi Rhythm section that often turned good songs into classics, and he sang with the conviction and talent that provided the final component in an artistically and commercially satisfying union. —*Ron Wynn*

Gets Next to You / 1971 / The Right Stuff ✦✦✦✦
After the shaky start of *Green Is Blues*, Al Green and producer Willie Mitchell established that classic sound with Green's second album, *Gets Next to You*. The main difference is in the rhythm section. Abandoning the gritty syncopations of deep Southern soul, the Hi Rhythm section plays it slow and seductive, working a sultry, steady pulse that Green

exploits with his remarkable voice. Alternating between Sam Cooke's croon and Otis Redding's shout, Green develops his own distinctive style, and *Gets Next to You* only touches the surface of its depth. Although the album is filled with wonderful moments, few are as astonishing as Green and Mitchell's reinterpretation of the Temptations' "I Can't Get Next to You," which turns the original inside out. —*Stephen Thomas Erlewine*

Let's Stay Together / Feb. 1972 / The Right Stuff ✦✦✦✦
Green's third album for Hi and the first of a string of brilliant releases. The title song was the big hit, but an extended version of the Bee Gees' "How Can You Mend a Broken Heart?" remained a staple for years. —*Rob Bowman*

☆ **I'm Still in Love with You** / Dec. 1972 / The Right Stuff ✦✦✦✦✦
I'm Still in Love with You shares many surface similarities to its predecessor, *Let's Stay Together*, from Al Green and Willie Mitchell's distinctive, sexy style to the pacing and the song selection. Despite those shared traits, *I'm Still in Love with You* distinguishes itself with its suave, romantic tone and its subtly ambitious choice of material. Green began exploring country music with this album, performing a startling version of Kris Kristofferson's "For the Good Times," as well as a wonderful, slow re-interpretation of Roy Orbison's "Oh Pretty Woman." And the soul numbers are more complex than they would appear; listen to how the beat falls together at the beginning of "Love and Happiness," or the sly melody of the title track. There's not a wasted track on *I'm Still in Love with You*, and in many ways it rivals its follow-up, *Call Me*, as Green's masterpiece. —*Stephen Thomas Erlewine*

☆ **Call Me** / Jul. 1973 / The Right Stuff ✦✦✦✦✦
Three R&B Top Ten hits (the title song, "Here I Am (Come and Take Me)," and "You Ought to Be with Me") dominate what is probably his finest album. Once again he tackles some country-soul, turning in moving versions of Hank Williams' "I'm So Lonesome I Could Cry" and Willie Nelson's "Funny How Time Slips Away." Green also returns to the gospel vein on "Jesus Is Waiting." —*Rob Bowman*

Livin' for You / Dec. 1973 / The Right Stuff ✦✦✦
A cut below the albums listed above, *Livin' for You* is still mighty fine. The title cut and "Let's Get Married" were both Top Ten R&B hits. —*Rob Bowman*

Al Green Explores Your Mind / 1974 / The Right Stuff ✦✦✦
Only one hit single this time out, "Sha-La-La (Make Me Happy)." *Explores Your Mind* also contains what may have become Green's best-known song, "Take Me to the River." —*Rob Bowman*

★ **Al Green's Greatest Hits** / Apr. 1975 / The Right Stuff ✦✦✦✦✦
Upon its original release in 1975, *Al Green's Greatest Hits* pretty much summed up everything about Green, containing his ten biggest hits up to that point. A few years later it was followed by a second volume, which contained hit singles that had charted since the release of the first collection. In 1995 the Right Stuff reissued *Al Green's Greatest Hits*, adding six of the highlights from the second volume of greatest hits as bonus tracks. The result was a definitive single-disc compilation featuring 16 of Green's absolute best songs, including "Tired of Being Alone," "Let's Stay Together," "I'm Still in Love with You," "Call Me," "Here I Am," "Sha-La-La (Make Me Happy)," and "L-O-V-E (Love)." The original version of *Greatest Hits* was great, but the revision made it nearly perfect. —*Stephen Thomas Erlewine*

Al Green Is Love / Oct. 1975 / The Right Stuff ✦✦✦
Two more Top Ten hits with "L-O-V-E (Love)" and "Oh Me, Oh My (Dream's in My Arms)." —*Rob Bowman*

Full of Fire / Apr. 1976 / Hi ✦✦✦
Wonderfully sung, expertly produced and performed '70s soul by a vocal master and a superb support combo. Al Green and Willie Mitchell were so solidly attuned to each other that Green's albums were truly collaborative affairs, with the superb Hi Rhythm section filling in behind and underneath him effortlessly. —*Ron Wynn*

Have a Good Time / Dec. 1976 / Hi ✦✦✦
Al Green was riding right along, still singing with confidence, power, and authority. Although this was kind of a transition effort, with Green beginning to head toward gospel, his vocals retained their edge and relaxed fire. Mitchell and Hi Rhythm did their usual excellent supporting job. —*Ron Wynn*

Al Green's Greatest Hits, Vol. 2 / Jul. 1977 / Motown ✦✦✦✦
As good as *Volume 1*, augmented by nonchart items that might have been hits anyway, like "Love and Happiness," "Take Me to the River," and "For the Good Times." —*Rob Bowman*

The Belle Album / Dec. 1977 / The Right Stuff ✦✦✦✦
Al Green severed his ties with longtime producer Willie Mitchell in 1977, establishing his own backup band and seizing the production reins. But he hadn't yet made the final break with soul; this was the last secular work he would make for many years, and it was brilliant, even though it didn't come close to equaling his previous commercial heights. In retro-

spect, many just didn't understand where he was going, while others were turned off by the blurred lyrical focus of songs like "Belle." But "I Feel Good" had as much danceable energy and soulful fire as any Green uptempo tune, and "Lovin' You" and "Dream" were sorely underrated compositions. —*Ron Wynn*

Truth & Time / 1978 / Hi ✦✦✦
Returning to the formula of his classic Hi albums, Al Green assembled a fine collection of originals and covers for *Truth & Time*. Although Green is in good voice, and his version of "Say a Little Prayer" is impressive, the album feels a bit like a holding pattern, simply repeating ideas that were more fruitful the first time around. Given the generally listless nature of *Truth & Time*, and how Green sounds vaguely uninterested in the material, it's not a surprise that it was his last secular record for a very long time. —*Stephen Thomas Erlewine*

The Lord Will Make a Way / 1980 / Myrrh ✦✦✦✦
One of the best gospel albums by Rev. Green. The R&B and pop hits had stopped coming but the sacred peaks were the equal of any of his secular material. In 1992 Green was still performing the title song and "In the Holy Name of Jesus." —*Rob Bowman*

Tokyo Live / 1981 / The Right Stuff ✦✦✦✦
A wonderful live set that serves as both a retrospective and a defining release showing that Green sang the same way regardless of musical and lyrical content. He did many of his greatest soul hits, performing them with the relaxed, powerful grace that made him the '70s' finest soul vocalist and the '80s' best male gospel artist. —*Ron Wynn*

Higher Plane / Feb. 1981 / Hi ✦✦✦✦
Another superior sacred recording, most notable for a stellar version of the Impressions' "People Get Ready." —*Rob Bowman*

He Is the Light / 1985 / A&M ✦✦✦✦
At the time of writing, this was Green's last truly great recording. Back with Willie Mitchell, the Hi Rhythm section, and the Memphis Horns, Green has great material and delivers the goods. —*Rob Bowman*

Love Ritual / 1989 / MCA ✦✦✦✦
Don't let the title lead you into thinking that these are second-rate leftovers, because this album (originally compiled for the British Demon label) is loaded with gems. Highlights are hard to pin down, but one surprise is a spirited version of the Beatles' "I Want to Hold Your Hand"; it should've been a single. Every track except "Ride Sally Ride" has been digitally remixed from the original multitracks. The sound is great, being faithful to the spirit of Willie Mitchell's production and mixing style, and the disc includes detailed liner notes. All in all, Green fans should pick this up. —*Rick Clark*

I Get Joy / May 1989 / A&M ✦✦✦✦
Some exuberant, rocking gospel and slower, less energetic, but equally reverent material from Rev. Al Green. Although he's not doing soul, Green still slips in some of the vocal maneuvers, sliding falsetto effects, and mannerisms that made his secular material electrifying. His '80s gospel albums were no less moving. —*Ron Wynn*

One in a Million / 1990 / Word ✦✦✦✦
A compilation from Green's gospel recordings, it reveals the emotional depth of his religious work. —*Brian Mansfield*

Love Is Reality / 1992 / Word ✦✦✦
After years of refusing to sing anything but gospel, Green decided the time had finally come to fuse the godly and the secular elements of his soul. *Love Is Reality* made an overt play for the mainstream R&B market. Unfortunately, Christian dance-pop producer Tim Miner works from formulas, while Green runs on inspiration. Green sounded great, but the final result paled in comparison to the rest of his catalog. —*Brian Mansfield*

Your Heart's in Good Hands / Nov. 7, 1995 / MCA ✦✦✦
Designed as Al Green's triumphant comeback to the R&B mainstream, *Your Heart's in Good Hands* is a mixed blessing. Although Green's voice is still astonishing, the album is undermined by a sterile urban R&B production that fails to capture the sensuality inherent in his music. As a result, *Your Heart's in Good Hands* is quite frustrating—you can hear Green hit new heights with his performance, but the music is constantly reined in by the lifeless production and the lackluster songs. —*Stephen Thomas Erlewine*

Anthology / Feb. 11, 1997 / Capitol ✦✦✦
Theoretically, an Al Green box set should be easy to assemble, given the overall excellence of his material, but the four-disc *Anthology* is a botch job. Instead of simply condensing the best of Green's prolific output, including all of the hits, the compilers were concerned with telling a story—literally. Three of the discs are spiked with lengthy interview segments; furthermore, most of the rarities are concert tracks, which means classics like "I Can't Get Next to You," "How Can You Mend a Broken Heart," "Love and Happiness," and "Sha-La-La (Make Me Happy)" are presented in inferior live versions. The live cuts, interviews, and rarities cut severely into the set's pacing, and they don't make *Anthology* useful

for the fan who wants one, definitive collection; their appeal is solely to collectors, who already have the material elsewhere. Consequently, *Anthology* isn't useful for either the casual or dedicated fan, both of whom would be better off with the original albums and the *Greatest Hits* collection, which does contain the essence of Al Green, and most of his hits, on one disc. —*Stephen Thomas Erlewine*

Vernon Green

b. 1953, Los Angeles, CA
Doo Wop
The Medallions, a Los Angeles doo wop quartet with a predilection for songs about speedy cars, formed in 1953. Their first single, "The Letter"/ "Buick '59," on the Dootsie Williams Dootone label, was a regional hit, coupling a dreamy ballad with a joyriding rocker complete with automotive sound effects by the group. (Encores in the same vein included "Speedin'," "Pushbutton Automobile," and "Coupe DeVille Baby"; there was even a "'59 Volvo"!). Williams' renamed Dooto label handed Green an opportunity to sing soul in 1973, and he recently reemerged with some doo wop offerings on the Classic Artists imprint. —*Bill Dahl*

● **Golden Classics** / Collectables ✦✦✦✦
This Los Angeles doo wop aggregation specialized in "rocking car songs" during the mid '50s. —*Bill Dahl*

The Greenberry Woods

f. 1989, Baltimore, MD
Alternative Pop-Rock, Power Pop
Matt Huseman and Ira Katz (both vocals and guitars) formed the Greenberry Woods in the late '80s at the University of Maryland. They later added Matt's twin brother, Brandt, for the bass, and drummer Miles Rosen. Signed by Sire Records in 1993, the band, influenced by the Beatles, the Byrds, and Big Star, have recorded two albums for the label. —*John Bush*

Rapple Dapple / Feb. 8, 1994 / Sire/Reprise ✦✦✦✦
● **Big Money Item** / Jul. 25, 1995 / Sire ✦✦✦✦
The Greenberry Woods' instrumentation and yearning vocal style tend to the emotionally manipulative, heart-on-sleeve side, but lyrics often rise above the vacuous boy-girl stuff that defines the genre. "Love Songs" surveys the cliched landscape with a sly, knowing eye while working completely within the musical formula. At 18 tracks, most hovering under the three-minute mark, *Big Money Item* serves up a dizzying over-abundance of sugary riches. While some selections remain lightweight trifles, enough substantial moments overflow the cone to coat the listener in captivating sticky goo. "Invisible Threads" combines sudden gear shifts with a phased, baroque pop underpinning. There's the stately soft-psych of "Parachute," and a dew-eyed tip of the hat to Crowded House balladry in "For You." "Nervous" pumps up the fuzz for some garage-y power-pop, while "Go Without You" breaks into Bay City Roller handclaps. "Oh Janine"'s soaring chorus recalls both the Beach Boys and Eric Carmen's Raspberries. Even at its most superficial and derivative and unapologetically nerdy, *Big Money Item* is just so chock full of fatal hooks that . . . well . . . life almost starts to feel that fresh and innocent again. —*Roch Parisien*

Clive Gregson

b. Jan. 4, 1955, Manchester, England
Folk, Singer-Songwriter, Folk-Rock, Pop-Rock, Adult Alternative Pop-Rock, Contemporary Folk
Clive Gregson and Christine Collister were the most moving and memorable UK folk-rock duo to emerge since Richard and Linda Thompson. Gregson's wry tales of the ins and outs of love, sung in Collister's heartbreaking voice, have earned the duo (and subsequent solo work) respect and a devoted following, though commercial success and mainstream recognition have eluded them.

Gregson (b.Jan. 4, 1955) was the founder of Any Trouble, a pub-rock/ new wave quartet, in Manchester in 1975. The band's sound, and Gregson's songwriting and singing, reminded some of Elvis Costello, and Any Trouble was signed by Stiff, Costello's label. The band made several well remembered but poor-selling albums, then split up in 1984.

In 1984 Gregson discovered Collister singing in a folk club and, impressed by her talents, offered to work with her on future projects. Gregson had already begun an association with Richard Thompson, initially singing backup on the classic *Shoot Out the Lights* in 1982. While working on Thompson's *Hand of Kindness*, Gregson suggested using Collister for additional backup vocal duties. The formula worked, and the two continued for years as integral parts of the Richard Thompson touring band, arguably the finest live band he's assembled. In 1985 Gregson made a solo album, *Strange Persuasions*, with Collister singing backup on a few tracks. The two began performing as a duo on the folk club circuit shortly thereafter. The duo's first release was a homemade tape sold at gigs, later released as *Home and Away*. It was followed by their first formal album, *Mischief,* in 1988, and by *Change in the Weather* in 1990. *Love in a Strange Hotel,* released later the same year, was an album of cover versions of Gregson and Collister's favorite songs. By 1992 the stress of constant touring and working together without substantial success finally took its toll on them. The two decided to go their separate ways after one parting shot, *The Final Word,* and one final tour. They both continued as solo acts. Gregson eventually relocated to Nashville and has been the more active of the two, releasing the live "official bootleg" *Carousel of Noise* on his own label in 1994, *People and Places* in 1995, and *I Love This Town* in 1996 for Compass Records in addition to various production work and side collaborations with Boo Hewardine. Christine Collister continued to play the folk circuit, releasing a live album, *Live,* in 1995 and a new studio album, *Blue Aconite* in 1997. *—Chris Woodstra and William Ruhlmann*

Strange Persuasions / 1985 / Compas ✦✦✦
Strange Persuasions came out in England in 1985, but it wasn't released in North America until 1995. After leaving his group Any Trouble, Gregson made his name in the States as a member of Richard Thompson's band and later as half of the Gregson and Collister duo. *Strange Persuasions* provides a missing link between his pub/pop days with Any Trouble and the more subtle, folkier tendencies of his later work. Some tracks sound like L.A. pop productions with a dash of Squeeze thrown in, while others, "Jewel in Your Crown," for example, offer his sophisticated ballad writing. Perhaps this is what Ralph McTell would have sounded like had he chosen a more produced musical road; the melodies are often rooted in the late-'60s and '70s folk singer-songwriter genre with enough pop to make things interesting. While there is nothing revelatory here—Gregson would perfect the formula later—*Strange Persuasions* is a good album. *—Chris Woodstra and Richard Meyer*

Home & Away / 1986 / Flying Fish ✦✦✦✦
Home & Away is a collection of songs recorded during an early acoustic tour in 1986; originally a cassette-only release to be sold at gigs, reportedly it cost under $60 to make. Despite the low budget and seemingly disposable nature of a release like this, the album has become a favorite among fans for its faithful representation of the duo's charming acoustic shows. The duo run through new originals, some songs from Gregson's Any Trouble days, and a few well chosen covers in a warm, intimate setting. *—Chris Woodstra*

Mischief / 1987 / Rhino ✦✦✦
Clive Gregson's songs treat romance with ironic charm. "We're Not Over Yet" is a compendium of reasons why they ought to be over, and "Everybody Cheats on You" is about more than romantic infidelity. Christine Collister gives the songs a depth that often keeps them from being too glib and clever, as do the folk-pop arrangements. *— William Ruhlmann*

• **A Change in the Weather** / 1989 / Rhino ✦✦✦✦
The self-insight continues in Gregson's lyrics, but the concerns are expanded. Collister does a fine job covering "Tryin' to Get to You." *—William Ruhlmann*

Welcome to the Workhouse / 1990 / Special Delivery ✦✦✦✦
Welcome to the Workhouse is a collection of Gregson's home demos and outtakes, and while most albums of this sort appeal only to the diehard fans, this one stands out as one of his finest recorded moments, working surprisingly well as an album. The recordings span 1980 to 1985 and provide a good bridge between his work with Any Trouble and his partnership with Christine Collister. *—Chris Woodstra*

Love Is a Strange Hotel / Nov. 1990 / Rhino ✦✦✦
A departure from the expansive arrangements of the previous two albums, *Love Is a Strange Hotel* is a low-key acoustic collection of covers. Even unlikely choices like Aztec Camera's "How Men Are" and 10cc's "Things We Do for Love" are pulled off in their own subtle and charming way. *—Chris Woodstra*

The Last Word / Mar. 24, 1992 / Rhino ✦✦✦✦
By 1992 the Gregson & Collister team had fallen apart, and the two had decided to record one more album before calling it quits. *Last Word* gives all the intimate details of a dissolving relationship, packed with real emotion and a dignified, stylish execution. In many ways, the duo tied things up with the high point of their career. Their extraordinary harmonies and cool mix of folk, jazz, country, and blues have never sounded better. And though the subject matter doesn't stray far from Gregson's usual themes, knowing the circumstances of the recording brings a new dimension to the songs, making the statements all the more powerful and touching. *—Chris Woodstra*

Carousel of Noise / 1995 / Gregsongs ✦✦✦
This mail-order-only "official bootleg" release serves as something of a sequel to *Home and Away,* this time with Gregson alone tackling old favorites like the Any Trouble classic "Second Choice" in an intimate live setting. As with *Home and Away, Carousel of Noise* is a charming document, essential for his devoted following. *—Chris Woodstra*

People & Places / Apr. 25, 1995 / Compas ✦✦✦
One hears more of Elvis Costello and Richard Thompson's influence on this release. Still the songs are strong and the production crisp with enough unusual dynamics to keep you listening. His literate lyrics are short domestic stories told in a generally straightforward way ("Mary's Divorce" or "My Eyes Gave the Game Away"). The Ralph McTell comparison still stands, and it's meant as a compliment. *—Richard Meyer*

I Love This Town / Aug. 20, 1996 / Compass ✦✦✦✦
Clive Gregson's solo work and collaborations with Christine Collister were marked by craftsmanlike quality, always subtle and tasteful. Despite the consistency of his output, there was always an unspoken desire among elements of his fan base for him to return to the pop days of Any Trouble. With *I Love This Town,* Gregson makes this return, pulling out a batch of upbeat, musically irresistible tunes. Certainly the album is more AAA-oriented than the new wave/pub-rock of the Any Trouble days, but the change of pace is welcome. *—Chris Woodstra*

Grifters

f. 1990, Memphis, TN
Alternative Pop-Rock, Lo-Fi, Indie Rock
If Guided by Voices are the Beatles of the mid-'90s lo-fi scene, then the Grifters' big, bluesy racket could certainly qualify as the Stones. Deliberately noisy, sloppy, and out-of-tune, the band masks melodies under a heavy static fuzz of distortion. Based in Memphis, and definitely influenced by their surroundings, the Grifters recall as well the proto-lo-fi musings of Royal Trux and Half Japanese—unlike GbV, who arrived at the lo-fi sound by simply recording pop songs at home on sub-standard equipment. Formed in the late '80s, initially as A Band Called Bud, with vocalist/guitarist Scott Taylor, bassist Tripp Lamkins, and drummer Dave Shouse, the band released only a single and an obscure tape consisting of front-room recordings. By the turn of the decade, Shouse had begun sharing songwriting and guitar chores with Taylor, when Stan Gallimore replaced him on drums. The four-piece debuted on vinyl with the 1990 single "Disfigurehead" on Doink Records. In 1992 the band issued their debut album, *So Happy Together,* on the evidently likeminded Sonic Noise label. The LP continued the Sonic Youth approach to punk prevalent on the initial recordings, though the following year's *One Sock Missing* showed a more mature Grifters; that is, the songs were slower, but no less skewered with distortion and tape splices. The album was the first released on their own Shangri-La label, which has also issued a single from A Band Called Bud as well as recordings from Taylor's side project, Hot Monkey.

With the ascension of Pavement and the emergence of Guided by Voices, the lo-fi scene became much more viable by 1994, especially in the world of indie-rock. The Grifters' third album, *Crappin' You Negative,* emphasized the bluesy swagger that had been understated before, and with the addition of somewhat proper melodies—actually the repetition of jagged riffs—the album became an underground hit. The band signed with Sub Pop later that year, and after the release of 1995's *Eureka* EP, issued *Ain't My Lookout* in 1996. *—John Bush*

• **One Sock Missing** / 1993 / Shangri-La ✦✦✦✦
There's a point during the second song, "She Blows Blasts of Static," where the Grifters sound like a bad bootleg of Stones' demos. This especially caustic version of lo-fi indie-pop might be too much for some listeners. *—John Bush*

Crappin' You Negative / May 16, 1994 / Shangri-La ✦✦✦✦

Ain't My Lookout / Feb. 1996 / Sub Pop ✦✦✦
Ain't My Lookout is the Grifters' tightest and cleanest record to date, but that's only a relative term; the band's previous records were so noisy and sloppy that it was occasionally difficult to discern melodies and hooks within the songs. Apart from the band's sharper attack, things haven't changed that much on *Ain't My Lookout.* The songs are still based in rootsy, Stonesy rock 'n' roll, but run through the shredder, making the riffs jagged and the chords angular. Although it has slightly higher production values than their early singles, the sound remains endearingly lo-fi and ragged. The Grifters haven't changed their sound enough to be labeled a sell-out by their indie fans, but they may have opened it up enough to welcome in new fans. *—Stephen Thomas Erlewine*

The Groundhogs

f. 1963, England
Blues-Rock, Hard Rock, British Blues
The Groundhogs were not British blues at their most creative; nor were they British blues at their most generic. They were emblematic of some of the genre's most visible strengths and weaknesses. They were prone to jam too long on basic riffs, they couldn't hold a candle to American blues singers in vocal presence, and their songwriting wasn't so hot. On the other hand, they did sometimes stretch the form in unexpected ways, usually at the hands of their creative force, guitarist/songwriter/vocalist T.S. (Tony) McPhee. For a while they were extremely popular in Britain, landing three albums in that country's Top Ten in the early '70s. The Groundhogs' roots actually stretch back to the mid-'60s, when

McPhee helped form the group, named after a John Lee Hooker song (the band was also known briefly as John Lee's Groundhogs). In fact, the Groundhogs would back Hooker himself on some of the blues singer's mid-'60s British shows, and back him on an obscure LP. They also recorded a few very obscure singles with a much more prominent R&B/soul influence than their later work. In 1966 the Groundhogs evolved into Herbal Mixture, which (as if you couldn't guess from the name) had a more psychedelic than blues flavor. Their sole single, "Machines," would actually appear on psychedelic rarity compilations decades later. The Groundhogs/Herbal Mixture singles, along with some unreleased material, has been compiled on a reissue CD on Distortions.

After Herbal Mixture folded, McPhee had a stint with the John Dummer Blues Band before re-forming the Groundhogs in the late '60s at the instigation of United Artists A&R man Andrew Lauder. Initially a quartet (bassist Pete Cruickshank also remained from the original Groundhogs lineup), they'd stripped down to a trio by the time of their commercial breakthrough, Thank Christ for the Bomb, which made the UK Top Ten in 1970. The Groundhogs' power-trio setup, as well as McPhee's vaguely Jack Bruce-like vocals, bore a passing resemblance to the sound pioneered by Cream. They were blunter and less inventive than Cream, but often strained against the limitations of conventional 12-bar blues with twisting riffs and unexpected grinding chord changes. McPhee's lyrics, particularly on Thank Christ for the Bomb, were murky, sullen anti-establishment statements that were often difficult to decipher, both in meaning and content. They played it straighter on the less sophisticated follow-up, Split, which succumbed to some of the period's blues-hard-rock indulgences, putting riffs and flash over substance.

McPhee was always at the very least an impressive guitarist, and a very versatile one, accomplished in electric, acoustic, and slide styles. Who Will Save the World? The Mighty Groundhogs! (1972), their last Top Ten entry, saw McPhee straying further from blues territory into somewhat progressive realms, even adding some Mellotron and harmonium (though the results were not wholly unsuccessful). The Groundhogs never became well known in the US, where somewhat similar groups like Ten Years After were much bigger. Although McPhee and the band have meant little in commercial or critical terms in their native country since the early '70s, they've remained active as a touring and recording unit since then, playing to a small following in the UK and Europe. —Richie Unterberger

● **Thank Christ for the Bomb** / 1970 / BGO ✦✦✦✦
Their most popular album, and probably their most representative, although Who Will Save the World? may be more imaginative. McPhee's guitar playing is impressive, and the songs, if not compelling, at least take some lyrical and instrumental chances, building off of a blues-rock base instead of being a slave to it. McPhee seems to be struggling with some very ambitious concepts here, but lacks clarity and vision to fashion an out-of-the-ordinary statement. —Richie Unterberger

Split / 1971 / BGO ✦✦✦
Closer to the British blues norm than some of their previous work, this boasts some of the lesser crowd-pleasing annoyances of the age—basic bluesy thumpers and extended, not-brilliant riffing. McPhee's songwriting suffered, and the band devoted half of the eight-song record to the four-part title track. That didn't prevent the album from being a big hit in Britain, but it hasn't dated well, unless you have an uncritical yen for middling 1970-era blues-rock/hard-rock hybrids. —Richie Unterberger

Who Will Save the World? / 1972 / BGO ✦✦✦
McPhee took the unusual step of adding progressive rock elements on this album, especially in his use of Mellotron and harmonium. Blues-rock and progressive rock is not exactly a fashionable combination among critics these days, but McPhee at least deserved credit for trying something a little bit different, instead of endlessly recycling the blues-rock cliches he'd mastered. Lyrically, he reached back to the socially conscious (if not terribly clear) musings on war, peace, and philosophy that had preoccupied him on the Thank Christ for the Bomb album. It wasn't gripping enough to add up to something notable, and the band were still prone to wander off into headache-inducing extended riffs, as on the closing track,"The Grey Maze." —Richie Unterberger

Groundhogs Best 1969-72 / One Way ✦✦✦✦

Guadalcanal Diary

f. 1981, Georgia, db. 1989
Alternative Pop-Rock, Jangle-Pop
Thanks to R.E.M., there was no shortage of Southern guitar pop bands in the early '80s, but Guadalcanal Diary was different from the rest. While their songs were as melodic and approachable as R.E.M. and the Byrds or any of their imitators, singer/guitarist Murray Attaway's lyrics were bizarre treatises on his favorite obsessions—American history and mythology, religion, and the supernatural. What kept them from becoming unbearly precious was their pop sense and eclecticism, which added a musical variety to the diverse and strange subject matter. After four albums, the group disbanded in 1989. —Stephen Thomas Erlewine

Walking in the Shadow of the Big Man / 1984 / Elektra ✦✦✦
Like R.E.M., the B-52s, and Pylon, this fine band hailed from the unlikely independent-rock hotbed of Athens, GA. The long jangle-pop shadow of R.E.M. is extremely strong on this release, with seven of the ten tracks showing either full or partial influence of that group. Fortunately, the songs here are excellent, exhibiting much variety within this style. "Trail of Tears," a haunting antiwar number, sounds the most like their Athens counterparts. "Fire from Heaven" is more uptempo, intense, and dynamic, while "Sleepers Awake" is an ominous, slowly unfolding song. "Ghost on the Road" is primarily a fast country-punk number that saves its R.E.M. stylings for its yearning chorus. "Gilbert Takes the Wheel" and the title track are jangly instrumentals, the former being a fast rocker with a thudding beat, the latter being a lengthy slow-tempo selection exhibiting noticeable psychedelic traits. Other territory is touched on as well. "Pillow Talk" is a winsomely energetic Everly Brothers-influenced song. The brilliant "Watusi Rodeo" is a jumpy pop number sporting over-the-top surf guitar licks and inspired hilarious-yet-uncomfortable lyrics about "Ugly American" cowboys in Africa. There's also an eccentric cover of the missionary hymn "Kum Ba Yah," complete with background audience shouting, an energetic drum solo, and extreme contrasts of loud and soft dynamics (sometimes within the same verse line). This odd, yet strong, album is well worth hearing. —David Cleary

Jamboree / 1986 / Elektra ✦✦✦
The first six selections on this release encompass some of the best R.E.M.-style songs never written by that band. "Michael Rockefeller" is a breathlessly rushed masterpiece with echoes of that other Athens band's "West of the Fields." "Pray for Rain" is a howling, intense number that snitches the opening two chords of Jefferson Airplane's "3/5 of a Mile in 10 Seconds" for its own beginning. Weighty concerns about religion are voiced in the ringing "Fear of God"; this song borrows the opening guitar riff from "I Call Your Name" by the Beatles. "Spirit Train" is a slower, intensely foreboding selection that suggests a highly charged version of R.E.M.'s "Old Man Kensey." What follows all this are a clutch of songs with bizarre or puckish lyrics in a wild array of pop styles. "T.R.O.U.B.L.E." is a hot jazz-influenced track with goofy lyrics about sibling rivalry. "I See Moe" is a jumpy country-punk number that compares the speaker's personality to that of the Three Stooges. "Dead Eyes" is a hard-rocking cut with threatening verses about unknown terrors and things that go bump in the night, resulting likely from too much booze. And "Cattle Prod" has to go down as one of the strangest pop songs ever written, a grindingly grandiose number with arena-rock touches that has lyrics about bestiality. This is an excellent, if sometimes bewildering, album very much worth hearing. —David Cleary

● **2x4** / 1987 / Elektra ✦✦✦✦
This wonderful, hard-rocking release shows Guadalcanal Diary moving away from the obvious R.E.M. influences exhibited on their first two releases. Only "Where Angels Fear to Tread" and "Winds of Change" (both excellent songs) sound like the music of their Georgia cousins. Styles explored here are surprisingly diverse. "Let the Big Wheel Roll" is a souped-up rockabilly-influenced number with nutty lyrics that make fun of junk-pop culture in general and television commercials in particular; appropriately enough, the Monkees song "For Pete's Sake" is closely referenced in the song's chorus. "3 AM" is an affectingly haunting and beautiful low-key stunner about alcoholism. Touches of funk and psychedelic-era Beatles inform the driving "Lips of Steel." "Under the Yoke" weds booming arena-rock touches to a growled vocal, wailing harmonica, and oppressive lyrics. John Lennon and Greg Lake are the obvious touchstones for the uneasy slow-tempo song about paranoia and superstition entitled "Little Birds." "Things Fall Apart" comes across as a stumbling quintuple-meter burlesque of Jethro Tull's more bombastic numbers. And the soaring "Litany" is a powerfully exuberant selection with a walloping drum beat and vibrant guitar work. This fine album is well worth purchasing. —David Cleary

Flip-Flop / 1989 / Elektra ✦✦✦
Guadalcanal Diary's final album is simultaneously their most stylistically consistent and their least effective. Most of the songs on this release uneasily mix walloping rock, arena stylings, and ringing R.E.M. touches; most have clearer, somehow less effective lyrics, some of which (most notably in "The Likes of You") are riddled with cliches. The temptation to think that the band is going for chart success in a big way is very strong here. A few off-style excursions can be found, all but one showing strong ties to songs on earlier albums. "Ten Laws" has the slow, ominous feel of "Spirit Train." " . . . Vista" mixes musical elements of "Country Club Gun" and "T.R.O.U.B.L.E." in an uneasy alliance with nonsense lyrics. And "Fade Out" (probably the album's best track) is a further excursion into paisley-period Beatles that recalls "Lips of Steel." The one surprise here is the power-pop selection "Always Saturday." A number of the songs on this release have sour, angry lyrics excoriating such things as out-of-control drunks ("Whiskey Talk") and women both snooty ("The Likes of You") and vacuous ("Pretty Is as Pretty Does"). In

short, the group seems to be stagnating. Fans of this band will likely find this release to be a letdown from earlier efforts. —*David Cleary*

The Guess Who

f. 1963, Winnipeg, Manitoba, Canada, **db.** 1976
Pop-Rock
While the Guess Who did have several hits in America, they were superstars in their home country of Canada during the 1960s and early '70s. The band grew out of vocalist/guitarist Chad Allan (born Allan Kobel) and guitarist Randy Bachman's Winnipeg-based group Chad Allan and the Expressions, originally known as the Silvertones and then the Reflections. The remainder of the lineup featured bassist Jim Kale, pianist Bob Ashley, and drummer Garry Peterson. The Expressions recorded a cover of Johnny Kidd and the Pirates' "Shakin' All Over" in 1965, which became a surprise hit in Canada and reached the US Top 40. When the Expressions recorded an entire album of the same name, its record company, Quality, listed their name as "Guess Who?" on the jacket, hoping to fool record buyers into thinking that the British Invasion-influenced music was actually by a more famous group in disguise. Ashley had been replaced by keyboardist/vocalist Burton Cummings, who became lead vocalist when Allan departed in 1966. The Guess Who embarked on an unsuccessful tour of England and returned home to record commercials and appear on the television program *Let's Go*, hosted by Chad Allan. However, further American success eluded the Guess Who until the 1969 Top Ten hit "These Eyes"; the recording session for the accompanying album, *Wheatfield Soul*, was paid for by producer Jack Richardson, who mortgaged his house to do so. *Canned Wheat Packed by the Guess Who* produced three Top 40 singles later that year. In 1970 the Guess Who released the cuttingly sarcastic riff-rocker "American Woman," which, given its anti-American putdowns, ironically became their only US chart-topper. The album of the same name became their first US Top Ten and first gold album, and the group performed for President and Mrs. Nixon and Prince Charles at the White House. (Pat Nixon requested that "American Woman" be dropped from the set list.) Trouble was brewing on the horizon, though. Guitarist Bachman, having recently converted to Mormonism, took issue with the band's typical rock 'n' roll lifestyle, leading to clashes with Cummings. Finding the atmosphere unbearable, Bachman left the group in July 1970 and formed Brave Belt with Chad Allan, which later evolved into Bachman-Turner Overdrive. His place in the Guess Who was taken by Kurt Winter and Greg Leskiw, and the title track from their next album, "Share the Land," climbed into the Top Ten later that year, and several more singles charted afterwards. The group returned to the Top Ten one last time in 1974 with the novelty single "Clap for the Wolfman," featuring dialogue by deejay Wolfman Jack. Burdened by shifting personnel and loss of direction, Cummings broke up the band in 1975 and tried a solo career. The lineup from the Guess Who's glory years reunited in 1983, and a version of the group with constantly shifting musicians (occasionally original members) continues to tour. —*Steve Huey*

Shakin' All Over / 1965 / Scepter ♦♦
Aside from the title track (itself not as good as the Johnny Kidd original), the Guess Who's American debut was a thin and hasty effort typical of the period, padding the hit single with various covers and a few Randy Bachman originals. "Stop Teasing Me" is one of the most accurate Merseybeat imitations ever waxed, but on the whole this sounds a lot closer to Gerry & the Pacemakers than the group would have liked to admit a few years later. —*Richie Unterberger*

Canned Wheat / 1969 / RCA ♦♦♦♦
The group's second album, and probably their best long-player, with a couple of hits surrounded by some lyrical, well-crafted album tracks. —*Bruce Eder*

Share the Land / 1970 / RCA ♦♦♦
Hot on the heels of the hit *American Woman* album (whose title track was a number one stateside hit), the Guess Who delivered *Share the Land*, the band's most cohesive collection of pop-smart rock songs. Includes the hits "Do You Miss Me Darlin'?," "Hand Me Down World," "Hang On to Your Life," and "Share the Land." —*Rick Clark*

● **The Best of Guess Who** / 1971 / RCA ♦♦♦♦
A fine single-disc collection of most of the band's hits, it's perfect for listeners who don't want to invest in the double-disc *Track Record.* —*AMG*

So Long, Bannatyne / 1971 / RCA ♦♦
The Guess Who changed direction, away from their hard pop-rock, and came up with a more pianistic set of songs, like the orchestrated numbers "Sour Suite," "Goin' a Little Crazy," and jazzy "Grey Day." "Pain Train," not found on the excellent *Track Record*, is a highlight, as well as the hit single "Rain Dance." —*Rick Clark*

Live at the Paramount / 1972 / RCA ♦♦
An okay, but unexceptional, document of their stage performances from the post-Bachman era. —*Bruce Eder*

Track Record: The Guess Who Collection / 1988 / RCA ♦♦♦♦
A perfect collection, covering the band's whole history on two CDs. Includes the hits "These Eyes," "Laughing," "Undun," "No Time," "American Woman/No Sugar Tonight," "Share the Land," and the novelty-ish "Clap for the Wolfman." —*Bruce Eder*

Ultimate Collection / Jan. 28, 1997 / RCA ♦♦♦♦
A seemingly well-assembled package that fails to go quite as far as it should, sticking closely to the charted material and rarely delving into the vaults for interesting oddities. Three rehearsal takes are tacked onto the end of the third disc in the set, providing little of interest to collectors or to the curious. The booklet does a workmanlike job of tracking the progress of the band, but there are few insights to be found in the difficult-to-read text. The set is built around the A and B sides of singles, with album cuts salted in between. This is effective in charting the band's progression from melodic popsters to hard rockers and back to the pop-inflected music that closed out their career. The highlights are scattered throughout—"American Woman," of course; "Rain Dance," with its unnerving echoes of American massacres; the funky, improvised live "Truckin' Off Across the Sky"; even the goofy "Clap for the Wolfman," which came when the Guess Who were all but finished. *The Ultimate Collection* works well as an introduction to the Guess Who, but will not gratify anyone with more than a basic need to know. On a sonic level, the set sounds good, however. —*Steven McDonald*

Guided by Voices

f. 1985, Dayton, OH
Alternative Pop-Rock, Lo-Fi, Indie Rock
Inspired equally by jangle-pop and arty post-punk, Guided by Voices created a series of trebly, hissy indie-rock records filled with infectiously brief pop songs that fell somewhere between the British Invasion and prog-rock. After recording six self-released albums between 1986 and 1992, the Dayton, OH-based band attracted a handful of fans within the American indie-rock underground. With the 1994 release of *Bee Thousand*, the group became an unexpected alternative rock sensation, winning positive reviews throughout the mainstream music press and signing a larger distribution deal with Matador Records. Despite all the attention, the band never changed their aesthetic, continuing to record their albums on cheap four-tracks tape decks, thereby limiting their potential audience; but that devotion to lo-fi indie-rock helped Guided by Voices maintain a sizable cult during the late '90s.

Schoolteacher Robert Pollard formed Guided by Voices in the early '80s. Throughout the group's history, Pollard was at the center, writing the majority of the songs and leading each incarnation of the band. During the '80s, Pollard was frequently joined by his brother Jim, who continued to write songs for the group even after his departure in the late '80s. Guided by Voices didn't become a full-fledged band until guitarist Tobin Sprout and bassist Dan Toohey joined in 1985. A year later the group released an EP, *Forever Since Breakfast*, on the local indie I Wanna Records. Guided by Voices released their first full-length album, *Devil Between My Toes*, on their own G Records in 1987; it was followed several months later by *Sand Box*, which appeared on Halo. *Self-Inflicted Aerial Nostalgia*, was released on Halo in 1989 and *Same Place the Fly Got Smashed*, appeared on Rocket No.9 Records in 1990.

During the latter half of the '80s, Guided by Voices was essentially a hobby. The band rarely performed, and a wide array of musicians appeared on the group's albums; according to some estimations, nearly 40 musicians passed through the band during its first decade. Nearly all of the Guided by Voices albums before *Vampire on Titus* were recorded in Steve Wilbur's eight-track studio in his garage; Wilbur occasionally played guitar and bass on the records. Guided by Voices added Mitch Mitchell (rhythm guitar) and Kevin Fennell (drums) around the time of *Propeller* (1992), which was released on Rockathon Records.

Before 1993's *Vampire on Titus*, all of Guided by Voices' records were essentially interchangeable musically, and none was widely available. *Vampire on Titus* was the first album the band released on the Cleveland-based indie label Scat, and the wider distrubtion meant the record was heard by a larger audience. Soon, the group had won fans like fellow Dayton native Kim Deal (Pixies, Breeders) and Sonic Youth's Thurston Moore. Later in 1993 the band began playing live for the first time in several years, with Greg Demos replacing bassist Toohey. By the spring of 1994 Scat had entered a national distribution deal with Matador Records. *Bee Thousand* was the first album released under the deal, and it became a surprise word-of-mouth hit, earning positive reviews from mainstream publications like *Rolling Stone* and *Entertainment Weekly*. Pollard had quit teaching shortly before the spring release of *Bee Thousand*, and the group toured heavily behind the album, appearing on the second stage at several Lollapalooza dates. By fall, GBV's video for "I Am a Scientist" was aired a handful of times on MTV. Demos left the band in late 1994 to study law and was replaced by music journalist Jim Greer. By the release of 1995's *Alien Lanes*, the group had joined Matador's official roster; their contract with Scat was completed with the spring release of *Box*, a five-disc box set containing the band's pre-*Propeller* albums. *Alien Lanes* was greeted with positive reviews upon its March release, and the group embarked on its first full-scale American tour. Greer left the band before the recording for *Under the Bushes, Under the Stars*, which was released in spring of 1996. That fall, Robert Pollard and Tobin Sprout both released solo albums on the same day; the records were followed by an album-length EP a month after their release. As the solo albums indicated, Pollard and Sprout had a falling out during the group's tour earlier that year, which resulted in Robert's firing the rest of the group. At the end of 1996, Pollard recorded the next Guided by Voices record, *Mag Earwhig*, supported by the Cleveland garage-punk band Cobra Verde. —*Stephen Thomas Erlewine*

Vampire on Titus / 1993 / Scat ✦✦✦✦
After years of impressive but flawed records, *Vampire on Titus* was Guided by Voices' first consistent record, with more than half of the 18 songs being blessed with memorable melodies or hooks. The CD version includes *Propeller*, which showed Robert Pollard's songwriting becoming more refined and accessible. —*Stephen Thomas Erlewine*

● **Bee Thousand** / Jun. 20, 1994 / Scat ✦✦✦✦
Sonically, *Bee Thousand* isn't that different from Guided by Voices' previous albums. The band still is creating minimalistic homages to British Invasion pop and art-rock, except the songs are better constructed, with hooks that are immediately memorable. —*Stephen Thomas Erlewine*

Box / Feb. 28, 1995 / Scat ✦✦✦
Compiling all of Guided by Voices' '80s albums—*Devil Between My Toes, Sandbox, Self-Inflicted Aerial Nostalgia*, and *Same Place the Fly Got Smashed* (the vinyl version includes *Propeller*, which was on the *Vampire on Titus* CD)—and adding a collection of rarities called *King Shit and the Golden Boys*, *Box* is a bit of an intimidating listen for some devoted fans, let alone beginners. Guided By Voices packs their records full of brief songs; if they reach the three-minute mark, it's an epic for the band. While that can make such a massive collection of music rather daunting, it all seems to speed by without much distinction if you're listening casually; but on closer inspection, it withstands repeated listens. The first records, *Devils* and *Sandbox*, are unpolished versions of R.E.M.'s *Murmur*. On the next two albums, the group's distinctive, British Invasion-inspired abbreviated pop begins to coalesce; their music sounds more like messages than songs, albeit messages that are driven by undeniable hooks. Retailing for under $50, *Box* is a worthwhile investment for dedicated fans. —*Stephen Thomas Erlewine*

Alien Lanes / Mar. 28, 1995 / Matador ✦✦✦
Featuring a slightly cleaner production and more straightforward melodies, *Alien Lanes*, the first record Guided by Voices released since their breakthrough *Bee Thousand*, is only slightly less impressive than their previous record. —*Stephen Thomas Erlewine*

Under the Bushes, Under the Stars / Mar. 26, 1996 / Matador ✦✦✦
Only Guided by Voices devotees can distinguish between their albums, but that doesn't make them any less enjoyable. *Under the Bushes, Under the Stars* delivers all of the standard GBV trademarks—the sharp, catchy melodies and hooks, the brief songs, the defiant lo-fi sound—without improving on the formula. Nevertheless, the album isn't any weaker than the previous *Alien Lanes;* in fact, it might even be a bit more consistent, with a stronger batch of songs. *Under the Bushes, Under the Stars* isn't the kind of album that will win the band new fans, but it will certainly fulfill the wishes of the many existing ones. —*Stephen Thomas Erlewine*

Mag Earwhig! / May 20, 1997 / Matador ✦✦✦✦
After the *Under the Bushes, Under the Stars* tour, Robert Pollard and Tobin Sprout had a falling out, resulting in Pollard's completely overhauling Guided by Voices' lineup. He recorded the majority of *Mag Earwhig!* with Cleveland garage-punk band Cobra Verde, and on a few tracks, they certainly give his songs a tougher backbone, with louder guitars and pounding backbeats. Cobra Verde prove equally adept at Pollard's lo-fi jangle, which means that *Mag Earwhig!* has the feeling of an epic; it encapsulates all of GBV's past, while pushing forward. Not coincidentally, Pollard has structured the album as a rock-opera about his childhood, and while his lyrics are too damn elliptical to tell a story, the ambition distinguishes the record from previous GBV efforts. It also makes Sprout's absence—he contributes only one track on the record—evident, since Pollard's songs sound too samey over the course of a full record, especially when some of the harder songs ("I Am a Tree," "Bulldog Skin") simply grind away aimlessly. Still, *Mag Earwhig!* has a stronger, more distinctive set of songs than any album since *Bee Thousand*, even if it suffers from the same inconsistencies as any other Guided by Voices record. —*Stephen Thomas Erlewine*

Gun Club

f. 1980, Los Angeles, CA, **db.** 1996
Blues-Rock, Punk, Alternative Pop-Rock
Tribal, psychobilly blues is the best way to describe Gun Club's ener-

getic death rock, but the band's career seemed doomed from the get-go by leader Jeffrey Lee Pierce's reputation as an unreliable wildman, and well publicized bouts of drunkenness dogged him throughout his career. Formed in Los Angeles in the early '80s, the band were vaguely aligned with similarly roots inspired groups like X and the Blasters, but later relocated to the Lower Eastside, resting more comfortably around the New York downtown set and Pierce's mentors, Debbie Harry and Chris Stein. Their 1981 debut, *Fire of Love*, was a punk/blues hybrid; intense energy fueled Pierce's exorcism-in-progress delivery and the band's (Ward Dotson, guitar; Rob Ritter, bass; and Terry Graham, drums) frenetic style. In 1982 *Miami* had the band allied with Blondie's Stein at the boards. Pierce had once been the president of Blondie's US fanclub, which sparked the liaison. The 1985 EP *Death Party* is a swingin' piece of punkabilly with Dee Pop on drums and Jim Duckworth of Panther Burns on guitar. For *Las Vegas Story* in 1984, the Club won over drummer Kid Congo Powers from the Cramps and Patricia Morrison (the Bags) on bass. Pierce launched his solo career in 1985 with the EP *Flamingo* and the *Wildweed* album for the Statick label. But it wasn't quite over; in 1987 Pierce came back with a realigned Club. *Mother Juno* (Fundamental) earned them a wider following than ever. In 1996, after drying-out, but suffering from persistent health problems, Pierce passed away from a brain hemorrhage. Morrison went on to play with Sisters of Mercy, Powers formed his own lounge group, and Dotson formed the Pontiac Brothers. —*Denise Sullivan*

● **Fire of Love** / 1981 / Slash ✦✦✦✦
Punkabilly blues, more soulful than the Cramps because singer and songwriter Jeffrey Lee Pierce brings a boatload of personal suffering to the table. "Sex Beat," "She's Like Heroin to Me," and "For the Love of Ivy" best capture the band's frenetic energy, which is never kept at bay—quite the opposite. Is it possible Pierce coined a phrase; "All dressed up like an Elvis from hell?" —*Denise Sullivan*

Miami / 1982 / IRS ✦✦✦
Produced by Blondie's Chris Stein and featuring harmonies by Deborah Harry, *Miami* widens the Gun Club's net to ensnare folk, country, and even pop-rock; however, the power of Jeffrey Lee Pierce's songs is compromised by an oddly pristine mix that overemphasizes his vocals while diluting the effects of Ward Dotson's gritty guitar work. —*Jason Ankeny*

Death Party [EP] / 1983 / Animal ✦✦✦
Some potent stuff, all right. Jeffrey Lee Pierce slowed down the tempo for the garage-rock dirge "Death Party," while "Come Back Jim" hearkens back to the debut album, and "The House on Highland Ave" is a modern-day murder ballad set to a straightahead rock melody. Always death-obsessed, Pierce may have been at his lowest ebb personally, but this EP set the stage for his strong solo work to come. —*Denise Sullivan*

The Birth, The Death, The Ghost / 1984 / ABC ✦✦
The first of two live Gun Club collections released in 1984, *The Birth, the Death, the Ghost* is also the better of the pair; recorded with guitarist Kid Congo Powers, back in the fold after a tenure with the Cramps, the set focuses on recently released material, and includes a number of otherwise unissued compositions as well. —*Jason Ankeny*

The Las Vegas Story / 1984 / IRS ✦✦✦
Original guitarist Kid Congo Powers returned to the Gun Club for *The Las Vegas Story*, an ambitious effort that lifts up the rock covering America's seamy underbelly to see what crawls out. A swamp-rock opus that bears a considerable debt to John Fogerty, Jeffrey Lee Pierce's reach often exceeds his grasp; while some of his cultural insights hit the mark, others offer only a hint of truth. Covers of Pharoah Sanders' "Master Plan" and George Gershwin's "My Man's Gone Now" (from *Porgy and Bess*) serve only to further blur whatever statement the album is attempting to make. —*Jason Ankeny*

Sex Beat 81 / 1984 / Lolita ✦✦
The flurry of live Gun Club material continued unabated with *Sex Club 81*, a badly recorded and rather uninspired collection documenting the group's first recorded lineup performing songs from *Fire of Love* and *Miami*. —*Jason Ankeny*

Danse Kalinda Boom / 1985 / Roadrunner ✦✦
Recorded in 1983, *Danse Kalinda Boom: Live in Pandora's Box* suffers from abysmal sound quality, although the performances are electric; Jeffrey Lee Pierce and Kid Congo Powers sound like men possessed on scorching readings of "Sleeping in Blood City" and a cover of Robert Johnson's "Preaching the Blues." —*Jason Ankeny*

Two Sides of the Beast / 1985 / Dojo ✦✦
Another stopgap collection released during one of the Gun Club's frequent dissolutions, *Two Sides of the Beast* is a double-LP set spanning both studio and live material. —*Jason Ankeny*

Mother Juno / 1987 / Red Rhino ✦✦✦✦
Produced in Berlin by the Cocteau Twins' Robin Guthrie, *Mother Juno* is a significant return to form; the single "Breaking Hands" is darkly beautiful and delicate, but the remainder is straightforward and lean, with

"Thunderhead" and "Yellow Eyes" reclaiming the grim intensity of the group's best work. —*Jason Ankeny*

Pastoral Hide and Seek / 1990 / Fire ✦✦✦✦
Recorded in Brussels, *Pastoral Hide and Seek* continues the Gun Club's sudden resurgence; "Emily's Changed" is a provocative and gripping character study, while the country-inflected "I Hear Your Heart Singing" is one of Jeffrey Lee Pierce's most moving songs to date. —*Jason Ankeny*

Divinity / 1991 / New Rose ✦✦✦
Noisy and intricate, *Divinity* ranks among the Gun Club's most ambitious efforts; however, the dissonant production often tends to muddy Jeffrey Lee Pierce's songs, which, conversely, are some of his most simple and straightforward. —*Jason Ankeny*

Live in Europe / 1992 / Triple X ✦✦✦
The first live Gun Club release in some years, *Live in Europe* concentrates on material from later efforts like *Mother Juno* and *Pastoral Hide and Seek*, although the group occasionally dips into its past to tackle songs like "Sex Beat" and "Preaching the Blues." —*Jason Ankeny*

In Exile / May 4, 1992 / Triple X ✦✦✦✦
In Exile compiles tracks from the Gun Club albums *Mother Juno*, *Pastoral Hide and Seek* and *Divinity*; among the highlights are "Breaking Hands," "Lupita Screams," "I Hear Your Heart Singing," and the previously unreleased "Pastoral Hide and Seek," recorded for (but not featured on) the LP of the same name. —*Jason Ankeny*

Lucky Jim / 1994 / Triple X Entertainment ✦✦✦
The final collection of new Gun Club material released prior to Jeffrey Lee Pierce's 1996 death, *Lucky Jim* is a spare, haunted work; the absence of Kid Congo Powers strips away the group's usual dominant elements, leaving Pierce's ghostly vocals to assume center stage. —*Jason Ankeny*

Guns N' Roses

f. 1985, Los Angeles, CA
Hard Rock, Heavy Metal

At a time when pop was dominated by dance music and pop metal, Guns N' Roses brought raw, ugly rock 'n' roll crashing back into the charts. They were not nice boys; nice boys don't play rock 'n' roll. They were ugly, misogynist, violent; they were also funny, vulnerable, and occasionally sensitive, as their breakthrough hit "Sweet Child o' Mine" showed. While Slash and Izzy Stradlin ferociously spit out dueling guitar riffs worthy of Aerosmith or the Stones, Axl Rose screeched out his tales of sex, drugs, and apathy in the big city; bassist Duff McKagan and drummer Steven Adler were a limber rhythm section that kept the music loose and powerful. Guns N' Roses' music was basic and gritty, with a solid hard, bluesy base; they were dark, sleazy, dirty, and honest—everything that good hard rock and heavy metal should be.

Guns N' Roses released their first EP in in 1986, which led to a contract with Geffen; the next year the band released their debut album, *Appetite for Destruction*. They started to build a following with their numerous live shows, but the album didn't start selling until almost a year later, when MTV started playing "Sweet Child o' Mine." Soon the album shot to No. 1, and Guns N' Roses became one of the biggest bands in the world. By the end of 1988, they released *G N' R Lies*, which paired four new, acoustic-based songs with their first EP.

Guns N' Roses began to work on the follow-up to *Appetite* at the end of 1990. In October of that year, the band fired Adler, claiming that his drug dependency caused him to play poorly; he was replaced by Matt Sorum from the Cult. During recording, the band added Dizzy Reed on keyboards. By the time the sessions were finished, the new album had become two new albums. After being delayed for nearly a year, the albums, *Use Your Illusion I* and *II*, were released in the fall of 1991. The *Illusions* showcased a more ambitious band; while there were still a fair number of full-throttle guitar rockers, there were stabs at Elton John-style balladry, acoustic blues, horn sections, female backup singers, ten-minute songs with several different sections, and a good number of introspective, soul-searching lyrics. In short, they were now making art; amazingly, they were successful at it. While the albums sold very well initially, the band soon fell out of favor. Stradlin left by the end of 1991, and with his departure the band lost their best songwriter. Once Nirvana's *Nevermind* hit the top of the charts in early 1992, there was a distinct division between what was cool in hard rock and what wasn't; Guns N' Roses—with all of their pretensions, impressionistic videos, models, and rock star excesses—were very uncool. The band didn't fully grasp the change until 1993, when they released their album of punk songs, *The Spaghetti Incident?*; it received some good reviews, but the band failed to capture the reckless spirit of not only the original versions, but their own *Appetite for Destruction*. By the middle of 1994, rumors were flying that the band was about to break up, since Rose wanted to pursue a new, more industrial direction and Slash wanted to stick with their blues-inflected hard rock. —*Stephen Thomas Erlewine*

★ **Appetite for Destruction** / 1987 / Geffen ✦✦✦✦✦
Guns N' Roses' debut *Appetite for Destruction* was a turning point for hard rock in the late '80s; it was a dirty, dangerous, and mean record in a time when heavy metal meant nothing but a good time. On the surface, Guns N' Roses may appear to celebrate the same things as their peers—namely, sex, liquor, drugs, and rock 'n' roll—but there is a nasty edge to their songs, since Axl Rose doesn't see much fun in the urban sprawl of LA and its parade of heavy metal thugs, cheap women, booze, and crime. The music is as nasty as the lyrics, wallowing in a bluesy, metallic hard rock borrowed from Aerosmith, AC/DC, and countless faceless hard-rock bands of the early '80s. It's a primal, sleazy sound that adds grit to already grim tales. It also makes Rose's misogyny, fear, and anger hard to dismiss as merely an artistic statment. This is music that sounds lived-in. And that's exactly why *Appetite for Destruction* is such a powerful record; not only does Axl have fears, but he is vulnerable, particularly on the power-ballad "Sweet Child o' Mine." He also has a talent for conveying the fears and horrors of the decaying inner city, whether it's on the charging "Welcome to the Jungle," the heroin ode "Mr. Brownstone," or "Paradise City," which simply wants out. But as good as Axl's lyrics and screeching voice are, they wouldn't be nearly as effective without the twin-guitar interplay of Slash and Izzy Stradlin, who spit out riffs and solos better than any band since the Rolling Stones, and that's what makes *Appetite for Destruction* the best metal record of the late '80s. —*Stephen Thomas Erlewine*

G N' R Lies / 1989 / Geffen ✦✦✦
Once *Appetite for Destruction* finally became a hit in 1988, Guns N' Roses bought some time by delivering the half-old/half-new LP *G N' R Lies* as a followup. Constructed as a double-EP, with the "indie" debut *Live ?!*@ Like A Suicide* coming first and four new acoustic-based songs following on the second side, *G N' R Lies* is where the band metamorphosized from genuine threat to joke. Neither recorded live nor released by an indie label, *Live ?!*@ A Suicide* is competent bar-band boogie, without the energy or danger of *Appetite for Destruction*. The new songs are considerably more problematic. "Patience" is Guns N' Roses at their prettiest and their sappiest, the most direct song they have recorded to date. Its emotional directness makes the misogyny of "Used to Love Her (But I Had to Kill Her)" and the pitiful slanders of "One in a Million" sound genuine. Although the cover shrugs them off as a "joke," Axl's venom is frightening; there's little doubt that he truly does believe "faggots" come to America from another country, and that "niggers" should stay out of his way. Since he wasn't playing a character on the remainder of the album, there's little doubt that this is from the heart as well. And what makes it harder to dismiss is the musical skills of the band, who make the country-fried boogie of "Used to Love Her," the bluesy revamp of "You're Crazy," and the tough, paranoid fever-dream of "One in a Million" indelible. So, you either listen to the music and are satisfied, or listen to the lyrics and become disturbed, not only by Axl's intentions, but the millions of record-buyers who identified with him. —*Stephen Thomas Erlewine*

Use Your Illusion I / Sep. 1991 / Geffen ✦✦✦✦
The "difficult second album" is one of the perennial rock 'n' roll cliches, but few second albums ever were as difficult as *Use Your Illusion, Pts. I & II*. Not really conceived as a double album, but impossible to separate as individual works, *Use Your Illusion* is a shining example of a suddenly successful band getting it all wrong and letting their ambitions run wild. Taking nearly three years to complete, the recording of the album was clearly difficult, and tensions between Slash, Izzy Stradlin, and Axl Rose are evident from the start. The two guitarists, particularly Stradlin, are trying to keep the group closer to their hard-rock roots, but Axl has pretensions of being Queen and Elton John, which is particularly odd for a notoriously homophobic Midwestern boy. Conceivably, the two aspirations could have been divided between the two records, but instead they are just thrown into the blender; it's just a coincidence that *I* is a harder-rocking record than *II*. Stradlin has a stronger presence on *I*, contributing three of the best songs—"Dust N' Bones," "You Ain't the First," and "Double Talkin' Jive"—which help keep the album in Stonesy Aerosmith territory. On the whole, the album is stronger than *II*, even though there's a fair amount of filler, including a song that takes its title from the Osmonds' biggest hit and a dippy psychedelic collaboration with Alice Cooper. But it also has two ambitious set-pieces, "November Rain" and "Coma," which find Axl fulfilling his ambitions, as well as the ferocious metallic "Perfect Crime" and the original version of the power ballad "Don't Cry." Still, it can be a chore to find the highlights on the record amid the overblown production and endless filler. —*Stephen Thomas Erlewine*

Use Your Illusion II / Sep. 1991 / Geffen ✦✦✦✦
Use Your Illusion II is more serious and ambitious than *I*, but it's also considerably more pretentious. Featuring no less than four songs that run over six minutes, *II* is heavy on epics, whether it's the charging funk-metal of "Locomotive," the anti-war "Civil War," or the multi-part "Estranged." As if an attempt to balance the grandiose epics, the record is loaded with an extraordinary amount of filler. "14 Years" may have a lean, Stonesy rhythm, and Duff McKagan's Johnny Thunders homage

"So Fine" may be entertaining, but there's no forgiving the ridiculous "Get in the Ring," where Axl threatens rock journalists *by name* because they gave him bad reviews, the misinterpretation of Dylan's "Knockin' on Heaven's Door," another version of "Don't Cry," and the bizarre closer "My World," which probably captures Axl's instability as effectively as the tortured poetry of his epics. There are numerous strengths to *Use Your Illusion II*—for all their pretensions, the overblown epics are effective, and a couple of songs have a nervy energy—but the pompous production and poor pacing make the album a tiring listen for anyone who's not a dedicated listener. —*Stephen Thomas Erlewine*

The Spaghetti Incident? / Nov. 23, 1993 / Geffen ✦✦
As punk albums go, *The Spaghetti Incident?* lacks righteous anger and rage. As Guns N' Roses albums go, it's a complete delight, returning to the ferocious, hard-rocking days of *Appetite for Destruction*. The Gunners play Stooges and New York Dolls songs exactly as they do Nazareth—as straightahead, driving riff-rockers. After the epic *Use Your Illusions*, the band sounds like it's having fun, not caring about making "art" like "November Rain" or "Estranged." Unfortunately, the tacked-on Charles Manson song leaves a bad aftertaste, but not because of the song itself; the inclusion of the song seems like a publicity-seeking stunt, a way to increase their sales while trying to regain their street credibility. And as *The Spaghetti Incident?* proves, they didn't need to stoop so low. —*Stephen Thomas Erlewine*

Arlo Guthrie

b. Jul. 10, 1947, Coney Island, NY
Guitar, Vocals / Folk, Singer-Songwriter, Folk-Rock, Contemporary Folk
Like his father Woody Guthrie, Arlo Guthrie has carved out a career as a folksinger and songwriter with a social conscience who leavens political messages with humor. Though Woody Guthrie was hospitalized for much of Arlo's youth, the youngster nevertheless grew up in a musical community that included Pete Seeger, Leadbelly, and Cisco Houston. He learned to play the guitar at age six and was performing in coffeehouses by his late teens. Guthrie's early fame was based on his anti-Establishment shaggy-dog story in song, "Alice's Restaurant," actually a comic monolog about the singer's troubles with the police and the draft board that was extremely timely when it appeared on record in 1967. The *Alice's Restaurant* album became Guthrie's only gold record, but he made a series of folk-rock records through the '70s, filling them with his own songs and those of his contemporaries, notably Steve Goodman's "The City of New Orleans," which became Guthrie's sole hit single in 1972. Guthrie's commercial fortunes, like those of most folkies, declined by the end of the '70s, and he made his last album for Warner Bros. in 1981. Since then he has launched his own label, Rising Son, which has reissued his Warner albums and released his new recordings. He continues to tour extensively and to work for such causes as environmentalism. —*William Ruhlmann*

☆ **Alice's Restaurant** / 1967 / Reprise ✦✦✦✦✦
In 1967 when this LP came out it was totally radical, directly political, and so deliciously funny that it deflated a great deal of the seriousness of the growing anti-war movement. In this one stroke Guthrie established himself as more than the son of the famous man and major star. People often forget about the "Motorcycle Song" and "Chillin' of the Evening" on side two. —*Richard Meyer*

Arlo / 1968 / Rising Son ✦✦✦
On this LP Guthrie continued his monologue with an extended "Motorcycle Song" and other originals. —*Richard Meyer*

Running Down the Road / 1969 / Reprise ✦✦✦
More of a rock 'n' roll record with the hit "Coming into Los Angeles." —*Richard Meyer*

Washington County / 1970 / Reprise ✦✦✦
This album is more homey and roots-flavored, with cuts like "Valley to Pray" with Doc Watson and "Lay Down Little Doggies." It's a good, relaxed effort. —*Richard Meyer*

Hobo's Lullaby / 1972 / Rising Son ✦✦✦✦
It contains his hit version of "City of New Orleans" and "1913 Massacre." —*Richard Meyer*

The Last of the Brooklyn Cowboys / 1973 / Rising Son ✦✦✦
A strong collection, it has good versions of "Ramblin' Round," "Gypsy Davey," "Love Sick Blues," and "Gates of Eden." —*Richard Meyer*

25th Anniversary Edition / 1974 / Rising Sun ✦✦✦

Together in Concert / 1975 / Reprise ✦✦✦✦
Separately and together, Arlo Guthrie and Pete Seeger delight in a live setting. —*William Ruhlmann*

Amigo / 1976 / Rising Son ✦✦✦✦
An excellent, rocking collection including Guthrie's adaptation of "Guabi, Guabi," a song about Victor Jara, and a knockabout cover of the Rolling Stones song "Connection." —*William Ruhlmann*

The Best of Arlo Guthrie / 1977 / Reprise ✦✦✦✦
This includes "Alice's Restaurant," the equally comic "Motorcycle Song," "Coming into Los Angeles," and "City of New Orleans." —*William Ruhlmann*

● **Precious Friend** / 1982 / Reprise ✦✦✦✦
A second excellent collection by Pete Seeger and Arlo Guthrie, veterans of two generations. —*William Ruhlmann*

Mystic Journey / Feb. 1996 / Rising Son ✦✦✦
On his first studio album of new original material in a decade, Arlo Guthrie turned out a recording to fit in well with his existing catalog. His chief musical influences continued to be Bob Dylan and the Beatles, circa 1966, as he made melodic folk-rock anchored by his acoustic guitar and augmented by a rock rhythm section, other stringed instruments, and keyboards, frequently played by his son and co-producer Abe Guthrie. The lyrics also had a Dylanish twinge in their poetic, sometimes obscure language, though Guthrie commented on a variety of contemporary issues including the experiences of veterans ("When a Soldier Makes It Home"), child and spouse abuse, and gentrification. Just as often, however, singing in his resonant, half-spoken voice, which had begun to be reminiscent of Willie Nelson, Guthrie adopted an elegiac, fatalistic tone, expressing spiritual concerns in nearly apocalyptic terms. That too had long been a feature, but on *Mystic Journey*, unleavened by humor, it was the dominant theme. —*William Ruhlmann*

Guy

f. 1987, New York, NY
Vocals / Urban, Club/Dance, New Jack R&B
This seminal R&B trio was the first group to sport the new jack swing sound, essentially traditional soul vocals melded to hip-hop beats, with credit for the genre's invention going to founder, multi-instrumentalist, and superproducer Teddy Riley. Riley formed his first band, Wreckx-N-Effect, while still a teenager, with brothers Markell Riley and Brandon Mitchell; Guy followed a few years later in 1987. Its first incarnation featured vocalists Aaron Hall and Timmy Gatling. Their self-titled debut album was an instant smash, producing the R&B hits "I Like," "Groove Me," "Spend the Night," and "Teddy's Jam." Meanwhile, Riley found himself in strong demand as a songwriter and producer; in 1988 Riley produced Bobby Brown's *Don't Be Cruel*, the album that helped new jack swing cross over into the pop mainstream. Riley has also worked with Kool Moe Dee, Michael Jackson (*Dangerous*), Stevie Wonder, Keith Sweat, Jane Child, and SWV, among others. In between albums, Guy contributed songs to the soundtracks of *Do the Right Thing* and *New Jack City*. By 1989, Guy was in turmoil; Riley's brother Brandon Mitchell was killed in a shooting, and Guy became involved in an acrimonious split with manager Gene Griffin over money. In 1990 *The Future* featured Hall's brother Albert Damion Hall in place of Gatling and spawned R&B hits in "Let's Chill," "Do Me Right," "D-O-G Me Out," and "Long Gone." However, by the time Riley and Guy finally started to attract media attention for their innovative and influential work, the trio had broken up. Riley concentrated on his production and songwriting career for several years before forming the band Blackstreet with vocalists Chauncey "Black" Hannibal, Dave Hollister, and Levi Little. The quartet released a self-titled debut in 1994. Aaron Hall released his solo debut, *The Truth*, in 1993; brother Damion followed in 1994 with *Straight to the Point*. —*Steve Huey*

● **Guy** / 1988 / MCA ✦✦✦✦
The hottest trend of the late '80s was new jack swing, in which hip-hop production met vintage R&B/soul singing. The man credited with perfecting this style, of course, was Guy's Teddy Riley. The New York City threesome roared out of the chute with this album, which eventually became a platinum success, and the hit "I Like" was extremely influential. "Spend the Night" and "Teddy's Jam" were other strong singles, but the key hit was "Groove Me," one of the year's hottest records and Guy's finest single. It had hypnotic beats, was superbly produced, and featured riveting vocals. —*Ron Wynn*

The Future / 1990 / Uptown/MCA ✦✦✦
New jack swing, a hard-edged, high-tech blend of funk, R&B, and rap/hip-hop, has been milked for all it's worth and run into the ground by Guy's numerous imitators in the late '80s and early– to mid-'90s. But in the hands of Guy, its highly influential orginators, it sounded fresh and inspired. Though not as strong as the debut album of 1988, *The Future* is one of the more appealing—and certainly more authentic—examples of new jack swing. Lead by the ubiquitous producer/songwriter Teddy Riley, the trio brings a definite urgency to both grinding, forceful funk like "Teddy's Jam 2" and "Her" and such slow jams as "Do Me Right" and "Tease Me Tonight" (both of which recall the Gap Band a la "Outstanding"). Especially riveting is the all-rap number "Total Control," a brutally honest commentary on exploitation in the music business. For those who understandably complain about the glut of faceless new jack swing artists saturating the market, it's important to absorb Guy's music and realize that it wasn't always cheap and formulaic. —*Alex Henderson*

H

Sammy Hagar

b. Oct. 13, 1947, Monterey, CA

Guitar, Vocals / Hard Rock, Heavy Metal, Arena Rock

After spending several years as the lead vocalist and rhythm guitarist for the mid-'70s hard rock band Montrose, Sammy Hagar began a solo career that produced several hits and made him an album rock favorite. Hagar became a true star once he joined Van Halen in 1985, but he was a popular hard rocker ever since his first album with Montrose.

After giving up a boxing career, Hagar began singing in the late '60s, performing with various California bands including Skinny, the Fabulous Catillas, Justice Brothers, and Dust Cloud. During this time, he built up a solid reputation in the Californian hard-rock scene. Former Edgar Winter guitarist Ronnie Montrose asked Hagar to join his band, Montrose, in 1973. Hagar recorded two albums with Montrose before going solo in 1976, taking the group's bassist Bill Church. Montrose's drummer Denny Carmassi later joined Hagar's band, along with keyboardist Geoff Workman. Hagar's self-titled *Sammy Hagar* was his first chart entry; it eventually went gold. In 1979, he created a new supporting band featuring Workman, Church, guitarist Gary Pihl, and drummer Chuck Ruff. This lineup played on Hagar's most popular solo albums, including 1981's platinum *Standing Hampton* and 1982's gold *Three Lock Box*. After *Three Lock Box* and its No. 13 hit single "Your Love Is Driving Me Crazy," Hagar toured with guitarist Neal Schon, bassist Kenny Aaronson, and drummer Mike Shrieve; the group recorded a live album under the name HGAS, as well as a studio version of Procol Harum's "A Whiter Shade of Pale." His 1984 album *VOA* contained the hit single "I Can't Drive 55," which peaked at No. 26.

In 1985, Hagar replaced David Lee Roth in Van Halen; his first album with the group was 1986's *5150*. Hagar released his last solo album, *Sammy Hagar*, in 1987; the title of the record was changed to *I Never Said Goodbye* in a MTV contest, but no copies of the record were ever issued with that name. Hagar stayed with Van Halen through the remainder of the '80s and half of the '90s. During that time, the band had four other multiplatinum albums—*OU812* (1988), *For Unlawful Carnal Knowledge* (1991), *LIVE: Right Here, Right Now* (1993), *Balance* (1995)—before tensions began to surface between Hagar and the rest of the band. In the summer of 1996, Hagar either quit Van Halen or was fired, as the band had Roth return to sing two tracks on *Best of, Vol. 1* before hiring former Extreme vocalist Gary Cherrone as Sammy's replacement. The entire incident became a media sensation, ensuring that Hagar's 1997 solo album *Marching to Mars*—his first in 10 years—would be greeted with much media-generated fanfare. *—Stephen Thomas Erlewine*

All Night Long / 1978 / One Way ♦♦♦

All Night Long is better than most hard rock live albums not only because Sammy Hagar is at his best when he's on stage, but because the set list includes only his best songs, eliminating the filler that tends to clutter his albums. *—Stephen Thomas Erlewine*

Standing Hampton / 1982 / Geffen ♦♦♦♦

After releasing several competent but more or less undistinguished albums on Capitol, Sammy Hagar switched to Geffen in 1981 and released *Standing Hampton*, a polished but tough record that showed a surprising amount of pop songcraft. The added production gloss and improved melodic sense proved commercially successful—the album was his first million-seller and it cracked the Top 30—and artistically successful as well; the record was the most consistent and memorable album he recorded to date, featuring the singles "I'll Fall in Love Again," "Baby's on Fire," and "There's Only One Way to Rock." *—Stephen Thomas Erlewine*

Rematch / 1982 / Capitol ♦♦♦♦

As Sammy Hagar's career was at its height in the early '80s, Capitol, his '70s record label, released *Rematch*, a compilation of highlights from his six albums with the label. Like *All Night Long* before it, *Rematch* cuts away all the fat from Hagar's '70s catalog, leaving only his best rockers, including the scorching "I've Done Everything for You," "Plain Jane," "Turn Up the Music," and "Trans Am (Highway Wonderland)." Even though the track listing is well chosen, his Capitol records weren't as impressive as his albums for Geffen, meaning *Rematch* is only the best of a specific era of Hagar's career, not his entire career. *—Stephen Thomas Erlewine*

Three Lock Box / 1983 / Geffen ♦♦♦♦

Continuing the sleek, driving pop-oriented sound of Hagar's breakthrough *Standing Hampton*, *Three Lock Box* equals its predecessor, featuring such highlights as the double entendres of the title track and the hit single "Your Love Is Driving Me Crazy." *—Stephen Thomas Erlewine*

VOA / 1983 / Geffen ♦♦♦♦

VOA was the last album Hagar recorded before he became the lead singer of Van Halen, and the record shows why he was invited to join the band. With songs like "I Can't Drive 55" he adds a simple melody to the song which never distracts from the all-important, hard-driving riff. On "Two Sides of Love," he shows that he has the ability to pull off a power ballad, wrenching every bit of feeling out of the song. Like Hagar himself, *VOA* is never subtle, but in hard rock, that's a positive attribute. *—Stephen Thomas Erlewine*

Sammy Hagar / 1987 / One Way ♦♦♦

Sammy Hagar, the singer's last solo album, was released a year after his first album with Van Halen, 1986's *5150*. Although it charted the highest of any of his records, peaking at No. 14, it wasn't as successful as his three previous albums, suffering from a slick, synthesized production and a lack of consistent material. The power ballad "Give to Live" was a hit and a couple of the rockers raised above the pedestrian level, yet the overall product was rather faceless. Perhaps sensing the lackluster quality of the record, Hagar launched an MTV promotion to re-title the record; the winning entry was *I Never Said Goodbye*. No copies were released with the new title, although the 1994 *Unboxed* compilation called the album *I Never Said Goodbye*, not *Sammy Hagar*. *—Stephen Thomas Erlewine*

● **Unboxed** / Jan. 1994„ MARC / Geffen ♦♦♦♦

Collecting the best of Hagar's prime years at Geffen, *Unboxed* has most of his hits from the early '80s—including "I Can't Drive 55," "There's Only One Way to Rock," "Three Lock Box," and "Give to Live"—but there's a noticeable absence of "Your Love Is Driving Me Crazy," which was his biggest hit. Nevertheless, *Unboxed* is a good introduction to his best years. *—Stephen Thomas Erlewine*

Marching to Mars / 97 / MCA ♦♦♦♦

Evidently, being kicked out of Van Halen revitalized Sammy Hagar, since *Marching to Mars* is among his best solo albums. A lean, tough collection of by-the-books hard-rockers, *Marching to Mars* stands out because of its immediate sound and Hagar's sense of purpose. He's out to prove himself, to illustrate that he wasn't just Van Halen's mouthpiece or a blowhard. Subtlety still remains a weak point with Hagar, but he's rarely sounded quite as convincing as he does here, tearing through a set of surprisingly well-written songs with such guest artists as Huey Lewis, Slash, Mickey Hart, and Bootsy Collins. There's still a handful of weak moments, but the record is one of his strongest, and with bluesy cuts like "Little White Lie," it's also one of his more ambitious. *—Stephen Thomas Erlewine*

The Best of Sammy Hagar / NOVE6Feb. 19 / Capitol ✦✦✦✦
A CD-era collection of Hagar's Capitol work that supplants *Rematch*, *The Best of Sammy Hagar* has a nearly identical track listing as the previous collection and suffers from the same flaws. —*Stephen Thomas Erlewine*

Nina Hagen

b. Mar. 11, 1955, Berlin, Germany
Vocals / Alternative Pop-Rock
Born in East Germany, Nina Hagen had already gained a reputation as a flamboyant rock singer by the time she emigrated to the West in 1976, where she formed a band, signed to CBS Germany, and released their debut album, *Nina Hagen Band*, in 1978. It was followed in 1980 by *Unbehagen*. Hagen's first US release was a four-song EP consisting of songs drawn from her two German releases, *Nina Hagen Band EP* (1980). She moved to New York and made her first English-language LP, *Nunsexmonkrock*, in 1982. That and its follow-up, the Giorgio Moroder-produced *Fearless* (1983), charted briefly, and "New York New York" was a Top Ten dance club hit. But Hagen left CBS after *Nina Hagen in Ekstacy* (1985). In 1988, she celebrated her marriage with the EP *Punk Wedding*, released in Canada, and in 1989 she returned to the German market with *Nina Hagen*. —*William Ruhlmann*

● **14 Friendly Abductions: Best Of** / Feb. 1996,, MARC / Columbia/Legacy ✦✦✦✦
Nina Hagen is a unique vocalist, ranging from a coloratura soprano to a guttural alto and phrasing in surprising, dramatically changing ways, so that her performances are musical roller coasters, full of sudden shifts in mood and volume. Singing alternately in German and English, Hagen is backed by rock tracks leaning toward punk on some songs, and by producer Giorgio Moroder's signature Eurodisco synth-dance sounds on others on this 14-track, 74-minute compilation. Want to hear a German-language version of the Tubes' "White Punks on Dope"? How about a performance of "My Way" (also in German) that rivals Sid Vicious' for outrageousness? Ultimately, Nina Hagen may be a period novelty act of the early '80s, a mixture of Toni Basil, Falco, and a hyena. But she gets your attention. —*William Ruhlmann*

Haircut 100

f. 1980, Beckenham, England, **db.** 1983
New Wave, Pop-Rock
Combining light funk with frothy pop, Haircut 100 was one of the cleanest and most accessible new wave groups. Formed in 1980, the British band's core members were vocalist Nick Heyward, bassist Les Nemes, and guitarist Graham Jones; the following years drummer Memphis Blair Cunningham, saxophonist Phil Smith, and percussionist Mark Fox joined the group. Once the band was signed to Arista Records, they were put in the direction of producer Bob Sargeant, who helped them polish their stylish pop. Released in late 1981, Haircut 100's first single, "Favourite Shirts (Boy Meets Girl)," managed to reach number four in the UK, establishing the group's widespread appeal. The band released their debut album, *Pelican West*, in early 1992. Their next single, "Love Plus One," was a bigger hit, making the band one of the hottest British pop groups of the year. However, their momentum crashed to a halt when Heyward decided to pursue a solo career. Fox became the lead vocalist in early 1984, yet Haircut 100 could not replicate their previous success; they broke up after the release of their second album, 1984's *Paint on Paint*. —*Stephen Thomas Erlewine*

Paint & Paint / 1983 / Polydor ✦✦
Nick Heyward left Haircut 100 for a solo career shortly after the success of *Pelican West*, so the group decided that percussionist Mark Fox would be an adequate lead vocalist for their second album, *Paint and Paint*. In many ways they were right, since Fox has a pleasantly thin voice that blends easily into the band's lightly jazzy pop and funk. However, he lacks both the fey wit and easy melodicism of Heyward and, as a result, the group fails to produce anything as effortlessly catchy and memorable as "Love Plus One." It's no surprise that the group disappeared shortly after the release of *Paint and Paint*. —*Stephen Thomas Erlewine*

● **Best of Haircut One Hundred** / 1994 / Alex ✦✦✦✦
The Best of Haircut One Hundred is a 14-track collection featuring all of the lite new wave group's biggest hits, including "Favourite Shirts (Boy Meets Girl)" and "Love Plus One," plus several of Nick Heyward's solo singles, like "Whistle Down the Wind." Track-for-track, it's the most consistent album by either Haircut One Hundred or Heyward, even though several of the cuts are little more than pleasant artifacts from the early '80s. However, the three previously mentioned singles are all minor new wave classics, and it's nice to have them collected on one disc. —*Stephen Thomas Erlewine*

Pelican West / 982 / Arista ✦✦✦✦
Haircut 100's debut album *Pelican West* is a widely uneven concoction of lite-funk and jazzy new wave pop. Although the group's music was frequently so light it virtually disappeared, they did record a pair of classic new wave singles with the effervescent "Love Plus One" and "Favourite Shirts (Boy Meets Girl)." Although much of the record lacks the hooks of those two tracks, there's a handful of enjoyably breezy pop songs on *Pelican West*, such as "Fantastic Day" and "Snow Girl," that makes it worth investigating for new wave fetishists. Still, there's no denying that Haircut 100's material was often inadequate—a situation that is only emphasized on the American edition of the album, which places the singles at the front—and that the record sounded like a period piece just a few years after its release. —*Stephen Thomas Erlewine*

Bill Haley (William John Clifton Haley)

b. Jul. 6, 1925, Highland Park, MI, **d.** Feb. 9, 1981, Harlingen, TX
Guitar, Vocals / Rock 'n' Roll, Western Swing, Rockabilly
The Bill Haley and the Comets recording of "Rock Around the Clock," which topped the charts for eight weeks in 1955, is remembered as the beginning of the rock era. Though it also represented Haley's peak as a performer, his career had begun some time before and would continue for a long time after. Born in Michigan, Haley began leading western swing bands under various names in the late '40s, slowly starting to incorporate elements of R&B. Soon after he began recording for Essex in the early '50s, his backup band was named the Comets.

Because of his somewhat square image and his undeniably white sound, Haley, it could be argued, has been short-changed by latter-day rock historians. He was among the first performers—perhaps he was even the very first—of any color to combine R&B and C&W in a way that can readily be identified by listeners of any era as bona fide rock 'n' roll. Although their initial impact was regional, his early '50s sides rank among his most exciting, steering country and Western and big band forms into uncharted regions that were more frenetic and reckless. Haley also wrote much of his own material, and one of his compositions, "Crazy, Man, Crazy," became one of the first Top 20 rock 'n' roll hits in 1953. In 1954, he moved to the major Decca label, where his sides became increasingly formulaic, though for a time very successful, after "Rock Around the Clock."

It is his Decca sides, however, that are his most famous. In 1954, he went to number 12 with "Shake, Rattle and Roll," and in 1955 he hit with "Dim, Dim, the Lights," "Mambo Rock," and "Birth of the Boogie." But it was "Rock Around the Clock," previously recorded and released as a B-side in 1954 and reissued as the theme song for the movie *Blackboard Jungle*, that became his biggest hit. At that time the band consisted of Haley on guitar and vocals, Danny Cedrone on lead guitar, Joey D'Ambrose on sax, Billy Williamson on steel guitar, Johnny Grande on piano, Marshall Lytle on bass, and Dick Richards on drums.

Following the success of "Rock Around the Clock," Haley and the Comets placed nine more records in the Top 40 over the next three years, among them the Top Tens "Burn That Candle" and "See You Later, Alligator." Haley was largely eclipsed as the king of rock 'n' roll by Elvis Presley and other more flamboyant performers who followed him from 1956 on. Nevertheless, he continued to perform overseas and in oldies shows in the US, and "Rock Around the Clock" even got back into the Top 40 in 1974. —*William Ruhlmann & Richie Unterberger*

Greatest Hits / 1985 / MCA ✦✦✦
The mini-skirted go-go dancers pictured on the cover reveal the year of release, a considerable distance from Haley's classic period, and it is amazing that Decca didn't have a hits compilation out earlier. The songs speak for themselves, and loudly, however—apart from "Rock Around the Clock" and "Shake Rattle and Roll," the highlights include "Thirteen Women," a delightfully surreal end-of-the-world rockabilly fantasy about a man on a post-nuclear world who finds himself the only male to service 13 fertile female survivors. —*Bruce Eder*

★ **From the Original Master Tapes** / 1985 / MCA ✦✦✦✦✦
This is it—the Bill Haley record to own! Compiled by producer Steve Hoffman from the original session masters (you even get studio chatter ahead of "Rock Around the Clock"), this 20-song collection is the definitive Haley hits collection, with every song of consequence that he recorded for Decca Records during the years 1954-56. The sound is extraordinary—you haven't really heard Haley's music till you've heard this disc—and the sessionography adds a great deal to our knowledge of the players. From "Rock Around the Clock" and "Thirteen Women" to "Don't Knock the Rock," this is the best representation of Haley's peak years. —*Bruce Eder*

The Decca Years & More / 1991 / Bear Family ✦✦✦✦

Rock the Joint! / Apr. 5, 1995 / Schoolkids ✦✦✦✦
A 22-track collection that collects sides from 1951-53. Those who haven't heard this material before will be astonished to discover bona fide rock 'n' roll dating from three to four years earlier than the era

('54-55) more commonly associated with the music's birth. Haley's sound is similar to the country-boogie of the late '40s, retaining the steel guitar prominent in much of the era's country music, but it's clearly more driving and forward-looking. The songs owe a lot to jump R&B, but are transformed into the basic model of rock 'n' roll with slapping bass, ricky-tick drums, and extended electric guitar riffing. Listen to his version of Jackie Brenston's "Rocket 88" (which has itself been pegged as one of the first rock 'n' roll records) and you'll be astounded to note the basics of rockabilly already in place—in 1951. The low buzzing, distorted guitar on "Green Tree Boogie" (also from 1951) is also a revelation, as is the guitar solo on 1952's "Rock the Joint," which is almost identical to the much more famous one on "Rock Around the Clock" a couple of years later. The later sides introduce a honking sax, which would become such a prominent feature in '50s rock 'n' roll. Includes "Crazy Man Crazy," one of the first rock 'n' roll songs to make the Top 20. —*Richie Unterberger*

Half Japanese

f. 1977, Maryland
Alternative Pop-Rock, Experimental, Post-Punk, Indie Rock
Depending on your point of view, Half Japanese is either a celebration of the pure, amateurish do-it-yourself rock 'n' roll spirit, or a pretentious, highly irritating example of noisy, self-conscious experimental rock at its most extreme. Formed by Jad and David Fair in 1977, the group started bashing out music in their parents' basement in Maryland, recording their debut EP by themselves. By the time the Fairs recorded their debut album, the three-record box set *1/2 Gentlemen/ Not Beasts*, they had acquired a full-time drummer plus a saxophonist, yet their music was no less noisy and primitive; if anything, it was more atonal and difficult than before.

For the rest of their career, the band has proudly displayed nothing approaching instrumental virtuosity. David Fair left the band after their third record, rejoining briefly for 1988's *Charmed Life*. Throughout the years, the lineup has changed frequently—at times it has included Velvet Underground drummer Maureen Tucker and guitarist Don Fleming, as well as occasional contributions from Fred Frith and John Zorn—but Jad Fair has remained. That doesn't necessarily mean the music hasn't changed; their later records are slightly more musically varied and accessible, yet no less challenging. Fair has released a few solo albums that are stranger (believe it or not) than the typical Half Japanese release. —*Stephen Thomas Erlewine*

Half Gentlemen, Not Beasts [Box Set] / 1980 / Armageddon ✦✦✦✦
As with any album that is three records long, *1/2 Gentlemen/Not Beasts* unwittingly shows Half Japanese's true roots. Over the three records, the band "covers" such minimalists as the Velvet Underground, the Stooges, and Jonathan Richman, as well as deconstructing such wordsmiths as Bruce Springsteen and Bob Dylan. Although they would have you believe that their untuned, almost unlistenable, instrumental clatter is the result of being so enthusiastic that they didn't bother to learn how to play their instruments, it's just the logical, inevitable intellectual extension of Richman's naivete and the Velvet Underground's stripped-down guitar. Half Japanese is consciously primitive and amateurish. —*Stephen Thomas Erlewine*

Loud / 1981 / Armageddon ✦✦✦
On the aptly titled *Loud*, Half Japanese travels into improvisational free-jazz territory; along with free-associative freakouts like "I Know How It Feels . . . Bad," there's also a funereal cover of the Doors' "The Spy." —*Jason Ankeny*

Music to Strip By / 1987 / 50 Skidillion Watts ✦✦✦
Produced by Kramer, *Music to Strip By* finds Jad Fair working without brother David for the group's most coherent and accessible outing to date. Scattered among the usual chaos ("My Sordid Past," "Stripping for Cash," "Sex at Your Parents' House," "Ouija Board Summons Satan") are telling covers of Fats Domino's "Blue Monday," Willie Dixon's "Hidden Charms," and "La Bamba." —*Jason Ankeny*

● **Charmed Life** / 1988 / 50 Skidillion Watts ✦✦✦✦
While *Charmed Life* is the band's most accessible record, it doesn't even come close to the mainstream's concept of what constitutes pop music. Yet when Jad Fair sings about love and joy on *Charmed Life*, he is as straightforward and direct as he ever gets. —*Stephen Thomas Erlewine*

The Band That Would Be King / 1989 / 50 Skidillion Watts ✦✦✦✦
Featuring contributions from John Zorn and Fred Frith, *The Band That Would Be King* is one of the most diverse and challenging records Half Japanese has recorded. It's also one of their most rewarding. —*Stephen Thomas Erlewine*

We Are They Who Ache with Amorous Love / 1990 / T.E.C. Tones/ Elemental Music ✦✦✦
Spirited and noisy, *We Are They Who Ache With Amorous Love* ranks as one of Half Japanese's most self-indulgent efforts. Much of the record

is overly aggressive and abrasive, a series of improvisational pieces that don't go anywhere; even the more cogent tracks, including a cover of "Gloria," are too lo-fi to be listenable. —*Jason Ankeny*

● **Greatest Hits** / Mar. 13, 1995 / Safe House ✦✦✦✦
Half Japanese began their career with a three-LP box set, so it's little wonder that their *Greatest Hits* encompasses two CDs. Under the guidance of Jad Fair, the group has become more accessible over the years, but that's only a relative term. Fair has remained doggedly amateurish and noisy, letting the twisted pop structures peak out only every once in awhile. There's a lot of subtle differences between albums, which only fans can tell, so *Greatest Hits* serves as a good introduction to Half Japanese as well as a kind of road map of their career. —*Stephen Thomas Erlewine*

Hall & Oates

f. 1972, Philadelphia, PA
Soft Rock, Folk-Rock, Pop-Rock, Blue-Eyed Soul
From their first hit in 1974 through their heyday in the '80s, Daryl Hall and John Oates' smooth, catchy take on Philly soul brought them enormous commercial success—including six No. 1 singles and six platinum albums—yet little critical success. Hall & Oates' music was remarkably well-constructed and produced; at their best, their songs were filled with strong hooks and melodies that adhered to soul traditions without being a slave to them by incorporating elements of new wave and hard rock.

Daryl Hall began performing professionally while he was a student at Temple University. In 1966, he recorded a single with Kenny Gamble and the Romeos; the group featured Gamble, Leon Huff and Thom Bell, who would all become the architects of Philly soul. During this time, Hall frequently appeared on sessions for Gamble and Huff. In 1967, Hall met John Oates, a fellow Temple University student. Oates was leading his own soul band at the time. The two students realized they had similar tastes and began performing together in an array of R&B and doo wop groups. By 1968, the duo had parted ways, as Oates transferred schools and Hall formed the soft-rock band Gulliver; the group released one album on Elektra in the late '60s before disbanding.

After Gulliver's breakup, Hall concentrated on session work again, appearing as a backup vocalist for the Stylistics, the Delfonics, and the Intruders, among others. Oates returned to Philadelphia in 1969, and he and Hall began writing folk-oriented songs and performing together. Eventually they came to the attention of Tommy Mottola, who quickly became their manager, securing the duo a contract with Atlantic Records. On their first records—*Whole Oates* (1972), *Abandoned Luncheonette* (1973), *War Babies* (1974)—the duo were establishing their sound, working with producers like Arif Mardin and Todd Rundgren, and removing much of their folk influences. At the beginning of 1974, the duo relocated from Philadelphia to New York. During this period, they only managed one hit—the No. 60 "She's Gone" in the spring of 1974.

After they moved to RCA in 1975, the duo landed on its successful mixture of soul, pop and rock, scoring a Top Ten single with "Sara Smile." The success of "Sara Smile" prompted the re-release of "She's Gone," which rocketed into the Top Ten as well. Released in the summer of 1976, *Bigger than the Both of Us* was only moderately successful upon its release. The record took off in early 1977, when "Rich Girl" became the duo's first No. 1 single.

Although they had several minor hits between 1977 and 1980, the albums Hall & Oates released at the end of the decade were not as successful as their mid-'70s records. Nevertheless, they were more adventurous, incorporating more rock elements into their blue-eyed soul. The combination would finally pay off in late 1980, when the duo released the self-produced *Voices*, the album that marked the beginning of Hall & Oates' greatest commercial and artistic success. The first single from *Voices*, a cover of the Righteous Brothers' "You've Lost That Lovin' Feeling," reached No. 12, yet it was the second single, "Kiss on My List," that confirmed their commercial potential by becoming the duo's second No. 1 single; its follow-up, "You Make My Dreams" hit No. 5. They quickly released *Private Eyes* in the summer of 1981; the record featured two No. 1 hits, "Private Eyes" and "I Can't Go for That (No Can Do)," as well as the Top Ten hit "Did It in a Minute." "I Can't Go for That (No Can Do)" also spent a week at the top of the R&B charts—a rare accomplishment for a white act. *H20* followed in 1982 and it proved more successful than their two previous albums, selling over two million copies and launching their biggest hit single, "Maneater," as well as the Top Ten hits "One on One" and "Family Man." The following year, the duo released a greatest hits compilation, *Rock 'N Soul, Part 1*, that featured two new Top Ten hits—the No. 2 "Say It Isn't So" and "Adult Education."

In April of 1984, the Recording Industry Association of America announced that Hall & Oates had surpassed the Everly Brothers as the most successful duo in rock history, earning a total of 19 gold and platinum awards. Released in October of 1984, *Big Bam Boom* expanded their number of gold and platinum awards, selling over two million copies and launching four Top 40 singles, including the No. 1 "Out of Touch." Following their contract-fulfilling gold album *Live at the Apollo with David Ruffin & Eddie Kendrick*, Hall & Oates went on hiatus. After the lukewarm reception for Daryl Hall's 1986 solo album, *Three Hearts in the Happy Ending Machine*, the duo regrouped to release 1988's *Ooh Yeah!*, their first record for Arista. The first single, "Everything Your Heart Desires," went to No. 3 and helped propel the album to platinum status.

However, none of the album's other singles broke the Top 20, indicating that the era of chart dominance had ended. *Change of Season*, released in 1990, confirmed that fact. Although the record went gold, it only featured one Top 40 hit—the No. 11 single, "So Close." The duo hasn't released an album since 1990. —*Stephen Thomas Erlewine*

Whole Oates / 1972 / Atlantic ♦♦♦

Hall & Oates' debut album was a tentative effort, with the two singers hesitantly working their way around slick but relatively undistinguished material that displayed their folk roots more than any other record they would later make. —*Stephen Thomas Erlewine*

Abandoned Luncheonette / 1973 / Atlantic ♦♦♦♦

Abandoned Luncheonette, Hall & Oates' second album, was the first indication of the duo's talent for sleek, soul-inflected pop-rock, featuring the single "She's Gone," which would become a big hit in 1975, when it was re-released following the success of "Sara Smile." —*Stephen Thomas Erlewine*

War Babies / 1974 / Atlantic ♦♦

After crafting the fitfully accomplished blue-eyed Philly soul-pop of *Abandoned Luncheonette*, Hall & Oates retreated to a more rock-oriented sound on *War Babies*, recorded with producer Todd Rundgren. Some of the tracks work, but the duo's performance sounds forced through much of the record. —*Stephen Thomas Erlewine*

Daryl Hall & John Oates / 1976 / RCA ♦♦♦♦

Switching to RCA, Daryl Hall & John Oates recorded a self-titled album that fulfilled their early promise as pop-savvy, blue-eyed soul craftsmen. A few of the tracks fall flat—including the reggae-tinged "Soldering" and the pompous "Ennui on the Mountain"—but much of the album is lush and catchy, featuring ballads and mid-tempo numbers that are nearly as engaging as their breakthrough single "Sara Smile." —*Stephen Thomas Erlewine*

Bigger than the Both of Us / 1977 / RCA ♦♦

Bigger Than the Both of Us continued the gold success of its predecessor by adding a cleaner, more pop-oriented gloss to the production, as well as fine songwriting that builds on the bright pulse of "Rich Girl." —*Stephen Thomas Erlewine*

No Goodbyes / 1977 / Atlantic ♦♦

Released after the success of their first RCA album, *No Goodbyes* is a compilation of their three Atlantic albums that includes three unreleased tracks. *No Goodbyes* concisely sums up the high points of the duo's early years (in particular, the soaring single "She's Gone"), and confirms the fact that the pair were still developing their signature style. —*Stephen Thomas Erlewine*

Beauty on a Back Street / 1977 / RCA ♦♦♦

Beauty on a Back Street isn't quite as accomplished as its two predecessors, yet it is more ambitious and diverse, as Hall & Oates begin to add some arena-rock conventions to their sound, particularly distorted guitars and anthemic choruses. On *War Babies*, they had tried a similar attack, but on *Beauty on a Back Street* the duo's songwriting was stronger, which meant that the instrumental approach didn't overwhelm the actual songs. —*Stephen Thomas Erlewine*

Along the Red Ledge / Sep. 1978 / RCA ♦♦♦

Continuing the more rock-oriented approach of *Beauty on a Back Street*, *Along the Red Ledge* is more successful than its predecessor, as the duo landed on a polished melodic pop-rock style that managed to retain their Philly soul influences without drowning their voices in distorted guitar flourishes. They would refine this sound two years later on *Voices*, the record that established them as pop-rock superstars. —*Stephen Thomas Erlewine*

X-Static / 1979 / RCA ♦♦

After coming up with a sleek and soulful template on *Along the Red Ledge*, Hall & Oates took a temporary detour on *X-Static*, concentrating on disco rhythms. A few tracks were successful—in particular, "Wait for Me"—but the record sounds unfocused and misguided. —*Stephen Thomas Erlewine*

Voices / 1980 / RCA ♦♦♦♦

This is the album that took Hall & Oates from being a successful '70s pop duo to being one of the four biggest singles acts of the '80s (the others: Michael Jackson, Prince, and Madonna). The sound is a wonderful pop pastiche, from the Beatlesque "How Does It Feel to Be Back" to

the neo-Philadelphia soul of the hits "Kiss on My List" and "You Make My Dreams." —*William Ruhlmann*

Private Eyes / 1981 / RCA ♦♦♦♦

Voices brought Hall & Oates into the new wave era, establishing their sleek fusion of synthesizers, Philly soul, mechanical beats, and pop hooks, but they didn't quite perfect it until *Private Eyes*. Powered by no less than three Top Ten singles, the album is filled with effortlessly catchy hooks and a handful of great songs that don't stop at the hits. Sure, "Private Eyes," "I Can't Go for That (No Can Do)," and "Did It in a Minute" all have remarkably graceful melodies, but what's unexpected is how flat-out terrific the pounding soul of "Looking for a Good Sign" is, or how deftly the arena-rock hooks of "Head Above Water" are executed. There's still a bit of filler, highlighted by John Oates' supremely silly "Mano a Mano," but Hall & Oates never made a record quite as good as *Private Eyes* ever again. —*Stephen Thomas Erlewine*

H2O / 1982 / RCA ♦♦♦♦

From the Motown beat of "Maneater" to the lush ballad "One on One," Hall & Oates continue to make the top pop of the early '80s. Also contains "Family Man." —*William Ruhlmann*

★ **Rock 'n' Soul Pt. 1: Greatest Hits** / 1983 / RCA ♦♦♦♦♦

Not a perfect hits collection but nonetheless an excellent compilation, *Rock 'n' Soul, Pt. 1: Greatest Hits* contains nine of Hall & Oates' biggest hits from 1974's "She's Gone" to 1983's "One on One," adding new songs—the wonderful "Say It Isn't So" and "Adult Education"—plus a live take of "Wait for Me" for good measure. While several terrific singles are missing—particularly "Did It in a Minute" and ""Family Man"—all the essential items are here, and they illustrate the duo's expertise in crafting soulful pop songs, making a convincing argument that Hall & Oates were the last great blue-eyed soul group. —*Stephen Thomas Erlewine*

Big Bam Boom / 1984 / RCA ♦♦♦

The last of the major Hall & Oates albums of the '80s features more of their patented soul-rock sound on the hits "Out of Touch" and "Method of Modern Love." —*William Ruhlmann*

Live at the Apollo / 1985 / RCA ♦♦

Hall & Oates' second live album was a better effort than 1978's *Livetime*, containing a collection of performances that are altogether more convincing, yet ironically, it fails to sound as exciting as their meticulously crafted studio albums. —*Stephen Thomas Erlewine*

Ooh Yeah! / 1988 / Arista ♦♦

Ooh Yeah!, Hall & Oates' first album for Arista Records, was their weakest studio effort since *X-Static*, both commercially and artistically. Although they still rely on their signature pop-soul sound, the duo's material is simply not up to par. Not that *Ooh Yeah!* is a total washout—the single "Everything Your Heart Desires" is as good as their early '80s hits—but the whole album is rather undistinguished. —*Stephen Thomas Erlewine*

Change of Season / 1990 / Arista ♦♦

Apart from the hit "So Close," *Change of Season* is largely undistinguished, relying more on sound than song craft. Not surprisingly, it was Hall & Oates' lowest-charting album of original material since 1974's *War Babies*, even if it did go gold. —*Stephen Thomas Erlewine*

Atlantic Collection / Jan. 23, 1996 / Rhino ♦♦♦♦

Drawing from Hall & Oates' four Atlantic albums and adding one previously unreleased song, *Atlantic Collection* is a definitive overview of the duo's early years. Although they only had one hit during this period—"She's Gone," which is included here in its full-length album version—their early recordings contained some of their richest, most diverse music. Much of the material is based in soul, particularly the smooth Philly soul of the early '70s, yet it also has strong folk overtones, as well as distinct pop-rock leanings. Within these 21 tracks, it is possible to hear the roots of their later hits, as well as directions they never wound up pursuing. For serious Hall & Oates fans, *The Atlantic Collection* can be a revelatory listen. —*Stephen Thomas Erlewine*

Kristen Hall

b. Atlanta, GA
Guitar, Vocals / Folk, Singer-Songwriter, Contemporary Folk

Atlanta based singer-songwriter Kristen Hall has built a strong reputation in folk circles with her infectious Indigo Girls style of acoustic folk-rock. Her raspy-voiced delivery of highly personal lyrics are the center of attention and often times accompanied only by acoustic guitar. While her first album, *Real Life Stuff*, released independently, consisted of minimalistic arrangements of nearly demo quality, subsequent releases (1991's *Fact and Fiction* and 1994 *Be Careful What You Wish For*) have been bigger productions featuring high-profile guests such as Emily Saliers of Indigo Girls, Cindy Wilson of the B-52's, and Jules Shear. —*Chris Woodstra*

Real Life Stuff / 1990 / Dog Gone ◆◆◆
An outstanding independent release from this Atlanta-based singer-songwriter. Her debut, a self-produced, low-key folk album centered around Hall's raspy voice and guitar, gives the blueprint for her later releases. Well worth seeking out. —*Chris Woodstra*

● **Fact and Fiction** / 1991 / High Street ◆◆◆◆
This mainly acoustic album ranges from introspective ballads to catchy upbeat folk-rock anthems. Hall's world-weary voice, both rough and delicate, tells reflective tales of yearning and love lost while retaining an uplifting spirit. Guests include Emily Sailers (Indigo Girls), and Cindy Wilson (B-52's). —*Chris Woodstra*

Be Careful What You Wish For / Jun. 14, 1994 / High Street ◆◆◆◆
Kristen Hall has a gutsy voice that never sounds forced. The rocking guitar-based arrangements have a sound not unlike some of John Hiatt's recent records. These are very personal songs, some with political centers such as "Proud Man," sung with commitment and deep emotion. The opening cut, "Cry Tomorrow," sets the tone of the album; she maintains the drive and quality through to the end. —*Richard Meyer*

Terry Hall

b. Mar. 19, 1959, Coventry, England
In the strictest sense, Terry Hall isn't a musician. He doesn't play an instrument and his singing is generally flat and detached. But Terry Hall is a great pop star, with a perfect look, a cooly laconic voice, and a knack for anticipating pop trends. As the frontman for the Specials, Hall shot to stardom in Britain in the early '80s, singing such classic ska-revival singles as "Gangsters," "Nite Club," and "Ghost Town" before leaving with the group's other vocalists to form the new wave pop group the Fun Boy Three. That trio began a long line of projects Hall pursued over the next decade. None of his groups recorded more than two albums, and each had a taste of British success. Of all these, the Fun Boy Three was the most successful, but he disbanded them within two years to form Colourfield, which led to Terry, Blair, and Anouchka and then a duo with David Stewart, called Vegas. Each group led Hall closer to the pop mainstream, yet he remained an outsider, since he had no desire for stardom. While his polished recordings only bore a slight resemblance to his seminal work with the Specials and the Fun Boy Three, Hall's presence was stronger than ever in the mid-'90s, as a new generation of alternative artists, including Blur and Tricky, acknowledged his influence. All the praise coincided with the release of *Home*, Hall's first official solo album, which appeared in 1995, well over 15 years after he began his career.

Hall was singing with a new wave band called the Squad when Jerry Dammers recruited him to sing with the Specials. "Gangsters," the first single the Specials released, went into the Top Ten upon its release, establishing both the group and its independent label 2-Tone as a major pop force in England. For the next two years, the Specials were one of the most popular and influential bands in the UK, scoring a streak of seven straight Top Ten singles. Their popularity culminated with the prophetic "Ghost Town," which spent three weeks at No. 1 in the summer of 1981. The "Ghost Town" single was the last to feature Terry Hall and the original lineup—after its release, Hall split with the group's other two vocalists, Lynval Golding and Neville Staples, to form the Fun Boy Three.

Where the Specials were a ska-revival band, the Fun Boy Three was a new wave pop group with distinctly weird, skeletal, and experimental overtones. The band released their first single, "The Lunatics (Have Taken Over the Asylum)," shortly after they departed from the Specials. The single peaked at No. 20 late in 1981. Early in 1982, the group charted again with "It Ain't What You Do (It's the Way That You Do It)," a duet with Bananarama on an old Jimmie Lunceford song. The Fun Boy Three finally released their eponymous debut in the spring of 1982. That summer, they had a hit with a cover of George Gershwin's "Summertime." The group recorded a second album with Talking Heads leader David Byrne late in 1982. The resulting album, *Waiting*, appeared in the spring of 1983, concurrently with the Top Ten singles "The Tunnel of Love" and "Our Lips Are Sealed," a song Hall wrote with Jane Wiedlin, who already made it into a hit the previous year with her group, the Go-Go's.

By the summer of 1983, the Fun Boy Three were peaking in popularity and Hall disbanded the group. Hooking up with ex-Swinging Cats members Toby Lyons and Karl Shale, Terry Hall moved to Manchester and formed the Colourfield, a more lush and melodic outfit than the Fun Boy Three. In January of 1984, the band released their first single, "The Colourfield," which just missed the Top 40. It was followed later that summer with "Take," which didn't even come close to the Top 40. The Colourfield had its first hit in January of 1985, when "Thinking of You" reached No. 12. It was followed by "Castles in the Air," another failed single that preceded the release of their debut album, *Virgins and Philistines*, by just a few weeks. Like the band's

singles, *Virgins and Philistines* failed to gain a large audience for the Colourfield. The band released a second album, *Deception*, in the spring of 1987. During the sessions, Lyons left the band, leaving Hall to finish the album by himself; to complete the album, Hall hired Raquel Welch's band.

After the Colourfield imploded, Terry Hall formed a trio with an American actress called Blair Booth and a jeweler called Anouchka Groce. Terry, Blair, and Anouchka explored Hall's love for '60s pop, as well as kitschy mainstream pop, as evidenced on the trio's cover of Captain & Tennille's "Love Will Keep Us Together." "Missing," the group's first single, was released in the fall of 1989 and it didn't make much of an impact, peaking at No. 75 on the British charts. The trio's second single, "Ultra Modern Nursery Rhyme," didn't even chart. Terry, Blair, and Anouchka's debut album, also called *Ultra Modern Nursery Rhyme*, was released in February of 1990 to little attention.

Two years later, Terry Hall returned with Vegas, a one-shot collaboration with Dave Stewart from the Eurythmics. Vegas' eponymous album was released in the fall of 1992 and yielded three minor UK hits—"Possessed," "She," and "Walk into the Wind." Vegas wasn't particularly successful and the duo disbanded in early 1993.

Terry Hall released his first official solo, *Home*, in the spring of 1995 to mild interest. After its release, Hall collaborated on a new single, "Chasing a Rainbow," with Blur's Damon Albarn. The single was a minor hit and was added to a re-release of *Home* later in the year. Early in 1996, Terry Hall was featured in Tricky's side-project, *Nearly God*, singing on the single "Poems." —*Stephen Thomas Erlewine*

● **Terry Hall: The Collection** / Jul. 13, 1993 / Chrysalis ◆◆◆◆
The Collection compiles 22 highlights from Terry Hall's long, eclectic career, spanning from his groundbreaking work with the Specials to his '90s collaboration with Dave Stewart, Vegas. In between, all of the major hits Hall has sung with are covered—from the Specials' "Gangsters," "Nite Klub," and "Ghost Town" to the Fun Boy Three's "The Lunatics (Have Taken Over the Asylum)," "It Ain't What You Do (It's the Way That You Do It)," "Summertime" and "Our Lips Are Sealed," as well as Colourfield's "Thinking of You." Several failed singles from the Colourfield, Terry, Blair, and Anouchka and Vegas are included, as are interesting B-sides and rarities. And even with these rarities, *The Collection* remains the definitive compilation of Terry Hall's career, since it boils down an uneven, but always interesting, career to the essentials. —*Stephen Thomas Erlewine*

Home / 1995 / Anxious ◆◆◆
Home, Terry Hall's first solo album, is a surprisingly polished collection of mainstream pop-rock produced by the Lightning Seeds' Ian Broudie. Theoretically, the setting is entirely too smooth for Hall's limited vocal skills, but the results are quite enjoyable, since he and Broudie have cleverly arranged each song to emphasize the strengths of Terry's detached vocals. While there is a bit of filler scattered throughout the album, the record is supported by pleasantly jangling pop songs that help make *Home* Hall's strongest effort since the Colourfield. —*Stephen Thomas Erlewine*

Hampton Grease Band

f. 1968, Atlanta, GA, **db.** 1973
Psychedelic, Art-Rock/Progressive Rock, Blues-Rock
Hampton Grease Band may have ultimately been a band easier to appreciate in concept than to listen to in practice. They are also, for most listeners, a band that's much more fun to read about than to hear. For a brief period, though, they were offering some of the wackiest rock ever to be found on a major label. Clearly influenced by both Zappa and Beefheart, but more grating and even less accessible to the rock underground, they took early-'70s avant-rock aesthetics near their extremes. This guaranteed an eternal cult reputation for the group, but also ensured that their commercial success in their own time was virtually nil.

Hampton Grease Band began as a blues-rock-oriented outfit in the late '60s in Atlanta, where the underground rock scene was barely big enough to support them. They managed to carve a reputation at a local underground club, as well as by playing support to psychedelic/progressive acts like the Grateful Dead, Jimi Hendrix, Procol Harum, and the Allman Brothers. The group steadily developed a more original sound, emphasizing intricate, Zappa-esque guitar lines and Bruce Hampton's off-the-cuff, nonsequitur lyrics, usually shouted in a throaty, scratchy wheeze that made Beefheart sound like Pavarotti. The band often betrayed the Zappa influence in their theatrical, sometimes confrontational stage show, in which Hampton would throw chairs at the audience, or sing while standing on a pizza. Their polarized audiences, to say the least; they were pelted with cups of ice at one memorable gig that found them playing to a crowd of 10,000 as the warmup act for Three Dog Night (a bill that must have been devised by Salvador Dali).

Hampton Grease Band generated enough of a reputation, though, to pique the interest of Columbia Records, whose curiosity incited Allman

Brothers manager Phil Walden to sign the group. The Grease Band quickly recorded two albums worth of material that could in no way be construed as having money-making potential. Half the songs, to begin with, weighed in at around the 20-minute mark; the silvery guitar work of Glenn Phillips and Harold Kelling often took its cues from improvised jazz, while the songs lurched unpredictably between melodies and tempos, all executed with impeccable finesse by the musicians. The crowning touch was Hampton, whose amelodic rants crossbred soapbox preachers with bleacher bums. The lyrics took the Dadaist bent of Zappa/Beefheart to more inscrutable levels, most notoriously on "Hendon," with Hampton reading many of the words off the label of a can of spray paint. Phillips' silly faux-Latin miniature "Maria" was a much more radio-friendly novelty, but Hampton Grease Band were obviously going to be a much tougher sell than the Allman Brothers.

Confronted with the tapes, Columbia reacted most unpredictably, deciding to make the band's debut (and, as it turned out, only) record a double album, *Music to Eat*. Legend has it that it was, at the time of its release, the second-lowest selling LP in the Columbia catalog (beaten only by a yoga record). Columbia itself didn't help matters by marketing *Music to Eat* as a comedy album. Shortly after its release, Hampton Grease Band began to disintegrate, with the departure of guitarist Harold Kelling. Despite a well-received show at the Fillmore East with Frank Zappa, CBS dropped the group, which then signed with Zappa's Bizarre/Straight label. It seemed like a logical combination, but nothing came of it record-wise, and the band finally broke up in 1973 when Hampton left to, ironically, unsuccessfully audition for a job as Zappa's lead vocalist.

All of the members of the quintet that recorded *Music to Eat* remained active in music, especially Hampton (who recorded albums with the Aquarium Rescue Unit) and Phillips (who has released nearly a dozen instrumental records, including some for the influential alternative rock indie label SST). As is so often the case with the most interesting cult bands, interest in the band actually grew in the decades after their breakup, culminating in the reissue of *Music to Eat* on CD in 1996—on Columbia, the same label that had dumped them when they supposedly sold less copies than anyone else who had ever recorded for the company. —*Richie Unterberger*

● **Music to Eat** / 1971 / Columbia ✦✦✦✦
Hampton Grease Band's only album, now reissued as a double CD, is a one-of-a-kind item, drawing upon jazz, progressive/psychedelic guitar rock, and a generally surrealist bent to back Bruce Hampton's idiot-savant ravings. Comparisons with Zappa and Beefheart are really inevitable, though Hampton Grease Band really weren't on the level of those two fellow weirdos. They were definitely on their own wavelength, though, carving out a more guitar-oriented sound that skirted even closer to the lunatic fringe. The reissue's enhanced with a lengthy history by guitarist Glenn Phillips that's crammed with believe-it-or-not anecdotes from the group's fascinating career. —*Richie Unterberger*

Hanson

f. 1992, Tulsa, OK
Pop-Rock
Sounding like a revamped Jackson 5 for the '90s, Hanson came storming out of Tulsa, OK, in 1997, blessed with photogenic looks and a surprisingly infectious sense of melody. Hanson had a sunny pop sense that stood in direct contrast to the gloomy grunge that dominated the '90s, yet they also arrived with hip credentials—a handful of the cuts on their debut were produced by the Dust Brothers (Beastie Boys, Beck, Sukia), and the rest were produced by Steve Lironi, who helmed Black Grape's debut. Along with the hip production, the record was comprised of songs co-written by the band with professsional songwriters like Barry Mann & Cynthia Weil and Desmond Child. It had the sound of a hip recording and the craft of professional pop record, making *Middle of Nowhere* the best of both worlds.

Hanson were certainly reminiscent of an earlier era, namely the early '70s, when teens could rule the top of the charts. Like the Jackson 5, the Cowsills, and the mythological Partridge Family, all of the members of Hanson were brothers. Isaac, age 16 at the time of their debut, played guitar; 13-year-old Taylor sang lead and played keyboards; drummer Zac was 11 years old. As children in Tulsa, OK, they sang around the dinner table, often '50s and '60s rock and R&B standards and gospel songs. Eventually, the group began playing around Tulsa, performing at local festivals, at school, around town. The brothers first attempted to break into the music industry around 1992, when they approached music attorney Christopher Sabec and sang a cappella for him. Impressed with their talents, he became their manager and began shopping them to major labels. Between 1992 and 1995, five labels passed on Hanson. The group decided to release a pair of indie records while waiting. The album *Boomerang*, which was filled with slick pop, appeared in 1995. Following the release of *Boomerang*, Hanson began

playing their own instruments, which strengthened their writing considerably, as shown on the single "MMMBop," the song that signalled that they were moving towards a fresher, hip-hop and soul-influenced direction. The group signed with Mercury Records on the strength of "MMMBop," and they were hooked up with producer Steve Lironi, who helped the band with arrangements. Over the next year, the group worked on their album with a variety of collaborators, including co-writers like Barry Mann & Cynthia Weil, Desmond Child, and Mark Hudson; nine of the 13 tracks on the final album featured contributions from professional writers. They also recorded a handful of tracks with the Dust Brothers, who were riding high on the success of Beck's *Odelay*.

Prior to the spring 1997 release of their debut album, *Middle of Nowhere*, Mercury put the publicity machine in full gear, hiring Tamara Davis (Sonic Youth, Luscious Jackson) to direct the video for "MMMBop" and courting the press and radio. The efforts worked, as "MMMBop" debuted at No.13 on the US charts upon its April release, and the album earned positive reviews. —*Stephen Thomas Erlewine*

Middle of Nowhere / Apr. 1996 / Mercury ✦✦✦✦
Sounding like a post-alternative version of the Jackson 5—complete with effervescent harmonies, sunny melodies, rolling hip-hop beats and dense, layered productions—Hanson is positively bubbling energy throughout their surprisingly infectious and melodic debut, *Middle of Nowhere*. It's hard not to hear the lead single "MMMBop," or the similarly infectious "Where Is the Love," and not get caught up in the joy of making music. Although the boys co-wrote nine of the 13 songs with professional writers, and the producers do offer a distinctive stamp, the personalities that shine through are Hanson's—youthful, exuberant, and positively joyous. A few of the songs may run on a bit too long, and there are a couple of borrowed melodies and silly lyrics, but *Middle of Nowhere* is a delight. —*Stephen Thomas Erlewine*

Happy Mondays

f. 1985, Manchester, England, **db.** 1992
Alternative Pop-Rock, Club/Dance, Alternative Dance, House
Along with the Stone Roses, the Happy Mondays were the leaders of the late '80s/early '90s dance club-influenced Manchester scene, experiencing a brief moment in the spotlight before collapsing in 1992. While the Stone Roses were based in '60s pop, adding only a slight hint of dance music, the Happy Mondays immersed themselves in the club and rave culture, eventually becoming the most recognizable band of that drug-fueled scene. The Mondays' music relied heavily on the sound and rhythm of house music, spiked with '70s soul licks, and swirling '60s psychedelia. It was bright, colorful music that had fractured melodies that never quite gelled into cohesive songs.

Unwittingly or not, the Happy Mondays personified the ugly side of rave culture. They were thugs, pure and simply—they brought out the latent violence that lay beneath the surface of any drug culture, even one as seemingly beatific as England's late '80s/early '90s rave scene. Under the leadership of vocalist Sean Ryder, the group sounded and acted like thugs, especially in comparison with their peace-loving peers, the Stone Roses. Ryder's lyrics were twisted and surrealistic, loaded with bizarre pop culture refrences, drug slang, and menacing sexuality. Appropriately, their music was as convoluted as The Happy Mondays were one of the first rock bands to integrate hip-hop techniques into their music. They didn't sample, but they borrowed melodies and lyrics and, in the process, committed rock blasphemy. For a band that celebrated their vulgarity and excessiveness, the Happy Mondays appropriately came undone by their addictions, but they left behind a surprisingly influential legacy, apparent in everyone from dance bands like the Chemical Brothers to rock 'n' rollers like Oasis.

With their second album, 1988's *Bummed*, the Happy Mondays became British superstars, particularly lead singer Shaun Ryder. *Pills 'n' Thrills and Bellyaches*, released in 1990, marked the height of the band's popularity, creativity, and influence; although the record made the Top 100 albums chart in America, it didn't establish them as stars in the US.

After that, the fall was quick. By the time they released their last studio album, *Yes, Please*, Manchester had disappeared from public consciousness; it sold respectably, but the group didn't have the commercial impact that they had just two years before. Besides the lack of public interest, Shaun Ryder had become addicted to heroin, tearing the band apart in the process. At a high-level record contract meeting, Ryder walked out for some "Kentucky Fried Chicken," which was the band's slang for heroin. Ryder never returned and the group quickly fell apart.

Shaun Ryder and the Mondays' full-time dancer Bez re-emerged in the mid-'90s with Black Grape. The band released their critically acclaimed debut, *It's Great When You're Straight ... Yeah!*, late in the summer of 1995. Black Grape's sound pursued the same direction as the Mondays, only with a harder, grittier edge to their sound and lyrics. —*Stephen Thomas Erlewine*

Squirrell & G Man Twenty Four Hour Part People Plastic Face Carnt Smile / Apr. 1987 / Factory ♦♦
Produced by John Cale, Happy Mondays' debut album is a haphazard affair that concentrates on bare-boned funk exercises, only occasionally landing on the colorful, swirlingly eclectic mixture of funk, hip-hop, and pop that would become the band's signature sound. —*Stephen Thomas Erlewine*

Bummed / Nov. 1988 / Elektra ♦♦♦♦
The Happy Mondays first essayed their fusion of dance-club beats, hip-hop, funk, and rock 'n' roll on *Bummed*. A considerable improvement from the unfocused *Squirrel and G-Man*, *Bummed* is slightly inconsistent, but the group's sound is beginning to gel. In particular, Shaun Ryder's incoherent bluster of non sequiturs, surreal imagery, and verbal threats is coming into its own, and it adds a sense of menace to dark grooves like "Lazy Itis," "Mad Cyril," and "Wrote for Luck." The latter was remixed by Vince Clarke after the album's release and the new version, which was included on later pressings, was the hardest dance the group had yet attempted, suggesting the direction they would follow on their next album. —*Stephen Thomas Erlewine*

● **Pills 'n' Thrills & Bellyaches** / Apr. 1990 / Elektra ♦♦♦♦
A swirling, neo-psychedelic kaleidoscope of hallucinogenic drugs, trippy beats, borrowed hooks, and veiled threats, *Pills 'n' Thrills & Bellyaches* is the Happy Mondays' masterpiece and the peak of the entire Madchester craze. Where the Stone Roses were pop classicists, the Happy Mondays pushed pop into the Ecstasy age. The Mondays' cut-and-paste rhythms and melodies are clearly influenced by hip-hop and electronic dance music, and their songs have the same sort of twisted internal logic, subverting conventional pop song structures while reinterpreting oldies, occasionally stealing entire songs and claiming them as their own (John Kongos' "He's Gonna Step on You Again" is transformed into "Step On," LaBelle's "Lady Marmalade" provides the basis for "Kinky Afro"). Most of the musical collage is the creation of producers Paul Oakenfold and Steve Osborne, but the vision of *Pills 'n' Thrills & Bellyaches* belongs to Shaun Ryder, who reveals himself as a surreally gifted lyricist. Lifting melodies at will, Ryder paints a bizarre vision of modern urban life, fueled by sex, drugs, violence, and dead-end jobs—and instead of lamenting the state of affairs, he celebrates them in his hoarse, arrhythmic, tuneless holler. His thuggishly surreal sense of humor and appropriation of hooks became enormously influential on British rock 'n' roll in the '90s, particularly on Oasis' sense of style. —*Stephen Thomas Erlewine*

Live / Nov. 19, 1991 / Elektra ♦♦
While the band frequently sounds stiff and Ryder frequently sounds stoned, *Live* is a better proposition than it sounds. Instead of relying strictly on the studio arrangements, the Happy Mondays open up their grooves some and play some new songs. It's an intriguing album, especially for dedicated fans, but it's not as convincing as *Pills 'n' Thrills* or *Bummed*. —*Stephen Thomas Erlewine*

Yes, Please / Oct. 22, 1992 / Elektra ♦
By the time of 1992's *Yes, Please*, The Happy Mondays had succumbed to the excessive lifestyle they had so enthusiastically promoted. Lead singer Shaun Ryder, who had always acted as both the mouthpiece and musical visionary for the band, sounds as if he couldn't be bothered, and the music reflects his disinterest. In the hands of Chris Frantz and Tina Weymouth (Talking Heads, Tom Tom Club), the group's music loses much of its distinctive, thuggish edginess, as well as its reliance on current dance trends, becoming faceless, undistinguished dance-pop sludge. *Yes, Please* was not a particularly good way to say goodbye. —*Stephen Thomas Erlewine*

Double Easy: The US Singles / Sep. 14, 1993 / Elektra ♦♦♦
The Happy Mondays' drug-soaked vision worked best on individual songs, so the concept of a singles collection seems ideal. However, the band's two groundbreaking and popular albums—*Bummed* and *Pills 'n' Thrills & Bellyaches*—have distinct musical visions, and work better as records than *Double Easy*, which fails to be a captivating listen, even though it includes nearly every one of their finest songs. —*Stephen Thomas Erlewine*

Loads (& Loads More) / Oct. 30, 1995 / London ♦♦♦♦
With the exception of *Pills 'n' Thrills & Bellyaches*, the Happy Mondays had difficulty expanding their ideas into full albums, which makes the singles compilation, *Loads*, all the more useful. It contains all of the band's hit singles—"Step On," "Kinky Afro," "Hallelujah," "Lazyitis," "W.F.L.," "Tokoloshe Man," "Loose Fit," "Bob's Yer Uncle," "24 Hour Party People," "Mad Cyril"—plus several important album tracks, making it an excellent distillation of the band's career; as an album, only *Pills 'n' Thrills* provides better listening, and *Loads* is arguably just as good as an introduction, especially for casual fans. The first 10,000 copies of *Loads* included an extra disc, *Loads More*, a compilation of

remixes making their debut appearance on CD, including Bernard Sumner's "Freaky Dancing," Mike Pickering's "Delightful," Martin Hannett's "Lazyitis," and Vince Clarke's "W.F.L."; all of the remaining mixes are by Paul Oakenfold. Since the remixes date from the height of Happy Mondays' career, they provide useful insight on the band's talents as a dance group. —*Stephen Thomas Erlewine*

Tim Hardin

b. Dec. 23, 1941, Eugene, OR, **d.** Dec. 29, 1980
Guitar, Vocals / Folk, Singer-Songwriter, Folk-Rock
A gentle, soulful singer who owed as much to blues and jazz as folk, Tim Hardin produced an impressive body of work in the late '60s without ever approaching either mass success or the artistic heights of the best singer-songwriters. When future Lovin' Spoonful producer Erik Jacobsen arranged for Hardin's first recordings in the mid-'60s, Tim was no more than an above-average white blues singer, in the mold of many fellow folkies working the East Coast circuit. By the time of his 1966 debut, however, he was writing confessional folk-rock songs of considerable grace and emotion. The first album's impact was slightly diluted by incompatible string overdubs (against Hardin's wishes), but by the time of his second and best LP, he'd achieved a satisfactory balance between acoustic guitar-based arrangements and subtle string accompaniment. It was the lot of Hardin's work to achieve greater recognition through covers from other singers, such as Rod Stewart (who did "Reason to Believe"), Nico (who covered "Eulogy to Lenny Bruce" on her first album), Scott Walker (who sang "Lady from Baltimore"), Fred Neil ("Green Rocky Road" has been credited to both him and Hardin), and most especially Bobby Darin, who took "If I Were a Carpenter" into the Top Ten in 1966. Beleaguered with a heroin habit since early in his career, Hardin's drug problems became grave in the late '60s; his commercial prospects grew dimmer, and his albums more erratic, although he did manage to appear at Woodstock. His end was not a pretty one: due to accumulated drug and health problems, as well as a scarcity of new material, he didn't complete any albums after 1973, dying of a drug overdose in 1980. —*Richie Unterberger*

Tim Hardin 1 / 1966 / Verve ♦♦♦
Hardin's official debut introduced a vocalist and composer of some talent, most effective on the gentle confessional tunes and least effective on the blues. Occasionally it suffered from inappropriate ornamental string arrangements, but it included some of his finest compositions, including "Reason to Believe," "How Can We Hang on to a Dream," and "Don't Make Promises." —*Richie Unterberger*

Tim Hardin 2 / 1967 / Verve ♦♦♦
Probably his best single album, on which he eschewed blues nearly entirely and forged a distinctive, folk-rock voice, occasionally embellished by tasteful full arrangements. "Lady Came from Baltimore," "Red Balloon," and especially "If I Were a Carpenter" rank among his best and most famous songs. —*Richie Unterberger*

This Is Tim Hardin / 1967 / Edsel ♦♦♦
Hardin's very earliest recordings from approximately 1964, not issued until the late '60s, when he had achieved some success with his albums for Verve. Accompanied by nothing besides his own guitar, Hardin's arrangements are far sparser and bluesier than his folk-rock work for Verve. Over half of the ten tracks are traditional blues numbers like "Hoochie Coochie Man" and "House of the Rising Sun," and even the four originals (one co-written by future Holy Modal Rounder Steve Weber) are in a very similar straight blues style. The material isn't nearly as distinctive as the best of Hardin's work, but the performances rank with Dave Van Ronk and Fred Neil as the best white blues/acoustic folk to emerge from the early-'60s Greenwich scene (indeed, Hardin covers Neil's "Blues on the Ceiling" here). The hollow, reverbed, one-man-sitting-alone-in-an-empty-room production gives this album a haunting, somber feel (though not to its detriment). While not as good as Fred Neil's similar material from this era, it's still well worth tracking down. —*Richie Unterberger*

Live in Concert / 1968 / Polydor Chronicles ♦♦♦♦
Originally titled *Tim Hardin 3*, this set was recorded live in 1968 with a backing band comprised primarily of jazz musicians. The support crew is a bit tentative—it's evident that they hadn't played much with Hardin, and in places the tempo comes close to breaking down. It's still a good, effective performance; Hardin is in good voice (a condition which apparently couldn't be readily counted on, even in his early days), and on the songs that had already been released on his first two albums, the arrangements vary from the recorded versions in interesting fashions. *Live in Concert* includes renditions of most of his best early compositions ("If I Were a Carpenter," "Red Balloon," "Reason to Believe," "Misty Roses," "Lady Came from Baltimore," "Black Sheep Boy"), and half-a-dozen Hardin originals that didn't make it onto his first pair of albums. The best of these is the Lenny Bruce tribute, "Lenny's Tune," which Nico covered on her first solo album (where it was retitled "Eulogy to Lenny Bruce"). The 1995 CD reissue of this

album adds three previously unreleased bonus tracks from the same concert. —*Richie Unterberger*

Tim Hardin 4 / 1969 / Verve ✦✦

● **Reason to Believe** / Oct. 25, 1990 / PolyGram ✦✦✦✦
The great early work of this top-flight '60s singer-songwriter includes the title track, "If I Were a Carpenter," and "Misty Roses." —*Kenneth M. Cassidy & William Ruhlmann*

● **Hang On to a Dream: The Verve Recordings** / Feb. 22, 1994 / Polydor ✦✦✦✦
Double-CD set of 47 tracks that Hardin recorded for Verve between 1964 and 1966. His expressive, blues-inflected vocals and confessional songwriting are heard on covers and famous compositions like "If I Were a Carpenter," "Lady Came from Baltimore," and "Reason to Believe." The compilation includes every studio recording that Hardin released on the Verve label, as well as two alternate takes and 15 previously unreleased tracks. —*Richie Unterberger*

Simple Songs / Sep. 3, 1996 / Columbia/Legacy ✦✦✦✦
Hardin's Columbia period, lasting from the late '60s to the early '70s, was a troubled one that saw his songwriting muse wither and his personal life start to dissolve. Although his best work was behind him, he was still capable of recording good material. This 17-song collection is a good distillation of the highlights of his three Columbia LPs, which largely still found his voice in good shape. Original tunes were more of a problem: although the best of his compositions were on a rough par with his Verve work, by the time of 1972's *Painted Head*, he was devoting himself entirely to covers of songs by others. The *Painted Head* selections are the least impressive on this anthology, the spare folk-rock of the earlier Columbia sessions giving way to slicker arrangements that don't highlight his sad, wavering voice nearly as effectively. The remainder is pretty good, with the significant bonus of his sole chart single, a 1969 cover of Bobby Darin's "Simple Song of Freedom," and five decent (if sometimes unpolished) previously unreleased outtakes from late 1968. *Simple Songs of Freedom* is the one album of post-Verve Hardin music to own. —*Richie Unterberger*

John Wesley Harding

b. Oct. 22, 1965, Hastings, England
Guitar / Urban-Folk, Singer-Songwriter, Alternative Pop-Rock, Contemporary Folk
John Wesley Harding may take his name from a Bob Dylan album and he's a modern-day folk singer, but with the biting, cynical observations in his songs, and sharp sense of humor combined with winning melodies, he shows his true forefathers are Elvis Costello and Nick Lowe with a hint of Billy Bragg. Far from being a follower or strict revivalist, however, Wes draws on a wide assortment of musical influences, pushing the boundaries of the all-too-often formulaic singer-songwriter tag to create something all his own.
Wesley Harding Stace was born in Hastings, East Sussex, England in 1965. He taught himself guitar, picking out songs by John Prine, Loudon Wainwright, and Bob Dylan, and eventually began writing on his own as a teenager. In 1988, he cut short his Ph.D. studies at Cambridge University in favor of a career in music. An opening slot for John Hiatt attracted the attention of Demon Records who signed him and released the live *It Happened One Night* the same year.
In 1990, he teamed up with producer Andy Paley and members of Elvis Costello's Attractions (the association would cause Costello comparisons that would continue to haunt him) to record *Here Comes the Groom* for Sire. He supported the album alone in the US where his spirited live shows attracted a great deal of word-of-mouth attention and strong cult following, especially in alternative and college radio. In 1991 he followed with *The Name Above the Title* and *Why We Fight* in 1992. While he received consistently good reviews, expanded on his cult following through constant touring, and finally shook (for the most part) the Elvis Costello comparisons, lack of a substantial push from Sire led to his leaving the label by the mid-'90s. The self-financed *John Wesley Harding's New Deal* was finished in 1996 and picked up for release by Rhino's Forward label. —*Chris Woodstra*

It Happened One Night / 1988 / Rhino ✦✦✦✦
This solo acoustic outing, recorded live in England in 1988, seems like an odd choice for a debut, but it comes off very well. Capturing both John Wesley Harding's folk roots and a wonderful sense of humor, *It Happened One Night* gives a very representative picture of the singer-songwriter. Included are early versions of songs appearing on the following two albums as well as unreleased gems such as his fun account of Live Aid ("July 13th, 1985") and a cover of Prince's "Kiss." —*Chris Woodstra*

● **Here Comes the Groom** / 1989 / Sire ✦✦✦✦
His second album has him working in the studio with a band called the Good Liars, including Pete Thomas, and Bruce Thomas of the Attractions. Not surprisingly, *Here Comes the Groom* has a feel similar

to classic Elvis Costello. Harding's articulate and biting vocal delivery, also reminiscent of Costello, retains a good dark sense of humor. —*Chris Woodstra*

God Made Me Do It: The Christmas EP / Nov. 1989 / Sire ✦✦✦
God Mad Me Do It—the Christmas EP features "Here Comes the Groom," from the LP of the same name, the not-so-festive but typically sharp "Talking Christmas Goodwill Blues," a thankfully nonironic folky take of Madonna's "Like a Prayer," the non-LP "The Rent," and a fun interview "conducted" by Viv Stanshall. —*Chris Woodstra*

The Name Above the Title / Feb. 19, 1991 / Sire ✦✦✦
The follow-up to *Here Comes the Groom* continues in the same direction. This time the arrangements are filled out with horn sections and strings, but the overall folky feel remains. —*Chris Woodstra*

Why We Fight / Mar. 1992 / Sire ✦✦✦
This 1992 release is more low-key and moody than any of his previous work. The subject matter is darker, though the melodies are still catchy and instantly memorable as always, this time with smoother production. From a discussion about Hitler in the bizarre fantasy of "Hitler's Tears" is musically irresistible, placing him in the ranks of Nick Lowe and Elvis Costello. —*Chris Woodstra*

Pett Levels: The Summer EP / Jul. 13, 1993 / Sire ✦✦
His second "seasonal" EP (and final release for Sire) features four otherwise unavailable tracks: the bright and bouncy "Summer Single," the *Why We Fight* outtake "Your New Clothes," "One Shot," an acoustic version of "When the Sun Comes Out," and "The End of Something," a preview of an album that never happened. —*Chris Woodstra*

John Wesley Harding's New Deal / Feb. 13, 1996 / Rhino ✦✦✦
Four years have passed since John Wesley Harding's last full-length album and it seems he spent the time "growing up" a bit, shaking once-and-for-all the image of Elvis Costello's smart-ass kid brother. *John Wesley Harding's New Deal* (the title presumably referring to his parting of ways with Sire and his new signing to Forward Records) finds a gentler Harding doing some soul searching on his most introspective outing to date. Continuing in the trend set by 1992's *Why We Fight*, the album's warmer production—bare-boned arrangements consisting mainly of acoustic guitar with subtle use of violin, cello, hammond organ, and pedal steel—create the appropriate intimate setting for the subject matter. Thankfully, the new John Wesley Harding's songs are still as clever as ever and, in a different way, just as catchy and memorable. —*Chris Woodstra*

Dynablob / Jun. 1996 / Mod Lang ✦✦✦
Dynablob is a collection of previously unreleased studio recordings from John Wesley Harding's first recording session in 1986 to 1994 with track-by-track commentary by Wes himself. This is obviously an essential purchase for fans, but it is also surprisingly consistent enough to offer a good listen and a good look at the artist in a more traditional singer-songwriter setting. Points should also be given for the detail of the Dylan-esque cover design. —*Chris Woodstra*

Francoise Hardy

b. Jan. 17, 1944, Paris, France
Guitar, Vocals / Pop, Girl-Group
Usually thought of as a middle-of-the-road popular singer, Francoise Hardy—at the beginning of her career, at least—covered more stylistic ground and owed more debts to pop-rock than she's given credit for. Immensely popular in her native France, the chanteuse first displayed her breathy, measured vocals in the early- and mid-'60s. Her (mostly self-penned) recordings from that era draw from French pop traditions, lightweight '50s teen-idol rock, girl groups, and sultry jazz and blues—sometimes in the same song. The material is perhaps too unreservedly sentimental for some (in the French tradition), but the songs are invariably catchy and the production, arrangements, and near-operatic backup harmonies excellent, at times almost Spector-esque. Fans of Marianne Faithfull's mid-'60s work can find something of a French equivalent here, though Hardy's material was stronger and her delivery more confident.
In the 1950s, Hardy was inspired by early rock recordings to pick up guitar, and was already writing her own songs by the time she was a teenager. By the age of 17, she was already singing her own compositions in French clubs, and successfully auditioned for Vogue Records in France in late 1961. Her debut EP appeared the following year, inaugurating a series of successful EPs and albums that would last through the '60s.
Hardy sang of young love with both fetching moodiness and unrestrained ebullience; although she often wrote both her music and lyrics, she often co-wrote tunes with others as well. She was greatly aided by a number of talented arrangers who seemed to be attempting (usually successfully) to blend American and British production sophistication with a Continental European sensibility. Charles Blackwell was the most notable and effective of these figures; in 1964, interestingly,

she recorded some tracks under the direction of the great American R&B guitarist Mickey Baker (yes, the same one who played on Mickey & Sylvia's "Love Is Strange"), who was then based in France.

Starting in 1964, Hardy made periodic attempts to capture the international market with English recordings. Although these weren't entirely unsuccessful ("All over the World" was actually a British Top 20 hit in 1965), by the late '60s she was concentrating on more mainstream, middle-of-the-road material and arrangements on both her French and English sessions. She has remained popular in France until the present. —*Richie Unterberger*

Ma Jeunesse Fout Le Camp / 1967 / Virgin [Vogue] ✦✦✦
Hardy moved toward a more adult, sedate form of orchestrated pop balladry on this 1967 album. Nothing wrong with that per se; what makes it less exciting than her previous work, though, was that in general the material lacked the bounce and melodic strength of her best recordings. "Il N'y a Pas D'Amour Heureux" ("There Is No Happy Love") she sings in one of the tracks, and that sets the mournful tone for much of the tunes (half of which were written by herself), which often deal with sentimental themes of sad farewells. Still, it's delivered with classy grace and ornate period production, and the uplifting "Voila" (easily the best cut here) is one of her top classics. John Paul Jones (presumably the same guy as the future Led Zeppelin bassist) was one of the arrangers. —*Richie Unterberger*

Comment Te Dire Adieu / 1968 / Virgin [Vogue] ✦✦✦
This may not rate as highly as her best mid-'60s recordings, which are less MOR-oriented. That stated, it's about as good as late-'60s MOR Continental pop gets, with tastefully imaginative orchestration, strong melodies, and sexy vocals. It's perhaps even sadder and more sentimental than was the norm for Francoise—she perpetually seems to be singing as though she's gazing out of a deserted chateau on a rainy afternoon. She largely forsakes original material here (although a couple of cuts bear her writing credit), and offers fine, haunting French interpretations of Leonard Cohen's "Suzanne," Phil Ochs' "There But for Fortune," and Ricky Nelson's "Lonesome Town." —*Richie Unterberger*

Francoise Hardy En Anglais / 1969 / Sonopress ✦✦
English covers of rock, folk, and pop tunes on this rather heavily orchestrated album, which may be Hardy's most marginal '60s recording. The renditions of Tim Hardin's "Hang on to a Dream" and Phil Ochs' "There But for Fortune" aren't bad, but the torpid interpretations of "Will You Love Me Tomorrow," "Let It Be Me," "That'll Be the Day," and Elvis Presley's "Loving You" really lay on the schmaltz. In both arrangement and material (there are no Hardy originals), there is little of what made the singer special here. Incidentally, one of the better tracks, the Europop-flavored "Empty Sunday," was reworked in part from a tune recorded earlier on a solo single by Yardbirds singer Keith Relf ("Shapes in My Mind"). —*Richie Unterberger*

Soleil / 1970 / Virgin ✦✦✦
One of Hardy's less colorful efforts. The orchestration leans toward MOR at times, and she only had a hand in writing about half the material, which zigzags between rock, sad ballads, sentimental pop, and chirpy show-biz. It can't be written off, though, as it contains one of her best-ever songs, "Fleur de Lune," with its beautifully moody melody, descending guitar lines, and sultry vocal. Actually, most of the rest isn't bad, whether it's the acoustic balladry of "Soleil," the pensive "L'Ombre," or the unexpectedly forceful "Le Crabe." —*Richie Unterberger*

La Question / 1971 / Virgin [Sonopresse] ✦✦✦✦
Throughout her career, most of Hardy's arrangements have tended toward the lush, though in a good way. This record is lush, too, but it's one of her most sparsely produced efforts, usually finding her voice accompanied by little more than an acoustic guitar, touches of bass, and very subtle orchestration. Much of the record's lights-low ambience could be attributed to Tuca (no last name given), who played guitar, coarranged, and cowrote most of the tunes (though Hardy did contribute to the composition of a few tracks). It may be her best post-'60s effort, songs like "Chanson D'O" and "Le Martien" featuring some of her most whispery, seductive vocals. As fireside romantic music goes, it beats the hell out of Jose Feliciano. —*Richie Unterberger*

Et Si Je M'en Vais Avant Toi / 1972 / Virgin [Sonopresse] ✦✦
One of her weaker efforts, frequently characterized by a happy-go-lucky, pedestrian country-blues flavor. It's nice to know that she was keeping her ears open to outside influences. Yet we Yankees who love Francoise listen to her, at least in part, *because* of her oh-so-very French qualities. If you want to hear lame L.A.-style early-'70s mellow rock, there are plenty of alternatives to turn to before you head for the import bins. It would be nice to lay the blame with some wrongheaded producer, but actually Hardy wrote almost all of the material herself. Yet it's not entirely dismissable. The most pop-oriented productions—"Ou Est-Il?," the title track, and the gorgeous "Bowm Bowm

Bowm"—are delicately tuneful and sensitively performed, even if they're incongruous with the rest of the album. —*Richie Unterberger*

All over the World / 1988 / Vogue ✦✦
Several French stars attempted to cross over into broader international success by recording in English. Usually these failed due to clumsy pronunciation and disinterest in American and British markets. Francoise Hardy was more successful than most, both artistically and commercially. Her accent is slight and her phrasing accomplished on these English re-recordings of 18 of her most popular mid-'60s tunes. One of these, "All over the World," actually cracked the British Top 20 in 1965. And she actually managed to release several albums of English material in the States, though she never took off commercially. These performances are respectable, but you're still better off with the original French versions. Her native tongue lends itself better to her romantic and melodramatic melodies and arrangements, which remain distinctly French in spite of their liberal debts to American girl group pop and production. The backing tracks are unchanged or only slightly altered on these re-recordings; the CD remastering is a bit awkward, placing her voice way up front. —*Richie Unterberger*

Story 1962-64 / 1989 / Vogue ✦✦✦
The *Story* series, with three separate volumes covering the period from 1962-1967, presents this immensely popular French chanteuse at her best. This first volume, which features 20 songs, is perhaps the most innocuous of the lot, which isn't to say it isn't good. Her 1962 single "Le Temps de L'Amour" is perhaps her best recording, featuring snakey spy guitars and a minor-key melody in an unlikely but wonderful marriage of early-'60s rock and a film-noirish atmosphere. —*Richie Unterberger*

● **Story 1964-65** / 1989 / Vogue ✦✦✦✦
Perhaps Hardy's finest compilation, although *Story 1962-64* is almost as good. This 20-song CD finds her at her most girl group-influenced; you don't need to understand French to catch the infectious melodies and sultry, almost hushed vocals. Highlights include the magnificently moody ballad "Tu Peux Bien"; "Non Ce N'est Pas un Reve," with melodramatic Spectorish production that recalls the Righteous Brothers at their peak; and the tense, romantic yearning of "Il Se Fait Tard." All of these *Story* discs have apparently been remixed for CD release, although the differences are slight, giving more prominence to the percussion and Hardy's vocals. —*Richie Unterberger*

Story 1965-67 / 1989 / Vogue ✦✦✦
The third 20-song anthology of work from Hardy's early (and best) years is perhaps the least essential of the trio. Several of the ballads and acoustic numbers are unmemorable, suffering from weak material and/or soppy, orchestrated arrangements. These sometimes recall a modified Petula Clark, which can be good or (more often) bad. But the best cuts here stand up to her best material from the decade. "Surtout Ne Vous Retournez Pas" and "Qu'ils Sont Hereux" are among her best ballads; "Je Ne Suis La Pour Personne" is a snappy folk-rocker; and "Voila" is her best grandiose, heart-on-the-sleeve orchestral production. All of the aforementioned highlights were Hardy originals. In the late '60s, Hardy moved towards more middle-of-the-road material (often sung in English), perhaps in an attempt to crack the international market; the three volumes of *Story* remain her most impressive work. —*Richie Unterberger*

L'integrale Disques Vogue 1962/1967 (The Complete Vogue Recordings) / 1995 / Vogue ✦✦✦✦
Four-CD, 83-track box retrospective of her first five (and best) years on record (1962-1967), including everything except the English-language versions she recorded for foreign markets. It's expensive, and hard to find in the US. But it's worth the investment for Hardy fans, as her early material was very consistent, and has usually been reissued in piecemeal fashion; this puts it all in one place, chronologically sequenced. —*Richie Unterberger*

Le Danger / Sep. 12, 1996 / Virgin ✦✦✦
Francoise Hardy is mostly known as a pop chanteuse with mild rock influences. It comes as something of a shock, then, to stick this into the CD player and hear her backed by assertive, guitar-oriented modern rock arrangements. Hardy's delivery hasn't changed much; it's still a mixture of fetching sensuality and composed reserve. What has changed is the music, with its emphasis upon gutsy guitar textures that sound influenced by '90s alternative rock—a bit of grungetone here, some Britpop energy there, some rootsy slide work (on "Ici Ou La?") in the mold of Ry Cooder. Many middle-aged pop singers move from gritty rock to lighthearted MOR. Hardy, unusually, seems determined to move in exactly the opposite direction. It's not as good as, or very similar to, the charming sentimental pop of her youth. Yet it's not at all embarrassing, with a couple of tunes ("Dix Heures En Ete" and "Contre-Jour") that would have definite hit potential, in the best sense of the word, were they sung in English. Whatever you think, one would be hard-pressed to name other rock singers in their early fifties, from

France or anywhere else, that managed to sound unassumingly contemporary in the mid-'90s. —*Richie Unterberger*

Wynonie Harris

b. Aug. 24, 1915, Omaha, NE, d. Jun. 14, 1969, Los Angeles, CA
Drums, Vocals / R&B, Jump Blues

No blues shouter embodied the rollicking good times that he sang of quite like raucous shouter Wynonie Harris. "Mr. Blues," as he was not-so-humbly known, joyously related risque tales of sex, booze, and endless parties in his trademark raspy voice over some of the jumpingest horn-powered combos of the postwar era.

Those wanton ways eventually caught up with Harris, but not before he scored a raft of R&B smashes from 1946 to 1952. Harris was already a seasoned dancer, drummer, and singer when he left Omaha for L.A. in 1940 (his main influences being Big Joe Turner and Jimmy Rushing). He found plenty of work singing and appearing as an emcee on Central Avenue, the bustling nightlife strip of the Black community there. Wynonie Harris' reputation was spreading fast—he was appearing in Chicago at the Rhumboogie Club in 1944 when bandleader Lucky Millinder hired him as his band's new singer. With Millinder's orchestra in brassy support, Harris made his debut on shellac by boisterously delivering "Who Threw the Whiskey in the Well" that same year for Decca. By the time it hit in mid-1945, Harris was long gone from Millinder's organization and back in L.A.

The shouter debuted on wax under his own name in July of 1945 at an L.A. date for Philo with backing from drummer Johnny Otis, saxist Teddy Edwards, and trumpeter Howard McGhee. A month later, he signed on with Apollo Records, an association that provided him with two huge hits in 1946: "Wynonie's Blues" (with saxist Illinois Jacquet's combo) and "Playful Baby." Harris' own waxings were squarely in the emerging jump blues style then sweeping the West Coast. After scattered dates for Hamp-Tone, Bullet, and Aladdin (where he dueled it out with his idol Big Joe on a two-sided "Battle of the Blues"), Harris joined the star-studded roster of Cincinnati's King Records in 1947. There his sales really soared.

Few records made a stronger seismic impact than Harris' 1948 chart-topper "Good Rockin' Tonight." Ironically, Harris shooed away its composer, Roy Brown, when he first tried to hand it to the singer; only when Brown's original version took off did Wynonie cover the romping number. With Hal "Cornbread" Singer on wailing tenor sax and a rocking, socking backbeat, the record provided an easily followed blueprint for the imminent rise of rock 'n' roll a few years later (and gave Elvis Presley something to place on the A side of his second Sun single).

After that, Harris was rarely absent from the R&B charts for the next four years, his offerings growing more boldly suggestive all the time. "Grandma Plays the Numbers," "All She Wants to Do Is Rock," "I Want My Fanny Brown," "Sittin' on It All the Time," "I Like My Baby's Pudding," "Good Morning Judge," "Bloodshot Eyes" (a country tune that was first released on King by Hank Penny), and "Lovin' Machine" were only a portion of the ribald hits Harris scored into 1952 (13 in all)—and then his personal hit parade stopped dead. It certainly wasn't Harris' fault—his King output rocked as hard as ever under Henry Glover's supervision—but changing tastes among fickle consumers accelerated Wynonie Harris' sobering fall from favor.

Sides for Atco in 1956, King in 1957, and Roulette in 1960 only hinted at the raunchy glory of a short few years earlier. The touring slowed accordingly. In 1963, his chauffeur-driven Cadillacs and lavish New York home a distant memory, Harris moved back to L.A., scraping up low-paying local gigs whenever he could. Chess gave him a three-song session in 1964, but sat on the promising results. Throat cancer silenced him for good in 1969, ending the life of a bigger-than-life R&B pioneer whose ego matched his tremendous talent. —*Bill Dahl*

Everybody Boogie! / Aug. 2, 1945-Dec. 1945 / Delmark ✦✦✦✦
This is one marvelous collection of 1945 recordings made for Apollo Records with Harris' powerhouse vocals backed by jump blues bands led by jazz greats Illinois Jacquet, Oscar Pettiford, and Jack McVea. No real honking and bar walking going on here; quite the opposite, as the Pettiford have bop lines creeping in throughout. But Harris seems oblivious to it all as tracks like "Time to Change Your Town," "Here Come the Blues," "Stuff You Gotta Watch," and "Somebody Changed the Lock on My Door" are on an equal par for sheer bravado and intensity with the best of his later work for King. A welcome compilation. —*Cub Koda*

☆ **Good Rocking Tonight** / 1990 / Charly ✦✦✦✦
Equally splendid compilation of the raspy shouter's King label output from the British Charly logo. Contains 20 sides, including a few essentials that Rhino didn't bother with: a roaring "Rock Mr. Blues" that grants Harris vocal group backing; the lascivious rocker "I Want My Fanny Brown" and "Lollipop Mama," and a celebratory "Mr. Blues Is Coming to Town." Harris and King always used inexorably swinging bands—saxists include Red Prysock, David Van Dyke (who duel it out

on the amazing "Quiet Whiskey"), Big John Greer, Hal Singer, and Tom Archia. —*Bill Dahl*

★ **Bloodshot Eyes: the Best of Wynonie Harris** / 1993 / King/Rhino ✦✦✦✦
Wynonie Harris was a hard-living, rousing R&B shouter who made some of the most sexually explicit songs in modern popular music history. Harris didn't leave much to the imagination, but he also possessed a booming voice with wonderful tone and range, and the comedic skill to execute these tunes without becoming raunchy. There are many hilarious cuts on this 18-track anthology, among them "I Like My Baby's Pudding," "Grandma Plays the Numbers," and "Good Morning Judge." Harris roars, struts, and wails over equally feverish arrangements, and earns a draw with Joe Turner on "Battle of the Blues." These songs give a good portrait of a delightful, often spectacular vocalist who could be both provocative and compelling. —*Ron Wynn*

Women, Whiskey & Fish Tails / 1993 / Ace ✦✦✦✦
British compiler Ray Topping focuses on Harris' 1952-1957 King output on this 21-song collection, when he was undeniably on the downside as far as making hits. But there was still plenty of wind in the shouter's sails, judging from "Greyhound," "Christina," "Shake That Thing" (an update of an ancient blues theme), "Git to Gittin' Baby," and "Mr. Dollar." Harris even supplied a savvy sequel to one of his immortal numbers with "Bad News Baby (There'll Be No Rockin' Tonite)." —*Bill Dahl*

George Harrison

b. Feb. 25, 1943, Liverpool, England
Guitar, Vocals / Singer-Songwriter, Pop-Rock

As lead guitarist for the Beatles, George Harrison provided the band with a lyrical style of playing in which every note mattered. Harrison was one of millions of young Britons inspired to take up the guitar by British skiffle king Lonnie Donegan's recording of "Rock Island Line." But he had more dedication than most, and with the encouragement of a slightly older school friend—Paul McCartney—he advanced quickly in his technique and command of the instrument. Harrison developed his style and technique slowly and painstakingly over the several years, learning everything he could from the records of Carl Perkins, Duane Eddy, Chet Atkins, Buddy Holly, and Eddie Cochran. By age 15, he was allowed to sit in with the Quarry Men, the Liverpool group founded by John Lennon, of which McCartney was a member; by 16 he was a full-fledged member of the group.

The Beatles finally coalesced around Lennon, McCartney, Harrison, and drummer Ringo Starr in 1962, with Harrison established on lead guitar. The Beatlemania years, from 1963 through 1966, were a mixed blessing for Harrison. The Beatles' studio sound was generally characterized by very prominent rhythm guitar parts, and on many of the Beatles' early songs, Harrison's lead guitar was buried beneath the chiming chords of Lennon's instrument. Additionally, he was thwarted as a songwriter by the presence of Lennon and McCartney—the quality and prolificacy of their output left very little room on the group's albums for songs by anyone else. Despite these problems, Harrison grew markedly as a musician between 1963 and 1966, writing a handful of good songs and one classic ("If I Needed Someone"), and also making his first acquaintance of the sitar, an Indian instrument whose sound fascinated him.

In 1966, Harrison finally seemed to find his voice, with two of his songs on the *Revolver* album, "Taxman" and "Love You Too." In the wake of the group's decision to stop touring, Harrison's playing and songwriting grew exponentially. The period from 1968 onward was Harrison's richest with the Beatles. He displayed a smooth, elegant slide guitar technique that showed up on their last three albums, and contributed two classic songs, "While My Guitar Gently Weeps" and "Here Comes the Sun," along with "Something," which became the first Harrison song on the A-side of a Beatles single.

Although never known as a strong singer, Harrison's vocals were always distinctive, especially when placed in the right setting—for his first solo record following the group's 1970 breakup, *All Things Must Pass*, Harrison collaborated with producer Phil Spector, whose so-called "wall of sound" technique adapted well to Harrison's voice. *All Things Must Pass* and the accompanying single "My Sweet Lord" had the distinction of being the first solo recordings by any of the Beatles to top the charts following their breakup. Unfortunately, Harrison was later successfully sued by the publisher of the 1962 Chiffons hit "He's So Fine," which bore a striking resemblance to "My Sweet Lord."

Harrison followed *All Things Must Pass* with rock's first major charity event, *The Concert for Bangladesh*, which was staged as two shows at New York's Madison Square Garden in 1971 to help raise money for aid to that famine-ravaged nation. The second of the two all-star shows was released as a movie and a live triple album. Harrison's next studio album, *Living in the Material World*, initially sold well, but its leaner, less opulent production lacked the majestic force of *All Things Must Pass*, and it lacked the earlier album's mass appeal. Subsequent Harrison albums from the 1970s into the '80s always had an audience, but except for *Somewhere in England* (1981), released in the wake of the murder of John Lennon with the memorial song "All Those Years Ago," none seemed terribly well-crafted or executed. During this same period, Harrison embarked on a successful career as a movie producer with the founding of Handmade Films.

In 1987, Harrison made a return to the top of the charts with his album *Cloud Nine*, which featured his most inspired work in years, most notably a cover of an old Rudy Clark gospel number called "Got My Mind Set on You," which reached No. 1 on the charts. In 1988, Harrison, Bob Dylan, Tom Petty, Jeff Lynne, and Roy Orbison formed the Traveling Wilburys, who have since released two very successful albums. —*Bruce Eder*

Wonderwall Music / Dec. 2, 1968 / Capitol ✦✦
The first-ever solo album by a Beatle (although John Lennon's *Two Virgins* preceded it in the US) is a film soundtrack combining Indian-influenced music (some of it played by Indian musicians) with more conventional pop. It's no more essential than most film scores away from the films themselves, but demonstrates the range of Harrison's musical taste. —*William Ruhlmann*

Electronic Sound / May 26, 1969 / Apple ✦✦
On his second non-Beatles side project (one could hardly call them solo albums), Harrison produces two sidelong instrumental tracks using a variety of sound effects, edits, and other studio wizardry. A trifle. —*William Ruhlmann*

★ **All Things Must Pass** / Nov. 27, 1970 / Capitol ✦✦✦✦✦
Without a doubt, Harrison's first solo recording, originally issued as a triple album, is his best. Drawing on his backlog of unused compositions from the late Beatle era, Harrison crafted material that managed the rare feat of conveying spiritual mysticism without sacrificing his gifts for melody and grand, sweeping arrangements. Enhanced by Phil Spector's lush orchestral production and Harrison's own superb slide guitar, nearly every song is excellent: "Awaiting on You All," "Beware of Darkness," the Dylan collaboration "I'd Have You Anytime," "Isn't It a Pity," and the hit singles "My Sweet Lord" and "What Is Life" are just a few of the highlights. A very moving work, with a very significant flaw: the jams that comprise the final third of the album are entirely dispensable, and have probably only been played once or twice by most of the listeners that own this record. —*Richie Unterberger*

The Concert for Bangladesh / Dec. 20, 1971 / Capitol ✦✦✦
A unique live document showcasing Harrison near his best, with ex-Beatle Ringo Starr, Eric Clapton, and many other superstars. It has less-than-perfect sound but overall fine re-creations of his best work, with work by Bob Dylan as an added bonus. —*Bruce Eder*

Living in the Material World / May 30, 1973 / Capitol ✦✦✦
Harrison had a lot of songs stored up for his first major solo work, *All Things Must Pass*, and it launched his post-Beatles career with a bang. Two and a half years later, he released its follow-up, which, although it contained some good playing by his band of superstar friends and some good tunes, notably the number one hit "Give Me Love (Give Me Peace on Earth)," indicated that the first album had contained his best effort and the most he'd be able to do in the future was to repeat it. —*William Ruhlmann*

Dark Horse / Dec. 9, 1974 / Capitol ✦✦
Rushed through in the preparations for Harrison's first (and last) North American tour, his third solo album found him with a strained throat and not enough first-rate material. Most embarrassing was a rewrite of "Bye Bye Love" in which he commented on the romantic triangle between himself, his wife, and his best friend, Eric Clapton (who later married her). The title track and "Ding Dong, Ding Dong" were Top 40 hits. —*William Ruhlmann*

Extra Texture / Sep. 22, 1975 / Capitol ✦✦
"You," a Top 20 hit, was a terrific pop song, but much of this album is expendable, including an update of the old Beatles song "While My Guitar Gently Weeps" called "This Guitar (Can't Keep from Crying)." From the superstar status of *All Things Must Pass*, Harrison had declined rapidly. —*William Ruhlmann*

The Best of George Harrison / Nov. 8, 1976 / Capitol ✦✦✦
The Harrison material is matched with some Beatles numbers in a good but routine collection. —*Bruce Eder*

33 & 1/3 / Nov. 24, 1976 / Dark Horse ✦✦✦✦
Having suffered the humiliation of being sued successfully over "My Sweet Lord," Harrison turned the ordeal into music, writing "This Song," a Top 25 hit. Even better was "Crackerbox Palace," which would have fit in nicely on any Beatles album. The rest was slight, although Harrison covering Cole Porter's "True Love" is an interesting idea. This was Harrison's first album on his Dark Horse custom label, formed after the completion of his contract with EMI/Capitol in June 1976 and initially distributed by A&M. —*William Ruhlmann*

George Harrison / Feb. 14, 1979 / Dark Horse ✦✦
Harrison's sixth solo studio album (released after a two-year hiatus) was another slight affair, boasting the Top 20 single "Blow Away," but otherwise unremarkable. "Not Guilty" was a Beatles-era song once short-listed for their *White Album*. "Here Comes the Moon" was a tepid sequel to "Here Comes the Sun." —*William Ruhlmann*

Somewhere in England / Jun. 1, 1981 / Dark Horse ✦✦
Harrison had trouble getting Warner Brothers Records, which now distributed his Dark Horse label, to accept this album (an early, rejected version even turned up in collecting circles). It finally appeared, heavily revised, featuring a song originally intended for Ringo Starr and with different lyrics, "All Those Years Ago." Now pitched as a tribute to the late John Lennon, the song (featuring Starr and Paul McCartney) became a substantial hit and carried the mediocre album, which also features two Hoagy Carmichael songs. —*William Ruhlmann*

Gone Troppo / Oct. 27, 1982 / Dark Horse ✦✦
Although George Harrison's solo career had faded from its early promise, through 1981 he could be counted on to turn in a gold-selling, Top 20 album containing a Top 20 single every year or so. Then came the disastrous *Gone Troppo*, a half-baked affair led by the minor single "Wake Up My Love" that failed to make the Top 100 LPs. Clearly, Harrison could no longer treat his musical career as a part-time stepchild to his interests in car racing and movie producing if he wanted to maintain it. As it turned out, he didn't; this was his last album for five years. —*William Ruhlmann*

Cloud Nine / Nov. 2, 1987 / Dark Horse ✦✦✦✦
Teaming with legendary Beatles obsessive Jeff Lynne, George Harrison crafted a remarkably consistent and polished comeback effort with *Cloud Nine*. Lynne adds a glossy production, reminiscent of ELO, but what is even more noticeable is that he's reined in Harrison's indulgences, keeping the focus on a set of 11 snappy pop-rock numbers. The consistency of the songs remains uneven, but the best moments—"Devil's Radio," "Cloud 9," "Just for Today," "Got My Mind Set on You," and the tongue-in-cheek Beatles pastiche "When We Was Fab"—make *Cloud 9* one of his very best albums. —*Stephen Thomas Erlewine*

The Best of Dark Horse (1976-1989) / Oct. 1989 / Dark Horse ✦✦✦✦
George Harrison's albums have been notoriously uneven, but despite the rough patches, his talent for songcraft never really left him, as the compilation *The Best of Dark Horse (1976-1989)* proves. A 15-song retrospective covering five albums, *The Best of Dark Horse* contains nearly every gem from *33 1/3*, *George Harrison*, *Somewhere in England*, *Gone Troppo*, and *Cloud Nine*, including "Crackerbox Palace," "All Those Years Ago," "Got My Mind Set on You," "Cloud 9," "When We Was Fab" and the lovely "Blow Away." For most casual fans, the record will be a welcome summation of a hit-and-miss era of Harrison's career. —*Stephen Thomas Erlewine*

Live in Japan / Jul. 1992 / Dark Horse ✦✦
George Harrison returned to the stage for the first time in years in 1991; that Japanese tour is documented on the fine double-disc set *Live in Japan*. Backed by a stellar supporting band led by Eric Clapton, Harrison turns in surprisingly strong versions of his best solo material; it easily surpasses Paul McCartney's double-disc *Tripping the Live Fantastic* or *Paul Is Live*. Not bad for a guy who doesn't like to give concerts. —*Stephen Thomas Erlewine*

Beware of Abkco! / 1994 / Strawberry [Bootleg] ✦✦✦✦
Probably demos recorded shortly prior to the sessions for *All Things Must Pass*, this is Harrison playing solo, unaccompanied by anything but his voices and guitar, sometimes electric, but usually acoustic. The fidelity is absolutely marvelous, at the point of the top of the pyramid for an unreleased recording. The performances are very interesting, if often tentative; the 15 songs are divided equally between versions of some of the better *All Things Must Pass* tracks ("Art of Dying," "Run of the Mill," "Let It Down," "Beware of Darkness," "If Not for You"), and songs that didn't end up making the final cut. Some of these were obviously too weak for inclusion on the final album, but others are good, or would have been strong contenders for the LP with more polishing of the songwriting and production ("Nowhere to Go," "Beautiful Girl," and "Tell Me What Has Happened to You" are standouts). One regrets that Harrison didn't take the time to work these into shape for the third disc of *All Things Must Pass*, instead of filling out the triple album with half-baked jams. —*Richie Unterberger*

All Things Must Pass: Acetate / 1994 / Black Dog [Bootleg] ✦✦✦
Also packaged as *Songs for Patti*, this isn't as essential an item as *Beware of Abkco!*, but is still a nifty addendum to the official *All Things Must Pass* release. Features alternate versions of songs from the LP, some of them substantially different early mixes (vocal and instrumental) without some layers of overdubs, some of them different takes entirely. Also includes a couple of songs that didn't make the final

album; the haunting, though unfinished, "I Still Love You" is a noteworthy find. Sound ranges from good to outstanding. —*Richie Unterberger*

Wilbert Harrison

b. Jan. 5, 1929, Charlotte, NC, **d.** Oct. 26, 1994, Spencer, NC
*Guitar, Piano, Drums, Vocals / Soul, R&B, Rock 'n' Roll, East Coast
Blues*

Perceived by casual oldies fans as a two-hit wonder (his 1959 chart-topper "Kansas City" and a heartwarming "Let's Work Together" a full
decade later), Wilbert Harrison actually left behind a varied body of
work that blended an intriguing melange of musical idioms into something quite distinctive. Country and gospel strains filtered into Wilbert
Harrison's consciousness as a youth in North Carolina. When he got out
of the Navy in Miami around 1950, he began performing in a calypso-
based style. Miami entrepreneur Henry Stone signed Harrison to his
Rockin' logo in 1953; his debut single, "This Woman of Mine," used the
same melody as his later reading of "Kansas City" (the first rendition of
the Jerry Leiber/Mike Stoller composition by pianist Little Willie Little-
field came out in 1952, doubtless making an impression). Its flip, a country-tinged "Letter Edged in Black," exhibited Harrison's eclectic mindset.
    After moving to Newark, NJ, Harrison wandered to the headquar-
ters of Savoy Records one fortuitous day and was snapped up by producer Fred Mendelsohn. Harrison recorded several sessions for Savoy,
beginning with a catchy cover of Terry Fell's country tune "Don't Drop
It." Top New York sessioneers—arranger Leroy Kirkland, saxist Buddy
Lucas, and guitarists Mickey Baker and Kenny Burrell—backed Harrison on his 1954-56 Savoy output, but hits weren't forthcoming.
    That changed instantly when Harrison waxed his driving "Kansas
City" for Harlem entrepreneur Bobby Robinson in 1959. With a barbed-
wire guitar solo by Wild Jimmy Spruill igniting Harrison's no-frills
piano and clenched vocal, "Kansas City" paced both the R&B and pop
charts soon after its issue on Fury Records (not bad for a $40 session).
Only one minor problem: Harrison was still technically under contract
to Savoy (though label head Herman Lubinsky had literally run him
out of his office some years earlier!), leading to all sorts of legal wrangles that finally went Robinson's way. Momentum for any Fury follow-
ups had been fatally blunted in the interim, despite fine attempts with
"Cheatin' Baby," the sequel "Goodbye Kansas City," and the original
"Let's Stick Together." Harrison bounced from Neptune to Doc to Constellation to Port to Vest with little in the way of tangible rewards
before unexpectedly making a comeback in '69 with his infectious
"Let's Work Together" for Juggy Murray's Sue imprint. The two-part single proved a popular cover item—Canned Heat revived it shortly thereafter, and Bryan Ferry chimed in with his treatment later on. Alas, it
was an isolated happenstance—apart from "My Heart Is Yours," a bot-
tom-end chart entry on SSS International in '71, no more hits were in
Wilbert's future. But Harrison soldiered on, sometimes as a one-man
band, for years to come. —*Bill Dahl*

Let's Work Together / 1969 / Sue ✦✦✦
Quickie album supervised by Juggy Murray to cash in on the unexpected success of Harrison's "Let's Work Together," but not a bad effort
all the same. Harrison brings his unique vocal delivery to oldies such
as "Blue Monday," "Stagger Lee," "Louie Louie," and "Stand by Me,"
imparting his own personal stamp to each. This LP deserves digital
reissue somewhere down the line. —*Bill Dahl*

Listen to My Song / 1987 / Savoy ✦✦✦✦
Harrison's first label association of any endurance commenced when
he signed with Herman Lubinsky's Savoy logo in 1954 for a two-year
stretch. Top New York sessioneers like guitarists Mickey Baker and
Kenny Burrell and saxists Buddy Lucas and Budd Johnson help out on
these 16 Savoy tracks (still unavailable on CD). He liked that C&W;
Terry Fell's "Don't Drop It" is a tremendously catchy hillbilly tune given
an R&B flavor by the young singer. —*Bill Dahl*

Greatest Classic R&B Hits / 1989 / Grudge ✦✦✦✦
This is the only available CD for Harrison's late-'60s material, long
after his 1959 classic "Kansas City." —*Bill Dahl*

● **Kansas City** / 1992 / Relic ✦✦✦✦
Finally, paydirt! Harrison smashed the charts in 1959 with his massive
hit "Kansas City" for Bobby Robinson's Fury logo. Here we have 22 fine
sides from the Fury hookup, some in stereo and many with Wild
Jimmy Spruill on lead guitar. "Cheatin' Baby," "C.C. Rider," "1960," and
the inevitable sequel "Goodbye Kansas City" are prime examples of
Harrison's slightly off-kilter approach to his craft, while this infectious
"Let's Stick Together" developed into the more worldly "Let's Work
Together" toward the end of the decade. —*Bill Dahl*

P.J. Harvey

b. Oct. 9, 1969, Yeovil, England
Alternative Pop-Rock, Singer-Songwriter
During the early-'90s alternative rock explosion, several female singer-

songwriters rose to prominence, but few were as distinctive or as
widely praised as Polly Jean Harvey. Over the course of three albums,
Harvey established herself as one of the most individual and influential songwriters of the '90s, exploring themes of sex, love, and religion
with unnerving honesty, dark humor, and a twisted theatricality. At the
outset of her career, she led the trio PJ Harvey, who delivered her stark
songs with bruisingly powerful, punkish abandon, as typified by her
1992 debut, *Dry.* Following the noisy, uncompromising follow-up *Rid
of Me,* the trio fell apart, and PJ Harvey became the sole property of
Polly Harvey. Her next record, 1995's *To Bring You My Love,* became
her mainstream critical breakthrough, confirming her status as one of
the cornerstone figures of '90s alternative rock.
    Polly Jean Harvey was raised on a sheep farm in Yeovil, England,
where she was raised by her quarryman father and her mother, who
was an artist. As a child, she learned how to play guitar and saxophone,
and when she was a teenager, she played in a variety of bands as a
sideman. In 1991, she formed PJ Harvey with bassist Steve Vaughn and
drummer Robert Ellis, and the trio recorded its debut record for under
$5,000. The band signed with the British indie label Too Pure and
released "Dress" that fall. "Dress" became a indie rock sensation, as did
its follow-up "Sheela-Na-Gig," with both singles receiving lavish praise
in the UK music press. Although Harvey was a reluctant interviewee,
she cannily used the press to her advantage, whether it was through
her candid interviews or startling, occasionally disturbingly sexy photo
sessions, which subverted traditional concepts of female sexuality.
    PJ Harvey's debut *Dry* was released in spring 1992 to considerable
praise; it was distributed in America by Island Records. The trio followed it with an extensive tour, culminating with an appearance at that
summer's Reading Festival. Shortly after the tour, Harvey moved to
London, where she nearly suffered a nervous breakdown due to the
extraordinary pressure and expectation surrounding her second album.
The group hired former Big Black frontman Steve Albini (Pixies,
Breeders), as the producer of their second album, *Rid of Me.* Albini
imposed his trademark noisy, guitar-heavy sound on the record, which
mirrored its harder-edged themes. *Rid of Me* was a major critical success and expanded Harvey's cult greatly. She supported the album with
a tour featuring herself in a fake leopard-skin coat and a feather boa,
signaling her developing interest in theatricality. At the end of the year,
Harvey released *4-Track Demos,* a collection of her original versions of
the songs on *Rid of Me.*
    Following the *Rid of Me* tour, Ellis and Vaughn parted ways with
Harvey, and she recorded her third album as a solo artist, augmented
by producer Flood, bassist Mick Harvey, and guitarists John Parish and
Joe Gore. Harvey developed a richer, bluesier sound with the expanded
band, and the resulting record, *To Bring You My Love,* was hailed as a
masterpiece by many critics upon its February 1995 release. Thanks to
considerable press attention, as well as strong support from MTV and
modern rock radio for the single "Down By the Water," *To Bring You
My Love* became a moderate hit, entering the US charts at No. 40. Harvey spent all of 1995 touring the album, and spent the following year
in relative seclusion. During 1996, she was relatively quiet, only
appearing twice on record: once in a duet with Nick Cave on his *Murder Ballads* album—the pair were reportedly romantically involved—
and singing on John Parish's *Dance Hall at Louse Point.* —*Stephen
Thomas Erlewine*

Dry / Jun. 30, 1992 / Too Pure/Indigo ✦✦✦✦
Polly Jean Harvey arrives fully formed as a songwriter on PJ Harvey's
debut album, *Dry.* Borrowing its primitive attack from post-punk guitar-rock and its form from the blues, *Dry* is a forceful collection of brutally emotional songs, highlighted by Harvey's deft lyricism and startling voice, as well as her trio's muscular sound. Her voice makes each
song sound like it was an exposed nerve, but her lyrics aren't quite that
simple. Shaded with metaphors and the occasional biblical allusion,
Dry is essentially an assault on feminine conventions and expectations,
and while there are layers of dark humor, they aren't particularly evident since Harvey's singing is shockingly raw. Her vocals are perfectly
complimented by the trio's ferocious pounding, which makes even the
slow ballads sound like exercises in controlled fury. And that's the key
to *Dry:* the songs, which are often surprisingly catchy—"Dress" and
"Sheela-Na-Gig" both have strong hooks—are as muscular and forceful
as the band's delivery, making the album a vibrant and fully realized
debut. —*Stephen Thomas Erlewine*

Rid of Me / May 4, 1993 / Island ✦✦✦✦
Dry was shockingly frank in its subject and sound, as Polly Harvey
delivered post-feminist manifestos with a punkish force. PJ Harvey's
second album, *Rid of Me,* finds the trio, and Harvey in particular, pushing themselves to extremes. This is partially due to producer Steve
Albini, who gives the album a bloodless, abrasive edge with his exacting production; each dynamic is pushed to the limit, leaving absolutely
no subtleties in the music. Harvey's songs, in decided contrast to
Albini's approach, are filled with grey areas and uncertainties, and are
considerably more personal than those on *Dry.* Furthermore, they are

lyrically and melodically superior to the songs on the debut, but their merits are obscured by Albini's black-and-white production, which is polarizing. It may be the aural embodiment of the tortured lyrics, and therefore a supremely effective piece of performance art, but it also makes *Rid of Me* a difficult record to meet halfway. But anyone willing to accept its sonic extremities will find *Rid of Me* to be a record of unusual power and purpose, one that has few peers in its unsettling emotional honesty. —*Stephen Thomas Erlewine*

4-Track Demos / Nov. 1993 / Island ✦✦✦
Since Steve Albini gave *Rid of Me* such an uncompromisingly noisy finish, it may have made sense for Polly Harvey to release her original demos, augmented by several unreleased songs, six months later as an album. After all, the initial British pressings of *Dry* came with a bonus disc of her demos. Still, the official, independent release of *4-Track Demos* suggests that Harvey wanted to give these songs another chance for listeners that found *Rid of Me* too abrasive. Even for those that enjoyed *Rid of Me*, *4-Track Demos* is a revelatory experience, since it arguably captures the raw emotion of the songs better than the official record. A handful of songs from the record aren't repeated in demo form—namely "Missed," "Man-Size," "Highway 61 Revisited," "Dry," and "Me-Jane"—but they're replaced by the previously unreleased "Reeling," "Driving," "Hardly Wait," "Easy," "M-Bike" and "Goodnight," most of which are easily the equal of the songs that were actually released, and that's what makes *4-Track Demos* necessary for every Harvey fan, not just collectors. —*Stephen Thomas Erlewine*

● To Bring You My Love / Feb. 28, 1995 / Island ✦✦✦✦
Following the tour for *Rid of Me*, Polly Harvey parted ways with Robert Ellis and Stephen Vaughn, leaving her free to expand her music from the bluesy punk that dominated PJ Harvey's first two albums. It also left her free to experiment with her style of songwriting. Where *Dry* and *Rid of Me* seemed like they were brutally honest, *To Bring You My Love* feels theatrical, with each song representing a grand gesture. Relying heavily on religious metaphors and imagery borrowed from the blues, Harvey has written a set of songs that are lyrically reminiscent of Nick Cave and Tom Waits' literary excursions into the gothic American heartland. Since she was a product of post-punk, she's nowhere as literally bluesy as Cave or Waits, preferring to embellish her songs with shards of avant-guitar, eerie keyboards, and a dense, detailed production. It's a far cry from the primitive guitars of her first two albums, but Harvey pulls it off with style, since her songwriting is tighter and more melodic than before; the menacing "Down By the Water" has genuine hooks, as does the psycho-stomp of "Meet Ze Monsta," the wailing "Long Snake Moan" and the stately "C'Mon Billy." The clear production by Harvey, Flood, and John Parish makes these growths evident, which in turn makes *To Bring You My Love* her most accessible album, even if the album lacks the indelible force of its predecessors. —*Stephen Thomas Erlewine*

Hassles

f. 1964, Long Island, NY
Rock 'n' Roll, Blue-Eyed Soul
The Hassles found their place in music history as Billy Joel's first recorded moment, but musically, they deserve more. Though they only released two albums, the Hassles were a pretty proficient, highly enjoyable, though not particularly groundbreaking act that saw a fair amount of local attention in the Long Island area.
    The Hassles were a blue-eyed soul band, modeled somewhat after the Rascals, formed in Long Island in 1964 by drummer Jon Small, singer John Dizek, organist Harry Webber, and guitarist Richie McKenna. Webber was fired from the band in 1966 due to erratic behavior and Billy Joel, who had earned a local reputation as a keyboardist with the Echoes, the Lost Souls, and the Commandos (as Billy Joe Joel), was enlisted to take his place on the condition that the band also take on bassist Howie Blauvelt. Though still a teenager, Joel was also able to add prodigiously soulful lead vocals and harmony. The group's new sound quickly found a following through constant gigging throughout Long Island. United Artists signed the band in 1967, releasing their self-titled debut by November the same year. The single, a cover of Sam & Dave's "You've Got Me Hummin' " made it to Billboard's No. 112, but the album failed to make an impact outside of the band's local following. In 1968, they followed with the more psychedelically-inclined *Hour of the Wolf*.
    The group disbanded the following year when Small and Joel left to form the heavier organ-and-drums duo, Attila. Attila released one album for Epic in early 1970 that went justifiably unnoticed at the time and remains an embarrassment for Joel to this day. Joel went on to an incredibly successful solo career and Small went on to become a video producer. —*Chris Woodstra*

● Hassles / 1967 / United Artists ✦✦✦✦
On the Hassles' self-titled debut, the band displayed a naive enthusiasm and a slightly better-than-average blue-eyed soul, covering several

hits and standards like "A Taste of Honey," "Fever," and "You've Got Me Hummin,'" as well as "Coloured Rain" (before Traffic recorded it) in standard Rascals style. Most of the album is nothing spectacular, but a pair of Billy Joel's tracks—"Every Step I Take (Every Move I Make)" and "I Can Tell"—show a budding songwriting talent, with the material fitting in quite nicely alongside established songs. [In 1992, the album was reissued on CD as part of EMI's "Legends of Rock & Roll" series with a generous eight bonus tracks recorded around the same time. The disc was pulled off the market shortly after its release at the request of Joel, who still seems embarrassed by his juvenilia despite the charm of the album.] —*Chris Woodstra*

Hour of the Wolf / 1968 / United Artists ✦✦✦
Hour of the Wolf showed a great leap in ambition and moved away from blue-eyed soul in favor of hippyish near-psychedelia, this time with Joel handling the songwriting himself (with a couple of cowrites with bandmates). Some of the stuff is certainly cringe-worthy—none so much as the title track, a 12-minute epic which boasts lyrics like "...God has loosed a hellhound freed to feed upon the prey of his desire/Death is borne alive akin to a creature with eyes of burning fire..." (There's even a middle bit featuring the band imitating wolf noises.) Embarrassing? Yes, but probably no more so than much of the other music from the era. Musically, the album shows the group dabbling in several styles, at times hinting at the more singer-songwriter-oriented direction Joel would take in the early '70s, as well as displaying his strong melodic sense. [*Hour of the Wolf* was set for release on CD in 1992, presumably with bonus tracks like the first album, but it was cancelled at the last minute when *The Hassles* was pulled.] —*Chris Woodstra*

Juliana Hatfield

b. Jul. 27, 1967, Wiscasset, ME
Bass, Guitar, Vocals / Alternative Pop-Rock, Pop-Rock
After Juliana Hatfield disbanded the jangle-pop trio the Blake Babies in 1990, she launched a solo career, performing a similarly melodic indie guitar-pop. Singing in an endearingly thin voice, Hatfield married her ringing hooks to sweet, lovelorn pop and startlingly honest confessional songs. Her 1992 solo debut *Hey Babe* became a college radio hit, and its follow-up, 1994's *Become What You Are*, was primed to become a crossover success in the wake of the commercialization of alternative rock. Although Hatfield had a handful of modern rock hits, including "Spin the Bottle," she never managed to gain the mainstream audience of peers like the Lemonheads, and by the late '90s, she had settled into a cult following.
    Juliana Hatfield was raised in an upper-middle-class home in Massachusetts; her father was a doctor and her mother was a fashion editor for *The Boston Globe*. As a child, she learned how to play piano, and during high school, she played guitar in a covers group called the Squids before discovering alternative rock through the Velvet Underground. Following high school, she attended the Berklee College of Music in Boston, where she studied voice. While at Berklee, she met guitarist John Strohm and drummer Freda Boner, with whom she formed the Blake Babies in 1986. Over the next six years, the Blake Babies and their charming jangle-pop became college radio favorites. Hatfield left the band in 1990, and Strohm and Boner formed Antenna.
    Immediately following her departure from the Blake Babies, Hatfield contributed several lyrics to Susanna Hoffs' debut album. The following year, she played bass on the Lemonheads' *It's a Shame About Ray*, which turned out to be the band's commercial breakthrough. The success of *It's a Shame About Ray* in 1992 stirred interest in Hatfield's solo debut, *Hey Babe*. Released on Mammoth Records, the album was very similar to the Blake Babies, yet the songs were more personal and confessional. *Hey Babe* was critically praised and became a college radio and MTV hit, leading to a major-label contract for Hatfield with Atlantic.
    In 1992, Hatfield formed the Juliana Hatfield Three with bassist Dean Fisher and drummer Todd Phillips, and the group recorded its debut for Atlantic with R.E.M.'s producer, Scott Litt. As she worked on the record, Hatfield became a minor media sensation; her songs were accepted as friendly, more accessible distillations of the feminist alternative rock movement known as riot grrrl. Hatfield appeared in fashion layouts in *Vogue* and *Sassy*, and she became the subject of gossipy tidbits about her speculated romance with Lemonhead Evan Dando and her assertion that she was still a virgin at the age of 25. In light of such exposure, many observers expected her 1993 album *Become What You Are* to be her mainstream breakthrough. A heavier record than its predecessor, *Become What You Are* was a moderate hit, as "My Sister" and "Spin the Bottle" earned heavy airplay on MTV and modern rock radio. Nevertheless, the album failed to make her a star.
    Only Everything followed in the spring of 1995, as alternative rock was beginning to decline in popularity. The album was received with mixed reviews, and only "Universal Heartbeat" managed to make

much headway on radio or MTV, causing the album to slip down the charts quickly. Hatfield was scheduled to deliver her fourth album in the summer of 1997. —*Stephen Thomas Erlewine*

● **Hey Babe** / Mar. 17, 1992 / Mammoth ✦✦✦✦
Hey Babe is Juliana Hatfield's terrific solo debut, filled with effortless melodies and catchy guitar riffs. Hatfield's thin, girlish voice can be slightly wearing over the course of an entire album, but her intelligent, hook-laden songs make up for that minor flaw. —*Stephen Thomas Erlewine*

Become What You Are / Aug. 3, 1993 / Mammoth/Atlantic ✦✦✦
Although she desperately tries to hide behind a grungier guitar sound, Hatfield is still a talented practitioner of girlish power-pop. Because she tries so hard to put the innocent pleasures of her debut behind her, *Become What You Are* isn't as satisfying. Most of the loud rave-ups betray her true gifts with a melody, which most definitely has not disappeared; her hooks are so strong that she can bring over such cringe-inducing lyrics as those of "For the Birds" and "Mabel" rather effortlessly. Hatfield's strongest points are apparent on "Supermodel," "My Sister," and "Spin the Bottle"—catchy, honest, and incisive portraits of adolescence, rendered truthful by her girlish, sing-song vocals. Fortunately, her talents are strong enough to carry the album over the weak spots. —*Stephen Thomas Erlewine*

Only Everything / Mar. 28, 1995 / Mammoth/Atlantic ✦✦✦
The Juliana Hatfield Three folded soon after the supporting tour for *Become What You Are*, yet Hatfield hasn't abandoned the basic approach of the band—she still rocks out, supporting her sing-song melodies with massive, grungy guitars. If anything, her new backing band rocks harder than the Hatfield Three, with a better, looser sense of rhythm as well. Even with the improved musicianship, Hatfield isn't able to deliver consistently impressive songs, occasionally relying on her cuteness to cover underdeveloped lyrics and pedestrian melodies. Most of the record doesn't drag, however—it's a fun, engaging pop album, yet its best moments follow the strengths of her earlier songs, without doing much to expand her formula. —*Stephen Thomas Erlewine*

Donny Hathaway

b. Oct. 1, 1945, Chicago, IL, d. Jan. 13, 1979, New York City, NY
Piano, Keyboards, Vocals / Soul
Donny Hathaway was a marvelous composer and vocalist. His sound, delivery, and timbre have influenced singers from Stevie Wonder to George Benson, while his compositions have been recorded by an array of artists from Cold Blood to Jerry Butler, the Staple Singers, Carla Thomas, and Aretha Franklin. Hathaway was born in Chicago, but grew up in St. Louis and began singing gospel at age three. He attended Howard University on a fine arts scholarship and was a classmate of Roberta Flack. He began recording for Curtis Mayfield's Curtom label in 1969, then signed with Atco. His single "The Ghetto" was a mild hit, but the duet "You've Got a Friend" with Flack was his first Top Ten R&B hit. The duo would later score two number one hit duets, "Where Is the Love" and "The Closer I Get to You," each of which was also a Top Ten pop hit. The duo had two final hits, "You Are My Heaven" and "Back Together Again," in 1980, after Hathaway stunned everyone by committing suicide in 1979 at age 33. —*Ron Wynn*

● **Collection** / Apr. 1990 / Atlantic ✦✦✦✦
Boasting many of his essential offerings, this CD underscores the fact that Donny Hathaway was one of the most riveting male soul singers of the 1970s. Hathaway's social concerns are illustrated by "To Be Young, Gifted and Black," a powerful live version of Marvin Gaye's "What's Goin' On" and his hit "The Ghetto," but more often than not, romance is his topic of choice. Indeed, R&B ballad singing doesn't get much more powerful than the Chicagoan's interpretations of Leon Russell's "A Song for You" and the remorseful "Giving Up" (an early Gladys Knight & the Pips hit written by Van McCoy of "The Hustle" fame). Hathaway and Roberta Flack usually made for a strong combination, and this holds true on duets ranging from the melancholy "Where Is the Love" to the ethereal "The Closer I Get to You" to the catchy "Back Together Again." Most of Hathaway's Atlantic albums are well worth hearing, but for novices, this CD is the most logical starting point. —*Alex Henderson*

Richie Havens (Richard Pierce Havens)

b. Jan. 21, 1941, Brooklyn, NY
Guitar, Vocals / Folk, Singer-Songwriter, Folk-Rock
Born in the Bedford-Stuyvesant section of Brooklyn, Richie Havens moved to Greenwich Village in 1961 in time to get in on the folk boom then taking place. Havens had a distinctive style as a folksinger, appearing in such clubs as the Cafe Wha? His guitar set to an opening tuning, he would strum it while barring chords with his thumb, using it essentially as percussion while singing rhythmically in a gruff voice for

a mesmerizing effect. Havens was signed to Douglas Records in 1965 and recorded two albums that gained him a local following. In 1967, the Verve division of MGM Records formed a folk section (Verve Forecast) and signed Havens and other folk-based performers. The result was Havens' third album, *Mixed Bag*. It wasn't until 1968 and the *Something Else Again* album, however, that Havens began to hit the charts—actually, Havens' fourth, third, and second albums charted that year, in that order. In 1969 came the double album *Richard P. Havens 1983*. Havens' career benefited enormously from his appearance at the Woodstock festival in 1969 and his subsequent featured role in the movie and album made from the concert in 1970. His first album after that exposure, *Alarm Clock*, made the Top 30 and produced a Top 20 single in "Here Comes the Sun." These recordings were Havens' commercial high-water mark, but by this time he had become an international touring success. By the end of the '70s, he had abandoned recording and turned entirely to live work.

Havens came back to records with a flurry of releases in 1987: a new album, *Simple Things*; an album of Bob Dylan and Beatles covers; and a compilation. In 1991, Havens signed his first major-label deal in 15 years when he moved to Sony Music and released *Now*. —*William Ruhlmann*

Mixed Bag / 1967 / Verve ✦✦✦✦
Havens' first major-label album, and his best, featuring his distinctive interpretations of such songs as Dylan's "Just Like a Woman" and the scathing antiwar anthem "Handsome Johnny." (It should be noted that, while it is his best overall collection, *Mixed Bag* is a also characteristic album: If you like it, you'll probably like other Havens records, which adopt much the same style.) —*William Ruhlmann*

Collection / 1987 / Rykodisc ✦✦✦
A compilation of Havens' '60s and early-'70s material. It leaves out some of his signature material, but it does include his version of "Here Comes the Sun." —*William Ruhlmann*

● **Resume: Best of** / Apr. 6, 1993 / Rhino ✦✦✦✦
Havens' output has been so extensive that picking tunes for a single-disc anthology would be a difficult task for any label. Rhino has done a respectable job in compiling 17 selections, although there was no material from the LPs *Stonehenge* or *1984*, and while he certainly performed them his way, neither Ray Charles' "Drown in My Own Tears" nor Billie Holiday's "God Bless the Child" were among Havens' best songs. By comparison, "Handsome Johnny," "Freedom," "Here Comes the Sun," "The Klan" and "Just Like a Woman" had a strength and power that came partly from being ideally suited for Havens' style. This isn't the comprehensive or qualitative anthology Havens deserves; just a decent hits collection. —*Ron Wynn*

Dale Hawkins

b. Aug. 30, 1938, Goldmine, LA
Guitar, Vocals / Rock 'n' Roll, Rockabilly
This Louisiana guitarist's 1957 hit "Suzy Q," with its crackling bluesy guitar and insistent cowbell, was one of the most exciting early rockabilly singles. Recording for Chess (as one of its few white artists) between 1956 and 1961, Hawkins never quite duplicated its success, either commercially or artistically, but came close enough on a number of occasions to warrant respect as one of the better rockabilly singers. His drawling delivery, sense of humor, affinity for blues, and sharp guitar work (which was actually provided by such ace players as Roy Buchanan, Scotty Moore, and James Burton) are heard to good effect on his 1958 album and a number of nonhit singles. Hawkins went on to become a producer of some note in the 1960s, working with the Five Americans and Bruce Channel. —*Richie Unterberger*

Susie Q / 1958 / Chess ✦✦✦
A way-above-average '50s rock 'n' roll album, including both sides of Dale's first four singles. Highlights are "Suzie Q," its killer B-side ("Don't Treat Me This Way"), and the goofy "See You Soon Baboon" and "Mrs. Mergitory's Daughter." —*Richie Unterberger*

My Babe / 1987 / Argo ✦✦✦
Rare singles and other interesting material that Hawkins cut, mostly for Chess, between 1958 and 1962. Includes his sole Top 40 hit besides "Suzie-Q" ("La-Do-Dada") and some fine rockabilly interpretations of blues hits. —*Richie Unterberger*

● **Oh Suzy Q** / Oct. 24, 1995 / Chess ✦✦✦✦
Eighteen tracks from Hawkins' Chess prime, all but one from the late '50s. Includes "Susie Q" and some obscure rockabilly cuts that are nearly as good, such as "Don't Treat Me This Way," "Liza Jane," and "Ain't That Lovin' You Babe." James Burton, Roy Buchanan, and Scotty Moore are the most prominent of the excellent guitarists to be heard on these sides. One could quibble over the absence of "Mrs. Mergitory's Daughter," "Yea Yea (Class Cutter)," and the post-Chess single "Stay at Home Lulu," but this is definitely the best Hawkins compilation ever assembled. —*Richie Unterberger*

Daredevil / Norton ✦✦✦✦

These 12 tracks, compiled from Hawkins' own personal stash of well-worn acetates, brings together the rarest of the rare of this Louisiana rockabilly songwriter/producer. The centerpiece of this 12-track collection is the first-time appearance of the original 1956 demo version of Dale's big hit, "Susie-Q." Recorded by country songwriter Merle Kilgore—then a disc jockey at KENT in Shreveport—the original demo is looser and faster than the better-known hit version, moved along with two raw guitar solos from a 16-year-old James Burton (this now becoming his debut recording) and a surprise solo from sax man Sheldon Bazelle. The sound is raw and overamped, the feel of a band taking a bandstand jam and trying to shape it into something that would fit onto one side of a phonograph record. The flip side of this scratchy 78 acetate is perhaps an even bigger surprise, Hawkins and band playing an impromptu slow blues entitled "If You Please Me" with Burton spraying licks all over the place, Dale mumbling a hastily assembled vocal, and no clear-cut ending. Equally fine is a version of Tarheel Slim's "Number Nine Train" featuring explosive guitar work from Carl Adams and the rare appearance of a slappin' upright bass (played by Bossier Strip regular Shorty Tony) on a Dale Hawkins record). This collection also features Hawkins in a supporting role picking guitar behind local boy vocalist Donnie Ray White and Nashville buddy Roger Miller, while his original band moonlights behind Maylon Humphries on "Weep No More," another cowbell rocker, this time in a minor key. Another noteworthy inclusion is "Superman," featuring Margaret Lewis on backup vocal, Roy Buchanan on guitar, and D.J. Fontana on drums. The title track, a wild instrumental with Adams driving the band on an agitated riff, later became the blueprint for "Lovin' Bug." Later cuts from the early 1960s flesh things out (the gospel-styled "Everglades," "On Account of You," "Hey Pretty Baby," "Mumbly Peg"), but these half dozen tracks—and especially the "Susie-Q" demo—are the main reasons to grab this one and add it to the MCA-Chess best-of compilation. —*Cub Koda*

Ronnie Hawkins

b. Jan. 10, 1935, Huntsville, AL
Guitar, Vocals / Rock 'n' Roll, Rockabilly
Hawkins is a rockabilly singer who formed his original backing band, the Hawks, while attending the University of Arkansas. After auditioning unsuccessfully for Sun in 1957, he started working regularly in Canada the following year, eventually taking up permanent residence there. After one release on the Canadian Quality label, he signed with Roulette in New York in 1959, having hits with "Forty Days" and "Mary Lou." The live fervor of Hawkins (known as Mr. Dynamo) & the Hawks' show continued in Canada after all the original members except Levon Helm headed back to the US. Hawkins quickly hired Canadian players Robbie Robertson, Garth Hudson, Rick Danko, and Richard Manuel as the new Hawks. They stayed with him until 1963, but later became Bob Dylan's backing group and went on to a career of their own as the Band. Hawkins has remained a legend in Canada, recording unrepentant rockabilly sides and gigging constantly. He's still the original Mr. Dynamo, capable of shaking the walls down any old time he feels like it. —*Cub Koda*

● **The Best of Ronnie Hawkins & His Band** / Jun. 1990 / Rhino ✦✦✦✦
In the late 1950s and early 1960s, Ronnie Hawkins was one of the few rock 'n' rollers committed to performing and recording unapologetic rockabilly while others were returning to their country roots or going the teen-idol route. This 18-song compilation focuses mostly on his initial burst of activity for Roulette in 1959 and 1960, with a few later odds and ends thrown in. While he deserves respect for keeping the torch of rock 'n' roll's roots burning during some of its leaner years, he didn't match the greatness of rockabilly's kingpins. His voice and performance were energetic but not brilliant; his material was a bit pedestrian. The best of these tunes are "Mary Lou" (his sole Top 30 hit), "Forty Days" (an update of Chuck Berry's "Thirty Days"), and "One of These Days" (later covered by the Searchers). What he's really known for, of course, is giving a bunch of mostly Canadian kids their start as his backing band, the Hawks. A later edition of the Hawks eventually toured with Bob Dylan and evolved into the Band. Only two of these songs, though, feature that lineup (the 1963 single "Bo Diddley"/"Who Do You Love"). On "Who Do You Love" especially, Robbie Robertson lets rip with a roaring solo that's a good few years ahead of its time in its manic distorted intensity. It's by far the most exciting track on this compilation of a respectable but minor performer from rock's early days. —*Richie Unterberger*

Screamin' Jay Hawkins

b. Jul. 18, 1929, Cleveland, OH
Vocals / R&B, Rock 'n' Roll, Jump Blues
Screamin' Jay Hawkins was the most outrageous performer extant during rock's dawn. Prone to emerging out of coffins onstage, a flaming

skull named Henry his constant companion, Screamin' Jay was an insanely theatrical figure long before it was even remotely acceptable.

Hawkins' life story is almost as bizarre as his onstage shtick. Originally inspired by the booming baritone of Paul Robeson, Hawkins was unable to break through as an opera singer. His boxing prowess was every bit as lethal as his vocal cords; many of his most hilarious tales revolve around Jay beating the hell out of a musical rival!

Hawkins caught his first musical break in 1951 as pianist/valet to veteran jazz guitarist Tiny Grimes. He debuted on wax for Gotham the following year with "Why Did You Waste My Time," backed by Grimes and his Rockin' Highlanders (they donned kilts and tam o' shanters on stage). Singles for Timely ("Baptize Me in Wine") and Mercury's Wing subsidiary (1955's otherworldly "[She Put The] Wamee [On Me]," a harbinger of things to come) preceded Hawkins' immortal 1956 rendering of "I Put a Spell on You" for Columbia's Okeh imprint.

Hawkins originally envisioned the tune as a refined ballad. After he and his New York session aces (notably guitarist Mickey Baker and saxist Sam "The Man" Taylor) had imbibed to the point of no return, Hawkins screamed, grunted, and gurgled his way through the tune with utter drunken abandon. A resultant success despite the protests of uptight suits-in-power, "Spell" became Screamin' Jay's biggest seller ("Little Demon," its rocking flip, is a minor classic itself).

Hawkins cut several amazing 1957-58 follow-ups in the same crazed vein—"Hong Kong," a surreal "Yellow Coat," the Jerry Leiber/Mike Stoller-penned "Alligator Wine"—but none of them clicked the way "Spell" had. Deejay Alan Freed convinced Screamin' Jay that popping out of a coffin might be a show-stopping gimmick by handing him a $300 bonus (long after Freed's demise, Screamin' Jay Hawkins is still benefiting from his crass brainstorm).

Hawkins' next truly inspired waxing came in 1969 when he was contracted to Philips Records (where he made two albums). His gross "Constipation Blues" wouldn't garner much airplay, but remains an integral part of his legacy to this day.

The cinema has been a beneficiary of Screamin' Jay's larger-than-life persona in recent years. His featured roles in *Mystery Train* and *A Rage in Harlem* have made Hawkins a familiar visage to youngsters who've never even heard "I Put a Spell on You." Hawkins remains musically active, though his act doesn't seem all that bizarre anymore. —*Bill Dahl*

● **Voodoo Jive: The Best of Screamin' Jay Hawkins** / Feb. 1990 / Rhino ✦✦✦✦
Some maintain that Hawkins was a one-hit fluke and a one-dimensional performer with a limited singing voice and no other discernible skills. Others insist that Hawkins was a decent R&B and blues singer and an excellent entertainer and personality whose real talents were overshadowed by the success of "I Put a Spell on You." This anthology doesn't convincingly answer the argument, but it does collect 17 Hawkins singles from Okeh, Enrica, and Phillips, including all of his major hits. The high (or low) point is perhaps 1969's "Constipation Blues." —*Ron Wynn*

Ted Hawkins

b. 1936, Biloxi, MS, d. Jan. 1, 1995, Los Angeles, CA
Guitar, Vocals / Soul, Soul Blues, Modern Acoustic Blues, Singer-Songwriter
Overseas, he was a genuine hero, performing to thousands. But on his L.A. hometurf, sand-blown Venice Beach served as Ted Hawkins' makeshift stage. He'd deliver his magnificent melange of soul, blues, folk, gospel, and a touch of country all by his lonesome, with only an acoustic guitar for company. Passersby would pause to marvel at Hawkins' melismatic vocals, dropping a few coins or a greenback into his tip jar on the way by.

That was the way Ted Hawkins kept body and soul together until 1994, when DGC/Geffen Records issued *The Next Hundred Years*, his breakthrough album. Suddenly, Hawkins was poised on the precipice of stardom. And then, just after Christmas that same year, in a bout of cruel irony, he died of a stroke.

Ted Hawkins' existence was no day in the park. Born into abject poverty in Mississippi, an abused and illiterate child, Hawkins was sent to reform school when he was 12 years old. He encountered his first musical inspiration there from New Orleans pianist Professor Longhair, whose visit to the school moved the lad to perform in a talent show. But it wasn't enough to keep him out of trouble. At age 15, he stole a leather jacket and spent three years at Mississippi's infamous state penitentiary at Parchman Farm.

Roaming from Chicago to Philadelphia to Buffalo after his release, Hawkins left the frigid weather behind in 1966, purchasing a one-way ticket to L.A. Suddenly, music beckoned; he bought a guitar and set out to locate the ex-manager of Sam Cooke (one of his idols). No such luck, but he did manage to cut his debut 45, "Baby"/"Whole Lot of Women," for Money Records. When he learned no royalties were forthcoming from its sales, Hawkins despaired of ever making a living at his music and took to playing on the streets. Fortunately, producer Bruce Bromberg was interested in Hawkins' welfare, recording his delightfully original material in 1971 both with guitarist Phillip Walker's band ("Sweet Baby" was issued as a single on the Joliet label) and in a solo acoustic format (with Ted's wife Elizabeth occasionally adding harmonies). The producer lost touch with Hawkins for a while after recording him, Hawkins falling afoul of the law once again. In 1982, those tapes finally emerged on Rounder as *Watch Your Step*, and Hawkins began to receive some acclaim (*Rolling Stone* gave it a five-star review). Bromberg corralled him again for the 1986 encore album *Happy Hour*, which contained the touching "Cold & Bitter Tears."

At the behest of a British deejay, Hawkins moved to England in 1986 and was treated like a star for four years, performing in Great Britain, Ireland, France, even Japan. But when he came home, he was faced with the same old situation. Once again, he set up his tip jar on the beach, donned the black leather glove he wore on his fretting hand, and played for passersby—until DGC ever so briefly propelled him into the major leagues.

Ted Hawkins was a unique talent, unclassifiable and eminently soulful. For a year or so, he was even a star in his own country. *—Bill Dahl*

Watch Your Step / 1982 / Rounder ◆◆◆
Guitarist/vocalist Ted Hawkins was an instant sensation when this session was originally released in 1982. At a time when slick, heavily produced urban contemporary material was establishing its domination on the R&B scene, Hawkins' hard-edged, rough, cutting voice, plus his crisp acoustic guitar accompaniment and country blues roots, seemed both dated and extremely fresh. This 15-track CD includes four numbers with Hawkins backed by Phillip Walker and his band, and others ranging from the humorous "Who Got My Natural Comb?" to the poignant "If You Love Me" and two versions of the title track. He also teamed with his wife Elizabeth on "Don't Lose Your Cool" and "I Gave It All I Had" for moving duets. *—Ron Wynn*

● **Happy Hour** / 1987 / Rounder ◆◆◆◆
Guitarist/vocalist Ted Hawkins' second Rounder record enhanced his reputation. *Happy Hour* features Hawkins' memorable compositions, plus a wonderful version of Curtis Mayfield's "Gypsy Woman." Hawkins' vocals were even more gritty and striking, as was his acoustic guitar backing and chording. He teamed with his wife Elizabeth on "Don't Make Me Explain It," "My Last Goodbye," and "California Song," and with guitarist Night Train Clemons on "Gypsy Woman" and "You Pushed My Head Away." Hawkins blended soul and urban blues stylings with country and rural blues inflections and rhythms, making another first-rate release. *—Ron Wynn*

The Next Hundred Years / Mar. 29, 1994 / DGC ◆◆◆
The former L.A. street musician's major label breakthrough was in a great many ways a far weaker outing than what came before, largely due to a plodding band unwisely inserted behind Hawkins that tends to distract rather than enhance his impassioned vocals and rich acoustic guitar strumming. Mostly originals ("There Stands the Glass" returns, as does "Ladder of Success") that would have sounded so much better in an intimate solo context. *—Bill Dahl*

Songs from Venice Beach / Oct. 1995 / Evidence ◆◆◆◆
Blending every form of roots music imaginable into his own singular soulful stew, the incomparable Ted Hawkins stuck mostly to R&B covers on this splendid 1985 solo outing—songs by Sam Cooke (his idol), Jerry Butler, Bobby Bland, the Temptations, and Garnet Mimms receive gorgeous readings by the acoustic guitarist. But even though he only contributed one original, the touching "Ladder of Success," to the set, Hawkins wasn't content to remain in one genre—his commanding revival of Webb Pierce's hillbilly weeper "There Stands the Glass" ranks with the disc's very best moments (of which there are many). *—Bill Dahl*

Hayden

b. 1971, Toronto, Ontario, Canada
Vocals / Alternative Pop-Rock
Hayden's *Everything I Long For* is bound to draw comparisons with alternative faves like Beck, J Mascis, and Palace; the low, prematurely wizened vocals, the plain acoustic (though not quite lo-fi) arrangements, the downbeat whimsy. The post-punk gloom is leavened by the sweetly melancholic guitars (something like Neil Young's *Four Way Street* version of "Cowgirl in the Sand") and heartfelt, sometimes heartrending throaty vocals with shades of Tom Waits and Captain Beefheart. Despite the abundant reference points, it's an original sound, and one whose left-field charm is likely to cause a warranted stir in the alternative audience. *—Richie Unterberger*

Everything I Long For / May 21, 1996 / Outpost ◆◆◆◆
Solitary, rootsy post-punk of the best kind, delving into somewhat dark and twisted terrrain, but invested with a lot of passion and unflinching

grit. The sparse and haunting arrangements put acoustic guitars at the forefront, but vary the pace with occasional searing licks, eerie solo piano, and harmony vocals. It's one of the relatively few releases of this type that will find a comfortable home in the collections of those with an ear for either stark folk-rock or grunge. *—Richie Unterberger*

Isaac Hayes

b. Aug. 6, 1942, Covington, TN
Piano, Saxophone, Vocals / Soul, Funk, Disco, R&B
Few figures exerted greater influence over the music of the 1960s and 1970s than Isaac Hayes; after laying the groundwork for the Memphis soul sound through his work with Stax-Volt Records, Hayes began a highly successful solo career which predated not only the disco movement but also the evolution of rap.

Hayes was born on August 6, 1942, in Covington, TN; his parents died during his infancy, and he was raised by his grandparents. After making his public debut singing in church at the age of five, he taught himself both piano, orga,n and saxophone before moving to Memphis to perform on the city's club circuit in a series of short-lived groups like Sir Isaac and the Doo-Dads, the Teen Tones, and Sir Calvin and His Swinging Cats. In 1962, he began his recording career, cutting sides for a variety of local labels.

Two years later, Hayes began playing sax with the Mar-Keys, which resulted in the beginning of his long association with Stax Records. After playing on several sessions for Otis Redding, Hayes was tapped to play keyboards in the Stax house band, and eventually established a partnership with songwriter David Porter. Under the name the Soul Children, the Hayes-Porter duo composed some 200 songs, reeling off a string of hits for Stax luminaries like Sam and Dave (the brilliant "When Something Is Wrong with My Baby," "Soul Man," and "Hold On, I'm Comin'"), Carla Thomas ("B-A-B-Y") and Johnnie Taylor ("I Got to Love Somebody's Baby," "I Had a Dream").

In 1967, Hayes issued his debut solo LP *Presenting Isaac Hayes*, a loose, jazz-flavored effort recorded in the early-morning hours following a raucous Stax party. With the release of 1969's landmark *Hot-Buttered Soul*, he made his commercial breakthrough, as the record's adventuresome structure (comprising four lengthy songs), ornate arrangements and sensual grooves—combined with the imposing figure cut by his shaven head, omnipresent sunglasses and fondness for gold jewelry—made Hayes one of the most distinct figures in music.

After a pair of 1970 releases, *The Isaac Hayes Movement* and *To Be Continued*, he reached his commercial zenith in 1971 with the release of *Shaft*, the score from the Gordon Parks film of the same name. Not only did the album win Hayes an Academy Award for Best Score (the first African-American composer to garner such an honor), but the single "Theme from 'Shaft,'" a masterful blend of prime funk and pre-rap monologues, became a No. 1 hit.

After 1971's superb *Black Moses and 1973's Joy*, Hayes composed two 1974 soundtracks, *Tough Guys* and *Truck Turner* (in which he also starred); by 1975, relations with Stax had disintegrated following a battle over royalties, and soon he severed his ties with the label to form his own Hot Buttered Soul imprint. Although both 1975's *Chocolate Chip* and 1976's *Groove-a-thon* went gold, his records of the period attracted considerably less attention than prior efforts; combined with poor management and business associations, Hayes had no choice but to file for bankruptcy in 1976.

After the 1977 double-LP *A Man and a Woman*, recorded with Dionne Warwick, Hayes began a comeback on the strength of the hit singles "Zeke the Freak," "Don't Let Go," and "Do You Wanna Make Love." Following the success of his 1979 collection of duets with Millie Jackson titled *Royal Rappin's*, he issued a pair of solo records, 1980's *And Once Again* and 1981's *Lifetime Thing*, before retiring from music for five years. After returning in 1986 with the LP *U Turn* and the Top Ten R&B hit "Ike's Rap," Hayes surfaced two years later with *Love Attack* before again dropping out of music to focus on acting.

In 1995, fully enshrined as one of the forefathers of hip-hop, Hayes emerged with two concurrent releases, the vocal *Branded* and instrumental *Raw and Refined*. Under the official name Nene Katey Ocansey I, he also served as a member of the royal family of the African nation of Ghana while continuing simultaneous careers as an actor, composer, and humanitarian. *—Jason Ankeny*

Presenting Isaac Hayes / 1968 / Stax ◆◆◆
Isaac Hayes' earliest single efforts, and he hadn't yet perfected his lengthy raps and symphonic soul formula. These were rather the same type of songs he and David Porter turned into classics for many other Stax artists. They were mostly short, gospel and country-tinged soul ballads, vamps, and uptempo numbers. Hayes sang them well, his domineering baritone revealing itself as a potent weapon. While none of them did that well, the album revealed the enormous potential Hayes would begin to fulfill with his next album. *—Ron Wynn*

☆ **Hot Buttered Soul** / 1969 / Stax ✦✦✦✦✦
Isaac Hayes had already co-written many immortal soul singles in the late '60s when he began forging a solo career. Hayes helped focus attention on the album as a creative source in soul and R&B. This seminal album went against the grain in several ways. There were only four cuts, three of them at least nine minutes. There were two with extensive monologues, and he used symphonic backing and elaborate production. The album went gold, cracked the Top 100, and helped usher soul and R&B into the concept album era. It also featured some superb vocals and fine keyboard work by Hayes. —*Ron Wynn*

Isaac Hayes Movement / 1970 / Stax ✦✦✦✦
His second huge hit album and a great follow-up to the superb *Hot Buttered Soul*. Those critics who thought there was no way Hayes could repeat that triumph got fooled. He included a brilliant remake of Jerry Butler's "I Stand Accused" and also did a 12-minute version of the Beatles' "Something," complete with a wailing violin solo from jazz-rocker John Blair. This album showed that Hayes was going to be around for a long time and perform just as consistently on his own as he did teaming with Porter. —*Ron Wynn*

To Be Continued / 1970 / Stax ✦✦✦
The third consecutive smash hit album for Isaac Hayes, with more anthemic raps and elaborate symphonic soul. This time he did his production/rap/movement routines remaking the songs "The Look of Love" and "You've Lost That Lovin' Feelin'." Once more, Hayes combined inspired vocals with equally creative production and arrangements, getting his third straight platinum album, something that was then unprecedented in R&B and soul circles for albums. —*Ron Wynn*

Black Moses / 1971 / Stax ✦✦✦
Isaac Hayes followed his Oscar-winning soundtrack LP *Shaft* with another two-record set blending remakes of soul and pop hits, extended monologues, symphonic orchestrations and backing, and other production devices that made him one of the 1970s' most successful producers and performers. Although *Black Moses* wasn't nearly as commercially dominant as earlier albums, it did make the Top Ten briefly and was on the charts for over 30 weeks. But it was also an indication that he was beginning to run a bit dry in the material department. —*Ron Wynn*

Shaft / 1971 / Stax ✦✦✦✦
Isaac Hayes surprised many in the film and R&B/soul world when he produced, arranged and composed the music for *Shaft*. Only three of the 15 tracks featured vocals, and Hayes displayed a finesse and capability with strings and mood pieces that his fans already knew he possessed from earlier albums, but which the general audience might have missed. This was a No. 1 pop LP, and eventually earned Hayes an Oscar. It's also held up much better than the film. —*Ron Wynn*

Joy / Dec. 1973 / Stax ✦✦
Isaac Hayes came close to recapturing his production and performance magic on this mid-'70s work. The title cut was a fine single, although it had to be split in two to fit radio formats. Otherwise, the songs alternated between classy ballads and fine uptempo cuts, neither of which did as well as expected. —*Ron Wynn*

Double Dynamite / 1974 / Stax ✦✦✦
Isaac Hayes not only was an innovative composer, songwriter, producer, and performer in the '60s and '70s, he was also an actor and appeared in several "blaxploitation" films during the early '70s. Hayes did double duty on these projects, writing and conducting the soundtracks for several, including the two featured on this twin-CD reissue. Neither *Truck Turner* nor *Tough Guys* was a particularly memorable film, but Hayes' effective use of symphony orchestras and strings against a vocal backdrop often made the music the best part of the movie. —*Ron Wynn*

Chocolate Chip / 1975 / HBS ✦✦✦
A fine mid-'70s album on which Isaac Hayes adapted to the disco era. His productions were already ideal for dance floors, and he now updated his charts to include some stomping segments with horns and layered beats, while maintaining his soulful vocals on both uptempo tunes and ballads. This album got two Top 20 hits for Hayes, and was his last really big hit LP in the '70s. —*Ron Wynn*

Best of Isaac Hayes, Vol. 1 / 1986 / Stax ✦✦✦
A decent attempt to present some of Isaac Hayes' past hits on an anthology. But as one of R&B and soul's first concept and album artists, it's impossible to appreciate his contributions out of sequence. His early—and mid-'70s albums helped change the course of contemporary black music production approaches, and that can't be understood by listening to condensed versions of hit singles, or even just by hearing the singles themselves removed from the album context. —*Ron Wynn*

Best of Isaac Hayes, Vol. 2 / 1986 / Stax ✦✦✦✦
These two compilations dutifully boil down Isaac Hayes' sometimes long-winded albums to their essential parts—in other words, they're both singles collections, highlighted by '70s landmarks such as "Theme

from Shaft" and "By the Time I Get to Phoenix." Fanatics may want to investigate *Hot Buttered Soul* and *Black Moses*. —*John Floyd*

● **Greatest Hit Singles** / Jun. 11, 1991 / Stax ✦✦✦✦
The place to start (and probably the place to end), with nearly an hour of music and 12 of his best-known singles, including "Theme from 'Shaft,'" "By the Time I Get to Phoenix," "Walk on By," "Never Can Say Goodbye," "Do Your Thing," and "Joy (Part 1)." There's a separate, two-volume series of Stax Hayes hits for those who want a little more, but this is the essential dose. —*Richie Unterberger*

The Best of Polydor Years / Feb. 6, 1996 / Polygram ✦✦✦✦

Roy Head

b. Jan. 9, 1943, Three Rivers, TX
Vocals / R&B, Rock 'n' Roll, Traditional Country
Actually a country and rock vocalist rather than an R&B star, Roy Head nevertheless cut one of the great pieces of uptempo soul in the mid-'60s. "Treat Her Right" on Back Beat made it to No. 2 on the R&B charts and No. 2 pop, and the fact that Head was white was soft-pedaled in R&B circles while the song made its way up the charts. That performance alone was enough to qualify Head as one of the finest blue-eyed soul singers of the 1960s. But in fact, Roy was one of the most versatile stylists of the era, capable of hard R&B/rock tunes (even cutting material with a pre-fame Johnny Winter on backup guitar), mournful, soul-tinged country, and straight R&B and blues covers. Head was also an excellent entertainer, and his live shows of the period even included some fancy footwork clearly under the influence of James Brown. The Texan singer is remembered as a one-shot artist, but he actually cut many records (some under the auspices of noted producer Huey Meaux) throughout the 1960s on a confusing variety of labels. A few of these were tiny hits in the wake of "Treat Her Right," only a couple ("Just a Little Bit" and "Apple of My Eye") sneaking into the Top 40. Quite a few of his records were dynamic, sleek hybrids (in varying degrees) of soul, rock, and country, all featuring Head's cocky, confident vocals. In a sense, though, he was damned by his versatility, not fitting comfortably into any niche or marketing plan; the tiny labels he recorded for lacked national promotional muscle in any case. In the 1970s, after several years without success in the rock or R&B fields, Head returned to country, and landed quite a few chart hits in the arena between 1974 and 1985. —*Ron Wynn & Richie Unterberger*

Treat Me Right / 1965 / Bear Family ✦✦✦✦
Read the title carefully; it's not "Treat Her Right," the title of Head's 1965 megasmash, but *Treat Me Right*, an entirely different song. Yes indeed, this is an exploitation release of material Head cut for a different label than the one that issued "Treat Her Right," repackaged after the hit to capitalize on its unexpected success. The final punchline is that, as exploitative as this LP is, it's quite good. The ten songs—mostly revved-up R&B, with a bit of country soul thrown in—are solid evidence of Head's stature as one of the finest white soul singers of the '60s. The small combo R&B arrangements are spare and tight, investing even overdone standards like "Money" with excitement. Long out of print, it still shows up in the used bins from time to time and is worth picking up. —*Richie Unterberger*

Slip Away: His Best Recordings / Aug. 5, 1993 / Collectables ✦✦✦
Not only are these *not* his best recordings by a long shot—this package also matches the shoddiest standards of the Collectables label, a company often (justly) criticized for a variety of inadequacies. The documentation on these 14 tracks is totally nonexistent—not a clue as to when they were first released or recorded. A good many came out in the mid-'60s (though "Treat Her Right" and most of the other best Back Beat singles are absent); others have a heavier soul/blues feel that sounds as though they might date from a few years later, or even much later. What's more, a few tracks that appear (in better fidelity) on the Varese Sarabande compilation are presented here with different track titles, although you might mistakenly think at a glance that it doesn't duplicate anything from that anthology. There *are* a few very good cuts here that aren't on *The Best of Roy Head*, such as the talking soul rap "Slip Away," the deep soul ballad "The Feeling Is Gone," and the zany psychedelic/jazz-flavored "Easy Loving Girl" (written by Johnny Winter, who plays fuzz guitar on the song). Just be warned that this is a carelessly assembled package, much inferior to the Varese Sarabande compilation, if you only want one disc. —*Richie Unterberger*

● **Treat Her Right: Best of Roy Head** / Aug. 29, 1995 / Varèse Vintage ✦✦✦✦
A long overdue anthology of Head's best sides, mostly recorded for the Back Beat label in the mid-'60s. Besides "Treat Her Right," it has all five of his other singles that dented the charts at the time. These aren't necessarily the highlights of these 18 tracks; "Pain" is country-soul moan at its best (although it's a thinly veiled rewrite of Lonnie Mack's "Why"), "To Make a Big Man Cry" is his best foray into country-pop from the period, and "You're (Almost) Tuff" is one of his toughest rockers, with a

sound that almost verges on Texas garage. This collection is the most solid evidence of Head's superb talents, which were never rewarded with the consistent material or national recognition he deserved. —*Richie Unterberger*

Heart

f. 1973, Seattle, WA
Hard Rock, Pop-Rock

Sisters Ann and Nancy Wilson were the creative spark behind Heart, a hard rock group that initially found success in the mid-1970s, only to reach greater heights after engineering a major comeback about a decade later. The daughters of a Marine Corps captain, Ann (born June 19, 1950) and Nancy (born March 16, 1954) grew up in both Southern California and Taiwan before the Wilson family settled in Seattle, WA. Throughout their formative years, both were interested in folk and pop music; while Ann never took any formal music lessons as a child (she later learned to play several instruments), Nancy took up guitar and flute. After both sisters spent some time at college, they decided to try their hand as professional musicians, and while Nancy began performing as a folksinger, Ann joined the all-male vocal group Heart.

Based in Vancouver, BC, Heart was actually formed in 1963 by bassist Steve Fossen and brothers Roger and Mike Fisher; initially dubbed the Army, they later became White Heart before settling on simply Heart at the beginning of the 1970s. After her arrival in the group, Ann became romantically involved with guitarist Roger; when Nancy joined in 1974, she in turn began a relationship with Mike, who had subsequently retired from active performing to become the band's sound engineer. After gaining a following in Vancouver, Heart was approached by Shelly Siegel, the owner of the Canadian label Mushroom; augmented by keyboardist Howard Leese and drummer Michael Derosier, they recorded their debut album, *Dreamboat Annie*, in 1975.

After selling more than 30,000 copies north of the border, Mushroom issued the LP in the US, where it quickly achieved platinum status on the strength of the hit singles "Crazy on You" and "Magic Man." In 1977, Heart jumped ship to the CBS affiliate Portrait, resulting in a protracted legal battle with Siegel, who in 1978 released the unfinished LP *Magazine* on Mushroom shortly after the band issued its true follow-up *Little Queen* on Portrait. The single "Barracuda" was another massive hit, and like its predecessor, *Little Queen* sold over a million copies.

After 1978's *Dog and Butterfly*, both of the Wilson/Fisher romances ended, and Roger left the group. In 1980, Heart issued *Bebe Le Strange*; following a lengthy US tour, both Fossen and Derosier exited, and were replaced by ex-Spirit and Firefall bassist Mark Andes and former Gamma drummer Denny Carmassi. After 1982's *Private Audition* and 1983's *Passionworks* slumped, the group was largely written off by industry watchers, and moved to Capitol Records.

In 1985, however, Heart emerged with a self-titled effort, which ultimately sold more than five million copies on its way to launching four Top Ten hits—"What About Love?," "Never," the chart-topping "These Dreams" and "Nothin' at All." 1987's *Bad Animals* continued their comeback success; "Alone" was another No. 1 hit, and both "Who Will You Run To" and "There's the Girl" achieved considerable airplay as well. *Brigade*, issued in 1990, featured the No. 2 smash "All I Want to Do Is Make Love to You," as well as the Top 25 hits "I Didn't Want to Need You" and "Stranded."

In the early '90s, the Wilson sisters took a brief hiatus from Heart to form the Lovemongers, an acoustic quartet fleshed out by Sue Ennis and Frank Cox; in 1992, they issued a four-song EP, which included a cover of Led Zeppelin's "The Battle of Evermore." Heart returned in 1993 with *Desire Walks On*, on which Andes and Carmassi were replaced with bassist Fernando Saunders and drummer Denny Fongheiser. With 1995's *The Road Home*, Heart enlisted onetime Led Zep bassist John Paul Jones to produce a live, acoustic set reprising hits like "Dreamboat Annie," "Crazy on You," and "Barracuda." —*Jason Ankeny*

Dreamboat Annie / Mar. 1976 / Capitol ✦✦✦✦
In the 1980s and '90s, numerous women have recorded blistering rock, but things were quite different in 1976—when female singers tended to be pigeonholed as soft-rockers and singer-songwriters and were encouraged to take after Carly Simon, Melissa Manchester, or Joni Mitchell rather than Led Zeppelin or Black Sabbath. Greatly influenced by Zep, Heart did its part to help open doors for ladies of loudness with the excellent *Dreamboat Annie* (reissued on a gold audiophile CD by DCC Compact Classics in 1995). Aggressive yet melodic rockers like "Sing Child," "White Lightning and White," and the rock radio staples "Magic Man" and "razy on You" led to the tag "the female Led Zeppelin." And in fact, Robert Plant did have a strong influence on Ann Wilson. But those numbers and caressing, folkish ballads like "How Deep It Goes" and the title song also make it clear that the Wilson sisters had their own identity and vision early on. —*Alex Henderson*

Little Queen / May 1977 / Portrait ✦✦✦✦
After acquiring a substantial following with *Dreamboat Annie*, Heart solidified its niche in the hard rock and arena rock worlds with the equally impressive *Little Queen*. Once again, loud-and-proud, Led Zeppelin-influenced hard rock was the thing that brought Heart the most attention. But while "Barracuda" and "Kick It Out" are the type of sweaty rockers one thought of first when Heart's name was mentioned, hard rock by no means dominates this album. In fact, much of *Little Queen* consists of such folk-influenced, acoustic-oriented fare as "Treat Me Well" and "Cry to Me." Anyone doubting just how much Heart's ballads have changed over the years need only play "Dream of the Archer" next to a high-volume power ballad like "Waiting for an Answer" from 1990's *Brigade*. —*Alex Henderson*

Magazine / Apr. 1978 / Capitol ✦✦
A collection of early demos and outtakes released when the group changed record labels, *Magazine* accentuates Heart's folkie roots, but that's not what makes the album such an unengaging listen. Instead, the album is mediocre because most of the material is underdeveloped and directionless. —*Stephen Thomas Erlewine*

Dog & Butterfly / Sep. 1978 / Portrait ✦✦✦

Bebe Le Strange / Feb. 1980 / Epic ✦✦✦✦

Heart Greatest Hits/Live / Nov. 1980 / Epic ✦✦✦✦
This set includes all of the significant rock radio hits that made Heart such a staple during the '70s and early '80s, such as "Barracuda," "Crazy on You," "Straight On," "Dreamboat Annie," "Even It Up," "Magic Man," "Heartless," and "Dog & Butterfly." Filling out the disc are six live tracks, including versions of Led Zeppelin's "Rock and Roll" and the Beatles' rave-up "I'm Down." —*Rick Clark*

Private Audition / May 1982 / Epic ✦✦

Passionworks / Aug. 1983 / Epic ✦✦

Heart / Jun. 1985 / Capitol ✦✦✦✦
Just when it seemed that Heart was yesterday's news on the radio, they changed labels and experienced a resurgence of huge success with this, their self-titled Capitol debut. Includes the hits "If Looks Could Kill," "What About Love?," "Never," "Nothin' at All," and "These Dreams." —*Rick Clark*

Bad Animals / May 1987 / Capitol ✦✦✦
Switching from Epic to Capitol with 1985's *Heart* proved to be a wise move for the Wilson sisters, who experienced a major resurgence in popularity and gained many new followers. Heart's arena rock sound had become even glossier, and the band was selling more albums than ever. But for all its production gloss (courtesy of Ron Nevison) and pop slickness, *Bad Animals* comes across as sincere rather than formulaic or cynical. From the rockers "You Ain't Too Tough" and "Easy Target" to the power ballads "Alone" and "Wait for an Answer," all of the songs are quite memorable. The folk elements and acoustic leanings that characterized many of Heart's early ballads were long gone, and the Wilson sisters keep the volume high however slow the tempo. —*Alex Henderson*

Brigade / Mar. 26, 1990 / Capitol ✦✦
Heart entered the 1990s with *Brigade*, which isn't quite as strong as *Heart* or *Bad Animals*, but is nonetheless a respectable effort that has more pluses than minuses. While producer Richie Zito's approach is undeniably slick and glossy, he maintains enough rough edges to keep things interesting on songs ranging from the aggressive hard rock of "Call of the Wild" (not to be confused with the Ted Nugent/Amboy Dukes classic), "Wild Child," and "The Night" to the arena-oriented powerful ballads like "Stranded" and "Secret." Heart unintentionally generated some controversy with the hit "All I Want to Do (Is Make Love to You)," a tale of an intimate encounter with a hitchhiker. The "Thought Police" argued that the song encouraged women to endanger themselves by picking up hitchhikers—overlooking the fact that the song, like a romance novel, is pure fantasy. Though *Heart* or *Wild Animals* would serve as a better introduction to Heart's Capitol output, *Brigade* is an album that diehard fans shouldn't overlook. —*Alex Henderson*

Desire Walks On / Nov. 1993 / Capitol ✦✦
Without a strong single, *Desire Walks On* dissolves into a puddle of spineless contemporary AOR that Heart has performed much better on their recent albums. —*AMG*

The Road Home / Nov. 1995 / Capitol ✦✦✦
On *The Road Home*, Heart re-records some of their biggest hits acoustically live in concert. It's interesting to hear these arena-rock and AOR standards—including "Barracuda," "Crazy on You," "Dreamboat Annie," and "All I Wanna Do Is Make Love to You"—recast as intimate numbers; Heart manages to find new layers in all of these warhorses, partially due to the sublime production of John Paul Jones. The result is Heart's best album in years—the old material sounds more alive than anything they have written in a decade. —*Stephen Thomas Erlewine*

● **Greatest Hits** / Mar. 11, 1997 / Capitol ◆◆◆◆
Heart's two decades of rock hits are compiled on this collection combining original studio recordings and live renditions. Among the featured cuts are the smashes "Crazy on You," "Barracuda (Live)," "Magic Man," "Straight On (Live)," "What About Love?," "Dreamboat Annie," "Dog and Butterfly (Live)" and "These Dreams." —*Jason Ankeny*

The Heartbeats

f. 1955, Jamaica, NY, **db.** 1961
Doo Wop
Lead singer James "Shep" Sheppard co-wrote a series of velvety doo wop ballads for the Heartbeats during the mid-'50s; one entry, "A Thousand Miles Away," was a huge R&B seller in 1956. The Queens, NY, quintet began their string of street-corner classics with "Crazy for You" and "Darling How Long," culminating with "A Thousand Miles Away." The Heartbeats recorded for Hull, Rama, Roulette, Gee, and Guyden before packing it in. In 1961 the lead singer formed a new trio, Shep & the Limelites, and scored on the charts with a heartwarming sequel to his first hit, "Daddy's Home," for Hull. "Our Anniversary" also sold well for the trio the next year, but they broke up soon thereafter. Sheppard was found dead in his auto on the Long Island Expressway in 1970. —*Bill Dahl*

● **The Best of the Heartbeats** / Apr. 1990 / Rhino ◆◆◆◆
This silky smooth New York quintet appeared from the mid-'50s. The album includes five tracks by lead James Sheppard's early-'60s vocal trio, Shep & the Limelites. —*Bill Dahl*

Hearts & Flowers

f. California
Country-Rock, Folk-Rock
Of the many folk-rock groups in southern California in the 1960s, Hearts & Flowers were one of the relatively few that were closer to "folk" than "rock." Founding guitarist Larry Murray was a member of the Scottsville Squirrel Barkers bluegrass group in the late '50s and early '60s; Chris Hillman and Bernie Leadon were also members of that group for a time. Murray teamed up with David Dawson and Rick Cunha to form Hearts & Flowers, a self-described "Georgia country-folk meets Hawaiian ukulele folk-rock" group, in the mid-'60s. They released a couple albums of pleasant but inessential country-folk-rock in the late '60s. —*Richie Unterberger*

Now Is the Time for Hearts and Flowers / 1967 / Capitol ◆◆◆◆
This debut album is an overlooked precursor to country-rock, echoing the late-'60s Byrds, Stone Poneys, Gene Clark, and most especially, as Brian Hogg points out in his lengthy liner notes, the Dillards. Earnest vocals and conscientious harmonies on this subdued acoustic and countrified take on folk-rock, with mild Eastern/psychedelic dabs of autoharp. The songs mix original tunes with covers of Donovan, Tim Hardin, Hoyt Axton, Kaleidoscope, and Carole King. There's little to criticize, but it lacks the innovative spark that characterizes the best folk-rock of the time. —*Richie Unterberger*

Of Horses, Kids and Forgotten Women / 1968 / Capitol ◆◆◆◆
Future Flying Burrito Brother/Eagle Bernie Leadon replaced Rick Cunha for the group's second and final album, which is actually a considerably more L.A. pop-flavored production than their debut. Country-seasoned folk-rock remains at the core of the group's sound, but producer Nik Venet provides occasional tasteful, psychedelic-tinged orchestral arrangements. The material—about half original—is fairly strong, especially their covers of Arlo Guthrie's "Highway in the Wind" and Jesse Lee Kincaid's "She Sang Hymns Out of Tune" (also covered by Harry Nilsson on his first album). The unquestioned highlight is Larry Murray's "Ode to a Tin Angel"; by far the group's most psychedelic slice of folk-rock, with its swimming strings, tripped-out lyrics, and sweet harmonies, it's also their most atypical track. A slicker, but better, album than their first effort. —*Richie Unterberger*

● **Now is the Time for Hearts and Flowers/Of Horses, Kids and Forgotten Women** / Oct. 1995 / Edsel ◆◆◆◆
Edsel does '60s collectors a favor by combining both of Hearts & Flowers' hard-to-find LPs onto one compact disc, which puts the group's entire repertoire in one place. —*Richie Unterberger*

Heaven 17

f. Oct. 1980, Sheffield, England
Synth-pop, New Wave, New Romantic
Taking their name from the Anthony Burgess novel *A Clockwork Orange*, the UK techno-pop trio Heaven 17 grew out of the experimental dance project the British Electric Foundation, itself an offshoot of the electro-pop outfit Human League. The core of Heaven 17 was comprised of Martyn Ware and Ian Craig Marsh, a pair of onetime computer operators who first teamed in 1977 as the Dead Daughters, a duo that integrated synthesizer patterns with a heavy reliance on tape

loops. Soon, Ware and Marsh were joined by Philip Oakey and Adi Newton and changed their name to the Human League, where they remained before exiting together in 1980.

As a means of establishing the synthesizer as an expressive, human instrument, Marsh and Ware formed the British Electric Foundation, a production project that employed a variety of musicians and singers including Tina Turner, Sandie Shaw, and Gary Glitter. The B.E.F.'s debut, 1980's *Music of Quality and Distinction, Vol. 1*, also included vocalist Glenn Gregory, a former photographer whom Ware and Marsh met at a Sheffield drama center; in 1981, the duo enlisted Gregory for Heaven 17, the first and most successful B.E.F. alter ego, and debuted with the single "(We Don't Need This) Fascist Groove Thang," a minor hit banned by the BBC over its title. An album, *Penthouse and Pavement*, followed the same year.

By the release of 1983's *The Luxury Gap*, the B.E.F. had fallen by the wayside, and Heaven 17 had become Ware and Marsh's primary focus; the LP proved highly successful, spawning the hit singles "Temptation," "Come Live with Me," "Crushed by the Wheels of Industry," and "Let Me Go." The follow-up, *How Men Are*, was another British hit, but the group receded from view after its release; when they returned in 1986 with the album *Pleasure One*, it was with a number of guest musicians and vocalists.

After the commerical failure of 1988's *Teddy Bear, Duke & Psycho*, Heaven 17 officially disbanded; Ware focused on production chores, and worked on Terence Trent D'Arby's debut *Introducing the Hardline According to Terence Trent D'Arby*. In 1990, he and Marsh resurrected the B.E.F. aegis, releasing *Music of Quality and Distinction, Vol. 2* the following year; in 1997, a reformed Heaven 17 returned with *Bigger than America*. —*Jason Ankeny*

● **The Best of Heaven 17: Higher & Higher** / Aug. 24, 1993 / Virgin ◆◆◆◆
The Best of Heaven 17: Higher & Higher is an extensive, 17-track collection that contains all of the group's best moments, including "Temptation" and "(We Don't Need This) Fascist Groove Thang," plus several album tracks, lesser-known singles, and remixes of their two greatest hits. It's too much music for casual fans, especially since the sequencing is slightly illogical, and it's not comprehensive enough for dedicated collectors, but *Higher & Higher* remains an adequate overview of the synth-pop band's career. —*Stephen Thomas Erlewine*

Heavy D & the Boyz

f. 1986, Mt. Vernon, NY
Hip Hop, Urban, Pop-Rap
Jamaican-born Heavy D (born Dwight Myers) sports a 260-pound frame, but can move and dance with agility and verve. He wisely chose sensitivity, rather than obesity or verbosity, as his framework, and many of his lyrics emphasize his search for a mate of similar qualities. He's also done good cover songs and penned cultural awareness tunes and tributes to Black women.

Heavy D. has managed perhaps the ultimate balancing act. He's remained a positive figure with close ties to his mother, and is arguably the most admired male rap figure among African-American feminists. At the same time, he's been willing to take chances musically, never embracing hardcore gangsta-rap, but yet able to include snatches of pop, R&B, reggae, and funk into his music without being assaulted with cries of sellout. He's even survived the tragic death of longtime friend and original Boyz member Troy Dixon aka T-Roy in 1990.

During the early '90s, Heavy D began to expand his business opportunities, launching not only an acting career, but also beginning to develop his skills as a music industry mogul; by 1996, he had become one of the presidents of Uptown Records. He didn't abandon his recording career, even though his albums weren't quite as popular as they were in the late '80s. Both 1992's *Blues Funk* and 1994's *Nuttin' But Love* were moderate hits, with both albums reaching gold status. Even though his success was consistent, it wasn't splashy, so it came as a bit of a surprise that his sixth album *Waterbed Hev* debuted in the Top 10 upon its spring 1997 release. Such a placing confirmed that Heavy D was one of the few hip-hop stars from the late '80s that neither burned out nor faded away—he has become one of the few rap artists able to carve out a lasting career. —*Ron Wynn*

Living Large / 1987 / Uptown ◆◆◆
This offers his first hit, a smartly done remake of "Mr. Big Stuff," plus charming romantic entries, though he sometimes overdoes the "overweight lover" routine. —*Ron Wynn*

Big Tyme / Jun. 1989 / Uptown ◆◆◆◆
Like Whodini, Heavy D. has managed to appeal to both R&B audiences and rap's hardcore. Indeed, Heavy shows strong R&B leanings on *Big Tyme*, his second album, which is definitely softer and more congenial than what one would have expected from Ice-T or Public Enemy that year. But the Long Island MC has a lot of technique—a fact that hardcore hip-hoppers couldn't overlook when hearing him let loose on such

numbers as "Here We Go Again, Y'all," "More Bounce" and "You Ain't Heard Nuttin' Yet." Residents of the hood may have viewed the commercial appeal that "Somebody for Me" had suspiciously, but they couldn't ignore Heavy's obvious technique. Although not remarkable, *Big Tyme* is an enjoyable effort that works well as escapist party music. —*Alex Henderson*

● **Peaceful Journey** / Jul. 2, 1991 / Uptown ✦✦✦✦
Heavy D. maintained his high visibility in both the R&B and rap markets with his third album, *Peaceful Journey*. The title says a lot about Heavy's outlook—he was never an inflammatory, confrontational rapper, and generally sought to entertain rather than challenge. While most of this melodic, very R&B-ish album (which includes his remake of the Gamble & Huff classic "Now That We've Found Love") is fun and escapist in nature, the self-proclaimed Overweight Lover shows himself to be a noteworthy and effective social commentator on the title song, "Letter to the Future" (which urges a teenage criminal to change his ways) and "Sister Sister"—a salute to Black women clearly written in response to misogyny in rap. Whether being sociopolitical or simply aiming to entertain, Heavy still makes it clear that he has a lot of technique. —*Alex Henderson*

Blue Funk / 1992 / Uptown ✦✦✦
Although it didn't have a big hit, *Blue Funk* was another solid album of pop-oriented, R&B-tinged rap from Heavy D. —*AMG*

Nuttin But Love / May 24, 1994 / Uptown ✦✦✦✦

Waterbed Hev / Apr. 22, 1997 / Uptown/Universal ✦✦✦
By the time Heavy D released *Waterbed Hev*, his audience had dwindled significantly and he was more of an icon than a vital artist. Unfortunately, *Waterbed Hev* provides several reasons why this was so. Heavy D was never a graceful rapper, but he sounds labored throughout the record, especially when paired with the pedestrian beats and grooves. There's still something charming about his persona, paritcularly on the single "Big Daddy" and the album's title track, a remake of the classic Waterbed Kev too, but he can't save such bland music with his mere presence—the songs have to be there, as well. —*Stephen Thomas Erlewine*

Helium

f. 1992, Boston, MA
Alternative Pop-Rock, Indie Rock
Helium is essentially the project of Mary Timony, formerly of the girl-punk band Autoclave. Helium formed with Brian Dunton on bass and Shawn King Devlin in 1992, and started releasing seven-inches like "The American Jean" in 1993. 1994 saw the band release the *Pirate Prude* EP, an interesting but somewhat inaccessible exercise in mixing radical feminism with punk rock. *The Dirt of Luck*, released in 1995, was an improvement and embellishment of the sound laid forth in *Pirate Prude:* Heavy, sluggish guitars, spooky keyboards, and Timony's breathy alto laid over an understated rhythm section. That year, Polvo's Ash Bowie also joined the lineup, replacing Dunton on bass; in 1997, the group returned with the *No Guitars* EP. Helium are a challenging listen, but also a rewarding one. —*Heather Phares*

Pirate Prude / Apr. 5, 1994 / Matador ✦✦✦
The group's debut EP is an uncompromising introduction to Mary Timony's mix of radical feminism and warped pop sensibilities. Songs like "XXX," "OOO," and "Baby Vampire Made Me" are alluring and vicious, made all the more startling by their sonically droning and lyrically violent contrasts. Timony murmurs sentiments like "your love is a fad/and you're gonna pay me with your life" in a schoolgirlish alto, adding to the intriguing contradictions in her work. Though it requires some concentrated listening, *Pirate Prude* ultimately rewards its listeners. —*Heather Phares*

● **The Dirt of Luck** / Apr. 1995 / Matador ✦✦✦✦
Helium's first full-length album expands on Timony's feminist lyrical bent and adds more colors to the band's musical palette. Full of what Timony calls "cartoon and monster movie music," *The Dirt of Luck* is a tight, focused album that is also diverse. The sludgy "Pat's Trick" mingles with the sweet-sounding and sweetly named "Honeycomb," which shares space with the nasty-sultry sounds of "Medusa" and the shimmery drone-pop of "Baby's Going Underground." It's tied together by the album's spacious sound and Timony's singing, which is fuller and richer than on the group's debut. —*Heather Phares*

No Guitars [EP] / Apr. 8, 1997 / Matador ✦✦✦✦

Richard Hell

b. Oct. 2, 1949, Lexington, KY
Punk, Proto-Punk
Some people will tell you Richard Hell was the main catalyst behind the birth of New York punk and its sensibilities. That's hardly true, but he's been around forever and did influence a number of budding

punks (the Sex Pistols among them). In 1971 Hell and former high school buddy, Tom Verlaine, formed a group called the Neon Boys, who later became Television; he also cofounded the Heartbreakers with ex-New York Doll Johnny Thunders. In 1976, Hell formed the Voidoids, a caustic congregation that included guitarists Ivan Julian and Robert Quine and soon-to-be Ramones drummer Marc Bell. Hell's apocalyptic lyrics were steeped in alienated poetry, and his anguished howl of a voice set the pattern for scores of Bowery rockers. —*John Floyd*

● **Blank Generation** / 1977 / Sire ✦✦✦✦
Hell's debut isn't a masterpiece but it manages to recreate the intensity and exhilaration of the burgeoning days of American punk. "Love Comes in Spurts" defines Hell's romantic outlook, and the title cut is a classic piece of angst rock. —*John Floyd*

Destiny Street / 1982 / Razor & Tie ✦✦✦
It took five years for Hell to follow his debut, but *Destiny Street* is a moderately successful extension of *Blank Generation.* Some of the energy from the old days had disappeared, but Hell compensates with some fine ballads and another screwball classic, "The Kid with the Replaceable Head." —*John Floyd*

R.I.P.: The ROIR Sessions / 1984 / Combat ✦✦✦
Since Hell didn't record all that much, this cassette collection of live tracks and studio outtakes is an illuminating collection of antiques and curios. —*John Dougan*

Helmet

f. 1989, New York, NY
Alternative Pop-Rock, Heavy Metal, Alternative Metal
Led by ex-Band of Susans guitar monster and university-trained musician Page Hamilton, Helmet boils away nearly all of the excess of hard rock and heavy metal and serves up a thick wad of aural assault that values power, volume, and simplicity. It's a concept that makes for compelling music, and Hamilton does a great job of creating songs that emphasize lacerating riffs, hypnotically repetitive distortion, and, at times, slower-than-a-lingering-death tempos. When the gears mesh on this monstrous machine, Helmet is one intimidating proposition. But by distilling hard rock to its feral core without the wit and panache that mark the careers of other, better, like-minded bands (e.g., Motörhead, the Melvins), one may not need a lot of Helmet to live a long and happy life. Hamilton does deserve credit for coming up with one killer record and scoring a sizable contract with a major label after the buzz surrounding their 1990 indie-label debut, *Strap It On.* Their 1992 major label bow *Meantime* won critical acclaim, and was followed by 1994's *Betty* and 1997's *Aftertaste.* —*John Dougan*

Strap It On / Nov. 1991 / Interscope ✦✦✦
Helmet's debut isn't as accomplished or powerful as *Meantime*, but it still provides enough gut-busting crunch to satisfy their fans. —*AMG*

● **Meantime** / Jun. 1992 / Interscope ✦✦✦✦
This is all the Helmet you will ever need. *Meantime* is a ferocious, sonic onslaught akin to hearing multiple explosions or living through a series of train accidents. Intense beyond description, *Meantime* will, with few exceptions, destroy nearly everything in its path, including Helmet's two other records. —*John Dougan*

Betty / Jun. 1994 / Interscope ✦✦✦✦
Although I cannot imagine wanting more Helmet than *Meantime*, if you've become a volume junkie and want a new fix, *Betty* might do the trick. Not as brutal or overpowering as *Meantime*, it has its moments, but indicates that Helmet's rage and fury may be changing into something slightly less aggressive. —*John Dougan*

Aftertaste / Mar. 18, 1997 / Interscope ✦✦
Helmet pushed at the boundaries of their sound with *Betty*, perhaps too much for their audience's liking—the album stiffed in comparison to *Meantime.* As a result, the band returned to straightforward Helmet territory with *Aftertaste*, restoring grinding guitars and pummeling rhythms to prominence. Theoretically, this approach should have made *Aftertaste* a more immediate, visceral record, but it is simply numbing. Without the invention of *Betty* or the gut-level force of *Meantime*, Helmet is simply a bland alternative metal band, lacking riffs, hooks, and purpose, and relying only on volume. It's a shocking and disheartening turn of events for one of the more intriguing metal bands of the '90s. —*Stephen Thomas Erlewine*

Jimi Hendrix

b. Nov. 27, 1942, Seattle, WA, d. Sep. 18, 1970, London, England
Guitar, Vocals / Rock 'n' Roll, Blues-Rock, Hard Rock, Psychedelic
In his brief four-year reign as a superstar, Jimi Hendrix expanded the vocabulary of the electric rock guitar more than anyone before or since. Hendrix was a master at coaxing all manner of unforeseen sonics from his instrument, often with innovative amplification experiments that produced astral-quality feedback and roaring distortion. His

frequent hurricane blasts of noise, and dazzling showmanship—he could and would play behind his back and with his teeth, and set his guitar on fire—has sometimes obscured his considerable gifts as a songwriter, singer, and master of a gamut of blues, R&B, and rock styles.

When Hendrix became an international superstar in 1967, it seemed as if he'd dropped out of a Martian spaceship, but in fact he'd served his apprenticeship the long, mundane way in numerous R&B acts on the chitlin circuit. During the early and mid-'60s, he worked with such R&B/soul greats as Little Richard, the Isley Brothers, and King Curtis as a backup guitarist. Occasionally he recorded as a session man (the Isley Brothers' '64 single "Testify" is the only one of these early tracks that offers even a glimpse of his future genius). But the stars didn't appreciate his show-stealing showmanship, and Hendrix was straightjacketed by sideman roles that didn't allow him to develop as a soloist. The logical step was for Hendrix to go out on his own, which he did in New York in the mid-'60s, playing with various musicians in local clubs, and joining while blues-rock singer John Hammond, Jr.'s, band for a while.

It was in a New York club that Hendrix was spotted by Animals bassist Chas Chandler. The first lineup of the Animals was about to split, and Chandler, looking to move into management, convinced Hendrix to move to London and accept a solo act in England. There a group was built around Jimi, also featuring Mitch Mitchell on drums and Noel Redding on bass, that was dubbed the Jimi Hendrix Experience. The trio became stars with astonishing speed in the UK, where "Hey Joe," "Purple Haze," and "And the Wind Cries Mary" all made the Top 10 in the first half of 1967. These tracks were also featured on their debut album, *Are You Experienced?*, a psychedelic meisterwerk that became a huge hit in the US after Hendrix created a sensation at the Monterey Pop Festival in June 1967.

Are You Experienced? was an astonishing debut, particularly from a young R&B veteran who had rarely sung, and apparently never written his own material, before the Experience formed. What caught most people's attention at first was his virtuosic guitar playing, which employed an arsenal of devices, including wah-wah pedals, buzzing feedback solos, crunching distorted riffs, and lightning, liquid runs up and down the scales. But Hendrix was also a first-rate songwriter, melding cosmic imagery with some surprisingly pop-savvy hooks and tender sentiments. He was also an excellent blues interpreter and passionate, engaging singer (although his gruff, throaty vocal pipes were not nearly as great assets as his instrumental skills). *Are You Experienced?* was psychedelia at its most eclectic, synthesizing mod pop, soul, R&B, blues, Dylan, and the electric guitar innovations of British pioneers like Jeff Beck, Pete Townshend, and Eric Clapton.

Amazingly, Hendrix would only record three fully conceived studio albums in his lifetime. *Axis: Bold as Love* and the double-LP *Electric Ladyland* were more diffuse and experimental than *Are You Experienced?* On *Electric Ladyland* in particular, Hendrix pioneered the use of the studio itself as a recording instrument, manipulating electronics and devising overdub techniques (with the help of engineer Eddie Kramer in particular) to plot uncharted sonic territory. Not that these albums were perfect, as impressive as they were; the instrumental breaks could meander, and Hendrix's songwriting was occasionally half-baked, never matching the consistency of *Are You Experienced?* (although he exercised greater creative control over the later albums).

The final two years of Hendrix's life were turbulent ones musically, financially, and personally. He was embroiled in enough complicated management and record company disputes (some dating from ill-advised contracts he'd signed before the Experience formed) to keep the lawyers busy for years. He disbanded the Experience in 1969, forming the Band of Gypsies with drummer Buddy Miles and bassist Billy Cox to pursue funkier directions. He closed Woodstock with a sprawling, shaky set, redeemed by his famous machine-gun interpretation of "The Star-Spangled Banner." The rhythm section of Mitchell and Redding were underrated keys to Jimi's best work, and the Band of Gypsies ultimately couldn't measure up to the same standard, although Hendrix did record an erratic live album with them. In early 1970, the Experience re-formed again—and disbanded again shortly afterwards. At the same time, Hendrix felt torn in many directions by various fellow musicians, record-company expectations, and management pressures, all of whom had their own ideas of what Hendrix should be doing. Coming up on two years after *Electric Ladyland*, a new studio album had yet to appear, although Hendrix was recording constantly during the period.

While outside parties did contribute to bogging down Hendrix's studio work, it also seems likely that Jimi himself was partly responsible for the stalemate, unable to form a permanent lineup of musicians, unable to decide what musical direction to pursue, unable to bring himself to complete another album despite jamming endlessly. A few months into 1970, Mitchell—Hendrix's most valuable musical collaborator—came back into the fold, replacing Miles in the drum chair,

although Cox stayed in place. It was this trio that toured the world during Hendrix's final months.

It's extremely difficult to separate the facts of Hendrix's life from rumors and speculation. Everyone who knew him well, or claimed to know him well, has different versions of his state of mind in 1970. Critics have variously mused that he was going to go into jazz, that he was going to get deeper into the blues, that he was going to continue doing what he was doing, or that he was too confused to know what he was doing at all. The same confusion holds true for his death: contradictory versions of his final days have been given by his closest acquaintances of the time. He'd been working intermittently on a new album, tentatively titled *First Ray of the New Rising Sun*, when he died in London on September 18, 1970, from drug-related complications.

Hendrix recorded a massive amount of unreleased studio material during his lifetime. Much of this (as well as entire live concerts) were issued posthumously; several of the live concerts were excellent, but the studio tapes have been the focus of enormous controversy for over 20 years. These initially came out in haphazard drabs and drubs (the first, *The Cry of Love*, was easily the most outstanding of the lot). In the mid-'70s, producer Alan Douglas took control of these projects, posthumously overdubbing many of Hendrix's tapes with additional parts by studio musicians. In the eyes of many Hendrix fans, this was sacrilege, destroying the integrity of the work of a musician known to exercise meticulous care over the final production of his studio recordings. Even as late as 1995, Douglas was having ex-Knack drummer Bruce Gary record new parts for the typically misbegotten compilation *Voodoo Soup*. After a lengthy legal dispute, the rights to Hendrix's estate, including all of his recordings, returned to Al Hendrix, the guitarist's father, in July of 1995. This may or may not mean that greater care will be exercised in packaging Jimi's legacy in the future. —*Richie Unterberger*

☆ **Are You Experienced?** / 1967 / MCA ✦✦✦✦✦
One of the most stunning debuts in rock history, and one of the definitive albums of the psychedelic era. On *Are You Experienced?*, Hendrix synthesized various elements of the cutting edge of 1967 rock into music that sounded both futuristic and rooted in the best traditions of rock, blues, pop, and soul. It was his mind-boggling guitar work, of course, that got most of the ink, building upon the experiments of British innovators like Jeff Beck and Pete Townshend to chart new sonic territories in feedback, distortion, and sheer volume. It wouldn't have meant much, however, without his excellent material, whether psychedelic frenzy ("Foxy Lady," "Manic Depression," "Purple Haze"), instrumental freakout jams ("Third Stone from the Sun"), blues ("Red House," "Hey Joe"), or tender, poetic compositions ("The Wind Cries Mary") that demonstrated the breadth of his songwriting talents. Not to be underestimated were the contributions of drummer Mitch Mitchell and bassist Noel Redding, who gave the music a rhythmic pulse that fused parts of rock and improvised jazz. Many of these songs are among Hendrix's very finest; it may be true that he would continue to develop at a rapid pace throughout the rest of his brief career, but he would never surpass his first LP in terms of consistently high quality. The British and American versions of the album differed substantially when they were initially released in 1967; MCA's 17-song CD reissue does everyone a favor by gathering all of the material from the two records in one place, adding a few B-sides from early singles as well. —*Richie Unterberger*

☆ **Axis: Bold as Love** / 1967 / MCA ✦✦✦✦✦
When the Experience recorded their second album, they were in the process of solidifying their international stardom. That meant access to more studio time and more sophisticated technology, but not, alas, a great deal of time to write the material. That may be why *Axis* isn't quite as much of a tour de force as *Are You Exerienced?*, but it's nevertheless another major effort, showing Hendrix continue to grow, particularly in his increasing mastery of the studio and more sophisticated lyrics. Soul and R&B influences are more prominent here than on his debut, though psychedelic experimentalism ran rampant (to great effect) on "If 6 Was 9," "Spanish Castle Magic," "Up from the Skies," "You Got Me Floatin'," and "Castles Made of Sand" all had funky grooves that gave the spiraling guitars and crunchy rhythm section a much-needed buoyancy. The best song, though, might have been the mellowest: "Little Wing" was Hendrix at his most delicate, and perhaps his most personal. —*Richie Unterberger*

Smash Hits / Jan. 1968 / Reprise ✦✦✦✦
Smash Hits is a solid collection of his most popular radio tracks, as well as featuring the bluesy "Red House" and "Stone Free," which were not found on previous albums. —*Rick Clark*

☆ **Electric Ladyland** / Feb. 1968 / MCA ✦✦✦✦✦
With *Electric Ladyland*, Hendrix took psychedelic experimentation as far as he could within the original Experience trio format. That meant pushing the barriers of late-'60s studio technology as far as they could bend, particularly with regard to multitracking and effects that could

only be achieved through certain treatments and manipulation of the tape itself. It also meant greater freedom and looseness in the playing and the songwriting, which could be both a plus and a drawback, as the compositions became both less constricted and less concise. Not all of the material here is top-of-the-line, but certainly much of this is Hendrix at his best: the dreamy wah-wah guitars of "Rainy Day, Dream Away" were only matched by the dreaminess of the lyrics, and "Have You Ever Been (to Electric Ladyland)" and "Gypsy Eyes" were also standouts. "1983...(A Merman I Should Turn to Be)" and "Voodoo Chile" were lengthy cuts dominated by jam-like instrumental passages; "Crosstown Traffic" and a cover of Dylan's "All Along the Watchtower," by contrast, were two of his catchiest and most pop-friendly tunes. "Voodoo Chile," "Voodoo Child (Slight Return)," and a cover of Earl King's "Come On" are three of his most determined forays into the blues, albeit the blues as fed through a nearly avant-garde filter. Originally released as a double album, the CD reissue fits the entire recording onto one 75-minute disc. —*Richie Unterberger*

Band of Gypsies / 1970 / Capitol ✦✦✦✦
Hendrix, sans the Experience, hooked up with bassist Billy Cox and drummer Buddy Miles to record this hard electric funk outing live at the Fillmore East in New York on December 31, 1969. While the rhythm section may have lacked the chops for wild free-form excursions, they provided Hendrix with a no-nonsense groove for his funkier R&B experiments. "Machine Gun," the album's highlight, features some of Hendrix's greatest playing. His dramatically violent soundscapes convey the horror of the war experience, with brilliantly controlled use of feedback and rapid-fire bursts of notes. —*Rick Clark*

The Cry of Love / 1971 / Reprise ✦✦✦✦
The posthumously released *The Cry of Love* revealed Hendrix turning toward a more subdued, less psychedelic style, with songs like "Night Bird Flying" and "Angel." Hendrix does deliver a few strong rockers with "Freedom," "Ezy Ryder," and "Astro Man." —*Rick Clark*

Plays Monterey / 1986 / Reprise ✦✦✦✦
Hendrix's show at the 1967 Monterey Pop Festival was the performance that broke him in the United States. While half of this was previously available as one side of an LP that also featured a side of live Otis Redding from the same event, this has his whole performances. Jimi and the Experience were in fine, lean, fiery form on this nine-song set, which showcased the most well-known tunes from the *Are You Experienced?* album and covers of "Killing Floor," "Like a Rolling Stone," "Rock Me Baby," and "Wild Thing." —*Richie Unterberger*

Live at Winterland / 1987 / Rykodisc ✦✦✦✦
Jimi Hendrix's sonic assaults and attacks hypnotized, frightened, and amazed audiences in the late '60s. His studio recordings helped him attain his reputation, but his live works validated it. That's the case on the 13 songs from a 1968 Winterland concert that made their way onto CD in 1987. Whether he was doing short, biting songs like "Fire" or stretching out for sprawling blues statements like "Red House" and "Killing Floor," Jimi Hendrix turned the guitar into a battering ram, forcing everyone to notice and making every solo and note a memorable one. —*Ron Wynn*

Radio One / 1989 / Rykodisc ✦✦✦✦
Seventeen songs from 1967 BBC broadcasts, when the Experience had yet to burn out from the wheel of constant touring, management hassles, and internal strife. They're in good, enthusiastic form as they run through early gems like "Hey Joe," "Foxy Lady," "Fire," and "Stone Free," the lack of studio polish giving these versions a loose feel. The Experience studio albums are still considerably superior to this set, but it's certainly worth acquiring by any serious Hendrix fan, not least because it has several covers that didn't make it onto the three proper Experience LPs. Several of these ("Hoochie Koochie Man," "Killing Floor," "Catfish Blues") reveal his sometimes overlooked affinity for Chicago-style electric blues; there are also a couple of surprises ("Hound Dog" and "Day Tripper"). With good sound, it's a solid addition to the Hendrix library, demonsrating his versatility in various rock, soul, and blues styles. —*Richie Unterberger*

● **The Ultimate Experience** / Apr. 27, 1993 / MCA ✦✦✦✦
As a single-disc compilation, *The Ultimate Experience* is hard to beat. Drawing from all of the original Jimi Hendrix Experience albums, the 20-track collection hits all of the major highpoints—"Purple Haze," "All Along the Watchtower," "Little Wing," "Red House," "The Wind Cries Mary," "Highway Chile," "Angel"—and gives an accurate impression of why Hendrix was so revolutionary and influential. All three of Hendrix's completed studio albums are mandatory listening, but *The Ultimate Experience* is a terrific introduction to the guitarist. —*Thom Owens*

Jimi Hendrix: Blues / Apr. 26, 1994 / MCA ✦✦✦
While Hendrix remains most famous for his hard rock and psychedelic innovations, more than a third of his recordings were blues-oriented. This CD contains eleven blues originals and covers, eight of which

were previously unreleased. Recorded between 1966 and 1970, they feature the master guitarist stretching the boundaries of electric blues in both live and studio settings. Besides several Hendrix blues-based originals, it includes covers of Albert King and Muddy Waters classics, as well as a 1967 acoustic version of his composition "Hear My Train a-Comin.' " —*Richie Unterberger*

Jimi Hendrix: Woodstock / Aug. 2, 1994 / MCA ✦✦✦
Hendrix's entire legendary set at Woodstock is featured on this set for the first time. Hardcore Hendrix fans may enjoy this good-sounding set, but it's a lot of endless jamming and general noodling for even the average fan to ingest. Besides his incendiary reading of "The Star Spangled Banner" and moments where the playing really comes together, better live Hendrix sets can be found elsewhere, like *Jimi Hendrix in the West.* —*Rick Clark*

Jimi by Himself: The Home Recordings / 1995 / Berkshire Studio ✦✦✦
This CD is only available (quite legitimately) with the hardback comic/graphic biography *Voodoo Child: The Illustrated Legend of Jimi Hendrix.* Be warned that if you're primarily (or only) interested in this half-hour disc of previously unreleased material, it only comes at a high price ($35 or so). If you want to take the plunge, you'll find the music—recorded unaccompanied by Hendrix in New York around April of 1968—quite worthwhile. The guitar is electric, but this is basically *Hendrix Unplugged,* with much quieter, reflective, and personal versions of songs that would get the full-on electric treatment on *Electric Ladyland* and other albums. "1983," "Gypsy Eyes," "Voodoo Chile," and "Angel" are particularly fascinating to experience in this context, as we hear Jimi tentatively working out (and sometimes fumbling through) skeletal versions of these compositions, with some different lyrics appearing on occasion. What this lacks in typical Hendrix firepower, it makes up for in poetic delicacy. In some respects, these performances bring us closer to the tender heart of his work than the famous official versions of these classics. —*Richie Unterberger*

Voodoo Soup / Apr. 1995 / MCA ✦✦✦
Voodoo Soup was supposed to be the outtake album that got it right. Instead, it was another in a line of botched attempts to re-create Jimi Hendrix's unfinished final studio album. For most fans, the re-recorded drum tracks by the drummer of the Knack was the most unforgivable sin, yet the album is also poorly sequenced and lacks several important tracks. The sound is polished to a disturbingly bright sheen, while the cover art is garishly retro. —*Stephen Thomas Erlewine*

First Rays of the New Rising Sun / Apr. 22, 1997 / MCA ✦✦✦✦
At the time of his death, Jimi Hendrix was working on a new studio album tentatively titled *First Rays of the Rising Sun.* Contents of those sessions were initially released as *The Cry of Love,* and were scattered throughout official releases and bootlegs over the next 20 years. 1995's *Voodoo Soup* was the first CD-era attempt to compile all these outtakes into an official album, but it was plagued by odd sequencings, omissions, and several overdubbed tracks. Once Hendrix's family regained control of his catalog in 1995, they assembled *First Rays of the Rising Sun* and released it in the spring of 1997. This edition is the closest anyone will ever get to the final Hendrix album, and while it has flaws—the sound is a little too crisp, and the sequencing is debatable—it's hard to imagine this material being assembled any better. *First Rays of the Rising Sun* still has all of the hallmarks of a posthumous release, but this is the first time such seminal songs as "Angel," "Room Full of Mirrors" and "Freedom" have been presented logically, making the record truly the last word on Hendrix's final studio sessions. —*Stephen Thomas Erlewine*

Nona Hendryx

b. Oct. 4, 1944, Trenton, NJ
Vocals / Soul, Disco
One-third of the pop-soul act Labelle (their big hit was "Lady Marmalade"), Nona Hendryx, by far and away, made the hippest solo records of any member of that group (the others being Patti LaBelle and Sarah Dash). After Labelle called it quits in 1976, Hendryx released her self-titled debut record, which was an amazingly strong amalgam of soul and hard rock. It also went almost completely ignored by critics, soul fans, and even Labelle fans, and Hendryx took her strong, clear, booming voice and did lots of session work in the late '70s and early '80s. It was here that she fell in with a hip crowd of musicians, specifically as a result of her time singing backup for Talking Heads. This association with David Byrne led to her working with Bill Laswell, who, along with his band Material, helped her put together a second solo record entitled *Nona.* A strong album that's not as wild-eyed as her debut, *Nona* did spark greater interest in Hendryx's considerable talents, and since then, her solo career has been flourishing to the point where she no longer needs studio work to supplement her income. Although some of her late-'80s records sound a little formulaic, Nona Hendryx is a dynamic, daring, and extremely talented performer, who, as is often

the case, doesn't receive the credit she's due. But unlike Patti Labelle, who has chosen a career as the most histrionic singer in MOR soul/pop, or the relative invisibility of Sarah Dash, who sings backup for Keith Richards' X-Pensive Winos, Hendryx has taken the road less traveled, and that has meant a more aesthetically rewarding and interesting career. —*John Dougan*

Nona Hendryx / 1977 / Epic ✦✦✦✦
Wearing skintight pants, black leather, and brandishing a Bowie knife on the LP cover, Nona Hendryx announces her intentions loudly and clearly on her debut record. At the time, this record was unpromotable (hell, it would be today), mainly because the record company and radio stations didn't know what to do with a huge-voiced, African-American woman who was comfortable and capable of singing hard rock as well as soul music. So, as usual, they turned their backs on the record and it disappeared almost as quickly as it was released. Which is a shame, because it's a nasty, relentless chunk of hard-edged rock 'n' soul that was just a bit ahead of its time. Long out of print, but worth searching for. —*John Dougan*

Nona / 1983 / RCA ✦✦
After a few years doing session work, Hendryx, with help from the band Material, came up with this winner that drops the hard rock of her debut for a more Talking Heads-tinged pop/funk. Although the songwriting could be a little sharper, Hendryx's powerful voice gives the record focus and always commands your attention. Extra musical emphasis provided by Sly Dunbar, Jamaladeen Tacuma, and Nile Rodgers. —*John Dougan*

● **Skindiver** / Jul. 1989 / Private Music ✦✦✦✦
A transitional album from the word go, Hendryx plays synthesizer and works with producer and former Tangerine Dream member Peter Baumann, and the result is this lush (at times too lush) pop record that sounds unlike anything else Hendryx recorded. Fans of her previous work may be taken aback by this record, but the dense, almost ambient, soundscapes she constructs and her always great singing make this a satisfying foray into uncharted territory. —*John Dougan*

Don Henley

b. Jul. 22, 1947, Gilmer, TX
Drums, Keyboards, Vocals, Guitar / Singer-Songwriter, Pop-Rock
Out of all of the Eagles, Don Henley had the most successful solo career. After the group broke up in 1982, Henley released his first solo album, *I Can't Stand Still*. Although it wasn't as successful as an Eagles record, the album peformed respectably, launching the No. 3 single "Dirty Laundry" and going gold. *Building the Perfect Beast* followed two years later and established Henley as a solo star in his own right. Featuring the Top 10 hits "Boys of Summer" and "All She Wants to Do Is Dance," as well as the Top 40 singles "Not Enough Love in the World" and "Sunset Grill," the album sold over two million copies and stayed on the charts for over a year. Henley's third album, 1989's *The End of the Innocence*, was his most ambitious record yet, as well as his most commercially successful. The album sold over three million copies and stayed on the charts for nearly three years, launching the hit singles "The End of the Innocence," "Heart of the Matter," "New York Minute," "How Bad Do You Want It?," and "The Last Worthless Evening." Henley reunited with the Eagles in 1994, embarking on a worldwide tour. The group released a live album culled from an appearance on *MTV Unplugged* called *Hell Freezes Over;* the record also featured a handful of new studio tracks. *Hell Freezes Over* was a major success, selling over five million copies by the summer of 1995. However, the group decided not to pursue any more projects together and Henley continued working on his fourth solo album in 1995. —*Stephen Thomas Erlewine*

I Can't Stand Still / 1982 / Asylum ✦✦✦
This crisply produced and well-conceived debut is highlighted by "The Unclouded Day," "Johnny Can't Read," and "Dirty Laundry." —*John Floyd*

Building the Perfect Beast / 1984 / Geffen ✦✦✦✦
His commercial breakthrough defined his solo formula with songs like "The Boys of Summer" and "All She Wants to Do Is Dance," which responded to political and romantic breakdowns. —*John Floyd*

The End of the Innocence / Jun. 1989 / Geffen ✦✦✦
A conceptual elaboration on his *Beast* album, this frames some wonderfully sarcastic rockers around "The Heart of the Matter," one of the finest ballads of the '80s. —*John Floyd*

● **Actual Miles: Henley's Greatest Hits** / Nov. 21, 1995 / Geffen ✦✦✦✦
Although it is drawn from only three albums (with only one track, "Dirty Laundry," from *I Can't Stand Still*), *Actual Miles* was a well-chosen best-of from an artist who had had just enough hits to justify one. Five tracks each came from *Building the Perfect Beast* and *The End of the Innocence*, and they included all of Don Henley's Top 40 hits. The album was filled out with a cover of Leonard Cohen's "Everybody

Knows" and two new tracks, among them the ambitious "The Garden of Allah," which seemed to be an attempt to create a new allegorical masterpiece along the lines of "Hotel California," but managed to be only pretentious. Still, the bulk of this album was the sound of AOR radio in the mid-1980s. That, of course, was the catch—this album should have come out about four years before it did, and probably would have if Henley hadn't been suing Geffen Records. Though destined to be a successful catalog item, in 1995 it was more a historical artifact than a major release. —*William Ruhlmann*

Clarence "Frogman" Henry

b. Mar. 19, 1937, Algiers, LA
Piano, Trombone, Vocals / R&B, New Orleans R&B
He could sing like a girl, and he could sing like a frog. That latter trademark croak, utilized to the max on his 1956 debut smash "Ain't Got No Home," earned good-natured Clarence Henry his nickname and jump-started a rewarding career that endures to this day around the Crescent City.

Naturally, Fats Domino and Professor Longhair were young Clarence Henry's main influences while growing up in the Big Easy. He played piano and trombone with Bobby Mitchell & the Toppers from 1952 to 1955 before catching on with saxist Eddie Smith's band. Henry improvised the basic idea behind "Ain't Got No Home" on the bandstand one morning in the wee hours; when the crowd responded favorably, he honed it into something unique. Paul Gayten (New Orleans A&R man for Chess Records) concurred, hustling Henry into Cosimo Matassa's studio in September of 1956. Local deejay Poppa Stoppa laid the "Frogman" handle on the youngster when he spun the 45 (issued on the Chess subsidiary Argo), and it stuck.

Despite some fine follow-ups—"It Won't Be Long," "I'm in Love," the inevitable sequel "I Found a Home"—Frog sank back into the marsh, sales-wise, until 1960, when Allen Toussaint's updated arrangement melded beautifully with a country-tinged Bobby Charles composition called "(I Don't Know Why) But I Do." Henry's rendition of the tune proved a huge pop smash in early 1961, as did a Domino-tinged "You Always Hurt the One You Love" later that year.

Frogman continued to record a variety of New Orleans-styled old standards and catchy originals for Argo (Chess assembled a Henry album that boasted what may be the worst cover art in the history of rock 'n' roll, even recording at one point with Nashville saxist Boots Randolph and pianist Floyd Cramer). But the hits dried up for good after 1961. Henry opened 18 concerts for the Beatles across the US and Canada in 1964, but his main source of income came from the Bourbon Street strip, where he played for 19 years. You'll likely find him joyously reviving his classics at the New Orleans Jazz & Heritage Festival every year come spring—and his croak remains as deep and melodious as ever. —*Bill Dahl*

But I Do / 1994 / Charly ✦✦✦✦
Twenty Argo waxings by the roly-poly pianist—much duplication with the easier-to-locate MCA disc as far as the hits go, though the inclusion of the sequel "I Found a Home" and the lesser-known rockers "Steady Date," "Oh Why," and "Live It Right" certainly make this one worth looking for. —*Bill Dahl*

● **Ain't Got No Home: Best of Clarence "Frogman" Henry** / 1994 / MCA ✦✦✦✦
The New Orleans R&B singer with the joyous frog's croak in his voice is served well by this 18-song collection of his 1956-1964 output for the Chess subsidiary Argo Records. Begins with his definitive "Ain't Got No Home," follows with his vicious Crescent City rockers "Troubles, Troubles," "It Won't Be Long," and "I'm in Love," and visits his comeback hits "But I Do" and "You Always Hurt the One You Love." —*Bill Dahl*

Joe Henry

b. North Carolina
Guitar, Vocals / Singer-Songwriter, Americana
Joe Henry is best known for his two country-influenced albums, 1992's *Short Man's Room* and 1993's *Kindness of the World*, both of which feature members of the country-rock band the Jayhawks, but his musical direction has actually changed several times over the course of his recording career, reflecting his restless, adventurous spirit.

Henry was born in North Carolina, grew up in Michigan, spent the early part of his music career in New York City, and finally settled in Los Angeles in 1990 with his wife and son. After his little-heard 1986 debut, *Talk of Heaven*, Henry debuted on A&M in 1989 with the rock 'n' roll album *Murder of Crows*, which was produced by Anton Fier and featured Mick Taylor on guitar.

From there, he pared down to the quiet, entirely acoustic moods of *Shuffletown* (1990) before shifting into the country- and folk-influenced territory of "Short Man's Room" and "Kindness of the World." The latter two albums earned him an excellent reputation among fans of alternative rock and country as a superb singer and songwriter. He followed *Kindness* with the five-song EP *Fireman's Wedding* a year later.

Henry's lyrics are a central focus of his songwriting, but even though he often writes in the first person, his songs are not "personal" in the manner of musicians who are often called singer-songwriters (a genre he doesn't like to be associated with). He's recorded some excellent country covers, but he's equally interested in soul, funk, and rock 'n' roll.

On *Trampoline,* released in 1996, Henry veered his music in an edgier, more rhythm-oriented direction. While he still employs acoustic instruments and even a pedal-steel guitar on several songs, "Trampoline" (much of which Henry recorded at a studio he set up in his garage) is more clearly defined by its drum loops, loud electric guitars, mysterious voices, and curious sonic textures. For this album, Henry recruited guitarist Page Hamilton from the band Helmet and drummer Carla Azar from the band Edna Swap. —*Kurt Wolff*

Talk of Heaven / 1986 / Profile ♦♦

Murder of Crows / 1989 / Mammoth ♦♦
Major label release, a name producer, noted session men, this album couldn't lose, right? Well, not quite. Although time has caught up with *Murder of Crows,* sometimes Joe Henry gets lost amidst all the busy work and fancy arranging of his songs. True, there are some great songs here, notably "Six Feet in the Country," "Here and Gone" and "Step Across the Mountain," which will remind one a lot of Counting Crows. Here is a glimpse at a young songwriter being pushed too quickly to come up with the goods. Sometimes, the waiting *is* the hardest part . . . —*James Chrispell*

Shuffletown / Aug. 1990 / A&M ♦♦♦
All-acoustic album with a quiet, laidback, late-night vibe. Recorded live to two-track and produced by T-Bone Burnett. The lineup includes jazz trumpeter Don Cherry. —*Kurt Wolff*

● **Short Man's Room** / Jun. 16, 1992 / Mammoth ♦♦♦♦
A stunning collection of beautiful country—and folk-inflected songs that shift and sway with spare acoustic arrangements. While the songs are not autobiographical per se, the lyrics are a central focus, bringing a rich assortment of complex characters to life with abstract but vividly rendered details. The band includes Gary Louris and Marc Perlman from the Jayhawks. —*Kurt Wolff*

Kindness of the World / Sep. 28, 1993 / Mammoth ♦♦♦♦
On this album of more strong songs, some have definite country leanings. Henry covers Tom T. Hall's "I Flew over Our House Last Night," and he wrote "She Always Goes" with George Strait in mind. —*Brian Mansfield*

Fireman's Wedding / Feb. 15, 1994 / Mammoth ♦♦
This CD-5 contains the title track (originally from *Kindness of the World*) and four live recordings, including versions of A.P. Carter's "Hello Stranger" and Merle Travis' "Dark as a Dungeon." —*Brian Mansfield*

Trampoline / Mar. 26, 1996 / Mammoth ♦♦♦
On *Trampoline,* Joe Henry moves away from the country-rock that earned his reputation in the early '90s. Though there are still some remnants of his Gram Parsons and Neil Young influences, Henry attempts a more atmospheric, rock-based sound on *Trampoline,* which explains his choice of Helmet guitarist Page Hamilton as musical collaborator. The shift in sound is effective, but it does sound as if the singer-songwriter is still trying to become comfortable with his new direction. It doesn't help that the album is slightly uneven, as Henry tries to write more literate lyrics, making his songs almost into short stories. When his ambitions do work, *Trampoline* is a stark, affecting listen, and even when they don't, the album is admirable. —*Stephen Thomas Erlewine*

Herman's Hermits

f. 1964, Manchester, England, **db.** 1970
British Invasion, Pop-Rock
Herman's Hermits began life in 1963 in Manchester, England, as the Heartbeats, the group consisting of Keith Hopwood (b. Oct 26, 1946, Manchester, England) (guitar), Karl Green (b. Jul 31, 1947, Salford, England) (guitar, harmonica), Derek Leckenby (b. May 14, 1945, Leeds, England) (guitar), and Barry Whitwam (b. Jul 21, 1946, Manchester, England) (drums). They got the name Herman's Hermits when they were joined by 16-year-old TV actor Peter Noone (b. Nov 5, 1947, Manchester) (vocals, piano, guitar), who was thought to resemble the Sherman character on the *Rocky & Bullwinkle* TV cartoon. Pop producer Mickie Most, induced to see the group by their managers, thought Noone looked like a young John Kennedy and agreed to sign them. Most chose the group's material, from revamped oldies and pub songs to tunes submitted by professional songwriters like Gerry Goffin

and Carole King, and produced the recordings, generally using Noone as singer and a group of studio musicians.

The result was two years of solid hits, starting with "I'm into Something Good," which topped the UK charts and broke the group in America. There were 11 Top Ten hits in the US through 1967, among them the No. 1 gold singles "Mrs. Brown You've Got a Lovely Daughter" and "I'm Henry VIII, I Am." Herman's Hermits had ten Top Ten hits in Britain through 1970. Inevitably, the group's teenage heartthrob appeal waned, and they never became the kind of self-sustaining musical unit that could outlive that initial infatuation. The group split in 1970, though it has re-formed, with and without Noone, for oldies performances. —*William Ruhlmann*

● **Their Greatest Hits** / 1973 / ABKCO ♦♦♦♦
Basic hits package, but too brief and under par sound-wise. (Originally released as a 15-track LP In 1973, *Their Greatest Hits* was reissued as a 16-track CD in 1987.) —*Jeff Tamarkin*

The EP Collection / Jan. 1990 / See For Miles ♦♦♦♦
This 22-track CD also features most of the major Herman hits, with a handful of obscurities thrown in. —*Jeff Tamarkin*

The Collection / Jun. 1990 / Castle ♦♦♦♦
All of the hits by Peter Noone and company, with room to spare for some nice surprises. —*Jeff Tamarkin*

Kristin Hersh

b. Aug. 7, 1966, Atlanta, GA
Guitar, Vocals / Singer-Songwriter, Alternative Pop-Rock
Kristin Hersh, the lead singer-songwriter of Throwing Muses, released her first solo album, the acoustic *Hips and Makers,* in early 1994; she followed it a couple of months later with the *Strings* EP, which featured versions of selected songs from the album recorded with a string quartet. After releasing the record, Hersh did a solo tour and finished the next Throwing Muses record, *University,* which was released in February 1995. —*Stephen Thomas Erlewine*

● **Hips and Makers** / Feb. 1, 1994 / Sire/Reprise ♦♦♦♦
Hersh dug into her backlog of compositions for material of an intensely personal nature that she felt wouldn't be suitable for her band on her solo debut, *Hips and Makers.* In stark contrast to her work with Throwing Muses, *Hips and Makers* is almost entirely acoustic. Hersh embellishes her waifish voice and acoustic guitar with touches of cello and piano on this album, which offers a despairing and introspective tone that fails to submerge her considerable inner strength and fortitude. Recorded in a mere two weeks, this collection of haunting and confessional songs was produced by ex-Patti Smith Group guitarist Lenny Kaye, who has also produced Suzanne Vega. Hersh's voice and lyrical tone, however, are considerably brittler and coarser than Vega's. The opening track, "Your Ghost," features a duet with R.E.M. singer Michael Stipe. —*Richie Unterberger*

Strings / Jun. 14, 1994 / Sire ♦♦♦♦
A beautiful EP featuring several tracks that didn't make *Hips and Makers,* as well as excellent re-recorded versions of several of the tracks that did. —*Stephen Thomas Erlewine*

Richard X. Heyman

b. New York City, NY
Guitar, Vocals, Keyboards, Drums, Bass / Power Pop, Singer-Songwriter
Richard X. Heyman is one of the sadly overlooked pop craftsmen of the '90s. His two albums are, however, widely regarded in power-pop circles as instant classics. Heyman began recording in the late '80s in the tradition of the studio nerd/one man band, playing all instruments himself in his upper west side Manhattan apartment living room, named Brontasaurus, presumably after the classic song by the Move. He released the independent *Actual Size* EP in 1987 and followed with the full-length *Living Room!!* in 1988. Considerable word-of-mouth exposure led to the album being reissued by Cypress Records in 1990 in slightly modified form. He signed to Sire in 1990 and released one album for the label, the Andy Paley-produced *Hey Man!* in 1991. Poor sales led to him being dropped by the label, but he has continued recording (several albums' worth by his estimations) while shopping for the elusive new deal. *Cornerstone* was completed by 1996 and is awaiting release. —*Chris Woodstra*

Living Room!! / 1988 / Cypress ♦♦♦
This homemade debut effort shows Heyman's fully formed command of '60s Brit-pop and Byrds-style jangle. Material-wise, Heyman seems to lack focus. Heyman's voice, at times, lands somewhere between Petty, Hiatt, and Costello. Highlights include "Call Out for the Military" and "Wouldn't That Be a Riot?" —*Rick Clark*

● **Hey Man!** / May 28, 1991 / Sire ♦♦♦♦
Heyman delivers a fine collection of largely self-performed tunes. His drumming is particularly fine, especially on "Sidetracked." "Falling

Away" is a great power-pop song in the classic mid-'60s Anglo tradition. Other standouts include the Byrds/Petty-ish "In the Scheme of Things," the upbeat rocker "Private Army," the Beatley "Loud," and "Bad Business in Town." — *Rick Clark*

John Hiatt

b. 1952, Indianapolis, IN

Guitar, Piano, Vocals / Rock 'n' Roll, Country-Rock, Singer-Songwriter, Americana

John Hiatt's sales never quite matched his reputation. Hiatt's songs were covered successfully by everyone from Bonnie Raitt, Ronnie Milsap, and Dr. Feelgood, to Iggy Pop, Three Dog Night, and the Neville Brothers, yet it took him 13 years to reach the charts himself. Of course, it nearly took him that long to find his own style. Hiatt began his solo career in 1974, and over the next decade, he ran through a number of different styles from rock 'n' roll to new wave pop before he finally settled on a rootsy fusion of rock 'n' roll, country, blues and folk with his 1987 album *Bring the Family*. Though the album didn't set the charts on fire, it became his first album to reach the charts, and several of the songs on the record became hits for other artists, including Raitt and Milsap. Following its success, Hiatt became a reliable hit songwriter for other artists, and he developed a strong cult following that continued to gain strength into the mid-'90s.

While he was growing up in his hometown of Indianapolis, IN, John Hiatt played in a number of garage bands. Initially, he was inspired by the Rolling Stones and Bob Dylan, and the music of those two artists would echo strongly throughout his work. Out of all the bar bands he played with in the late '60s, a group called the White Ducks was the one that received the most attention. Following his high school graduation, he moved to Nashville at the age of 18, where he landed a job as a songwriter for Tree Publishing. For the next several years, he wrote and performed at local clubs and hotels. Within a few years, his songs were being recorded by several different artists, including Conway Twitty, Tracy Nelson, and Three Dog Night, who took Hiatt's "Sure as I'm Sittin' Here" to No. 16 in the summer of 1974. Eventually, his manager secured him an audition at Epic Records, and the label signed him in 1974, releasing his debut album *Hangin' Around the Observatory* later that year. Despite their critical acclaim, neither *Hangin' Around the Observatory* nor its 1975 follow-up *Overcoats* sold many copies, and he was dropped by the label. By the end of the year, Tree Publishing had let him go as well.

Following his failure in Nashville, Hiatt moved out to California. By the summer of 1978 he had settled in Los Angeles, where began playing in clubs and opening for folk musicians like Leo Kottke. With Kottke's assistence, Hiatt hired a new manager, Denny Bruce, who helped him secure a record contract with MCA Records. *Slug Line*, his first record for MCA, was released in the summer of 1979. Where his first two records were straightahead rock 'n' roll and folk-rock, *Slug Line* was in the new wave vein of angry English singer-songwriters like Elvis Costello, Graham Parker, and Joe Jackson, as if Hiatt was vying for the role of the American angry young man. The new approach earned some strong reviews, yet it failed to generate any sales. *Two Bit Monsters*, his second MCA album, faced the same situation. Although it was well-received critically upon its 1980 release, it made no impression on the charts, and the label dropped him.

Apart from working on *Two Bit Monsters*, Hiatt spent most of 1980 as a member of Ry Cooder's backing band, playing rhythm guitar on the *Borderline* album and touring with the guitarist. Hiatt stayed with Cooder throughout 1981, signing a new contract with Geffen Records by the end of the year. Produced by Tony Visconti (David Bowie, T. Rex), his Geffen debut *All of a Sudden* was released in 1982, followed by the Nick Lowe/Scott Matthews & Ron Nagel-produced *Riding with the King* in 1983. As with his previous records for Epic and MCA, neither of his first two Geffen releases sold well. By this time, Hiatt's personal life was beginning to spin out of control as he was sinking deep into alcoholism. Around the time he completed 1985's *Warming Up to the Ice Age*, his second wife committed suicide. Following the release of *Warming Up to the Ice Age*, Hiatt was dropped by Geffen. By the end of 1985, he had entered a rehabilitation program. During 1986, he remarried and signed a new deal with A&M Records.

For his A&M debut, Hiatt assembled a small band comprised of his former associates Ry Cooder (guitar), Nick Lowe (bass), and Jim Keltner (drums). Recorded over the course of a handful of days, the resulting album *Bring the Family* had a direct, stripped-down rootsy sound that differed greatly from his earlier albums. Upon its summer 1987 release, *Bring the Family* received the best reviews of his career and, for once, the reviews began to pay off, as the album turned into a cult hit, peaking at 107 on the US charts; it was his first charting album. Hiatt attempted to record a follow-up with Cooder, Lowe and Keltner, but the musicians failed to agree on the financial terms for the sessions. Undaunted, he recorded an album with John Doe, David Lindley, and Dave Mattacks, but he scrapped the completed project, deciding that

the result was too forced. Hiatt's final attempt at recording the follow-up to *Bring the Family* was orchestrated by veteran producer Glyn Johns, who had him record with his touring band, the Goners. Despite all of the behind-the-scenes troubles behind its recording, the follow-up album, *Slow Turning*, actually appeared rather quickly, appearing in the summer of 1988.

Slow Turning, like *Bring the Family* before it, received nearly unanimous positive reviews and it was fairly well-received commercially, spending 31 weeks on the US charts and peaking at 98. Within the next year, Hiatt successfully toured throughout America and Europe, strengthening his fan base along the way. Inspired by the success of Hiatt's two A&M albums, Geffen released the compilation *Y'All Caught? The Ones That Got Away 1979-85* in 1989. That same year, other artists began digging through Hiatt's catalog of songs, most notably Bonnie Raitt, who covered "Thing Called Love" for her multiplatinum comeback album, *Nick of Time*.

In 1990, Hiatt returned with *Stolen Moments*, which was nearly as successful as *Slow Turning*, both critically and commercially. "Bring Back Your Love to Me," an album track from *Stolen Moments* that was also recorded by Earl Thomas Conley, won BMI's 1991 Country Music Award. By the time "Bring Back Your Love to Me" won that award, it had become a standard practice for artists to cover Hiatt's songs, as artists as diverse as Bob Dylan, Ronnie Milsap, Suzy Bogguss, and Iggy Pop all covered his songs in the early '90s. In 1993, Rhino Records released *Love Gets Strange: The Songs of John Hiatt*, which collected many of the cover versions that were recorded during the '80s and '90s.

During 1991, the group that recorded *Bring the Family*—Hiatt, Cooder, Lowe, and Keltner—re-formed as a band called Little Village, releasing their eponymous debut in early 1992. Based on the success of *Bring the Family* and Hiatt's A&M albums, expectations for Little Village were quite high, yet the record and its supporting tour were considered a major disappointment. Later, the individual members agree that the band was a failure, mainly due to conflicting egos.

Hiatt decided to back away from the superstar nature of Little Village for his next album, 1993's *Perfectly Good Guitar*. Recorded in just two weeks with a backing band comprised of members of alternative rock bands School of Fish and Wire Train, the album was looser than any record since *Bring the Family*, but it didn't quite have the staying power of its two predecessors, spending only 11 weeks on the charts and peaking at No. 47. The following year, he released his first live album, *Hiatt Comes Alive at Budokan?*. Hiatt left A&M Records after the release of the record, signing with Capitol Records the following year.

Walk On, Hiatt's first Capitol album, was recorded during his supporting tour for *Perfectly Good Guitar* and featured guest appearances by the Jayhawks and Bonnie Raitt. *Walk On* entered the charts at 48, but slipped off the charts in nine weeks, indicating that his audience had settled into a dedicated cult following. — *Stephen Thomas Erlewine*

Hangin' Around the Observatory / 1974 / Epic ♦♦♦
John Hiatt mixed pop, folk, rock, R&B, country, and gospel on his debut album, immediately becoming an uncategorizable (and thus uncommercial) entity. Although this album was cut in Nashville, it owes more to Van Morrison than it does to Conway Twitty, and like the Belfast bluesman, Indianian Hiatt came to his influences somewhat secondhand, however sincerely he evoked them. What he really was, of course, was a singer-songwriter, albeit not in a style easily recognizable in 1974. The title indicates his position: Hiatt's songs show him an acute observer. But the performances require him to dig in, and although he does so with alacrity, the result is too diffuse. Nevertheless, Hiatt earned critical kudos for this album, and Three Dog Night (who knew good songwriting when they heard it) covered "Sure As I'm Sittin' Here," getting a Top 40 single out of it. — *William Ruhlmann*

Overcoats / 1975 / Epic ♦♦
John Hiatt is better at imitating Howlin' Wolf than he is James Taylor, and that he tries both here as well as Bob Dylan and Ben E. King is some indication of his ambition, if not his accomplishment. Conversely, be began to become more himself on his second album, at least on such songs as "I'm Tired of Your Stuff" and "I Killed an Ant with My Guitar," if not on the more lugubrious numbers, such as "Distance" or on the ones that sounded like publishing demos for a more popular singer, such as "Down Home." — *William Ruhlmann*

Slug Line / 1979 / MCA ♦♦♦
Conventional wisdom at the time was that MCA Records had signed John Hiatt (who had languished without a record contract for four years) with the idea that he would be their Elvis Costello—a singer-songwriter in the fashionable punk/new wave style. Certainly, Hiatt has stripped down and roughed up from his Epic records here, fronting a straightahead guitar rock band (that was capable, of course, of playing the obligatory reggae number), eschewing the stylistic diversity he reveled in before, and throwing out snappy, aphoristic lyrics in a highly

processed voice. None of this quite turns him into Elvis Costello, although the mean streak he reveals would serve him well later. — *William Ruhlmann*

Two Bit Monsters / 1980 / MCA ✦✦✦

At the time of its release, *Two Bit Monsters* was perceived by critics who had caught up with John Hiatt on *Slug Line* as a less impressive follow-up to that record. In retrospect, it may be the better of the two albums, boasting an even more simplified musical approach and such notable songs (and future Rosanne Cash covers) as "Pink Bedroom" and "It Hasn't Happened Yet." Hiatt here was starting to emerge from the "new Elvis Costello" tag that had been affixed to him with *Slug Line*, but his reviewers, however well-meaning, seemed determined to keep him in that category. (In any case, record buyers were paying little attention—*Slug Line* was Hiatt's fourth straight album to miss the charts, and MCA dropped him as Epic had before.) — *William Ruhlmann*

All of a Sudden / 1982 / Geffen ✦✦✦

Hiatt's fifth album and his first for Geffen, his third record label, was given a somewhat inappropriate big-gloss production (all shimmering keyboards and filtered vocals) by Tony Visconti, known for his work with David Bowie. What counts with Hiatt, though, is the songs, and this album contains "I Look for Love," as knowing a dissection of the dating scene as anyone has yet attempted. — *William Ruhlmann*

Riding with the King / 1983 / Geffen ✦✦✦✦

One half of Hiatt's best Geffen album is played by him and Scott Matthews, while the other half features a band including Paul Carrack and Nick Lowe. But what matters is the songs: Hiatt's trenchant observations on life and love, especially the perceptive and painfully funny "She Loves the Jerk." — *William Ruhlmann*

Warming Up to the Ice Age / Jan. 1985 / Geffen ✦✦✦

Hiatt turned to veteran country producer Norbert Putnam here, but the result still rocked hard, with the occasional soul touch (notably those obnoxious thumb-struck bass lines that are so prevalent in '80s music). Highlights here are "The Usual," later covered by Bob Dylan, and "She Said the Same Things to Me." There is also an odd duet with Elvis Costello on the old Spinners hit "Living a Little, Laughing a Little" (try and tell them apart). Critics' darling or not, when this album went into the tank, Geffen became the third label to drop Hiatt. — *William Ruhlmann*

★ Bring the Family / May 1987 / A&M ✦✦✦✦✦

Not only is the small-band playing impeccable, but this is Hiatt's best collection of songs, which is saying a lot for so talented a writer. "Memphis in the Meantime" is a knowledgeable look at the fame game, "Your Dad Did" perfectly skewers domestic life, and "Have a Little Faith in Me" is a touching evocation of persistent love. And that's just three of them. — *William Ruhlmann*

Slow Turning / 1988 / A&M ✦✦✦✦

Only a notch below *Bring the Family*, with such strong songs as "Drive South" and the wild criminals-on-the-loose song "Tennessee Plates." — *William Ruhlmann*

Y' All Caught? The Ones That Got Away 1979-1985 / Sep. 1989 / Geffen ✦✦✦

Though John Hiatt's three records for Geffen were all quite strong, none of them received much attention other than a handful of good reviews at the time of release. After *Bring the Family* brought Hiatt to a wider audience, Geffen compiled *Y'All Caught? The Ones That Got Away*, a collection of the highlights from his three Geffen records that attempted to win over his new fans. Though the new wave overtones of the production won't appeal to some of his roots rock fans, *Y'All Caught?* still features an abundance of first-rate songs, including "Radio Girl," "Riding with the King," "She Said the Same Things to Me," "It Hasn't Happened Yet," "Slug Line," and "She Loves the Jerk," making it an excellent sampler for fans of Hiatt's latter-day work. — *Stephen Thomas Erlewine*

Stolen Moments / Jun. 1990 / A&M ✦✦✦

John Hiatt's highest charting album yet is a step down from the dizzy heights of *Bring the Family* and *Slow Turning*, as he abandons his more acid commentaries and turns in a self-deprecating set full of promises of reformation and celebrations of marriage and family life. But the observations remain acute, and Hiatt's singing (so much camouflaged in his early days) is becoming his secret weapon. — *William Ruhlmann*

Perfectly Good Guitar / Sep. 7, 1993 / A&M ✦✦

Perfectly Good Guitar is clearly a John Hiatt rock album, harking back to his mid-period *Riding with the King* days. It might disappoint some ardent admirers of the more subtle roots approach that defined Hiatt's peak "highway" twin-pack *Bring the Family* and *Slow Turning*, but most listeners should not be deterred by this perfectly good release. — *Roch Parisien*

Hiatt Comes Alive at Budokan? / Nov. 22, 1994 / A&M ✦✦✦

John Hiatt's first live album was recorded during a 1994 winter-spring tour of the US. (the title is a joke) and finds the singer-songwriter backed by the Guilty Dogs, a guitar-bass-drums trio. He doesn't need any more ammunition than that, not when he's got a set of 15 songs drawn from his last four critically acclaimed albums, including "Thing Called Love" and "Tennessee Plates." Hiatt gives his songs a rougher treatment than some of those who have covered them, his throaty voice giving even love songs like "Angel Eyes" an unsentimental force. In the absence of an A&M best-of, *Hiatt Comes Alive at Budokan?* makes a good sampler of his work, 1987-1993. — *William Ruhlmann*

Walk On / Oct. 24, 1995 / Capitol ✦✦✦

Walk On is a classic "road" album in the sense that its songs largely seem written to or about people who are not present, either because the singer is away from them, he is singing about the past, or they are dead. John Hiatt exploits the resulting feelings of longing, anger, and mourning inherent in that premise, sometimes, as in "I Can't Wait," singing about wanting to be back home, sometimes, as in the odd love song "Ethylene," wishing for a departed lover, sometimes, as in "Dust Down a Country Road," reflecting as in a dream on the past. He employs rustic nature imagery, but frequently for ominous effects rather than gentle ones, and he is supported by spare, guitar-dominated backup that is alternately soothing and disturbing. Hiatt's label debut for Capitol (though they didn't do much to promote it), *Walk On* is not among Hiatt's more consistent or more accessible works, but he remains a highly imaginative and craftsmanlike writer who can startle you. The raucous "Shredding the Document" is among the half dozen best songs of the year, if not the decade. — *William Ruhlmann*

Living a Little, Laughing a Little / Jun. 4, 1996 / Raven ✦✦✦✦

Living a Little, Laughing a Little does a good job as an early-career summary, drawing material from each of his albums released from 1974 to 1985—*Hangin' Around the Observatory*, *Overcoats*, *Slug Line*, *Two Bit Monster*, *All of a Sudden*, *Riding with the King*, and *Warming Up to the Ice Ages*. For those who are only familiar with his critically acclaimed work from the late '80s on, this provides an introduction to the formative years and a fascinating look at an man finding his voice—from an average '70s-style singer-songwriter to a rocker a la Elvis Costello to the first hints of his better known, later rootsy incarnation. A 1985 interview and a track Hiatt contributed to the *Cruisin'* soundtrack have been added as bonuses to those who already have the albums. — *Chris Woodstra*

The High Llamas

f. 1991, London, England
Alternative Pop-Rock, Post-Rock/Experimental
Although the High Llamas are nominally a group, they're pretty much the brainchild of singer and guitarist Sean O'Hagan. O'Hagan did some time in the London-by-way-of-Dublin band Microdisney, in which he was the songwriting partner of Cathal Coughlan. After Microdisney split in 1988 (Coughlan forming Fatima Mansions), O'Hagan released a couple of import-only solo albums before forming the High Llamas. The Llamas issued their debut, *Gideon Gaye*, in 1994 to high praise in the British press; it was released in the States a year later almost as an afterthought, with virtually no fanfare. Comparisons of the High Llamas/O'Hagan to Brian Wilson/the Beach Boys are unavoidable, and not just from arcane critics. Anyone with a large Beach Boys collection will detect the uncanny resemblance to 1966-70 Beach Boys, with the sophisticated melodies, the beautiful harmonies, and the elaborate production, with the emphasis on layered keyboards and orchestration. Echoes of *Pet Sounds*, *Smile*, *Wild Honey*, and *Surf's Up* predominate, though O'Hagan also claims Burt Bacharach as a major inspiration. At this point, however, the strong resemblance to Wilson's meisterwerks place O'Hagan closer to imitation than originality. Considering that he's been making records for about a decade, he might want to start aiming his sights higher. — *Richie Unterberger*

Apricots / 1992 / Plastic Records ✦✦✦

Gideon Gaye / 1994 / Alpaca Park/Epic ✦✦✦

Despite what Don Was, Van Dyke Parks, and others might be claiming, Brian Wilson is *not* going to return to the peak of his powers. In his absence, Sean O'Hagan might be the best available substitute. He's obviously done his homework, listening not only to all the albums between *Pet Sounds* and *Surf's Up*, but the widely circulated *Smile* bootlegs as well. Cheeky references to cuts like "Let's Get Away for a While" and "Surf's Up" pop up from time to time on this lush set, which takes its cues from both Wilson's most melodic and most eccentric qualities (though the ten-minute flute solo on "Track Goes By" does this to excess). It's an impressive outing that sounds like little else in the alternative rock world of the mid-'90s. But it only establishes O'Hagan and his various pals as charming emulators, rather than true innovators. — *Richie Unterberger*

● **Hawaii** / 1996 / Alpaca Park ✦✦✦✦

Jessie Hill

b. Dec. 9, 1932, New Orleans, LA
Vocals / New Orleans R&B, R&B
Loose and wild, Jessie Hill cut a New Orleans party classic with his crazed "Ooh Poo Pah Doo." The two-sided single, a 1960 Allen Toussaint production on Minit, has Hill shouting the nearly unintelligible lyrics over a strong Crescent City groove, while the flip is an instrumental featuring saxist David Lastie. Hill cut several more boisterous outings with Toussaint at the helm before heading to the West Coast, where he made a disappointing album for Blue Thumb in 1970. —*Bill Dahl*

● **Golden Classics** / 1989 / Collectables ✦✦✦✦
Good-time New Orleans R&B from the early '60s, produced by prolific pianist Allen Toussaint. —*Bill Dahl*

His Name Is Alive

f. 1989, Livonia, MI
Alternative Pop-Rock, Experimental, Dream-Pop
His Name Is Alive create some of the most beautiful and complex independently released music in recent memory, ranging from simple, folky ballads to electrifying guitar maelstroms. The brainchild of guitarist Warren Defever (also of shockabilly group Elvis Hitler), His Name Is Alive features the voices of Karin Oliver, Melissa Elliott, Denise James, and Karen Neal, and the drumming of Damian Lang and Trey Many (also of Licorice). The band's sound is as ever-changing as its lineup; each of the group's releases, from the haunting, near-Gothic *Livonia* (named after the group's Michigan hometown) to the sunny-sounding *Mouth by Mouth*, shows innovation and continual change. *Stars on ESP* followed in 1997. —*Heather Phares*

Livonia / 1990 / Rykodisc ✦✦✦
The group's artiest release, *Livonia*, was recorded when Defever was a mere 19 years old. Karin Oliver's wide vocal range and elegant harmonies mix with Defever's guitar maelstroms and tape loops in a unique and usually successful way. "E-Nicolle," "How Ghosts Affect Relationships" and "Caroline's Supposed Demon" are good examples of *Livonia*'s mix of sonic beauty and experimentalism. —*Heather Phares*

Home Is in Your Head / Jul. 23, 1992 / Rykodisc ✦✦✦✦
Home Is in Your Head completes His Name Is Alive's moody, neo-gothic period. A dark and disturbing but also very beautiful record, *Home Is in Your Head* features song titles like "Put Your Finger in Your Eye," "Why People Disappear," "Chances Are We Are Mad" and "Are We Still Married?" The album is musically diverse, ranging from gentle folk ballads to ethereal instrumentals to harsh guitar blasts. The Rykodisc re-release also includes the group's *The Dirt Eaters* EP, which contains a creepy remix of "Are We Still Married?" as well as one of His Name Is Alive's best songs, "We Hold the Land in Great Esteem." —*Heather Phares*

King of Sweet / 1993 / Perdition Plastics ✦✦✦
This release, on the miniscule Perdition Plastics label, is a limited edition of 2000. Nevertheless, it's an interesting collection of HNIA's odds and sods, including previously unreleased tracks and alternate takes and mixes of other songs. Sampling and tape loops are emphasized more on *King of Sweet* than on any of the band's previous releases, so its novelty and collector's value make it a must for fans of this unique and mesmerizing band. —*Heather Phares*

● **Mouth by Mouth** / Apr. 13, 1993 / 4AD ✦✦✦✦
His Name Is Alive's third release is actually half HNIA songs and half Dirt Eaters (HNIA's sister band) songs. The two groups' songs work together brilliantly, creating one of the best and most varied albums in alternative music. The Dirt Eaters' songs, like "Baby Fish Mouth," "In Every Ford," "Sick," and "The Dirt Eaters" are loud, catchy art-pop songs with lots of fuzzy, distorted guitars. His Name Is Alive's tunes, in contrast, feature the pristine harmonies and crisp cellos of "Cornfield," the pseudo-gamelan on "Sort Of," and the disturbing dead calm of "Can't Go Wrong Without You" and "Ear." The light and shadow that the bands create with their harmonious yet distinct styles make *Mouth by Mouth* fascinating and rewarding on each listen. —*Heather Phares*

Stars on ESP / Jul. 1996 / 4AD ✦✦✦✦
As usual, Michigan-based sonic envelope-pushers His Name Is Alive continue to boggle expectations with their beautiful, exciting music. On their fourth album for 4AD, *Stars on ESP*, the group mixes dub, dream-pop, surf, country and *Pet Sounds*-era Beach Boys into something altogether unique. The songs range from the deceptively simple, folky "Answer to Rainbow at Midnight" and "Famous Goodbye King" to bouncy pop like "Bad Luck Girl," "The Bees," and "Across the Street." Then there are songs that defy easy description, like the beautiful, lilting "Dub Love Letter," and the "Good Vibrations" pastiche "Universal Frequencies." On the whole, *Stars on ESP* is their most acoustic since

1992's *Home Is in Your Head* and their brightest sounding since *Mouth by Mouth*. However, the trademark strange, spacey noises that peppered the band's other releases can still be found on this album, particularly on "What Else Is New List" and "Wall of Speed." An eclectic, unique album—it even includes a gospel song—from an eclectic, unique band, *Stars on ESP* features His Name Is Alive at their most accessible and exciting. —*Heather Phares*

Robyn Hitchcock

b. Mar. 3, 1953, London, England
Guitar, Vocals / Singer-Songwriter, Alternative Pop-Rock, Folk-Rock, Neo-Psychedelia
Robyn Hitchcock is one of England's most enduring contemporary singer-songwriters and live performers, although he's been branded with the tags eccentric and quirky during the course of his long career. Born in London in 1953, Hitchcock started his recording career with the Soft Boys, including Andy Metcalfe on bass and Morris Windsor on drums, in 1976. The punk-era band specialized in melodic pop merged with comedic lyrics, and were primarily responsible for keeping the Rickenbacker guitar sound alive in the years between the Byrds and R.E.M. R.E.M.'s guitarist Peter Buck and the Replacements claimed Hitchcock and the Soft Boys to be one of their greatest influences, thereby explaining the band's resurgence in the mid-'80s, as well as Hitchcock's prolific '80s solo output. Hitchcock's voice veers between John Lennon and Syd Barrett, helping to nurture his madman reputation, but his true influences lie more in English folk-rock; his guitar and vocal style and lyrical inanities recall Incredible String Band or Roy Harper.

His solo debut, 1981's *Black Snake Diamond Role*, helped consolidate Hitchcock's reputation as an oddball, and was followed by the psychedelia of *Groovy Decay* in 1982 and the all-acoustic *I Often Dream of Trains* in 1984. By 1985, Hitchcock rounded up his old Soft Boys mates, as well as Roger Jackson on keyboards, to form the Egyptians and released *Fegmania*, the album where Hitchcock's penchant for zaniness and songsmithing coalesced. It is often cited as the most beloved record among Hitchcock afficionados. From countless tours of America with his band and as a solo artist, Hitchcock's cult following grew and established him as a consistent live entertainer. The recording and release of a live album in 1986, *Gotta Let This Hen Out*, with the Egyptians was no mean feat for a cult act. That year also saw *Element of Light*, the apex of a string of iconoclastic albums. By 1988, aided by his association with R.E.M., Hitchcock landed his first major US label contract with A&M Records and released *Globe of Frogs* in 1988 and *Queen Elvis* in 1989. *Eye* was an acoustic one-off for Twin-Tone in 1990, and then it was back to A&M for *Perspex Island* in 1991 and *Respect* in 1993. He sustained and probably even grew his career; however, by this time, critical approval had fallen off for his work. Simultaneously, a number of his songs were compiled and released as rarities discs; *Groovy Decoy*, an alternate version of *Groovy Decay* with additional tracks, was released in 1985, *Invisible Hitchcock* in 1986 and *You and Oblivion* in 1995. It wasn't until the 1996 release of *Moss Elixir* that Hitchcock returned to form and fully embraced his folk roots, leaving the madman behind and instead drawing on his years of solid songcrafting, yielding his 15th album of solo material. —*Denise Sullivan*

Black Snake Diamond Role / 1981 / Rhino ✦✦✦
Robyn Hitchcock's first album after leaving the Soft Boys isn't that far removed from the edgy, warped guitar pop of his former band, which isn't surprising, considering the presence of former Soft Boys bassist Andy Metcalfe and drummer Morris Windsor. However, *Black Snake Diamond Role* removes much of the sharp, cutting guitars of *Underwater Moonlight* and replaces them with friendlier, ringing riffs. But that doesn't mean Hitchcock has gone soft—he's just refined his technique. And that doesn't mean his songwriting has improved. Cut by cut, *Black Snake Diamond Role* is weaker than *Underwater Moonlight*, but that's relative—the album contains pretty and twisted pseudo-psychedelic pop like "Brenda's Iron Sledge," "Acid Bird," "The Man Who Invented Himself," and "Do Policemen Sing?," which all rank among his finest songs. —*Stephen Thomas Erlewine*

Groovy Decay / 1982 / Combat ✦✦
For his second solo album, Robyn Hitchcock decided to work with producer Steve Hillage, a former member of Gong. Under his guidance, Hitchcock made an album that smoothed out his rough edges and obscured his quirks under layers of saxophones, trumpets, and processed guitars. Beneath the stilted production lay some of Hitchcock's weakest songs, most of which were under-developed melodically and lyrically. Some of the songs are worthwhile—"The Cars She Used to Drive" is the best stab at slick new wave pop, while "Fifty Two Stations" and "St. Petersburg" are powerful—but most of the album is simply lifeless. After its release, Hitchcock retired from music for nearly three years. In 1986, he released an alternate version of *Groovy Decay*,

comprised mostly of songwriting demos, called *Groovy Decoy*. —*Stephen Thomas Erlewine*

I Often Dream of Trains / 1984 / Rhino ✦✦✦✦
Hitchcock was so shaken by the entire *Groovy Decay* disaster that he retired from recording for two years. When he returned in 1984 with *I Often Dream of Trains*, it was clear that the time off had affected his music. A collection of spare, acoustic-based pop-folk songs, *I Often Dream of Trains* is one of Hitchcock's most introspective and charming records. Instead of creating an impenetrably personal album, the stripped-down instrumentation actually opens up the songwriter's world, allowing the ballads ("Trams of Old London," "Cathedral," "Flavour of Night") to sit comfortably next to the jokes ("Uncorrected Personality Traits"). Alternating between acoustic guitars and solo piano, the music is never fragile, adding a strong support to Hitchcock's eccentric lyrics. —*Stephen Thomas Erlewine*

Fegmania! / Mar. 1985 / Rhino ✦✦✦✦
After the stripped-back collection *I Often Dream of Trains*, Hitchcock slowly formed a backing band called the Egyptians with ex-Soft Boys Andy Metcalfe and Morris Windsor and keyboardist Roger Jackson over the course of the next year. *Fegmania!*, the Egyptians' first album, was a distinct departure from both the Soft Boys and Hitchcock's previous solo work, featuring layered, intertwining guitars and keyboards that created lush and thick sonic textures. Even with the more detailed arrangements, the songs remained twitchy and off-kilter, with melodies that usually went in willfully unpredictable directions, yet remained catchy all the while. *Fegmania!* was Hitchcock's most consistent work to date, featuring such highlights as the Eastern-tinged "Egyptian Cream," the creepy "My Wife & My Dead Wife," and the relatively straightforward "The Man with the Lightbulb Head." —*Stephen Thomas Erlewine*

● **Gotta Let This Hen Out** / Oct. 1985 / Rhino ✦✦✦✦
Recorded at the Marquee in London shortly after the release of *Fegmania!*, the live *Gotta Let This Hen Out!* is a tense and exciting record, finding the raw energy that usually goes untapped in Hitchcock's music. Although the album makes the Egyptians sound more like a rock 'n' roll band than they actually were—they never played with such wreckless abandon before or since—the driving performances don't wreck the melodic and lyrical eccentricities of the songs; instead, the increased vigor gives the music a searing power, obliterating the notion that his songs are delicate and precious. The set list also accentuates Hitchcock's strengths, relying on his most accessible and melodic material, whether it's recent material like "Egyptian Cream," "Sometimes I Wish I Was a Pretty Girl," and "Acid Bird" or Soft Boys' tracks like "Kingdom of Love," "Only the Stones Remain," "The Face of Death," and "Leppo and the Jooves." —*Stephen Thomas Erlewine*

Groovy Decoy / Dec. 1985 / Relativity ✦✦
Four years after its release, Robyn Hitchcock pulled *Groovy Decay* from circulation, replacing it with *Groovy Decoy*, an alternate version of the record assembled mainly from demos he recorded with Soft Boys bassist Matthew Seligman; the album included some versions that are identical to the *Decay* material, as well as a handful of new songs. By and large, *Groovy Decoy* is a better record, with more immediate and gripping versions of the songs that comprised the original album, but the material remains some of the weakest Hitchcock has written. —*Stephen Thomas Erlewine*

Element of Light / 1986 / Rhino ✦✦✦✦
Element of Light, Hitchcock's second studio album with the Egyptians, remains one of his finest moments and offers a convincing argument for his talents as a pop craftsman. Using John Lennon's work for *Revolver* and *The Beatles* as a template, Hitchcock wrote an elegant set of songs for *Element of Light*, songs that contained all of his cryptic lyrical sensibilities, yet featured more refined melodies and song structures. The Egyptians play with a subtle grace, moving between the stately "Winchester" and light psychedelia of "If You Were a Priest" to the bracing attack of "Tell Me About Your Drugs," with ease. While it sacrifices some of the edgy tension of Hitchcock's earlier work, *Element of Light* is his most melodic and eerily beautiful record. —*Stephen Thomas Erlewine*

Invisible Hitchcock / 1986 / Rhino ✦✦✦
As the reference to the Soft Boys' rarities collection, *Invisible Hits*, suggests, *Invisible Hitchcock* gathers together a selection of obscurities and nonalbum tracks Robyn Hitchcock recorded between 1980 and 1986. Granted, the material is a bit uneven, but the album holds together well, as it emphasizes Hitchcock's gift for warped wordplay and appealingly convoluted melodies. Upon its original release, the running order for *Invisible Hitchcock* was considerably different in Britain and America; Rhino's 1995 reissue standardized the album, including all the material from both versions of the album (with the exception of "Grooving on a Inner Plane," which appeared as a bonus track on the company's reissue of *Black Snake Diamond Role*), as well

as adding two songs that never appeared on either version of the record. —*Stephen Thomas Erlewine*

Globe of Frogs / 1988 / A&M ✦✦✦✦
Hitchcock's first foray into US major-label territory disappointed some critics, but helped expand his audience beyond the realm of college radio, thanks to the radio-friendly "Balloon Man." Aided by his band the Egyptians, it's the production that mars this record, along with half of the songs. "Sleeping with Your Devil Mask," "Chinese Bones," and "Flesh Number One (Beatle Dennis)," which features Peter Buck on guitar and Squeeze's Difford and Tilbrook on vocals, are the reasons to own this record. —*Denise Sullivan*

Queen Elvis / 1989 / A&M ✦✦✦✦
Hitchcock redeemed himself on this collection—song for song more vital than *Globe of Frogs*. "Madonna of the Wasps" is a timeless pop song, but the record is mired in modern-rock production and synthesizer sounds. "One Long Pair of Eyes" remains a Hitchcock standard, and the bizarre "Wax Doll" and "Veins of the Queen" kept Hitchcock at the fore of eccentric rock, making him the only appropriate heir to the English king-loony throne formerly occupied by Syd Barrett. —*Denise Sullivan*

Eye / 1990 / Rhino ✦✦✦✦
Robyn Hitchcock recorded *Eye*, his fourth proper solo album, after the disappointing *Queen Elvis*. *Eye* marked a return to the acoustic-oriented folk-pop of *I Often Dream of Trains*, featuring a collection of his most personal songs. Where *I Often Dream of Trains* was a kaleidoscopic journey through a colorfully twisted world, *Eye* sounds more confessional, although Hitchcock's exact lyrical sentiments can be difficult to sort out through his dense and willfully obscure imagery. Nevertheless, the immediacy of the music—which is delivered on acoustic guitars and piano—and the simple, delicate grace of Hitchcock's melodies make even the most cryptic lines sound direct and straightforward. —*Stephen Thomas Erlewine*

Perspex Island / Aug. 6, 1991 / A&M ✦✦
By this time, Hitchcock could be counted on for a couple of exceptional songs per album plus a preponderance of less than astonishing material. "So You Think You're in Love" was the keeper from this set, a rollicking, cautionary tale about the joys of early love. Wisely, Hitchcock and the Egyptians gave up producing themselves, but Paul Fox's attempt was still muddled and misguided and ultimately didn't showcase the band to the best of their abilities—although the lack of quality material could also explain the lapse. —*Denise Sullivan*

Respect / Feb. 23, 1993 / A&M ✦✦
Through his years of leading influential psychedelic rockers the Soft Boys, his solo work, and seven releases with current combo the Egyptians, Robyn Hitchcock has earned recognition as a literate tunesmith in the tradition of great British eccentrics. Hitchcock uses conventional pop structures as a launching pad for whimsical, sometimes abstract, and often wildly imaginative flights. *Respect* is true to form, although his lyrics are at his most accessible here. Instrumentally, Hitchcock's layers of acoustic and electric guitars are accompanied not only by bass, keyboards, and drums, but also—when called upon—by water jug, cheese grater, and frying pans. The intelligence and emotion of Robyn Hitchcock's work continues to reward. —*Roch Parisien*

Gravy Deco / Jan. 1995 / Rhino ✦✦
When Rhino reissued Robyn Hitchcock's catalog in 1995, the record company combined the material from *Groovy Decoy* and *Groovy Decay* onto one disc titled *Gravy Deco*. In any form, it's the weakest music he ever recorded, with a couple of songs—particularly the haunting "St. Petersburg," "Fifty Two Stations," and "America"—that make it worthwhile for dedicated fans. —*Stephen Thomas Erlewine*

You & Oblivion / Mar. 1995 / Rhino ✦✦
Released as part of Rhino's 1995 series of Robyn Hitchcock reissues, *You & Oblivion* is the second collection of Hitchcock rarities, featuring demos, live tracks, and studio outtakes. Unfortunately, much of the material is second rate, and some of the songs sound unfinished. Accentuating the frustratingly inconsistent musical quality of the record is the lack of liner notes and nonchronological sequencing, which makes the record confusing for casual listeners and exasperating for hardcore fans. There are a handful of intriguing performances among the 22 tracks, yet most of *You & Oblivion* is a chore to listen to. —*Stephen Thomas Erlewine*

Moss Elixir / Aug. 1996 / Warner Brothers ✦✦✦
Wisely, Hitchcock chucked the band sound (though longtime associates Morris Windsor and Andy Metcalfe continue to lend their services on some tracks) and returned to the spare singer-songwriter format for his best set of songs in more than ten years. Everything is here: the quirky on "Man with a Woman's Shadow," the elegant on "Beautiful Queen," and the straightahead Beatlesque music in which Hitchcock excels in the perfect pop of "Alright, Yeah." Finally, Hitchcock embraced his folk-guitar roots, which hearken back to the days of the Incredible String

Band and Roy Harper, while imprinting his indelible lyrical and vocal stamp, one of the true leading lights of contemporary alternative music. —*Denise Sullivan*

● **Greatest Hits** / Sep. 9, 1996 / A&M ✦✦✦✦
Covering Robyn Hitchcock & the Egyptians' four albums for A&M, *Greatest Hits* features many of Hitchcock's best-known songs, including "Balloon Man," "Madonna of the Wasps," and "So You Think You're in Love," as well as several rare B-sides and single mixes, designed to bait the dedicated collector. Even with the presence of these handful of rarities, *Greatest Hits* remains targeted to casual Hitchcock fans who just want to have his late-'80s and early-'90s modern rock radio hits. Consequently, it functions as a streamlined introduction to some of Hitchcock's most memorable and melodic music. —*Stephen Thomas Erlewine*

Susanna Hoffs

b. Jan. 17, 1961, Newport Beach, CA
Guitar, Vocals / Pop-Rock
After the Bangles disbanded in 1989, vocalist/guitarist Susanna Hoffs began her own solo career. Two years after the band's demise, she released *When You're a Boy,* which featured songs written by Cyndi Lauper, Juliana Hatfield, and Diane Warren. As the wide array of songwriters suggest, the album was a little unfocused—alternating between jangling guitar-pop and synth-laden mainstream pop—but it did generate the Top 40 hit, "My Side of the Bed."

Following the release of *When You're a Boy,* Hoffs took several years off to concentrate on domestic life. She returned to recording in 1996 with *Susanna Hoffs,* her first release for London Records. While the album failed to launch a hit single, it received stronger reviews than her debut. —*Stephen Thomas Erlewine*

When You're a Boy / Feb. 1991 / Columbia ✦✦✦

● **Susanna Hoffs** / Sep. 24, 1996 / Polygram ✦✦✦✦
Delivered five years after her botched solo debut, Susanna Hoffs' eponymous second album is a remarkably accomplished and catchy collection of mature jangle-pop, power-pop, and ballads. Combining originals with well-chosen covers like the Lightning Seeds' "All I Want," the album is an infectious and engaging set of melodic pop that also happens to be Hoffs' most introspective and personal record to date. The combination of sweet melodies and reflective songwriting makes *Susanna Hoffs* a remarkable artistic comeback from a performer that many would have thought was past her prime. —*Stephen Thomas Erlewine*

Hole

f. 1989, Los Angeles, CA
Alternative Pop-Rock, Grunge, Riot Grrrl
Throughout Hole's career, vocalist/guitarist Courtney Love's notorious public image has overshadowed her band's music. In its original incarnation, Hole was one of the noisiest, most abrasive alternative bands performing in the early '90s. By the time of their second album, 1994's *Live Through This,* the band had smoothed out many of their rougher edges, as well as adding more melody and hooks to their songwriting. Through both versions of Hole, Love's combative, assaultive persona permeated both the group's music and lyrics, giving the band a tense, unpredictable edge even at their quietest moments.

Love formed Hole in Los Angeles in 1989, recruiting guitarist Eric Erlandson through a newspaper ad. Love had played with numerous bands before Hole, including an early version of Babes in Toyland and Faith No More. Erlandson and Love eventually drafted bassist Jill Emery and drummer Caroline Rue into the band, recording their first album with producer Kim Gordon, the bassist of Sonic Youth. The violent and uncompromising *Pretty on the Inside,* Hole's debut record, was released on Caroline Records in 1991, to numerous positive reviews, especially in the British weekly music press.

In early 1992, Courtney Love married Kurt Cobain, the lead singer-songwriter of Nirvana. For a couple of months, the couple were the king and queen of the new rock world; soon, that world came crashing in. Cobain became addicted to heroin and the couple fought to keep custody of their baby after a piece in *Vanity Fair* accused Love of shooting heroin while pregnant, charges which she vehemently denied at the time; she would later admit that she had taken small quanities of the drug. By 1993, their private world had settled down somewhat, with Cobain and Love recording new albums with their respective bands.

Halfway through 1993, Love reassembled Hole with Erlandson, adding bassist Kristen M. Pfaff and drummer Patty Schemel. Hole was set to release their first major-label album, the more pop-oriented *Live Through This,* on DGC Records in April of 1994. Advance word on the album was overwhelmingly positive, with many critics calling it one of the best records of the year. Four days before the album was released,

Kurt Cobain's body was discovered in the couple's Seattle home; he died of a self-inflicted shotgun wound three days before.

Two months after Cobain's death, Kristen M. Pfaff was found dead of a heroin overdose in a Seattle apartment. Two months later, Hole began touring again, with bassist Melissa Auf Der Maur taking Pfaff's place. "Doll Parts" was released as a single late in 1994, climbing into the Top 60 by the beginning of 1995. *Live Through This* topped many critics' polls at the end of the year, including *Rolling Stone* and *the Village Voice.* After *Live Through This* went gold in the summer of 1995, Hole toured with the fifth Lollapalooza tour. —*Stephen Thomas Erlewine*

Pretty on the Inside / Jul. 1, 1991 / Caroline ✦✦✦
With the assistance of producers Kim Gordon and Don Fleming, Hole records a brutally uncompromising debut with *Pretty on the Inside.* The jagged white noise and buzzing guitars articulate Courtney Love's pent-up rage as well as her lyrics, and while that might make the album difficult to absorb in one sitting, it also makes it a singular achievement. —*Stephen Thomas Erlewine*

● **Live Through This** / Apr. 12, 1994 / DGC ✦✦✦✦
Courtney Love completely revamped Hole before recording their second album, keeping only Eric Erlandson in the lineup. That is one of the reasons why *Live Through This* sounds so shockingly different from *Pretty on the Inside,* but the real reason is Love's desire to compete in the same commercial alternative-rock arena as her husband, Kurt Cobain. In fact, many rumors have claimed that Cobain ghostwrote a substantial chunk of the album, and while that's unlikely, there's no denying that his patented stop-start dynamics, bare chords and punk-pop melodies provide the blueprint for *Live Through This.* Love adds her signature rage and feminist rhetoric to the formula, but the lyrics that truly resonate are the ones the unintentionally predict Cobain's suicide. For all the raw pain of the lyrics, *Live Through This* rarely sounds raw, because of the shiny production and the carefully considered dynamics. Despite this flaw, the album retains its power because it was one of the few records patterned on *Nevermind* that gets the formula right, with a set of gripping hooks and melodies that retain their power even if they follow the predictable grunge pattern. —*Stephen Thomas Erlewine*

The Hollies

f. 1962, Manchester, England
British Invasion, Pop-Rock
One of the best and most commercially successful pop-rock acts of the British Invasion, when the Hollies began recording in 1963, they relied heavily upon the R&B/early rock 'n' roll covers that provided the staple diet for countless British bands of the time. They quickly developed a more distinctive style of three-part harmonies (heavily influenced by the Everly Brothers), ringing guitars, and hook-happy material, penned by both outside writers (especially Graham Gouldman) and themselves, eventually composing most of their repertoire on their own. The best early Hollies records evoke an infectious, melodic cheer similar to that of the early Beatles, although the Hollies were neither in their class (not an insult: nobody else was) nor demonstrated a similar capacity for artistic growth. They tried, though, easing into somewhat more sophisticated folk-rock and mildly psychedelic sounds as the decade wore on, especially on their albums (which contain quite a few overlooked highlights).

Allan Clarke (lead singer) and Graham Nash (vocals, guitar) had been friends since childhood in Manchester, and formed the nucleus of the Hollies in the early '60s with bassist Eric Haydock. In early 1963, EMI producer Ron Richards signed the group after seeing them at the famous Cavern Club in Liverpool. Guitarist Vic Steele left before the first session, to be replaced by 17-year-old Tony Hicks. Drummer Don Rathbone only lasted for a couple of singles before being replaced by Bobby Elliott, who had played with Hicks in his pre-Hollies group, the Dolphins. The lineup changes were most fortuitous: Hicks contributed a lot to the group with his ringing guitar work and songwriting, and Elliott was one of the very finest drummers in all of pop-rock.

Although their first singles were R&B covers, the Hollies were no match for the Rolling Stones (or for that matter the Beatles) in this department, and were much more at home with pop-rock material that provided a sympathetic complement to their glittering harmonies. They ran off an awesome series of hits in the UK in the '60s, making the Top 20 almost 20 times. Some of their best mid-'60s singles, like "Here I Go Again," "We're Through," and the British No. 1 "I'm Alive," passed virtually unnoticed in the US, where they couldn't make the Top 40 until early 1966, when Graham Gouldman's "Look Through Any Window" did the trick. In 1966, Eric Haydock left the group under cloudy circumstances, replaced by Bernie Calvert.

The Hollies really didn't break in America in a big way until "Bus Stop" (1966), their first Stateside Top Tenner; "On a Carousel," "Carrie Ann," and "Stop Stop Stop" were also big hits. Here the Hollies were providing something of a satisfying option for pop-oriented listeners that found the increasingly experimental outings of groups like the Beatles and Kinks too difficult to follow. At the same time, the production and harmonies were sophisticated enough to maintain a broader audience than more teen- and bubblegum-oriented British Invasion acts like Herman's Hermits. Their albums showed a more serious and ambitious side, particularly on the part of Graham Nash, without ever escaping the truth that their forte was well-executed pop-ock, not serious statements.

Nash, however, itched to make an impression as a more serious artist, particularly on the "King Midas in Reverse" single (1967). Its relatively modest commecial success didn't augur well for his influence over the band's direction, and their next 45s were solidly in the more tried-and-true romantic tradition. By 1968, though, Nash really felt constrained by the band's commercial orientation, and by the end of the year he was gone, leaving for the States to help found Crosby, Stills, & Nash. His departure really marked the end of the group's peak era.

In 1969, the band tried to have their cake and eat it too by doing a whole album of Hollie-ized Dylan songs, which was received poorly by some critics, although it was a decent seller in Britain. Nash was replaced by Terry Sylvester (formerly of Liverpool bands the Escorts and Swinging Blue Jeans), and the hit streak continued for a while. "He Ain't Heavy, He's My Brother," in fact, was one of their biggest international singles. But the group was really reaching a cul de sac; they'd managed a remarkably long run at the top considering that they hadn't changed their formula much since the mid-'60s, adding enough sophistication to the lyrics and arrangements to avoid sounding markedly dated. It was apparent they really weren't capable of producing long-playing works striking enough to appeal to the album audience, though, and their singles, though still hits on occasion, weren't as memorable as their best '60s work.

A modest slide in the early '70s was arrested by "Long Cool Woman in a Black Dress," a Creedence Clearwater Revival-type rocker that made No. 2 in the States in 1972. The timing wasn't ideal; by the time it became a smash, Clarke, who had sung lead on the single, had left to go solo, to be replaced by Swedish vocalist Mikael Rikfors. Clarke rejoined in mid-1973, and the group had one last international monster, "The Air That I Breathe," which made No. 6 in the US in 1974. The Hollies recorded several other albums in the 1970s and 1980s, and toured often; Graham Nash even rejoined them for a 1983 album. Their post-mid-'70s output, however, is only for fanatics; it's the '60s classics that continue to hold an enduring appeal. —*Richie Unterberger*

Stay with the Hollies / 1964 / Beat Goes On ♦♦
In *The Rolling Stone Illustrated History of Rock'n' Roll*, Lester Bangs wrote of the Hollies, "During the British invasion, they were mostly just bad, grinding out sloppy covers of 'Stay,' 'Do You Love Me,' 'Lucille,' and 'Memphis' in the most shamelessly churn-'em-up, bash-'em out Liverpudlian manner." While this is an unfair overgeneralization, it's basically an accurate assessment of their first album, which contains all of the above-mentioned cuts. The group stuck to the tried-and-true rock/R&B cover staples of dozens, if not hundreds, of British bands circa 1963 on this 14-cut LP, which featured only one original composition. The Hollies' harmonic blend was yet to fully coalesce; there's plenty of energy, but the voices are adenoidal (and not always in perfect key) and the performances almost embarassingly callow. Nonetheless, the album was a huge hit in Britain, reaching No. 2 and staying in the Top Ten for 18 weeks. "Stay" itself had been their first UK Top Ten hit in late 1963, and the album's best track, the edgy R&B/harmony rendition of "Watcha Gonna Do 'Bout It," was one of their better early cuts. The group also covers Ray Charles, Roy Orbison, Conway Twitty, "Rockin' Robin," and "Mr. Moonlight" (before the Beatles) on this set. —*Richie Unterberger*

In the Hollies Style / 1964 / Beat Goes On ♦♦♦♦
Released only ten months after their debut album, *Stay with the Hollies*, their second LP was a huge leap forward in every respect. Their famous airtight harmonies were now in place, and the sloppiness of the instrumental attack gone. Most important, the group developed enormously as songwriters. Eight of the twelve tracks were Hollies originals, and quite skillful in their mastery of the British Invasion essentials of driving, catchy melodies and shining harmonies. A couple of the covers are duds, but the "Nitty Gritty/Something's Got a Hold of Me" medley is first-rate, and the version of "It's in His Kiss" (retitled "It's in Her Kiss") respectable. The Hollies weren't from Liverpool (though Manchester is fairly close), but this nonetheless ranks as one of the very best Merseybeat albums not released by The Beatles themselves. It doesn't include any British or American hits, but "Come On Home," "To You My Love," "Don't You Know," and "What Kind of Boy" (the last of which was written by one Big Dee Irwin) will appeal to any British Invasion fan. Surprisingly, none of the tracks were ever released in the United States, making the reissue all the more desirable an item for British Invasion collectors from US shores, who most likely missed it entirely the first time around. —*Richie Unterberger*

Hollies / 1965 / BGO ♦♦♦
The Hollies' third album saw a band in the throes of transition between the Merseybeat and rock 'n' roll with which they established themselves, and the folk-rock and soul music that was blowing the strongest winds of change in 1965. They clean up their backlog of cover staples with versions of tunes by Lloyd Price, Buddy Holly, and Roy Orbison, and delve into soul by taking on The Miracles' "Mickey's Monkey" and Curtis Mayfield's "You Must Believe Me." Their attempt at "Fortune Teller" won't make you forget The Rolling Stones' version; nor, for that matter, are any of the other covers impressive. That leaves five reasonably good originals, the best of which are the gorgeous "So Lonely" and the excellent Merseybeat knockoff "When I Come Home to You." They also sound Beatlesque on "I've Been Wrong," but "Too Many People" and their cover of Peter, Paul & Mary's "Very Last Day" hearken to a folk-rock direction. The album was issued in the US as *Hear! Here!*, replacing "Mickey's Monkey" with their No. 1 British hit "I'm Alive." —*Richie Unterberger*

Would You Believe / 1965 / Beat Goes On ♦♦♦
One of the less essential '60s albums by the Hollies, whose capabilities were arguably stretched by the two-album-a-year-pace-in-addition-to-three-hit-singles model established by the Beatles during this time. Their version of Paul Simon's "I Am a Rock" is nice, but the soul and early rock covers of Sam & Dave, Otis Redding, and Chuck Berry are pretty dispensable; the Hollies were not the Stones or the Animals, lacking their soul and interpretative imagination. Some of the originals are pretty ho-hum too (including the pathetic "Fifi the Flea," which was covered by the Everly Brothers). But every Hollies album of the '60s has some strong overlooked tracks. On this one, they're the surprisingly tough folk-rockers "Hard, Hard Year" and "I've Got a Way of My Own." The ultra-catchy "Don't You Even Care," written by Clint Ballard Jr. (also responsible for their No. 1 British hit "I'm Alive," as well as "The Game of Love" and "You're No Good"), is the real obscure gem here, and could have well been a hit under its own steam. The album's last song, "I Can't Let Go," was a big hit in Britain (and a small one in the US) and one of the Hollies' best performances. The record was issued in America, in a slightly amended version, as *Beat Group! —Richie Unterberger*

For Certain Because / 1966 / Beat Goes On ♦♦♦
One gets the feeling that, as 1966 drew to a close amidst an incredible acceleration of innovations in the pop and rock world, the Hollies felt the need to prove themselves capable of artistic growth despite having established a very winning formula. *For Certain Because* was their first album entirely composed of original material, and echoed pop's increased sophistication with fuller, more adventurous arrangements and more personal, folk-rock-influenced compositions. Such was the intense competition of the time that this record couldn't hope to take on *Revolver, Aftermath,* or *Face to Face,* but it nevertheless remains an admirable effort that may stand as the group's most accomplished album (greatest hits packages excepted) of the '60s. The Hollies were very much a pop group, and didn't let their somewhat more sober and introspective compositions stand in the way of their glittering harmonies and jangling guitars. Occasional brass, banjo, bells, and vibrating piano embellish their basic rock instrumentation on this pleasant, if hardly earthshaking, work. The circus-like "Stop! Stop! Stop!," with its manic banjo, was a hit on both sides of the Atlantic; the good-natured "Pay You Back with Interest" a Top 30 hit in America; and the jazzy "Tell Me to My Face" was one of their best '60s album tracks. The LP was released as *Stop! Stop! Stop!* in the US. —*Richie Unterberger*

Evolution / 1967 / Beat Goes On ♦♦
The title of the album, along with the psychedelic shirts and artwork on the cover, sound a clarion call that The Hollies were aiming to keep up with the times on this mid-1967 release. Actually, they don't deviate too much from their formula of high harmonies and catchy tunes on this release, which stands as one of their less memorable '60s albums. If there are any expanded ambitions here, they're found in the eight cuts that feature modest orchestral arrangements directed by former Manfred Mann member Mike Vickers. When the band tries to stretch it a bit with clips of hard fuzz guitars and the embarrassingly dated "underwater" vocals of "Lullaby to Tim," it doesn't come off well. A couple of the better cuts are "Rain on the Window," a kind of downbeat sequel to "Bus Stop" with its Graham Gouldman-influenced melody line, and "Leave Me," which actually hearkens back to earlier British Invasion days with its strong Zombies influence. "Have You Ever Loved Somebody" is a good tune that was done better in cover versions by the Searchers and the Everly Brothers. No hits were featured on this LP, which was released in a slightly truncated form in the US. —*Richie Unterberger*

Butterfly / 1967 / Beat Goes On ♦♦♦
This late-1967 album found The Hollies making some modest adjustments to the psychedelic era: occasionally trippy studio effects, a sitar on their most psychedelic track ("Maker"), songs that didn't always deal

with boy-girl relationships. In fact, however, the group's focus remained where it usually was: modest but pleasing, similar-sounding catchy tunes with high harmonies and strumming guitars. It's not remarkable or essential, but it's certainly pleasant enough, and a bit better than their earlier 1967 LP, *Evolution*, with some of their better album-only cuts ("Postcard," "Pegasus," "Butterfly," "Away Away Away"). With some track alterations, the record was issued in the US as *Dear Eloise/King Midas in Reverse;* the UK edition, as collectors should note, has a few songs that were never released in the States ("Pegasus," "Elevated Observations?," "Try It"). *—Richie Unterberger*

Confessions of the Mind / Dec. 1970 / Beat Goes On ◆◆◆
The group's first album of original material after Nash's departure was a competent but unremarkable affair. The harmonies and concise execution were still intact, and the material still brightly pop-oriented, if increasingly serious in lyrical content and slightly more sophisticated in production. The Hollies were now becoming somewhat of an anachronism in a world of progressive album-oriented rock. Their considerable melodic strengths and professionalism ensured that their efforts were never embarrassing. But the hooks weren't as sharp as their vintage hits, and their content wasn't deep enough to establish them with an older rock audience. Most of the songs were issued in the US on the Epic LP *Morning Finger*, which had a slightly different track lineup. *—Richie Unterberger*

Distant Light / Dec. 1971 / Beat Goes On ◆◆◆
The Hollies continued to tread water as the early '70s progressed. *Distant Light* offered nothing particularly new or unexpected, but the harmonies and songwriting remained at a high enough standard to refute any accusations of decline. Too pop for the album-oriented audience, and not light and frothy enough for the pop market, it would have been totally overlooked if not for the surprise success of the Creedence Clearwater Revival soundalike "Long Cool Woman in a Black Dress." Released in the States almost as an afterthought, it became (deservedly) their biggest American hit, reaching No. 2. Its success inspired the return of Allan Clarke to the fold, after he had left the group to briefly pursue a solo career. *—Richie Unterberger*

What Goes Around / 1983 / Atlantic ◆◆◆
Graham Nash rejoined the Hollies for one album for the first time in 15 years, which certainly beefed up their harmonies. He also coproduced, but he didn't bring any songs along, which makes this something less than one might have hoped. The group did get its first US hit in eight years and last so far with a remake of the Supremes' "Stop in the Name of Love." *—William Ruhlmann*

Not the Hits Again / Feb. 1986 / See For Miles ◆◆
A 22-track selection of lesser-known songs from the '60s, inessential for a couple of reasons. The selection is surprisingly uninspired, largely opting for a bunch of routine covers, and passing over many fine originals that could have been picked. And virtually all of the cuts have been reissued on CD. Typically, there's one rarity that makes this essential for Hollies completists. "Honey and Wine," a fine moody (and quite obscure) Goffin-King composition, only appeared on a 1965 British EP; this ragtag compilation marks its only reissue. *—Richie Unterberger*

The EP Collection / Apr. 1987 / See For Miles ◆◆◆
The British have an odd yen for album-length collections of tracks that appeared on EPs in the '60s, even if some or most of them also appeared on LPs and singles. The contents of this 22-song anthology of items from 1964-'66 Hollies EPs are pretty good, but almost everything is available on CD now, in the better context of album or greatest hits reissues. Frustratingly, it does include two fine Merseyish originals from their debut 1964 EP, "What Kind of Love" and "When I'm Not There," that never made it onto LP otherwise. Except, that is, for the British 1978 LP compilation *The Best of the Hollies' EPs*, which duplicates the track listing of this disc almost exactly. *—Richie Unterberger*

● **Epic Anthology** / Jun. 1990 / Epic ◆◆◆◆
A 20-track compilation that picks up when the Hollies signed with Epic in 1967 and presents their biggest hits plus select album tracks and rarities through 1975. Includes "Carrie-Anne," "He Ain't Heavy, He's My Brother," "Long Cool Woman (in a Black Dress)," and "The Air That I Breathe." *—William Ruhlmann*

● **All Time Greatest Hits** / Sep. 1990 / Curb ◆◆◆◆
A 12 track all-singles compilation that includes the Hollies' biggest US hits on both Imperial ("Bus Stop," "Stop, Stop, Stop") and Epic Records from 1964 to 1975. *—William Ruhlmann*

Thirtieth Anniversary Collection 1963-1993 / 1993 / EMI America ◆◆◆◆
This three-CD, 57-track box set does a good if imperfect job of encapsulating the legacy of one of the British Invasion's better bands. This includes all of the Hollies' singles, A–and B-sides, from the '60s, as well as five previously unreleased tunes. The hits—"I'm Alive," "Bus Stop," "On a Carousel," and others—contain some of the finest beat

harmonizing not done by the Beatles. The B-sides—many of them originals, some of them never before available in the United States—are often nearly equal in quality to the classic material. The compilation wisely touches upon only the essentials of their post-1970 singles ("Long Cool Woman" and "The Air That I Breathe"), and unwisely closes with three forgettable tracks from the early '90s. Don't be misled, however, that this box contains all of their best material—their early albums, though inconsistent, featured a fair number of strong original tunes which remain little known beyond collector circles. It's a good set, with an excellent booklet and thoroughly annotated discography, but not definitive. *—Richie Unterberger*

Brenda Holloway

b. Jun. 21, 1946, Atascadero, CA
Vocals / Soul, Motown
This sultry '60s addition to the Motown roster waxed several memorable ballads for the firm. One of Motown's first Los Angeles signings, Holloway's Tamla debut, "Every Little Bit Hurts," was a soaring ballad that sailed up the pop charts in 1964, while Smokey Robinson wrote and produced Holloway's 1965 smash "When I'm Gone." The voluptuous vocalist opened several concerts for the Beatles on their 1965 US tour, including their Shea Stadium show. In 1967, Holloway co-wrote and recorded the original version of "You've Made Me So Very Happy," later a gigantic hit for Blood, Sweat & Tears. *—Bill Dahl*

● **Greatest Hits & Rare Classics** / Oct. 14, 1991 / Motown ◆◆◆◆
Brenda Holloway was Motown's second big solo female star, but she spent even less time at the label than Mary Wells. A hard-edged, gospel-tinged belter, Holloway scored two Top 20 hits in the mid-'60s with "Every Little Bit Hurts" and "When I'm Gone," and her single "You've Made Me So Very Happy" was later a huge smash for Blood, Sweat & Tears. Holloway lasted on Motown until 1967, then departed after becoming a born-again Christian. This album includes her biggest singles for Tamla, plus some other good, though not necessarily classic, 1960s soul numbers. *—Ron Wynn*

Buddy Holly (Charles Hardin Holley)

b. Sep. 7, 1936, Lubbock, TX, **d.** Feb. 3, 1959, Mason City, IA
Guitar, Vocals / Rock 'n' Roll, Rockabilly, Pop-Rock
An enormously important and influential performer, Buddy Holly started in his native Texas doing country music with boyhood friend Bob Montgomery, eventually adding R&B numbers to the set list after meeting Elvis Presley. He recorded early rockabilly sides in Nashville, resulting in the Decca singles "Blue Days, Black Nights" (April 1956) and "Modern Don Juan" (December 1956). But success didn't come until he formed the Crickets and recorded in Norman Petty's New Mexico studio, producing the No. 1 hit "That'll Be the Day" (May 1957). Holly and Petty experimented in the studio, utilizing double-tracking ("Words of Love" [June 1957]), different forms of echo ("Peggy Sue" [September 1957], a second gold-selling Top Ten hit), and close-miking techniques, now commonplace in the industry. Holly recorded under his own name and the name of the Crickets interchangeably ("That'll Be the Day" was credited to the group, "Peggy Sue" to him alone). With the Crickets, he had the further chart hits "Oh, Boy!" (October 1957) (another Top Ten), "Maybe Baby" (February 1958), and "Think It Over"/ "Fool's Paradise" (May 1958), while "Rave On" (April 1958) was a Holly "solo" hit.

Holly went solo for real during 1958, however, marrying and relocating to New York. He charted with "Early in the Morning" (July 1958) and "Heartbeat" (November 1958), and released "It Doesn't Matter Anymore"/"Raining in My Heart" (January 1959) before embarking on the Winter Dance Party package tour, during which, on February 3, he, the Big Bopper, and Ritchie Valens were killed in an airplane crash.

After Holly's death, much of his earlier pre-Crickets music was overdubbed by Petty, using the Fireballs, to keep up with fan demand for more product. In England, where "It Doesn't Matter Anymore" went to No. 1 in the wake of his death, Holly continued to score hits through the mid-'60s, and he exerted tremendous influence on the developing beat groups both for his music and for his self-contained approach to his work—writing his own songs, playing them with his own group. As late as 1978, Holly could still top the UK charts with a hits collection, *20 Golden Greats.*

Buddy Holly's moment in the spotlight lasted barely 18 months, and the movie version of his life story only got it about half right, but his music still sounds fresh and continues to influence musicians to this day. *—Cub Koda & William Ruhlmann*

☆ **The Chirping Crickets** / 1957 / MCA ◆◆◆◆◆
The debut album by the Crickets and the only one featuring Buddy Holly released during his lifetime, *The "Chirping" Crickets* contains the group's No. 1 single "That'll Be the Day" and its Top 10 hit "Oh, Boy!" Other Crickets classics include "Not Fade Away," "Maybe Baby," and "I'm Looking for Someone to Love." The rest of the 12 tracks are not up

to the standard set by those five, but those five are among the best rock 'n' roll songs of the 1950s or ever, making this one of the most significant album debuts in rock 'n' roll history, ranking with *Elvis Presley* and *Meet the Beatles*. — *William Ruhlmann*

That'll Be the Day / 1958 / Decca ♦♦
This album consists of material Buddy Holly recorded prior to his breakthrough with "That'll Be the Day" in 1957. On songs like "Blue Days—Black Nights," he adopts a distinctly rockabilly feel, though "Rock Around with Ollie Vee" is a lost classic. The album also includes the earlier, more country-oriented version of "That'll Be the Day." There is practically no Holly that is without merit, but this skimpy album is largely of historical interest. (Originally released on LP by Decca Records [as Decca 8707] in April 1958, *That'll Be the Day* was reissued, with the song "Ting-a-Ling" deleted, under the title *The Great Buddy Holly* on the Decca subsidiary Vocalion [as Vocalion 73811] in October 1967. It was reissued on CD under its second title on MCA [as MCA 31037] in June 1988.) — *William Ruhlmann*

Buddy Holly / 1958 / MCA ♦♦♦♦
When Buddy Holly and the Crickets broke through nationally in 1957, they were marketed by Decca Records as two different acts whose records were released on two different Decca subsidiaries—Brunswick for Crickets records, Coral for Holly records. But there was no real musical distinction between the two, except perhaps that the "Crickets" sides had more prominent backup vocals. Nevertheless, coming three months after *The "Chirping" Crickets*, this was the debut album credited to Buddy Holly. It featured Holly's Top 10 single "Peggy Sue" plus several songs that have turned out to be standards—"I'm Gonna Love You Too," "Listen to Me," "Everyday," "Words of Love," and "Rave On." The rest of the 12 tracks weren't as distinctive, though Holly's takes on such rock 'n' roll hits as "Ready Teddy" and "You're So Square (Baby, I Don't Care)" provide an interesting contrast with the more familiar versions by Elvis Presley. This was the final new album featuring Holly to be released during his lifetime. Every subsequent album was an archival or posthumous-collection. (Originally released on LP by Coral Records [as Coral 57210] on February 20, 1958, *Buddy Holly* was reissued on CD by MCA Records in 1988.) — *William Ruhlmann*

The Great Buddy Holly / 1968 / MCA ♦♦
This ten-song, 22-minute album consists of material Buddy Holly recorded prior to his breakthrough with "That'll Be the Day" in 1957. On songs like "Blue Days—Black Nights," he adopts a distinctly rockabilly feel, though "Rock Around with Ollie Vee" is a lost classic. The album also includes the earlier, more country-oriented version of "That'll Be the Day." There is practically no Holly that is without merit, but this skimpy album is largely of historical interest. (Originally released as an 11-track LP under the title *That'll Be the Day* by Decca Records [as Decca 8707] in April 1958, *The Great Buddy Holly* was reissued, with the song "Ting-a-Ling" deleted, on the Decca subsidiary Vocalion [as Vocalion 73811] in October 1967. It was reissued on CD under its second title on MCA [as MCA 31037] in June 1988.) — *William Ruhlmann*

20 Golden Greats / 1978 / MCA ♦♦♦♦
Originally released in Great Britain, where it topped the charts, *20 Golden Greats* helped lead the Buddy Holly revival of the late 1970s that also included a biography and a feature film. It is a good, concise collection of Holly's best-known recordings and, at the time of its release, was much needed in the American market, though it has since been superseded by the 1993 double-CD *The Buddy Holly Collection*. (Originally released in the UK in February 1978, and in the US in July 1978.) — *William Ruhlmann*

☆ **The Complete Buddy Holly** / 1979 / MCA ♦♦♦♦♦
In the wake of the No. 1 British ranking for *20 Golden Greats* in 1978 and the release of the feature film *The Buddy Holly Story*, MCA UK assembled this six-LP box set (which finally was released in the US in February 1981). It traces Buddy Holly's career from his country & western duo with Bob Montgomery in 1954/1955 to his 1956 Nashville sessions for Decca Records, the Clovis, New Mexico, recordings with the Crickets and producer Norman Petty that launched his career in 1957, the New York sessions of 1958, the final 1958 demo recordings, the various posthumously overdubbed versions of the demos, and other assorted rarities. In other words, all the material that Decca/MCA previously had spread across seven LPs—*The "Chirping" Crickets*, *Buddy Holly*, *That'll Be the Day*, *Reminiscing*, *Showcase*, *Holly in the Hills*, and *Giant*—between 1957 and 1969 (not counting the many compilations) was here, plus more. The box also contained an extensive scrapbook, lots of liner notes, and a detailed discography. It was, thus, the state of the art in box sets just prior to the CD era, and given Holly's importance in the history of rock 'n' roll, an essential album for any serious collector. With the passing of the LP era, it is out of print, and MCA claims to be gathering more unreleased material for some comparable box set, though years go by without its appearing. Meanwhile, if you needed one record album to demonstrate what the most popular

music of the second half of the 20th century sounded like, this would be it. — *William Ruhlmann*

For the First Time Anywhere / 1983 / MCA ♦♦♦♦
When this album was originally released in 1983, it was a major revelation in collector's circles. Here were the original, undubbed versions of eight songs that had appeared on posthumous Holly albums like *Reminiscing*, *Showcase* and others with overdubbed backing provided by the Fireballs and producer Norman Petty, along with two rarities to pad things out. And hearing the stripped-down Holly minus the audio coverups and beefups revealed strong (and sometimes superior) efforts all by themselves without the assistance. With future Cricket Jerry Allison on drums, a set of revolving bass players, and Sonny Curtis handling lead guitar chores on three tracks, Holly blasts through some bona fide Texas rockabilly here. Four of the eight tracks come from Buddy's pen, and these early efforts ("Rock-a-Bye Rock," "Because I Love You," "Changing All Those Changes," and "I'm Gonna Set My Foot Down") are sign pointers toward his later, more commercial style; in this case we get stripped-down, elemental pop tunes disguised as rockabilly ravers and country ballads. The collection is bookended with two more tracks, the original studio swipe of "Maybe Baby" and "That's My Desire," a ballad from the 1958 New York session that produced "Rave On." Although the overdubbing done to Holly's music made sense from a commercial standpoint at the time, this collection only whets your appetite to hear more of the real thing. — *Cub Koda*

★ **From the Original Master Tapes** / 1985 / MCA ♦♦♦♦♦
From the Original Master Tapes is the best single-disc collection of Buddy Holly, featuring 20 of his biggest hits. Although the songs aren't presented in chronological order, the disc flows well, running through every one of his hits and all of his best-known songs—"That'll Be the Day," "Peggy Sue," "Oh, Boy!," "Maybe Baby," "Rave On," "Think It Over," "Heartbeat," "It Doesn't Matter Anymore," "Raining in My Heart," "Everyday," "Not Fade Away," "Well . . . All Right," and many others. A few terrific songs are missing, but *From the Original Master Tapes* remains a first-rate introduction and a nearly definitive retrospective of Holly's brief career. — *Stephen Thomas Erlewine*

☆ **The Buddy Holly Collection** / Sep. 28, 1993 / MCA ♦♦♦♦♦
The first comprehensive, remastered CD retrospective of Holly's work, including early tracks recorded in the Holly family garage, the Owen Bradley-produced singles, all the rockin' hits, orchestrated ballads, and tracks overdubbed with instrumentation after Holly's tragic death. Two discs, solid liner notes. — *Roch Parisien*

Hollywood Flames

f. 1949, Los Angeles, CA
Doo Wop
Long-lasting Los Angeles doo wop aggregation with a very fluid personnel roster. Bobby Day was one of the group's founders in 1950, and they recorded prolifically for Hollywood, Specialty, Lucky, Swingtime, Money, and other firms before cutting their one major hit, the rocking "Buzz Buzz Buzz," in 1957 for Ebb Records. Earl Nelson, who was later half of Bob And Earl, sang lead on the tune, and some of their subsequent Ebb 45s were rocking novelties. Day went on to solo success with "Rockin' Robin," and the group managed one more chart item, "Gee," for Chess in 1961 with Donald Height as lead. — *Bill Dahl*

● **The Hollywood Flames** / Aug. 3, 1992 / Specialty ♦♦♦♦
Though not in a class with the Moonglows, the Five Satins, or the Platters, the Hollywood Flames were a solid doo wop group that should have been much better known. The only song on this CD that was a major hit is the infectious "Buzz Buzz Buzz." Otherwise, listeners are treated to excellent material that fell through the cracks, which ranges from invigorating uptempo songs like "Strollin' on the Beach," "A Little Bird," and "Crazy," to such engaging ballads as "Give Me Back My Heart," "A Star Fell," and "My Confession." While "Frankenstein's Den" shows that the Flames could be as much fun as the Coasters, the atypical and previously unreleased "This Heart of Mine" is as brooding as something Bobby "Blue" Bland would do. For doo wop aficionados who only know the Flames for "Buzz Buzz Buzz," this collection demonstrates that they had many other inspired moments. — *Alex Henderson*

Eddie Holman

b. Jun. 3, 1946, Norfolk, VA
Vocals / Soul
Holman's 1970 No. 2 smash "Hey There Lonely Girl," with its creamy falsetto vocals and lush Philadelphia soul arrangement, is one of the most well-remembered one-shot soul hits. Actually, Holman had been recording since the early '60s, scoring some minor hits with "This Can't Be True" (1965) and "Am I a Loser (From the Start)" (1966). In 1969, he hooked up with Philadelphia producer Peter DeAngelis, best known for his work with teen idols Fabian and Frankie Avalon. His arrange-

ments for Holman, however, rivaled Gamble & Huff's in quality, yielding some other minor R&B hits in 1969 and 1970 with "I Love You," "Don't Stop Now," and "Cathy Called," as well as a decent album in 1970. Most identified with his rich falsetto, Holman actually sang in a much more traditional vocal range on much of his material, some of which was written by himself or his wife Sheila. He largely vanished from sight after 1970, though he recorded for several labels in the 1970s. —*Richie Unterberger*

● **I Love You** / 1970 / Varese Sarabande ◆◆◆◆
First-class romantic soul, featuring Holman's swooping vocals and lush Philly string and backup vocal arrangements. Includes "Hey There Lonely Girl" and his other minor R&B hits from the same period. The CD reissue adds three non-LP cuts from 1969 and 1970 singles. —*Richie Unterberger*

Holsapple-Stamey

f. 1991
Power Pop, Jangle-Pop
During the early '80s, guitarist/vocalist Chris Stamey and keyboardist/guitarist/vocalist Peter Holsapple led the dB's, one of the premier jangle-pop bands of the American pop universe. Stamey left the group in 1983, but Holsapple led the band until its final album, 1987's *The Sound of Music*. Four years after the dB's broke up, Holsapple and Stamey reunited to record an album that was in the vein of their previous collaborations. Released in 1991, *Mavericks*—the only album they ever released as a duo—received good reviews but didn't sell well. After the release of *Mavericks*, Stamey returned to his solo career and Holsapple formed the Continental Drifters with his wife Susan Cowsill. In 1994, Holsapple re-formed the dB's and the group released *Paris Avenue* later in the year. —*Stephen Thomas Erlewine*

Mavericks / 1991 / Rhino ◆◆◆◆
A charming, low-key, power-pop effort, "Geometry" is a perfect Gary Lewis & the Playboys-style sendup. "Angels" is pure power-pop magic. The softer acoustic numbers, "Close Your Eyes" and "Anymore," recall the duo's work on *Repercussions*. —*Rick Clark*

Honey Cone

f. 1969, Los Angeles, CA, **db.** 1972
Soul
This female trio formed in Los Angeles in 1969. They were all experienced background vocalists. Carolyn Willis had been in the Girlfriends and Bob B. Soxx & the Blue Jeans; Edna Wright was Darlene Love's sister and had sung in the Blossoms and Bob B. Soxx & the Blue Jeans, and Shellie Clark had been an Ikette and regular on *The Jim Nabors Hour* in 1969 and 1970. They were signed by legendary songwriters Holland-Dozier-Holland to their Hot Wax label. They had their first major hit in 1969 with "Girls It Ain't Easy," then garnered two consecutive R&B chart toppers in 1971 with "Want Ads" and "Stick-Up." "Want Ads" proved a '70s standard, also topping the pop charts. The Honey Cone scored two more R&B hits, "One Monkey Don't Stop No Show" and "The Day I Found Myself" in 1971 and 1972, before things began to slow down. They continued on Hot Wax through 1972. Wright later recorded as a solo act. —*Ron Wynn*

● **Greatest Hits** / 1990 / Fantasy ◆◆◆◆
One of the finest girl groups of the early '70s, Honey Cone was often compared to Martha & the Vandellas for a number of reasons. The fact that the label they recorded for, Hot Wax/Invictus, was owned by former Motown producers/songwriters Holland/Dozier/Holland made it an obvious comparison. And also, the robust nature of Honey Cone's harmonies certainly bring the Vandellas to mind. On "Want Ads," "Stick Up," "One Monkey Don't Stop No Show," and other hits included on this superb CD, the singers effectively combine sweetness and grit—pop sleekness and gospel-influenced soulfulness. To be sure, Honey Cone could pack quite a punch emotionally and harmonically. But as much potential as Honey Cone had, its success was short-lived—and the singers were gone from the charts by 1974. With its albums long out of print, *Greatest Hits* can serve as a fine introduction to Honey Cone's soul/pop legacy. —*Alex Henderson*

The Honeycombs

f. 1963, London, England, **db.** 1967
British Invasion
Mostly renowned for their 1964 Top Five hit "Have I the Right," the Honeycombs were pretty much a front for producer Joe Meek and their songwriting-management team of Ken Howard and Alan Blaikley. With bee-sting guitar leads and lead singer Dennis O'Dell's wobbling vocals, which sounded like a Gene Pitney unable to hold notes, "Have I the Right" was a single that you either loved or hated, but couldn't forget. The relatively faceless group afforded Meek perhaps his fullest artistic expression in the studio; all the Honeycombs' singles and

albums feature vari-speed vocals, ghostly organ, unpredictable clavoline runs, majestically thudding drums, and super-compressed sonics. The group managed a couple more minor American hits, "Is It Because" and the thrilling "I Can't Stop," as well as another British Top 20 hit, "That's the Way," and cut quite a few singles and two albums before Meek's death in early 1967 effectively finished the group as well. The Honeycombs' material can be annoyingly cloying and lightweight, but the eerie melodies and production continue to fascinate. —*Richie Unterberger*

● **The Honeycombs** / 1964 / Repertoire ◆◆◆◆
Most famed for their 1964 one-shot British Invasion hit "Have I the Right" and for being the first rock band of any renown to feature a female drummer, the Honeycombs recorded a surprising amount of material in the mid-'60s. Even for collectors, this definitely falls into the "guilty pleasure" category. Lead singer Dennis O'Dell's wobbly voice sounds like a speeded-up Gene Pitney, and the material, though peppy and catchy, is exceedingly trite and innocuous. The group's chief asset, actually, was producer Joe Meek, who found the band to be a perfect vehicle for his eccentric production techniques. Meek used compression to the point of squashing, and used all manners of odd vari-speed vocals, bee-stinging guitars, tinny keyboards, and echo to achieve a sound that was quite otherworldly by 1964 standards. Besides "Have I the Right," this 1964 debut LP includes the British Top 20 hit "That's the Way" (featuring drummer Honey Lantree on vocals) and the ghostly ballads "Without You It Is Night" and "This Too Shall Pass Away," though most of the rest of the material is slight. This 1990 reissue adds seven bonus tracks from non-LP singles, including a German recording of "Have I the Right" and the manic, irresistible "I Can't Stop," which was a minor hit for the band in the US. —*Richie Unterberger*

All Systems Go / 1965 / Repertoire ◆◆◆
Despite downwardly spiraling commercial fortunes, the Honeycombs recorded a second album in 1965 that featured as many intriguing production flourishes and oddball British pop songs as their first effort. No hits were included on this LP—and be warned that the version of their minor hit single "I Can't Stop" (probably their best song) featured here is an inferior, drastically slower remake. This album also includes a mighty obscure ballad by Ray Davies, "Emptiness," that was never recorded by the Kinks (or any other artist but the Honeycombs, for that matter). It's not much of a song, but it's a find for Kinks fanatics. The record's highlights are the sparkling guitars of "Love in Tokyo" and the soulful ballad "Something I Got to Tell You" (featuring drummer Honey Lantree on vocals), which sounds like an honest-to-God hit-that-never-was. The CD reissue of the album adds six non-LP cuts from 1965-66 singles. The best of these are the tense, overwrought ballad "Should a Man Cry?" and the uptempo "Can't Get Through to You," on which producer Joe Meek took his vari-speed vocals and neurotic rhythms to their farthest extremes. —*Richie Unterberger*

Best of the Honeycombs / 1988 / PRT ◆◆◆
The German Repertoire label has reissued both of the Honeycombs' studio LPs with bonus tracks; oddly, they don't include quite a few of the group's A-sides. All six of those missing singles can be found on this reissue, along with most of their other best-known songs. Two of these A-sides are standouts: "Is It Because," a small hit in the UK, is a driving number, and "Eyes" one of the spookiest productions from a man (Joe Meek) who specialized in them. If you pick this up thinking you'll forego the fanatically repackaged CDs for a 14-song greatest hits collection of this interesting but minor British Invasion band, be warned: the version of "I Can't Stop," the minor US hit that was their best song, included here is not the original, but an inferior remake from their second album. —*Richie Unterberger*

The Hoodoo Gurus

f. 1981, Sydney, Australia
Alternative Pop-Rock, Power Pop
Like most bands, Australia's Hoodoo Gurus were largely the product of their influences; unlike most bands, however, the Hoodoos channeled their inspiration from the vast entirety of the American pop cultural landscape, drawing on such disparate sources as B-movies, bad sitcoms, and junk food—in tandem with the usual suspects like garage rock, power pop and surf—to create a distinctly kitschy and catchy sound.

Formed in Sydney in 1981, Le Hoodoo Gurus (as they were originally dubbed) were led by singer-songwriter Dave Faulkner, who along with drummer James Baker previously served as a member of the short-lived Perth punk unit the Victims (best known for the autobiographical single "Television Addict"). Ex-Scientist Rod Radalj and Kimble Rendall rounded out the group's initial lineup, and their unique sound (three guitars, no bass)—along with Faulkner's infectious songs—quickly earned them a record deal. After issuing the 1982 debut single "Leilani," both Radalj and Rendall quit, and were replaced by former Super-K guitarist Brad Sheppard and bassist Clyde Bramley.

In 1983, the Hoodoo Gurus (having dropped the French article) recorded their excellent debut record *Stoneage Romeos;* dedicated to luminaries like *F-Troop's* Larry Storch and *Green Acres'* pig Arnold Ziffel, the album offered such trash-pop treats as the single "I Want You Back,"In the Echo Chamber," and "I Was a Kamikaze Pilot." Mark Kingsmill replaced Baker in 1985, leaving Faulkner the band's sole founding member. He responded by writing an even stronger batch of tunes for 1985's college-radio smash *Mars Needs Guitars!,* an album highlighted by the superb single "Bittersweet" and marked by a widening scope that touched base with demented hillbilly humor ("Hayride to Hell") and crazed surf ("Like Wow—Wipeout").

With 1987's *Blow Your Cool,* the Hoodoos appeared poised for the big time; their tourmates, the Bangles, even contributed to the singles "What's My Scene" and "Good Times." However, the album failed to register beyond alternative radio, and Bramley exited, replaced by onetime Divinyl Rick Grossman. 1989's *Magnum Cum Louder* didn't fare much better—although the singles "Come Anytime," "Another World," and "Baby Can Dance" all garnered significant airplay—while 1991's *Kinky* featured "Miss Freelove '69," a smirking look at flower-power romance, which was the latest in a long line of near-hits. After a three-year hiatus, the Hoodoo Gurus returned with the harder-edged *Crank,* produced by Ed Stasium; *Blue Cave* followed in 1996. *—Jason Ankeny*

Stoneage Romeos / 1983 / A&M ✦✦✦✦
Their debut effort is '60s garage-punk heaven. Highlights include the raveups "Let's All Turn On" and "Tojo"; "Dig It Up," a Cramps-style rocker; "My Girl," a slice of '60s girl/boy guitar pop; and the grunge-ola "I Was a Kamikaze Pilot." Highly recommended. *—Rick Clark*

● **Mars Needs Guitars** / 1985 / Elektra ✦✦✦✦
This is the album that gave this Aussie band their break on the American college radio market, thanks to some classic tracks, "Bittersweet," "Poison Pen," "Death Defying," and "Like Wow, Wipeout." The production is a little unfocused, lacking some of the punch the material demands and the trashy sparks of *Stoneage Romeos.* Nevertheless, the songs reflect considerable growth in the band's vision. *—Rick Clark*

Blow Your Cool! / 1987 / Elektra ✦✦✦✦
The Gurus alternate between appealing tuneful updates of Turtles-style guitar pop ("Good Times," "What's My Scene") and wild workouts like "Where Nowhere Is" and "Hell for Leather." The anthemic "I Was the One" is a standout. The Bangles assist on backup harmonies on this effort. All in all, it's a solid effort. *—Rick Clark*

Magnum Cum Louder / Jun. 1989 / RCA ✦✦✦
The Gurus continue their once-every-two-year release schedule with this consistent effort that showcases vocalist Dave Faulkner's solid songwriting. "Come Anytime" is primo Gurus and the moody "Shadow Me" is also a highlight. Even though *Magnum Cum Louder* doesn't shine as brightly as previous efforts, it's still a stronger album than many efforts by groups mining this genre. *—Rick Clark*

Kinky / Apr. 1991 / RCA ✦✦✦
Kinky blasts out of the gate with pedal-to-the-metal speed, on the hard-rocking put-down of substance abuse, "Head in the Sand." No doubt the inebriated fraternity crowd that worships this band will appreciate Faulkner's sentiments. All in all, this is one of the band's very best releases. *Kinky* portrays a band straddling their playful '60s garage-rock esthetic with issues of adulthood, all the while playing as fiercely as ever. *—Rick Clark*

● **Electric Soup: The Singles Collection** / 1992 / RCA ✦✦✦✦
Electric Soup is a 19-track, Australian-only collection of the band's best singles. And though the Hoodoo Gurus made several fine albums, this collection shows the band in the best light, with their catchiest and best-loved songs. An excellent distillation and the best introduction to this sorely underrated brand of Aussie-pop. *—Chris Woodstra*

Gorilla Biscuit: The B-Sides and Rarities / 1993 / RCA ✦✦✦
Gorilla Biscuits, a companion to the singles collection *Electric Soup,* features another 20 songs, all B-sides and rarities. And though the songs are often not as instantly endearing as the singles, they're certainly not throwaways either, making it essential for hardcore fans and at least interesting for casual listeners. *—Chris Woodstra*

Crank / Sep. 13, 1994 / Zoo ✦✦

Blue Cave / Aug. 1996 / Zoo ✦✦✦
By the time the Hoodoo Gurus released their seventh album, *Blue Cave,* in 1996, the band had settled into a fairly predictable pattern for their records—namely, they hadn't changed their psychedelic, jangly guitar-pop much at all. Occasionally, they add louder guitars to the mix, but they are essentially the same band they were in 1986. That's not necessarily a bad thing—the Hoodoo Gurus have a way with crafting a solid hook. The problem with *Blue Cave* is that they just didn't come up with enough of them. A few songs stand out, but by and large

the album is just a standard Hoodoo Gurus album, albeit an enjoyable one. *—Stephen Thomas Erlewine*

Hootie & the Blowfish

f. 1989, Columbia, SC
Pop-Rock, Adult Alternative Pop-Rock
Hootie & the Blowfish's mainstream pop variation of blues-rock brought the band to the top of the charts in 1995. Formed at the University of South Carolina, the group features lead vocalist/guitarist Darius Rucker, Mark Bryan, Dean Felber, and Jim "Soni" Sonefeld; the name refers to two friends of the band, not Rucker and the group itself. *Cracked Rear View,* the group's first album, was released in the fall of 1994 and a single, "Hold My Hand," worked its way into the Top Ten by the beginning of 1995. Its success propelled the album to No. 1, as well as launching a second hit, "Let Her Cry," which was quickly followed by "Only Wanna Be With You."

Cracked Rear View had become a massive success by the fall of 1995, going platinum several times over. By the time the group released their second album, *Fairweather Johnson,* in the spring of 1996, the debut had sold 13 million copies in the US alone. *Fairweather Johnson* initially didn't replicate that success. It entered the charts at No. 1 and sold two million copies within its first four months of release, but it didn't produce any hit singles on the level of the debut's "Hold My Hand" or "Let Her Cry." *—Stephen Thomas Erlewine*

● **Cracked Rear View** / Jul. 5, 1994 / Atlantic ✦✦✦✦
Hootie and the Blowfish's debut album *Cracked Rear View* was *the* success story of 1994/1995, selling over 12 million copies. It's a startling large number, especially for a new band, but in some ways, the success of the record isn't that surprising. Although Hootie and the Blowfish aren't innovative, they deliver the goods, turning out an album of solid, rootsy folk-rock that have simple, powerful hooks. "Hold My Hand" has a sing-along chorus that epitomizes the band's good-times vibes. None of the tracks transcend their generic status, but they are strong songs for their genre, with crisp chords and bright melodies. Still, the songs wouldn't be convincing without the emotive vocals of Darius Rucker, whose gruff baritone has more grit than the actual songs. At their core, Hootie and the Blowfish is a bar band, but they managed to convince millions of listeners that they were the local bar band, and that's why *Cracked Rear View* was a major success. *—Stephen Thomas Erlewine*

Fairweather Johnson / Apr. 1996 / Atlantic ✦✦✦
Following up a debut as successful as *Cracked Rear View* would be intimidating for most groups, but it had to be especially daunting for such a direct, straightforward combo as Hootie & the Blowfish. What made *Cracked Rear View* such a success was its very unpretentiousness; how each song sounded like it was the crowd-pleaser from the local bar band. Hootie & the Blowfish haven't lost that universal appeal on their second album, *Fairweather Johnson,* but they have been able to add more weight to their music. While the essential formula of Hootie's music hasn't changed—Darius Rucker still belts out anthemic choruses over interweaving acoustic guitars—the band is stronger and more muscular, giving their simple, direct melodies powerful support. They also have learned how to shade their music with varying dynamics and subtle arrangements, which also adds depth to the band. And behind the bright, sing-along melodies, Rucker has hidden some surprisingly introspective and searching lyrics, tackling everything from racism to heartbreak. Hootie & the Blowfish still have a bit of trouble coming up with a set of consistently engaging songs, but the weakest moments on *Fairweather Johnson* resonate more than those on *Cracked Rear View,* while the best moments eclipse those on the debut. It's a surprisingly assured and effective second album. *—Stephen Thomas Erlewine*

Mary Hopkin

b. May 3, 1950, Pontardawe, Wales
Vocals / Pop, Folk-Rock
It was the British supermodel Twiggy who alerted Paul McCartney to the Welsh singer Mary Hopkin when Apple Records was looking for talent in 1968. The waifish soprano scored a huge, worldwide smash with her first Apple single, the melancholy but rabble-rousing ballad "Those Were the Days," in late 1968; it actually knocked the Beatles' own "Hey Jude" out of the No. 1 position in the UK. Paul McCartney lent Hopkin a further hand by producing her first album, and writing her second single, "Goodbye," which was also a hit. More comfortable with refined, precious ballads and folky pop than rock, Hopkin scored several more hit singles in the UK, although she never entered the American Top 40 again. Her commercial success diminished as Apple's fortunes dwindled in the early '70s. *—Richie Unterberger*

● **Post Card** / 1969 / Apple ✦✦✦✦
Paul McCartney produced this debut album of twee but pretty, roman-

tic pop-folk. Besides "Those Were The Days," the highlights are Donovan's "Lord of the Reedy River" and "The Honeymoon Song," which Paul himself had sung with the Beatles way back in 1963 on the BBC. —*Richie Unterberger*

Earth Song, Ocean Song / 1971 / Apple ✦✦✦✦
More folk-oriented than her first effort, Mary Hopkin's lilting voice soothes the listener like hot tea with honey. Included in this set, which was produced by Tony Visconti, are her interpretations of Ralph McTell's "Streets of London," Cat Stevens' "The Wind" and Gallagher & Lyle's "International." —*James Chrispell*

Those Were the Days / 1972 / Apple ✦✦✦
A greatest hits compilation with all the highlights of Hopkin's career presented. From the title cut, which is worth the price alone, through the lightweight "Goodbye," a song the Beatles passed on, right on through to the end, Mary Hopkin delivers what she is best known for. —*James Chrispell*

Bruce Hornsby

b. Nov. 23, 1954, Williamsburg, VA
Vocals, Piano / Adult Contemporary, Pop-Rock
Hornsby was born in Williamsburg, VA, and grew up in that combination college town and tourist center, later attending the University of Miami and the Berklee School of Music. He then spent years playing in bars and sending demo tapes to record companies. In 1980, he and his brother (and songwriting partner) John Hornsby moved to Los Angeles, where they spent three years writing for 20th Century Fox. There Bruce Hornsby met Huey Lewis, who would eventually produce him and record his material. Hornsby finally signed his band, the Range, to RCA in 1985.

Their debut album, *The Way It Is*, was released in August 1986. It eventually produced three Top 20 hits, the biggest of which was the socially conscious "The Way It Is," which featured Hornsby's characteristically melodic right-hand piano runs. The album stayed in the charts almost a year and a half, and sold two million copies. Hornsby and the Range won the Best New Artist Grammy Award for 1986.

Hornsby's second album, *Scenes from the Southside*, was not as successful as his debut, though it sold a million copies, and produced the Top Ten single "The Valley Road." Hornsby also began to make his mark as a songwriter for others: Huey Lewis had a hit with his "Jacob's Ladder," as did Don Henley with "The End of the Innocence."

Hornsby's third album, *A Night on the Town* (1990), found him trying to break out of his signature sound into other areas. It was less successful than its predecessors but, along with the pianist's extensive session work, it signaled his determination to tackle new musical challenges.

Hornsby worked extensively as a producer and sideman in the early '90s, notably doing temporary duty in the Grateful Dead after their keyboardist, Brent Mydland, died in July 1990, and producing a comeback album for Leon Russell, an idol of Hornsby's. He also became the father of twin sons. This musical turned in his fourth album, *Harbor Lights*, for release in 1993. This solo album, which did not feature his backup band, the Range, went gold, and Hornsby toured the US and Canada through the end of the year. He followed it with a similar effort, *Hot House*, in July 1995. — *William Ruhlmann*

● **The Way It Is** / Aug. 1986 / RCA ✦✦✦✦
One of the best collections of new songs released in the 1980s, performed to perfection by a versatile band led by a seasoned (if new to the listener) artist. The songs provide an American panorama, in terms both of landscape and social mores. This is smart, compassionate music for thinking adults . . . and you can dance to it, too. Includes "The Way It Is" and "Mandolin Rain." — *William Ruhlmann*

Scenes from the Southside / 1988 / RCA ✦✦✦✦
The Way It Is, part two, featuring some wonderful story songs, not only on the hits "Jacob's Ladder" and "The Valley Road," but also "Defenders of the Flag" and "The Road Not Taken." Hornsby continues to mine a rich American vein on this album. — *William Ruhlmann*

A Night on the Town / Jun. 1990 / RCA ✦✦✦
Hornsby's third album found him trying to break out of his signature sound into other areas. It was less successful than its predecessors but, along with the pianist's extensive session work, it signaled his determination to tackle new musical challenges. — *William Ruhlmann*

Harbor Lights / Apr. 6, 1993 / RCA ✦✦✦
Bruce Hornsby dumped the Range with barely any public notice. Yet there is a difference in the music; more than any other Hornsby record, *Harbor Lights* is about playing. It's short on memorable songs and heavy on jazz improvisations. In short, Hornsby has taken the chops he has always had, honed them during his live shows with the Grateful Dead, and applied what he learned to adult contemporary radio. —*Stephen Thomas Erlewine*

Hot House / Jul. 18, 1995 / RCA ✦✦✦
With 1993's *Harbor Lights*, Bruce Hornsby began abandoning the conventional pop-rock structures that had dominated his songwriting, turning toward an open-ended jazz-pop fusion. *Hot House* continues that direction, abandoning the three-to-four minute singles for longer pieces that showcase his musical skills. It's an impressive exercise that would be even more engaging if the actual songs had stronger melodies. —*Stephen Thomas Erlewine*

Hot Tuna

f. Oct. 1970, San Francisco, CA
Rock 'n' Roll, Blues-Rock, Folk-Rock
Hot Tuna (formed October 1970) was an offshoot group led by Jefferson Airplane guitarist Jorma Kaukonen and bassist Jack Casady. The group's self-titled debut was a live recording that covered versions of old blues songs by Rev. Gary Davis and Jelly Roll Morton, as well as some originals that became required listening for those inclined toward the Airplane or Grateful Dead's more laidback material. By the third album, *Burgers*, Hot Tuna increasingly drew upon their rock background, performing extended jams built around Casady's wide, lumbering bass sound and Kaukonen's tastefully texturous lead work. Even though the band seemed perpetually stuck in medium tempo, they were quite capable of generating sparks, which made them a popular concert draw for a number of years. —*Rick Clark*

Hot Tuna / 1970 / RCA ✦✦✦✦
This live set includes some solid originals, in particular the instrumental "Mann's Fate," and versions of tunes by Mississippi John Hurt and the Rev. Gary Davis. Jorma Kaukonen contributes exceptionally tasteful acoustic guitar work. Highlights include "Hesitation Blues" and "Death Don't Have No Mercy." RCA's CD reissue adds five previously unreleased tracks from the same shows that produced the original album, increasing the disc's length by half. The new tracks include Tuna favorites like "Keep Your Lamps Trimmed and Burning" and "Candy Man," both from Davis' songbook, as well as Lightnin' Hopkins' "Come Back Baby." All three would turn up electrified on Tuna's second album, while a studio version of "True Religion" would lead off the third album. —*Rick Clark & William Ruhlmann*

First Pull Up, Then Pull Down / 1971 / RCA ✦✦✦
While the first Hot Tuna album had been an acoustic trio album featuring Jorma Kaukonen, Jack Casady, and Will Scarlet, this second album added violinist Papa John Creach and drummer Sammy Piazza, and most significant, it added electricity. Now, the sound was closer to Kaukonen's features in Jefferson Airplane. The highlight was the eight-minute "Keep Your Lamps Trimmed and Burning," although "Candy Man" also became a concert favorite. — *William Ruhlmann*

● **Burgers** / 1972 / RCA ✦✦✦✦
On this third effort, Hot Tuna turned in some blistering jams with "Sea Child" and "Sunny Day Strut." "Water Song" is a gorgeous instrumental, featuring some wonderful acoustic guitar and electric-bass interplay. David Crosby guests on background vocals. "Keep on Truckin' " was a moderate underground FM hit. —*Rick Clark*

The Phosphorescent Rat / 1973 / RCA ✦✦✦
Hot Tuna's first album made after the breakup of Jefferson Airplane found Jorma Kaukonen taking a firm hand: he's the author of nine out of ten songs. The walking tempos and familiar soaring, psychedelic guitar solos are in place, but much of the music is given over to Kaukonen's reflective lyrics, sung in his matter-of-fact voice, and there are strings on a couple of tracks. The group's fans, devoted as they were to its extended versions of blues standards, seem to have been unimpressed: the album was Hot Tuna's lowest-charting among those released during its 1970-1978 heyday. Probably a lack of enthusiasm at RCA, due to the demise of Jefferson Airplane, didn't help in the album's promotion, either. — *William Ruhlmann*

America's Choice / 1975 / RCA ✦✦✦
Hot Tuna returned to a heavier sound on their fifth album, which, although it again was dominated by Jorma Kaukonen's compositions, leaned more heavily on extended electric-guitar solos and even included a Robert Johnson classic, "Walkin' Blues." Drummer Bob Steeler replaced Sammy Piazza as of this release. The result was a modest recovery from the disappointing sales of *The Phosphorescent Rat*, although not a complete return to form. — *William Ruhlmann*

Yellow Fever / 1975 / RCA ✦✦✦
Hot Tuna's second album of 1975 began with a cover of Jimmy Reed's "Baby, What You Want Me to Do" rendered in the group's characteristic noisy electric-guitar style, an approach that was typical of this more-of-the-same album. By this point, Jorma Kaukonen seemed to have found a balance between his songwriting ambitions and the need to provide springboards for the group's boogie-all-night improvisations. Here, "Sunrise Dance with the Devil" and "Bar Room Crystal Ball" feature

good lyrics and excellent hooks, yet still fit into Hot Tuna's heavy approach. — *William Ruhlmann*

Hoppkorv / 1976 / Grunt ✦✦✦
Unlike recent Hot Tuna albums, *Hoppkorv* found the group acting less as a mouthpiece for guitarist Jorma Kaukonen's compositions and more as a heavy rock cover band, handling such familiar material as Buddy Holly's "It's So Easy" and Chuck Berry's "Talkin' 'Bout You," although "Watch the North Wind Rise" was one of Kaukonen's better tunes. Even on the originals, the tempo had picked up, the arrangements were shorter; nothing here ran as long as five minutes, and the sound had been filled out by the occasional addition of keyboards, second guitar, and background vocals. So, *Hoppkorv* was closer to a straightforward pop-rock album than many Hot Tuna releases, and for that, predictably, it got higher marks from critics, who appreciated the variety, and lower marks from Tuna fans, who found less music to boogie to. — *William Ruhlmann*

Double Dose / 1978 / Grunt ✦✦✦
Hot Tuna, now a quartet with the official addition of keyboardist Nick Buck, released this two-LP live album, its first concert material in seven years, and having thus summed things up, broke up as the album hit record stores. *Double Dose* gave a good sense of mature Hot Tuna as a vehicle for the musical interests of Jorma Kaukonen, who used the entire first side as an acoustic solo set, then included the excellent "Genesis" from his solo album *Quah* on side B. Elsewhere, the electrified group alternated between Kaukonen's best Hot Tuna compositions and blues and rock standards. It was produced by Felix Pappalardi (Cream, Mountain), who gave Hot Tuna its best recorded sound; even though it's a "live" record, there seems to have been a lot of studio overdubbing. — *William Ruhlmann*

Splashdown / 1984 / Relix ✦✦✦
This archival release is taken from a broadcast on New York radio station WQIV-FM on July 25, 1975, and features the duo of guitarist Jorma Kaukonen playing acoustic and bassist Jack Casady performing at the station. At the time, Hot Tuna recently had released its *America's Choice* album, but this set harks back to the group's 1970 debut album, *Hot Tuna*, both in its acoustic format and in the selection of mostly folk-blues standards. The performance also has an informality and intimacy that rivals the debut. Casual fans are likely to find the album redundant, but more fervent followers rejoiced when this album appeared nine years after the broadcast occurred and five years after the group's apparent demise. The album's title is derived from the re-entry of an Apollo spacecraft during the broadcast, which is mixed in with the performance of "Police Dog Blues." — *William Ruhlmann*

Historic Hot Tuna / 1985 / Relix ✦✦
Relix's second Hot Tuna release was another archival work, its two sides containing two KSAN-FM radio broadcasts from the spring and summer of 1971; one side was taped at the station, the other chronicles the band's appearance at the closing of the Fillmore West. In his liner notes, Jorma Kaukonen acknowledges that the band has encountered criticism for releasing such "so-called antique material," but counters that "If you like it, you like it . . . if you don't, you don't." Hardcore Tuna fans will be pleased with the existence on record of these performances by a Hot Tuna that featured Kaukonen (acoustic guitar on side one, electric on side two), Jack Casady, Papa John Creach, and Sammy Piazza. Others may find that the rudimentary sound quality and the generally restrained performing level render this inessential. — *William Ruhlmann*

Pair a Dice Found / Oct. 1990 / Epic ✦✦
Hot Tuna's first new album release in more than a decade, *Pair a Dice Found* was perhaps the band's most commercial, yet poorest-selling major-label effort. Unlike the Hot Tuna of the 1970s, this edition, again fronted by guitarist Jorma Kaukonen and bassist Jack Casady, was not a groove-oriented showcase for Kaukonen's songwriting and guitar prowess on old blues standards. Instead, Kaukonen had only three compositions on the record, while the closest thing to the old repertoire was the Jesse Fuller nugget "San Francisco Bay Blues." Second guitarist Michael Falzarano, in contrast, had five songs, and there was even a cover of the old Barry McGuire folk-rock protest hit "Eve of Destruction." Tuna fans ignored the release, and Epic failed to woo the new audience for whom the record seemed to be intended. — *William Ruhlmann*

Classic Acoustic / Apr. 23, 1996 / Relix ✦✦✦
In 1985, Relix Records released the LP *Historic Hot Tuna*, which consisted of a side's worth of tracks recorded at KSAN-FM on April 30, 1971, with the band in an "acoustic" format, i.e., with Jorma Kaukonen on acoustic guitar, and a side's worth of tracks recorded at the closing of the Fillmore West on July 3, 1971, with the band in an "electric" format. Eleven years later, the label released more complete versions of the two performances on separate CDs. This one presents a 53-minute version of the April 1971 radio show. The material is drawn from the band's first two albums, *Hot Tuna* and *First Pull Up, Then Pull Down*,

the differences being that the former was recorded without drummer Sammy Piazza and violinist Papa John Creach and that the latter was recorded electric. For fans of the first Hot Tuna album, this will be an enjoyable, if nonessential part two. — *William Ruhlmann*

Classic Electric / Apr. 23, 1996 / Relix ✦✦✦
In 1985, Relix Records released the LP *Historic Hot Tuna*, which consisted of a side's worth of tracks recorded at KSAN-FM on April 30, 1971, with the band in an "acoustic" format, i.e., with Jorma Kaukonen on acoustic guitar, and a side's worth of tracks recorded at the closing of the Fillmore West on July 3, 1971, with the band in an "electric" format. Eleven years later, the label released more complete versions of the two performances on separate CDs. This one presents a 56-minute version of the July 1971 concert. The material is drawn from the band's first two albums, *Hot Tuna* and *First Pull Up, Then Pull Down*, the latter recorded only three months earlier. For fans of *First Pull Up, Then Pull Down*, this will be an enjoyable, if nonessential alternate version. — *William Ruhlmann*

House of Freaks
. . . .
f. 1986, Richmond, VA
Group / Rock, Alternative Pop-Rock
House of Freaks were a completely original two-man act—Bryan Harvey and Johnny Hott—who played only guitar and drums, respectively, but achieved a full band sound. Formed in Richmond, VA, in the late '80s, the Freaks specialized in Southern Gothic, provided by Harvey's literary lyrics with references to regional culture. The band debuted on Rhino in 1987 with the *Bottom of the Ocean* EP and quickly followed with *Monkey on a Chain Gang* (Rhino 1987). The more cohesive follow-up, *Tantilla*, showcased their songwriting and unique style. An uneven EP, *To Our Friends*, followed in 1990 and finally gave way to a major-label deal with Giant and *Cakewalk* in 1991. House of Freaks eventually disbanded, but Harvey and Hott continued to work together, chiefly in Gutterball, a side project for them as well as Steve Wynn, formerly of Dream Syndicate, and Bob Rupe of the Silos, which has yielded two albums. — *Denise Sullivan*

Monkey on a Chain Gang / 1987 / Rhino ✦✦✦
Instantly likable pop, strong vocals, and beautiful melodies made it a wonder this two-man band didn't explode during the late '80s. Drummer Johnny Hott's style has a military beat, appropriate to the band's historical, Southern bent. Singer Bryan Harvey is incredibly original and confident. The record still sounds completely fresh. — *Denise Sullivan*

● **Tantilla** / 1989 / Rhino ✦✦✦✦
Folk and pop melodies drive this magnificent album from start to finish. The chorus to "Sun Gone Down" holds up against any great hook, from Nick Lowe to Tommy James. *Tantilla* is pure Southern Gothic, as subjects from religion to the Civil War are addressed and set to a roots-music beat that is handy, tight pop-rock at the core. After so many years, this record has worn quite well. — *Denise Sullivan*

All My Friends / Oct. 1989 / Rhino ✦✦
All their friends joined Bryan Harvey and Johnny Hott in the studio for an inconsequential six-song EP. Harvey reveals a nice knack for the Delta blues on the spare "This Old Town," which could have been at least three times its miniscule, throwaway-track length. — *Denise Sullivan*

Cakewalk / Jan. 1991 / Giant/Reprise ✦✦✦
Still mining Southern gothic for inspiration and making modern roots music, House of Freaks were a bit early for the No Depression movement; "Rocking Chair" would sound just dandy beside anything by Wilco or Son Volt. Yet, on this record, the group tried to push the envelope of what their brand of folk and roots music was about and ended up sounding a little generic, perhaps due to producer Dennis Herring's Timbuk 3 touch. Nonetheless, the charming, Jules Shear-like "Honor Among Lovers" and the Waitsian drinking song "Remember Me Well" stand out. — *Denise Sullivan*

House of Love
. . . .
f. 1986, London, England, **db.** 1994
Alternative Pop-Rock
The post-Smiths guitar-pop of the House of Love was popular for a short time in the late '80s, as many college and alternative rock fans became converts to their mixture of shiny ringing guitars, pseudo-psychedelic melodies, and bursts of noise. The British group formed in 1986; it featured Guy Chadwick (vocals, guitar), Terry Bickers (guitar), Andrea Heukamp (vocals, guitar), Pete Evans (drums), and Chris Groothuizen (bass). Their demo tape attracted the attention of Alan McGee, the head of Creation Records. McGee signed the band for a single, "Shine On," which was released in May of 1987 to some critical acclaim; it and its follow-up, "Real Animal," both sold poorly. Following a tour supporting the singles, Heukamp left the group. Instead of

replacing her, the House of Love continued as a quartet, releasing their untitled debut album in the spring of 1988. Many UK critics called it one of the finest records of the year, and the band built up a cult audience.

The following year the band moved over to PhonoGram Records (PolyGram in the US) and released two singles, "Never" and "I Don't Know Why I Love You," that failed to crack the British Top 40. By the end of 1989, Bickers left the group; he was replaced by Simon Walker. The House of Love's second untitled album (commonly called *Fontana*) was released in early 1990 to lukewarm sales and reviews; the band's revivalist guitar-pop didn't fit in with England's club-conscious pop scene, spearheaded by the Stone Roses and Happy Mondays. After the group's 1990 tour, Walker left the group and was replaced by Andrea Heukamp. The House of Love returned in early 1992 with *Babe Rainbow*, which received favorable reviews, but had weak sales. The continuing lack of commercial success began to wear on the band, leading to their disbandment in 1994. — *Stephen Thomas Erlewine*

● **House of Love ['88]** / 1988 / Creation ✦✦✦✦
This brilliant debut established a pattern oft-imitated: a layered, swirling guitar sound and outstanding songs as well. — *Steve Aldrich*

House of Love ['90] / 1990 / Fontana ✦✦✦
A strong second album, it never quite reaches the highs of their debut. — *Steve Aldrich*

Spy in the House of Love / 1990 / Fontana ✦✦✦
This is a collection of B-sides, outtakes, etc. — *Steve Aldrich*

Babe Rainbow / Aug. 18, 1992 / Fontana ✦✦✦
Three albums back, House of Love was among the first to mine that distinctively British sound of fragile pop harmonies coupled to fuzzy, feedback-drenched guitars. Now that every other UK alternative music group is doing that very thing, House of Love has evolved. Superb, understated melodies still dominate *Babe Rainbow*, but the instrumentation is much more free-flowing and accessible. *Babe Rainbow* is the soundtrack to one of those grey-mood days that leaves you hanging in the balance somewhere between elation and despair. — *Roch Parisien*

House of Pain

f. 1990, Los Angeles, CA
Hip Hop, East Coast Rap, Hardcore Rap
"Jump Around," an impossibly infectious and catchy single, instantly elevated House of Pain from an unknown white hip-hop group to near-stars when it became a massive crossover hit in 1992. It made the band and it also broke the band, consigning them to the level of one-hit wonders. House of Pain continued to release records after their eponymous '92 debut and "Jump Around," yet none of them gained much attention, partially because of the band's self-consciously loutish behavior. Led by rapper Everlast, the group celebrated their Irish-American heritage by wearing green, drinking prodigious amounts of beer, and swearing constantly. It certainly earned them attention at the outset, particularly when it was tied to a single like "Jump Around," but the bottom quickly fell out of their career. The group's second album, 1994's *Same as It Ever Was*, went gold, but it failed to generate a hit single, and by the time of 1996's *Truth Crushed to Earth Shall Rise Again*, the band had been forgotten.

Everlast (b. Erik Schrody, August 18, 1969) became fascinated by hip-hop while he was in high school, eventually becoming part of Ice-T's Rhyme Synidacte. His association with Ice-T led to a contract with Warner Bros., who released his debut album *Forever Everlast* in 1990. After the record bombed, Everlast formed House of Pain with his high school friend Danny Boy (b. Daniel O'Connor) and DJ Lethal (b. Leor DiMant), a Latvian immigrant. Released on Tommy Boy Records, the group's eponymous 1992 debut was co-produced by DJ Muggs, who masterminded Cypress Hill's groundbreaking debut. Muggs gave "Jump Around" its distinctive, incessant beat which merged a deep bass groove with drum loops and Public Enemy-styled sirens. On the back of Kris Kross' spring hit "Jump," "Jump Around" became a huge hit in the summer of 1992, peaking at number three on the pop charts. Both the single's video and the remainder of *House of Pain* celebrated the group's Irish heritage in a tongue-in-cheek fashion that quickly became schtick. Throughout their 1993 tour, the group ran into trouble with promoters and the law, culminating in Everlast's March arrest for possessing an unregistered, unloaded pistol at Kennedy Airport. He was sentenced to community service, and later that year, the group began work on their second album.

Like its predecessor, 1994's *Same As It Ever Was* was produced by DJ Muggs. Upon its summer release, the record was greeted with surprisingly strong reviews and sales, debuting at number 12 on the charts. However, the sales quickly slowed as "On Point" failed to become a hit. Most of the next two years were spent in seclusion, and the group returned in the fall of 1996 with *Truth Crushed to Earth*

Shall Rise Again, a record that was ignored by both the press and the public. — *Stephen Thomas Erlewine*

● **House of Pain** / Jul. 21, 1992 / Tommy Boy ✦✦✦✦
It would be hard for nearly anyone to top the explosive, insanely catchy "Jump Around," so it's no great surprise to find that House of Pain isn't up to the task. At times, HOP comes close to duplicating the intoxicating power of their slamming single, but for the most part, their debut album is a repetitive circle of similar beats, misogyny, racism, and posturing lyrics. But the perfection of "Jump Around" almost makes up for the numerous faults. — *Stephen Thomas Erlewine*

Same as It Ever Was / Jun. 28, 1994 / Tommy Boy ✦✦✦✦
House of Pain's self-titled album had its moments, but on the whole, wasn't very memorable. However, the Irish-American group really blossomed on its far superior and much more hardcore second album, *Same as It Ever Was*. With this album, Everlast changed his style of rapping considerably and unveiled a much more distinctive and recognizable approach. Sounding twisted, damaged, and maniacal, Everlast grabs the listener's attention and refuses to let go on such wildly entertaining fare as "Back from the Dead," "Over There Shit" and "Runnin' Up on Ya." House of Pain's subject matter—namely, their superior rapping skills and the threat they pose to sucker MCs—is far from groundbreaking. But an abundance of strong, clever hooks and Everlast's psycho-like rapping make *Same as It Ever Was* consistently appealing. — *Alex Henderson*

Truth Crushed to Earth Shall Rise Again / Oct. 22, 1996 / Tommy Boy ✦✦✦
Having found its voice on *Same as It Ever Was*, House of Pain delivered an equally captivating effort with its third album, *Truth Crushed to Earth Shall Rise Again*. Being Anglo rappers in a genre that had grown increasingly hostile toward whites, Everlast and Danny Boy encountered their share of racism and bigotry. And they responded by being unapologetically street and hardcore, while bragging about their Irish heritage. On the whole, the album's subject matter isn't very substantial—the group still spends too much time boasting. But as was also the case with *Same as It Ever Was*, the LP is impossible to resist thanks to House of Pain's insanely captivating hooks and Everlast's twisted style of rapping. — *Alex Henderson*

The Housemartins

f. 1984, Hull, England, db. Jun. 1988
Alternative Pop-Rock, Pop-Rock
One of Britain's more popular indie guitar pop groups of the late '80s, the Housemartins' post-Smiths guitar jangle and subtle updating of catchy, melodic British beat groups earned the Hull-based quartet a substantial critical and popular following within the UK. Though the group never gained much more than a cult following in America, their balance of simple, memorable melodies and cutting sarcasm helped them rise into the British Top Ten, as well as earn consistently strong reviews. The Housemartins broke up in 1988, just before they fully broke into the mainstream. The group's lead songwriter, Paul Heaton, formed the Beautiful South the following year, and his new band capitalized on the success of the Housemartins to become one of the more popular UK groups of the early '90s.

Paul Heaton (vocals, guitar) formed the Housemartins with Ted Key (guitar), Stan Cullimore (bass), and Hugh Whitaker (drums) in 1984. From the outset, the group cultivated a distinctly English image, blending a cynical sense of humor with leftist political leanings and low-key, commonplace appearance. In 1985, they signed with Go! Discs and by the end of the year, Key was replaced by Norman Cook. "Happy Hour," the Housemartins' third single, became the group's first hit in the summer of 1986, climbing all the way to No. 3. *Hull 4, London 0*, their debut album, followed shortly afterward and, like the single, it cracked the British Top Ten. At the end of the year, the a cappella "Caravan of Love" became a No. 1 hit.

Due to their success in 1986, the Housemartins were awarded the BPI award for Best Newcomers. Before they recorded their second album, Hugh Whitaker left the band and was replaced by Dave Hemmingway. *The People Who Grinned Themselves to Death* followed later in 1987, spawning the hit singles "Five Get Over Excited" and "Me and the Farmer." Though the Housemartins were developing into one of the most popular bands within Britain, they broke up in the summer of 1988, claming they only intended to stay together for three years. In reality, Heaton and Cook were suffering from creative tensions, as the singer wanted to move into sophisticated jazz-pop while the bassist was eager to explore dance music. This difference in taste became apparent in the groups they formed immediately after the disbandment of the Housemartins. Cook formed Beats International, who had a few hits in the early '90s before Cook became a full-time remixer. With drummer Hemmingway, Heaton formed the Beautiful South, which carried on the aesthetic of the Housemartins, but added more complex melodies and arrangements. Toward the end of 1988, a compilation of Housemartins singles and rarities called *Now That's What I Call Quite Good!* was released. In 1993, original drummer Hugh Whitaker was imprisoned for wounding with intent and arson attacks on a business partner. *—Stephen Thomas Erlewine*

● **London 0 Hull 4** / 1986 / Go! Discs ✦✦✦✦
The Housemartins had a bouncy pop-rock sound that was reminiscent of the British beat groups of the mid-'60s. This album is full of catchy tunes, although the lyrics are sometimes more serious than the music might suggest. *— William Ruhlmann*

The People Who Grinned Themselves to Death / 1987 / Go! Discs ✦✦✦✦
Not quite on par with their debut, their second album nevertheless contains some bright moments of bouncy Brit-pop. The band takes a more abstract lyrical approach but the song craftsmanship can't be denied. The band broke up shortly after its completion. *—Chris Woodstra*

Now That's What I Call Quite Good / 1988 / Go! Discs ✦✦✦✦
A solid collection of singles, B-sides and rarities released only in the UK which, when combined with the two proper albums, represents nearly all of the band's recorded output. Clocking in at over 70 minutes and hitting a lot of the band's highpoints, *Now That's What I Call Quite Good* works quite well as an introduction, though the actual albums should be heard as well. *—Chris Woodstra*

Cissy Houston

b. 1932, Newark, NJ
Vocals / Soul
A terrific soul singer who is known primarily as Whitney Houston's mother rather than for her own considerable talents, Houston was born Emily Drinkard, and began her career as a member of her family's gospel group, the Drinkards. In the early '60s, she joined forces with a floating group of singers, known simply as "the Group" (including at various points Doris Troy and Dee Dee Warwick), to provide backup vocals on numerous soul, pop, and rock sessions. They contributed to many Atlantic sessions in particular, and Atlantic executive Jerry Wexler signed the act to the label in 1967. Named the Sweet Inspirations, they recorded some excellent gospel-flavored soul in the late '60s, managing a few hits (as well as continuing to back up other artists, most notably Aretha Franklin) before Cissy left to go solo at the end of 1969.

Houston recorded an impressive album for Commonwealth United in 1970, *Presenting Cissy Houston*, which yielded a couple small R&B/pop hits, "I'll Be There" and "Be My Baby." Much in the manner of the Sweet Inspirations, although the material consisted of fairly well-worn soul, rock, and pop tunes, the state-of-the-art arrangements and gospelish vocals made them sound fresh. Her contract was sold to Janus Records later in the year, and while she issued a few fine singles until the middle of the 1970s, she never received the support and promotion she deserved. A case in point was her little-known original version of "Midnight Train to Georgia," taken to the top of the charts about a year later by Gladys Knight & the Pips. Houston recorded several albums for Private Stock beginning in the late '70s, as well as continuing her regular work on sessions and commercial jingles. She recorded a duet with daughter Whitney ("I Know Him So Well") in 1987, and cut a duet album with veteran soul singer Chuck Jackson in 1992. *—Richie Unterberger*

● **Midnight Train to Georgia: The Janus Years** / Apr. 25, 1995 / Ichiban Soul Classics ✦✦✦✦
Fine 21-track compilation of almost everything she recorded between 1970 and 1975, including most of her 1970 album *Presenting Cissy Houston*, ten songs that were previously available only on singles, and a couple that were previously unreleased in the US. Highlights include excellent interpretations of two Bacharach-David classics ("I Just Don't Know What to Do with Myself," "This Empty Place") and Tim Hardin's "Hang on to a Dream," as well as the original version of "Midnight Train to Georgia." *—Richie Unterberger*

Penelope Houston

b. San Francisco, CA
Autoharp, Vocals, Melodica / Singer-Songwriter, Alternative Pop-Rock
Houston is one of the most shocking reincarnations from the original punk era. She was the lead singer of the San Francisco band the Avengers, one of the very first full-out American punk acts, opening for the Sex Pistols on the last show of their legendary US tour. After the group broke up in 1979, Houston worked for a time with Howard Devoto, and released a 1986 single fronting the short-lived -30-, finally releasing her debut album in 1988. To the shock of those who remembered her work with the Avengers, Houston had transformed into a folk-rock singer-songwriter with alternative rock sensibilities. As a solo act, her material emphasizes acoustic textures, haunting melodies, and her gentle soprano voice. Popular as a performing act in San Francisco, she has had trouble finding recording deals. Her similar, somewhat more fully

produced second album did not appear until 1993 (a couple cassette-only releases mixing live and studio material appeared in the interim). Fans of singer-songwriters like Suzanne Vega, Shawn Colvin, and Christine Lavin looking for something similar but darker would do well to check Houston out. *—Richie Unterberger*

● **Birdboys** / 1988 / Subterranean ✦✦✦✦
A moody, melodic debut that evokes the spirit of Nick Drake and Sandy Denny with its brooding images of loss. Mandolins, accordion, acoustic bass, and sparse percussion (usually tambourines and bells) almost qualify this as a contemporary folk album, but Houston's biting and somber approach draws from her punk and alternative-rock roots. The writing is inconsistent, and Houston's fragile voice is sometimes not as forceful as the material seems to demand, but overall this is one of the more underrated alternative music statements of the late 1980s. *—Richie Unterberger*

500 Lucky Pieces / 1992 / ID ✦✦✦
One of the tapes Houston released on her own label while she was without a recording contract. This professionally recorded set includes a number of songs that would be re-recorded for 1996's *Cut You*, including "Sweetheart," "White Out," "Fall Back," and "Glad I'm a Girl." A slightly folkier set than usual, it's good, but mostly of interest to serious fans, as much of the material is more widely available in similar versions on CD. If you're interested, though, the tape is available by contacting Id Records at PO Box 422163, San Francisco, CA 94142. *—Richie Unterberger*

The Whole World / Aug. 24, 1993 / Heyday ✦✦✦
Similar in tone to her debut, but bouncier and more engaging, prominently featuring her husband Mel Pappas on mandolin. Mature and introspective works that do their best to examine romance, innocence, aging, and compassion without sounding hackneyed, but it doesn't quite match the haunting power of her first album. *—Richie Unterberger*

Karmal Apple / 1994 / Normal ✦✦✦
One of Houston's more subdued efforts, with characteristically eclectic arrangements sprinkled with autoharp, melodica, mandolin, violin, and cello. There's a constant sense of uneasy suspicion, worry, failed romance, and vague dissatisfaction simmering underneath the pleasing modern folk-rock melodies. These elements alone imbue the set with a lot more interest than the average contemporary folk recording. It's not her best album, but it's a typically solid one, with an occasional light (only occasional, and very light) country touch. Still only available in Europe as of 1996. *—Richie Unterberger*

Cut You / Mar. 5, 1996 / Reprise ✦✦✦
A curious disc in that it's more of a career survey than a collection of newly minted material, although all of these tracks were recorded shortly before the album was issued, as is the standard for new releases. Many of the songs were released in different versions on previous albums, some as long ago as 1988. This could be because it's Houston's first effort to benefit from major-label distribution, meaning that it will mark the first time that many listeners outside of the San Francisco Bay Area will be exposed to her material. That may make it a disappointment for those who've followed her career and have the original versions. But it's a solid set of melodic and inventively arranged folk-rock, with arrangements that differ from the originals in interesting ways that avoid redundancy. It also offers proof that Houston helped pioneer the melodic-yet-hard-hitting alternative rock currently mined by such performers as Liz Phair and Aimee Mann. Ironically, because of the timing of the release, it may be perceived as being just the opposite. *—Richie Unterberger*

Whitney Houston

b. Aug. 9, 1963, Newark, NJ
Vocals / Dance-Pop, Urban, Adult Contemporary, Pop-Rock, Club/Dance
Coming from a solid musical background, this daughter of soul singer Cissy Houston and cousin of Dionne Warwick debuted in 1985. Her first album, *Whitney Houston*, was the first in *Billboard* chart history by a woman to enter at No. 1; it sold 14 million copies. She scored heavily on MTV with classy videos, helping to break the "color barrier" originally knocked down by Michael Jackson. Her second album, *Whitney*, was just as popular, scoring seven consecutive number ones in the US, shattering the previous record held by the Beatles.

After the disappointing performance of her third album, *I'm Your Baby Tonight*, Houston rocketed back to the top of the charts in late 1992 with the soundtrack from her first movie, *The Bodyguard*. The love theme from the movie, a version of Dolly Parton's "I Will Always Love You," broke all previous sales and airplay records, becoming the biggest single in pop music history; it also won her an almost innumerable amount of awards, including several Grammies. With pure pop music melded to stunning beauty, Houston's star shines bright whether she is singing ballads, uptempo dance material, the national anthem, or cola commercials. Almost ten years after her first album, she is one of the biggest stars in pop music. —*Cub Koda & Stephen Thomas Erlewine*

● **Whitney Houston** / 1985 / Arista ◆◆◆◆
The legend of Whitney Houston began with this self-titled album. It marked her shift away from the experimental songs she did with the group Material and a move into heavily produced, very slick urban contemporary and adult pop. Although Houston had learned her craft working in New York nightclubs and singing in a Baptist church in Newark, she was steered into radio-friendly ballads that emphasized style over substance. The album did yield an unprecedented string of No. 1 hits, but "Saving All My Love for You" and "How Will I Know" created an impression of an incredibly talented vocalist using only a minimum of her skills. It also contained one of her few legitimate soul workouts in "The Greatest Love of All." —*Ron Wynn*

Whitney / 1987 / Arista ◆◆◆◆
Whitney Houston became an international star with this album. It sold more than 13 million copies around the world, yielded a string of number hit singles across the board like "How Will I Know," "Saving All My Love for You," and "You Give Good Love," and established Houston as the era's top female star. She has since gone to more than solidify that status, with other hit albums and now a budding film career. While this is a far cry from soul, it's the ultimate in polished, super-produced urban contemporary material. —*Ron Wynn*

I'm Your Baby Tonight / 1990 / Arista ◆◆
While Houston's voice always provides some interesting listening, this is somewhat of a disappointing release, with very few memorable songs. While she attempts to make a larger foray into dance music, she fails to make the crossover impact of artists such as Mariah Carey and Taylor Dayne. The two high points she does reach on this album come in the form of ballads—the uplifting tale of another's love being enough to provide happiness in "All the Man That I Need" and the powerful verses surrounding a love lost through one's own devices in "Miracle." —*Ashley S. Battel*

H.P. Lovecraft

f. 1967, Chicago, IL, **db.** 1969
Psychedelic, Garage Rock
Featuring two strong singers (who often sang dual leads), hauntingly hazy arrangements, and imaginative songwriting that drew from pop and folk influences, H.P. Lovecraft were one of the better psychedelic groups of the late '60s. The band was formed by ex-folkie George Edwards in Chicago in 1967. Edwards and keyboardist Dave Michaels, a classically trained singer with a four-octave range, handled the vocals, which echoed the Jefferson Airplane's in their depth and blend of high and low parts. Their self-titled 1967 LP was an impressive debut, featuring strong originals and covers of early compositions by Randy Newman and Fred Neil, as well as one of the first underground FM radio favorites, "White Ship." The band moved to California the following year; their second and last album, *H.P. Lovecraft II*, was a much more sprawling and unfocused work, despite some strong moments. A spin-off group, Lovecraft, released a couple LPs in the '70s that bore little relation to the first incarnation of the band. —*Richie Unterberger*

H.P. Lovecraft / 1967 / Philips ◆◆◆◆
With the exception of a couple of badly dated tracks, this is one of the best second-division psychedelic albums, with strong material that shows the immediately identifiable Edwards-Michaels vocal tandem at its best. According to the LP notes, the songs were largely inspired by novelist H.P. Lovecraft's "macabre tales and poems of Earth populated by another race." It's more haunting than gloomy, though, with deft touches of folk, jazz, and horns. —*Richie Unterberger*

H.P. Lovecraft II / 1968 / Philips ◆◆◆
Much more progressive than their first effort, the album also showed the band losing touch with some of their most obvious strengths, most notably their disciplined arrangements and incisive songwriting. The arrangements are more swirling and far denser on this follow-up. Not surprisingly, the more concise, dual-harmony numbers that bear the closest resemblance to the first album work best, especially "At the Mountains of Madness." —*Richie Unterberger*

● **At the Mountains of Madness** / 1988 / Edsel ◆◆◆◆
A superb double-album package of all of their studio material. Includes both LPs, historical liner notes, and a 1967 non-LP single (released prior to their debut) that is much poppier than their albums. —*Richie Unterberger*

Live May 11, 1968 / 1991 / Sundazed ◆◆◆
A most impressive document of the band in concert at the Fillmore West, with good, clear sound. Unlike many other groups of the era, H.P. Lovecraft could successfully replicate their fairly intricate vocal and instrumental arrangements on stage. The eight-song set (six from the

first LP, two from the second) features all of their best songs; the extended versions of "Wayfaring Stranger" and "The Drifter" (clocking in at ten and eight minutes, respectively) successfully embellish the original arrangements without succumbing to meandering jamming. Recorded between the first and second albums, the addition of bassist Jeff Boyan's backing harmonies creates subtle differences between the live and studio versions of tunes from the first LP. Lengthy liner notes top off a fine package. —*Richie Unterberger*

The Hudson Brothers

f. 1970, Portland, OR
Power Pop
Those that remember the Hudson Brothers usually think of them as a bubblegum act of sorts, due to the fact that they hosted some comedy-variety TV shows in the mid-'70s. But they were in fact a real group, extremely Anglophile in orientation, with heavy debts to the Beatles and Beach Boys, and occasional hints of the Kinks. In these respects, as well as their harmonies and superficial vocal resemblances to Lennon and McCartney, they echoed other players in the sub-Beatle game, like Badfinger, the Move, and ELO. That might be raising your expectations too high: they weren't nearly as deep or clever as the Move, as infectious or energetic as Badfinger, or even as ambitious as ELO. During their brief mid-'70s vogue, they recorded a few albums for Elton John's Rocket label (some of which were produced by Elton's songwriting partner Bernie Taupin), and managed a few small hits, "So You Are a Star," "Lonely School Year," and "Rendezvous." —*Richie Unterberger*

● **So You Are a Star: The Best of the Hudson Brothers** / 1995 / Varese Sarabande ◆◆◆◆
All three of their mid-chart hits, selections from their 1974-1980 albums, an unreleased song, a 1967 garage single they recorded as The New Yorkers, and three 1994 recordings. —*Richie Unterberger*

Human League

f. 1977, Sheffield, England
Dance-Pop, Synth-pop, New Wave, Club/Dance, New Romantic
The Human League scored a number of hits in the '80s that crossed the line between post-new wave rock and dance-pop, though that was a very different style from the music the group played at first. The Human League was formed in Sheffield, England, in 1977 by synthesizer players Martin Ware (b. May 19, 1956) and Ian Marsh (b. Nov 11, 1956), along with Addy Newton and singer Philip Oakey (b. Oct 2, 1955). Newton was soon replaced by Adrian Wright and the lineup held for the first two Human League albums, *Reproduction* (1979) and *Travelogue* (1980).

Ware and Marsh left the Human League in October 1980 (they subsequently formed Heaven 17). Oakey and Wright recruited bassist Ian Burden (b. Dec 24, 1957) and backup singers Joanne Catherall (b. Sep 18, 1962) and Susanne Sulley (b. Mar 22, 1963), resulting in a much more pop-sounding version of the band. Synth player Jo Callis (b. May 2, 1955) was added to the group.

The Human League's third album, *Dare*, was its commercial and international breakthrough. Released in October 1981 in the UK and in February 1982 in the US, it went to No. 1 in England and No. 3 in the US, largely on the strength of the single "Don't You Want Me," which topped the charts in both countries. Subsequent hits in 1982 and 1983 included "(Keep Feeling) Fascination" and "Mirror Man."

Hysteria (1984), was far less successful, and the group agonized over a follow-up. *Crash* appeared in 1986, produced by Jimmy Jam and Terry Lewis (responsible for Janet Jackson's *Control*, among other hits). Largely a studio creation, it was nevertheless successful, producing the No. 1 hit "Human." The Human League's sixth album, *Romantic?*, was released in 1990. —*William Ruhlmann*

Travelogue / 1980 / Virgin ◆◆
The Human League's second album, *Travelogue*, was its first to be released in the US. (Not that you would have noticed at the time, given the limited distribution; the album subsequently was picked up for reissue by Virgin/Atlantic in 1988). It was also the last to feature the nearly original lineup of Martyn Ware, Ian Marsh, Philip Oakey, and Adrian Wright. Already, the band's synthesizer textures and Oakey's mannered voice were starting to lean in a pop direction, but much of this album retained the austere tone of earlier synthesizer groups such as Kraftwerk and Tangerine Dream. The conflicting musical directions led to a split in the band after this album, with Ware and Marsh forming Heaven 17 and Oakey and Wright reorganizing a new version of the Human League. Ironically, both ventures were more pop-oriented than before. —*William Ruhlmann*

Dare / 1981 / A&M ◆◆◆◆
Martin Rushent's fresh, clean production keeps the synthesized music from being too cluttered, while Philip Oakey's voice is used for its self-consciously melodramatic effect and contrasted with the untrained

singing of Joanne Catherall and Susanne Sulley. The hits are "Don't You Want Me" and (in England) "The Sound of the Crowd," "Love Action (I Believe in Love)," and "Open Your Heart," but the album also works as a consistent piece. — *William Ruhlmann*

Love and Dancing / 1982 / A&M ✦✦
Credited to "The League Unlimited Orchestra" in homage to Barry White's Love Unlimited Orchestra, *Love and Dancing* carried a sleeve note that read, "This album contains instrumental versions of previously released songs by the Human League specially remixed and produced by Martin Rushent." (Actually, one song was new, and there are a few vocal choruses.) The songs had been released previously on *Dare* so if you always thought "Don't You Want Me" was a great track with obnoxious vocals, this is the album for you. — *William Ruhlmann*

Fascination! / 1983 / A&M ✦✦✦
Instead of following *Dare*, its internationally successful third album, with another full-length effort, the Human League re-emerged with this under-27-minute, six-track EP, which consists of the one new track on its *Love and Dancing* remix album, plus the A—and B-sides of its post-*Dare* singles "(Keep Feeling) Fascination" (in two versions) and "Mirror Man." Both those songs were hits in the pop-synthesizer style of *Dare*, but the group's failure to produce a new album after 19 months was an indication of the instability it would suffer for the rest of its career. — *William Ruhlmann*

Hysteria / 1984 / Virgin ✦✦✦
The Human League's two-and-a-half-year effort to come up with a follow-up to *Dare* resulted in *Hysteria*, which tinkered with the hit formula, demoting producer Martin Rushent to computer programmer on only a few cuts. It was probably a mistake to release the politically oriented "The Lebanon" as the first single, especially in the US, where the country is called merely "Lebanon" and where the band was known primarily for the romantic "Don't You Want Me." That song wasn't typical of the album, which featured a remake of the earlier hit ("Don't You Know I Want You"), but was mostly filled with nondescript synhesizer dance tracks that barely deserved to be called songs. *Hysteria* was the Human League's opportunity to consolidate their worldwide success with *Dare;* instead, they slumped slightly at home and put their career in jeopardy in America. — *William Ruhlmann*

Crash / 1986 / A&M ✦✦✦
The Human League turned to American R&B producers Jimmy Jam and Terry Lewis in the wake of their success with Janet Jackson's *Control,* and the combination brought the group its second No. 1 hit with the Jam-Lewis composition "Human," which harked back to the earlier "Don't You Want Me," albeit with a gentler tone. The album's second single, the *Control*-soundalike "I Need Your Loving," was also a Jam-Lewis song (as was the UK-only third single, "Love Is All That Matters"), but the bulk of the album was made up of group-written songs with appealing backing tracks that maintained their dance appeal while eschewing the overtly synthesized sound of previous albums. That made *Crash* an improvement over the lackluster *Hysteria,* but still not on a par with *Dare*. — *William Ruhlmann*

● **Greatest Hits** / 1988 / A&M ✦✦✦✦
Greatest Hits reminds that popular tracks like "Don't You Want Me" successfully bridged the gap between dance, pop, and rock audiences. With "Being Boiled," the 16-strong collection even offers a token sample of the League's earliest, more experimental machine music approach—although their atmospherically funereal cover of the Righteous Brothers' "You've Lost That Loving Feeling" should also have made the cut. Includes the rather engaging new recording "Stay with Me Tonight" from the currently active version of Phil Oakey and friends. — *Roch Parisien*

Romantic? / Sep. 1990 / A&M ✦✦
The Human League reorganized in the four years it took to follow *Crash,* stripping down to a trio of singers, Philip Oakey, Joanne Catherall, and Susan Ann Sulley, then adding guitarist Russell Dennett and keyboard player Neil Sutton. They also shed producers Jimmy Jam and Terry Lewis, returning to old friend Martin Rushent on a couple of tracks, among them the Top 40 hit "Heart like a Wheel." But eight years after "Don't You Want Me," the group's pop-synthesizer sound seemed dated. Although some songs showed a little spirit, especially when Catherall and Sulley were used more prominently, all of this had been done before, and better. *Romantic?* spent only two weeks in the British charts and didn't chart at all in America. — *William Ruhlmann*

Octopus / Jan. 27, 1995 / East West ✦✦✦
The Human League hadn't learned any new tricks in the four-plus years it took to craft another one of their synth-pop collections. The best track was the most unusual, when Philip Oakey took a backseat and let one of his fellow vocalists—probably Joanne Catherall, though her singing is interchangeable with Susan Ann Sulley's—handle a delicately arranged love song, "One Man in My Heart." But more typical was the song that followed it, "Words," in which Oakey whined at con-

siderable length about undetailed wrongs done to him in childhood. Even with a good dance beat, such stuff was hard to stomach, and most of the blips and blats that filled up the tracks had been used to better purpose on earlier recordings. — *William Ruhlmann*

Humble Pie
....

f. 1968, Essex, England, **db.** 1975
Blues-Rock, Hard Rock
A showcase for former Small Faces frontman Steve Marriott and onetime Herd guitar virtuoso Peter Frampton, the hard rock outfit Humble Pie formed in Essex, England, in 1969. Also featuring ex-Spooky Tooth bassist Greg Ridley along with drummer Jerry Shirley, the fledgling group spent the first several months of its existence locked away in Marriott's Essex cottage, maintaining a relentless practice schedule. Signed to the Immedtate label, Humble Pie soon issued their debut single "Natural Born Boogie," which hit the British Top Ten and paved the way for the group's premiere LP, *As Safe as Yesterday Is.*

After touring the US in support of 1969's *Town and Country,* Humble Pie returned home only to discover that Immediate had declared bankruptcy. The band recruited a new manager, Dee Anthony, who helped land them a new deal with A&M; behind closed doors, Anthony encouraged Marriott to direct the group towards a harder-edged, grittier sound far removed from the acoustic melodies favored by Frampton. As Marriott's raw blues shouting began to dominate subsequent LPs like 1970's eponymous effort and 1971's *Rock On,* Frampton's role in the band he cofounded gradually diminished; finally, after a highly charged US tour, which yielded 1971's commercial breakthrough *Performance—Rockin' the Fillmore,* Frampton exited Humble Pie to embark on a solo career.

After enlisting former Colosseum guitarist Dave "Clem" Clempson to fill the void, Humble Pie grew even heavier for 1972's *Smokin',* their most successful album to date. However, while 1973's ambitious double studio/live set *Eat It* fell just shy of the Top Ten, its 1974 follow-up *Thunderbox* failed to crack the Top 40. After 1975's *Street Rats* reached only No. 100 before disappearing from the charts, Humble Pie disbanded; while Shirley formed Natural Gas with Badfinger alum Joey Molland, and Clempson and Ridley teamed with Cozy Powell in Strange Brew, Marriott led Steve Marriott's All-Stars before joining a reunited Small Faces in 1977.

In 1980, Marriott and Shirley reformed Humble Pie with ex-Jeff Beck Group vocalist Bobby Tench and bassist Anthony Jones. After a pair of LPs, 1980's *On to Victory* and the following year's *Go for the Throat,* the group mounted a troubled tour of America: after one injury-related interruption brought on when Marriott mangled his hand in a hotel door, the schedule was again derailed when the frontman fell victim to an ulcer. Soon, Humble Pie again dissolved; while Shirley joined Fastway, Marriott went into seclusion. At the dawn of the 1990s, he and Frampton made tentative plans to begin working together once more, but on April 20, 1991, Marriott died in the fire that destroyed his 16th-century Arkesden cottage. He was 44 years old. — *Jason Ankeny*

As Safe As Yesterday Is / 1969 / Immediate ✦✦✦
Even though many think of Humble Pie as a boogie-rock band, their first two efforts, originally released on Immediate Records, possessed a healthy dose of tasty acoustical instrumentation. Steve Marriott and Peter Frampton applied themselves, through months of rehearsals, and came up with a solid collection of songs. Even though *Safe as Yesterday Is* is a little stronger than the pastoral *Town and Country,* both albums are worth seeking out. In 1972, they were sold as a double-record set titled *Lost and Found,* which is now out of print. — *Rick Clark*

Rock On / 1971 / A&M ✦✦✦
By 1971, Humble Pie had taken on a much harder electric direction. Of their post-Immediate studio albums, this is probably their best. — *Rick Clark*

Performance: Rockin' at the Fillmore / 1971 / A&M ✦✦✦✦
This live, extended-play effort, recorded at the Fillmore, showcased the band in its element, with Steve Marriott's stratospheric wail and Peter Frampton's lyrical lead work in fine form. Frampton split to pursue a successful solo career after this album. — *Rick Clark*

Smokin' / 1972 / A&M ✦✦✦
With Marriott firmly in control, *Smokin'* featured grittier blues-based hard rock, with tracks like "Hot & Nasty," "C'mon Everybody," and the FM hit "Thirty Days in the Hole." — *Rick Clark*

Lost and Found / 1973 / A&M ✦✦✦✦
After the Top Ten success of *Smokin',* A&M prepared *Lost and Found,* which collected Humble Pie's first two albums in one package. The marketing ploy was a success and the record charted in the Top 40. — *Stephen Thomas Erlewine*

Eat It / 1973 / A&M ✦✦✦
Although the quality of the material is decidedly uneven, the double album *Eat It* is the last Humble Pie record to capture the rough and tumble spirit of their heyday. Nevertheless, all of side four—which was recorded live in Glasgow—is worthless. *—Stephen Thomas Erlewine*

Thunderbox / 1974 / A&M ✦✦
With *Thunderbox*, it's clear that most of the inspiration has left Humble Pie, as the band turns in a set of by-the-numbers boogie. *—Stephen Thomas Erlewine*

Street Rats / 1975 / A&M ✦✦
Even more undistinguished than *Thunderbox*, the limp blues-rock of *Street Rats* illustrates why Humble Pie threw in the towel after the release of this record. *—Stephen Thomas Erlewine*

On to Victory / 1980 / Atco ✦✦
Five years after breaking up Humble Pie, Steve Marriott formed a new version of the band—featuring drummer Jerry Shirley, guitarist Bobby Tench, and bassist Anthony Jones—and recorded *On to Victory*. Unfortunately, *On to Victory* picks up exactly where *Street Rats* left off—it's a rote set of competent but faceless blues boogie *—Stephen Thomas Erlewine*

Go for the Throat / 1981 / Atco ✦
Peaking at No. 60, the resurrected Humble Pie's first album *On to Victory* was surprisingly successful, allowing the group to have another chance to record an album. The ensuing record, *Go for the Throat*, was nearly identical to *On to Victory*, as the band ran through a set of bland, arena-ready blues-rock. The only difference was that the songs weren't as good as the last album, and those weren't very good to begin with. *—Stephen Thomas Erlewine*

The Best of Humble Pie / 1982 / A&M ✦✦✦✦
A brief but entertaining collection of Humble Pie's finest moments, *The Best of Humble Pie* is an effective introduction to the group's loud boogie. *—Stephen Thomas Erlewine*

● **Classics, Vol. 14** / 1987 / A&M ✦✦✦✦
If you are looking for the one place to go for Humble Pie, this best-of collection covers the essentials, such as "I Don't Need No Doctor," "Stone Cold Fever," "30 Days in the Hole," "Hot 'n' Nasty," "C'Mon Everybody," and "Take Me Back." *—Rick Clark*

Hot N' Nasty—the Anthology / Jun. 7, 1994 / A&M ✦✦✦✦
Album rock artists that never made great albums, Humble Pie are well served by *Hot N' Nasty*, a double-disc set that collects the hits and highlights from throughout their career. *—Stephen Thomas Erlewine*

Early Years / Oct. 27, 1994 / Castle ✦✦✦

Ian Hunter

b. Jun. 3, 1946, Shrewsbury, Shropshire, England
Guitar, Vocals / Rock 'n' Roll, Hard Rock
With Mott the Hoople, guitarist/vocalist Ian Hunter established himself as one of the toughest and most inventive hard rock songwriters of the early '70s, setting the stage for punk rock with his edgy, intelligent songs. As a solo artist, Hunter never attained the commercial heights of Mott the Hoople, but he cultivated a dedicated cult following.

Hunter was born in Shrewsbury but raised in cities throughout England, since his father worked in the British Intelligence agency called MI5 and had to move frequently. Eventually, the family returned to Shrewsbury, where the teenaged Hunter joined a band called Silence in the early '60s. Silence released an album, but it received no attention. In the years following Silence, Hunter played in a handful of local bands and worked a variety of jobs.

In 1968, Hunter began playing bass with Freddie "Fingers" Lee and the duo played around Germany. Shortly afterward, Hunter became the vocalist for Mott the Hoople. During the next six years, Hunter sang and played piano and guitar with the band, becoming its lead songwriter within a few albums. Although few of their records sold, Mott the Hoople was one of the most popular live bands in England. In 1972, David Bowie produced their breakthrough album, *All the Young Dudes*, which brought the band into the British Top Ten and the American Top 40. For the next two years, the group had a consistent stream of hits in both the UK and the US.

Toward the end of 1973, the band began to fall apart, as founding member and lead guitarist Mick Ralphs left the band. Hunter carried through another album, but he left the group in late 1974, taking along former Bowie guitarist Mick Ronson, who had just joined Mott. Just prior to leaving the group, Hunter published *Diary of a Rock Star*, an account of his years leading Mott the Hoople, in June of 1974.

Hunter moved to New York, where he and Ronson began working on his solo debut. Released in 1975, *Ian Hunter* spawned "Once Bitten, Twice Shy," a Top 20 UK hit. Following its release, Hunter and Ronson embarked on a tour. After its completion, the pair parted ways, although they would reunite later in the '80s. *All-American Alien Boy*, Hunter's second solo album, was recorded with a variety of all-star and

session musicians, including members of Queen. Released in the summer of 1976, *All-American Alien Boy* was a commercial failure. It was followed in 1977 by *Overnight Angels*, an album that saw Hunter moving closer to straightforward rock 'n' roll; disappointed with the completed album, Hunter decided to leave the album unreleased in America.

Following the mainstream approach of *Overnight Angels*, Hunter became involved with England's burgeoning punk rock movement, producing Generation X's second album, 1979's *Beyond the Valley of the Dolls*. For Hunter's next solo album, he reunited with Mick Ronson, who produced and arranged 1979's *You're Never Alone with a Schizophrenic*. The album was a hit, especially in America where it peaked at number 35. Hunter and Ronson set out on another tour, which resulted in the 1980 double live album, *Ian Hunter Live / Welcome to the Club*. In 1981, Hunter released *Short Back N' Sides*, which was produced by the Clash's Mick Jones.

Two years later, he released *All of the Good Ones Are Taken*. After the release of *All of the Good Ones Are Taken*, Ian Hunter became a recluse, spending the next six years in silence; occasionally, he contributed a song to a movie soundtrack. In 1989, Hunter resumed recording, releasing *YUI Orta* with Mick Ronson. After its release, Hunter remained quiet during the '90s, appearing only on Ronson's posthumous 1994 album *Heaven and Hull* and at tribute concerts for Ronson in 1994 and Freddie Mercury in 1992. Hunter returned to recording with *Artful Dodger*, which was released in Britain and Europe in the spring of 1997. *—Stephen Thomas Erlewine*

Ian Hunter / 1975 / Columbia ✦✦✦✦
A spotty debut, but "Once Bitten Twice Shy," "Who Do You Love," and "I Get So Excited" rank with the best Mott the Hoople material. *—John Floyd*

All American Alien Boy / 1976 / Columbia ✦✦✦
Ian Hunter's second solo album lacked the consistently impressive songwriting of his first, and it suffered from overly slick production, yet it had a handful of songs that made it worthwhile. *—Stephen Thomas Erlewine*

Overnight Angels / 1977 / Columbia ✦✦
For most of *Overnight Angels*, Ian Hunter sounds a bit uninspired—the music follows his patented literate hard rock formula, only without the stylistic embellishments and variations that made *Ian Hunter* and *All American Alien Boy* compelling listens. Nevertheless, there are a handful of tracks that make the record worthwhile for dedicated fans. *—Stephen Thomas Erlewine*

Shades of Ian Hunter / 1979 / Chrysalis ✦✦✦✦
A fine, if somewhat inconsistent, collection that features highlights from the early part of Ian Hunter's solo career as well as selections from Mott the Hoople's catalog, *Shades of Ian Hunter* is a good introduction to his work, even if it doesn't feature many of his best songs. *—Stephen Thomas Erlewine*

● **You're Never Alone with a Schizophrenic** / 1979 / Razor & Tie ✦✦✦✦
Hunter's post-punk return salutes the genre he helped spawn and brings that old Mott crunch to a fine set of energetic, if somewhat dated, rock 'n' roll. *—John Floyd*

Ian Hunter Live / Welcome to the Club / 1980 / Chrysalis ✦✦✦
Recorded with guitarist Mick Ronson, *Ian Hunter Live / Welcome to the Club* is a tough, hard-rocking album that features material from both Ronson and Hunter. *—Stephen Thomas Erlewine*

Short Back and Sides / 1981 / Chrysalis ✦✦✦✦
Ian Hunter had been revitalized by punk rock, as *Short Back and Sides* shows. Featuring the Clash's Mick Jones on guitar, the music is a tougher and spikier take on Hunter's rock 'n' roll, and his songwriting is at a near-peak. *—Stephen Thomas Erlewine*

All of the Good Ones Are Taken / 1983 / Columbia ✦✦✦
With its slightly dated and stiff sound, *All of the Good Ones Are Taken* is a step down from the vibrant *Short Back and Sides*, yet a handful of songs manage to break free of the restrictions placed on them by the production. *—Stephen Thomas Erlewine*

Yui Orta / 1989 / Mercury ✦✦✦✦
Overlooked upon its release, this is Hunter's most lyrically ambitious and mature disc, with tight rockers and melancholy ballads working gloriously off one another. *—John Floyd*

Artful Dodger / Mar. 1997 / Citadel ✦✦✦
As Ian Hunter's first record since his 1989 collaboration with Mick Ronson, *Artful Dodger* appropriately offers a tribute to the late guitarist in "Michael Picasso," but a greater tribute to the guitarist is the fact that the album could have used some of his focused production skills. Hunter still has his cynical wit and skill for catchy, intelligent rockers, but the material on the record is disarmingly uneven, considering that it took him seven years to make the album. A sharper production could have saved the weaker moments, but the sound is a bit too pedestrian

and the focus a bit too fuzzy to make the record a true return to form. —*Stephen Thomas Erlewine*

Ivory Joe Hunter

b. Oct. 10, 1914, Kirbyville, TX, **d.** Nov. 8, 1974, Memphis, TN
Piano, Vocals / R&B, Piano Blues, West Coast Blues
Bespectacled and velvet-smooth in the vocal department, pianist Ivory Joe Hunter appeared too much mild-mannered to be a rock 'n' roller. But when the rebellious music first crashed the American consciousness in the mid-'50s, there was Ivory Joe, deftly delivering his blues ballad "Since I Met You Baby" right alongside the wildest pioneers of the era.

Hunter was already a grizzled R&B vet by that time who had first heard his voice on a 1933 Library of Congress cylinder recording made in Texas (where he grew up). An accomplished tunesmith, he played around the Gulf Coast region, hosting his own radio program for a time in Beaumont before migrating to California in 1942. It was a wise move; Hunter (whose real name was Ivory Joe, incidentally—perhaps his folks were psychic!) found plenty of work pounding out blues and ballads in wartime California. He started his own label, Ivory Records, to press up his "Blues at Sunrise" (with Johnny Moore's Three Blazers backing him), and it became a national hit when leased to Leon Rene's Exclusive imprint in 1945. Another Hunter enterprise, Pacific Records, hosted a major hit in 1948 when the pianist's "Pretty Mama Blues" topped the R&B charts for three weeks.

At whatever logo Hunter paused from the mid-'40s through the late '50s, his platters sold like hotcakes. For Cincinnati-based King in 1948-49, he hit with "Don't Fall in Love with Me," "What Did You Do to Me," "Waiting in Vain," and "Guess Who." At MGM, then new to the record biz, he cut his immortal "I Almost Lost My Mind" (another R&B chart-topper in 1950), "I Need You So" (later covered by Elvis), and "It's a Sin." Signing with Atlantic in 1954, he hit big with "Since I Met You Baby" in 1956 and the two-sided smash "Empty Arms"/"Love's A Hurting Game" in 1957.

Hunter's fondness for country music reared its head in 1958. Upon switching to Dot Records, he scored his last pop hit with a cover of Bill Anderson's "City Lights." Hunter's Dot encores went nowhere; neither did typically mellow outings for Vee-Jay, Smash, Capitol, and Veep. Epic went so far as to recruit a simmering Memphis band (including organist Isaac Hayes, trumpeter Gene "Bowlegs" Miller, and saxist Charles Chalmers) for an LP titled *The Return of Ivory Joe Hunter* that hoped to revitalize his career, but it wasn't meant to be. The album's cover photo—a closeup of Hunter's grinning face with a cigarette dangling from his lips—seems grimly ironic in the face of his death from lung cancer only a few years later. —*Bill Dahl*

● **Since I Met You Baby: The Best of Ivory Joe Hunter** / Oct. 19, 1994 / Razor & Tie ✦✦✦✦
Bespectacled pianist Ivory Joe Hunter's crooning blues balladry made him a hot commodity from the late '40s through the late '50s, but he could rock reasonably convincingly hard, too. He does both on this wonderful survey of his 1949-1958 MGM and Atlantic sides—"I Need You So," "I Almost Lost My Mind," and the title item are sophisticated and mellow, while "Rockin' Chair Boogie," "Love Is a Hurting Game," and "Shooty Booty" find the pianist in decidedly unsentimental moods. —*Bill Dahl*

Jumping at the Dew Drop / Route 66 ✦✦✦
A European import slab of vinyl offering an overview of Hunter's 1947-1952 pre-Atlantic days. Emphasis on jump entries ("Are You Hep?," "She's a Killer," "We're Gonna Boogie," "Old Man's Boogie") is a welcome change-of-pace from Hunter's better-known propensity for velvety blues ballads. —*Bill Dahl*

Hunters & Collectors

f. 1981, Melbourne, Australia
Alternative Pop-Rock
Hunters & Collectors developed a cult following in the American and Australian underground in the '80s. Originally, the band sketched out a noisy punk and funk fusion reminiscent of the Fall and Gang of Four, except with horns added into the mix. In the middle of the decade, the band turned into a driving, hard-hitting rock 'n' roll band with a flair for pop melodies. The band formed in Melbourne, Australia, in 1981; over the years, numerous members went through the lineup, but the group's mainstays were Mark Seymour (vocals, guitar), Martin Lubran (guitar), John Archer (bass), Geoff Crosbie (keyboards), Doug Falconer (drums), Jeremy Smith (keyboards, saxophone), Greg Perano (percussion), Michael Waters (trombone), and Jack Howard (trombone). Hunters & Collectors released their debut single in 1982 and quickly followed it with two EPs and a self-titled, full-length record; the band was briefly on A&M Records in America before switching to Slash. By the late '80s, the group had earned a cult following in America and their native Australia, as their sound became progressively more direct and

melodic. However, they were never able to attain any commercial success, and the band quietly disappeared in the early '90s. —*Stephen Thomas Erlewine*

Hunters & Collectors / 1983 / Virgin ✦✦✦
Fireman's Curse / 1983 / Virgin ✦✦
Jaws of Life / 1984 / Epic ✦✦
Way to Go Out / 1985 / White Label ✦✦
Human Frailty / 1986 / IRS ✦✦✦✦
As the title suggests, the band loses some of the edge of earlier releases on *Human Frailty*, revealing a softer, nearly vulnerable side. A more mainstream pop album, it includes the great love song "Throw Your Arms Around Me." —*Chris Woodstra*

Fate / 1988 / IRS ✦✦✦✦
The finest moment of their later period, *Fate* is a cohesive and tightly produced album with an edge. "Back on the Breadline" received some attention through college and "Modern Rock" radio, making this the closest thing to an American breakthough the band has seen yet. —*Chris Woodstra*

Ghost Nation / Apr. 1990 / Atlantic ✦✦
Ghost Nation is a pleasant, though not distinctive album. Failing to build on the the previous effort, a lack of direction seems to hold the band back from being anything other than a second-string Midnight Oil. —*Chris Woodstra*

● **Collected Works** / Aug. 1990 / IRS ✦✦✦✦
A good collection of the band's recordings for IRS records in the mid-to-late '80s. This poppier side of the band is easily the most palatable of their work, though not definitive. Their varied career deserves better. —*Chris Woodstra*

Cut / 1993 / Mushroom ✦✦✦
Australia's Hunter's & Collectors have long been the source of some of down-under's most stately, dignified rock, while never forsaking an element of challenge. The group spices the standard instrumental lineup with trumpet, trombone, and french horn, which are used to create an almost-string-section-like moody canvas upon which the other instruments dance and paint. Mark Seymour's strong lyrics tackle several topical subjects, but are most successful when dealing with personal politics—especially the quest for self-purpose. While "Head Above Water" will be the party favorite, "Holy Grail" and "Closer Angel of Mercy" have an epic feel where all H&C's lyric and instrumental strengths converge. —*Roch Parisien*

Demon Flower / Jul. 18, 1995 / Shake ✦✦✦

Hüsker Dü

f. 1978, Minneapolis, MN, **db.** Jan. 1988
Alternative Pop-Rock, Hardcore Punk
Hüsker Dü and R.E.M. were the two American post-punk bands of the '80s that changed the direction of rock 'n' roll. R.E.M. became superstars; Hüsker Dü never was more than a cult favorite. Nevertheless, their albums between between 1981 and 1987 have proven remarkably influential; they provided the sonic blueprint for the roaring punk-pop hybrid that crossed over into the mainstream in the early '90s. Not only did they shape the sound of the music, they shaped the way independent bands made the transition to the major labels; they showed other bands that it was possible to record uncompromising music on a major label without losing any integrity or creative control. From the Replacements to Nirvana, the Pixies to Superchunk, nearly every major and minor band that appeared in the alternative underground in the late '80s and '90s owed a major debt to Hüsker Dü, whether they were aware of it or not.

The band's two songwriters, guitarist Bob Mould and drummer Grant Hart, both had a knack for writing songs that essentially followed conventional pop structures, complete with memorable melodies, but were still punk songs. Hüsker Dü took the Buzzcocks' pioneering punk pop and made it harder, both musically and lyrically. Throughout their career, Hüsker Dü never lost their edge, never turned down their amplifiers, never compromised their music. While Hart and bassist Greg Norton were an unflailingly strong rhythm section, Mould would prove to be one of the most influential guitarists of the decade. With his slashing rhythms, distorted strumming, and blazing leads, he set the stage for the alternative guitar heroes of the late '80s and the '90s.

Hüsker Dü formed in Minneapolis, MN, in 1979. Guitarist/vocalist Bob Mould was studying at Macalester College in St. Paul, MN, and working at a record store, which is where he met drummer/vocalist Grant Hart and bassist Greg Norton. The three musicians had diverse tastes, but all shared a love for hardcore punk rock. Naming themselves Hüsker Dü after a '50s Swedish boardgame (the name means "do you remember?"), the trio began rehearsing in Norton's basement. In the early '80s, Hüsker Dü developed a strong local following—nearly every local band, from the Replacements to Soul Asylum, sounded like the Hüskers. Both Mould and Hart wrote songs and sang lead. In 1981, they released their first single, "Statues," on the local label Reflex, which was quickly followed by their debut album, *Land Speed Record*, which was released on New Alliance Records. Recorded live, *Land Speed Record* boasted 17 songs that lasted a full 26 minutes. Later that year, they released an equally fast and hard EP, *In a Free Land*.

In 1982, they moved backed to Reflex, where they released *Everything Falls Apart*, their first album recorded in a studio. By this time, Hüsker Dü had begun touring the US relentlessly, travelling across the country in a van and playing small clubs throughout the country. Along with the Minutemen, R.E.M., Black Flag, the Meat Puppets, and the Replacements, Hüsker Dü formed the core of a group of independent rock 'n' roll bands that carved out a reputation by touring ceaselessly and getting their records played through college radio stations—they formed the core of the American rock underground in the mid-'80s. Hüsker Dü concerts were a nonstop barrage: The band rarely spoke to the audience and each song segued directly into the next, without interruption. In addition to touring constantly, Hüsker Dü was recording quickly, turning out the *Metal Circus* EP in 1983.

After *Metal Circus*, Hüsker Dü developed musically at a rapid pace, with Mould and Hart coming into their own as songwriters on 1984's *Zen Arcade*, their first album for SST Records and their critical breakthrough. *Zen Arcade* was a double album—something that was completely unheard of in the underground—that showed the band stretching out musically, writing sharper pop songs, as well as lengthy abrasive instrumentals. Critics embraced the record, as did independent rock fans. At the end of 1984, they released "Eight Miles High," a cover of the Byrds' song that was only available as a single.

Hüsker Dü continued to record at tour at a blindingly fast speed throughout 1984 and 1985. Mould and Hart were beginning to develop an unspoken rivalry, as well as a dependency on alcohol and speed. Nevertheless, the group was at their peak in 1985, turning out two albums. The first, *New Day Rising*, was released in the spring and showed the band moving closer to concise pop songwriting while accentuating their fierce sonic barrage. *Flip Your Wig*, released late in 1985, featured their cleanest, most accessible production, without making any concessions to mainstream rock. Both albums received excellent reviews, both in fanzines and in some mainstream rock publications.

Following the release of *Flip Your Wig*, Hüsker Dü became the first of the mid-'80s independent post-punk bands to sign a contract with a major label, as they closed a deal with Warner Brothers. *Candy Apple Grey*, the band's first major-label album, appeared in 1986. During that year, tensions between Bob Mould and Grant Hart escalated. Mould began to clean up and Hart continued to sink further into drug and alcohol addiction. Nevertheless, they managed to write and record another double album, *Warehouse: Songs and Stories*. Although Warner didn't want the band to release another double record, *Warehouse* was released in the spring of 1987, to uniformly positive reviews.

Hüsker Dü was preparing to launch a series of concerts to support *Warehouse* when their manager, David Savoy, committed suicide the night before the start of the tour. Hüsker played the tour anyway—they ran through the new album in order every night, without interruption—but Savoy's suicide helped the interband turmoil reach a peak. Hart showed no signs of sobering—he was developing a heroin addiction—while Mould was clean. Following the *Warehouse* tour, the band played no more concerts for the rest of the year, which caused speculation that the group was breaking up. Those rumors were confirmed in January of 1988, when Hart was fired and the band broke up.

Hart would released a solo EP, *2541*, on SST later that year, followed by a full-length album called *Intolerance* a year later. After its release, Hart shook loose his addictions and formed a new band, Nova Mob. Nova Mob released their debut album, *The Last Days of Pompeii*, in 1991; a self-titled second album appeared in 1994. Greg Norton became a chef in Minneapolis.

Immediately after the breakup of Hüsker Dü, Bob Mould embarked on a solo career. After releasing two solo albums—*Workbook* (1989) and *Black Sheets of Rain* (1990)—he formed a trio called Sugar in 1992. Between 1992 and 1994, Sugar released two albums—*Copper Blue* (1992) and *File Under: Easy Listening* (1994). Mould broke up the band in 1995 and returned to a solo career the following year. —*Stephen Thomas Erlewine*

Land Speed Record / 1981 / SST ♦♦

A brief live EP, *Land Speed Record* races through its songs without regard for melody or riffs. As a sonic blitzkrieg, it's quite impressive, yet little of the record makes a lasting impression. —*Stephen Thomas Erlewine*

Everything Falls Apart / 1982 / Reflex ♦♦♦

On their first studio recording *Everything Falls Apart*, Hüsker Dü demonstrate a sharper sense of purpose than on their live debut, *Land Speed Record*, but that doesn't necessarily make the album a breakthrough. Indeed, the trio demonstrates that they're capable of powerful

noise, but not songcraft—the only song with a discernible hook is their thrashing cover of Donovan's "Sunshine Superman." Still, the band's hardcore is better than many of their contemporaries because their grasp of noise is superior. Even with the inconsistent songwriting, *Everything Falls Apart* rages with layers of blistering guitars and scorching rhythms, which are exciting in their own right. —*Stephen Thomas Erlewine*

Metal Circus / 1983 / SST ♦♦♦

A five-song EP bristling with energy and pummeling guitars, *Metal Circus* is the first indication of Hüsker Dü's greatness. With these five songs, the band shows more invention, skill, and melody than they did over the course of a full album with *Everything Falls Apart*, and both Mould and Hart emerge as significant songwriters. While they both stay within hardcore conventions on *Metal Circus*, their songs illustrate that they would break free of its constrictions on their subsequent, masterful double album, *Zen Arcade*. —*Stephen Thomas Erlewine*

☆ **Zen Arcade** / 1984 / SST ♦♦♦♦♦

In many ways, it's impossible to overestimate the impact of Husker Du's *Zen Arcade* on the American rock underground in the '80s. It's the record that exploded the limits of hardcore and what it could achieve. Hüsker Dü broke all of the rules with *Zen Arcade*. First and foremost, it's a sprawling concept album, even if the concept isn't immediately clear or comprehensible. More important are the individual songs. Both Bob Mould and Grant Hart abandoned the strict "fast, hard, loud" rules of hardcore punk with their songs for *Zen Arcade*. Without turning down the volume, Hüsker Dü tries everything—pop songs, tape experiments, acoustic songs, pianos, noisy psychedelia. Hüsker Dü willed themselves to make such a sprawling record—as the liner notes state, the album was recorded and mixed within 85 hours and consists almost entirely of first takes. That reckless, ridiculously single-minded approach does result in some weak moments—the sound is thin and the instrumentals drag on a bit too long—but it's also the key to the success of *Zen Arcade*. Hüsker Dü sounds phenomenally strong and possessed, as if they could do anything. The sonic experimentation is bolstered by Mould and Hart's increased sense of songcraft. Neither writer is afraid to let their pop influences show on *Zen Arcade*, which gives the songs—from the unrestrained rage of "Something I Learned Today" and the bitter, acoustic "Never Talking to You Again" to the eerie "Pink Turns to Blue" and anthemic "Turn on the News"—their weight. It's music that is informed by hardcore punk and indie-rock ideals without being limited by it. —*Stephen Thomas Erlewine*

★ **New Day Rising** / 1985 / SST ♦♦♦♦♦

For *New Day Rising*, the follow-up to their breakthrough double-album *Zen Arcade*, Hüsker Dü replaced concept with conciseness, concentrating on individual songs delivered as scalding post-hardcore pop. *New Day Rising* is not only a more vicious and relentless record than *Zen Arcade*, it's more melodic. Bob Mould and Grant Hart have written tightly crafted, melodic pop songs that don't compromise Hüsker's volcanic, unchecked power. Mould and Hart's songs owe a great deal to '60s pop, as the verses and choruses ebb and flow with immediately catchy hooks. Occasionally, the razor-thin production and waves of noise mean that it takes a little bit of effort to pick out the melodies, but more often the furious noise and melodies fuse together to create an overwhelming sonic force. It's possible to hear the rivalry between Mould and Hart on the album itself—each song is like a game of one-upmanship, as Mould responds to "The Girl Who Lives on Heaven Hill" with "Celebrated Summer." Neither songwriter slips—both turn in songs that are catchy, clever, and alternately wracked with pain or teeming with humor. *New Day Rising* is a positively cathartic record and ranks as Hüsker Dü's most sustained moment of pure power. —*Stephen Thomas Erlewine*

☆ **Flip Your Wig** / 1985 / SST ♦♦♦♦♦

Spot—SST's house producer who manned the boards for *Zen Arcade* and *New Day Rising*—didn't produce *Flip Your Wig*, Hüsker Dü's second album of 1985, and the difference is immediately noticeable. Everything on *Flip Your Wig* is cleaner and brighter than on its two immediate predecessors, which is appropriate, considering that Bob Mould and Grant Hart have only increased their debt to '60s pop. The hooks and melodies are on the surface, right from the kick-start call-and-response of the title track. On paper, it might sound as if Hüsker Dü have watered down their hardcore ideals, but it doesn't play that way. *Flip Your Wig* is pop played as punk, as if this is the only time these songs could ever be heard. Which means Hart's love song "Green Eyes" and Mould's pure pop single "Makes No Sense at All" are delivered with the same rage and passion as Mould's blistering "Divide and Conquer" and Hart's "Keep Hanging On," or the pair of surging, neopsychedelic and noise-wracked instrumentals that close the album. *Flip Your Wig* would be a remarkable record on its own terms, but the fact that it followed *New Day Rising* by a matter of months and *Zen Arcade* by just over a year is simply astonishing. —*Stephen Thomas Erlewine*

Candy Apple Grey / 1986 / Warner Brothers ✦✦✦
Moving to a major label doesn't affect Hüsker Dü's sound greatly—although the production is more full-bodied than Spot's razor-thin work, the Hüskers don't change their blazing attack at all. Much of *Candy Apple Grey* charges along on the same frenzied beat that propelled *New Day Rising* and *Flip Your Wig*, and both Mould and Hart are in fine form, spinning out fine punk-pop with "Sorry Somehow" and "Don't Want to Know If You Are Lonely." However, the sound is beginning to seem a bit tired, which is what makes Mould's two acoustic numbers, "Too Far Down" and "Hardly Getting Over It," so welcome. Demonstrating that punks can mature without losing their edge, Mould inverts the rules of conventional confessional singer-songwriter songs with these two haunting numbers, and in doing so, he illustrates the faults with the relatively staid post-hardcore punk that dominates the remainder of the record. —*Stephen Thomas Erlewine*

☆ **Warehouse: Songs & Stories** / 1987 / Warner Brothers ✦✦✦✦✦
It's cleaner and more produced than any of their records, which is one reason why many Hüsker Dü fans have never fully embraced their second double-album, *Warehouse: Songs and Stories*. Granted, *Warehouse* boasts a fuller production—complete with multitracked guitars and vocals, various percussion techniques and endless studio effects—that would have seemed out of place a mere two years before its release. However, *Flip Your Wig* and *Candy Apple Grey* both suggested this full-fledged pop production, and it's to Hüsker Dü's credit that they never sound like they are selling out with *Warehouse*. What they do sound like is breaking up. Although there was a schism apparent between Bob Mould and Grant Hart on *Candy Apple Grey*, they don't even sound like they are writing for the same band on *Warehouse*. But the individual songs on the album are powerhouses in their own right, as both songwriters exhibit a continuing sense of experimentation—Hart writes a sea shanty with "She Floated Away" and uses bubbling percussion on "Charity, Chastity, Prudence and Hope," while Mould nearly arrives at power-pop with "Could You Be the One?" and touches on the singer-songwriter-styled folk-rock with "No Reservations." *Warehouse* doesn't have the single-minded sense of purpose or eccentric sprawl of *Zen Arcade*, but as a collection of songs, it is of the first order. Furthermore, its stylish production—which makes pop concessions without abandoning a punk ethos—pointed the way to the kind of "alternative" rock that dominated the mainstream in the early '90s. In all, it was a fine way for one of the most important bands of the '80s to call it a day. —*Stephen Thomas Erlewine*

Everything Falls Apart and More / 1993 / Rhino ✦✦✦
Rhino's reissue of Hüsker Dü's shattering first studio album includes a couple of rare singles, making it a must-have for the band's fans, as well as anyone interested in hardcore punk rock. Anyone unfamiliar with Hüsker Dü's early work should brace themselves for a breakneck force like no other. Not for the faint of heart. —*Stephen Thomas Erlewine*

The Living End / Oct. 1994 / Warner Brothers ✦✦✦
Recorded on their final tour, *The Living End* is an invigorating document of Hüsker Dü's blistering live power, highlighted by a couple unreleased songs and a manic cover of "Sheena Is a Punk Rocker." —*Stephen Thomas Erlewine*

I

Ian & Sylvia

f. 1960, Toronto, California, **db.** 1973
Folk, Folk-Rock

One of the most popular acts of the early-'60s folk revival, Canadian duo Ian Tyson (b. 1933) and Sylvia Tyson (b. 1940) made several fine albums that spotlighted their stirring harmonies on a mixture of traditional and contemporary material. While these recordings can seem a tad earnest and dated today, they were overlooked influences upon early folk-rockers such as the Jefferson Airplane, the We Five, the Mamas and the Papas, and Fairport Convention, all of whom utilized similar blends of male/female, lead/harmony vocals. They were also inspirations to fellow Canadian singer-songwriters such as Neil Young, Joni Mitchell, and Gordon Lightfoot. Like most acoustic folkies, after the mid-'60s they moved into folk-rock and country-rock, though the results were less impressive than their early work.

Tyson took up folk music in his 20s while convalescing from a rodeo injury, and teamed up with Fricker after moving to Toronto in the late '50s. In 1960, they moved to New York, where they were signed by Albert Grossman, famous for managing Bob Dylan and Peter, Paul, and Mary. Their self-titled debut (1962) began a successful series of recordings for Vanguard, on which they helped expand the range of folk by adding bass (sometimes played by Spike Lee's father Bill) and mandolin to Ian's guitar and Sylvia's autoharp. Just as crucially, they ranged far afield for their repertoire, which encompassed not just traditional folk ballads, but bluegrass, country, spirituals, blues, hillbilly, gospel, and French-Canadian songs.

Ian & Sylvia were among the first to cover songs by Dylan, Lightfoot, Joni Mitchell, and Phil Ochs, and also began writing material of their own. Although original compositions were never at the forefront of their early LPs, a couple of them would become very influential indeed. Tyson's "Four Strong Winds" would be covered by the Searchers and (in the '70s) Neil Young, and Fricker's "You Were on My Mind," given a far poppier treatment by the We Five, became one of the first big folk-rock hits.

By 1966, Ian & Sylvia had started to rely primarily on original material, and begun to use electric instruments. While some of these tracks were outstanding, generally their folk-rock lacked the focus and consistency of their acoustic recordings. In the late 1960s, they would take stabs at country-rock and straight country music, even hooking up with young producer Todd Rundgren for the 1970 album *Great Speckled Bird*. The quality of their records, and the size of their audience, declined steadily after they ended their association with Vanguard in 1967. In the '70s, they split up, professionally and personally (they had married in 1964). Both have since pursued solo careers: Tyson's was far more successful, as he moved into country music, recording albums of songs with cowboy and rodeo themes that received much popular and critical acclaim in Canada. *—Richie Unterberger*

Ian & Sylvia / 1962 / Vanguard ♦♦♦
Ian & Sylvia's debut album is their most standard affair, and indeed a fairly typical folk recording for the era, with such traditional warhorses as "Rocks And Gravel" (also recorded, but not released, by Dylan during this time), "C.C. Rider," and "Handsome Molly." What made the pair immediately distinctive was their superb vocal dueting, which was definitely a case of the sum being greater than its parts. Blended together, they canceled each other's weaknesses and gave the material great freshness and vigor. Ian's guitar and Sylvia's autoharp are backed by stellar playing from guitarist John Herald and string bassists Bill Lee (director Spike Lee's father) and Art Davis. *—Richie Unterberger*

Four Strong Winds / 1964 / Vanguard ♦♦♦♦
Ian & Sylvia hit their stride on their second LP, which features the first in a line of talented second guitarists (John Herald) they would use to augment their original guitar-autoharp-bass lineup. The album featured an assortment of largely traditional material that was unsurpassed in its time, encompassing bluegrass, spirituals, gospel, hillbilly, the French-Canadian standard "V'La L'bon Vent," a British prison song, and two tunes from the Cecil Sharp collection of Southern mountain folk songs of British origin. Two of the most impressive cuts, however, were contemporary compositions. One was their version of Bob Dylan's "Tomorrow Is a Long Time," one of the first obscure Dylan tunes to be committed to vinyl. The title cut, an Ian Tyson original, would prove to be the duo's first song to influence rock musicians, as the Searchers covered it shortly afterwards with a reverent version that was quite close to the original; Neil Young revived it in the late '70s. *—Richie Unterberger*

Northern Journey / 1964 / Vanguard ♦♦♦
The duo continue to fill out their sound on another collection of mostly traditional material, with John Herald (guitar), Monte Dunn (mandolin and guitar), and Eric Weissberg and Russ Savakus (bass) backing Ian & Sylvia's own guitar and autoharp. The few originals stand out much more than the traditional updates on this LP; Tyson's "Four Rode By" and "Some Day Soon" clearly point toward his future C&W/cowboy direction, and Fricker's "You Were on My Mind" remains his best (and best-known) song. *—Richie Unterberger*

Early Morning Rain / 1965 / Vanguard ♦♦♦
Side one of their fourth LP continues in the eclectic folkie style of their earlier albums, containing only one original (Tyson's "Marlborough Street Blues"). The other cuts include the fine Gordon Lightfoot title track, a Johnny Cash cover ("Come in Stranger") that heralded their increasing interest in country and western music, one of their finest interpretations of a bona fide traditional warhorse ("Nancy Whiskey"), and "Darcy Farrow," a fine obscure composition that could pass for a traditional standard (written for the duo by an unknown Californian singer-songwriter pair). Side two, however, with the exception of one traditional tune and another Lightfoot cover, is composed entirely of originals. The most notable of these is Tyson's "Song for Canada" (written with Pete Gzowski). A bittersweet plea for greater communication between French—and English-speaking Canadians, it could just as well be heard as a comment on any sort of deteriorating relationship. *—Richie Unterberger*

Play One More / 1966 / Vanguard ♦♦♦
Ian & Sylvia rely mostly on original material for the first time on this erratic record. For the first time, they employ full modern arrangements on four of the tracks, which sometimes works (their cover of Bacharach-David's "24 Hours from Tulsa") and sometimes doesn't (unfortunately for them, on one of their best compositions, "The French Girl"). They also cover songs by Phil Ochs and Scott McKenzie, and their own tunes range from solid numbers in their proven contemporary folk style ("Short Grass") to mediocre. Future Cream producer Felix Pappalardi plays bass. *—Richie Unterberger*

So Much for Dreaming / 1967 / Vanguard ♦♦♦
Ian & Sylvia's adjustment to folk-rock was sometimes fine, sometimes awkward, and this was another inconsistent, though generally worthwhile, effort. Highlights include "Circle Game," one of the very first recorded covers of a Joni Mitchell composition. Tyson's "Wild Geese" and "Child Apart" count as some of their better unheralded tunes, and the occasional muted orchestration worked well on "Circle Game" and the melancholy title track. On the other hand, the attempts at blues were abominable, the traditional ballads anachronistic, and some of

the material (especially Fricker's) undistinguished. —*Richie Unterberger*

● **Greatest Hits** / 1987 / Vanguard ✦✦✦✦
This compilation (CVSD 5/6) captures much of their best work. Do not confuse it with the identically titled Vanguard album 73114, which includes only half the material found on this set. —*William Ruhlmann*

Long Long Time / Oct. 25, 1994 / Vanguard ✦✦✦
After leaving Vanguard in 1967, Ian & Sylvia spent the next few years recording in a much more countrified style for MGM, Ampex (as figureheads of the band Great Speckled Bird), and Columbia. This compilation—ironically on Vanguard—draws from five albums they released between 1967 and 1971. While the duo's ambitions to expand their artistic horizons were admirable, the fact is that they were much more effective as eclectic folkies than country-pop-folk-rockers. The harmonies remained intact, but the material (mostly original) is often humdrum, the arrangements sometimes lackadaisical. A few cuts, like "Salmon in the Sea" and "Last Lonely Eagle," are reasonably strong; the higlights are the 1967 versions of "Hang on to a Dream" and "Reason to Believe," which were among the first Tim Hardin covers ever recorded. —*Richie Unterberger*

Live at Newport / Jun. 18, 1996 / Vanguard ✦✦✦
Divided about equally between material from their appearances at the 1963 and 1965 Newport Folk Festivals, these 14 tracks present concert versions of many of the duo's best songs, including "You Were on My Mind," "Someday Soon," "Song for Canada," and "Four Strong Winds." Eric Hord adds lead acoustic guitar on the 1963 cuts; Rick Turner does the same on the ones from 1965. Ian & Sylvia recorded studio versions of all of the songs on their '60s Vanguard albums, which makes this disc a sort of souvenir that's essential only for big fans, although the sound and performances are decent. —*Richie Unterberger*

Janis Ian (Janis Eddy Fink)

b. Apr. 7, 1951, New York City, NY
Guitar, Vocals / Singer-Songwriter, Folk-Rock, Contemporary Folk
A singer-songwriter both celebrated and decried for her pointed handling of taboo topics, Janis Ian enjoyed one of the more remarkable second acts in music history; after first finding success as a teen, her career slumped, only to enter a commercial resurgence almost a decade later. The child of a music teacher, Janis Eddy Fink was born on May 7, 1951, in New York City; she studied piano as a child, and, drawing influence from Edith Piaf, Billie Holiday, and Odetta, wrote her first songs at the age of 12. She soon entered Manhattan's High School of Music and Art, where she began performing at school functions; after adopting the surname Ian (her brother's middle name), she quickly graduated to the New York folk circuit.

When she was just 15, she recorded her self-titled debut; the LP contained "Society's Child (Baby I've Been Thinking)," a meditation on interracial romance written by Ian while waiting to meet with her school guidance counselor. While banned by a few radio stations, the single failed to attract much notice until conductor Leonard Bernstein invited its writer to perform the song on his television special *Inside Pop: The Rock Revolution*. The ensuing publicity and furor over its subject matter pushed "Society's Child" into the upper rungs of the pop charts, and made Ian an overnight sensation.

Success did not agree with her, however, and she soon dropped out of high school; in rapid succession, she recorded three more LPs—1967's *For All the Seasons of Your Mind*, 1968's *The Secret Life of J. Eddy Fink* and 1969's *Who Really Cares*—but gave away the money she earned to friends and charities. After meeting photojournalist Peter Cunningham at a peace rally, the couple married, and at age 20, she announced her retirement from the music business. The marriage failed, however, and she returned in 1971 with the poorly-received *Present Company*. After moving to California to hone her writing skills in seclusion, Ian resurfaced three years later with *Stars*, which featured the song "Jesse," later a Top 30 hit for Roberta Flack.

With 1975's *Between the Lines*, Ian eclipsed all of her previous success; not only did the LP achieve platinum status, but the delicate single "At Seventeen" reached the Top Three and won a Grammy. While subsequent releases like 1977's Latin-influenced *Miracle Row*, 1979's *Night Rains*, and 1981's *Restless Eyes* earned acclaim, they sold poorly; Ian was dropped by her label, and spent 12 years without a contract before emerging in 1993 with *Breaking Silence* (the title a reference to her recent admission of homosexuality), which pulled no punches in tackling material like domestic violence, frank eroticism, and the Holocaust. Similarly, 1995's *Revenge* explored prostitution and homelessness. —*Jason Ankeny*

Janis Ian / Jan. 1967 / Verve ✦✦✦✦
An amazingly precocious set of songs, including the civil rights anthem "Society's Child" and songs touching on religion, prostitution, politics, and other urban concerns, all from the viewpoint of an intelligent teenager. —*William Ruhlmann*

For All the Seasons Of Your Mind / Oct. 1967 / Verve ✦✦✦
Sixteen-year-old Janis Ian's second album continues to probe a series of unusually mature issues, notably on the single "Insanity Comes Quietly to the Structured Mind," a meditation on suicide, and "Shady Acres," which is about old age. Producer Shadow Morton found interesting musical contexts for Ian's pronouncements, none of which was sufficiently provocative to score with the impact of "Society's Child." —*William Ruhlmann*

The Secret Life of J. Eddie Fink / Jul. 1968 / Verve ✦✦
Janis Fink is Ian's real name, and her concerns moved more toward the personal on her third album. "42nd St. Psycho Blues" was her unhappy commentary on what having a pop music career had been like, while "When I Was a Child" found her reminiscing regretfully about what had happened to her. Other songs waxed poetic, and producer Shadow Morton kept recreating the folk-rock sound of "Society's Child," but nothing here caught fire, and this album failed to chart, seeming to confirm that Ian would be a one-hit wonder, over the hill at 17. With a few years to think about it, of course, she'd have some trenchant things to say about that age. —*William Ruhlmann*

Present Company / 1971 / One Way ✦✦
Janis Ian's muse had subsided to a series of pretty-sounding but pedestrian piano tunes with sensitive-seeming but vague lyrics by the time of this, her fifth album, released the year she turned 20 by Capitol Records. Although the sound, when combined with far more substantial songs, would reinvigorate her career several years hence, *Present Company* went practically unnoticed when it came out, and it marked the end of Ian's juvenile efforts. —*William Ruhlmann*

Stars / 1974 / One Way ✦✦✦
From precocity to an accelerated maturity, Ian ruefully comments on the fame business in the title track, then turns deeply romantic on "Jesse," a hit for Roberta Flack. —*William Ruhlmann*

● **Between the Lines** / Mar. 1975 / Columbia ✦✦✦✦
"At Seventeen" is only one of a group of beautifully written, tastefully performed, and very moving songs. —*William Ruhlmann*

Aftertones / 1975 / Columbia ✦✦✦
Following only nine months after Ian's masterpiece, *Between the Lines*, *Aftertones* was something of a coda to that album, again tastefully produced by Brooks Arthur and featuring songs in the same mood. Although none came up to the standard of "At Seventeen," "I Would Like to Dance" presents much the same delicacy of expression. —*William Ruhlmann*

Miracle Row / 1977 / Columbia ✦✦✦
Janis Ian's career in the 1970s paralleled her career in the '60s—stimulated by a major hit early on, she made a series of albums that were successively less accomplished and less commercially successful. This, her second follow-up to the top-selling *Between the Lines*, is a disturbing collection of tastefully written and performed songs about loneliness, desperation, drinking, and promiscuity. There was nothing as focused as "At Seventeen" or some of the songs on *Aftertones*, but the overall portrait of the singer was as painful, in a more mature way, as the one Ian presented in her later albums as a teenager. —*William Ruhlmann*

Janis Ian / 1978 / Columbia ✦✦
Janis Ian may have intended to signal a creative rebirth by using her own name as this album's title, the second time in her career she did so, but although the record was a more direct, low-key effort than its predecessor, *Miracle Row*, it didn't indicate any new directions. "Hotels & One-Night Stands" found the singer once again reflecting on life in the music business, while "Do You Wanna Dance?" used dancing as a metaphor for a desired romance for the umpteenth time. More extended metaphors, such as "The Bridge," were even less effective. With its piano textures and tasteful string arrangements, *Janis Ian* retained the artist's pretty sound, but much of the time the singer came off less confessional than merely self-involved. —*William Ruhlmann*

Night Rains / 1979 / Columbia ✦✦
When Janis Ian's self-titled 1978 album failed to crack the Top 100, it was clear that changes were in order. Here, she turns to producer Ron Frangipane and a surprising songwriting partner, Eurodisco maven Giorgio Moroder, who brings in his dance tracks for "Fly Too High," which was intended for the motion picture *Foxes*. More appropriately, Ian also pairs with Albert Hammond for the leadoff track, "The Other Side of the Sun." Even on her own, however, she is attempting a more timely pop style: "Memories" is as much of a disco cut as the Moroder one. That makes the album more engaging on the surface than her recent releases, but less compelling. As a commercial move, all this was a failure: *Night Rains* failed to chart, a major comedown for an artist who had topped the chart only four years earlier. —*William Ruhlmann*

Restless Eyes / 1981 / Columbia ✦✦
Janis Ian turned to producer Gary Klein and a backup group of L.A. session aces after the commercial failure of *Night Rains*, and they gave

her the kind of pop-rock album that people like Carly Simon turned out regularly. Despite the liner notes by former *New York Times* music critic Robert Shelton, little here was distinctive, and when the album failed to restore Ian's commercial fortunes, she retired for the second time at the age of 30. — *William Ruhlmann*

Breaking Silence / Jun. 8, 1993 / Morgan Creek ✦✦✦✦
Breaking Silence finds Ian ditching her past waifishness for a confident, mature, contemporary acoustic approach relying mostly on spare guitar and piano textures. Opening with "All Roads to the River" (also recorded by John Mellencamp), *Breaking Silence* includes among its highlights the Holocaust-survivor tale "Tattoo" and the dramatic half-a cappella, half-syncopated-rocker title track. — *Roch Parisien*

Revenge / May 16, 1995 / Grapevine ✦✦✦
The second album of Janis Ian's third career as a recording artist found her singing love songs full of violent imagery and story songs about desperate characters. Opening with "Ready for War," Ian used metaphors of armed struggle to describe romantic interaction, following with "Take No Prisoners" and later, in "Stolen Fire," depicting infidelity in Promethean terms. And even when she employed more conventional imagery, as in "Take Me Walking in the Rain," the album's catchiest song with its familiar rock 'n' roll chord progression (think "Every Breath You Take," "Billie Jean," and countless others), Ian gave the song a demanding, erotic edge that made love seem less appealing than urgent. "Love," she noted in the album-closing "When Angels Cry," "is a four letter word" (a statement no less powerful for having been made 30 years earlier by Bob Dylan). And so, she added, was hope: In songs like "Davy," "Ruby," and "The Mission," she painted sympathetic portraits of homelessness and prostitution. The effect, when set to her typically restrained, melodic tunes and sung in her precise, sometimes clipped voice, was of a tough, adult worldview. Of course, that was not so far removed from the view Ian had held in the songs she wrote back when she was a teenager. — *William Ruhlmann*

Society's Child: the Verve Recordings / Aug. 22, 1995 / Polydor ✦✦✦✦
The 41 songs on this double CD contain almost everything from the four albums that the singer-songwriter recorded for Verve in the late '60s. While it is true that Ian's early work may have been unduly savaged by unsympathetic rock critics, it's also true that the magnitude of her talent isn't large enough to merit a box set. As others have pointed out over the years, these compositions are often overly wordy, didactic, and self-absorbed, though these flaws are understandable (to a degree) given that Ian was in her mid—and late teens when they were recorded. At the same time, the grooves make a fairly strong case that Ian is underrated, if hardly a major figure; some of the songs are affecting, the arrangements (especially the early ones by Shangri-Las producer Shadow Morton) have a '60s-period charm, and she's a pretty strong singer. Although some Laura Nyro fans might find the comparison insulting, there's a similarity to be found in Ian's bluesier and more soulful vocals, especially on her later Verve records. So while this couldn't be classified as a milestone of the early singer-songwriter era, it's more enjoyable and impressive than a lot of listeners would expect, although two-and-a-half hours is too much to take at once. — *Richie Unterberger*

Ice Cube

b. Jun. 15, 1969, Los Angeles, CA
Vocals / Hip Hop, Gangsta Rap, West Coast Rap
Ice Cube was the first member of the seminal Californian rap group N.W.A. to leave, and he quickly established himself as one of hip-hop's best and most controversial artists. From the outset of his career, he courted controversy, since his rhymes where profane and political. As a solo artist, his politics and social commentary sharpened substantially, and his first two records, *AmeriKKKa's Most Wanted* and *Death Certificate*, were equally praised and reviled for their lyrical stance, which happened to be considerably more articulate than many of his gangsta peers. As his career progressed, Ice Cube's influence began to decline, particularly as he tried to incorporate elements of contemporary groups like Cypress Hill into his sound, but his stature never diminished, and he remained one of the biggest rap stars throughout the '90s.

For such a revolutionary figure, Ice Cube (b. O'Shea Jackson) came from a surprisingly straight background. Raised in south central Los Angeles, where both of his parents had jobs at UCLA, Cube didn't become involved with B-Boy culture until his late teens. He began writing raps while in high school, including "Boyz N Da Hood." With his partner Sir Jinx, Cube began rapping in a duo called CIA at parties hosted by Dr. Dre, and he eventually met Eazy-E, then leading a group called HBO, through Dre. Eazy asked Cube to write a rap, and he presented them with "Boyz N Da Hood," which was rejected. Eazy-E decided to leave CIA and he, Ice Cube, and Dr. Dre formed the first incarnation of N.W.A. Cube left to study architectural drafting at Phoe-

nix, Arizona, in 1987, returning the following year after he obtained a one-year degree. He arrived just in time for N.W.A.'s debut album, *Straight Outta Compton*. Released late in 1988, *Straight Outta Compton* became an underground hit over the course of 1989, and its extreme lyrical content—which was over-the-top both lyrically and politically—attracted criticism, most notably from the FBI.

N.W.A. may have been rivaling Public Enemy as the most notorious group in hip-hop, but Ice Cube was having deep conflicts with their management, resulting in him leaving the band in late 1989. He went to New York with his new posse, Da Lench Mob, and recorded his first solo album with Public Enemy's production team, the Bomb Squad. Released in the spring of 1990, his debut *AmeriKKKa's Most Wanted* was an instant hit, going gold within its first two weeks of release. While the record's production and Cube's rhythmic skills were praised, his often violent, homophobic, and misogynist lyrics were criticized, particularly by the rock press and moral watchdogs. Even amidst such controversy, the album was hailed as a groundbreaking classic within hip-hop, and it established Cube as an individual force. He began his own corporation, which was run by a woman, and he produced the debut album from his female protegee, Yo-Yo. At the end of 1990, he released the EP *Kill at Will*, which was followed in the spring by Yo-Yo's debut, *Make Way for the Motherlode*. That summer, his acting debut in John Singleton's acclaimed urban drama *Boyz N the Hood* was widely praised.

AmeriKKKa's Most Wanted may have been controversial, but it paled next to the furor surrounding Cube's second album, *Death Certificate*. Released late in 1991, *Death Certificate* was simultaneously more political and vulgar than its predecessor, it caused more outrage. In particular, "No Vaseline," a vicious attack on N.W.A. manager Jerry Heller, was perceived as antisemitic, and "Black Korea" was taken as a racist invocation to burn down all Korean-owned grocery stores. The songs provoked a public condemnation from the trade publication *Billboard*. It was the first time an artist had been singled-out by the magazine. The furor over *Death Certifacate* didn't prevent it from reaching No. 2 and going platinum. During 1992, he toured with the second Lollapalooza tour in a successful attempt to consolidate his white rock audience. He also converted to the Nation of Islam during 1992, which was evident on his next album, *The Predator*. Upon its release in December 1992, *The Predator* became the first album to debut at number one on both the pop and R&B charts. The steady-rolling single "It Was a Good Day" and the Das Efx collaboration "Check Yo Self" made the album Cube's most popular.

However, Ice Cube's hold on the mass rap audience was beginning to slip. His former colleague, Dr. Dre, was dominating hip-hop with his stoned G-Funk, and Cube tried to keep pace with 1993's *Lethal Injection*. While the album debuted at No. 5 and went platinum, its funkier sound wasn't well-received. *Lethal Injection* was Cube's last offical album for several years. In 1994, he wrote and produced Da Lench Mob's debut *Guerillas in the Mist*, and produced Kam's debut *Neva Again*, releasing a remix and rarities collection *Bootlegs & B-Sides* at the end of the year. In 1995, he kept quiet, appearing in Singleton's film *Higher Learning* and making amends with Dre on their duet "Natural Born Killaz." The following year, he acted in the comedy *Friday*, which he wrote himself. He also formed the Westside Connection with Mack 10 and WC, releasing their debut album, *Bow Down*, at the end of the year. It went gold within its first month of release. In the spring of 1997, Cube starred in the surprise hit horror film, *Anaconda*. — *Stephen Thomas Erlrewine*

☆ **AmeriKKKa's Most Wanted** / May 1990 / Priority ✦✦✦✦✦
After leaving N.W.A. on anything but good terms with Dr. Dre and Eazy-E, Ice Cube launched his solo career with the hard-hitting and impressive *AmeriKKKa's Most Wanted*. While the Angelino continued to embrace gangster rap—a style in which MCs provide violent, graphic, first-person portrayals of thugs, gang members, drug dealers, etc.—there's a lot more to this riveting CD than that controversial approach. As much as Cube thrives on the shocking and the profane, it's clear that he isn't glamorizing the harsh urban realities he raps about, but rather, protesting them. "Once Upon a Time in the Projects" is about being arrested for being in the wrong place (a crack house) at the wrong time (during a drug bust), while "Endangered Species" (a duet with Public Enemy leader Chuck D) is a sobering reflection on the high mortality rate among young African-American males. On some of his subsequent recordings, Cube would, artistically speaking, become a victim of his own anger. But on *AmeriKKKa's Most Wanted*, a more lucid Cube quite effectively articulates just how bad things are in the America's inner cities—and how badly things need to change. —*Alex Henderson*

Kill at Will / 1990 / Priority ✦✦✦✦
Ice Cube's riveting debut album, *AmeriKKKa's Most Wanted* was still burning up the charts when Priority Records released this EP, which lacks that album's overall excellence but has its moments. With *Kill at Will*, Cube unveiled his engaging "The Product" and "Dead Homiez," a

poignant lament for the victims of Black-on-Black crime that is among the best songs he's ever written. Enjoyable but not essential are remixes of "Endangered Species (Tales from the Darkside)" and the outrageous "Get Off My D****" and Tell Yo B****" to Come Here." Clearly, *Kill at Will* was intended for hardcore fans rather than casual listeners—who would do well to stick with *AmeriKKKa's Most Wanted* and *Death Certificate*. —Alex Henderson

★ **Death Certificate** / Oct. 31, 1991 / Priority ✦✦✦✦✦
Death Certificate is even harder and angrier than *AmeriKKKa's Most Wanted*, which is both a good and a bad thing, depending on your politics. If you're inclined to see Ice Cube as a spokesman and social commentator, *Death Certificate* will support your claims—it continues the sharp insights and unflinching looks at contemporary urban lifestyles that his solo debut only hinted at; in short, it's hardcore without any gangsta posturing. If you're inclined to see Ice Cube as a bigoted, misogynistic rabble-rouser, *Death Certificate* will also support your claims—"No Vaseline" contains explicit anti-semitic taunts directed at his former manager, there are homophobic slurs scattered throughout the album, and women are frequently are either bitches or whores. However, if you look beyond the surface—no matter what political viewpoint you happen to have—you will find that Cube's rhymes do promote self-awareness and education. In short, they are some of the most incisive raps about life as a young Black man since the advent of Public Enemy. Considering this, it's not surprising that *Death Certificate* bears the mark of Public Enemy's dense, abrasive soundscapes—it's a funkier, noisier, and more musically effective album than *AmeriKKKa's Most Wanted*. Ice Cube had never before created a statement of purpose as coherent and incendiary as *Death Certificate* and, sadly, he never did again. —Leo Stanley

The Predator / Nov. 17, 1992 / Priority ✦✦✦
Although Ice Cube makes a lot of noise throughout *The Predator*, he never actually says anything. For the most part, *The Predator* is Ice Cube by the numbers, spouting his standard line about women, police, drugs, and gangsters. The album doesn't sound weak at all; it's full of strong beats and muscular rhymes. Das EFX invigorate "Check Yo Self," "Wicked" is a classic single, and the light '70s groove of "It Was a Good Day" proves that Ice Cube doesn't need hardcore beats to succeed. If Ice Cube hadn't just blustered grandiosely, *The Predator* might have ranked among his previous efforts. —Stephen Thomas Erlewine

Lethal Injection / Dec. 7, 1993 / Scarface ✦✦
It's difficult to explain the dip in quality of Ice Cube's recent CDs. Where Cube was once among hip-hop's most acerbic, gripping rappers, his voice sounds unconvincing and devoid of fury on such ostensibly political numbers as "Cave Bitch" and "Ghetto Bird." He takes repeated cheap shots at Christianity, but his pitch for Islam on "When I Get to Heaven" doesn't convey any sense of that religion's alternative views or allegedly superior stances. It's only on standard gangsta tracks that Cube comes close to resembling the incendiary figure who recorded *Kill At Will* and *Amerikkka's Most Wanted*. It's hard to believe, but could Ice Cube possibly be running out of things to say after only four solo albums? —Ron Wynn

Bootlegs & B-Sides / Nov. 22, 1994 / Priority ✦✦✦
It's nothing but a collection of remixes and flip sides, but Ice Cube's *Bootlegs & B-Sides* proves that he has always remained in step with the times and, more importantly, often set the standards for hip-hop. In fact, the record almost functions as an alternate best-of; none of the original single versions are included, but the material is so strong, it doesn't matter—these songs are essential listening, no matter what mix they are heard in. —Stephen Thomas Erlewine

Ice-T

b. 1959, Newark, NJ
Vocals / Hip Hop, Gangsta Rap, Hardcore Rap, Old School Rap, West Coast Rap
Ice-T (born Tracy Morrow) has proven to be one of hip-hop's most articulate and intelligent stars, as well as one of its most frustrating. At his best, the rapper has written some of the best portraits of ghetto life and gangsters, as well as some of the best social commentary hip-hop has produced. Just as often, he can slip into sexism and gratuitous violence, and even then his rhymes are clever and biting. Ice-T's best recordings have always been made in conjunction with strong collaborators, whether it's The Bomb Squad or Jello Biafra. With his music, Ice-T has made a conscious effort to win the vast audience of white male adolescents, as his frequent excursions with his heavy metal band Body Count show. All the while, he has withstood a constant barrage of criticism and controversy to become a respected figure not only in the music press, but the mainstream media as well.

Although he was one of the leading figures of Californian hip-hop in the '80s, Ice-T was born in Newark, NJ. When he was a child, he moved from his native Newark to California after his parents died in an auto accident. While he was in high school, he became obsessed with rap

while he went to Crenshaw High School in south central Los Angeles. Ice-T took his name from Iceberg Slim, a pimp that wrote novels and poetry. Ice-T used to memorize lines of Iceberg Slim's poetry, reciting them for friends and classmates. After he left high school, he recorded several undistinguished 12-inch singles in the early '80s. He also appeared in the low-budget hip-hop films *Rappin', Breakin',* and *Breakin' II: Electric Boogaloo* as he was trying to establish a career.

Ice-T finally landed a major label record deal with Sire Records in 1987, releasing his debut album, *Rhyme Pays.* On the record, he is supported by DJ Aladdin and producer Afrika Islam, who helped create the rolling, spare beats and samples that provided a backdrop for the rapper's charismatic rhymes, which were mainly party-oriented; the record wound up going gold. That same year, he recorded the theme song for Dennis Hopper's *Colors,* a film about inner-city life in Los Angeles. The song—also called "Colors"—was stronger, both lyrically and musically, and more incisive than anything he had previously released. Ice-T formed his own record label, Rhyme Syndicate (which was distributed through Sire/Warner) in 1988, and released *Power. Power* was a more assured and impressive record, earning him strong reviews and his second gold record. Released in 1989, *The Iceberg/Freedom of Speech ... Just Watch What You Say* established him as a true hip-hop superstar by matching excellent abrasive music with fierce, intelligent narratives and political commentaries, especially about hip-hop censorship.

Two years later, Ice-T began an acting career, starring in the updated blaxploitation film *New Jack City;* he also recorded "New Jack Hustler" for the film. "New Jack Hustler" became one of the centerpieces of 1991's *O.G.: Original Gangster,* which became his most successful album to date. *O.G.* also featured a metal track called "Body Count" recorded with Ice-T's band of the same name. Ice-T took the band out on tour that summer, as he performed on the first Lollapalooza tour. The tour set up increased his appeal with both alternative music fans and middle-class teenagers. The following year, the rapper decided to release an entire album with the band, also called *Body Count.*

Body Count proved to be a major turning point in Ice-T's career. On the basis of the track "Cop Killer"—where he sang from the point-of-view of a police murderer—the record ignited a national controversy; it was protested by the NRA and police activist groups. The record company initially supported Ice-T, yet they refused to release his new rap album, *Home Invasion,* on basis of the record cover. Ice-T and the label parted ways by the end of the year. *Home Invasion* was released on Priority Records in the spring of 1993 to lukewarm reviews and sales. Somewhere along the way, Ice-T had begun to lose most of his original hip-hop audience; now he appealed primarily to suburban white teens. In 1994, he wrote a book and released the second Body Count album, *Born Dead,* which failed to stir up the same controversy as the first record—indeed, it failed to gain much attention of any sort. Nevertheless, Body Count was successful in clubs and Ice-T continued to tour with the band.

In the summer of 1996, Ice-T released his first rap album since 1993, *Return of the Real.* The album was greeted by mixed reviews and it failed to live up to commercial expectations. —Stephen Thomas Erlewine

Rhyme Pays / 1987 / Sire ✦✦
Ice-T made his initial pop impact with this 1987 album. It earned him his first gold record, and while there were still lighter numbers like "I Love Ladies," it was also an early indication that the graphically violent images and sexist language of such songs as "Squeeze the Trigger," "Sex," and "Pain" would appeal across racial and economic lines. Ice-T was also trimming and tightening his rap approach, putting more menace in his tone and more edge in his rhymes. —Ron Wynn

Power / 1988 / Sire ✦✦✦✦
His second release is a quantum-leap improvement over his debut—better samples, a more pronounced and developed rapping style, and smarter material. Ice-T does marvelous homage to Curtis Mayfield with an excellent adaption of "I'm Your Pusherman" from the vintage *Superfly* soundtrack. —Ron Wynn

☆ **The Iceberg/Freedom of Speech ... Just Watch What You Say** / Oct. 1989 / Sire ✦✦✦✦✦
Ice-T threw listeners quite a curve ball with his riveting third album, *The Iceberg/Freedom of Speech ... Just Watch What You Say*—arguably the closest hip-hop has come to George Orwell's *1984.* Instead of focusing heavily on gangster rap, Ice-T made First Amendment issues the CD's dominant theme. Setting the album's tone is the opener "Shut Up, Be Happy," which finds guest Jello Biafra (former leader of punk band Dead Kennedys) envisioning an Orwellian America in which the goverment controls and dominates every aspect of its citizens' lives. Though there are a few examples of first-rate gangster rap here—including "The Hunted Child" and the chilling "Peel Their Caps Back"—Ice's main concern this time is censorship and what he views as a widespread attack on free speech in the US. As angry and lyrically

intense as most of *The Iceberg* is, Ice enjoys fun for its own sake on "My Word Is Bond" and "The Girl Tried to Kill Me"—an insanely funny rap/rock account of an encounter with a dominatrix. —*Alex Henderson*

★ **O.G. Original Gangster** / May 14, 1991 / Sire ✦✦✦✦✦
After placing gangster rap on the back-burner on *The Iceberg*, Ice-T returned to it with thrilling results on his fourth album, *O.G. Original Gangster*. In 1991—four years after the release of Ice's debut album, *Rhyme Pays*—hip-hop was saturated with a glut of unimaginative gangster rappers who lacked even a fraction of Ice's inventiveness. But in his hands, the style could still be arresting, insightful, and informative. When he provides nightmarish, first-person accounts of inner-city L.A.'s ugly realities on such disturbing rhymes as "Midnight" and "New Jack Hustler," he isn't glorifying the life of the gangbanger or the street hustler, but instead, sending out a message that crime is a dead end. Ice-T generated some controversy in hip-hop circles with "Escape from the Killing Fields," which asserts that moving away from the violence and the poverty of the ghetto isn't "selling out"—it's self-preservation. —*Alex Henderson*

Home Invasion / Mar. 23, 1993 / Priority ✦✦✦
Given the fact that most of *Home Invasion* was recorded during and after the "Cop Killer" media firestorm, it comes as no surprise that the album is an uneven, muddled affair, not the clean, focused attack of *O.G. Original Gangster*. Instead of producing an album that illustrates his confusion through the music (like Public Enemy's claustrophobic "Welcome to the Terrordome"), Ice-T made a confused album, unsure in its musical and lyrical direction. *Home Invasion* does have some flashes of brilliance (about a third of the album, particularly the tribute to the gang truce, "Gotta Lotta Love"), but it takes a little digging to find the best material. —*Stephen Thomas Erlewine*

The Classic Collection / May 4, 1993 / Rhino ✦✦
Ice-T's early sound was far different from the material that later earned him fame and controversy. His voice was higher, his cadence less assured, his commentary and ideas rough and evolving, and his backdrops less sophisticated, with straight scratches rather than multiple edits and song samples. While he did rap about social problems, Ice-T was then just as concerned with proving his manhood on the mike as many East Coast types, and had to overcome initial skepticism about a West Coast rapper not being inherently soft. This collection reissues formative Ice-T, including such seminal raps as "6 in the Mornin'," "Killers," "Body Rock," and a 1992 autobiographical review of the old days, "Ice-a-Mix." It's also interesting to remember just how little furor there was in the mid-'80s over things that get people easy headlines in the 1990s. —*Ron Wynn*

Return of the Real / Jun. 1996 / Priority ✦✦✦
As the title says, Ice-T returns to the street and the hardcore beats with his sixth album, *Return of the Real*. In fact, the return isn't just to hardcore—it's to hardcore that happened before gangsta rap, before the message and the music became diluted with endless B-boy posturing and loping P-Funk beats. In concept, the album is brilliant—Ice-T has always had an eye for lyrical detail and has always been a vocal supporter of hardcore, street-oriented hip-hop; at the very least, his rejection of G-funk/post-NWA gangsta rap is a bold political move. However, *Return of the Real* doesn't quite re-establish Ice-T as a force, mainly because the production sounds a bit dated. Sure, there are the occasional contemporary flourishes—usually in the guise of a Wu-Tang-style soundscape—but for the most part, Ice sounds like he's in his own world. Unfortunately, that doesn't mean that he has created a unique sonic world; it just means that he hasn't progressed far since 1991. Of course, there are a number of tracks that sound vibrant and alive, but *Return of the Real* can't help escape a creeping sense of stagnation that permeates through the entire album. —*Stephen Thomas Erlewine*

Icicle Works

f. 1980, Liverpool, England, db. 1990
New Wave, Pop-Rock, Neo-Psychedelia
A product of the same Liverpool neo-psychedelic community that gave rise to Echo & the Bunnymen and the Teardrop Explodes, the Icicle Works formed in 1980 from the ashes of local bands like City Limits and the Cherry Boys. A trio originally comprised of singer/guitarist Ian McNabb, bassist Chris Layhe and drummer Chris Sharrock, the Icicle Works (who nicked their name from an obscure sci-fi novel) issued their debut single "Ascending" in 1981. After the success of subsequent efforts like 1982's "Nirvana," the band earned a deal with the Beggars Banquet label, and scored a UK Top 15 hit with "Love Is a Wonderful Colour."

The Icicle Works' self-titled debut appeared in 1984 and reached the US Top 40 on the strength of the excellent single "Birds Fly (Whisper to a Scream)." The superior 1985 follow-up *The Small Price of a Bicycle* failed to match their earlier success, however, and neither the 1986 hits

collection *Seven Singles Deep* nor 1987's *If You Want to Defeat Your Enemy Sing His Song* failed to generate much interest either.

Prior to recording 1988's *Blind*, both Layhe and Sharrock left the band, and were replaced by bassist Roy Corkhill and drummer Zak Starkey, the son of Ringo Starr. Minus Starkey, the Icicle Works (now rounded out by guitarist Mark Revell, keyboardist Dave Baldwin, and drummer Paul Burgess) completed one final album, *Permanent Damage*, before disbanding in 1990. McNabb continued on as a solo artist. —*Jason Ankeny*

Icicle Works / 1984 / Beggars Banquet ✦✦✦
The internationally successful debut includes their two biggest hits. —*Steve Aldrich*

Small Price of a Bicycle / 1985 / Beggars Banquet ✦✦✦✦
This is huge, wide-screen music; Icicle Works throw everything at the wall and most of it sticks. —*Steve Aldrich*

Understanding Jane / 1986 / Beggars Banquet ✦✦
Who Do You Want for Your Love? / 1986 / Beggars Banquet ✦✦
If You Want to Defeat Your Enemy Sing His Song / 1987 / Beggars Banquet ✦✦✦
This uneven album still has strong moments. —*Steve Aldrich*

Blind / 1988 / Beggars Banquet ✦✦
This is the final album with original lineup. —*Steve Aldrich*

Permanent Damage / 1990 / Epic ✦✦
Ian McNabb with short-lived second lineup. —*Steve Aldrich*

● **Best of the Icicle Works** / 1995 / Beggars Banquet ✦✦✦✦
The Best of the Icicle Works gives a good overview of the band and stands as the best introduction for newcomers. A second disc, *Best Kept Secrets*, is added as bonus and collects several B-sides, live tracks, and other rarities. —*Chris Woodstra*

Billy Idol (William Broad)

b. Nov. 30, 1955, Middlesex, England
Vocals / Hard Rock, Pop-Rock
Billy Idol represents the bridge between punk rock and hard rock/metal, a logical enough connection that somehow seemed unlikely until he made the transition. Idol left Sussex University in 1976 to join the punk movement, specifically the group of rabid Sex Pistols fans called the Bromley Contingent. Many of the members formed their own bands, and Idol began Generation X with Tony James. Generation X became a moderate success during the punk heyday of the late '70s, especially in England, with Idol on snarling lead vocals.

When the band split in 1981, Idol went to New York and hooked up with manager Bill Aucoin (who had handled Kiss, among others). This resulted in Idol's grooming as more of a mainstream rock figure. His debut album, *Billy Idol*, came out in 1982 and spent two years on the charts as the result of such video hits as "White Wedding" and "Hot in the City." But it was Idol's second album, *Rebel Yell*, that was his big breakthrough, selling two million copies and spawning hits in the raucous title track and the ballad "Eyes without a Face." Idol followed it up with *Whiplash Smile* in 1986 and *Charmed Life* in 1990.

Idol's first commercial failure came in 1993, with *Cyberpunk*, his stab at techno-influenced rock. —*William Ruhlmann*

Billy Idol / Jul. 1982 / Chrysalis ✦✦✦✦
Billy Idol's self-titled debut album was a snarling take on hard rock, injected with the spite and attitude of punk and new wave. While the record is spotty, Idol pulls it all together on the classic single "White Wedding." —*Stephen Thomas Erlewine*

● **Rebel Yell** / 1983 / Chrysalis ✦✦✦✦
Tight rock arrangements featuring Steve Stevens' slashing guitar playing and Idol's vocal sneer. The dance-rock of "Rebel Yell" is alternated with power-ballads like "Eyes without a Face" for a well-rounded pop package. —*William Ruhlmann*

Whiplash Smile / 1986 / Chrysalis ✦✦✦
While *Whiplash Smile* is Idol's most ambitious album, it only comes to life on hard-rocking pseudo-rockabilly like "I Forgot to Be Your Lover." Unfortunately, there aren't many songs that are as good as that single on this album. —*Stephen Thomas Erlewine*

Vital Idol / 1986 / Chrysalis ✦✦
Dance remixes of Idol's hits, plus a live cover of "Mony Mony" that topped the charts. —*William Ruhlmann*

Charmed Life / 1990 / Chrysalis ✦✦✦✦
Like any Billy Idol album, *Charmed Life* is wildly inconsistent, but it has enough strong songs—like the gloriously tongue-in-cheek hard rock of "Cradle of Love"—to make most of the filler on the record forgivable. —*Stephen Thomas Erlewine*

Cyberpunk / Jun. 29, 1993 / Chrysalis ✦
Cyberpunk, Idol's attempt to restyle himself as a futuristic cyber-rocker, only works when he falls back on his effortlessly catchy guitar hooks

and melodies of his past hits (the first single, "Shock to the System," for instance). Unfortunately, most of the album is padded with pretentious speeches, sampled dialog, and underdeveloped songs. Especially noteworthy is his techno-dance interpretation of the Velvet Underground's "Heroin" (featuring a repeated Patti Smith quote), which is one of the worst covers ever recorded. —*Stephen Thomas Erlewine*

The Impressions

f. 1958, Chicago, IL, **db.** 1983
Soul, R&B

The first Impressions hit, "For Your Precious Love," was an anachronism when released in 1958. Jerry Butler's robust, yearning vocal was a throwback to deep-South gospel, and Curtis Mayfield's arrangement was decidedly barebones. But this song also precipitated the changes coming in R&B; you can hear the groundwork for soul music being laid, from the melisma of Butler's phrasing to Mayfield's skeletal guitar. The song literally flew in the face of then-popular doo wop formulas.

Butler left the group in 1960, but the pared-down trio, led by Mayfield, cut a path that altered the R&B map. Mayfield's high falsetto and the trade-off vocals of Fred Cash and Sam Gooden framed a new kind of R&B: smooth and graceful, at times lilting, soaked in the history of gospel, and, thanks to Mayfield's lyrical examinations of racism and urban decay, the catalyst for the wave of socially aware Black hits recorded in the '70s.

The group's hits varied from supple statements of affirmation ("It's All Right," "People Get Ready") and romantic declarations ("Talking About My Baby," "I'm So Proud") to songs that were sociopolitical ("Choice of Colors," "This Is My Country") or mystical ("Gypsy Woman"). Mayfield's outside production work yielded similar-sounding hits for the likes of Major Lance, Walter Jackson, and Billy Butler (and the sound of the Impressions was imitated by the likes of the Viscounts and the Knight Brothers). Their chart run ended by the late '60s, as did Mayfield's Midas touch; after recording the brilliant *Superfly* in 1972, his talents ran dry. Nonetheless, Mayfield's reputation as one of soul's supreme innovators cannot be exaggerated. —*John Floyd*

The Impressions / 1963 / Paramount ++++
A landmark soul date, one of the Impressions' finest albums. They showed once and for all that they would succeed as a trio, and also revealed to any who weren't aware Curtis Mayfield's brilliance as a composer. The hits came pouring out of Mayfield in the mid-'60s, and "It's All Right" was just the first of many gems he would write, produce, sing lead vocals on, and arrange. A fabulous album. —*Ron Wynn*

Keep on Pushing / 1964 / Paramount +++
The Impressions moved over to Paramount in 1964, but had absolutely no problems continuing their soul dominance. Mayfield's title track and "I've Been Trying" were among the many monster tunes on this release. The Impressions had jelled and had the perfect combination of Mayfield's gripping leads and flickering guitar, plus perfect support by Sam Gooden and Fred Cash. —*Ron Wynn*

One by One / 1965 / Paramount ++++
The Impressions continued a great run of hit singles and fine albums with this outstanding release, one of three that were issued on ABC in 1965. The structure by now was both fixed and marvelous; songs revolved around Mayfield's leads, superb production and arrangements, guitar licks and riffs anchoring the backdrop, and Fred Cash and Sam Gooden interacting with Mayfield on the choruses, bridges, and turnarounds. —*Ron Wynn*

The Young Mods' Forgotten Story / 1969 / Curtom ++++
Curtis Mayfield was almost ready to leave The Impressions and began a remarkable solo career when they cut the brilliant *Young Mods' Forgotten Story*, which fully displays Mayfield's splendid skills as a lead vocalist, songwriter, and arranger. He penned both moving love songs and provocative message tracks, with "Choice oOf Colors" and "Mighty, Mighty (Spade & Whitey)" challenging audiences across the color line to address their prejudices. Mayfield managed to cram his ideas and sentiments into the restrictive pop frameworks of the time (no song longer than three minutes). —*Ron Wynn*

The Complete Vee-Jay Recordings / Nov. 22, 1993 / Vee-Jay ++++
The Impressions' early music has taken a back seat to what they did after Jerry Butler departed and Mayfield began doing the lead vocals, writing, producing, and arranging. This excellent 18-track disc helps put the early years into focus, with Butler showcased on seven cuts and Mayfield on eight. The Impressions weren't a bad five-member harmony unit; they just were not a great one in an era when you had to be fantastic simply to break out of the pack. These are mostly nice love songs, and they aren't lyrically different from thousands of similar tracks, but they did deserve a better fate than to be dropped from the Vee-Jay label in 1959. —*Ron Wynn*

Keep on Pushing/People Get Ready / Mar. 19, 1996 / Kent ++++
Two good Impressions albums from the mid-'60s, combined onto one CD, making them handier to collect in this fashion than hunting down good-quality copies of the rare original vinyl editions. As usual, the singles ("Keep on Pushing," "People Get Ready," "Amen," "I've Been Trying," "Woman's Got Soul," "You Must Believe Me") overshadow the LP-only cuts. But the Impressions made a higher standard of albums than most '60s soul groups, investing a lot of care in the songwriting and production, making this a decent pickup for those who want to go beyond the greatest-hits anthologies. —*Richie Unterberger*

This is My Country/The Young Mods' Forgotten Story / Apr. 24, 1996 / Sequel ++++
Two fine late-'60s albums, combined onto one CD, including some hits and a wealth of good, overlooked Mayfield compositions that touched on sensitive racial issues as well as romance. Offering excellent value, the CD is a recommended alternative to tracking down the hard-to-find original vinyl editions. —*Richie Unterberger*

Further Impressions: More Soulful Classics / Jul. 1996 / HIPP ++++
Featuring a selection of 14 songs making their compact disc debut, *Further Impressions: More Soulful Classics* fills in the gaps left by the single-disc MCA *Greatest Hits* collection and the more comprehensive double-disc anthology. Only four R&B hits are present, but the remaining ten songs are all first-rate album tracks that are nearly equal in quality. *Further Impressions* doesn't overlap at all with MCA's two previous Impressions sets, so it is a necessary addition to any fan's CD library. —*Stephen Thomas Erlewine*

● **Very Best Of** / Feb. 4, 1997 / Rhino ++++
A good 16-track anthology for the moderate Impressions fan, sticking to their most famous smashes—"Gypsy Woman," "It's All Right," "Keep on Pushing," "Amen," "People Get Ready," "We're a Winner," "Choice of Colors," "Check Out Your Mind," and so forth. Most of it's from the '60s, but it does end with three hits from the mid-'70s, after Mayfield's departure from the group. —*Richie Unterberger*

The Incredible String Band

f. 1965, Glasgow, Scotland, **db.** 1974
Folk, Folk-Rock, British Folk, Psychedelic

Hippie mystics or cosmic fools? In the late '60s, the Incredible String Band mixed folk and psychedelia in ways that could be innovative, irritating, or both. The folk was always more prominent than the psychedelic, though, for the ISB's two mainstrays, Scottish singer-songwriters Robin Williamson (b. 1943) and Mike Heron (b. 1942).

Williamson, who had occasionally played with fellow Scotsman Bert Jansch before Jansch established himself as a solo act, began the Incredible String Band with Clive Palmer in the mid-'60s. (Palmer owned the Incredible Folk Club in Glasgow, hence the Incredible String Band.) The jugband duo were soon joined by Mike Heron, and as a trio, they recorded their debut for Elektra in 1966. Though the debut is tame in comparison with later outings, the group's ambitious blend of British folk, American folk, and miscellaneous exotic influences was already evident. The influence of the contemporary music of the 1960s was felt in the fairytale ambience of the songwriting and the melismatic, almost raga-like vocals, two traits that would both charm and annoy listeners depending upon individual tastes.

Soon after the LP's release, this iteration of the band broke up. Palmer, whose contributions to the first LP were marginal in any case, traveled to India; Williamson also took off, for Morocco. Williamson returned from North Africa while Heron was touring as a solo act, and the pair reunited for the second Incredible String Band album, *The 5000 Spirits or the Layers of the Onion* (1967). Psychedelic influences were apparent in the music as well as the title, and these cosmic ambitions would be pushed further on *The Hangman's Beautiful Daughter*, which is usually cited as their most innovative album. In the UK, it was also their most successful, reaching No. 5.

The Williamson-Heron era is seen as the ISB's peak. In the late '60s, Christina McKenzie and Rose Simpson joined, and the music became less concise and more airy-fairy. The Incredible String Band, at least, could not be accused of standing still. Some of their later records were considerably more rock-oriented; the 1970 album *U* was performed with a mime troupe when it was presented onstage.

But like an overdose of chocolate (or of acid, for that matter), the Incredible String Band's charm began to wilt after its initial novelty. Like fellow Scotlander Donovan, the fantasy world detailed by the ISB seemed increasingly silly and trivial. Unlike Donovan, the ISB didn't have much straight pop appeal, which consigned them to a much smaller audience, especially in the US, when they were known only to underground cultists. They did gain an unlikely fan in Led Zeppelin's Robert Plant, who once credited them (in a Led Zeppelin tour booklet) as having inspired his band's occasional digressions into folk (though it must be said that these don't sound a whole lot like the Incredible String Band).

With some further musical chairs in personnel, the Incredible String Band continued releasing albums through the mid-'70s. Williamson and Heron had begun separate recording careers in the early '70s, and it was little surprise when the increasingly anachronistic group dissolved. Williamson has had a much more active solo career than Heron, releasing a few solo albums, and attaining a higher American profile after moving to Los Angeles. —*Richie Unterberger*

The Incredible String Band / 1966 / Rykodisc ✦✦✦
As much a showcase for individual performances as group ones, The ISB's debut was their most traditional effort, though Williamson and Heron modernized traditional British Isles music with their whimsical songwriting and vari-pitch vocals. It also has minor contributions from guitarist Clive Palmer, who would leave the group after this album. —*Richie Unterberger*

5,000 Spirits or the Layers of The Onion / 1967 / Hannibal ✦✦✦✦
For their second album, the ISB officially reduced to the duo of Mike Heron and Robin Williamson. Lumped in with the psychedelic movement, that categorization was probably more due to the trippy cover graphics, the occasional Indian influences, and the whimsical, sometimes fantasy-ridden lyrical images than the music. It's more like a slightly cosmic version of traditional British folk than psychedelic rock. Although their next album, *The Hangman's Beautiful Daughter*, is usually considered their most adventurous, some listeners may find this to be the more accessible effort. It also featured what is probably Williamson's best-known song, "First Girl I Loved" (also familiar via Judy Collins' cover version, "First Boy I Loved"). —*Richie Unterberger*

● **Hangman's Beautiful Daughter** / 1968 / Hannibal ✦✦✦✦
The ISB most ambitious album, with Williamson and Heron employing an arsenal of unusual instruments (sitar, gimbri, pan pipe, oud, chahanai, and more), and Dolly Collins adding a couple of the more dignified arrangements. It's usually considered their most important effort by critics, but there were also traces of the sprawling, occasionally grating lack of focus that would increasingly come to characterize their work. —*Richie Unterberger*

Wee Tam / 1969 / Elektra ✦✦✦
Mixing English and American folk with what we now call "world music," the multi-instrumental Scottish duo of Robin Williamson and Mike Heron achieve a whimsical, delicate style that has never been duplicated. It reaches a peak here with such songs as "You Get Brighter." (*Wee Tam* is sometimes packaged with the simultaneously released *The Big Huge*, which is also recommended.) —*William Ruhlmann*

Relics of the Incredible String Band / 1970 / Elektra ✦✦✦✦
The ISB's prolific output makes a compilation a virtual necessity, and this two-record set selects wisely from the seven albums the group released in the US between 1967 and 1970. From Robin Williamson's "First Girl I Loved" (covered by Judy Collins) and "Way Back in the 1960s" (recorded in 1967), to Mike Heron's "Air," and "This Moment," the ISB's eclectic, fanciful acoustic style is well portrayed. —*William Ruhlmann*

No Ruinous Feud / 1973 / Edsel ✦✦✦
The ISB began to change its approach in 1971, cutting back on its sometimes open-ended song structures and adding a rock rhythm section to selected tracks. But it wasn't until this album that everything came together, resulting in a delightful collection of songs that range from reggae to light pop, along with the traditional folk styles that had always been the group's strong suit. —*William Ruhlmann*

Indigo Girls

f. 1985, Decatur, GA
Singer-Songwriter, Folk-Rock, Adult Alternative Pop-Rock
While they came into prominence as part of the late-'80s folky singer-songwriter revival, the Indigo Girls have had staying power where other artists from the same era quickly faded. Their two-women-with-guitars formula may not seem very revolutionary on paper, but the combination of two distinct personalities and songwriting styles provides a tension and an interesting balance—Emily Saliers, hailing from the more traditional Joni Mitchell school, has the gentler sound, is more complex musically, and often leans toward the abstract and spiritual, while Amy Ray draws heavily from the singer-songwriter aspects of punk rock, citing influences such as the Jam, the Pretenders, and Hüsker Dü for her more abrasive and direct approach. In more than a decade of recording, they have managed respectable mainstream success as well as keeping their rabid core following.

Amy Ray and Emily Saliers first took the name Indigo Girls while living in Atlanta in 1985, although they had been performing together since the early '80s, at times under the name the B-Band. In 1986, they recorded an independent, self-titled EP and followed in 1987 with the

full-length *Strange Fire*—only 7,000 copies were pressed and very little interest was generated. Things changed quickly in 1988 when, in the wake of the success of Suzanne Vega, Tracy Chapman, and 10,000 Maniacs, they seemed to fit nicely into "the next big thing." Epic Records was quick to sign them.

Indigo Girls, released in 1989, was an excellent national debut. Featuring a guest vocal by R.E.M.'s Michael Stipe ("Kid Fears") gave them initial college radio credibility and the single "Closer to Fine" was a hit—the album eventually broke the Top 30 and earned a Grammy for Best Folk Recording that year. By the end of 1991, it achieved platinum sales. *Strange Fire* was reissued in the fall with a cover of "Get Together," replacing one of the original tracks.

The follow-up, 1990's *Nomads Indians Saints*, didn't fare quite as well. It was nominated for a Grammy and eventually reached gold status, but the material wasn't nearly as strong. A live EP, *Back on the Bus, Y'All*, was released in 1991 while they regrouped. It was also certified gold and was nominated for a Grammy.

In spring of 1992, they made a comeback with *Rites of Passage*, which debuted at No. 22 and went platinum by year's end. The album showed an increasing diversity and some of their strongest songs to date. Almost exactly two years later, *Swamp Ophelia* was released and entered the charts at No. 9; it went gold by the end of the year. A double-live album, *1200 Curfews*, was released in 1995 and the much-awaited follow-up to *Swamp Ophelia, Shaming of the Sun*, followed in 1997.

In addition to her work as part of the Indigo Girls, Amy Ray also set up and presides over Daemon Records, a nonprofit label to nurture new talent with an emphasis on like-minded singer-songwriters. The label's releases include albums by Kristen Hall, Ellen James Society, James Hall, a remake of *Jesus Christ Superstar* (which includes performances by both Ray and Saliers), and a gun control benefit. —*Chris Woodstra*

Strange Fire / 1987 / Epic ✦✦
Their first proper album, *Strange Fire*, hints at future greatness with the duo's lush harmonies and shining acoustic guitars blending nicely for highly likeable folk-pop. The album has its inpired moments, but, for the most part, their sound isn't fully formed yet. —*Chris Woodstra*

● **Indigo Girls** / 1989 / Epic ✦✦✦✦
This major-label debut is a strong showcase for this duo's harmonic skills and songwriting virtues. "Closer to Fine" (No. 52) was a moderate hit. Emily Saliers' "History of Us" is particularly affecting. Other highlights include "Secure Yourself," "Tried to Be True," and "Kid Fears," which featured R.E.M. vocalist Michael Stipe on backups. Hothouse Flowers also provides support. —*Rick Clark*

Nomads Indians Saints / Sep. 1990 / Epic ✦✦✦✦
Not as dynamic as *Indigo Girls*, this effort includes a few nice songs with "Welcome Me," "Watershed," and "Southland in the Springtime." The dichotomy between Ray's occasionally abrasive vocal strain and Saliers' delicately earthy alto is more apparent, making their delivery feel less focused. Their overreaching lyrics also undermined the success of this outing. —*Rick Clark*

Live: Back on the Bus Y'all / Jun. 4, 1991 / Epic ✦✦
A spirited live set with Saliers and Ray backed by a full band, it features live and studio versions of their radio hit "1 2 3," and a version of Dylan's "All Along the Watchtower." —*Rick Clark*

Rites of Passage / Feb. 1992 / Epic ✦✦✦
Not straying too far from their nearly formulaic sound, *Rites of Passage*, shows great strides in songwriting maturity. The tension between Amy Ray's harsher rock style and Emily Sailers' sweeter melodic sense makes for a beautiful combination. Only a ridiculous reading of Dire Straits' "Romeo and Juliet" misses the mark. —*Chris Woodstra*

Swamp Ophelia / May 10, 1994 / Epic ✦✦✦
The most sophisticated sounding Indigo Girls production to date, *Swamp Ophelia* features some fine material, like "Touch Me Fall," "Mystery," "Language or the Kiss," "Power of Two," and "Least Complicated." For the most part, Amy Ray's occasional over-the-top stridency is fortunately restrained, while Emily Saliers' warm, earthy voice continues to pull the listener into considering her lyrical sentiments. As usual, when the two sing together, it's a wonderful sound. —*Rick Clark*

4.5 the Best Of / 1995 / Epic ✦✦✦
4.5 is a 15-track import collection covering the Indigo Girls' career from their self-titled Epic Records debut to *Swamp Ophelia*. While it certainly does the job of introducing the band to the foreign market, its lack of rarities and prohibitive import price make it unnecessary for the US—the self-titled album is still the best place to start. —*Chris Woodstra*

1200 Curfews / Oct. 24, 1995 / Epic ✦✦✦✦
1200 Curfews is a double live album recorded on the *Swamp Ophelia* tour from 1994 to 1995, covering the duo's best-loved songs as well as some inspired covers of classics from Bob Dylan, Neil Young, and Joni

Mitchell. And while this is obviously directed at the Indigo Girls' insatiable cult following, even casual fans will find the album engaging since the live performances are often more spirited and direct than the studio versions. —*Chris Woodstra*

Shaming of the Sun / Apr. 29, 1997 / Sony ✦✦✦

James Ingram

b. Feb. 16, 1956, Akron, OH
Keyboards, Vocals / Soul, Urban, Adult Contemporary
Ingram began performing with the band Revelation Funk in the early '70s, moving from Akron, OH, to Los Angeles in 1973. During the '70s, Ingram supported Ray Charles on the road with backup vocals and piano, played keyboards behind the Coasters on Dick Clark's oldies revues, and was Leon Haywood's musical director. After hearing a demo of him singing "Just Once," Quincy Jones asked Ingram to perform on his new album. Released in 1980 on *The Dude,* the No. 17 "Just Once" was Ingram's first success, resulting in three Grammy nominations—Best New Artist, Best Pop Male Vocal, and Best R&B Vocal—winning in the two latter categories. Throughout the '80s, Ingram had steady popular success singing duets, but all of his solo albums failed to make a dent in the charts; in 1990 he scored his first solo hit, "I Don't Have the Heart." —*Stephen Thomas Erlewine*

● **The Power of Great Music: Best of James Ingram** / Sep. 24, 1991 / Qwest ✦✦✦✦
Includes his Top 40 duets—"Yah Mo B There" (recorded with Michael McDonald), "Somewhere Out There" (recorded with Linda Ronstadt), "Baby, Come to Me" (recorded with Patti Austin), and his first solo hit, "I Don't Have the Heart"—as well as songs that have scored the urban charts. —*Ron Wynn*

Luther Ingram

b. Nov. 30, 1944, Jackson, TN
Vocals / Soul, Urban
This Jackson, TN, Southern-soul singer was one of the top artists at Stax during the early '70s. Hooking up with producer Johnny Baylor's tiny KoKo label, Ingram appeared regularly on the R&B charts after Baylor brought his firm into the Stax fold in 1969. Ingram's intimate vocal approach was well suited to ballads, and his 1970 hit revival of "Ain't That Loving You (For More Reasons than One)" set the stage for his R&B chart-topping classic "(If Loving You Is Wrong) I Don't Want to Be Right" two years later. Long after Stax had folded, Ingram was still releasing hit singles—clear into 1987. —*Bill Dahl*

● **Greatest Hits** / Apr. 1996 / The Right Stuff ✦✦✦✦

The Ink Spots

f. 1938, Indianapolis, IN
R&B, Pop
The Ink Spots played a large role in pioneering the Black vocal group-harmony genre, helping to pave the way for the doo wop explosion of the '50s. The quavering high tenor of Bill Kenny presaged hundreds of street-corner leads to come, and the sweet harmonies of Carlie Fuqua, Deek Watson, and bass Hoppy Jones (who died in 1944) backed him flawlessly.
   Kenny's impeccable diction and Jones' deep drawl were both prominent on the Ink Spots' first smash on Decca in 1939, the sentimental "If I Didn't Care." From there through 1951, the group was seldom absent from the pop charts, topping the lists with "We Three (My Echo, My Shadow, and Me)" (1940), "I'm Making Believe," and "Into Each Life Some Rain Must Fall" (both in 1944), and "The Gypsy" and "To Each His Own" (both in 1946).
   Watson eventually split to form his own group, the Brown Dots, and appeared in numerous low-budget film musicals, while Kenny attempted a solo career, notching a solo hit in 1951 with the uplifting "It Is No Secret." Countless groups masquerading as the Ink Spots have thrived across the nation since the '50s. —*Bill Dahl*

★ **The Greatest Hits 1939-46** / 196 / MCA ✦✦✦✦✦
Greatest Hits 1939-46 is a 15-track collection of the Ink Spots' hits for Decca Records. During this era, the vocal group was at the height of their popularity, and most of the group's best-known songs—"If I Didn't Care," "Whispering Grass," "Maybe," "Java Jive," "Street of Dreams," "Gypsy," "To Each His Own"—are collected on this excellent compilation. —*Stephen Thomas Erlewine*

Tetsu Inoue

b. Tokyo, Japan
Synthesizer, Sequencer / Electronica, Ambient
A native of Tokyo, Japan, Tetsu Inoue is an ambient composer whose solo and collaborative works with the likes of Pete Namlook, Jonah Sharp, and Atom Heart are important documents of new school ambi-

ent and experimental electronic. Inoue began playing music in high school, starting on guitar in pop-rock cover bands. He began experimenting with synthesizers and early monophonic sequencers, inspired by the fusion of pop, psychedelic rock, and experimental electronic pioneered by groups like Pink Floyd, Tomita, and particularly Yellow Magic Orchestra, and by the mid-'80s was scoring for ballet and small dance groups. Tetsu Inoue moved to New York around 1986, securing an apartment before heading for an extended stay in San Francisco, where he played guitar in karaoke bands and began working with SF-based composer Naut Humon. He returned to New York soon after, continuing to amass demo material, and headed for Germany in the late '80s, where he met Uwe Schmidt (Atom Heart,) and Pete Namlook. Although ostensibly on vacation, Inoue recorded his first work for release while in Frankfurt (*Station Rose,* a collaboration with Schmidt, on *Cyclotron*) and, upon his return to New York, began working with Namlook on a number of different projects. Although dabbling in dance music styles such as techno and trance during this period, he was moving increasingly toward strictly ambient composition, and Namlook's noted Fax label would release several of his albums through the early- to mid-'90s. Most of his best solo and collaborative works appear there, including *2350 Broadway* and *Shades of Orion* with Namlook, *Electro Harmonix* with Jonah Sharp, and *Ambiant Otaku, Organic Cloud,* and *Slow and Low* as a solo artist. His mature aesthetic centers around a fusion of by turns haunting and contemplative soundscapes layered with heavily treated samples and field source materials, and occasional, usually sparse percussion. It's most elegantly stated on such works as *MU* (with Atom Heart as Masters of Psychedelic Ambiance) and *World Receiver.* —*Sean Cooper*

2350 Broadway / 1993 / Fax ✦✦✦✦
A seminal, almost fabled release spanning two CDs and recorded in real time (no pre—or post-production and no overdubs). Remarkably engaging for its simplicity, the set was subsequently reissued by popular demand and spawned a pair (and counting) of follow-ups in the series. —*Sean Cooper*

Shades of Orion / 1994 / Fax ✦✦✦✦
Tetsu Inoue's second full-length collaboration with Pete Namlook splits evenly between beatless and beat-oriented ambient, with spacey, immersive textures and subtle arrangments. High production values and the wealth of creative territory covered make for one of the finest early Fax releases. —*Sean Cooper*

Ambiant Otaku / 1994 / Fax ✦✦✦✦
Tetsu Inoue's first solo work on Fax and a highly sought-after collectible. Some of the tracks bear a passing resemblance to Brian Eno's early generative experiments (*Discreet Music, Evening Star*) but Inoue's take is decidedly contemporary, with pillowy, mellifluous synth passages occasionally accented by subtle beats and lilting melodies. —*Sean Cooper*

Organic Cloud / 1995 / Fax ✦✦✦✦
Mere austere than *Otaku,* it's also less varied, although the album ranks among his finest works. Sprawling but focused soundscapes with breathy atmospherics and subtle, complex rhythms. —*Sean Cooper*

Slow and Low / 1995 / Fax ✦✦✦
Tetsu Inoue's experimental tendencies take full reign on his third Fax solo work. Heavily hacked samples and field recordings abound, and though not as immediately engaging as his early work, it repays close attention with a depth of shape and color. —*Sean Cooper*

Time2 / 1996 / Fax ✦✦✦
Although it's always hard to tell who's leading and who's following in a Namlook production, it's safe to say this latest collaboration between Namlook and N.Y. producer Tetsu Inoue has benefited from both musicians' recent excursions to the more beat-oriented side of the tracks (Namlook with *Ozoona* and *Amp,* Inoue with *Hat, Ondas,* and *Instant Replay*). Most of *Time2* is dominated by skittery jungle-esque rhythms reminiscent of Atom Heart (particularly on the Namlook/Atom Heart Fax release *Jet Chamber 2*), although Inoue's signature hand-picked synth patches are in equal evidence. —*Sean Cooper*

● **World Receiver** / Jun. 11, 1996 / Instinct ✦✦✦✦
An engulfing combination of *Slow and Low*'s brazen experimentalism, and *Otaku* and *Cloud*'s concentrated ambiance and subtle melodiousness. Ostensibly a concept album integrating field recordings gathered from his travels around the world, the album is much more integrated and involved than much of his early solo work. His best work to date. —*Sean Cooper*

Insect Trust

f. 1966, **db.** 1970
Rock 'n' Roll, Jazz-Rock, Art-Rock/Progressive-Rock, Folk-Rock, Experimental, Psychedelic
One of the more interesting one-shot bands in rock 'n' roll, the Insect

Trust's most famous member was writer/critic/ethnomusicologist Robert Palmer, who played alto sax and clarinet. Less famous, but still a notable member, was guitarist/songwriter Luke Faust, who went on to add creative input for the Holy Modal Rounders' string of wonderful early- to mid-'70s records. Although the Insect Trust released two albums, their 1968 debut on Capitol remains a mystery to me: never seen it, never heard it. In fact, I wasn't aware of their second and final LP, *Hoboken Saturday Night*, until nearly a decade after its release and a few more years spent scrounging around used record stores before coming across a copy. Along with the loose-limbed music, *Hoboken Saturday Night* features musical contributions by heavy hitters (no pun intended) such as drummers Elvin Jones and Bernard "Pretty" Purdie, guitarist Hugh McCracken, and novelist Thomas Pynchon. The music ranges from surreal folk-rock (à la the Holy Modal Rounders and Fugs) to Booker T.-like pop-soul, to flat-out free jazz. Twenty-five years after its release, *Hoboken Saturday Night* sounds a bit dated, but its charm is irresistible, especially when Nancy Jefferies sings and the band cranks up its raucous onslaught of reeds and percussion. Never intended to be a traditional pop act, the Insect Trust should be best remembered for extending rock's boundaries and taking the genre to a much hipper level without resorting to a lot of banal technique. Good luck locating their records. —*John Dougan*

Insect Trust / 1968 / Capitol ✦✦✦

● **Hoboken Saturday Night** / 1970 / Atco ✦✦✦✦
Ebullient, warm, and wonderful, *Hoboken Saturday Night* is a long-forgotten piece of rock trivia that deserves to be rescued from the archives of oblivion and reissued. When the band wasn't indulging in a bit of jarring, jazzy dissonance, they were coughing up some intelligent folk-rock ("Trip on Me") or kicking out some serious Booker T.-style jams ("Ducks"). Robert Palmer's horn blowing is mighty fine, as is Nancy Jeffries' wan, but oddly seductive, vocalizing. Long out-of-print, it would be sad if this were lost forever. —*John Dougan*

Inspiral Carpets

f. 1986, Manchester, England, **db.** 1994
Alternative Pop-Rock, Alternative Dance
Of all of the Manchester bands of the early '90s, Inspiral Carpets were arguably the least interesting. They didn't explore the deep psychedelia of the rave scene as thoroughly as the Happy Mondays, nor did they have the classic pop skills of the Stone Roses. What the band did have was some massive organ hooks, courtesy of Clint Boon; the organ recalled the classic garage punk of the '60s. When the Inspiral Carpets could write a song that matched the sheer pleasure of their sound—and they managed at least two on each album, as well as their UK hit singles—the group made some wonderful pop gems; unfortunately, their hit-miss ratio was too low to make their albums consistent. When the Manchester fad passed, the Inspiral Carpets were still around and managed to keep scoring hits in the UK by losing some of the dated club beats and experimenting with their music slightly, including a collaboration with Mark E. Smith of the Fall on their 1994 album. —*Stephen Thomas Erlewine*

Life / Oct. 1990 / Elektra ✦✦✦✦
An impressive but inconsistent debut that recalled '60s British pop more strongly than the current Manchester dance craze, *Life* nevertheless had some fine dance tracks that were made to be played in clubs. —*Stephen Thomas Erlewine*

Beast Inside / May 7, 1991 / Elektra ✦✦✦
Inspiral Carpets' second album relies more on their organ-driven garage psychedelia than the previous *Life*, and the result is an engagingly diverse set of dance-oriented modern pop. —*Stephen Thomas Erlewine*

Revenge of the Goldfish / Oct. 13, 1992 / Elektra ✦✦✦
Inspiral Carpets continue to get further away from their club-oriented dance roots on their third album; fortunately, their pop songwriting continues to improve, which is why *Revenge of the Goldfish* never sounds like the work of a bunch of has-beens. —*Stephen Thomas Erlewine*

● **Singles** / Sep. 18, 1995 / Mute ✦✦✦✦
Inspiral Carpets couldn't really sustain their vision over the course of an entire album, yet they made a number of infectious Madchester singles, which became fairly big hits in England. The *Singles* collects all of the group's UK hits, from the swirling, sunny "Joe" to "I Want You," a duet with the Fall's Mark E. Smith that has previously been unavailable on album. Over the course of 17 tracks, nearly every one of the band's great moments ("This Is How It Feels," "Dragging Me Down," "She Comes in the Fall," "Saturn 5," "Uniform") is featured, making *Singles* a definitive overview of the laid-back, baggy band's career. —*Stephen Thomas Erlewine*

INXS

f. 1977, Sydney, Australia
Rock 'n' Roll, New Wave, Pop-Rock, Alternative Dance
INXS hailed from the pubs of Australia, which is part of the reason they never comfortably fit in with new wave. Even when the band branched out into synth-pop on its early recordings, they were underpinned by a hard, Stonesy beat and lead singer Michael Hutchence's Jaggeresque strut. Ultimately, these were the very things that made INXS into international superstars in the late '80s. By that time, the group had harnessed their hard rock, dance, and new wave influences into a sleek, stylish groove that made their 1987 album *Kick* into a multimillion-selling hit. While that sound was their key to stardom, it also proved to be their undoing; the group became boxed in by their Stonesy pop-funk in the early '90s, when their audience became entranced by harder-edged alternative rock. In spite of declining sales, INXS soldiered on, continuing to tour and record for a dedicated fan base into the late '90s.

Appropriately for a band that featured three brothers, INXS had its roots in a family act, the Farriss Brothers. The group came together while Andrew Farriss (keyboard, guitar), the middle brother, was in high school with Michael Hutchence (vocals). The two formed a band with Garry Gary Beers (bass). Simultaneously, Tim Farriss (guitar) was playing in various groups with his friend, Kirk Pengilly (guitar, saxophone). Eventually the two groups merged in 1977, with Jon Farriss joining as drummer. Two years later, when Jon graduated from high school, the band renamed itself INXS, moved from Perth to Sydney, and began to play pubs in Australia's capital. Within a year, the group landed an Australian record contract, releasing an eponymous debut on Deluxe in 1980.

INXS and *Underneath the Colours* (1981) became Australasian hits, leading the band to an American contract with Atco Records. In 1983, they released their US debut, *Shabooh Shoobah*, and embarked on an extensive tour which, thanks to the hit single "Don't Change," made them minor new wave stars. For their next album, INXS recorded a few sessions with producer Nile Rodgers, which resulted in the sleek, funky "Original Sin," the first inclination that the band was making a move toward a fusion of Stonesy rock and dance music. "Original Sin" made 1984's *The Swing* a minor hit, yet the group didn't have a genuine mainstream breakthrough until 1985's *Listen Like Thieves*, which climbed to number 11 in the US on the strength of the single "What You Need."

Listen Like Thieves laid the groundwork for *Kick*, the album that made INXS international superstars. Released late in 1987, *Kick* worked its way to multiplatinum status over the course of 1988, as four singles—the No. 1 "Need You Tonight," "Devil Inside," "New Sensation," and "Never Tear Us Apart"—climbed into the US Top Ten. In the wake of the album's success, Hutchence was hailed in some quarters as the heir to Mick Jagger's throne, and the group was considered to rival U2 in terms of international popularity. However, such success went to the group's heads. Hutchence released the "experimental" side project *Max Q* in early 1990, and the record tanked. *X*, INXS' follow-up to *Kick*, appeared in the fall of 1990 to mostly negative reviews. While the album generated several hits, including "Disappear" and "Bitter Tears," only its first single, "Suicide Blonde," reached the Top Ten in the US, and the sales of *X* were disappointing when compared to *Kick*.

X hurt INXS' momentum considerably. Although the group was still quite popular on its accompanying tour—the 1991 live album *Live Baby Live* was recorded at Wembley Stadium— the group could no longer be considered in the same league as U2, or now R.E.M. Hutchence continued to live a jet-setting lifestyle, dating Kylie Minogue and various supermodels, which did not wear well in the wake of alternative rock's commercial breakthrough in 1992. By the time INXS released *Welcome to Wherever You Are*, the group's most adventurous record, they were out of date in 1992, and even a rash of reviews that compared the record favorably to U2's *Achtung Baby* couldn't make it a hit. *Full Moon, Dirty Hearts* followed in 1993, and it was generally ignored. Following its release, the group left Atlantic, releasing *Greatest Hits* as its last album for the label.

INXS signed with PolyGram in 1994, yet it took them three years to release a new album. During that time, Hutchence was involved in several tabloid scandals, most notably his love affair with British TV personality Paula Yates (which brought an end to her marriage to Bob Geldof), and he hinted that he was recording a solo album. That record didn't materialize, but INXS returned in the spring of 1997 with *Elegantly Wasted*. While the album was greeted with poor reviews, its hedonistic dance-rock was better suited to the late '90s than the early '90s, which made the record the group's biggest hit since *X* —*Stephen Thomas Erlewine*

INXS / 1980 / Atco ✦✦
At the time of their debut album, INXS had not developed a signature style, playing a competent but unremarkable variation on droning new

wave synth-pop. Although Michael Hutchence already exuded a powerful vocal charisma, the only time *INXS* springs to life is when the group hints at the R&B and dance roots that would form the basis of their biggest hits. —*Stephen Thomas Erlewine*

Underneath the Colours / 1981 / Atco ✦✦✦
Underneath the Colours, INXS' second album, was a nearly identical continuation of the new wave pop of their debut, yet the record featured better arrangements and songs, including the Australian hit "The Loved One." —*Stephen Thomas Erlewine*

Shabooh Shoobah / 1982 / Atco ✦✦✦
On *Shabooh Shoobah*, INXS finally hit upon a smooth, stylish fusion of new wave synth-pop and rock 'n' roll that drew equally from the Stones' dirty R&B-inspired rhythms and AC/DC's loud crunch. However, the group hits their stride only on a handful of tracks. The droning synth riff of "Don't Change" masks a hard, funky groove, and "The One Thing" is an infectious, catchy pop single, yet most of the album lacks memorable songwriting. —*Stephen Thomas Erlewine*

Dekadance / 1983 / Atco ✦✦
Over the course of four remixed tracks from *Shabooh Shoobah,* the *Dekadance* EP accentuates INXS' flair for catchy rhythms, yet the record only comes to life on the six-minute remix of "The One Thing," simply because it has a stronger melody than anything else on the EP. —*Stephen Thomas Erlewine*

The Swing / 1984 / Atco ✦✦✦
Consolidating the strengths of *Shabooh Shoobah, The Swing* is the first consistently impressive INXS album. With the Nile Rodgers-produced "Original Sin" acting as the centerpiece, *The Swing* retains the new wave pop sense and rock attack of their earlier albums, while adding a stronger emphasis on dance rhythms. At the same time, the group's songwriting had improved, with more than half of the album featuring memorable hooks. —*Stephen Thomas Erlewine*

Listen like Thieves / 1985 / Atlantic ✦✦✦✦
INXS completes its transition into an excellent rock 'n' roll singles band with this album. Unfortunately, the new configuration only works for three songs: "What You Need," "Listen like Thieves," and "Kiss the Dirt (Falling Down the Mountain)." But these three songs are so strong that the album cannot be dismissed completely. The album is worth its price just for "What You Need," a strong Stonesy groove with Michael Hutchence singing more warmly than he ever has. —*Stephen Thomas Erlewine*

Kick / 1987 / Atlantic ✦✦✦✦
Kick, INXS's commercial and artistic breakthrough, overflows with hit singles, including "Need You Tonight," "Devil Inside," "New Sensation," and "Never Tear Us Apart." The band's mix of Stonesy rock 'n' roll, melodic pop, and dance-oriented beats has never sounded fresher—even the album tracks are fully developed songs that never seem like filler. It's easily their best album. —*Stephen Thomas Erlewine*

X / Sep. 1990 / Atlantic ✦✦✦
The seventh album from Australia's INXS basically sticks to the formula set up on *Kick*, mixing solid remixable dance-floor beats with slightly quirky production tricks, Michael Hutchence's rough-edged, bluesy vocals, and some good solid song hooks. The most immediate numbers are, of course, the two singles, "Suicide Blonde" and "Disappear," but other tracks stand out as potential hit material as well, including the anthemic "The Stairs." The biggest problems with the album are a tendency to play it safe, sticking to the tried and true—echoing a line in the thumping "Who Pays the Price," when Hutchence sings "it's all been felt before"—and the fact that there's very little in the way of subtlety on the entire album. All of the songs are designed for immediate radio contact—they don't really give you a chance to grow into them, they just grab you by the throat and start shaking. "Know the Difference," as an example, threatens to be sneaky, but immediately switches to an obvious assault instead. In the finish, the overwhelming lack of subtlety and sense of sameness overcomes the album as a whole. It's not that's it's a bad album. It's just nowhere near as good as it could—and should—have been. —*Steven McDonald*

Live Baby Live / 1991 / Atlantic ✦
Recorded during their international 1990 tour, *Live Baby Live* is a lifeless live album. INXS sounds professional—they never miss a note—and that's part of the problem. All of the performances sound like the studio versions, stripped of their excitement and savvy productions, which were essential factors in making the songs hit singles. Consequently, the album is a thoroughly unengaging affair and the worst record INXS have recorded. —*Stephen Thomas Erlewine*

Welcome to Wherever You Are / Aug. 4, 1992 / Atlantic ✦✦✦✦
Although INXS needed to experiment badly, their attempt at self-reinvention, *Welcome to Wherever You Are*, didn't even come close to gaining commercial or critical acceptance. From the start of the album, it's clear that INXS is out to confuse the standard perceptions of the band;

the first instrument on the album is an Eastern-flavored horn. Special recording effects and exotic rhythms and sounds are abundant on the album. Evidently, the pop audience didn't care about INXS anymore, since nobody bought the album. And that is a shame, since it is one of their strongest. —*Stephen Thomas Erlewine*

Full Moon, Dirty Hearts / Nov. 2, 1993 / Atlantic ✦
Following the surprisingly adventurous and artistically successful *Welcome to Wherever You Are, Full Moon, Dirty Hearts* sounds tired and as calculated as *X*. While most of the exotic trappings of *Welcome* have been pared down, there is still the same sense of the band experimenting as a way to stay current. INXS sounds energetic throughout the album, but the experimentation is poorly executed and there is a serious lack of strong songs and singles, apart from two duets: "Please (You Got That . . .)" with Ray Charles and the title track, which features Chrissie Hynde. —*Stephen Thomas Erlewine*

● **The Greatest Hits** / 1994 / Atlantic ✦✦✦✦
While INXS have made a few consistent albums, singles are the best format for the group's stylish dance-rock. Throughout the '80s and early '90s, the group racked up nine Top 40 hits and seven of those singles hit the Top Ten. *Greatest Hits* collects all of those hits—including "Need You Tonight," "What You Need," "Devil Inside," "New Sensation," "Disappear," "Suicide Blonde," and "Never Tears Us Apart"—adding minor hits like "Original Sin" and "Listen like Thieves," but curiously bypassing the pivotal "Don't Change" and excellent "Bitter Tears," which was a bigger hit than several songs on the record. Nevertheless, *Greatest Hits* lives up to its title and provides a fine introduction to the band. —*Stephen Thomas Erlewine*

Elegantly Wasted / Apr. 15, 1997 / Polygram ✦✦
INXS stumbled greatly in the early '90s, since their slick, professional fusion of disco and the Stones was singularly out of place in the grunge era. On the heels of U2's discovery of irony and the dance floor and Oasis' popularizing rock 'n' roll hedonism again, INXS seemed to be better suited to the late '90s, but *Elegantly Wasted*, their first new studio album in four years, proves that theory wrong. The band does dabble in contemporary dance on *Elegantly Wasted*, but it all comes out sounding like the lite funk-n-roll of *Kick*, only without the energy. And without the tunes. Throughout *Elegantly Wasted*, INXS goes through the motions, coming up with a record nearly as weak as *Full Moon, Dirty Hearts*. The really unfortunate thing is, it sounds like they were trying this time around. —*Stephen Thomas Erlewine*

Iron Butterfly

f. 1966, San Diego, CA, **db.** 1971
Hard Rock, Psychedelic, Heavy Metal, Acid Rock
The heavy, psychedelic acid rock of Iron Butterfly may seem dated to some today, but the group was one of the first hard rock bands to receive extensive radio airplay, and their best-known song, the 17-minute epic "In a Gadda Da Vida," established that more extended compositions were viable entries in the rock marketplace, paving the way for progressive AOR. The track was written by vocalist, organist, and bandleader Doug Ingle, who formed the first incarnation of Iron Butterfly in 1966 in San Diego with drummer Ron Bushy. After the group moved to Los Angeles and played the club scene, it secured a recording contract and got national exposure through tours with the Doors and Jefferson Airplane. Following the release of their 1968 debut album, *Heavy*, original members Jerry Penrod (bass), Darryl DeLoach (vocals), and Danny Weis (guitar) left the band and were replaced by guitarist Erik Braunn and bassist Lee Dorman. Weis went on to join Rhinoceros. The new lineup recorded *In a Gadda Da Vida* later that year, which sold four million copies, spent over a year in the Top Ten, and was the first album to receive platinum certification after the RIAA instituted the award. (The title has been translated as "in the garden of Eden" or "in the garden of life.") A shortened version of the title track, which contained extended instrumental passages with loud guitars and classical/Eastern-influenced organ, plus a two-and-a-half-minute drum solo, reached No. 30 on the singles charts. The follow-up, *Ball*, showed greater musical variety and went gold, but it also marked the beginning of the band's decline. Erik Braunn left the group and was replaced by guitarists Mike Pinera and Larry "Rhino" Reinhardt, but the group's success was largely over. Iron Butterfly broke up in 1971; Braunn and Bushy re-formed the group in the mid-'70s without success. —*Steve Huey*

Heavy / 1968 / Atco ✦✦✦
Iron Butterfly's 1968 debut album *Heavy* established the band's trademark sound, relying on plodding, heavy guitar riffs and thundering drums. Most of the album was not particularly well-written—the riffs *were* the songs, not their foundation—but the band's overwhelmingly loud, sonic attack occasionally made up for the weakness in the material. —*Stephen Thomas Erlewine*

● **In a Gadda Da Vida** / 1968 / Atco ✦✦✦✦
With its endless, droning minor-key riff and mumbled vocals, "In a Gadda Da Vida" is arguably the most notorious song of the acid-rock era. According to legend, the group was so stoned when they recorded the track that they could neither pronounce the title "In the Garden of Eden" or end the track, so it rambles on for a full 17 minutes, which to some listeners sounds like eternity. But that's the essence of its appeal—it's the epitome of heavy psychedelic excess, encapsulating the most indulgent tendencies of the era. Iron Butterfly never matched the warped excesses of "In a Gadda Da Vida," either on their debut album of the same name or the rest of their catalog, yet they occasionally made some enjoyable fuzz-guitar-driven psychedelia that works as a period piece. The five tracks that share space with their magnum opus on *In a Gadda Da Vida* qualify as good artifacts, and the entire record still stands as the group's definitive album, especially since this is the only place the full-length title track is available. — *Stephen Thomas Erlewine*

Ball / 1969 / Atco ✦✦✦
Following the huge success of their second record, *In-a-Gadda-Da-Vida*, Iron Butterfly scored a second straight Top Five album with *Ball*. While it didn't have any acid-rock freak-out to compare with the epic "In a Gadda Da Vida," *Ball* was a more ambitious album, as the group experimented with shorter, more melodic songs. Like any Iron Butterfly album, the quality of the material is wildly inconsistent, yet cut-for-cut, *Ball* is a more consistent album than their two previous records, as the group trimmed away some of the acid-rock excesses of their earlier records while retaining their brutally loud trademark heavy guitars. — *Stephen Thomas Erlewine*

Metamorphosis / 1970 / Atlantic ✦✦✦
On *Ball*, Iron Butterfly began to expand their sound, attempting to write more concisely. On *Metamorphosis*, the group continued their musical explorations, adding a layered production to their sound. However, only keyboardist/vocalist Doug Ingle was enthusiastic about the band's new musical direction and most of the group refused to participate in the recording of the album, claiming it strayed too far from Iron Butterfly's signature sound. The truth of the matter is the rest of the band was right—under Ingle's direction, the group tries stylistic diversions that they do not have the ability to accomplish, including funk and acoustic ballads. Nevertheless, this ambition makes for an interesting listen, since Iron Butterfly's albums can be weighed down by their relentless heaviness. Despite a handful of strong tracks—particularly the single "Easy Rider (Let the Wind Pay the Way)"—most of the album doesn't hold up on repeated plays. — *Stephen Thomas Erlewine*

Scorching Beauty / 1975 / MCA ✦✦
Five years after their breakup, Iron Butterfly reunited in 1975 and released *Scorching Beauty*, an undistinguished album that fell between the group's heavy acid-rock and mid-'70s arena rock conventions. — *Stephen Thomas Erlewine*

Sun and Steel / 1976 / MCA ✦
If the 1975 comeback *Scorching Beauty* was faceless, Iron Butterfly's 1976 follow-up, *Sun and Steel*, was an outright disastrous attempt at reshaping the band's signature sound to '70s hard rock conventions, lacking even the curiosity value of *Scorching Beauty*. — *Stephen Thomas Erlewine*

Light and Heavy: The Best of Iron Butterfly / Jan. 19, 1993 / Rhino ✦✦✦✦
Although the compilation is quite generous, featuring 21 tracks on CD, *Light and Heavy: The Best of Iron Butterfly* isn't all that entertaining, due to Iron Butterfly's difficulties with producing compelling material. All of the group's highlights from 1968-1970 are included, although the career-making, 17-minute "In a Gadda Da Vida" is presented in its three-minute single edit. Since that is the only Iron Butterfly song most listeners know, the lack of the full-length version could potentially sink the album, but the fact of the matter is, "In a Gadda Da Vida" gets quite repetitive over the course of nearly 20 minutes. While the quality of the rest of *Light and Heavy* is spotty—ranging from heavy psychedelic rock to light psychedelic pop—it is a more intriguing listen than *In a Gadda Da Vida*, even if it doesn't have the period-piece charm of the original hit record. — *Stephen Thomas Erlewine*

Iron Maiden

f. 1976, London, England
Heavy Metal, British Metal
From their origins as a bar band in the mid-'70s to the present, England's Iron Maiden has become one of the most imitated bands in heavy metal. The man who has held the group together through the rough times is bassist Steve Harris. Some of their theatrics were somewhat tacky in the early days, but by the late '70s they were already gaining a respectable following. EMI released their self-titled debut

album in 1980, featuring Paul Di'Anno on vocals and Dave Murray on guitar. In the US, the album was released on Harvest.
The band's second album helped them gain a huge following all over Europe and America, but within the band there were problems. Out went Di'Anno and in came Bruce Dickinson, former vocalist for the band Samson. Another change was the addition of guitarist Adrian Smith (who joined just before the *Killers* album, replacing Dennis Stratton), and it was this lineup (along with drummer Clive Burr) that took them over the top. The band's impact has been immense, selling millions, and their sound has easily distinguished them from other bands. — *John Book*

Iron Maiden / 1980 / Capitol ✦✦✦✦
This is the debut album that started it all for this band; many of the songs remain all-time metal classics, including "Sanctuary" and "Running Free." — *John Book*

Killers / 1981 / Capitol ✦✦✦✦
Album No. 2 by Iron Maiden is not as aggressive or as addicting as their self-titled debut, but still an essential part of their career. This was the last studio album to feature vocalist Di'Anno; he later formed Paul Di'Anno's Battlezone. — *John Book*

Maiden Japan / 1981 / Capitol ✦✦
A live EP recorded in Japan, this was the last Iron Maiden record to feature vocalist Paul Di'Anno. — *John Book*

The Number of the Beast / 1982 / Capitol ✦✦✦✦
The first Maiden album to feature ex-Samson vocalist Bruce Dickinson, this is powerful with some great guitar work from Dave Murray and Adrian Smith and fantastic bass playing from Steve Harris. This is the album that brought the band success in the US, and it features the classics "Run to the Hills" and the title track. — *John Book*

Piece of Mind / 1983 / Capitol ✦✦✦✦
The first Maiden album to feature drummer Nicko McBrain, *Peace of Mind* is easily one of their best efforts. Lead guitarists Adrian Smith and Dave Murray play their most creative work here, and the whole band is in top form. — *John Book*

Powerslave / 1984 / Capitol ✦✦✦
Iron Maiden gets more into lyrical themes this time around, featuring the 13-minute classic "Rime of the Ancient Mariner." — *John Book*

Live After Death (The World Slavery Tour) / 1985 / Capitol ✦✦✦✦
Documenting the band at their peak, this is a great live double album with a wide range of songs, going as far back as their first album. It's also available as a home video. — *John Book*

Somewhere in Time / 1986 / Capitol ✦✦
A somewhat controversial album, the band prominently used keyboards and synthesizers in their sound. It has lots of great songs, including "Heaven Can Wait." — *John Book*

Seventh Son of a Seventh Son / 1988 / Capitol ✦✦✦✦
The band's first attempt at a concept album includes keyboardist/synthesizer sounds, but is not as annoying as the *Somewhere in Time* album. A good set of songs includes "Can I Play with Madness?," "The Clairvoyant," and the haunting title track. — *John Book*

No Prayer for the Dying / 1990 / Epic ✦✦
The band's first label move since signing to EMI in 1979, it's probably their weakest album, songwise, but Bruce Dickinson shows that he is one of the best vocalists in heavy metal. — *John Book*

Fear of the Dark / May 12, 1992 / Epic ✦✦
On their tenth album, the band shows that they haven't lost their edge or power. No surprises—it's just what you'd expect from Iron Maiden. — *AMG*

X Factor / Oct. 10, 1995 / CMC International ✦✦

● **The Best of the Beast** / Sep. 24, 1996 / Castle ✦✦✦✦
Over the course of two CDs, *The Best of the Beast* hits all of Iron Maiden's biggest hits, from "Run to the Hills" and "Wasted Years" to "Two Minutes to Midnight," "Aces High," and a live version of "Rime of the Ancient Mariner." In addition to the classic Maiden cuts, there are several rare tracks, including two unreleased songs from the Soundhouse Tapes, the unreleased "Strange World," and a new single called "Virus." *The Best of the Beast* works because Iron Maiden was always at its best on individual songs, despite their series of concept albums. This compilation gathers nearly all of their finest moments, providing an excellent introduction to one of the most popular and influential heavy metal bands of the early '80s. — *Stephen Thomas Erlewine*

Chris Isaak

b. Jun. 26, 1956, Stockton, CA
Guitar, Vocals / Roots-Rock, Pop-Rock, Americana
Chris Isaak clearly loves the reverb-laden rockabilly and country of Sun Studios. In particular, he transfers the sweeping melancholy of Roy Orbison's sweeping, classic melancholy Monument singles ("Crying,"

"Oh, Pretty Woman," "In Dreams") to the more stripped-down, rootsy sound of Sun. His stylized take on '50s and '60s rock 'n' roll eventually made him into a star in the early '90s, thanks to the hit single "Wicked Game."

Isaak began performing after he graduated from college, forming the rockabilly band Silvertone. The group, which featured guitarist James Calvin Wilsey, bassist Rowland Salley, and drummer Kenney Dale Johnson, would become the singer-guitarist's permanent supporting band. Isaak released his first album, *Silvertone*, on Warner Brothers Records in 1985. It was critically well-received, yet it didn't sell. Two years later, he released *Chris Isaak*, which managed to scrape into the Top 200 album charts. After its release, the singer began an acting career with a bit part in Jonathan Demme's 1988 film, *Married to the Mob;* he would later have parts in *Wild at Heart* and *The Silence of the Lambs*. Released in 1989, *Heart Shaped World* initially sold more than *Chris Isaak*, yet it didn't manage to break big until late 1990, when the single "Wicked Game" was featured in David Lynch's *Wild at Heart*. Soon, the single became a Top Ten hit; the album also made it into the Top Ten and sold over a million copies. Both 1993's *San Francisco Days* and 1995's *Forever Blue* mine essentially the same vein as *Heart Shaped World*, yet both went gold and spawned a handful of hits. In 1996, Isaak released *The Baja Sessions.* — *Stephen Thomas Erlewine*

Silvertone / 1985 / Warner Brothers ✦✦✦✦
Chris Isaak's debut album, *Silvertone*, named after his three-piece backup group, sets the pattern for his subsequent albums in its meticulously constructed retro sound. Isaak enters a time machine and emerges around 1960, when Roy Orbison is ruling the charts with his melodramatic ballads and Elvis Presley has just returned from the Army. Of course, what passed for a style 25 years before is in Isaak's hands stylization, and when he wails in an Orbison falsetto of romantic desperation, then does a flat, Presley-like recitation in the album-closing "Western Skies," it all seems over the top. But he is just about sincere enough to pull it off, and James Calvin Wilsey is a strong enough guitarist to keep the arrangements on track. So, to the extent that you can resist the "Is this guy kidding?" impression, the music is appealing. — *William Ruhlmann*

Chris Isaak / Dec. 1986 / Warner Brothers ✦✦✦
Chris Isaak moves up about five years from his usual stylistic focus by covering the Yardbirds' 1965 hit "Heart Full of Soul," but on his original tunes he remains in the Roy Orbison orbit, using his sob-filled voice and James Calvin Wilsey's Duane Eddy-like twangy guitar work to evoke the romantic angst of the early 1960s. Listening to him is still an oddly dislocating experience, but he does what he does so thoroughly it's hard not to go along if only for the running time of the record. — *William Ruhlmann*

● **Heart Shaped World** / Jun. 1989 / Reprise ✦✦✦✦
The album that really broke Isaak through to a mainstream audience, this features the title cut, "I'm Not Waiting," "Wrong to Love You," a driving rendition of "Diddley Daddy," and the surprise No. 6 hit "Wicked Game." Brooding and intense. — *Cub Koda*

San Francisco Days / Apr. 13, 1993 / Reprise ✦✦✦✦
Chris Isaak's records are eerily out of time; the production is too clean and sterile to sound as if it was recorded at Sun Studios (a sound he clearly admires), but his music doesn't fit neatly into the sounds of contemporary radio. Accordingly, his sound is original yet familiar, appealing both to fans of early-'60s rock 'n' roll and a modern audience. At times, Isaak tries too hard to emulate his idols—for instance, his strained Orbison-esque falsetto on "Two Hearts"—but when he doesn't try too hard, the results are often startling. *San Francisco Days* is Isaak's most musically diverse album yet. — *Stephen Thomas Erlewine*

Forever Blue / May 23, 1995 / Warner Brothers ✦✦✦
Chris Isaak's albums all follow the same basic formula, yet he adds a grittier edge to *Forever Blue*. Kicking off with the bluesy stomp of "Baby Did a Bad Thing," where Isaak tries to sound like John Lee Hooker, the album is another piece of expertly crafted rock 'n' roll, carefully crafted to sound like the early '60s. It's enjoyable, yet it never is as consistent as *Heart Shaped World* or *San Francisco Days*. — *Stephen Thomas Erlewine*

Baja Sessions / Oct. 8, 1996 / Reprise ✦✦✦
The Baja Sessions is Chris Isaak's rootsiest record since *Silvertone*, alternating between loose versions of some of his earliest tracks and roughed-up, improved covers of recent hits like "Two Hearts." In addition to the older cuts, there are two new songs—"I Wonder" and "Return to Me"—which are fine additions to his catalog. — *Stephen Thomas Erlewine*

Ken Ishii

b. Tokyo, Japan
DJ / Techno, Club/Dance, Electronica
Japanese techno artist Ken Ishii is among the most innovative, experi-

mental composers in contemporary techno. Although working in and drawing from a decidedly dancefloor-oriented, Detroit-derived framework, Ishii's exploration of avant-garde compositional techniques like chromaticism and the prominent influence of digital synthesis figures him as strongly deviant from Motor City aesthetic tradition. A Tokyo native, Ishii's work is most resonant in feel perhaps to the work of Derrick May, though the influence of more artful electronic experimentalists like Yellow Magic Orchestra and Haruomi Hosono also figure prominently. Although Ishii has only been releasing music since the early '90s—recording under his own name for the R&S label, as well as Rising Sun (for ESP), Utu (Plus 8), Flare (Sublime), and Yoga (ESP)—his '93 and '94 R&S works, as well as his Sublime CD *Reference to Difference*, are all benchmarks of techno futurism. Incorporating elements of British bleep and breakbeat techno, as well as elements of the 20th century avant-garde, Ishii's finest work expands on techno's rigid rhythmic structure, wedging in elements of chaos and disruption. Like the Black Dog, B12, and other armchair experimentalists, Ishii's music is often praised by DJs who nonetheless refuse to give his often challenging records much play. Although until only recently unknown in Japan and just a step above obscure on the global techno scene, Ishii's 1995 release *Jelly Tones* opened his work out onto a larger audience, prompting a world tour and growing repute as composer and DJ. In addition to a continuous performance and DJing schedule, Ishii has also remixed tracks for Keiichi Suzuki, Tokyo Skaparadise Orchestra, Cova, and Masatoshi Nagase. — *Sean Cooper*

Tangled Notes / 1994 / R&S ✦✦✦✦
A relentless, cacophonous collection of outbound experimental techno, with a clanging, bleeting harmonic wallop edged on by disjointed rhythms and complex arrangements. A masterpiece of future-form techno and criminally underacknowledged. — *Sean Cooper*

Reference to Difference / 1994 / Sublime ✦✦✦
Unexpectedly atmospheric, with ambient and environmental textures filling out just under an hour of lyrical, mid-tempo experimental techno. Originally a Japan-only release, Sublime issued *Reference* worldwide in 1995 on vinyl and CD with extra tracks. — *Sean Cooper*

● **Innerelements** / 1994 / R&S/Sony ✦✦✦✦
Collects the best material from his earlier "Deep Sleep," "Pneuma," and "Tangled Notes" releases for R&S/Apollo and adds three new tracks. Reissued by Sony, the album is an excellent, relatively easy-to-find introduction to Ishii's oeuvre. — *Sean Cooper*

The Isley Brothers

f. 1954, Cincinnati, OH
Soul, Funk, R&B, Urban, Quiet Storm
First formed in the early '50s, the Isley Brothers enjoyed one of the longest, most influential and most diverse careers in the pantheon of popular music. The first generation of Isley siblings were born and raised in Cincinnati, OH, where they were encouraged to begin a singing career by their father, himself a professional vocalist, and their mother, a church pianist who provided musical accompaniment at their early performances. Initially a gospel quartet, the group was comprised of Ronald, Rudolph, O'Kelly and Vernon Isley; after Vernon's 1955 death in a bicycling accident, tenor Ronald was tapped as the remaining trio's lead vocalist.

In 1957, the brothers went to New York City to record a string of failed doo wop singles. While performing a spirited reading of the song "Lonely Teardrops" in Washington, DC, in 1959, they interjected the line "You know you make me want to shout," which inspired frenzied audience feedback. An RCA executive in the audience saw the concert, and when he signed the Isleys soon after, he instructed that their first single be constructed around their crowd-pleasing catch-phrase; while the call-and-response classic "Shout" failed to reach the pop Top 40 on its initial release, it eventually became a frequently-covered classic.

Still, success eluded the Isleys, and only after they left RCA in 1962 did they again have another hit, this time with their seminal cover of the Topnotes' "Twist and Shout." Like so many of the brothers' early R&B records, "Twist and Shout" earned greater commercial success when later rendered by a white group—in this case, the Beatles; other acts who notched hits by closely following the Isleys' blueprint were the Yardbirds ("Respectable," also covered by the Outsiders), the Human Beinz ("Nobody But Me"), and Lulu ("Shout"). During a 1964 tour, they recruited a young guitarist named Jimmy James to play in their backing band; James—who later shot to fame under his given name, Jimi Hendrix—made his first recordings with the Isleys, including the single "Testify," issued on the brothers' own T-Neck label.

The Isleys signed to the Motown subsidiary Tamla in 1965, where they joined forces with the famed Holland-Dozier-Holland writing and production team. Their first single, the shimmering "This Old Heart of Mine," was their finest moment yet, and barely missed the pop Top Ten. The record was their only hit on Motown, however, and when the song hit No. 3 in Britain in 1968, the Isleys relocated to England in order to sustain their flagging career; after years of writing their own material, they felt straitjacketed by the Motown assembly-line production formula, and by the time they returned stateside in 1969, they had exited Tamla to resuscitate the T-Bone label.

Their next release, the muscular and funky "It's Your Thing," hit No. 2 on the US charts in 1969, and became their most successful record. That year, the Isleys also welcomed a number of new members as younger brothers Ernie and Marvin, brother-in-law Chris Jasper, and family friend Everett Collins became the trio's new backing unit. Spearheaded by Ernie's hard-edged guitar leads, the group began incorporating more and more rock material into its repertoire as the 1970s dawned, and scored hits with covers of Stephen Stills' "Love the One You're With," Eric Burdon & War's "Spill the Wine," and Bob Dylan's "Lay Lady Lay."

In 1973, the Isleys scored a massive hit with their rock-funk fusion cover of their own earlier single "Who's That Lady," retitled "That Lady (Part I);" the album $3 + 3$ also proved highly successful, as did 1975's *The Heat Is On*, which spawned the smash "Fight the Power (Part I)." As the decade wore on, the group again altered its sound to fit into the booming disco market; while their success on pop radio ran dry, they frequently topped the R&B charts with singles like 1977's "The Pride," 1978's "Take Me to the Next Phase (Part 1)," 1979's "I Wanna Be with You (Part 1)," and 1980's "Don't Say Goodnight."

While the Isleys' popularity continued into the 1980s, Ernie and Marvin, along with Chris Jasper, defected in 1984 to form their own group, Isley, Jasper, Isley; a year later, they topped the R&B charts with "Caravan of Love." On March 31, 1986, O'Kelly died of a heart attack; Rudolph soon left to join the ministry, but the group reunited in 1990. Although the individual members continued with solo work and side projects, the Isley Brothers continued on in one form or another throughout the decade; in 1996, now consisting of Ronald, Marvin and Ernie, they released the album *Mission to Please*. —*Jason Ankeny*

Twist & Shout! / 1962 / Sundazed ✦✦✦
On this album, the Isleys tried to mine the "Twist & Shout" groove for all it was worth. Produced by Bert Berns, over half the material was written or co-written by "Russell"; the same Russell who co-wrote "Twist And Shout," it was a pseudonym for Berns himself. Not that this was always necessarily a bad thing; "Twist And Shout" was a stone classic, and many of the other tunes do their best to emulate its groove with Latin rhythms and the Isleys' frayed, gospelish vocals. Some of the tracks, though, do little more than rework the basic riff, and even the ones that aren't blatant rewrites don't measure up to the hit. The ballad "Time After Time" is a nice change of pace, and the brothers are never less than energetic and entertaining, but this is really not that strong as a whole. The CD reissue on Sundazed includes three bonus tracks: the previously unreleased (and unremarkable) "Crazy Love" and the cool singles "Twistin' with Linda" and "Nobody But Me," which are easily available on Rhino's *Story* compilation. —*Richie Unterberger*

Doin' Their Thing / 1969 / Motown ✦✦✦✦
An underrated masterpiece. This album really began the $3 + 3$ relationship between the older brothers and the younger generation. The single "It's Your Thing" became a national catch phrase and later turned up in a film the brothers financed. More importantly, they now saw that they could expand their stylistic frontiers and start doing funk and rock along with the soul. —*Ron Wynn*

3 Plus 3 / 1973 / T Neck ✦✦✦✦
A masterpiece, one of the defining albums for '70s Black music. The original Isley frontline of Ronald, Rudolph, and O'Kelly merged with the next generation featuring younger brothers Marvin and Ernie, plus cousin Chris Jasper. The lead single "That Lady" established their new sound and identity on Epic, and was just one of four monster songs that came from the album. —*Ron Wynn*

The Isley Brothers Live It Up / 1974 / T Neck ✦✦✦✦
The album that cemented the revolution begun by the $3 + 3$ LP. The title song was a blazing triumph, landing them on *Soul Train* and getting widespread pop and club attention, although it didn't prove to be their biggest hit in those areas. Ernie Isley made his first significant impact as a guitar soloist, and the group also began attracting fans who hadn't heard their earlier cuts, while alerting the faithful they were really back on the scene. —*Ron Wynn*

The Heat Is On / 1975 / T Neck ✦✦✦✦
Another spectacular album. The Isley Brothers had refined rock/disco and now had it down to a science. The uptempo tunes had extended vamps, slithering, driving backbeats, and funky rhythms, while the ballads were smooth and sentimental. Ernie Isley would get a track to blaze away on guitar, and the whole thing revolved around the group's nonstop excitement and intensity. —*Ron Wynn*

Harvest for the World / 1976 / T Neck ✦✦✦
The Isley Brothers kept their great string of hits going with this mid-'70s release. They enjoyed two more Top 10 R&B singles and several

club smashes, and were making enjoyable, delightful music, both the uptempo songs and the ballads. —*Ron Wynn*

Showdown / 1978 / T Neck ✦✦✦
The Isley Brothers had perfected their rock/disco format by the late '70s, and each album had a set pattern. There were the hit singles, with their chunking beat, synthesized underpinning, and energetic collective vocals. Then came the album cuts, sentimental ballads wonderfully sung by Ronnie Isley. Then there was a cut designed to show off Ernie Isley's blistering guitar, which reflected the group's rock legacy and the influence of Jimi Hendrix. This contained another chart-topper in "Take Me to the Next Phase." —*Ron Wynn*

Winner Takes All / 1979 / T Neck ✦✦✦
This was the last great Isley Brothers album in the rock/disco style. Their vocals still retained the energy and exuberance of earlier works, Ernie Isley hadn't become so disgruntled that he simply recycled Hendrix cliches, and the group's production, songs, and arrangements weren't yet becoming stagnant. —*Ron Wynn*

Go All the Way / 1980 / T Neck ✦✦✦
Although regarded as the beginning of their decline, this 1980 album did get the Isley Brothers three more chart hits. But they were so locked into their uptempo dance/R&B, ballad, rock guitar solo format that each LP became more and more predictable. The internal difficulties that finally tore the group apart were also surfacing with this album. —*Ron Wynn*

Grand Slam / 1981 / T Neck ✦✦✦
Despite getting three more hits, including one Top 10 R&B song, the bloom was definitely off the Isley Brothers' rose. Stagnation and internal bickering were taking their toll, and the innocent, energetic air that sparked their '70s albums was gone. It had been replaced by a calculating, indifferent attitude that clearly affected their music. —*Ron Wynn*

Between the Sheets / 1983 / T Neck ✦✦✦
The title track was a huge ballad hit for The Isley Brothers and marked the end of an era. The great $3 + 3$ collaboration between the brothers Ronnie, Rudolph, and O'Kelly and the second generation of younger brothers, Marvin and Ernie, plus cousin Chris Jasper, finally splintered over artistic differences. Neither ever attained the same levels apart as they did together. —*Ron Wynn*

Greatest Hits & Rare Classics / Feb. 1991 / Motown ✦✦✦✦
Although the Isleys recorded some good stuff for Motown in the late '60s, it's generally true that the label's attempts to fit them into the standard Motown production line inhibited their creativity and individuality. This 22-track retrospective of their Motown days is dominated by material from in-house songwriters like Eddie Holland, Smokey Robinson, and Ivory Joe Hunter, and doesn't rank among the Isleys' best work, though it's respectable enough. The best tracks—the Top Ten hit "This Old Heart of Mine," "Behind a Painted Smile," and "Take Some Time Out for Love"—are available on the Rhino best-of, but Isleys fans will find this a worthwhile summary of their brief Motown stay. Includes the original versions of two of their biggest hits cut for other labels, "Twist & Shout" and "It's Your Thing." —*Richie Unterberger*

The Complete UA Sessions / Mar. 26, 1991 / EMI America ✦✦✦
After the Isleys left Scepter, they recorded for United Artists for a year, a period that produced no hits but a wealth of muscular R&B. Although there's some overlap with the first volume of Rhino's anthology, this one is essential for fans of the Isleys. —*Stephen Thomas Erlewine*

★ **The Isley Brothers Story, Vol. 1** / Apr. 2, 1991 / Rhino ✦✦✦✦✦
Ranging from major hits to obscurities, *The Isley Bros. Story, Vol. 1* can serve as a most impressive introduction to the Isley Brothers' early years. One thing this CD won't be accused of is predictability. The North Jersey group is heard on everything from frenzied, gospel-drenched performances like "Shout," "Twistin' with Linda," and "Twist and Shout" to smoother Motown recordings such as "This Old Heart of Mine" and "I Guess I'll Always Love You." One of the biggest surprises here is 1964's "Who's That Lady," an Impressions-influenced pearl that received little attention at the time, but later evolved into the 1973 mega-hit "That Lady." Recorded that same year is "Testify," which employs a then-unknown guitarist named Jimi Hendrix. —*Alex Henderson*

★ **The Isley Brothers Story, Vol. 2** / Apr. 2, 1991 / Rhino ✦✦✦✦
Summarizing 16 years of history by a group as consistently exciting as the Isley Brothers on two CDs may not be the most realistic undertaking on earth, but Rhino generally makes wise and insightful selections on this compilation, which traces the Isleys' evolution from raw hits of the late '60s and early '70s like "It's Your Thing," "Work to Do" and "Pop That Thang" to the sleeker work they did as a sextet from 1973 to 1984. Most of their essential hits as a sextet—everything from the hypnotic "That Lady," the haunting "Footsteps in the Dark," and the sentimental "For the Love of You" to such angry sociopolitical smokers as "Fight the Power" and "Livin' in the Life"—is included. Both the scorching funk of "The Pride" and "Take Me to the Next Phase" and the dreamy romanti-

cism of "Between the Sheets" and "Don't Say Goodnight" illustrate the type of excellence the Isleys so often achieved. —*Alex Henderson*

Shout: the RCA Sessions / Jul. 1996 / RCA ✦✦✦✦
The Isley Brothers spent a year at RCA Records, during which time they only had one hit—"Shout"—which barely scraped the charts. Of course, Joey Dee & the Starliters would later take the song into the Top Ten, but at the time it was an inauspicious beginning to a long, illustrious career. "Shout" and the rest of the recordings the Isleys made for RCA Records are collected on *Shout: RCA Sessions*. Although it's only a single-disc collection, the material is too uneven to be a thoroughly compelling listen, although it is certainly valuable as a historical compilation. —*Stephen Thomas Erlewine*

The Iveys

f. 1968, England, **db.** 1969
Pop-Rock
Essentially the same group as Badfinger, the Iveys landed on the Beatles' Apple label in late 1968 after Beatle personal assistant Mal Evans encouraged them to submit tapes to Paul McCartney. Their bright, melodic, and harmony-filled pop-rock sound immediately drew comparisons to the Beatles, and to the work of McCartney in particular.

Their sole album (*Maybe Tomorrow*,) released in Europe in mid-1969, was an accomplished if somewhat lightweight collection of original material, reflecting the heavy influence of both McCartney and Ray Davies (indeed, the latter had expressed interest in producing the group before Apple picked them up). The LP gathered little attention, but after a name change to Badfinger, the replacement of bassist Ron Griffiths by Joey Molland, a commission to score the Peter Sellers/Ringo Starr film *The Magic Christian*, and a McCartney-penned hit single from the movie ("Come and Get It"), the group were on their way. Half a dozen of the tunes from *Maybe Tomorrow* ended up on Badfinger's first proper album, *Magic Christian Music*. —*Richie Unterberger*

Maybe Tomorrow / 1969 / Capitol ✦✦✦
Issued at long last in the US in 1992, this is decent late-'60s British pop-rock, if somewhat less developed and more precious than Badfinger's prime efforts. Six of the better tracks were used on *Magic Christian*. The ones that got left behind are certainly not an embarrassment, with "Yesterday Ain't Coming Back," "Angelique," and "I've Been Waiting" (by far the album's hardest-rocking tune) ranking as the standouts. The CD reissue adds four rare cuts, two of them previously unreleased. —*Richie Unterberger*

J

The Jackson 5

f. 1966, Gary, IN
Soul, Motown, Philly Soul

The Jackson 5 was Motown's last great pop group and among the most successful singles acts of the '70s. The group consisted of five brothers—Jackie (b. May 4, 1951), Tito (b. Oct. 15, 1953), Jermaine (b. Dec. 11, 1954), Marlon (b. Mar. 12, 1957), and Michael Jackson (b. Aug. 29, 1958). They grew up in Gary, IN, and were first organized as a group by their father, Joe Jackson, in 1966. In essence, the group was a vocal ensemble centered on Michael, who, though the youngest, was clearly the most talented. The group came to the attention of Motown and was signed in 1969. Their first four singles, "I Want You Back," "ABC," "The Love You Save," and "I'll Be There," all hit No. 1 in 1970; "Mama's Pearl" and "Never Can Say Goodbye" did almost as well in 1971. In 1972, Motown launched both Michael Jackson and Jermaine Jackson as solo acts, and the group's efforts were gradually less successful in the following years, though "Dance Machine" was a big hit in 1974. In 1975, Jackie, Tito, Marlon, and Michael signed to Epic Records, adding brother Randy (b. Oct. 29, 1961), and became the Jacksons (the name the Jackson 5 was owned by Motown). (Although Jermaine stayed at Motown, he rejoined the group in 1984.) —*William Ruhlmann*

ABC / 1970 / Motown ✦✦✦✦
A fabulous album, arguably their best on Motown. While the debut LP established the group's sound, this one cemented it and also made it clear that Michael was going to be a huge star for a long time. His blend of gentility, soul, and innocence sparkled on the title cut and throughout the album, while the songs, production, arrangement, and musical support were superb. —*Ron Wynn*

Third Album / 1970 / Motown ✦✦✦
The Jackson 5 solidified the audience they enjoyed with their first two albums by turning in a consistently produced and occasionally exciting third record. It included the fine ballad "I'll Be There" and another hit in "Mama's Pearl"; the group hadn't yet become hardened by Motown manipulation or troubled by internal dissension. Michael Jackson was still widely beloved and seen as the 1970s' Frankie Lymon, and this LP became their third Top Ten album in a row. —*Ron Wynn*

Maybe Tomorrow / 1971 / Motown ✦✦✦
Another fine album, with Michael Jackson displaying surprising conviction and earnestness on the title track. The group was rolling along with a strong mix of novelty/dance hits, ballads, and soul covers, scoring massive pop success and turning up all over the airwaves. —*Ron Wynn*

Lookin' through the Windows / 1972 / Motown ✦✦✦
The Jackson 5 were still an engaging, delightful family unit when this album was released. They hadn't yet lost their innocent qualities and were also continuing to get first-rate material, production, and arrangements. They were three years away from the bitter fights that marred their exit from Motown, and Michael hadn't yet become a huge star. —*Ron Wynn*

Skywriter / 1973 / Motown ✦✦
The Jackson 5 slipped a bit with this album, although they still had two pop and R&B hits. But it wasn't anywhere near as dominant or popular an album as their earlier ones and wound up being one of their final three releases for Motown. They later did some recording with Stevie Wonder, Michael cut some solo material, and everyone except Jermaine headed for Columbia. —*Ron Wynn*

Get It Together / 1973 / Motown ✦✦
Although they were still getting hits, there were some problems creeping into the Jackson 5's Motown albums. The main one was that the company was no longer in the forefront of Black music production, and their '60s-style efforts were sounding dated. Only Michael Jackson's individual brilliance and the group's polished performances salvaged much of this material, and they soon openly expressed their disapproval. —*Ron Wynn*

Dancing Machine / 1974 / Motown ✦✦✦✦
For a brief time, it seemed as if the magic was back between Motown and the Jackson 5. The title track was their best uptempo hit since "ABC," and put them back on top of the R&B charts for the first time in three years. It just missed topping the pop charts as well, peaking at No. 2. They even got a second chart hit from the album, and it restored their position within the pop and R&B communities. —*Ron Wynn*

The Jacksons / 1976 / Epic ✦✦✦
Epic turned the Jacksons over to Philly soul producers Kenny Gamble and Leon Huff for this smooth, danceable label debut featuring the discofied hit "Enjoy Yourself." —*William Ruhlmann*

☆ **Anthology** / 1976 / Motown ✦✦✦✦✦
This three-LP set contains all 18 of the Jackson 5's pop-chart hits, plus solo hits by Jermaine and Michael Jackson, among its 33 cuts. It's the definitive collection and a good sampler of the sound of pop/R&B, circa 1969–1975. (Originally released as a 33-track, three-LP set by Motown on June 15, 1976, as Motown 868, *Anthology* was reissued as a 40-track, two-CD set in August 1986 as Motown 6194.) —*William Ruhlmann*

Goin' Places / 1977 / Epic ✦✦✦
The Jacksons' move to Epic regenerated their enthusiasm and spirit for several years. The Gamble/Huff team brought them fresh material and new production ideas, as well as better tracks and arrangements than they'd gotten in quite a while on Motown. This album got them R&B and pop hits and kept the family act in the spotlight for a little while longer. —*Ron Wynn*

Destiny / 1978 / Epic ✦✦✦✦
The Jacksons are finally turned loose to write and produce themselves, and the result is their best (non-hits collection) ever. The dance tracks still sound fresh; "Blame It on the Boogie," "Shake Your Body (Down to the Ground)"; and the ballads are heartfelt and smooth. This album is a dry run for Michael Jackson's adult solo career. —*William Ruhlmann*

Triumph / 1980 / Epic ✦✦✦✦
An excellent follow-up, featuring the hits "Can You Feel It" and "Heartbreak Hotel." —*William Ruhlmann*

Victory / 1984 / Epic ✦✦✦
Victory has the distinctions of being the only Jacksons album to feature all six brothers and the last Jacksons album to feature Michael Jackson. In the four years that had passed since the last Jacksons studio album, *Triumph*, Michael had become the biggest pop star in the world because of 1982's *Thriller*. He had little excuse, other than family ties, to work with his brothers again, but he agreed to a final album and tour. So, here one has the ludicrous situation of an album in which Marlon Jackson has as prominent a role as Michael Jackson. That's how it sounded to listeners in 1984, anyway, and they weren't fooled—"State of Shock," on which Michael shared vocals with Mick Jagger, was a gold Top Ten hit, and "Torture," which teamed Michael with Jermaine, made the Top 40, while the album went platinum. But the tracks by other group members went virtually ignored. In retrospect, *Victory* is a competent album of slick contemporary R&B, occasionally goosed toward greatness by the appearance of one of pop music's most identifiable voices. Which is the same thing you can say about nearly the entire Jackson 5/Jacksons catalog. —*William Ruhlmann*

2300 Jackson Street / 1989 / Epic ♦♦♦
This was the final gathering of the entire Jackson family, and it turned out to have both historical significance and some musical value. The team of L.A. and Babyface, then emerging as major producers, spearheaded the track "Nothin' Compares to U," and the title track was a nice autobiographical/family outing song. —*Ron Wynn*

Greatest Hits / 1995 / Epic ♦♦♦
While they were with Epic, the Jacksons mainly recorded disco and dance-pop, with a few romantic ballads thrown in for good measure. *Greatest Hits* collects the majority of their hit singles from the late '70s and early '80s, although *Destiny* and *Triumph* remain more consistent and enjoyable albums than this compilation. —*Stephen Thomas Erlewine*

Soulsation! / Jun. 27, 1995 / Motown ♦♦♦♦
Nineteen years after the release of *Anthology*, Motown finally tops that 33-track, three-LP compilation with this 82-track, four-and-a-half-hour, four-CD/cassette box set. The Jackson 5 were long overdue for box set treatment, and this one is well-done. All the hits by the group as well as those by Michael and Jermaine Jackson are here (that is, from 1969-1975, the J5's tenure at Motown), along with a representative sampling of album cuts. The J5's albums were afterthoughts to their singles, but some of these songs are nevertheless interesting, whether the group is covering Sly and the Family Stone or Jackson Browne (!). An entire disc is given over to previously unreleased or rare tracks from the Motown vaults. Taken together, it may be more than all but the most diehard fan wants to hear, which may be why Motown rushed out yet another single-disc hits collection, *The Ultimate Collection*, a couple of months later. But if you want the Jackson 5 on Motown, a big chunk of it is here. —*William Ruhlmann*

★ **The Ultimate Collection** / Aug. 15, 1995 / Motown ♦♦♦♦♦
Not quite as extensive as the 40-song *Anthology*, this 21-song single disc does include the group's biggest Motown hits, as well as early solo hits by Michael Jackson and Jermaine Jackson. *Anthology* is still the best way to go for those whose interest isn't deep enough to spring for the *Soulsation!* box. However, if you're on a budget, this does nail down most or all of the key cuts that most listeners want or need. —*Richie Unterberger*

Pre-History: The Lost Steeltown Recordings / Jun. 4, 1996 / Brunswick ♦♦

Chuck Jackson

b. Jun. 22, 1937, Latta, SC
Vocals / Soul, R&B
He's relatively forgotten today, and his brand of "uptown" soul is dismissed by the relatively vocal clique of critics who prefer their soul deep and down-home. But Chuck Jackson was a regular visitor to the R&B charts (and an occasional one to the pop listings) in the early '60s with such early pop-soul concoctions as "I Don't Want to Cry," "Any Day Now," and "Tell Him I'm Not Home." His records were very much of a piece with New York pop-rock-soul production, with cheeky brass, sweeping strings, and female backup vocalists. Those production trills make his work sound dated to some listeners, and his hoarse, emotional vocals weren't as subtle or commanding as peers like Ben E. King or Wilson Pickett. On its own terms, though, his best work is quite good, whether you prefer pop to soul or vice versa.

　　Jackson sang with one of the best doo wop groups, the Dell-Vikings, for a while in the late '50s (although he doesn't appear on their hit singles). Spotted by Scepter Records while performing with Jackie Wilson's Revue, he started recording for the label in 1961. As was the case with labelmates Dionne Warwick and the Shirelles, Jackson's early-'60s arrangements blended pop, R&B, and New York session professionalism. Like Warwick, Jackson was one of the first singers to successfully record Bacharach-David material; one of his best singles, "I Keep Forgettin'" (1962), was written and produced by Leiber-Stoller. Chuck had some success with some duets with Maxine Brown in the mid-'60s, but he left Wand in 1967 for Motown, at the urging of Smokey Robinson. Jackson was (perhaps understandably) lost in the shuffle during his four years at Motown, and he's barely been heard from since, although he remains a favorite on England's "Northern soul" scene. —*Richie Unterberger*

Mr. Emotion / 1984 / Kent ♦♦♦
A fairly haphazard survey of Jackson's '60s prime, mixing some of his most well-known Wand cuts ("I Keep Forgettin'," "Any Day Now," "Tell Him I'm Not Home") with a clutch of also-rans, and not coming close to consolidating his best material. There's good stuff here, but there's no reason to seek it out now that better Jackson anthologies are on the market. —*Richie Unterberger*

● **The Great Recordings** / 1995 / Tomato ♦♦♦♦
This 46-song, double-CD compilation of Wand-era recordings is the most extensive Jackson retrospective, though it doesn't include every

last worthwhile track. It does contain his most important songs, as well as a few of his duets with Maxine Brown, but the programming leaves something to be desired, inserting some half-baked instrumentals, live cuts, and Elvis Presley covers among the prime stuff. —*Richie Unterberger*

Something You Got: the Best of Chuck Jackson / Jun. 1996 / Soul Classics/Ichiban ♦♦♦
All 20 of the duet tracks that Jackson recorded with Maxine Brown for the Wand label between 1965 and 1967, comprising the entirety of their two albums for the company. It's reasonable pop-soul, but not nearly as memorable as the best male-female soul duets of the era (like the ones by Marvin Gaye and various Motown partners, or by Otis Redding and Carla Thomas). Highlights are the early compositions by the Jo Armstead-Nick Ashford-Valerie Simpson team, including a version of "Let's Go Get Stoned" that was recorded (though not released) before Ray Charles' more famous hit rendition. —*Richie Unterberger*

J.J. Jackson

b. New York City, NY
Soul
One of the most interesting obscure figures of '60s soul, Jackson scored a mammoth R&B hit in 1966 with one of the most infectious dance smashes of the decade, "But It's Alright." The New Yorker had worked as an arranger for Jack McDuff and Jimmy Witherspoon before his manager arranged for Jackson to come to England in 1966. Though "But It's Alright," with its classic stuttering guitar riff and sharp horn charts, sounded as authentic as any Stax/Volt single, it was actually recorded in the UK with British session musicians. Jackson—a mammoth, nearly 300-pound man who also played organ—was a grainy, good-natured belter in the mold of Otis Redding. A talented songwriter who penned much of his own material, he wrote the A-side of one of The Pretty Things' best mid-'60s R&B/raunch singles ("Come See Me"). Jackson never matched the success of "But It's Alright," but cut some singles that are highly valued by English "Northern Soul" connoisseurs. His hard-to-find 1969 and 1970 albums found him exploring, in the manner of most other soul stars of the time, increased social consciousness in his songwriting and increasingly sophisticated horn and string arrangements. He later surfaced as a Los Angeles disc jockey, leading to a cameo appearance in the film *Car Wash* that has been sampled by numerous rappers. —*Richie Unterberger*

● **The Great J.J. Jackson** / 1989 / See For Miles ♦♦♦♦
A reissue of his 1966 album, recorded in England with British producer Miki Dallon. Includes "But It's Alright," his version of "Come See Me" (actually recorded after the Pretty Things' rendition), and the effervescent, boastful "I Dig Girls." Much more solid than the average '60s soul album, it shows Jackson as a fine songwriter and infectiously throaty vocalist on a mixture of uptempo ravers and deep soul ballads. Somewhat similar to Otis Redding, but more pop-oriented, which is not necessarily a bad thing when you can make it work as well as J.J. does. —*Richie Unterberger*

Janet Jackson

b. May 16, 1966, Gary, IN
Vocals / Dance-Pop, Urban, Adult Contemporary, Pop-Rock, Club/Dance
Janet Jackson is the ninth and last child in the musically talented Jackson family that includes the Jackson 5, Michael Jackson, and Jermaine Jackson. Janet Jackson performed on stage with her brothers at the age of seven. At ten, she acted in the TV series *Good Times* and was later seen in *Diff'rent Strokes* and *Fame*. She released her first album, *Janet Jackson*, in 1982 and her second, *Dream Street*, in 1984, but neither of these records was notably successful. Then, in 1985, Jackson turned to the production team of Jimmy Jam and Terry Lewis (formerly of the Time) for the album *Control*, which, ironically, emphasized the artist's new maturity and independence, even though most of the songs were co-compositions of the three. *Control* was a massive hit: it topped the charts, selling more than four million copies, and spawned five Top Ten hits, including the No. 1 "When I Think of You." The follow-up, *Rhythm Nation 1814*, did even better, spawning seven Top Ten hits, among them the No. 1s "Miss You Much," "Escapade," and "Black Cat." In 1991, Jackson signed a new recording contract with Virgin Records for a reported $32 million.

　　1993's *janet.* proved to be as successful as her previous two releases, featuring a series of Top Ten singles including "If" and "That's the Way Love Goes." —*William Ruhlmann*

Janet Jackson / 1982 / A&M ♦♦
On her eponymous debut album, Janet Jackson demonstrated no distinctive musical personality of her own, which wasn't surprising considering that she was in her teens. If her producers had concocted a sharper set of songs and more interesting beats, *Janet Jackson* might

have been a pleasant set of sunny dance-pop, but as it stands, only "Young Love" stands out among the undistinguished, sub-disco thumpers and drippy ballads. *—Stephen Thomas Erlewine*

Dream Street / 1984 / A&M ✦✦
After a style switch, this features more light rock and polished pop tunes. Includes the stellar cut, "You Don't Stand Another Chance." *—Bil Carpenter*

Control / 1986 / A&M ✦✦✦✦
Jam and Lewis tailor their contemporary dance-pop to the emerging personality of Jackson, who is attempting to take "Control" of her life on this record. In the course of that attempt, she comes across as an aggressive, independent woman, notably on "What Have You Done for Me Lately." But the album is primarily a production showcase; it may be tailored to Jackson's persona, but the real artists are Jam and Lewis. *—William Ruhlmann*

Rhythm Nation 1814 / 1989 / A&M ✦✦✦✦
After shocking the R&B world with 1986's *Control*—a gutsy, risk-taking triumph that was a radical departure from her first two albums—Michael and Jermaine Jackson's younger sister reached an even higher artistic plateau with the conceptual *Rhythm Nation 1814*. Once again, she enlists the help of Time graduates Jimmy Jam & Terry Lewis (one of the more soulful production/songwriting teams of 1980s and '90s R&B) with wildly successful results. In 1989, protest songs were common in rap, but rare in R&B—Jackson, following rap's lead, dares to address social and political topics on "The Knowledge," the disturbing "State of the World," and the poignant ballad "Living in a World" (which decries the reality of children being exposed to violence). Jackson's voice is wafer-thin, and she doesn't have much of a range—but she definitely has lots of soul and spirit, and uses it to maximum advantage on those gems as well as nonpolitical pieces ranging from the Prince-influenced funk-pop of "Miss You Much" and "Alright" to the caressing, silky ballads "Someday Is Tonight," "Alone," and "Come Back to Me" to the pop-rock smoker "Black Cat." For those purchasing their first Janet Jackson release, *Rhythm Nation* would be an even wiser investment than *Control*—and that's saying a lot. *—Alex Henderson*

Janet. / May 18, 1993 / Virgin ✦✦✦
Janet Jackson returns with *janet.,* a long (75 minutes), ambitious album declaring her sexual maturity. There are good moments here, but it's marred by the torturously long running time and the intros cluttering the entire album. With a CD player, it's possible to program these excesses out and enjoy *janet.* as a solid successor to *Control* and *Rhythm Nation 1814*. *—Stephen Thomas Erlewine*

★ **Design of a Decade 1986-1996** / Oct. 10, 1995 / A&M ✦✦✦✦✦
Design of a Decade: 1986/1996 is a misleading title. The bulk of Janet Jackson's greatest hits collection concentrates on *Control* and *Rhythm Nation 1814*, simply by contractual necessity. That is far from a fatal flaw. The hits from those two albums were state-of-the-art, dance-pop productions at the time of their release, filled with bottomless beats and memorable, catchy hooks. None of the songs have lost any of their impact, from the funk of "Miss You Much" and "What Have You Done for Me Lately" to the ballads "Let's Wait Awhile" and "Come Back to Me." In addition to all 13 Top 40 hits from *Control* and *Rhythm Nation*—all but one went into the Top Five—*Design of a Decade* includes the biggest and best hit from *janet.*, the sultry "That's the Way Love Goes," and two new songs, "Runaway" and "Twenty Foreplay." It's a credit to Janet Jackson that the two new numbers feel like genuine hits, not tacked-on filler, and help make the album a compulsively listenable greatest hits collection. *—Stephen Thomas Erlewine*

Joe Jackson

b. Aug. 11, 1955, Burton-upon-Trent, England
Piano, Keyboards, Vocals / Singer-Songwriter, New Wave, Pop-Rock
Of the three angry young men that emerged in the British new wave movement of the early '80s, Joe Jackson was perhaps the most idiosyncratic. Not content with being a pop songwriter, Jackson went to considerable lengths to prove himself as a composer—often, he even seemed to have contempt for pop music itself. Appearing a few years after Elvis Costello and Graham Parker, Joe Jackson was doomed to always live in their shadow. Jackson was considerably more ambitious than Parker, rivaling Costello in his stylistic detours. After establishing himself as a gifted songwriter with a pair of edgy new wave pop records, he quickly set out to prove his eclecticism, recording album-length tributes to reggae, jump blues, traditional pop, and jazz. While such diversity earned him critical praise and a cult following, it didn't result in widespread acclaim until 1982's *Night and Day*, which launched the jazzy hits "Steppin' Out" and "Always Something Breaking Us in Two." Once he had a taste of success, Jackson didn't become more accessible—he became weirder, crafting a number of self-consciously difficult records intended to push the boundaries of pop. Following his 1987 classical

album *Will Power*, Jackson's audience began to decline, and by the early '90s, his cult was a fraction of its size a decade earlier. Despite his shrinking audience, Jackson was even less compromising in the '90s than he was in the '80s, eventually abandoning pop altogether.

Jackson began playing music as child, learning violin at the age of 11 and convincing his parents to invest in a piano by the time he was a teenager. He began writing songs as an adolescent, and he studied percussion and oboe in school as well. Following high school, he received a scholarship for London's Royal Academy of Music, and he studied composition at the institution between 1971 and 1974. Following his graduation, he performed with a band named Arms and Legs, and was then hired as the musical director for the Portsmouth Playboy Club. Within a few years, he recorded a demo album of original songs that landed him a publishing deal with Albion Music. By 1978, he had secured a record contract with A&M.

Released in early 1979, at the height of new wave, Jackson's debut album *Look Sharp!* was a collection of nervy, edgy pop songs recorded in just a week and a half. Highlighted by the Top 25 single "Is She Really Going Out with Him?," *Look Sharp!* was widely praised and became a Top 20 hit in the UK. Jackson followed it six months later with *I'm the Man*, a record that closely resembled the debut. Not wanting to be pigeonholed as an Elvis Costello-style pop songwriter, Jackson took a detour on his next record, 1980's *Beat Crazy*, recording a full-fledged reggae and ska album. The album received mixed reviews and weak sales, but it played well with his cult audience. Jackson followed the reggae experiments of *Beat Crazy* in 1981 with *Jumpin' Jive*, a collection of swing and jump blues. He supported the album with a tour featuring a big band, and the record became a cult hit.

Following *Jumpin' Jive*, Jackson moved to New York, where he attempted to write a jazzy, sophisticated pop album in the vein of Cole Porter. The resulting album, *Night and Day*, was widely praised upon its 1982 release, and the album proved to be his commercial breakthrough, as "Steppin' Out" reached the US Top Ten and the ballad "Always Something Breaking Us in Two" also became a hit. Jackson delved further into jazz with the record's follow-up, *Body and Soul*. Boasting a cover modeled on a Coleman Hawkins sleeve, *Body and Soul* was even jazzier than its predecessor, and it produced the Top 20 hit "You Can't Get What You Want (Til You Know What You Want)." Breaking away from his sophisticated pop leanings, Jackson conceived his next record as a live album of entirely new material, recorded directly to two-track, and performed in front of a live audience who would not be audible on the recording. The album was also conceived as one seamless piece, designed for a compact disc—it was released as a double album on vinyl, but one side was blank. The resulting record, 1986's *Big World*, received decidedly mixed reviews and was a only a moderate hit.

The artistic contrivance of *Big World* was only the beginning of Jackson's wild deviations from the norm. He had already proven himself an idiosyncratic musician, yet few observers would have predicted that his next album would be a full-fledged symphony. *Will Power* was poorly received upon its 1987 release, and Jackson, who was contemptuous of the bad reviews, nevertheless backed away from its complexities on his next album. Following the double-disc set *Live 1980/86* in 1988, Jackson released *Blaze of Glory*, a collection of pop songs designed to tell a semi-autobiographical story, in 1989. *Blaze of Glory* was moderate hit, producing the album-rock hits "Down to London" and the title track. It was also his last album for A&M—he signed to Virgin for 1991's straightahead pop-rock record, *Laughter & Lust*. Despite strong reviews, *Laughter & Lust* wasn't the hit it was designed to be, and Jackson abandoned pop music once and for all with 1994's *Night Music*, a fusion of classical music and show tunes that was greeted with mixed reviews and poor sales. *—Stephen Thomas Erlewine*

★ **Look Sharp!** / Apr. 1979 / A&M ✦✦✦✦✦
Hyperactive new wave rock overlaid with the intelligent, caustic worldview of a man as angry as any punk, but far more perceptive. Includes the hit "Is She Really Going Out with Him?" *—William Ruhlmann*

I'm the Man / Oct. 1979 / A&M ✦✦✦✦
Nearly a rewrite of *Look Sharp*, and capturing all of its brilliance, *I'm the Man* is pure power-pop—hook-filled, concise, and fun. Includes the wonderful "It's Different for Girls," a marginal hit in both the US and UK. *—Chris Woodstra*

Beat Crazy / 1980 / A&M ✦✦✦✦
Credited to the Joe Jackson Band, *Beat Crazy* completes Jackson's power-pop period. Jackson begins to stretch a bit stylistically, flirting with reggae and more experimental styles while in the confines of the three-minute form he would later dismiss. Every bit as charming as the first two. *—Chris Woodstra*

Jumpin' Jive / 1981 / A&M ✦✦✦✦
A delightful trip back to '40s and '50s jump blues and big-band swing. With faithful covers of Louis Jordan and Cab Calloway, Jackson

appears to be having fun, while helping a new generation discover these classics. —*Chris Woodstra*

Night & Day / 1982 / A&M ✦✦✦✦
Since Jackson has already demonstrated his broad musical tastes by turning from rock to "jumpin' jive" on his last album, that he was able to incorporate Latin, dance, and sophisticated ballad styles into his music wasn't so surprising. But that he could do it all so well was delightful. Includes "Steppin' Out" and "Breaking Us in Two." —*William Ruhlmann*

Body & Soul / 1984 / A&M ✦✦✦
Continuing in his move away from pop music that began with *Night and Day*, Jackson shows his love of '50s jazz with detail best represented by the cover photo (nearly identical to the Sonny Rollins album of the same name). Features his last US hit, "You Can't Get What You Want" and the beautiful "Be My Number Two." —*Chris Woodstra*

Big World / 1986 / A&M ✦✦✦
A brilliant collection of songs, running over an hour, finds Jackson as biting as ever as he surveys the world, but also tenderly reflective on "Home Town." —*William Ruhlmann*

Will Power / 1987 / A&M ✦✦
Joe Jackson finally becomes the "serious composer" on *Will Power*. A good exercise in self-indulgence but little of anything else. —*Chris Woodstra*

Live ... 1980-1986 / 1988 / A&M ✦✦✦
A double-disc live collection, *Live ... 1980-1986* manages to effectively trace the development of Joe Jackson's diverse career. Drawing from four different periods in the songwriter's career—with each period featuring a new backing band—*Live* captures Jackson with his original new wave trio, a 1983 quintet that was dominated by keyboards, a horn-driven group from 1984, and a 1986 quartet that specialized in straightahead rock 'n' roll. The resulting album highlights his musical diversity, not his songwriting, which means the record is more intriguing as a historical document than as casual listening —*Stephen Thomas Erlewine*

Blaze of Glory / 1989 / A&M ✦✦✦
A loose concept album about a second-generation rock 'n' roller struggling to come to terms with maturity, *Blaze of Glory* holds together fairly well, as the story takes a backseat to individual songs. While that does mean that the concept is never fleshed out, the approach results in a handful of brisk, stylish pop songs—including "Nineteen Forever" and "Down to London"—that are more compelling than the story itself. —*Stephen Thomas Erlewine*

Laughter & Lust / Apr. 30, 1991 / Virgin ✦✦✦
Jackson's work has sometimes been too didactic for its own good, but on *Laughter & Lust* he managed to balance the agenda with a nice blend of humor and heart. His perpetual disdain for the pop music industry found full flower in "Hit Single," in which Jackson finds himself in "pure pop heaven," where angels only want to hear the hits, but not "the whole damn album." Other highlights are the classic acidic Jackson-style rocker "Obvious Song," the hyperkinetic "Jamie G," a faithful remake of Fleetwood Mac's "Oh Well," and Jackson's ode to the dynamics of love in "Stranger than Fiction." —*Rick Clark*

Night Music / Oct. 4, 1994 / Virgin ✦
Joe Jackson's second attempt at "serious" composition, *Night Music* is an insufferable song cycle about writers' block. Jackson's lyrics are ponderous and elusive, his vocals are smug and self-important, and the unmemorable, low-key music is stiffly executed on a dry, lifeless synthesizer. What sinks *Night Music* is the total lack of involving music. *Will Power* may have been just as indulgent, yet the album had the occasional interesting twist in melodic lines and arrangements. On *Night Music*, everything from the production to the performance sounds processed, devoid of any defining characteristics. —*Stephen Thomas Erlewine*

Greatest Hits / May 7, 1996 / A&M ✦✦✦✦

This Is It! The A&M Years / Feb. 1997 / A&M ✦✦✦✦
This Is It! The A&M Years is a double-disc, 37-track collection covering Joe Jackson's commercial and creative heyday. Over the course of two discs, *This Is It!* runs through all of his biggest hits—"Is She Really Going Out with Him?," "It's Different for Girls," "Steppin' Out," "Breaking Us in Two," "You Can't Get What Want (Till You Know What You Want)"—plus a number of significant album tracks and lesser-known singles, making it a comprehensive retrospective of Jackson's pop-oriented work. While it's unfortunate that the compilation stops just short of his last pop album, 1991's *Laughter & Lust*, because it was released on Virgin Records, the great majority of his best work is here, making it a perfect choice for fans who want something more—and better assembled—than *Greatest Hits*, and those who don't want to dig as deep as the actual albums. —*Stephen Thomas Erlewine*

Michael Jackson

b. Aug. 29, 1958, Gary, IN
Vocals / Soul, Dance-Pop, Funk, Urban, Motown, Pop-Rock, New Jack R&B

As part of the Jackson 5, a group made up of his brothers, Michael Jackson was among the most popular singing stars of the '70s. On his own, he was the biggest pop star of the '80s. Jackson was always the visual and vocal focus of the Jackson 5, who broke through to national success on the Motown label in 1970, when he was 11, with the first of four straight No. 1 hits, "I Want You Back." Jackson was also promoted as a solo artist, and he scored his first hit, "Got to Be There," in 1971. Subsequent hits included his remake of "Rockin' Robin" and "Ben" in 1972.

Jackson's and the Jackson 5's fortunes declined somewhat after the early '70s, and the group moved to Epic at mid-decade, with Michael temporarily abandoning his solo career and subsuming his group leadership to other members of what was now called the Jacksons. The group gradually built back its popularity by writing its own material. Jackson returned to solo work in 1979 with *Off the Wall*, a mature combination of driving dance songs ("Don't Stop 'til You Get Enough") and feelingly sung ballads ("She's Out of My Life") that outsold any previous group or solo effort, and spawned four Top Ten hits.

Jackson again recorded and toured with the Jacksons, but his next album, *Thriller* (1982), became a musical phenomenon. It was the biggest-selling album of all time, moving 20 million copies in the US alone and including seven Top Ten hits. Clearly Jackson had grown beyond his brothers, but he stayed with them for one more album and tour in 1984.

His follow-up album, *Bad* (1987), accompanied by a solo world tour, sold six million copies domestically. Only six of its seven singles hit the Top Ten, but five in a row hit No. 1.

In late 1991, Jackson returned with *Dangerous*, which, by mid-1992, had sold four million copies and spawned the hits "Black and White," "Remember the Time," "In the Closet," and "Jam." Jackson's second world tour, launched in Europe in June 1992, continued into 1993.

Although numerous rumors had circled around Jackson throughout his career, his reputation remained clean. It wasn't until 1993 that he suffered serious damage to his image. Jackson was accused of child abuse by a teenage friend, sparking a major media frenzy. Through it all, Jackson vehemently denied the accusations. The civil case was settled out of court in early 1994. Jackson began working on *HIStory* soon after the settlement. *HIStory* contained one disc of Jackson's greatest hits and one disc of new material. It was released on June 20, 1995. —*William Ruhlmann*

☆ **Off the Wall** / 1979 / Epic ✦✦✦✦✦
If you were listening to The Jacksons' *Destiny* from the previous year, maybe you were less surprised than many that Michael Jackson was capable of making an album this accomplished and assured. From the first moments, he seems bursting with the wide range of music included, from the first side's clutch of irresistible dance tracks ("Don't Stop 'til You Get Enough," "Rock with You," "Working Day and Night") to the light pop and ballads ("She's Out of My Life," "Off the Wall") of side two. Throughout, Jackson's flexible tenor coos and growls by turns, always goosing the songs along. Deservedly a massive hit, this is less dated today than much of the dance music of that era. —*William Ruhlmann*

The Best of Michael Jackson / 1981 / Motown ✦✦✦
Michael Jackson's greatest hits, 1971-1975, emphasize his waiflike charm and youth (he was 13 when the first of these songs appeared) in ballads such as "Got to Be There," "Ben" (even if it is a love song to a rat), and "I Wanna Be Where You Are." The upbeat cover of "Rockin' Robin" is equally appealing. —*William Ruhlmann*

★ **Thriller** / 1982 / Epic ✦✦✦✦✦
What impresses after a decade is Jackson's range of musical expression, one that touches the schmaltzy pop of Paul McCartney (his duet partner on "The Girl Is Mine") on one side and the hard rock of Van Halen (whose guitarist, Eddie Van Halen, is heard on "Beat It") on the other, with plenty of mainstream rock/pop and dance music in between. It's no accident that the record found a home in so many record collections—there's good music here for everyone. And of course, by summing up the state of pop music, Jackson also redefined it—this was a high-water mark for pop music never equaled since, even in his subsequent music. —*William Ruhlmann*

Anthology / 1986 / Motown ✦✦✦✦
Michael Jackson's greatest hits (1971-1975) emphasize his waiflike charm and youth (he was 13 years old when the first of these songs appeared) in ballads such as "Got to Be There," "Ben" (even if it is a love song to a rat), and "I Wanna Be Where You Are." The upbeat cover of "Rockin' Robin" is equally appealing. The digitally remastered, double-CD version includes a few additional tracks. —*William Ruhlmann*

Bad / 1987 / Epic ✦✦✦✦
A partially successful attempt to remake *Thriller*. Interestingly, Jackson did not turn to a softer, more broadly commercial approach, but instead upped the dance-rock ante. Songs such as "Dirty Diana" and "Smooth Criminal" found him striding forward in terms of rhythm and beat. And with seven hit singles out of ten tracks (five at No. 1), this, like *Thriller*, is in effect a Michael Jackson greatest-hits record, covering 1987-1989. — *William Ruhlmann*

Dangerous / 1992 / Epic ✦✦✦
Wisely, Jackson altered his creative process here, jettisoning producer Quincy Jones in favor of Teddy Riley and bringing in several songwriting collaborators. The result is an updated dance-floor success (the drums are way up in the mix), though the songwriting sometimes seem schematic. When Jackson is left more or less to himself, he is less R&B-oriented, notably on the pop ballad "Heal the World" and the guitar-driven pop-rock song "Black or White" (a Stones riff, though taken at a tempo the Stones never attempted). Rather than resting on his laurels, Jackson continues to work hard to maintain and further the quality of his work. — *William Ruhlmann*

History: Past, Present and Future, Book 1 / Jun. 20, 1995 / Epic ✦✦✦
Michael Jackson's double-disc *HIStory: Past, Present, and Future, Book I* is a monumental achievement of ego. Titled *HIStory Begins*, the first disc is a collection of his post-Motown hits, featuring some of the greatest music in pop history including "Billie Jean," "Don't Stop Til Ya Get Enough," "Beat It," and "Rock with You." It leaves some hits out—including the No. 1s "Say Say Say" and "Dirty Diana"—yet it's filled with enough prime material to be thoroughly intoxicating. That can't be said for the second disc, called *HIStory Continues* and consisting entirely of new material—which also happen to be the first songs he released since being accused of child molestation. *HIStory Continues* is easily the most personal album Jackson has recorded. References to the scandal permeate almost every song, creating a thick atmosphere of paranoia. If Jackson's music had been the equal of *Thriller* or *Bad*, the nervous, vindicative lyrics wouldn't have been quite as overbearing. However, *HIStory Continues* reiterates musical ideas Jackson has been exploring since *Bad*. Jackson certainly tries to stay contemporary, yet he has a tendency to smooth out all of his rougher musical edges with show-biz schmaltz. Occasionally, Jackson produces some well-crafted pop that ranks with his best material: R. Kelly's "You Are Not Alone" is seductive, "Scream" improves on the slamming beats of his earlier single "Jam," and "Stranger in Moscow" is one of his most haunting ballads. Nevertheless, *HIStory Continues* stands as his weakest album since the mid-'70s. — *Stephen Thomas Erlewine*

Blood on the Dance Floor: History in the Mix / May 20, 1997 / Sony ✦✦
Despite its heavy promotion, *HIStory* was a considerable sales disappointment, largely because it buried an album of new material with a greatest hits collection, causing the new record to get buried. Although the new album was unfocused, it had its moments, which may be why Michael Jackson refused to let *HIStory* die. He remixed eight of its songs for *Blood on the Dance Floor: History in the Mix*, and then saddled that record with five new songs, which meant that he repeated the same mistake by burying the new songs yet again. This time, however, it wasn't such a loss, since all the songs on *Blood on the Dance Floor* are embarrassingly weak, sounding tired, predictable, and bloodless. The title track, a bleak reworking of "Jam" and "Scream," is indicative of the weakness of the album, but it only touches on how sad the whole affair is. It would be one thing if Jackson wasn't relevant to the late '90s and ignored all contemporary innovations, since he could make good music on his own terms. However, he flaunts his ignorance aggressively, as if sheer willpower will return him to the charts, making it all the more apparent because he can no longer craft good melody or beat. And, for one of the greatest musicians of the late '70s and early '80s, that's quite a depressing state of affairs. — *Stephen Thomas Erlewine*

Walter Jackson

b. Mar. 19, 1958, Pensacola, FL, **d.** Jun. 20, 1983
Vocals / Soul, R&B
Walter Jackson was '60s Chicago soul at its sweetest and, occasionally, most mainstream. In the mid-'60s, he had a brace of solid R&B hits—"Suddenly I'm All Alone," "It's an Uphill Climb (to the Bottom)," "Speak Her Name," "Welcome Home," "A Corner in the Sun"—without ever rising higher than the lower reaches of the Top 100. Recording for the OKeh stable, which was home to the top Chi-town soul talent, he benefited for a time from the production services of local masters Carl Davis and Curtis Mayfield, who handled the Impressions, Major Lance, Gene Chandler, and others. His sides employed similar punchy brass and strings, but in a smoother, more urbane fashion; Jackson was also comfortable with occasional outings into pure supper-club pop with nary a trace of R&B. Jackson had already recorded for Columbia (and

unsuccessfully auditioned for Motown) when OKeh A&R director Davis saw him at a Detroit piano bar in 1962. Stricken with polio as a young boy, Jackson had never let his disability get in the way of his musical ambitions, performing on crutches. Impressed with his commanding voice, Carl Davis thought of Walter as a Nat "King" Cole type of singer, and procured material for Jackson from Mayfield, Van McCoy, Chip Taylor, and other top-notch songwriters.

Despite the obvious pop crossover potential of Jackson's recordings, he remained obscure to white listeners. During the latter part of his stay with OKeh, he was reassigned from Davis' stable to producer Ted Cooper. Jackson had a few hits with Cooper, but there was little success after the late '60s, although he recorded for a few more labels before dying of a cerebral hemorrhage in 1983. — *Richie Unterberger*

● **The Best of Walter Jackson: Welcome Home: The Okeh Years** / Jun. 4, 1996 / Epic/Legacy ✦✦✦✦
Fifteen tracks from his artistic and commercial peak (1964-67), including his slew of R&B chart hits, highlights from LPs, and a flop single version of "My Ship is Comin' In." Commercial pop-soul with elaborate production, reaching deeply enough into the gloss on occasion to rate as a vague precursor to the "quiet storm" music of subsequent decades. — *Richie Unterberger*

Wanda Jackson

b. Oct. 20, 1937, Maud, OK
Vocals / Traditional Country, Rockabilly, CCM, Country Gospel
Wanda Jackson was only halfway through high school when, in 1954, country singer Hank Thompson heard her on an Oklahoma City radio show and asked her to record with his band, the Brazos Valley Boys. By the end of the decade, Jackson had become one of America's first major female country and rockabilly singers.

Jackson was born in Oklahoma, but her father Tom—himself a country singer who quit because of the Depression—moved the family to California in 1941. He bought Wanda her first guitar two years later, gave her lessons, and encouraged her to play piano as well. In addition, he took her to see such acts as Tex Williams, Spade Cooley, and Bob Wills, which left a lasting impression on her young mind. Tom moved the family back to Oklahoma City when his daughter was 12 years old. In 1952, she won a local talent contest and was given a 15-minute daily show on KLPR. The program, soon upped to 30 minutes, lasted throughout Jackson's high school years. It's here that Thompson heard her sing. Jackson recorded several songs with the Brazos Valley Boys, including "You Can't Have My Love," a duet with Thompson's bandleader, Billy Gray. The song, on the Decca label, became a national hit, and Jackson's career was off and running. She had wanted to sign with Capitol, Thompson's label, but was turned down so she signed with Decca instead.

Jackson insisted on finishing high school before hitting the road. When she did, her father came with her. Her mother made and helped design Wanda's stage outfits. "I was the first one to put some glamour in the country music—fringe dresses, high heels, long earrings," Jackson says of these outfits. When Jackson first toured in 1955 and 1956, she was placed on a bill with none other than Elvis Presley. The two hit it off almost immediately. Jackson says it was Presley, along with her father, who encouraged her to sing rockabilly.

In 1956, Jackson finally signed with Capitol, a relationship that lasted until the early '70s. Her recording career bounced back and forth between country and rockabilly; she did this by often putting one song in each style on either side of a single. Jackson cut the rockabilly hit "Fujiyama Mama" in 1958, which became a major success in Japan. Her version of "Let's Have a Party," which Elvis had cut earlier, was a US Top 40 pop hit for her in 1960, after which she began calling her band the Party Timers. A year later, she was back in the country Top Ten with "Right or Wrong" and "In the Middle of a Heartache." In 1965, she topped the German charts with "Santa Domingo," sung in Dutch. In 1966, she hit the US Top 20 with "The Box It Came In" and "Tears Will Be the Chaser for the Wine." Jackson's popularity continued through the end of the decade.

Jackson toured regularly, was twice nominated for a Grammy, and was a big attraction in Las Vegas from the mid-'50s into the '70s. She married IBM programmer Wendell Goodman in 1961, and instead of quitting the business—as many women singers had done at the time—Goodman gave up his job in order to manage his wife's career. He also packaged Jackson's syndicated TV show, *Music Village*. In 1971, Jackson and her husband discovered Christianity, which she says saved their marriage. She released one gospel album on Capitol in 1972, *Praise the Lord*, before shifting to the Myrrh label for three more gospel albums. In 1977, she switched again, this time to Word Records, and released another two.

In the early 1980s, Jackson was invited to Europe to play rockabilly and country festivals and to record. She's since been back numerous times. More recently, American country artists Pam Tillis, Jann Browne, and Rosie Flores have acknowledged Jackson as a major influence. In 1995, Flores released a rockabilly album, *Rockabilly Filly*, and invited Jackson, her longtime idol, to sing two duets on it with her. Jackson embarked on a major US tour with Flores later that year. It was her first secular tour in this country since the '70s, not to mention her first time back in a nightclub atmosphere. —*Kurt Wolff*

There's a Party Goin' on / 1959 / Capitol ✦✦✦
While this doesn't have most of Wanda's best rockabilly sides (check the compilation *Rockin' with Wanda* for those), it's a pretty solid and energetic set. About half of it is taken up with retreads of the "Let's Have a Party" theme and covers of early rock hits like "Tweedlee Dee" and "Kansas City," which are, admittedly, well done. "Fallin' " and, especially, "Hard Headed Woman" are really fine cuts that rank among her best rock 'n' roll performances. The real surprise of this album is the lightning-speed rockabilly riffing by Roy Clark; his playing on "Hard Headed Woman" is downright savage, almost enough to redeem all those horrible *Hee-Haw* programs. —*Richie Unterberger*

Rockin' with Wanda / 1960 / Capitol ✦✦✦✦
Absolutely the best collection of her rockabilly recordings, including her key 1956-60 singles—"Fujiyama Mama," "Mean Mean Man," "Hot Dog! That Made Him Mad," and others. A leading candidate for the best female rock 'n' roll album of the 1950s. The British reissue adds four worthwhile bonus cuts, including the essential "Let's Have a Party." —*Richie Unterberger*

● **Rockin' in the Country: Best of Wanda Jackson** / Jun. 1990 / Rhino ✦✦✦✦
Perhaps the greatest of the rockabilly women, Wanda Jackson later turned to pure country. Rhino's *Best of Wanda Jackson—Rockin' in the Country* presents the best of both eras here on this 18-track collection. —*Jeff Tamarkin*

Vintage Collection Series / Jan. 23, 1996 / Capitol ✦✦✦✦
This 20-track anthology of Jackson's early work is roughly equal to Rhino's *Rockin' in the Country* in value. *Rockin' in the Country* offers a considerably wider range, chronologically speaking. *Vintage Collections*, on the other hand, focuses on 1956-61 recordings, affording greater depth for what is acknowledged as her most fertile period. Although it's issued on Capitol Nashville, it mixes rockabilly and straight country, including her biggest hits in each style ("Let's Have a Party," "Fujiyama Mama," "Right or Wrong") and some worthy obscurities. Those with an appetite for both rock 'n' roll and country will find this the best compilation of her work; those who want just the rock 'n' roll should look for the harder-to-find *Rockin' with Wanda* instead. —*Richie Unterberger*

Mick Jagger

b. Jul. 26, 1943, Dartford, Kent, England
Guitar, Harmonica, Keyboards, Vocals / Rock 'n' Roll, Pop-Rock
As the lead singer for the Rolling Stones, Mick Jagger was one of the most popular and influential frontmen in the history of rock 'n' roll. Jagger fronted the Rolling Stones for over 20 years before he began a solo career in 1985. At the time of the release of his debut solo album, *She's the Boss*, it appeared that the Stones may have been approaching the end of their career, but it soon transpired that Jagger's solo career would run concurrently with that of the band's. Over the next decade, he released a string of solo albums, none of which achieved the commercial success of the Stones' less popular releases.

During the early '80s, Jagger and Keith Richards—the rhythm guitarist and co-songwriter in the Rolling Stones—conflicted over the musical direction of the band. Jagger wanted to move the band in a more pop and dance-oriented direction while Richards wanted to stay true to the band's rock 'n' roll and blues roots. By 1984, Jagger had begun recording a solo album where he pursued a more mainstream, dance-inflected pop direction. The resulting album, *She's the Boss*, was released in 1985. Jagger filmed a number of state-of-the-art videos for the album, which all received heavy airplay from MTV, helping propel the record's first single, "Just Another Night," to No. 12 and the album to platinum status. "Lucky In Love," the second single from the album, scraped the bottom of the Top 40. In the summer of 1985, Jagger and David Bowie recorded a cover of Martha & the Vandellas' "Dancing in the Street" for the Live Aid organization. The single peaked at No. 7 on the US pop charts; all the proceeds from its sale were donated to Live Aid.

Around the same time the Rolling Stones released their 1986 album, *Dirty Work*, Jagger released the theme song from the movie *Ruthless People* as a single and told Richards that the Stones would not tour to support *Dirty Work*. For the next few years, Jagger and Richards barely spoke to each other and sniped at each other in the press. During this time, Jagger tried to make his solo career as successful as the Rolling Stones, pouring all of his energy into his second solo album, 1987's *Primitive Cool*. Although the album received stronger

reviews than *She's the Boss*, only one of the singles—"Let's Work"—scraped the bottom of the Top 40 and the record didn't go gold.

Following the commercial failure of *Primitive Cool*, Jagger returned to the fold of the Rolling Stones in 1989, recording, releasing, and touring the *Steel Wheels* album. *Steel Wheels* was a massively successful venture and after the tour was completed, the Stones entered a slow period, where each of the members pursued solo projects. Jagger recorded his third solo album with Rick Rubin, who had previously worked with the Beastie Boys and Red Hot Chili Peppers. The resulting solo album, *Wandering Spirit*, was released in 1993 and received the strongest reviews of any of Jagger's solo efforts. The album entered the US charts at No. 11 and went gold the year it was released. A year after the release of *Wandering Spirit*, the Stones reunited and released *Voodoo Lounge*, supporting the album with another extensive international tour. —*Stephen Thomas Erlewine*

She's the Boss / 1985 / Columbia ✦✦✦
Jagger employs a Who's Who including Herbie Hancock, Pete Townshend, and Jeff Beck for an album that replaces the familiar sound of the Stones with a more sophisticated but no less hard rock sound. And the voice *is* familiar. Features the hit "Just Another Night." —*William Ruhlmann*

Primitive Cool / 1987 / Rolling Stones ✦✦✦
For his second solo album, Mick Jagger teamed up with producer Dave Stewart (Eurythmics), turning in a more adventurous and ambitious record. Of course, "adventurous" and "ambitious" are relative terms. In comparison to the carefully constructed, state-of-the-art, pop-rock of *She's the Boss*, *Primitive Cool* sounds lively, as Jagger puts some genuine conviction behind the funky "Peace for the Wicked" and the country stylings of "Party Doll." Nevertheless, the album, like *She's the Boss* before it, is designed to establish Mick Jagger as a solo star in his own right, and *Primitive Cool* is filled with attempts at contemporary rock and dance-pop. The nadir of his stabs at modern pop is the appalling single "Let's Work," where the rock star tells his fans to get off their asses and start working, all to a bouncy, aerobicized beat. However, most of the album is more appealing than the single, even if Jagger's writing seems forced on the numbers designed with the Top 40 in mind ("Shoot Off Your Mouth," in particular). Not surprisingly, the best moments on *Primitive Cool* occur when he stops seeing the album as a way to jump-start his solo career and he concentrates on the music. While his emotionally unguarded songs ("War Baby" and "Party Doll") are the most affecting tracks on the record, songs like "Let's Work" are more indicative of Jagger's true feelings. —*Stephen Thomas Erlewine*

● **Wandering Spirit** / Feb. 9, 1993 / Atlantic ✦✦✦✦
Jagger doesn't show any signs of wear on his third—and by far best—solo album. If anything, his voice seems to have developed a deeper bottom end without sacrificing any of the highs. This is not always an advantage—the forced falsetto and rhythmic pulse of "Sweet Thing" causes a nightmarish flashback to the Stones' disco flirtations in the mid-'70s. But more times than not, this disc works. A lot of the credit goes to Jagger's backing band and producer Rick Rubin who keep things lean, mean, and simple. The economy of performance allows Jagger to remain credible on a wide variety of styles—he delivers a groovin', sultry version of Bill Withers' soul classic "Use Me," a passionate country ballad on "Evening Gown," and even pulls off an Irish traditional folk piece with "Handsome Molly." —*Roch Parisien*

Jags

f. 1977, England, db. 1981
New Wave, Power Pop, Mod-Revival
Like so many of their peers, the Jags were a one-hit wonder of the UK power-pop explosion of the late '70s. The quartet was formed by the songwriting team of Nick Watkins (vocals) and John Adler (guitar), who enlisted the help of Steve Prudence (bass) and Alex Baird (drums). The band's debut for Island Records in 1979 was the memorable, though highly derivative, "Back of My Hand," which reached the UK Top 20. The follow-up, "Woman's World," barely scraped its way on to the charts. *Evening Standards* (1980) sold fairly well, but as steam ran out of the power-pop craze, the band faded into obscurity, releasing only one more album, *No Tie Like the Present*, in 1981. —*Chris Woodstra*

● **Evening Standard** / 1980 / Island ✦✦✦✦
The "Back of My Hand" single showed a lot of promise. Unfortunately, the debut album put an end to those hopes with its only slightly better-than-average watered down version of power-pop. The album is not completely without merit—just a disappointment. —*Chris Woodstra*

No Ties to the Present / 1981 / Island ✦✦
The second album by the Jags is great, fun listening. Starting out with a cover of the Tremelos' "Here Comes My Baby," it rolls on through a series of very English-sounding pop tunes written by band members. Very reminiscent of the early '80s, it nevertheless has a lot of

spunk—check out the surfer instrumental "Silver Birds" and you won't be disappointed. —*James Chrispell*

Jale

f. Apr. 1992, Halifax, Nova Scotia
Indie Rock
A product of the same Halifax, Nova Scotia, musical community that spawned Sloan and Eric's Trip, the sparkling indie-pop band Jale formed in April 1992 while its members were attending art school. Dubbing themselves Jale as an acronym of the first names of guitarist Jennifer Pierce, drummer Alyson MacLeod, bassist Laura Stein and guitarist Eve Hartling (all of whom shared vocal and songwriting chores), the group borrowed their instruments from friends and played their first show less than five weeks after forming. Soon they issued their debut single "Aunt Betty," followed by an appearance on the Sub Pop label's double seven-inch Halifax sampler *Never Mind the Molluscs*.

After a few more singles, Jale officially signed with Sub Pop to record 1994's *Dreamcake*, a stunning collection spotlighting the group's infectious melodies and shimmering harmonies. After the LP's release, the band recorded the 1995 EP *Closed*, followed by MacLeod's decision to exit to assume bass duties with Halifax's Hardship Post. With new drummer Mike Belitsky, Jale travelled to Chicago to work with producer Brad Wood and resurfaced a year later with the stellar *So Wound*, highlighted by the should-have-been hit "All Ready." In early 1997, Hartling left the band to focus on raising a family. —*Jason Ankeny*

Dream Cake / Jul. 12, 1994 / Sub Pop ✦✦✦
● **So Wound** / Jun. 4, 1996 / Sub Pop ✦✦✦✦
Jale's utterly infectious *So Wound* is a manic pop thrill, a superb collection of sweet-and-sour songs laced with wit, intelligence, and poignancy. Crisply produced by Brad Wood, the record's 14 tracks (13 listed, one bonus) are fresh and sassy, combining the sweet harmonies and gleaming songcraft of the girl-group era with post-punk attitude and edge; while each song is a gem, the chiming "All Ready," the buzzing "Ali," and the snotty "Over You" are standouts. —*Jason Ankeny*

The Jam

f. 1975, Woking, England, **db.** 1982
Rock 'n' Roll, Punk, Pop-Rock, Mod-Revival
The Jam were the most popular band to emerge from the initial wave of British punk rock in 1977; along with the Sex Pistols, the Clash, and the Buzzcocks, the Jam had the most impact on pop music. While they could barely get noticed in America, the trio became genuine superstars in Britain, with an impressive string of Top Ten singles in the late '70s and early '80s. The Jam could never have a hit in America because they were thoroughly and defiantly British. Under the direction of guitarist/vocalist/songwriter Paul Weller, the trio spearheaded a revival of mid-'60s mod groups, in the style of the Who and the Small Faces. Like the mod bands, the group dressed stylishly, worshipped American R&B, and played it loud and rough. By the time of the group's third album, Weller's songwriting had grown substantially, as he was beginning to write social commentaries and pop songs in the vein of the Kinks. Both his political songs and his romantic songs were steeped in British culture, filled with references and slang in the lyrics, as well as musical allusions. Furthermore, as the Jam grew more popular and musically accessible, Weller became more insistent and stubborn about his beliefs, supporting leftist causes and adhering to the pop aesthetics of '60s British rock without ever succumbing to hippie values. Paradoxically, that meant even when their music became more pop than punk, they never abandoned the punk values—if anything, Weller stuck to the strident independent ethics of 1977 more than any other punk band just by simply refusing to change.

Weller formed the Jam with drummer Rick Buckler, bassist Bruce Foxton, and guitarist Steve Brookes while they were still in school in 1975; Brookes quickly left the band and they remained a trio for the rest of their career. For the next year, the band played gigs around London, building a local following. In February 1977, the group signed a record contract with Polydor Records; two months later, they released their debut single, "In the City," which reached the UK Top 40. The following month, the group released their debut album, also called *In the City*. Recorded in just 11 days, the album featured a combination of R&B covers and Weller originals, all of which sounded a bit like faster, more ragged versions of the Who's early records. Their second single, "All Around the World," nearly broke into the British Top Ten and the group embarked on a successful British tour. During the summer of 1977, they recorded their second album, *This Is the Modern World*, which was released toward the end of the year. "The Modern World" made it into the Top 40 in November, just as the Jam were beginning their first American tour. Although it was brief, the tour was not successful, leaving bitter memories of the US in the minds of the band. *This Is the Modern World* peaked in the British charts at No. 22, yet it

received criticism for repeating the sound of the debut. The band began a headlining tour of the UK, yet it was derailed shortly after it started when the group got into a nasty fight with a bunch of rugby players in a Leeds hotel. Weller broke several bones and was charged with assault, although the Leeds Crown Court would eventually acquit him. The Jam departed for another American tour in March of 1978 and it was yet another unsuccessful tour, as they opened for Blue Öyster Cult. It did nothing to win new American fans, yet their star continued to rise in Britain. Bands copying the group's mod look and sound popped up across Britain and the Jam itself performed at the Reading Festival in August. *All Mod Cons*, released late in 1979, marked a turning point in the Jam's career, illustrating that Weller's songwriting was becoming more melodic, complex, and lyrically incisive, resembling Ray Davies more than Pete Townshend. Even as their sound became more pop-oriented, the group lost none of their tightly controlled energy. *All Mod Cons* was a major success, peaking at number six on the UK charts, even if it didn't make a dent in the US. Every one of the band's singles were now charting in the Top 20, with the driving "Eton Rifles" becoming their first Top Ten in November 1979, charting at No. 3.

Setting Sons, released at the end of 1979, climbed to number four in the UK and marked their first charting album in the US, hitting No. 137 in spring of 1980. At that time, the Jam had become full-fledged rock stars in Britain, with their new "Going Underground" single entering the charts at No. 1. During the summer, the band recorded their fifth album, with the "Taxman"-inspired "Start" released as a teaser single in August; "Start" became their second straight No. 1. Its accompanying album, the ambitious *Sound Affects*, hit No. 2 in the UK at the end of the year; it was also the band's high-water mark in the US, peaking at No. 72. "That's Entertainment," one of the standout tracks from *Sound Affects*, charted at No. 21 in the UK charts as an import single, confirming the band's enormous popularity.

"Funeral Pyre," the band's summer 1981 single, showed signs that Weller was becoming fascinated with American soul and R&B, as did the punchy, horn-driven "Absolute Beginners," which hit No. 4 in the fall of the year. As the Jam were recording their sixth album, Weller suffered a nervous breakdown, which prompted him to stop drinking. In February 1982, the first single from the new sessions—the double-A-sided "Town Called Malice"/"Precious"—became their third No. 1 single and the band became the first group since the Beatles to play two songs on BBC's *Top of the Pops*. *The Gift*, released in March of 1982, showcased the band's soul infatuation and became the group's first No. 1 album in the UK. "Just Who Is the 5 O'Clock Hero" hit No. 8 in July, becoming the group's second import single to make the UK charts.

Although The Jam was at the height of its popularity, Paul Weller was becoming frustrated with the trio's sound and made the decision to disband the group. On the heels of the No. 2 hit "The Bitterest Pill," the Jam announced their breakup in October of 1982. The band played a farewell tour in the fall and their final single, "Beat Surrender," entered the charts at No. 1. *Dig the New Breed*, a compilation of live tracks, charted at No. 2 in December of 1982. All 16 of the group's singles were re-released by Polydor in the UK at the beginning of 1983; all of them re-charted simultaneously. Bruce Foxton released a solo album, *Touch Sensitive*, and Rick Buckler played with the Time UK; neither of the efforts were as noteworthy as the Jam biography the two wrote in the early '90s, which contained many vicious attacks on Paul Weller.

Immediately after the breakup of the Jam, Weller formed the Style Council with Mick Talbot, a member of the Jam-inspired mod-revival band the Merton Parkas. After a handful of initial hits, the Style Council proved to be a disappointment and Weller fell out of favor, both critically and commercially. At the end of the decade, he disbanded the group and went solo in the early '90s; his solo albums have been both artistic and popular successes, returning him to the spotlight in the UK. The legacy of the Jam is apparent in nearly every British guitar-pop band of the '80s and '90s, from the Smiths to Blur and Oasis. More than any other group, the Jam kept the tradition of three-minute, hook-driven British guitar-pop alive through the '70s and '80s, providing a blueprint for generations of bands to come. —*Stephen Thomas Erlewine*

In the City / May 20, 1977 / Polydor ✦✦✦✦
On their debut, the Jam offered a good balance between the forward looking, "destroy everything" aggression of punk with a certain reverence for '60s beat and R&B. In an era that preached attitude over musicianship, the Jam bettered the competition with good pop sense, strong melodies, and plenty of hooks that compromised none of punk's ideals or energy, with youth culture themes and an abrasive, ferocious attack. Even though the band would improve exponentially over the next couple of years, *In the City* is a remarkable debut and stands as one of the landmark punk albums. —*Chris Woodstra*

This Is the Modern World / Nov. 18, 1977 / Polydor ✦✦✦
As is so often the case with overnight successes, the Jam rush-recorded their sophomore effort during a hurried schedule to capitalize on the debut. This, combined with Weller's various personal distractions and

temporary lack of interest, led to less-than-satisfying results, especially in comparison to *In the City*. *This is the Modern World* can be faulted for borrowed Who licks, pale rewrites of the debut, somewhat cliched sloaganeering, and unfinished ideas, but there were still some moments of inspiration, especially in Weller's more introspective songs like "Life from a Window" and "I Need You (for Someone)"—both songs feature personal sentiments that the debut was clearly missing. *This is the Modern World* is a flawed album by Jam standards, but it would have received certain praise had it been released by another band. [The US edition added the single "All Around the World" with a different track order.] —*Chris Woodstra*

☆ **All Mod Cons** / Nov. 3, 1978 / Polydor ✦✦✦✦✦
The band regrouped and refocused for *All Mod Cons*, an album that marked a great leap in songwriting maturity and sense of purpose. For the first time, Weller built upon rather than falling back on his influences, carving a distinct voice all his own, employing a story-style narrative, with invented characters and vivid British imagery a la Ray Davies to make incisive social commentary—all in a musically irresistible package. The youthful perspective and empassioned delivery on *All Mod Cons* first earned Weller the "voice of a generation" tag, and it certainly captures a moment in time, but really the feelings and sentiments expressed on the album just as easily speak to any future generation of young people. Terms like "classic" are often bandied about but in the case of *All Mod Cons*, it is certainly deserved. —*Chris Woodstra*

☆ **Setting Sons** / Nov. 16, 1979 / Polydor ✦✦✦✦✦
Setting Sons was originally planned as a concept album about three childhood friends who, upon meeting after some time apart, discover how they've grown apart and in different directions. Though only about half of the songs ended up following the concept due to a rushed recording schedule, where it does, Weller vividly depicts British life, male relationships, and coming to terms with entry into adulthood. Weller's observation on society are more pointed and pessimistic than ever but at the same time, he's employed stronger melodies with a slicker production and comparatively fuller arrangements, even using heavy orchestration for a reworked version of Foxton's "Smithers-Jones." *Setting Sons* often reaches brilliance and stands among their best albums, but the inclusion of a number of throwaways and knock-offs (especially the out-of-place cover of "Heat Wave" that closes the album) mars an otherwise perfect album. —*Chris Woodstra*

☆ **Sound Affects** / Nov. 28, 1980 / Polydor ✦✦✦✦✦
Unhappy with the slicker approach of *Setting Sons*, the Jam got back to basics, using the direct, economic playing of *All Mod Cons* and "Going Underground," the simply brilliant single which preceded *Sound Effects* by a few months. Thematically though, Weller arrives a more indirect path, leaving behind (for the most part) the story-song narratives in favor of more abstract dealings in spirituality and perception—the approach stemming from his recent readings of Blake and Shelley (who was quoted on the sleeve) but more specifically Geoffrey Ash, whose *Camelot and the Vision of Albion* made a strong impression. Musically, Weller drew upon *Revolver*-era Beatles as a primary source (the bass line on "Start," which comes directly from "Taxman," being the most obvious occurrence), incorporating the occassional odd sound and sometimes echoed vocal, which implied psychedelia without succumbing to its excesses. Beginning to end, the songs are pure, clever, infectious pop—probably their catchiest—with "That's Entertainment and "Man in the Corner Shop," the should-have-been-a-single, standing out. —*Chris Woodstra*

The Gift / Mar. 12, 1982 / Polydor ✦✦✦
As good mods, the Jam always had a healthy respect for R&B and soul—even the first album featured the revved-up Northern Soul of "Non-Stop Dancing." With *The Gift*, however, Weller seems to have become completely absorbed in it, and more specifically, in Stax-styled soul with more than a hint of psychedelia a la "Psychedelic Shack." An uneven album marked by over-indulgence like the instrumental "Circus" and unnecessarily long songs, *The Gift* has no shortage of terrific songs like the simply sublime "Ghost," "Town Called Malice" (the hit), and the funk workout of "Precious." Weller can obviously do "soulful"—his voice has never sounded better—but unfortunately, *The Gift*, with its excesses and marginal tracks, doesn't show his talents in the proper light. Points for ambition, but ultimately this is their least consistent since *This Is the Modern World*. —*Chris Woodstra*

Dig the New Breed / Dec. 10, 1982 / Polydor ✦✦✦
A postumous collection of live tracks from throughout their career, *Dig the New Breed* manages to chronicle the band's rapid progression quite nicely from the agressive early days through to the more polished last tour. Most notable for the inclusion of the non-LP cover of Eddie Floyd's "Big Bird" as well as a particularly moving reading of "Ghosts," which betters the album version, the collection serves to show what a terrific and consistent live act they were. —*Chris Woodstra*

★ **Snap!** / Oct. 14, 1983 / Polydor ✦✦✦✦✦
Snap! collects all of the Jam's singles, from "In the City" to "Beat Surrender," including several B-sides (" 'A' Bomb in Wardour Street," "Dreams of Children") and a handful of rarities, like a demo of "That's Entertainment" and the rock version of "Smithers-Jones." For its compact disc release, several songs were trimmed, but *Snap!* remains a brilliant summation of why the Jam were one of the most important and beloved British bands of their era. The latter-day collection *Greatest Hits* covers much the same ground as *Snap!*, but the earlier compilation remains preferable because of sequencing and its inclusion of essential items like " 'A' Bomb in Wardour Street" and "Dreams of Children." —*Stephen Thomas Erlewine*

Greatest Hits / Jul. 1, 1991 / Polydor ✦✦✦✦
Greatest Hits covers nearly the same ground as *Snap!*, with all the tracks but "Just Who Is the Five O'Clock Hero" included on the previous compilation. Granted, "That's Entertainment" is presented in the album version and "Funeral Pyre" in its original mix, but the album isn't quite as strong as *Snap!*. Nevertheless, it has all of their hit singles, making it a thoroughly entertaining record, as well as an effective introduction to the group. —*Stephen Thomas Erlewine*

Extras: A Collection of Rarities / Apr. 6, 1992 / Polydor ✦✦✦✦
Extras offers 26 B-sides, rarities, and unreleased tracks that, while far from complete (the wonderful "See Saw" is absent for instance), is a fan's dream come true. This is a fans' album to be sure, but for fans, the never-before heard demos (like "Burning Sky" and "Thick as Thieves") have a certain spine-tingling effect and the covers (like "So Sad About Us," "And Your Bird Can Sing," and "Disguises") are undeniably fun—often more so than the covers they chose to include on the proper albums. *Extras* is not a good introduction, to be sure, but for the converted, this is essential. —*Chris Woodstra*

Wasteland / Oct. 1992 / Pickwick ✦✦
Wasteland is a budget-line import that collects 16 tracks from throughout the Jam's career, mostly focusing on album tracks, but it also includes a couple of singles. Though they had no shortage of great material and the songs here are all great, the song selection (and order for that matter) seem to have been done at random. *Wasteland* is ultimately a waste of time. —*Chris Woodstra*

Beat Surrender [Collection] / May 1993 / Karussell ✦✦
Just like *Wasteland*, the odd collection that preceded it by a year, *Beat Surrender* combines a couple of hits with poorly chosen album cuts for an incoherent and certainly far from comprehensive package. The Jam had a lot of great album tracks that were unfairly overshadowed by the singles, but *The Jam Collection* (released in 1996) offers better proof to that fact. —*Chris Woodstra*

Live Jam / Oct. 25, 1993 / Polydor ✦✦
Repeating none of the songs on *Dig the New Breed*, *Live Jam* is an energetic, exciting collection of concert material recorded during the band's early-'80s glory days. While it's an entertaining album, it's worthwhile listening only for dedicated fans. —*Stephen Thomas Erlewine*

Jam Collection / Oct. 22, 1996 / Polydor ✦✦✦
The Jam Collection is basically a purposeless compilation. Pulling a handful of album tracks from each of the group's records and throwing a few B-sides into the mix, it is neither a greatest hits nor rarities disc—it simply spotlights some tracks you might have missed. While that approach may seem logical on the surface, it actually falls apart under any scrutiny. The Jam were one of the definitive single bands, as collections like *Snap!*, *Greatest Hits*, and the B-sides comp *Extras* proved. *The Jam Collection* ignores those singles completely for tracks that usually work better in their original album context, no matter how terrific they are as a song. Furthermore, it appears that the compilers didn't consider their selections carefully. While some songs like "English Rose," "Liza Radley," and "The Butterfly Collector" are obvious selections, the inclusion of several songs seems arbitrary. There are certainly a number of fine songs on *The Jam Collection*, but dedicated fans will have everything on here (or they should purchase the original albums) and casual fans are better served by *Snap!*, *Greatest Hits*, or even *All Mod Cons*, *Setting Sons*, and *Sound Affects*. —*Stephen Thomas Erlewine*

☆ **Direction Reaction Creation** / May 26, 1997 / Polydor ✦✦✦✦
Direction Reaction Creation is the ultimate Jam package, offering 117 tracks over five discs—essentially the band's complete studio recordings. With a strict adherence to chronological order, the box presents each single followed by its B-side(s) (six of which appear on CD for the first time, including the brilliant "See Saw"), followed by the proper album tracks—oddly, though, the album versions of the singles are chosen in most places. Unfortunately, this approach sometimes disrupts the flow of the albums, especially in the case of *All Mod Cons*, which loses three tracks to the treatment, and *Setting Sons*, which loses "Eton Rifles" to a separate disc. This is a small point for purists to debate—the

difference is really unnoticeable in light of the truly great music found on the discs. In addition to the regular studio tracks, Disc Five offers over an hour of studio demos—22 previously unreleased tracks of considerably different takes of better-known material, a few never-before-heard Weller and Foxton originals, and some interesting covers like "Rain," "Dead End Street," and "Every Little Bit Hurts." A lavish, 88-page booklet accompanies the set with great liner notes, an extensive band chronology and discography, and the band's complete gig list, along with plenty of rare photos and memorabilia. The Jam, simply put, were one of the finest bands in rock 'n' roll history, and *Direction Reaction Creation* offers the proof, showing both their remarkable rapid growth and their incredible consistency. —*Chris Woodstra*

James

f. 1982, Manchester, England
Alternative Pop-Rock, Adult Alternative Pop-Rock
As one of the first groups to be dubbed "the next Smiths," James became an institution on the British alternative music scene of the '80s and '90s with their pleasant folk-pop. Early in their career, James was blessed by praise from their idol Morrissey, which turned out to be both a blessing and a curse. The group was pegged as second-rate Smiths, yet continued to tour and record, eventually gaining a sizable following. In the late '80s, the group, like many of their British peers, became involved in the acid-house-inspired "baggy" scene and recorded the baggy-inspired "Sit Down," which became their breakthrough hit. Shortly after "Sit Down," James became more experimental, culminating in a collaboration with Brian Eno that resulted in their biggest American album, *Laid*, in 1993. James took four years to follow *Laid*, by which time their audience had returned to a cult following.

James formed in Manchester in 1982, when Paul Gilbertson (guitar), Jim Glennie (bass), and Gavan Whelan (drums) met Tim Booth (vocals) at Manchester University and asked him to join their fledgling band. During the next year, the band became regulars on the local club circuit, and by 1983, they had signed to Factory, releasing their debut EP, *Jimone*, later that year. Two years later, their second EP, *James II*, was released and Morrissey, the lead singer of the Smiths, publicly endorsed the group, asking them to open for his group. By the summer of 1985, Larry Gott had replaced Gilbertson and the group signed to Sire Records. Working with producer Lenny Kaye, the group recorded their debut, *Stutter*, that year, releasing it in early 1986 to generally positive reviews.

Over the next two years, James toured constantly, building up a solid fan base. They released their second album, the folky *Strip Mine*, in 1988. The record failed to capitalize on their live following, and the band departed Sire the following year, signing with the independent Rough Trade. On their new label, James released the moderately successful "Sit Down" and the live album *One Man Clapping*, which climbed to No. 1 on the indie charts. In 1990, Whelan was replaced by David Baynton-Powell, and James expanded to a septet with the addition of keyboardist Mark Hunter, violinist Saul Davies, and trumpeter Andy Diagram. The new lineup signed to Fontana Records and released *Gold Mother* in the fall. Following a handful of minor hit singles, *Gold Mother* finally became a breakthrough success in the spring of 1991, when a re-recorded version of "Sit Down"—now boasting a contemporary baggy beat—climbed to No. 2 on the UK charts and became a staple on US modern rock radio. Although the success of "Sit Down" was a blessing, it was also a curse, as the single became all James was known for. The band began to rebel in concert, playing almost nothing but new material, and their next album, 1992's *Seven*, was perceived as a misguided stab at big arena-rock.

For the follow-up to *Seven*, James stripped away Diagram and Davies and worked with producer Brian Eno. The resulting record, *Laid*, was a quieter, more ambitious album, and it received some of the band's best reviews. While the album was ignored in the U., it was an alternative rock hit in the US on the strength of the title track, which became a crossover hit. During the *Laid* sessions, James recorded another album's worth of experimental music with Eno that was released in the fall of 1994 as *Wah Wah*. The album received mixed reviews and the group took an extended break throughout 1995. In 1996, Tim Booth recorded a collaboration with composer Angelo Badalamenti (*Twin Peaks, Blue Velvet*) entitled *Booth and the Bad Angel*, which received generally positive reviews. James returned in early 1997 with *Whiplash*, a more straightforward record that was greeted with mixed reviews. —*Stephen Thomas Erlewine*

Stutter / 1986 / Blanco y Negro/Sire ✦✦
In spite of the group's overarching ambition, particularly in the grandiose voice with which Tim Booth sings his preening lyrics, James' debut album is an engaging collection of folk-pop, finding the group exploiting the Smiths' jangling guitars in an endearing fashion. —*Stephen Thomas Erlewine*

Strip-Mine / 1988 / Blanco y Negro/Sire ✦✦✦
Boasting a more detailed production than its predecessor, *Strip-Mine* accentuates James' more anthemic tendencies, but it's generally a stronger album than the first, featuring such charming folk-pop gems as "Stripmining." —*Stephen Thomas Erlewine*

One Man Clapping / 1989 / One Man/Rough Trade ✦✦✦
Released after James was dropped from Blanco Y Negro, *One Man Clapping* is a rather entertaining live album featuring highlights from the group's first two albums, but it's somewhat undone by Tim Booth's overly theatrical performance. —*Stephen Thomas Erlewine*

Gold Mother / Aug. 1990 / Fontana ✦✦✦✦
James completely revamped their lineup for *Gold Mother*, adding a violinist, a keyboardist, and a trumpeter to the band and attempting to write grand, ambitious arena-rock that recalled U2 and the Waterboys. Although a few of the tracks captured the sprawling, epic splendor that James wished to achieve, they have difficulty writing convincing material, and they aren't nearly as interesting as they were when they concentrated on jangling folk-pop. [*Gold Mother* was reissued in 1991 after a re-recorded version of "Sit Down" became a hit. "Sit Down" and "Lose Control" replaced "Crescendo" and "Hang On," but the baggy beats of the new songs sat uncomfortably with the sprawling, anthemic rock of *Gold Mother*.] —*Stephen Thomas Erlewine*

Seven / Mar. 17, 1992 / Fontana/Mercury ✦✦✦✦
Instead of following the Madchester leanings of "Sit Down," James carried on with the anthemic rock of *Gold Mother* on its follow-up, *Seven*. While *Seven* may indulge in the same arena-rock excesses as its predecessor, the group's writing and playing is controlled and textured, making a captivating exercise in grand, sprawling rock 'n' roll. —*Stephen Thomas Erlewine*

● **Laid** / Oct. 5, 1993 / Mercury ✦✦✦✦
Teaming up with producer Brian Eno had a considerable effect on James. Instead of pursuing the grandiose inclinations of *Gold Mother* and *Seven*, the group reduced their scale, choosing to explore texture in a dark, atmospheric, and intimate setting. As a result, *Laid* is by far the most subdued album the band has ever made, and it benefits as a result—rarely have Tim Booth's vocal theatrics and poetics sounded so affecting. But what really makes *Laid* resonate is James' subtle, textured playing, which gives the record a quiet, graceful power. —*Stephen Thomas Erlewine*

Wah Wah / Oct. 1994 / Mercury ✦✦✦
Recorded during the *Laid* sessions but released a year later, *Wah-Wah* is a collaborative effort between James and producer Brian Eno. Where *Laid* concentrated on songs, *Wah-Wah* is about sound, and frequently it's fascinating, as its 23 songs float between ambient soundscapes, worldbeat, and pop songs. Although it's an atypical record for James, the band's music has rarely been as captivating as it is here. —*Stephen Thomas Erlewine*

Whiplash / Feb. 25, 1997 / Mercury ✦✦✦
Retreating from the experimental tendencies of *Laid* and *Wah-Wah*, James return to straightforward anthemic folk-rock with *Whiplash*. Although the album isn't a retread of *Seven* or *Gold Mother*, it is considerably more rock-oriented than its two predecessors, particularly because the group has incorporated some elements of Brit-pop into their music. "She's a Star," the record's first single, soars on a slide guitar and heavy riff that falls somewhere between Suede and Oasis, as well as a distinctive falsetto from Tim Booth. It is a small song that aims big, which makes it surprisingly graceful, and it's a trick that James only pulls off a couple more times on the album. While *Whiplash* does find them on more familiar territory, it doesn't have the layered sonics and consistently excellent songwriting that made *Laid* a breakthrough. In fact, if *Whiplash* is anything, it's a bit of a step backward—it's an album that will appeal to their cult, not a large audience. —*Stephen Thomas Erlewine*

James Gang

f. 1966, Cleveland, OH, db. 1976
Rock 'n' Roll, Hard Rock, Boogie Rock
For a brief period in the early '70s, the James Gang was one of the top hard rock acts in America, thanks to the songwriting and inventive instrumental work of singer/guitarist Joe Walsh. The band was founded in Cleveland by drummer Jim Fox; its first lineup was fleshed out by bassist Tom Kriss and guitarist Glen Schwartz. The group toured the Midwest and built a name for itself, but Schwartz left the band in 1969. Walsh stepped in admirably, and word of the new guitar phenom spread quickly; the James Gang recorded its debut, *Yer Album*, later that year. The follow-up, *The James Gang Rides Again*, proved to be arguably the group's strongest and contained their best-known song, "Funk No.49" (they never had a hit single). The album went gold, as did their next two, and hit the Top 20. James Gang fan Pete Townshend invited the group to open for the Who on a European tour in 1971;

shortly thereafter, Walsh left the group, feeling constrained by the power-trio formula. He first formed Barnstorm; later, he recorded several solo albums and joined the Eagles for *Hotel California* and *The Long Run.* Dominic Troiano served as guitarist until 1973, when he joined the Guess Who; Tommy Bolin played on the *Bang* and *Miami* albums, but when he left to join Deep Purple, it essentially spelled the end of the James Gang, whose sales declined steadily following Walsh's departure. The James Gang finally broke up for good in 1976. —*Steve Huey*

Yer' Album / 1969 / One Way ✦✦✦
Yer' Album, the James Gang's first album, was a strong debut, thanks to the presence of guitarist Joe Walsh. Walsh helped bring the loud, bracing attack of British hard rock to American Southern rock-boogie with his loud, crunching power chords and concise, biting leads. Most of the original songs on *Yer' Album* are underdeveloped and lack memorable melodies, yet the sound of the band is invigorating and forceful. —*Stephen Thomas Erlewine*

● Rides Again / 1970 / MCA ✦✦✦✦
With their second album *The James Gang Rides Again,* the James Gang came into their own. Under the direction of guitarist Joe Walsh, the group—now featuring bassist Dale Peters—began incorporating keyboards into their hard rock, which helped open up their musical horizons. For much of the first side of *Rides Again,* the group tears through a bunch of boogie numbers, most notably the heavy groove of "Funk No. 49." On the second side, the James Gang departs from their trademark sound, adding keyboard flourishes and elements of country-rock to their hard rock. Walsh's songwriting had improved, giving the band solid support for their stylistic experiments. What ties the two sides of the record together is the strength of the band's musicianship, which burns brightly and powerfully on the hardest rockers, as well as on the sensitive ballads. —*Stephen Thomas Erlewine*

Thirds / 1971 / One Way ✦✦✦✦
Thirds wasn't quite as satisfying as *The James Gang Rides Again,* lacking the consistently strong songwriting of the previous album. Nevertheless, the interplay between the musicians is impressive throughout the record and whenever Walsh turns in a killer song, like "Walk Away" or "Midnight Man," the band drives it home for all it's worth. —*Stephen Thomas Erlewine*

Live in Concert / 1971 / One Way ✦✦✦
The James Gang earned a great number of fans through their live performances, so it made sense that they would release a live record within months of their successful third album. *Live in Concert* captures much of the energy of their live performances, with Joe Walsh's guitar solos catching fire on nearly every song. However, the record also makes it clear that he was beginning to outgrow the confines of the James Gang, as Fox and Peters struggled to keep up with his imaginative playing for most of the album. —*Stephen Thomas Erlewine*

Straight Shooter / 1972 / One Way ✦✦
Following the departure of Joe Walsh, drummer Jim Fox and bassist Dale Peters recruited guitarist Dominic Troiano and vocalist Roy Kenner and set about recording the James Gang's fourth studio album, *Straight Shooter.* Although Troiano was a competent player, he lacked Walsh's fiery passion and knack for crafting melodic solos. In addition to Troiano's workmanlike performances, the band was saddled by a noticeable lack of strong material, since none of the members could write songs with memorable hooks. —*Stephen Thomas Erlewine*

Passin' Thru / 1972 / ABC ✦✦
Passin' Thru continued James Gang's dry period, as the band suffered from a dearth of memorable songs and Troiano exhausted his supply of guitar licks. Troiano left after the release of *Passin' Thru* and was replaced with ex-Zephyr guitarist Tommy Bolin, who helped revitalize the band. —*Stephen Thomas Erlewine*

Bang / 1973 / Atco ✦✦✦
Bang was the first record the James Gang recorded with Tommy Bolin, a former member of Zephyr. While the songs were still fairly undistinguished, Bolin's playing was imaginative and captivating, making the lack of interesting material forgivable. —*Stephen Thomas Erlewine*

The Best of the James Gang / 1973 / ABC ✦✦✦✦
A good collection of their innovative hard rock features "Walk Away" and "Funk 49." —*Dan Heilman*

Miami / 1974 / Atco ✦✦✦
Like *Bang* before it, *Miami* was a success solely because of the presence of guitarist Tommy Bolin. Bolin's energetic, muscular playing reinvigorated the James Gang, sparking the rest of the band into giving lively performances. Again, there was a noticeable lack of memorable songs, but *Miami* is worthwhile for guitar aficionados. —*Stephen Thomas Erlewine*

Rick James (James Johnson)
b. Feb. 1, 1952, Buffalo, NY
Bass, Guitar, Vocals / Funk, Urban, Quiet Storm

In the late '70s, when the fortunes of Motown Records seemed to be flagging, Rick James came along and rescued the company, providing funky hits that updated the label's style and saw it through into the mid-'80s. Actually, James had been with Motown earlier, though nothing had come of it. After growing up in Buffalo and running away to join the Naval Reserves, he ran away from the Navy to Toronto, where he was in a band with future Buffalo Springfield members Neil Young and Bruce Palmer, and with Goldy McJohn, later of Steppenwolf. As the Mynah Birds, they signed to Motown and recorded, though no record was ever released.

James had a journeyman's career playing bass in various groups before signing again to Motown as an artist, songwriter, and producer. His first single, "You and I" (May 1978), topped the R&B charts and reached the pop Top 40. "Mary Jane" (September 1978) was another hit. Both were on James' debut album, *Come and Get It!* (June 1978), which went gold. Subsequent efforts were not as successful, though *Bustin' Out of L Seven* (January 1979) featured the R&B hit "Bustin' Out" (April 1979). James returned to form with the No. 1 R&B hit "Give It to Me Baby" (March 1981), featured on the million-selling *Street Songs* (April 1981), which also featured the hit "Super Freak."

James turned his production attention to resuscitating the career of the Temptations, recently returned to Motown, and "Standing on the Top" (April 1982), credited to "The Temptations Featuring Rick James," was an R&B Top Ten. (He also produced recordings by Teena Marie and the Mary Jane Girls.) James' follow-up to *Street Songs* was the gold-selling *Throwin' Down* (May 1982), which featured the hit "Dance wit' Me." The title song of *Cold Blooded* (August 1983) became James' third R&B No. 1, and the album also featured his hit duet with Smokey Robinson, "Ebony Eyes." James' greatest hits album *Reflections* (August 1984) featured the new track "17" (June 1984), which also became a hit. *Glow* (April 1985) contained Top Ten R&B singles in the title track and "Can't Stop," which was featured in the summer movie blockbuster *Beverly Hills Cop. The Flag* (June 1986) featured the hit "Sweet and Sexy Thing" (May 1986).

James left Motown for the Reprise division of Warner Bros. Records as of the album *Wonderful* (July 1988), which featured his No. 1 R&B hit "Loosey's Rap," on which he was accompanied by rapper Roxanne Shante. Nevertheless, his "punk funk" didn't seem to rest comfortably with the trend toward rap/hip-hop. In 1989, James charted briefly with a medley of the Drifters hits "This Magic Moment" and "Dance with Me." In 1990, M.C. Hammer scored a massive hit with "U Can't Touch This," which consisted of his rap over the instrumental track of "Super Freak." That should have made for a career rebirth, but James has been plagued by drug and legal problems that have found him more frequently in court and in jail than in the recording studio. —*William Ruhlmann*

Come Get It! / 1978 / Motown ✦✦✦
An excellent debut set, "Mary Jane" was very risqué for its time. —*Rick A. Bueche*

Bustin' Out of L Seven / 1979 / Gordy ✦✦✦✦
Rick James' second album, *Bustin' Out of L Seven,* maintained his status among R&B fans, almost topping the Black LP chart and spawning hits in the title track, "High on Your Love Suite," and "Fool on the Street," though none of them matched the popularity of the debut album's "You and I" or "Mary Jane." James managed an effective amalgam of recent R&B big-band styles, from Sly and the Family Stone to Earth, Wind and Fire and Funkadelic, overlaying the result with his jeeringly rendered sex-and-drugs philosophy. What was missing this time was a real pop crossover—if *Come Get It!* had suggested he could have the pop success of Earth, Wind and Fire, *Bustin' Out of L Seven* threatened that his work would find as restricted an audience as Funkadelic, and without the critical cachet. —*William Ruhlmann*

Fire It Up / 1979 / Gordy ✦✦✦
Rick James' third album in 18 months may have spread the funk a little thin (or saturated the market), since *Fire It Up* was not as effective as his first two efforts. The usual mix of rock and R&B had some disco added, which dulled the music's edge and made it more formulaic. At the same time, James' single-entendre come-ons, notably the album's biggest single, "Love Gun," were beginning to sound less provocative than just smutty. James had all the weapons for success in his arsenal, but he hadn't yet figured out a unified plan of attack, and *Fire It Up* was a holding action. —*William Ruhlmann*

3 Times in Love / 1980 / Gordy ✦✦✦

Garden of Love / 1980 / Motown ✦✦
Rick James was riding high in the early '80s, although this album was the weakest of his hit string. Although he did get a couple of Top 20 R&B singles, this album was more of a formula job than either its pre-

decessor or successor, and had less exuberant vocals and more repetitive production and arrangements. But it didn't hurt James' then-soaring career much, and in retrospect was much better than some LPs he did later in the decade. —*Ron Wynn*

Street Songs / 1981 / Motown ✦✦✦✦
Rick James peaked on this album. His vocals were never more aggressive or better produced than on the singles "Super Freak" and "Give It to Me Baby." James became a crossover sensation, as the LP peaked at No. 3 on the pop album chart and eventually went platinum. "Give It to Me Baby" topped the R&B charts for five weeks, while "Super Freak" was also a Top Ten single. —*Ron Wynn*

Throwin' Down / 1982 / Gordy ✦✦
Cold Blooded / 1983 / Motown ✦✦
The last gasp for Rick James, at one time the king of '80s punk-funk. He was close to the end by the time this came out, but got some fresh life from a surprising source. A ballad between James and Smokey Robinson, possibly the two least compatible male vocalists around, proved a big hit and regenerated James as a single artist for a few more years. But the remainder of the album marked his continual deterioration as a producer, arranger, songwriter, and performer. —*Ron Wynn*

Bustin' Out: The Very Best Of / May 17, 1994 / Motown ✦✦✦✦
Over the course of 27 tracks and two discs, *Bustin' Out: The Very Best Of* runs through nearly all of Rick James' biggest hits for Gordy/Motown Records. Although there may be too much music for casual fans, no essential items are missing from the set, making it a definitive retrospective for the serious fan, featuring not only the obvious hits like "Mary Jane," "Bustin Out," "Cold Blooded," and "Super Freak," but a number of fine lesser-known singles and album tracks as well. —*Stephen Thomas Erlewine*

● **Ultimate Collection** / Mar. 25, 1997 / Motown ✦✦✦✦
This excellent overview of Rick James' Motown hits features seven Top Ten hits, including the seminal "Super Freak" as well as "Cold Blooded," "Give It to Me Baby," "You and I," "Mary Jane," "Dance Wit' Me" and "Bustin' Out." —*Jason Ankeny*

Tommy James & the Shondells

f. 1966, Dayton, OH, db. 1970
Pop-Rock, Bubblegum, Brill Building Pop
During the last half of the '60s, Tommy James & the Shondells were one of America's most successful pop acts, generating 14 Top 40 hits between 1966 and 1969. James formed the original Shondells at the age of twelve, in 1960. In 1963, they recorded a Jeff Barry-Ellie Greenwich song called "Hanky Panky" for the Snap label. Two years later, a Pittsburgh DJ picked up on the song and made it into a regional hit. James and the original Shondells parted ways because the band members didn't want to relocate from Indiana, and James formed a new Shondells by taking on a group called the Raconteurs. In 1966 they signed to Morris Levy's Roulette, which reissued "Hanky Panky" (it became a No. 1 million-seller).

For the next two years, they embodied lightweight chewy pop with hits like "I Think We're Alone Now" and "Mirage." The group developed a heavier sound with the percussive 1968 hit "Mony Mony." In keeping with the times, they became more psychedelic, best captured in their No. 1 "Crimson and Clover." The Shondells continued to chart until James left for a moderately successful solo career in 1970. James' biggest hit was "Draggin' the Line." The Shondells changed their name to Hog Heaven to no appreciable success. During the '80s, the Shondells' material enjoyed a resurgence of popularity among various pop and rock artists. Joan Jett scored with "Crimson and Clover," while Billy Idol's version of "Mony Mony" and Tiffany's "I Think We're Alone Now" took turns at the No. 1 position in November of 1987. —*Rick Clark*

● **Anthology** / 1990 / Rhino ✦✦✦✦
James and his band had a remarkable string of hits from the mid-'60s to the early '70s, largely because of an uncanny ability to keep current with fast-changing pop trends, from their first garage-band hit, "Hanky Panky," to their psychedelicized songs like "Crimson and Clover." Even more remarkable, the music holds up entertainingly today, and this well-annotated, 27-track compilation contains all the hits and more. —*William Ruhlmann*

The Solo Years (1970-81) / Feb. 1, 1991 / Rhino ✦✦✦✦
Crimson & Clover/Cellophane / Aug. 27, 1991 / Rhino ✦✦✦
One of the most flexible units in late-'60s rock, Tommy James & the Shondells could go from teen-oriented power pop to way-out psychedelic experimentation without sounding derivative of anyone or allowing their own identity to become obscured. Generously combining two of their classic albums, *Cellophane Symphony* and *Crimson & Clover*, on a single CD, this reissue reminds us just how unpredictable the rockers could be. This was a band that managed to appeal to Beach Boys aficionados as well as the hippies who fancied Jefferson Airplane, the Doors, and Cream. Whether digging into psychedelic rock on

"Crimson & Clover" (a major hit), "Cellophane Symphony" and the goofy "I Am a Tangerine," sugary power pop on "Do Something to Me" or smooth blue-eyed soul on "Crystal Blue Persuasion," the group consistently comes across as honest and true to itself. —*Alex Henderson*

The Very Best of Tommy James / Apr. 20, 1993 / Rhino ✦✦✦✦

Jan & Dean

f. 1958, Los Angeles, CA, db. Apr. 1966
Surf, Pop-Rock
Besides the Beach Boys, no other vocal group captured the sound of California surf music with as much success—both commercial and artistic—as Jan & Dean. The duo actually began as a doo wop-soaked harmony act in the late '50s, reaching the Top Ten with the goofy "Baby Talk" and scoring minor hits with doo wop updates of standards like "A Sunday Kind of Love" and "Heart and Soul." When the Beach Boys began their climb to superstardom, Jan & Dean changed gears and followed suit with a series of surf and hot rod hits that featured falsetto harmonies, chugging guitars, and Jan Berry's clean production. Brian Wilson himself sang backup vocals on their biggest hit (which he co-wrote with Jan), "Surf City," in 1963.

While they lacked the Beach Boys' depth and capacity for artistic growth, Jan & Dean's hits from 1963 and 1964—which also included "The Little Old Lady (From Pasadena)," "Drag City," "Honolulu Lulu," and the mini-soap opera "Dead Man's Curve"—are in the same class as the Beach Boys' early work in their infectious, energetic invocation of good times and California sunshine. They added an irresistibly reckless humor to the genre, and were well cast as the fun-loving hosts of the classic 1964 rock 'n' roll hootenanny film *The T.A.M.I. Show* (for which they performed the rip-roaring theme, "(Here They Come) From All over the World"). The duo's success, already on the wane a bit, was tragically cut short by Jan Berry's near-fatal auto accident in April 1966, which had been eerily foreshadowed by the lyrics of "Dead Man's Curve." —*Richie Unterberger*

● **Surf City: The Best of Jan & Dean** / 1990 / EMI America ✦✦✦✦
Remembered mostly for their surfing hits, Jan & Dean had a bit more range than they're generally given credit for. Their roots were in doo wop, and after scoring surf and hot rod hits, they also cut some decent straight pop-rock songs and zany singles that verged on pop satire. *Surf City* includes just about all the material you'd want from the duo. The 22 songs include the big hits "Surf City," "Dead Man's Curve," and "The Little Old Lady (From Pasadena)," of course, but also feature nifty smaller successes like "Honolulu Lulu," "The New Girl In School," and "Ride the Wild Surf." The pair was second only to the Beach Boys in blending high, soaring harmonies with driving vocal surf 'n' hot rod sounds. Of course, they weren't nearly as talented as Brian Wilson's group, but even their minor material has an irrepressible sense of fun and sparking L.A. pop-rock production and melodies. Other highlights include their rearrangement of the old standard "Linda" and the 1965 Top 40 hit "I Found a Girl," written by P.F. Sloan and Steve Barri. Sloan-Barri also penned their infectious theme for the classic rock film *The T.A.M.I. Show*, "(Here They Come) From All over the World," which deserved to be a bigger hit than it was. The only major omissions of this well-packaged set are their early, heavily doo wop-influenced hits "Jennie Lee," "Baby Talk," and "Heart and Soul," which weren't recorded for EMI. —*Richie Unterberger*

Teen Suite 1958-1962 / Jul. 4, 1995 / Varese Sarabande ✦✦✦
When Jan & Dean hit it big with "Surf City," they'd actually already been active on the L.A. pop-rock scene for a good five years, recording numerous singles for small labels that owed much more to doo wop and teen-idol styles than surf music. This has over 20 selections from the era, most taken from rare singles, including five from 1958 that were billed to Jan & Arnie (Jan's original partner was Arnie Ginsburg, who left shortly after their debut single and Top hit, "Jennie Lee"). This is mawkish, primitively recorded stuff, but not without its charm and even importance. With their white doo wop harmonies, Jan & Dean's early records were a clear influence on the Beach Boys; the best of their energetically naive, fashion-conscious singles (which Jan Berry often helped write) were a vague, but definite, forerunner of garage rock and '60s California pop-rock; and even at this point, they had a zany and infectious sense of humor, especially on their go-for-broke doo wop updates of the standards "Clementine" and "Heart and Soul." Most listeners should stick with the EMI anthology, but more specialized tastes will find a lot of this enjoyable, the hits ("Baby Talk," "Jennie Lee," "Clementine") being the standouts, though songs like "Baggy Pants" and "Something a Little Bit Different" are surprisingly goofy and satirical for the era. —*Richie Unterberger*

Golden Hits, Vols. 1-3 / Jan. 19, 1996 / One Way ✦✦✦
One Way combined all three of Jan & Dean's original hits collections for EMI onto a double-disc collection that features 36 tracks. Though it has more tracks than the single-disc *Surf City: The Best of Jan & Dean*, it isn't necessarily a better one. Not only is *Surf City* sequenced better,

giving a better overview of the duo's career, it has a more thoughtful selection of tracks. Because Jan & Dean did record their fair share of filler, most listeners will be satisfied with a 22-track collection, since it does have all the hits and completists will be better served by the reissues of the original albums. Still, the double-disc set has all the hit singles and it is reasonably well-packaged, featuring the original album covers, if not a new set of liner notes, so it isn't a bad purchase. It's just that there are better bargains. — *Stephen Thomas Erlewine*

Jan & Dean / May 21, 1996 / Era ✦✦✦✦
While their surf and hot-rod sides have been anthologized and reissued ad infinitum, someone found a hole in the Jan & Dean discography and decided to reissue their debut album as originally released on the Dore label plus all the 45s that didn't make the album to bring it up to a solid 18 tracks. True, eight of them already show up on Varese Sarabande's excellent *Teen Suite* compilation (including "Baggy Pants," "Clementine," and "Jeanette Get Your Hair Done"), but the other ten are more than worthy additions to that Jan & Dean collection you've been so diligently assembling. Jan & Dean were a doo wop duo during this period, there's really no other explanation for the sound they give out with on these sides, check out their stab at the Crescendos' "Oh Julie" and you'll see what I mean. Actually, this fills in a nice section of the guys' career, after the early Jan and Arnie sides and before the surf, the hot rods and "Dead Man's Curve." — *Cub Koda*

Golden Summer Days / Jul. 1996 / Varese Sarabande ✦✦✦
The bulk of *Golden Summer Days* is drawn from the original soundtrack to the television movie *Dead Man's Curve*, which was based on the story of Jan & Dean. Much of the music is performed by a group of surf music superstars and studio musicians—including Dean Torrence, Brian Wilson, Mike Love, Bruce Johnston, John Cowsill, and Gary Griffin—who perform under the name the Legendary Masked Surfers. Most of the music on *Golden Summer Days* was intended for use in the film, but didn't survive the final cut. It's a fun listen, but basically the album is just a curiosity for surf fans. — *Thom Owens*

● **All the Hits—From Surf City to Drag City** / Nov. 12, 1996 / EMI ✦✦✦✦
Two discs, each running over 70 minutes, of the duo's most celebrated performances from the late '50s through the mid-'60s. If you're stacking this up against the *Legendary Masters Series* compilation, the advantage of getting this one is that it adds their doo wop-influenced, pre-Liberty hits ("Baby Talk," "Heart and Soul," "A Sunday Kind of Love"), as well as the pre-Jan & Dean smash by Jan & Arnie ("Jennie Lee"). It also has a few good tunes not on the previous anthology, like "My Mighty G.T.O." and the original version of "Bucket 'T' " (covered by the Who in 1966). And it's stuffed with alternate takes of some of their most famous tunes, which could be viewed as either a boon or an irrelevance. Some of their flop singles were really cringe-worthy: "The Universal Coward" is a stupid parody of "Universal Soldier," and "A Beginning from an End," a melodrama in which the singer's wife dies in childbirth (!) against a typically sunny Top 40 arrangement, is downright tasteless fare. Collectors will appreciate these bonuses mightily, but less intense fans, if they're not determined to have "Baby Talk" and "Jennie Lee," will probably be better off with the more focused and consistent *Legendary Master Series* disc. — *Richie Unterberger*

Jane's Addiction

f. 1984, Los Angeles, CA, **db.** 1991
Hard Rock, Alternative Pop-Rock, Heavy Metal, Alternative Metal
Jane's Addiction were one of the most hotly pursued rock bands when they gained notice in Los Angeles in the mid-'80s, with record companies at their feet. Flamboyant frontman Perry Farrell, formerly of the band Psi Com, has an undeniable charisma and an interest in provocative art (he designed the band's album covers) and Jane's Addiction plays a hybrid of rock music—metal with strains of punk, folk, jazz, or you-name-it.

The quartet comprising Farrell, bassist Eric Avery, drummer Stephen Perkins, and guitarist Dave Navarro had already released their debut album as well, in the form of a live recording from the Roxy in Hollywood. Finally, Warner Brothers won the bidding war and released *Nothing Shocking* in 1988. The band's abrasive sound and aggressive attitude (typified by the nude sculpture on the cover) led to some resistance, but Jane's Addiction began to break through to an audience: the album spent 35 weeks in the charts.

Ritual de lo Habitual followed in 1990 and was the band's commercial breakthrough, reaching the Top 20 and going gold. Farrell designed the travelling rock festival Lollapalooza as a farewell tour for Jane's Addiction. After the tour was completed at the end of the summer of 1991, the group split. Farrell would continue to be involved with the organization of the annual Lollapalooza festival for the next several years; he also formed Porno for Pyros with Perkins in 1992, releasing their debut record the following year. After a couple of quiet years—which included forming Deconstruction, a band that didn't

release any records until 1994, with Avery—Navarro joined the Red Hot Chili Peppers at the end of 1993. — *William Ruhlmann*

Jane's Addiction / 1987 / Triple X ✦✦✦
When this live date was recorded at Hollywood's famous Sunset Strip club the Roxy in 1987, Jane's Addiction hadn't yet become the darlings of alternative-rock culture. The L.A. band's unorthodox fusion of Led Zeppelin-influenced hard rock, dark Velvet Underground-ish imagery and stream-of-consciousness art rock wasn't as focused or confident as it would be on the commanding *Ritual de Lo Habitual*. But even so, the band showed considerable potential. As erratic and self-indulgent as this set gets, many of the songs are quite memorable. Lead singer/composer Perry Farrell was always fascinated with the dark side of the human psyche, and that fascination serves him well on "Pigs in Zen," the twisted "Whores," and the alternative rock favorite "Jane Says." And things get enjoyably trashy on covers of the Velvet Underground's "Rock N' Roll" and the Rolling Stones' "Sympathy for the Devil." But while this CD will interest completists, more casual listeners should stick to *Ritual de Lo Habitual*. — *Alex Henderson*

Nothing's Shocking / 1988 / Warner Brothers ✦✦✦✦
The cover (a sculpture of two naked females joined at the hips with their hair ablaze) screams that this is an artsy album, and it is. Jane's Addiction, under the direction of lead vocalist Perry Farrell, brings the aesthetics of performance art to heavy metal. Some of the results are provoking, but the group's ambitions are usually irritating. Farrell's voice wears thin after a few songs, and it's not helped much by the post-Zeppelin stumble of the band—Dave Navarro may be a fluid guitarist, but he can't write riffs as powerful and catchy as Jimmy Page. Nevertheless, *Nothing's Shocking* works on occasion, particularly "Summertime Rolls" and the re-recorded version of "Jane Says." — *Stephen Thomas Erlewine*

● **Ritual de lo Habitual** / Aug. 1990 / Warner Brothers ✦✦✦✦
Throughout the first half of *Ritual*, Jane's Addiction manages to groove, creating the best rock 'n' roll of their short career. The two Bo Diddley knock-offs, "Stop!" and "Been Caught Stealing," in particular, sound tight and exciting, but on the second half, the indulgent ten-minute songs are hauled out, beginning with the insufferable *menage à trois* magnum opus "Three Days." Still, the band manages to salvage the album with the majestic "Classic Girl," one of their best songs. — *Stephen Thomas Erlewine*

Japan

f. 1974, London, England, **db.** 1982
Art-Rock/Progressive-Rock, New Wave, New Romantic
Japan's evolution from rather humble glam-rock beginnings into stylish synth-pop (and beyond) made the British group one of the more intriguing and successful artists of their era. Formed in London in 1974, Japan began its existence as a quintet comprised of singer-songwriter David Sylvian, bassist Mick Karn, keyboardist Richard Barbieri, drummer (and Sylvian's brother) Steve Jansen, and guitarist Rob Dean. In their primary incarnation, the group emulated the sound and image of glam-rockers like David Bowie and the New York Dolls; Sylvian's over-the-top vocals, much in the vein of Bryan Ferry, also earned Japan frequent (if derisive) comparisons to Roxy Music.

After winning a label-sponsored talent contest, they were signed to Germany's Ariola-Hansa Records in 1977 and debuted a year later with a pair of LPs, *Adolescent Sex* and *Obscure Alternatives*, which received little notice at home or in the US, but did find favor among Japanese audiences. With 1979's *Quiet Life*, Japan made a tremendous leap into more sophisticated stylistic and subtle territory; a subsequent hit single covering Smokey Robinson's "I Second That Emotion" further underscored the newfound soulfulness of their music.

1980's *Gentlemen Take Polaroids* continued to broaden Japan's scope, incorporating a variety of exotic influences into their increasingly atmospheric sound. With 1982's *Tin Drum* (recorded minus Dean), the band peaked: tapping sources as diverse as funk and Middle Eastern rhythms, the album moved beyond pop confines into experimental tones and textures, and scored a UK smash with the single "Ghosts."

However, *Tin Drum* also proved to be Japan's swan song: long-simmering differences among the band members came to a head when Karn's girlfriend moved in with Sylvian, and the group disbanded in 1982. The individual members quickly forged ahead with their projects: Sylvian began a successful solo career and also entered into a series of collaborations with performers like Ryuichi Sakamoto, Holger Czukay, and Robert Fripp, while Karn issued a 1982 solo LP, *Titles*, before launching the short-lived duo Dali's Car with Bauhaus' Peter Murphy. In 1986, meanwhile, Jansen and Barbieri issued *Worlds in a Small Room* under their own names before recording together as the Dolphin Brothers.

In 1987, Karn released *Dreams of Reason Produce Monsters*, a solo LP that featured contributions from Sylvian and Jansen, spurring rumors of a reunion that came to fruition in 1989 when the four principal members reteamed under the name Rain Tree Crow. By the time an eponymously-titled album appeared in 1991, however, relations had again dissolved in acrimony, and the musicians went their separate ways; while Sylvian continued working independently, as the decade wore on Karn, Jansen, and Barbieri occasionally reunited in various projects while also maintaining solo careers. —*Jason Ankeny*

Adolescent Sex / 1978 / Ariola ✦✦✦✦
The debut album is vastly different from later work. —*Steve Aldrich*

Obscure Alternatives / 1978 / Ariola ✦✦✦
Continuing artsy glam-rock formula of debut. —*Steve Aldrich*

Quiet Life / 1979 / Fame ✦✦✦
This transitional album turned the group from their original glam-rock style to the later Roxy Music-influenced sound. —*Steve Aldrich*

● **Gentlemen Take Polaroids** / 1980 / Blue Plate ✦✦✦✦
This was the first fully realized album in the group's latter-day phase. —*Steve Aldrich*

Tin Drum / 1981 / Blue Plate ✦✦✦✦
A highly atmospheric effort, this early-'80s classic was strongly influenced by folk music of their namesake country. —*Steve Aldrich*

Assemblage / 1981 / Hansa ✦✦✦
First of the collections of Hansa-era tracks. —*Steve Aldrich*

Oil on Canvas / 1983 / Blue Plate ✦✦✦
An outstanding live album, it focused on *Tin Drum-* and *Polaroids*-era material. —*Steve Aldrich*

Exorcising Ghosts / 1984 / Virgin ✦✦✦
This is a compilation of Virgin-era material. —*Steve Aldrich*

Jason & the Scorchers

f. 1981, Nashville, TN
Rock 'n' Roll, Country-Rock, Roots-Rock
A country/hard-rock band formed by Illinois native Jason Ringenberg in 1981, Jason and the Scorchers came careening onto the indie-rock scene seemingly out of nowhere (truth was, it was Nashville) with a debut EP whose most killer track (among a slew of killer tracks) was a fire-breathing cover of Bob Dylan's "Absolutely Sweet Marie." This amalgam of speedy hard rock fused with Ringenberg's decidedly country twang, along with the band's ability to deftly negotiate between Rolling Stones-style stomps and quieter, more melodic acoustic country music, led to Jason and the Scorchers becoming a critically lauded and fairly popular '80s band. Capitalizing quickly on the notoriety brought by their debut EP, the Scorchers kicked out two fine LPs (*Lost & Found* and *Still Standing*) that sounded perfect for radio, but not so slick as to sound manufactured. With Ringenberg's yowling voice pushed way up front, the band's sonic power came from the synchronous playing of Nashville rock veterans Warner Hodges (guitar), Jeff Johnson (bass), and Perry Baggs (drums). Sharing similar musical backgrounds that valued the music of Hank Williams and Johnny Cash as much as the Stones or Beatles, these guys could crank out mega-amped hard rock one minute and sound like the Flying Burrito Brothers the next, all of it done with great skill and excitement.

Despite their obvious talent, by the release of 1986's *Still Standing*, it seemed as though the band wasn't going anywhere. They had achieved a modicum of success, but weren't able to break through to mass acclaim, partly because they came along just before the explosion of country radio in the late '80s/early '90s. Hence, rock radio was reluctant to play them because they sounded too country, and country radio thought they were too rock; it's an old story that usually spells doom for the band in question. After a three-year break that saw Johnson's departure, the Scorchers released a desultory third album (*Thunder and Fire*) that sounded like a desperate attempt at hard rock credibility. They broke up soon after. Ringenberg went on to record country-oriented solo work, re-formed the original Scorchers in 1994, and released a modest reunion record (*A Blazing Grace*) that sounded like the Scorchers of old. Two years later, the reunited Scorchers released *Clear Impetuous Morning*. —*John Dougan*

Fervor / 1983 / EMI America ✦✦✦✦
Their debut EP has "Absolutely Sweet Marie" (which you'll play over and over and over), as well as some wonderful country-rock like "Hot Nights in Georgia." Ringenberg's twangy voice is a hoot to listen to, and Warner Hodges plays some great guitar. A wonderful, if too brief, record and a harbinger of some great rock 'n' roll to come. R.E.M.'s Michael Stipe contributes a song ("Both Sides of the Line") and some backup vocals. —*John Dougan*

Lost & Found / 1985 / EMI America ✦✦✦✦
Of the Scorchers' three full-length LPs, this is by far the best. There is so much pent-up energy and excitement on this record, it sounds as if it will fly off your turntable (assuming you still have a turntable) at any moment. With Hodges (as usual) driving this machine, Ringenberg's

wild-eyed country-punk persona is here in full fury, and the good times never let up. This should have been the album that made them stars, but it did solidify their audience and place them in larger concert venues, where they tore it up. —*John Dougan*

Still Standing / 1986 / EMI ✦✦✦
Produced by veteran hard rock producer Tom Werman, *Still Standing* is a fine record, but also shows subtle signs of the band in decline: the hard-rock is stiffer, Hodges' guitar is smoother and more akin to the anonymous hard rock/heavy metal guitar sound that defined AOR radio in the '80s. That notwithstanding, there are still songs like "Golden Ball and Chain," which sounds like an outtake from *Exile on Main Street*, and continuing with the Rolling Stones motif, a ripsnortin' cover of "19th Nervous Breakdown." A teensy bit disappointing in comparison to *Lost and Found*, but by no means a bad record or one to ignore. If you've liked the Scorchers up to this point, you'll want *Still Standing*. —*John Dougan*

Thunder & Fire / Dec. 1989 / A&M ✦✦✦
With the release of *Thunder & Fire*, Jason & the Scorchers should have been set for the top. Unfortunately, that didn't happen. They broke up instead. But the record they left behind does have its moments. Hard-hitting rockers like "Now That You're Mine" and "6 Feet Underground" fit snugly alongside "Close Up the Road," a country-tinged weeper and "Bible & a Gun," which recalls the best things about the roots-rock movement of the late '80s. —*James Chrispell*

● **Essential, Vol. 1 (Are You Ready for the Country)** / Oct. 20, 1992 / Capitol ✦✦✦✦
Essential, Vol. 1 (Are You Ready for the Country) compiles Jason & the Scorchers' first EP, *Fervor*, and their debut LP *Lost & Found*, adding four bonus tracks for good measure. It's an excellent way to acquire their best records, yet it was replaced four years later by the nearly identical *Both Sides of the Line*, which featured the EP and LP without the bonus tracks. —*Stephen Thomas Erlewine*

Blazing Grace / Feb. 7, 1995 / Mammoth ✦✦✦
Jason & the Scorchers came "blazing" back with this rockin' barrelhouse of a release. Containing sure-fire rockers in "Where Bridges Never Burn" and "Cry by Night Operator," the Scorchers never sounded better. But also check out their hard-drivin' covers of both John Denver's "Take Me Home, Country Roads" and George Jones' "Why Baby Why." They're great! Coming back with just the original four members, Jason & the Scorchers prove that there is life after punk, or were they roots-rock, or maybe cowpunk, or.... Ah, you get the picture. A *Blazing Grace* is superb! —*James Chrispell*

Both Sides of the Line / Sep. 1996 / EMI ✦✦✦✦
CD reissue combines the *Fervor* EP and *Lost & Found* album onto one disc, and thus offers the best way to collect their early material. —*Richie Unterberger*

Clear Impetuous Morning / Oct. 1996 / Mammoth ✦✦✦
Here comes yet another steam-rolling country-rock release from Jason & the Scorchers. Pushin' the pedal to the metal, *Clear Impetuous Morning* sounds a lot like a band that has just found an open stretch of highway and is jammin' in high gear. Just about everything here rocks out in fine form including a cover of the Byrds' "Drug Store Truck Drivin' Man." Emmylou Harris even drops by to guest on "Everything Has a Cost" to great effect. You won't be disappointed if you choose to get a hold of this disc. —*James Chrispell*

Jay & the Americans

f. 1961, New York, NY
Pop-Rock, Brill Building Pop
Though they had a bunch of hits in the 1960s, Jay & the Americans were a throwback to a previous era in their doo wop influenced vocals, neatly groomed, short-haired appearance, and mix of pop-rock with operatic schmaltz. Built around the neck-bulging, upper-register vocals of Jay Black, their biggest hits—"She Cried," "Cara Mia," "Come a Little Bit Closer," and "Let's Lock the Door (And Throw Away the Key)"—came off as a sort of hit parade version of *West Side Story*. The group also relied on outside songwriters for their material, drifting into MOR covers of oldies by the end of the '60s, and were generally a sort of textbook of unhipness during a time when self-contained rock bands were becoming the norm. Now that there's no pressure to disparage them in favor of more authentic acts, we can appreciate them for what they were—purveyors, at their best, of enjoyable kitsch with little depth.

Jay Black wasn't even in the band when they got their first big hit, "She Cried," which went to No. 5 in 1962. Produced by Leiber and Stoller, the booming percussion and soaring strings, as well as the sad melody, was reminiscent of their work with the Drifters, though in a much whiter mold. Jay Black had replaced lead singer Jay Traynor by the time of their second hit in 1963, "Only in America" (neither of them, by the way, were actually named Jay; their first names were conveniently changed to fit the band's billing). Not coincidentally, perhaps, "Only in America" had originally been offered to the Drifters, whose version remained unreleased until 1996. In the hands of Jay & the Americans, the Barry Mann-Cynthia Weil tune—originally designed as a subtle (probably too subtle) protest of sorts—became a rather gauche patriotic statement, complete with mariachi trumpets.

That odd Mexican feel reappeared on two of their biggest mid-'60s hits, "Come a Little Bit Closer" and "Cara Mia," which transplanted Roy Orbison's operatic sensibilities to the heart of the Bronx. "Cara Mia" in particular was a rather astonishing exercise in sheer top-range vocal power by Black, if not one to everyone's taste. The less memorable "Sunday and Me," from 1965, was notable in that it was Neil Diamond's first major success as a songwriter. Out of the Top Forty for a few years after 1966, Jay and the boys resurfaced in 1969 and 1970 with smooth hit updates of the Drifters' "This Magic Moment" and the Ronettes' "Walkin' in the Rain" before heading to the oldies circuit. Interestingly, future Steely Dan leaders Walter Becker and Donald Fagen played in the Americans' backup group for a time in the early '70s. —*Richie Unterberger*

● **Come a Little Bit Closer: The Best of Jay & the Americans** / 1990 / United Artists ✦✦✦✦
Jay Black possesses one of the most remarkable voices in rock 'n' roll. On *Come a Little Bit Closer—The Best of Jay & the Americans*, an exhaustive 28-song collection, you get all of the hits in superb fidelity, and plenty of bonuses. —*Jeff Tamarkin*

Jayhawks

f. 1985, Minneapolis, MN, **db.** 1996
Alternative Country-Rock, Americana
Led by the gifted songwriting, impeccable playing, and honeyed harmonies of vocalists/guitarists Mark Olson and Gary Louris, the Jayhawks' shimmering blend of country, folk, and bar-band rock made them one of the most widely acclaimed artists to emerge from the alternative country scene. The group sprung up in 1985 out of the fertile Minneapolis, MN, musical community, where Olson had been playing stand-up bass in a rockabilly band called Stagger Lee until his desire to write and perform his own country-folk material prompted him to begin a solo career. He enlisted Marc Perlman, the guitarist for a local band called the Neglecters, whom Olson then convinced to take up the bass; after the addition of drummer Norm Rogers, the group first played in front of a crowd of less than a dozen people. One of those patrons, however, was Gary Louris, a veteran of the local bands Safety Last and Schnauzer; after the show, he and Olson began talking, and by the end of the evening Louris, a guitarist famed locally for his innovative, pedal steel-like sound, had become a member of the group, eventually named the Jayhawks.

Drawing on influences like Gram Parsons, the Louvin Brothers, Tim Hardin, and *Nashville Skyline*-era Bob Dylan, the Jayhawks quickly became a local favorite, honing their sound in Twin Cities clubs before releasing their eponymous debut in 1986. Issued in a pressing of just a few thousand copies, the album was well-received by those who heard it; a major recording deal did not follow, however, so the band continued to polish their craft live, with more and more of their songs bearing writing credits belonging to both Olson and Louris. In October 1988, after a line-up change that saw the departure of Rogers (who joined the Cows) followed by the addition of drummer Thad Spencer, Louris was nearly killed in an auto accident, and the Jayhawks went on hiatus. At much the same time, however, executives at the Minneapolis independent label Twin/Tone decided to issue the demos the group had been stockpiling over the past few years, and after some overdubbing and remixing, *The Blue Earth* appeared in 1989. Richer in sound and more complex in its themes and concerns, the record's release brought the group considerable attention, and also brought Louris back into the fold. After another drummer switch (Spencer for Ken Callahan), the band hit the road for a national tour.

The Jayhawks were signed to major label (Def) American Records after producer George Drakoulias heard *The Blue Earth* playing in the background during a phone call to Twin/Tone's offices. With Drakoulias in the producer's seat, the band recorded their breakthrough album *Hollywood Town Hall* in 1991; a mainstay of critics' annual "best of" lists, the album generated the alternative radio hits "Waiting for the Sun," "Take Me with You (When You Go)," and "Settled Down Like Rain." After a tour that saw the permanent addition of Minneapolis pianist Karen Grotberg, the individual band members guested on albums from Counting Crows, Soul Asylum, Maria McKee, Joe Henry, and others. Before recording the fourth Jayhawks album, Callahan departed, and was replaced by session drummer Don Heffington. The resulting record, 1995's *Tomorrow the Green Grass*, was the group's finest, a beautiful collection of songs led off by the elegiac single "Blue," the recipient of significant airplay. A tour followed, but after some months on the road, Olson announced he was quitting the band.

In 1997, the Jayhawks—now consisting of Louris, Perlman, Grotberg, and drummer Tim O'Reagan—released the album *Sound of Lies*. —*Jason Ankeny*

The Jayhawks / 1986 / Bunkhouse ✦✦✦
Though lacking the almost telepathic interplay later developed by frontmen Mark Olson and Gary Louris, the Jayhawks' self-titled debut—issued in a tiny pressing of just a few thousand copies—is a fair indication of the remarkable things still to come from the band. Complete with song titles that could have been cribbed from old Replacements records—"Six Pack on the Dashboard," "The Liquor Store Came First," "I'm Not in Prison," and so forth—the record owes a clear debt to the group's Minneapolis stomping grounds, but evidence of the Jayhawks' own distinct identity can be found in the fluid guitar work as well as in Olson and Louris' harmonies, which even this early in the game are graceful and rich. —*Jason Ankeny*

Blue Earth / 1989 / Twin/Tone ✦✦✦
The songs that make up *Blue Earth* originated as demos, and save for some minor studio tinkering, are presented here in their original, embryonic state. As a consequence, the record lacks punch; spare and economical, the songs are simply too primitive to come to life in this setting. Nonetheless, the growth of the band's songwriting skills over their debut is substantial; while many of the themes—drifting, drinking, and lost love—remain the same, they're handled with greater insight and clarity than before, with a keen eye for detail and nuance. —*Jason Ankeny*

Hollywood Town Hall / Sep. 15, 1992 / Def American ✦✦✦✦
Hollywood Town Hall is the Jayhawks' breakthrough record, a uniformly strong collection heralding a dramatic leap in maturity and depth over the band's earlier work. Benefitting greatly from the increased production values afforded by their newfound major label status, the group's songs—a handful of them redone from the earlier *Blue Earth*—shimmer like never before; the guitars crackle with energy, and Mark Olson and Gary Louris' harmonies lock together so organically that at times it's impossible to distinguish where one voice ends and the other begins. —*Jason Ankeny*

● **Tomorrow the Green Grass** / Feb. 14, 1995 / American ✦✦✦✦
The Jayhawks' final record with singer-songwriter Mark Olson, *Tomorrow the Green Grass* is also the group's finest. While the band's earlier efforts perfected a more traditonal brand of country-rock, their fourth record is marvelously eclectic, both musically and emotionally; never before had they rocked as hard as on "Real Light," dug as painfully deep as on "Two Hearts," or hit quite the same peaks of exuberance as on "Miss Williams' Guitar," a tribute to Olson's new wife, neo-folkie Victoria Williams. The addition of keyboardist Karen Grotberg brings rich new layers to the Jayhawks' sound, as does the inclusion of a string section on cuts like "Blue" and "I'd Run Away," a soaring pop song that's quite possibly the best thing the group ever recorded. A fitting legacy, indeed. —*Jason Ankeny*

Sound of Lies / Apr. 22, 1997 / Warner Brothers ✦✦✦
Following Mark Olson's amicable departure, the remaining Jayhawks reconvened under the direction of Gary Louris to record *Sound of Lies*, the band's most ambitious album to date. Like Wilco's *Being There*, *Sound of Lies* uses country-rock as a foundation and wanders off into a variety of different sonic territories, including surf-rock and Beatlesque pop, bringing the music closer to the sound of adult-alternative pop-rock. Although the surface of the album is pleasant and melodic, Louris has written a uniformly harrowing set of songs, inspired both by the dissolution of his partnership with Olson and a recent divorce. The lyrics have a naked, emotional honesty, which would have been more affecting if the music echoed its sentiment, yet the record still has a subtle grace and power, proving that the Jayhawks remain a distinctive band without Olson. —*Thom Owens*

The JB's

f. 1964
Soul, R&B, Soul Jazz, Funk
Maceo Parker joined James Brown's fabled band in 1964, Alfred "Pee Wee" Ellis joined the fold two years later, and Fred Wesley came on board in 1968. Ellis co-wrote such classics as "Cold Sweat" and "Say It Loud—I'm Black and I'm Proud," and both he and Wesley at various points were musical director of the JB's. Parker was immortalized in Brown's famous incantation "Maceo, come blow your horn." Ellis also served as musical director for Van Morrison, while Wesley and Parker were part of the Parliament/Funkadelic gang at their peak in the mid-and late '70s. The three of them have recorded in various permutations as Maceo and All the King's Men, Maceo and the Macks, the JB's, Fred Wesley and the New JB's, Fred Wesley and the Horny Horns, the John Book Horns, and simply under any one of their individual names. In the '80s and early '90s, with the resurgence of interest in James Brown and Parliament/Funkadelic, the three horn men have been involved in

a plethora of recordings. (Note: All of the albums made by Parker, Ellis, and Wesley in their various permutations have been included here; the artist credited with the album appears at the end of the review.) —*Rob Bowman*

Doing It to Death / 1973 / People ✦✦✦✦
Extended live "funkafizing" including a ten-minute version of the No.1 R&B hit "Doing It to Death." Written, produced, and arranged by James Brown. —*Rob Bowman*

A Blow for Me: a Toot for You / 1977 / Atlantic ✦✦✦✦
Produced by George Clinton and Bootsy Collins and recorded with the company of much of the P-Funk Mob, *A Blow for Me, a Toot for You* showcases a new, slinkier, more produced and less hard-edged edition of the J.B. Horns. The lead cut, a remake of Parliament's "Up for the Down Stroke," received a little R&B airplay. —*Rob Bowman*

New Friends / 1990 / Antilles ✦✦✦
Wesley and Parker in the company of jazz musicians Gerri Allen, Anthony Cox, and Robin Eubanks. This is by far the jazziest of Fred, Maceo, and Pee Wee's recordings, covering the likes of Thelonious Monk, Duke Ellington, and Dizzy Gillespie. Wesley also proves himself to be a fine jazz writer; "For the Elders" is particularly notable. —*Rob Bowman*

● **Funky Good Time: the Anthology** / Feb. 28, 1995 / Polydor/A&M ✦✦✦✦
The JB's recorded under various billings in the early '70s, including the JB's, Fred Wesley & the JB's, Maceo & the Macks, the First Family, the Last Word, and others. This double CD gathers 30 of the prime tracks by all of the above configurations from the first half of the '70s, including all nine of their chart hits and quite a few rare singles and long versions. Often, James Brown himself chirps in with incidental vocals (though this is mostly instrumental) and keyboards. The two-and-a-half-hour program can start to sound monotonous if taken all at once, but it's prime, often riveting funk, jammed with lockstep grooves that vary between basic R&B vamps and imaginative, almost jazzy improvisation. —*Richie Unterberger*

The JB Horns / Rhino ✦✦✦
On an album made up of eleven originals, the three horn men turn in a fine, if undistinguished, mix of jazz and funk. Worth hearing just for Fred's rapping, the gently swinging "Mother's Kitchen," and the sly "Everywhere Is Out of Town." —*Rob Bowman*

Jefferson Airplane

f. 1965, San Francisco, CA, **db.** 1973
Rock 'n' Roll, Psychedelic, Folk-Rock

Jefferson Airplane was the first of the San Francisco psychedelic rock groups of the 1960s to achieve national recognition, and in its later configurations, billed as Jefferson Starship or simply Starship, it remained a significant popular recording act well into the 1980s. The band was organized in the summer of 1965 by singer-songwriter Marty Balin (b. Jan. 30, 1943, Cincinnati), who recruited a band to play at the Matrix, a club he was planning to launch in San Francisco. Balin brought in guitarist/singer Paul Kantner (b. Mar. 12, 1941, San Francisco), guitarist/singer Jorma Kaukonen (b. Dec. 23, 1940, Washington, DC), and singer Signe Anderson (b. Sept. 15, 1941, Seattle). After the original rhythm section didn't work out, Balin persuaded guitarist Skip Spence (b. Apr. 18, 1946, Ontario, Canada) to switch to drums, and Kaukonen invited his friend Jack Casady (b. Apr. 13, 1944, Washington, DC) to join on bass.

RCA signed the Airplane and released their debut album, *Jefferson Airplane Takes Off* (Sep. 1966), to little commercial response. Anderson and Spence then left the group. Spence (who went on to form Moby Grape) was replaced by Spencer Dryden (b. Apr. 7, 1943). In Anderson's place, the group invited in the lead singer of a rival group, Grace Slick (b. Oct. 30, 1939, Chicago) of the Great Society. The new lineup released *Surrealistic Pillow* (Feb. 1967), a gold-selling Top Ten hit that spawned the Top Ten singles "Somebody to Love" (which Slick brought with her from the Great Society) and "White Rabbit" (which Slick wrote). This success made Jefferson Airplane the top San Francisco group during the 1967 Summer of Love and helped touch off the national craze for psychedelic music, the hippie lifestyle, and youthful drug-taking.

After Bathing at Baxter's (Nov. 1967) was a more experimental effort that was less successful. But *Crown of Creation* (Sep. 1968) was another gold-selling Top Ten hit, despite the lack of a successful single. *Bless Its Pointed Little Head* (Feb. 1969) was a live album, followed by *Volunteers* (Nov. 1969), another gold studio album. At this point, Dryden left and was replaced by Joey Covington. Violinist Papa John Creach (b. May 28, 1917, Beaver Falls, PA, d. Feb. 22, 1994) joined in the fall of 1970, and Balin quit in early 1971. The group began to release solo and offshoot albums including Kantner's *Blows Against the*

Empire (Dec. 1970) (co-credited to a group of friends he dubbed "Jefferson Starship") and recordings by Kaukonen and Casady's Hot Tuna.

The next Airplane album was *Bark* (Aug. 1971), which went gold, as did its follow-up, *Long John Silver* (Jul. 1972) (by which time Covington had been replaced by John Barbata). Ex-Quicksilver Messenger member David Freiberg was brought in to belatedly replace Balin as male lead singer, and the group made a second live album, *Thirty Seconds over Winterland* (Apr. 1973).

Kaukonen and Casady then left, and were replaced by guitarist Craig Chaquico (b. Sep. 26, 1954, Sacramento) and (after a brief stint by Kaukonen's brother Peter) bassist Pete Sears (b. England), as the group name was changed to Jefferson Starship. This new aggregation made *Dragon Fly* (Oct. 1974), a gold-selling hit that included one song sung by Marty Balin. Balin joined Jefferson Starship full-time for *Red Octopus* (Jul. 1975), contributing "Miracles," which hit the Top Ten as the album topped the charts. The next two albums, *Spitfire* (Jun. 1976) and *Earth* (Feb. 1978), were Top Ten million-sellers.

Then Slick, Balin, and Barbata left the group. Veteran drummer Aynsley Dunbar (b. Jan. 10, 1946, Liverpool) and ex-Elvin Bishop Group singer Mickey Thomas (b. Cairo, GA) joined, and the next album, *Freedom at Point Zero* (Nov. 1979), went gold and reached the Top Ten. Slick rejoined for *Modern Times* (Mar. 1981), which was followed by *Winds of Change* (Oct. 1982), after which Don Baldwin replaced Dunbar. *Nuclear Furniture* (May 1984) was the group's final album, after which Kantner (the last original Airplane member) and Freiberg left and the remaining lineup of Slick, Thomas, Chaquico, Sears, and Baldwin carried on as Starship. (See Starship.)

In 1989, Jefferson Airplane reunited with original members Balin, Kantner, Kaukonen, Casady, and Slick for a tour and an album, *Jefferson Airplane* (Sep. 1989). In 1995, a new edition of Jefferson Starship featuring Kantner, Balin, and Casady released *Deep Space/Virgin Sky*. —*William Ruhlmann*

Takes Off / Sep. 1966 / RCA ✦✦✦
The debut Jefferson Airplane album was dominated by singer Marty Balin, who wrote or co-wrote all the original material and sang most of the lead vocals in his heart-breaking tenor with Paul Kantner and Signe Anderson providing harmonies and backup. (Anderson's lead vocal on "Chauffeur Blues" indicated she was at least the equal of her successor, Grace Slick, as a belter.) The music consisted mostly of folk-rock love songs, the most memorable of which were "It's No Secret" and "Come Up the Years." (There was also a striking version of Dino Valenti's "Get Together" recorded years before the Youngbloods' hit version.) Jorma Kaukonen already displayed a talent for mixing country, folk, and blues riffs in a rock context, and Jack Casady already had a distinctive bass sound. But the Airplane of Balin-Kantner-Kaukonen-Anderson-Casady-Spence is to be distinguished from the Balin-Kantner-Kaukonen-Casady-Slick-Dryden version of the band that would emerge on record five months later chiefly by Balin's dominance. Later, Grace Slick would become the group's vocal and visual focal point. On *Takes Off*, the Airplane was Balin's group. (*Jefferson Airplane Takes Off* was released as RCA 3584 in September 1966. It was reissued as RCA 66797 on January 30, 1996, as a CD that contained both the stereo and mono versions and that added back the track "Runnin' 'Round This World," which had been deleted from all but initial copies due to the sexual and perceived drug references of the line, "The nights I've spent with you have been fantastic trips." But the included version still eliminated the word "trips.") —*William Ruhlmann*

★ **Surrealistic Pillow** / Feb. 1967 / RCA ✦✦✦✦✦
Their groundbreaking folk-based psychedelic album hit like a shot heard round the world. From "White Rabbit" and "Somebody to Love" to the sublime "3/5 of a Mile in 10 Seconds," the sensibilities are fierce, the material is melodic, and the performances, sparked by new member Grace Slick on most of the lead vocals, are magnificent and inspired. —*Bruce Eder*

After Bathing at Baxter's / Dec. 1967 / RCA ✦✦✦
Jefferson Airplane's third album was both a further exploration of the more unusual aspects of their second album, *Surrealistic Pillow*, and a reaction against that album's more conventional aspects and its commercial success. *After Bathing at Baxter's* was dominated by rhythm guitarist/singer Paul Kantner, who wrote or co-wrote six of the 11 selections, including the two singles "The Ballad of You & Me & Pooneil" and "Watch Her Ride." While Grace Slick wrote and sang the bizarre "rejoyce" (based on James Joyce's writings) and "Two Heads" (songs well to the left of the already-daring "White Rabbit"), the album also marked the emergence of the bass/guitar team of Jack Casady and Jorma Kaukonen, whose nine-minute instrumental "Spare Chaynge" foreshadowed their spinoff group Hot Tuna. *After Bathing at Baxter's* was the album on which the Airplane, touted as the leaders of the San Francisco acid-rock scene, actually tried to catch up to the movement. Unlike other psychedelic exponents, they had been primarily song-

based rather than performance-based; despite the studio gimmicks and self-indulgence, they remained so. —*William Ruhlmann*

Crown of Creation / Sep. 1968 / RCA ✦✦✦
An impressive but meandering journey through the drugged-out sensibilities of 1967. The science fiction content gives it some cohesiveness, but not enough. —*Bruce Eder*

Bless Its Pointed Little Head / Feb. 1969 / RCA ✦✦✦
Jefferson Airplane's first live album demonstrated the group's development as concert performers, taking a number of songs that had been performed in concise, pop-oriented versions on their early albums—"3/5's of a Mile in 10 Seconds," "Somebody to Love," "It's No Secret," "Plastic Fantastic Lover"—and rendering them in arrangements that were longer, harder rocking, and more densely textured, especially in terms of the guitar and bass lines constructed by Jorma Kaukonen and Jack Casady. The group's three-part vocal harmonizing and dueling was on display during such songs as a nearly seven-minute version of Fred Neil's folk-blues standard "The Other Side of This Life," here transformed into a swirling rocker. The album emphasized the talents of Kaukonen and singer Marty Balin over the team of Paul Kantner and Grace Slick, who had tended to dominate recent records: the blues song "Rock Me Baby" was a dry run for Hot Tuna, the band Kaukonen and Casady would form in two years, and Balin turned in powerful vocal performances on several of his own compositions, notably "It's No Secret." Jefferson Airplane was still at its best in concise, driving numbers, rather than in the jams on Donovan's "Fat Angel" (running 7:35) or the group improv "Bear Melt" (11:21); they were just too intense to stretch out comfortably. But *Bless Its Pointed Little Head* served an important function in the group's discography, demonstrating that their live work had a distinctly different focus and flavor from their studio recordings. —*William Ruhlmann*

Volunteers / Nov. 1969 / RCA ✦✦✦
The band's most political album is a somewhat-dated statement but also a very joyous and rewarding one. "We Can Be Together" is still a compelling anthem. —*Bruce Eder*

Blows Against the Empire / 1970 / RCA ✦✦✦

Bark / Sep. 1971 / RCA ✦✦✦
By the time of *Bark*, personnel changes had gutted much of the original vision of the group, especially with the departure of Marty Balin. Paul Kantner and Grace Slick remained, but their compositions were growing increasingly ill-focused, and Jorma Kaukonen and new drummer Joey Covington were ill-equipped to pick up the songwriting slack. The result was an album that bore hallmarks of the classic Airplane sound, but lacked any classic Airplane songs. That said, the record isn't as bad as many reviewers have made it out to be. It's just mediocre, with little that sticks in the memory, despite occasional nice moments in cuts like Covington's "Pretty as You Feel" and Kantner's delicate "Third Week in the Chelsea." —*Richie Unterberger*

Long John Silver / Jul. 1972 / RCA ✦✦
The band's final studio album other than their abominable 1989 reunion record, *Long John Silver* continued the group's descent into inoffensive mediocrity. The aircraft burned on pretty low fuel on this low-key set, although most of the principal members were still around. Kantner and Slick wrote most of the material, and while it's far from awful, it sounds more like a set of outtakes than anything approaching their glory days. —*Richie Unterberger*

Thirty Seconds over Winterland / Apr. 1973 / RCA ✦✦
Well-produced document of the final days of the Airplane before it evolved into the Jefferson Starship. The singing and playing are all inspired, and the repertory is surprisingly melodic, considering the direction in which the group had been going. The highlight is a live version of the science fiction anthem "Have You Seen the Saucers." —*Bruce Eder*

Early Flight / Apr. 1974 / RCA ✦✦
A beguiling collection of bluesy, druggy, and idealistic leftovers from the group's recorded output, partly supplanted by *2400 Fulton Street*, and sure to be further devalued by the upcoming boxed set, but still a handy little disc to have around. —*Bruce Eder*

● **2400 Fulton Street: An Anthology** / Mar. 1987 / RCA ✦✦✦✦
A more-than-adequate retrospective on the group, with every major song and a lot of oddball favorites as well, all remastered from sources far superior to those used on the original albums. Some of it will be redundant (virtually the whole *Surrealistic Pillow* album is here), but the quality and the order of the programming is rewarding. —*Bruce Eder*

Jefferson Airplane / Sep. 1989 / Epic ✦
Reuniting Slick, Kantner, Balin, Kaukonen, and Cassidy for this project should have struck gold. Unfortunately, "Jefferson Airplane" became just a sorry footnote in an otherwise stellar career. Only Marty Balin's "Summer of Love," which looks back on those late-'60s shows, offers any glimpse of the old Airplane magic and it's muted at that. Not recommended for anyone who remembers "White Rabbit" or "Somebody to Love." —*James Chrispell*

Jefferson Airplane Loves You / Oct. 1992 / RCA ✦✦✦
A three-disc box set loaded with rarities, *Jefferson Airplane Loves You* is necessary for hardcore fans, but the double-disc *2400 Fulton Street* offers a better portrait of the band and is the essential purchase for casual fans. —*Stephen Thomas Erlewine*

Jefferson Starship

f. 1974, San Francisco, CA, **db.** 1984
Pop-Rock, Arena Rock

With their 1974 metamorphosis into the Jefferson Starship, the group once known as the Jefferson Airplane underwent a radical facelift, which resulted not only in a change of name but also a new lineup and a new musical identity. Formerly torch-bearers of the Haight-Ashbury counterculture, famed for psychedelic-era landmarks including *Surrealistic Pillow* and *Volunteers*, as the Starship the group reached even greater heights of success, forging a more mainstream sound and attitude, which established them as one of the predominant hard rock units of the 1970s.

The new group's origins actually dated back to 1970, when Airplane guitarist Paul Kantner issued the album *Blows Against the Empire*, credited to "Paul Kantner and the Jefferson Starship." Featuring guest appearances from Jerry Garcia, David Crosby, and Graham Nash, the record reflected Kantner's fascination with science fiction, and became the first musical work ever nominated for the sci-fi field's Hugo Awards; when, four years later, the Airplane decided to relaunch after a series of personnel shifts, the Starship name was permanently installed to draw a clear line of demarcation between the band's past and its future. In addition to Kantner, the initial Jefferson Starship roster featured vocalist Grace Slick, bassist David Freiberg, violinist Papa John Creach, and drummer John Barbata, all holdovers from the final incarnation of the Airplane; rounding out the lineup was 19-year-old guitarist Craig Chaquico, an alumnus of the group Steelwind.

After the addition of bassist/keyboardist Pete Sears, Jefferson Starship entered the studio to record their 1974 debut *Dragon Fly;* after former Airplane vocalist/guitarist Marty Balin guested on the track "Caroline," he signed on as a permanent member in the early weeks of 1975. The follow-up, *Red Octopus*, became the Starship's most successful effort, topping the charts off and on throughout the year on the strength of Balin's Top Three ballad "Miracles." Despite Slick's protests that the music was growing too commercial—prompting a new round of conflicts with Balin, with whom she'd repeatedly battled during their Airplane days—the band continued to hone a more mainstream identity on 1976's *Spitfire*, their first platinum-selling release.

In 1976, Slick and Kantner's lengthy romance ended, and in November she married the band's lighting director, Skip Johnson. In the midst of considerable interpersonal difficulties, Jefferson Starship recorded 1978's *Earth*, another smash which spawned the Top Ten hit "Count on Me." However, in the wake of the record's release Slick's long-standing drinking problem spun out of control, and she left the group during a European tour. Balin exited later in 1978, leaving the Starship without a lead singer; finally, in 1979 the remaining members recruited vocalist Mickey Thomas, best known for his lead turn on the Elvin Bishop hit "Fooled Around and Fell in Love." Aynsley Dunbar, a session drummer best known for his work with Frank Zappa and David Bowie as well as a tenure with Journey, replaced Barbata prior to 1979's *Freedom at Point Zero*, which launched the hit "Jane."

In 1980, Kantner—now the group's lone original member—suffered a massive cerebral hemorrhage which, remarkably, left no permanent damage. After a period of recovery, he reassembled the Starship for 1981's *Modern Times*, which featured a cameo appearance by Slick. She rejoined the group full-time for the following year's *Winds of Change*, which scored hits with "Be My Lady" and the title track. After 1984's *Nuclear Furniture*, Kantner—who had long been vocally dissatisfied with his diminishing role in the group and their glossy mainstream sound—exited the Starship's ranks; a battle ensued over rights to the band name, with Kantner finally awarded custody of the "Jefferson" prefix. The remaining members continued on as simply Starship, scoring the hits "We Built This City," "Sara," and "Nothing's Gonna Stop Us Now."

In 1989, Slick, Kantner, and Balin reteamed with former bandmates Jack Casady and Jorma Kaukonen in a revived Jefferson Airplane; Starship broke up soon after, but when the revitalized Airplane fizzled as well, Kantner reclaimed the now-dormant Jefferson Starship name and in 1991 formed a new lineup of the group featuring Creach and Casady as well as new vocalist Darby Gould, formerly of the band World Entertainment War. Balin signed on in 1992, and the band—dubbed "Jefferson Starship—The Next Generation"—mounted a tour; in 1995, along with guest Slick, they recorded *Deep Space/Virgin Sky*, a live collection of original material as well as new versions of Airplane and Starship favorites. —*Jason Ankeny*

● **Red Octopus** / 1975 / RCA ✦✦✦✦
The masterpiece, and a massive seller, too. Grace Slick sings expressively, especially on "Fast Buck Freddie" and "Play on Love," but the real story is the integration of Marty Balin fully into the band, and again he brings a timeless ballad along in the hit "Miracles." —*William Ruhlmann*

Freedom at Point Zero / 1979 / Grunt ✦✦✦
Amazingly enough, the band survives the departure of Grace Slick and Marty Balin, adding Mickey Thomas on vocals and scoring hits with "Jane" and Kantner's "Girl with the Hungry Eyes." —*William Ruhlmann*

Gold / 1979 / RCA ✦✦✦✦
Well-chosen best-of covering the years 1974-1979, after which the band personnel changed significantly. —*William Ruhlmann*

Modern Times / 1981 / RCA ✦✦✦
Slick comes back for one song, and "Find Your Way Back" becomes a hit. Also included is "Stairway to Cleveland," as gutsy a statement of purpose as any in rock. —*William Ruhlmann*

Jeru the Damaja

b. Brooklyn, NY
Hip Hop, East Coast Rap, Hardcore Rap
Speaking out against what he saw as a decline in rap during the mid-'90s, Jeru the Damaja came to the fore as a self-proclaimed prophet and the savior of hip-hop, much as KRS-One had done almost ten years before. Jeru first appeared as a guest on Gang Starr's *Daily Operations* album, and his own deal with Payday/FFRR appeared soon after, resulting in 1994's *The Sun Rises in the East*. Though he made few friends in the rap world—given his outspoken criticism of such popular figures as the Fugees and Sean "Puffy" Combs—he proved a vital force in the emergence of the new rap consciousness of the late '90s.

Raised Kendrick Jeru Davis in Brooklyn, the Damaja began writing rhymes at the age of ten. At high school, he met Guru and DJ Premier of Gang Starr, and first guested on Gang Starr's "Who the Man," from the 1992 album *Daily Operation*. Jeru toured with the group during 1993 and released his solo debut, "Come Clean," for Gang Starr's Illkids label. The single became an underground sensation and led to his contract with Payday Records. He recorded *The Sun Rises in the East* with DJ Premier producing, and released the album in 1994. Though the album was well-received, Jeru got some flak for the song "Da Bichez"—though he explicitly stated that most girls did not fit into the category. During 1994, he appeared on Digable Planets' second album (*Blowout Comb*) and recorded his follow-up, *Wrath of the Math*, with DJ Premier and Guru once again helping out with production. —*John Bush*

● **The Sun Rises in the East** / Dec. 22, 1994 / Payday ✦✦✦✦
Resting halfway between the sultry swagger of gangsta and the classy tones of jazz-rap, Jeru began his career guesting for Guru on a few tracks. Although Gang Starr are listed as executive producers, *The Sun Rises in the East* has already established The Damaja as a unique voice in hip-hop. His inner-city lyrics on songs "You Can't Stop the Prophet" and "Ain't the Devil Happy," work well with his flowing sing-speak delivery. "Da Bichez" might offend some, even with the line: "I'm not talking about the queens, but the bitches." Nevertheless, *The Sun Rises in the East* is an amazing debut. —*John Bush*

Wrath of the Math / Oct. 1996 / Payday/London ✦✦✦✦
Wrath of the Math proved almost as effective as Jeru the Damaja's debut LP, even though little had changed—DJ Premier once again provides his customary scratchy, minimalist production and Jeru's lyrical themes focus either on hip-hop itself (as on "One Day") or the state of life on the streets ("Revenge of the Prophet"). *Wrath of the Math* just can't sustain the power of Jeru's message, however, since it includes five more tracks than on his debut. "Ya Playin' Yaself," "Not the Average" and "Me or the Papes" (which attempts to atone for the sins of "Da Bichez" from *The Sun Rises in the East*) are great songs, but the album just runs out of steam by the end. —*John Bush*

The Jesus & Mary Chain

f. 1984, East Kilbride, Scotland
Alternative Pop-Rock, Post-Punk
Like the Velvet Underground, their most obvious influence, the chart success of the Jesus and Mary Chain was virtually nonexistent, but their artistic impact was incalculable; quite simply, the British group made the world safe for white noise, orchestrating a sound dense in squalling feedback which served as an inspiration to everyone from My Bloody Valentine to Dinosaur Jr.

Though the supporting players drifted in and out of focus, the heart of the Mary Chain remained vocalists and guitarists William and Jim

Reid, Scottish-born brothers heavily influenced not only by underground legends like the Velvets and the Stooges, but also by the sonic grandeur and pop savvy of Phil Spector and Brian Wilson. In the Jesus and Mary Chain, which the Reids formed outside of Glasgow in 1984 with bassist Douglas Hart and drummer Murray Dalglish (quickly replaced by Bobby Gillespie), these two polarized aesthetics converged; equal parts bubblegum and formless guitar distortion, their sound both celebrated pop conventions and thoroughly subverted them.

In late 1984, the band issued its seminal debut single, "Upside Down," a remarkable blast of livewire feedback anchored by a caveman-like drumbeat; the record made the Mary Chain an overnight sensation in the UK, as did their nascent live shows, 20-minute sets of confrontational noise (performed with the band's members backs to the audience), which frequently ended in rioting. The follow-up, "You Trip Me Up," further perfected the formula, and led to their 1985 debut LP *Psychocandy*, which gift-wrapped sweet, simple pop songs in ribbons of droning guitar fuzz.

After a two-year layoff (during which time Gillespie exited to form Primal Scream, and was replaced by John Moore), the Jesus and Mary Chain returned with *Darklands*, a dramatic shift in approach which stripped away the feedback to expose the skeletal guitar-pop at the music's core. After a sprawling 1988 collection of singles, B-sides, and demos titled *Barbed Wire Kisses*, they emerged with *Automatic*, which introduced a more tightly-coiled brand of feedback while jettisoning Moore's live drums in favor of synthesized beats.

After another long absence, the Mary Chain (minus Hart) resurfaced in 1992 with *Honey's Dead*, and earned greater US visibility thanks to a spot on that summer's Lollapalooza lineup; the first single "Reverence" also won them renewed notoriety at home when *Top of the Pops* banned the song because of its opening lines "I wanna die just like Jesus Christ" and "I wanna die just like JFK." With 1994's gentle, largely acoustic *Stoned and Dethroned*, they even reached the US pop charts thanks to the lovely single "Sometimes Always," a duet with Mazzy Star's Hope Sandoval. Another collection of scattered sides, *The Jesus and Mary Chain Hate Rock 'n' Roll*, followed a year later, highlighted by the single "I Hate Rock 'n' Roll," a scabrous swipe which reclaimed the pure noise attack of their earliest work. —*Jason Ankeny*

● **Psychocandy** / 1985 / Blanco y Negro/Reprise ✦✦✦✦
The album that launched a thousand shoegazer bands, the visceral power of *Psychocandy* has diminished not one whit in the years since it made its bow. Still far and away the Mary Chain's defining moment, standout cuts like "Just Like Honey," "The Hardest Walk" and "You Trip Me Up" represent the purest fusion of the Jekyll-and-Hyde mindset that dominates the group—in subsequent years, they've been a noise band at times, while at others they've been a pop band, but here, they're both, and it's glorious. —*Jason Ankeny*

Darklands / 1987 / Blanco y Negro/Warner Brothers ✦✦✦✦
It's completely emblematic of the Mary Chain's perversity that they followed up the dissonant squalor of *Psychocandy* with the minimal, almost gentle guitar-pop of *Darklands*. Here, the melodies which the previous album's squalls of feedback threatened to rip open are left to their own devices; the results are quite stunning, with songs like "Deep One Perfect Morning," "Cherry Came Too" and the title track revealing unforeseen layers of beauty. —*Jason Ankeny*

Barbed Wire Kisses / 1988 / Blanco y Negro/Warner Brothers ✦✦
Despite the overall inconsistency of *Barbed Wire Kisses*, a collection of singles, B-sides, and other rarities, the record does contain more than enough superior moments to make it an essential purchase for all serious Mary Chain aficionados. Chief among them is "Upside Down," the group's feedback-mad debut single and the purest distillation of their aesthetic they ever recorded. Other highlights include the menacing "Kill Surf City," a brutal deconstruction of "Surfin' USA." and the sleek single "Sidewalking." —*Jason Ankeny*

Automatic / Oct. 1989 / Blanco y Negro/Warner Brothers ✦✦✦
Too much of *Automatic* is just that—formulaic, uninspired, and essentially rote music recorded with the aid of a drum machine. Splitting the difference between the feedback pyrotechnics of *Psychocandy* and the gentle pop of *Darklands*, the record sports a metallic, glossy guitar sheen that complements the synthetic beats all too well: robotic and processed, much of *Automatic* is simply lifeless. Even at their most lackluster, however, the Reid brothers can still spit out some terrific songs—both the menacing "Blues from a Gun" and "Head On" (later covered by the Pixies) are twisted, infectious gems. —*Jason Ankeny*

Honey's Dead / May 1992 / Blanco y Negro/Def American ✦✦✦✦
A vast improvement over the preceding *Automatic*, *Honey's Dead* teams the Mary Chain with engineer/mixer Alan Moulder, who layers the album with a more organic and aggressive guitar sound than the Reid brothers have enjoyed in some time. The opening "Reverence"—a live-wire feedback fever-dream stretched across a loping dance rhythm—quickly establishes the tone: *Honey's Dead* brings the noise, but it also emphasizes the group's unerring pop instincts, as further evi-

denced by such gems as "Far Gone and Out," "Rollercoaster," and "Sugar Ray." —*Jason Ankeny*

Stoned & Dethroned / Aug. 23, 1994 / Blanco y Negro/American ✦✦✦
More subdued than any of their previous records, the Jesus & Mary Chain explore a calmer, almost acoustic-oriented direction for part of *Stoned & Dethroned*. Apart from the hit duet with Mazzy Star's Hope Sandoval, "Sometimes Always," the fuzz-drenched pseudo-psychedelic pop that has become the group's trademark is more effective than any of the band's musical experiments. —*Stephen Thomas Erlewine*

Jesus & Mary Chain Hate Rock N' Roll / Sep. 26, 1995 / Blanco y Negro/American ✦✦
The Jesus & Mary Chain Hate Rock N' Roll was the group's second collection of rarities and B-sides. Like *Barbed Wire Kisses*, the album is fitfully entertaining, but only the scathing "I Hate Rock N' Roll" is an essential addition to their catalog. —*Stephen Thomas Erlewine*

The Jesus Lizard

f. 1987, Chicago, IL
Alternative Pop-Rock
Willfully abrasive and atonal, the Jesus Lizard emerged in the early '90s as a leading noise-rock band in the American independent underground. During the first part of the decade, the band turned out a series of independent records filled with scathing, disemboweling, guitar-driven pseudo-industrial noise, all of which received positive reviews in underground music publications and heavy college radio play. By the mid-'90s, the group's following had grown large enough to convince a major label, Capitol Records, to sign the band.

The Jesus Lizard was formed by guitarist Duane Denison and vocalist David Yow and David Sims, two former members of the Austin-based post-hardcore noise group, Scratch Acid. After Scratch Acid disbanded, Sims joined Rapeman, an abrasive indie-rock group led by Steve Albini. The recording and performing schedule of Rapeman was rather erratic, so Sims formed the Jesus Lizard with Yow and Denison in 1987. Originally, the group performed with a drum machine, much like Albini's previous band, Big Black. Albini produced the group's debut EP, *Pure*, which was released on Touch & Go in 1989; the producer would work on every Jesus Lizard release on Touch & Go.

The Jesus Lizard added a human drummer, Mac McNeilly, in late 1989 and he appeared on the band's first full-length album, 1990's *Head*. The following year, the group released their second album, *Goat*, which received positive reviews from mainstream music publications such as *Spin*. By the time of the release of *Goat*, the band had cultivated a large cult following among the American indie-rock underground, based on both the group's records and their notoriously reckless, occasionally violent and vulgar, live performances.

In 1992, the Jesus Lizard released a split single with Nirvana ("Puss" [Jesus Lizard] / "Oh the Guilt" [Nirvana]), who had just broken into the rock 'n' roll mainstream with their second album, *Nevermind*. That same year, the band released their third album, *Liar*. In 1993, the group was relatively quiet, releasing only the "Lash" single.

Early in 1994, the Jesus Lizard released a one-shot EP on Giant Records called *Show*. The EP was their first appearance on a major label. The fact that the Jesus Lizard released a record on a major label caused tension between the band and their longtime producer Steve Albini, who was notorious for his indie-centric beliefs. Although he produced *Down*, the group's final Touch & Go album, he severed ties with the band by the time the record was released in the fall of 1994.

In 1995, the Jesus Lizard signed with Capitol Records and before they recorded their full-length, major-label debut, the band toured with Lollapalooza 1995. At one of the shows on the tour, David Yow was arrested for exposing himself on stage. Later in 1995, the group recorded their major-label debut. The resulting album, *Shot*, was released on Capitol in the spring of 1996. —*Stephen Thomas Erlewine*

Pure / 1989 / Touch & Go ✦✦
A five-song debut EP produced by Steve Albini, the Jesus Lizard's *Pure* expanded on the uncompromising hardcore of Scratch Acid while adding touches of Big Black's galvanizing pseudo-industrial rhythms. —*Stephen Thomas Erlewine*

Head / 1990 / Touch & Go ✦✦✦
Head, the Jesus Lizard's first full-length album, featured looser rhythms and a greater dynamic range than their debut EP, but that in no way diluted the impact of David Yow's manic vocals or the bracing force of Duane Denison's crushingly loud riffs. —*Stephen Thomas Erlewine*

● **Goat** / 1991 / Touch & Go ✦✦✦✦
Building upon the intense, spirited noise-rock of their two previous records, *Goat* is the album where Jesus Lizard's twisted, post-hardcore punk comes into its own. Denison's acerbic guitar provides an appropriate setting for Yow's ranting tales of decadence and degradation. The Jesus Lizard never make a commentary about the urban filth they

depict in their music—they're down in the grime because they like it there. —*Stephen Thomas Erlewine*

Liar / May 1992 / Touch & Go ✦✦✦✦
Jesus Lizard's third album, *Liar*, is their most focused set of bleak, grinding noise-rock, yet it lacks the wild abandon that made *Goat* so frightening. —*Stephen Thomas Erlewine*

Show / Apr. 1994 / Collision Arts/Giant ✦✦
A scathing but inessential live EP, *Show* was the first recording the Jesus Lizard released in association with a major record label. Although the record's release was barely promoted and it made only a small impact in the American underground, it prompted the band's long-time producer, Steve Albini, to sever ties with the band by the end of the year, simply because the Jesus Lizard released an album on a major label. —*Stephen Thomas Erlewine*

Down / Oct. 1994 / Touch & Go ✦✦✦
Although the Jesus Lizard is in fine form throughout *Down*, the record is essentially a retread of *Goat* or *Liar*, featuring a slightly more accessible production. However, accessibility is a liability in the case of the Jesus Lizard, and the overall impact of *Down* suffers accordingly. —*Stephen Thomas Erlewine*

Shot / Apr. 1996 / Capitol ✦✦
The big difference between the Jesus Lizard's first major-label album, *Shot*, and their independent records mainly lies in the fact that their long-time producer, Steve Albini, is no longer behind the boards. Albini was reportedly infuriated that the band decided to make the plunge to a major label for their brief EP for Giant Records, so he cut off all associations with the band. The Jesus Lizard hired GGGarth Richardson, who had previously cut albums for the Melvins and L7, so his noise-rock credentials should theoretically all be in place. But they're not, at least on *Shot*. The album sounds too similar to a conventional, major-label alternative hard rock album with pushing rhythms and distorted guitars with clean attacks. David Yow still screams his vocals and Duane Denison's guitar riffs are appropriately gnarled and twisted, but the album is in desperate need of the grit that Albini's abrasive lo-fi productions lent to the band's earlier records. Furthermore, the Jesus Lizard hasn't progressed musically since the early '90s—they still churn out the same, noisy post-Butthole Surfers/Big Black indie-rock as before. Since the music doesn't have the same scathing kick as it did on *Goat* or *Liar*, *Shot* just sounds like a pointless exercise in treading water. —*Stephen Thomas Erlewine*

The Jet Set

f. 1979, London, England, **db.** 1988
Mod-Revival
The Jet Set were one of the oddest footnotes in British pop music history. Loosely associated with the mod-revival of the late '70s, they took the revival one step further. Not only did they recreate the sounds of '60s pop, but they also attempted to mirror the careers and myths of their idols with near-Rutles-esque devotion, attempting a media blitz which included a proposed television series, Christmas greeting flexi-singles, comic strips, trading cards, and an array of fake Jet Set-related products. Though they never really made it out of the underground and have been forgotten by all but mod/pop fetishists, the Jet Set left behind an impressive body of work.

The band was formed in 1979 by teenage friends Paul Bevoir and Melvyn J. Taub. After recording a few demos with Secret Affair's Paul Bultitude, Bevoir and Taub pulled together a makeshift band for promotional photos. When record companies began to show an interest, they enlisted keyboardist Angus Nanan and drummer Paul Bonin as the "real" band for an open slot for Secret Affair. Bultitude signed the band to his own Dance Network label in 1983, releasing their debut, *The Best of the Jet Set* EP. With the release, they began their marketing attack, creating the Jet Set myth and concept—the EP included stills from their forthcoming TV show and the "Jet Set Theme." Zany Beatlesque interviews and antics combined with support from mod underground magazines helped to cultivate a strong cult following for the band. *There Goes the Neighborhood*, their first full-length album, was released in 1985. The album received a great deal of acclaim in the UK and eventually the band attempted to crack the States with Bevoir making a brief promo tour. After 1986's *Go Bananas*, an album that featured commercials for Jet Set products between songs, Bevoir retired from touring to concentrate on his songwriting and studio craft. In 1987, the band, under Bevoir's direction and growing Beatles obsession, sought to create their own *Sgt. Pepper* with the lushly orchestrated and painstakingly-produced *Vaudeville Park*, recreating not only the album's sound but also its packaging. True to form, they followed with the reactionary back-to-basics recording sessions where Bevoir and Taub found they could no longer work together due to creative differences. The band was dissolved and their final album, *Five*, was pieced together from the sessions. Bevoir formed Smalltown Parade in 1990 and resumed a solo career in 1994. —*Chris Woodstra*

The Best of the Jet Set [EP] / 1983 / Dance Network ✦✦✦
There Goes the Neighborhood / 1985 / Dance Network ✦✦✦
Go Bananas / 1986 / Dance Network ✦✦✦
Vaudville Park / 1987 / Dance Network ✦✦✦✦
Five / 1988 / Dance Network ✦✦✦✦
● The Best of the Jet Set [CD] / 1995 / Tangerine ✦✦✦✦
Best of the Jet Set gives a 27-track career overview of the band that
wanted more than anything to be the Beatles. While their determina-
tion and ambition makes for fascinating story—detailed in the exten-
sive booklet—their music had a naive charm and enough hooks to
please any power pop aficionado. —Chris Woodstra

The Best of the Jet Set Too! / 1995 / Tangerine ✦✦✦✦
A companion disc to the first Best of, Best of Too! offers another 22
songs. In addition to the album tracks, a handful of rarities are
included. Those who were won over by the first collection will
undoubtedly need this one as well—the material is just as strong.
—Chris Woodstra

Jethro Tull

f. 1967, Blackpool, England
Blues-Rock, Hard Rock, Art-Rock/Progressive-Rock
Jethro Tull was a unique phenomenon in popular music history. Their
mix of hard rock, folk melodies, blues licks, surreal, impossibly dense
lyrics, and overall profundity defied easy analysis, but that didn't dissuade fans from giving them 11 gold and five platinum albums. At the
same time, critics rarely took them seriously, and they were off the cutting edge of popular music since the end of the 1970's. But no record
store in the country would want to be without multiple copies of each
of their most popular albums or their various "best of" compilations,
and few would knowingly ignore their newest releases. As co-founded
and led by wildman-flautist-guitarist-singer-songwriter Ian Anderson,
the group carved a place all its own in popular music.
Tull had its roots in the British blues boom of the late '60s. Anderson's first band was called the Blades, with Michael Stephens on guitar,
Jeffrey Hammond-Hammond on bass and John Evans on drums, playing a mix of jazzy blues and soulful dance music on the northern club
circuit. In 1965, they changed their name to the John Evan Band (Evan
having dropped the "s" in his name at Hammond's suggestion) and
later the John Evan Smash. By the end of 1967, Glenn Cornick had
replaced Hammond-Hammond on bass. After moving to the London
area—the center of the British blues boom—the band began to fall
apart; there Anderson and Cornick met guitarist/singer Mick Abrahams and drummer Clive Bunker, who had previously played together
in the Toggery Five and were now members of a local blues band
called McGregor's Engine. In December of 1967, the four of them
agreed to form a new group. They began playing two shows a week,
trying out different names, including Navy Blue and Bag of Blues.
One of the names that they used, Jethro Tull—borrowed from an
18th-century farmer/inventor—stuck, and in January of 1968, they cut
a rather derivative pop-folk single called "Sunshine Day" on MGM
(under the misprinted name "Jethro Toe"). The single went nowhere,
but the group managed to land a residency at the Marquee Club in
London, where they became very popular. At the time, a lot of blues
enthusiasts didn't accept wind instruments at all—especially the flute—
as seminal to the sound they were looking for, and as a group struggling for success and recognition, Jethro Tull was just a little too
strange in that regard. Abrahams was a hardcore blues enthusiast, and
he was pushing for a more traditional band configuration, which
would've put him and his guitar out front; his blues sensibilities were
impeccable, but the audience for British blues by itself couldn't elevate
Jethro Tull any higher than being a top club act—Anderson's antics on
stage, and his use of folk sources as well as blues and jazz, gave the
band the potential to grab a bigger audience and some much-needed
press attention.
By the end of the summer of 1968, Tull had a recording contract
with Island Records. The resulting album, This Was, was issued in
November. By this time, Anderson was the dominant member of the
group on stage, and at the end of the month Abrahams exited the band.
The group went through two hastily recruited and rejected replacements, future Black Sabbath guitarist Tony Iommi (who was in Tull for
a week, just long enough to show up in their appearance on the Rolling
Stones' Rock 'N Roll Circus extravaganza), and ex- Nice guitarist Davy
O'List, before naming Martin Barre, a former architecture student, as
the permanent replacement. In May of 1969, Barre's first recording
with the group, "Living in the Past," reached the British No. 3 spot; their
next album, Stand Up, reached the top spot the next month. Stand Up
also contained the first orchestrated track by Tull, "Reasons for Waiting," which featured strings arranged by David Palmer, a Royal Academy of Music graduate and theatrical conductor who would play an

increasingly large role in subsequent albums, and finally join the group
officially in 1977.
Meanwhile, "Sweet Dream," issued in November, rose to No. 7, and
was the group's first release on the newly-formed Chrysalis label. Their
next album, Benefit, marked their last look back at the blues, and
marked the final appearance of John Evan. Benefit reached the No. 3
spot in England, but, much more important, it ascended to No. 11 in
America. By the following December, Cornick had decided to leave the
group, and was replaced on bass by Jeffrey Hammond-Hammond.
Early the following year, they began working on their magnum opus,
Aqualung; here the blues influences were muted almost to non-exist-
ence, but the hard rock passages were searing and the folk influences
provided a refreshing contrast. After Bunker was replaced by Barriemore Barlow in late 1971 Tull began work on their next album, Thick
as a Brick. Structurally more ambitious than Aqualung, and supported
by an elaborately designed jacket in the form of a newspaper, this
record was essentially one long song steeped in surreal imagery, social
commentary, and Anderson's newly solidified image as a wildman-
sage.
Thick as a Brick was a major success, and at this point, it seemed as
though Jethro Tull could do no wrong. For the critics, however, the
group's string ran out in July of 1973 with the release of A Passion Play,
another extended song running the length of the album, this time
steeped in fantasy and religious imagery far denser than Aqualung.
This time, the critics were hostile toward Anderson and the group,
attacking the album for its obscure lyrical references and excessive
length. The real venom, however, didn't start to flow until the group
went on tour that summer. By this time, their sets ran to two-and-a-half
hours, and included not only the new album done in its entirety but
Thick as a Brick and the most popular songs off Aqualung and their
earlier albums.
It was 16 months until the group's next album, WarChild—conceived as part of a film project that never materialized—was released,
in November of 1974. The expectations surrounding the album gave it
pre-order sales sufficient to get it certified gold upon release, and it was
also Tull's last platinum album, reaching No. 2 in America and No. 14
in England. During this period, Anderson became involved with producing an album by Steeleye Span, a folk-rock group that was also
signed to Chrysalis, and who had opened for Tull on one of their American tours. Their music slowly began influencing Anderson's songwriting over the next several years, as the folk influence grew in prominence; by the next Tull album, 1975's Minstrel in the Gallery, the
dominant theme was Elizabethan minstrelsy, within an electric rock
and English folk context.
In January of 1976, Hammond-Hammond left the band to pursue a
career in art. His replacement, John Glascock, joined in time for the
recording of Too Old to Rock 'n Roll, Too Young to Die, an album made
up partly of songs from an unproduced play proposed by Anderson
and Palmer. In late 1976, a Christmas E.P. entitled "Ring Out Solstice
Bells" appeared; this song later turned up on their next album, the
folky Songs from the Wood. Having lasted into the late 1970's, Jethro
Tull now found itself competing in a new musical environment, as
journalists and, to an increasing degree, fans became fixated on the
growing punk rock phenomenon. The group's next album, 1978's
Heavy Horses, was Anderson's most personal work in several years, the
title track expressing his regret over the disappearance of England's
huge shire horses as casualties of modernization. In the fall of 1978,
their first full-length concert album, the double-LP Live-Bursting Out,
was released to modest success, accompanied by an international television broadcast from Madison Square Garden.
1979 was a pivotal and tragic year for the group. Glascock died from
complications of heart surgery on November 17, five weeks after the
release of Stormwatch. Although Tull was lucky enough to acquire the
services of Dave Pegg, the longtime bassist for Fairport Convention,
Glascock's death led to Anderson's decision to record a solo album during the summer of 1980. The record, A, was eventually released as a
Jethro Tull album in September of 1980, but even the Tull name didn't
do much for its success. Barlow, Evan, and Palmer, however, were
dropped from the group line-up with the recording of A, and it was
with yet another new line-up—including Barre, Pegg, Fairport Convention alumnus Gerry Conway (drums) and Peter-John Vettese (keyboards)—that The Broadsword and the Beast wasrecorded in 1982.
In 1983, Anderson confined his activities to his first official solo
album, Walk Into Light; following its lackluster performance, Anderson revived Jethro Tull for the 1984 album Under Wraps. No further
Tull albums were to be released until the Grammy-winning Crest of a
Knave in 1987, as a result of Anderson's intermittent throat problems.
After 1989's Rock Island, Tull returned in 1990 with Catfish Rising;
And A Little Light Music, their own "unplugged" release, was taped on
their summer 1992 European tour. —Bruce Eder

This Was / 1968 / Chrysalis ✦✦✦

Jethro Tull was very much a blues band on their debut album, vaguely reminiscent of the Graham Bond Organization only more cohesive, and with greater commercial sense. The revelations about the group's roots on *This Was* —which was recorded during the summer of 1968—can be astonishing, even 30 years after the fact. Original lead guitarist Mick Abrahams contributed to the songwriting and the singing, and his presence as a serious bluesman is felt throughout, often for the better: "Some Day the Sun Won't Shine for You," an Ian Anderson original that could just as easily be credited to Big Bill Broonzy or Robert Johnson; "Cat's Squirrel" (Abrahams' big showcase, where he ventures into Eric Clapton territory); and "It's Breaking Me Up," which also features some pretty hot guitar from Abrahams. Roland Kirk's "Serenade to a Cuckoo" (the first song Anderson learned to play on flute), their jazziest track ever, is one of the best parts of the album. The drum solo on "Dharma for One" now seems like a mistake, but is understandable in the context of the time in which it was done. The one number here that everybody knows, "A Song for Jeffrey," almost pales amid these surroundings, but at the time it was a superb example of commercial psychedelic blues. This would be the last album of its kind by the group, as Abrahams' departure and the lure of more fertile inspiration tugged them toward English folk music. Curiously, the audio mix here is better than that on their second album, with a much stronger, harder group sound overall. *—Bruce Eder*

Stand Up / 1969 / Chrysalis ✦✦✦

The group's second album, with Anderson (vocals, flute, acoustic guitars, keyboards, balalaika), Martin Barre (electric guitar, flute), Clive Bunker (drums), and Glen Cornick (bass), solidified the group's sound. There is still an element of blues, but except for "A New Day Yesterday," it is far more muted than on their first album, as Mick Abrahams' blues stylings are largely absent from Martin Barre's playing. The influence of folk music also began to manifest itself ("Look into the Sun"). The instrumental "Bouree," which could've been an early Blood, Sweat & Tears track, became a favorite concert number, although at this point Anderson's flute playing on stage needed a lot of work—by his own admission, he just wasn't that good. Bassist Cornick would last only one more album, but got his best moments here, on "Bouree." As a story-song with opaque lyrics and jarring tempo changes, "Back to the Family" is the forerunner to *Thick as a Brick*. The only major flaw in this album is the mix, which divides the electric and acoustic instruments and fails to find a solid center. The Mobile Fidelity audiophile CD (out-of-print), in addition to superior sound, re-creates the original LP's "pop up" jacket interior. *—Bruce Eder*

Benefit / 1970 / Chrysalis ✦✦✦

Benefit was the album on which the Tull sound solidified around folk music, abandoning blues as a major source. Beginning with the opening number, "With You There to Help Me," Anderson adopted his now-familiar slightly mournful folk singer/sage persona—his acoustic guitar carried the melody, joined by Martin Barre's electric instrument for the crescendos. This would be the model for much of the material on *Aqualung* and, especially, *Thick as a Brick*, although the acoustic/electric pairing would be executed more effectively on those albums. Most of the songs here display pleasant, delectably folk-like melodies, with Barre's guitar adding enough wattage to keep the rock listeners interested. "To Cry You a Song," "Son," and "For Michael Collins, Jeffrey and Me" all defined Tull's future sound: Barre's amp cranked up to 10 (especially on "Son"), coming in above Anderson's acoustic strumming, a few unexpected changes in tempo, and Anderson spouting lyrics filled with dense, seemingly profound imagery and statements. As on *Stand Up*, the group was still officially a quartet, with future member John Evan appearing as a guest on keyboards. *—Bruce Eder*

● **Aqualung** / 1971 / Chrysalis ✦✦✦✦

Released at a time when a lot of bands were embracing pop-Christianity (*a la Jesus Christ, Superstar*), *Aqualung* was a bold statement for a rock group, a pro-God, anti-church tract that probably got lots of teenagers wrestling with these ideas for the first time in their lives. This was the album that made Jethro Tull a fixture on FM radio, with riff-heavy songs like "My God," "Hymn 43," "Locomotive Breath," "Cross-Eyed Mary," "Wind Up," and the title track. And from there, they became a major arena act, and a fixture at the top of the record charts for most of the 1970s. Mixing hard rock and folk melodies with Ian Anderson's dour musings on faith and religion (mostly how organized religion had restricted man's relationship with God), the record was extremely profound for a No. 7 chart hit, one of the most cerebral albums ever to reach millions of rock listeners. Indeed, from this point on, Anderson and company were compelled to stretch the lyrical envelope right to the breaking point. As a compact disc, *Aqualung* has gone through numerous editions, mostly owing to problems finding an original master tape when the CD boom began. When the album was issued by Chrysalis through Columbia Records in the mid-1980s, the source tape was an LP production master, and the first release was crit-

icized for thin, tinny sound; Columbia remastered it sometime around 1987 or 1988, in a version with better sound. Chrysalis later switched distribution to Capitol-EMI, and they released a decent-sounding CD that is currently available. Chrysalis also issued a 25th anniversary edition in 1996. *—Bruce Eder*

Thick As a Brick / 1972 / Chrysalis ✦✦✦✦

Jethro Tull's first LP-length epic is a masterpiece in the annals of progressive rock, and one of the few works of its kind that still holds up 25 years later. Mixing hard rock and English folk music with classical influences, set to stream-of-consciousness lyrics so dense with imagery that one might spend weeks pondering their meaning—assuming one feels the need to do so—the group created a dazzling tour-de-force, at once playful, profound, and challenging, without overwhelming the listener. The original LP was the best-sounding, best-engineered record Tull had ever released, easily capturing the shifting dynamics between the soft all-acoustic passages and the electric rock crescendos surrounding them. The sound on the original Columbia Records CD (not identified as such, but recognizable by a "VK" prefix in its catalog number) was harsh and thin, and left a lot to be desired in terms of richness—the Mobile Fidelity audiophile disc (out-of-print) solved those problems, and the current Chrysalis disc is an improvement as well. *—Bruce Eder*

Living in the Past / 1972 / Chrysalis ✦✦✦✦

Listen to this 20-song collection, put together to capitalize on the explosive growth in the group's audience after *Aqualung*, and it is easy to understand just how fine a group Jethro Tull was in the early '70s. Most of the songs, apart from a few heavily played album tracks ("Song for Jeffrey," etc.) and a pair of live tracks from a 1970 Carnegie Hall show, came off of singles and EPs that, apart from the title song, were scarcely known in America, and it's all so solid that it needs no apology or explanation. Not only was Ian Anderson writing solid songs every time out, but the group's rhythm section was about the best in progressive rock's pop division. Along with any of the group's first five albums, this collection is seminal and essential to any Tull collection, and the only compilation by the group that is a must-own disc. *—Bruce Eder*

A Passion Play / 1973 / Chrysalis ✦✦✦✦

Jethro Tull's second album-length composition, *A Passion Play*, is very different from—and not quite as successful as—*Thick as a Brick*. Ian Anderson utilizes reams of biblical (and biblical-sounding) references, interwoven with modern language, as a sort of rock equivalent to T.S. Eliot's *The Wasteland*. As with most progressive rock, the words seem important and profound, but their meaning is anyone's guess ("The ice-cream lady wet her drawers, to see you in the Passion Play. . . "), with Anderson as a dour but engaging singer/sage (who, at least at one point, seems to take on the role of a fallen angel). It helps to be aware of the framing story, about a newly deceased man called to review his life at the portals of heaven, who realizes that life on earth is preferable to eternity in paradise. But the music puts it over successfully, a dazzling mix of old English folk and classical material, reshaped in electric rock terms. The band is at its peak form, sustaining the tension and anticipation of this album-length piece across 45 minutes, although the music runs out of inspiration about five minutes before it actually ends. The sound on the CD is significantly brighter than the LP, bringing out the full impact of the electric instruments once the piece takes off, but also imparting more presence to the acoustic instruments (such as Anderson's guitar over the line "God of ages/Lord of time" and the sax part that follows). The only serious complaint about the compact disc is that it isn't indexed to separate the two halves of *A Passion Play* from the A.A. Milne-style interlude "The Story of the Hare That Lost His Spectacles," instead being treated as one long track. *—Bruce Eder*

War Child / 1974 / Chrysalis ✦✦✦

As a return to standard-length songs following two epic-length pieces (*Thick as a Brick* and *A Passion Play*) it was inevitable that the material on *War Child* would lack power. The music was no longer quite able to cover for the obscurity of Tull's lyrics: the title track is reasonably successful, but "Queen and Country" seems repetitive and pointless. "Ladies," by contrast, is one of Tull's folk-based pieces, and one of the prettiest songs on the record, beautifully sung and benefiting from some of Anderson's best flute playing to date. The band is very tight, but doesn't get to really show its stuff until "Back-Door Angels," after which the album picks up: "Sealion" is one of Anderson's pseudo-philosophical musings on life, mixing full-out electric playing and restrained orchestral backing, while "Skating Away on the Thin Ice of a New Day" is a beautiful, largely acoustic number that was popular in concert. "Bungle in the Jungle," with a title that went over well, got most of the radio play. *—Bruce Eder*

Minstrel in the Gallery / 1975 / Chrysalis ✦✦✦✦

Minstrel in the Gallery was Tull's most artistically successful and elaborately produced album since *Thick as a Brick*, and harkened back to that album with the inclusion of a 17-minute extended piece ("Baker Street Muse"). Although English folk elements abound, this is really a hard rock showcase on a par with—and perhaps even more aggressive—than anything on *Aqualung.* The title track is a superb showcase for the group, freely mixing folk melodies, lilting flute passages, an archaic, pre-Elizabethan feel, and the fiercest electric rock in the group's history—parts of it do recall phrases from *A Passion Play,* but all of it is more successful than anything on *War Child.* Martin Barre's attack on the guitar is as ferocious as anything in the band's history, and John Evan's organ matches him amp-for-amp, while Barriemore Barlow and Jeffrey Hammond-Hammond hold things together in a furious performance. Anderson's flair for drama and melody come to the fore in "Cold Wind to Valhalla," and "Requiem" is the loveliest acoustic number in Tull's repertory, featuring nothing but Anderson's singing and acoustic guitar, Glascock's bass, and a small string orchestra backing them. "Nothing at All" isn't far behind for sheer, unabashed beauty, but "Black Satin Dancer" is a little too cacophonous for its own good. "Baker Street Muse" recalls *Thick as a Brick* and *A Passion Play,* not only in its structure but a few passages—at slightly under 17 minutes, it's a tad more manageable than either of its conceptual predecessors, and it has all of their virtues, freely overlapping hard rock and folk material, classical arrangements (some of the most tasteful string playing on a Tull recording, surprising tempo shifts, and complex stream-of-consciousness lyrics (some of which clearly veer into self-parody) into a compelling whole. —*Bruce Eder*

Too Old to Rock N' Roll, Too Young To Die / 1976 / Chrysalis ♦♦
The nadir of Tull's 1970's releases, *Too Old to Rock 'n Roll,* was made up of songs salvaged from an unproduced stage work by Ian Anderson and David Palmer. Unfortunately, in the absence of the play itself—which seems to have been rather sketchily devised—the songs don't hang together, despite the presence of a plot synopsis in cartoon form. Worse still, they aren't terribly memorable as individual tracks. The playing is okay, and the singing isn't bad, but there's no real center or point to the album, which sold fairly well in America, but was an unmitigated disaster in England, where critics and audiences greeted it as a self-indulgent mess. —*Bruce Eder*

M.U.: The Best of Jethro Tull / 1976 / Chrysalis ♦♦♦
M.U. is a decent sampling of hits and album picks, but not definitive. —*Rick Clark*

Songs from the Wood / 1977 / Chrysalis ♦♦♦♦
Far and away the prettiest record Tull has released at least since *Thick as a Brick,* and a special treat for anyone with a fondness for the group's more folk-oriented material. Anderson had moved to the countryside sometime earlier, and it showed in his choice of source material. The band's aggressive rock interplay and Anderson's fascination with early British folk melodies produce a particularly appealing collection of songs—the seriousness with which the group took this effort can be discerned by the album's unofficial "full" title on the original LP: "Jethro Tull with Kitchen Prose, Gutter Rhymes, and Divers Songs from the Wood." The group's sound was never more carefully balanced between acoustic folk and hard rock—the result is an album that sounds a great deal like the work of Tull's Chrysalis Records label mates Steeleye Span (though Nigel Pegrum never attacked his cymbals—or his entire drum kit—with Barriemore Barlow's ferocity). The harmonizing on "Songs from the Wood" fulfills the promise shown in some of the singing on *Thick as a Brick,* and the delicacy of much of the rest, including "Ring Out, Solstice Bells" (where the group plays full out, but with wonderful elegance), "Hunting Girl," and "Velvet Green," set a new standard for the group's sound. "Pibroch (Cap In Hand)," which is dominated by Martin Barre's electric guitar in a stunning array of overlapping flourishes at full volume, is the only concession to the group's usual hard rock raveups, and even it has some lovely singing to counterbalance the bulk of the song. —*Bruce Eder*

Bursting Out / 1978 / Chrysalis ♦♦♦
Released just as punk was taking hold on the public's imagination in America and making groups like Tull seem like dinosaurs on their way to extinction, *Live—Bursting Out* became a seemingly perpetual denizen of the cutout bins for years afterward. However, it happened to be a good album, a more-than-decent capturing of a live Tull concert from Europe. The sound is remarkably good, given the group's arena-rock status at the time, and the repertoire is a solid representation of the group's history, going all the way back to "A New Day Yesterday" from their second album and up through 1977's *Songs from the Wood,* with stops along the way for "Bouree," "Aqualung," "Locomotive Breath," "Cross-Eyed Mary" and a compact reprise of *Thick as a Brick.* Some of these tracks work better than others—the tendency here is to play loud and hard, and sometimes that just doesn't translate well on record; seeing "Locomotive Breath" probably worked better than hearing it. —*Bruce Eder*

Heavy Horses / 1978 / Chrysalis ♦♦♦♦
Jethro Tull's 11th studio album is one of their prettier records, a veritable celebration of English folk music chock full of gorgeous melodies, briskly played acoustic guitars and mandolins, and Anderson's flute

lilting in the background, backed by the group in top form. This record is a fairly close cousin to 1977's *Songs from the Wood,* except that its songs are decidedly more passionate, sung with a rough, robust energy that much of Tull's work since *Thick as a Brick* had been missing, and surpassing even *Aqualung* in its lustiness. "No Lullaby" is the signature heavy riff song, a concert version of which opened *Live—Bursting Out.* Anderson sings it—and everything else here—as though it might be the last lines he ever gets to voice, with tremendous intensity. The band plays hard behind him throughout, with lead guitarist Martin Barre (most notably on "Weathercock") and bassist John Glascock showing up very well throughout. Anderson's production and Robin Black's engineering catch their every nuance without sacrificing the delicacy of his acoustic guitar and mandolin playing. "Acres Wild," "Rover," "One Brown Mouse," "Weathercock," and "Moths" (which makes this listener think of a folk version of Peter Gabriel's "Solsbury Hill"), the latter featuring some of David Palmer's most tasteful orchestral arrangements, are among the loveliest songs in the group's entire repertory. Curved Air's Darryl Way plays violin solo on the title track—a tribute to England's vanishing shire horses, which doesn't really take off until Way's instrument comes in on the break, with a marked tempo change—and on "Acres Wild." —*Bruce Eder*

Stormwatch / 1979 / Chrysalis ♦♦
Stormwatch marked the end of an era in Jethro Tull's history, as the last album on which longtime members Barriemore Barlow, John Evan, and David Palmer participated, and the final appearance of bassist John Glascock, who played on three of the cuts (Anderson supplied the bass elsewhere) and died following open-heart surgery a few weeks after its release. Anderson's inspiration seemed to be running out here, his writing covering environmental concerns ("North Sea Oil") and very scattershot social topical criticism ("Dark Ages"). The fire is still there in some of the hard rock passages, especially on "Dark Ages," but most of the songs generally lack the craftsmanship and inspiration of such albums as *Minstrel in the Gallery* or *Heavy Horses,* much less *Aqualung.* Just when "Something's on the Move" seems like it could be the most tuneless track in Tull's history, "Old Ghosts" and "Dun Ringill" follow it with even less memorable melodic material. The latter, in particular, proved that Anderson's well of folk-inspired tunes was also running dry, apart from the instrumental "Warm Sporran." —*Bruce Eder*

A / 1980 / Chrysalis ♦♦♦
Gone is the longtime Anderson image of the vagabond/sage (the group are clad in white jumpsuits on the cover)—also gone is the historical immersion of their music, and anything resembling Dickensian, much less Elizabethan, sensibilities. And nearly gone was Jethro Tull itself, for *A* started life as an Ian Anderson solo project but ended up as a Jethro Tull release, probably for commercial reasons. The difference is probably too subtle for most people to comprehend anyway. It is more reflective than Tull's usual work, but lacks the sudden, loud hard rock explosions that punctuate most of the group's albums. The death of bassist John Glascock in late 1979, and the departure of Anderson's longtime friend John Evans after the release of *Stormwatch,* as well as the exit of arranger/keyboard player David Palmer, led to some major lineup shifts—Fairport Convention's Dave Pegg's taking over Glascock's spot and the addition of Eddie Jobson, ex-Roxy Music/King Crimson violinist/keyboardman, all seem to have removed some of Anderson's impetus, at least for a time, for keeping the group going in the studio. What finally emerged is the first Tull record not to feature Anderson's acoustic guitar, yet it also has a more balanced sound than any of their prior records. Jobson's arrangements are leaner and more muscular than Palmer's, giving the music a stripped-down sound, a sort of *hard* folk-rock (reminiscent of Steeleye Span's *All Around My Hat*), augmented by synthesizer and electric violin, somewhat updating Anderson's music, and moving him into the "art-rock" category. Released in the midst of the punk/new wave boom in the United States, it didn't do too much for anyone's career, although it probably maintained Anderson's credibility better than any traditional Tull album would have. —*Bruce Eder*

The Broadsword & The Beast / 1982 / Chrysalis ♦♦
The cover of this first actual Jethro Tull album since 1979's *Stormwatch* depicts Ian Anderson as an elf-warrior, with wings and a sword, and a ship with a stylized Norse dragon's head. Anyone expecting a fantasy or heavy metal album was due for a disappointment, however, for most of the songs that have any identifiable references are about topical politics, more than anything else. Martin Barre's electric guitars share the spotlight for the first time with Peter-John Vettese's synthesizers, and Anderson is still playing lilting tunes on his flute and acoustic guitar. The band's electric sound, this time in the hands of ex-Yardbird Paul Samwell-Smith, is smoother, less heavy, and thinner textured than their past work, and there are times—most especially on "Flying Colours"—where Tull could almost pass for the latter day Moody Blues, something they never would have permitted in earlier days (though if

the Moodies could rock this hard and fast, it would be an achievement—for *them*). "Broadsword" and "Pussywillow" are easily the two best songs here, and, not coincidentally, the two that owe the most to traditional folk music in their structure. Most of the rest is little better than tuneless drivel. —*Bruce Eder* ✦

Under Wraps / 1984 / Chrysalis ✦

Crest of a Knave / 1987 / Chrysalis ✦✦✦
Ian Anderson and company seemed to make a conscious effort to update Jethro Tull's sound on this record. And, to the amazement (and distress) of many, it was voted the Grammy Award for Best Hard Rock/Heavy Metal Performance. Truth is, it isn't a bad album, with an opening track that qualifies as hard rock and pretty much shouts its credentials out in Martin Barre's screaming lead guitar line, present throughout. "Jump Start" and "Raising Steam" also rock hard, and no one can complain of too much on this record being soft, apart from the acoustic "The Waking Edge," and "Budapest," and "Said She Was a Dancer," Anderson's two aging rock-star's-eye-view accounts of meetings women from around the world. The anti-war song "Mountain Men" is classic Tull-styled electric folk, all screaming electric guitars at a pretty high volume by its end. Overall this is a fairly successful album, and arguably their best since 1978, even if it does seem a little insignificant in relation to, say, *Thick as a Brick*. By this time Tull was effectively a core trio of Anderson, Barre, and bassist Dave Pegg, augmented by whatever musicians (drummers Gerry Conway and Doane Perry, and Fairport Convention keyboard player Martin Allcock and violinist Ric Sanders) that they needed to fill out their sound. The result is a very lean sounding group, and a record probably as deserving of a Grammy as any other album of its year—in the cosmic scheme, it sort of made up for Tull's not winning one for *Thick as a Brick* or *Aqualung*, or for Dave Pegg's former band Fairport Convention never winning. —*Bruce Eder*

20 Years of Jethro Tull / 1988 / Chrysalis ✦✦✦
Fans of the Tull should enjoy this collection that amply documents the band's entire career. There are loads of live performances, TV appearances, and good interviews. The sound quality is quite good. —*Rick Clark*

20 Years of Jethro Tull: Highlights / 1988 / Chrysalis ✦✦✦✦
This is a distilled version of tracks taken from the Tull's boxed set. Broken down into four parts, it includes a smattering of hits, live tracks, and some key album sides. It might not be definitive, but it does give the listener a good idea of the band's musical range. —*Rick Clark*

Rock Island / 1989 / Chrysalis ✦✦
After the promise of their previous effort, this one comes off as more of the same, with band members sounding as though they were painting by numbers rather than showing any enthusiasm for what they're playing. Includes the novel "Another Christmas Song," along with the usual Tull performances, but overall, a ho-hum release. —*James Chrispell*

Catfish Rising / Sep. 10, 1991 / Chrysalis ✦✦✦
Jethro Tull's best album of the 1990s, a surging, hard-rocking monster (at least, compared to anything immediately before or since) that doesn't lose sight of good tunes or the folk sources that have served this band well. The lineup this time out is Anderson on acoustic and electric guitars, flute, and electric and acoustic mandolins, Martin Barre on electric guitar, Doane Perry on drums, Dave Pegg on bass, and Andrew Giddings on keyboards. The real difference between this and most of the group's output since the end of the 1970s lies in the songs, all of which are approached with serious energy and enthusiasm—the lyrics are completely forgettable, but for the first time since *War Child*, the band sounds like they're playing as though their lives depended on it. "Sparrow on the Schoolyard Wall" is at least as good a song as "Bungle in the Jungle" or "Skating Away on the Thin Ice of a New Day," and while that ain't exactly "My God," it's still better than most other recent Tull albums have done. "Still Loving You Tonight" and "Sleeping with the Dog" recall the group's blues roots, albeit not quite in bluesy enough fashion. There's still some dross, as there would almost have to be on an hour-long album, but overall this is the group's best album since the end of the 1970s. —*Bruce Eder*

25th Anniversary / Apr. 20, 1993 / Chrysalis ✦✦
Jethro Tull's four-CD celebration of their quarter of a century in the music business is only worth the time of hardcore Tull fans. Two discs are full-length live performances (both discs contain two of the same songs), one disc is full of alternate versions of their most famous tracks, and a final disc has new remixes of "classic" tracks (which includes the third appearance of "A Song for Jeffrey" on the four CDs). Casual fans are much better served by one of the smaller collections. —*Stephen Thomas Erlewine*

The Best of Jethro Tull: the Anniversary Collection / Jun. 29, 1993 / Chrysalis ✦✦✦✦
This double CD, containing about 150 minutes of music, was released around the same time as the 25th anniversary box, and outclasses it in

virtually every way possible. Instead of dwelling on rarities and live versions of songs, this collection simply assembles most of the best tracks on the group's records up through 1991. Of course, precisely what constitutes the "best" tracks is a matter of debate—the harder-rocking numbers get picked in favor of the folkier, more lyrical tracks on most of the group's albums. The earlier songs are also remastered, giving them a sharper sound and, even more important, a better blended sound between the group's electric and acoustic instruments than the complete albums, which were remastered at an earlier date. For the truly dedicated, it is simpler just to buy them all—and certainly *This Was, Benefit, Aqualung, Thick as a Brick,* and *A Passion Play* are priority items, as should be, but for more casual listeners, this is the best overview of the group's work, and infinitely superior to any of the prior "best of" or other anthologies of Tull's music. —*Bruce Eder*

Nightcap / 1994 / Import ✦✦✦
This double-CD was originally released in the early '90s and then disappeared for four years, until 1997. It is a true gift to hardcore fans, offering previously unseen glimpses of Jethro Tull when the group was at its absolute peak. Anyone else, however, may find the album rough going, for while the group was never tighter or more productive, the material isn't even second rate. Essentially, *Nightcap* is Jethro Tull's version of the Beatles' *Anthology* releases, only far less interesting, simply because we are talking about Tull and not the Beatles. The first disc consists of tracks that the band started to record during 1973 at the Chateau D' Herouville, abandoned due to health, business, and technical problems—the best parts of this material ended up being rewritten and incorporated into what became *A Passion Play*. Much of the rest is more noisy than interesting, and considering what the group started with, Anderson's strong reaction to the critical drubbing later accorded *A Passion Play* was understandable. The 1973 outtakes are pretty at times, but also unformed and distinctly unfinished—Anderson takes a gorgeous classical guitar solo on "First Post," for example, which goes absolutely nowhere, drifting into an attractive but similarly aimless harpsichord-dominated piece (both undoubtedly would have been edited into an appropriate piece on a finished album). "Tiger Toon" is an early version of the principal theme from "A Passion Play," not altered too much except in tempo—it must've been a real mess, however, because it is faded down on this release. "Law of the Bungle" repeats the same musical material, and "Critique Oblique" offers material that made up the louder, later sections of "A Passion Play," with some impressive playing from Martin Barre on lead guitar and John Evan on organ—except that it goes nowhere for nine minutes; "Post Last" is an early version of the "Passion Play" finale. Of the rest, "Look at the Animals" is pleasant in a folk-rock mode, with Anderson's wry mix of nonsense poetry and digressive images—but it doesn't justify this double CD set by itself. The 1974 outtakes and rare tracks that comprise the second disc are less problematic, because they are less fragmentary. "Piece of Cake" is one of the best pieces of straightahead rock 'n' roll that the band ever cut, so solid and straightforward that but for the presence of the flute, it might not even sound like Jethro Tull. "Crew Nights," "The Curse," and "Hard Rider" aren't far behind, and there are other fine tracks here, more than compensating for the aimless noodling and pointless profundity that rear their heads elsewhere. And "Broadford Bazzar" is about the prettiest free-standing folk-style tune Anderson and company ever came up with. (British import) —*Bruce Eder*

Roots to Branches / Sep. 12, 1995 / Chrysalis ✦✦
The latest Tull studio album has its good moments, mostly shadows of earlier work. All of the songs here have more of a mood of urgency than some of Tull's other recent albums, and a few even have memorable melodies—the title tune, "At Last, Forever" (which sounds like a *Thick as a Brick* outtake), "Rare and Precious Chain," "Dangerous Veils," and "Valley," which recall the best moments of Ian Anderson's mid-1970's work. There are also attempts to revive the band's one-time fixation on jazz influences (the opening of "Wounded, Old and Treacherous"), although this sort of thing came off better on *This Was*. Anderson's flute occasionally takes flight, Martin Barre's guitar still wails on the breaks, and Doane Perry (drums), Dave Pegg (bass), and Steve Bailey (bass) make up a decent rhythm section. Not nearly as strong as *Catfish Rising,* but better than anything else since *Heavy Horses*. —*Bruce Eder*

Joan Jett

b. Sep. 22, 1960, Philadelphia, PA
Guitar, Vocals / Rock 'n' Roll, Hard Rock
By playing pure and simple rock 'n' roll without making an explicit issue of her gender, Joan Jett became a figurehead for several generations of female rockers. Jett's brand of rock 'n' roll is loud and stripped down, yet with overpowering hooks—a combination of the Stones' tough, sinewy image and beat, AC/DC chords, and glam-rock hooks. As the numerous covers she has recorded show, she adheres both to

rock tradition and breaks with it—she plays classic three-chord rock 'n' roll, yet she also loves the trashy elements (in particular, Gary Glitter) of it as well, and she plays with a defiant sneer. From her first band, the Runaways, through her hit-making days in the '80s with the Black-hearts right until her unexpected revival in the '90s, she hasn't changed her music, yet she's kept her quality control high, making one classic single ("I Love Rock-n-Roll") along the way.

Jett was born in Philadelphia, PA; her family moved to Los Angeles when she was 12 years old. By the time she was 15, she had formed her first band and was performing around town. Kim Fowley, a Los Angeles record producer, discovered the band at one of their gigs and became their manager; soon, he renamed the all-female group the Runaways and secured them a contract with Mercury Records. The band released three albums that never had much commercial success in America, yet were very popular in Japan; the group were popular in both the Los Angeles hard rock and punk scenes, which led to Jett's production of the Germs' first record, G.I. The Runaways group broke up in 1980 and Jett moved to New York to begin a solo career.

Teaming up with producer/manager Kenny Laguna, Jett independently released her self-titled debut album in 1980 in America, since no labels were interested in signing her. The record was a more traditional rock 'n' roll record than the punky Runaways, yet it retained her previous band's defiant attitude. The record sold very well for an independent release, leading to a contract with Boardwalk Records, who reissued the album under the title Bad Reputation; it soon climbed to No. 51 on the American charts.

Jett formed the Blackhearts between Bad Reputation and her second album, 1981's I Love Rock-n-Roll; the group included guitarist Ricky Byrd, bassist Gary Ryan, and drummer Lee Crystal. Released at the end of 1981, I Love Rock & Roll became her greatest success, sending her into the Top Ten. Originally the B-side of an Arrows single, the title track was an enormous success, spending seven weeks at No. 1 in the spring of 1982. The follow-up single, a version of Tommy James & the Shondells' "Crimson and Clover," went Top Ten as well; a single of Gary Glitter's "Do You Wanna Touch Me (Oh Yeah)," taken from the Bad Reputation album reached No. 20 in the summer of 1982. Album, released in 1983, went gold yet it had no hits that compared with either "I Love Rock & Roll" or "Crimson and Clover."

Jett starred in Paul Schrader's 1987 film Light of Day, which featured the Top 40 title song, yet she didn't have another Top Ten hit until 1988, when "I Hate Myself for Loving You," taken from the Up Your Alley album, hit No. 8; the album became her second platinum record. After the album's success, her career had another slow period, with 1990's all-covers album The Hit List making it to No. 36 and 1991's Notorious failing to chart. Between Notorious and 1994's Pure and Simple, a new generation of female rockers came of age and everyone from hard alternative rockers like L7 to the minimalist, riot grrl punk rockers like Bikini Kill claimed Jett and the Runaways as an influence. As a consequence, Pure and Simple received more press and positive reviews than any of her albums since the mid-'80s. In 1995, Jett recorded the live album Evilstig with the remaining members of the Gits, a Seattle punk rock band whose lead singer, Mia Zapata, was raped and murdered in 1993. —Stephen Thomas Erlewine

Bad Reputation / 1981 / Blackheart ✦✦✦✦
Her debut suffers from a lack of one coherent sound, but it's an impassioned homage to her glitter-and-punk roots. —John Floyd

I Love Rock & Roll / 1981 / Blackheart ✦✦✦✦
I Love Rock & Roll, Joan Jett's first record with the Blackhearts, was a tougher, louder album than Bad Reputation, primarily because her new backing band gave her a more coherent sound. That dynamic, hard rock crunch is what made the title track into an international hit, but it also gives the album dimension—not only can Jett and the Blackhearts tear up heavy glam-rockers, but they also pull off the mock psychedelia of Tommy James & the Shondells' "Crimson and Clover" with aplomb. On the whole, I Love Rock & Roll doesn't have as many strong songs as its predecessor, but the band's muscular, gritty sound makes the album just as good as Bad Reputation. —Stephen Thomas Erlewine

Album / 1983 / Blackheart ✦✦✦✦
With her best set of songs and big-time production, this is an astonishing statement of purpose, full of gritty Rolling Stones-like boogie and a cover of Sly Stone's "Everyday People" that works better than you'd think. But it's all spectacular. —John Floyd

Glorious Results of a Misspent Youth / 1984 / Blackheart ✦✦✦✦
Another masterful blast of fury and celebration, it shifts from a blazing cover of the Runaways' "Cherry Bomb" to her best song, "I Got No Answers." Besides the Pretenders' early work, Glorious Results . . . ranks with the best rock of the '80s, focused through a female point of view. —John Floyd

Good Music / 1986 / Epic ✦✦✦
The production's a bit heavy, but Jett's formula is still a winner. "Black Leather" and the title cut are fine rock anthems. —John Floyd

Up Your Alley / 1988 / Epic ✦✦
"I Hate Myself for Loving You" is a strikingly complex take on relationships and was a hit, but aside from a whopping cover of Chuck Berry's "Tulane," this album is pretty thin. —John Floyd

The Hit List / 1990 / Epic ✦✦
From Sly Stone's "Everyday People" to Tommy James & the Shondell's "Crimson & Clover," cover songs have long been one of Joan Jett's strong points. Covers can be a waste of time in the hands of some rockers, but they've always worked well for Jett, who's been wise enough to make sure that her own personality never became obscured when recording other artists' material. The one-time member of the criminally neglected Runaways embraces covers exclusively on The Hit List, tackling everything from the Sex Pistols' "Pretty Vacant" to AC/DC's "Dirty Deed" to the Doors' "Love Me Two Times" with spirited, inspired results. While those investigating Jett's career would do better to start out with I Love Rock & Roll or Glorious Results of a Misspent Youth, The Hit List was a welcome addition to her catalogue. —Alex Henderson

Notorious / Aug. 20, 1991 / Epic ✦✦✦
Jett finally conceives an album where the ballads work as well as the barnburners. Included is a collaboration with Paul Westerberg of the Replacements. —John Floyd

● **Flashback** / 1994 / Blackheart ✦✦✦✦
While it includes a healthy share of rarities, nothing on Joan Jett's career overview, Flashback, is second-rate. Even though she vascillated between punky hard rock and smoothed-out arena-rock for much of the '80s, the disc accentuates her rebellious nature, making Flashback an effective introduction to her career. Besides, it rocks like hell. —Stephen Thomas Erlewine

Pure and Simple / Jun. 14, 1994 / Warner Brothers ✦✦✦
A strong record showing that she has lost very little of her power, Pure and Simple contained contributions by several of Jett's fans, including members of L7 and Bikini Kill. —Stephen Thomas Erlewine

Jewel

f. May 23, 1974, Homer, AK
Guitar, Vocals / Singer-Songwriter, Adult Alternative Pop-Rock
One of the most folk-based of alternative female singer-songwriters in the mid-'90s, Jewel moved from the coffeehouses to a major-label record deal before she turned 20. Born Jewel Kilcher on May 23, 1974, she grew up in Homer, AK. She began performing at the age of five, and studied singing for two years on a scholarship to the Interlochen Musical Academy in Michigan. After graduation, Jewel moved to San Diego to live with her mother, and began performing at a local coffeehouse. By 1994, the occasional shows became a packed Thursday-night residency, and Atlantic executives signed her to a contract. An EP was released in late 1994, and Jewel's debut album Pieces of You, appeared the following February. —John Bush

● **Pieces of You** / Feb. 28, 1995 / Atlantic ✦✦✦✦
Jewel's debut album is a charming collection of light alternative folk-rock from the teenage singer-songwriter. Her songs are occasionally naive, but her melodies can usually save her lyrics. —Sara Sytsma

The Jive Five

f. 1959, Brooklyn, NY
Soul, R&B, Doo Wop
Best known for the No. 1 R&B hit "My True Story," the Jive Five were one of the few vocal groups to survive the transistion from the '50s to the '60s. In the process, they helped move the music itself forward, providing a key link between doo wop and '60s soul.

Formed in Brooklyn, NY, the group originally consisted of Eugene Pitt (lead), Jerome Hanna (tenor), Richard Harris (tenor), Billy Prophet (baritone), and Norman Johnson (bass). The Jive Five's first hit, "My True Story," was their biggest, peaking at No. 1 on the R&B charts and No. 3 on the pop charts in the summer of 1961. None of the band's subsequent singles—including the minor R&B hit, 1962's "These Golden Rings"—were as popular, but the group managed to keep performing and recording. Under the direction of Eugene Pitt and Norman Johnson, the Jive Five refashioned themselves as a soul band in 1964, forming a new lineup with Casey Spencer (tenor), Webster Harris (tenor), and Beatrice Best (baritone). This new incarnation of the band signed to United Artists Records. The group only had one hit on UA, 1965's "I'm a Happy Man."

In 1966, the Jive Five left United Artists and signed with Musicor, where they had the 1968 R&B hit "Sugar (Don't Take Away My Candy)." They changed labels again in 1970, signing with Decca. That same year, they changed their name to the Jyve Fyve, in order to appear more contemporary. The Jyve Fyve had only one minor R&B hit, 1970's "I Want You to Be My Baby."

The group continued to perform and record for a variety of small labels during the '70s, but they never had another hit. Throughout the '70s and '80s, the only constant member was Eugene Pitt. In 1975, Pitt changed the name of the group to Ebony, Ivory, and the Jades, but this new incarnation failed to gain much attention. In 1982, Pitt changed the name of the group back to the Jive Five and the band recorded two albums for the indie label, Ambient Sound. For the rest of the '80s and the '90s, the Jive Five were regulars on the oldies circuit. —*Stephen Thomas Erlewine*

● **The Jive Five** / 1989 / United Artists ✦✦✦✦
A superb 20-track collection, it features the Jive Five's finest material, recorded in the early '60s for Lescay/Belton; songs include "Rain," "My True Story," "No Not Again," "What Time Is It?," and "Hurry Back." —*AMG*

Greatest Hits / Apr. 18, 1990 / Collectables ✦✦✦

My True Story / Feb. 1, 1991 / Relic ✦✦✦
These hard-hitting doo woppers testify on the title cut, "What Time Is It?," and on "Hully Gully Callin' Time." Eugene Pitts is one of the era's most evocative singers. —*John Floyd*

The Complete United Artists Recordings . . . / Oct. 20, 1992 / Capitol ✦✦✦✦
A superior 21-track collection, it highlights the Jive Five's material for United Artists, recorded in the mid-'60s. —*AMG*

Jodeci

f. 1990, Tiny Grove, NC
Urban, Club/Dance
If Boyz II Men are portrayed as a clean-cut, wholesome R&B vocal group, then Jodeci's wild, sexual, bad-boy image represents the other side of the coin. Made up of two sets of brothers, the group's name is a consolidation of three members' aliases: "JoJo" Hailey, Donald "DeVante Swing" DeGrate, and Cedric "K-Ci" Hailey; the group also includes Dalvin DeGrate. Natives of Charlotte, NC, all four members toured the South as young boys singing gospel music, even recording albums; both families belonged to the Pentecostal church, and the DeGrates' father was a minister. The boys were able to hear each other's gospel songs played on the radio, and eventually were introduced through girlfriends as teenagers. However, when they did meet, K-Ci was with a girl Dalvin had been dating, and a fight nearly broke out. The Hailey brothers and DeVante started hanging out together, partying and talking about making R&B records together, coming up with the name Jodeci at this time.

At age 16, DeVante ran away to Minneapolis to get a job in Prince's organization, but was refused. He returned to Charlotte, where he wrote a song and recorded JoJo singing it. The two planned on going to New York to shop the demo around by themselves, but both K-Ci and Dalvin decided to tag along at the last minute. By the time they got to New York, they had demo recordings of 29 songs, which they brought to the offices of Uptown Entertainment. They were almost rejected, but rapper Heavy D overheard the tape and talked Uptown president Andre Harrell into hearing the group. Harrell was impressed, and just like that, Jodeci signed a recording contract. In 1991, they recorded *Forever My Lady*, which featured the gold single "Come and Talk to Me" and went on to sell over three million copies. A minor feud resulted over the band's follow-up album, *Diary of a Mad Band*; Jodeci, unhappy with their treatment by Uptown, flirted with the idea of leaving for Dr. Dre's Death Row Records, which resulted in almost zero promotion for their new album. It didn't matter much, as *Diary* went platinum. The group's troubles got worse in 1993; DeVante and K-Ci were involved in an incident with a woman K-Ci met at a club and brought back to DeVante's apartment. The woman filed charges against the two, saying that K-Ci had threatened her and fondled her breast, while DeVante pointed a gun at her. Both pleaded guilty, but that wasn't all; shortly afterwards, DeVante's house was robbed of over $160,000 in jewelry and clothes as the singer was held with guns in his mouth and at the back of his head.

Jodeci's third album, *The Show, the After Party, the Hotel*, was released in the summer of 1995. DeVante also was afforded the opportunity to work with Al Green, one of his idols, writing and producing the song "Could This Be the Love." —*Steve Huey*

Forever My Lady / May 28, 1991 / Uptown/MCA ✦✦✦
A pair of brother acts combined forces to form Jodeci, a singing group with one foot in the future and the other squarely in the past. Dalvin and Devante Swing DeGrate teamed with Jo-Jo and K-Ci Hailey for a debut album that mixed vintage soul singing with New Jack production and bravado. But it wasn't the hip-hop-flavored songs that earned them popularity; instead, urban contemporary audiences embraced the love tunes "Come and Talk to Me" and the title track, signaling the

beginnings of a move away from New Jack Swing that's become a full-fledged retreat. —*Ron Wynn*

● **Diary of a Mad Band** / 1993 / Uptown/MCA ✦✦✦✦
Jodeci juggles New Jack Swing and vintage soul on their second album, and wind up with a jarring, mismatched release. The disc's love songs, particularly "Cry for You," "What About Us," and "My Heart Belongs to You," are tender, passionately sung, sincere expressions of romance and love. But they diminish these with a string of innuendo-laden come-on numbers, complete with explicit language, tired raps and samples, and the kind of sentiments and appeals better suited to a *Penthouse Forum* entry than an album. —*Ron Wynn*

The Show, the After Party, the Hotel / Jul. 18, 1995 / Uptown ✦✦✦
Although their songs imply otherwise, the Hailey brothers had extensive careers in gospel before turning to secular music. The wails, shouts, and yells that accompany most of their hits reaffirm that tradition, and it's clearly audible often on their latest Uptown entry. Again they employ a running storyline/theme through the disc, this time incorporating audio vignettes about life on and off stage during a concert that are interspersed through the disc, and help pad things out through what is a poorly edited and sequenced CD. Unlike many other urban and R&B groups, Jodeci doesn't really produce its material with singles in mind; there's not really one song here that works as a separate entity, even though several stations are playing edited cuts. Ironically, their refusal to emphasize radio hits, which in most cases would be deemed a sage creative ploy, frequently works against Jodeci. They let ballads drone on, uptempo tunes end awkwardly, and extend sections until they lose their impact. However Jodeci's earnestness and enthusiasm often helps them overcome cliched lyrics and melodramatic vocals, and there are enough good moments sprinkled throughout this disc to make it worthwhile for most urban contemporary listeners. —*Ron Wynn*

The Jody Grind

f. Atlanta, GA
Group / Alternative Pop-Rock
Before there was a Cocktail Nation and a mania for retro lounge music, Atlanta's Jody Grind were turning out jazzy renditions of Gershwin, Bacharach, and Dusty Springfield numbers, country & western standards, and original rock songs that hybridized those forms with alternative music. Singer Kelly Hogan distinguished the band (Bill Taft; guitars, Walter Brewer; drums and Robert Hayes; bass) from any number of alternative groups, as she was a real singer and used her beautiful voice to great effect. Long an Atlanta scene favorite, in 1990 DB Records released *One Man's Trash is Another Man's Treasure*. Followed by the more experimental *Lefty's Deceiver*, the band's career was cut short following a car accident that killed two members. Hogan continues to perform as a solo act in Atlanta and has released one record. —*Denise Sullivan*

● **One Man's Trash Is Another Man's Treasure** / 1990 / Ichiban ✦✦✦✦
The title track and "Eight-Ball" encapsulate the Jody Grind sound—from jazz to bossanova to soul shouting. It's a little discombobulated, but ultimately timeless. Kelly Hogan's voice is hard to resist, but the band's cool detachment never matches the singer's warmth. Sadly, the band did not stick around to enjoy the lounge-music revival. —*Denise Sullivan*

Lefty's Deceiver / Apr. 3, 1992 / Ichiban ✦✦✦
By the time the Jody Grind's second record came along, the band were drowning in their own hype, aided by Michael Stipe sightings at their frequent Athens, GA, appearances. What started out as a promising career as a neo-lounge band developed into a confusing lite-alternative/jazz/no wave/country experiment produced by percussionist Michael Blair with guitar by Peter Buck on "Third of July." Given a larger budget and proper direction, who knows how the talented band could have grown. Sadly, their career was cut short when two members died in a car crash. —*Denise Sullivan*

Billy Joel

b. May 9, 1949, Hicksville, Long Island, NY
Organ, Synthesizer, Harmonica, Piano, Keyboards, Vocals / Singer-Songwriter, Pop-Rock
Although Billy Joel never was a critic's favorite, the pianist emerged as one of the most popular singer-songwriters of the latter half of the '70s. Joel's music consistently demonstrates an affection for Beatlesque hooks and a flair for Tin Pan Alley and Broadway melodies. His fusion of two distinct eras made him a superstar in the late '70s and '80s, as he racked an impressive string of multi-platinum albums and hit singles.

Joel was raised in the Bronx suburb Levittown, where he learned to play piano as a child. Upon seeing the Beatles on *The Ed Sullivan Show* in 1964, Joel decided to pursue a musical career and set about finding a local band to join. Eventually, he found the Echoes, a group that specialized in British Invasion covers. Shortly after he joined the group, the Echoes became a popular New York attraction. While he was still a member of the group, Joel began playing recording sessions in 1965, playing piano on recordings George "Shadow" Morton produced as well as several records released through Kama Sutra Productions. Soon, his musical commitments occupied all of his time and Joel dropped out of high school, just a few months shy of his graduation. In 1967, he joined the Hassels, a Long Island rock 'n' roll band that had a recording contract with United Artists. Over the next year and a half, the Hassels released two albums and four singles, all of which failed commercially. In 1969, the Hassels broke up. Joel and the band's drummer, Jon Small, formed a heavy, psychedelic organ and drums duo called Attila. Epic released *Attila* early in 1970; sporting a cover featuring the duo dressed as barbarians, the album was a bomb and the band broke up. While the group was still together, Joel began a romance with Small's wife, Elizabeth; she would eventually leave the drummer and marry the pianist in 1973. After *Attila*'s embarrassing failure, Joel wrote rock criticism and played on commercial jingles.

Billy Joel signed a deal with Family Productions in 1971. Under the terms of the contract, Joel signed to the label's parent company, Ripp, for life; the pianist was unaware of the clause at the time. Joel refashioned himself as a sensitive singer-songwriter for his debut album, *Cold Spring Harbor*, which was released in November of 1971. Upon Joel's completion of a small US tour, Family Productions were experiencing signal and financial difficulties, which prevented Joel from recording an immediate follow-up. Early in 1972, he moved out to Los Angeles with Elizabeth. Joel adopted the name Bill Martin and spent half a year playing lounge piano at the Executive Room. Toward the end of the year, he began touring, playing various nightclubs across the country. Around the beginning of 1973, a Philadelphia radio station began playing a live version of "Captain Jack." Soon, record companies were eager to sign the pianist, and he eventually signed with Columbia Records. In order for Joel to sign with Columbia, the major label had to agree to pay Ripp Productions 25 cents for each album sold, plus display the Family and Remus logos on each record Joel released. By the end of 1973, Billy Joel's first album for Columbia Records, *Piano Man*, had been released. The record slowly worked its way up the charts, peaking at No. 27 in the spring of 1974. The title track—culled from experiences he had while singing at the Executive Room—became a Top 40 hit single. At the end of the summer, Joel assembled a touring band and undertook a national tour.

By the end of 1974, he had released his album, *Streetlife Serenade*, which reached No. 35 early in 1975. After its success, Joel signed a contract with James William Guercio and Larry Fitzgerald's management company, Caribou, and moved from California to New York, where he recorded his 1976 album *Turnstiles*. The sessions for *Turnstiles* were long and filled with tensions, culminating with Joel firing the album's original producer, Guercio, and producing the album himself. Once he fired Guercio, Joel also left Caribou, hired his wife as his new manager, and recorded his new album with his touring band.

Turnstiles stalled on the charts, only reaching No. 122. Billy Joel was at the make-or-break point for his career and the resulting album, *The Stranger*, catapulted him into superstardom. Produced by Phil Ramone, *The Stranger* was released in the fall of 1977—by the end of the year, it peaked at No. two and had gone platinum and, within the course of a year, it spawned the Top 40 singles "Just the Way You Are," "Movin' Out (Anthony's Song)," "She's Always a Woman," and "Only the Good Die Young." Joel followed *The Stranger* with *52nd Street*, which was released in the fall of 1978. *52nd Street* spent eight weeks at No. 1 in the US, selling over two million copies within the first month of its release. The album spawned the hit singles "My Life," "Big Shot," and "Honesty," and won the Grammy award for Album of the Year in 1980.

In the spring of 1980, Joel released *Glass Houses*, theoretically a harder-edged album that was a response to the punk and new wave movement. By the summer of 1980, *Glass Houses* had reached No. 1 in America, where it stayed for six weeks; the album spawned the Top 40 singles "You May Be Right," "It's Still Rock 'n' Roll to Me," "Don't Ask Me Why," and "Sometimes a Fantasy" and won the Grammy for Best Rock Vocal Performance, Male in 1981. In the fall of 1981, Joel released *Songs in the Attic*, a live album that concentrated on material written and recorded before he became a star in 1977.

Songs in the Attic bought Joel some time as he was completing an album he had designed as his bid to be taken seriously as a composer. The recording was long and plagued with problems, most notably Joel's divorce. The record, called *The Nylon Curtain*, was finally released in the fall. The album was a commercial disappointment, only selling a million copies, but it did earn him some of his better reviews, as well as spawning the Top 20 hits "Pressure" and "Allentown." Joel quickly followed the album in 1983 with the oldies pastiche *An Innocent Man*, which restored Joel to his multi-platinum status. The album also launched the hit singles "Uptown Girl," "Tell Her About It," "An Innocent Man," and "Keeping the Faith." During 1983 and 1984, Joel

became one of the first '70s stars to embrace MTV and music videos, shooting a number of clips for the album that were aired frequently on the network.

Billy Joel released a double-album compilation, *Greatest Hits, Vols. 1 & 2*, in the summer of 1985. Two new songs—including the Top Ten "You're Only Human (Second Wind)"—were added to the hits collection; the album itself peaked at No. 6. In the summer of 1986, Joel returned with the Top Ten single "Modern Woman," which was a teaser for his new album, *The Bridge*, which was released in August. *The Bridge* peaked, sold over two million copies, and launched the Top 40 hits "A Matter of Trust" and "This Is the Time." In the spring of 1987, Billy Joel embarked on a major tour of the USSR. His Leningrad concert was recorded and released in the fall of 1987 as the double-live album *Kohuept*.

Billy Joel fired his long-time manager and former brother-in-law Frank Weber in August of 1989, after an audit revealed that there were major discrepancies in Weber's accounting. Following Weber's dismissal, Joel sued Weber for $90 million, claiming fraud. Immediately after filing suit, Joel was hospitalized with kidney stones. All of this turmoil didn't prevent the release of his twelfth studio album, *Storm Front*, in the fall of 1989. It was preceded by the single "We Didn't Start the Fire," which became a No. 1 hit. *Storm Front* marked a significant change for Billy Joel—he fired his band, keeping only Liberty DeVito, and ceased his relationship with producer Phil Ramone, hiring Mick Jones of Foreigner to produce the album. *Storm Front* was another hit for Joel, reaching No. 1 in the US and selling over three million albums. During 1990, Joel embarked on a major US tour that ran well into 1991. In January, the court awarded Joel two million dollars in a partial judgement against Frank Weber. At the end of the year, the National Academy of Recording Arts and Sciences honored Billy Joel with a Grammy Living Legend award. Following the *Storm Front* world tour, Billy Joel spent the next few years quietly. Joel returned in the summer of 1993 with *River of Dreams*, which entered the charts at No. 1 and spawned the Top Ten title track. —*Stephen Thomas Erlewine*

Cold Spring Harbor / 1971 / Columbia ✦✦✦
Joel's debut solo album finds him sounding like a romantic singer-songwriter with a strong sense of melody. The album's single, "She's Got a Way," later turned up in his concerts. The original 1971 album released by Family Productions was mastered wrong and speeds up the tape; in 1984, Columbia Records released a corrected version. —*William Ruhlmann*

Piano Man / Nov. 1973 / Columbia ✦✦✦
Joel presents a personal perspective of middle-class teen life in the suburbs ("Captain Jack," "The Ballad of Billy the Kid") followed by life in a cocktail lounge ("Piano Man"), and concludes, "Worse comes to worst, I'll get along." But his already apparent sense of melody and supple singing voice indicate much more promise than that. —*William Ruhlmann*

Streetlife Serenade / Oct. 1974 / Columbia ✦✦✦
Extending a mean streak he'd already revealed more than once, Joel looks upon the star-making machinery that broke him the year before and scorns it. But he has such a gift for the putdown, notably in "Los Angelenos" and "The Entertainer," and the melodies are so good that you can't help singing along and agreeing with him. If you didn't already, that is. —*William Ruhlmann*

Turnstiles / May 1976 / Columbia ✦✦✦✦
Billy Joel's best, most consistent, most accessible record, even if not his best seller. From "Say Goodbye to Hollywood," which signals his return to the Big Apple with a drumbeat borrowed from the Ronettes, through the Sinatra ballad "New York State of Mind," the reflective "Summer, Highland Falls," and the hilarious "Miami 2017," Joel has never been more imaginative or more tuneful. Of course, "Angry Young Man" shows him to be as mean-spirited as ever, but the music carries even that one home. This record was the prototype to a virtual hit assembly line. —*William Ruhlmann*

The Stranger / Sep. 1977 / Columbia ✦✦✦✦
If *Turnstiles* was a creative breakthrough, *The Stranger* was where Billy Joel consolidated his skills into a commercial juggernaut. The difference isn't in melody or songcraft—*Turnstiles* exhibited those in abundance—but in presentation. Produced by Phil Ramone, *The Stranger* has a slick, glossy finish that coincides with Joel's shift towards more pop-oriented songwriting. Apart from the ballads "Just the Way You Are" and "She's Always a Woman," the songs represent a significant step forward from Joel's singer-songwriter roots. "Only the Good Die Young" bounces with a vigor unheard in his earlier albums, while "Movin' Out" and "The Stranger" are layered pop confections that nevertheless have serious lyrical undercurrents. In fact, it's clear that Joel intended *The Stranger* to be a concept album of sorts, writing songs about "the masks" people hide behind in their everyday lives—"The Stranger" theme is even reprised at the end fo the album—but he lacks the discipline or will to follow through on his

ambitions. Yet *The Stranger* stands as an excellent collection of songs, from the gospel stylings of "Everybody Has a Dream" to the center-piece "Scenes from an Italian Restaurant," which is constructed more like a Broadway show-stopper than the Springsteen-esque storytelling it is intended to be, and Joel rarely bettered it in terms of consistency. —*Stephen Thomas Erlewine*

52nd Street / Oct. 1978 / Columbia ✦✦✦✦
Joel consolidated his position with this somewhat harder rocking fol-low-up to *The Stranger,* which contained the hits "My Life," "Big Shot," and "Honesty." —*William Ruhlmann*

Glass Houses / Mar. 1980 / Columbia ✦✦✦
Billy Joel's response to punk, which, being a snotty kid himself, he felt a certain affinity with, and which allowed his usual belligerence unusu-ally free rein (an aspect of his work that can be tolerated only because it is unflinchingly honest and as often directed at himself as at others). Again, most of the best songs are on the *Greatest Hits,* but this is the only place you can get "Sometimes a Fantasy." —*William Ruhlmann*

Songs in the Attic / Sep. 1981 / Columbia ✦✦✦
Joel used his first live album to refocus attention on his pre-*Stranger* catalog, turning in new versions of worthy songs like "She's Got a Way" and "Say Goodbye to Hollywood," both of which now became Top 25 hits. —*William Ruhlmann*

The Nylon Curtain / Sep. 1982 / Columbia ✦✦✦✦
Upon release, Joel's eighth studio album was hailed by critics who had previously scorned him because he had decided to take on social con-cerns—the stress of modern life in "Pressure," unemployment in "Allen-town," and the Vietnam War in "Goodnight Saigon." In retrospect, those songs were the best of an uneven collection. —*William Ruhlmann*

An Innocent Man / Aug. 1983 / Columbia ✦✦✦
A brilliant evocation of popular styles of the early '60s, from doo wop to R&B, that is much more than a period exercise because it obviously is so deeply felt and because it is so well executed. And no one has sounded quite so guilty as the singer of the title track, whether he real-ized it or not. —*William Ruhlmann*

● **Greatest Hits, Vols. 1 & 2 (1973-1985)** / 1985 / Columbia ✦✦✦✦
Although it's missing a few important (not to mention big) hits, *Great-est Hits, Vols. 1 & 2* is an excellent retrospective of the first half of Billy Joel's career. Beginning with "Piano Man," the first disc runs through a number of early songs before arriving at the hit-making days of the late '70s; some of these songs, including "Captain Jack" and "New York State of Mind," weren't strictly hits, but were popular numbers within his stage show and became radio hits. Once the songs from *The Stranger* arrive halfway through the first disc, there's no stopping the hits (although "Scenes from an Italian Restaurant," an album track from *The Stranger,* manages its way onto the collection). In fact, over the next disc and a half, there are so many hits, it's inevitable that some are left off—to be specific, "Honesty," "Sometimes a Fantasy," "An Inno-cent Man," "Leave a Tender Moment," and "Keeping the Faith" aren't included. But all the other hits—including "Just the Way You Are," "Only the Good Die Young," "My Life," "You May Be Right," "It's Still Rock and Roll to Me," "Don't Ask Me Why," "Allentown," "Tell Her About It" and "Uptown Girl," among many others—*are* present and accounted for, as are two new songs ("You're Only Human (Second Wind)," "The Night Is Still Young") that became hits as well. In short, *Greatest Hits, Vols. 1 & 2* does its job perfectly, encapsulating exactly why Billy Joel was one of the most popular singer-songwriters of the late '70s and early '80s. —*Stephen Thomas Erlewine*

The Bridge / Jul. 1986 / Columbia ✦✦
The hits are "Modern Woman," "A Matter of Trust," and "This Is the Time," all melodic rockers in Joel's patented style. There is also "Baby Grand," a duet with Ray Charles. But, three years on, this wasn't a patch on *An Innocent Man* and suggested Joel's best work might be behind him. —*William Ruhlmann*

Kohuept (Live in Leningrad) / Oct. 1987 / Columbia ✦✦
Since Joel's concerts largely reproduce his studio recordings, and since he already has a greatest hits album out, a live record is inessential. The cachet of recording it in the old Soviet Union doesn't last over the years, and while the performances are fine, only completists need this record. Joel fans must have realized this, since the album was his first to miss the Top Ten in 11 years. —*William Ruhlmann*

Storm Front / Oct. 1989 / Columbia ✦✦
Joel caused a stampede for high school social science classes with the patter song "We Didn't Start the Fire," a cross between Gilbert and Sul-livan and rock 'n' roll that listed events in the news over the last 40 years, broken up by chants of the title. "I Go to Extremes" was a confes-sion of emotional instability set to a strong melody and a rocking beat. There was also minor entries, such as "The Downeaster 'Alexa,'" which was about Long Island fishermen, and "Shameless," which Garth Brooks turned into a country smash. And, as usual, there was about a side's worth of worthless filler. —*William Ruhlmann*

River of Dreams / Aug. 10, 1993 / Columbia ✦✦
Joel has reached middle age and he is still restless and angry. Fortu-nately, this results in some fine, adventurous music, making *River of Dreams* his strongest effort since *The Nylon Curtain.* Joel explores all of his favorite musical territory on this album, reaching back to doo wop, moving through Beatlesque pop, towards his trademark balladry. —*Stephen Thomas Erlewine*

David Johansen

b. Jan. 9, 1950, Staten Island, NY
Vocals / Rock 'n' Roll, Hard Rock
Best known for his tenure fronting the hugely influential New York Dolls, David Johansen was a true chameleon; throughout the course of a career which saw him transform from a lipstick-smeared proto-punk hero into an urbane blue-eyed soul man and finally into a tuxedo-clad lounge lizard, he remained a rock 'n' roll original, an unpredictable iconoclast, and a true cultural innovator.

Born January 9, 1950, in Staten Island, NY, Johansen joined his first band, the Vagabond Missionaries, in his mid-teens. A tenure with Fast Eddie and the Electric Japs, as well as an attempt to mount a career as a theatrical actor, followed before a club-hopping Johansen met bassist Arthur Kane, who extended an invitation to join his band Actress. After changing their name to the New York Dolls, the group began building a notorious reputation for their menacing, edgy music, drug-fueled life-style, and outrageously campy, drag queen-inspired glam image; although neither their eponymous 1973 debut nor 1974's *Too Much Too Soon* even cracked the Top 100, the Dolls established an enduring cult following, and their influence on the rise of punk was unmistak-able.

The Dolls officially broke up in 1975, although Johansen and guitar-ist Syl Sylvain continued performing under the group's name for two more years. Finally, in 1977, Johansen entered the recording studio with his support group, the Staten Island Boys, to cut his self-titled solo debut; while it sold no better than the Dolls' records, it did renew the critics' love affair with the singer and his gritty, soulful voice. With pro-ducer Mick Ronson, he returned in 1979 with the Motown-influenced *In Style,* followed in 1981 by the commercial-minded *Here Comes the Night.*

While 1982's concert set *Live It Up* won some airplay for its medley of the Animals hits "We Gotta Get Out of This Place," "It's My Life," and "Don't Bring Me Down," Johansen was forced to reassess his career when 1984's dance-flavored *Sweet Revenge* tanked. At the end of 1984, he resurfaced in the pompadoured guise of Buster Poindexter, a sup-posed ethnomusicologist armed with an expansive knowledge of R&B chestnuts. After debuting the Buster character at a series of mid-1980s downtown New York loft gigs with the Uptown Horns, Johansen con-tinued honing the identity in the piano bars of Manhattan, establishing a lounge swinger persona which predated the lounge-kitsch revival of the mid-1990s by a decade.

As Poindexter's popularity grew, he began fronting a large band dubbed the Banshees in Blue and building a devoted following on the New York club circuit. In 1987, he issued an LP, *Buster Poindexter,* which featured the party classic "Hot Hot Hot," an effervescent cover of an obscure 1984 soca hit. In addition to reviving Johansen's career as a musical performer, Buster also renewed his long-dormant acting bug, and he was tapped to co-star in the 1988 features *Married to the Mob* and *Scrooged.* The character remained Johansen's focus in subsequent years as well, as evidenced by the albums *Buster Goes Berserk* in 1989 and *Buster's Happy Hour* in 1994. —*Jason Ankeny*

David Johansen / May 1978 / Razor & Tie ✦✦✦✦
True, the best songs here ("Frenchette," "Funky but Chic," "Girls") are the ones Johansen brought with him from the Dolls. What's intriguing about his solo debut, though, is how well he pulls off ballads like "Donna" and "Pain in My Heart." And Johnny Rao's guitar work *almost* compensates for the absence of Johnny Thunders, the Dolls' guitarist. —*John Floyd*

Live / Oct. 1978 / Columbia/Legacy ✦✦✦

In Style / 1979 / Razor & Tie ✦✦✦
Despite the presence of guitarist Mick Ronson, David Johansen's sec-ond solo album *In Style* wasn't a collection of blistering glam-rock. Instead, Johansen began to expand the boundaries of his music, adding elements of disco, soul, and reggae. Occasionally, the soul inflections work, but the songs are by and large weaker than the ones on his first album, although any record with a song as beautiful as "Melody" is worthwhile. —*Stephen Thomas Erlewine*

Here Comes the Night / 1982 / Razor & Tie ✦✦
David Johansen returned to straightahead rock 'n' roll with his third album, *Here Comes the Night,* but the combination of uninspired mate-rial and slick, professional music made the record his weakest effort to date. —*Stephen Thomas Erlewine*

Live It Up / Jun. 1982 / Razor & Tie ✦✦✦✦

A scorching live set from 1982, it also works as a career-defining best-of. Johansen drives his roadhouse band through a few old Dolls hits, the best cuts from his solo albums, and a medley of Animals hits that damn near outstrips the originals. And don't miss the two Motown covers. —*John Floyd*

Sweet Revenge / 1984 / M.I.L. Multimedia ✦✦✦

The live album *Live It Up* gave David Johansen a surprise MTV hit with an Animals medley and he attempted to continue his success with *Sweet Revenge*. Unlike his previous albums, *Sweet Revenge* is driven by synthesizers, but Johansen hasn't abandoned hard rock. The synths add a stylish sheen to his slyly powerful songs, which have some of his cleverest lyrics and melodies. Overall, the record is his strongest since his debut. —*Stephen Thomas Erlewine*

The Live at the Bottom Line / Feb. 2, 1993 / CBS ✦✦✦

Live at the Bottom Line is taken from a late-'70s show at the famous New York club and it captures David Johansen in all of his hard rock glory, even if the album isn't quite as impressive as *Live It Up*. —*Stephen Thomas Erlewine*

● **From Pumps to Pompadour: The David Johansen Story** / Oct. 1995 / Rhino ✦✦✦✦

Drawing from all three phases of David Johansen's career, *From Pumps to Pompadours: The David Johansen Story* is a comprehensive retrospective of the hard rocker's career. Only three songs date from his influential days with the New York Dolls ("Trash," "Personality Crisis," "Babylon"), but that has been the most well-documented period of his career. While his biggest hits—in fact, his only hits—are the five Buster Poindexter tracks at the end of the disc, the middle portion of the album, which selects the highlights from his overlooked solo albums of the late '70s and early '80s, is where most of the best material lies. From the sleazy rush of "Funky But Chic" to the savage Animals medley "We Gotta Get out of This Place / Don't Bring Me Down / It's My Life," the 11 solo tracks make a case for Johansen being one of the finest hard rockers of his era. —*Stephen Thomas Erlewine*

John's Children

f. 1966, England, **db.** 1968
British Invasion, Psychedelic

Because Marc Bolan—soon to become T. Rex—was briefly a member, John's Children are perhaps accorded more reverence by '60s collectors and aficionados than they deserve. Still, they were an interesting, if minor, blip on the British mod and psychedelic scene during their relatively brief existence (1966-68), although they were perhaps more notable for their flamboyant image and antics than their music. Yardbirds manager Simon Napier-Bell recalled that they were "positively the worst group I'd ever seen" when he chanced upon them in France in 1966, yet he was conned into taking them on as clients. Not proficient enough to be trusted to play on their own records, their first single, "Smashed Blocked"/"Strange Affair," was recorded with sessionmen in late 1966. This disorienting piece of musical mayhem, opening with a crescendo of swirling organs and an otherworldly over-reverbed vocal, was one of the first overtly psychedelic singles. Their improbable saga was launched when the single actually reached the bottom depths of the US Top 100, cracking the Top Ten in some Florida and California markets. The group's US company, White Whale, requested an album, which it shelved when it received an LP with the then-unthinkable title, *Orgasm*. The actual album consisted of mediocre studio material smothered in audience screams lifted from the *A Hard Day's Night* soundtrack, and was, bizarrely, actually released in 1971 (and reissued a decade later). Their second single, "Just What You Want—Just What You'll Get"/"But You're Mine," reached the British Top 40, and featured a guitar solo by recently departed Yardbird Jeff Beck on the B-side. A brief German tour followed, during with they managed to upstage the headliners, the Who (with their theatrics, not their music).

At this point, Marc Bolan joined the group for a time as their principal singer and songwriter; details are hazy, but he recorded at least one single with the group, "Desdemona" (which was banned by the BBC for the line "lift up your skirt and fly"), as well as several unreleased cuts that have surfaced on reissues. Bolan departed in a squabble with Napier-Bell, and the group released a couple more flop singles before disbanding in 1968. Their halfdozen singles rank among the most collectible British '60s rock artifacts, and the group—who actually managed some decent modish power-pop, once they'd learned their way around their instruments a bit—were acclaimed as pre-glam rockers of sorts by historians. Andy Ellison (the group's lead singer except during Bolan's brief tenure) recorded some decent pop singles at the end of the '60s, and members of John's Children were involved with the obscure British groups Jook, Jet, and Radio Stars in the 1970s. —*Richie Unterberger*

Legendary Orgasm Album / 1982 / Cherry Red ✦✦✦

The first readily available edition of *Orgasm*. The skimpy, vaguely Who-ish songs are nearly buried under the mountainous overdubs of hysterical teenage screams, making this a true artifact—and nothing more—of an era. The reissue includes excellent liner notes and four bonus tracks—the fine psychedelic single "Smashed Blocked" and its decent follow-up, "Just What You Want—Just What You'll Get," the B-side of which ("But You're Mine") is an unabashed ripoff of the Who's "I Can't Explain." Be warned that the version of "Strange Affair" (the B-side of "Smashed Blocked") included here has, for some inexplicable reason, been presented backwards! —*Richie Unterberger*

Instant Action / 1985 / Hawkeye ✦✦✦

A hard-to-find collection of 18 rare and unreleased tracks by the band. It doesn't include three of the four songs on their first two singles, but it includes their ultra-rare follow-ups, as well as some rawer, unreleased versions of those later singles and some Andy Ellison solo 45s. The material borrows from the poppiest aspects of the Who and sprinkles in some campy British psychedelia; Bolan's songs and vocals are quite T. Rex-like, even at this early stage. They manage to get a bit tougher with "Jagged Time Lapse," with crashing drums and power chords aplenty. Ellison's solo singles are quite interesting, especially the oddball folk-psychedelic "Cornflake Zoo" and the bizarre lounge/soul version of the Beatles' "Help!" (unlisted on the sleeve). Includes voluminous liner notes. —*Richie Unterberger*

● **Midsummer Night's Scene** / 1987 / Bam Caruso ✦✦✦✦

The A—and B-sides of all of their singles, plus the Andy Ellison solo number "It's Been a Long Time." It's missing some interesting material from *Instant Action*, but it's generally the best anthology available, as well as the only readily obtainable one. Comes with another set of fine, exhaustive liner notes—has a minor band ever been as well-documented by loving liner notes as John's Children has? —*Richie Unterberger*

Midsummer Night's Scene [EP] / 1988 / Bam Caruso ✦✦✦

A four-song 12", with the title cut (a single from the Marc Bolan era that never made it past the test pressing stage) and three previously unreleased tracks: Ellison's nifty solo cuts "Help" and "Casbah Candy," and "Hippy Gumbo" (a Bolan composition with the whole group). One for the collectors. —*Richie Unterberger*

It's Child's Play / 1989 / Zonophone ✦✦✦

Yet more unreleased tracks. This four-song, seven-inch EP is actually fairly worthwhile, capturing a somewhat rawer and more rock-oriented sound than the official singles. Includes the Bolan compositions "Hot Rod Mama" and "Perfumed Garden," as well as a cover of the R&B tune "Daddy Rolling Stone," which the Who had covered in a similar bashing power-chord style on the B-side of their second single. —*Richie Unterberger*

Elton John (Reginald Dwight)

b. Mar. 25, 1947, Pinner, Middlesex, England
Piano, Vocals / Rock 'n' Roll, Singer-Songwriter, Adult Contemporary, Soft Rock, Pop-Rock

In terms of sales and lasting popularity, Elton John was the biggest pop superstar of the early '70s. Initially marketed as a singer-songwriter, John revealed he could craft Beatlesque pop and pound out rockers with equal aplomb. He could dip into soul, disco, and country, as well as classic pop balladry and even progressive rock. His versatility, combined with his effortless melodic skills, dynamic charisma, and flamboyant stage shows, made him the most popular recording artist of the '70s. Unlike many pop stars, John was able to sustain his popularity, charting a Top 40 single every single year from 1970 to 1996. During that time, he had temporary slumps in creativity and sales, as he fell out of favor with critics, had fights with his lyricist Bernie Taupin, and battled various addictions and public scandals. But through it all, John remained a remarkably popular artist and many of his songs—including "Your Song," "Rocket Man," "Goodbye Yellow Brick Road," and "Don't Let the Sun Go Down On Me"—became contemporary pop standards.

The son of a former Royal Air Force trumpeter, Elton John was born Reginald Kenneth Dwight in 1947. Dwight began playing piano at the age of four, and when he was 11, he won a scholarship to the Royal Academy of Music. After studying for six years, he left school with the intention of breaking into the music business. In 1961, he joined his first band, Bluesology, and divided his time between playing with the group, giving solo concerts at a local hotel, and running errands for a London publishing house. By 1965, Bluesology were backing touring American soul and R&B musicians like Major Lance, Doris Troy, and the Bluebells. In 1966, Bluesology became Long John Baldry's supporting band, and began touring cabarets throughout England. Dwight became frustrated with Baldry's control of the band and began searching for other groups to join. He failed his lead vocalist auditions with both King Crimson and Gentle Giant before responding to an advertisement by Liberty Records. Though he failed his Liberty audition, he was given a stack of lyrics Bernie Taupin, who had also replied to the ad, had left with the label. Dwight wrote music for Taupin's lyrics and began corresponding with him through mail. By the time the two met six months later, Dwight had changed his name to Elton John, taking his first name from Bluesology saxophonist Elton Dean and his last from John Baldry.

John and Taupin were hired by Dick James to become staff songwriters at his fledgling DJM in 1968. The pair collaborated at a rapid rate, with Taupin submitting batches of lyrics—he often wrote a song an hour—every few weeks. John would then write music without changing the words, sometimes completing the songs in under a half hour. Over the next two years, the duo wrote songs for pop singers like Roger Cook and Lulu. In the meantime, John recorded cover versions of current hits for budget labels to be sold in supermarkets. By the summer of 1968, he had begun recording singles for release under his own name. Usually, these songs were more rock- and radio-oriented than the tunes he and Taupin were giving to other vocalists, yet neither of his early singles for Phillips, "I've Been Loving You Too Long" and "Lady Samantha," sold well. In June of 1969, he released his debut album for DJM, *Empty Sky*, which received fair reviews, but no sales.

For his second album, John and Taupin hired producer Gus Dudgeon and arranger Paul Buckmaster, who contributed grandiose string charts to *Elton John*. Released in the summer of 1970, *Elton John* began to make inroads in America, where it appeared on MCA's Uni subsidiary. In August, he gave his first American concert at the Troubadour in Los Angeles, which received enthusiastic reviews, as well as praise from Quincy Jones and Leon Russell. Throughout the fall, *Elton John* continued to climb the charts on the strength of the Top 10 single, "Your Song." John followed it quickly in February 1971 with the concept album *Tumbleweed Connection*, which received heavy airplay on album-oriented radio in the US, helping it climb into the Top 10. The rapid release of *Tumbleweed Connection* established a pattern of frequent releases that John maintained throughout his career. In 1971, he released the live *11-17-70* and the *Friends* soundtrack, before releasing *Madman Across the Water* late in the year. *Madman Across the Water* was successful, but John achieved stardom with the followup, 1972's *Honky Chateau*. Recorded with his touring band—bassist Dee Murray, drummer Nigel Olsson, and guitarist Davey Johnstone—and featuring the hit singles "Rocket Man" and "Honky Cat," *Honky Chateau* became his first American No. 1 album, spending five weeks at the top of the charts.

Between 1972 and 1976, Elton John and Bernie Taupin's hit-making machine was virtually unstoppable. "Rocket Man" began a four-year streak of 16 Top 20 hits in a row; out of those 16—including "Crocodile Rock," "Daniel," "Bennie and the Jets," "The Bitch Is Back," and "Philadelphia Freedom"—only one, the FM hit "Saturday Night's Alright for Fighting," failed to reach the Top Ten. *Honky Chateau* began a streak of seven consecutive No. 1 albums—*Don't Shoot Me I'm Only the Piano Player* (1973), *Goodbye Yellow Brick Road* (1973), *Caribou* (1974), *Greatest Hits* (1974), *Captain Fantastic and the Brown Dirt Cowboy* (1975), *Rock of the Westies* (1975)—that all went platinum. John founded Rocket, a record label distributed by MCA, in 1973 in order to sign and produce acts like Neil Sedaka and Kiki Dee. John didn't become a Rocket recording artist himself, choosing to stay with MCA for a record-breaking $8 million dollar contract in 1974. Later in 1974, he co-wrote John Lennon's No. 1 comeback single, "Whatever Gets You Through the Night," and he persuaded Lennon to join him onstage at Madison Square Garden on Thanksgiving Day 1974; it would prove to be Lennon's last live performance. The following year, *Captain Fantastic* became the first album to enter the American charts at No. 1. After its release, he revamped his band, which now featured Johnstone, Quaye, Roger Pope, Ray Cooper, and bassist Kenny Passarelli; *Rock of the Westies* was the first album to feature this lineup.

Throughout the mid-'70s, John's concerts were enormously popular, as were his singles and albums, and he continued to record and perform at a rapid pace until 1976. That year, he revealed in an interview in *Rolling Stone* that he was bisexual; he would later admit that the confession was a compromise, since he was afraid to reveal that he was homosexual. Many fans reacted negatively to John's bisexuality, and his audience began to shrink somewhat in the late '70s. The decline in his record sales was also due to his exhaustion. After 1976, John cut his performance schedule drastically, announcing that he was retiring from live performances in 1977, and started recording only one album a year. His relationship with Taupin became strained following the release of 1976's double-album *Blue Moves*, and the lyricist began working with other musicians. John returned in 1978 with *A Single Man*, which was written with Gary Osborne; the record produced no Top 20 singles. That year, he returned to live performances, first by jamming at the *Live Stiffs* package tour, then by launching a comeback tour in 1979 accompanied only by percussionist Ray Cooper. "Mama Can't Buy You Love," a song he recorded with Philly soul producer

Thom Bell in 1977, returned him to the Top Ten in 1979, but that year's *Victim of Love* was a commercial disappointment.

John reunited with Taupin for 1980's *21 at 33*, which featured the Top 10 single "Little Jeannie." Over the next three years, John remained a popular concert artist, but his singles failed to break the Top 10, even if they reached the Top 40. In 1981, he signed with Geffen Records and his second album, *Jump Up!*, became a gold album on the strength of "Blue Eyes" and "Empty Garden (Hey Hey Johnny)," his tribute to John Lennon. But it was 1983's *Too Low for Zero* that began his last great streak of hit singles, with the MTV hit "I'm Still Standing" and the Top Ten single "I Guess That's Why They Call It the Blues." Throughout the rest of the '80s, John's albums would consistently go gold, and they always generated at least one Top 40 single; frequently, they featured Top 10 singles like "Sad Songs (Say So Much)" (1984), "Nikita" (1986), "Candle in the Wind" (1987), and "I Don't Want to Go on with You Like That" (1988). While his career continued to be successful, his personal life was in turmoil. Since the mid-'70s, he had been addicted to cocaine and alcohol, and the situation only worsened during the '80s. In a surprise move, he married engineer Renate Blauel in 1984; the couple stayed married for four years, although John later admitted he realized he was homosexual before his marriage. In 1986, he underwent throat surgery while on tour, but even after he successfully recovered, he continued to abuse cocaine and alocohol.

Following a record-breaking, five-date stint at Madison Square Garden in 1988, John auctioned off all of his theatrical costumes, thousands of pieces of memorabilia, and his extensive record collection through Sotheby's. The auction was a symbolic turning point. Over the next two years, John battled both his drug addiction and bulimia, undergoing hair replacement surgery at the same time. By 1991, he was sober and the following year, he established the Elton John AIDS Foundation; he also announced that he would donate all royalties from his single sales to AIDS research.

In 1992, John returned to active recording with *The One*. Peaking at No. 8 on the US charts and going double platinum, the album became his most successful record since *Blue Moves*, and sparked a career renaissance for John. He and Taupin signed a record-breaking publishing deal with Warner/Chappell Music in 1992 for an estimated $39 million. In 1994, John collaborated with lyricist Tim Rice on songs for Disney's animated feature *The Lion King*. One of their collaborations, "Can You Feel the Love Tonight," won the Academy Award for Best Original Song, as well as the Grammy for Best Male Pop Vocal Performance. John's 1995 album *Made in England* continued his comeback, peaking at No. 3 on the UK charts and No. 13 in the US; in America, the album went platinum. —*Stephen Thomas Erlewine*

Empty Sky / 1969 / MCA ✦✦
Although he had made a number of re-recordings of popular songs for a budget record label in the late '60s, *Empty Sky* was the first true solo album John recorded after leaving Bluesology; it also marked the beginning of his long and fruitful collaboration with lyricist Bernie Taupin. *Empty Sky* is quite indicative of the post-*Sgt. Pepper* era. With its ambitious arrangements and lyrics, it's clear that John and Taupin intended the album to be a major statement. Though it shows some signs of John's R&B roots, most of the album alternates between vaguely psychedelic rock and burgeoning pop songcraft, capped off by a bizarre reprise of brief moments of *all* of the songs on the record. There aren't any forgotten gems on *Empty Sky*, but it does suggest John's potential. (The CD reissue includes the bonus tracks "Lady Samantha," "All Across the Havens," "It's Me That You Need," and "Just Like Strange Rain.") — *Stephen Thomas Erlewine*

Elton John / Aug. 1970 / MCA ✦✦✦✦
Empty Sky was followed by *Elton John*, a more focused and realized record that deservedly became his first hit. John and Taupin's songwriting had become more immediate and successful; in particular, John's music had become sharper and more diverse, rescuing Taupin's frequently nebulous lyrics. "Take Me to the Pilot" might not make much sense lyrically, but John had the good sense to ground its willfully cryptic words with a catchy blues-based melody. Next to the increased sense of songcraft, the most noticeable change on *Elton John* is the addition of Paul Buckmaster's grandiose string arrangements. Buckmaster's orchestrations are never subtle, but they never overwhelm the vocalist, nor do they make the songs schmaltzy. Instead, they fit the ambitions of John and Taupin, as the instant standard "Your Song" illustrates. Even with the strings and choirs that dominate the sound of the album, John manages to rock out on a fair share of the record. Though there are a couple of underdeveloped songs, *Elton John* remains one of his best records. (The CD reissue includes the bonus tracks "Bad Side of the Moon," "Grey Seal," and "Rock 'n' Roll Madonna.") — *Stephen Thomas Erlewine*

☆ **Tumbleweed Connection** / Jan. 1971 / MCA ✦✦✦✦
Instead of repeating the formula that made *Elton John* a success, John and Taupin attempted their most ambitious record to date for the fol-

low-up to their breakthrough. A loose concept album about the American West, *Tumbleweed Connection* emphasized the pretensions that always lay beneath their songcraft. Half of the songs don't follow conventional pop song structures; instead, they flow between verses and vague choruses. These experiments are remarkably successful, primarily because Taupin's lyrics are evocative and John's melodic sense is at its best. As should be expected for a concept album about the Wild West, the music draws from country and blues in equal measures, ranging from the bluesy choruses of "Ballad of a Well-Known Gun" and the modified country of "Country Comfort" to the gospel-inflected "Burn Down the Mission" and the rolling, soulful "Amoreena." Paul Buckmaster manages to write dramatic but appropriate string arrangements that accentuate the cinematic feel of the album. (The CD reissue includes the bonus tracks "Into the Old Man's Shoes" and the original, stringless version of "Madman Across the Water.") — *Stephen Thomas Erlewine*

11-17-70 / Mar. 1971 / MCA ✦✦✦
Elton John's fourth album release in less than a year was a bootleg-beating live album culled from a concert broadcast on a New York radio station that also served the function of bridging the gap in the public perceptions of John as the soft balladeer of "Your Song" on the one hand and the piano-stool-throwing rock 'n' roller who was appearing in concert on the other. Here, John essayed songs like "Honky Tonk Women" and generally acted like a rock 'n' roll animal. — *William Ruhlmann*

Madman Across the Water / Nov. 1971 / MCA ✦✦✦✦
Trading the cinematic aspirations of *Tumbleweed Connection* for a tentative stab at prog-rock, Elton John and Bernie Taupin delivered another excellent collection of songs with *Madman Across the Water*. Like its two predecessors, *Madman Across the Water* is driven by the sweeping string arrangements of Paul Buckmaster, who gives the songs here a richly dark and haunting edge. And these are songs that benefit from grandiose treatments. With most songs clocking in around five minutes, the record feels like a major work, and in many ways it is. While it's not as adventurous as *Tumbleweed Connection*, the overall quality of the record is very high, particularly on character sketches "Levon" and "Razor Face," as well as the melodramatic "Tiny Dancer" and the paranoid title track. *Madman Across the Water* begins to fall apart toward the end, but the record remains an ambitious and rewarding work, and John never attained its darkly introspective atmosphere again. — *Stephen Thomas Erlewine*

☆ **Honky Chateau** / May 1972 / MCA ✦✦✦✦✦
Considerably lighter than *Madman Across the Water*, *Honky Chateau* is a rollicking collection of ballads, rockers, blues, country-rock, and soul songs. On paper, it reads like an eclectic mess, but it plays as the most focused and accomplished set of songs Elton John and Bernie Taupin ever wrote. The skittering boogie of "Honky Cat" and the light psychedelic pop of "Rocket Man" helped send *Honky Chateau* to the top of the charts, but what is truly impressive about the album is the depth of its material. From the surprisingly cynical and nasty "I Think I'm Gonna Kill Myself" to the moving ballad "Mona Lisas and Mad Hatters," John is at the top of his form, crafting immaculate pop songs with memorable melodies and powerful hooks. While Taupin's lyrics aren't much more comprehensible than before, John delivers them with skill and passion, making them feel more substantial than they are. But what makes *Honky Chateau* a classic is the songcraft, and the way John ties disparate strands of roots music into distinctive and idiosyncratic pop—it's one of the finest collections of mainstream singer-songwriter pop of the early '70s. — *Stephen Thomas Erlewine*

Don't Shoot Me I'm Only the Piano Player / Jan. 1973 / MCA ✦✦✦
Elton John became a true superstar with 1972's *Honky Chateau*. He followed that album with *Don't Shoot Me I'm Only the Piano Player*, his most direct, pop-oriented album to date. Designed as a pastiche of classic and contemporary pop styles, the album almost sounds like an attempt to demonstrate the diversity of the John/Taupin team. Though the hits are remarkable—"Daniel" is a moving ballad and "Crocodile Rock" is a sly take on '50s rock 'n' roll—the album is slightly uneven. Several of the album tracks, particularly the knowing "I'm Gonna Be a Teenage Idol" and the rocking "Elderberry Wine," are as strong as anything John had recorded, but there are too many melodies that simply don't catch hold. Nevertheless, the singles were strong enough to keep the album at the top of the charts and at its best, it is a very enjoyable piece of well-crafted pop-rock. (The CD reissue includes the bonus tracks "Screw You (Young Man's Blues)," "Jack Rabbit," "Whenever You're Ready (We'll Go Steady Again)," and the piano version of "Skyline Pigeon.") — *Stephen Thomas Erlewine*

Goodbye Yellow Brick Road / Oct. 1973 / MCA ✦✦✦✦
Goodbye Yellow Brick Road was where Elton John's personality began to gather more attention than his music, as it topped the American charts for eight straight weeks. In many ways, the double album was a recap of all the styles and sounds that made John a star. *Goodbye Yel-*

low Brick Road is all over the map, beginning with the prog-rock epic "Funeral for a Friend (Love Lies Bleeding)" and immediately careening into the balladry of "Candle in the Wind." For the rest of the album, John leaps between pop-craft ("Bennie and the Jets"), ballads ("Goodbye Yellow Brick Road"), hard rock ("Saturday Night's Alright for Fighting"), novelties ("Jamaica Jerk-Off"), Taupin's literary pretensions ("The Ballad of Danny Bailey"), and everything in between. Though its diversity is impressive, the album doesn't hold together very well. Even so, its individual moments are spectacular and the glitzy, crowd-pleasing showmanship that fuels the album pretty much defines what made Elton John a superstar in the early '70s. — *Stephen Thomas Erlewine*

Caribou / Jun. 1974 / MCA ✦✦
Glitzy showmanship is what fuels *Caribou*, the least successful collection to be reissued in this batch of albums. Though the shiny surface of the album is alluring, only a few tracks on the record rank among John's best work. "The Bitch Is Back" is one of his best hard rock cuts, and "Don't Let the Sun Go Down on Me" is one of his classic ballads, but the album tracks tend to be ridiculous filler on the order of "Solar Prestige a Gammon" or competent genre exercises like "You're So Static." There are a couple of exceptions—"Pinky" is a fine ballad and "Dixie Lily" is an endearing stab at country—but on the whole, *Caribou* is a disappointment. (The CD reissue includes the bonus tracks "Pinball Wizard," "Sick City," "Cold Highway," and "Step into Christmas.") — *Stephen Thomas Erlewine*

★ **Greatest Hits** / Nov. 1974 / MCA ✦✦✦✦✦
Rarely has a greatest hits collection been as effective as Elton John's first compilation of *Greatest Hits*. Released at the end of 1974, after *Goodbye Yellow Brick Road* and *Caribou* had effectively established him as a superstar, *Greatest Hits* is exactly what it says it is—it features every one of his Top 10 singles ("Your Song," "Rocket Man," "Honky Cat," "Crocodile Rock," "Daniel," "Goodbye Yellow Brick Road," "Bennie and the Jets," "Don't Let the Sun Go Down on Me"), plus the No. 12 "Saturday Night's Alright for Fighting" and radio and concert favorites "Border Song" and "Candle in the Wind." Despite the exclusion of a couple of lesser hits from this era, most notably "Levon" and "Tiny Dancer," *Greatest Hits* is a nearly flawless collection, offering a perfect introduction to Elton John and providing casual fans with almost all the hits they need. — *Stephen Thomas Erlewine*

Captain Fantastic & The Brown Dirt Cowboy / May 1975 / MCA ✦✦✦✦
Bernie Taupin's most ambitious lyrical effort, *Captain Fantastic & the Brown Dirt Cowboy* is an autobiographical song cycle that also drew an unusually strong musical effort from John, resulting in perhaps his strongest overall record since *Tumbleweed Connection*. — *William Ruhlmann*

Rock of the Westies / Oct. 1975 / MCA ✦✦
The title signals that this album is short on ballads and long on bouncers; the hit was "Island Girl," but the real key to this album's thinness is that it came a mere five months after its ambitious predecessor, and even for Elton and Bernie, that's a bit too soon to expect much quality. — *William Ruhlmann*

Here & There / May 1976 / MCA ✦✦
One side from a May 1974 London concert, one side from a November 1974 New York concert, released a year and a half later for the 1976 summer buying season when the artist didn't have a new studio recording ready, this second Elton John live album looks suspiciously like product and sounds like it, too. — *William Ruhlmann*

Blue Moves / Oct. 1976 / MCA ✦✦
An unprecedented year in the making, the two-record *Blue Moves* was Elton John's opening farewell, a dreary song cycle full of self-pity and recycled melodies by an artist who had finally run out of gas. The inevitable hit was "Sorry Seems to Be the Hardest Word," although "Tonight," the album's other memorable song, was just as indicative of the low emotional ebb of the John-Taupin team. As the Mamas and the Papas once said in an LP title, "Farewell to the first golden era." — *William Ruhlmann*

☆ **Greatest Hits, Vol. 2** / Sep. 1977 / MCA ✦✦✦✦✦
Greatest Hits, Vol. 2 rounds up the handful of singles that weren't included on Elton John's first *Greatest Hits* collection ("Levon," "Tiny Dancer") and adds the highlights from *Caribou*, *Captain Fantastic and the Brown Dirt Cowboy*, and *Rock of the Westies* ("The Bitch is Back," "Someone Saved My Life Tonight," "Island Girl," "Grow Some Funk of Your Own," "I Feel Like a Bullet (In the Gun of Robert Ford)"), plus two non-LP hit singles ("Lucy in the Sky with Diamonds," "Philadelphia Freedom") and John's version of "Pinball Wizard," taken from the soundtrack to *Tommy*. In short, it's an excellent continuation of the first collection and taken together, they function as an ideal singles retrospective of the most successful singles artist of the early '70s. — *Stephen Thomas Erlewine*

A Single Man / Oct. 1978 / MCA ✦✦✦
An unusually well-crafted album, and the beginning of John's come-back. "Part-Time Love" was the hit, but "Madness" and the instrumental "Song for Guy" were musical highlights. — *William Ruhlmann*

Victim of Love / 1979 / MCA ✦
As he had in 1977 with Thom Bell, Elton John turned to German disco producer Pete Bellotte in 1979, acting only as the singer over Bellotte's tracks. It was a disaster: there were no hits, and *Victim of Love* was John's first new studio album not to go gold. This was the bottom of the decline John had been in artistically and commercially since 1976. — *William Ruhlmann*

21 at 33 / May 1980 / MCA ✦✦✦
An ambitious songwriting effort featuring Tom Robinson's collaboration on "Sartorial Eloquence" and Gary Osborne's on "Little Jeannie," although the best songs are by the returning Bernie Taupin: "Chasing the Crown" and "Two Rooms at the End of the World." — *William Ruhlmann*

The Fox / 1981 / MCA ✦✦
Sounding like it contained outtakes from the superior *21 at 33, The Fox* found Elton John still hedging his bets, writing four songs with Bernie Taupin, but still collaborating with Gary Osborne, Tom Robinson, and James Newton Howard. And the album's No. 21 single, "Nobody Wins," was a Eurodisco cover. Altogether, a bump on the comeback road and not an auspicious beginning to John's tenure at Geffen Records. The album has since been acquired by MCA. — *William Ruhlmann*

Jump Up! / Apr. 1982 / MCA ✦✦✦
John began finding his greatest successes with ballads in the 1980s, and this album still finds him mixing collaborators, including Tim Rice (with whom he would write the 1994 soundtrack to *The Lion King*), this time to good effect: Gary Osborne contributes "Blue Eyes," while Bernie Taupin effectively eulogizes John Lennon in "Empty Garden." Originally on Geffen, this album has since been acquired by MCA. — *William Ruhlmann*

Too Low for Zero / May 1983 / Geffen ✦✦✦✦
With Taupin (and his old band) on board full-time, John turned out one of his best '80s albums—one full of remorse ("Cold as Christmas") and fierce reaffirmation ("I'm Still Standing"), not to mention such irresistible tunes as "Kiss the Bride" and "I Guess That's Why They Call It the Blues." — *William Ruhlmann*

Breaking Hearts / Jul. 1984 / Geffen ✦✦✦
This album was paced by its No. 5 big ballad hit, "Sad Songs (Say So Much)," one of Elton John's most memorable latter day tunes. There were also two more Top 40 entries in "Who Wears These Shoes?" and "In Neon," but in retrospect, this is one of John's slighter albums of the '80s. — *William Ruhlmann*

Ice on Fire / Nov. 1985 / Geffen ✦✦
Elton John's relationship with Geffen Records seems to have been deteriorating by this point, and his regular output of one album a year was becoming rote. This one contains the No. 7 ballad "Nikita," and a pleasant uptempo song, "Wrap Her Up," but is otherwise undistinguished. The CD added the single "Act of War," a raucous workout with Millie Jackson that immediately became the album's standout track. — *William Ruhlmann*

Leather Jackets / 1986 / Geffen ✦✦
This pedestrian throwaway of an album represents the end of Elton John's contractual commitment to Geffen Records and, as happens with these things, was buried, becoming perhaps the singer's worst-selling album ever. In retrospect, it deserved a better fate, but not much better. — *William Ruhlmann*

Elton John Live in Australia (With the Melbourne Symphony Orchestra) / Jun. 1987 / MCA ✦✦
The first mystery is why Elton John would decide to mark his return to MCA Records with a live album of some of his wimpiest music swamped in strings. The second mystery is why he pressed on with this plan even though his voice was in such terrible shape that, right after the concert, he underwent throat surgery. The final mystery is why the album did so well, and the answer to that may be that "Candle in the Wind," that wimpy tribute to Marilyn Monroe from *Goodbye Yellow Brick Road*, finally was released as a single in the US, where it soared to No. 6. So, go figure. — *William Ruhlmann*

Greatest Hits, Vol. 3 (1979-1987) / Sep. 1987 / Geffen ✦✦✦✦
Greatest Hits, Vol. 3 (1979-1987) is a 12-track that compiles the bulk of Elton John's biggest hits from the '80s, including such classic tracks as "Little Jeannie," "I Guess That's Why They Call It the Blues," "Empty Garden," "Blue Eyes," "I'm Still Standing" and "Sad Songs (Say So Much)." It also includes the previously unreleased "Heartache All Over the World," a new single that failed to make the Top 40, as well as "Too Low for Zero," which never was a single. *Greatest Hits, Vol. 3* went out

of print after John left Geffen for MCA, who issued a replacement package, *Greatest Hits 1976-1986*, which eliminates those two songs and adds "Sorry Seems to Be the Hardest Word," "Don't Go Breaking My Heart," and "Who Wears These Shoes?" to the remaining ten songs. — *Stephen Thomas Erlewine*

Reg Strikes Back / Jun. 1988 / MCA ✦✦
As Elton John's first album for MCA Records, *Reg Strikes Back* received a considerable amount of hype upon its release, but the results were considerably less-inspired than his early-'80s records for Geffen. It's always a bad sign when an artist re-records or re-interprets one of his classics, as John does here with "Mona Lisas and Mad Hatters, Pt. 2," but what really sinks *Reg Strikes Back* is the colorless tunes. Apart from the clenched dance-pop of "I Don't Wanna Go on with You Like That" and the simpy "A Word in Spanish," none of the melodies on the record are memorable, and even those aren't particularly strong. Instead of re-charging his career, *Reg Strikes Back* began a dry spell that ran for nearly five years. — *Stephen Thomas Erlewine*

The Complete Thom Bell Sessions / 1989 / MCA ✦✦✦
Elton John released a three-song EP from his abortive 1977 sessions with Philadelphia International producer Thom Bell in 1979. Ten years later, he issued a six-song EP containing the initial three tracks and three more that are unremarkable. The things an artist will do for record collectors . . . — *William Ruhlmann*

Sleeping with the Past / Aug. 1989 / MCA ✦✦
The past Elton John has in mind is the era of soul music of the mid-1960s to the mid-1970s, and although all the songs are new, he re-creates it well here. The album's most notable selection is the ballad "Sacrifice," which amazingly became his first-ever No. 1 hit in the UK. — *William Ruhlmann*

To Be Continued . . . / 1990 / MCA ✦✦✦✦
The inevitable Elton John box set is a four-disc, 68-track affair covering 25 years of the biggest pop star since the Beatles. Hit after hit is heard, plus good album tracks and rarities. There's a big booklet with commentary by John and his lyricist, Bernie Taupin. In a pinch, you can get by with the two MCA and one Geffen greatest hits collections, but for a complete overview of Elton John's career, this is the place to come. — *William Ruhlmann*

The One / Jun. 23, 1992 / MCA ✦✦
Elton John's latest album is a pleasant collection of adult-contemporary pop in the vein of the hit title track. —*AMG*

Rare Masters / Oct. 20, 1992 / PolyGram ✦✦✦✦
A two-disc collection of rarities from the early '70s, it includes B-sides and the entire *Friends* soundtrack, which has previously been unavailable on CD. *Rare Masters* is essential for any hardcore Elton John fan. —*AMG*

Greatest Hits, 1976-1986 / Nov. 10, 1992 / MCA ✦✦✦✦
When Elton John left Geffen for MCA, *Greatest Hits, 1976-1986* replaced *Greatest Hits, Vol. 3 (1979-1987)*. The newer collection is a better collection than its predecessor, since it trims the failed single "Heartache All Over the World," which was added as an incentive for hardcore collectors, and "Too Low for Zero," replacing them with "Sorry Seems to Be the Hardest Word," "Don't Go Breaking My Heart" and "Who Wears These Shoes?." Those three cuts are added to 10 songs that illustrate that John could still craft a killer pop single during the '80s. — *Stephen Thomas Erlewine*

Duets / Nov. 23, 1993 / MCA ✦✦
Unlike Frank Sinatra's album, John actually recorded in the studio with his duet partners, adding a spark to his album missing on Sinatra's *Duets*, even if his choices are nearly as bewildering. Some of the material doesn't work in the duet format, and his partners occasionally don't mesh with his current adult contemporary style. All of this makes *Duets* an ultimately disappointing record, even with the occasional successful track, like the kitschy number with drag queen RuPaul. — *Stephen Thomas Erlewine*

Chartbusters Go Pop! 20 Legendary Covers from 1969/70 as Sung by Elton John / 1994 / RPM ✦✦
The title is no joke, but dead-on truth in advertising. Circa 1970, Elton helped pay the rent and gain studio expertise as a session vocalist for British quickie budget exploitation LPs that "re-created" the sound of current hit singles. Elton takes on such vintage AM mothballs as "In the Summertime," "Up Around the Bend," "My Baby Loves Lovin'," "Yellow River," and "Signed Sealed Delivered" here, along with a few songs that were only hits in the UK. These records were never intended to be taken seriously as artistic statements, and one suspects that the studio players were having fun at someone else's expense on "In the Summertime," with farting raspberry noises and ridiculous orgiastic grunts by John during the instrumental break. Most of the time, though, he played it straight, his supple pipes proving to possess the necessary versatile anonymity required of such projects. This reissue, complete with scholarly liner notes, aspires to do nothing more than

preserve this footnote in the budding superstar's career, of interest mostly to completists and novelty seekers. As far as unintentionally funny moments go, the highlight has to be John extolling, "To be young, gifted, and black, that's where it's at!" on his cover of the Nina Simone classic. —*Richie Unterberger*

Made in England / Mar. 21, 1995 / Rocket ✦✦✦
Made in England could as easily be the follow-up to Elton John's self-titled 1970 album as his first recording since the success of his songs for *The Lion King* soundtrack. John has brought back some of his old associates, including percussionist Ray Cooper, guitarist Davey Johnstone, and, particularly, orchestrator Paul Buckmaster, who gave the *Elton John* album its distinctive sound 25 years ago and contributes four string charts here. John remains a musical jukebox: "Please" has a twangy guitar riff that sounds like the Searchers, circa 1965, while guest organist Paul Carrack brings a soulful Booker T-like feel to "Man." As usual, though, John's main vocal influence remains John Lennon, especially on the album's first single, "Believe," the lyrics to which also echo the tone of several of Lennon's solo ballads. Lyricist Bernie Taupin is unusually personal, writing mostly in short, simple, declarative sentences and giving his songs one-word titles—"House," "Cold," "Pain," etc. His overall theme posits a positive conclusion ("Blessed") eventually triumphing over adversity ("Lies"). John never works up much feeling for this concept, though he does come off alternately angry and solemn as the lyrics seem to require, though without ever upsetting the melodic flow. It sounds, in other words, as if Taupin had a lot to get off his chest this time around, but his mouthpiece, as usual, was more interested in the sound of the words than in their meaning. Which, given the predictability of the message, seems to have been just as well. —*William Ruhlmann*

Love Songs / Sep. 24, 1996 / MCA ✦✦✦
Not strictly a "greatest hits" collection, *Love Songs* contains Elton John's most famous ballads, from "Your Song" and "Don't Let the Sun Go Down on Me" to "Can You Feel the Love Tonight." Featuring two new songs, including the single "You Can Make History (Young Again)," *Love Songs* is designed for the casual John fan, who is familiar with his songs through adult contemporary radio. If you don't fall into that category, the compilation is bound to fall short of expectations, but the record nevertheless works well as a collection of ballads and soft rock. —*Stephen Thomas Erlewine*

1968 Nick Drake Session [bootleg] / Totonka ✦✦
The title looks like a joke, or a misprint: Elton John sings Nick Drake? Surely you jest, sir! But this session actually did take place, though in July 1970, not 1968, as the title indicates. Producer Joe Boyd organized these tracks as a publisher's demo to circulate the compositions of Drake, John & Beverly Martyn, Mike Heron, and Ed Carter. John actually only covers four Drake tunes; as someone who owns the Nick Drake box set, believe me when I say that John's versions are so different that I could hardly recognize the songs without looking at the titles. John strips the music of its odd melancholia; the results sound like, well, early Elton John records. So, despite the good fidelity, it's a curiosity for both Drake and John fans, nothing more. John also offers covers of other British folk songwriters on the disc, and some of the tracks feature Linda Thompson (then known as Linda Peters) rather than John on vocals. —*Richie Unterberger*

Eric Johnson

b. Austin, TX

Guitar / Instrumental Rock, Fusion, Pop-Rock
Very few post-Hendrix guitarists can match Eric Johnson's six-string magic. There's no hint of anger, angst, or sloppiness in any of his playing; instead, each note, each phrase, demonstrates his obsession with tone. Joyous celebrations, his solos seem to grow more magnificent with each listening. For years, esteemed players proclaimed Eric Johnson one of rock's most imaginative and tasteful guitarists. Despite the praise, Johnson labored in relative obscurity in Austin, TX, until the 1986 release of *Tones*. His goal was to produce music that entertains and heals, and his playing married deep emotion to mind-boggling finesse. The album's collage of guitar tones ran from purest-of-pure Strat to Hendrix-approved psychedelia and majestic, violinlike textures. Johnson spent nearly two years producing his 1990 follow-up, *Ah Via Musicom*. Full of fire, light, and swirling thunder, it's an artistic triumph, as powerful a statement for Eric Johnson as *Electric Ladyland* was for Jimi Hendrix. *Venus Isle* followed in 1996. —*Jas Obrecht*

Tones / 1986 / Reprise ✦✦✦
This is a landmark guitar recording. —*Jas Obrecht*

● **Ah Via Musicom** / Feb. 1990 / Capitol ✦✦✦✦
There are strong songs and exquisite tones here. —*Jas Obrecht*

Venus Isle / Sep. 3, 1996 / Capitol ✦✦✦
Eric Johnson is notorious for his perfectionism, but the six-year wait between his breakthrough *Ah! Via Musicom* and its follow-up *Venus*

Isle seems a little extravagant, especially considering the resulting album. In six years, it could be assumed that an artist would undergo a number of different phases, exploring several different musical genres and textures. Johnson didn't spend his six years exploring—he spent them refining. *Venus Isle* reveals no new insights about the guitarist, it only offers a new spin on the territory *Ah! Via Musicom* covered. In one respect, this isn't a bad thing. Johnson is a consummate guitarist, pulling out tones and licks from his instrument that no other musician can quite match. It is a joy to hear him play, but *Venus Isle* nevertheless seems like a lost opportunity because he never departs from his standard bag of tricks. There are the occasional jazzy grooves, a handful of blues, several fusion numbers, and a few stabs at prog-rock—all of the things that distinguished the album's predecessor. With playing as stylish and distinctive as Johnson's, it may seem churlish to complain about the lack of innovation, but given the large span of time between albums, it should have been more adventurous and unique. *Venus Isle* would have been a perfect follow-up if it had been released in 1992 or 1993, but as it stands it has to be ranked as a disappointment, no matter how enjoyable parts of it are. —*Stephen Thomas Erlewine*

Marv Johnson

b. Oct. 15, 1938, Detroit, MI, **d.** May 16, 1993
Vocals / Soul, R&B, Motown
Best remembered for a handful of hits including the Top Ten smashes "You Got What It Takes" and "I Love the Way You Love," Marv Johnson was also a seminal figure in the early history of Motown Records. Marvin Earl Johnson was born in Detroit, MI, in 1938, and was raised in a musical environment that mixed the gospel music of the Baptist church with the jump-jazz of Louis Jordan and his Tympany Five. By the time he was in high school he had joined a local singing group, playing carnivals and fairs. In 1958, he cut his first sides, "My Baby-O" and "Once Upon a Time"; the single failed to sell, but the recording session resulted in a meeting with songwriter and would-be record producer Berry Gordy.

After Johnson played his original song "Come to Me" for Gordy and his future wife Raynoma, the couple chose Johnson as the first artist for their fledgling record label, Tamla. Because the new label didn't have distribution outside of Detroit, "Come to Me" (credited to Gordy and Johnson) was released nationally by United Artists, and rose to No. 6 on the R&B charts and No. 30 on the pop charts. Gordy soon lost direct control of his first discovery after United Artists signed Johnson directly, but continued as the singer's manager. Johnson also toured with Motown acts such as the Miracles in addition to appearing on Alan Freed's rock 'n' roll revues and media venues such as *American Bandstand*, and joined early package tours and stage revues where he shared bills with his idols Sam Cooke and Jackie Wilson.

Johnson's second single fared poorly, but his third, 1959's "You've Got What It Takes," exploded onto the charts, becoming a Top Ten hit and earning a gold record. The 1960 follow-up "I Love the Way You Love" also landed in the Top Ten; among his subsequent singles, "You've Got to Move Two Mountains" was a more pop-flavored effort that reached the Top 20, while "Happy Days" got to No. 7 on the R&B charts late in 1960. "Merry-Go-Round," issued in early 1961, was Johnson's last chart success.

In 1965, with the British invasion in full swing, Johnson's contract was dropped by United Artists; he finally came "home" to Motown, joining the Gordy label, but never enjoyed another American hit, although he earned a British gold record with "I'll Pick a Rose for My Rose" for Tamla in 1968. He later worked in a front-office job for Motown, and also wrote songs for Tyrone Davis and Johnny Taylor. Johnson's recording career ended in the late 1960s, but he never stopped performing, and remained active on stage into the 1990s. —*Bruce Eder*

● **Marvelous Marv Johnson** / 1960 / Collectables ✦✦✦✦
Although he was one of the early artists who helped Motown become a pop and soul empire during the 1960s, Marv Johnson made better records while recording for United Artists in the late '50s and early '60s. This is one of several compilations chronicling his cuts prior to the Motown days. Although Berry Gordy produced a number of these, the ones that clicked weren't as clever, elaborate, or pop-oriented as Motown's finest cuts. Johnson had a soulful, flexible voice and is among the transitional artists who deserve more attention for their role in Motown's emergence. —*Ron Wynn*

More Marv Johnson / 1961 / United Artists ✦✦✦
Even many R&B and soul fans have overlooked the greatness of Marv Johnson, whose smooth, exuberant, and sometimes poignant style helped turn some weepy numbers into triumphant outings. He sounded uniformly great throughout this early '60s album, doing everything from light pop to anguished soul and singing with strength, conviction, and intensity. Unfortunately, with the exception of some

greatest hits anthologies, there's very little Marv Johnson on today's market except on the collector's circuit. —*Ron Wynn*

I Believe / 1966 / United Artists ✦✦✦

A wonderful, sorely overlooked late-'50s and '60s soul singer, Marv Johnson had the misfortune to have early hits on Tamla, then a tiny label and not the giant wing of Motown it would become by the mid-'60s. He was a dynamic, aggressive vocalist who excelled at heartache ballads, and, as these songs repeatedly show, was among the finest of his era in building and pacing a song, delivering a lyric, and wrenching emotion out of whatever he was singing. —*Ron Wynn*

● **You Got What It Takes: The Best of Marv Johnson** / Aug. 11, 1992 / EMI America ✦✦✦✦

A 24-song collection, remastered from original session tapes (several tracks in stereo for the first time), including all of the hits and every key single in Johnson's American output except for the first Kudo single. The best songs could pass for Motown releases of the early 1960's, and even the most overproduced numbers have a soulful, moody power. Excellent sound and superb notes. —*Bruce Eder*

Daniel Johnston

b. Austin, TX

Guitar, Vocals / Alternative Pop-Rock

As with other talented but troubled artists such as Syd Barrett, Brian Wilson, and Roky Erickson, Daniel Johnston fights a daily battle with the chronic mental illness that has plagued him nearly his entire life. However, despite recurrent bouts of delusional behavior during which he has physically endangered himself and others, Johnston has carved out a respectable, influential career as a singer-songwriter of extraordinary talent that has grown since his first crudely recorded cassette was released in 1980. He has become the singer-songwriter of choice of the alternative/underground rock scene, and at various times has had his work championed by members of Sonic Youth, Yo La Tengo, Butthole Surfers, Half Japanese, Nirvana (Kurt Cobain was often photographed wearing a Daniel Johnston T-shirt), and numerous others.

Until recently, Johnston's recording were basically homemade affairs, his plain voice accompanied by crude piano and guitar playing. His narrative concerns focused mainly on lost love, the pain of miscommunication, his love for the Beatles and comic-book superhero Captain America. Johnston's music is unflinchingly direct, almost embarrassingly and painfully honest. Because of this and his increasingly erratic behavior, he was considered a local hero in his home of Austin, TX (where he moved from rural West Virginia), but too extreme to engender the interest of a record label. That situation changed in 1985, when MTV filmed a program on the Austin music scene. Johnston's performance brought him almost overnight acclaim, and he went from local legend to national cult figure. Soon, many of his self-released cassette recordings (on his appropriately named Stress label) began showing up in hip record stores from Boston to L.A., and the buzz was that Daniel Johnston was the coolest. There was, however, a grim side to this "success," as if his mental illness was the primary component of his hipness; therefore, there was a feeling that those not close to him were marketing his illness as much as his talent. Sadly, Johnston's behavior wasn't helping, and he was institutionalized twice in the late '80s after his refusal to take medication led to two dangerous episodes.

In the late '80s, indie label Homestead issued some of Johnston's early recordings on vinyl and a full-blown appreciation of Johnston's work was well underway. Soon he was recording solo and with Half Japanese mastermind Jad Fair on the Shimmy Disc indie label, and most recently with Butthole Surfer Paul Leary, who may well be the best producer/musical accompanist Johnston has ever had. Johnston, to the amazement of virtually everyone, now records for Atlantic and, despite occasional behavioral lapses, seems more self-assured than ever. As a result, he has been recording some of the best music of his career: smart, ebullient pop with ringing guitars, primitive keyboards, and a wonderfully naive way of looking at the world. Although he sometimes becomes sad and bitter, cynicism and self-pity aren't his style, and that makes the little tragedies and epiphanies he writes about all the more compelling. Daniel Johnston's world may seem small, but it's much bigger and friendlier than that of our wildest imaginations. —*John Dougan*

Yip Jump Music / 1983 / Homestead ✦✦✦

As for his early music, this may be the best place to begin immersing yourself in the world of Daniel Johnston. Very primitively recorded with little instrumentation other than keyboards, Johnston's upbeat mood makes this a funny, sometimes moving exercise in obsessive behavior. Two things he thinks about a lot, the Beatles and Casper the Friendly Ghost, are the subject of songs, along with his usual examinations of unattainable love. Not the easiest record in the Johnston canon, but a rewarding one nonetheless. —*John Dougan*

Hi, How Are You / 1983 / Homestead ✦✦✦✦

As with *Yip/Jump Music, Hi, How Are You* was a reissue of a cassette recording Johnston made in 1983, and as such it reflects the most fertile period of his early development. Like its predecessor, this is a friendly record marked by his increasing skill as a pop songwriter and his increasingly comfortable singing. His mood here is good, especially during the defiant "Keep Punching Joe," which eschews bitterness for personal resolve. Another important release. —*John Dougan*

● **Fun** / Sep. 13, 1994 / Atlantic ✦✦✦✦

Johnston's major label debut is, arguably, his finest moment. With considerable help from Butthole Surfer Paul Leary, Johnston has never sounded so self-assured or confident before. Some of the songs are more polished, but they're never slicked up to such a degree that this sounds like a user-friendly approximation of Johnston's style; in fact, there are plenty of tracks that return Johnston to the keyboards ("Delusion & Confusion" and "My Little Girl") for his freewheeling, primitive workouts. Exhibiting some of his strongest songwriting to date, *Fun* is a rewarding record that never loses its initial, visceral appeal. —*John Dougan*

Freedy Johnston

b. Kinsley, Kansas

Guitar, Vocals / Singer-Songwriter, Folk-Rock, Adult Alternative Pop-Rock, Americana

Pitting acute, evocative portraits of outsiders and beautiful losers against fragile, shimmering country-pop melodies, the acclaimed work of Freedy Johnston earned him a reputation as one of the brightest singer-songwriters to emerge in the 1990s. Born and raised on his family's farm in the small town of Kinsley, KS, Johnston bought his first guitar at the age of 16; because there was no local music store, he was forced to order the instrument through a mail-order service. After entering college in nearby Lawrence, he began composing his first songs, and was soon focusing all of his energies on becoming a musician. In 1985, he moved to New York, where one of his demos earned him a recording contract.

In 1990, Johnston issued his debut LP, *The Trouble Tree*, which attracted a cult following domestically while becoming a sizable hit abroad, especially in the Netherlands, where he became a star. However, Johnston remained a struggling musician at home, and in order to complete his 1992 sophomore effort *Can You Fly?*, he was forced to sell the family farm, which he had inherited from his grandfather. The resulting recording, however, was a critical smash that ended up on a number of prominent year-end lists, and after another EP, *Unlucky*, he was signed to Elektra Records. His 1994 major-label debut, the Butch Vig-produced *This Perfect World*, proved to be Johnston's most satisfying release to date; its first single, "Bad Reputation," even earned him significant airplay on alternative radio formats. In 1996, he composed the score for the film comedy *Kingpin;* the full-length LP *Never Home* surfaced in early 1997. —*Jason Ankeny*

Trouble Tree / 1990 / Bar/None ✦✦✦✦

Johnston's debut, though not without its rough edges, firmly established him as a talent to be reckoned with—even his earliest songs are marked by great maturity and insight. —*Jason Ankeny*

Can You Fly / Apr. 14, 1992 / Bar/None ✦✦✦✦

"Well I sold the dirt to feed the band" goes the opening line of Johnston's sophomore effort, a reference to the sale of his family farm, a measure necessary to pay for the record's completion. The move was a risky one, but *Can You Fly* was worth it; this is a uniformly excellent collection of songs, highlighted by the lilting "Tearing Down This Place" and "Down in Love," a beautiful duet with Syd Straw. —*Jason Ankeny*

Unlucky / 1993 / Bar/None ✦✦✦

The six-song EP *Unlucky* features *Can You Fly*'s tale of Las Vegas woe, "The Lucky One," in both its completed and demo forms. In addition to three new Johnston originals, it also contains a terrific cover of Jimmy Webb's "Wichita Lineman." —*Jason Ankeny*

● **This Perfect World** / Jun. 28, 1994 / Elektra ✦✦✦✦

The songwriting gifts of Freedy Johnston grow in depth and resonance with each effort, and with *This Perfect World*, he makes his biggest leap yet. Richly produced by Butch Vig, the record is a collection of poignant character studies, finely etched portraits of alienation, loneliness, and rejection. —*Jason Ankeny*

Never Home / Feb. 25, 1997 / Elektra ✦✦✦✦

From the propulsive opener "On the Way Out" to the lilting closer "Something's Out There" (about, of all things, a UFO abduction), the sparkling *Never Home* is Johnston's most musically and emotionally expansive outing to date. Finding a sympathetic ear in producer and guitarist Danny Kortchmar, Johnston's songs transcend their dark themes to reveal unexpected and heretofore unseen moments of warmth and sentimentality; even edgy, Randy Newman-like character studies such as "He Wasn't Murdered" and "Gone to See the Fire" offer moments of tenderness which their subjects (suicide and arson, respectively) can't suppress. —*Jason Ankeny*

Gloria Jones

Soul

When the name of Gloria Jones comes up in rocktalk, it's usually as a trivia question. In the mid-'60s, she recorded the original version of "Tainted Love," which was covered by Soft Cell for a huge international hit in 1982. She was also the girlfriend of British glam rocker Marc Bolan, in addition to singing and playing keyboards in his T. Rex band. Her considerable talent as as a soul singer gets lost in the shuffle, especially because few of her recordings are currently available.

Jones earns a spot in rock history on the merits of "Tainted Love" alone. This propulsive mid-'60s soul stomper, wholly dissimilar to Soft Cell's wimpy synth-pop cover, is one of the great '60s hits that never was. "Heartbeat" was another throbbing near-miss, recorded with, oddly enough, producer Ed Cobb, who was more renowned for his work with garage-pop groups like the Standells and the Chocolate Watch Band. Both "Heartbeat" and "Tainted Love" were written by Cobb as well, although Jones was not without songwriting talent, co-writing Marvin Gaye and Diana Ross' 1974 hit duet, "My Mistake." Jones never had more than regional success, and (like several other minor American soul singers) moved to Great Britain, where the cultish devotion of Northern Soul fans ensured regular work.

In 1974, Jones joined T. Rex (which by that time was fading rapidly) as a keyboardist and backing vocalist. Becoming romantically involved with the singer, she also helped sway him into a more soul/dance-oriented direction. Bolan in turn helped her out on her solo album *Vixen*, playing guitar and writing songs. After having a child, their time together came to a tragic end when Bolan was killed in a car accident in 1977, with Jones at the wheel. —*Richie Unterberger*

● **Come Go with Me** / Uptown ✦✦✦✦
Competent but unexceptional commercial mid-'60s soul with a strong, brassy Motown flavor. Jones was clearly a powerhouse singer, but wasn't getting the material her talents deserved. "Heartbeat," by far the best track on the album, was reissued in better company in Rhino's *Soul Shots* series. —*Richie Unterberger*

Howard Jones (John Howard Jones)

b. Feb. 23, 1955, Southampton, Hants, England
Keyboards, Vocals / Synth-pop, New Wave, Pop-Rock
Howard Jones was one of the defining figures of mid-'80s synth-pop. Jones' music merged the technology-intensive sound of new wave with the cheery optimism of hippies and late-'60s pop. Jones racked up a string of hits in the mid- and late '80s before he retreated into being a cult figure in the '90s.

A native of Southampton, England, Jones learned to play piano at the age of seven. By the time he was a teenager, his family had relocated to Canada, which is where he joined his first band, a progressive-rock group called Warrior. Eventually, Jones moved back to England, where he played in a number of different groups. In the mid-'70s, he enrolled in the Royal Northern College of Music. After he dropped out of college, he played with a variety of local Southampton jazz and funk bands. Eventually, Jones began performing as a solo artist. At these solo shows, Jones performed only with synthesizers and drum machines. For these one-man concerts, Jones had a mime called Jed Hoile perform. After a few years of solo performing, Jones attracted the attention of John Peel, who offered the keyboardist a BBC session. Soon, Jones was opening for new wave synth-pop acts across England. By 1983, he had signed with WEA in England and Europe; in America, he signed to Elektra.

Howard Jones released his first single, "New Song," in England in the fall of 1983 and it became a big hit, peaking at No. 3. His second single, "What Is Love," was released a few months later and it reached No. 2. *Humans Lib*, Jones' debut album, was released in the spring of 1984 and quickly rose to No. 1 in England. Thanks to repeated exposure on MTV, the album became a moderate hit in the US. Later in 1984, "New Song" and "What Is Love" became American Top 40 hits, while "Pearl in the Shell" became his third British Top Ten single.

In 1985, Jones phased Hoile out of his live show, formed a touring band, and released his second album, *Dream into Action*. The record became his most successful album, reaching No. 10 and going platinum in the US and spawning the hit singles "Things Can Only Get Better," "Like to Get to Know You Well," "Life in One Day," and "Look Mama." In the spring of 1986, he released *Action Replay*, an EP of remixes that featured a new version of "No One Is to Blame" from *Dream into Action*. "No One Is to Blame" became Jones' biggest US hit, peaking at No. 4. The relatively weaker chart placement of No. 16 in the UK was indicative of his future in England—his next single, "You

Know I Love You . . . Don't You?," taken from his third album *One to One*, became his last British Top 40 hit.

Jones released his fourth album, *Cross That Line*, in the spring of 1989. The first single from the album, "Everlasting Love," became a No. 1 adult contemporary hit in America, reaching No. 13 pop. However, the album stalled at No. 65. Jones returned three years later with *In the Running*, a set that saw him abandoning synthesizers for piano. The album didn't make the charts. Following the release of *The Best of Howard Jones* in 1993, Elektra dropped him. Instead of seeking a new record contract with another major label, Jones hit the road in 1994, performing acoustic shows. At the 1994 shows, he sold *Working in the Backroom*—an album he recorded at his home studio and released on his own label, Dtox Records—at his concerts. For the next two years, Jones continually toured America and Europe. In 1996, he released *Live Acoustic America* on PLM Records. —*Stephen Thomas Erlewine*

Human's Lib / 1984 / Elektra ✦✦✦✦
His debut album is almost entirely performed on synthesizers. The material on *Human's Lib*, like all of the following albums, is very inconsistent; Jones either writes hits or flops, with very little in between. Contains two of Jones' best songs, "New Song" and "What Is Love?" —*Iotis Erlewine*

Dream into Action / 1985 / Elektra ✦✦✦✦
This album shows the synthesizer pop idol at the height of his creativity—*Dream into Action* is definitely the most interesting of Jones' albums. It contains some of his best songs—"Things Can Only Get Better," "Life in One Day," and "No One Is to Blame." The CD includes two bonus tracks, "Bounce Right Back" and "Like to Get to Know You Well," both of which are worthwhile additions. —*Iotis Erlewine*

Action Replay / 1986 / Elektra ✦✦
This is a six-track mini-album that includes an updated version of "No One Is to Blame" featuring Phil Collins on percussion. This album really isn't worth buying, especially if you have the other Jones albums. —*Iotis Erlewine*

One to One / 1986 / Elektra ✦✦
This is Jones' most musically mature and toned-down album. The synthesizers are less overbearing than on the previous albums, yet the songs are mediocre. *One to One* reached No. 10 in the UK, but did not fare as well in the US, peaking at No. 56. This album features the revamped "No One Is to Blame," which is inferior to the original version. —*Iotis Erlewine*

Cross That Line / 1989 / Elektra ✦✦✦
After a three-year wait, this album was a bit of a disappointment. Musically, it is his best yet, but it lacked a certain energy that the others had. The songs seemed to replace vivacity with length. The album didn't do very well on the charts; the No. 13 single (US), "Everlasting Love," was the biggest hit. Ironically, the best song on this album, "Out of Thin Air," does not use a single synthesizer but instead is a solo piano piece performed by Jones himself. After all those years of electronic music, a song featuring a real instrument is a welcome relief. —*Iotis Erlewine*

In the Running / Apr. 14, 1992 / Elektra ✦✦
On his fifth album, *In the Running*, Howard Jones backs away from his trademark bouncy synth-pop in an attempt to secure a position in the adult-contemporary market. While his graceful keyboard playing is still impressive, he hasn't written a set of songs that supports his talent. Most of the record lacks strong hooks and melodies, making it nothing more than a pleasant, but bland and unmemorable, album. —*Stephen Thomas Erlewine*

● **The Best of Howard Jones** / Jun. 29, 1993 / Elektra ✦✦✦✦
The Best of Howard Jones successfully distills all the hits and highlights from his albums onto one disc. It could be all the Howard Jones you'll ever need. —*AMG*

Live Acoustic America / Feb. 13, 1996 / Plump ✦✦✦
In 1992, coinciding with the release of his album, *In The Running*, Howard Jones undertook a tour of the US accompanying himself on acoustic piano with only a percussionist in support. The tour doesn't seem to have had the desired effect of successfully promoting his current album, which became his first to miss the charts in the US and the UK (despite the hit "Lift Me Up") and ended his career as a major-label act. But it was artistically satisfying for an artist usually consigned to the synth-pop category, who could emphasize his melodies and hopeful lyrics, not to mention his instrumental virtuosity and elastic voice, in the format. This recording was made early in the tour, on April 28, at the Variety Arts Theater in Los Angeles. Jones plays all of his hits and a representative sampling of songs from his five albums. Jones' hits collection may make a better sampler, but this set demonstrates that he can generate his own electricity even when his machines are unplugged. —*William Ruhlmann*

Marti Jones

b. Ohio

Vocals / Singer-Songwriter, Pop-Rock, Jangle-Pop

Pop singer Marti Jones first emerged as the frontwoman of the group Color Me Gone before issuing her solo debut *Unsophisticated Time*—produced by future husband Don Dixon—in 1985. Though the recipient of widespread critical acclaim, Jones found little commercial success with LPs like 1986's *Match Game* (recorded with guests Mitch Easter, T-Bone Burnett, and Darlene Love) and 1988's *Used Guitars* (featuring contributions from Marshall Crenshaw and Janis Ian), and she was dropped by her label A&M. After signing to RCA for 1990's *Any Kind of Lie*, Jones disappeared from sight before signing to Sugar Hill and returning in 1996 with a pair of new releases, *Live from Spirit Square* and *My Long-Haired Life. —Jason Ankeny*

Unsophisticated Time / 1985 / A&M ✦✦✦✦

Marti Jones' debut firmly establishes the winning formula of all her solo work—superb singing, excellent song selection (including compositions from the dB's and the Bongos), and tastefully simple musical backing and production (courtesy of future husband Don Dixon). —*Jason Ankeny*

Match Game / 1986 / A&M ✦✦✦

For the all-star *Match Game*, Marti Jones and producer Don Dixon are joined by guests including Marshall Crenshaw, Mitch Easter, T-Bone Burnett, Darlene Love, Richard Barone, and Paul Carrack; the song selection is similarly impressive, drawing from the pens of David Bowie ("Soul Love") and Free ("Soon I Will Be Gone") as well as Crenshaw, the dB's, and the Bongos. Nonetheless, the album is Jones' show, and her rich, expressive performances never relinquish the spotlight. —*Jason Ankeny*

● **Used Guitars** / 1988 / A&M ✦✦✦✦

Marti Jones' best effort to date, *Used Guitars* expands on her folk-pop foundations to stretch into soul ("Twisted Vines") and piano ballads (the stunning "Ruby," co-written by Janis Ian). Again, the songs are astutely chosen, and feature contributions from John Hiatt, Graham Parker and Jackie DeShannon; Jones' own compositions, penned with Don Dixon, are especially strong—the breezy opener "Tourist Town" is a stunner. —*Jason Ankeny*

Any Kind of Lie / Apr. 1990 / RCA ✦✦✦

With *Any Kind of Lie*, Marti Jones strives for autonomy; keeping the covers to a minimum (only Clive Gregson's "Second Choice" and Loudon Wainwright's "Old Friend" make the cut), she and Don Dixon write the nine remaining songs themselves. The results are mixed: while none of the couple's originals are weak, Jones' greatest strength as a performer is as an interpreter of other people's work—*Any Kind of Lie* is an impressive accomplishment, but it lacks the eclectic fun of her best efforts. —*Jason Ankeny*

Live at Spirit Square / Mar. 19, 1996 / Sugar Hill ✦✦✦

Appearing more than five and a half years after it was recorded, *Live at Spirit Square* chronicles a Marti Jones performance from August 29, 1990, made during her promotional tour for her fourth studio album, *Any Kind of Lie*. Not surprisingly, eight of the seventeen songs in the set come from that album, with five from its predecessor, *Used Guitars*, and two each from *Match Game* and *Unsophisticated Time*. That means the album is not the perfect live compilation of Jones' best material, with the missing including such first-album favorites as "(If I Could) Walk Away" and "Lonely Is (as Lonely Does)." But you can't complain too loudly when the featured material is of the caliber of "I've Got Second Sight" and "Follow You All Over the World" (not to mention covers of songs by John Hiatt, Elvis Costello, and Loudon Wainwright III). Jones leads a five-piece band that is, of course, anchored by her husband, producer, co-songwriter, and comic foil Don Dixon. That means the pop-folk-rock is accomplished and infectious, and that the onstage patter and interplay give the album an engagingly comfortable feeling. Play this album back to back with Dixon's live one, *Chi-Town Budget Show*, and it'll be a fun evening. —*William Ruhlmann*

My Longhaired Life / Oct. 15, 1996 / Sugar Hill ✦✦✦

Jones' first new studio effort in six years returns to the covers-heavy format of her earlier work, drawing from a wonderfully eclectic pool of material including Joe Tex's "You Got What It Takes," Squeeze's "Black Coffee in Bed," Joni Mitchell's "Songs to Aging Children Come," and Elvis Costello's "Sleep of the Just." —*Jason Ankeny*

Rickie Lee Jones

b. Nov. 8, 1954, Chicago, IL

Guitar, Keyboards, Vocals / Singer-Songwriter, Folk-Rock

Once touted as the natural successor to Joni Mitchell, singer-songwriter Rickie Lee Jones proved no less idiosyncratic or mercurial; like Mitchell, Jones experienced significant commercial success at the outset of her career, but a restless creative spirit—combined with a stubborn

refusal to fit comfortably into any one musical niche—sealed her ultimate destiny as that of a highly regarded cult heroine. Jones was born on November 8, 1954, in Chicago, but the volatile relationship between her mother and father resulted in an upbringing that led her everywhere from Phoenix, AZ, to Olympia, WA, where an expulsion ended her school career. As a teen, Jones began drinking heavily, and eventually she left home and began drifting up and down the West Coast before settling in Los Angeles in the mid-1970s. There she worked a series of waitressing jobs while occasionally performing in area clubs, where she sang and honed her unique, Beat-influenced spoken word monologues. She also began a relationship with fellow boho Tom Waits.

Her first measure of success was as a songwriter; after her friend Ivan Ulz sang Jones' composition "Easy Money" over the phone to Lowell George, the ex-Little Feat frontman included it on his album *Thanks I'll Eat It Here*. Then, in 1978 Jones' four-song demo came to the attention of Warner Brothers executive Lenny Waronker, who enlisted Russ Titleman to co-produce her self-titled 1979 debut LP. Spurred by the success of the jazz-flavored hit single "Chuck E's in Love," *Rickie Lee Jones* became a smash both commercially and critically, earning praise for Jones' elastic vocals, vivid wordplay, and unique fusion of folk, jazz, and R&B.

With 1981's follow-up, *Pirates*, she gave early notice that her music would not sit still; employing longer and more complex song structures, her lyrics tackled themes of evolution, change, and death. Two years later, she returned with *Girl at Her Volcano*, an EP collection of live jazz standards and studio outtakes; with 1984's *The Magazine*, she made another left turn, teaming with composer James Newton Howard for her most slick, synth-driven outing to date.

Problems with alcohol, business difficulties, and the birth of a daughter effectively sidelined Jones for much of the decade; she did not resurface until 1989's sterling *Flying Cowboys*, produced by Steely Dan's Walter Becker and recorded with the aid of the wonderful Scottish trio the Blue Nile. Don Was took over the production reins for 1991's *Pop Pop*, on which Jones covered ballads ranging in origin from Tin Pan Alley to the Haight-Ashbury while backed by jazz players including Charlie Haden and Joe Henderson. After 1993's *Traffic from Paradise*, she embarked on an acoustic tour; *Naked Songs*, a document of those unplugged shows, followed in 1995. —*Jason Ankeny*

★ **Rickie Lee Jones** / Mar. 1979 / Warner Brothers ✦✦✦✦✦

One of the most impressive debuts for a singer-songwriter ever, this infectious mixture of styles not only features a strong collection of original songs (the hits are "Chuck E's in Love" and "Young Blood," but "Danny's All-Star Joint" and "Coolsville" are just as good) but also a singer with a savvy, distinctive voice that can be streetwise, childlike, and sophisticated, sometimes all in the same song. —*William Ruhlmann*

Pirates / Jul. 1981 / Warner Brothers ✦✦✦✦

If the songs are less immediately accessible than on Jones' first album, repeated listenings are likely to lead to even greater rewards. Open-ended song structures allow Jones to explore more fully her closely observed portraits of lowlife characters, and her singing remains entrancing. —*William Ruhlmann*

Girl at Her Volcano / 1983 / Warner Brothers ✦✦✦✦

This seven-song EP originally was released as a 10-inch record. It's a charming collection featuring Billy Strayhorn's standard "Lush Life," as well as the Left Banke hit "Walk Away Renee," which should give some sense of Jones' breadth. A minor, but enjoyable change of pace. —*William Ruhlmann*

The Magazine / Sep. 1984 / Warner Brothers ✦✦

The reason *The Magazine* was such a disappointment was that Jones had proven herself a major artist with her first two albums and turned into a self-conscious, pretentious, minor one on this, her third. Once, she made art by observing street people and describing them carefully; now she tried to make "Art" by navel-gazing. What a letdown. —*William Ruhlmann*

Flying Cowboys / Sep. 1989 / Geffen ✦✦✦✦

Five years after the disappointing *The Magazine*, Rickie Lee Jones returned to form with *Flying Cowboys*, which shared much of the playful, childlike charm of her debut, *Rickie Lee Jones*, and some of the musically diffuse, lyrically ambitious form of its follow-up, *Pirates*. From the opening track, "The Horses," which suggested a mother's delight with her child as much as a lover's devotion, Jones reintroduced the joyous tone of her early work as well as establishing the western theme that would run through the album—cowboys, rodeos, horses, deserts—without adding up to an actual story line. The easy rhythms and lazy, flexible singing on the first few songs were reminiscent of Laura Nyro's work with Labelle on their *Gonna Take a Miracle* album, after which Jones branched out into reggae and folk-blues, coming up with an affectionate bluesman voice on "Ghost Train." "Satellites," the college radio hit, used the sprung rhythms and surprising choral parts familiar from her popular early songs. If Jones could be obscure and unfocused as a writer, that weakness was also her strength, since it was an expression of the imagination that also produced her most striking musical effects. Producer Walter Becker may have helped keep things from getting as grandiose as they had on *The Magazine*, but it was really the artist herself who managed to rein in from that album's self-importance. If what resulted was not as accomplished as *Pirates*, it was the most accessible and enjoyable music Jones had made since her debut. —*William Ruhlmann*

Pop Pop / Aug. 1991 / Geffen ♦♦♦

Traffic from Paradise / Sep. 14, 1993 / Geffen ♦♦♦♦
"Just give me many chances . . . time to learn to crawl," sings Rickie Lee Jones on this, her fifth album of new material in 14 years. Clearly, she's had a lot of chances already, and some have paid off big. Here, however, Jones has made a record of what sound like rough performances of musical ideas that might at some point become songs and then, with some work, acceptable recordings. As it is, the record is vague and unfocused, only aspiring to coherence when someone other than Jones is heard from, such as the two songs co-written by Leo Kottke. Too much of the time, Jones sounds like she's singing half-forgotten songs, and the result is wispy and fragmentary. —*William Ruhlmann*

Naked Songs / Sep. 19, 1995 / Reprise ♦♦♦♦
Rickie Lee Jones "unplugged"—in fact, solo with an acoustic guitar or piano on all but a couple of tunes—*Naked Songs* is otherwise a retrospective concert album on which Jones cherrypicks songs from her five studio albums, including the hits "Chuck E's in Love" and "Young Blood," and others from her breakthrough debut record. The studio album arrangements always tried to support and augment Jones' idiosyncratic writing and playing style, which sounds less unusual when she is simply accompanying herself, and in many ways more effective. "Altar Boy," a previously unreleased song, strays into Leonard Cohen territory, mixing religion with eroticism. —*William Ruhlmann*

Tom Jones (Thomas Jones Woodward)

b. Jun. 7, 1940, Pontypridd, South Wales, England
Vocals / Pop, Pop-Rock, Country-Pop
Tom Jones became one of the most popular vocalists to emerge from the British Invasion. Since the mid-'60s, Jones has sang nearly every form of popular music—pop, rock, show tunes, country, dance, and techno, he's sung it all. His actual style—a full-throated, robust baritone that had little regard for nuance and subtlety—never changed, he just sang over different backing tracks. On stage, Jones played up his sexual appeal; it didn't matter whether he was in an unbuttoned shirt or a tuxedo, he always radiated a raw sexuality, which earned him a large following of devoted female fans who frequently threw underwear on stage. Jones' following never diminished over the decades; he was able to exploit trends, earning new fans while retaining his core following.

Born Thomas Jones Woodward, Tom Jones began singing professionally in 1963, performing as Tommy Scott with the Senators, a Welsh beat group. In 1964 he recorded a handful of solo tracks with record producer Joe Meek and shopped them to various record companies to little success. Later in the year, Decca producer Peter Sullivan discovered Tommy Scott performing in a club and directed him to manager Phil Solomon. It was a short-lived partnership and the singer soon moved back to Wales, where he continued to sing in local clubs. At one of the shows, he gained the attention of former Viscounts singer Gordon Mills, who had become an artist manager. Mills signed Scott, renamed him Tom Jones, and helped him record his first single for Decca, "Chills and Fever," which was released in late 1964. "Chills and Fever" didn't chart, but "It's Not Unusual," released in early 1965, became a No. 1 hit in the UK and a Top Ten hit in the US. The heavily orchestrated, over-the-top pop arrangements perfectly meshed with Jones' swinging, sexy image, guaranteeing him press coverage, which translated into a series of hits, including "Once upon a Time," "Little Lonely One," and "With These Hands." During 1965, Mills also secured a number of film themes for Jones to record, including the Top Ten hit "What's New Pussycat?" (June 1965) and "Thunderball" (December 1965).

Jones' popularity began to slip somewhat by the middle of 1966, causing Mills to redesign the singer's image into a more respectable, mature tuxedoed crooner. Jones also began to sing material that appealed to a broad audience, like the country songs "Green, Green Grass of Home" and "Detroit City." The strategy worked, as he returned to the top of the charts in the UK and began hitting the Top 40 again in the US. For the remainder of the '60s, he scored a consistent string of hits in both Britain and America. At the end of the decade, Jones relocated to America, where he hosted the television variety program, "This Is Tom Jones." Running between 1969 and 1971, the show was a success and laid the groundwork for the singer's move to Las Vegas in the early '70s. Once he moved to Vegas, Jones began recording less,

choosing to concentrate on his lucrative club performances. After Gordon Mills died in the late '70s, Jones' son, Mark Woodward, became the singer's manager. The change in management prompted Jones to begin recording again. This time, he concentrated on the country market, releasing a series of slick Nashville-styled country-pop albums in the early '80s that earned him a handful of hits.

Jones' next image makeover came in 1988, when he sang Prince's "Kiss" with the electronic dance outfit, the Art of Noise. The single became a Top Ten hit in the UK and reached the American Top 40, which led to a successful concert tour and a part in a recording of Dylan Thomas' voice play, *Under Milk Wood*. The singer then returned to the club circuit, where he stayed for several years. In 1993, Jones performed at the Glastonbury Festival in England, where he won an enthusiastic response from the young crowd. Soon, he was on the comeback trail again, releasing the alternative-dance-pop album *The Lead and How to Swing It* in the fall of 1994; the record was a moderate hit, gaining some play in dance clubs. —*Stephen Thomas Erlewine*

Things That Matter Most to Me / 1987 / Mercury ♦♦♦♦
Things That Matter Most to Me compiles Jones' greatest country-pop hits. Taken in one sitting, the singles sound stronger than they do on the albums, and show that Jones can deliver country-flavored material convincingly. —*Stephen Thomas Erlewine*

● **The Complete Tom Jones** / Aug. 17, 1993 / PolyGram ♦♦♦♦
Collecting almost all of his hit singles on one album, *Complete Tom Jones* is the singer's most entertaining album, devoid of the filler that clutters all of his studio records. —*Stephen Thomas Erlewine*

Janis Joplin

b. Jan. 19, 1943, Port Arthur, TX, d. Oct. 4, 1970, Los Angeles, CA
Vocals / Rock 'n' Roll, Blues-Rock
The greatest white female rock singer of the 1960s, Janis Joplin was also a great blues singer, making her material her own with her wailing, raspy, supercharged emotional delivery. First rising to stardom as the frontwoman for San Francisco psychedelic band Big Brother & the Holding Company, she left the group in the late '60s for a brief and uneven (though commercially successful) career as a solo artist. Although she wasn't always supplied with the best material or most sympathetic musicians, her best recordings, with both Big Brother and on her own, are some of the most exciting performances of her era. She also did much to redefine the role of women in rock with her assertive, sexually forthright persona and raunchy, electrifying onstage presence.

Joplin was raised in the small town of Port Arthur, TX, and much of her subsequent personal difficulties and unhappiness has been attributed to her inability to fit in with the expectations of the conservative community. She'd been singing blues and folk music since her teens, playing on occasion in the mid-'60s with future Jefferson Airplane guitarist Jorma Kaukonen. There are a few live pre-Big Brother recordings (not issued until after her death), reflecting the inspiration of early blues singers like Bessie Smith, that demonstrate she was well on her way to developing a personal style before hooking up with the band. She had already been to California before moving there permanently in 1966, when she joined a struggling early San Francisco psychedelic group, Big Brother & the Holding Company.

Big Brother's story is told in more detail in their own entry. Although their loose, occasionally sloppy brand of bluesy psychedelia had some charm, there can be no doubt that Joplin—who initially didn't even sing lead on all of the material—was primarily responsible for lifting them out of the ranks of the ordinary. She made them a hit at the 1967 Monterey Pop Festival, where her stunning version of "Ball and Chain" (perhaps her very best performance) was captured on film. After a debut on the Mainstream label, Big Brother signed a management deal with Albert Grossman, and moved on to Columbia. Their second album, *Cheap Thrills*, topped the charts in 1968, but Joplin left the band shortly afterwards, enticed by the prospects of stardom as a solo act.

Joplin's first album, *I Got Dem Ol' Kozmic Blues Again Mama!*, was recorded with the Kozmic Blues Band, a unit that included horns and retained just one of the musicians that had played with her in Big Brother (guitarist Sam Andrew). Although it was a hit, it wasn't her best work; the new band, though more polished musically, were not nearly as sympathetic accompanists as Big Brother, purveying a soul-rock groove that could sound forced. That's not to say it was totally unsuccessful, boasting one of her signature tunes in "Try (Just a Little Bit Harder)."

For years, Joplin's life had been a roller coaster of drug addiction, alcoholism, and volatile personal relationships, documented in several biographies. Musically, however, things were on the upswing shortly before her death, as she assembled a better, more versatile backing outfit, the Full Tilt Boogie Band, for her final album, *Pearl* (ably produced by Paul Rothschild). Joplin was sometimes criticized for screeching at the expense of subtlety, but *Pearl* was solid evidence of her growth as a mature, diverse stylist who could handle blues, soul, and folk-rock. "Mercedes Benz," "Get It While You Can," and Kris Kristofferson's "Me and Bobby McGee" are some of her very best tracks. Tragically, she died before the album's release, overdosing on heroin in a Hollywood hotel in October 1970. "Me and Bobby McGee" became a posthumous No. 1 single in 1971, and thus the song with which she is most frequently identified. —*Richie Unterberger*

I Got Dem Ol' Kozmic Blues Again Mama / 1969 / Columbia ✦✦✦
Joplin's only solo album to be released during her lifetime heavily employs horns and an R&B band feel, but the dominant sound remains Joplin's impassioned singing on such songs as "Try." —*William Ruhlmann*

☆ **Pearl** / Feb. 1971 / Columbia ✦✦✦✦✦
Backed by a tight rock band, Full Tilt Boogie, Joplin puts her mark on everything from the bluesy "Cry Baby" to her hit version of Kris Kristofferson's "Me & Bobby McGee." —*William Ruhlmann*

In Concert / May 1972 / Columbia ✦✦✦
About half of this two-record set features Janis Joplin with Big Brother and the Holding Company in 1968, performing songs like "Down on Me" and "Piece of My Heart." The rest, recorded in 1970, finds her with her backup group, Full Tilt Boogie, mostly performing songs from *I Got Dem Ol' Kozmic Blues Again Mama!.* Joplin puts herself out on stage, both in terms of singing until her voice is raw and describing her life to her audiences. Parts of this album are moving, parts are heartbreaking, and the rest is just great rock 'n' roll. —*William Ruhlmann*

● **Janis Joplin's Greatest Hits** / Jul. 1973 / Columbia ✦✦✦✦
Well-chosen best-of gathers together tracks from Big Brother and the Holding Company and solo material. —*William Ruhlmann*

Farewell Song / 1982 / Columbia ✦✦✦
A ragtag collection of odds and ends, live and studio, from both the Big Brother and solo era. The best cuts are on the *Janis* box in different versions, but serious fans will find some interesting items here, especially the *Cheap Thrills*-era outtakes and live performances; "Misery 'N,' "Farewell Song," and "Catch Me Daddy" were easily good enough to have qualified for inclusion on that album. —*Richie Unterberger*

Janis / Nov. 23, 1993 / Columbia/Legacy ✦✦✦✦
This three-CD box set is the most thorough and valuable retrospective of Janis Joplin's career. Besides including all of her most essential recordings with and without Big Brother and the Holding Company, this 49-song package features quite a few enticing rarities; 18 of the tracks were previously unissued. These include a 1962 home recording of the Joplin original "What Good Can Drinkin' Do," which marked the first time her singing was captured on tape; a pair of acoustic blues tunes from 1965 with backup guitar by future Jefferson Airplane star Jorma Kaukonen, an acoustic demo of "Me and Bobby McGee," a 1970 birthday song for John Lennon, and live performances from her appearance on "The Ed Sullivan Show" in 1969. The real showstopper is the previously unissued, eight-minute version of "Ball and Chain" from Big Brother's first set at the 1967 Monterey Pop Festival (the cut on the *Monterey Pop* box set is from their second set). The more forgettable tracks from her solo albums are wisely excised, as are the Big Brother songs that did not feature her vocals. This is the rare multidisc set of a major artist, which manages to cover all the official milestones and present a bounty of worthwhile rarities at the same time. —*Richie Unterberger*

18 Essential Songs / Jan. 24, 1995 / Legacy/Columbia ✦✦✦✦
18 Essential Songs is a one-disc distillation of the triple-disc *Janis* box set. Running 70 minutes, it is a more extensive best-of than the ten-track 1973 *Janis Joplin's Greatest Hits* album. But it is denied "first pick" status because, unlike that album, it does not contain the hit version of Joplin's only No. 1 single, "Me and Bobby McGee." (It does, however, contain an alternate demo version of that song.) —*William Ruhlmann*

Journey

f. 1973, San Francisco, CA
Soft Rock, Pop-Rock, Arena Rock
During its 14-year existence (1973-1987), Journey altered its musical approach and its personnel extensively while becoming a top touring and recording band. The only constant factor was guitarist Neal Schon (b. Feb. 27, 1954), a music prodigy who had been a member of Santana in 1971-1972. The original unit, which was named in a contest on KSAN-FM in San Francisco, featured Schon, bassist Ross Valory, drummer Prairie Prince (replaced by Aynsley Dunbar), and guitarist George Tickner (who left after the first album). Another former Santana member, keyboard player and singer Gregg Rolie, joined shortly afterwards. This lineup recorded *Journey* (1974), the first of three moderate-selling jazz-rock albums given over largely to instrumentals.

By 1977, however, the group decided it needed a strong vocalist/frontman and hired Steve Perry (b. Jan. 22, 1953). The results were

immediately felt on the fourth album, *Infinity* (1978), which had sold a million copies by the end of the year. (By this time, Dunbar had been replaced by Steve Smith.) *Evolution* (1979) was similarly successful, as was *Departure* (after which Rolie was replaced by Jonathan Cain). After a live album, *Captured* (1981), Journey released *Escape*, which broke them through to the top ranks of pop groups by scoring three Top Ten hit singles, all ballads featuring Perry's smooth tenor: "Who's Crying Now," "Don't Stop Believin'," and "Open Arms." The album topped the charts and had sold seven million copies by 1989.

Frontiers (1983), featuring the hit "Separate Ways," was another big success, after which Perry released a successful solo album, *Street Talk* (1984). When the group got back together to make a new album, Valory and Smith were no longer in the lineup, and *Raised on Radio* (1986) was made by Schon, Perry, and Cain, who added other musicians for a tour.

Following the *Raised on Radio* tour, Journey disbanded. Perry went into a prolonged period of seclusion as Cain formed Bad English with vocalist John Waite. Bad English had several hit singles, including the No. 1 "When I See You Smile," before breaking up. Perry returned to recording in 1994, releasing *For the Love of Strange Medicine*. Although the album was a minor hit, it was a commercial disappointment, leading Perry to re-form Journey with Cain in 1996. That fall, Journey released *Trial By Fire*, which became a hit on adult contemporary radio. —*William Ruhlmann*

Journey / 1975 / Columbia ✦✦
On its eponymous debut album, Journey was still trying to find its signature sound. They were relying too much on prog-rock, filling the album with meandering jazz-rock instrumentals that never quite catch fire. Furthermore, their pop songs are ill-formed and lack hooks—in short, they are too mainstream for the progressive audience and too unfocused for the pop audience. —*Stephen Thomas Erlewine*

Look into the Future / 1976 / Columbia ✦✦
Journey's second album *Look Into the Future* is essentialy a reprise of their debut, and while the music has a sharper focus and better instrumental sections than its predecessor, it still lacks strong material and is a little too directionless to function as good jazz-rock. Still, it's a marginal improvement over the debut. —*Stephen Thomas Erlewine*

Next / 1977 / Columbia ✦✦
With *Next*, Journey began to break away from the jazzy, progressive-rock inclinations that dominated their first two albums, yet without a forceful lead vocalist like Steve Perry, the group lacks a focus and a pop sensibility, and their attempts at straightahead pop-rock suffer considerably as a result. —*Stephen Thomas Erlewine*

Infinity / 1978 / Columbia ✦✦✦
This was the first album with vocalist Steve Perry. "Wheel in the Sky" was the band's first US-charting single, followed by "Anytime" and "Lights." It was the beginning of their climb up the charts with the trademark tenor of Steve Perry. —*Donna DiChario*

Evolution / 1979 / Columbia ✦✦✦✦
Journey got major US radio airplay with "Just the Same Way," "Lovin', Touchin', Squeezin'," and "City of Angels." —*Donna DiChario*

In the Beginning / 1979 / Columbia ✦✦
Selecting the highlights from Journey's first three albums, *In the Beginning* illustrates that the band was better at pop-oriented arena-rock than attempts at jazz and art-rock that comprised their early records. —*Stephen Thomas Erlewine*

Departure / 1980 / Columbia ✦✦✦
Featuring the driving "Any Way You Want It" and the Top 40 hit "Walks Like a Lady," *Departure* didn't mark a departure from Journey's successful pop-rock formula, but overall the record was a little weaker than their previous two albums. —*Stephen Thomas Erlewine*

Captured / 1981 / Columbia ✦✦✦
A live double-album, it featured many of their late-'70s hits. —*Donna DiChario*

Escape / 1981 / Columbia ✦✦✦✦
Jonathan Cain (ex-Babys keyboardist) replaced Gregg Rolie on the band's most popular album to date. On the strength of the hits "Who's Crying Now" and "Don't Stop Believin'," this album spent more than a year in the Top 20. —*Donna DiChario*

Frontiers / 1983 / Columbia ✦✦✦✦
The ballads "Faithfully" and "Send Her My Love" reap the benefits of Steve Perry's crystal-clear vocals. —*Donna DiChario*

Raised on Radio / 1986 / Columbia ✦✦✦
Journey's ninth and last new studio album found the group reduced to a trio of guitarist Neal Schon, singer Steve Perry, and keyboard player Jonathan Cain. But even without their regular rhythm section, the group was able to re-create the accessible pop-rock sound perfected on earlier albums such as *Escape* and *Frontiers*. Schon's guitar still cut through the fat keyboard chords, and Perry's fluid tenor still gave the

songs an airy, melodic appeal. All of that was good for sales of two million copies and five chart singles, four of which made the Top 40 and one of which, "Be Good to Yourself," reached the Top Ten. That didn't match the seven-million-selling No. 1 *Escape*, but it confirmed that Journey's music had a large audience right to the end of its career. —*William Ruhlmann*

● **Greatest Hits** / 1988 / Columbia ◆◆◆◆
Greatest Hits is an excellent, thorough, 14-track collection containing all of Journey's big hits, from 1978's "Wheel in the Sky" to 1986's "I'll Be Alright without You." Although the songs aren't presented in chronological order and a handful of minor hits ("Suzanne," "Walks Like a Lady") aren't included, it doesn't matter, since every essential Journey single—"Only the Young," "Don't Stop Believin'," "Any Way You Want It," "Separate Ways," "Lovin', Touchin' Squeezin'," "Open Arms," "Send Her My Love"—is here, which means that it's all that most casual fans will ever need. —*Stephen Thomas Erlewine*

Time 3 / Dec. 1, 1992 / Columbia ◆◆◆
A three-disc box set of Journey is too much music for most listeners, although hardcore fans will be happy to know that all of their hits and best album tracks are included here. *Time 3* is more than comprehensive, but if you buy this you will never need to own another Journey album. —*AMG*

Trial by Fire / Oct. 22, 1996 / Sony ◆◆◆
After a ten-year hiatus, Journey returned to recording in 1996 with *Trial by Fire*, an album that sounds as if no time had passed between it and the band's last album, *Raised on Radio*. Journey has been completely unaffected by *any* trend in popular music, whether it's hair-metal, hip-hop, or alternative rock and, frankly, they're the better for it. *Trial by Fire* delivers exactly what any Journey fan wants—anthemic rockers and sweeping power ballads. Steve Perry sounds as powerful as ever, while Neal Schon's accomplished guitar licks remain as tasty as ever. The songwriting, as before, is slightly hit-and-miss, with singles like "When You Love a Woman" and "Message of Love" standing out from the handful of mediocre album tracks. Which means, if you've enjoyed Journey in the past, you're certain to enjoy the best moments of *Trial by Fire*, but if their arena rock had radio-ready ballads have never agreed with you, the album will not change your mind. —*Stephen Thomas Erlewine*

Joy Division

f. 1977, Manchester, England, **db.** May 18, 1980
Post-Punk
Formed in 1977 in the wake of the punk explosion in England, Joy Division became the first band in the post-punk movement by later emphasizing not anger and energy but mood and expression, pointing ahead to the rise of melancholy alternative music in the '80s. Though the group's raw initial sides fit the bill for any punk band, Joy Division later incorporated synthesizers (taboo in the low-tech world of '70s punk) and more haunting melodies, emphasized by the isolated, tortured lyrics of its lead vocalist, Ian Curtis. While the British punk movement shocked the world during the late '70s, Joy Division's quiet storm of musical restraint and emotive power proved to be just as important to independent music in the 1980s.

The band was founded in the fall of 1976, soon after the Sex Pistols had made their first appearance in Manchester. Guitarist Bernard Albrecht (b. Bernard Dicken, Jan. 4, 1956) and bassist Peter Hook (b. Feb. 13, 1956) had met while at the show and later formed a band called the Stiff Kittens; after placing an ad through a Manchester record store, they added vocalist Ian Curtis (b. July 15, 1956) and drummer Steve Brotherdale. Renamed Warsaw (from David Bowie's "Warszawa"), the band made its live debut the following May, supporting the Buzzcocks and Penetration at Manchester's Electric Circus. After the recording of several demos, Brotherdale quit the group in August 1977, prompting the hire of Stephen Morris (b. Oct. 28, 1957). A name-change to Joy Division in late 1977—necessitated by the punk band Warsaw Pakt—was inspired by Karol Cetinsky's World War II novel *The House of Dolls*. (In the book, the term "joy division" was used as slang for concentration-camp units wherein inmates were forced to prostitute themselves for the enjoyment of Nazi soldiers.)

Playing frequently in the north country during early 1978, the quartet gained the respect of several influential figures: Rob Gretton, a Manchester club DJ who became the group's manager; Tony Wilson, a TV/print journalist and owner of the Factory Records label; and Derek Branwood, a record executive with RCA Northwest, who recorded sessions in May 1978 for what was planned to be Joy Division's self-titled debut LP. Though several songs bounded with punk energy, the rest of the album showed at an early age the band's later trademarks: Curtis' themes of post-industrial restlessness and emotional despair, Hook's droning bass lines and the jagged guitar riffs of Albrecht.

The album should've been hailed as a punk classic, but when a studio engineer added synthesizers to several tracks—believing that the

punk movement had to move on and embrace new sounds—Joy Division scrapped the entire LP. (Titled *Warsaw* for a 1982 bootleg, the album was finally given wide issue ten years later.) The first actual Joy Division release came in June 1978, when the initial mid-1977 demos were released as the EP *An Ideal for Living*, on the band's own Enigma label. Early in 1979, the buzz surrounding Joy Division increased with a session recorded for John Peel's BBC radio show.

The group began recording with producer Martin Hannett and released *Unknown Pleasures* on old friend Tony Wilson's Factory label in July 1979. The album enjoyed immense critical acclaim and a long stay on the UK's independent charts. Encouraged by the punk buzz, the American Warner Bros. label offered a large distribution contract that fall. The band ignored it but did record another radio session for John Peel on November 26th. (Both sessions were later collected on the *Peel Sessions* album.)

During late 1979, Joy Division's manic live show gained many converts, partly due to rumors of Curtis' ill health. An epilepsy sufferer, he was prone to breakdowns and seizures while onstage—it soon grew difficult to distinguish the fits from his usual on-stage jerkiness and manic behavior. As the live dates continued and the new decade approached, Curtis grew weaker and more prone to seizures. After a short rest over the Christmas holiday, Joy Division embarked on a European tour during January, though several dates were cancelled because of Curtis. The group began recording its second LP after the tour ended (again with Hannett), and released "Love Will Tear Us Apart" in April. The single was again praised but failed to move beyond the independent charts. After one gig in early May, the members of Joy Division were given two weeks of rest before beginning the group's first US tour. Four days before the scheduled flight, however, Curtis was found dead in his home, the victim of a self-inflicted hanging.

Before Curtis' death, the band had agreed that Joy Division would cease to exist if any member left, for any reason. Ironically though, the summer of 1980 proved to be the blooming of the band's commercial status, when a re-release of "Love Will Tear Us Apart" rose to No. 13 on the British singles chart. In August, the release of *Closer* finally united critics' positivity with glowing sales, as the album peaked at No. 6. Before the end of the summer, *Unknown Pleasures* was charting as well.

By January of the following year, Hook, Morris, and Albrecht (now Bernard Sumner) had formed New Order, with Sumner taking over vocal duties. Also in 1981, the posthumous release of *Still*—including one side of rare tracks and one of live songs—rose to No. 5 on the British charts. As New Order's star began to shine during the '80s, the group had trouble escaping the long shadow of Curtis and Joy Division. "Love Will Tear Us Apart" charted for the third time in 1983, and 1988 also proved a big year for the defunct band: the reissued single "Atmosphere" hit No. 34 and a double-album compilation entitled *Substance* reached No. 7 in the album charts. Seven years later, the 15th anniversary of Curtis' death was memorialized with a new JD compilation (*Permanent: Joy Division 1995*), a tribute album (*A Means to an End*), and a biography of his life (*Touching from a Distance*) written by his widow, Deborah Curtis. —*John Bush*

☆ **Unknown Pleasures** / 1979 / Qwest ◆◆◆◆◆
Raw and vital, Joy Division's full-length debut juxtaposes the taut, visceral energy of the group's evolving sound with the ghostly presence of vocalist Ian Curtis, whose grasp on the corporeal world seems to diminish with each passing song. While as claustrophobic and remote as any of the band's records, *Unknown Pleasures* is informed by a sense of punk-influenced aggression absent from Joy Division's later work; the album's tangible tension derives from the efforts of the primal rhythm battery of Peter Hook and Stephen Morris to breathe life into the music at the same time that the vortex of Curtis' soul threatens to suck it all out. Remarkable. —*Jason Ankeny*

☆ **Closer** / 1980 / Qwest ◆◆◆◆◆
Released in the wake of Ian Curtis' suicide, *Closer* travels through the looking glass into a cold, hopeless world of menace and loss. The opener "Atrocity Exhibition" sets both the sonic and emotional tone of the record: brutal and distant, the music is stripped bare of its humanity, finding its foothold instead in metallic rhythms, damaged synth patterns and jagged guitars. Looming over the proceedings are Curtis' disembodied vocals, which grip the songs from seemingly beyond the physical plane; while the singer dominates *Closer*, his presence is remote and ephemeral—while he can be felt at every moment, in truth he was already gone. —*Jason Ankeny*

Still / 1981 / Qwest ◆◆◆
Still collects outtakes and rarities along with a live set recorded on May 2, 1980, just over two weeks prior to Ian Curtis' death. In addition to the atmospheric "Glass" and the haunting funeral march "Dead Souls," the studio sides include four leftover tracks from the sessions for *Unknown Pleasures*, while the concert set includes performances of

seminal tracks such as "Transmission," "Isolation," and "A Means to an End." Although neither as cogent nor as indispensable as the band's two studio records or the *Substance* compilation, *Still* is nonetheless a valuable chronicle of Joy Division's remarkable evolution, a growth charted by the inclusion of an early live cover of the Velvet Underground's "Sister Ray" to the only recorded version of the hypnotic "Ceremony," the ultimate Ian Curtis composition, which later resurfaced as the first single from New Order. —*Jason Ankeny*

★ **Substance** / 1988 / Qwest ◆◆◆◆◆
Collecting some riveting and rare material previously available only on singles and compilations, this offers a more diverse portrait of the band and works as both an introduction and a supplement to the original release. —*John Floyd*

Warsaw / 1994 / Intermusic ◆◆◆◆
What was planned to be Joy Division's first LP (unreleased until 1994, except in bootleg form) sounds like an album from the punk era—raw and edgy, undisciplined but tuneful, unlike the group's proper debut, *Unknown Pleasures*. All of the tracks were later seen in different form, but *Warsaw* still manages to captivate through its pure energy. In addition to the twelve tracks from the bootleg recordings, the album also includes five tracks from July 1977, the most punk-inspired songs in the group's discography. —*John Bush*

Permanent / Aug. 15, 1995 / Warner Brothers ◆◆◆
Featuring selected highlights from *Unknown Pleasures* and *Closer*, *Permanent* contains some of Joy Division's best songs, but the compilation isn't as useful as *Substance*, which featured early demos and B-sides, nor is it as mesmerizing as the band's two original studio albums. Consequently, *Permanent* is not only useless for dedicated fans, it's an incomplete and misleading introduction for casual fans, even though it contains a wealth of brilliant music. —*Stephen Thomas Erlewine*

Judas Priest

f. 1973, Birmingham, England, db. 1993
Hard Rock, Heavy Metal, British Metal

Judas Priest was one of the most influential heavy metal bands of the '70s, spearheading the "new wave of British heavy metal" late in the decade. Decked out in leather and chains, the band fused the gothic doom of Black Sabbath with the riffs and speed of Led Zeppelin, as well as adding a vicious two-lead guitar attack; in doing so, they set the pace for much popular heavy metal from 1975 until 1985, as well as laying the groundwork for the speed- and death-metal of the '80s.

Formed in Birmingham, England, in 1970, the group's core members were guitarist K.K. Downing and bassist Ian Hill. Joined by Alan Atkins and drummer John Ellis, the band played their first concert in 1971. Atkins' previous band was called Judas Priest, yet the members decided it was the best name for the new group. The band played numerous shows throughout 1971; during the year, Ellis was replaced by Alan Moore; by the end of the year, Chris Campbell replaced Moore. After a solid year of touring the UK, Atkins and Campbell left the band in 1973 and were replaced by vocalist Rob Halford and drummer John Hinch. They continued touring, including a visit to Germany and the Netherlands in 1974; by the time the tour was completed, they had secured a record contract with Gull, an independent UK label.

Before recording their debut album, *Rocka Rolla*, Judas Priest added guitarist Glenn Tipton. They released the record in September of 1974 to almost no attention. The following year they gave a well-received performance at the Reading Festival and Hinch departed the band; he was replaced by Alan Moore. Later that year, the group released *Sad Wings of Destiny*, which earned some positive reviews. However, the lack of sales were putting the band in a dire financial situation, which was remedied by an international contract with CBS Records.

Sin After Sin (1977) was the first album released under that contract; it was recorded with Simon Phillips, who replaced Moore. The record received positive reviews and the band departed for their first American tour, with Les Binks on drums. When they returned to England, Judas Priest recorded 1978's *Stained Class*, the record that established them as an international force in metal. Along with 1979's *Hell Bent for Leather* (*Killing Machine* in the UK), *Stained Class* began the "new wave of British heavy metal" movement. A significant number of bands adapted Priest's leather-clad image and hard, driving sound, making their music harder, faster, and louder.

After releasing *Hell Bent for Leather*, the band recorded the live album *Unleashed in the East* (1979) in Japan; it became their first platinum album in America. Les Binks left the band in 1979; he was replaced by former Trapeze drummer Dave Holland. Their next album, 1980's *British Steel*, entered the British charts at No. 3, launched the hit singles "Breaking the Law" and "Living After Midnight," and was their

second American platinum record; *Point of Entry*, released the following year, was nearly as successful.

At the beginning of the '80s, Judas Priest was a top concert attraction around the world, in addition to being a best-selling recording artist. Featuring the hit single "You've Got Another Thing Comin'," *Screaming for Vengeance* (1982) marked the height of their popularity, peaking at No. 17 in America and selling over a million copies. Two years later, *Defenders of the Faith* nearly matched its predecessor's performance, yet metal tastes were beginning to change, as Metallica and other speed/thrash-metal groups started to grow in popularity. That shift was evident on 1986's *Turbo*, where Judas Priest seemed out of touch with current trends; nevertheless, the record sold over a million copies in America on the basis of name recognition alone. However, 1987's *Priest...Live!* was their first album since *Stained Class* not to go gold. *Ram It Down* (1988) was a return to raw metal and returned the group to gold status. Dave Holland left after this record and was replaced by Scott Travis for 1990's *Painkiller*. Like *Ram It Down*, *Painkiller* didn't make an impact outside the band's diehard fans, yet the group was still a popular concert act. In the late '80s, Rob Halford began his own thrash band, Fight, and soon left Judas Priest. The rest of the band quietly faded away. —*Stephen Thomas Erlewine*

Rocka Rolla / 1974 / RCA ◆◆◆
While Judas Priest was still trying to find their footing on *Rocka Rolla*, the group managed to turn in an effective, lean debut album that suggested their potential. —*Stephen Thomas Erlewine*

Sad Wings of Destiny / 1976 / RCA ◆◆◆
Vintage Judas Priest from the mid-'70s, it's an excellent example of British heavy metal coming into its own and of a band beginning to gain acceptance on both sides of the Atlantic. The album includes "The Ripper" and "Victim of Changes," the latter of which demonstrates the full vocal range of Rob Halford. —*John Book*

Sin After Sin / 1977 / Columbia ◆◆◆
Sin After Sin was Judas Priest's first album for Columbia Records and it marked a noticeable improvement in their songwriting, as well as indicating the group was beginning to develop a signature sound. —*Stephen Thomas Erlewine*

Stained Class / Apr. 1978 / Columbia ◆◆◆◆
Judas Priest came into its own on *Stained Class*, a lean and lethal collection of brutal riffs. Halford's lyrics were deliberately morbid—"Beyond the Realms of Death" and "Saints in Hell" are about as bleak as heavy metal gets—but he sang them with a salacious glee, as the band hammered out a series of relentless power chords. *Stained Class* sounded like nothing else in heavy metal at the time and it sowed the seeds of the death-metal movement of the '80s. —*Stephen Thomas Erlewine*

Hell Bent for Leather / Mar. 1979 / Columbia ◆◆◆◆
In 1979, Judas Priest was growing more and more influential. And as the 1980s progressed, it would become crystal clear that the British headbangers—who influenced everyone from Iron Maiden to Metallica to King Diamond—had every bit as great an impact as fellow British headbangers Black Sabbath. One of the Priest's strongest albums, *Hell Bent for Leather* cannot be described in anything less than glowing terms. Although gothic themes are present on such treasures as "The Green Manalishi (With the Two-Pronged Crown)"—originally recorded by Fleetwood Mac—"Evil Fantasies" and "Before the Dawn," the album generally isn't as dark or morbid as *Stained Class* or *Sin After Sin*. But musically, the band is as aggressive and brutally intense as ever. The two-guitar attack of Glenn Tipton and KK Downing is characteristically blistering, and lead singer Rob Halford never sounded more inspired. For those with even a casual interest in metal, *Hell Bent for Leather* is essential listening. —*Alex Henderson*

Unleashed in the East (Live in Japan) / Oct. 1979 / Columbia ◆◆◆◆
Recorded live in Japan, this was the album that helped Judas Priest finally break through in America with support from critics and radio airplay. The album is an exceptional live performance. The songs chosen are a good example of their material from the '70s. —*John Book*

● **British Steel** / 1980 / Columbia ◆◆◆◆
British Steel added something that *Stained Class* and *Hell Bent for Leather* were missing—melody. Halford had managed to write some strong pop hooks for the album, particularly on the driving "Breaking the Law" and "Living After Midnight." Instead of diluting the group's power, the melodic hooks made them more forceful, arguably making *British Steel* their finest moment. —*Stephen Thomas Erlewine*

Point of Entry / 1981 / Columbia ◆◆◆
Point of Entry was another major-league success for Judas Priest. With well-written songs, solid musicianship from the entire band, and powerful vocals from Rob Halford, Judas Priest helped define heavy metal in the '80s. Included is "Heading Out to the Highway," "Hot Rockin'," and "Don't Go." —*John Book*

Screaming for Vengeance / 1982 / Columbia ◆◆◆◆

Screaming for Vengeance was Judas Priest's most successful album, featuring the hit single "You've Got Another Thing Comin'." While the group had backed away from the blitzkrieg attack of their late-'70s albums, they had increased the volume, turning in a set of thundering, heavy riffs that managed to stay melodic and catchy. The result was one of the band's finest albums; along with *British Steel*, it is their most accessible and memorable work. —*Stephen Thomas Erlewine*

Defenders of the Faith / 1984 / Columbia ◆◆◆

Defenders of the Faith was just as heavy as *Screaming for Vengeance*, but it lacked the well-constructed songs that made the previous record so impressive. Nevertheless, Judas Priest sounds tight and powerful throughout the record, which is one of the reasons why the album was another platinum success for the band. —*Stephen Thomas Erlewine*

Turbo / 1986 / Columbia ◆◆◆

Lacking the overwhelming power and heaviness of Judas Priest's two previous albums, *Turbo* was a streamlined collection that emphasized the group's pop leanings. However, the group's songs weren't quite as well written as their earlier material, making the record a muddled, unfocused affair. —*Stephen Thomas Erlewine*

Priest…Live! / 1987 / Columbia ◆◆

Judas Priest's first live album, *Unleashed in the East*, was a power-house, but *Priest…Live!* was a sad, lackluster document of an aging heavy metal band desperately trying to hold on to their glory days. No matter how hard they tried, the group could not hide the fact that their power was declining rapidly. —*Stephen Thomas Erlewine*

Ram It Down / 1988 / Columbia ◆◆

Ram It Down recaptured some of the force of *British Steel* and *Screaming for Vengeance*, yet Judas Priest's songwriting was the weakest since *Sin After Sin*. Even though the guitars were as bracing as anything on *Defenders of the Faith* and the group performed with conviction, they could not save the album from mediocrity. —*Stephen Thomas Erlewine*

Painkiller / Aug. 1990 / Columbia ◆◆

After going in a more commercial direction during much of the 1980s on albums like *Turbo*, Judas Priest responded to thrash metal's challenge with the brutal *Painkiller*—clearly its heaviest album in at least a decade and one of its best offerings ever. The Priest was taking no prisoners this time. Pop embellishments are avoided altogether, and the veteran headbangers go for the type of intensity and brute force associated with Metallica and Slayer. While *Painkiller* was undeniably fresh-sounding, it also represented a return to basics for the band. Indeed, when Priest toured with Testament and Megadeth in 1990, Rob Halford & Co. proclaimed their commitment to heaviness in a major way. But unfortunately, Priest suffered a major blow when Halford left the band the following year. —*Alex Henderson*

● **Metal Works '73-'93** / May 18, 1993 / Columbia ◆◆◆◆

Over two discs, *Metal Works '73-'93* winds its way through Judas Priest's 20-year career, hitting most of the high points as well as the low points and somehow managing to overlook seven of their eleven UK hits. Still, there isn't a better place to get acquainted with the band, which really was one of the most important metal acts of the late '70s and early '80s. —*AMG*

Phil Judd

b. Mar. 23, 1953, Hastings, New Zealand
New Wave

A founding member and early creative force behind New Zealand's Split Enz, Phil Judd quickly became disillusioned with the music industry and dropped out of the band in 1977. After rejoining Split Enz and leaving again, he spent a short time with two legendary New Zealand punk bands—Suburban Reptiles and Enemy—eventually setting up his own three-piece band, Swingers. Swingers had some minor success in their homeland (including a No. 1 hit with the unforgettable "Counting the Beat"), but fell apart by the early '80s. Judd released his first and only solo album in 1982, *Private Lives* (edited down to *The Swinger* EP in the US). It was virtually ignored and Judd changed directions, focusing more on composing film music and pursuing art. In 1986, he joined with former Split Enz bandmates Nigel Griggs and Noel Crombie, along with guitarist Michael Den Elzen, to form Schnell Fenster. After two albums, the group broke up in 1992. Judd has since returned to film music along with rumored future solo projects in the works. Despite consistently producing some really terrific music, Judd's eccentric approach to pop music and skewed outlook have sadly been overlooked. —*Chris Woodstra*

The Swinger / 1983 / MCA ◆◆◆

A six-song EP drawn from the Australian *Private Lives* LP. *The Swinger* picks up where Judd's previous band, the Swingers, left off. Quirky pop songs with slightly odd subject matter are the focus but

with a more polished, radio-ready production. Unfortunately overlooked, this is his only solo work to date. —*Chris Woodstra*

● **Private Lives** / 1983 / Mushroom ◆◆◆◆

Sadly, Judd's only full-length album, *Private Lives* never saw release outside of Australia/New Zealand, but fans of his work with Swingers or Split Enz should seek this one out rather than the inferior, edited version—*The Swinger*. —*Chris Woodstra*

Jules & the Polar Bears

f. 1978, db. 1980
Rock 'n' Roll, New Wave

After the demise of the Funky Kings, singer-songwriter Jules Shear formed his own band consisting of Stephen Hague (keyboards and, later, a noted producer), Richard Bredice (guitar), David White (bass), and David Beebe (drums). They were signed to Columbia Records in 1978 solely on the basis of Shear's demos—at the time, the band had never played live together. They recorded their first LP, *Got No Breeding*, in 1978, which quickly found critical acclaim, drawing favorable comparisons to Jackson Browne, the Kinks, Bob Dylan, and Bruce Springsteen. Unfortunately, it failed to sell when Columbia tried to lump the band in with its new wave promotion. 1979's *Fenetiks*, another fine effort, went virtually unnoticed as well. A third LP, *Bad for Business*, was recorded, but Columbia decided to pass on it and the band folded. Shear moved on to a distinguished, though commercially unsuccessful, solo career, and Hague focused on production. The albums, especially *Got No Breeding*, remain cult favorites. *Bad for Business* was finally released in late '96 by Columbia/Legacy. —*Chris Woodstra*

Bad for Business / Sep. 3, 1996 / Sony/Legacy ◆◆◆

Deemed not commercially viable and rated a bit on the weird side by the powers that be at Columbia Records in 1980, *Bad for Business*, the third album from Jules and the Polar Bears, remained in the Columbia vaults for 16 years before being issued in 1996. *Bad for Business* still seems somewhat quirky after all these years, although not really much more than its predecessor *Fenetiks*, with which it shares a similar sound thanks to Stephen Hague's keyboards. The real treat in Columbia's decision to release the record is its batch of hook-laden tunes and the frenetic spurts of lyrics from Jules Shear. Songs such as the driving pop of "In Love with the Ballet" and the sweet but edgy "Only the Motion" show Shear to be in fine form on *Bad for Business*. This is a chance to further discover a terrific songwriter and one of the criminally overlooked bands of the late '70s. —*Brett Hartenbach*

The Jungle Brothers

f. 1986, Brooklyn, NY
Hip Hop, Alternative Rap, Jazz-Rap

Although they predated the jazz-rap innovations of De La Soul, A Tribe Called Quest and Digable Planets, the Jungle Brothers were never able to score with either rap fans or mainstream audiences, perhaps due to their embrace of a range of styles—including house music, Afrocentric philosophy, a James Brown fixation, and of course, the use of jazz samples—each of which has been the sole basis for the start-up of a rap act. Signed to a major label for 1989's *Done by the Forces of Nature*, the JB's failed to connect on that album—hailed by some as an ignored classic—or the follow-up, *J Beez Wit the Remedy*.

Mike Gee (b. Michael Small; Harlem, NY), DJ Sammy B (b. Sammy Burwell; Harlem, NY), and Baby Bam (b. Nathaniel Hall; Brooklyn, NY) came together as the Jungle Brothers in the mid-'80s and began their recording career at the dance label Idler's. The result of the sessions, *Straight Out the Jungle*, was released in early 1988. The album's Afrocentric slant gained the Jungle Brothers entry into the Native Tongue Posse, a loose collective formed by hip-hop legend Afrikaa Bambaataa including Queen Latifah (and, later, De La Soul and A Tribe Called Quest). The album's most far-out cut was a remix by British DJ Todd Terry of "I'll House You," an early experiment in what later became known as hip-house.

Though *Straight Out the Jungle* had not sold in large quantities, Warner Bros. signed the trio in 1989 and released a second album, *Done by the Forces of Nature*, that same year. Though it was issued around the time of De La Soul's groundbreaking *3 Feet High and Rising* LP and gained just as many positive reviews, the album was overlooked by most listeners. The Jungle Brothers' chances of mainstream acceptance weren't helped at all by a four-year absence after the release of *Done by the Forces of Nature*, inspired mostly by Warner Bros. marketing strategies. Finally, in the summer of 1993, *J Beez Wit the Remedy* appeared, complete with a sizeable push from Warner Bros.; unfortunately, the large amount of promotion failed to carry the album. Obviously not learning from their earlier mistakes, Warner Bros. also delayed the release of the group's fourth album, *Raw Deluxe*, until mid-1997. —*John Bush*

Straight Out the Jungle / 1988 / Warlock ✦✦✦✦
The trio's debut is powered by muscular funk riffs underpinned by an Afrocentric sensibility and a sharp sense of humor. —*John Floyd*

Done by the Forces of Nature / Nov. 1989 / Warner Brothers ✦✦✦✦
By injecting some vocal delicacy and some clever samples into their moderately militant message, they made a second album that elaborates on their own winning formula. —*John Floyd*

J. Beez Wit the Remedy / Jun. 22, 1993 / Warner Brothers ✦✦✦
Nearly four years after *Done By the Forces of Nature*, the Jungle Brothers return with a hazy, funky album, filled with their brand of literate hip-hop. Although they've made some stylistic progressions since the last record, it wasn't enough to be a completely groundbreaking release, nor was it commericial enough to break them out of their critically acclaimed/cult status. Instead, it was another solid, inventive album that didn't receive the attention it deserved. —*Stephen Thomas Erlewine*

Mickey Jupp

b. 1940, Exxex, England
Guitar, Vocals / Rock 'n' Roll, Pub Rock
Like Dave Edmunds, guitarist/pianist/vocalist Mickey Jupp was a champion of traditional rock 'n' roll during the late '70s, a time when it had been all but discarded. Unlike Edmunds, Jupp wrote the majority of his own material, which updated '50s rock 'n' roll with a tongue-in-cheek irony.

Jupp began his career with the Essex-based British R&B group the Orioles in the early '60s. The band earned a devoted local following in the early '60s, yet they never had the opportunity to record. The Orioles broke up late in 1965, after Jupp was arrested for not making alimony payments to his wife. Three years later, he returned to music, forming Legend, who laid the groundwork for the English pub rock of the early '70s. Following the release of their third album in 1971, Legend disbanded, and Jupp took another lengthy break from music. When he was coaxed back into performing in 1975 by Lee Brileaux, the lead singer of Dr. Feelgood, pub rock was in its last days, yet Jupp was well-respected in the scene, since both Ducks Deluxe and Dr. Feelgood had recorded versions of his songs ("Cheque Book" and "Down at the Doctors," respectively).

Jupp released his first solo single, "Nature's Radio," on Arista Records in 1978. The single led to a contract with Stiff Records, who released the "Old Rock N Roller" single and the *Juppanese* album in 1978; the bulk of *Juppanese* was recorded with Rockpile and produced by Nick Lowe. Released the same year as his debut, *Mickey*

Jupp's Legend featured material from his previous band. Following the release of *Juppanese*, Jupp joined Stiff's Rail Tour, although he left the lineup before it hit the US because he was afraid of flying. Shortly afterward, he left Stiff Records and signed with Chrysalis in 1979. The same year he released *Long Distance Romancer*, which was produced by for 10cc members Kevin Godley and Lol Creme; like *Juppanese*, it failed to gain a large audience. Jupp moved over to A&M Records in 1982, releasing *Some People Can't Dance*. After releasing one more record on A&M, 1983's *Shampoo Haircut and Shave*, he was dropped from the label. Jupp spent the rest of the '80s and '90s touring the UK, releasing the occassional album on independent labels. —*Stephen Thomas Erlewine*

● **Juppanese** / 1978 / Stiff ✦✦✦✦
Before he released his first solo album in 1978, Mickey Jupp's reputation as a songwriter had begun to grow, as pub rockers like Dr. Feelgood and Ducks Deluxe were covering his compositions. As a performer, Jupp didn't fare as well. The main problem with *Juppanese*, his first solo album, is his lifeless vocals. The first half of *Juppanese* was recorded with Rockpile, the rock 'n' roll group fronted by guitarist Dave Edmunds and bassist Nick Lowe. Because Jupp's strength is standard three-chord rock 'n' roll, the first side of the album works the best; while it never captures the joyous energy of Rockpile's best moments, it is considerably tighter and rawer than the slick second side, where Jupp's nondescript voice struggles to be heard amid the studio professionalism. Even though it features several of Jupp's finest songs, including "You'll Never Get Me up in One of Those" and "Old Rock 'n' Roller," *Juppanese* doesn't include "Switchboard Susan," arguably his best song. Rockpile recorded the backing track for the album, yet Jupp refused to sing on it. Nick Lowe kept the tape, recording his own vocals for the song; his version is included on his 1979 album *Labour of Lust*. —*Stephen Thomas Erlewine*

Long Distance Romancer / 1979 / Line ✦✦✦
Long Distance Romancer, Jupp's first release for Chrysalis Records, continued the polished rock 'n' roll of the second half of *Juppanese*, except it bettered it. Unlike Gary Brooker, producers Godley and Creme could exploit the slick, synth-based sound that Jupp was beginning to mine. However, the highly produced sound doesn't mesh with Jupp's main strength—direct, simple rock 'n' roll. Instead of being powered by a driving beat, "Switchboard Susan" winds up sinking in the layers of keyboards and processed guitars. Yet the production does manage to save slight songs like "You Made a Fool out of Me," creating an album of pleasant pop-rock that never manages to really sink in. —*Stephen Thomas Erlewine*

K

Ernie K-Doe

b. Feb. 22, 1936, New Orleans, LA
Vocals / New Orleans R&B, R&B

New Orleans vocalist Ernest Kador, Jr., had one unforgettable R&B hit in 1961, aided by Benny Spellman's authoritative bass vocal. "Mother-In-Law" topped the charts for five weeks, and was recorded for Minit. K-Doe originally sang with The Blue Diamonds, who recorded for Savoy in 1954. Their ranks included Huey "Piano" Smith, Billy Tate, Frank Fields, and Earl Palmer. "Te-Ta-Te-Ta-Ta" did reasonably well as a follow-up single, peaking at No. 21. It would be six years before K-Doe would get another chart hit; the singles "Later for Tomorrow" and a remake of "Until the Real Thing Comes Along" each gained only marginal success for Duke in 1967, his last releases to make any national noise. —*Ron Wynn*

● **Burn! K-Doe, Burn!** / 1989 / Charly ◆◆◆◆

Kajagoogoo

f. 1982, Hertfordshire, England, **db.** 1985
New Wave, New Romantic

Kajagoogoo's light synth-pop and pretty, photogenic look made the group an instant sensation in the early days of MTV. Led by vocalist Limahl (born Chris Hamill), the group also featured Steve Askew (guitar), Nick Beggs (vocals, bass), and Stuart Crawford (vocals, synthesizer). Produced by Duran Duran's Nick Rhodes, Kajagoogoo's debut single "Too Shy" hit No. 1 in the UK in early 1983; it peaked at No. 5 in the US. "Too Shy" and the following album *White Feathers* proved the band may have shared some similarities with Duran Duran and Naked Eyes—they were pretty and they played immediately accessible, polished pop—yet Kajagoogoo was essentially a synth-pop variation of a bubblegum group. Like a bubblegum group, they were destined to have only one big hit; "Ooh to Be Ah" and "Hang on Now"; both were Top 15 UK hits, yet neither made an impact in the US. At the end of the 1983, Limahl left for a solo career. Kajagoogoo continued with Nick Beggs as the lead vocalist, releasing *Islands* in 1984; it disappeared from the charts quickly. Meanwhile, Limahl scored a hit with the theme song from *The Neverending Story*. Perhaps in an attempt to gain some credibility, the group shortened their name to Kaja and released *Crazy People's Right to Speak*. It was a sales disaster and the band broke up the following year. Limahl continued to record, albeit without much chart success; eventually, his records were not released in either the US or the UK—his last album, 1992's *Love Is Blind*, was only released in Germany. —*Stephen Thomas Erlewine*

White Feathers / 1983 / One Way ◆◆◆◆

"Too Shy" was one of the flimsiest singles of the new wave era, a cloying and catchy bubblegum tune disguised as synth-pop. Kajagoogoo never quite matched those heights again—in fact, they rarely even came close. Their debut album *White Feathers* is filled with similarly lightweight synth-pop like "Magician Man," "Ooh to Be Ah," "Eronomics," "This Car Is Fast" and the theme song "Kajagoogoo." All of these are pleasantly danceable in a sub-Duran Duran fashion, but they are also frequently inane and ridiculous, and are of no use to anyone but hardcore new wave fetishists. —*Stephen Thomas Erlewine*

Islands / 1984 / EMI ◆◆◆

Limahl departed Kajagoogoo at the earliest opportunity, leaving the group to pursue the stardom that was destined to be his. Of course, fate decided that Limahl would be banished to obscurity after recording the theme for *The Neverending Story*, but his former band joined the ranks of the forgotten much sooner. Replacing Limahl with vocalist Nick Beggs, the group replicated the lightweight, danceable synth-pop of its debut on their second album, *Islands,* with one crucial difference—this time, there's no hooks. And without hooks or Limahl's campy, fey star appeal, Kajagoogoo's music just disappears into thin air. —*Stephen Thomas Erlewine*

● **Too Shy: The Singles . . . & More** / Sep. 7, 1993 / EMI ◆◆◆◆

As this collection proves, Kajagoogoo was a one-hit wonder. Only "Too Shy" stands out amidst the slick, bouncy new wave synth-pop that dominates the compilation, which covers material from all of the band's albums, as well as lead singer Limahl's solo career. Most of the music on the rest of the collection is pleasant, but none of it is memorable. However, "Too Shy" is one of the best pop singles of the new wave era, driven by layers of bubbly synths, an inanely catchy chorus, and Limahl's thin, airy vocals. —*Stephen Thomas Erlewine*

Kaleidoscope

f. 1964, England, **db.** 1970
Psychedelic

No relation to the far better known American Kaleidoscope, though this British group was also psychedelic, and was active at almost exactly the same time in the late '60s. Highly esteemed by some collectors, Kaleidoscope epitomized certain of the more precious traits of British psychedelia with their fairytale lyrics and gentle, swirling folky sound. At times they sound like a far more melodic and accessible Incredible String Band. Their folky ballads have aged best, and although there's some period charm to be found throughout their two albums, it's all a bit too cloying to rank among the finest unknown psychedelia. Although they had a solid underground reputation in Britain, they never found wide success, and evolved into a similar group, Fairfield Parlour, by the end of the '60s. —*Richie Unterberger*

● **Tangerine Dream** / 1967 / Fontana ◆◆◆◆

Probably has the edge as the best of their two albums, but not by much. Includes several of their best songs: "Flight from Ashiya," "Dive into Yesterday," "The Murder of Lewis Tollani," and especially the fragile ballad "Please Excuse My Face." —*Richie Unterberger*

Faintly Blowing / 1969 / Fontana ◆◆◆

There's really not much difference between this and their debut album: if you like one, you'll like the other. It's perhaps more fully produced than their maiden effort, the standout being the ballad "Poem," which vies with "Please Excuse My Face" as their best composition. —*Richie Unterberger*

Kaleidoscope

f. 1966, Berkeley, CA, **db.** 1970
Psychedelic, Folk-Rock

Kaleidoscope were arguably the most eclectic band of the psychedelic era, weaving together folk, blues, Middle Eastern, and acid more often and seamlessly than any other musicians. The California group were formed under the nucleus of multi-instrumentalists David Lindley and Chris Darrow in the mid-'60s. Adding fiddle, banjo, and various exotic string instruments such as the oud and saz to the traditional rock lineup, Kaleidoscope complemented their experimental sounds with taut and witty (if lyrically eccentric) songwriting. Other important members were Solomon Feldthouse, who specialized in the Turkish-style instruments, and Chester Crill, who, to make documentation just that much more difficult, sometimes used odd pseudonyms like Fenrus Epp.

With the exception of their mawkish forays into old-timey music, Kaleidoscope's work holds up well. Their first three albums were their best, highlighted by the lengthy tracks "Taxim" and "Seven-Ate Sweet," which are groundbreaking fusions of Middle Eastern music and rock. Kaleidoscope were a popular live act, even incorporating some flamenco and belly dancers into their performances. But in commercial terms, their very eclecticism probably worked against them. Hit singles, too, were a difficult proposition for such a versatile group to get to grips with, although several of their 45s were pretty good. One of the best, "Nobody," was a most unusual fusion of R&B and psychedelia that found the group backing veteran rock and blues greats Larry Williams and Johnny "Guitar" Watson.

Kaleidoscope's eclecticism may have been a by-product of numerous personnel changes throughout the last half of the '60s that would make the construction of a family tree a most unwieldy task. Darrow, in fact, only lasted a couple of albums; in 1970, shortly after their fourth album, they split up. Several of the group's more important contributors reunited for an album in 1975 (although Lindley played only a small part); there was another reunion record in 1988. —*Richie Unterberger*

Side Trips / Jun. 1967 / Epic ✦✦✦✦

A Beacon from Mars / Jan. 1968 / Epic ✦✦✦

The Incredible Kaleidoscope / Jun. 1969 / Epic ✦✦✦
Coming out of the San Francisco scene of the late '60s, Kaleidoscope melds rock, blues, and middle eastern rhythms together to form a rather interesting kaleidoscope of sound. This release includes a cover of Howlin' Wolf's "Killing Floor" along with what would become something of a highlight from this band called "Seven-Ate Sweet." Oh, and for those who are interested, Kaleidoscope boasts David Lindley as a member. Good, but now sounding dated, it is worth your while. —*James Chrispell*

Bacon from Mars / Aug. 1983 / Edsel ✦✦✦
The most intelligent compilation of their more accessible songs. Includes highlights of their first three albums, three tracks from non-LP singles, and a lengthy history of the band. —*Richie Unterberger*

Rampe Rampe / Jun. 1984 / Edsel ✦✦✦
Focusing on the more experimental and Middle Eastern-influenced side of the band, this five-track LP includes all three of their groundbreaking, ten-minute-plus jams—"Taxim," "Seven-Ate Sweet," and "Beacon from Mars"—as well as a couple of nifty shorter tunes that were left off the *Bacon from Mars* compilation. —*Richie Unterberger*

● **Egyptian Candy (A Collection)** / 1990 / Epic ✦✦✦✦

Big Daddy Kane

b. Brooklyn, NY
Vocals / Hip Hop
Brooklyn-ite Big Daddy Kane (born Antonio Hardy, KANE is an acronym for King Asiatic Nobody's Equal) has been able to balance nicely his image as the ultimate hipster with the requisite solemnity and air of indignation and anger necessary to creditably deliver messages of Afrocentric awareness and Muslim reverence. He's done alternately inspirational, prophetical, ridiculous, and scandalous raps over his career, and has also managed to include duets with the maestro of love Barry White and legendary comedian Rudy Ray Moore, aka Dolemite, who laid waste to Kane in a dozens (insult-swapping) classic.

Big Daddy Kane has been a high profile figure the past couple of years. Not only has he appeared in such films as *Posse* and *Gunmen*, but he also posed in Madonna's controversial photo book *Sex*, and issued a defiant disc *Looks Like a Job for Big Daddy Kane* that offered no apologies for past actions and ridiculed unnamed individuals he claimed were fronting as gangsters.—*Ron Wynn*

Looks Like a Job for Big Daddy / May 25, 1993 / Cold Chillin' ✦✦✦
Looks Like a Job for Big Daddy Kane was a solid comeback record by Kane, bringing him back to the harder beats of his earlier albums. His rapping hasn't lost its spark, and the music is sparse and funky. However, it didn't have the same flair or innovation of *Long Live the Kane* and *It's a Big Daddy Thing*, and it fell off the charts quickly. —*Stephen Thomas Erlewine*

Kansas

f. 1970, Topeka, KS, **db.** 1983
Art-Rock/Progressive-Rock, Pop-Rock, Arena Rock
Popular prog-rock group from Topeka, whose ranks included Steve Walsh (vocals, keyboards), Kerry Livgren (guitar, keyboards), Rich Williams (guitar), Robby Steinhardt (violin), Dave Hope (bass), and Phil Ehart on percussion. Kansas' music leaned more towards progressive arena rock than the artsier, more symphonic music of other groups like Yes and King Crimson. Hits like "Carry On Wayward Son" and "Point of Know Return" cemented that reputation and resulted in multi-platinum success in the late '70s. Walsh, unhappy with the more commercial direction the band had taken, left the group in the early '80s and recorded a solo album. He was replaced by John Elefante. Without Walsh, their primary songwriter, the band lost direction and broke up in 1983. Livgren subsequently became a contemporary Christian artist. Walsh, Williams, and Ehart re-formed in 1986 with ex-Dixie Dregs gui-

tarist Steve Morse and bassist Billy Greer joining the band. —*Steve Huey*

Kansas / 1974 / Kirshner ✦✦✦✦
This encouraging debut reflected an infatuation with English art-rock. —*Rick Clark*

Song for America / 1975 / Kirshner ✦✦✦
The title cut comprises some beautiful passages. While they never really attained the intensity of art-rock bands like Yes, this album is possibly Kansas' most fully realized artistic effort at testing the possibilities of the genre. —*Rick Clark*

Leftoverture / 1976 / Kirshner ✦✦✦✦
The rock hit "Carry On Wayward Son" catapulted Kansas (and this album) into the big arena rock circuit. —*Rick Clark*

Point of Know Return / 1977 / Kirshner ✦✦✦

Audio-Visions / 1980 / Legacy/Epic ✦✦✦
By the time of its eighth album, *Audio-Visions*, Kansas had entered the post-platinum, solo-album phase of the typical successful rock group's career. Leaders Kerry Livgren and Steve Walsh were devoting time to making their own records, and Kansas was becoming a part-time occupation. The two divided up the songwriting chores on *Audio-Visions*, alternating Livgren's always spiritual and by now explicitly religious lyrical sentiments and ornate musical structures with Walsh's earthier, and harder-rocking concerns. Livgren's Christian-themed "Hold On" ("Outside the door He is waiting") made the Top 40, and Walsh's "Got to Rock" was a singles-chart entry, but nothing here matched the music from the group's late-'70s heyday. *Audio-Visions* was the last of seven straight Kansas albums to go gold or platinum and the last album made by the group's most successful lineup. In 1981, Walsh quit. —*William Ruhlmann*

Vinyl Confessions / 1982 / Legacy/Epic ✦✦✦
Replacing Steve Walsh with singer/keyboard player John Elefante, Kansas demonstrated that it could carry on by scoring its biggest hit in four years with the Top 20 "Play the Game Tonight," the leadoff track from *Vinyl Confessions*. Like now-undisputed group leader Kerry Livgren, Elefante was a born-again Christian, however, and his involvement in the songwriting turned the group decisively toward religious lyrical sentiments, often of a judgmental, we versus you nature. It's possible that fans who had been happy to accept the notion that "we are dust in the wind" were less patient with the ideas expressed in Elefante's "Face It" ("How many times do I have to tell you") or Livgren's "(You're Standing on the) Borderline." Or maybe it was just that it was getting hard to distinguish Kansas from Foreigner and Journey. In any case, *Vinyl Confessions* was Kansas' first album since its debut not to go gold. —*William Ruhlmann*

Drastic Measures / Jul. 1983 / Legacy/Epic ✦✦
John Elefante, who had joined Kansas for 1982's *Vinyl Confessions*, dominated its next album, *Drastic Measures*, writing six of nine songs. Elefante seemed a little unnerved by the new attention ("Everybody's My Friend"), while bandleader Kerry Livgren seemed burned out by the pressure to sell records ("Mainstream"). In that attempt, Kansas turned toward more of a hard rock/heavy metal sound. But the group's enervation was palpable, and it spread to their fans: *Drastic Measures* was the least successful Kansas album since the group's debut. Unsurprisingly, it was also the last album Kansas made before disbanding. Kerry Livgren became a solo Contemporary Christian artist, and John Elefante became his producer. —*William Ruhlmann*

● **The Best of Kansas** / 1984 / Epic ✦✦✦✦
It contains the essential rock radio hits "Dust in the Wind," "Carry on Wayward Son," and "Point of Know Return," as well as improved remastering from the original tapes. —*Rick Clark*

Power / 1986 / MCA ✦✦✦

In the Spirit of Things / 1988 / MCA ✦✦✦
Pink Floyd producer Bob Ezrin gives Kansas a sonically impressive sound. Fans of orchestral mainstream rock will like this, particularly "One Man, One Heart," "One Big Sky," "House on Fire," and "The Preacher." Ex-Dixie Dregs guitarist Steve Morse and vocalist Steve Walsh shine. —*Rick Clark*

Box Set / Jul. 12, 1994 / Epic ✦✦✦✦

Katrina & the Waves

f. 1981, England
New Wave, Pop-Rock
Led by ex-Soft Boy guitarist Kimberly Rew, Katrina and the Waves effortlessly evoked the irresistibly catchy guitar-pop of the mid-'60s with their first three albums in the early '80s. Not only could Rew write songs that were instantly memorable ("Goin' Down to Liverpool" and "Walking on Sunshine"), but the band had a dynamic lead singer with the Kansas-born Katrina Leskanich, who could sound sweet or tough according to the material. After scoring a hit single with "Walking on

Sunshine" in 1985, the band began to add a little bit of soul on their next album, *Waves*. While the experimentation was flawed, what really hurt the record was the fact that Rew only contributed two songs. *Waves* marked a downturn in their commercial fortunes, which was fixed with 1989's *Break of Hearts*, when the band turned into indistinguishable commercial hacks; they were rewarded with a Top 20 hit, "That's the Way." Following *Break of Hearts*, Katrina and the Waves drifted for a number of years. In 1993, they began performing reunion gigs, but it wasn't until 1997 that the band bounced back, when they won that year's Euro-vision song contest. —*Stephen Thomas Erlewine*

Walking on Sunshine / 1983 / Attic ✦✦✦✦
Ex-Soft Boy Kimberley Rew would find the perfect band to showcase his formidable songwriting talents in Katrina and the Waves; erstwhile lead singer Katrina Leskanich can belt, croon, or plead with the best in business. The group's first release is an almost perfect album of timeless pure pop songs. The tunes are hook-laden and memorable, and they're performed with a flawless mix of energy and lightness. "Going Down to Liverpool" is a great, infectiously bouncy song that would be covered later by the Bangles and other groups. The title track is rushed-tempo perfection, irresistibly bubbly and frothy. "Machine Gun Smith" is a nervously memorable number with chattering guitar accompaniment and ironic lyrics critical of terrorists. "I Really Taught Me to Watusi" exhibits an itchily danceable Latin influence and gives the instrumentalists a chance to do solos, while "Ain't No Money" is an energetic soul-styled song. "Spiderman" and "Don't Take Her Out of My World" show glimmers of a fuller power-pop approach that the band would explore more fully on subsequent albums. This release is an absolute must if you can find it. —*David Cleary*

Katrina & The Waves 2 / 1984 / Attic ✦✦✦✦
Katrina and her mates come up big again with their second album, which explores a number of different wrinkles in Kimberley Rew's basic pop approach. "He's a Charmer" exhibits a bit of Motown influence, while "Game of Love" is an eminently danceable 1950s-flavored tune. "Cry for Me" and "The Sun Won't Shine" are slow, gutsy belters that recall Janis Joplin. "Maniac House" is a goofy mid-tempo hoot propelled by a walloping drum beat. "Red Wine and Whisky" is simply a great driving pop song with a stunningly memorable chorus. And "She Loves to Groove" is an infectiously bubbly confection that would fit in perfectly with the pure pop selections from *Walking on Sunshine*. Bassist Vince de la Cruz shows some ace songwriting ability of his own with the memorable, rushed "Mexico" and the intense power-pop number "Do You Want Crying?" This top-quality album is not to be passed up if found. —*David Cleary*

● **Katrina & the Waves** / 1985 / Capitol ✦✦✦✦
Instead of recording a new batch of songs for their major-label debut, Katrina and the Waves elected to redo ten songs from their first two albums (given the criminal lack of dissemination these two fine platters apparently received, this decision made a lot of sense). All were re-recorded in an aggressive power-pop style; surprisingly, most all these fine songs hold up extremely well under this approach. A few of these tunes, notably "Going Down to Liverpool" and "Walking on Sunshine," lose a bit of their original sparkle and purity as a result—but just as one cannot obliterate the taste of a great hunk of prime rib with a little sauce, so too one cannot ruin these amazing songs by adding a little extra oomph. Other tunes gain surprising virtues this way. "Red Wine and Whisky" and "Do You Want Crying" [sic] become desperately driven and urgent tuneful rockers, while "Game of Love" transforms into a rollicking party platter of the first magnitude. And "Cry for Me" and "The Sun Won't Shine" regenerate as blueslike shouting numbers of apocalyptic intensity. This great album is an essential purchase, especially since the two Attic Records releases that precede it seem to be impossible to find nowadays. —*David Cleary*

Waves / 1985 / Capitol ✦✦✦
Break of Hearts / Jul. 1989 / SBK ✦✦
● **Anthology** / Apr. 25, 1995 / One Way ✦✦✦✦
Like most One Way collections, *Anthology* doesn't offer a comprehensive overview of the group. Instead, it resequences Katrina And The Waves' first American album and adds a couple of hits and album tracks from their second. While the compilation is haphazard, it does contain most of the group's best material, making it a worthwhile purchase. —*Stephen Thomas Erlewine*

K.C. & the Sunshine Band

f. 1973, Miami, FL
Disco
In the early '70s, two white men, Harry "KC" Casey (b. Jan. 31, 1951) and Richard Finch (b. Jan. 25, 1954), created a racially integrated disco band that based its music on various soul styles. They became one of the most commercially successful groups of the early disco era. KC & the Sunshine Band's disco was funky enough to be a staple in the clubs, while remaining melodic and sweet enough to be huge pop hits. The group continued to have hits until the early '80s; their last hit single, "Give It Up," was credited to KC in the US. —*Bil Carpenter*

● **The Best of KC & the Sunshine Band** / Jun. 1990 / Rhino ✦✦✦✦
A percussive mix of steel drums, whistle flutes, and funky group harmonies, this most soulful disco set includes all of their hits—"Get Down Tonight," "Please Don't Go," "That's the Way (I Like It)," "I'm Your Boogie Man," "(Shake, Shake, Shake) Shake Your Booty," and KC's solo hit, "Give It Up." —*Bil Carpenter*

Tommy Keene

b. , Bethesda, MD
Guitar, Vocals / Alternative Pop-Rock, Power Pop, Pop-Rock, Jangle-Pop
Hailing from Bethesda, MD, Tommy Keene is a guitarist-singer-songwriter who plays and writes melodic guitar-based pop-rock. As a child, Keene played classical piano before picking up guitar and drums. He spent his teenage years drumming in a rock trio called Blue Steel, whose original guitar player Mike Lofgren was the younger brother of Nils Lofgren. Consequently, Keene's first notable gig was when Blue Steel opened for Lofgren's band Grin. In 1977, while attending the University of Maryland, Keene switched to guitar and formed the short-lived band the Rage with songwriter Richard X Heyman. During this period, Keene left the Rage to join a popular Washington, DC, rock band called the Razz, who opened for such notable acts as the Ramones, Devo, and Patti Smith. It was in the Razz that Keene met bass player Ted Niceley, who would work with him throughout the '80s. After the Razz, Keene embarked on a European tour as a sideman for new wave singer Suzanne Fellini, before cofounding a band called Pieces in New York. Unhappy with the music, Keene decided to form his own group with Nicely and drummer Doug Tull also from the Razz, plus a guitar player named Michael Colburn, who was soon replaced by Billy Connelly. Using Keene's name, they released *Strange Alliance* on their own Avenue label in 1982, before being picked up by the Dolphin label out of North Carolina. Keene recorded two EPs there before being signed to Geffen, who released two full albums, *Songs from the Film* and *Based on Happy Times*, as well as *Run Now*, a six-song EP of previously recorded material, before dropping Keene from its roster. With a new backup band that included bassist/vocalist Brad Quinn and drummer John Richardson, Keene inked a deal with Matador in the early '90s, recording the EP *Sleeping on a Roller Coaster* and a full-length album entitled *Ten Years After* in 1996. In 1993, Alias released *The Real Underground*, a retrospective of Keene's career that included a wealth of unreleased tracks and out-of-print material from the '80s. In addition to recording and touring behind his records, Tommy Keene spent some of the '90s as a guitar-for-hire, on the road with both Velvet Crush and Paul Westerberg. As of this printing, only the Alias and Matador titles are in print. —*Jack Leaver*

Strange Alliance / 1982 / Avenue ✦✦✦
Places That Are Gone / 1984 / Dolphin ✦✦✦✦
This six-song set became one of 1984's top-selling and critically acclaimed independent releases. Although the reissued version of his 1981 debut album *Strange Alliance* received a lot of press, it wasn't readily available even within a couple of years of its release, so this magnificent collection of intelligent, guitar-based pop was the first glimpse many got of the much-written-about great pop hope from Washington, DC. Shades of the Who, the Byrds, and Big Star shine through in memorable, hook-laden songs and strong vocal harmonies, with Keene's fluid guitar work adorning every track. Containing five irresistible Keene originals plus an ardent cover of Alex Chilton's "Hey! Little Child," the original and best version of the melodic title track is also the leadoff song. Rave reviews of the EP in *Rolling Stone* and the *Village Voice* helped Keene gain national exposure and catch the attention of major record labels. But similar to Marshall Crenshaw, Keene's critical accolades never translated to record sales, even though he would continue to release truly great and artistically consistent pop-rock records. —*Jack Leaver*

Back Again (Try . . .) [EP] / 1984 / Dolphin ✦✦✦✦
With its luscious harmonies and cheerful hooky chorus, "Back Again" had all the makings to be a hit single. Unfortunately, it never happened. "Back Again" was produced by T-Bone Burnett and Don Dixon and was originally intended to be part of Tommy Keene's second album *Songs From the Film*, with its melancholy flip-side "Safe in the Light," a leftover from the *Places That Are Gone* sessions. More positive reviews in *Rolling Stone*, plus an enormous amount of college airplay, made this a good-selling indie release. Once again, fine vocal performances and gorgeous guitar work deliver two great tunes from the Keene catalog. Also included were two interesting live covers: Roxy Music's "All I Want Is You" and the Rolling Stones' "When the Whip Comes Down." —*Jack Leaver*

Songs from the Film / 1986 / Geffen ✦✦✦✦
In what seemed like an attempt by Geffen to make a "big" pop record and endear Keene to an audience wider than critics and a small cult of discerning record buyers, renowned producer Geoff Emerick (Elvis Costello, Beatles) only succeeded at rounding the edges, thus stealing the spark from Keene's performance. The drums are buried in the mix and Keene's distinctive vocals obscured behind a wash of studio processing, but fortunately, Keene's talent shines through in memorable songwriting and biting guitar solos. "In Our Lives" and "Goldtown" are classic Tommy Keene melodic power rockers, while "The Story Ends" stands among his best Beatlesque ballads. But the infectious "Places That Are Gone," which opens side one, sounds awkwardly sped up and doesn't come close to matching the quiet intensity of the version that appeared as the title track of the 1984 Dolphin EP. The story has it that Geffen rejected the original *Songs From the Film* sessions, produced by T-Bone Burnett and Don Dixon, to make this record, although the label at least momentarily came to their senses and released tracks from those sessions later that year on the excellent *Run Now* EP. —*Jack Leaver*

Run Now / 1986 / Geffen ✦✦✦✦
Containing the song "Run Now," produced by Bob Clearmountain and included in the Madonna film *Out of Bounds*, four of the other five tracks here were culled from the T-Bone Burnett and Don Dixon sessions cut in 1984 for the original version of *Songs from the Film*. In contrast to the album Geffen ended up releasing, the Burnett/Dixon tracks reveal an effort to capture the subtle nuances and characteristics of Keene's unique guitar sound and style. Thankfully, the drum sound in these recordings belies the typical bigger-than-life studio reverberation found on commercial recordings of the day; Burnett and Dixon opted to keep the foundation for these tracks simple. The title cut—produced by Bob Clearmountain—is okay, but it pales next to songs like "They're in Their Own World" and "Back Again," which appeared in 1984 as a 12" single. A plus is the killer live version of Lou Reed's "Kill Your Sons," which is much better than the studio rendition released on *Songs from the Film*. —*Jack Leaver*

Based on Happy Times / 1989 / Geffen ✦✦✦✦
Much like 1986's *Songs from the Film*, Geffen seemed bent on making Keene's music bigger than life with *Based on Happy Times*, but this time the overall production sounds less forced and truer to capturing the purity and aggressiveness of Keene's live sound. Recorded at Ardent Studios in Memphis with Joe Hardy and John Hampton at the helm, *Based on Happy Times* brought together the best elements of Keene's previous work, including excellently crafted pop songs, delicious guitar figures, and tight ensemble playing. Among the collection's strongest cuts: the sadly beautiful "This Could Be Fiction," which fades with a lovely string passage, the powerful "When Our Vows Break," and the haunting album closer "A Way Out," featuring R.E.M.'s Peter Buck on mandolin. And as usual, Keene can pick interesting cover tunes; this time around doing a quirky and fun take on a Beach Boys' obscurity "Our Car Club," which also includes a guitar cameo by Buck. Perhaps if this superb record had been given the promotion it deserved, Tommy Keene would have the name recognition of the aforementioned artists. —*Jack Leaver*

Sleeping on a Roller Coaster / 1992 / Matador ✦✦✦✦
After a less than ideal tenure at Geffen Records, Keene emerged undaunted in the '90s with a rockin' new band and a strong batch of fresh songs, as evidenced on this five-song EP. Produced by Keene and Steve Carr—who engineered a good share of Keene's work in the '80s, including the magnificent *Places That Are Gone* EP—*Sleeping on a Roller Coaster* contains some of Keene's most dynamic and powerful pop-rock performances to date. With muscular grooves provided by Brad Quinn on bass, vocals, and piano, and drummer John Richardson, along with a guest guitar appearance from Justin Hibbard on two tracks, Keene—who also doubles on keyboards—delivers an irresistibly melodic guitar assault and inspired singing throughout the set. —*Jack Leaver*

● **Real Underground** / Aug. 2, 1993 / Alias ✦✦✦✦
A well-done and welcome retrospective of a talented guitarist/singer-songwriter, *The Real Underground* boasts 23 tracks, all of which are currently out of print in their original packaging or previously unreleased. Although this is a great collection, unfortunately it does not include anything from the two fine albums Keene made for Geffen, or the excellent tracks that company released on the *Run Now* EP. Regardless, fans will delight in having the outstanding Dolphin EP *Places That Are Gone* in its entirety, as well as singles and previously unreleased demos from 1982-92. Some of the fun in those unreleased tracks comes from great covers, such as the Who's "Tattoo" and the Flamin' Groovies' "Shake Some Action." —*Jack Leaver*

Driving into the Sun / 1995 / Alias ✦✦✦✦

Ten Years After / Feb. 13, 1996 / Matador ✦✦✦✦
The first full-length album since 1989's *Based on Happy Times*, *Ten Years After* comes closer to capturing the raw energy of a Tommy Keene

live show than any of his previous studio recordings. Kicking off with a hard guitar assault in "Going Out Again," the intensity and emotion is sustained throughout the rest of this superb 12-song collection. Keene's voice has never sounded better, and his guitar lines are fluid and inspired. The strength of lyric and melody in songs such as "We Started Over Again" and "Turning on Blue" assure that Keene's songwriting craft is still in top form. *Ten Years After* contains a memorable hook at every turn, whether it's in the drive of the delicate acoustic guitar in the folky "Silent Town" or the thunderous eloquence of "Your Heart Beats Alone." And Keene's band is particularly impressive; bassist/ vocalist Brad Quinn and drummer John Richardson rock hard, yet still provide the right rhythmic footing for each of the guitarists' musical detours—for example, the country flavoring of "You Can't Wait for Time." A must for longtime fans, as well as anyone who appreciates intelligent and well-crafted pop-rock that maintains a sharp edge. —*Jack Leaver*

Paul Kelly

b. Jan. 12, 1955, Adelaide, Australia
Rock 'n' Roll, Folk-Rock
One of Australia's foremost singer-songwriters and lyricists, Paul Kelly has drawn comparisons to a more folk- and pop-oriented Graham Parker. Kelly began performing in the coffeehouses of his native Adelaide, but moved to Melbourne to form a backing band, the High Rise Bombers, in 1977. A new backing band, the Dots, took shape the following year, and Kelly recorded the albums *Talk* and *Manila* in 1981 and 1982, also scoring a minor Australian hit with "Billy Baxter." The band's revolving-door membership proved troublesome, and Kelly took three years to return with the solo acoustic *Post*. The album drew on the conditions of inner-city Melbourne for its subject matter and received favorable notices. Kelly responded by putting together a permanent backing band, originally called the Coloured Girls, which featured guitarist Steve Connolly, saxophonist Chris Coyne, keyboardist Pedro Bull, bassist Michael Armiger, and drummer Michael Barclay. 1987's *Gossip* was Kelly's first album to be released in the US; the Coloured Girls were referred to as the Messengers to avoid racist connotations, and the band eventually kept the name permanently. *Under the Sun* and *So Much Water So Close to Home*, with the latter's title track borrowing from a short story by Raymond Carver, were released to further acclaim, but Kelly's strongly Australian subject matter and frame of reference prevented widespread popularity in America and Europe. He has continued to record and remains quite popular in his homeland. —*Steve Huey*

Talk / 1981 / Mushroom ✦✦

Manila / 1982 / Mushroom ✦✦✦

Post / 1985 / Mushroom ✦✦

● **Gossip** / 1987 / A&M ✦✦✦✦
Their US debut offers 17 sublime examples of Kelly's compassionate and witty songwriting as well as the group's flexibility and charm. Highlights include "White Train," the gentle "Renwick Bells," "Darling It Hurts," and "Don't Ever Harm the Messenger." —*John Floyd & Kit Kiefer*

Under the Sun / 1988 / A&M ✦✦✦✦
This covers a lot of stylistic ground, including rockabilly, country, and punk throwbacks. A beautifully arranged set runs the gamut from Hoodoo Gurus-style raveups ("Dumb Things") to country-rock shuffles ("To Her Door") and pointed social criticism ("Bicentennial"), not to mention the golden title track. —*John Floyd & Kit Kiefer*

So Much Water, So Close to Home / Aug. 1989 / A&M ✦✦✦
A somewhat light release, but Kelly's writing continues to dazzle with a song written from the perspective of an abused wife and a touching interpretation of a Raymond Carver story. —*John Floyd*

Comedy / 1992 / Doctor Dream ✦✦✦✦
A diverse, startling record full of everything from folky social protest ("From Little Things Big Things Grow") to gorgeous pop ("Brighter"), it features a dazzling out-of-left-field homage to Jimmie Dale Gilmore's "Dallas from a DC-9" ("Sydney from a 727"). —*Kit Kiefer*

Wanted Man / Sep. 1994 / Vanguard ✦✦✦
Paul Kelly had disbanded the Messengers by the time of his fifth US release, and as a solo performer his musical approach was more diverse. He led the album off with a string chart on the stately "Summer Rain," cruised to Bakersfield for "Maybe This Time" (attention Buck Owens), to Memphis for "Ball and Chain" (attention Carl Perkins), and to Jamaica for "We've Started a Fire," while "Lately" sounded like an intended theme for a *film noir* of the 1940s. But for the most part, this still was familiar folk-rock, with Kelly singing romantic lyrics over acoustic and electric guitars and a rhythm section. *Wanted Man* was less ambitious lyrically than some of Kelly's earlier albums, but it served to distinguish him musically and suggested a transition from his band days to a broader stylistic base. —*William Ruhlmann*

Deeper Water / Sep. 12, 1995 / Vanguard ✦✦✦
Without reconvening the Messengers, Paul Kelly nevertheless worked with a steady backup band on *Deeper Water*, resulting in a more consistent musical style than he had employed on *Wanted Man*. He did try South African mbaqanga on "Madeleine's Song" and a kind of Eno-like ambience on "Gathering Storm," but most of the songs had folk-rock arrangements, and most concerned romantic subjects, within which Kelly's primary concerns were lust and betrayal. On the best songs, he took a different tack or found a twist: The title tune was a rite of passage metaphor about generational commitment and "I'll Forgive But I Won't Forget" found new ways to talk about infidelity by focusing on the friend rather than the straying lover and delaying the news of the crime until the last verse. Such songs marked Kelly as a craftsman with a sense of surprise, and raised *Deeper Water* a cut above the more diffuse *Wanted Man*. — *William Ruhlmann*

Live at Continental & Esplanade / Jul. 23, 1996 / Vanguard ✦✦✦

R. Kelly

b. , Chicago, IL
Urban, Club/Dance, Hip-Hop, Adult Contemporary
Urban R&B producer/vocalist/multi-instrumentalist/songwriter R. Kelly and his supporting band Public Announcement began recording in 1992 at the tail end of the New Jack Swing era, yet he was able to keep much of its sound alive while remaining commercially successful. While he's created a smooth, professional mixture of hip-hop beats, soul-man crooning, and funk, the most distinctive element of Kelly's music is its explicit carnality. Over the course of two albums, the singer has been able to make songs like "Sex Me," "Bump n' Grind," and "Your Body's Callin' " into hits because his production has been seductive enough to sell such blatant come-ons.

Kelly and Public Announcement released their debut album, *Born into the '90's*, at the beginning of 1992. It was an instant R&B smash, while earning a fair amount of pop airplay; "Honey Love" and "Slow Dance (Hey Mr. DJ)" were No. 1 R&B hits, while "Dedicated" was his biggest pop hit at No. 31. *12 Play*, released in the fall of 1993, established R. Kelly as an R&B superstar. The first single pulled from the album, "Sex Me (Parts I & II)," became a gold single and the second, "Bump n' Grind" hit No. 1 on both the pop and R&B charts in 1994; "Bump N' Grind" stayed on the top of the R&B charts for an astonishing 12 weeks, while it logged four weeks at the top of the pop charts. "Your Body's Callin' " was another gold single for Kelly, peaking at No. 13 on the pop charts. In 1994, he also produced *Age Ain't Nothin' But a Number*, the debut album for Aaliyah, a 15-year-old R&B singer from Detroit; it featured two Top Ten pop singles, "Back & Forth" and "At Your Best (You Are Love)". Late in 1994, it was revealed that Kelly and Aaliyah had wed in August. The news sparked a small storm of controversy in the media, yet it didn't appear to hurt the careers of either singer. Kelly wrote and co-produced "You Are Not Alone," the second single from Michael Jackson's *HIStory* album, which was released in the summer of 1995. — *Stephen Thomas Erlewine*

Born into the 90's / Jan. 14, 1992 / Jive ✦✦✦
One of the last popular new jack groups, this East Coast unit had some smash singles in 1992 doing both conventional R&B/soul and hip-hop/New Jack tracks. They did both originals and covers, had an enthusiastic attitude, were well produced, and stayed on the urban contemporary outlets throughout the year. — *Ron Wynn*

● **12 Play** / Nov. 9, 1993 / Jive ✦✦✦✦
New jack swing may be on its way out as a primary R&B sound, but R. Kelly hasn't lost any points by employing it here. Kelly skillfully mixes '70s-style funk beats, '90s hip-hop production, and his own raps, as well as those of Deandre Boykins and Carey Kelly. Sometimes things come perilously close to sounding corny and dated, but he manages to bring things off successfully. Kelly is a competent vocalist, but a master at striking and maintaining a heated mood, keeping a light touch no matter how explicit the language gets and giving this album distinction even as it mines territory that's essentially played out. — *Ron Wynn*

R. Kelly / Nov. 14, 1995 / Jive ✦✦✦✦
With the salacious *12 Play*, R. Kelly established himself as one of the top R&B hitmakers of the mid-'90s, rivalled only by Babyface and Dr. Dre for overall consistency. *12 Play* was marred by occasionally slight tunes, which were obscured by the explicit sexuality of the lyrics. *R. Kelly* isn't hampered by those flaws, although it isn't a perfect record by any means. Throughout the album, Kelly relies on melody and grooves instead of overtly carnal imagery. But that doesn't mean he has cleaned up—Kelly remains a sly, seductive crooner, and his sexiness is more effective when it is suggestive. Nevertheless, his lyrics and music are never subtle—even on the ballads that dominate this album—which can make *R. Kelly* tiresome if taken as a whole. Taken as individual songs, the album works better than anything he has recorded to date. — *Stephen Thomas Erlewine*

Kenickie

f. Aug. 1994, England
Alternative Pop-Rock, Brit-Pop, Punk-Pop
Refining the riot grrrl aesthetic to a simple, bratty attitude, Kenickie were one of a rash of British teenage punk-pop bands that emerged in the wake of Supergrass' success in the mid-'90s. More indebted to indie rock than either Supergrass or their peers Ash, but considerably less strident, amateurish, and cutesy than the Bis, Kenickie's music wasn't necessarily revolutionary, but it had an invigorating energy that earned them a cult following within the UK music press before the release of their 1997 debut album, *At the Club*.

Schoolmates Lauren Laverne (vocals, guitar), Marie Du Stantiago (guitar), and Emmy-Kate Montroe (bass) formed Kenickie in August 1994 as they were studying in secondary school. All three were 16 years old. Laverne's older brother, Johnny X, was recruited as drummer, and the band chose to call themselves Kenickie, naming themselves after John Travolta's sidekick from *Grease*. Over the next few months, they wrote a batch of songs, made a demo, and by late 1994, they had begun playing indie clubs. Creation Records' Alan McGee approached the band in February of 1995, but they rejected his offer, preferring to release a series of indie singles. John Peel played their demo *Catsuit City* well before its April 1995 release by the Newcastle-based indie label, Slampt. The seven-inch *Catsuit City* EP created a buzz around Kenickie but because of their studies and "A" level tests, they didn't release their second single, "Come Out 2 Nite," until nearly a year later. The song was the lead track on their second EP, *Skillex*, which appeared on the hip Fierce Panda label in the spring of 1996. A few months later, the band had signed to Emidisc, a subsidiary of EMI headed by St. Etienne's Bob Stanley and Pete Wiggs.

In the latter half of 1996, Kenickie released two singles—"Punka" and "Millionaire Sweeper"—which reached Nos. 44 and 60, respectively, and substantially expanded their following. Early in 1997, they had their first Top 40 hit with the No. 24 "In Your Car." The single was followed in April by the band's full-length debut, *At the Club*. — *Stephen Thomas Erlewine*

● **At the Club** / Apr. 1997 / Warner Brothers ✦✦✦✦
Like Ash before them, Kenickie has an adolescent exuberence that makes *At the Club* a joyous, infectious debut. Kenickie are self-styled adolescents, making a big deal of their age, not only in their surprisingly funny lyrics, but in the way their guitars and drums bounce off of each other, creating a wonderful cacophony. And just as wonderful are the songs themselves, filled with hooks and melodies that ring in the head, especially since they're delivered with ragged, invigorating enthusiasm. "Punka," "Come Out 2nite," "PVC" and "In Your Car" all date from early singles, yet they've lost none of their power. More importantly, Kenickie has come up with another batch of originals that are just as strong, making *At the Club* a terrific punk-pop debut. — *Stephen Thomas Erlewine*

Chris Kenner

b. Dec. 25, 1929, Kenner, LA, **d.** Jan. 25, 1976
Vocals / New Orleans R&B, R&B
Kenner wrote a number of enduring New Orleans R&B classics, although subsequent cover versions eclipsed all but "I Like It like That," his Grammy-nominated greatest hit in 1961. Kenner co-wrote "Sick and Tired" with Fats Domino and charted with it in 1957 on Imperial, but Domino's version blew it out of the water. Signing with Joe Babashak's Instant label, Kenner's "I Like It like That," "Land of 1000 Dances," and "Something You Got" sported Allen Toussaint's rolling piano behind Kenner's raw vocals. — *Bill Dahl*

Land of a Thousand Dances / 1966 / Atlantic ✦✦✦✦
Slashing soul by the writer of the title cut, this is one of the great forgotten albums. — *David Szatmary*

● **I Like It like That: Golden Classics** / 1987 / Collectables ✦✦✦✦
Vocalist Kenner's early-'60s sides for Instant, with Allen Toussaint laying down rolling piano behind him, represent New Orleans R&B at its most infectious. — *Bill Dahl*

Nik Kershaw

b. Mar. 1, 1958, Bristol, England
Guitar, Vocals / Synth-pop, New Wave, Pop-Rock
During the mid-'80s Nik Kershaw managed to score a handful of pop hits and, in doing so, establish himself as a profitable commercial songwriter. Kershaw began his musical career by learning to play guitar when he was a teenager. In 1974, he joined his first band, Half Pint Hogg, which played nothing but Deep Purple covers. However, his musical ideas were not limited to heavy metal; after he left school, he joined a jazz-funk band called Fusion. Fusion released one album, *'Til I Hear from You*, in the late '70s. Once the group broke up, Kershaw signed to

MCA Records with the help of Nine Below Zero's manager, Micky Modern.

Kershaw released his first solo single, "I Won't Let the Sun Go Down on Me," in 1983; it peaked at No. 47 on the UK charts. His next single, "Wouldn't It Be Good," hit No. 5 in the UK and charted at No. 46 in the US Its success led to stardom in Britain for Kershaw; "I Won't Let the Sun Go Down on Me" was re-released in summer of 1984 and charted at No. 2, leading to a series of hit singles. Released in 1986, his third album, *Radio Musicola*, wasn't as successful as his previous albums. Kershaw subsequently retreated from performing and recording regularly. Although he released *The Works* in 1990, Kershaw's main musical contribution since the late '80s is as a songwriter; he's written several songs for other artists, including Chesney Hawke's hit single "The One and Only." *—Stephen Thomas Erlewine*

Human Racing / 1983 / MCA ✦✦✦
His debut, although rough around the edges, showed talent and promise, and includes "Wouldn't It Be Good." *—Scott Bultman*

The Riddle / 1984 / MCA ✦✦✦✦
Kershaw's second album, containing a remixed "Wouldn't It Be Good" finally garnered some deserved attention. The rest is his unique style of well-crafted synth-pop. *—Scott Bultman*

Radio Musicola / 1986 / MCA ✦✦

The Works / 1990 / MCA ✦✦✦

Best Of / 1994 / Import ✦✦✦✦
More comprehensive than the US *Anthology*, the British *Best of Nick Kershaw* covers Kershaw's career from begining. Where it fails however, is in its exclusion of the single versions of some of the hits (including "Wouldn't It Be Good") in favor of 12" remixes. *—Chris Woodstra*

● **Anthology** / Jan. 31, 1995 / One Way ✦✦✦✦
Nik Kershaw's albums have always been somewhat spotty, which is what makes *Anthology* a welcome event. By concentrating only on the singer's best material and biggest hits, the disc is an entertaining listen and arguably the only album most casual fans will ever need. *—Sara Sytsma*

Chaka Khan

b. Mar. 23, 1953, Great Lakes, IL
Vocals / Soul, Funk, Urban, Club/Dance, Quiet Storm
The lead singer of the R&B band Rufus from 1972 to 1978, Khan went solo with *Chaka* and the single "I'm Every Woman." Since 1978 she has released several solo albums. The Grammy-winning Khan has also done vocal work for Prince, Steve Winwood, David Bowie, and Quincy Jones. *—William Ruhlmann*

Chaka Khan / 1982 / Warner Brothers ✦✦✦✦
An excellent album from Chaka Khan, mixing tingling uptempo tunes with her characteristic soaring, glorious vocals. "Got to Be There" reached No. 5 on the R&B charts, but it actually wasn't the album's high point. That was the marvelous "Be Bop Medley," which later led hardcore jazz purist Betty Carter to proclaim Khan the one female singer working outside the jazz arena with legitimate improvising credentials. *—Ron Wynn*

● **I Feel for You** / 1984 / Warner Brothers ✦✦✦✦
Smoothly produced funk outing features the Prince-composed title track, an R&B No. 1, and two more R&B Top 20 hits, "This Is My Night" and "Through the Fire." *—William Ruhlmann*

Destiny / 1986 / Warner Brothers ✦✦✦
Another fine, although more uneven than usual, album from Chaka Khan. "Love of a Lifetime" was the latest in her string of definitive singles, while she also elevated several otherwise mundane ballads and uptempo cuts. No matter what her personal situation, Khan seldom made a misstep on any of her albums during the early and mid-'80s, and this one might have been the least distinguished of the batch. *—Ron Wynn*

C.K. / 1988 / Warner Brothers ✦✦✦✦
A first-class release, despite the fact that it didn't pack the normal commercial punch. But it had excellent production, many outstanding selections, and uniformly dazzling, booming, triumphant vocals from Khan. She currently speaks with disdain about the record business, and it's probably due to the relative failure of great records like this to break out and really enjoy the success they merit that's disillusioned her. *—Ron Wynn*

Life Is a Dance (The Remix Project) / Jun. 1989 / Warner Brothers ✦✦
In lieu of a desperately needed greatest hits album, we'll have to settle for this reconfiguration of such Khan hits as "I'm Every Woman" and "Clouds." *—William Ruhlmann*

The Woman I Am / Apr. 14, 1992 / Warner Brothers ✦✦✦
In the early to mid-1990s, many of the great soul singers of the '70s were struggling. Chaka Khan's popularity had decreased, but she was better off than some—at least she still had a record deal. And from an A&R standpoint, Warner Bros. did right by her with *The Woman I Am*. Although not quite in a class with *Whatcha Gonna Do for Me* or *I Feel for You*, this is a solid and commendable offering that fans of the singer shouldn't overlook. The production—handled by Marcus Miller, Arif Mardin, and the late Wayne Braithwaite, among others—is high-tech, yet warm instead of mechanical. And on songs ranging from the melancholy "Telephone" to the introspective title song and the appealing single "Love You All My Lifetime," it's clear that Khan was given strong material to work with. *—Alex Henderson*

● **Epiphany: The Best of Chaka Khan, Vol. 1** / Nov. 12, 1996 / Warner Brothers ✦✦✦✦
Epiphany: Best of Chaka Khan, Vol. 1 is a long-overdue collection of Khan's greatest hits, ranging from "Ain't Nobody" and "I'm Every Woman" with Rufus to "I Feel for You." Though Rufus' mid-'70s hits for ABC aren't included, all of her big hits for Warner are present. What nearly sinks the collection is the addition of no less than five new songs, including the Me'Shell Ndegeocello duet "Never Miss the Water," which aren't nearly as strong as the original hits. Even with the addition of the new cuts, *Epiphany* remains a fine compilation and is the best way to get caught up with Khan. *—Leo Stanley*

Kid Creole & the Coconuts

f. Aug. 12, 1950, Montreal, Quebec, Canada
New Wave, Disco
After leaving Dr. Buzzard's Original "Savannah" Band in 1980, August Darnell (born Thomas August Darnell Browder) conceived the Kid Creole persona: a kitschy lounge lizard that played disco, reggae, salsa, calypso—any kind of dance-derived music, really. With the help of Coati Mundi (born Andy Hernandez), Darnell developed a band that could fuse the disparate musical elements convincingly.

Releasing their first album, *Off the Coast of Me*, in 1980, Kid Creole and the Coconuts built up a cult following during the first half of the decade. Their popularity had peaked by 1982, when their third album *Wise Guy* peaked at No. 145 on the US charts. Nevertheless, the band remained new wave and dance club favorites until 1984, when their audience began to shrink. The group continued to release albums until 1990's *Private Waters in the Great Divide*, which barely made any impact. Since that album, Darnell and his band have been silent. *—Stephen Thomas Erlewine*

Off the Coast of Me / Aug. 1980 / Antilles ✦✦✦✦
Mixing disco, Caribbean music, and strains of big-band jazz, Kid Creole engages in a self-deprecating dialogue with his backup singers, the Coconuts, who dismiss him as "Mister Softee" and plead, "Can You Get Me into Studio 54?" on this hilarious debut album. *—William Ruhlmann*

Fresh Fruit in Foreign Places / Jun. 1981 / ZE ✦✦✦✦
Musical gumbo of esoteric lilting, jazzy laidback disco, an acquired taste. *—Bil Carpenter*

Wise Guy / Jun. 1982 / Sire ✦✦✦✦
The ongoing adventures of Kid Creole continue on this bouncy collection that produced three British Top Ten hits, including "Annie, I'm Not Your Daddy" and "I'm a Wonderful Thing, Baby." *—William Ruhlmann*

Doppelganger / 1983 / ZE ✦✦✦

In Praise of Older Women & Other Crimes / 1985 / Sire ✦✦

I Too Have Seen the Woods / 1987 / Sire ✦✦

Private Waters in the Great Divide / Mar. 1990 / Columbia ✦✦✦

You Shoulda Told Me You Were / Aug. 13, 1991 / Columbia ✦✦

● **Kid Creole Redux** / Mar. 17, 1992 / Sire ✦✦✦✦
Featuring the great majority of Kid Creole's singles, *Kid Creole Redux* is the perfect introduction to the eccentric dance-pop artist. *—Sara Sytsma*

To Travel Sideways / May 5, 1995 / Hot Productions ✦✦✦

Kiss Me Before the Light / Jun. 6, 1995 / Hot Productions ✦✦✦

Kid 'n Play

f. 1987, Queens, NY, db. 1993
Pop-Rap, Hip Hop
Among the first groups to tame rap's hardcore mentality into a positive, message-oriented music suitable for teens and mass audiences, Kid 'n Play debuted in 1988 with the platinum album *2 Hype*, which the duo later spun into a deal involving films and a Saturday-morning cartoon show, the first involving a rap act. Though their recording activity became limited during the gangsta-dominated '90s—1991's *Face the Nation* was their last album—the group managed two sequels to their original *House Party* film, as well as the 1991 teen flick *Class Act*.

Kid (b. Christopher Reid; Bronx, NY) and Play (b. Christopher Martin; Queens, NY) first met while performing in rival high-school groups (the

Turnout Brothers and Super Lovers, respectively) and initially teamed up as Fresh Force. Play's former bandmate, Hurby "Luv Bug" Azor, became the duo's manager and signed Kid 'n Play to Select Records in 1987. Despite the predominance of James Brown samples during the mid-'80s, Azor gave *2 Hype* a production job more rooted in disco and pop; thanks to the near Top Ten R&B hit "Rollin' with Kid 'n Play," the album eventually reached platinum status. Though many rappers were more successful at the time, Kid 'n Play became film stars due to their clean-cut image—Kid's six-inch eraserhead hairstyle, which seemed outrageous to white audiences, was vindicated by his honest, well-scrubbed face. The film *House Party* became a moderate success upon its release in 1990, and the duo even managed a proper LP that same year, *Funhouse*. During 1991, two Kid 'n Play films appeared: a sequel to *House Party* and *Class Act*. That same year, the album *Face the Nation* showed a growing reluctance to pander to pop audiences, but the duo were already entrenched in their style. A second sequel to *House Party* appeared in 1993, and little has been heard from them since. —*John Bush*

● **2 Hype** / 1988 / Select ✦✦✦✦
A solid debut with snatches of house, dance, and go-go. Despite minimal rapping abilities, the duo quickly captured a chunk of the hip-hop audience. —*Ron Wynn*

Funhouse / 1990 / Select ✦✦✦

Kid 'N Play's Fun House / 1990 / Select ✦✦✦
One of two releases from the twosome in 1990, this one has new cuts with funkier, looser foundations and more ambitious adult lyrics and rapping style. —*Ron Wynn*

House Party [O.S.T.] / 1990 / Motown ✦✦✦
Not strictly, or even mainly, their album, it does contain the singles "Funhouse" and "Kid vs. Play (The Battle)." Its prime importance was as the soundtrack from an extremely successful film of the same name, which launched the duo into cinematic stardom. —*Ron Wynn*

Face the Nation / Sep. 24, 1991 / Select ✦✦

Johnny Kidd & the Pirates

f. Dec. 23, 1939, Willesden, London, **db.** Oct. 7, 1966, Radcliff
Rock 'n' Roll, British Invasion
One of England's top rock 'n' roll outfits before the Beatles led the early-'60s Beat Boom, Johnny Kidd & the Pirates are best remembered today for one international rock classic ("Shakin' All Over") and as a seminal influence on several more famous groups, most notably the Who.

Johnny Kidd (b. Frederick Heath) had formed his first band, a skiffle group called the Five Nutters, in 1957. They quickly outgrew their skiffle roots and, after a short period fronting the Fred Heath Combo, he joined Alan Caddy (guitar), Tony Docherty (rhythm guitar), and Ken McKay (drums) in early 1958 in an outfit that was dubbed Johnny Kidd & the Pirates, who were spotted by an EMI Record representative and signed to the label.

The group cut their first record, the outstanding "Please Don't Touch," in April 1959, highlighted by Heath's menacing vocals, which reached No. 26 on the British charts. The group's subsequent records were an uneven mix of solid R&B-based rock juxtaposed with awkwardly covered "standards."

In May 1960, however, the band was in the studio to record one of those standards, "Yes Sir, That's My Baby," with an original B-side that they hadn't fully worked out. That B-side, a Heath original called "Shakin' All Over," became the A-side of a No. 1 single that became the first original rock song in England to achieve the status of an international rock standard. Driven by Caddy's guitar and a mournful, ominous lead vocal by Heath, the song topped the charts and completely astonished everybody who heard it that such a track could have come from an English rock 'n' roll band.

Unfortunately, like every other British label of the era, EMI was never sure how best to deal with rock 'n' roll success, and the group was made to record any amount of dross in the wake of this success, amid some superb follow-up numbers. Several membership changes followed, most notably the addition of Mick Green on lead guitar. The group was among the finest rock combos of the early '60s, with a wild stage act that had them playing in pirate regalia, but it never had enough consistent chart success to put it back in the top ranks of Britain's rock hierarchy, though they received a great deal of respect from the younger generation of rock 'n' rollers.

Early in their career, the Who played on the same bill as Johnny Kidd & the Pirates, and it was through watching the Pirates at work that they arrived at their own sound of a solo singer backed by a guitar, bass, and drums; the band also added "Shakin' All Over" to their repertory. Heath and his band struggled onward into the mid-'60s, even remaking "Shakin' All Over." Green left in 1964 (replaced by John Weider) to take over as a member of the Dakotas, Billy J. Kramer's backup band, and Heath put together a new combo during this period. The mid-'60s

seemed to be a more favorable period for Heath's brand of R&B-based rock 'n' roll. He put together a group called the New Pirates, and was about to embark on a new phase of his career, when he was killed in a car crash on October 7, 1966. The New Pirates continued on for a time, with Johnny Carroll fronting the group until mid-1967, when they called it quits.

During the 1970s, however, the Pirates, with Mick Green back in the lineup, began playing together again, and they have continued to perform to this day in England, and recorded a handful of albums during the 1970s and '80s, featuring Johnny Kidd-era material as well as new songs in their stage show. Among the New Pirates, bassist Nicky Simper went on to become a founding member of Deep Purple. —*Bruce Eder*

● **Hits & Rarities** / 1983 / See For Miles ✦✦✦✦
This collection is the best of three now available. It contains the strongest of Kidd's singles plus superb vault finds. Considered too rough for release in the '60s, they hold up splendidly. —*Bruce Eder*

Complete Johnny Kidd / 1994 / EMI ✦✦✦✦
A double CD of everything this underrated band ever recorded, assembled chronologically and beautifully remastered and annotated (with great pictures, too). This is the collection to own, especially since it has been issued at mid-price. And fans of the Who or the Small Faces can double the priority of owning this collection. —*Bruce Eder*

Greg Kihn

b. 1952, Baltimore, MD
Guitar, Vocals / Rock 'n' Roll, Singer-Songwriter, New Wave, Power Pop, Pop-Rock
Greg Kihn began his career in his hometown of Baltimore, MD, working in the singer-songwriter mold, but switched to straightforward rock 'n' roll when he moved to San Francisco in 1974. The following year, he became one of the first artists signed to Matthew Kaufman's now legendary Beserkley Records. Along with Jonathan Richman, Earthquake, and the Rubinoos, Kihn helped to carve the label's sound—melodic pop with a strong '60s pop sensibility—a refreshing alternative to the bloated prog-rock of the time. In 1976, after his debut on the compilation *Beserkley Chartbusters*, he recorded his first album with his own band consisting of Ronnie Dunbar (guitar), Steve Wright (bass), and Larry Lynch (drums). Through the '70s, he released an album each year and built a strong cult following through constant touring, becoming Beserkley's biggest seller. In 1981, he earned his first bonafide hit with the Top 20 single, "The Breakup Song (They Don't Write 'Em)," from the *Rockihnroll* album. He continued in a more commercial vein through the '80s with a series of pun-titled albums; *Kihntinued* (1982), *Kihnspiracy* (1983), *Kihntageous* (1984), and *Citizen Kihn* (1985). He scored his biggest hit with 1983's "Jeopardy" (No. 2) from the *Kihnspiracy* album. One more single broke the Top 40, 1985's "Lucky," but by the time *Love and Rock and Roll* was released in 1986, the puns had run out and so had the hits. Kihn has kept a relatively low profile throughout the '90s, releasing *Mutiny* in 1994 and *Horror Show* in 1996. —*Chris Woodstra*

Greg Kihn / 1976 / Beserkley ✦✦✦
This record has it all: good songs (mostly written by Kihn) with strong vocals and tight harmonies. If you only know Kihn from the hits, you owe it to yourself to go back and track this record down. If you're only just discovering him, start here and grow with the band. —*Jim Worbois*

Greg Kihn Again / 1977 / Beserkley ✦✦✦✦
A fine follow-up to *Greg Kihn* as Kihn continues to grow as an artist and songwriter. His version of "For You" received some favorable comments from *Kihnspiracy* as well as first dibs on an original Springsteen tune for a later album. —*Jim Worbois*

Next of Kihn / 1978 / Beserkley ✦✦✦
For the first time, Kihn has written all the songs and, with the first track, has adopted a harder edge to his sound, at least on that particular track. Overall, not a bad record but more of a lateral move as an artist than a step forward. —*Jim Worbois*

With the Naked Eye / 1979 / Beserkley ✦✦✦
The awaited Springsteen cover finally pops up on this record, as does a cover of labelmate Jonathan Richman's "Roadrunner." The former allows some of the Kihn magic to shine through, but the latter is just a straight read with none of the fun of the original. In between are some pleasant songs but nothing really memorable. —*Jim Worbois*

Glasshouse Rock / 1980 / Beserkley ✦✦

Rockihnroll / 1981 / Beserkley ✦✦✦✦
With this album Kihn finally has the hit he long ago deserved ("Breakup Song"). He also manages to recapture some of what made the early records so enjoyable. Once again, with both the material and the performance, Kihn sounds as if he is enjoying himself. —*Jim Worbois*

Kihntinued / 1982 / Beserkley ✦✦✦✦
A couple of the tracks, like "Everyday/Saturday" and "Testify," are more memorable than nearly anything on the previous record, but still not up to the potential Kihn hinted at on his first couple of albums. —*Jim Worbois*

Kihnspiracy / 1983 / EMI/Beserkley ✦✦
With the help of the hit single ("Jeopardy" and saturation MTV airplay, *Kihnspiracy* became Kihn's highest-charting album to date—eventually breaking the Top 20. Unfortunately, Kihn continued his decline into mediocrity with this overall uninspired effort. —*Sara Sytsma*

Kihntagious / 1984 / Beserkley ✦✦✦

Citizen Kihn / 1985 / EMI ✦✦
Kihn made his last appearance in the pop charts with this album. The single "Lucky" was a Top 40 hit, but the remainder of the album is second rate. —*Sara Sytsma*

Love & Rock & Roll / 1986 / Beserkley ✦✦
Something of a return to form, Kihn delivers his finest album in years with a batch of solid originals and some well-chosen covers (including the Only Ones classic "Another Girl, Another Planet"). Unfortunately, by 1986, no one was all that interested anymore and the album went unnoticed. —*Sara Sytsma*

● **Kihnsolidation: The Best of Greg Kihn** / Jul. 1989 / Rhino ✦✦✦✦
A fine sampling of Kihn's pop sensibility. Drawing from each of his albums, it includes the hits "The Breakup Song" and "Jeopardy" as well as his better album cuts. —*Chris Woodstra*

Unkihntrollable (Greg Kihn Live) / 1991 / Rhino ✦✦

Horror Show / Nov. 5, 1996 / Clean Cuts ✦✦✦
Horror Show is the title of Greg Kihn's first novel. Appropriately, the concept of the same name is a neo-gothic collection of British Invasion pop-rock and folk-rock, complete with the occasional string and woodwind arrangements. Kihn doesn't limit himself to his own song, working Ray Davies' "Waterloo Sunset" and the traditional "Come Back Baby" and "Trials, Troubles, Tribulations" into the concept. Though *Horror Show* never really tells a story, it is one of Kihn's most enjoyable latter-day albums, simply because of the variety of styles and its sense of purpose. —*Stephen Thomas Erlewine*

Killing Joke

f. 1978, London, England
Alternative Pop-Rock, New Wave, Post-Punk
Heavy and slow, Killing Joke (at least early in their career) was a quasi-metal band dancing to a tune of doom and gloom. They eventually became less heavy and more arty (the latter seems almost impossible)—more danceable even—but early on they made some urgent slabs of molten dynamite that oozed with the power of thick guitars, thudding drums, and over-the-top singing. The origins of Killing Joke lay in the Matt Stagger Band. Paul Ferguson was drumming for the group when he met Jaz Coleman (vocals, keyboards) in the late '70s. Coleman joined the Matt Stagger Band briefly, but soon he and Ferguson split to form Killing Joke in late 1978. The duo recruited bassist Youth (born Martin Glover Youth), who had previously played with the punk group the Rage, and guitarist Geordie (born K. Walker) to complete the band's lineup. Killing Joke moved to Notting Hill Gate and recorded their debut EP, *Turn to Red*, with money borrowed from Coleman's girlfriend of the time. BBC disc jockey John Peel was impressed by the EP and offered the group a session on his show, which became one of the most popular shows he broadcast in the late '70s. By the end of 1979, the group had signed with Island Records, who allowed them to set up their own label, Malicious Damage.

Killing Joke released "Wardance," their debut single on Malicious Damage, in February of 1980. Following its release, Killing Joke and Malicious Damage switched from Island Records to EG and began their eponymous debut album. The group began playing shows regularly throughout England and gained a reputation for being controversial. Their artwork often featured repulsive or inflammatory images, and after one of their concert posters pictured the Pope blessing legions of Nazis, the group was banned from performing a concert in Glasgow. Despite the controversy, the group began amassing a following of both punk and disco fans with hard-edged but danceable singles like "Psyche" and "Follow the Leader." The band released their second album, *What's This For . . . !* in 1981.

After recording and releasing the group's third album, 1982's *Revelations*, Jaz Coleman—who had developed an obsession with the occult—decided that the apocalypse was near, so he left the group and ran away to Iceland with Geordie. While in Iceland, Coleman and Geordie worked with a number of Icelandic bands, most notably Theyr, which would later evolve into the Sugarcubes. Youth followed Coleman to Iceland shortly after his departure. After a few months with no sign of the end of the world, Youth returned to England and formed Brilliant with Ferguson. However, Ferguson left shortly after the group's forma-

tion and moved to Iceland with Killing Joke's new bassist, Paul Raven. Youth continued playing with Brilliant, while Killing Joke's new lineup—featuring Coleman, Geordie, Ferguson, and Raven—worked in Iceland for a brief period. Soon, the group returned to England and recorded *Fire Dances*, which was released in 1983. *Fire Dances* demonstrated a calmer, more straightforward band than the one showcased on the group's earlier records.

For the rest of the '80s, Killing Joke continued to release albums, all of which failed to regain the audience they had in the early '80s. After 1988's *Outside the Gate*, the group broke up, only to reunite two years later for *Extremities, Dirt, & Various Repressed Emotions*. *Extremities* featured a new drummer, Martin Atkins, and returned the band to the noisy dance experiments of their earlier records. Following its release, the group took a four-year break. In 1994, Killing Joke re-formed as a trio with Coleman, Geordie, and Youth and the group released *Pandemonium*, a harder-edged, heavier album than their previous records. Two years later, the band released *Democracy*. —*Stephen Thomas Erlewine & John Dougan*

Killing Joke / May 1981 / EG ✦✦✦✦
Killing Joke's self-titled debut album is a throttling merger of heavy metal, new wave, and noise. It's a dense, claustrophobic record that basically sketched out the path the band would follow over the next decade. —*Stephen Thomas Erlewine*

What's This for / Jul. 1981 / EG ✦✦✦

Revelations / Jun. 1982 / EG ✦✦

Fire Dances / 1983 / EG ✦✦✦✦

Night Time / 1985 / EG ✦✦✦

Brighter Than a 1000 Suns / 1986 / Virgin ✦✦✦

Outside the Gate / 1988 / EG ✦✦

Extremities, Dirt & Various Repressed Emotions / 1990 / Noise ✦✦✦✦

● **Incomplete Collection 1980-85** / 1990 / EG ✦✦✦✦

Laugh? I Nearly Bought One! / Sep. 18, 1992 / Plan 9/Caroline ✦✦✦✦

Pandemonium / Aug. 2, 1994 / Zoo ✦✦

Democracy / Apr. 1996 / Zoo ✦✦
Democracy, the second consecutive reunion album to feature the original lineup, is a slightly more cohesive effort than the previous *Pandemonium*, boasting a more streamlined, powerful attack. Nevertheless, they haven't recaptured the raw aggression of their early releases—instead, they've refashioned themselves into a techno-informed heavy metal band. They haven't come up with enough hooks to sell themselves to the mainstream alternative audience, but they have enough aggression to appeal to post-alternative metal fans. Ironically, there's just not much on *Democracy* to appeal to their original fans. —*Stephen Thomas Erlewine*

King Crimson

f. 1969, England
Group / Art-Rock/Progressive-Rock
If there is one group that embodies progressive rock, it is King Crimson. Led by guitar/Mellotron virtuoso Robert Fripp, during its first five years of existence the band stretched both the language and structure of rock into realms of jazz and classical music, all the while avoiding pop and psychedelic sensibilities. The absence of mainstream compromises and the lack of an overt sense of humor ultimately doomed the group to nothing more than a large cult following, but made their albums among the most enduring and respectable of the prog-rock era.

King Crimson originally grew out of the remnants of an unsuccessful trio called Giles, Giles & Fripp. Michael Giles (drums, vocals), Peter Giles (bass, vocals), and Robert Fripp (guitar) had begun working together in late 1967 after playing in a variety of bands: Fripp's resume included tenures with the League of Gentlemen and the Majestic Dance Orchestra, while the Giles brothers had played with Trendsetters, Ltd.

After signing to Deram, the trio recorded their debut single, "One in a Million," and began cutting a follow-up album, *The Cheerful Insanity of Giles, Giles & Fripp*, during the summer of 1968.

Even as the album was in the works, however, the group's lineup was changing: ex-Infinity singers/guitarists Ian McDonald and Peter Sinfield joined late in 1968, and Judy Dyble, who had passed through the first Fairport Convention lineup, signed on briefly as a singer. This lineup recorded demos of "I Talk to the Wind" and "Under the Sky," but soon dissolved: Peter Giles exited the scene in November of 1968, and Fripp's childhood friend, vocalist/bassist Greg Lake, joined two days later. The new roster of Fripp, Lake, McDonald, and Michael Giles—with satellite member Sinfield writing their lyrics and later running their light show, among other functions—officially became King Crimson on January 13, 1969, deriving the name from Sinfield's lyrics for the song "Court of the Crimson King." In July of 1969, the group debuted in front of 650,000 people at a free concert in London's Hyde Park on a bill with the Rolling

Stones; later that month, King Crimson ultimately recorded and produced their first album. *Court of the Crimson King* was one of the most challenging albums of the entire fledgling progressive rock movement, but somehow it caught the public's collective ear at the right moment and hit No. 5 in England in November of 1969—four months later, the album climbed to No. 28 on the American charts. Ironically, at the peak of the LP's success the original band broke up: McDonald and Giles were becoming increasingly unhappy with the music's direction, as well as the strain of touring. By November they decided to leave—Fripp was so shaken that he even offered to exit if they would stay. The original group played its last show in December 1969; Greg Lake, having joined the group last, was uncomfortable with the idea of staying on with two replacement members, and had also been approached by Keith Emerson of the Nice about the possibility of forming a new group. He soon decided to leave Crimson as well, but agreed to stay long enough to record vocals for the next album.

Whether there would even be a next album was debatable for a time after Fripp was offered the chance to replace Peter Banks in Yes. Finally, a new single ("Catfood") and album (*In the Wake of Poseidon*) were recorded early in 1970: essentially a Fripp-dominated retake of *Court of in the Crimson King*, Lake sang on all but one of the songs, Fripp played the Mellotron as well as all of the guitars, and a new singer, Fripp's boyhood friend Gordon Haskell, debuted on "Cadence and Cascade." Fripp spent the month of August rehearsing a new King Crimson lineup, consisting of himself, Haskell (bass, vocals), saxman/flautist Mel Collins (who had played on *Poseidon*), and Andy McCullough (drums). This group, augmented by pianist Keith Tippett, guest vocalist Jon Anderson of Yes, and oboist/English horn virtuoso Marc Charig, recorded the next Crimson album, *Lizard*, in the fall of 1970, but Haskell and McCullough both walked out soon after it was finished; with Fripp busy putting a new band together, Peter Sinfield took over the final production chores.

In December of 1970, Ian Wallace joined on drums, and after auditioning several aspiring singers including Bryan Ferry, Fripp chose Boz Burrell as the group's new vocalist. The latest Crimson lineup of Fripp, Burrell, Collins, and Wallace emerged on stage in April of 1971, and for the next year, King Crimson was a going concern, playing gigs across the globe. The only casualty during the remainder of the year was Sinfield, who split in December after Fripp asked him to leave. Their new album, *Islands*, got to No. 30 in England, and No. 76 in America; the band might've succeeded had it lasted for another album to make its case, but in April of 1972, this latest lineup broke up after Wallace, Collins, and Burrell moved as a trio to join Alexis Korner in a band called Snape. (Burrell later became the bassist with Bad Company.)

It seemed as though King Crimson had finally come to an end. Then, in July of 1972, Fripp put together a new band consisting of ex-Yes drummer Bill Bruford, ex-Family member John Wetton on bass and vocals, David Cross on violin and Mellotron, and Jamie Muir on percussion. Sinfield's successor as lyricist was Richard Palmer-James, who was otherwise invisible in the lineup. This group recorded their debut album, *Larks' Tongues in Aspic*, and made its debut in Frankfurt in October of 1972. Muir was out of the lineup by early 1973, but as a quartet the band toured England, Europe and America while *Larks' Tongues* made it all the way to the Top 20 in England. In January of 1974, King Crimson cut a new album, *Starless and Bible Black*, thus becoming the first lineup to remain intact for more than one American tour and more than one album (discounting the departed Muir).

Alas, by July of 1974 even this long-lasting King Crimson lineup had begun to splinter. This time Cross was the one to exit, following a performance in New York. With King Crimson reduced to a trio of Fripp, Wetton, and Bruford, one more album, *Red*, was completed that summer with help from David Cross and former members Mel Collins and Ian McDonald (who would go on to fame and fortune as the co-founder of the arena band Foreigner). Fripp disbanded the group on September 25, 1974, seemingly for the last time. Wetton later passed through the lineup of Uriah Heep before going on to international success as the lead singer of Asia, while Cross later turned up on the Mellotron multi-artist showcase album *The Rime of the Ancient Sampler*.

In June of 1975, 11 months after their last public concert, a live album called *USA* was issued, followed four months later by Fripp's first solo album, *Exposure*. Finally, in April of 1981, Fripp formed a new group called Discipline with Bruford, bassist Tony Levin, and guitarist/singer Adrian Belew. By the time their album was released in October of that year, the group's name had been changed to King Crimson. This band, with a sound completely different from any of the other lineups to use that name, toured and recorded regularly over the years, including full-length video productions. —*Bruce Eder*

★ **In the Court of the Crimson King** / 1969 / EG ✦✦✦✦✦
The group's definitive album, and one of the most daring debut albums ever recorded by anybody. At the time, it blew all of the progressive/psychedelic competition (the Moody Blues, the Nicem, etc.) out of the running, although it was almost too good for the band's own good—it took them nearly four years to come up with a record as strong or concise.

Ian McDonald's Mellotron is the dominant instrument, along with his saxes and Fripp's guitar, making this a somewhat different-sounding record from everything else they ever did. And even though that Mellotron sound is muted and toned down compared to their concert work of the era (see *Epitaph*, below), it is still fierce and overpowering—coupled with some strong songwriting, most of it filled with dark and doom-laden visions, the strongest singing of Greg Lake's entire career, and Fripp's guitar playing (a strange mix of elegant classic, Hendrix-like rock explosions, and jazz noodling), the mix was overpowering. Fripp would be the only survivor on their subsequent records. Note: Be sure the CD you buy indicates it was made or distributed by Caroline Records—earlier versions sounded awful. —*Bruce Eder*

In the Wake of Poseidon / 1970 / EG ✦✦✦✦
King Crimson opened the year 1970 scarcely in existence as a band, having lost two key members (McDonald, Giles) with a third (Lake) about to leave. The second album, made up of material salvaged from their stage repertory ("Pictures of a City," "The Devil's Triangle") and Fripp's songwriting (having taken over that duty from the departed Lake and McDonald), is actually better produced and better sounding than their first. Surprisingly, Fripp's guitar is not the dominant instrument—he also took over the Mellotron chores from the departed McDonald, and that instrument, played even better than McDonald did, still comprises the band's signature. The record doesn't tread enough new ground to rival that first album, although Fripp has made an impressive show of transmuting material that worked on stage ("Mars," aka "The Devil's Triangle") into viable studio creations, and "Cadence and Cascade" may be the prettiest song the group ever cut. —*Bruce Eder*

Lizard / 1970 / EG ✦✦✦
This was to have been Crimson's first proper album since their first, the second having been patched together by Fripp and various former and future band members. Instead, *Lizard* was practically an orphan from the time it was recorded, the band that recorded it having broken up (at least, the singer walked) soon after finishing the sessions. The music is more consciously jazz-oriented (Miles Davis' influence is especially strong), and so are the progressive tendencies—the songs are longer and have more ornate subjects and lyrics, and if anything, the Mellotron is a stronger presence here than it was on the first two albums, with the music's doom-laden mood just as strong. What's missing is a sense of humor. Jon Anderson of Yes guests on one number as well. *Lizard* is an acquired taste to all but hardcore prog-rock fanatics, though perhaps one worth acquiring. —*Bruce Eder*

Islands / 1971 / EG ✦✦✦
The weakest Crimson studio album from their first era, by the most stable lineup the early group ever had (this band, featuring Mel Collins on saxes and flute and Boz Burrell on bass and vocals, actually did a couple of tours). The songs are mostly pretty, and sometimes raunchy and even surprising (Beatle-type harmonies turn up on the nearly lewd "Ladies of the Road"), but they generally run way too long for their content, and not even the guitar pyrotechnics of "A Sailor's Tale" make up for the wasted time elsewhere. It's still a good record, and if anyone but Crimson had issued it, *Islands* would probably seem like a fair effort. —*Bruce Eder*

Earthbound / 1972 / Polydor ✦✦
The nadir of King Crimson's recorded output, a live album recorded along their final US tour that suffers from such poor fidelity, that its release can be presumed to have been motivated by contractual obligation. Only "Schizoid Man" and "A Sailor's Tale" (all two minutes of that) stand out, amid some aimless and noisy improvisations. Atlantic declined to release it in America, and only "Schizoid Man" has ever surfaced on CD. (Out of print, British import) —*Bruce Eder*

Larks' Tongues in Aspic / 1973 / EG ✦✦✦✦
King Crimson reborn—the newly configured band makes its debut with a violin (courtesy of David Cross) sharing center stage with Fripp's guitars and Mellotron, which is pushed into the background. The music is the most experimental of Fripp's career up to this time, and John Wetton is the strongest singer/bassist since Greg Lake's departure. What's more, this version of King Crimson quickly established themselves as the most powerful performing band since the first lineup. —*Bruce Eder*

Red / 1974 / EG ✦✦✦
King Crimson falls apart once more, seemingly for the last time, as David Cross walks away during the recording of this album. It became Fripp's last thoughts on this version of King Crimson, a bit noisier and less subtle than its predecessors, and a little thin—though "Starless," a cousin to the title track of the preceding album, is a superb swan song—but still impressive. —*Bruce Eder*

Starless & Bible Black / 1974 / EG ✦✦✦✦
The first Crimson follow-up album to match its predecessor for content and quality. The music is even more powerful than the material on *Larks' Tongues*, and it's only slightly more obscure, the only reason the earlier album gets first choice over records by this version of the band.

Fripp's guitar and Cross' violin seemed like the ultimate progressive rock instrumental duo here. —*Bruce Eder*

USA / 1975 / Atlantic ✦✦✦
The group was disbanded, but at least two bootleg live albums (drawn from live FM radio broadcasts along their last tour) were circulating, and it was obvious there was some kind of audience, so *USA* was released. The performances are good, though *The Great Deceiver* box proved there was better material and there were better ways of treating these tapes. Eddie Jobson subs for David Cross on the violin on several of these cuts. (Out of print) —*Bruce Eder*

Young Person's Guide to King Crimson / 1976 / Island ✦✦✦✦
Two years after the group's breakup, Robert Fripp prepared this double-LP compilation, which included rare singles ("Groon"), Giles, Giles & Fripp-era outtakes ("I Talk to the Wind") and a booklet giving about the fullest account of the group's history ever done up to that point. Supplanted by later CD boxes, but as good a collection as one could have hoped for at the time. (Out of print, British import) —*Bruce Eder*

Discipline / 1981 / EG ✦✦✦✦
The new King Crimson, harder and heavier. —*Bruce Eder*

Beat / 1982 / EG ✦✦✦✦
A superior mid-'80s follow-up with better material. —*Bruce Eder*

3 of a Perfect Pair / 1984 / Warner Brothers ✦✦✦
The final chapter? Don't bet on it, but this would be a good way to end, if so. —*Bruce Eder*

Frame by Frame / 1991 / Caroline ✦✦✦✦
Frame by Frame is a four-disc box set, compiled by bandleader Robert Fripp, that does a good job providing primo samples of each of Crimson's musical periods. Sonically, the excellent remastering makes this the best this band has ever sounded on disc. Three of the discs cover their studio work, while the fourth is a collection of live work, spanning the band's entire career. Enclosed is a richly detailed diary (written by Fripp) of Crimson's entire history, plus interviews with band members, and glowing and disparaging reviews from critics. Typical of Crimson, precious little of the music on this set would qualify for casual listening. However, those whose taste run towards the dark side of prog-rock will find this set rewarding. —*Rick Clark*

The Great Deceiver (Live 1973-1974) / Oct. 30, 1992 / Caroline ✦✦✦✦
Four CDs full of live King Crimson from 1973 and 1974, an era that many consider their best. Although some songs are repeated, they're never played the same way twice. If you're a King Crimson fan, that's enough of an incentive for purchase; if you're not, the musical expertise of the band might convert you, providing you have the money for a box set. —*Stephen Thomas Erlewine*

Vroom / 1995 / Discipline ✦✦
Thrak / Apr. 1995 / Virgin ✦✦✦
King Crimson returned with a new record in 1995. With *Thrak*, the group picks up right where they left off; although they incorporate a couple of new technical tricks, the heart of the album echoes back to the early '80s with its dense, guitar-dominated sonic textures. —*Sara Sytsma*

Thrakattak / Jun. 25, 1996 / DPL ✦✦✦
Thrakattak is a collection of live, improvised pieces the 1995 edition of King Crimson performed during their fall tour. Often, the group delves into dense, treacherous waters, heading into the unknown with reckless abandon. Sometimes, this results in soaring, majestic music, but occasionally it means that the band meanders directionlessly for far too long. And that means that even though this is filled with great, challenging music, there is simply too much mediocre material for anyone but diehard Crimson fans. —*Stephen Thomas Erlewine*

Epitaph / Apr. 15, 1997 / Discipline ✦✦✦✦

King Curtis (Curtis Ousley)

b. Feb. 7, 1934, Fort Worth, TX, d. Aug. 14, 1971, New York City, NY
Sax (Tenor) / R&B, Groove, East Coast Blues
King Curtis was the last of the great R&B tenor sax giants. He came to prominence in the mid-'50s as a session musician in New York, recording, at one time or another, for most East Coast R&B labels. A long association with Atlantic/Atco began in 1958, especially on recordings by the Coasters. He recorded singles for many small labels in the '50s—his own Atco sessions (1958-1959), then Prestige/New Jazz and Prestige/TruSound for jazz and R&B albums (1960-1961). Curtis also had a No. 1 R&B single with "Soul Twist" on Enjoy Records (1962). He was signed by Capitol (1963-1964), where he cut mostly singles, including "Soul Serenade." Returning to Atlantic in 1965, he remained there for the rest of his life. He had solid R&B single success with "Memphis Soul Stew" and "Ode to Billie Joe" (1967). Beginning in 1967, Curtis started to take a more active studio role at Atlantic—leading and contracting sessions for other artists, producing with Jerry Wexler and later on his own. He also became the

leader of Aretha Franklin's backing unit, the Kingpins. He compiled several albums of singles during this period. All aspects of his career were in full swing at the time he was murdered in 1971. —*Bob Porter*

Country Soul / 1962 / Capitol ✦✦
This album of country standards was intended to be Curtis Knight's answer to Ray Charles' *Modern Sounds in Country and Western Music.* It never sold remotely as well as Charles' album, primarily because of Curtis' more perfunctory singing and some unwise choices of music to cover—"Night Train to Memphis," "Raunchy" (which *is* an instrumental), and "I'm Movin' On" work as R&B instrumentals, with the latter benefiting from some sizzling interplay between the guitars, the trumpets, and Curtis' sax. But "High Noon" and "'Home on the Range" are a lot less convincing, conceptually as well as in execution. There are a few surprises, however, such as a version of "Your Cheatin' Heart" that tries desperately to transform itself into "Stand By Me." (out of print) —*Bruce Eder*

Soul Serenade / 1964 / Capitol ✦✦✦✦
Curtis' second Capitol album is a triumph on every level. The tragedy is that, apart from the hit title track, almost nothing off of this superb album was heard by the public—most of the singles he was doing were very different from this material. The album featured Curtis' covers of songs like the Bill Doggett co-authored "Honky Tonk," Chuck Berry's "Memphis," the hottest, most soulful version of the Champs' old hit "Tequila" ever recorded, and Herbie Hancock's "Watermelon Man," as well as a re-recording of his hit "Soul Twist," and a version of his "Night Train," a big hit for Jimmy Forrest. Maybe the biggest surprise here is the cover of the blues standard "Hide Away," written by Curtis' old friend Freddie King. Sharing the spotlight with Curtis' sax throughout this record is Cornell Dupree on lead guitar, adding just the right accompaniment variously as a lead and rhythm instrument—the two make the oft-heard cover of "Hide Away" by John Mayall and Eric Clapton sound like a poor demo. There's not a wrong or wasted note. —*Bruce Eder*

Plays Hits Made by Sam Cooke / Mar. 9, 1965+Mar. 11, 1965 / Capitol ✦✦✦✦
This is about the only Sam Cooke tribute record—other than individual songs cut by Otis Redding—that one could imagine Cooke himself not only would have approved of fully, but might have enjoyed himself, had it been recorded under other circumstances. One could even visualize him dancing to the versions of "Shake," which does have a few echoes of "Night Train" in it, or "Twistin' the Night Away" or "Good Times." Curtis had known and worked with Cooke, and the singer's shooting death late in 1964 affected the saxophonist deeply, as it did millions of people. This album was the result, a dozen covers that blow away most any other Sam Cooke tribute album (including the still highly collectible Supremes' *We Remember Sam Cooke*). (Out of print) —*Bruce Eder*

Blow Man, Blow! / 1992 / Bear Family ✦✦✦✦
Seventy-one songs spread among three CDs, covering King Curtis' tenure at Capitol from 1962 until 1965. This wasn't the most productive period in Curtis' career, but it was his first chance to make records on more than a piecemeal basis under his own name; the result is a dazzling array of sounds and songs. Hidden among the country covers and abortive early sides on disc one is a lot of gold, most notably "Slow Drag" and the previously unreleased "New Dance," which features some killer guitar; the early unissued material is superb, including the Curtis original "Frisky," a slow version of "Alexander's Ragtime Band," the beguiling "Sukiyaki," and a gorgeous bossa nova called "Amorosa." (Many of these tracks feature guitarist Cornell Dupree, who was to figure in Curtis' most successful records for Capitol.) Disc two is where things start to cook: from "More Soul" on through to the previously unreleased "Hung Over," there's not a note of filler on the disc, which encompasses all of the *Soul Serenade* album as well as a brace of unreleased songs and some very fine singles, including a dazzling cover of the Acker Bilk standard "Stranger on the Shore," and a soulful recomposition of Jackie Gleason's "Melancholy Serenade." Disc three comprises material ranging from reinterpretations of pop standards like "Moon River" and "The Girl From Ipanema" through a dozen covers of Sam Cooke songs, all worthwhile. —*Bruce Eder*

● **Instant Soul: The Legendary King Curtis** / Oct. 19, 1994 / Razor & Tie ✦✦✦✦
King Curtis has never been served with a comprehensive collection until *Instant Soul*, which features the best instrumental singles the distinctive, soulful, and influential tenor saxophonist ever recorded. —*Stephen Thomas Erlewine*

Best of King Curtis / Aug. 1996 / Capitol ✦✦✦✦
Best of King Curtis collects the bulk of King Curtis' singles for Capitol, plus selected album tracks. Although he didn't have many hits while on Capitol—only "Soul Serenade" hit the charts—this collection demonstrates the depths of Curtis' talents, showcasing his stabs at jazz and blues in addition to his trademark R&B. *Instant Soul* remains a stron-

ger introduction, but for fans that want to dig a little deeper, *The Best of King Curtis* is an excellent purchase. —*Stephen Thomas Erlewine*

Ben E. King

b. Sep. 23, 1938, Henderson, NC
Vocals / Soul, R&B, Brill Building Pop

Swirling strings, subtly shaded orchestrations, and Ben E. King's assured baritone were a blueprint for uptown soul success during the early '60s. King and his vocal group, the Five Crowns, were in the right place at the right time when, in 1959, the manager of the Drifters decided to sack his entire group and solicit replacements. As new lead singer for the Drifters, King crooned the soulful smashes "There Goes My Baby," "Save the Last Dance for Me," and "I Count the Tears" before heading out on his own in 1960. The vocalist's own Atco singles mirrored the sumptuous production of his Drifter sides, and "Spanish Harlem," "Don't Play That Song (You Lied)," and the R&B chart-topping "Stand by Me" were all huge successes. King remained with Atco through 1969, then triumphantly returned to Atlantic in 1975 with another No. 1 soul hit, "Supernatural Thing (Part 1)."

With the re-release of "Stand by Me" as the theme to the 1986 film of the same title, King was in demand all over again, the stirring song improbably scaling the charts for a second time, despite being a quarter-century old. —*Bill Dahl*

The Ultimate Collection / 1987 / Atlantic ✦✦✦✦
The rich baritone of this ex-Drifter lead is matched by the majestic, violin-drenched, uptown soul arrangements on these early-'60s classics. —*Bill Dahl*

● **Anthology** / Apr. 20, 1993 / Rhino ✦✦✦✦
This two-disc, 50-song box set thoroughly documents the recordings that Ben E. King cut for Atlantic. Starting as the lead voice of the Drifters on such hits as "There Goes My Baby" and "Save the Last Dance for Me," King went on to a successful solo career with a string of singles that matched his smooth, sexy baritone with tastefully arranged string sections and Latin rhythms. All of those early hits—"Stand By Me" and "Spanish Harlem"—were the biggest—are included here, along with non-hit 45s by the likes of Leiber/Stoller, Doc Pomus, Mort Shuman, Phil Spector, and Goffin/King that were nearly equal in worth. As the '60s progressed, King moved toward a more mainstream, heavier soul sound and less distinctive material, culminating in his parting from Atlantic in 1969. He returned to the label in the mid-'70s for a string of mainstream R&B successes. This compilation includes 16 non-LP singles from the '60s, which together with the hits constitute the definitive overview of this influential soul singer's work. —*Richie Unterberger*

Anthology One: Spanish Harlem / 1997 / Sequel ✦✦✦✦
The first installment of Sequel's ambitious retrospective of Ben E. King's entire output for Atlantic/Atco—in which an original album is fleshed out with numerous bonus tracks—is one of the best installments in the series, featuring his earliest hits, including "Spanish Harlem." While the quality of the songs are uneven, there are more good cuts than poor, making it useful for serious King collectors. —*Thom Owens*

Anthology Two: Songs for Soulful Lovers / 1997 / Sequel ✦✦✦
The second installment of Sequel's seven-volume retrospective of Ben E. King's Atco/Atlantic recordings concentrates on his versions of pop standards and includes four live bonus tracks. Although King sings very well throughout the disc, the material is weaker than that on *Spanish Harlem* and it lacks any major hits, making it one of the lesser entries in the series. —*Thom Owens*

Anthology Three: Don't Play That Song / 1997 / Sequel ✦✦✦✦
Chronicling the peak of Ben E. King's career, *Don't Play That Song* is the finest volume of Sequel's seven-disc retrospective of his Atlantic/Atco recordings. King's biggest hits, including "Stand By Me" and "Don't Play That Song," are included, and while several of the tracks are merely filler, the majority of the collection is first rate. —*Thom Owens*

Anthology Four: Seven Letters / 1997 / Sequel ✦✦✦
Seven Letters, the fourth installment of Sequel's seven-volume anthology of Ben E. King's Atco/Atlantic recordings, doesn't have many big hits and indicates that his orchestrated soul formula was beginning to run out of steam, yet it still offers many fine moments. —*Thom Owens*

Anthology Five: What is Soul / 1997 / Sequel ✦✦✦
The fifth volume of Sequel's seven-disc Ben E. King *Anthology, What Is Soul,* finds the singer at a crossroads, as he begins to abandon the pop-R&B stylings of his best-known work for a harder-hitting soul approach. While the results aren't always successful, there's enough good material to make the disc a worthwhile purchase for dedicated fans. —*Thom Owens*

Anthology Six: Supernatural / 1997 / Sequel ✦✦✦
Supernatural, the sixth volume of Sequel's seven-disc *Anthology,* picks up Ben E. King's Atco/Atlantic career in 1975, when he was attempting to blend in with the smooth soul and disco trends of the mid-'70s. King was surprisingly successful at making himself sound contemporary, and

while the material is uneven, the sound of the record is appealing, meaning that it was a respectable comeback. —*Thom Owens*

Anthology Seven: Benny and Us / 1997 / Sequel ✦✦✦
Benny and Us was Ben E. King's last album of consequence, and as the final installment in Sequel's seven-volume *Anthology* series, it functions as solid, if unremarkable, closer to the series. King recorded the record with the Average White Band, and the pairing is a good one—they are funky and soulful, even on the weaker numbers. Nevertheless, the music isn't as substantive as King's earliest work, and it isn't as immediate as those on *Supernatural,* which makes the disc appealing only to hardcore collectors. —*Thom Owens*

Carole King

b. Feb. 9, 1942, Brooklyn, NY
Synthesizer, Guitar, Piano, Keyboards, Vocals / Singer-Songwriter, Adult Contemporary, Soft Rock, Pop-Rock, Brill Building Pop

While the landmark album *Tapestry* earned her superstar status, singer-songwriter Carole King had already firmly established herself as one of pop music's most gifted and successful composers, with work recorded by everyone from the Beatles to Aretha Franklin. Born Carole Klein on February 9, 1942, in Brooklyn, NY, she began playing piano at the age of four, and formed her first band, the vocal quartet the Co-Sines, while in high school. A devotee of the composing team of Jerry Lieber and Mike Stoller (the duo behind numerous hits for Elvis Presley, the Coasters, and Ben E. King), she became a fixture at influential DJ Alan Freed's local rock 'n' roll shows; while attending Queens College, she fell in with budding songwriters Paul Simon and Neil Sedaka as well as Gerry Goffin, with whom she forged a writing partnership.

In 1959, Sedaka scored a hit with "Oh! Carol," written in her honor; King cut an answer record, "Oh! Neil," but it stiffed. She and Goffin, who eventually married, began writing under publishers Don Kirshner and Al Nevins in the famed pop songwriting house the Brill Building, where they worked alongside the likes of Doc Pomus, Mort Shuman, Jeff Barry, Ellie Greenwich and countless others. In 1961, Goffin and King scored their first hit with the Shirelles' chart-topping "Will You Love Me Tomorrow"; their next effort, Bobby Vee's "Take Good Care of My Baby," also hit No. 1, as did "The Locomotion," recorded by their baby-sitter, Little Eva. Together, the couple wrote over 100 chart hits in a vast range of styles, including the Chiffons' "One Fine Day," the Monkees' "Pleasant Valley Sunday," the Drifters' "Up on the Roof," the Cookies' "Chains" (later covered by the Beatles), Aretha Franklin's "(You Make Me Feel) Like a Natural Woman," and the Crystals' controversial "He Hit Me (and It Felt like a Kiss)."

King also continued her attempts to mount a solo career, but scored only one hit, 1962's "It Might as Well Rain Until September." In the mid-1960s she, Goffin, and columnist Al Aronowitz founded their own short-lived label, Tomorrow Records; Charles Larkey, the bassist for the Tomorrow group the Myddle Class, eventually became King's second husband after her marriage to Goffin dissolved. She and Larkey later moved to the West Coast, where in 1968 they founded the City, a trio rounded out by New York musician Danny Kortchmar. The City recorded one LP, *Now That Everything's Been Said,* but did not tour due to King's stage fright; as a result, the album was a commercial failure, although it did feature songs later popularized by the the Byrds ("Wasn't Born to Follow"), Blood, Sweat and Tears ("Hi-De-Ho") and James Taylor ("You've Got a Friend").

Taylor and King ultimately became close friends, and he encouraged her to pursue a solo career. 1970's *Writer* proved a false start, but in 1971, she released *Tapestry,* which stayed on the charts for over six years and was the best-selling album of the era. A quiet, reflective work which proved seminal in the development of the singer-songwriter genre, *Tapestry* also scored a pair of hit singles, "So Far Away" and the chart-topping "It's Too Late," whose flip-side, "I Feel the Earth Move," garnered major airplay as well. 1971's *Music* also hit No. 1, and generated the hit "Sweet Seasons;" 1972's *Rhymes and Reasons* reached No. 2 on the charts, and 1974's *Wrap Around Joy,"* which featured the hit "Jazzman," hit the No. 1 spot.

In 1975, King and Goffin reunited to write *Thoroughbred,* which also featured contributions from James Taylor, David Crosby, and Graham Nash. After 1977's *Simple Things,* she mounted a tour with the backing group Navarro, and married her frequent songwriting partner Rick Evers, who died a year later after a heroin overdose. 1980's *Pearls,* a collection of performances of songs written during her partnership with Goffin, was her last significant hit, and King soon moved to a tiny mountain village in Idaho, where she became active in the environmental movement. After 1983's *Speeding Time,* she took a six-year hiatus from recording before releasing *City Streets,* which featured guest Eric Clapton. 1993's *Colour of Your Dreams* included a cameo from Guns N' Roses guitarist Slash; a year later, King made her Broadway debut in the drama *Bloodbrothers.* —*Jason Ankeny*

★ **Tapestry** / Mar. 1971 / Epic ✦✦✦✦✦
In the world of popular music, the word "classic" gets bandied about like the word "improved" on ad campaigns, ceasing to mean anything after a while. *Tapestry*, however, is a *classic*, no two ways about it. King (already a very successful songwriter) assembled a collection of her best-known songs, plus some new ones, and gave them intimate heartfelt readings. King's voice had a warm earthy quality, with just the right amount of urgency. Listing highlights is fairly pointless, as the whole album is stunning. —*Rick Clark*

Music / Dec. 1971 / Epic ✦✦✦✦
Without the reserve of self-penned standards to draw upon, *Music* lacked the powerful resonance of its predecessor, *Tapestry*. Nevertheless, songs like "Sweet Seasons," "Brother Brother," "Some Kind of Wonderful," and "Song of Long Ago" make this one of her better efforts. —*Rick Clark*

Rhymes & Reasons / Nov. 1972 / Epic ✦✦✦
On her second follow-up to *Tapestry* and third new album in less than two years, King turned entirely to new compositions; most of them co-written with Toni Stern; rather than relying partly on songs from her back catalog. The result was a thinner collection than *Tapestry* or *Music*, although the album still went to No. 2 and featured the Top 25 hit "Been to Canaan," as well as the warm love song "The First Day in August." —*William Ruhlmann*

Fantasy / Jun. 1973 / Epic ✦✦✦
By this time, King's work recalled the detached craftsmanship of her days as a professional tunesmith. As a result, many of her post-*Tapestry* efforts lack a certain sense of emotional investment in their performances. Regardless, *Fantasy* (an improvement over the previously released *Rhymes and Reasons*) produced three hits with "Believe in Humanity," "Corazon," and "You Light Up My Life." Other highlights include "A Quiet Place to Live" and "Directions." —*Rick Clark*

Wrap Around Joy / Sep. 1974 / Epic ✦✦✦
More upbeat and rockin' than her last couple of efforts, *Wrap Around Joy* contains much of the jazz-tinged rock King was becoming known for. Here, she found chart action with "Jazzman" as well as the title track. A good, solid effort, as usual, from one of America's finest songwriters. —*James Chrispell*

Really Rosie / 1975 / Caedmon ✦✦✦✦
This winning soundtrack collaboration for a children's TV special (with children's author Maurice Sendak) was a return to form for King. *Really Rosie* contains some of King's best solo material. This is an enjoyable listening experience for children and adults alike. —*Rick Clark*

Thoroughbred / Jan. 1976 / Epic ✦✦✦
After a series of solid but unexceptional albums, King re-collaborated with her first husband Gerry Goffin and produced her best album since *Tapestry*. Like *Tapestry*, much of *Thoroughbred* reflect a rich soulfulness. The only thing lacking is *Tapestry*'s amazing collection of standards. The emotive "Only Love Is Real" became a substantial hit. —*Rick Clark*

Simple Things / Jul. 1977 / Capitol ✦✦
Carole King moved to Capitol Records with this release and introduced as her lyric collaborator Rick Evers, who became her third husband. The new associations, however, did not signal an impressive new phase in her work. The rollicking "Hard Rock Cafe," which anticipated the chain of restaurants by a decade, was the only moderate hit here, with most of the music well-meaning but lacking the distinctiveness of King's previous pop classics. Similarly, Navarro, her backup band, was adequate but no more. Despite the stimulus of a new label, *Simple Things* became King's first album since her breakthrough with *Tapestry* to peak below the Top 10. —*William Ruhlmann*

Welcome Home / 1978 / Capitol ✦✦
After seven straight gold-selling, Top 20 albums, *Welcome Home* demonstrated thoroughly that Carole King was on the wrong track. Her third husband, Rick Evers, who wrote lyrics for some of her songs and is pictured with her on the record cover, died of a drug overdose after this album was recorded in January 1978, but before it was released in May, which seems emblematic of the problems here. They include "Venusian Diamond," a song that deliberately borrows gimmicks from Beatles records, and "Disco Tech." That's right, Carole King goes disco. There were no hits, although "Morning Sun" made a brief appearance in the adult contemporary chart, and there was certainly nothing that was up to King's usual standards. The album failed to make the Top 100 and effectively removed King from the top echelon of pop artists. —*William Ruhlmann*

Her Greatest Hits / Mar. 1978 / Epic ✦✦✦✦
All of King's major hits are here, plus a few key album tracks. It's a decent starting place for the uninitiated, but *Tapestry* is a richer listening experience. —*Rick Clark*

Touch the Sky / 1979 / Capitol ✦✦
Continuing on a downhill curve, this record did little for Carole King's career. Recorded in Austin, TX, with a group of musicians who had been backing Jerry Jeff Walker at the time, the main failing is that King only plays piano on three tracks, and then not as well as she's known for. The songs don't hold up either, and that's a shame, for while nothing here is great, given some of her old backing musicians, she could have had a much better chance at making this release better. Not one of her best. —*James Chrispell*

Pearls: Songs of Goffin and King / 1980 / Scarface ✦✦✦
King reprises the early-'60s pop gems she wrote with Gerry Goffin, with fine results. —*Dan Heilman*

One to One / 1982 / Atlantic ✦✦

Speeding Time / 1983 / Atlantic ✦✦

City Streets / Apr. 1989 / Capitol ✦✦
Carole King's first album in six years also marks her return to Capitol Records, for whom she recorded from 1977 to 1980. She tries updating her sound, with aggressive guitars played on a couple of cuts by Eric Clapton, synthesizers, and drum machines, while singing lyrics that declare her renewed passion and hope. King was never one of pop's deep thinkers, which got her into trouble when she started going cosmic in the late '70s, but here she restricts herself to a kind of willed optimism and determination, and she sings as though she means it. *City Streets* is thus King's most engaging record since her early '70s hits, and even if it's too late for her to reclaim her place in pop music, that's encouraging. —*William Ruhlmann*

Colour of Your Dreams / Mar. 16, 1993 / Rhythm Safari ✦✦
The success of "Now and Forever," which was used as the opening-credits music for the summer 1992 film *A League of Their Own*, seems to have earned Carole King another shot at record-making, albeit with an indie label. That song turns out to be one of the few highlights of a varied collection in which King sings some love songs and then turns to more serious fare, with dubious results. The best new songs here are two that reunite King with old partner Gerry Goffin, who still has a way with a romantic lyric. —*William Ruhlmann*

● **A Natural Woman: The Ode Collection (1968-1976)** / Sep. 13, 1994 / Ode ✦✦✦✦
Carole King had already written an enormous amount of pop classics by the time she began her solo career in earnest in the late '60s. With her second album, *Tapestry*, King became one of the most popular and artistically successful singer-songwriters of the early '70s. King never matched the consistent brilliance of *Tapestry*, yet managed to record many fine songs during the rest of the decade. *A Natural Woman* collects all of her finest moments over the course of two discs. *Tapestry* is included in its entirety, along with the highlights from her other albums, making *A Natural Woman* the one essential King album—apart from *Tapestry* itself, of course. —*Stephen Thomas Erlewine*

Carnegie Hall Concert: June 18 1971 / Oct. 29, 1996 / Sony ✦✦✦✦
This 17-song set was recorded on June 18, 1971, just as *Tapestry* was topping the charts and making King a superstar. Featuring most of *Tapestry* and a few songs from *Writer* and *Music*, this is in a sense Carole King unplugged (although that terminology was not yet in use). King performs the first half-dozen songs alone at the piano; bassist Charles Larkey, guitarist Danny Kortchmar, and a string quartet back her (in varying combinations) throughout the rest of the program. *Tapestry* wasn't exactly a high-wattage affair to begin with, so these rearrangements aren't radical, but they're different enough from the studio versions to merit attention by serious King fans. James Taylor, then at the peak of his own popularity, joins King on vocals for a medley of some of her old Brill Building hits, "Will You Still Love Me Tomorrow"/"Some Kind of Wonderful"/"Up on the Roof." —*Richie Unterberger*

Evelyn Champagne King

b. Jun. 29, 1960, Bronx, NY
Vocals / Soul, House, Disco, Quiet Storm
Once a sparkling, youthful star who seemed to be emerging as a perennial winner, Evelyn "Champagne" King didn't completely fulfill the potential she showed in her early records, but still became a very successful artist. She was reportedly discovered while subbing for her sister as a cleaning woman at Sigma Studios in her teens. Producer T. Life heard King singing Sam Cooke's "A Change Is Gonna Come." He took her to RCA, where her debut single vaulted King into prominence in 1978; both "Shame" and "I Don't Know If It's Right" were triumphant, explosive tunes that deserved their Top Ten R&B status. King kept making hits into the mid-'80s, topping the charts with "I'm in Love" and "Love Come Down," both spectacular vocals that elevated good arrangements into great ones. "Betcha She Don't Love You" and "Your Personal Touch" were her final RCA hits, and King moved to EMI-Manhattan in 1988. The song "Flirt" returned her to hit status, peaking at No. 3 R&B. RCA issued a greatest hits/retrospective CD in 1993. —*Ron Wynn*

● **Love Come Down: The Best Of . . .** / Mar. 1993 / RCA ✦✦✦✦
Before the term "disco diva" was universally adopted, Evelyn "Champagne" King was hailed as dance music's reigning female vocalist. King was a sensation in disco's heyday, and she survived the backlash and prospered during the genre's evolution into dance music. She enjoyed a string of hits into the mid-'80s and was able to excel on rhythm-dominated material and sentimental ballads. This 15-track anthology includes her finest uptempo cuts ("Shame," "I'm In Love," and "Love Come Down," all done at the original hit length), plus underrated numbers such as "Don't Hide Our Love" and "Give Me One Reason." Those who remember King's hits will savor this collection, while others who missed her prime period will hear why she was so dominant. — *Ron Wynn*

The Kingsmen

f. 1957, Portland, OR
Rock 'n' Roll, Garage Rock
A rock 'n' roll band from Portland, OR, the Kingsmen's one big hit "Louie, Louie" defined the garage-band style and became one of the all-time classics. The original lineup included Jack Ely (lead singer and guitar), Lynn Easton (drums), Mike Mitchell (lead guitar), Bob Nordby (bass), and Don Galucci (piano). After Ely had "incorrectly" taught the rest of the band the Wailers version of Richard Berry's "Louie Louie" (thus altering the basic rhythm into the now famous duh-duh-duh, duh-duh, duh-duh-duh, duh-duh riff that has become the only way anyone has played it since), they recorded it for fifty dollars at a primitive local recording studio with only three mikes, Ely hollering the lyrics into an overhead boom mike suspended ten feet in the air. Released on a local label, the record went nowhere after Paul Revere & the Raiders quickly covered it in the Northwest market, although it had quickly become a standard for all teen bands in that area. In 1964, the record started to break nationally, causing the breakup of the original lineup when Easton copyrighted the group's name, informing the other members that he was now sole owner of the Kingsmen and its new lead singer. Ely formed his own Kingsmen, touring at the same time as Easton, who was lip-synching the record whenever possible. Only Easton and Mitchell were left from the original lineup, but they kept scoring big with frat-band versions of "Money" and "Little Latin Lupe Lu," reaching their peak with "The Jolly Green Giant," while Ely languished in relative obscurity and Gallucci formed Don & the Goodtimes. By the early '90s, history had redressed itself somewhat. While replacement members from the Easton version of the band toured as the "original" Kingsmen, Jack Ely finally received some of his due, headlining the 30th Anniversary Louie Louie tour. Though the song itself has been covered repeatedly, the version by Ely and the original lineup remains definitive. — *Cub Koda*

The Kingsmen in Person / 1963 / Sundazed ✦✦✦
CD reissue of the group's first album, including the rock anthem "Louie Louie," issued here for the first time minus the annoying overdubbed crowd noises. Also nice is the inclusion of three bonus tracks. — *Cub Koda*

The Kingsmen, Vol. 2 / 1964 / Sundazed ✦✦✦
Supposedly another "live" album, finally issued here without the audience overdubs. Highlights include "Little Latin Lupe Lu," "Long Green," and "David's Mood," plus two CD bonus tracks. — *Cub Koda*

The Kingsmen, Vol. 3 / 1965 / Sundazed ✦✦✦
The group's third album, again issued here without the overdubbed crowd noises. This features their hit "Jolly Green Giant" plus three CD bonus tracks. — *Cub Koda*

The Kingsmen on Campus / 1965 / Sundazed ✦✦

Up and Away / 1966 / Sundazed ✦✦

● **The Best of the Kingsmen** / 1989 / Rhino ✦✦✦✦
Although the Kingsmen's original albums are enjoyable as artifacts, they're unnecessary for anyone but hardcore collectors. For most listeners, Rhino's *The Best of the Kingsmen* will be all the Kingsmen they'll ever need to hear. Over the course of 18 tracks, all of the garage-rock band's greatest hits—not just "Louie Louie," but trashy gems like "Little Latin Lupe Lu," "Death of an Angel," "The Jolly Green Giant," "Annie Fanny," "Killer Joe," and "The Climb"—are featured, along with several fine album tracks that make this the definitive compilation. — *Stephen Thomas Erlewine*

Since We've Been Gone / Oct. 21, 1994 / Sundazed ✦✦✦

The Kinks

f. 1963, London, England
Rock 'n' Roll, Hard Rock, British Invasion, Pop-Rock
Although they weren't as boldly innovative as the Beatles or as popular as the Rolling Stones or the Who, the Kinks were one of the most influential bands of their era. Like most bands of their era, the

Kinks began as an R&B/blues outfit. Within four years, the band had become the most staunchly English of all their contemporaries, drawing heavily from British music hall and traditional pop, as well as incorporating elements of country, folk, and blues.

Throughout their long, varied career, the core of the Kinks remained Ray (b. June 21, 1944) and Dave Davies (b. February 3, 1947), who were born and raised in Muswell Hill, London. In their teens, the brothers began playing skiffle and rock 'n' roll. Soon, the brothers recruited a schoolmate of Ray's, Peter Quaife, to play with them; like the Davies brothers, Quaife played guitar, but he switched to bass. By the summer of 1963, the group had decided to call itself the Ravens and had recruited a new drummer, Mickey Willet. Eventually, their demo tape reached Shel Talmy, an American record producer who was under contract to Pye Records. Talmy helped the band land a contract with Pye in 1964. Before signing to the label, the Ravens replaced drummer Willet with Mick Avory.

The Ravens recorded their debut single, a cover of Little Richard's "Long Tall Sally," in January 1964. Before the single was released, the group changed their name to the Kinks. "Long Tall Sally" was released in February of 1964 and it failed to chart, as did their second single, "You Still Want Me." The band's third single, "You Really Got Me," was much noisier and dynamic, featuring a savage, fuzz-toned, two-chord riff and a frenzied solo from Dave Davies. Not only was the final version the blueprint for the Kinks' early sound, but scores of groups used the heavy power chords as a foundation. "You Really Got Me" reached No. 1 within a month of its release; released on Reprise in the US, the single climbed into the Top Ten. "All Day and All of the Night," the group's fourth single, was released late in 1964 and it rose all the way to No. 2; in America, it hit No. 7. During this time, the band also produced two full-length albums and several EPs.

Not only was the group recording at a breakneck pace, they were touring relentlessly, as well, which caused much tension within the band. At the conclusion of their summer 1965 American tour, the Kinks were banned from re-entering the United States by the American government for unspecified reasons. For four years, the Kinks were prohibited from returning to the US, which not only meant that the group was deprived of the world's largest music market, but that they were effectively cut off from the musical and social upheavals of the late '60s. Consequently, Ray Davies' songwriting grew more introspective and nostalgic, relying more on overtly English musical influences such as music hall, country, and English folk, than the rest of his British contemporaries. The Kinks' next album, *The Kinks Kontroversy*, demonstrated the progression in Davies' songwriting. "Sunny Afternoon" was one of Davies' wry social satires and the song was the biggest hit of the summer of 1966 in the UK, reaching No. 1. "Sunny Afternoon" was a teaser for the band's great leap forward, *Face to Face*, a record that featured a vast array of musical styles. In May of 1967, they returned with "Waterloo Sunset," a ballad that reached No. 2 in the UK in the spring of 1967. Released in the fall of 1967, *Something Else* continued the progressions of *Face to Face*. Despite the Kinks' musical growth, their chart performance was beginning to stagnate. Following the lackluster performance of *Something Else*, the Kinks rushed out a new single, "Autumn Almanac," which became another big UK hit for the band. Released in the spring of 1968, the Kinks' "Wonderboy" was the band's first single not to crack the Top Ten since "You Really Got Me." They recovered somewhat with "Days," but the band's commercial decline was evident by the lack of success of *The Village Green Preservation Society*.

Released in the fall of 1968, *Village Green Preservation Society* was the culmination of Ray Davies' increasingly nostalgic tendencies. While the album was unsuccessful, it was well-received by critics, particularly in the US.

Peter Quaife soon grew tired of the band's lack of success, and he left the band by the end of the year, being replaced by John Dalton. In early 1969, the American ban on the Kinks was lifted, leaving the band free to tour the US for the first time in four years. Before they began the tour, the Kinks released *Arthur (or the Decline and Fall of the British Empire)*. Like its two predecessors, *Arthur* contained distinctly British lyrical and musical themes, but it was a modest success. As they were recording the follow-up to *Arthur*, the Kinks expanded their lineup to include keyboardist John Gosling. The first appearance of Gosling on a Kinks record was "Lola." Featuring a harder rock foundation than their last few singles, "Lola" was a Top Ten hit in both the UK and the US. Released in the fall of 1970, *Lola Versus Powerman and the Money-goround, Part One* was their most successful record since the mid-'60s in both the US and UK, helping the band become concert favorites in the US.

The band's contract with Pye/Reprise expired in early 1971, leaving the Kinks free to pursue a new record contract. By the end of 1971, the Kinks had secured a five-album deal with RCA Records, which brought them a million-dollar advance. Released in late 1971, *Muswell Hillbillies*, the group's first album for RCA, marked a return to the nostalgia of the Kinks' late-'60s albums, only with more pronounced country and music hall influences. The album failed to be the commercial block-buster RCA had hoped for. A few months after the release of *Muswell Hillbillies*, Reprise released a double-album compilation callled *The Kink Kronikles*, which outsold their RCA debut. *Everybody's in Show-biz* (1973), a double-record set consisting of one album of studio tracks and another of live material, was a disappointment in the UK, although the album was more successful in the US.

In 1973, Ray Davies composed a full-blown rock opera called *Preservation*. When the first installment of the opera finally appeared in late 1973, it was harshly criticized and given a cold reception from the public. *Act 2* appeared in the summer of 1974; the sequel received worse treatment than its predecessor. Davies began another musical, *Starmaker*, for the BBC; the project eventually metamorphosed into *Soap Opera*, which was released in the spring of 1975. Despite poor reviews, *Soap Opera* was a more commercially successful record than its predecessor. In 1976, the Kinks recorded Davies' third straight rock opera, *Schoolboys in Disgrace*, which rocked harder than any album they released on RCA.

During 1976, the Kinks left RCA and signed with Arista Records. On Arista, the band refashioned themselves as a hard rock band. Bassist John Dalton left the group near the completion of their debut Arista album; he was replaced by Andy Pyle. *Sleepwalker*, the Kinks' first album for Arista, became a major hit in the US. As the band was completing the follow-up to *Sleepwalker*, Pyle left the group and was replaced by the returning Dalton. *Misfits*, the band's second Arista album, was also a US success. After a British tour, Dalton left the band again, along with keyboardist John Gosling; bassist Jim Rodford and keyboardist Gordon Edwards filled the vacancies. Soon, the band was playing arenas in the United States. Even though punk rockers like the Jam and the Pretenders were covering Kinks songs in the late '70s, the group was becoming more blatantly commercial with each release, culminating in the heavy rock of *Low Budget* (1979), which became the group's biggest American success, peaking at No. 11. The Kinks' next album, *Give the People What They Want*, appeared in late 1981; the record peaked at No. 15 and went gold. For most of 1982, the band was on tour. In spring of 1983, "Come Dancing" became the group's biggest American hit since "Tired of Waiting for You," thanks to the video's repeated exposure on MTV; in the US, the song peaked at No. 6, in the UK it climbed to No. 12. *State of Confusion* followed the release of "Come Dancing," and it was another success, peaking at No. 12 in the US. For the remainder of 1983, Ray Davies worked on a film project, *Return to Waterloo*, which caused considerable tension between himself and his brother. Instead of breaking up, the Kinks merely reshuffled their lineup, but there was a major casualty—Mick Avory, the band's drummer for 20 years, was fired and replaced by Bob Henrit. As Ray finished post-production duties on *Return to Waterloo*, he wrote the next Kinks album, *Word of Mouth*. Released in late 1984, the album was similar in tone to the last few Kinks records, but it was a commercial disappointment and began a period of decline for the band—they never released another record that cracked the Top 40.

Word of Mouth was the last album they would record for Arista Records. In early 1986, the band signed with MCA Records in the US, London in the UK. *Think Visual*, their first album for their new label, was released in late 1986. It was a mild success, but there were no hit singles from the record. The following year, the Kinks released another live album, appropriately titled *The Road*, which spent a brief time on the charts. Two years later, the Kinks released their last studio record for MCA, *UK Jive*. During 1989, keyboardist Ian Gibbons left the band. The Kinks were inducted into the Rock & Roll Hall of Fame in 1990, but the induction did not help revive their career. In 1991, a compilation of their MCA records, *Lost & Found (1986-1989)*, appeared, signalling that their contract with the label had expired. Later in the year, the band signed with Columbia Records and released an EP called *Did Ya*, which didn't chart. The Kinks' first album for Columbia, *Phobia*, arrived in 1993 to fair reviews but poor sales. By this time, only Ray and Dave Davies remained from the original lineup. In 1994, the band was dropped from Columbia Records, leaving the group to release the live *To the Bone* on an independent label in the UK; the band was left without a record label in the US.

Despite a lack of commercial success, the band's public profile began to rise in 1995, as the group was hailed as an influence on several of the most popular British bands of the decade, including Blur and Oasis. Ray Davies was soon on popular television shows again, acting as these band's godfather and promoting his autobiography, *X-Ray*, which was published in early 1995 in the UK. Dave Davies' autobiography, *Kink*, was published in the spring of 1996. —*Stephen Thomas Erlewine*

You Really Got Me / 1964 / Rhino ◆◆
The highlight of this rather spotty debut (consisting of a sampling of originals and covers the Kinks churned out at gigs) was, without a doubt, the title track, which single-handedly pioneered riff-oriented hard rock. "Stop Your Sobbing," a song later recorded by the Pretenders, was

also a standout track, but producer Shel Talmy's "Bald Headed Woman" was an absolute low point. —*Rick Clark*

Kinda Kinks / 1965 / Rhino ◆◆◆
Album No. 2 featured a rewrite of "You Really Got Me," with the equally fine "All Day and All of the Night." Ray Davies, however, delivered a strong set of tunes that went beyond riff-rockers with the exuberant "Come on Now" and "You Shouldn't Be Sad." His penchant for memorable melodies emerged with tracks like "Something Better Beginning" and "Tired of Waiting for You." —*Rick Clark*

Kink-Size/Kinkdom / 1965 / Rhino ◆◆◆◆
This Rhino reissue contains the Kinks' third and fourth albums, *Kink-Size* and *Kinkdom*, respectively, plus some nonalbum sides from the same period. *Kink-Size* featured the hit "Set Me Free," another Kinks classic, as well as "Everybody's Gonna Be Happy." By the release of *Kinkdom*, the Kinks had developed an instantly identifiable sound, built around Davies' wavering lower tenor and the group's airy falsetto background vocals and ragged garage rock-like ensemble work. "Dedicated Follower of Fashion," a noisy dance-hall rocker, was a wonderful poke at a Carnaby Street fop in his "frilly nylon panties." Other hits included "Who'll Be the Next in Line?" and "A Well Respected Man." This disc also includes the assertive "I'm Not Like Everybody Else" (originally written as a pitch for the Animals, and the B-side to "Sunny Afternoon"). —*Rick Clark*

Kink Kontroversy / 1965 / PRT ◆◆◆
This great album is still only available as a British import. The Kinks sludge out some fine trashy rockers with "Where Have All the Good Times Gone?" (later re-recorded by Van Halen) and "Till the End of the Day," a moderate hit. Other highlights included "It's Too Late," "You Can't Win," and "I'm on an Island." —*Rick Clark*

☆ **Face to Face** / 1966 / Reprise ◆◆◆◆◆
The Kink Kontroversy was a considerable leap forward in terms of quality, but it pales next to *Face to Face*, one of the finest collections of pop songs released during the '60s. Conceived as a loose concept album, *Face to Face* sees Ray Davies' fascination with English class and social structures flourish, as he creates a number of vivid character portraits. Davies' growth as a lyricist has coincided with the Kinks' musical growth. *Face to Face* is filled with wonderful moments, whether it's the mocking Hawaiian guitars of the rocker "Holiday in Waikiki," the droning eastern touches of "Fancy," the music-hall shuffle of "Dandy," or the lazily rolling "Sunny Afternoon." And that only scratches the surface of the riches of *Face to Face*, which offers other classics like "Rosy Won't You Please Come Home," "Party Line," "Too Much on My Mind," "Rainy Day in June," and "Most Exclusive Residence for Sale," making the record one of the most distinctive and accomplished albums of its time. —*Stephen Thomas Erlewine*

Live at Kelvin Hall / 1967 / Reprise ◆◆◆
Outside of the Rolling Stones' *Got Live If You Want It* and the Beatles' *Live at the Hollywood Bowl*, this is the only readily available concert document of a British Invasion-era band, complete with all of the screaming fans. The Kinks slog through a version of "The Batman Theme," "I'm on an Island," "Milk Cow Blues," and a smattering of hits. —*Rick Clark*

☆ **Something Else by the Kinks** / 1967 / Reprise ◆◆◆◆◆
Face to Face was a remarkable record, but its follow-up *Something Else* expands its accomplishments, offering 13 classic British pop songs. As Ray Davies' songwriting becomes more refined, he becomes more nostalgic and sentimental, retreating from the psychedelic and mod posturings that had dominated the rock world. Indeed, *Something Else* sounds like nothing else from 1967. The Kinks never rock very hard on the album, preferring acoustic ballads, music-hall numbers, and tempered R&B to full-out guitar attacks. Part of the album's power lies in its calm music, since it provides an elegant support for Davies' character portraits and vignettes. From the martial stomp of "David Watts" to the lovely, shimmering "Waterloo Sunset," there's not a weak song on the record, and several—such as the allegorical "Two Sisters," the Noel Coward-esque "End of the Season," the rolling "Lazy Old Sun" and the wry "Situation Vacant"—are stunners. And just as impressive is the emergence of Dave Davies as a songwriter. His Dylanesque "Death of a Clown" and bluesy rocker "Love Me Til the Sun Shines" hold their own against Ray's masterpieces, and help make *Something Else* the endlessly fascinating album that it is. —*Stephen Thomas Erlewine*

☆ **The Village Green Preservation Society** / 1968 / Reprise ◆◆◆◆◆
Ray Davies' sentimental, nostalgic streak emerged on *Something Else*, but it developed into a manifesto on *The Village Green Preservation Society*, a concept album lamenting the passing of old-fashioned English traditions. As the opening title song says, the Kinks—meaning Ray himself, in this case—were for preserving "draft beer and virginity," and throughout the rest of the album, he creates a series of stories, sketches, and characters about a picturesque England that never really was. It's a lovely, gentle album, evoking a small British country town,

and drawing the listener into its lazy rhythms and sensibilities. Although there is an undercurrent of regret running throughout the album, Davies' fondness for the past is warm, making the album feel like a sweet, hazy dream. And considering the subdued performances and the detailed instrumentations, it's not surprising that the record feels more like a Ray Davies solo project than a Kinks album. The bluesy shuffle of "Last of the Steam-Powered Trains" is the closest the album comes to rock 'n' roll, and Dave's cameo on the menacing "Wicked Annabella" comes as surprise, since the album is so calm. But calm doesn't mean tame or bland—there are endless layers of musical and lyrical innovation on *The Village Green Preservation Society*, and its defiantly British sensibilities became the foundation of generations of British guitar-pop. —*Stephen Thomas Erlewine*

☆ **Arthur or the Decline and Fall of the British Empire** / 1969 / Reprise ◆◆◆◆◆
Arthur (Or the Decline and Fall of the British Empire) extends the British-oriented themes of *Village Green Preservation Society*, telling the story of a London man's decision to move to Australia during the aftermath of World War II. It's a detailed and loving song cycle, capturing the minutiae of suburban life, the numbing effect of bureaucracy, and the horrors of war. On paper, *Arthur* sounds like a pretentious mess, but Ray Davies' lyrics and insights have rarely been as graceful or deftly executed, and the music is remarkable. An edgier and harder-rocking affair than *Village Green*, *Arthur* is as multilayered musically as it is lyrically. "Shangri-La" evolves from English folk to hard rock, "Drivin' " has a lazy grace, "Young and Innocent Days" is a lovely, wistful ballad, "Some Mother's Son" is one of the most uncompromising anti-war songs ever recorded, while "Victoria" and "Arthur" rock with simple glee. The music makes the words cut deeper, and the songs never stray too far from the album's subject, making *Arthur* one of the most effective concept albums in rock history, as well as one of the best and most influential British pop records of its era. —*Stephen Thomas Erlewine*

Lola vs. the Powerman & the Money-Go-Round, Part One / 1970 / Reprise ◆◆◆◆
Thanks to the No. 9 hit single "Lola" (about an encounter with a transvestite), *Lola vs. the Powerman & the Money-go-round, Part One* became a comeback of sorts for the Kinks. Overall, this album is a Davies eye view of life as an artist coping with the road ("This Time Tomorrow") and the music industry, which includes blackly humorous portrayals of the musician's union ("Get Back in Line"), music publishers ("Denmark Street"), making it big ("Top of the Pops"), and greed ("Money-go-round"). This might be a whinefest from a successful pop artist, but his observations aren't that far off base. Musically, the Kinks still had their ragged delivery, but they increasingly employed more acoustic instrumentation, giving the arrangements a slightly folky quality at times. —*Rick Clark*

Percy [O.S.T.] / 1971 / Pye ◆◆
Ray Davies and company had already participated in one failed television musical when the movie *Percy* came along—it wasn't as original as *Arthur*, nor did Ray Davies have nearly as much to do with its creation, but he still outdid himself given the material at hand. Directed and co-produced by Ralph Thomas, who had been responsible for some brilliant thrillers (*The Clouded Yellow, Above Us the Waves*) and very popular comedies (*Doctor in the House*) in past decades, *Percy* was the story of the world's first penis transplant (it was probably inspired, or at least justified, by big-budget efforts of the period like *Myra Breckinridge*). Although virtually unseen in the United States, it was still popular enough to yield a sequel (*Percy's Progress*), but its real impact came from its soundtrack. Davies wrote some hauntingly beautiful ballads and some solid blues and country as well—"God's Children" and "Animals in the Zoo" have turned up on some career anthologies, but there's a lot more to *Percy* than those two tracks. "Completely" is as fine a slow blues as the band ever recorded, with a sizzling performance by Dave Davies, and "Dreams" is a pretty solid rocker, even up alongside "Animals in the Zoo." To this day, the album has never appeared in the US catalog—recorded at the tail-end of their contract with Pye Records in England and Warner/Reprise in America, and connected with a movie that was never going to see much exposure in the USA, Reprise passed on it at the time. —*Bruce Eder*

Muswell Hillbillies / 1971 / Rhino ◆◆◆◆
For their first outing on the RCA label, the Kinks adopted a more laid-back rootsy sound that even sported traces of country ("Holloway Jail") and dancehall/cabaret theater styles ("Skin and Bones," "Holiday," "Alcohol"). "Twentieth Century Man" is a nice medium-tempo rocker, but lacks the reckless fire of their earlier efforts. —*Rick Clark*

Everybody's in Show-Biz / 1972 / Rhino ◆◆◆
One half of this release is a document of the Kinks' spirited live slopfest, including versions of "Top of the Pops," "Holiday," and the "Banana Boat Song." The other half contains a couple of gems like "Celluloid Heroes" and "Sitting in My Hotel," as well as "Motorway," and "Maximum Consumption." —*Rick Clark*

★ **The Kink Kronikles** / 1972 / Reprise ◆◆◆◆◆
Strictly speaking, the double-album compilation *The Kink Kronikles* isn't a greatest hits collection. Covering the years 1966 through 1970, *The Kink Kronikles* is comprised of album tracks, non-LP singles, B-sides, unreleased tracks, solo singles, and the handful of hits the Kinks had in the latter half of the '60s; out of the album's 28 tracks, only nine were hits in the UK or the US. Even though it isn't packed with hits, *The Kink Kronikles* is a definitive overview of this era, which was one of Ray Davies' most productive songwriting periods and although much of this music wasn't heard outside of the group's cult, it proved to be some of the most influential British music of its time. It's hard to imagine how a a better compilation of the Kinks' latter-day recordings for Pye could be assembled. Apart from the hits—the lazy, sardonic "Sunny Afternoon," the gorgeous "Waterloo Sunset," and the 1970 comeback hits "Lola" and "Apeman"—there is a wealth of music that ranks among their very best material and much of it isn't available on any other album. First off, non-LP British hit singles like the music-hall raver "Dead End Street" and the wry "Autumn Almanac" are included, as are Dave Davies' two solo hits, "Death of a Clown" and "Suzannah's Still Alive." Then there are the wealth of non-LP singles and B-sides that *didn't* make the British charts: "Wonderboy," "Mr. Pleasant," "Polly," "Big Black Smoke" and Dave Davies' wonderful "Mindless Child of Motherhood." There are also unreleased songs ("Berkeley Mews," "Did You See Him Name") that are genuinely worthy items, and obscurities like "This is Where I Belong," "She's Got Everything" and the lovely "God's Children," which rank among the group's finest songs. And the album tracks—including minor hits like the Chuck Berry-styled tribute to "Victoria" and acknowledged classics like the droning "Fancy" and the title track to *Village Green*, but also superb neglected songs like "Get Back in Line" and the absurdist rocker "Holiday In Waikiki"—each demonstrate another side of the Kinks' musical versatility and Davies' abilities. The key to the success of *The Kink Kronikles* is how the singles and rarities complement each other and, taken together, present a full portrait. It's the rare compilation that is equally valuable to the collector and to the neophyte fan. —*Stephen Thomas Erlewine*

The Great Lost Kinks Album / 1973 / Reprise ◆◆◆◆
An aptly titled collection; out of print for many years, there are even some Kinks cultists who have never been able to hear this ragtag but worthy collection of late-'60s and early-'70s outtakes and rarities. Most of these were recorded around the same time as the 1968 LP *Village Green Preservation Society*; these low-key, wry, bouncy tunes would have fit in well with that record. Lyrically, they're on the whole slighter than much of their late-'60s work, which is perhaps why the group did not deign to release them at the time. Still, songs like "Rosemary Rose," "Misty Water," and "Mr. Songbird" would have hardly embarrassed the group, and rank as the highlights of this anthology. Besides 1969-era outtakes, it includes the single "Plastic Man," a couple of okay way-obscure B-sides featuring Dave Davies, and some songs penned for long-forgotten film and television productions. It also has the dynamite 1966 B-side "I'm Not Like Everybody Else," though that's easily available on reissue these days. That's not the case for most of the rest of this album; Kinks fans will find it quite worthwhile, and should be on the lookout for it in the used bins. —*Richie Unterberger*

Preservation: Acts 1 & 2 / 1973 / Rhino ◆◆◆
Initially intended as an extension of *The Village Green Preservation Society*, *Preservation* offered relatively little in the way of great songwriting or spirited performances, something *Village Green* had in spades. "Money Talks" is a nice mid-tempo rocker. The Rhino CD includes the single, "Preservation." —*Rick Clark*

The Kinks Present Schoolboys in Disgrace / 1975 / Rhino ◆◆
As the last of the Kinks' overt conceptual excercises, *Schoolboys* was further proof that Ray Davies' best "plays" happened when he focused his observational skills into singular songs, rather than fleshing out an idea over the course of a whole album. Like *Soap Opera*, this is only recommended for hardcore completists. —*Rick Clark*

The Kinks Present a Soap Opera / 1975 / Rhino ◆◆
Davies' obsession with concept albums reached a nadir with *Soap Opera*. At this point, Davies and company were so busy pandering to their live audiences, they seemed to forget how to make truly memorable music. The lifeless production, indicative of this era of their music, didn't help matters either. Nevertheless, "You Make It All Worthwhile," "Face in the Crowd," and "Everybody's a Star" were highlights from this spotty set. —*Rick Clark*

The Kinks' Greatest: Celluloid Heroes / 1976 / RCA ◆◆◆
This is a good collection comprising the cream of The Kinks' RCA years. It includes "Sitting in My Hotel," "Twentieth Century Man," "Alcohol," and "Everybody's a Star." —*Rick Clark*

Sleepwalker / 1977 / Arista ◆◆◆
Arista had made it clear they would not accept any concept albums from the Kinks, and *Sleepwalker*, their first effort for the label, makes good on the band's promise. Comprised entirely of glossy arena-rockers and

power ballads, the album is more of a stylistic exercise than a collection of first-rate songs. Davies contributed a handful of fairly strong songs, highlighted by the exceptional "Juke Box Music," which sees Ray in a shockingly resigned frame of mind, claiming that rock 'n' roll is just rock 'n' roll, and nothing more. Unfortunately, he chose to illustrate that fact by loading the rest of *Sleepwalker* with competent but undistinguished mainstream rock. While that might have made the album a hit at the time, its processed sound and weak songs sound dated today, especially compared to the lively arena-rock the Kinks later released. —*Stephen Thomas Erlewine*

Misfits / 1978 / Arista ✦✦✦✦
The Kinks became arena-rockers with *Sleepwalker*, and its follow-up, *Misfits*, follows in the same vein, but it's a considerable improvement on its predecessor. Ray Davies has learned how to write within the confines of the arena-rock formula, and *Misfits* is one of rock 'n' roll's great mid-life crisis albums, finding Davies considering whether he should even go on performing. "Misfits," a classic outsider rallying cry, and "Rock and Roll Fantasy" provide the two touchstones for the album—Davies admits that he and the Kinks will never be embraced by the rock 'n' roll mainstream, but after Elvis' death, he's not even sure if rock 'n' roll is something for mature adults to do. Over the course of *Misfits*, he finds answers to the question, both in his lyrics and through the band's muscular music. Eventually, he discovers that it is worth his time, but the search itself is superbly affecting—even songs like the music-hall shuffle "Hay Fever," which appear as filler as first, have an idiosyncratic quirk that make them cut deeper. Although Ray would return to camp on their next album, *Misfits* is a moving record that manages to convey deep emotions while rocking hard. The Kinks hadn't made a record this good since *Muswell Hillbillies*. —*Stephen Thomas Erlewine*

Low Budget / 1979 / Arista ✦✦✦
Even though the Kinks enjoyed their most consistently satisfying album-chart success during their years at Arista, so much of this lacks the vision and execution of their work found on Reprise. Regardless of all that, the disco-influenced pop-rocker "(Wish I Could Fly Like) Superman" was a No. 41 hit. —*Rick Clark*

One for the Road / 1980 / Arista ✦✦
By this time, the Kinks enjoyed quite a bit of FM rock success, enough to make this servicable live album a hit. A singalong performance of "Lola" even resurrected itself to No. 81 on the pop charts. —*Rick Clark*

Give the People What They Want / 1981 / Arista ✦✦✦
Riding high on the success of *Low Budget*, the Kinks turned out another collection of hard-driving, arena-ready rock 'n' roll with *Give the People What They Want*—in short, they delivered exactly what the title suggests. Throughout the record, the band kicks up a storm, rocking out with a surprising amount of precision, and although Ray Davies' writing isn't as strong as it was on the group's two previous albums, he has contributed a set of professional hard rock that is distinguished by solid hooks and a clever sense of humor. After all, there's a certain charm in hearing him rework "All Day and All of the Night" into the paranoid "Destroyer," or his pure cynicism on the title track. But the minor masterpiece of the album is "Better Things," a sweet piece of charming sentimentalism that is the only time Davies lets his guard down during the entire album. —*Stephen Thomas Erlewine*

State of Confusion / 1983 / Arista ✦✦✦
State of Confusion had its share of glossy hard rock in the vein of "Low Budget" and "Destroyer," but the record came to life on the quieter numbers, whether it's the elegiac "Don't Forget to Dance," the wistful pop of "Long Distance," or the buoyant nostalgia of "Come Dancing," which became the group's biggest hit since "Tired of Waiting for You." —*Stephen Thomas Erlewine*

Word of Mouth / 1984 / Arista ✦✦
State of Confusion gave the Kinks their biggest single in nearly 20 years, but they didn't try to replicate the music hall-tinged pop of "Come Dancing" on its follow-up *Word of Mouth*, preferring to concentrate on straightahead hard rock. Most of the material was well-crafted, but only a few songs were distinctive, particularly the circular, synth-spiked minor hit "Do It Again." —*Stephen Thomas Erlewine*

Come Dancing with the Kinks: The Best of the Kinks 1977-1986 / Jul. 1986 / Arista ✦✦✦✦
A sampling of their Arista years (1977-1986), most of the essential tracks are here, including all of their hits from that period. "Come Dancing," "A Rock 'n' Roll Fantasy," "Juke Box Music," "Destroyer," and "(Wish I Could Fly Like) Superman" are among the titles found here. —*Rick Clark*

Think Visual / Dec. 1986 / MCA ✦✦
Think Visual, the band's first album for MCA Records, represented an artistic dead end for the Kinks, as Ray Davies continued to crank out a series of competent, but undistinguished hard rockers. Out of all the loud, riff-driven numbers, only Dave Davies' "Rock N' Roll Cities" made a lasting impression. Ray's gentler songs weren't among his most mem-

orable, relying on slight melodies and underdeveloped lyrics. —*Stephen Thomas Erlewine*

The Kinks Live: the Road / 1988 / MCA ✦✦
The Kinks' second album for MCA was *The Kinks Live: The Road*, a tepid document of their workman-like arena-rock shows from 1987. At the time of recording, the group couldn't fill the arenas they were packing in the early '80s, so they began moving back to theaters. Perhaps the band resented being sent back to smaller venues, since they exhibited very little passion or excitement as they ran through their recent hits and old warhorses. The album also included a new, studio-recorded song called "The Road," which was a chronicle of the band's typical touring experiences. Like the rest of the record, the song wasn't anything special. —*Stephen Thomas Erlewine*

★ **Greatest Hits, Vol. 1** / 1989 / Rhino ✦✦✦✦✦
Featuring a total of 18 highlights from the Kinks' early career, Rhino's *Greatest Hits* is the definitive compilation of the group's hit singles from the mid-'60s. Beginning with "You Really Got Me" and ending with "Sunny Afternoon," all of the Kinks' essential garage-rockers and British Invasion singles are here—"All Day and All of the Night," "Till the End of the Day," "Tired of Waiting for You," "A Well Respected Man," "Stop Your Sobbing," "Dedicated Follower of Fashion," "I'm Not Like Everybody Else," "Where Have All the Good Times Gone." Only the ambitious, Indian-tinged British hit "See My Friends" is missing, but it isn't a major oversight, especially since the disc distills the group's uneven early albums into manageable form for many fans. While *Kinkdom, Kontroversy*, and *Face to Face* have many excellent album tracks in their own right, *Greatest Hits* remains a terrific summation of the group's earliest, hardest-rocking work. —*Stephen Thomas Erlewine*

UK Jive / Sep. 1989 / MCA ✦✦
Even though the album was weighed down by its adherence to late-'80s state-of-the-art studio techinques, *UK Jive* was a noticeable improvement over the lackluster *Think Visual*. Featuring only a handful of hard rockers—including the excellent, snarling "Aggravation"—the album was comprised of pop songs that painted an unfocused portrait of modern British life. Although many of Ray Davies' finest songs were based on a similar concept, his songwriting on *UK Jive* was frustratingly inconsistent, ranging from the infectious bop of the title track to the ham-fisted anthem "Down All Days (to 1992)." With the loping "Looney Balloon," Davies wrote one of his finest songs of the '80s, but the only track that equalled its conviction was his brother Dave's spiteful protest "Dear Margaret." —*Stephen Thomas Erlewine*

Lost & Found (1986-89) / Aug. 27, 1991 / MCA ✦✦
The Kinks were on MCA Records for a remarkably brief time, recording three albums in three years, including one live record. During these three years, Ray Davies' songwriting was frequently uninspired and formulaic. Not surprisingly, the records didn't feature enough highlights to form an engaging compilation and *Lost & Found* is certainly the weakest of their "best-of" collections, featuring no hit singles at all. Although *Lost & Found* is a better album than either *Think Visual* or *The Kinks Live: The Road*, it isn't as consistent or engaging as *UK Jive*, which remains the only worthwhile record from their time at MCA. —*Stephen Thomas Erlewine*

Phobia / Apr. 13, 1993 / Columbia ✦✦
Ray Davies continues to turn out three or four brilliant songs on albums that barely anyone will ever hear. For Kinks fans, that's enough to justify the purchase of any of their recent albums, and the harder-edged *Phobia* is no exception to that rule. —*AMG*

You Really Got Me [Karussell] / 1994 / Karussell ✦✦✦✦
Okay, so there are better compilations, but at $9 list for 18 songs and a whopping 53 minutes, covering repertory from the title track through "Days," and all in glittering sound, it's hard to ignore this budget-priced gem. The emphasis is somewhat weighted toward the group's earlier Pye recordings, but there's just enough of the later stuff to make it an almost fair cross-section of the group's sound and its development. The real treat is the sound—Karussell must've gotten access to the remastered tapes, because there's not a passage, whether it is electric or acoustic, that doesn't leap out and fill the room, and that's at normal volume; cranked up, this record is a great party album or a lease-buster. Otherwise, the notes are decent if a little perfunctory, and the selection is weird enough to be enjoyable, looping all over the map from 1964 through 1970, and zigzagging through the likes of "Shangri-La," "Long Tall Sally," "God's Children," "Too Much Monkey Business," "Days," and "Cadillac." It's even more fun if you set your CD player to "scramble." (German import) —*Bruce Eder*

To the Bone / Oct. 1994 / Grapevine ✦✦✦
Since the mid-'70s, The Kinks have not been able to stop themselves from attempting their own variations on pop music trends, taking stabs at everything from bombastic heavy metal to sleek disco-flavored pop. On *To the Bone*, the group became another one of the scores of veteran rock acts to record an acoustic, "unplugged" album. However, the

group's American popularity was at an all-time low in the mid-'90s and the band wasn't able to score a major-label record deal, let alone land a spot on MTV's prime-time ratings bonanza, *Unplugged.* So, the group financed their acoustic greatest hits record *To the Bone* themselves, releasing it on the UK independent label Grapevine. Naturally, Ray Davies' songs work well in such a stripped-back setting, but the album is nothing more than a pleasant diversion, featuring a lovely version of "Waterloo Sunset," possibly the most beautiful song of the rock 'n' roll era. —*Stephen Thomas Erlewine*

Good Luck Charm [bootleg] / Scorpio ✦✦✦✦

It's got no label or catalog number, and it ain't easy to find, but if you're a Kinks fanatic, you should try to get a hold of this. It has some rare BBC/ live material from the mid—and late '60s, highlighted by the never-released R&B/rock original "All Aboard" and three songs from a 1967 Dave Davies solo broadcast (one of which, "Good Luck Charm," was also never released officially). Then there are a few nifty folk-rockish songs from Dave's aborted late-'60s solo LP, which remains a sort of holy grail for Kinks fans; the Ray Davies-penned calypso "And I Will Love You," and a few late-'60s songs from official releases that have only shown up on obscure import anthologies. The five live songs from 1970 have lousy fidelity, but otherwise this collates a lot of interesting stuff that is hard to come by elsewhere. —*Richie Unterberger*

Kollektable Kinks [bootleg] / Reprieve ✦✦✦✦

This double LP of rare studio material is a bit less of a tour de force now than it was when it first came out around 1983, as some of the cuts have surfaced on official releases and CD bootlegs. Still, one could hardly ask for a better compilation of B-sides, import-only tracks, alternate versions, and the like. Highlights include the Dave Davies '60s non-LP solo singles, the sanitized version of "Lola" (where Ray Davies sings "cherry cola" instead of "Coca Cola" to avoid a BBC ban), a Denmark-only (and better) version of "Apeman," the sarcastic "Father Christmas" single, and the "Preservation" 45. Best of all are five unreleased demos of Davies compositions from 1965, including a stark Ray-and-piano version of "I Go to Sleep," as well as the beautifully melancholic ballads "Tell Me Now So I'll Know" and "There's a New World Just Opening for Me." With excellent sound quality, this isn't just for manic collectors; any old Kinks fan will enjoy this. —*Richie Unterberger*

Kinks Kontraband [bootleg] / Reprieve ✦✦✦

Not as essential as *Kollektable Kinks,* but still a solid highlight as far as Kinks bootlegs go. About half of this features BBC recordings from the mid-'60s in good quality, though the takes don't differ much from the studio versions (actually, they're substantially less powerful). The major highlight of the broadcasts is the typically laconic and moody Ray Davies original "This Strange Effect," which the Kinks never recorded in the studio (although Dave Berry had a European hit with a cover version). Other goodies are a raw demo of the unreleased Ray original "All Night Stand" (given to the obscure British band the Thoughts), a song which would have fit in well on *Face To Face,* and the garagey studio outtake "Time Will Tell," yet another mid-'60s Davies composition that the band never released. The rest of the disc is pretty much filler, presenting some unfinished instrumental backing tracks from the '60s, and some marginally different live/alternate studio recordings from much later in the group's career. —*Richie Unterberger*

Kevn Kinney

Vocals / Folk, Country-Rock, Singer-Songwriter, Folk-Rock

Kevn Kinney is the lead singer of the Atlanta rock band Drivin' n' Cryin', but since the band's 1986 inception he's released two spare acoustic records on his own, often collaborating with R.E.M. guitarist Peter Buck.

MacDougal Blues for Island in 1990 announced the rocker's arrival on the folk scene with the engaging title cut and nine more acoustic tracks produced by Buck and mostly played by his bandmates from Drivin' n' Cryin'. Though often cited as a working-class lyricist, Kinney cannot easily be thrown into the same bag as Springsteen, Mellencamp, or Dave Alvin. Instead, his is a unique spin on class, not urban yet not completely rural—he's lived and worked in the urban center, Atlanta. Yet there is a gentleness and deeply humanistic thread to his work, and his use of traditional instruments enhances his words' warmth. His follow-up, *Down Out Law* (Mammoth 1994), is a little more of a downer and less a celebration of folk music than a revealing, melancholy personal treatise, unaccompanied except by himself on guitar, save for one track. Continuing to record with Drivin' n' Cryin', Kinney also tours as a solo act, often assisted by Buck or his brother. —*Denise Sullivan*

● **Mac Dougal Blues** / Jan. 1990 / Island ✦✦✦✦

Drivin' n' Cryin's Kevn Kinney joins the folk fray with a stunning solo acoustic debut backed by the band and producer Peter Buck. The classic case of a brilliant songwriter stuck within the confines of an okay band, Kinney came bursting forth as a great new talent on the new folk scene with songs like the emotional "Not Afraid to Die" and lilting "The House Above Tina's Grocery." This release was mostly unheard by those who

might have appreciated Kinney's unique spin on southern culture. —*Denise Sullivan*

Down Out Law / Jan. 25, 1994 / Mammoth ✦✦✦✦

With less instrumentation than his first solo outing, this makes for a tough listen for those not completely appreciative of Kinney's unique southern rock voice or the solo folk-blues idiom. The title cut is outstanding, as is "Shindig with the Lord"; the song recalls the excitement of a revival tent set up on the outskirts of town as it winds up and down. It's a sight often seen in the rural South, but as in his other songs, the sight seems to be taken from Kinney's fertile imagination, delivered with his usual urbanity. —*Denise Sullivan*

Kiss

f. 1973, New York City, NY
Hard Rock, Heavy Metal, Hair Metal, Arena Rock

Rooted in the campy theatrics of Alice Cooper and the sleazy hard rock of glam rockers the New York Dolls, Kiss became an favorite for American teenagers in the '70s. Most kids were infatuated with the look of Kiss, not their music. Decked out in outrageously flamboyant costumes and makeup, the band fashioned a captivating stage show featuring dry ice, smoke bombs, elaborate lighting, blood spitting, and fire breathing that captured the imaginations of thousands of kids. But Kiss' music shouldn't be dismissed out of hand—it was a commercially potent mix of anthemic, fist-pounding hard rock driven by sleek hooks and ballads powered by loud guitars, cloying melodies, and sweeping strings. It was a sound that laid the groundwork for both arena rock and the pop/metal that dominated rock in the late '80s.

Kiss was the brainchild of Gene Simmons (bass, vocals) and Paul Stanley (rhythm guitar, vocals), former members of the New York-based hard rock band Wicked Lester; the duo brought in drummer Peter Criss through his ad in *Rolling Stone* and guitarist Ace Frehley responded to an advertisement in *The Village Voice.* Even at their first Manhattan concert in 1973, the group's approach was quite theatrical; Flipside producer Bill Aucoin offered the band a management deal after the show. Two weeks later, the band was signed to Neil Bogart's fledgling record label Casablanca. Kiss released their self-titled debut in February of 1974; it peaked at No. 87 on the US charts. By April of 1975, the group had released three albums and had toured America constantly, building up a sizable fan base. Culled from those numerous concerts, *Alive!* (released in the fall of 1975) made the band rock 'n' roll superstars; it climbed into the Top Ten and its accompanying single, "Rock 'N' Roll All Nite," made it to No. 12. Their follow-up, *Destroyer,* was released in March of 1976 and became the group's first platinum album; it also featured their first Top Ten single, Peter Criss' power ballad "Beth."

A 1977 *Gallup* poll named Kiss the most popular band in America. Kiss mania was in full swing and thousands of pieces of merchandise hit the marketplace. The group had two comic books published by Marvel, they had pinball machines, makeup and masks, board games, and an animated television special, *Kiss Meet the Phantom of the Park.* The group was never seen in public without wearing their makeup, and their popularity was growing by leaps and bounds; the membership of the Kiss Army, the band's fan club, was now in the six figures. Even such enormous popularity had its limits and the band reached them in 1978, when all four members released solo albums on the same day in October. Simmons' record was the most successful, reaching No. 22 on the charts, yet all of them made it into the Top 50. *Dynasty,* released in 1979, continued their streak of platinum albums, yet it was their last recorded with the original lineup—Criss left in 1980.

Kiss Unmasked, released in the summer of 1980, was recorded with session drummer Anton Fig; Criss' permanent replacement, Eric Carr, joined the band in time for their 1980 world tour. *Kiss Unmasked* was their first record since *Destroyer* to fail to go platinum and 1981's *Music from the Elder,* the first album recorded with Carr, didn't even go gold—it couldn't even climb past No. 75 on the charts. Ace Frehley left the band after its release; he was replaced by Vinnie Vincent in 1982. Vincent's first album with the group, 1982's *Creatures of the Night,* fared better than *Music from the Elder,* yet it couldn't make it past No. 45 on the charts.

Sensing it was time for a change, Kiss dispensed with their makeup for 1983's *Lick It Up.* The publicity worked, as the album became their first platinum record in four years. *Animalize,* released the following year, was just as successful and the group had recaptured its niche. Vincent left after *Animalize* and was replaced by Mark St. John; St. John was soon taken ill with Reiter's Syndrome and left the band. Bruce Kulick became Kiss' new lead guitarist in 1984. For the rest of the decade, Kiss turned out a series of best-selling albums, culminating in the early 1990 hit ballad "Forever," which was their biggest single since "Beth."

Kiss were scheduled to record a new album with their old producer Bob Ezrin in 1990 when Eric Carr became severely ill with cancer; he died in November of 1991 at the age of 41. Kiss replaced him with Eric

Singer and recorded *Revenge* (1992), their first album since 1989; it was a Top Ten hit and went gold. Kiss followed it with the release of *Alive III* the following year; it performed respectably, but not up to the standards of their two previous live records. In 1996, the original lineup of Kiss—featuring Simmons, Stanley, Frehley, and Criss—reunited to perform an international tour, complete with their notorious makeup and special effects. The tour was one of the most successful of 1996. — *Stephen Thomas Erlewine*

Kiss / Apr. 1974 / Casablanca ✦✦✦✦
Compared to their later albums, Kiss' self-titled debut is a raw, riveting dose of heavy metal. At the time of its recording, the group was still working out their sound, trying to develop their loud, lumbering guitar riffs into sleek, melodic heavy hooks. Kiss only succeeds in streamlining their bombast on a couple of tracks—"Deuce," "Black Diamond," "Firehouse," "Strutter"—but the rest of the record sounds vigorous and forceful, making up for the lapses in songwriting quality. — *Stephen Thomas Erlewine*

Hotter Than Hell / Nov. 1974 / Casablanca ✦✦✦
Hotter than Hell is nearly an identical replica of Kiss' first album, which isn't surprising, considering how quickly it was recorded after their debut. *Hotter than Hell* has a few highlights—"Parasite," "Let Me Go, Rock and Roll," "Got to Choose," and the title track—but overall the riffs aren't as catchy and the songs aren't as well-written as *Kiss*. — *Stephen Thomas Erlewine*

Dressed to Kill / Apr. 1975 / Casablanca ✦✦✦✦
With *Dressed to Kill*, Kiss began to write songs that delivered on the promise of their live shows. Driven by the pounding, but catchy, hooks of "Rock 'n' Roll All Nite" and "She," the album increases the amount of melody Kiss works into their songs. Kiss also increases their sleaze content, delivering obvious, leering double entendres like "Room Service," "Love Her All I Can," and "Ladies in Waiting" throughout the record. But the hooks make the sleaze appealing, and when they can't come up with convincing melodies, the group has polished their sound enough to make the filler enjoyable. — *Stephen Thomas Erlewine*

★ **Alive!** / Oct. 1975 / Casablanca ✦✦✦✦✦
Given the wildly inconsistent quality of Kiss' first three albums, the high quality of *Alive!* comes as somewhat of a surprise. Then again, Kiss were showmen, not songwriters, which means they were always at their best when they were on stage. Part of that show—the makeup, the explosions, the lights, the dry ice—could not be replicated on record, but the group was invigorated by the live setting, adding passion and conviction to their thunderously loud riffs. Of course, some of the material still falls flat, but most of *Alive!* seethes with energy, making their finest moments—"Rock 'n' Roll All Nite," "Deuce," "Strutter," "Black Diamond," "She," "Hotter than Hell"—seem like hard rock classics. — *Stephen Thomas Erlewine*

Destroyer / 1976 / Casablanca ✦✦✦✦
Kiss followed the breakthrough Top Ten success of *Alive!* with *Destroyer*, the most pop-oriented record they had ever recorded. Under the direction of producer Bob Ezrin (Alice Cooper), the group's recorded sound became as theatrical as their live shows, featuring strings, sound effects, multilayered guitars and vocals. That doesn't necessarily mean *Destroyer* is a better record than *Dressed to Kill*—it means the album is a set of slick pop-rock that hides its lack of improved songwriting with stylish production flourishes. Despite the presence of the throttling "Shout It Out Loud" and "Detroit Rock City," none of the rockers are quite as distinct and memorable as "Rock 'n' Roll All Night," but that's remedied by the heavily orchestrated proto-power-ballad "Beth." — *Stephen Thomas Erlewine*

Rock and Roll Over / 1976 / Casablanca ✦✦✦✦
Rock and Roll Over was Kiss' second straight No. 11 album, and it was a marginally better album than the previous *Destroyer*, featuring a harder, more direct production and improved songwriting, as illustrated by the hit singles "Calling Dr. Love" and "Hard Luck Woman." — *Stephen Thomas Erlewine*

Love Gun / Jul. 1977 / Casablanca ✦✦✦✦
By the time of *Love Gun*, Kiss had perfected their gimmick, turning in a set of sleek, slick, hard rock that celebrated its silly, tongue-in-cheek jokes and grotesque imagery. The group had polished all of the rough edges out of their sound, leaving a collection of hard-driving riffs that were more catchy than heavy. Songwriting was still a problem for the band, but *Love Gun* was one of their most consistent albums, featuring the concert staples "Christine Sixteen," "Plaster Caster," and "Love Gun." — *Stephen Thomas Erlewine*

Alive II / Nov. 1977 / Casablanca ✦✦✦
Kiss recorded *Alive!* after the release of their first three albums. *Alive II* appeared after *Love Gun*, their sixth studio album, giving the band three albums of new material for their new live record. Even with all the fresh material—including a side of new songs recorded in the studio—*Alive II* isn't nearly as energetic as Kiss' first live album. The prob-

lem with *Alive II* lies with the fact that the three albums that followed *Alive!* were better produced than their first three records. Since the songs on *Destroyer*, *Rock and Roll Over*, and *Love Gun* were crafted in the studio, they weren't as raw or rocking as the songs that comprised Kiss' first albums, and consequently they didn't work quite as well on stage, where they were divorced from the detailed production of the original records. Nevertheless, songs like "Detroit Rock City," "Shout It Out Loud," and "Calling Dr. Love" benefitted from the live setting, with their riffs coming across more forcefully than in the studio versions. Overall, *Alive II* doesn't match the sheer power of Kiss' first live record. — *Stephen Thomas Erlewine*

Double Platinum (Greatest Hits) / 1978 / Casablanca ✦✦✦✦
Double Platinum (Greatest Hits) is a double-album, 20-track collection that gathers all of Kiss' biggest hits ("Rock and Roll All Nite," "Shout It Out Loud," "Beth," "Detroit Rock City," "Calling Dr. Love," "Love Gun"), but what makes it an essential retrospective and introduction is how it doesn't overlook key album tracks and concert favorites like "Cold Gin," "Deuce," "Black Diamond" and "She." If "Strutter" was represented by the original version instead of a pointless 1978 remake—which was recorded only to entice collectors into buying an album of music they already owned—*Double Platinum* would have been a definitive collection, but as it stands, it's simply a very, very good overview. — *Stephen Thomas Erlewine*

Dynasty / 1979 / Casablanca ✦✦✦
Although *Dynasty* was another Top Ten platinum success for Kiss, it marked the beginning of their turn-of-the-decade decline. Featuring a noticeable lack of memorable songs—only the hits "I Was Made for Lovin' You" and "Sure Know Something" stand out amidst the scores of undistinguished numbers—the record's main weakness is the workmanlike performance of the band, which adds no style to their limp material. — *Stephen Thomas Erlewine*

Kiss Unmasked / 1980 / Casablanca ✦✦
Kiss Unmasked was the group's first album since *Destroyer* to not go platinum, and it's easy to see why. Driven by pedestrian riffs and melodies, none of the songs are memorable, and the group sounds uninspired throughout the record. Peter Criss left during the recording of the album; session drummer Anton Fig completed the record after Criss' departure. The change in drummers isn't evident in the music, but what the music does make clear is that it was time for Kiss to change their act. — *Stephen Thomas Erlewine*

Music from "The Elder" / 1981 / Casablanca ✦✦
On *Music from the Elder*, the first album the band recorded with Eric Carr, Kiss reworked their trashy metal aesthetic into a more ambitious and pretentious variation on hard rock. Recorded with an orchestra and a choir, the record sounded like nothing else in the band's catalog. While Kiss' desire to change musical directions was admirable, the stilted results aren't successful—in fact, they're frequently embarrassing. — *Stephen Thomas Erlewine*

Creatures of the Night / 1982 / Casablanca ✦
Ace Frehley left the band after *Music from the Elder* and the guitarist was replaced with Vinnie Vincent for *Creatures of the Night*, a return to the bombastic hard rock of Kiss' glory years. Although Vincent's playing is impressive, the group failed to write distinctive material, making the album sound like the work of a band well past their prime. — *Stephen Thomas Erlewine*

Lick It Up / 1983 / Mercury ✦✦✦
Kiss had been left scarred by the failures of *Music from the Elder* and *Creatures of the Night*, and they knew it was time for a makeover. So, for *Lick It Up*, the band removed their makeup and costumes for the first time in their careers, ensuring themselves a great deal of media coverage. The ploy worked, but what made *Lick It Up* a platinum success was the quality of the songwriting. While it wasn't up to the standards of *Dressed to Kill* and *Destroyer*, *Lick It Up* was state-of-the-art melodic heavy metal that returned the band to platinum status. — *Stephen Thomas Erlewine*

Animalize / 1984 / Mercury ✦✦
Animalize was more successful than the previous *Lick It Up*, but that's only because its predecessor had accomplished the job of restoring the band's reputation among adolescents. While it followed the same pattern as *Lick It Up*, most of the songs were second-rate, with the noticeable exception of the smoldering "Heaven's on Fire." — *Stephen Thomas Erlewine*

Asylum / 1985 / Mercury ✦✦
Sonically, Kiss retained their revitalized roar throughout *Asylum*, turning in a tough, but supple performance that would have been more impressive if the songs were stronger. — *Stephen Thomas Erlewine*

Crazy Nights / 1987 / Mercury ✦✦✦
Like most of Kiss' '80s albums, *Crazy Nights* was an inconsistent set of power ballads and streamlined, polished hard rockers, but the hooks on

the album were the strongest the band had written since *Lick It Up*. —*Stephen Thomas Erlewine*

Smashes, Thrashes & Hits / 1988 / Casablanca ✦✦✦✦
The companion volume to the above, from their later makeup-less period, including "Lick It Up," "Let's Put the X in Sex," and "Love Gun." —*Dan Heilman*

Hot in the Shade / Oct. 1989 / Mercury ✦✦
Hot in the Shade continued Kiss' late-'80s winning streak, thanks to the hit power ballad "Forever." The rest of the album followed the familiar Kiss blueprint, with only a couple of the tracks meeting the standard of the hit single. —*Stephen Thomas Erlewine*

Revenge / 1992 / Mercury ✦✦✦
Revenge was supposed to be a triumphant return to Kiss' glory days of the mid-'70s, as the band reunited with producer Bob Ezrin, who was responsible for *Destroyer*. However, drummer Eric Carr died in 1991, making the whole affair more somber and reflective than it was originally intended to be. Kiss replaced Carr with Eric Singer and proceeded to record the album that became *Revenge*. *Revenge* was the most brutal record they had recorded since the mid-'70s, driven by throttling riffs and relentless rhythms. Even though their sound had been considerably beefed up, their songwriting had only improved slightly, with "Heart of Chrome" a particular standout. —*Stephen Thomas Erlewine*

Alive III / May 18, 1993 / PolyGram ✦✦
Judged against Kiss' previous *Alive!* albums, *Alive III* doesn't hold up particularly well. Instead of relying on raw energy and ridiculous but dynamic showmanship, the band plays like the professionals they are, performing a competent set that never catches fire. However, if *Alive III* is judged against Kiss' late '80s and early '90s records, it holds up very well. By cutting away the filler that plagued their studio records, the band is left with a consistently entertaining batch of songs, served up with style. It might not be as exciting as the first two *Alive* albums, but *Alive III* provides more thrills than most of the group's records of the previous decade. —*Stephen Thomas Erlewine*

Unplugged / Mar. 12, 1996 / Mercury ✦✦✦
Kiss always were masters of marketing, so it comes as no surprise that the band began celebrating their 25th anniversary with *Unplugged*, the conventional way to revive a career in the '90s. Drawing from their extensive catalog of hits and adding a few choice rarities, the band sounds unexpectedly vibrant—they sound like they're having fun and that vibe is infectious. For most fans, the highlight of the record is the appearance of the reunited original lineup for four tracks, including their classic power ballad, "Beth," but the entire record is an energetic, joyous, and appropriately sleazy celebration of a long, popular career. —*Stephen Thomas Erlewine*

You Wanted the Best You Got the Best / Jun. 25, 1996 / Polygram ✦
Talk about a misleading title! Judging by the title alone, *You Wanted the Best, You Got the Best* sounds like it would be the definitive Kiss retrospective, or at least an enjoyable collection of hits. But it's not—it's a rip-off album, pure and simple. It doesn't matter that the majority of the tracks are live recordings of their best-known songs, because Kiss always sounded better live than they did in the studio and these versions—which were taken from *Alive* and *Alive II*—are definitive. It's the fact that the release is baited with the live, unreleased "Room Service," "Take Me," "Let Me Know," and "Two Timer," and the rest of the disc is padded with an absurd, 17-minute interview with the four original band members conducted by Jay Leno. There is simply no reason for this to exist—dedicated fans would prefer a full, unreleased live album or an interview disc, while casual fans would be better served by the original *Alive* album if they're about to purchase their first Kiss record. With this album, you may have wanted the best, but you didn't get it—you just got exploited. —*Stephen Thomas Erlewine*

● **Greatest Kiss** / Apr. 8, 1997 / Polygram ✦✦✦✦
Greatest Kiss is a fine, 16-track collection of the group's biggest hits presented in their original studio versions, with the notable exception of a live version of "Shout It Out," a track recorded at the opening of the group's 1996 reunion tour that was added to entice dedicated collectors. Ignoring "Shout It Out," *Greatest Kiss* lives up to its billing, since it captures the band's most familiar material—"Rock & Roll All Night," "Strutter," "Beth," "Cold Gin"—on one disc, making it and *Alive* the only necessary albums for casual Kiss fans. —*Stephen Thomas Erlewine*

The KLF

f. 1987, England, **db.** May 5, 1992
Ambient, Alternative Pop-Rock, Acid House, Techno, Club/Dance
More than any pop band in history, the KLF ripped off the music industry for a bucketful of loot and got away with it—as illustrated in their own guidebook to creating number one singles, *The Manual*. Bill Drummond and Jimi Cauty applied the tactics of punk shock-terrorism to late-'80s acid-house and became one of Britain's best-selling artists just before their retirement in 1992. The duo then deleted their entire

back catalogue—a potential loss in the millions of pounds—and declared they wouldn't release another record until peace was declared throughout the world.

The son of a Scottish preacher, Bill Drummond (b. William Butterworth; April 29, 1953; South Africa) had played with Big in Japan and formed the Zoo Records label with Dave Balfe before he recorded the 1986 solo album *The Man* for Creation. After a brief retirement from the music industry, he called up an old friend, Brilliant's Jimi Cauty (b. 1954), and the two recorded a sample-heavy pastiche as the JAMS. The single, released that May, was followed a month later by an album, *1987—What the Fuck Is Going On?*, which continued the sonic piracy with long passages lifted from the Beatles, Led Zeppelin, and ABBA. By September, the Copyright Protection Society demanded that all copies be recalled and destroyed. Later that year, the JAMS released an edited version of the album called *1987 (The JAMS 45 Edits)*, with specific instructions on how to recreate the original *1987* at home.

A second album, *Who Killed the JAMS?*, appeared early in 1988, but it was superseded by the May release of "Doctorin' the Tardis" (recorded as the Timelords). Incorporating samples from Gary Glitter, Sweet and the theme to *Dr. Who*, the single hit No. 1 in the British charts and eventually became one of the most popular sports anthems of all time. Six months later, Cauty and Drummond compiled their knowledge of popular success and the music industry, publishing *The Manual* with a statement of purpose included in the subtitle: "How to have a number one the easy way—The Justified Ancients of Mu Mu reveal their zenarchistic method used in making the unthinkable happen."

Instead of focusing on the lucrative pop market, however, the duo played a major part in the development of the '90s boom in ambient music by retaining the samples and effects of their previous work, but without the house beats. Cauty and Drummond recorded the classic *Chill Out* album in late 1989, mixing source material from two DAT machines onto a cassette recorder during a live session.

Obviously, the KLF's ambient recordings weren't going to top the charts, so later in 1990 Cauty and Drummond moved back to acid-house, subsequently earning the greatest success of their career. The single "What Time Is Love?" hit No. 5 on the UK singles charts in August 1990. "3 A.M. Eternal" took over the No. 1 spot in January 1991, and *The White Room* LP topped the album charts upon its release in March. A third single, "Last Train to Trancentral," also made Top Ten that year. The KLF's success carried into Europe during 1991, and even the Americans caught on by September, pushing "3 A.M. Eternal" to No. 5 and *The White Room* into the Top 40 album charts. The US-only "America: What Time Is Love?" reached No. 57 in November 1991, and early in 1992 "Justified and Ancient"—the surprising pairing of the KLF with country queen Tammy Wynette—almost reached the American Top Ten. Cauty and Drummond, the best-selling singles act in the world during 1991, were on the verge of becoming superstars.

The duo had other plans in mind, though. Voted Best British Group by BPI and the BRIT Awards, the KLF were scheduled to perform at a London awards ceremony on February 13, 1992. Cauty and Drummond did show up, but horrified the formal audience with a hardcore thrash version of "3 A.M. Eternal" (performed with the justifiably named Extreme Noise Terror) that also included Drummond spraying the crowd with blanks from an automatic rifle and the post-performance announcement, "The KLF have left the music industry." The industry and press reaction was overwhelmingly negative, but Cauty and Drummond had already made their mint. Promising that no more releases were forthcoming until peace reigned around the world, they officially retired from music in May 1992. To convince the public that it wasn't simply a scam to sell more records, Drummond and Cauty deleted the entire back catalogue of KLF Communications. Despite recording one single as the K Foundation and appearing on the *HELP* charity compilation as the One World Orchestra, the duo refused to resume recording. Instead, Cauty and Drummond used the proceeds from their massive success to perpetrate bizarre stunts—including the burning of a million pounds—which functioned as commentaries on the art world. —*John Bush*

1987 (What the Fuck is Going On?) / May 1987 / KLF Communications ✦✦✦

The History of the JAMs a.k.a. The Timelords / 1988 / TVT ✦✦✦
Interesting more for its sample-and-scatter philosophy than the thick Scottish brogue with which Drummond tries to emulate Run-D.M.C., *The History of the JAMs a.k.a. The Timelords* takes no prisoners—Dave Brubeck's familiar saxophone riff from "Take Five" is looped onto the James Brown-style jam "Don't Take Five (Take What You Want)," Whitney Houston "guests" on the hilarious "Whitney Joins the JAMs" (a dry run for the later, actually *live*, appearance of Tammy Wynette) and assorted other stars of the past who also make appearances (including the Beatles, MC5, Jimi Hendrix, and Petula Clark). Aside from the novelty tracks—which wear as thin as their production values quite soon—this is the only available KLF full-length containing "Doctorin' the Tardis," which later became a popular sports anthem. —*John Bush*

Who Killed the Jams? / Jan. 1988 / KLF Communications ✦✦✦

Shag Times / Jan. 1989 / Discipline ✦✦✦

The What Time is Love Story / 1990 / KLF Communications ✦✦✦

Chill Out / Jan. 1990 / Wax Trax! ✦✦✦✦

Space / Jul. 1990 / Space-KLF Comm. ✦✦✦

● The White Room / Mar. 1991 / Arista ✦✦✦✦
After the incredible success of their "Doctorin' the Tardis" single in 1988 (better known as that theme from *Dr. Who*), Drummond and Cauty had plenty of money to hire talented musicians (instead of merely sampling them, as on their early recordings). *The White Room* is the result, an album bursting with hit singles that nevertheless flows as well as any concept album. Often overlooked as a classic from the acid-house era (mostly because of the KLF's retirement one year later), *The White Room* represents the commercial and artistic peak of late-'80s club culture. —*John Bush*

KMFDM

f. 1984, Germany
Industrial, Alternative Pop-Rock, Club/Dance
KMFDM was one of Wax Trax's first industrial superstars, combining the corrosive scratching of their guitars with a hard, throbbing hip-hop-derived beat. In the late '80s, the German trio (originally a quartet) became an underground sensation not only in America but in much of Europe; clubs became devoted to playing their style of abrasive, distorted guitar-driven dance music. KMFDM continues to be one of the major industrial bands of the '90s, with their recordings becoming even more aggressive, both musically and politically, as evidenced by releases including 1995's *Nihil* and *Juke-Joint Jezebel* as well as 1996's *XTORT*. —*Stephen Thomas Erlewine*

● Naive / 1990 / Wax Trax! ✦✦✦✦
KMFDM's fourth full-length album is their strongest release to date. It's a claustrophobic wall of noise, driven by a relentless jackhammer beat. —*Stephen Thomas Erlewine*

Money / 1992 / Wax Trax! ✦✦✦

Sucks / May 25, 1993 / Wax Trax! ✦✦

Angst / Oct. 13, 1993 / Wax Trax! ✦✦✦

Nihil / Apr. 4, 1995 / Wax Trax! ✦✦

Xtort / Jun. 25, 1996 / TVT ✦✦✦
XTORT doesn't sound markedly different than KMFDM's other releases—there are still the bruising mechanical drum beats and numbingly drilling guitars, combined with barked vocals. What's noticeable about *XTORT*—their first album since industrial broke into the Top 40 with Nine Inch Nails' *The Downward Spiral*—is how the band made no concessions to the pop-rock mainstream whatsoever. They are still the same grimy, dank heavy dance band they were in the '80s. For some listeners, that means they're keeping the flame burning and, to a certain extent, they'd be right—KMFDM sounds as good as they ever have, and several tracks rank among their best. But, over a decade into their career, it would be nice to hear the band branch out and start to experiment a little bit more. —*Stephen Thomas Erlewine*

The Knack

f. 1978, Los Angeles, CA, db. 1981
New Wave, Power Pop
Forming in Los Angeles in the late '70s, the Knack (Doug Fieger, vocals/guitar; Berton Averre, lead guitar; Prescott Niles, bass; and Bruce Gary, drums) were neither punk nor rock, but pure simple pop, standing out amongst the musical dross that littered the Sunset Strip. Signing with Capitol after a feeding frenzy of label offers, the Knack released their debut, *Get the Knack*, in 1979. With its leadoff single "My Sharona," the Knack climbed both the album and singles charts (eventually selling millions of copies around the globe), gained wide commercial acceptance, and regenerated the power-pop scene that had laid dormant for half a decade.
The Knack's image, or lack thereof, was often unfavorably compared to the Beatles, but their music relied on the rough punchiness of the Kinks and the Who rather than the Fab Four. Their refusal to do interviews turned critics against them, and by the time they released their second album, *. . . But the Little Girls Understand*, less than a year after the debut, the backlash had already begun. The Knack began a quick spiral downward that they were never to recover from. Their third album, *Round Trip*, was adventurous and daring and received favorable reviews, but the band decided to split up soon after the album was released.
Due to their continuing underground popularity, the Knack resurfaced almost a decade later (minus Bruce Gary) and recorded the abysmal *Serious Fun* before hiding out once again to lick their wounds. Due to the appearance of "My Sharona" on soundtracks and compilations,

the Knack have never really gone away. Still playing the L.A. club scene with Bruce Gary back on the skins, the band may yet again have another stab at the limelight. —*Spaz Schnee*

● Get the Knack / 1979 / Capitol ✦✦✦✦
The band attempted to update the Beatles sound for the new wave era on their debut. A good idea that was well executed, but critics cried "foul" when millions sold after Capitol's pre-release hype (it went gold in 13 days and eventually sold five million copies, making it one of the most successful debuts in history). *Get the Knack* is at once sleazy, sexist, hook-filled, and endlessly catchy—above all, it's a guilty pleasure and an exercise in simple fun. When is power-pop *legitimate* anyway? Includes the unforgettable hits "My Sharona" and "Good Girls Don't." —*Chris Woodstra*

. . . But the Little Girls Understand / Dec. 1979 / Razor & Tie ✦✦✦
Mike Chapman summed it up best in the liner notes—"The songs are an assortment of feelings and emotions expressed redundantly as only the Knack can . . . This record is very dear to me and my bank manager." The self-deprecating title (which quotes Willie Dixon's "Back Door Man") isn't really an attempt to apologize but rather to let people know that they were in on the joke all along—and they're laughing all the way to the bank. This is essentially a rewrite of the debut, especially evident on the lead-off single "Baby Talks Dirty." It's not as good as *Get the Knack* and didn't sell nearly as well, but it *is* a good time for those who don't take rock 'n' roll too seriously. —*Chris Woodstra*

Round Trip / 1981 / Capitol ✦✦
By the time their third album was released in 1981, the *Knuke the Knack* backlash had been long forgotten, but so had skinny ties. A slightly more low-key effort, *Round Trip* is a pleasant though unmemorable collection from a fast-fading era. The commercial failure of this album prompted the band to call it quits until reuniting in 1991. —*Chris Woodstra*

Serious Fun / Jan. 16, 1991 / Charisma ✦✦
Nearly a decade since the failure of *Round Trip*, *Serious Fun* marks the reunited band's attempt at credibility through a harder-rocking sound. Though "Rocket O' Love" stirred up some regional radio interest, the album is their least fun to date. —*Chris Woodstra*

Retrospective: The Best of the Knack / Nov. 16, 1992 / Capitol ✦✦✦✦
A fine greatest hits set that collects the best from their debut and their two weaker follow-ups. —*Stephen Thomas Erlewine*

The Knickerbockers

f. 1964, Bergenfield, NJ, db. 196?
Pop-Rock
In early 1966, the Knickerbockers hit the Top 20 with "Lies," the best and most accurate early Beatle imitation ever recorded; the lead vocals were a dead ringer for John Lennon, and the whole production could have fit in snugly on the second side of *A Hard Day's Night*. Actually a frat-rock band from New Jersey who didn't write much of their own material, they never made anything else as successful or good. A couple of decent follow-ups, "One Track Mind" and the similarly mock British Invasion "High on Love," were small hits, but their albums were even blander than many of the era's other one-shot artists. Their three noteworthy singles were all featured in Rhino's *Nuggets* series, and everyone but '60s completists would be advised to stick with those tracks. Drummer and singer Jimmy Walker briefly replaced Bill Medley in the Righteous Brothers. —*Richie Unterberger*

Jerk & Twine Time / 1965 / Sundazed ✦✦
Even if you're a dedicated collector, you should think twice about chasing down this album, which consists almost entirely of British Invasion and R&B covers in the frat-rock style, and not done especially well. The CD reissue has three bonus tracks, and an interview with a couple of band members. —*Richie Unterberger*

Lies / 1965 / Sundazed ✦✦
Recorded in Hollywood, with songwriting contributions from such top session men of the day as Glen Campbell, Jim Seals, and Dash Crofts, this is, aside from the first-rate title track, an extremely generic mid-'60s set, with only one group original other than "Lies." The Knickerbockers never found an identity, alternating between frat-rock, flaccid pop-rock, and strange wall-of-sound productions in which the producers apparently had visions of turning them into the Walker Brothers. The CD reissue has three bonus tracks, and an interview with a couple of band members. —*Richie Unterberger*

● The Fabulous Knickerbockers / 1988 / Sundazed ✦✦✦✦
This [best-of] collection includes the hits "Lies" (one of the greatest mid-'60s singles) and "One Track Mind." Tracks like "I Can Do It Better," "Rumors, Gossip, Words Untrue," and "High on Love" are more period highlights. This set contains ample annotation and great sound. —*Rick Clark*

The Great Lost Album / Sep. 27, 1994 / Sundazed ✦✦✦✦
Those into the camp aspects of pop culture will enjoy the idealistic "The Coming Generation," or adolescent swinger fantasy poppers "Playgirl" and "The Pad and How to Use It"—complete with cheesy organ and garage rock guitar leads. —*Rick Clark*

Knickerbockerism!: Hits, Rarities, Unissued Cuts & More... / Feb. 24, 1997 / Sundazed ✦✦✦
Though its modern-day connotation means something quite the opposite in terms of flattery, the Knickerbockers in their heyday were the ultimate bar band. With a stripped-down lineup of guitar, bass, drums, and tenor saxophone and all four members singing, their repertoire truly "covered the waterfront." Their harmonies were gorgeous, fuller, and sharper than your average self-contained bands, and their collective ear for mimicry was unparalleled. When they recorded a deadly accurate Beatle soundalike original, "Lies," for the tiny Challenge label, it started zooming up the charts, and the band seemed poised for multitalented stardom. Alas, it was not to be, but certainly not for lack of talent. This definitive 36-track, two-disc set documents—if not the best the group had to offer—at the very least, the best they were allowed to commit to magnetic tape, and spotlights their many strong points (impeccable harmonies, a solid-as-a-brick rhythm section, and a willingness to adapt to different types of material thrust upon them). We'll never really know what the Knickerbockers were ultimately capable of, but this collection shows that even when their rockin' locomotive was put on a single direction track, they still had much to contribute. A one-hit group, perhaps, but one with more talent than chart success, that much is obvious. —*Cub Koda*

Gladys Knight

b. May 28, 1944, Atlanta, GA
Soul, Dance-Pop, R&B, Motown
One of the great soul singers, Gladys Knight was a performer from her childhood years, forming the Pips with her brother Merald and a couple cousins. They made the Top Ten in 1961 with the heavily doo wop-influenced "Every Beat of My Heart," and recorded some fine, nowadays overlooked, pop-soul sides for the Fury and Maxx labels in the early and mid-'60s, sometimes under the direction of songwriter Van McCoy. A couple singles from this period, "Letter Full of Tears" and "Giving Up," made the Top 40, but Knight didn't hit her commercial stride until she moved to Motown in 1966. Steeped in the gospel tradition, like so many soul singers, Knight & the Pips developed into one of Motown's most dependable acts, although they never quite scaled the commercial or artistic heights of fellow stars on the label like the Supremes, Marvin Gaye, and the Temptations. With Norman Whitfield providing the production and much of the songwriting, the Pips fit into the mainstream of Motown's machine well, scoring big hits with some rabble-rousers (like "Friendship Train" and the original version of "I Heard It Through the Grapevine"), mainstream mid-tempo soul ("It Should Have Been Me" and "The End of Our Road"), and smooth ballads like "If I Were Your Woman."

In 1973, Knight had her biggest Motown hit with "Neither One of Us," which made No. 2; shortly afterwards, she and the Pips left Motown for Buddah. The group were briefly superstars in 1973-74, reeling off the smashes "Midnight Train to Georgia" (their only No. 1), "I've Got to Use My Imagination," and "Best Thing That Ever Happened to Me." This ranked as some of their best material, but Knight soon moved toward an easy listening, adult contemporary direction, one that she's maintained to this day. Now performing separately from the Pips (who have retired), her days as a high-charting star ended after the mid-'70s, although she remains fairly popular. —*Richie Unterberger*

● **Anthology** / 1974 / Motown ✦✦✦✦
Atlanta family-group Gladys Knight & the Pips had performed together for 14 years before signing with Motown in 1966. Earlier recordings for Huntom (the master recordings were later sold to Vee-Jay), Fury, and Maxx had generated five chart hits, including the Top Ten R&B smashes "Every Beat of My Heart" and "Letter Full of Tears," but it was on the Motown subsidiary Soul that Gladys Knight and company hit their stride. This compilation more than adequately covers this period of the Pips' career. Working primarily with producer Norman Whitfield from 1967 through 1969, the group created such Motor City classics as "Everybody Needs Love," "I Heard It Through the Grapevine," "The End of Our Road," and "Friendship Train." From 1970 through 1973, the Pips worked with a variety of Motown producers, concentrating on ballads. Although they were perhaps a little less consistent, there was no shortage of hits, the most notable being 1970's "If I Were Your Woman" and 1973's "Neither One of Us (Wants to Be the First to Say Goodbye)." The updated double-CD version of *Anthology,* featuring digitally remastered sound, replaces about a dozen songs with different ones, though this 40-track collection still contains all of the essential hits and adds lengthy liner notes. Be aware that the three early-'60s hits that lead off

the volume (on both versions of *Anthology*) are Motown re-recordings, not the originals. —*Rob Bowman*

Every Beat of My Heart / 1989 / Chameleon ✦✦✦
The best collection of Knight's pre-Motown sides, including both of their big early-'60s hits (the title track and "Letter Full of Tears"), but concentrating more heavily on their mid-'60s sessions. These were overseen by Van McCoy, who supplied the group with several of his own compositions as well. McCoy was one of the most melodically ambitious pop-soul composers of the era, and his songs on this compilation—"Either Way I Lose," "Why Don't You Love Me," "Lovers Always Forgive"—are achingly beautiful and rife with unexpected key changes. His "Stop and Get a Hold of Myself," on the other hand, is a more conventional (but equally first-rate) uptempo soul stomper. If there's any criticism of these sides, it's that Knight and the group don't establish a strong identity, handling doo wop-like ballads, girl-group-tinged pop, McCoy's idiosyncratic songs, and more modern pop-soul with chameleon-like skill. In the end, that doesn't detract from the strength of this CD, which is a collection of fine early to mid-'60s pop-soul. The major flaw is the inexplicable omission of the McCoy composition "Giving Up," a Top 40 hit for the group in 1964. —*Richie Unterberger*

● **Soul Survivors: The Best of Gladys Knight & the Pips 1973-1988** / Oct. 1990 / Rhino ✦✦✦✦
Soul Survivors—The Best of Gladys Knight & the Pips picks up where the Motown anthology left off, containing the most important singles that Gladys Knight And The Pips recorded for Buddah, Columbia, and MCA from the early '70s until the late '80s. The Buddah tracks, highlighted by the Jim Weatherly-written "Midnight Train to Georgia" and "Best Thing That Ever Happened to Me," contain some of Knight's most impassioned vocal performances. —*Rob Bowman*

Every Beat of My Heart [U.K. Reissue Compilation] / 1992 / Charly ✦✦✦✦
Twenty-track compilation of Knight's pre-Motown material, including most of the songs from the US anthology of the same name (on Chameleon). This has the slight edge, mostly due to the inclusion of the Top 40 single "Giving Up," and an odd version of Holland-Dozier-Holland's "Come See About Me" that is very different than the hit rendition by the Supremes. Unfortunately, the packaging is ugly, and the liner notes nonexistent. —*Richie Unterberger*

Blue Lights in the Basement / Apr. 1996 / RCA ✦✦✦
Knight's stint for the Buddah label in the mid-'70s found her commercial success at its peak, landing hits like "Midnight Train to Georgia," "Best Thing That Ever Happened to Me," "Part Time Love," and "The Way We Were" (all included here). But this 17-track survey of 1973-78 material is not nearly as artistically satisfying as her Motown and Vee Jay recordings, finding her and the Pips easing into a middle-of-the-road sound that helped pave the way for mellow urban contemporary music. What's more, this compilation is not truly representative of the era, omitting the huge hit "I've Got to Use My Imagination," presumably because it's too uptempo to find a place on an anthology geared toward the Quiet Storm audience. —*Richie Unterberger*

Buddy Knox (Wayne Knox)

b. Jul. 20, 1933, Happy, TX
Guitar, Vocals / Rock 'n' Roll, Rockabilly, Pop-Rock
The brand of Texas rockabilly that Buddy Knox cooked up around 1957 wasn't quite as raw as that of his Memphis cohorts at Sun, but it was just as commercially potent. Knox sported a light, almost gentle vocal style, and his band, the Rhythm Orchids, obliged with upbeat backing that suited him well. Formed at West Texas State University, the Rhythm Orchids also included Jimmy Bowen on upright bass, and it was Bowen's equally lighthearted vocal on "I'm Stickin' with You" that originally graced the flip side of Knox's first smash, "Party Doll." Roulette Records astutely picked up the master from the tiny Triple-D logo, separated the sides, and the fledgling label enjoyed two giant hits for the price of one.

"Party Doll" soared to the very top of the pops, and Knox encored with the equally tuneful "Rock Your Little Baby to Sleep" and "Hula Love," which he performed in the 1957 rock flick *Jamboree.* Knox waxed the fine rockabilly-based "Swingin' Daddy," "Devil Woman," and a cover of Ruth Brown's "Somebody Touched Me" for Roulette before moving to Liberty and hitting with a pop-flavored rendition of the Clovers' song "Lovey Dovey" in 1960. Over three decades later, the Texas rocker remains a popular act on the oldies front. —*Bill Dahl*

● **The Best of Buddy Knox** / Jun. 1990 / Rhino ✦✦✦✦
Rhino's *The Best of Buddy Knox* is a definitive, 18-track compilation featuring all of the hits the light rockabilly cat ever had, including "Party Doll," "Rock Your Little Baby to Sleep," "Hula Love," "Swingin' Daddy," "Somebody Touched Me," "Teasable, Pleasable," "That's Why I Cry," "I Think I'm Gonna Kill Myself," "Lovey Dovey" and "Ling-Ting-Tong." —*Stephen Thomas Erlewine*

The Complete Roulette Recordings / May 7, 1996 / Sequel ✦✦✦
Knox only has one-half of this double CD; the second disc is devoted to tracks by his friend and contemporary, Jimmy Bowen. The approach isn't as odd as it seems: When Knox and Bowen began their recording careers, they were both part of the Rhythm Orchids, and a similar lineup of Orchids backs each solo singer on their respective recordings. Most listeners will be much better off with Rhino's briefer, more selective Knox best-of. Completists, however, will find all 30 of Knox's 1956-60 Roulette tracks on disc one of this two-pack. Including five previously unreleased songs, it's pleasant Tex-Mex rockabilly, tamer than Buddy Holly, but far gutsier than the Jimmy Bowen solo cuts that take up all of disc two. —*Richie Unterberger*

Chris Knox

b. Sep. 2, 1952, Invercargill, New Zealand
Alternative Pop-Rock, Lo-Fi
Possibly the most important figure in New Zealand alternative/indie/post-punk rock, Chris Knox has been an integral figure of three of the country's more important rock bands (Tall Dwarfs, Toy Love, the Enemy), as well as recording prolifically as a solo artist. He sang with one of the country's very first punk acts, the Enemy, in the late '70s. The Enemy didn't record, but his next group, the more new wave-poppish Toy Love, had hit singles in New Zealand. However, they broke up in 1980 after an attempt to crack a more international market by moving to Australia proved fruitless.

By this time, Knox, notorious for Iggy Pop-style onstage self-laceration, wished to move from punk/new wave into more subtle, experimental underground rock. Sharing this desire was guitarist Alec Bathgate, who had played with Knox in the Enemy and Toy Love. Together they formed the duo Tall Dwarfs, lo-fi experimentalists with a penchant for both pop and psychedelia. Tall Dwarfs (whose activities are detailed in a separate entry) were instrumental in developing the quirky aesthetic picked up by most artists on the Flying Nun label, the top New Zealand indie that counted Tall Dwarfs as one of its first signees.

Although Knox has worked with Bathgate on Tall Dwarfs records since the early '80s, he has also maintained a less active, but ongoing, solo career in which he writes, performs, and records without Bathgate's assistance. Knox has had an ample opportunity to work alone given that he and Bathgate, because of their different living circumstances, are usually only able to record together for short, infrequent bursts of time. Undoubtedly, Knox's solo albums are more personal in nature than his group projects, yet in all honesty it can be difficult to find much difference between them and the Tall Dwarfs records. Working independently, Knox still staunchly adheres to a lo-fi, home recording ethic; he also favors songs that alternate between acoustic pop, post-psychedelia, and bursts of fuzzy garage noise, just as Tall Dwarfs do.

Consequently, Tall Dwarfs fans will undoubtedly find Knox's records worth checking out, though on the whole the best of Tall Dwarfs is a better place to start investigating Knox's music. Within each Knox solo record there is a great deal of diversity, although it must be cautioned that there isn't a notable difference in approach from recording to recording. This can make his extensive discography less rewarding than those of pop auteurs who take greater care to vary their palette from release to release, such as England's Martin Newell. —*Richie Unterberger*

Not Given Lightly/Guppiplus / 1989 / Flying Nun ✦✦✦
Side one of this 12-inch plays at 45 rpm and is devoted solely to a song from the *Seizure* album, "Not Given Lightly," which is one of his most accessible (not to say Lennonesque) songs. Fans will be more concerned with the ten songs on side two, which plays at 33 rpm. Eight of the tracks are taken from his 1983 solo debut, *Songs for Cleaning Guppies*. These are more primitive and subdued than much of his later work, but just as experimental, and in some intangible way feel more personal. The disc is filled out with a couple of cuts from obscure New Zealand compilations. —*Richie Unterberger*

Seizure / 1989 / Flying Nun ✦✦✦
There's really little to distinguish this from a Tall Dwarfs record of the same period. Knox may be writing and playing everything, but it's very close in tone and tune to what he makes with Alec Bathgate—eclectic, psychedelic noise with lo-fi production values. If you need to differentiate, this seems to be somewhat cruder and more noise-oriented than the Tall Dwarfs projects; song titles like "The Woman Inside of Me" and "Rapist" are indication enough that the subjects stray just as far from the hit parade. If you like Tall Dwarfs well enough to pick up their albums every time you see one, you will want this as well, but if your interest is more casual, you'd be better off sticking with one or two Tall Dwarfs records. —*Richie Unterberger*

Polyfoto, Duck Shaped Pain & "Gum" / 1993 / Communion ✦✦✦
Recorded on a Walkman between 1990 and 1992, although you wouldn't really know from the quite listenable clarity of the results; fidelity-wise, it's no worse than other Knox/Tall Dwarfs product, and

quite possibly better than some. More important is the content, a typically Knoxian journey through such varied topics as rape, Rodney King, distorted self-images, cosmetic surgery, and ruminations inspired by contemporary cultural theorists. The music is still pop-rock-experimentalism, sometimes approaching (as in "Trim Milk") his best melodies. It's not *so* outstanding, however, that the herky-jerky nature of the exploration can't start to get exhausting. With nearly 70 minutes, it may well have worked better in a somewhat edited fashion. —*Richie Unterberger*

Meat / Apr. 16, 1995 / Communion ✦✦✦

● **Songs of You & Me** / May 16, 1995 / Caroline ✦✦✦✦
Although this isn't a good deal different than his other work (both with the Tall Dwarfs and on his own), this may be Knox's best album, simply by virtue of the sheer amount of territory it covers over 21 songs. The fidelity is also somewhat better than most of his other releases, and although Knox has often championed the virtues of cheap home recording, this is a considerable virtue. A bit of clarity, without coming at the expense of slickness, simply makes the stuff easier to listen to. The disc is also the strongest evidence of Knox's talents as one of the more interesting lyricists working in indie rock, examining psychological conflict with a complexity that takes several listenings to grip. —*Richie Unterberger*

Cub Koda

b. Oct. 1, 1948, Detroit, MI
Guitar, Vocals / Rock 'n' Roll, Electric Chicago Blues, Blues-Rock, Rockabilly
Best known as the leader of Brownsville Station and composer of their hit, "Smokin' in the Boys Room," Cub Koda has proven that his roots went far deeper, both before the band's formation, during its days in the sun, and long after its demise. His high school band, the Del-Tinos, was dipping into blues and rockabilly as far back as 1963—not only pre-Butterfield, but pre-Beatles. Similarly, he recorded legendary home tapes during his off hours from Brownsville, before the rockabilly revival had uttered its first hiccup, and later teamed with Hound Dog Taylor's former rhythm section, the Houserockers, to play the blues in the '80s. Along the way he cranked out a monthly column ("The Vinyl Junkie") and recorded a series of albums that kept roots music of all kinds alive without ever treating it like a museum piece.

Originally a drummer at age five, Koda switched over to guitar when he formed his first band, the Del-Tinos, a teenage garage combo equally influenced by rock 'n' roll, blues, and rockabilly. The group cut their first single—Roy Orbison's "Go Go Go"—in the fall of 1963, and released two more 45s independently before they disbanded in 1966. By this time, Koda had become so immersed in the blues, that the last Del-Tinos' single had the trio doing Muddy Waters' "I Got My Mojo Workin' " on one side and Robert Johnson's "Ramblin' on My Mind" on the other.

After a couple of bands in the late '60s that largely went unrecorded, Koda formed Brownsville Station in early 1969. After playing local Midwest gigs and releasing a handful of singles, the band released their first album in 1970. But it wasn't until "Smokin' in the Boys Room" that Brownsville had a genuine hit. Released as a single in the fall of 1973, "Smokin' " climbed all the way to No. 3, eventually selling two million copies.

But Koda began to back away from the group's loud, overdriven rock sound—at least in private. He purchased a multitrack tape recorder and started producing one-man-band tapes, where he overdubbed all the instruments and vocals. For the next several years, Koda made home recordings of rockabilly, blues, R&B, country, jazz, and early rock 'n' roll—the exact opposite of Brownsville's heavy rock stance; the rockabilly tapes were eventually released as *That's What I Like about the South* in the early '80s, with other tracks showing up on compilations as late as 1993.

When Brownsville disbanded in 1979, Cub began writing a column, "The Vinyl Junkie" for *Goldmine* magazine, now being published in *DISCoveries*. Through the column's success, Koda established himself as an expert record collector and critic—eventually, Cub would compile and write liner notes for a number of projects, including three volumes in Rhino's acclaimed *Blues Masters* series.

In 1980, Koda worked with Hound Dog Taylor's backing band, the Houserockers. Over the next 15 years, Koda, guitarist Brewer Phillips, and drummer Ted Harvey performed and recorded together, with their first album, *It's the Blues*, appearing in 1981 and their latest, *The Joint Was Rockin',* being released in 1996.

Throughout the '80s and '90s, Koda has continued to divide his time equally between touring, recording, and writing. 1993 saw the twin release of *Smokin' in the Boy's Room: The Best of Brownsville Station* on Rhino and *Welcome to My Job*, a retrospective of his non-Brownsville material on Blue Wave, followed a year later by *Abba Dabba Dabba: A Bananza of Hits* on Schoolkids' Records. —*Stephen Thomas Erlewine*

Cub Koda & the Points / 1980 / Fan Club ✦✦✦✦
Koda's first solo album after Brownsville Station. Highlights include "Jail Bait" and "Welcome to My Job." —*Stephen Thomas Erlewine*

It's the Blues / 1981 / Fan Club ✦✦✦
The addition of bass and special guests Left Hand Frank and Lefty Dizz only distract from the chemistry beween Cub and the Houserockers (even more obvious on their belated live follow-up), but this is a strong session, with the ex-stadium boogie boy sounding totally at home with these blues veterans. His vocal duet with Brewer Phillips on J.B. Lenoir's "Talk to Your Daughter" is a joy, and thankfully not every note is perfectly in place—or in the case of Brewer's guitar, in tune. Added treats: Koda's big-toned harp on "Rockin' This Joint Tonight" and humorous dialog with Frank on "Dirty Duck Blues." —*Dan Forte*

Cub Digs Chuck / 1989 / Garageland ✦✦✦
Koda's tribute album to Chuck Berry, featuring blistering versions of "Johnny B. Goode," "Maybellene," and others. —*Stephen Thomas Erlewine*

● **Live at B.L.U.E.S. 1982** / 1991 / Wolf ✦✦✦✦
What's wrong with this picture? The sawed-off bespectacled singer/guitarist from Brownville Station fronting the late Hound Dog Taylor's ex-rhythm section, the Houserockers—blasphemy, you say? Get a life. Koda smokes like he's: 1) out to dispel any doubts about his legitimacy, and 2) having the time of his life. Opening with Howlin' Wolf's "Highway 49" (a rather tall order), the Cubmaster grabs the Chicago crowd by its collective neck and shakes it into submission. His guitar trade-offs with Brewer Phillips (no bass in this band) are a delight, and by "You Can't Sit Down" drummer Ted Harvey is blowing his police whistle—signalling that things be rockin'! Eddie Clearwater sits in on one tune, and Koda tips his hat to the guitarist with a stellar rendition of Eddie's "Hillbilly Blues." This is worthy of wider release, not to mention an encore. —*Dan Forte*

Cub Digs Bo / 1991 / Garageland ✦✦✦✦
Koda's tribute album to Bo Diddley, including powerhouse renditions of "Mumblin' Guitar," "Roadrunner," and "Background to a Music." —*Stephen Thomas Erlewine*

● **Welcome to My Job: The Cub Koda Collection 1963-93** / 1993 / Blue Wave ✦✦✦✦
Covering everything from his pre-Brownslide Station days to two brand-new songs, *Welcome to My Job* is the definitive collection of Cub Koda's versatile solo career. —*Stephen Thomas Erlewine*

Abba Dabba Dabba: A Bonanza of Hits / Jul. 19, 1994 / Schoolkids ✦✦✦✦
Cub Koda's first album for Schoolkids' Records is his wildest, funniest, and simply best album in years. —*Stephen Thomas Erlewine*

Joint Was Rockin' / 1996 / Deluxe ✦✦✦✦

Kool & the Gang

f. 1964, Jersey City, NJ
Soul, Funk, Urban, Pop-Rock
One of the leading funk outfits of the '70s and '80s, with gold and platinum platters galore. Formed by bassist Robert "Kool" Bell (b. 1950) as the Jazziacs in Jersey City, the Gang also featured his brothers Robert and Ronald Bell. The crew signed with De-Lite Records in 1969 and began churning out massively funky grooves, hitting full stride in 1973-1974 with "Jungle Boogie," "Hollywood Swinging," and "Higher Plane." The Gang topped the soul charts in 1979 with the high-stepping disco favorite "Ladies Night"—the same year they hired J.T. Taylor as their new lead singer. "Celebration," a staple of every respectable wedding reception of the last dozen years, went platinum for the group in 1980, and their nonstop string of incendiary successes stretched into the mid-'80s with "Fresh" and "Cherish." Taylor went solo in 1988, although the remaining members of the group continued performing throughout the next decade. —*Bill Dahl*

● **Everything Is Kool & the Gang: Greatest Hits** / Jul. 25, 1988 / Mercury ✦✦✦✦
Kool And The Gang's long run as a recreated pop act in the '80s formally ended with this release of this late-'80s anthology. It contained all the smooth pop winners sung by J.T. Taylor, who had already made his exit. It demonstrated how smooth, slick, yet also engaging a lead singer he'd been, and how the efforts of such producers as Deodato had successfully turned Kool and the Gang into superstars by erasing the funk beats, making the arrangements mellow and subdued, and also providing catchy, hook-filled songs like "Celebration" and "Ladies Night." —*Ron Wynn*

● **The Best of Kool & the Gang** / May 18, 1993 / Mercury ✦✦✦✦
Although Kool & the Gang became pop superstars in the 1980s on the strength of J.T. Taylor's silky voice and several catchy arrangements, R&B fans regard their true glory days as the 1970s. The New Jersey-based ensemble patented a jazz-tinged funk approach keyed by Robert

"Kool" Bell's bass lines, red-hot horn lines, chunky keyboards and guitar riffs, and functional vocals. Although they seldom ventured beyond the R&B charts during this era, their music had far more bite than their later pop hits. These 16 cuts pay homage to Kool & the Gang's funk roots, and should be a revelation to those who only know them as the light ensemble behind J.T. Taylor. —*Ron Wynn*

Funk Essentials Series: Celebration—Best of (1979-87) / 1994 / Mercury ✦✦✦✦

Kool Moe Dee

b. 1963, Harlem, NY
Vocals / Hip Hop, Old School Rap
A member of one of the original hip-hop crews, the Treacherous 3, Kool Moe Dee later became a solo star in his own right in 1986 by teaming with a teenaged Teddy Riley (later famed as the king of new jack swing) on the crossover hit "Go See the Doctor." The single earned him a contract with Jive Records, for which he recorded three successful late-'80s albums, dominated by his skillful speed-raps. A long-running feud with LL Cool J—who stole his aggressive stance and rapping style, he claims—gained Kool Moe Dee headlines for awhile, but he began to fade by the early '90s.

Born Mohandas Dewese in 1963, Dee was an early hit at local block parties, MCing with high-school buddies L.A. Sunshine, Special K, and DJ Easy Lee as the Treacherous 3. Introduced to longtime producer Bobby Robinson (Gladys Knight, the Orioles) by Spoonie Gee, the Treacherous 3 debuted on wax in 1980 with "The New Rap Language," released on Robinson's Enjoy Records. "Body Rock" and "Feel the Heartbeat" followed during 1980-81 before Robinson sold the group's contract to Sugarhill Records. The Treacherous 3 recorded several singles for Sugarhill, but broke up by the mid-'80s.

Instead of climbing aboard the solo wagon after the breakup, Kool Moe Dee enrolled in college. After earning a communications degree from SUNY, he enlisted an unknown producer for his solo debut, "Go See the Doctor." The 17-year-old Teddy Riley more than vindicated himself, though, and the single became an underground hit. By 1986, Kool Moe Dee was signed to Jive Records, and his self-titled debut album appeared that same year.

With 1987's *How Ya Like Me Now*, Dee struck back at the brash young generation who had forsook their forebears; the cover featured a red Kangol hat—the prominent trademark of LL Cool J—being crushed by the wheel of a Jeep. The album went platinum and was followed two years later by the gold-certified *Knowlege Is King*, for which Dee became the first rapper to perform at the Grammy Award ceremonies. Also in 1989, Dee worked on two important projects: the single "Self-Destruction," recorded in conjunction with KRS-One's Stop the Violence Movement; and Quincy Jones' all-star *Back on the Block* LP, which united hip-hop stars with their musical forebears.

Kool Moe Dee's fourth album, *Funke, Funke Wisdom* was a bit of a disappoinment when compared to his earlier successes, and Jive/RCA dropped him after releasing his *Greatest Hits* package in 1993. Hardly washed up, though, Dee recorded a Treacherous 3 reunion album in 1993 and signed to DJ Easy Lee's label for the 1994 album, *Interlude*. The title wasn't quite prophetic, however, it being his last album. —*John Bush*

I'm Kool Moe Dee / 1986 / Jive ✦✦✦
By the time he recorded this self-titled debut solo album, Kool Moe Dee was considered a veteran by hip-hop standards. The graduate of the Treacherous Three made no secret of the fact that he was among the founders of rap's old school—a term used to describe Kurtis Blow, Grandmaster Flash & the Furious Five,the Sugarhill Gang, Spoony G, and others who'd been rapping since the late '70s. This engaging album proved that Dee still had considerable technique, and could be a commanding storyteller. Lyrically, he is undeniably blunt, and this bluntness works to his advantage on such gems as "Little John," a reflection on an inner-city youth's life of crime; the anti-cocaine number "Monster Crack"; and the commentary on venereal disease "Go See the Doctor." Kool Moe Dee's infectious hit "Do You Know What Time It Is" was accused of being sexist, but such knee-jerk reactions to the song missed its point—the Harlem native was attacking materialistic women, not women in general. One of this album's producers is Teddy Riley, who went on to enjoy quite a bit of recognition a few years later as a member of the highly influential new jack swing outfit Guy. —*Alex Henderson*

How Ya Like Me Now / 1987 / Jive ✦✦✦✦
Kool Moe Dee resented the fact that in the mid-to-late-'80s, most of rap's founding fathers were enjoying little attention. But Dee himself was one of the few exceptions, and the old-school survivor had a major hit with his sophomore effort, *How Ya Like Me Now*. Dee would have done better to devote more time to storytelling and less time to boasting, but he definitely brings plenty of soul and spirit (as well as technique) to this material. Though not as strong as his first album, it definitely has its share of classics, including "Wild Wild West," a reflection on the nitty-

gritty environment that surrounded rap during its early years; his denunciation of materialism "No Respect"; and the infectious title song, which was clearly inspired by Dee's feud with L.L. Cool J. A few years later, much of the rap world was sick to death of hearing about the feud, but in 1987, it was a major topic of conversation in hip-hop. —*Alex Henderson*

The Best / 1987 / Jive ✦✦✦✦
The value of this compilation has been diminished by the release of a superior 1993 hits package. This contains several of Kool Moe Dee's big records from the early '80s, and is a blueprint for both his rise and the emergence of the Kool Moe Dee/LL Cool J rivalry. —*Ron Wynn*

★ **Greatest Hits** / 1989 / Sequel ✦✦✦✦✦
As much as any single performer, Kool Moe Dee epitomized rap's rise from an East Coast underground genre to a national youth sound, and has been unceasing in his demands for respect and recognition. Dee was also among the first able to bring social significance to his material without being pedantic, and his songs (with the exception of "They Need Money") weren't littered with sexist and misogynistic rhetoric. This 15-song collection covers his biggest recordings, from novelty-type fare ("The Wild Wild West" and "Whosgotdaflava") to the safe sex number "Go See the Doctor," cultural battle cries like "Rise 'N' Shine" and "No Respect," and his "war" with L.L. Cool J that peaked with "Death Blow" and "How Ya Like Me Now." —*Ron Wynn*

Knowledge Is King / May 1989 / Jive ✦✦✦
What was true of *How Ya Like Me Now* is certainly true of Kool Moe Dee's third solo album, *Knowledge Is King*—the hardcore rapper spends too much time boasting and doesn't devote enough time to his real strength: meaningful storytelling. Nonetheless, his soulful spirit and considerable technique make this effort worthwhile—not remarkable, but certainly engaging. The CD's strongest offerings include "Pump Your Fist," an angry denunciation of social injustice; "The Avenue," a description of a day in the hood; and the controversial attack on materialistic women "They Want Money." The latter was accused of being sexist, but Dee rightly countered that criticizing women who judge men by the size of their wallets rather than the size of their hearts or their brains isn't sexist—it's honest. —*Alex Henderson*

Funke, Funke Wisdom / Jun. 4, 1991 / Jive ✦✦✦
Kool Moe Dee's popularity had faded considerably by 1991, when Jive/RCA released *Funke Funke Wisdom*. This is hardly his finest hour. Featuring sociopolitical commentators Chuck D (Public Enemy's leader) and KRS-One, the inspiring "Rise N' Shine" is a gem. But most of the album falls short of that song's excellence, and Dee often sounds like he's coasting on his talent. This isn't a terrible album by any means, but Dee is capable of much more. Though it's hard to miss just how much technique he has, it doesn't serve as well this time. And his boasting lyrics sound very routine. Dee overdoes it with James Brown samples, which by 1991, had long since become a very tired cliché in hip-hop. —*Alex Henderson*

Interlude / Nov. 8, 1994 / Ichiban ✦✦

Jive Collection Series, Vol. 2 / Jun. 27, 1995 / Jive ✦✦✦✦
Kool Moe Dee's installment of the *Jive Collection Series* contains all of the rapper's groundbreaking singles from the early '80s, plus a selection of lesser-known album tracks and singles. The album isn't as consistently entertaining as his previous *Greatest Hits* compilation, but *Jive Collection Series* remains a good introduction to his pioneering career. —*Stephen Thomas Erlewine*

Kraftwerk

f. 1970, Dusseldorf, Germany
Electronic, Art-Rock/Progressive Rock, Kraut-Rock
In the mid-'70s, the German quartet Kraftwerk laid the groundwork for most of the electronic and synth-rock bands that followed them in the next two decades. Each of the members played synthesizers, creating a cold, precise, almost mechanical music that was hypnotic in its repetitiveness. For the rest of the '70s, the band was on the cutting edge of rock and dance music, influencing numerous musicians in the process. As the '80s progressed, the group's records became less and less innovative, but they still made a number of albums that were very impressive; the band continues to record in the '90s.
Echoes of Kraftwerk's music can be heard in everyone from David Bowie and Tangerine Dream to Depeche Mode and the Human League. Hip-hop is also unwittingly in debt to the band's innovative use of electronics. But the underground techno scene of the '80s and '90s owes a great debt to Kraftwerk, as artists like Aphex Twin, Orbital, Vapourspace, and the Orb bring the band's trance-like electronics to new heights, adding a warm, human dimension that Kraftwerk never had when they recorded *Autobahn* in 1974. —*Stephen Thomas Erlewine*

Kraftwerk 1 / 1971 / Philips ✦✦

Kraftwerk 2 / 1972 / Philips ✦✦✦
The synthesis of man and machine was forged in the "power station," aka Kraftwerk. Ralf Hutter and Florian Schneider took the *sturm und drang* of the industrial revolution and implanted it into a musical core that consisted of electronic soundscapes and metronomic rhythmic pulsations. The future sound of industrial music was fashioned on these two albums, in addition to the primal pulse that was later to become punk. —*Archie Patterson*

★ **Autobahn** / 1974 / Warner Brothers ✦✦✦✦✦
Although Kraftwerk's first three albums were groundbreaking in their own right, *Autobahn* is where the group's hypnotic electro-pulse genuinely came into its own. The main difference between *Autobahn* and its predecessors is how it develops an insistent, propulsive pulse, which makes the repeated rhythms and riffs of the shimmering electronic keyboards and trance-like guitars all the more hypnotizing. The 22-minute title track, in a severely edited form, became an international hit single and remains the peak of the band's achievements—it encapsulates the band and why they are important within one track—but the rest of the album provides soundscapes equally as intriguing. Within *Autobahn*, the roots of electro-funk, ambient, and synth-pop are all evident—it's a pioneering album, even if its electronic trances might not capture the attention of all listeners. —*Stephen Thomas Erlewine*

Trans-Europe Express / 1977 / Capitol ✦✦✦✦
Kraftwerk may not have enjoyed multi-platinum success in the US—in fact, many American pop, rock, and R&B fans have never even heard of the visionary, seminal West German group—but its influence was tremendously far-reaching. Having employed synthesizers and drum machines long before electronic instrumentation became so widespread, the innovators directly or indirectly influenced everyone from Whodini to Donna Summer to Berlin to Skinny Puppy. Melodically, harmonically, and rhythmically, Kraftwerk reached its creative peak with 1977's *Trans Europe Express*. The infectious title song, which rapper Afrika Bambaataa used as the basis for his 1982 hit "Planet Rock," enjoyed quite a bit of dance club exposure. Equally innovative are the eerie "The Hall of Mirrors," the amusing "Showroom Dummies" and the oddly charming "Europe Endless." The historic importance of this bold and risk-taking music cannot be overstated. —*Alex Henderson*

The Man Machine / 1978 / Capitol ✦✦✦✦
Like the equally synthesizer-oriented *Trans Europe Express*, *The Man Machine* begged the question: is this the future of music? The answer is yes and no. Yes, technology would define much of the music that was to come—especially in R&B, hip-hop, and dance music. But the use of real instruments remained a crucial part of rock and jazz. Technology, to be sure, has often been used in a knee-jerk fashion, but in Kraftwerk's hands, it was bold, risk-taking, and consistently creative. If one were to own only two Kraftwerk CDs, the logical choices would be *Trans Europe Express* and this impressive follow-up—which ranges from the strangely funky "The Robots" to the eerie "Metropolis" to "Neon Lights" (a number that, like "Europe Endless," is charming in its own strange way). Anyone who has ever enjoyed the use of synthesizers and drum machines owes it to himself/herself to hear *The Man Machine*. —*Alex Henderson*

The Mix / Jun. 11, 1991 / Elektra ✦✦✦
By the early '90s, it was quite apparent just how far-reaching Kraftwerk's influence had been. From techno to hip-hop to industrial music to house, numerous others were undeniably indebted to the group. Dance clubs had long been a key part of Kraftwerk's following, and the dance market was the obvious target of *The Mix*—a collection of highly enjoyable, often clever remixes. While novices would do better to start out with *Trans Europe Express* or *The Man Machine*, hardcore Kraftwerk followers shouldn't pass up these remixes of such classics as "Trans Europe Express," "The Robots," "Autobahn" and "Radioactivity." One could nitpick about the absence of "Neon Lights" and "Europe Endless," but the bottom line is that this CD was a welcome addition to the Kraftwerk catalogue. —*Alex Henderson*

The Capitol Years / Oct. 18, 1994 / Cleopatra ✦✦✦✦

Billy J. Kramer & the Dakotas

f. Aug. 19, 1943, Bootle, England
Vocals / British Invasion, Pop-Rock
One of the most popular Mersybeat singers, Billy J. Kramer (born Billy Ashton) was one of the most mild-mannered rockers of the entire British Invasion. He wasn't that noteworthy a singer, either, and more likely than not would have never been heard outside of northern England if he hadn't been fortunate enough to become a client of Beatles manager Brian Epstein. Even more crucially, he was gifted with several Lennon-McCartney songs in 1963 and 1964, several of which the Beatles never ended up recording. That gave him his entrance into the charts on both sides of the Atlantic, but Kramer couldn't sustain his success after the supply of Lennon-McCartney tunes dried up. Significant? No. Enjoy-

able? Yes. Even tossing aside the considerable value of hearing otherwise unavailable Lennon-McCartney compositions, his best singles were enjoyably wimpy, melodic pop-rock, offering a guilty pleasure comparable to taking a break from Faulkner and diving into some superhero comics.

It's been reported that George Martin was reluctant to produce Kramer because of the latter's vocal deficiencies, making sure to hide the cracks in his upper register with loud piano notes in Billy's cover of "Do You Want to Know a Secret." No matter—the song made it to No. 2 in the UK in mid-1963, followed by another Lennon-McCartney effort, "Bad to Me." "I'll Keep You Satisfied" and "From a Window" were other gifts from the Beatles camp that gave Kramer solid hits; one Beatle reject, "I'll Be On My Way," was even relegated to a B-side (the Beatles' own BBC version was finally released in 1994). All these tunes, it should be noted, represented Lennon-McCartney at their lightest and most facile, which to a large degree explains why they didn't record the numbers for their own releases, deeming them more suitable for Kramer's fairly bland approach.

Billy J. actually landed his biggest hit, the corny pop ballad "Little Children," without assistance from his benefactors; the single also broke him, briefly, as a star in the United States, where it and its flipside ("Bad to Me") both made the Top Ten. He appeared in the legendary 1964 *The T.A.M.I. Show* rockumentary film, and the Dakotas recorded some instrumental rock on their own, getting a Top Twenty British hit with the Ventures-ish "The Cruel Sea." Early British guitar hero Mick Green, formerly with Johnny Kidd & the Pirates, was even a Dakota briefly. But after 1965's cover of Bacharach-David's "Trains Boats and Planes," the hits ceased, as the Beatles and Epstein's attention was lost. Kramer continued recording throughout the '60s, even venturing into hard psychedelic-tinged rock briefly, without much success, and has toured often on the oldies circuit. —*Richie Unterberger*

● **Best of Billy J. Kramer** / Oct. 8, 1991 / EMI America ✦✦✦✦
A strong collection that presents all of his best—including a number of songs written by John Lennon and Paul McCartney—in excellent sound. —*Bruce Eder & Jeff Tamarkin*

Lenny Kravitz

b. May 26, 1964, New York, NY
Bass, Guitar, Drums, Vocals / Rock 'n' Roll, Pop-Rock
As a musician and a producer, Lenny Kravitz is unquestionably gifted. He can successfully recreate the sound and feeling of countless groups from the past; his music recalls everyone from Lennon, Hendrix, and Bowie to the Velvet Underground, Curtis Mayfield, and Prince. What Kravitz can't do is synthesize these influences into a distinctive style—every song on each of his albums sounds like it was recorded by a different artist. However, that's not entirely a bad thing, because Kravitz *can* reproduce the sound of his favorite artists exactly; "It Ain't Over 'Til It's Over" sounds like it was recorded in 1972, "Are You Gonna Go My Way" sounds like a forgotten track from 1968. His music might not be original, but it is quite enjoyable. Since his 1989 debut, *Let Love Rule*, Kravitz's songwriting and production skills have been consistently improving. His second album, *Mama Said*, gave him a No. 2 hit with "It Ain't Over 'Til It's Over." *Are You Gonna Go My Way*, Kravitz's third album, was released in 1993; it was a stronger album than anything he had released in the past and was his most commercially successful record yet. —*Stephen Thomas Erlewine*

Let Love Rule / Sep. 1989 / Virgin ✦✦✦✦
In many ways, Lenny Kravitz's *Let Love Rule* is a thoroughly impressive debut. Like Prince, he plays nearly every instrument on the record, yet makes it sound organic and alive. Musically, it's a startlingly accurate replication of late-'60s psychedelia, crossed with a Princely groove and a heavy John Lennon fixation. Kravitz has no desire to move forward, he only wants to recreate classic rock, and as a result, *Let Love Rule* is an enormous, guilty pleasure. His songcraft may be derivative, but it's catchy—the title track has a lean groove and a colorful chorus, "Sittin' on Top of the World" and "Does Anybody Out There Even Care" have strong hooks, and while the stately psychedelia of "I Build This Garden for Us" can sound like a parody, it is quite effective. Kravitz stumbles when he gets preachy (the awkward "Mr. Cab Driver") or flowery ("Flower Child"), but that doesn't diminish the pleasures of *Let Love Rule*. —*Stephen Thomas Erlewine*

Mama Said / Apr. 2, 1991 / Virgin ✦✦✦
Moving forward a couple years from the psychedelic fixations of his debut, *Mama Said* finds Lenny Kravitz in the early '70s, trying to graft Curtis Mayfield and Jimi Hendrix influences to his Prince and Lennon obsessions. This time around, he synthesizes his influences better; it's essentially a seamless record, with all of its classic rock homages so carefully produced that it sounds as if it could have been released in 1972. Kravitz's songcraft has gotten better as well, with the swirling Philly soul of "It Ain't Over Till It's Over" and the rampaging Sly Stone-meets-Hendrix "Always on the Run" standing out as instantly addictive

singles. Still, some of the joy that informed *Let Love Rule* has worn off, largely because it's more polished and studied than its predecessor. That, however, doesn't prevent *Mama Said* from being another thoroughly enjoyable guilty pleasure—its sweet soul and fuzzy hard rock are slyly seductive. Ironically for such an inviting record, *Mama Said* is Kravitz's divorce album, yet it never quite conveys any true pain or emotion, since he puts sound over substance. Essentially, the lyrics are afterthoughts, but with a record as immaculately produced and sonically pleasurable as *Mama Said*, it doesn't really matter that it's talking loud and saying nothing, because it sounds good while it's talking. —*Stephen Thomas Erlewine*

● **Are You Gonna Go My Way?** / Nov. 22, 1993 / Virgin ✦✦✦✦
The cover indicates that *Are You Gonna Go My Way?* is Lenny Kravitz's bid for rock stardom. Designed in the style of an early-'70s record, it features Kravitz in hippie clothing, apparently exposing himself to a photographer—in other words, he's a dangerously sexy counterculture rebel. That may have been true in 1970, but in 1993, he simply sounds like a weird sideshow exhibit, the man who lived past 1973. Of course, it's easy to make such potshots, but Kravitz opens himself up to such attacks. No other artist, especially a successful one, has been quite so devoted to the past and ignorant of the present. Since he has considerable talent for songcraft and production, Kravitz isn't nearly as bad as could be, and *Are You Gonna Go My Way* is just as enjoyable and more accomplished than its predecessors. This time around, Hendrix is his chief influence, as evidenced by the roaring title track, and he does expand that with his traditional Lennon, Curtis Mayfield, and Prince obsessions. Song for song, it's his most consistent album, although by the end of the record, his painstaking reproduction of classic rock sounds begins to appear a bit too studied, suggesting that Kravitz may have hit a creative wall. Nevertheless, that does nothing to diminish the enjoyment of this record. —*Stephen Thomas Erlewine*

Circus / Sep. 12, 1995 / Virgin ✦✦
After the fuzz-rock revivalism of *Are You Gonna Go My Way*, Lenny Kravitz seems to have settled into a comfortable groove, alternating between early-'70s album rock and early-'70s soul, with the occasional Prince flourish thrown in for good measure. *Circus* is the weakest of Kravitz's albums, simply because he didn't change his style in a distinctive manner, replicating the sound of *Are You Gonna Go My Way* instead. To compound his problems, Kravitz kicks off the record with "Rock N' Roll Is Dead," a workmanlike rewrite of "Are You Gonna Go My Way" that lacks hooks. However, after one more half-hearted rocker, *Circus* begins to open up, as Kravitz turns in a series of ballads and lightly psychedelic mid-tempo pop numbers, which prove to be his real strength. —*Stephen Thomas Erlewine*

Kula Shaker

f. 1995, England
Rock 'n' Roll, Alternative Pop-Rock, Brit-Pop, Neo-Psychedelia
By reviving the swirling, guitar-heavy sounds of late '60s psychedelia and infusing it with George Harrison's Indian mysticism and spirituality, Kula Shaker became one of the most popular British bands of the post Brit-pop era. More musically adept and experimental than Cast, Kula Shaker nevertheless worked the same vaguely spiritual lyrical territory, but musically they brought the overpowering rush of Oasis to psychedelia, a genre that the Mancunians had previously avoided. The band's classicalist approach to rock 'n' roll earned them both critical praise and derision, as they quickly rocketed to the top of the British charts.

Led by vocalist/guitarist Crispian Mills (b. January 18, 1973; the son of '60s actress Hayley Mills and film director Roy Boulting), Kula Shaker was initially a psychedelic quartet called the Kays, which formed in 1993. In addition to Mills, the Kays featured his teenaged friend Alonza Bevan. The two had previously played together in a band named Objects of Desire; during that time they also ran a psychedelic nightclub in the back of an ice rink. Following the dissolution of Objects of Desire, Mills made a spiritual pilgrimage to India, and upon returning he formed the Kays with bassist Bevan, drummer Paul Winterhart, and vocalist Saul Dimont. Within a year, Dimont had left and organistist Jay Darlington had joined the band; prior to joining the group, Darlington had played in several mod revival bands. After spending two years touring and recording, releasing two EPs on Gut Reaction Records, the group had not made any headway. According to Mills, the band changed their name and direction in the spring of 1995, when he had an epiphany that the group should be called Kula Shaker after a ninth-century emperor and pursue a more spiritual direction. For the next three months, they performed as Kula Shaker, and they quickly received a record contract with Columbia, who were eager to sign another band that had the multi-platinum, crossover appeal of Oasis.

"Grateful When You're Dead," Kula Shaker's debut single, was released in the spring of 1996 to moderate success, but it was the followup single, "Tattva," that established the band. Peaking at No. 4 on the charts, "Tattva" had a chorus that was adapted from an ancient Sanskrit text and a colorful organ and guitar riff, which essentially encapsulated the band's sound. The single also set the stage for the band's debut, *K*, which appeared in September of 1996. Upon its release, *K* entered the charts at No. 1, becoming the fastest-selling British debut album since Oasis' *Definitely Maybe*. The album received reviews that ranged from enthusiastic to derisive, but the band continued to gain momentum, which eventually translated to a strong word-of-mouth in America. Kula Shaker wasn't able to replicate their British success in America, but "Tattva" became a Top 10 modern rock hit in late 1996, and the group received uniformly positive reviews. — *Stephen Thomas Erlewine*

● **K** / Oct. 22, 1996 / Sony ✦✦✦
By the mid-'90s, most bands had abandoned the sounds and sensibilities of late '60s psychedelia, which is what makes Kula Shaker's debut album *K* such a weird, bracing listen. The band doesn't simply revive the swirling guitar and organ riffs of psychedelia, they embrace the mysticism and eastern spirtuality that informed the music. On both "Tattva" and "Govinda," lead singer Crispian Mills has adapted portions of Sanskrit text for the lyrics, chanting Indian mantras without a hint of embarrassment. Similarly, Kula Shaker is unashamed about their devotion to Hendrix, Traffic, and the Beatles, cutting their traditionalist tendencies with an onslaught of volume, overdriven guitars, and catchy melodies—though they have a song called "Grateful When You're Dead," all of their psychedelic sensibilities derive from British rock, not the more experimental American counterpart. Kula Shaker may play well—they have a powerful rush that makes you temporarily forget how traditionalist their music actually is—but they still have trouble coming up with hooks. About half the record ("Hey Dude," "Tattva," "Govinda," "Grateful When You're Dead") has strong melodies, while the rest just rides by on the band's instrumental skills. Consequently, much of *K* doesn't stick around once the record is finished, but the singles remain excellent blasts of colorful neo-psychedelia. — *Stephen Thomas Erlewine*

Kursaal Flyers

f. England
Rock 'n' Roll, New Wave, Power Pop, Pub Rock
The Kursaal Flyers bridged the gap between pub rock and power-pop, turning out a handful of fine albums and great singles in their brief two-year career. Comprised of Paul Shuttleworth (vocals), Graeme Douglas (guitar), Vic Collins (guitar, steel guitar, vocals), Riche Bull (bass, vocals), and Will Birch (drums), the band released their first album *Chocs Away* in 1975; it was followed soon afterward by *The Great Artiste*. Both records showed a grasp of country and roots-rock, as well as pure pop. They would begin to emphasize their pop elements with 1976's *Golden Mile*, released by CBS Records. The union with the major label helped the single "Little Does She Know" reach the British Top 20. Douglas left to join Eddie & the Hot Rods before the recording of their final album, *Five Live Kursaals* (1977); he was replaced by Barry Martin. The band broke up after the release of punk- and power-pop-injected *Five Live Kursaals*. Out of the members, only Will Birch and John Wicks stayed active—they formed the Records immediately after the Kursaal Flyers' disbandment. The Kursaal Flyers reunited in 1988, recording *A Former Tour de Force Is Forced to Tour,* which picks up right where they left off in 1977. — *Stephen Thomas Erlewine*

Chocs Away / 1975 / UK ✦✦

Great Artiste / 1975 / UK ✦✦✦

Golden Mile / 1976 / CBS ✦✦✦✦

Five Live Kursaals / 1977 / CBS ✦✦✦

● **In for a Spin: The Best of the Kursaal Flyers** / 1985 / Edsel ✦✦✦✦
In for a Spin: The Best of the Kursaal Flyers is a comprehensive overview of the band's brief and underappreciated career, comprised of highlights from their three albums, plus the terrific non-LP single "Television Generation" and five previously unreleased tracks. — *Stephen Thomas Erlewine*

A Former Tour De Force Is Forced to Tour / 1988 / Waterfront ✦✦✦

L

L7

f. 1985, Los Angeles, CA
Hard Rock, Alternative Pop-Rock, Heavy Metal, Grunge, Riot Grrrl
L7's heavy, punk-inflected, riff-oriented guitar grind—a mix of the Ramones, Motorhead, and Joan Jett—was what earned them a dedicated following of fans in the early '90s, not the fact that they were female. While the band is strongly feminist, they never let their rhetoric stand in the way of their roaring guitars. L7 always relies on the sheer sonic aggression of rock, not its lyrical power.

When the group was on Sub Pop early in the '90s, the band sounded punkier and more abrasive; signing to a major label didn't cause them to lose that aggression—they just had a better production, courtesy of Butch Vig (Nirvana, Smashing Pumpkins, Sonic Youth). Featuring "Pretend We're Dead," 1992's *Bricks Are Heavy* was a major alternative hit; their second major-label album, the coarse *Hungry for Stink*, was released right before L7 toured with 1994's Lollapalooza. The acclaimed *Beauty Process: Triple Platinum* followed in 1997. —*Stephen Thomas Erlewine*

L7 / 1990 / Epitaph ✦✦✦
L7's major-label debut brings Riot Grrl polemic into the mainstream. Despite the most superficial similarities, this clearly ain't the Runaways as nobody's pulling their strings. And somebody tell me if there hasn't been a better election-year battle cry than "Pretend We're Dead." —*Steve Aldrich*

Smell the Magic / Jul. 12, 1991 / Sub Pop ✦✦✦✦
A wonderfully abrasive set of thrashing guitars and growling vocals. —*Stephen Thomas Erlewine*

● **Bricks Are Heavy** / Apr. 14, 1992 / Slash ✦✦✦✦
While their major-label debut is hampered by Butch Vig's rather tame production, it does show that L7 has some strong pop sensibilities underneath their burning guitars, as "Pretend We're Dead" and "Everglade" prove. —*Stephen Thomas Erlewine*

Hungry for Stink / Jul. 12, 1994 / Slash/Reprise ✦✦
While L7 sounds tremendous on *Hungry for Stink*, the band has neglected to write any songs. But when you're caught in the middle of a massive guitar grind this good, songs don't matter much. —*Stephen Thomas Erlewine*

Beauty Process: Triple Platinum / Feb. 25, 1997 / Warner Brothers ✦✦✦
Jennifer Finch left L7 after the completion of *The Beauty Process: Triple Platinum*, which is appropriate—the album feels like the end of an era. L7 still have enough attitude to make them underground rockers, but they continue to move closer to heavy metal biker territory with each record. *The Beauty Process* has a bigger, harder kick than *Hungry for Stink*, and it also has its fair share of hooks—they just don't play them for pop effect as they did on *Bricks Are Heavy*. Which means that *The Beauty Process* will appeal to old-time fans and fans of Motorhead and AC/DC. In other words, it's a good hard-rock record, but it'll make some fans yearn for the days when L7 appeared revolutionary, not just keepers of the flame. —*Stephen Thomas Erlewine*

The La De Das

f. New Zealand
Garage Rock, Pop-Rock
Aside from, perhaps, Ray Columbus & the Invaders, the La De Das were New Zealand's most popular rock group of the 1960s. As big fish in a very small pond, their work doesn't hold up to scrutiny in the company of the era's top American and English acts. But they did record some fine garage/pop numbers in the spirit of the Rolling Stones in the mid-'60s. A few of these ("How Is the Air up There?," "All Purpose Low") were big N.Z. hits, and they reached the Top Ten with covers of John Mayall's "On Top of the World" and a lame version of Bruce Channel's "Hey Baby." In 1968, they recorded a psychedelic-tinged children's concept LP, *The Happy Prince;* while ahead of its time, it sounds unbearably twee today. After a failed attempt to crack the British market, the group soldiered on for quite some time with pedestrian hard rock that—like even the best of their early work—was very derivative of overseas trends. —*Richie Unterberger*

Rock 'n' Roll Decade 1964-'74 / 1981 / EMI Australia ✦✦✦
A hefty double-album compilation, including most of their mid-'60s singles, the entire *The Happy Prince* LP, and a mixture of live and studio hard-rock material from the late '60s and early '70s. Includes exhaustive liner notes from Australian rock authority Glenn A. Baker, and their rare, fine 1965 punk debut 45 "Little Girl," but the final three sides of this two-fer are pretty tedious going. —*Richie Unterberger*

● **La De Das/Find Us a Way** / CBS ✦✦✦✦
A double-LP reissue of their first two albums, covering their 1966-67 material, including nearly all of their best songs. Their debut (*La De Das*) is almost solely composed of R&B covers, with the exception of the hit "How Is the Air up There?" *Find Us a Way* is better, with more original compositions and a more mature soulful rock approach, including the snarling singles "Find Us a Way" and "All Purpose Low." —*Richie Unterberger*

The La's

f. 1986, Liverpool, England
Alternative Pop-Rock
When the La's released their debut album in 1990, it made immediate waves in the British pop scene, as well as American college radio. Drawing from the hook-laden, ringing guitars of mid-'60s British pop as well as the post-punk pop of the Smiths, the La's self-titled first album had a timeless, classic feel. It seemed like effortless music, yet that was not the case. From their inception in 1986 to the present day, lead singer/guitarist/songwriter Lee Mavers has been a perfectionist with a nearly obsessive eye for detail. Consequently, the La's were never able to totally fulfill their promise.

Mavers formed the group in Liverpool with bassist John Power, guitarist Paul Hemmings, and drummer John Timson. On the strength of their demo tapes, Go! Discs signed the band in 1987, releasing the single "Way Out"; it received good reviews, yet it wasn't a chart success. Similarly, the following year's "There She Goes" received good press yet stalled on the charts. With a new lineup featuring bassist James Joyce, guitarist Cammy (born Peter James Camell), and Lee's brother Neil on drums, the La's began recording their debut album that same year. The record didn't appear until 1990. Even though Myers claimed it was rush-released, the Steve Lillywhite-produced *The La's* received glowing reviews and strong sales; a re-released "There She Goes" entered the UK Top 20 and hit No. 49 in America. For most of 1991, the band was on tour. At the end of the year, they went back to the studio to record their follow-up. This time, Lee Mavers was in complete control and he took his time to perfect the album, re-recording tracks and rewriting songs. The La's disappeared without a trace from the pop music scene. Mavers and a reconstituted band resurfaced in the spring of 1995, playing a handful of supporting concerts that featured a couple of new songs; the band began recording their second album the following summer. —*Stephen Thomas Erlewine*

The La's / 1990 / London ✦✦✦✦
The La's were one of the few English alternative groups to keep traditional British guitar-pop alive during the late '80s and early '90s. Drawing heavily from the punchy British Invasion sound of early Beatles, the Hollies, the Searchers, and Small Faces, the group's eponymous debut is a swirling array of ringing guitar hooks and strong, undeniable pop melodies. Throughout the record, chief songwriter Lee Mavers turns out small, well-crafted gems, highlighted by the hit single "There She Goes," whose jangling hooks and sighing melodies simply scratch the surface of the abundance of pleasures on the record. While Mavers claimed at the time that the label forced him to release *The La's*, it's hard to imagine the record being any more infectious. As it stands, *The La's* was a refreshing slice of classicist guitar-pop at the time of its release, and its charms have not faded over the years. —*Stephen Thomas Erlewine*

Labelle

f. 1970, Philadelphia, PA, db. 1977
Soul, Funk, Disco, R&B
A girl group from Philadelphia, they formed in 1962. Initially known as the Blue Belles, and then Patti LaBelle and the Bluebelles, the group's personnel consisted of Patti LaBelle, Cindy Birdsong, Sarah Dash, and Nona Hendryx. The quartet scored six R&B hits from 1962 through 1967 before Birdsong departed to join Diana Ross and the Supremes. Continuing as a trio, for the next seven years the group languished in obscurity. British manager Vicki Wickham remade their image in the early '70s and shortened the name to Labelle. Decked out in ersatz futuristic garb, the threesome appeared as whirling dervishes delivering an explosive gospel-funk hybrid. Between late 1974 and late 1976, Labelle enjoyed five R&B hits, the first, "Lady Marmalade," reaching the No. 1 spot on the R&B and pop charts. Labelle split up in early 1977. —*Rob Bowman*

Nightbirds / 1974 / Epic ✦✦✦✦
The finest of the three Labelle albums, *Nightbirds* was recorded in New Orleans with funkmeister Allen Toussaint handling the production chores and, one assumes, members of the Meters taking care of the session work. Worth the price of admission for the Bob Crewe-written "Lady Marmalade" alone, the album veers between the strutting New Orleans, horn-laden singles and more mainstream pop material. —*Rob Bowman*

Lady Marmalade: The Best of Patti and Labelle / Feb. 28, 1995 / Epic/Legacy ✦✦✦✦
Lady Marmalade: The Best of Labelle features eight of the group's best tracks—including their two hits, "Lady Marmalade" and "What Can I Do for You?"—as well as eight of Patti LaBelle's R&B hits from the late '70s, which were among the funkiest tracks she ever recorded. —*Stephen Thomas Erlewine*

● **Something Silver** / Feb. 11, 1997 / Warner Brothers ✦✦✦✦
Most of the past LaBelle CD-era compilations have been poorly assembled, but this one is an exception. Whereas those other sets usually consist of a measly ten songs and some of their weaker commercial ventures, this set features their only major mainstream commercial hit, "Lady Marmalade," and 14 underappreciated, stellar songs. Most of these songs were culled from the trio's two acclaimed Warner Brothers albums and a single RCA set in the 1971-73 period. Some of the selections demonstrate Nona Hendryx's flare for poignantly creative lyrics and intricate melodies on such confessionals as "Can I Speak To You Before You Go To Hollywood?" and "Sunday's News." However, the set also features their rock-funk-edged high-voltage covers of Aretha Franklin's "Runnin' Out of Fools," Cat Stevens' "Moon Shadow" and the Rolling Stones' "Wild Horses," among others. This set more than any other honestly reveals what we lost when the group disbanded in 1976. —*Bill Carpenter*

You Are My Friend: Ballads / Feb. 11, 1997 / Sony ✦✦✦
You Are My Friend: Ballads collects 13 ballads Patti LaBelle and Labelle recorded during the '70s, including "You Turn Me On," "Find the Love," "Quiet Time," "Isn't It A Shame," and "Come What May." Although the albums sounds as if it is a greatest hits compilation, very few of these songs were hits, yet that doesn't detract from the disc's worth. It's designed for Patti LaBelle fans who want to dig a little deeper into her catalog without purchasing the actual albums, and they'll find several songs to cherish, even though the song selection is slightly uneven. —*Leo Stanley*

Patti LaBelle (Patricia Holt)

b. May 24, 1944, Philadelphia, PA
Vocals / Soul, Dance-Pop, Urban, Quiet Storm
Born Patricia Holt in Philadelphia, Patti LaBelle has enjoyed a 30-year-plus career, having sung early-'60s girl group material, soul, funk, and '80s ballad and dance music. From 1962-1976 she was a

founding member of both Patti LaBelle & the Blue Belles and Labelle. She began her solo career in 1977. Over the ensuing six years, she scored a number of lower-rung R&B hits with Epic, coming into her own on Gamble and Huff's Philadelphia International label in 1984 with the No. 1 R&B hit, "If Only You Knew." She has been a consistent chartmaker ever since, renowned for a gospel-trained voice with stunning power and range, capable of exhilarating aural gymnastics. One of the most gifted, idiosyncratic voices in R&B. —*Rob Bowman*

Patti LaBelle / 1977 / Epic ✦✦✦
Patti LaBelle's solo debut for Epic closed the book on a 15-year collaboration with Nona Hendryx and Sarah Dash. She mixed light pop and soul covers on this outing, turning in earnestly sung renditions of "You Are My Friend" and the Skyliners' "Since I Don't Have You," but also doing curious material like "Dan Swift Me" and "You Can't Judge a Book by the Cover." LaBelle was still finding her niche and hadn't yet become comfortable or established her now commonplace tendencies, such as the drawn-out lyric emphasis and the embellishments and lengthy holding of notes. —*Ron Wynn*

The Best of Patti LaBelle / 1986 / Epic ✦✦✦✦
This anthology includes the biggest pop hit that the trio Labelle scored, the classic "Lady Marmalade," plus other staples from Patti LaBelle's solo phase, including "You Are My Friend," "Joy to Have Your Love," and "I Don't Go Shopping." LaBelle didn't make her best or most successful records while on Epic, so these aren't the tunes associated with her. They were decently produced and often well performed, but lack the depth of her best MCA cuts. —*Ron Wynn*

Winner in You / 1986 / MCA ✦✦✦
Patti LaBelle enjoyed the biggest hit of her solo career when she switched labels from Philadelphia International to MCA. None of her albums had consistently clicked since she'd gone solo in 1977, but LaBelle's 1986 MCA debut topped the pop album charts, anchored by the huge hit "On My Own." The duet with Michael McDonald dominated both the pop and R&B scenes, staying atop the R&B charts for four weeks and giving LaBelle her first No. 1 pop single as a solo artist. She even earned a second Top 40 hit with "Oh, People," even though there was another fine single on the LP, "Kiss Away the Pain," that was ignored. Still, this album gave LaBelle the elusive solo stardom she'd sought since 1977. —*Ron Wynn*

The Best of the Bluebelles / Apr. 14, 1994 / Relic ✦✦✦✦
This anthology collects the early, often charming, and sometimes overly cute singles from Patti LaBelle and the Bluebelles. Besides the classic "I Sold My Heart to the Junkman" (which was really LaBelle backed by the Starlets), there are lesser-known numbers like "Down the Aisle (The Wedding Song)" and "I'm Still Waiting." Overall, this is competent period-piece material, but it's clear that LaBelle and company preferred more aggressive and assertive material and were never quite comfortable with most of these songs. —*Ron Wynn*

Over the Rainbow: The Atlantic Years / Aug. 23, 1994 / Ichiban ✦✦✦✦
The Bluebelles' stint with Atlantic in the '60s was not a great commercial success, yielding only a couple of minor R&B hits ("I'm Still Waiting" and "Take Me for a Little While," both included here), but that wasn't due to any shortcomings on the records themselves, either in performance or material. Patti and the group recorded fine sides in pop-soul, Motown, Aretha Franklin, and early Philly soul styles, making full use of their powerful gospel-derived lead vocals and harmonies. This 22-track anthology features most of the singles (many previously non-LP) and some key album tracks that they recorded for Atlantic between 1965 and 1969, using top-notch writers like Carole Bayer, Pam Sawyer, Lori Burton, Bert Berns, Jeff Barry, Bacharach-David, Lorraine Ellison, Spooner Oldham, Dan Penn, and Curtis Mayfield (who produced some of the later sides), as well as the Bluebelles' own Nona Hendryx and Sarah Dash. Highlights include the original version of "Groovy Kind of Love" (a big hit for the Mindbenders), the Supremes-like "Tender Words," the dramatic "All or Nothing," and the moody Oldham-Penn ballad "Dreamer." —*Richie Unterberger*

● **Greatest Hits** / 1996 / MCA ✦✦✦✦
The first Patti LaBelle compilation to span her work from the '60s to the '90s. It's weighted toward her pop-R&B material from the '80s and '90s, with hits like "New Attitude," "On My Own," and "Feels Like Another One." It leads off with the version of "Over the Rainbow" that she recorded with the Bluebelles in the '60s, and also has four Labelle cuts, including the chart-topping "Lady Marmalade." —*Richie Unterberger*

Laika

f. 1993, England
Dream-Pop, Indie-Rock
Like their namesake—the dog rocketed into orbit by the Soviets

renowned as the first living creature to exit the earth's atmosphere—Laika travelled the spaceways, forging a distinct and wildly experimental fusion of hip-hop, jazz, electronica, dub, and Krautrock without earthly precedent. A kind of Too Pure label all-star team comprising former Moonshake vocalist/programmer Margaret Fiedler and bassist John Frenett, onetime PJ Harvey drummer Rob Ellis and noted producer Guy Fixsen, as well as ex-God percussionist Lou Ciccotelli and saxophonist/flautist Louise Elliott, Laika formed in London during the autumn of 1993; their debut EP *Antenna* appeared the following summer. *Silver Apples of the Moon*, the group's acclaimed full-length debut, followed in late 1994; after a hiatus and the departure of Frenett, Laika resurfaced with *Sounds of the Satellites* in early 1997. —*Jason Ankeny*

● **Silver Apples of the Moon** / 1995 / Too Pure ◆◆◆◆
A visionary debut, *Silver Apples of the Moon* channels the full scope of modern music: hip-hop, dub, jungle, acid-jazz, electronica—you name it, it's here. Contradictions and ironies fuel the record: a featherlight surface sheen masks a dark, complex rhythmic undertow, while Margaret Fiedler's gentle, whispery vocals act as camouflage for the perversity and malice at the heart of highlights like "Marimba Song," "44 Robbers," and "Honey in Heat." —*Jason Ankeny*

Sounds of the Satellites / Feb. 24, 1997 / Too Pure ◆◆◆◆

Lamb

f. 1994, Manchester, England
Techno, Jungle/Drum 'N' Bass, Electronica
Mancunian down-tempo/drum'n'bass duo Lamb were one of the first groups to add a lyrics-based vocalist to steadfastly jungle-based productions. Unlike other vocal-based groups (such as Everything But The Girl and the Sneaker Pimps) who've dabbled in rolling breaks as a quiet accompaniment to a clearly dominant vocal lead, Lamb dwell in brash musical contrasts and, occasionally, contradictions that make their songs as musically complex and exploratory as they are vocally catchy. Formed in 1994 by producer Andrew Barlow and vocalist Louise Rhodes (the former an in-house engineer for So What management, the latter a daughter of folk-singer parents and a budding songstress), Lamb nailed a contract with Mercury subsidiary Fontana almost straight out of the gate.

The group's calling card, the "Cotton Wool" single, already showed field-leaders such as Gerald Simpson and Fila Brizillia were on their side (each contributed a remix). But if anything it was the untouched title track that illustrated Lamb's commitment to keeping the music interesting (the track rows along on a thick double-bass sample and absolutely brutalizing drum sequences) while filling it out with a big dose of tunefulness. An additional single ("Gold") followed, with Lamb's self-titled debut released in the Fall of '96 to widespread acclaim. Like the previous singles, much of *Lamb* explores song-oriented deployments of jungle, but the album also adds elements of downtempo and ambient-ish electro-jazz as well, making for one of the most diverse, stylistically mature debuts in recent memory. Most recently, Rhodes lent her vocals to Sheffield legends 808 State's *Don Solaris* LP (on the track "Azura"), and the success of Lamb's debut has also brought a fair amount of remix work their way. The pair have also added touring to their repertoire (*Lamb*'s release was followed by a European tour with labelmates Galliano), combining their electronics-heavy productions with live instrumentalists. —*Sean Cooper*

● **Lamb** / May 13, 1997 / Fontana ◆◆◆◆
Using the post-modern torch music of Portishead as a foundation, Lamb spins out into new sonic territories on its eponymous debut album. Lamb sports a heavier techno influence, incorporating the buzzing rhythms of drum n' bass into their music in particular, yet they cut their modernistic electronic influences with a dark sense of melodicism. Most of the album is devoted to jazzy songs that are broken apart by Andrew Barlow's synthesizers and sampler, and are anchored by Louise Rhodes' seductive vocals, which prevent the electronics from becoming cold. It's sophisticated urban music, miles away from the avant-garde sensibilities of Tricky and the haunted romanticism of Portishead, or even the pop leanings of Sneaker Pimps and the soul-inflected grooves of Morcheeba. Instead, Lamb is classy, detached, and cool—a more club-oriented and less melodic variation of Everything But the Girl's *Walking Wounded*. Although *Lamb* may run a little long, it's one of the more hypnotic byproducts of trip-hop yet released. —*Stephen Thomas Erlewine*

Lambchop

f. Nashville, TN
Indie Rock, Alternative Country-Rock
One of the hands-down weirdest groups to appear on the alternative scene in the mid-'90s (although they had been active for some years

before that), it's hard to tell whether Lambchop play alternative rock with a heavy Nashville country influence, straight country music with a heavy alternative rock influence, or whether the whole thing is just an ironic joke. The group are actually from Nashville, and number about ten members (although the lineup fluctuates). The chief of this zany crew, however, is singer-songwriter/guitarist Kurt Wagner, whose stream-of-consciousness laments are distinctly at odds with the (usually) comfortably normal-sounding country-pop arrangements.

Musically, Lambchop can (and often does) offer a reasonable facsimile of the MOR Nashville country devised by producers such as Billy Sherrill (who handled Charlie Rich's most popular work, and worked with Tammy Wynette and Tanya Tucker in the '70s). It is doubtful, however, that any release on the Merge label (also home to acts like Magnetic Fields and Superchunk) is aimed at the mainstream country music audience. Lambchop subverts the cliches of Nashville country with lyrics about suicide, bowling, and Theodore Dreiser-ish narratives about mundane everyday activities. There are also occasional interjections of post-punk guitar, thrash, clarinets, organ, and recorders that will not find a home in many trailer parks. Nor will Wagner's uneasy mumbling vocal style, which has more in common with Morrissey than Garth Brooks.

This is not the solace that most listeners turn to country-pop for as a respite from their day-to-day activities; it *is* their day-to-day activities, rendered too unflinchingly for comfort. Nor is it, despite considerable critical acclaim, the art statement some make it out to be, with plenty of what's-the-point lyrics and a nagging suspicion that the whole thing is a tongue-in-cheek art-school project that's gotten out of hand. Of their two albums, the debut is by far the more rock-influenced; 1995's *How I Quit Smoking* embraces mushy country production values much more wholeheartedly, without much alteration to the off-kilter, unsettling (and occasionally profane) tone of the lyrics. —*Richie Unterberger*

I Hope You're Sitting Down [aka Jack's Tulips] / Sep. 1994 / Merge ◆◆◆
A mix of post-modernism and straight (not roots) country music. The spooky organ fills, saxes, clarinets, and cello make this sound at times like the Art Ensemble of Chicago-as-country-band. Kurt Wagner's morose, resigned lyrics and dry, almost spoken delivery can get hard to take over the course of the hour-plus disc. "Soaker in the Pooper," a song about suicide in the bathroom, gave Wagner almost instant notoriety, and many of the other songs deal with similarly downbeat matters, although usually not as directly. —*Richie Unterberger*

● **How I Quit Smoking** / Jan. 30, 1996 / Merge ◆◆◆◆
Bona fide string arrangements give Lambchop's second album a much more "authentic" Nashville country feel than the first—meaning, ironically, that it sometimes sounds as gloppy, sentimental, and superficial as "real" Nashville country records. The arrangements are more inventive as well, mixing conventional country instruments like steel and acoustic guitars with saxes, clarinet, cornet, banjo, tin whistle, and more, along with the same kind of off-center organ featured on the first album. Wagner continues to mine the same offbeat lyrical territory, though unlike other audio verité talents like (say) Lou Reed, he doesn't bring much passion to his inner monologues. —*Richie Unterberger*

The Lambrettas

f. 1978, Brighton, England, **db.** 1981
New Wave, Power Pop, Pop-Rock, Mod-Revival
This Brighton-based band featuring Jez Bird (guitar/vocals), Doug Saunders (guitar), Mark Ellis (bass), and Paul Wincer (drums), jumped on the mod-revival bandwagon of the late '70s, dressing in matching mohair suits and naming themselves after one of the mod-favored motor scooters. Led by Bird's catchy songwriting, the Lambrettas proved to be more (if only slightly more) than just Jam soundalikes, leaving behind mod-life arrogance/elitism in favor of a pure pop sensibility. The band signed to Elton John's Rocket Records in 1979 and after one failed single, "Go Steady," had a UK hit with their cover of Leiber and Stoller's "Poison Ivy." The follow-up singles "D-a-a-ance" and "Another Day (Another Girl)" also charted in the UK. The latter (originally titled "Page Three"), with its not-so-thinly veiled jabs at *The Sun* newspaper's practice of placing photos of topless women on page three, earned them some notoriety when the newspaper threatened legal action. *Beat Boys in the Jet Age*, their debut LP, released in 1979, collected the early singles and other similar-sounding originals. Though it did make it into the British charts, the mod revival was fading fast. Subsequent singles and a second album, 1981's *Ambience*, were commercial flops despite efforts to break from the mod mold. The band called it quits in 1981 and faded quickly into obscurity. Bird regrouped the band in the '90s, playing

small venues in England, and recorded several demos for a new album yet to be released. —*Chris Woodstra*

Beat Boys in the Jet Age / 1980 / Rocket ✦✦✦✦
The band's debut picks up on all of the elements that made the early Jam albums brilliant—a certain reverence for '60s pop with a youthful, forward-looking attitude, punk's high-charged energy, and strong songwriting. *Beat Boys in the Jet Age* is an unfortunately forgotten album which features some of the era's best teen anthems and serves as a high point of the often disappointing mod-revival. The CD version adds three bonus tracks. —*Chris Woodstra*

Ambience / 1981 / Rocket ✦✦✦
As the mod-revival was running out of steam, the band took a step away from the sound for a more mature and varied album. No longer are their main concerns motor scooters, girls, and living for today, as evident in the haunting "Good Times" and "Decent Town." Though it failed commercially, *Ambience* is a fine collection of Britpop worth seeking out. —*Chris Woodstra*

● **Best of the Lambrettas: The Singles Collection** / 1995 / Dojo ✦✦✦✦
Like so many bands of the era, the Lambrettas are best represented by their singles; *Best of the Lambrettas* collects all of the A—and B-sides (as well as a newly recorded demo) in one place for the first time, providing the best introduction to the band. The songs are certainly of the time, but they've aged well, sounding as fresh as they did originally. —*Chris Woodstra*

Major Lance

b. Apr. 4, 1941, Chicago, IL, **d.** Sep. 3, 1994
Vocals / Soul
Blessed with a warm, sweet voice, Major Lance was one of the leading figures of Chicago soul during the '60s and the top-selling artist for OKeh Records during the decade. Lance not only had a lovely voice, but his material was excellent. During the height of his success, the majority of his songs were written by Curtis Mayfield and produced by Carl Davis, and the pair developed a smooth, Latin-flavored sound that was punctuated by brass and layered with vocal harmonies, usually from the Impressions. It was urban, uptown soul and while it was considerably less gritty than its Southern counterpart, its breezy rhythms and joyous melodies made songs like "The Monkey Time" and "Um, Um, Um, Um, Um, Um" some of the most popular good-time R&B of its era. Major Lance's career declined significantly after he parted ways with Mayfield and Davis in the late '60s, but his classic OKeh recordings remain some of the best-loved soul music of the decade.

Born in Winterville, MS, Major Lance moved to Chicago as a child, where he was initially raised on the west side of the city, before he moved near the north. While studying at Wells High School—where Curtis Mayfield and Jerry Butler also attended—Lance began boxing, but his attention soon turned to music and he formed the Floats with Otis Leavill. Although the Floats never released any records, his dancing earned him a spot on a local *American Bandstand*-styled program hosted by disc jockey Jim Lounsbury. The DJ helped Lance secure a one-shot single for Mercury Records in 1959, and the singer recorded "I Got a Girl," which was written and produced by Mayfield. The single disappeared and Lance spent the next three years working odd jobs.

In 1962, Lance was signed to the revived OKeh Records, based on his connections with Otis Leavill and, especially, Curtis Mayfield, who signed with the Impressions to ABC Records and was having hits with his own group. Later that year, Lance recorded his first single, "Delilah," for the label. Like most of the Major's material, the song was written by Mayfield who, along with OKeh president Carl Davis and arranger Johnny Pate, developed a distinctive, Latin-tinged sound for the record, filled with sliding trombones and a light-stepping rhythms in order to distinguish Chicago soul from its counterparts in the South, New York, Detroit, and California. Though "Delilah" wasn't a hit, Lance's second single, "The Monkey Time," was a monster. Released in the summer of 1963, "The Monkey Time" reached No. 2 on the R&B charts and No. 8 pop, establishing not only Lance as a singer but the revitalized OKeh Records as a pop music force. "Hey Little Girl" was a Top 15 pop and R&B hit later that year, followed by the Top Ten "Um, Um, Um, Um, Um, Um" early in 1964.

"The Monkey Time" and "Um, Um, Um, Um, Um, Um" proved to be the height of Lance's popularity. Over the next year and a half, he continued to turn out a series of Mayfield-written and Davis-produced singles, nearly all of which reached the R&B Top 40, but only a handful—"The Matador" (which Mayfield didn't write), "Rhythm," "Come See"—were pop hits. Following the summer 1965 release of the Top 20 R&B hit "Ain't It A Shame," Pate departed for ABC Records and Mayfield began concentrating on his group, but Lance and Davis continued to mine the same Chicago sound, using guitarist Gerald Sim as a songwriter and co-producer. After releasing a few

singles, including the R&B hit "Too Hot to Hold" and the Van McCoy-written "Everybody Loves a Good Time," Davis left OKeh Records due to arguments with his superiors at Epic Records and Lance was sent to work with Billy Sherrill in Nashville. Out of these sessions, "It's the Beat" became Lance's only Top 40 hit. Since the teaming with Sherrill wasn't working out, Lance worked with a number of producers during 1966 and 1967, with only "Without a Doubt" scraping the R&B charts in 1968. He left OKeh shortly after that single, moving to Daka Records the following year, where he had the Top 40 R&B hit "Follow the Leader." Within a year, he moved to Mayfield's Curtom label, which resulted in his last two Top 40 R&B hits—the No. 13 "Stay Away From Me (I Love You too Much)" and "Must Be Love Coming Down."

Lance left Curtom later in 1971 and he moved through a variety of labels, including Volt and Columbia, over the next several years without much success. In 1972, he relocated to England, where Northern Soul—a phenomenon of dance clubs playing rare, underappreciated and just plain obscure American soul and R&B records—was in full force. For the next two years, Lance was a staple on the Northern Soul circuit, eventually returning to Atlanta in 1974. He signed with Playboy and released a disco version of "Um, Um, Um, Um, Um, Um" that became a minor hit, which was followed by a pair of minor hits in 1975. Shortly afterward, his career entered a downward spiral, and in 1978 he hit rock bottom when he was convicted of selling cocaine. Lance spent the next four years in prison. Upon his release, he began playing the Beach Music circuit on the Carolina coast, but a 1987 heart attack prevented him from launching a full-scale comeback. In 1994, Lance gave a final, triumphant performance at the Chicago Blues Festival, which turned out to be his last. He died of heart failure on September 3, 1994 at the age of 55, leaving behind a recorded legacy that stands among the best midwestern soul of the '60s. —*Stephen Thomas Erlewine*

● **Everybody Loves a Good Time!: The Best of Major Lance** / Feb. 28, 1995 / Epic/Legacy ✦✦✦✦
Delightful 40-song, double-CD compilation of Lance's best work for OKeh between 1962 and 1967, including all of the chart singles, quite a few misses and B-sides, five previously unreleased cuts, and some Curtis Mayfield songs from his debut LP. The later tracks, recorded after producer Carl Davis and songwriter Mayfield had moved on to other projects, suffer in comparison with Lance's 1963-65 output, as he tried to keep abreast of contemporary soul trends, especially Motown. For many listeners, a briefer best-of Lance compilation will suffice. But for soul fans, this is prime stuff, dominated by the classic Latin-influenced Chicago soul sound of the Davis-produced tracks. —*Richie Unterberger*

Mark Lanegan

b. Nov. 25, 1964, Ellensburg, WA
Guitar, Vocals / Alternative Pop-Rock
Mark Lanegan's solo albums are sufficiently dissimilar in tone from those of the group he usually fronts, Screaming Trees, to make listeners wonder where his true interests lie. His two records to date employ a much more acoustic tone, and address much more serious, personal concerns. Quite a few critics and listeners find them more impressive than the Screaming Trees' efforts, although he apparently has no plans to quit the band for a solo career. When Lanegan was planning his first solo recording, the original plan was to do an EP of blues songs with Nirvana's Kurt Cobain and Chris Novoselic, as well as Screaming Trees drummer Mark Pickerel. That didn't work out, and the first album ended up being recorded with Pickerel, guitarist Mike Johnson (later bassist in Dinosaur Jr.), and noted producer Jack Endino on bass. Despite a good reception from the underground, it took over three years for the follow-up, *The Winding Sheet*, to surface, again featuring Johnson in a prominent role. —*Richie Unterberger*

The Winding Sheet / 1990 / Sub Pop ✦✦✦✦
A dark side of this Screaming Trees vocalist. —*Robert Gordon*

● **Whiskey for the Holy Ghost** / Jan. 18, 1994 / Sub Pop ✦✦✦✦
As a member of the Washington state alternative rock group Screaming Trees, Lanegan sings a somewhat lightweight and goofy blend of punk, hard rock, and psychedelia. On his own, he pursues an altogether more somber, acoustic, and bluesier vision. Like his debut release *The Winding Sheet*, Lanegan's second effort features his deep, husky-voiced musings, evocative mystic imagery, and brooding meditations on mortality. His dark but passionate vision is underscored by forceful acoustic guitars, harmonica, and occasional female backup harmonies. Sonically, Lanegan strongly resembles post-punk god Nick Cave, but his vision is ultimately more optimistic and accessible. —*Richie Unterberger*

Daniel Lanois

b. Sep. 19, 1951, Hull, Quebec, Canada
Guitar, Percussion, Vocals / Alternative Pop-Rock
Canadian Daniel Lanois has made a name for himself as a producer of very ambient albums. He has worked on successful projects with U2, Bob Dylan, the Neville Brothers, and Chris Whitley. Since his relocation to New Orleans, his thoughtful solo work reflects his fascination with the French Cajun rhythms. —*Rick Clark*

Acadie / Sep. 1989 / Opal ✦✦✦✦
Producer Lanois imbues this solo debut with his trademark otherworldly ambience on classics like "Still Water" and "Amazing Grace." Originals like the mystical "The Maker" and the soft French folk melodicism of "O Marie" are other highlights. —*Rick Clark*

● **For The Beauty of Wynona** / Mar. 23, 1993 / Warner Brothers ✦✦✦✦
This remarkable follow-up to his great debut shows Lanois growing as a singer and songwriter. His production is as weirdly magical as ever. "Brother L.A." and "Lotta Love to Give" are highlights among the many delights this album offers. —*Rick Clark*

The Last Poets

f. May 16, 1969, Harlem, NY
Poetry / Rap, Fusion
With their politically-charged raps, taut rhythms, and dedication to raising African-American consciousness, the Last Poets almost single-handedly laid the groundwork for the emergence of hip-hop. The group arose out of the prison experiences of Jalal Mansur Nuriddin, a US Army paratrooper who chose jail as an alternative to fighting in Vietnam; while incarcerated, he converted to Islam, learned to "spiel" (an early form of rapping), and befriended fellow inmates Omar Ben Hassan and Abiodun Oyewole.

Upon the trio's release from prison, they returned to the impoverished ghettos of Harlem, where they joined the East Wind poetry workshop and began performing their fusion of spiels and musical backing on neighborhood street corners. On May 16, 1969—Malcolm X's birthday—they officially formed the Last Poets, adopting the name from the work of South African Little Willie Copaseely, who declared the era to be the last age of poets before the complete takeover of guns. After a performance on a local television program, the group was signed by jazz producer Alan Douglas, who helmed their eye-opening eponymous debut LP in 1970. A collection condemning both white oppression ("White Man's Got a God Complex") and black stasis ("Niggas Are Scared of Revolution"), *The Last Poets* reached the US Top Ten album charts, but before the group could mount a tour, Oyewole was sentenced to 14 years in prison after being found guilty of robbery, and was replaced by percussionist Nilajah.

After the 1971 follow-up *This Is Madness* (which landed them on President Richard Nixon's counter-intelligence programming lists), Hassan joined a southern-based religious sect. Jalal recruited former jazz drummer Suliaman El Hadi for 1972's *Chastisement*, which incorporated jazz-funk structures to create a sound the group dubbed "jazzoetry." Following the 1973 Jalal solo concept album *Hustler's Convention* (recorded under the alias Lightnin' Rod), the Last Poets issued 1974's *At Last*, a foray into free-form jazz; after its release, Nilajah exited, and with the exception of 1977's *Delights of the Garden*, the group kept a conspicuously low profile for the remainder of the decade.

By the 1980s, however, the proliferation of rap—and the form's acknowledged debt to the Last Poets—made their early records sought-after collectors' items; finally, in 1984 the group resurfaced with the LP *Oh, My People*, followed in 1988 by *Freedom Express*. Another splinter ensued, during which time Omar Ben Hassan issued a solo LP, 1993's *Be Bop or Be Dead* and Jalal mentored the British acid jazz unit Galliano. In 1995, two splinter groups simultaneously reclaimed the Last Poets name; while Jalal and Suliaman El Hadi teamed for the single "Scatterrap," Hassan and Abiodun Oyewole issued the LP *Holy Terror*. —*Jason Ankeny*

Delights in the Garden / 1977 / Charly ✦✦✦✦
Reactionist/revolutionist/humanist poets on fire. Highly recommended. With drummer Bernard Purdie. —*Michael G. Nastos*

Oh My People / 1984 / Celluloid ✦✦✦
Updated sound, same powerful message. —*Michael G. Nastos*

Right On! / Dec. 28, 1990 / Collectables ✦✦✦✦
The foundation work for latter-day rappers—Afrocentric themes, improvisational vocal styles, obscenity, and a political slant. —*Ron Wynn*

This Is Madness / Nov. 13, 1992 / Celluloid ✦✦✦✦
A legendary set featuring a group of extremely controversial street poets. The Last Poets used offensive language brilliantly, talked in

graphic detail about America's social and racial failures, and helped expose a wider audience to the sentiments of the '70s black nationalists. They were the forerunners of today's Afrocentric rappers, and also showed the way to a jazz/rap union now being explored on both sides of the Atlantic. This has been reissued on CD. —*Ron Wynn*

Holy Terror / 1994 / P-Vine ✦✦✦
Best of the Prime Time Rhyme of the Last Poets / Jun. 1, 1995 / On The One ✦✦✦

● **The Legend: the Best of the Last Poets** / Mar. 19, 1996 / M.I.L. Multimedia ✦✦✦✦
The Legend: The Best of the Last Poets is a 35-track, two-disc overview of the group's career. The first covers "The Beginnings," while the second's focus is "The Real Rap Masters." —*Jason Ankeny*

The Time Has Come / Apr. 15, 1997 / Polygram ✦✦✦✦
Picking up where *Holy Terror* and Omar Ben Hassan's solo album *Be Bop or Be Dead* left off, *The Time Has Come* is a scalding blend of avant-jazz, bebop and hip-hop, highlighted by cameos from Chuck D and Pharoah Sanders. These two guests may be impressive, but they don't steal the show—they merely demonstrate that the Last Poets are too diverse and way too smart to be pigeonholed into one particular category. Occasionally, the record may be a bit unfocused, and its relentless barrage of avant-poetry may be headache-inducing to some, but few records are as politically powerful and articulate as this. —*Leo Stanley*

Latimore

b. Sep. 7, 1939, Charleston, TN
Keyboards, Vocals / Soul, Funk, Disco, Soul Blues, Urban
Deep-voiced Latimore's sultry mid-'70s output for Miami's Glades label was a steamy marriage of soul and blues. Initially billed as Benny Latimore, the Tennessean began recording for Miami mogul Henry Stone in 1965, and his late-'60s Dade singles are solid deep-soul. Dropping his first name on Glades, Latimore finally found stardom in 1973 with a jazzy reading of T-Bone Walker's "Stormy Monday." He topped the soul lists in 1974 with the anguished "Let's Straighten It Out," a simmering soul-blues hybrid, and encored with the incendiary "Keep the Home Fires Burnin'" the next year. Most of Latimore's Glades sides were produced in Miami by Steve "Every Day I Have to Cry" Alaimo, and when he wasn't cutting his own hits, Latimore acted as a house pianist for parent TK Records. Latimore moved to Malaco during the '80s, his appeal undiminished. —*Bill Dahl*

● **Straighten It Out: The Best of Latimore** / Sep. 19, 1995 / Rhino ✦✦✦✦
All of Latimore's greatest hits are included on this 17-track collection *Straighten It Out: The Best of Latimore*, making the album the best overview of the seductive '70s soul balladeer's career. —*Stephen Thomas Erlewine*

Latin Playboys

f. 1994, Los Angeles, CA
Experimental
David Hidalgo and Louie Perez of Los Lobos hooked up with Tchad Blake and producer Mitchell Froom for this side project, a twisted and avant-garde take on roots music. Latin Playboys draw from blues, border music, experimental studio trickery, and cinematic sound textures on their ambitious self-titled 1994 album. All of the material was composed by Hidalgo and Perez, and shows a considerably more experimental direction than their work with Los Lobos. —*Richie Unterberger*

Latin Playboys / Mar. 8, 1994 / Slash ✦✦✦
These are hardly "songs" in the conventional sense; more like eccentric sketches that create haunting moods. The players bounce back and forth between scratchy traditional Latin music, free-associating blues numbers, and spaced-out honky-tonk. Grounded in roots music, the lyrics and song structures are almost impressionistic in tone, creating an effect similar to listening to your car radio as stations drift in and out of reach while you drive along the Mexican border. —*Richie Unterberger*

Cyndi Lauper

b. Jun. 20, 1953, Queens, NY
Guitar, Vocals / New Wave, Pop-Rock
Cyndi Lauper was one of the biggest stars of the early MTV era, selling five million copies of her debut album, *She's So Unusual*, as well as scoring a string of four Top Ten hits from the record, including the major hits "Girls Just Want to Have Fun" and "Time After Time." Lauper's thin, girlish voice and gleefully rag-tag appearance became one of the most distinctive images of the early '80s, which helped lead

her not only to the top of the charts, but also to stardom. Throughout America, there were numbers of teenage girls dressing like Lauper and using "Girls Just Want to Have Fun" as an anthem, a call to arms for self-expression. At first, her music was a bright, colorful new wave fusion of a number of styles, including new wave, post-punk, reggae, pop, and funk. Both her music and her appearance helped popularize—and just as importantly, sanitize—the image of punk and new wave for America, making it an acceptable part of the pop land-scape. Lauper didn't follow through on the success of *She's So Unusual*, choosing to turn toward middle-of-the-road balladry and mainstream pop, but her first album remains a benchmark for the early '80s.

Born in Queens, NY and raised in the neighboring borough of Brooklyn, Cyndi Lauper (b. June 22, 1953) dropped out of high school in her late teens, choosing to sing in a number of local cover bands instead. Eventually, her voice was so strained she turned to voice les-sons from Katherine Agresta, a well-known vocal teacher in New York. In 1977, Lauper began writing her own material with keyboard-ist John Turi. The duo formed Blue Angel that same year. Over the next few years, the group built up a solid following in New York, cul-minating in the release of an eponymous debut album on Polydor in 1980. The Blue Angel record flopped and shortly afterward, Lauper filed for bankruptcy, which led to the disbanding of Blue Angel.

Following the breakup of the group, Lauper sang in local clubs and restaurants. In 1983, her manager and boyfriend David Wolff managed to secure her a contract with Portrait. At the end of the year, she released her debut album, *She's So Unusual*. Helped by heavy MTV support of the album's first single/video "Girls Just Want to Have Fun," *She's So Unusual* became a major hit in the spring of 1984, eventually climbing to No. 4 on the US charts; it would wind up going platinum five times, as well as becoming a hit in the UK and Europe. "Girls Just Want to Have Fun" peaked at No. 2, while its follow-up, the ballad "Time After Time," reached No. 1; two other songs, "She Bop" and "All Through the Night," went Top Ten.

With the success of *She's So Unusual* under her belt, Lauper was an official star, yet she wasn't able to maintain her popularity. Dur-ing 1985 she worked on her follow-up album; her only release of the year was "The Goonies 'R' Good Enough," the theme song from the children's adventure film, *The Goonies*. Her second album, *True Col-ors*, appeared in the fall of 1986, and while it was successful—the title track went to No. 1, while the album peaked at No. 4 and went platinum—its softer, adult-contemporary sound lost Lauper some fans.

Lauper's career continued to lose momentum, as her feature film debut in 1988's comedy *Vibes* bombed. *A Night to Remember*, her third album, was released to weak reviews in 1989 and although it spawned the Top Ten hit "I Drove All Night," it suffered from disap-pointing sales, peaking at No. 37. The next year, she severed her rela-tionship with Wolff and married actor David Thornton.

After taking a few years off, Lauper returned in 1993 with *Hat Full of Stars*, an album for which she co-produced and co-wrote all of the tracks. The record stiffed, peaking at 112. The following year, the hits compilation *12 Deadly Cyns and Then Some* was released in the UK; the album reached No. 2, while a remixed "Girls Just Want to Have Fun" became a No. 1 hit. *12 Deadly Cyns* was released in Amer-ica the following year to less attention. Lauper released *Sisters of Avalon*, her first album of new material in four years, in the spring of 1997 to generally positive reviews, yet the record didn't chart. —*Stephen Thomas Erlewine*

● **She's So Unusual** / 1984 / Portrait ✦✦✦✦
This quirky diva created a musical and MTV sensation with her pop-feminist "Girls Just Want to Have Fun" and her tender ballad "Time After Time." She won the 1984 Grammy for Best New Artist. —*Donna DiChario*

True Colors / 1986 / Portrait ✦✦✦
Included is the Top Five title track ballad and her Top 20 faithfully remade cover of Marvin Gaye's "What's Going On." Also included is the harder-edged "Change of Heart." —*Donna DiChario*

A Night to Remember / 1989 / Epic ✦✦
On *True Colors*, Cyndi Lauper began to edge her way into adult con-temporary territory, but it was on her third album, *A Night to Remember*, that she concentrated all of her attention on becoming a self-consciously "mature" singer-songwriter. *A Night to Remember* doesn't work, but not because she's incapable of performing pol-ished, well-crafted middle-of-the-road material—"Time after Time" and "True Colors" prove that she could convincingly deliver ballads. Instead, the album is a failure because it assumes that labored arrangements and precisely detailed production are tantamount to musical sophistication. Far from sounding sophisticated, *A Night to Remember* is bland and tedious, with only the seductive "I Drove All Night" making a lasting impression. —*Stephen Thomas Erlewine*

A Hat Full of Stars / 1992 / Epic ✦✦
A Night to Remember was a dull, unengaging affair, but Lauper's fol-low-up, *A Hat Full of Stars*, was even more repetitious and undistin-guished, lacking a hit single like "I Drove All Night" to break the syn-thesized, sterile MOR tedium. —*Stephen Thomas Erlewine*

12 Deadly Cyns / Jul. 18, 1995 / Epic ✦✦✦✦
Thankfully bypassing the Top Ten hit "The Goonies 'R' Good Enough," *12 Deadly Cyns* features almost all of Cyndi Lauper's Top 40 hits, tacking on a handful of new tracks at the end, including "Hey Now (Girls Still Wanna Have Fun)," an updated version of her breakthrough hit single, "Girls Just Wanna Have Fun." As hits collec-tions go, the album is fine, but with the exception of the ballad "True Colors" and the pop confection "Change of Heart," all of her finest songs and biggest hits were on *She's So Unusual*, which is a more consistent and entertaining album. —*Stephen Thomas Erlewine*

Sisters of Avalon / Apr. 1, 1997 / Sony ✦✦✦
Cyndi Lauper made a valiant effort to jump-start her career with the varied and eclectic *Sisters of Avalon*. Working with producer Mark Saunders, Lauper attempts to work world beat, adult alternative, and even trip-hop influences into her trademark adult-contemporary pop, and while the results aren't always successful, the record is the most intriguing and rewarding album she has made since *True Colors*. —*Stephen Thomas Erlewine*

Amanda Lear

b. England
Vocals / Disco, Euro-Dance
Amanda Lear first surfaced in the early '70s as a fetishistically-clothed album-cover model for Roxy Music. She was said to be a transsexual but, as she told *Interview* magazine, that was just a ruse dreamed up by her sponsor, David Bowie, to draw attention. Her importance to disco fans, however, began in 1977 when, in Germany, with production help from Tony Monn, she recorded *I Am a Photo-graph*, the first of six sleazy, hard-to-find albums in which she flaunts a voice so heavy with low notes you wonder if she really isn't a man after all. But no, Lear's slow notes are simply an exaggeration of the whisky-voiced sultriness created by Marlene Dietrich. Which isn't to say that Lear's lyrics—or the music's inverted proportions—don't exploit her mythology as a kinky concoction to the bursting point. —*Michael Freedberg*

I Am a Photograph / 1977 / Chrysalis ✦✦✦✦
Lear, previously known as a Roxy Music album cover model and a protégé of Salvador Dali, appears here as a cabaret countess. She enunciates sexually naughty suggestions in a smoke-and-velvet rasp. Her best subversions hit a dancer's most salacious fantasies dead on. Most of these songs support their studied lewdness with absurdly dif-ferent music, creating tangible friction (i.e. "Alligator"—funk bottom, frothy violins on top) that makes Lear's tape-loop voice feel even naughtier. All of Lear's tempos assault disco norms, either as sleaze or ultra-fast high-energy. An album not to be missed. —*Michael Freedberg*

Sweet Revenge / 1978 / Chrysalis ✦✦✦✦
Producer Anthony Monn parades every effect known to Euro-dream imagery in support of Lear as disco vamp: whispers from inside a tunnel, rhythms that filter in subliminally, themes that scale up to soprano range, choirs of angels singing, guitar rhythm rock-ons, and, of course, Lear's voice. Lear's singing is perhaps Monn's greatest effect: androgynous, sultry, out of reach and horny at the same time, Lear works hard to pretend at playing the merciless siren. She can't properly sing even one note, but what's that got to do with anything? —*Michael Freedberg*

● **Super 20** / Ariola ✦✦✦✦

The Leaves

f. 1965, San Fernando Valley, CA, **db.** 1967
Garage Rock, Folk-Rock
One of the first L.A. folk-rock groups to spring up in the wake of the Byrds in the mid-'60s, the Leaves are most remembered for record-ing the first—and one of the most successful—rock versions of "Hey Joe," which reached the Top 40 (and was a huge Californian hit) in 1966. None of their other releases approached this success (although "Too Many People" was a local hit), but the group recorded a fair number of strong covers and original songs during their brief exist-ence. More explicitly Stones and Beatles-influenced than the Byrds, they didn't project as strong an identity as competitors like the Byrds or Love, despite displaying considerable talent for harmony rockers in both the folk-rock and British Invasion styles. After cutting some singles and a decent album for the tiny Mira label, they moved to Capitol, and disbanded after a disappointing follow-up (*All the Good That's Happening*, 1967) that offered less distinguished material and

a more diluted sound. Leaves bassist Jim Pons went on to join the Turtles for a while in the late '60s. —*Richie Unterberger*

Hey Joe / 1966 / One Way ♦♦♦
Their spotty first album includes the hit title track, the strong beat ballad "Just a Memory," the Bo Diddley-esque folk-rocker "Dr. Stone," "Back on the Avenue" (a ripoff of the Stones' "2120 South Michigan Avenue"), and a pre-Monkees version of "Words." The CD reissue on One Way adds five bonus tracks. —*Richie Unterberger*

● **1966** / 1982 / Fan Club ♦♦♦♦
Somewhat hard to find these days, this well-chosen best-of compilation includes the best cuts from the *Hey Joe* album and a clutch of fine rare and unreleased tracks. Highlights among these are the raw, original 45 version of "Too Many People," the Beatlesque B-side "Funny Little World," a Byrds-like folk-rock cover of Dylan's "Love Minus Zero," and "Be with You," a superb rip-off of the Byrds' "All I Really Want to Do." Liner notes by Leaves member Jim Pons top off a fine package. —*Richie Unterberger*

Led Zeppelin

f. Jul. 1968, England, **db.** Dec. 1980
Electric British Blues, Blues-Rock, Hard Rock, Heavy Metal
Led Zeppelin was the definitive heavy metal band. It wasn't just their crushingly loud interpretation of the blues—it was how they incorporated mythology, mysticism, and a variety of other genres (most notably world music and British folk)—into their sound. Led Zeppelin had mystique. They rarely gave interviews, since the music press detested the band. Consequently, the only connection the audience had with the band was through the records and the concerts. More than any other band, Led Zeppelin established the concept of album-oriented rock, refusing to release popular songs from their albums as singles. In doing so, they established the dominant format for heavy metal, as well as the genre's actual sound.

Led Zeppelin formed out of the ashes of the Yardbirds. Jimmy Page had joined the band in its final days, playing a pivotal role on their final album, 1967's *Little Games*, which also featured string arrangements from John Paul Jones. During 1967, the Yardbirds were fairly inactive. While the Yardbirds decided their future, Page returned to session work in 1967. In the spring of 1968, he played on Jones' arrangement of Donovan's "Hurdy Gurdy Man." During the sessions, Jones requested to be part of any future project Page would develop. Page would have to assemble a band sooner than he had planned. In the summer of 1968, the Yardbirds' Keith Relf and James McCarty left the band, leaving Page and bassist Chris Dreja with the rights to the name, as well as the obligation of fulfilling an upcoming fall tour. Page set out to find a replacement vocalist and drummer. Initially, he wanted to enlist Procol Harum's singer Terry Reid and the band's drummer B.J. Wilson, but neither musician was able to join the group. Reid suggested that Page contact Robert Plant, who was singing with a band called Hobbstweedle.

After hearing him sing, Page asked Plant to join the band in August of 1968, the same month Chris Dreja dropped out of the new project. Following Dreja's departure, John Paul Jones joined the group as its bassist. Page recommended that Plant hire John Bonham, the drummer for Plant's old band, the Band of Joy. Bonham had to be persuaded to join the group, as he was being courted by other artists who offered the drummer considerably more money. By September, Bonham agreed to join the band.

Performing under the name the New Yardbirds, the band fulfilled the Yardbirds' previously booked engagements in late September 1968. The following month, they recorded their debut album in just under 30 hours. Also in October, the group switched their name to Led Zeppelin. The band secured a contract with Atlantic Records in the United States before the end of the year. Early in 1969, Led Zeppelin set out on their first American tour, which helped set the stage for the January release of their eponymous debut album. Two months after its release, *Led Zeppelin* had climbed into the US Top Ten. Throughout 1969, the band toured relentlessly, playing dates in America and England. While they were on the road, they recorded their second album, *Led Zeppelin II*, which was released in October of 1969. Like its predecessor, *Led Zeppelin II* was an immediate hit, topping the American charts two months after its release and spending seven weeks at No. 1. The album helped establish Led Zeppelin as an international concert attraction, and for the next year, the group continued to tour relentlessly.

Led Zeppelin's sound began to deepen with *Led Zeppelin III.* Released in October of 1970, the album featured an overt British folk influence. The group's infatuation with folk and mythology would reach fruition on the group's untitled fourth album, which was released in November of 1971. *Led Zeppelin IV* was the band's most musically diverse effort to date, featuring everything from the crunching rock of "Black Dog" to the folk of "The Battle of Evermore," as

well as "Stairway to Heaven," which found the bridge between two genres. "Stairway to Heaven" was an immediate radio hit, eventually becoming the most played song in the history of album-oriented radio; the song was never released as a single. Despite the fact that the album never reached No. 1 in America, *Led Zeppelin IV* was their biggest album ever, selling well over 16 million copies over the next two and a half decades.

Led Zeppelin did tour to support both *Led Zeppelin III* and *Led Zeppelin IV*, but they played fewer shows than they did on their previous tours. Instead, they concentrated on only playing larger venues. After completing their 1972 tour, the band retreated from the spotlight and recorded their fifth album. Released in the spring of 1973, *Houses of the Holy* continued the band's musical experimentation, featuring touches of funk and reggae among their trademark rock and folk. *Houses of the Holy* debuted at No. 1 in both America and Britain, setting the stage for a record-breaking American tour. Throughout their 1973 tour, Led Zeppelin broke box-office records—most of which were previously held by the Beatles—across America. The group's concert at Madison Square Garden in July was filmed for use in the feature film *The Song Remains the Same*, which was released three years later. After their 1973 tour, Led Zeppelin spent a quiet year during 1974, releasing no new material and performing no concerts. They did, however, establish their own record label, Swan Song, which released all of Led Zeppelin's subsequent albums, as well as records by Dave Edmunds, Bad Company, the Pretty Things, and several others. *Physical Graffiti*, a double album released in the spring of 1975, was the band's first release on Swan Song. The album was an immediate success, topping the charts in both America and England. Led Zeppelin planned to launch a large American tour in the late summer of 1975 when Robert Plant and his wife suffered a serious car crash while vacationing in Greece. Plans for the tour were cancelled and Plant spent the rest of the year recuperating from the accident.

Led Zeppelin returned to action in the spring of 1976 with *Presence*. Although the album debuted at No. 1 in both America and England, the reviews for the album were lukewarm, as was the reception to the live concert film *The Song Remains the Same*, which appeared in the fall of 1976. The band finally returned to tour America in the spring of 1977. A couple of months into the tour, Plant's six-year-old son Karac died of a stomach infection. Led Zeppelin immediately cancelled the tour and offered no word whether or not it would be rescheduled, causing widespread speculation about the band's future. For a while, it did appear that Led Zeppelin was finished. Robert Plant spent the latter half of 1977 and the better part of 1978 in seclusion. The group didn't begin work on a new album until late in the summer of 1978, when they began recording at ABBA's Polar studios in Sweden. A year later, the band played a short European tour, performing in Switzerland, Germany, Holland, Belgium, and Austria. In August of 1979, Led Zeppelin played two large concerts at Knebworth; the shows would be their last English performances.

In Through the Out Door, the band's much-delayed eighth studio album, was finally released in September of 1979. The album entered the charts at No. 1 in both America and England. In May of 1980, Led Zeppelin embarked on their final European tour. In September, Led Zeppelin began rehearsing at Jimmy Page's house in preparation for an American tour. On September 25, John Bonham was found dead in his bed—following an all-day drinking binge, he had passed out and choked on his own vomit. In December of 1980, Led Zeppelin announced they were disbanding, since they could not continue without Bonham.

Following the breakup, the remaining members all began solo careers. John Paul Jones never released a solo album. Instead, he returned to producing and arranging. After recording the soundtrack for *Death Wish II*, Jimmy Page compiled the Zeppelin outtakes collection, *Coda*, which was released at the end of 1982. That same year, Robert Plant began a solo career with the *Pictures at Eleven* album. In 1984, Plant and Page briefly reunited in the all-star oldies band the Honeydrippers. After recording one EP with the Honeydrippers, Plant returned to his solo career and Page formed the Firm with former Bad Company singer Paul Rogers. In 1985, Led Zeppelin reunited to play Live Aid, sparking a flurry of reunion rumors; the reunion never materialized. In 1988, the band re-formed to play Atlantic's 25th Anniversary Concert. During 1989, Page re-mastered the band's catalog for release on the 1990 box set, *Led Zeppelin*. The four-disc set became the biggest selling multi-disc box set of all time. In 1994, Jimmy Page and Robert Plant reunited to record a segment for *MTV Unplugged*, which was released as *Unledded* in the fall of 1994. Although the album went platinum, the sales were disappointing considering the anticipation of a Zeppelin reunion. The following year, Page and Plant embarked on a successful international tour. —*Stephen Thomas Erlewine*

☆ **Led Zeppelin [I]** / Jan. 12, 1969 / Swan Song ✦✦✦✦✦
Led Zeppelin had a full-formed, distinctive sound from the outset, as their eponymous debut illustrates. Taking the heavy, distorted electric blues of Jimi Hendrix, Jeff Beck, and Cream to an extreme, Zeppelin created a majestic, powerful guitar-rock constructed around simple, memorable riffs and lumbering rhythms. But the key to the group's attack was subtlety—it wasn't just an onslaught of guitar noise, but it was shaded and textured, filled with alternating dynamics and tempos. As *Led Zeppelin* proves, the group was capable of such multilayered music from the start. Although the extended psychedelic blues of "Dazed and Confused," "You Shook Me," and "I Can't Quit You Baby" often gather the most attention, the remainder of the album is a better indication of what would come later. "Babe I'm Gonna Leave You" shifts from folky verses to pummeling choruses, "Good Times Bad Times" and "How Many More Times" have groovy, bluesy shuffles," "Your Time Is Gonna Come" is an anthemic hard-rocker, "Black Mountain Side" is pure English folk, and "Communication Breakdown" is a frenzied rocker with a nearly punkish attack. Although the album isn't as varied as some of their later efforts, it nevertheless marked a significant turning point in the evolution of hard rock and heavy metal. —*Stephen Thomas Erlewine*

☆ **Led Zeppelin II** / Oct. 22, 1969 / Swan Song ✦✦✦✦✦
Recorded quickly during Led Zeppelin's first American tours, *Led Zeppelin II* provided the blueprint for all the heavy metal bands that followed it. Since the group could only enter the studio for brief amounts of time, the material that *II* comprises is almost entirely reworked blues and rock 'n' roll standards that the band were performing onstage at the time. Not only did the short amount of time result in a lack of original material, it made the sound more direct. Jimmy Page still provided layers of guitar overdubs, but the overall sound of the album is heavy and hard, brutal and direct. "Whole Lotta Love," "The Lemon Song," and "Bring It on Home" are all based on classic blues songs, only the riffs are simpler and louder, and each song has an extended section for instrumental solos. Out of the remaining six songs, two sport light acoustic touches ("Thank You," "Ramble On"), but the other four are straight-ahead heavy rock, following the formula of the revamped blues songs. While *Led Zeppelin II* doesn't have the eclecticism of their debut, it was arguably more influential. After all, nearly every one of the hundreds of Zeppelin imitators used this record, with its lack of dynamics and its pummeling riffs, as a blueprint. —*Stephen Thomas Erlewine*

☆ **Led Zeppelin III** / Oct. 5, 1970 / Swan Song ✦✦✦✦✦
On their first two albums, Led Zeppelin issued a relentless assault of heavy blues and rockabilly riffs, and *Led Zeppelin III* provided the band with the necessary room to grow musically. While there are still a handful of metallic rockers, *III* is built on a folky, acoustic foundation that gives the music extra depth. And even the rockers aren't as straightforward as before—the galloping "Immigrant Song" is powered by Plant's banshee wail, "Celebration Day" turns blues-rock inside out with a warped slide guitar riff, and "Out on the Tiles" lumbers along with a tricky, multi-part riff. Nevertheless, the heart of the album lies on the second side, when the band delves deeply into English folk. "Gallows Pole" updates a traditional tune with a menacing flair, and "Bron-Y-Aur Stomp" is an infectious acoustic romp, while "That's the Way" and "Tangerine" are shimmering songs with graceful country flourishes. The band hasn't left the blues behind, but the twisted bottleneck blues of "Hats Off to (Roy) Harper" actually outstrips the epic "Since I've Been Loving You," which is the only time Zeppelin sound a bit set in their ways. —*Stephen Thomas Erlewine*

★ **Led Zeppelin IV** / Nov. 8, 1971 / Swan Song ✦✦✦✦✦
Encompassing heavy metal, folk, pure rock 'n' roll, and blues, Led Zeppelin's untitled fourth album is a monolithic record, defining not only Led Zeppelin but the sound and style of '70s hard rock. Expanding the breakthroughs of *III*, Zeppelin fuses its majestic hard rock with a mystical, rural English folk that gives the record an epic scope. Even at its most basic—the muscular, traditionalist "Rock & Roll"—the album has a grand sense of drama, which is only deepened by Plant's burgeoning obsession with mythologies, religion, and the occult. Plant's mysticism comes to a head in the eerie folk ballad "The Ballad of Evermore," a mandolin-driven song with haunting vocals from Sandy Denny, and on the epic "Stairway to Heaven." Of all of Zeppelin's songs, "Stairway to Heaven" is the most famous, and not unjustly—building from a simple finger-picked acoustic guitar to a storming torrent of guitar riffs and solos, it encapsulates the entire album in one song. Which, of course, isn't discounting the rest of the album. "Going to California" is the group's best folk song, and the rockers are endlessly inventive, whether it's the complex, multi-layered "Black Dog," the pounding hippie satire "Misty Mountain Hop," or the funky riffs of "Four Sticks." But the closer, "When the Levee Breaks," is the one song truly equal to "Stairway," helping give *IV*

the feeling of an epic. An apocalyptic slice of urban blues, "When the Levee Breaks" is as forceful and frightening as Zeppelin ever got, and its seismic rhythms and layered dynamics illustrate why none of their imitators could ever equal them. —*Stephen Thomas Erlewine*

☆ **Houses of the Holy** / Mar. 28, 1973 / Swan Song ✦✦✦✦✦
Houses of the Holy follows the same basic pattern as *Led Zeppelin IV*, but the approach is looser and more relaxed. Jimmy Page's riffs rely on ringing, folky hooks as much as thundering blues-rock, giving the album a lighter, more open atmosphere. While the pseudo-reggae of "D'Yer Mak'er" and the affectionate James Brown send-up "The Crunge" suggest that the band was searching for material, they actually contribute to the musical diversity of the album. "The Rain Song" is one of their finest moments, featuring a soaring string arrangement and a gentle, aching melody. "The Ocean" is just as good, starting with a typically heavy, but funky, guitar groove before slamming into an a cappella section and ending with a swinging, doo wop-flavored raveup. With the exception of the rampaging opening number "The Song Remains the Same," the rest of *Houses of the Holy* is fairly straightforward, ranging from the foreboding "No Quarter" and the strutting hard rock of "Dancing Days" to the epic folk-metal fusion "Over the Hills and Far Away." Throughout the record, the band's playing is excellent, making the eclecticism of Page and Plant's songwriting sound coherent and natural. —*Stephen Thomas Erlewine*

☆ **Physical Graffiti** / Feb. 24, 1975 / Swan Song ✦✦✦✦✦
Led Zeppelin returned from a nearly two-year hiatus in 1975 with the double album *Physical Graffiti*, their most sprawling and ambitious work. Where *Led Zeppelin IV* and *Houses of the Holy* integrated the influences on each song, the majority of the songs on *Physical Graffiti* are individual stylistic workouts. The highlights are when Zeppelin incorporate influences together and stretch out into new stylistic territory, most notably on the tense, Eastern-influenced "Kashmir." "Trampled Underfoot," with John Paul Jones' galloping keyboard, is their best funk-metal workout, while "Houses of the Holy" is their best attempt at pop, and "Down By the Seaside" is the closest they've come to country. Even the heavier blues—the 11-minute "In My Time of Dying," the tightly-wound "Custard Pie," and the monstrous epic "The Rover"—are louder, and more extended and textured than their previous work. Also, all of the heavy songs are on the first record, leaving the rest of the album to explore more adventurous territory, whether it's acoustic tracks or grandiose but quiet epics like the affecting "Ten Years Gone." The second half of *Physical Graffiti* feels like the group is cleaning the vaults out, issuing every little scrap of music they set to tape in the past few years. That means that the album is filled with songs that aren't quite filler, but don't quite match the peaks of the album, either. Still, even these songs have their merits—"Sick Again" is the meanest, most decadent rocker they ever recorded, and while the folky acoustic rock 'n' roll of "Boogie with Stu" and "Black Country Woman" may be tossed off, they have a relaxed, offhand charm that Zeppelin never matched. It takes a while to sort out all of the music on the album, but *Physical Graffiti* captures the whole experience of Led Zeppelin at the top of their game better than any of their other albums. —*Stephen Thomas Erlewine*

The Song Remains the Same / 1976 / Swan Song ✦✦
Led Zeppelin's initial popularity was based as much on their concerts as their albums, so it's strange that the group's only official live album is such an uninspired, boring affair. Released in conjunction with the pseudo-documentary film of the same name, *The Song Remains the Same* reproduces the very things that made Zeppelin concerts legendary—lengthy solos, intertwining interplay between Page and Plant, and ridiculously long songs ("Dazed and Confused" is nearly an entire half hour)—but the group's performance is not intoxicating, it's long-winded. As scores of bootlegs prove, Led Zeppelin could produce magic with the same formula, but *The Song Remains the Same* is excruciatingly dull. —*Stephen Thomas Erlewine*

Presence / 1976 / Swan Song ✦✦✦
Presence scales back the size of *Physical Graffiti* to a single album, but it retains the grandiose scope of the double album. If anything, *Presence* has more majestic epics than its predecessor, opening with the surging ten-minute "Achilles Last Stand" and closing with the meandering, nearly ten-minute "Tea for One." In between, Zeppelin adds the lumbering blues workout "Nobody's Fault but Mine" and the terse, menacing "For Your Life," which is the best song on the album. These four tracks take up the bulk of the album, leaving three lighthearted throwaways to alleviate the foreboding atmosphere of the epics, as well as their pretensions. If all of the throwaways were as focused and funny as those on *Physical Graffiti* or *Houses of the Holy*, Zeppelin would have had another classic on their hands. However, the Crescent City love letter of "Royal Orleans" sags in the middle, and the ersatz rockabilly of "Candy Store Rock"

doesn't muster up the loose, funky swagger of "Hots on for Nowhere," which it *should* in order to work. The three throwaways are also scattered haphazardly throughout the album, making it seem more ponderous than it actually is, and the result is the weakest album they had yet recorded. —*Stephen Thomas Erlewine*

In Through the Out Door / 1979 / Swan Song ✦✦✦

Between *Presence* and *In Through the Out Door*, disco, punk, and new wave had overtaken rock 'n' roll, and Led Zeppelin chose to tentatively embrace the pop revolutions, adding synthesizers to the mix and emphasizing Bonham's inherent way with a groove. The album's opening number "In the Evening," with its stomping rhythms and heavy, staggered riffs, suggests that the band hasn't strayed from their course, but by the time the rolling shuffle of "South Bound Suarez" kicks into gear, it's apparent that the group have regained their sense of humor. After "South Bound Suarez," the group try a variety of styles, whether it's an overdriven homage to Bakersfield country called "Hot Dog," the layered, Latin-tinged percussion and pianos of "Fool in the Rain," or the slickly seductive ballad "All My Love." "Carouselambra," a lurching, self-consciously ambitious synth-driven number, and the slow blues "I'm Gonna Crawl" aren't quite as impressive as the rest of the album, but the record is a graceful way to close their career, even if it wasn't intended as the final chapter. —*Stephen Thomas Erlewine*

Coda / 1982 / Swan Song ✦✦✦

An odds-n-sods collection assembled after Bonham's death, *Coda* is predictably a hit-or-miss affair. The best material comes from later in their career, including the ringing folk stomp of "Poor Tom," the jacked-up '50s rock 'n' roll of "Ozone Baby," and their response to punk rock, the savage "Wearing and Tearing." The rest of the album, sadly including the Bonham showcase "Bonzo's Montreux," is average, despite the presence of some stellar playing, especially on the early blues-rock blitzkrieg "I Can't Quit You Baby" and "We're Gonna Groove." —*Stephen Thomas Erlewine*

Led Zeppelin [Box Set] / Sep. 1990 / Swan Song ✦✦✦

Led Zeppelin's primary method of artistic expression was their albums. Although they had a handful of hit singles, and selected album tracks were played endlessly on the radio, the true range of their music is only evident on the original albums, which were carefully sequenced and assembled. Consequently, the notion of a Led Zeppelin anthology is a bit strange—their records worked as individual pieces. Nevertheless, the four-disc box set *Led Zeppelin* includes most of their best and most famous material. Jimmy Page determined the set's running order, taking the songs out of their familiar contexts and placing them in a new, occasionally jarring, sequence, providing new insights into the band's music that dedicated fans will appreciate. *Led Zeppelin* is the only album in their catalog to include the classic B-side "Hey Hey What Can I Do," as well as their unreleased version of Robert Johnson's "Travelling Riverside Blues" and a live medley of Page's "White Summer/Black Mountain Side." Most fans will find these three tracks essential, but will balk at the price, especially since all of Zeppelin's albums have been re-mastered since the original release of the box set. While the box contains a wealth of brilliant music, all of it is better heard in its original incarnation. —*Stephen Thomas Erlewine*

Led Zeppelin Remasters / Feb. 21, 1992 / Swan Song ✦✦✦

A collection of most of Zeppelin's best-known tracks, this double-disc set gives only a slight idea of what the band accomplished in its career; stick with the original albums instead. —*Stephen Thomas Erlewine*

Boxed Set 2 / Mar. 19, 1993 / Swan Song ✦✦✦

Rounding up all of the studio tracks that didn't appear on the first box (as well as the pleasant, but unremarkable, "Baby Come on Home"), *Boxed Set 2* is the perfect way to complete a Led Zeppelin library begun with the first box set. —*Stephen Thomas Erlewine*

Complete Studio Recordings / Sep. 24, 1993 / Swan Song ✦✦✦

Collecting all of Led Zeppelin's groundbreaking studio albums (as well as a reworked *Coda*) in one unattractive box, *The Complete Studio Recordings* is only necessary for hardcore fans wishing to replace their old records. Although the artwork inside the package is lavish, the box features no new material or re-mastering, making it completely irrelevant for those who already own the first two box sets. The music here is brilliant, but it's available in better, more attractive, and less expensive packages. —*Stephen Thomas Erlewine*

Brenda Lee (Brenda Mae Tarpley)

b. Dec. 11, 1944, Lithonia, GA

Vocals / Rock 'n' Roll, Country-Pop, Pop, Nashville Sound/Countrypolitan

One of the biggest pop stars of the early '60s, Brenda Lee hasn't attracted as much critical respect as she deserves. She is sometimes inaccurately characterized as one of the few female teen idols. More crucially, the credit for achieving success with pop-country crossovers usually goes to Patsy Cline, although Lee's efforts in this era were arguably of equal importance. While she made few recordings of note after the mid-'60s, the best of her first decade is fine indeed, encompassing not just the pop ballads that were her biggest hits, but straight country and some surprisingly fierce rockabilly.

Lee was a child prodigy, appearing on national television by the age of ten, and making her first recordings for Decca the following year (1956). Her first few Decca singles, in fact, make a pretty fair bid for the best pre-teen rock 'n' roll performances this side of Michael Jackson. "BIGELOW 6-200," "Dyamite," and "Little Jonah" are all exceptionally powerful rockabilly performances, with robust vocals and white-hot backing from the cream of Nashville's session musicians (including Owen Bradley, Grady Martin, Hank Garland, and Floyd Cramer). Lee would not have her first big hits until 1960, when she tempered the rockabilly with teen idol pop on "Sweet Nothin's," which went to the Top Five.

The comparison between Lee and Cline is to be expected, given that both singers were produced by Owen Bradley in the early '60s. Naturally, many of the same session musicians and backup vocalists were employed. Brenda, however, had a bigger in with the pop audience, not just because she was still a teenager, but because her material was more pop than Cline's, and not as country. Between 1960 and 1962, she had a stunning series of huge hits—"I'm Sorry," "I Want to Be Wanted," "Emotions," "You Can Depend on Me," "Dum Dum," "Fool No. 1," "Break It to Me Gently," and "All Alone Am I" all made the Top Ten. Their crossover appeal is no mystery. While these were ballads, they were delivered with enough lovesick yearning to appeal to adolescents, and enough maturity for the adults. The first-class melodic songwriting and professional, orchestral production guaranteed that they would not be ghettoized in the country market.

Lee's last Top Ten pop hit was in 1963, with "Losing You." While she still had hits through the mid-'60s, these became smaller and less frequent with the rise of the British Invasion (although she remained very popular overseas). The best of her later hits, "Is It True?," was a surprisingly hard-rocking performance, recorded in 1964 in London with Jimmy Page on guitar. 1966's "Coming on Strong," however, would prove to be her last Top 20 entry.

In the early '70s, Lee reunited with Owen Bradley and, like so many early white rock 'n' roll stars, returned to country music. For a time she was fairly successful in this field, making the country Top Ten half a dozen times in 1973-74. Although she remained active as a recording and touring artist, for the last couple of decades she's been little more than a living legend, directing her intermittent artistic efforts to the country audience. —*Richie Unterberger*

Brenda Lee / 1960 / Decca ✦✦✦✦

Brenda Lee's nickname at 15 was "Miss Dynamite" and it's no lie. Some of her early hits are included—"Sweet Nothin's," "That's All You Gotta Do," plus "I'm Sorry," a great rocking reworking of "Weep No More My Lady," the bluesy "Be My Love Again," and "Just Let Me Dream." —*George Bedard*

Miss Dynamite / 1961 / Brunswick ✦✦✦✦

Brenda Sings Songs Everybody Knows / 1964 / Decca ✦✦✦

The Brenda Lee Story (Her Greatest Hits) / 1974 / MCA ✦✦✦✦

This 22-song, two-LP set included the bulk of her biggest hits, although it misses somes some significant singles (like "Is It True?"). The two-volume *Anthology* CD, with nearly twice as much material, is a much better investment. —*Richie Unterberger*

★ Anthology, Vols. 1 & 2 (1956-1980) / 1991 / MCA ✦✦✦✦✦

A 40-song, two-CD collection, this proves Lee was the best white female rock singer of the pre-Beatles '60s. By the time she turned 18, Lee had hit the pop Top Ten 11 times. All of those cuts are here, from the innocently salacious "Sweet Nothin's" to the string-laden "I'm Sorry" and her remake of Earl "Fatha" Hines's "You Can Depend on Me." Her best country singles, "Johnny One Time" and "Big Four Poster Bed," are also included. The compilers wisely passed over some minor hits in favor of obscure sides like the odd rockabilly "Let's Jump the Broomstick," a cover of Edith Piaf's "If You Love Me (Really Love Me)," and "Is It True?," a middling hit from 1964, which features guitarist Jimmy Page (who is 11 months older than Lee). *Anthology* thoroughly traces Lee's development as a vocalist, from early-childish exuberance to mature, graceful phrasing. —*Brian Mansfield*

Rock the Bop / 1995 / Radio Archives ✦✦✦✦

A 30-track CD of mysterious origin. The name of the label (Radio Archives) implies that these might be illicitly issued radio broadcasts, but in fact these are all legitimate early Decca recordings, presented in fine fidelity. For the most part, this is Brenda at her most rockabilly-influenced, spanning 1956 to 1960. There are a few early hits ("Sweet Nothin's," "Emotions," "I Want to Be Wanted"), but most of these cuts, which include supremely tough rockabilly like "Bigelow 6-2000" and "Little Jonah," didn't get much national exposure. It's a good survey of her earliest work, but not the most sensible option for the serious Lee fan, given its hefty price and the fact that the material is available on the far more thorough Bear Family box set. —*Richie Unterberger*

Little Miss Dynamite / 1997 / ✦✦✦✦

Those coming to her music with a passing interest would be well directed towards MCA's excellent two-CD *Anthology* set, covering all her hits and running a time frame from 1956 to 1980. But fans with deeper appreciation for her multi-genre artistry (and the deeper wallets such patronage will require) will want to make a beeline straight for this absolutely gorgeous deluxe four-disc box. Running her full discography from her earliest recordings in 1956 straight through into March of 1962, Bear Family puts 122 tracks. Arguably this is Brenda's peak period of creativity, with all the sides of her musical personality well-documented here. Kicking from her early country sides as an 11-year-old wonder ("Jambalaya" from her first session is jaw-droppingly amazing), we move into her rockabilly and rock 'n' roll period with classics like "Sweet Nothin's" and scorchers like "Bigelow 6-2000" straight into her ballad and pop material period from 1959 into the early '60s. Eschewing their standard album-sized booklet, this box goes the extra mile, featuring a bound, hardcover 85-page *book* on glossy stock, taking you through her early life and triumphs and every recording session she made during that six-year period, capped off with a full discography and a reprint of her 1957 souvenir album program. As Ms. Lee recorded during this period almost exclusively for Decca Records in Nashville (save for a stray New York session in January of 1957 that produced "One Step at a Time" and execrable "Fairyland"), the sound of the original mono and stereo masters from producer Owen Bradley's studio is crisp and full and the transfers here are exemplary. As a definitive hits roundup, it falls short by its self-imposed time frame, almost begging for a second volume covering the years 1962 to 1968 just to anthologize hits like "All Alone Am I," "As Usual," "Too Many Rivers," "Coming on Strong," and her lone British session which produced the hard-rocking "Is It True?" featuring Jimmy Page on guitar. But as a deluxe documentation of her ascension to becoming the most popular female vocalist during the time frame covered here, you couldn't really ask for much more, and certainly—based on sheer talent alone—few artists deserve it more. —*Cub Koda*

Laura Lee

b. Mar. 9, 1945, Detroit, MI
Vocals / Soul

A tough '60s soul singer with a salty sense of humor (aimed mostly at the men in her life), Laura Lee recorded at Rick Hall's FAME studio in Muscle Shoals for the Chess label, and later for Hot Wax. In songs like "Wanted: Lover, No Experience Necessary," "A Man with Some Backbone," and the anthemic "Women's Love Rights," the female experience was brazenly discussed, debated, kicked around, and, finally, celebrated. Her music laid the groundwork for artists like Millie Jackson and Denise LaSalle to expand this proud, sexy, brash-talking corner of "women's" soul music. Lee had a country-soul, romantic side as well, as shown on her splendid version of the Penn-Oldham classic "Uptight Good Man." Lee is a fine, versatile, saucy singer whose work deserves more attention. —*Christine Ohlman*

That's How It Is: Chess Years / 1990 / Chess ✦✦✦✦

Her '60s Chess recordings feature bone-chilling vocals. —*Richard Pack*

● **Greatest Hits** / Jul. 1, 1991 / Fantasy ✦✦✦✦

Like the music of Honey Cone, Freda Payne, 100 Proof (Aged in Soul), and the Chairmen of the Board, Laura Lee's *Greatest Hits* underscores the fact that the demise of Holland/Dozier/Holland's Hot Wax label in 1974 wasn't due to a lack of strong material. Essentially, distribution problems killed the company, where former gospel singer turned brassy soul shouter Lee recorded some of her best work. The big-voiced Lee was best known for humorous yet biting songs encouraging women to demand respectful treatment in relationships—a theme that makes for powerful listening on such classics as "Wedlock Is a Padlock," "Crumbs Off the Table," and her best-known hits "Rip Off" and "Women's Love Rights." Lee's Hot Wax output has all of the trademarks of a Holland/Dozier/Holland project—tough, gospel-influenced belting is combined with a sleek production style. In fact, Lee's heartfelt singing is no less gritty than Carla Thomas' work at Stax; the main difference lies in the approach to production. But as talented as she was, Lee faded into obscurity after Hot Wax's demise. —*Alex Henderson*

The Left Banke

f. 1966, New York City, NY, **db.** 1969
Pop-Rock

This New York group pioneered "Baroque 'n' Roll" in the '60s with their mix of pop-rock and grand, quasi-classical arrangements and melodies. Featuring teenage prodigy Michael Brown as keyboardist and chief songwriter, the group scored two quick hits with "Walk Away Renee" (No. 5) and "Pretty Ballerina" (No. 15). Chamber-like string arrangements, Steve Martin's soaring, near-falsetto lead vocals, and tight harmonies that borrowed from British Invasion bands like the Beatles and the Zombies were also key elements of the Left Banke sound. Though their two hits are their only well-remembered efforts, their debut album (*Walk Away Renee/Pretty Ballerina*) was a strong, near-classic work that matched the quality of their hit singles in songwriting and production.

The group's internal dynamic wasn't nearly as harmonious as their sound, and their history goes some way toward explaining their short career. Initially, the group made some recordings that were produced by Brown's father, Harry Lookofsky. When these recordings failed to interest companies in signing the band, the Left Banke broke up, Brown moving to California with the group's original drummer. A backing track for "Walk Away Renee" had already been completed, and the other members overdubbed vocals in Brown's absence. The song was released on Smash and became a hit, and the musicians reunited to tour and continue recording.

Unfortunately, the group, which showed such tremendous promise, was quickly torn asunder by dissension. Due to the nature of their music (which often employed session musicians), the Left Banke's sound was difficult to reproduce on the road, and one could sympathize with Brown's wishes to become a Brian Wilson-like figure, concentrating on writing and recording while the rest of the musicians took to the road. A variety of guitarists, as both session musicians and ostensible group members, flitted in and out of the lineup; Rick Brand, credited as the guitarist on the first LP, actually plays on only one of the album's songs. Adding fuel to the fire, Brown's bandmates wanted to oust Brown's father as the act's manager. In early 1967, Brown went so far as to record a Left Banke single without them, using vocalist Bert Sommer.

That single ("And Suddenly") flopped, and for a brief time in September 1967 the original members were recording together again. After just one single ("Desiree"), though, Brown left for good. Most of the group's second and final album, *The Left Banke Too*, was recorded without him. While it still sported baroque arrangements and contained some fine moments, Brown's presence was sorely missed, and the record pales in comparison to their debut. Brown went on to form a Left Banke-styled group, Montage, which released a fine and underappreciated album in the late '60s. He later teamed up to form Stories with vocalist Ian Lloyd.

There were some confusing son-of-Left Banke recordings over the next few years, although the band really came to a halt in 1969, after the second album. Brown, Martin, and unknown musicians made a few recordings in late 1969; then, oddly, the original group reformed for a fine early '71 single on Buddha ("Love Songs in the Night"/"Two By Two"), although the record itself was credited to Steve Martin. And the original group, minus its key visionary Michael Brown, made an album's worth of ill-advised reunion recordings in 1978. —*Richie Unterberger*

● **There's Gonna Be a Storm: Complete Recordings 1966-69** / 1992 / Mercury ✦✦✦✦

Though it's missing a few rarities—namely the Steve Martin single for Buddha that reunited him with Michael Brown—this is the most definitive Left Banke compilation. It features the entirety of their two late-'60s albums, as well as a couple of singles that didn't make it onto LPs at the time (though they later appeared on Rhino's *History*) and a previously unissued cut, "Men Are Building Sand." Their debut 1967 LP, *Walk Away Renee/Pretty Ballerina*, is an underrated classic of the time, matching smart harmonies and pop hooks to baroque orchestration. Its brilliance casts a bit of a shadow over the rest of this collection. The group's 1968 album *Too* suffered from bloated production and, more importantly, the absence of chief songwriter/arranger Michael Brown. In turn, the 1967 single Brown cut under the Left Banke moniker with singer Bert Sommer suffers from the absence of lead vocalist Steve Martin. By the time Brown and Martin tenuously reunited for a late-1969 single, some of the spark had gone. All of the aforementioned highs and lows of this prodigiously talented but strife-ridden group are on this disc. —*Richie Unterberger*

Leiber & Stoller

Songwriters / R&B, Rock 'n' Roll, Pop-Rock, Brill Building Pop

A complete biography of the lives of Jerry Leiber and Mike Stoller and their contribution to rock 'n' roll could easily take up the rest of this book. Very simply, Mike Leiber and Jerry Stoller are two of the most important songwriters of the early days of rock 'n' roll. Although they had penned songs for R&B artists such as Jimmy Witherspoon, Floyd Dixon, and Charles Brown in the early '50s, Leiber and Stoller more or less exploded onto the rock scene in 1953 by writing "Hound Dog" for Big Mama Thornton (later to be covered by Elvis). From that point on, the duo composed and produced a string of hits that include some of the most instantly recognizable songs in rock history. They were also pushing the art of rock songwriting (and record production) into, at the time, uncharted territory. As is noted by critic Greg Shaw in the *Rolling Stone Illustrated History of Rock and Roll:* "They were the true architects of pop-rock . . . Their signal achievement was the marriage of rhythm & blues in its most primal form to the pop tradition."

Few songwriters of this era had the Midas touch as did Leiber and Stoller. A partial list of their credits include "Riot in Cell Block No.9" (1953), "Love Me" (1956), "Charlie Brown" (1959), "Stand By Me" (1961), "On Broadway" (1963), and numerous songs for Elvis, including songs for the films *Jailhouse Rock* and *King Creole.* Along with wedding R&B with the pop tradition, Leiber and Stoller also introduced string arrangements to R&B records (the Drifters featuring Ben E. King, "There Goes My Baby") and by doing so created the foundation for a new era of soul music production that would come on the heels of the fading doo wop style. Among the many artists and writers they influenced, few were more important than Phil Spector, who cut his teeth learning production techniques from them while they painstakingly assembled the great early Drifters tracks.

In 1964, Leiber and Stoller started their own record label, Red Bird, devoted to girl groups. Wisely, they also hired the talented songwriting duo of Ellie Greenwich and Jeff Barry, who were at their peak powers, composing some of the most lasting songs of the albeit brief heyday of girl group music, including the Shangri-Las' "Leader of the Pack" and the Dixie Cups' "Chapel of Love." Leiber and Stoller, however, became disinterested in the business side of Red Bird and sold the label two years later, just as the girl group sound was on the wane. So, too, were the hit-making days of Leiber and Stoller on the wane. They continued to write songs, mostly for the Coasters, but they no longer dominated the pop and R&B charts the way they once did. Still, they survived, taking on the august role of rock 'n' roll elder statesmen, eventually landing a spot in the Rock and Roll Hall of Fame in 1987. More recently, their songs were the basis of a successful Broadway musical entitled *Smokey Joe's Cafe*, which revived interest in their great body of work, and also brought the music of Jerry Leiber and Mike Stoller to a whole new audience. Not bad for a couple of guys who, in the words of Mike Stoller, never wanted to write rock 'n' roll songs, just good R&B. —*John Dougan*

★ **There's a Riot Goin' On! The Rock 'N' Roll Classics of Leiber and Stoller** / 1991 / Rhino ✦✦✦✦✦
Sure, you can spend a lot of dough buying CD reissues of all the bands Leiber and Stoller wrote songs for. And while that would give you a great record collection (especially of Drifters and Coasters material), you might want to start with this indispensable 18-track collection. All the big hits are here, as are the songs that show off Leiber and Stoller's melodramatic way with a song ("I Who Have Nothing") and their deft comic touch ("Charlie Brown"). The essence of Leiber and Stoller's genius is here, and I'm willing to wager you'll recognize nearly every one of these songs as soon as they start. Memory can be a wonderful thing. —*John Dougan*

Lemon Pipers

f. 1967, Cincinnati, OH, **db.** 1969
Psychedelic, Pop-Rock, Bubblegum
The Lemon Pipers included singer Ivan Browne, guitarist William Bartlett, keyboardist R.G. Nave, bassist Steve Walmsley, and drummer William Albaugh. The group is best known for their No. 1 bubblegum hit "Green Tambourine" and several follow-ups, all written by the team of Paul Leka and Shelley Pinz. The group actually wanted to play more psychedelic music; they only recorded "Green Tambourine" because their label would have dropped them had they refused. They eventually got the artistic control they wanted and ended up dropping off the charts for good with their first self-produced album. They broke up in 1969, with Bartlett joining Ram Jam. —*Steve Huey*

● **The Lemon Pipers** / 1990 / Sequel ✦✦✦✦
This 20-song compilation of late '60s material is effectively a "best-of" from a group that only had one hit. Whether intentionally or not, on much of the material supplied to them by outside songwriters (i.e., "Love Beads and Meditation"), the impression is that of late-'60s AM radio trying to co-opt suitably freaky aspects of the psychedelic sound. On the cuts they wrote themselves, the group play in a far more guitar-oriented and gutsy style that's nonetheless pleasantly

anonymous American freakbeat, in search of both an identity and (even more crucially) hooks. Translation: nothing here's nearly as good or lasting as the No. 1 single "Green Tambourine," which is included on this disc, but can be found on numerous oldies collections that provide superior value. —*Richie Unterberger*

The Lemonheads

f. 1984, Boston, MA
Alternative Pop-Rock, Hardcore Punk, Pop-Rock, Alternative Country-Rock, Punk-Pop
The Lemonheads' evolution from post-Hüsker Dü hardcore punk rockers to teenage heart-throbs is one of the strangest sagas in alternative music. Initially, the group was a punk-pop trio formed by three teenage Boston suburbanites, but over the years, the band became a vehicle for Evan Dando. Blessed with good looks and a warm, sweet voice, Dando became a teen idol in the early '90s, when Nirvana's success made alternative bands commercially viable. While his simple, catchy songs were instantly accessible, they tended to hide the more subversive nature of his lyrics, as well as his gift for offbeat covers and devotion to country-rock father Gram Parsons. After developing his signature blend of pop, punk, and country-rock on several independent records in the late '80s, Dando moved the Lemonheads to Atlantic Records in 1990. Two years later, *It's A Shame About Ray* made the group into media sensations, as Dando's face appeared on music and teen magazines across America and Britain. Though the Lemonheads were poised to become superstars, the band never quite found the right breakthrough single, and their popularity peaked in the early '90s. Around the same time, Dando descended into severe drug abuse that he curbed by the 1996 release of *Car Button Cloth.* However, he had missed his chance at stardom—though the group retained their cult, much of their audience had already slipped away.

The son of a Boston attorney and a fashion model, Evan Dando (vocals, guitar, drums) formed the Lemonheads with his high school classmates Ben Deily (vocals, guitar, drums) and Jesse Peretz (bass). Initially, the group was called the Whelps, but by the time the band made their debut EP, *Laughing All the Way to the Cleaners*, they had changed their name to the Lemonheads. Recorded the day after their high school graduation, *Laughing All the Way to the Cleaners* was released on the group's own label Huh-Bag. The EP gained the attention of the Boston-based indie label Taang!, who signed the band later that same year. By the beginning of 1987, Doug Trachten had become the band's full-time drummer, leaving Dando and Peretz to share guitar and vocal duties. *Hate Your Friends*, a speedy hardcore LP that fell halfway between Hüsker Dü and the Replacements, was released in 1987. Trachten left after the record's release, and the band made 1988's *Creator* with Blake Babies drummer John Strohm.

Released in 1989, *Lick* expanded the Lemonheads' cult, thanks to a loud, power-pop cover of Suzanne Vega's "Luka." Following the release of *Lick*, Dando and Diely had a vicious dispute over the leadership of the Lemonheads, resulting in a temporary breakup. Dando briefly played with the Blake Babies before forming a new version of the Lemonheads with drummer David Ryan. The Lemonheads signed with Atlantic Records in 1990, releasing *Lovey*, their most accomplished, melodic and eclectic record to date, later that year. Dando's interest in the band began to wander the following year, as he recorded the solo EP *Favourite Spanish Dishes.* In 1992, he recorded *It's a Shame About Ray*, which featured Blake Baby Juliana Hatfield on bass and harmony vocals.

It's a Shame About Ray would prove to be the Lemonheads' breakthrough album, but it didn't become a hit until a cover of Simon & Garfunkel's "Mrs. Robinson" was added to the album several months after its initial release. By the end of 1992, the record had gained momentum, and Dando was being touted as the next alternative star. By the fall release of 1993's *Come On Feel the Lemonheads*, Dando had become a minor celebrity, appearing in gossip columns frequently and hanging out with fellow Gen-X icons, including actors like Johnny Depp and musicians like Hole's Courtney Love. His fame was large enough to spark the creation of an anti-Dando fanzine, *I Hate Evan Dando.* Recorded with the band's new bassist Nic Dalton, *Come On Feel* was hyped as the album that would make the band superstars, but Dando's antics received more press than the record received airplay, even though "Into Your Arms" nearly scraped the pop charts. During the press junket to promote the album, he confessed to heavy use of hard drugs, including an escapade where he smoked enough crack to ruin his voice for several weeks. His addiction deepened throughout 1994, and he was frequently seen in a drug-induced haze on Oasis' fall tour of Britain. Early in 1995, he launched a solo tour of the US with Epic Soundtracks, after which he was booed at the Glastonbury Festival after appearing several hours late. Dando sobered up during the remaining months of 1995, though he hadn't completely stopped drinking by the time he recorded *Car Button Cloth* with a new lineup of the Lemonheads featuring former Dinosaur Jr. drummer Murph, guitarist John Strohm, and bassist Bill Gibson. The album was greeted with mixed reviews upon its fall 1996 release and failed to generate a hit single. —*Stephen Thomas Erlewine*

Hate Your Friends / 1987 / Taang! ♦♦
The Lemonheads' debut album is a bit unfocused, spending most of its time thrashing around in post-Hüsker Dü hardcore punk, but its best moments ("Second Chance," "Fed Up") show that Evan Dando has a natural knack for pop hooks. —*Stephen Thomas Erlewine*

Creator / 1988 / Taang! ♦♦
Demonstrating an increased sense of pop, not only in their songwriting but also in their relatively measured performances, the Lemonheads turn in a winning second album with *Creator*. Although they still spend a little too much time mucking around with sub-hardcore noise, Evan Dando's gentler pop numbers are quite appealing, even when he treads a little too closely to dippy hippie cliches, and they certainly point the way to the engaging punk-pop of *Lick*. —*Stephen Thomas Erlewine*

Lick / 1989 / Taang! ♦♦♦♦
Although it's fairly incoherent, bouncing back and forth between punk-pop and folky pop, *Lick* is a thoroughly engaging record. The tensions between Evan Dando and Ben Deily are fairly evident throughout the albums, especially since Dando's songs, with their immediate hooks and melodies, outshine his bandmates, but that unevenness makes the record endearingly messy. Also, the mess makes the group's best songs, including an inspired electric cover of Suzanne Vega's "Luka," shine all the more brightly. —*Stephen Thomas Erlewine*

Create Your Friends / 1989 / Taang! ♦♦
Create Your Friends combines the Lemonheads' first two albums for Taang!, *Hate Your Friends* and *Creator*, on one compact disc. While this material is fairly inconsistent, the hardcore numbers are enjoyable Husker Du and Replacements rip-offs, and several of the songs illustrate Evan Dando's talent for simple pop hooks. —*Stephen Thomas Erlewine*

Lovey / 1990 / Atlantic ♦♦♦
Moving to a major label didn't affect the Lemonheads' sound as much as the departure of Ben Deily; without him, Evan Dando was free to let his sensitive side run wild, which is exactly what he does on *Lovey*. Dando never completely abandons punk-pop on *Lovey*, but he does balance it with excursions into jangle-pop and country-rock, many of which contain his best songwriting to date. By now, he has begun to develop a signature voice, a distinctly suburban and middle-class voice that embraces the mundane details of every day life. That gives songs like "Stove" and "Lil' Seed" an off-kilter sensibility, which is made all the more appealing by his gift for simple hooks. Even though Dando has made significant strides forward, the most affecting moment on the record remains his stark and very pretty cover of Gram Parsons' "Brass Buttons." —*Stephen Thomas Erlewine*

● **It's a Shame About Ray** / Jun. 2, 1992 / Atlantic ♦♦♦♦
If *Lovey* captured Evan Dando as he found his signature blend of punk-pop, jangle-pop, and folk-rock, *It's a Shame About Ray* is where he perfected that style. Breezing by in under a half hour, the album is a simple collection of sunny melodies and hooks, delivered with typical nonchalance by Dando. None of the songs are about anything major, nor do they have astonishing original melodies, but that's part of their charm—they're immediately accessible and thoroughly catchy. Dando's laidback observations of middle-class outcasts are minor gems. The heartbroken title track or "Confetti," the crushes of "Bit Part in Your Life," the love letter to substances "My Drug Buddy," or the wonderful "Alison's Starting to Happen," in which a girl finds herself as she discovers punk rock, capture the laconic rhythms of suburbia, and its warm, friendly voice, which is offset by Juliana Hatfield's girlish harmonies, gives the songs an emotional resonance. [*It's a Shame About Ray* was later re-released with a competent punk-pop remake of Simon & Garfunkel's "Mrs. Robinson" added as a bonus track. As Dando approached stardom, the album was repressed again with the title of "My Drug Buddy" truncated to "Buddy." It was later restored to its original title.] —*Stephen Thomas Erlewine*

Come on Feel the Lemonheads / Oct. 12, 1993 / Atlantic ♦♦♦
Come on Feel the Lemonheads should have been the album that propelled the trio and Evan Dando to stardom, but instead of delivering a concise pop record in the vein of *It's a Shame About Ray*, they made a messy record that never quite found its focus. That's not to say that *Come On Feel* is without merit, because that's hardly the case. In many ways, it's the most interesting record that the Lemonheads have released, because it finds Dando confused about every-

thing, particularly his burgeoning fame and love, both for girls and drugs. There are moments of self-indulgence—whether it's the aimless piano instrumental "The Jello Fund" or two versions of the drug-obsessed "Style"—yet they are as essential to the album's desperate tone as the heartbreaking acoustic ballad of "Favorite T." Between those two extremes are some of the finest power-pop and country-rock Dando's ever written. He still has a tendency to be too cutesy, as on the otherwise winning country-rock "Being Around" and "Big Gay Heart," but the hooky rush of "The Great Big No," the bright "I'll Do It Anyway," and the lovely simplicity of "Into Your Arms" are irresistible. *Come On Feel* may not be as consistent or immediate as *It's a Shame About Ray*, but finding its pleasures is quite rewarding. —*Stephen Thomas Erlewine*

Car Button Cloth / Oct. 15, 1996 / Atlantic ♦♦♦
If *Come on Feel the Lemonheads* was a bit confused, *Car Button Cloth* is positively a mess, filled with perfect pop, stoned rock, and rambling country-rock, which is alternately ingratiating and infuriating. Evan Dando may have (relatively) sobered up between the two records, but the sound of *Car Button Cloth* is even wearier than before—his voice is beginning to show signs of abuse, while the tempos often sag and lurch, occasionally becoming burdened with lead guitars that steal directly from J. Mascis. The turgid grunge that wears at the fringes of the record actually makes the gems all the more endearing. "If I Could Talk I'd Tell You" is one of Dando's finest three-chord sing-alongs; the self-deprecating "The Outdoor Type" is excellent country-rock; the stop-start verses of "It's All True" are fleshed out by Dando's weary croak, and the grunge interpretation of "Knoxville Girl" is actually very affecting. However, only dedicated fans will be willing to sort through the hubris to actually find these songs, which is unfortunate, because at its best, *Car Button Cloth* is as good as anything Dando has yet recorded. —*Stephen Thomas Erlewine*

John Lennon

b. Oct. 9, 1940, Liverpool, England, **d.** Dec. 8, 1980, New York City, NY
Guitar, Piano, Keyboards, Vocals / Rock 'n' Roll, Singer-Songwriter, Pop-Rock

Out of all the Beatles, John Lennon had the most interesting—and frustrating—solo career. Lennon was capable of honest, brutally honest confessional songwriting and melodic songcraft; he also had a tendency to rest on his laurels, churning out straight-ahead rock 'n' roll without much care. But the extremes, both in his music and his life, were what made him fascinating. Where Paul McCartney was content to be a rock star, Lennon dabbled in everything from revolutionary politics to the television talk-show circuit during the early '70s. After releasing a pair of acclaimed albums, *John Lennon/Plastic Ono Band* and *Imagine*, in the early '70s, Lennon sunk into an infamous "lost weekend" where his musical output was decidedly uneven and his public behavior was often embarrassing. Halfway through the decade, he sobered up and retired from performing to become a house-husband and father. In 1980, he launched a comeback with his wife Yoko Ono, releasing the duet album *Double Fantasy* that fall. Just as his career was on an upswing, Lennon was tragically assassinated outside of his New York apartment building in December of 1980. He left behind an enormous legacy, not only as a musician, but as a writer, actor, and activist.

Considering the magnitude of his achievements with the Beatles, Lennon's solo career is relatively overlooked. Even during the height of Beatlemania, Lennon began exploring outside of the group. In 1964, he published a collection of his writings called *In His Own Write*, which was followed in 1965 by *A Spaniard in the Works*, and in 1966, he appeared in Dick Lester's comedy *How I Won the War*. He didn't pursue a musical career outside of the group until 1968, when he recorded the experimental noise collage *Unfinished Music, No. 1: Two Virgins* with his new lover, avant-garde artist Yoko Ono. *Two Virgins* caused considerable controversy, both because of its content and its cover art, which featured a nude photograph of Lennon and Ono. The couple married in Gibraltar on March 20, 1969. For their honeymoon, the pair staged the first of many political demonstrations with their "Bed-In for Peace" at the Amsterdam Hilton. Several months later, the avant-garde records *Unfinished Music, No. 2: Life with the Lions* and *The Wedding Album* were released, as was the single "Give Peace a Chance," which was recorded during the Bed-In. During September of 1969, Lennon returned to live performances with a concert at a Toronto rock 'n' roll festival. He was supported by the Plastic Ono Band, which featured Ono, guitarist Eric Clapton, bassist Klaus Voormann, and drummer Alan White. The following month, Lennon and the Plastic Ono Band released "Cold Turkey," which was about his battle with heroin addiction. When the single failed to make the Top Ten in Britain and America, Lennon sent his MBE back to the Queen, protesting Britain's involvement in

Biafra, America's involvement in Vietnam, and the poor chart performance of "Cold Turkey."

Before the release of "Cold Turkey," Lennon had told the Beatles that he planned to leave the group, but he agreed not to publicly announce his intentions until after Allen Klein's negotiations with EMI on behalf of the Beatles were resolved. Lennon and Ono continued with their campaign for peace, spreading billboards with the slogan "War Is Over! (If You Want It)" in 12 separate cities. In February of 1970, he wrote, recorded, and released the single "Instant Karma" within the span of one week. The single became a major hit, reaching the Top Ten in both the UK and the US. Two months after "Instant Karma," Paul McCartney announced that the Beatles were splitting up, provoking the anger of Lennon. Much of this anger was vented on his first full-fledged solo album, *John Lennon/Plastic Ono Band*, a scathingly honest confessional work inspired by his and Ono's primal scream therapy. Lennon supported the album with an extensive interview with *Rolling Stone*, in which he debunked many of the myths surrounding the Beatles. Early in 1971, he released another protest single, "Power to the People," before moving to New York. That fall, he released *Imagine*, which featured the Top Ten title track. By the time *Imagine* became a hit album, Lennon and Ono had returned to political activism, publicly supporting American radicals like Abbie Hoffman, Jerry Rubin, and John Sinclair. Their increased political involvement resulted in the double album *Sometime in New York City*, which was released in the summer of 1972. Recorded with the New York hippie band Elephant's Memory, *Sometime in New York City* consisted entirely of political songs, many of which were criticized for their simplicity. Consequently, the album sold poorly and tarnished Lennon's reputation.

Sometime in New York City was the beginning of a three-year downward spiral for Lennon. Shortly before the album's release, he began his long, involved battle with US Immigration, who refused to give him a green card due to a conviction for marijuana possession in 1968. In 1973, he was ordered to leave America by Immigration, and he launched a full-scale battle against the department, frequently attacking them in public. *Mind Games* was released in late 1973 to mixed reviews; its title track became a moderate hit. The following year, he and Ono separated, and he moved out to Los Angeles, beginning his year-and-a-half-long "lost weekend." During 1974 and 1975, Lennon lived a life of debauchery in Los Angeles, partying hard with such celebrities as Elton John, Harry Nilsson, Keith Moon, David Bowie, and Ringo Starr. *Walls and Bridges* appeared in November of 1974, and it became a hit due to the inclusion of "Whatever Gets You Through the Night," a song he wrote with Elton John. At the end of the year, John helped reunite Lennon and Ono, convincing the ex-Beatle to appear during one of his concerts; it would be Lennon's last performance.

Rock & Roll, a collection of rock oldies recorded during the lost weekend, was released in the spring of 1975. A few months before its official release, a bootleg of the album called *Roots* was released by Morris Levy, who Lennon later sued successfully. Lennon's immigration battle neared its completion on October 7, 1975, when the US court of appeals overturned his deportation order; in the summer of 1976, he was finally granted his green card. After he appeared on David Bowie's *Young Americans*, co-writing the hit song "Fame," Lennon quietly retired from music, choosing to become a house-husband following the October birth of his son, Sean Lennon.

During the summer of 1980, Lennon returned to recording, signing a new contract with Geffen Records. Comprising equally material by Lennon and Ono, *Double Fantasy* was released in November to positive reviews. As the album and its accompanying single, "(Just Like) Starting Over," were climbing the charts, Lennon was assassinated on December 8 by Mark David Chapman. Lennon's death inspired deep grief from the entire world; on December 14, millions of fans around the world participated in a ten-minute silent vigil for Lennon at 2 p.m. EST. *Double Fantasy* and "(Just Like) Starting Over" both became No. 1 hits in the wake of his death. In the years after his death, several albums of unreleased recordings appeared, the first of which was 1984's *Milk & Honey*. *— Stephen Thomas Erlewine*

Two Virgins: Unfinished Music No. 1 / Nov. 11, 1968 / Apple ✦✦
At the time of its release, this duo album by John Lennon and Yoko Ono gained its greatest notice for its cover, a photograph that depicted the two standing before the camera naked. The recording, too, can be described as naked, in that it contains no music that would interfere with one's ability to hear the normal sounds of life. The record is not unlike what you might get if you turned on a tape recorder for a random half hour in your home—snatches of inaudible conversation far away from the microphone, footsteps, wind, etc. Conceptual "music" in the Cageian sense, yes, but not popular music of the kind with which John Lennon had been previously associated in any sense at all. *— William Ruhlmann*

Life with the Lions: Unfinished Music #2 / May 26, 1969 / Apple ✦✦
John Lennon and Yoko Ono's second collaborative album consists of five tracks. All of side one is taken up by "Cambridge 1969," a live recording at Lady Mitchell Hall in Cambridge of Lennon playing an electric guitar backup to Ono's singing and screaming. Side two includes an a cappella rendering by Ono of "No Bed For Beatle John," which discusses the refusal of a hospital to give Lennon a bed so he could stay during his wife's troubled pregnancy; "Baby's Heartbeat," which is what it says it is; "Two Minutes Silence" in commemoration of Ono's miscarriage, which also is what it says it is; and "Radio Play," 12 minutes of a radio dial being turned back and forth to pick up random stations. If, as they suggested, their lives were their art, then this is, too. Maybe. *— William Ruhlmann*

Live Peace in Toronto 1969 / Dec. 12, 1969 / Capitol ✦✦✦
Impromptu concert appearance, with Lennon singing a few rock 'n' roll oldies plus his then-new single, "Cold Turkey," backed by guitarist Eric Clapton. Also 17-plus minutes of Yoko Ono screaming and singing over guitar feedback. *— William Ruhlmann*

Wedding Album / 1969 / Apple ✦✦
The third and last of John Lennon and Yoko Ono's experimental albums to be released within a one-year period, *Wedding Album*, like *Unfinished Music No. 1—Two Virgins*, was in some ways more notable for its packaging than for its content. It came in a box containing a facsimile of the Lennons' wedding certificate and a photograph of a piece of wedding cake. The record itself contained two selections, one of which consisted of nearly 25 minutes of Yoko Ono's wailing, while the other, "John and Yoko," featured the two, one in each stereo speaker, calling out the other's name for more than 22 minutes. Employing such limited lyrics, Lennon is the more expressive, Ono the more penetrating. *— William Ruhlmann*

☆ **John Lennon/Plastic Ono Band** / Dec. 11, 1970 / Capitol ✦✦✦✦✦
The cliché about singer-songwriters is that they sing confessionals direct from their heart, but John Lennon exploded the myth behind that cliché, as well as many others, on his first official solo record, *John Lennon/Plastic Ono Band*. Inspired by his primal scream therapy with Dr. Arthur Janov, Lennon created a harrowing set of unflinchingly personal songs, laying out all of his fears and angers for everyone to hear. It was a revolutionary record—never before had a record been so explicitly introspective, and very few records made absolutely no concession to the audience's expectations, daring the listeners to meet all the artist's demands. Which isn't to say that the record is unlistenable. Lennon's songs range from tough rock 'n' rollers to piano-based ballads and spare folk songs, and his melodies remain strong and memorable, which actually intensifies the pain and rage of the songs. Not much about *Plastic Ono Band* is hidden. Lennon presents everything on the surface, and the song titles—"Mother," "I Found Out," "Working Class Hero," "Isolation," "God," "My Mummy's Dead"—illustrate what each song is about, and chart his loss of faith in his parents, country, friends, fans, and idols. It's an unflinching document of bare-boned despair and pain, but for all its nihilism, it is ultimately life-affirming; it is unique not only in Lennon's catalog, but in all of popular music. Few albums are ever as harrowing, difficult, and rewarding as *John Lennon/Plastic Ono Band*. *— Stephen Thomas Erlewine*

☆ **Imagine** / Sep. 9, 1971 / Capitol ✦✦✦✦
After the harrowing *Plastic Ono Band*, Lennon returned to calmer, more conventional territory with *Imagine*. While the album had a softer surface, it was only marginally less confessional than its predecessor. Underneath the sweet strings of "Jealous Guy" lies a broken and scared man; the jaunty "Crippled Inside" is a mocking assault at an acquaintance; and "Imagine" is a paean for peace in world with no gods, possessions, or classes, where everyone is equal. And Lennon doesn't shy away from the hard rockers—"How Do You Sleep" is a scathing attack on Paul McCartney, "I Don't Want to Be a Soldier" is a hypnotic anti-war song, and "Give Me Some Truth" is bitter hard rock. If *Imagine* doesn't have the thematic sweep of *Plastic Ono Band*, it is nevertheless a remarkable collection of songs that Lennon would never be able to better. *— Stephen Thomas Erlewine*

Sometime in New York City / Jun. 12, 1972 / Capitol ✦✦
The first album co-billed to John Lennon and Yoko Ono to actually contain recognizable pop music, *Sometime in New York City* found the Lennons in an explicitly political phase, expounding on such topical subjects as the Attica prison riot and the treatment of activists John Sinclair and Angela Davis. Especially in the case of Lennon's songs, there is an appealing rock style to the material, even if the lyrics limit the record's appeal. *Sometime in New York City* was originally released with a free bonus disc that contained a live medley of Lennon's "Cold Turkey" and Ono's "Don't Worry Kyoko," and an appearance by the Lennons at a Mothers of Invention concert. This slight material now makes the album a two-CD set, and it is priced accordingly. *— William Ruhlmann*

Mind Games / Nov. 2, 1973 / Capitol ✦✦✦✦

After the hostile reaction to the politically charged *Sometime in New York City*, John Lennon moved away from explicit protest songs and returned to introspective songwriting with *Mind Games*. Lennon didn't leave politics behind—he just tempered his opinions with humor on songs like "Bring on the Lucie (Freda People)," which happened to undercut the intention of the song. It also indicated the confusion that lies at the heart of the album. Lennon doesn't know which way to go, so he tries everything. There are lovely ballads like "Out of the Blue" and "One Day (At A Time)," forced ham-fisted rockers like "Meat City" and "Tight As," sweeping Spectoresque pop on "Mind Games," and many mid-tempo, indistinguishable pop-rockers. While the best numbers are among Lennon's finest, there's only a handful of them, and the remainder of the record is simply pleasant. But compared to *Sometime in New York City*, as well as the subsequent *Walls and Bridges*, *Mind Games* sounded like a return to form. —*Stephen Thomas Erlewine*

Walls and Bridges / Sep. 26, 1974 / Capitol ✦✦✦

Walls and Bridges was recorded during John Lennon's infamous "lost weekend," as he exiled himself in California during a separation from Yoko Ono. Lennon's personal life was scattered, so it isn't surprising that *Walls and Bridges* is a mess itself, containing equal amounts of brilliance and nonsense. Falling between the two extremes was the bouncy Elton John duet "Whatever Gets You Thru the Night," which was Lennon's first solo No. 1 hit. Its bright, sunny surface was replicated throughout the record, particularly on middling rockers like "What You Got" but also on enjoyable pop songs like "Old Dirt Road." However, the best moments on *Walls and Bridges* come when Lennon is more open with his emotions, like on "Going Down on Love," "Steel and Glass," and the beautiful, soaring "No.9 Dream." Even with such fine moments, the album is decidedly uneven, containing too much mediocre material like "Beef Jerky" and "Ya Ya," which are weighed down by weak melodies and heavy overproduction. It wasn't a particularly graceful way to enter retirement. —*Stephen Thomas Erlewine*

Rock 'n' Roll / Feb. 17, 1975 / Capitol ✦✦✦

It was a common practice in the early 1970s for artists to satisfy record companies' demands for frequent LP releases by recording albums of cover songs (see the Band's *Moondog Matinee* and David Bowie's *Pinups* for more examples). The story of John Lennon's covers album is a little more complicated, but the result is the same, with the artist tackling songs from the '50s by many of his favorites, from Gene Vincent to Lloyd Price. Of course, these are the kinds of songs that turned up on early Beatles albums, and while Lennon doesn't reinvent them as strikingly as his old group did, he gives them an affectionate, knowing treatment. —*William Ruhlmann*

Shaved Fish / Oct. 24, 1975 / Capitol ✦✦✦✦

Although superseded by *The John Lennon Collection* (see below), this greatest-hits album is the only place to find such singles as "Cold Turkey" and "Happy Xmas (War Is Over)." —*William Ruhlmann*

Double Fantasy / Nov. 17, 1980 / Capitol ✦✦✦✦

On an album made shortly before his death, Lennon explores his retirement, his artistic rebirth, and his relationship with his family on such songs as "(Just Like) Starting Over," "Woman," and "Watching the Wheels," all of which were Top Ten hits. Lennon's songs are interspersed with surprisingly accessible contributions from Ono. —*William Ruhlmann*

★ **The John Lennon Collection** / Nov. 10, 1982 / Capitol ✦✦✦✦✦

Six of the seven Lennon tracks from *Double Fantasy*, plus nine of his best songs from 1969 to 1974, among them the singles "Give Peace a Chance," in its only album appearance, and "Instant Karma!" The CD version, released in 1989, adds four tracks, including the B-side single "Move Over Ms. L," making this album all the more necessary. —*William Ruhlmann*

Milk & Honey / Jan. 27, 1984 / Polydor ✦✦✦

Posthumous followup to *Double Fantasy*, featuring sometimes rough takes of perhaps unfinished songs that nevertheless sparkle with Lennon's wit and exuberance, among them the Top Five hit "Nobody Told Me." (Again, Ono's songs are interspersed with Lennon's contributions.) —*William Ruhlmann*

Live in New York City / Feb. 10, 1986 / Capitol ✦✦✦

This benefit concert, recorded August 30, 1972, marked John Lennon's last full-length concert appearance. The 55-minute video released 13 years later finds Lennon and wife Yoko Ono leading the band Elephant's Memory in a set of songs taken from Lennon's solo albums of the time, some of them with a heavily political theme. Nevertheless, hits like "Imagine" and "Instant Karma!" are also included, and Lennon is as witty and charismatic as ever. —*William Ruhlmann*

Menlove Ave. / Nov. 3, 1986 / Capitol ✦✦✦

John Lennon is heard in outtakes from the sessions for the albums

Walls and Bridges and *Rock 'N' Roll*, including alternate versions of songs that turned up on those albums, as well as such original songs as "Rock and Roll People," previously heard only in a version by Johnny Winter. —*William Ruhlmann*

Imagine: John Lennon [O.S.T.] / Oct. 10, 1988 / Capitol ✦✦✦✦

A two-disc set containing a selection of Lennon's work with the Beatles and as a solo artist. This is the original soundtrack album. —*William Ruhlmann*

☆ **Lennon** / 1990 / Capitol ✦✦✦✦✦

Lennon is given a solid box-set treatment with this four-disc, 73-track collection. The set is so complete that there is essentially no need to go out and obtain any of his albums on disc. *Lennon* runs chronologically, from the Plastic Ono Band's "Give Peace a Chance," to "Grow Old with Me" from 1984's *Milk and Honey*. All the best stuff from *Live Peace in Toronto 1969* is here, as well as his live (with Elton John) versions of "I Saw Her Standing There" and "Lucy in the Sky with Diamonds." The book contains a generous collection of photos and lyrics to all of the songs. The A-to-Z color-coded index is overkill in lieu of any track information detailing where and when the songs were cut and who played on them. —*Rick Clark*

Annie Lennox

b. Dec. 25, 1954, Aberdeen, Scotland
Keyboards, Vocals / Adult Contemporary, Pop-Rock, Club/Dance
Following the disbanding of the Eurythmics in 1991, vocalist Annie Lennox began a solo career that rivaled the Eurythmics' in terms of crossover popularity.

Born and raised in Aberdeen, Scotland, Annie Lennox began playing music as child, learning how to play both the piano and flute. In her late teens, she won a scholarship to London's Royal Academy of Music but she dropped out of the school before she took her finals. For the next several years after she quit school, she worked around London, performing various jobs during the day and singing at night. In the late '70s, she met guitarist Dave Stewart through a friend. Stewart, who had previously played with Longdancer, asked Lennox to join a new band he was forming with a songwriter called Peet Coombes. The band was named the Tourists; they released three albums between 1979 and 1980, scoring a No. 4 UK hit with a cover of Dusty Springfield's "I Only Want to Be With You."

While they were collaborating together in the Tourists, Lennox and Stewart became lovers. Soon, tensions within the band grew and by 1980, the pair had left the band to begin the Eurythmics. During the early '80s, the sleek synth-pop of the Eurythmics became one of the most popular sounds of new wave, racking up a number of hits in both the US and UK, including "Sweet Dreams (Are Made of This)," "Love Is A Stranger," "Who's That Girl," and "Here Comes The Rain Again." Midway through their career, Eurythmics began pursuing a harder, more straightforward rock 'n' roll sound.

In 1990, following the release of the Eurythmics' commercial disappointment *We Too Are One*, Lennox announced that she was taking a two-year sabbatical to have a child. During this time, the group quietly dissolved, Lennox had a baby, and she began working on her first solo album. *Diva*, her solo debut, arrived in 1992 and it showcased a calmer, more mature vocalist designed to cross over into the adult contemporary audience. On the strength of the singles "Walking on Broken Glass" (No. 14) and "Why" (No. 34), *Diva* sold over two million copies in the US alone; the album was also nominated for three Grammy awards.

Annie Lennox delivered her second solo album, a covers collection entitled *Medusa*, in 1995. Peaking at No. 11, *Medusa* spawned the hit single "No More I Love You's" and went platinum by the end of 1995. —*Stephen Thomas Erlewine*

● **Diva** / Apr. 28, 1992 / Arista ✦✦✦✦

Those expecting Annie Lennox to come out full guns blazing for her solo debut with the high energy Euro-electro-pop-meets-American-R&B of her Eurythmics work may have to wind their pacemakers down a notch. The enigmatic vocalist who made a career toying with different notions of gender now plays on the concept of fame—Lennox dressing up in the persona of a solitary *Diva* trapped by counterfeit glory. The framework offers an effective stage for Lennox's husky voice, showcasing her as much more of a chanteuse than in the past. But the music is strangely muted and understated. In fact, the album almost works best as one integrated mood-piece rather than a collection of individual songs. While Lennox succeeds in carving out a personality distinct from her Eurythmics days with *Diva*, one can't help but crave a shot of former partner Dave Stewart's musical muscle. —*Roch Parisien*

Medusa / Mar. 14, 1995 / Arista ✦✦

Annie Lennox's second solo album reprises the slick R&B-pop approach of *Diva*, complete with sophisticated arrangements and impressive vocal workouts. Unfortunately, it was applied to a set of songs that are considered pop classics and Lennox's interpretations add nothing except the sheen of upper-class glamour. —*Stephen Thomas Erlewine*

Let's Active

f. 1981, Chapel Hill, NC, **db.** 1988
Power Pop, Jangle-Pop
Mitch Easter carved his place in music history as a hip producer in the '80s, most notably for the early R.E.M. albums *Murmur* and *Reckoning;* unfortunately, these achievements often overshadowed and distracted him from giving his full commitment to his own recording career with Let's Active, a band that, between 1983 and 1988, released some of the finest Southern power-pop/jangle-pop of the decade.

After a short stint with the Sneakers, a band he formed with future dB's Chris Stamey in North Carolina in the late '70s, Mitch Easter set up his legendary Drive-In Studios in 1981 and formed Let's Active with bassist Faye Hunter and drummer Sara Romweber. The trio released a six-song EP, 1983's *Afoot*, on IRS Records. In 1984, the band released the more experimental *Cypress*. While the EP and album sold modestly, they found a strong following in the emerging alternative/"college rock" audience. Hunter and Romweber left shortly after the release, leaving Let's Active as essentially a solo project for Easter. Romweber later went on to join Snatches of Pink.

Easter recruited drummers Eric Marshall and Rob Ladd, along with multi-instrumentalist Angie Carlson (Hunter returned temporarily for bass duties) for *Big Plans For Everybody* in 1986, another critically praised yet commercially undervalued album. The harder-edged *Every Dog Has His Day*, which replaced Hunter with a full-time bassist, John Heames, was released in 1988. Following a small-scale promotional tour of college campuses, the band hung in limbo—no subsequent albums were recorded. Easter has continued producing into the '90s while infrequently playing with other bands, including Velvet Crush and Vinyl Devotion. —*Chris Woodstra*

Afoot / 1983 / IRS ◆◆◆◆
Afoot, their six-song debut EP, features Mitch Easter's own brand of Southern power-pop. With infectious, hook-filled songs, Easter proves to be a master of the three-minute form, especially on the classic "Every Word Means No." —*Chris Woodstra*

Cypress / 1984 / IRS ◆◆◆◆
The band stretch out a bit on their first proper LP. While it is still every bit a jangly guitar-pop effort, Easter seems to be enjoying the powers of his studio, experimenting in different electronic sounds and neo-psychedelic textures. "Waters Part," the failed single from the album, is still one of his finest moments as a songwriter. —*Chris Woodstra*

Big Plans for Everybody / 1986 / IRS ◆◆◆
Essentially a Mitch Easter solo project, *Big Plans for Everybody* moves into darker territory than the previous album. Though Easter's trademark bright production and quirky songwriting still stand out, the mood is decidedly melancholy. —*Chris Woodstra*

Every Dog Has His Day / Aug. 22, 1988 / IRS ◆◆◆
Every Dog Has His Day features some of Easter's strongest songs in a harder-edged setting. Almost completely ignored, this was the band's last effort before disbanding indefinitely. —*Chris Woodstra*

● **Cypress/Afoot** / Jun. 1989 / IRS ◆◆◆◆
This CD combines their first EP, *Afoot*, and their first album, *Cypress*. Featuring highly memorable songs like "Every Word Means No" and "Waters Part," this perfect Southern power-pop is worth seeking out. —*Chris Woodstra*

Level 42

f. 1980, Manchester, England
Synth-Pop, New Wave, Pop-Rock
At the beginning of their career, Level 42 were a jazz-funk fusion band, following in the footsteps of such pioneers as Stanley Clarke. By the end of the '80s, they were a pop-R&B band with a number of hit singles to their credit. Featuring Mark King (bass, vocals), Phil Gould (drums), Boon Gould (guitar), and Mark Lindup (keyboards), the band formed in 1980. Before they released their first single, "Love Meeting Love," the band was pushed to add vocals to their music in order to give it a more commercial sound; they complied, with King becoming the lead singer. Released in 1981, their self-titled debut album was a slick soul-R&B collection that charted in the UK Top 20, resulting in the release of *The Early Tapes* by their former record label, Polydor. Level 42 had several minor hit singles before 1984's "The Sun Goes Down (Living It Up)" hit the British Top Ten. Released in late 1985, *World Machine* broke the band worldwide; "Lessons in Love" hit No. 1 in Britain and "Something About You" hit No. 7 in America. Their next two records, *Running in the Family*

(1987) and *Staring at the Sun* (1988), were a big success in the UK, yet made only some headway in the US. Both of the Gould brothers left the band in late 1987; they were replaced by guitarist Alan Murphy and drummer Gary Husband. Murphy died of AIDS in 1991; he was replaced by the renowned fusion guitarist Allan Holdsworth for 1991's *Guaranteed*. The band followed *Guaranteed* in 1995 with *Forever Now*. —*Stephen Thomas Erlewine*

Level 42 / 1981 / Polydor ◆◆◆◆
The album was produced by label owner Andy Sojka. Highlights include "Love Meeting Love," "Wings of Love," "Love Games," "Turn It On," and "Starchild." —*Bil Carpenter*

Pursuit of Accidents / 1982 / Polydor ◆◆◆
Although they didn't really begin to have dance-pop hits until later in the '80s, the English group Level 42 provided some fine performances on this album. While vocals weren't their strong suit, they did a reasonable job of harmonizing and at least getting through the melodies, while the production and arrangements helped embellish and compensate for their singing inadequacies. Although such groups as the Pet Shop Boys and even Thompson Twins do this type of thing better, Level 42 at least isn't irritating or self-indulgent. —*Ron Wynn*

True Colours / 1983 / Polydor ◆◆◆
Level 42 was steadily perfecting and evolving their dance-pop, funk, and rock mix during the '80s, and when they hit the big time, the label began reissuing their earlier, less successful material. It's hard to understand why this didn't do as well as later albums like *World Machine*, *Running in the Family*, and *Staring at the Sun*, although the obvious reason would be that no singles ever broke that compared with the ones from those releases. But it was just as well-produced, the songs were almost as cutely performed, and the arrangements are very similar. —*Ron Wynn*

● **Level Best** / 1989 / Polydor ◆◆◆◆
This hits CD draws heavily from *Running in the Family* (1987) and *World Machine* (1985) but offers a good introduction to this band. —*Scott Bultman*

Barbara Lewis

b. Feb. 9, 1943, South Lyon, Michigan
Vocals / Soul
Pop-soul doesn't get much better than Barbara Lewis, whose seductive, emotive croon took "Hello Stranger" to No.3 in 1963. The Michigan native had been writing songs since the age of nine, and began recording as a teenager with producer Ollie McLaughlin, who'd also had a hand in the careers of Del Shannon, and Deon Jackson. Lewis wrote all of the songs on her debut LP (including "Hello Stranger"), and confidently handled harmony soul numbers (some with backing by the Dells) and more pop-savvy tunes, some of which, like "Hello Stranger," were driven by an organ and a bossa nova-like beat.

Follow-ups to "Hello Stranger" didn't sell nearly as well (although one of her singles, "Someday We're Gonna Love Again," was covered by the Searchers for a British Invasion hit). In the mid-'60s, she began doing some recordings in New York City, with assistance from producers like Bert Berns and Jerry Wexler, that employed more orchestral arrangements and pop-conscious material. The approach clicked, both commercially and artistically: "Baby I'm Yours" and "Make Me Your Baby" were both big hits, and both among the best mid-'60s girl-group style productions.

Lewis cut an album in the late '60s for Stax (on the Enterprise subsidiary) that, as one would expect, gave her sound a grittier approach, without compromising the smooth and poppy elements integral to the singer's appeal. It passed mostly unnoticed, though, and Lewis withdrew from the music business after a few other singles. The "beach music" scene of the Carolinas remains a bastion of appreciation for Lewis' records, which continue to enjoy popularity and airplay there decades after their original release. —*Richie Unterberger*

Snap Your Fingers / 1964 / Atlantic ◆◆◆
Not much. Lewis sings a variety of standards like "Twist and Shout" and even "Turn on Your Love Light." Nice music, but not great Barbara Lewis. —*Michael Erlewine*

Baby, I'm Yours / 1966 / Atlantic ◆◆◆◆
Here is a classic Barbara Lewis album with four tunes written by Lewis herself. "Baby, I'm Yours," and "Hello Stranger" we all know, but "Puppy Love" and "Think a Little Sugar" are also fine. The song "How Can I Say Goodbye" is wonderful. Most of these are available on compilations. —*Michael Erlewine*

It's Magic / 1966 / Atlantic ◆◆◆
An album of standards like "Yesterday" and "A Taste of Honey." Not the Lewis that most of us hunger for, although the cut "He's So Bad" is very good. —*Michael Erlewine*

Many Grooves of Barbara Lewis / 1969 / Stax ✦✦✦✦

Although this late-'60s album isn't nearly as well known as her pop-pier mid-'60s hits, this is excellent sweet soul that avoids slickness. Still working with producer Ollie McLaughlin, Lewis recorded this set of strong soul-pop in Chicago. The slightly updated, gutsier tone of the arrangements did nothing to obscure her characteristically smooth and assured delivery. The CD reissue adds three bonus tracks from singles. —*Richie Unterberger*

★ **Hello Stranger: The Best of Barbara Lewis** / Jul. 19, 1994 / Rhino ✦✦✦✦✦

At last! Twenty great Barbara Lewis songs in glorious remastered digital sound. In fact, the sound is so good it's like hearing these classic sides for the first time. The only significant omission is the song "On Bended Knee," but then again, I would have liked a two-disc compilation. Thank you Rhino! —*Michael Erlewine*

Gary Lewis & the Playboys (Gary Levital)

b. Jun. 31, 1946, Los Angeles, CA
Drums, Vocals / Pop-Rock

The son of comedian Jerry Lewis formed this American rock group in 1964. After landing a gig at Disneyland, they were immediately signed to Liberty Records and handed over to pop production genius Snuff Garrett. Utilizing the best songwriters and studio players available, Garrett fashioned five Top Five hits in a matter of 18 months (15 in the Hot 100 by 1969) around Lewis' meager abilities, sometimes augmenting his voice in the studio with backup singers doubling his part. Lewis pretty well held his own against the British invasion, but the combination of his draft call in late 1966 and the rising tide of psychedelia brought his days on the charts to an end. Still active on the oldies circuit, he fronts various backup bands under the name the Playboys. —*Cub Koda*

● **Legendary Masters Series** / 1990 / Capitol ✦✦✦✦

One of the most engaging pop acts of the mid-'60s, The Playboys benefited from strong songwriting (Al Kooper cowrote "This Diamond Ring") and studio personnel (courtesy of Leon Russell). It's still light, catchy pop with the enjoyable, unaffected vocals of Gary Lewis on top, and still fun. —*William Ruhlmann*

Greatest Hits [Curb] / Apr. 5, 1994 / Curb ✦✦

Gary Lewis is not the kind of artist that inspires meticulous completeness. Therefore, it's quite likely that many Lewis fans will not even notice the absence of some minor hits on this 10-song collection, which includes the biggest of the biggies ("This Diamond Ring," "She's Just My Style," "Everybody Loves a Clown"). The *Legendary Masters Series*, however, offers much more content, making this a much less desirable alternative. —*Richie Unterberger*

Huey Lewis

b. Jul. 5, 1950, New York, NY
Pop-Rock

Huey Lewis and the News were a bar band that made good. With their simple, straightforward rock 'n' roll, the San Francisco-based group became one of America's most popular pop-rock bands of the mid-'80s. Inspired equally by British pub-rock and '60s R&B and rock 'n' roll, the News had a driving, party-hearty spirit that made songs like "Workin' for a Livin'," "I Want a New Drug," "The Heart of Rock & Roll," "Hip to Be Square" and "The Power of Love" yuppie anthems. At their core, the group were a working band, and they knew how to target their audience, writing odes to 9-to-5 jobs and sports. As the decade progressed, the group smoothed out their sound to appeal to the aging baby boomers that adopted them, but by the beginning of the '90s, the appeal of their formula had decreased. Nevertheless, the group remained a popular concert attraction, and continued to have radio hits on adult contemporary stations.

The roots of Huey Lewis & the News lay in Clover, an early '70s country-rock band from San Francisco that featured Lewis (vocals, harmonica) and keyboardist Sean Hopper. Clover moved to England in 1976 upon the urging of Nick Lowe, who believed they could fit into the UK's pub-rock scene. In a short time, the group cultivated a small following. Lowe produced the group's first single, "Chicken Funk," which featured lead vocals by Lewis, and the following year the band, minus Lewis, supported Elvis Costello on his debut album, *My Aim is True*. Polygram released two Clover albums that failed to find an audience and when their leader, John McFee, left the group to join the Doobie Brothers, the band broke up and returned to California. Before returning to the States, Lewis played harmonica on Lowe's *Labour of Lust* and Dave Edmunds' *Repeat When Necessary*, which also featured Lewis' song "Bad Is Bad."

Upon their return to America, Lewis and Hopper began jamming at a Marin County bar called Uncle Charlies, which is where they formed American Express with Mario Cipollina (bass), Johnny Colla

(saxophone, guitar) and Bill Gibson (drums), who had all played in Soundhole, one of Van Morrison's backing bands in the late '70s. American Express recorded a disco version of "Theme from Exodus," calling it "Exodisco." Mercury released the single, which was ignored. In 1980, the group added lead guitarist Chris Hayes and were offered a contract by Chrysalis who requested that the band change their name. The members chose Huey Lewis and the News and the band's eponymous debut was released later that year to little attention.

Picture This, the group's second album, was released early in 1982 and the record became a hit on the strength of the Top Ten single "Do You Believe in Love," which was written by former Clover producer Robert John "Mutt" Lange. A couple other minor hits, "Hope You Love Me Like You Say You Do" and "Workin' for a Livin'," followed and the band began building a strong following by touring heavily. *Sports*, the group's third album, was released in the fall of 1983 and it slowly became a multi-platinum success, thanks to touring and a series of clever, funny videos that received heavy MTV airplay. "Heart and Soul" (No. 8, 1983), "I Want a New Drug" (No. 6, 1984), "The Heart of Rock & Roll" (No. 6, 1984) and "If This Is It" (No. 6, 1984) all became Top Ten hits, and *Sports* climbed to No.1 in 1984; it would eventually sell over seven million copies. Late in 1984, Lewis sued Ray Parker Jr., claiming that his song "Ghostbusters" plagiarized "I Want a New Drug." The suit was settled out of court. The News had their first No. 1 single in 1985 with "The Power of Love," taken from the soundtrack to *Back to the Future*.

Huey Lewis and the News returned with their fourth album, *Fore!*, in 1986. The record sailed to No. 1 on the strength of five Top Ten singles: "Stuck With You" (No. 1, 1986), "Hip to Be Square" (No. 3, 1986), "Jacob's Ladder" (No. 1, 1987), "I Know What I Like" (No. 9, 1987), and "Doing It All for My Baby" (No. 6, 1987). The band was riding high on the charts when they decided to expand their musical reach with 1988's *Small World*, dipping tentatively into various American roots musics. While the record produced the Top Ten hit "Perfect World," it was a commercial disappointment after two chart-topping, multi-platinum albums, stalling at No. 11 on the charts and only going platinum.

The News took three years to follow up *Small World* with *Hard at Play*, which was released on their new label, EMI. *Hard to Play* failed to break the Top 20 and only produced one hit, "Couple Days Off." The group's commercial heyday had clearly passed, and the group took the remainder of the '90s rather easy, touring sporadically and releasing the covers album *Four Chords & Several Years Ago* in 1994. Their first release for Elektra Records, the album generated one adult contemporary radio hit, "But It's Alright," and failed to go gold. —*Stephen Thomas Erlewine*

Huey Lewis & the News / 1980 / Chrysalis ✦✦✦

On their eponymous debut, Huey Lewis & the News essentially act as a pub-rock band, turning out hard-driving covers and originals in a workmanlike fashion. While that usually makes for great club gigs, it only occasionally makes for great records, and the debut suffers from an uneven selection of material and a somewhat stiff production, mainly because the group can't quite reproduce their sound in the studio. Even with such flaws, the album shows signs of promise, particularly in the charging anthem "Working for a Living." —*Stephen Thomas Erlewine*

Picture This / 1982 / Chrysalis ✦✦✦✦

Huey Lewis & the News sound considerably more focused on their second album, *Picture This*. By incorporating stronger elements of R&B and doo wop (their cover of "Buzz Buzz Buzz" is first-rate) and embracing pop to a much greater extent, the News find their own distinctive sound—clean-cut, steady middle-class rock 'n' roll. They still suffer from uneven material, but "Do You Believe In Love?" is a stunner, a tight set of polished, anthemic hooks that is one of the best mainstream pop singles of the early '80s. —*Stephen Thomas Erlewine*

Sports / 1983 / Chrysalis ✦✦✦✦

Picture This found Huey Lewis & the News developing a signature sound, but they truly came into their own on their third album, *Sports*. It's true that the record holds together better than its predecessors because it has a clear, professional production, but the real key is the songs. Where their previous albums were cluttered with generic filler, nearly every song on *Sports* has a huge hook. And even if the News aren't bothered by breaking new ground, there's no denying that the craftsmanship on *Sports* is pretty infectious. There's a reason why well over half of the album ("Heart of Rock & Roll," "Heart and Soul," "I Want a New Drug," "Walking on a Thin Line," "If This Is It") were huge American hit singles—they have instantly memorable hooks, driven home with economical precision by a tight bar band, who are given just enough polish to make them sound like superstars. And that's just what *Sports* made them. —*Stephen Thomas Erlewine*

Fore! / 1986 / Chrysalis ✦✦✦

Sports was one of the rare mainstream pop-rock albums where everything worked—the songs were catchy and the sound was inviting, and it all sounded perfect on the radio. It would have been tough for Huey Lewis & the News to match its quality with its follow-up *Fore!*, and it comes as little surprise that *Fore!* suffers from an overdose of the very things that made *Sports* nearly irresistible. Where the songs on *Sports* were so straightforward that they seemed inevitable, much of *Fore!* sounds labored, particularly when the News try to write a middle-class anthem. It's one thing to celebrate "The Heart of Rock & Roll," but it's quite another to proclaim it's "Hip to Be Square," especially if you're supported by a chorus of football players. And "Hip to Be Square," as well as "Stuck With You," where a married yuppie couple can't divorce 'cause it would simply be too much hassle, makes Lewis' complacent tendencies all too clear. That wouldn't be a big problem if the songs were as catchy as "If This Is It" or "Heart and Soul," but they aren't, and the sound of the record is so sterile that the News no longer sound like a working band. *Fore!* is a reasonably enjoyable facsimile of the pleasures of *Sports*, yet it lacks the gleeful sense of fun that made that record, as well as portions of *Picture This*, so enjoyable. —*Stephen Thomas Erlewine*

Small World / 1988 / Chrysalis ✦✦

Small World was another platinum hit for Huey Lewis & the News, but the album was noticeably weaker than their previous three records. Lewis tries to position himself as a socially-conscious rocker—no less than three tracks have the word "world" in their title—writing songs about the perilous state of the environment and urging everybody to live together peacefully, since "there ain't no livin' in a perfect world." Such sanctimonious and simple lyrical platitudes would be acceptable if the band had written a set of catchy pop to support them. Instead, the group decided to stretch out, exploring rootsy American music like the zydeco of "Bobo Tempo" and the bluesy "Old Antone's." None of the musical diversions work as well as the bouncy Top Ten hit "Perfect World." However, "Perfect World" is the only song that ranks with the group's best material—as "Give Me the Keys (And I'll Drive You Crazy)" proves, the News had failed to come up with hooks that rivaled their earlier hits. —*Stephen Thomas Erlewine*

Hard at Play / Jan. 1991 / EMI America ✦✦✦

As the title indicates, *Hard at Play* is a return to the straigh-ahead blues-inflected pop-rock that made Huey Lewis & the News superstars in the early '80s. While the material wasn't as consistently strong as *Sports* or *Picture This*, the band rocked with a renewed vigor, and a handful of songs, including the anthemic hit "Couple Days Off," were as catchy as their older hits. —*Stephen Thomas Erlewine*

The Heart of Rock & Roll: The Best of Huey Lewis & the News / Nov. 18, 1992 / Chrysalis ✦✦✦✦

For four years, the UK compilation *The Heart of Rock & Roll: The Best of Huey Lewis & the News* was the only hits collection available on the San Franciscan bar band, and in some ways it's a better overview than the American retrospective, *Time Flies*. Although it does include a live version of "Workin' for a Livin'" and overlooks "Doing it All for My Baby" and "I Know What I Like," it contains several key tracks that aren't on *Time Flies*: "Hip to Be Square," "Back in Time" (which is only available on the *Back to the Future* soundtrack), "Jacob's Ladder," "Perfect World," the *We Are the World* track "Trouble in Paradise," and the terrific LP cut "Some of My Lies Are True." These tracks are added to the familiar hits to make *The Heart of Rock & Roll* a more thorough retrospective and, in many ways, a better introduction than *Time Flies*. —*Stephen Thomas Erlewine*

Four Chords & Several Years Ago / Nov. 1, 1994 / Elektra ✦✦

Four Chords & Several Years Ago was a set of well-performed R&B covers by Huey Lewis & the News. While it lacked the polished energy of their *Sports*-era hits ("The Heart of Rock & Roll," "I Want a New Drug," "The Power of Love"), the album was filled with pleasant, professional performances that proved the band still knew how to construct a hit single—both "(She's) Some Kind of Wonderful" and "It's Alright" were minor hits. Even though it was a well-crafted record that managed to avoid the group's tendency for bombast, *Four Chords & Several Years Ago* never managed to be a compelling listen; it sounded better on the radio than it did on the stereo. —*Stephen Thomas Erlewine*

● **Time Flies: The Best of Huey Lewis** / Oct. 29, 1996 / Elektra ✦✦✦✦

Theoretically, it should be easy to assemble a greatest-hits collection from Huey Lewis & the News, since they spent most of the '80s in the Top Ten. *Time Flies... The Best of Huey Lewis & the News* proves that assumption false. Although many of the band's biggest hits are here—"Do You Believe in Love," "Workin' for a Livin'," "Heart and Soul," "I Want a New Drug," "The Heart of Rock & Roll," "If This Is It," "The Power of Love," "Stuck with You," and "Doing It All for My Baby"—the selection is remarkably uneven, bypassing many

major hits from *Fore!* ("Hip to be Square," "Jacob's Ladder," "I Know What I Like") and neglecting the latter-day hit singles "Perfect World" and "Couple Days Off" completely, both of which were the only things worth salvaging from their respective albums. In their place are four new songs, which are pleasant but unremarkable. Even though it is flawed, *Time Flies* remains a useful compilation, since it gathers all of the very best singles, particularly the ones from *Sports* and *Picture This*, in one place. However, the group could use an even better retrospective in the future. —*Stephen Thomas Erlewine*

Jerry Lee Lewis

b. Sep. 29, 1935, Ferriday, LA
Piano, Vocals / Rock 'n' Roll, Traditional Country, Honky Tonk

Is there an early rock 'n' roller that has a crazier reputation than the Killer, Jerry Lee Lewis? His exploits as a piano-thumping egocentric wild man with an unquenchable thirst for living have become the fodder for numerous biographies, film documentaries, and a full-length Hollywood movie. Certainly few other artists came to the party with more ego and talent than he and lived to tell the tale. And certainly even fewer could successfully channel that energy into their music and prosper doing it as well as Jerry Lee. When he broke on the national scene in 1957 with his classic "Whole Lotta Shakin' Goin' On," he was every parents' worst nightmare perfectly realized: a long-blonde-haired Southerner who played the piano and sang with uncontrolled fury and abandon, while simultaneously reveling in his own sexuality. He was rock 'n' roll's first great wild man and also rock 'n' roll's first great eclectic. Ignoring all manner of musical boundaries is something that has not only allowed his music to have wide variety, but to survive the fads and fashions as well. Whether singing a melancholy country ballad, a lowdown blues or a blazing rocker, Lewis' wholesale commitment to the moment brings forth performances that are totally grounded in his personality and all singularly of one piece. Like the recordings of Hank Williams, Louis Armstrong and few others, Jerry Lee's early recorded work is one of the most amazing collections of American music in existence.

He was born to Elmo and Mamie Lewis on September 29, 1935. Though the family was dirt poor, there was enough money to be had to purchase a third-hand upright piano for the family's country shack in Ferriday, LA. Sharing piano lessons with his two cousins, Mickey Gilley and Jimmy Lee Swaggart, a ten-year-old Jerry Lee showed remarkable aptitude for the instrument. A visit from piano-playing older cousin Carl McVoy unlocked the secrets to the boogie-woogie styles he was hearing on the radio and across the tracks at Haney's Big House, owned by his uncle, Lee Calhoun and catering to Blacks exclusively. Lewis mixed that up with gospel and country and started coming up with his own style. He even mixed genres in the way he syncopated his rhythms on the piano; his left hand generally played a rock-solid boogie pattern while his right played the high keys with much flamboyant filigree and showiness, equal parts gospel fervor and Liberace showmanship. By the time he was 14, by all family accounts, he was as good as he was ever going to get. Jerry Lee was already ready for prime time.

But his mother Mamie had other plans for the young family prodigy. Not wanting to squander Jerry Lee's gifts on the sordid world of show business, she enrolled him in a bible college in Waxahatchie, Texas, secure in the knowledge that her son would now be exclusively singing his songs to the Lord. But legend has it that the Killer tore into a boogie-woogie rendition of "My God Is Real" at a church assembly that sent him packing the same night. The split personality of Jerry Lee, torn between the sacred and the profane (rock 'n' roll music), is something that has eaten away at him most of his adult life, causing untold aberrant personality changes over the years with no clear-cut answers to the problem. What is certain is that by the time a 21-year-old Jerry Lee showed up in Memphis on the doorstep of the Sun studios, he *had* been thrown out of bible college, been a complete failure as a sewing-machine salesman, been turned down by most Nashville-based record companies *and* the Louisiana Hayride, been married twice, in jail once and burned with the passion that *he* truly was the next big thing.

Sam Phillips was on vacation when he arrived, but his assistant Jack Clement put Roland Janes on guitar and J.M. Van Eaton on drums behind Jerry Lee, whose fluid left hand made a bass player superfluous. This little unit would become the core of Jerry Lee's recording band for almost the entire seven years he recorded at Sun. The first single, a hopped-up rendition of Ray Price's "Crazy Arms," sold in respectable enough quantities that Phillips kept bringing Lewis back in for more sessions, astounded by his prodigious memory for old songs and his penchant for rocking them up. A few days after his first single was released, Jerry Lee was in the Sun studios earning some Christmas money, playing backup piano on a Carl Perkins session that yielded the classics "Matchbox" and "Your True Love." At the tail end of the recording, Elvis Presley showed up, Clement turned on the tape machine, and the impromptu *Million Dollar Quartet* jam session ensued, with Perkins, Presley, and Lewis all having the time of their lives.

With the release of his first single, the road beckoned and it was here that Jerry Lee's lasting stage persona was developed. Discouraged because he couldn't dance around the stage strumming a guitar like Carl Perkins, he stood up in mid-song, kicked back the piano stool and, as Carl has so saliently pointed out, "a new Jerry Lee Lewis was born." This new-found stage confidence was not lost on Sam Phillips. While he loved the music of Carl Perkins and Johnny Cash, he saw neither artist as a true contender to Elvis' throne; with Jerry Lee he thought he had a real shot. For the first time in his very parsimonious life, Sam Phillips threw every dime of promotional capital he had into Jerry Lee's next single, and the gamble paid off a million times over. "Whole Lotta Shakin' Goin' On" went to No. 1 on the country and the R&B charts, and was only held out of the top spot on the pop charts by Debbie Reynolds' "Tammy." Suddenly Jerry Lee was the hottest, newest, most exciting rock 'n' roller out there. His television appearances and stage shows were legendary for their manic energy, and his competitive nature to outdo anyone else on the bill led to the story about how he once set his piano on fire at set's end to make it impossible for Chuck Berry to follow his act. Nobody messed with the Killer.

Jerry Lee's follow-up to "Shakin'" was another defining moment for his career, as well as for rock 'n' roll. "Great Balls of Fire" featured only piano and drums, but sounded huge with Phillips' production behind it. It got him into a rock 'n' roll movie (*Jamboree*) and his fame was spreading to such a degree that Johnny Cash and Carl Perkins left Sun to go to Columbia Records. His next single, "Breathless," had a promotional tie-in with Dick Clark's Saturday night "Bandstand" show, making it three hits in a row for the newcomer.

But Jerry Lee was sowing the seeds of his own destruction in record time. He sneaked off and married his 13-year-old cousin, Myra Gale Brown, the daughter of his bass-playing uncle, J.W. Brown. With the Killer insisting that she accompany him on a debut tour of England, the British press got wind of the marriage and proceeded to crucify him in the press. The tour was canceled and Jerry Lee arrived back in the US to find his career in absolute disarray. His records were banned nationwide by radio stations and his booking price went from $10,000 a night to $250 in any honky tonk that would still have him. Undeterred, he kept right on doing what he had been doing, head unbowed and determined to make it back to the bigs, Jerry Lee Lewis style. It took him almost a dozen years to pull it off, but finally, with a sympathetic producer and a new record company willing to exact a truce with country disc jockeys, the Killer found a new groove, cutting one hit after another for Smash Records throughout the late '60s into the '70s. Still playing rock 'n' roll onstage whenever the mood struck him (which was often) while keeping all his releases pure country struck a creative bargain that suited Lewis well into the mid-'70s.

But while his career was soaring again, his personal life was falling apart. The next decade and a half saw several marriages fall apart (starting with his 13-year-long union with Myra), the deaths of his parents and oldest son, battles with the I.R.S., and bouts with alcohol and pills that frequently left him hospitalized. Suddenly the Ferriday Fireball was nearing middle age and the raging fire seemed to be burned out. The mid-'80s saw another jumpstart to his career. A movie entitled *Great Balls of Fire* was about to be made of his life and Lewis was called in to sing the songs for the soundtrack. Showing everyone who was the real Killer, Jerry Lee sounded energetic enough to make you believe it was 1957 all over again with the pilot light of inspiration still burning bright. He also got a boost back to major-label land with a one-song appearance on the soundtrack for *Dick Tracy*. With box sets and compilations, documentaries, a bioflick and his induction to the Rock & Roll Hall of Fame all celebrating his legacy, Jerry Lee still continues to record and tour, delivering work that vacillates from tepid to absolutely inspired. While his influence will continue to loom large until there's no one left to play rock 'n' roll piano anymore, the plain truth is that there's only *one* Jerry Lee Lewis and American music will never see another like him. —*Cub Koda*

Jerry Lee Lewis / 1957 / Rhino ✦✦✦✦
Jerry Lee Lewis' debut album was a virtual greatest hits album, featuring "Whole Lotta Shakin' Goin' On." —*AMG*

Jerry Lee's Greatest / 1961 / Rhino ✦✦✦
Jerry Lee's second record followed the same formula as the first, mixing singles—including "Great Balls of Fire"—with album tracks that were nearly as good as the hits. —*AMG*

The Greatest Live Show on Earth / 1964 / Bear Family ✦✦✦✦
Combining two live albums originally issued in the '60s, Lewis proves that the onslaught of the British Invasion hadn't lowered his rocking quotient one single bit. Blazing performances. —*Cub Koda*

☆ **Live at the Star Club** / 1965 / Rhino ✦✦✦✦
The rock 'n' roll landscape changed dramatically between the mid-'50s and 1964, when this five-star performance was recorded in Hamburg, Germany. The British Invasion was in full swing, and '50s icons like Chuck Berry, Little Richard, Elvis Presley, and Bill Haley were no longer considered cutting-edge. Be that as it may, Lewis would continue to make live audiences sweat for decades to come. Amazingly, *Live at the Star Club* was only released in West Germany in the '60s and didn't come out in the US until 1992. At 29, the Killer spares no passion whatsoever on frenzied versions of "Great Balls of Fire," "Whole Lotta Shakin' Goin' On," "Hound Dog," and other '50s classics. Though Lewis would record more and more country in the '60s, the only honky-tonk treasure embraced here is Hank Williams' "Your Cheatin' Heart." For both hardcore Lewis devotees and more casual listeners, this stunning CD is essential. —*Alex Henderson*

★ **18 Original Sun Greatest Hits** / 1984 / Rhino ✦✦✦✦
Solid single-disc collection of the records that got Lewis into the Rock & Roll Hall of Fame on the first ballot: "Whole Lotta Shakin' Goin' On," "Great Balls of Fire," "High School Confidential," and "Breathless" being merely the tip of the iceberg. —*Cub Koda*

Milestones / 1985 / Rhino ✦✦✦✦
There are so many Jerry Lee Lewis compilations out, ranging from single-disc Sun retrospectives to mammoth German imports documenting a few years in particular, that it's easy to lose track of what the best ones are. All you need to know about this double LP is that it's a good selection of his most famous material, properly emphasizing the late-'50s classics, with excellent liner notes. It also throws on enough of his most notable post-Sun cuts ("What's Made Milwaukee Famous," "Me and Bobby McGee") to make rock-oriented listeners feel that they have a sense of his post-rockabilly career without boring them to death. Those looking for one Jerry Lee album should get Rhino's *All Killer, No Filler* anthology instead. Those who are satisfied with *Milestones* as supplying all the Jerry Lee they want have no need to replace it. —*Richie Unterberger*

Classic / 1989 / Bear Family ✦✦✦✦
Eight-disc box set of Lewis' complete output for Sun Records. Along with Muddy Waters' Chess recordings, Louis Armstrong's *Hot Fives & Sevens*, and Hank Williams' undubbed MGM sides, this box comprises one of the finest bodies of American music ever recorded. —*Cub Koda*

★ **All Killer, No Filler: The Anthology** / May 18, 1993 / Rhino ✦✦✦✦✦
Out of all of the Jerry Lee Lewis compilations available on the market, only *All Killer, No Filler* contains material from all of the different labels he recorded for. Although there are 12 Sun tracks (including all of the major hits), the set doesn't draw enough from those early years; but then again, that's the intent. *All Killer, No Filler* is out to prove to an audience only familiar with his Sun singles that his country material is as brilliant as his rock 'n' roll, and it succeeds. Stick with the *18 Original Sun Greatest Hits* if you only want rock 'n' roll. If you want an idea of the scope of Lewis' talents and how consistently rich his music was throughout his career, you can't go wrong here. —*Stephen Thomas Erlewine*

Locust Years . . . And the Return to the Promised Land / Nov. 29, 1994 / Bear Family ✦✦✦✦
Picking up where the eight-CD set *Classic* left off, the eight-CD box *The Locust Years . . . and the Return to the Promised Land* rivals its predecessor in musical quality. Tracing Jerry Lee Lewis' '60s career at Smash Records, the first two discs find the pianist trying to replicate his rock 'n' roll success; while the performances were good, it was clear he was out of touch with the times. During the third disc, he begins to concentrate on country music. The fourth, fifth, and sixth discs match his Sun recordings for consistently brilliant performances; several of the songs became big hits on the country charts, establishing him as a country star. The seventh disc chronicles an exciting unreleased show, while the eighth disc is an unexceptional interview. For dedicated Jerry Lee Lewis fans, *The Locust Years* is every bit as essential as *Classic*. —*Stephen Thomas Erlewine*

● **Killer Country** / 1995 / Mercury ✦✦✦✦
Killer Country is a well-chosen selection of Jerry Lee Lewis' biggest and best country hits between 1963 and 1977, which feature some of his finest performances, including "Another Place, Another Time," "What's Made Milwaukee Famous," "She Still Comes Around (To Love What's Left of Me)," and "She Even Woke Me Up to Say Goodbye." —*Stephen Thomas Erlewine*

Young Blood / May 23, 1995 / Sire ✦✦
Jerry Lee Lewis made a comeback effort in 1995 with *Young Blood*. Although the Killer's performance is impressive—his voice continues to weather well with age and he hasn't lost much of his instrumental prowess—the selection of material is fairly uninspired and predictable. This wouldn't have been a problem if Jerry Lee was allowed to

work with a top-notch backing band, elevating the pedestrian material to a new level. Instead, *Young Blood* was made like most albums in the mid-'90s—each song was constructed track-by-track, with the musicians laying down their parts at different times. Consequently, the record is stripped of most of its potential power, leaving behind a well-produced but thoroughly unengaging album. —*Stephen Thomas Erlewine*

Smiley Lewis

b. Jul. 5, 1913, DeQuincy, LA, **d.** Oct. 7, 1966, New Orleans, LA
Guitar, Vocals / R&B, Piano Blues, New Orleans Blues, New Orleans R&B

Dave Bartholomew has often been quoted to the effect that Smiley Lewis was a "bad luck singer," because he never sold more than 100,000 copies of his Imperial singles. In retrospect, Lewis was a lucky man in many respects—he enjoyed stellar support from New Orleans' ace sessioneers at Cosimo's, benefited from top-flight material and production (by Bartholomew), and left behind a legacy of marvelous Crescent City R&B. We're lucky he was there, that's for sure.

Born with the unwieldy handle of Overton Lemons, Lewis hit the Big Easy in his mid-teens, armed with a big, booming voice and some guitar skills. He played clubs in the French Quarter, often with pianist Tuts Washington (and sometimes billed as "Smiling" Lewis). By 1947, his following was strong enough to merit a session for DeLuxe Records, which issued his debut 78, "Here Comes Smiley." Nothing happened with that platter, but when Lewis signed with Imperial in 1950 (debuting with "Tee-Nah-Nah") things began to move.

As the New Orleans R&B sound developed rapidly during the early '50s, so did Lewis, as he rocked ever harder on "Lillie Mae," "Ain't Gonna Do It," and "Big Mamou." He scored his first national hit in 1952 with "The Bells Are Ringing," but enjoyed his biggest sales in 1955 with the exultant "I Hear You Knocking" (its immortal piano solo courtesy of Huey Smith). Here's where that alleged bad luck rears its head—pop chanteuse Gale Storm swiped his thunder for any pop crossover possibilities with her ludicrous whitewashed cover of the plaintive ballad.

But Storm wouldn't dare come near its roaring flip, the Joe Turnerish rocker "Bumpity Bump," or some of Smiley Lewis' other classic mid-'50s jumpers ("Down the Road," "Lost Weekend," "Real Gone Lover," "She's Got Me Hook, Line and Sinker," "Rootin' and Tootin'"). In front of the Crescent City's hottest players (saxists Lee Allen, Clarence Hall, and Herb Hardesty usually worked his dates), Lewis roared like a lion.

Strangely, Fats Domino fared better with some of Smiley Lewis' tunes than Lewis did ("Blue Monday" in particular). Similarly, Elvis Presley cleaned up the naughty "One Night," and hit big with it, but Lewis' original had already done well in 1956 (as had his melodic "Please Listen to Me"). His blistering "Shame, Shame, Shame" found its way onto the soundtrack of the steamy Hollywood potboiler *Baby Doll* in 1957 but failed to find entry to the R&B charts.

After a long and at least semi-profitable run at Imperial, Lewis moved over to OKeh in 1961 for one single, stopped at Dot in 1964 just long enough to make a solitary 45 (produced by Nashville deejay Bill "Hoss" Allen) and bowed out with an Allen Toussaint-produced remake of "The Bells Are Ringing" for Loma in 1965. By then, stomach cancer was eating the once-stout singer up. He died in the autumn of 1966, all but forgotten outside his New Orleans homebase.

The ensuing decades have rectified that miscarriage of justice, however. Smiley Lewis' place as one of the greatest New Orleans R&B artists of the 1950s is certainly assured. —*Bill Dahl*

★ **The Best of** / Nov. 3, 1992 / Capitol ✦✦✦✦✦
Smiley Lewis made several fabulous singles, had a booming, terrific voice, and received the same great backing and support that defined the city's R&B sound. But Lewis' records seldom made it outside New Orleans, even though they were frequently brilliant. This great 24-track anthology contains the four that did make it to the charts, among them the signature song "I Hear You Knocking." It shows Lewis doing first-rate novelty tracks, ballads, weepers, uptempo wailers and blues, and making wonderful recordings. The set also includes a thorough discography and good notes and is superbly mastered. It's magnificent, exuberant R&B, and deserved a much better national fate than it enjoyed. —*Ron Wynn*

Shame, Shame, Shame / 1993 / Bear Family ✦✦✦✦
Booming-voiced Smiley may have never enjoyed his share of breaks (as his producer Dave Bartholomew never tires of pointing out), but he sure left behind a legacy of blistering 1950s New Orleans R&B. This four-disc boxed set contains every track Lewis cut for Imperial, along with a handful of obscurities issued on Okeh, Dot, and Loma not long before his untimely demise. If EMI's single disc retrospec-

tive isn't enough for you, this exhaustively annotated, beautifully presented package is the ultimate source. —*Bill Dahl*

LFO

f. 1988, Sheffield, England
Acid House, Techno, Electronica, Club/Dance

The Sheffield techno duo of Mark Bell and Jez Varley have a reputation that, at first glance, might seem to exceed them. Having released only two records and not many more singles in their eight years together, the pair's apparently meager contribution would hardly seem to bear out the claim that they've been one of British techno's most important, agenda-setting groups. Nonetheless, early singles such as "We Are Back," "Freeze," and "Love Is the Message" from their debut *Frequencies*, as well as "Tied Up" from the more recent *Advance*, have indelibly marked British techno with Detroit's progressiveness, electro's funk, and an unflinching, uniquely British experimentalism. Taking their name from the foundational component of the synthesizers—the low frequency oscillator (kind of like calling a rock group Power Chord)—the pair were approached by the London-based Warp label in the late '80s, after tapes the pair had put together on some junky, second-hand equipment caught the ears and dance floors of local clubs and DJs. Both Bell and Varley admit to roots in the early- and mid-'80s hip-hop and electro invasions as well as the more obvious British acid house explosion, and their affectation for thick electronic breaks, vocoder samples, and sparse, modal melodies derive largely from that source. (LFO are also one of only a few—with 808 State and Coldcut—to find domestic reissue through the New York-based hip-hop label Tommy Boy, making obvious a connection between British experimental techno and American hip-hop and electro-funk that hasn't been followed up on until very recently.) Releasing their bass-heavy debut in 1991 to universal acclaim, the pair were silent for the next five years, with rumors of a follow-up surfacing from time to time, but failing to produce anything. Reportedly working with early Depeche Mode member Alan Wilder and Karl Bartos of Kraftwerk (none of that material's ever seen light), LFO finally resurfaced in 1995 with the ironically titled "Tied Up," followed several months later by *Advance*. The group have also recently re-mixed tracks for Bjork and the Sabres of Paradise. —*Sean Cooper*

● **Frequencies** / Oct. 1, 1991 / Tommy Boy ✦✦✦✦
Definitive collection of the new style electro-techno, with composition and dynamics taking equal play with groove and DJ-friendliness. Reissued by Tommy Boy in the US, the hip-hop connection was apparent in the few breakbeat tracks, but for the most part the record leans more toward acid house and techno for its cues. Recommended. —*Sean Cooper*

Advance / 1996 / Warp ✦✦✦✦
Nearly legendary as the album-that-almost-never-happened, *Advance* was a full five years in the making, with hardly a peep over new material in between. The result isn't as essential as their debut, but growth and maturity are evident, particularly in the focus and depth of composition. The material flows nicely, with the heavier, more body-oriented material broken up by contemplative, atmospheric ambient interludes. —*Sean Cooper*

Gordon Lightfoot

b. Nov. 17, 1938, Orillia, Ontario, Canada
Guitar, Piano, Vocals / Folk, Singer-Songwriter, Folk-Rock

Canadian Gordon Lightfoot first began to gain recognition in the mid-'60s as a songwriter when his compositions "For Lovin' Me" and "Early Morning Rain" became hits for Peter, Paul & Mary, and Marty Robbins topped the country charts with "Ribbon of Darkness." Lightfoot's own style was understated, his tasteful folk arrangements topped by a gentle burr of a voice. His albums began to appear in 1966, but it was not until the start of the '70s that he became a big success as a performer, scoring in 1970 with *Sit Down Young Stranger*, which contained his hit "If You Could Read My Mind," a song with a typically flowing melodic line and gently poetic lyrics.

Thereafter, the first half of the '70s were his. Lightfoot hit a peak in 1974 with *Sundown*, which went to No. 1, as did the title song when released on a single. Though he had developed a timeless style, Lightfoot was caught by the popular decline of folk-based music in the latter half of the 1970s, and has performed and recorded less frequently since, sometimes trying to conform to perceived commercial trends without success. But concert appearances in the early '90s confirmed that he remains an engaging performer and that his catalog of original songs is hard to match. —*William Ruhlmann*

Lightfoot / Mar. 1966 / United Artists ✦✦✦✦
Lightfoot was already 27 at the time of his solo debut, which might have accounted in part for the unusually fully developed maturity

and confidence on this recording, in both his songwriting and vocals. Contains some of his best compositions, including "Early Mornin' Rain," "I'm Not Sayin'," "The Way I Feel," "Lovin' Me," and "Ribbon of Darkness." At this point Lightfoot was still including some covers in his repertoire, and he handles numbers by Phil Ochs ("Changes"), Ewan McColl ("The First Time Ever I Saw Your Face"), and Hamilton Camp ("Pride of Man") well. The whole album is included on *The United Artists Collection.* —*Richie Unterberger*

The Way I Feel / Apr. 1967 / United Artists ✦✦✦✦
Lightfoot had used additional guitar and bass on his debut, but for his second LP he went for a fuller band sound, using a couple of the noted Nashville sessionmen (Charlie McCoy and Ken Buttrey) who had played on Bob Dylan's *Blonde on Blonde.* The result was a brighter and more accessible sound, with the country elements more to the fore. The songs weren't quite as impressive as his first batch, but they were still very good, highlighted by the epic "Canadian Railroad Trilogy" and an electrified remake of "The Way I Feel." The whole album is included on *The United Artists Collection.* —*Richie Unterberger*

Did She Mention My Name / Jan. 1968 / United Artists ✦✦✦✦
Every '60s singer-songwriter of note expanded their instrumental approach as time went on, and Lightfoot was no exception. For his third album, he worked with John Simon (who would handle the Band and Big Brother), and occasionally used low-key orchestration. Though a tad more erratic than his earlier efforts, his songwriting remained remarkably consistent. His characteristically bright, uplifting outlook became more diverse as well, allowing for the chilling "Black Day in July" (written in response to the 1967 Detroit riots), the odd "Pussywillows, Cat-Tails" (an unusual and successful detour into baroque orchestral pop), and the ambiguous sobriety of "Does Your Mother Know." The whole album is included on *The United Artists Collection.* —*Richie Unterberger*

Back Here on Earth / Nov. 1968 / United Artists ✦✦✦
After the mild experimentation of *Did She Mention My Name?*, *Back Here on Earth* was a retrenchment of sorts, recorded in Nashville with a three-piece acoustic lineup and a more countrified approach. It's not quite as outstanding as his first three albums, lacking highlights on the order of "Early Mornin' Rain" or "Black Day in July." Lightfoot never offered weak material on his United Artists efforts, however, and *Back Here on Earth* is still a very solid set, certainly worth acquiring if you like his other UA LPs. And all of the UA studio LPs, of course, are available on the two-disc *The United Artists Collection.* —*Richie Unterberger*

Sunday Concert / 1969 / Beat Goes On ✦✦✦
Recorded at a March 1969 concert in Toronto, this holds more interest than the usual live album because about half of the songs are Lightfoot compositions that had not been previously recorded in the studio. Accompanied by Red Shea on lead guitar and Rick Haynes on bass, he also mixed old favorites like "I'm Not Sayin'" and "Canadian Railroad Trilogy" with the new material on this set, which has good (though not outstanding) sound. These then-new songs aren't among his classics, but are up to the generally high standard of his '60s work, with the socially conscious "The Lost Children" and the poetic "Leaves of Grass" standing out as lyrical highlights. This is the only one of Lightfoot's '60s United Artists albums that is not included on *The United Artists Collection;* EMI reissued it on CD in 1996. —*Richie Unterberger*

Sit Down Young Stranger / 1970 / Reprise ✦✦✦✦
Lightfoot's Reprise albums are always tastefully constructed, with their careful finger-picking, restrained rhythm sections, and subtle string arrangements serving as a bed for the singer's sturdy baritone. What distinguishes the albums is the quality of Lightfoot's songwriting, and this one, featuring the title track as well as "Approaching Lavender" and "If You Could Read My Mind," has the best overall selection. —*William Ruhlmann*

Summer Side of Life / 1971 / Reprise ✦✦✦
This extraordinary release doesn't have big hits on it but contains some of his finest songwriting, from the political song "Miguel," to the wistful songs about divorce, "Same Old Loverman" and "Talking in Your Sleep," to the joyous "Cotton Jenny." This is highly recommended. —*Richard Meyer*

Sundown / 1974 / Reprise ✦✦✦✦
Lightfoot's commercial peak came with this album, which topped the US charts, containing both the No. 1 title song and the Top Ten hit "Carefree Highway." But songs like "Somewhere USA" and "High and Dry" are textured, catchy folk-rock on a par with the better-known tunes. —*William Ruhlmann*

Gord's Gold / 1975 / Reprise ✦✦✦
Following the success of *Sundown,* Gordon Lightfoot continued his success by releasing a greatest-hits compilation. A double album

(now a single CD), it contained his most popular songs from his Warner Bros. years on disc two and he re-recorded many of his early songs for side one of disc one. Although not as good, perhaps, as the originals, this did bring them up to date with his current style. Just about all the favorites are here. A good overview of a strong talent. —*James Chrispell*

Summertime Dream / 1976 / Reprise ✦✦✦
Due to Lightfoot's tendency to re-record his hits when preparing compilations (the warning "caveat emptor" applies to the two volumes of *Gord's Gold*), this is the only place to find the original version of his No. 2 "Wreck of the Edmond Fitzgerald." —*William Ruhlmann*

Waiting for You / Apr. 13, 1993 / Reprise ✦✦✦
Anyone fearing that sobriety and serenity might dull Gordon Lightfoot's creative edge can rest at ease. Having apparently freed himself of several personal demons, *Waiting for You* delivers the most consistent Lightfoot to be heard since the late '70s. While most tracks feature bass, drums, electric guitar, and/or keyboards (the synth washes sometimes overpower), for the most part the instrumentation is used sparingly, for color. The overwhelming feeling one derives from *Waiting for You* is of an intimate back porch session soaking up the sounds of a rejuvenated Gordon Lightfoot and his guitar. —*Roch Parisien*

★ **The United Artists Collection** / Oct. 5, 1993 / EMI ✦✦✦✦✦
This double CD contains all four of the Toronto singer-songwriter's '60s studio albums (the live LP *Sunday Concert*, not included here, was also released in the '60s). On these records, his resonant vocals, lyrical ambition, and melodic strengths produced as close a rival to Bob Dylan as Canada ever fashioned during that decade, and foreshadowed work by other major Canadian singer-songwriters of the late '60s, such as Joni Mitchell, Neil Young, and Leonard Cohen. "Early Mornin' Rain" (covered by fellow Canadian folkies Ian & Sylvia), the folk-rock protest number "Black Day in July," the epic "Canadian Railroad Trilogy," and his cover of Ewan McColl's "The First Time Ever I Saw Your Face" are all present, and are among the most popular tracks Lightfoot has issued during his long career. Featuring both acoustic and folk-rock recordings, this neatly bundles Lightfoot's early work into a listenable and fairly inexpensive package. —*Richie Unterberger*

Lightning Seeds

f. 1989, Liverpool, England
Pop-Rock
The wispy pop outfit the Lightning Seeds were essentially the solo project of noted producer Ian Broudie. Born August 4, 1958 in Liverpool, England, Broudie first emerged as a member of Big in Japan, a product of the same Liverpudlian post-punk scene which gave rise to Echo and the Bunnymen, the Teardrop Explodes and Icicle Works. After Big in Japan split in 1979, Broudie followed a brief tenure in the Original Mirrors by producing the first two Bunnymen LPs, *Crocodiles* and *Heaven Up Here*, as well as work by the Fall, Wah! and Frazier Chorus.

Seeking to return to performing, in 1982 Broudie teamed with Wild Swans vocalist Paul Simpson; under the name Care, the duo released a series of shimmering singles which pointed in the direction Broudie followed in the Lightning Seeds, a one-man band backed by pop luminaries and session players. After scoring an international hit with the lush single "Pure," the Lightning Seeds issued their debut LP *Cloudcuckooland* in 1989. Still, despite the record's success, Broudie again returned to production, helming albums for groups like the Primitives, Sleeper, Alison Moyet and the Frank & Walters.

In 1992, Broudie revived the Lightning Seeds guise for *Sense*, on which he made synth programmer Simon Rogers (formerly of the Fall) a full musical partner; for 1994's *Jollification*, he formed a touring band (comprising keyboardist Ali Kane, former Rain bassist Martin Campbell and ex-Icicle Works drummer Chris Sharrock) to play his first live shows since serving in the Original Mirrors over a decade ago. The British chart hits "Ready or Not" and "Three Lions on a Shirt" followed in 1996. —*Jason Ankeny*

● **Cloudcuckooland** / 1989 / MCA ✦✦✦✦
Bouncy pop by Ian Broudie, producer of such groups as the Fall and Echo & the Bunnymen. —*David Szatmary*

Pure / Mar. 23, 1990 / Virgin ✦✦✦✦
Pure is an 18-track UK-only collection, covering the Lightning Seeds' biggest hits as well as some of their lesser-known, though just as pleasing, songs. —*Chris Woodstra*

Sense / Feb. 18, 1992 / MCA ✦✦✦
There's a certain school of distinctly British pop music characterized by a reserved, dignified demeanor and pretty, fragile melodies. The Lightning Seeds is one exponent of the genre that also includes such

groups as Beautiful South and Trashcan Sinatras. The Seeds, mainly the one-man project of Liverpool artist-producer Ian Broudie, have more of a groove than their peers. Many of the songs tend to fall in the New Order camp, except that the vocals are more up-front than the rhythm tracks. —*Roch Parisien*

Jollification / Dec. 20, 1994 / Trauma/Interscope ♦♦♦

Dizzy Heights / 1996 / Epic ♦♦♦

Lil' Kim

b. , Brooklyn, NY
Hip Hop, East Coast Rap, Hardcore Rap
After making her presence known on Junior M.A.F.I.A.'s debut album *Conspiracy*, Lil' Kim launched a solo career in 1996 with the release of her first record, *Hard Core*. As the album's title implies, Lil' Kim was a rarity among female rappers—one that not only concentrated on edgy, hardcore rap, but also explicit sexuality, two territories that had long been the province of male rappers. Of course, Lil' Kim's near-pornographic sexuality and hard-edged rhythms made her an anomaly within hip-hop, but *Hard Core* proved that she was no novelty, as it garnered positive reviews and strong sales.

A native of Bedford-Stuyvesant, Brooklyn, Lil' Kim was raised by her parents until they split up when she was nine years old. Following their separation, she lived with her father, yet he threw her out of the house when she was a teenager. As a teen, she lived with her friends and, occasionally, on the streets. Eventually, she and her rhyming skills came to the attention of Biggie Smalls, who helped her cultivate her career. Smalls helped her become a member of the Junior M.A.F.I.A., and Lil' Kim was a key part of the group's hit debut single, "Player's Anthem." Lil' Kim also made a big impression on the remainder of the Junior M.A.F.I.A.'s 1995 debut album, *Conspiracy*.

Following the release of *Conspiracy*, Lil' Kim appeared on records by Mona Lisa, the Isley Brothers, Total, and Skin Deep. For her debut album, she worked with a variety of producers, including Sean "Puffy" Combs, High Class, Jermaine Dupri, and Pretige. The result, entitled *Hard Core*, was released in late 1996. Lil' Kim's marketing campaign for the album was quite provocative—she was dressed in a skimpy bikini and furs in the advertisements, as well as the album covers—but instead of resulting in a backlash, the album became a hit, debuting at No. 11 on the pop charts. The first single from the album, "No Time," a duet with Sean "Puffy" Combs, became a No. 1 rap single. —*Stephen Thomas Erlewine*

● **Hardcore** / Nov. 12, 1996 / Undeas/Big Beat ♦♦♦♦
After making her presence felt on Junior M.A.F.I.A.'s hit debut album, Lil' Kim broke out on her own, refashioning herself as a hardcore and defiantly sexy female rapper. Working with producers like Sean Combs and the Notorious B.I.G., Lil' Kim has developed a sleek but hard sound that is positively dripping with attitude and sex. When she slips into conventional, seductive R&B the record loses some steam, but her filthy, hard-driving tracks are stunning—it's hardcore in more than one sense of the word. —*Stephen Thomas Erlewine*

Liliput

f. 1978, Zurich, Switzerland, **db.** 1983
Alternative Pop-Rock, Post-Punk
During the punk rock era of the late '70s, there were three bands composed of women who made some of the best, most adventurous, most exhilarating, and most critically derided music of the time. Two were the English bands the Slits and the Raincoats, and the third band, from Switzerland, was Liliput. Fans of all three bands will argue ad infinitum as to who was the better. As far as I'm concerned, they were equals, and depending on what day you asked me, I might give you a different answer as to who was better, but one thing is for certain: Liliput was an amazing band that recorded amazing music, and comparing what they accomplished to that of another band is a useless intellectual exercise. Besides, it detracts from valuable listening time.

Formed in Zurich in 1978 by guitarist Marlene Marder and bassist/vocalist Klaudia Schiff, they began with the name Kleenex until the threat of a lawsuit by corporate giant Kimberly-Clark (who had copyrighted the name Kleenex) forced them to become Liliput in 1980. Recording for the great English indie label Rough Trade, the then-Kleenex produced jumpy, aggressive, clamorous punk-noise that featured Marder's scratchy, semi-melodic guitar and Schiff's yelping vocals. Not punk rock in the fast, loud, economical sense, Liliput were forging a different kind of punk, one that was gleefully anarchic, avant-garde, unrestrained, and suffused with a giddy, almost palpable sense of joy. Listening to this music now, one gets the sense that there was a near-rapturous enjoyment that went into these recordings. Their tenure at Rough Trade was short, as was their interest in exploring career options beyond Europe. (I may be wrong, but I don't believe they ever toured America, nor did they release any

music domestically.) By 1982, when they released their only LP, they seemed perfectly happy remaining in Switzerland, running the band as part of numerous other artistic projects (painting, writing, etc.) they pursued. By the end of 1983, Liliput had disbanded, and the music they had recorded quickly achieved legendary, but mostly unheard, status. As for the band, they seemed destined to be relegated to the status of feminist-inspired punk rock footnote. All of this changed in 1993, when the Swiss label Off Course released a double-disc, 46-track compilation of the entire recorded output of Kleenex/Liliput. The result was one of the great reissues of the decade. The exuberance and excitement of Liliput's breathtaking music can be enjoyed once again, and a band that was almost forgotten returns with some of the most artful, contemporary, truly alternative music to be recorded under the genre identifier of punk rock. Also, fans of riot grrrl rock take note: this was a tremendously influential band. Although they eschewed extreme confrontation, there is a compelling sense of self that imbues this music and lit the way for a new generation of female musicians. —*John Dougan*

● **Liliput** / 1982 / Rough Trade ♦♦♦♦
Little more needs to be said, other than that this is a tremendous, absolutely essential recording of feminist post-punk, loaded with scratchy, distorted guitars, elemental rhythms, and gleefully unhinged, screeching singing. The only way you can get it is to send $30 to Off Course Records, P.O. Box 241, CH-8025, Zurich, Switzerland. I suggest you do it immediately. —*John Dougan*

Bob Lind

b. Nov. 25, 1944, Baltimore, MD
Vocals / Singer-Songwriter, Pop, Folk-Rock
Bob Lind's "Elusive Butterfly" was one of the most successful one-shots of the mid-'60s folk-rock boom, reaching the Top Five in early 1966. He never came close to matching that early triumph, although other acts brought his songs to a wider audience with their covers of Lind compositions like "Cheryl's Going Home" (Blues Project), "Counting" (Marianne Faithfull), and "Mr. Zero" (Yardbirds' lead singer Keith Relf). The beauty of Jack Nitzsche's intricate production on Lind's two 1966 LPs, favoring acoustic guitars and pretty string arrangements, is admirable, but Lind himself hasn't worn that well. His songs are wordy and on the didactic side; his voice is nervous and lacks emotional range; his melodies are pretty, but not enormously so. —*Richie Unterberger*

● **The Best of Bob Lind: You Might Have Heard My Footsteps** / Jun. 29, 1993 / EMI ♦♦♦♦
This 25-song compilation includes the entire contents of his two 1966 LPs, as well as a 1967 single and two previously unreleased tracks. This period piece is highlighted by "Elusive Butterfly," the original versions of "Counting" and "Cheryl's Goin' Home," "Mr. Zero" (covered by Yardbird lead singer Keith Relf on a flop single), and the previously unreleased, gorgeous baroque rock song "English Afternoon." —*Richie Unterberger*

Lindisfarne

f. 1968, Newcastle-on-Tyne, England
Art-Rock/Progressive-Rock, Folk-Rock, Pub-Rock, British Folk
During the early '70s, Lindisfarne was one of the hottest folk-based rock bands in England. With a sound that mixed plaintive folk-like melodies, earthy but well-sung harmonies, and acoustic and electric textures, the group seemed poised for international success, but a series of unfortunate artistic decisions, followed by a split in their lineup, left them bereft of audience and success.

Singer/guitarist Alan Hull, guitarist Simon Cowe, mandolin player Ray Jackson, bassist/violinist Rod Clements, and drummer Ray Laidlaw all hailed from Newcastle-on-Tyne, England, and the surrounding area. At one point, they were known as Downtown Faction, eventually becoming Brethren. After becoming a popular act on the college circuit, in 1968 they discovered that an American group was already using the name Brethren, and rechristened themselves Lindisfarne, taking the name from an island off the coast of Northern England. The new name fit the times and the group's sound, which was evolving in the direction of folk-style music. The group signed to Charisma Records in 1970, and released their first album, *Nicely Out of Tune*, that same year. The album and single "Lady Eleanor" failed to chart, but the group's live shows grew in popularity. 1971's *Fog on the Tyne*—a collection of earthy, folk-type pub songs—marked their commercial breakthrough: after the single "Meet Me on the Corner" climbed to No. 1 on the charts, the album suddenly rose to the No. 1 spot. Within a matter of weeks, *Nicely Out of Tune* entered the charts for the first time and eventually hit No. 8; "Lady Eleanor," reissued in June of 1972, made it to No. 3. Lindisfarne became media darlings, and later in 1972, they released their third album, *Dingly Dell*. After the band had a falling-out with producer Bob Johnston over the LP, they re-mixed it themselves immediately prior to release; the result was a more mainstream hard rock sound than their previous two efforts. Unfortunately, this was not the move that the critics had wanted or expected; additionally, the songwriting was sub-par. Reviewers and journalists seemed bent on revenge for the group's failure to rise to the praise lavished on them over the previous year, and the record was universally savaged, although it yielded one modest hit, "All Fall Down."

Cowe, Laidlaw, and Clements exited the band in early 1973 and formed a new group called Jack the Lad. A live Lindisfarne album, featuring the original lineup and songs mostly off of the first three albums, was issued in 1973, but it was at best a holding action. Later that year, Hull and Jackson were back leading a new Lindisfarne lineup, featuring Ken Craddock on guitar, keyboards, and vocals, Charlie Harcourt on guitars, Tommy Duffy on bass and vocals, and Paul Nichols on drums. Their first album, *Roll On Ruby*, was a critical and commercial failure; Hull embarked on a solo recording career at around this same time, which seemed to draw away still more of Lindisfarne's original audience. The band switched to Warner Bros. for their next album, *Happy Daze*, but it fared no better. By 1977, Jack the Lad had called it quits and Cowe, Clements, and Laidlaw were back with Lindisfarne. Hull also recorded with Laidlaw and Craddock under the group name Radiator, releasing *Isn't It Strange*. Lindisfarne switched labels again to Mercury and debuted with a double live album, *Magic in the Air*. The band remained intact for two more long-players, 1978's *Back and Fourth* (which yielded a pair of modest hits in "Run for Home" and "Warm Feeling") and 1979's *The News*, all to little lasting commercial success. Still, they remained a reasonably popular concert attraction into the early '80s, and continued to record and reunite for concerts periodically in later years. —*Bruce Eder*

Nicely out of Tune / 1970 / Elektra ◆◆◆◆
Easily the best album the group ever recorded, *Nicely Out Of Tune* is one of the prettiest folk-rock albums of the late 1960s. If Lindisfarne had never recorded anything else, they'd be one of the most fondly remembered acts of their era just for this album. "Lady Eleanor" is a very pretty tune that manages to incorporate elegant mandolin over some heavy rock riffing. "Road To Kingdom Come" is closer in spirit to the group's usual pub-rock sound, a sing-along-type number with lots of really crunchy harmonica, mandolin, and fiddle, and a really catchy chorus—"Jackhammer Blues" is pretty nearly as good a rocker. But "Winter Song" is one of the gentlest, most haunting folk ballads of its period, almost too pretty to have come from a rock band, and "Alan In The River With Flowers" isn't far behind. The rest is in the same class and league, and as a bonus the CD contains two lost B-sides, "Knackers Yard Blues" and "Nothing But The Marvelous Is Beautiful"—they're not bad, either. —*Bruce Eder*

Fog on the Tyne / 1971 / Elektra ◆◆◆◆
The album that turned Lindisfarne into a chart-topping act, and made their tour of the US a foregone conclusion. This is an earthier album, a piece of urban English folk-rock with a gentle, easygoing feel very different from the first album. "Meet Me On The Corner" has one of the most delectable sing-along choruses of any rock song you'll ever hear. Additionally, the lyrics of this song, as well as those of "Together Forever" and "Fog On The Tyne," display a clarity, vivid imagery, and emotional subtlety just about worthy of Bob Dylan, and it is easy to see how "Meet Me On The Corner" could've reached the No. 4 spot. "January Song" is nearly as pretty as "Winter Song" on the first album. And the record is worth the price just for the instrumental break on "Fog on the Tyne." —*Bruce Eder*

Dingly Dell / 1972 / Elektra ◆◆◆
The record that more or less broke the spell of Lindisfarne's first two albums, but it isn't really that bad an album, just not as wildly inventive or accessible as its two predecessors. "All Fall Down" made the English charts, and it does sound rather like a leftover track from the previous album (though Ray Jackson's mandolin is really pretty here). "Don't Ask Me" is about the ballsiest rocker this version of the band ever cut, with some really high-powered guitar and a thunderous beat. Some of the rest just sounds a little lethargic next to the previous albums, but none of this should have been a career-ending move. —*Bruce Eder*

Lindisfarne Live / 1973 / Charisma ◆◆◆
Cut along the tour that preceded the breakup of the original group, this record features some fair performances by the band, though one surprise is the absence of "Lady Eleanor" and also the minimal presence of material off of *Nicely Out Of Tune*. Not that it's bad to have stuff off of the two subsequent albums, especially *Fog on the Tyne*. (out of print) —*Bruce Eder*

Roll on Ruby / 1973 / Elektra ◆◆
The reformed Lindisfarne, trying hard to pick up where the original quintet left off and definitely not succeeding. For completists only. —*Bruce Eder*

Finest Hour / 1975 / Charisma ◆◆◆◆
A 16-song best-of, marking the end of the group's Charisma Records era. The CD equivalent *The Best of Lindisfarne: 16 Classic Tracks* is readily available. —*Bruce Eder*

Back and Fourth / 1978 / Atco ◆◆◆
Something of a comeback for the group, highlighted by the hard-rocking "Run For Home," which was a hit. This album made the English charts as well, and reintroduced the group. —*Bruce Eder*

Sleepless Nights / 1982 / LMP ◆◆
The group's first recording for their own label, not as inspired as some of the intervening material. —*Bruce Eder*

Peel Sessions / 1988 / Dutch East India ◆◆◆◆
Long before MTV's Unplugged sessions, deejay John Peel and the BBC would get acts on the air strumming away on acoustic or low-amplification electric instruments. Lindisfarne made the appearance at which the four cuts here ("Poor Old Ireland," "Mandolin King," "Lady Eleanor," "Road to Kingdom Come") were broadcast on May 8, 1972, when the group was still at its peak. The two songs off *Dingly Dell* fare pretty well, but the earlier numbers really shine. The sound is excellent, with really sharp resolution on the strummed guitars, and it's only a pity there wasn't more recorded, though what is here is fine, especially "Lady Eleanor." —*Bruce Eder*

● **The Best of Lindisfarne** / 1989 / Virgin ◆◆◆◆
The history is a little sketchy, but this collection does distill down the best of the group's first three Charisma Records albums. The only problems are that *Nicely Out of Tune* and *Fog on the Tyne* should be in any fan's collection complete, and that later, post-Charisma hits like "Run For Home" are not here. This disc is a good introduction to the group, however, and an easy way for the neophyte to see if Lindisfarne is really for them. —*Bruce Eder*

Lindisfarne Live 1990 / Jul. 5, 1994 / Demon ◆◆◆
The compact disc version of the 1990 live concert actually works slightly better, as the group sounds better than they come off on screen, especially on "Anyway the Wind Blows," "Meet Me on the Corner," and "Lady Eleanor." That having been said, there are enough gaps in the repertory here (both of the rival live CDs currently available feature "Run for Home") to leave this last on the list for a live disc. —*Bruce Eder*

Caught in the Act / Oct. 13, 1994 / Castle ◆◆◆
Recorded (and videotaped) at Newcastle City Hall (where the group have played over 125 shows) in December of 1982, this somewhat uneven concert album caught Lindisfarne in pretty fair form at the tail end of a UK tour. Among the newer songs, "Ode To a Taxman" is a decent rocker, with crunchy guitars and a pretty catchy chorus. "Lady Eleanor" fares well, as does "Meet Me On The Corner," but nothing beats the explosive power of "Fog On The Tyne" as performed here, which has become to Lindisfarne (especially when playing to Newcastle fans) what "Bo Diddley" is to Bo Diddley. Hull's "Nights" has a pleasing classic rock sound, although most of the newer material (the exceptions are the Jackson/Harcourt "Warm Feeling" and Hull's Springsteen-like "Run For Home") pales next to the older stuff here. The audio is crisp and clean, capturing the harmonies and the different guitar (and mandolin) voices very well, and the mix puts the band very close. Until the live albums from Charisma and Mercury show up, this will have to do, and it makes a decent career best-of-substitute. —*Bruce Eder*

Another Fine Mess / 1995 / Grapevine ◆◆◆◆
The group succeeds on its fourth official try at a live album, recorded at Newcastle City Hall on July 2, 1995, 130 performances and 25 years to the day after their group's first performance there. The lineup this time out includes Alan Hull (lead vocals, acoustic guitars), Marty Craggs (lead vocals, saxes, flute, harmonica), Ray Laidlaw (drums), Rod Clements (lead guitar, slide guitar, mandolin, fiddle, vocals), Dave Denholm (guitars, vocals), and Ian Thomson (bass), and they're pretty tight all the way around. This is the only live album by the group to include "Lady Eleanor," "Fog On The Tyne," *and* "Meet Me on the Corner" *and* "Run for Home," and it also features other early songs like "All Fall Down" and "Road to Kingdom Come." This is a strong album, and the definite first choice for anyone seeking a live disc or a definitive hits collection by the band that includes "Run for Home." The sound is good, too, and overall it's worth the few extra dollars. —*Bruce Eder*

Little Anthony & the Imperials

b. 1958, Brooklyn, NY
Vocals / R&B, Doo Wop

Featuring the high-pitched vocals of Anthony Gourdine and a brace of solid material, Little Anthony & the Imperials had a much longer chart run than the majority of doo wop from the '50s. When the dust finally settled, the group clocked in with a total of ten entries in the

Hot 100 between 1958 and 1974, including "Tears on My Pillow," "Two People in the World," "Wishful Thinking," "Oh Yeah," "So Much," "Shimmy Shimmy Ko Ko Bop" (not to be confused with the similarly titled "Shimmy Shimmy Ko Ko Wop" by the El Capris), "When You Wish Upon a Star," "Going Out of My Head," "Better Use Your Head," and "Hurt So Bad."

Gourdine formed the group in the mid-'50s after his previous group, the Duponts, disbanded. Grabbing friends Clarence Collins, Ernest Wright, Tracy Lord, and Nat Rogers, the group was originally called the Chesters, but had their name changed to the Imperials by popular New York disc jockey Alan Freed. Gourdine's vocal similarities to the popular Frankie Lymon-inspired "kiddie group" sound, coupled with a tendency to chop up syllables and overstress lyrics, made theirs a style deceptively simple yet enduring. After revamping the group down to a quartet in 1964, the sound changed from doo wop to a harder, more uptown R&B sound, best exemplified on hits like "I'm on the Outside Looking In." Still touring and from all reports, *still* knockin' em dead into their fourth decade together as a group, for many lovers of the genre, Little Anthony & the Imperials are simply New York-styled doo wop at its smoothest and finest. —*Cub Koda*

● **The Best of Little Anthony & the Imperials** / Oct. 1989 / Rhino ✦✦✦✦

"Little" Anthony Gourdine's angst-ridden leads were ideal for tearjerkers and heartache ballads. Although this Brooklyn group began in the doo wop era, they were much more effective on soul songs, where group harmonies were low-key and Gourdine's voice was the major focus. This anthology includes "Hurt So Bad," "I'm on the Outside Looking In," and "Take Me Back," arguably their three finest hits, plus several others with equally theatrical vocals, but dissimilar chart performances. —*Ron Wynn*

The Best of Little Anthony & The Imperials [EMI] / May 28, 1996 / EMI ✦✦✦

Unlike the collection of the same name on Rhino, this focuses solely on their mid-to-late-'60s recordings for Veep and United Artists. That means you don't get any doo wop, but slickly arranged pop-soul that sometimes borders on easy listening, featuring string charts and Little Anthony's choked vocals (which could bring to mind an effeminate Johnny Mathis). The best and biggest of these cuts are also on the Rhino comp ("I'm on the Outside Looking In," "Goin' Out of My Head," "Hurt So Bad"), which gets the edge for its wider chronology. This is a satisfactory alternative, though, for those who prefer the Imperials' later phase, or want a more extensive sampler of their '60s stuff. —*Richie Unterberger*

Little Eva

b. Jun. 29, 1943, Bellhaven, NC
Vocals / Girl Group, Brill Building Pop

Little Eva Narcissus Boyd was a babysitter for Carole King and Gerry Goffin when the songwriting team was inspired to write "Locomotion," a song based on a dance that Eva would do around the house. Eva also got to sing on their demo, which impressed Don Kirshner enough to release it as it was. One of the greatest girl-group hits, "Locomotion," hit No. 1 in 1962; the follow-up, "Keep Your Hands Off My Baby," was also written by Goffin-King. Almost as good as her debut, it reached the Top 20, and was even covered by the Beatles on stage in their early days (though they never recorded it in the studio). Unfortunately, Eva was then pigeonholed as a dance-craze singer and given inferior material. She never again reached the soulful heights of her first two singles; "Let's Turkey Trot" (1963) was her only other Top 20 hit. —*Richie Unterberger*

● **The Best of Little Eva** / 1988 / Murray Hill ✦✦✦✦

Fifteen songs, most cut for the Dimension label between 1962 and 1964. Includes all the hits and some pleasant girl group flops in a more lightweight style than "Locomotion." —*Richie Unterberger*

The Loco-Motion / Feb. 27, 1996 / Rhino ✦✦✦

Some collectors will be glad to have some Little Eva available on CD domestically. At only ten cuts (and no liner notes), however, it's on the skimpy side, and "Let's Turkey Trot" is unexpectedly missing. The 15-song best-of on Murray Hill is considerably more extensive and well annotated (albeit getting harder to find). On the other hand, this Rhino comp does have seven songs not on the Murray Hill LP (including some obscure Goffin/King compositions), although some of these are covers of popular early '60s hits. —*Richie Unterberger*

Little Feat

f. 1969, Los Angeles, CA
Rock 'n' Roll, Blues-Rock, Southern Rock

Though they had all the trappings of a Southern-fried blues band, Little Feat were hardly conventional. Led by songwriter/guitarist Lowell George, Little Feat was a wildly eclectic band, bringing together strains of blues, R&B, country, and rock 'n' roll. The group was exceptionally gifted technically and their polished professionalism sat well with the slick sounds coming out of Southern California during the '80s. However, Little Feat were hardly slick—they had a surreal sensibility, as evidenced by George's idiosyncratic songwriting, which helped the band earn a cult following among critics and musicians. Though the band earned some success on album-oriented radio, the group was derailed after George's death in 1979. Little Feat re-formed in the late '80s, and while they were playing as well as ever, they lacked the skewed sensibility that made them cult favorites. Nevertheless, their albums and tours were successful, especially among American blues-rock fans.

However, Little Feat wasn't conceived as a straight-ahead blues-rock group. Its founding members, Lowell George (vocals, guitar, slide guitar) and Rob Estrada (bass), were veterans of Frank Zappa's Mothers of Invention. George had a long musical career before joining the Mothers. As a child, he and his brother Hampton performed a harmonica duet on television's *Ted Mack's Original Amateur Hour*. During high school, he learned how to play flute, which led to him appearing as an oboist and baritone saxophonist on several Frank Sinatra recording sessions. He formed the folk-rock group the Factory with drummer Richard Hayward in 1965. The Factory released on album on Uni Records before disbanding. Following the group's demise, George joined the Mothers of Invention where he met Estrada. Zappa convinced George to form his own band after hearing "Willin'," but the guitarist was reluctant to begin a band until he participated in a brief Standells reunion.

George and Estrada formed Little Feat in 1969 with Hayward and keyboardist Billy Payne. Neither its eponymous first album (1971) nor 1972's *Sailin' Shoes* were commercial successes, despite strong reviews. As a result, the group temporarily disbanded, with Estrada leaving music to become a computer programmer. When the group reconvened later in 1972, he was replaced by New Orleans musician Kenny Gradney. In its second incarnation, Little Feat also featured guitarist Paul Barrere and percussionist Sam Clayton, who gave the music a funkier feeling, as demonstrated by 1973's *Dixie Chicken*. The band toured heavily behind the record, building a strong following in the South and on the East Coast. Nevertheless, the group remained centered in Los Angeles, since the members did a lot of session work on the side.

Though the band was earning a cult following, several members of the group were growing frustrated by George's erratic behavior and increasing drug use. Following 1974's *Feats Don't Fail Me Now*, Barrere and Payne became the band's primary songwriters and they were primarily responsible for the jazzy fusions of 1975's *The Last Record Album*. Little Feat continued in that direction on *Time Loves A Hero* (1977), the double-live album *Waiting for Columbus* (1978), and *Down on the Farm* (1979). Frustrated with the band's increasingly improvisational and jazzy nature, George recorded a solo album, *Thanks I'll Eat It Here*, which was released in 1979. Following its release, George announced that Little Feat had broken up, and he embarked on a solo tour. Partway through the tour, he died of an apparent heart attack. *Down on the Farm* was released after his death, as was the rarities collection, *Hoy-Hoy!* (1981).

After spending seven years as sidemen, Payne, Barrere, Hayward, Gradney, and Clayton re-formed Little Feat in 1988, adding vocalist/guitarist Craig Fuller and guitarist Fred Tackett. The heavily-anticipated *Let It Roll* was released in 1988 to mixed reviews, but it went gold. The group's subsequent reunion albums—*Representing the Mambo* (1990), *Shake Me Up* (1991), *Ain't Had Enough Fun* (1995)—each sold progressively worse, but the band remained a popular concert attraction. —*Stephen Thomas Erlewine*

Little Feat / 1971 / Warner Brothers ✦✦✦

Debut album finds Lowell George's songwriting, singing, and playing style in place on his signature song, "Willin'," as well as "Truck Stop Girl" and "Crazy Captain Gunboat Willie." —*William Ruhlmann*

Sailin' Shoes / 1972 / Warner Brothers ✦✦✦✦

A near-peak of songwriting ("Easy to Slip," "Cold, Cold, Cold," "Sailin' Shoes") distinguishes this second album, on which the band finds a perfect second-line groove and Lowell George sings and plays with blues authority. —*William Ruhlmann*

★ **Dixie Chicken** / 1973 / Warner Brothers ✦✦✦✦✦

A reconfigured group adds greater depth to the percussion, along with a rhythm guitarist, who frees Lowell George to slide his way to heaven, and the songs—especially the title track, "Two Trains," and "Fat Man in the Bathtub"—are among George's best. —*William Ruhlmann*

Feats Don't Fail Me Now / 1974 / Warner Brothers ✦✦✦✦

Whereas earlier albums were carried by Lowell George, this one finds the band as a whole at a writing and performing peak, with Bill Payne and Paul Berrere especially standing out on such songs as

"Rock and Roll Doctor," "Oh Atlanta," and "Skin It Back." —*William Ruhlmann*

The Last Record Album / 1975 / Warner Brothers ✦✦✦
From this point on, Lowell George's role in Little Feat seems to have diminished, with the group's direction increasingly left in the capable, if less inspired hands, of Bill Payne and Paul Barrere. The album does, however, contain two excellent George originals in "Down Below the Borderline" and "Long Distance Love." —*William Ruhlmann*

Time Loves a Hero / 1977 / Warner Brothers ✦✦✦
Lowell George's gradual disappearance from his own group continued here, with the album containing only one of his solo compositions, "Rocket in My Pocket," which wasn't one of his best. The title track and "Hi Roller," among other tracks, show Paul Barrere and Bill Payne to be talented substitutes, but this album, the original group's final studio effort, does not show them at their best. —*William Ruhlmann*

Waiting for Columbus / 1978 / Warner Brothers ✦✦✦✦
Excellent double-disc live album. —*William Ruhlmann*

Down on the Farm / 1979 / Warner Brothers ✦✦
A scraped-together, post-breakup, contractual obligation album, for charitable fans only. —*William Ruhlmann*

Hoy-Hoy / 1981 / Warner Brothers ✦✦✦✦
Compilation of best songs and odds and ends makes a good wrap-up to the Lowell George years. —*William Ruhlmann*

Let It Roll / Jul. 1988 / Warner Brothers ✦✦✦

Representing the Mambo / 1989 / Warner Brothers ✦✦
Having demonstrated on *Let It Roll* that they could produce an effective Little Feat soundalike record, the reconstituted band should have stopped while they were ahead. This follow-up shows a decline in songwriting, making the absence of Lowell George unmistakably apparent. —*William Ruhlmann*

Shake Me Up / Sep. 24, 1991 / Morgan Creek ✦✦
With this pedestrian third reunion album, Little Feat should have lost the right to use its noble name. Little of the band's original spark remained. —*William Ruhlmann*

Ain't Had Enough Fun / Apr. 25, 1995 / Zoo ✦✦✦
The members of the group that has the legal right to call itself "Little Feat" perhaps are to be complimented for their realization, after three albums, that having Craig Fuller imitate the voice of the band's deceased founder, Lowell George, was ethically suspect. Or maybe they didn't realize; this album's liner notes say only that "mister fuller decided that the road life was not for him." In any case, the surviving "featsters" have cast against type, recruiting one Shaun Murphy, who can't imitate George but certainly can imitate long-time Feat booster Bonnie Raitt. The addition of a female voice allows for greater variety in lyric-writing and some entertaining call-and-response singing; however, and more importantly, it begins to free the group from the ghost of Lowell George. The featsters locate themselves more than ever in the mythology of New Orleans, alternating second-line rhythms with John Lee Hooker boogie. One may still wish they had found another name to distinguish themselves from George's group, but *Ain't Had Enough Fun* is a worthy addition to their catalog on its own terms. —*William Ruhlmann*

Live from Neon Park / Jun. 18, 1996 / Zoo ✦✦✦
Live from Neon Park is an exhaustive double-disc live set recorded on the tour supporting *Ain't Had Enough Fun*, the first Little Feat album that featured vocalist Shaun Murphy. The double-disc features all of the band's best-known material, from "Dixie Chicken" to "Let It Roll." The Feat have always been one of the best live rootsy rock bands, so they naturally give inspired performances, even if they occasionally sound like they've performed these songs one too many times. Dedicated Little Feat fans will find this to be an entertaining memento of the latter-day edition of the band. —*Thom Owens*

Little Richard (Richard Wayne Penniman)

b. Dec. 5, 1935, Macon, GA
Piano, Vocals / R&B, Rock 'n' Roll, New Orleans R&B
Little Richard may or may not have been "the king of rock 'n' roll," as he eagerly proclaims to this day. But of all the major rock 'n' rollers of the 1950s, he was certainly the most flamboyant. Merging the fire of gospel with New Orleans R&B, he pounded the piano and wailed with gleeful abandon, brandishing a six-inch pompadour and mascara that were downright outlandish for the time—and more than a little threatening. Although he was only a hitmaker for a couple of years or so, his influence upon both the soul and British Invasion stars of the 1960s was vast, and he remains one of the yardsticks by which sheer rock 'n' roll outrageousness is measured. Heavily steeped in gospel music while growing up in Georgia, when

Little Richard began recording in the early '50s, he played unexceptional jump blues/R&B that owed a lot to his early inspirations Billy Wright and Roy Brown. In 1955, at Lloyd Price's suggestion, Richard sent a demo tape to Specialty Records, who were impressed enough to sign him and arrange a session for him in New Orleans. That session, however, didn't get off the ground until Richard began fooling around with a slightly obscene ditty during a break. With slightly cleaned-up lyrics, "Tutti Frutti" was the record that gave birth to Little Richard as we know him—the ecstatic trilling "woo!," the furious piano playing, the sax-driven, pedal-to-the-metal rhythm section. It was also his first hit, although, ridiculous as it now seems, Pat Boone's cover version outdid Richard's on the hit parade.

Pat Boone would also try to cover Richard's next hit, "Long Tall Sally," but by that time it was evident that audiences Black *and* white much preferred the real deal. In 1956 and 1957, Richard reeled off a string of classic hits—"Long Tall Sally," "Slippin' and Slidin'," "Jenny, Jenny," "Keep a Knockin'," "Good Golly, Miss Molly," "The Girl Can't Help It"—that remain the foundation of his fame. While Richard's inimitable mania was the key to his best records, he also owed a lot of his success to the gutsy playing of ace New Orleans session players like Lee Allen (tenor sax), Alvin Tyler (baritone sax), and especially Earl Palmer (drummer), who usually accompanied the singer in both New Orleans and Los Angeles studios. Richard's unforgettable appearances in early rock 'n' roll movies, especially *The Girl Can't Help It*, also did a lot to spread the rock 'n' roll gospel to the masses.

Little Richard was at the height of his commercial and artistic powers when he suddenly quit the business during an Australian tour in late 1957, enrolling in a bible college in Alabama shortly after returning to the States. Richard had actually been feeling the call of religion for a while before his announcement, but it was nonetheless a shock to both his fans and the industry. Specialty drew on unreleased sessions for a few more hard-rocking singles in the late '50s, but Richard virtually vanished from the public eye for a few years. When he did return to recording, it was as a gospel singer, cutting a few little-heard sacred sides for End, Mercury, and Atlantic in early '60s.

By 1962, though, Richard had returned to rock 'n' roll, touring Britain to an enthusiastic reception. Among the groups that supported him on those jaunts were the Rolling Stones and the Beatles, whose vocals (Paul McCartney's especially) took a lot of inspiration from Richard's. In 1964, the Beatles cut a knockout version of "Long Tall Sally," with McCartney on lead, that may have even outdone the original. It's been speculated that the success of the Beatles and other British Invaders who idolized Richard finally prompted the singer into making a full-scale comeback, as an unapologetic rock 'n' roller. Hooking up with Specialty once again, he had a small hit in 1964 with "Bama Lama Bama Loo." These and other sides were respectable efforts in the mold of his classic '50s sides, but tastes had changed too much for Little Richard to climb the charts again. He spent the rest of the '60s in a continual unsuccessful comeback, recording for Vee-Jay (accompanied on some sides by Jimi Hendrix, who was briefly in Richard's band), OKeh, and Modern (for whom he even tried recording in Memphis with Stax session musicians).

It was the rock 'n' roll revival of the late '60s and early '70s, though, that really saved Richard's career, enabling him to play on the nostalgia circuit with great success (though he had one last small hit, "Freedom Blues," in 1970). Constant entertaining appearances on television talk shows seemed to ensure his continuing success as a living legend, yet by the late '70s he'd returned to the church again. Somewhat predictably, he'd eased back into rock and show business by the mid-'80s. Since then, he's maintained his profile with a role in *Down and Out in Beverly Hills*, and guest appearances on soundtracks, compilations, and children's rock records. At this point it's safe to assume that he never will get that much-hungered-for comeback hit, but he remains one of rock 'n' roll's most colorful icons, still capable of turning on the charm and charisma in his infrequent appearances in the limelight. —*Richie Unterberger*

★ **18 Greatest Hits** / 1985 / Rhino ✦✦✦✦✦
18 Greatest Hits is the definitive single-disc collection of Little Richard's Specialty singles, especially for listeners who only want the hits. Every one of Richard's biggest hits—"Tutti Frutti," "Long Tall Sally," "Slippin' and Slidin'," "Rip It Up," "Ready Teddy," "The Girl Can't Help It," "Lucille," "Send Me Some Lovin'," "Keep A-Knockin'," "Good Golly Miss Molly"—plus singles like "Heeby-Jeebies," "She's Got It," "Ooh! My Soul," "Miss Ann," "Kansas City/Hey Hey Hey," and "Bama Lama Bama Loo" that were bigger hits on the R&B charts than the pop charts. All of the singles are presented in chronological order and the disc simply rips it up from beginning to end. It's a definitive collection. —*Stephen Thomas Erlewine*

The Specialty Box Set / 1989 / Specialty ✦✦✦✦
Dig it—a collection of all 73 songs that Little Richard cut for Specialty Records from 1955 through 1959, including early working versions of hits including "Long Tall Sally" and "Slippin' and Slidin,'" may seem like overkill to the casual listener, but if you're thinking of buying this three-CD box, chances are you're not a casual listener. And if you're not thinking about it, then you should be. A product of British-based Ace Records, this set covers only four years in Little Richard's career, but manages to sum up virtually everything you need to know about him (his earlier sides, available on Bear Family, are an interesting appendix, but of his later stuff, only the early—and mid-'60s material, with Jimi Hendrix on guitar, hold any significance, mostly as a curiosity). Not only does the music make you want to get up and dance, but the notes—spread out on a lavishly illustrated booklet and the individual jewel boxes—tell the whole story of Specialty Records and the people behind it, including Art Rupe, Bumps Blackwell, Dave Bartholomew, and, of course, Richard Penniman himself. The session information alone could keep owners busy for a week. The sound is nothing less than breathtaking, loud and raunchy but razor sharp, and the price of this set—about $42 retail—makes it competitive with other Little Richard single-disc sets as well as more attractive than the price of boxes devoted to Elvis Presley and Chuck Berry. The only complaint: why couldn't the producers list the songs on the individual jewel boxes? —*Bruce Eder*

The Formative Years 1951-53 / Jul. 1989 / Bear Family ✦✦✦✦
Early Richard, pre-"Tutti Frutti." —*Cub Koda*

★ **The Georgia Peach** / Aug. 5, 1991 / Specialty ✦✦✦✦✦
Perhaps the greatest of Little Richard's greatest hits compilations, the 25-track *Georgia Peach* features all of his biggest hits in chronological order, as well as terrific singles that never were as big as "Tutti Frutti" and "Good Golly Miss Molly." On top of the sublime song selection and sound, the liner notes by compiler Billy Vera are splendid and insightful. —*Stephen Thomas Erlewine*

Shag on Down by the Union Hall / Feb. 13, 1996 / Specialty ✦✦✦✦
For those who want more classic Little Richard than a greatest-hits collection but aren't devoted enough to spring for the expensive box sets, this is an excellent anthology of 24 of his best lesser-known tracks. Most of it dates from his classic era at Specialty (1955-57), with alternate takes of a lot of his hits and some decent B-sides; there are also a few songs that he cut for the label during his 1964 comeback, including the minor hit "Bama Lama Bama Loo." —*Richie Unterberger*

Little River Band

f. Mar. 1975, Melbourne, Australia
Pop-Rock, Soft Rock
Little River Band (formed 1975) enjoyed an impressive string of hits during the late '70s and early '80s with their rather mellow harmony-laden MOR pop. The original lineup included lead singer Glenn Shurrock; guitarists Rick Furmoru, Beeb Birtles, and Graham Goble; Rugo McLachlan on bass; and Derek Pellicci on drums. Later members included David Briggs (guitar), George McArdle (bass), and lead singer John Faraham. —*Rick Clark & Larry Lapka*

● **Greatest Hits** / 1982 / Capitol ✦✦✦✦
All of their best are included—"Reminiscing," "Lady," "Lonesome Loser," "Cool Change," "The Night Owls," and "Take It Easy on Me.". —*Larry Lapka*

Reminiscing: The 20th Anniversary Collection / 1995 / Rhino ✦✦✦✦

Little Willie John (William Edgar john)

b. Nov. 15, 1937, Cullendale, AK, d. May 26, 1968, Walla Walla Prison, WA
Vocals / Soul, R&B
He's never received the accolades given to the likes of Sam Cooke, Clyde McPhatter, and James Brown, but Little Willie John ranks as one of R&B's most influential performers. His muscular high timbre and enormous technical and emotional range belied his early age (his first hit came when he was 18), but his mid-'50s work for Syd Nathan's King label would play a great part in the way soul music would sound. Everyone from Cooke, McPhatter, and Brown to Jackie Wilson, B.B. King, and Al Green has acknowledged his debt to this most overlooked of rock and soul pioneers. His debut recording, a smoking version of Titus Turner's "All around the World" from 1955, set the pattern for a remarkable string of hits: "Need Your Love So Bad," "Suffering with the Blues," "Fever," "Let Them Talk," and his last, "Sleep," from 1961. His version of "Fever" was copied note for note by Peggy Lee and Elvis Presley, both of whom had bigger hits with it; John's version, however, remains definitive. His second hit,

"Need Your Love So Bad," contains one of the most intimate, tear-jerking vocals ever caught on tape.

John had a volatile temper, fueled by a taste for liquor and an insecurity regarding his slight height (5 ft 4 in). He was known to pack a gun and knife; in 1964, he stabbed a man and was sent to the Washington State penitentiary, where he died of pneumonia in 1968. James Brown recorded a tribute album to John that year, and his material has been recorded by scores of artists from the Beatles to Fleetwood Mac to the Blasters. Nevertheless, Little Willie John remains a stranger to most listeners and has never received the respect his talent deserves.

Little Willie John was one of the first artists featured in Rhino's King reissues series. *Fever* was issued late in 1993, and the single-disc, 20-track anthology included such John releases as "Need Your Love So Bad," "Suffering with the Blues," and the title cut. —*John Floyd*

Live

f. 1988, York, PA
Alternative Pop-Rock, Post-Grunge
Live rose to chart success on the strength of its anthemic music and idealistic, overtly spiritual songwriting, two hallmarks that earned the group frequent comparisons to U2. Live first formed in the early '80s in their hometown of York, Pennsylvania, when future members Chad Taylor (guitar), Patrick Dahlheimer (bass), and Chad Gracey (drums) began playing together under the name First Aid while attending middle school. After losing an area talent contest, they decided to enlist singer Ed Kowalczyk, and as a foursome the group played under a series of names before settling on Public Affection.

After earning a rabid local following, in 1989 Public Affection released a cassette, *The Death of a Dictionary,* on their own Action Front label. After graduating to CBGB and other famed New York clubs, they earned a demo deal with Giant Records, which proved unsuccessful; the completed demo earned them a deal with Radioactive, however, and before drawing their new name out of a hat, Live recruited Talking Head Jerry Harrison to produce their 1991 debut, *Mental Jewelry.* A collection of songs based on the writings of Indian philosopher Jiddu Krishnamurti, the record made Live one of the key players in the post-Nirvana alternative music scene thanks to singles like "Operation Spirit (The Tyranny of Tradition)" and "Pain Lies on the Riverside."

Three years later, Live returned with the muscular *Throwing Copper,* which lingered a number of months on the charts before pushing the group into the rock mainstream; after a series of popular singles like "Selling the Drama" and "I Alone," the album's slow build climaxed with the funereal "Lightning Crashes," which propelled the album to the top of the charts and paved the way for the hits "White, Discussion" and "All Over You." *Secret Samadhi,* the third Live LP, followed in early 1997. —*Jason Ankeny*

Mental Jewelry / Dec. 31, 1991 / Radioactive ✦✦✦✦
Live's debut album was an impressive set of righteous, hard-driving alternative rock; *Mental Jewelry* was in the vein of such college-radio favorites as U2, but was more vulnerable and less sanctimonious. —*Stephen Thomas Erlewine*

● **Throwing Copper** / Apr. 19, 1994 / Radioactive ✦✦✦✦
Not only did Live's songwriting improve on their second album, *Throwing Copper,* but their sound was much stronger; their hooks were powerful and memorable, and their melodies were carefully crafted and catchy. The result was a major crossover hit, thanks to the singles "Selling the Drama," "I Alone," and "Lightning Crashes." —*Stephen Thomas Erlewine*

Secret Samadhi / Feb. 18, 1997 / Radioactive ✦✦✦
Throwing Copper made Live stars, but it didn't necessarily earn them respect. Evidently, the band thought that the problem lay with Jerry Harrison's crisp, commercial production, so they've hired Jay Healey as a co-producer and set out to make a messy, hard-edged visionary statement. Unfortunately, *Secret Samadhi* fails like most self-conscious grand statements. Borrowing heavily from Jimmy Page's bag of tricks, Live spikes *Secret Samadhi* with Eastern-tinged strings, sitars, and powerful, overdubbed guitars. However, Ed Kowalczyk's lyrics and singing remain indebted to early U2—he wants to say something big in a big way. The two approaches sit together uncomfortably, especially since Live's spirituality is ill-defined and the songs lack hooks. "Lakini's Juice" is propelled by a slide guitar riff out of *Physical Graffiti,* but there isn't a vocal melody, and that's symptomatic of the album's failure. While the scope of Live's ambition is admirable, the music falls flat in execution, especially when compared to the clear-headed, earnest, arena-oriented alterna-rock of *Throwing Copper.* —*Stephen Thomas Erlewine*

The Lively Ones

f. California
Surf

One of the best of the many instrumental surf bands working the Southern Californian region in 1963, the Lively Ones' recordings were built around storming, reverb-drenched Fender guitars, embellished by occasional raunchy sax breaks. Originality was not the Lively Ones' forte: over a period of about 12 months, they ground out about five albums, filled out with many covers or retitled numbers based on other rock and R&B compositions. They had a couple of hits in the L.A. area in 1963 ("Surf Rider" and "Rik-A-Tik"), but their best moment was probably "Goofy Foot," whose staccato gunfire of riffs deservedly propelled the track onto several modern best-of-surf anthologies. They ranged far and wide for source material, giving the surf treatment to "Telstar," "Exodus," "Rawhide," and Cole Porter's "Night and Day." Even the overdone standards are arranged and executed with panache. One best-of compilation is all you need, but anyone who likes Dick Dale will dig the Lively Ones' similar sleek arrangements and prototypically twangy, classy surf guitar leads. —*Richie Unterberger*

Surf Rider / 1963 / Del Fi ✦✦✦
Decent surf LP, even if it does often sound like a second-tier Dick Dale (indeed, a few of the songs are Dick Dale covers). Eight of the 12 tracks, are also available on Del-Fi's 24-song *Best of the Lively Ones*, which is the recommended alternative. —*Richie Unterberger*

Bugalu Party / 1967 / MGM ✦✦
The Lively Ones otherwise were a surf band (except for another group called the Lively Ones on Word Records). *Bugalu Party* is never terrible, but neither is it ever exciting. It should be considered for the boogaloo (New York Latin soul of the late 1960s) completist only. There is none of the guitar flamboyancy of the surf records. —*Tony Wilds*

● **Hang Five!!! The Best of the Lively Ones** / Jan. 17, 1995 / Del Fi ✦✦✦✦
A well-chosen 24-song retrospective, with six pages of informative liner notes by surf authority Domenic Priore. Includes "Goofy Foot," "Surf Rider," "Rik-A-Tik," and lots of other highlights from their Del-Fi releases, as well as a rare single they did for Smash. —*Richie Unterberger*

Living Colour

f. 1984, New York City, NY
Hard Rock, Heavy Metal

All-Black metal band comprising bandleader/guitarist Vernon Reid (a co-founder of New York City's Black Rock Coalition), singer Corey Glover, bassist Muzz Skillings, and drummer William Calhoun. Reid originally formed the band in 1984 as a trio. Mick Jagger was an early fan and helped them secure a deal with Epic. Living Colour's brand of metal also includes elements of jazz and funk, plus Reid's messy-but-lightning-fast guitar solos; the band drew praise from critics for its genre-straddling hybrid and political lyrics. Their debut album, *Vivid*, was a Top Ten smash. Skillings left the band in 1992 and was replaced by Doug Wimbish. Living Colour disbanded early in 1995. —*Steve Huey*

Vivid / 1988 / Epic ✦✦✦✦
Major record companies tended to stereotype Black artists as urban contemporary singers or rappers. But Living Colour refused to be pigeonholed, and excelled by sticking to its guns. Although *Vivid* can be described as heavy metal or hard rock, the album is far removed from the headbanger recordings that were popular at the time. Angrily sociopolitical, LC boldly and fearlessly questions the impact charismatic politicians can have ("Cult of Personality"), attacks heartless landlords ("Open Letter (To a Landlord)") and questions life in the fast lane ("Desperate People"). When the album went gold, the record-company executives who turned Living Colour away were sent an important message: a sense of adventure and commercial success aren't mutually exclusive. —*Alex Henderson*

Time's Up / Aug. 1990 / Epic ✦✦✦
Though it falls short of *Vivid*'s excellence, *Time's Up* is an enjoyable and ambitious, if a bit uneven, sophomore effort, boasting guests ranging from Little Richard to Maceo Parker to rappers Queen Latifah and Doug E. Fresh. Lyrically, the hard rock-metal unit is still uncompromising, and can be quite thought-provoking at times. "Information Overload" seriously questions the impact technology is having on people's lives, while "This Is Your Life" encourages listeners to make the most of their lives, as tough and disappointing as they may be. And LC takes quite a few chances musically as well, incorporating elements of jazz, rap, and African pop. The least coherent song here is the very talked-about "Elvis Is Dead," which decries tabloid and trash journalism's unending obsession with Elvis Presley,

but comes across as exploitative itself. Nonetheless, this CD's strengths by far outweigh its weaknesses. While *Vivid* would be a better introduction to Living Colour, there's a lot to admire on this album. —*Alex Henderson*

Biscuits / Jul. 16, 1991 / Epic ✦✦✦
A generally impressive assortment of rarities, *Biscuits* will be of interest primarily to more hardcore Living Colour devotees rather than casual listeners. Highlights of this diverse EP range from a rock-funk cover of James Brown's "Talkin' Loud and Sayin' Nothing'" to a soulful reggae-influenced remake of Jimi Hendrix's "Burning of the Midnight Lamp" to invigorating live versions of "Desperate People" and "Memories Can't Wait." Al Green's "Love and Happiness" has seldom been transformed into a rock song, but that's exactly what happens here—and with likable results. But as much as *Biscuits* has going for it, those new to LC should start out with *Vivid*. —*Alex Henderson*

Stain / Mar. 2, 1993 / Epic ✦✦✦
With the addition of new bassist Doug Wimbish, Living Colour turns in a harder-edged effort with *Stain*, a record driven more by the shattering metal-jazz fusion riffs of Vernon Reid than any of their other albums. While the sheer sonic force of the album is impressive, the songs don't match the power of the music; nevertheless, the music is so strong that it usually overshadows the inadequate songwriting. —*Stephen Thomas Erlewine*

● **Pride** / Nov. 14, 1995 / Epic ✦✦✦✦
After three albums, Living Colour disbanded in 1995, releasing a retrospective collection called *Pride*. Featuring a total of 17 tracks, including four previously unreleased songs, the album includes every one of the band's biggest hits and best songs. From "Cult of Personality" to "Type," all of the band's best-known moments are present, making it not only the perfect disc for casual fans, but also their most consistent album. —*Stephen Thomas Erlewine*

LL Cool J (James Smith)

b. Aug. 16, 1968, Queens, NY
Vocals / Hip Hop, East Coast Rap, Crossover Rap

Hip-hop is notorious for short-lived careers, but LL Cool J is the inevitable exception that proves the rule. Releasing his first single "I Can't Live Without My Radio" in 1985 when he was just 19 years old, LL Cool J initially was a hard-hitting, street-wise B-Boy with spare beats and ballistic rhymes. He quickly developed an alternate style, a romantic—and occasionally sappy—lover's rap epitomized by his mainstream breakthrough single, "I Need Love." LL's first two albums, *Radio* and *Bigger and Deffer*, made him a star, but he strived for pop stardom a little too much on 1989's *Walking With A Panther*. By 1990, his audience had declined somewhat, since his ballads and party raps were the opposite of the chaotic, edgy political hip-hop of Public Enemy or the gangsta rap of N.W.A., but he shot back to the top of the charts with *Mama Said Knock You Out*, which established him as one of hip-hop's genuine superstars. By the mid-'90s, he had starred in his own television sitcom, *In the House*, appeared in several films, and racked up two of his biggest singles with "Hey Lover" and "Doin' It." In short, he had proven that rappers could have long-term careers.

Of course, that didn't seem likely when he came storming out of Queens, New York when he was 16 years old. LL Cool J (b. James Todd Smith; his stage name is an acronym of "Ladies Love Cool James") had already been rapping since the age of nine. Two years later, his grandfather—he had been living with his grandparents since his parents divorced when he was four—gave him a DJ system and he began making tapes at home. Eventually, he sent these demo tapes to record companies, attracting the interest of Def Jam, a fledgling label run by New York University students Russell Simmons and Rick Rubin. Def Jam signed LL Cool J and released his debut single, "I Need A Beat," as their first single in 1984. The record sold over 100,000 copies, establishing both the label and the rapper.

LL dropped out of high school and recorded his debut album, *Radio*. Released in 1985, *Radio* was a major hit and it earned considerable praise for how it shaped raps into recognizable pop song structures. On the strength of "I Can't Live Without My Radio" and "Rock the Bells," the album went platinum in 1986. The following year, his second album *Bigger and Deffer* shot to No. 1 due to the ballad "I Need Love," which became one of the first pop-rap crossover hits.

LL Cool J's knack for making hip-hop as accessible as pop was one of his greatest talents, yet it was also a weakness, since it opened him up to accusations of him being a sellout. Taken from the *Less Than Zero* soundtrack, 1988's "Goin' Back to Cali" walked the line with ease, but 1989's *Walking With A Panther* was not greeted warmly by most hip-hop fans. Although it was a Top Ten hit and spawned the gold single "I'm That Type of Guy," the album was perceived as a pop sellout effort, and on a supporting concert at the Apollo, he was booed. LL Cool J didn't take the criticism lying down—he struck back with 1990's *Mama Said Knock You Out*, the hardest record he ever made. LL supported the album with a legendary, live acoustic performance on *MTV Unplugged*, and on the strength of the Top Ten R&B singles "The Boomin' System" and "Around the Way Girl" (No. 1, pop) as well as the hit title track, *Mama Said Knock You Out* became his biggest-selling album, establishing him as a pop star in addition to a rap superstar. He soon landed roles in the films *The Hard Way* (1991) and *Toys*, and he also performed at Bill Clinton's Presidential Inauguration in 1993. *Mama Said Knock You Out* kept him so busy that he didn't deliver the follow-up, *14 Shots to the Dome*, until the spring of 1993. Boasting a harder, gangsta-rap edge, *14 Shots* initially sold well, debuting in the Top Ten, but it was an unfocused effort that generated no significant hit singles. Consequently, it stalled at gold status and hurt his reputation considerably. Following the failure of *14 Shots to the Dome*, LL Cool J began starring in the NBC sitcom *In the House*. He returned to recording in 1995, releasing *Mr. Smith* toward the end of the year. Unexpectedly, *Mr. Smith* became a huge hit, going double platinum and launching two of his biggest hits with the Boyz II Men duet "Hey Lover" and "Doin' It." At the end of 1996, he released the greatest hits album, *All World*. —*Stephen Thomas Erlewine*

☆ **Radio** / 1985 / Def Jam/Columbia ✦✦✦✦✦
LL Cool J's debut, produced by Rick Rubin, is a brilliant mix of hardcore street anthems ("I Can't Live Without My Radio," "Rock the Bells") and updated twists on the dozens ("That's a Lie"), with a couple of ballads thrown in. —*John Floyd*

Bigger and Deffer / 1987 / Def Jam/Columbia ✦✦
On his second album, LL Cool J's ego goes to his head, resulting in a weak album of mild beats and inflated bragging, which is only partially saved by his first successful ballad, the syrupy "I Need Love." —*Stephen Thomas Erlewine*

Walking with a Panther / 1989 / Def Jam/Columbia ✦✦✦✦
A sprawling follow-up to his stinko second album, it's his most ambitious. LL Cool J not only regroups the strengths that made his debut a winner, but shows a musical expansion of his art that bodes well for the future. Includes "I'm That Type of Guy," "Going Back to Cali," and "Big Ole Butt." —*John Floyd*

Mama Said Knock You Out / Aug. 1990 / Def Jam/Columbia ✦✦✦✦
Most of the "Second Generation" rappers who emerged in the mid-'80s—including Run-D.M.C., Whodini, and the Fat Boys—had seen their popularity decrease considerably by the end of the decade. But LL Cool J has enjoyed greater longevity than most rappers, and was still going strong in 1990. With *Mama Said Knock You Out*, LL kept the momentum going thanks to such captivating hits as the erotic "Jingling Baby," the anthemic "The Boomin' System," and "Around the Way Girl," LL's R&B-flavored ode to the ladies of the hood. On "Illegal Search," he candidly addresses the issue of police excesses without stereotyping law enforcement or being unnecessarily inflammatory. Still exhibiting considerable technique, he tends to overdo it with boasting lyrics—which can wear thin quickly. Even so, *Mama* is a generally enjoyable (though not outstanding) album that has more pluses than minuses. —*Alex Henderson*

14 Shots to the Dome / 1993 / Def Jam/Columbia ✦✦
It's not the tour de force of *Mama Said Knock You Out*, but *14 Shots to the Dome* is a solid effort finding LL Cool J maturing gracefully and strongly, without selling out. *14 Shots* may not have sold as well as *Mama* either, but at least half of the album ranks with his best work. —*Stephen Thomas Erlewine*

Mr. Smith / Nov. 1995 / Def Jam ✦✦✦
On the strength of the slow-burning Boyz II Men duet "Hey Lover," LL Cool J returned to the top of the charts with *Mr. Smith*, meaning the album is somewhat of a comeback for the veteran rapper. LL Cool J's skills had never deserted him, but his previous album, *14 Shots to the Dome*, was a exercise in hardcore that worked only in fits and spurts. There are a couple of hard moments on *Mr. Smith*, but the album is at its most successful when he concentrates on his seductive, romantic side. LL has gotten a bit dirtier since the teenage days of "I Need Love," but he never steps over into the explicit, lewd come-ons of R. Kelly, preferring to suggest everything with a series of double entendres, metaphors, and analogies. *Mr. Smith* isn't a perfect record—there are too many slack moments for it to qualify as one of his best—but it proves that LL Cool J remains vital a decade after his debut. —*Stephen Thomas Erlewine*

★ **All World: Greatest Hits** / Nov. 5, 1996 / Def Jam ✦✦✦✦✦
All World: Greatest Hits is an excellent compilation of LL Cool J's greatest hits, featuring 16 of his biggest and best singles, including "I Can't Live Without My Radio," "Rock the Bells," "I'm Bad," "I Need Love," "Going Back to Cali," "I'm That Type of Guy," "Jingling Baby," "The Boomin' System," "Mama Said Knock You Out," "Around the Way Girl" and "Hey Lover." It's a definitive retrospective of one of the greatest rappers to ever record and if you doubt that statement's true, just take a listen to this collection. —*Stephen Thomas Erlewine*

Locust

b. London, England
Ambient, Experimental
Locust's Mark Van Hoen occupies the shadier, more melancholic side of contemporary ambient, assembling records of unmistakable beauty out of shards of dark, somewhat foreboding textures and arrangements. A London native active in the film and commercial music business before concentrating full-time on recording for release, Van Hoen has produced a string of highly thought-of releases for the R&S subsidiary Apollo in a relatively short period of time. He's quoted Steve Reich, David Sylvian, Kraftwerk, and Brian Eno as early influences, but more recently has been attempting to pursue paths of creative conception opened up by John Coltrane and Karlheinz Stockhausen. Although earlier releases focused on sprawling, mostly beatless experimental soundscapes, his more recent work has incorporated elements of breakbeat styles such as trip-hop and jungle—mostly in terms of production techniques, as opposed to aesthetic qualities, and with decidedly Locust flair. *Truth Is Born of Arguments* was the first release of this sort, and included heavy, distorted percussion and complex, looping polyrhythms similar to (although much more sluggish than) those found in drum'n'bass.

Not always the ambient misanthrope, Van Hoen splits his creative activity between Locust and a pair of ongoing collaborative ventures: Autocreation (techno) and Involution (post-techno experimental electronic), the latter with Seefeel frontman Daren Seymour. Van Hoen also completed a number of re-mixes for Seefeel and As One, among others, and has recently incorporated elements of multimedia and performance art into his live appearances. —*Sean Cooper*

In Remembrance of Times Past / 1994 / Apollo ✦✦✦
Collects demos, four-track experiments, and otherwise unreleased material recorded during the mid—to late '80s. —*Sean Cooper*

● **Truth is Born of Arguments** / 1995 / Apollo ✦✦✦✦
A collection of austere, somewhat paranoid beat-oriented experimental ambient, similar in feel and tone to his earlier material, though with decidedly deviant stylistic features. Song titles include gems like "I Feel Cold Inside Because of the Things You Say," "I Believe in a Love I May Never Know," and "Inside I Am Crying." —*Sean Cooper*

The Last Flowers from the Darkness / 1996 / Touch ✦✦✦
Although it appears under his own name (on the English Touch label), Mark Van Hoen's *Last Flowers from the Darkness* is not so far off from his Locust and Scala material, combining resonant, somewhat dark ambient with fractured beats and detailed rhythmic and melodic textures. The first eight pieces on *Flowers* are the head-nodders of the lot—a mixture of downbeat breaks and fast, jungly rhythms—with the ninth and final track a sprawling, more-than-20-minute opus of minimalist environmental ambient. —*Sean Cooper*

Nils Lofgren

b. Jun. 21, 1951, Chicago, IL
Guitar, Vocals / Rock 'n' Roll
While singer/guitarist Nils Lofgren is better known for his work with Neil Young and Bruce Springsteen, his own solo career has produced a worthwhile, if inconsistent, body of work. Lofgren learned to play the accordion at age five and studied jazz and classical music as a child. He switched to rock guitar at 15 and formed the band Grin in 1969 with bassist Bob Gordon, drummer Bob Berberich, and later his brother Tom Lofgren on guitar. The group quickly built a reputation around Washington, DC, and Neil Young and Crazy Horse guitarist Danny Whitten caught wind of them while touring in the area. Young invited Lofgren to play piano and sing on 1970's *After the Gold Rush*, and he also played on and wrote two songs for Crazy Horse's debut album the following year. Instead of remaining with Young, Lofgren used the resulting exposure to get Grin a record contract. The group recorded three albums from 1971 to 1972, garnering critical praise but no sales. A move to A&M produced the lackluster *Gone Crazy*, which proved to be Grin's swan song; Lofgren accepted an invitation from Young to tour in 1973 and play on his *Tonight's the Night* album. Grin officially disbanded in mid-1974 owing to lack of success and financial problems. Lofgren was rumored to be under consideration as a replacement for Mick Taylor in the Rolling Stones; instead, he signed to A&M as a solo artist. His first two solo efforts, *Nils Lofgren* and *Cry Tough*, were all-around successes, and Lofgren made a name for himself on supporting tours through stunts such as performing while jumping on a trampoline. Subsequent releases failed to develop Lofgren's sound any further, and he became more viable as a sideman than a solo performer. Following 1983's *Trans* tour with Young, Lofgren joined Bruce Springsteen's E Street Band,

replacing Little Stevie Van Zandt in 1984, and remaining there until
the unit was dissolved in 1991. Lofgren returned to solo recording
that year with *Silver Lining*, which featured guest appearances from
Springsteen and members of Ringo Starr's band. *—Steve Huey*

● **Nils Lofgren** / 1975 / A&M ✦✦✦✦
After dismantling Grin in 1974, Lofgren signed a solo deal with
A&M, releasing a self-titled debut that neatly showcased his
strengths as a singer-songwriter and multi-instrumentalist. His reading of Carole King's wistful chestnut "Goin' Back" is a highlight, as
are fiery originals like "Keith Don't Go" (a tribute to The Stones'
Keith Richards) and "Rock & Roll Crook," with its wonderfully convoluted twin-guitar interplay. "Back It Up" is another gem. *—Rick Clark*

Back It Up (Authorized Bootleg) / 1975 / A&M ✦✦✦

Cry Tough / 1976 / A&M ✦✦✦
Lofgren's only bout of worthwhile record. A little forced on the song-
writing side, but delivered with enough panache to make it work.
—John Dougan

I Came to Dance / 1977 / A&M ✦✦

Night After Night [Live] / 1977 / A&M ✦✦✦

Nils / 1979 / A&M ✦✦✦✦
Lofgren rebounded, after several spotty albums, with this effort,
which featured some of the strongest writing in his career, particularly "Shine Silently," "A Fool like You," "Steal Away," and the powerful ballad "No Mercy." *—Rick Clark*

Night Fades Away / 1981 / MCA ✦✦

Wonderland / 1983 / MCA ✦✦✦
Unfortunately, this one got totally buried. "Across the Tracks," the sin-
gle, should have been given the push it deserved. A remake of Bobby
Womack's "It's All Over Now" is another highlight. *—Rick Clark*

Flip / 1985 / Columbia ✦✦✦

Classics, Vol. 13 / 1987 / A&M ✦✦✦✦
A solid 15-song compilation that gives a good sense of Lofgren's
career, but *Nils Lofgren* is a better introduction. *—Stephen Thomas
Erlewine*

Silver Lining / 1991 / Rykodisc ✦✦

Crooked Line / 1992 / Rykodisc ✦✦✦
Crooked Line evokes Lofgren's Youngian (not Jungian) roots, and it's
therefore appropriate that original mentor Neil guests on the sessions. Mr. Young adds distinctive background vocals and harmonica
to the country-folk ramble "You," and lets loose with some grungy
electric guitar for "Drunken Driver." Not that he steals any of the
limelight from Lofgren, who offsets his trademark tough but melodic
string-bending with tasteful acoustic pop forays like "Shot At You."
The guitarist leaves flashy pyrotechnics to others, preferring to cut
his material with direct, slashing simplicity. *—Roch Parisien*

Collection / Oct. 13, 1994 / Castle ✦✦✦

Everybreath / 1995 / Permanent ✦✦

Live on the Test / Oct. 10, 1995 / Windsong ✦✦✦

Damaged Goods / Oct. 17, 1995 / Transatlantic ✦✦✦

Steal Your Heart / 1996 / A&M ✦✦✦

Soft Fun Tough Tears / Feb. 11, 1997 / Raven ✦✦✦✦

Loggins & Messina

f. 1970, California, **db.** Jul. 1976
Folk-Rock, Pop-Rock, Soft Rock
Kenny Loggins and Jim Messina were the most successful pop-rock
duo of the first half of the '70s. Loggins was a staff songwriter who
had recently enjoyed success with a group of songs recorded by the
Nitty Gritty Dirt Band when he came to the attention of Messina, a
record producer and former member of Buffalo Springfield and Poco.
Messina agreed to produce Loggins' first album, but somewhere
along the way it became a duo effort that was released in 1972 under
the title *Kenny Loggins with Jim Messina Sittin' In*. The album was a
gold-seller that stayed in the charts more than two years. In the next
four years, Loggins & Messina released a series of gold or platinum
albums, most of which hit the Top Ten. They were all played in a
buoyant country-rock style with an accomplished band. *Loggins &
Messina* (1972) featured the retro-rock hit "Your Mama Don't Dance."
Full Sail (1973), *On Stage* (a double live album, 1974), and *Mother
Lode* (1974) all hit the Top Ten. *So Fine* was an album of '50s cover
songs. The pair's last new studio album, *Native Sons,* came out at the
start of 1976. Loggins & Messina split for two solo careers by the end
of that year, their catalog completed by a greatest-hits album, *Best of
Friends,* and a live record, *Finale.* *—William Ruhlmann*

Sittin' in / Jan. 1972 / Columbia ✦✦✦✦
This debut album was credited to "Kenny Loggins with Jim Messina"

because the project had begun as a solo record by Loggins being produced by Messina. By the time it was finished, however, Messina had
written or co-written six of the 11 songs, contributed "first guitar,"
and shared lead vocals on many tracks. Messina's "Nobody but You"
and "Vahevala," co-written by Loggins' brother Dave, were the singles chart entries, but today everybody remembers the album for
Loggins' "House at Pooh Corner," which had earned Loggins his
record contract, and "Danny's Song," which Anne Murray took into
the Top Ten the following year. The only thing wrong with this
record is that it was too perfect—with their infectious blend of country, folk, rock and Caribbean music,L&M started out at the top of
their game, and although they were able to match some of the material and performances on later records, the team never got any better
than this. *—William Ruhlmann*

Loggins & Messina / Oct. 1972 / Columbia ✦✦✦✦
The first full-fledged L&M album found the duo in good form as
songwriters, with Messina turning in the sparkling "Thinking Of
You" and the two collaborating on the hit single "Your Mama Don't
Dance" and "Angry Eyes." Their backup band was anchored by multi-
instrumentalist Al Garth and also featured keyboardist Michael
Omartian and Poco steel guitarist Rusty Young. *—William Ruhlmann*

Full Sail / Oct. 1973 / Columbia ✦✦✦
This is every inch a follow-up to *Loggins And Messina*, including a
'50s rock 'n' roll pastiche in the style of "Your Mama Don't Dance"
called "My Music" that hit No. 16 as a single. Other notable material
included Messina's island-rock anthem "Lahaina" and one of Loggins'
sensitive-but-generic ballads, typically called "A Love Song." But then,
the charm of L&M was that they could get away with something this
sappy. Balance is the key to L&M albums, and it's the chief talent
(among many) that producer Messina brings to them. Here, as on
L&M's first two albums, he achieves a musical flow that's exhilarating, and the record is only denied a "finest" rating because the quality of the songwriting doesn't quite match those LPs. *—William Ruhlmann*

On Stage / Apr. 1974 / Columbia ✦✦✦
Having assembled a strong backup band, L&M were at their best in
concert, and this two-LP set catches all of their diverse talents, from
the tight, intricate rockers devised by Messina to the sensitive ballad
skills of Loggins and the band's ability to stretch out on the sidelong
"Vahevala." *—William Ruhlmann*

Mother Lode / Oct. 1974 / Columbia ✦✦✦
From its brown-toned cover to its contents, Loggins & Messina's
fourth studio album is a sober, low-key, reflective affair. The band's
music, with its single flute, violin, and horn lines, directed by Messina's intricate guitar and mandolin playing, serves a series of mid-
tempo tunes expressing a lot of quiet dissatisfaction signaled by titles
like "Be Free," "Changes," and "Move On." As usual in a Jim Messina
production, all of this is elegantly, tastefully accomplished, but one
could hardly come away from the record feeling that all was well in
the L&M camp. *—William Ruhlmann*

Native Sons / Jan. 1976 / Columbia ✦✦✦
Loggins And Messina's fifth and last album of new studio material
was also their least. No hit singles issued from a collection that featured a new backup band and extensive use of strings on a set of
mediocre material. L&M's breakup at the end of the tour promoting
this record seemed confirmation that they had exhausted the possibilities of their partnership. *—William Ruhlmann*

● **The Best of Friends** / Nov. 1976 / Columbia ✦✦✦✦
The Best of Friends contains ten of Loggins & Messina's best-known
songs, not only including all of their big hits ("Vahevala," "Your
Mama Don't Dance," "Thinking of You," "Watching the River Run"),
but also key album tracks like "House at Pooh Corner," "Danny's
Song," "Peace of Mind," and "Angry Eyes." *—Stephen Thomas
Erlewine*

Finale / 1977 / Columbia ✦
Loggins And Messina's five-year partnership produced five albums of
original material, one album of covers, a greatest hits album, and,
with this post-breakup release, two double-LP live albums. The first
of them, 1974's *On Stage*, displayed their concert abilities at the
height of their career. This one, a profit-taking redundancy probably
released because double live albums were fashionable in the wake of
Peter Frampton's *Frampton Comes Alive*, chronicles their less-interest-
ing last couple of years. Songs are contracted into medleys to get
them over with, and even the ones at full length are better heard on
the studio albums. *—William Ruhlmann*

Kenny Loggins

b. Jan. 7, 1948, Everette, WA
Guitar, Keyboards, Vocals / Soft Rock, Pop-Rock
Singer, songwriter, and guitarist Kenny Loggins was born in Everett,

WA, and moved to Los Angeles in his teens. He got a job as a staff writer and wrote four songs used on a Nitty Gritty Dirt Band album in 1970, among them the hit "House at Pooh Corner." This brought him to the attention of former Poco member Jim Messina, now a staff producer at CBS, who intended to produce Loggins' debut album. The two ended up in a duo, however, and Loggins & Messina made a series of successful albums during the '70s.

Loggins & Messina broke up in 1976, and Loggins went on to solo stardom with such million-selling albums as *Celebrate Me Home*, *Nightwatch* (which included the hit "Whenever I Call You Friend"), and *Keep the Fire*, all in the cheerful, sensitive style he had displayed in Loggins & Messina. Loggins also became known as the king of the movie soundtrack songs, scoring Top Ten hits with "I'm Alright" (from *Caddyshack*), "Footloose" (from *Footloose*), "Danger Zone" (from *Top Gun*), and "Nobody's Fool" (from *Caddyshack II*). His own albums sold less well (and came less frequently) throughout the '80s. — *William Ruhlmann*

Celebrate Me Home / Apr. 1977 / Columbia ✦✦✦
This features the hit single "I Believe in Love." "Lady Luck," "Why Do People Lie?," and the title cut are highlights on this relatively light MOR debut. — *Rick Clark*

Nightwatch / Jun. 1978 / Columbia ✦✦✦
This super-slick sophomore effort was Loggins' biggest chart success, aided in no small part by the singles "Whenever I Call You Friend," which featured a duet with Stevie Nicks, and "Easy Driver." "Wait a Little While," and remakes of the Doobies' hit "What a Fool Believes" and Billy Joe Royal's "Down in the Boondocks" were further highlights. — *Rick Clark*

Keep the Fire / Oct. 1979 / Columbia ✦✦✦
Produced by Tom Dowd (Rod Stewart, Aretha Franklin, Allman Brothers), Loggins beefs up his sound a little with "Love Has Come of Age." He also enjoys more hits with "This Is It" and the title cut. — *Rick Clark*

Kenny Loggins Alive / Sep. 1980 / Columbia ✦✦✦✦
This extended live effort arrived on the wings of Loggins' No. 7 hit "I'm Alright," from the movie soundtrack of *Caddyshack*. The concert version included here is much better, stripped of some of the cute studio tricks found on the single. Most of the material comes from previously released studio tracks, which are given faithful (but livelier) readings. — *Rick Clark*

High Adventure / Sep. 1982 / Columbia ✦✦✦✦
Loggins continued his successful string of hit albums with this release. A light mainstream rock duet with Journey lead singer Steve Perry, titled "Don't Fight It," reached No. 17, while Loggins turned in a couple of MOR hits with "Heart to Heart" and "Welcome to Heartlight." As with all of his albums to this point, his sound is pleasant and well crafted. — *Rick Clark*

Vox Humana / Mar. 1985 / Columbia ✦✦
Kenny Loggins turns to a more techno approach and stubs his toe commercially. He had established himself as a singles and soundtrack star (notably in 1984's *Footloose*) with this kind of uptempo, synthesized material, but in so doing lost his connection with his album audience and, by taking such a stylistic sidetrack on his first regular LP in two-and-a-half years, failed to reconnect with fans who still remembered him from "House At Pooh Corner." In retrospect, they were wise; *Vox Humana* is ambitious but unaccomplished. — *William Ruhlmann*

Back to Avalon / 1988 / Columbia ✦✦✦
The title might have implied a return to form, but Kenny Loggins' commercial decline continued here, despite the inclusion of "Nobody's Fool," the Top Ten theme from *Caddyshack II*, "Meet Me Half Way," the No. 11 theme from *Over the Top*, and a cover of the Exciters' "Tell Him [Her]." Instead of addressing the concerns of his longtime fans, Loggins proceeded further into contemporary sounds, employing multiple producers of the likes of Patrick Leonard (Madonna) and Peter Wolf (Starship), all to little effect. This was Loggins' first solo album to miss gold certification and made his career crisis official. — *William Ruhlmann*

Leap of Faith / Sep. 10, 1991 / Columbia ✦✦
Kenny Loggins seems to have thought long and hard during the three years between *Back To Avalon* and this album, during which he underwent a divorce. The results can be heard on what is undoubtedly his most mature and heartfelt effort. He embraces environmental issues here, and tells his side of the unhappy marriage. He still isn't a cerebral sort, so the subject matter clashes somewhat with his typically simple expressions, but the effort helped him reconnect with his fans, who made this album something of a sleeper hit: although it was his lowest charting effort ever, it stayed in the charts longer than any album he'd made since the heyday of Loggins and Messina and went gold. — *William Ruhlmann*

Outside: From the Redwoods / Aug. 10, 1993 / Columbia ✦✦✦
On his second live album, Kenny Loggins puts together a special show consisting of rearranged versions of old favorites like "What A Fool Believes" (complete with co-author Michael McDonald on vocals) and "Your Mama Don't Dance." It's Loggins' version of an "unplugged" performance (despite a substantial backup band), and as such a turning away from the technology-happy days of albums like *Back To Avalon* (which, by the way, is forgotten in a catalog promotion in the CD booklet), without quite returning to the more homegrown quality of early albums like *Celebrate Me Home*. The real question in Loggins' career is what will happen with his next set of new material, but as a placeholder, this release should be welcomed by his fans, who may find even "Footloose" tolerable in a barrel-house piano arrangement. — *William Ruhlmann*

● **Yesterday Today Tomorrow: Greatest Hits** / Mar. 25, 1997 / Sony ✦✦✦✦
Yesterday Today Tomorrow compiles Loggins' biggest solo hits, including the chart-topping "Footloose" theme, "Danger Zone" (from *Top Gun*) and "I'm Alright" (from the classic *Caddyshack*), along with the newly recorded single "For the First Time." — *Jason Ankeny*

Lone Justice

f. 1984, Los Angeles, CA, **db.** 1986
Country-Rock, Roots-Rock
The roots-rock band Lone Justice was formed in Los Angeles by guitarist Ryan Hedgecock and singer Maria McKee. The half-sister of Bryan MacLean, a member of the seminal psychedelic outfit Love, McKee's involvement in the L.A. club scene dated back to her infancy; at the age of three, she joined MacLean at a performance at the famed Whisky-a-Go-Go and was befriended by Frank Zappa and members of the Doors. As a teen, she studied musical theatre, and briefly performed in duos with MacLean and local blues singer Top Jimmy. McKee and Hedgecock first met while dabbling in the L.A. rockabilly scene, and their mutual affection for country music inspired them to found Lone Justice in 1982.

Initially, the group was strictly a cover band, but the additions of veteran bassist Marvin Etzioni and Don Heffington, a former drummer in Emmylou Harris' Hot Band, prompted McKee to begin composing original material inspired by Dust Bowl-era balladry. Gradually, elements of rock began creeping into the Lone Justice sound, and soon the band became a local favorite. At the urging of Linda Ronstadt, they were awarded a contract with Geffen Records; their self-titled debut appeared in 1985, followed by a tour in support of U2. Still, despite good press and media hype, *Lone Justice* failed to sell; slickly produced by the band's manager Jimmy Iovine, it failed to connect with either country or rock audiences. In the record's wake, Hedgecock, Etzioni and Heffington all exited the band, leaving McKee to lead Lone Justice alone. After enlisting guitarist Shayne Fontayne, bassist Greg Sutton, drummer Rudy Richardson, and keyboardist Bruce Brody, Lone Justice recorded its second LP, *Shelter*. Shortly after the record's release, McKee broke up the band for good and went on to a solo career. Heffington became a successful session drummer, while Etzioni recorded under the guise Marvin the Mandolin Man. After a decade removed from the music industry, Hedgecock returned in 1996 as half of the duo Parlor James. — *Jason Ankeny*

● **Lone Justice** / 1985 / Geffen ✦✦✦✦
Maria McKee has one of those aching, little-girl voices (not unlike Stevie Nicks'), and it's heard to great effect on these country-rock tunes, especially Tom Petty and Mike Campbell's "Ways to Be Wicked." — *William Ruhlmann*

Shelter / 1986 / Geffen ✦✦✦

The Long Ryders

f. 1981, Los Angeles, CA
Country-Rock, Roots-Rock, Paisley Underground
Although they played the same clubs as most of Los Angeles' "paisley underground" bands (i.e., Dream Syndicate, Rain Parade) and even featured Dream Syndicate leader Steve Wynn in an early lineup, the Long Ryders were actually more a roots-rock group strongly influenced by Gram Parsons. The group was founded by Kentucky native Sid Griffin, a Parsons devotee who moved to Los Angeles after hearing about that city's punk scene, with guitarist Stephen McCarthy, the only two members to remain throughout the group's tenure. The group's first rhythm section featured bassist Barry Shank and drummer Matt Roberts; they, along with Griffin, had previously been members of the Unclaimed. The band's 1983 debut EP, *10-5-60*, was a blend of punk attitude, '60s rock, and traditional country (Griffin played steel guitar, autoharp, and mandolin). Their first full-length album, the following year's *Native Sons*, was

also arguably their best, and featured guest vocals from former Byrd Gene Clark. Subsequent albums failed to find an audience and, unhappy with their label's promotional efforts but unable to secure a release from their contract, the Long Ryders called it quits in 1987. McCarthy formed Gutterball and, along with Griffin, contributed to the 1993 Gram Parsons tribute album *Commemorativo*. Griffin, meanwhile, moved to London and formed the Coal Porters; today he works as a music critic and writer, foreshadowed by his definitive 1985 biography of (who else?) Gram Parsons. —*Steve Huey*

10 5 60 EP / 1983 / PVC ✦✦✦

Native Sons / 1984 / Frontier ✦✦✦✦
This updates the Byrds and Gram Parsons. —*Robert Gordon*

● **The State of Our Union** / 1985 / Island ✦✦✦✦
American country-tinged rock 'n' roll. —*Robert Gordon*

Two Fisted Tales / 1987 / Island ✦✦✦
Two Fisted Tales, the last album by the Long Ryders, pulls together all the various elements that had distinguished them from the rest of the jangly, '60s revisionist rock bands of the mid-'80s. The Long Ryders' sound was a unique blending of McGuinn-esque guitar figures with well-defined parameters that encompassed Gram Parsons' country-rock sensibilities and the various tenets of traditional roots-rock. Highlights include the kick-off track "Gunslinger Man," a powerful guitar assault that displays the band's ability to rock strong and hard. In contrast, "I Want You Bad," a Terry Adams-penned tune, also covered by Dave Edmunds, is a melodic song of long-distance desire. Here the vocal quality is particularly expressive and fitting to the song's message. On the other hand, formative years in the South are reflected on Sid Griffin's "Harriet Tubman's Gonna Carry Me Home." The overall instrumentation, which includes mandolin, autoharp, lap steel, and a guest accordion by David Hidalgo from Los Lobos, reflects their allegiance to traditional Americana music. Unfortunately *Two Fisted Tales* was to be the Long Ryders' swan song. However, in the '90s there are still those who recall the pioneering spirit of the Long Ryders. —*Jack Leaver*

Metallic B.O. / 1989 / Long Ryders Fan Club ✦✦✦

BBC Radio 1 Live in Concert / 1995 / Windsong ✦✦✦

Los Bravos

f. 1965, Spain
Pop-Rock
In 1966, this Spanish quintet became one of the very few rock groups from a non-English-speaking country to have an international smash with "Black Is Black," which got to No. 4 in the US and No. 2 in the UK. Lead singer Mike Kogel's overwrought, pinched vocals sounded so much like Gene Pitney that many listeners assumed that "Black Is Black" was a Pitney single, and the strong resemblance remained intact throughout Los Bravos' career, both in the singing and arrangements. Indeed, with their brassy pop-rock songs and production, which sounded about halfway between New York mid-'60s pop-soul and Jay & the Americans, Los Bravos sounded far more like a mainstream American pop-rock group than a Spanish or British one. Most of their records were sung in English, and although they never made the American Top 20 again, they were far more popular in Europe, even placing another single in the British Top 20 in late 1966 with "I Don't Care." —*Richie Unterberger*

● **All the Best** / (no label) ✦✦✦✦
There's no label for this CD (though, oddly, it has the catalog No.21670), but rest assured that it's easily available in specialty shops and mail-order collector catalogs, and in fact is much easier to locate than their original LPs. Good value, with 30 songs (about 90% of them in English), including "Black Is Black" and "I Don't Care," and a host of little-known tunes that usually follow the melodramatic, elaborately produced pop-rock mold of their hits. Fairly strong stuff, if not especially compelling. —*Richie Unterberger*

Los Lobos

f. 1973, East Los Angeles, CA
Tex-Mex, Roots-Rock, Adult Alternative Pop-Rock, Americana, Blues-Rock
Los Lobos were one of America's most distinctive and original bands of the '80s. They may have had a hit with "La Bamba" in 1987, yet that cover barely scratches the surface of their talents. Los Lobos are eclectic in the best sense of the word. While they draw equally from rock, Tex-Mex, country, folk, R&B, blues, and traditional Spanish and Mexican music, their music never sounds forced or self-conscious. Instead, all of their influences became one graceful, gritty sound. From their very first recordings their rich musicality was apparent; on nearly every subsequent record they have found ways to redefine

and expand their sound, without ever straying from the musical traditions that form the heart and soul of the band.

After releasing an independent EP in the late '70s and an EP in 1983, Los Lobos delivered their first major-label album, *How Will the Wolf Survive*, in 1984; it received an enormous amount of critical acclaim, as well as a dedicated following of fans. In the next four years, they released a marginally successful attempt to make their wildly eclectic sound palatable to a pop audience (*By the Light of the Moon*), a soundtrack of old Ritchie Valens songs that was a hit (*La Bamba*), and an album of traditional Mexican music (*La Pistola y El Corazon*). The band took two years off and returned with *The Neighborhood* in 1990; the album was a varied and powerful rock 'n' roll record that was better than anything they had released in six years. *Kiko*, released in 1992, brought the band into more experimental territory, without ever abandoning their graceful songwriting.

Los Lobos released a career retrospective, *Just Another Band from East LA: A Collection*, in 1993. The following year, David Hidalgo and Louie Pereze released a side project called *Latin Playboys*, which also featured producers Mitchell Froom and Tchad Blake. In 1995, the group released a children's album called *Papa's Dream*. In the spring of 1996, Los Lobos released *Colossal Head*, the proper follow-up to *Kiko*. —*Stephen Thomas Erlewine*

....and a Time to Dance / 1983 / Slash ✦✦✦
Only seven songs, but they're a perfect summation of what the band does and why it's important. This perfectly seamless fusion of Tex-Mex, R&B, and rock 'n' roll has powerhouse covers of the Ritchie Valens hit "Come On, Let's Go" and the norteño classic "A Te Dejo en San Antonio" thrown in for good measure. —*Kit Kiefer*

How Will the Wolf Survive? / 1984 / Slash/Warner Brothers ✦✦✦✦
A broader spectrum of music without a measure of the all-out joy of ... And a Time to Dance, How Will the Wolf Survive? features at least two raveup rockers ("Don't Worry Baby" and "I Got Loaded"), an irresistible shuffle ("Evangeline"), two traditional Mexican numbers ("Seranata Norteña" and "Corrida No.1"), and a stirring title tune. The album is well-rounded and fully realized. —*Kit Kiefer*

By the Light of the Moon / 1987 / Slash/Warner Brothers ✦✦✦
A very gentle, very Catholic album, it's summed up by the trilogy of sad songs ("River of Fools," "The Mess We're In," "Tears of God") that closes out the record. —*Kit Kiefer*

La Bamba [O.S.T.] / Jun. 1987 / Slash/Warner Brothers ✦✦✦
After two critically acclaimed but only moderately selling albums, Los Lobos was hired to record songs for the film biography of Hispanic '50s rocker Ritchie Valens, resulting in this soundtrack album, which, in addition to eight Los Lobos recordings, features tracks by Marshall Crenshaw, Brian Setzer, and others. Los Lobos' remake of the title song topped the charts, as did this album, which went on to sell two million copies. The result has been something of a career dilemma for the band, which went back to being a critically acclaimed, modest seller afterwards. —*William Ruhlmann*

La Pistola y El Corazon / Sep. 1988 / Slash/Warner Brothers ✦✦✦
Los Lobos used the commercial breakthrough represented by *La Bamba* to turn to its first love, Mexican folk music, and recorded this excellent collection of norteño songs. If this is a band that seems to do too many things well, in a sense they are at their best when they narrow their focus, and they are certainly masters of their style here. —*William Ruhlmann*

The Neighborhood / Aug. 1990 / Slash/Warner Brothers ✦✦✦
Recharged by their set of Mexican music, Los Lobos return with arguably their finest straight rock 'n' roll record. *The Neighborhood* effortlessly combines rock, R&B, blues, and country into a singular, powerful sound that manages to be as darkly funky as "I Walk Alone" and "Georgia Slop" and as gently moving as "Emily." —*Stephen Thomas Erlewine*

Kiko / May 1992 / Slash/Warner Brothers ✦✦✦✦
With its highly textured layers of sound, *Kiko* sounds like nothing else Los Lobos has done. Although their sound is still based in roots music of all kinds (rock, folk, Mexican, country), the band has shaped it into a dense, impressionistic wall of sound that intensifies the emotions behind such carefully constructed and moving songs as "Two Janes," "Angels with Dirty Faces," and "Kiko and the Lavender Moon." It's certainly their most ambitious album, and it's arguably their best. —*Stephen Thomas Erlewine*

● **Just Another Band from East L.A.: A Collection** / Aug. 31, 1993 / Slash/Warner Brothers ✦✦✦✦
Just Another Band from East L.A.: A Collection is a splendid double-disc collection that draws an accurate picture of Los Lobos, one of the most musically versatile bands of the 1980s. Featuring all of the band's hits and best-known songs, as well as several rare and previously unreleased tracks, there isn't a weak spot among the compilation's 41 songs. —*Stephen Thomas Erlewine*

Colossal Head / Mar. 19, 1996 / Warner Bros. ✦
Producer Mitchell Froom and his engineer Tchad Blake marred Los Lobos' 1992 album *Kiko* with their patented collection of arbitrary junkyard percussion and gimmicky sound processing; they completely ruin its follow-up. It is amazing that a band with as much craft and feeling in their music as Los Lobos should willingly submit that music to men whose goal is to create a flat sound in which clashing, isolated instruments compete in the creation of cacophony, while the vocals are so compressed and distorted they sound like they're coming out of a cheap transistor radio. (It is equally amazing that a major record label would willingly and repeatedly entrust a band with proven commercial potential to a production team that, however trendy, has never had a hit.) Somewhere on *Colossal Head* may be songs of some value, but it's impossible to tell through the distracting soundscape that renders listening to the album a singularly unpleasant experience. —*William Ruhlmann*

Lothar & the Hand People

f. New York City, NY
Psychedelic
One of the weirder psychedelic groups of the late '60s, the New York–based Lothar & the Hand People took special pride in augmenting many of their tunes with the theremin, a then-futuristic instrument most famous for its use in horror movies (as well as the Beach Boys' "Good Vibrations"). Playing eccentric satirical rock, good-time folk-rock, and experimental psychedelia, their material wasn't nearly strong enough to elevate them to the rank of innovators. Although their first album is their best, they are most fondly remembered for the trance-inducing "Space Hymn," an FM radio favorite for many years. —*Richie Unterberger*

Presenting . . . Lothar & The Hand People / Aug. 23, 1994 / One Way ✦✦✦
This group may be one of the more fondly remembered psychedelic cult bands of the late '60s, but their debut album hasn't dated that well. Their determinedly freaky material has some period charm, but the songwriting and singing really aren't all that hot. There are other problems: the frequent use of "Lothar," the group's theremin, sounds gimmicky rather than futuristic. They vacillate between good-time New York psychedelia in the style of the Youngbloods (who did it much better) and satirical shock-rock of the Mothers (who also did it much better), and the styles don't mix especially well. What sounded adventurous and far-out at the time can be a bit flat and embarrassing out of the context of the era. The saving grace of the CD reissue is the addition of six bonus cuts from their first three singles. Of variable quality, they nonetheless show the Hand People playing it straighter and, for the most part, the psychedelic folk-rock on these rare tracks was more effective and tuneful than the material on their LPs. The undoubted highlight is the fabulous "L-O-V-E (Ask For It By Name)," an explosive slice of pop-psychedelia that ranks as one of the best hit-singles-that-never-were of the late '60s. —*Richie Unterberger*

Loud Family

f. 1991, San Francisco, CA
Alternative Pop-Rock, Power Pop
After dissolving Game Theory, Scott Miller formed Loud Family, releasing their first album, *Plants and Birds and Rocks and Things*, in early 1992 on Alias Records. *Plants and Birds and Rocks and Things* received good reviews and maintained Miller's cult following, as did the subsequent EP, 1993's *Slouching Towards Liverpool*. In 1994, Loud Family released their second album, *The Tape of Only Linda*. The group's third album, *Interbabe Concern*, appeared in the late summer of 1996. —*Stephen Thomas Erlewine*

● **Plants and Birds and Rocks and Things** / 1992 / Alias ✦✦✦✦
Former Game Theory frontman Scott Miller returns with a new band and his classic style of power-pop. With a sound similar to the experimental *Lolita Nation*, Miller builds on his former band's strong points while leaving behind much of its excesses. *Plants and Birds and Rocks and Things* will be pleasantly familiar to old fans and will no doubt inspire newcomers to seek out Game Theory albums. —*Chris Woodstra*

Tape of Only Linda / Oct. 25, 1994 / Alias ✦✦✦

Interbabe Concern / Jul. 1996 / Alias ✦✦✦

John D. Loudermilk

b. Mar. 31, 1934, Durham, NC
Trombone, Trumpet, Drums, Saxophone, Vocals / Rock 'n' Roll, Traditional Country, Pop-Rock
Although his music isn't exactly weird, John D. Loudermilk is one of the weirdest figures of early rock 'n' roll. Much more famous as a

songwriter than as a performer (although he made plenty of records), his material was incredibly erratic. He could range from the most mindless, sappy pop to a hard-bitten, bluesy tune that rang with as much authentic grit as a Mississippi Delta blues classic. That tune was "Tobacco Road," and if he'd written nothing else, Loudermilk would have been worth a footnote in any history of popular music.

Loudermilk wrote plenty of other songs, though, in a lengthy career that saw him straddling the fields of rock, pop, and country. Originally striving to be a performer in a very mild pop-rockabilly style, he found his first success as a songwriter, when George Hamilton IV took "A Rose and a Baby Ruth" into the Top Ten in 1956. Recording as Johnny Dee, Loudermilk made a few singles for the small Colonial label in North Carolina. The best and most successful of these was "Sittin' in the Balcony," which made the Top 40 in 1957. Eddie Cochran's cover, based closely on Loudermilk's version (though performed with more force and style), stole most of John's thunder when it outsold the original by a wide margin, making the Top 20.

Johnny Dee changed his name back to John Loudermilk when he signed with Columbia in 1958, and also decided to concentrate on songwriting when he relocated to Nashville, eventually working for Chet Atkins at RCA. Although Loudermilk had a pleasantly passable voice, his early records aren't worth much, often purveying material that was mindlessly lightweight or, worse, idiotically humorous ("Asiatic Flu"). "Tobacco Road" was a different story—a stark, stomping tale of hard-bitten Southern poverty, it had a strong blues flavor that was virtually absent from most of his material. It took a one-shot British Invasion group, the Nashville Teens, to fully realize the song's menace in their magnificent, hard-rocking 1964 cover, which made the US Top 20. The song was also covered by Lou Rawls, the Jefferson Airplane, Edgar Winter, and others.

"Tobacco Road" was far from Loudermilk's only success. In the late '50s and early '60s, he supplied material for country stars, teen idols, and pop-rock singers, including "Waterloo" (Stonewall Jackson), "Angela Jones" (Johnny Ferguson), "Ebony Eyes" (the Everly Brothers), "Norman" (Sue Thompson), and "Abilene" (George Hamilton IV). In the mid-'60s, he was briefly in vogue in Britain: the Nashville Teens did both "Tobacco Road" and "Google Eyes" (the latter of which was a hit in the UK, though a flop stateside), and Marianne Faithfull had a British hit with the moody "This Little Bird."

Loudermilk continued to record on his own, though more as an afterthought than as a specialty, reserving most of his focus for writing songs for other performers. Much of his material followed a fainthearted, goofy pop-novelty thread, which made his somber efforts seem all the more incongruous. His last big songwriting success was another of his serious-minded tunes, "Indian Reservation," which topped the charts for Paul Revere & the Raiders in 1971 (it had previously been a hit for British singer Don Fardon). He withdrew from professional activities to spend most of the last two decades studying ethnomusicology. —*Richie Unterberger*

12 Sides of / 1962 / RCA Victor ✦✦
Although this contains some of Loudermilk's own versions of some of his most famous songs, it's a surprisingly disposable effort. The production is period Nashville pop-lite, Loudermilk's voice is almost devoid of character, and the songs themselves are usually downright dippy in their slightness. Much of this is Loudermilk at his worst—chipper, mindless romantic trifles, or trivial tunes about characters who are, one would guess, supposed to be laughably eccentric, though the results are about as funny as your average prime-time sitcom. Includes versions of "Angela Jones," "Google Eye," and "This Little Bird" (here titled, for some reason, "The Little Bird"), all of which were big hits in the hands of others. Beware, though—the version of "Tobacco Road" here is not the original, basic thumper on Loudermilk's 1960 Columbia single, but a vastly inferior remake with an inappropriately jaunty arrangement. —*Richie Unterberger*

Blue Train / 1989 / Bear Family ✦✦✦✦

It's My Time / 1989 / Bear Family ✦✦✦✦

● **Sittin' in the Balcony** / Jul. 5, 1995 / Bear Family ✦✦✦✦
A 23-song collection of his earliest material from 1957-60. Includes both sides of all five singles he recorded for Colonial (when he was known as Johnny Dee), and early Columbia singles, as well as three previously unreleased songs from the early Columbia era. "Sittin' in the Balcony" and the original, stark version of "Tobacco Road" are the clear highlights here. Most of the rest is timid rockabilly-pop, with songwriting that's riddled with goody-goody teen cliches; the novelty "Asiatic Flu" and "The Happy Wanderer (Val-De-Ri Val-De-Ra)" are downright unbearable. Still, it's probably Loudermilk's best work, considering that from 1960 on he principally worked as a songwriter, recording his own work only as a sideline. The previously unissued "The Angel of Flight 509" stirs mild interest, as it's a prototype of sorts for "Ebony Eyes," minus the tragic elements. —*Richie Unterberger*

Love

f. 1965, Los Angeles, CA, db. 1974
Psychedelic, Folk-Rock

One of the best West Coast folk-rock-psychedelic bands, Love may have also been the first widely acclaimed cult-underground group. During their brief heyday—lasting all of three albums—they drew from Byrdsish folk-rock, Stonesish hard rock, blues, jazz, flamenco, and even light orchestral pop to create a heady stew of their own. They were also one of the first integrated rock groups, led by genius singer-songwriter Arthur Lee, one of the most idiosyncratic and enigmatic talents of the 1960s. Stars in their native Los Angeles, and an early inspiration to the Doors, they perversely refused to tour until well past their peak. This ensured their failure to land a hit single or album, though in truth the band's vision may have been too elusive to attract mass success anyway.

Love was formed by Lee in the mid-'60s in Los Angeles. Although only 20 at the time, Lee had already scuffled around the fringes of the rock and soul business for a couple of years. In addition to recording some flop singles with his own bands, he wrote and produced a single for Rosa Lee Brooks that Jimi Hendrix played on as session guitarist. Originally calling his outfit the Grass Roots, Lee changed the name to Love after another Los Angeles group called the Grass Roots began recording for Dunhill. Love's repertoire would be largely penned by Lee, with a few contributions by guitarist Bryan Maclean.

Inspired by British Invasion bands and local peers the Byrds, Love built up a strong following in hip L.A. clubs. Soon they were signed by Elektra, the noted folk label that was just starting to get its feet wet in rock (it had recorded material by early versions of the Byrds and the Lovin' Spoonful, and had just released the first LP by Paul Butterfield). Their self-titled debut album (1966) introduced their marriage of the Byrds and the Stones on a set of mostly original material, and contained a small hit, their punkish adaptation of Bacharach-David's "My Little Red Book."

Love briefly expanded to a seven-piece for their second album, *Da Capo* (1967), which included their only Top 40 hit, the corkscrew-tempoed "7 and 7 Is." The first side was psychedelia at its best, with an eclectic palette encompassing furious jazz structures, gentle Spanish guitar interludes, and beautiful baroque pop with dreamlike images ("She Comes in Colors"). It was also psychedelia at its most reckless, with the whole of side two taken up by a meandering 19-minute jam. It was still a great step forward, but by mid-'67, the band was threatening to disintegrate due to drugs and general disorganization.

The group was in such sad shape, apparently, that Elektra planned to record their third album with session men backing Lee (on his compositions) or Maclean (on his compositions). Work on two tracks actually commenced in this fashion, but the shocked band pulled itself together to play their own material, resulting in one of the finest rock albums of all time, *Forever Changes*. An exceptionally strong set of material graced by captivating lyrics and glistening, unobtrusive horn and string arrangements, it was not a commercial hit in the US (though it did pretty well in Britain), but remains an all-time favorite of many critics.

Just at the point where they seemed poised to assert themselves as a top band, Love's first and best lineup was broken up in early 1968, at Arthur Lee's instigation. Several albums followed in the late '60s and early '70s which, though credited to Love, are in reality Arthur Lee and backup musicians—none of whom had skills on the level of Bryan Maclean or the other original Love men. Lee largely forsook folk-rock for hard rock, with unimpressive results, even when he was able to get Jimi Hendrix to play on one track. The problems ran deeper than unsympathetic accompaniment: Lee's songwriting muse had largely deserted him as well, and nothing on the post-*Forever Changes* albums competes with the early Elektra records. Lee released a solo album in the early '70s, and then put another Love together for one last effort in 1974, but basically Love/Lee (the two had in effect become synonymous) ground to a halt in the mid-'70s. Lee has sporadically recorded and performed since then without coming up with anything resembling a unified full-length studio statement, though some scattered live and studio recordings have appeared, the most recent being a 1994 single on the tiny Distortions label. —*Richie Unterberger*

Love / 1966 / Elektra ◆◆◆◆
Their debut is both their hardest-rocking early album, and their most Byrds-influenced. Lee's songwriting muse hadn't fully developed at this stage, and in comparison with their second and third efforts, this is the least striking of the LPs featuring their classic lineup, with some similar-sounding folk-rock compositions and stock riffs. A few of the tracks are great, though: their punky rendition of Bacharach/David's "My Little Red Book" was a minor hit, "Signed D.C." and "Mushroom Clouds" were superbly moody ballads, and Bryan Maclean's "Softly to Me" served notice that Lee wasn't the only songwriter of note in the band. —*Richie Unterberger*

Da Capo / 1967 / Elektra ◆◆◆◆
Love broadened their scope into psychedelia on their sophomore effort, Lee's achingly melodic songwriting gifts reaching full flower. The six songs that the first side of this album comprised when it was first issued are a truly classic body of work, highlighted by the atomic blast of pre-punk rock "7 and 7 Is" (their only hit single), the manic jazz tempos of "Stephanie Knows Who," and the enchanting "She Comes in Colors," perhaps Lee's best composition (and reportedly the inspiration for the Rolling Stones' "She's a Rainbow"). It's only half a great album, though; the seventh and final track, "Revelation," is a tedious 19-minute jam that keeps *Da Capo* from attaining truly classic status. —*Richie Unterberger*

★ **Forever Changes** / 1967 / Elektra ◆◆◆◆◆
It wasn't a hit, but *Forever Changes* continues to regularly appear on critics' lists of the top ten rock albums of all time, and it had an enormously far-reaching and durable influence that went way beyond chart listings. The best fusion of folk-rock and psychedelia, it features Lee's trembling vocals, beautiful melodies, haunting orchestral arrangements, and inscrutable but poetic lyrics, all of which sound nearly as fresh and intriguing upon repeated plays. One of rock's most organic, flowing masterpieces, every song has a lingering, shimmering beauty, including the two penned by the band's other talented songwriter-guitarist-singer, Bryan Maclean. —*Richie Unterberger*

Four Sail / 1969 / Elektra ◆◆◆
Lee and Love started to lose focus by turning up the volume on this album. Hardly memorable. —*Jeff Tamarkin*

Out Here / 1969 / One Way ◆◆
Out *there* would have been more like it. This quasi-metal hour-plus recording has little in common with earlier Love. —*Jeff Tamarkin*

False Start / 1970 / One Way ◆◆
Clearly influenced by Hendrix at this stage, Arthur Lee began to lose sight of what Love once was. Some sparks but mostly misfires. Appropriately titled. —*Jeff Tamarkin*

Reel to Real / 1974 / RSO ◆◆

Love Live / Studio / 1982 / One Way ◆◆
Just like the title says—some live Fillmore East tracks and some studio stragglers. Nothing special. —*Jeff Tamarkin*

● **Love Story 1966-1972** / 1995 / Rhino ◆◆◆◆
Double-CD box contains most of their classic first three albums (including the entirety of *Forever Changes*), all three non-LP tracks from their 1966-68 prime, and highlights of the post-Bryan Maclean albums from the late '60s and early '70s. Great booklet of liner notes and photos, but considering that all of those first three albums remain easy to find, and that the post-*Forever Changes* material is much inferior to the early recordings, it's not an essential purchase. The absence of "Revelation" from *Da Capo* is no big deal, but a few tracks from the debut are missing, including one of the better ones, "Mushroom Clouds." —*Richie Unterberger*

Love and Rockets

f. 1984, Northampton, England
Alternative Pop-Rock, Goth-Rock

Love and Rockets comprised guitarist/vocalist Daniel Ash, bassist/vocalist David J, and drummer Kevin Haskins, all former members of the pioneering goth band Bauhaus. However, the group didn't sound very similar to their first group. Instead, Love and Rockets emphasized the strains of psychedelia and glam rock that appeared underneath Bauhaus' gloomy drone, adding elements of pop song craft, folk and R&B, as well as cryptic, self-important lyrics. For most of the late '80s, the group had a devoted cult following, resulting in a surprise Top Ten hit single, "So Alive," in 1989. During the early '90s, the group's audience steadily declined, although they still retained a number of loyal fans. After Bauhaus broke up in 1983, David J recorded a solo album and collaborated with the Jazz Butcher, while Daniel Ash concentrated on a side project, Tones on Tail. Haskins soon joined Tones on Tail, but the group folded in 1984. Haskins and Ash then attempted to reunite Bauhaus. David J agreed to the project but the band's lead vocalist Peter Murphy refused. Instead of pursuing an incomplete Bauhaus reunion, Ash, J, and Haskins formed Love and Rockets, taking their name from the underground comic book written by Jaime and Gilbert Hernandez.

Love and Rockets released their first album, *Seventh Dream of Teenage Heaven*, in 1985; it received mixed reviews but it began to build their following. *Express*, released the following year, was more successful, charting in both the US and the UK. On *Earth Sun Moon* (1987) the band retreated to more atmospheric musical territory, with the notable exception of the alternative-college radio hit "No New Tale to Tell," which helped the increase the group's fan base. *Love and Rockets*, released in 1989, broke the band into the mainstream, thanks to the T. Rex-inspired Top Ten single "So Alive." The album was nearly as successful, breaking into the Top 15 and going gold. After the success of *Love and Rockets*, the members of the band concentrated on solo projects for nearly half a decade. Love and Rockets returned to recording in 1994 with *Hot Trip to Heaven*, which failed to make any inroads on the pop or alternative charts. In 1996, they returned again with *Sweet F.A.—Stephen Thomas Erlewine*

Seventh Dream of Teenage Heaven / 1985 / Beggars Banquet/RCA
✦✦✦
From behind the black shrouds and smoky din of Bauhaus—very much in contrast to their dark, gothic angst, very much like a night-time liftoff—arises Love and Rockets. Their debut *Seventh Dream of Teenage Heaven*, a vast divergence from the Bauhaus sound, is marked by an ethereal quality, as much by the transcendental lyrics as the richly layered depth of the production: the atmosphere is one of reflection, yet all the while remaining enlightened, without the somber negativity often induced by such a journey into the mind. The title track sounds like a hot night under blue neon, and is totally addicting, as are many of the tracks; perhaps the most distinctive is the instrumental "Saudade," remarkable in its almost pastoral beauty. Another track, "Haunted When the Minutes Drag," starts deep in a funk, with overwhelming vocals pulling you into the song, yet shifts subtly to a feel of self-affirmation. Symbolizing the band's transition from gothic negativity to fields of thought and light, this is truly an album to attach memories to. *—Bob Sakomano*

Express / 1986 / Beggars Banquet/Big Time ✦✦✦✦
Rich in sonic detail, the neo-psychedelic *Express* offers a listening experience like no other album—guitars spiral to dizzying heights from beds of sound, arrangements swirl, songs change and mutate. "Kundalini Express" typifies Love and Rockets' approach, chugging along for several verses before breaking open and ascending into the heavens; Anglo-fied Eastern religious imagery and philosophy predominate lyrically and, in tandem with the psychedelic music, offer an almost quasi-religious experience. John A. Rivers (who also co-produced Love and Rockets' first album) outdoes himself with the sound on this disc, offering a huge, unique canvas for the band to paint its sound on: crystalline acoustic guitars cut through thick, distorted tones, and the bass is an equal player to the guitars and drums. "Yin & Yang the Flower Pot Man" is ecstatically upbeat, offering a propulsive rhythm, flailing guitars, and insistent bass—a compulsively danceable and bliss-inducing track. "An American Dream," meanwhile, is an anthem of sorts, with distinct sections setting apart the moods of hope, disillusionment, and acceptance. *—Jonathan Ball*

● **Earth, Sun, Moon** / 1987 / Beggars Banquet/Big Time ✦✦✦✦
Earth, Sun, Moon reins in the rampant excesses of *Express* while remaining psychedelic; the near-white-out of the cover gives a clue to the music, as many of the songs emerge from a soup of white-noise guitar distortion. Much of the record addresses, in the group's nebulous fashion, hope and disappointment; the title track and "Youth" are two of their most simple, yet most affecting, songs. Not a "normal" pop record by any means, it is more straight-ahead than their previous work and includes the upbeat single "No New Tale to Tell," a college radio hit which set the stage for their popular breakthrough a year later. *—Jonathan Ball*

Love and Rockets / Apr. 1989 / Beggars Banquet/RCA ✦✦✦
Featured is their only US hit, "So Alive." *—Steve Aldrich*

Hot Trip to Heaven / Sep. 27, 1994 / American ✦✦
Returning from a four-year absence, Love and Rockets attempts to update their sound with *Hot Trip to Heaven*. Adding several elements of the British house and ambient dance scenes to their sound doesn't make Love and Rockets sound hip. Instead, they sound like they're trying to figure out what the hell is going on. *—Stephen Thomas Erlewine*

Sweet F.A. / Mar. 19, 1996 / American ✦✦
In an attempt to sell themselves to the '90s alternative audience, Love and Rockets refashioned their sound with *Sweet F.A.* Throughout the album, the band is less concerned with creating atmospheric soundscapes or terse, edgy pop songs; instead, they try to rock hard. Using louder guitars and borrowed ideas from industrial bands like Ministry, the group sounds directionless—they haven't been able to incorporate these elements into their music, they simply regurgitate them. Consequently, *Sweet F.A.* is exactly what the title says it is. *—Stephen Thomas Erlewine*

Love Sculpture

f. 1966, England, **db.** 1970
Blues-Rock, Art-Rock/Progressive-Rock, Roots-Rock
A British blues-rock band of the late '60s that, despite being very good, would normally be relegated to footnote status if it were not for the fact that the lead guitarist of this trio was the soon-to-be-famous Dave Edmunds. Like many similar bands of the times, Love Sculpture

was really a showpiece for Edmunds' guitar playing talents (which on the first LP are considerable), and little else. The covers are well chosen, slightly revved-up, but mostly reverent versions of blues classics. They had a fluke hit in 1968 with a cover of the classical piece "Sabre Dance" rearranged for guitar. After two LPs, Love Sculpture split up in 1970. Edmunds went on to solo success ("I Hear You Knockin'") and a long, sometimes contentious relationship with ex-Brinsley Schwarz bassist Nick Lowe, which culminated in the great band Rockpile. Still, Love Sculpture, though slightly dated, is a hoot to listen to today. And Edmunds, full of youthful bravado and dazzling technique, certainly knows his way up and down a fretboard. *—John Dougan*

Blues Helping / 1968 / Rare Earth ✦✦✦✦
As hyperkinetic blues albums by white English kids go, this is a good one. Dave Edmunds, armed only with a 1959 Gibson 335 and a 100-watt Marshall stack, cranks through these recognizable blues covers (with one original instrumental) with reckless abandon and gobs of technique. Backup support is handled by bassist John Williams and drummer Congo Jones, who do their best to keep up and provide a rhythmic foundation for Edmunds to wail over. Edmunds also handled nearly all the vocals, and as blues singers go, he's merely serviceable, but what makes this LP worthwhile is the revved-up guitar playing, especially when Edmunds shreds both Freddy King's "The Stumble" and Willie Dixon's "Wang Dang Doodle." *—John Dougan*

Forms & Feelings / 1969 / Parrot ✦✦✦
Forms & Feelings essentially replicates the high-voltage attack of *Blues Helping*, only with a notable lack of energy and an eye on the charts. It's no coincidence that the group chose to revamp *L'Arlesienne*'s "Farandole," given that "Sabre Dance" was the only thing that distinguished Love Sculpture from the legions of British blues bands. But this time around, "Farandole" and all of *Forms & Feelings* sounded tired and redundant, with only a fraction of the passion that made the debut worthwhile. *—Stephen Thomas Erlewine*

● **Singles A&B's** / 1990 / Harvest ✦✦✦✦
Singles A&B's is a useful overview of Love Sculpture's brief career, containing the majority of their best moments and proving that there was more to this British blues group than their gimmicky cover of "Sabre Dance." *—Stephen Thomas Erlewine*

Love Tractor

f. 1980, Athens, GA, **db.** 1989
Group / Alternative Pop-Rock, Jangle-Pop
Beginning as an instrumental group, Athens, GA band Love Tractor ultimately found their greatest success on the dance floor. Their beat-driven sound was similar to Pylon's, but it's safe to say they were a genre unto themselves. *Love Tractor*, their 1982 debut for the DB label, is an all-instrumental affair. On *Around the Bend*, their 1983 record for the same label, they added vocals, mostly by Mike Richmond. In an unusual move, Mark Cline and Armistead Wellford traded guitar and bass chores; Kit Schwartz was the drummer. Two collections of odd bits followed—1984's *Till The Cows Come Home* EP for DB and *Wheel of Pleasure* for Armageddon in 1985. *This Ain't No Outerspace Ship* for Big Time in 1987 was just what the title implied—it's a funkin' dance party that includes their surprising cover of the Gap Band's "Party Train." The band left us with one more light collection of grooves in *Themes from Venus* in 1989. Though well-loved and everyone's favorite party band in their hometown of Athens (after Pylon called it quits), Love Tractor didn't really connect with folk outside the small college burg. Wellford went on to play in Gutterball with Steve Wynn, Bob Rupe, and the House of Freaks. *—Denise Sullivan*

Love Tractor / 1982 / DB ✦✦✦

Around the Bend / 1983 / DB ✦✦✦
A gentle collection of songs with the distinctly Athens rural beat, in the mold cast by the B-52's and Pylon, and somehow related to surf music. Love Tractor augment their previously all-instrumental agenda with some obscured, tentative vocals. An acquired taste, to be sure. *—Denise Sullivan*

Til the Cows Come Home / 1984 / DB ✦✦✦

Wheels of Pleasure / 1985 / DB ✦✦✦✦

Double Play (Love Tractor/Around the Bend) / 1986 / DB ✦✦✦✦

This Ain't No Outer Space Ship / 1987 / Big Time ✦✦✦

● **Themes from Venus** / 1989 / DB ✦✦✦✦

Darlene Love (Darlene Wright.)

b. Jul. 26, 1938, Los Angeles, CA
Vocals / R&B, Girl Group
Amazingly, Darlene Love, a superb vocalist, hasn't had much of a track record as a solo singer, at least not in terms of hits. Love was a

founding member of the Blossoms in 1957. They did several sessions and were resident singers on the television show *Shindig*. Love sang lead vocals on "He's a Rebel," which was credited to the Crystals, and "Zip-A-Dee-Doo-Dah," which was issued as Bob B. Soxx and the Blue-jeans. She cut six singles for Spector's Phillies label, with "Wait Till My Bobby Gets Back Home" the most successful. Love became busy as an actress, but reunited with Spector for the 1977 single "Lord, If You're a Woman." Love appeared in all three *Lethal Weapon* films, and was also in the Royal Shakespeare Company's co-production of Stephen King's *Carrie*. Her 1990 LP, *Paint Another Picture*, failed to chart in America. Love later toured as a background vocalist with Cher. She appeared briefly on the soap opera *Another World* in 1993. —*Ron Wynn*

● **The Best of Darlene Love** / Sep. 22, 1992 / ABKCO ✦✦✦✦
A terrific compilation of Love's Phil Spector-produced hits, it includes "(Today I Met) the Boy I'm Gonna Marry," "Wait Till My Bobby Gets Back Home," and the hits she sang for the Crystals, "He's a Rebel" and "He's Sure the Boy I Love." —*AMG*

Loverboy

f. 1978, Vancouver, B.C., Canada, **db.** 1989
Hard Rock, Pop-Rock
With a string of three multi-platinum albums, Loverboy was one of the most successful mainstream hard rock groups of the early '80s. Comprising vocalist Mike Reno, guitarist Paul Dean, bassist Scott Smith, keyboardist Doug Johnston, and drummer Matthew Frenette, the band formed in Toronto, Canada, in 1980 and immediately signed with CBS Records. Later that year, their Bruce Fairbairn-pro-duced debut album appeared. Featuring the slick, hard-rocking sin-gles "Turn Me Loose" and "The Kid Is Hot Tonite," the album went platinum in both Canada and America.
Loverboy recorded the follow-up, *Get Lucky*, in 1981. Driven by the anthemic "Working for the Weekend," the Fairbairn-produced record was a major success in the US and Canada, yet it failed to gain an audience anywhere in Europe. Nevertheless, the band was a staple on AOR stations across North America, as well as a popular concert attraction. The band's good fortunes continued with the 1983 album *Keep It Up*. Again, Loverboy worked with Fairbairn, who kept their melodic yet tough sound intact; the album featured the hit sin-gle "Hot Girls In Love."
Loverboy's fortunes began to slip with 1985's *Lovin' Every Minute of It*, which was produced by Tom Allom (Judas Priest). Allom gave the band a harder edge, which didn't prove as commercially success-ful as their past records; nevertheless, the band's fans managed to make the album go platinum. Fairbairn returned from working with Bon Jovi to produce 1987's *Wildside*, yet the combination didn't prove as potent as before. After an extensive two-year tour, the band returned to Canada. In 1989, their greatest-hits record, *Big Ones*, was released. The same year Reno and Dean announced plans to make solo records, which effectively put an end to the group. —*Stephen Thomas Erlewine*

Loverboy / 1980 / Columbia ✦✦✦✦
Their debut, with guitar-heavy pop-metal, included the Top 40 hit "Turn Me Loose" and the signature Loverboy tune, "The Kid is Hot Tonite." —*Donna DiChario*

Get Lucky / 1981 / Columbia ✦✦✦✦
Although occasionally overblown, songs like "Lucky Ones" and "Working for the Weekend" were made for blasting on the radio. —*Donna DiChario*

Keep It Up / 1983 / Columbia ✦✦✦✦
Loverboy kept up their string of multi-platinum albums with their third record, *Keep It Up*. Although it wasn't as consistent as *Get Lucky*, its finest moments were as good as anything on its predeces-sor, including the driving "Hot Girls in Love" and the Top 40 hit "Queen of the Broken Hearts." —*Stephen Thomas Erlewine*

Lovin' Every Minute of It / 1985 / Columbia ✦✦✦
While it was another platinum album, *Lovin' Every Minute of It* was slightly weaker than Loverboy's first three records, due to a slip in songwriting quality. Although hits like "Lovin' Every Minute of It," "Dangerous," and "This Could Be the Night" were well-constructed arena-rock numbers, none of the album tracks were quite as catchy, resulting in the group's weakest record since their debut. —*Stephen Thomas Erlewine*

Wildside / 1987 / Columbia ✦✦
Although it went gold, *Wildside* made it clear that Loverboy's pol-ished hard rock formula was running out of gas. The band wasn't able to come up with strong hooks for most of the record, with the Top 40 hit "Notorious" providing the only memorable moment on the album. —*Stephen Thomas Erlewine*

Big Ones / Oct. 1989 / Columbia ✦✦✦✦
Loverboy's biggest and best hits include "Turn Me Loose," "Lovin' Every Minute of It," "This Could Be the Night," "Hot Girls in Love," "Heaven in Your Eyes," and "Working for the Weekend." —*AMG*

● **Loverboy Classics** / Oct. 11, 1994 / Columbia ✦✦✦✦
Like *Big Ones*, *Loverboy Classics* doesn't contain all of the band's sin-gles, but it does feature a greater selection of hits and album rock favorites, including Mike Reno's duet with Ann Wilson, "Almost Para-dise," making it a better introduction to the group. —*Stephen Thomas Erlewine*

Lyle Lovett

b. Nov. 1, 1957, Klein, TX
Guitar, Vocals / Singer-Songwriter, Alternative Country
Lyle Lovett was one of the most distinctive and original singer-song-writers to emerge during the '80s. Though he was initially labeled as a country singer, the tag never quite fit him. Lovett had more in com-mon with '70s singer-songwriters like Guy Clark, Jesse Winchester, Randy Newman, and Townes Van Zandt, combining a talent for inci-sive, witty lyrical detail with an eclectic array of music, ranging from country and folk to big-band swing and traditional pop. Lovett's liter-ate, multilayered songs stood out among the formulaic Nashville hit singles of the late '80s, as well as the new traditionalists that were beginning to take over country music. Drawing from alternative country and rock fans, Lovett quickly built up a cult following which began to spill over into the mainstream with his second album, 1988's *Pontiac*. Following *Pontiac*, his country audience declined but his reputation as a songwriter and musician continued to grow, and he sustained a dedicated cult following well into the '90s.
Born in Klein, Texas—a small town named after his great-grandfa-ther (a Bavarian weaver called Adam Klein) that later became a Houston suburb—Lyle Lovett was raised on his family's horse ranch. Lovett didn't begin his musical career until he began writing songs while he attended Texas A&M University in the late '70s, where he studied journalism and German. While he was a student, he per-formed covers and original songs at local folk festivals and clubs. As a graduate student, he traveled to Germany to study and continued to write and play while he was in Europe. However, he didn't begin to pursue a musical career in earnest until he returned to America in the early '80s.
Upon his return to the States, Lovett played clubs throughout Texas, eventually landing a spot in the 1983 Mickey Rooney TV-movie, *Bill: On His Own*. The following year Nanci Griffith, who Lovett had interviewed for a school paper while he was in college, recorded his "If I Were the Woman You Wanted" on her *Once in a Very Blue Moon* album. He also sang on the album, as well as her 1985 record, *Last of the True Believers*. Guy Clark heard a demo tape of Lovett's songs in 1984 and directed it toward Tony Brown of MCA Records. Over the next year, MCA worked out the details of a record contract with Lovett. In the meantime, he made his first recorded appearance on *Fast Folk Musical Magazine, Vol. 2: No.8* later in the year.
Lovett signed with MCA/Curb in 1986, releasing his eponymous debut later in the year. *Lyle Lovett* received excellent reviews and five of its singles—"Farther Down the Line," the Top Ten "Cowboy Man," "God Will," "Why I Don't Know" and "Give Back My Heart"—reached the country Top 40. Despite his strong showing on the country charts, it was clear from the outset that Lovett's musical tastes didn't rely on country, though the genre provided the founda-tion of his sound. Instead, he incorporated jazz, folk, and pop into a country framework, pushing the musical boundaries of each genre. *Pontiac*, his second album, revealed exactly how eclectic and literate Lovett was. Greeted with overwhelmingly positive reviews from both country and mainstream publications upon its early 1988 release, *Pontiac* expanded his audience in the pop and rock markets. The album charted in the lower reaches of the pop charts and slowly worked its way toward gold status. While his pop audience grew, his country fan base began to shrink—"She's No Lady" and "I Loved You Yesterday" both made the Top 30, but after those two songs, none of his other singles cracked the country Top 40.
It didn't matter that Lovett's country audience was disappear-ing—*Pontiac* had gained enough new fans in the pop mainstream to guarantee him a strong cult following. To support *Pontiac*, he assem-bled His Large Band, which was a modified big band complete with guitars, a cellist, a pianist, horns, and a gospel-trained backup singer named Francine Reed. Lovett recorded his third album, *Lyle Lovett & His Large Band*, with his touring band. Like its two predecessors, the album was well-received critically upon its early 1989 release and it performed well commercially, peaking at No. 62 and eventually going gold. Perhaps because of the album's eclectic, jazzy sound, the album produced only one minor country hit in "I Married Her Just

Because She Looks like You," but his straight rendition of Tammy Wynette's "Stand by Your Man" received a great deal of attention in the media.

Following the release of *His Large Band*, Lovett settled out in California, which signaled that he was abandoning country. After settling in Los Angeles, he spent the next two years collaborating and working on his fourth album. In 1990, he produced Walter Hyatt's *King Tears* album; the following year, he sang on Leo Kottke's *Great Big Boy* and donated a cover of "Friend of the Devil" to the Grateful Dead tribute album, *Dedicated*. Also in 1991, he made his acting debut in Robert Altman's *The Player*, which was released in the spring of 1992. A few months after *The Player* hit the theaters, Lovett's fourth album, *Joshua Judges Ruth*, was released. Boasting a heavy gospel and R&B influence, *Joshua Judges Ruth* was his most successful album to date, peaking at No. 57 and going gold. On the whole, the album was ignored by country radio, but pop audiences embraced the record and Lovett became a staple on adult alternative radio and VH-1.

Despite the success of *Joshua Judges Ruth*, Lyle Lovett became a near-superstar for a completely different reason in 1993—his surprise marriage to actress Julia Roberts. Upon the announcement of their marriage, Lovett became the subject of many gossip segments and tabloid stories, elevating him to a level of fame he had not experienced before. Lyle's first project after his marriage was a role in Altman's 1993 film *Short Cuts*. He didn't release another album until the fall of 1994, when *I Love Everybody* hit the stores. A collection of songs Lovett wrote in the late '70s and early '80s, *I Love Everybody* continued his move away from country, and it was the first record he had released that didn't expand his audience in some way. After it entered the charts at No. 26, it disappeared 13 weeks later, failing to go gold.

Lovett and Roberts divorced in the spring of 1995 and Lyle began to retreat from the spotlight somewhat, spending the remainder of the year touring and writing. Lovett re-emerged with *The Road to Ensenada*, the first album since *Pontiac* to be dominated by country songs, in the summer of 1996. In addition to performing well on the pop charts, where it entered at a career peak of No. 24, *The Road to Ensenada* performed strongly on the country charts, entering at No. four. —*Stephen Thomas Erlewine*

Lyle Lovett / 1986 / Curb ✦✦✦✦
Lyle Lovett has an ironic overview of the world, expressed in songs he sings with the dead seriousness of the true comic. But he also has a finely defined sense of romantic troubles that sometimes isn't funny at all. Songs like "God Will" and "If I Were the Man You Wanted" mark him as one of the best new writers of the decade. —*William Ruhlmann*

★ **Pontiac** / 1987 / Curb ✦✦✦✦✦
Lovett's best overall collection of songs includes the gently absurd "If I Had a Boat," the subtly murderous "L.A. County," and the Henny Youngman-style "She's No Lady," among other gems. —*William Ruhlmann*

Lyle Lovett & His Large Band / 1989 / Curb ✦✦✦✦
On his third album, Lovett continues to explore a synthesis of country and big band. Included is his version of Tammy Wynette's country classic on "Stand by Your Man" and the bittersweet "I Married Her Just Because She Looks Like You." —*Rick Clark*

Joshua Judges Ruth / Mar. 31, 1992 / Curb ✦✦✦
Lyle Lovett goes folk-gospel. To be fair, the country tag was never a comfortable fit for Lovett's eclectic musings. *Joshua Judges Ruth* distances him from the category without firmly boxing him into any new ones. There is a southern-fried gospel feel throughout much of the album, even if it's sometimes irreverent. "Church" best displays Lovett's surreal, dry wit, recounting a hunger-driven church rebellion complete with full gospel backing vocals. "She's Leaving Me," featuring guest vocals from Emmylou Harris, is the one sop offered to traditional country. Overall, though, the mood is somber bordering on bleak. Like the album cover and insert photos, *Joshua* deals in shades of gray and themes of loneliness and death. What one misses the most on this release is the infrequent surfacing of Lovett's weird, playful sense of humor. —*Roch Parisien*

I Love Everybody / Sep. 27, 1994 / Curb ✦✦✦
A collection of odds and ends that Lyle Lovett has written over the years (some of the tunes date back to the late '70s), *I Love Everybody* doesn't have the self-conscious artistic importance of *Joshua Judges Ruth*, and it's all the better for it. Instead, Lovett offers a set of relaxed, casual songs, accentuating his infamous, off-kilter sense of humor ("Skinny Legs," "Penguins"). At the same time, the songs offer hints of Lovett's sly, subtle sense of menace, particularly "Creeps Like Me." —*Stephen Thomas Erlewine*

Road to Ensenada / Jun. 18, 1996 / Curb ✦✦✦✦
Since *Pontiac*, Lyle Lovett has been experimenting with different sounds, whether it was the big band posturing of *& His Large Band*, the gospel overtones of *Joshua Judges Ruth*, or the '70s singer-songwriter flourishes of *I Love Everybody*. With *The Road to Ensenada*, he hunkers down and produces his most straightforward album since *Pontiac*. As it happens, it is also his best record since that breakthrough album. Lovett strips the sound of the album down to the bare country essentials, allowing it to drift into western swing, country-rock, folk, and honky-tonk when necessary. He also decides to balance his weightier material ("Private Conversation," "Who Loves You Better," "It Ought to Be Easier," "I Can't Love You Anymore," "Christmas Morning") with fun, light-hearted numbers like "Don't Touch My Hat," "Fiona," and "That's Right (You're Not from Texas)," which are funny without being silly. In fact, *The Road to Ensenada* is the lightest album Lyle Lovett has ever made—the darkness that hung around the fringes of *Pontiac*, *Joshua Judges Ruth*, and *I Love Everybody* has drifted away, leaving his wry sense of humor and a newly found empathetic sentimentality. The combination of straightforward instrumentation and lean, catchy, and incisive songwriting results in one of the best albums of his career—he's just as eclectic and offhandedly brilliant as always, but on *The Road to Ensenada* he's more focused and less flashy about his own talent than he's ever been. —*Stephen Thomas Erlewine*

Lene Lovich

b. Mar. 30, 1949, Detroit, MI
Saxophone, Vocals / New Wave
One of the more offbeat and memorable figures in new wave, Lene Lovich certainly drew much of her widely varied approach from her unconventional early experiences. Born of a Yugoslavian father and British mother, she spent much of her childhood in Detroit, MI. At age 13, she moved to Hull, England, with her mother. She ran away to London shortly thereafter, where she worked several odd jobs ranging from bingo caller to go-go dancer to street busker. Around this time, she developed an interest in art and theater, enrolling at the Central School of Art. She took up the saxophone and, after a brief stint in a soul-funk band (with future collaborator Les Chappell), Lovich wrote a string of songs for French disco star Cerrone. In 1978, Stiff Records signed her after hearing her first recording, a remake of "I Think We're Alone Now." She quickly became one of Stiff's brightest stars, headlining package tours and earning several UK hits over the next three years with the unforgettable "Lucky Number," "Say When," "Bird Song," and "New Toy." Unfortunately, her theatrical quirkiness didn't translate well into LP length and as new wave dissolved, she disappeared from the music scene. After an eight-year absence, she returned in 1990 with *March*. It failed to ignite any further interest and she again went into retirement. —*Chris Woodstra*

● **Stateless . . . Plus** / 1979 / Rhino ✦✦✦✦
Stateless, her aptly titled 1978 debut, is a new wave cult classic. Featuring her offbeat vocals and quirky synth-heavy production, this is her finest moment. Includes the great single, "Lucky Number." Now reissued on CD as *Stateless . . . Plus* with five extra tracks and extensive liner notes. —*Chris Woodstra*

Flex . . . Plus / 1980 / Rhino ✦✦✦
Flex shows Lovich staying true to her unique sound, though it is somewhat watered down with super-slick production. And while it doesn't quite match the debut, the new wave classic, "New Toy" (written by Thomas Dolby), makes it worthwhile. The CD reissue, *Flex . . . Plus*, offers six bonus tracks. —*Chris Woodstra*

The Lovin' Spoonful

f. 1965, New York, NY, **db.** 1968
Folk-Rock, Pop-Rock
Right on the tails of the Beau Brummels and the Byrds, the Lovin' Spoonful were among the first American groups to challenge the domination of the British Invasion bands in the mid-'60s. Between mid-1965 and the end of 1967, the group was astonishingly successful, issuing one classic hit single after another, including "Do You Believe in Magic?," "You Didn't Have to Be So Nice," "Daydream," "Summer in the City," "Rain on the Roof," "Nashville Cats," and "Six O'Clock."

Like most of the folk-rockers, the Lovin' Spoonful were more pop and rock than folk, which didn't detract from their music at all. Much more than the Byrds, and even more than the Mamas & the Papas, the group exhibited a brand of unabashedly melodic, cheery, and good-time music, though their best single, "Summer in the City," was uncharacteristically riff-driven and hard-driving. More influenced by blues and jug bands than other folk-rock acts, their albums were spotty and their covers at times downright weak. As glorious as their singles were, the group lacked the depth and innovation of the Byrds, their chief competitors for the crown of best folk-rock band, and their legacy hasn't been canonized with nearly as much reverence as their West Coast counterparts.

Leader and principal songwriter John Sebastian was a young veteran of the Greenwich Village folk scene when he formed the band in 1965 with Zal Yanovsky, who'd already played primitive folk-rock of a sort with future members of the Mamas & the Papas in the Mugwumps. Sebastian already had some recording experience under his belt, playing harmonica (his father was a virtuoso classical harmonica player) on sessions by folkies like Tom Rush and Fred Neil. The Spoonful were rounded out by Steve Boone on bass and Joe Butler on drums. After some tentative interest from Phil Spector (who considered producing them), they ended up signing with Kama Sutra. Sebastian's autoharp (which would also decorate several subsequent tracks) helped propel "Do You Believe in Magic" into the Top Ten in late 1965.

The Lovin' Spoonful were torn asunder by a drug bust in 1967. Boone and Yanovsky were arrested in California for marijuana possession, and evidently got out of trouble by turning in their source. This didn't sit well with the burgeoning counterculture, which called for a boycott of Spoonful product, although the effect on their sales may have been overestimated; most of the people who bought Spoonful records were average teenage Americans, not hippies. Yanovsky left the band in mid-1967, to be replaced by Jerry Yester, former producer of the Association.

The band had a few more mild hits, but couldn't survive the loss of John Sebastian, who effectively closed the chapter by leaving in 1968, although the group straggled on briefly under the helm of Butler. Sebastian went on to moderate success as a singer-songwriter in the 1970s. — *Richie Unterberger*

Do You Believe in Magic / 1965 / Kama Sutra ✦✦✦✦
By the time of its release, the Lovin' Spoonful's debut album was already a significant record because of the inclusion of its title track, John Sebastian's timeless anthem to love and music, which had been one of the major hits of the summer of 1965. The album elaborated upon Sebastian's gentle, winning songwriting style with the humorous "Did You Ever Have to Make up Your Mind," which was released as a single in the spring of 1966 and became another Spoonful hit, and the wistful "Younger Girl," which became a chart hit for the Critters. The album also revealed the group's jug band roots in its arrangements of traditional songs like "Fishin' Blues" and "Wild About My Lovin'," and revealed that lead guitarist Zal Yanovsky and drummer Joe Butler, while not quite in Sebastian's league, were good singers as well....The Spoonful would be remembered as a vehicle for Sebastian's songwriting, but *Do You Believe in Magic* was a well-rounded collection that demonstrated their effectiveness as a group. — *William Ruhlmann*

What's up Tiger Lily? [O.S.T.] / 1966 / Kama Sutra ✦✦
This marks one of the first times a rock band wrote the whole score for a movie that they weren't starring in. There's lots of whimsy, mostly instrumental, and it includes the hit "Pow." "Introduction to Flick" is a brief monologue from the film's producer, Woody Allen. — *Gary Mollica*

Hums / 1966 / Pair ✦✦✦
Their third "real" album and their fourth in 13 months, is quieter than previous efforts. There are eleven Sebastian originals, three of which became huge hits: "Summer in the City," "You and Me and Rain on the Roof" (as it's called on the label), and "Nashville Cats," along with "Lovin' You," later a hit for Bobby Darin. The album also features tributes to Fred Neil ("Coconut Grove") and Howlin' Wolf ("Voodoo in My Basement"). — *Gary Mollica*

Daydream / May 1966 / One Way ✦✦✦
The band's second LP was very strong; this time, most of the tunes are originals, with the exception of a cover of "Bald Headed Lena." Joe Butler and Yanovsky are featured on some lead vocals, and the album includes two more hits, "You Didn't Have to Be So Nice" and "Didn't Want to Have to Do It." Strangely enough, this has been the only Spoonful LP reissued on CD in the States. — *Gary Mollica*

You're a Big Boy Now / 1967 / Kama Sutra ✦✦✦
Director Francis Ford Coppola hired Lovin' Spoonful leader John Sebastian to compose music for his romantic comedy, *You're a Big Boy Now*, and Sebastian brought his band in to perform many of the songs, including the ballad "Darling Be Home Soon," which became the Spoonful's next hit. Most of the rest of the score consisted of instrumentals, many augmented by an uncredited orchestra, but Sebastian's title song was also impressive. — *William Ruhlmann*

Everything Playing / 1968 / Kama Sutra ✦✦✦
The Lovin' Spoonful's fourth album, *Everything Playing*, was made under trying circumstances. Musically, the *Sgt. Pepper*/Summer of Love era had made The Spoonful's good-time, jug band approach obsolete, and chief songwriter John Sebastian had to try to keep up.

Personally, the group had suffered the disaster of a drug bust that resulted in the departure of lead guitarist Zal Yanovsky, who was replaced in August 1967 by Jerry Yester. Despite these problems, Sebastian was able to turn out a good album paced by its three Top 40 hits, "Six O'Clock," "She Is Still a Mystery," and the deceptively comic "Money," in which he castigated financial aspects of the music industry. Also excellent were "Boredom" and "Younger Generation," which Sebastian later would sing at Woodstock. When Sebastian wasn't at the mike, the singing could be mediocre, and the group was often all over the map in its attempt at musical sophistication, but the record was saved by Sebastian's writing and singing. Then he too jumped ship. — *William Ruhlmann*

Revelation Revolution '69 / 1968 / Kama Sutra ✦✦
The band is billed here as "the Lovin' Spoonful Featuring Joe Butler." Just when everybody had written them off after Sebastian's departure, this flawed gem came out of left field. Butler's smooth voice had graced a few tracks on all of the past LPs, in addition to having a few of his own tunes included. He comes into his own here, but unfortunately, his three originals are the weakest songs on the LP, especially the ultra-hip sound collage "War Games." However, the great pop team of Bonner and Gordon came up with three strong tunes, including the hit "Me About You" (previously done by The Turtles) and the fine "(Till I) Run with You" (the title of the LP as written on the label), with John Stewart supplying the best track, the gorgeous "Never Going Back." — *Gary Mollica*

★ **Anthology** / Jan. 1990 / Rhino ✦✦✦✦✦
Unquestionably the finest collection of a major band that did much to launch American folk-rock in the mid-'60s. *Anthology* jams 26 cuts onto a single CD, including all of their hits and some of their strongest album tracks, drawing mostly from their 1965-66 prime. As for the more interesting non-smashes, these include the original version of John Sebastian's "Younger Girl," which was a hit in a more commercial version by the Critters; the minor 1967 hit "She Is Still a Mystery," a dreamily psychedelic number that holds its own with their other standards, but has somehow been forgotten by oldies radio; and "Good Time Music," recorded early in 1965 for an obscure Elektra sampler (and a small hit in a cover version by the Beau Brummels). The most overlooked find here is the instrumental "Lonely (Amy's Theme)," from the early Francis Ford Coppola film *You're a Big Boy Now*, a lushly orchestrated, melancholy tune featuring Sebastian's wistful harmonica. There are also little-known Sebastian originals, with vocals, from *You're a Big Boy Now* and Woody Allen's early screen venture *What's Up, Tiger Lily?* The accompanying booklet features comments from Sebastian himself about some of the group's most famous songs. — *Richie Unterberger*

Nick Lowe

b. Mar. 25, 1949, Woodchurch, Suffolk, England
Guitar, Bass, Vocals / Rock 'n' Roll, Country-Rock, New Wave, Pop-Rock, Pub Rock
As the leader of the seminal pub rockers Brinsley Schwarz, a producer, and a solo artist, Nick Lowe held considerable influence over the development of punk rock. With the Brinsleys, Lowe began a back-to-basics movement that flowered into punk rock in the late '70s. As the house producer for Stiff, he recorded many seminal records by the likes of the Damned, Elvis Costello, and the Pretenders. His rough, ragged production style earned him the nickname "Basher," and also established the amateurish, DIY aesthetics of punk. Despite his massive influence on punk rock, Lowe never really was a punk rocker. Lowe was concerned with bringing back the tradition of three-minute pop singles and hard-driving rock 'n' roll, but he subverted his melodic songcraft with a nasty sense of humor. His early solo singles and albums *Jesus of Cool* and *Labour of Lust* overflowed with hooks, bizarre jokes, and an infectious energy that made them some of the most acclaimed pop records of the new wave era. As new wave began to fade away in the early '80s, Lowe began to explore roots-rock, eventually becoming a full-fledged country-rocker in the '90s. While he never had another hit after 1980's "Cruel to Be Kind," his records found a devoted cult audience, and often were critically praised.

The son of a British Royal Air Force officer, Nick Lowe spent part of his childhood stationed in the Middle East before his family settled in Kent. As a teenager, he played in a variety of bands, including Three's A Crowd and Sounds 4 Plus 1, with his friend, guitarist Brinsley Schwarz. In 1965, the pair formed the guitar-pop band Kippington Lodge, which landed a contract with Parlophone Records the following year. Over the next four years, the group released five singles, none of which received much attention. In 1969, Kippington Lodge evolved into the country-rock band Brinsley Schwarz, who secured a record contract with United Artists the following year. At the outset of their career, the Brinsleys attempted to gain fame by holding a showcase concert at the Fillmore East, but the publicity stunt backfired, making the band outcasts from the British music scene by the time their first album was released. Over the next five years, the group slowly built a following as the leading exponents of pub-rock, a back-to-basics movement of good-time rock 'n' roll that earned a niche in the early '70s.

With their unassuming appearance and unpretentious music, pub-rockers set the stage for punk rock in the late '70s, not only by relying on three-chord rock 'n' roll, but also establishing a circuit of pubs to play. Of all the old-guard pub-rockers, Lowe was the most significant in the development of punk rock. By the time Brinsley Schwarz broke up in 1975, he had already gained a reputation as an excellent, eccentric songwriter, and he was beginning to produce artists like Graham Parker, Dr. Feelgood, and the Kursaal Flyers. At the time, his songwriting was veering away from the country-rock and bluesy rock that distinguished his Brinsley work, and he was beginning to write inventive pop songs. Lowe wanted to leave United Artists, but the label refused to let him go, so he proceeded to record a series of deliberately unmarketable singles in hopes of getting kicked off the label. The first was "Bay City Rollers We Love You," a tongue-in-cheek tribute to the teen-pop sensations credited to the Tartan Horde. Inexplicably, the single became a hit in Japan—the Japanese branch of UA even asked for a full album—and the label kept him as an artist. However, after "Let's Go to the Disco," credited to the Disco Brothers, UA dropped him from the label.

After leaving UA, Lowe became the first artist on Jake Riviera and Dave Robinson's fledgling independent label Stiff Records, as well as the label's in-house producer. Recorded for just 65 pounds and released in the summer of 1976, "So It Goes"/"Heart of the City" became the first British proto-punk single of the late '70s, earning glowing reviews if not sales. Lowe began producing records at a rapid rate, helming the Damned's debut album *Damned Damned Damned*—the first British punk album—and Elvis Costello's *My Aim is True* in 1977; he would produce all of Costello's albums between *My Aim Is True* and 1981's *Trust*. Lowe also produced singles by Wreckless Eric, the Rumour, and Alberto y Los Trios Paranoias, as well as Graham Parker's early albums. In the summer of 1977, he became part of Dave Edmunds' touring band Rockpile, which would become his backing band within a year. He also released the *Bowi* EP (a play on the title of David Bowie's *Low* LP) in 1977, and toured with the Stiff package tour Live Stiffs before leaving the label with Costello to join Riviera's new label, Radar Records.

Lowe released his debut album, *Jesus of Cool* (retitled *Pure Pop for Now People* for its American release), in 1978, which featured his first British Top Ten hit, "(I Love the Sound Of) Breaking Glass." The single "American Squirm" was released in the fall of 1978 to little success. After producing the Pretenders' debut single "Stop Your Sobbing," Lowe recorded his second album, *Labour of Lust*, supported by Rockpile; Edmunds' *Repeat When Necessary* was recorded at the same session. *Labour of Lust* featured Lowe's one big American hit, "Cruel to Be Kind," which was a reworked version of an old Brinsley Schwarz song. Between the recording and touring in 1979, Lowe married Carlene Carter, the stepdaughter of Johnny Cash; he would produce her albums *Musical Shapes* (1980) and *Blue Nun* (1981).

Lowe and Edmunds toured with Rockpile to support their respective 1979 albums, and the pair were the subject of the BBC documentary "Born Fighters" later that year. Rockpile's shows became notorious for their wild, frequently drunken performances, and the group's spirited selection of originals and obscure covers. In 1980, the band decided to record an album together, but the sessions were plagued by tension between Lowe and Edmunds. *Seconds of Pleasure*, the group's lone album, was released in the fall of 1980 to mixed reviews; it generated one hit single, the Lowe-written "Teacher Teacher." Rockpile split only months after the release of *Seconds of Pleasure*, with the remaining members choosing to support Edmunds on his solo album.

Lowe returned with *Nick the Knife* in February of 1982, supporting the album with a band featuring guitarist Martin Belmont and keyboardist Paul Carrack; the group was first called the Chaps, but their name changed to Noise to Go during the American tour. *Nick the Knife* was a moderate hit, but its follow-up, 1983's *The Abominable Showman*, was a flop. Lowe retaliated by shifting his music toward roots-rock on his 1984 album *And His Cowboy Outfit*. Both *Cowboy Outfit* and its 1985 successor *Rose of England* were greeted with positive reviews and improved sales; the former featured his last UK hit, "Half A Boy Half A Man" and the latter featured his last US hit, a reworking of his chestnut "I Knew the Bride (When She Used to Rock & Roll)." In 1986, he reunited with Elvis Costello to produce *Blood & Chocolate*. The album was one of many records—including efforts by the Fabulous Thunderbirds, John Hiatt, and Paul Carrack—he produced in the '80s. During much of the mid-'80s, Lowe suffered from alcohol abuse, but with the assistance of his old mates Costello and Riviera he recovered and gave up looking for a crossover pop hit, concentrating on country-rock and roots-rock. *Pinker and Prouder Than Previous* (1988) was the first indication of this shift in style, but the record went largely unnoticed. Produced by Dave Edmunds, *Party of One* (1990) became his first charting album since 1985. Later that year, Lowe divorced Carter. The following year, he formed the supergroup Little Village with John Hiatt, Ry Cooder, and Jim Keltner; all of the musicians played on Hiatt's 1987 breakthrough album, *Bring the Family*. Little Village was fraught with tension and their eponymous 1992 album and its supporting tour suffered as a result. The group disbanded upon the tour's conclusion. While he was working on material for a new album, Lowe's Brinsley Schwarz composition "(What's So Funny 'Bout) Peace, Love and Understanding," which had previously been a hit for Elvis Costello, was covered by Curtis Stigers for the soundtrack to Whitney Houston's film *The Bodyguard*. The album became the biggest-selling soundtrack album in history and, in the process, Lowe unexpectedly became a millionaire from the songwriting royalties.

Lowe made a comeback in 1994 with the straight country album, *The Impossible Bird*. Hailed as his finest effort in years, the album became a hit in the burgeoning Americana movement in the US, and he supported the album with his first solo tour in five years; his touring band featured former Commander Cody guitarist Bill Kirchen. —*Stephen Thomas Erlewine*

★ **Pure Pop for Now People** / 1978 / Columbia ✦✦✦✦✦
For his first solo album, *Pure Pop for Now People*, Nick Lowe completely abandoned the rootsy underpinnings of his work with Brinsley Schwarz and refashioned himself as a pop craftsman or, as the original British title put it, the *Jesus of Cool*. Lowe tries anything and everything on the record, from the sweet pop of "Tonight" to the blinding rock of "Heart of the City." It's a veritable tour de force of his songwriting talent, as well as his wit. Not only does he turn in a set of wildly eclectic pop songs, he writes lyrics that slyly and gleefully subvert and pervert rock 'n' roll tradition. *Pure Pop for Now People* sounds like '60s pop from an alternate universe, where hit singles are about actresses who are eaten by their pet dogs, castrating Castro, and grown men who write odes to teen idols. He also writes about the sleaziness of the music business itself with unrestrained joy. If Lowe's sense of humor wasn't so sharp and his melodies weren't so catchy, the amalgam of pop music and pop culture wouldn't have been so successful. However, he not only can write pop songs, he knows how to record them—each song sounds like an individual single and the cheap production means that the album sounds like it's coming out of tinny radio speakers. And that also means that it doesn't matter what sequence these songs are put in—the album is like a jukebox, where different musical styles can follow each other and it all makes perfect sense. —*Stephen Thomas Erlewine*

☆ **Labour of Lust** / 1979 / Demon ✦✦✦✦✦
Jesus of Cool was a jukebox, spinning out a series of perfectly crafted—and decidedly quirky and subversive—pop singles. In contrast, Nick Lowe's second album *Labour of Lust* is the work of a bar band, in this case Rockpile, playing the hell out of the same type of songs. Naturally, the result is a more coherent sound that may be a little less freewheelingly eclectic, but it is no less brilliant. Recorded simultaneously with Dave Edmunds' *Repeat When Necessary*, *Labour of Lust* benefits from the muscular support of Rockpile, who make Lowe's songs crackle with vitality. Working primarily in the roots-rock vein of Brinsley Schwarz, but energizing his traditionalist tendencies with strong pop melodies, a sense of humor, and an edgy new wave sensibility, Lowe comes up with one of his best sets of songs. Not only is his only hit, the propulsively hook-laden "Cruel to Be Kind," here, but so are the rampaging outsider anthem "Born Fighter," the tongue-in-cheek, Chuck Berry-style "Love So Fine," the wonderful pure pop of "Dose of You," the haunting "Endless Grey Ribbon," the druggy "Big Kick, Plain Scrap!," and the terrific "Cracking Up," as well as his definitive version of Mickey Jupp's "Switchboard Susan." It's an exceptional collection of inventive pop songs, delivered with vigor and energy, making it one of the great records of the new wave. —*Stephen Thomas Erlewine*

Nick the Knife / 1982 / Demon ✦✦✦
Lowe's first album since the breakup of Rockpile was a casually rocking record that recalled his former band, which isn't surprising, considering that both Billy Bremner and Terry Williams provide instrumental support. —*Stephen Thomas Erlewine*

The Abominable Showman / 1983 / Demon ✦✦
Caught between the desire for another big pop hit and his burgeoning re-interest in country music, Nick Lowe made the most confused album of his career with *The Abominable Showman*. Although Lowe's craftsmanship hasn't abandoned him, he isn't particularly inspired on *Abominable Showman*. Furthermore, much of the album

is hampered by stiff, dated new wave production, which makes amiable throwaways like "Saint Beneath the Paint" irritating. Still, Lowe manages to break through the tedium with charming, clever pop-rockers like "We Want Action," "Time Wounds All Heels," "(For Every Woman Who Ever Made a Fool of a Man There's a Woman Who Made A) Man of the Fool," and the silly doo wop of "Tanque-Rae." But a song as sharp as "Ragin' Eyes," with its wryly observed lyrics and infectious melody, make it clear that the rest of the album is lacking. — *Stephen Thomas Erlewine*

Nick Lowe & His Cowboy Outfit / 1984 / Demon ✦✦✦

The title isn't entirely in jest—*Nick Lowe & His Cowboy Outfit* does represent Lowe's reinvention as a roots-rocker, as he delves into Tex-Mex, country-rock, garage rock, and, of course, pop. After the muddled *The Abominable Showman*, *Cowboy Outfit* sounds positively vibrant, thanks in no small part to Lowe's backing band, composed largely of veteran pub-rockers. The songs are also more consistently memorable, from the Farfisa-driven "Half a Boy and Half a Man" to the sublime covers of Mickey Jupp's "You'll Never Get Me Up In One of Those" and Sandie Shaw's "Breakaway." The rest of the album's pleasures, however, are subtle. "Maureen" and "God's Gift to Women" are charming yet slight, and the songs become increasingly lightweight as the album approaches its close. Even with the uneven songs, the Cowboy Outfit make the material appealing, and Lowe certainly sounds more appealing—and comfortable—as a roots-rocker than as an aging new wave popster. — *Stephen Thomas Erlewine*

The Rose of England / 1985 / Demon ✦✦✦✦

Following through on the roots-rock leanings of *Cowboy Outfit*, Nick Lowe delivered the delightful *The Rose of England*. While some of the material is still rather lightweight—"Lucky Dog" and "Bo Bo Ske-diddle" are defiant and thoroughly entertaining throwaways—much of the record is clever and charming, delivered with laidback confidence from the Cowboy Outfit. "Darlin' Angel Eyes" and "The Rose of England" are minor classics in the Lowe canon, while his cover of John Hiatt's "She Don't Love Nobody" and the revival of the rockabilly standard "7 Nights to Rock" keep the album moving. Still, it's his stark take on Elvis Costello's lovely "Indoor Fireworks" that gives the album an anchor, and it's a performance so affecting that it makes the neutered reworking of "I Knew the Bride" completely forgivable. — *Stephen Thomas Erlewine*

Pinker and Prouder than Previous / 1988 / Demon ✦✦✦

Abandoning the Cowboy Outfit but not roots-rock, Nick Lowe followed the winning *The Rose of England* with the amiable but muddled *Pinker and Prouder Than Previous*. Working with the same blend of classic pop, rock 'n' roll, and country-rock, Lowe gets things off to a roaring start with the driving "(You're My) Wildest Dream," but the record quickly bogs down in mediocre material. Many of the songs are certainly not bad, yet they rarely distinguish themselves from each other—only "Lover's Jamboree," John Hiatt's "Love Gets Strange," and Graham Parker's "Black Lincoln Continental" stand out, and they would have been second-string songs on *The Rose of England*. That doesn't necessarily make *Pinker and Prouder Than Previous* a bad record; it's just not particularly memorable. — *Stephen Thomas Erlewine*

• Basher: The Best of Nick Lowe / Sep. 1989 / Columbia ✦✦✦✦

Containing no less than 25 tracks, *Basher: The Best of Nick Lowe* is an excellent overview of Lowe's solo career, detailing how he evolved from a quirky, innovative new wave pop craftsman to a fine roots-rocker. All of Lowe's absolutely essential songs—from "So It Goes" and "Heart of the City" through "Cracking Up," "Born Fighter," and "Cruel to Be Kind" to "American Squirm," "The Rose of England," "Half a Boy and Half a Man," and "Raging Eyes"—are here, and while *Jesus of Cool* and *Labour of Lust* are essential in their own right, *Basher* is a terrific introduction to his body of work. — *Stephen Thomas Erlewine*

Party of One / 1990 / Upstart ✦✦

Nick Lowe settled a long-standing feud with Dave Edmunds with *Party of One*, hiring his former Rockpile mate to produce the album. Edmunds gives Lowe a sharper sound than before, keeping a tight rein on the performances and the songs—for the first time, there are no covers on a Nick Lowe album. Theoretically, that wouldn't be a problem, but Lowe was in a songwriting slump at the time of *Party of One*. "All Men Are Liars," with its weird jab at dance-pop idol Rick Astley, is symptomatic of the record's flaws—ingratiating melodies are undercut by forced humor and bland support. Even the best moments—"(I Want To Build a) Jumbo Ark," "What's Shakin' on the Hill," "I Dont' Know Why You Keep Me On"—are undercut by stiff, colorless performances. From an artist who is defined by his relaxed charm, the stilted *Party of One* comes as an unwelcome surprise. — *Stephen Thomas Erlewine*

The Wilderness Years / 1991 / Demon ✦✦✦✦

Between the disbanding of Brinsley Schwarz in 1974 and the formation of Rockpile in 1977, Nick Lowe recorded a lot, attempting to settle on a sound. Simultaneously, he became the house producer at Stiff Records, where he became notorious for his raw, quickly produced records. That attitude shines through on *The Wilderness Years*, a compilation of singles, outtakes, covers, rarities, and demos Lowe recorded during this year. With the exception of *Pure Pop/Jesus of Cool*, no other record captures Lowe's sense of humor or love of pop music quite as well. Divided equally between gems and glorious throwaways, *The Wilderness Years* is all over the place, but that's its charm. It has the notorious songs Lowe wrote to break his contract with United Artists ("Bay City Rollers We Love You," "Let's Go to the Disco," "Rollers Show"), both sides of his first Stiff single ("So It Goes," "Heart of the City"), his "erstwhile Stiff advertising jingle" "I Love My Label," terrific covers of "Halfway to Paradise" and Sandy Posey's "Born a Woman," plus forgotten gems like the demo for "Endless Sleep" and "Heart," "Fool Too Long" (which was written for Dr. Feelgood), and "I Got a Job," a song Nick claims he doesn't remember writing or recording. In fact, Nick doesn't think much of any of this material, but an artist isn't always the best judge of his own work—he rarely got any better than he did here. — *Stephen Thomas Erlewine*

The Impossible Bird / Nov. 29, 1994 / Upstart ✦✦✦✦

Nick Lowe's best records have always been full of clever lyrics and undeniable pop craftsmanship; the exception is *The Impossible Bird*. For most of the 1980s, Lowe had been appropriating country and R&B influences, but *The Impossible Bird* is where he fully incorporates those styles into his songwriting. Lowe doesn't abandon his gift for melody; "Soulful Wind" and "12-Step Program (To Quit You Babe)" are as catchy as anything he's ever written. The difference is haunting songs like "The Beast in Me" and "Withered on the Vine," two rich, sad, introspective numbers that Lowe would never have put on previous albums. And that's what makes *The Impossible Bird* his best album since *Labour of Lust*—it's the most focused, mature, personal music of his career, without a single throwaway. — *Stephen Thomas Erlewine*

Live! On the Battlefield / Jul. 5, 1995 / Upstart ✦✦✦

Essentially not much more than a CD single for "Love on the Battlefield," *Live! On the Battlefield* contains the album version of the title track, a song from an Arthur Alexander tribute record and two live tracks, all recorded with the Impossible Birds. "Love on the Battlefield" is one of the finest moments on *The Impossible Bird*, and Alexander's "In the Middle of it All" is similarly charming, with Lowe's performance doing justice to one of Alexander's best songs. The live tracks are tight and exciting, but no better than the album versions, making the EP necessary only for completists. — *Stephen Thomas Erlewine*

Lulu (Marie MacDonald McLaughlin Lawrie)

b. Nov. 3, 1948, Lennox Castle, Glasgow
Vocals / British Invasion, Pop-Rock, Girl Group

Most Americans first heard of Lulu when she soared to the top of the charts with the pop ballad "To Sir with Love," the theme to the film of the same name, in 1967. Actually, the Scottish singer—born Marie McDonald McLaughlin Lawrie—had been a star in Britain since 1964, when she hit the Top Ten with a raucous version of "Shout." Lulu's mid-'60s recordings (which included a version of "Here Comes the Night" that preceded Them's hit rendition) were often surprisingly rowdy and R&B-influenced. Although she didn't match Dusty Springfield, her Brenda Lee-like rasp could be quite gutsy and soulful. Her career was headed in a determinedly middle-of-the-road direction by the late '60s, which saw her hosting a British variety show and marrying Bee Gee Maurice Gibb (they have since divorced). Recording intermittently ever since, she raised a few eyebrows by traveling to Muscle Shoals studios to record her 1970 album *New Routes*, and releasing a single of David Bowie tunes (which Bowie also played on and co-produced) in 1973. — *Richie Unterberger*

Something to Shout About / 1965 / Decca ✦✦✦

Reissue of a 1965 LP, with many bonus tracks. In the UK, Lulu first reached stardom as a gutsy belter of R&B tunes, delivered with a maturity and soulfulness that belied her teenage years. This 20-song compilation of material from 1964 to 1966 is the best CD reissue of her early work, although it's missing some of her better cuts. It includes her two mid-'60s British Top Ten hits, a cover of the Isley Brothers' "Shout," and the mid-tempo pop-soul tune "Leave a Little Love." Elsewhere, you get the spunky "I'll Come Running Over," which features Jimmy Page on guitar, and a raunchy cover of the obscure Rolling Stones song "Surprise Surprise" (also featuring Page). Most intriguing of all is the original version of "Here Comes the Night," later a hit for Them. Lulu performs it as an overwrought, pull-out-all-the-stops orchestral ballad; it's not nearly as successful as Van Morrison's rendition, but it's worth hearing. Unfortunately, this compilation doesn't include her surprisingly superb cover of "Heat Wave" from the same era. —*Richie Unterberger*

From Lulu . . . with Love / 1967 / Parrot ◆◆◆
Rush-released by Parrot to capitalize on the success of "To Sir with Love," this album may have been deceptively titled—it doesn't include "To Sir with Love," and the material dates from the mid-'60s, before she switched labels to Epic. But it's nonetheless a pretty good cross section of her early sides, which saw her concentrating on rock and R&B rather than orchestrated pop ballads. Besides the British hits "Shout" and "Leave a Little Love," it has Bert Berns' "Here Comes the Night," which she recorded before Them's hit version; "I'll Come Running," one of her raunchiest tracks, which features Jimmy Page on guitar; "Surprise, Surprise," an unlikely cover of an obscure Rolling Stones tune; and gutsy covers of the Knickerbockers' "Lies," Jerry Butler and Curtis Mayfield's "She Will Break Your Heart," and Van McCoy's "Take Me as I Am." —*Richie Unterberger*

Melody Fair / 1970 / Atlantic ◆◆◆
Since Lulu's most soulful qualities had usually been repressed or smothered by MOR-conscious material and production, this 1970 album seemed to have all the right ingredients for a blue-eyed soul triumph along the lines of Dusty Springfield's late-'60s LPs. The same label that midwifed those Springfield sessions was now doing the same for Lulu, matching her with backing by the Dixie Flyers, the Sweet Inspirations, and the Memphis Horns. Atlantic honchos Jerry Wexler, Tom Dowd, and Arif Mardin produced; the material included compositions by Gary Bonds, Leiberand Stoller, Randy Newman, and Bacharach-David. Yet the results, as is so often the case when the menu seems tasty, were rather underwhelming, the sum failing to add up to the parts. It's not at all bad, just unexciting. The songs aren't special enough, the arrangements never catch fire, and there are a couple of ill-advised detours into cheery pop tunes by the Beatles and Bee Gees. But it's not all bad timing; Lulu herself never seemed to let it all hang out and belt as she had occasionally in the past, except for a few funky moments. —*Richie Unterberger*

● **From Crayons to Perfume: The Best of Lulu** / Nov. 15, 1994 / Rhino ◆◆◆◆
By far the most wide-ranging retrospective of a singer who never found the consistently good material that her considerable talents deserved. Starting with her 1964 British hit cover of "Shout," it also includes the No. 1 single "To Sir with Love" and a few of her other British Top Ten hits from the '60s, including the nice '65 soul ballad "Leave a Little Love" and the chirpy 1967 Neil Diamond tune "The Boat That I Row" (the flip side of "To Sir with Love," which wasn't a hit at all in the UK). Unfortunately, it gives short shrift to the raunchy R&B she recorded in the mid-'60s, but it does include the sadly neglected, moody "Dreary Nights and Days" (penned by "To Sir with Love" author Mark London) and the Top 40 orchestrated ballad "Best of Both Worlds," co-arranged by future Led Zepper John Paul Jones. You also get nifty covers of Tim Rose's "Morning Dew" and Nilsson's "Without Him," along with a few songs she recorded with Atlantic (some with the Dixie Flyers) that gave her more sympathetic soul material than she was accustomed to, including the hit "Oh Me Oh My." There's also her semi-legendary 1974 single "Watch That Man"/ "The Man Who Sold the World," a double-sided 45 of David Bowie covers produced by Bowie himself, and the theme song to the James Bond film *The Man with the Golden Gun*. This 20-song compilation doesn't gather together all her fine material by any means, but it's the only one to cover most of her career. —*Richie Unterberger*

World of Lulu [Karussell] / 1996 / Karussell ◆◆◆◆◆
The packaging on this 20-track British import may not be so hot, but it's the best compilation to date of her mid-'60s Decca material, when she was at her most soulful and raunchy. Besides the hits "Shout" and "Leave a Little Love," and her version of "Here Comes the Night," it has quite a few excellent tracks that are hard or impossible to come by on other reissues, like Van McCoy's "Take Me as I Am," Goffin-King's stomping "Can't Hear You No More," and the Motown covers "Heatwave," "What's Easy for Two Is So Hard for One," and "Stubborn Kind of Fellow." —*Richie Unterberger*

Shout [dutch] / 1996 / Disky ◆◆
An 18-song collection that concentrates on her more pop/MOR-inclined recordings of the late '60s, with a few sides from the mid-'70s and mid-'80s thrown in. While some of this material is hard to come by in the US, it's not necessarily working seeking. The 1969 Top Five UK single "Boom Bang-a-Bang," the winner of that year's Eurovision Song contest, is a piece of kiddie fluff that ultimately may have done her a lot more harm than good. "I'm a Tiger" and "Let's Pretend" are other late-'60s British hits that are hard to locate stateside, but they aren't so hot either, though not as disgraceful as "Boom

Bang-a-Bang." The best numbers, including "To Sir With Love," "Without Him," and "Best of Both Worlds," are all on Rhino's best-of compilation. Also be aware that the version of her first hit, "Shout," is not the 1964 original, but a sub-par 1986 re-recording; the abominable cover of "My Boy Lollipop" sounds like it dates from the same session. —*Richie Unterberger*

Luna

f. 1991, New York City, NY
Alternative Pop-Rock, Dream-Pop
After Dean Wareham disbanded Galaxie 500 in the early '90s, he formed Luna, which followed in the same dreamy, slow style of his previous group, except the new band had a tendency to accentuate their melodies more frequently; in short, it was a lot like the Velvet Underground's third album, but not in a bad way at all. —*Stephen Thomas Erlewine*

Lunapark / Aug. 18, 1992 / Elektra ◆◆◆
Luna's first album doesn't sound that different from Galaxie 500, except that Dean Wareham's pop sensibilites come to the forefront with his new band, which makes *Lunapark* more enjoyable than most of his old band's albums. —*Stephen Thomas Erlewine*

Slide EP / Mar. 30, 1993 / Elektra ◆◆◆
The *Slide* EP is an engaging six-song collection of odds and ends, featuring the album version of the title track, the new "Rollercoaster," a demo of "Hey Sister," and three entertaining covers—the Velvet Underground's "Ride Into the Sun," Steve Wynn's "That's What You Always Say," and Beat Happening's "Indian Summer." —*Stephen Thomas Erlewine*

● **Bewitched** / Mar. 1, 1994 / Elektra ◆◆◆◆
While it doesn't sound all that much different than their debut, Luna's second album is a stronger record, featuring improved playing and songwriting. —*Stephen Thomas Erlewine*

Penthouse / Aug. 8, 1995 / Elektra ◆◆◆◆
Penthouse isn't as entracing as *Bewitched*, since Dean Wareham is suffering a slight songwriting slump, yet the group's lush, droning guitars remain enchanting, and they're effectively fleshed out by primitive keyboards and strings. None of the songs are that dissimilar from each other, yet the washes of airy melodies and guitars make *Penthouse* quite listenable. And the album does feature one terrific bonus track with "Bonnie and Clyde," a cover of a Serge Gainsbourg and Brigitte Bardot song performed in French by Wareham and Laetitia Sadier of Stereolab. —*Stephen Thomas Erlewine*

Luscious Jackson

f. 1991, New York City, NY
Alternative Pop-Rock
With their dark hip-hop-influenced alternative rock, Luscious Jackson recreates the dense, multicultural bohemian world of New York in a collage of sound, where Spanish guitars, jazzy keyboards, funky beats, and breathy, singsong vocals combine into one. Like the Beastie Boys, Luscious Jackson's eclecticism doesn't acknowledge boundaries; instead, it takes freely from every kind of music. Luscious Jackson's first two recordings, 1993's *In Search of Manny* and 1994's *Natural Ingredients*, earned them a cult following and positive critical reviews.

The core of Luscious Jackson—Kate Schellenbach (drums), Jill Cunniff (vocals, bass), and Gabby Glaser (vocals, guitar)—all met as teenagers on the New York post-punk scene of the early '80s. Schellenbach was the drummer in the original hardcore punk incarnation of the Beastie Boys; she met Cunniff when Jill interviewed the Beasties for her fanzine, *The Decline of Art*. Eventually, the trio began hanging out, seeing bands that ranged from hardcore and arty post-punk to reggae and hip-hop. When the members graduated from high school, they went their separate ways. Schellenbach stayed in New York, where she drummed with Hippies with Guns and attended college, while Cunniff and Glaser attended art school in San Francisco, where they both played in a punk band called Jaws; Jill continued to edit her fanzine.

In 1991, Cunniff and Glaser returned to New York and began writing songs. Eventually, the duo recruited Schellenbach and Jill's friend, Vivian Trimble, to form Luscious Jackson, taking their name from a '60s basketball player for the Philadelphia 76ers. The following year, the group released their debut EP, *In Search of Manny*, on the Beastie Boys' record label, Grand Royal; it was reissued the following year on Capitol/Grand Royal. *In Search of Manny* received very positive reviews and the group quickly became a hip name to drop in alternative rock circles.

Natural Ingredients, the group's first full-length album, was released in the late summer of 1994 to generally favorable reviews. "City Song" became a minor modern rock hit in the fall of that year.

Before the release of *Natural Ingredients*, Luscious Jackson spent the summer of 1994 on the second stage of Lollapalooza, per the request of the Beastie Boys. Following the release of *Natural Ingredients*, the group spent most of 1995 on the road, including a stint opening for R.E.M. on the *Monster* tour. *Natural Ingredients* eventually sold almost 200,000 copies. Early in 1996, Schellenbach and Cunniff released a side project entitled *Ko-Stars*. At the time, Luscious Jackson was continuing work on their second album, working with producer Daniel Lanois. The result, *Fever In Fever Out*, was released in the fall of 1996. —*Stephen Thomas Erlewine*

● **In Search of Manny EP** / 1992 / Grand Royal/Capitol ✦✦✦✦
A darkly funky, atmospheric EP where hip-hop is used as a basis for the folk-tinged songs, which paint detailed, textured portraits of the New York bohemian slacker scene. An impressive debut from this New York quartet. —*Stephen Thomas Erlewine*

Natural Ingredients / Aug. 23, 1994 / Grand Royal/Capitol ✦✦✦
Luscious Jackson's first full-length album, *Natural Ingredients*, features a brighter, more open sound than *In Search of Manny*, without losing the funky, organic feel of the EP. Musically, the band continue to refine their hip-hop influenced pop, adding stronger hooks and denser grooves. *Natural Ingredients* isn't as consistent or edgy as *In Search of Manny*, but the record fulfills their initial promise. —*Stephen Thomas Erlewine*

Fever in Fever Out / Oct. 29, 1996 / Grand Royal/Capitol ✦✦✦✦
For all of its sunny eclecticism, *Natural Ingredients* lacked the darkly funky urban soundscapes that made *In Search of Manny* so engaging. *Fever In Fever Out* brings that dark funkiness while keeping the pop hooks that made *Natural Ingredients* a step forward. Producer Daniel Lanois keeps his ambient tendencies to a minimum, providing just enough atmosphere to make songs as catchy as the jazzy, intricate "Naked Eye" surprisingly haunting. But what really impresses is the sense of forward motion Luscious Jackson displays on *Fever In Fever Out*, how their eclecticism is becoming more seamless as their songs grow stronger. —*Stephen Thomas Erlewine*

Lush

f. Oct. 1988, London, England
Alternative Pop-Rock, Shoegazing, Brit-Pop, Dream-Pop
Meshing dreamy, feedback-drenched guitars with airy, catchy melodies, Lush were one of the most prominent shoegazing bands of the early '90s. Led by guitarists Miki Berenyi and Emma Anderson, the British band earned a cult following within the British and American undergrounds with their first EPs, yet they never quite attained the critical respect given to their peers My Bloody Valentine and Ride. Even so, the group lasted longer than any other their contemporaries (with the exception of the Boo Radleys), developing sharp pop skills as their career progressed. By the time of their final album, 1996's *Lovelife*, the band had converted themselves into a power-pop band with dream-pop overtones, which resulted in the greatest chart success of their career. Their success was dealt a blow when drummer Chris Acland committed suicide in the fall of 1996, putting the band's future in doubt.

Mikie Berenyi, Emma Anderson, Chris Acland, Steve Rippon (bass), and Meriel Barham (guitar) formed Lush in 1987 in London, England. Prior to the group's formation, school friends Berenyi and Anderson had collaborated on a fanzine together, as well as played in a number of other bands individually; Anderson, who had been working as a DHSS clerical assistant, had played bass with the Rover Girls, while Berenyi had been a member of I-Goat, Fuhrer Five and the Lillies. Berenyi's then-boyfriend Acland had previously played with several other groups as well, including Panik, Infection, and A Touch of Hysteria. Barham left Lush soon after the band's formation to form the Pale Saints, and the remaining members began playing around London, quickly earning a number of fans, including Robin Guthrie of the Cocteau Twins. Guthrie helped the band secure a contract with 4AD Records, and the band released its acclaimed debut EP *Scar* in 1989. Lush supported the EP with opening tours for Loop and the Darling Buds, and by 1990, they had graduated to headlining tours of their own.

Throughout 1990, the band's reputation in the British music press began to grow, as they released the acclaimed EPs *Mad Love* and *Sweetness and Light*, played high-profile gigs like the Glastonbury Festival, and became favorites of the music weeklies' gossip columns. *Gala*, an album compiling their three EPs, became the band's first American release at the end of 1990. Lush spent most of 1991 recording their debut album, releasing the *Black Spring* EP in the spring. Rippon left the band during the sessions, and was replaced by Phillip King, a former picture researcher for the *NME* and a previous member of Felt, Servants, and Biff Bang Pow. Lush finally released their delayed debut album *Spooky* in the spring of 1992. While the album sold well, reaching the British Top Ten and topping

the UK indie charts, it was criticized in the press for Robin Guthrie's heavy-handed production. The band supported the album in America by appearing on the second Lollapalooza Tour, but their dream-pop wasn't well-received by an audience hungry for metal. Lush released their second album, *Split*, in the summer of 1994 to mixed reviews. *Split* was lost in the twin waves of Brit-pop and American post-grunge, even through the band's songwriting was more pop-oriented than ever. After regrouping during 1995, Lush returned in early 1996 with *Lovelife*, an album that showcased a debt to the pop-single ideals of Brit-pop. The musical changeover paid off, as "Single Girl" and "Ladykiller" became their two biggest hit singles, and the album became a British Top 20 hit; in America, it was their highest-charting album, even if it just scraped the charts at No. 189. Lush had completed their supporting tours and summer festival appearances when Chris Acland unexpectedly hanged himself in his parent's house on October 17, 1996. Devastated by his death, the remaining members of Lush went into a long period of mourning, and by early 1997, it appeared as if the band was on the verge of breaking up. —*Stephen Thomas Erlewine*

Gala / Dec. 1990 / 4AD/Reprise ✦✦✦✦
Anyone who believes that music loosely defined as "alternative rock" has to be forceful and abrasive hasn't heard Lush, which delights in melodies that are rich, intoxicating, and—as its name indicates—lush. Singer Miki Berenyi doesn't have a great range by any means, but her fragility and sweetness serve their purpose on this striking CD. As atmospheric as *Gala* is, it's far from redundant, and hardly qualifies as lightweight background music. In fact, treasures ranging from "Thoughtforms" to "Hey Hey Helen" to "Scarlet" are quite substantial. Blending pop sweetness and folk delicacy with rock edginess, *Gala* is an album of contrasts that is as impressive as it is unpredictable. —*Alex Henderson*

● **Spooky** / Jan. 1992 / 4AD/Reprise ✦✦✦✦
While Lush features fragile, dual-female vocals layered over hypnotic melodies, the group has always taken a minimalist approach to its music. The vocal tracks are just as likely to be wedded to fuzzy guitar riffs and pounding rhythms. Everything kind of blurs and merges together in an urgent, often disturbing mix that belies the vocal sweetness. There are exceptions. Lush softens its stance on several fragile acoustic tracks, notably "Tiny Smiles," "For Love," and "Monochrome." Then like a shattered mirror, "Superblast!" and "Laura" offer a harsher extreme, shards of glass splintering through the songs without mercy. While Lush's bittersweet soundscapes will never grace mainstream dance floors or Top 40 radio, *Spooky* does make fascinating listening under headphones in the dark. —*Roch Parisien*

Split / Jun. 1994 / 4AD/Reprise ✦✦✦✦
One of the original British "shoe-gazer" bands shoots eons beyond the competition thanks to stunningly confident vocals that maintain the requisite waifish innocence, combined with instrumentation that shimmers and slices in enchanting, three-chord wonder. —*Roch Parisien*

Lovelife / Mar. 5, 1996 / 4AD/Reprise ✦✦✦✦
Lovelife represents a major shift in style for Lush. Nearly abandoning the trancy melodies and droning guitars that were their trademark, the band has crafted an album full of sharp hooks and melodies, one that owes a great deal to the Brit-pop mania of 1995. From the circular melody of the opening "Ladykillers," it's clear that Lush had been influenced by the direct, jagged pop of Elastica, but they also have reached back into '60s pop. All of the ballads on *Lovelife* are rooted in the hazy dream-pop of the early '90s, but they are given stylish, mod arrangements complete with muted brass. Even more startling is the Nancy Sinatra/Lee Hazlewood pastiche of "Ciao!," an irresistible duet between Miki Berenyi and Pulp's Jarvis Cocker. *Lovelife* would have simply been an embarrassing attempt to seem fashionable if Lush hadn't succeeded in updating their sound. However, they have been able to re-create themselves as a pop band and the result is their most direct—and arguably their most rewarding—album. —*Stephen Thomas Erlewine*

Frankie Lymon

b. Sep. 30, 1942, Harlem, NY, d. Feb. 28, 1968, Harlem, NY
Doo Wop
Frankie Lymon (1942-1968) & the Teenagers were a New York doo wop group consisting of Joe Negroni, Herman Santiago, Jimmy Merchant, and Sherman Garnes, but centered around the extraordinary talents of their lead singer, thirteen-year-old Frankie Lymon. Lymon was credited with their first big hit, "Why Do Fools Fall in Love." (In the early '90s, a federal judge ruled—after a lengthy trial—that Lymon hadn't written "Why Do Fools Fall in Love"—another member of the Teenagers had.) His wise-beyond-his-years vocal and performing abilities not only made the Teenagers a group several notches above the competition but made Lymon the first Black teenage pop star. Though only together for a brief 18-month period,

Lymon & the Teenagers exerted an enormous influence, spawning several "kid" vocal groups and providing initial inspiration to Berry Gordy to model his entire Motown production approach around Lymon's original vocal style. Inexplicably, the group split into two factions at the height of their success, and neither had a hit again. Lymon died from a drug overdose at age 25. Diana Ross, Smokey Robinson, Len Barry, and his principal protégé, Michael Jackson (whose early recordings with the Jackson 5 are virtual re-creations of the early Lymon sound, merely updated) all show the influence of Frankie Lymon & the Teenagers' groundbreaking work. — *Cub Koda*

★ The Best of Frankie Lymon & the Teenagers / 1990 / Rhino ✦✦✦✦✦
Frankie Lymon wrote "Why Do Fools Fall in Love?" at 13 and led his group, the Teenagers, to a brief stardom. They remain one of the finest examples of New York vocal group singing, and all of the essentials are on this album. — *Jeff Tamarkin*

Barbara Lynn

b. Jan. 16, 1942, Beaumont, TX
Guitar, Vocals / Soul, R&B, New Orleans R&B
A bluesy southpaw guitarist from Beaumont, TX, Barbara Lynn Ozen wrote her own ticket to hitdom with the 1962 smash "You'll Lose a Good Thing," an R&B chart-topper. Texas producer Huey Meaux brought Lynn to Cosimo's studio in New Orleans to cut the atmospheric downbeat tune, her debut single on the Jamie label. Followups included the bouncy "Oh! Baby (We Got a Good Thing Goin')"—better remembered through the Rolling Stones' faithful cover—and her minor 1966 hit on the often-covered "You Left the Water Running." Barbara Lynn resurfaced again in 1994, this time recording for Bullseye Blues. Her CD *So Good* included a new version of "This Is the Thanks I Get," but no reprise of "You'll Lose a Good Thing." Lynn remains active, currently recording for Antone's. — *Bill Dahl*

You'll Lose a Good Thing / 1962 / Jamie ✦✦✦✦
Barbara Lynn Ozen's smoky voice and fine guitar playing made one of the better blends of soul vocals and blues embellishment. Huey P. Meaux produced this early-'60s record, which featured the classic title track. Other Lynn numbers, like "I'll Suffer," were equally outstanding; Lynn was sometimes tough and confrontational, at other times tender, inviting, or anguished. Meaux didn't clutter the works with unnecessary firepower; his arrangements and charts were just enough to augment Lynn's sturdy vocals. Lynn also wrote ten of the 12 songs. — *Ron Wynn*

● **Barbara Lynn** / 1989 / Goodthing ✦✦✦✦
Yet another Barbara Lynn anthology, this one is more complete than its counterparts in that it includes her material on Jamie and other labels, as well as the Atlantic hits. Lynn actually recorded "You'll Lose A Good Thing" for Jamie, but it was later included on an Atlantic release. This has 17 songs from Jamie, Atlantic, and Tribe sessions, including some that weren't big hits but should have been, like "This Is The Thanks I Get" and "It's Better To Have It." — *Ron Wynn*

The Best of Barbara Lynn: the Atlantic Years / Nov. 22, 1994 / Ichiban/Soul Classics ✦✦✦
This 20-track collection gathers most of Lynn's output for Atlantic between 1968 and 1973, including most of her 1968 *Here Is Barbara Lynn* album and several non-LP singles. Commercially, Lynn's stay at Atlantic was not fruitful, yielding only a couple of moderate R&B hits, the self-penned "This Is The Thanks I Get" and "Until Then, I'll Suffer" (both included). Artistically, this is fairly solid period soul, but a bit faceless. It seems as though Atlantic tried to fit Lynn into current soul trends; many of the 1968 tracks are quite derivative of Motown, and many of the later sides take a Memphis/Muscle Shoals approach. Those are fine influences, of course, but Lynn's strengths were her original songwriting and bluesy Southern phrasing. The most outstanding tracks are from her first Atlantic single, "This Is The Thanks I Get" and "Ring Telephone Ring," when much of her original relaxed Texas/New Orleans R&B style was still in evidence. The version of "You'll Lose A Good Thing" here, incidentally, is a remake, not the original 1962 hit. — *Richie Unterberger*

Lynyrd Skynyrd

f. 1965, Jacksonville, FL
Southern Rock, Hard Rock, Blues-Rock
Lynyrd Skynyrd was the definitive Southern Rock band, fusing the overdriven power of blues-rock with a rebellious Southern image and a hard-rock swagger. Skynyrd never relied on the jazzy improvisations of the Allman Brothers. Instead, they were a hard-living, hard-driving rock 'n' roll band—they may have jammed endlessly on stage, but their music remained firmly entrenched in blues, rock, and country. For many, Lynyrd Skynyrd's redneck image tended to obscure the songwriting skills of its leader, Ronnie Van Zant.

Throughout the band's early records, Van Zant demonstrated a knack for lyrical detail and a down-to-earth honesty that had more in common with country than rock 'n' roll. During the height of Skynyrd's popularity in the mid-'70s, however, Van Zant's talents were overshadowed by the group's gritty, greasy blues-rock. Sadly, it wasn't until he was killed in a tragic plane crash in 1977 along with two other band members that many listeners began to realize his talents. Skynyrd split up after the plane crash, but they reunited a decade later, becoming a popular concert act during the early '90s.

While in high school in Jacksonville, Florida, Ronnie Van Zant (vocals), Allen Collens (guitar), and Gary Rossington (guitar) formed My Backyard. Within a few months, the group added bassist Leon Wilkeson and keyboardist Billy Powell, and changed their name to Lynyrd Skynyrd, a mocking tribute to their gym teacher Leonard Skinner, who was notorious for punishing students with long hair. With drummer Bob Burns, Lynyrd Skynyrd began playing throughout the South. For the first few years, the group had little success, but producer Al Kooper signed the band to MCA after seeing them play at an Atlanta club called Funocchio's in 1972. Kooper produced the group's 1973 debut, *Pronounced Leh-Nerd Skin-Nerd*, which was recorded after former Strawberry Alarm Clock guitarist Ed King joined the band. The group became notorious for their triple guitar attack, which was showcased on "Free Bird," a tribute to the recently-deceased Duane Allman. "Free Bird" earned Lynyrd Skynyrd their first national exposure and it became one of the staples of album-rock, still receiving airplay nearly 25 years after its release.

"Free Bird" and an opening slot on the Who's 1973 *Quadrophenia* tour gave Lynyrd Skynyrd a devoted following, which helped its second album, 1974's *Second Helping*, become its breakthrough hit. Featuring the hit single "Sweet Home Alabama"—a response song to Neil Young's "Southern Man"—*Second Helping* reached No. 12 and went multi-platinum. At the end of the year, Artimus Pyle replaced drummer Burns and King left the band shortly afterward. The new sextet released *Nuthin' Fancy* in 1975, and it became the band's first Top Ten hit. The record was followed by the Tom Dowd-produced *Gimme Back My Bullets* in 1976, which failed to match the success of its two predecessors. However, the band retained its following through its constant touring, which was documented on the double-live album *One More from the Road*. Released in late 1976, the album featured the band's new guitarist Steve Gaines and a trio of female backup singers, and it became Skynyrd's second Top Ten album.

Lynyrd Skynyrd released its sixth album, *Street Survivors*, on October 17, 1977. Three days later, a privately chartered plane carrying the band between shows in Greenville, SC and Baton Rouge, LA crashed outside of Gillsburg, MS. Ronnie Van Zant, Steve Gaines, and his sister Cassie, one of the group's backing vocalists, died in the crash; the remaining members were injured. The cause of the crash was either fuel shortage or a fault with the plane's mechanics. The cover for *Street Survivors* had pictured the band surrounded in flames; after the crash, the cover was changed. In the wake of the tragedy, the album became one of the band's biggest hits. Lynyrd Skynyrd broke up after the crash, releasing a collection of early demos called *Skynyrd's First . . . and Last* in 1978. The album had been scheduled for release before the crash. The double-album compilation, *Gold and Platinum*, was released in 1980. Later in 1980, Rossington and Collins formed a new band that featured four surviving members. Two years later, Pyle formed the Artimus Pyle Band. Collins suffered a car crash in 1986, killing his girlfriend and leaving him paralyzed. Four years later, he died of respiratory failure. In 1987, Rossington, Powell, King, and Wilkeson reunited Lynyrd Skynyrd, adding vocalist Johnny Van Zant and guitarist Randall Hall. The band embarked on a reunion tour, which was captured on the 1988 double-live album, *Southern by the Grace of God/Lynyrd Skynyrd Tribute Tour—1987*. The re-formed Skynyrd began recording in 1991, and for the remainder of the decade, the band toured frequently, putting out albums occasionally. The reunited Skynyrd frequently switched drummers, but it had little effect on their sound. — *Stephen Thomas Erlewine*

Pronounced Leh-Nerd Skin-Nerd / 1973 / MCA ✦✦✦✦
With the release of this debut album, Skynyrd was immediately recognized as one of the South's premier bands. The album's highlight is "Free Bird," a song that, over time, has become one of the most requested rock songs in the history of radio. "Simple Man," "Gimme Three Steps," and "Tuesday's Gone" are several other standards from this classic album. — *Rick Clark*

☆ **Second Helping** / 1974 / MCA ✦✦✦✦✦
The appropriately titled follow-up to their debut was equally impressive, containing their highest-charting hit, "Sweet Home Alabama." Unlike many albums, where the hit is the highlight, *Second Helping* is chock-full of great tunes like "Working for MCA," "Call Me the Breeze," "Don't Ask Me No Questions," and "Ballad of Curtis Loew." — *Rick Clark*

Nuthin' Fancy / 1975 / MCA ✦✦✦
Frazzled by too much endless roadwork and too little songwriting preparation, *Nuthin' Fancy* is a step down from its impressive predecessor. Nevertheless, "Saturday Night Special," the album's opener, is a classic rocker. Other standouts include the Free-style "On the Hunt," "Whiskey Rock-A-Roller," and "Am I Losin'." —*Rick Clark*

Gimme Back My Bullets / 1976 / MCA ✦✦✦
On their first production with the legendary Tom Dowd (Rod Stewart, Eric Clapton, Allman Brothers), Skynyrd sounds relatively uninspired, even as they indignantly call for a return to platinum status with the Free-influenced title cut. Nevertheless, Van Zant's gift for plain-speaking lyrics and the band's undeniable chemistry help this record hold up better than many late-'70s AOR rock acts. —*Rick Clark*

One More from the Road / 1976 / MCA ✦✦✦
Recorded at Atlanta's Fox Theater and produced by Tom Dowd, Skynyrd returned to their original three-guitar lineup concept with the addition of Steve Gaines. Some might complain that *One More* failed to capture the energy of the band's shows, but overall it ranks as one of rock's finest live releases. When it was first reissued on CD, MCA abridged the album, cutting out some key tracks and dialog. However, the 1996 two-CD edition includes everything from the original album, resequences it to correspond with the original running order of the sets, and adds three previously unreleased tracks from the concerts. —*Rick Clark*

Street Survivors / 1977 / MCA ✦✦✦✦
The addition of lead guitarist and singer Steve Gaines goaded Ronnie Van Zant and the band into a dramatic rebirth. *Street Survivors* featured tighter songs, strong melodies, and an exciting element of vocal interplay between Van Zant and Gaines ("You Got That Right"). The contrast between Gaines' clean lead style, Collins' flash, and Rossington's thick-toned lyrical phrasing is something to behold. Without a doubt, it's Skynyrd's most cohesive body of work since *Second Helping*. —*Rick Clark*

Skynyrd's First And . . . Last / 1978 / MCA ✦✦✦
Pre-Al Kooper Skynyrd, recorded in Muscle Shoals, it may not be their best work, but shows without a doubt that this Jacksonville band was already head and shoulders above many major-label bands, even before they were signed. —*Rick Clark*

★ **Gold & Platinum** / 1980 / MCA ✦✦✦✦✦
Gold and Platinum was compiled by Gary Rossington and Allen Collins, the two surviving members of Lynyrd Skynyrd. Though many years have elapsed since its 1980 release, the double-record set remains the best, most concise compilation of the groundbreaking Southern rock band. Over the course of two albums, all of Skynyrd's hits—"Sweet Home Alabama," "Free Bird," "Saturday Night Special," "What's Your Name," "You Got That Right"—are featured, as well as essential album tracks like "The Ballad of Curtis Loew," "That Smell," "Down South Jukin'," "Gimme Three Steps," "I Know A Little," and "Tuesday's Gone." Some great songs like "Working for MCA" are missing, and the four-disc box set may be more comprehensive, but it's hard to imagine a better, more concise greatest hits collection than *Gold and Platinum*. —*Stephen Thomas Erlewine*

Legend / Oct. 5, 1987 / MCA ✦✦
Southern by the Grace of God: Lynyrd Skynyrd Tribute Tour, Vol. 1 / 1988 / MCA ✦✦✦

Lynyrd Skynyrd 1991 / Jun. 11, 1991 / Atlantic ✦✦
After the 1987 Tribute Tour, this re-formed lineup of Skynyrd inked a deal with Atlantic and cut this album in Memphis with Tom Dowd producing. As a playing unit, the band still had a formidable delivery, but with the absence of Van Zant and Collins, it is obvious that there was a shortage of strong songs with a distinctive point of view—a given throughout all of their pre-plane crash albums. However, "Smokestack Lightning," "Backstreet Crawler," and "Pure & Simple" (later re-mixed for the country market) are highlights. —*Rick Clark*

Lynyrd Skynyrd [Box Set] / Nov. 12, 1991 / MCA ✦✦✦✦
This attractively packaged and well-chosen collection of the band's most popular tracks also includes early demos and other unreleased tracks. —*Rick Clark*

The Last Rebel / Feb. 16, 1993 / Atlantic ✦✦
Although it should please diehard fans, the reconstituted Lynyrd Skynyrd's second studio record does little to expand the group's horizons. Aside from a few longer songs that allow the group to stretch out, most of *The Last Rebel* is by-the-book Southern rock, further undermined by Johnny Van Zant's cliche-riddled lyrics. —*Jason Ankeny*

Endangered Species / Aug. 9, 1994 / Capricorn ✦✦✦✦
Okay, it's the latter-day band with lots of replacement members, but this is a great record, and this time out there are no repertory problems. This is Skynyrd's "unplugged" album, with the band performing most of its best-known songs without amplification, on an array of instruments that includes mandolin. The songs come off very strong and surprisingly natural in this setting, and it's all good enough and different enough to make *Endangered Species* a necessary addition to the collection of any fan of the original band. —*Bruce Eder*

Free Bird: The Movie / Aug. 13, 1996 / MCA ✦✦✦
Despite its title, *Free Bird: The Movie* does *not* contain a series of variations on the title song (granted, only four versions of "Free Bird" could have fit on a standard-play compact disc). Instead, it captures a number of highlights from the soundtrack of *Free Bird: The Movie*, a documentary about Lynyrd Skynyrd's final tour. In addition to a dynamite version of "Free Bird," the album contains a number of rare Skynyrd live cuts, including the first released live takes of "What's Your Name" and "That Smell." For dedicated fans, it's a live memento worth seeking out and cherishing. —*Stephen Thomas Erlewine*

Twenty / Apr. 29, 1997 / CMC International ✦✦
As the title says, *Twenty* is the twentieth album from Lynyrd Skynyrd, but perhaps a more relevant yardstick is that it is the fifth record the group has released since reuniting in the late '80s. Prior to recording *Twenty*, the group added two new members—ex-Blackfoot Ricky Medlocke and former Outlaw Hughie Thomasson—making the group a virtual Southern rock supergroup, and that's part of the problem. There are too many egos involved to make the album truly captivating—especially since the songwriting is usually undistinguished—but occasionally, the star power gels and results in some hot rock 'n' roll. In other words, specialists and aficionados will find plenty of stuff to enjoy here, but most casual fans will think that it's all been said before. —*Stephen Thomas Erlewine*

The Lyres

f. 1979, Boston, MA
Punk, Garage Rock
Few bands in Boston rock 'n' roll history have lasted as long, and made as much good music, as the Lyres. Led by garage-rock obsessive, record collector, Farfisa organ king, and world-class megalomaniac Jeff "Monoman" Connolly, the Lyres rose from the ashes of Connolly's first band, DMZ. Sporting a similar high-energy trash-rock sound indebted to the Seeds, ? and the Mysterians, the Stooges, and the early British Invasion (especially early Kinks), the Lyres, for a brief, shining moment, were the kingpins of Boston's punk rock scene. Resembling venerable British blues-rockers Savoy Brown because of a constantly changing lineup (something like 40 musicians have passed through the ranks), the Lyres (or more specifically, Monoman) gleefully party on, oblivious of trends or the assorted vagaries of the alternative rock marketplace. A dinosaur in his own right? Perhaps, but as long as Jeff Connolly has his organ, a few guys behind him and a place to play, the simple joy that can only be had through rock 'n' roll will exist in this world—hipness be damned! —*John Dougan*

AHS: 1005 / 1981 / Ace of Hearts ✦✦✦✦
On Fyre / 1984 / Ace of Hearts ✦✦✦✦
Simply their best. *On Fyre* is a nonstop raveup from the opening salvo of "Don't Give It up Now." Garage rock fans will want for nothing here: blistering tempos, manic intensity, hyperactive vocals, ultra-cheesy organ; it's a knock-down, drag-out rock 'n' roll party, Lyres-style. —*John Dougan*

Lyres Lyres / 1986 / New Rose ✦✦✦
More emotionally complex and reflective than *On Fyre*, this could well be one of the most mature garage rock records ever recorded. That doesn't mean that energy and excitement are sacrificed for dour introspection—far from it. This is a total joy from start to finish, and a great place to hang out after a thousand or so spins of *On Fyre*. —*John Dougan*

Live at Continental / 1987 / Pryct ✦✦
A Promise Is a Promise / 1988 / Ace of Hearts ✦✦✦
The Lyres Live 1983: Let's Have a Party!! / 1989 / Pryct ✦✦✦
Recorded live in the studio for Emerson College's great Boston music show Metrowave, these 13 slices of reckless abandon get about as close as one can to the "majesticity" (according to the guy introducing them) of a typical Lyres gig. Includes great versions of "Never Met a Girl Like You" and "Gonna Find a New Love." BYOB and crank it up! —*John Dougan*

● **Some Lyres** / Mar. 11, 1994 / Taang! ✦✦✦✦
An excellent, if brief (12 tracks) part-career retrospective, part-collection of oddities that includes their 1979 debut single "How Do You Know" b/w "Don't Give it Up Now." Packaged as a parody of The Rolling Stones' controversial *Some Girls*, *Some Lyres* proves to be a valuable introduction. —*John Dougan*

Those Lyres / Apr. 25, 1995 / Norton ✦✦✦
Early Years Live 1979-1983 / Jan. 21, 1997 / Crypt ✦✦✦✦

M

Kirsty MacColl

b. Oct. 10, 1959, London, England
Guitar, Vocals / Singer-Songwriter, Folk-Rock, Pop-Rock, Adult Alternative Pop-Rock

Kirsty MacColl, daughter of folk singer-songwriter Ewan MacColl, began her own musical career while still in her teens, singing in a band called the Addix, and eventually signed to the legendary Stiff Records. Her first single, the modern girl group gem "They Don't Know," was released in 1979. Though it failed in the charts, it was later a major hit for Tracey Ullman. She switched to Polydor in the '80s and landed a UK Top 20 hit with the novelty song "There's a Guy Works Down the Chip Shop (Swears He's Elvis)." She followed the single with her first LP, *Desperate Character*, in 1981. In 1984, she married producer Steve Lillywhite and put her solo career on hold, raising their two children and working as a backup singer. MacColl returned in 1989 with a more mature effort, *Kite*, which reached the UK Top 20. Since then, she has released two more albums, *Electric Landlady* (1991) and *Titanic Days* (1993), displaying great talent and diversity and, above all, good pop sensibilities. —*Chris Woodstra*

Desperate Character / 1981 / Polydor ✦✦✦

Kite / 1989 / Charisma ✦✦✦
After nearly a decade's absence as solo performer, MacColl released the low-key *Kite*, a decidedly more mature effort. Her literate and sharp vocals are perfectly matched with lush, textured folk-pop arrangements. Johnny Marr contributes his distinctive guitar playing on several tracks. —*Chris Woodstra*

Electric Landlady / Jun. 25, 1991 / Charisma ✦✦✦✦
MacColl is in peak form on the more experimental *Electric Landlady*. Playing with a different band on nearly every track, she effortlessly moves from the hip-hop of "Walking Down Madison," to the Latin-tinged "My Affair," to the Smiths' sound-alike "Children of the Revolution" (co-written by Smiths guitarist Johnny Marr). Overall, she builds on the folk-pop of her previous effort with much stronger material. Her lyrics have become more personal, mainly focusing on her relationship with, and the recent death of, her father. —*Chris Woodstra*

The Essential Collection / 1993 / Stiff ✦✦✦✦
A fine collection of Kirsty MacColl's early singles for Stiff Records in the late '70s. She wrote effortlessly melodic three-minute pop singles that managed to recast the classic girl group sound of the '60s into a style that was contemporary and timeless, in much the same way that Rockpile energetically recast '50s and '60s rock 'n' roll. Not only were these singles some of the best she's ever written, they were among the best pop songs of the era, including the original version of Tracey Ullman's hit "They Don't Know" and the infectious "There's a Guy Works Down the Chip Shop (Swears He's Elvis)." —*Chris Woodstra*

Titanic Days / Oct. 5, 1993 / IRS ✦✦✦
MacColl delivers another brilliant album with 1993's *Titanic Days*. The arrangements have become more ambitious, as evident in the jazzy "Bad" and the heavily orchestrated "Soho Square." The lyrics are still sharp with biting commentary, this time backed by a more dance-oriented pop. —*Chris Woodstra*

● **Galore** / Jan. 24, 1995 / IRS ✦✦✦✦
Eighteen-track compilation. The strength of these collected forces may just be sufficient to overcome Kirsty MacColl's two fatal commercial "flaws": she spreads herself all over the musical map, and writes intelligent, often dryly humorous lyrics about life and relationships that never pander to chart sentimentality. MacColl oozes a pure, fresh-scrubbed, girl-next-door quality that belies the sophistication of her songwriting without ever resorting to vacant innocence. —*Roch Parisien*

The Mad Lads

f. 1963, Memphis, TN
Soul, R&B

One of the few vocal groups on the Stax roster during the '60s, the Mad Lads' doo wop-influenced harmonies were more akin to what you might find in Philadelphia soul acts than to those of their native Memphis. Featuring the high, innocent tenor of John Gary Williams, the group were still in high school when they were signed to Stax in late 1964. In the mid-'60s, they enjoyed solid R&B hits with "Don't Have to Shop Around," "I Want Someone," and "I Want a Girl," although they never would cross over to the pop audience. Williams and fellow Mad Lad William Brown were drafted in 1966, and their recording career was suspended while they were in the service (although the other members carried on live with replacements). After their discharge, Williams and Brown were told by fellow original members Julius Green and Robert Philips that they didn't want Brown in the group; Brown and Stax co-owner Jim Stewart forced them to reinstate Williams, but their subsequent efforts were more in the Stax soul-funk formula, and not as memorable as their more atypical mid-'60s singles. They did return to the R&B Top 30 in 1968 with "Whatever Hurts You." —*Richie Unterberger*

● **Don't Have to Shop Around** / Aug. 2, 1995 / Stax ✦✦✦✦
Career-spanning disc of material recorded between the mid-'60s and early '70s, including the hits "Don't Have to Shop Around," "I Want Someone," and "I Want a Girl," as well as more modern-styled cuts from the late '60s and early '70s. Good second-division soul, although it's missing their 1968 hit "Whatever Hurts You." —*Richie Unterberger*

Madness

f. 1978, Camden, London, England, db. 1986
New Wave, Ska-Revival, Pop-Rock

Along with the Specials, Madness were one of the leading bands of the ska revival of the late '70s and early '80s. As their career progressed, Madness branched away from their trademark "nutty sound" and incorporated large elements of Motown, soul, and British pop. Although the band managed one crossover American hit in 1983, they remained a British phenomenon, influencing several successive generations of musicians and becoming one of the most beloved groups the country produced during the '80s.

The origins of Madness lie in a ska group known as Morris and the Minors, which was formed by Mike Barson, Chris Foreman, and Lee Thompson in 1976. By 1978, the band had changed their name to the Invaders and had added Graham "Suggs" McPherson, Mark Bedford, Chas Smash, and Dan Woodgate to the group. Later in 1978, they changed their name to Madness, in homage to one of their favorite Prince Buster songs. The following year, Madness released their debut single, a tribute to Prince Buster entitled "The Prince," on Two-Tone. The song was a surprise success, reaching the British Top 20. Following its success, the band signed a record contract with Stiff Records and released another Prince Buster song, "One Step Beyond," which climbed to No. 7.

Madness quickly recorded their debut album, also titled *One Step Beyond*, with producers Clive Langer and Alan Winstanley. Released toward the end of the year, the album peaked at No. 2 in Britain and it stayed on the charts for well over a year. At the beginning of 1980, the band's third single, "My Girl," peaked at No. 3. For the next three years, the group had a virtually uninterrupted run of 13 Top Ten singles, during which time they were one of the most popular bands in Britain, rivaled only by the Jam in terms of widespread popularity. Where the Jam appealed to teenagers and young adults, Madness had a broad fan base, reaching from children to the elderly. Which didn't mean their music was diluted—they continued to expand their sound, both musically and lyrically.

In the spring of 1980, Madness released the *Work Rest and Play* EP, which reached No. 6 on the strength of the EP's lead song, "Night Boat to Cairo." Also during the spring, *One Step Beyond* was released in the US, where it peaked at No. 128. Madness' second album, *Absolutely*, was released in the fall of 1980. The record peaked at No. 2 on the British charts, but stalled at No. 146 in the US. Sire dropped the band after the commercial disappointment of *Absolutely*, leaving Madness without an American record contract for several years.

Back in England, Madness continued to gain momentum, as the group began playing matinee shows on their tours so children under 16 years old could attend the concert. In the fall of 1981, the band released their third album, *Seven*, which peaked at No. 5. In January of 1982, Madness hit No. 4 with a cover of Labi Siffre's "It Must Be Love." In March, their streak of Top Ten hits was interrupted when "Cardiac Arrest" stalled at No. 14 on the charts, due to radio's reluctance to play the tune. The band bounced back a few months later with "House of Fun," their first No. 1 single. That same month, the hits compilation, *Complete Madness*, reached No. 1.

Madness returned in the late summer of 1982 with *The Rise and Fall*, their full-fledged shift to pop. Like their previous albums, it was a UK hit, reaching the Top Ten, but it also contained the seeds of their brief US success with the Top Five British single "Our House." The single was released in America on the group's new label, Geffen, and it received heavy airplay from MTV. The music-video television network had previously played the videos for "House of Fun," "It Must Be Love," and "Cardiac Arrest" when the band's albums were unreleased in the US, thereby setting the stage for "Our House" to become a massive hit. With "Our House," Madness had MTV exposure coincide with a record release for the first time, which sent the single into the US Top Ten in the summer of 1983. The success of the single brought the US compilation album, *Madness*, to No. 41. Madness managed one more US Top 40 hit that fall, when "It Must Be Love" peaked at No. 33.

At the end of 1983, Mike Barson—the band's key songwriter—left the group to settle down with his wife. Although Madness was able to stay near the top of the charts with their first post-Barson release, "Michael Caine," the band's fortunes began to decline over the course of 1984. Upon its release in the spring, *Keep Moving* hit No. 6 on the UK charts; in America, the record reached No. 109. In June, the group released its final single for Stiff Records, "One Better Day," which peaked at No. 17. In the fall, Madness formed their own record label, Zarjazz. Madness released "Yesterday's Men," their first recording on Zarjazz, in September of 1985, nearly a year after the label's formation. The record peaked at No. 18 and its parent album, *Mad Not Mad*, reached No. 16 upon its October release. Their chart decline continued early in 1986, when their cover of Scritti Politti's "Sweetest Girl" peaked at No. 35. For most of 1986, the group was quiet. In September, Madness announced they were disbanding. Two months later, their farewell single, "Waiting for the Ghost Train," was released, charting at No. 18.

After staying dormant for a year and a half, the group reunited at the beginning of 1988 as a quartet called the Madness, releasing its comeback single, "I Pronounce You," in March. The Madness featured Chris Foreman, Lee Thompson, Chas Smash, and Suggs, and was augmented by the Specials' keyboardist Jerry Dammers, and Steve Nieve (keyboards) and Bruce Thomas (bass) of the Attractions. "I Pronounce You" reached No. 44 on the UK charts and its accompanying album stiffed upon its spring release. The group disbanded for a second time that fall.

In the summer of 1992, the original lineup of Madness reunited to perform two outdoor concerts at London's Finsbury Park. The group dubbed the event "Madstock" and released a recording of the shows on Go! Records. Madstock became an annual event for the next four years—every summer the band would reunite and headline an outdoor festival at Finsbury Park. Suggs launched a solo career in 1995 with *The Lone Ranger*, which performed respectably in the UK charts. In 1996, Madness played the final Madstock and announced they planned not to reunite for future concerts. —*Stephen Thomas Erlewine*

One Step Beyond / 1979 / Sire ✦✦✦✦

Madness made a name for themselves early on with a silly image and irresistible novelty-dance numbers like "One Step Beyond" and the similar-sounding "Night Boat to Cairo." They did that extremely well on their debut—certainly these singles are among the finest of the era—but what made *One Step Beyond* such a remarkable record was not only the fun-time music they created, but also the diversity they displayed. Combining ska with distinctly British flavors of music-hall and '60s pop along with soul and even a hint of punk, Madness created a unique sound that, while very much a part of the 2-Tone ska revival, also managed to transcend it. *One Step Beyond* is a charming album packed with some terrific songs, and it arguably stands as the high point of their distinguished career. —*Chris Woodstra*

Absolutely / Oct. 1980 / Sire ✦✦✦

For their second album, Madness continued the bright and bouncy fun of their debut. *Absolutely* placed slightly more emphasis on their novelty aspect, creating something of a fun-house atmosphere with stray sounds, exaggerated accents, faster tempos, and often unintelligible lyrics rattled off by Suggs at breakneck speed. Although the album shows a dip in quality control and much less diversity than *One Step Beyond*, it is nevertheless a charming romp with its share of inspired moments, like the classic singles "Baggy Trousers" and "Embarrassment." —*Chris Woodstra*

Seven / Sep. 1981 / Stiff ✦✦✦

Their "nutty sound" seems to fall to the background somewhat on this move toward more mature songwriting. Expanding beyond the limited scope of ska, this is a fine pop effort, at times dabbling in more experimental sounds such as sitars and Arabic rhythms. Includes the splendid single "It Must Be Love." —*Chris Woodstra*

Madness Present the Rise and Fall / 1982 / Stiff ✦✦✦✦

Madness Present the Rise and Fall marks the band's most mature effort and artistic statement. Completely devoid of their early ska influence, they paint a picture of British life in the spirit of the Kinks' *Village Green Preservation Society*. Though it was never released in the US, several tracks were later placed on the compilation *Madness*, including "Our House," their biggest Stateside hit. —*Chris Woodstra*

★ Complete Madness / 1982 / Stiff ✦✦✦✦✦

The 16-track compilation *The Complete Madness* compiles all of the group's early singles—from "The Prince" to "House of Fun"—and adds a handful of classic album tracks and concert favorites like "In the City," "Bed and Breakfast Man," and "Madness." It's a thorough and thoroughly entertaining collection, encapsulating exactly why Madness were significant and, more importantly, how much fun their "nutty sound" was. Furthermore, *The Complete Madness* isn't just an introduction—since it contains a wealth of non-LP singles like "Cardiac Arrest" and "House of Fun," it's essential for any Madness collectors. This compilation is definitive proof that Madness were one of the great singles acts of their era. —*Stephen Thomas Erlewine*

Madness / 1983 / Geffen ✦✦✦✦

Madness is a US compilation released to capitalize on the success of "Our House." Aside from a handful of earlier singles like "Night Boat to Cairo," "It Must Be Love," "Cardiac Arrest," and "House of Fun," the collection's real focus is on material from the previous year's *Madness Present the Rise and Fall*, which wasn't released in America. The collection suffers from a mixture of two distinct periods in the band's career and some glaring omissions, but there is no shortage of great material, making for a pretty good, though far from perfect, introduction. —*Chris Woodstra*

Keep Moving / 1984 / Geffen ✦✦

By 1986, the Clive Langer/Alan Winstanley production team had become synonymous with an all-too-slick approach. And despite their previous, well-tempered work with the band, *Keep Moving* falls into the same formulaic pitfalls of the period, incorporating the overused Afrodiziak and TKO horns, as well as a full gospel choir and even a cameo from Michael Caine. Overbearing production aside, this is well-crafted Brit-pop that explores a brighter, though decidedly less memorable side than the previous album. (The American issue replaces the lesser "Waltz Into Mischief" with the stray singles "Wings of a Dove" and "The Sun and the Rain," along with "Prospects" and "Samantha," making it the preferable version of the album.) —*Chris Woodstra*

Mad Not Mad / 1985 / Geffen ✦✦

Utter Madness / 1986 / Zarjazz ✦✦✦

Picking up where *Complete Madness* left off, this collection includes all of the key singles from 1982 to 1986. A good collection, though listeners will probably be better served by simply sticking to *Rise and Fall* for a representation of this period. —*Chris Woodstra*

The Business / 1992 / Virgin ✦✦✦

The Business is not the comprehensive, one-stop shopping solution for Madness that it appears to be based on the track listing. The three-disc box does contain all of the singles and B-sides, but the inclusion of spoken bits between and overlapping into the songs makes for an awkward listen. Certainly the goal of this package was to tell the story of the band, but both the band and the listener would be better served by letting the music speak for itself. —*Chris Woodstra*

Divine Madness / 1992 / Virgin ✦✦✦✦

This UK-only collection attempts to condense the band's career onto a single disc—from the early singles to 1985's *Mad Not Mad*. Though the two distinct periods lead to a somewhat disjointed listen, the chronological sequencing works as an adequate career survey, and the offering of the non-LP "Driving in My Car" and "(Waiting) For the Ghost Train" are a nice touch. *Complete Madness* is still the best collection, but this one isn't bad either, despite a few omissions. —*Chris Woodstra*

Madonna

b. Aug. 16, 1958, Rochester, MI

Vocals / Dance-Pop, Adult Contemporary, Pop-Rock, Club/Dance

After a star reaches a certain point, it's easy to forget what they became famous for and concentrate solely on their persona. Madonna is such a star. Madonna rocketed to stardom so quickly in 1984 that it obscured most of her musical virtues. Appreciating her music became even more difficult as the decade wore on, as discussing her lifestyle became more common than discussing her music. However, one of Madonna's greatest achievements is how she manipulated the media and the public with her music, her videos, her publicity, and her sexuality. Arguably, Madonna was the first female pop star to have complete control of her music and image.

Madonna moved from her native Michigan to New York in 1977, with dreams of becoming a ballet dancer. She studied with choreographer Alvin Ailey and modelled. In 1979, she became part of the Patrick Hernandez Revue, a disco outfit who had the hit "Born to Be Alive." She traveled to Paris with Hernandez; it was there that she met Dan Gilroy, who would soon become her boyfriend. Upon returning to New York, the pair formed the Breakfast Club, a pop-dance group. Madonna originally played drums for the band, but she soon became the lead singer. In 1980, she left the band and formed Emmy with her former boyfriend, drummer Stephen Bray. Soon, Bray and Madonna broke off from the group and began working on some dance-disco-oriented tracks. A demo tape of these tracks worked its way to Mark Kamins, a New York-based DJ/producer. Kamins directed the tape to Sire Records, who signed the singer during 1982.

Kamins produced Madonna's first single, "Everybody," which became a club and dance hit at the end of 1982; her second single, 1983's "Physical Attraction," was another club hit. In June of 1983, she had her third club hit with the bubbly "Holiday," which was written by Jellybean Benitez. Madonna's self-titled debut album was released in September of 1983; "Holiday" became her first Top 40 hit the following month. "Borderline" became her first Top Ten hit in March of 1984, beginning a remarkable string of 17 consecutive Top Ten hits. While "Lucky Star" was climbing to number four, Madonna began working on her first starring role in a feature film, Susan Seidelman's *Desperately Seeking Susan*. Madonna's second album, the Niles Rodgers-produced *Like a Virgin*, was released at the end of 1984. The title track hit No. 1 in December, staying at the top of the charts for six weeks; it was the start of a whirlwind year for the singer. During 1985, Madonna became an international celebrity, selling millions of records on the strength of her stylish, sexy videos and forceful personality. After "Material Girl" became a No. 2 hit in March, Madonna began her first tour, supported by the Beastie Boys. "Crazy for You" became her second No. 1 single in May. *Desperately Seeking Susan* was released in July, becoming a box office hit; it also prompted a planned video release of *A Certain Sacrifice*, a low-budget erotic drama she filmed in 1979. *A Certain Sacrifice* wasn't the only embarrassing skeleton in the closet dragged into the light during the summer of 1985—both *Playboy* and *Penthouse* published nude photos of Madonna that she had posed for in 1977. Nevertheless, her popularity continued unabated, with thousands of teenage girls adopting her sexy appearance—and being dubbed "Madonna Wannabes." In August 1985, she married actor Sean Penn; the couple had a rocky marriage that ended in 1989.

Madonna began collaborating with Patrick Leonard at the beginning of 1986; Leonard would co-write most of her biggest hits in the '80s, including "Live to Tell," which hit No. 1 in June of 1986. A more ambitious and accomplished record than her two previous albums, *True Blue* was released the following month, to both massive commercial success (it was No. 1 in both the US and the UK, selling over five million copies in America alone) and critical acclaim. "Papa Don't Preach" became her fourth No. 1 hit in the US. While her musical career was thriving, her film career took a savage hit with the November release of *Shanghai Surprise*. Starring Madonna and Sean Penn, the comedy received terrible reviews, which translated into disastrous box office returns.

At the beginning of 1987, she had her fifth No. 1 single with "Open Your Heart"—the third No. 1 from *True Blue* alone. "La Isla Bonita," taken from the soundtrack of her third feature film, *Who's That Girl?*, was another Top Five hit, although the film itself was another box office bomb; the title track from the movie became her sixth No. 1 single. 1988 was a relatively quiet year for Madonna, as she spent the first half of the year acting in David Mamet's *Speed the Plow* on Broadway. In the meantime, she released the re-mix album *You Can Dance*. After withdrawing the divorce papers she filed at the beginning of 1988, she divorced Penn at the beginning of 1989.

Like a Prayer, released in the spring of 1989, was her most ambitious and far-reaching album, incorporating elements of pop, rock, and dance. It was another No. 1 hit and launched the No. 1 title track, as well as "Express Yourself," "Cherish," and "Keep It Together," three more Top Ten hits. In April 1990, she began her massive *Blonde Ambition* tour,

which ran throughout the entire year. "Vogue" became a No. 1 hit in May, setting the stage for her co-starring role in Warren Beatty's *Dick Tracy*; it was her most successful film appearance since *Desperately Seeking Susan*. Madonna released a greatest hits album, *The Immaculate Collection*, at the end of the year. It featured two new songs, including the No. 1 single "Justify My Love," which sparked another controversy with its sexy video; the second new song, "Rescue Me," became the highest-debuting single by a female artist in US. chart history, entering the charts at No. 15. *Truth or Dare*, a documentary of the *Blonde Ambition* tour, was released to positive reviews and strong ticket sales at the end of 1991.

Madonna returned to the charts in the summer of 1992 with the No. 1 "This Used to Be My Playground," a single featured in the film *A League of Their Own*, which featured the singer in a small part. Later that year, Madonna released *Sex*, an expensive, steel-bound soft-core pornographic book that featured hundreds of erotic photographs of herself, several models, and other celebrities—including Isabella Rossellini, Big Daddy Kane, Naomi Campbell, and Vanilla Ice—as well as selected prose. *Sex* received scathing reviews and enormous negative publicity, yet that didn't stop the accompanying album, *Erotica*, from selling over two million copies. *Bedtime Stories*, released two years later, was a more subdued affair than *Erotica*. Initially, it didn't chart as impressively, prompting some critics to label her a has-been, yet the album spawned her biggest hit, "Take a Bow," which spent seven weeks at No. 1. It also featured the Bjork-penned "Bedtime Stories," which became her first single not to make the Top 40; its follow-up, "Human Nature," also failed to crack the Top 40. Nevertheless, *Bedtime Stories* marked her seventh album to go multi-platinum.

Beginning in 1995, Madonna began one of her most subtle image makeovers as she lobbied for the title role in the film adaptation of Andrew Lloyd Webber's *Evita*. Backing away from the overt sexuality of *Erotica* and *Bedtime Stories*, Madonna recast herself as an upscale sophisticate, and the compilation *Something to Remember* fit into the plan nicely. Released in the fall of 1995, around the same time she won the coveted role of Evita Peron, the album was composed entirely of ballads, designed to appeal to the mature audience that would also be the target of *Evita*. As filming was completed, Madonna announced she was pregnant; her daughter, Lourdes, was born late in 1996, just as *Evita* was scheduled for release. The movie was greeted with generally positive reviews and Madonna began a campaign for an Oscar nomination that resulted in her winning the Golden Globe for Best Actress (Musical or Comedy), but not the coveted Academy Award nomination. The soundtrack for *Evita*, however, was a modest hit, with a dance re-mix of "Don't Cry for Me Argentina" and the newly-written "You Must Love Me" both becoming hits. —*Stephen Thomas Erlewine*

Madonna / 1983 / Sire ✦✦✦✦

Madonna's self-titled debut was one of the strongest dance records of the early '80s, featuring a state-of-the-art production and a handful of great songs. Although her voice was still quite thin at this point, Madonna projected a powerful charisma, bringing slight material like "Everybody," "Physical Attraction," and "Burning Up" to life. However, it was on well-constructed pop songs like "Borderline," "Lucky Star," and "Holiday" that the record became truly impressive, as the material matched Madonna's performance. All three of the songs became hits and wrote the blueprint for dance-pop divas that dominated much of the remaining decade. —*Stephen Thomas Erlewine*

Like a Virgin / 1984 / Sire ✦✦✦

Armed with the talents of producer Nile Rodgers, Madonna surpassed the excellence of her self-titled debut album with its superb, hit-laden follow-up *Like a Virgin*—arguably, the album that really made Miss Ciccone a superstar. While Rodgers' early projects outside of Chic (including Sister Sledge and Diana Ross) sounded very much like that seminal disco group, that was no longer the case in the mid-'80s (when he was working with everyone from David Bowie to Duran Duran). *Virgin* never sounds like anything but a Madonna album, although Rodgers' gift for sleek, seductive dance music (Chic's specialty) is evident on such gems as "Dress You Up," "Angel," and the Motownish title song. Though R&B and dance music are dominant, Madonna obviously wasn't content to focus on the urban-contemporary market exclusively, and she embraces quirky, new wave-ish pop with likeable results on "Over and Over" and the infectious "Material Girl." Everything on *Virgin* is well worth hearing, including nonhits like Madonna's pleasant ballad "Shoo Be Doo" and her remake of Rose Royce's "Love Don't Live Here Anymore." All too many dance-floor divas are never heard outside the clubs—a fate that Madonna, like Donna Summer before her, guarded against. With *Virgin*, Madonna became one of the 1980s' bestselling pop icons without losing her sizeable club following. —*Alex Henderson*

True Blue / 1986 / Sire ✦✦✦✦

A staggering album from an artist known for hot singles, the hits include "Papa Don't Preach," "Open Your Heart," and "True Blue." "Live to Tell," her best, is also to be found here. —*John Floyd*

Who's That Girl / 1987 / Sire ✦✦
In the strictest sense, *Who's That Girl* isn't a Madonna album—it's a soundtrack album to her 1987 comedy, featuring competent but uninspiring dance-pop by Club Nouveau, Scritti Politti, Coati Mundi, Michael Davidson, and Duncan Favre. Madonna has four new tracks on the record, including the No. 1 "Who's That Girl" and the No. 2 "Causing a Commotion." Those two hits aren't among her finest singles—neither song made her greatest-hits compilation, *The Immaculate Collection*—making it her weakest album. —*Stephen Thomas Erlewine*

You Can Dance / 1987 / Sire ✦✦✦
A decent assortment of extended dance remixes, it's ideal for parties. —*John Floyd*

☆ **Like a Prayer** / 1989 / Sire ✦✦✦✦✦
Out of all of Madonna's albums, *Like a Prayer* is her most explicit attempt at a major artistic statement. Even though it is apparent that she is trying to make a "serious" album, the kaleidoscopic variety of pop styles on *Like a Prayer* is quite dazzling. Ranging from the deep funk of "Express Yourself" and "Keep It Together," to the haunting "Oh Father" and "Like a Prayer," Madonna displays a commanding sense of songcraft, making this her best and most consistent album. —*Stephen Thomas Erlewine*

★ **The Immaculate Collection** / 1990 / Sire ✦✦✦✦✦
On the surface, the single-disc hits compilation *The Immaculate Collection* appears to be a definitive retrospective of Madonna's heyday in the '80s. After all, it features 17 of Madonna's greatest hits, from "Holiday" and "Like a Virgin" to "Like a Prayer" and "Vogue." However, looks can be deceiving. It's true that *The Immaculate Collection* contains the bulk of Madonna's hits, but there are several big hits that aren't present, including "Angel," "Dress You Up," "True Blue," "Who's That Girl," and "Causing a Commotion." The songs that are included are frequently altered. Everything on the collection is remastered in Q-sound, which gives an exaggerated sense of stereo separation that often distorts the original intent of the recordings. Furthermore, several songs are faster than their original versions and some are faded out earlier than either their single or album versions, while others are segued together. In other words, while all the hits are present, they're simply not in their correct versions. Nevertheless, *The Immaculate Collection* remains a necessary purchase, because it captures everything Madonna is about and it proves that she was one of the finest singles artists of the '80s. Until the original single versions are compiled on another album, *The Immaculate Collection* is the closest thing to a definitive retrospective. —*Stephen Thomas Erlewine*

Dick Tracy: "I'm Breathless" (Music from & Inspired by the Film) [st] / May 1990 / Sire ✦✦
A collection of songs featured in or inspired by the comic-book-turned-movie *Dick Tracy*, *I'm Breathless* is essentially Madonna's take on popular music from the '40s, particularly big band pop. Although her singing shows a surprising amount of range, the material tends to be nothing more than cutesy novelty numbers, like the double entendre-laden hit "Hanky Panky." *I'm Breathless* approaches greatness only on "Vogue," a hit single tacked on to the end of the record. Featuring an endlessly deep house groove and an instantly memorable melody, "Vogue" is a detached, affectionate celebration of transcendent pop and gay culture and stands as Madonna's finest single moment. —*Stephen Thomas Erlewine*

Erotica / Oct. 20, 1992 / Maverick ✦✦✦
While it didn't set the charts on fire like her previous albums, the ambitious *Erotica* contains some of Madonna's best and most accomplished music (including the hit singles "Deeper and Deeper" and "Rain"), even if it runs a bit long. —*Stephen Thomas Erlewine*

Bedtime Stories / Oct. 25, 1994 / Maverick ✦✦✦✦
Perhaps Madonna correctly guessed that the public overdosed on the raw carnality of her book *Sex*. Perhaps she wanted to offer a more optimistic take on sex than the distant *Erotica*. Either way, *Bedtime Stories* is a warm album, with deep, gently pulsating grooves; the album's title isn't totally tongue-in-cheek. The best songs on the album ("Secret," "Inside of Me," "Sanctuary," "Bedtime Story," "Take a Bow") slowly work their melodies into the subconscious as the bass pulses. In that sense, it does offer an antidote to *Erotica*, which was filled with deep but cold grooves. The entire production of *Bedtime Stories* suggests that she wants listeners to acknowledge that her music isn't one-dimensional. She has succeeded with that goal, since *Bedtime Stories* offers her most humane and open music; it's even seductive. —*Stephen Thomas Erlewine*

Something to Remember / Nov. 7, 1995 / Maverick ✦✦✦✦
Something to Remember is Madonna's second greatest hits collection, compiling a selection of the singer's ballads. Several of her biggest hits are included, including the No. 1 songs "Crazy for You," "Live to Tell," "This Used to Be My Playground," and "Take a Bow," as well as a handful of first-rate album tracks (a re-mixed "Love Don't Live Here Any-

more," "Something to Remember," "Oh Father"), and three new tracks, most notably a version of Marvin Gaye's "I Want You" recorded with the British trip-hop group Massive Attack. Only two tracks on the album overlap with *The Immaculate Collection*, and the disc also marks the first appearance of "This Used to Be My Playground" and "I'll Remember" on one of Madonna's albums. Throughout the album, Madonna proves that she's a terrific singer whose voice has improved over the years. Not one of the tracks is second-rate, and the best songs on *Something to Remember* rank among the best pop music of the '80s and '90s. —*Stephen Thomas Erlewine*

Evita [original Soundtrack] / Nov. 12, 1996 / Warner Brothers ✦✦✦
Madonna staked much of her career on *Evita*, gambling that it would establish her as a proper movie star and respected actress, as well as revive her slumping musical career. Both the film and the soundtrack, while worthy efforts, fall just short of their goals, despite their numerous strong points. The double-disc soundtrack to *Evita*—which essentially is an audio document of the entire film, since there is no dialogue in the movie—is an exquisitely produced and expertly rendered version of Andrew Lloyd Webber and Tim Rice's rock-inspired musical, yet it remains curiously unengaging. Part of the reason is Madonna's performance. While she gives a startlingly accomplished and nuanced performance—her voice actually sounds like it matures over the course of the album—it is impossible to listen to her without getting the impression that she is trying *really* hard to be credible, which makes it difficult to connect with her. It doesn't help that her supporting cast of Jonathan Pryce and Antonio Banderas are only fitfully successful; Banderas' performance, in particular, suffers from being removed from the visuals. Even with the faults, *Evita* has its merits, including the written-for-film ballad "You Must Love Me," and is worth investigating. It just isn't the definitive work that it wishes to be. —*Stephen Thomas Erlewine*

Magazine

f. 1977, Manchester, England, **db.** 1981
Post-Punk
After leaving the Buzzcocks in 1977, vocalist Howard Devoto formed Magazine with guitarist John McGeoch, bassist Barry Adamson, keyboardist Bob Dickinson, and drummer Martin Jackson. One of the first post-punk bands, Magazine kept the edgy, nervous energy of punk, adding elements of art-rock, particularly with their theatrical live shows and shards of keyboards. Devoto's lyrics were combinations of social commentary and poetic fragments, while the band alternated between cold, jagged chords and gloomy, atmospheric sonic landscapes.

Magazine performed their first concert in the fall of 1977 and were signed to Virgin Records by the end of the year; by that point, Dickinson had left the group. The band recorded their first single, "Shot by Both Sides," as a quartet; Devoto had written the song with his former Buzzcocks partner, Pete Shelley. Appearing in early 1978, the single gathered good reviews on both sides of the Atlantic and charted in the UK, peaking at No. 41. Before they recorded their debut album, keyboardist Dave Formula joined the lineup. *Real Life*, released later in 1978, continued the confrontational, arty pop-punk of "Shot by Both Sides." Following their first tour, Jackson left the group and was replaced by John Doyle. The new lineup recorded the band's second album, *Secondhand Daylight* (1979). *Secondhand Daylight* was something of a departure from the debut, featuring more keyboards, smoother rhythms, and streamlined lyrics from Devoto. Despite its ambitiousness, the record was poorly received by the press. During this time, McGeoch played with Siouxsie & the Banshees and Adamson, Formula, and McGeoch were part of Visage, along with Steve Strange. At the beginning of 1980, the band released their third album, *The Correct Use of Soap*.

In the summer of 1980, Magazine released "Sweetheart Contract," which became their second and last British chart hit, peaking at No. 54. After it hit the charts, McGeoch left the band to become a full-time member of Siouxsie & the Banshees; he was replaced by Robin Simon. Magazine toured America and Australia, recording a live album called *Play*, which was released at the end of 1980. Simon left at the end of the tour, with former Amazorblades guitarist Bob Mandelson taking his place. *Magic, Murder and the Weather* was released in the spring of 1981; it proved to be Magazine's last album. Devoto left the group in May of 1981 to pursue a solo career and the band broke up shortly afterward. —*Stephen Thomas Erlewine*

Real Life / Apr. 1978 / Blue Plate ✦✦✦✦
Magazine's debut album *Real Life* is an edgy collection of terse punk-pop songs that are turned inside out by complex, unpredictable arrangements and shards of atonal keyboards. The undeniable peak is the classic "Shot by Both Sides," but the entire album, with its cerebral fusion of concise pop songs and dark, evocative instrumental textures, helped establish the difference between punk and post-punk. —*Stephen Thomas Erlewine*

Secondhand Daylight / 1979 / Blue Plate ✦✦✦

The Correct Use of Soap / 1980 / Blue Plate ✦✦✦✦
Magazine returned to complex pop songs on *The Correct Use of Soap* after taking a detour toward gloomy electronics with their second album, *Secondhand Daylight*. Howard Devoto's songs remain nervous, dense with wordplay and tight melodies, and the increasingly impressive band fleshes the songs out with unpredictable, funk-inflected rhythms and layers of guitars and keyboards. It's a little less accessible than the first album, but *The Correct Use of Soap* nevertheless surprises with its immediate performances and melodies. —*Stephen Thomas Erlewine*

Play. / 1980 / IRS ✦✦
Play. documents an Australian concert from 1980 that finds Magazine in fine form, spitting out their unsettling, edgy post-punk songs with controlled energy. By this point, guitarist John McGeoch had been replaced by Robin Simon, and although there are some weak patches on the record, he fits into the group's dense interplay remarkably well. *Play.*, however, remains a record for the collector, especially since their best-known song, "Shot by Both Sides," isn't on the record and an awkward cover of Sly Stone's "Thank You (Falletinme Be Mice Elf Again)" is. —*Stephen Thomas Erlewine*

Magic Murder & the Weather / Sep. 1981 / IRS ✦✦✦
Magazine's final studio album, *Magic, Murder and the Weather*, finds Dave Formula's washes of cold, brittle keyboards dominating the bitter and cynical music. Occasionally, Howard Devoto's weary lyrics surface through the icy mix, but it's clear that Devoto and Magazine have both had better days. It's not a graceful way to bow out, but the album has enough strong moments to prevent it from being an embarrassment, as well. —*Stephen Thomas Erlewine*

After the Fact / 1982 / IRS ✦✦✦
Released after Magazine disbanded in 1981, *After the Fact* was designed as a career overview for its British release, collecting the group's singles and selected highlights from their four albums. In its American incarnation, *After the Fact* was radically different. Instead of functioning as an overview, it collected several B-sides, augmenting them with album tracks, and only a few of those overlapped with its UK counterpart. So, the British version (which has a green cover) is for the neophyte, and the American version (red cover) is for the collector, which is a strange state of affairs for this distinctly British post-punk band. —*Stephen Thomas Erlewine*

● **Rays & Hail** / 1987 / Virgin ✦✦✦✦
A comprehensive compilation that samples from all of the band's albums, as well as including the original single version of "Shot By Both Sides." —*Stephen Thomas Erlewine*

Scree (Rarities 1978-81) / Mar. 8, 1991 / Blue Plate ✦✦✦
Scree (Rarities 1978-81) compiles all of Magazine's B-sides plus their non-LP singles, offering a useful, 15-track collection of the group's most obscure items. —*Stephen Thomas Erlewine*

Magnapop

f. 1987, Athens, GA
Alternative Pop-Rock
This Athens, Georgia band creates high-energy punk-pop with catchy hooks and literate lyrics. Formed in 1987 by singer Linda Hopper, guitarist Ruthie Morris, drummer David McNair, and bassist Shannon Mulvaney, the group recorded a demo album with their friend Michael Stipe in 1992, which was released on Caroline Records. In 1994 the group released their "official" debut, *Hot Boxing*, on Priority. *Hot Boxing* was produced by another of the band's friends, Bob Mould, and features a more streamlined, intense approach than the quirky, off-kilter demos do; *Rubbing Doesn't Help* followed in 1996. What makes Magnapop interesting (and different from many of the punk-pop bands out there) is the combination of Hopper's smooth, unhurried vocals and the furious lashings of Morris' guitar—it creates a tension that makes the group's songs all the more dramatic. An intelligent, underappreciated band. —*Heather Phares*

Magnapop / Oct. 16, 1992 / Play It Again Sam/Priority ✦✦✦✦
This is a collection of demos and early singles produced by the band's friends, Michael Stipe and Bob Mould. *Magnapop* unveils the band as a punk-pop group with an arty bent, especially on songs like "Spill It" and "Favorite Writer." The cover of Big Star's "13" is a welcome addition to this good beginning. —*Heather Phares*

● **Hot Boxing** / Jul. 5, 1994 / Play It Again Sam/Priority ✦✦✦✦
On their official debut, Magnapop iron out the kinks of their sound and come out a tighter but slightly less interesting band for it. The group are at their best on "Lay It Down," "Piece of Cake," and "The Crush," where they mix punk-fueled energy and wistful lyrics. —*Heather Phares*

Rubbing Doesn't Help / May 21, 1996 / Play It Again Sam/Priority ✦✦✦
For their third album, Magnapop sand away even more of their punk edges, leaving behind a competent, and occasionally engaging, post-

grunge pop-punk band. The production on *Rubbing Doesn't Help* is too big for the songs, with echoing drums and fat, loud guitars, but there are enough strong songs scattered throughout the album to indicate that the group's talent for tuneful yet intense pop hasn't abandoned them. They just don't know how to articulate their ideas very well on *Rubbing Doesn't Help*. —*Stephen Thomas Erlewine*

Magnetic Fields

f. 1989, Boston, MA
Alternative Pop-Rock, Lo-Fi, Indie Rock
The Magnetic Fields are a bona fide band, but in most essential respects they are the project of studio wunderkind Stephin Merritt. Merritt writes, produces, and (lately) sings all of their material, as well as plays many of the instruments, concocting a sort of indie-pop synth-rock. While the Magnetic Fields may draw upon the electronic textures of vintage acts like ABBA, Kraftwerk, Roxy Music with Eno, Joy Division, and Gary Neuman, Merritt's vision is far more pointed toward the alternative rock underground. His songs are also far warmer and more purely pop-oriented than the above reference points might lead you to believe, sounding at times like late-20th-century equivalents to Phil Spector or Brian Wilson.

Merritt had been recording on his own four-track from a very young age, but didn't issue the first Magnetic Fields album until 1990, when he was well into his twenties. The first pair of discs featured the choirgirl vocals of Susan Amway, and are probably the most accessible offerings for general listeners wary of electro-rock.

On subsequent releases, Merritt handled the vocals himself in a deep croon not far removed from his European influences. The synth-pop quotient also became heavier, although Merritt has always taken care to mix in quite a few natural instruments with the electronic ones, often with the help of Claudia Gonson (percussion) and Sam Davol (cello, flute). The emphasis has always remained on the pop hooks and eccentric, romantically reflective lyrics rather than the bedrock synthetic rhythms and textures.

In addition to his work with Magnetic Fields, Merritt has involved himself in several side projects, the most notable being the 6ths' *Wasps Nests* album (1995). Merritt sang only one track himself on this disc, for which he acted as composer/producer/multi-instrumentalist, employing well-known alternative lead singers like Barbara Manning, Dean Wareham (Luna), Lou Barlow, Georgia Hubley (Yo La Tengo), Chris Knox, and Robert Scott (the Bats) to handle the lead vocals. —*Richie Unterberger*

Distant Plastic Trees / 1990 / Red Flame ✦✦✦
The Magnetic Fields' debut unveiled an unusually skilled indie-rock auteur in Stephin Merritt, aided by the sometimes overlooked contributions of the other band members on cello, horns, vocals, and percussion. Although not quite as polished as later Magnetic Fields releases, it's a decent set of tunes guided by Merritt's inventive pop melodies and unexpectedly imaginative facility with cheap synthesizers. Merge has combined this album and its successor, *The Wayward Bus*, onto one disc with its CD reissue. —*Richie Unterberger*

The Wayward Bus / 1991 / Feel Good All Over ✦✦✦✦
The last of the two Magnetic Fields albums to feature Susan Amway as lead singer, this has Merritt's most gorgeous melodies and most pop-friendly production, strongly recalling Phil Spector in particular (more than one of the songs quotes the opening "Be My Baby" rhythms). Merge has combined this album and its predecessor, *Distant Plastic Trees*, onto one disc with its CD reissue. —*Richie Unterberger*

Holiday / 1994 / Feel Good All Over ✦✦✦✦
Starting with this album Merritt, who had never sung on previous Magnetic Fields discs, took over the vocal chores with the departure of Susan Amway. His low and somewhat sober tones are less accessible, and the music began to move in a more percolating electro-pop direction as well. This is probably the most enjoyable of their Merritt-sung efforts, though, with a couple of real standouts in "The Trouble I've Been Looking For" and "In My Car." —*Richie Unterberger*

The Charm of the Highway Strip / 1994 / Merge ✦✦✦
Merritt took more of a narrative approach than usual on this album, which was in part inspired (as the title indicates) by on-the-road experiences, and exhibited a (very slight) country influence. Not as good as *Holiday*, although it has characteristically agile songwriting and production. —*Richie Unterberger*

● **The Wayward Bus/Distant Plastic Trees** / Jan. 23, 1995 / Merge ✦✦✦✦
The group's first two albums are combined onto one CD for this reissue, which effectively summarizes the period in which all of the Magnetic Fields' material was sung by Susan Amway, rather than Stephin Merritt. There are reservations attached to recommending this as the first purchase, since the subsequent albums, on which Merritt handles all of the vocals, are obviously a more accurate reflection of his auteurist vision. The fact is, however, that the Amway-sung albums are more immedi-

ately attractive to most listeners, especially *The Wayward Bus.* —*Richie Unterberger*

Get Lost / Oct. 24, 1995 / Merge ✦✦✦
Merritt's homespun (although not carelessly lo-fi) approach to electronic pop is a big part of the Magnetic Fields' charm, but he may be starting to stretch it to the limit with *Get Lost.* The most electro-oriented of their releases to date, it's also perhaps their least engaging, although the brooding ballad "Don't Look Away" is one of their best songs. They may want to start thinking about varying their synthetic percussions and patterns more, as these are starting too sound a little too boxy and similar for comfort. —*Richie Unterberger*

The Main Ingredient

f. 1966, Harlem, NY
Soul, R&B
Originally formed in 1964 as the Poets, this New York soul group (Donald McPherson, Luther Simmons, Jr., and Tony Sylvester) recorded for Red Bird before changing their name in 1966. After McPherson's death in 1971, Cuba Gooding became the lead singer, and the band scored three Top 40 hits, including "Everybody Plays the Fool," which went to No. 3.

The Main Ingredient tried it again in 1986, with Cuba Gooding returning to his lead spot. They recorded for Zakia, but didn't get much response to "Do Me Right." They kept trying, cutting a song on Polydor in 1989. Longtime group member Luther Simmons, who had left in 1975 to become a stockbroker and then come back in 1980, returned to Wall Street and was replaced for this session by Jerome Jackson. —*Bil Carpenter & Stephen Thomas Erlewine*

● **The All-Time Greatest Hits** / Oct. 25, 1990 / RCA ✦✦✦✦
It wasn't until 1971 that the Main Ingredient's fortunes changed; when Cuba Gooding replaced Donald McPherson, his engaging voice helped make them part of the "sweet" soul trend. Gooding's leads made "Spinning Around (I Must Be Falling in Love)" and "Everybody Plays the Fool" huge hits, as well as "Just Don't Want to Be Lonely" and "Happiness Is Just Around the Bend." These and several other hits are featured on this anthology covering their prime years on RCA. —*Ron Wynn*

A Quiet Storm / Apr. 1996 / RCA ✦✦✦✦
Be cautioned that this 20-track retrospective of material spanning the late '60s to the mid-'70s is not a best-of, although it does include some of their biggest hits ("Just Don't Want to Be Lonely," "Everybody Plays the Fool"). As the title indicates, this focuses on the mellow and romantic side of the group. As the Main Ingredient largely specialized in mellow and romantic songs, this ends up being close to something of a best-of anyway. The relentless soft-pillow ambience of the tracks can become wearisome; in this context, the easygoing "Everybody Plays the Fool" sounds more like a blitzkrieg than a "quiet storm." —*Richie Unterberger*

The Mamas & the Papas

f. 1964, New York, NY, **db.** 1972
Folk-Rock, Pop-Rock
The leading California-based vocal group of the '60s, the Mamas & the Papas epitomized the ethos of mid- to late-'60s pop culture: live free, play free, and love free. Their music, built around radiant harmonies and a solid electric-folk foundation, was gorgeous on its own terms, but a major part of its appeal lay in the easygoing Southern California lifestyle it endorsed.

Founder and leader John Phillips came out of early rock roots and a partly successful folk career, as did Cass Elliott and Denny Doherty, while Phillips' wife Michelle was an ex-model who also sang. They got together out of several failed folk groups just as the music was going electric, pulled up stakes in New York and headed west, where they signed with Lou Adler and wowed the world with a song called "California Dreamin."

Phillips was a pop poet with a commercial edge, and a good arranger. The group had enviable chart success, lived well, and indulged themselves lavishly yet retained credibility with the counterculture. But it all came apart in a couple of years, as the quartet's intertwining romantic entanglements, coupled with their chemical excesses (detailed in separate books by John and Michelle Phillips), strangled their ability to work. By 1971 they were a fond memory, although a reconstituted version of the quartet has done well on the oldies circuit in the late '80s and early '90s. —*Bruce Eder*

If You Can Believe Your Eyes and Ears / 1966 / MCA ✦✦✦✦
Bursting with great songs and gorgeous four-part harmonies, the first Mamas & Papas album is a true delight. From the kickoff of "Monday Monday" right on through to the last track, a cover of "The In Crowd," nothing fails to delight. A rightful smash! —*James Chrispell*

The Mamas & the Papas / 1966 / MCA ✦✦✦
Their second album isn't as packed with famous songs as their debut, but the quality remains at the same level, with strong original material

from John Phillips and imaginative, well-executed harmonies. "Trip, Stumble & Fall," "Words of Love," and "I Saw Her Again" are among their best songs. If you have *Creeque Alley*, you should be warned that half of these cuts show up on that anthology. If you're a big fan of the group, though, it's worth picking up, as the remaining tracks are pretty solid harmony numbers as well. —*Richie Unterberger*

Deliver / 1967 / MCA ✦✦✦
The hits just kept on coming and by this time, it looked as though the Mamas & the Papas could do no wrong. Songs as strong as "Look Through My Window" and "Creeque Alley" were standouts on a record that had no bad cuts (again!). They truly did "Deliver." —*James Chrispell*

● **16 Greatest Hits** / 1970 / MCA ✦✦✦✦
A great overview of the music from this group, one of the founders of the California sound in the late '60s. This is a good collection of their unforgettable electric folk-pop songs, including "Monday, Monday" and "California Dreamin." (Originally released in August 1969 by Dunhill Records as *16 of Their Greatest Hits*, it was reissued on CD by MCA Records in 1986.) —*AMG*

Monterey International Pop Festival / 1971 / One Way ✦✦
A live concert curio, with uneven performances and recording quality, but it is unique. —*Bruce Eder*

Creeque Alley / Mar. 12, 1991 / MCA ✦✦✦✦
They weren't the most important folk-rock group of the mid-'60s; the Byrds and others produced more enduring music. Yet the Mamas & the Papas were undoubtedly the most commercially successful folk-rock group of their time, racking up an astonishing nine Top 30 hits in little more than a year and a half. This 43-song double CD is by far the most comprehensive document of their legacy. It draws most heavily from their two 1966 albums (nine songs originate from their debut album *If You Can Believe Your Eyes and Ears* alone), when John Phillips' songwriting talent had yet to exhaust itself. Beyond the hits, the material is variable. Quite a few album tracks—especially "Got a Feelin'," "Straight Shooter," "Go Where You Wanna Go," "Once Was a Time I Thought," and their cover of Lennon-McCartney's "I Call Your Name"—were strong enough to have been hits under their own steam. Their slowed-down, California-ized versions of rock oldies were more problematic. And there's no doubt that their later material is less spirited and memorable than their initial burst of glory. The set includes various late-'60s and '70s solo recordings by each of the group's members (including small hit singles by John Phillips and Cass Elliott). Perhaps the most intriguing rarities are from the members' pre-Mamas days. These include commercial folk by the Big Three (featuring Cass Elliott) and primitive pop-folk-rock by the Mugwumps (including Elliott, Denny Doherty, and future Lovin' Spoonful member Zal Yanovsky). —*Richie Unterberger*

Mandrill

f. 1968, Brooklyn, NY
Soul, Funk, R&B
Mandrill may have been the most musically ambitious of all the funk bands, something that hurt them commercially. Mandrill albums blended lengthy jazz-oriented pieces with danceable ditties and merged soul, blues, rock, and Afro-Latin elements. The Wilson brothers Louis, Richard, and Carlos were the creative core of the Brooklyn group, aided by Omar Mesa, Claude "Coffee" Cave, Charlie Pardo, and Fudgie Kae. The seven members played over 20 instruments. They recorded for Polydor from 1972 to 1974, then resurfaced on Arista in 1977. They remained there until 1982, then cut a final session for Montage. Mandrill's best songs weren't easily condensed or edited into singles, and only one tune, "Fencewalk" in 1973, cracked the Top 20. But such songs as "Funky Monkey" and "Can You Dig It" scored in the clubs. —*Ron Wynn*

● **The Best of Mandrill** / 1975 / Polydor ✦✦✦✦
A fine, unpredictable band that was too eclectic for its own good. This Brooklyn group merged jazz, rock, funk, Latin, and R&B, were fine singers, and made some sensational extended jams and fine album cuts, as well as some hits, like "Hang Loose" and "Fencewalk." While you can't get the full range of their material from the anthology, it's a fine introduction to how creative and dynamic some '70s funk bands were. —*Ron Wynn*

Fencewalk: Anthology / Feb. 4, 1997 / Polygram ✦✦✦✦
Fencewalk is a definitive two-disc set of Mandrill's oft-sampled funk hits, including "Hang Loose," "Mango Meat," "Funky Monkey," and the title cut. The 31-track collection also includes "Echoes in My Mind," popularized by the cult film *The Warriors.* —*Jason Ankeny*

Manfred Mann

f. 1964, London, England
British Invasion, Art-Rock/Progressive-Rock, Pop-Rock
An R&B band that only played pop to get on the charts, Manfred Mann ranked among the most adept British Invasion acts in both styles. South

African-born keyboardist Manfred Mann was originally an aspiring jazz player, moving toward R&B when more blues-oriented sounds became in vogue in England in the early '60s. Original Manfred Mann singer Paul Jones was one of the best British Invasion singers, and his resonant vocals were the best feature of their early R&B sides, which had a slightly jazzier and smoother touch than the early work of the Rolling Stones and the Animals. It was a couple of covers of obscure girl group songs, "Do Wah Diddy Diddy" (the Exciters) and "Sha La La" (the Shirelles), that broke the group internationally—"Do Wah Diddy Diddy" reached No.1 in the States, and "Sha La La" just missed the Top Ten. The Paul Jones lineup never duplicated this success, although "Come Tomorrow" and "Pretty Flamingo" were smaller hits. From 1964 to 1966, they took the approach of playing gutsy pop-rock on their singles (including the original version of "My Little Red Book"), and soul and R&B on their albums, with occasional detours into jazz, Dylan (their cover of his then-unreleased "If You Gotta Go, Go Now" was a big British hit), and competent original material.

Jones left for a solo career and acting in 1966, and the group reformed around singer Mike D'Abo (Beatle friend Klaus Voormann was also in this aggregation on bass). Adopting an even more pop-oriented approach for the singles, with occasional psychedelic and progressive touches, the band ran off a string of Top Ten hits in their homeland until 1969, although the only one to hit the jackpot in the US was their cover of another unreleased Dylan song, "The Mighty Quinn."

Mann dissolved the D'Abo lineup in 1969 to form Manfred Mann Chapter Three with drummer Mike Hugg, who had been in the band since the beginning. The outfit's early jazz-rock efforts were interesting, but not very popular, and Mann steered the ship back toward mainstream rock by forming yet another incarnation, Manfred Mann's Earth Band. The heavier, more synthesizer-oriented outfit made quite a few albums in the 1970s; 1976's The Roaring Silence made the Top Ten, and featured the No. 1 hit "Blinded by the Light" (Mann also made the Top 40 with another Springsteen cover, "Spirit in the Night"). Ironically, despite Mann's oft-proclaimed preference for serious explorations of jazz, blues, and progressive music, it's his pop-rock recordings that hold up best, and for which he'll be remembered most. —Richie Unterberger

The Manfred Mann Album / 1964 / Ascot ✦✦✦
Manfred Mann's debut full-length US platter was probably their strongest, and indeed one of the stronger British Invasion albums of the very competitive year of 1964. Besides the smash "Do Wah Diddy Diddy," it contained a number of fine soul and R&B covers. Standouts were the versions of "Untie Me" and Ike & Tina Turner's "It's Gonna Work Out Fine," as well as the strong pounding Paul Jones original, "Without You." —Richie Unterberger

The Five Faces of Manfred Mann / 1965 / Ascot ✦✦✦
The band's second LP was slightly less impressive than their first, but was still a respectable mix of R&B and pop. For pop, there were "Sha La La" and "Come Tomorrow," two of their biggest mid-'60s hits, and "She," one of their best self-penned efforts in that vein. For R&B, there was the original "Hubble Bubble (Toil and Trouble)," a British hit, and some good covers, notably "I'm Your Kingpin," "Groovin'," and "Dashing Away with the Smoothing Iron." The group also flaunted its eclecticism with forays into jazz (a version of "Watermelon Man") and folk (the traditional "John Hardy"). The album has now been combined with the first LP on one CD release (on EMI 37067). —Richie Unterberger

Soul of Mann / 1967 / See For Miles ✦✦✦
Amidst their pop-rock, blues, and folk-rock, Manfred Mann peppered their early recordings with jazzy instrumentals that faintly suggested a jazz-rock direction. Soul of Mann, never issued in the US, is a compilation of most of these early instrumental efforts, which originally appeared on various singles, EPs, and LPs between 1963 and 1966 (though one song, "L.S.D.," is actually a blues-rocker with a Paul Jones vocal). Instrumentals were not the band's forte, but this collection is more interesting than you might think. No one would put Manfred Mann on the level of genuine American jazz acts like Oscar Peterson, but these cuts are executed with a surprising amount of style and wit. And Mann and his men were nothing if not eclectic, producing downright strange instrumental takes on "Satisfaction," "I Got You Babe," and "My Generation." There are straighter (but still imaginative) versions of songs by the Yardbirds and Cannonball Adderly, as well as their own originals (the bluesy stomper "Mr. Anello" is a standout). Manfred Mann fans will find this worth picking up, especially given that several of the tracks never came out in the US, such as the aforementioned "Mr. Anello," and all of the pop covers they did for the 1966 EP Instrumental Asylum. —Richie Unterberger

The Roaring Silence / 1976 / Warner Brothers ✦✦✦✦
A later edition of Mann's band, which had a '70s hit with Bruce Springsteen's "Blinded by the Light" (on this album). —William Ruhlmann

The R&B Years / 1982 / See For Miles ✦✦✦✦
The Manfreds always took great pains to point out that their true loves were R&B and jazz, not the pop-rock they sang on their hit singles,

although they should have realized that their fans dug both approaches. Anyway, this 20-song compilation is a good taste of their purer sounds, taken from LPs, EPs, and singles cut by the band during the Paul Jones era (1963-66). Look to EMI's fine Best of Manfred Mann CD for the big hits; this has covers of R&B and soul cuts by the likes of Willie Dixon, Muddy Waters, and Screamin' Jay Hawkins, as well as some more-than-competent group originals in the same vein. "I'm Your Kingpin," "Without You," and "Hubble Bubble (Toil and Trouble)" rank among the better early self-penned British R&B, and their cover of Ben E. King's "Groovin'" is a stormer. Although Manfred Mann weren't quite as fine R&B interpreters as fellow British Invaders the Stones, the Yardbirds, and the Animals, they were quite respectable, and this is a good complement to the more wide-ranging EMI anthology. —Richie Unterberger

Best Of: The Definitive Collection / Jun. 2, 1992 / Capitol ✦✦✦✦
For a guy who claimed to be a jazz buff and to despise pop, Manfred Mann (the keyboard player) sure knew a pop hit when he heard one. And here they are, including "Do Wah Diddy Diddy" and "Pretty Flamingo." —William Ruhlmann

Chapter Two: The Best of the Fontana Years / Oct. 11, 1994 / Fontana ✦✦✦
The departure of Paul Jones for a solo career in 1966 spelled major reorganization for Mann and his troops, who recruited lead vocalist Mike D'Abo and bassist (and Beatle chum) Klaus Voormann. To the surprise of many, the new lineup rattled off seven Top Ten British hits in the next three years in a far less R&B-oriented style. Emphasizing harmonies and Manfred Mann's inventiveness as arranger and keyboardist (often employing the then-futuristic Mellotron), this represented the group's most commercial phase, with an upbeat approach that bordered on downright chipper. These 20 tracks include all the key singles from this time, as well as a few LP cuts. Frankly, this rather lightweight, prototypically cheery late-'60s British pop—sounding rather like a more commercial version of the Odessey & Oracle-era Zombies—hasn't aged nearly as well as their far gutsier Paul Jones-era recordings. Only one of these songs was a hit in the US, but it was a big one—their great 1968 arrangement of the then-unreleased Bob Dylan song "The Mighty Quinn." —Richie Unterberger

● **The Best of the EMI Years** / Jan. 23, 1996 / Griffin ✦✦✦✦
This double CD replaces EMI's Best Of anthology (1992) as the collection of choice for their British Invasion years due to its slightly more extensive length (34 tracks), including most of the tracks on the previous compilation. It has all of the British and American hits, as well as some standout B-sides and album tracks, some of which have been quite hard to come by on reissues. Classic British Invasion music by one of the most versatile bands of the era, comfortable with both straight pop-rock and jazz-tinged R&B. —Richie Unterberger

Manfred Mann Album/Five Faces of Manfred Mann / Feb. 20, 1996 / Capitol ✦✦✦✦
A CD reissue of their first two albums, with a few bonus tracks, most notably a previously unreleased version of "Sticks and Stones" and the instrumental "Mr. Anello," which was included on their UK debut LP, but left off its stateside counterpart. Very good British Invasion music, though most of the best songs are available on Griffin's The Best of the EMI Years. —Richie Unterberger

The Manhattans

f. 1964, Jersey City, NJ
Soul, Urban, Doo Wop, Quiet Storm
A venerable soul quintet from New Jersey, whose career has spanned the dawn of soul and the death of disco, although they have steadfastly preferred ballads over the years. Led initially by George Smith, who died in 1970, the Manhattans first charted in 1965 with "I Wanna Be (Your Everything)." After a string of solid R&B sellers on Carnival and DeLuxe, Gerald Alston replaced the late Smith and the group moved to Columbia. In 1976 they struck paydirt with the elegant platinum-selling ballad "Kiss and Say Goodbye," which topped both the pop and soul lists. Several more huge R&B hits preceded their uplifting 1980 gold record "Shining Star," and still more followed. —Bill Dahl

For You & Yours: Golden Carnival Classics, Pt. 2 / Apr. 24, 1990 / Collectables ✦✦✦✦
For many Manhattans fans, their earliest singles for Carnival were their greatest. These featured the wondrous George "Smitty" Smith, a young Blue Lovett, and some classic heartbreak and anguished soul singles, such as the divine "I Wanna Be (Your Everything)." These haven't been available on anthologies very often, and haven't been available anywhere since the early days of the Solid Smoke series. While Collectables' reissues sometimes leave a lot to be desired in the sound category, these songs are so good and so rare that any anthology featuring them has to get the highest recommendation, regardless of technical merit. This is the second of two volumes covering this era. —Ron Wynn

● **Dedicated to You: Golden Carnival Classics, Pt. 1** / Apr. 24, 1990 / Collectables ♦♦♦♦

The first of two superb volumes covering the Manhattans' early years on the Carnival label, the period many regard as their greatest. While they didn't come close to equaling the crossover-pop success they would enjoy with Columbia in their second incarnation, these were the pure soul works. The group featured both a glorious George "Smitty" Smith and young Blue Lovett, and their songs were produced solely with soul/R&B audiences in mind. There was little of the slick, polished orchestrations or smooth arrangements that were the hallmark of the Columbia hits. Instead, Smith's aching, soaring leads and the group's alternately mellow and frenzied harmonies were the high points. No matter what the sound quality, both this album and its counterpart are essential purchases for soul fans. —*Ron Wynn*

● **The Best of the Manhattans: Kiss and Say Goodbye** / Oct. 31, 1995 / Sony ♦♦♦♦

The Best of the Manhattans: Kiss and Say Goodbye is a terrific, 19-song overview of the Manhattans' recordings for Columbia in the '70s. All but two of the group's Top Ten R&B hits for the label are featured—there's no "We Never Danced to a Love Song" or "Crazy," but "There's No Me Without You," "Don't Take Your Love," "Hurt," "Kiss and Say Goodbye," "I Kinda Miss You," "It Feels So Good to Be Loved So Bad," "Am I Losing You," and "Shining Star" are all present—and several fine lesser-known singles and album tracks are added for good measure. Although the collection might be a bit too extensive for casual fans, it's the definitive overview of the Manhattans' time as a smooth soul group, illustrating how they helped develop the quiet storm sub-genre. —*Stephen Thomas Erlewine*

Manic Street Preachers

f. 1991, Blackwood, Gwent, South Wales
Hard Rock, Alternative Pop-Rock, Brit-Pop

Dressed in glam clothing, wearing heavy eyeliner, and shouting political rhetoric, the Manic Street Preachers emerged from their hometown of Blackwood, Wales in 1991 as self-styled "Generation Terrorists." Fashioning themselves after the Clash and the Sex Pistols, the Manics were on a mission, intending to restore revolution to rock 'n' roll at a time when Britain was dominated by trancy shoegazers and faceless, trippy acid-house. Their self-consciously dangerous image, leftist leanings, crunching hard rock, and outsider status made them favorites of the British music press and helped them build a rabidly dedicated following. For much of the band's early career, it was impossible to separate the rhetoric from the music and even from the members themselves—the group's image was forever associated with lyricist-guitarist Richey James carving the words "4 Real" into his arm during an early interview. As the British pop music climate shifted toward Brit-pop in the wake of Suede, the Manics didn't achieve fame, but they had notoriety. Legions of followers emerged, including many bands that formed the core of the short-lived New Wave of New Wave movement. But as the group climbed toward stardom, the story didn't get simpler—it got weirder. James' behavior became increasingly bizarre, culminating on the group's harrowing 1994 album, *The Holy Bible*. Early in 1995, James disappeared, leaving no trace of his whereabouts. The remaining trio carried on with 1996's *Everything Must Go*, the album that established them as superstars in England, yet that came at the expense of the arrogant, renegade gender-bending and revolutionary rhetoric that earned them their initial fan base.

It was a bizarre, unpredictable journey for a band that once proclaimed that all bands should break up after releasing one album. James Dean Bradfield (vocals, guitar), Nicky Wire (born Nick Jones; bass), Sean Moore (drums) and rhythm guitarist Flicker formed Betty Blue in 1986. Within two years' time, Flicker had left the band and the group had changed their name to the Manic Street Preachers. In the summer of 1988, a fellow student of Wire's at Swansea University, Richey James (born Richey Edwards), who had been the group's driver, joined the band as rhythm guitarist. They began recording demos, eventually releasing the single "Suicide Alley" in August. "Suicide Alley" boasted a cover replicating that of the Clash's first album, which indicated the sound of the group at the time—equal parts punk and hard rock. A year after the single's release, the *NME* gave it an enthusiastic review, citing James' press release—"We are as far away from anything in the '80s as possible."

Indeed, the Manics were one of the key bands of the early '90s, and their career didn't get rolling until 1991. The *New Art Riot* EP appeared in the summer of 1990, followed by a pair of defining singles—"Motown Junk" and "You Love Us"—in early 1991 on Heavenly Records. The singles and the band's incendiary live shows, where they wrote slogans on their shirts, created a strong buzz in the music press, which only escalated in May. James gave an interview to Steve Lamaq for the *NME* in which Lamaq questioned the group's authenticity; after an argument, James responded by carving the words "4 Real" on his arm. The incident

became a sensation, attracting numerous magazine articles, as well as a major-label contract with Sony. Many observers interpreted the action as a simple stunt, but over the next few years, it became clear that the self-mutilation was the first indication of James' mental instability.

"Stay Beautiful" was the Manics' first release for Sony, and it climbed into the British Top 40 late in the summer of 1991, followed early in 1992 by a re-recorded "You Love Us," which peaked in the Top 20. By the time the group released their much-hyped debut album, *Generation Terrorists*, in February 1992—a record they claimed would outsell Guns N' Roses' *Appetite for Destruction*—they had already cultivated a large and devoted following, many of which emulated their glammy appearance and read the same novels and philosophers the group namedropped. The Manics had been claiming that they would disband following the release of their debut, yet it became clear by the fall, when a non-LP cover of "Suicide is Painless (Theme from 'MASH')" became their first Top Ten hit, that they would continue performing. Nicky Wire and Richey James had become notorious for their banter throughout the British music press, and while it earned them countless articles, it also painted the group into a corner. Comparatively more polished and mainstream than its predecessor, *Gold Against the Soul*, the group's second album, appeared in the summer of 1993 to mixed reviews.

Shortly after the release of *Gold Against the Soul*, the Manics' support began to slide as the group began to splinter amid internal tensions, many of them stemming from James. Nicky Wire ran into trouble over onstage remarks about R.E.M.'s Michael Stipe dying of AIDS, but Richey James was in genuine trouble. Suffering from deepening alcoholism and anorexia, James entered prolonged bouts of depression, highlighted by incidents of self-mutilation—most notoriously at a concert in Thailand, when he appeared with his chest slashed open by knives a fan gave him. Early in 1994, he entered a private clinic, and the band had to perform a number of concerts as a trio. James' mental illness surfaced on the group's third album, *The Holy Bible*. Reportedly recorded in a red-light district in Wales, *The Holy Bible* was a bleak, disillusioned record that earned considerable critical acclaim upon its late summer release in 1994.

Although the Manics' critical reputation was restored and James was playing with the band, even giving numerous interviews with the press, all was not well. Prior to the American release of *The Holy Bible* and the band's ensuing tour, James checked out of his London hotel on February 1, 1995, drove to his Cardiff apartment, and disappeared, leaving behind his passport and credit cards. Within the week he was reported missing and his abandoned car was found on the Severen Bridge outside of Bristol, a spot notorious for suicides. By the summer, the police had presumed he was dead. Broken, but not beaten, the remaining Manics decided to carry on as a trio, working the remaining lyrics James left behind into songs.

The Manic Street Preachers returned in December 1995, opening for the Stone Roses. In May 1996, they released *Everything Must Go*, which was preceded by the number two single, "A Design for Life." Their most direct and mature record to date, *Everything Must Go* was greeted with enthusiastic reviews, and the group became major stars in England. Throughout 1996, the band toured constantly, and most UK music publications named *Everything Must Go* Album of the Year. Despite their growing success, several older fans expressed distress at the group's increasingly conservative image, yet that didn't prevent the album from going multi-platinum. —*Stephen Thomas Erlewine*

Generation Terrorists / Feb. 1992 / Columbia ♦♦♦♦

Debut albums rarely come as ambitious as the Manic Street Preachers' *Generation Terrorists*. Released in England as a double album (it was trimmed to the length of a single record in America), the album teemed with slogans, political rhetoric, and scarily inarticulate angst. Since the Manics deliver these charged lyrics as heavy guitar-rockers, the music doesn't always hit quite as forcefully as intended. The relatively polished production and big guitar sound occasionally sell the music short, especially the lesser songs, yet the Manics' passion is undeniable, even on the weaker cuts. While the album is loaded with a little bit too much unrealized material in retrospect, its best moments—the fiery "Slash N' Burn," "Little Baby Nothing," the incendiary "Stay Beautiful," the sardonic "You Love Us," and the haunting "Motorcycle Emptiness"—capture the Manics in all their raging glory. —*Stephen Thomas Erlewine*

Gold Against the Soul / Jun. 1993 / Columbia ♦♦♦

Taking the hard-rock inclinations of *Generation Terrorists* to an extreme, the Manic Street Preachers delivered a flawed but intriguing second album with *Gold Against the Soul*. Inspired by Guns N' Roses, the Manics decided to rework their working-class angst as heavy arena rock; they seize upon the latent politicism of Guns N' Roses' tortured white-trash metal, interpreting it as a call to arms. Since the Manics are more intellectual and revolutionary than the Gunners, *Gold Against the Soul* burns with inspired, if confused, rhetoric. The Manics, however, aren't quite as gifted with hooks at this stage—their power derives from their self-belief, which they can't quite translate into songs. They are given a bigger, louder production on *Gold Against the Soul*, which makes the album a more visceral listen than *Generation Terrorists*, but the songs aren't as consistently compelling as those on the debut. "From Despair to Where" is a vibrant anthem, and "Drug Drug Druggy," "Roses in the Hospital," "Yourself," and "Sleepflower" all have a similar energy, but the peaks don't arrive quite as frequently as before. Nevertheless, the rage is more articulate and the sound is stronger, making *Gold Against the Soul* a flawed but worthy step forward. —*Stephen Thomas Erlewine*

The Holy Bible / Aug. 1994 / Epic ✦✦✦✦
It's difficult not to look at *The Holy Bible* as Richey James' last will and testament, yet that only makes the record all the more powerful. A remarkable step forward from the Manic Street Preachers' first two records, *The Holy Bible* is a tense, harrowing collection of tortured, cryptic declarations of depression—the diary of anorexia "4st 7lb" is one of the most chilling songs in rock 'n' roll. James' lyrics, which are punctuated by Nicky Wire's political tirades, are unflinching in their bleakness. Every song has a passage frightening in its imagery. Although the music itself isn't as scarily intense, its tight, terse hard rock and glam hooks accentuate the paranoia behind the songs, making the lyrics cut deeper. —*Stephen Thomas Erlewine*

● Everything Must Go / May 1996 / Epic ✦✦✦✦
Months after the release of the harrowing *The Holy Bible*, Manic Street Preachers guitarist Richey James disappeared, leaving no trace of his whereabouts or his well-being. Ultimately, the remaining trio decided to carry on, releasing their fourth album *Everything Must Go* in 1996. Considering the tragic circumstances that surrounded it, *Everything Must Go* is the strongest, most focused, and certainly the most optimistic album the Manics ever released. Five of the songs feature lyrics James left behind before his disappearance, and while offering no motivation for his actions, they do hint at the depths of his despair. Nicky Wire wrote the remaining lyrics, and his songs give the record its weight and balance, confronting the issue of James' disappearance in a roundabout way, never explicitly mentioning the topic but offering a gritty dose of realistic optimism—offering the hope that things *will* get better; after the nihilism of *The Holy Bible*, the outlook is all the more inspiring. Furthermore, the Manics' musical attack has become leaner; their music still rages, but it's channeled into concise, anthemic rock songs that soar on their own belief. Above all, *Everything Must Go* is a cathartic experience—it is genuinely moving to hear the Manics offering hope without sinking to mawkish sentimentality or collapsing under the weight of their situation. —*Stephen Thomas Erlewine*

Barry Manilow

b. Jun. 17, 1946, Brooklyn, NY
Piano, Vocals / Adult Contemporary, Pop, Soft Rock
Although he has never earned the respect of either the critics or much of the public, Barry Manilow was one of the most successful recording artists of the '70s. Manilow began his pop music career by writing advertising jingles in the '60s; during this time, the Juilliard-trained musician honed his pop instincts, as evidenced by the sheer number of successful advertisements he wrote. In 1972, he began accompanying Bette Midler on piano as she performed in New York City's gay bathhouses. Manilow arranged her first two albums, which helped earn him a record contract with Bell. His self-titled first album was a flop, yet his second featured the No. 1 ballad "Mandy."

"Mandy" began a decade's worth of polished MOR hits for Manilow, which included the No. 1 singles "I Write the Songs" and "Looks Like We Made It," as well as Top Ten singles "Could It Be Magic," "Copacabana (At the Copa)," and "I Made It Through the Rain." Manilow also became a popular live act during this time. By the mid-'80s, he decided to broaden his musical horizons by making records of jazz and pop standards. At the end of the decade, the widow of Johnny Mercer invited him to set music to a number of the great songwriter's unpublished lyrics; some of the results appeared on *Showstoppers*. Manilow continued in a similar vein on the records *Singin' with the Big Bands* (1994) and *Another Life* (1995), before he made the nostalgia-drenched *Summer of '78* in 1996. —*Stephen Thomas Erlewine*

Barry Manilow II / Oct. 1974 / Arista ✦✦✦✦
Barry Manilow's second album was his breakthrough, since it contained his No. 1 gold single "Mandy," as well as the No. 12 "It's A Miracle." With its lush sound and appealing pop songs, this album set the pattern for Manilow's ongoing easy-listening success through the rest of the 1970s and into the '80s. —*William Ruhlmann*

Live / May 1977 / Arista ✦✦✦✦
Live was Manilow's only No. 1 album. The performances are so seamless that it's practically a faithfully performed greatest-hits album. It includes the hit "Daybreak." —*Rick Clark*

● Greatest Hits, Vol. 1 / Nov. 1978 / Arista ✦✦✦✦
Manilow has had a load of albums, but essentially he is a singles artist. This first *Greatest Hits* collection is the place to start, for those desiring

an introduction to one of the most successful MOR singers of all time. Among the songs included in this collection are "Mandy," "Looks Like We Made It," "Can't Smile Without You," "Tryin' to Get the Feeling Again," and "Daybreak." —*Rick Clark*

Greatest Hits, Vol. 2 / Nov. 1983 / Arista ✦✦✦✦
Included are "Could It Be Magic," "This One's for You," "Weekend in New England," "Copacabana (At the Copa)," and "I Write the Songs." —*Rick Clark*

2:00 AM Paradise Cafe / Nov. 1984 / Arista ✦✦✦✦
With his contemporary pop career in decline and "classic pop" on the rise, Barry Manilow began to position himself as a long-term show business talent in the tradition of, say, Mel Torme, who turns up here to do a duet with him. So does Sarah Vaughan, and even when Manilow isn't hobnobbing with great singers of an earlier era, he's leading a band of jazz veterans like Shelly Manne and Gerry Mulligan in what are supposed to be new jazz-pop standards. So, can Barry Manilow become Harry Connick, Jr.? Well, not quite, but it's a nice try. —*William Ruhlmann*

Swing Street / 1987 / Arista ✦✦✦✦
Barry Manilow takes another stab at traditional jazz-pop, again enlisting support from those who have made a career at it, such as Diane Schuur. This time he includes some covers, such as "Summertime," the Schuur duet that also includes some sax from Stan Getz. But there are also his own originals, which don't compare, and he even adds lyrics to "Stompin' At The Savoy," firm evidence that he hasn't got the respect for tradition to make the transition from sweet to hot. —*William Ruhlmann*

Greatest Hits, Vol. 3 / 1989 / Arista ✦✦✦✦
Vol. 3 isn't as consistently strong as the first two, since it consists mainly of his less successful tracks. This set contains "The Old Songs," "Memory," "Let's Hang On," "Somewhere Down the Road," "I Made It Through the Rain," and his Top Ten version of Ian Hunter's "Ships." —*Rick Clark*

Summer of '78 / Nov. 19, 1996 / Arista ✦✦✦
Barry Manilow decided to follow the success of *Singing with the Big Bands* with an album saluting *another* great lost era—*The Summer of '78*. Even on the newly-written title song, it's never quite clear *why* Manilow chose to single out the summer of 1978 out of the entire decade—after all, the album comprises songs written throughout the '70s—but the exact reason doesn't matter: as much as its predecessor, this is an exercise in nostalgia, pure and simple. Of course, it's very entertaining nostalgia, as Manilow has chosen soft-rock songs (Dan Hill's "Sometimes When We Touch," Leo Sayer's "When I Need You," Bob Seger's "We've Got Tonight") that perfectly suit his style. It's a minor entry in Manilow's catalog to be sure, but *The Summer of '78* is a perfectly executed and entertaining slice of nostalgia. —*Stephen Thomas Erlewine*

Aimee Mann

b. Aug. 9, 1960, Richmond, VA
Bass, Guitar, Vocals / Singer-Songwriter, Pop-Rock
During the '80s, Aimee Mann led the post-new wave pop group, Til Tuesday. After releasing three albums with the group, Mann broke up the band and embarked on a solo career. Her first solo album, *Whatever*, was a more introspective, folk-tinged effort than Til Tuesday's albums and received uniformly positive reviews upon its release in the summer of 1993. However, the album was only a small hit, spending just seven weeks on the American charts, where it peaked at 127. Nevertheless, *Whatever* rejuvenated her career—after its release, critics were praising her songwriting, as were peers like Elvis Costello, Difford & Tilbrook, and Andy Partridge.

Early in 1995, Mann had a modest hit with "That's Just What You Are," a song included on the soundtrack to the television series, *Melrose Place*. Following the success of the single, Mann was set to release her second solo album in the spring of 1995, but her record label, Imago, filed for bankruptcy before its release. She signed a contract with Reprise Records after Imago went under, but Imago prevented her from releasing any records. For most of 1995, Mann battled Imago in an attempt to free herself from the label, eventually winning her independence at the end of the year. After her dispute with Imago was settled, she signed with DGC Records. Mann's second album, *I'm with Stupid*, was released in England in the late fall of 1995 and in January of 1996 in America. Again, it was greeted with positive reviews, but weak sales. —*Stephen Thomas Erlewine*

● Whatever / May 11, 1993 / Geffen ✦✦✦✦
Led by the instantly memorable power-pop of "I Should've Known," Aimee Mann's first solo album, *Whatever*, is a strong collection of pure pop singles and folk-tinged ballads, proving that she is a very talented songwriter with a gift for melody, as well as a fine lyricist. —*Stephen Thomas Erlewine*

I'm with Stupid / Nov. 1995 / Geffen ♦♦♦
From the opening of "Long Shot," with its rolling hip-hop-derived beat and its nonchalant profanity, it's clear that Aimee Mann is trying to appeal to a wider audience with her second solo album, *I'm with Stupid*. Taking her cues from Liz Phair and Beck, she adds alternative rock flourishes to her music but she never abandons her love of the basic, three-minute pop single. Mann builds from the more pop-oriented songs on *Whatever*, incorporating her confessional singer-songwriter instincts into the pop songs while working with a more adventurous production and instrumentation. Occasionally, the fusion is a bit awkward, but the best moments on *I'm with Stupid*—the sighing "Choice in the Matter," the nearly perfect "That's Just What You Are," featuring backing vocals by Glenn Tilbrook, and the Bernard Butler collaboration "Sugarcoated"—surpass even the best moments on *Whatever*. However, *I'm With Stupid* falls short of matching Mann's debut for consistent song quality—there are several tracks that are pleasant, but simply don't lead anywhere. Nevertheless, the album confirms that she is a distinctive, talented songwriter. At her best, she is as capable of melding melody with intelligent lyrics as her idols Elvis Costello, Difford/Tilbrook, and Ray Davies. —*Stephen Thomas Erlewine*

Mansun

f. Chester, England
Arriving in the aftermath of Brit-pop, Mansun was one of the first British guitar bands to depart from the prevailing styles of the mid-'90s, leaving both light, Beatlesque pop and studied trad-rock behind. Mansun had more in common with early '90s bands like Suede and the Manic Street Preachers, groups that stood defiantly outside of the pop spotlight, yet managed to cultivate a devoted fan base. By combining a dark, grandiose vision with the driving intensity of hard rock and the stylish swagger of New Romanticism, Mansun didn't sound a thing like their contemporaries. While their first singles earned a devoted audience, the British music press didn't focus heavily on the group, so it came as a surprise when their debut album, *Attack of the Grey Lantern*, debuted at No. 1 in early 1997, knocking the long-awaited Blur comeback off the top of the charts. But by that time, Mansun had been hailed as one of the best new bands of 1997, and the record was praised throughout the UK music press, making the group one of the most respected and popular new groups of 1997.

Led by guitarist-vocalist Paul Draper, Mansun formed in Chester, England in the mid-'90s. Draper met Stove King (bass) at Wrexham Art College, discovering that they shared a fondness for New Wave acts like Duran Duran and ABC, as well as Prince, Pink Floyd, and David Bowie. The pair, who worked at a photo laboratory together, met Dominic Chad (lead guitar) at a local pub he was managing. Forming under the name Grey Lantern, the trio began playing, supported by a series of drummers. After being told by an acquaintance that Grey Lantern was the worst name he had ever heard, the group changed their name to Mansun, which was a truncation of a Verve B-side, "A Man Called Sun."

Early in 1996, the group released the limited-edition single "Take It Easy Chicken" on their own Sci Fi Hi Fi label, and it entered the play list for Radio 1. Shortly afterward, Andy Rathbone became their permanent drummer. Initially, the UK music weeklies tagged Mansun as one of the crowd of post-Oasis, lad-rock bands, primarily because of Chad's heavy drinking and alcohol-fueled antics. Over the course of the year, the guitarist sobered up and the band released a series of singles, each more ambitious than the one before. By the end of the year, they had earned their first *Melody Maker* cover. In February of 1997, Mansun released their debut album *Attack of the Grey Lantern* on Parlophone Records. It unexpectedly entered the charts at No. 1, earning enthusiastic reviews in the process. —*Stephen Thomas Erlewine*

● **Attack of the Grey Lantern** / Feb. 1997 / Parlophone ♦♦♦♦
Opening with the swirling, cinematic strings of "The Chad Who Loved Me," Mansun's debut album *Attack of the Grey Lantern* is anything but a conventional Brit-pop record. Few debut records are this assured, especially when a group is developing such an idiosyncratic, individual style. Mansun recalls many artists—Suede, Manic Street Preachers, Tears for Fears, David Bowie, ABC, Blur, Prince—without sounding exactly like any of them. *Attack of the Grey Lantern* is a grandiose, darkly seductive blend of new wave and '90s indie-rock, filled with phased guitars, drum machines, and subversive, off-kilter song structures, many of which wind past five minutes. No song is ever quite what it seems—"Mansun's Only Love Song" balances between soul and fractured pop, "Stripper Vicar" has new wave backing vocals and hard-rock chords, while "Taxloss" marries Suede's dark glam-rock with uneasy psychedelia. It's an ambitious, even pretentious, record, but Mansun has enough confidence and skill to make it an astonishingly original debut. —*Stephen Thomas Erlewine*

Mantronix

f. 1984, New York, NY
Hip Hop, Club/Dance, Electro-Funk, Old School Rap
Combining rap, funk, pop, reggae, and electronics, Mantronix was one of the most innovative hip-hop groups of the mid-'80s. Formed in 1984, the New York group comprised DJ-keyboardist Mantronik (born Curtis Khaleel) and rapper MC Tee (born Tooure Embden). Mantronix's demo tape gained the attention of William Socolov, the head of the independent record label Sleeping Bag. The group released their first single, "Fresh Is the Word," in 1985; it was a big hit on the street and in the clubs, as was their debut album, *Mantronix*. The duo enhanced their reputation by producing Joyce Sims and 12.41. However, their second record, 1986's *Music Madness*, showed them in a holding pattern; soon afterward, their audience began to shrink and by the beginning of the '90s they had faded away. —*Stephen Thomas Erlewine*

● **The Album** / 1985 / Sleeping Bag ♦♦♦♦
Mantronix's finest album remains this intriguing mid-'80s debut, when Curtis "Mantronik" Kahleel and rapper M.C. Tee scored with what was then an imaginative and unusual mix of dance and hip-hop production styles and sensibility with soul and R&B vocals. They weren't house, or rap, or urban contemporary, but a wonderful hybrid of all these and more, including touches of dancehall reggae and even pop and funk. The album had two fine singles in "Bassline" and "Ladies" and made Mantronix a hot property. —*Ron Wynn*

This Should Move Ya / 1987 / Capitol ♦♦♦
Mantronix switched labels in the late '80s, moving from the independent Sleeping Bag to the major label Capitol. This was their second Capitol album, and it worked out fine. Although the lineup had now changed, with Bryce Luvah and D.J.D. on board rather than M.C. Tee, the group had another strong single in "Got To Have Your Love," and Capitol was providing Curtis "Mantronik" Kahleel with a bigger push and sharper production and sound. But the underground spirit that permeated Mantronix's Sleeping Bag albums was missing, as was the quirky air that marked their past singles. —*Ron Wynn*

In Full Effect / 1988 / Capitol ♦♦♦
The Capitol debut for Curtis "Mantronik" Kahleel, and the final album featuring rapper M.C. Tee. This album skirted the lower regions of the pop charts and had a less abrasive, smoother sound, although the patented dance/hip-hop/urban contemporary fusion hadn't been affected. But overall, it wasn't quite as risky or spirited as their Sleeping Bag records, which may have been the reason Tee departed. —*Ron Wynn*

The Incredible Sound Machine / Mar. 18, 1991 / Capitol ♦♦
Mantronix's high-tech and futuristic approach fared better in clubs and dance music circles than among b-boys and hip-hoppers, but make no mistake: the New York group created some of the most memorable rap of the mid-'80s. Unfortunately, things began unraveling for Mantronix artistically when it left the small (and now defunkt) Sleeping Bag Records for Capitol. A pedestrian effort that, surprisingly, favors R&B, new jack swing, and house music over rap, *The Incredible Sound Machine* contains nothing that's even a fraction as imaginative as Mantronix's Sleeping Bag recordings. Rapper MC Tee is gone, and leader-producer Curtis "Mantronik" Khaleel is joined by singer Jade Trini, among others. Trini's singing isn't bad—it's the material that's so forgettable and generic. A much wiser purchase would be *Mantronix: The Album*. —*Alex Henderson*

Bass Machine Re-Tuned / 1997 / Oxygen Music Works ♦♦♦
One half of innovative hip-hop/electro duo Mantronix (namely, Curtis "Mantronik" Khaleel) back behind the "Bass Machine" for this '90s-style update. The three-track single includes re-mixes of the electro classic by Riz Maslen (of Neotropic) and Florida-based producer Omar Santana, whose mid-'80s electro and funky breaks-based tracks were as influential as Mantronix's own. Great stuff. —*Sean Cooper*

The Mar-Keys

f. 1958, Memphis, TN
Soul
Before Booker T. & the MG's, there were the Mar-Keys, who literally laid the groundwork for the Memphis Sound with their powerfully economic early-R&B instrumental sound. They enjoyed only one real hit with the No. 3 "Last Night," which was released in 1961 on Satellite Records, the predecessor to Stax.

Besides including Steve Cropper and "Duck" Dunn in the lineup, the Mar-Keys also had Wayne Jackson, who later formed the Memphis Horns, and Don Nix, who had a fairly successful career as a solo artist and producer. —*Rick Clark*

The Markeys / 1961 / Atlantic ♦♦♦
Do the Pop-Eye / 1962 / Atlantic ♦♦♦

Back to Back / 1967 / Atlantic ✦✦✦✦
Recorded live at Paris in 1967, when the Stax-Volt Revue was touring Europe, this CD is split between cuts by Booker T. & the MG's, and cuts by the Mar-Keys. This is just about exactly what you'd expect: solid, straight-ahead live versions of the instrumental groups' best-known tunes, in good sound. Booker T. & the MG's take seven of album's ten tracks, including their hits "Green Onions" and "Hip Hug-Her"; the Mar-Keys do "Last Night" and a couple of other numbers. —*Richie Unterberger*

Damifiknew / 1969 / Stax ✦✦✦
For this session, the Mar-Keys were basically Booker T. & the MG's, augmented by trumpeter Wayne Jackson and tenor saxophonist Andrew Love (who would soon become the Memphis Horns). It's not quite fair to call this laidback set easy listening, but it's certainly not much more than background listening, as they wind their way through a mix of originals and covers of shopworn '60s tunes like "Mustang Sally," "Soul Man," and "Daydream." It's pleasant and executed with the expected precision, but it has to rate among the musicians' more secondary efforts, whether they're calling themselves the MG's or something else. The album was combined with the 1971 Mar-Keys LP *Memphis Experience* on a single-CD reissue in 1994. —*Richie Unterberger*

Memphis Experience / 1971 / Stax ✦✦
The Mar-Keys had a history of strange personnel changes; their previous LP (1969's *Damifiknow!*) had basically been Booker T. & the MG's-plus-horn-section playing under the Mar-Keys name. Yet *Memphis Experience* was even stranger, demonstrating that the Mar-Keys at this point meant nothing more to Stax than a name that could be exploited. Three of the seven cuts were Bar-Kays outtakes that were scrapped when that band underwent one of its numerous reorganizations. The rest of the album was recorded by an assortment of Memphis musicians. The result was serviceable period instrumental soul-funk, occasionally creeping into psychedelia (especially on the nine-minute "Cloud Nine," with several minutes of weird screams and whispers). It's an oddity in the Stax discography, related to the rest of the Mar-Keys' releases in name only, and not worth paying attention to unless you're determined to track down every available Stax recording. The album was combined with the 1969 Mar-Keys LP *Damifiknow!* on a single-CD reissue in 1994. —*Richie Unterberger*

Damifiknow!/Memphis Experience / May 20, 1994 / Stax ✦✦✦
A two-for-one disc combining a couple of strange releases, neither of which was truly the Mar-Keys. *Damnifiknow!* was played by Booker T. & the MG's, supplemented by a horn section that would become the Memphis Horns; *Memphis Experience* combined Bar-Kays outtakes with instrumentals by Memphis musicians with no connection to prior Mar-Keys lineups. It's a convenient way for major Stax/soul collectors to pick up two of the group's odder records, but it's not a representative reflection of the Mar-Keys. Nor is the music especially noteworthy: *Damifiknow!* is easygoing, rather humdrum soul instrumentals that don't pack nearly the punch of the MG's at their best, while *Memphis Experience* is average wordless early '70s soul-funk with occasional psychedelic-hard rock tinges. —*Richie Unterberger*

The Marcels

f. Pittsburgh, PA
Doo Wop
This Pittsburgh ensemble deserved a much better fate than being known primarily for a novelty-tinged cover of "Blue Moon." Baritone vocalist Richard F. Knauss teamed with Fred Johnson, Gene J. Bricker, Ron Mundy, and lead vocalist Cornelius Harp, an integrated ensemble. They named themselves after Harp's hairstyle, the marcel. The group did a string of covers as demo tapes that were sent to Colpix. The label's A&R director had them cut several oldies at RCA's New York studios in 1961, one of them being "Blue Moon." They used the bass intro arrangement from the Cadillacs' "Zoom" and the results were a huge hit. It eventually topped both the pop and R&B charts, and also was an international smash.

The group eventually appeared in the film *Twist Around the Clock* with Dion and Chubby Checker, and recorded an 18-cut LP for Colpix. Alan Johnson and Walt Maddox later replaced Knauss and Gene Bricker, making the Marcels an all-Black unit. The group did score another Top Ten pop single with "Heartaches," another cover of a pre-rock single. This peaked at No. 7 pop and No. 19 R&B in 1961. They continued recording on Kyra, Queen Bee, St. Clair, Rocky, and Monogram with varying lineups, but never again equaled their past success. —*Ron Wynn*

● **The Best of the Marcels** / Apr. 1990 / Rhino ✦✦✦✦
An outstanding vocal ensemble that is exceptional on nonsense-novelty tunes like "Blue Moon." —*Ron Wynn*

Complete Colpix Sessions / Apr. 16, 1995 / Sequel ✦✦✦✦

Marillion

f. 1978, Aylesbury, England
Hard Rock, Art-Rock/Progressive-Rock
Marillion emerged from the short-lived progressive rock revival of the early '80s to become one of the most enduring cult acts of the era. The group formed in Aylesbury, England in 1978, and adopted their original name, Silmarillion, from the title of a J.R.R. Tolkien novel. Initially, Marillion comprised guitarist Steve Rothery, bassist Doug Irvine, keyboardist Brian Jelliman, and drummer Mick Pointer, but after recording "The Web," an instrumental demo, they recruited vocalist Fish (born Derek Dick) and bassist Diz Minnett.

Prior to recording their debut single "Market Square Heroes," keyboardist Mark Kelly and bassist Pete Trewavas replaced Jelliman and Minnett; Marillion issued its debut album *Script for a Jester's Tear* in 1983, and on the strength of their relentless touring schedule the group won a loyal following. With new drummer Ian Moseley (formerly of Curved Air) firmly in place, they returned to the studio for 1984's *Fugazi*, which streamlined the intricacies of the group's prog-rock leanings in favor of a more straightahead hard rock identity; the refinements paid off, and both "Assassin" and "Punch and Judy" became British hits.

With 1985's *Misplaced Childhood*, an elaborate conceptual album reflecting Fish's formative experiences, Marillion earned its greatest success to date; the lush ballad "Kayleigh" reached the No. 2 position on the UK charts, and became a hit in the US as well. The follow-up, "Lavender," was also a smash, but the group began crumbling: Fish developed alcohol and drug problems, and egos ran rampant. After 1987's *Clutching at Straws*, Fish left the band for a solo career, and after the 1988 live effort *The Thieving Magpie*, it appeared that Marillion's days were numbered.

Instead, they recruited ex-Europeans vocalist Steve Hogarth for their 1990 comeback effort *Seasons End;* although Marillion did not return to the peaks of the mid-1980s heyday, they did continue on successfully through albums like 1991's *Holidays in Eden*, 1994's *Brave*, and 1995's *Afraid of Sunlight*, scoring hit singles including "Sympathy," "The Hollow Man," and "Alone Again in the Lap of Luxury." —*Jason Ankeny*

Script for a Jester's Tear / 1983 / Capitol ✦✦✦✦
Their strong debut shows the influence of Peter Hammill, Pink Floyd, Rick Wakeman, and Jethro Tull, and the much-ballyhooed resemblance to Genesis. —*Michael P. Dawson*

Fugazi / 1984 / Capitol ✦✦✦✦
Gut-wrenchingly powerful lyrics and dynamic prog-rock performance make this a classic! —*Michael P. Dawson*

Misplaced Childhood / 1985 / Capitol ✦✦✦✦
A masterpiece of articulate and emotional lyrics, it has exciting and colorful musical settings. The songs form a continuous album-length suite. —*Michael P. Dawson*

Clutching at Straws / Jun. 19, 1987 / Capitol ✦✦✦
The follow-up to *Misplaced Childhood* is even more personal and often disturbing with its ruminations on alcohol abuse and self-betrayal. —*Michael P. Dawson*

The Thieving Magpie (la Gazza Ladra) / 1988 / Capitol ✦✦✦
A fine double-CD live set from their 1984 and 1987 tours, this was Fish's last recording with Marillion and was named for the Rossini piece they open their shows with. —*Michael P. Dawson*

Season's End / 1989 / Capitol ✦✦
An uneven but still tasty album, it features Steve Hogarth taking over for the irreplaceable Fish. —*Michael P. Dawson*

● **Six of One, Half-Dozen of the Other** / Jul. 14, 1992 / IRS ✦✦✦✦
A fine collection of Marillion's best and most popular tracks, *Six of One, Half-Dozen of the Other* offers a good introduction to the art-rock group. —*Stephen Thomas Erlewine*

Biz Markie

b. Apr. 8, 1964, Harlem, NY
Vocals / Hip Hop
Biz Markie's inclination toward juvenile humor and his fondness for goofy, tuneless, half-sung choruses camouflaged his true talents as a freestyle rhymer. The Biz may not have been able to translate his wild rhyming talents to tape, but what he did record was worthwhile in its own way. With his silly humor and inventive, sample-laden productions, he proved that hip-hop could be funny and melodic, without sacrificing its street credibility. His distinctive style made his second album, *The Biz Never Sleeps*, a gold hit and its single "Just A Friend" into a Top Ten pop single. While its success made Biz Markie a semi-star, it also cursed him. Not only was he consigned as a novelty act, but it brought enough attention to him that Gilbert O'Sullivan sued him over the unauthorized sample of "Alone Again (Naturally)" on Biz's 1991 album, *I Need A Haircut*. The lawsuit severely cut into Markie's career and 1993's *All Samples Cleared* was the last record he released during the '90s. However,

his reputation was restored somewhat in the mid-'90s, as the Beastie Boys championed him, and other alternative-rap groups showed some debt to his wild, careening music.

A native of New York, Biz Markie (born Marcel Hall) first came to prominence in the early '80s, when he began rapping at Manhattan nightclubs like the Funhouse and the Roxy. The Biz met producer Marley Marl in 1985, and later that year, he recorded his first set of demos. By 1988, he had signed with Cold Chillin', and later that year he released his debut, *Goin' Off*, which became a word-of-mouth hit based on the underground hit singles "Vapors," "Pickin' Boogers," and "Make the Music With Your Mouth, Biz." A year later, Markie broke into the mainstream when "Just A Friend," a single featuring rapped verses and out-of-tune sung choruses, reached the pop Top Ten and its accompanying album, *The Biz Never Sleeps*, went gold.

The Biz Never Sleeps put Biz Markie near the top of the hip-hop world, but he fell from grace as quickly as he achieved it. Markie's third album, *I Need A Haircut*, was already shaping up to be a considerable sales disappointment when he was served a lawsuit from Gilbert O'Sullivan, who claimed that the album's "Alone Again" featured an unauthorized sample of his hit "Alone Again (Naturally)." Sullivan won the case in a ruling that drastically changed the rules of hip-hop. According to the ruling, Warner Bros., Cold Chillin's parent company, had to pull *I Need A Haircut* from circulation and all companies had to clear samples fully before releasing a hip-hop record. The Biz countered with his 1993 album *All Samples Cleared!*, but his career had already been hurt by the lawsuit, and the record bombed. For the remainder of the decade, he kept a low profile, occasionally guesting on records by the Beastie Boys and filming a freestyle television commercial for MTV2 in 1996. The alliance with the Beasties raised his profile considerably, but as of 1997, Biz Markie had not released an album of new material in four years. — *Stephen Thomas Erlrewine*

Goin' Off / Feb. 23, 1988 / Cold Chillin' ♦♦♦♦
Biz Markie's debut album introduced his absurdly comical and extremely inventive musical style. While he talked about "Pickin' Boogers," and hanging out at "Albee Square Mall," and made music with his mouth, The Biz never kept the music similar, with Marley Marl's production covering all of the bases, concentrating on a deeply funky R&B-dance beat. It was a funny, surrealistic minor masterpiece. — *Stephen Thomas Erlewine*

The Biz Never Sleeps / Oct. 10, 1989 / Cold Chillin' ♦♦♦♦
Biz Markie's madcap humor was effectively utilized on this release. Markie relied on puns, quips, bad jokes, and his disjointed rap style, creating material quite different from the hard-edged fare that now rules hip-hop. Some of it was funny, some of it stupid, but none of it vicious or offensive. The album contained the hits "Just a Friend" and "Spring Again." — *Ron Wynn*

I Need a Haircut / Aug. 27, 1991 / Cold Chillin' ♦♦♦
Biz Markie, rap's clown prince, can usually be counted on to deliver goofy humor, and *I Need a Haircut* is as wildly entertaining as anything he's ever done. The Biz isn't one to rap about his sexual prowess, drive-by shootings near the projects, or Louis Farrakhan's ideology. In contrast to the sobering gangster rap of N.W.A. and Ice-T, the angry political protests of Public Enemy and Boogie Down Productions, and the machismo of LL Cool J, Biz Markie seeks only to amuse, entertain, and have fun. Indeed, rap doesn't get much sillier than "T.S.R. (Toilet Stool Rap)" and "Kung Fu." The Brooklyn native's third album also contains "Alone Again"—the song that incorporated Gilbert O'Sullivan's pop hit "Alone Again Naturally" (allegedly without the pop singer's permission) and inspired a major lawsuit. — *Alex Henderson*

All Samples Cleared / Jun. 22, 1993 / Cold Chillin' ♦♦
Biz Markie made sure he had permission for every sample featured on this album. Unfortunately, it seemed that the effort to get clearances took its toll on the creative process. The bizarre humor that made his earlier releases so entertaining was much less evident, as Markie now strained for results and mostly came up short. — *Ron Wynn*

● **Biz's Baddest Beats** / Jul. 1, 1994 / Cold Chillin' ♦♦♦♦
Biz's Baddest Beats collects all of Biz Markie's hit singles, making the album a good introduction to his bizarrely humorous hip-hop. — *Stephen Thomas Erlewine*

The Marshall Tucker Band

f. 1971, Spartanburg, SC
Country-Rock, Southern Rock
One of the major Southern-rock bands of the '70s, the Marshall Tucker Band was formed in Spartanburg, SC in 1971 by singer Doug Gray; guitarist Toy Caldwell (born1948); his brother, bassist Tommy Caldwell (born 1950, died April 4, 1980); guitarist George McCorkle; drummer Paul Riddle; and reed player Jerry Eubanks. The group's style combined rock, country, and jazz, and featured extended instrumental passages on which lead guitarist Toy Caldwell shone. The band was signed to Capri-

corn Records and released its debut album, *The Marshall Tucker Band*, in March 1973. They gained recognition through a tour with the Allman Brothers Band and found significant success during the course of the '70s, with most of their albums going gold. Their peak came with the million-selling album *Carolina Dreams* and its Top 15 single "Heard It in a Love Song" in 1977. The band was slowed down by the death of Tommy Caldwell in a car accident in 1980, and it faded from the album charts after 1982. Toy Caldwell left for a solo career, and by the early '90s, Marshall Tucker consisted of Doug Gray, Jerry Eubanks, guitarist Rusty Milner, bassist Tim Lawter, drummer Ace Allen, and pianist Don Cameron. — *William Ruhlmann*

The Marshall Tucker Band / 1973 / AJK ♦♦♦♦
With flute and the occasional blast of horns, the Marshall Tucker Band were one of the most laidback Southern country-rock outfits of the late '70s. Their first album easily demonstrates this, and it still holds up well, with "Take the Highway," "Can't You See," and "Ramblin'" sounding particularly strong. — *Stephen Thomas Erlewine*

A New Life / 1974 / AJK ♦♦♦♦
On their second release, the Marshall Tucker Band becomes slightly rootsier and bluesier without sacrificing any of the relaxed charm of their first record. Overall, it is a stronger, more consistent album, highlighted by "Southern Woman," "Blue Ridge Mountain Sky," and "Too Stubborn." — *Stephen Thomas Erlewine*

Where We All Belong / 1974 / AJK ♦♦♦♦
Although it runs a little long, *Where We All Belong* captures the sound of the Marshall Tucker Band coming into its own. Half the album consists of new studio recordings, which are more focused than their previous releases; the other half is a harder-edged, jam-oriented live set. Taken together, they show that the band was progressing musically. — *Stephen Thomas Erlewine*

Searchin' for a Rainbow / 1975 / AJK ♦♦♦♦
With *Searchin' for a Rainbow*, the Marshall Tucker Band retreats somewhat from the grittier sounds of *Where We All Belong* without abandoning their country and blues roots. — *Stephen Thomas Erlewine*

Long Hard Ride / 1976 / AJK ♦♦♦
On *Long Hard Ride*, the Marshall Tucker Band's country influences come to the fore, resulting in a strong record that failed to gain many hits. Still, the final product is well worth listening to—it's one of their better releases. Be sure to listen for Charlie Daniels' guest appearance. — *Stephen Thomas Erlewine*

Carolina Dreams / 1977 / AJK ♦♦♦
Carolina Dreams marks a retreat from the more pronounced country leanings of *Long Hard Ride* to the more successful country-tinged pop-rock of "Heard It In a Love Song" and "Fly Like An Eagle." They gathered more hits with this approach, and although the hits hold up well, the rest of the album doesn't live up to their quality. — *Stephen Thomas Erlewine*

● **Greatest Hits** / 1978 / AJK ♦♦♦♦
If you are looking for a place to start with this band, *Greatest Hits* covers all the main bases. Included are "Can't You See," "Heard It in a Love Song," "Fire on the Mountain," and "This Ol' Cowboy." — *Rick Clark*

Together Forever / 1978 / AJK ♦♦♦
Together Forever boasts a more mainstream rock approach than any of its predecessors, halfway between the country-tinged *Long Hard Ride* and the pop-oriented *Carolina Dreams*. Although the band sounds good, the songs don't match the strength of their performances. — *Stephen Thomas Erlewine*

Best Of . . . The Capricorn Years / 1995 / ERA ♦♦♦♦
Country Tucker / Aug. 1996 / K-Tel ♦♦♦♦
Country Tucker compiles tracks from the Marshall Tucker Band's mid-'70s heyday. As the title implies, all of the songs included on this collection lean toward the group's country roots—many of them, including "Heard It In A Love Song," were minor country hits. In fact, *Country Tucker* works as a greatest hits collection, since it does feature pop hits like "Fire on the Mountain" (presented in its original single version) and "Can't You See" that nevertheless demonstrate strong country leanings. In short, it's a useful introduction and a nearly definitive compilation that should satiate the desires of most casual fans. — *Stephen Thomas Erlewine*

Martha & the Vandellas

f. 1963, Detroit, MI, **db.** 1972
Soul, Motown, Girl Group
Along with the Supremes, Martha & the Vandellas defined the distaff side of the Motown sound in the 1960s; their biggest hits, including "Heat Wave," "Dancing in the Street," and "Nowhere to Run," remain among the most potent and enduring dance records of the era. The vocal group was led by Martha Reeves, who along with fellow Detroit, MI natives Annette Sterling Beard, Gloria Williams, and Rosalind Ash-

ford founded the Del-Phis in 1960. After Reeves landed a secretarial position at the offices of Motown Records, the Del-Phis were tapped to record a one-off single for the label's Melody imprint, which they cut under the name the Vels.

The single fizzled, and Williams exited, reducing the group to a trio. After backing Marvin Gaye on the superb 1962 record "Stubborn Kind of Fellow," they were renamed Martha & the Vandellas, taking inspiration from Detroit's Van Dyke Street and Reeves' heroine Della Reese. When singer Mary Wells failed to show up for a recording date, musicians' union rules demanded that a vocalist be found to fulfill contractual obligations; as a result, Reeves was yanked from the secretarial pool and laid down what would become Martha & the Vandellas' first record, 1963's "I'll Have to Let Him Go."

The Top 30 success of the ballad "Come and Get These Memories" brought the group the attention of Motown's hit-making production team Holland-Dozier-Holland, who crafted their next smash, the galvanizing Top 5 classic "Heat Wave," which perfected the mix of impassioned call-and-response vocals, pulsing rhythms, and full-bodied horns that became the trio's trademark. Following another Top Ten hit, "Quicksand," Beard retired, and was replaced by former Velvelette Betty Kelly. After singer Kim Weston turned down the Marvin Gaye/Ivy Jo Hunter/Mickey Stevenson composition "Dancing in the Street," the song was shuttled to Martha & the Vandellas; refashioned by Holland-Dozier-Holland to fit the group's formula, the anthem became their biggest hit and definitive statement, reaching No. 2 in the summer of 1964. A year later, they returned with another smash, the savage "Nowhere to Run," followed by "I'm Ready for Love."

In 1967, Kelly exited, and was replaced by Reeves' younger sister Lois; on subsequent releases, the group was billed as Martha Reeves and the Vandellas. 1967's "Jimmy Mack" and "Honey Chile" were the last records overseen by the Holland-Dozier-Holland team before their defection from Motown, and were also the final significant Vandellas hits; in 1968, Martha Reeves fell seriously ill, and in 1969 Ashford departed, with another former Velvelette, Sandra Tilley, assuming her position. The trio continued unsuccessfully for a few more years before breaking up in the wake of a December, 1972 farewell performance at Detroit's Cobo Hall. After Motown relocated its corporate offices to Los Angeles (a move Reeves denied she was privy to), the singer, who had begun a solo career, sued to have her contract with the label annulled; in her 1994 autobiography *Dancing in the Street*, she charged that the Vandellas' career, though highly successful in its own right, could have been even greater had Motown founder Berry Gordy Jr. given their music the same obsessive attention he afforded to Diana Ross and the Supremes.

Reeves recorded her debut solo effort, *Martha Reeves: Produced by Richard Perry*, for MCA in 1974; though a few more LPs followed, including 1976's *The Rest of My Life* and 1978's *We Meet Again*, she received little notice on her own, and eventually suffered a pair of nervous breakdowns that led to a brief period of institutionalization. Lois Reeves, meanwhile, went on to work with Al Green, while Sandra Tilley retired from music; she died in 1982 following surgery on a brain tumor. In 1989, Martha Reeves, Annette Beard, and Rosalind Ashford successfully sued Motown for back royalties, and occasionally reunited for performances in the 1990s. Reeves also continued as a solo artist, and in addition performed with a Vandellas unit consisting of Lois and a third sister, Delphine. —*Jason Ankeny*

Come and Get These Memories / 1963 / Motown ✦✦✦
Their debut album finds The Vandellas in a more lightweight and pop-oriented style than they would become known for, with some girl group and doo wop roots still in evidence. As was often the case during this era, the best tracks were the singles: the title track (the group's first big hit), "There He Is (At My Door)," and The Shirelles-like "I'll Have To Let Him Go." Most of the material was written by Holland-Dozier-Holland, but beyond the singles, there aren't any exceptionally noteworthy cuts. —*Richie Unterberger*

Heat Wave / 1963 / Motown ✦✦✦
Martha And The Vandellas began making their first noise on the pop and soul charts with this 1963 album. The title song was a classic, while there were also decent remakes of such vintage tunes as "Mocking Bird" and "My Boyfriend's Back." These proved that the group was a singles rather than an album act, and that a little more effort needed to be extended toward finding more material (they even put "Danke Schoen" on this album). But no one really cared, since "Heat Wave" was such a triumph. —*Ron Wynn*

Dance Party / 1965 / Motown ✦✦✦✦
Another collection of singles rather than a unified album, but who cared when the songs included "Dancing In The Street" and "Nowhere To Run," as well as "Wild One"? Martha Reeves was singing with as much energy, sensuality and joy as any Motown performer during the mid-'60s, and at least the filler for this record was "Hitch Hike" and "Jerk" instead of "Danke Schoen." —*Ron Wynn*

Watchout! / 1966 / Motown ✦✦✦
The creative well was already starting to run a bit dry for Martha And The Vandellas, mainly because they were a singles band and seldom made a whole album worth a second listen. This proved no different, with the great singles "I'm Ready For Love" and "Jimmy Mack" anchoring an otherwise forgettable collection of filler, although "No More Tearstained Make Up" was a decent bit of period-piece heartache soul and "What Am I Going To Do Without Your Love" brushed the low end of the pop and soul charts. —*Ron Wynn*

★ **Live Wire! The Singles (1962-1972)** / Sep. 7, 1993 / Motown ✦✦✦✦✦
This two-CD box set includes all of the top singles and many of the flipsides that Martha Reeves and the Vandellas cut for Motown. All the hits are here, of course; the collector will be especially interested in the B-sides and non-hit singles, many of which employed the songwriting talents of Motown regulars like Holland-Dozier-Holland and Mickey Stevenson. There's also the rare single (featuring Gloria Williamson on lead vocals) cut by the Vells in 1962, before Reeves took top billing and the group changed their name. Eight of these cuts have never been released on album before. Among the non-hits, there isn't anything to match "Heat Wave" or "Dancing in the Street," but Reeves' astonishingly powerful voice never falters. She was arguably Motown's most talented female singer, but the label's investment in her seemed to flag as the decade progressed. The later material lacks the distinction of her classic period, though the 1970 album track "I Should Be Proud" is a little-known (if somewhat heavy-handed) protest against the Vietnam War. —*Richie Unterberger*

● **Milestones** / 1995 / Motown ✦✦✦✦
Featuring 18 of Martha & The Vandellas' biggest hits and finest songs, *Milestones* is an inexpensive introduction to one of Motown's best girl groups. —*Stephen Thomas Erlewine*

The Marvelettes

f. 1960, Inkster, MI, **db.** 1971
Soul, Motown, Girl Group
Probably the most pop-oriented of Motown's major female acts, the Marvelettes didn't project as strong an identity as the Supremes, Mary Wells, or Martha Reeves, but recorded quite a few hits, including Motown's first No. 1 single, "Please Mr. Postman" (1961). "Postman," as well as other chirpy early '60s hits like "Playboy," "Twistin' Postman," and "Beechwood 4-5789," were the label's purest girl group efforts. Featuring two strong lead singers, Gladys Horton and Wanda Young, the Marvelettes went through five different lineups, but maintained a high standard on their recordings. After a few years, they moved from girl group sounds to up-tempo and mid-tempo numbers that were more characteristic of Motown's production line. They received no small help from Smokey Robinson, who produced and wrote many of their singles; Holland-Dozier-Holland, Berry Gordy, Mickey Stevenson, Marvin Gaye, and Ashford-Simpson also got involved with the songwriting and production at various points. After the mid-'60s, Wanda Young assumed most of the lead vocal duties, Gladys Horton departing the group in the late '60s. While the Marvelettes didn't cut as many monster smashes as most of their Motown peers after the early '60s, they did periodically surface with classic hits like "Too Many Fish in the Sea," "Don't Mess with Bill," and "The Hunter Gets Captured by the Game." There were also plenty of fine minor hits and misses, like 1965's "I'll Keep Holding On," which is just as memorable as the well-known Motown chart-toppers of the era. The group quietly disbanded in the early '70s after several years without a major hit. —*Richie Unterberger*

Deliver: The Singles (1961-1971) / Sep. 7, 1993 / Motown ✦✦✦✦
Forty-one songs, featuring most of both the A-sides and B-sides, nine of which had never been issued on album before. The ace Motown songwriting and production stable was involved in virtually every one of these tracks, making for a surprisingly strong and consistent collection. Includes all the chart hits, as well as rarities like the Phil Spector-style single they released in 1963 as the Darnells. —*Richie Unterberger*

● **Motown Milestones** / Jul. 25, 1995 / Motown ✦✦✦✦
For those who don't want to invest in the two-CD *Deliver* anthology, this 20-song best-of is a good alternative. Contains all of their major pop hits, as well as some obscure low-charting singles. —*Richie Unterberger*

Marvin & Johnny

R&B
One of the first notable rhythm and blues duos, Marvin & Johnny weren't so much a permanent act as they were Marvin Phillips (born Oct. 23, 1931) and a series of partners that he would name "Johnny." Although Emory Perry was the most frequent of these, Phillips also duetted with Jesse Belvin, (reaching No. 2 in the R&B chart as Jesse & Marvin with "Dream Girl"), Carl Green, and others, though Phillips called Perry "my main Johnny." Whoever was singing, Marvin & Johnny were significant, if not major, figures in the transition from West Coast

jump blues to hotter sax-driven R&B sides that began to approach rock 'n' roll; they were also forerunners of doo wop with their appealingly grainy harmonies and occasional sly sense of humor. Recording for Specialty and Modern, they had a couple of Top Ten R&B hits, "Baby Doll" (1953) and "Tick Tock"/"Cherry Pie" (1954), and also issued several other strong singles, sometimes in a sort of updated Louis Jordan style. They faded after the mid-'50s, although they would also record for Aladdin and several other small Los Angeles labels. —*Richie Unterberger*

● **Flipped Out** / 1992 / Specialty ✦✦✦✦
Twenty-five early-to-mid-'50s tracks cut for the Specialty label, some previously unissued, varying between loose uptempo grooves and ballads. "Baby Doll" was the hit, but the pounding boogie of "Wine Woogie" and the sassy dueting on "Boy Loves Girl" are other highlights of a pretty strong set of early '50s R&B. But it doesn't have material they recorded during the same era for Modern, including their most famous single, "Tick Tock"/"Cherry Pie." —*Richie Unterberger*

Barbara Mason

b. 1949, Philadelphia, PA
Vocals / Soul
An interesting minor soul performer, Mason initially focused on songwriting when she entered the music business in her teens. As a performer, though, she had a huge hit in 1965 with her self-penned "Yes, I'm Ready" (No. 5 pop, No. 2 R&B), a fetching soul-pop confection that spotlighted her high, girlish vocals. One of the first examples of the sweet, lush sound that came to be called Philly soul, she had modest success throughout the rest of the decade on the small Arctic label, reaching the pop Top 40 again in 1965 with "Sad, Sad Girl."

In the early and mid-'70s, Mason toughened her persona considerably, singing about sexual love and infidelity with a frankness that was uncommon for a female soul singer in songs like "Bed and Board," "From His Woman to You," and "Shackin' Up." Sweet soul continued to be her groove, and she continued to write some of her material. But the production, as it was throughout soul in the '70s, was more funk-oriented, and at times Mason would interrupt her singing to deliver some straight-talkin' raps about romance. Curtis Mayfield produced her on a cover of Mayfield's "Give Me Your Love," which restored her to the pop Top 40 and R&B Top Ten in 1973; "From His Woman to You" and "Shackin' Up" were also solid soul sellers in the mid-'70s. After leaving Buddha Records in 1975, she only dented the charts periodically, with "I Am Your Woman, She Is Your Wife" (1978), "Another Man" (1984), and a couple of other singles. —*Richie Unterberger*

Yes, I'm Ready / 1965 / Artic ✦✦✦✦

Oh How It Hurts / 1968 / Artic ✦✦✦✦

● **The Very Best of Barbara Mason** / 1996 / Sequel ✦✦✦✦
Most of this 15-track comp deals with her 1972-75 stint on Buddah, ending with a few tracks from the late '70s and early '80s. Those who prefer '60s soul to '70s soul will prefer her early work, but at the time of its release this was the best CD compilation of her material available, including the hits "Give Me Your Love," "From His Woman to You," and "Shackin' Up." The version of "Yes, I'm Ready" here, by the way, is not the 1965 original, but an early-'70s remake. —*Richie Unterberger*

Dave Mason

b. May 10, 1944, Worcester, England
Guitar, Vocals / Pop-Rock
After serving as road manager for the Spencer Davis Group and meeting Steve Winwood, singer-guitarist Dave Mason found fame as one of the founding members of the jazz-rock-pop fusion group Traffic. However, conflicts between Winwood and Mason over the group's direction led to the latter's departure in 1969 after three albums. Mason moved to Los Angeles and joined Delaney and Bonnie before beginning his solo career. His 1970 solo debut, *Alone Together*, went gold and has proven to be arguably his best album. Mason next collaborated with Mama Cass Elliott for *Dave Mason & Cass Elliott*, but its reception was lukewarm at best. Mason settled permanently in America in 1973 and signed a long-term contract with CBS, recording a series of moderately successful, often inconsistent pop-rock albums featuring originals and a sprinkling of covers. Mason scored his biggest solo hit in 1977 with "We Just Disagree," which reached No. 12. New Mason material was scarce in the 1980s, except for a beer commercial; Mason continued to tour, though, and joined Fleetwood Mac in 1994. —*Steve Huey*

Alone Together / 1970 / MCA ✦✦✦✦
Mason's debut solo album remains his best effort, due to well-crafted tracks like the hit "Only You Know & I Know" and an appealing easygoing rock sound that presents a nice blend of acoustic and electric instrumentation. —*Rick Clark*

Let It Flow / Apr. 1977 / Columbia ✦✦✦✦
On *Let It Flow*, Mason delivered a super-slick bid for radio-friendly pop. He succeeded with three hits, "So High (Rock Me Baby and Roll Me

Away)," "Let It Go, Let It Flow," and the richly harmonic "We Just Disagree." —*Rick Clark*

● **Long Lost Friend: The Best of Dave Mason** / Jun. 6, 1995 / Columbia/Legacy ✦✦✦✦
The Best Of Dave Mason At Columbia would be a more accurate title, as this doesn't include work from his early-'70s LPs for Blue Thumb. The 19 tracks spotlight selections from seven albums that he recorded for Columbia. Including the hits "We Just Disagree," "Let It Go, Let It Flow," and "Will You Still Love Me Tomorrow," it charts his move from easygoing early-'70s FM rock to a more mainstream AOR pop sound. —*Richie Unterberger*

Massive Attack

f. 1988, Bristol, England
Alternative Pop-Rock, Club/Dance, Trip-Hop
Massive Attack was one of the pioneers of the British dance genre labelled "trip-hop," a dark, seductive combination of hip-hop beats, atmospheric reverb-laden guitars and samples, soul hooks, deep bass grooves, and ethereal melodies. Released in 1991, *Blue Lines* set the pace for much of the nontechno British dance of the decade, including that of Portishead and former Massive Attack member Tricky. Both of these acts managed to score more commercial success, including alternative hits in America, but much of their work builds on the concepts of Massive Attack. *Protection*, the group's second album, was a critical and underground hit in England during 1994, yet it made little impact in the US when it was released early in 1995. —*Stephen Thomas Erlewine*

● **Blue Lines** / Aug. 6, 1991 / Virgin ✦✦✦✦
At the time of its 1991 release, *Blue Lines* was a startlingly fresh album. Before Massive Attack, few dance collectives attempted to fuse hip-hop rhythms with hypnotic, trance-like pop melodies and soul instrumentation. All of the album has a dark, muted quality, making the tracks blend together seamlessly. While that might mean the songs are indistinguishable from each other, Massive Attack offer enough subtle variations in the rhythms and arrangements to keep the record a mesmerizing listen. —*Stephen Thomas Erlewine*

Protection / 1994 / Virgin ✦✦✦✦
While it wasn't as fresh and innovative as *Blue Lines*, Massive Attack's second album, *Protection*, was a fine album that refined the group's atmospheric fusion of soul, pop, and hip-hop, yet it offered no new musical ideas. —*Stephen Thomas Erlewine*

No Protection / 1995 / Circa ✦✦✦✦
Protection was widely considered a disappointing follow-up to Massive Attack's groundbreaking debut, *Blue Lines*. Whereas their debut bent all of the conventional hip-hop, dub reggae, and soul rules, *Protection* essentially delivered more of the same. Perhaps that's the reason why Mad Professor's re-mix of the album, *No Protection*, was welcomed with open arms by both Massive Attack fans and critics. Mad Professor has returned the group to their experimental, cut-and-paste dub reggae and hip-hop roots. He has gutted the songs—twisting and reassembling the vocal tracks, giving the songs deeper, fuller grooves and an eerily seductive atmosphere. In other words, he has made *Protection* into a more daring and fulfilling album with his re-mixes. —*Stephen Thomas Erlewine*

Matching Mole

f. 1971, Canterbury, England, **db.** 1972
Art-Rock/Progressive-Rock
Between his departure from the Soft Machine and the proper beginning of his solo career, Robert Wyatt steered Matching Mole, an outfit whose work bore much similarity to his later work with Soft Machine. Indeed, the name Matching Mole was chosen as a subtle pun on Soft Machine (the English phrase "matching mole" sounds very similar to the French translation of "soft machine," *machine molle*). However, Matching Mole didn't measure up to either his best Soft Machine work or his best solo outings. Although Wyatt occasionally let his vocal charm and humor shine, in the main Matching Mole were an outlet for the improvisational talents of the band, which often veered from inspiration into dated fusionoid noodling.

The first lineup of Matching Mole also included former Caravan member David Sinclair on keyboards, Phil Miller on guitar, and Bill MacCormick. Wyatt wrote most of the material on the 1972 self-titled debut. By the follow-up, *Little Red Book* (also 1972), Sinclair had been replaced by David MacRae, and the group had become a more democratic enterprise, with all the members contributing material more or less equally. Robert Fripp produced the second LP, and Eno guested on synthesizer on one track, though neither celebrity dramatically affected or improved the band's sound. Never destined to be a commercial enterprise, Matching Mole had folded by the end of 1972; Wyatt began his lengthy solo career, and Phil Miller went on to two other Canterbury art-rock bands, Hatfield & the North and National Health. —*Richie Unterberger*

● **Matching Mole** / 1972 / BGO ✦✦✦✦
The opening track, "O Caroline," is indicative of Wyatt at his best: art-rock with a human face, a playful vocal, and soul. Much of the record is instrumental improvisation, though, with the humor largely confined to the song titles ("Instant Pussy," "Dedicated to Hugh, But You Weren't Listening"). For every nifty passage (the extended melancholy Mellotron solo on "Immediate Curtain," the goofy scat vocals on "Signed Curtain"), there's equal or greater instrumental patter. Some art-rock devotees really get behind this album, but it doesn't count among the more enduring statements by the Canterbury crowd. —*Richie Unterberger*

Little Red Record / 1972 / BGO ✦✦
Maybe it's because Wyatt relinquished his firm upper hand on the songwriting (everybody in the band pens material) and production (Robert Fripp takes over), but this is a distinct comedown from Matching Mole's debut. The fusion rock chops assert themselves much more strongly on this largely instrumental set, though not to any great effect or purpose. It's not just difficult listening, but a bit of a bore, which is probably not what they intended. Another great song title, though, in "Starting in the Middle of the Day We Can Drink Our Politics Away." —*Richie Unterberger*

Material Issue

f. 1986, Chicago, IL, **db.** 1996
Alternative Pop-Rock, Power Pop
Material Issue's music is a return to the classic power-pop formula: catchy, melodic songs driven by loud, jangly guitars and usually paying tribute to girls and teenage love. The inevitable Beatles/Big Star/Cheap Trick/Tom Petty comparisons sparked intense interest in the band from power-pop fans and critics, and the group's musical allegiances were further underscored when ex-Shoes member Jeff Murphy produced their first two records, and Cheap Trick's Rick Nielsen guested on 1994's *Freak City Soundtrack*. The group was formed in Chicago by vocalist-guitarist Jim Ellison, an early member of Green, and his friend Ted Ansani (bass); they located drummer Mike Zelenko through a want ad. They released a self-titled EP in 1987 and attracted some local attention through a 1989 single. Their 1991 debut for Mercury, *International Pop Overthrow*, was hailed as pure power-pop in all its glory and earned the group a fan base; several songs became hits on modern-rock radio. *Destination Universe* tended to follow an identical formula and was not as well-received. *Freak City Soundtrack* utilized a more streamlined, '70s hard rock production and consolidated the group's standing as critics' darlings, but when the album failed to sell, Mercury dropped the group. Sadly, Ellison committed suicide on June 20, 1996, suffocating himself in his garage with carbon monoxide fumes from his moped. —*Steve Huey*

● **International Pop Overthrow** / Feb. 5, 1991 / Mercury ✦✦✦✦
Produced by Jeff Murphy of the Shoes, this major-label debut contained some power-pop gems like "Renee Remains the Same," "Dianne," "Valerie Loves Me," and the title cut. Fans of Cheap Trick and early Who should love much of this. Also check out their self-titled EP, which preceded this album. —*Rick Clark*

Destination Universe / Mar. 1992 / Mercury ✦✦✦
Freak City Soundtrack / Mar. 8, 1994 / Mercury ✦✦✦
Energetic pop-rock abounds on Material Issue's third album. "Goin' Through Your Purse" kicks things off, sounding like a garage punk version of "Ballroom Blitz"-era Sweet. The single, "Kim the Waitress," fuses Byrds-style 12-string guitars and electric sitar with rich vocal harmonies. Other highlights include "Funny Feeling" and "The Fan." —*Rick Clark*

Telecommando Americano / May 20, 1997 / Rykodisc ✦✦✦
It's hard not to listen to *Telecommando Americano* and feel a sense of loss, given that guitarist-songwriter Jim Ellison committed suicide shortly after completing the recording of these 11 songs. Technically, the record would have been demos for Material Issue's fourth album, but they are all that he left behind, and they demonstrate that he had a gift for both jangly and fuzzy power-pop hooks. No matter how good these are, there's a sense that Ellison took his life before he reached his full potential, and that's really what makes *Telecommando Americano* so sad—he had the gift, but he hadn't completely mastered it yet. (*Telecommando Americano* also features the trio's eponymous 1987 debut EP, which is the first time the record has been available on compact disc.) —*Stephen Thomas Erlewine*

Johnny Mathis

b. 1935, San Francisco, CA
Guitar, Vocals / Pop, Traditional Pop
One of the last in a long line of male pop vocalists who emerged before the rock-dominated 1960s, Johnny Mathis concentrated on romantic

readings of jazz and pop standards for the ever-shrinking adult-contemporary audience of the '60s and '70s. Though he debuted with a flurry of singles-chart activity, Mathis later made it big in the album market, where 13 of his LPs hit gold or platinum and 68 total made the charts. While he concentrated on theme-oriented albums of show tunes and popular favorites during the '60s, he began incorporating soft rock by the '70s and remained a popular concert attraction well into the '90s.

Though Johnny Mathis made his name singing exclusively romantic ballads for the pop market, he actually debuted in a jazz mode. Born John Royce Mathis (Sept. 30, 1935; San Francisco, CA), he was an exceptional athlete during high school, but was wooed away from a promising track career by the chance to sing. In 1956, Mathis moved to New York, where he was discovered by George Avakian at Columbia Records. Mathis' debut, a jazzy self-titled album released in 1957, was mostly ignored upon release, so Columbia A&R executive Mitch Miller—known for his desperately pop-slanted *Singalong* albums and TV show—switched him to singing pop ballads. The formula worked like a charm: the LP *Wonderful! Wonderful!* spawned a Top 20 hit later in 1957 with its title track, which was followed by the No. 5 "It's Not for Me to Say" and Mathis' first No. 1, "Chances Are." From that point on, he concentrated strictly on lush ballads for adult-contemporary listeners.

Though he charted consistently, hit singles were rare for Johnny Mathis during the late '50s and '60s—half of his career Top Ten output had occurred in 1957 alone—so he chose to focus instead on the burgeoning album market, much like Frank Sinatra, his main rival during the late '50s for most popular male vocalist. Mathis moved away from show tunes and traditional pop into soft rock during the '70s, and found his second No. 1 single, "Too Much, Too Little, Too Late," in 1978. Recorded as a duet with Deniece Williams, the single prompted Mathis to begin trying duets with a variety of partners (including Dionne Warwick, Natalie Cole, Gladys Knight, and Nana Mouskouri), though none of the singles enjoyed the success of the original. Mathis continued to release and sell albums throughout the '90s, in his fifth decade of recording for Columbia. —*John Bush*

★ **Johnny's Greatest Hits** / 1962 / Columbia ✦✦✦✦✦
The original greatest-hits package, which stayed on the charts for ten years, includes "Chances Are," "It's Not for Me to Say," "Wonderful! Wonderful!" and "The Twelfth of Never." It seldom gets more romantic than this. —*Cub Koda*

40th Anniversary Collector's Set [box] / May 7, 1996 / Columbia/Legacy ✦✦✦✦

Dave Matthews Band

Guitar, Vocals / Rock 'n' Roll, Adult Alternative Pop-Rock, Folk-Rock
The South African vocalist-guitarist Dave Matthews formed the Dave Matthews Band in Virginia in the early '90s. Featuring Matthews, Stefan Lessard, Leroi Moor, Boyd Tinsley, and Carter Beauford, the group's music presents a more pop-oriented version of the Grateful Dead, crossed with the world beat explorations of Paul Simon and Sting. The band built up a strong word-of-mouth following in the early '90s by touring the country constantly, concentrating on college campuses. In addition to amassing a sizable following, their self-released album *Remember Two Things* sold well for an independent release; soon, they were attracting the attention of majors. Signing with RCA, the Dave Matthews Band released their major-label debut, *Under the Table and Dreaming*, in the fall of 1994. By spring of 1995, the record had launched the hit single "What Would You Say" and sold over a million copies.

A year and a half after the release of *Under the Table & Dreaming*, the record had sold over four million copies in the US alone. In April of 1996, the Dave Matthews Band released *Crash*, which entered the charts at No. 2 and quickly went platinum. Throughout 1996, the group toured behind *Crash*, sending it to double-platinum status. Also in 1996, Matthews launched an attack on bootleggers in conjunction with the federal government, targeting stores that were selling semi-legal discs of live performances. The efforts of Matthews, his band, and his management resulted in an unprecedented crackdown on bootleggers in early 1997, when nearly all of the major foreign bootlegging companies were arrested by the US, thereby putting a moratorium on the entire underground industry. —*Stephen Thomas Erlewine*

Remember Two Things / 1993 / Bama Rags ✦✦✦
Although the Dave Matthews Band's debut album *Remember Two Things* is hindered by a number of long-winded jams and an unfocused production, the record is an impressive showcase for their instrumental prowess. —*Stephen Thomas Erlewine*

● **Under the Table & Dreaming** / Apr. 1994 / RCA ✦✦✦✦
On their major-label debut, *Under the Table & Dreaming*, the Dave Matthews Band is helped by the lean production of Steve Lillywhite, who manages to rein in the group's tendency to meander. The result is a set of eclectic pop-rock accentuated by bursts of instrumental virtuosity instead of being ruled by it. That also means that the Dave Matthews

Band is capable of turning out pop songs, and as the hit single "What Would You Say" and "Ants Marching" illustrate, they have a flair for catchy hooks. —*Stephen Thomas Erlewine*

Crash / Apr. 1996 / RCA ♦♦♦
Under the Table & Dreaming, the Dave Matthews Band's first major label album, was their popular breakthrough, bringing their mildly eclectic sound to a mass audience. Although the group appeals to the same audience as Blues Traveler, Hootie & the Blowfish, and the Spin Doctors, the Dave Matthews Band has more influences than its peers. Fusing together folk-rock, world beat, jazz, and pop, the band is arguably the most musically adept of all their contemporaries. However, they have trouble coming up with engaging hooks, as their third album, *Crash*, proves. Although the band continues to get better—their musical cross-breeding is effortless and seamless—they often don't have an attractive frame for their skills. Strangely, the lack of memorable melodies doesn't particularly hurt the album—it actually emphasizes the band's instrumental talents. Nevertheless, since there's a lack of strong pop hooks, *Crash* is an album that will please fans, but not novices. —*Stephen Thomas Erlewine*

Eric Matthews

b. 1969, Gresham, OR
Singer-Songwriter, Alternative Pop-Rock
The work of Eric Matthews was a direct reaction to the lo-fi recording practices so prevalent throughout the alternative music scene of the 1990s; while many of the decade's artists trafficked in a defiantly ragged, do-it-yourself aesthetic, Matthews' records grew out of orchestral theories and practices, and reveled in the stately elegance of warm harmonies and lush arrangements. A native of Gresham, OR, Matthews was born in 1969, and fell in love with the symphonic pop of the Beach Boys, Burt Bacharach, and the Bee Gees at an early age; John Williams' score for *Star Wars* steered him into orchestral music, and he picked up his first instrument, the trumpet, while in elementary school.

After attending a San Francisco conservatory to hone his craft, he moved to the Boston area to further pursue his songwriting and performing. There he met Sebadoh's Lou Barlow and Bob Fay, and under the name Belt Buckle they teamed for a four-song EP in 1993. Through Fay, Matthews also struck up a friendship with Richard Davies, an Australian-born singer-songwriter best known for fronting the cult band the Moles. Together they formed the duo Cardinal, a forum for Davies' wry songwriting and Matthews' arranging skills and instrumental talents (which now included a mastery of piano, organ, harpsichord, and marimba), and released a stunning self-titled debut in 1994. Internal difficulties resulted in Cardinal's brief lifespan, however, and Matthews soon resurfaced as a solo artist. In 1995, he issued his debut, *It's Heavy in Here*, an ornate, complex collection highlighting his emerging vocal and composing skills. —*Jason Ankeny*

● **It's Heavy in Here** / Sep. 26, 1995 / Sub Pop ♦♦♦♦
Sounding like Lou Barlow singing Nick Drake songs, Eric Matthews constructs an impressive debut with *It's Heavy In Here*, and construct is the right word. Matthews composes and arranges his songs, using string sections, arpeggiated guitars, trumpets, and whispered vocals—it's orchestral pop for the post-Nirvana generation. *It's Heavy In Here* works both as a mood piece and as individual songs—the individual tracks balance each other, providing different shades, textures, and variations on one theme. Matthews' sighing melodies reflect beautiful melancholy, not a haunting despair, and that's why *It's Heavy in Here* is such a refreshing debut. —*Stephen Thomas Erlewine*

Ian Matthews

b. Jun. 1946, Lincolnshire, England
Guitar, Vocals / Folk, Singer-Songwriter, Folk-Rock, British Folk
Ian Matthews (now spelled Iain to reflect his Celtic roots) has had a widely varied and complex recording career. He began as the lead singer for Fairport Convention after a short stint as the vocalist for a London-based surf band, Pyramid in 1966. During Fairport's 1969 *Unhalfbricking* sessions, he decided to leave due to growing musical differences with the band. After making his first solo album, *Matthews Southern Comfort*, he released two albums with a band of the same name. They had a hit with a version of "Woodstock."

Matthews left in 1971 for a second chance at a solo career, releasing two fine folk-rock albums for Vertigo. He then formed Plainsong while finishing the contractual obligation album, *Journey from Gospel Oak*—one of his finest recorded moments despite the conditions. Plainsong released one critically acclaimed album on Elektra and then disbanded while recording the second. His stay at Elektra ended after two more acclaimed yet overlooked country-folk albums— *Valley Hi* (1973) and *Some Days You Eat the Bear Some Days the Bear Eats You* (1974). He began experimenting in different styles for the rest of the '70s, often

with uninspired and unsuccessful results. He did, however, have a US Top Ten hit in 1978 with "Shake It" from the *Stealin' Home* album.

The '80s were a relatively slow period for Matthews. Recording intermittently, he spent a few years as an A&R man for Island and later worked for Windham Hill. He relocated permanently to the US in the late '80s. The '90s have found him reviving his solo career, signing to Watermelon Records, and returning to his folk-rock roots. Plainsong reunited in 1993, releasing two more albums. Matthews has since formed another group, Hamilton Pool, for one album. —*Chris Woodstra*

Matthews Southern Comfort / 1969 / Decca ♦♦♦
This is a transitional album for Matthews. Having recently exited Fairport Convention, this record pays tribute to that period of his career both in material ("A Castle Far") and in the choice of musicians who back him (many of them from Fairport Convention). At the same time, songs like "A Commercial Proposition" indicate where Matthews is headed on 1971's *Later that Same Year*. —*Jim Worbois*

Second Spring / 1969 / Line ♦♦♦
With this album, Matthews' Southern Comfort is a real band and, in addition to Matthews, includes Roger Swallow (ex-Marmalade) and Marc Griffiths (ex-Spooky Tooth). Though there is really nothing that makes this a memorable record, it's still quite a nice record overall. If you already know his work on Elektra, Mooncrest, or even *Later that Same Year*, it would be well worth your while to search this record out. —*Jim Worbois*

1 2 3 Too Good / 1970 / MCA ♦♦

Later That Same Year / Dec. 1970 / Line ♦♦♦
Best known for the hit "Woodstock," this is really the album on which Matthews first finds his direction. A nice mix of covers and originals, this record has held up nicely over the years. —*Jim Worbois*

If You Saw Thro' My Eyes / Jan. 1971 / Vertigo ♦♦♦♦
After leaving Southern Comfort, Matthews reunited with Fairport Convention members Richard Thompson and Sandy Denny and made one of his finest albums. Though the material and playing are superior to his previous work, this album was unfortunately overlooked at the time. Now combined with his follow-up, *Tigers Will Survive* on CD (German import only), this is a must-have for fans. —*Chris Woodstra*

Tigers Will Survive / Nov. 1971 / Vertigo ♦♦♦
Recorded during two different periods of time broken up by a US tour, his follow-up to *If You Saw Through My Eyes* lacks the focus of its predecessor. Still worthwhile if only for "Morning Star," one of Matthews' most beautiful originals. —*Chris Woodstra*

Journeys from Gospel Oak / 1972 / Mooncrest ♦♦♦♦
Billed as a contractual obligation record by the artist, *Journeys from Gospel Oak* is easily as good as Matthews' best work. It is most assuredly a companion piece to Plainsong's *In Search of Amelia Earhart* (an album loosely based on the disappearance of Amelia Earhart), this time loosely based around the night Hank Williams died. This album includes such solid tracks as Gene Clark's "Polly," "Bride 1945" by Paul Siebel, and the haunting Jimmy Webb tune, "Met Her on a Plane." A strong (but often overlooked record) and well worth the effort it takes to find a copy. —*Jim Worbois*

Valley Hi / 1973 / Elektra ♦♦♦♦
Often regarded as his best solo album, *Valley Hi* finds Matthews combining his folk-rock expertise with producer Mike Nesmith's country leanings. Highlights include the Nesmith-penned "Propinquity" and Jackson Browne's "These Days." —*Chris Woodstra*

Some Days You Eat the Bear Some Days the Bear Eats You / 1974 / Elektra ♦♦♦
His final LP recorded for Elektra continues in the country spirit of *Valley Hi*, with a stronger pop sensibility. Includes a brilliant rendition of Tom Waits' "Old 55" and the touching tribute to Hank Williams, "A Wailing Goodbye." —*Chris Woodstra*

Go for Broke / 1975 / Columbia ♦
More a hodge-podge than a proper album, Matthews gives us a mix of originals and mostly uninspired covers. One exception to the covers is one from the often overlooked Tim Moore (whose first two albums on Asylum are worth looking for). Still, this is mediocre at best. —*Jim Worbois*

Hit and Run / 1976 / Columbia ♦♦
This rather directionless record has Matthews covering himself ("Tiger Will Survive"), sounding like David Crosby (Terry Reid's "The Frame"), and affecting a disco beat on a song that's very reminiscent of "Lady Marmalade" ("Times"). Still, long-time fans shouldn't write this one off. —*Jim Worbois*

Stealin' Home / 1978 / Line ♦♦
This album features Matthews' highest-charting single ("Shake It") which, on its own, isn't a bad song. It, along with one or two others, was written by John Boylan, an under-appreciated songwriter of the late '70s (he wrote some nice stuff, but his career never really took off like those

of some of his peers). While not one of Ian's stronger records, it is pleasant overall. —*Jim Worbois*

Siamese Friends / 1979 / Line ✦✦
Saddled with late-'70s production techniques, there is nothing, on the surface, to recommend this record. A close look at the songwriting credits, though, will reveal a beginning of Matthews' fascination with the work of great Jules Shear. (Matthews would later do an entire album of Shear's songs, *Walking a Changing Line*.) Still, even this track is burdened by a cheesy David Sanborn-style sax line. —*Jim Worbois*

Discreet Repeat / 197 / Rockburgh ✦✦
This is a nice cross-label compilation that features some of his best work (stuff recorded for Vertigo, Elektra, and Mooncrest) as well as some of his least interesting work. If you are a fan of Matthews, you likely own all these records already. If not, this compilation will help you decide which areas of his career you will need to concentrate on in order to build your Ian Matthews collection. —*Jim Worbois*

Spot of Interference / 1980 / Rockburgh ✦✦✦
Matthews' makes an attempt at new wave and power-pop on this 1980 album. Surprisingly, he pulls it off quite well. Not his strongest work but certainly of interest to fans. Jules Shear's "Driftwood from Disaster" and the Wilde-Ainsworth (later the Rembrandts') "I Survived the 70's" stand out. —*Chris Woodstra*

Shook / 1983 / Line ✦✦
On this, the first vocal album for Windham Hill, Matthews pays tribute to the songwriting of Jules Shear. While the song selection is first rate as always, the typical Windham Hill musical indulgences take away from the enjoyment of this disc. Worthwhile for curious fans of Matthews or Shear. —*Chris Woodstra*

Pure & Crooked / Aug. 1990 / Watermelon ✦✦✦
Matthews' move from the freeways of L.A. to the active but relatively less jaded musical oasis of Austin also saw a return to his own songwriting after a five-year hiatus. The results married Matthews' honey tenor to a mostly uptempo blend of pop, folk, and rock that evokes his best '70s work. His knack for a crisp, plaintive melody is keenly honed. If all this wasn't enough, the reissue adds five previously unreleased tracks, including an a cappella pair and a live version of Danny Whitten's "I Don't Want To Talk About It" recorded in Hamburg, Germany. —*Roch Parisien*

● **Best of Matthews' Southern Comfort** / Mar. 10, 1992 / MCA ✦✦✦✦
A fine 16-track collection drawing from Matthews' first solo effort and the two Matthews' Southern Comfort albums. Includes the band's hit version of "Woodstock." —*Chris Woodstra*

Orphans & Outcasts, Vol. 1 / 1993 / Dirty Linen ✦✦✦
An exceptional collection of demos, rarities, and outtakes from Matthews' '70s period, *Orphans & Outcasts* is essential for fans. —*Chris Woodstra*

● **The Soul of Many Places** / May 11, 1993 / Elektra ✦✦✦✦
The Soul of Many Places compiles the best moments from Matthews' recording high point for Elektra (1972-1974). Featuring selections from *Valley Hi*, *Some Days You Eat the Bear . . .*, and Plainsong's *The Search for Amelia Earhart*, this is the best introduction to Matthews' finest work (all currently out-of-print in the US.). The inclusion of non-LP tracks makes this essential for fans as well. —*Chris Woodstra*

Skeleton Keys / May 18, 1993 / Rhino ✦✦✦
Matthews emerges from his experimental '80s period with a return to his classic acoustic country-folk sound. With his first album composed solely of originals, he shows more focus than he has in nearly two decades. —*Chris Woodstra*

Orphans & Outcasts, Vol. 2 / 1994 / Dirty Linen ✦✦✦
Volume 2 of the series, essentially a demos collection of the late '70s/ early '80s material, is more interesting than the actual albums of the time. Fans of Matthews' folky early-'70s albums who couldn't connect with this somewhat misdirected phase of his career should find this much more enjoyable. —*Chris Woodstra*

Dark Ride / Jun. 7, 1994 / Watermelon ✦✦
A gentle, country-inflected set. While his music may reflect midwestern America these days, his lyrics tend to take a more cosmopolitan approach, with songs touching New York or London more often than Ohio or Kansas. Matthews is in fine form throughout. —*Steven McDonald*

Scion / 1995 / Band of Joy ✦✦✦

God Looked Down / Aug. 13, 1996 / Watermelon ✦✦✦

Seattle Years 1978-1984 / Oct. 8, 1996 / Varese ✦✦✦✦
Between 1978 and 1984, Ian Matthews relocated to Seattle, and shed the acoustic folkiness and introspection he had become known for in favor of a more contemporary, commercial sound; *The Seattle Years* collects the highlights from the four solo albums he recorded during this

period—*Stealin' Home*, *Siamese Friends*, *Spot of Interference*, and *Shook* (unfortunately, the one album he did with Hi-Fi in the same period is sadly unrepresented). Though Matthews is best remembered for his work just prior to this period, the collection presents the high points in a highly listenable fashion and, in retrospect, his take on ultra-slick soft-rock stands up against the best of the genre. Included is his biggest hit, "Shake It," as well as lesser-known but well-executed album tracks like a new wave/power-pop reading of the Left Banke classic "She May Call You Up Tonight" and Jona Lewie's "The Baby She's On the Street." —*Chris Woodstra*

John Mayall

b. Nov. 29, 1933, Macclesfield, Cheshire, England
Organ, Guitar, Harmonica, Piano, Harmonium, Harpsichord, Keyboards, Tambourine, Ukulele, Vocals / Electric British Blues, Blues-Rock, British Blues

The elder statesman of British blues, it is Mayall's lot to be more renowned as a bandleader and mentor than as a performer in his own right. Throughout the '60s, his band, the Bluesbreakers, acted as a finishing school for the leading British blues-rock musicians of the era. Guitarists Eric Clapton, Peter Green, and Mick Taylor joined his band in a remarkable succession in the mid-'60s, honing their chops with Mayall before going on to join Cream, Fleetwood Mac, and the Rolling Stones, respectively. John McVie and Mick Fleetwood, Jack Bruce, Aynsley Dunbar, Dick Heckstall-Smith, Andy Fraser (of Free), John Almond, and Jon Mark also played and recorded with Mayall for varying lengths of times in the '60s.

Mayall's personnel have tended to overshadow his own considerable abilities. Only an adequate singer, the multi-instrumentalist was adept at bringing out the best in his younger charges (Mayall himself was in his thirties by the time the Bluesbreakers began to make a name for themselves). Doing his best to provide a context in which they could play Chicago-style electric blues, Mayall was never complacent, writing most of his own material (which ranged from good to humdrum), revamping his lineup with unnerving regularity, and constantly experimenting within his basic blues format. Some of these experiments (with jazz-rock and an album on which he played all the instruments except drums) were forgettable; others, like his foray into acoustic music in the late '60s, were quite successful. Mayall's output has caught some flak from critics for paling next to the real African-American deal, but much of his vintage work—if weeded out selectively—is quite strong, especially his legendary 1966 LP with Eric Clapton, which both launched Clapton into stardom and kick-started the blues boom into full gear in England.

When Clapton joined the Bluesbreakers in 1965, Mayall had already been recording for a year, and had been performing professionally long before that. Originally based in Manchester, Mayall moved to London in 1963 on the advice of British blues godfather Alexis Korner, who thought a living could be made playing the blues in the bigger city. Tracing a path through his various lineups of the '60s is a daunting task. At least 15 different editions of the Bluesbreakers were in existence from January 1963 through mid-1970. Some notable musicians (like guitarist Davy Graham, Mick Fleetwood, and Jack Bruce) passed through for little more than a cup of coffee; Mayall's longest-running employee, bassist John McVie, lasted about four years. The Bluesbreakers, like Fairport Convention or the Fall, was more a concept than an ongoing core. Mayall, too, had the reputation of being a difficult and demanding employer, willing to give musicians their walking papers as his music evolved, although he also imparted invaluable schooling to them while the associations lasted.

Mayall recorded his debut single in early 1964; he made his first album, a live affair, near the end of the year. At this point the Bluesbreakers had a more pronounced R&B influence than would be exhibited on their most famous recordings, somewhat in the mold of younger combos like the Animals and Rolling Stones. Quite respectable it was too, but the Bluesbreakers would take a turn for the purer with the recruitment of Eric Clapton in the spring of 1965. Clapton had left the Yardbirds in order to play straight blues, and the Bluesbreakers allowed him that freedom (or stuck to well-defined restrictions, depending upon your viewpoint). Clapton began to inspire reverent acclaim as one of Britain's top virtuosos, as reflected in the famous "Clapton is God" graffiti that appeared in London in the mid-'60s.

In professional terms, though, 1965 wasn't the best of times for the group, which had been dropped by Decca. Clapton even left the group for a few months for an odd trip to Greece, leaving Mayall to struggle on with various fill-ins, including Peter Green. Clapton did return in late 1965, around the time an excellent blues-rock single, "I'm Your Witchdoctor" (with searing sustain-laden guitar riffs), was issued on Immediate. By early 1966, the band were back on Decca, and recorded their landmark *Bluesbreakers* LP. This was the album that, with its clean, loud, authoritative licks, firmly established Clapton as a guitar hero, on both reverent covers of tunes by the likes of Otis Rush and Freddie King, and decent originals by Mayall himself. The record was also an unexpected commercial success, making the Top Ten in Britain. From that point on, in fact, Mayall became one of the first rock musicians to depend primarily upon the LP market; he recorded plenty of singles throughout the '60s, but none of them came close to becoming a hit.

Clapton left the Bluesbreakers in mid-1966 to form Cream with Jack Bruce, who had played with Mayall briefly in late 1965. Mayall turned quickly to Peter Green, who managed the difficult feat of stepping into Clapton's shoes and gaining respect as a player of roughly equal imagination and virtuosity, although his style was quite distinctly his own. Green recorded one LP with Mayall, *A Hard Road*, and several singles, sometimes writing material and taking some respectable lead vocals. Green's talents, like those of Clapton, were too large to be confined by sideman status, and in mid-1967 *he* left to form a successful band of his own, Fleetwood Mac.

Mayall then enlisted 19-year-old Mick Taylor; remarkably, despite the consecutive departures of two star guitarists, Mayall maintained a high level of popularity. The late '60s were also a time of considerable experimentation for the Bluesbreakers, which moved into a form of blues-jazz-rock fusion with the addition of a horn section, and then a retreat into mellower, acoustic-oriented music. Mick Taylor, the last of the famous triumvirate of Mayall-bred guitar heroes, left in mid-1969 to join the Rolling Stones. Yet in a way Mayall was thriving more than ever, as the US market, which had been barely aware of him in the Clapton era, was beginning to open up for his music. In fact, at the end of the 1960s, Mayall moved to Los Angeles. 1969's *The Turning Point*, a live, all-acoustic affair, was a commercial and artistic high point.

In America at least, Mayall continued to be pretty popular in the early '70s. His band was no more stable than ever; at various points some American musicians flitted in and out of the Bluesbreakers, including Harvey Mandel, Canned Heat bassist Larry Taylor, and Don "Sugarcane" Harris. Although Mayall has released numerous albums since and remained a prodigiously busy and reasonably popular live act, little of his post-1970 output is worthy of discussion. Following collaborations with an unholy number of guest celebrities, in the early 1980s he reteamed with a couple of his more renowned vets, John McVie and Mick Taylor, for a tour. It's the '60s albums that you want, though there's little doubt that over the past decades Mayall has done a great deal to popularize the blues all over the globe, whether or not the music has meant much on record. — *Richie Unterberger*

John Mayall Plays John Mayall / Mar. 26, 1965 / Decca ◆◆◆
Recorded live at the British club Klooks Kleek in late 1964 before Clapton joined (Roger Dean plays lead guitar), this is a fine set of early British R&B with a more pronounced rock feel (akin to the Rolling Stones) than Mayall's other '60s work. Mayall wrote all but one of the songs on this overlooked but driving, highly enjoyable LP that is recommended to connoisseurs of early British blues-rock. — *Richie Unterberger*

★ **Bluesbreakers with Eric Clapton** / Jul. 1966 / Deram ◆◆◆◆◆
One of the seminal blues albums of the '60s with the Bluesbreakers, capturing Clapton on a series of blues standards, after the pop leanings of the Yardbirds and before the heavy indulgence of Cream. — *William Ruhlmann*

A Hard Road / Feb. 17, 1967 / Deram ◆◆◆
Eric Clapton is usually thought of as Mayall's most important right-hand man, but the case could also be made for his successor, Peter Green. The future Fleetwood Mac founder leaves a strong stamp on his only album with the Bluesbreakers, singing a few tracks and writing a couple, including the devastating instrumental "Supernatural." Green's use of thick sustain on this track clearly pointed the way to his use of this feature on Fleetwood Mac's hits "Albatross" and "Black Magic Woman," as well as providing a blueprint for Carlos Santana's style. Mayall acquits himself fairly well on this mostly original set (with occasional guest horns), though some of the material is fairly mundane. Highlights include the uncharacteristically rambunctious "Leaping Christine" and the cover of Freddie King's "Someday After a While (You'll Be Sorry)." — *Richie Unterberger*

Crusade / Sep. 1, 1967 / London ◆◆◆◆
The personnel changes in John Mayall's Bluesbreakers continued on his fourth album, and although Mayall had vowed not to, he had added two permanent horn players. Perhaps because he was putting out his second album within a year, Mayall wasn't able to fill up the record with his own compositions and turned to blues standards, which certainly didn't hurt the record overall. Mayall's heroes included Buddy Guy, Otis Rush, Freddie King, and Sonny Boy Williamson, and he did them proud. The album became his third straight UK Top Ten and, following the Bluesbreakers' first US tour in the summer of 1967, his first charting album in America. — *William Ruhlmann*

The Blues Alone / Nov. 1967 / Deram ◆◆◆
The Blues Alone was the first Mayall "solo" album (without the Bluesbreakers). Mayall played and overdubbed all instruments except drums, which were handled by Bluesbreaker Keef Hartley. The album also tried

to serve notice that, despite his band being a spawning ground for several British stars by now, the real star of the group was its leader. But it didn't quite prove that, since Mayall, while certainly competent on harmonica, keyboards, and guitars, doesn't display the flair of an Eric Clapton or Peter Green, and the overdubbing, as is so often the case, robs the recording of any real sense of interplay. — *William Ruhlmann*

Blues from Laurel Canyon / 1968 / Deram ◆◆◆
Blues from Laurel Canyon has a couple of nice passages, but the album suffers from poor songwriting and indulgent solos, from both Mayall and his newly acquired L.A. sidemen. — *Thom Owens*

Bare Wires / Jun. 21, 1968 / Deram ◆◆◆
Bare Wires was the first Bluesbreakers album of new studio material since *A Hard Road*, released 16 months before. In that time, the band had turned over entirely, expanding to become a septet. Mayall's musical conception had also expanded—the album began with a 23-minute "Bare Wires Suite," which included more jazz influences than usual and featured introspective lyrics. In retrospect, all of this is a bit indulgent, but at the time it helped Mayall out of what had come to seem a blues straitjacket (although he would eventually return to a strict blues approach). It isn't surprising that he dropped the "Bluesbreakers" name after this release. (The album was Mayall's most successful ever in the UK, hitting No. 3.) — *William Ruhlmann*

The Turning Point / 1969 / Deram ◆◆◆◆
Recorded just after Mick Taylor departed for the Stones, Mayall eliminated drums entirely on this live recording. With mostly acoustic guitars and John Almond on flutes and sax, Mayall and his band, as his typically overblown liner notes state, "explore seldom-used areas within the framework of low volume music." But it does work. The all-original material is flowing and melodic, with long jazzy grooves that don't lose sight of their bluesy underpinnings. Lyrically, Mayall stretches out a bit into social comment on "The Laws Must Change" on this fine, meditative mood album. — *Richie Unterberger*

Looking Back / Aug. 1969 / Deram ◆◆◆
Reasonably interesting collection of non-LP singles from 1964 to 1968, featuring almost all of the notable musicians that passed through the Bluesbreakers throughout the decade. "Sitting in the Rain" (with Peter Green) showcases fine fingerpicking, the haunting "Jenny" is one of Mayall's best originals, and "Stormy Monday" is one of the few cuts from the 1966 lineup that briefly featured both Eric Clapton and Jack Bruce. The rest is largely pleasant and doesn't rank among Mayall's finest work. — *Richie Unterberger*

Thru the Years / 1971 / Deram ◆◆◆◆
A grab bag of rare tracks from the '60s, some of which stand among Mayall's finest. His debut 1964 single "Crawling up a Hill" is one of his best originals; this comp also includes a couple of 1964-65 flipsides that were never otherwise issued in the US. The eight songs featuring Peter Green include some top-notch material that outpaces much of the only album recorded by the Green lineup (*A Hard Road*), particularly the Green originals "Missing You" and "Out of Reach," a great B-side with devastating, icy guitar lines and downbeat lyrics that ranks as one of the great lost blues-rock cuts of the '60s. The set is filled out with a few songs from the Mick Taylor era, the highlight being the vicious instrumental "Knockers Step Forward." Look for the CD reissue and not the early-'70s double US album of the same name, which includes a lot of superfluous material and omits the three 1964-65 songs from British 45s. — *Richie Unterberger*

Latest Edition / 1974 / Polydor ◆◆◆
The title makes a virtue of necessity, as John Mayall introduces another all-new lineup (actually, bassist Larry Taylor is returning from an older edition). Two guitarists, Hightide Harris and Randy Resnick, lead the band in more of an uptempo R&B style than has been used in much of Mayall's music during the past several years, starting with the timely "Gasoline Blues" (1974 was the year of the gas lines, remember?) and going on to "Troubled Times" (which advises impeaching President Nixon). Still, this was a lackluster set, which is only appropriate since it was Mayall's swan song with Polydor, and the album became his first to miss the charts in the US since 1967. — *William Ruhlmann*

A Sense of Place / Mar. 1990 / Island ◆◆◆
A Sense of Place represents Mayall's full-fledged return to major-label record-making, with all the good and bad things that implies, from a high-profile producer, R.S. Field, to the introduction of such cover material as Wilbert Harrison's "Let's Work Together" and J.J. Cale's "Sensitive Kind." Field uses a spare production style, light on atmosphere and heavy, as is the current fashion, on unusual percussion. This makes for an identifiable sound, to be sure, but you can't help thinking that it isn't what The Bluesbreakers sound like on a good night in a small club. The result, as intended, was Mayall's first chart appearance in 15 years, but as a commercial comeback, the record ultimately failed. — *William Ruhlmann*

● **London Blues (1964-1969)** / Oct. 20, 1992 / PolyGram ✦✦✦✦
Featuring 40 tracks over two discs, *London Blues* is an excellent collection of most of the best moments from Mayall and the Bluesbreakers' early recordings, a time when Eric Clapton, Peter Green, and Mick Taylor all passed through the band. —*Stephen Thomas Erlewine*

Room to Move (1969-1974) / Oct. 20, 1992 / Polydor ✦✦✦✦
The majority of Mayall and the Bluesbreakers' best material from the early '70s is collected on this 29-track, double-disc set. Although Clapton appears on a couple of songs, the playing on *Room to Move* isn't as universally breathtaking as it is on *London Blues*, but the collection is thoroughly listenable, and it does feature many fine musicians. —*Stephen Thomas Erlewine*

Wake up Call / Apr. 6, 1993 / Jive/Novus ✦✦✦
Fuelled by Coco Montoya's searing but economical string-slashing, drummer Joe Yuele, and bassist Rick Cortes, John Mayall has managed to keep a stable core of Bluesbreakers together in recent years. Mayall rarely does the same album twice, and *Wake up Call* finds him returning to a basic, physical sound after 1990s more progressive/highly produced *A Sense of Place*. The harp whiz has rarely flirted with the pop charts over the decades, a track record that will likely handicap the title track—a potential hit featuring guest vocalist Mavis Staples and some take-charge riffing from former mate Mick Taylor. For pure guitar joy though, Montoya turns the trick all on his own with barnburners "Loaded Dice" and "Nature's Disappearing". —*Roch Parisien*

Curtis Mayfield
....
b. Jun. 3, 1942, Chicago, IL
Guitar, Vocals / Soul, Funk, R&B, Quiet Storm
Perhaps because he didn't cross over to the pop audience as heavily as Motown's stars, it may be that the scope of Curtis Mayfield's talents and contributions have yet to be fully recognized. Judged merely by his records alone, the man's legacy is enormous. As the leader of the Impressions, he recorded some of the finest soul vocal group music of the 1960s. As a solo artist in the 1970s, he helped pioneer funk, and helped introduce hard-hitting urban commentary into soul music. "Gypsy Woman," "It's All Right," "People Get Ready," "Freddie's Dead," and "Superfly" are merely the most famous of his many hit records.

But Curtis Mayfield isn't just a singer. He wrote most of his material, at a time when that was not the norm for soul performers. He was among the first—if not the very first—to speak openly about African-American pride and community struggle in his compositions. As a songwriter and a producer, he was a key architect of Chicago soul, penning material and working on sessions by notable Windy City soulsters like Gene Chandler, Jerry Butler, Major Lance, and Billy Butler. In this sense, he can be compared to Smokey Robinson, who also managed to find time to write and produce many classics for other soul stars. Mayfield was also an excellent guitarist, and his rolling, Latin-influenced lines were highlights of the Impressions' recordings in the '60s. During the next decade, he would toughen up his guitar work and production, incorporating some of the best features of psychedelic rock and funk.

Mayfield began his career as an associate of Jerry Butler, with whom he formed the Impressions in the late '50s. After the Impressions had a big hit in 1958 with "For Your Precious Love," Butler, who had sung lead on the record, split to start a solo career. Mayfield, while keeping the Impressions together, continued to write for and tour with Butler before the Impressions got their first Top 20 hit in 1961, "Gypsy Woman."

Mayfield was heavily steeped in gospel music before he entered the pop arena, and gospel—as well as doo wop—influences would figure prominently in most of his '60s work. Mayfield wasn't a staunch traditionalist, however. He and the Impressions may have often worked the call-and-response gospel style, but his songs (romantic and otherwise) were often veiled or unveiled messages of Black pride, reflecting the increased confidence and self-determination of the African-American community. Musically he was an innovator as well, using arrangements that employed the punchy, blaring horns and Latin-influenced rhythms that came to be trademark flourishes of Chicago soul. As the staff producer for the OKeh label, Mayfield was also instrumental in lending his talents to the work of some Chi-town soul singers who went on to national success. With Mayfield singing lead and playing guitar, the Impressions had 14 Top 40 hits in the 1960s (five made the Top 20 in 1964 alone), and released some above-average albums during that period as well.

Given Mayfield's prodigious talents, it was perhaps inevitable that he would eventually leave the Impressions to begin a solo career, as he did in 1970. His first few singles boasted a harder, more funk-driven sound; singles like "(Don't Worry) If There's a Hell Below, We're All Gonna Go" found him confronting ghetto life with a realism that had rarely been heard on record. He really didn't hit his artistic or commercial stride as a solo artist, though, until *Superfly*, his soundtrack to a 1972 blaxploitation film. Drug deals, ghetto shootings, the death of young Black men before their time: all were described in penetrating detail. Yet Mayfield's

irrepressible falsetto vocals, uplifting melodies, and fabulous funk-pop arrangements gave the oft-moralizing material a graceful strength that few others could have achieved. For all the glory of his past work, *Superfly* stands as his crowning achievement, not to mention a much-needed counterpoint to the sensationalistic portrayals of the film itself.

At this point Mayfield, along with Stevie Wonder and Marvin Gaye, was the foremost exponent of a new level of compelling auteurism in soul. His failure to maintain the standards of *Superfly* qualifies as one of the great disappointments in the history of Black popular music. Perhaps he'd simply reached his peak after a long climb, but the rest of his '70s work didn't match the musical brilliance and lyrical subtleties of *Superfly*, although he had a few large R&B hits in a much more conventional vein, such as "Kung Fu," "So in Love," and "Only You Babe."

Mayfield had a couple of hits in the early '80s, but the decade generally found his commercial fortunes in a steady downward spiral, despite some intermittent albums. On August 14, 1990, he became paralyzed from the neck down when a lighting rig fell on top of him at a concert in Brooklyn, NY. In the mid-'90s, a couple of tribute albums consisting of Mayfield covers appeared, with contributions by such superstars as Eric Clapton, Bruce Springsteen, and Gladys Knight. These tributes are no substitute for the man himself, but they are an indication of the enormous regard in which Mayfield is still held by his peers. —*Richie Unterberger*

☆ **Curtis** / Sep. 1970 / Curtom ✦✦✦✦✦
A masterpiece, and still one of the greatest urban soul albums of all time. Curtis Mayfield stepped into the spotlight and immediately showed that he would have no trouble away from the Impressions. While he had done many transcendent singles with them, he'd never made a song as searing in its indictments or immediately compelling as "(Don't Worry) If There's a Hell Below We're All Gonna Go." That was just one of many classic tunes, which retain their impact 25 years later. Those who don't think there were great message songs before the hip-hop era should check this one out and then come up with better songs done by Public Enemy, Ice-T, Boogie Down Productions, or anyone else. —*Ron Wynn*

Roots / 1971 / Charly ✦✦✦✦
A fine follow-up to his hit debut album as a solo artist. Although he only scored one smash single, "Get Down," there were plenty of superb selections, expertly produced numbers, and fine arrangements. Mayfield, Marvin Gaye, Stevie Wonder, and Isaac Hayes were among the innovative composer/producer/performers that helped usher in the album age on the R&B/soul circuit. Mayfield was now doing concept works with a thematic unity and sophisticated style, rather than stringing together singles in the manner of '50s and '60s LPs. —*Ron Wynn*

☆ **Superfly** / Jul. 1972 / Curtom ✦✦✦✦✦
A post-Impressions Curtis Mayfield recorded one dynamic solo project after another in the 1970s, but if a listener could own only one of them, *Superfly* would be the ideal choice. The sleek yet earthy soundtrack to one of the '70s' most celebrated blaxploitation films, *Superfly* is full of riveting, sometimes chilling sociopolitical commentary reflecting on the drugs, violence, and crime plaguing the inner city. Unlike so many soundtracks, this outstanding CD can be fully appreciated whether or not one has seen the film. From the infectious title song to "Freddie's Dead" (a reflection on a junkie's tragic life as troubling as it is poignant) to the hard-hitting "Pusherman" (brilliantly interpreted by rapper Ice-T in 1988), *Superfly* is clearly Mayfield's finest hour. —*Alex Henderson*

Curtis in Chicago / 1973 / Curtom ✦✦✦✦
In the midst of a great run of superb albums, Curtis Mayfield cranked out a fine live set displaying how penetrating his music was in concert. He headed a fine combo, performed extended versions of several hits, sang with authority, earnestness, and conviction, and got an equally intense response from the audience. Sadly, this album is currently not available on CD. —*Ron Wynn*

Back to the World / May 1973 / Curtom ✦✦✦✦
Another stirring album by Curtis Mayfield, now in a groove on his own label. Mayfield's works issued challenges across the board, urging everyone to examine his or her prejudices and then seek a solution. While he always included one or two wonderful love songs for balance, these albums were largely examinations of American issues in the 1970s. He scored three R&B chart hits, with "Future Shock" just missing the Top Ten, but that was icing on the cake. Mayfield's music had far more importance than simply getting hits. —*Ron Wynn*

Got to Find a Way / 1974 / Curtom ✦✦✦
Curtis Mayfield continued his run of excellent albums in the '70s with this follow-up to the huge hit *Superfly* soundtrack. This album had more love songs than some of his earlier material, although he didn't tone down his searing attacks on American injustice and hypocrisy. His vocals continued to be alternately poignant, urgent, and accusatory, while his lyrics, production, and arrangements were once again magnificent. —*Ron Wynn*

Sweet Exorcist / 1974 / Curtom ✦✦✦

Curtis Mayfield hit a stride during the '70s that was unparalleled among R&B-soul performers from an album standpoint. He was writing, producing, arranging, and performing on great album after great album, then distributing them on his own label as well. This one included the big hit "Kung Fu," plus the title song, and once more perfectly blended rigorous message tracks and steamy love songs. Sadly, it hasn't been reissued on CD and isn't on the list to be at this time. —*Ron Wynn*

There's No Place Like America Today / 1975 / Curtom ✦✦✦✦

Curtis Mayfield continued his string of powerful, assertive message albums with this mid-'70s release, but, as luck would have it, the only hit the album scored came with a love tune, "Only You, Babe." Still, the title tune, "Hard Times," "When Seasons Change," and "Blue Monday People" were unrelenting, unapologetic statements of frustration and anger. Mayfield also included "So In Love" and "Love to the People" to balance the menu, but the finest cuts addressed the inequities and injustices he saw being ignored. —*Ron Wynn*

Live in Europe / Jul. 1987 / Curtom ✦✦✦

Although Curtis Mayfield's album sales had decreased significantly by the late '70s, the smooth Chicago soul veteran remained a popular live attraction well into the '80s. Audiences still longed to hear both gems from his years with the influential Impressions and his early solo hits, and he gives them exactly what they want on this album (released as both a single CD and a two-CD set). Mayfield reminds us just how great the Impressions were on heartfelt versions of such '60s classics as "Gypsy Woman" (which greatly influenced the Isley Brothers), "It's Alright," and the inspirational "People Get Ready," and is equally captivating on incisive, early-'70s sociopolitical hits like "Pusherman," "Freddie's Dead," and "If There's a Hell Below." *Live in Europe's* main flaw isn't Mayfield's performances, but a band that, although decent, just doesn't go that extra mile or do this superb material justice. Horns, a main ingredient of many of his hits, are sorely missed—especially on "Move on Up"—and Buzz Amato's keyboards simply can't take their place. —*Alex Henderson*

Of All Time: Classic Collection / 1990 / Curtom ✦✦✦✦

This anthology spotlights Curtis Mayfield's biggest hits as a solo star since 1970. It includes his first hit as a lead artist, "(Don't Worry) If There's a Hell Below We're All Gonna Go," plus "Superfly," "Freddie's Dead," "So in Love," and many other classics recorded for his Curtom label. Mayfield penned many masterful sociopolitical and protest tunes, but could also write poignant, expressive love songs. —*Ron Wynn*

Take It to the Street / Feb. 1990 / Curtom ✦✦✦

In the 1980s and '90s, some soul veterans turned to high-tech urban-contemporary sounds in an effort to appeal to black radio. Curtis Mayfield, however, continued to deliver rewarding albums by remaining true to himself and sticking with the type of classic soul approach that put him on the map. *Take It to the Streets* falls short of the unmitigated excellence of *Superfly* or *Sweet Exorcist*, but is a respectable effort, demonstrating that he could still pack a punch as a vocalist, composer, and producer. There's much to savor and admire here, including "Homeless" (which makes it clear that Mayfield hadn't lost his touch when it came to biting sociopolitical commentary), "He's a Fly Guy," the charismatic "Who Was That Lady," and an engaging remake of "On and On" (a gem he wrote for Gladys Knight & the Pips in 1973). With the re-emergence of hard-hitting "blaxploitation" (black exploitation) films in the late '80s, the gritty imagery of "I'm Gonna Get You Sucka" and the haunting "He's A Fly Guy" proved quite timely. While this material could have used some horns, Mayfield generally employs technology in a soulful way—employing "real instruments" along with keyboards and drum machines, and never letting his production sound stiff, unnatural, or forced. —*Alex Henderson*

★ **The Anthology 1961-1977** / Dec. 8, 1992 / MCA ✦✦✦✦✦

An absolutely wonderful collection, it includes both the Impressions' '60s hits and Curtis Mayfield's early-'70s solo recordings on his Curtom label. All of the music on the two CDs (including "It's Alright," "People Get Ready," "Superfly," and "Freddie's Dead") is superb and the liner notes are excellent; it's the definitive Mayfield collection. —*AMG*

Living Legend / Aug. 1, 1995 / Curtom ✦✦✦

Living Legend is a double-disc collection of some of Curtis Mayfield's finest solo material from the '70s, but it contains too much mediocre material to function as an effective introduction to the soul great. —*Stephen Thomas Erlewine*

People Get Ready: The Curtis Mayfield Story / Feb. 27, 1996 / Rhino ✦✦✦✦

Like most large box sets, this three-CD, 51-song production is too extensive for the casual fan, and sacrifices consistency in an attempt to span an entire career. The focus is on Mayfield's solo work; much of the first disc is devoted to his most popular work with the Impressions, but the remainder of the compilation surveys his solo output, from 1970 to 1990. The Impressions tracks are uniformly excellent, but the Mayfield-only cuts are more problematic. The best of these—the *Superfly* highlights, of course, and early '70s singles like "(Don't Worry) If There's a Hell Below We're All Going to Go" and "Beautiful Brother of Mine"—are as good as anything he ever did. But even in the early '70s, he was erratic, and after *Superfly* (his career summit), nothing he did smacked of brilliance. Some of the post-*Superfly* stuff is okay, but considering that this period takes up half of disc two and all of disc three, it means you're in for a pretty swift downhill slide over the last half of the box. Mayfield never lost his vocal abilities, or his production skills, but after the late '70s his material was simply unimpressive, getting into pedestrian dance music and romantic urban contemporary. For a Mayfield retrospective, you're much better off with MCA's two-disc *Anthology*, which goes into the Impressions period with much greater depth, and includes the cream of his '70s solo recordings. —*Richie Unterberger*

New World Order / Oct. 1, 1996 / Warner Brothers ✦✦✦

New World Order is a touching, moving comeback from Curtis Mayfield. As the first new music Mayfield has recorded since he was paralyzed in 1990, the album engenders a lot of good will—it's undeniably affecting to hear him sing again, especially with the knowledge that his performances had to be recorded line-by-line, due to his paralysis. The joy of hearing him sing makes the inconsistency of the album forgivable, especially since he is in good voice. Narada Michael Walden, Daryle Simmons, and Organized have all contributed productions that are sensitive but strong, which gives the album added weight. The songs are hit-and-miss, but the main strength of the record is that it illustrates that Mayfield can make music that is still vital. —*Leo Stanley*

Percy Mayfield

b. Aug. 12, 1920, Minden, LA, d. Aug. 11, 1984, Los Angeles, CA

Piano, Vocals / Soul, R&B, Piano Blues, West Coast Blues, Urban Blues

A masterful songwriter whose touching blues ballad "Please Send Me Someone to Love," a multi-layered universal lament, was a No. 1 R&B hit in 1950, Percy Mayfield had the world by the tail until a horrific 1952 auto wreck left him facially disfigured. That didn't stop the poet laureate of the blues from writing in prolific fashion, though. As Ray Charles' favorite scribe during the '60s, he handed the Genius such gems as "Hit the Road Jack" and "At the Club."

Like so many of his postwar L.A. contemporaries, Mayfield got his musical start in Texas but moved to the coast during the war. Surmising that Jimmy Witherspoon might like to perform a tune he'd penned called "Two Years of Torture," Mayfield targeted Supreme Records as a possible buyer for his song. But the bosses at Supreme liked his own gentle reading so much that they insisted he wax it himself in 1947 with an all-star band that included saxist Maxwell Davis, guitarist Chuck Norris, and pianist Willard McDaniel.

Art Rupe's Specialty logo signed Mayfield in 1950 and scored a solid string of R&B smashes over the next couple of years. "Please Send Me Someone to Love" and its equally potent flip "Strange Things Happening" were followed in the charts by "Lost Love," "What a Fool I Was," "Prayin' for Your Return," "Cry Baby," and "Big Question," cementing Mayfield's reputation as a blues balladeer of the highest order. Davis handled sax duties on most of Mayfield's Specialty sides as well. Mayfield's lyrics were usually as insightfully downbeat as his tempos; he was a true master at expressing his innermost feelings, laced with vulnerability and pathos (his "Life Is Suicide" and "The River's Invitation" are two prime examples).

Even though his touring was drastically curtailed after the accident, Mayfield hung in there as a Specialty artist through 1954, switching to Chess in 1955-56 and Imperial in 1959. Charles proved thankful enough for Mayfield's songwriting genius to sign him to his Tangerine logo in 1962; over the next five years, the singer waxed a series of inexorably classy outings, many with Brother Ray's band (notably "My Jug and I" in 1964 and "Give Me Time to Explain" the next year).

It's a rare veteran blues artist indeed who hasn't taken a whack at one or more Mayfield copyrights. Mayfield himself persisted into the '70s, scoring minor chart items for RCA and Atlantic while performing on a limited basis until his 1984 death. —*Bill Dahl*

My Jug and I / 1962 / Tangerine ✦✦✦✦

Mayfield's gentle vocal delivery and the big, brassy sound of Ray Charles' orchestra were a match made in heaven. Mayfield brought some first-class material to this party (which begs for CD reissue): "My Jug and I," "Stranger in My Own Home Town" (later covered by Elvis Presley), the untypically jumping "Give Me Time to Explain," and a handful of Specialty remakes. —*Bill Dahl*

Bought Blues / 1969 / Tangerine ✦✦✦✦

Another elegant, beautifully arranged collection fraught with brilliant, sometimes heartbreaking material: "Ha Ha in the Daytime," "We Both Must Cry," "My Bottle Is My Companion." —*Bill Dahl*

★ **Poet of the Blues** / 1990 / Specialty ✦✦✦✦✦

The insightful songwriting skills of this West Coaster were matched by his wry, plaintive vocal delivery (Mayfield was usually his own best interpreter). The 25 sides here date from his hit-laden 1950-1954 stay at Art Rupe's Specialty logo and include his universal lament "Please Send Me Someone to Love," the resolutely downbeat "Strange Things Happening" and "Lost Love," and an ironic "The River's Invitation." Saxman Maxwell Davis led the horn-powered combos providing sympathetic support behind Mayfield. —*Bill Dahl*

For Collectors Only / Apr. 6, 1992 / Specialty ✦✦✦
As the title suggests, this gives a deeper look at Mayfield's early career. Alternate takes and unissued material are included. —*Hank Davis*

Memory Pain / Sep. 17, 1992 / Specialty ✦✦✦✦
Twenty-five more nuggets from the voluminous Specialty vaults, including alternate takes of some of his biggest smashes, a plethora of unissued stuff, and both sides of his 1957 single for the firm that showed him coping subtly with the rocking changes sweeping the R&B world, and ending with a 1960 demo of his classic "Hit the Road, Jack." —*Bill Dahl*

Maze Featuring Frankie Beverly

f. 1976, San Francisco, CA
Soul, Funk, Urban
Frankie Beverly & Maze may be the ultimate urban contemporary group, though they're much more soulful and funky than many of their counterparts. They began in Philadelphia as the Butlers, and later became Raw Soul. They moved to San Francisco in the mid-'70s, and switched identities again to Maze. The lineup was lead singer Frankie Beverly, Wayne Thomas, Sam Porter, Robin Duke, Roame Lowry, McKinley Williams, and Joe Provost. Ahaguna G. Sun later replaced Provost, and Sun was subsequently replaced by Billy "Shoes" Johnson. Ron Smith replaced Thomas, and Phillip Woo was added on keyboards in 1980. Though they've had only one No. 1 R&B hit in their long tenure ("Back in Stride" in 1985), Maze's popularity is unquestioned, especially as a live act. They recorded for Capitol from 1977 until 1989, when they moved to Warner Brothers and issued another smash LP in *Silky Soul*. Their most recent release was *Back to Basics* in 1993. —*Ron Wynn*

Live in New Orleans / 1981 / Capitol ✦✦✦✦
A superb live album, one of the finest soul-funk concert dates ever released. Frankie Beverly and Maze managed to capture on this two-album set the energy, spontaneity, and nonstop excitement of their concerts, which have always been among the finest on the R&B/soul/funk circuit. The set functioned as both a greatest hits work and a wonderful introduction to people who'd never seen their live show. The album version of "Joy and Pain" became an international hit, and led to other singles being pulled and re-released in extended versions. —*Ron Wynn*

Maze / 1982 / Capitol ✦✦✦
Formerly known as Raw Soul, Frankie Beverly and his band took a new name when they relocated from Philadelphia to San Francisco, and broadened their style from mainly standard soul to a funk-soul hybrid. They signed with Capitol in the mid-'70s, and their first album under the new pact was their finest set, with Beverly's energetic lead vocals and an excellent band that included keyboardists Phillip Woo and Sam Porter, bassist Robin Duhe, and guitarist Ron Smith. They made an immediate impact with their hard-driving sound, not as strictly on the beat as the Dayton bands like the Ohio Players or Slave, but just as soulful. —*Ron Wynn*

Silky Soul / Sep. 1989 / Warner Brothers ✦✦✦
After being on Capitol through much of the 1970s and '80s, Maze moved to Warner Brothers in 1989 and scored immediate dividends with this album, containing some of the group's finest ballads ever. The title track was a poignant tribute to Marvin Gaye, a supporter and advocate of the group. Beverly also paid homage to Nelson Mandela, but didn't overdo the political message material. There were plenty of breezy and superbly crafted romantic numbers, while "Love's on the Run" was a decent uptempo number. The album helped re-establish the group as a major urban contemporary act and got them back on the charts for the first time in three years. —*Ron Wynn*

The Greatest Hits of Maze . . . Lifelines, Vol. 1 / Nov. 8, 1989 / Capitol ✦✦✦✦
When the Philadelphia band Raw Soul moved to San Francisco in the mid-'70s, they changed their name to Maze and made Frankie Beverly their lead singer. Beverly's personality and exuberance and their evolution into one of the tightest bands on the soul scene turned Maze into an institution. This collects formative hits from their years on Capitol, including "Golden Time of Day" and "Joy and Pain." It shows that they were both an enjoyable uptempo and funk band and a convincing ballad and love song ensemble. —*Ron Wynn*

● **Anthology** / Jan. 23, 1996 / Capitol ✦✦✦✦
Maze have been a fan favorite since the mid-'70s; while they've received little critical notice or adulation except among soul and R&B scribes, Maze have seldom been out of the charts since making their debut on Capitol. Lead singer Frankie Beverly's roots extend back to classic doo

wop and East Coast soul; although he made the transition to funk, then urban material, Beverly always had plenty of soul and passion in his vocals. Maze also blazed their own musical trail; when such competitors as Earth, Wind & Fire, the Bar-Kays, Con Funk Shun, and Slave were featuring surging horn sections and jazz-tinged arrangements with heavy bass lines, Beverly and company favored rock-influenced guitar parts juxtaposed with soulful organ riffs or synthesizer riffs and just a trace of reggae and/or Latin rhythm. Beverly enjoyed several hits on Capitol, but became dissatisfied with their inability to break the group beyond the R&B-funk market. They departed Capitol in the late '80s, and resurfaced on Warner Bros., where they continued making strong, distinctive releases. *Anthology* gathers the best (at least most of the best) singles the band did for Capitol, among them classics like "Southern Girl," "Before I Let Go," the complete "Joy and Pain," and "Happy Feeling." Despite being only an 18-cut, single-disc release, there's a completeness not often available in a single CD set. British journalist David Nathan's notes are comprehensive, and nicely combine anecdotal and discographical references. While it would be good if Capitol and Warner Bros. could combine on a multi-disc set, until (or if) that happens, here's a fine tribute to one of R&B's most underrated and consistently enjoyable bands. —*Ron Wynn*

Mazzy Star

f. 1989, Santa Monica, CA
Alternative Pop-Rock, Adult Alternative Pop-Rock, Dream-Pop
If psychedelic music has a voice in '90s post-punk, Mazzy Star may be its strongest reincarnation. That doesn't necessarily mean that fans of the Jefferson Airplane and the Grateful Dead will find the band to their liking, however. Mazzy Star much prefer the dark side of psychedelia, as exemplified by the most distended tracks of the Doors and the Velvet Underground. Their fuzzy guitar workouts and plaintive folky compositions are often suffused in a dissociative ennui that is very much of the 1990s, however much their textures may recall the drug-induced states of vintage psychedelia.

Although Mazzy Star are nominally a full band, they're basically the core duo of guitarist David Roback and singer Hope Sandoval with backing musicians. Roback boasts a long history in the paisley underground, with the Rain Parade and Opal. He came across Sandoval after hearing a tape she had made as part of a folky duo, Going Home. (The Going Home album that Roback subsequently produced remains unissued, although its eventual release has been rumored for some time.) Sandoval ended up replacing Kendra Smith on Opal's final tours. After Opal dissolved, Roback and Sandoval continued to work together as Mazzy Star, and released their first album for Rough Trade, *She Hangs Brightly*, in 1990.

Rough Trade's US branch went under shortly afterwards, but luckily Mazzy Star were picked up by Capitol, who kept the debut in print and issued their follow-up, 1993's *So Tonight That I Might See*. There isn't much to differentiate the two albums, though that's not necessarily a criticism. Both share similar strengths and weaknesses: appealingly dreamy and atmospheric arrangements, rambling distorted guitar workouts, and lyrics that mix the haunting and the meaninglessly vague. *Tonight That I Might See* had been around for about a year before it suddenly got hot, reaching the Top 40, and spinning off a small hit single, "Fade into You." Even in the wake of this surprise success, Roback and Sandoval remained as enigmatic and aloof as their music, rarely submitting to interviews, and offering mysterious, unhelpful replies when journalists did manage to talk with them. —*Richie Unterberger*

She Hangs Brightly / 1990 / Capitol ✦✦✦
Roback and Sandoval slog through a collection of Velvet Underground-style psychedelia and comatose folk. Sandoval's pleasantly detached vocal delivery complements the cold, highly reverberant production. It's good for encouraging numb disconnection from the planet. —*Rick Clark*

● **So Tonight That I Might See** / Sep. 27, 1993 / Capitol ✦✦✦✦
Treading a similar path as on their debut, Mazzy Star generally succeed in their efforts to create an otherworldly, dream-state-like buzz with their lulling songs and layers of droning guitars. The duo offers a considerably warmer and more authentic persona on the pretty, acoustic-dominated songs than on the droning trance-rock exercises. With its socially detached self-absorption, this CD is like a definitive soundtrack for the slacker elements of Generation X. —*Richie Unterberger*

Among My Swan / Oct. 29, 1996 / Capitol ✦✦✦✦
The similarity between *Among My Swan* and *So Tonight That I Might See* is all the more mind-boggling when considering the four years it took to record the album. Stylistically, there is no difference between the records—it is still the same crawling, trancey acoustic-folk—but that's not necessarily a bad thing. Mazzy Star has a pleasant sound and their songwriting is always consistent, making their records enjoyable. However, *Among My Swan* lacks any standouts on the level of "Fade Into

You," which makes it a less compelling listen, especially on repeated plays. In other words, it's a holding pattern, which should appeal to the converted, without making any new fans. — *Stephen Thomas Erlewine*

MC5

f. 1966, Detroit, MI, **db.** 1971
Hard Rock, Proto-Punk
This Detroit rock 'n' roll band's musical and political stance helped sow the seeds of the British punk movement of the late '70s. Original members included Wayne Kramer (guitar), Rob Tyner (vocals), Bob Gaspar (drums), Pat Burrows (bass), and Fred "Sonic" Smith (guitar). They played around their native Detroit ca. 1966 as the Motor City Five. Both Gaspar and Burrows, who had shaped much of the band's early rhythmic drive, left before the band ever recorded and were replaced by Dennis Thompson (drums) and Michael Davis (bass). After two local singles went nowhere, manager John Sinclair (of the revolutionary White Panther Party) got them signed to Elektra, who recorded them live at Detroit's Grande Ballroom, where they enjoyed a fanatical local following. Troubles with the album's lyrical content (based in large part around the band's revolutionary sex, drugs, and rock 'n' roll rhetoric) and Sinclair's conviction on drug charges saw the band tone down its image for their second album, released on Atlantic. By the time their third album was released in 1971, the band was plagued by drugs and personal problems, and they broke up shortly thereafter. Though never commercially successful, the MC5 personified the Detroit high-energy sound and approach to rock 'n' roll, and their style lives on in the work of punk and alternative bands around the world. — *Cub Koda*

★ **Kick out the Jams** / 1969 / Elektra ✦✦✦✦✦
The band in full cry at the Grande Ballroom, 1968; one of the most exciting live albums ever recorded. Highlights include the title track (uncensored on CD), "Ramblin' Rose," and "Borderline." — *Cub Koda*

Back in the U.S.A. / 1970 / Rhino ✦✦✦
Their second album is not so wild but still exciting. Great original material is included, like "Shakin' Street" (featuring vocals by Fred "Sonic" Smith), "The American Ruse," "The Human Being Lawnmower," and "Looking at You," which featured some fiery lead-guitar work by Wayne Kramer. — *Rick Clark*

High Time / 1971 / Rhino ✦✦✦✦
Their last studio album, with "Sister Anne" and "Baby, Won't Ya" as principal highlights. — *Cub Koda*

Babes in Arms / 1983 / ROIR ✦✦✦
Rare and unreleased sides. This includes their first singles, previously unavailable on album. — *Cub Koda*

American Ruse / 1994 / Total Energy ✦✦
Previously unreleased pre-production rehearsals for *Back in the USA*, recorded in July 1969. In the liner notes, original MC5 manager John Sinclair goes on at considerable length at how *Back in the USA* producer Jon Landau ruined the material by substituting pop production for raw power. It's not at all certain, though, that all listeners, or even all MC5 fans, will agree. Certainly the approach is more stripped-down, but the sound quality is boxy, on par with a reasonable-fidelity bootleg. Also, many of the songs are in an unfinished state, with no vocals having been added to the instrumental backing tracks. MC5 diehards will certainly find it interesting, and perhaps even preferable to *Back in the USA* in certain aspects, but for general listening purposes it doesn't rate as a valid alternative to the official LP. The CD also includes a couple of lo-fi cuts from a live show in September 1968. — *Richie Unterberger*

Teenage Lust / Apr. 1996 / Alive ✦✦✦
The existence of an early board tape captures the MC5 in all their rocking glory, recorded live at the Saginaw Civic Center, January 1, 1970. This show falls in between the two studio releases for Atlantic (*Back In The USA* and *High Time*), finding the band restyling themselves for mass consumption while remaining a very potent force as a live act. The set list reflects this, combining tunes from their live album ("Ramblin' Rose," "Rama Lama Fa Fa Fa," and a medley of "Starship" and "Kick Out The Jams") with harder takes of songs from *Back In The USA* than what appear on the studio release. Although this has been around for a number of years as a bootleg release with dubious fidelity, this is its first official release. — *Cub Koda*

MC Hammer

b. Mar. 30, 1962, Oakland, CA
Vocals / Hip Hop, West Coast Rap, Crossover Rap, Pop-Rap
Considered either the ultimate success story or consummate fraud, Oakland's MC Hammer, a one-time jack-of-all-trades for the Oakland Athletics baseball team, dominated the charts in 1990 with *Please Hammer Don't Hurt 'Em*. The single "U Can't Touch This," despite a rather feeble rap and recycle job on Rick James' single "Superfreak," was an enormous crossover smash. Hammer live puts on a fine show as far as dancing, sound, light effects, production, and such. But from a technical

standpoint, everything, from his rhymes to his enunciation, qualifies as the ultimate in "wack" (weak) performance. He does have great taste in cover songs, picking choice items from Marvin Gaye, B.B. King, the Chi-Lites, and Prince, among others. He's since dropped the MC from his name.

After staying in the limelight as a racehorse owner and Evander Holyfield's promoter, Hammer returned to the rap wars in 1994 with *The Funky Headhunter*. It featured a leaner, harder sound, with assistance and material provided by gangsta-rap producers, and featured Hammer sporting a more street look. He previewed the new style on Arsenio Hall's show early in the year, then issued the CD in March. It debuted at No. 2 on *Billboard's* R&B charts, then dipped the next week to No. 6. Skeptics voiced their doubts about the new Hammer, especially in the hip-hop press. — *Ron Wynn*

● **Greatest Hits** / Oct. 1, 1996 / Capitol ✦✦✦✦
Despite being one of the best-selling rappers of all-time, none of MC Hammer's albums were very consistent—the singles stood out like sore thumbs among the filler on each record, which is why *Greatest Hits* is such a good bargain. *Greatest Hits* compiles 12 of Hammer's biggest hits for Capitol Records, including "U Can't Touch This," "Pump It Up," "Turn This Mutha Out," "They Put Me in the Mix," "Have You Seen Her," "Pray," "Here Comes the Hammer," "2 Legit 2 Quit," "Do Not Pass Me By," and "Addams Groove." It's not only an excellent introduction to MC Hammer, it's the best album in his entire catalog. — *Stephen Thomas Erlewine*

McAlmont & Butler

f. 1995, London, England, **db.** 1996
Brit-Pop, Alternative Pop-Rock
After Bernard Butler left Suede following the group's second LP *Dog Man Star*, the guitarist joined forces with the British soul diva David McAlmont. In 1996, the duo released the album *The Sound of McAlmont & Butler;* while it was a huge hit in the UK, the two acrimoniously dissolved their partnership before they could record a follow-up. — *Jason Ankeny*

● **The Sound of McAlmont & Butler** / Jan. 1996 / Hut ✦✦✦
The complete works of David McAlmont and Bernard Butler's stormy, short-lived collaboration are collected on *The Sound of McAlmont & Butler*. Featuring all the songs from their two singles, "Yes" and "You Do," the disc illustrates why the collaboration didn't last more than a few months in 1995. Both of the musicians are extremely talented—McAlmont's voice soars like few other contemporary soul and pop singers, while Butler has a talent for grandiose, majestic songs and arrangements that his contemporaries generally disdain—but both are prone to indulgence, which is exactly what happened. Instead of achieving the dark, theatrical beauty of *Dog Man Star*, his last album with Suede, Butler throws literally everything into the mix—all of his songs sound like extensions of his magnum opus with Suede, "Stay Together," without the precise vision of Brett Anderson to temper his more outlandish tendencies. That's because McAlmont has a tendency for the outlandish too—he's just as likely to collapse into vocal histrionics as he is to reach new sonic heights. Consequently, the songs on *The Sound of McAlmont & Butler* are about *sound*, not about melody. There are selected highlights—the duo fulfills their ambitions on the gorgeous "Yes"—but for the most part, the album is disappointingly tedious and frustratingly unengaging. In short, a wasted opportunity. — *Stephen Thomas Erlewine*

Paul McCartney

b. Jun. 18, 1942, Liverpool, England
Bass, Guitar, Piano, Keyboards, Vocals / Soft Rock, Pop-Rock
Of all the former Beatles, Paul McCartney has had by far the most successful solo career, maintaining a constant presence in the UK and American charts during the '70s and '80s. In America alone, he had nine No. 1 singles and seven No. 1 albums during the first 12 years of his solo career. Although he sold records, McCartney never attained much critical respect, especially when compared to his former partner John Lennon. Then again, he pursued a different path than Lennon, deciding early on that he wanted to be in a rock band. Within a year after the Beatles' breakup, McCartney had formed Wings with his wife Linda, and the group remained active for the next 10 years, racking up a string of hit albums, singles, and tours. By the late '70s, many critics were taking pot-shots at McCartney's effortlessly melodic song craft, but that didn't stop the public from buying his records. His sales didn't slow considerably until the late '80s, and he retaliated with his first full-scale tour since the '70s, which was a considerable success. During the '90s, McCartney recorded less frequently, concentrating on projects like his first classical recording, a techno album, and the Beatles' *Anthology*.

Like Lennon and George Harrison, Paul McCartney began exploring creative avenues outside the Beatles during the late '60s, but whereas his bandmates released their own experimental records, McCartney confined himself to writing and production for other artists, with the exception of his 1966 soundtrack to *The Family Way*. Following his marriage to Linda Eastman on March 12, 1969, McCartney began working at his home studio on his first solo album. He released the record, *McCartney*, in April 1970, two weeks before the Beatles' *Let It Be* was scheduled to hit the stores. Prior to the album's release, he announced that the Beatles were breaking up, which was against the wishes of the other members. As a result, the tensions between him and the other three members, particularly Harrison and Lennon, increased and he earned the ill will of many critics. Nevertheless, *McCartney* became a hit, spending three weeks at the top of the American charts. Early in 1971, he returned with "Another Day," which became his first hit single as a solo artist. It was followed several months later by *Ram*, an even homemade collection, this time featuring the contributions of his wife Linda.

By the end of 1971, the McCartneys had formed Wings, which was intended to be a full-fledged recording and touring band. Former Moody Blues guitarist Denny Laine and drummer Denny Seiwell became the group's other members, and Wings released their first album, *Wild Life*, in December 1971. *Wild Life* was greeted with poor reviews and was a relative flop. McCartney and Wings, which now featured former Grease Band guitarist Henry McCullough, spent 1972 as a working band, releasing three singles—the protest "Give Ireland Back to the Irish," the reggae-fied "Mary Had a Little Lamb" and the rocking "Hi Hi Hi"—in England. *Red Rose Speedway* followed in the spring of 1973, and while it received weak reviews, it became his second American No. 1 album. Later in 1973, Wings embarked on their first British tour, at the conclusion of which McCullough and Seiwell left the band. Prior to their departure, McCartney's theme to the James Bond movie *Live and Let Die* became a Top Ten hit in the US and UK. That summer, the remaining Wings proceeded to record a new album in Nigeria. Released late in 1973, *Band on the Run*, was simultaneously McCartney's best-reviewed album and his most successful, spending four weeks at the top of the US charts and eventually going triple platinum.

Following the success of *Band on the Run*, McCartney formed a new version of Wings with guitarist James McCulloch and drummer Geoff Britton. The new lineup was showcased on the 1974 British single "Junior's Farm" and the 1975 hit album *Venus and Mars*. *At the Speed of Sound* followed in 1976, and it was the first Wings record to feature songwriting contributions by the other band members. Nevertheless, the album became a monster success on the basis of two McCartney songs, "Silly Love Songs" and "Let 'Em In." Wings supported the album with their first international tour, which broke many attendance records and was captured on the live triple-album *Wings over America* (1976). After the tour completed, Wings rested a bit during 1977, as McCartney released an instrumental version of *Ram* under the name Thrillington and produced Denny Laine's solo album, *Holly Days*. Later that year, Wings released "Mull of Kintyre," which became the biggest-selling British single of all time, selling over two million copies. Wings followed "Mull of Kintyre" with *London Town* in 1978, which became another platinum record. After its release, McCulloch left the band to join the re-formed Small Faces and Wings released *Back to the Egg* in 1979. Though the record went platinum, it failed to produce any big hits. Early in 1980, McCartney was arrested for marijuana possession at the beginning of a Japanese tour; he was imprisoned for 10 days and released, without any charges being pressed.

Wings embarked on a British tour in the spring of 1980 before McCartney recorded *McCartney II*, which was a one-man-band effort like his solo debut. The following year, Denny Laine left Wings because McCartney didn't want to tour in the wake of John Lennon's assassination; in doing so, he effectively broke up Wings. McCartney entered the studio later that year with Beatles producer George Martin to make *Tug of War*. Released in the spring of 1982, *Tug of War* received the best reviews of any McCartney record since *Band on the Run* and spawned the No. 1 single "Ebony and Ivory," a duet with Stevie Wonder that became McCartney's biggest American hit. In 1983, McCartney sang on "The Girl is Mine," the first single from Michael Jackson's blockbuster album *Thriller*. In return, Jackson dueted with McCartney on "Say Say Say," the first single from McCartney's 1983 album *Pipes of Peace* and the last No. 1 single of his career. The relationship between Jackson and McCartney soured considerably when Jackson bought the publishing rights to the Beatles' songs from underneath McCartney in 1985.

McCartney directed his first feature film in 1984 with *Give My Regards to Broad Street*. While the soundtrack, which featured new songs and re-recorded Beatles tunes, was a hit, generating the hit single "No More Lonely Nights," the film was a flop, earning terrible reviews. The following year he had his last American Top Ten with the theme to the Chevy Chase/Dan Aykroyd comedy *Spies Like Us*. *Press to Play* (1986) received some strong reviews but the album was a flop. In 1988, he recorded a collection of rock 'n' roll oldies called *Choba B CCCP* for release in the USSR; it was given official release in the US and UK in 1991. For 1989's *Flowers in the Dirt*, McCartney co-wrote several songs

with Elvis Costello; the pair also wrote songs for Costello's *Spike*, including the hit "Veronica." *Flowers in the Dirt* received the strongest reviews of any McCartney release since *Tug of War* and was supported by an extensive international tour, which was captured on the live double album *Tripping the Live Fantastic* (1990). For the tour, McCartney hired guitarist Robbie McIntosh and bassist Hamish Stuart, who would form the core of his band through the remainder of the '90s.

Early in 1991, McCartney released another live album in the form of *Unplugged*, which was taken from his appearance on MTV's acoustic concert program of the same name; it was the first *Unplugged* album to be released. Later that year, he unveiled *Liverpool Oratorio*, his first classical work. Another pop album, *Off the Ground*, followed in 1993, but the album failed to generate any big hits, despite McCartney's successful supporting tour. Following the completion of the "New World" tour, he released another live album, *Paul is Live*, in December of 1993. In 1994, he released an ambient techno album under the pseudonym the Fireman. McCartney premiered his second classical piece, "The Leaf," early in 1995, and then began hosting a Westwood One radio series called *Oobu Joobu*. But his primary activity in 1995, as well as 1996, was the Beatles' *Anthology*, which encompassed a lengthy video documentary of the band and the multi-volume release of Beatles outtakes and rarities. After *Anthology* was completed, he released *Flaming Pie* in the spring of 1997. *—Stephen Thomas Erlewine*

McCartney / Apr. 20, 1970 / Capitol ✦✦✦✦
Paul McCartney retreated from the spotlight of the Beatles by recording his first solo album at his home studio, playing nearly all of the instruments himself. Appropriately, *McCartney* has an endearingly ragged, homemade quality that makes even its filler—and there is quite a bit of filler—rather ingratiating. Only a handful of songs rank as full-fledged McCartney classics, but those songs—the light folk-pop of "That Would Be Something," the sweet, gentle "Every Night," the ramshackle Beatles leftover "Teddy Boy" and the staggering "Maybe I'm Amazed" (not coincidentally the only rocker on the album)—are full of all the easy melodic charm that is McCartney's trademark. The rest of the album is charmingly slight, especially if it is read as a way to bring Paul back to earth after the heights of the Beatles. At the time the throwaway nature of much of the material was a shock, but it has become charming in retrospect. Unfortunately, in retrospect it also appears as a harbinger of the nagging mediocrity that would plague McCartney's entire solo career. *—Stephen Thomas Erlewine*

Ram / May 17, 1971 / Capitol ✦✦✦
Compared to *McCartney*, Paul McCartney's second solo album *Ram*—which was credited as a collaboration with his wife Linda—is a more substantial and produced effort, yet it has much of the same homemade charm as its predecessor. Divided between simple pop-rockers and cleverly constructed mini-suites like "Uncle Albert/Admiral Halsey" and "Back Seat of My Car," *Ram* doesn't gel into any major statement, but it has many pleasurable detours. McCartney layers the ramshackle rhythm tracks with odd sound effects and off-kilter arrangements. While the production might not always work, it does make for pleasant ear candy, not only on lovely songs like "Heart of the Country," but also on throwaway numbers like the hard-rocking "Smile Away" and "Monkberry Moon Delight." Unfortunately, most of *Ram* is composed of filler, and while it's *enjoyable* filler, it prevents the record from being much more than pleasurable diversion. *—Stephen Thomas Erlewine*

Wild Life / Dec. 7, 1971 / Capitol ✦✦
The first album credited to Paul McCartney's group Wings is a collection of slight material (most of it written by Paul and Linda McCartney). Worst is the lyrically challenged "Bip Bop," which even comes with a reprise! This was the album that gave evidence to anyone who'd ever dismissed McCartney as a lightweight. (The CD version of the album added four non-LP singles tracks: "Oh Woman, Oh Why," which had been the B-side of McCartney's first solo single, "Another Day," and both sides of the single "Mary Had a Little Lamb"/"Little Woman Love.") *—William Ruhlmann*

Red Rose Speedway / 1973 / Capitol ✦✦
After the debacle of *Wild Life*, Paul McCartney spent 1972 rebuilding his reputation with a series of one-off singles, then released this, his fourth post-Beatles album, which restored his commercial fortunes by hitting No. 1 and spawning the No. 1 single "My Love." Like *Ram*, the album is awash in interesting musical ideas, most of which aren't finished off, and what sound like dummy lyrics that were never replaced with good ones. The only substantive song other than the single is the lead-off track, "Big Barn Bed." (The CD version adds three non-LP B-sides: "I Lie Around," "Country Dreamer," and "The Mess." The last, a live cut that was the B-side of "My Love," is the best uptempo rocker of McCartney's solo career up to this point.) *—William Ruhlmann*

Band on the Run / Dec. 5, 1973 / Capitol ✦✦✦✦
Neither the dippy, rustic *Wild Life* nor the slick AOR flourishes of *Red Rose Speedway* earned McCartney much respect, so he made the self-consciously ambitious *Band on the Run* to rebuke his critics. On the

surface, *Band on the Run* appears to be constructed as a song cycle in the vein of *Abbey Road,* but subsequent listens reveal that the only similarities the two albums share are simply superficial. McCartney's talent for songcraft and nuanced arrangements is on ample display throughout the record, which makes many of the songs—including the nonsensical title track—sound more substantial than they actually are. While a handful of the songs are excellent—the surging, inspired surrealism of "Jet" is by far one of his best solo recordings, "Bluebird" is sunny acoustic pop, and "Helen Wheels" captures McCartney rocking with abandon—most of the songs are more style than substance. Yet McCartney's melodies are more consistent than on any of his previous solo records, and there are no throwaways; the songs just happen to be not very good. Still, the record is enjoyable, whether it's the minor-key "Mrs. Vanderbilt" or "Let Me Roll It," a silly response to John Lennon's "How Do You Sleep," which does make *Band on the Run* one of McCartney's finest solo efforts. However, there's little of real substance on the record. No matter how elaborate the production is, or how cleverly his mini-suites are constructed, *Band on the Run* is nothing more than a triumph of showmanship. —*Stephen Thomas Erlewine*

Venus & Mars / 1975 / Capitol ✦✦✦
A highly polished band album featuring the No. 1 hit "Listen to What the Man Said," as well as "Letting Go" and "Venus and Mars/Rock Show," which served to introduce the McCartney & Wings world tour of 1975-1976. —*William Ruhlmann*

Wings at the Speed of Sound / 1976 / Capitol ✦✦
Released the same month as the start of Paul McCartney's first post-Beatles tour of the US, this album stayed at No. 1 seven weeks and featured the No. 1 single "Silly Love Songs" and the Top Ten "Let 'Em In." Without the hoopla, it's actually a mediocre effort not helped by having other members of Wings contribute songs, although it contains one of those lost McCartney gems, the rocker "Beware My Love." (The CD contains three bonus tracks culled from non-LP singles: "Walking in the Park with Eloise," "Bridge on the River Suite," and "Sally G.") —*William Ruhlmann*

Wings over America / Dec. 11, 1976 / Capitol ✦✦✦
McCartney made a favorable impression on his 1976 US tour, convincing skeptics he could rock out when he chose and effectively mixing solo hits with Beatles oldies. This live album, originally issued on three LPs and now on two CDs, was more than a souvenir, containing an entire concert (edited from various shows), and finding McCartney performing effective versions of everything from "Lady Madonna" and "Yesterday" to "Hi Hi Hi" and "My Love." "Soily" is otherwise unavailable. "Maybe I'm Amazed" became a Top Ten hit, and the album was McCartney's fifth straight No. 1. —*William Ruhlmann*

London Town / Mar. 31, 1978 / Capitol ✦✦
London Town found Wings once again reduced to the trio of the McCartneys and Denny Laine. It was typically successful, hitting No. 2 and selling a million copies, with the bouncy single "With a Little Luck" topping the charts and the follow-ups "I've Had Enough" and "London Town" making the Top 40. But the best tracks were "Deliver Your Children" and "Girlfriend," the latter discovered by Michael Jackson, who put it on his *Off the Wall* album the following year. (The CD contains the bonus track "Girls' School," which was a Top 40 single just prior to the album's release.) —*William Ruhlmann*

Wings Greatest / Nov. 22, 1978 / Capitol ✦✦✦✦
Most of McCartney & Wings' biggest hits, 1971-1978, among them the singles "Another Day," "Live and Let Die," "Junior's Farm," "Hi Hi Hi," and "Mull of Kintyre," which had not previously appeared on an album. —*William Ruhlmann*

Back to the Egg / May 24, 1979 / Capitol ✦✦
Back to the Egg was Paul McCartney's attempt to get back to rock 'n' roll after the soft-rock of *London Town.* Assembling a new lineup of Wings, McCartney led the group through a set of his most undistinguished songs, ranging from the forced arena-rock of "Old Siam Sir" to the formulaic adult contemporary pap of "Arrow Through Me"—and those are two of the more memorable cuts on the record. Part of the problem is the weak sound of the record and Wings' faceless performances, but the true problem is the songs, which have no spark whatsoever. On the basis of *Back to the Egg,* it's no wonder that McCartney returned to solo recordings after its relative failure. —*Stephen Thomas Erlewine*

McCartney II / May 21, 1980 / Capitol ✦✦✦
Entitled *McCartney II* because its one-man-band approach mirrors that of his first solo album, McCartney's first record since the breakup of Wings was greeted upon its release as a return to form, especially since its synth-heavy arrangements seemed to represent his acceptance of new wave. In retrospect, the record is muddled and confused, nowhere more so than on the frazzled sequencing of "Temporary Secretary," in which McCartney spits out ridiculous lyrics with a self-consciously atonal melody over gurgling synths. Things rarely get worse than that, and occasionally, as in the effortless hooks of "Coming Up," the record is

quite enjoyable. Nevertheless, the majority of *McCartney II* is forced, and its lack of memorable melodies is accentuated by the stiff electronics, which were not innovative at the time and are even more awkward in the present. Nevertheless, *McCartney II* at least finds Paul in an adventurous state of mind, which is a relief after years of formulaic pop. In some ways, the fact that he was trying was more relevant than the fact that the experiments failed. —*Stephen Thomas Erlewine*

Tug of War / Apr. 26, 1982 / Capitol ✦✦✦✦
McCartney turns to Beatles producer George Martin for a carefully constructed blockbuster album that features the No. 1 duet with Stevie Wonder, "Ebony and Ivory," and the Top Ten hit "Take It Away," plus McCartney's tribute to John Lennon, "Here Today." —*William Ruhlmann*

Pipes of Peace / Jan. 1983 / Capitol ✦✦
This was Paul McCartney's first new studio album, either as a member of the Beatles or as a solo artist, to miss the American Top Ten—ever—and this was despite the inclusion of the long-running No. 1 duet with Michael Jackson, "Say Say Say." Explicitly pitched as a follow-up to *Tug of War, Pipes of Peace* was not as carefully crafted as its predecessor, despite the presence of producer George Martin. But that doesn't explain the commercial disappointment. Hereafter, McCartney would struggle to maintain the mass audience he had previously taken for granted. —*William Ruhlmann*

Give My Regards to Broad Street / Jan. 1984 / Capitol ✦✦
McCartney's soundtrack to his poorly received feature film, this album contains re-recordings of Beatles songs and solo tunes, plus the hit single "No More Lonely Nights." —*William Ruhlmann*

Press to Play / Sep. 19, 1986 / Capitol ✦✦
This was Paul McCartney's first new studio album, either as a member of the Beatles or as a solo artist, not to go gold (i.e., sell half a million copies) upon initial release. It typically ranged from symphonic pop ("Only Love Remains") to rockers ("Pretty Little Head"), but was not one of McCartney's more impressive efforts. —*William Ruhlmann*

● **All the Best [U.S.]** / 1987 / Capitol ✦✦✦✦
Unfortunately, this second greatest-hits collection repeats many of the tracks from the first. But it does add the singles "C Moon" and "Goodnight Tonight" (previously unavailable on an album) and some of the bigger '80s hits, such as "Say Say Say" and "No More Lonely Nights." —*William Ruhlmann*

Flowers in the Dirt / May 1989 / Capitol ✦✦✦
A well-constructed comeback album on which McCartney collaborates with Elvis Costello for the Top 30 hit "My Brave Face," recalls his father on "Put It There," rocks out on "Figure of Eight," and turns in one of those lovely McCartney ballads on "This One." —*William Ruhlmann*

Tripping the Live Fantastic / Oct. 1990 / Capitol ✦✦
Paul McCartney's return to the stage in 1989 for the *Flowers in the Dirt* tour was heavily hyped, since it not only was his first extensive tour since the '70s, but also marked the first time he incorporated large portions of the Beatles catalog into his set list. The double-disc, 37-track *Tripping the Live Fantastic* documents the tour, and it's a pleasant, if ultimately inconsequential, nostalgia trip that puts the weaknesses of *Flowers in the Dirt* in a little too sharp of a relief. In fact, most of McCartney's flaws are on display throughout the album, whether it's his excessive cuteseness (the album opens with Paul and the boys being told "heidy-ho, it's time for the show"), his fondness for oldies, and his persistent desire to charm the daylights out of the entire crowd. Nevertheless, he often *does* charm the crowd, whether it's through the effortlessly dazzling performances or his thoroughly winning catalog of pop classics. The new songs may pale next to the classics from his Beatles and solo days, and those classics may be delivered in versions that are a little too studied, but *Tripping the Live Fantastic* is a fine exercise in nostalgia. —*Stephen Thomas Erlewine*

Liverpool Oratorio / 1991 / Angel ✦✦
Paul McCartney was commissioned by the Royal Liverpool Philharmonic Orchestra to compose a work to mark its 150th anniversary, and collaborated with composer-conductor Carl Davis on this 90-minute classical piece,which features soloists Kiri Te Kanawa and Jerry Hadley in a vaguely autobiographical story of a Liverpudlian named Shanty. While ambitious for an untaught musician like McCartney, the assignment didn't inspired him to any heights of melodic or lyrical achievement. In both areas, the piece plods, suggesting that McCartney hasn't so much taken on the unfamiliar form as surrendered to it. Maybe he should have worked with George Martin (who scored "Yesterday" and "Eleanor Rigby") instead. —*William Ruhlmann*

Unplugged (The Official Bootleg) / May 1991 / Capitol ✦✦✦✦
Released after the studied, meticulous *Flowers in the Dirt,* the live acoustic concert album *Unplugged* was a breath of fresh air, and it remains one of the most enjoyable records in McCartney's catalog. Running through a selection of oldies—not only his own, but Beatles and rock 'n' roll chestnuts—McCartney is carefree and charming, making

songs like "Be-Bop-a-Lula" and "Blue Moon of Kentucky" (which finds Paul melding Bill Monroe with Elvis) sound fresh. But the real revelations of the record are the songs McCartney hauls out from his debut—"That Would Be Something," "Every Night" and "Junk"—which sound lovely and timeless, restoring them to their proper place in his canon. They help make *Unplugged* into a thoroughly enjoyable minor gem. —*Stephen Thomas Erlewine*

Choba B CCCP / Oct. 28, 1991 / Capitol ✦✦
This album of rock 'n' roll oldies—"Lucille," "Twenty Flight Rock," etc.—was recorded in two days in July, 1987, and released exclusively in the Soviet Union in 1988. It finally saw release in the US in 1991 with one extra track, "I'm in Love Again," added. McCartney gives a spirited reading to the songs, which, it may be noted, are in some cases ("Ain't That a Shame," "Just Because") the same ones chosen by John Lennon for his similar *Rock 'N' Roll* album. But McCartney is characteristically more eclectic, including such ringers as "Summertime" and "Don't Get Around Much Anymore." —*William Ruhlmann*

Paul Is Live / Jan. 1, 1993 / Capitol ✦✦
McCartney's fourth live album in four years (including *Tripping the Live Fantastic—The Highlights*) is arguably his weakest yet, full of competent but utterly unnecessary versions of Beatles classics and recent McCartney numbers. Really, does anyone need to hear a live version of "Biker Like An Icon"? And after putting out two separate live albums from his previous tour, it smacks of overkill to release this record, which has the exact same band and tone as *Tripping the Live Fantastic*. —*Stephen Thomas Erlewine*

Off the Ground / Feb. 1993 / Capitol ✦✦
Paul McCartney gets an extra star for the song "Looking for Changes" from his latest *Off the Ground*. Its potent animal-rights message is married to a good tune, some sinewy playing, and a believable sense of commitment. Beyond this, the news is not as good. The advance hype pegged this release as a "return" to a harder, angry edge for cuddly Paul. The basic tracks were recorded live in the studio to impart an urgent feel. McCartney's social conscience may be active on songs like "Hope of Deliverance," "C'mon People," and "Peace in the Neighbourhood," but—more often than not—the album is awash in lame, gummy music and mawkish sentiment. —*Roch Parisien*

Flaming Pie / May 27, 1997 / Capitol ✦✦✦
According to McCartney, working on the Beatles *Anthology* inspired him to record an album that was stripped-back, immediate and fun, one that was less studied and produced than most of his recent work. In many ways, *Flaming Pie* fulfills those goals. A largely acoustic collection of simple songs, *Flaming Pie* is direct and unassuming, and at its best, it recalls the homely charm of *McCartney* and *Ram*. McCartney still has a tendency to wallow in trite sentiment, and his more ambitious numbers, like the string-drenched epic "Beautiful Night" or the silly Beatlesque psychedelia of "Flaming Pie," tend to fall flat. But when he works on a small scale, as on the waltzing "The Song We Were Singing," "Calico Skies," "Great Day," and "Little Willow," he's gently affecting, and the moderately rocking pop of "The World Tonight" and "Young Boy" is more ingratiating than the pair of aimless bluesy jams with Steve Miller. Even with the filler, which should be expected on any McCartney album, *Flaming Pie* is one of his most successful latter-day efforts, mainly because McCartney is at his best when he doesn't try so hard and lets his effortless melodic gifts rise to the surface. —*Stephen Thomas Erlewine*

James McCarty

b. Jul. 25, 1943, Liverpool, England
Guitar, Keyboard / Pop-Rock
James McCarty was one of the founding members of one of the seminal British Invasion groups, the Yardbirds. After leaving the group, he formed the progressive rock outfit Renaissance with Yardbirds vocalist Keith Relf. McCarty left Renaissance in 1973; he wrote material for Dave Berry and Dave Clark, among others, before attempting to re-form Renaissance in 1976. Sadly, the band's plans were destroyed by Relf's death in 1976; the group continued as Illusion. In 1983, he joined former Yardbirds Chris Dreja and Paul Samwell-Smith as Box of Frogs. In the late '80s, McCarty launched his own solo album, which has produced four albums that meld his blues-rock heritage with new age philosophies and musical textures. —*Stephen Thomas Erlewine*

● **Out of the Dark** / Feb. 7, 1994 / Higher Octave ✦✦✦✦
The are few modern albums that reflect the real spirit of the music in the 1960s. The haunting effect of something like Procol Harum's "A Whiter Shade of Pale" is hard to find today. James McCarty has survived a long musical journey through the 1960s and beyond to the 1990s with his message quite intact. The whole album has an other—or futureworld feel and yet no fussiness. There is real clarity here. The title cut is remarkable. —*Michael Erlewine*

Kathy McCarty

Alternative Pop-Rock
Singer-songwriter-guitarist Kathy McCarty helped make her former band Glass Eye one of the most interesting—if not commercially successful—bands to come out of the Austin, TX music scene. When they disbanded in 1993, McCarty decided to record an entire album dedicated to the songs of another local favorite, Daniel Johnston.

Johnston's songs possess the honesty and pain of the blues and the charm of the best pop music. Most of his recordings, done on a boombox with crude piano, guitar and even chord organ, are primitive while his songs range from sophisticated to almost child-like.

Because of Johnston's continuing battle with mental illness, it was unsure if he would ever record again. Being both a friend and a fan, McCarty decided to record the album as a "labor of love." —*Brett Hartenbach*

● **Dead Dog's Eyeball: The Songs of Daniel Johnston** / 1992 / Bar/None ✦✦✦✦
With the release of *Dead Dog's Eyeball*, Kathy McCarty has done the pop music world a great service; she has made the songs of Daniel Johnston accessible to all of those who may not have been able to get past the odd voice, bad recording, and less than polished performances of his homemade albums. McCarty fleshes out Johnston's music without covering up its original charm. She seems to grasp both the inherent darkness and irresistible poppiness in his songs. Check out the hooks she pulls out of songs like "Walking the Cow," "Rocket Ship," and "Museum of Love," as well as the pretty and sweet "Golly Gee," the troubled, jazzy "Desperate Man Blues," and the dissonant rocker "Sorry Entertainer." Highly recommended. —*Brett Hartenbach*

Sorry Entertainer [EP] / Nov. 21, 1995 / Bar/None ✦✦✦
Seven-song EP featuring three songs from *Dead Dog's Eyeball* (the previously available *Sorry Entertainer* and *Rocket Ship*, along with a terrific live version of *The Creature*), as well as interpretations of three other Daniel Johnston tunes, and a cut from McCarty's former band Glass Eye. Any of the new Johnston material would fit nicely on *Dead Dog's Eyeball*, but only *Love Wheel* could hold its own with the best tracks. Fans of Glass Eye will enjoy the addition of *Exodus Song*, although it seems to detract from the cohesiveness of the record as a whole. —*Brett Hartenbach*

The McCoys

f. 1963, Union City, IN
Pop-Rock
This Indiana group were still in high school when they were tapped by the Strangeloves production team of Feldman-Goldstein-Gottehrer as a vehicle for their material in 1965. Their first effort, "Hang on Sloopy," was a monster No. 1 smash, built around a riff and chorus that ranks with "Louie Louie" and "La Bamba" as a garage band perennial with its compelling, elemental simplicity. Featuring the lead vocals and lead guitar of a young Rick Derringer, they went on to cut a lot of similar chunky, innocuous pop-rock over the next couple of years with fair success. The "Hang on Sloopy" soundalike "Fever" was their only other Top Ten entry, and the Ritchie Valens cover "C'Mon Let's Go" their only other Top 40 hit.

The McCoys recorded very little original material during their early years at Bang Records; most of it was supplied by the Feldman-Goldstein-Gottehrer production team, much of which consisted of unexceptional derivations of the "Hang on Sloopy" prototype. Notable exceptions were the folky "Sorrow," covered for a Top Ten hit by the Merseys in Great Britain (and covered by David Bowie on *Pin Ups* a decade later), and the adventurous Middle Eastern-tinged garage psychedelia of "Don't Worry Mother," their best cut besides "Hang on Sloopy." The McCoys proved unusually durable after their career as a teen pop band; in the late '60s, they broke from their Bang producers to record psychedelic and progressive rock for Mercury. Most of the group joined Johnny Winter's backup band in the early '70s, and in 1973 Rick Derringer joined the Edgar Winter group as lead guitarist and vocalist, after which he had a successful hard rock solo career. —*Richie Unterberger*

● **Hang on Sloopy: The Best of the McCoys** / Jun. 6, 1995 / Legacy/Epic ✦✦✦✦
22-track compilation of their best mid-'60s material, including all the hits and tracks from their two Bang LPs, non-album singles, and a couple of previously unissued cuts. Much of this is rather forgettable if inoffensive, other than "Hang on Sloopy," "Fever," "Sorrow," and "Don't Worry Mother." —*Richie Unterberger*

Michael McDonald

b. 1952, St. Louis, MO

Vocals, Keyboards / Soul, Adult Contemporary, Pop-Rock

With his husky, soulful baritone, Michael McDonald became one of the most distinctive and popular vocalists to emerge from the laidback California pop/rock scene of the late '70s. McDonald found the middle ground between blue-eyed soul and smooth soft-rock, a sound which made him a star. He initially essayed his signature style with the Doobie Brothers, ushering in the group's most popular period with hits like "What a Fool Believes" and "Taking It to the Streets." McDonald disbanded the group in 1982 to pursue a solo career, which was initially quite successful, but by the end of the decade, his popularity had faded away, since he was reluctant to work regularly and hesitant to update his sound to suit shifting popular tastes.

After singing backup on several Steely Dan albums in the mid-'70s, Michael McDonald joined the Doobie Brothers in 1977. He was largely responsible for moving the group away from boogie-rock and toward polished, jazzy blue-eyed soul. Prior to the Doobies' farewell tour in 1982, he sang harmony on several hit single, including tracks by Donna Summer, Toto, Kenny Loggins, and Christopher Cross. As it turned out, McDonald's solo work was a cross between the Doobie Brothers' white-bread soul and Cross' adult contemporary ballads.

McDonald released his solo debut, *If That's What It Takes*, in 1982. The record climbed to No. 6 on the strength of the No. 4 single "I Keep Forgettin' (Every Time You're Near)," which also crossed over into the R&B Top Ten. In 1983, he had another Top 20 pop hit (and a Top Ten R&B hit) with his duet with James Ingram, "Yah Mo B There." McDonald didn't deliver his second solo album, *No Lookin' Back*, until 1985. The record wasn't as successful as its predecessor, producing only one moderate hit in its title track. He bounced back the following year, when his duet with Patti LaBelle, "On My Own," shot to No. 1 and "Sweet Freedom," his theme for the Billy Crystal/Gregory Hines comedy *Running Scared*, climbed into the Top Ten.

Instead of capitalizing on his revitalized success, McDonald didn't release another album until 1990. The resulting *Take It To Heart* was a bomb, peaking at No. 110. Two years later, his fortunes were revived somewhat when he sang on Aretha Franklin's minor hit, "Ever Changing Times," and he toured with Donald Fagen's *New York Rock and Soul Revue*. The following year, he released *Blink of an Eye*, which was ignored. In 1994, "I Keep Forgettin' (Every Time You're Near)" was sampled heavily in Warren G's smash hit "Regulate." By 1996, McDonald had returned to the Doobie Brothers, touring the oldies circuit with the reunited group. The following year, McDonald released *Blue Obsession*, his first album of new material in three years. —*Stephen Thomas Erlewine*

● **Sweet Freedom: The Best of Michael McDonald** / 1986 / Warner Brothers ✦✦✦✦

A solid collection that features all of McDonald's greatest hits from the early '80s. —*Stephen Thomas Erlewine*

Roger McGuinn

b. Jul. 13, 1942, Chicago, IL

Guitar, Vocals / Rock 'n' Roll, Country-Rock, Folk-Rock, Pop-Rock

As the frontman of the Byrds, Roger McGuinn and his trademark 12-string Rickenbacker guitar pioneered folk-rock and, by extension, country-rock, influencing everyone from contemporaries like the Beatles to acolytes like Tom Petty and R.E.M. in the process. James Joseph McGuinn was born on July 13, 1942 in Chicago, where by his teenage years he was already something of a folk music prodigy. After touring with the Limelighters, in 1960 he signed on as an accompanist with the Chad Mitchell Trio, appearing on the LPs *Mighty Day on Campus* and *Live at the Bitter End;* frustrated with his limited role in the group, he soon joined Bobby Darin's group when the singer moved from pop to folk.

After appearing on sessions for Hoyt Axton, Judy Collins and Tom & Jerry (soon to be known as Simon & Garfunkel), McGuinn began playing solo dates around the Los Angeles area, where he soon formed the Jet Set with area musicians David Crosby and Gene Clark. After a failed single under the name the Beefeaters, the group recruited bassist Chris Hillman and drummer Michael Clarke, changed their name to the Byrds, and set about crystallizing McGuinn's vision of merging the poetic folk music of Bob Dylan with the miraculous pop sounds heard via the British Invasion. McGuinn was the only member of the Byrds to play on their landmark debut single "Mr. Tambourine Man," but his jangly guitar work quickly became the very definition of the burgeoning folk-rock form; still, despite the Byrds' immediate success, both commercially and critically, the group was plagued by internal strife, and following the release of their 1968 country-rock breakthrough *Sweet-*

heart of the Rodeo, McGuinn was the only founding member still in the band.

Under the direction of McGuinn—who had changed his first name to Roger after a flirtation with the Subud religion—the Byrds soldiered on, delving further into country and roots music before finally dissolving in February 1973. That same year, McGuinn issued his self-titled solo debut, and ambitious, eclectic affair which explored not only folk and country but surf and even space rock. 1974's *Peace on You* and 1975's *Roger McGuinn and Band* preceded a stint with Bob Dylan's Rolling Thunder Revue before helping revitalize his standing within the musical community. 1976's *Cardiff Rose* was regarded as his best solo effort to date, but the next year's *Thunderbyrd*, which featured a cover of Tom Petty's "American Girl," failed to connect with audiences.

In late 1977, McGuinn reunited with Byrds mates Chris Hillman and Gene Clark; the resulting LP, 1979's *McGuinn, Clark & Hillman*, notched a Top 40 pop hit with the McGuinn-penned "Don't You Write Her Off." Midway through recording the follow-up, 1980's *Home*, Clark departed, and the album was released under the name Roger McGuinn and Chris Hillman featuring Gene Clark. Following another effort, 1981's *McGuinn/Hillman*, they went their separate ways. After undergoing another religious conversion, this time becoming a born-again Christian, McGuinn spent the remainder of the 1980s without a recording contract and performing solo dates.

The appearance of a faux-Byrds led by Michael Clarke prompted McGuinn to reform the group with Hillman and David Crosby in 1989, resulting in a series of club performances, an appearance at a Roy Orbison tribute , and a handful of new recordings for inclusion on a box set retrospective. In 1991—the same year the Byrds were inducted into the Rock and Roll Hall of Fame—McGuinn issued his first new solo recordings in over a decade, the all-star *Back to Rio*, which was met with great public and critical acclaim. *Live from Mars*, a retrospective of songs and stories, appeared in 1996.

Roger McGuinn / 1973 / Columbia ✦✦✦

Peace on You / 1974 / Columbia ✦✦✦

Roger McGuinn & His Band / 1975 / Columbia ✦✦✦

Cardiff Rose / 1976 / Columbia ✦✦✦✦

Thunderbyrd / 1977 / Columbia ✦✦✦

Back from Rio / 1990 / Arista ✦✦✦✦

This comeback effort put McGuinn together with Tom Petty & the Heartbreakers, former Byrds Chris Hillman and David Crosby, and other guest artists eager to pay tribute, like Michael Penn and Timothy B. Schmit. "King of the Hill" was a substantial FM rock hit. Other highlights include Elvis Costello's "You Bowed Down" and a fine version of Jules Shear's "If We Never Meet Again." The mainstream AOR production values make McGuinn sound like he's guesting on a Tom Petty record—which is not a bad thing, just an observation. —*Rick Clark*

● **Born to Rock & Roll** / Mar. 1992 / Columbia ✦✦✦✦

A well-chosen overview of McGuinn's post-Byrds solo work, it includes "American Girl," "I'm So Restless," "Lover of the Bayou," "My New Woman," and "Peace on You." —*Rick Clark*

Nitty Gritty Dirt Band-Roger McGuinn Live / 1994 / Javelin ✦✦✦✦

Someday someone may put out a full live Roger McGuinn album with 16 or 20 songs from across his repertory and history, but in the meantime, these four songs ("Turn, Turn, Turn," "Mr. Spaceman," "Mr. Tambourine Man," "Tiffany Queen") recorded at Little Darlin's Rock N' Roll Palace in Kissimmee, Florida will have to do. They're very well recorded, with McGuinn in excellent voice, backed by an uncredited band—the latter-day Byrds didn't do them much differently, though Clarence White's presence is missed (as it always will be). An announcer intro sort of blows the opening of "Mr. Tambourine Man," but otherwise this is a decent concert vignette. —*Bruce Eder*

Live from Mars / Nov. 19, 1996 / Hollywood ✦✦✦

Taking his cue from Ray Davies' "Storyteller" tour to support his autobiography *X-Ray*, Roger McGuinn constructed his live performances of the mid-'90s as a series of greatest hits, new songs, neglected gems, and witty, affectionate anecdotes of his life in the music industry. *Live from Mars* replicates one of these concerts, featuring classics like "Mr. Tambourine Man," "Turn, Turn, Turn," and "So You Want to Be a Rock "N" Roll Star" intercut with humorous stories and two new songs, "May the Road Rise to Meet You" and "Fireworks." For fans, *Live from Mars* is a small treasure, since it is one of McGuinn's friendliest and most relaxed recordings. —*Stephen Thomas Erlewine*

Barry McGuire

b. Oct. 15, 1935, Oklahoma City, OK
Vocals / Folk-Rock

Barry McGuire achieved one-hit-wonder status for the 1965 folk-rock protest song "Eve of Destruction," which topped the charts. He began his career in folk music earlier in the decade and had been a member of the New Christy Minstrels, for whom he co-wrote the hit "Green, Green." McGuire was unable to follow up "Eve Of Destruction" despite several subsequent releases, but he found success in the Christian music field in the 1970s. He now devotes his time to a charity that sponsors poor children in Third World countries. — *William Ruhlmann*

● **Anthology** / 1994 / One Way ✦✦✦✦
Althogh the packaging leaves something to be desired, all of Barry McGuire's hits, including "Eve of Destruction" and many similar-sounding protest folk-rockers, are featured on *Anthology.* — *Stephen Thomas Erlewine*

Maria McKee

b. Aug. 17, 1964, Los Angeles, CA
Guitar, Vocals / Rock 'n' Roll, Country-Rock, Alternative Pop-Rock

While she was with Lone Justice, Maria McKee always showed promise; her gritty, soulful mix of R&B, rock, and country helped distinguish the band from the multitude of '80s roots rockers. When she released her first solo album in the late '80s, it suffered from the same problem as Lone Justice—lots of potential, but no delivery. However, 1993's *You Gotta Sin to Get Saved* showed McKee making good on her promise, with an album of impassioned rockers and ballads. Three years later, McKee released her third solo album, *Life Is Sweet,* an album that marked a departure from her roots-rock roots and a movement toward alternative and art-rock. — *Stephen Thomas Erlewine*

Maria McKee / Jun. 1989 / Geffen ✦✦✦
Three years after Lone Justice's last album, Maria McKee released her self-titled debut, which showed that her skills as a songwriter had grown considerably since her first band. Not only were her songs better, but McKee's singing had improved; while it was still a little thin, her voice had grown grittier and more soulful, which made her songs all the more convincing. Unfortunately, most of McKee's musical growth was obscured by Mitchell Froom's mushy overproduction. — *Stephen Thomas Erlewine*

● **You Gotta Sin to Get Saved** / Jun. 22, 1993 / Geffen ✦✦✦✦
A few years after an underappreciated solo album, former Lone Justice leader Maria McKee returns with *You Gotta Sin to Get Saved,* her best album yet. With Black Crowes and Jayhawks producer George Drakoulias at the helm, *You Gotta Sin to Get Saved* evokes the country-rock vibe of the early '70s (much like the aforementioned groups) without sounding like a studied replica. McKee sings a dynamic mix of originals and covers with genuine conviction, making *You Gotta Sin to Get Saved* an album that demands repeated plays. — *Stephen Thomas Erlewine*

Life is Sweet / Mar. 26, 1996 / Geffen ✦✦✦
For most of her career, Maria McKee has never deviated from country-rock, but *Life Is Sweet* is a bold departure from her trademark sound, taking her into new sonic territories. Although the loud, distorted guitars are the first noticeable change, it soon becomes apparent that what makes the album sound so different are its latent progressive-rock influences. Throughout the album, McKee weaves complex, layered arrangements of strings, guitars, and keyboards. Appropriately, her melodies are more convoluted than ever before, yet they never become too obscure. Lyrically, she has become more cryptic and angry, but that is all part of the plan—*Life Is Sweet* is McKee's bid to be taken seriously as an artist. For some reason, that means she has constructed a hybrid of the prog-rock arrangements that dominate the first half of the album and the confessional songwriting that is prominent on the second. Fortunately, the results sound better than they read, primarily because beneath all of the bombastic arrangements, McKee has retained her keen sense of songcraft. Still, with its art-rock tendencies and naked ambition, *Life Is Sweet* may not appeal to fans that have become attached to McKee's country-rock. For those willing to accept her pretensions, it is a frustrating but rewarding album. — *Stephen Thomas Erlewine*

Sarah McLachlan

b. Jan. 28, 1968, Halifax, Nova Scotia, Canada
Guitar, Piano, Vocals / Singer-Songwriter, Alternative Pop-Rock, Folk-Rock, Adult Alternative Pop-Rock

Sincer her debut in 1988, Sarah McLachlan's atmospheric folk-pop has gained a devoted following of fans not only in Canada, where she has established star status, but also in the US and UK. Each album has shown her growing both as a musician and songwriter, continually rede-

fining herself and emerging as a major voice in the growing Adult Alternative Pop format.

Sarah McLachlan was born on January 28, 1968 in Halifax, Nova Scotia where she took vocal training in addition to classical piano and guitar lessons as a child. After a year of art training at the Nova Scotia School of Design, while fronting a new wave band, October Game, Nettwerk Records approached her for a solo deal. She initially turned it down in favor of continued studies, but took them up on the offer in late 1987 and relocated to Vancouver. On the strength of her debut, 1988's *Touch,* she was signed to Arista for international distribution. The album eventually reached gold status in Canada and was reissued worldwide in 1989. In 1991, she followed up with *Solace,* an impressive collection that showed a great leap in song craft and built a strong cult following in the US.

In September 1992, following a 14-month promotional tour, McLachlan traveled to Cambodia and Thailand for work on a Canadian-sponsored documentary on poverty and child prostitution, *World Vision.* Inspired by her experiences, she retreated to a secluded house outside of Montreal to write material for her next album. After six months in a Montreal studio with collaborator/producer Pierre March-and, *Fumbling Toward Ecstasy,* her strongest and most personal effort to date, was released in late 1993. The album peaked in the US charts at No. 50 and by the end of 1994, it reached platinum status after 62 weeks on the chart. "Possession," the single from the album, broke the Top 100 and received considerable airplay, especially on modern rock radio, where it reached No. 14. "Good Enough" also found a home in that format, reaching No. 16. *The Freedom Sessions,* consisting mainly of alternate versions of tracks from *Fumbling,* was released in 1995, and *Rarities, B-Sides and Other Stuff,* a collection of non-LP tracks and re-mixes, was issued in Canada in 1996. In 1997, McLachlan began work on her fourth album. In addition to her own albums, she has contributed tracks to several cause-related releases, provided the theme for the film *Brothers McMullen* ("I Will Remember You"), and organized the Lilith tour, a package tour focusing on emerging women singer-songwriters. — *Chris Woodstra*

Touch / 1989 / Arista ✦✦✦
On her debut effort, McLachlan sets the stage for future greatness. While only in her early twenties, she shows insights beyond her years with highly personal and introspective lyrics. — *Chris Woodstra*

Solace / Sep. 10, 1991 / Arista ✦✦✦✦
With her second album, McLachlan shows a marked improvement in songwriting. Yearning lyrics flow perfectly with her 12-string guitar, a tight rhythm section, and strong Celtic influences. A fine folk-pop effort. — *Chris Woodstra*

Live EP / Oct. 27, 1992 / Nettwerk ✦✦
An engaging live EP, replete with soaring vocals, sweeping sounds, and hypnotic percussion. McLachlan's music draws on a variety of influences, including pop and folk, but the hybrid result is something unique to her. McLachlan is a truly mesmerizing singer-songwriter. — *Steven McDonald*

● **Fumbling Towards Ecstasy** / Feb. 1, 1994 / Arista ✦✦✦✦
From the heavy dance beats of the opening single, "Possession," to the more delicate "Good Enough," McLachlan explores self-awareness and sensuality as well as a new world view in ways unrivaled by her previous efforts. Lush arrangements back her powerful vocals to build a highly rewarding album. — *Chris Woodstra*

The Freedom Sessions / Mar. 28, 1995 / Nettwerk ✦✦✦
A nice companion piece to *Fumbling Towards Ecstasy, The Freedom Sessions* offers seven early versions of songs from that album in a more stripped-down form. Also included is a cover of Tom Waits' "Ol' 55." — *Chris Woodstra*

Rarities, B-Sides, and Other Stuff / 1996 / Nettwerk ✦✦✦
In the time it took her to release her first three proper albums, Sarah McLachlan has put out nearly as much music as B-sides singles, or as stray tracks for compilations and soundtracks, leaving no easy job for fans wanting her entire output. *Rarities, B-Sides, and Other Stuff* collects 13 of these non-album tracks, including "I Will Remember You" from the *Brothers McMullen* soundtrack, "Dear God," the song she contributed to an XTC tribute album, a cover of Joni Mitchell's "Blue," and several re-mixes. While this by no means empties the vaults or even collects all the necessary B-sides (her spot-on version of Peter Gabriel's "Solsbury Hill," for instance, is not included), *Rarities'* focus on re-mixes *does,* in the end, provide an interesting and highly listenable alternate view of the artist. — *Chris Woodstra*

Don McLean

b. Oct. 2, 1945, New Rochelle, NY
Guitar, Vocals / Folk, Singer-Songwriter

Famed for—and ultimately defined by—his perennial "American Pie," singer-songwriter Don McLean was born October 2, 1945 in New Rochelle, NY. After getting his start in the folk clubs of New York City during the mid-'60s, McLean struggled for a number of years, building a small following through his work with Pete Seeger on the *Clearwater*, a sloop that sailed up and down the eastern seaboard to promote environmental causes.

Still, McLean was primarily singing in elementary schools and the like when in 1970 he wrote a musical tribute to painter Vincent Van Gogh; the project was roundly rejected by a number of labels, although MediaArts did offer him a contract to record a number of his other songs under the title *Tapestry*. The album fared poorly, but Perry Como earned a hit with a cover of the track "And I Love Her So," prompting United Artists to pick up McLean's contract. He returned in 1971 with *American Pie*; the title track, an elegiac eight-and-a-half-minute folk-pop epic inspired by the tragic death of Buddy Holly, became a No. 1 hit, and the LP soon reached the top of the charts as well.

The follow-up, "Vincent," was also a smash, and McLean even became the subject of the Roberta Flack hit "Killing Me Softly With His Song"; however, to his credit—and to his label's horror—the singer refused to let the success of "American Pie" straitjacket his career. After a time, he stopped performing the song live, and subsequent records like 1972's self-titled effort and 1974's *Playin' Favorites* deliberately avoided any attempts to re-create the "American Pie" flavor; not surprisingly, his sales plummeted, and the latter release even failed to chart. After 1974's *Homeless Brother* and 1976's *Solo*, United Artists dropped McLean from his contract; he resurfaced on Arista the next year with *Prime Time*, but when it too fared poorly, he spent the next several years without a label.

McLean enjoyed a renaissance of sorts with 1980's *Chain Lightning*, his first Top 30 LP in close to a decade, it spawned a Top Ten smash with its cover of Roy Orbison's classic "Crying," and his originals "Castles in the Air" and "Since I Don't Have You" both also reached the Top 40. However, 1981's *Believers* failed to sustain the comeback, and after 1983's *Dominion* he was again left without benefit of label support. McLean spent the remainder of his career primarily on the road, grudgingly restoring "American Pie" to his set list and drawing inspiration from the country market; in addition to a number of live sets and re-recordings of old favorites, he also returned to the studio for projects like 1990's *For the Memories* (a collection of classic pop, country, and jazz covers) and 1995's *River of Love* (an LP of original material). —*Jason Ankeny*

Tapestry / 1970 / MediaArts ◆◆◆
It took the success of Don McLean's second album, *American Pie*, to stimulate interest in his debut record, *Tapestry*. But once the new fans looked, they found that the album contained the same high level of pop-folk songwriting, if in a somewhat less epic form. "Castles in the Air" became a hit, and the album also contained McLean's version of his song "And I Love You So," which Perry Como successfully covered in 1973. —*William Ruhlmann*

American Pie / Oct. 1971 / EMI America ◆◆◆◆
The album that made McLean famous. The title track is the only real rocker, but the rest is intelligently produced and at times quite haunting, if a little angst-ridden. —*Bruce Eder*

Don McLean / 1972 / United Artists ◆◆◆◆
Don McLean's follow-up to the overwhelmingly successful *American Pie* inevitably fell short of its predecessor, but it was a strong collection, containing the chart entry "If We Try" and "Dreidel," which should have been a hit, too. —*William Ruhlmann*

Homeless Brother / 1974 / United Artists ◆◆◆
McLean turned in more of a light pop effort here, with the charming "Wonderful Baby" topping the adult contemporary chart, an excellent cover of "Crying In The Chapel," and another strong original in "La La Love You." —*William Ruhlmann*

Solo / 1976 / United Artists ◆◆◆
A surprisingly rewarding and personal live double-album. —*Bruce Eder*

Prime Time / 1977 / Arista ◆◆
McLean went in a dozen directions on this 1977 release. There are wild tunes like "Jump" (with great piano playing by Howie Wyeth), solemn ones like "The Statue," that is a solo vocal and string quartet (15 years before Elvis Costello's *The Juliet Letters*), and back-to-the-roots banjo playing on "Redwing." McLean has always believed in the power of melody and worked against the stereotype he was saddled with because of "American Pie." His albums are generally not commanding, but they demonstrate a loving breadth of material and his committed enthusiasm. —*Richard Meyer*

● **Greatest Hits Then & Now** / 1987 / Capitol ◆◆◆◆
For most fans, the single-disc *Greatest Hits Then & Now* will be all the Don McLean they need, since it compiles all of his hits and best-known songs on one concise disc. —*Stephen Thomas Erlewine*

Favorites & Rarities / 1992 / EMI America ◆◆◆◆
Fans of Don McLean should be thrilled with this comprehensive, digitally re-mastered, 42-track, double-disc set covering his hits, like "Ameri-

can Pie," "Castles in the Air," "Vincent," and "Everyday." There are also 18 previously unreleased tracks. Also included is an excellent set of liner notes, track annotations, and numerous photos from McLean's collection. —*Rick Clark*

River of Love / Oct. 24, 1995 / Curb ◆◆◆
In his liner notes to his first new studio album in quite a while, Don McLean recalled his earliest efforts to make music, when he was 15 in 1960. It was an appropriate memory, since on the album he seemed to be trying to write and sing the kind of light, romantic pop tunes typical of the pre-rock 1950s. While the tracks had blues and rock elements, the swooping strings turned the clock back, and the simple sentiments McLean sang of cemented the retro impression. There was a sense that the singer had found domestic contentment and religious faith after a rough period. But this happy state was expressed in terms so idealized and superficial it was hard to credit. —*William Ruhlmann*

Greatest Hits Live / Feb. 25, 1997 / Hip-O ◆◆◆
Recorded in London on October 4, 1980, this double CD presents 20 tracks dominated by McLean originals, with occasional oldies covers of the likes of Bobby Darin, Buddy Holly, and Roy Orbison. It's a sturdily executed set, some tracks embellished by a string section. Partially due to its length, it's an extraneous release, serious McLean fans being the target audience. —*Richie Unterberger*

Clyde McPhatter

b. Nov. 15, 1932, Durham, NC, **d.** Jun. 13, 1972, Teaneck, NJ
Vocals / R&B
As the lead singer for Billy Ward & His Dominoes and the Drifters, Clyde McPhatter was one of the most important R&B vocalists of the '50s. His high, passionate vocals were charged with gospel inflections, as well as blues—his fusion of the sacred and the secular was crucial in the development of R&B and soul. While his recordings with Ward and the Drifters were his most influential, McPhatter's solo records were equally excellent, as well as popular—his first nine solo singles were all Top Ten R&B hits, and three of those—"Treasure of Love," "Long Lonely Nights," "A Lover's Question"—were No. 1. However, his career began to slide in the '60s as he became increasingly dependent on alcohol. His abuse eventually led to his early death in 1972, yet Clyde McPhatter's legacy could be heard throughout the soul and R&B of the '60s and '70s, particularly in the seductive smooth soul of Al Green and the Spinners.

Clyde McPhatter first came to prominence as the lead singer for Billy Ward & the Dominoes. Ward had the teenaged McPhatter join the group in 1950, and over the next year, the group had no less than three major hits—"Do Something for Me," "I Am With You," and "Sixty-Minute Man." McPhatter's dynamic, gospel-flavored vocals were charged with sexual energy, and that certainly helped the singles become a hit. Furthermore, "Sixty-Minute Man" was one of the first R&B singles to cross over into the pop charts, establishing McPhatter's star power. He stayed with the group through 1952, as they racked up Top Ten hits with "Have Mercy Baby," "The Bells," "I'd Be Satisfied," and "These Foolish Things Remind Me of You."

In 1953, he formed the Drifters under the encouragement of Atlantic Records' Ahmet Ertegun. McPhatter found his future bandmates—David Baughan, William Anderson, David Baldwin, and James Johnson—singing with the Mount Lebanon Singers in a Harlem church, and the group formed shortly afterward. Because of McPhatter's established stardom, the Drifters were immediately a hit, but they stayed at the top of the R&B charts, and made a number of inroads on the pop charts, through a combination of excellent records and extraordinary live performances. "Money Honey," "Such a Night," "Honey Love," "White Christmas," and "Whatcha Gonna Do" all reached the top two slots on the R&B charts, and the Drifters' live shows, which featured passionate performances and stylized dance routines, were equally popular. The group was at the height of their popularity when McPhatter was drafted into the army late in 1954.

The Drifters continued without McPhatter, but his own career was sidelined for over a year. He returned late in 1955, initially with "Love Has Joined Us Together," a duet with Ruth Brown, which hit No. 8 on the R&B charts. Even though he had been away for a while, McPhatter's star power hadn't diminished, and between 1956 and 1959 he consistently hit the R&B Top Ten with "Seven Days," "Treasure of Love," "Without Love (There Is Nothing)," "Just To Hold My Hand," "Long Lonely Nights," "Come What May," and "A Lover's Question," many of which also reached the pop Top 20, as well. During the late '50s, it became apparent that his distinctive vocal style had influenced Sam Cooke and Elvis Presley, and soon McPhatter became overshadowed by those he had influenced. "A Lover's Question" became his first pop Top Ten hit in early 1959, and several Top 15 R&B singles—including "Lovey Dovey" and "You Went Back on Your Word"—followed that year, but his career was beginning to run out of steam. McPhatter left Atlantic for MGM early in 1960, switching to Mercury later that year. "Ta Ta," his first single for

Mercury, was a Top Ten R&B hit in the summer of 1960 and a year later "I Never Knew" reached number 17, but "Lover Please," a Top Ten pop hit in 1962, was his last significant hit. During the mid-'60s he only had one hit single, "Crying Won't Help You Now," and he began to succumb to alcoholism. In 1968, he moved to England, but despite his constant touring, he found little success there. Two years later, he returned to America and recorded the *Welcome Home* LP for Decca. It would prove to be his last recording. In 1972, McPhatter died of a heart attack which was aggravated by his alcohol abuse. Although he was neglected at the time of his death, his importance had been acknowledged by the end of the decade, and he was one of the first inductees to the Rock & Roll Hall of Fame in 1987. *—Stephen Thomas Erlewine*

★ **Deep Sea Ball: The Best of Clyde McPhatter** / Oct. 1, 1991 / Atlantic ◆◆◆◆◆
This 19-track compilation contains all of the top hits that McPhatter scored between 1956 and 1959. He also charted singles on MGM and Mercury, but the bulk of his best-remembered work is here, including "A Lover's Question" and "Treasure of Love." *—William Ruhlmann*

Meat Puppets

f. 1980, Tempe, AZ
Rock 'n' Roll, Alternative Pop-Rock, Hardcore Punk
Out of all of the bands that made SST Records a towering force in the American underground during the mid-'80s, the Meat Puppets lasted the longest, surviving where other bands fell apart. The Meat Puppets never had the dedicated following of Hüsker Dü or the Minutemen—two fellow SST bands that played the same circuit as the Puppets—but they were able to carve out a long career where other hardcore bands could not because they always drew from conventional hard rock as well as punk. Not only did they play hard, loud, and fast, but they also had elements of the blues-rock of ZZ Top, the ambling folk-rock of the Grateful Dead, and Neil Young's country-rock and hard rock. As they grew older, the band matured musically, developing an accomplished instrumental technique and moving closer to the traditional hard rock that was always underneath their punk; but they never quite abandoned their punk roots, even when they briefly broke into the mainstream in the early '90s.

The core of the Meat Puppets was Curt (guitar; born Jan. 10, 1959) and Cris Kirkwood (bass; born Oct. 22, 1960), a pair of brothers born and raised in Phoenix, AZ. As teenagers, the Kirkwoods played in local rock 'n' roll bands, primarily playing mainstream rock and hard rock. After graduating from a Jesuit prep school, the brothers formed the Meat Puppets in 1980 with drummer Derrick Bostrom. Unlike the Kirkwoods' earlier bands, the Meat Puppets were directly inspired by punk rock—they were so committed to keeping the music punk that they refused to rehearse.

A little over a year after their formation, the Meat Puppets released their first EP, *In a Car*, on World Imitation. At this point in their career, the band was at its noisiest, playing furious hardcore with avant-garde leanings. Greg Ginn, the lead guitarist for Black Flag and the head of SST Records, heard the record and offered the Meat Puppets a contract with SST. In 1982, the band released their full-length eponymous debut album on SST, which continued in the experimental vein of their EP.

The Meat Puppets didn't develop their own distinctive voice until their second album, *Meat Puppets II*, which was released in 1984. On *Meat Puppets II*, the band created a fusion of punk and country that sounded unlike anything else in the American underground. With their second album and constant touring, the Meat Puppets began to cultivate a dedicated cult following across the US that continued to grow throughout the rest of the decade. In 1985, the group released their third album, *Up on the Sun*, which earned them their first reviews in mainstream music publications. *Up on the Sun* also demonstrated that the band was beginning to streamline their sound, moving closer to traditional blues-rock, country-rock, and psychedelia. This shift toward conventional hard rock continued throughout the late '80s, as the band gradually sanded away their rougher, punk edges.

After releasing an EP called *Out My Way* in 1986, the Meat Puppets released two critically acclaimed albums—*Mirage* and *Huevos*—in 1987. By the release of *Mirage*, the Meat Puppets had established themselves as college radio stars, as well as popular attractions on the American underground circuit. *Monsters*, their final album for SST Records, was released in 1989 and its heavy rock attack foreshadowed the approach the band would adopt in the following decade. The straightforward sound of *Monsters* wasn't greeted favorably by the band's cult following and the record stiffed at college radio.

Following the weak reception of *Monsters*, the Meat Puppets broke up. In 1991, they re-formed and signed a major-label deal with London Records. Before they recorded their first album for London, SST issued the compilation *No Strings Attached* in 1990. The following year, *Forbidden Places*, the group's major-label debut, appeared in the stores.

Forbidden Places was neither a commercial nor an underground success.

For two years after the release of *Forbidden Places*, the Meat Puppets were relatively quiet, playing a couple of gigs every once in a while. In 1993, they re-emerged as an opening act on Nirvana's *In Utero* tour. Toward the end of the tour, Nirvana taped an appearance for *MTV Unplugged*, during which they covered three songs from *Meat Puppets II* with the Meat Puppets themselves. The exposure on *MTV Unplugged* helped set the stage for the commercial breakthrough of the band's second major-label album, 1994's *Too High to Die*. Released around the same time as *MTV Unplugged* originally aired, *Too High to Die* didn't gather much attention at first, but after Kurt Cobain's suicide in April, the record and its first single, "Backwater," began to move. This was due to radio's acceptance of "Backwater," but also to MTV's constant airings of Nirvana's *Unplugged*. By the summer of 1994, "Backwater" was a genuine hit, climbing to No. 2 on the album rock charts and just missing the pop Top 40. None of the other singles from *Too High to Die* performed quite as well, but the album was a success, becoming the group's first gold album. The Meat Puppets released *No Joke!*, their follow-up to *Too High to Die*, in the fall of 1995. The album received mediocre reviews and little airplay, and disappeared from the charts and radio a few months after its release. *—Stephen Thomas Erlewine*

Meat Puppets / 1982 / SST ◆◆◆
Considering what they sound like these days, it's hard to imagine what an explosively noisy trio the Pups were around the time of their debut. There are bits and pieces of the country, folk and blues stylings that would show up on later recordings, but the first time out there was plenty of noise, feedback, arrhythmic bashing, and screeched vocals. In other words, if you've become a Meat Pups fan on the strength of their last few records, this one will set your head spinning. It ain't nothing like anything else they've ever done. *—John Dougan*

● **Meat Puppets II** / 1983 / SST ◆◆◆◆
More traditional songs, less noise, more great Curt Kirkwood guitar and vocals, this LP has been referred to as a seminal slice of country-punk, and who am I to argue? This record was a startling mini-masterpiece, primarily because their debut record hadn't prepared anyone for this sudden stylistic shift. And, in typical Meat Puppets fashion, they pulled it off without batting an eye, as if they'd been recording music like this for many years. One of the great rock records of the '80s. *—John Dougan*

Up on the Sun / 1985 / SST ◆◆◆◆
Moving even farther away from the dissonance of their debut, the Pups at this juncture were sounding more and more like a (gasp!) regular old rock band. But only a fool would consider their debut the best record of their career; clearly there was much more to this band than what met the ear(s). *Up on the Sun* continues the postmodern country punk of *II* and offers up great greasy globs of guitar thanks to Curt Kirkwood's rapidly improving playing. There are some moments on this record that even leave rock behind in favor of folkie quietude, but for Meat Pups fans, they were turning into a formidable band unjustly ignored by the world. *—John Dougan*

Out My Way / 1986 / SST ◆◆◆◆
Out My Way is a six-song EP that finds the Meat Puppets expanding their punky, psychedelicized country-rock with tougher, grittier grooves that border on funk. Furthermore, their songwriting has improved, which means their chaotic deconstruction of "Good Golly Miss Molly" isn't the most impressive thing here. *—Stephen Thomas Erlewine*

Mirage / 1987 / SST ◆◆◆
Mirage signals the start of the period of the Meat Pups' career when they began the transformation (subtle though it was) from a wonderfully messy punk band to a slightly less messy rock band. As usual, Curt's guitar is the star and at times he sounds like the psychedelic hippie-punk offspring of Doc Watson on tracks like "Confusion Fog." Still, the Pups were, in terms of playing, songwriting, and production, light years beyond the first album, and that was a good thing. Unlike many maturing bands, the Meat Puppets are one of the few that remain consistently good without sounding as though they are pandering to an audience. *—John Dougan*

Huevos / 1987 / SST ◆◆◆◆
With *Huevos*, the Meat Puppets crafted a tribute to ZZ Top that was only slightly ironic. Curt Kirkwood had been listening to a lot of the Texas trio, and that came through on *Huevos* in fat slabs of loud, richly distorted Les Pauls and the country-fried boogie rhythms. Of course, the direct attack had some longtime fans branding the Meat Puppets as sellouts, but the group's impressive leaps in technical skills and songwriting are the only logical conclusion to the progression they started with *Meat Puppets II*. *—Stephen Thomas Erlewine*

Monsters / 1989 / SST ◆◆◆
I lump *Huevos* and *Monsters* together mainly because they are built around a similar "big rock" guitar sound. Curt had been listening to a lot of ZZ Top at this point (not a bad thing to do, I might add!) and the effect

on the music of the Meat Puppets was obvious. Now playing Les Paul guitars and fancying a louder, more aggressive, fat, distorted wall of sound, the Pups sounded like world beaters on these two records. Old-time fans and purists were decidedly distraught when these records came out, for it sounded as though the Pups had simply decided to sound like just another country/blues-tinged hard rock band, but that was only true on the more mediocre songs; the reality was that the Pups were now diamond hard and airtight. The proof of this is in songs like "Bad Love," "Sexy Music," and "I Can't Be Counted On" (from *Huevos*) and "Attacked by Monsters," "Meltdown," and "Party Til the World Obeys" (from *Monsters*). At this point (later borne out by Kurt Cobain during Nirvana's *Unplugged* gig) the Pups had become a tremendously influential American rock band. *—John Dougan*

No Strings Attached / 1990 / SST ✦✦✦
An extremely well-thought-out two-LP sampler of the Pups from their SST days. Tracks go up to and include material from *Monsters*. SST released this after the band left the venerable indie label for London in 1990. An excellent anthology. *—John Dougan*

Forbidden Places / Jul. 9, 1991 / London ✦✦✦
Few of the best bands that recorded for SST in the '80s (Hüsker Dü, Minutemen, Black Flag) stayed with the label as long as did the Meat Puppets, and as a result, their leaving for a major label in 1990 seemed anti-climactic. *Forbidden Places*, while not as immediately gripping as some of the Meat Pups' better records, is a consistently enjoyable slice of psychedelic hard rock. The record's opening track, the annoying "Sam," got a lot of airplay on alternative rock stations, but it was not nearly as good as (or indicative of) the rest of the music. It should be noted that Curt Kirkwood's singing, never a strength, sounds improved here. Had he been taking voice lessons? *—John Dougan*

Too High to Die / Jan. 25, 1994 / London ✦✦✦✦
Still crazy after all these years, the Pups sound in fine fettle on this appropriately named recording, but a touch of sameness is starting to creep in, making *Too High* probably the least essential of the band's later recordings. Being a laidback rock band can be cool, but it can also mean that falling into a rut is easier than taking on new challenges. But if the history of the Meat Puppets teaches us anything, it's that this band is capable of surprises—and plenty of them! *—John Dougan*

No Joke! / Oct. 3, 1995 / London ✦✦
Too High to Die was a surprise success in 1994, so it's not a big surprise that the Meat Puppets didn't mess with the formula for their follow-up, *No Joke!* Not that the band's essential sound has changed all that much over the years—it's still a warped, sun-fried amalgam of punk, Southern rock, heavy metal, and country. For *Too High to Die*, they had not only streamlined their approach enough to appeal to a wider audience, but the music world had changed enough to make them seem like a mainstream rock 'n' roll band. *No Joke!* might have a heavier production than its predecessor, but the tunes and riffs are cut from the same mold as before. It's an extremely competent album and is frequently enjoyable, but it doesn't have the same wild spark as their mid-'80s classics, nor does it have the bizarre sense of humor—which makes *No Joke!* just an average Meat Puppets record. *—Stephen Thomas Erlewine*

Meat Loaf

b. Jan. 22, 1946, Dallas, TX
Pop-Rock
Marvin Lee Aday was a singer and occasional actor who, for reasons never definitively answered, recorded under the name Meat Loaf. In all likelihood a childhood nickname, the tag stuck, and many puns followed as the performer—who tipped the scales at well over 300 pounds—became one of the biggest chart acts of the 1970s before enjoying a commercial renaissance two decades later.

Meat Loaf was born in Dallas, TX. The product of a family of gospel singers, he moved to L.A. in 1967 and formed a group known as both Meat Loaf Soul and Popcorn Blizzard. The band earned some renown through opening gigs in support of the Who, the Stooges, and Ted Nugent before Meat Loaf won a role in a West Coast production of the musical *Hair*. During a tour stop in Detroit, he and a fellow cast-mate named Stoney teamed to record the 1971 LP *Stoney and Meat Loaf* for Motown's Rare Earth imprint.

After a tenure in the off-Broadway production *Rainbow (In New York)*, Meat Loaf earned a slot in *More Than You Deserve*, a musical written by classically-trained pianist Jim Steinman. An appearance in the cult film *The Rocky Horror Picture Show* followed, and in 1976 Meat Loaf also handled vocal duties on one side of Nugent's LP *Free-for-All*. Soon, Meat Loaf re-teamed with Steinman for a tour with the National Lampoon Road Show, after which Steinman began composing a musical update of the Peter Pan story titled *Never Land*.

Ultimately, much of what Steinman composed for *Never Land* became absorbed into 1977's *Bat out of Hell*, the album that made Meat Loaf a star. Produced by Todd Rundgren, the record was pure melodrama, a teen rock opera that spawned three Top 40 singles—"Two Out

of Three Ain't Bad," "Paradise by the Dashboard Light," and "You Took the Words Right out of My Mouth"—on its way to becoming one of the best-selling albums of the decade.

A sequel was planned, but in 1981 Steinman issued his own solo debut, *Bad for Good*. After Meat Loaf released his own follow-up, *Dead Ringer*, rumors began flying, and it was reported that Loaf had been unable to record the songs comprising the Steinman album due to physical and emotional problems. Eventually, Steinman filed suit against Meat Loaf and his label, Epic, and none of his songs appeared on the 1983 Meat Loaf effort *Midnight at the Lost and Found*. After subsequent records like 1984's *Bad Attitude* and 1986's *Blind Before I Stop* bombed, the singer declared bankruptcy and began physical and psychological rehabilitation to restore his road-ravaged voice.

After several years in relative obscurity, Meat Loaf and Jim Steinman reunited in 1993 for *Bat out of Hell II: Back into Hell*, which continued the original's story-line and duplicated its thunderous sound. The follow-up proved even more successful than the first *Bat out of Hell*, selling over ten million copies within its first three months of release alone and yielding a massive hit single with "I'd Do Anything for Love (But I Won't Do That)."

Without Steinman, he returned in 1995 with *Welcome to the Neighborhood. —Jason Ankeny*

● **Bat Out of Hell** / 1978 / Epic ✦✦✦✦
Meat Loaf's powerful, passionate voice serves as the messenger for Jim Steinman's over-the-top rock songs, which treat teenage angst in practically Wagnerian terms, while Todd Rundgren provides a clean, well-articulated Wall of Sound production in this kitsch masterpiece, which includes "Two Out of Three Ain't Bad" and "Paradise by the Dashboard Light." *—William Ruhlmann*

Meatloaf (Featuring Stoney) / 1979 / Prodigal ✦✦
In 1971, Meat Loaf was signed to Motown Records' Rare Earth subsidiary in a vocal duo with a woman named Stoney, and Rare Earth released a couple of singles and an album (*Stoney and Meatloaf*, September 1971, Rare Earth 529), getting some minor chart action out of one of the singles. Six years later, Meat Loaf became a success with *Bat out of Hell*, and in October 1978, Motown's Prodigal subsidiary unearthed six tracks from the *Stoney and Meatloaf* LP, added three previously unreleased tracks, and released *"Meatloaf" Featuring Stoney and Meatloaf*. Meat Loaf's distinctive dramatic tenor is identifiable on these hard rock tracks, but the material is in no way comparable to the style he later developed for *Bat out of Hell*. *—William Ruhlmann*

Dead Ringer / 1981 / Epic ✦✦✦
Although it took Meat Loaf and composer Jim Steinman another 12 years to come up with the marketing gimmick of positioning an album as a deliberate follow-up to the multi-platinum *Bat out of Hell*, *Dead Ringer* was the *real Bat II*. Once again, Steinman wrote extended, operatic songs with hyperbolic lyrics ("I'll Kill You If You Don't Come Back" was one title) and organized a backup band anchored by E Street Band members Max Weinberg (drums) and Roy Bittan (keyboards), while Meat Loaf sang with a passion all the more compelling for its hint of the ridiculous. In the US, with four years separating *Bat* and *Dead Ringer*, nobody cared much. But in the UK, where *Bat* was still going strong, *Dead Ringer* topped the charts, and the title track, featuring a perfectly cast Cher as duet singer, went Top Ten. In retrospect, the missing ingredient in the album is Todd Rundgren's pop sensibility as producer; he was the one who knew how long the compositions could go for maximum dramatic impact without becoming exhausting. It was Rundgren who made *Bat out of Hell* a fiery listening experience—producing himself, Meat Loaf often sounded only warmed over. *—William Ruhlmann*

Midnight at the Lost & Found / 1983 / Epic ✦✦
Singer Meat Loaf and composer Jim Steinman tried to do without producer Todd Rundgren, who had handled their masterpiece, *Bat out of Hell*, on its follow-up, *Dead Ringer*, and they managed okay. But then Meat Loaf tried to do without Steinman on the third album, *Midnight at the Lost and Found*, and didn't even come close. Meat Loaf was in typically impassioned form, but the material just didn't scale the heights of Steinman's incredible hubris. The US had long since lost interest, but even in the UK, where Meat Loaf was loved, the album was a step down commercially. *—William Ruhlmann*

Hits Out of Hell / 1984 / Epic ✦✦✦
Since Meat Loaf's *Bat out of Hell* album is vastly better than its follow-ups, *Dead Ringer* and *Midnight at the Lost and Found*, the idea of doing a hits compilation culling familiar tracks from the three albums is not really a good one. But the second and third albums did feature UK hits, and *Hits* does contain the four key tracks from *Bat*—the title track, "Two Out of Three Ain't Bad," "You Took the Words Right out of My Mouth," and "Paradise by the Dashboard Light." A few tracks from *Dead Ringer*, notably "Read 'Em and Weep" and "I'm Gonna Love Her for Both of Us," are in the same spirit, but the songs from *Midnight* are simply inferior. *—William Ruhlmann*

Bad Attitude / 1984 / Fame ✦✦✦
Meat Loaf collects a couple of Jim Steinman songs and he, Paul Jacobs, and Mack work at re-creating the Todd Rundgren production sound for an album of high-voltage rock. (Originally released on Arista Records in the UK in October 1984, *Bad Attitude* was released in the US on RCA Records in April 1985.) —*William Ruhlmann*

Blind Before I Stop / 1986 / Arista ✦✦
Rather than aping the grandiose rock 'n' roll style pioneered by Jim Steinman and Todd Rundgren on Meat Loaf's landmark *Bat out of Hell* album, German producer Frank Farian opts for a standard-issue heavy metal approach on *Blind Before I Stop*, emphasizing a heart-stoppingly loud rhythm section (sometimes playing at Eurodisco tempo), icy keyboards in the mid-range, and endlessly diddling high-pitched guitar solos on a series of forgettable tunes. Somewhere in the back of the mix, Meat Loaf exercises his adenoids, but all of his usual distinctiveness is lost in the sludge. —*William Ruhlmann*

Bat Out of Hell II: Back into Hell / 1993 / MCA ✦✦✦✦
Although Meat Loaf has made several albums since *Bat out of Hell* (most of them never released in the US), *Bat out of Hell II: Back into Hell* is an explicit sequel to that milestone of '70s pop culture. Reprising the formula of the original nearly to the letter, *Back into Hell* is bombastic and has too much detail, thanks to the pseudo-operatic splendor of Jim Steinman's grandly cinematic songs. From the arrangements to the length of the tracks, everything on the album is overstated; even the album version of the hit single, "I Would Do Anything for Love (But I Won't Do That)," is 12 minutes long. Yet that's precisely the point of this album, and also why it works so well. No other rock 'n' roller besides Meat Loaf could pull off the humor and theatricality of *Back into Hell* and make it seem real. In that sense, it's a worthy successor to the original. —*Stephen Thomas Erlewine*

Welcome to the Neighbourhood / Nov. 14, 1995 / Virgin ✦✦✦
After having scored a surprising commercial comeback with 1993's *Bat out of Hell II: Back into Hell*, his reunion with songwriter Jim Steinman, Meat Loaf tried to make it on his own, just as he had from 1983 to 1993, and with similarly disappointing results. As with albums like *Bad Attitude*, a couple of Steinman songs were tossed in, in this case the minor "Original Sin" (copyright 1989) and "Left in the Dark" (copyright 1980), a song previously cut by Barbra Streisand. But most of the album's songwriting was provided by a team of people, including pop songwriter Diane Warren, Van Halen lead singer Sammy Hagar, and ex-E Streeter Steven Van Zandt, plus producer Ron Nevison, trying to clone the flamboyant Steinman style and failing to do so. In particular, the Warren material (which sounded more like the kind of thing she tends to write for Michael Bolton) lacked Steinman's gothic excess, sly humor, and lyrical reach. Meat Loaf, as usual, sang like his life depended on it, while a band that was less distinctive than it should have been given such notable participants as Kenny Aronoff and Kasim Sulton churning out sub-metal riffs. The resulting sales fall-off was not as great as it had been before, but it remained true that Meat without Steinman was only half a loaf. —*William Ruhlmann*

Live Around the World / 1996 / Tommy Boy ✦✦✦
Deliberately theatrical, over the top, and overblown, Meat Loaf's unapologetically '70s-sounding arena rock is exactly the type of music rock critics love to loathe. But what separates Meat Loaf's music from so much corporate rock is the amount of conviction he brings to it. *Live Around the World* may be campy, but it's an honest campiness—never does this live two-CD set come across as contrived or formulaic. When Meat Loaf rips into "Paradise by the Dashboard Light," "Rock and Roll Dreams Come True," "Bat out of Hell," and other odes to the suburban adolescent experience, his sincerity is hard to miss. Even so, the package is unlikely to change anyone's mind—Meat Loaf lovers will find much to admire, his detractors much to lash out at. —*Alex Henderson*

Joe Meek
....

b. 1929, Glouster, England, **d.** Feb. 3, 1967, London, England
Pop-Rock
Not an artist in the traditional sense of the term—he couldn't play or sing at all—producer Joe Meek has nonetheless been belatedly recognized as an important, even inimitable, figure of early British rock 'n' roll. Like Phil Spector, Meek developed idiosyncratic production techniques that, much more than the artists he worked with, stamped a vision of mad genius on his recordings. In Meek's case, this usually amounted to super-compressed sound, wavering sped-up vocals, ghostly backing violins and choruses, spooky echo and reverb, ticky-tack vari-speed piano, and all manner of Halloween and outer-space sound effects. The recordings were all the more remarkable for being produced not in a state-of-the-art studio, but in Meek's own bedroom-sized facility, located over a shop within the flat he rented.

Meek couldn't rightly be compared to Phil Spector—he favored gawky, dippy teen-idol fare for gawky, dippy teen idols, not the gutsy soul and R&B-infused Wall of Sound. But he was a trailblazer in his own

right—even before Spector, he set up shop as rock 'n' roll's very first independent producer of note, making recordings on his own terms and leasing them to labels for distribution. In the US, he only scored big with the Tornados' "Telstar" (the first British rock 'n' roll record to top the American charts, a year before the Beatles) and the Honeycombs' "Have I the Right." In the UK, he produced scores of records—many of them flops, and many others hits—for the Tornados, Honeycombs, Screaming Lord Sutch, John Leyton, Heinz, the Outlaws (featuring Ritchie Blackmore for a time), and many more. Highly prized by some collectors, these range from brilliant to insufferably insipid, though, as none other than Jello Biafra noted in the book *Incredibly Strange Music Volume 2*, "you can tell a Joe Meek record a mile away."

Meek's business and production methods may have been ahead of his time, but his actual musical tastes actually started to run behind the times with the advent of the self-contained groups of the British Invasion. He actually recorded a few respectable efforts in the R&B-mod vein, but his career was in a severe spiral by the time his life ended in tragic circumstances in early 1967, when he shot his landlady and himself. The existing CD compilations of his work don't actually do him justice; it's better to seek out the greatest hits collections of the artists mentioned above. John Repsch's book *The Legendary Joe Meek* (published in the UK only) is a good biography of this fascinating figure. —*Richie Unterberger*

Joe Meek Story, Vol. 1 / 1991 / Line ✦✦✦
Although one can hear the genesis of some of Meek's unique methods on this 20-track collection of 1960 releases, the material and performances are fairly insufferable, exhibit A in the lameness of much pre-Beatle British rock. Includes the super-rare (and silly) science fiction EP about intelligent life in outer space that he created with then-futuristic sound effects and tape manipulation under the moniker "The Blue Men." —*Richie Unterberger*

Joe Meek Story: The Pye Years / 1991 / Sequel ✦✦✦
Forty-eight-track double CD of Meek productions released on the British Pye label between 1960 and 1966 give a surprisingly scattershot and fragmented overview of his work, with an overabundance of weak early '60s-type teen idol and instrumental fare, despite some strong tracks by the Honeycombs, Riot Squad, and Glenda Collins. —*Richie Unterberger*

I Hear a New World / 1991 / RPM ✦✦✦
In 1960, Meek—already thinking in terms that couldn't be constrained by the limits of the day's technologies and marketing strategies—devised a "concept LP" of sorts that speculated about the nature of life on the moon (this was almost ten years before Apollo 11, remember). Working with a group of musicians he dubbed the Blue Men, this "outer space music fantasy" tried to conjure the mood of the cosmos with the clavioline, a Hawaiian guitar, a rinky-dink piano, and then-futuristic electronic noises and sound effects. Listening today, the largely instrumental work sounds futuristic in a very dated way, especially the Chipmunk-like electronically sped-up voices that were meant to simulate those little green men. As Monty Python would say, it all sounds a bit silly, but it's an interesting insight into his unique production techniques—the sounds he sculpted for "Magnetic Field," for instance, are a clear forerunner of the electronic pulses that open and close "Telstar." Only four tracks from the opus were released at the time, on a super-rare EP; 30 years later, this CD presented the full work to the public for the first time. —*Richie Unterberger*

Work in Progress: The Triumph Sessions / 1994 / RPM ✦✦
Twenty-seven outtakes, demos, and previously unissued tracks that Meek recorded at his Triumph label in 1959 and 1960. Most of these are unfinished (sometimes they're not even close to finished); the West Five and the Fabulous Flee-Rakkers get about half the tracks, and such fellow no-names as Chick Lewis, Ricky Wayne, Yolanda, Lee Sutton, and Eve Boswell fill out the compilation (John Leyton, who did eventually get some hits, has one track). Stylistically it's all over the board, from instrumental '50s rock to rockabilly to pop ballads and awful lounge piano singing, as well as a couple of demos featuring Meek's own off-key vocals. It's been assembled not for the general listener, but for the Meek scholar, who knows full well that the quality of both the audio and the actual songs isn't up to what you'll find on most CDs, by Meek or anybody else. It's patchy, sometimes embarrassingly so, but it does provide insights into the man's methods at a time when he was just spreading his wings. Sometimes it's kinda cool, especially when Meek plays around with echo and odd effects/arrangements. Mostly, though, it's only of use to the Joe Meek fan club, which is no slur upon the label that compiled the disc—that's exactly the kind of audience for which it was intended. —*Richie Unterberger*

● **It's Hard to Believe: The Amazing World of Joe Meek** / Oct. 1995 / Razor & Tie ✦✦✦✦
Twenty of Meek's most notable hit singles and misses from 1960 to 1966. Includes his biggest hit productions (the Tornados' "Telstar," the Honeycombs' "Have I the Right," Heinz' "Just like Eddie," Mike Berry's "Tribute to Buddy Holly," John Leyton's "Johnny Remember Me"). Just as

intriguing, though, are the more obscure items, some of which are hard or impossible to find on other compilations. Among these are the wild horror-rock of Screaming Lord Sutch's "'Til the Following Night," the super-creepy Moontrekkers instrumental "Night of the Vampire," the soul-pop of the Riot Squad (with Mitch Mitchell on drums), brassy femme pop by Glenda Collins, and a couple of excerpts from *I Hear a New World*, his bizarre outer-space opus. There are many other interesting Meek discs out there for those who want to go further, but this is an excellent introduction. —*Richie Unterberger*

Let's Go! Joe Meek's Girls / 1996 / RPM ✦✦✦

When you take the plunge into a Joe Meek rarity CD, you have fair warning that you're not going to encounter many lost masterworks. This compilation of 29 tracks by female singers he worked with in the early and mid-'60s, though, is one of the better ones on the market. None of these—by the likes of Jenny Moss, Gunilla Thorn, Kim Roberts, and Yolanda—were hits (ten tracks weren't even previously released), and frankly they didn't deserve to be, due to the extremely innocuous and slight nature of the material. That's not, however, what Meek connoisseurs are seeking with these archival releases. You want examples of Meek's inimitable outer space bathroom production techniques, whether highly polished or in progress, and you get them here, via the Casper-the-ghost strings, compressed percussion, and spooky keyboards. Which makes it a not half-bad document if you've got the Meek bug, even if the songs themselves are completely overshadowed by their embellishments, although the odd tune (Jenny Moss' "Hobbies," Pamela Blue's "Hey There Stranger," and especially Glenda Collins' dramatic "Baby It Hurts") carried some hit potential. —*Richie Unterberger*

Megadeth

f. 1983, Los Angeles, California
Thrash, Heavy Metal, Speed Metal
After he left Metallica in 1983, guitarist/vocalist Dave Mustaine formed the thrash metal quartet Megadeth. Though Megadeth followed the basic blueprint of Metallica's relentless attack, Mustaine's group distinguished themselves from his earlier band by lessening the progressive-rock influences, adding an emphasis on instrumental skills, speeding the tempo up slightly, and making the instrumental attack harsher. By streamlining the classic trash-metal approach and making the music more threatening, as well as making the lyrics more nihilistic, Megadeth became one of the leading bands of the genre during the mid- and late '80s. Each album they released went at least gold and they continually sold out arenas across America, in addition to developing a strong following overseas. By the early '90s, they had toned their music down slightly, but that simply increased their following—both 1992's *Countdown to Extinction* and 1994's *Youthanasia* debuted in the US Top Ten.

Throughout Megadeth's many lineup changes, the two core members have been bassist Dave Ellefson and guitarist-vocalist Dave Mustaine (born Sept. 13, 1961), who is the band's official leader. Mustaine grew up in the suburbs of Southern California, where he was raised by his mother in a broken home; frequently, his mother left him to be raised by aunts and uncles, who never encouraged his musical inclinations and often belittled him for his fondness for heavy metal. In 1981, he formed Metallica with James Hetfield and Lars Ulrich. Mustaine spent two years with Metallica, developing a strong cult following in California's underground metal scene, before he was kicked out of the group, allegedly over his substance abuse. Immediately following his firing, he formed Megadeth with Ellefson. The pair recruited guitarist Chris Poland and drummer Gars Samuelson to round out the lineup.

For the next few years, Megadeth toured and gained a following, eventually signing with the independent label Combat in 1985. Later that year, the group released their debut, *Killing Is My Business... And Business Is Good!*, which received strong reviews, not only in metal-oriented publications, but also in mainstream music magazines. The album sold very well for an independent release, which attracted the attention of major record labels. By the end of the year, the group had signed with Capitol. Megadeth's first major-label album, *Peace Sells... But Who's Buying?* was released in the fall of 1986. Like its predecessor, *Peace Sells* was greeted with strong reviews and sales; it eventually went platinum.

Although the band's fortunes were on the upswing, Mustaine was beginning to sink deeper into drug abuse, as he began using heroin. Soon, his addictions began to affect his work. Many stories concerning his erratic behavior were circulating within the metal community, and they seemed to be proven correct when he fired both Poland and Samuelson before the recording of the band's third album; they were replaced by Jeff Young and Chuck Behler, respectively. The new lineup debuted on *So Far, So Good... So What!*, released early in 1988. *So Far, So Good* peaked at No. 28 on the charts and went gold, and featured a cover of the Sex Pistols' "Anarchy in the UK."

In the years immediately following the release of *So Far, So Good... So What!*, Mustaine was impaired by his drug addictions. In early 1990, he was arrested for driving under the influence and entered a rehabilitation program. By the end of the year, he was not only sober, but he had reconvened the band—firing Young and Behler and replacing them with guitarist Marty Friedman and drummer Nick Menza—and recorded Megadeth's fourth album, *Rust in Peace*. The record peaked at No. 23 on the American charts and went gold.

Countdown to Extinction was released two years later, entering the charts at No. 2; the record went platinum, confirming that the band retained its audience in the wake of grunge. Megadeth followed the album with *Youthanasia* in 1994. *Youthanasia* entered the charts at No. 4 and, like its predecessor, it went platinum. The following year, the group released *Hidden Treasures*, a rarities collection that entered the charts at its peak position of 90. —*Stephen Thomas Erlewine*

Killing Is My Business... and Business Is Good! / 1985 / Combat ✦✦✦

After his exit from Metallica, Dave Mustaine regrouped with his own band on this debut album, accentuating his own chaotic, driving rhythm guitar work and careening, lightning-fast solos. The music here is as raw as Megadeth gets, and that can be both good and bad—Megadeth's later precise, complex riffing and composition aren't completely developed, but the music is performed with a great deal of raw energy, while Mustaine's vocals (never his strong point) are amateurish at best. Highlights include a retooled version of Nancy Sinatra's "Boots" and "Mechanix," a Mustaine composition written with Metallica that turned into the latter's "The Four Horsemen." —*Steve Huey*

● Peace Sells... But Who's Buying? / 1986 / Capitol ✦✦✦✦

Arguably Megadeth's strongest effort and a classic of early thrash, *Peace Sells* combines a punkish political awareness with a dark, threatening, typically heavy-metal worldview, preoccupied with evil, the occult, and the like. The anthemic title track and "Wake Up Dead" are the two major standouts, and there is also a cover of Willie Dixon's "I Ain't Superstitious," which takes on an air of supernaturally induced paranoia in the album's context. The lines between hell and earth are blurred throughout the album, and the crashing, complex music backs up Mustaine's apocalyptic vision of life as damnation—his limited vocal style is used to great effect, growling and snarling in a barely intelligible fashion under all the complicated guitar work. Vital, necessary thrash. —*Steve Huey*

So Far, So Good... So What! / 1988 / Capitol ✦✦✦

A largely uninspired effort recorded with a new guitarist and drummer, *So Far, So Good... So What!* lacks the conceptual unity and musical bite of *Peace Sells*, which helps push much of its lyrical material into the realm of self-parody, as Mustaine rants about the P.M.R.C., the apocalypse, ex-girlfriends, and other people he is angry with, while hinting at the depth of his substance abuse problem with "502," a paean to driving drunk. The album wants to sound threatening but mostly comes off as forced and somewhat juvenile; typical is the embarrassing cover of "Anarchy in the UK," which is played in Megadeth's tightly controlled riffing style and without the looseness of the original, making it sound stilted and stiff—and Mustaine doesn't even get the lyrics right. This one is for diehards only. —*Steve Huey*

Rust in Peace / Sep. 24, 1990 / Capitol ✦✦✦✦

A sobered-up Mustaine returns with yet another lineup, this one featuring ex-Cacophony guitar virtuoso Marty Friedman and drummer Nick Menza, for what is easily Megadeth's strongest musical effort. As Metallica was then doing, Mustaine accentuates the progressive tendencies of his compositions, producing rhythmically complex, technically challenging thrash suites that he and Friedman burn through with impeccable execution and jaw-dropping skill. Thanks to Mustaine's focus on the music rather than his sometimes clumsy lyrics, *Rust In Peace* arguably holds up better than any other Megadeth release, even for listeners who think they've outgrown heavy metal. While the whole album is consistently impressive, the obvious highlight is the epic, Eastern-tinged "Hangar 18." —*Steve Huey*

Countdown to Extinction / Jul. 14, 1992 / Capitol ✦✦✦✦

Megadeth guns for arena-thrash success and gets it on *Countdown to Extinction*. Following the lead of 1991's *Metallica*, Megadeth trades in their lengthy, progressive compositions for streamlined, tightly written and played songs more conducive to radio and MTV airplay. Cries of "sellout" seem pointless when the results are artistically (as well as commercially) successful; songs like the mega-hit "Symphony of Destruction," "Skin o' My Teeth," "Foreclosure of a Dream," and "Sweating Bullets" are among the band's best. —*Steve Huey*

Youthanasia / Nov. 1, 1994 / Capitol ✦✦✦

Megadeth's follow-up to the hit *Countdown to Extinction* lacks the focus of its predecessor, but *Youthanasia* makes up the difference with more accessible, radio-friendly production, and tighter riffs. Unfortunately, they have abandoned some of the more experimental, progressive elements in their music, but those are hardly missed in the jackhammer riffs of tracks like "Train of Consequences." —*Stephen Thomas Erlewine*

Hidden Treasures / Jul. 18, 1995 / Capitol ✦✦
Culled from various soundtracks and tribute albums, and featuring a new cover of the Sex Pistols' "Problems," *Hidden Treasures* may have a number of rare tracks, but it doesn't have many first-rate songs, with only "99 Ways to Die" making much of an impression. —*Stephen Thomas Erlewine*

The Mekons

f. 1979, Leeds, England
Alternative Pop-Rock, Post-Punk
More than any band that came out of late-'70s England, the Mekons (the name taken from the popular low-tech British sci-fi show *Dr. Who*) have perhaps the most devoted fans of any band even remotely connected to punk rock. And why not? After 16 years together, this band, with an ever-shifting lineup (only Jon Langford and Tom Greenhaigh remain from the original lineup), has produced some of the best rock 'n' roll on the planet; be it amateurish rock-noise, cool synth-driven pop, guitar raveups, or post-modern country & western, the Mekons have done it all and done it with style, grace, and a ribald sense of humor.

Emerging from the same Leeds University "scene" that begat the Gang of Four, the Mekons weren't as overtly political as their Marxist-inspired brethren, but their punk-rock pedigree and unsubtle anti-Thatcherisms and anti-Reaganisms did set them apart from the post-punk world's innumerable careerists and posers. Their early recordings were exceedingly low-fi affairs that valued emotion and energy over anything that remotely resembled musical proficiency. Songs like "Never Been in a Riot" and "32 Weeks" sound as if the band entered the studio, arbitrarily decided who was going to play what, and started the tapes rolling. It was fun, challenging, and anarchic—principles to which the band has clung, musical genre notwithstanding, since their inception.

From the time of their debut album, *The Quality of Mercy Is Not Strained*, the Mekons had turned into a slightly more accomplished post-punk band, who, like their pals in the Gang of Four, wielded trebly guitars and shouted vocals over semi-funky rhythm tracks. The songs lacked focus, but this was a bizarre record that, for all of its oddly ingratiating music, offered little insight as to who was making it. This remained true for a couple of years or so as the band (basically Langford, Greenhaigh, Kevin Lycett and whoever else they could rope into a session) made one exciting, enigmatic and extremely difficult-to-find record after another.

In 1985, after it seemed the earth had swallowed them whole, the Mekons released the startling *Fear and Whiskey*, a ragged country album influenced by the ghosts of Hank Williams and Gram Parsons that was unlike anything they'd ever recorded. Thus began the second coming of the Mekons, who finally began to reach an underground-alternative rock audience that had missed them the first time around.

Soon they began touring more frequently, putting on clamorous, exciting shows. Talented new members jumped on board, like violinist Susie Honeyman and singer Sally Timms, and even former Pretty Thing Dick Taylor was a Mekon for a while; records started coming out with more frequency and, despite considerable trouble from major labels that sent them back to the indies, could be found in nearly any record store. In the interim between *Fear and Whiskey* and their most recent record *Retreat from Memphis*, the Mekons have continually reinvented themselves: sodden country band, wise-ass folk-rock band, cranked-up guitar band, trouble-making punk band; whatever the scenario, what has remained consistent throughout the Mekons' existence has been great, great music. —*John Dougan*

The Quality of Mercy Is Not Strained / 1979 / Caroline ✦✦✦
Here's where it all began. Not the best Mekons album available, but *Quality*, along with their second album, *Devils, Rats and Piggies*, and A *Special Message from Godzilla* (Red Rhino, 1980, now out of print) shows off the Mekons' noisy, avant-garde side. It's abrasive and not as user-friendly as their later records, but this was an exciting time for British punk-rock, and this music, as dense and difficult as it may be, reflects punk's seemingly limitless possibilities. Issued by Blue Plate on CD in 1990. —*John Dougan*

Fear and Whiskey / 1985 / Sin ✦✦✦✦
A startling, unexpected record that sounds as wonderful now as it did when it was released. *Fear and Whiskey* uses American country music as its foundation, and the Mekons (ever the playful band) screw around with the genre, alternating between an honest-to-God reverence and flat-out parody. Don't expect sharply executed singing and playing; that's never been the Mekons' style. Instead, plan on a rambling, sodden opus of cowpunk with Hank Williams' ghost lurking in the shadows. In 1989, *Fear and Whiskey* was issued on CD by the Minneapolis-based indie label Twin/Tone with extra material and re-titled *Original Sin*. —*John Dougan*

Edge of the World / 1986 / Sin ✦✦✦✦
Hot on the heels of *Fear* came this terrific follow-up that mined the same cowpunk terrain as its predecessor. The new members (Timms, et al.) sound fully integrated into the lineup, and the manic intensity doesn't let up for an instant. It's a party, but a very weird one indeed. —*John Dougan*

Honky Tonkin' / 1987 / Loud ✦✦✦✦
Finally, nearly a decade after the first Mekons release and after years of purchasing high-priced English imports, one of America's coolest indie labels manages to unleash the mighty Mekons domestically. The wonderful *Honky Tonkin'* marks the Mekons' last overt country-cowpunk record as they slowly shifted into more guitar-oriented rock. Its title taken from the classic Hank Williams song, this is slightly less essential than *Fear* or *Edge*, but with songs as great as "If They Hang You" and the goofy "Sympathy for the Mekons," you most certainly need it as you build your Mekons collection. —*John Dougan*

New York / 1987 / Combat ✦✦✦✦
You know a band is great when they release odds and ends that are better than most other bands' painstakingly rendered studio efforts. *New York* is a shambling ode to life on the road that features live tracks, band commentary (including snoring), and a ratty version of the Band's "The Shape I'm In." Upon its release, I thought *New York* the province of Mekons fanatics, that the casual fan or curious would tire of its casual attitude, lack of focus, and its audio-verité documentary approach. Now I think that if you like the Mekons, there is no good reason not to possess this recording. Originally released on cassette, *New York* was reissued on CD by ROIR/Important in 1990. —*John Dougan*

So Good It Hurts / 1988 / Twin/Tone ✦✦✦
The second release for Twin/Tone showed the Mekons putting a bit of reggae and Latin rhythms into the more-folk-than-country mix. *So Good* sounds a tad subdued in comparison to earlier records, but that does not indicate a lackadaisical attitude or a softening of the band after nearly a decade of recorded work. In fact, its best moments ("Sometime I Feel Like Fletcher Christian") live up to the album's title. —*John Dougan*

● **The Mekons Rock 'n' Roll** / Sep. 1989 / A&M ✦✦✦✦
Asking a Mekons fan to select a favorite Mekons record is crazy—there isn't one, there are many. But, if the situation were such that a choice had to be made, this might be the record. Loud, unruly guitars, pissed-off vocals—the Mekons have made an unregenerate, unapologetic punk rock record. This is a dark record, one that comfortably negotiates the dark recesses of rock 'n' roll. They rip the messianic aspirations of U2's Bono ("Blow Your Tuneless Trumpet"), sing a tale of substance abuse that is both cautionary and parodic ("Cocaine Lil"), all the while cranking up a sonic tar pit of guitar noise. Bands this far on in a career don't, generally speaking, make records this good. But *The Mekons Rock 'n' Roll* is one of those cathartic records that only righteously indignant, justifiably pissed-off, grizzled veterans could make. Sadly, and perhaps unsurprisingly, it sold next to nothing and precipitated the band's departure from A&M, who didn't want to release another record like this one. —*John Dougan*

Curse of the Mekons / 1991 / Blast First ✦✦✦✦
It's amazing that as down and out as the Mekons were at this point, they could manage to summon up the emotional wherewithal to make a record as excellent as *Curse*, but they did. The title most definitely reflects the band's mindset at this time, but this is not the music of self-pity and despair ("We're right in all we distrust" yelps Greenhaigh on the title track); in fact, if it weren't for *Rock 'n' Roll*, this might be the Mekons' finest moment. Politically charged songs despairing about communism and capitalism, a return to C&W (Sally Timms' passionate reading of John Anderson's "Wild and Blue"), and a dig at America's status as the world's only post-Cold War superpower ("100% Song"). Heady stuff, and not all happy, but remarkably assured and very rewarding. —*John Dougan*

The It Falleth like Gentle Rain from Heaven—The Mekons Story / 1993 / CNT ✦✦
Originally released in 1982, *The Mekons Story* (also known as *It Falleth like the Gentle Rain from Heaven*) is a collection of singles, odd tracks, and assorted effluvia recorded between 1977 and 1982, that was thankfully reissued as a limited edition CD by Chicago-based indie label Feel Good All Over. With a drunken-sounding David Spencer providing a between-cuts "history" of the band, this, more than any other Mekons recording, shows their crucial and comic post-punk development. After hearing this, you'll never believe it's the same band recording today. —*John Dougan*

I Love Mekons / Oct. 18, 1993 / Quarterstick ✦✦✦✦
A series of rancorous disagreements with the high and mighty at Warner Bros. subsidiary Loud forced the Mekons into an unanticipated two years of silence that nearly scuttled this record and ended the band's career. Eventually, Warner relented (they had maintained the record was

not good enough to release), and the increasingly restless Mekons fans were able to judge for themselves that this was another terrific Mekons record. More traditionally rock-oriented and less prone to stylistic leaps than before, *I Love Mekons* is a strong, confident record that should have placed the Mekons at the forefront of the growing "alternative rock" market. It didn't, but often there's no accounting for taste. —*John Dougan*

Retreat from Memphis / May 2, 1994 / Quarterstick ✦✦✦
Retreat came hot on the heels of *I Love* and was a similar-sounding (almost too-similar) record, and while that might have dismayed the purists, it was obvious to those who'd paid attention that the Mekons couldn't make a bad record even if they tried, especially one this tuneful and stuffed to the gills with rampaging guitars. *Retreat* might not be the first Mekons record I'd buy, but as with virtually all of their recorded output, there is no earthly reason not to want this record. —*John Dougan*

Melanie

f. Feb. 3, 1947, Queens, NY
Guitar, Vocals, Singer / Folk, Singer-Songwriter, Pop, Folk-Rock, Pop-Rock
No talent who came out of Woodstock and who continued actively performing more than a quarter century later remained as closely associated with the 1960s and "flower power" than Melanie. Born Melanie Safka in Astoria, Queens in 1947, she made her first public appearance at age four on a radio show, later studying at the New York Academy of Fine Arts. After mounting a singing career while in college, she later sang in clubs in Greenwich Village, and was signed to a publishing contract in 1967. She recorded her first single, "Beautiful People," for Columbia Records that same year. Her relationship with the record company was short-lived, however, and after one more single she left the label.

In 1969, she chanced to meet producer Peter Schekeryk, and after a hastily arranged audition, he took charge of her career. Her first album, *Born to Be*, was recorded and released by Buddah later that same year. On August 16, Melanie took the stage at the Woodstock Music & Art Festival in Bethel, New York; her song "Birthday of the Sun" was later released on the *Woodstock 2* album, and 20 years later it was released on video as part of *Woodstock: The Lost Performances*, alongside the work of Janis Joplin, Crosby, Stills & Nash, and the Who.

Soon afterward, she cut her second album, *Affectionately Melanie*, which did slightly better than her first; however, her commercial breakthrough came 11 months after Woodstock, when she released the song "Lay Down (Candles in the Rain)," recorded with the Edwin Hawkins Singers. The song, written as a tribute to the audience at Woodstock and displaying the feel of a gospel hymn, rose to No. 6 on the US charts, while the accompanying LP, entitled *Candles in the Rain*, reached the Top 20.

After 1970's *Leftover Wine*, a live album recorded at a Carnegie Hall concert, she issued a plaintive version of the Rolling Stones' "Ruby Tuesday." In January of 1971, Melanie's own version of "What Have They Done to My Song, Ma," a recent smash for the New Seekers, got to No. 39 in Britain, where she emerged as a major star. In March, however, her new release *The Good Book* peaked on the US charts at just No. 80, despite the presence of several impressive tracks, among them a hauntingly beautiful cover of Phil Ochs' prophetic, doom-laden self-eulogy "Chords of Fame."

At around this time, Melanie rebelled against her contract with Buddah, which required her to supply albums more or less on demand—she'd had four LPs released in half as many years, and wanted more control over her work and career. With help from Schekeryk, whom she had married, she organized her own label, Neighborhood Records, during the summer of 1971. Her first subsequent single, "Brand New Key," hit No. 1 on the US charts while on its way to becoming a million-seller; thanks to its not-so-subtle sexual undertones, the song became a kind of "in" dirty joke in some circles, and was even censored on some radio stations, but it also made Melanie one of the top-selling artists of the year 1971.

The accompanying album, *Gather Me*, was the best-produced long-player she had ever released, and reached a chart position of No. 15, earning a gold record in the process. This huge success prompted Buddah to release *Garden in the City*, consisting of previously unreleased outtakes. At the same time that 1971's *Gather Me* spawned the single "Ring the Living Bell," Buddah decided to capitalize more directly on Melanie's catalog and released "The Nickel Song"; the presence of two singles in release simultaneously from two different labels and distributors—each competing for radio play and listener dollars—damaged both releases, and they effectively cancelled each other out.

Garden in the City rose to No. 19, but her next new album on Neighborhood, *Stoneground Words*, only got to No. 70 late in 1972. In June of 1973, her double concert album, *Live at Carnegie Hall*, recorded the previous year, didn't even make the Top 100. By this time, Melanie had withdrawn from the stage, and was devoting her time to more personal

and domestic concerns, having the first of three children in as many years. She re-emerged in 1974 for a short series of concerts, but her new album of that period, *Madrugada*, barely made it onto the charts, and her subsequent two LPs, *As I See It Now* and *Sunset and Other Beginnings*, released in 1975, barely sold. Neighborhood Records was later closed down.

A year later, *Photograph* was released to lackluster sales on Atlantic; the follow-up, *Photogenic*, also failed to chart, and her last album for the next five years, *Ballroom Streets*, appeared on the Tomato label in 1977. In 1982, Melanie cut a comeback album, *Arabesque*, for RCA; a year later, her single "Every Breath of the Way" scraped the middle of the British charts and led to a series of concerts in England. Neighborhood was soon reactivated just long enough for Melanie to release one last album, *Seventh Wave*.

At the end of the 1980s, she re-emerged once again with her theme music for the popular television series *Beauty and the Beast*. By that time, Woodstock nostalgia was beginning to be stoked by the media and concert promoters, and Melanie appeared at one of the 20th anniversary events. She continued to periodically perform at clubs in the US and larger festivals in Europe, where her association with the 1960s made her a major draw, and every so often released an album of new songs and re-recordings of her classic numbers. —*Bruce Eder*

Candles in the Rain / 1970 / Buddah ✦✦✦✦
Apart from the title track, this album also contains her superb cover of the Rolling Stones' "Ruby Tuesday" and her own "What Have They Done to My Song, Ma." —*Bruce Eder*

Gather Me / 1971 / Neighborhood ✦✦✦✦
Melanie's most accomplished and best-produced studio album, containing the hits "Brand New Key" and "Ring the Living Bell." —*Bruce Eder*

The Good Book / 1971 / Buddah ✦✦✦✦
Another surprising record, most notably for Melanie's wonderful cover of Phil Ochs' "Chords of Fame," which is superior in many ways to Ochs' own, good as that is. The packaging, which includes a cover photo and small-size booklet with lyrics in the center of the jacket, makes this a difficult record to find completely intact two or three decades later. —*Bruce Eder*

● **The Best of Melanie** / 1990 / Rhino ✦✦✦✦
Eighteen songs from her 1968-1974 heyday, including all six of her Top 40 hit singles, and her unexpectedly passionate cover of the Rolling Stones' "Ruby Tuesday." —*Richie Unterberger*

From Woodstock to the World / 1994 / Laserlight ✦✦✦
A double-CD set made in the studio and in concert in Europe. The live set is made up of her old songs from the 1960s and early '70s, while the studio stuff is newer. The sound is good, but none of the material here is going to replace the original versions, especially as Melanie has modernized her style. —*Bruce Eder*

John Cougar Mellencamp (John Mellencamp)

b. Oct. 7, 1951, Seymour, IN
Guitar, Vocals / Rock 'n' Roll, Pop-Rock
Throughout his career, John Mellencamp has had to fight, whether it was for the right to record under his own name or for respect as an artist. Of course, he never made it easy on himself. Mellencamp began his career in the late '70s as a Bruce Springsteen clone called Johnny Cougar. As his career progressed, his music became more distinctive, developing into a Stonesey blend of hard rock and folk-rock. His musical development coincided with his growth in popularity—by the time "Hurts So Good" and "Jack and Diane" became hits in 1982, Mellencamp had created his own variation of the heartland rock of Springsteen, Tom Petty, and Bob Seger. While he had the record sales, it took several years before rock critics took him seriously. For some artists, this would be easy to ignore, but Mellencamp had the desire to be a serious social commentator, chronicling the times and trials of Midwestern baby boomers. *Scarecrow*, released in 1985, fulfilled his wish of being taken seriously, and every record he released after it was greeted warmly by critics. Furthermore, he sustained his popularity into the late '90s, only occasionally experiencing dips in record sales.

A prolonged, acclaimed career seemed an impossibility when Mellencamp released his first album under the name Johnny Cougar in 1976. As a child in Seymour, Indiana, Mellencamp had suffered a number of setbacks, including being born with a neural tube defect called spina bifida that necessitated a lengthy hospitalization as a baby. As a teenager, he was rebellious, often getting in trouble with the law. He formed his first band at the age of 14, and continued to play throughout his teens. When he was 17, he eloped with Pricilla Esterline, his pregnant girlfriend, and proceeded to try to support his family by working a series of blue-collar jobs. By the time he was 24, he had decided to move to New York City to attempt to break into the music industry.

In New York, Mellencamp became a client of David Bowie's manager Tony DeFries, who signed him to a lucrative contract with Mainman/

MCA. Mellencamp recorded an album of covers called *Chestnut Street Incident*. Upon receiving the finished album in 1976, he was infuriated to learn that DeFries had billed the singer as Johnny Cougar. *Chestnut Street Incident* was a bomb and MCA immediately dropped the singer. The fiasco of his first album was enough to sour Mellencamp toward the industry for the remainder of his career. Two years later, he signed with Riva Records, releasing *A Biograpay* (1978) to little attention. However, *Johnny Cougar* (1979) spawned the Top 40 hit "I Need a Lover," which also became an AOR hit for Pat Benatar a few years later. Steve Cropper produced 1980's *Nothin' Matters and What If It Did*, which contained the Top 30 hits "This Time" and "Ain't Even Done With the Night."

John Mellencamp's next album, 1982's *American Fool*, became his breakthrough, both commercially and musically. More focused than his earlier records, *American Fool* rocketed to No. 1 on the strength of the No. 2 hit "Hurts So Good" and the No. 1 single "Jack & Diane," both of which were supported by videos that became MTV favorites. The success of *American Fool* meant that he could add "Mellencamp" to his stage name, and 1983's *Uh-Huh* became the first album credited to John Cougar Mellencamp. *Uh-Huh* was released while *American Fool* was still high on the charts, and it became a No. 9 hit, generating the Top Ten hits "Crumblin' Down" and "Pink Houses," as well as the Top 15 "Authority Song." He supported the album with his first headlining tour.

While he had commercial success, Mellencamp made his bid for critical acclaim with his next album, 1985's *Scarecrow*. *Scarecrow* displayed a greater social conscious and musical eclecticism, resulting in his best-reviewed—as well as his biggest—album to date. Peaking at No. 2, *Scarecrow* generated the Top Ten singles "Lonely Ol' Night," "Small Town," and "R.O.C.K. in the USA." Following the release of *Scarecrow*, Mellencamp became an outspoken advocate of the American farmer, organizing Farm Aid with Willie Nelson and Neil Young. He also became known for his anti-corporate stance, refusing to accept tour sponsorship offers from beer and tobacco companies.

Mellencamp continued to explore social commentary and new musical avenues with 1987's *The Lonesome Jubilee*. Featuring a distinct Appalachian folk and country influence, *The Lonesome Jubilee* was a melancholy elegy for forgotten middle America, and while it was more adventurous than its predecessors, it was another hit, peaking at No. 6 and generating the hits "Paper in Fire," "Cherry Bomb" and "Check it Out." Mellencamp continued to explore American roots music on *Big Daddy* (1989). While the album received generally good reviews and peaked at No. 7, it failed to produce a big single. Two years later, he returned with *Whenever We Wanted*, which was another moderate hit, peaking at No. 17. *Human Wheels* (1993) received some of Mellencamp's strongest reviews, yet the record didn't generate a hit single and quickly fell down the charts after debuting at No. 7.

Mellencamp bounced back into the Top Ten in 1994, when his duet with Me'Shell NdegeOcello on Van Morrison's "Wild Night" peaked at No. 3. Its accompanying album, *Dance Naked*, became his biggest album since *Big Daddy*, going gold months after its release. Mellencamp planned to support the album with an extensive tour, but he suffered a major heart attack in late 1994 that necessitated its cancellation. Mellencamp spent 1995 recuperating, re-emerging in 1996 with *Mr. Happy Go Lucky*. Produced by Junior Vasquez and demonstrating a slight dance influence, *Mr. Happy Go Lucky* was greeted with positive reviews and featured the minor hit single "Key West Intermezzo (I Saw You First)," which helped the album go gold. —*Stephen Thomas Erlewine*

Chestnut Street Incident / 1976 / Rhino ✦

John Mellencamp began his career as Johnny Cougar, on the advice of his manager Tony DeFries. Cougar's debut, *Chestnut Street Incident*, was released in 1976 in a whirlwind of hype, which the album simply didn't deserve. At best, the record is a competent collection of Stonesy rockers, infused with a blue-collar Bruce Springsteen/Bob Seger attitude, but Cougar's music and lyrics aren't memorable and are often laughable. —*Stephen Thomas Erlewine*

Biography / 1978 / Riva ✦

Since neither *Chestnut Street Incident* or *The Kid Inside* generated much attention, John Cougar's third album, *A Biography*, wasn't released in America. Ironically, it was his best effort yet, featuring a harder and genuinely rocking backbeat and, in the silly but catchy "I Need a Lover," his first good song. The rest of the album didn't even come close to matching those heights, yet the song indicated that Mellencamp had talent—he just wasn't sure how to access it. —*Stephen Thomas Erlewine*

John Cougar / 1979 / Riva ✦

Once "I Need a Lover" became an Australian hit, Riva in America decided to release John Cougar's eponymous fourth album, adding the song to the record as well. Essentially, *John Cougar* is sonically similar to *A Biography*, but apart from the tacked-on "I Need a Lover," none of the songs hit the mark. —*Stephen Thomas Erlewine*

Nothin' Matters & What If It Did / 1980 / Riva ✦✦

Although the title suggested the nihilism that would underpin Mellencamp's best work in the '80s, *Nothin' Matters and What if It Did* came across as posturing, since its lyrics are silly, juvenile cliches and the music simply recycled Stones, Springsteen, and Seger. In other words, it gave little indication of the breakthrough that would occur with *American Fool*. —*Stephen Thomas Erlewine*

American Fool / 1982 / Mercury ✦✦✦

John Cougar's first albums were so bereft of strong material that the lean swagger of *American Fool* came as a shock. The difference is evident from the opening song "Hurts So Good," a hard, Stonesy rocker with an irresistibly sleazy hook. Cougar had never written anything as catchy as this before, nor had his romantic vision of small-town America resonated like it did on "Jack & Diane," a minor and remarkably affecting sketch of dead-end romance. These two songs are the only true keepers on *American Fool*, but the rest of the record works better than his previous material because his band is tighter than ever before, making his weaker moments convincing. Besides, songs like "Hand to Hold On to" and "China Girl," for all their faults, do indicate that his sense of craft is improving considerably. —*Stephen Thomas Erlewine*

Uh-Huh / 1983 / Mercury ✦✦✦✦

Since *American Fool* illustrated that John Cougar was becoming an actual songwriter, it was only proper that he reclaimed his actual last name, Mellencamp, for the follow-up, *Uh-Huh*. After all, now that he had success, he wanted to be taken seriously, and *Uh-Huh* reflects that in its portraits of broken-hearted life in the Midwest and its rumbling undercurrent of despair. Although his lyrics still had the tendency to be a little too vague, they were more effective than ever before, as was his music; he might not have changed his style at all—it was still a fusion of the Stones and Springsteen—except that he now knew how to make it his own. *Uh-Huh* runs out of steam toward the end, but the first half—with the dynamic rocker "Crumblin' Down," his best protest song, "Pink Houses," the punky "Authority Song," the melancholy "Warmer Place to Sleep," and the garage-rocker "Play Guitar"—makes the record his first terrific album. —*Stephen Thomas Erlewine*

● Scarecrow / 1985 / Mercury ✦✦✦✦

Uh-Huh found John Mellencamp coming into his own, but he perfected his Heartland rock with *Scarecrow*. A loose concept album about lost innocence and the crumbling of small-town America, *Scarecrow* says as much with its tough rock and gentle folk-rock as it does with its lyrics, which remain a weak point for Mellencamp. Nevertheless, his writing has never been more powerful: "Rain on the Scarecrow" and "Small Town" capture the hopes and fears of middle America, while "Lonely Ol' Night" and "Rumbleseat" effortlessly convey the desperate loneliness of being stuck in a dead-end life. Those four songs form the core of the album, and while the rest of the album isn't quite as strong, that's only a relative term, since it's filled with lean hooks and powerful, economical playing that make *Scarecrow* one of the definitive blue-collar rock albums of the mid-'80s. —*Stephen Thomas Erlewine*

The Lonesome Jubilee / 1987 / Mercury ✦✦✦✦

John Mellencamp's fascination with the American heartland came into full flower on *Scarecrow*, but with its follow-up, *The Lonesome Jubilee*, he began exploring American folk musics, adding fiddle, accordions, and acoustic guitars to his band, which allowed him to explore folk and country. The expansion of his band coincided with his continuing growth as a songwriter. Song for song, *The Lonesome Jubilee* is Mellencamp's strongest album, the record on which he captured his romantic, if decidedly melancholy, vision of working-class America. He may recycle the same lyrical ideas as before, but he captures them better than ever, and his music is richer, which gives the album resonance. Again, there are a few moments where Mellencamp's reach exceeds his grasp, but "Paper in Fire," "Check It Out," "Cherry Bomb," "Empty Hands," and "Hard Times for an Honest Man" make the record his best. —*Stephen Thomas Erlewine*

Big Daddy / May 1989 / Mercury ✦✦✦

Continuing with the folk inclinations of *The Lonesome Jubilee*, John Mellencamp recorded his most ambitious and serious-minded album with *Big Daddy*. Mellencamp produced the record himself, giving the album a concise and stripped-down sound, which help give his songs the appearance of being gritty statements of truth. Unfortunately, Mellencamp isn't saying nearly as much as he believes he is, since his lyrics tend to be cliched and half-baked, making much of the album feel pompous and self-serving. This is only reinforced by the lack of rockers on *Big Daddy*, since he saves the most carefree moment—a ripping cover of the Hombres' "Let It Out (Let It All Hang Out)"—for an unlisted bonus track. Still, when he does hit his target, like on the gentle "Jackie Brown," the stuttering, fiddle-driven "Sometimes a Great Notion," and even the self-pitying "Pop Singer," Mellencamp proves that his talents haven't abandoned him. —*Stephen Thomas Erlewine*

Whenever We Wanted / Oct. 8, 1991 / Mercury ✦✦✦
Mellencamp took his signature blend of Stonesy rock and folk as far as it could go on *Big Daddy*, so he wisely returned to straightahead rock 'n' roll with *Whenever We Wanted*. *Uh-Huh* was the last record he had made that rocked as hard and consistently as this, and his songwriting had improved considerably in the years since that breakthrough release. Which means, of course, that *Whenever We Wanted* is more consistent than the earlier record, but it never reaches the highs of *Uh-Huh*. Even its best moments ("Love and Happiness," "Get a Leg Up," "Whenever We Wanted," "Again Tonight") shine because of their craftmanship, failing to achieve the kinetic energy of his earlier work. *Whenever We Wanted* remains a solid record, but it's one that feels like a holding pattern. —*Stephen Thomas Erlewine*

Human Wheels / Sep. 7, 1993 / Mercury ✦✦✦✦
Following the stripped-down rock 'n' roll of *Whenever We Wanted*, the somber *Human Wheels* comes as a bit of shock. Throughout his mid-'80s peak, Mellencamp infused his best work with despair, but he never has sounded as beaten and broken as he does on *Human Wheels*. It's not just that the record sounds murky and bleak, but his singing is weary and the lyrics are filled with resignation. Consequently, *Human Wheels* isn't a particularly easy listen, even though it doesn't depart from his signature sound, but it is a rewarding one, and the record is arguably his most affecting. —*Stephen Thomas Erlewine*

Dance Naked / Jun. 21, 1994 / Mercury ✦✦✦
A short, stripped-down collection of basic rock 'n' roll, *Dance Naked* isn't quite as powerful as *Human Wheels*, but it has more good songs in its 30 minutes than most 70-minute albums. —*Stephen Thomas Erlewine*

Mr. Happy Go Lucky / Sep. 10, 1996 / Mercury ✦✦✦
John Mellencamp responded to his massive heart attack and close call with death with *Mr. Happy Go Lucky*, the most overtly ambitious album in his career. Mellencamp has always been a bit of a fatalist, so it isn't any great surprise that there is an undercurrent of dark mortality running through most of his songs. What is a surprise is his musical approach. Although he hasn't abandoned the essential elements of his music—the rootsy instrumentation, the violins, the simple song structures, the gritty folk-rock— he has augmented it with the help of Junior Vasquez, a noted dance producer. Vasquez doesn't push Mellencamp into dance, but he adds certain dynamics and techniques from club music to *Mr. Happy Go Lucky* which occasionally give the album a greater depth. It's a gentle change, not a forceful one—nothing sounds like dance music, but there are deeper rhythms and bass throughout the album, which breathe life into well-crafted songs like "Key West Intermezzo." Since he doesn't pursue dance completely on *Mr. Happy Go Lucky*, Mellencamp doesn't end up alienating his fans, but the reluctance to give himself over to dance makes the album uneven. Ironically, the tracks that exhibit Vasquez's influence are the least successful—they simply sound like Mellencamp is going through the motions. Nevertheless, *Mr. Happy Go Lucky* proves that Mellencamp has more surprises in him than many listeners would have expected and suggests that he is in the process of revitalizing his career. —*Stephen Thomas Erlewine*

Harold Melvin & the Blue Notes

b. Jun. 25, 1939, Philadelphia, PA, **d.** Mar. 24, 1997
Soul, Doo Wop, Philly Soul
Starting out in 1954 in Philadelphia as a doo wop group with Harold Melvin as lead singer, the Blue Notes first recorded for the New York-based Josie label two years later. They debuted on the R&B charts in 1960 on the Value label with "My Hero." A 1965 release, "Get Out," with a lead vocal by John Atkins, also charted R&B Top 40 on Landa. But it was not until 1972, when drummer Teddy Pendergrass took over lead vocal chores and the group came under the wing of Kenny Gamble and Leon Huff and their Philadelphia International label, that Harold Melvin & the Blue Notes became consistent chart-makers.

Pendergrass' vocals smoldered with sensuality. Combined with the smooth group harmonies that had always been a Blue Note trademark, Gamble and Huff's superior writing, and lush productions, the superb TSOP house band records, such as "I Miss You," "If You Don't Know Me by Now," and "The Love I Lost" were staples on both Black and white radio from 1972 to 1975. Pendergrass went solo in 1975 and the Blue Notes' glory days came to an end. Recording subsequently for a number of labels (including ABC, Source, MCA, and Philly World), Harold Melvin & the Blue Notes hit the R&B charts another ten times, often with lead vocals by Sharon Paige. Three of those 45s entered the Top 20, and one (1977's "Reaching for the World") reached as high as No. 6. The latter was the only one of the Blue Notes' post-Pendergrass recordings to break the Pop Hot 100. —*Rob Bowman*

★ **The Best of Harold Melvin & the Blue Notes** / Feb. 28, 1995 / Epic/ Legacy ✦✦✦✦✦
Although the ten-track disc is criminally brief, *The Best of Harold Melvin & the Blue Notes* contains most of their biggest hits and offers a good portrait of one of the finest soul groups of the '70s. —*Stephen Thomas Erlewine*

Melvins

f. 1985, Aberdeen, WA
Alternative Pop-Rock, Heavy Metal, Grunge
The Melvins were the first post-punk band to revel in the slow, sludgy sounds of Black Sabbath. Their music is oppressively slow and heavy, only without any of the silly mystical lyrics or the indulgent guitar solos—it's just one massive, oozing pile of dark slime. The Melvins' first record was released in 1987; they've released several albums since then, but it wasn't until 1993 that they went to a major label, thanks to their protégé, Kurt Cobain.

While the Melvins can be dull and repetitive, their place in rock history is interesting, even if it is just a minor footnote. The band formed in Aberdeen, WA, the same town that produced Nirvana's Cobain and Chris Novaselic. For Nirvana and many other Seattle-area bands, the Melvins' sludge was inspirational; the younger bands took the Sabbath-styled heaviness of the Melvins, while adding an equally important pop song structure, which the group tended to lack. While all of their disciples became famous after Nirvana broke big in 1991 (including Mudhoney, which featured former Melvin bassist, Steve Turner), the Melvins only expanded their cult slightly. They did earn a major-label contract with Atlantic, but after releasing three records for the label, they were dropped in late 1996, and the group returned to indie status. —*Stephen Thomas Erlewine*

Gluey Porch Treatments / 1987 / Boner ✦✦✦
When it comes to heavy music, the Melvins are the reigning kings. This essential debut is mandatory for those into aggressive songs, the majority of which are played in a slow fashion, and those who want to hear power chords stretched beyond compare. It includes such songs as "Oh," "Steve Instant Newman," and "Over From Under the Excrement." —*John Book*

Ozma / 1989 / Boner ✦✦✦
The band's long-awaited second album was definitely worth the wait. With the band relocated in San Francisco, *Ozma*—which was released exactly the same time the Seattle music scene exploded in Europe—became an underground favorite. Fierce guitar work from Osborne, intense drumming from Crover, and mind-numbing bass work from Lori Black make *Ozma* one of the hardest (and harshest) albums of 1989. The CD version includes *Gluey Porch Treatments* in its entirety as a bonus. —*John Book*

Bullhead / 1991 / Boner ✦✦✦
Either a progression or a disappointment, *Bullhead* represented a slightly different sound for the group. The material on this album made an attempt at being actual "songs" rather than short examples of guitar execution, and the production is not as overpowering as on their first two albums. But the progression of playing slightly faster songs did appeal to those who thought the band were running in molasses every day. —*John Book*

Eggnog / 1991 / Boner ✦✦✦✦
Eggnog delivers on the goods, an EP that supplies what *Bullhead* failed to give. This record serves as a centerpiece for the Melvins, showing what they've accomplished in the past and what they intend to execute in the future. The future lies in the 12-minute opus "Charmicarmicat." A holiday recording not recommended for the kids, or adults for that matter. —*John Book*

Lysol / 1992 / Boner ✦✦✦
The Melvins take the Jethro Tull route by recording one lengthy song and releasing it as a full-length album. *Lysol* is a progressive song in the vein of Jethro Tull's "Thick as a Brick" and "A Passion Play," as the band go through different tempo changes, musical moods, and emotions during its 31-minute duration. This release also returns to the large sound they created on their first two albums; this takes heaviness to an all-new plateau. The band's last album on an independent label. —*John Book*

Houdini / Sep. 21, 1993 / Atlantic ✦✦✦✦
The Melvins changed nothing when they went to a major label. They still grind out the same slow, fuzzy, heavy sludge that remains the final word on "grunge." For those who have been wondering what all of the fuss is about, *Houdini* is a good way to catch up. —*Stephen Thomas Erlewine*

Prick / Aug. 5, 1994 / Reptile ✦✦
Even by Melvins standards, *Prick* is difficult to listen to. Filled with loud, distorted guitars but no discernable hooks or melodies, *Prick* is the band at their most experimental. The only problem is that the band isn't good at experimenting; they're good at making sludge rock. Even hardcore fans may find *Prick* rather tedious. —*Stephen Thomas Erlewine*

● **Stoner Witch** / Oct. 1994 / Atlantic ✦✦✦✦
Before The Melvins released *Stoner Witch*, they cleared out their systems by recording the defiantly unlistenable *Prick*. Everything *Prick*

was, *Stoner Witch* isn't. For the first time, The Melvins' songwriting abilities match their ability for making noise, making *Stoner Witch* their finest moment to date. — *Stephen Thomas Erlewine*

Stag / Jul. 15, 1996 / Atlantic ✦✦✦✦
The Melvins haven't ever been in the habit of change their sonic sludge, so the musical variety of *Stag* comes as a bit of a surprise. Not that the group has abandoned grunge—their heavy riffing is still the foundation of the music. What's changed is the details, from the sharper rhyhms to the occasional trumpet or sitar. Even more impressive is the acoustic "Cottonmouth," which would have been unthinkable on their earlier records. And it isn't change for the sake of change—the Melvins sound more energetic, committed, and versatile than ever before, which makes their occasionally weak songwriting forgivable. Few of their albums have ever been as listenable as *Stag*. — *Stephen Thomas Erlewine*

Honky / May 5, 1997 / Amphetamine Reptile ✦✦

Members

f. 1977, Surrey, England, **db.** 1984
New Wave, Ska-Revival
Formed in Surrey, England, in the summer of 1977, the Members were among the new wave of British bands jumping on the punk bandwagon. The band—composed of Nicky Tesco (vocals), Jean-Marie Caroll (guitar), Gary Baker (guitar), Adrian Lillywhite (drums), and Chris Payne (bass)—was among the first to successfully blend reggae rhythms with punk's attitude and aggression. Stiff Records saw some promise in the band and signed them early in 1978, releasing their first single, "Solitary Confinement." The success of the single led to their signing with Virgin Records in 1979. Their Virgin debut single, "Sound of the Suburbs," made it into the British Top 20, but subsequent singles failed to match its success. After replacing Baker with Nigel Bennett, they recorded their first LP, *Live at the Chelsea Nightclub*, which also made a brief appearance in the lower reaches of the UK charts. Around this time, the Two-Tone movement was stealing much of their limelight and their popularity began to fade. After one more album for Virgin in 1980, *1980 The Choice Is Yours*, they were dropped by the label. After a brief layoff, they returned in 1982 with *Uprhythm, Downbeat* (released in 1983 in the UK as *Going West*), broadening their sound with horns and a more serious attitude. "Working Girl" from the album became a cult classic in the US through MTV exposure, but mainstream acceptance eluded them on both sides of the Atlantic. The band called it quits the following year. — *Chris Woodstra*

At the 1980 Chelsea Night Club / 1979 / Caroline ✦✦✦✦
The only Members album worth owning, *Chelsea Nightclub* plays into the band's strengths and is loaded with their strongest songwriting (e.g., "Stand up and Spit," "Off-Shore Banking Business"). — *John Dougan*

1980 the Choice Is Yours / 1980 / Virgin ✦✦
The band's sophomore effort finds them slipping drastically after a fine debut. It has its moments, but the overall impression is one of a lack of inspiration and direction. — *Chris Woodstra*

Uprhythm, Downbeat / 1982 / Arista ✦✦✦
After the flop of *1980 the Choice Is Yours*, the band took two years off to regroup and change strategies; the resulting *Uprhythm, Downbeat* (retitled *Going West* and released a year later in the UK) shows a more serious band (now a seven-piece with a horn section) with a fuller sound. Their punk edges have been smoothed over, leaving a slick reggae-funk-pop sound. While it fit nicely with the new wave era, it hasn't aged very well. Only the classic "Working Girl" leaves a lasting impression. — *Chris Woodstra*

● **Sound of the Suburbs: A Collection of the Members' Finest Moments** / Apr. 18, 1995 / Caroline ✦✦✦✦
True to its subtitle, this 18-track collection compiles the finest moments of the band's two-year stay at Virgin Records (1979-1980). While this period was the strongest for the band, it would have been nice to include a track or two from their final album, *Uprhythm, Downbeat*, such as the near-hit "Working Girl." — *Chris Woodstra*

Men at Work

f. 1979, Melbourne, Australia, **db.** 1985
New Wave, Pop-Rock
Men at Work were one of the more surprising success stories of the new wave era, rocketing out of Australia in 1982 to become the most successful artist of the year. With its Police-styled rhythms, catchy guitar hooks, wailing saxophones, and off-kilter sense of humor, the band's debut album *Business as Usual* became an international blockbuster, breaking the American record for the most weeks a debut spent at the top of the charts. Their funny, irreverent videos became MTV favorites, helping send "Who Can It Be Now?" and "Down Under" to No. 1. Men at Work's momentum sustained them through their second album, 1983's *Cargo*, before the bottom fell out of the band's popularity. After releas-

ing *Two Hearts* in 1985, Men at Work broke up, becoming one of the better-remembered phenomena of New Wave.

Colin Hay (lead vocals, guitar), a native of Scotland who moved to Australia at the age of 14, formed Men at Work as an acoustic duo with Ron Strykert (guitar, vocals) in Melbourne, Australia in 1979. Within a few months, the duo had expanded to a full group with the addition of John Rees (bass), Greg Ham (saxophone, flute, keyboards), and Jerry Speiser (drums). Over the next two years, the band became regulars at the Cricketer's Arms Hotel bar and on Australia's pub circuit, eventually becoming the highest-paid unsigned band in the country. By 1981, they had landed a contract with Australian Columbia, who released "Who Can It Be Now?" by the end of the year. The single became an huge hit, as did their debut album, *Business as Usual*, upon its spring 1982 release. Featuring contributions by Hay, Strykert, and Ham, *Business as Usual* spent ten weeks at the top of the Australian charts, beating a record held by Split Enz's *True Colours*. The album was released in America in the summer, and within a few weeks "Who Can It Be Now?" began its climb to the top of the US charts. In November, *Business as Usual* hit the top of the charts, where it would stay for 15 weeks. "Down Under" became the group's second American No. 1 early in 1983, and it became the band's first British hit single; the song reached No. 1 in both countries simultaneously. In February, the band was named the Best New Artist of 1982 at the Grammys.

Men at Work's second album, *Cargo*, had been recorded during the summer of 1982, but its release was delayed because of the remarkable success of the debut. Largely written by Hay, *Cargo* reached No. 3 in the US and generated the Top Ten singles "Overkill" and "It's a Mistake." Following an extensive tour, during which the group co-headlined the US Festival with the Clash and the Stray Cats, Men at Work took an extended break in 1984, which caused Speiser and Rees to leave the band. They were replaced by session musicians for the group's third album, 1985's *Two Hearts*. Though the record went gold in the US, it was a considerable commercial disappointment, failing to generate one Top 40 single. Following the release of *Two Hearts*, the band broke up. Out of the remaining members, Hay was the only one to pursue a solo career, but neither of his two American solo albums—*Looking for Jack* (1987) and *Wayfaring Sons* (1990)—was a success. Hay continued to release albums in Australia during the '90s; he also began an acting career. — *Stephen Thomas Erlewine*

● **Business as Usual** / 1981 / Columbia ✦✦✦✦
Business as Usual became a surprise international hit on the basis of "Who Can It Be Now?" and "Down Under," two excellent singles that merged straightahead pop-rock hooks with a quirky new wave production and an offbeat sense of humor. Colin Hay's keening vocals uncannily recall Sting, and the band's rhythmic pulse and phased guitars also bring to mind a bar-band version of the Police. And that helps make the remainder of *Business as Usual* enjoyable. There's a fair amount of filler on the record, but "Be Good Johnny," "I Can See It In Your Eyes," and "Down By the Sea" are all fine New Wave pop songs, making *Business as Usual* one of the more enjoyable mainstream-oriented efforts of the era. — *Stephen Thomas Erlewine*

Cargo / 1983 / Columbia ✦✦✦✦
Cargo was bashed out fairly quickly, but it its release was delayed because of the success of Men at Work's debut, *Business as Usual*. Though it was recorded on the road, *Cargo* is considerably more diverse—but not necessarily more ambitious—than its predecessor. Again, the album is anchored by two extraordinary singles. Fortunately, the soaring ballad "Overkill" and the satiric, anti-nuclear "It's a Mistake" aren't rewrites of "Who Can It Be Now?" and "Down Under," demonstrating more depth than anything on the debut. Despite this growth, the remainder of *Cargo* is weighed down by filler. "Doctor Heckyll and Mr. Jive" might be goofy fun, and "High Wire" and "Blue for You" are tight pop songs, but the rest are simply pleasant, occasionally embarrassing ("I Like To," "Settle Down My Boy"), new wave pop. — *Stephen Thomas Erlewine*

Two Hearts / 1985 / Columbia ✦✦
By the time of their third album, Men at Work's music had become a bland, synthesized variation on mainstream pop, featuring none of the melodic sensibilities or subtle humor of their first two albums. Although the album went gold, it featured no Top 40 singles. The commercial performance of *Two Hearts* was a considerable disappointment after their first two multi-platinum records and the band broke up shortly after its release. — *Stephen Thomas Erlewine*

Contraband: The Best Of / Mar. 26, 1996 / Sony/Legacy ✦✦✦✦
Men at Work's records were always somewhat uneven affairs. Certainly, the singles were the highlights, but they had a handful of first-rate album tracks that made the records necessary for dedicated fans, even if the overall album was inconsistent. *Contraband: The Best of Men at Work* does a terrific job of consolidating all of their highlights on one disc. From hits like "Who Can It Be Now?," "Down Under," "Overkill," and "It's a Mistake" to slightly neglected album tracks like "Be Good

Johnny," *Contraband* has every great track from the Australian new wave band. For most fans, it will be the only disc they need. —*Stephen Thomas Erlewine*

Men Without Hats

f. 1980, Memphis, TN
New Wave, Pop-Rock

The new wave synth-pop collective Men Without Hats was formed in 1980 by brothers Ivan and Stefan Doroschuk. Ivan was the leader of the group, writing the majority of the songs and providing the lead vocals; Stefan was the guitarist; and the other members changed frequently throughout the course of the band's career. The group independently released their debut EP, *Folk of the 80's*, in 1980; it was reissued the following year by Stiff in Britain.

During 1982, the band consisted of Ivan, Stefan, and keyboardist Colin Doroschuk, along with drummer Allan McCarthy; this is the lineup that recorded Men Without Hats' 1982 debut album *Rhythm of Youth*. Taken from their debut, the single "The Safety Dance" became a major hit, peaking on the American charts at No. 3 in 1983. Driven by an insistent three-chord synthesizer riff, the song was one of the biggest synth-pop hits of the new wave era. The group wasn't able to exploit its success, however. *Folk of the '80s (Part III)* stalled at No. 127 on the charts in America and made even less of an impact in other parts of the world. Thanks to the minor hit title track, 1987's *Pop Goes the World* was a bigger success, yet it didn't recapture the audience their first album had gained. Released two years later, *The Adventures of Women & Men Without Hats in the 21st Century* failed to chart, as did its follow-up, 1991's *Sideways*. The two albums' lack of success effectively put an end to Men Without Hats' career. —*Stephen Thomas Erlewine*

Rhythm of Youth / 1982 / Backstreet ◆◆◆◆
Men Without Hats' debut album *Rhythm of Youth* was a set of catchy, appealing synth-pop. Although the material on the album was wildly inconsistent, the group's energy was infectious, making up for the weaker songs. And when the band managed to write a solid melody—such as the hit single "The Safety Dance"—the results were quite memorable. —*Stephen Thomas Erlewine*

Folk of the '80s (Part III) / 1984 / MCA ◆◆◆
Men Without Hats' follow-up to their successful first album repeated the same formula as the debut, with essentially the same results. Though *Folk of the '80s (Part III)* has its share of tedious material, the best songs on the album are as fun and charming as the finest moments from the debut. However, the band's audience had declined since the release of the first record, and *Folk of the '80s (Part III)* stiffed. —*Stephen Thomas Erlewine*

Pop Goes the World / 1987 / Mercury ◆◆◆
Men Without Hats made a minor comeback with 1987's *Pop Goes the World*, which featured the ingratiating electro-pop hit title track. Most of the songs on the record weren't as catchy as the hit, as the rest of the material emphasized beats and textures over hooks and melodies. —*Stephen Thomas Erlewine*

The Adventures of Women & Men Without Hate in the 21st Century / Oct. 1989 / PolyGram ◆◆

Sideways / 1991 / PolyGram ◆◆

● **Collection** / Feb. 20, 1996 / Oglio ◆◆◆◆
Men Without Hats were never an album-oriented band, so *Collection* does the casual fan a favor by compiling all of their hits—namely "The Safety Dance" (included in its original single mix) and "Pop Goes the World"—onto one disc. While many of the songs aren't as strong as those two singles, they are enjoyable new wave artifacts, making the compilation a fun nostalgia trip. Still, some casual fans will be disappointed that there aren't any lost classics on *Collection*, but less-discerning listeners will be pleased. —*Stephen Thomas Erlewine*

Menswear

f. 1994, Camden, England
Brit-Pop

Menswear signed a record contract before they played more than five gigs. That alone tells you everything you need to know about the band. Menswear were an outgrowth of the post-Blur pop scene in London, England, a group of charming, handsome young men that wanted to be in a pop group more than they wanted to play music. Consequently, they received their fair share of detractors, but the band weathered the storm, becoming one of the most popular Brit-pop bands of 1995.

The members of Menswear—vocalist Johnny Dean (born Dec. 12, 1971), guitarist Simon White, guitarist Chris Gentry (born Feb. 23, 1977), bassist Stuart Black, and drummer Matt Everett—told everyone around Camden, London that they were in a band before they had actually rehearsed. Toward the end of 1994, they decided to actually start playing music, choosing the name Menswear and writing Elastica- and Blur-inspired pop songs.

The group's first single, "I'll Manage Somehow," received good notices in the *NME* and *Melody Maker*, and their second single, "Daydreamer," peaked at No. 14. —*Stephen Thomas Erlewine*

● **Nuisance** / Oct. 24, 1995 / London ◆◆◆◆
Perhaps Menswear was always destined to be a footnote in pop history, a product of the heady good times of London in 1994 and 1995. Reportedly signed after only three shows, the band was never given the chance to fully develop before they recorded their debut album, *Nuisance*. At the time of their first single, they appropriated the sound of Blur and the style of Pulp; by the time *Nuisance* was released, they also incorporated the sound of Elastica and Oasis, making the band a virtual Cliff Notes of Brit-pop. Naturally, Menswear doesn't quite have the skills or panache of any of their idols, but that doesn't mean they are lacking in charm. Like Oasis and Blur, Menswear appropriates sections of pop history, claiming them as their own. However, they aren't half the songwriters that Noel Gallagher and Damon Albarn are, which means many of their ideas are never developed. Nevertheless, when they assimilate them fully—as in the intoxicating rush of "Around You Again" or the sweeping ballad "Being Brave," which lifts the intro to Pink Floyd's "Comfortably Numb"—the band is an undeniable guilty pleasure. When pressed, the 'swear can come up with irresistibly infectious pop gems, from the frazzled Monkees pop of "Sleeping In" to the flat-out great single "Daydreamer," which sounds more like Wire than Elastica, only funnier, even if it may be unintentional. Even funnier are Johnny Dean's lyrics, from the groupie saga of "125 West 3rd Street" to "Stardust," a silly attack on Primal Scream's Bobby Gillespie. In all, *Nuisance* is the perfect product from a band that is better known for being seen than being heard. —*Stephen Thomas Erlewine*

Natalie Merchant

b. Oct. 26, 1963, Jamestown, NY
Piano, Vocals / Singer-Songwriter, Pop-Rock, Adult Alternative

Natalie Merchant was the lead singer for 10,000 Maniacs from their inception in the early '80s to her departure in early 1994. Merchant began a solo career the following year, releasing her solo debut, *Tiger Lily*, in the summer of 1995. —*Stephen Thomas Erlewine*

Tigerlily / Jun. 20, 1995 / Elektra ◆◆◆◆
Tigerlily, Natalie Merchant's first solo record, does sound different than 10,000 Maniacs. Instead of relying strictly on jangly folk-rock, Merchant continues opening her music up as she did on *Our Time in Eden*, her last album with the Maniacs. From the understated groove of "Carnival" to the rolling "San Andreas Fault," the added emphasis on rhythmic texture works, creating an intimate but not exclusive atmosphere that holds throughout the record, even when her occasionally sophomoric, sentimental poetry threatens to sink the album in the weight of its own preciousness (as in "River," her tribute to the late actor River Phoenix). —*Stephen Thomas Erlewine*

Mercury Rev

f. Buffalo, NY
Alternative Pop-Rock, Psychedelic, Indie Rock, Neo-Psychedelia, Dream-Pop

Not so much a band as a long, strange trip, the chaotic avant-pop pranksters Mercury Rev formed in Buffalo, NY in the late 1980s. Originally comprising vocalist David Baker, vocalist-silver pickup guitarist Jonathan Donahue, guitar shaper and single-exhaust clarinetist Grasshopper (born Sean Mackowiak), rooster tail bass flautist Suzanne Thorpe, bass explorer Dave Fridmann, and mojo stick drummer Jimy Chambers, the sextet—always rife with personality conflicts—interacted with one another infrequently, and their first recordings evolved simply as a means of creating soundtracks for the members' experimental student films as well as for Howard Nelson's *Lite-Brite* and Marco Fogg's *Sugardaddy Sea*.

Encouraged to further their music by academic mentor Tony Conrad—a minimalist composer and multimedia artist who had performed with John Cale, LaMonte Young, and Faust—the loosely-connected aggregate dubbed Mercury Rev (a name whose inspiration was variously attributed to an imaginary Russian ballet dancer, a sharp rise in temperature, or a revved-up auto) began to emerge, and eventually the group recorded a demo onto a reel of 35mm magnetic film. At the same time, Donahue was working as a concert promoter, and scheduled a Butthole Surfers gig; after the show, he befriended the support act, Oklahoma's like-minded Flaming Lips, and soon joined the tour as a guitar technician. Ultimately, Donahue—under the alias "Dingus"—became the Lips' lead guitarist, and with them recorded 1990's *In a Priest Driven Ambulance*, an album produced by Fridmann.

With Mercury Rev effectively in limbo and its members scattered across the country, their demo tape somehow made its way to the British offices of the Rough Trade label, which contacted Baker about signing the group. Soon, the band convened to record their debut *Yerself Is Steam*, an LP cut at the same time Donahue and Fridmann were also working on the Flaming Lips' major-label bow *Hit to Death in the Future Head*. A brilliantly melodic and free-form set highlighted by distorted art-pop epics like "Chasing a Bee," "Coney Island Cyclone," and "Frittering," *Yerself Is Steam* was issued to widespread acclaim in 1991; however, within weeks of the LP's release Rough Trade's American branch declared bankruptcy, aborting any hopes of proper distribution or promotion.

Still, a British tour followed, and not without incident; the performances, mounted without any practice sessions, constantly teetered on the brink of disintegration—set lists were nonexistent, and Baker frequently hopped off the stage (in mid-song, no less) to grab a drink. Additionally, the group was reportedly banned from air travel after Donahue attempted to gouge out Grasshopper's eye with a spoon in mid-flight. Following the tour, Mercury Rev again went their separate ways; the members found menial jobs, moved in with their parents, or earned money by participating in medical experiments. Finally, Sony signed the group and reissued *Yerself Is Steam* along with an extra track, the sublime single "Car Wash Hair" (recorded with the aid of Luna's Dean Wareham after Fridmann—much to his bandmates' dismay—spent all of their advance money to fund a Bermuda vacation package for his mother).

Amid considerable tension, Mercury Rev set up studio space in a barn to craft their second album; after completing the principal recording sessions, the group collected samples from sites as far-ranging as Times Square and NASA's Cape Canaveral to flesh out the music's dense, prismatic sound. Following the release of the stunning 1993 LP, dubbed *Boces* in honor of an upstate New York school for children, Mercury Rev again toured, even playing the second stage at Lollapalooza; ultimately, the band was kicked off the bill during the festival's Denver stop due to excessive noise—the electricity to the stage was cut off in mid-performance, and concert security removed their soundman in a headlock. Additionally, an elaborate video for the single "Something for Joey" was shot with the notorious porn star Ron Jeremy, but the clip's suggestive space-age sexcapades and visual double entendres made mainstream airplay a moot point.

After relations soured to the point where Baker was travelling to gigs apart from his bandmates, he was dismissed from Mercury Rev's ranks; under the name Shady, he returned in 1994 with *World*, an excellent solo LP recorded with luminaries from the Boo Radleys, Rollerskate Skinny, and St. Johnny. With their newly-perfected Tettix Wave Accumulator (patent pending) in tow, the remaining quintet returned to the studio to record 1995's *See You on the Other Side*, a beautiful, shimmering effort that found the group—newly freed of Baker's darker impulses—exploring increasingly diverse stylistic territory with newfound emotional depth. Under the name Harmony Rockets, Mercury Rev also issued 1995's *Paralyzed Mind of the Archangel Void*, a 40-minute improvisational excursion into ambient noise. —*Jason Ankeny*

Yerself Is Steam / 1991 / Columbia ✦✦✦✦
One of the most original debuts in years, Mercury Rev's *Yerself Is Steam* could be classified as '70s art-rock played with '90s postmodern sensibilities, but the band refuses to stay in one place. Instead of the self-absorbed excesses of Pink Floyd, there are elements of psychedelia, punk, free jazz, and warped pop. *Yerself Is Steam* only hints at the band's potential. Columbia's CD reissue includes the Velvet Underground pop of "Car Wash Hair" as a bonus track. —*Stephen Thomas Erlewine*

● **Boces** / Jun. 1, 1993 / Columbia ✦✦✦✦
Boces, Mercury Rev's second album, is an even stronger affair than their first, showcasing the possibilities of their truly mind-bending neo-psychedelic guitar rock. All of their flights into the netherworld are fascinating; even the 11-minute songs seem too short. —*Stephen Thomas Erlewine*

See You on the Other Side / Sep. 19, 1995 / Work ✦✦✦✦
Without David Baker, Mercury Rev opens up, relying on the bright psychedelia of Jonathan Donahue's songwriting. While that means the band has a greater tendency to indulge themselves in noisy, free-form jams that don't lead anywhere, it also means that the music is more accessible, since Baker's dark hallucinations no longer dominate the group's experimental instrumental section. However, the music on *See You on the Other Side* isn't quite as compelling without the tension between Donahue's colorful pop and Baker's haunting voice and lyrics—which means that although they've progressed musically, they've lost an essential element of what made their first two records distinctive. —*Stephen Thomas Erlewine*

The Merry-Go-Round

f. Los Angeles, CA, **db.** 1969
Pop-Rock
Like the Left Banke, the Merry-Go-Round were teen pop-rock prodigies who combined British Invasion pop melodies with baroque-pop studio polish. The L.A. group, dominated by singer and songwriter Emmitt Rhodes, had a couple of huge local hits, "Live" and "You're a Very Lovely Woman," but achieved little national success before disbanding in 1969. A Paul McCartney soundalike and lookalike, Rhodes was blatantly influenced by McCartney's *Magical Mystery Tour*-era compositions, as one listen to "Pardon Me" (a ringer for "Fool on the Hill") will attest. Rhodes achieved modest commercial and critical recognition with his solo recordings in the early '70s. —*Richie Unterberger*

● **Best of the Merry-Go-Round** / 1985 / Rhino ✦✦✦✦
A 14-song compilation of songs from their sole album, plus a few rare singles. Highlights include "Live," "Come Ride," "Time Will Show the Wiser" (covered by Fairport Convention on their first album), and especially the gorgeous, haunting string ballad "You're a Very Lovely Woman." Solid, melodic late-'60s pop-rock with sophisticated arrangements, though it's sometimes lightweight. —*Richie Unterberger*

The Merseybeats

f. 1963, Liverpool, England, **db.** 1966
British Invasion
The Merseybeats were one of the better Liverpool bands of the British Invasion, scoring several major and minor hits in the UK, although they made no impact whatsoever in America. Friends of the Who (with whom they shared management for a time) and the Beatles, the band leaned toward mid-tempo harmony numbers, with the occasional ballad and raver thrown in. Not nearly as distinguished as top-line British Invasion pop-rockers like the Hollies and the Searchers, the Merseybeats did have classy taste in cover material, recording the original version of Bacharach-David's "Wishin' and Hopin'" (a hit in the US for Dusty Springfield), reaching the UK Top 40 with "I Stand Accused" (covered by Elvis Costello), and releasing covers of "Mr. Moonlight" and "Fortune Teller" before the Beatles and the Stones recorded their more famous versions. Like many of the original Liverpool bands, they were crippled by a lack of songwriting talent. After breaking up in 1966, members Tony Crane and Billy Kinsley formed the Merseys, who landed a huge British hit with "Sorrow" (covered by David Bowie on *Pin Ups*) the same year. —*Richie Unterberger*

The Merseybeats / 1964 / Fontana ✦✦✦
A very well-programmed 18-song collection representing the band's good and bad sides. The former includes crisp pop-rock ditties like "Don't Turn Around," "Last Night," and "It's Love That Really Counts," while the latter is mostly an over-reliance on show tunes. —*Bruce Eder*

● **Beat & Ballads** / 1982 / Edsel ✦✦✦✦
All of their British hits, and indeed most of the A—and B-sides they cut between 1963 and 1965—"I Think of You," "Don't Turn Around," "Wishin 'N' Hopin'," "I Stand Accused." Also includes the 1964 single "Last Night," which flopped, but is one of the best obscure British invasion pop-rockers. —*Richie Unterberger*

The Merton Parkas

f. 1978, Merton, England, **db.** 1980
New Wave, Power Pop, Mod-Revival
The Merton Parkas, taking their name from their home in South London (Merton) and the classic mod-wear (the parka), are another footnote in the British mod-revival of the late '70s (which itself was merely a footnote in music history). Formed by brothers Mick Talbot (keyboards) and Danny Talbot (vocals) along with Neil Wurrel (bass) and Simon Smith (drums) in 1978, they became one of the first third-wave mod-revivalists to release an album, *Face in the Crowd*, which featured the hit single "You Need Wheels." While many of the movement's followers took a more serious approach, the Merton Parkas tapped into the novelty side of the genre, becoming something of a mod version of Madness, though less innovative (and less interesting). Mick Talbot later teamed up with Paul Weller to form the Style Council in 1983. —*Chris Woodstra*

● **Face in the Crowd** / 1979 / Beggars Banquet ✦✦✦✦
The band's sole LP, while certainly flawed, offers a lightweight, novelty approach to the Jam-inspired mod-revival. A little too derivative to be taken seriously, but there are some fun songs nonetheless, such as the UK hit "You Need Wheels," "Plastic Smile," and the title track. —*Chris Woodstra*

Metallica

f. 1981, Los Angeles, CA
Thrash, Heavy Metal, Speed Metal
Metallica was easily the best, most influential heavy metal band of the '80s, responsible for bringing the music back to earth. Instead of playing the usual rock star games of metal stars of the early '80s, the band looked and talked like they were from the street. Metallica expanded the limits of thrash, using speed and volume not for their own sake, but to enhance their intricately structured compositions. The release of 1983's *Kill 'Em All* marked the beginning of the legitimization of heavy

metal's underground, bringing new complexity and depth to thrash metal. With each album, the band's playing and writing improved; James Hetfield developed a signature rhythm playing that matched his growl, while lead guitarist Kirk Hammett became one of the most copied guitarists in metal. Lars Ulrich's thunderous, yet complex drumming clicked in perfectly with Cliff Burton's innovative bass playing.

After releasing their masterpiece *Master of Puppets* in 1986, tragedy struck when the band's tour bus crashed in Sweden, killing Burton. When the band decided to continue, Jason Newsted was chosen to replace Burton; two years later, the band released the conceptually ambitious *...And Justice for All*, which hit the Top Ten without any radio play and very little support from MTV. But Metallica completely crossed over into the mainstream with 1991's *Metallica*, which found the band trading in their long compositions for more concise song structures; it resulted in a No. 1 album that sold over seven million copies in the US alone. The band launched a long, long tour that kept them on the road for nearly two years. By the '90s, Metallica had changed the rules for all heavy metal bands; they were the leaders of the genre, respected not only by headbangers, but by mainstream record buyers and critics. No other heavy metal band has ever been able to pull off such a trick.

However, the group lost some members of their core audience with their long-awaited follow-up to *Metallica*, 1996's *Load*. For *Load*, the band decided to move toward alternative rock in terms of image—they cut their hair and had their picture taken by Anton Corbijn. Although the album was a hit upon its summer release—entering the charts at No. 1 and selling three million copies within two months—certain members of their audience complained about the shift in image, as well as the group's decision to headline the sixth Lollapalooza. —*Stephen Thomas Erlewine*

☆ **Kill 'Em All** / 1983 / Elektra ✦✦✦✦✦
The true birth of thrash. On *Kill 'Em All*, Metallica fuses the tight, controlled riffing of N.W.O.B.H.M. bands like Judas Priest, Iron Maiden, and Diamond Head with the velocity of Motörhead and punk and hardcore bands. James Hetfield's technical rhythm guitar style drives most of the album, especially on classic tracks like "The Four Horsemen," "Jump in the Fire," and "Seek and Destroy." Unlike later releases, there isn't much variation (apart from a lyrical bass solo from Cliff Burton), but the band's jaw-dropping power makes up for it. An Elektra reissue added the cover songs "Blitzkrieg" and "Am I Evil?" from the European *Creeping Death* EP, which have since been deleted but are worth tracking down. —*Steve Huey*

Ride the Lightning / 1984 / Elektra ✦✦✦✦
An incredibly ambitious follow-up, *Ride the Lightning* finds Metallica aggressively expanding their compositional technique and range of expression. The material ranges from blasts of fury ("Fight Fire with Fire") to tight, concise groove-rockers ("For Whom the Bell Tolls," "Escape") to the extended title track, but perhaps the strongest single song is the slow, haunting, partially acoustic suicide lament "Fade to Black," which also illustrates the band's move away from traditional metal theatrics toward more serious fare. While it is a transitional album, *Ride the Lightning*'s experiments push the boundaries of metal in consistently intriguing ways. —*Steve Huey*

★ **Master of Puppets** / 1986 / Elektra ✦✦✦✦✦
Without question Metallica's finest album, and that says something. The extended, progressive compositions (eight songs in just under one hour) vary enough in texture, tempo, and mood to hold interest throughout; taken as a whole, the album is a masterpiece, and the first half in particular is absolutely flawless. The subject matter is fairly cohesive; in general, *Master of Puppets* addresses the misuse of power in various ways. Even though it follows much the same pacing as *Ride the Lightning*, *Master* is more focused, and the band sounds more in control of its innovations. It stands as one of the best heavy metal albums ever recorded; some critics have called it *the* best. —*Steve Huey*

Garage Days Re-Revisited / 1987 / Elektra ✦✦✦
Following Cliff Burton's death, Metallica took some time off and initiated new bassist Jason Newsted with a raw, unpolished EP of covers originally recorded by Diamond Head, Holocaust, Killing Joke, Budgie, and the Misfits. Most fit the band's style quite well; only "Last Caress" sounds out of place, as the original seemed looser and more dangerous. As a showcase for some strong metal riffs and material by mostly underground bands, the EP works quite well. —*Steve Huey*

...And Justice for All / 1988 / Elektra ✦✦✦✦
The first thing a listener will notice about *...And Justice for All* isn't the ever-growing sophistication of Metallica's compositions or the chilling, apocalyptic lyrics—it's the terrible production, which unfortunately overshadows some of the band's brilliance. The guitars buzz thinly, the drums click more than pound, and Newsted's bass is nearly inaudible. That said, *...And Justice for All* is Metallica's most complex, ambitious work; every song is an expanded suite, with none clocking in at under five minutes. While not as consistently focused as *Master of Puppets*, the best moments here are at least its equal. Based on Dalton Trumbo's anti-

war novel *Johnny Got His Gun*, "One" is a tour de force and possibly the band's best song, combining spooky arpeggios, an oddly haunting melody, and a structure building up to the pummeling "machine-gun" section and wild guitar solo that close the track. The abundance of good material here makes the poor sound that much more frustrating. —*Steve Huey*

Metallica / Aug. 1991 / Elektra ✦✦✦✦
Longtime fans may call this one a sellout but that's hardly the case. Instead, the group has increased the bottom end of their sound and keeps the riff-per-song limit down to about two. This may keep *Metallica* from alienating staunch metal-haters, but it's the quality of the songs—hits such as "Enter Sandman" and the ballad "Nothing Else Matters," but also "Holier Than Thou"—that has made this their most successful (and best) album to date. —*John Floyd*

Live Shit...Binge and Purge / Nov. 23, 1993 / Elektra ✦✦✦
Weighing in at three CDs and three videos, plus a bunch of tour memorabilia, the sheer bulk of *Live Shit...Binge and Purge* scares off anyone but the most devoted fans, which is too bad. Although it is exhausting, this box provides ample proof of the brutal power of Metallica in concert—the entire program of a Mexico City concert is included, and it is awe-inspiring. For hardcore fans, *Live Shit* is a godsend. —*Stephen Thomas Erlewine*

Load / Jun. 1996 / Elektra ✦✦✦
Delivered five years after their eponymous "black" album in 1991, *Load* captures Metallica settling into an uneasy period of maturation. Under the guidance of producer Bob Rock, Metallica have streamlined their sound, cutting away most of the twisting, unpredictable time signatures and the mind-numbingly fast riffs. What's left is polished—and disappointingly straightforward—heavy metal. Metallica's attempts at expanding their sonic palette have made them seem more conventional than they ever had before. They add in Southern boogie rock, country-rock, and power ballads to their bag of tricks, which make them sound like '70s arena rock holdovers. Metallica's idea of opening up their sound is to concentrate on relentless mid-tempo boogie—over half the album is dedicated to songs that are meant to groove, but they simply don't swing. Metallica sounds tight, but with the material they've written, they should sound loose. That becomes apparent as the songs drag out over the album's nearly 80-minute running time—there are only so many times that a band can work the same tempo *exactly the same way* before it becomes tedious. It isn't surprising to hear Metallica get stodgier and more conservative as they get older, but it is nonetheless depressing. —*Stephen Thomas Erlewine*

The Meters

f. 1966, New Orleans, LA, db. 1977
Instrumental / Soul, Funk, R&B, New Orleans R&B
The Meters defined New Orleans funk, not only on their own recordings, but also as the backing band for numerous artists, including many produced by Allen Toussaint. Where the funk of Sly Stone and James Brown was wild, careening, and determinedly urban, the Meters were down-home and earthy. Nearly all of their own recordings were instrumentals, putting the emphasis on the organic and complex rhythms. The syncopated, layered percussion intertwined with the gritty grooves of the guitar and organ, creating a distinctive sound that earned a small, devoted cult during the '70s, including musicians like Paul McCartney and Robert Palmer, both of whom used the group as a backing band for recording. Despite their reputation as an extraordinary live band, the Meters never broke into the mainstream, but their sound provided the basis for much of the funk and hip-hop of the '80s and '90s.

Throughout their career, the Meters were always led by Art Neville (keyboard, vocals), one of the leading figures of the New Orleans musical community. As a teenager in high school, he recorded the seminal "Mardi Gras Mambo" with his group, the Hawketts, for Chess Records. The exposure with the Hawketts led to solo contracts with Specialty and Instant, where he released a handful of singles that became regional hits in the early '60s. Around 1966, he formed Art Neville and the Sounds with his brothers Aaron and Charles (both vocalists), guitarist Leo Nocentelli, drummer Joseph "Zigaboo" Modeliste, and bassist George Porter. The band grew out of informal jam sessions the musicians held in local New Orleans nightclubs. After the band spent a few months playing under the Sounds name, producer Allen Toussaint and Marshall Sehorn hired the instrumentalists—without the vocalists—to be the house band for their label Sansu Enterprises.

As the house band for Sansu, the Meters played on records by Earl King, Lee Dorsey, Chris Kenner, and Betty Harris, as well as Toussaint himself. They also performed and recorded on their own, releasing danceable instrumental singles on Josie Records. "Sophisticated Cissy" and "Cissy Strut" became Top Ten R&B hits in the spring of 1969, followed by the No. 11 hits "Look-Ka Py Py" and "Chicken Strut" a year later. The Meters stayed at Josie until 1972, and throughout that time they reached the R&B Top 50 consistently, usually placing within the

Top 40. In 1972, the group moved to Reprise Records, yet they didn't sever their ties with Sansu, electing to keep Toussaint as their producer and Sehorn as their manager. Ironically, the Meters didn't have nearly as many hit singles at Reprise, but their profile remained remarkably high. If anything, the group became hipper, performing on records by Robert Palmer, Dr. John, Labelle, King Biscuit Boy, and Paul McCartney. By the release of 1975's *Fire on the Bayou,* the Meters had a Top 40 hit with *Rejuvenation*'s "Hey Pocky A-Way" (1974), and they had gained a significant following among both rock audience and critics. *Fire on the Bayou* received significant praise, and the group opened for the Rolling Stones on the British band's 1975 and 1976 tours.

During 1975, the Meters embarked on the Wild Tchoupitoulas project with the Nevilles' uncle and cousin, George and Amos Landry, two members of the Mardi Gras ceremonial black Indian tribe, the Wild Tchoupitoulas. The Meters, the Landrys, and the Neville Brothers—Aaron, Charles, Art, and Cyril—were all involved in the recording of the album, which received enthusiastic reviews upon its release in 1976. Cyril joined the Meters after the record's release. Despite all of the acclaim for *The Wild Tchoupitoulas,* its adventurous tendencies indicated that the group was feeling constrained by its signature sound. Such suspicions were confirmed the following year, when they separated from Toussaint and Sehorn, claiming they needed to take control of their artistic direction. Following the split, the Meters released *New Directions* in 1977, but shortly after its appearance, Toussaint and Sehorn claimed the rights to the group's name. Instead of fighting, the band broke up; Art and Cyril formed the Neville Brothers with Aaron and Charles, while the remaining trio became session musicians in New Orleans. Modeliste, in particular, became a well-known professional musician, touring with the New Barbarians in 1979 and moving to L.A. during the '80s.

The Meters reunited as a touring unit in 1990, with Russell Batiste taking over the drum duties from Modeliste. Four years later, Nocentelli left the band, allegedly because he and Art Neville disagreed whether the band should be paid for samples hip-hop groups took from their old records; he was replaced by Brian Stoltz, who had played with the Neville Brothers. The Meters continued to tour throughout the '90s. *—Stephen Thomas Erlewine*

The Meters / 1969 / Josie ✦✦✦

While this isn't an album in the strictest sense, but a collection of singles, it was certainly welcomed when it was released. This featured some prime cuts from the Meters, the great New Orleans funk ensemble who began doing their own sessions in the late '60s. They only cut two albums for Josie, and both were monsters. Both were later deleted, although the hit singles have since been reissued. *—Ron Wynn*

Look: Ka Py Py / 1970 / Rounder ✦✦✦✦

The Meters' great 1960s singles anticipated the coming of funk. They made short, catchy tunes and scored occasional hits, particularly the single "Look-Ka-Py-Py," one of 12 outstanding tunes on this CD. These were the ultimate party-dance records, and they also showed the link between traditional African rhythms, New Orleans shuffle, second line sounds, soul, and funk. Marvelous rhythm music at its hottest. *—Ron Wynn*

Cissy Strut / 1974 / Island ✦✦✦✦

The Meters made their anthemic funk cuts on Josie in the late '60s. The New Orleans crew backed Fats Domino, Lee Dorsey, and Aaron Neville before they started jamming on their own in the late '60s. Island issued this anthology of Josie material in the mid-'70s. It came out in the US too. Rounder has since reissued some of this material. *—Ron Wynn*

Rejuvenation / 1974 / Reprise ✦✦✦

A nice, but not as definitive, mid-'70s Meters session. Their Reprise albums were never as transcendent, energetic, or freewheeling as the Josie tracks, but were better produced and engineered. This was one of the better sessions, and sometimes the Meters seemed to recapture that old New Orleans funk energy. But Reprise's attempts to bring them crossover success inevitably disrupted their chemistry, as they tried to blend a formulaic rock sensibility with the group's close-knit funk. *—Ron Wynn*

Best of the Meters / 1975 / Virgo ✦✦✦

A good collection of this quintessential New Orleans funk group's best '70s singles for the Reprise label. Of course they did their finest cuts for Josie, but turned in some reasonably good work on Reprise in a more rock-funk direction. "Hey, Pokey-A-Way" was probably the Reprise cut closest to matching the superb Josie singles. But these are the songs that got them gigs with the Rolling Stones and work with Paul McCartney and Robert Palmer, so they did have some value. *—Ron Wynn*

New Directions / 1977 / Warner Brothers ✦✦

This was perhaps the weakest Meters album, with rather mediocre vocals and songs, decent production and arrangements, but little of the fire or zeal that characterized their fine Josie dates and their earlier rock-funk Reprise material. They were nearing the end of the line as a group anyhow, something that this material reflects. *—Ron Wynn*

Good Old Funky Music / 1990 / Rounder ✦✦✦

There are some good moments on this disc, culled from unissued material from the Meters' Josie heyday in the late '60s and early '70s, but there's too much filler. *—Bill Dahl*

The Meters Jam / Mar. 1, 1992 / Rounder ✦✦

The 10 songs on this CD are a mixed bag, mainly because The Meters insisted on singing and simply weren't great vocalists. Their leads and harmonies on "Come Together" and "Bo Diddley," among others, were exuberant, but didn't add much to the proceedings. On the other hand, there haven't been many groups in any style that clicked any more smoothly and soulfully. Their inspired, funky playing almost overshadows the tepid vocals. *—Ron Wynn*

★ **Funkify Your Life** / Feb. 28, 1995 / Rhino ✦✦✦✦✦

Two discs of the Meters is a lot to ask of most casual fans, yet for the devoted few, *Funkify Your Life* is essential. Featuring tracks from both their Josie and Warner years, the double-disc set captures some of the rawest New Orleans funk recorded in the Crescent City. *—Stephen Thomas Erlewine*

George Michael

b. Jun. 26, 1963, Bushey, England
Guitar, Vocals / Dance-Pop, Adult Contemporary, Pop-Rock

Yorgos Kyriatou Panayioutou (George Michael) achieved fame in the duo Wham! in his native UK in 1982. Through 1986, he and his partner, Andrew Ridgeley, scored hit after hit in a variety of styles from rap to uptempo pop to slow ballads. As songwriter and lead singer, Michael gradually overshadowed his partner, and by the time they split, he was ready for a massively successful solo career. This began with the 1987 album *Faith,* which featured a series of chart-topping hit singles and sold more than seven million copies. That Michael had not achieved a similar critical success was evident from the title of his follow-up album, *Listen Without Prejudice—Vol. 1,* which—though it sold a million copies, included two Top Ten hits, and hit No. 2—must be considered a major commercial disappointment. With *Vol. 2* apparently shelved, Michael contributed several songs to the charity album *Red Hot + Dance* in 1992, and one of them, "Too Funky," reached the Top 20.

After the failure of *Listen Without Prejudice,* Michael engaged in a bitter legal battle with his record company, accusing them of not properly promoting the album and asking them to release him from his contract; he stated that he would refuse to release any records if he lost the lawsuit. He lost. After losing an appeal, Michael bought his way out his Columbia contract and signed with the music division of Dreamworks, a fledgling entertainment corporation founded by Steven Spielberg, Jeffrey Katzenberg, and David Geffen. In 1996, he released *Older. —William Ruhlmann*

★ **Faith** / 1987 / Columbia ✦✦✦✦✦

George Michael certainly looked like the biggest pop star to emerge in the second half of the '80s when he released this debut album after his years in Wham! It wasn't just that the music topped the charts for 12 weeks and sold seven million copies and that six of its nine tracks were Top Ten hits (four No. 1s, a No. 2, and a No. 5); it was that Michael, who wrote, arranged, and produced, seemed to have a broad understanding of all aspects of pop, from the rockabilly of the title track and the heartfelt ballad "Father Figure" to the R&B dance grooves of "I Want Your Sex" (indeed, the album also got to No. 2 on the Black charts). *—William Ruhlmann*

Listen Without Prejudice, Vol. 1 / Aug. 1990 / Columbia ✦✦✦✦

Michael's follow-up to the massive success of *Faith* found him turning inward, trying to gain critical acclaim as well as sales. *Listen Without Prejudice* is not an entirely successful effort; Michael has cut back on the effortless hooks and melodies that crammed not only *Faith* but also his singles with Wham!, and his socially conscious lyrics tend to be heavy-handed. But the highlights—the light, Beatlesque harmonies of "Heal the Pain," the plodding No. 1 "Praying for Time," "Waiting for That Day," and the Top Ten "Freedom '90"—make a case for his talents as a pop craftsman. *—Stephen Thomas Erlewine*

Older / Apr. 1996 / DreamWorks ✦✦✦

Older is the album that many observers initially believed *Listen Without Prejudice, Vol. 1* to be—a relentlessly serious affair, George Michael's bid for artistic credibility. It's an album that makes *Listen Without Prejudice* sound like *Faith.* Michael has dispensed with the catchy, frothy dance-pop numbers that brought him fame, concentrating on stately, pretentious ballads—even "Fastlove," the album's one dance track, lacks the carefree spark of his earlier work. Although Michael's skills as a pop craftsman still shine through—several songs are well-constructed ballads that rank with his best material—his earnestness sinks the album. It is one thing to be mature and another to be boring. Too often, Michael mistakes slight melodies for mature craftsmanship and *Older* never quite recovers. When melodies do pop up, he doesn't deliver them with enough force to make an impact, and the album slowly disappears as a result. —*Stephen Thomas Erlewine*

Lee Michaels

b. Nov. 24, 1945, Los Angeles, CA
Piano, Vocals / Psychedelic, Pop-Rock
One of the most interesting second-division California psychedelic musicians, keyboardist Lee Michaels was one of the most soulful white vocalists of the late '60s and early '70s. Between 1968 and 1972, he released half a dozen accomplished albums on A&M that encompassed baroque psychedelic pop and gritty white, sometimes gospelish R&B with equal facility. A capable songwriter, Michaels was blessed with an astonishing upper range, occasionally letting loose some thrilling funky wails. In 1971, he landed a surprise Top Ten single with "Do You Know What I Mean," one of the best and funkiest AM hits of the early '70s.

But Michaels was really much more of an album-oriented artist, from the time he began recording in the late '60s. Michaels started playing music in Southern California, where he was in a band with future members of Moby Grape, the Turtles, and Canned Heat. By the time he signed to A&M, however, he'd moved to San Francisco, joining the management stable of Matthew Katz (which also included, at various times, Jefferson Airplane, Moby Grape, and It's a Beautiful Day). Michaels was unusual for a San Francisco act in that he mostly relied on an organ-based sound, especially after the first pair of albums, when for a time he played, live and in the studio, with the mammoth drummer "Frosty" as his only accompanist.

"Do You Know What I Mean," ironically, was a throwaway tune that Michaels wrote hurriedly. Though Lee himself didn't think much of it, the song was a first-rate blast of white boy soul; around this time, the gospel influence that had often informed his sound come to the fore. His albums in the mid-'70s for Columbia, however, were both critical and commercial disappointments. Michaels moved to Hawaii for an extended retirement from the music business; aside from a self-released album in the early '80s, little's been heard from him since. —*Richie Unterberger*

Carnival of Life / 1968 / One Way ♦♦♦
A strong, cheerful debut, awash in the Summer of Love vibe, but featuring tight songs and arrangements. Although Lee played fewer instruments himself here than he would on his subsequent work, it introduces his organ-piano-harpsichord blend, heard to best effect on the uplifting opening track, "Hello." —*Richie Unterberger*

Recital / 1968 / One Way ♦♦♦
Michaels produced his second album himself and took over all the keyboard chores (he had played only sporadically on his first LP), accompanied by top-flight L.A. session players. Quite similar in sound and direction to his debut, it does show him expanding his songwriting horizons on tracks like "Grocery Soldier" and "The War." —*Richie Unterberger*

Lee Michaels / 1969 / A&M ♦♦♦♦
An abrupt but fairly successful change in direction, Lee's third album was recorded in a mere seven hours with drummer Frosty as his sole sideman, and is basically a reflection of his live set at the time. Far bluesier than his first two albums, side one is a 20-minute medley; side two features his superb interpretation of "Stormy Monday" and one of his best good-time numbers, "Heighty Hi." Some superb organ playing and thrilling high vocal trills, although Frosty's drum solo on the 20-minute track is tough to sit through. —*Richie Unterberger*

Fifth / 1971 / One Way ♦♦♦
Michaels went for a sparse, heavily soul—and gospel-influenced approach on this album, which includes his only big hit, "Do You Know What I Mean." For that matter, it also includes his only small hit, "Can I Get a Witness." But it's not among his best efforts, due to the similar arrangements and compositions, most of which echo the clanky piano-organ approach of "Do You Know I Mean" less effectively. —*Richie Unterberger*

● **The Collection** / Jul. 14, 1992 / Rhino ♦♦♦♦
Good 18-track overview of his A&M work, drawing from all six of the albums he released between 1968 and 1972. Includes "Do You Know What I Mean," "Stormy Monday," "Heighty Hi," "Hello," "The War," and "Carnival Of Life," as well as the 1969 non-LP B-side "Goodbye, Goodbye," and his only Top 40 single besides "Do You Know What I Mean," a cover of "Can I Get A Witness." —*Richie Unterberger*

Mickey & Sylvia

f. 1956, db. 1965
R&B, Rock 'n' Roll
Although this duo is primarily remembered as a one-hit act—for "Love Is Strange," which reached No. 11 in 1957—they actually recorded quite a few exciting hybrids of R&B and rock 'n' roll in the mid- and late '50s. Playing on countless '50s sessions for various labels (especially Atlantic and OKeh), Mickey Baker was one of the greatest guitar players of early

rock 'n' roll. With his partner (and former guitar student) Sylvia Robinson, he got to stretch out a bit from his usual role, with some trailblazing piercing, lean, and bluesy leads. Vocally, Mickey & Sylvia had an engagingly playful, occasionally sly 'n' sassy repartee that makes up in charm for what it might lack in smoke and firepower. Their recordings were inconsistent, but at their best they offered a fetching blend of blues, Bo Diddley, calypso, and doo wop.

After "Love Is Strange," whose devastating licks inspired countless guitarists, the duo notched a couple more substantial R&B hits. But although they recorded as late as 1965, they never approached the Top 20 again. Mickey Baker recorded as a solo artist and enjoyed a fairly successful career as an expatriate sessionman in France. Sylvia Robinson unexpectedly re-emerged with the No. 3 pre-disco hit "Pillow Talk" in 1973, and co-founded the pioneering rap label Sugar Hill in the late '70s. —*Richie Unterberger*

Love Is Strange [Bear Family] / 1990 / Bear Family ♦♦♦
This two-CD, 60-song (!) set includes many alternate takes and a fair amount of previously unreleased material, spanning 1955 to 1964. A lot of the obscurities are in the close harmony, doo wop vein, and are disappointingly short on verbal sparring and scorching Baker guitar. Lovingly packaged, but everyone except hardcore specialists should stick with the RCA compilation. —*Richie Unterberger*

● **"Love Is Strange" & Other Hits** / Mar. 1990 / RCA ♦♦♦♦
Unless you're a major R&B collector, it's likely you've never heard anything by this duo besides "Love Is Strange," their only major hit (and a great one). With 20 cuts from 1956-60, this disc reissues the bulk of their most interesting work. "Love Is Strange" will remain their most memorable tune after you've heard this, but on the whole, this is way-above-average '50s R&B-rock. If you're hungering for more great solos like the ones in "Love Is Strange," you'll find some here, especially in "There Oughta Be a Law" and the instrumental "Shake It Up," although Baker's virtuosity doesn't dominate most of the songs. Some of these tunes are routine doo wop, but a little over half the material is strong, ranging from the calypso-rock they're best remembered for to ballads to straightahead R&B shouters, with King Curtis on sax. —*Richie Unterberger*

The Willow Sessions / 1995 / Sequel ♦♦♦
Mickey & Sylvia are properly thought of as '50s rock 'n' rollers, but they actually did a good deal of recording in the '60s, though without much notable commercial success. Most of this 19-track CD was recorded in the early '60s for their own label, Willow; only one song, "Baby You're So Fine," was a hit, making the R&B Top 30. The album doesn't have the fire of their best sides for RCA in the '50s, but it's not bad, usually purveying a groove similar to their early work, though tamer. Occasionally Mickey brandishes blues-rock chops to show that he can still cut deep with his axe, especially on "Darling (I Miss You So)" and the previously unissued instrumentals "Sylvia's Blues" and "Mickey's Blues." There are also a few curious (but fairly respectable) cuts dating from the late '60s that Sylvia recorded for the All Platinum label in a much more contemporary soul vein. —*Richie Unterberger*

Bette Midler

b. Dec. 1, 1945, Patterson, NJ
Vocals / Nostalgia, Adult Contemporary, Pop, Soft Rock, Show Tunes
Bette Midler counts singing as only one of her talents; at times, since 1972, when she first came to national recognition, it has seemed to be the least of her talents. Still, she has managed to score a number of major hits in a roller-coaster career as a recording artist. Born in Patterson, NJ, and raised in Hawaii, Midler early on showed an interest in singing and acting, and by the '60s she had moved to New York and gotten a role in the long-running Broadway hit *Fiddler on the Roof*. Midler developed a nightclub act that included comedy and singing of a variety of kinds of material, including show tunes, pop hits, and even a takeoff on the Andrews Sisters, and appeared with increasing frequency in New York with her accompanist, Barry Manilow. She was signed to Atlantic Records and released *The Divine Miss M* (1972), which went gold and included a Top Ten single cover of the Andrews Sisters' "Boogie Woogie Bugle Boy." *Bette Midler* (1973) was similarly successful.

Midler's album sales fell off during the rest of the '70s, though her records always reached the Top 100 in the album chart. But in 1979 she starred in the film *The Rose*, a fictional account of the life of Janis Joplin, and the title track became a Top Ten hit. 1980 saw the release of Midler's concert film, *Divine Madness*, and her best-selling book, *A View from a Broad*. Her next film, *Jinxed* (1982), however, was a major flop, and subsequent records didn't fare well. Midler made a cinematic comeback with *Down and Out in Beverly Hills* (1986), but it wasn't until 1989 that she had another pop hit, when her version of "Wind Beneath My Wings" from her film *Beaches* became a No. 1 hit. This rejuvenated her singing career, and 1990's *Some People's Lives* became a Top Ten, million-selling album, with the song "From a Distance" hitting No. 2. Midler's soundtrack album to her 1991 film *For the Boys* was also a gold-selling hit. — *William Ruhlmann*

The Divine Miss M / 1972 / Atlantic ♦♦♦♦
Midler's early camp style is captured in this debut album, which features her torchy version of "Do You Want to Dance?", the bubbly remake of "Boogie Woogie Bugle Boy," and Buzzy Linhart's "Friends," all Top 40 hits. — *William Ruhlmann*

Bette Midler / 1973 / Atlantic ♦♦♦
This is an earthy mix of blues, R&B, and '40s boogie-woogie. — *Bil Carpenter*

Songs for the New Depression / 1976 / Atlantic ♦♦♦♦
Notable for a duet with Bob Dylan on "Buckets of Rain" and an excellent version of Tom Waits' "Shiver Me Timbers." — *William Ruhlmann*

The Rose / 1979 / Atlantic ♦♦♦♦
The soundtrack to Midler's successful film, with the title track written by Amanda McBroom. — *William Ruhlmann*

Divine Madness / 1980 / Atlantic ♦♦♦♦
This record showcases Midler at her liveliest, during a concert at Pasadena Civic Auditorium. — *Larry Lapka*

No Frills / 1983 / Atlantic ♦♦♦
Top-40 pop and light rock. — *Bil Carpenter*

For the Boys / Nov. 12, 1991 / Atlantic ♦♦♦
A film placing Midler in the Andrews Sisters' milieu of WWII was an inspired choice, and the soundtrack shows her abilities on period material as well as giving her a chance to sing a touching version of the Beatles' "In My Life." — *William Ruhlmann*

● **Divine Collection** / Jun. 22, 1993 / Atlantic ♦♦♦♦
Bette Midler's first compilation features most of her hits, including "Wind Beneath My Wings," "The Rose," "Boogie Woogie Bugle Boy," "From a Distance," and her version of "One More for My Baby (And One More for the Road)," recorded on one of the final episodes of *The Tonight Show* starring Johnny Carson. *Divine Collection* is the greatest-hits collection that Midler has needed for quite some time. — *AMG*

Midnight Oil

f. 1975, Sydney, Australia
Alternative Pop-Rock
Australia's Midnight Oil brought a new sense of political and social immediacy to pop music: not only did incendiary hits like "Beds Are Burning" and "Blue Sky Mine" bring global attention to the plight of, respectively, aboriginal settlers and impoverished workers, but the group also put its money where its mouth was—in addition to mounting benefit performances for groups like Greenpeace and Save the Whales, frontman Peter Garrett even ran for the Australian Senate on the Nuclear Disarmament Party ticket.

The band formed in Sydney in 1971 as Farm, and originally comprised guitarists Jim Moginie and Martin Rotsey, drummer Rob Hirst, and bassist Andrew "Bear" James; Garrett, a law student known for his seven-foot-tall stature and shaven head, assumed vocal duties in 1975, and the group soon rechristened itself Midnight Oil. After months of sporadic gigs, they began making the rounds to area record companies; following a string of rejections, the group formed its own label, Powderworks, and issued their self-titled debut—a taut, impassioned collection of guitar rock that quickly established the Midnight Oil sound— in 1978.

After declaring their independence from the music industry, the Oils grew increasingly active and outspoken in the political arena; after performing in opposition to uranium mining, they supported the Tibet Council before turning their attentions to the unfair practices of the local music industry, and formed their own booking agency in response to the monopoly exerted by area agents and promoters. With their 1979 sophomore effort *Head Injuries*, the band scored their first hit single, "Cold Cold Change," and earned a gold record. James left the band the following year due to health problems; with new bassist Peter Gifford, they cut the EP *Bird Noises*, another chart success.

With 1981's *Place Without a Postcard* (recorded with producer Glyn Johns), Midnight Oil achieved platinum status on the strength of the smash "Armistice Day," which won the group an American deal with Columbia Records. Their follow-up, 1982's *10, 9, 8, 7, 6, 5, 4, 3, 2, 1,* spent over two years in the Australian Top 40; after 1984's *Red Sails in the Sunset,* Garrett made his run at the Senate, losing by only a narrow margin. Participation in the Artists United Against Apartheid project followed, leading directly into Midnight Oil's increased interest in the battles of Australia's aboriginal settlers and a tour, dubbed "Black Fella White Fella," with the aborigine group the Warumpi Band.

The aborigines' plight came to the fore on 1987's *Diesel and Dust,* the Oils' breakthrough record: sparked by the hit single "Beds Are Burning," the album reached the US Top 20, and made Midnight Oil a household name. After bassist Dwayne "Bones" Hillman (ex-Swingers) replaced Gifford, Midnight Oil returned with 1990's *Blue Sky Mining,* which they followed with a concert outside of the Exxon corporation's Manhattan offices in protest of the company's handling of the Alaskan oil spill. (A film of the performance, titled *Black Rain Falls,* was later released, with profits going to Greenpeace.) The album *Earth and Sun and Moon* appeared in 1993, followed three years later by *Breathe.* — *Jason Ankeny*

Midnight Oil / 1978 / Columbia ♦♦
Generally speaking, Midnight Oil records pre-*10, 9, 8, 7, 6, 5, 4, 3, 2, 1* are the sound of a band honing its skills, trying to find itself, and succeeding infrequently. Their debut is worth mentioning only because it's a virtually worthless record. In fact, the leap they made between their first release and their great mid-'80s output is all the more astounding. Sounding clumsy and unsure of themselves, the Oil's debut sounds like a record they were told to make rather than one they wanted to make. —*John Dougan*

Head Injuries / 1979 / Columbia ♦♦♦♦
Fortunately, the same was not true on their second release, *Head Injuries* (great title). From start to finish this is a stoked and smokin' piece of punk-inspired hard rock with Garrett wailing away as though his life depended on it. Furious, relentless, chocked to the brim with solid songs and fierce playing, *Head Injuries* is hands-down the best of the Oil's early output. —*John Dougan*

Bird Noises / 1980 / Columbia ♦♦♦
On this four-song EP, Midnight Oil tried some musical variations after two albums of hard rock. "Let's rock," declared Peter Garrett at the outset of "No Time for Games" (a lament for the loss of childhood in the modern world), but the music in fact was restrained, and the group tried acoustic instruments and a moody instrumental, for an intriguing change of pace from their usual style. (Originally released in November 1980 in Australia on Powderworks Records, *Bird Noises* was released in 1990 in the US on Columbia Records as Columbia 46136.) —*William Ruhlmann*

Place Without a Postcard / 1981 / Columbia ♦♦♦
Place Without a Postcard, produced by the usually reliable Glyn Johns, is so-so, but a real letdown after the intensity of *Head Injuries.* The songs are very good, and at its best, it hints at the consistency that was to mark the rest of their recorded work, but it never coalesces into a whole. Even after repeated plays, *Place Without a Postcard* is too much of a mess to recommend unequivocally. —*John Dougan*

10, 9, 8, 7, 6, 5, 4, 3, 2, 1 / 1983 / Columbia ♦♦♦♦
Midnight Oil's first album to have a full-scale production, this album effectively brings out the band's driving rock sound, Peter Garrett's impassioned vocals, and the band's forthright political standpoint. —*William Ruhlmann*

Red Sails in the Sunset / 1984 / Columbia ♦♦♦♦
Midnight Oil's second international release found them ambitiously taking on a variety of lyrical causes in a variety of musical styles. Their basic approach, with its martial rhythms, chanted vocals, and guitar textures, served as a jumping-off place, but they always sounded more assured when they stuck to that, rather than trying other things. And the unrelentingly judgmental tone of the lyrics, sung with dead seriousness by Peter Garrett, tended to douse the album's potential enjoyment, too. It's hard to dance when you're being lectured to. It wasn't much of a surprise when Garrett decided to run for the Australian Senate shortly after this album's release. (Originally released on CBS Records Australia in 1984, *Red Sails in the Sunset* was released on Columbia Records in the US in July 1985.) —*William Ruhlmann*

Species Deceases / 1985 / Columbia ♦♦♦
Midnight Oil marked the 40th anniversary of the dropping of the atomic bomb on Hiroshima by cutting this four-song EP of driving rock 'n' roll songs on international political themes. "Some say it's progress, I say it's cruel," Peter Garrett sang in "Progress," a song that disparaged "third world infanticide" and "junk in the stratosphere." Environmentalism gave way to war protest on "Blossom and Blood," which referred specifically to Hiroshima. *Species Deceases* efficiently presented Midnight Oil's usual lyric concerns and musical style in miniature form, and at an EP price, it made a good short sampler of the group. (Originally released by CBS Records Australia in 1985, *Species Deceases* was released by Columbia Records in the US in 1990.) —*William Ruhlmann*

● **Diesel and Dust** / Aug. 1987 / Columbia ♦♦♦♦
A thematic album dealing with the plight of Aborigines in Australia, *Diesel and Dust* contains Midnight Oil's most focused and compelling music. Its single most impressive song, "The Dead Heart," works powerfully, both as agit-pop and as moving rock music. Also included is the anthemic hit single "Beds Are Burning." (Originally released by CBS Records Australia in August 1987, *Diesel and Dust* was released on Columbia Records in the US in January 1988.) —*William Ruhlmann*

Blue Sky Mining / Feb. 1990 / Columbia ♦♦♦
Diesel and Dust, only with less aggression. It's still a solid record. —*John Dougan*

Scream in Blue Live / May 5, 1992 / Columbia ✦✦

Scream In Blue Live is, thankfully, a very worthy addition to the group's catalogue. The Oils' music has always had more edge and power in a live setting, and this captures it perfectly. All that's missing is the visual dimension of frantic and imposing front-man Peter Garrett stalking the stage. Great songs that were delivered too tamely in their studio incarnations—"Dreamworld" from *Diesel and Dust* and "Stars of Warburton" from *Blue Sky Mining*, for example—erupt in full bloom live from the Brisbane Boondall Centre. Other highlights include "Progress," recorded in 1990 at a protest rally in front of Exxon head offices on 6th Avenue in New York, and a passionate plea for aboriginal rights that serves as an introduction to "Beds Are Burning." —*Roch Parisien*

Earth and Sun and Moon / Apr. 1993 / Columbia ✦✦✦✦

After the slightly uninspired *Blue Sky Mining*, Midnight Oil sound revitalized on *Earth and Sun and Moon*. Their most melodic, nearly Beatlesque effort is arguably their best yet. Unfortunately, the album was generally overlooked. —*Chris Woodstra*

Breathe / Oct. 15, 1996 / Sony ✦✦✦

Breathe strips away some of the big, detailed production of *Earth and Sun and Moon*, replacing it with a more direct sound while keeping the anthemic melodicism of the group's more recent records intact. The result is an album that is less ambitious than its predecessor, yet also more forceful, and Midnight Oil sounds enlivened in this less constricted setting. *Breathe* may not have the overall impact of *Diesel and Dust* and *Earth and Sun and Moon*, but it remains one of the group's best latter-day records. —*Stephen Thomas Erlewine*

Mighty Baby

f. 1965, Liverpool, England, db. 1971

Group / Art-Rock/Progressive-Rock, Psychedelic

The British psychedelic band Mighty Baby grew out of the Action, the Liverpool-based R&B outfit signed to Parlophone by George Martin in 1965. Long considered one of Martin's best discoveries this side of the Beatles, the Action consisted of Reggie King (vocals), Alan King (guitar), Pete Watson (guitar), Mike Evans (bass), and Roger Powell (drums). After Watson left in 1967, he was succeeded by keyboardist Ian Whiteman and blues guitarist Martin Stone, a veteran of the Savoy Brown Blues Band. This new lineup evolved beyond the R&B-soul sound that the original Action had played, and into a topflight experimental group, incorporating the kinds of long jams and folk-blues influences that the West Coast bands were starting to export around the world.

They hooked up with ex-Yardbirds manager Giorgio Gomelsky in 1967 and recorded an album's worth of material that went unreleased. Reggie King was gone by early 1968 to record a solo album, and the remaining members went through a number of name changes, at one point calling themselves Azoth. In 1968, they hooked up with the managers who represented Pink Floyd and T. Rex, and cut a new series of demo recordings, featuring Whiteman (who wrote most of the songs) and Alan King on lead vocals. These demos were even more ambitious than the 1967 sides, extending the structure of the group's songs with long, beautiful guitar progressions and soaring choruses. Unlike a lot of R&B outfits that tried the psychedelic route and failed, they were suited to the new music by inclination and temperament.

The president of the band's new record label, Head Records, for reasons best known to himself, chose "Mighty Baby" as the group's new name. The self-titled album that followed was a masterpiece of late psychedelic rock, with long, fluid guitar lines and radiant harmonies; still, *Mighty Baby* didn't sell very well, although the group continued to play live shows to enthusiastic audiences. Their record label folded in 1970, and the group eventually signed to the Blue Horizon label, where they released a respectable if not wholly successful second album, *A Jug of Love*. It was clear by then, however, that their moment had passed, both personally and professionally. Mighty Baby broke up in 1971, although several of the members periodically played together on various projects—Evans and Whiteman even played backup to Richard and Linda Thompson in the late 1970's. —*Bruce Eder*

● **Mighty Baby** / 1969 / Head ✦✦✦✦

This hour-long CD is one of the best bodies of British psychedelia ever released. It contains the complete *Mighty Baby* album from Head Records, expanded to 13 tracks with the addition of five tracks cut by the Action during its 1967 transition period. The opening number, "Egyptian Tomb," sets the tone for the entire album—in terms of content, structure, and beat, it sounds like the early Allman Brothers, or maybe the Grateful Dead in one of their harder-rocking moments, jamming with Crosby, Stills, Nash & Young on an impromptu version of CSN's "Pre-Road Downs." The beauty of the original *Mighty Baby* album tracks is that they're psychedelia with a solid beat, none of that noodle-rock that drugged-up Brits usually engaged in. "A Friend You Know But Never See" might have passed muster on the Byrds' *Notorious Byrd Brothers* album. Other songs noodle around too much, but overall this is some of the most energetic psychedelia to come out of England, and

anyone who enjoys psychedelic guitar will love Martin Stone's and Alan King's work on this album. The bonus tracks, all "lost" demos, are even better: highly rhythmic, driving rock (check out "Understanding Love") with lots of spacy guitar and tougher-than-normal flower-power introspective lyrics, with some gorgeous harmonies dressing it all up—a near perfect meld of garage rock and psychedelic sensibilities. —*Bruce Eder*

The Mighty Mighty Bosstones

f. Boston, MA

Hard Rock, Alternative Pop-Rock, Third Wave Ska-Revival

With their party-ready mix of heavy metal and ska, the Mighty Mighty Bosstones gained a strong following across America in the early '90s, particularly on college campuses. While their records are usually fun, the band hasn't completely captured their kinetic energy on disc. —*Stephen Thomas Erlewine*

● **Devils Night Out** / 1990 / Taang! ✦✦✦✦

The Bosstones' debut is an energetic, skankin' party album fusing ska with punk and hard rock, with more of an emphasis on ska than the band would show on later records. The band shifts freely between styles, making *Devils Night Out* their most spirited, freewheeling collection of ska-core. Highlights include the humorous "Hope I Never Lose My Wallet," "A Little Bit Ugly," and "The Bartender's Song." —*Steve Huey*

More Noise & Other Disturbance / 1992 / Taang! ✦✦✦

As the title indicates, the Bosstones' second LP begins to downplay their ska influences in favor of punk and hard rock. The songwriting has also slipped a bit, a problem that would plague the band throughout its career. Nevertheless, there are enough good moments here to make it worthwhile for fans of the group's party-hearty, so-called "plaid" sound. —*Steve Huey*

Where'd You Go? / 1992 / Taang! ✦✦✦

Never officially titled, this EP is also referred to as simply *Mighty Mighty Bosstones*. Two originals, including the title track, are present, as well as several punked-out hard rock covers—Aerosmith's "Sweet Emotion," Metallica's "Enter Sandman," and Van Halen's "Ain't Talkin' 'Bout Love." Logically, this one emphasizes the punk-metal components of the Bosstones' sound over their ska influence. —*Steve Huey*

Don't Know How to Party / Mar. 1993 / Mercury ✦✦

An attempt to mainstream the Bosstones' sound and accentuate their metal influences backfires in a lackluster debacle. Their connection to ska has sometimes seemed tenuous at best, but on *Don't Know How to Party*, the ska is reduced to a mere stylistic quirk punctuating a set of tepid, half-baked metal songs. "Holy Smoke" and a cover of the Stiff Little Fingers' "Tin Soldiers" do manage to rise above the murk, and "Someday I Suppose" is recycled (in an inferior version), but the poor songwriting renders this album necessary for diehards only. —*Steve Huey*

Question the Answers / 1994 / Mercury ✦✦✦✦

A skanking return to form for the Bosstones, sporting probably the band's best songwriting since its debut album. Their ska, funk, punk, and metal influences blend together in seamless, exciting ways, using the horn section in unexpected places, and the melodies are undeniably strong. Highlights include "Pictures to Prove It," "Bronzing the Garbage," "Toxic Toast," and "Hell of a Hat." —*Steve Huey*

Ska-Core, the Devil & More / Mar. 8, 1994 / Mercury ✦✦✦

This mini-album contains the definitive version of the Bosstones' signature song, "Someday I Suppose," plus covers of early Bob Marley ("Simmer Down") and hardcore bands like Minor Threat, Angry Samoans, and SSD. Aside from the jazzy Marley cover and the well-crafted fusion of "Someday I Suppose," most of the songs—true to the title—essentially sound like thrashy hardcore with horn breaks. —*Steve Huey*

Let's Face It / Mar. 11, 1997 / Mercury ✦✦

By the time the Mighty Mighty Bosstones released their fifth album, *Let's Face It*, they must have felt that this was their last chance at the big time. After all, No Doubt and Rancid had both had hits with their own variation of ska-punk, and it seemed that these two younger groups had paved the way for a mass audience for the Bosstones. However, those groups had a lighter touch than the Bosstones, who always tempered their skank with metal, and nowhere is that more evident than on the slick surfaces of *Let's Face It*. Producers Paul Q. Kolderie and Sean Slade give the band a shiny, radio-oriented production, which dilutes the power of the music. Unfortunately, the group didn't have many strong songs to begin with, and the glossy production only makes *Let's Face It* that much more ineffectual. —*Stephen Thomas Erlewine*

Steve Miller

b. Oct. 5, 1943, Milwaukee, WI

Guitar, Vocals / Blues-Rock, Psychedelic, Pop-Rock

Steve Miller's career has encompassed two distinct stages: first, as one of the top San Francisco blues-rockers during the late '60s and early '70s, and second, as one of the top-selling pop-rock acts of the mid- to-late '70s and early '80s with hits like "The Joker," "Fly like an Eagle," "Rock'n Me," and "Abracadabra."

Miller was turned on to music by his father, who worked as a pathologist but knew stars such as Charles Mingus and Les Paul, who he brought home as guests; Paul taught the young Miller some guitar chords and let him sit in on a session. Miller formed a blues band, the Marksmen Combo, at age 12 with friend Boz Scaggs; the two teamed up again at the University of Wisconsin in a group called the Ardells, later the Fabulous Night Trains. Miller moved to Chicago in 1964 to get involved in the local blues scene, teaming with Barry Goldberg for two years. He then moved to San Francisco and formed the first incarnation of the Steve Miller Blues Band, featuring guitarist James "Curly" Cooke, bassist Lonnie Turner, and drummer Tim Davis. The band built a local following through a series of free concerts and backed Chuck Berry in 1967 at a Fillmore date later released as a live album. Scaggs moved to San Francisco later that year and replaced Cooke in time to play the Monterey Pop Festival; it was the first of many personnel changes. Capitol signed the group as the Steve Miller Band following the festival.

The band flew to London to record *Children of the Future*, which was praised by critics and received some airplay on FM radio. It established Miller's early style as a blues-rocker influenced but not overpowered by psychedelia. The follow-up, *Sailor*, has been hailed as perhaps Miller's best early effort; it reached No. 24 on the *Billboard* album charts and consolidated Miller's fan base. A series of high-quality albums with similar chart placements followed; while Miller remained a popular artist, pop radio failed to pick up on any of his material at this time, even though tracks like "Space Cowboy" and "Brave New World" had become FM rock staples. 1971's *Rock Love* broke Miller's streak, with a weak band lineup and poor material, and Miller followed it with the spotty *Recall the Beginning... A Journey from Eden*. Things began to look even worse for Miller when he broke his neck in a car accident and subsequently developed hepatitis, which put him out of commission for most of 1972 and early 1973.

Miller spent his recuperation time reinventing himself as a blues-influenced pop-rocker, writing compact, melodic, catchy songs. This approach was introduced on his 1973 LP *The Joker* and was an instant success, with the album going platinum and the title track hitting No. 1 on the pop charts. Now an established star, Miller elected to take three years off. He purchased a farm and built his own recording studio, at which he crafted the wildly successful albums *Fly like an Eagle* and *Book of Dreams* at approximately the same time. *Fly like an Eagle* was released in 1976 and eclipsed its predecessor in terms of quality and sales (over four million copies), in spite of the long down time in between. It also gave Miller his second No. 1 hit with "Rock'n Me," plus several other singles. *Book of Dreams* was almost as successful, selling over three million copies and producing several hits as well. All of the hits from Miller's first three pop-oriented albums were collected on *Greatest Hits 1974-1978*, which to date has sold over six million copies and remains a popular catalog item.

Miller again took some time off, not returning again until late 1981 with the disappointing *Circle of Love*. Just six months later, Miller rebounded with *Abracadabra*; the title track gave him his third No. 1 single and proved to be his last major commercial success. None of his remaining '80s albums were consistent enough to be critically or commercially successful. A box set covering most of Miller's career was compiled by the artist himself in 1994. —*Steve Huey*

Children of the Future / 1968 / Capitol ✦✦✦✦
Recorded in England with producer Glyn Johns (the Who, the Faces), this debut effort presented Miller as someone who was not only immersed in the blues but also fascinated with sound effects and sequencing, not unlike the Moody Blues or Pink Floyd. As a whole, this album flows nicely. Among the album's many highlights are "Baby's Callin' Me Home" (written by Boz Scaggs), "Stepping Stone," "Roll with It," "Junior Saw It Happen," and the spacey Mellotron-heavy ballad "In My First Mind." —*Rick Clark*

Sailor / 1968 / Capitol ✦✦✦✦
Less than six months after *Children of the Future*, Miller's solid follow-up proved that he wasn't a flash in the pan. Like its predecessor, *Sailor* dabbled in neat segues and effects, but to a lesser degree. Miller shines on the gently acoustic "Quicksilver Girl" and haunting "Dear Mary." *Sailor* has a couple of great rockers with "Living in the USA" (Miller's first hit at No. 94) and "Dime a Dance Romance," penned by soon-to-be-departing member Boz Scaggs. —*Rick Clark*

Your Saving Grace / 1969 / Capitol ✦✦✦
This effort is a little more subdued than *Brave New World*, with cuts like "Baby's House" and "Feel So Glad." However, Miller does lay down an authoritative groove on "Don't Let Nobody Turn You Around," while "Little Girl" features some excellent, tasty lead guitar work. Miller also included a spacey reworking of "Motherless Children." Lonnie Turner's

daft "Last Wombat in Mecca" is the album's only low point. Considering this was the fourth album Miller released in two years, the weakness is hardly worth mentioning. —*Rick Clark*

Brave New World / 1969 / Capitol ✦✦✦✦
From the anthemic opening title cut, accelerating through to the crash-and-burn closer, "My Dark Hour" (featuring Paul McCartney ghosting on drums, bass, and vocals under the pseudonym of Paul Ramon), *Brave New World* is a tour de force. Other standout tracks include Miller's atmospheric "Seasons," "Kow Kow," and "Space Cowboy," an FM rock classic. —*Rick Clark*

Number Five / 1970 / Capitol ✦✦✦
For this effort Miller went to Nashville, among other places, and recorded a wide range of material that covered everything from waxing poetic about eating hot chili to railing at the industrial military complex. In spite of this album's uneven material, it possesses many strong tunes, including "Going to Mexico," "Good Morning," and "Going to the Country." It also includes "Steve Miller's Midnight Tango." —*Rick Clark*

Rock Love / 1971 / Capitol ✦

● **Anthology** / 1972 / Capitol ✦✦✦✦
This is a smartly assembled best-of collection that provides a good introduction to Miller's work up to this point. Those interested in digging deeper than this should check out *Brave New World, Sailor, Children of the Future,* and *Your Saving Grace,* in that order. —*Rick Clark*

Recall the Beginning: A Journey From Eden / 1972 / Capitol ✦✦✦
After the miserable album *Rock Love,* Miller rebounded somewhat with *Recall the Beginning—A Journey from Eden.* One side is largely throwaway stuff, but the other half features a string of dreamy compositions that culminates with the haunting "Journey from Eden." "Love's Riddle," another track from that grouping, is also fine. —*Rick Clark*

The Joker / 1973 / Capitol ✦✦✦
While not as strong as some of his earlier work, *The Joker's* title cut (built from a simple guitar riff) was Miller's first huge No. 1 single. "Sugar Babe" and "Something to Believe In" were also highlights. Nevertheless, Miller's focus on basic catchy material laid the groundwork for his incredibly successful late-'70s albums. —*Rick Clark*

Fly Like an Eagle / 1976 / Capitol ✦✦✦✦
In his effort to create the ultimate playable album, Miller re-incorporated his interest in spacey sound effects and neat segues and synthesized them with a batch of tightly crafted light pop-rock tunes. The result generated a load of seamless hits like "Take the Money and Run," "Rock'n Me," and the title track. —*Rick Clark*

Book of Dreams / 1977 / Capitol ✦✦✦✦
Recorded at the same time as *Fly like an Eagle,* this album repeated the same formula, with the same big results. Hits included "Jet Airliner" (a slight reworking of an old R&B tune by Paul Pena), "Jungle Love," and "Swingtown." —*Rick Clark*

● **Greatest Hits 1974-1978** / 1978 / Capitol ✦✦✦✦
Greatest Hits 1974-1978 collects the majority of Steve Miller's biggest hits—"The Joker," "Take the Money and Run," "Rock'n Me," "Fly Like An Eagle," "Jet Airliner," "Jungle Love," "Swingtown"—and seven album tracks that received a fair amount of airplay as album rock tracks. The collection only covers a total of three albums—*The Joker, Fly Like An Eagle, Book of Dreams*—with the latter two providing the bulk of the material. Because of this, "Living in the USA," one of Miller's biggest hits of the late '60s/early '70s, isn't included but it isn't missed, since all of his other hits of the '70s are included. The thoroughness of *Greatest Hits 1974-1978* makes it an excellent introduction to Miller and for many casual fans, it also means that they can confine their Steve Miller collection to one disc. —*Stephen Thomas Erlewine*

Circle of Love / 1981 / Capitol ✦✦✦
After a four-year layoff, Miller returns with a truly weird album. One half of it is a wandering space-funk jam called "Macho City," the other half featured a couple of decent tunes, which were singles, "Heart Like a Wheel" and "Circle of Love." —*Rick Clark*

Abracadabra / 1982 / Capitol ✦✦✦
Even though the catchy title track became a No. 1 hit, returning Miller to the limelight, this album lacked the focus and strong material to provide more staying power. —*Rick Clark*

Steve Miller Band: Live! / 1983 / Capitol ✦✦
This decent live album features a cross-section of hits, including "Living in the USA." —*Rick Clark*

Italian X Rays / 1984 / Capitol ✦✦

Living in the 20th Century / Dec. 15, 1987 / Capitol ✦✦
Miller does a half-assed return to his blues roots with this outing, which was dedicated to Jimmy Reed. Among the more promising numbers was "Nobody but You Baby," but heavily processed rhythm tracks marred what might have been a strong album. —*Rick Clark*

Born 2B Blue / 1988 / Capitol ✦✦✦
After a string of incredibly spotty albums, Miller quits noodling around with synthesizers and gimmicky effects, and knuckles down with a smooth collection of jazz standards. Utilizing the formidable talents of vibe player Milt Jackson, Phil Woods (alto sax), and Ben Sidran (keys and co-production), Miller creates an album that is playful and sophisticated. While his guitar playing is downplayed, Miller shines on "Just a Little Bit," "God Bless the Child," and the swinging "Red Top." —*Rick Clark*

The Best of Steve Miller (1968-1973) / 1990 / Capitol ✦✦✦✦
Some duplication with *Anthology*, but this is a better initiation to the early days, including some cuts from *The Joker*. —*John Floyd*

Wide River / Jun. 8, 1993 / Polydor ✦✦
Steve Miller returns to the bluesy pop-rock sound that made his career so successful with *Wide River*, a pleasant collection of new songs that will appeal greatly to fans of "The Joker," "Take the Money and Run," and "Rock'n Me." —*AMG*

Steve Miller Band [Box Set] / Jul. 26, 1994 / Capitol ✦✦✦✦
This is one case where the project would have, more than likely, been better served if it were compiled without the help of the artist. This three-disc set is broken down into pre-"Joker" (vol. 1), post-"Joker" (vol. 2), and "Blues" (vol. 3). While Miller aced Vol. 2's song selection, and the third disc is enjoyably playable, it's obvious he holds much of his earlier work in disregard. It's hard to justify why he would perform horrible editing jobs and fade-outs on some of his best early work. Why didn't Miller just include *Anthology*, with a couple of extra cuts, as disc one? The set does feature great sound, and the liner notes and the pictures in the booklet are first-rate. —*Rick Clark*

Garnet Mimms

b. Nov. 16, 1933, Ashland, VA
Piano, Vocals / Soul, R&B
With his backing band the Enchanters in the early '60s, Garnet Mimms cut several fine, underrated R&B singles, including the hit "Cry Baby." After the Enchanters fell apart in 1964, Mimms pursued a solo career that merged a sophisticated R&B backing with his gospel-influenced singing. He made many terrific records that never hit the charts; it wasn't until 1977 that he had another hit, "What It Is." But in the '60s, Mimms made many records that should have been hits; they remain criminally unheard, but fans of '60s soul and R&B should seek them out. —*Stephen Thomas Erlewine*

Cry Baby / Sep. 20, 1963 / United Artists ✦✦✦✦
Mimms' debut album was a well-above-average effort for soul LPs of the era. Besides the title smash, it featured solid material that married Mimms' gospel feel with uptown New York soul production; "Anytime You Want Me," "Wanting You," and "Baby Don't You Weep" were some of his finest songs. It's been reissued in its entirety, along with 14 other cuts, on the British CD *Cry Baby/Warm & Soulful;* most of the songs are on the domestic compilation *The Best of Garnet Mimms.* —*Richie Unterberger*

● **The Best of Garnet Mimms/Cry Baby** / 1993 / EMI ✦✦✦✦
Excellent compilation of this early soul singer, whose influence extended beyond his one big hit, the 1963 title track. Emerging from a gospel background and obscure doo wop groups, Mimms invested the increasingly sophisticated R&B sound of the mid-'60s with both emotion and supple pipes. He never hit the top ten after "Cry Baby," but rang off a string of minor hits like "Baby Don't You Weep," "For Your Precious Love," "It Was Easier to Hurt Her," and "I'll Take Good Care of You." Grittier than Motown, but not as down-home as Stax, Mimms married his vocals to the uptown production values and pop songwriting savvy of his producer Jerry Ragavoy to produce some of the more memorable early soul recordings. This 25-track anthology, covering his recordings for United Artists between 1963 and 1966, is unerringly consistent. It features all of his hit singles, highlights from the three albums he released during this period, and the original versions of "Cry Baby" (later one of Janis Joplin's signature tunes) and "Anytime You Want Me" (covered by the Who on a B-side in 1965). —*Richie Unterberger*

Cry Baby/Warm & Soulful / 1995 / Beat Goes On ✦✦✦✦
This 26-track compilation of Mimms' work between 1963 and 1966 (including his entire '63 debut LP) is roughly equal in merit to the US *The Best of Garnet Mimms* compilation. Each focuses upon the singer's prime; each largely duplicates the other's track selection; and each has some songs that are not on the other. The most notable item here that isn't on the American compilation is "It Won't Hurt (Half as Much)," which was also recorded by Them in the mid-'60s. The US anthology, however, rates a slight edge: it's easier to locate (in North America, that is), and has the crucial track "Cry Baby" (covered by Janis Joplin), which is missing from this British comp. —*Richie Unterberger*

Ministry

f. 1981, Chicago, IL
Industrial, Alternative Pop-Rock, Heavy Metal
When Ministry released their first EP in 1981, it seemed impossible that the band would become one of the biggest industrial terrorists of the late '80s and '90s. On their first album and EP, the band was a synth-funk duo, more similar to the Human League than to Einsturzende Neubauten. Yet lead singer-guitarist Al Jourgensen was smart enough to abandon that sound and begin constructing a terrifying new form of dance music. Using heavy guitar, synthesizers, samples, distorted vocals, massive drums, noise, and tape effects, Ministry created some of the first industrial dance records to cross over to a mass audience. And it wasn't because Jourgensen diluted the power of the music. Although the band sometimes approached conventional song structures that were simply fueled by jack-hammer guitars, the real reason Ministry appealed to heavy metal fans as much as to the alternative crowd is because of how the band looked. Instead of the faceless, abrasive drone of KMFDM or Skinny Puppy, Ministry acted like rock stars, dressing in leather and sunglasses, playing a relentlessly heavy guitar rock that happened to have a dance beat and synthesizers. After years of slowly building a large fan base, the band completed their crossover into the mainstream with 1992's *Psalm 69;* the album's success confirmed that Ministry was one of the most popular hard rock and industrial bands of the early '90s. —*Stephen Thomas Erlewine*

With Sympathy / 1983 / Arista ✦✦
Twitch / 1986 / Sire ✦✦
Twelve Inch Singles (1981-1984) / 1987 / Wax Trax! ✦✦✦
Included are all of their best-known hits and great songs before they got signed by a major label (Sire). Early techno-industrial music from the early '80s. —*John Book*

● **The Land of Rape and Honey** / 1988 / Sire ✦✦✦✦
Considered to be one of Ministry's best albums, this is the one that crossed them over from the industrial-alternative scene into the heavy metal crowds. It's very heavy and enjoyable from start to finish. —*John Book*

The Mind Is a Terrible Thing to Taste / Nov. 1989 / Sire ✦✦✦✦
In Case You Didn't Feel Like Showing Up (Live) / Sep. 4, 1990 / Sire ✦✦
A live album recorded during their most recent tour, *In Case You Didn't Feel Like Showing Up (Live)* demonstrates that a band that used a lot of technological wizardry in the studio is fully capable of playing its music on stage. It's also available as a home video on Warner/Reprise. —*John Book*

Psalm 69: The Way to Succeed & The Way to Suck Eggs / Jul. 14, 1992 / Sire ✦✦✦✦
Although this is Ministry's most accessible album, it is not a sellout. Al Jourgensen and company never let the intensity up, with the machine-like grind of the rhythm section constantly driving the same sixteenth-note rhythms again and again. "Just One Fix" is the best track on a remarkable, intense album, which also includes the single "Jesus Built My Hotrod." —*Stephen Thomas Erlewine*

Filth Pig / 1995 / Sire ✦✦
Distracted by drugs, arrests, and replacing nearly the entire lineup of Ministry, Al Jourgenson took nearly four years to complete *Filth Pig*. Instead of being a carefully constructed masterpiece, the record is a monotonous attack of relentless guitar noise. And although Jourgenson does keep his promise of reducing the number of samplers and synthesizers used on the album, the new approach sounds like a retreat into heavy metal, not a brave step forward. Slowing the songs down slightly and turning up the guitars results in a muddled quagmire. Without the blitzkrieg barrage of samples and clean metallic attack, Ministry sounds strangely castrated, and it doesn't help that Jourgenson's songs are neither catchy nor powerful. *Psalm 69* may have been too concise for long-time Ministry fans, but at least it packed a punch. On the surface, *Filth Pig* is noisier, but it has no power. —*Stephen Thomas Erlewine*

Minor Threat

f. 1980, Washington, D.C., db. 1983
Hardcore Punk
Minor Threat was the definitive Washington, DC hardcore punk band, setting the style for the straight-edge punk movement of the early '80s. Led by vocalist Ian MacKaye, the band was staunchly independent and fiercely sober. Through their songs, the group rejected drugs and alcohol, espoused anti-establishment politics and led a call for self-awareness. Every song was fast, sharp, and lethal, often clocking in at just around a minute. Their speed and fury often hid their fairly catchy melodies, but the band's main function was to vent rage. Over the course of three years, Minor Threat released two EPs, one album, and several singles, all of which were quite popular in the American punk under-

ground. Their records and concerts helped spawn straight-edge, an American punk lifestyle based on the group's intense, clean-living ideology. Following the disbanding of Minor Threat, MacKaye formed Fugazi, who became one of the more popular American indie-rock bands of the late '80s and '90s.

The origins of Minor Threat lay in the Teen Idles, Ian MacKaye's first band. MacKaye formed the Teen Idles while he was attending Wilson High School in Washington, DC, and after he graduated in 1980, he founded the Dischord record label with the intent of putting out his group's records through the label. Shortly after graduation, the Teen Idles broke up and MacKaye formed Minor Threat with former Teen Idles drummer Jeff Nelson, former Government Issue bassist Brian Baker, and guitarist Lyle Preslar. By the end of the year, Minor Threat had released the singles "Minor Threat" and "Straight Edge," and had played many concerts along the east coast. Throughout 1981, they followed this same pattern, playing a lot of concerts and releasing seven-inch singles. That year, they also released two EPs, *Minor Threat* and *In My Eyes*, both of which compiled their singles.

In 1982, bassist Baker left and was replaced by Steve Hansen; Baker later played with the Meatmen, Junkyard and Dag Nasty. With Hansen on board, the group recorded their only full-length album, *Out of Step*. Upon its 1983 release, the album became popular within the underground and Minor Threat were becoming alternative stars, which didn't sit well with MacKaye. By the end of the year, he broke up the band. MacKaye and Nelson continued to run Dischord, which thrived well into the '90s. The pair also played together in another band, Egg Hunt. Following the disbanding of Egg Hunt, Nelson played with a variety of bands—including Three, Skewbald, and Senator Flux—before devoting his energies to running Dischord. MacKaye played with Embrace and Pailhead before forming Fugazi, who carried on the aesthetic, if not the sound, of Minor Threat. *— Stephen Thomas Erlewine*

★ **Complete Discography** / 1988 / Dischord ✦✦✦✦✦
Complete Discography compiles Minor Threat's entire body of recordings on a single compact disc. Hardcore, as a rule, wasn't particularly musically diverse, but Minor Threat were one of the genre's groundbreaking acts and their music has held up better than that of most of their contemporaries. As the de facto leaders of the Washington, DC hardcore scene, the band pioneered the straight-edge mentality by emphasizing impossibly fast tempos, brief songs, political lyrics, and a drug—and alcohol-free lifestyle. Besides setting the precedent for several generations of punk rockers with their music and ideals, Minor Threat were simply a better band than most hardcore groups. They had a tight, distinctive sound that wasn't as heavy as that of their Californian counterparts, and therefore was often more bracing and effective. Although some of the music on *Complete Discography*, like much of hardcore in general, hasn't aged particularly well—with its cheap production, rigid song structures, and political concerns, it is very much a piece of the early '80s—the sound remains invigorating; the band possessed a visceral energy matched by only a handful of their peers. *Complete Discography*, in fact, is not only one of the cornerstones of any hardcore collection, it's not a bad way to become acquainted with hardcore. *— Stephen Thomas Erlewine*

Minutemen

f. 1980, San Pedro, CA, **db.** 1986
Alternative Pop-Rock, Hardcore Punk
More than any other hardcore band, the Minutemen epitomized the free-thinking independent ideals that formed the core of punk-alternative music. Wildly eclectic and politically revolutionary, the Minutemen never stayed in one place too long—they moved from punk to free jazz to funk to folk at a blinding speed. And they toured and recorded at blinding speed—during the early '80s, they were constantly on the road, turning out records whenever they had a chance. Like their peers Black Flag, Hüsker Dü, R.E.M., Sonic Youth, and the Meat Puppets, the Minutemen built a large, dedicated cult following throughout the United States through their relentless touring. Like their fellow American indie bands, the trio was poised to break into the world of major labels in 1986, and they would have if it wasn't for the tragic death of guitarist-vocalist D. Boon in December of 1985. Even though bassist Mike Watt and drummer George Hurley carried on with fIREHOSE in the late '80s, the legacy of the Minutemen overshadowed the new band in the late '80s and early '90s, as the San Pedro trio influenced several generations of musicians.

D. Boon and Mike Watt began playing music when they were teenagers in the mid-'70s, covering '70s hard rock standards. After they graduated from high school in 1976, they heard their first punk rock records, which marked a significant change in their musical development. Once Boon and Watt heard punk, they began writing their own songs and decided to form their first full-fledged rock 'n' roll band. In 1980, the pair assembled a quartet called the Reactionaries, which featured drummer Frank Tonche and a second guitarist. Within a few months, their second

guitarist left and the band changed their name to the Minutemen, since most of their songs were not much longer than a minute in duration. They recorded one single with Tonche before he was replaced by George Hurley. After Hurley joined the band, the Minutemen recorded *Paranoid Time*, their first EP; the record was released on SST Records in 1981. From the start, the band was eclectic and political, but they didn't find their voice until their first full-length album, 1981's *The Punch Line*.

Following the release of *The Punch Line*, the Minutemen embarked on a punishing touring schedule, driving across America and playing any city where they could get a gig. They were recording frequently, too. All of their major records appeared on SST Records, but they also issued selected tracks and EPs for other independent labels, beginning with 1982's *Bean-Spill* EP, which appeared on Thermidor Records. The band's second full-length album, 1983's *What Makes a Man Start Fires?*, earned them considerable critical acclaim throughout the underground and alternative press. Later in 1983, they released their third album, *Buzz or Howl Under the Influence of Heat*.

By the end of 1983, the Minutemen had become one of the most popular bands in the American underground, a status they only built upon during 1984. That year, they delivered the double album *Double Nickels on the Dime*. The length of the album was a response to Hüsker Dü's 1984 double album *Zen Arcade*, but the expanded length gave the group an opportunity to stretch out and showcase their increasing musical depth and vision. *Double Nickels on the Dime* was a considerable underground hit, earning substantial college radio play and critical praise; many critics named it one of the best albums of the year. Also in 1984, the band released a collection of outtakes and unreleased material called *The Politics of Time* on New Alliance Records.

Throughout 1985, the Minutemen churned out recordings, beginning with the *Tour-Spiel* EP on Reflex Records. It was followed by the cassette-only retrospective *My First Bells*, which was released on SST. After *My First Bells*, the group issued another EP, *Project Mersh*, which featured covers of "commercial" arena rock bands several long original "spiels." Around the same time, the group recorded the *Minuteflag* EP, a one-off collaboration with Black Flag. Finally, the Minutemen released the full-length follow-up to *Double Nickels on the Dime*, *3-Way Tie (For Last)*, toward the end of the year. Like its predecessor, *3-Way Tie (For Last)* received overwhelmingly positive reviews, including notices in mainstream publications.

In December of 1985, D. Boon and his girlfriend were driving home from a concert when they suffered a fatal automobile accident. For the first part of 1986, Mike Watt and George Hurley were trying to decide whether they would continue playing music. During this time, the live *Ballot Result* was compiled and released. After a few months, both Watt and Hurley had decided to quit music when they were convinced to continue playing by a passionate Minutemen fan and guitarist called Ed Crawford. Watt, Hurley, and Crawford formed fIREHOSE in 1986 and later in the year, the new band released their debut album, *Ragin', Full-On*. fIREHOSE toured and recorded for the next seven years, signing with the major label Columbia in 1991. *— Stephen Thomas Erlewine*

Paranoid Time / 1980 / SST ✦✦✦
The Minutemen's debut EP *Paranoid Time* is a startlingly coherent set of primal minimalism—a cross between Californian hardcore punk and the succinct experimentalism of Wire. It speeds by too quickly for any particular song to stand out, but the band's terse, frenetic energy is invigorating, as are their imaginative ideas. *— Stephen Thomas Erlewine*

Punch Line / 1981 / SST ✦✦✦
With lyrics that sound lifted from William Carlos Williams' poetry, this is a hit of punk rock unlike anything else available at the time. With dense, compact songs (18, and the record isn't even 30 minutes long) that spin off into the stratosphere in their jagged, funky way, it's an exhilarating, totally original record—one that alleged alternative rockers of today probably would never think of making. A bold indication of the great music that was to come. *— John Dougan*

Buzz or Howl Under the Influence of Heat / 1983 / SST ✦✦✦✦
Not wasting an instant, the Minutemen recorded *Buzz or Howl* in a near-improvisatory frenzy. The arrangements seem looser and the lyrics more Beat-inspired in their harsh, epigrammatic imagism ("Dreams Are Free, Motherfucker"). With only eight tracks, this record began a larger critical examination of the Minutemen due to its dazzling music. The racket and wailing kicked up by Boon, Watt, and Hurley was indisputably great—and original. It was clear from this recording that it was only a matter of time (the next record to be exact) before the Minutemen exploded with a major work(s). *— John Dougan*

What Makes a Man Start Fires? / 1983 / SST ✦✦✦✦
At the time this record was released, nothing in punk rock (or in any kind of rock, for that matter) sounded like the Minutemen. And although their earlier EPs and singles had provided glimpses at what kind of band they were, *What Makes a Man...* was an amazingly confident display of talent proving that this was one of the best young

bands in America, and that punk rock (or in this instance, hardcore) could no longer be defined simply as yowling guitar rant. On this record, Boon's guitar is all over the place, as Hurley and Mike Watt begin to assert themselves as punk rock's greatest rhythm section. As usual, brevity is the soul of the Minutemen's wit, but unlike earlier recordings, the songs here are more expansive and complex. —*John Dougan*

Politics of Time / 1984 / SST ✦✦✦

Not a follow-up to *Double Nickels* as much as it was an interesting assortment of odds and ends recorded during the band's infancy and pre-Minutemen days when they were called the Reactionaries. Unsurprisingly, the quality of some of these recordings is less than high, but the energy and excitement come through. Side two is arguably the most interesting, with Martin Tamburovich on lead vocals; this is perhaps the most exhaustive collection of Reactionaries material on record. Perhaps not an essential record, but a good one nonetheless. —*John Dougan*

★ **Double Nickels on the Dime** / 1984 / SST ✦✦✦✦✦

Today it seems hard to believe that a record as amazing as this was released the same month as Hüsker Dü's *Zen Arcade*, and it seemed that many critics at the time were knee-deep in either record. An astonishing record, *Double Nickels* remains the Minutemen's finest moment. It was on this record that the music, political activism, and band chemistry coalesced into a forceful document of rage during the height of the Reagan Administration's marketable "me-first" jingoism. Boon's guitar sputters, clanks, and cajoles, while Watt and Hurley explode in rhythmic splendor. The songs, now more explicitly political, question US covert military operations in Central America and challenge accepted approaches to American political history, as well as the crassness and narcissism of popular culture and the business machinations of corporate rock 'n' roll. Daring, justifiably pissed-off, and accusatory, this is a benchmark work of the era that hasn't lost an ounce of power since the day it was released. In fact, it gets better with age. —*John Dougan*

My First Bells / 1985 / SST ✦✦✦✦

A superb collection of all Minutemen recordings from their first EP (*Paranoid Time*) up to and including *What Makes a Man Start Fires*. Rather than going crazy looking for those hard-to-find bits of vinyl, here's the whole shootin' match from 1980-83 in one spot. Cheap at twice the price. —*John Dougan*

Project: Mersh / 1985 / SST ✦✦✦✦

"Mersh" is San Pedro slang for commercial, and as the hilarious cover art by D. Boon indicates, the Minutemen were a long way from establishing any kind of toehold in the commercial rock marketplace. But that didn't slow them down from recording, nor did it force them to reevaluate what they had done up to this point. The Minutemen were true punk rockers, and commercial success (and I'm talking huge mega-unit-selling success here, not simply making a solid middle-class life for oneself) was treated more as an accident than as an aspiration. *Mersh* is only a six-song EP, but it sated the appetites of hungry Minutemen fans awaiting the first full-length record in the wake of *Double Nickels*. This proved that there was plenty more good stuff on the way, especially in Mike Watt's "Take out Test" and Boon's incredible "The Cheerleaders" and "King of the Hill." Added bonus is a hilarious run-through of Steppenwolf's "Hey, Lawdy Mama." —*John Dougan*

3-Way Tie (For Last) / Oct. 1985 / SST ✦✦✦✦

D. Boon's death in December 1985 was one of rock's most tragic occurrences. And, a decade later, I find that it still affects the way I listen to this, the "final" Minutemen record. Boon was hitting his stride here; the songs were emphatic, smart, and marked by his increasing sociopolitical awareness. Boon did not suffer fools gladly, and this record (as does the best of the Minutemen) retains a strong sense of moral indignation (listen to "The Price of Paradise" and "The Big Stick"). One fact that shouldn't be lost in eulogizing over Boon was the significant role Mike Watt was playing in the band. This hadn't happened overnight, but with each successive record Watt's confidence as a bass player and songwriter was growing, and, by the time of *3-Way Tie*, his skills were in full flower—so much so that one side of the record is called Side D., the other Side Mike. Dense and driving, this is a bittersweet moment closing an excellent band's career. —*John Dougan*

Ballot Result / 1987 / SST ✦✦✦

Originally, this was to be a major work entitled *3 Dudes/6 Sides/3 Studio/3 Live*. For the live recording, ballots were enclosed in copies of *3-Way Tie* and Minutemen fans were given the chance to vote on the 30 songs they'd like to hear on the three live sides. Unfortunately, Boon's death scuttled the project, but Hurley and Watt managed to piece together this two-LP set based on the ballots that were sent in. A fine collection of live tracks that go back to 1980, this is a classy way to say goodbye, and proves what muscle the Minutemen had onstage. —*John Dougan*

Post-Mersh, Vol. 1 (Punch Line/What Makes a Man Start Fires) / 1987 / SST ✦✦✦✦

Minutemen's *Post-Mersh* is a valuable series, collecting all of the group's

official discography—with the exception of *Double Nickels on the Dime, 3-Way Tie (For Last)*, and *Ballot Result*—over the course of three discs. *Post-Mersh, Vol. 1* starts at the beginning, combining the trio's first two albums, *The Punch Line* (1981) and *What Makes A Man Start Fires?* (1983), on one disc. —*Stephen Thomas Erlewine*

Post-Mersh, Vol. 2 (Buzz or Howl under the Influence of Heat) / 1987 / SST ✦✦✦✦

Picking up where the first volume left off, *Post-Mersh, Vol. 2* contains the Minutemen's 1983 *Buzz or Howl Under the Influence of Heat* LP and the 1985 *Project Mersh* EP. —*Stephen Thomas Erlewine*

Post-Mersh, Vol. 3 / 1989 / SST ✦✦✦✦

The third and final volume of *Post-Mersh* crams an extraordinary amount of music onto one disc, compiling the EPs *Paranoid Time* (1980), *Bean-Spill* (1982), and *Tour-Spiel* (1985), the 1981 "Joy" single, and the 1984 rarities and outtakes collection *The Politics of Time*. —*Stephen Thomas Erlewine*

The Misfits

f. 1976, New Jersey, db. 1983
Hardcore Punk

Long before Danzig (the band) sold tons of records and showed up with regularity on MTV, Glenn Danzig (the guy) sang for the Misfits. Crawling out of the swamps of New Jersey in the late '70s, the Misfits were part of the early hardcore scene populating New York's trend-setting underground rock Bowery hangout, CBGB's. But while other bands favored skinheads and Doc Martens boots, Danzig and pals drew their look from early goth-punks like the Damned's Dave Vanian. Playing tuneful, ferocious speed-punk, Danzig's big baritone bellowed lyrics that sounded torn from '50s and '60s grade-Z gore flicks (e.g. "Mommy, Can I Go Out and Kill Tonight?," "Vampira," "Last Caress"). As scary as they tried to be, there was always something cartoonish about the Misfits, and that made their horror-punk less shocking and more tastelessly funny (and sometimes just tasteless). Still, they were a potent rock band, capable of some thunderously good music. Some would argue the Misfits are an underappreciated band, but with Glenn Danzig now so successful, he's probably having the last laugh. Danzig split up the Misfits in 1983 and then formed the gloomier, more ghoulish (and not nearly as good) Samhain. Danzig (the band) debuted in 1988.

The original lineup of guitarist Doyle Wolfgang Von Frankenstein, bassist Jerry Only and drummer Dr. Chud reunited in 1997 with new vocalist Michale Graves to release *American Psycho* on Geffen Records. —*John Dougan*

Walk Among Us / 1982 / Ruby ✦✦✦✦

With imagery lifted from sci-fi flicks and gory horror films, Glenn Danzig and Co. sound all revved up and ready to go on their debut record. With Ramones-influenced punk that occasionally veers into speedy, unintelligible hardcore, this is a ferocious, relentless record that makes no apologies for its capacity to alienate listeners. Ugly, unrepentantly nasty, and essential. Issued on CD in 1988. —*John Dougan*

Earth A.D. / 1983 / Plan 9/Caroline ✦✦✦

Legacy of Brutality / 1985 / Plan 9/Caroline ✦✦✦

A collection of outtakes released two years after the band called it a day, *Legacy* is a pretty intimidating proposition that provides an excellent historical overview. Going back to 1978 for some tracks, this collection has its inconsistent moments, but its strengths overshadow its weaknesses. —*John Dougan*

● **Misfits** / 1986 / Plan 9/Caroline ✦✦✦✦

Purists may disagree, but for the benighted, this is the best place to start. A 20-track anthology that gives you the most Misfits for your money. Everything that made the Misfits great is here, including the odd remix, alternate take, and re-edited version. The band is loud and defiant, as is Danzig, whose considerable vocal chops are well displayed here. The perfect music for an evening of headbanging or watching gore films. —*John Dougan*

Die Die My Darling / 1987 / Plan 9/Caroline ✦✦✦

Box Set / Feb. 27, 1996 / Caroline ✦✦✦✦

The Misfits' self-titled box set is designed for the collector, not the casual fan. Featuring a selection of tracks from their five official albums, the set is full of rarities, including the entire *Static Age* album— which has never been released—plus 30 other rarities, ranging from outtakes to alternate takes. Of course, this means that *The Misfits* won't be of interest to anyone but the diehard fans, but for those fans, it's an indispensable, rare treasure. —*Stephen Thomas Erlewine*

American Psycho / May 13, 1997 / Geffen ✦✦✦

The Misfits were always the most ridiculous of all hardcore bands, but age has only made them sillier, as the reunion album *American Psycho* proves. Without Danzig, the group loses much of their menace, and new vocalist Michale Graves helps the band turn into a kitschy goth-punk outfit that relies more on metal than hardcore. Since they have trouble writing catchy riffs, the Misfits rely on their campy persona to make the album listenable, and on occasion—such as "Hate the Living, Love the Dead," "Abominable Dr. Phibes," "Dig Up Her Bones," and "Don't Open Til Doomsday"—they are so over-the-top they're funny. However, the majority of *American Psycho* is simply labored and uninvolving, and in that respect, it's no different than most reunion albums. —*Stephen Thomas Erlewine*

Missing Persons

f. 1980, Los Angeles, CA, **db.** 1986
New Wave, Pop-Rock
Famed as much for their video-ready space-age image as for their music, the L.A.-based New Wave outfit Missing Persons formed in 1980, a year after the marriage of singer Dale Bozzio and her drummer husband Terry. A onetime member of Frank Zappa's backing band, Terry Bozzio met the former Dale Consalvi (an ex-Playboy Bunny) at a Hollywood recording studio; after founding Missing Persons—initially dubbed US Drag—the couple recruited fellow Zappa alumni Warren Cuccurullo on guitar and Patrick O'Hearn on bass, and with classically-trained keyboardist Chuck Wild in tow, they began playing area clubs.

In 1981, the band released its self-titled debut EP; after signing to Capitol, the label reissued the record in 1982, and the singles "Words" and "Destination Unknown" both nearly hit the Top 40. Their videos also helped Missing Persons find success on the fledgling MTV network, where Dale Bozzio's hiccuping voice and campy look (composed of shocking-pink hair and sci-fi outfits capped off with Plexiglass bras) combined with the group's synth-driven songs to make them naturals for heavy rotation. Later in 1982, the group issued its first full-length album, *Spring Session M* (an anagram of their name), which launched the underground smash "Walking in L.A."

After 1984's *Rhyme and Reason* notched only a minor hit with the single "Give," Missing Persons enlisted Chic's Bernard Edwards to produce 1986's dance-pop effort *Color in Your Life;* the album stiffed, however, and both the band and the Bozzios themselves broke up. While Dale Bozzio issued one solo album on Prince's Paisley Park label, Terry Bozzio went on to work with Jeff Beck; Cuccurullo, meanwhile, joined Duran Duran, O'Hearn recorded several instrumental new age albums, and Wild composed music for films and television. —*Jason Ankeny*

Missing Persons / 1982 / Capitol ◆◆◆

Spring Session M / 1982 / One Way ◆◆◆◆

Rhyme & Reason / 1984 / Capitol ◆◆◆

Color in Your Life / 1986 / Capitol ◆◆

● **The Best of Missing Persons** / 1987 / Capitol ◆◆◆◆
The two main qualities of this band, heard on this compilation taken from their three albums and one EP, are the untutored singing of Dale Bozzio and the technical facility of the musicians, expressed in the inventive guitar and keyboard arrangements. High-quality '80s rock. —*William Ruhlmann*

Mission of Burma

f. 1980, Boston, MA, **db.** 1983
Punk, Post-Punk
Of all the punk-inspired bands that came out of Boston in the early '80s, none were better than Mission of Burma. Arty without being too pretentious, capable of writing gripping songs and playing with ferocious intensity, guitarist Roger Miller, bassist Clint Conley, drummer Peter Prescott, and tapehead Martin Swope galvanized the city's alternative rock scene, and despite a too-short existence, set a standard for excellence that has rarely been equaled.

Burma's music is vintage early-'80s post-punk: jittery rhythms, odd shifts in time, declamatory vocals; an aural assault similarly employed by bands such as the Gang of Four, Mekons, and Pere Ubu—Burma's peers as well as their influences. Also conspicuously present in the mix was the proto-punk of the Stooges and Velvet Underground (with just a dash of Led Zeppelin and Roxy Music), bands that inspired Burma's darker songwriting impulses and tendencies toward longish, repetitive jams capable of boring holes into your skull. What Burma added was a sonic texture through the use of extreme volume. Roger Miller's guitar enveloped the band in thick, distorted, cascading chords, erupting into squealing solos and (intentional) squalls of feedback. With Prescott and Conley furiously bashing in support, the band's sound was extremely physical (ask anyone who saw them live) to the point of leaving you feeling slightly bruised, battered, but extremely happy.

After releasing an explosive single ("Academy Fight Song," still one of punk rock's greatest songs) on Boston's then-hippest indie label Ace of Hearts, Burma released two excellent records in just over a year: The *Signals, Calls and Marches* EP and their only full-length studio album, *VS.* The former was poppier, but in a breathtakingly intense way; the latter dark and ominous, lacking in riff-heavy punch, but still delivering a wicked blast of aural chaos. Unbeknownst to fans, this was the begin-

ning of the end. The massive volume, a key element in Burma's sound, had taken its toll on the band members, especially Miller, who developed a severe case of tinnitus that hastened the band's demise. (Always the trooper, Miller played the band's final tour wearing a protective headset used on shooting ranges to prevent his ears from absorbing more punishment.) After a bittersweet farewell tour in 1983, the shows were released as a live LP entitled *The Horrible Truth About Burma,* an occasionally thrilling example of their considerable stage prowess.

Miller has since gone on to a career as a solo artist and with his nontouring band Birdsongs of the Mesozoic. Prescott formed the wonderful Volcano Suns, who released a half-dozen records all worth checking out, before starting a new band, Kustomized, with ex-Bullet Lavolta singer Yukki Gipe. Clint Conley produced the first Yo La Tengo record and then left the music business. He now reportedly works as a television producer in New Jersey. —*John Dougan*

Vs. / 1982 / Ace of Hearts ◆◆◆◆
Mission of Burma becomes a harder-rocking, more obviously punk-oriented band in their first full-length release. Songs such as "That's How I Escaped My Certain Fate," "Secrets," "Learn How," and "The Ballad of Johnny Burma" are slices of gutsy, inspired hardcore. Unusual wrinkles on this basic style can be seen in "New Nails," which delves into the goofy side of punk, and "Fun World," which is a feedback-drenched number that is almost danceable in places. Other songs explore different territory. "Train" is a chaotic, somewhat experimental rock number. "Weatherbox" is a slow, gritty song with grindingly distorted guitar and stuttering tape effects. There's a very noticeable Joy Division influence in "Trem Two." And the excellent "Einstein's Day" is a slow, tenacious, loud production number with a big arcing vocal line. This is an excellent album well worth buying. —*David Cleary*

The Horrible Truth About Burma [EP] / 1985 / Ace of Hearts ◆◆
Now re-released on CD, it's a wonderful sample of the power of Mission of Burma live. An assaultive "Peking Spring" and great covers of the Stooges' "1970" and Pere Ubu's "Heart of Darkness" make this essential listening. —*John Dougan*

Mission of Burma [EP] / 1987 / Taang! ◆◆

Forget / 1987 / Taang! ◆◆◆

● **Mission of Burma** / 1988 / Rykodisc ◆◆◆◆
A stunning, long (80 minutes) career overview of this magnificent band that includes all of *Signal Calls and Marches, VS.* and the single "Academy Fight Song." Only two tracks from *Horrible Truth* are here, and recent converts will want to find the original album to hear Burma's sonic madness in its entirety. Very simply a great release from a great band, whose best moments have served as inspiration for hundreds of younger bands. —*John Dougan*

Let There Be Burma / 1990 / Taang! ◆◆◆
With so little material available, it's common for outtakes and assorted ephemera to be released to a ravenous horde of uncritical fans. These are interesting, but nonessential releases. The Rykodisc release serves as the most exhaustive and authoritative document. Caveat Emptor: *Let There Be Burma* is a re-release of *Mission of Burma* (not to be confused with the Rykodisc release) and *Forget* on one disc. —*John Dougan*

The Mission UK

f. 1986, Leeds, England
Alternative Pop-Rock, Goth-Rock
Derided by critics as pompous, melodramatic, and bombastic, the Mission, as they were known in their native UK (their name had to be changed in America owing to a Philadelphia R&B band with the same moniker), nonetheless attracted a core audience of goth-rock fans and continues to record today. The Mission was formed in 1986 by guitarist-singer Wayne Hussey and bassist Craig Adams, who both left the Sisters of Mercy to do so. (Hussey had also played with the Walkie Talkies and Dead or Alive.) The two recruited Artery guitarist Simon Hinkler and former Red Lorry Yellow Lorry drummer Mick Brown, and called themselves the Sisterhood, to which Sisters of Mercy leader Andrew Eldritch objected strenuously. The Mission released two successful independent singles in the UK and signed to Mercury in 1986. The group soon completed its debut album, *God's Own Medicine*, which critics lambasted as ponderous and derivative of Led Zeppelin and Yes, but the album produced several UK hits anyway. The band toured extensively in the UK and America; Adams had to return home from the latter after suffering from exhaustion. Produced by Led Zeppelin bassist John Paul Jones, *Children* widened the band's audience, reaching No. 2 on the UK album charts. 1990's *Carved in Sand* shed some of the Mission's Zep fascination for more refined songwriting. Hinkler left the band mid-way through the supporting tour and was eventually replaced permanently by Paul Etchells. Meanwhile, several Mission members backed Slade members Noddy Holder and Jim Lea on the Christmas charity single "Merry Xmas Everybody." By 1992, Hussey was the only original mem-

ber left; following the 1994 *Sum and Substance* retrospective, he recorded the album *Neverland* with a new Mission lineup. —*Steve Huey*

God's Own Medicine / 1986 / Mercury ✦✦✦✦
The debut by ex-Sisters of Mercy members engages in puffy synth-heavy pomp rock. Regardless, this effort produced a handful of British hits. "Bridges Burning" is an overwrought highlight. —*Rick Clark*

The First Chapter / 1987 / Mercury ✦✦✦

Children / 1988 / Mercury ✦✦✦✦

Carved in Sand / Feb. 1990 / Mercury ✦✦✦

Grains of Sand / Nov. 1990 / Mercury ✦✦✦✦
This continues what "God's Own Medicine" started, with weaker songs, except for "Hands Across the Ocean" (one of their best). Maybe XTC member Andy Partridge's production was the difference. —*Rick Clark*

Masque / Dec. 1991 / Mercury ✦✦✦

● **Sum & Substance** / May 17, 1994 / Polygram ✦✦✦✦

The Misunderstood

f. 1963, Riverside, CA, **db.** 1967
Psychedelic, Garage Rock
Of the thousands of US garage bands that struggled in the 1960s without achieving international success, the Misunderstood were not only among the very best, but among the very few to progress beyond basic garage sounds to music that has been (belatedly) recognized as nearly as accomplished and innovative as that of the British Invasion bands that touched off the garage explosion in the first place. Formed in Riverside, CA in 1963, the group began as a basic R&B-rock combo in the tradition of the Stones and the Animals. After the addition of steel guitarist Glenn Campbell, they rapidly moved toward a proto-psychedelic sound with guitar feedback, sustain, Middle Eastern influences, and exploratory song structures that strongly echoed the Yardbirds. With the encouragement of local expatriate British radio announcer John Ravenscroft (who would shortly become one of Britain's most influential DJs as John Peel, a designation he holds to this day), the band moved to England in 1966 in an attempt to find a sympathetic audience. The group cut six songs (a few of which were issued as extremely rare singles) that found them anticipating the early innovations of groups like Pink Floyd and Jimi Hendrix. The group were praised by the British press and up-and-coming acts like Pink Floyd and the Move, but were hounded by US draft authorities and internal problems, and disbanded in confusion around early 1967. Campbell kept the Misunderstood name alive briefly with a couple of unimpressive singles before forming Juicy Lucy, who had a small British hit with a cover of "Who Do You Love?" The group's other guitarist, Tony Hill (actually a British man who joined the band after they arrived in England), joined High Tide, who recorded some progressive rock albums. The Misunderstood finally gained some measure of the respect due them with a well-packaged reissue of their best material in the early '80s. —*Richie Unterberger*

● **Before the Dream Faded** / 1982 / Cherry Red ✦✦✦✦
One of the great lost '60s albums. Side one includes all six of the tracks they recorded in England in 1966, with magnificent guitar work and nervy, ambitious (if a bit overtly cosmic) songwriting that combines some of the best aspects of the Jeff Beck-era Yardbirds and Syd Barrett's Pink Floyd. Remember that Pink Floyd and Hendrix had yet to record when these sides were waxed; they aren't derivations, but genuinely innovative and groundbreaking performances. Side two contains seven pre-psychedelic demos from their US garage days in the mid-'60s that, while not nearly as important as their 1966 work, are solid, crunching R&B-soaked rock in the tradition of their chief British influences. —*Richie Unterberger*

Golden Glass / 1984 / Cherry Red ✦✦✦
Only Glenn Campbell remains from the original lineup on this album of 1969 material. Competent blues-rock, with some commendable steel guitar work by Campbell, it's nonetheless a pale shadow of the group's psychedelic recordings. Instead of picking this up, be on the lookout for a three-song EP (also called *Golden Glass*) that includes wild psychedelic covers of "Shake Your Money Maker" and "I'm Not Talkin'" by the original lineup in early 1966, and the eight-minute 1969 track "Golden Glass," which is probably the best cut from the last version of the band. —*Richie Unterberger*

Joni Mitchell

b. Nov. 7, 1943, Fort McLeod, Alberta, Canada
Guitar, Piano, Keyboards, Vocals / Singer-Songwriter, Folk-Rock
When the dust settles, Joni Mitchell may stand as the most important and influential female recording artist of the late 20th century. Uncompromising and iconoclastic, Mitchell confounded expectations at every turn; restlessly innovative, her music evolved from deeply personal folk stylings into pop, jazz, avant-garde and even world music, presaging the multicultural experimentation of the 1980s and 1990s by over a decade.

Fiercely independent, her work steadfastly resisted the whims of both mainstream audiences and the male-dominated recording industry—while Mitchell's records never sold in the same numbers enjoyed by contemporaries like Carole King, Janis Joplin, or Aretha Franklin, none experimented so recklessly with artistic identity or so bravely explored territory outside of the accepted confines of pop music, resulting in a creative legacy that paved the way for performers ranging from Patti Smith and Chrissie Hynde to Madonna and Courtney Love.

Born Roberta Joan Anderson in Saskatchewan, Canada on November 7, 1943, she was stricken with polio at the age of nine; while recovering in a children's hospital, she began her performing career by singing to the other patients. After later teaching herself to play guitar with the aid of a Pete Seeger instruction book, she went off to art college, and became a fixture on the Alberta, Calgary folk music scene. After relocating to Toronto, she married folksinger Chuck Mitchell in 1965, and began performing under the name Joni Mitchell.

A year later the couple moved to Detroit, Michigan, but separated soon after; Joni remained in the Motor City, however, and won significant press acclaim for her burgeoning songwriting skills and smoky, distinctive vocals, leading to a string of high-profile performances in New York City. There she became a cause celebre among the media and other performers; after she signed to Reprise in 1967, David Crosby offered to produce her debut record, a self-titled acoustic effort that appeared the following year. Her songs also found great success with other singers: in 1968, Judy Collins scored a major hit with the Mitchell-penned "Both Sides Now," while Fairport Convention covered "Eastern Rain" and Tom Rush recorded "The Circle Game."

Thanks to all of the outside exposure, Mitchell began to earn a strong cult following; her 1969 sophomore effort *Clouds* reached the Top 40, while 1970's *Ladies of the Canyon* sold even better on the strength of the single "Big Yellow Taxi." It also included her anthemic composition "Woodstock," a major hit for Crosby, Stills, Nash and Young. Still, the commercial and critical approval awarded her landmark 1971 record *Blue* was unprecedented: a luminous, starkly confessional set written primarily during a European vacation, the album firmly established Mitchell as one of pop music's most remarkable and insightful talents.

Predictably, she turned away from *Blue's* incandescent folk with 1972's *For the Roses*, the first of the many major stylistic turns she would take over the course of her daring career. Backed by rock-jazz performer Tom Scott, Mitchell's music began moving into more pop-oriented territory, a change typified by the single "You Turn Me On (I'm a Radio)," her first significant hit. The follow-up, 1974's classic *Court and Spark*, was her most commercially successful outing: a sparkling, jazz-accented set, it reached the No. 2 spot on the US album charts and launched three hit singles—"Help Me," "Free Man in Paris," and "Raised on Robbery."

After the 1974 live collection *Miles of Aisles*, Mitchell emerged in 1975 with *The Hissing of Summer Lawns*, a bold, almost avant-garde record that housed her increasingly complex songs in experimental, jazz-inspired settings; "The Jungle Line" introduced the rhythms of African Burundi drums, placing her far ahead of the pop world's mid-1980s fascination with world music. 1976's *Hejira*, recorded with Weather Report bassist Jaco Pastorius, smoothed out the music's more difficult edges while employing minimalist techniques; Mitchell later performed the album's first single, "Coyote," at the Band's *Last Waltz* concert that Thanksgiving.

Her next effort, 1977's two-record set *Don Juan's Reckless Daughter*, was another ambitious move, a collection of long, largely improvisational pieces recorded with jazz players Larry Carlton and Wayne Shorter, Chaka Khan, and a battery of Latin percussionists. Shortly after the record's release, Mitchell was contacted by the legendary jazz bassist Charles Mingus, who invited her to work with him on a musical interpretation of T.S. Eliot's *Four Quartets*. Mingus, who was suffering from Lou Gehrig's disease, sketched out a series of melodies to which Mitchell added lyrics; however, Mingus died on January 5, 1979 before the record was completed. After Mitchell finished their collaboration on her own, she recorded the songs under the title *Mingus*, which was released the summer after the jazz titan's passing.

Following her second live collection, 1980's *Shadows and Light*, Mitchell returned to pop territory for 1982's *Wild Things Run Fast;* the first single, a cover of the Elvis Presley hit "(You're So Square) Baby I Don't Care," became her first chart single in eight years. Shortly after the album's release, she married bassist-sound engineer Larry Klein, who became a frequent collaborator on much of her subsequent material, including 1985's synth-driven *Dog Eat Dog*, co-produced by Thomas Dolby. Mitchell's move into electronics continued with 1988's *Chalk Mark in a Rain Storm*, featuring guests Peter Gabriel, Willie Nelson, Tom Petty, and Billy Idol.

Mitchell returned to her roots with 1991's *Night Ride Home*, a spare, stripped-down collection spotlighting little more than her voice and acoustic guitar. Prior to recording 1994's *Turbulent Indigo*, she and Klein separated, although he still co-produced the record, which was her most acclaimed work in years. In 1996, she compiled a pair of anthologies, *Hits* and *Misses*, which collected her chart successes as well as underappreciated favorites. —*Jason Ankeny*

Joni Mitchell / Mar. 1968 / Reprise ✦✦✦
David Crosby produced this debut album, on which Mitchell sings in a formal, restrained manner and writes in a wordy, poetic style, which is nevertheless touching on such songs as "I Had a King" and "Michael from Mountains." —*William Ruhlmann*

Clouds / May 1969 / Reprise ✦✦✦
Contains Mitchell's version of "Both Sides Now," as well as the exuberant "Chelsea Morning" and such vulnerable love songs as "I Don't Know Where I Stand." Grammy Award-winner for best folk performance. —*William Ruhlmann*

Ladies of the Canyon / Apr. 1970 / Reprise ✦✦✦✦
Contains several Mitchell standards, including "For Free," "Big Yellow Taxi," "Woodstock," and "The Circle Game." —*William Ruhlmann*

☆ **Blue** / Jun. 1971 / Reprise ✦✦✦✦✦
Sad, spare, and beautiful, *Blue* is the quintessential confessional singer-songwriter album. Forthright and poetic, Mitchell's songs are raw nerves, tales of love and loss (two words with relative meaning here) etched with stunning complexity; even tracks like "All I Want," "My Old Man" and "Carey"—the brightest, most hopeful moments on the record—are darkened by bittersweet moments of sorrow and loneliness. At the same time that songs like "Little Green" (about a child given up for adoption) and the title cut (a hymn to salvation supposedly penned for James Taylor) raise the stakes of confessional folk-pop to new levels of honesty and openness, Mitchell's music moves beyond the constraints of acoustic folk into more intricate and diverse territory, setting the stage for the experimentation of her later work. Unrivaled in its intensity and insight, *Blue* remains a watershed. —*Jason Ankeny*

For the Roses / Nov. 1972 / Asylum ✦✦✦✦
Mitchell rails against the music industry and defends the position of the artist in isolation, at the same time moving toward more of a pop sound, notably on the Top 25 hit "You Turn Me on, I'm a Radio." —*William Ruhlmann*

★ **Court & Spark** / Jan. 1974 / Asylum ✦✦✦✦✦
Mitchell reached her commercial high point with *Court and Spark*, a remarkably deft fusion of folk, pop, and jazz that stands as her best-selling work to date. While as unified and insightful as *Blue*, the album—a concept record exploring the roles of honesty and trust in relationships, romantic and otherwise—moves away from confessional songwriting into evocative character studies: the hit "Free Man in Paris," written about David Geffen, is a not-so-subtle dig at the machinations of the music industry, while "Raised on Robbery" offers an acutely funny look at the predatory environment of the singles bar scene. Much of *Court and Spark* is devoted to wary love songs: both the title cut and "Help Me," the record's most successful single, carefully measure the risks of romance, while "People's Parties" and "The Same Situation" are fraught with worry and self-doubt (standing in direct opposition to the music, which is smart, smooth, and assured from the first note to the last). —*Jason Ankeny*

Miles of Aisles / Nov. 1974 / Asylum ✦✦✦
Like most live albums, this two-record set was a profit-taking release on which the artist re-presented many of her old songs for a new acceptance now that she had a larger pop audience. Backed by the pop-jazz ensemble the L.A. Express, Mitchell reprised the best from her first five albums, pointedly ignoring *Court and Spark* and including two new cuts, "Love or Money" and "Jericho." —*William Ruhlmann*

The Hissing of Summer Lawns / Nov. 1975 / Asylum ✦✦✦✦
Mitchell evolved from the smooth jazz-pop of *Court and Spark* to the radical *The Hissing of Summer Lawns*, an adventurous work that remains among her most difficult records. After opening with the graceful "In France They Kiss on Main Street," the album veers sharply into "The Jungle Line," an odd, Moog-driven piece backed by the rhythms of the warrior drums of Burundi—a move into multiculturalism that beat the likes of Paul Simon, Peter Gabriel, and Sting to the punch by a decade. While not as prescient, songs like "Edith and the Kingpin" and "Harry's House—Centerpiece" are no less complex or idiosyncratic, employing minor-key melodies and richly detailed lyrics to arrive at a strange and beautiful fusion of jazz and shimmering avant-pop. —*Jason Ankeny*

Hejira / Nov. 1976 / Asylum ✦✦✦
Spare recordings prominently featuring the bass of Jaco Pastorius. Mitchell sings of life on the road, literally and figuratively. —*William Ruhlmann*

Don Juan's Reckless Daughter / Dec. 1977 / Asylum ✦✦
A big chunk of the pop audience Mitchell had earned with *Court and Spark* in 1974 deserted her in 1975 and 1976 when the follow-ups, *The Hissing of Summer Lawns* and *Hejira*, proved more difficult works.

With this pretentious double album, Mitchell lost many of the loyal fans who'd stuck with her from the beginning but who now, as she spread her obscure poetic observations and thin melodies across whole sides of the album, found her disengaged from the close, personal observations that filled her best songs. This was Mitchell's last album to go gold. —*William Ruhlmann*

Mingus / Jun. 1979 / Asylum ✦✦✦
Mitchell sets lyrics to Charles Mingus' last melodies in collaboration with the composer and a Who's Who of prominent jazz musicians. —*William Ruhlmann*

Shadows & Light / Sep. 1980 / Warner Brothers ✦✦
On her second double live album, Mitchell fronted a band that included fusion-jazz stars Pat Metheny, Lyle Mays, Michael Brecker, and Jaco Pastorius, who gave considerable validity to the jazzy compositions she had been writing over the last five years. —*William Ruhlmann*

Wild Things Run Fast / Oct. 1982 / Geffen ✦✦✦
On her first new studio album of original material in five years and her debut for Geffen Records, Joni Mitchell achieved more of a balance between her pop abilities and her jazz aspirations, meanwhile rediscovering a more direct, emotional lyric approach. The result was her best album since the mid-'70s. —*William Ruhlmann*

Dog Eat Dog / Oct. 1985 / Geffen ✦✦
Joni Mitchell here turned to guests like Michael McDonald, Thomas Dolby, Don Henley, James Taylor, and Wayne Shorter, continuing to straddle the worlds of California folk/pop and fusion jazz. Musically, it worked, although as a lyricist, Mitchell again took off after abstractions (one song railed against "the three great stimulants of the exhausted ones/Artifice, brutality and innocence"), such that, even when you could figure out what she was talking about, you didn't care. —*William Ruhlmann*

Chalk Mark in a Rain Storm / Mar. 1988 / Geffen ✦✦✦
Long before Frank Sinatra made his *Duets* album, Joni Mitchell cast a variety of name singers in prominent roles for the songs on *Chalk Mark in a Rainstorm*. Peter Gabriel sings with her on the lead-off track, "My Secret Place," Don Henley is heard on "Lakota" and "Snakes and Ladders," Billy Idol and Tom Petty have roles in "Dancin' Clown," and Willie Nelson brings his dry phrasing to "Cool Water," while ex-Cars singer Benjamin Orr and ex-Prince associates Wendy Melvoin and Lisa Coleman also sing backup parts. Mitchell uses the vocal firepower over spare tracks heavy on percussion (by Manu Katche) and programming to tell stories and comment on social issues. "Lakota" deals with Native American and environmental matters, "Cool Water" (a Mitchell rewrite of the Bob Nolan original) discusses water pollution, "The Tea Leaf Prophecy (Lay Down Your Arms)" and "The Beat of Black Wings" tell war-related tales. But Mitchell's main theme, which encompasses those topics, concerns the evils of contemporary culture in which one struggles to be "Number One," rises and falls like a game of "Snakes and Ladders," and suffers "The Reoccurring Dream" brought on by advertising. *Chalk Mark in a Rainstorm* rarely makes these points personally enough to stir the listener, and the trendy percussion sound (popular with artists like Gabriel and Kate Bush in the '80s) is already beginning to sound dated. But the songwriting and Mitchell's voice remain impressive, especially when she recalls her past with a revised version of "Corrina, Corrina" at the end. —*William Ruhlmann*

Night Ride Home / Feb. 19, 1991 / Geffen ✦✦✦

Turbulent Indigo / Oct. 25, 1994 / Warner Brothers ✦✦✦
Joni Mitchell returned to the relatively spare style of albums like *Hejira* and her early folk collections on *Turbulent Indigo*, emphasizing her acoustic guitar strumming and singing on a series of songs that detail the political and social discontent she had previously explored on *Dog Eat Dog* and *Chalk Mark in a Rainstorm*. In the brief opener, "Sunny Sunday," a woman tries to shoot out a streetlight with a pistol and misses every night, a metaphor for the individual's futile struggle against civilization, and Mitchell repeats much the same message in songs like "Sex Kills," a generalized criticism of everything from lawyers to the hole in the ozone layer; "Turbulent Indigo," which describes the inability of people to understand artists; "Last Chance Lost," which treats romantic disappointment, and "Not to Blame," about spousal abuse. The low-key music and restrained vocals stand in contrast to the lyrics—over and over, Mitchell's imagery refers to guns and violence. *Turbulent Indigo* provides a disturbing view of modern life made all the more compelling by its calm presentation. —*William Ruhlmann*

Hits / Oct. 29, 1996 / Reprise ✦✦✦✦
The album is a long overdue anthology of one of Canada's most celebrated ex-pats, Joni Mitchell. She sanctioned the release only on the condition that she be allowed to compile the companion album *Misses*. While the 15-strong *Hits* focuses on the her earlier folk-pop crossover successes, many made famous initially by others ("Both Sides Now," Woodstock," "The Circle Game"), *Misses* is a personal cross-section of her more challenging early material and more recent recordings—the

riveting "The Wolf That Lives in Lindsey" from *Mingus* is especially enlightening. One should not pick up one disc without the other. With the flood of box sets released in recent years for far less deserving artists, it's odd that Reprise didn't go all out and make this a more elaborate tribute. —*Roch Parisien*

Misses / Oct. 29, 1996 / Reprise ◆◆◆

Misses intends to round up the best of Joni Mitchell's failed singles and forgotten album tracks, which is a daunting task, to be sure. In a career as acclaimed, idiosyncratic, and prolific as Mitchell's, it's problematic to boil all the forgotten favorites down to one disc, but the task is made all the more difficult by the fact that the songwriter herself compiled the collection and she has an agenda. Mitchell is out to prove that her neglected Geffen recordings during the '80s were as consistent as her classic '70s albums for Reprise. Although she is correct in her assessment that the albums should be given more respect, her execution could have been better. The bulk of *Misses* comprises the Geffen recordings, which were frequently difficult to appreciate, and in this presentation, they aren't any easier to digest. "A Case of You," which probably should have been on *Hits*, is added as bait, but casual fans of that song won't find the rest of *Misses* as illuminating as *Blue*. In fact, only the converted will be willing to make an effort with the bulk of *Misses*, and they'll probably find the individual albums more rewarding. So, the record doesn't appeal to its intended audience, leaving it without one. —*Stephen Thomas Erlewine*

Lennie and Dom Songs (Early On) / [Bootleg] ◆◆◆

Early Joni Mitchell bootlegs are pretty thin on the ground; from the sounds of things, this one was recorded live around 1970. It's not remarkably different from her studio takes, except that all of the songs are performed solo, on guitar and piano. A good cross-section of material from her early LPs, including "Chelsea Morning," "Marcie," "Night in the City," and "Both Sides Now." Almost an hour in length, too, neat bonuses including a cover of "Get Together," and what sounds like a studio version of "Urge for Going," probably her best-loved song that was not included, for whatever reason, on her first albums. —*Richie Unterberger*

Mobb Deep

f. 1992, Queens, NY

Hip Hop, Club/Dance, East Coast Rap, Hardcore Rap

The duo known as Mobb Deep—Prodigy and Havoc—met at a Queens high school in the early '90s and soon became friends. After writing a few raps together, they hung out around the Def Jam headquarters waiting to get noticed. After attracting the attention of Q-Tip from A Tribe Called Quest, the duo gained a record deal with 4th & Broadway by 1993 and released their debut album, *Juvenile Hell*, the same year. The LP wasn't very successful, but Mobb Deep resurfaced on Loud Records the same year, with the single "Temperature's Rising." Prodigy and Havoc's debut album for the label, *Infamous*, was released in 1995. It hit the Top 20 and went gold, thanks in part to the rap Top Ten single, "Shook Ones Part II." Mobb Deep's second album *Hell on Earth* debuted at No. 6 in early December 1996. —*John Bush*

Juvenile Hell / Apr. 13, 1993 / Fourth & Broadway ◆◆◆

● **Infamous** / Apr. 25, 1995 / Loud ◆◆◆◆

Hell on Earth / Nov. 19, 1996 / Loud/RCA ◆◆◆◆

Mobb Deep's second album, *Hell on Earth*, surpasses the group's debut in nearly every respect—lyrically, thematically, and musically, it's a towering effort. Though the duo hasn't abandoned gangsta rap, they have made it harder and more convincing. Whereas most of their contemporaries deal entirely in cliches, Mobb Deep takes it to hyper-reality, where the beats and production are as bleak and threatening as the hardcore lyrics. Though the beats are slow and smoked-out, they carry a menacing violence that makes the lyrics cut even deeper. —*Leo Stanley*

Moby

b. 1967, New York

Synthesizer, Vocals / Ambient, Alternative Pop-Rock, Techno, Club/Dance, Electronica

Moby was one of the most controversial figures in techno music, alternately praised for bringing a face to the notoriously anonymous electronic genre, and scorned by hordes of techno artists and fans for diluting and trivializing the form. In either case, Moby was one of the most important dance music figures of the early '90s, helping bring the music to a mainstream audience both in England and America. Moby fused rapid disco beats with heavy distorted guitars, punk rhythms, and detailed productions that drew equally from pop, dance, and movie soundtracks. Not only did his music differ from both the cool surface textures of ambient music and the hedonistic world of house music, but so did his lifestyle—Moby was infamous for his devout, radical Christian beliefs, as well as his environmental and vegan activism. "Go" became a British Top Ten hit in 1991, establishing him as one of the premier

techno DJs. By the time he came to the attention of American record critics with 1995's *Everything Is Wrong*, his following from the early '90s had begun to erode, particularly in Britain. Nevertheless, he remained one of the most recognizable figures within techno, even after he abandoned the music for guitar-rock with 1996's *Animal Rights*.

Born Richard Melville Hall, Moby received his nickname as a child; it derives from the fact that Herman Melville, the author of *Moby Dick*, is his great-great granduncle. Moby was born and raised in Darien, Connecticut, where he played in a hardcore punk band called the Vatican Commandos as a teenager. Later, he briefly sang with Flipper, while their singer was serving time in jail. He briefly attended college before he moved to New York City, where he began DJing in dance clubs. During the late '80s and 1990, he released a number of singles and EPs for the independent label Instinct. In 1991, he set the theme from David Lynch's television series *Twin Peaks* to an insistent, house-derived rhythm and titled the result "Go." The single became a surprise British hit single, climbing into the Top Ten. Following its success, Moby was invited to re-mix a number of mainstream and underground acts, including Michael Jackson, Pet Shop Boys, Brian Eno, Depeche Mode, Erasure, the B-52's, and Orbital.

Moby continued to DJ various dances and raves throughout 1991 and 1992, culminating in a set at 1992's *Mixmag* awards where he broke his keyboards at the end of his concert. *Moby*, his first full-length album, appeared in 1992. In 1993, he released the double A-side single "I Feel It" / "Thousand," which became a moderate UK hit. According to the *Guinness Book of Records*, "Thousand" is the fastest single ever, appropriately clocking in at 1000 beats a minute. That same year, Moby signed a record contract with Mute and his first release was *Ambient*, which compiled unissued material recorded between 1988 and 1991. Later that year, *The Story So Far*, a collection of singles released on Instinct, appeared. In 1994, the single "Hymn"—one of the first fusions of gospel, techno, and ambient music—was released.

In 1994, Moby signed a major-label contract with Elektra Records in the US. *Everything Is Wrong*, his first album released under the deal, appeared in the spring of 1995 to uniformly excellent reviews, especially in the American press, who had previously ignored him. Despite the promotional push behind the album and his popular sets at the 1995 Lollapalooza, the album wasn't a commercial success. The following year, Moby suddenly abandoned techno to record an album of heavy guitar rock, *Animal Rights*. The album received mixed reviews. —*Stephen Thomas Erlewine*

Moby / 1992 / Instinct ◆◆◆◆

After a string of singles on the Instinct label, Moby released a self-titled album of his brand of high-energy techno. Though the beats aren't terribly original, the instrumentation is, and added vocal samples freshen the songs. This is challenging, decidedly nonrepetitive music, and Moby's take on the *Twin Peaks* theme in "Go" is magnificent. —*John Bush*

Early Underground / Apr. 28, 1993 / Instinct ◆◆◆

A 15-track compilation of Moby's early career, collected from seven releases, this album fails to show the diversity that makes his self-titled LP such a joy. The tracks here are acceptable techno, but they won't appeal to those who think repetition is a sign of artistic deficiency. Most of the vocal samples are typical house-techno fare, but "Go (Original)" is a worthy song. —*John Bush*

Ambient / Aug. 17, 1993 / Instinct ◆◆◆

Hoping to cash in on the ambient-house craze, Instinct Records released a collection of Moby's softer tracks. (To his credit, he had recorded these songs long before.) The album is quite good; it showcases his talent for majestic orchestral sounds and melodic synth layered over slower beats and percussion. —*John Bush*

Mixmag Live, Vol. 7 / 1995 / Mixmag ◆◆◆◆

Moby and Slam's Orde Mekle mixed this seventh volume (cassette only) in *Mixmag*'s series of DJ compilations. —*John Bush*

● **Everything is Wrong** / Mar. 14, 1995 / Elektra ◆◆◆◆

For his first major label album, Moby pulled out all the stops, trying to fit as many different styles as possible into 50 minutes. From fast breakbeats to pseudo-industrial trash, ambient trance to dance-pop, Moby tries it all. It's not quite a statement of genius—for all the bluster, there really isn't that much difference among his songs, which are nearly all standard three-chord progressions; it's all in the production. What ties everything together is Moby's understanding of the beat. The pulse holds steady throughout the record, making it sound like a very good night at a club. —*Stephen Thomas Erlewine*

Rare: Collected B-Sides / Aug. 1996 / Instinct ◆◆◆

Rare: Collected B-sides isn't just for the diehard Moby fan. Compiling a number of B-sides and non-LP singles on a single disc, *Rare* features a few run-of-the mill re-mixes, but usually these alternate versions offer a significantly new spin on the songs. More importantly, tracks like the notorious "Thousand"—which zips by at the impossibly fast speed of a thousand beats per minute—are included, making it a necessary listen for any dedicated fan of Moby. —*Stephen Thomas Erlewine*

Animal Rights / Feb. 11, 1997 / Elektra ✦✦

Just as the rock mainstream was turning its attentions toward techno, Moby abandoned electronic music to refashion himself as an alternative rocker—sort of like a cross between Nine Inch Nails and Smashing Pumpkins—for *Animal Rights*. Moby attempted rock on *Everything is Wrong*, but on *Animal Rights*, his thin, pseudo-industrial guitar riffs dominate the proceedings, with his ambient soundscapes being pushed to the back of the record. Though Moby could be commended for having the courage to diversify, he simply isn't very good at alternative rock—his voice is thin and undistinguished, his rhythms are too tight, his guitars sound anemic, and he can't write a hook. In fact, he even buries the hook in his ill-conceived cover of Mission of Burma's post-punk classic "That's When I Reach for My Revolver." Consequently, *Animal Rights* ranks as one of the classic failed albums, right alongside Sinead O'Connor's big-band *Am I Not Your Girl*. (The American edition of *Animal Rights* contained five bonus tracks not available on the original British version, which was released in the fall of 1996.) —*Stephen Thomas Erlewine*

Moby Grape

f. Sep. 1966, San Francisco, CA
Rock 'n' Roll, Country-Rock, Psychedelic, Folk-Rock

One of the best '60s San Francisco bands, Moby Grape were also one of the most versatile. Although they are most often identified with the psychedelic scene, their specialty was combining all sorts of roots music—folk, blues, country, and classic rock 'n' roll—with some Summer of Love vibes and multilayered, triple-guitar arrangements. All of those elements only truly coalesced, however, for their 1967 debut LP. Although subsequent albums had more good moments than many listeners are aware of, a combination of personal problems and bad management effectively killed off the group by the end of the 1960s.

Many San Francisco bands of the era were assembled by recent immigrants to the area, but Moby Grape had even more tenuous roots in the region than most when they formed. Matthew Katz, who managed the Jefferson Airplane in their early days, helped put together Moby Grape around Skip Spence. Spence, a legendarily colorful Canadian native whose first instrument was the guitar, had played drums in the Airplane's first lineup at the instigation of Marty Balin. Spence left the Airplane after their first album, and reverted to his natural guitarist and songwriting role for the Grape (the Airplane had already recorded some of his compositions). Guitarist Jerry Miller and drummer Don Stevenson were recruited from the Northwest bar band the Frantics; guitarist Peter Lewis had played in Southern California surf bands like the Cornells; and bassist Bob Moseley had also played with outfits from Southern California.

The group's relative unfamiliarity with each other may have sown seeds for their future problems, but they jelled surprisingly quickly, with all five members contributing more or less equally to the songwriting on their self-titled debut (1967). *Moby Grape* remains their signature statement, though the folk-rock and country-rock worked better than the boogies; "Omaha," "Sittin' by the Window," "Changes," and "Lazy Me" are some of their best songs. Columbia Records, though, damaged the band's credibility with over-hype, releasing no fewer than five singles from the LP simultaneously. Worse, three members of the group were caught consorting with underage girls. Though charges were eventually dropped, the legal hassles, combined with an increasingly strained relationship with manager Katz, sapped the band's drive.

Moby Grape's follow-up, the double LP *Wow*, was one of the most disappointing records of the '60s, in light of the high expectations fostered by the debut. The studio half of the package had much more erratic songwriting than the first recording, and the group members didn't blend their instrumental and vocal skills nearly as well. The "bonus" disc was almost a total waste, consisting of bad jams. Spence departed while the album was being recorded in New York in 1968, as a result of a famous incident in which he entered the studio with a fire axe, apparently intending to use it on Stevenson. Committed to New York's Bellevue Hospital, he did re-emerge to record a wonderful acid-folk solo album at the end of 1968, but that would be his only notable post-Grape project; he struggles with mental illness to this day.

Another unexpected blow was dealt when Moseley, despite his membership in a band that emerged from the Haight-Ashbury psychedelic scene, joined the Marine Corps at the beginning of 1969. The band did struggle on and release a couple more albums during that year, and the best tracks from these (particularly the earlier one, *Moby Grape '69* proved they could still deliver the goods, though usually in a more subdued, countrified fashion than on their earliest material. The group broke up at the end of the '60s, although they would periodically reunite for nearly unheard albums over the next two decades, in lineups featuring varying original members. Their problems were exacerbated by

Matthew Katz, who has sometimes prevented the original members from using the name when they worked together. —*Richie Unterberger*

Moby Grape / Jun. 1967 / San Francisco Sound ✦✦✦✦

Some consider this 1967 debut to be the most impressive of the San Francisco rock revolution. Not a wasted moment, and the Grape do jam. —*Jeff Tamarkin*

Wow/Grape Jam / 1968 / San Francisco Sound ✦✦✦

Could Moby Grape live up to the hype following the release of their first album? The answer was "No." That fact alone nearly broke up the band. They went back into the studio and recorded a flawed but essential gem that they titled *Wow*. Great R&B and blues workouts co-existed alongside hallucinogenic raveups and introspective ballads. Production gimmicks did mar such near-classic cuts as "The Place and the Time" and "Bitter Wind," but on the whole, this album is well worth the time. *Grape Jam* is just that, a jam between Moby Grape members and famous friends such as Mike Bloomfield and Al Kooper, essentially making things up as they went along. For historical purposes only. —*James Chrispell*

Truly Fine Citizen / 1969 / Columbia ✦✦

Recorded in just three days down in Nashville, *Truly Fine Citizen* was little more than a contractual obligation with the Grape pared down to a trio. Augmented by sessionmen, it does have its moments. "Right Before My Eyes" has a relaxed country feel to it and the title track rocks out like the old days, if only briefly. The end of Moby Grape came about just as the "country-rock" sound was about to become the Next Big Thing. —*James Chrispell*

Moby Grape '69 / 1969 / Columbia ✦✦✦

20 Granite Creek / 1971 / Reprise ✦✦✦✦

Re-grouping with all the original members, Moby Grape attempted a comeback that fell just short of its mark. The move to the country was highlighted in several tracks, but couldn't mask their R&B-rock roots. Although uneven, this set has flashes of the ol' Grape electricity interwoven with short country ditties. Sort of a poor man's "Workingman's Dead." —*James Chrispell*

Moby Grape '84 / 1984 / San Francisco Sound ✦✦✦

The Grape go country-rock and pull it off. —*Jeff Tamarkin*

● **Vintage: The Very Best of Moby Grape** / May 11, 1993 / Columbia/ Legacy ✦✦✦✦

It's hard to imagine a better-produced package of Moby Grape's work than this two-disc, 48-track condensation of their best late-'60s recordings. The first disc of this set centers around their entire 1967 self-titled debut LP (included in its entirety), which mixed blues, country, and folk influences with hard-charging psychedelic rock 'n' roll. The result was one of the Summer of Love's more enduring works. The second disc boils their wildly inconsistent 1968-69 material down to a fairly strong and coherent selection. While it doesn't match the peak of the group's initial burst, it features some strong folk and country-rock originals that wear much better in the absence of the bloated jams and half-baked hard rock that could make their albums a chore to sit through. Each disc includes interesting demos, outtakes, and live performances that round out the legacy of this prodigiously talented but ill-fated band, which was overcome by internal strife and label/management difficulties after their promising debut. —*Richie Unterberger*

Modern English

f. 1979, Colchester, England, db. 1991
New Wave

British punk quintet from Colchester formed in 1979 and featuring singer and guitarist Robbie Grey, guitarist Gary McDowell, bassist Mick Conroy, keyboard player Stephen Walker, and drummer Richard Brown. By 1990, personnel changes had left the group a trio of Grey and Conroy, with keyboardist, guitarist, and singer Aaron Davidson. —*William Ruhlmann*

Mesh & Lace / 1981 / 4AD ✦✦✦

● **After the Snow** / 1982 / 4AD ✦✦✦✦

Modern English had evolved into a synthesizer-driven power-pop band by the release of this second album, which features their signature hit, "I Melt with You." Ignore the 1990 remake on Tee Vee Toons. —*William Ruhlmann*

Ricochet Days / 1984 / Sire ✦✦✦✦

Stop Start / 1986 / Sire ✦✦✦

Pillow Lips / May 1990 / TVT ✦✦✦

The Mojo Men

f. San Francisco, CA
Psychedelic, Garage Rock, Pop-Rock

One of the earliest San Francisco rock bands, the Mojo Men had local hits on the Autumn label with "Dance with Me," "She's My Baby," and a cover of the Rolling Stones' "Off the Hook" in the mid-'60s. Their early sides displayed a raunchy but thin approach taken from the mold of British Invasion groups like the Stones and Them. In 1966, after female drummer Jan Errico joined from the San Francisco folk-rock group the Vejtables, they moved to Reprise and pursued folkier psychedelic pop directions, and had a Top 40 hit with a baroque arrangement of Buffalo Springfield's "Sit Down I Think I Love You" in 1967. In their later days, they developed more intricate arrangements and harmonies that reflected the influence of the Mamas & the Papas and the Jefferson Airplane, although they weren't in the same leagues as those groups. Their many singles never fully displayed the band's considerable songwriting and vocal talents, and after changing their name to the Mojo and finally just Mojo, they disbanded in the late '60s. —*Richie Unterberger*

Dance with Me / 1984 / Eva ✦✦✦
A ragtag collection, drawn from their first seven singles and a few unreleased tracks. The later tracks, featuring Errico, are much more ornate productions that sound like a somewhat less refined Mamas & the Papas. A wealth of unreleased material (much of it original) that has circulated among collectors shows them to be a much more interesting group than this album would indicate; unfortunately, this anthology focuses on their more simplistic and derivative numbers. —*Richie Unterberger*

Sly Stone & The Mojo Men / 1993 / WPC ✦✦
A deceptively packaged collection of early work, most of which is not Sly himself but the Mojo Men, a minor San Francisco rock band that he worked with in the mid-'60s as a producer. It's the same as another dubious collection of early Sly/Mojo Men work (*Family Affair*), though it's missing one Sly track, "Seventh Son," which does appear on *Family Affair* and other murky reissues of early Sly material. —*Richie Unterberger*

Why's Ain't Supposed to Be / 1995 / Sundazed ✦✦✦
This 21-track disc covers the Mojo Men's first incarnation, when they were a pop-garage group, not the pop-folk-rock act they would evolve into when Jan Errico joined. "She's My Baby" and "Dance with Me" made some noise regionally, "Dance with Me" making the middle of the national charts, but Autumn Records folded before the group got the chance to do any albums. Assembled from a handful of Autumn 45s and many previously unissued recordings, this could be considered the Mojo Men's lost album. But it's really not worth getting excited about, even if you're a garage fan. The thumping, monotonous drums and rinky-dink organ patterns can grate, and worse, the material is often so thin as to be puerile. Juvenile lyrics are a mainstay of many garage recordings, but the Mojo Men's compositions could be downright annoying. Their emulations of the Rolling Stones, the Kinks, and the Animals were pale, though some promise could be heard in a few moodier, folk-rock influenced cuts. —*Richie Unterberger*

● **Sit Down . . . It's the Mojo Men** / Nov. 14, 1995 / Sundazed ✦✦✦✦
An 18-song compilation of material from their 1966-68 hitch with Reprise, combining several singles with five tracks from an unreleased album. This fully documents the second phase of the band, when they added drummer Jan Errico and changed from a second-rate garage band into a better (but not fully first-rate) pop-folk-rock group. This isn't half bad for the genre, but you can see why they never really distinguished themselves from the San Francisco crowd. It's way too pop to be associated with the Haight-Ashbury scene, a little too weird to be compared to, say, The Association (with the occasional sudden blasts of psychedelic fuzz guitar and baroque production), not as accomplished as the Mamas & the Papas, and gussied up with too many conventional pop string arrangements. Van Dyke Parks arranged a few of the singles, including their lone hit, "Sit Down I Think I Love You" (which is here). Most of the material was written by Errico and bassist Jim Alaimo, and although it's a pleasantly worthwhile archival collection, it's not a major find. —*Richie Unterberger*

The Mojos

f. Liverpool, England
British Invasion
Known mostly (if at all) in the States for doing the original version of "Everything's Alright" (covered by David Bowie on his *Pin Ups* album), the Mojos were one of the best Liverpool groups of the British Invasion. Besides "Everything's Alright"—a Top Five raver in the UK—they never scored any other British hits of note, though a couple squeezed into their Top 30. At times, they could be pretty wimpy, with jerky vocals and material that would have been at home with Gerry & the Pacemakers. But at other times, with their electric keyboard-driven sound, they echo the much tougher Manfred Mann. Way below the Beatles and even the Searchers in terms of quality, they were, except for the Swinging Blue Jeans and maybe the Merseybeats, the best of the rest in their home city. —*Richie Unterberger*

● **Working** / 1982 / Edsel ✦✦✦✦
This compilation includes 16 tracks recorded by the group between 1963 and 1965, taken from rare singles and their sole EP. This stuff isn't exactly timeless, but it has a giddy Merseybeat enthusiasm that remains infectious. Comes with a detailed history of the band. —*Richie Unterberger*

Moloko

f. 1993, Sheffield, England
Club/Dance, Trip-Hop, Alternative Pop-Rock, Electronica
Mark Brydon worked with the UK house team House Arrest and Cloud 9 before forming Moloko with Roison Murphy. Moloko's musical goal was to combine the best aspects of house and acid jazz with elements of funk and hip-hop. The Sheffield-based duo issued the debut EP *Where Is the What If the What Is in the Why?*. After its release, they signed to Echo Records; their debut album, *Do You Like My Tight Sweater?*, appeared in 1995. —*John Bush*

● **Do You Like My Tight Sweater?** / Nov. 1995 / Echo Label ✦✦✦✦
Moloko's debut album *Do You Like My Tight Sweater?* is a swirling, neo-psychedelic blend of trip-hop, G-funk, drum 'n' bass, and pop. Combining samplers with cheap keyboards, rolling beats, and Roisin Murphy's thin but seductive vocals, Moloko concocts an intoxicating, infectious, and original dance music, one that fits comfortably between adventurous techno and floor-shaking grooves designed for dance clubs. Although it runs a little long, *Do You Like My Tight Sweater?* is one of the finest by-products of the mid-'90s dance music renaissance, especially for pop-oriented listeners. —*Stephen Thomas Erlewine*

The Moments

f. 1968, Hackensack, NJ, **db.** 1978
Soul, R&B, Old School Rap, Quiet Storm
One of the most consistent R&B aggregations of the '70s, the Moments enjoyed a string of major hits throughout the decade. The Hackensack, NJ trio introduced themselves and the Stang label with "Not on the Outside" in 1968, and topped the R&B charts in 1970 with the gold-plated "Love on a Two-Way Street," produced by Sylvia Robinson (one half of Mickey & Sylvia). Other major soul smashes by the Moments included "If I Didn't Care" and "All I Have" in 1970, "Sexy Mama" in 1973, and another No. 1 R&B item, "Look at Me (I'm in Love)," in 1975. Members Harry Ray, Al Goodman, and William Brown changed their billing to Ray, Goodman & Brown in 1978 and topped the soul lists the next year with the slickly harmonized "Special Lady" on Polydor. The renamed trio remained potent soul hitmakers through the '80s. —*Bill Dahl*

● **Love on a Two-Way Street: Best of the Moments** / Jul. 15, 1996 / Rhino ✦✦✦✦
The 18-track collection *Love on a Two-Way Street: Best of the Moments* is a definitive retrospective, featuring all of the group's Top 20 R&B hits, from "Sunday" and "I Do" in the late '60s to "Look At Me (I'm In Love)" and "With You" from the late '70s. —*Stephen Thomas Erlewine*

Money Mark

f. Detroit, MI
Trip-Hop
Money Mark was Mark Ramos Nishita, a keyboardist whose funky, retro-flavored riffs earned him the unofficial title of the fourth Beastie Boy. Born in Detroit to a Japanese-Hawaiian father and a Chicano mother, Nishita moved to the West Coast when he was six; some years later, he hooked up with the Dust Brothers production team, and began overdubbing keyboards for the Delicious Vinyl label. While working as a handyman, Nishita accepted a job repairing the Beastie Boys' Silverlake, California home; soon, he became a pivotal member of the group's Grand Royal Posse, and performed on both 1992's *Check Your Head* and 1994's *Ill Communication*.

Recorded at his home studio, Money Mark's solo debut *Mark's Keyboard Repair*—a loose, infectious collection of fuzzy organ noodlings performed on vintage equipment—appeared in 1995 as a set of three ten-inch records issued on the L.A.-based label Love Kit. Although the small pressing sold out almost instantly, the first record in the series found its way to Britain and the offices of Mo'Wax founder James Lavelle, who quickly flew to L.A. to meet with Nishita; a deal was struck, and *Mark's Keyboard Repair* was reissued in late 1995. —*Jason Ankeny*

● **Mark's Keyboard Repair** / 1995 / MoWax' ✦✦✦✦
Money Mark was the keyboardist on the Beastie Boys' *Check Your Head* and *Ill Communication*. Both albums demonstrated his influence, with his thick, funky organ appearing all over the place. On his own, Money Mark creates music that is quite similar to the instrumental tracks on the two Beastie albums, but his music is grittier and jazzier. *Mark's Keyboard Repair* sounds like a lo-fi, indie rock variation of '60s soul-jazz, particularly the records of Jimmy Smith and John Patton. Mark's attention span is extremely short—some of the songs don't last a minute—but

the songs keep the same laidback groove flowing throughout the album. *Mark's Keyboard Repair* features a full 30 songs on its American release—the original English version clocked in with 20—but it is rarely boring. Only the groove is important on the album, and Money Mark never lets it stop. —*Stephen Thomas Erlewine*

Eddie Money

b. Mar. 2, 1949, Brooklyn, NY
Keyboards, Saxophone, Vocals / Pop-Rock
Eddie Money arrived in the late '70s at the height of album-rock's popularity. While Money didn't have a remarkable voice, he had a knack for catchy, blue-collar rock 'n' roll, which he delivered with a surprising amount of polished, radio-friendly finesse. He was able to survive in the early MTV era by filming a series of funny narrative videos, something his AOR peers were reluctant to do. However, he wasn't able to resist the temptations of a rock 'n' roll lifestyle, and his popularity dipped in the mid-'80s as he struggled with various addictions. Once he sobered up, he made a remarkable comeback in the late '80s, with singles like "Take Me Home Tonight" and "Walk on Water" reaching the Top Ten. It proved to be Money's last string of hits—during the early '90s, his popularity faded and he retired to the oldies circuit.

Initially, Eddie Mahoney was going to follow in his father's footsteps and become a Brooklyn cop. He attended the New York Police Academy during the early '70s, but at night, he sang in rock 'n' roll bands under the name Eddie Money. After a few years, he decided to pursue rock 'n' roll as a career and quit the Academy, moving to Berkeley, California. Money became a regular at Bay Area clubs, where he eventually got the attention of legendary promoter Bill Graham, who signed the singer to his management company. Graham also secured him a contract with Columbia Records, and Money released his eponymous debut in 1977.

During the late '70s, Eddie Money had a handful of album-rock hits, and wound up crossing over into the Top 40 with songs like "Baby Hold On" and "Maybe I'm a Fool." During the early '80s, Money began to make funny narrative videos, which became staples on early MTV and made "Shakin'" and "Think I'm In Love" hits. His career hit a slump during the mid-'80s, as he struggled with various drug addictions, but he made a comeback in 1986 with *Can't Hold Back*. Featuring the hit duet with Ronnie Spector "Take Me Home Tonight," as well as the Top 20 "I Wanna Go Back," the album became a Top Ten smash, re-establishing Money as a successful blue-collar rocker. Money followed the album in 1988 with *Nothing to Lose*, which featured the Top Ten "Walk on Water." Two years later, "Peace in Our Time," taken from the 1989 *Greatest Hits: Sound of Money*, reached No. 11.

"Peace in Our Time" proved to be Money's last big hit. During the early '90s, his audience slowly faded away, as both 1991's *Right Here* and 1992's *Unplug It In* were ignored. Columbia dropped him in the mid-'90s, and he spent the remainder of the decade touring the oldies circuit. —*Stephen Thomas Erlewine*

Eddie Money / 1977 / Columbia ✦✦✦✦
The debut album of his raspy-voiced, pop-rock tunes charted in the Top 40 and went platinum. —*Donna DiChario*

Life for the Taking / 1978 / Columbia ✦✦✦
Eddie Money's second album wasn't as consistent as his debut, featuring a slicker production that relied heavily on current pop trends, including disco and arena rock. Nevertheless, the record had a couple of good tracks, including the single "Can't Keep A Good Man Down." —*Stephen Thomas Erlewine*

Playing for Keeps / 1980 / Columbia ✦✦
If *Life for the Taking* made concessions to pop trends, *Playing for Keeps* was sunk by Eddie Money's attempt to fit into the mainstream. While his production had never been raw, the sound of the album was entirely too glossy for album rock radio, which meant Money couldn't write songs with enough memorable hooks to earn him radio play. The result was one of his weakest albums. —*Stephen Thomas Erlewine*

No Control / 1983 / Columbia ✦✦✦
On *No Control*, Eddie Money found the perfect middle ground between AOR production and pop hooks, with the singles "Think I'm In Love" and "Shakin'" sending the rocker back into platinum territory. —*Stephen Thomas Erlewine*

Where's the Party / 1985 / Columbia ✦✦
After the comeback of *No Control*, Money produced the lackluster *Where's the Party?* Although the album replicated the formula of its predecessor, it lacked a collection of hook-filled songs, which made *Where's the Party?* Money's lowest-charting record to date. —*Stephen Thomas Erlewine*

Can't Hold Back / 1986 / Columbia ✦✦✦✦
It featured his biggest-selling single—"Take Me Home Tonight," an upbeat duet with Ronnie Spector of the Ronettes. —*Donna DiChario*

Nothing to Lose / 1988 / Columbia ✦✦✦
Throughout his career, Eddie Money has followed a successful album with another record that sounded remarkably similar to its predecessor and *Nothing to Lose* was no exception to the rule. However, *Nothing to Lose* was marginally better than *Playing for Keeps* and *Where's the Party?*, featuring a handful of well-crafted mainstream pop songs, including the Top Ten hit "Walk on Water." —*Stephen Thomas Erlewine*

● **Greatest Hits: Sound of Money** / Oct. 1989 / Columbia ✦✦✦✦
Money's albums are often uneven combinations of solid tracks and filler. This collection has all the hits with none of the misses, including "Baby Hold On," "Two Tickets to Paradise," and "No Control." —*Donna DiChario*

Unplug It In / Nov. 3, 1992 / Columbia ✦✦
Eddie Money was one of the first rockers to attempt to capitalize on MTV's successful *Unplugged* series, releasing this record in 1992. Like any "unplugged" recording, the album features a collection of the rocker's biggest hits performed acoustically. However, Money's songs have always been big, anthemic pop-rockers that benefited from their slick studio production, which doesn't make them good candidates for acoustic treatments. *Unplug it In* confirms this fact, as even his best songs sound limp in these stripped-back arrangements. —*Stephen Thomas Erlewine*

Love and Money / May 30, 1995 / Wolfgang ✦✦

The Monkees

f. 1965, Los Angeles, CA, db. 1969
Pop-Rock
Formed primarily for the purpose of starring in a television series, the Monkees were on the one hand a cynically manufactured group, devised to cash in on the early Beatles' success by applying the most superficial aspects of the British Invasion formula to capture a preteen audience. On the other hand, they weren't devoid of musical talent, and at their best managed to craft some enduring pop-rock hits. "I'm a Believer," "Last Train to Clarksville," "A Little Bit Me, a Little Bit You," "Pleasant Valley Sunday," "Stepping Stone," "Take a Giant Step," "Valleri," "Words"—all were pleasantly jangling, harmony rock numbers with hooks big enough for a meat locker, and all were huge hits in 1966-68. Scorned at their peak by hipsters for not playing on many of their own records, the group gained some belated critical respect for their catchy, good-time brand of pop. It would be foolish to pretend, however, that they were a band of serious significance, despite the occasional genuinely serious artistic aspirations of the members.

The Monkees were the brainchild of television producers Bert Schneider and Bob Rafelson, who decided to emulate the zany, madcap humor of the Beatles' *A Hard Day's Night* for the small screen. In September 1965, they placed in ad in *Variety* for four "folk & rock musicians" to appear in a TV series. Over 400 applied for the job, including Stephen Stills and Harry Nilsson, but as it turned out only one of the four winners, guitarist and songwriter Michael Nesmith, actually saw the ad. Mickey Dolenz (who would play drums), Davy Jones (who would sing), and Peter Tork (bass) found out about the opportunity from other sources. Nesmith and Tork had experience in the folk scene; Dolenz and Jones were primarily actors (although Nesmith and Jones had already made some obscure solo recordings).

From the outset, it was made clear that the Monkees were hired to be television actors first, and musicians a distant second. There would be original material generated for them to sing in the series, mostly by professional songwriters like Tommy Boyce, Bobby Hart, Carole King, Gerry Goffin, and Neil Diamond. There would be records, as well—had to be, with that kind of weekly exposure, to promote the tunes—but the group wouldn't do much more than sing, although the series would give the impression that they played their own instruments.

The TV show was a big hit with young audiences between 1966 and 1968, with slapstick comedy, super-fast editing, and thin plots that could be banded together by almost surreal humor. It wasn't *A Hard Day's Night*, but it was, in its way, innovative relative to the conventions of television at the time. The irony was that, by the time the series debuted in September 1966, the Beatles themselves had just released *Revolver*, and had evolved way beyond their moptop phase into psychedelia.

Also in September 1966, their debut single "Last Train to Clarksville" became their first big hit, reaching No. 1, as did the followup, "I'm a Believer." They were quickly one of the most popular acts in the business, yet they were not allowed to play anything on most of their first records, only to sing; the instruments would be handled by session players. This was particularly hard for Mike Nesmith, a serious musician and songwriter, to swallow, although he did manage to place a few of his own tunes on their records from the start.

Eventually the Monkees revealed that they didn't play on most of their own records, and Nesmith in particular incited the group to wrest control of their recordings into their own hands. Partly to deflect criticism of the group as nothing more than puppets, and partly to effect control over their musical destiny (some of their early recordings had been packaged and released without their consent), the Monkees did indeed play and write much of the music on their third album, *Headquarters* (1967), with a lot of help from producer Chip Douglas. It didn't prove the band to be hidden geniuses, in fact sounding not much different from their previous releases, but as a hard-won victory to establish their own identity, it was a major point of pride. They would continue, however, to rely upon industry songwriters for the rest of their hit singles, and frequently employ session musicians throughout the rest of their career.

Despite the questions surrounding their musical competence, the Monkees did tour before live audiences. They made their own contribution to rock history by enlisting Jimi Hendrix, then barely known in the US, as an opening act for a 1967 tour; Hendrix lasted only a few shows before everyone agreed that the combination was a mismatch (to put it mildly). But the Monkees were always a lot hipper personally than many assumed from their bubblegum packaging. Their albums are strewn with rather ambitious, even mildly psychedelic, cuts, some rather successful ("Porpoise Song," Nesmith's "Circle Sky"), some absolutely awful. In 1968, they gained their freak credentials with the movie *Head*, a messy, indulgent, occasionally inspired piece of drug-addled weirdness that was co-written and co-produced by Jack Nicholson (before he had broken through to stardom with *Easy Rider*).

By 1968, the Monkee phenomenon was drawing to a close. The show's final episode aired in March 1968, and *Head*, released in November, was not a commercial success, confusing the teenyboppers and confounding the critics (not many people saw it to begin with in any case). Surprisingly, it was not Nesmith, but Tork who was the first to leave the group, at the end of 1968. They carried on as a trio, releasing a couple of fairly dismal albums in 1969, as well as producing a little-seen TV special. By the end of the '60s, Nesmith—who had established his credentials as a songwriter with "Different Drum," which was taken into the Top 20 by Linda Ronstadt and the Stone Poneys—was also gone, to start a lengthy solo career that finally allowed him to stretch out as a serious artist. That left only Dolenz and Jones, who fulfilled the Monkees contract with the pointless *Changes* in 1970.

When enough years separated the music from the hype, the Monkees underwent a critical rehab of sorts, as listeners fondly remembered their singles as classy, well-executed, fun pop-rock. That led to a predictable clamor for a reunion, especially after their albums were reissued to surprisingly swift sales in the mid-'80s, and their series was rerun on MTV. Nesmith was having none of it; by this time he was a respected and hugely successful music video mogul with his Pacific Arts company. The other three did reunite to tour and record a predictably horrendous album, *Pool It!* (Nesmith did join them once onstage in 1989). Rhino has treated the Monkee catalog with a respect usually accorded to Charlie Parker outtakes, reissuing all of their original albums on CD with added unreleased/rare bonus tracks, and even assembling a box set. *—Richie Unterberger*

The Monkees / Oct. 1966 / Rhino ✦✦✦
The Monkees did virtually nothing besides sing lead vocals on their full-length debut; poor Peter Tork didn't even get to do that, his contribution being limited to one of the six guitar parts on "Papa Gene's Blues." Given that it wasn't a project of high integrity, it wasn't bad—in fact, much of this is reasonably gutsy pop-rock, including their TV theme song, the hits "Last Train to Clarksville" and "Take a Giant Step," and various decent songs by top Brill Building tunesmiths like Goffin/King, Boyce/Hart, and David Gates. Nesmith was allowed one composition ("Papa Gene's Blues") that indicated his country-rock direction. The CD reissue includes unremarkable bonus tracks of alternate versions of the Monkees theme and a couple of songs that would turn up on subsequent LPs. *—Richie Unterberger*

More of the Monkees / Jan. 10, 1967 / Rhino ✦✦✦
Second album, same as the first, virtually: a huge single ("I'm a Believer"/"Steppin' Stone"), a couple of token Mike Nesmith songs (including "Mary, Mary," previously recorded by the Paul Butterfield Blues Band and a rap hit for Run-D.M.C. in 1988), tunes by Boyce/Hart, Goffin/King, Neil Diamond, Jeff Barry, Neil Sedaka, and Carole Bayer; no participation from the group other than lead vocals. The band was quite upset at their lack of input at the time, but it's relatively decent (if quite harmless) pop-rock, featuring one of their best album tracks, "She." Like all of the Rhino CD reissues, it adds marginally interesting bonus tracks of unreleased alternate versions, including an early take of "I'm a Believer." *—Richie Unterberger*

Headquarters / May 22, 1967 / Rhino ✦✦✦
For their third album, the Monkees were determined to wrest control of the creative process, and with producer Chip Douglas functioning as frequent bassist and auxiliary member, they were indeed able to play most of the instruments and write much of the material. It would be nice to report that the result far exceeded previous efforts and established the group as visionary artists, but in fact this was, again,

pleasantly inoffensive pop-rock. There was more of a country flavor and a sense of personal involvement, though the group still tapped songwriting pros like Boyce/Hart and Mann/Weil for about half the songs. Standouts included Nesmith's "You Just May Be the One," one of his best Monkees tunes, and Tork's "For Pete's Sake," which became the show's closing theme. The CD reissue includes six unreleased tracks and alternate takes, a couple of which (Nilsson's "All of Your Toys" and Nesmith's "The Girl I Knew Somewhere") rank among their finest. *—Richie Unterberger*

Pisces, Aquarius, Capricorn & Jones Ltd. / Nov. 14, 1967 / Rhino ✦✦✦✦
One of their better efforts, featuring the double-sided hit "Pleasant Valley Sunday"/"Words," and some of their best album tracks, like "She Hangs Out," "Star Collector," and "Cuddly Toy," the last of which was one of the first Nilsson songs to be covered by a major artist. As usual, some of the country-rockers and half-baked psychedelic tunes are tedious, though a couple of tracks are notable for featuring some of the first uses of a Moog synthesizer on a rock record. The CD reissue adds some previously unissued alternate mixes, as well as the killer soulful B-side "Goin' Down," which ranks as one of their very best tracks despite its obscurity. *—Richie Unterberger*

The Birds, the Bees & the Monkees / Apr. 22, 1968 / Rhino ✦✦
Not one of their better efforts, dominated almost wholly by session musicians (with the occasional songwriting and instrumental contribution by Mike Nesmith) and containing too many sickly sweet Davy Jones-sung numbers. It does have the hits "Daydream Believer" and "Valleri," as well as Nesmith's "Tapioca Tundra," which just inched into the Top 40, but overall the material is pretty weak. The CD adds some previously unissued songs and alternate takes, the only one of interest being Peter Tork's "Lady's Baby," which sounds like a Buffalo Springfield outtake with its laidback country-folk-rock flavor. *—Richie Unterberger*

Head / Dec. 1, 1968 / Rhino ✦✦✦✦
Like the film from which it came, the soundtrack to *Head* was far from a masterpiece, but had some inspired moments. These include the spacy "Porpoise Song," written by Gerry Goffin and Carole King; the toughrocking "Circle Sky," probably the best song Mike Nesmith wrote for the group; "Can You Dig It," one of Peter Tork's best contributions; and "As We Go Along" and "Daddy's Song," little-known songs by Carole King and Nilsson, respectively. As a listening experience, it's made more difficult by the juxtaposition of music and dialogue from the film. The CD reissue adds bonus unissued jingles and alternate takes, highlighted by a live version of "Circle Sky." *—Richie Unterberger*

Instant Replay / Feb. 15, 1969 / Rhino ✦✦
By 1969's *Instant Replay*, it was all over but the funeral. Peter Tork had already left the fold and the songs were little more than disjointed solo vehicles for the remaining three, combined with older unreleased tracks from the vaults. This afforded far too much rope for schmaltzy Jones ballads, although Nesmith salvages the day once again with tasty country inflections on the wistful "Don't Wait for Me" and "While I Cry." This otherwise slight collection—for intensive Monkees fans only—is at least beefed up by some interesting previously unreleased songs, rather than just alternate mixes. *—Roch Parisien*

The Monkees Present / Oct. 1969 / Rhino ✦✦
Like *Instant Replay, The Monkees Present* was an incoherent collection of pop and country-rock. Although most of the album was well-produced but bland, Mike Nesmith's contributions, particularly "Listen to the Band," indicated that he was continuing to grow as a songwriter. However, his handful of songs couldn't save the album from being a rather desultory affair. After the record's release, Nesmith left the band to pursue a solo career. *—Stephen Thomas Erlewine*

Changes / Jun. 1970 / Rhino ✦
For all intents and purposes, The Monkees had broken up before the recording of *Changes*, their final record. Peter Tork and Mike Nesmith had left the band, leaving only Mickey Dolenz and Davy Jones. Although Dolenz was a relatively accomplished songwriter, he only contributed one song to *Changes*, which meant both he and Jones were vehicles for a variety of professional songwriters, particularly Jeff Barry, who also produced the majority of the album. Most of the material was bland pop, featuring a couple of R&B and soul inflections to liven up the sound. Neither Dolenz or Jones sounds inspired by the material, which isn't surprising—out of the 12 songs, only Boyce and Hart's "I Never Thought It Peculiar" makes any sort of impression. The lack of worthwhile material and the slick, passionless production easily make *Changes* the weakest record the Monkees released. Until they reunited for *Pool It*, that is. *—Stephen Thomas Erlewine*

Pool It / 1986 / Rhino ✦
Failed '80s reunion album is more "fake" sounding than anything from their prime. Stick to the originals. *—Jeff Tamarkin*

Missing Links / 1987 / Rhino ✦✦✦
A fine selection of rarities and oddities that every Monkee maniac with more than a passing interest should own. —*Jeff Tamarkin*

Missing Links 2 / 1990 / Rhino ✦✦✦
Nineteen rare and unreleased tracks that, like the rest of the Monkees' output, ranges from excellent to insufferable, with plenty of mediocre material between. The highlights are the sprightly pop-rocker "All the King's Horses" (a 1966 Mike Nesmith original) and alternate versions of two of the group's best singles, "Words" and "Valleri." These alternate takes aren't exactly better, but they are definitely different and less elaborately produced. Most of the rest is either lightweight 1966 pop-rock or weedy 1968 Mike Nesmith country-rock tunes that foreshadow his solo work; several cuts are alternate versions of songs that were hardly notable efforts in the first place. An exception is the live 1968 recording of the unusually forceful Nesmith original "Circle Sky," which was featured in their movie *Head* (although a studio version was substituted on the actual soundtrack album). Odds and ends like an instrumental banjo piece by Peter Tork and a Spanish Christmas carol are pleasant but inessential. A thoughtfully compiled CD, it nonetheless really gives this group more respect than they're due by treating these artifacts with such importance. —*Richie Unterberger*

Listen to the Band / Sep. 24, 1991 / Rhino ✦✦✦✦
A four-CD box set that includes every Monkees track a fan could want, and probably much more. Excessive, but a collector's dream. —*Jeff Tamarkin*

● **Greatest Hits** / Nov. 1995 / Rhino ✦✦✦✦
Twenty-song collection includes all of their big chart hits, as well as key album tracks like "(Theme From) the Monkees" and "Mary, Mary," and the ace B-side "Goin' Down." The slightly more extensive Arista anthology still has the edge, due to the inclusion of two good cuts ("Take a Giant Step" and "She") that are somehow omitted from this Rhino compilation. On the other hand, if you're still in the market for just one Monkees album, this will do just fine. Good, extensive liner notes, though the last two songs (from 1987 singles that only featured Dolenz and Tork) are a waste. —*Richie Unterberger*

Missing Links 3 / Mar. 26, 1996 / Rhino ✦✦✦
Rhino treats the Monkees catalog with a seriousness akin to the Beatles' *Anthology* series, but it's nonsense to pretend that the group's outtakes and rarities are deserving of such fanatical scrutiny. There are a lot more than anyone suspected, though, and volume three of the *Missing Links* presents 24 more, again proving that the bottom of the Monkees' barrel has the same mixture of fun and boredom as hiding in a barrel as a stowaway. There are too many trivial cuts here from the late '60s—that goes for both the slight pop-rockers and Nesmith's less-slight country-rockers. On the other hand, there are some good 'uns, like the Dolenz-sung acoustic 1967 demo "She'll Be There," which recalls early British Invasion acts like Peter & Gordon; different/rare mixes/takes of "Circle Sky" (one of Nesmith's best compositions), Jeff Barry's "She Hangs Out," and Neil Diamond's "Love to Love"; "How Insensitive," Nesmith's imaginative country rearrangement of an Antonio Carlos Jobim (!) standard; and "Merry Go Round" and "Zor and Zam," insanely experimental outings for a teenybopper group. Thrown into the mix are novelties like commercials and an Italian version of the Monkees' theme, icing the cake on an inconsistency that makes the nearby presence of a CD remote button a necessity. —*Richie Unterberger*

Justus / Oct. 15, 1996 / Rhino ✦✦✦
As the final reunion album from the Monkees—and the first one featuring Mike Nesmith, who produced the record—*Justus* isn't bad. Nesmith occasionally steers the group toward country-rock, but the record is largely composed of nondescript pop-rock that is neither remarkable nor unpleasant. Frequently, the Monkees show their age with strained vocals, but *Justus* is far from the disaster of *Pool It*, and it may stir warm, nostalgic memories from many long-term fans—if they're willing to sift through the mediocre songs that form the bulk of the album. —*Stephen Thomas Erlewine*

The Monks

f. 1964, Germany, db. 1967
Rock 'n' Roll, Garage Rock
One of the strangest stories in rock history, the Monks were formed in the early '60s by American G.I.'s stationed in Germany. After their discharge, the group stayed on in Germany as the Torquays, a fairly standard "beat" band.

After changing their name to the Monks in the mid-'60s, they also changed their music, attitude, and appearance radically. Gone were standard oldie covers, replaced by furious, minimalistic original material that anticipated the blunt, harsh commentary of the punk era. Their insistent rhythms recalled martial beats and polkas as much as garage rock, and the weirdness quotient was heightened by electric banjo, berserk organ runs, and occasional bursts of feedback guitar. To prove that they meant business, the Monks shaved the top of their heads and performed their songs—crude diatribes about the Vietnam war, dehumanized society, and love/hate affairs with girls—in actual monks' clothing.

This was pretty strong stuff for 1966 Germany, and their shocking repertoire and attire were received with more confusion than hostility or warm praise. Well known in Germany as a live act, their sole album and several singles didn't take off in a big way, and were never released in the US because, it was rumored, the lyrical content was deemed too shocking. They disbanded in confusion around 1967, but their album—one of the most oddball constructions in all of rock—gained a hardcore cult following among collectors, and has ironically made them much more popular and influential on an international level than they were during their performing years. Bassist Eddie Shaw's 1994 autobiography, *Black Monk Time*, is a fascinating narrative of the Monks' stranger-than-fiction story. —*Richie Unterberger*

● **Black Monk Time** / 1966 / Infinite Zero/American ✦✦✦✦
The Monks' only album is packed with angst anthems on the order of "Shut Up," "I Hate You," and "Drunken Maria." One of the strangest recordings of all time, it's now finally available in the US as a 1997 CD reissue on Infinite Zero. The repackage is made all the more appealing with the inclusion of their two later non-LP singles, the live 1966 "Monk Chant," and a couple of 1965 demos, making it the definitive document of the Monks' recorded legacy. —*Richie Unterberger*

The Monochrome Set

f. 1978, London, England
Alternative Pop-Rock, New Wave
When the British art-school punk band the B-Sides changed their name and direction to become Adam & the Ants, guitarist-vocalist Bid and guitarist Lester Square opted out to form their own group, the Monochrome Set. Founded in London in 1978, the band (also comprising ex-Gloria Mundi and Mean Street bassist Jeremy Harrington and former Art Attacks drummer J.D. Crowe) was quickly snapped up by the Rough Trade label, and during 1979 issued three singles—"He's Frank," "Eine Symphonie des Grauens," and their signature number, "Monochrome Set"—each completely different in content and stylistic approach.

After former B-Sides bassist Andy Warren grew tired of life in Adam & the Ants, he rejoined bandmates Bid and Square, replacing Harrington. In 1980 the Monochrome Set released their debut album, the cabaret-flavored *Strange Boutique*, followed later that year by the singles "405 Lines" and "Apocalypso" as well as another, more accessible full-length effort, *Love Zombies*. Complete with new guitarist Foz, keyboardist Carolne Booth, and drummer Nick Wesolowski, they returned in 1982 with a cleaner, more melodic sound on the LP *Eligible Bachelors;* "The Jet Set Junta," a satiric jab at the Falklands Islands conflict, became a significant hit the next year.

Following the departure of Square, the Monochrome Set veered even closer to light pop fare on singles like 1985's "Jacob's Ladder"; the sound subsequently crystallized on the nostalgically-themed LP *The Lost Weekend*. When the record met with dismal commercial response, the group disbanded, only to reform in 1989 around the nucleus of Bid, Square, and Warren along with new keyboardist Orson Presence. The 1990 album *Dante's Casino* did little to raise the Monochrome Set's chart visibility, but the band soldiered on, releasing *Charade* in 1993, *Misere* in 1994, and *Trinity Road* in 1995. —*Jason Ankeny*

Strange Boutique / 1980 / Dindisc ✦✦✦

Love Zombies / 1981 / Dindisc ✦✦✦✦

Eligible Bachelors / 1982 / Cherry Red ✦✦✦

Volume! Brilliance! Contrast! / 1983 / Cherry Red ✦✦✦✦

The Lost Weekend / 1985 / Blanco y Negro ✦✦✦

Fin / 1986 / el/Cherry Red ✦✦

Colour Transmission / 1988 / Virgin ✦✦✦
The Monks' only album is packed with angst anthems on the order of "Shut Up," "I Hate You," "Complication," and "Drunken Maria." One of the strangest recordings of all time, it's now finally available in the US as a 1997 CD reissue on Infinite Zero. The repackage is made all the more appealing with the inclusion of their two later non-LP singles, the live 1966 "Monk Chant," and a couple of 1965 demos, making it the definitive document of the Monks' recorded legacy. —*Richie Unterberger*

Westminster Affair / 1988 / Cherry Red ✦✦✦

Dante's Casino / 1990 / Vinyl Japan ✦✦

B & W Minstrels / 1995 / Cherry Red ✦✦✦

● **Tomorrow Will Be Too Long: the Best of the Monochrome Set** / Apr. 25, 1995 / Caroline ✦✦✦✦

Chris Montez

b. Jan. 17, 1943, Los Angeles, CA
Vocals / Rock 'n' Roll
One of the leading rockers in the Los Angeles Hispanic community after the tragic death of Ritchie Valens, Chris Montez later mellowed out under the tutelage of Herb Alpert and tallied several MOR-style hits. His first smash was on Monogram in 1962, "Let's Dance." It was a grinding rocker with roller-rink organ. Montez changed his attitude after signing with A&M. With Alpert producing, Montez adopted an easygoing approach on "Call Me," "The More I See You," and "Time after Time," all solid sellers in 1966. The formula quickly faded, however, and his final chart entry came the following year with "Because of You." —*Bill Dahl*

● **All-Time Greatest Hits** / 1991 / DCC ✦✦✦
Montez began as a Ritchie Valens-style rocker and re-emerged as a crooner of pop ballads in the mid-'60s. He excelled at both styles, each of which is amply documented here. —*Jeff Tamarkin*

The Moody Blues

f. 1964, Birmingham, England
Art-Rock/Progressive-Rock, British Invasion, Pop-Rock
Although they're best known today for their lush, lyrically and musically profound (some would say bombastic) psychedelic-era albums and singles, the Moody Blues started out as one of the better R&B-based combos of the British Invasion. The Moody Blues' history began in Birmingham, England, where one of the more successful bands during that time was El Riot and the Rebels, co-founded by Ray Thomas (harmonica, vocals) and Mike Pinder (keyboards, vocals). Pinder left the band for a gig with Jackie Lynton and then a stint in the Army. In May of 1963, he and Thomas reunited under the auspices of the Krew Cats. They were good enough to get overseas bookings in Germany, where English rock bands were the rage. Upon their return to Birmingham in November of 1963, the entire English musical landscape was occupied by 250 groups, all of them vying for gigs in perhaps a dozen clubs. Thomas and Pinder decided to try and go professional, recruiting members from some of the best groups working in Birmingham. This included Denny Laine (vocals, guitar), Graeme Edge (drums), and Clint Warwick (bass, vocals). The Moody Blues made their debut in Birmingham in May of 1964, and quickly earned the notice and later the services of manager Tony Secunda. A major tour was quickly booked, and the band landed an engagement at the Marquee Club, which resulted in a contract with England's Decca Records less than six months after their formation. The group's first single, "Steal Your Heart Away," released in September of 1964, didn't touch the British charts.

Their second single "Go Now," released in November of 1964, fulfilled every expectation and more, reaching No. 1 in England; in America, it peaked at No. 10. Following it up was easier said than done. Despite their fledgling songwriting efforts and the access they had to American demos, this version of the Moody Blues never came up with another single success. By the end of the spring of 1965, the frustration was palpable within the band. The group decided to make their fourth single, "From the Bottom of My Heart," an experiment with a different sound. Unfortunately, the single only reached No. 22 on the British charts following its release in May of 1965. Ultimately, the grind of touring coupled with the strains facing the group, became too much for Warwick, who exited in the spring of 1966, and by August of 1966 Laine had left as well. Warwick was replaced by John Lodge. His introduction to the band was followed in late 1966 by the addition of Justin Hayward.

The reconstituted Moody Blues set about keeping afloat financially, mostly playing in Europe, recording the occasional single. Their big break came from Deram Records, an imprint of their Decca label, which in 1967 decided that it needed a long-playing record to promote its new "Deramic Stereo." The Moody Blues were picked for the proposed project, a rock version of Dvorak's *New World Symphony*, and immediately convinced the staff producer and the engineer to abandon the source material and permit the group to use a series of its own compositions that depicted an archetypal "day," from morning to night. Using the tracks laid down by the band, and orchestrated by conductor Peter Knight, the resulting album *Days of Future Passed* became a landmark in the band's history. The mix of rock and classical sounds was new, and at first puzzled the record company, but eventually the record was issued. This album, and its singles "Nights in White Satin" and "Tuesday Afternoon," hooked directly into the musical side of the Summer of Love and its aftermath. *In Search of the Lost Chord* (1968) abandoned the orchestra in favor of the Mellotron, which quickly became a part of their signature sound.

By the time of 1969's *To Our Children's Children's Children*, the group found themselves painted into something of a corner. Working in the studio with the process of overdubbing, they'd created albums that were essentially the work of 20 or 30 Moody Blues. Beginning with *A Question of Balance* (1970), the group made the decision to record albums that they could play in concert, reducing their reliance on over-

dubbing and toughening up their sound. By the release of *Seventh Sojourn* (1972), the strain of touring and recording steadily for five years was beginning to take its toll, and following an extended international tour, the band decided to take a break from working together, which ultimately lasted five years. During this era, Hayward and Lodge recorded a very successful duet album, *Blue Jays* (1975), and all five members did solo albums. By 1977, however, the group members had made the decision to reunite, a process complicated by the fact that Pinder had moved to California during that period. Although all five participated in the resulting album, *Octave* (1978), there were stresses during its recording, and Pinder was ultimately unhappy enough with the LP to decline to tour with the band. The reunion tour was a success, with Patrick Moraz brought in to replace Pinder on the keyboards, and the album topped the charts.

The group's follow-up record, *Long Distance Voyager* (1981), was even more popular, though by this time a schism was beginning to develop between the band and the critical community. Although they continued to reach the middle levels of the charts, and even ascended reasonably close to the top with the Hayward single "In Your Wildest Dreams" (1986), the Moody Blues were no longer anywhere near the cutting edge of music. By the end of the 1980s, they were perceived as a nostalgia act, albeit one with a huge audience. In 1994, a four-CD set called *Time Traveller* was released. In early 1995, the group—having completed a US tour—began work on another studio album. —*Bruce Eder*

Go Now/Moody Blues #1 / 1965 / London ✦✦✦
The first and only US album by the first, rhythm-and-blues-inspired incarnation of the Moody Blues, led by Denny Laine, is an okay compilation of early singles and B-sides, but has long since been supplanted by better collections. The title song and "From the Bottom of My Heart" are killer tracks, however. —*Bruce Eder*

The Magnificent Moodies / 1965 / Polydor ✦✦✦
The definitive collection of the band's rhythm-and-blues period, containing every track known to exist. All—except for "Go Now," which sounds very tinny here—are beautifully re-mastered, and annotated with great (if occasionally inaccurate) detail. About a dozen of the 20-odd songs here are among the finest R&B tracks recorded during the British Invasion. Out of print in America, but worth finding. —*Bruce Eder*

Days of Future Passed / 1967 / Polydor ✦✦✦✦
The reconstituted Moody Blues, with Justin Hayward and John Lodge established on guitar, bass, and vocals, venture into progressive rock territory with the London Festival Orchestra and have their first major success, with both the album and the singles "Nights in White Satin" and "Tuesday Afternoon." The material seems pretentious but really rocks pretty hard, and the orchestral interludes, courtesy of the late Peter Knight, have an epic sweep that still dazzles the ear. In 1967, a lot of people hungry for something to put on the turntable after *Sgt. Pepper* turned to this, and turned it into an international hit with good reason. —*Bruce Eder*

In Search of the Lost Chord / 1968 / Polydor ✦✦✦
The Moody Blues discover drugs and mysticism as a basis for songwriting, and come up with a compelling psychedelic album, filled with songs about Dr. Timothy Leary, the astral plane and other psychedelic-era concerns, all resplendent in sweeping choruses and an elegant mix of conventional rock instruments augmented by flutes, sitars, tablas, cellos, and electronic orchestrations. Beautiful and elegant. —*Bruce Eder*

On the Threshold of a Dream / 1969 / Polydor ✦✦✦✦
Mysticism gives way to science fiction on this album, which abandons Indian sitars and tablas in favor of more traditional-sounding orchestrations (created on the Mellotron), and also rocks a little harder in spots than their previous records. —*Bruce Eder*

To Our Children's Children's Children / 1969 / Polydor ✦✦✦
The Moody Blues' most personal album was also, oddly enough, the poorest seller among their psychedelic period releases, taking longer to go gold. The material here dwells on time, space, and distance, with a curious mood of loneliness on several of the songs. The last of the band's "studio"-based albums (that is, built up with multiple overdubs, regardless of the difficulty in recreating the material on stage), it has a very lush, rich sound, although the group avoids extended suites of the kind on their previous two albums. And Hayward's "Gypsy" and "Watching and Waiting" are among the best songs in their history. —*Bruce Eder*

Question of Balance / 1970 / Polydor ✦✦✦
A return to a harder-rocking sound in the studio, beginning with the rippling "Question" and including the oft-overlooked "Tortoise and the Hare" (a great rock number in concert), as well as the gorgeous "And the Tide Rushes In." —*Bruce Eder*

● **Every Good Boy Deserves Favour** / 1971 / Polydor ✦✦✦✦
The most well-realized of the band's psychedelic era albums, filled with gorgeous melodies, superbly crafted songs, and a dazzling array of key-

board and guitar pyrotechnics—"Emily's Song," "Nice to Be Here," and "My Song" are among the best work the group has ever done, and "The Story in Your Eyes" is the best rock number they've ever cut, with a riveting beat and the kind of insights one expected more out of George Harrison at his best. —*Bruce Eder*

Seventh Sojourn / 1972 / Polydor ✦✦✦
The group's hardest-rocking album, and one that closed their psychedelic period. The songs generally lack the rich Mellotron orchestrations of the earlier records, and most of the songs are built around John Lodge's and Graeme Edge's driving rhythm section—"New Horizons" was the most romantic number the band had debuted since "Nights in White Satin," while "I'm Just a Singer in a Rock 'n Roll Band" showed the sudden emergence of John Lodge as a major songwriter in the group. —*Bruce Eder*

This Is the Moody Blues / 1974 / Polydor ✦✦✦✦
A double-CD best-of covering the group's 1967-1972 period, its tapes recompiled and re-mastered for the compact disc reissue. The selection is reasonably complete, although it leaves out one excellent number for every two that are included, and the individual CDs are probably a better investment. The new liner notes by John Tracy are thoughtful and informative. —*Bruce Eder*

In the Beginning / 1975 / Deram ✦✦✦
A deliberately misleading attempt to resell the "Go Now"-era R&B material in a psychedelic style package. Protests from the band, coupled with a nasty reaction from fans, resulted in its being deleted very quickly, making it a genuine rarity. —*Bruce Eder*

Dream / 1977 / Decca ✦✦✦✦
Although this isn't too easy to locate, Moody Blues fans may find this double-LP, 29-song set of early recordings worth the search. It includes every track the band released prior to *Days of Future Passed*, with the unfortunate exception of "Time Is on My Side." All of the Denny Laine tracks are available on the *Magnificent Moodies* CD reissue, but three of the four songs from non-LP 1967 singles recorded after Laine's departure are only available here or on the pricey *Time Traveller* box. The remaining B-side, "Really Haven't Got the Time," makes one of its few (if not its only) LP reissue appearances here. And besides that, the music is pretty good, although the post-Laine singles are only adequate. —*Richie Unterberger*

Caught Live + 5 / 1977 / PolyGram ✦✦✦✦
The Moody Blues put out this collection, a live concert augmented by some previously unreleased studio cuts, once they'd decided to re-form at the end of the 1970s, to get some product out. They never liked the concert much as a document (the unofficial word is that several of the group members were under the influence of controlled substances during the show, and thus less sharp than they might otherwise have been), which is one reason why they didn't authorize its release on CD until 1996. The 1969 Royal Albert Hall show sounds a lot better than it did on the LP, with a closeness that was never evident before—Justin Hayward's guitar and Michael Pinder's various Mellotrons, in particular, sound really close, and the singing comes out with more detail. The songs come primarily from *Days of Future Passed*, *Lost Chord*, and *Threshold of a Dream;* they rock hard on "Legend of a Mind" and "Ride My See-Saw," and "Tuesday Afternoon" is a highlight as well. As for the studio cuts, they're salvaged from failed album sessions in 1967 and 1968—not bad, but definitely filler. —*Bruce Eder*

Octave / 1978 / Polydor ✦✦✦
The group's first post-reunion album is uneven in spots, but Justin Hayward's songwriting and singing maintain a haunting romantic edge, and John Lodge shows a newly prominent and energetic voice as a composer. Keyboard player Mike Pinder exited after finishing this album, leaving behind one song on the record. —*Bruce Eder*

Long Distance Voyager / 1981 / Polydor ✦✦✦
The group's biggest-selling album of the '80s also marked a turning point in their fortunes, where they began losing even the mainstream critics. The music has drive, and is extremely well played and produced (this was the only album the band ever got to do at their own, custom-designed Threshold Studios), but also seemed very dated in its time, with a '60s sensibility that was out of place. —*Bruce Eder*

The Present / 1983 / Polydor ✦✦
The group's best years were clearly behind them, as evidenced by this record, which lacked much of the energy of their previous efforts and seemed predictable throughout. Reasonably well played but very much limited in interest to the band's hardcore fans. —*Bruce Eder*

Voices in the Sky: The Best of the Moody Blues / 1985 / Polydor ✦✦✦✦
A good sampling of the Moody Blues' greatest hits from the 1960s and '70s; it's fine for those who only want the hits. —*Stephen Thomas Erlewine*

A Compleat Collection / 1985 / Compleat ✦✦
A 19-track retrospective of the Denny Laine era. The reissue of *The Magnificent Moodies* captures this period with more thoroughness, and is packaged much better. —*Richie Unterberger*

The Other Side of Life / 1986 / Polydor ✦✦✦
The group's best album in several years benefited mostly from the presence of the Top Ten single "Your Wildest Dreams," which managed to turn their status as dinosaurs from the '60s psychedelic era into a plus, with a great beat to boot and a very entertaining video featuring young British psychedelic rockers the Mood Six playing the young Moody Blues. The rest was fairly routine, alas, but the single was strong enough on its own terms to revive interest in the group one more time out. —*Bruce Eder*

Prelude / 1987 / Polydor ✦✦✦
A collection of little known "transitional" period tracks in the group's history, dating from the period after guitarist-vocalist Denny Laine exited, and after Justin Hayward and John Lodge replaced them, but before the band had fully hit upon a new sound. Some of the stuff is surprisingly Beatlesque, and "Love and Beauty" marks the group's first use of the Mellotron and the layered vocals that would define their later psychedelic-era sound. And all of this is rounded out by the presence of the late-'60s studio tracks that filled out their 1978 compilation *Caught Live + Five*. This disc, out of print in America, is worth tracking down for fans as an import. —*Bruce Eder*

In Search of the Lost Song [bootleg] / 1989 / JVB ✦✦✦
There aren't many Moody Blues bootlegs, and this may be the only one really worth searching for, containing as it does extremely rare material from the dawn of their career. Side one has rare, pre-Moodies singles by Justin Hayward and the Wilde Three (a mid-'60s group that included Hayward), an unreleased 1963 demo by El Riot & The Rebels (which featured Ray Thomas, John Lodge, and Mike Pinder), and a 1964 demo by the Carpet Baggers (written by then-Carpet Bagger John Lodge). This material is lightweight but ingratiating in a chipper, very early British Invasion fashion; Hayward's "Day Must Come," with its ballroom orchestration, strongly hints at the direction the Moodies would take just after he joined the band. The problem with these sides is the fidelity, seemingly taken from an old radio program; the tape hiss is at such a high level as to be distracting, even by bootleg standards, and the speed seems too fast. Couldn't anyone at least have located actual copies of the Justin Hayward singles to dub from, instead of tapes of tapes of tapes? The rest of the material, performed by the Moodies as a group, dates from the mid—and late '60s, and is fairly good, comprising Coca-Cola commercials (with both the Denny Laine and Hayward lineups), BBC sessions (including the rare singles "Love and Beauty" and "Leave This Man Alone"), a cover of the Animals' "Don't Let Me Be Misunderstood," and TV performances of some of the highlights from *Days of Future Passed* and *Lost Chord*. It's not a bad thing to have if you want more Moodies from their prime era; just be aware that there are some severe sonic deficiencies. —*Richie Unterberger*

Greatest Hits / Nov. 1989 / Polydor ✦✦✦✦
All of the Moody Blues' best songs and biggest hits from the 1980s are collected on *Greatest Hits;* it's the most mainstream pop-oriented material the band has ever recorded. —*Stephen Thomas Erlewine*

Keys of the Kingdom / Jun. 25, 1991 / Polydor ✦
Disappointing studio album from the band—now reduced officially to a quartet with the departure of Patrick Moraz from the keyboard spot. The melodies lack freshness and invention, the lyrics are predictable in the worst possible way, and the band fails to generate any excitement or interest on this record. —*Bruce Eder*

A Night at Red Rocks with the Colorado . . . / 1993 / Polydor ✦✦✦
Having succeeded in the '80s by drawing on '60s nostalgia with a song ("Your Wildest Dreams") and video, the Moody Blues in the '90s began tailoring entire shows to recapture their '60s glory days—and they succeeded. Performing on tour with a series of regional orchestras, they brought the majesty of their old studio sound onto the stage for the first time on songs like "Nights in White Satin" and "Tuesday Afternoon," and audiences responded by turning them into one of the top concert draws of the decade. This album and the accompanying video are beautifully recorded (and the video looks gorgeous, too) and performed, and the group—caught amid the splendor of one of the prettiest outdoor concert venues in the West (Stevie Nicks has also done a video there) and with the orchestra backing them up on half the numbers, rise to the occasion with a drive and eloquence that they haven't shown on stage in many years. An essential recording and video for any fan of the group. —*Bruce Eder*

Time Traveller / Sep. 27, 1994 / PolyGram ✦✦✦✦
When the Moody Blues were due for the box set treatment, it would have been uncharacteristic for the production to be lacking in overstated grandiosity. On that count, this four-CD retrospective does not disappoint, including the bulk of their most famous work (from their

1967-72 albums), lots from their later records and side projects, and a few rarities. There's not a great deal of reason for anyone but fanatics to fork out for this package; the albums (which were specifically programmed to work as separate entities) remain readily available, there's too much late stuff and Hayward/Blue Jays tracks, and there's nothing from the Denny Laine era. The three non-LP 1967 cuts that open the set are available on the double import LP *A Dream* (still possible to find), an album that also has the additional 1967 B-side "Really Haven't Got the Time," which somehow doesn't make it onto *Time Traveller*. As consolation, the liner notes are pretty good and extensive, and the first printings of the box include a bonus disc of a 1992 concert with the Colorado Symphony Orchestra. —*Richie Unterberger*

● **Best Of** / Jan. 28, 1997 / Polygram ✦✦✦✦
The 17-track *The Best of the Moody Blues* contains all of the group's biggest hits, from 1964's "Go Now" to 1988's "I Know You're Out There Somewhere." Between those two songs, all of the Moodies' best-known songs are featured, including "Nights in White Satin," "Tuesday Afternoon," "Ride My See-Saw," "Story in Your Eyes" and "Your Wildest Dreams," making the compilation an excellent choice for casual fans. —*Stephen Thomas Erlewine*

The Moonglows

f. 1951, Louisville, KY
R&B, Doo Wop
Among the most seminal R&B and doo wop groups of all time, the Moonglows' lineup featured some of the genre's greatest pure singers. The original lineup from Louisville included Bobby Lester, Harvey Fuqua, Alexander Graves, and Prentiss Barnes, with guitarist Billy Johnson. They were originally called the Crazy Sounds, but were renamed by disc jockey Alan Freed as the Moonglows. The group also cut some recordings as the Moonlighters. Their first major hit was the No. 1 R&B gem "Sincerely" for Chess in 1954, which reached No. 20 on the pop charts. They enjoyed five more Top Ten R&B hits on Chess from 1955 to 1958, among them "Most of All," "We Go Together," "See Saw," and "Please Send Me Someone to Love," as well as "Ten Commandments of Love." Fuqua, the nephew of Charlie Fuqua of the Ink Spots, left in 1958. He recorded "Ten Commandments of Love" as Harvey & the Moonglows with Marvin Gaye, Reese Palmner, James Knowland, and Chester Simmons before founding his own label, Tri-Phi. Fuqua created and produced the Spinners in 1961 and wrote and produced for Motown until the early '70s. The Moonglows disbanded in the '60s, then reunited in 1972 with Fuqua, Lester, Graves, Doc Williams, and Chuck Lewis. They recorded for RCA and a re-worked version of "Sincerely" eventually charted, but wasn't a major hit. —*Ron Wynn*

● **Blue Velvet: The Ultimate Collection** / Dec. 7, 1993 / Chess ✦✦✦✦
Few rivaled the Moonglows in musical sophistication, inventiveness, or flair. They could sing gorgeous heartache ballads, rollicking uptempo rhythm tunes, creditable period-piece novelty numbers, wonderful pop covers, or shattering originals. This two-disc set contains 44 outstanding numbers, with every major Moonglows anthem and several others that weren't big hits but deserved to be, such as "Penny Arcade" and "Love Is a River." This collection updates and expands the *Greatest Sides* single LP release, briefly available when Sugar Hill had the Chess catalog in the 1970s. It wisely restricts its material to the era when they were at their best, the 1950s, and includes an excellent booklet. —*Ron Wynn*

● **Their Greatest Hits** / May 20, 1997 / MCA ✦✦✦✦

Gary Moore

b. Apr. 4, 1952, Belfast, Ireland
Guitar / Blues-Rock, Hard Rock
Belfast native Gary Moore first achieved renown as the lead guitarist of hard rockers Thin Lizzy. Moore's first band, Skid Row, featured bassist Brendan Shields, drummer Noel Bridgeman, and singer Phil Lynott, who left to form Thin Lizzy while Moore remained to pursue a record deal with the help of Fleetwood Mac guitarist Peter Green. Skid Row recorded three albums before Moore left for a solo career, releasing his first album, *Grinding Stone*, in 1973. Lynott then invited Moore to join Thin Lizzy as a replacement for guitarist Eric Bell; Moore stayed for a short time before leaving to pursue session work, which he has continued off and on throughout his career. Moore joined the fusion outfit Colosseum II in 1975 and rejoined Thin Lizzy in 1977 as a full-time member, appearing on their 1979 album *Black Rose*. In the middle of a 1979 American tour, Moore left Thin Lizzy again to form the unsuccessful G-Force; his single "Parisienne Walkways," from the solo LP *Back on the Streets*, became a UK hit that May.

Moore recorded a series of moderately successful albums during the 1980s and had popular UK numbers with "Empty Rooms" in 1985 and a collaboration with Lynott, "Out in the Fields." 1989's *After the War* showed the influence of Celtic music, but Moore's breakthrough came with the following year's *Still Got the Blues*. Toning down the hard rock

feel of many of his previous recordings, Moore mixed traditional blues standards with a sprinkling of originals and delivered a superb performance vocally and instrumentally, and the album became a critical and commercial success. Moore followed his surprise success with *After Hours*, which featured guest spots from B.B. King and Albert Collins and solidified Moore's reputation as a blues-rocker of note. Moore recorded a side project called BBM in 1994 with former Cream rhythm section Jack Bruce and Ginger Baker, and in 1995, he released a tribute album to his idol, Peter Green, composed entirely of Green originals played on a guitar Green had given him years ago. —*Steve Huey*

Back on the Streets / 1979 / Grand Slamm ✦✦

Corridors of Power / 1982 / Mirage ✦✦✦
Corridors of Time offers several distinct musical styles by New Age music pioneer Steven Halpern. His two "Fantasy" pieces for spatially expanded piano (lots of pedal and echo) create a drone effect with undulating waves of octaves and embellishments. Spacy synthesizer effects add other drones and mind-bending sounds and dimensions. The effect is very relaxing, like floating. Halpern's synthesizer pieces use percolating and unfolding electronic sequences with deep "aum" drones to keep the mind anchored. These pieces differ from Halpern's typical relaxation sound (i.e., the gentle clarion), but they are meditative in their own way. "Diana's Dream Theme" features Diana Allen's enchantingly echoed voice, which seems to lasso across the heavens. Even more variety from Halpern as the title cut features even sharper synthesized sequences; "Round Midnight in Marrakesh" features Middle Eastern rhythms. As Halpern points out in the tape's liner notes, this album is not one of his "Anti-Frantic Alternative" series. It is meant for meditation and visual mind tripping, and an enjoyable excursion it is, too. —*Carol Wright*

After the War / 1989 / Virgin ✦✦✦

● **Still Got the Blues** / May 1990 / Charisma ✦✦✦✦
Relieved from the pressures of having to record a hit single, he cuts loose on some blues standards as well as some newer material. Moore plays better than ever, spitting out an endless stream of fiery licks that are both technically impressive and soulful. It's no wonder *Still Got the Blues* was his biggest hit. —*David Jehnzen*

After Hours / Mar. 10, 1992 / Charisma ✦✦✦✦
Not wanting to leave a good thing behind, Moore reprises *Still Got the Blues* on its follow-up, *After Hours*. While his playing is just as impressive, the album feels a little calculated. Nevertheless, Moore's gutsy, impassioned playing makes the similarity easy to ignore. —*David Jehnzen*

Blues Alive / Jul. 1, 1992 / Virgin ✦✦✦

Live at the Marquee Club / Jul. 1, 1992 / Castle ✦✦

Blues for Greeny / 1995 / Charisma ✦✦✦
Gary Moore's tribute to Fleetwood Mac guitarist Peter Green, *Blues for Greeny*, is more of a showcase for Moore's skills than Green's songwriting. After all, Green was more famous for his technique than his writing. Consequently, Moore uses Green's songs as a starting point, taking them into new territory with his own style. And Moore positively burns throughout *Blues for Greeny*, tearing off licks with ferocious intensity. If anything, the album proves that Moore is at his best when interpreting other people's material—it easily ranks as one of his finest albums. —*Stephen Thomas Erlewine*

Ballads & Blues 1982-1994 / Mar. 21, 1995 / Charisma ✦✦✦✦

Melba Moore

b. Oct. 27, 1945, New York, NY
Vocals / Soul
Melba Moore has been an extremely successful actress and performer since her early days in such plays as *Hair* and *Purlie*. She began recording for Buddah in 1975, and has continued with Epic, EMI, and Capitol. She has done duets with Lilo Thomas, Kashif, and Freddie Jackson, and was instrumental in helping to discover and get Jackson started by signing her to Hush Productions, a firm run by her husband Beau Higgins. Moore's flamboyant, octave-leaping style has been featured on ballads and dance-disco material, but her biggest hits were "A Little Bit More" (with Freddie Jackson) and "Falling," both R&B chart-toppers in 1986, recorded for Capitol. Other R&B Top Ten hits include "Love's Comin' at Ya" for EMI in 1982, "Livin' for Your Love" in 1984, "Love the One I'm With (A Lot of Love)" with Kashif in 1986, and "It's Been So Long" in 1987, all three for Capitol. —*Ron Wynn*

● **Little Bit Moore: Magic of Melba Moore** / Jan. 28, 1997 / EMI ✦✦✦✦
A selection of 14 tracks from her 1980s albums, usually sticking to a mainstream urban contemporary vein. Includes the hits "Falling," "I'm in Love," "Underlove," "Livin' for Your Love," "A Little Bit More," and "I Can't Complain," the last two of which are duets with Freddie Jackson. —*Richie Unterberger*

Moose

f. 1990, London, England

Alternative Pop-Rock, Shoegazing, Dream-Pop

Not so much underrated as unheard, Moose grew up in Britain's distortion-heavy shoegazing movement of the early '90s but soon shed the fuzzy wash of their compatriots to embrace a clean, acoustic-based style—inspired by '60s icons Burt Bacharach and Tim Buckley as well as jangle merchants like the Byrds and R.E.M.—that still relied on the intense guitar effects that characterized the band's early works. Moose was formed in early 1990 by the songwriting team of Kevin (K.J.) McKillop and Russell Yates (Yates had appeared in an early incarnation of Stereolab), plus drummer Damien Warburton and bassist Jeremy Tishler. The group signed to Hut Records (also the British home of Smashing Pumpkins and the Verve) in 1990, and began recording with producer Guy Fixsen (later of Laika).

After the release of three EPs during 1991, both Warburton and Tishler left the band; Moose then added drummer Richard Thomas and the brothers Fong, Lincoln on bass and Russell on guitar and sometimes production. Hut Records had just formed an alliance with the major label Virgin, which condensed Moose's past material onto a seven-track EP, *Sonny and Sam.* (It served as an American primer for the band, but proved to be their only stateside release.) Hut financed a full-length album, ...XYZ, in 1992 and recruited Mitch Easter for production and Dolores O'Riordan of the Cranberries for harmony vocals on one track. The album sold poorly, however, and Hut dropped the band by early 1993. Not fazed in the least, Moose came back with the *Liquid Make Up* EP for their own Cool Badge label. Its lead-off track, "I Wanted to See You to See If I Wanted You," was a charming piece of pop, their best single yet. Signed to Belgium's Play It Again Sam Records, the band released their second album, *Honey Bee,* in early 1994. It wisely included a different version of "I Wanted to See You to See If I Wanted You," but Moose appeared to be verging on overkill with yet another carbon-copy version included on the *Bang Bang* EP several months later. Perhaps signaling a stall in creativity, their third album, *Live a Little, Love a Lot,* was released with no attaching single, though the Cocteau Twins' Liz Fraser did lend her vocals to one track. *—John Bush*

Sonny and Sam [EP] / Jan. 1992 / Virgin ✦✦✦

An out-of-print American EP, it summarizes Moose's first three EPs for the British label Hut. The band's shoegazing roots are easily seen on blissed-out tracks such as "This River Will Never Run Dry" and "Do You Remember?" *—John Bush*

● **...Xyz** / Sep. 1992 / Hut ✦✦✦✦

Moose's debut album (produced by Mitch Easter) shows the band moving toward a pop-oriented style, sacrificing much of the ethereal guitar effects of the shoegazers. Highlights include "Little Bird," "Sometimes Loving Is the Hardest Thing," and a beautiful cover of "Everybody's Talking." Dolores O'Riordan of The Cranberries makes a guest appearance. *—John Bush*

Live a Little, Love a Lot / Feb. 1996 / Play It Again ✦✦✦

Morcheeba

f. 1995, London, England

Alternative Pop-Rock, Club/Dance, Trip-Hop, Electronica

The most groove-oriented act in the mid-'90s female-fronted electronica crowd, Morcheeba rely on the sweet, fluid vocals of Sky Edwards and a laidback mix of fusion, funk and blues produced by brothers Paul and Ross Godfrey, on beats/scratches and guitar/keyboards respectively. The trio was formed in 1995 when the Godfreys decided to go out on their own after touring as part of David Byrne's backup band. They submitted several tapes of their instrumental demos to labels around London, but received little interest in them. After hooking up with vocalist Edwards at a party, however, their music began to gel and Morcheeba signed to the China label. After the release of two EPs (*Trigger Hippie* and *Music That We Hear*), the trio issued their debut album, *Who Can You Trust?* It appeared on the American Discovery label in late 1996, and Morcheeba toured the US with Live and Fiona Apple the following year. *—John Bush*

Who Can You Trust? / Sep. 24, 1996 / Discovery ✦✦✦✦

Slower, smoother, and more soulful than Portishead and less pop-oriented than the Sneaker Pimps, Morcheeba has an alluringly dark sound that nevertheless remains accessible. As their debut *Who Can You Trust?* illustrates, the trio has a keen sense of how to make a pop melody seem dangerous and foreign by having it crawl out of the murk of creeping beats and ominous samples. Although the group lacks the visionary spark of Tricky and Portishead, and their songs aren't as bracing as those of the Sneaker Pimps, Morcheeba has a distinctive, idiosyncratic sound that makes *Who Can You Trust?* entrancing. Although the latter half of the album tends to sound a little samey, without many beats or hooks to distinguish each song, the album remains a haunt-

ingly atmospheric—and quite terrific—debut. *—Stephen Thomas Erlewine*

Alanis Morissette

b. Jun. 1, 1974, Ottawa, Ontario, Canada

Vocals / Alternative Pop-Rock, Pop-Rock

Alanis Morissette (b. June 1, 1974, Ottawa, Canada) was one of the most unlikely stars of the mid-'90s. A former child actress turned dance-pop diva, Morissette transformed herself into a confessional alternative singer-songwriter, in the vein of Liz Phair and Tori Amos. However, she added enough pop sensibility, slight hip-hop flourishes, and marketing savvy to that formula to become a superstar with her third album, *Jagged Little Pill.*

Morissette was born and raised in Ottawa, Canada. In her childhood, she began playing piano and writing songs. At the age of ten, she joined the cast of *You Can't Do That on Television,* a children's television program.

Using money that she earned on the show, Morissette recorded an independent single, "Fate Stay with Me," which was released when she was ten. After leaving the show, she concentrated on a musical career, signing a music publishing contract when she was 14. The publishing contract led to a record deal with MCA/Canada. In 1991, she moved to Toronto and released her debut album, *Alanis.*

Alanis was a collection of pop-oriented dance numbers and ballads that was successful in Canada, selling over 100,000 copies, and leading to a Juno Award for Most Promising Female Artist. However, no other country paid any attention to the record. In 1992, she released *Now Is the Time,* an album that closely resembled her debut. Like its predecessor, it was a success in Canada, even if it sold half of what *Alanis* did. Following the release of *Now Is the Time,* Morissette relocated to Los Angeles, where she met Glen Ballard in early 1994. Ballard had previously written Michael Jackson's hit "Man in the Mirror," produced Wilson Phillips' hit debut album, and worked with David Hasselhoff. Despite the duo's mainstream pop pedigree, they decided to pursue an edgier, alternative rock-oriented direction. The result was *Jagged Little Pill,* which was released on Maverick Records, Madonna's label.

On the strength of the single "You Oughta Know," *Jagged Little Pill* gained attention upon its release in the summer of 1995. Soon, the single received heavy airplay from both alternative radio and MTV, sending the album into the Top Ten and multi-platinum status. The second and third singles from *Jagged Little Pill,* "Hand in My Pocket" and "All I Really Want," kept the album in the Top Ten. In early 1996, Morissette was nominated for six Grammys. Shortly after the nominations, she released her fourth single, "Ironic," which proved to be her biggest crossover success. Morissette won several Grammy awards in 1996, including Album of the Year and Record of the Year. *—Stephen Thomas Erlewine*

● **Jagged Little Pill** / Jun. 13, 1995 / Maverick/Reprise ✦✦✦✦

Alanis Morissette knows the pain of love—you can tell from the caterwauling single "You Oughta Know." Over a grinding alterna-funk groove, Morissette rails against her ex-lover who's left her for someone "older" than her and wonders "is she perverted like me?" Morissette doesn't understand why she's been left alone, since he said he would "hold me until you died, until you died/But you're still alive!" Every song on *Jagged Little Pill* reads exactly like that—it sounds like the writings of a dejected college sophomore, so perhaps it isn't surprising that the majority of *Jagged Little Pill* was written when she was 19 years old. In that sense, it is a pseudo-concept album on which a confused teenager, inspired by Liz Phair, begins to grow up, learning about sex, relationships, drugs, and life in general. Morissette doesn't have a great, or even good voice—it's herky-jerky, making the octave jumps of Sinead O'Connor but without the sense of pitch. Her lyrics are too personal to connect with universal truths—when she tells one ex-boyfriend "You took me out to wine dine 69 me / But didn't hear a damn word I said . . . Now that I'm Miss Thing / Now that I'm a zillionaire / You scan the credits for your name / And wonder why it's not there," it's hard to gather much sympathy for her. And, despite the presence of superstar musicians like Benmont Tench, Flea, and Dave Navarro, the album sounds like the work of studio hacks. It's enjoyable in small doses—"You Oughta Know" is ingratiatingly catchy, as is the opener "All I Really Want"—yet her music is merely a vehicle for her hackneyed prose. *—Stephen Thomas Erlewine*

Morphine

f. 1990

Rock 'n' Roll, Alternative Pop-Rock

Morphine is a rarity—a bluesy, bare bones rock 'n' roll without any guitars. Instead of guitar riffs, the trio relies on sliding two-string bass lines, raucous saxophones, and wry, ironically detached vocals. During the mid-'90s, Morphine gained a sizable cult following in America, primarily due to good word of mouth, heavy college airplay, and positive reviews.

Morphine was formed in 1990 by bassist-vocalist Mark Sandman, who had previously played with the bluesy alternative rock band Treat Her Right, and Dana Colley (tenor and baritone saxophone), a former member of the local Boston group, Three Collers. Sandman and Colley added drummer Jerome Dupree to complete the lineup. The group released their debut album, *Good*, on the independent Accurate-Distortion in 1991; it was reissued on Rykodisc Records in 1992. *Good* received substantial airplay on American college radio stations, as well as favorable reviews in alternative publications across the country. After the release of *Good*, Dupree left the band and was replaced by Billy Conway, who had previously played with Sandman in Treat Her Right.

The positive reception for *Good* set the stage for 1993's *Cure for Pain*, which received good reviews from a variety of music and mainstream publications upon its spring release. Morphine supported *Cure for Pain* with an extensive American and European tour that lasted throughout 1994, which helped the album sell over 300,000 copies—an impressive feat for an independent release. In 1995, Morphine released their third album, *Yes*, which also received favorable reviews and helped the band sustain their large cult following.

The success of *Cure for Pain* and *Yes* also attracted the attention of major record labels, and in late 1996, Dreamworks bought out the majority share of Morphine's contract from Rykodisc. *Like Swimming*, the group's debut for Dreamworks, was released in the spring of 1997 to generally favorable reviews, yet it failed to break the band out of cult status. *—Stephen Thomas Erlewine*

Good / Sep. 8, 1992 / Rykodisc ✦✦✦
While somewhat uneven, the stark simplicity of the band's stripped-down approach and the barking exchanges between the sliding bass and baritone sax make Morphine's debut album a worthwhile listen. *—Stephen Thomas Erlewine*

Cure for Pain / Sep. 1993 / Rykodisc ✦✦✦✦
With stronger songwriting and a darker, more menacing atmosphere, Morphine's second album improves on their debut. *—Stephen Thomas Erlewine*

● **Yes** / Mar. 1995 / Rykodisc ✦✦✦✦
From the start of *Yes*, it's clear that Morphine have stripped away a lot of their pretenses and have just set out to rock. Well, that's not entirely true. *Yes* still is highly stylized, with Mark Sandman sounding like an English major that took his Charles Bukowski to heart, and the band adhering to its no-guitar/no-keyboard policy (with the exception of a couple of acoustic guitar ballads, that is). But Morphine rocks out more fearlessly than before, making the music sound alive, not the product of a conscious conceit. From the growling "Honey White" to the dirty "Super Sex," it provides an immediate gratification that previous Morphine records never quite delivered. *—Stephen Thomas Erlewine*

Like Swimming / Mar. 11, 1997 / DreamWorks ✦✦✦

Van Morrison

b. Aug. 31, 1945, Belfast, Ireland
Guitar, Harmonica, Keyboards, Saxophone, Vocals / Singer-Songwriter, Adult Contemporary, Soft Rock, Folk-Rock, Pop-Rock, Blue-Eyed Soul, Jazz-Rock
Van Morrison is one of the most critically acclaimed pop music singer-songwriters to have emerged in the 1960s. His bluesy voice and jazzy sense of improvisation have resulted in a three-decade career full of outstanding albums and concert performances. Morrison's father was a fan of American music, and he grew up listening to records by Leadbelly, Woody Guthrie, Jelly Roll Morton, and Jimmy Rodgers, among others, spanning the genres of blues, folk, jazz, and country. As a teen, Morrison took up guitar and saxophone and played in a series of local bands, culminating in the formation of Them, an R&B quintet, in 1964. Signed to Decca Records (the catalog is now controlled by PolyGram), Them released two albums, *Them* (issued under the title *The Angry Young Them* in the US) and *Them Again*, and scored Top Ten hits in the UK with "Baby Please Don't Go" and "Here Comes the Night" in 1965. In the US, Them also charted with two Morrison-composed songs, "Gloria" (which became a rock standard) and "Mystic Eyes." But the group disbanded in 1966.

Morrison signed to Bang Records, a label set up by songwriter Bert Berns, who had written "Here Comes the Night," and in March 1967, recorded eight tracks in New York intended for single release. The first result of the session was "Brown-Eyed Girl," which became a US Top Ten hit, prompting Bang to release the singles session as Morrison's first solo album, *Blowin' Your Mind!* (July 1967), though Morrison had not approved the release, the title, or the trendy psychedelic cover. Nevertheless, Morrison returned to the studio in the fall and cut eight more songs for Bang, which took five of them, culled five from the previous album, and released the deceptively titled *The Best of Van Morrison* (November 1967). With that, Morrison negotiated to get off the label, a process made

easier by the sudden death of Berns in December 1967. Morrison agreed to turn over his next ten compositions to Bang, but submitted a tape of unusable off-the-cuff improvisations finally released in 1994 on *Payin' Dues*. (The Bang material has been reissued endlessly, the most complete version being Epic/Legacy's 1991 *Bang Masters*.)

Morrison then signed to Warner Bros. Records and recorded *Astral Weeks* (November 1968), which failed to chart but seems to have made every critic's all-time Top Ten list ever since. Living in Woodstock, NY, and later in Marin County, CA, with his wife Janet Planet, Morrison adopted a more commercial country-pop sound, and his second Warner Bros. album, *Moondance* (February 1970), was more of a sales success, spawning a Top 40 hit in "Come Running" and eventually selling over a million copies. Its follow-up, *His Band and the Street Choir* (October 1970), featured chart singles in "Domino" (which hit the Top Ten), "Blue Money," and "Call Me Up in Dreamland." Completing a trilogy of country-pop successes, *Tupelo Honey* (October 1971) produced chart singles in the title song and "Wild Night" and eventually went gold. Morrison took a more soul-oriented approach on *Saint Dominic's Preview* (July 1972), characterized by the album's first single, "Jackie Wilson Said (I'm in Heaven When You Smile)." *Hard Nose the Highway* (July 1973), released around the time of the breakup of his marriage, found a more introspective Morrison crooning such material as *Sesame Street* puppet Kermit the Frog's "(It isn't easy bein') Green," but he bounced back with a powerful double live album, *It's Too Late to Stop Now* (February 1974), then made his most reflective album since *Astral Weeks* in *Veedon Fleece* (October 1974) before disappearing from record stores for two and a half years, reportedly due to writer's block. He returned with *A Period of Transition* (March 1977), an R&B-tinged effort that paired him with Dr. John. More assured was *Wavelength* (September 1978), whose title track was his biggest chart single in more than six years. *Into the Music* (August 1979) explicitly looked back on earlier styles and revealed an increasing religious interest, while the pastoral *Common One* (September 1980) was filled with references to English poets.

Morrison's albums of the 1980s and '90s largely repeated the musical styles and spiritual lyric themes he had developed in the 1970s, though they frequently contained moving performances. In 1984, Morrison switched from Warner Bros. Records to PolyGram, which had been distributing his albums outside the US since 1979 on its Mercury label. He recorded with the Chieftains on the traditional album *Irish Heartbeat* (June 1988), a change of pace. In 1990, he experienced a career resurgence when Mercury/PolyGram released *The Best of Van Morrison*, which quickly became his biggest seller, at two million copies and counting. In his concert performances of the 1990s, Morrison increasingly relied on a band led by British jazz organist Georgie Fame and introduced guest singers, among them his daughter Shana. A typical performance was captured on *A Night in San Francisco* (June 1994). Morrison also continued to release new albums almost annually: *Days Like This* (June 1995) was his 22nd studio album of new, mostly original material in 28 years. It was followed at the end of the year by *How Long Has This Been Going On?*, a jazz album recorded with Fame. A year later, he assembled *Songs of Mose Allison: Tell Me Something*, a tribute to the jazz pianist recorded with Morrison and his band, Ben Sidran and Allison himself. Early in 1997, he released *The Healing Game*, which was his first album of original material since *Days Like This*. *— William Ruhlmann*

Blowin' Your Mind! / 1967 / Bang ✦✦✦
Although his first solo album is remembered for containing the immortal pop hit "Brown-Eyed Girl," *Blowin' Your Mind!* is actually a dry run for Van Morrison's masterpiece, *Astral Weeks*. Songs like "Who Drove The Red Sports Car" look to that song cycle, even as "Midnight Special" nods to Morrison's R&B past. But it is the agonizing "T.B. Sheets"—all nine-and-three-quarters minutes of it—that dominates this record and belies its trendy title and pop association. "T.B. Sheets" takes the blues and reinvents it as noble tragedy and humiliating mortality. It is where Van Morrison emerges as an artist. (*Blowin' Your Mind!* was superseded by *Bang Masters*, which contains all of its tracks except "He Ain't Give You None," presented in an alternate take, plus Morrison's other recordings for Bang, in 1991.) *— William Ruhlmann*

☆ **Astral Weeks** / Nov. 1968 / Warner Brothers ✦✦✦✦✦
Astral Weeks is generally considered one of the best albums in pop music history. For all that renown, *Astral Weeks* is anything but an archetypal rock 'n' roll album: In fact, it isn't a rock 'n' roll album at all. Employing a mixture of folk, blues, jazz, and classical music, Van Morrison spins out a series of extended ruminations on his Belfast upbringing, including the remarkable character "Madame George" and the climactic epiphany experienced on "Cyprus Avenue." Accompanying himself on acoustic guitar, Morrison sings in his elastic, bluesy voice, accompanied by a jazz rhythm section (Jay Berliner, guitar, Richard Davis, bass, Connie Kay, drums), plus reeds (John Payne) and vibes (Warren Smith, Jr.), with a string quartet overdubbed. An emotional outpouring cast in delicate musical structures, *Astral Weeks* has a unique musical power. Unlike any record before or since, it nevertheless

encompasses the passion and tenderness that have always mixed in the best postwar popular music, easily justifying the critics' raves. —*William Ruhlmann*

☆ **Moondance** / Feb. 1970 / Warner Brothers ✦✦✦✦✦

After *Astral Weeks*, Morrison switched gears for *Moondance*, a flawless collection of more accessible R&B-rooted material, which drew from easygoing swing ("These Dreams"), upbeat shuffles ("Come Running"), gospel-influenced song structures like "Crazy Love," and "Caravan," the latter a celebration of radio that didn't pander to that medium's more self-congratulatory nature. The jazzy title cut is a classic, as is "Into the Mystic," a song that essentially encapsulated Morrison's artistic bent. *Moondance*'s tasteful production imbued the music with a timeless quality. —*Rick Clark*

His Band & Street Choir / Oct. 1970 / Warner Brothers ✦✦✦✦

After the brilliant one-two punch of *Astral Weeks* and *Moondance*, *His Band and Street Choir* brings Morrison back down to earth, both literally and figuratively. While neither as innovative nor as edgy as its predecessors, *His Band and Street Choir* also lacks their overt mysticism; at heart, the album is simply Morrison's valentine to the rhythm and blues that inspired him, resulting in the muscular and joyous tribute "Domino" as well as the bouncy "Blue Money" and "Call Me Up in Dreamland." —*Jason Ankeny*

Tupelo Honey / Oct. 1971 / Warner Brothers ✦✦✦✦

Tupelo Honey is typical of Morrison's early-1970s work in both sound and structure; after dispensing with the requisite hit—here, the buoyant, R&B-inflected "Wild Night"—he truly gets down to business, settling into a luminously pastoral drift typified by the nostalgic "Old Old Woodstock." At the heart of the record are a pair of stunning love songs, "You're My Woman" and the hymn-like title cut, one of Morrison's most enduring and transcendent compositions. —*Jason Ankeny*

Saint Dominic's Preview / 1972 / Warner Brothers ✦✦✦✦

While less thematically and sonically cohesive than Morrison's prior albums, *Saint Dominic's Preview* nonetheless hangs together on the strength of its songs, an intriguingly diverse collection that draws together the disparate threads of the singer's recent work into one sterling package. The opener, "Jackie Wilson Said (I'm in Heaven When You Smile)" is pure R&B jubilation, while the title cut, although essentially a rewrite of "Tupelo Honey," is stunning gospel-pop; both "Listen to the Lion" and "Almost Independence Day," meanwhile, mark a return to the epic mystical explorations of Morrison's earlier work, and offer a pair of his most primal performances. —*Jason Ankeny*

Hard Nose the Highway / Aug. 1973 / Warner Brothers ✦✦✦

Although it marks a decline from the astonishing run of five great albums Van Morrison had made from 1968 through 1972, *Hard Nose the Highway* is still a respectable, if uneven, effort, notably containing "Snow in San Anselmo" (which features the Oakland Symphony Chamber Chorus) and "Warm Love." Nevertheless, it marked the end of Morrison's greatest period of creativity and accomplishment. —*William Ruhlmann*

It's Too Late to Stop Now / Jan. 1974 / Warner Brothers ✦✦✦✦

While Morrison is, to be kind, an erratic and temperamental live performer, he's in stellar form throughout the double LP *It's Too Late to Stop Now*, a superb concert set that neatly summarizes his career from his days with Them (represented by scorching renditions of "Gloria" and "Here Comes the Night") through 1973's *Hard Nose the Highway* ("Warm Love," "Wild Children"). In addition to the hits, including "Caravan," "Domino," and "Into the Mystic" (the final line of which gives the album its title), Morrison even pulls out a handful of R&B chestnuts ("Bring It on Home to Me," "Ain't Nothin' You Can Do") before capping off the collection with a show-stopping rendition of *Astral Weeks*' "Cyprus Avenue." An engaging, warm portrait of the Man at the peak of his powers. —*Jason Ankeny*

Veedon Fleece / Feb. 1974 / Warner Brothers ✦✦✦✦

The final album of Morrison's remarkably prolific and innovative 1968-1974 period (followed by three years of silence), *Veedon Fleece* brings the singer full circle, returning him to the introspection and poignancy of *Astral Weeks*. Composed following his sudden divorce from wife Janet Planet and subsequent retreat from the US, the songs are subtle and spartan, the performances deeply felt; though less tortured and cathartic than *Astral Weeks*, it's a record fraught with emotional upheaval, as evidenced by such superior moments as "Linden Arden Stole the Highlights," "Who Was That Masked Man," and "You Don't Pull No Punches, But You Don't Push the River." —*Jason Ankeny*

A Period of Transition / 1977 / Warner Brothers ✦✦✦

On paper, the collaboration of Morrison with Dr. John looked awfully good. While *A Period of Transition* failed to live up to the potential, it did have some wonderful songs, like "Heavy Connection" and "It Fills You Up" (a particular favorite). The flat-sounding mixes tend to rob the

sparks out of the music, making some of this album's more expressive moments sound forced. —*Rick Clark*

Wavelength / 1978 / Warner Brothers ✦✦✦

The self-produced *Wavelength* marked an improvement over *A Period of Transition*, producing a near-hit with the title cut. Other highlights included "Santa Fe," co-written with Jackie DeShannon. —*Rick Clark*

Into the Music / 1979 / Warner Brothers ✦✦✦✦

Five years after Van's last great album (*Veedon Fleece*), he returns one of his finest albums, *Into the Music*, which fuses the earthly with the spiritual. Highlights include "Bright Side of the Road," "Full Force Gale," "Angelou," and a version of "It's All in the Game." Not the first place to go to discover Morrison, it's a masterful album nonetheless. —*Rick Clark*

Common One / 1980 / Warner Brothers ✦✦✦

Van Morrison's most meditative album since *Veedon Fleece*, *Common One* paints a pastoral portrait dominated by such extended pieces as "Summertime in England" and "When the Heart Is Open," each of which is more than 15 minutes long. The result can be soothing, but also enervating. —*William Ruhlmann*

Beautiful Vision / 1982 / Warner Brothers ✦✦✦

Beautiful Vision improved upon its meandering predecessor, *Common One*, first by having some stronger melodies, and second by having a song as mystically upbeat as "Cleaning Windows." —*Rick Clark*

The Inarticulate Speech of the Heart / Mar. 1983 / Warner Brothers ✦✦✦

Van Morrison's final album for Warner Brothers Records was one of his more uncompromising efforts, including the two-part instrumental title track and "Rave On, John Donne," a spoken tribute to one of Morrison's influences. —*William Ruhlmann*

A Sense of Wonder / 1985 / Mercury ✦✦✦

Van Morrison's US label debut with PolyGram (which had issued his *Live at the Opera House Belfast* album in England earlier) is a strong effort, mixing some of his familiar influences—R&B, poetry, mysticism—on such characteristic tracks as "Tore Down A La Rimbaud." It might be fair to say that, by now, Morrison's fans had heard what he had to say and the rest was just repetition, but he continued to write and perform at a high level at this mature stage in his career. —*William Ruhlmann*

Live at the Grand Opera House Belfast / 1985 / Polydor ✦✦✦✦

Not as fiery as *It's Too Late to Stop Now*, it's still an enjoyable set, featuring "It's All in the Game," "Cleaning Windows," and other tracks from this period. —*Rick Clark*

No Guru, No Method, No Teacher / Jul. 1986 / Mercury ✦✦✦

With "Ivory Tower," Van Morrison produced another excellent rocker in his familiar style, while "In the Garden" took him to one of his more spiritual, religious spaces. —*William Ruhlmann*

Poetic Champions Compose / 1987 / Mercury ✦✦✦✦

The hypnotic string arpeggios and rolling rhythms of "The Mystery," the gentle exhortation of "Did Ye Get Healed," and even reverberant cocktail-jazz instrumentals like "Spanish Steps" help make the meditative *Poetic Champions Compose* one of Morrison's better albums during the '80s. —*Rick Clark*

Irish Heartbeat / 1988 / Mercury ✦✦✦✦

Although still purposeful, Van Morrison's '80s albums were becoming repetitive when he took a break for this collaboration with the Chieftains on traditional Irish songs. The result takes him back to his earliest days and finds him singing with renewed conviction. This album should appeal to all fans of Irish music as well as Morrison lovers. —*William Ruhlmann*

Avalon Sunset / Jun. 1989 / Polydor ✦✦✦✦

Avalon Sunset's evocative melodies and almost prayerful sentiments make this one of Morrison's finest albums during the '80s. Some might find this album's rich orchestration a little too close to easy listening, but repeated listenings reveal it adds a quiet, dignified elegance and atmospheric unity to the proceedings not unlike the strings on Marvin Gaye's transcendent *What's Going On*. "I'm Tired Joey Boy," "Orangefield," "Have I Told You Lately?", "I'd Love to Write Another Love Song," and the supplicatory "When Will I Learn to Live in God?" are among the many highlights. *Avalon Sunset* is the mature, timeless work of an artist beyond fashion. —*Rick Clark*

★ **The Best of Van Morrison [Mercury]** / Jan. 1990 / Mercury ✦✦✦✦✦

This is a strong collection of many of Van Morrison's best songs. Of particular note is the inclusion of "Wonderful Remark," previously only available on *The King of Comedy* soundtrack. That alone makes this worth having. Many of the key Them tracks are here ("Gloria," "Here Comes the Night"), as is Morrison's classic "Brown-Eyed Girl." Even though it's a strong sampler, it fails to draw a complete-enough picture of the depth of his work. Sonically, this CD is quite impressive. —*Rick Clark*

Enlightenment / Feb. 1990 / Mercury ✦✦✦
Morrison dispensed with the super-reflective spirit that dominated many of his albums from the '80s and returned to a more relaxed, almost playful effort with *Enlightenment*. "In the Days before Rock 'n' Roll" is a particular highlight. Not one of his best albums, it's still a nice change of pace. —*Rick Clark*

The Bang Masters / Feb. 26, 1991 / Epic ✦✦✦✦
With excellent sound and packaging of Morrison's work at Bert Bern's Bang label, the tracks range from the morose "T.B. Sheets," to his pop standard "Brown-Eyed Girl." This is a must for fans who want to go deeper than just obtaining his obviously classic albums. —*Rick Clark*

Hymns to the Silence / Sep. 24, 1991 / Polydor ✦✦✦

The Best of Van Morrison, Vol. 2 / Mar. 9, 1993 / PolyGram ✦✦✦✦
No big hit singles are here, or even familiar songs for that matter. Van Morrison compiled *The Best Of, Volume 2* himself, leaning heavily toward his recent work. As an anthology, it doesn't completely work, since it's uneven and lacking a sense of scope; what makes the album fascinating is to see how Morrison views himself. Although there are many good (even great) songs here, *The Best Of, Volume 2* only works as an introduction to Morrison's idiosyncratic recent work, not to his entire career. —*Stephen Thomas Erlewine*

Too Long in Exile / Jun. 8, 1993 / Polydor ✦✦
Too Long in Exile marks a welcome return to the earthy secular world, an embrace of rootsy R&B and smoky jazz, a street album that ranks with Morrison's best. He weaves a kind of magic with a funky "Good Morning Little Schoolgirl" and the confessional blues of "Bigtime Operator," a story-song recounting some harrowing early experiences within the music industry. Instrumentally, the album is driven by a smooth horn section, Van's harmonica, and British vet Georgie Fame's virtuoso Hammond B-3. The proceedings stall briefly toward the end with a pair of vapid jazz pieces and noodling instrumental backing that does little justice to a W.B. Yeats text, but the searing closer "Tell Me What You Want" moves things right back into club territory. —*Roch Parisien*

A Night in San Francisco / May 17, 1994 / Polydor ✦✦✦
Van Morrison's third commercially-released live album takes a show format that frequently spotlights the backup band, led by organist-singer Georgie Fame and featuring singers Brian Kennedy and James Hunter, as well as saxophonist Candy Dulfer and blues singers John Lee Hooker, Junior Wells, and Jimmy Witherspoon. Even Morrison's daughter Shana comes on to sing his "Beautiful Vision." The material is not limited to Morrison compositions, either. In fact, it isn't so much that Morrison & Co. cover a variety of rock, pop, blues, R&B, and jazz standards, as that many pieces are medleys that contain complete songs and quotes from others, rather in the way that a jazz soloist will suddenly throw in a few bars of a familiar tune. Those who want to see Morrison as an esoteric singer-songwriter rather than a showman may find this album a mongrel creation, but it's undeniably lively, and that's the first requirement of a live album. —*William Ruhlmann*

Payin' Dues / Nov. 1, 1994 / Charly ✦✦✦
A most fascinating double disc. The first contains the tracks found on *Bang Masters;* the bonus CD contains 31 previously unreleased acoustic ditties. The word ditties is a description, not a value judgment. According to one account, Morrison cut these purely out of necessity to fulfill his Bang contract, delivering the most unusable material possible. All of the cuts are between 45 and 90 seconds, divided between the inane (numerous nonsensical variations on "La Bamba," "Twist and Shout," and "Hang on Sloopy") and the viciously uncommercial ("The Big Royalty Check," "Ring Worm," "Blow in Your Nose"), along with a few silly variations on "Madame George." Along with Lou Reed's *Metal Machine Music*, this ranks as the least commercial music recorded by a major rock artist, and a spit in the eye of commercial expectations and contractual obligations. It's more listenable than *Metal Machine Music*, and funnier. If you haven't picked up the *Bang Masters* collection, this off-the-wall material (which may never find release in the US) makes *Payin' Dues* a recommended alternative. —*Richie Unterberger*

How Long Has This Been Going On? / 1995 / Polygram ✦✦
Throughout his career, Van Morrison has incorporated jazz phrasing and techniques into his singing, so it was only a matter of time before he released a full-fledged jazz record. Recorded with his longtime pianist Georgie Fame, *How Long Has This Been Going On?* is Morrison's jazz album, and it is a muddled affair. Alternating between standards and reinterpreted originals, the album is too casual to be a pop album and too restrained to be a jazz album. Fame's charts aren't particularly original or compelling, but Morrison deserves a fair share of the blame as well—he mistakes jazziness for jazz. —*Stephen Thomas Erlewine*

Days Like This / Jun. 20, 1995 / Polydor ✦✦
Van Morrison is a songwriter. He's paid to write about romance. We know this because he tells us on "Songwriter." A list of clichés, presumably intended to be ironic, the song unintentionally reveals the real problem with *Days like This*—Van Morrison is going through the

motions. *Days like This* smooths over the rougher edges of the R&B-dominated *Too Long in Exile* without returning to the meditative, jazzy explorations of his '80s works. Instead, the ensuing album is a completely competent yet completely uninspired pop-R&B workout, with Van sounding as if he couldn't care less about the words leaving his mouth. And that, in a way, explains the empty rhymes of "Songwriter"—it's just a job and Van will get paid no matter what he turns out. —*Stephen Thomas Erlewine*

Songs of Mose Allison: Tell Me Something / Oct. 8, 1996 / Polygram ✦✦✦
Songs of Mose Allison: Tell Me Something is a tribute record to Mose Allison coordinated by Van Morrison, who brought in his long-time sideman Georgie Fame, Ben Sidran, and Allison himself to record a selection of Mose's best songs. That doesn't necessarily mean his most famous, even though many of his best-known songs are here. Instead, the musicians are interested in capturing the laidback, idiosyncratic spirit of Allison's music by combining famous numbers with lesser-known tunes, and performing them a warm, relaxed manner. The approach works, and it is a better, jazzier record than *How Long Has This Been Going On?* —*Stephen Thomas Erlewine*

The Healing Game / Mar. 4, 1997 / Polygram ✦✦✦

Morrissey

b. May 22, 1959, Manchester, England
Vocals / Alternative Pop-Rock
With the Smiths, singer-songwriter Morrissey established himself as a post-punk hero, becoming the spokesman for millions of disaffected teenagers and young adults with his literate, biting, and sensitive lyrics and dramatic vocals. After the band broke up in 1987, he pursued a solo career, releasing his first album the following year. While he released several excellent singles in the late '80s, he ultimately began to sink into his persona without producing enough quality songs. After 1991's self-absorbed *Kill Uncle*, many critics considered him a has-been, with his best work in the past. Thanks to the explosive, Mick Ronson-produced *Your Arsenal*, Morrissey regained his credibility; it was almost universally acclaimed as one of the best albums of the year and many said it was his best work since the Smiths' masterpiece *The Queen Is Dead.* His fan base continued to grow, both in size and devotion. With 1994's *Vauxhall and I*, he even had a hit single ("The More You Ignore Me, the Closer I Get") scrape the Top 50 singles chart in America, which would have been unthinkable when "Hand in Glove" was released a decade earlier. —*Stephen Thomas Erlewine*

Viva Hate / 1988 / Sire ✦✦✦✦
Following the breakup of the Smiths, Morrissey needed to prove that he was a viable artist without Johnny Marr, and *Viva Hate* fulfilled that goal with grace. Working with producer Stephen Street and guitarist Vini Reilly (of the Durutti Column), Morrissey doesn't drastically depart from the sound of *Strangeways, Here We Come,* offering a selection of 12 jangling guitar-pop sounds. One major concession is the presence of synthesizers—which is ironic, considering the Smiths' adamant opposition to keyboards—but neither the sound, nor Morrissey's wit, is diluted. And while the music is occasionally pedestrian, Morrissey compensates with a superb batch of lyrics, ranging from his conventional despair ("Little Man, What Now?", "I Don't Mind If You Forget Me") to the savage political tirade of "Margaret on a Guillotine." Nevertheless, the two master strokes on the album—the gorgeous "Everyday is Like Sunday" and the infectious "Suedehead"—were previously singles, and both are on the compilation *Bona Drag.* —*Stephen Thomas Erlewine*

Bona Drag / Dec. 1990 / Sire ✦✦✦✦
As he was toiling on *Kill Uncle,* Morrissey released *Bona Drag,* a compilation of singles and B-sides, including "Everyday is Like Sunday" and "Suedehead" from *Viva Hate.* While the record conveniently overlooks some rarities, the selections on *Bona Drag* are uniformly first-rate and many of the songs—"Piccadilly Palare," "Interesting Drug," "November Spawned a Monster," "The Last of the Famous International Playboys," "Lucky Lisp," "Disappointed," "He Knows I'd Love to See Him" and "Ouija Board, Ouija Board"—are Morrissey classics, making *Bona Drag* arguably a more consistent and entertaining record than *Viva Hate.* —*Stephen Thomas Erlewine*

Kill Uncle / Mar. 5, 1991 / Sire ✦✦
With *Kill Uncle,* Morrissey descended into the ranks of self-parody, churning out a series of pleasant but tired alternative jangle-pop songs that had neither melody nor much wit to distinguish them. Part of the problem lies with his choice of collaborators. Producers Clive Langer and Alan Winstanley don't provide the appropriately sympathetic backdrop for Morrissey's sly humor, while guitarist Mark E. Nevin is incapable of developing hooks. A few cuts, such as "(I'm) The End of the Family Line" and "There's a Place in Hell for Me and My Friends," stand out, but *Kill Uncle* is Morrissey's least distinguished record. —*Stephen Thomas Erlewine*

● **Your Arsenal** / Jul. 28, 1992 / Sire ✦✦✦✦
Morrissey bounced back from the lackluster *Kill Uncle* with the terrific *Your Arsenal*. A dynamic, invigorating fusion of glam-rock and rockabilly, *Your Arsenal* rocks harder than any other record Morrissey ever made. Guitarist Alan Whyte's riffs swagger with a self-absorbed arrogance, and producer Mick Ronson gives the music a tough, stylish sheen—it may be a break from Morrissey's jangle-pop, but the music is sharper than it has been since the Smiths, and so is Morrissey's pen. Running through his trademark litany of emotional, social, and personal observations, Morrissey is viciously clever and occasionally moving. And the songs—whether it's the rush of "You're Gonna Need Someone on Your Side," the menacing "We'll Let You Know," the spare rockabilly bop of "Certain People I Know," the gospel-tinged "I Know It's Gonna Happen Someday" or "Tomorrow"—are uniformly excellent, forming the core of Morrissey's finest solo record and his best work since *The Queen Is Dead*. —*Stephen Thomas Erlewine*

Beethoven Was Deaf / May 11, 1993 / EMI ✦✦✦
Recorded on the English *Your Arsenal* tour, the 16-track album *Beethoven Was Deaf* is an effective argument for Morrissey's capabilities as a live performer. Although none of the songs, which are all drawn from his solo career, are drastically different than their original studio incarnation, they are performed with skill by Morrissey's pseudo-rockabilly band, giving the singer ample opportunity to flaunt his charisma. But it's not just charisma—Morrissey is a powerful, if unconventional vocalist, capable of squeezing out all the wit and exaggerated emotion from each song. While many of his great solo songs are here ("Suedehead," "Certain People I Know," "Sister I'm a Poet"), it relies a little too heavily on *Your Arsenal* to be a good career overview, yet it remains a fine souvenir for hardcore fans. —*Stephen Thomas Erlewine*

Vauxhall & I / Mar. 22, 1994 / Sire ✦✦✦✦
While it isn't a gutsy rock 'n' roll record like *Your Arsenal*, *Vauxhall and I* is equally impressive. Filled with carefully constructed guitar-pop gems, the album contains some of Morrissey's best material since the Smiths. Out of all of his solo albums, *Vauxhall and I* sounds the most like his former band, yet the textured, ringing guitar on this record is an extension of his past, not a replication of it. In fact, with songs like "Now My Heart Is Full" and "Hold on to Your Friends," Morrissey sounds more comfortable and peaceful than he ever has. And "The More You Ignore Me, the Closer I Get," "Speedway," and "Spring-Heeled Jim" prove that he hasn't lost his vicious wit. —*Stephen Thomas Erlewine*

World of Morrissey / Feb. 21, 1995 / Sire ✦✦✦
Released to coincide with Morrissey's brief winter tour of England in 1995, *World of Morrissey* follows none of the accepted rules for compilations. It's not a hits collection, nor is it a "best of"—the disc is filled with album cuts, live tracks, a couple of B-sides, and a new single, all of which dedicated Morrissey fans already own. However, the choice of songs does mean something—the choice of the vaguely threatening "Spring-Heeled Jim" over "Now My Heart Is Full" and the sad "Billy Budd" over "The More You Ignore Me, the Closer I Get" makes the calm *Vauxhall & I* seem darker than it is. But that melancholy is cut by the sly taunt of "Have-A-Go Merchant" and the perennial "Last of the Famous International Playboys," as well as a long, bizarre crawl through "Moon River." Only hardcore fans will notice such subtle matters as running orders; for them, *World of Morrissey* is a mix tape. —*Stephen Thomas Erlewine*

Southpaw Grammar / Aug. 1995 / Reprise ✦✦
If *Vauxhall & I* represented a more mature Morrissey, *Southpaw Grammar* superficially presents a more rough & tumble version of the singer. As his previous single, "Boxers," indicated, Morrissey's fascination with boxing and violence has reached full fruition. The music appropriately reflects this, with growling, distorted guitars and martial rhythms. But *Southpaw Grammar* doesn't rock as hard or with as much style as the rockabilly-inflected *Your Arsenal*—instead, it's his art-rock album, complete with strings, drum solos, and two ten-minute songs. Of these, the winding, menacing "The Teachers Are Afraid of the Pupils" works the best, and it represents a significant change in Morrissey's outlook; instead of the children being outsiders, the teachers are. Throughout *Southpaw Grammar*, the privileged are oppressed by their fortunes, while working-class toughs are celebrated for their violence. However, there is no cohesive glue to the record. "The Teachers" uses its 11 minutes effectively, but "Southpaw" is merely ponderous. "Reader Meet Author" and "Dangenham Dave" are classic three-minute pop songs, but "Do Your Best and Don't Worry" is strictly by the books. Nevertheless, there is plenty of enjoyable music on the record, even if the concept is flawed. —*Stephen Thomas Erlewine*

The Motels

f. 1973, Berkeley, CA, **db.** 1987
New Wave, Pop-Rock, Arena Rock
By the time the Motels scored with their 1982 hit album *All Four One* (No. 16), they had spent ten years in Los Angeles' alternative scene, going through enough lineup changes (particularly drummers) to make

Spinal Tap proud. At the time of their self-titled 1979 debut album, the Motels featured dramatic vocalist Martha Davis, guitarist Jeff Jourard, keyboardist-saxophonist Martin Jourard, bassist Michael Goodroe, and drummer Brian Glascock. *The Motels* earned positive reviews upon its release, but the group wasn't able to translate the critical success into commercial success. During the recording sessions for their second album, 1980's *Careful*, Jeff Jourard was replaced by Davis' boyfriend Tim McGovern, formerly of Captain Kopter and the Fabulous Twirlybirds. Although the album sold more copies than their debut, it didn't break the band into the mainstream.

All Four One, released in 1982, was their commercial breakthrough, spawning the Top Ten single "Only the Lonely" and going gold. Featuring the Top Ten hit "Suddenly Last Summer," the Motels' 1983 follow-up, *Little Robbers*, was equally successful. On *Shock* (1985), the group had succumbed to a West Coast mainstream rock sound. Although the album produced the minor hit "Shame," it was clear that the band was running out of steam. The Motels broke up two years later. —*Rick Clark*

The Motels / 1979 / Capitol ✦✦✦
The Motels' eponymous debut is a generally undistinguished collection of overblown AOR rockers highlighted by "Atomic Cafe" and "Anticipating," but even those can't excuse the ludicrous "Porn Reggae." —*Stephen Thomas Erlewine*

Careful / 1980 / Capitol ✦✦✦
Careful, the Motels' second album, is a marginal improvement over the group's debut, demonstrating a sharper pop sense, but remains a lukewarm effort due to half-baked songs and overheated production. —*Stephen Thomas Erlewine*

All 4 One / 1982 / Capitol ✦✦✦✦
The Motels' third album *All 4 One* finds the group working the fine line between mainstream arena-rock and quirky new wave pop. Their roots lie in the sleek, polished Californian hard rock that dominated late-'70s and early-'80s album-oriented radio, but *All 4 One* has a shiny new wave production, complete with keyboards and processed guitars. Still, it plays like arena rock, especially since Martha Davis over-sings each track, but its best moments—"Take the L" (out of lover and it's over) and the single "Only the Lonely"—are embarrassingly catchy guilty pleasures that make the album an entertaining nostalgia piece. One Way's CD reissue is even more attractive, since it adds the group's two other big singles, "Suddenly Last Summer" and "Shame," as bonus tracks. —*Stephen Thomas Erlewine*

Little Robbers / 1983 / Capitol ✦✦✦✦
Little Robbers, the follow-up to the Motels' commercial breakthrough *All 4 One*, is nearly as consistent as its predecessor, finding the perfect balance between mainstream rock conventions and quirky new wave flourishes. Again, the singles are the best parts of the record, with the hazy "Suddenly Last Summer" deservedly reaching the Top Ten and "Remember the Nights" being a fine AOR workout, but the remainder of the album suffers from undistinguished material and a distinct lack of hooks. —*Stephen Thomas Erlewine*

Shock / 1985 / Capitol ✦✦
With *Shock*, the Motels attempted to move squarely into the MTV-sponsored pop-rock mainstream, adding harder guitars and bigger hooks. Although their makeover isn't entirely successful, the best moments on the album—"Shame," "Cries and Whispers," and the title track—are enjoyable mainstream rock. —*Stephen Thomas Erlewine*

Policy / 1987 / Capitol ✦✦
Policy, the Motels' final album, is pretty much a disaster, as the group attempts to find a voice in the late '80s. The record tries to refashion their arena-sized hooks to no avail, since they still sound as if they are stuck in the early '80s, and their songs aren't nearly as memorable as they used to be. It's little surprise that the group broke up shortly after the release of *Policy*. —*Stephen Thomas Erlewine*

● **The Best of the Motels: No Vacancy** / 1990 / Capitol ✦✦✦✦
All five of the Motels' albums are well worth acquiring—even 1985's more commercial *Shock*. But for an introductory overview of the often dark and unsettling band's legacy, *No Vacancy* is highly recommended. This superb CD boasts all of the songs the Motels were best known for, including the dreamy "Suddenly Last Summer," the clever "Little Robbers" and the melancholy hits "Only the Lonely" and "Take the L." But as *No Vacancy* illustrates, they had many more artistic triumphs than those hits. Often compared to the Doors, the Motels didn't sound very much like Jim Morrison & Co.—but paralleled that fellow L.A. band in that they were experts when it came to depicting Hollywood's darker side. Classics like "So L.A.," "Apocalypso," and the troubling "Celia" brilliantly capture the type of emotional desperation that's prevalent in Tinseltown. Meanwhile, Pat Benatar is a valid comparison on "Cries and Whispers" and "Shame," both examples of the slicker, more commercial direction the Motels were taking in the end. But even at her most commercial, the charismatic Martha Davis sounds soulful and inspired. —*Alex Henderson*

Mother Love Bone

f. 1988, Seattle, WA
Hard Rock, Heavy Metal

When other Seattle bands were releasing singles and EPs of hard garage grunge, Mother Love Bone had their sights set on the arenas, making a grandiose heavy metal that recalled Zeppelin and Aerosmith with a slight punk fervor; in a sense, the band was a response to Guns N' Roses' sleazy guitar boogie. Considering that guitarist Stone Gossard and bassist Jeff Ament formed the rhythmic core of the Stooges-soaked Green River, it was a little strange that the band played it so safe, but that was mainly due to the lead vocalist, Andrew Wood. Wood was a modern-day hippie, preaching love and understanding, as well as a healthy dose of sex. Most of the hooks came from Gossard and Ament, but Wood was the focal point. The band was set to make their stab at the big time with 1990's *Apple*, but Wood died of a heroin overdose before it was released; the *Temple of the Dog* album, featuring Gossard, Ament, Soundgarden's Matt Cameron and Chris Cornell, and vocalist Eddie Vedder, was released as a tribute to him.

Gossard and Ament went on to form Pearl Jam, which took many of the hard rock elements of Mother Love Bone, except it was rawer and more honest. Also, Pearl Jam had a distinctive lead vocalist and lyricist in Eddie Vedder, who easily eclipsed the macho posturings of Wood. —*Stephen Thomas Erlewine*

● **Stardog Champion** / 1990 / Stardog ✦✦✦✦
Released after the phenomenal success of Pearl Jam, *Mother Love Bone* collects everything Mother Love Bone ever released. Their resurrection of the epic hard rock of the 1970s was quite good, but also derivative. While Wood was a fine singer, he wasn't a very original vocalist and often sounded very similar to Robert Plant. *Mother Love Bone* is the definitive collection of the band, and worth the time of fans of Pearl Jam and the Seattle scene. —*Stephen Thomas Erlewine*

Mötley Crüe

f. 1981, Los Angeles, CA
Hard Rock, Heavy Metal, Hair Metal

As far as commercial appeal goes, Mötley Crüe was one of the top heavy metal bands in the '80s, exploiting every trend in metal and hard rock without seeming crass or opportunistic. *Shout at the Devil* had them embracing a theatrical, Kiss-styled Satanism; *Theater of Pain* saw them ride the line between glam and pop-metal; *Girls Girls Girls* had them toughening up their image with leather and harder guitars, reaching for street credibility; *Dr. Feelgood* had them sharpening the guitars of the previous album while adding a pop sensibility that took them straight to the top of the charts. Throughout their changes, the Crüe remained joyously sleazy and stupid, with their Zeppelin/Aerosmith-based hard rock making them high school favorites across the country. After the success of *Dr. Feelgood*, singer Vince Neil was fired from the band. When the band re-emerged in 1994 with their new vocalist John Corabi, they had changed their image again, falling somewhere between Ministry, Stone Temple Pilots, and Soundgarden in an attempt to recapture the new alternative metal audience. *Mötley Crüe*, the new lineup's first album, was a commercial disappointment, spending ten weeks on the charts and only going gold. —*Stephen Thomas Erlewine*

Too Fast for Love / 1981 / Elektra ✦✦
Sleazy heavy metal before all the hype took over their home of Los Angeles, their debut album was re-mixed from the original on their own Leathür label. —*John Book*

Shout at the Devil / 1983 / Elektra ✦✦✦
Possibly the best mainstream heavy metal band of the '80s, and their best album to date. —*John Book*

Theater of Pain / 1985 / Elektra ✦✦✦✦
Powered by a sneering remake of Brownsville Station's "Smokin' in the Boys Room" and the classic power ballad "Home Sweet Home," *Theater of Pain* was Mötley Crüe's biggest hit up to that point, even if the rest of the album wasn't as strong as its hit singles. —*Stephen Thomas Erlewine*

Girls, Girls, Girls / 1987 / Elektra ✦✦✦✦
With *Girls, Girls, Girls*, Mötley Crüe toughens up their music as well as their image, turning in an album of greasy, sleazy hard-rock boogie that, at its best, rivals Aerosmith. —*Stephen Thomas Erlewine*

Dr. Feelgood / Sep. 1989 / Elektra ✦✦✦✦
Mötley Crüe's albums were a lot like episodes of *Married with Children* in the sense that they may not be great works of art, but can be darn entertaining. With Bob Rock serving as producer, the L.A. headbangers savor the joys of trashy, unapologetically decadent fun on *Dr. Feelgood*—an album that makes no pretense at being anything else. While nothing here is quite as commanding as "Shout at the Devil," "Wild Side," or "Live Wire," such hook-oriented MTV smashes as "Kickstart My Heart," the amusing "Don't Go Away Mad (Just Go Away)," and the title

song are infectious and hard to resist. Unfortunately, the album would be lead singer Vince Neil's last album with the band. Neil's departure—and pop-metal's decline in popularity in the mid-'90s—proved to be severe blows to Mötley Crüe. —*Alex Henderson*

● **Decade of Decadence** / 1991 / Elektra ✦✦✦✦
Elektra Entertainment drew on the five albums Mötley Crüe had recorded in the 1980s and threw in a few new songs as well when assembling the best-of collection *Decade of Decadence*. The title couldn't be more appropriate—whether the subject matter is strippers ("Girls, Girls, Girls") or the occult ("Shout at the Devil"), Crüe delights in some of rock's sleaziest decadence since Kiss and Sweet. Diehard aficionados will already be more than familiar with such headbanger classics as "Looks That Kill," "Wild Side," and "Piece of Your Action," but for those new to the band's metal and hard rock, the album isn't a bad introduction at all. The previously unreleased material includes a live version of "Kickstart My Heart" and an ironic cover of the Sex Pistols' "Anarchy in the UK." In the '70s, the punk and metal audiences were hardly the best of friends; but in the '80s, it became downright fashionable for headbangers to embrace punk. —*Alex Henderson*

Mötley Crüe / Mar. 15, 1994 / Elektra ✦✦
On *Mötley Crüe*, their first album recorded without vocalist Vince Neil, the band revamped their trademark dirty but melodic heavy metal, adding elements of '90s grunge and alternative metal. The group's new vocalist John Corabi is a hoarse shouter without the charisma of Vince Neil, so he wasn't able to put a distinctive spin on the pedestrian grind the rest of the band churned out. The Crüe seem to have equated grunge with seriousness, since very few of the songs on the record recall the hedonistic atmosphere of their '80s albums. Unfortunately, this also means the group have neglected to write memorable hooks and riffs, which makes *Mötley Crüe* the weakest effort in their catalog. —*Stephen Thomas Erlewine*

Motörhead

f. 1975, London, England
Hard Rock, Thrash, Heavy Metal, British Metal

Motörhead's overwhelmingly loud and fast style of heavy metal was one of the most groundbreaking styles the genre had to offer in the late '70s. Though the group's leader Lemmy Kilminster had his roots in the hard-rocking space-rock band Hawkwind, Motörhead didn't bother with his old group's progressive tendencies, choosing to amplify the heavy biker-rock elements of Hawkwind with the speed of punk rock. Motörhead wasn't punk rock—they formed before the Sex Pistols and they loved the hell-for-leather imagery of bikers too much to conform with the safety-pinned, ripped T-shirts of punk—but they were the first metal band to harness that energy and, in the process, they created speed-metal and thrash-metal. Unlike many of their contemporaries, Motörhead continued performing well into the '90s. Although the band changed its lineup many, many times—Kilminster was its only consistent member—they never changed their raging sound.

The son of a vicar, Lemmy Kilminster (born Ian Fraiser Kilminster, Dec. 24, 1945) first began playing rock 'n' roll in 1964, when he joined two local Blackpool, England R&B bands, the Rainmakers and the Motown Sect. Over the course of the '60s, he played with a number of bands—including the Rockin' Vickers, Gopal's Dream, and Opal Butterfly—as well as briefly working as a roadie for Jimi Hendrix. In 1971, he joined the heavy prog-rock band Hawkwind as a bassist. Kilminster was originally slated to stay with the band only six months, yet he stayed with the group for four years. During that time, he wrote and sang several songs with the band, including their signature song, the No. 3 UK hit "Silver Machine" (1972).

Kilminster was kicked out of Hawkwind in the spring of 1975, after he spent five days in a Canadian prison for drug possession. Once he returned to England, Kilminster set about forming a new band. Originally, it was to have been called Bastard, but he soon decided to call the band Motörhead, named after the last song he wrote for Hawkwind. Kilminster drafted in Pink Fairies guitarist Larry Wallis and drummer Lucas Fox to round out the lineup. Motörhead made its debut supporting Greenslade in July. Two months later, the group headed into the studio to make its debut album for United Artists with producer Dave Edmunds. Motörhead and Edmunds clashed over the direction of recording, resulting in the group firing the producer and replacing him with Fritz Fryer. At the end of the year, Fox left the band and Kilminster replaced him with his friend, Philthy Animal (born Philip Taylor), an amateur musician.

Motörhead delivered its debut album to UA early in 1976, but the label rejected the album. Shortly afterward, former Blue Goose and Continuous Performance guitarist "Fast" Eddie Clarke joined the band. Following one rehearsal as a four-piece, Wallis left the band, leaving Motörhead as a trio; this was the lineup through what would later be recalled as the group's classic period. However, the band spent most of 1976 struggling, performing without a contract or manager, and generating little money. At the end of the year, they cut a single, "White Line Fever" / "Leavin' Here," for Stiff Records, which wasn't released until two years later. By the summer of 1977, the group had signed a one-record contract with Chiswick Records, releasing their eponymous debut in June; it peaked at No. 43 on the UK charts. A year later, the band signed with Bronze Records.

Overkill, Motörhead's first album for Bronze, was released in the spring of 1979. The album peaked at No. 24, while its title track became the band's first Top 40 hit. Motörhead continued to gain momentum, as their concerts were selling well and *Bomber*, the follow-up to *Overkill*, reached No. 12 upon its fall release. The band was doing so well that UA released the rejected album at the end of the year as *On Parole*. *Ace of Spades*, released in the fall of 1980, became a No. 4 hit, while the single of the same name reached No. 15.

Ace of Spades became Motörhead's first American album, yet the group was making little headway in the US, where they only registered as a cult act. Back in England, the situation could hardly have been more different. Motörhead was at the peak of its popularity in 1981, releasing a hit collaboration with the all-female group Girlschool as a group called Headgirl and entering the charts at No. 1 with their live album, *No Sleep 'Til Hammersmith*. Though the group was rising commercially, there was tension within the band, particularly between Clarke and Kilminster. Clarke left the band during the supporting tour for 1982's *Iron Fist*, reportedly angered by Kilminster's planned collaboration with Wendy O. Williams. Former Thin Lizzy guitarist Brian Robertson replaced Clarke.

The new lineup released *Another Perfect Day* in the summer of 1983. *Another Perfect Day* was a disappointment, only reaching No. 20 in the UK. Robertson left two months later, being replaced by two guitarists—former Persian Risk member Phillip Campbell and Wurzel (born Michael Burston). Shortly afterward, Taylor left to join Robertson's band Operator, and was replaced by former Saxon drummer Pete Gill. This lineup released a single, "Killed by Death," in September of 1984, but shortly afterward the group left Bronze and the label filed an injunction against the band. As a result, Motörhead was prevented from releasing any recordings—including a bizarre collaboration between Lemmy and page-three girl Samantha Fox—for two years.

Motörhead finally returned to action in 1986, first with a track on the charity compilation *Hear N Aid* and later with the Bill Laswell-produced *Orgasmatron*, which was released on their new label, GWR. *Orgasmatron* was successful with the band's still-dedicated cult audience in England and America, and received some of the group's best reviews to date. The following year, they released *Rock 'N' Roll*, which was equally successful. In 1988, the live *No Sleep at All* appeared, and Lemmy made his acting debut in the comedy *Eat the Rich*. Two years later, the band signed to WTG and released *The Birthday Party*.

Taylor briefly rejoined the band in 1991, appearing on that year's *1916*, before Mikkey Dee, formerly of King Diamond, took over on drums. Dee's first album with the band was 1992's *March or Die* which didn't chart in the US, yet played into their UK cult following. WTG dropped the band after its release and the band started their own label, appropriately called Motörhead, which was distributed through ZYX. Their first album for the label was 1994's *Bastards*.

For the remainder of the '90s, Motörhead concentrated on touring more than recording. Outside of the band, Lemmy appeared in insurance commercials in Britain. He also acted in *Hellraiser 3* and had a cameo in the porno movie *John Wayne Bobbit Uncut*. In 1997, the group moved to the metal-oriented indie label Receiver and released *Stone Dead Forever*. —*Stephen Thomas Erlewine*

Motörhead / 1977 / Roadrunner ✦✦✦

Overkill / 1979 / Roadrunner ✦✦✦✦
Motörhead's second album followed the same pattern as the first—it was a relentless collection of fast, loud, and simple heavy metal—but the songwriting was more melodic and consistent than on the debut. —*Stephen Thomas Erlewine*

Bomber / 1979 / Roadrunner ✦✦✦✦
By the time of Motörhead's third album *Bomber*, it was clear that the band had one basic sound and nothing else. However, that didn't mean the group was boring—the lethal attack of their buzzing guitars and Lemmy's hoarse vocals never became tedious because of the immediacy of the group's sound, as well as their talent for coming up with memorable riffs and tightly written songs. *Bomber* sounded no different than Motörhead's two previous albums, but the group had lost none of its impact and the album featured "Dead Men Tell No Tales," one of their finest songs. —*Stephen Thomas Erlewine*

Ace of Spades / 1980 / Roadrunner ✦✦✦✦
The forefathers of thrash on one of their better-known albums, *Ace of Spades* features guitarist "Fast" Eddie Clark, who later left and formed Fastway. Highlights include "(We Are) the Road Crew" and the title track. —*John Book*

No Sleep 'Til Hammersmith / 1981 / Roadrunner ✦✦✦✦
No Sleep 'Til Hammersmith is arguably Motörhead's finest album, featuring an unrelenting barrage of fast, furious punk-injected metal. The group's classic lineup tears through material from their first four albums, including "Bomber" and "Ace of Spades." If any record captures the pure, riveting energy of Motörhead at the top of its power, it's *No Sleep 'Til Hammersmith*. (The 1996 Castle reissue includes a bonus four-track EP.) —*Stephen Thomas Erlewine*

Iron Fist / 1982 / Roadrunner ✦✦✦✦
Five years after its self-titled debut album, Motörhead wasn't compromising or softening its approach one iota. *Iron Fist* is state-of-the-art Motörhead—bombastic, abrasive, and thoroughly captivating. Having done more than its part to define the emerging thrash metal genre, Motörhead was known for taking no prisoners. And songs like "Speedfreak" (which could be considered a Motörhead manifesto), "Go To Hell," and the title song made it clear that it wasn't about to stop. The last album by the Lemmy/Fast Eddie Clark/Philthy Animal Taylor edition of the band, *Fist* was reissued on CD in 1990 with the obscure "Remember Me, I'm Gone" added. —*Alex Henderson*

★ **No Remorse** / 1984 / Roadrunner ✦✦✦✦✦
A best-of anthology that was first released as a two-LP set in 1984 and reissued on a single CD in 1990, *No Remorse* is essential listening for anyone with even a casual interest in thrash metal—a genre Motörhead did so much to define. *No Remorse* may not tell the whole story, but it does tell a good bit of it. Many of the most celebrated and revered Motörhead gems—everything from "Ace of Spades," "Snaggletooth," and "Killed by Death" to "Iron Fist," "Overkill," and "We Are the Road Crew"—are included. The CD configuration omits "Louie, Louie" and "Leaving Here," but even so, this isn't a disc to pass up. For those who haven't experienced the pleasures of Motörhead, *No Remorse* can serve as an exhilarating introduction to the godfathers of thrash. —*Alex Henderson*

Orgasmatron / 1986 / Sinclair ✦✦✦✦
For *Orgasmatron*, Motörhead enlisted producer Bill Laswell, who assisted the band in achieving a dense wall of sound, which sounded a little too compressed. Highlights include "Built for Speed," "Deaf Forever," and the title track, an incredible aural sludgefest that borders on psychedelic. —*Rick Clark*

Rock 'N' Roll / 1987 / Sinclair ✦✦✦

1916 / Feb. 26, 1991 / WTG ✦✦✦✦
Lemmy Kilminster had been leading Motörhead for 16 years by the time *1916* was recorded in 1991. Over the years, Motörhead had experienced more than its share of personnel changes—and in fact, Kilminster was its only remaining original member. But the band's sound hadn't changed much, and time hadn't made its sledgehammer approach any less appealing. As sobering as his reflections on the horrors of World War I are on the title song, he's unapologetically amusing on "Going to Brazil," "Angel City" (an ode to the "beautiful" party people of L.A.), and "Ramones" (which salutes the New York punk band). Whether the subject matter is humorously fun or more serious, Motörhead is as inspired as ever on *1916*. —*Alex Henderson*

March or Die / Jul. 14, 1992 / WTG ✦✦
The year 1992 seems to be the one of accessibility for veteran heavy metallurgists. Lemmy Kilminster and his hoary band of rockers Motörhead remain as dependable as ever on their 15th outing *March or Die*. The original punk-metal fusion band (going back to 1977) continues to play it raw as sushi. But, like many old-time noise-mongers, Motörhead have come out this summer with their most user-friendly and well-produced work. The toned-down fury even allows for an emotive ballad-duet with Ozzie Osbourne on "I Ain't No Nice Guy," with guest guitar courtesy of Slash from Guns N' Roses. The pile-driving "Name in Vain," a bulldozer cover of Ted Nugent's "Cat Scratch Fever," and the title track's ominous, death-metal rap will please the hardcore following. —*Roch Parisien*

Fistful of Aces: Best of Motörhead / Sep. 6, 1994 / Griffin Music ✦✦✦✦

Live 1983 / Oct. 27, 1994 / Castle ✦✦✦

Overnight Sensation / Oct. 15, 1996 / CMC International ✦✦✦

Stone Dead Forever / Mar. 4, 1997 / Receiver ✦✦✦

Motors

f. 1977, db. 1979
Rock 'n' Roll, New Wave, Power Pop, Pub Rock
After several years in England's pub-rock scene, ex-Duck Deluxe members Nick Garvey and Andy McMaster formed the Motors in 1977 with vocalist Bram Tchaikovsky and drummer Ricky Slaughter. Their first album was a splendid piece of guitar-driven pop-rock highlighted by the single "Dancing the Night Away." *Approved by the Motors* was the album that earned them the UK hits "Airport" and "Forget About You";

the record saw the band's songwriting improving, with forceful melodies and invigorating performances. After that record, the Motors split up; Garvey and McMaster used the band's name for the 1980 album *Tenement Steps*, which didn't equal the spark of their first two records. —*Stephen Thomas Erlewine*

Motors 1 / 1977 / Virgin ✦✦✦
Their debut features a re-worked version of pub rock with an edgier punk feel. Includes the catchy single "Dancing the Night Away," the high point of the album. —*Chris Woodstra*

Approved by the Motors / 1978 / Virgin ✦✦✦✦
Their second album shows a marked improvement over the debut, with a stronger melodic base and catchier songs, including the British hits "Airport" and "Forget About You." The CD version adds three bonus tracks. —*Chris Woodstra*

Tenement Steps / 1980 / Virgin ✦✦
The band, now reduced to Nick Garvey and Andy McMaster, is a little too ambitious and overproduced. While not their best album, it does include one of their finest songs, "Love and Loneliness," making it worthwhile for those who liked the first two albums. Essential for collectors if only for the uniquely shaped sleeve. —*Chris Woodstra*

● **Airport: The Motors' Greatest Hits** / Apr. 25, 1995 / Caroline ✦✦✦✦
A solid collection of the band's best moments, *Airport* provides a good introduction for the uninitiated, drawing from the brilliant first two albums and the lesser *Tenement Steps*. —*Chris Woodstra*

Mott the Hoople

f. 1969, Hereford, England, **db.** 1976
Rock 'n' Roll, Hard Rock
Mott the Hoople are one of the great also-rans in the history of rock 'n' roll. Though the band scored a number of album-rock hits in the early '70s, they never quite broke through into the mainstream. Nevertheless, their nasty fusion of heavy metal, glam-rock, and Bob Dylan's sneering hipster cynicism provided the groundwork for many British punk bands, most notably the Clash. At the center of Mott the Hoople was lead vocalist-pianist Ian Hunter, a late addition to the band who developed into its focal point as his songwriting grew. Hunter was able to subvert rock 'n' roll conventions with his lyrics, and the band, led by guitarist Mick Ralphs, had a tough, muscular sound that kept the band firmly in hard-rock territory, even when they flirted with homosexual imagery and glammy makeup. However, the group's lack of success meant that they inevitably splintered apart in the '70s, with Ralphs forming Bad Company and Hunter launching a cult solo career.

Mick Ralphs (lead guitar, vocal), Verden Allen (organ), Overend Pete Watts (bass), and Dale "Buffin" Griffin (drums) formed Silence in 1968 and began playing around their hometown of Hereford, England. Early in 1969, the band added vocalist Stan Tippens and landed a record contract with Island (Atlantic in the US), heading to London to record with producer Guy Stevens, whose first move was to change the band's name to Mott the Hoople, after a Willard Manus novel. By the summer, Tippens was fired, later becoming the band's road manager, and was replaced by Ian Hunter. Mott the Hoople's eponymous debut album was released in the fall of 1969 and it became an underground hit, known for its fusion of *Blonde on Blonde*-era Dylan and heavy metal, as well as for its straight cover of Sonny Bono's "Laugh at Me" and its pounding instrumental version of the Kinks' "You Really Got Me."

Despite all of the attention *Mott the Hoople* received, it didn't sell well and neither did its poorly-reviewed 1970 follow-up, *Mad Shadows*. The band returned in 1971 with the country-tinged *Wildlife*, which was their least-popular record to date. Despite their lack of sales, Mott the Hoople had gained a cult following in Britain through their consistent touring. At a concert at the Royal Albert Hall in July 1971, the band sparked a mini-riot that led the venue to ban rock concerts for a number of years. More than any of their previous releases, *Brain Capers* (1971) demonstrated the band's live power, but when it failed to sell, the group was prepared to disband.

Just as the band was about to split, David Bowie intervened and convinced the group to stay together. Riding at the height of his Ziggy Stardust popularity, Bowie agreed to produce the band's next album and offered them "Suffragette City" to record. Mott refused the song, asking for "Drive-In Saturday" instead. They eventually settled for "All the Young Dudes," which became the group's breakthrough hit. An explicitly gay anthem recorded by a heterosexual band, "All the Young Dudes" became the anthem for the glam-rock era, becoming a No. 3 hit in the UK and a Top 40 summer in the US in the summer of 1972. An album of the same name was released on Columbia Records in the fall, and it became a hit in the UK and the US. Allen left the band before the recording of the group's follow-up to *All the Young Dudes*, citing Hunter's reluctance to record his songs. A concept album about a rock band struggling for success, *Mott*, released in summer 1973, expanded the band's success, receiving good reviews and peaking at No. 7 in Britain and No. 35 in America. "All the Way from Memphis" and "Roll Away

the Stone" became Top Ten hits in the UK, confirming the band's status as one of the leaders of the glam-rock movement. In the summer of 1974, Hunter published *Diary of a Rock Star* to great acclaim in the UK.

While the band was finally experiencing the success that they had desired, the group was beginning to fall apart. Frustrated with Allen's departure, as well as the fact that his song "Can't Get Enough" was out of Hunter's range, Ralphs left Mott in late 1973 to form Bad Company with Paul Rodgers. He was replaced by former Spooky Tooth guitarist Luther Grosvenor, who changed his name to Ariel Bender upon joining the band; keyboardist Morgan Fisher also joined the group. The new lineup toured in late 1973, and the concerts were documented on 1974's *Mott the Hoople Live*. The live record was released after *The Hoople* appeared in the spring, peaking at No. 11 in the UK and No. 28 in the US on the strength of the singles "The Golden Age of Rock and Roll" and "Foxy Foxy." Former David Bowie guitarist Mick Ronson replaced Bender in the fall of 1974 upon Hunter's request. Within a few months, the pair left the band to begin working as a duo. The remaining members of Mott the Hoople added guitarist Ray Major and vocalist Nigel Benjamin, truncating their name to Mott. The new incarnation of the group released *Drive On* (1975) and *Shouting and Pointing* (1976) to little attention before adding John Fiddler as their lead singer and changing their name to British Lions. They split up two years later.

Though the allegiance between Ian Hunter and Mick Ronson was short-lived, it was well received, and the two would continue to sporadically work together until Ronson's death in 1993. Hunter pursued a moderately successful solo career, highlighted by his eponymous 1975 album and 1979's *You're Never Alone With a Schizophrenic*. Hunter's "Ships" was covered by Barry Manilow in 1975, while Great White took his "Once Bitten, Twice Shy" into the Top Ten in the early '90s. —*Stephen Thomas Erlewine*

Mott the Hoople / 1969 / Atlantic ✦✦✦✦
Mott the Hoople, with its hard-rock variation of Dylan's *Blonde on Blonde* sound, stands as one of the band's better efforts. This debut sported some fine originals, particularly "Backsliding Fearlessly" and "Rock and Roll Queen," as well as some unusual (but hip) song covers, like Sonny Bono's "Laugh at Me" and Doug Sahm's "At the Crossroads." The Kinks' garage-riff standard "You Really Got Me" gets a high-octane instrumental treatment. Only on the middle section of the lengthy "Half Moon Bay" does *Mott the Hoople* lose momentum. The fidelity on this disc (and *Brain Capers*) rivals the sound of a good vinyl import version. —*Rick Clark*

Mad Shadows / 1970 / Atlantic ✦✦

Wildlife / 1971 / Atlantic ✦✦

Brain Capers / 1971 / Atlantic ✦✦✦✦
After a couple of fairly dismal efforts, Mott rebounded with one of the great lost hard rock albums of the '70s. Released with practically no fanfare whatsoever, *Brain Capers* sank without a trace. Certainly, in the decade that produced Styx and Journey, *Brain Capers* (from the audaciously titled "Death May Be Your Santa Claus," to the closing "The Wheel of the Quivering Meat Conception") convincingly drew a line in the sand, revealing most everything called "rock" to be a fraud. Some of this was due, in part, to the return of Guy Stevens at the production helm. Among the album's highlights are versions of Dion's "Your Own Backyard," the Youngbloods' "Darkness Darkness," and Ian Hunter's powerful "The Journey," "Sweet Angeline," and the previously mentioned "Death . . . ." —*Rick Clark*

All the Young Dudes / 1972 / Columbia ✦✦✦✦
Just as Mott was about to pack it in due to their amazing lack of public acceptance, David Bowie entered the picture, and with the recording of a few cannily conceived songs, containing strong gay allusions (Bowie's "All the Young Dudes" and Mott's "Sucker" and "One of the Boys"), Mott went from potential has-beens to avatars of the glam rock movement. The Bowie-produced album contained a version of Lou Reed's "Sweet Jane" and Mick Ralphs' "Ready for Love," one of his finest bits of writing to date. As on many albums of that genre, the production sounds stiff and dry. Nevertheless, Mott makes the proceedings rock fairly convincingly. —*Rick Clark*

☆ **Mott** / 1973 / Columbia ✦✦✦✦✦
Regarded by many to be their finest album, this self-produced effort was a loosely conceived concept album about the ups and downs of rock 'n' roll success. *Mott* contained two UK hits with "All the Way from Memphis" and "Honaloochie Boogie." Other highlights were "The Ballad of Mott the Hoople," "Whizz Kid," "Violence," and "Drivin' Sister." The sound of this reissue is a little on the muddy side. Nevertheless, of their Columbia-period albums, this is the one to get. —*Rick Clark*

The Hoople / 1974 / Columbia ✦✦✦✦

Mott the Hoople Live / 1974 / Columbia ✦✦✦

Drive On / 1975 / Columbia ✦

Greatest Hits / 1975 / Columbia ✦✦✦

★ **The Ballad of Mott: A Retrospective** / Jun. 15, 1993 / Columbia ✦✦✦✦✦

Mott the Hoople were punks without realizing it. Combining a heavy-metal roar with the sneering hipster stance of 1965 Bob Dylan, Mott the Hoople made some of the best, most original rock 'n' roll of the early '70s. This two-disc set chronicles their Columbia recordings, with four tracks from their early Atlantic albums thrown in for good measure. Because of David Bowie's production of *All the Young Dudes* and their stage costumes, Mott was tossed into the glam rock scene, but their music was often wittier and meaner than other glam rock bands. This made the group an enormous element in the punk-new wave movement. Although it isn't definitive because it doesn't contain enough material from *Mott the Hoople* or *Brain Capers*, *The Ballad of Mott* is all the Mott most people will need. Nearly all of the songs from their two classic Columbia albums, *All the Young Dudes* and *Mott*, are included, as is a generous selection of tracks from *The Hoople* and a number of B-sides and unreleased tracks. While the band didn't receive much attention at the time, their music still sounds vital over 20 years later. —*Stephen Thomas Erlewine*

Backsliding Fearlessly: the Early Years / Apr. 19, 1994 / Rhino ✦✦✦✦

A compilation of 16 songs from their first four albums, covering their strongest material from the records pre-dating their *All the Young Dudes* breakthrough. This shows the band casting about, sometimes wildly, for an identity. The earliest tunes (including a cover of Sonny Bono's "Laugh at Me") are perhaps the most blatant imitations of Dylan's *Blonde on Blonde* period ever attempted. Subsequent efforts found them getting into boogie and hard rock, with a few Stones riffs copped here and there. The gut-stomping "Death May Be Your Santa Claus" is a highlight, and Ian Hunter's piano-based ballad "When My Mind's Gone" hints at the more complex psychological territory he'd explore during Mott's prime. This isn't bad and is often interesting, but it is neither very similar to Mott's best work, nor nearly as good as Mott's best stuff. Weirdest cut: a cover of Melanie's "Lay Down." But where is their instrumental version of "You Really Got Me"? —*Richie Unterberger*

Bob Mould

b. 1961, Lake Placid, NY
Guitar, Vocals / Singer-Songwriter, Alternative Pop-Rock
Guitarist-singer-songwriter Bob Mould was initially a member of Hüsker Dü, one of the most influential American bands of the '80s. Hüsker Dü was a post-hardcore punk band that helped define the sound and ideals of alternative rock.

After Hüsker Dü broke up, Bob Mould signed a solo contract with Virgin Records in 1988. The following year, he released his first solo album, *Workbook*, which represented a major shift in sonic direction. *Workbook* was an introspective collection, featuring keyboards, acoustic guitars, and even strings. The album received excellent reviews and spent 14 weeks on the charts, peaking at No. 127; "See a Little Light" became a Top Ten modern rock hit. Mould returned to loud, guitar-driven rock on his second solo album, 1990's *Black Sheets of Rain*. Featuring the Top Ten modern rock hit "It's Too Late," *Black Sheets of Rain* received mixed reviews.

Frustrated with the business operations of major record labels, Mould left Virgin after the release of *Black Sheets of Rain;* they would later release a compilation of the two albums, *Poison Years*. Mould then formed an independent record company, SOL (Singles Only Label), which released 45s from new, developing bands as well as cult bands. In 1992, he formed a new trio, Sugar, with bassist David Barbe and drummer Malcolm Travis; the band signed with Rykodisc in the US, Creation in the UK.

Sugar's first album, *Copper Blue*, was released in the fall of 1992 to enthusiastic reviews and it became Mould's most successful project to date. *Copper Blue* nearly went gold and spawned several alternative radio and MTV hits, including "Helpless" and "If I Can't Change Your Mind." In the spring of 1993, Sugar released the mini-LP *Beaster*, a more abrasive collection than *Copper Blue* that was recorded at the same sessions.

Around the time of the release of *Beaster*, Mould was forced out of the closet by various gay publications, with hopes that he would embrace their political cause; he rejected their requests.

Mould wrote the material for the second Sugar album during 1993. The band began recording in the spring of 1994, but the sessions ground to a halt and the tapes were erased. Mould decided to give the album one more try and it was recorded quickly late that spring. The album, *File Under: Easy Listening*, appeared in the fall of 1994. Although it received good reviews and was moderately successful commercially, it didn't match the performance of *Copper Blue*.

In the spring of 1995, it was announced that Sugar was on hiatus. *Besides*, a collection of rarities and B-sides, was released that summer. By the fall, Mould had broken up the band and begun to work on a third

album entirely by himself. Mould played all of the instruments on his self-titled third album, which was released in the spring of 1996. —*Stephen Thomas Erlewine*

● **Workbook** / Apr. 1989 / Virgin ✦✦✦✦

Arriving after years of sonic bombast in Hüsker Dü, the reflective, acoustic nature of Bob Mould's first solo album, *Workbook*, was a bold statement of renewal. Like all of Mould's work, it's an intensely introspective record, finding him purging demons left over from the dissolution of Hüsker Dü. Instead of relying on raging guitars, Mould explores a wide variety of styles, from pure pop ("See a Little Light") to reflective folk laced with cellos. It's an astonishing array of styles, and the songs are among Mould's finest. For many observers, the record established him as a major songwriter, but it also established a way for underground post-punk artists to mature—echoes of *Workbook* could be heard throughout the '90s, from R.E.M.'s elegiac *Automatic for the People* to Nirvana's use of cellos on *In Utero* and *Unplugged*. But *Workbook* remains a stunning work of individuality, marrying a distinctive body of songs with an original musical vision. Occasionally, the production is a little too pristine, but the power of the songs can not be diminished. —*Stephen Thomas Erlewine*

Black Sheets of Rain / May 1990 / Virgin ✦✦✦

A scalding, monolithic collection of soul-baring lyrics and primal guitars, *Black Sheets of Rain* is extremely powerful musically, but is also slightly monotonous. Nevertheless, the record features several inspired songs from Mould, including the catchy single "It's Too Late." —*Stephen Thomas Erlewine*

Poison Years / Jul. 26, 1994 / Virgin ✦✦✦

Drawing heavily from *Black Sheets of Rain*, this anthology of Mould's time at Virgin doesn't give enough space to the brilliant *Workbook*, but it does have several fiery live tracks, including a harrowing version of Richard Thompson's "Shoot Out the Lights." —*Stephen Thomas Erlewine*

Bob Mould / Apr. 30, 1996 / Rykodisc ✦✦✦✦

As he was promoting the last Sugar album, *File Under: Easy Listening*, Bob Mould hinted that he was tired of working with a band and was fascinated by the simple, four-track recordings of Sebadoh and Guided By Voices. So, it didn't come as a complete surprise when he disbanded Sugar a year after the release of *FU:EL* and began working on a record by himself. *Bob Mould*, his third solo album, was recorded entirely by Mould, but it doesn't sound like a lo-fi project—it doesn't have the professional production of Sugar's records, but it has all their sonic detail. What has changed is the details themselves. *Bob Mould* may not surge on waves of loud guitars like Hüsker Dü or Sugar, but Mould is reaching into new territory, using distortion as a coloring device and exploring trancier melodies. And Mould sounds revitalized throughout the album—although it is clear that this isn't a collection of first takes, his obsession with making the album entirely on his own makes the music fierce and alive. Mould may be heading further into singer-songwriter territory with each album he releases, but he keeps his music away from stodginess by continually changing his approach and delving into new sonic territories. It also doesn't hurt that his increasingly bitter lyrics are gut-wrenchingly provocative and his melodies are consistently engaging. —*Stephen Thomas Erlewine*

Mountain

f. 1969, Long Island, NY, db. 1972
Hard Rock
Hard-rock band Mountain was formed in 1969 by guitarist Leslie West and bassist and former Cream producer Felix Pappalardi. The two met while West was a member of a Long Island R&B band, the Vagrants, local heroes who never broke nationally; when West left to record the solo album *Leslie West—Mountain*, Pappalardi produced for him. The results were satisfying enough for the two to form a partnership, and Mountain's first lineup included drummer N.D. Smart and keyboardist Steve Knight. The group played its fourth live performance ever at Woodstock, after which Smart was replaced by Corky Laing. Their debut album, 1970's *Mountain Climbing*, went gold, thanks in part to the hard rock classic "Mississippi Queen." *Nantucket Sleighride* was equally successful, but the group failed to progress with its next album, and after *Mountain Live* in 1972, the group broke up. Pappalardi, whose hearing had been damaged by Mountain's excessive in-concert volume, returned to production, while West and Laing teamed up with ex-Cream bassist Jack Bruce under the name West, Bruce and Laing. A brief reunion featuring only West from the group's original lineup took place in 1974. In subsequent years, West and Laing revived the group for live shows, sometimes joined by Pappalardi; West also performed with his own Leslie West Band. Pappalardi was shot and killed by his wife in 1983. Two years later, West and Laing regrouped with Mark Clarke on bass and recorded an album before once again calling it quits. Laing has served as PolyGram's A&R vice president since 1989. —*Steve Huey*

Mountain Climbing! / 1970 / Columbia/Legacy ✦✦✦✦
This includes the hit "Mississippi Queen." All in all, this is Mountain's strongest studio effort. —*Rick Clark*

Nantucket Sleighride / 1971 / Columbia ✦✦✦

Flowers of Evil / Nov. 1971 / Columbia/Legacy ✦✦✦
Counting Leslie West's July 1969 solo album, *Flowers of Evil* was the fourth album in 28 months for West and Felix Pappalardi's Mountain, and the pace was catching up with them: *Flowers of Evil* was only half of a studio album, four new songs, its second side filled up with a live 25-minute rock 'n' roll medley and encore of Mountain's sole Top 40 hit, "Mississippi Queen." This was unmistakable evidence that Mountain had run its course. There would be live albums, compilations, and reunions over the succeeding years, but *Flowers of Evil* marked the creative end of a surprisingly short-lived enterprise. (Originally released in November 1971 as Windfall 5501, *Flowers of Evil* was reissued on April 16, 1996, as Columbia/Legacy 52749.) —*William Ruhlmann*

Mountain Live / 1972 / Windfall ✦✦

The Best of Mountain / 1973 / Columbia ✦✦✦✦
This collection contains most of the band's recorded highlights, except for the curious omissions of "Dreams of Milk and Honey" (from the debut *Leslie West—Mountain*) and "Silver Paper" (from *Mountain Climbing*). Included are "Mississippi Queen" (No. 21), "The Animal Trainer and the Toad" (No. 76), "For Yasgur's Farm" (No. 107), and their version of Jack Bruce's "Theme for an Imaginary Western." —*Rick Clark*

Avalanche / 1974 / Columbia ✦✦

Twin Peaks / 1974 / Columbia ✦✦

Over the Top / Apr. 11, 1995 / Columbia/Legacy ✦✦✦✦
Over the Top is right. Two discs of Mountain—complete with all the AOR hits, unreleased tracks, three newly recorded songs, a nearly six-minute guitar solo, and a twenty-minute jam—is a bit much for anyone but the most devoted Leslie West fans, yet the number of rarities and classy packaging make the set a necessary item for the dedicated. —*Stephen Thomas Erlewine*

Mouse & the Traps

f. Tyler, TX
Psychedelic, Garage Rock, Pop-Rock
This Tyler, TX group from the mid-'60s is most known for their uncanny imitation of *Highway 61*-era Dylan, "A Public Execution." Featured on the *Nuggets* compilation, it is to Dylan what the Knickerbockers' "Lies" is to the Beatles: one of the few rip-offs so utterly accurate that it could easily fool listeners into mistaking it for the original article. Spearheaded by singer and songwriter Ronnie Weiss, the group actually recorded quite a few decent singles between 1965 and 1969, without approaching any sort of national recognition. "Mouse" never got as explicitly Dylanesque again, but there's no doubt that Weiss often recalled a nonatonal Dylan with his nasal delivery, and several of their singles were a much more melodic, pop-oriented extension of Dylan's mid-'60s sound. Recording almost exclusively original material, they were one of the better regional groups of the time, and also waxed some capable Texas punk-psychedelia and good-time pop-rockers. —*Richie Unterberger*

Public Execution / 1982 / Eva ✦✦✦✦
This 19-song compilation includes most of their '60s singles, as well as the 1966 single they recorded under the name Positively Thirteen O'Clock with singer Jimmy Rabbit. Most of the songs are original material of a pretty high standard; a good buy for '60s specialists. —*Richie Unterberger*

Mouse on Mars

f. 1993, Germany
Techno, Electronica
German post-techno duo Mouse on Mars are among a growing number of electronic music groups dabbling in complex, heavily hybridized forms that include everything from ambient, techno, and dub to rock, jazz, and jungle. The combined efforts of Andi Toma and Jan St. Werner (of Koln and Dusseldorf, respectively), MOM formed in 1993, reportedly after Werner and Toma met at a death metal concert. Working from Werner's studio, the pair fused an admiration for the early experiments of Kraut-rock outfits like Can, Neu!, Kluster, and Kraftwerk into an offbeat update including influences from the burgeoning German techno and ambient scenes. A demo of material found its way to London-based guitar-ambient group Seefeel, who passed it on to the offices of their label, Too Pure. MOM's first single, "Frosch," was released by the label soon after, and was also included on the debut album, *Vulvaland*. Immediately hailed for its beguiling, inventive edge that seemed to resist all efforts at easy "schublade" (an even less flattering approximation of the English "pigeonhole"), *Vulvaland* was reissued in 1995 by (oddly) Rick Rubin's American Recordings label, who also released their

follow-up, *Iaora Tahiti*, soon after. More upbeat and varied than their debut, the album made some inroads into the American marketplace, but the group's somewhat challenging complexity and steadfast refusal to pander make widespread popularity unlikely. Although re-mixes are rare, the group have been appearing with increasing frequency on compilations of experimental electronic music, including Volume's popular *Trance Europe Express* series. They were also prominently featured on a pair of tribute albums—*Folds And Rhizomes* and *In Memoriam*—dedicated to French post-structuralist philosopher Gilles Deleuze. Werner also records as Aurobindo with Seefeel's Daren Seymor and as Microstoria with Oval's Markus Popp, both of whom have issued album-length releases. —*Sean Cooper*

Vulvaland / 1994 / Too Pure/American ✦✦✦✦
A wibbly, barely digital match of ambient texturology with experimental strains of techno, dub, and Kraut-rock. While the flip relies too heavily on four-on-the-floor ambient house cliches, the A-side is a prize, cultivating a weird, electronics-based avant-pop vibe as successful as it is unique. —*Sean Cooper*

Iaora Tahiti / Oct. 3, 1995 / Too Pure/American ✦✦✦✦
More upbeat and with far greater detail than the debut, *Tahiti* proves Werner and Toma haven't stood still. The pair's fondness for all things lo-fi follows them here, but just as evident is a depth and punch lacking in their earlier material. Jungle-style programming pops up on the first single, "Bib," as well as elements of dub, funk, industrial, film soundtracks, and musique concrete. Their finest work to date. —*Sean Cooper*

Cache Coeur Naif / 1997 / Too Pure ✦✦✦✦
In 1997, while American bands were struggling to incorporate the trendy gadgetry of electronica into their acts and major labels were running around trying to sign Their Own Private Chemical Brothers, many of the European scene's more stalwart experimentalists (Aphex Twin, Warp Records, Mark Van Hoen, Witchman) were drawing on the catchiness of the pop tradition by adding vocalists, quoting '70s soul and jazz in their music, and/or (in Warp's case) signing jazz-funk (Jimi Tenor, Red Snapper) and rock (Broadcast) acts to their rosters. Mouse On Mars make their bid on the former with "Cache Coeur Naif," a four-track EP (and the group's first release under their own name in more than two years) featuring Stereolab vocalists Mary Hansen and Laetitia Sadier. While only one of the songs features vocals in anything like a "pop" sense (verse-chorus-etc.), each incorporates at least a Hansen whisper or a Sadier purr (en Francaise, natch) wrapped around gloriously off-kilter, bleached-out dub-electro rhythms and the usual Mars-bound assortment of wheezy bleeps, whirrs, and crackles. An excellent return. —*Sean Cooper*

The Move

f. 1966, Birmingham, England, **db.** 1972
Art-Rock/Progressive-Rock, Pop-Rock
The Move were the best and most important British group of the late '60s that never made a significant dent in the American market. Through the band's several phases (which were sometimes dictated more by image than musical direction), their chief asset was guitarist and songwriter Roy Wood, who combined a knack for Beatlesque pop with a peculiarly British, and occasionally morbid, sense of humor. On their final albums (with considerable input from Jeff Lynne), the band became artier and more ambitious, hinting at the orchestral rock that Wood and Lynne would devise for the Electric Light Orchestra. The Move, however, always placed more emphasis on the pop than the art, and never lost sight of their hardcore rock 'n' roll roots.

Formed in the mid-'60s, the Move were so named because the five musicians from the original lineups were moving from established Birmingham groups into a new band. Most of the Move, in fact, had previously recorded flop singles in average, unremarkable British Invasion styles as members of other outfits. Taken under the wing of manager Tony Secunda, the group moved to London and crafted an explosive act, heavily influenced by the Who, which found them destroying televisions on stage. The Move's early singles were also heavily influenced by mod pop in their chunky chords and oddball character sketches, although Roy Wood's songs were much poppier and bouncier than those of Pete Townshend.

With Wood handling all of the writing, the group's first four singles ("Night of Fear," "I Can Hear the Grass Grow," "Flowers in the Rain," and "Fire Brigade") all made the British Top Ten in 1967-68. Despite the strength of the music (and a solid debut album in 1968), management and press gave more attention to their flamboyant stage antics, clothes, and outrageous publicity stunts. The most famous of these—a publicity mailing for "Flowers in the Rain" picturing British Prime Minister Harold Wilson in an embarrassing state of undress—backfired badly when the band lost royalties from the single in a subsequent libel suit.

Bassist Ace Kefford (never an essential part of the band except for image purposes) left the Move in 1968. After a couple of less successful singles, they topped the British charts for the only time in 1969 with one of their best songs, "Blackberry Way," a kind of black-humored flipside to "Penny Lane." Guitarist Trevor Burton, who had moved to bass after Kefford left, split too just after "Blackberry Way." Rick Price was brought in to replace Burton, and the group's second album, *Shazam* (1970), was one of their best, allowing them to stretch out in more progressive and experimental directions than they could within the format of hit singles. After a misguided venture into the cabaret circuit, singer Carl Wayne left, leaving the lead vocal chores primarily in the hands of Roy Wood.

The rapid succession of personnel changes would have stopped most bands in their tracks, but the Move, if anything, became a more interesting group in the early '70s. This was due primarily to the replacement of Wayne by Jeff Lynne, previously with the cutesy but interesting pop-rock group the Idle Race. Lynne would be the only member of the Move other than Wood to contribute notable songs and help shape the band's vision. On *Looking On* (1971) and *Message from the Country* (1972), Lynne's cheerier pop inclinations would effectively counterpoint Wood's darker and more ironic compositions, in the manner of great rock collaborations like Lennon-McCartney and Stills-Young. Their best work from this period, though, is actually contained on their singles, several of which ("Brontosaurus," "California Man," and "Tonight") were British hits.

The Move remained unknown in the US (where they had barely toured), and concentrated primarily on studio work after Lynne joined. Their arrangements became denser and more ambitious, particularly as Wood developed proficiency on a number of common and exotic instruments. As a result of their increasing fascination with orchestral rock, Wood, Lynne, and drummer Bev Bevan discontinued the Move in the early '70s to form the Electric Light Orchestra. ELO's remake of one of the Move's final singles, "Do Ya" (which had scraped the bottom of the US charts in 1972) would become a hit in 1977. By that time, though, Wood was long gone from ELO—he had left in 1972 to pursue a career as a leader of Wizzard and as a solo artist. And for all ELO's massive worldwide success, they never matched the intriguing blend of pop and experimentation that characterized the best work of the Move. —*Richie Unterberger*

The Move / 1968 / Repertoire ✦✦✦✦
The Move's debut album was a solid effort of mod-pop-psychedelia, boasting a number of fine Roy Wood compositions: the British hits "Flowers in the Rain" and "Flower Brigade," the original version of "Cherry Blossom Clinic," and the lesser-known but equally worthy "Yellow Rainbow" and "Walk Upon the Water." The three routine covers (of Eddie Cochran, the Coasters, and Moby Grape) that pad the album dilute it only slightly. The German CD reissue adds seven bonus tracks from late-'60s singles, but if you can live with vinyl, you should still seek out the A&M double LP compilation *The Best of the Move*, which has the entire debut album and even more of their late-'60s and early-'70s 45s. —*Richie Unterberger*

Something Else from the Move / 1968 / Regal Zonophone ✦✦✦
When the Move were reaching the peak of their popularity after a burst of fine psychedelic-tinged power pop singles, they issued this rather odd live five-song, 12-inch EP consisting entirely of covers. If nothing else, it proves the Move were a dynamic live act with an eclectic range, to say the least, as they cover tunes by the Byrds, Love, Eddie Cochran, Jerry Lee Lewis, and Spooky Tooth on this set. They really burn it up, in fact, on the Byrds' "So You Want to Be a Rock and Roll Star" and Love's "Stephanie Knows Who," with spinning and frenetic guitar work. The rest of the set is more routine, coming off more as a tribute to some of their idiosyncratic favorites. —*Richie Unterberger*

☆ **Shazam** / 1970 / Repertoire ✦✦✦✦✦
The single most accomplished album to be recorded by any of the Birmingham rock bands (which include the Moody Blues), *Shazam* is sort of *Sgt. Pepper* with an attitude, a mixture of expansive progressive rock worthy of the Beatles and high-energy music honed by years of playing loud on stage. The rendition of Tom Paxton's "The Last Thing on My Mind" pushes these guys simultaneously into Byrds and Jimi Hendrix territory, while "Beautiful Daughter" is one of the most unabashedly pretty records of this era, and "Cherry Blossom Clinic Revisited" is defiantly strange. The album only exists as an import from Japan, paired up on one CD with the earlier *Flowers in the Rain* album (all songs in print domestically or on a better German version filled out with five live tracks from London's Marquee Club, off of the super-rare *Something Else* EP). —*Bruce Eder*

Looking On / 1971 / Capitol ✦✦
Probably their weakest album, finding the group trying to blend progressive elements with lumpy hard rock boogie on obscure, extended tracks. The songs do look forward to the Electric Light Orchestra, for good or ill, in the helium-like high harmonies and the wide palette of instruments. Most of the multi-instrumentation is provided by Roy Wood, who picks up oboe, sitar, slide guitar, cello, and saxophone in

addition to his usual guitar chores. Includes the British Top Ten single "Brontosaurus." —*Richie Unterberger*

Message from the Country / 1971 / One Way ✦✦✦
The group's last good album, weaker than *Shazam* but pleasant enough in its sub-*White Album* way. —*Bruce Eder*

Split Ends / 1972 / United Artists ✦✦✦
Basically an improved version of *Message from the Country*, replacing that album's weakest tracks with some fine British singles, especially "Tonight," "Chinatown," and "Do Ya." With the release of all of these tracks and the entire *Message from the Country* album on the 1994 reissue *Great Move!*, fans no longer have to seek out this package. —*Richie Unterberger*

The Best of the Move [A&M] / 1974 / A&M ✦✦✦✦
Really the best of the group's early period, ranging from delightfully trippy ("Here We Go Round the Lemon Tree," "Flowers in the Rain") to downright weird ("Zing Went the Strings of My Heart," "Night of Fear") singles and album sides that helped establish the group's reputation for eccentricity. —*Bruce Eder*

Black Country Rock / 1993 / Gold Standard ✦✦✦
This quasi-legal compilation of 26 BBC performances from the late 1960s, in reasonable to excellent fidelity, shows the Move's astonishing versatility and range of influences. Ten of these are live-in-the-studio run-throughs of original material, including most of their early British hits—"Night of Fear," "Fire Brigade," "Flowers in the Rain," "I Can Hear the Grass Grow," and "Blackberry Way." More interesting from a historical perspective are the 16 covers, showing an eclectic range that must have been the equal of any major group of the time—the Byrds, Simon & Garfunkel, Tim Rose, Love, Jerry Lee Lewis, Eddie Cochran, Neil Diamond, Jackie Wilson, Janis Joplin, Johnny Cash, Moby Grape, and the Beach Boys all come in for the Move's accomplished chunky rock, harmony-laden treatment. The covers of the Byrds' "Goin' Back" and Paul Simon's "Sounds of Silence" are particularly nifty. It's not recommended to anyone except serious fans, but that small audience could hardly wish for a better collection of rarities from the group's salad days. —*Richie Unterberger*

BBC Sessions / 1994 / Band of Joy ✦✦✦
This is exactly the same (in content and fidelity) as the quasi-legal *Black Country-rock* compilation on Gold Standard, with the notable omission of one of the best songs, a cover of Simon & Garfunkel's "The Sounds of Silence." —*Richie Unterberger*

★ **Great Move! The Best of the Move** / Jun. 15, 1994 / EMI ✦✦✦✦✦
The title is really a misnomer; it includes much of the best of the Move, but can hardly stake a claim as a definitive collection, as it only covers their final years in the early '70s. Which isn't to say it isn't good. This is basically a spruced-up version of their final album, *Message from the Country* (1971), with the addition of five bonus tracks from early-'70s singles. *Message from the Country* itself was an erratic affair, alternating between lumbering forays into hard rock, revivalist roots rock and country, and some of Roy Wood and Jeff Lynne's most inspired Beatlesque progressive compositions. The singles, most of which were previously issued on the *Split Ends* compilation, include some of their most memorable moments. "Tonight" (a British hit) is Roy Wood at his most tuneful, wistful, and folk-rockish; "Chinatown," though not quite as good (and not quite as big a British hit), is in much the same vein; and "Do Ya," redone with much more success by ELO, is one of their catchiest all-out rockers. Wood also gets into heavy sounds on the Top Ten British hit "California Man." Includes informative liner notes by respected rock critic Ira Robbins. —*Richie Unterberger*

Alison Moyet

b. Jun. 18, 1961, Basildon, Essex , England
Vocals / Pop-Rock
Alison Moyet, a British pop singer with a remarkably bluesy voice, began her professional career with synth-pop duo Yazoo (Yaz in the US) in the early '80s. In 1983, Moyet began a solo career, releasing her debut album, *Alf* the following year. *Alf* was a major success in Britain, hitting No. 1 on the charts and launching the hit singles "Invisible," "All Cried Out," and "Love Resurrection"; it was a minor hit in the US, with "Invisible" cracking the Top 40. During 1985, Moyet toured with a jazz band led by John Altman; the group recorded a version of Billie Holiday's "That Ole Devil Called Love," which became her biggest British hit, even though the group received poor reviews.

In 1986, Moyet had another major UK hit with "Is This Love?", which was released while she was recording her second solo album. *Raindancing* appeared in 1987 and it was another big British hit, peaking at No. 2 and featuring the Top Ten hits "Weak in the Presence of Beauty" and "Love Letters." The record wasn't quite as successful in the US, peaking at No. 94. In 1991, she released her third album, *Hoodoo*, which was her most musically ambitious collection to date. However, it didn't match the commercial success of her previous albums, failing to chart in

America. *Essex*, her fourth album, appeared in 1994 and she released a greatest hits collection, *Singles*, the following year. *—Stephen Thomas Erlewine*

Alf / 1984 / Columbia ✦✦✦✦
Moyet's debut attempted a gradual transition from the electronic-pop backgrounds of her Yaz work. She succeeded to the tune of three UK hits—"Love Resurrection," "All Cried Out," and "Invisible." *— William Ruhlmann*

Raindancing / 1987 / Columbia ✦✦✦

Hoodoo / Aug. 27, 1991 / Columbia ✦✦✦✦
Moyet's voice has never sounded bigger or more expressive than it does on this disc. The arrangements span popular African-American music from the Delta to the dance floor, and every tune is delivered with an amazing emotional intensity. *—J. Poet*

Essex / Mar. 22, 1994 / Columbia ✦✦✦

● **Singles** / Jun. 27, 1995 / Columbia ✦✦✦✦
Singles collects all of Alison Moyet's biggest hits and best-known songs, providing an excellent and concise overview of her career, as well as a terrific introduction to her sophisticated, bluesy jazz-pop. *—Stephen Thomas Erlewine*

Mu

f. California
Art-Rock/Progressive-Rock, Psychedelic
This intriguing early '70s Southern Californian group featured the talents of singer-songwriter Merrell Fankhauser (who was also at the helm of cult classics in the '60s by Fapardokly and HMS Bounty) and Jeff Cotton, previously slide guitarist with Captain Beefheart. Their sole album (from 1971) is a gem of the late hippie era, combining the fractured blues-based tangents of Beefheart with the loose flow and stoned lyricism of bands like the late '60s Grateful Dead. After a couple more singles, Mu moved to Maui and cut a fair amount of unreleased material before breaking up around 1974. Their eponymous album, as well as a lot of their unreleased material, was reissued in the 1980s. *—Richie Unterberger*

● **Mu** / 1971 / Reckless ✦✦✦✦
One of the best overlooked albums of the early '70s. Daring rhythms and song structures that build off the blues without following the standard three-chord/12-bar progressions, occasional modal jazzy sax by Cotton, and great slide guitar combine to form one of the most unclassifiable recordings of the time, with a high-spirited lightness that avoids the heavy excesses that sometimes burdened late-period psychedelia. *—Richie Unterberger*

End of an Era / 1988 / Reckless ✦✦✦
Seventeen songs recorded after their relocation to Maui in 1974. More subdued and acoustic than the *Mu* LP, but still worthwhile, with Crosby, Stills, & Nash-like harmonies, melancholy melodies, and almost prototypically hippie-ish lyrics about visitations from other planets, searches for lost lands, mystical love, and the like. *—Richie Unterberger*

Mu-Ziq (μ-Ziq)

Ambient Techno, Experimental, Electronica, Jungle/Drum 'N Bass
Michael Paradinas is the character behind Mu-Ziq, who has surprised the music world with his distorted style of industrial-techno. *Tango 'N Vectif*, his first album, appeared in mid-'94, and quickly became out-of-print. Follow-up *Bluff Limbo*, limited to 500 copies, also disappeared, while the buzz about him grew. His first US release, *Mu-Ziq Vs. The Auteurs*, increased the hype, and Virgin UK signed him to a multi-album deal in early 1995. His prolific output continued on efforts including 1995's *Salsa with Mesquite* and *In Pine Effect*, as well as 1997's *Urmur Bile Trax*. *—John Bush*

Tango N' Vectif / 1993 / Rephlex ✦✦✦✦
This album immediately paired the young bedroom rat as a contemporary of Richard "Aphex Twin" James, on whose label it appeared. The offbeat, envelope-pushing themes and occasionally heavily distorted percussion see the comparison through, but that's where the similarity ends. His only full-length work with former bandmate Francis Naughton. *—Sean Cooper*

Mu-Ziq Vs. the Auteurs / 1994 / Hut/Astralwerks ✦✦✦✦
An album of re-mixes of material by solemn British pop group the Auteurs, from their 1993 album *I Wish I Were a Cowboy*. Unlike re-mix projects that pair track with doting (or at least neutral-to-positive) fan, this one is notable for Paradinas' well-publicized disdain for the music. He shows as much on the thorough hatchet job to which he submits four of the album's tracks. *—Sean Cooper*

● **In Pine Effect** / Oct. 31, 1995 / Astralwerks ✦✦✦✦
His most stylistically developed album under the Mu-Ziq name to date. Although Paradinas is big on insisting his music isn't for dancing, most

of the tracks here feature a familiar dance-floor pulse, with alternately arresting and sidesplitting melodies floating above signature percussion and some interesting brass work. "Phiesope" even samples Kristen Hersh! *—Sean Cooper*

Bluff Limbo / 1996 / Rephlex ✦✦✦✦
Historically interesting from the standpoint of his later work—shades of Jake Slazenger and Kid Spatula can be heard here—*Limbo* is nonetheless overly repetitive, relying heavily on the distortion-pedal aesthetic by now a cliche of Rephlex artists (Aphex Twin, Cylob, Kinaesthesia). The album was originally issued promo-only in 1994 (and then with different track listings across formats!) and finally saw proper release in mid-'96. *—Sean Cooper*

Urmur Bile Trax, Vols. 1 & 2 / Jan. 1997 / Astralwerks ✦✦✦✦
The first attempt at jungle rhythms for Mike Paradinas, *Urmur Bile Trax* is an extended double EP, clocking in at just under 70 minutes on its American CD issue. The eight-tracker sees Paradinas in a much more experimental form than on his earlier "queasy listening" releases as Jake Slazenger and Gary Moscheles; in fact, he sounds refreshed, working with break-beats. Still less uncompromising than old pal Aphex Twin's skittery drum 'n' bass noodling on *Richard D. James Album*, Mu-Ziq comes closer to straight-ahead jungle than the other electronica experimentalists—Plug, Squarepusher, and Aphex—working at the time. *—John Bush*

Mudhoney

f. 1988, Seattle, WA
Alternative Pop-Rock, Grunge
With their fuzzed-out guitars and Mark Arm's straining vocals, Mudhoney defined '80s and '90s grunge rock. In fact, their 1988 debut single "Touch Me, I'm Sick" is the definitive grunge song—an obnoxious, dirty song driven by massively distorted guitars and a screaming vocal. It was a terrific, invigorating song that the band rewrote on each album that followed, but that's alright because Mudhoney only has one other song—a slow, sludgy Stooges grind. But their limitations are ultimately endearing; the band is a punk band, not like a '70s or '80s group, but like a '60s garage band, kicking out the same three chords with an unbridled enthusiasm. Leave the serious themes to Nirvana, Pearl Jam, Soundgarden, and Alice in Chains—Mudhoney takes the same themes but makes them sleazy and trashy, like the Russ Meyers film they named themselves after. Their records are inconsistent but when they are good, they are great. *—Stephen Thomas Erlewine*

● **Superfuzz Bigmuff (& Early Singles)** / 1988 / Sub Pop ✦✦✦✦
Combining the band's first EP with a handful of early singles, highlighted by the classic "Touch Me, I'm Sick," this disc showcases Mudhoney at their most furious and fine. *Superfuzz Bigmuff* keeps the overextended riffing and hyper-vocalizing down to a minimum, focusing on maximum-torque, metallic garage raunch. A release that provides as much bite as bark. *—John Dougan & Meredith Erlewine*

Mudhoney / Jul. 1989 / Sub Pop ✦✦✦
Mudhoney's first full-length album cut away the acid-rock excesses of their debut EP, concentrating on a tighter, punkier sound, highlighted by the raging "You Got It (Keep It out of My Face)." *—Stephen Thomas Erlewine*

Every Good Boy Deserves Fudge / Jul. 26, 1991 / Sub Pop ✦✦✦✦
It's no great stylistic breakthrough, but what Mudhoney record is? Instead, it's another solid album of fuzzed-out three-chord garage rockers. There's nothing as great as "Touch Me, I'm Sick" or "In 'n' out of Grace," but song for song, it's their most consistent album. *—Stephen Thomas Erlewine*

Piece of Cake / Oct. 1992 / Reprise ✦✦✦
While their first major-label album isn't as raw as their earlier singles, Mudhoney haven't lost their apathetic, slacker attitude. Full of short jokes between tracks (ranging from a rip on techno music to 28 seconds of flatulence), *Piece of Cake* is a muddled album showing flashes of brilliance. The thundering opener, "No End in Sight," and the pulverizing single "Suck You Dry" fill the hammering grunge quotient, while the band veers off into slower territory on other tracks and is almost equally successful. The fuzz guitars never let up. *—Stephen Thomas Erlewine*

Five Dollar Bob's Mock Cooter Stew / Oct. 26, 1993 / Reprise ✦✦✦
A stopgap EP that sounds like it was recorded in a garage, *Five Dollar Bob's Mock Cooter Stew* has some of Mudhoney's rawest and best rock 'n' roll. *—Stephen Thomas Erlewine*

My Brother the Cow / Mar. 28, 1995 / Reprise ✦✦✦✦
Mudhoney doesn't have an expansive musical vocabulary, they're all about grunge. Naturally, they don't abandon it now that it's no longer hip—they just keep going and going. In fact, they make it harsher and nastier, stripping melody off of the songs. The guitar hooks growl, occasionally sinking their teeth in, and Mark Arm has never sounded quite so pissed off. *My Brother the Cow* isn't much for songs—it's nearly all

sneering attitude—yet the sound is positively galvanizing. —*Stephen Thomas Erlewine*

Maria Muldaur

b. Sep. 12, 1943, New York, NY
Vocals / Dance-Pop, Pop, Pop-Rock
Singer Maria Muldaur was born Maria D'Amato in New York City. In the 1960s, she was a member of the New York-based Even Dozen Jug Band and later of the Boston-based Jim Kweskin Jug Band, which also included her husband, Geoff Muldaur, from whom she was divorced in 1972. She found solo success with the sultry single "Midnight at the Oasis," which was featured on her debut solo album, *Maria Muldaur*, in 1973, and she followed with several similar albums, though her commercial success declined. In the 1980s, Muldaur began performing as a Christian artist. She continues to work the club circuit successfully while issuing records like 1994's *Meet Me at Midnite* and 1996's *Fanning the Flames*. —*William Ruhlmann*

● **Maria Muldaur** / 1974 / Reprise ✦✦✦✦

Waitress in a Donut Shop / 1974 / Reprise ✦✦✦
Maria Muldaur's follow-up to her gold-selling debut album includes her second (and final) hit single, "I'm A Woman," and presents a pleasant folk-blues mixture of material including everything from contemporary songs by Wendy Waldman and Anna McGarrigle to Skip James blues tunes and Fats Waller's "Squeeze Me," all given Muldaur's earthy, enthusiastic treatment. —*William Ruhlmann*

Sweet Harmony / 1976 / Reprise ✦✦✦✦

Southern Winds / 1978 / Reprise ✦✦

Open Your Eyes / 1979 / Reprise ✦✦

Louisiana Love Call / Aug. 24, 1992 / Black Top ✦✦✦✦

Sunny Side of the Street / Oct. 27, 1992 / WEA ✦✦✦

Meet Me at Midnite / Aug. 30, 1994 / Black Top ✦✦✦

Jazzabelle / Aug. 15, 1995 / Stony Plain ✦✦
Maria Muldaur's *Jazzabelle* is a set of jazz and blues material recorded with piano trios, which are fronted by David Torkanowsky, Dave Matthews, and John R. Burr. —*Stephen Thomas Erlewine*

Fanning the Flames / Aug. 1996 / Telarc ✦✦✦
With *Fanning the Flames*, Maria Muldaur delves deeper into the blues than she ever has before, trying her hand at a variety of different blues and R&B styles. Muldaur is at her best when she doesn't try to belt out a song—her pipes simply aren't equipped for bold, brassy shouting—and when she lays back with soulful numbers like "Stand by Me." Even though much of the album features such low-key efforts, it is undone by its sterile production and the lifeless playing of Muldaur's backing band. —*Thom Owens*

The Mumps

f. New York, NY
New Wave
The Mumps were one of the most obscure, but distinctive, New York bands of the late '70s, performing an absurdly theatrical fusion of pop, punk, and glam rock. Led by vocalist Lance Loud, the group's music was an affectionate satire of '70s kitsch culture, predating the similar obsessions of the B-52's by a number of years. The Mumps rocked as hard as the New York Dolls, while writing clever pop hooks that updated trashy garage and bubblegum singles of the '70s.

Although they never even earned a large underground following, the group was a favorite of many punk rockers of the era (including the Ramones, Blondie, the New York Dolls, X, Television, the Cramps, Devo, and the Go-Go's), as well as '80s alternative rockers like R.E.M., Game Theory, and Sparks.

In addition to Lance Loud, the core lineup of the Mumps also featured keyboardist Kristiann Hoffman, guitarist Rob Duprey, bassist Kevin Kiely, and drummer Paul Rutner. Over the years, the lineup changed slightly, with Loud, Hoffman, and Duprey remaining the constant members in each incarnation of the band. The Mumps only released two singles while they were active in the late '70s, but in 1994 Eggbert Records released a CD called *Fatal Charms* that compiled everything the band ever recorded, including outtakes, alternate takes, and live rehearsals. *Fatal Charms* proves that the Mumps' music remains vibrant, creative, and intoxicatingly bizarre nearly 20 years after it was recorded. —*Stephen Thomas Erlewine*

Fatal Charm / 1994 / Eggbert ✦✦✦✦
Fatal Charm compiles essentially the complete recorded works of the quirky New York band, including the simply wonderful "Crocodile Tears," as well as some equally spirited outtakes and live rehearsals. Though very little of the Mumps' music was released during their five years together as a band, their live shows were legendary, influencing many of the next generation of new wave and alternative rockers; *Fatal*

Charm helps explain why bands continue to namedrop them 20 years later. —*Chris Woodstra*

Peter Murphy

b. Jul. 11, 1957, Northampton, England
Vocals / Alternative Pop-Rock, Goth-Rock, Post-Punk
Despite having a successful solo career as a cult artist, vocalist Peter Murphy remains best known as the lead vocalist for Bauhaus, the pioneering post-punk goth-rock band of the early '80s.

After disbanding Bauhaus in 1983, Murphy formed Dali's Car with former Japan member Mick Karn. Dali's Car only released one album, *The Waking Hour*, in 1984. Following its release, the duo broke up and Murphy hesitantly began a solo career with a cover of Magazine's "The Light Pours out of Me," which was featured on a 1985 Beggars Banquet compilation called *The State of Things*. In 1986, he released his first full-fledged solo album, *Should the World Fail to Fall Apart*, which featured a number of guest artists, including former Bauhaus member Daniel Ash. Two years later, Murphy released his second solo album, *Love Hysteria*. Like its predecessor, *Love Hysteria* received lukewarm reviews but sold well to his dedicated fan base.

With 1990's *Deep*, Murphy had a surprise hit—the first single from the record, the Bowie-esque "Cuts You Up," became the American modern rock hit of the year, spending seven weeks at the top of the US charts and crossing over to AOR radio and the pop charts, where it peaked at No. 55. Following its success, *Deep* reached No. 44 on the album charts. Murphy wasn't able to sustain that success with his next album, 1992's *Holy Smoke*, which only reached No. 108 on the charts, despite the No. 2 modern rock hit, "The Sweetest Drop."

In 1995, Murphy released *Cascade*, which was greeted with weak reviews. The album failed to chart in either America or Britain. —*Stephen Thomas Erlewine*

Should the World Fail to Fall Apart / 1986 / Beggars Banquet ✦✦✦
Peter Murphy's first solo effort makes a determined effort to shake off any residual goth-rock elements; written and produced in tandem with guitarist-keyboardist Howard Hughes, *Should the World Fail to Fall Apart* is an understated, muted record that opts against dark theatrics in favor of more subtle textures. Still, while you can take the singer out of Bauhaus, you can't take Bauhaus out of the singer; regardless of his intentions, Murphy remains a highly melodramatic vocalist, and set against such a minimal backdrop his voice becomes disconcertingly predominant, especially on awkward covers of Pere Ubu's "Final Solution" and Magazine's "The Light Pours Out of Me." —*Jason Ankeny*

Love Hysteria / 1988 / Beggars Banquet ✦✦✦
With *Love Hysteria*, Peter Murphy's music began to move in an increasingly commercial direction; produced by keyboardist Simon Rogers, the record is glossy and slick, clearly influenced by mid-'70s era David Bowie (the cover of the Bowie/Iggy Pop collaboration "Funtime" is a dead giveaway). More taut and concise than the languid *If the World Should Fail to Fall Apart*, its songs are melodic and accessible—both "All Night Long" and "Indigo Eyes" were near hits—but the album's mainstream sheen quickly grows tiresome and sterile. —*Jason Ankeny*

● **Deep** / 1990 / Beggars Banquet ✦✦✦✦
Peter Murphy's newfound mainstream tendencies bore fruit with *Deep*, which launched the hit single "Cuts You Up." Like its predecessor *Love Hysteria*, the record is bright and sophisticated, and Murphy seems more confident in his diverse new settings—tracks like "Seven Veils," "The Line Between the Devil's Teeth," and "Roll Call" flirt with dance-pop, while "A Strange Kind of Love" and "Marlene Dietrich's Favourite Poem" are beautifully melancholy ballads. —*Jason Ankeny*

Holy Smoke / Apr. 14, 1992 / Beggars Banquet ✦✦
Holy Smoke continues in the pop vein of Peter Murphy's then-current work: the title of "Hit Song" is a fair barometer of the record's aims—again, Murphy sacrifices content in favor of a slick, overtly commercial sound frequently at odds with the preciousness of his songwriting. In the absence of memorable melodies, the record relies on production excess—"The Sweetest Drop" is overblown rock opera, while "Kill the Hate" mistakes attitude for content; although *Holy Smoke* occasionally catches fire (as on the opening "Keep Me from Harm"), its peaks are too few and far between to make it worthwhile to anyone outside of Murphy's devout fan base. —*Jason Ankeny*

Cascade / Apr. 11, 1995 / Beggars Banquet ✦✦✦✦
Having hit a creative and commercial wall with *Holy Smoke*, Peter Murphy returns to form with *Cascade*, a more consistent and ambitious work that largely sheds the mainstream veneer of his recent LPs to restore the singer to the drama of his strongest work. Produced by Pascal Gabriel, much of the record is enigmatic and atmospheric; "Subway," "Huuvola," and the title cut rank among Murphy's most experimental work in ages, while the "infinite guitar" work of the reliably brilliant Michael Brook adds much-needed ambience and edge to even the most mainstream moments. —*Jason Ankeny*

Music Explosion

f. Mansfield, OH
Pop-Rock, Bubblegum

One-hit-wonder Ohio garage band that reached No. 2 in 1967 with "Little Bit O'Soul," a great gutsy pop-rock number with a classic bass-organ riff. Whatever personality they may have had was created in the studio by producers Jeffrey Katz and Jerry Kasenetz, who would soon help create bubblegum with acts like the 1910 Fruitgum Co. and the Ohio Express. The Music Explosion didn't have nearly as juvenile a sound as those groups, but they never latched onto another piece of material nearly as attention-grabbing as "Little Bit O'Soul," entering the Top 100 only once more with the tiny hit "Sunshine Games." —*Richie Unterberger*

Little Bit o' Soul / 1986 / Performance ✦✦✦
Fourteen tracks taken from their sole album and several nonhit singles. Nothing comes close to matching the ultra-catchy "Little Bit o' Soul," and in fact, on the whole it's quite mediocre and unmemorable. —*Richie Unterberger*

● **Anthology** / Apr. 25, 1995 / One Way ✦✦✦✦
Although it could have been packaged and sequenced with more care, One Way's 21-track *Anthology* provides all the material a hardcore fan could want from a Music Explosion collection, and far more than the average listener needs. While "Little Bit O' Soul" is an incredible single, the remainder of the group's songs are generally undistinguished, ranging between competent garage covers and pleasant, but unmemorable, '60s pop-rock, making *Anthology* unnecessary for anyone but dedicated '60s collectors. —*Stephen Thomas Erlewine*

The Music Machine

Psychedelic, Garage Rock

Most famous for "Talk Talk," a Top 20 single from 1966 that was one of the most manic '60s garage-punk hits, the Music Machine had much more depth and songwriting talent than the typical one-hit-wonders of the day. Lead singer and songwriter Sean Bonniwell's strangled lyrics and dark, verbose vision paced the group's wiry psychedelic guitar lines and ominous, minor-key Farfisa organ. Only one album was released with the original lineup, and the group's ferocious energy was diluted on subsequent recordings. Despite chalking up only one more minor hit single ("The People in Me"), the Music Machine recorded quite a few excellent, imaginatively produced singles and album tracks that found them exploring the darker side of psychedelia with compelling intensity and imagination. —*Richie Unterberger*

(Turn on) The Music Machine / 1966 / Performance ✦✦✦
The Music Machine's debut would have been a lot better if they'd let Sean Bonniwell write all of the songs. Yet it was, as was often the case at the time, divided between fine Bonniwell originals and dispensable covers of current rock hits. Which means that, side by side with excellent Bonniwell originals like "Talk Talk," "The People in Me," and "Trouble," you'll find lukewarm covers of Neil Diamond's "Cherry Cherry," the Beatles' "Taxman," and "96 Tears" (though the slow, moody reading of "Hey Joe" is nice). Most of the Bonniwell songs were issued in much better company on the Rhino anthology, although one good one, the typically tortuous "Wrong," is only available on this album. —*Richie Unterberger*

Bonniwell Music Machine / 1968 / Warner Brothers ✦✦✦
The Music Machine were renamed the Bonniwell Music Machine when they went to Warner Brothers, as the original lineup disbanded at some point, leaving only chief singer and songwriter Sean Bonniwell. Much of the material on Warner, however, was recorded by the original group, and this album was pasted together from some singles (some of which had appeared on Original Sound in 1967) and other tracks, both by the original incarnation and a second outfit that was pretty much a Sean Bonniwell solo vehicle. Accordingly, the tone of the album is pretty uneven, but much of the material is excellent. In fact, some of the songs rate among their best; a few are also found on the Rhino anthology, but other first-rate tunes ("Bottom of the Soul," "Talk Me Down," "The Trap") are not. Some of the cuts (presumably those recorded after the first lineup broke up) find Bonniwell branching out from psych-punk into a poppier and more eclectic direction, sometimes with very good results, sometimes not. Long out of print and difficult to find, the entire album is included on the Sundazed CD reissue *Beyond the Garage*, meaning that it's no longer necessary to search for an original copy. —*Richie Unterberger*

● **The Best of the Music Machine** / 1984 / Rhino ✦✦✦✦
Besides "Talk Talk" and "The People in Me," this features the best cuts from their first LP, some fine non-LP singles that rank among the best obscure gems of the psychedelic era, and some decent previously unissued cuts. The package is enhanced by detailed liner notes by Sean Bonniwell. —*Richie Unterberger*

Beyond the Garage / Nov. 14, 1995 / Sundazed ✦✦✦✦
Although the material the Music Machine recorded for Warner Brothers (released under the name Bonniwell Music Machine) is little known, it's almost up to the high standards of their Original Sound sides. It's also been extremely hard to find, until this excellent 20-track reissue. This contains the entire contents of the 1968 *Bonniwell Music Machine* album (some of which had actually been released on the Music Machine's 1967 singles for Original Sound), plus various rare singles and a couple of unreleased tunes. Though a bit erratic, the best of this is thrilling stuff, as exciting as experimental garage rock ever got. "Bottom of the Soul," "The Eagle Never Hunts the Fly," "Talk Me Down," and "Double Yellow Line" all count among their toughest pop-psych punkers. Tracks like "Tin Can Beach," "The Trap," and "Discrepancy" also show songwriter and lead singer Sean Bonniwell expanding from the pounding guitar-organ prototype into more eclectic, but equally compelling, directions with touches of folk and orchestration. Inventive studio arrangements and lyrical wordplay are constants throughout. You won't find Bonniwell's name mentioned in many standard rock reference books, but this CD further bolsters his credentials as one of the most underappreciated innovators of late-'60s rock. —*Richie Unterberger*

My Bloody Valentine

f. 1984, Dublin, Ireland
Alternative Pop-Rock, Shoegazing, Dream-Pop

Like the Velvet Underground, Sonic Youth, and the Jesus & Mary Chain before them, My Bloody Valentine redefined what noise meant within the context of pop songwriting. Led by guitarist Kevin Shields, the group released several EPs in the mid-'80s before recording the era-defining *Isn't Anything* in 1988, a record that merged lilting, ethereal melodies of the Cocteau Twins with crushingly loud, shimmering distortion. Though My Bloody Valentine rejected rock 'n' roll conventions, it didn't subscribe to the precious tendencies of anti-rock art-pop bands. Instead, it rode crashing waves of white noise to unpredictable conclusions, particularly since their noise wasn't paralyzing like the typical avant-garde noise-rock band: It was translucent, glimmering, and beautiful. Shields was a perfectionist, especially when it came to recording, as much of My Bloody Valentine's sound was conceived within the studio itself. Nevertheless, the band was known as a formidable live act, even though they rarely moved, or even looked at the audience, while they were on stage. Their notorious lack of movement was branded "shoegazing" by the British music press, and soon there were legions of other shoegazers—Ride, Lush, the Boo Radleys, Chapterhouse, Slowdive—that, along with the rolling dance-influenced Madchester scene, dominated British indie-rock of the late '80s and early '90s. As shoegazing reached its peak in 1991, My Bloody Valentine released *Loveless*, which broke new sonic ground and was hailed as a masterpiece. Though the band was poised for a popular breakthrough, they disappeared into the studio and didn't emerge over the next five years, leaving behind a legacy that proved profoundly influential in the direction of '90s alternative rock.

Born in Queens, New York, Kevin Shields' family moved to Dublin, Ireland when he was six years old. In his teens, he became obsessed with pop music, eventually playing in Complex with his childhood friend Colm O'Ciosoig. In 1984, Shields and O'Ciosig formed My Bloody Valentine with vocalist Dave Conway and keyboardist Tina, taking their name from a slasher horror film. The group relocated to Berlin, where they released the Birthday Party-influenced EP *This Is Your Bloody Valentine* on the Tycoon label in 1985 to little notice. The following year, the band moved to London, where they added bassist Debbie Googe. By the summer, they had signed to Fever and had released the EP *Geek!*, which again was ignored. Later that year, the group moved to Kaleidoscope Sound, releasing *The New Record By My Bloody Valentine* EP, which illustrated a Jesus & Mary Chain influence. The following year, the band moved to the Primitives' Lazy Records, releasing *Sunny Sundae Smile* early in the year. That EP was the first My Bloody Valentine record to mesh airy melodies with grinding guitars, but the two EPs that followed in 1987—*Strawberry Wine* and *Ecstasy*—were more focused and acclaimed. Conway left the band by the end of the year and was replaced by vocalist-guitarist Belinda Butcher, whose breathy vocals fit the group's evolving sound more appropriately.

My Bloody Valentine's new sound coalesced with the group's first full-fledged album, 1988's *Isn't Anything*. Released on Creation Records, *Isn't Anything* was greeted with enthusiastic reviews in the UK music press and the band's following increased dramatically by the end of the year; in fact, their reputation had become large enough to attract the attention of Sire/Warner Bros. in the US, who became the group's American label. Two other EPs, *Feed Me With Your Kiss* and *You Made Me Realise*, were also quite popular, and by the beginning of 1989, bands that based their sound on My Bloody Valentine's droning swirl began to appear. The group retreated to the studio in 1989 to record their follow-up, which meant that only one EP, *Glider*, was released during that year. By the spring of 1990, it was becoming clear that the follow-up to *Isn't Anything* wouldn't be appearing anytime soon, and reports about

Shields' growing perfectionism began to circulate in the UK weekly music press. Soon, it became apparent that the band's lengthy recording sessions were crippling Creation Records, but the group's audience was still passionate, despite the inactivity: The *Tremelo* EP was released at the end of 1990 to considerable acclaim, and managed to climb into the UK Top 40.

When My Bloody Valentine's second album, *Loveless,* finally appeared in late 1991, it was greeted with uniformly excellent reviews and it became a hit within the UK, reaching No. 24 on the charts. In America, the group made significant inroads, particularly by supporting Dinosaur Jr. Despite the band's acclaim and growing audience, *Loveless* didn't sell in numbers to recoup its reported $500,000 recording cost and Creation dropped the band from their label; Creation wouldn't fully recover until 1994, when they signed Oasis. My Bloody Valentine signed with Island and entered the studio at the end of 1992 to record a new album. In 1993, the group contributed a James Bond cover to a charity compilation.

And then . . . nothing happened.

Shields built a home studio with his Island advance and reportedly completed two separate albums, but scrapped them both. Often, the studio ran into technological problems. Between 1993 and 1997, both Googe and O'Ciosoig left the band, leaving only Shields and Butcher; after driving a cab for about a year, Googe formed Snowpony in 1996. There were signs that My Bloody Valentine were emerging from hiding in 1996, when the group contributed to the Wire tribute album *Whore* and Shields played on Experimental Audio Research's *Beyond the Pale,* but as of the spring of 1997, there was no new My Bloody Valentine album. —*Stephen Thomas Erlewine*

This Is Your Bloody Valentine / 1985 / Tycoon ++
My Bloody Valentine's debut album *This Is Your Bloody Valentine* is an unfocused and derivative collection of post-punk goth-rock that offers no indication of the revolutionary guitar sound the group would later create. —*Stephen Thomas Erlewine*

Isn't Anything / 1988 / Creation/Sire ++++
The first of My Bloody Valentine's two landmark albums, *Isn't Anything,* combines delicate, brittle melodies and big guitars. "Lose My Breath" and "No More Sorry" highlight Belinda Butcher's understated but charismatic voice, while guitars take the spotlight on "Cupid Come." Songs like "Sue Is Fine" and the seminal "Feed Me with Your Kiss" point toward the band's future sound of fuzzed-out, multi-tracked guitars and blissful male-female vocal harmonies. An underrated and surprisingly accessible album. —*Heather Phares*

Ecstasy & Wine / 1989 / Lazy +++
Ecstasy & Wine combines the 1987 EPs *Strawberry Wine* and *Ecstasy* on one compact disc. *Strawberry Wine* finds the band moving closer to their lush, shimmering neo-psychedelia, while *Ecstasy* finds the group incorporating dissonance and layers of feedback into sound established by *Strawberry Wine,* and thereby offering a rough blueprint for *Isn't Anything.* —*Stephen Thomas Erlewine*

Glider / 1989 / Sire ++++
The *Glider* EP finds My Bloody Valentine exploring the different harmonics in their dissonances and distortion, creating floating layers of sound that are hypnotic in their ebb and flow. The first song, "Soon," is one of the group's greatest sound paintings, filled with evocative textures and eerie, disembodied rhythms, while the title track is nearly as fascinating, making *Glider* an essential addition to a My Bloody Valentine library. —*Stephen Thomas Erlewine*

★ **Loveless** / 1991 / Sire +++++
One of the best and most influential albums in '90s alternative rock, *Loveless* puts the band's innovative sonic style over lyrical substance. And the sonic styles of *Loveless* change constantly: Drums bludgeon the listener's ears and fade into nothingness; guitars whine like chainsaws and hum like cellos. The intricate mix of feedback, guitar washes, and dreamy harmonies on songs like "Til Here Knows When" and "Blown a Wish" is awe-inspiring; though it takes My Bloody Valentine many years of work to complete their albums, it's easy to understand why when the results are this breathtaking. —*Heather Phares*

My Life Story

f. 1990, Camden, England
Alternative Pop-Rock, Brit-Pop
My Life Story was one of many orchestral British pop groups that appeared in the wake of Pulp and Suede. Led by Jake Shillingford, the group comes across as a low-rent Neil Hannon (the Divine Comedy), the group never won the critical respect of its influences—or even contemporaries like the Divine Comedy—but they won a hardcore following of diehard Anglophiles.

Jake Shillingford (born May 15, 1966), for all intents and purposes, is My Life Story. Born in Southend-on-Sea, Shillingford formed his first band in 1980, but he didn't begin a career until the late '80s. During the

mid-'80s, he briefly attended the Southend Art College, after which he held a job at Dingwalls in Camden. He worked during the day and ran the Panic Station club at night, often playing with his band, My Life Story. After a few years he grew bored and he departed to America in 1989 on a mission to find himself. He returned the following year, convinced that he would remodel My Life Story as a string-laden, orchestral pop band. Over the course of 1990, he assembled a new version of the band, re-hiring former MLS drummer Aaron Cahill as musical arranger, drummer Steave Searley, bassist Jon King, keyboardist Helen Caddick, violinists Alison Gabriel and Ellie Newton, cellist Judith Fleet, Rob Spriggs on viola, and Rachel Simnett, who played various brass instruments. Playing concerts in underground London clubs, the band slowly built a small following, self-releasing their indie debut EP *Big* at the end of the year. By 1992, the band consisted of a total of 11 musicians, and they were regularly playing clubs like the 100 Club and the Marquee.

During 1993, My Life Story's profile began to rise considerably, as they contributed strings to the Wonder Stuff's "Welcome to the Cheap Seats." That fall, they signed to Mother Tongue records, releasing the single "Girl A, Girl B, Boy C" by the end of the year. Produced by Giles Martin, the son of the legendary Beatles producer George Martin, the record was named Single of the Week by both *Melody Maker* and *NME,* and My Life Story opened for both Blur and Pulp during the winter of 1994. In February, the group's second single, "Funny Ha Ha," was released. A year later, "You Don't Sparkle (In My Eyes)" reached the indie Top Ten, followed by the February 1995 release of their debut album, *Mornington Crescent.* Although the record received positive reviews, its release was hampered by threatened legal action from London Underground due to breach of copyright, but the issue vanished quickly. *Melody Maker* named *Mornington Crescent* one of the year's best albums, but the record didn't sell in large numbers. Distraught, Shillingford decided to have My Life Story perform a month-long residency at Dingwalls during February 1996, and if the band wasn't signed to a major label at the end of the four-Sunday stint, he was going to disband the group. Following the group's Dingwalls residency, My Life Story was signed to Parlophone Records.

As they recorded their major-label debut during the spring and summer, My Life Story played a series of high-profile gigs that increased their profile substantially. Late that summer, the group's first Parlophone single, "12 Reasons Why I Love Her" was released. It was followed by "Sparkle" in October and "The King of Kissingdom" in February, both of which received mixed reviews in the music press. *The Golden Mile,* My Life Story's long-delayed major label debut, was finally released in March of 1997. Although the band's audience was larger than ever, a critical backlash had begun, and the reviews for *The Golden Mile* were frequently harsh—*Select* labeled the record "the worst album ever made." —*Stephen Thomas Erlewine*

Mornington Crescent / Feb. 6, 1995 / Mother Tongue +++
My Life Story's debut album *Mornington Crescent* is a fitfully engaging collection of grandiose, orchestral pop. Jake Shillingford sounds like a bizarre cross between Martin Fry and Scott Walker, and while he occasionally has the wit and melodic skills to make his grand ambitions work—"Girl A, Girl B, Boy C" soars with its strings and wry lyrical observations—he too often relies on style, not substance, ultimately making *Mornington Crescent* a frustrating debut. —*Stephen Thomas Erlewine*

● **The Golden Mile** / Mar. 10, 1997 / Parlophone +++
With a bigger budget to support his delusions of grandeur, Jake Shillingford takes My Life Story completely over the top with their major-label debut, *The Golden Mile.* Shillingford hasn't grown much as a lyricist—if anything, his witticisms and asides are cutesier and more banal than before—but his sense of melody has sharpened, making the single "12 Reasons Why I Love Her" and "Sparkle" shimmer. Unfortunately, these are the exceptions, not the rule. Too often, the music is weighed down by Shillingford's preciousness and its own pretentiousness, which has the effect of making the weakest moments on the record—"You Can't Uneat the Apple," "Mr. Boyd," the matching "April 1st" and "November 5th," and the ludicrous "The King of Kissingdom"—seem positively comical. Even so, the lush, glossy production helps make such flaws more tolerable than the half-baked music of *Mornington Crescent,* and *The Golden Mile* consequently sounds like a qualified step forward for the band. —*Stephen Thomas Erlewine*

The Mystic Tide

f. 1965, Long Island, NY, db. 1967
Psychedelic, Garage Rock
Of the many garage bands who released unrecognized and obscure singles in the mid-'60s, the Mystic Tide were one of the very best. The Long Island group released four singles on their own labels in 1966 and 1967, mostly for distribution at their own gigs (and apparently they didn't sell too well there either). While the production on these is fairly raw, the group had genuine original talent, pursuing a dark, psychedelic vision

with overloaded, distorted guitar breaks. Their tunes (all written by guitarist Joe Docko) combined the minor-key melodies of British Invasion groups like the Zombies with the raunch of acts like Them. Unlike most other American groups following this path, however, they added a mysterioso (at times vaguely Middle Eastern) element that echoed the innovations of groups like the Doors, the Velvet Underground, and the very early Pink Floyd and Soft Machine, though the Mystic Tide most likely didn't hear any of these groups. Their sound and outlook were perhaps too foreboding for even local success, and the group disbanded in 1967, ironically finding a much greater audience when their singles were reissued for psych/garage collectors in the 1980s. —*Richie Unterberger*

● **Solid Ground** / 1994 / Distortions ✦✦✦✦

Both sides of their four singles, plus three earlier demos in a lighter, more Zombies-like style. The grinding "Frustration" and the ominous "Running Through the Night," featuring Docko's prickly psychedelic guitar, are garage classics; the lengthy instrumental "Psychedelic Journey" anticipates Pink Floyd's "Interstellar Overdrive"; and "I Search for a New Love" has delightful interweaving harmonies. The final seven tracks on this 18-cut disc were recorded by Docko over two decades later, with a lumbering sub-Hendrix approach (including two Mystic Tide remakes). Fortunately, their placement at the end of the CD means that they can be ignored with ease by discriminating listeners. —*Richie Unterberger*

N

Naked Eyes

f. 1981, **db.** 1984
Synth-pop, New Wave, New Romantic
A key figure in the synth-pop movement of the early '80s, the New Romantic duo Naked Eyes formed in Britain in 1981. Comprised of former schoolmates Pete Byrne (vocals) and Rob Fisher (keyboards), Naked Eyes debuted in March 1983 with the LP *Burning Bridges*, reissued in the US a month later (minus several tracks) as a self-titled effort. The lead single, a majestic cover of the Burt Bacharach-Hal David perennial "Always Something There to Remind Me," emerged as a hit on both sides of the Atlantic, reaching the US Top Ten on the strength of its video, which received heavy airplay on the fledgling MTV network. The American follow-up "Promises, Promises" (not the Bacharach/David composition) was also a major hit, and Naked Eyes' future looked bright; however, 1984's *Fuel for the Fire* fared poorly, its lone single "(What) In the Name of Love" barely scraping into the Top 40. The duo disbanded soon after; in 1988 Fisher resurfaced as one half of the pop duo Climie Fisher. —*Jason Ankeny*

Naked Eyes / 1983 / EMI America ◆◆◆◆
Naked Eyes were in peak form for their debut, showing a highly likable, warmer side to the often cold and detached synth-duo form. The songs they're best known for, "Always Something There to Remind Me," "Promises, Promises," and "When the Lights Go Down," are all included here, though the album can also be found in its entirety (save for one track) on the more readily available *Promises, Promises: The Very Best of Naked Eyes*. For some reason, Naked Eyes' debut was released in slightly different forms on either side of the Atlantic. *Naked Eyes*, released a month after its British counterpart, *Burning Bridges*, was given new artwork and dropped two tracks. Both tracks were reinstated for the *Very Best Of* collection. —*Chris Woodstra*

Burning Bridges / 1983 / EMI ◆◆◆◆
The synth duo's debut and finest moment was released in the UK as *Burning Bridges* a month before it was offered to US audiences in a slightly edited and rearranged form. The key tracks (namely the hits) are shared by both, but both versions have been made redundant by the *Very Best of* collection, which collects all but one track, "Could Be." "Could Be" can be found on the other collection, *Best of Naked Eyes*, released in 1991. —*Chris Woodstra*

Fuel for the Fire / 1984 / EMI America ◆◆
By late 1984, most synth-pop acts attempted to redefine themselves rather than be trapped by the genre's limited scope. Naked Eyes, however, didn't give up the fight, instead opting to re-create the formula of their debut. The results were predictably less interesting on the first outing, but *Fuel for Fire* did manage to recapture the magic at least once with "(What) In the Name of Love." All but two tracks were compiled on *Promises, Promises: The Very Best of Naked Eyes*. —*Chris Woodstra*

The Best of Naked Eyes / Apr. 31, 1991 / EMI America ◆◆◆◆
Best of Naked Eyes offers fifteen tracks of the synth-pop duo's best moments from their two US albums, 1983's *Naked Eyes* and 1984's *Burning Bridges*. The collection is surpassed by the more extensive *Very Best Of* from 1994, but is notable for the inclusion of one track, "Could Be," which the second collection excluded. —*Chris Woodstra*

● **Promises, Promises: The Very Best of Naked Eyes** / Apr. 19, 1994 / EMI America ◆◆◆◆
It seems odd that a group which really only released two albums' worth of material in the span of about 18 months should warrant two best-of collections released only three years apart. Nevertheless, *Promises, Promises: The Very Best of Naked Eyes* beats the competition by offering 20 tracks, including all four of the hits, most of the album tracks, a few

B-sides, and two versions of "Promises, Promises"—nearly all of the duo's recorded output. And while anything more than four songs is probably overkill for all but the new wave-obsessed, it is nice to have it all available in one package. —*Chris Woodstra*

Nas

b. Long Island, NY
Vocals / Hip Hop, East Coast Rap
Long Island rapper Nas, born Nasir Jones, immersed himself in hip-hop and street culture at age nine, the fruits of which can be heard on his 1994 debut, *Illmatic*. Nas got his big break when former 3rd Bass rapper MC Serch included his "Half Time" on the soundtrack of the film *Zebrahead*, which led to a deal with Serch's production company. *Illmatic* was released on Columbia in 1994 and attracted attention for its depiction of ghetto life and Nas' refusal to include much of the misogyny and violence of standard gangsta-rap, not to mention his admiration of Michael Jackson and the Jackson 5.

Nas' second album, *It Was Written*, was an immediate hit upon its release in the summer of 1996, entering the charts at No. 1, which far eclipsed the No. 12 peak of *Illmatic*. —*Steve Huey*

● **Illmatic** / Apr. 19, 1994 / Columbia ◆◆◆◆
Nas' debut album, *Illmatic*, is a dynamic display of unparalleled lyrical virtuosity, demonstrating his deep rhyming skills and his eye for lyrical detail. Married to a set of spare yet funky soundscapes produced by everyone from Pete Rock and Q-Tip to DJ Premier, Nas' rhymes are vital and alive, touching not only on portraits of ghetto life, but dreams and good times as well. Occasionally, the music sounds a little too similar, but there's no denying that *Illmatic* is a debut of monumental proportions. —*Leo Stanley*

It Was Written / Jul. 2, 1996 / Columbia ◆◆◆◆
For his second album, *It Was Written*, Nas has hired a bunch of hip-hop's biggest producers—including Dr. Dre, DJ Premier, Stretch, and Trackmasters—to help him create the musical bed for his daring, groundbreaking rhymes. Although that rhyme style isn't as startling on *It Was Written* as it was on his debut, *Illmatic*, Nas has deepened his talents, creating a complex series of rhymes that not only flow, but manage to tell coherent stories as well. Furthermore, Nas often concentrates on creating vignettes about life in the ghetto that never are apolitical or ambivalent. This time around, the production is more detailed and elaborate, which gives the music a wider appeal. Sometimes this is a detriment—Nas sounds better when he tries to keep it at street-level—but usually, Nas' lyrical force cuts through the commercial sheen. Combined with the spare but deep grooves, his rhymes have a resonance unmatched by most of his mid-'90s contemporaries. Because no matter how deep his lyrics are, his grooves are just as deep, and that bottomless funk and spare beats are what make *It Was Written* so compulsively listenable. —*Leo Stanley*

Johnny Nash

b. Aug. 19, 1940, Houston, TX
Vocals / Soul, Reggae, Pop-Rock
Native-Texan Johnny Nash experienced his first chart success in 1958 with the No.23 hit "A Very Special Love." By the end of the '60s, Nash had begun recording in Jamaica and formed his own record labels, Joda and Jad. He became one of the first artists to bring reggae into the pop mainstream, with the 1968 No.5 hit "Hold Me Tight," 1972's No.1 "I Can See Clearly Now," and a 1973 No.12 version of Bob Marley's "Stir It Up." —*Rick Clark*

I Can See Clearly Now / 1972 / Epic ✦✦✦✦
This is West Indian music for a pop audience, rhythmic and melodic. Nash helped open the mass-market doors to reggae. The title song and "Stir It Up" are winners. —*Hank Davis*

The Reggae Collection / Sep. 21, 1993 / Epic ✦✦✦✦
Nash was the first American singer to incorporate reggae rhythms, and as such deserves a lot of credit for paving the way for the acceptance of bona fide Jamaican performers. His own pop-soul-reggae concoctions, though, were often rather watery in comparison to the real thing. This brings together 20 of the reggae-style tracks he cut between 1968 and the mid-'70s, including his hits "Hold Me Tight," "Cupid," and "Stir It Up"; the version of "I Can See Clearly Now" is an alternate take. This leans too heavily on his 1972-75 Epic material without enough of his late-'60s work; the small hit "You Got Soul" is missing, and the delightfully light and soaring "Hold Me Tight" towers over most everything else here. Almost half the tracks were previously unreleased or previously unavailable in the US. —*Richie Unterberger*

● **The Best of Johnny Nash** / 1996 / Columbia ✦✦✦✦
The Best of Johnny Nash is a terrific collection of Johnny Nash's early-'70s pop-reggae crossover hits, highlighted by "Stir It Up" and "I Can See Clearly Now." —*Stephen Thomas Erlewine*

The Nashville Teens

f. Weybridge, Surrey, England
British Invasion
The Nashville Teens' "Tobacco Road" was one of the British Invasion's better one-shot hits. Their 1964 rearrangement of John Loudermilk's folkish tune, built around insistently hammering riffs and soulful dual lead vocals, was their only Top 20 entry in the US. Although they never had another hit in America and only had one other sizable hit in the UK (Loudermilk's "Google Eye"), the group continued to record singles throughout the rest of the '60s. The Teens never came close to matching their one taste of glory, commercially or aesthetically. Their ragged R&B covers didn't remotely match the Stones, Yardbirds or Pretty Things, and without any songwriting talent to speak of, they drifted rather aimlessly in search of an identity or style, stabbing at straight pop, folk-rock, and hard rock. Keyboardist John Hawken joined Renaissance in the late '60s. —*Richie Unterberger*

Tobacco Road / 1964 / One Way ✦✦✦
A representative album by the group, with lots of loud R&B, but not rough or tough enough to compete with the Rolling Stones, Kinks, et al. —*Bruce Eder*

Nashville Teens / 1974 / New World ✦✦✦
A mid-'70s reissue with some hard-to-find tracks that are actually superior to much of the released tracks from the 1960s. Probably the best single album by this band. —*Bruce Eder*

Remembering / 197 / Decca ✦✦✦

Live at the Red House / 1984 / Shanghai ✦✦

● **Best of the Nashville Teens** / 1993 / EMI ✦✦✦✦
The group recorded a fair amount of material in the '60s, almost all of which is included on this 24-track anthology, which contains their sole album (from 1964) and several singles. They had no songwriting talent (only two of these tunes are originals), and they drifted rather aimlessly in search of an identity and style, stabbing at straight pop, folk-rock, and hard rock. Some Shel Talmy-produced numbers from 1966 are of mild interest, as are some nicely arranged folk-pop tunes from 1965 (which suffer from mediocre vocals), but even British Invasion completists will be unimpressed by this collection. As a final insult, the mix of "Tobacco Road," which leads off this set, is notably inferior to the familiar hit vinyl version. —*Richie Unterberger*

Naughty by Nature

f. East Orange, NJ
Gangsta Rap, East Coast Rap
One of the finest new rap posses received some help from Queen Latifah on their 1991 debut and landed a huge hit with the naggingly incessant "O.P.P." Naughty By Nature scored another huge hit with their next release. *19 Naughty III* featured "Hip Hip Hooray," which rivaled "O.P.P." as a crossover smash and national catchphrase in 1993. —*John Floyd*

● **Naughty by Nature** / Sep. 3, 1991 / Tommy Boy ✦✦✦✦
This leering trio's first single, "O.P.P.," dominated the airwaves in the fall of 1991 on the strength of its home-truth bedroom message and its butt-hugging beat. Fans of the single will find plenty more in NBN's rollicking debut album. —*John Floyd*

19 Naughty III / Feb. 23, 1993 / Tommy Boy ✦✦✦✦
With its slamming beats and infectious hooks (exemplified by the hit single "Hip Hop Hooray"), *19 Naughty III*, Naughty by Nature's second album, proves that they're not a one-hit-wonder group. Although the

music is terrific, the lyrical posturing and misogyny can grow tiresome. —*Stephen Thomas Erlewine*

Poverty's Paradise / May 2, 1995 / Tommy Boy ✦✦✦
For their third album, Naughty by Nature do little to truly change their style. Some of the beats are a little slower and funkier, some of the rhymes are more dexterous, some of the rhythms are a little more complex—yet nothing distinguishes *Poverty's Paradise* from the group's two previous, and superior, records. —*Stephen Thomas Erlewine*

The Nazz

f. 1967, Philadelphia, PA, **db.** 1969
Psychedelic, Power Pop
The Nazz (named after a Yardbirds song, "The Nazz Are Blue") was a Philadelphia-based quartet formed in 1967 by guitarist and songwriter Todd Rundgren, bassist Carson Van Osten, drummer Thom Mooney, and vocalist and keyboard player Robert "Stewkey" Antoni. Rejecting the free-form psychedelic rock and hippie fashions of the day, the group harked back a couple of years to the British Invasion, performing short, catchy pop songs, mostly written by Rundgren (sometimes with a hard rock edge), and sporting suits and Beatle haircuts. They released their debut album, *Nazz*, in 1968 and scored a minor hit single with Rundgren's plaintive ballad "Hello, It's Me" in 1969 (it recharted in 1970, and Rundgren had a Top Five hit with a new version in 1973). Critics and a growing audience were charmed but the Nazz fell apart in 1969, largely because of Rundgren's ascendancy. Predictably, he went on to his greatest success after the split. —*William Ruhlmann*

Nazz / 1968 / Rhino ✦✦✦✦
Even though the voice of the Nazz was Robert "Stewkey" Antoni, it is hard not to think of the group as a dry run for guitarist Todd Rundgren's successful solo career. On their debut album, Rundgren wrote all but one of the songs and sang with Stewkey on several of them. The album featured the group's chart single, Rundgren's ballad "Hello It's Me," which would become a signature song for him after he re-recorded it in 1972. But that lush, romantic pop tune is not indicative of the Nazz's style. In fact, no one style is apparent on *Nazz:* Just as Rundgren would prove to be a pop chameleon, the Nazz absorbed and re-created various styles of the late '60s. The lead-off track, "Open My Eyes," was a complex pop-rock anthem. Many songs had a fashionable blues-based hard rock sound: "Back of Your Mind" was like Cream, "Wildwood Blues" like Blue Cheer, "When I Get My Plane" like the Who, "Lemming Song" like the Jimi Hendrix Experience. "But If That's the Way You Feel" was another delicate, Beach Boys-style ballad, complete with strings and harmonizing backup vocals. The Nazz imitated existing styles well, but at this point Rundgren wasn't ready to move beyond imitation, and the album's diversity must have confused the teenyboppers who bought it on the basis of "Hello It's Me." —*William Ruhlmann*

Nazz Nazz / 1969 / Rhino ✦✦✦
Unlike the Nazz's first album, which found them veering from one style to another in succeeding songs, the group's second album, *Nazz Nazz*, clearly was the work of a particular entity. Unfortunately, in choosing one dominant musical direction, the Nazz had opted to return to the psychedelic pop sound of 1967, with its lightness, eclecticism, and whimsical humor. Keyboard textures dominated songs devoted to such subjects as a pig named "Meridian Leeward," sung in unison falsetto, and the album concluded with the 11-minute, multipart "A Beautiful Song," which boasted a string arrangement and lots of Todd Rundgren guitar playing. (There were still forays into other styles, though, notably the Chicago blues sound of "Kiddie Boy" and "Featherbedding Lover," complete with horns, and two attempts to re-create the hit ballad style of "Hello It's Me" in "Gonna Cry Today" and "Letters Don't Count.") As a result, a group that had sounded overly trendy on its first album sounded way out-of-date on its second. Rundgren wrote all the songs, but having to come up with another album's worth of tunes in six months may have strained even his prolific nature; the material was thin. —*William Ruhlmann*

Nazz III / 1970 / Rhino ✦✦✦
Nazz III was recorded at the same time as *Nazz Nazz* and intended to be the second record in a two-LP set. It also featured the lead vocals of guitarist Todd Rundgren rather than the Nazz's usual singer, Robert "Stewkey" Antoni. But *Nazz Nazz* was pared down to a single LP, the group split with Rundgren and bassist Carson Van Osten departing, and Antoni re-recorded the vocals himself, with the album not seeing release until November 1970. For all that turmoil, *Nazz III* marks a real development in composer Rundgren's previously imitative style; songs like "Some People" and "Only One Winner" could easily fit on one of his solo albums. And this is the band's most diverse album, from the cover of Paul Revere & the Raiders' "Kicks" to the parody of Archie Bell & the Drells' "Tighten Up," of course called "Loosen Up." —*William Ruhlmann*

● **The Best of Nazz** / 1983 / Rhino ✦✦✦✦
Contains good examples of the band's powerful uptempo material
("Open My Eyes"), the kind of Rundgren ballad material that defined the
group to its pop audience ("Hello, It's Me"), and some interesting covers
("Kicks," a previously unreleased "Train Kept A-Rollin'"). —*William
Ruhlmann*

Fred Neil

b. 1937, St. Petersburg, FL
Guitar, Vocals / Folk, Singer-Songwriter, Folk-Rock
Moody, bluesy, and melodic, Fred Neil was one of the most compelling
folk-rockers to emerge from Greenwich Village in the mid-'60s. His
albums showcased his extraordinarily low, rich voice on intensely personal and reflective compositions, sounding like a cross between Tim
Buckley and Tim Hardin. His influence was subtle but significant;
before forming the Lovin' Spoonful, John Sebastian played harmonica
on Neil's first album, which also featured guitarist Felix Pappalardi, who
went on to produce Cream. The Jefferson Airplane featured Neil's "Other
Side of This Life" prominently in their concerts, and dedicated a couple
of songs ("Ballad of You and Me and Pooneil" and "House at Pooneil
Corner") to him. On the B-side of "Crying" is Neil's "Candy Man," one of
Roy Orbison's bluesiest efforts. Stephen Stills has mentioned Neil as an
influence on his guitar playing. Most famously, Nilsson took Fred's
"Everybody's Talkin'" into the Top Ten as the theme to the movie *Midnight Cowboy*.
For all his tangential influence, Neil himself has remained an enigmatic, mysterious figure. His recorded output was formidable but
sparse. His drumless debut, *Little Bit of Rain* (which did have additional
instruments), is one of the best efforts from the era in which folk was
just beginning its transition to folk-rock. The bluesiest of his albums, it
contained some of his best songs, including the title track, "Other Side of
This Life," and "Candy Man." His true peak was his follow-up, *Fred Neil*,
which made a full transition to electric instruments. Less bluesy in tenor,
it featured "Everybody's Talkin'," as well as an equal gem in "The Dolphins."
Neil's subsequent slide into obscurity was strange and quick. *Sessions*, from 1968, was a much more casual and slapdash affair that
included some instrumental jamming. Always a recluse, he retreated to
his home in Coconut Grove, FL, after achieving cult success, and hasn't
released anything since a live album in 1971. His current obscurity is
enforced by an absence of domestic compact-disc reissues of his best
work, a situation that should be rectified. —*Richie Unterberger*

Bleecker & MacDonald / 1964 / Elektra ✦✦✦✦
Neil's Greenwich Village coffeehouse roots are in strongest evidence on
this album (later retitled *Little Bit of Rain*). The drummerless (but not
entirely acoustic) LP is also his bluesiest recording. The uniformly
strong tracks include "Other Side of This Life" and "Candy Man."
—*Richie Unterberger*

● **Very Best of Fred Neil** / 1986 / See For Miles ✦✦✦✦
It doesn't include any of his Elektra tracks, but this is a good compilation
of his Capitol work, including all of the 1967 album *Fred Neil* (which
featured Stephen Stills) and four tracks from his follow-up LP *Sessions*.
Contains "Everybody's Talkin'," "Green Rocky Road," and the beautiful
"The Dolphins." —*Richie Unterberger*

Rick Nelson (Eric Hilliard Nelson)

b. May 8, 1940, Teaneck, NJ, **d.** Dec. 31, 1985, Dallas, TX
*Guitar, Vocals / Rock 'n' Roll, Country-Rock, Rockabilly, Pop-Rock,
Teen Idol*
Rick Nelson was one of the very biggest of the '50s teen idols, so it took
a while for him to attain the same level of critical respectability as other
early rock greats. Yet now the consensus is that he made some of the finest pop-rock recordings of his era. Sure, he had more promotional push
than any other rock musician of the '50s; no, he wasn't the greatest
singer; and yes, Elvis, Gene Vincent, Carl Perkins, and others rocked
harder. But Nelson was extraordinarily consistent during the first five
years of his recording career, crafting pleasant pop-rockabilly hybrids
with ace session players, and projecting an archetype of the sensitive,
reticent young adult with his accomplished vocals. He also played a
somewhat underestimated role in rock 'n' roll's absorption into mainstream America—how bad could rock be if it was featured on one of
America's favorite family situation comedies on a weekly basis?
Nelson entered professional entertainment before his tenth birthday,
when he appeared with father Ozzie (once a jazz musician), mother Harriet, and brother David on a radio comedy series based around the family. By the early '50s, the series was on television, and Ricky grew into a
teenager in public. He was just the right age to have his life turned
around by rock 'n' roll in 1956, and started his recording career almost
accidentally the following year. The story's sometimes been told that he
had no professional singing ambitions until he recorded his debut single
to impress a girlfriend. The single, a cover of Fats Domino's "I'm

Walkin'," that went to No. 4, was helped immensely (as all of his early
singles would be) by plugs on the *Ozzie and Harriet* TV show.
So far the script was adhering to the Pat Boone teen idol prototype—a
whitewash of an R&B hit stealing the thunder from the pop audience,
sung by a young, good-looking fella with barely any musical experience
to speak of. What happened next was easy to predict commercially, but
surprisingly satisfying musically as well. Nelson was a fairly hip kid
who preferred the rockabilly of Carl Perkins and Elvis Presley to the fodder dished out for teen idols, and over the next five years he would offer
his own brand of rockabilly music, albeit one with some smooth Hollywood production touches and occasional pure pop ballads. Nelson
recruited one of the greatest early rock guitarists, James Burton, to supply authentic licks (another great guitarist, Joe Maphis, played on some
early sides). Some of his best and toughest songs ("Believe What You
Say," "It's Late") were written by Johnny and/or Dorsey Burnette, who
had previously been in one of the best rockabilly combos, the Johnny
Burnette Rock 'N Roll Trio. Ricky could rock pretty hard when he
wanted to, as on "Be-Bop Baby" and "Stood Up," though in a polished
fashion that wasn't quite as wild and threatening as rockabilly's Southern originators.
Nelson really hit his stride, though, with midtempo numbers and ballads that provided a more secure niche for his calm vocals and narrow
range. From 1957 to 1962, he was about the highest-selling singer in the
US except for Elvis, making the Top 40 about 30 times. "Poor Little Fool"
and "Lonesome Town" (1958) were early indications of his ballad style;
in the early '60s, "Travelin' Man," "Young World," "Teen Age Idol," and
other hits pointed to a more countrified, mature style as he honed it on
his 21st birthday (by which time he would shorten his billing from
"Ricky" to "Rick"). He could still play rockabilly from time to time, the
most memorable example being "Hello, Mary Lou" (co-written by Gene
Pitney), with its electrifying James Burton solos.
Nelson was lured away from the Imperial label by a mammoth 20-
year contract with Decca in 1963 (which would be terminated prematurely in the mid-'70s), and for a year or so the hits continued, at a less
frenetic pace. Early 1964's "For You," however, would be his last big
smash of the '60s. The fault wasn't all the Beatles and changing music
trends—on both singles and albums, much of the material was either
substandard pop or dusty Tin Pan Alley standards, although isolated
tracks still generated some sparks. He wasn't exactly starving, as he continued to appear on *Ozzie and Harriet*. But by the mid-'60s even that
institution was declining in popularity, leading to its cancellation in
1966.
Nelson had a strong country feel to much of his material from the
beginning, and by the late '60s it was becoming dominant. He covered
straight country material by the likes of Willie Nelson and Doug Kershaw, and formed one of the earliest country-rock groups, the Stone
Canyon Band, with musicians who had played (or would play with)
Poco, Buck Owens, Little Feat, and Roger McGuinn. A cover of Bob
Dylan's "She Belongs to Me" made the Top 40 in 1970, but his country-
rock outings attracted more critical acclaim than commercial success,
until 1972's "Garden Party." A rare self-composed number, based around
the frosty reception granted his contemporary material at a rock 'n' roll
oldies show, it became his last Top Ten hit.
Nelson would continue to record off and on for the next dozen years,
and toured constantly, yet he was unable to capitalize on his assets. A
big part of the problem was that although Nelson wanted to play contemporary music, he didn't write much of his own material, which was a
basic precept of self-respecting rock acts after the advent of the Beatles.
Nor did he tap into good outside compositions, and there's little of interest on the albums he recorded over the last decade or so of his life. He
died (along with his fiancée) in a private plane crash on December 31,
1985, on his way to a New Year's Eve gig in Dallas, at the age of 45.
—*Richie Unterberger*

Hey Pretty Baby / 1986 / Rockstar ✦✦✦
If you're looking for Imperial-era material that's not on the EMI best-of
compilation CDs, this 16-track British import offers a good selection.
Much of this is not present on those domestic CDs, and the collection
emphasizes his more rocking side, with James Burton frequently contributing his tasty licks. But it doesn't compare with the best of his vintage material, though it's pleasant enough (and quite innocuous); most
listeners would be content to pick up the greatest-hits comps and leave it
at that. —*Richie Unterberger*

★ **Legendary Masters** / 1990 / EMI America ✦✦✦✦✦
Legendary Masters compiles all of the hits Ricky Nelson released for
Imperial Records in the late '50s, including "Be-Bop Baby," "Stood Up,"
"Lonesome Town," "It's Late," "Poor Little Fool," "Sweeter Than You,"
"Just a Little Too Much," "Never Be Anyone Else but You," and "Believe
What You Say." A few essential items are missing—such as the Verve
sides "A Teenager's Romance" and "I'm Walking"—and it would have
been nice if the disc had extended into the early '60s, so songs like "Trav-
elin' Man" and "Mary Lou" could have been included, but *Legendary*

Masters remains a vital collection from one of the most undervalued early rock 'n' rollers. —*Stephen Thomas Erlewine*

Best of 1963-1975 / 1990 / MCA ✦✦✦
No longer Rockin' Ricky, but Responsible Rick, his Decca output was wildly inconsistent. The early efforts like "Fools Rush In" and "String Along" still feature guitarist James Burton prominently. —*Bill Dahl*

Best of Rick Nelson, Vol. 2 / Mar. 26, 1991 / Capitol ✦✦✦
Focusing primarily on Rick's early-'60s material for Imperial, this 27-cut disc is not quite as rocking as Vol. 1, but still offers plenty of worthy moments. It includes all of his massive, mid-tempo teen-idol ballad hits of the era: "Young World," "A Wonder like You," "Teenage Idol," "It's Up to You," and the No.1 hit "Travelin' Man." Teen ballads they might have been, but James Burton's masterful guitar licks and Nelson's assured, committed delivery placed them leagues above other teen-idol hits of the period. Of more interest to serious fans are the inclusion of several minor hit singles and covers of R&B tunes. And of course, there's the first-class rockabilly hit "Hello Mary Lou" (penned by Gene Pitney), perhaps his best recording of the decade. His surprisingly raucous cover of "Summertime" features, amazingly, the same bass line used as a hook on the Blues Magoos' psych-pop-garage hit "We Ain't Got Anything Yet" years later. The pleasures of this CD are modest but consistent. —*Richie Unterberger*

Collection / Jul. 1, 1992 / Castle ✦✦✦

Stay Young: The Epic Recordings / Aug. 31, 1993 / Epic ✦✦✦
Stay Young is an entertaining overview of Rick Nelson's country-tinged years at Epic, proving that he recorded plenty of worthwhile material in the '70s. —*Stephen Thomas Erlewine*

Rockin' with Ricky / 1996 / Ace ✦✦✦✦
Originally released as an LP in 1984, the CD version of this collection of Nelson's hardest-rocking early material doubles in length to include a whopping 32 tracks (on one disc) from the late '50s and early '60s. This has most of his uptempo smashes, a la "Be-Bop Baby," "Waitin' in School," and "Believe What You Say," with a host of LP tracks, many of them covers of songs made famous by Elvis, Carl Perkins, Roy Orbison, and the like. The two volumes of greatest hits on EMI are more well-rounded, and on the whole better, retrospectives of his classic era. This is pretty good proof that he could rock respectably, though, with some good cuts that are hard to find on reissues, like "You're So Fine" and "Poor Loser." —*Richie Unterberger*

The Neon Philharmonic

f. 1967, Nashville, TN, **db.** 1975
Psychedelic
Such was the influence of psychedelic music in the late '60s that even pop-based acts like the Fifth Dimension, Kenny Rogers, and the Association felt obliged to put in their two cents' worth. Such was the case with the Neon Philharmonic, which was primarily a vehicle for songwriter/arranger/keyboardist Tupper Saussy. Also featuring singer Don Gant, the group had an easy-going, not-too-memorable Top 20 pop hit in mid-1969, "Morning Girl." Their debut album, *The Moth Confesses*, was a much stranger piece of work, sounding something like Jimmy Webb on acid. For all of its ambitious orchestral arrangements and operatic lyrical reach, it has dated in the most embarrassing and silly of fashions, sounding like the aural equivalent of the middle-class accountant who decides to take acid with his kids in a misguided attempt to get with it.

The Nashville-based Saussy's primary credit prior to the Neon Philharmonic was his contributions to *The Swinger's Guide to Mary Poppins*, which featured jazz renditions of songs from the children's film. This, and even the "Morning Girl" single, weren't exactly the sort of resume credits that led one to expect an ambitious song cycle. That's what he cooked up with *The Moth Confesses*, however, though the bloated arrangements, Gant's white-bread vocals, and the overwrought, sentimental lyrics came closer to Rod McKuen than Van Dyke Parks. The NH did manage another album, as well as a few singles, and were active as late as 1975. Gant was a session vocalist before dying in the mid-'80s. Saussy, as befitting a man with such unpredictable interests, became an anti-tax activist, going underground to avoid Federal authorities in the 1980s. —*Richie Unterberger*

● **The The Moth Confesses** / 1996 / Sundazed ✦✦✦
A timepiece in the less impressive sense of the term, seeking to fuse the conceptual ambition and sophisticated production of *Pet Sounds* and *Song Cycle* with MOR pop. It doesn't work that well, particularly since songwriter Tupper Saussy is clearly more well-versed in (and comfortable with) MOR pop. The collision of grandoise romantic songs, rococo string arrangements, and a touch of psychedelic experimentation is so bizarre that it exerts a strange fascination, but it doesn't make for durable music. The album included the hit single, "Morning Girl"; the CD reissue adds six bonus cuts from non-LP singles that are more straightforward than the bulk of *The Moth Confesses*. —*Richie Unterberger*

The Nerves

f. 1975, **db.** 1984
New Wave, Power Pop
They could've been contenders had they stayed together long enough, but the Nerves, despite their brief existence, were one of the most exciting bands in power pop. Formed by Jack Lee, Peter Case, and Paul Collins in 1975, their career was over by 1978, but they produced a great EP that featured the power-pop classic "Hanging on the Telephone," which was later recorded (and wonderfully so) by Blondie. Ultimately, having three talented songwriters in one band hurried the demise of the Nerves, and all three principles found greater happiness and success with their new bands, although Jack Lee (arguably the most talented songwriter of the three) had the shortest career and eventually dropped out of sight after a fine solo record (*Jack Lee's Greatest Hits, Vol. 1*) in 1981. Case went on to form the Plimsouls, who recorded two good records and a transcendent pop song, "A Million Miles Away." After breaking up in 1984, Case recorded as a roots-rock solo act for the rest of the decade and into the '90s, although there is a rumor he's put the Plimsouls back together. Collins formed the Beat (later Paul Collins' Beat), who were merely OK, and has done little since the mid-'80s. —*John Dougan*

● **Nerves [EP]** / 1976 / Nerves ✦✦✦✦
There was only one EP; it had four songs, and each one is great. Although I'm sure this record has vanished from the face of the earth, if you run across it, snatch it up; it's wonderful. Best song: Paul Collins' "Working Too Hard." There is a French import release from 1986 that includes outtakes and some related ephemera. But, sadly, this EP stands as the sum total of a great band. —*John Dougan*

Notre Demo / 1981 / Good Vibration ✦✦✦

Michael Nesmith

b. Dec. 30, 1943, Houston, TX
Guitar, Vocals / Country-Rock, Singer-Songwriter, Folk-Rock
Even when he was a member of the '60s teen sensation the Monkees, Michael Nesmith was a respected songwriter and musician. Before he joined the group in 1966, he had written several singles, and two of his songs—"Different Drum" and "Mary Mary"—were recorded, respectively, by the Stone Poneys and Paul Butterfield. In the Monkees, Nesmith was the only member to consistently write songs and he was the only one who knew how to play an instrument proficiently. So, it isn't surprising that after he left the Monkees in 1969, he was the only member to sustain a solo career. What is surprising is that his late-'60s and early-'70s works were among the most groundbreaking country-rock recordings of the era. Throughout the 1970s, '80s and '90s, Nesmith continued to record sporadically, in addition to pioneer the concept of music video with his communications company, Pacific Arts.

Nesmith was born December 30, 1943, in Houston, Texas. He listened to the blues and played saxophone while growing up, but after spending two years in the Air Force, Nesmith became fascinated with folk and learned to play the guitar. He played around the area, but then moved to Memphis to play back-up guitar on recordings for Stax-Volt. Nesmith moved to Los Angeles in the mid-'60s and formed the folk-rock duo Mike and John with John London. He also recorded several singles as a solo act before auditioning to join the Monkees in 1965.

The Monkees TV show ran from 1966 to 1968. During its first few years, the show was a big hit in America, especially with teenagers. The group's popularity with teenagers and its fabricated origins didn't earn them respect within much of the rock 'n' roll intelligencia, nor did the fact that the members did not play any instruments on their first three records. Nesmith led the fight to have the Monkees play on their own records, as well as contribute some songs to each release. Colgems, the band's record label, acquiesced and the first album to feature the Monkees playing their own instruments was 1967's *Headquarters*. In 1968, Nesmith recorded a solo album called *Wichita Train Whistle Songs* for Dot Records, and left the band—then only a trio—one year later.

Nesmith's first act independent of the Monkees was the formation of the First National Band, with old friend John London on bass, John Ware on drums, and one of country music's best steel guitarists, Red Rhodes. The group signed to RCA Victor and released two albums in 1970, *Magnetic South* and *Loose Salute*. The single "Joanne" hit the pop Top 25, and "Silver Moon" also charted later in the year. Nesmith added younger members for 1971's *Nevada Fighter*, and credited it to the Second National Band. The title track skirted the bottom of the charts for several weeks, but Nesmith provided the Nitty Gritty Dirt Band with their hit, "Some of Shelly's Blues." The following year, the National Band released *Tantamount to Treason*.

Michael Nesmith dropped the group credit later that year, recording *And the Hits Keep Comin'* as a solo artist—though Red Rhodes continued to play with him. Nesmith's 1973 album *Pretty Much Your Standard Stash* was his last for RCA Victor, as he formed the music/communications label Pacific Arts in 1974. The following year he released *The Prison* and co-wrote Olivia Newton-John's hit "Let It Shine." Nesmith re-entered the charts with 1977's *From a Radio Engine to a Photon Wing;* the single "Rio" was a hit in the UK, and a filmed version of the song helped develop the concept of music video.

In 1977, Nesmith furthered his efforts in the field of music video by creating a TV chart show called *Popclips;* Warner bought the idea from him and later developed it into MTV. A stop-gap live album (*Live at the Palais*) appeared in 1978, while *Infinite Rider on the Big Dogma* (Nesmith's last solo album for 13 years) was released the following year. During the '80s, Pacific Arts became the most important video publishing company in America. Nesmith moved into film and TV production, winning the first Video Grammy award in 1981 for *Elephant Parts*. He returned to the music business in 1989, appearing with the Monkees once on stage during their reunion tour. Nesmith also released a compilation of rare solo tracks called *The Newer Stuff* for England's Awareness Records. Rhino Records followed two years later with the best of his early-'70s material called *The Older Stuff*. In 1992, Nesmith released his first album of new material in 13 years, *...Tropical Campfire's....* Four years later, he reunited with the Monkees again, to record *Justus*, which was the first Monkees album since 1968 to feature all four original members. —*John Bush*

Mike Nesmith Presents the Wichita Train Whistle Sings / 1968 / Dot ♦♦
Nesmith stepped away from the Monkees for this instrumental rendering of many of the songs he'd written for the Monkees. Looking back on the record, with its experimentation with musical styles, it seems to point to some of the music Nesmith would make on Pacific Arts. For that reason, the album is somewhat interesting, though it's certainly not a necessity for your Nesmith collection. —*Jim Worbois*

Loose Salute / 1970 / Pacific Arts ♦♦♦
With this record, Nesmith's momentum builds as this album is even better than the first. While the single from this album didn't do as well as his previous hit, it was a better song and kicks off the album nicely. Also, steel player extraordinaire "Red" Rhodes is beginning to take a more dominant role in the sound of the band. Of special interest are Nesmith's third go at recording "Listen to the Band," a fine cover of Patsy Cline's "I Fall to Pieces," and his renewed interest in Latin rhythms. —*Jim Worbois*

Magnetic South / 1970 / Pacific Arts ♦♦♦♦
This fine collection not only features Nesmith originals (and his first solo hit) but one of the most interesting versions of "Beyond the Blue Horizon" ever committed to vinyl. For nearly six minutes we follow a day in the life of the singer, from the minute he wakes in the morning and goes off to work on his tractor until the time he returns at day's end. Also, at least two of the Nesmith originals were songs from his Monkees days but the Monkees versions of these songs would not be heard until the issue of the *Missing Links* series nearly 20 years later. —*Jim Worbois*

Nevada Fighter / 1971 / Pacific Arts ♦♦♦
This album stands in contrast to the previous two, in part because of the use of several members of Elvis' band, which gives the album a slightly different sound. Also notable is the fact that Nesmith only wrote half of the tracks. Still, the songs he wrote were as strong as anything he'd written to this point, and the covers he chose fit well with the feel and spirit of his own material. —*Jim Worbois*

Tantamount to Treason / 1972 / Pacific Arts ♦♦♦
Tantamount to Treason has a lazy feel to it, perhaps inspired by the beer recipe Papa Nes includes in the album's liner notes. That laziness is the reason the album is not as listenable as the previous three records, since you almost need to be "in the mood" to put this one on. That said, it's still quite a nice album and is worth tracking down. —*Jim Worbois*

And the Hits Just Keep on Comin' / 1972 / Pacific Arts ♦♦♦♦
If you don't own this record, there is a huge hole in your collection. Nesmith's own version of "Different Drum" (a song that introduced Linda Ronstadt to many of us back in 1968 and that most of us had only heard Nesmith do as a speeded up, mumbled "audition" on an old Monkees episode) may be the key to lure you in, but every song is a gem. This is easily some of Nesmith's finest work as both a songwriter and an artist. Also, between Nesmith and Red Rhodes, the sound is so full that it's easy to forget that a full band wasn't used in creating this record. —*Jim Worbois*

Pretty Much Your Standard Ranch Stash / 1973 / Pacific Arts ♦♦♦♦
Despite the comment inside the cover that "After two or three months this album may lose potency although some of the aroma may linger," this record holds up some 20 years later as one of Nesmith's finest. He continues to mix originals and a nice selection of covers as before, but somehow this record feels more "comfortable" than his previous efforts. This seems to be, in part, due to the strong musical bond between

Nesmith and steel player Red Rhodes. If the "Buy This Record" inducement on the front cover doesn't make this a must for your collection, one listen to the music inside will. —*Jim Worbois*

The Prison / 1974 / Pacific Arts ♦♦
If Nesmith's albums are listened to in chronological order, this record is startling in how different it is to his previous work, especially the previous two records. It may even be a little off-putting. Accepted on its own, it's actually a nice album. That said, it's not one of those records one feels compelled to listen to more than a few times. —*Jim Worbois*

From a Radio Engine to the Photon Wing / 1977 / Pacific Arts ♦♦
"Rio" is probably the best-known song on this album as well as the most memorable. It seems that most of the tracks are meant to evoke a mood rather than be actual songs and, for that reason, they tend to be a bit more interesting on their own rather than as a collection. —*Jim Worbois*

Live at Palais / 1978 / Pacific Arts ♦♦
On this album, which was recorded while on tour in Australia in 1977, Nesmith reintroduces some of the music from his years on RCA. These are not mere copies though each song is performed differently, and, in each case, is presented as a longer version than the original. These songs obviously still mean something to their writer. —*Jim Worbois*

Infinite Rider on the Big Dogma / 1979 / Pacific Arts ♦♦♦
This is easily Nesmith's most interesting record from the '70s Pacific Arts material, and the one that most often calls for repeated listenings. By this time, he was getting heavily into video, so a number of these tracks were also turned into music videos (check out the Grammy-winning *Elephant Parts*). While not a must, it's still a record worth searching out. —*Jim Worbois*

Newer Stuff / 1989 / Rhino ♦♦♦
This compilation of later solo material is often glossy and overreaching but still quite impressive. —*Jeff Tamarkin*

The Older Stuff: Best of Michael Nesmith (1970-1973) / 1991 / Rhino ♦♦♦♦
Post-Monkees country-oriented material is proof that at least one member of the "pre-fab four" possessed genuine musical talent. —*Jeff Tamarkin*

Tropical Campfires / Oct. 27, 1992 / Pacific Arts ♦♦♦
Nesmith plays desert music—quiet, contemplative, dignified—embellished, as the album title suggests, with splashes of lush tropical rhythms. His yearning vocals are ably supported by a cast of crack sessioneers, including the legendary Red Rhodes on pedal steel. Nesmith pens nine of the disc's 12 tracks, the others being covers of the samba chestnut "Brazil" and two Cole Porter tunes. Somehow, *Tropical Campfires* makes for exceedingly pleasant (if mellow) listening overall. The disc's highlight is Nesmith's weepy "Moon over the Rio Grande"; close your eyes and hear the campfire crackle and the coyotes wail. —*Roch Parisien*

● **Complete** / Sep. 28, 1993 / Pacific Arts ♦♦♦♦
All of Michael Nesmith and the First National Band's three albums are collected on this superb two-disc set, proving what a surprisingly inventive musician the former Monkee is. —*Stephen Thomas Erlewine*

Garden / 1994 / Rio Royal ♦♦

Neu!

f. 1971, Dusseldorf, Germany, db. 1975
Electronic, Kraut-Rock
While little-known and relatively unheralded during their brief existence, the Krautrock duo Neu! cast a large shadow over later generations of musicians, and served as a major influence on artists as diverse as David Bowie, Sonic Youth, Pere Ubu, Julian Cope and Stereolab.

Neu! formed in Dusseldorf, Germany in 1971 after multi-instrumentalists Michael Rother and Klaus Dinger both split from Kraftwerk. Recorded in the space of four days with Can producer Conrad Plank, the duo's self-titled debut appeared early in 1972, and quickly established their affection for minimalist melodies and lock-groove rhythms. While virtually ignored throughout the rest of the world, the album sold extremely well in West Germany, resulting in a tour with support from Guru Guru's Uli Trepte and Eberhard Krahnemann.

Rother and Dinger returned to the studio in 1973 for *Neu! 2*, where a shortfall of cash allowed the duo to complete only two songs, "Super" and "Neueschnee," which they subsequently remixed at varying and disorienting speeds in order to flesh out a full-length album. After the record's release, Rother joined Dieter Moebius and Joachim Roedelius of Cluster to form Harmonia, but Neu! officially reunited in 1975 to record *Neu! 75*. After its release, they again disbanded; Rother continued on as a solo performer, while Dinger and drummer Hans Lampe formed La Dusseldorf. In the mid-'80s, Rother and Dinger reformed yet again, although the recording sessions, titled *Neu! 4*, did not officially surface until 1996. —*Jason Ankeny*

Neu / 1972 / Billingsgate ✦✦✦✦
Neu!'s visionary debut is an intensely visceral record that reinvents rock in its own visage: a shifting soundscape of drones, feedback, proto-ambient textures, processed effects, and industrial rhythms hung upon minimalist melodies, the album has few precedents, and the fingerprints of its influence are still smeared across experimental music decades later. —*Jason Ankeny*

Neu 2 / 1973 / United Artists ✦✦✦✦
A perverse effort, *Neu! 2* mocks the very concept of recorded music: when a lack of cash forced the group to curtail their studio sessions after finishing only a handful of songs, they simply remixed the singles "Super" and "Neueschnee" at various speeds—complete with scratches and pops—to ensure enough material for a full-length LP. Other tracks consist simply of music being played back in the studio, ending when the needle is pulled off the turntable; another concludes with the sound of a cassette being eaten by a tape machine. Confrontational, subversive, and brilliant. —*Jason Ankeny*

Neu 75 / 1975 / United Artists ✦✦✦
A work of polar extremes, *Neu! 75* is essentially a group record in name only; anticipating the duo's imminent breakup, the album splits evenly between the diametrically opposed work of Klaus Dinger and Michael Rother, resulting in a jarring juxtaposition of Rother's ambient minimalism and Dinger's proto-punk abrasion. —*Jason Ankeny*

72 Live! / 1996 / Captain Trip ✦✦✦

Neu! 4 / 1996 / Captain Trip ✦✦✦
Recorded sometime in the mid-'80s but not released until over a decade later, *Neu! 4* picks up where the duo left off in 1975, exploring the extremes of both white noise and ambient beauty. Like *Neu! 2*, the album fills out with remixes of the basic tracks, but where the earlier effort simply varied playback speeds, the material on *Neu! 4* undergoes radical, even alien transformations. Much of the record predates 1990s electronic music with remarkable foresight: "Fly Dutch II" is a spacey techno loop that stakes out territory later claimed by Mouse on Mars, "Danzing" is a brutal electro experiment, and "86 Commercial Trash" is constructed around samples from German television advertisements. —*Jason Ankeny*

Neutral Milk Hotel

f. 1989, Ruston, LA
Lo-Fi, Indie Rock
The self-described "fuzz-folk" project Neutral Milk Hotel was one of the primary outgrowths of the Elephant 6 Recording Company collective, a coterie of like-minded, lo-fi indie groups—including the Apples (in stereo), the Olivia Tremor Control and Secret Square—who shared musicians, ideas and sensibilities. While ranging in sound and concept from solo acoustic work to full band performances, Neutral Milk Hotel essentially remained the work of Jeff Mangum, a singer-songwriter from the remote town of Ruston, Louisiana.

Ruston was also home to Robert Schneider (later of the Apples), as well as William Cullen Hart and Bill Doss (who formed the Olivia Tremor Control); throughout high school, the aspiring musicians—all influenced by the likes of the Beatles, the Beach Boys, the Zombies, Pink Floyd and Sonic Youth—exchanged home recordings and played in each other's bands. Neutral Milk Hotel first took shape in 1989 as a noise-rock trio which played its debut gig at a local laundromat; a year later Mangum, Hart and Doss moved to Athens, Georgia to form the group Cranberry Life Cycle, which later became Synthetic Flying Machine (and ultimately the Olivia Tremor Control) after Mangum's departure.

In 1993, he and Schneider relocated to Denver, Colorado, where Schneider soon founded the Apples (in stereo). Eventually, Mangum gravitated to New York, and resumed recording under the Neutral Milk Hotel aegis. After a series of singles, cassettes and compilation tracks, Mangum travelled back to Denver to record the critically-acclaimed 1996 album *On Avery Island* on Schneider's four-track machine; in the spring of 1997, he again returned to Colorado to begin work on the follow-up. —*Jason Ankeny*

● **On Avery Island** / Mar. 26, 1996 / Merge ✦✦✦✦
Like their Elephant 6 labelmates and kindred spirits Olivia Tremor Control's *Music from the Unrealized Film Script "Dusk at Cubist Castle,"* Neutral Milk Hotel's debut *On Avery Island* is an inscrutable concept album, a chronicle of an insular world told in a remarkably universal language. A fuzzy masterpiece of experimental lo-fi recording, the album wraps its ragged pop songs in ribbons of loops, marching-band squawks, and Casio noodling; the opener "Song Against Sex" is as much a manifesto as a kickoff, a self-propelled marvel hopped up on rapid-fire wordplay and a stunningly ramshackle melody punctuated by bloated trombone moans. Throughout the record, Jeff Mangum's wheels threaten to fly off at any point—his songs are cryptic and crazed, his ideas fast and furious, and together they force the home-recording concept out of the basement and into a brave new world. —*Jason Ankeny*

The Neville Brothers

f. 1977, New Orleans, LA
Soul, Funk, R&B, New Orleans R&B
Throughout their long careers as both solo performers and as members of the group which bore their family name, the Neville Brothers proudly carried the torch of their native New Orleans' rich R&B legacy. Although the four siblings—Arthur, Charles, Aaron and Cyril—did not officially unite under the Neville Brothers aegis until 1977, all had crossed musical paths in the past, while also enjoying success with other unrelated projects: eldest brother Art was the first to tackle a recording career, when in 1964 his high school band the Hawketts cut "Mardi Gras Mambo," a song which later became the annual carnival's unofficial anthem. Both Aaron and Charles sang with the Hawketts as well, and when Art joined the Navy in 1958, he handed Aaron the group's vocal reins.

Two years later, Aaron scored his first solo hit, "Over You;" in 1966, he notched a pop smash with the classic "Tell It Like It Is," a lush ballad showcasing his gossamer vocals. Art, meanwhile, returned from the service to begin his own solo career, and recorded a series of regional hits like "Cha Dooky Doo," "Zing Zing" and "Oo-Whee Baby." In 1967, he formed Art Neville and the Sounds, which included both Aaron and Charles as featured vocalists and quickly became a sensation on the local club circuit.

In 1968 producer Allen Toussaint hired the group as the house band for his Sansu Enterprises; minus Aaron and Charles, the Sounds evolved into a highly-regarded rhythm section which backed artists as diverse as Lee Dorsey, Robert Palmer and Labelle before eventually finding fame on their own as the Meters. Consequently, Aaron resumed his solo career, although with only sporadic success; as a result, he also worked as a dock hand. Charles, meanwhile, relocated to New York City, where his skills as a saxophonist led to tenures with a variety of jazz units; after returning to New Orleans, he was arrested for possession of marijuana and served a three-year sentence at the Angola Prison Farm.

In 1975, the Meters backed the Wild Tchoupitoulas, a group led by the Nevilles' uncle, George "Big Chief Jolly" Landry. Both Aaron and Charles were enlisted for the session, as was youngest brother Cyril; when the Meters disbanded the following year, the four brothers backed the Tchoupitoulas on tour, and in 1977 they officially banded together as the Neville Brothers. Despite their gift for intricate four-part harmonies, their self-titled 1978 debut unsuccessfully cast the vocal quartet as a disco band, and following a dismal response they were dropped by their label, Capitol.

The Nevilles spent the following three years without a contract, but after signing with A&M, fan Bette Midler helped secure the services of producer Joel Dorn for 1981's superior *Fiyo on the Bayou*, which spotlighted Aaron's angelic tenor on standards like "Mona Lisa" and "The Ten Commandments of Love" along with renditions of "Iko Iko" and "Brother John." Despite widespread critical acclaim, the album sold poorly, and again the Nevilles were cut loose from their contract. After signing to the tiny Black Top label, they issued 1984's *Neville-ization,* an incendiary live set recorded at the Crescent City landmark Tipitina's which featured Duke Ellington's "Caravan" and Aaron's perennial "Tell It Like It Is" alongside the brothers' own "Africa" and "Fear, Hate, Envy, Jealousy."

After another concert album, 1987's *Live at Tipitina's,* the Nevilles signed with EMI and returned to the studio in 1987 with *Uptown,* which again met with commercial failure despite cameo appearances from Keith Richards, Jerry Garcia and Carlos Santana. In 1989, they resigned to A&M and recruited the services of famed New Orleans producer Daniel Lanois; the atmospheric *Yellow Moon,* the group's finest hour, finally earned them success on the charts, thanks in part to the anthemic single "Sister Rosa." 1990's *Brother's Keeper* fared even better, no doubt spurred by Aaron's concurrent success with Linda Ronstadt on the smash duet "Don't Know Much."

In subsequent years, Aaron reignited his solo career while also remaining with his brothers; while the Nevilles retained their cult following with LPs like 1992's *Family Groove,* 1994's *Live on Planet Earth* and 1996's *Mitakuye Oyasin Oyasin/All My Relations,* Aaron scored a Top Ten hit in 1991 with the single "Everybody Plays the Fool," taken from the Ronstadt-produced *Warm Your Heart.* In 1993, he notched a minor hit with "Don't Take Away My Heaven" from the LP *The Grand Tour;* a year later, he found success with "I Fall to Pieces," a duet with country star Trisha Yearwood. In 1990, Charles issued the jazz collection *Charles Neville and Diversity.* In addition, a second generation of Nevilles also began making their mark on music; in 1988, Aaron's son Ivan, a member of Keith Richards' backing band the X-Pensive Winos, released his solo debut, *If My Ancestors Could See Me Now.* —*Jason Ankeny*

Fiyo on the Bayou / Apr. 1981 / A&M ✦✦✦✦
A brilliant updating of the New Orleans R&B sound to include strains of Cajun, rock, and reggae on standards ranging from "Hey Pocky Way" to

"The Ten Commandments of Love" and "Sitting in Limbo." — *William Ruhlmann*

Neville-Ization / Jun. 1984 / Black Top ✦✦✦
It took Black Top Records two years to put this record out after the Neville Brothers recorded it live at Tipitina's in New Orleans in September 1982, and one reason may be that it presents a mediocre, going-through-the-motions set. At their best, the Nevilles achieve a transcendent musical mixture, and even at the level of mere professionalism they're an impressive unit, but this just isn't the live album of which they are capable. — *William Ruhlmann*

★ **Treacherous: A History of the Neville Brothers** / 1986 / Rhino ✦✦✦✦✦
The music of the Neville Brothers was more a matter of rumor than documentation to most record buyers outside the New Orleans area until 1986, when Rhino Records finally gathered together their various solo and group records dating back 30 years and presented their story coherently on this two-disc set. Suddenly, it all makes sense, and the Nevilles' mixture of styles emerges as a singular American genre unto itself. This record is a revelation. — *William Ruhlmann*

Uptown / Mar. 1987 / EMI America ✦✦
The Neville Brothers displayed their eclecticism on this lone EMI album. They played with some high-class guest stars, including Branford Marsalis, Jerry Garcia, Ronnie Montrose, Carlos Santana, and Keith Richards. But despite these excellent musicians and the Nevilles' usual tight playing and exuberant collective vocals, once more, the album failed to either get them a huge hit or faithfully re-create the quality of their live shows. — *Ron Wynn*

Yellow Moon / 1989 / A&M ✦✦✦✦
The Neville Brothers made a bid for pop-rock stardom with this well-produced album for A&M, their first under a new pact with the label inked in the late '80s. It was certainly as solid as any they cut for A&M; the vocals were both nicely arranged and expertly performed, the arrangements were basically solid, and the selections were intelligently picked and sequenced. The album charted and remained there for many weeks, while the Nevilles toured and generated lots of interest. It didn't become a hit, but it did respectably and represents perhaps their finest overall pop LP. — *Ron Wynn*

Brother's Keeper / Jul. 1990 / A&M ✦✦✦
All of the Neville Brothers' recent albums for A&M have been frustrating, uneven propositions, with great performances followed by disjointed numbers, and the studio productions seldom convey the excitement and fire this group routinely generates in concert. The same holds true for this release, even though it got more pop exposure and chart penetration than any previous Neville Brothers album. But despite their energetic vocals and often superb instrumental interaction, this release still didn't come close to presenting the Neville Brothers on a good night, much less a great one. — *Ron Wynn*

Treacherous Too: A History of the Neville Brothers, Vol. 2 (1955-1987) / Feb. 1, 1991 / Rhino ✦✦✦✦
Okay, there's no such thing as secondhand revelation, but the Neville Brothers had more than enough stray tracks from their decades of local music-making around New Orleans to justify this second, single-disc follow-up to Rhino's first Nevilles history. There's more of an emphasis on novelty material here, but once again you can hear the roots of the Nevilles' cross-genre appeal in pop, R&B, and soul music dating back to the 1950s. Since most of these songs were recorded as singles, they have an immediate surface appeal, but repeated listenings also bring out the sounds of the tight session bands (including members of the Meters) who backed the Nevilles up. Actually, it's only the five 1980s tracks from just-okay albums like *Neville-ization* and *Uptown* that keep this collection from classic status, not the older stuff. — *William Ruhlmann*

Live on Planet Earth / Apr. 19, 1994 / A&M ✦✦✦
Clearly, this is intended to be the definitive live document of a band that has always been defined by its live work. Clocking in at 71 minutes, the album was culled from a world tour. The rhythm section of drummer Willie Green and bassist Tony Hall keeps up a steady groove from song to song, and the Nevilles trade off lead and harmony vocals on original songs that range across their career and add everything from Bob Marley compositions to "Love the One You're With" and "Amazing Grace." They Neville-ize all comers, throwing them into the pot and coming out with a tasty gumbo. If there's anything missing, it's the small club atmosphere from which the Nevilles emerged: this is a wide-screen treatment of a music that gained impact from its intimacy but now seeks to form a global conga line. — *William Ruhlmann*

Mitakuye Oyasin Oyasin/All My Relations / May 14, 1996 / A&M ✦✦✦
The Neville Brothers have made a family affair of their first studio album in four years, writing much of the material themselves and co-producing the record with James Stroud. As a result, they are making less of an effort to secure a pop hit this time, even though they do throw

in a little rap and a funky cover of Bill Withers' "Ain't No Sunshine." But part of the reason they tend to be more interesting live than on record is that, beyond being well-meaning, they haven't got much to say. Most of the songs here are homilies to brotherhood, responsibility, and environmentalism, set against tracks that evoke Brazilian music, mbaqanga, reggae, R&B, and soul and are heavy on percussion and horns. Occasionally, as on the respectable cover of the Grateful Dead's "Fire of the Mountain," with guest guitarist Bob Weir, or on Aaron Neville's typically ethereal "Saved by the Grace of Your Love," the music transcends both the message and the groove. But this is an album of small pleasures rather than the larger statement it seems intended to be. — *William Ruhlmann*

● **Very Best of the Neville Brothers** / Jan. 14, 1997 / Rhino ✦✦✦✦
Sixteen-track compilation focusing almost exclusively on the period spanning the late '70s to the late '80s. A couple of Aaron Neville's big '60s hits ("Tell It like It Is" and "Over You") are thrown in as well, as are a couple of cuts from the Wild Tchoupitoulas' 1976 album. Some may argue that the Nevilles' sprawling output is too difficult to condense into a single disc. On the other hand, given how often they're criticized for underachieving on record, this is a pretty suitable purchase for someone whose interest only runs deep enough for one anthology. — *Richie Unterberger*

Aaron Neville

b. Jan. 24, 1941, New Orleans, LA
Vocals / Soul, R&B, Adult Contemporary, Pop-Rock, New Orleans R&B
Although Neville is often compared to singer Sam Cooke in terms of sheer vocal refinement, he has a voice and style uniquely his own. Today he is well known as part of the New Orleans sound of the Neville Brothers. Yet, aside from the 1967 No. 1 R&B hit "Tell It Like It Is," few have heard his incredible early solo recordings. Many of the first recordings of Aaron Neville, in the early and mid-'60s, were arranged, produced, and often written by the brilliant Allen Toussaint—another talent only now being really appreciated. Most of these sides were cut for the Minit (and later) Parlo labels. Songs like "She Took You for a Ride" and "You Think You're So Smart" on Parlo are masterpieces. While his more recent work, including that with Linda Ronstadt, makes for pleasant listening, it lacks the sheer persuasion of his early songs. Aaron has re-recorded his early work often, and it is important to hear the originals. The early sides of Aaron Neville are just waiting to be heard.

Aaron Neville has been venturing more into other waters besides R&B. 1993's *The Grand Tour* included a remake of a George Jones song that got Neville a little country attention, and he announced plans in 1994 to do a complete country album. He was also one of several R&B artists who teamed with country stars for the *Rhythm, Country and Blues* session. Neville was paired with Trisha Yearwood, and the duo also performed together in a benefit concert for the LP held in Los Angeles in April 1994. The LP made history by debuting in the Top Ten on the pop, R&B, and country charts. — *Michael Erlewine and Ron Wynn*

● **Tell It Like It Is** / 1967 / Curb ✦✦✦✦
Eleven of Neville's best Parlo cuts, including those mentioned above, are included on one CD. His biggest solo smash from 1966, plus more songs in the same style. Sublime stuff. — *Bill Dahl*

Like It 'Tis / Oct. 14, 1967 / EMI America ✦✦✦
An excellent vinyl compilation of Neville's early-'60s Allen Toussaint-produced Minit singles, this includes the amusingly macabre 1960 rocker "Over You." — *Bill Dahl*

Orchid in the Storm / Dec. 1986 / Rhino ✦✦✦✦
Aaron Neville's wondrous singing on this poorly distributed EP was overlooked by many still unaware of his stunning falsetto. But Neville covered doo wop, soul, and even country on this project, singing with a soaring conviction and poignancy that made it a delightful, though short, set. Rhino has thankfully reissued it on CD. It's actually closer to representing Neville's real style than his recent much-hyped, overproduced pop records. — *Ron Wynn*

● **Tell It Like It Is: Golden Classics** / 1989 / Collectables ✦✦✦✦
One of many collections covering Aaron Neville's superb early R&B and soul classics. The burly Neville, whose delicate, feathery voice stands in vivid contrast to his muscular body, made great heartache ballads, uptempo wailers, and brilliantly sung originals for tiny New Orleans labels, often not even getting widespread soul airplay. Now that's he's hot property, the domestic anthologies are coming out left and right. This one is as good as any other, although for my money the import labels have still done a better job on early Neville than the American companies. — *Ron Wynn*

Show Me the Way / Aug. 1989 / Charly ✦✦✦
Here are 22 of his early Minit recordings, many of them incredible. — *Michael Erlewine*

The My Greatest Gift / 1991 / Rounder ✦✦✦
The songs that made Neville famous among soul and R&B fans were done years before he became a recognized star for tiny Southern labels. The 12 tracks on this anthology were recorded in the late '60s, when Neville's soaring falsetto, emphatic delivery, and gut-wrenching treatments were locked out of the pop mainstream. Although this isn't the definitive version of "Tell It Like It Is," it's far from a throwaway. On "Love Letters," "Hercules," "Mojo Hannah," and "Where Is My Baby," Aaron Neville tackled the soul mountain and conquered it. —*Ron Wynn*

Warm Your Heart / Jun. 11, 1991 / A&M ✦✦✦
This new set finds Neville's wavering vocals as elegant as ever on a ballad-oriented program. —*Bill Dahl*

Aaron Neville's Soulful Christmas / Oct. 5, 1993 / A&M ✦✦✦
Neville doesn't stray too far from tradition with his mellowly crooned R&B, gospel, and doo wop inflected renditions. Neville really breaks into his own for the Cajun-flavored toe-tapper "Louisiana Christmas Day" and the swingin' "Such a Night." —*Roch Parisien*

New Colony Six

f. 1964, Chicago, IL
Garage Rock, Pop-Rock
Chicago's New Colony Six originally emerged as a tough, British Invasion-styled outfit prominently featuring Farfisa organ and a novel (at the time) Lesley guitar. Scoring a huge local hit with "I Confess," their early recordings—exemplified by their 1966 debut album, *Breakthrough*—featured first-class original material that gave the sound of Them and the Yardbirds a more commercial, American garage-based, vocal harmony approach. The rest of the '60s saw the band gradually abandoning their roots for middle-of-the-road pop with horns and strings. Continuing to rack up major local hits and minor national ones, they finally cracked the US Top 30 with "Love You So Much" (1968) and "Things I'd Like to Say" (1969). —*Richie Unterberger*

Breakthrough / 1966 / Sentar ✦✦✦✦
Breakthrough was one of the very finest American garage LPs, fusing Midwestern guitar-organ pop with the raunch of British Invasion groups, and stressing well-written original material. It is also extremely rare, and extremely expensive should you locate an original copy. But take heart—ten of the 12 tracks have been reissued on Sundazed's *At the River's Edge* CD. The two other songs are routine, dispensable covers of the Yardbirds' "Mr., You're a Better Man than I" and the McCoys' "Hang On, Sloopy," so you shouldn't fret about their absence from your collection. —*Richie Unterberger*

● **At the River's Edge** / 1993 / Sundazed ✦✦✦✦
Twenty-two tracks, including all of the worthwhile songs from their classic *Breakthrough* album, a non-LP single, and most of their second album, *Colonization*. The only New Colony Six package worth owning. —*Richie Unterberger*

Colonized! The Best of New Colony Six / Apr. 6, 1993 / Rhino ✦✦
In the mid—and late '60s, the New Colony Six were one of Chicago's most successful pop-rock groups, scoring many regional hits and hitting the national Top 30 with "I Will Always Think About You" and "Things I'd Like to Say." Both of those tracks are included on this 20-track retrospective, which documents the group's evolution from masterful garage rockers to pop-rock softies. In this case, this was certainly not a change for the better. The Six's 1966 LP *Breakthrough* was one of the finest obscure rock albums of the 1960s, marrying American pop hooks and harmonies to tough organ-dominated British R&B in the spirit of Them. Four songs from that album are included on this compilation, as well as a non-LP single (a cover of Bo Diddley's "Cadillac") from the same period. With personnel changes, the group devolved into a pedestrian mainstream pop-rock outfit that owed more to Gary Puckett than their gritty British Invasion roots. Discriminating listeners are advised to stick with their early material. —*Richie Unterberger*

New Edition

f. 1982, Boston, MA
Hip Hop, Urban, Pop-Rock, New Jack R&B
When Maurice Starr assembled New Edition in the early '80s, he never could have guessed that the group would produce some of the biggest, most influential urban R&B stars of the following decade. At the time of their first record, Bobby Brown, Ralph Tresvant, Ricky Bell, Mike Bivins, and Ronald Davoe were barely in their teens, yet they had impressive voices and a natural charisma that sent them to the charts with their first single, "Candy Girl." Their second album was even bigger, featuring the No. 2 single "Cool It Now." New Edition's songs were either light funk or sweet ballads, yet they followed their formula well, even if much of it seems quaint now, especially compared to their groundbreaking solo work.
Brown left the band after their third album, being replaced by Johnny Gill. The band released two more albums before splitting. After the

group was finished, they each became successful as solo artists in the late '80s.
New Edition reunited in 1996, releasing a new album in the fall of that year. —*Stephen Thomas Erlewine*

Candy Girl / 1983 / Warlock ✦✦✦✦
When Maurice Starr uncovered the talents of a Roxbury vocal group in the early '80s, he envisioned a second Jackson 5. That was the direction he took New Edition in its early days, and this album includes such overt Jackson 5 rip-offs as "Candy Girl" and the title track. None of the toughness or street touches that emerged on their later material were evident on this slick, pop-oriented session. Ralph Tresvant, Ronald DeVoe, Michael Bivins, Ricky Bell, and Bobby Brown were all aged 13 to 15 when this was released. —*Ron Wynn*

New Edition / 1984 / MCA ✦✦✦✦
Maurice Starr's vision peaked with this second album by New Edition. They were now thoroughly Jackson 5 clones and were reaping similar commercial dividends thanks to the teen angst cuts "Cool It Now" and "Mr. Telephone Man." They earned their first platinum album, one Top Ten hit, and another Top 20 pop single (both songs topped the R&B charts) and were among the hottest acts in either pop or R&B during this stretch. —*Ron Wynn*

All for Love / 1985 / MCA ✦✦✦
New Edition's voices and focus were changing in the late '80s. They'd moved away from the kiddie pop-soul of the early '80s and were singing harder, adult love material and cutting uptempo funk tracks, although there weren't many of those on this session. While sometimes things got a bit sappy lyrically and seemed repetitive at other times, the group compensated with their strongest harmonies and vocal performances to date. —*Ron Wynn*

Under the Blue Moon / 1986 / MCA ✦✦✦
Changes were on the horizon for New Edition. They had become enormously successful by aping the Jackson 5, but were undergoing internal trauma as original member Bobby Brown bolted amid rumors of dissatisfaction with the group's direction. This album featured their covers of '50s and '60s standards and was among early examples of the retro trend now so prominent in urban contemporary camps. While they didn't do this type of material nearly as well as the Force MD's, they at least brought fresh attention to such songs as "Earth Angel" and "Tears on My Pillow." —*Ron Wynn*

Heart Break / 1989 / MCA ✦✦✦
The arrival of Johnny Gill's lusty baritone and the production tactics of Jimmy Jam and Terry Lewis temporarily revived the sagging careers of New Edition. Jam and Lewis gave them current beats, let Gill take the lead on romantic numbers, and put punch and edge into their arrangements. This proved New Edition's biggest album since 1985's *All for Love*, and such songs as "Can You Stand the Rain," "If It Isn't Love," and the autobiographical "Where It All Started" signaled the end of the Jackson 5 ties. But it was also the precursor to more internal dissension. —*Ron Wynn*

● **Greatest Hits, Vol. 1** / Oct. 1, 1991 / MCA ✦✦✦✦
For anyone who missed New Edition in either its Jackson 5 imitation phase or final days as a funkier, more aggressive urban contemporary vocal group with a slight dance influence, this collection contains examples of both incarnations. Kiddie-pop hits such as "Candy Girl," "Cool It Now," and "Mr. Telephone Man" are included, along with their final hits "If It Isn't Love," "Can You Stand the Rain," and the appropriately titled "Is This the End?" This anthology shows how dominant New Edition was during the '80s and early '90s. —*Ron Wynn*

Home Again / Sep. 10, 1996 / MCA ✦✦✦✦
When Bobby Brown, Ralph Tresvant, Ricky Bell, Michael Bivins, Ronnie DeVoe, and Johnny Gill entered the studio for a full-fledged New Edition reunion in 1996, reactions ranged from excitement to skepticism. Would the chemistry still be there? With Brown, Tresvant, and Gill (the only one who wasn't an original member) having put so much energy into their solo careers and the other three having enjoyed success as Bell Biv DeVoe, could they make a cohesive statement as a sextet? But in fact, they did prove cohesive on *Home Again*, the first New Edition album since 1988's *Heartbreak* and Brown's first with the group since 1986's *Under the Blue Moon*. Not remarkable but certainly decent, this CD is a long way from the type of Jackson Five-influenced bubblegum soul-pop Edition was recording in the '80s. Listeners wondered whether Brown or BBD's album would have the greatest impact on this project, and the truth is that both were influential. Some of the songs bring to mind BBD's in-your-face aggression, while others benefit from Brown's charisma. A few of the songs sound contrived, but in general, *Home* makes us glad the singers decided to reunite. —*Alex Henderson*

New Edition's Solo Hits / Dec. 3, 1996 / MCA ✦✦✦✦
A 12-track compilation of four tracks each by spin-off acts of New Edition seems like a strange way to pick up their work, to say the least. Still, if you want some hits by Bobby Brown, Bell Biv DeVoe, and Ralph Tres-

vant, and are for some reason uninterested in scoping out their albums or waiting for their one-artist-only greatest-hits collections, this is a succinct mini-primer of one of the most successful clans in urban contemporary music. —*Richie Unterberger*

New Order

f. 1980, Manchester, England
Dance-Pop, Synth-pop, Alternative Pop-Rock, New Wave, Post-Punk, Club/Dance, Alternative Dance

Of all of the synth-based post-punk bands that emerged in the '80s, New Order is the most important. After Ian Curtis hung himself, the remaining members of Joy Division—Bernard Sumner, Peter Hook, and Stephen Morris—picked up the pieces and formed New Order, adding keyboardist Gillian Gilbert. While the group alleviated some of Curtis' most morbid tendencies, their music still was serious; the band also adhered to pop melodies and structure more frequently than Joy Division. New Order exploited synthesizers and electronics to their fullest, creating a detached, yet strangely human soundscape that managed to convey the emotional alienation of the Thatcher and Reagan era. The band was also not afraid to use disco as the basic rhythm in their music, laying the groundwork for the house scene in the UK at the end of the decade, as well as the cold, detached synth-dance pop that dominated the charts in America and the UK for most of the beginning of the decade. In the UK, New Order were stars, yet they never developed anything larger than a cult following in America.

After 1991's *Technique*, the band members concentrated on solo projects (Sumner in Electronic, Hook in Revenge, Gilbert and Morris in the Other Two), fueling rumors that they had broken up. In 1993, they returned with *Republic*, which earned them their first genuine hit single in America, "Regret." After a tension-filled tour, the members resumed their solo projects, again sparking rumors of the band's split. —*Stephen Thomas Erlewine*

Movement / 1981 / Factory ✦✦✦
New Order's debut album *Movement* bridges the gap between the dance-rock the group would later develop and Joy Division's languid, morbid drone. *Movement* pointed the way toward New Order's future by featuring more synthesizers than any of Joy Division's records, as well as more accessible hooks and melodies. —*Stephen Thomas Erlewine*

Power Corruption and Lies / 1983 / Qwest ✦✦✦✦
Synthesized dance music at moderate tempos, plus calmly sung, distanced lyrics, makes for an entrancing effect. —*William Ruhlmann*

Low Life / 1985 / Qwest ✦✦✦✦
New Order's messages are no less dire here, but the tempos are faster, the singing more engaged, and the melodies more distinct. In fact, "Love Vigilantes" is positively catchy. —*William Ruhlmann*

Brotherhood / 1986 / Qwest ✦✦✦✦
Brotherhood repeated the formula of *Low-Life*, but instead of being a mere retread of its predecessor, the new album was a refinement of the innovations of the previous album, when the group's songwriting became tighter and more accessible, as the single "Bizarre Love Triangle" proved. —*Stephen Thomas Erlewine*

☆ **Substance** / 1987 / Qwest ✦✦✦✦✦
Substance is a double-disc set collecting New Order's singles, including several songs that were never available on the group's albums, at least in these versions. While there are a couple of re-recordings of earlier singles, most of *Substance* consists of 12-inch single mixes designed for dance club play. Arguably, these 12-inch mixes represent New Order's most groundbreaking and successful work, since they expanded the notion of what a rock 'n' roll band, particularly an indie-rock band, could do. *Substance* collects the best of their remixes and in the process it showcases not only the group's musical innovations, but also their songwriting prowess—"Temptation," "Blue Monday," "Bizarre Love Triangle," and "True Faith" are some of the finest pop songs of the '80s. Although it is a double disc set, *Substance* isn't overly long. Instead, it offers a perfect introduction to New Order, while providing collectors with an invaluable collection of singles. —*Stephen Thomas Erlewine*

Technique / 1989 / Qwest ✦✦✦✦
Technique expands New Order's trademark sound by adding elements of dense acid house rhythms, the occasional acoustic guitar, and a greater reliance on pop melody. All of the subtle experimentation made *Technique* one of their most intriguing and successful records. —*Stephen Thomas Erlewine*

Republic / May 11, 1993 / Qwest ✦✦✦
New Order's most pop-oriented record actually resulted in a hit single in the US, the pleasantly catchy "Regret." However, most of the album finds New Order repeating ideas that are now almost a decade old. —*Stephen Thomas Erlewine*

★ **Best of New Order** / Mar. 14, 1995 / Qwest ✦✦✦✦
Instead of presenting New Order as a progressive dance band as *Substance* did, *(The Best Of) New Order* showcases New Order the pop band, condensing most of their hit singles onto one disc. A couple of remixes are thrown in (Shep Pettibone takes over "Blue Monday") and several classics, including "Temptation" and "Ceremony," are missing, but it is still a concise explanation of why the group was one of the most important bands of the '80s. —*Stephen Thomas Erlewine*

The New York Dolls

f. 1971, New York, NY, **db.** 1977
Rock 'n' Roll, Hard Rock, Glam Rock, Proto-Punk

The New York Dolls created punk rock before there was a term for it. Building on the Rolling Stones' dirty rock 'n' roll, Mick Jagger's adrogeny, girl group pop, the glam rock of David Bowie and T. Rex, and the Stooges' anarchic noise, the New York Dolls created a new form of hard rock that presaged both punk rock and heavy metal. Their drug-fueled, shambolic performances influenced a generation of musicians in New York and London, who all went on to form punk bands. And although they self-destructed quickly, the band's two albums remained two of the most popular cult records in rock 'n' roll history.

All of the members of the New York Dolls played in New York bands before they formed in late 1971. Guitarists Johnny Thunders and Rick Rivets, bassist Arthur Kane and drummer Billy Murcia were joined by vocalist David Johansen. Early in 1972, Rivets was replaced by Syl Sylvian and the group began playing regularly in lower Manhattan, particularly at the Mercer Arts Center. Within a few months, they had earned a dedicated cult following, but record companies were afraid of signing the band because of their cross-dressing and blatant vulgarity.

Late in 1972, the New York Dolls embarked on their first tour of England. During the tour, drummer Murcia died after mixing drugs and alcohol. He was replaced by Jerry Nolan. After Nolan joined the band, the Dolls finally secured a record contract with Mercury Records. Todd Rundgren—whose sophisticated pop seemed at odds with the band's crash and burn rock 'n' roll—produced the band's eponymous debut, which appeared in the summer of 1973. The record received overwhelmingly positive reviews, but it didn't stir the interest of the general public—the album peaked at No. 116 on the US charts. The band's follow-up, *Too Much Too Soon*, was produced by the legendary girl group producer George "Shadow" Morton. Although the sound of the record was relatively streamlined, the album was another commercial failure, only reaching No. 167 upon its early summer 1974 release.

Following the disappointing sales of their two albums, Mercury Records dropped the New York Dolls. No other record labels were interested in the band, so they decided to hire a new manager, the British Malcolm McLaren, who would soon become famous for managing the Sex Pistols. With the Dolls, McLaren began developing his skill for turning shock into invaluable publicity. Although he made it work for the Pistols just a year later, all of his strategies backfired for the Dolls. McLaren made the band dress completely in red leather and perform in front of the USSR's flag—all of which meant to symbolize the Dolls' alleged communist allegiance. The new approach only made record labels more reluctant to sign the band and members soon began leaving the group.

By the middle of 1975, Thunders and Nolan left the Dolls. The remaining members, Johansen and Sylvain, fired McLaren and assembled a new lineup of the band. For the next two years, the duo led a variety of different incarnations of the band, to no success. In 1977, Johansen and Sylvain decided to break up the band permanently. Over the next two decades, various outtakes collections, live albums, and compilations were released by a variety of labels and the New York Dolls' two original studio albums never went out of print.

Upon the Dolls' break up, David Johansen began a solo career that would eventually metamorphose into his lounge-singing alter-ego Buster Poindexter in the mid-'80s. Syl Sylvain played with Johansen for two years before he left to pursue his own solo career. Johnny Thunders formed the Heartbreakers with Jerry Nolan after they left the group in 1975. Over the next decade, the Heartbreakers would perform sporadically and Thunders would record the occasional solo album. On April 23, 1991, Thunders—who was one of the more notorious drug abusers in rock 'n' roll history—died of a heroin overdose. Nolan performed at a tribute concert for Thunders later in 1991; a few months later, he died of a stroke at the age of 40. —*Stephen Thomas Erlewine*

★ **The New York Dolls** / 1973 / Mercury ✦✦✦✦✦
There are hints of girl group pop and more than a hint of the Rolling Stones, but *The New York Dolls* doesn't really sound like anything that came before it. It's hard rock with a self-conscious wit, a celebration of camp and kitsch that retains a menacing, malevolent edge. The New York Dolls play as if they can barely keep the music from falling apart, and David Johansen sings and screams like a man possessed. *The New York Dolls* is a noisy, reckless album that rocks and rolls with a ven-

geance. The Dolls rework old Chuck Berry and Stones riffs, playing them with a sloppy, violent glee. "Personality Crisis," "Looking for a Kiss," and "Trash" strut with confidence, while "Vietnamese Baby" and "Frankenstein" sound otherworldly, working the same frightening drone over and over again. *The New York Dolls* was the definitive proto-punk album, even more so than anything the Stooges released. It plunders history while celebrating it, creating a sleazy urban mythology along the way. *—Stephen Thomas Erlewine*

☆ **Too Much, Too Soon** / 1974 / Mercury ✦✦✦✦✦
After the clatter of the New York Dolls' first album failed to bring them to a wide audience, the group hired producer Shadow Morton to work on their second album, *Too Much, Too Soon*. The differences are immediately noticeable as soon as the ferocious "Babylon" kicks the album into gear. Not only are the guitars cleaner, there are waves of studio sound effects and girl backup singers. Ironically, instead of making the Dolls safer, all the added frills just emphasizes how gleefully sleazy and reckless the band sounds. Throughout the album, the band sounds on the verge of falling apart, with Johnny Thunders and Syl Sylvian relentlessly trading buzz-saw riffs with David Johansen singing, shouting, and sashaying on top of the racket. On *Too Much, Too Soon*, the Dolls' originals—which included bluesy ravers like "It's Too Late" and the noisy girl-group pop of "Puss N' Boots," as well as the Thunders showcase "Chatterbox"—were rounded out by obscure R&B and rock 'n' roll covers that sounded like they were designed for the Dolls. Johansen camps it up throughout Leiber & Stoller's "Bad Detective," Archie Bell's "(There's Gonna Be A) Showdown," and the Cadets' "Stranded in the Jungle" with affection and as much grit as he gives Sonny Boy Williamsons' "Don't Start Me Talkin'"—he really means it, man. The whole record collapses in the scathing "Human Being," where a bunch of cross-dressing misfits defiantly declare that it's OK that they want too many things, cause they're human beings, just like you—three years later, the Sex Pistols never came up with anything quite so musically visceral and dangerous. Perhaps that's why the Dolls never found their audience in the early '70s—not only were they punk rock before punk rock was cool, they remained weirder and more idiosyncratic than any of the bands that followed. And they rocked harder, too. *—Stephen Thomas Erlewine*

Rock & Roll / Oct. 18, 1994 / Mercury ✦✦✦✦
Rock & Roll contains all of the original material from the Dolls' two classic albums and adds a couple of outtakes and rarities. So why isn't it as much fun as *New York Dolls* or *Too Much Too Soon?* For starters, the Dolls' versions of "Pills," "Stranded in the Jungle," "Don't Start Me Talkin'," and "(There's Gonna Be A) Showdown" weren't filler, they were essential to the overall feeling of the albums. And that brings us to the main problem of *Rock & Roll*—it isn't sequenced in an inviting manner. Instead of showcasing the New York Dolls in all of their trashy glory, the disc manages to make them sound rather tedious, which is something their proper albums certainly aren't. Nevertheless, there's plenty of fine music here, and hardcore fans will want the rarities. But the original albums remain the best way to hear the Dolls. *—Stephen Thomas Erlewine*

Martin Newell

Alternative Pop-Rock, Pop-Rock
One of the great eccentrics of modern English pop-rock, Martin Newell's songs are recommended listening for anyone who enjoys the peculiarly British eccentricities of Ray Davies, Andy Partridge, Syd Barrett, and the like. His grasp of the pop hook has been second to few throughout the 1980s and '90s; his arrangements favor a guitar jangle, but are usually infused with a whimsical eclecticism full of goofy sound effects and unusual garnishes of unexpected percussion and string instruments. His voice is winningly quizzical, but his chief assets are his compositions, which reflect contemporary English life with a wry combination of affection and cynicism.

For most of the 1980s, Newell was the mainstay of Cleaners from Venus, who recorded most of their albums at home for cassette-only self-release, although they eventually put out some vinyl product. After a short stint as head of the similar Brotherhood of Lizards, Martin started a solo career in the 1990s that was essentially a continuation of the territory he'd explored in the 1980s; sometimes he re-recorded songs from the previous decade. The difference, if any, was that he was concentrating on the proper official album market instead of the cassette underground, with somewhat higher (though not slick) production values.

Newell's most acclaimed album was 1993's *The Greatest Living Englishman*, which was produced by Andy Partridge of XTC. *The Off White Album* (1995) was a bit more baroque in approach, with occasional string arrangements. Newell has co-written material with Captain Sensible, and is a poet/humorist of some renown in Britain, publishing his own prose with a good deal of success, and writing humorous pieces for the *Independent* newspaper. Ironically, his music is virtually unknown on his home turf, although he enjoys a considerable cult fol-

lowing in Germany, Japan, France, and on certain American college radio stations. *—Richie Unterberger*

● **The Greatest Living Englishman** / Nov. 1993 / Pipeline ✦✦✦✦
As it was produced by XTC's Andy Partridge (who also plays most of the drums), this was Newell's first project to receive any semblance of mainstream media attention in the US. What he was presenting, however, differed little in essence from what he'd been doing since *Cleaners from Venus* started in the early '80s: tuneful pop with heart and clever lyrics that could be joyfully optimistic, whimsically satirical, or dourly cynical. In fact, a few of these songs are remakes of things that Newell had done in the Cleaners days, such as "Home Counties Boy," the very Kinks-like "A Street Called Prospect," and "Christmas in Suburbia." The production was more in line with state-of-the-art standards, but really the results were no worse or better than on Newell's '80s recordings; less idiosyncratically homespun, perhaps, but more accessible to a wider audience. Playing, as always, like a snapshot of English life, it's the most suitable introduction to Newell's work, not in the least because it's one of his few albums that's reasonably obtainable without a major effort. *—Richie Unterberger*

The Off White Album / 1995 / Humbug ✦✦✦
Newell's second widely distributed album (he self-released some tapes under his own name in the 1980s) is a bit more precious and ornate than *The Greatest Living Englishman*, particularly when the songs employ string arrangements. At these times especially, this sounds a bit like Elvis Costello's unplugged/string quartet releases. Newell's phrasing, too, is getting more deliberate in a way that also faintly recalls Costello, though Martin doesn't sound as calcuated in his delivery. As far as the songs go, it's largely more of the same: witty, affecting vignettes about British characters, simultaneously evoking a glorious past and a somewhat unsettling, frustrating present. It's not his best record, but it's still more inventive, intelligent British pop than what you hear from most other such artists that try to carry this kind of thing off. *—Richie Unterberger*

Martin Newell's Box of Old Humbug / 1996 / Humbug ✦✦✦✦
A three-CD box set containing *The Greatest Living Englishman*, *The Off White Album*, and the four-song CD single *Let's Kiosk!* The single, which is available separately, has "The Jangling Man" (from *The Greatest Living Englishman*) and three otherwise unavailable tracks that are quite up to the standards of his albums, although they wouldn't be standouts on them. If you're interested enough in Newell in the first place to find *any* of his work, you're more likely than not devoted enough to check out *anything* he's done. So if you haven't gotten any of this stuff yet, it makes sense to splurge and get the whole danged package at once. Here's as good a place as any to mention that Newell uses incidental noises of schoolchildren and birds as well as anybody in rock; the best track on the single "I Will Haunt Your Room" is an outstanding example of this. *—Richie Unterberger*

Randy Newman

b. Nov. 28, 1943, New Orleans, LA
Piano / Singer-Songwriter, Brill Building Pop, Pop-Rock
Randy Newman was an anomaly among early '70s singer-songwriters. Though he was slightly influenced by Bob Dylan, his music owed more to New Orleans R&B and traditional pop than folk. Newman developed an idiosyncratic style that alternated between sweeping, cinematic pop and rolling R&B, which were tied together by his nasty sense of humor. Where his peers concentrated on confessional songwriting, Newman drew characters, creating a world filled with misfits, outcasts, charlatans, and con-men. Though he occasionally showed sympathy for his characters, he became well-known for his biting sense of satire, highlighted by his fluke 1978 hit "Short People" and his parody of '80s yuppies, "I Love L.A." While Newman's records consistently received strongly positive reviews, he made his money through composing film scores for films like *Ragtime* and *The Natural*. His albums may never have sold in large amounts, but his work influenced several generations of songwriters, including Lyle Lovett and Mark Knopfler.

Born into a musical family—his uncles Alfred and Lionel were both noted film composers—Randy Newman had become a professional songwriter by the time he was 17, working for a Californian publishing house. Newman pursued a B.A. in music from UCLA, but he dropped out of college when his friend Lenny Waronker landed him a record contract with Reprise Records. His eponymous debut album received little attention upon its 1968 release, but over the next few years, his reputation as a songwriter grew as Judy Collins, Dusty Springfield and Peggy Lee recorded his songs. Three Dog Night took his "Mama Told Me Not To Come" to No. 1 in 1970, the same year Harry Nilsson recorded an entire album of Randy's songs, *Nilsson sings Newman*. The pianist toured with Nilsson, eventually earning a cult following across America, especially on college campuses.

Newman's second album, 1970's *12 Songs*, was widely-praised upon its release, but the record failed to sell. *Live* repeated the same pattern in

1971, but 1972's *Sail Away* became a moderate hit, due to positive reviews and Newman's constant touring. He followed the record album in 1974 with *Good Old Boys*, an ambitious concept album about the South that received excessive controversy over its song, "Rednecks," whose ironic sense of humor was misunderstood by many. The song set the stage for 1977's "Short People," a simple satire of bigotry and prejudice taken from *Little Criminals*. While the irony in "Short People" was barely hidden, the song offended many listeners, and the ensuing furor helped the single reach No. 2 on the charts. Newman supported the album with his first tour since 1974.

In 1979, he returned with *Born Again*, which received mixed reviews, and Newman began a career as a film composer two years after its release. His first score was for Milos Forman's *Ragtime*, and his work was nominated for two Academy Awards. Newman released *Trouble In Paradise* to strong reviews in 1983, and the album spawned "I Love L.A.," a parody of shallow yuppie culture that was misinterpreted and became an anthem for '80s greed. Newman didn't release another album until 1988's *Land of Dreams*, which contained his first attempts at personal songwriting. Like most of his records, the album was greeted warmly by the critics, yet it failed to sell; "It's Money That Matters," a re-write of "I Love L.A.," did become a minor hit.

Newman spent most of the '90s composing film scores and working on a musical adaptation of *Dr. Faust*. The resulting musical, *Faust*, was initially released as a concept album in the fall of 1995 to mixed reviews. A stage version of *Faust* opened the same month as the album's release, and it received better reviews. Newman another Oscar nomination in 1996 for "You've Got a Friend," which was featured in the Disney computer-animated film, *Toy Story*. —*Stephen Thomas Erlewine*

Randy Newman / 1968 / Reprise ✦✦✦✦
"Randy Newman creates something new under the sun," read the banner on the back of Newman's debut album, but it wasn't so much that, in keeping with the intended irony of the statement, Newman was intent upon taking clichés and using them to satirize social conventions, a popular parlor game in the late '60s. Thus, we have "Love Story" (predating the sappy book/movie of the same title), in which the lovers retire to Florida and pass away; "So Long Dad," in which a son squares things with his old man; and "Davy the Fat Boy," in which an affectionate friend exploits the title character. But there were also songs like "Living Without You" and "I Think It's Gonna Rain Today," which were so painfully lonely you wished they weren't so sincere. Taken together, this was an audacious first album by a major, if extremely quirky, talent. —*William Ruhlmann*

★ **12 Songs** / 1970 / Reprise ✦✦✦✦✦
Randy Newman's droll humor and ability to render ludicrous settings (through the eyes of protagonists who were obviously not playing with full decks) made *12 Songs* an instant classic to the handful of people lucky enough to hear it. The bare-bones production, along with assistance from guitarist Ry Cooder, gave the record a homey immediacy. Highlights are hard to single out, but "Mama Told Me Not to Come" (later a hit for Three Dog Night), "Yellow Man," "Lucinda," and "Uncle Bob's Midnight Blues" are great. —*Rick Clark*

Randy Newman Live / 1971 / Reprise ✦✦✦
This live set basically reprises much of his first two albums, without adding much to their interpretation. There are a few new tunes, the only standout being a song that Frank Sinatra passed on, called "Lonely at the Top." —*Rick Clark*

☆ **Sail Away** / 1972 / Reprise ✦✦✦✦✦
Sail Away was Newman's first synthesis of his satirical writing and his impressive orchestral arrangement skills. The result was one of his very best albums. The title cut was a brilliantly twisted take on slaves coming on a ship from Africa, set to a score that owed much to Stephen Foster. "Burn On," Newman's sentimental-sounding ode to the polluted Cuyahoga River (in Cleveland, OH), and his perverse "You Can Leave Your Hat On" are among the many great songs to be found on *Sail Away*. —*Rick Clark*

☆ **Good Old Boys** / 1974 / Reprise ✦✦✦✦✦
On *Good Old Boys*, Newman increasingly focused his obsessions on the South, but his slant seemed to be rooted more in Steppin' Fetchit and Shirley Temple *Little Rebel* Hollywood films than in reality. As distorted as viewing things through that particular lens may be, the South in *Good Old Boys* is undeniably poignant. "Louisiana 1927" is an affecting account of a spring flood, while "Marie" (a love song from a drunk) is one of the most touching songs written in popular music. The grand, sweeping melodies and arrangements are quite simply beautiful. Newman's sloppy, soulful mumble and understated piano keep this great record from tumbling into drippy sentimentality. —*Rick Clark*

Little Criminals / 1977 / Reprise ✦✦✦
On *Little Criminals*, Newman's penchant for satirically illuminating the quirks in human nature earned him a million-selling No. 2 hit with "Short People," a song that dealt with the issue of bigotry. It also earned him the loathing of thousands of short people who failed to get the mes-

sage. Aside from that controversy, *Little Criminals* was relatively tame by Newman standards. "Baltimore," "Sigmund Freud's Impersonation of Albert Einstein in America," and "Rider in the Rain" were among the standout tracks. —*Rick Clark*

Born Again / 1979 / Reprise ✦✦✦
It was on his sixth studio album that Newman's caustic humor seemed to become mean-spirited. His characters had always been small-minded creeps, but on *Born Again*, they weren't presented with any sympathy, and the hand of the author was apparent. Newman was as clever as ever, just crueler than usual. Except for "The Story of a Rock and Roll Band," his trashing of the Electric Light Orchestra, that is. They deserved it. —*William Ruhlmann*

Trouble in Paradise / 1983 / Reprise ✦✦✦✦
After the mean-spirited 1979 release *Born Again*, Newman regrouped and released *Trouble in Paradise*, an album that employed more lyrical subtlety and was more successful at skewering its terminally character-disordered targets ("Christmas in Capetown," "Song for the Dead," "My Life Is Good"). "The Blues," a dryly humorous duet with Paul Simon, was a moderate hit at No. 51. "I Love L.A." failed to chart, in spite of extensive exposure. Musically, Newman downplayed the timeless feel of his best work in favor of a trendier, clean West Coast-pop sound. As a result, this effort doesn't age so well. *Trouble in Paradise* may not be Newman's best work, but fans will enjoy it. —*Rick Clark*

● **Retrospect** / 1983 / WEA ✦✦✦✦
To date, Warner Brothers in the US has not released a compilation of Randy Newman's best work, but the UK division has, and here it is. From "Political Science" to "God's Song," these 16 songs should show any listener the depth of Randy Newman's talent as a songwriter and provide some big horse laughs along the way. —*William Ruhlmann*

Land of Dreams / 1988 / Reprise ✦✦✦✦
After a five-year layoff, Newman returned with the solid *Land of Dreams*, an album that was by turns gentle and reflective ("Something Special," "Falling in Love") or subtly scathing. Among the topics explored in *Land of Dreams* are Newman's childhood memories in New Orleans ("Dixie Flyer," "New Orleans Wins the War"), a beautifully twisted ode to patriotism ("Follow the Flag"), and an explanation from a father to his son ("I Want You to Hurt Like I Do"), concerning the passing down of abusive ways. The cynical "It's Money That Matters" barely dented the charts at No. 80. Interestingly, Jeff Lynne helped produce this album; only two albums earlier, Newman was skewering Lynne's band ELO for representing some of the worst elements of the music biz. —*Rick Clark*

Faust / Sep. 19, 1995 / Reprise ✦✦
Since Randy Newman has always borrowed from Hollywood and Broadway musicals in his songwriting, it's not surprising that he wrote his own full-blown musical with *Randy Newman's Faust*. Adapting Goethe's classic morality play for the '90s, Newman has his God and Devil vying for the soul of a Harvard college student. However, neither wins because they can't keep abreast of modern times—the Devil tempts the student with a recording contract, while the student wants his own video game company since that's where the money is. On paper, the reworking of the story is fairly intriguing, but the actual execution is heavily flawed. Newman's humor is forced and not all that funny, while his eye for detail isn't as sharp as it is on his classic albums; furthermore, he sacrifices strong melodies for the lyrics. The bombastic production—featuring large orchestras and choirs as well as guest artists James Taylor (God), Don Henley (Student), Elton John, Bonnie Raitt, and Linda Ronstadt—emphasizes the lack of subtlety in the lyrics and the lack of compelling melodies, making *Randy Newman's Faust* no more than a noble failure. —*Stephen Thomas Erlewine*

Olivia Newton-John

b. Sep. 26, 1948, Cambridge, England
Vocals / Pop-Rock, Soft Rock

Olivia Newton-John skillfully made the transition from popular country-pop singer to popular mainstream soft-rock singer, becoming one of the most successful vocalists of the '70s in the process. The transition itself wasn't much of a stretch—her early '70s hits "I Honestly Love You" and "Have You Never Been Mellow" were country only in the loosest sense—yet the extent of her success in both fields was remarkable. As a country singer, her first five charting singles all went Top Ten in the US; as a pop singer, she had no less than 15 Top Ten hits, including five No. 1 singles, highlighted by "Physical," which spent 10 weeks at No. 1 in 1981-82. Newton-John's sweet voice suited both country-pop and soft-rock perfectly, which is what kept her at the top of the charts until the mid-'80s. After 1984, she was no longer able to reach the Top 40, partially because of shifting musical tastes and partially because she was unable to successfully record sexy dance-pop, no matter how hard she tried. Nevertheless, her '70s and '80s hits remained soft-rock and adult contemporary staples into the '90s, when she was no longer recording frequently

Although she was born in Cambridge, England, Olivia Newton-John was raised in Melbourne Australia, where her father was the headmaster of Ormond College (her grandfather, Max Born, won the Nobel Prize for physics). She tenatively entered show business at the age of 12, when she won a local Haley Mills-lookalike contest. A few years later, she formed an all-female vocal group called the Sol Four with three school friends. Once the Sol Four disbanded, Newton-John entered a television talent contest, winning the grand prize of a trip to London, England. Once in London, she formed a duo with Pat Carroll, another Australian-based vocalist, and tried to work her way into the music industry. Though her partenership with Carrol was short-lived—Pat was sent back to Australia once her visa expired—Olivia was making inroads in the business. Following Carrol's departure, Newton-John recorded and released her first single, a version of Jackie DeShannon's "Till You Say You'll Be Mine." Shortly afterward, she became a member of Toomorrow, a bubblegum group assembled by Don Kirshner in hopes of creating a British version of the Monkees.

Toomorrow appeared in a science-fiction movie of the same name and had one minor British hit single, "I Could Never Live Without Your Love," in early 1970 before the group quietly disbanded. Following the failure of Toomorrow, Newton-John became part of Cliff Richard's touring show, appearing both as an opening act at his concerts and on his British television series, *It's Cliff!* The exposure as a singer and comedienne on the show helped Olivia's career immersurably, and her first single for Uni Records, a version of Bob Dylan's "If Not For You" became a Top Ten hit in the UK in the spring of 1971; in America, it was surprisingly successful, spending three weeks at the top of the Adult Contemporary charts and peaking at No. 25 on the pop charts. For the next two years, Newton-John's success was primarily contained in Britain, where she had a string of lesser hits with covers of George Harrison's "What Is Life" and John Denver's "Take Me Home Country Roads." In America, her career was stalled—her followup single, "Banks of the Ohio," barely scraped the lower reaches of the Top 100. On the other hand, she didn't release a full-length album in the US until 1973, when *Let Me Be There* appeared. The title track from the record became a huge hit, going gold in early 1974 and peaking in the Top Ten country and pop charts. "Let Me Be There" was so successful it won the Grammy award for Best Country Vocal Performance, Female, much to the consternation of many members of Nashville's music industry.

"Let Me Be There" was followed by four other Top Ten hits—"If You Love Me (Let Me Know)" (No.2 country, No.5 pop, 1974), "I Honestly Love You" (No.6 country, No.1 pop, 1974), "Have You Never Been Mellow" (No.3 country, No.1 pop, 1975), and "Please Mr. Please" (No.5 country, No.3 pop, 1975). Newton-John moved to Los Angeles late in 1974, and early the following year, she won the Female Vocalist of the Year award from the Country Music Association. As a protest, several members of the CMA quit the organization. Ironically, Olivia Newton-John was already planning to move away from country. During 1976 and 1977, she had a number of minor hits with soft-rock songs. Though none of these were big pop successes, they began to establish her as a pop singer, not a country-pop singer.

Olivia Newton-John's transformation into a mildly sexy pop singer was complete in 1978, when she starred in the movie version of the popular Broadway musical *Grease.* Also starring John Travolta, *Grease* was an international hit and it spawned three huge hit singles—"Hopelessly Devoted to You," "Summer Nights" and "You're the One That I Want;" the latter two were duets between Newton-John and Travolta. "You're The One That I Want," in particular, was a massive success, reaching No. 1 in both America and Britain; in the UK, it spent a staggering nine weeks at No. 1. During 1979, Olivia released the *Totally Hot* album, which boasted a mixture of soft rock and light disco. The record was another hit, with the first single "A Little More Love" peaking at No. 3 on the US pop charts and going gold. Early in 1980, Newton-John starred in the roller-disco fantasy film *Xanadu.* While the movie was an unqualified bomb, the soundtrack was a huge hit. "Magic" spent four weeks at the top of the US pop charts, while the ELO duet "Xanadu" reached No. eight and her duet with Cliff Richard, "Suddenly," peaked at No. 20.

With her next album, *Physical,* Newton-John continued to rework her image, re-inventing herself as a sexy aerobics fanatic. The first single from the record, the suggestive "Physical," was a huge hit, spending ten weeks at No. 1 during the fall and winter of 1981-82. *Physical* spawned two other Top Ten hits—"Make a Move On Me" and "Heart Attack"—and became her most successful record. Following the album's success, she was awarded with an Order of the British Empire. In 1983, Newton-John again starred with Travolta, this time in the comedy *Two of a Kind.* The movie was a bomb, but a song she recorded for the soundtrack, "Twist of Fate," became a Top Ten hit in early 1984.

By the end of 1984, Newton-John had married actor Matt Lattanzi. The following year, she released the *Physical* clone *Soul Kiss,* which produced only one minor hit with its title track. In 1986, she had a

daughter named Chloe and opened a clothing store chain called Koala Blue. Newton-John attempted to launch a comeback in 1988 with *The Rumour,* but the album was ignored. She signed with Geffen the following year, releasing the children's album *Warm and Tender.* During the late '80s and '90s, she devoted herself to her family and business, as well as several environmental activist organizations. In 1992, Koala Blue folded and Newton-John was diagnosed with breast cancer. Over the next year, she successfully underwent treatment for the disease. In 1994, she returned to recording with the indepently-released and self-produced album *Gaia. —Stephen Thomas Erlewine*

● **Back to Basics** / Jun. 9, 1992 / Geffen ✦✦✦✦
An artist well-defined by her hit singles, Olivia Newton-John has had a stylistically varied career, as is illustrated on *Back to Basics: The Essential Collection 1971-1992,* a set that ranges from her teary ballad "I Honestly Love You" to that bouncy paean to getting horizontal, "Physical." Fans may quibble that such hits as "Let Me Be There" and "Make a Move on Me" are not included, but Newton-John's two greatest-hits albums are out of print, and this is the only collection to combine both her good-girl and bad-girl personas. *—William Ruhlmann*

The Nice

f. 1967, London, England, **db.** 1970
Keyboards / Art-Rock/Progressive-Rock
One of the first art-rock bands to experiment with classical forms and fusion, the Nice was an early vehicle for the talents of keyboard virtuoso Keith Emerson, who plundered Mozart, Sibelius, and Tchaikovsky for his extended rock instrumental forays. The group began as the backing band for British soul singer P.P. Arnold and also featured guitarist David O'List, drummer Brian "Blinky" Davison, and bassist Lee Jackson. In October 1967, only two months after formation, the group split from Arnold, christened itself the Nice, and released a single called "The Thoughts of Emerlist Davjack," which became the title track of their 1968 debut album. The Nice quickly built a reputation as an exciting, theatrical live band thanks to Emerson, who dressed in gold lame, hurled knives into his Hammond organ to produce strange sounds, and mimed masturbation onstage. Emerson's antics spawned controversy with *Ars Longa Vita Brevis,* which contained a cover of Leonard Bernstein's *West Side Story* song "America." The Nice performed it at the Royal Albert Hall while burning an American flag, and Bernstein subsequently attempted to stop the song's release in the US. Emerson had emerged as the star of the group, both in terms of instrumental skill and showmanship, and the fed-up O'List had departed the group by the time of the album's release to join Roxy Music. *Nice* and *Five Bridges Suite* became big hit albums in Britain, but the group never broke through in America. In 1969, Emerson met Greg Lake, then with King Crimson, on a US tour, and broke up the Nice in frustration in 1970 due to its lack of success. He, Lake, and drummer Carl Palmer formed the much more popular Emerson, Lake and Palmer, which expanded on Emerson's innovations with the Nice. The remaining Nice members went on to several short and/or unsuccessful stints with other groups before fading away. *—Steve Huey*

The Thoughts of Emerlist Davjack / 1967 / Columbia ✦✦✦
An okay, but unambitious first album, heavily influenced by Jimi Hendrix. Lacking discipline, but full of surprises. *—Bruce Eder*

Ars Longa Vita Brevis / 1968 / Columbia ✦✦✦
Leonard Bernstein, Bach, and Sibelius interpreted through a musical lens forged by Brubeck, Monk, and a mad keyboard player named Keith Emerson. *—Bruce Eder*

● **Nice** / 1969 / Columbia ✦✦✦✦
Their final statement, with rippling organ passages and a great lineup of songs, plus 20 minutes of a legendary Fillmore live gig. *—Bruce Eder*

Elegy & Five Bridges / 1975 / Mercury ✦✦✦
A farewell record of live cuts and outtakes, not showing the band to its best advantage. A good appendix to their superior Immediate recordings on Columbia. *—Bruce Eder*

● **The Best of the Nice** / Jun. 6, 1995 / Griffin Music ✦✦✦✦

Stevie Nicks

b. May 6, 1948, Phoenix, AZ
Vocals / Pop-Rock
Famed for her mystical chanteuse image, singer-songwriter Stevie Nicks enjoyed phenomenal success not only as a solo artist but also as a key member of Fleetwood Mac. Stephanie Lynn Nicks was born May 26, 1948 in Phoenix, Arizona; the granddaugher of a frustrated country singer, she began performing at the age of four, and occasionally sang at the tavern owned by her parents. Nicks started writing songs in her midteens, and joined her first group, the Changing Times, while attending high school in California.

During her senior year, Nicks met fellow student Lindsey Buckingham, with whom she formed the band Fritz along with friends Javier

Pacheco and Calvin Roper. Between 1968 and 1971, the group became a popular attraction on the West Coast music scene, opening for Jimi Hendrix, Janis Joplin and Creedence Clearwater Revival. Ultimately, tensions arose over the amount of attention paid by fans to Nicks' pouty allure, and after three years Fritz disbanded; Buckingham remained her partner, however, and soon became her lover as well.

After moving to Los Angeles, the duo recorded their 1973 debut LP, *Buckingham-Nicks*. Despite a cover which featured the couple nude, the album flopped; however, it caught the attention of the members of Fleetwood Mac, who invited Buckingham and Nicks to join their ranks in 1974. In quick time, the revitalized group achieved unparalled success: after the LP *Fleetwood Mac* topped the charts in 1975, they recorded 1977's *Rumours*, which sold over 17 million copies and stood for several years as the best-selling album of all-time.

Major hit singles like "Dreams" and "Rhiannon" made Nicks a focal point of Fleetwood Mac, and in 1981 she took time off from the group to record her solo debut, *Bella Donna*, which hit No. 1 on the strength of the Top 20 hits "Stop Draggin' My Heart Around" (a duet with Tom Petty and the Heartbreakers), "Leather and Lace" (a duet with Don Henley) and "Edge of Seventeen (Just Like the White Winged Dove)." After a return to Fleetwood Mac for the 1982 album *Mirage* (which featured her hit "Gypsy"), Nicks released her second solo effort, *The Wild Heart*, highlighted by the Top Five smash "Stand Back." *Rock a Little*, which featured the single "Talk to Me," followed in 1985.

After a long hiatus (during which time Nicks was treated for a chemical dependency problem), Fleetwood Mac reunited for the album *Tango in the Night; The Other Side of the Mirror*, Nicks' first solo record in four years, followed in 1989. After a series of line-up changes and dropping sales figures, she left Fleetwood Mac in 1993, and issued *Street Angel* a year later. —*Jason Ankeny*

Bella Donna / 1981 / Modern ✦✦✦✦
Stevie Nicks' solo career was off to an impressive, if overdue, start with *Bella Donna*, which left no doubt that she could function quite well without the input of her colleagues in Fleetwood Mac (a band she would remain a member of until 1993). The album yielded a number of hits that seemed omnipresent in the '80s, including the moving "Leather and Lace" (which unites Nicks with Don Henley), the poetic "Edge of Seventeen," and her rootsy duet with Tom Petty, "Stop Draggin' My Heart Around." But equally engaging are less exposed tracks like the haunting "After the Glitter Fades." Hit producer Jimmy Iovine wisely avoids overproducing, and keeps things sounding organic on this striking debut. —*Alex Henderson*

The Wild Heart / 1983 / Modern ✦✦✦
Stevie Nicks was following both her debut solo album, *Bella Donna* (1981), which had topped the charts, sold over a million copies (now over four million), and spawned four Top 40 hits, and Fleetwood Mac's *Mirage* (1982), which had topped the charts, sold over a million copies (now over two million), and spawned three Top 40 hits (including her "Gypsy"), when she released her second solo album, *The Wild Heart*. She was the most successful American female pop singer of the time. Not surprisingly, she played it safe: *The Wild Heart* contained nothing that would disturb fans of her previous work and much that echoed it. As on *Bella Donna*, producer Jimmy Iovine took a simpler, more conventional pop-rock approach to the arrangements than Fleetwood Mac's inventive Lindsey Buckingham did on Nicks' songs, which meant the music was more straightforward than her typically elliptical lyrics. Iovine did get a Mac-like sound on "Nightbird," in which Nicks repeated her invocation to "the white winged dove" from *Bella Donna's* "Edge of Seventeen," and on "Sable on Blond," a "Gypsy" soundalike. His most daring effort was the album's lead-off single, "Stand Back," which boasted a disco tempo. Elsewhere, the songs were largely interchangeable with those on *Bella Donna*, even down to the obligatory duet with Tom Petty. Nicks seemed to know what she was up to—one song was called "Nothing Ever Changes." As a result, *The Wild Heart* sold to the faithful—it made the Top Ten, sold over a million copies, and spawned three Top 40 hits ("Stand Back," "Nightbird," and "If Anyone Falls"). And that was appropriate: If you loved *Bella Donna*, you would like *The Wild Heart* very much. —*William Ruhlmann*

Rock a Little / 1985 / Modern ✦✦✦✦
In contrast to the earthy, rootsy qualities of *Bella Donna*, Stevie Nicks took a slicker, more high-tech approach on her third solo album, *Rock a Little*. But for all its glossiness, this pop-rock CD comes across as sincere and heartfelt rather than formulaic or contrived. From the catchy "I Can't Wait" to the intense "No Spoken Word" to the dark "The Nightmare," everything on *Rock a Little* is as honest as it is memorable. Assisting Jimmy Iovine and Rick Nowels with the production, Nicks wisely sees to it that technology adds to her songs instead of smothering or overpowering them. —*Alex Henderson*

The Other Side of the Mirror / May 1989 / Modern ✦✦✦
Stevie Nicks' fourth solo album received more than its share of negative reviews from rock critics, who seemed to mistake her poetic and not

always terribly discernable lyrics for pretentiousness. Although not as strong as Nicks' three previous solo dates, *The Other Side of the Mirror* is a decent CD that has many more pluses than minuses. While there are a few less than memorable moments, some of the songs—including "Long Way to Go," "Ghosts," and "Whole Lotta Trouble"—are fairly strong. Nicks' more devoted followers will want this album, which should be purchased only if one already has *Bella Donna*, *The Wild Heart*, and *Rock a Little*. —*Alex Henderson*

● **Timespace: Best of Stevie Nicks** / Sep. 3, 1991 / Modern ✦✦✦✦
Uniting the familiar and the unfamiliar, best-of collections can present a problem for an artist's more devoted fans, who are forced to spend money on songs they already have in order to obtain a few new ones. That's certainly true of *Timespace*, a 1991 CD containing three new songs that are well worth hearing ("Sometimes It's a Bitch," "Desert Angel," and "Love's a Hard Game to Play") in addition to such well-known gems as "Stand Back," "Edge of Seventeen," and "I Can't Wait." But while one can argue that Modern should have waited until Stevie Nicks' next album to release the new songs, this collection presents a fine overview of her solo career. For those purchasing their first Nicks CD, *Timespace* is the ideal place to start. —*Alex Henderson*

Street Angel / Sep. 21, 1993 / Modern ✦✦
From 1981 through 1993, Stevie Nicks successfully juggled a solo career and membership in Fleetwood Mac. But in 1993, she left Mac for good and became strictly a solo artist. Quite similar to *Bella Donna* and *The Wild Heart* but not as strong, *Street Angel* found Nicks taking a fairly rootsy approach and avoiding the type of high-tech production gloss one hears on *Rock a Little* and *The Other Side of the Mirror*. The CD (Nicks' first since departing Mac) contains a few gems, including the single "Blue Denim," the free-spirited "Love Is Like a River," and the earthy "Listen to the Rain." But most of the songs, although generally decent, fall short of the excellence Nicks so often achieved in the 1980s. Nicks' hardcore devotees will want *Angel*, but it's far from essential. —*Alex Henderson*

Maybe Love Will Change Your Mind / May 26, 1994 / Atlantic ✦✦✦

Nico (Christa Paffgen)

b. Oct. 16, 1938, Cologne, Germany, **d.** Jul. 18, 1988
Harmonium, Vocals / Alternative Pop-Rock, Art-Rock/Progressive-Rock, Experimental, Euro-Dance
One of the most fascinating figures of rock's fringes, Nico hobnobbed, worked, and was romantically linked with an incredible assortment of the most legendary entertainers of the 1960s. The paradox of her career was that she herself never attained the fame of her peers, pursuing a distinctly individualistic and uncompromising musical career that was uncommercial, but wholly admirable and influential. Nico first rose to fame as a European supermodel, also landing a bit part in Fellini's *La Dolce Vita* film and giving birth to a son by Alain Delon. In 1965, she attracted the attention of Rolling Stones manager Andrew Loog Oldham, who gave her a chance to record for his Immediate label, though the resulting single, which also featured Brian Jones and Jimmy Page on guitars, flopped. Shortly afterwards, she moved to New York, where Andy Warhol installed her as a vestigial presence and occasional lead singer for the Velvet Underground. The band never really accepted her as a bonafide member, and she departed in 1967, but not before contributing unforgettable deadpan vocals to three of the songs on their classic 1967 debut album.

Nico embarked on a solo career, recording folk-rock flavored songs for her debut *Chelsea Girl* album with assistance from Jackson Browne, Lou Reed, and John Cale. Her 1969 follow-up, *The Marble Index*, was a dramatic departure that unveiled her doom-laden, gothic persona, produced by Cale and prominently featuring her deep vocals, impenetrable lyrics, and ghostly harmonium. Her subsequent 1970s albums explored much the same territory, with assistance from Cale and influential artrockers like Eno and Phil Manzanera. Her career fell into disarray during the rest of the '70s and the '80s, as she struggled with a massive drug habit and tangled personal life. She released several live albums on various labels, but the ill-planned *Drama of Exile* and the more successful *Camera Obscura* were her only coherent studio efforts until she died of a cerebral hemorrhage in Ibiza in 1988.

The original goth-rocker, Nico's albums are demanding and bleak, but map a unique and starkly powerful vision that has become more influential with age. An intimate of Bob Dylan, Jackson Browne, the Velvets, the Stones, Jim Morrison, Iggy Pop, and others, her fascinating story is recounted in the biography *Nico: The Life & Lies of an Icon*, by Richard Witts, published in Great Britain by Virgin books; *The End*, by James Young, is a seedy look at her drug-addled final years by a member of her touring band. —*Richie Unterberger*

● **Chelsea Girl** / 1967 / Polydor ✦✦✦✦
Nico's distanced, German-accented voice is presented over austere strings and, in one case, electric guitar on a series of songs reminiscent of her work with the Velvet Underground and written by Velvets John

Cale and Lou Reed. Other songs (some unrecorded elsewhere) were written by a young Jackson Browne. — *William Ruhlmann*

The Marble Index / 1969 / Elektra ✦✦✦
The quirky, orchestrated folk-rock of Nico's 1968 debut album *Chelsea Girl* in no way prepared listeners for the stark, almost avant-garde flavor of her 1969 follow-up, *The Marble Index*. Produced by former Velvet Underground partner John Cale, the chanteuse presented an uncompromisingly bleak, gothic soundscape on her second album. Dominated by spare harmonium and Nico's deep, brooding vocals, this album unveiled her singularly morose songwriting (her first record featured none of her compositions). Owing more to European classical and folk music than rock, it found little favor with 1969 audiences. But like the work of the Velvet Underground, it proved to be quite influential in the long run on a future generation of black-clad goth-rockers. The 1991 reissue of this recording adds two previously unreleased songs, "Roses in the Snow" and "Nibelungen." — *Richie Unterberger*

Desert Shore / 1971 / Reprise ✦✦✦✦
John Cale produces, arranges, and plays almost all the instruments on this atmospheric collection of songs well suited to Nico's droning delivery. — *William Ruhlmann*

The End / 1974 / Island ✦✦✦
The most remote and Teutonic of Nico's studio albums features Roxy Music guitarist Phil Manzanera, Brian Eno on synthesizer, and John Cale (who also produced) on a dozen instruments. After five Nico originals, it concludes with chilling readings of the Doors' "The End" and "Das Lied Der Deutschen." — *Richie Unterberger*

Drama of Exile / 1981 / Aura ✦

Do or Die! / 1982 / ROIR ✦✦

Camera Obscura / 1985 / Beggars Banquet ✦✦

(Live) Heroes / 1986 / Performance ✦✦✦
A six-track mini-album, four songs recorded live, including David Bowie's title track, which is perfectly suited to the Nico treatment. — *William Ruhlmann*

Peel Sessions / 1988 / Dutch East India ✦✦✦
In February 1971, Nico recorded a four-song session for the BBC that included songs from three of her solo albums. "No One Is There" and "Frozen Warnings" had appeared on 1969's *The Marble Index*, and "Janitor of Lunacy" on 1970's *Desert Shore*; "Secret Side" would appear on 1974's *The End*. Frequently bootlegged over the years, this official release presents the performance at the right speed in pristine sound. These renditions are about as bare-boned as they come, with no accompaniment save Nico's own harmonium. In both material and performance, she leans toward the more wistful and gothic of her numbers. They don't differ drastically from the LP versions, but it's an interesting addition to fans' collections. — *Richie Unterberger*

Hanging Gardens / 1990 / Restless ✦✦✦

Heroine / 1995 / Anagram ✦✦

Icon / Apr. 1996 / Cleopatra ✦✦✦
A hodgepodge of recordings from the early 1980s, including the "Saeta"/"Vegas" single along with live material, outtakes, and interviews, released on the heels of the acclaimed 1995 documentary *Nico/Icon.* — *Jason Ankeny*

Night Ranger

f. 1981, San Francisco, CA, db. 1989
Hard Rock, Pop-Rock, Heavy Metal, Hair Metal, Arena Rock
Featuring ex-Ozzy Osbourne guitarist Brad Gillis and former Montrose keyboardist Alan Fitzgerald, Night Ranger was one of the most popular mainstream hard rock bands of the mid-'80s. The group formed in the early '80s in San Francisco; in addition to Gillis and Fitzgerald, the members included Jack Blades (vocals, bass), Jeff Watson (guitar), and Kelly Keagy (drums). After a few local gigs, promoter Bill Graham managed to get them supporting slots on Judas Priest, Santana, and Doobie Brothers concerts. Night Ranger's first album, *Dawn Patrol* (1982), reached No. 38 on the US charts, yet it was 1983's *Midnight Madness* that established the band as a commercial force. Featuring the AOR hit "(You Can Still) Rock in America" and the No. 5 single "Sister Christian," the record peaked at No. 15 and sold over a million copies. 1985's *7 Wishes* was just as successful, reaching No. 10 on the charts. Night Ranger's audience began to diminish after 1987's *Big Life*. Fitzgerald left the following year and the band released their last album, *Man in Motion*, which failed to go gold or spawn any Top 40 singles. Night Ranger broke up the next year. Jack Blades joined the supergroup Damn Yankees, which also featured Ted Nugent and Tommy Shaw. — *Stephen Thomas Erlewine*

● **Night Ranger's Greatest Hits** / Jun. 1989 / Camel ✦✦✦✦
Night Ranger's albums were usually hit-or-miss affairs. Without exception, the strongest songs on the records were the singles, which com-

bined their hard rock crunch with pop hooks. *Greatest Hits* collects all of their Top 40 singles, including "Sister Christian," "When You Close Your Eyes," and "Sentimental Street," as well as lesser hits "(You Can Still) Rock in America" and "Sing Me Away" and album rock radio hits like "Restless Kind" and "Eddie's Comin' Out Tonight," making it a definitive compilation. — *Stephen Thomas Erlewine*

Harry Nilsson

b. Jun. 15, 1941, Brooklyn, NY, **d.** Jan. 15, 1994, Agoura Hills, CA
Piano, Vocals / Singer-Songwriter, Pop-Rock
Although he synthesized disparate elements of both rock and pop traditions, singer-songwriter Harry Nilsson was at heart a maverick whose allegiance belonged to neither. His initial series of albums in the late '60s made him a personal favorite of the Beatles, who found a natural affinity with his knack for catchy melodies, witty lyrics, and extraordinary vocal range. Thought of as a songwriter first and a performer second, he became a pop star himself in the late '60s and early '70s with "Everybody's Talking" and "Without You." He lost some of his original audience, however, with subsequent detours into pre-rock styles of pop, and did little recording over the last 15 years of his life.

Nilsson had been struggling to make inroads into the music business for over five years before his critically acclaimed 1967 album, *Pandemonium Shadow Show*. He made demos, sang commercial jingles, and shopped songs, all the while keeping his job at a Los Angeles-area bank. In the mid-'60s he wrote a few songs with Phil Spector that were recorded by the Ronettes and the Modern Folk Quartet; occasionally he released records of his own. The Monkees recorded his "Cuddly Toy," and the Yardbirds did "Ten Little Indians" on a single in their waning days. But Nilsson didn't quit his bank job until after the release of *Pandemonium Shadow Show*, which gave him creative rein in the studio for the first time, and showcased his three-and-a-half-octave voice to full advantage.

The album caught the attention of the Beatles (helped, no doubt, by its ingenious medley of classic Beatle tunes, "You Can't Do That"). John Lennon and Paul McCartney named him as their favorite American singer at a press conference, an extraordinary accolade for an unknown. (Nilsson was sometimes even rumored to be joining the group.) Three Dog Night took Harry's "One" into the Top Ten in 1969, and Nilsson's second LP, *Aerial Ballet*, continued the ambitious pop-rock direction of his debut, marrying his slightly eccentric, bouncy (if sometimes precious) tunes to baroque orchestral production. When one of its songs, "Everybody's Talkin'," was used as the theme for the *Midnight Cowboy* film, Nilsson had his first Top Ten hit. The irony was that, although Nilsson was primarily identified as a singer-songwriter, the song was actually a cover of a composition by folk-rocker Fred Neil.

But Nilsson would never be content to be pigeonholed into definite categories, as demonstrated by his two 1970 albums. One was devoted entirely to covers of songs by Randy Newman (then just emerging as a performer); another was his soundtrack to an animated children's special, *The Point* (including the hit "Me and My Arrow"). And it was another cover (of a Badfinger album track) that gave him his biggest single, the No.1 smash "Without You." Yet Nilsson didn't cash in on his stardom in a conventional manner; he never performed in concert (there were occasional television appearances), preferring to craft his artistry in the studio.

"Without You" appeared on *Nilsson Schmilsson*, which included a couple of other hits, the faux-tropical "Coconut" and the surprisingly gritty "Jump into the Fire," which rates as his hardest-rocking cut. During the first half of the 1970s, he continued to broaden his range from the well-crafted, peppy, sensitive tunes that had dotted his early releases, cutting some tougher, more sour work. He lost some of his constituency, however, with 1973's *A Little Touch of Schmilsson in the Night*, a collection of pre-rock pop standards with an orchestra conducted by arranger Gordon Jenkins (most noted for his work with Frank Sinatra). His affection for the music wasn't entirely surprising, as there had always been a strong Tin Pan Alley flavor to much of his writing, but it wasn't exactly in step with the times.

Much of Nilsson's notoriety stems from a period in the mid-1970s when he was a drinking buddy of John Lennon in Los Angeles (where Lennon was living during a separation from Yoko Ono). The drunken pair were thrown out of L.A.'s Troubadour club in a well-publicized incident, following which Lennon offered to produce Nilsson's next album. The timing was not opportune; Nilsson lost his voice during the sessions, rupturing one of his vocal cords, keeping it a secret out of fear that Lennon would abandon the project. Released as *Pussycats*, it was his last album to make the Top 100. During the same period, he also embarked on a project with another L.A.-based ex-Beatle, Ringo Starr, acting and writing music for the little-seen *Son of Dracula* film.

The upper register of Nilsson's voice, which was ultimately his greatest asset, had been permanently (though not irredeemably) damaged. After a few rather unsuccessful late '70s album, Nilsson withdrew from the studio into family life and other business ventures, spending much of his energies campaigning for gun control after Lennon was shot in 1980. In failing health in the 1990s, diagnosed with diabetes and suffering a massive heart attack, he died in early 1994, just after finishing the vocal tracks for a new album. —*Richie Unterberger*

Pandemonium Shadow Show / 1967 / RCA ✦✦✦✦
It's no wonder that Nilsson was taken up by members of the Beatles after they heard this album, which demonstrated that the singer understood better than most the eclectic whimsy that had given birth to *Sgt. Pepper's Lonely Hearts Club Band*. Contains the bittersweet "1941" and "Cuddly Toy," which was covered by the Monkees. —*William Ruhlmann*

Aerial Ballet / 1968 / RCA ✦✦✦✦
Nilsson's second effort is on the lightweight side; the tunes are always clever, but often cloying, sounding at times like a rock album for little kids (which he would indeed produce shortly afterwards with *The Point*). The influence of Tin Pan Alley and the lighter elements of Lennon-McCartney hover over the piano-dominated compositions, which could often use a little more guts. When he does reach for a little more complexity and melancholy, he comes up with some of his strongest material: his effervescent interpretation of Fred Neil's "Everybody's Talkin'" (which became a Top Ten hit), "One" (a smash for Three Dog Night), and a couple of more obscure gems in the pensive and melodic "Don't Leave Me" and "Together." —*Richie Unterberger*

Harry / 1969 / RCA ✦✦✦

Nilsson Sings Newman / Feb. 1970 / RCA ✦✦✦✦
Nilsson turns out to be a wonderful interpreter of the work of Randy Newman, his light voice making Newman's satiric humor even drier than when the composer himself sang the songs. —*William Ruhlmann*

The Point / 1971 / RCA ✦✦✦

Aerial Pandemonium Ballet / 1971 / RCA ✦✦✦
Nilsson selected tracks from his 1967 album *Pandemonium Shadow Show* and his 1968 album *Aerial Ballet*, and did some re-recording and remixing to produce this 1971 reconfiguration. Whatever you make of it, it does contain a version of "Everybody's Talkin'," plus Nilsson's recording of his composition "One," which was a hit for Three Dog Night. —*William Ruhlmann*

Nilsson Schmilsson / Nov. 1971 / RCA ✦✦✦✦
Nilsson's most successful album was a bouncy Richard Perry production, whose catchy songs were deepened by the singer's puckish humor. Contains the hits "Without You," "Jump into the Fire," and "Coconut." —*William Ruhlmann*

Son of Schmilsson / Jul. 1972 / RCA ✦✦✦✦
The humor is starting to take over on this follow-up, but the songs are still entertaining, and the session players, including "George Harrysong" and "Richie Snare," make for a great backup band. Contains the hits "Spaceman" and "Remember (Christmas)," as well as the ultimate put-down song, "You're Breaking My Heart." —*William Ruhlmann*

A Little Touch of Schmilsson in the Night / 1973 / RCA ✦✦
Nilsson was nearly a decade ahead of Linda Ronstadt and other nouveau crooners in hiring a conductor/arranger of the pre-rock era (in this case Gordon Jenkins) and recording an album of standards before a full orchestra. And he did it better than most, proving to be a marvelous interpreter of songs like "What'll I Do?" and "Makin' Whoopee!" His version of "As Time Goes By" became a minor hit. —*William Ruhlmann*

Son of Dracula / Apr. 1, 1974 / RCA ✦✦
This was a soundtrack to the movie Nilsson made with Ringo Starr. Eerily gothic in nature, the music was a mishmash of some of Harry's familiar songs, along with the usual soundtrack instrumentals. The highlight of this set is the fantastic, rockin' "Daybreak." As with all movie soundtracks, if you loved the movie, the soundtrack makes a nifty souvenir, but it's really intermittently good. —*James Chrispell*

Pussy Cats / Aug. 19, 1974 / RCA ✦✦✦
A dark, disjointed album of covers (including "Subterranean Homesick Blues," "Rock Around the Clock," and "Many Rivers to Cross"), the John Lennon-produced *Pussy Cats* is the strangest album Nilsson ever recorded; it's an aural document of Lennon and Nilsson's notorious, alcohol-soaked "lost weekend"—the sheer chaos of the album effectively evokes their aimless hedonism. —*Stephen Thomas Erlewine*

Sandman / 1975 / RCA ✦✦

That's the Way It Is / 1976 / RCA ✦✦

Knnillssonn / 1977 / RCA ✦✦

● **All-Time Greatest Hits** / 1978 / RCA ✦✦✦✦
Nilsson's albums tended to hang together well, but that didn't keep him from throwing off singles, at least in the late '60s and early '70s. This collection contains all ten of his chart singles (including "Everybody's Talkin'"), plus his version of his song "One," which was a hit for Three Dog Night. —*William Ruhlmann*

Nilsson '62: The Debut Sessions / 1995 / RPM ✦
Harry Nilsson does indeed sing on these 21 tracks, recorded at one fell swoop during a 1962 demo session. But it could not be considered either a proper Nilsson album, or a stellar moment in the singer-songwriter's career. The somewhat complicated story is this: in 1962, unknown Los Angeles guitarist and songwriter Scott Turner met Nilsson. Impressed with his voice, he arranged to have Harry demo many of his tunes. Harry helped write a couple of the songs, but this was Turner's show. The material, some written with John Marascalco (who had penned some stuff for Little Richard) or actor Audie Murphy (!), was bland, wimpy early-'60s pop. At its worst, it recalled such insufferable teen idols as Mark Dinning ("Teen Angel"). This in itself was bad enough, but Turner compounded the damage by overdubbing most of the original demos with hack Nashville country backing in 1977 and 1994. This strategy never leads to positive results, and although Harry does indeed sing well, the tunes and overdubs are so poor as to make listening painful, of interest only for purely historical reasons. Seven of the songs were spared the Nashville treatment; five were overdubbed in 1962 by Los Angeles session aces like James Burton, Leon Russell, Herb Alpert, and Hal Blaine, and just two were left untouched. These tracks may have higher "integrity," such as it is, but still there's not a single thing here worth hearing unless you're a Nilsson scholar. —*Richie Unterberger*

Personal Best: The Harry Nilsson Anthology / Feb. 28, 1995 / RCA ✦✦✦✦
Spanning two discs, *Personal Best: The Harry Nilsson Anthology* is a comprehensive overview of Nilsson's varied career, including all of the hits and many significant album tracks, yet it offers too much material for the casual fan, who would be better served by *All-Time Greatest Hits*. —*Stephen Thomas Erlewine*

Nine Inch Nails

f. 1989, Cleveland, OH
Industrial, Alternative Pop-Rock, Industrial Metal
Nine Inch Nails, the one-man band of Trent Reznor, brought industrial music to the masses with 1989's *Pretty Hate Machine*. With its electronic rush, incessant beats, and distorted guitars, the album appeared to be like much industrial music on the surface, yet Reznor wrote pop songs, not the soundtrack to a personal horror movie. NIN's scarred, harsh soundscapes were bleak enough, yet Reznor's lyrics raise the despair and self-loathing to new heights; at times, his relentless darkness can veer dangerously close to self-parody.

Pretty Hate Machine wasn't a hit when it was released; it charted in 1990 and stayed on the charts for years afterward. By the time Reznor assembled a band for the first Lollapalooza tour in 1991, the group had a sizable following that only grew with NIN's ferocious performances on the tour. Legal troubles with his record company delayed the release of a second album; in 1992, he released a stop-gap EP, *Broken*, that was harder and more abrasive than the debut, yet still conformed to conventional song structures; it debuted in the *Billboard* Top Ten. With their second full-length album, Reznor showed his true roots–'70s progressive rock. *The Downward Spiral* was promoted as a concept album, a cohesive piece of work; it also featured ex-King Crimson guitarist Adrian Belew. Still, NIN is able to straddle two seemingly opposing genres easily, gaining alternative and mainstream hard rock fans alike; whether he likes it or not, Trent Reznor is the man that made industrial palatable for pop fans. —*Stephen Thomas Erlewine*

● **Pretty Hate Machine** / Nov. 1989 / TVT ✦✦✦✦
The reason *Pretty Hate Machine* gained a huge cult following is that Trent Reznor didn't make an industrial album in the strict sense of the term; his songs are pop songs played in an industrial style. Meanwhile, he constructs a towering monument of angst and hatred in his lyrics, perfect for legions of alienated adolescents. As Reznor says, "I'd rather die than give you control," and he proves it throughout *Pretty Hate Machine*. Full of hooks, beats, and abrasive noise, *Pretty Hate Machine* gave a generation of adolescents a martyr as well as a great way to vent anger. —*Stephen Thomas Erlewine*

Broken / Sep. 22, 1992 / Interscope ✦✦✦✦
After the unexpected success of *Pretty Hate Machine*, Trent Reznor found himself unable to enjoy it. Instead, he became embroiled in an ugly lawsuit with his record company, which prevented him from releasing any new material for three years. Although *Broken* is only an EP, the wait was more than worth it. Those who fell in love with the pseudo-industrial *Pretty Hate Machine* will likely be alienated by the raging, angry assault of *Broken*. Instead of blaming everyone else for his troubles, Reznor turns his anger inward. "Wish" and "Happiness in Slavery" are busier, angrier, and noisier than anything on *Pretty;* the songs still have hooks, but the hooks are the noise. The anger on *Broken* is real, not feigned; for those who can stomach undiluted rage, *Broken* is a masterpiece. —*Stephen Thomas Erlewine*

Fixed / Nov. 1992 / Interscope ✦✦✦

Even more than *Broken*, the limited-edition *Fixed* EP sounds like an attempt by Reznor to whittle down the size of his audience. The remixes on *Fixed* totally distort all of the original meanings and intents of the original versions on *Broken;* it's the closest Reznor has come to pure industrial music. While the remixes completely rearrange the songs, *Fixed* is additional proof that NIN is not a flash in the pan. A bold artistic move, and not for the faint of heart. —*Stephen Thomas Erlewine*

The Downward Spiral / Mar. 8, 1994 / Interscope ✦✦✦

Although Trent Reznor designed *The Downward Spiral* as a concept album about despair and anger, these are familiar themes for Nine Inch Nails; it's up to the music to carry the album. And it does carry the album, featuring harder guitars and more brutal beats. However, the songwriting has slipped, and the aggression sounds forced. —*Stephen Thomas Erlewine*

Further Down the Spiral / May 30, 1995 / Nothing/Interscope ✦✦

While it's marketed as an EP, *Further down the Spiral* is essentially the single for "Hurt," which is included here in its live version, the same version that's used in the video. However, what makes the disc worth investigating is the remixes. Like *Fixed* before it, *Further down the Spiral* deconstructs and reassembles the tracks from the platinum *The Downward Spiral*, reconfiguring the music in ways that are frequently more interesting and challenging than the original versions. —*Stephen Thomas Erlewine*

Nirvana

f. 1987, Aberdeen, WA, **db.** 1994
Alternative Pop-Rock, Grunge

Prior to Nirvana, alternative music was consigned to specialty sections of record stores and major labels considered it to be, at the very most, a tax write-off. After the band's second album, 1991's *Nevermind*, nothing was ever quite the same, for better and for worse. Nirvana popularized punk, post-punk and indie-rock, unintentionally bringing it into the American mainstream like no other band before it. While its sound was equal parts Black Sabbath (as learned by fellow Washington underground rockers, the Melvins) and Cheap Trick, Nirvana's aesthetics were strictly indie-rock. They covered Vaselines songs, they revived New Wave cuts by Devo, and leader Kurt Cobain relentlessly pushed his favorite bands—whether it was art-punk of the Raincoats or the country-fried hardcore of the Meat Puppets—as if his favorite records were always more important than his own music. While Nirvana's ideology was indie-rock and their melodies were pop, the sonic rush of their records and live shows merged the post-industrial white noise with heavy metal grind. And that's what made the group an unprecedented multi-platinum sensation. Jane's Addiction and Soundgarden may have proven to the vast American heavy metal audience that alternative could rock, and the Pixies may have merged pop sensibilities with indie-rock white noise, but Nirvana pulled at all together, creating a sound that was both fiery and melodic. Since Nirvana was rooted in the indie aesthetic, but loved pop music, they fought their stardom while courting it, becoming some of the most notorious anti-rock stars in history. The result was a conscious attempt to shed their audience with the abrasive *In Utero*, which only partially fulfilled the band's goal. But by that point, the fate of the band and Kurt Cobain had been sealed. Suffering from drug addiction and manic depression, Cobain had become destructive and suicidal, though his management and label were able to hide the extent of his problems from the public until April 8, 1994, when he was found dead of a self-inflicted shotgun wound. Cobain may not have been able to weather Nirvana's success, but the band's legacy stands as one of the most influential in rock 'n' roll history.

Kurt Cobain (vocals, guitar) met Krist Novoselic (bass) in 1985 in Aberdeen, Washington, a small logging town 100 miles away from Seattle. While Novoselic came from a relatively stable background, Cobain's childhood had been thrown into turmoil when his parents divorced when he was eight. Following the divorce, he lived at the homes of various relatives, developing a love for the Beatles and then heavy metal in the process. Eventually, American hardcore punk worked its way into dominating his listening habits and he met the Melvins, an Olympia-based underground heavy punk band. Cobain began playing in punk bands like Fecal Matter, often with the Melvins' bassist Dale Crover. Through the Melvins' leader Buzz Osbourne, Cobain met Novoselic, who also had an intense interest in punk, which meant that he, like Cobain, felt alienated from the macho, redneck population of Aberdeen. The duo decided to form a band called the Stiff Woodies, with Cobain on drums, Novoselic on bass and a rotating cast of guitarists and vocalists. The group went through name changes as quickly as guitarists, before deciding that Cobain would play guitar and sing. Re-named Skid Row, the new trio featured drummer Aaron Burkhart, who left the band by the end of 1986 and was replaced by Chad Channing. By 1987, the band was called Nirvana. Nirvana began playing parties in Olympia, gaining a cult following. During 1987, the band made ten demos with producer

Jack Endino, who played the recordings to Jonathan Poneman, one of the founders of the Seattle-based indie label Sub Pop. Poneman signed Nirvana, and in December of 1988, the band released their first single, a cover of Shocking Blue's "Love Buzz." Sub Pop orchestrated an effective marketing scheme, which painted the band as back-woods, logging-town hicks, which irritated Cobain and Novoselic. While "Love Buzz" was fairly well-received, the band's debut album, *Bleach*, was what began the ball rolling. Recorded for just over $600 and released in the spring of 1989, *Bleach* slowly became a hit on college radio, due to the group's consistent touring. Though Jason Everman was credited as a second guitarist on the sleeve of *Bleach*, he didn't appear on the record; he only toured in support of the album before leaving the band at the end of the year to join Soundgarden and then Mindfunk. *Bleach* sold 35,000 copies and Nirvana became favorites of college radio, the British weekly music press and Sonic Youth, Mudhoney and Dinosaur Jr., which was enough to attract the attention of major labels.

During the summer, Nirvana released "Sliver" / "Dive," which was recorded with Mudhoney's Dan Peters on drums and was produced by Butch Vig. The band also made a six-song demo with Vig, which was shopped to major labels, who soon began competing to sign the group. By the end of the summer, Dave Grohl, formerly of the DC-based hardcore band Scream, had become Nirvana's drummer and the band signed with DGC for $287,000. Nirvana recorded their second album with Vig, completing the record in the summer. Following a European tour supporting Sonic Youth in the late summer, *Nevermind* was released in September, supported by a quick American tour. While DGC was expecting a moderately successful release, in the neighborhood of 100,000 copies, *Nevermind* immediately became a smash hit, quickly selling-out its initial shipment of 50,000 copies and creating a shortage across America. What helped the record become a success was "Smells Like Teen Spirit," a blistering four-chord rocker that was accompanied by a video that shot into heavy MTV rotation. By the beginning of 1992, "Smells Like Teen Spirit" had climbed into the American Top Ten and *Nevermind* bumped Michael Jackson's much-touted comeback album *Dangerous* off the top of the album charts; it reached the British Top Ten shortly afterward. By February, the album had been certified triple platinum.

Nirvana's success took the music industry by surprise, Nirvana included. It soon become apparent that the band wasn't quite sure how to handle their success. Around the time of *Nevermind's* release, the band was into baiting their audience—Cobain appeared on MTV's *Headbanger's Ball* in drag, the group mocked the tradition of miming on the BBC's *Top of the Pops* by Novoselic throwing his bass into the air constantly, and Cobain sang his live vocals in the style of Ian Curtis, and their traditional live destruction of instruments was immortalized on a *Saturday Night Live* performance that ended with Novoselic and Grohl sharing a kiss—but by the spring, questions had begun to arise about the band's stablity. Cobain married Courtney Love, the leader of the indie-rock/foxcore band Hole, in February of 1992, announcing that the couple was expecting a child in the fall. Shortly after the marriage, rumors that the couple were heavy heroin users began to circulate, and the strength of the rumors only increased when Nirvana cancelled several summer concerts and refused to mount a full-scale American tour during the summer. Cobain complained that he was suffering from chronic stomach troubles, which seemed to be confirmed when he was admitted to a Belfast hospital after a June concert. But, heroin rumors continued to surface, especially in the form of a late-summer *Vanity Fair* article which implied that Love was using during her pregnancy. Both Love and Cobain denied the article's allegations, and publicly harrassed and threatened the article's author. Love delivered France Bean Cobain, a healthy baby, on August 18, 1992, but the couple soon battled with Los Angeles' children's services, who claimed they were unfit parents on the basis of the *Vanity Fair* article. The couple was granted custody of their child by the beginning of 1993.

Since Cobain was going through such well-documented personal problems, Nirvana was unable to record a followup to *Nevermind* until the spring of 1993. In the meantime, DGC released the odds-and-ends compilation *Incesticide* late in 1992; the album reached No. 39 in the US and No. 14 UK. As the group prepared to make their third album, they released "Oh, the Guilt" as a split-single with the Jesus Lizard on Touch & Go Records. Choosing Steve Albini (Pixies, Breeders, Big Black, Jesus Lizard) as their producer, Nirvana recorded their third album *In Utero* in two weeks during the spring of 1993. Following its completion, controversy began to surround Nirvana again. Cobain suffered a heroin overdose on May 2, but the event hidden from the press. The following month, Love called police to their Seattle home after Cobain locked himself in the bathroom, threatening suicide. Prior to debuting *In Utero* material during the New Music Seminar at New York's Roseland Ballroom in July, Cobain had another covered-up overdose. By that time, reports began to circultate, including an article in *Newsweek*, that DGC was unhappy with the forthcoming album, accusing that the band deliberately made an uncommercial record.

Both the band and the label denied such allegations. Deciding that Albini's production was too flat, Nirvana decided to remaster the album with R.E.M.'s producer, Scott Litt.

In Utero was released in September of 1993 to positive reviews and strong initial sales, debuting at the top of the US and UK charts, and Nirvana supported it with a fall American tour, hiring former Germs member Pat Smear as an auxiliary guitarist. While the album and the tour were both successful, sales weren't quite as strong as expected, with several shows not selling out until the week of the concert. As a result, the group agreed to play MTV's acoustic *Unplugged* show at the end of the year, and sales of *In Utero* picked up after its December airing. After wrapping up the US tour on January 8, 1994 with a show at the Center Arena in Seattle, Nirvana embarked on a European tour in February. Following a concert in Munich on February 29, Cobain stayed in Rome to vacation with Love. On March 4, she awakened to find that Cobain had attempted suicide by overdosing on the tranquilizer Rohypnol and drinking champagne. While the attempt was initially reported as an accidental overdose, it was known within the Nirvana camp that the vocalist had left behind a suicide note.

Cobain returned to Seattle within a week of his hospitalization, and his mental illness began to grow. On March 18, the police had to again talk the singer out of suicide after he locked himself in a room threatening to kill himself. Love and Nirvana's management organized an intervention program that resulted in Cobain's admission to the Exodus Recovery Center in LA on March 30, but he escaped from the clinic on April 1, returning to Seattle. His mother filed a missing persons report on April 4. The following day, Cobain shot himself in the head at his Seattle home. His body wasn't discovered until April 8, when an electrician contracted to install an alarm system at the Cobain house stumbled upon the body. After his death, Kurt Cobain was quickly anointed as a spokesman for Generation X, as well as a symbol of its tortured angst.

Novoselic and Grohl planned to release a double-disc live album at the end of 1994, but sorting through the tapes proved to be too painful, so *MTV Unplugged in New York* appeared in its place. The album debuted at the top of the British and American charts. In 1996, its electric counterpart, *From the Muddy Banks of the Wishkah*, was released, debuting at the top of the US charts. Following Cobain's death, Grohl formed the Foo Fighters, who released their debut album in the summer of 1995. Novoselic formed the trio Sweet 75, who released their debut in the spring of 1997. —*Stephen Thomas Erlewine*

Bleach / 1989 / Sub Pop ✦✦✦
At the time, *Bleach* is a stellar piece of Seattle sludge, state-of-the-art indie-rock. Although it still stands as one of the best albums in the Sub Pop catalog, it pales next to their other work. *Bleach* is clearly a debut album; there is a fair amount of filler, and the band sometimes collapses into a sub-Sabbath murk, but "School," "Love Buzz," "Blew," and "Negative Creep" are outstanding, furious rockers, and the gorgeous, Beatlesque ballad "About a Girl" signals the heights the band would reach on their next album. —*Stephen Thomas Erlewine*

★ **Nevermind** / Sep. 24, 1991 / DGC ✦✦✦✦✦
If "Smells like Teen Spirit" was the only good song on *Nevermind*, the album wouldn't have inspired the popular revolution that it did. Although the "Louie Louie"-meets-the-Pixies teen angst of "Teen Spirit" is what crossed Nirvana over, what made the album so remarkable was the quantum leap in Kurt Cobain's songwriting. The throttling punk rockers "Breed" and "Territorial Pissings" demolish anything on *Bleach*, and the haunting "Something in the Way" and "Polly" show Cobain's full range. Even better are "In Bloom," "Drain You," "On a Plain," and "Lithium," which fully combine both the melodicism and the sonic roar that Nirvana do so well. And the record wouldn't sound half as good as it does without Dave Grohl, who pushes every song to the limit. —*Stephen Thomas Erlewine*

Incesticide / Dec. 1992 / DGC ✦✦✦✦
More than anyone else, Nirvana itself was caught completely off guard by the overwhelming success of *Nevermind*. While Cobain wondered what to do next, the band put out *Incesticide*, a collection of B-sides, live performances, outtakes, demos, and "rare" singles. The first half of the album is terrific, but after "Beeswax" the entire enterprise collapses into half-baked ideas and outtakes that deserved to stay that way. The first half is filled with BBC sessions previously only available on the Japanese import *Hormoaning*, the B-sides "Been a Son" and "Son of a Gun," and a Sub Pop single. The price of the CD is justified by the first two tracks, the "Dive"/"Sliver" single, which was released just before *Nevermind* was recorded. —*Stephen Thomas Erlewine*

☆ **In Utero** / Sep. 21, 1993 / DGC ✦✦✦✦✦
Despite all of the pre-release rumors predicting a noisy all-out sonic assault, *In Utero* is not an alienating alternative rock monster. Instead, *In Utero* retains all of the melodic splendor of *Nevermind*, injecting it with a raw roar louder and harder than anything on *Bleach*. However, Kurt Cobain remains a pop songwriter, and the melodies don't get buried under Steve Albini's sonic assault, as "Heart-Shaped Box" and "Pen-

nyroyal Tea" prove. The songs are among Cobain's best, making *In Utero* a successful follow-up to a landmark, groundbreaking album. —*Stephen Thomas Erlewine*

☆ **MTV Unplugged in New York** / Nov. 1, 1994 / DGC ✦✦✦✦✦
Sadly, *MTV Unplugged* stands as Nirvana's last album. While it's an album of covers and old songs, it ranks as one of the band's most cohesive records. Instead of relying on the trio's overpowering sonic force, *Unplugged* concentrates on Kurt Cobain's subtly shaded songwriting and Nirvana's deceptively simple musical power. Every version of their previously recorded songs, with the possible exception of "On a Plain," dramatically improves the original, and the covers reveal more about Cobain than he intended. By the time Nirvana close with a wrenching, spine-chilling version of Leadbelly's "Where Did You Sleep Last Night?" the emotional complexity of Nirvana's music is clear. It's also clear that they could have made even greater music. —*Stephen Thomas Erlewine*

From the Muddy Banks of the Wishkah / Oct. 1, 1996 / Geffen ✦✦✦✦
Assembled from a variety of live tapes recorded between 1989 and 1994, *From the Muddy Banks of the Wishkah* captures the scathing power of Nirvana in concert at the peak of their powers. Compiled by Krist Novoselic and Dave Grohl, the album features many of the band's hits—"Smells like Teen Spirit," "Lithium," and "Heart Shaped Box" are all here—but it relies on B-sides and album tracks like "Drain You," "Aneurysm," and the 1992 Reading performance of "Tourette's," infamously introduced as "The Eagle Has Landed." Musically, the album offers no great revelations—if you didn't know that Nirvana was a great rock band from listening to their studio albums, you weren't paying attention—but it does confirm their greatness, and on occasion, the band eclipses the studio versions, such as on early songs like "Blew" and "School." —*Stephen Thomas Erlewine*

Mojo Nixon

b. Aug. 2, 1957, Chapel Hill, NC
Vocals / Alternative Pop-Rock, Rockabilly Revival
Mojo Nixon parlayed an irrepressible personality, a wicked sense of humor, and a taste for high-energy rockabilly into success on a series of novelty albums, and even a place as an MTV VJ. The latter was surprising, since Nixon had first gained notice for a song on his and Skid Roper's second album, *Frenzy* (1986), called "Stuffin' Martha's Muffin," an ode to the joys of intimate contact with MTV VJ Martha Quinn. The song was typical of Nixon's lyrical approach, which he followed with relentless mirth through the course of four albums on which Roper (a mostly silent partner) contributed incidental instrumental backup. *Bo-Day-Shus!!!* (1987), for example, contained "Elvis Is Everywhere," one of the more outrageous tributes to The King. Debunking famous names came more naturally to Nixon, however, and *Root Hog or Die* was introduced by the *National Enquirer*-headline leadoff song "Debbie Gibson Is Pregnant with My Two Headed Love Child." Gibson didn't comment, but when Nixon (now separated from Roper) issued his first solo album, *Otis*, containing the song "Don Henley Must Die," the ex-Eagle was heard to say that the singer needed a laxative. —*William Ruhlmann*

Mojo & Skid / 1985 / IRS ✦✦
Get Out of My Way / 1986 / Restless ✦✦✦
Frenzy / 1986 / IRS ✦✦✦
Arguably the duo's best album, highlights include "I'm Living with the Three-Foot Anti-Christ," "The Amazing Bigfoot Diet," and two songs any working musician should understand, "Where the Hell's My Money?" and "I Hate Banks." By the way, the *Get Out of My Way* mini-LP, which included some of Nixon's Christmas tunes, is also part of the *Frenzy* CD. —*Rick Clark*

Bo-Day-Shus!!! / 1987 / Enigma ✦✦✦✦
On *Bo-Day-Shus!!!*, Nixon and Roper want you to know that "Elvis Is Everywhere" (but you knew that anyway—right??). They explore the junk-food underbelly of American culture with thoughtful odes like "B.B.Q.USA.," "I'm Gonna Dig Up Howlin' Wolf," and "We Gotta Have More Soul." Declarative odes like "I Ain't Gonna Piss in No Jar" and "Don't Want No Foo-Foo Haircut on My Head" are indications of the duo's sensitivity to politically correct issues. —*Rick Clark*

Root Hog or Die / 1989 / IRS ✦✦✦✦
With the help of producer Jim Dickinson and a few sidemen, Skid Roper and Mojo Nixon plow through thoughtful numbers like "Debbie Gibson Is Pregnant with My Two-Headed Love Child," "She's Vibrator Dependent," and "Louisiana Liplock." Nixon indulges his Elvis fixation with "(619) 239-KING," and a version of "This Land Is Your Land" mutates into a pitch for Mojo World. —*Rick Clark*

● **Unlimited Everything** / 1990 / Enigma ✦✦✦✦
This fairly complete overview of Nixon and Roper's most popular work is a good place to start for the uninitiated. —*Rick Clark*

Otis / 1990 / IRS ✦✦✦
After *Root Hog or Die*, Mojo went solo and enlisted a primo group of rude rock sidemen from the Del-Lords, X, Beat Farmers, and Dash Rip Rock. Nixon did a good job making the transition from the bare-bones duo approach to a full band. His put-down of "serious" pop rockers like Don Henley ("Don Henley Must Die") gained quite a bit of publicity. —*Rick Clark*

Gadzooks / Jan. 28, 1997 / Needletime ✦✦✦
Gadzooks is a 17-cut retrospective of Nixon's career, which spans his very first recorded song to five new tracks. Additionally, the set includes demos and rare material found only on singles, compilations, and flexi-discs. —*Jason Ankeny*

No Doubt

f. 1987, Anaheim, CA
Alternative Pop-Rock, Third Wave Ska-Revival, Ska-Metal
With the return of the punks in the mid-'90s came a resurgence of their slightly more commercial rivals, new wave bands. No Doubt found a niche as a new wave/ska band, on the strength of vocalist Gwen Stefani's persona—alternately an embrace of little-girl-lost innocence and riot grrl feminism—exemplified on the band's breakout single, "Just a Girl."

Formed in early 1987 as a ska band inspired by Madness, the lineup of No Doubt initially comprised John Spence, Gwen Stefani and her brother Eric. While playing the party-band circuit around Anaheim, the trio picked up bassist Tony Kanal, a native of India. Hardened by the suicide of Spence in December 1987, No Doubt nevertheless continued; Gwen became the lone vocalist and the group added guitarist Tom Dumont and drummer Adrian Young.

No Doubt's live act began to attract regional interest, and Interscope Records signed them in 1991. The band's debut a year later, an odd fusion of '80s pop and ska, sank without a trace in the wake of the grunge movement. As a result, Interscope refused to support No Doubt's tour or further recordings. The band responded by recording on their own during 1993-94; the result was the self-released *The Beacon Street Collection*, much rawer and more punk-inspired than the debut. Eric Stefani left just after its release, later working as an animator for *The Simpsons*. By late 1994, Interscope allowed recordings to resume, and *Tragic Kingdom* was released in October 1995. The album served as a document of the breakup of Gwen Stefani and Kanal, whose relationship had lasted seven years. Thanks to constant touring and the appearance of "Just a Girl" and "Spiderwebs" on MTV's Buzz Bin, the album hit the Top Ten in 1996. Stefani, who has made no secret of her pop ambitions, became a centerpiece of attention as an alternative to the crop of tough girls prevalent on the charts. By the end of the year, *Tragic Kingdom* hit No. 1 on the album charts, almost a year after its first release. —*John Bush*

No Doubt / Mar. 17, 1992 / Interscope ✦✦✦
Despite No Doubt's punk influences, they weren't included in the grunge boom of the early '90s. Much of the cause is due to the band's debut album, a work of polished production inspired more by '80s synth than No Doubt's heritage. Compared to Southern California's accepted ska/punk fusion, the album is overly pop-oriented, with new wave keyboards and punchy brass proving a foil to the basically ska framework. Stefani's extroverted vocals rescue the affair, however. —*John Bush*

Beacon Street Collection / Mar. 1995 / Beacon Street ✦✦✦✦
When No Doubt's debut album proved a disappointment to Interscope executives, the label withdrew support from the band and refused to release them from their contract. The group's self-produced reply, recorded during several sessions from 1993 to early 1995, is their finest album. The synth and new wave influences of the debut are pushed to the background and replaced by a raw sound inspired more by punk. —*John Bush*

● **Tragic Kingdom** / Oct. 10, 1995 / Trauma/Interscope ✦✦✦✦
Led by the infectious, pseudo-new wave single "Just a Girl," No Doubt's major-label debut *Tragic Kingdom* straddles the line between '90s punk, ska-revival, and new wave pop sensibility. In other words, it's a mess but it can be an *enjoyable* mess. No Doubt is at their best when they fuse their edgy energy with pop melodies, but that doesn't happen frequently enough to make the album a consistently entertaining listen. When everything does click—and it does several times, most noticeably on "Just a Girl"—the record is pure fun, but the rest of the album makes you wish they could sustain that energy throughout the record. —*Stephen Thomas Erlewine*

The Notorious B.I.G.

b. May 21, 1972, Brooklyn, NY, d. Mar. 9, 1997, Los Angeles, CA
Vocals / G-Funk, Gangsta Rap
The Brooklyn-born rapper the Notorious B.I.G. (born Chris Wallace) first gained attention for his work on Mary J. Blige's "What's the 411?" When

he delivered his debut album, *Ready to Die*, in 1994, it became one of the most popular hip-hop releases of the year. In June of 1995, his single "One More Chance" debuted at No. 5 in the pop singles chart, tying Michael Jackson's "Scream / Childhood" as the highest-debuting single of all time. *Ready to Die* continued to gain popularity throughout 1995, eventually selling two million copies. With its success, the Notorious B.I.G. became the most visable figue in East Coast hip-hop, and he became a target in the heated feud between the two coasts; especially, he and Tupac Shakur, a former ally, became vicious rivals.

As the Notorious B.I.G. was preparing his second album, Shakur was shot and killed in Las Vegas. Many in the media speculated that Biggie's camp was responsible for the shooting, accusations that he and his produces, Sean "Puffy" Combs, vehemently denied. However, the wheels had been set in motion for another tragedy. Early on the morning of March 9, the Notorious B.I.G. was returnign to his hotel in Los Angeles after a Soul Train Award party when another car pulled up aside his car and opened fire, killing him instantly. Shakur had been killed just six months earlier.

The Notorious B.I.G.'s second album, the double-disc *Life After Death*, was released three weeks later, debuting at No. 1 on the charts. —*Stephen Thomas Erlewine*

● **Ready to Die** / Sep. 13, 1994 / Arista ✦✦✦✦
With the galvanizing deep funk of *Ready to Die*, The Notorious B.I.G. scores one of the most impressive rap debuts since Dr. Dre's seminal *The Chronic*. While *Ready to Die* takes its throbbing bass grooves from that P-Funk-saturated album, the Notorious B.I.G. writes more acute and evocative lyrics, as well as being a more skillful rapper. —*Stephen Thomas Erlewine*

Life After Death / Mar. 25, 1997 / Bad Boy/Arista ✦✦✦✦
Life After Death will always be haunted by the death of the Notorious B.I.G., who was murdered merely three weeks before his second album was released. Certain songs, and certainly the title, have a different, sadder aura in the wake of his death, but there's no denying that the double album is a triumphant effort, one that follows through on the achievements of his debut, *Ready to Die*. That doesn't necessarily mean that it is a consistent album—after all, it's hard to sustain attention over the course of over two hours, especially since Biggie Smalls worked with nearly every major hip-hop producer in order to ensure his commercial viability. While that means some cuts fall flat—including, surprisingly, his collaborations with R. Kelly and Bone Thugs-N-Harmony—it also means there's a wealth of excellent music, from Puffy Combs-produced funk extravaganzas to edgy cuts with RZA and Havoc. *Life After Death* is impossible to digest all at once, but its very best moments vividly and poignantly illustrate the Notorious B.I.G.'s deep talents as a musician and lyricist. —*Stephen Thomas Erlewine*

NRBQ (New Rhythm & Blues Quintet)

f. 1967, Miami, FL
Rock 'n' Roll, Roots-Rock
NRBQ (the New Rhythm and Blues Quartet) have amassed a fanatical cult following over more than two decades of recording and touring with their incredibly versatile eclecticism; their music might veer from country to rockabilly to pop to bar-band R&B to blues to free jazz, all in the same album. The group's wacky, sometimes corny sense of humor and in-concert unpredictability (the band sometimes vows to play whatever song audience members request) have endeared them to fans, even if some find them a bit precious. The band was formed in Miami in 1967 by keyboardist Terry Adams, guitarist Steve Ferguson (both former members of Merseybeats USA), singer Frank Gadler, drummer Tom Staley, and bassist/singer Joey Spampinato. After moving to New Jersey and playing clubs, NRBQ attracted immediate attention with their wide-ranging musicianship and were signed to Columbia. On their 1969 self-titled debut, the band covered rockabilly and Sun Ra on one record and pulled it off; not surprisingly, rave reviews followed. NRBQ followed it with *Boppin' the Blues*, a collaboration with rockabilly singer Carl Perkins; it too received critical praise, but Columbia was unhappy with the group's sales and dropped it. Ferguson left the group and was replaced by former Wildweeds guitarist Al Anderson; Gadler left in 1972, and in 1974, drummer Tom Ardolino replaced Staley. This lineup carried on through 1994, recording albums for labels including Kama Sutra, Rounder, and Mercury (*At Yankee Stadium*), as well as their own Red Rooster. NRBQ and its members have worked with Skeeter Davis (1985's *She Sings, They Play*), John Sebastian, jazz artist Carla Bley, and even unofficial manager and wrestling star Captain Lou Albano, who appeared on 1986's *Lou and the Q*. Joey Spampinato appeared in the Chuck Berry film *Hail! Hail! Rock and Roll* as a member of the backing band. In 1989, the band got another one-album major-label deal with Virgin, which resulted in *Wild Weekend*, their first album to make the charts since the debut record. Al Anderson joined a Nashville publishing house in 1991 and had songs recorded by several major country artists, including Alabama, Carlene Carter, and Ricky Van Shelton; he left the

group in 1994 and was replaced by Spampinato's brother Johnny for the album *Message for the Mess Age.* —*Steve Huey*

NRBQ / 1969 / Columbia ✦✦✦
The Q's debut is as succinct a summation of what this band was about than perhaps anything they've released since. After opening the record with a storming version of Eddie Cochran's "C'mon Everybody," they take a breath and leap headlong into a raucous version of Sun Ra's "Number 9." Add to that a songwriting collaboration between Terry Adams and jazz composer Carla Bley, and the great guitar playing of Steve Ferguson (really great on "Stomp"), and you've got the makings of a tremendously important record by a furiously eclectic and always wonderful band. —*John Dougan*

Scraps / 1972 / Polydor ✦✦✦
A spotty album, it contains a few necessary gems, like "Magnet" and "It's Not So Hard." —*John Floyd*

Workshop / 1973 / Kama Sutra ✦✦✦

Scraps/Workshop / 1976 / Annuit ✦✦✦✦
When vinyl was still the prevailing form of sound reproduction, these two long-lost records were re-released in this fantastic double set, which is probably out of print, but (assuming it hasn't been issued on CD) is worth ferreting out. Both records feature the debut of Al Anderson's superb guitar, and, (trivia buffs take note) *Scraps* is the only time in the band's history they were a quintet with lead vocalist Frank Gadler (who's very good). Both records are chock-full of classic Q: "Howard Johnson's Got His Hojo Working on Me," "C'Mon If You're Comin'," "Get That Gasoline," and "Magnet." Also making these records indispensable is Joey Spampinato's best-ever Beatles impression "It's Not So Hard," maybe the best pop song the Q ever recorded. Buyer's note: Parts of *Workshop*, along with an assortment of outtakes, were issued by Rounder in 1986 as an album entitled *RC Cola & a Moon Pie.* —*John Dougan*

All Hopped Up / 1977 / Rounder ✦✦✦
A fairly consistent and ballsy offering, it contains early classics such as "Ridin' in My Car" and "That's Alright." —*John Floyd*

● **NRBQ at Yankee Stadium** / 1978 / Mercury ✦✦✦✦
More than just NRBQ's best record, but one of the great records of the '70s (maybe ever!). This album contains the strongest batch of new Q songs on one record, several of them the best and most memorable songs in the band's long and storied career. Starting with Terry Adams' herky-jerky "Green Lights" to the rollicking "I Want You Bad," the band has rarely sounded better. The record's gem, however, is an Al Anderson song left over from their previous record (*All Hopped Up on Red Rooster*), "Ridin' in My Car." A song about lost love and blown chances, it has Anderson's characteristic wry sensibility and (nonfatal) heartache, all wrapped up in an ebullient pop package driven by Terry Adams' melodic keyboard riffing and Tom Ardolino's amazingly assertive drumming. *Yankee Stadium* should have been a huge album, but Mercury booted it and never capitalized on the band's fanatical support base. Caveat emptor: When this record was issued by Mercury on CD just a couple of years back, they inexplicably left off "Ridin' in My Car." As to whether that idiotic oversight has been rectified, I haven't a clue. —*John Dougan*

Kick Me Hard / 1979 / Rounder ✦✦✦✦
This is a decent mix of tough rockers and cheesy pop. —*John Floyd*

Tiddlywinks / 1980 / Rounder ✦✦✦✦
After being unceremoniously dumped by Mercury after *Yankee Stadium*, NRBQ returned to the warm embrace of Rounder and recorded a string of fine records that started with *Kick Me Hard.* This lineup was to remain intact for nearly 20 years, but here, fairly early on, the synchronicity among the quartet was apparent; it was if they'd been playing together forever, and the music excelled as a result. The songwriting was getting better too: Al, Terry, and Joey were dividing the chores but never losing the group's cohesiveness. At times, Terry's songs would be a little too goofy, and Joey's heartfelt pop might dip into saccharine sweetness now and again, but never so much that it becomes a huge problem. Of these two excellent records, *Kick Me Hard* lives up to its title, especially during the bluesy organ workout "Don't You Know" and the riff-happy "All Night Long" (great solo by Al). *Tiddlywinks* is carried by "Me and the Boys" (later to be recorded by Bonnie Raitt) and Anderson's beautiful "Never Take the Place of You." —*John Dougan*

Grooves in Orbit / 1983 / Bearsville ✦✦✦
Back to a major label, NRBQ came up with a solid record that, again, didn't significantly increase their audience, even though many musicians (Elvis Costello, Bonnie Raitt) were singing their praises. Although very good, *Grooves* is not significantly better (actually it's not any better) than *Kick Me Hard* or *Tiddlywinks.* Both sides end with a whimper rather than a bang, and it seems that the band was developing an over-reliance on recycling material (their cover of Johnny Cash's "Get Rhythm" shows up on *Yankee Stadium*). Still, the crucial stuff ("Rain at the Drive-In" and "Smackeroo") fit the bill. —*John Dougan*

Tap Dancin' Bats / 1983 / Rounder ✦✦✦
While the Q was recording *Grooves* for Bearsville, Rounder released this bizarre chunk of odds and sods that featured the band's experimental side. Ask anyone who's ever gone to an NRBQ gig and they'll tell you that the Q are as likely to play Sun Ra as they are Carl Perkins, or sometimes fuse the two. *Tapdancin' Bats* has such supremely strange moments: their paean to wrestler/actor Lou Albano, "Captain Lou," a crazy novelty song from the '50s; "Rats in My Room," some straightahead (but slightly skewed) rock 'n' roll; and the title track, a dissonant jazz blurt that sounds like Ornette Coleman. Truly inspiring stuff. —*John Dougan*

She Sings, They Play / 1985 / Rounder ✦✦✦
During the mid-'80s, bassist Joey Spampinato married country music legend Skeeter Davis, and what better way to celebrate than with a record that featured Skeeter's great voice with the Q backing her up. To those who have little patience for classic country performers, and who simply want to hear NRBQ rock, this is probably a minor work. But, for the rest of us, it's an unfettered joy. —*John Dougan*

RC Cola & a Moon Pie / 1986 / Rounder ✦✦
This abridged version of *Workshop* (one of their finest early albums) includes some previously unreleased and rare material. —*John Floyd*

Lou and the Q / 1986 / Rounder ✦✦
Silliness abounds on this wacky meeting of the "Q" with pro-wrestling manager Lou Albano. —*Jeff Tamarkin*

God Bless Us All / 1987 / Rounder ✦✦✦
Go figure this: Rounder decides to release two live recordings in succession. Granted, NRBQ had long been known for great live shows, but these records, while certainly enjoyable, seem a little perfunctory, and only hint at the kind of excitement the band was capable of generating live. Still, on *God Bless Us All*, Al tears through an inspired "Crazy Like a Fox" and the whole band cranks on "Shake, Rattle and Roll." *Diggin'* has a pounding "It Comes to Me Naturally" and the country standard "Scarlet Ribbons." Both records are fun, but neither is essential unless you're a completist. —*John Dougan*

Diggin' Uncle Q (Live) / 1988 / Rounder ✦✦
1988's *Diggin' Uncle Q* is NRBQ's second consecutive live release, recorded largely in Providence, Rhode Island. Given their über-bar band aesthetic, the live setting typically represents the Q at their best; it's where their rock and R&B roots really shine through. This set—which includes the fan-favorites "Rocket in My Pocket" and "It Comes to Me Naturally" but otherwise focuses on new material—is no exception. —*Jason Ankeny*

Wild Weekend / Sep. 1989 / Virgin ✦✦
Another year, another shot with a major label. Actually, of all the recent Q releases, *Wild Weekend* got the most ink and promotional support out of the box. Helping it along was a video for the title track, as well as mostly favorable critical notices. It's a good record, but not a great one. The good stuff rocks with the power, swing, and sway of classic Q, whereas the bad stuff (not really bad, just mediocre) serves as filler. Another great Al Anderson song ("Boys' Life") and a wonderful, whimsical one from Terry ("Little Floater"). —*John Dougan*

● **Peek-A-Boo: Best of NRBQ (1969-1989)** / Oct. 1990 / Rhino ✦✦✦✦
A two-CD set that does a great job of hitting the band's high spots, without sacrificing any of the freewheeling stylistic leaps or engaging lunacy that has made NRBQ one of America's longest-lived bands. If you're interested in a career overview and little more, this is the ideal release. However, it is my considered opinion that anyone who loves this stuff (and to emphatically use a double negative, there's nothing not to love) will have their appetite whetted for more. Not a slow spot, ill-chosen track, or bad decision among the 35 songs, this is as great a statement for NRBQ as one of the best rock bands America has ever produced. Few bands, genre notwithstanding, have been able to effortlessly recombine styles, be so defiantly off-the-wall, and rock like all get-out for so long and still sound so good. God bless them all. —*John Dougan*

Honest Dollar / Jul. 10, 1992 / Rykodisc ✦✦
If legendary American rockers NRBQ would issue an album of songs as wistful and infectious as *Honest Dollar*'s opener "Ridin' in My Car," they would be huge stars. But then they wouldn't be NRBQ, the band for which repetition and predictability equals death. *Honest Dollar* features 17 wildly diverse live tracks spanning the last decade's worth of NRBQ life on the road, 11 of which have never previously been set to disc by the group. The collection serves as a perfect introduction to NRBQ's rootsy, off-center pop fused with blues, jazz, country, and rockabilly. NRBQ are obviously too spontaneous and diverse for their own commercial good, but offer a heady experience for anyone willing to ride this musical roller coaster with an open mind. —*Roch Parisien*

Stay with We: The Best of NRBQ / May 11, 1993 / Columbia ✦✦✦
Featuring 24 songs including eight unreleased tracks, *Stay with We* is the definitive compilation of NRBQ's early years at Columbia. —*Stephen Thomas Erlewine*

Message for the Mess Age / Feb. 22, 1994 / Forward ✦✦✦
Sadly, the last record with Al on guitar (he's since been replaced by Joey's brother Johnny, ex-guitar slinger for the Incredible Casuals and Four Star Combo) isn't a knockout, but the material is strong and makes one optimistic for the Q's next 25 years. Al does contribute another achingly beautiful song, "A Better Word for Love," and even the goofy moments ("Girl Scout Cookies" and the spell-my-name-right-anthem "Spampinato") don't sound nearly as forced as they occasionally have in the past. We're lucky to still have 'em around. —*John Dougan*

Tokyo: Recorded Live at on Air West Tokyo / Feb. 11, 1997 / Rounder ✦✦✦

Ted Nugent

b. 1948, Detroit, MI
Guitar / Hard Rock, Heavy Metal, Arena Rock
Nugent started in a local Detroit teen band, the Lourds, and formed the Amboy Dukes in late 1965 or early 1966. He scored his first hit with "Journey to the Center of Your Mind" in 1968. Several albums using the Amboy Dukes tag followed, with the personnel changing with almost every album. Nugent went solo in 1975, marking his greatest success to date with one album after another in the charts; he put his solo career on hold to become a member of the group Damn Yankees in 1990. He resumed his solo career in 1995 with *Spirit of the Wild.* A powerful, high-decibel guitarist, Nugent's energy more than makes up for whatever subtleties he lacks. —*Cub Koda*

Free for All / 1976 / Epic ✦✦✦✦
Ted Nugent's career kicked into gear with his second solo album, *Free-for-All*, which was a collection of storming hard rockers sung by Meat Loaf, who had yet to establish himself as a star in his own right. —*Stephen Thomas Erlewine*

Cat Scratch Fever / 1977 / Epic ✦✦✦✦
Driven by a set of hard-driving, catchy riffs and numerous gut-wrenching solos, *Cat Scratch Fever* remains Ted Nugent's best studio album. —*Stephen Thomas Erlewine*

Weekend Warrior / 1978 / Epic ✦✦✦
Weekend Warriors, Nugent's follow-up to the career peaks of *Cat Scratch Fever* and *Double Live Gonzos!,* isn't quite as strong as his two previous albums, but it remains one of his better albums, featuring a handful of prime hard rockers. —*Stephen Thomas Erlewine*

Double Live Gonzo / 1978 / Epic ✦✦✦✦
This is the ultimate document of Nugent's mountain-man persona. —*Dan Heilman*

● **Great Gonzo: The Best of Ted Nugent** / 1981 / Epic ✦✦✦✦
Featuring all of his hard-rock standards from the 1970s, *Great Gonzos: The Best of Ted Nugent* is a better collection than the double-disc *Out of Control*, since there isn't a bit of filler. —*Stephen Thomas Erlewine*

● **Ted Nugent and the Amboy Dukes** / 1987 / DCC ✦✦✦✦
Featuring the psychedelic classic "Journey to the Center of the Mind," as well as several other similar-sounding acid-rockers, *Ted Nugent and the Amboy Dukes* is the best record Nugent made with his first band. —*Stephen Thomas Erlewine*

Out of Control / Jun. 22, 1993 / Epic ✦✦✦✦
Out of Control is two CDs of prime Nugent, covering his days with the Amboy Dukes as well as his lengthy solo career. It's the definitive collection of the Motor City Madman. —*AMG*

Spirit of the Wild / May 2, 1995 / Atlantic ✦✦✦✦
Spirit of the Wild ranks as one of Ted Nugent's finest moments because it cuts away the filler and keeps the wildman's tendency for indulgence in check. A fair amount of the material does concern itself with the wilderness, which fits right in with his '90s reinvention as a conservative family-values spokesman. That doesn't mean that it's a tame record—it means that Nugent sounds committed again, since that passion for hunting and family flows throughout his performance. —*Stephen Thomas Erlewine*

Live at Hammersmith 1979 / Mar. 11, 1997 / Sony ✦✦✦✦
Originally broadcast on the *King Biscuit Flower Hour,* this 1979 set recorded at London's Hammersmith Odeon as the finale to Nugent's European tour has crowd favorites including "Cat Scratch Fever," "Gonzo," "Motor City Madhouse," and "Free-for-All." —*Jason Ankeny*

Gary Numan (Gary Webb)

b. 1958, Hammersmith, London, England
Synthesizer, Vocals / Synth-pop, Electronic, New Wave, New Romantic
Gary Numan managed to incorporate the electronic innovations of Kraftwerk, Brian Eno, and David Bowie into pop music, creating some of the first synth-pop hits of the new wave era. Numan originally performed under the name Tubeway Army, which had a chart-topping British single with "Are 'Friends' Electric?" The first record he released

under his own name, 1979's *Pleasure Principle,* featured the international hit "Cars"; the single hit No. 1 in the UK and reached the US Top Ten. Throughout the early '80s, Numan was one of the most popular artists in the UK, amassing several Top Ten hits and two No. 1 albums. Around 1983, his career began to slip, as each record became indistinguishable from the other. Even as he fell out of the Top Ten, Numan held on to his diehard fans. He continued to record into the '90s. —*Stephen Thomas Erlewine*

Tubeway Army / Nov. 1978 / Beggars Banquet ✦✦✦
Gary Numan's first album, recorded with his backup band Tubeway Army and released under their name, is a tentative but intriguing effort, as the keyboardist works synthesizers and electronic textures into basic, guitar-driven post-punk song structures. —*Stephen Thomas Erlewine*

Replicas / 1979 / Atco ✦✦✦✦
On *Replicas,* Gary Numan took top billing over Tubeway Army, which was appropriate, considering that Numan's synthesizers were now the dominant instruments in the band's music. The new direction was successful, both artistically and commercially, with the cold, catchy single "Are 'Friends' Electric?" reaching the top of the UK charts. —*Stephen Thomas Erlewine*

● **The Pleasure Principle** / Sep. 1979 / Arista ✦✦✦✦
Gary Numan perfected his combination of Kraftwerk-influenced synth-drone and pop melodies on *The Pleasure Principle,* the first album he released under his own name. —*Stephen Thomas Erlewine*

Telekon / 1980 / Atco ✦✦✦✦
After the synthesized triumph of *The Pleasure Principle,* Gary Numan brought some guitars back into his sound on *Telekon.* Unlike *Tubeway Army,* which was dominated by guitars, the instrument is used to flesh out the keyboard-created textures on *Telekon,* which makes the album one of his most intriguing and creative records. —*Stephen Thomas Erlewine*

I Assassin / 1982 / Atco ✦✦✦✦
Although it showcases his trademark sound to a fine effect, the repetitive, formulaic songwriting of *I, Assassin* suggests that Gary Numan had hit a brick wall with his robotic, synthesized pop. —*Stephen Thomas Erlewine*

Ghost: Exhibition Tour 1987 / 1987 / Numa ✦✦✦
A live double LP originally released through the Numan fan club, later reissued on CD through his revived record company. Energetic renditions of Numan material up to *Strange Charm.* —*Steven McDonald*

The Best Of: 1984-1992 / 1997 / Emporio ✦✦✦
Gary Numan had stopped having hits several years before 1984, which is where *The Best of: 1984-1992* chooses to begin. During the late '80s, Numan began to concentrate more on sonic textures, creating glassy, shimmering soundscapes with his synthesizers and abandoning the robotic funk that made "Cars" and "Are Friends Electric?" into hits. While the latter is included in a stilted live version, none of his best moments are featured on this collection. Nevertheless, it does feature the cream of a highly uneven era, and that alone makes it a worthwhile addition to his catalog. For many casual fans, *The Best of: 1984-1992* will be all they need from Numan's latter-day recordings, if they need it at all. —*Stephen Thomas Erlewine*

N.W.A.

f. 1986, Compton, CA, **db.** 1991
Hip Hop, Gangsta Rap, Hardcore Rap, West Coast Rap
N.W.A., the unapologetically violent and sexist pioneers of gangsta rap, is in many ways the most notorious group in the history of rap. Emerging in the late '80s, when Public Enemy had rewritten the rules of hardcore rap by proving that it could be intelligent, revolutionary and socially aware, N.W.A. capitalized on PE's sonic breakthroughs while ignoring their message. Instead, the five-piece crew celebrated the violence and hedonism of the criminal life, capturing it all in blunt, harsh language. Initially, the group's relentless attack appeared to be serious, vital commentary, and it even provoked the FBI to caution N.W.A.'s record company, but following Ice Cube's departure late 1989, the group began to turn to self-parody. With his high-pitched whine, Eazy-E's urban nightmares now seemed like comic book fantasies, but that fulfilled the fantasies of the teenage, white suburbanites that had become their core audience, and the group became more popular than ever. Nevertheless, clashing egos prevented the band from recording a third album, and they fell apart once producer Dr. Dre left for a solo career in 1992. Although the group was no longer active, their influence—from their funky, bass-driven beats to their exaggerated lyrics—was evident throughout the '90s.
Ironically, in its original incarnation NWA was hardly revolutionary. Eazy-E (b. Eric Wright), a former drug dealer who started Ruthless Records with money he earned by pushing, was attempting to start a rap empire, by building a roster of successful rap artists. However, he wasn't having much success until Dr. Dre—a member of the World Class

Wreckin' Cru—and Ice Cube (b. O'Shea Jackson) began writing songs for Ruthless. Eazy tried to give one of the duo's songs, "Boyz N The Hood," to Ruthless signees HBO and when the group refused, Eazy formed NWA—an acronym for Niggaz With Attitude—with Dre and Cube, adding World Class Wreckin' Cru member DJ Yella (b. Antoine Carraby), the Arabian Prince and the D.O.C. to the group.

N.W.A's first album, *N.W.A. and the Posse,* was a party-oriented jam record that largely went ignored upon its 1987 release. In the following year, the group added MC Ren and revamped their sound, bringing in many of the noisy, extreme sonic innovations of Public Enemy and adopting a self-consciously violent and dangerous lyrical stance. Late in 1988, N.W.A. delivered *Straight Outta Compton,* a vicious hardcore record that became an underground hit with virtually no support from radio, the press or MTV. N.W.A. became notorious for their hardcore lyrics, especially those of "Fuck Tha Police," which resulted in the FBI sending a warning letter to Ruthless and its parent company Priority, suggesting that the group should watch their step.

Most of the group's political threat left with Ice Cube when he departed in late 1989 admist many financial disagreements. A nasty feud between N.W.A. and Cube began that would culminate with Cube's "No Vaseline," an attack on the group's management released on his 1991 *Death Certificate* album. By the time the song was released, N.W.A., for all intents and purposes, was finished.

In the two years between Ice Cube's departure and the group's dissolution, N.W.A. was dominated by Eazy-E's near-parodic lyrics and Dr. Dre's increasingly subtle and complex productions. The group quickly released an EP, *100 Miles and Runnin',* in 1990 before following it up early the next year with *Efil4zaggin* ("Niggaz 4 Life" spelled backward). *Efil4zaggin* was teeming with dense, funky soundscapes and ridiculously violent and misogynist lyrics. Naturally, the lyrics provoked outrage from many critics and conservative watchdogs, but that only increased the group's predoiminately male, white suburban audience. Even though the group was at the peak of their popularity, Dre began to make efforts to leave the crew, due to conflicting egos and what he perceived as an unfair record deal.

Dre left the group to form Death Row Records with Suge Knight in early 1992. According to legend, Knight threatened to kill NWA's manager Jerry Hibbler if he refused to let Dre out of his contract. Over the next few years, Dre and Eazy engaged in a highly-publicized feud, which included both of the rappers attacking each other on their respective solo albums. MC Ren and Yella both released solo albums, which were largely ignored, and Eazy-E continued to record albums that turned him into a complete self-parody until his tragic death from AIDS in March 1995. Before he died, Dre and Cube both made amends with Eazy. With his first solo album, 1992's *The Chronic,* Dr. Dre established himself as the premier hip-hop producer of the mid-'90s, setting the pace for much of hardcore rap with its elastic bass and deep, rolling grooves. Gangsta rap established itself as the most popular form of hip-hop during the '90s—in other words, N.W.A's amoralistic, hedonistic stance temporarily triumphed over the socially conscious, self-award hip-hop of Public Enemy, and it completely rewrote the rules of hip-hop for the '90s. —*Stephen Thomas Erlrewine*

N.W.A. and the Posse / 1987 / Priority ✦✦✦✦

Hip-hop was still very much dominated by New York in 1987, when Macola Records (a company that distributed numerous Los Angeles rap labels in the 1980s, including Eazy-E's Ruthless Records) distributed N.W.A's groundbreaking debut album *N.W.A and the Posse.* Ice-T was among the few West Coast rappers enjoying national exposure, and gangsta rap was far from the phenomenon it would become a few years later. A number of the songs—including the brutally honest "Dopeman"—would be reissued on *Straight Outta Compton,* while Eazy-E's first single, "Boyz-N-Tha-Hood," would be included on his 1988 solo album, *Eazy-Duz-It.* And the entire album would be reissued by Priority in 1989. This CD ranges from those early and seminal examples of gangsta rap to songs that are pure, unapologetic fun, such as the outrageously humorous "Fat Girl" and N.W.A. associates the Fila Fresh Crew's "Drink It Up," an infectious ode to booze employing the melody from the Isley Brothers' "Twist and Shout." One of the Crew's members was the D.O.C., who Dr. Dre and Eazy-E took to the top of the charts in 1989. Though not quite on a par with *Straight Outta Compton,* this is an engaging and historically important CD that's well worth acquiring. —*Alex Henderson*

★ Straight Outta Compton / 1989 / Priority ✦✦✦✦✦

Unapologetically frightening, N.W.A's *Straight Outta Compton* is one of the most seminal albums in the history of rap and greatly influenced countless gangsta rappers. N.W.A didn't invent gangsta rap—Ice-T and Schoolly D had already embraced first-person narratives focusing on the harsh realities of ghetto life—but the Los Angeles group made it even more violent. Portraying gang members and other felons, Dr. Dre, Ice Cube, MC Ren, and Eazy-E take listeners on an arresting journey through Los Angeles' tough Compton ghetto. Critics of this highly controversial album contended that N.W.A was glamorizing Black-on-Black

crime. The rappers countered that they weren't encouraging violence, but rather, were presenting an audio-documentary of life as they knew it growing up in Compton. Subsequently, gangsta rap would be plagued by numerous soundalike MCs who lacked even a fraction of N.W.A or Ice-T's originality. But in the innovative hands of N.W.A, it was bold, inspired, and arresting. —*Alex Henderson*

100 Miles and Runnin' / Aug. 1990 / Priority ✦✦✦

Like the Sex Pistols, N.W.A. had a major impact despite being together for only a few years. And like the British punk band, N.W.A. was so explosive, so volatile, so angry that it seemed destined to self-destruct. When Ice Cube left N.W.A. on anything but good terms in early 1990 to pursue a solo career, there was much doubt as to whether or not the controversial gangsta rap group would continue. But Dr. Dre, Eazy-E, MC Ren, and DJ Yella carried on without him, and continued to make worthwhile recordings for another year or so. *100 Miles and Runnin',* an EP, falls short of *Straight Outta Compton's* brilliance, but proved that there was indeed life after Cube for N.W.A. With "Real Niggaz" and the title song, N.W.A. offered more no-holds-barred depictions of the ugliness of ghetto life—while "Just Don't Bite It" (an explicit and insanely funny number that, to be sure, isn't for everyone) inspires comparisons to Rudy Ray Moore's X-rated humor. And Dre's imaginative production alone is worth the price of admission. —*Alex Henderson*

Niggaz4life / May 30, 1991 / Priority ✦✦✦

By the time N.W.A. recorded its third album, *Niggaz 4 Life* (fourth if you count the EP *100 Miles and Runnin'*), in 1991, gangsta rap had become ubiquitous. First-person narratives in which MCs portrayed thugs and felons and rapped about their misdeeds were more than plentiful. But the majority of gangsta rappers who debuted in the early '90s weren't even a fraction as interesting or distinctive as those who originated the style—namely, Ice-T, Schoolly D, and N.W.A. While the post-Cube album isn't as outstanding as *Straight Outta Compton,* N.W.A's graphic and unapologetically vulgar depictions of ghetto life remained quite riveting. The group pulls no punches; these first-person narratives make it abundantly clear just how hellish a nightmare life in the gang-infested, crack-ridden inner cities of Los Angeles could be. And true to form, Dr. Dre's aggressive yet melodic production is consistently imaginative. Unfortunately, *Niggaz 4 Life* would be N.W.A's last album. Eazy-E and Dr. Dre had a bitter falling out (much as they'd both turned against Ice Cube), and parted company for good. —*Alex Henderson*

Greatest Hits / Jul. 1996 / Ruthless ✦✦✦✦

N.W.A's career isn't necessarily one that lends itself well to anthologies. Though they had important singles, especially in the underground hip-hop community in the late '80s, they never received any support from radio or MTV, which meant they never had any official "hits." Instead, their albums were more important, popular, and influential than singles, even if individual tracks—"Fuck tha Police," "Straight Outta Compton," "Gangsta Gangsta," "Express Yourself"—became the focus of attention. And, if you notice, all those songs were from *Straight Outta Compton,* the only good album the group ever made. *Greatest Hits* does include all of the high points from that album (the title track is present in a previously unavailable remix), plus a scattershot sampling of raw early singles and the highlights from *100 Miles and Runnin'* and *Niggaz4Life.* It's nice to have the good tracks isolated from the group's latter-day efforts, but *Greatest Hits* is unnecessary—all you need is *Straight Outta Compton.* —*Stephen Thomas Erlewine*

Laura Nyro

b. Oct. 18, 1947, Bronx, NY, d. Apr. 9, 1997
Piano, Vocals / Singer-Songwriter, Pop-Rock

Laura Nyro was one of pop music's true originals: a brilliant and innovative composer, her songs found greater commercial success in the hands of other performers, but her own records—intricate, haunting works highlighting her singularly powerful vocal phrasing, evocative lyrics and alchemical fusion of gospel, soul, folk and jazz structures—remain her definitive artistic legacy.

The daughter of a jazz trumpeter, she was born Laura Nigro on October 18, 1947, and composed her first songs at the age of eight. After attending Manhattan's famed High School of Music and Art, she began performing in area clubs, drawing on influences as diverse as Bob Dylan and John Coltrane. In 1966, Nyro issued her first LP, *More Than a New Discovery;* though commercially unsuccessful, the album was a treasure trove of material for other artists—the Fifth Dimension scored with "Wedding Bell Blues" and "Blowin' Away," Barbra Streisand covered "Stoney End," and Blood, Sweat and Tears tackled "And When I Die."

In 1967, Nyro made just her second major live appearance to date at the Monterey Pop Festival; her idiosyncratic performance baffled the crowd, and she was booed off the stage. Then-music agent David Geffen caught her set, however, and was so impressed that he quit his current position to become her manager. He also won Nyro a contract with Columbia, and in 1968 she returned with the extraordinary *Eli and the*

Thirteenth Confession; while the album earned vast critical acclaim, she again found commercial success not with her own recordings, but with covers of *Eli's* songs as the Fifth Dimension reached the charts with renditions of "Stoned Soul Picnic" and "Sweet Blindness," while "Eli's Comin'" became a major hit for Three Dog Night.

New York Tendaberry, released in 1969, fared better thanks to the strong word-of-mouth now trailing her work; the record's "Time and Love" and "Save the Country" soon emerged as two of her most well-regarded and popular songs. With 1970's *Christmas and the Beads of Sweat*, she continued her exploration of soul music, enlisting Muscle Shoals staples like Barry Beckett, Roger Hawkins and Eddie Hinton; "Beads of Sweat" also featured guitar work from Duane Allman. 1971's *Gonna Take a Miracle*, recorded with Labelle and the production team of Kenny Gamble & Leon Huff, marked a dramatic left turn; Nyro's lone album of non-original material, it featured her tributes to Motown ("Jimmy Mack," "Nowhere to Run"), doo wop ("The Bells," "Spanish Harlem") and the girl-group era ("I Met Him on a Sunday").

At the age of 24, Nyro announced her retirement; she married, severed her industry connections, and moved to a small community in New England. However, the marriage ended in divorce, and in 1975 she resurfaced with *Smile;* a subsequent tour yielded the 1977 live set *Season of Lights*. However, the long layoff derailed whatever chart momentum her music had accrued, and after the dismal sales of 1978's *Nested*, she again retreated from the music business.

When Nyro finally returned from her self-imposed exile in 1984 with *Mother's Spiritual*, her music had grown more reserved and introspective; as the title indicated, her own motherhood provided considerable inspiration for her new work, as did her rustic New England lifestyle. While she did not make any overt declarations of retirement, Nyro waited another five years before issuing her next LP, *Live at the Bottom Line*, recorded at the legendary New York club; *Walk the Dog and Light the Light*, her first collection of new material in nearly a decade, followed in 1993. Nyro died of ovarian cancer on April 9, 1997. *—Jason Ankeny*

More than a New Discovery / 1967 / Verve/Forecast ✦✦✦
A collection given over to the more conventional, if high-quality, early Nyro songs that later became hits (and standards) in the hands of other performers. The album includes "Wedding Bell Blues," "Stoney End," and "And When I Die." (Also released under the title *The First Songs* and reissued on Columbia Records in 1973.) *—William Ruhlmann*

● **Eli and the 13th Confession** / 1968 / Columbia ✦✦✦✦
The hits (for others) keep coming—"Sweet Blindness," "Eli's Comin'," and "Stoned Soul Picnic" are all here, sung by their author—but Nyro not only proves herself a powerful singer in her own right, comfortable in styles from jazz to gospel-R&B to stark balladry, she also begins to turn to a more introspective, personal writing and singing which no one will be able to replicate. *—William Ruhlmann*

New York Tendaberry / 1969 / Columbia ✦✦✦✦
A stunning musical journey through love, loss, religion, and eroticism, by turns passionate, inspired, and suicidal, this is Nyro's most accomplished, most idiosyncratic record, and one of the greatest singer-songwriter works ever made. Using a wide vocal range and her often delicate piano work with deftly added instrumental touches, Nyro creates an aural landscape that spans the extremes of human emotion. It's not listed as her "pick" album only because it's not the place to start; rather, it's the logical conclusion of her musical development. *—William Ruhlmann*

Gonna Take a Miracle / 1971 / Columbia ✦✦✦✦
A joyous change of pace, this album presents inspired readings of pop-R&B hits of the '60s, songs like "Jimmy Mack" and "Nowhere to Run," produced by creamy-smooth soul producers Gamble & Huff and sung rapturously by Nyro, with gorgeous backing by Patti LaBelle, Sarah Dash, and Nona Hendryx. *—William Ruhlmann*

The First Songs / 1973 / Columbia ✦✦✦
Columbia Records acquired Laura Nyro's 1967 debut album from Verve Forecast and reissued it in 1973, by which time such songs as "Wedding Bell Blues," "Stoney End," and "And When I Die" had become enormously successful copyrights for Nyro. *—William Ruhlmann*

Smile / 1976 / Columbia ✦✦✦
This warm comeback album is Laura Nyro's *Double Fantasy*, a return to action by a mature artist, who retains her emotional power but has worked through her problems and beaten back her demons to emerge as a "Sexy Mama." *—William Ruhlmann*

Season of Lights . . . Laura Nyro in Concert / 1977 / Columbia ✦✦
Trying to make the most of Laura Nyro's comeback, Columbia Records released this live album, most of whose songs come from her trio of stunning records of 1968-1970, *Eli and the Thirteenth Confession, New York Tendaberry*, and *Christmas and the Beads of Sweat*. There's not really much hope of besting those performances, but this is a decent effort, even if not essential. *—William Ruhlmann*

Nested / 1978 / Columbia ✦✦✦

Mother's Spiritual / 1984 / Columbia ✦✦
Laura Nyro's romantic passion has been replaced by motherly nurturing, a respectable if less compelling development in the work of an artist whose concerns are always private and personal. Political concerns for women's rights and environmentalism, while clearly deeply felt, are neither well integrated into her overall perspective or particularly insightful. *—William Ruhlmann*

Live at the Bottom Line / 1990 / Cypress ✦✦✦
Laura Nyro's first album in five years, reflecting another return to action in the music business, is a pleasant mixture of her own hits ("Stoned Soul Picnic"), other people's, and promising new material such as "The Japanese Restaurant Song." *—William Ruhlmann*

Walk the Dog & Lite the Lite (Run the Dog Darling Lite Delite) / Aug. 17, 1993 / Columbia ✦✦✦
Laura Nyro effectively re-creates her emotional, piano-based sound on her first new studio album in nine years. By now, the political stands are a part of her persona, expressed as directly as her emotional ones, and this is a well-rounded portrait of a mature artist. *—William Ruhlmann*

Stoned Soul Picnic: Best of Laura Nyro / Feb. 18, 1997 / Sony ✦✦✦✦
A double-CD, career-spanning retrospective that offers little in the way of surprises: it's a tastefully selected overview of her career highlights, heaviest (and justifiably so) on her late '60s albums. There's the inevitable feeling of letdown as disc two progresses; her post-early '70s material is far less interesting than her earliest work, even if it's inoffensive. All of the first five albums (through 1971's *Gonna Take a Miracle*) are now on CD, so this is most suitable for the fan who isn't passionate enough to be a completist. Includes a couple of previously unreleased live tracks from the 1990s; the version of "Sweet Blindness," unfortunately, is not the original late-'60s recording, but from a late-'70s live album. *—Richie Unterberger*

O

___

Oasis

f. 1993, Manchester, England
Rock 'n' Roll, Alternative Pop-Rock, Pop-Rock, Brit-Pop

Oasis shot from obscurity to stardom in 1994, become one of Britain's most popular and critically acclaimed bands of the decade; along with Blur and Suede, they are responsible for returning British guitar-pop to the top of the charts. Led by guitarist/songwriter Noel Gallagher, the Manchester quintet adopts the rough, thuggish image of the Stones and the Who, crosses it with Beatlesque melodies and hooks, distinctly British lyrical themes and song structures like the Jam and the Kinks, and ties it all together with a massive, loud guitar roar, as well as a defiant sneer that draws equally from the Sex Pistols' rebelliousness and the Stone Roses' cocksure arrogance. Gallagher's songs frequently rework previous hits from T. Rex ("Cigarettes and Alcohol" borrows the riff from "Bang a Gong") to Wham! ("Fade Away" takes the melody from "Freedom"), yet the group always puts the hooks in different settings, updating past hits for a new era.

Originally, the group was formed by school mates Liam Gallagher (vocals), Paul "Bonehead" Arthurs (guitar), Paul McGuigan (bass), and Tony McCaroll (drums). After spending several years as the guitar technician for the Stone Roses-inspired group the Inspiral Carpets, Noel Gallagher returned to Manchester to find that his brother had formed a band. Noel agreed to join the band if he could have complete control of the group, including contributing all the songs; the rest of the band agreed and under the new name Oasis, they began a year of intensive rehearsing.

After playing a handful of small club gigs, the band cornered Alan McGee, the head of Creation Records, and forced him to listen to their demo. Impressed, he signed the band. The group released their first single, "Supersonic," in the spring of 1994; it edged its way into the charts on the back of positive reviews. With a melody adapted from "I'd Like to Teach the World to Sing," "Shakermaker" became a bigger hit in the early summer. Released a month before their debut album, the soaring ballad "Live Forever" became a major hit in England. The group's first record, *Definitely Maybe*, became the fastest-selling debut in British history, entering the charts at No. 1. Oasis mania continued throughout 1994, as the group began playing larger theaters and each new single outperformed the last. However, tensions in the group began to build—Liam and Noel refused to do joint interviews because they always fought—and Noel Gallagher briefly left the band at the end of a difficult fall American tour; he soon rejoined and the band headed back to England. As "Supersonic" began to climb the US album rock and modern rock charts, the non-LP, string-laden "Whatever" hit No. 2 over the British Christmas season.

At the beginning of 1995, the group concentrated on America, promoting the single "Live Forever." The song became a major hit on MTV, album rock, and modern rock radio stations, peaking at No. 2 and *Definitely Maybe* went gold in the US. Returning to England after a sold-out American tour, the group recorded a new single, "Some Might Say." On the eve of its release, drummer Tony McCaroll parted ways with the band, with Alan White taking his place. "Some Might Say" entered the charts at No. 1 upon its May release; its success led to all of their previous singles re-entering the indie charts. Oasis spent the rest of the summer completing their second album, *(What's the Story) Morning Glory?*, which was released in October of 1995. Upon its release, the album shot to No. 1 in England, becoming the fastest-selling in the UK since Michael Jackson's *Bad*.

Over the course of 1996, *(What's the Story) Morning Glory?* became the second biggest-selling British album in history, as Oasis became international phenomenons. On the strength of the single "Wonderwall," *Morning Glory* became a Top Ten success in America,

eventually being certified quintuple platinum; it also reached the Top Ten throughout Europe and Asia. During 1996, the Gallaghers' combative relationship frequently made newspapers and gossip columns, particularly when they suddenly pulled out of their late summer US tour, which followed the group's two concerts at Knebworth, which broke records for being the biggest outdoor concert in England. After Oasis abandoned their American tour, they concentrated on recording their third album. Where their first two albums were quickly recorded, they took several months to record the third, finally completing the album in the spring of 1997. The album, *Be Here Now*, was released in late August, with the single "D'You Know What I Mean" preceding the full-length record in July. —*Stephen Thomas Erlewine*

● **Definitely Maybe** / Aug. 1994 / Epic ✦✦✦✦

Definitely Maybe manages to encapsulate much of the best of British rock 'n' roll, from the Beatles to the Stone Roses, in the space of eleven songs. Their sound is louder and more guitar-oriented than any British band since the Sex Pistols, and the band is blessed with the excellent songwriting of Noel Gallagher. Gallagher writes perfect pop songs, offering a platform for his brother Liam's brash, snarling vocals. Not only does the band have melodies, but they have the capability to work a groove with more dexterity than most post-punk groups. But what makes *Definitely Maybe* so intoxicating is that it already resembles a greatest-hits album. From the swirling rush of "Rock 'n' Roll Star," through the sinewy "Shakermaker," to the heartbreaking "Live Forever," each song sounds like an instant classic. —*Stephen Thomas Erlewine*

(What's the Story) Morning Glory / Oct. 3, 1995 / Epic ✦✦✦✦

If *Definitely Maybe* was an unintentional concept album about wanting to be a rock 'n' roll star, *(What's the Story) Morning Glory?* is what happens after the dreams come true. Oasis turns in a relatively introspective second record, filled with big, gorgeous ballads instead of ripping rockers. Unlike *Definitely Maybe*, the production on *Morning Glory* is varied enough to handle the range in emotions; instead of drowning everything with amplifiers turned up to 12, there are strings, keyboards, and harmonicas. This expanded production helps give Noel Gallagher's sweeping melodies an emotional resonance that he occasionally can't convey lyrically. However, that is far from a fatal flaw; Gallagher's lyrics work best in fragments, where the images catch in your mind and grow, thanks to the music. Gallagher may be guilty of some borrowing, or even plagiarism—a track called "Step Out" had to be pulled at the last minute because it sounded too similar to Stevie Wonder's "Uptight"—but he uses the familiar riffs as building blocks. This is where Gallagher's genius lies: he's a thief and doesn't have many original thoughts, but as a pop-rock melodicist he's pretty much without peer. Likewise, as musicians, Oasis are hardly innovators, yet they have a majestic grandeur in their sound that makes ballads like "Wonderwall" or rockers like "Some Might Say" positively transcendent. Alan White does add authority to the rhythm section, but the most noticeable change is in Liam Gallagher. His voice sneered throughout *Definitely Maybe*, but on *Morning Glory* his singing has become more textured and skillful. He gives the lyric in the raging title track a hint of regret, is sympathetic on "Wonderwall," defiant on "Some Might Say," and humorous on "She's Electric," a bawdy rewrite of "Digsy's Diner." It might not have the immediate impact of *Definitely Maybe*, but *Morning Glory* is just as exciting and compulsively listenable. —*Stephen Thomas Erlewine*

Definitely Maybe Singles Box Set / Dec. 6, 1996 / Creation ✦✦✦✦

Noel Gallagher wanted Oasis to be a definitive singles band, much like his idols the Jam and the Smiths, so he made sure that his band had worthwhile B-sides on each of its singles. That had an unexpected, and perhaps intentional, end result—many of Oasis' very best songs were stranded on their singles instead of showcased on their albums. Once Oasis became superstars in the UK, Creation packaged each of their singles from their two albums in two separate four-CD box sets that were shaped like a Benson & Hedges cigarette pack. (The extraordinary "Whatever," a non-LP homage to "All You Need Is Love," was left off the set.) Although the singles for Oasis' debut *Definitely Maybe* weren't as consistent as those for *Morning Glory*, there's still a remarkable number of highlights. *Supersonic* features "I Will Believe," a wonderful reinterpretation of the Stone Roses, as well as Noel's first solo acoustic ballad, "Take Me Away." *Shakermaker* features another fine solo number from Noel, the deceptively bouncy "D'Yer Wanna Be a Spaceman?," while *Live Forever* has an acoustic version of "Up in the Sky" again sung by Noel and spiked with slide guitars. But *Cigarettes & Alcohol* is the one perfect single on the collection, not only featuring their primal deconstruction of "I Am the Walrus," but also another fine introspective number from Noel ("Listen Up") and the monumental "Fade Away," where the melody for Wham's "Freedom" is twisted into a storming lament for lost childhood dreams. — *Stephen Thomas Erlewine*

(What's the Story) Morning Glory? Singles Box Set / Dec. 6, 1996 / Creation ◆◆◆◆

Many of the songs on Oasis' second album *(What's the Story) Morning Glory?* illustrated that Noel Gallagher's songwriting skills had deepened considerably, but the depth of his talent becomes evident when the B-sides of the album's singles are also considered. Almost every song from those four singles—which Creation conveniently packaged in one box set in the wake of *Morning Glory*'s success—is at least the equal of what was on the actual album, and several songs are actually far better than several songs on the official record. The three flip-sides for *Some Might Say* all were worthy of inclusion on the album. "Acquiesce," which Oasis used as the opener on their 1996 tour, is an astonishing hard-rocker, where Liam and Noel trade the verse and chorus in a song about their notorious love-hate relationship. The throttling "Headshrinker" is fine, but "Talk Tonight" is the other gem, a spare Noel showcase that finds him disarmingly letting down his emotional guard. The two keepers from *Roll with It* are a little less assuming, but the rolling acoustics of "It's Better People" is charming, and "Rockin' Chair," with its haunting melody and Liam's nuanced vocal, is an overlooked gem. While the full-length instrumental "The Swamp Song" on *Wonderwall* is a bit tedious, "Round Are Way" is fantastic, sounding like *Definitely Maybe* crossed with Madness, and the string-drenched "The Master Plan" is as effective an epic as "Champagne Supernova." Oasis begin to run out of steam on *Don't Look Back in Anger*, resorting to a cover of Slade's "Cum on Feel the Noize" to round out the three B-sides. While that is actually heavier than Quiet Riot's hit cover, the hyper-active "Step Out"—which was pulled from *Morning Glory* at the last minute—totally demolishes it, and the neo-psychedelic "Underneath the Sky" is a lovely change of pace. There's an album's worth of fresh material scattered throughout these singles, and it's no exaggeration to say that these songs form an album as good as *(What's the Story) Morning Glory?*, which makes you wish Noel Gallagher showed a little more control in deciding what went on the album and what was reserved for the B-sides. —*Stephen Thomas Erlewine*

Ocean Colour Scene

f. 1990, England
Brit-Pop, Rock 'n' Roll

Falling between the energetic pop-rock of mod revival and the psychedelic experimentations of Traffic, Ocean Colour Scene came to be one of the leading bands of the traditionalist, post-Oasis British rock of the mid-'90s. Although they had formed in the late '80s and had several hits during the height of "Madchester" in the early '90s, the band didn't earn a large following until 1996, when their second album *Mosley Shoals* became a multi-platinum success story in the UK. Their ascent was greatly aided by Paul Weller and Oasis' Noel Gallagher, who both publicly praised Ocean Colour Scene for keeping the flame of real rock 'n' roll burning during the '90s. And, according to one specific definition, they were right, since Ocean Colour Scene was nothing if not rock 'n' roll traditionalists, drawing heavily from British Invasion pop, psychedelia, soul, R&B and blues-rock to create a reverential homage to classic rock. Their devotion to trad-rock may have earned them decidedly mixed-reviews, but that was the very thing that earned them a sizable following.

Ocean Colour Scene is comprised of Steve Cradock (lead guitar, keyboards, vocals), Simon Fowler (lead vocals, guitar), Damon Minchella (Bass) and Oscar Harrison (drums). Prior to forming in 1990, the members of the band had played in a variety of other groups. During the late '80s, Cradock played in a mod revival band called the Boys. Though they released an independent EP called *Happy Days* and supported former Small Faces frontman Steve Marriot, the band never gained much of an audience. At the same time the Boys were active, Fowler and Minchella were in a Velvet Underground-influenced group called the Fanatics, who released an EP, *Surburban Love Songs*, on the independent label Chapter 22 in the spring of 1989. Following the release of the single, the group's original drummer, Caroline Bullock, was replaced by Harrison, who had previously played with a reggae/soul band called Echo Base. Shortly after Harrison joined the Fanatics, the group split up. Several months after their disbandment, Fowler, Minchella and Harrison formed Ocean Colour Scene with Cradock, who they met at a Stone Roses concert.

Appropriately, Ocean Colour Scene was intially heavily influenced by the Stone Roses. After performing a few concerts, the group built a small fanbase and signed with a local indie label, !Phfft. Shortly after signing with !Phfft, Ocean Colour Scene became hyped as "the next big thing" by the British music weekly press, as their live shows and debut single, "Sway," earned extremely positive reviews during the first half of 1990. In the spring of 1991, they headed into the studio to record the debut album with Jimmy Miller, who worked on the Rolling Stones' classic albums of the late '60s and early '70s. Instead of concentrating on work, the band essentially drank away their hours in the studio, resulting in a batch of uneven recordings. Unsatisfied by the tapes, the band headed back into the studio with Hugo Nicolson, who was had previously worked with Primal Scream.

By the time they completed the record, !Phfft had been acquired by Fontana Records, who bought the indie with the intent of owning the rights to Ocean Colour Scene. Despite their enthusiasm for the band, the label's head of A&R, Dave Bates, rejected the group's first attempt at the album and asked them to re-enter the studio to re-record most of the album with another producer, Tim Palmer, who had previously worked with Tin Machine. Palmer also remixed the remaining cuts, resulting in a slick, over-produced debut album that was delivered belatedly in the spring of 1992. By that time, the music press had abandoned the "madchester" scene that the Stone Roses spawned and, in turn, they rejected the return of Ocean Colour Scene. The public also refused to buy the record and it sank upon its release. The band made some headway on an American tour, but tensions with Fontana continued to increase throughout the year.

Ocean Colour Scene returned to England halfway through the year, planning to record a new album quickly, but Bates rejected their new material. Soon, the band sued to get out of its Fontana contract. By the time it was settled in early 1993, the group owed hundreds of thousands of pounds to the label and they were back on the dole. Ocean Colour Scene continued to rehearse, often supported by their manager (and Steve's father) Chris Cradock, who put the family house up for mortgage. The band converted their rehearsal space into a recording studio and began recording constantly, but their break didn't arrive until they played a gig supporting Paul Weller's new band in early 1993. Weller was impressed with Steve Cradock's playing, and asked him to play on his forthcoming single, "The Weaver." Cradock gradually became part of Weller's backing band, performing on much of Weller's second solo album, *Wild Wood.* However, the guitarist didn't abandon Ocean Colour Scene—all the money he was making was funneled back into the band, and he landed Fowler a gig as a backing vocalist for Weller. By the end of the 1993, Cradock, Fowler and Minchella were all playing in Weller's band.

The next break for Ocean Colour Scene arrived in late summer of 1994, when Noel Gallagher, the leader of Oasis, heard the band's tape in the offices of his record label. Gallagher offered OCS the opening slot for Oasis' breakthrough fall 1994 tour, which provided the group with needed exposure. Soon, the group was subject to a bidding war among several major labels, all of whom wanted the band to change their name. Eventually, the band signed with MCA in the summer of 1995; they were one of the few labels not to insist that the group change their name.

During early 1996, the hype machine began to go into overdrive for Ocean Colour Scene, as Gallagher proclaimed them the best band in Britain in several interviews and Chris Evans, a DJ on BBC's Radio 1, constantly played OCS's comeback single "The Riverboat Song," essentially using it as his theme song. "The Riverboat Song" entered the charts at No. 15 early in 1996. *Mosley Shoals*, the band's second album, was released in April of 1996, unexpectedly entering the charts at No. 2. The album was a fixture in the British Top Ten throughout 1996, spending six months total in the upper regions of the charts. Two subsequent singles from the record, "You've Got it Bad" and "The Day We Caught the Train," reached the Top Ten and the album continued to sell strongly throughout 1996, going multi-platinum in the UK. Ocean Colour Scene also became a popular live attraction in Britain, selling out concerts during their summer tour. *Moseley Shoals* was released in America during the summer, but it failed to make much of an impact in the US. —*Stephen Thomas Erlewine*

Ocean Colour Scene / Sep. 8, 1992 / Fontana ✦✦✦
Ocean Colour Scene's eponymous debut album suffered from botched production, one that smoothed all the edges out of the group's fusion of classic rock, R&B. and Madchester grooves. Occasionally, the band's personality peaks through the polished sound, such as on the terrific single "Sway," but the record is stifled by radio-friendly production, which prevents the group from stretching out musically, as well as wildly inconsistent songwriting. —*Stephen Thomas Erlewine*

● **Moseley Shoals** / Apr. 1996 / MCA ✦✦✦✦
By the time the Ocean Colour Scene released their debut album in 1992, they were already considered has-beens. The band had formed during the height of Madchester, but they never released their first album until the scene was already dead, which left them without a following. But between their debut and their second album, 1996's *Moseley Shoals*, a strange thing happened—the band was taken under the wings of two of Britain's biggest pop stars, Paul Weller and Noel Gallagher. The band suddenly catapulted back into the spotlight because of their superstar connections, but the music actually deserved the attention. The Ocean Colour Scene had spent the time between their two albums improving their sound. On *Moseley Shoals*, they are looser, funkier, and have a strong, organic R&B vibe that was inherited from the Small Faces and Weller's solo recordings. They sprinkle Beatlesque and Stonesy flourishes throughout the album, as well as the odd prog-rock flair, adding an even more eclectic flavor to their traditionalist pop -rock. The Ocean Colour Scene is still developing their songwriting skills—the sound is more impressive than the songs throughout *Moseley Shoals*—but their second album is an unexpectedly enjoyable record. —*Stephen Thomas Erlewine*

B-Sides: Seasides & Freerides / Mar. 1997 / MCA ✦✦✦✦
Rounding up all the B-sides, demos, and rarities Ocean Colour Scene released over the course of 1996, when the band was riding the crest of their popularity, *B-Sides: Seasides & Freerides*, for all its inconsistency, illustrates the depth of their ambition, as well as their flaws. Primarily comprising acoustic material, including a demo of "The Circle" and a fine, stripped-down version of "The Day We Caught the Train," the 16 tracks on *B-Sides* can tend to sound a little samey, but when the group branches out to the neo-prog-rock of the very English "Huckleberry Grove" or to the funky instrumental "Chicken Bones and Stones," they sound better than ever, and a couple of early songs by the pre-Ocean Colour Scene band the Fanatics are interesting. Still, about half of the songs suggest that OCS may be a little too reverent in their appreciation for late-'60s rock, since they come across as only stylistic exercise, not full songs. And their live cover of "Day Tripper," featuring Noel Gallagher on guitar and Liam Gallagher on vocals, is an embarrassment, simply because Liam's restrained vocals slay Simon Fowler's bellowing. But this is an isolated moment on *B-Sides: Seasides & Freerides*, since it contains enough first-rate material to make it necessary for dedicated fans. —*Stephen Thomas Erlewine*

Billy Ocean

b. 1950, Trinidad, West Indies
Vocals / Soul, Adult Contemporary, Pop-Rock
Born in Trinidad, Billy Ocean emigrated to the UK as a child. He worked as a tailor while pursuing music on the side in the '60s, then broke through with the Motown-flavored "Love Really Hurts without You," which hit No. 3 in the UK in 1976. Ocean continued to have UK hits through the end of the '70s but didn't achieve mass success in the US until 1984, when "Caribbean Queen (No More Love on the Run)" became a No. 1 hit, the first of seven Top Ten hits over the next four years. —*William Ruhlmann*

Nights (Feel Like Getting Down) / 1981 / Epic ✦✦✦
Billy Ocean was on his way to superstardom with this album, his first big hit release on Epic. The title song was his first R&B Top Ten record, and he got another couple of chart singles before beginning his run of R&B and pop hits. It also demonstrated his equal ability doing exuberant uptempo dance tunes and convincing, if at times oversung and vapid, ballads. Epic was later left red-faced when an act they developed moved over to Jive/RCA and went platinum. —*Ron Wynn*

Inner Feelings / 1982 / Epic ✦✦
Billy Ocean went from international superstar to falling completely off the charts in one of the most amazing rise and fall stories of the 1980s and early '90s. This was an early, introductory self-produced session for Epic, with Ocean still feeling his way around in America after having enjoyed huge success on Britain's club circuit. There were some decent ballads and uptempo dance tunes, but little to suggest that Ocean was on his way to becoming Britian's pop-dance king and an urban contemporary and pop superstar in America as well. —*Ron Wynn*

Suddenly / 1984 / Jive ✦✦✦✦
Billy Ocean vaulted into international stardom with this album in 1984. The album peaked at No. 9, was on the charts for over a year and a half, and yielded him three R&B hits that were all also pop smashes. Ocean would sing on the soundtrack for the film *The Jewel of the Nile*, make sellout appearances around the world, and appear regularly on television and videos. At this point he was a bigger pop star than R&B artist, as two of his three hits did better as crossover vehicles than R&B tunes. —*Ron Wynn*

Love Zone / 1986 / Jive ✦✦✦✦
Billy Ocean was riding atop the charts when he issued this album in '86. The title track contained both a fine arrangement and Ocean's emphatic lead vocal, and was a huge hit. He topped the R&B charts twice that year with both "Love Zone" and "There'll Be Sad Songs (To Make You Cry)," each of which was also a huge pop smash, the latter topping the pop chart. This was arguably his finest album, and was certainly his most successful. —*Ron Wynn*

Tear Down These Walls / 1988 / Jive ✦✦✦
Things were beginning to slip a bit for Billy Ocean in the late '80s. While he was still a successful attraction, this album wouldn't reach the multiplatinum levels of its predecessors. Ocean's voice also lacked the resonance and authority it had on earlier dance tunes and wasn't as convincing or confident on ballads. He still landed a couple more hits, and one additional chart topper (R&B and pop) with "Get Outta My Dreams, Get into My Car," but the decline was starting. —*Ron Wynn*

● **Greatest Hits** / Oct. 1989 / Jive ✦✦✦✦
Contains this cool '80s disco hits "Caribbean Queen" and "Get Outta My Dreams, Get into My Car" and piano-based ballads like "There'll Be Sad Songs to Make You Cry." —*Bil Carpenter*

Phil Ochs

b. Dec. 19, 1940, El Paso, TX, d. Apr. 9, 1976, Far Rockaway, NY
Guitar, Vocals / Folk, Singer-Songwriter, Folk-Rock
Singer-songwriter Phil Ochs was a self-coined "singing journalist" when he began performing in New York in the early '60s. Like Bob Dylan, the rival who always outpaced him, Ochs made his reputation singing topical protest songs. He stayed with them much longer than Dylan (and indeed would never really abandon them), but eventually he too would follow Dylan into electric music and more personal, abstract, and romantic compositions. Ochs came off as a perennial second-best to critics during his heyday. It was only after his tragic tailspin and eventual death that he was properly appreciated as one of the most sincere and humane songwriters of his day, whether detailing political atrocities or more poetic concerns.

Ochs moved from Ohio to New York in the early '60s, and was soon a prolific writer of the topical, left-leaning protest songs then in vogue. His initial recording efforts, heard on compilations for Broadside, Folkways, and Vanguard, were rather dry and instantly dated. By the time made his Elektra debut in 1964 with *All the News That's Fit to Sing*, Ochs was finding his own voice—more melodic than Dylan (if not as lyrically innovative), its strident accusations tempered by a warm delivery and underlying compassion. With second guitar by Danny Kalb (later of the Blues Project), his first album was highlighted by "Power and the Glory" and "Bound for Glory," as well as an adaptation of Edgar Allan Poe's "The Bells." The similar follow-up *I Ain't Marching Any More* (1965) gave the anti-war movement two rallying calls with the title track and "Draft Dodger Rag," along with a moving civil-rights piece, "Here's to the State of Mississippi."

Ochs addressed all manner of anti-war, civil rights, labor, and social justice issues on his first albums, the best of which was *In Concert* (1966). Ochs' social criticism was deepening in acuity, as heard on "Canons of Christianity," "Cops of the World," and the satirical "Love Me, I'm a Liberal." But he also began to move into nonpolitical subjects with equal or greater effect, as on "There But for Fortune" and "Changes," his most famous love song.

In Concert was Ochs' final acoustic album. He'd already moved into electric rock with a fine (though flop) single-only version of "I Ain't Marching Anymore." In 1967, he broke from his acoustic folk troubadour image with a vengeance, leaving Elektra for A&M and moving to Los Angeles. There he plunged into baroque folk-rock, with mixed results. Some of the tracks on his late-'60s A&M records are among the best he ever did, especially the devastating social apathy parody "Outside a Small Circle of Friends." On others, he seemed to be overreaching or straining for highbrow poetry. The L.A. session production sometimes enhanced his musical settings, but the more elaborate and pretentious arrangements worked against the material just as often.

Ochs hadn't forsaken his political commitments, appearing at the violence-riddled 1968 Democratic Convention in Chicago. By 1969's *Rehearsals of Retirement*, some weariness and disenchantment with idealism was beginning to seep into both his compositions and his singing. The problems became more acute with 1970's facetiously titled *Greatest Hits*, when the standard of his material began to drop noticeably.

Although it wasn't foreseen at the time, *Greatest Hits* was his last studio album. Ochs did remain active, recording a live LP (initially released only in Canada) that excited controversy with its strange mix of original songs and unexpected covers of old rock 'n' roll tunes by Elvis Presley and Buddy Holly, performed in a gold lamé suit. The '50s revival act was received poorly by an audience accustomed to a folkie troubadour, but that was among the least of Ochs' obstacles. His well of original compositions had run dry, and he was developing severe alcohol and psychological problems. In a mysterious mugging incident in Africa, his voice was permanently damaged.

Ochs did record a couple of flop singles in the early '70s, but by the middle of the decade he was largely inactive, and afflicted with serious depression. In early 1976, he hanged himself at his sister's suburban home. —*Richie Unterberger*

All the News That's Fit to Sing / 1964 / Hannibal ✦✦✦
All the News That's Fit to Sing is his bittersweet debut and is a vital and topical album of its time. —*Bruce Eder & William Ruhlmann*

I Ain't Marching Anymore / 1965 / Carthage ✦✦✦✦
A strident, searching, and haunting echo of the '60s. —*Bruce Eder*

Phil Ochs in Concert / 1966 / Elektra ✦✦✦✦
It's since been revealed that some or all of these tracks were not "in concert" at all, but recorded in the studio, with audience noise dubbed on afterwards. Nevertheless, this is Ochs' finest acoustic album. As a lyricist, he was moving from the singing journalist mode to more abstract symbolism, but still attacked US imperialism, knock-kneed bleeding hearts, and even organized religion with an uncompromising sensitivity. Some haunting, wistful ballads transcended topical concerns entirely, including the beautiful love song "Changes" and "There but for Fortune" (a British hit for Joan Baez). —*Richie Unterberger*

★ **Pleasures of the Harbor** / 1967 / A&M ✦✦✦✦✦
Moving from his acoustic base to elaborate musical arrangements, Ochs also turns largely away from his topical material to more lyrical and poetic songs, though the caustic "Outside a Small Circle of Friends" and the apocalyptic "The Crucifixion" clearly retain his social and political focus. —*William Ruhlmann*

Tape from California / 1968 / A&M ✦✦✦
A somewhat manic production, highlighted by reasonably successful straightforward rock (the title track) and one of the great '60s anti-war songs, "The War Is Over," a perfect combination of droll commentary with jaunty backing. Most of the rest of the tracks fall into the over-orchestrated malaise that, to a lesser degree, afflicted *Pleasures of the Harbor*. —*Richie Unterberger*

Rehearsals for Retirement / 1969 / A&M ✦✦✦
Ochs' final album to feature top-notch original material continued his move to poetic abstraction, as can be guessed from titles like "William Butler Yeats Visits Lincoln Park and Escapes Unscathed." The Los Angeles session musician production values resulted in indifferent arrangements that were downright bland at worst. In hindsight, the muted tone of much of the material contained some seeds of Ochs' loss of boisterous idealism. More to the point, it doesn't have as many outstanding songs as his other '60s albums, though the standard of writing remained fairly solid. The *Live in Vancouver 1968* CD contains higher-charged acoustic versions of six of the songs, and many listeners may find those interpretations superior. —*Richie Unterberger*

Phil Ochs's Greatest Hits / 1970 / Edsel ✦✦✦
Not really his greatest hits (the title was intended as irony). This is his final, troubled studio album, and a good companion to *Gunfight at Carnegie Hall*. —*Bruce Eder*

Gunfight at Carnegie Hall / 1975 / Mobile Fidelity ✦✦✦✦
Most unusual. Ochs does Elvis and Buddy Holly songs exceptionally to an angry audience and plays out his own internal conflicts at the same time. —*Bruce Eder*

Chords of Fame / 1976 / A&M ✦✦✦✦
A fine collection on vinyl only, but worth having for the liner notes. Note that this out-of-print double LP is the only album to combine Ochs' Elektra work (1964-1966) with his A&M work (1967-1970). The two CD samplers cover the same ground separately. —*Bruce Eder & William Ruhlmann*

A Toast to Those Who Are Gone / 1987 / Rhino ✦✦✦
Fourteen previously unreleased demos, all of excellent fidelity; while no dates or sources are given for these sessions, an educated guess would put them in his earliest, most topical period, circa 1964-65. Most of these feature just Phil and acoustic guitar, and sound as strong as the material officially released on his first Elektra LPs. The other, equally fine cuts seem to date from a later period, and show

him delving into intensely personal, nonpolitical concerns. —*Richie Unterberger*

War Is Over: The Best of Phil Ochs / 1988 / A&M ✦✦✦
Not his best by a long shot, but a cross-section of his better A&M recordings. —*Bruce Eder*

The Broadside Tapes 1 / 1989 / Smithsonian/Folkways ✦✦✦
This album of previously unreleased songs was recorded casually in the 104th St. Offices of Broadside Magazine. They were intended as demos for transcription but are in fact quite good performances. —*Richard Meyer*

There and Now: Live in Vancouver / 1990 / Rhino ✦✦✦✦
Definitive Ochs (along with *Gunfight at Carnegie Hall*). A "lost" 1968 concert featuring his most beloved songs. The real "best-of." —*Bruce Eder*

Live at Newport / Mar. 12, 1996 / Vanguard ✦✦✦
A dozen songs from Ochs' performances at the 1963, 1964, and 1966 Newport Folk Festivals. Four of these cuts were previously available on the *Newport Broadside* and *Evening Concerts, Vol. 1* anthologies, but the rest were previously unreleased. While all of these songs are available on his studio albums, Ochs was in good form for these shows, so these are good supplementary versions. Especially noteworthy are the 1966 tracks; four of the five songs would appear in far more elaborately produced arrangements on his *Pleasures of the Harbor* and *Tape from California* albums. These solo acoustic performances are interesting contrasts, putting the voice and the lyrics at the forefront, in the best unplugged tradition. —*Richie Unterberger*

Sinéad O'Connor

b. Dec. 12, 1966, Dublin, Ireland
Guitar, Keyboards, Vocals / Alternative Pop-Rock
From Dublin, Ireland, Sinéad O'Connor came onto the music scene in 1987 with a powerful image of a woman who could express great sensitivity while not losing any qualities of inner strength. In public, O'Connor's seemingly audacious pronouncements about the state of the world around her may have put off those unaccustomed to a woman so forthright with her feelings; nevertheless, it's that courageousness that has endeared her to millions of fans. O'Connor's second album, *I Do Not Want What I Haven't Got*, was a worldwide hit. Musically, O'Connor draws from hard synth-rock, Celtic folk, and funk. Her dramatic alto explores sound in much the same way Peter Gabriel applies varied tonal dynamics. After the success of *I Do Not Want What I Haven't Got*, O'Connor seemed a bit directionless. Two years later, she released an album of big-band covers, *Am I Not Your Girl?*, a strange record that was a commercial disappointment. Even worse, the singer suffered a tidal wave of bad publicity when she tore a photo of The Pope on *Saturday Night Live*, saying "Fight the Real Enemy." For the next year, O'Connor laid low, recording a new album which was released in the fall of 1994. —*Rick Clark*

The Lion and the Cobra / 1987 / Ensign ✦✦✦✦
The Lion and the Cobra was an impressive showcase for this Dubliner's vocal and writing skills. On this self-produced effort, O'Connor incorporates bits of hard rock, folk, synth-pop, and light funk onto standout tracks like "I Want Your (Hands on Me)," "Jerusalem," and "Mandinka," a wonderful synth-rocker. —*Rick Clark*

● **I Do Not Want What I Haven't Got** / Mar. 1990 / Ensign ✦✦✦✦
O'Connor's debut might have been a strong showing, but her follow-up, *I Do Not Want What I Haven't Got*, was a stunner. Her songwriting skills were much more incisive and, vocally, O'Connor exhibited a greater range of interpretive skills. Highlights include "The Emperor's New Clothes," "I Am Stretched on Your Grave," "Jump in the River," "Black Boys on Mopeds," and the international hit "Nothing Compares 2 U," which was penned by Prince. —*Rick Clark*

Am I Not Your Girl? / Sep. 22, 1992 / Ensign ✦✦
Based on O'Connor's version of "You Do Something to Me" (a highlight on the *Red Hot & Blue* album), an album of pop standards performed with a big band might have actually worked. At times, such as on "Success Has Made a Failure of Our Home" and "Don't Cry for Me, Argentina," *Am I Not Your Girl?* does work. However, O'Connor runs into trouble with acknowledged standards and songs heavily identified with other vocalists. She doesn't offer a new perspective on these songs, and her airy voice is buried under overwrought string arrangements. Plus, there's O'Connor's bizarre two-minute rant on love, hatred, herself, and the Catholic church. —*Stephen Thomas Erlewine*

Universal Mother / Sep. 13, 1994 / Ensign ✦✦✦
O'Connor's first album of original material since her breakthrough *I Do Not Want What I Haven't Got* is nearly as confused as her big-band album, *Am I Not Your Girl?* O'Connor has lost her sense of conceptual unity, which makes her most extreme moments quite embarrassing ("Red Football" and the white hip-hop of "Famine"). Every so often, she manages to pull off a number that shows why her first two

albums were so startling and captivating, but through most of *Universal Mother*, O'Connor sounds lost and confused. —*Stephen Thomas Erlewine*

Offspring

f. Orange County, CA
Hard Rock, Alternative Pop-Rock, Punk Revival
Offspring's metal-inflected punk became a popular sensation in the 1994, selling over a four million copies on an independent record label. While the group's credentials and approach follows the indie-rock tradition of the '80s, sonically they sound more like an edgy, hard-driving heavy metal band, with their precise, pulsing power chords and Brian "Dexter" Holland's flat vocals.

Featuring Holland, guitarist Kevin "Noodles" Wasserman, bassist Greg Kriesel, and drummer Ron Welty, the Offspring released their first album, *Ignition*, in 1993. It was an underground hit, setting the stage for the across-the-board success of 1994's *Smash*. The Nirvana-soundalike "Come out and Play," the first single from the album, became an MTV hit in the summer of 1994, which paved the way to radio success. The band was played on both alternative and album rock stations, confirming their broad-based appeal. "Self Esteem," the second single, followed the same soft verse/loud chorus fomula and stayed on the charts nearly twice as long as "Come out and Play." The group got offers from major labels, yet they chose to stay with Epitaph. While they were able to play arenas in the US, their success didn't translate in foreign countries. Nevertheless, the band's popularity continued to grow in America, as "Gotta Get Away" became another radio/MTV hit in the beginning of 1995. The Offspring recorded a version of the Damned's "Smash It Up" for the *Batman Forever* soundtrack in the summer of that year; it kept the band on the charts as they worked on their third album.

Following a prolonged bidding war and much soul-searching, the Offspring decided to leave Epitaph Records in 1996 for Columbia Records. The move was particularly controversial within the punk community, and many artists on the Epitaph roster, including Pennywise and owner Brett Gurewitz, criticized the band. After much delay, the Offspring finally released their Columbia debut, *Ixnay on the Hombre*, in February of 1997. Expectation for the record was high and it did receive good reviews, but *Ixnay on the Hombre* failed to become a crossover hit on the level of *Smash*, and the group also lost a significant portion of their hardcore punk audience, due to the album's major-label status.—*Stephen Thomas Erlewine*

Offspring / 1989 / Nemesis ♦♦♦
The Offspring's self-titled debut album is a rawer, harder-edged collection than their breakthrough set *Smash*, but that doesn't necessarily mean it's a better record. Although it makes a more convincing argument for the band's punk credibility—the record lacks the metal guitar crunch that dominated *Smash—The Offspring* doesn't have any songs driven by hooks as catchy as "Keep 'Em Separated" or "Self Esteem," nor does it have the consistency of *Smash*. A handful of tracks make a lasting impression, but most of *The Offspring* is notable for its surface style, not its substance. —*Stephen Thomas Erlewine*

Ignition / Mar. 8, 1993 / Epitaph ♦♦♦♦

● **Smash** / Aug. 23, 1994 / Epitaph ♦♦♦♦
The Offspring's second album for Epitaph did the impossible: it landed in the Top Five, unheard of for independent records. The Offspring crossed over due to the raucous, Eastern-tinged single "Come out and Play (Keep 'Em Separated)," which stopped and started just like Nirvana, only without the Seattle trio's recklessness. The record stayed in the charts because the Offspring sounded relentlessly heavy, no matter how much the band claimed to be punk. Their tempos are slower than traditional hardcore, and their attack is as heavy as Metallica. But they acted like they were punk, with odes to no "Self Esteem" and singing about fighting in school. Nothing on the album matches the incessant catchiness of the singles, but *Smash* is a solid record, filled with enough heavy riffs to keep most teenagers happy. —*Stephen Thomas Erlewine*

Ixnay on the Hombre / Feb. 4, 1997 / Sony ♦♦♦
The Offspring may have been a product of the Southern California hardcore scene, but their instincts have always been more metal than punk. Their guitars plod along with a heavy backbeat, and even their speedier numbers are weighed down by clumsy riffs, which is evident on *Ixnay on the Hombre*, the follow-up to the group's unexpected hit *Smash*. Despite Jello Biafra's opening assertation of the Offspring's punk credentials, *Ixnay on the Hombre* sounds like a competent hard-rock band trying to torch themselves to the post-grunge bandwagon. The riffs don't have hooks, and Dexter Holland yelps his vocals tunelessly. Of course, much hardcore followed this formula, but it got by on its self-righteousness and visceral forward force. Since Offspring *slows down the tempo* of hardcore, it doesn't have either the undiluted rage of hardcore, or the four-on-the-floor groove of hard rock.

Also, they haven't come up with a ridiculous hook on the level of "Come out and Play (Keep 'Em Separated)" or "Self Esteem," which leaves *Ixnay on the Hombre* as a tedious, turgid mess of anemic punk-metal. —*Stephen Thomas Erlewine*

Mary Margaret O'Hara

b. Toronto, Ontario
Singer-Songwriter
Though the subject of great critical acclaim, to date singer-songwriter Mary Margaret O'Hara has issued only one LP. The sister of comedienne Catherine O'Hara (best known for her work in the groundbreaking sketch comedy series *SCTV* and the *Home Alone* movies), she was born in Toronto; after graduating from the Ontario Art College, she joined her first band, the soul-pop outfit Dollars. In 1976 O'Hara signed on with the group Songship—soon renamed the Go Deo Chorus—and began writing much of the group's material.

She left the band in 1983, but not before recording the demos which subsequently earned her a contract with Virgin Records. After a series of delays and label battles, in 1988 O'Hara finally issued her lone full-length album, *Miss America*, which she co-produced with the innovative guitarist Michael Brook; a four-song holiday release, *The Christmas EP*, followed in 1991. O'Hara subsequently appeared with a diverse range of artists, contributing vocals to recordings from Morrissey, Gary Lucas, the Henrys, This Mortal Coil and John & Mary. In 1996, she also contributed a song to the benefit album *Sweet Relief II: The Gravity of the Situation: The Songs of Vic Chestnutt*. An occasional actress, she appeared in the films *The Hunter* (1980), *Candy Mountain* (1987) and *The Events Leading Up to My Death* (1992). —*Jason Ankeny*

● **Miss America** / 1988 / Virgin ♦♦♦♦
Originally recorded in 1984 and not released until 1988, *Miss America* still sounds light years ahead of its time: Mary Margaret O'Hara is a force of nature, a remarkable singer and composer whose crystal-clear soprano acrobatics and hypnotic songs defy accepted conventions. Flirting intermittently with country ("Anew Day," "Dear Darling") and jazz ("Keeping You in Mind"), O'Hara works primarily with pop dynamics, but deconstructs and reassembles the form according to her own blueprint: "Year in Song" is jaggedly intense, "To Cry About" is gorgeously ambient, and "Body's in Trouble" is delicately gripping, yet none conform easily to such facile assessments, with hairpin turns in mood and atmosphere that blindside expectations. Following instead its own abstract internal logic, *Miss America* is a work of mad-scientist genius, and it remains a singular experience. —*Jason Ankeny*

Ohio Express

f. 1968, Mansfield, OH, db. 1969
Bubblegum
Ohio Express and the 1910 Fruitgum Co. were two of the leading late-'60s bubblegum rock groups. Under the aegis of producers Jerry Kasenetz and Jeff Katz, both of these rather anonymous bands surfaced repeatedly on the late-'60s pop charts for Buddah Records, spearheading the bubblegum rock craze. With Joey Levine taking the vocals on their early hits, The Ohio Express roared up in 1968 with "Yummy Yummy Yummy" and "Chewy Chewy," a pair of million-sellers. Future 10CC leader Graham Gouldman fronted the Express on their final chart bow in 1969, "Sausalito (Is the Place to Go)."

At the same time, another Kasenetz-Katz discovery, New Jersey's 1910 Fruitgum Co., was bubbling over with the obnoxiously catchy "Simon Says," "1,2,3, Red Light," and "Indian Giver," another gold record triumvirate. Like their labelmates, their mercurial chart run was history before 1969 was over. —*Bill Dahl*

● **Golden Classics** / Mar. 21, 1994 / Collectables ♦♦♦♦
Although the sound is poor and the packaging is skimpy, *Golden Classics* is a perfectly reasonable 17-track collection of the Ohio Express' Buddah singles, featuring the majority of their hits, including "Yummy Yummy Yummy," "Down at Lulu's," "Chewy Chewy," "Sweeter Than Sugar," "Mercy," "Pinch Me (Baby, Convince Me)," and "Sausalito (Is the Place to Go)." —*Stephen Thomas Erlewine*

The Ohio Players

f. 1959, Dayton, OH
Soul, Funk
Originally formed in 1959 as an instrumental R&B group, the Ohio Untouchables (as they were then known) provided backup on the Falcons' records. After the Untouchables broke up, two of the members (Clarence "Satch" Satchell and Marshall "Rock" Jones) formed a new outfit called the Ohio Players and began working as the house band at Compass Records. In the early '70s, the Ohio Players had a steady stream of funky, sexual hit singles, including the No. 1s "Fire" and

"Love Rollercoaster." As the decade progressed, their sound gradually transformed into a throbbing disco pulse and their sales slowly tapered off; even so, they continued recording through the 1990s. —*Stephen Thomas Erlewine*

Pain / 1972 / Westbound ✦✦✦
The Ohio Players perked up ears around the soul world with their early -'70s debut. This was prototype jazz-rock/funk, particularly the title cut, with its layered bass lines, Marvin Pierce's crackling trumpet solo, and Sugarfoot's prickly guitar accompaniment. While the arrangements had a skeletal sound due to Westbound's rather meager engineering, the energy, flip/flamboyant attitude, and vocal assertiveness provided an early read on what would prove to be one of the 1970's finest funk bands. —*Ron Wynn*

Ecstacy / 1973 / Westbound ✦✦✦

Pleasure / 1973 / Westbound ✦✦✦
This was the first Ohio Players album to get sizable mileage and attract some attention. "Funky Worm" was their initial No. 1 R&B hit, got them into the pop Top 20, and alerted the funk and R&B community to the group's mix of sizzling beats, a jazz-rock sensibility, and exuberant collective vocals. They were almost ready to break, and this was an early indication of the band's potential. —*Ron Wynn*

Climax / 1974 / Westbound ✦✦✦
This was the lull before the storm. The Ohio Players had left Westbound, where they perfected their shuddering funk sound, and moved to Mercury. In just a few short weeks, they would explode with their greatest album and begin a string of classic funk records. Meanwhile, Westbound issued this vintage session, in which their older material seemed a little thin and light, but was still enjoyable. It would quickly be eclipsed by what came next. —*Ron Wynn*

Skin Tight / 1974 / Mercury ✦✦✦✦
Skin Tight was a major turning point for the Ohio Players, who had enjoyed several hits on Black radio (including "Pain," "Funky Worm," "Varee Is Love," and "I Wanna Hear from You"), but hadn't been huge. Switching from Westbound to Mercury, the Dayton funksters became exactly that—huge—and went from enjoying a cult following to being one of the most celebrated funk bands of the 1970s. With *Skin Tight*, the band's erotic album covers went from employing bizarre S&M/bondage imagery to being more *Playboy*-ish, and its music became less abstract (but remained quite risk-taking and unpredictable). The title song and "Jive Turkey" are down and dirty funk classics, and the jazz-influenced "Heaven Must Be like This" illustrates the fact that the Players could also be captivatingly romantic. —*Alex Henderson*

Rattlesnake / 1975 / Westbound ✦✦✦

Fire / 1975 / Mercury ✦✦✦✦
After greatly increasing its visibility with *Skin Tight*, the Ohio Players became even more visible with *Fire*—an unpredictable masterpiece that boasted such explosive horn-driven funk jewels as "Smoke" and the wildly addictive title song. The Players were always best known for their hard-edged funk, but, in fact, there was much more to their legacy. "I Want to Be Free," the almost innocent "Together," and the remorseful "It's All Over" demonstrate that their ballads and slower material could be first-rate soul treasures. The influence of gospel imagery and the Black church experience had asserted itself on *Skin Tight*'s "Is Anybody Gonna Be Saved?" and does so once again on the intense "What the Hell" and the hit "Runnin' from the Devil." Without question, *Fire* was one of the Ohio Players' greatest triumphs—both commercially and artistically. —*Alex Henderson*

Honey / 1975 / Mercury ✦✦✦✦
Honey may have had the most controversial LP cover of 1975. Its erotic cover, which depicted a nude model covered in honey, was protested by feminists when it was alleged that the model had become stuck to the floor during the photo shoot. Some retailers, in fact, refused to carry it. All the controversy certainly didn't hurt the album commercially. In 1975, the Ohio Players were one of R&B's most successful acts, and were inescapable for anyone who listened to Black radio at the time. The album kept the band's commercial momentum going thanks to such hard-driving funk as "Love Rollercoaster" (a song that was sampled to death by rappers in the 1980s and '90s and covered by the Red Hot Chili Peppers in 1996) and "Fopp" and the playfully jazz-influenced hit "Sweet Sticky Thing." While the Players' outstanding contributions to funk would continue to have an enormous impact long after the band's popularity faded, it's important to stress that only about half of *Honey* falls into the funk category. In fact, lead singer Sugarfoot's moving performance on the remorseful "Alone" makes one wish that the Players' ballads were discussed more often. —*Alex Henderson*

★ **Ohio Players Gold** / 1976 / Mercury ✦✦✦✦✦
When it gets right down to it, the Ohio Players' albums were as memorable for their risque album covers as they were for their music. Sure, there were some seriously funky individual tracks, but the Play-

ers couldn't keep the momentum up throughout the course of an entire album. And that's why *Ohio Players Gold* is such a useful collection, even in light of more comprehensive latter-day collections. *Ohio Players Gold* has the good stuff and absolutely no filler. From the scorching "Fire" and the wild "Love Rollercoaster" to the sly "Jive Turkey" and "Who'd She Coo?," nearly every one of the group's finest songs are present and accounted for on *Gold*. Naturally, there are some omissions—"Funky Worm" really should have been on the collection, especially since it was their first No. 1 R&B hit—but this album should satisfy most listeners that just want the hits. If you want to dig a little deeper into their catalog without sampling their albums, try *Funk on Fire: The Mercury Anthology* but otherwise, stick with the *Gold* and you'll reap its rewards. —*Leo Stanley*

Contradiction / 1976 / Mercury ✦✦✦
Although not in a class with *Skin Tight, Fire*, or *Honey, Contradiction* is a varied, sometimes risk-taking effort that has a lot going for it. The album was best known for the insistent funk hit "Who'd She Coo?," but equally appealing are the Spanish-influenced "Little Lady Maria," the ominous "Far East Mississippi," and the poetic title song. Unfortunately, Mercury/PolyGram's CD configuration of *Contradiction* is missing the lyric sheet that came with the original LP version. Enjoyable but not essential, the LP was the last Players album to include a major hit—by the time *Angel* was released in 1977, the band's popularity had decreased considerably. —*Alex Henderson*

Angel / 1977 / Mercury ✦✦
Arguably the greatest of the Dayton funk bands, the Ohio Players had peaked by the time this album was issued in the late '70s. Internal dissent would soon split them apart, and it seemed that they had run out of catchy funk hits and inspiration. There were remnants of the old spirit, fire, and energy, but often the collective vocals sounded detached, and the classic horn lines and guitar/bass/keyboards interaction stiff. They still made great album covers. —*Ron Wynn*

Mr. Mean / 1977 / Mercury ✦
This album hit the charts after the group was defunct, and had sentimental value if little musical distinction. They had long since lost the magic and cohesion that made them the definitive Dayton funk ensemble. The vocals, even Sugar's Sly Stone/Bar-Kays inflections, were bland, while everything else, from production to arrangements and vocals, were a shell of past works. —*Ron Wynn*

Jass-Ay-La-Dee / 1978 / Mercury ✦
The group was already in massive decline by the time this album was released. They had officially disbanded, and this album was rushed out by Mercury to fill the void. It sounded like a wrap job as well; their vocals were never great, but they were at least exuberant. Now, they were lifeless, as were the arrangements, horn charts, musical backing, and compositions. Only Ohio Players completists ever purchased it, and they're the only ones who would ever own it. —*Ron Wynn*

Tenderness / 1981 / Boardwalk ✦✦
The Ohio Players were near the end of the line when they issued this album for the Boardwalk label. It featured the same roster that had made so many strong hits for Mercury, but they sounded tentative and unfocused, which was probably justified, since most of the songs were undistinguished and the production and arrangements were muddled. This proved a completely forgettable proposition all around. —*Ron Wynn*

Funk on Fire: the Mercury Anthology / Jun. 6, 1995 / Mercury Funk Essentials ✦✦✦✦

The O'Jays

f. 1958, Canton, OH
Soul, R&B, Urban, Philly Soul, Quiet Storm
Perhaps the reigning vocal group of the '70s and '80s, the O'Jays began in Canton as the Triumphs in 1958. The original lineup was Eddie Levert, Walter Williams, William Powell, Bobby Massey, and Bill Isles. They recorded as the Mascots for King in 1961 and were renamed by Cleveland disc jockey Eddie O'Jay. Isles departed in 1965 and Massey left in 1971 to become a producer, making the group a trio. They got their first chart single in 1963 for Imperial, for whom they recorded until 1967. The O'Jays' first major hit was "I'll Be Sweeter Tomorrow (Than I Was Today)" for Bell in 1967, which reached No. 8 on the R&B charts. They continued on Bell and Neptune until they attained stardom in 1972 on Philadelphia International. "Back Stabbers" was the first of eight No. 1 R&B hits they would get on the label from 1972-1987. Others included "Love Train, " "Give the People What They Want," "I Love Music," "Livin' for the Weekend," "Message to Our Music," "Use Ta Be My Girl," "Darlin' Darlin' Baby (Sweet, Tender, Love)" and "Lovin' You." They also had eight other Top Ten R&B hits and four other Top Ten pop smashes, while "Love Train" also topped the pop charts in 1973. They moved to EMI

in 1987 and continued recording. Their most recent release was *Heart-breaker* in 1993. —*Ron Wynn*

Comin' Through / 1965 / Imperial ✦✦✦
The O'Jays were a fledgling five-member outfit when they issued their debut album in 1965. They generated a little attention with the dance/novelty tune "Do the Wiggle," and also issued a pair of good ballads in "Lonely Drifter" and "Lipstick Traces." None of these songs were as masterfully produced or arranged as the epic Gamble/Huff material, but it did reveal the potential they had for R&B stardom. This album has been out of print for years, although some of the songs have surfaced on anthologies. —*Ron Wynn*

Back on Top / 1968 / Bell ✦✦✦
A fine album, their last for the Bell label. George Kerr was still working with them, and they were now down to three members. The harmonies weren't quite polished, and Eddie Levert, Walter Williams, and William Powell hadn't rounded into form, although at times they flashed signs that things were coming together. But this album has more nostalgic than musical value, although those who only heard the O'Jays on Philadelphia International should check it out to discover their roots in '50s doo wop and '60s soul. —*Ron Wynn*

O'Jays in Philadelphia / 1969 / Philadelphia International ✦✦✦✦
Contrary to what its title suggests, *The O'Jays in Philadelphia* isn't a live album. Rather, the title of this studio date refers to the beginning of their association with Philly's R&B scene and producers/songwriters Kenny Gamble & Leon Huff. What they didn't know in 1969 was just how long and fruitful that association would end up being. This album wasn't the major hit that *Back Stabbers* would be, but not for lack of strong material. From "One Night Affair" to "Let Me in Your World," this superb album is quintessential Philly soul. While Eddie Levert's gospel-influenced belting is as gritty as anything that came from Stax Records, the production is as notably sleek. A few years later, Gamble & Huff would produce a longer, heavily syncopated version of "Affair" for Jerry Butler that some soul historians exalt as the first disco single. The main problem with the CD configuration of this classic is its skimpiness—Legacy could have easily added at least another half hour of material. —*Alex Henderson*

☆ **Back Stabbers** / 1972 / Philadelphia International ✦✦✦✦✦
A major turning point for the O'Jays, *Back Stabbers* took the group to the top of the charts and made them household names in the R&B world. The O'Jays had been paying serious dues since the late '50s, and their perseverance paid off in a major way when the unsettling title song, the infectious "Time to Get Down," and the uplifting "Love Train" became their biggests hits up to that point. Indeed, this album did more than its part to help establish Gamble & Huff's Philadelphia International Records as the most successful soul label since Stax and Motown. The problem with the CD configuration of *Back Stabbers* that Legacy/Sony released in 1996 isn't the music—which is consistently superb—but its length. Couldn't Legacy have either combined *Back Stabbers* and another O'Jays album on a single CD or come up with some type of rarities? Be that as it may, the album is essential listening for fans of Philly soul. —*Alex Henderson*

Ship Ahoy / 1973 / Philadelphia International ✦✦✦✦
The "other" O'Jays album masterpiece, *Ship Ahoy* combined shattering message tracks and stunning love songs in a fashion matched only by Curtis Mayfield's finest material. From the album cover showing a slave ship to the memorable title song and incredible "For the Love of Money," Gamble and Huff addressed every social ill from envy to racism and greed. Eddie Levert's leads were consistently magnificent, as were the harmonies, production, and arrangements. "Put Your Hands Together" and "You Got Your Hooks in Me" would be good album cuts, but on *Ship Ahoy* they were merely icing on the cake. —*Ron Wynn*

Survival / 1975 / Philadelphia International ✦✦✦✦
The O'Jays followed the spectacular *Backstabbers* and *Ship Ahoy* with the good, but not on the same level, *Survival*. It was unrealistic to expect masterpieces every time out, and the LP included many strong ballads and good message tracks. But while it may not have been as epic in its performances and compositions, it was certainly the other albums' equal in sales strength. The group had two No. 1 R&B hits in 1975, "Give the People What They Want" and "I Love Music (Part 1)." In addition, the title track made the charts as the B-side to "Let Me Make Love to You," another rousing ballad. —*Ron Wynn*

Family Reunion / 1975 / Philadelphia International ✦✦✦
In the 1970s, Philadelphia International Records could seemingly do no wrong where the O'Jays were concerned. The Cleveland trio recorded one gem after another under Gamble & Huff's direction, and *Family Reunion* was no exception. Nothing on this CD has the angry bite of "Back Stabbers," "Don't Call Me Brother," or "Rich Get Richer," and the mood is upbeat and optimistic on everything from the uplifting "Unity" to the ballad "Stairway to Heaven" (not to be confused

with the Led Zeppelin song) to the escapist party anthem "Livin' for the Weekend." With the intoxicating "I Love Music," the O'Jays stressed the soul side of disco and provided one of the most appealing hits of the disco era. From start to finish, *Family Reunion* was a valuable addition to a catalog that already had its share of treasures. —*Alex Henderson*

★ **Collector's Item** / 1977 / Philadelphia International ✦✦✦✦✦
After enjoying an impressive string of gold and platinum albums, the O'Jays had this collection of their biggest hits on Philadelphia International released in 1978. There was no way to lose with such songs as "Back Stabbers," "Love Train," "For the Love of Money," and "I Love Music." Unfortunately, Philadelphia International haphazardly sequenced the collection, ignoring chronological and stylistic considerations and just sticking tracks on the two sides without any attention to pacing. That gaffe aside, it's a worthy anthology for the casual listener, although the hardcore fan should look elsewhere. —*Ron Wynn*

So Full of Love / 1978 / Philadelphia International ✦✦✦
This was the biggest hit album the O'Jays ever enjoyed, even though it wasn't as aesthetically transcendent as *Ship Ahoy*. But it came at the right time; there weren't many great group albums being produced in R&B at the time, and that's what this really was, even if Eddie Levert took most of the leads. "Use Ta Be My Girl" was a triumphant success, while "Brandy" was the prototype album cut that became a hit through popular demand. —*Ron Wynn*

● **Greatest Hits** / 1984 / Philadelphia International ✦✦✦✦
When The O'Jays left Columbia for EMI, the company promptly issued this greatest-hits package, although they opted to put fewer tracks on it than on the 1978 *Collector's Items*. So, the logical question would be, why would anyone want it? Probably because they've made *Collector's Items* extremely difficult to locate, and also because this mid-'80s release had better mastering of such seminal O'Jays items as "Love Train" and "For the Love of Money." While it has gaping holes as a single-disc anthology, this release provides an acceptable overview of the group's Epic/Philadelphia International/TSOP material. —*Ron Wynn*

● **Love Train: The Best of the O'Jays** / Aug. 9, 1994 / Epic/Legacy ✦✦✦✦
All of the band's monster 1972-76 Philadelphia International hits are here, as well as a couple of small ones. The essay by Robert Palmer is good, but at a mere ten tracks, the selection is unaccountably skimpy. —*Richie Unterberger*

Let Me Make Love to You / Jan. 24, 1995 / Epic/Legacy ✦✦✦
Like *Give the People What They Want*, *Let Me Make Love to You* is a concept compilation, collecting ten of the O'Jays' most under-appreciated love ballads, including the title track, which was a minor hit, "Stairway to Heaven," and "Listen to the Clock on the Wall." Again, the disc is not a hits collection, but a sampling of some of the group's finest album tracks and forgotten singles, and in that context, it's very enjoyable. —*Stephen Thomas Erlewine*

Give the People What They Want / Feb. 28, 1995 / Epic/Legacy ✦✦✦
In addition to liner notes, a major problem with the first CD configurations of the classic O'Jays albums like *Ship Ahoy* and *Family Reunion* was their brevity. By LP standards, roughly 35-40 minutes was generous; but for CDs, it's undeniably skimpy. In 1995, Sony's reissue-oriented Legacy label was fairly generous when assembling *Give the People What They Want*, a CD containing material from those gems as well as *Back Stabbers* and *Survival*. Everything here is first-rate—from the angry sociopolitical commentary of "Give the People What They Want" and "Rich Get Richer" to the romantic optimism of "(They Call Me) Mr. Lucky," the CD reminds us how consistently superb the O'Jays were during the '70s. It also reminds us of another important fact: under Gamble & Huff, the group's albums tended to contain very little, if any, filler. Most of these pearls—including the moving "How Time Flies" and the biting "Shiftless, Shady, Jealous Kind of People"—weren't even released as singles. —*Alex Henderson*

In Bed with the O'Jays: Greatest Love Songs / Aug. 20, 1996 / EMI ✦✦✦
As if you couldn't guess, this compilation targets the group's most romantic, urban contemporary-oriented efforts, spanning 1976 to 1991. It's not the group at its peak, nor is it an accurate reflection of their diverse output. But it does have a few massive R&B hits, including "Lovin' You," "Darlin' Darlin' Baby (Sweet, Tender, Love)," and "Used to Be My Girl." Most unusual item: their cover of Bob Dylan's "Emotional Yours," from the 1991 album of the same name. —*Richie Unterberger*

Olivia Tremor Control

f. 1992, Athens, GA
Lo-Fi, Indie Rock
As much a concept as a band, the Olivia Tremor Control was one of the most visible and innovative members of the Elephant 6 Recording

Company collective, a coterie of like-minded, lo-fi indie groups—including the Apples (in stereo), Neutral Milk Hotel and Secret Square—who shared musicians, ideas and sensibilities. The Olivia Tremor Control was led by singers/songwriters/multi-instrumentalists William Cullen Hart and Bill Doss, natives of the small, isolated town of Ruston, Louisiana, where they struck up friendships with fellow outsiders Robert Schneider (who went on to front the Apples) and Jeff Mangum (the auteur behind Neutral Milk Hotel).

Throughout high school, the aspiring musicians—all influenced by the likes of the Beatles, the Beach Boys, the Zombies, Pink Floyd and Sonic Youth—exchanged home recordings and played in each other's bands. Hart and Doss later attended Louisiana Tech University together, where they tenured as college-radio deejays and furthered their musical educations and ambitions. In 1990 Hart, Doss and Mangum moved to Athens, Georgia to form the group Cranberry Life Cycle; when Mangum exited, they enlisted John Fernandes and became Synthetic Flying Machine. After Doss' temporary defection to Chocolate USA, Synthetic Flying Machine mutated into the Olivia Tremor Control at much the same time both Schneider and Mangum relocated to Denver, Colorado to start their own respective projects.

In 1995, the OTC (later fleshed out by Pete Erchick and "technical advisor" Eric Harris) debuted with the EP California Demise, the first chapter in an ongoing series of high-concept recordings built around the surreal plot of an imaginary film conceived by Hart and Doss. The follow-up seven-inch, "The Giant Day," led directly into the group's 1996 debut double-LP, Music from the Unrealized Film Script 'Dusk at Cubist Castle', a sprawling collection of Beatlesque psychedelia, popcraft and tape loops culled from some 200 unrecorded songs. The first few thousand copies of the album also included a bonus disc of ambient "dream sequences." —Jason Ankeny

Dusk at Cubist Castle / Aug. 1996 / Flydaddy ✦✦✦✦
Not the Beatles, but an incredible facsimile: on their sprawling 27-song debut opus Music from the Unrealized Film Script "Dusk at Cubist Castle," the Olivia Tremor Control manage to summon not only the sound of the White Album-era Fab Four, but also the unfettered creativity. The soundtrack to an as-yet unmade film about a pair of women named Olivia and Jacqueline and a massive earthquake dubbed the California Demise, the album incorporates a slew of influences and textures (including Beach Boys-flavored pop, psychedelia, Krautrock, noise, and folk-rock) and synthesizes them into a distinct home brew of shimmering harmonies, guitar drones, backwards tape loops, and inventive effects. As an added bonus, the first few thousand copies come with a bonus CD of ambient "dream sequences"—titled Explanation II—which, when played simultaneously with the first disc, realizes true quadraphonic sound. Amazing. —Jason Ankeny

The 101'ers

f. May 1974, London, England, **db.** Jun. 1976
New Wave, Pub Rock
Primarily known as the band Joe Strummer was in before he joined the Clash, the 101'ers were part of the last wave of British pub rock bands of the mid-'70s. The group never released any recordings while they were together, yet they were among the important transitional figures in the metamorphosis of pub rock into punk rock.

Joe Strummer formed the 101'ers formed in May of 1974, recruiting guitarist Clive Timperley, bassist Dan Kelleher and drummer Richard Dudanski; according to legend, the group either named themselves after the torture room in George Orwell's 1984 or the building where they lived. By the end of the summer, the group had performed their first concert, playing Brixton's Telegraph pub. For the next year and a half, the 101'ers worked the pub rock circuit. During 1975 and early 1976, the group laid down some demos. In the first half of 1976, the 101'ers had been opening for the Sex Pistols on selected dates. Inspired by the Pistols and the burgeoning punk movement, Strummer decided to quit the 101'ers in June 1976 and form the Clash. Within a month, the group's only single, "Keys to Your Heart," was released on Chiswick Records.

Following the demise of the 101'ers, Dudanski played with the Raincoats and, later, Public Image Limited; Timperley joined the Passions and Kelleher became a member of the Derelicts. In 1981, after the Clash had become stars, Strummer allowed a 101'ers compilation called Elgin Avenue Breakdown to be released. —Stephen Thomas Erlewine

Elgin Ave Breakdown / 1981 / Andalucia ✦✦✦
Elgin Avenue Breakdown compiles nearly all of the recordings that the 101'ers left behind. There are three demo sessions, dating from 1975 and 1976, a handful of home-taped live performances, and an alternate version of their only single, "Keys to Your Heart." Though the sound quality is rough, there is plenty of enjoyable, driving Stonesy

rock 'n' roll on the album, making it worthwhile for pub rock and Clash completists. —Stephen Thomas Erlewine

Alexander O'Neal

b. Nov. 14, 1953, Minneapolis, MN
Vocals / Soul, Urban
This Minneapolis soul man cut his teeth in The Time but was bounced (for looking "too Black") before they signed with Warner Brothers. His tough, ballsy voice has the same grain and range as Otis Redding's. Like that master, O'Neal is comfortable with pumping dance-floor burners and slinky couch-cuddlers. He's certainly the best singer Jimmy Jam and Terry Lewis have ever produced, and the strength of his material and his robust voice can be heard on releases including 1986's Hearsay, 1991's All True Love and 1997's Lovers Again. —John Floyd

Alexander O'Neal / 1985 / Tabu ✦✦✦
Former Time member Alexander O'Neal made a smashing debut as a lead artist in the mid-'80s. The Jam/Lewis duo found the ideal balance for O'Neal between dance/funk uptempo tunes and urgent urban contemporary ballads. They scored with "If You Were Here Tonight" and "A Broken Heart Can Mend," as well as "Innocent." Suddenly, O'Neal was among the top male urban artists, and continued to have hits into the '90s. —Ron Wynn

Hearsay / 1986 / Tabu ✦✦✦✦
Alexander O'Neal almost achieved the breakout he needed for crossover success with his second album. It cracked the Top 30 on the pop album chart, earned a gold record, and included O'Neal's two strongest uptempo tunes, "Fake" and "Criticize." Jam and Lewis linked the material with "party" dialogue and patter, providing their finest and tightest production for any O'Neal record. The beats were catchy, the songs hook-laden, and O'Neal's voice alternately explosive, sensitive, and bemused. —Ron Wynn

All Mixed Up / 1988 / Tabu ✦✦
This lengthy and intelligently programmed set of remixed hits is culled mostly from Hearsay. —John Floyd

All True Love / 1991 / Tabu ✦✦✦
Most soul and R&B male vocalists excel at slow, simmering love tunes and merely execute uptempo ones; Alexander O'Neal reverses the process. So it was no surprise that All True Love contained several excellent dance-based tunes and no memorable love ballads. Despite some production clutter with multi-tracked female vocalists and overblown strings, O'Neal scored on such numbers as "What Is This Thing Called Love?" and "All True Man," prime Jimmy Jam/Terry Lewis numbers. For some reason, Jam and Lewis sought to thematically link several songs on the CD into a portrait of '90s urban angst, without success. —Ron Wynn

All True Man / Jan. 24, 1991 / Tabu ✦✦✦
In the '80s and early '90s, Jimmy Jam and Terry Lewis have been the closest thing R&B has had to a Gamble and Huff or a Holland/Dozier/Holland. Although not in a class with those legends, the Time graduates can usually be counted on to produce high-quality albums—a good example being Alexander O'Neal's All True Man. While this isn't the gritty Minneapolis soul shouter's best album and contains nothing as outstanding as "Innocent," "Fake," or "The Way You Look Tonight," it's a respectable effort that's far superior to most of 1991's contrived R&B releases. O'Neal reminds us just how gutsy and heartfelt his singing can be on sweaty funk smokers like "Time Is Running Out" and "The Yoke (G.U.O.T.T.)"—both of which demonstrate his willingness to tackle social issues—and such vulnerable balladry and slow material as "The Morning After," "Sentimental," and the haunting "Shame." Those exploring O'Neal's music for the first time would do better to purchase Alexander O'Neal or Heresay, but for his hardcore followers, All True Man is definitely worth hearing. —Alex Henderson

Love Makes No Sense / Feb. 9, 1993 / Tabu ✦✦✦

● **This Thing Called Love: Greatest Hits of** / Apr. 6, 1993 / CBS ✦✦✦✦
While it can be argued that Alexander O'Neal's track record doesn't merit any greatest hits or best-of compilations, that didn't deter Tabu from issuing this compilation. It presented O'Neal's finest uptempo and ballad singles, displaying his ferocity on such cuts as "Fake" and "Criticize," plus his range and passion on "Never Knew Love Like This." —Ron Wynn

The Best of Alexander O'Neal / Oct. 1995 / Tabu ✦✦✦✦

The Only Ones

f. 1977, South London, England
Punk, New Wave, Power Pop
Led by the raffish and slightly scuzzy romance-obsessed Peter Perrett, the Only Ones were one of the punk era's most underrated bands. Not as confrontational as the Sex Pistols, as politically indulgent as the

Clash, or as stripped-down as the Ramones, the Only Ones played not-so-fast guitar rock that sounded deeply indebted to the New York Dolls and other mid-'70s proto-punks. Singing his intelligently crafted pop songs in a semi-tuneful whine of a voice and backed by a band that effectively combined youthful exuberance with gracefully aging veterans (non-punk drummer Mike Kellie had done time with early-'70s clod-rockers Spooky Tooth, bassist Alan Mair was nearly 40!), Perrett was an astute chronicler of the vagaries of modern, dysfunctional love. Despite a career that lasted from 1978-1981 and one certifiable "hit" song to their credit (the brilliant "Another Girl, Another Planet") the Only Ones became the archetypal contenders that never broke big, despite assurances from fans and critics that they couldn't miss.

Although they split up in 1981 after only three records, the Only Ones, due in large part to "Another Girl, Another Planet," became more influential than one would have guessed. Listen to Paul Westerberg and you'll hear more than a little Peter Perrett (in fact, the Replacements covered "Another Girl"); look at the number of Only Ones releases over the past decade (a half-dozen at least) and you soon realize that a significant cult surrounding the band grew after their breakup. Ironically, it was the posthumous release of the sessions for John Peel's BBC show that, more than any of the proper studio releases, accurately displayed the muscle and smarts of this fine band. There have been many rumors surrounding Perrett's life after the Only Ones, many of them involving an alleged heroin addiction. Perrett did continue to record and release solo projects during the '80s, eventually reuniting the Only Ones as the Ones in the mid-'90s. —John Dougan

The Only Ones / Apr. 1978 / CBS ✦✦✦✦
"Another Girl, Another Planet" is here, but then again, it surfaces on a number of Only Ones records. The best of their studio releases, this record is a tuneful anomaly of mid-'70s rock that stands in stark contrast to the prevailing punk zeitgeist. Still, the band (even the old guys) play with an infectious enthusiasm, and Perrett, despite his tendency toward adenoidal Dylanesque vocals, is particularly winning. —John Dougan

● **Special View** / 1979 / Epic ✦✦✦✦
In America, Epic couldn't decide whether or not to release any Only Ones recordings, so they came up with this half-way measure: a sampler. Special View took the strongest tracks from their debut, added tracks from their so-so second album, Even Serpents Shine, and the result was (surprise) a great record. All these years later, Special View is as good a sampler of early Only Ones as anyone could have hoped for and should be considered an important purchase, although I think it's no longer in print. —John Dougan

Even Serpents Shine / 1979 / CBS ✦✦✦✦
Only a shade removed from the standard of debut LP. —Steve Aldrich

Baby's Got a Gun / Jun. 1980 / Epic ✦✦✦
Less consistent than their first two efforts, it's still rewarding. —Steve Aldrich

Remains / 1984 / Closer ✦✦
Included are demos and unfinished studio tracks. —Steve Aldrich

Peel Sessions / 1989 / Dutch East India ✦✦✦✦
Frankly, one could argue an eloquent case either way as to why Special View or the Peel Sessions are the most important Only Ones recordings. I tend to recommend the Peel Sessions, because it's rougher, a little meaner, and the Only Ones were in the midst of their 15 minutes of fame as a rock band; plus, there's a swagger here that's missing on other recordings. —John Dougan

Live / 1989 / Edsel ✦✦✦
Not essential, but if you've fallen under Peter Perrett's spell, you owe it to yourself to hear what a fine live band they were. Recorded in London in 1977 in the Ones' pre-CBS days, this is a "punkier" sounding band, a little ragged, but wonderful. To no one's surprise, "Another Girl" is here and it's great. —John Dougan

Live in London / 1990 / Skyclad ✦✦✦
Essentially a greatest-hits live package, this contains many of the aforementioned tracks, but adds bits and some hots-on guitar spuzz. —John Dougan

The Immortal Story / 1992 / CBS ✦✦✦
The "Official" compilation consists of best-ofs, including alternate takes and rare tracks. —Steve Aldrich

Yoko Ono

b. Feb. 18, 1933, Tokyo, Japan
Pop-Rock, Experimental
Over the years, Yoko Ono has received an unfair treatment in the press. From being pegged as the reason The Beatles broke up to being called talentless, Ono has been dragged through the press more times than any one person deserves. And she did have talent,

although it was primarily as a conceptual and visual artist. As a musician, she is allegedly influential on many post-punk bands, though it is highly unlikely anyone outside of The B-52s actually listened to her records. With her abrasive, frequently atonal pop and rock experimentations, Ono did predict, if not influence, the sound of some experimental post-punk bands, including Public Image Limited. Ono could be even more effective when she conformed to pop songwriting, turning in some surprisingly moving straightforward pop-rock. If you can wade through the pretensions—as well as grow accustomed to her shrill voice—you may find some rewarding music among her many records. —Stephen Thomas Erlewine

Yoko Ono/Plastic Ono Band / 1970 / Apple ✦✦✦✦
Recorded concurrently with John Lennon's Plastic Ono Band album, Yoko's features the same musicians, namely John, Ringo Starr, and Klaus Voormann along with the Ornette Coleman Quartet on one cut. Unlike John's record, however, Yoko's Plastic Ono Band is much more a "jam"-sounding record. And while there are definite songs, lyrics are mainly vocal improvisations. Still, if avant-garde is your cup of tea, then check this one out. It's good, if only to hear John Lennon really get the guitar cranking on the opening cut "Why." —James Chrispell

Fly / 1971 / Apple ✦✦✦
A double-album release from Mrs. Lennon. While the first disc contains real songs, such as the rockin' "Midsummer New York" and the gentle love ballad, "Mrs. Lennon," disc two contains more avant-garde doodlings that Yoko was known for at the time. The side-long cut entitled "Fly" is soundtrack material from John and Yoko's film of the same name. If you tend to ignore her weird stuff, stick to disc one, because there are some good tunes to be found there. All in all, a split decision. —James Chrispell

Feeling the Space / 1973 / Apple ✦✦
On Feeling the Space, Yoko took complete control of her product for the first time. John Lennon only played as a side musician on one cut, with the rest of the songs ably abetted by some of New York's finest studio cats. This is a feminine record dedicated to "the sisters who died in pain and sorrow for being unable to survive in a male society." The best term to describe the music here is "angry." Yoko finds no love or sweetness where the male population is concerned, and it shows. Shortly after this was released, however, Yoko reconciled with John, and son Sean was born. But here, her anger comes through loud and clear. —James Chrispell

Approximately Infinite Universe / 1973 / Apple ✦✦
Written and recorded in New York City with Elephant's Memory, Yoko Ono has finally come into her own write and draw. Showing off her rock capabilities, she finds the hard spot with such cuts as "Yang Yang" and "I Felt like Smashing My Face in a Clear Glass Window." But she shows gentle sentiment in cuts such as "Song for John" and the wonderful "Looking over from My Hotel Window." Although this record, another double on vinyl, could have used some editing, it is well worth delving into. —James Chrispell

Walking on Thin Ice / 1981 / Geffen ✦✦✦

Seasons of Glass / 1981 / Geffen ✦✦✦✦
After John Lennon's murder, Yoko took her anguish into the recording studio and emerged with this raw collection of songs. From the gunshots before the cut "No, No, No" to the bloody glasses of John's on the cover, this is harrowing stuff indeed. But it's surprisingly good if only for the fact that the whole world was feeling similarly at the time. One of the most essential Yoko Ono releases, it's powerful and chilling. —James Chrispell

It's Alright (I See Rainbows) / 1982 / Polydor ✦✦
Although still mourning the death of John Lennon, Yoko found herself looking toward the future with It's Alright. With a more upbeat pop approach, Yoko found herself played on some radio stations with the cut "Never Say Goodbye," even if it contained soundbites from John calling out her name. She'd gone through hell and now was finding her own place in the world of rock music. —James Chrispell

Starpeace / 1985 / Polydor ✦✦

Ono Box / Jan. 28, 1992 / Rykodisc ✦✦✦✦
Although it inspires countless jokes, the music on the six-disc Onobox is, by and large, quite impressive. In terms of experimental rock 'n' roll, Ono was certainly one of the leaders in the 1970s, creating intense, almost atonal rock that demanded to be accepted on its own terms. Nearly 20 years later, some of the music sounds dated, but much of it sounds remarkably contemporary. Nevertheless, the box is rarely dull and makes a strong case for her musical talents. —Stephen Thomas Erlewine

● **Walking on Thin Ice Compilation** / Mar. 20, 1992 / Rykodisc ✦✦✦✦
A single-disc distillation of the Onobox which covers everything the curious listener needs to know. —Stephen Thomas Erlewine

New York Rock [original Cast] / May 2, 1995 / Capitol ✦✦✦

Rising / Nov. 7, 1995 / Capitol ✦✦✦

"The making of the album served as a purging of my angst, pain and fear," writes Yoko Ono in a sleeve note to her first new album in a decade. "I hope it will for you, too." The angst, pain, and fear she cites come both from her childhood in war-torn Japan and such current-day scourges as AIDS. Ono returns to primal screaming on some tracks to express those feelings, and the album's music, played by IMA, a trio featuring her son Sean Ono Lennon, matches her fury with hard rock and funk worthy of the Red Hot Chili Peppers. In the '80s, Ono turned to pop-rock without achieving a commercial breakthrough. Here, she returns to the abrasive style of her '70s work, which has turned out to be more influential on a generation of alternative rockers. — *William Ruhlmann*

Rising Mixes / Mar. 5, 1996 / Capitol ✦✦✦

This 58-minute disc takes four of the tracks from the Yoko Ono/IMA album *Rising*—"Talking to the Universe," "Ask the Dragon," "Where Do We Go from Here?," and "Rising"—and assigns remix duties to, respectively, Cibo Matto, Ween, Tricky, and Sonic Youth's Thurston Moore. Of course, "remix" is a restrained word for what the remixers do. For example, Cibo Matto adds two drum sets, extra keyboards and samples, and a rap by Miho Hatori to "Talking to the Universe," resulting in an extensively revised version of the song. Gene and Dean Ween and Andrew Weiss also play along with "Ask the Dragon," retaining only Yoko Ono's arch spoken vocal. The album also includes "The Source," credited to ABA Allstars, who are led by the Beastie Boys' Adam Yauch, which contains some of Ono's patented screaming, and the 30-minute "Franklin Summer," which is not a special mix, but rather a new soundscape by Ono and IMA consisting of her ululating voice (and, halfway in, some improvised singing), acoustic guitars, and percussion. — *William Ruhlmann*

Opal

f. 1984, db. 1988

Alternative Pop-Rock, Psychedelic, Neo-Psychedelia, Dream-Pop

The neo-psychedelic group Opal formed in the mid-'80s, featuring former Rain Parade guitarist David Roback and former Dream Syndicate bassist Kendra Smith. Initially, the group was called Clay Allison, yet the group dropped the name after one single; Roback, Smith, and drummer Keith Mitchell released the remaining Clay Allison tracks underneath their own name in 1984, on the *Fell from the Sun* EP. After its release, the group adopted the name Opal and released an EP, *Northern Line*, in 1985. *Happy Nightmare Baby*, their first full-length album, followed in 1987. Smith left the group during the *Happy Nightmare* tour, effectively putting an end to the band. Roback continued with vocalist Hope Sandoval; the group then metamorphosed into Mazzy Star. — *Stephen Thomas Erlewine*

● **Happy Nightmare Baby** / 1987 / SST ✦✦✦✦

Transcending the limitations of its psychedelic-era inspirations, Opal's one and only LP goes beyond nostalgia to forge its own distinct and swirling tapestry of moody drones and guitar washes. Edgier and darker than the group's earlier singles, *Happy Nightmare Baby* is also considerably more rock-oriented; the opening "Rocket Machine" recalls T. Rex, while the keyboard textures bear the influence of another mind-expanding Los Angeles band, the Doors. Still, the record has an ambience all its own—Kendra Smith is a singularly evocative vocalist, and David Roback's guitar work is powerful and expressive. — *Jason Ankeny*

Early Recordings / 1989 / Rough Trade ✦✦✦✦

While Opal's *Happy Nightmare Baby* is more representative of the group's richly textured brand of neo-psychedelia, the stripped-down *Early Recordings* compilation is an even better example of David Roback and Kendra Smith's remarkable songcraft. Released in the wake of the group's breakup, the album collects the majority of tracks from the *Fell from the Sun* and *Northern Line* EPs, along with a handful of outtakes and unreleased cuts, all spotlighting Opal's more subdued, acoustic-folk side. Peeling away the mystical haze that enshrouded *Happy Nightmare Baby*, the songs are plaintive and stark, exposing the emotional complexity at the band's core—the wistful "Empty Box Blues" and the haunting "Harriet Brown," both previously unissued, are unmatched in their beauty and grace. — *Jason Ankeny*

Orange Juice

f. 1976, Glasgow, Scotland, db. 1985

Alternative Pop-Rock, Blue-Eyed Soul

The leaders of the Scottish neo-pop uprising, Orange Juice formed in Glasgow in late 1976. Originally dubbed the Nu-Sonics, the group comprised vocalist/guitarist Edwyn Collins, guitarist James Kirk, bassist David McClymont and drummer Steven Daly; following the formation of the Postcard label by Collins protege Alan Horne, the quartet

renamed itself Orange Juice in 1979, adopting the new moniker as well as an aura of romantic innocence as a direct reaction to the increasingly macho aggression of punk.

As Postcard's flagship band, Orange Juice quickly distinguished the label as a leading proponent of independent pop music; their 1980 debut single "Falling and Laughing," recorded for less than 100 pounds, garnered massive critical acclaim, and subsequent releases like "Blueboy," "Simply Thrilled Honey" and "Poor Old Soul" further established the group as a major new talent. Soon, sessions began for a full-length album; however, in the midst of recording, Orange Juice left Postcard to sign to Polydor, which funded the LP's completion. After the 1982 release of the album, titled *You Can't Hide Your Love Forever*, ex-Josef K guitarist Malcolm Ross joined the group, hastening the exit of Kirk and Daly (who went on to form Memphis) and paving the way for Zimbabwe-born drummer Zeke Manyika.

Manyika's addition gave Collins the new capability of exploring a more complex fusion of pop and blue-eyed soul; consequently, 1982's *Rip It Up* was a more ambitious affair than its predecessor, veering from the buoyant Motown tribute "I Can't Help Myself" to the energetic pop of the title track, Orange Juice's lone Top Ten single. However, subsequent releases failed to chart, and relations between the group and Polydor began to disintegrate; amid these tensions, both Ross and McClymont quit, with Ross later resurfacing in Aztec Camera. Reduced to the duo of Collins and Manyika, Orange Juice enlisted reggae producer Dennis Bovell to record the 1984 EP *Texas Fever*.

After a makeshift tour, Collins and Manyika returned to the studio to record a dark, ambitious full-length effort; released in 1984, neither *The Orange Juice* nor its singles "What Presence?!" and "Lean Period" charted, and Collins was dropped from his contract, although Polydor kept Manyika on as a solo act. Only in 1995 did the stunning single "A Girl Like You" finally win Collins the commercial respect that had so long eluded him and his former bandmates. — *Jason Ankeny*

● **The Very Best of Orange Juice** / Oct. 1995 / Polydor ✦✦✦✦

Released in the wake of Edwyn Collins' surprise success with "A Girl like You," *The Very Best of Orange Juice* contains all of the Scottish pop group's biggest hit singles, offering an excellent introduction to their career, as well as rounding up all the highlights from their often incoherent records. — *Stephen Thomas Erlewine*

The Orb

f. 1989, London, England

Ambient House, Club/Dance, Ambient Dub, Electronica

The Orb virtually invented the electronic genre known as ambient-house, resurrecting slower, more soulful rhythms and providing a soundtrack for early-morning ravers once the dance clubs had closed their doors. The group popularized the genre as well, by appearing on the British chart show *Top of the Pops* and hitting No. 1 in the UK with the 1992 album *U.F.Orb*. Frontman Dr. Alex Paterson's formula was quite simple: he slowed down the rhythms of classic Chicago house and added synthwork and effects inspired by '70s ambient pioneers such as Brian Eno and Tangerine Dream. To make the whole a bit more listenable—as opposed to danceable—obscure vocal samples were looped, usually providing a theme for tracks which lacked singing.

Paterson had worked as a roadie for Killing Joke during the '80s, and began to be influenced by the explosion of Chicago house music in England during the mid-to-late-'80s. After recording an uptempo house EP called *The Kiss* in 1989, Paterson's first foray into ambient-house appeared in October 1989 on the WAU!/Mr. Modo label. Recorded with Jimi Cauty (of the KLF), the 22-minute single "A Huge Ever Growing Pulsating Brain That Rules from the Centre of the Ultra-world" actually hit the UK charts in late 1989. The single became popular with indie-kids as well as club DJs, and earned Paterson and Cauty the chance to re-record the song in December 1989 for a John Peel session.

In the meantime, Alex Paterson had been working with Youth (from Killing Joke) on the new track "Little Fluffy Clouds," with a melody incorporated from composer Steve Reich. The single appeared in November 1990, sparking the wrath of the sampled Rickie Lee Jones, whose dialogue with Levar Burton—from the PBS-TV children's program *Reading Rainbow*—was sampled for the chorus and title of the track; Big Life later settled out of court for an undisclosed sum. Though the single failed to place in the charts, its laidback vibe made it a big hit on the dancefloor.

Youth's other commitments made it unable for him to become a permanent member of the Orb, so Paterson decided to recruit Kris Weston (nicknamed Thrash for his punk/metal roots), a young studio engineer who worked on "Little Fluffy Clouds." The duo debuted in April 1991 with a full-length, *The Orb's Adventures Beyond the Ultraworld*. Given reams of critical acclaim, the album was pushed into Great Britain's Top 30 LP charts. By the end of the year, the Orb returned to the album charts with *The Aubrey Mixes*, a remix compilation with reworkings by Steve Hillage, Youth and Jimi Cauty.

In June 1992, the new single "Blue Room" hit the British Top Ten. The longest single in chart history at just under 40 minutes, it earned the Orb a spot on *Top of the Pops*, where they ruminated over a chess game and waved at the camera while a three-minute edit of the single played in the background. Released in July, the album *U.F.Orb* hit No. 1 on the British album charts, and also did well with critics, who praised it and the duo's sold-out tour of England.

Though the Orb had released several hours of recordings and many remixes during its first three years of existence, the beginning of 1993 prompted a dry spell of over a year and a half. The problem wasn't a lack of material; Paterson and Thrash continued to record, but Big Life Records had begun a controversial campaign to reissue several early singles. The Orb threatened to release no new material until the label promised to cease and desist, and negotiations stalled while the duo looked to opt out of their contract. In the meantime, Big Life reissued five CD singles and two other 12-inch releases, including "Little Fluffy Clouds" (which hit the British Top Ten), "Huge Ever Growing Pulsating Brain" and "Perpetual Dawn" (the second single from *Ultraworld*).

Paterson finally signed an international deal with Island in 1993 and released the stop-gap *Live 93* later that year. The Orb's first studio release for Island, the *Pomme Fritz* EP, appeared the following year but signalled a diminished role for Kris Weston. Taking up the slack from Weston's departure was Thomas Fehlmann. The Orb had previously remixed a single from his Sun Electric project, and most of *Pomme Fritz* was recorded at his Berlin studios. Finally, almost three years after *U.F.Orb*, the new and improved group released the Orb's third studio LP, *Orbus Terrarum*. With a concept and a sound rooted firmly on terra firma, the album's dense rhythms and return to natural samples heralded a turn away from the cosmic fascination within ambient-house—which had been nurtured in large part by *Ultraworld* and *U.F.Orb*. After the release of a double-disc remix compilation, the Orb returned to the great beyond with the spacey sounds of 1997's *Orblivion*. —*John Bush*

● **The Orb's Adventures Beyond the Ultraworld** / Aug. 1991 / Big Life ◆◆◆◆

Much like the early Orb-related project recorded as Space, *Ultraworld* simulates a journey through the outer realms—progressing from "Little Fluffy Clouds" and "Back Side of the Moon" (a veiled Pink Floyd reference) to "Into the Fourth Dimension," ending after two hours with a glorious live mix of "A Huge Ever Growing Pulsating Brain." A varied cast of samples (including *Flash Gordon*, space broadcasts, and foreign-language vocals) and warm synthesizer tones provide a convincing bed for the mid-tempo house beats and occasional ambience on *Ultraworld*. This is the album that defined the ambient-house movement. —*John Bush*

U.F.Orb / Mar. 1992 / Big Life ◆◆◆◆

So far, the Orb haven't made an album better than *U.F.Orb*, a hypnotic series of trance-inducing rhythms and interweaving synths that never grows boring, even at its 74-minute length. —*Stephen Thomas Erlewine*

Live 93 / Nov. 22, 1993 / Island ◆◆◆◆

Although the thought of an Orb live album may raise some eyebrows, the resulting two-CD set is amazing, a complete representation of the group in concert and living proof that techno is indeed a live, as well as recorded, art form. Besides, the consistent Pink Floyd jokes on the record (as well as the brilliant cover art) are hilarious. —*Stephen Thomas Erlewine*

Pomme Fritz Ep / Jul. 12, 1994 / Island Red ◆◆

After a long absence, Orb returned with this EP, a very experimental work that won't appeal to most listeners. Still, "Alles Ist Schoen" features a great ambient groove. —*John Bush*

Orbus Terrarum / Apr. 4, 1995 / Island ◆◆◆

The perfect response to a music scene swamped by what Paterson himself called "lame ambient noodling for seventy minutes." The melodies and dub lines of the first two albums are still in the mix, though they are overpowered by harsh percussion and noisy synth. This creates an unsettling effect on first listen, though, after repeated plays, the brilliance of *Orbus Terrarum* becomes clear. The hilarious vocal samples on "Slug Dub," taken from a children's story, make it the highlight of the disc. —*John Bush*

Auntie Aubrey's Excursions Beyond the Call of Duty / Aug. 1996 / Deviant ◆◆◆◆

A double-disc compilation of over two and a half hours of remixes, *Excursions* includes Orb reworkings of well-known bands (Primal Scream, Erasure, Depeche Mode, Killing Joke) and more obscure acts (Keiichi Suzuki, Love Kittens). Several mixes sound a bit dated, and the scattershot quality of the set can distract listeners, but the inclusion of several epiphanous moments (Material's "Praying Mantra," Primal Scream's "Higher than the Sun," and Sun Electric's "O'Locco") makes the album worthwhile for fans. Included is a thick book containing colorful discographies and an interesting essay. —*John Bush*

Orbscure Trax: The Rare Excursions / 1997 / Island ◆◆◆

Orbscure Trax was a digipak promo CD given away with purchased copies of the Orb's 1997 CD, *Orblivion*, primarily to boost sales during the group's spring '97 tour. Hardly a throwaway gimmick, however, the 70-minute-plus disc contains some extremely high-quality material, beginning with the Ganja Kru's hardstep take on *Orblivion's* first single, "Toxygene," and moving through unreleased mixes such as "Molten Love (Berlin Session Film Mix)" and "Bedouin," as well as rare versions of perennial faves such as "Little Fluffy Clouds," "Oxbow Lakes," and "Plateau." —*Sean Cooper*

Orblivion / Jan. 1997 / Island ◆◆◆◆

If the Orb's 1995 release *Orbvs Terrarvm* was an extended meditation on the earthbound, the band's follow-up in *Orblivion* rises from the muck of primordial ectoplasm for a guided tour of late-20th-century Western culture's more paranoid face. From the Cold War (the album kicks off with Kennedy's intoning of the immortal invective "Are you now, or have you ever been . . . "), to the pre-millenial ranting of David Thewlis' warped, apocalyptic monologue from Mike Leigh's *Naked* ("The bar code! The ubiquitous bar code!"), *Orblivion* does for post-industrial turn-of-the-century mania what earlier albums such as *The Orb's Adventures Beyond the Ultraworld* and *U.F.Orb* did for aliens and flying saucers. Like the previous record—an effusive mix of sprawling environmental textures, clanging, treated percussion, and humorous, trainspotterly samples—*Orblivion* brings with it another adjustment in mood, combining elements of downbeat, electro, and drum 'n' bass with dense, soupy amalgams of treated electronics and shimmering rhythms. *Orblivion* also evidences a renewed interest in the more immediately engaging, upbeat pop of "Perpetual Dawn"—and "Little Fluffy Clouds"-era Orb, with a deeper, more embellished sound marked, in all likelihood, by the first full-time contributions from former engineer Andy Hughes (who replaced Kris Weston after the latter's departure in 1994). Dub is still the organizing principle of the Orb's music, however, and whatever one's opinion of the actual album (reactions are likely to range from "genius" to "aimless") the production is undeniably amazing. —*Sean Cooper*

Roy Orbison

b. Apr. 23, 1936, Vernon, TX, d. Dec. 6, 1988, Madison, TN
Guitar, Vocals / Rock 'n' Roll, Rockabilly, Pop, Pop-Rock

Although he shared the same rockabilly roots as Carl Perkins, Johnny Cash, and Elvis Presley, Roy Orbison went on to pioneer an entirely different brand of country/pop-based rock 'n' roll in the early '60s. What he lacked in charisma and photogenic looks, Orbison made up for in spades with his quavering operatic voice and melodramatic narratives of unrequited love and yearning. In the process, he established rock 'n' roll archetypes of the underdog and the hopelessly romantic loser. These were not only amplified by peers such as Del Shannon and Gene Pitney, but also influenced future generations of roots rockers such as Bruce Springsteen and Chris Isaak, as well as current country stars the Mavericks.

Orbison made his first widely distributed recordings for Sun Records in 1956. Roy was a capable rockabilly singer, and had a small national hit with his first Sun single, "Ooby Dooby." But even then, he was far more comfortable as a ballad singer than as a hepped-up rockabilly jive cat. Other Sun singles met with no success, and by the late '50s he was concentrating primarily on building a career as a songwriter, his biggest early success being "Claudette" (recorded by the Everly Brothers).

After a brief, unsuccessful stint with RCA, Orbison finally found his voice with Monument Records, scoring a No. 2 hit in 1960 with "Only the Lonely." This established the Roy Orbison persona for good: a brooding rockaballad of failed love with a sweet, haunting melody, enhanced by his Caruso-like vocal trills at the song's emotional climax. These and his subsequent Monument hits also boasted innovative, quasi-symphonic production, with Roy's voice and guitar backed by surging strings, ominous drum rolls, and heavenly choirs of backup vocalists.

Between 1960 and 1965, Orbison would have 15 Top 40 hits for Monument, including such nail-biting mini-dramas as "Running Scared," "Crying," "In Dreams," and "It's Over." Not just a singer of tear-jerking ballads, he was also capable of effecting a tough, bluesy swagger on "Dream Baby," "Candy Man," and "Mean Woman Blues." In fact, his biggest and best hit was also his hardest-rocking: "Oh, Pretty Woman" soared to No. 1 in late 1964, at the peak of the British Invasion.

It seemed at that time that Roy was well-equipped to survive the British onslaught of the mid-'60s. He had even toured with the Beatles in Britain in 1963, and John Lennon has admitted to trying to emulate Orbison when writing the Beatles' first British chart-topper, "Please Please Me." But Orbison's fortunes declined rapidly after he left Monument for MGM in 1965. It would be easy to say that the major label couldn't replicate the unique production values of the classic Monument singles, but that's only part of the story. Roy, after all, was still writing most of his material, and his early MGM records were produced in a style that closely approximated the Monument era. The harder truth to face was that his songs were sounding to start like lesser variations of themselves, and that contemporary trends in rock and soul were making him sound outdated.

Orbison, like many early rock greats, could always depend on large overseas audiences to pay the bills. The two decades between the mid-'60s and mid-'80s were undeniably tough ones for him, though, both personally and professionally. A late-'60s stab at acting failed miserably. In 1966, his wife died in a motorcycle accident; a couple of years later, his house burned down, two of his sons perishing in the flames. Periodic comeback attempts with desultory albums in the 1970s came to naught.

Orbison's return to the public eye came about through unexpected circumstances. In the mid-'80s, David Lynch's *Blue Velvet* film prominently featured "In Dreams" on its soundtrack. That led to the singer making an entire album of re-recordings of hits, with T-Bone Burnett acting as producer. The record was no subsitute for the originals, but it did help restore him to prominence within the industry. Shortly afterwards, he joined George Harrison, Bob Dylan, Tom Petty, and Jeff Lynne in the Traveling Wilburys. Their successful album set the stage for Orbison's best album in over 20 years, *Mystery Girl*, which emulated the sound of his classic 1960s work without sounding hackneyed. By the time it reached the charts in early 1989, however, Orbison was dead, claimed by a heart attack in December 1988. —*Richie Unterberger*

Crying / 1962 / Columbia ♦♦
Roy Orbison's second album was above-average considering the slight standards of the time, but was a fairly slight effort nonetheless. In its favor, the album features nearly all original material by Orbison and some of the writers who frequently tailored songs for him, such as Boudleaux and Felice Bryant and Joe Melson. The trademark early Orbison production flourishes, with swooping strings and full vocal choruses, are also present. What's missing is truly first-rate songwriting. With the exception of "Love Hurts," the title track, and the epic hit "Running Scared," most of the cuts lean toward the Big O's more sentimental side, and are pleasantly forgettable. Of the obscure cuts here, the best are the uptempo "Nite Life" and "Let's Make a Memory," with its bouncing string arrangement, but neither could be classified among his best early work. —*Richie Unterberger*

There Is Only One / 1965 / Polygram ♦♦
Orbison explains in the liner notes that MGM will allow him "a new climate of freedom" as an artist, but the results of his first album for the label were unimpressive. He forsakes much of the rock 'n' roll foundation of his classic early-'60s hits for Nashville country and western on most of the LP, complete with barroom piano. The material (mostly written by Orbison with various collaborators) doesn't approach the magnificence of his best work, and his version of his composition "Claudette" isn't nearly as good as the Everly Brothers' hit rendition from 1958. The highlight is the strange, almost rambling minor hit single, "Ride Away." —*Richie Unterberger*

Fastest Guitar Alive / 1968 / Columbia ♦♦
Orbison's one bid for film stardom, *The Fastest Guitar Alive*, was an unqualified flop. The soundtrack fares slightly better, but only slightly. With ten songs clocking in at a mere 27 minutes, most of the tunes—which Roy composed with longtime collaborator Bill Dees—borrow from the cheesiest elements of cowboy music, with quasi-Mexican guitar riffs, silly Indian chants, and uneasy spaghetti-Western pathos. For all its ill-conceived failure, it includes what may be his best obscure tune, the little-anthologized "Whirlwind." With its galloping rhythm, emotive operatic vocals, swirling strings, and ghostly backing vocals, it recalls the best uptempo ballads that he recorded during his early-'60s heyday at the Monument label. In 1968, of course, few listeners were interested. —*Richie Unterberger*

All-Time Greatest Hits of Roy Orbison / 1976 / Monument ♦♦♦♦
The *All-Time Greatest Hits of Roy Orbison* is an essential collection. It rounds up 20 of the Big O's best '60s recordings, with some fine album tracks thrown in. —*John Floyd*

All-Time Greatest Hits of Roy Orbison, Vols. 1 & 2 / 1985 / Monument ♦♦♦
Although it's missing his early Sun hit "Ooby Dooby," the 20-track *All-Time Greatest Hits of Roy Orbison* contains every one of his big hits for Monument Records, including "Up Town," "Only the Lonely," "Blue Angel," "I'm Hurtin'," "Running Scared," "Crying," "Dream Baby," "Leah," "Working' for the Man," "Candy Man," "In Dreams," "Falling," "Mean Woman Blues," "Blue Bayou," "Pretty Paper," "It's

Over," and "Oh, Pretty Woman." In other words, it is nearly as complete as Rhino's 18-track *For the Lonely*. The main difference between the two collections is the fact that the Rhino disc contains some Sun material, which makes it the preferable retrospective. Nevertheless, *All-Time Greatest Hits* remains a first-rate collection, especially if you're just looking for hits. —*Stephen Thomas Erlewine*

★ **For the Lonely: 18 Greatest Hits** / 1988 / Rhino ♦♦♦♦♦
For the Lonely: Roy Orbison Anthology (1956-1965) offers the usual Monument hits along with a few Sun tunes—18 in all. Buyers beware: the vinyl version contains more cuts than the CD. —*John Floyd*

The Legendary Roy Orbison / 1988 / Sony ♦♦♦♦
While the Rhino set, *For the Lonely: Roy Orbison Anthology (1956-1965)*, is the most essential single-disc release of Orbison's work, *The Legendary Roy Orbison* tries to flesh out the picture considerably with a four-disc, 75-track boxed set. It may be overkill for some, and certain tracks feel like pointless inclusions, but fans who want more than just a hits collection should like this set. The enclosed booklet contains a wealth of photos and the annotation is passionate and informative. —*Rick Clark*

The Classic Roy Orbison (1965-1968) / 1989 / Rhino ♦♦♦
The hits dried up when Orbison left the Monument label for MGM in 1965. The 14 recordings here, taken from singles and LP tracks, feature arrangements and production not far removed from his classic Monument era. The singing is wonderful, but stacked up against his classic hits, a lot is missing. Lacking the ace songwriting of his best work, there's lots of midtempo, melodramatic rock balladry here, but somehow nothing nearly as gripping as his best compositions. —*Richie Unterberger*

Our Love Song / 1989 / Monument ♦♦
Skimpily assembled package of a dozen obscurities, most from the early—and mid-'60s Monument era. "(I Get So Sentimental)" and "Born on the Wind" count as some of his better unknown tunes from that time, but on the whole it's a poor and haphazard collection. —*Richie Unterberger*

Sun Years / 1989 / Rhino ♦♦♦♦
20-track compilation of Orbison's Sun sides, including both sides of all four of his official Sun 45s, and a dozen tracks he recorded for the label that remained unissued at the time. Orbison at this point was a decent but somewhat also-ran rockabilly singer, and not nearly as suited for the style as fellow Sun artists Elvis Presley, Jerry Lee Lewis, and Carl Perkins. He also had yet to find his songwriting or singing voice with balladeering pop-rock material, so this collection may disappoint those who expect something along the lines of Roy's famous Monument hits. It's not at all bad, though, with standout cuts such as "Ooby Dooby," "Rock House," and "Devil Doll"; it's just not Orbison at either his best or his most comfortable. —*Richie Unterberger*

Mystery Girl / 1989 / Virgin ♦♦♦♦
Roy's comeback is remarkable in that every song, from "You Got It" and "She's a Mystery to Me" to "The Only One," proves that the formula of his '60s stuff is still vital 30 years later. This album really deserved a follow-up. —*John Floyd*

The Sun Years 1956-58 / Apr. 1989 / Bear Family ♦♦♦♦
Roy Orbison wasn't among the great rockabilly cats, as his voice was a little too rich and his performances a little too mannered to truly rock with abandon. Nevertheless, he did cut a pair of terrific rockabilly singles for Sun with "Ooby Dooby" and "Domino." He never quite reached those heights again while he was on Sun, as Bear Family's single-disc collection *The Sun Years 1956-58* illustrates. Containing every track he recorded for the label, including alternate takes and undubbed mixes, the collection suffers from too much similar-sounding material. Apart from the previously mentioned singles, Orbison only made a handful of songs that really rocked, and they tend lose their impact when mixed in among the mediocre songs and minutely different alternate takes. For hardcore Orbison and rockabilly collectors, the very comprehensiveness of *The Sun Years 1956-58* makes the disc necessary, but most fans—especially those enamored with his grandiose, theatrical ballads—will find that this collection is overkill. —*Stephen Thomas Erlewine*

Singles Collection / Oct. 1990 / Polygram ♦♦♦
Overlooked at the time of its issue, as it was almost simultaneously released with Rhino's *The Classic Roy Orbison (1965-1968)*, this offers a more comprehensive look at his post-Monument recordings. That doesn't mean that it's better. Most of the 1965-68 cuts on this album are also on the Rhino one, though "She" and "Heartache," which are only on *Singles Collection*, are a couple of his better late-'60s songs. The post-1968 tracks that take up the rest of the anthology are a waste, an embarrassment at worst, as Orbison failed to either successfully incorporate contemporary influences or offer quality variations on his tested formula. Stick with the cheaper, more succinct,

and easier-to-find *The Classic Roy Orbison* for an overview of this era. —*Richie Unterberger*

King of Hearts / Oct. 20, 1992 / Virgin ✦✦✦
The posthumously released *King of Hearts* collects a handful of Orbison's final vocal tracks along with a few demos and non-LP singles, including the Jeff Lynne-produced "Heartbreak Radio." The highlight, however, is an amazing duet of "Crying" recorded with k.d. lang. —*Jason Ankeny*

Gold Collection / Dec. 3, 1996 / Tristar ✦✦✦
The Gold Collection is a 15-track hits compilation that contains most of Orbison's biggest hits, including "Only the Lonely," "Pretty Woman," "It's Over," "Blue Bayou," "Crying," and "Candy Man." While it hits most of the high points, it leaves out a handful of necessary tracks, and isn't as strong as Rhino's *For the Lonely* or Monument's *All-Time Greatest HIts.* Essentially, the reason to pick up *The Gold Collection* is the fact that it is a gold-disc, and while the sound is good on the disc, it isn't a dramatic improvement over the other discs on the market. —*Stephen Thomas Erlewine*

Orbital

f. 1987, Seven Oaks, London, England
Techno, Club/Dance, Ambient Techno, Electronica
Orbital became one of the biggest names in techno during the mid-'90s by solving the irreconcilable differences previously inherent in the genre: to stay true to the dance underground and, at the same time, force entry into the rock arena, where an album functions as an artistic statement—not a collection of singles—and a band's prowess is demonstrated by the actual performance of live music. Though the Hartnoll brothers first charted with a single, the 1990 British Top 20 hit "Chime," the duo later became known for critically praised albums. The LPs sold well with rock fans as well as electronic listeners, thanks to Orbital's busy tour schedule, which included headlining positions at such varied spots as the Glastonbury Festival, the Royal Albert Hall and Tribal Gathering.

The brothers Hartnoll—Phil (b. Jan. 9, 1964) and Paul (b. May 19, 1968)—grew up in Dartford, Kent, listening to early-'80s punk and electro. They began recording together in 1987 with a four-track, keyboards and a drum machine. In 1990, the duo gained a contract with FFRR Records for their first single, "Chime," and christened themselves Orbital in honor of the M25, the circular London expressway which speeded thousands of club-kids to the hinterlands for raves during the days of blissed-out acid-house. "Chime" hit No. 17 on the British charts in March 1990, and led to an appearance on the TV chart show *Top of the Pops*, where the Hartnolls stared at the audience from behind their synth banks. Second single "Omen" barely missed the Top 40 in September, but "Satan" made No. 31 early in 1991, with a sample lifted from the Butthole Surfers.

Orbital's 1991 self-titled debut, more of a collection of songs than a true full-length work, had a cut-and-paste attitude typical of many techno LPs of the time. After releasing two EPs the following year, the brothers entered 1993 ready to free techno from its club restraints, beginning in June with a second LP. Also untitled, but nicknamed the 'brown' album as an alternative to the 'green' debut, it unified the disjointed feel of its predecessor and hit No. 28 on the British charts. The Hartnolls continued the electronic revolution that fall during their first American appearances. On a tour with Moby and the Aphex Twin, Orbital proved to Americans that techno shows could actually be diverting for the undrugged multitudes. With no reliance on DATs (the savior of most live techno acts), Phil and Paul allowed an element of improvisation to the previously sterile field, making their live shows actually sound live. The concerts were just as entertaining to watch as well, with the Hartnolls' constant presence behind the banks—a pair of flashlights attached to each head, bobbing in time to the music—underscoring the impressive light shows and visuals. That summer proved to be the pinnacle of Orbital's performance ascent; an appearance at Woodstock 2 and a headlining spot at the Glastonbury Festival (both to rave reviews) confirmed the duo's status as one of the premier live acts in the field of popular music, period.

Orbital's third album, *Snivilization*, appeared in August 1994. The album pushed Orbital into the active world of political protest, focusing on the Criminal Justice Bill of 1994, which gave police greater legal action both to break up raves and prosecute the promoters and participants. A wider variety of styles signalled that this was Orbital's most accomplished work, and *Snivilization* also became the duo's biggest hit, reaching No. 4 in Great Britain's album charts.

During 1995, the brothers concerned themselves with touring, headlining the Glastonbury Festival in addition to the dance extravaganza Tribal Gathering. In May 1996, Orbital set out on quite a different tour altogether; the duo played untraditional, seated venues—including the prestigious Royal Albert Hall—and appeared on stage earlier in the night, much like typical rock bands. Two months

later, Phil and Paul released "The Box," a 28-minute single of orchestral proportions. It screamed of prog-rock excess—especially the inclusion of synth harpsichords—and appeared to be the first mistep in a very studied career. The resulting *In Sides*, however, became their most acclaimed album, with many excellent reviews in publications that had never covered electronic music. —*John Bush*

Orbital / Oct. 1991 / ffrr ✦✦✦✦
The US version of Orbital's debut album serves as a good primer to the group's early history, including standard versions of the early singles "Chime," "Omen," "Satan," and "Midnight," in addition to two B-sides that showed Phil and Paul's first stab at varying their Kraftwerk-inspired sound. "Belfast" (from the "Satan" single) is a warm, mid-tempo synth track inspired by Depeche Mode; "Choice," at the other extreme, is an aggro-house piece with vocal samples (i.e., "Wake Up!") that recall socially conscious punks like Crass. —*John Bush*

Orbital 2 / 1992 / ffrr ✦✦✦✦
Opening with a looped *Star Trek* sample, Orbital's second album progresses through eight tracks of warm, unrepetitive techno in what sounds more like a DJ mix album than an LP, with no bows to mainstream sensibilities. Here, the duo's acknowledged inspiration from Kraftwerk, present before but always in the background, came to the fore. The brilliant manner in which the Hartnolls weave several synth lines, samples, sung vocals, and percussion—mathematically precise but still beautifully orchestrated—updated Kraftwerk's mastery of minimalist electronic music. One of the highlight of the '90s techno movement, the "brown" album is still Orbital's most exciting work. —*John Bush*

● **Snivilisation** / Aug. 23, 1994 / ffrr ✦✦✦✦
The political commentary inherent in 1994's *Snivilization* extended even to the Top 30 single "Are We Here?," whose Criminal Justice Bill Mix voiced Phil and Paul's concern over what the bill might lead to—silence. Musically, the album delivers on the diverse promises of early B-sides "Choice" and "Belfast," more harbingers to their thrash background—especially on "Quality Seconds"—and the addition of a third member, vocalist Alison Goldfrapp, on two songs. The shuffling, quasi-Eastern jungle rhythms of "Are We Here?," a beautiful piano run to begin "Kein Trink Wasser," and the glorious ambient climax "Attached" also reflect the fact that *Snivilization* is Orbital's most varied LP. —*John Bush*

In Sides / Mar. 1996 / ffrr/London ✦✦✦✦
In Sides isn't Orbital's best album, or the most accomplished, but it is the most definitive. It pulses with the energy of the debut, the lush flow of the second, and the conceptual theme of *Snivilization*. The focus this time, though, is ecology. "The Girl with the Sun in Her Head" was recorded on a Greenpeace bus using only solar power, and "Dwr Budr" (Welsh for "dirty water") also criticizes the misuse of natural resources. Phil and Paul's respect for the jungle/drum 'n' bass movement showed in the moderate breakbeat rhythms on several tracks. —*John Bush*

Orchestral Manoeuvres in the Dark

f. 1978, Liverpool, England
Synth-pop, New Wave, New Romantic, Alternative Dance
Featuring the core members Paul Humphreys and Andy McCluskey, the Liverpudlian synth-pop group Orchestral Manoeuvers in the Dark formed in the late '70s. Humphreys and McCluskey began performing together in school, playing in the bands VCL XI, Hitlerz Underpantz, and the Id. After the Id split in 1978, McCluskey was with Dalek I Love You for a brief time. Once he left Dalek, he joined with Humphreys and Paul Collister to form Orchestral Manoeuvers In The Dark. The group released their first single "Electricity" on Factory Records; the record led to a contract with the Virgin's subsidiary Din-Disc. Using their record advance, McCluskey and Humphreys built a studio, which allowed them to replace their 4-track recorded with drummer Malcolm Holmes (formerly of the Id) and Dave Hughes (formerly of Dalek I Love You).

In 1980, the group released their self-titled debut album, which featured the UK Top Ten single "Enola Gay." *Organisation* appeared the same year; Hughes was replaced by Martin Cooper after its release. The band's next few albums—*Architecture and Morality* (1981), *Dazzle Ships* (1983), *Junk Culture* (1984)—found the band experimenting with their sound, resulting in several UK hit singles. Recorded with two new members, Graham and Neil Weir, *Crush*, their most pop-oriented album, found more success in America than in Britain, as the single "So in Love" hit No. 26 on the charts. "If You Leave," taken from the *Pretty in Pink* soundtrack was their biggest American hit, climbing to No. 4 in 1986. *The Pacific Age* was released the same year, yet America was the only country where it was popular. Shortly after its release, the Weir brothers left the band, followed by Holmes, Cooper, and Humphreys. McCluskey continued with the band, releasing *Sugar Tax* in 1991; in the meantime, Humphreys formed the Listening Pool.

After *Sugar Tax* failed to gain an audience, Orchestral Manoevres in the Dark returned with *Liberator* in 1993, which also was ignored. It was followed three years later with *Universal*. —*Stephen Thomas Erlewine*

Orchestral Manoeuvres in the Dark / 1980 / Virgin ✦✦✦✦
A very quirky, nervous album of clockwork synth-pop that avoided the lock-step imposed by primitive technology, mainly by dint of Andy McCluskey's twitchy, frantic bass and vocals and a quirky tape machine. Includes the re-recorded version of "Electricity" (their first single) as well as "Red Frame, White Light" and "Messages," two cuts that seem to promote muscle spasms as dance methodology. —*Steven McDonald*

Organisation / Nov. 1980 / Virgin ✦✦✦
OMD's second album *Organisation finds the group adding an actual drummer, which has the effect of deepening the band's dark, swirling synth-pop. While Organization* isn't as thoroughly impressive or unexpected as the debut, its best songs, most notably the single "Enola Gay," demonstrate that the band's craft is improving. —*Stephen Thomas Erlewine*

Architecture & Morality / Nov. 1981 / Virgin ✦✦✦✦
With their third album *Architecture & Morality,* Orchestral Manoeuvres in the Dark attempt to make their synth-pop sound organic, and the result is an uneven but fascinating collection of somber dance-pop highlighted by the eerie hit singles "Joan of Arc" and "Souvenir." —*Stephen Thomas Erlewine*

Dazzle Ships / 1983 / Virgin ✦✦✦
With *Dazzle Ships,* OMD push their sonic boundaries to the extreme, incorporating found sounds, studio effects, and altered tapes in attempt to create a concept album about the history of technology. Despite their efforts, the end result isn't very captivating since the group concentrated on texture, not songs, but some of those sounds are well worth investigating. —*Stephen Thomas Erlewine*

Junk Culture / 1984 / A&M ✦✦✦✦
Junk Culture finds OMD reintegrating crisp pop melodies to their sound while moving far away from pop song stucture. Instead, the group explores modern dance rhythms and production styles—there are more complex rhythm tracks on *Junk Culture* than any of their other albums, and "Tesla Girls" even incorporates hip-hop scratching. It's a fascinating, frequently captivating listen, and represents a significant comeback for the duo. —*Stephen Thomas Erlewine*

Crush / 1985 / A&M ✦✦✦✦
Following through on the pop inclinations of *Junk Culture,* OMD recorded a full-fledged mainstream pop album with *Crush.* Considerably calmer and more accessible than their previous records, the album may be less adventurous than their earlier work, but the breezy melodic charm of dance-pop singles like "So in Love" make *Crush* a thoroughly winning album. —*Stephen Thomas Erlewine*

The Pacific Age / 1986 / A&M ✦✦
OMD flirted with the mainstream on *Crush,* so some fans might find *The Pacific Age* a welcome return to esoteric, cryptic music. However, the album is loaded down with pompous, unrealized concepts and weak melodies, making it one of the most tedious and trying albums in their catalog. —*Stephen Thomas Erlewine*

● The Best of O.M.D. / 1988 / A&M ✦✦✦✦
The Best of OMD is a 16-track collection that features all of the group's hit singles, from "Enola Gay," "Souvenir," and "Joan of Arc" to "Tesla Girls," "So in Love," and "If You Leave," adding 12-inch mixes of "We Love You" and "La Femme Accident" for good measure. It's a thorough and entertaining retrospective, and it's all that most casual fans will need. —*Stephen Thomas Erlewine*

Sugar Tax / Jun. 11, 1991 / Virgin ✦✦✦
Sugar Tax is the first album OMD recorded without Paul Humphreys, and while the record is less adventurous than most of the group's previous albums, that's not necessarily due to his absence. Instead, OMD began a slow decline into lite soul-inflected synth-pop in the late '80s, and *Sugar Tax,* while thoroughly competent, is nothing more than predictably refined and pleasant dance-pop. —*Stephen Thomas Erlewine*

Liberator / Jun. 29, 1993 / Virgin ✦✦
OMD have rarely been as dance-oriented as they are on *Liberator,* a collection of retro-disco and contemporary '90s club cuts. While it is far from the experimental and edgy synth-pop that earned the group rave reviews in the early '80s, it is an enjoyable, lightweight collection of appealing dance-pop. —*Stephen Thomas Erlewine*

Universal / 1996 / Virgin ✦✦
Universal is a rote collection of synth-pop and dance-pop from OMD, demonstrating only a fraction of the sophisticated craft that made its

predecessor *Liberator* enjoyable, and none of the adventurous spirit of their '80s records. —*Stephen Thomas Erlewine*

The Originals
f. 1966, Detroit, MI
Soul, Motown
Detroit soul vocal group. Led by Freddie Gorman, the Originals took the R&B world by storm in 1969, although they had worked at Motown for years as invaluable background vocalists. Gorman recorded as a solo for Berry Gordy in 1961 and co-wrote "Please Mr. Postman" for the Marvelettes, and the Originals cut a version of Leadbelly's "Goodnight Irene" for Gordy's Soul subsidiary in 66 with ex-Falcon Joe Stubbs as lead. But Stubbs had split to form 100 Proof (Aged in Soul) by the time the quartet waxed the beautiful doowop throwback "Baby I'm for Real," a R&B chart-topper in '69 that was co-written and lushly produced by Marvin Gaye. The same combination also produced "The Bells," another major hit in 1970. Former solo act Ty Hunter joined the group in 1971, and the Originals continued to chart into the next decade. —*Bill Dahl*

● Motown Superstar Series, Vol. 10 / 1976 / Motown ✦✦✦✦
The Detroit-based Originals began singing in 1966, with tenor vocalists Crathman Spencer and Henry Dixon, bassist Freddie Gorman, and baritone Walter Gaines. Marvin Gaye helped bring them to Motown and later wrote or co-wrote three of their singles, including the anthemic "Baby, I'm For Real." That single, their other major hit, "The Bells," and the third Gaye single, "We Can Make It, Baby," are among the tunes on this anthology. They weren't a great group, but their two hits are as gripping and wonderfully produced and arranged as any Motown material. —*Ron Wynn*

The Orioles
f. 1948, Baltimore, MD, **db.** Dec. 9, 1957
R&B, Doo Wop
Led by Sonny Til, the Orioles were the first Black vocal group to sing music directly for a Black audience. Through their early recordings—which were made in the late '40s and early '50s—the band laid the groundwork for R&B vocal groups and doo wop. The Orioles fused traditional pop songs with gospel sensibilities and arranged blues and gospel material with smooth harmonies, designed to appeal to the broadest audience possible.

Based in Baltimore, MD, the Orioles consisted of lead vocalist Sonny Til (born Earlington Carl Tilghman, Augest 18, 1928; d. December 9, 1981), Alexander Sharp (tenor vocals), George Nelson (baritone vocals), Johnny Reed (bass vocals), and guitarist Tommy Gaither. Originally called the Vibranaires, the group formed when its members were teenagers. They came to the attention of Deborah Chessler, a local merchant that also wrote songs; she would write many of the group's subsequent hits. Chessler became the band's manager and she was able to get the Vibranaires a spot on Arthur Godfrey's *Talent Scouts* television show. Although the group lost to pianist George Shearing, they caught the eye of Jerry Blaine, a New York record company executive, while they were in town for the program.

Jerry Blaine signed the group to his newly created It's A Natural record label and had the band cut "It's Too Soon to Know," a ballad written by Chessler. After they signed their deal with It's A Natural, the band changed its name to the Orioles. In the late summer of 1948, "It's Too Soon to Know" was released on It's A Natural but shortly after the single's release National Records Blaine complained about the name of his new label, so he re-released the song on Jubilee Records, a record label he had previously used to release Yiddish comedy records. "It's Too Soon to Know" became a No. 1 R&B hit and crossed over to No. 13 on the pop charts. At the time of its release, no Black group had managed to cross over to the pop charts with what was then-known as a "race" record. The Orioles immediately followed the success of their debut single with the seasonal "(It's Gonna Be A) Lonely Christmas," which reached the R&B Top Ten at the end of 1948.

"Tell Me So" became the Orioles' second No. 1 R&B hit in the spring of 1949, beginning a streak of six hit R&B singles that year. In addition to "Tell Me So," the group charted with "A Kiss and a Rose" (No. 12, late summer), "I Challenge Your Kiss (No. 11, fall)," "Forgive and Forget" (No. 5, fall), a re-released "(It's Gonna Be A) Lonely Christmas" (No. 5, winter), and the B-side of "Lonely Christmas," "What Are You Doing New Year's Eve" (No. 9, winter).

Following their peak year of 1949, the group ran into tragedy. In 1950, Gaither, Nelson, and Reed suffered a automobile accident that killed Gaither and severely injured the other two members; Nelson quit the group later in the year. As Reed recovered from the accident, the group found replacements for Gaither and Nelson, finally settling on guitarist Ralph Williams and vocalist Gregory Carroll. The new lineup of the band had its first hit in 1952, when "Baby Please Don't

Go" reached No. 8 on the R&B charts. The following year, the group had their biggest hit with "Crying in the Chapel." Released in the summer of 1963, "Crying in the Chapel" spent five weeks on the R&B charts and reached No. 11 on the pop charts, eventually going gold; Elvis Presley had a hit with the song 12 years later. Toward the end of the year, the group had another Top Ten R&B hit with "In the Mission of St. Augustine." The single would turn out to be their last hit.

In 1954, the Orioles began to splinter, as Sharp and Reed left to join the Ink Spots. Sony Til assembled a new lineup, but the group didn't gain much attention. Til continued to lead various incarnations of the Orioles, performing concerts and re-recording the group's old hits, until his death in 1981. George Nelson died sometime in 1959 and Alexander Sharp died in the early '70s.

In 1995, 40 years after the original lineup of the group disbanded, the Orioles were inducted into the Rock & Roll Hall of Fame. *—Stephen Thomas Erlewine*

★ **Sing Their Greatest Hits** / Nov. 25, 1991 / Collectables ✦✦✦✦✦
This Orioles hit package is about equal to any other that's available, but pales next to the Bear Family boxed set. The now defunct Murray Hill also had a great Orioles box several years ago. Save your money and grab the Bear Family if you want the real story on The Orioles. *—Ron Wynn*

Jubilee Sides / 1993 / Bear Family ✦✦✦✦
This exhaustive six-CD box set shows you all the reasons why the Orioles, led by smooth-as-silk vocalist Sonny Til, were one of the most pivotal, if not the most important, of all the early Black vocal groups. The group's honey-smooth harmonies perfectly frame Til's soaring, sexy vocals against the simplest of backgrounds on their earliest sides, while later sessions with full orchestras surprisingly do little to intrude, with interesting results. With typical Bear Family completeness, this rounds up everything the group cut for Natural-Jubilee from two different tenures with the label. *—Cub Koda*

Orlando

f. 1994, London, England
Romo
Orlando was the most successful and visible band to emerge from the extremely brief Romo movement of the mid-'90s. Led by songwriter/keyboardist Dickon Edwards, Orlando combined the stylish, synthesized dance-pop of early '80s with Pulp's sense of purpose, the Manic Street Preachers' sense of outrage, Morrissey's sense of humor and an lyrical stance that bordered on the explicitly gay. Thanks to journalist Simon Price, the duo became a sensation on the pages of *Melody Maker*, who grouped Orlando with bands like Plastic Fantastic, DexDexter and Hollywood as Romo bands—i.e., bands that revived the stylistic sensibilities of New Romantics and crossed it with modernist art. Despite a huge push within the media, Romo failed miserably, with *Melody Maker's* package tour playing to audiences of less than 100 in early 1996. Most of the bands crashed and burned following the tour, but Orlando persevered, becoming one of only three Romo bands to actually release singles.

It's nearly impossible to separate Orlando's story from the saga of Dickon Edwards, the leading light behind the duo. Born in Bildeston, a small village in Suffolk, England, Edwards—who was named after a boy in the children's book *The Secret Garden*, even though his parents officially registered him as Richard, fearful of the torment he would receive as a strangely-monikered child—concerned himself with his studies and he was a good student until his last year, when he was in the Sixth form. At that time, he began questioning whether he wanted to go to college. Inspired by *Dead Poets Society*, he dropped out of school and ran away from home. Although he reconciled with his parents, he had left school for good and began studying theater, eventually enrolling in the Bristol Old Vic Theatre School in 1991. By that time, he had developed a fervent obsession with indie-rock, largely through the British music weeklies and John Peel. In the early '90s, he developed an obsession with the cute, twee-pop of Sarah Records and Heavenly in particular, following the band from gig-to-gig. By the mid-'90s, he was spending a lot of time in London, where he met Tim Chipping, who was heavily involved in the Camden Lurch scene. The two began attending concerts, seeing bands like Field Mice and Another Sunny Day.

In 1992, Dickon began publishing a fanzine called *Studbase Alpha*—a parody of the title of Saint Etienne's first album, *Fox Base Alpha*—which consisted primarily of his thoughts and poetry. Within the fanzine, he mentioned he had a band called Orlando, named after the Virginia Woolf novel. He didn't, actually, but soon after reading Kevin Pearce's book on Mod *Something Beginning with O*, he realized that Orlando was destined to become an actual band. Dickon had the concept of pulling the strings for a band fronted by an effeminate male, sending up the concept of the female-fronted indie-band.

Despite his dream, Orlando originally consisted of himself and his friend Simon Kehoe, and the duo began making spoken-word tapes at home. Soon, the duo added Chipping, who had been playing in a post-Huggy Bear and lo-fi band, formed an allegiance. With Tim on board, as well as guitarist Stephen Jefferis, Orlando nearly fulfilled Dickon's vision, but the group was becoming too guitar-oriented for his tastes. Eventually, Kehoe, Jeffris and Chipping all left the band.

Moving to London, Edwards revamped the band into a dance-pop band, with ideas of making Stock-Aitken-Waterman music with intellectual lyrics. Chipping rejoined as vocalist and Dickon began collaborating with keyboardist Sean Turner, who left the group after just one song, "Just for a Second," because he didn't like Edwards lyrics or Tim's flamboyant voice. Frustrated, the duo recorded some old songs under the name Shelley for Sarah, but the EP was ignored upon its spring 1995 release. Shortly afterward, Orlando was revived, with Neil Turner and Mike Austen providing instrumental support. Inspired by the success of Menswear and the despaired by the disappearance of Richey Edwards in the Manic Street Preachers, the duo decided to appeal to the middle ground between the two extremes, but wound up sounding like New Romantics. By networking throughout the Camden scene, the duo got the name of Orlando to all the right journalists and DJs, and they soon received a glowing review of their debut gig from Simon Price in *Melody Maker*. During October, *Melody Maker* ran a cover story about the Romo movement, of which Orlando was one of the most prominent bands, before any of the artists had even released a record. However, the spread led to a deal with Blanco Y Negro for Orlando. In the spring of 1996, Orlando's "Nature's Hated" was featured on a *Melody Maker* Romo giveaway tape.

In the summer of 1996, Orlando released their first single, "Just for a Second," which received decidedly mixed revews, ranging from Price's enthusiastic praise to several other publications who panned it. The *Magic* EP followed in the fall, and it received similar reviews. "Nature's Hated," the group's third single, was scheduled for spring release in 1997. *—Stephen Thomas Erlewine*

Just for a Second / 1996 / Blanco Y Negro ✦✦✦
Not quite the auspicious debut that it wants to be, "Just for a Second" crosses awkward, lite funk similar to latter-day Duran Duran with a synthesized, symphonic disco sweep, straight out of Euro-pop. Try as it may, it never quite develops a melody, especially since Tim Chipping's thin, quivering voice can't carry a tune, yet it still manages to make a definitive stylistic statement. Political statements are reserved for the piano-driven ballad "Something to Write Home About," one of the more explicitly gay anthems of the '90s, or "The Trouble With You," which consists of classical music in one channel, and an interview stating Orlando's modus operandi on the other. *—Stephen Thomas Erlewine*

● **Magic Ep** / 1996 / Blanco Y Negro ✦✦✦✦
A more diverse, but not necessarily more accomplished, affair than "Just for a Second," The Magic EP is the definitive Orlando recording, capturing the awkward gap between their pretensions and their achievements. "Don't Kill My Rage" is a boisterous disco number that has a tight arrangement, but is undercut by Tim's chirping, wavering, and tuneless falsetto. "Fatal" is a downright bizarre attempt to fuse Euro-disco with G-Funk that actually features Tim's best vocal. "Contained" is a spare, Northern Soul-styled R&B track, highlighted by percolating horns, and "Up Against It" is a grand, theatrical piano ballad much like "Something to Write Home About." Throughout it all, Dickon really tries to say something, usually to no avail. However, his botched imagery and poetry are endearing, and are perfectly suited for Tim's non-voice. *—Stephen Thomas Erlewine*

Beth Orton

b. Dec. 1970, Norwich, England
Singer-Songwriter, Trip-Hop
Singer-songwriter Beth Orton combined the passionate beauty of the acoustic folk tradition with the electronic beats of trip-hop to create a fresh, distinct fusion of roots and rhythm. Born in Norwich, England in December 1970, Orton debuted as one half of the duo Spill, a one-off project with William Orbit which released a cover of John Martyn's "Don't Wanna Know About Evil." She continued working with Orbit on his 1993 LP *Strange Cargo 3*, co-writing and singing the track "Water from a Vine Leaf" before appearing with the group Red Snapper on their first singles "Snapper" and "In Deep." In 1995 Orton teamed with the Chemical Brothers for "Alive: Alone," the ultimate track on their *Exit Planet Dust* LP. After assembling a backing band comprised of double bassist Ali Friend, guitarist Ted Barnes, keyboardist Lee Spencer and drummer Wildcat Will, she finally issued her 1996 debut EP *She Cries Your Name;* her stunning full-length bow *Trailer Park*, produced in part by Andrew Weatherall, followed later in the year. *—Jason Ankeny*

● **Trailer Park** / 1996 / Heavenly ✦✦✦✦
A folkie for the electronica age, Beth Orton brilliantly bridges the gap between acoustic songcraft and digital dance beats with her extraordinary debut album *Trailer Park*. Fusing the plaintive emotional power of the singer-songwriter tradition with the distanced cool of trip-hop rhythms, Orton creates a fresh, distinct, and surprisingly organic sound without obvious precedent; blessed with a warm, ethereal voice capable of adapting comfortably to spartan folk ("Whenever," a touching cover of the Spector/Greenwich/Barry-penned "I Wish I Never Saw the Sunshine"), buoyant pop ("Live As We Dream," "How Far"), and spacy, densely layered electronica ("Tangent," "Touch Me With Your Love"), she shifts gears with remarkable ease, the depth and clarity of her unique perspective connecting even the most disparate tracks together into a unified whole. Simply put, *Trailer Park* is one of the most promising and innovative debuts of its era. —*Jason Ankeny*

Ozzy Osbourne (John Osbourne)

b. Dec. 3, 1948, Birmingham, England
Vocals / Hard Rock, Heavy Metal
Ozzy Osbourne has been ridiculed over the years, yet he has had an immeasurable effect on heavy metal, while he was in Black Sabbath and as a solo artist. Osbourne doesn't have a great voice—it's thin and it doesn't have much range—yet he has a good ear and a great dramatic flair. Over the course of his career, his band has featured some of the most innovative and distinctive guitarists in hard rock, including the late Randy Rhoads. As a showman, his instincts are nearly as impeccable; his live shows have been over-wrought spectacles with gore and glitz that have endeared him to adolescents around the world. Indeed, Osbourne has managed to establish himself as an international superstar, capable of selling millions of records with each album and packing arenas across the world, capturing new fans with each record.
Ozzy Osbourne began his professional career with Black Sabbath, who released their first album in 1970. Throughout the '70s, the group carved out a distinctive brand of slow, gloomy heavy metal that became the essence of metal for many listeners. Osbourne left the band in 1979, embarking on a solo career. Supported by a band featuring ex-Uriah Heep drummer Lee Kerslake, former Rainbow bassist Bob Daisley, and ex-Quiet Riot guitarist Randy Rhoads, the singer recorded *Blizzard of Ozz;* the group would adopt the album's title as their name. Released in 1981, *Blizzard of Ozz* had some of the same ingredients of Black Sabbath—the lyrics focused on the occult and the guitars were loud and heavy—yet he was supported by a group that was more technically proficient and capable of pulling off varying the standard metal formulas. The record hit No. 7 on the UK charts; it peaked at No. 21 in the US, staying on the charts for over two years and going platinum. Before the band began their first US tour in 1981, Kerslake and Daisley left the band; they were replaced by former Pat Travers Band drummer Tommy Aldridge and ex-Quiet Riot bassist Rudy Sarzo. This is the group that recorded Osbourne's second album, *Diary of a Madman;* the album charted at No. 16 in the US and also became a platinum seller. Following its release, Daisley returned to the group and Aldridge left; former Rainbow keyboardist Don Airey was added to the lineup at this time, as well.
During Osbourne's 1982 tour, guitarist Randy Rhoads died in a bizarre plane accident, leaving a gaping hole in Osbourne's band, since Rhoads essentially determined the musical direction of the group. He was replaced by Brad Gillis, a former member of Night Ranger. Gillis' first record with Osbourne was *Speak of the Devil,* a live album of Black Sabbath material released to combat Sabbath's live album, *Live At Last.* After the release of *Speak of the Devil,* Osbourne reshaped the lineup of his band, adding guitarist Jake E. Lee. The new group recorded *Bark at the Moon,* which repeated the success of the first two records. For the rest of the decade, Osbourne's band continued to change, yet the only lineup changes that mattered were the guitarists. Lee left the band in 1987 and was replaced by Zakk Wylde, who led Osbourne's group into the '90s. Following a year of rest, Osbourne assembled the 1997 Ozzyfest package tour, which featured him as a solo headliner as well as the frontman for the reunited Black Sabbath. —*Stephen Thomas Erlewine*

Diary of a Madman / 1981 / Jet ✦✦✦✦
The follow-up was rushed, and it shows: Rhoads didn't even have time to lay down a real solo on "Little Dolls" (the solo used was intended only as a guide). Even so, his classical training manifests itself even more, and the compositions generally increase in sophistication (especially the epic title track). One wonders how much the Osbourne/Rhoads combination would have accomplished had Rhoads not been killed in a plane crash five months after this recording. —*Steve Huey*

Blizzard of Ozz / 1981 / Jet ✦✦✦✦
Osbourne's solo debut not only re-established him as a viable attrac-

tion, it also introduced the ample talents of guitarist Randy Rhoads, whose classically influenced style had a huge impact on rock guitar in the '80s. Say what you will about Ozzy Osbourne, but the music here is simply great: Osbourne/Rhoads collaborations like "Crazy Train," "Mr. Crowley," and "Revelation (Mother Earth)" still stand today as all-time heavy metal classics. —*Steve Huey*

Speak of the Devil / 1982 / Jet ✦✦
In fulfilling his contractual obligation to deliver a live album, Osbourne decided that it would be a disservice to the memory of Randy Rhoads to perform songs from the Blizzard of Ozz band's repertoire, so he delivered this album instead, which consists entirely of newly recorded versions of Black Sabbath numbers with Night Ranger's Brad Gillis on guitar. It's not bad, but it's not really necessary either, except for diehard Ozzy and Sabbath fans. —*Steve Huey*

Bark at the Moon / 1983 / Epic ✦✦✦
The unexpected death of guitar legend Randy Rhoads did not prevent Ozzy Osbourne from making another satisfying album that is just as interesting as ever. Songs such as the classic title track and the aggressive "Rock N' Roll Rebel" show that Osbourne has retained his songwriting and composing talents, the two key factors that make this album entertaining. Rhoads' replacement, guitarist Jake E. Lee, displays a style similar to his predecessor while adding his own enjoyable licks and riffs. Although *Bark at the Moon* may not be as memorable as *Blizzard of Ozz* or *Diary of a Madman,* it is still a very satisfying album that has enough rockin' tunes to please each and every Ozzy fan. —*Barry Weber*

The Ultimate Sin / 1986 / Epic ✦✦
Osbourne streamlines his approach to keep up with the emerging trend toward slick, radio-ready metal, but *The Ultimate Sin* is largely unsuccessful, as the performances are flat and uninspired and the material lacks much variety. There are some good moments, including the single "Shot in the Dark," but overall, *The Ultimate Sin* is unable to push past the level of mediocrity. —*Steve Huey*

● **Tribute** / 1987 / Epic ✦✦✦✦
This live double album, released five years after Randy Rhoads' death, showcases a hard rock guitarist whose all-around ability was arguably second only to Eddie Van Halen. Osbourne leads his best band lineup through the entire *Blizzard* repertoire, plus a few *Diary* and Sabbath numbers. Of special note are Rhoads' unaccompanied solos, leaving no doubts about his virtuosity, and the studio outtakes of his short solo piece, "Dee." Rhoads' entire output is absolutely essential for guitar freaks, but he sounds even better live than in the studio. —*Steve Huey*

No Rest for the Wicked / 1989 / Epic ✦✦✦
Things start to improve here, as Zakk Wylde replaces Jake E. Lee on guitar and Osbourne comes up with his best set since 1983. Again, it's not quite up to the level of excellence his Blizzard of Ozz band achieved, but Osbourne sounds somewhat rejuvenated, and Wylde is a more consistently interesting guitarist than Lee. Highlights include "Miracle Man" (in which Ozzy gloats about the downfall of the TV preachers who had long attacked him as an agent of Satan) and the MTV hits "Crazy Babies" and "Breaking All the Rules." —*Steve Huey*

Just Say Ozzy / Jan. 1990 / Epic ✦✦
This six-song mini-album contains live performances from the supporting tour for *No Rest for the Wicked,* featuring three songs from that album plus "Shot in the Dark." The performances aren't that special, but longtime fans will want to note that there are also two Black Sabbath songs included with none other than Geezer Butler on bass. —*Steve Huey*

No More Tears / Sep. 17, 1991 / Epic ✦✦✦✦
While looking for fresh inspiration, Osbourne started writing songs with Motorhead's Lemmy Kilmister, the kind of collaboration metal fans dream about. As a result, the songs on *No More Tears* are more compact, the sound denser, the musical payoffs more immediate. And not that Ozzy's mellowing in old age or anything, but *No More Tears* contains two of his best ballads—"Mama, I'm Coming Home" and "Time After Time." —*Brian Mansfield*

Live & Loud / 1992 / Epic ✦✦✦
Fans will be pleased with this live set from Osbourne, which isn't as consistent as *Tribute* but does feature a hot new band and songs that aren't available on any other live Osbourne album. —*AMG*

Ozzmosis / Oct. 24, 1995 / Epic ✦✦
Despite a never-ending succession of guitarists, Ozzy Osbourne hasn't changed his basic musical attack over the years. There are slight differences between the records, with the only noticeable distinctions being the production fads of the time. *Ozzmosis,* his sixth solo studio album, isn't all that different from his previous two records, *No More Tears* and *No Rest for the Wicked,* largely due to the still impressive skills of guitarist Zakk Wilde. However, even Wilde's prowess is diluted by the slick, modern-rock-conscious production by Michael Beinhorn

(Soul Asylum). Occasionally, the guitar is synthesized, which is indicative of the album's main flaw—on the surface, the music is hard and loud, but it actually sounds smooth and processed. Furthermore, there's a distinct lack of fully formed songs and riffs, which is what really sinks the record. Osbourne can survive bad production—he has for most of his career—but he can't survive without having anything to sing. —*Stephen Thomas Erlewine*

Ozzyfest, Vol. 1: Live / Apr. 29, 1997 / Red Ant ♦♦♦
Ozzfest, Vol. 1: Live captures Ozzy's 1996 return to the stage, when he launched an ambitious day-long festival of metal with such groups as Sepultura, Slayer, Powerman 5000, Biohazard, Fear Factory, and Cellophane. While Ozzy only contributes a handful of cuts on the album, his influence is apparent throughout the record, and the performances the supporting acts turn in are tough and forceful, making it a good sampler of post-alternative heavy metal. —*Stephen Thomas Erlewine*

The Outsiders [Dutch]

f. 1964, Amsterdam, Holland, **db.** 1970
Psychedelic, Garage Rock
Not to be confused with the Cleveland pop-rock group that had a Top Ten hit in 1966 with "Time Won't Let Me," these Outsiders (from Amsterdam, Holland) could issue a serious claim for consideration as the finest rock band of the '60s to hail from a non-English speaking nation. Led by singer and songwriter Wally Tax, the group were quite comparable to England's Pretty Things in their fine raw, punky R&B/pop with basic but riveting hooks. Like the Pretty Things, the Outsiders (who sang entirely in English) made similar psychedelic/progressive ventures in the late '60s that cut loose from their R&B roots without losing sight of them entirely. Recording several albums worth of material (consisting wholly of original compositions) between 1965 and 1969, the group tempered their punky, almost proto-hardcore ravers with melancholy, pensive folk-rockers and unpredictable production touches ranging from baroque mandolins and harpsichords to found radio static. The Outsiders' music was fraught with tension, the punkish rhythms playing against the melodic tunes, the R&B sensibilities against the pop hooks, often within the same song. Unknown on an international level to all but the most fervent '60s collectors, a lot of fine music awaits those who have yet to discover the Outsiders. Wally Tax moved to the US in the early '70s, where he recorded one album as the leader of the band Tax Free. —*Richie Unterberger*

The Outsiders / 1967 / Pseudonym ♦♦♦♦
Their super-raw debut album, a few songs of which were recorded live. Some of this is too melodically primitive and clumsy to survive the ages, but tracks like "Filthy Rich," "Won't You Listen," and "If You Don't Treat Me Right" are comparable to little else of the era with their savage, Pretty Things-on-speed mood and hyper-fast tempos. The CD reissue adds several bonus tracks. —*Richie Unterberger*

C.Q. / 1968 / Polydor ♦♦♦♦
Their final LP (now available on CD) is one of the finer unsung psychedelic records of the late '60s. Heavy echoes of Syd Barrett-era Pink Floyd, Hendrix, and psychedelic-era Pretty Things, with adroit shifts from crunching rock and soft, almost folky passages to spacy phaseshift bits and just plain dementia. The album has an ominous and creepy, but rocking, ambience that still cuts deep. —*Richie Unterberger*

● **The Best of the Outsiders** / 1979 / MFP ♦♦♦♦
16-song compilation collects most of their singles, ranging from raunchy cuts like "Touch" and "I'm Only Trying to Prove Myself" to tune-

ful, forceful folk-rockish cuts like "I've Been Loving You So Long" and "Summer Is Here." Very consistent and strong, only a couple of clunkers. —*Richie Unterberger*

C.Q. Sessions / 1994 / Pseudonym ♦♦♦
A double CD comprising 29 alternate takes, some instrumental and some vocal, of songs from the classic *C.Q.* album, one of the finest obscure psychedelic records. Besides one or two different alternate versions of each of the 13 songs from that record, it also has alternate versions of sides from non-LP singles they released around the same time ("Do You Feel Allright?" and "You Remind Me"), as well as four songs (some instrumental) that never made it onto any official release. Some of the tracks are quite close to the finished versions, and some are quite different, but it's a pretty fascinating look at works in progress, and the sound quality is uniformly excellent. The audience for this reissue is, to say the least, extremely specialized and limited, but if you're a fan of this group, it's worth picking up. It also includes five bonus tracks from excruciatingly rare (and quite good) earlier non-LP singles from 1965 and 1966, when they were a much more R&B/beat-oriented outfit. —*Richie Unterberger*

Oval

f. 1993, Germany
Techno, Experimental, Post-Rock/Experimental, Electronica
Although Oval are perhaps more well-known for how they make their music than for the music they actually make, the German experimental electronic trio have provided an intriguing update of some elements of avant-garde composition in combination with techniques of digital sound design, resulting in some of the most original, if somewhat challenging electronic music of the contemporary scene.

Composed of trio Markus Popp, Sebastian Oschatz, and Frank Metzger, the bulk of the group's work released through the Force Inc-related Mille Plateaux label incorporates elements of what could be described as "prepared compact disc"—manually marred and scarified CDs played and sampled for the resultant, somewhat randomly patterned rhythmic clicking. Layered together with subtle, sparse melodies and quirky electronics, the results are often as oddly musical as they are just plain odd. The trio brought this approach to bare on their first full-length releases—*Systemische* and *94 Diskont*—as well as a number of compilation tracks. Although a rung below marginal in their home country and even more obscure in the States, the group's remixes of Chicago post-rock group Tortoise brought Oval in contact with American audiences; Oval's most recent two albums, as well as Markus Popp's work as Microstoria (with Mouse on Mars' Jan St. Werner), were reissued domestically by Thrill Jockey in 1996. —*Sean Cooper*

● **94 Diskont** / 1994 / Mille Plateaux ♦♦♦♦
Oval's second proper collection of digitally damaged electronica adds a far wider range of sound and texture to the blender than the previous *Systemische*. The vinyl Mille Plateaux version included a bonus 12-inch of remixes by Scanner, Mouse on Mars, and Jim O'Rourke. —*Sean Cooper*

Systemische / 1995 / Mille Plateaux ♦♦♦
Slightly overbearing over the course of its 11 tracks, the best of *Systemische* is truly remarkable in its unlikely musicality. The group is at its best when the clickety-clackety rhythms are backgrounded to concentrate on melodic and thematic development. —*Sean Cooper*

P

The Pagans

f. 1977, Cleveland, OH

Punk

Of all the bands that burst out of Cleveland in the mid- to late-'70s punk explosion, one of the most unjustly ignored was the Pagans. Despite breaking up in 1979 (they have, however, reunited several times since), these grimy bohunks played fast 'n' loud piss-and-vinegar garage rock that valued alienation and, at times, extreme bad taste. Led by the honking rasp of Mike Hudson and the rapid-fire guitar of Mike "Tommy Gunn" Metoff, the Pagans never played it safe, nor did they enter the rock 'n' roll wars wanting to win any friends. And this, ultimately, was a good thing, for like their pals the Dead Boys, their antistar pose and *carpe diem* attitude meant that their best songs (and there are quite a few) sound as if they were set to autodestruct at the tune's end. Although their don't-give-a-shit attitude lends itself more than once to some sexist japes and homophobic ranting, the Pagans didn't care who they offended. In fact, listening to any of their vintage material (1977-79), you'd think that offending everyone was their *raison d'etre*. As Treehouse Records president, Mark Trehus, opines in the liner notes to the great collection *Buried Alive*, "the Pagans were as unwrought, impudent and gnarly a buncha rock'n'roll bedlamites as America's ever spewed outta its queasy underbelly." Little more need be said. —*John Dougan*

● **Buried Alive** / 1986 / Treehouse ♦♦♦♦
Nasty, loud, and vulgar, this is the best collection of the Pagans' music and one of the great, although almost forgotten, American punk rock records. After hearing such endearing "classics" as "What Is This Shit Called Love," you can see why Tesco Vee and his Meatmen covered it years later. Even better is the living-in-nowhere anthem "The Street Where Nobody Lives" and "Dead End America." Seventeen tracks, and each one's a killer, even the ones that make you wince. —*John Dougan*

The Painted Faces

f. 1965, Florida, db. 1968

Psychedelic, Garage Rock

A psychedelic garage band that prominently used ominous minor keys and organ, the Painted Faces recorded a few singles in 1967 and 1968 whose popularity was largely limited to their home state of Florida, where "Anxious Color" was a sizable hit. A garage band of average or a bit above-average worth, they featured mostly original material and sounded like a garage Doors at times, with some pop, soul, and folk-rock influences as well. They were moving in a more progressive-rock direction when their drummer was drafted in 1968, after which they disbanded. They achieved some notoriety in the 1980s when their singles "Anxious Color," "I Lost You in My Mind," and "I Think I'm Going Mad" showed up on '60s garage compilations. —*Richie Unterberger*

Anxious Color / 1994 / Distortions ♦♦♦
This 19-song compilation includes all seven of the tracks they released during their lifetime, as well as a dozen previously unreleased cuts from 1967 and 1968. A fair, though not remarkable, collection of a band that leaned toward the moodiest end of the garage-psych spectrum. Taken from copies of the singles and the like, the sound quality on some of the material (especially on side two) is even funkier than it usually is on compilations of this nature. —*Richie Unterberger*

Palace

f. 1992, Louisville, KY, db. 1997

Guitar, Vocals / Indie Rock, Alternative Country-Rock, Alternative Country

Will Oldham, the brains and brawn behind releases as Palace Brothers,

Palace Songs, Palace Music and just plain Palace, is loosely grouped with the '90s antifolk movement that also includes Bill Callahan of Smog, a label-mate of Oldham's on Chicago's Drag City Records. Often mistaken for an old man due to his cracking vocals, sparse guitar pickings, and Biblical dialect, Oldham has recorded since 1992 with a variety of sidemen—basically any friends or acquaintances that can play an instrument.

Raised in Louisville, KY, Will Oldham first became involved in acting; he starred in John Sayles' 1987 mining film, *Matewan*, playing—with considerable ease—an elderly miner who relates the action over a series of flashbacks. Two years later, he moved to TV for *Everybody's Baby: The Rescue of Jessica McClure*, and he returned to the cinema in 1991 for *Thousand Pieces of Gold*, another mining film. At the same time, Oldham was also involved in the fertile indie-rock scene in Louisville, picking up his first musical credit with Slint for the photograph on the cover of the band's 1991 album, *Spiderland*.

Will Oldham the musical artist debuted in 1992 with the single "Ohio River Boat Song" on Drag City Records. Though he's credited as Palace Songs on the single, Oldham's debut album the following year was filed under Palace Brothers—in part to denote the work of Todd Brashear. *There Is No-One What Will Take Care of You* introduced several of Oldham's continuing themes: drunkenness, sin in general, and the varied results of each.

Recording regularly during 1993-94, Oldham released several singles and an EP (*An Arrow Through the Bitch*) before his second album—self-titled, but also listed as *Days in the Wake*—was issued by Drag City in 1994. Again, Oldham followed with a string of limited-release singles and one EP, but mixed things up for late-1995's *Viva Last Blues* (as Palace Music); Oldham recruited a band, with guitarist Bryan Rich, organist Liam Hayes and bassist Jason Loewenstein (from Sebadoh). The following year's *Arise, Therefore* found Oldham back in a largely solitary setting. —*John Bush*

There Is No-One What Will Take Care of You / Jun. 14, 1993 / Drag City ♦♦♦
The name says it all. Dramatic, desperate country-indie rock that focuses on the dark side of life. —*Heather Phares*

Days in the Wake / Aug. 29, 1994 / Drag City ♦♦♦♦
Oldham's second is even more spartan and gaunt-sounding than Palace's debut. Strumming away on an acoustic guitar, his feeble voice barely topping a whisper, Oldham croaks out tunes of quiet despair like "Pushkin" and "I Am a Cinematographer." —*Heather Phares*

Mountain / Aug. 8, 1995 / Drag City ♦♦♦♦

Viva Last Blues / Aug. 21, 1995 / Drag City ♦♦♦
Viva Last Blues continues Oldham and company's trend of spare acoustic tunes with sad, world-weary themes. Palace seems to be refining and honing both their playing and songwriting skills with each album. —*Heather Phares*

Arise, Therefore / Apr. 1996 / Drag City ♦♦♦♦
Once again Will Oldham emerges out of the murky, Midwestern haze with another helping of lovely, low-key musings on his fourth full-length album, *Arise, Therefore*, this time recorded under the name Palace Music (previously Palace Brothers, Palace Songs, or just plain Palace). Much quieter than 1995's *Viva Last Blues* and less Appalachian in its folk spirit than Palace's earlier music, the songs on *Arise, Therefore* shift and moan with breathy cracks and shivers. Oldham's meandering, poet-speak vocals and guitar are accompanied by his brother Ned's bass, David Grubbs' piano, and (surprise!) a Maya Tone drum machine. The lyrics (included for the first time) are beautiful in their stark, pale honesty, often they are indecipherable. "I watch things painted on public walls, now but I see other things as well, behind but right fuck in front of

my spirit is how the real road's laid out in a line" he sings on "Kid of Harith." Don't ask for an interpretation: It will come with time, or it won't. —*Kurt Wolff*

● **Lost Blues & Other Songs** / Mar. 24, 1997 / Drag City ✦✦✦✦
Lost Blues and Other Songs collects various singles and rarities Will Oldham released under his various Palace incarnations during the early '90s. Nearly all of the it is haunting, spare acoustic-based material, drawing from traditional folk and country, but undercut by Oldham's detached postmodern sensibilities. Occasionally, his removed, affected vocals can make Palace's music seem emotionally distant, but it often works, and *Lost Blues and Other Songs* finds him at his very best. —*Stephen Thomas Erlewine*

Pale Saints

f. 1987, Leeds, England
Alternative Pop-Rock, Dream-Pop
This British band formed in 1987, and starting with their first full album in 1990, *The Comforts of Madness*, displayed a knack for writing tunes both effervescent and ethereal. The original lineup included Chris Cooper, Ian Masters, and Graeme Naysmith, to which current vocalist/guitarist Meriel Barham was added in late 1990. Masters left after 1992's *In Ribbons*, and despite the loss of its founding member and chief songwriter, Pale Saints has endured with Barham at the helm. Bassist Colleen Browne joined for 1994's strong third album, *Slow Buildings*. Pale Saints' songs range from whimsical, airy Britpop to elongated, droning soundscapes, but on the majority prove enjoyable. —*Heather Phares*

The Comforts of Madness / 1990 / 4AD ✦✦✦
The group's debut contains some of their finest jangly songs as well as some of their most evocative soundscapes. —*Heather Phares*

● **In Ribbons** / Apr. 14, 1992 / 4AD ✦✦✦✦
In Ribbons introduces Meriel Barham's sweet vocals and guitars to the Pale Saints. The group's second album continues their winning ways with light, delicate pop and ethereal melodies. A good introduction to Barham and Master's singing and songwriting. —*Heather Phares*

Slow Buildings / Aug. 30, 1994 / 4AD ✦✦✦
Pale Saint's third album finds them carrying on without Masters, who had previously written the bulk of the group's material. While his absence is noticeable, it's not disastrous. *Slow Buildings* is an album of competent pop like "Will You Be My Angel" and "Fine Friend" and some experimental instrumentals like "King Fade" and "Henry." —*Heather Phares*

Robert Palmer

b. Jan. 19, 1949, Batley, England
Vocals / Pop-Rock
The career of blue-eyed soul singer Robert Palmer was a study in style versus substance. While the performer's earliest work won praise for its skillful assimilation of rock, R&B, and reggae sounds, his records typically sold poorly, and he achieved his greatest notoriety as an impeccably-dressed lounge lizard. By the mid-'80s, however, Palmer became a star, although his popularity owed less to the strength of his material than to his infamous music videos: taking their cue from the singer's suave presence, Palmer's clips established him as a dapper, suit-and-tied ladies' man who performed his songs backed by a band composed of leggy models, much to the delight of viewers, who made him one of MTV's biggest success stories.

Born Alan Palmer on January 19, 1949 in Bentley, England, he spent much of his childhood living on the island of Malta before permanently returning to Britain at the age of 19 to sing with the Alan Bown Set. A year later he joined Dada, a 12-piece, Stax-influenced soul group that soon changed its name to Vinegar Joe; after three LPs with the band—a self-titled effort and *Rock 'n' Roll Gypsies*, both issued in 1972, and 1973's *Six Star General*—Palmer exited to mount a solo career and debuted in 1974 with *Sneakin' Sally Through the Alley*, recorded with members of Little Feat and the Meters.

With 1975's *Pressure Drop*, he tackled reggae, a trend furthered following a move to Nassau prior to 1978's *Double Fun*, which featured Palmer's first hit, "Every Kinda People." With 1979's self-produced *Secrets*, his music moved into more rock-oriented territory, as typified by the single "Bad Case of Loving You (Doctor, Doctor)." Palmer's stylistic experimentation continued with 1980's *Clues*, a foray into synth-pop aided by Gary Numan and Talking Heads' Chris Frantz, which yielded the club hit "Looking for Clues."

After 1983's *Pride*, Palmer teamed with the Duran Duran side project Power Station, scoring hits with the singles "Some Like It Hot" and "Get It On" (a T. Rex cover), which returned the singer to overt rock territory.

After exiting the band prior to a planned tour, Palmer recorded the 1985 solo album, *Riptide*, a sleek collection of guitar rock which scored

a No. 1 hit with "Addicted to Love," the first in a string of videos that offered him in front of a bevy of beautiful women.

The follow-up, "I Didn't Mean to Turn You On," continued to play with the sex-symbol image and hit No. 2, as did "Simply Irresistible," the first single from 1988's *Heavy Nova*. By 1990's *Don't Explain*, Palmer returned to the eclecticism of his earliest material; without any attendant soft-core videos, sales plummeted, but he stuck to his guns for 1992's *Ridin' High*, a collection of Tin Pan Alley and cabaret chestnuts. —*Jason Ankeny*

Sneakin' Sally Through the Alley / 1974 / Island ✦✦✦✦
On his debut solo album, Palmer employs members of the Meters and Little Feat for a musical gumbo enriched by his husky, percussive voice. —*William Ruhlmann*

Pressure Drop / 1976 / Island ✦✦✦✦
Palmer's own songs (especially the silky "Give Me an Inch" and "Work to Make It Work") and the backing of Little Feat help make this a worthy follow-up to *Sally*. —*William Ruhlmann*

Some People Can Do What They Like / 1976 / Island ✦✦✦✦
Palmer's "Keep in Touch," "Man Smart, Woman Smarter," and "Spanish Moon" (the latter by Little Feat's Lowell George) pace *Some People Can Do What They Like*, another terrific collection. —*William Ruhlmann*

Double Fun / 1978 / Island ✦✦✦
Palmer produces and writes more songs than usual, resulting in the hit "Every Kinda People" and a somewhat lighter, more pop approach. —*William Ruhlmann*

Secrets / 1979 / Island ✦✦✦✦
Palmer scores his biggest hit single of the '70s with the uptempo rocker "Bad Case of Loving You (Doctor, Doctor)" on an album that also includes a wonderful version of Todd Rundgren's ballad "Can We Still Be Friends." —*William Ruhlmann*

Clues / 1980 / Island ✦✦✦
A move toward fast-paced electronic dance-rock. It's successful about half the time, especially on Palmer's UK hits "Looking for Clues" and "Johnny and Mary." (Rod Stewart Xeroxed "Johnny and Mary" for his hit "Young Turks" the following year.) —*William Ruhlmann*

Maybe It's Live / 1982 / Island ✦✦
Five oldies recorded in concert and five new songs, among them Palmer's first big UK hit, "Some Guys Have All the Luck." (Rod Stewart had a US hit version two years later.) —*William Ruhlmann*

Pride / 1983 / Island ✦✦
Robert Palmer continued to move toward techno-rock here, cutting a cover of the System's "You Are in My System" that, for once, did little to illuminate the original. —*William Ruhlmann*

Riptide / Nov. 1985 / Island ✦✦✦✦
Palmer's commercial breakthrough, much of it in the hard-rock style of his one-shot band Power Station and featuring the hits "Discipline of Love," "Addicted to Love" (a No. 1 hit), "Hyperactive," and "I Didn't Mean to Turn You On." —*William Ruhlmann*

Heavy Nova / Jun. 1988 / EMI America ✦✦
Robert Palmer cloned his hard-rock *Riptide* style for its follow-up, his debut album on EMI, and was rewarded with the No. 2 hit "Simply Irresistible," even if the formula was beginning to sound thin. —*William Ruhlmann*

● **Addictions, Vol. 1** / Oct. 1989 / Island ✦✦✦✦
Thirteen-track compilation containing Palmer's biggest hits, not only the ones on Island but also the Power Station singles and "Simply Irresistible," from Palmer's first EMI album. —*William Ruhlmann*

Don't Explain / Oct. 1990 / EMI America ✦✦
Robert Palmer's second EMI album, which turned out to be a sales disappointment, seems to combine two different musical concepts in its 18 tracks. The first is a straightforward, rhythm-heavy Robert Palmer rock album that takes up about the first half of the record. The second is a soundtrack for a planned musical that a Palmer bio describes as "a futuristic comedy using telling songs from the '40s to the present day," some produced by jazzman Teo Macero. These include songs like Bob Dylan's "I'll Be Your Baby Tonight" (done reggae style), Marvin Gaye's "Mercy Mercy Me" and "I Want You," and Rodgers and Hammerstein's "People Will Say We're in Love." The idea looks forward to Palmer's next album, *Ridin' High*, which is comprised entirely of standards, but the mixture of rhythm tracks and string-filled arrangements here makes for a confusing mixture. —*William Ruhlmann*

Addictions, Vol. 2 / May 5, 1992 / Island ✦✦✦
Apart from "I Didn't Mean to Turn You On," there are no big hits, only album tracks and failed singles, all of which are quite good. Unfortunately, the majority of the material has been remixed, remade, or has new vocal tracks; the album may sound great, but it isn't an accurate retrospective. —*Stephen Thomas Erlewine*

Very Best of Robert Palmer / Jan. 28, 1997 / Capitol ✦✦✦✦

Pantera

f. 1982, Texas
Heavy Metal, Speed Metal

Pantera's massively brutal, aggressive, jagged heavy metal earned them a large cult following in the early '90s. During the early '80s, the band explored several different styles of hard rock; sometimes they sounded like Kiss and Aerosmith, others Def Leppard. After several years of struggling, the band changed their tune in 1988, becoming rougher and harder, much like Metallica. Guitarist Diamond Darrell (aka "Dimebag") rejected an offer to join Megadeth, concentrating on Pantera's new direction. The change in style proved successful; 1992's *A Vulgar Display of Power* became an underground metal hit, eventually scaling *Billboard's* Top 50. When their new album, *Far Beyond Driven*, was released in 1994, the band debuted at No. 1. Some chart watchers were surprised, but anyone that followed their rise from obscurity to *A Vulgar Display of Power* knew that Pantera was one of the most popular metal bands of the early '90s. *Great Southern Trendkill* was released in May 1996. —*Stephen Thomas Erlewine*

Power Metal / 1988 / Metal Magic ✦✦

Cowboys from Hell / Jul. 1990 / East West ✦✦✦✦
Technical thrash from Texas, this is the album that put them in the spotlight and opened the door for thrash bands who were a little different. —*John Book*

● **Vulgar Display of Power** / Feb. 25, 1992 / East West ✦✦✦✦
A burning, disemboweling collection of brutal riffs, pulverizing speed, and hoarse, shouted vocals, *Vulgar Display of Power* is the record that established Pantera as the most vicious and popular heavy-metal band of the early '90s. —*Stephen Thomas Erlewine*

Far Beyond Driven / Mar. 15, 1994 / East West ✦✦✦
Far Beyond Driven finds Pantera in a bit of a holding pattern. Although the riffs are still lethally fast, the band shows no signs of musical development, and the songs aren't any better than those on *Vulgar Display of Power*. Nevertheless, there's enough primal metal here to satisfy most of their fans. —*Stephen Thomas Erlewine*

Great Southern Trendkill / May 1996 / Atlantic ✦✦✦
Thankfully, Pantera have stopped attempting to outdo each successive album in terms of start-to-finish intensity, but that doesn't mean they don't try in spots. *Great Southern Trendkill* is burdened with passages in which Phil Anselmo's vocals cross the line into histrionics, making the band's trademark intensity sound dull, forced, and theatrical rather than sincere. The lyrics, which reached their apex with *Vulgar Display of Power's* focus on personal politics and integrity, have degenerated into half-baked rants against drugs and pop-culture media. But *Trendkill* is partially redeemed by trading Pantera's usual pound-then-pound-harder approach to albums for a greater variety of tempos and moods. Dimebag Darrell, while mostly sticking to his familiar riffing style, does coax some intriguing, unexpected sounds from his instrument. Ultimately, though, the ballads and slower tracks ("10's," "Suicide Note Pt. 1," "Floods") provide the album's most chilling, memorable moments and rank with their best material. Longtime Pantera fans will find plenty to enjoy here, and the band's expanding range bodes well, but overall *Trendkill* is an inconsistent outing. —*Steve Huey*

Graham Parker

b. Nov. 15, 1950, East London, England
Guitar, Vocals / Rock 'n' Roll, New Wave, Pop-Rock, Pub Rock

Stereotyped early in his career as the quintessential angry young man, Graham Parker was one of the most successful singer-songwriters to emerge from England's pub-rock scene of the early '70s. Drawing heavily from Van Morrison and the Rolling Stones, Parker developed a sinewy fusion of driving rock 'n' roll and confessional folk-rock, highlighted by his indignant passion, biting sarcasm, and bristling anger. At the outset of his career, his albums crackled with pub-rock energy, snide witticisms, and gentle insights, earning him a devoted following of fans and critics, who lavished praise on his debut, *Howlin' Wind*. Despite all of the positive word-of-mouth, Parker never managed to become a star, and he was soon overshadowed by the emergence of Elvis Costello, a singer-songwriter who shared similar roots. After delivering *Squeezing Out Sparks* in 1979, Parker attempted to make a few crossover albums before settling into a cult following in the late '80s and continuing to garner critical acclaim.

After spending much of his early adulthood working odd jobs, ranging from breeding mice and guinea pigs to working at a gas station, Parker began seriously pursuing a musical career in 1975. Until that time, he had played in a number of obscure pub-rock groups, including a cover band that had spent time playing in Morocco and Gibraltar. But it wasn't until 1975 that he began shopping his demos. That year, Dave Robinson, one of the cofounders of the new independent label Stiff, heard one of Parker's demo tapes and encouraged the songwriter, helping him assemble a backing band called the Rumour. Robinson rounded

up several stars of the pub-rock scene—guitarist Brinsley Schwarz and keyboardist Bob Andrews, both formerly of the leading pub rockers Brinsley Schwarz, former Ducks Deluxe guitarist Martin Belmont, former Bontemps Roulez drummer Steve Goulding, and bassist Andrew Bodnary—to form the Rumour, and the band was soon supporting Parker on the dying pub-rock scene. With the assistance of DJ Charlie Gillett, the group landed a record contract with Mercury by the end of 1975.

Parker and the Rumour headed into the studio to cut their debut album with producer Nick Lowe, who gave the resulting record, *Howlin' Wind*, an appealingly ragged edge. *Howlin' Wind* was greeted with enthusiastic reviews upon its summer release, as was the similar *Heat Treatment*, which followed in the fall. Despite the positive press, Parker was growing frustrated with Mercury, believing that the company was not properly promoting and distributing his records. His third album, *Stick to Me*, had to be re-recorded quickly after the original tapes were accidentally damaged prior to its scheduled release. As a result, *Stick to Me* received mixed reviews upon its fall 1977 release, which derailed Parker's momentum slightly. Furthermore, the concurrent success of Elvis Costello, a fellow pub-rock survivor who not only possessed a more pop-oriented style of songwriting, but also a more dangerous and media-friendly persona, soon eclipsed Parker in popularity. Frustrated by his career hitting a standstill, Parker released the live double album *The Parkerilla* in the summer of 1978 in order to get out of his contract. Following a short but intense bidding war, he quickly signed to Arista Records, where he released "Mercury Poisoning"—a blistering attack on his former record label—as the B-side of a promotional single as his first record for the label.

Squeezing Out Sparks, Parker's first album for Arista, put a halt to his decline. Sporting a slicker, new wave-oriented production—it was the first of his records not to be produced by Nick Lowe—the album was greeted with terrific reviews and, on the strength of radio hits like "Local Girls," it became his most successful album, reaching No. 40 on the American charts and selling over 200,000 copies. Parker was poised for a major breakthrough, but that didn't happen. He followed *Squeezing Out Sparks* in 1980 with the Jimmy Iovine-produced *The Up Escalator*, which was considerably slicker than its predecessor. *The Up Escalator* didn't sell, and Parker decided to ditch the Rumour, who had already begun a solo career. For 1982's *Another Grey Area*, he hired producer Jack Douglas and a team of session musicians, resulting in a radio-ready production that received mixed reviews, yet managed to peak at No. 51. *The Real Macaw*, which followed in 1983, suffered a similar fate. For 1985's *Steady Nerves*, Parker moved to Elektra Records and formed a backing band called the Shot with guitarist Brinsley Schwarz, who helped him deliver his most radio-ready collection. This time, the pop move paid off. "Wake Up (Next to You)" became his only Top 40 hit, and the album stayed on the charts for nearly as long as *Squeezing Out Sparks*.

Despite his moderate commercial success with *Steady Nerves*, the album wasn't widely praised, and he also ran into trouble with Elektra, leaving the label after just one record. He briefly moved to Atlantic Records, who dropped him without releasing a single record. Consequently, Parker wasn't able to deliver another album until 1988, when he signed with RCA and released *The Mona Lisa's Sister* in the spring. Hailed as a comeback by several critics upon its release, the album generated a college radio hit with "Get Started (Start a Fire)" and spent 19 weeks on the charts. Instead of being the beginning of a comeback, the album turned out to be a last gasp—it was the last time Parker was able to crack the Top 100. *Live! Alone in America* (1989) received positive reviews but was ignored, and 1990's mild worldbeat experiment *Human Soul* received mixed reviews and peaked at No. 165 on the charts. Parker's final album for RCA—and his last album to chart—was the stripped-down *Struck by Lightning* (1991), and while it was critically praised, it didn't find an audience outside of his cult. The following year, he switched to Capitol and released *Burning Questions*, which was ignored.

Following the release of 1993's double-disc anthology *Passion Is No Ordinary Word*, Parker made the leap to independent labels—he had spent time at all but one of the major labels (Columbia/Sony) with little success. In 1994, he released the *Christmas Cracker* EP on Dakota Arts, and then he signed with Razor & Tie, where he released *12 Haunted Episodes* in the spring. Like *The Mona Lisa's Sister* and *Struck By Lightning* before it, *12 Haunted Episodes* was hailed as a comeback, and it sold in respectable numbers for an indie release. Parker followed it with two albums in 1996, *Live From New York, NY* and *Acid Bubblegum*, which appeared within two months of each other late in the summer. Early in 1997, he released yet another album with the double-disc *The Last Rock N' Roll Tour*, which was recorded with the power-pop quartet the Figgs. —*Stephen Thomas Erlewine*

☆ **Howlin Wind** / Jul. 1976 / Mercury ✦✦✦✦✦
For most intents and purposes, Graham Parker emerged fully formed on his debut album, *Howlin' Wind*. Sounding like the bastard offspring

of Mick Jagger and Van Morrison, Parker sneers his way through a set of stunningly literate pub rockers. Instead of blindly sticking to the traditions of rock 'n' roll, Parker invigorates them with cynicism and anger, turning his songs into distinctively original works. "Back to Schooldays" may be reconstituted rockabilly, "White Honey" may recall Morrison's white R&B bounce, and "Howlin' Wind" is a cross of Van's more mystical moments and the Band, but the songs themselves are original and terrific. Similarly, producer Nick Lowe gives the album a tough, spare feeling, which makes Parker and the Rumour sound like one of the best bar bands you've ever heard. *Howlin' Wind* remains a thoroughly invigorating fusion of rock tradition, singer-songwriter skill, and punk spirit, making it one of the classic debuts of all time. — *Stephen Thomas Erlewine*

Heat Treatment / Oct. 1976 / Mercury ✦✦✦✦
On his second album *Heat Treatment*, Graham Parker essentially offered more of the same thing that made *Howlin' Wind* such a bracing listen. However, his songwriting wasn't as consistent, with only a handful of songs—like "Pourin' It All Out" and the title track—making much of an impression. Unfortunately, the record was also tamed by the production of Mutt Lange, who polishes the record just enough to make the Rumour sound restrained. Which means, of course, the sheer musicality of the band can't save the lesser material. *Heat Treatment* remains an enjoyable listen—at this stage of the game, Parker hadn't soured into a curmudgeon, and his weaker songs were still endearing—but it's a disappointment in light of its predecessor. — *Stephen Thomas Erlewine*

Stick to Me / Oct. 1977 / Mercury ✦✦✦✦
Graham Parker and the Rumour's third new studio album to be released in 18 months finds the bandleader running short of top-flight material; "Thunder and Rain" and "Watch the Moon Come Down" are up to his usual standards, but songs like "The Heat in Harlem" find him dangerously out of his depth. As a result, although fiercely played, this star-crossed release (it had to be re-recorded when the first version suffered technical problems) is a cut below Parker's first two albums. — *William Ruhlmann*

The Parkerilla/Live / 1978 / Mercury ✦✦
This is an ill-conceived live album (probably put out as a contract breaker with Mercury) on which Graham Parker and the Rumour sing songs from the substandard *Stick to Me* album and even use up a whole side of the original two-LP version on a studio re-recording of "Don't Ask Me Questions." With this release, what had seemed like one of the most promising careers of the second half of the 1970s suddenly seemed to be on the rocks. — *William Ruhlmann*

☆ **Squeezing Out Sparks** / Mar. 1979 / Arista ✦✦✦✦✦
Generally regarded as Graham Parker's finest album, *Squeezing Out Sparks* is a masterful fusion of pub rock classicism, new wave pop, and pure vitriol that makes even his most conventional singer-songwriter numbers bristle with energy. Not only does Parker deliver his best, most consistent set of songs, but he offers more succinct hooks than before—"Local Girls" and "Discovering Japan" are powered by quirky hooks that make them new wave classics. But Parker's new pop inclinations are tempered by his anger, which seethes throughout the hard rockers and even his quieter numbers. Throughout *Squeezing Out Sparks*, Graham spits out a litany of offenses that make him feel like an outsider, but he's not a liberal, he's a conservative. The record's two centerpieces—"Passion Is No Ordinary Word" and the anti-abortion "You Can't Be Too Strong"—indicate that his traditionalist musical tendencies are symptomatic of a larger conservative trend. But no one ever said conservatives made poor rock 'n' rollers, and Parker's ruminations over a lost past give him the anger that fuels *Squeezing Out Sparks*, one of the great rock records of the post-punk era. — *Stephen Thomas Erlewine*

The Up Escalator / May 1980 / Arista ✦✦✦✦
On his last album with the Rumour, Parker goes for mainstream rock success, employing the widescreen production style of Jimmy Iovine and such guests as Bruce Springsteen. It didn't sell, but it was a great try. — *William Ruhlmann*

Another Grey Area / Mar. 1982 / Razor & Tie ✦✦✦✦
Parker begins to make his peace with human imperfection (though he can still be sharp-tongued) and starts to look for love ("It's All Worth Nothing Alone"), backed by a smooth session band and a clean Jack Douglas production, which cool his usual fire without putting it out. — *William Ruhlmann*

The Real Macaw / Jul. 1983 / Razor & Tie ✦✦✦
Parker finds love and manages to write about it without losing his usual wit ("Last Couple on the Dance Floor"). He also re-employs Rumour guitarist Brinsley Schwarz and goes back to the uptempo pub rock of his '70s albums. — *William Ruhlmann*

Steady Nerves / Mar. 1985 / Elektra ✦✦✦
Graham Parker moves to his third record label (following stints at Mercury and Arista), forms a backup band called the Shot (again led by guitarist Brinsley Schwarz), and continues alternately arguing with exist-

ence ("Break Them Down") and praising his romantic life ("Wake Up [Next to You]"). — *William Ruhlmann*

The Mona Lisa's Sister / Apr. 1988 / RCA ✦✦
Graham Parker moves to his fourth record label (actually, his fifth, if you count Atlantic, which dumped him before releasing an album) for one of his less-inspired efforts. When he sings "Get Started, Start a Fire," he seems to be talking to himself, and when he resorts to covering the old Sam Cooke hit "Cupid," he seems to be grasping for material. — *William Ruhlmann*

Live! Alone in America / Jul. 1989 / RCA ✦✦✦
Graham Parker's second commercially released live album is a solo affair that finds him connecting with his audience and singing a lot of his 1970s favorites. — *William Ruhlmann*

Human Soul / Jan. 1990 / RCA ✦✦
On *Human Soul*, Graham Parker begins to retreat further into his domestic life, writing an album that includes a side of romantic ruminations and a side of social commentary. With a band that comprises guitarist Brinsley Schwarz, bassist Andrew Bodnar, and Attractions Steve Nieve (keyboards) and Pete Thomas (drums), Parker's music is subtly diverse, adding elements of worldbeat, reggae, pop, and folk to his R&B-fueled rock 'n' roll; however, most of the impact of the music is lost by the slick, radio-ready production. When Parker stays at home on the first half of *Human Soul*, he makes his most impressive music, from the sultry come-ons of "Call Me Your Doctor" to the reassuring "My Love's Strong." He tends to lose his focus on the latter half of the record, when he writes about subjects that don't directly affect his homelife. Taken in conjunction with the self-conscious musical eclecticism, the lyrical stretches make *Human Soul* an intriguing, but flawed, record. — *Stephen Thomas Erlewine*

Struck by Lightning / Feb. 1991 / RCA ✦✦✦
Struck by Lightning was the culmination of Graham Parker's previous two records, where he increasingly began to chronicle domestic tasks and affairs of the married heart. For such an intimate subject, Parker wisely decided to scale back the musical ambition of *Human Soul* on *Struck by Lightning*, recording a lean, stripped-down album that relies heavily on acoustic guitars. Appropriately, his lyrics were some of the most concise he has written in years, breathing life into tales like "The Kid with the Butterfly Net" and "Wrapping Paper." Parker's music is similarly simple and tuneful, making *Struck by Lightning* his best effort since the early '80s. — *Stephen Thomas Erlewine*

Burning Questions / Jul. 20, 1992 / Capitol ✦✦
After *Struck by Lightning*, Graham Parker was dropped by RCA Records. He moved to Capitol in 1992, releasing another installment in his musical diaries called *Burning Questions*. A more open and polished affair than the previous record, *Burning Questions* concentrates on broader issues than *Struck by Lightning*, yet the scope is similarly scaled-back. And it's clear from "Long Stem Rose," "Oasis," and "Mr. Tender" that his heart is with his home, not with the sputtering rage of "Here It Comes Again" and "Short Memories." — *Stephen Thomas Erlewine*

The Best of Graham Parker 1988-1991 / Sep. 1992 / RCA ✦✦✦
All of the highlights from Graham Parker's brief stint at RCA are here on this single-disc compilation. — *AMG*

Live Alone! Discovering Japan / 1993 / Demon ✦✦
Live Alone! Discovering Japan isn't all that different than *Live! Alone in America*. Parker runs through a set largely composed of his classics, adding some newer material in for good measure. It's an engaging disc—he remains not only a convincing performer but also somewhat of a showman, cracking jokes throughout the album—but it's only of interest to hardcore fans, who will find it a pleasant, but decidedly minor, addition to their collection. — *Stephen Thomas Erlewine*

● **Passion Is No Ordinary Word: The Graham Parker Anthology 1976-1991** / Sep. 21, 1993 / Rhino ✦✦✦✦
With its smart song selection and entertaining liner notes, *Passion Is No Ordinary Word* is an excellent two-CD anthology covering Parker's entire career, complete with such rarities as "Mercury Poisoning" and "I Want You Back (Alive)" among such signature songs as "White Honey" and "You Can't Be Too Strong." A terrific introduction to Parker's career. — *Stephen Thomas Erlewine*

12 Haunted Episodes / Mar. 14, 1995 / Razor & Tie ✦✦✦
12 Haunted Episodes, Graham Parker's first album recorded for an independent label, is appropriately intimate and warm, recalling the simplicity of *Struck by Lightning*, but with a gentler approach. Parker makes no concessions to commerical radio on the record, dispensing with the slick productions that tended to plague his albums for the past decade or so. That doesn't mean the record is raw—it means that it's more personal and intimate. At its core, *12 Haunted Episodes* is not that different than Parker's records since *The Mona Lisa's Sister:* Most of the songs are love songs to his wife and daughter, or they're tales of an aging rebel, trying to keep his youthful fire alive as he grows older. How-

ever, the songs are measured and reflective, signalling that he's settling gracefully into his middle age. When Parker does get bitter—such as his attack on capitalism, "Disney's America"—it doesn't seem vengeful, it seems regretful, which helps make *12 Haunted Episodes* his most mature album to date. —*Stephen Thomas Erlewine*

Live on the Test / Oct. 10, 1995 / Windsong ✦✦✦✦

Live from New York, NY / Aug. 20, 1996 / Razor & Tie ✦✦
Live from New York captures Graham Parker with his backing band 12 Haunted Episodes live in concert. Recorded at the Bottom Line in June of 1995, *Live from New York* features highlights from Parker's long career, spanning from "Stick to Me" to "Disney's America." Although he doesn't add anything new to the songs, Parker sounds charged on the newer material, bringing out an edginess on the material from his RCA albums and *12 Haunted Episodes* that wasn't necessarily on the original recordings. Still, that doesn't prevent the album from being more than a little predictable—after all, it is the *fifth* officially released live album in Parker's career (sixth, if you count the 1979 promo-only *Live Sparks*, which was officially released a couple of months after *Live in New York, NY*). For anyone but dedicated Parker fans, *Live in New York, NY* is unnecessary, although it is a pleasant, enjoyable listen (with the notable exception of a forced cover of Nirvana's "In Bloom"). —*Stephen Thomas Erlewine*

Acid Bubblegum / Sep. 24, 1996 / Razor & Tie ✦✦✦
Like *Struck by Lightning* before it, *12 Haunted Episodes* was a kind of artistic rebirth for Graham Parker, boasting a quiet set of intimate songs about simple, domestic concerns that had tenderness, even when he was bitter. Of course, *12 Haunted Episodes* was just the calm before the storm, since the follow-up *Acid Bubblegum* blasts out of the speaker with the snarly rage that distinguished his seminal late '70s albums. Unfortunately, it often sounds like a parody of classic Parker instead of an inspired return to form. Spitting out songs like "Bubblegum Cancer," "Turn It into Hate" and "Character Assasination," his voice is raw and snide, but it doesn't sounds passionate—it sounds like feigned energy. Similarly, the songs are all fairly perfunctory, following standard Parker patterns without ever catching fire. Moments of *Acid Bubblegum* sound good, with Parker and the Haunted Episodes bashing out tight, competent R&B-inflected garage rock, but it is alarmingly low in terms of content. —*Stephen Thomas Erlewine*

The Last Rock N' Roll Tour / Apr. 22, 1997 / Razor & Tie ✦✦✦
During the '90s, Graham Parker released a remarkable number of live albums, which is particularly odd for a performer known for his songwriting, not his performances. The double disc *The Last Rock N' Roll Tour* was presumably released because Parker intended his 1996 excursion with the Figgs to be his final time on the road with a rock 'n' roll band. With the Figgs doing their best Rumour impersonation, Parker runs through a number of his classic songs, as well as selections from recent albums like *12 Haunted Episodes* and *Acid Bubblegum*. Although the performances are solid, there's no real spark on the record, and therefore, none of these versions are particularly noteworthy. And considering that *The Last Rock N' Roll Tour* comes on the heels of four live records in as many years, it's puzzling why such a thoroughly average performance was released, especially as a double-disc set. —*Stephen Thomas Erlewine*

Robert Parker

b. Oct. 14, 1930, Crescent City, LA
Saxophone, Vocals / Soul, Disco, R&B
Parker's dance raver "Barefootin'" was one of the biggest hits to come out of New Orleans during the mid-'60s. Parker played sessions as a saxophonist back in 1949 with the legendary pianist Professor Longhair, and his 1959 solo debut for Ron, "All Night Long," was a scorching two-part instrumental. But Parker's underutilized vocal talents suddenly emerged in 1966, when his highly infectious "Barefootin'" became a giant hit on tiny Nola. Only one other Parker single, "Tip Toe," charted the next year, but Parker remains a popular attraction in his hometown. —*Bill Dahl*

● **Barefootin'** / 1966 / Collectables ✦✦✦✦
Originally issued in 1987 on vinyl by England's Charly, this collection includes Parker's main claim to fame, the 1966 R&B and pop dance smash "Barefootin'"; its flip side, "Let's Go Baby (Where the Action Is)"; both sides of a 1969 single Parker cut for Silver Fox; and a number of '70s recordings the erstwhile sax player waxed for Sansu Enterprises. Much of the CD, including the title cut, is infectious New Orleans R&B of a high caliber, but other tracks find Parker attempting to cut mainstream funk and disco, usually with less-than-inspiring results. If possible, find the Charly reissue, because Collectables, in their typically shoddy manner, do not bother to provide songwriting credits, let alone track credits or liner notes. A good policy is to buy Collectables only if there is no other anthology of the same material issued anywhere else in the world, no matter what the price difference. —*Rob Bowman*

Van Dyke Parks

b. Jan. 3, 1941, Mississippi
Synthesizer, Piano, Accordion, Keyboards, Vocals / Singer-Songwriter, Experimental
Composer, arranger, producer, and musician Van Dyke Parks has had a varied career in popular music without ever getting near the popular mainstream. Parks worked as a songwriter in the early '60s and became a producer, handling such mid-'60s acts as Harper's Bizarre. He was enlisted by Beach Boy Brian Wilson to write lyrics for what turned out to be an abortive album project called *Smile* (now one of the legendary lost albums of the '60s), resulting in such songs as the hit "Heroes and Villains." Parks released his own album, the eclectic *Song Cycle*, to critical acclaim and minimal sales in 1968. He then did session work with a variety of artists, not releasing his second album, *Discover America*, which revealed his immersion in Trinidadian music, until 1972. *Clang of the Yankee Reaper*, another eclectic collection, followed in 1975. But Parks maintained his "day job"—film work on scores by Ry Cooder and others, writing and arranging for Shelley Duvall's children's TV series, and other pursuits. Finally, in 1984, came the brilliant *Jump!*, a concept album based on the Uncle Remus tales of Joel Chandler Harris. It was followed in 1989 by *Tokyo Rose*, which concerned the state of American-Japanese relations. —*William Ruhlmann*

● **Song Cycle** / 1968 / Warner Brothers ✦✦✦✦
Parks demonstrated an audacious musical imagination on this debut album, which effectively deployed a full orchestra, along with electric instruments, balalaikas, accordions, and an "authentic folk choir," nature sounds and God knows what else to produce a unique soundscape. A unusual piece of music and a stunning accomplishment. —*William Ruhlmann*

Discover America / 1972 / Warner Brothers ✦✦✦✦
Parks turns to the music of Trinidad here, especially as it was heard in the '40s, which means tributes to "Bing Crosby" and "The Four Mills Bros.," not to mention "G-Man Hoover" and "FDR in Trinidad," played on steel drums and other indigenous instruments. A charming, idiosyncratic genre exercise. —*William Ruhlmann*

The Clang of the Yankee Reaper / 1975 / Warner Brothers ✦✦✦
Expanding the Caribbean approach he took with *Discover America*, Van Dyke Parks explores more arcane Americana on an album that ranges from New Orleans to the islands to the classics. Only the title track bears a co-composing credit for the artist, but Parks' exuberant, eclectic musical personality is the unifying force in a collection of music that varies from the Sandpipers' "Another Dream" to Pachelbel's "Canon in D." —*William Ruhlmann*

Jump! / Feb. 1984 / Warner Brothers ✦✦✦✦
An exhilarating song cycle based on the Uncle Remus tales. It incorporates the styles of Stephen Foster, ragtime, '30s movie-soundtrack music, you name it, all in the service of playful, touching lyrics that correspond to the source material, without actually aping it. A delight from start to finish. —*William Ruhlmann*

Tokyo Rose / Jul. 1989 / Warner Brothers ✦✦✦
One can hear "America" as played on a Japanese koto on this history of relations between East and West, which covers everything from the "Trade War" to baseball with Parks' typically eclectic and broad musical imagination. A charming album. —*William Ruhlmann*

Fisherman & His Wife / Jul. 1, 1991 / Windham Hill ✦✦✦

Idiosyncratic Path Best Of / Jul. 5, 1994 / Demon ✦✦✦✦

Parliament

f. 1970, Detroit, MI, **db.** 1980
Soul, Funk
Inspired during the late '60s by Motown's assembly line of sound, George Clinton gradually assembled a collective of over 50 musicians and recorded the ensemble during the '70s as both Parliament and Funkadelic. While Funkadelic pursued band-format psychedelic rock, Parliament engaged in a funk free-for-all, blending influences from the godfathers (James Brown and Sly Stone) with freaky costumes and themes inspired by '60s acid culture and science fiction. From its 1970 inception until Clinton's dissolving of Parliament in 1980, the band hit the R&B Top Ten several times but truly excelled in two other areas: large-selling, effective album statements and the most dazzling, extravagant live show in the business. In an era when Philly soul continued the slick sounds of establishment-approved R&B, Parliament scared off more white listeners than it courted.

By the time his on-the-move family settled in New Jersey during the early '50s, George Clinton (b. July 22, 1941, Kannapolis, NC) became interested in doo wop, which was just beginning to explode in the New York metro area. Basing his group on Frankie Lymon & the Teenagers, Clinton formed the Parliaments in 1955 with a lineup that gradually shifted to include Clarence "Fuzzy" Haskins, Grady Thomas, Raymond

Davis, and Calvin Simon. Based out of a barbershop backroom where Clinton straightened hair, the Parliaments released only two singles during the next ten years, but frequent trips to Detroit during the mid-'60s—where Clinton began working as a songwriter and producer—eventually paid off their investment.

After finding a hit with the 1967 single "(I Wanna) Testify," the Parliaments ran into trouble with Revilot Records and refused to record any new material. Instead of waiting for a settlement, Clinton decided to record the same band under a new name: Funkadelic. Founded in 1968, the group began life as a smoke screen, claiming as its only members the Parliaments' backing band—guitarist Eddie Hazel, bassist Billy Nelson, rhythm guitarist Lucius "Tawl" Ross, drummer Ramon "Tiki" Fulwood, and organist Mickey Atkins—but in truth including Clinton and the rest of the former Parliaments lineup. Revilot folded not long after, with the label's existing contracts sold to Atlantic; Clinton, however, decided to abandon the Parliaments name rather than record for the major label. One previously recorded Parliaments single, "A New Day Begins," was licensed to Atco in 1969 and became a No. 44 hit that May.

Funkadelic released five albums from 1970 through early 1974, and consistently hit the lower reaches of the R&B charts, but the collective pulled up stakes later that year and began recording as Parliament. Signing with the Casablanca label, Parliament's "Up for the Down Stroke" (No. 10 R&B, No. 63 pop) appeared in mid-1974 and reflected a more mainstream approach, with funky horn arrangements reminiscent of James Brown and a live feel that recalls contemporary work by Kool & the Gang. It became the biggest hit yet for the Parliament/Funkadelic congregation. "Testify," a revamped version of the Parliaments' 1967 hit, also charted in 1974. One year later, *Chocolate City* continued Parliament's success: the title track reached No. 24 R&B, and "Ride On" also charted.

Though keyboard player Bernie Worrell (b. April 19, 1944, Long Beach, NJ) had played on the original *Funkadelic* album, his first credit with the conglomeration appeared on Funkadelic's second album, 1970's *Free Your Mind... And Your Ass Will Follow.* Clinton and Worrell had known each other since the New Jersey barbership days, and Worrell soon became the most crucial cog in the P-Funk machine, working on arrangements and production for virtually all later Parliament/Funkadelic releases. His strict upbringing and classical training (at the New England Conservatory and Juilliard), as well as the boom in synthesizer technology during the early '70s, gave him the tools to create the synth runs and horn arrangements that later trademarked the P-Funk sound. Two years after the addition of Worrell, P-Funk added its second-most famed contributor, Bootsy Collins. The muscular, throbbing bassline of Collins (b. Oct. 26, 1951, Cincinnati, OH) had already been featured in James Brown's backing band (the J.B.'s) along with his brother, guitarist Catfish Collins. Bootsy and Catfish were playing in a Detroit dance club when George Clinton saw and hired them.

Clinton & Co. ushered in 1976 with the April release of the third Parliament LP in as many years: *Mothership Connection.* Arguably the peak of Parliament's power, the album made No. 13 on the pop charts and went platinum, sparked by three hit singles: "P. Funk (Wants to Get Funked Up)" (No. 33 R&B), "Tear the Roof off the Sucker (Give Up the Funk)" (No. 5 R&B, No. 15 pop) and "Star Child" (No. 26 R&B). In addition to Bootsy Collins, the album featured two other James Brown refugees: horn legends Maceo Parker and Fred Wesley. Just six months after the release of *Mothership Connection,* Clinton had another Parliament album in the can, *The Clones of Doctor Funkenstein.* Though it only reached gold status, the LP spawned the No. 22 R&B hit "Do That Stuff" and the No. 43 "Dr. Funkenstein."

Several internal squabbles during 1977 apparently didn't phase Clinton at all; the following year proved to be the most successful in Parliament's history. In January, "Flash Light"—from the Parliament album *Funkentelechy vs. the Placebo Syndrome*—became the collective's first No. 1 hit. It topped the R&B charts for three weeks, and was followed by the No. 27 single, "Funkentelechy." The LP reached No. 13 on the pop charts and became Parliament's second platinum album. Early in 1979, Parliament hit No. 1 yet again with "Aqua Boogie," from its eighth album, *Motor-Booty Affair.* The LP, which stalled at No. 23, nevertheless became the group's fifth consecutive album to go gold or better. Parliament's ninth album, *Gloryhallastoopid (Or Pin the Tale on the Funky),* was released later in 1979 and showed a bit of a slip in the previously unstoppable Clinton machine. The group charted in the R&B Top Ten twice during 1980 ("Theme from 'The Black Hole'" and "Agony of Defeet"), but Clinton began to be weighed down that year by legal difficulties arising from Polygram's acquisition of Casablanca. Jettisoning both the Parliament and Funkadelic names (but not the musicians), Clinton began his solo career with 1982's *Computer Games.* He and many former Parliament/Funkadelic members continued to tour and record during the '80s as the P. Funk All Stars, but the decade's disdain of everything to do with the '70s resulted in the neglect of critical and commercial opinion for the world's biggest funk band, especially one which in part had spawned the sound of disco. During the early '90s, the

rise of funk-inspired rap (courtesy of Digital Underground, Dr. Dre, and Warren G.) and funk-rock (Primus and Red Hot Chili Peppers) re-established the status of Clinton & Co., one of the most important forces in the recent history of black music. —*John Bush*

Osmium / 1970 / Invictus ++
An early Parliament release in which George Clinton and company are still perfecting their mix of straight soul and zany mythology. It's pretty tame compared to what would come in the future, but does reveal in bits and pieces the razor-sharp Clinton wit. —*Ron Wynn*

Up for the Down Stroke / 1974 / Casablanca ++++
The first album by Clinton's revamped Parliament remains a perfect introduction, although its best songs are on their *Greatest Hits.* —*John Floyd*

Chocolate City / 1975 / Casablanca +++
The title track was a masterpiece, one of George Clinton's satirical triumphs. Whether you think it was a political work or not, everything clicked—the production, comic lead vocals, lyrics, and arrangements. The remainder of the album wasn't quite that strong but was still excellent. It mixed every Clinton element: chaotic jamming, quirky outlook, hilarious vocals, and that sense of the casually absurd that Clinton championed. —*Ron Wynn*

Clones of Dr. Funkenstein / 1976 / Casablanca ++++
George Clinton had his otherworldly, controlled, chaotic vision well in gear for this album. He milked the Frankenstein notion, creating a mad scientist and sonically documenting his warped funk notions. Clinton got instrumental assistance from a crack corps that included keyboardist Bernie Worrell, saxophonist Maceo Parker, and trombonist Fred Wesley, plus numerous vocalists, guitarists, and instrumentalists. The album went gold, although it wasn't as inspired or successful as *Mothership Connection.* But such songs as "Dr. Funkenstein," "I've Been Watching You (Move Your Sexy Body)," and "Everything Is on the One" were quintessential Parliament jams. —*Ron Wynn*

☆ **Mothership Connection** / 1976 / Casablanca +++++
This was *the* Parliament masterpiece. It mixed creative and clever satirical takeoffs on James Brown, Sly Stone, and classic black radio with the kind of loose, inventive improvising seldom heard in R&B or soul circles. The narratives were swift and humorous and the music crackling, fast-moving and progressive. The title cut, "Tear the Roof off the Sucker (Give Up the Funk)," and others marked the beginning of Clinton and Parliament/Funkadelic's evolution into national celebrities. —*Ron Wynn*

☆ **Funkentelechy vs. the Placebo Syndrome** / 1977 / Casablanca +++++
Funkentelechy vs. the Placebo Syndrome offers an even better introduction to the group than the singles collection, by presenting the most intelligible and rhythmically unstoppable glimpse into Clinton's P-Funk world. —*John Floyd*

Live: P-Funk Earth Tour / 1977 / Casablanca +++
One of the few live sets that accurately depict the flavor of an epic event. George Clinton's massive P-Funk tour, with all the spin-off groups and support personnel, gave some incredible shows in the late '70s. Concerts would last three to four hours and run together in an amazing display of controlled chaos. Songs were open-ended, the pace was nonstop, and it was much more like a ritual than a concert. This album perfectly conveyed the concert's feel and quality. —*Ron Wynn*

Motor Booty Affair / 1978 / Casablanca +++
Another concept album, only this time the concept is about water, not being able to swim, and not wanting to swim. This album is worth hearing, in spite of its occasional Frank Zappa-isms. —*John Floyd*

Gloryhallastoopid / 1979 / Casablanca +++
Although at the time, this album was viewed as a disaster, there has been some critical reassessment in the past years. It was certainly not as inspired, brilliantly executed, or memorable as any of some many 1970s Parliament or Funkadelic gems, but it did have its own humorous/ bizarre outlook. Clinton was being torn in many directions and plagued by money problems, so he didn't give it the attention it probably needed. Still, it deserves a revisit by Clinton fans who tossed it aside in disgust the first time around. —*Ron Wynn*

Trombipulation / 1980 / Casablanca ++
The final album issued before Parliament temporarily disbanded. Clinton's empire was being besieged, and while he didn't completely lose his gifts, the impact could be heard on the album. The spontaneity, bizarre comic wit and wisdom, as well as the production and arranging greatness, weren't as evident. There were no epic jams, classic satirical numbers, or magnificent message tracks. Instead, it was more a worthy goodbye, one that fortunately hasn't been final. —*Ron Wynn*

Greatest Hits (The Bomb) / 1984 / Casablanca ++++
Treating Parliament as a singles band isn't entirely fair, since many of their greatest moments came when they pushed the boundaries of funk

and soul to their limits. However, George Clinton's vision was so sprawling that it was often best articulated as individual tracks within the studio, which is what makes *Greatest Hits (The Bomb)* such an effective record. Concentrating solely on Parliament's singles actually illustrates the depth of their vision and influence, since there are no half-baked ideas surrounding these ten stunning songs ("Up for the Down Stroke," "Chocolate City," "Give Up the Funk," "Bop Gun," "Flash Light," "Aqua Boogie"). Of course, their individual albums remain worthy, occasionally essential, listening, but as an introduction *Greatest Hits* does its job effectively, and for some casual fans, it may be all the Parliament they'll ever need. —*Stephen Thomas Erlewine*

☆ **Tear the Roof Off** / May 18, 1993 / Casablanca ✦✦✦✦✦
Two discs of the hardest funk ever recorded, *Tear the Roof Off* is essential for both the casual fan and the hardcore collector. In addition to the presence of the full-length versions of all their hits, several 12" mixes make their first appearances on CD here. Without the music on *Tear the Roof Off*, contemporary music would not sound as it does today. —*AMG*

Live 1972-1993 / 1994 / AEM ✦✦
A scatter-shot multi-disc collection, *Live 1972-1993* provides a good overview of the number of incarnations of Parliament/Funkadelic, even if it is a bit too inconsistent to be essential listening. —*Stephen Thomas Erlewine*

★ **The Best of Parliament: Give Up the Funk** / Jun. 6, 1995 / Mercury Funk Essentials ✦✦✦✦✦
To some, boiling Parliament's legacy down to a single-disc collection is the equivalent of heresy, since most fans treat each album as an individual work of art. Still, there is no denying that Parliament was an untouchable singles act, recording some of the greatest soul-funk singles of the '70s. For those listeners who just want an introduction or only need the hits, *The Best of Parliament: Give Up the Funk* is the ideal choice. A more complete and logical collection than the previous *Greatest Hits (The Bomb)*, *The Best of Parliament* supplies all of the great group's greatest hits, from "Up for the Down Stroke" and "Tear the Roof off the Sucker" to "Flash Light" and "Aqua Boogie." For those who can only handle the funk in moderation, there is no better collection. —*Leo Stanley*

Funkadelic Live 1976-1993 [box] / Apr. 25, 1996 / Sequel ✦✦✦

Alan Parsons Project

f. 1975, London, England
Art-Rock/Progressive-Rock, Soft Rock, Pop-Rock
As indicated by its name, the Alan Parsons Project was not a band so much as a concept overseen by the titular Parsons, a successful producer and engineer. Born in Britain on December 20, 1949, he began his musical career as a staff engineer at EMI Studios and first garnered significant industry exposure via his work on the Beatles' 1969 masterpiece *Abbey Road.* Parsons subsequently worked with Paul McCartney on several of Wings' earliest albums; he also oversaw recordings from Al Stewart, Cockney Rebel, and Pilot, but solidified his reputation by working on Pink Floyd's *Dark Side of the Moon.*

Influenced by his work on Stewart's concept album *Time Passages*, Parsons decided to begin creating his own thematic records; along with songwriter Eric Woolfson, he soon founded the Alan Parsons Project. Although Parsons played keyboards and infrequently sang on his records, the Project was designed primarily as a forum for a revolving collection of vocalists and session players—among them Arthur Brown, ex-Zombie Colin Blunstone, Cockney Rebel's Steve Harley, and the Hollies' Allan Clarke—to interpret and perform Parsons and Woolfson's conceptually linked, lushly synthesized music.

The Project debuted in 1975 with *Tales of Mystery and Imagination*, a collection inspired by the work of Edgar Allen Poe; similarly, the science fiction of Isaac Asimov served as the raw material for 1977's follow-up *I, Robot.* With 1980's *The Turn of a Friendly Card*, a meditation on gambling, the Alan Parsons Project scored a Top 20 hit, "Games People Play"; 1982's *Eye in the Sky* was their most successful effort, and notched a Top Three hit with its title track. While 1984's *Ammonia Avenue* went gold, the Project's subsequent LPs earned little notice, although records like 1985's *Vulture Culture*, 1987's *Gaudi* and 1996's *On Air* found favor with longtime fans. —*Jason Ankeny*

Tales of Mystery & Imagination / 1975 / Mercury ✦✦✦✦
This "project," led by former Beatles engineer Alan Parsons, was recorded at Abbey Road and featured a session group including Terry Sylvester and Arthur Brown (he of the "Crazy World"). It made its first and best album (if not its most popular one) by interpreting the ominous poems and stories of Edgar Allan Poe. Heavy on synthesized keyboards and dramatic choral parts, it's rock soundtrack music minus the film. The group went on to make a series of similar follow-ups, notably including *I Robot* and *Eye in the Sky*, but this is the place to start. —*William Ruhlmann*

I Robot / Jun. 1977 / Arista ✦✦✦✦
The Alan Parsons Project was established as a top record seller with *I, Robot*, their second album. Musically, the record continued the ideas of their debut. Thematically, the record was an exploration of the science-fiction concept of a world run by machines and mechanized human beings, particularly robots. —*Daevid Jehnzen*

Pyramid / Jun. 1978 / Arista ✦✦✦
Even though it didn't break into the Top Ten like its predecessor, *Pyramid* was another hit for the Alan Parsons Project, going gold and peaking at No. 26. Thematically, it was an exploration of mystic Middle Eastern myths and traditions, particularly pyramids and the like. —*Daevid Jehnzen*

Eve / Sep. 1979 / Arista ✦✦
Eve continued the Alan Parsons Project's string of best-selling albums, peaking at No. 13 and going gold. Musically, it reiterated the group's first three records, while thematically it explored the perplexing nature of women. Although the concept is certainly intriguing, Parsons' lyrical outlook is rather cold, opening him to charges of misogyny. —*Daevid Jehnzen*

The Turn of a Friendly Card / Nov. 1980 / Arista ✦✦✦✦
The Turn of a Friendly Card was the Alan Parson Project's second straight No. 13 album, but it proved more successful than either *Pyramid* or *Eve*, going platinum and spending over a year on the charts. Musically, the group had matured, offering intricate, carefully crafted pop songs that were exacting in detail. Thematically, the record seemed to be their slightest effort to date, as it superficially explored the medieval ramifications of a card game. Dig a little deeper, however, and the record reveals itself to be a rumination about destiny versus the choice of self-determination. It features the hit "Games People Play." —*Daevid Jehnzen*

Eye in the Sky / Jun. 1982 / Arista ✦✦✦✦
Eye in the Sky was the Alan Parsons Project's most successful record, peaking at No. 7 and going platinum, as the title track hit No. 3. Musically, it expanded the ideas of *Turn of a Friendly Card*, adding some softer edges and lusher textures; despite its hit single, the album worked better as a whole, not as a series of songs. Thematically, it was a snapshot of an Orwellian future, ruled by the all-seeing "Eye in the Sky," which watches over its populace with a calm, menacing glee. —*Daevid Jehnzen*

● **The Best of the Alan Parsons Project** / 1983 / Arista ✦✦✦✦
Although the Alan Parsons Project is a quintessential album-rock act, their most effective statements were made on singles, and this collection features their best songs, including "Eye in the Sky" and "Games People Play." —*Stephen Thomas Erlewine*

Ammonia Avenue / Feb. 1984 / Arista ✦✦✦
While it wasn't as successful as *Eye in the Sky*, *Ammonia Avenue* was yet another gold album for the Alan Parsons Project—even if it would turn out to be their last. Like the lilting single "Don't Answer Me," the album is filled with meticulously crafted, synthesized textures that straddle the line between conceptually sweeping art-rock and smooth, accessible pop. Thematically, *Ammonia Avenue* is the most simple and streamlined album the group recorded; it explored the decaying relations between the genders, as well as the rapidly deteriorating situations between people in general, as the modern world spins out of control, snapping off ties and lines between humans. However, Parsons and Woolfson offer a glimmer of hope with "Ammonia Avenue," which is where all the unvarnished answers lie. —*Daevid Jehnzen*

Vulture Culture / Mar. 1985 / Arista ✦✦
As the title suggests, *Vulture Culture* explores the tendencies the modern world has to feed off of each other, circling around for the losers, since you either "use it or you lose it." Musically, it's a bit tougher and more ambitious than *Ammonia Avenue*, though it basically reiterates the same themes as its predecessor, only in a more abstract way. —*Daevid Jehnzen*

Stereotomy / Nov. 1985 / Arista ✦✦
According to the *Random House Dictionary*, "stereotomy" is the technique of cutting solids, as stones, to specified forms and dimensions. On their album *Stereotomy*, the Alan Parsons Project paints a portrait of a man who has been cut into a specific shape according to the demands of society, as he thirsts after the "Limelight" but is consigned to "Urbania" and relies on "Beaujolais" to ease the pain. Most of the album is devoted to long, sweeping instrumental passages, which makes it one of the group's most ambitious records, but not one of their most accessible. —*Daevid Jehnzen*

Gaudi / 1987 / Arista ✦✦
One of Alan Parsons' most personal albums, *Gaudi* is a meditative tribute to and biography of the life of Antonio Gaudi, a Catalan architect. Gaudi's most ambitious and elaborate work was the Sagrada Familia Cathedral in Barcelona, which included in its architecture a timetable designed to run for hundreds of years; he is buried in this cathedral,

which was never finished. Fortunately, Alan Parsons was able to finish *Gaudi*, and it is breathtaking in its scope, if not in its accomplishment. Although the group does some amazing things musically, it doesn't quite work as a coherent album, which may be the reason it was one of the group's least commercially successful efforts. —*Daevid Jehnzen*

The Best of the Alan Parsons Project, Vol. 2 / 1988 / Arista ♦♦♦♦
The Alan Parsons Project didn't have as many hits between 1983 and 1988 as they did between 1976 and 1983, so the task of compiling a second volume of greatest hits was somewhat difficult. Instead of meeting this problem head on, the compilers ignored it, choosing a selection of album tracks from the group's first six albums as well as adding the hit "Don't Answer Me" and several tracks from *Stereotomy, Vulture Culture*, and *Ammonia Avenue*. It's an effective sampler of some of their more ponderous work. —*Daevid Jehnzen*

The Instrumental Works / 1988 / Arista ♦♦
Part of the charm of the Alan Parsons Project was always their gumption, how they dared to make albums that were linked together both by their synth-driven art-rock and by their lyrics, which almost always told a story. *Instrumental Works* selects all the instrumentals from their concept albums. Since these songs had a place on the original albums in their original sequence, they don't quite make as much sense on a different disc. Even so, the group shows its musical dexterity on these pieces. —*Daevid Jehnzen*

Try Anything Once / Oct. 26, 1993 / Arista ♦♦♦

Very Best Live / Jun. 27, 1995 / RCA Victor ♦♦

● ### Anthology / May 28, 1996 / Griffin Music ♦♦♦♦

On Air / Sep. 24, 1996 / A&M ♦♦♦
Though the title may lead you to believe that *On Air* is a live radio broadcast from the Alan Parsons Project, that is simply not the case. Instead, *On Air* is a rumination about man's desire to fly, and the album's soaring synthesizers and floating soundscapes accurately convey the blissful sadness of a wish that can never happen. Parsons' grasp of his material is so strong that even a pop vocalist like Christopher Cross adds to the music's richness. His vision is so deep, that it is extended to the bonus CD-ROM disc, which captures the music's bristling emotions through videos and literature. *On Air* is a welcome, and overdue, return to form from Alan Parsons, proving that his project shouldn't be put to rest just yet. —*Daevid Jehnzen*

Gram Parsons (Cecil Ingram Connor)

b. Nov. 5, 1946, Winterhaven, FL, d. Sep. 19, 1973, Joshua Tree, CA
Guitar, Vocals / Country-Rock
Gram Parsons is the father of country-rock. With the International Submarine Band, the Byrds, and the Flying Burrito Brothers, Parsons pioneered the concept of a rock band playing country music, and as a solo artist he moved even further into country music, blending the two genres to the point that they became indistinguishable from each other. While he was alive, Parsons was a cult figure who never sold many records, but influenced countless fellow musicians from the Rolling Stones to the Byrds. In the years since his death, his stature has only grown, as numerous rock and country artists build on his small, but enormously influential, body of work.

Gram Parsons was born Cecil Ingram Connor on November 5, 1946. Parsons was the grandson of John Snivley, who owned about one-third of all the citrus fields in Florida. Snivley's daughter married Coon Dog Connor. As a child, Parsons learned how to play the piano at the age of nine, the same year he saw Elvis Presley perform at his school; following that performance, Parsons decided to become a musician. When he was 12, Parsons' father committed suicide. After Connor's death, Parson and his mother moved in with her parents in Winter Haven, FL; a year after the move, his mother married Robert Parsons, who adopted Gram and the child legally changed his name to Gram Parsons.

At the age of 14, Parsons began playing in the local rock 'n' roll band the Pacers, which evolved into the Legends. During its time together, the Legends featured Jim Stafford and Kent Lavoie, who would later come to fame under the name Lobo. In 1963, Parsons formed a folk group called the Shilos who performed throughout Florida and cut two singles for Columbia Records. In 1965, Parsons graduated from high school; on the same day he graduated, his mother died of alcohol poisoning.

Following his graduation, Gram Parsons enrolled at Harvard, where he studied theology. Parsons only spent one semester at Harvard and while he was there, he spent more time playing music than attending classes. During this time he formed the International Submarine Band with guitarist John Nuese, bassist Ian Dunlop, and drummer Mickey Gauvin. After he dropped out of college, he moved to New York with the International Submarine Band in 1966. The group spent a year in New York, developing a heavily country influenced rock 'n' roll sound and cutting two unsuccessful singles for Columbia. The band relocated to Los Angeles in 1967, where they secured a record contract with Lee Hazlewood's LHI record label. The group's debut album, *Safe at Home*,

was released in early 1968, but by the time it appeared in the stores, the group had already disbanded.

Around the time the International Submarine Band dissolved, Parsons met Chris Hillman, the bassist for the Byrds. At that time, the Byrds were rebuilding their lineup and Hillman recommended to the band's leader, Roger McGuinn, that Parsons join the band. By the spring of 1968, Parsons had become a member of the Byrds and he was largely responsible for the group's shift toward country music with their album *Sweetheart of the Rodeo*. Originally, the album was going to feature Parsons' lead vocals, but he was still contractually obligated to LHI, so his voice had to be stripped from the record.

Gram Parsons only spent a few months with the Byrds, leaving the band in the fall of 1968 because he refused to accompany them on a tour of South Africa, allegedly because he opposed apartheid. Chris Hillman left the band shortly after him and the duo formed the Flying Burrito Brothers in late 1968. Parsons and Hillman enlisted pedal steel guitarist "Sneaky" Pete Kleinow and bassist Chris Ethridge to complete the band's lineup and recorded their debut album with a series of session drummers. *The Gilded Palace of Sin*, the Flying Burrito Brothers' debut album, was released in 1969. Although the album only sold a few thousand copies, the group gathered a dedicated cult following, which was mainly composed of musicians, including the Rolling Stones. In fact, by the time the album was released, Parsons had begun hanging around the Rolling Stones frequently, and he became close friends with Keith Richards. Prior to his time with the Stones, Parsons had experimented with drugs and alcohol, but in 1969 he dove deep into substance abuse, which he supported with his huge trust fund.

Parsons recorded a second album with the Flying Burrito Brothers, but by the time the record—titled *Burrito Deluxe*—appeared in the spring of 1970, he had left the band. Shortly after leaving the group, he recorded a handful of songs with producer Terry Melcher, but he never completed the album. Following these sessions, Parsons entered a holding pattern were he acted the role of being a rock star instead of actually playing music. He spent much of his time either hanging out with the Stones or ingesting large amounts of drugs and alcohol; frequently, he did a combination of the two. In 1971, he toured with the Rolling Stones in England, attended the recording of the band's *Exile on Main Street*, and it appeared that he would sign with the band's record label. Instead, he headed back to Los Angeles late in 1971, spending the rest of the year and the first half of 1972 writing material for an impending solo album. In 1972, he met Emmylou Harris through Chris Hillman and asked her to join his backing band; she accepted.

By the summer of 1972, he was prepared to enter the studio to record his first solo album. Parsons had assembled a band—which included Harris, guitarist James Burton, bassist Rick Grech, Barry Tashian, Glen D. Hardin, and Ronnie Tutt—and had asked Merle Haggard to produce the album. After meeting Parsons, Haggard turned the offer down, and Parsons chose Haggard's engineer, Hugh Davis, as the album's producer. The resulting album, *G.P.*, was released late in 1972 to good reviews but poor sales.

Following the release of *G.P.*, Parsons embarked on a small tour with his backing band, the Fallen Angels. After the tour was completed, they entered the studio to record his second album, *Grievous Angel*. The album was completed toward the end of the summer. A few weeks after the sessions, Parsons went on a vacation near the Joshua Tree National Monument in Arizona. He spent most of his time there consuming drugs and alcohol. On September 19, 1973, he overdosed on morphine and tequila and was rushed to the Yucca Valley Hospital—he was pronounced dead on arrival. According to the funeral plans, his body was to be flown back to New Orleans for a burial. However, Parsons' road manager stole the body after the funeral and carried it back out to the Joshua Tree desert, where he cremated the body. Phil Kaufman revealed that the cremation had been Parsons' wish. Kaufman could not be convicted for stealing the body, but he was arrested for stealing and burning the coffin.

In the two decades following Gram Parsons' death, his legacy continued to grow as both country and rock musicians built on the music he left behind. Everyone from Emmylou Harris to Elvis Costello has covered his songs, and his influence could still be heard well into the '90s. —*Stephen Thomas Erlewine*

Gram Parsons Int Sub Band (Safe at Home) / 1967 / Shiloh ♦♦♦
Safe at Home represents some of Gram Parsons' earliest recordings as a part of the International Submarine Band. Arguably the first country-rock album, this more than hints at Parsons' greatness to come. This charming document is essential listening. —*Chris Woodstra*

★ G.P./Grievous Angel / 1973 / Reprise ♦♦♦♦♦
Parsons' two best albums appear on one compact disc. Seeking to synthesize his own ideas with those of classic country and rock, Parsons hired Merle Haggard's recording engineer (he had approached Haggard himself about producing) and members of Elvis Presley's band, including pianist Glen D. Hardin and guitarist James Burton. The result had its roots in everything but sounded like nothing else. Parsons' songs were

the musings of a wounded soul, and his taste in others' material ran from Harlan Howard to the J. Geils Band. On *Grievous Angel*, Emmylou Harris emerges from the background to provide an angelic foil for Parsons' lost folkie voice. *—Brian Mansfield*

Sleepless Nights / 1976 / A&M ✦✦✦
Sleepless Nights is a collection of unreleased Gram Parsons material recorded while he was in the Flying Burrito Brothers. Most of the material are covers, yet the selection demonstrates how Parsons closed the gap between rock and country. *—Stephen Thomas Erlewine*

Gram Parsons & the Fallen Angels / 1981 / Sierra ✦✦✦✦
A good live document of Parsons' last tour, it was recorded at radio station WLIR in New York. *—Kenneth M. Cassidy*

Warm Evenings, Pale Mornings, Bottled Blues / 1992 / Raven ✦✦✦✦
Although all of Parsons' albums are essential, this import-only collection provides an excellent sampling of his entire career including his stints with the Shilos, the International Submarine Band, the Byrds (complete with Parsons' vocals restored), the Flying Burrito Brothers, and the solo years. *—Chris Woodstra*

Cosmic American Music / Jul. 18, 1995 / Sundown ✦✦
Cosmic American is a collection of demos made in various homes and hotel rooms in 1972. In an informal, sing-along environment, Parsons works through embryonic versions of songs and old favorites with friends Emmylou Harris, Barry Tashian, and Ric Grech (among others)—several songs never making it to the studio. Though the quality of the recordings can be off-putting to the casual fan, those who count themselves among GP's ever-growing cult will find this intimate look a compulsive listen. *—Chris Woodstra*

Billy Paul

b. Dec. 1, 1934, Philadelphia, PA
Vocals / Soul, Philly Soul
Billy Paul had a good run in the '70s as an R&B vocalist, though he'd been recording since the '50s when he debuted on Jubilee. Paul was featured on radio broadcasts in Philadelphia at age 11, and had an extensive jazz background. He worked with Dinah Washington, Miles Davis, and Roberta Flack, as well as Charlie Parker, before forming a trio and recording for Jubilee. His original 1959 recording of "Ebony Woman" for New Dawn was later re-recorded for Neptune as the title of his 1970 LP. He signed the next year with Philadelphia International and scored his biggest hit with "Me & Mrs. Jones" in 1972, topping both the R&B and pop charts. Paul had one other Top Ten R&B single, "Thanks for Saving My Life," in 1974. He remained on Philadelphia International until the mid-'80s. Paul recorded one LP for Total Experience in 1985, *Lately*, and another for Ichiban before announcing his retirement in 1989 in London. But he's since done several club dates, both in America and overseas. *—Ron Wynn*

● **Greatest Hits** / 1983 / Philadelphia International ✦✦✦✦

Pavement

f. 1989, Stockton, CA
Alternative Pop-Rock, Lo-Fi, Indie Rock
With their fractured songs, unexpected blasts of feedback, laconic vocals, cryptic, literate lyrics, and defiant low-fidelity, Pavement is one of the most influential and distinctive bands to emerge from the American underground in the '90s. Pavement, along with Sebadoh, were the leaders of the lo-fi movement that dominated US indie-rock in the early '90s. Initially conceived as a studio project between guitarists-vocalists Stephen Malkmus and Scott Kannberg in the '80s, Pavement gradually became a band during the early '90s. Along the way, their initial EPs and debut album, 1992's *Slanted and Enchanted*, earned a devoted following of musicians, indie fans and critics. Before long, the group's aesthetics—a combination of elliptic, cryptic underground American rock, unrepentant Anglophilia, a fondness for white noise, off-kilter arrangements and winding melodies, songs that frequently had shifting titles, and literate, clever lyrics—were imitated by underground bands throughout America and Britian. By that point, Pavement had become an actual band, one with a notorious acid-fried, ex-hippie drummer called Gary Young. Young left the band in 1993, as the band made the move to clean up their sound, if not their sensibility, on 1994's *Crooked Rain, Crooked Rain*. Their revamp resulted in a near-hit with "Cut Your Hair," but the mainstream decided Pavement was too strange for their tastes, and the band decided they preferred the underground, leaving the band as one of the most popular—and the most influential—American indie-rock bands of the '90s.

Stephen Malkmus (vocals, guitar) had finished studying history at the University of Virginia and returned to Stockton, CA, when he formed Pavement with childhood friend Scott Kannberg (guitar, vocals) in 1989. Pavement released their first seven-inch EP, *Slay Tracks: (1933-1969)*, by the summer of 1989. Recorded for $800 at the small local studio Louder Than You Think—which was owned by Gary Young, a 40-some-

thing drummer who appeared on the EP—and released on the duo's own indie label Treble Kicker, *Slay Tracks* demonstrated sonic debts to the Fall, R.E.M., the Pixies, and Sonic Youth. While there were only a couple hundred copies pressed of the EP, it managed to work its way to several influential people within the underground industry, including British DJ John Peel. Furthermore, the EP, which was credited only to "S.M." and "Spiral Stairs," became something of an enigma, since it was supported by no press releases or information about the band. By the 1990 release of *Demolition Plot J-7*, the band had begun to forge these influences into their own signature sound. Pavement moved to Drag City Records and added Young as a member during the recording of *Demolition Plot J-7*, but the band didn't perform any concerts until after the 1991 release of *Perfect Sound Forever*.

During preparation for their first concerts in 1991, Pavement added bassist Mark Ibold and, in order to bolster Young's shaky time-keeping, a second drummer named Bob Nastanovich, who had attended college with Malkmus. The new lineup appeared on the band's first full-length album, *Slanted and Enchanted*, although the group didn't record any of the album as a full band; instead, it was pieced together by Malkmus and Kannberg. Before it was released on Matador Records in the spring of 1992, *Slanted and Enchanted* created extremely good word-of-mouth praise; before the album was even available promotionally, critics were lavishly praising it in the press. Initially, the band's following was based upon critics and fellow musicians, but soon word began to spread on the street as well. Pavement supported the album with their first national tour, and while it didn't reach many cities, it became notorious for the band's sloppy sound and Young's grandstanding. He would greet the audience at the door, shaking their hands; he would perform handstands during the show; he would hand out salads at the door; and he would occasionally collapse drunk. Young was asked to leave the band during 1993; his last release with the group was the EP *Watery Domestic*, which was released in the fall of 1992. He was replaced by Steve West, a friend of Nastanovich. After West joined the band, the band's early EPs were compiled on Drag City's 1993 collection, *Westing (By Musket and Sextant)*.

Pavement's sound cleaned up somewhat after Young's departure; it was a combination of having a steady drummer and recording in real studios. Some pundits predicted that *Crooked Rain, Crooked Rain*, the 1994 follow-up to *Slanted and Enchanted*, would be Pavement's breakthrough into the mainstream. To a certain extent, it was. The album debuted on the US charts at No. 121 and "Cut Your Hair" became a Top Ten modern rock hit and MTV hit. But despite the album's overwhelmingly positive reviews, *Crooked Rain* simply expanded Pavement's cult dramatically, confirming their status as underground, not mainstream, stars. Following the release of *Crooked Rain*, Pavement recorded sporadically during 1994; Malkmus and Nastanovich also contributed to *Starlight Walker*, the second album by the Silver Jews, which was led by their college friend David Berman.

Pavement returned with their third album, *Wowee Zowee*, in the spring of 1995. More eclectic and inaccessible than either of its predecessors, *Wowee Zowee* was greeted in most quarters of the press by negative reviews, sparking a Pavement backlash that continued throughout the next two years. Nevertheless, the band landed a lucrative spot on the fifth Lollapalooza. After releasing the *Pacific Trim* EP early in 1996, the band spent the remainder of the year recording their fourth album with producer Mitch Easter. Released in February of 1997, *Brighten the Corners* was greeted with positive reviews and debuted at No. 70 on the American charts. *—Stephen Thomas Erlewine*

★ **Slanted & Enchanted** / May 1992 / Matador ✦✦✦✦✦
Slanted & Enchanted is a left-field classic, a record that came out of nowhere to help establish a new subgenre of rock 'n' roll. Pavement had already sketched out their sound, as well as their amateurish lo-fi aesthetic, on a series of indie singles before recording their debut, but *Slanted & Enchanted* is where they pulled all of their disparate sounds together into a distinctive style. At first, the primitive sound of the record is the most gripping thing about *Slanted*, but soon the true innovations of the record appear through the songs themselves. Stephen Malkmus and Spiral Stairs subvert conventional pop structures, turning melodies inside out, reinterpreting and reworking older songs, and blending genres together. It's a complex, enthralling record, filled with fractured riffs, strong and cryptic melodies, and with all the hiss and static, *Slanted & Enchanted* sounds like listening to a distant college radio station—melodies and hooks keep floating in and out of the mix, with individual lines instead of full lyrics surfacing through the murk. This unique song structure as much as the sound of the album itself makes *Slanted & Enchanted* an individual, signature work and one of the most influential records of the '90s. *—Stephen Thomas Erlewine*

Watery, Domestic / Nov. 1992 / Matador ✦✦✦
Released between *Slanted & Enchanted* and *Crooked Rain, Crooked Rain*, the *Watery, Domestic* EP captures Pavement in a transitional phase, as the band began to abandon the static-laden guitar-rock of their early recordings and started to move toward a cleaner sound. Most of

the innovations of *Watery, Domestic* have to do with recording techniques, yet the songs are certainly fine. The cleaner production brings Pavement's inherent fractured melodicism into sharper focus, which benefits "Texas Never Whispers," the wistful "Frontwards," and the bright, nearly jangly "Shoot the Singer," but the slow grind of "Lions (Linden)" would have been mesmerising regardless of the production, or the lack of it. —*Stephen Thomas Erlewine*

Westing (By Musket & Sextant) / Mar. 30, 1993 / Drag City ✦✦✦✦
A collection of all of Pavement's low-fidelity early singles and EPs, which features considerably less melody than *Slanted & Enchanted*. It's nice to have this rare material on one CD, although the music is defiantly anti-CD. Those who boarded the train with the acclaimed *Slanted & Enchanted* should catch up on what they've missed. —*Stephen Thomas Erlewine*

Crooked Rain, Crooked Rain / Feb. 1994 / Matador ✦✦✦✦
Although it's much calmer than the critically acclaimed *Slanted & Enchanted*, *Crooked Rain, Crooked Rain* shares the same spirit of the band's debut—it's a messy, impossibly catchy catalog of pop music and culture. On their second full-length album, Pavement have abandoned much of the lo-fi squalor of their earlier work, opting for a laidback, subdued sound that borders on country-rock and jazz-rock at times, and pure pop and rock 'n' roll at others. In other words, it's more accessible than *Slanted & Enchanted* but just as distinctive and original. Ultimately, *Crooked Rain, Crooked Rain* revamps rock history and reinvents it for the slacker generation. —*Stephen Thomas Erlewine*

Wowee Zowee / Apr. 1995 / Matador ✦✦✦✦
With its vast array of musical styles, *Wowee Zowee* isn't as accessible as *Crooked Rain, Crooked Rain* or as immediate as the bracing, noisy pop of *Slanted & Enchanted*. Pavement never abandon their warped pop aesthetic, they simply expand it, incorporating elements of folk-rock, English music hall, soul, jazz, and country, as well as adding asides to such contemporaries as Suede ("We Dance"), Ween ("Brinx Job"), and Stereolab ("Half a Canyon"). Alternating between majestic epics like "Grounded" and ragged narratives like "Rattled by the Rush" and "Father to a Sister of Thought" to song fragments like "Brinx Job" and the punkish "Serpentine Pad," the record might seem disjointed at first. After repeated listens, the songs play off each other, creating a dense collage of '90s rock 'n' roll that recasts the past and present into one rich, kaleidoscopic, and blissfully cryptic world view. —*Stephen Thomas Erlewine*

Brighten the Corners / Feb. 11, 1997 / Capitol ✦✦✦✦
There's a difference between accessibility and focus, which Pavement illustrate with their fourth album, *Brighten the Corners*. Arriving on the heels of the glorious mess of *Wowee Zowee*, the cohesive sound and laidback sarcasm of *Brighten the Corners* can give the record the illusion of being accessible or, at the very least, a retreat toward the songcraft of *Crooked Rain, Crooked Rain*. And the record is calm, with none of the full-out blasts of noise that marked all of their previous releases. It would be easy to dismiss the absence of noise as mere maturity or as a move toward more accessible songcraft, but neither statement is entirely true. *Brighten the Corners* is mature but wise-assed, melodic but complex—it's a record that reveals its gifts gradually, giving you enough information the first time to make you want to come back for more. At first, the dissonant sing-song verse of "Stereo" seems awkward, but it's all pulled into perspective with the gleeful, addictive outburst of the chorus, and that is a microcosm of the album's appeal. The first time around, the winding melody of "Shady Lane," the psycho jangle-pop of "Date with Ikea," the epic grace of "Type Slowly," and the speedy rush of "Embassy Row" make an impression, but repeated listens reveal sonic and lyrical details that make them indelible. Similarly, Malkmus' hip-hop inflections on "Blue Hawaiian" and the quiet beauty of "Transport is Arranged" unfold over time. While the preponderance of slow songs and laidback production make the album more focused than *Wowee Zowee*, it doesn't have the rich diversity of its predecessor—"Type Slowly" comes closest to the grand, melancholic beauty of "Grounded"—but it remains a thoroughly compelling listen. —*Stephen Thomas Erlewine*

Freda Payne

b. Sep. 19, 1945, Detroit, MI
Vocals / Soul
A Detroit soul/jazz/pop vocalist. Multitalented and beautiful, Payne crashed the soul and pop playlists in 1970 with a series of powerful sides for Holland-Dozier-Holland's Invictus imprint. Payne's early musical experience was quite varied, and she debuted on the jazz-oriented Impulse! label in 1965. Her 1970 blockbuster, "Band of Gold," made Payne a pop star with its strident message and insistent bassline, and she encored with "Deeper & Deeper." The controversial antiwar anthem "Bring the Boys Home" proved her biggest R&B seller the next year. Payne hosted a TV gabfest during the '80s. —*Bill Dahl*

● **Greatest Hits** / Jul. 1, 1991 / Fantasy ✦✦✦✦
Payne, an old childhood friend of Holland and Dozier, had already worked with Pearl Bailey, Duke Ellington, and Quincy Jones when she signed to Hot Wax/Invictus. Her biggest claim to fame was the No. 3 hit "Band of Gold," which eventually sold more than five million copies. Interestingly, Payne was reluctant to do the song. She garnered some moderate successes with the follow-up singles, "Deeper and Deeper" and "Cherish What Is Dear to You," but her heartfelt plea to end the Vietnam War, "Bring the Boys Home," hit a nerve with the public and became a No. 12 hit. —*Rick Clark*

Pearl Jam

f. 1990, Seattle, WA
Hard Rock, Alternative Pop-Rock, Grunge
Pearl Jam rose from the ashes of Mother Love Bone to become the most popular American rock 'n' roll band of the '90s. After vocalist Andrew Wood overdosed on heroin, guitarist Stone Gossard and bassist Jeff Ament assembled a new band, bringing in Mike McCready on lead guitar, Dave Krusen on drums, and vocalist Eddie Vedder. Naming themselves Pearl Jam, the band recorded their debut album, *Ten*, in the beginning of 1991. *Ten* didn't begin selling in significant numbers until early 1992, after Nirvana made mainstream rock radio receptive to alternative rock acts. Soon, Pearl Jam outsold Nirvana, which wasn't surprising. Pearl Jam fused the riff-heavy stadium rock of the '70s with the grit and anger of '80s post-punk, without ever neglecting hooks and choruses; "Jeremy," "Evenflow," and "Alive" fit perfectly into album rock radio stations that were looking for new blood.

Krusen left the band shortly after the release of *Ten;* he was replaced by Dave Abbruzzese. Pearl Jam's audience continued to grow during 1992, thanks to a series of radio and MTV hits, as well as a successful appearance on the second Lollapalooza tour. Despite their status as rock 'n' roll superstars, the band refused to succumb to the accepted conventions of the music industry. The group refused to release any videos or singles from their second album, 1993's *Vs.* Nevertheless, it was another multi-platinum success, debuting at No. 1 and selling nearly a million copies in its first week of release. On their spring 1994 American tour, the band decided not to play the conventional stadiums, choosing to play smaller arenas, including several shows on college campuses.

Pearl Jam cancelled their 1994 summer tour, claiming they could not keep ticket prices below $20 because Ticketmaster was pressuring promoters to charge a higher price. The band took Ticketmaster to the judicial department for unfair business practices. While the band fought Ticketmaster, they recorded a new album in the spring and summer of 1994. After the record was completed, the group fired Dave Abbruzzese, replacing him with former Red Hot Chili Peppers and Eleven drummer Jack Irons.

Vitalogy, the band's third album, appeared at the end of 1994. For the first two weeks, the album was only available as a limited vinyl-only release, but the record charted in the Top 60. Once *Vitalogy* was available on CD and cassette, the album shot to the top of the charts and quickly became multi-platinum. Pearl Jam continued to battle Ticketmaster in 1995, but the Justice Department eventually ruled in favor of the ticket agency. In early 1995, the band recorded an album with Neil Young. Vedder toured with his experimental side project, Hovercraft, in the spring of 1994, while Stone Gossard founded an independent record company. Mad Season, Mike McCready's side project with Layne Staley of Alice in Chains, released their first album, *Above*, in the spring of 1995. Composed entirely of Neil Young songs, *Mirror Ball* appeared in the summer under Young's name; although the individual members of the band were credited, the name Pearl Jam did not appear on the cover due to legal complications. Pearl Jam released a single culled from the sessions, "Mirror Ball," in the fall of 1995.

In late summer of 1996, Pearl Jam released their fourth album, *No Code*. —*Stephen Thomas Erlewine*

★ **Ten** / 1992 / Epic Associated ✦✦✦✦✦
The first Seattle band to hit the big time after Nirvana, Pearl Jam was not anyone's pick to be successful. Yet, Pearl Jam's brand of hard rock made them more accessible than any other Seattle band, including Nirvana. Pearl Jam's music is not as confused as Mudhoney, as melodic as Nirvana, as menacing as Alice in Chains, or as bloated as Soundgarden. *Ten* is remarkably clear-headed and clean, and very politically correct—a perfect soundtrack for the 1990s. The muscular, melodic rock of "Jeremy," "Alive," and "Evenflow" brought Pearl Jam crossover success, helping *Ten* climb into the Top Ten and sell over nine million copies. —*Stephen Thomas Erlewine*

Vs. / Oct. 12, 1993 / Epic Associated ✦✦✦
On the first listen, it appears that Pearl Jam's second album has no songs as instantly stunning as the best songs on *Ten*, but after a couple of plays, *Vs.* reveals its strengths. Instead of copying *Ten's* signature, clear, dark, hard rock, *Vs.* is rawer and more open, with a number of different textures. From the pulverizing assault of "Go," "Animal," and "Leash" to

the folkier, more reflective "Daughter," "Elderly Woman Behind the Counter in a Small Town," and "Indifference," Pearl Jam proves that their initial success was no fluke. Occasionally, the band falls into treacherous politically correct waters (the silly "Glorified G" and the meandering "W.M.A."), but for most of the album, Pearl Jam locks hold, and the best results are riveting. —*Stephen Thomas Erlewine*

Vitalogy / Dec. 1994 / Epic Associated ✦✦✦✦
Thanks to its stripped-down, lean production, *Vitalogy* stands as Pearl Jam's most original and uncompromising album. While it isn't a concept album, *Vitalogy* sounds like one. Death and despair shroud the album, rendering even the explosive celebration of vinyl "Spin the Black Circle" somewhat muted. But that black cloud works to Pearl Jam's advantage, injecting a nervous tension to brittle rockers like "Last Exit" and "Not For You" and especially to introspective ballads like "Corduroy" and "Better Man." In between the straight rock numbers and the searching slow songs, Pearl Jam contributes their strangest music—the mantra-funk of "Aye Davanita," the sub-Tom Waits accordion romp of "Bugs," and the chilling sonic collage "Hey Foxymophandlemama, That's Me." Pearl Jam are at their best when they're fighting, whether it's Ticketmaster, fame, or their own personal demons. —*Stephen Thomas Erlewine*

No Code / Aug. 27, 1996 / Epic/Sony ✦✦✦✦
A strange phenomenon with anthemic hard-rock bands is that when they begin to mature and branch out into new musical genres, they nearly always choose to embrace both the music and spirituality of the East and India, and Pearl Jam is no exception. Throughout *No Code*, Eddie Vedder expounds on his moral and spiritual dilemmas: where on previous albums his rage was virtually all consuming, it is clear on *No Code* that he has embraced an unspecified religion as a way to ease his troubles. Fortunately, that has coincided with an expansion of the group's musical palette. From the subtle, winding opener "Sometimes" and the near prayer of the single "Who You Are," the band reaches into new territory, working with droning, mantra-like riffs and vocals, layered exotic percussion, and a newfound subtlety. Of course, they haven't left behind hard rock, but, like any Pearl Jam record, the heart of *No Code* doesn't lie in the harder songs, it lies in the slower numbers and the ballads, which give Vedder the best platform for his soul-searching: "Present Tense," "Off He Goes," "In My Tree," and "Around the Bend" equal the group's earlier masterpieces. While a bit too incoherent, *No Code* is Pearl Jam's richest and most rewarding album, as well as its most human. They might be maturing in a fairly conventional method, but they still find new ways to state old truths. —*Stephen Thomas Erlewine*

Ann Peebles

b. Apr. 27, 1947, St. Louis, MO
Vocals / Soul
Ann Peebles was the queen of Willie Mitchell's Memphis-based Hi Records roster during the '70s, when Al Green was its undisputed king. Sung in a voice as bittersweet as it is riveting, her always-dramatic recordings include one undisputed masterpiece, "I Can't Stand the Rain," cited as a favorite by John Lennon and most recently covered by Tina Turner. Other covers abound—Robert Palmer took "I'm Gonna Tear Your Playhouse Down," and Bette Midler claimed "Breakin' Up Somebody's Home." Backed by the brilliant Hi rhythm section and flawlessly produced by Mitchell, Peebles sang and wrote (often in partnership with husband Don Bryant) of the feminine perspective on the darker side of love—sometimes untrusting love, but love for better or worse. Her work represents, with elegance and grit, some of the best of Memphis soul.
After a long absence from recording, Ann Peebles returned to the wars with the CD *Full Time Love* in 1992 for Bullseye/Rounder. While it didn't get much exposure or recognition in urban circles, it was a wonderfully sung and well-produced attempt at giving Peebles some contemporary tweaking without losing her gritty qualities. —*Christine Ohlman and Ron Wynn*

Part Time Love / 1971 / Hi ✦✦✦✦
The title track is a masterpiece, and everything else on this dynamic early '70s soul session is a jewel. Ann Peebles may have been the most overlooked great soul singer, male or female, who emerged in the '70s. Hi couldn't strike crossover gold twice, and Al Green was becoming a superstar. But Peebles deserved a better fate than obscurity, as this collection of soul wailers and weepers proves. —*Ron Wynn*

Straight from the Heart / 1972 / Hi ✦✦✦✦

I Can't Stand the Rain / 1974 / Hi ✦✦✦
The title song was an instant classic, and its lyrics are among the most moving and gripping in soul annals. This was Ann Peebles' finest album for Hi Records, and it should have been a massive success. Instead, while it's celebrated in Europe and now considered an anthem, it floundered and barely scraped the pop charts, although the single was her biggest R&B hit. —*Ron Wynn*

If This Is Heaven / 1978 / Hi ✦✦✦✦
Another exceptional album by Ann Peebles, who was cutting remarkable records for Hi in Memphis that no one noticed except for deep soul junkies. Her voice was alternately anguished, angry, defiant, and resigned, while Willie Mitchell and the Hi Rhythm Section provided minimal, yet spectacular backing. Peebles seldom toured, preferring to stay in Memphis around her family. But she had a voice only surpassed among female soul vocalists by Aretha Franklin and equalled by Carla Thomas. —*Ron Wynn*

Handwriting Is on the Wall / 1979 / Hi ✦✦✦
Some fabulous down-home, earthy soul from Ann Peebles, a Southern treasure. Peebles was the finest female singer to pass through the Hi Records operation, and Willie Mitchell achieved with her the same kind of wonderful records he made with Al Green, although they didn't get identical commercial success. Any and all of the albums Ann Peebles did with Hi are classics; sadly, most of them haven't been reissued. —*Ron Wynn*

● **The Best of the Hi Records Years** / Jul. 23, 1996 / Capitol ✦✦✦✦
The Best of the Hi Records Years collects all the highlights from Ann Peebles' creative and commercial heyday, featuring the majority of her hits for the label, including "I Can't Stand the Rain" and "Part Time Love," as well as several terrific lesser-known singles and album tracks. —*Stephen Thomas Erlewine*

Teddy Pendergrass

b. Mar. 26, 1950, Philadelphia, PA
Drums, Vocals / Soul, Urban, Club/Dance, Quiet Storm
In 1970, Pendergrass joined Harold Melvin and the Blue Notes as their drummer and lead vocalist; he sang on all of the group's Top 40 hits. Pendergrass left the group in 1976 and scored eight Hot 100 hits before he suffered an auto accident that left him partially paralyzed. He made a comeback two years later with *Heaven Only Knows*, which did not fare all that well commercially despite "Hold Me," a Top 50 duet with a young Whitney Houston. Subsequent albums also did not sell particularly well, although Pendergrass continued through 1993's *Believe in Love* and 1997's *You and I*. —*Stephen Thomas Erlewine*

Teddy Pendergrass / 1977 / Philadelphia International ✦✦✦✦
The skeptics had their suspicions allayed quickly when Teddy Pendergrass' debut album as a solo artist cracked the Top 40. Its lead single, "I Don't Love You Anymore," was among his best uptempo tunes, and the follow-up ballad "The Whole Town's Laughing at Me" ended any speculation that he was returning to Harold Melvin & the Blue Notes. While many thought the album would launch him to consistent R&B success, almost no one thought he would be R&B's biggest male star in a couple of years. —*Ron Wynn*

Life Is a Song Worth Singing / 1978 / Philadelphia International ✦✦✦✦
This was the album that convinced anyone who had doubts about the wisdom of Pendergrass leaving Harold Melvin and the Blue Notes that he had made a good decision. Although he only got one R&B hit from the album, there were enough strong ballads and uptempo cuts to show that Pendergrass had the sound, personality, and style to cut it on his own. He would shortly become R&B's greatest male attraction, but in the interim, Philadelphia International was laying the ground work. —*Ron Wynn*

Teddy Live / 1979 / Philadelphia International ✦✦
Until his tragic auto accident, Teddy Pendergrass was the number one male attraction on the R&B and urban contemporary circuit. His "For Women Only" concerts make Luther Vandross shows seem tame in comparison. He was a certified sex symbol and matinee idol. This album, recorded when he was at his peak in both popularity and appeal, shows why he was so beloved. His voice had a swagger and come-on quality, but he also had good range, knew how to project, and never rushed or hurried through a ballad. —*Ron Wynn*

Teddy / 1979 / Philadelphia International ✦✦✦
Teddy Pendergrass scored his greatest hit album with his third solo release, cementing his position at the end of the '70s as the reigning matinee idol and romantic balladeer among male R&B vocalists. This album cracked the pop Top Ten, dominated the R&B charts, and ruled the airwaves through much of 1979. While the overt sexual orientation of a song like "Turn Off the Lights" blinded some to the fact that Pendergrass' animated vocal was as soulful as you'd ever hear outside the gospel/blues/country axis of the South, this album confirmed that Pendergrass had found his niche and would be a dominant singer into the '80s. —*Ron Wynn*

It's Time for Love / 1981 / Philadelphia International ✦✦✦
Teddy Pendergrass showed no signs of slowing down in the early '80s. This was another R&B smash and crossover hit, again putting him in the Top 20. He got two good R&B singles, remained a popular concert attraction, and demonstrated good rapport with Stephanie Mills on sev-

eral duets. They teamed so well together that Pendergrass eventually appeared on stage with her during a tour of England. —*Ron Wynn*

This One's for You / 1982 / Philadelphia International ✦✦
In the immediate period after Teddy Pendergrass' tragic, near-fatal car accident, many wondered what would happen to his career. Philadelphia International rushed out a pair of albums containing unissued tracks that hadn't made the cut from past albums. This was the first one, released in the summer of 1982. It actually managed to have two singles crack the R&B Top 40, although neither moved very far beyond that. It was evident on several tracks why they hadn't been issued; the ballads weren't as powerful or sensual, and the uptempo numbers lacked style and hooks. —*Ron Wynn*

Heaven Only Knows / 1983 / Philadelphia International ✦✦
With Teddy Pendergrass undergoing tortuous rehabilitation from his near-fatal car crash, Philadelphia International was faced with the loss of its single greatest star. The company didn't sit back and mourn; they rushed out a pair of albums containing unissued tracks in both 1982 and 1983. This was the second release, and it had a few nice cuts, although it was evident why much of it hadn't been released in the first place. —*Ron Wynn*

Love Language / 1984 / Asylum ✦✦✦
Teddy Pendergrass delighted both R&B and music fans in general when he debuted on a new label with this album in 1984. It was his first album of fresh songs in two years, and Elektra put some muscle behind it. It also helped that he had a good duet with Whitney Houston, a song included in the film *D.A.R.Y.L.*, and generally better material than Philadelphia International had trotted out on the two albums of unissued vault tracks released in the interim. The album made it into the pop Top 40 and was a triumph of the spirit. —*Ron Wynn*

Workin' It Back / 1985 / Asylum ✦✦✦
A most appropriate title, as Pendergrass was making his comeback following the tragic car accident. The album took a long time to make an impact, but finally wound up a modest success. He wasn't able to generate much response to any single, but the fact that he continued his comeback was welcome news, owing to speculation that he was going to retire due to mixed response to his earlier release. —*Ron Wynn*

● **Greatest Hits** / 1987 / Philadelphia International ✦✦✦✦
This collection covers Pendergrass' run of big hits from the Philadelphia International era, including "I Don't Love You Anymore," "Close the Door" and "Turn Off the Lights." —*Ron Wynn*

Joy / 1988 / Elektra ✦✦✦
Teddy Pendergrass finally made it back to the top in 1988, when the title track from this album spent two weeks at the head of the R&B list. The song even got mild pop attention, and the album was the first since his accident to really reflect the new Pendergrass sound. He sang in a slower, somber yet appealing way quite different from the swaggering, openly sexual, macho posturing of the late '70s and early '80s. This was a weary but not beaten Pendergrass, whose manner and delivery underscored the resilient theme in *Joy*'s lyrics. —*Ron Wynn*

Truly Blessed / Mar. 5, 1991 / Elektra ✦✦✦
Teddy Pendergrass' return to recording and performing after the tragic accident that resulted in permanent paralysis was among the greatest stories of the 1980s. Pendergrass had to learn to sing all over again, with restraint, sensitivity, and control now his keys rather than volume and presence. This 1991 album wasn't quite as moving as 1988's *Joy*, but it still included several poignant numbers, especially the title track, which addressed his survival, neither downplaying the problems nor overstating his genuine happiness about still being alive. —*Ron Wynn*

You & I / Apr. 15, 1997 / Surefire ✦✦✦

The Penguins

f. 1954, Los Angeles, CA, db. 1959
Doo Wop
Best known for their hit single "Earth Angel," the doo wop quartet the Penguins were never able to replicate the success of their only Top 40 hit, but the song became a rock 'n' roll classic. The Penguins formed in 1954, when the members—Cleveland Duncan (lead vocal), Curtis Williams (tenor vocal), Dexter Tisby (baritone vocal), and Bruce Tate (tenor vocal)—were all attending Fremont High School in Los Angeles.

Although he wasn't the lead singer, Curtis Williams was the leader of the group. He learned "Earth Angel" from vocalist Jesse Belvin—some sources claim that Williams wrote the song alone, others say he co-wrote the song with Belvin, while others claim Gaynel Hodge, a member of the doo wop group the Turks, wrote the song with the duo (in fact, Hodge won a lawsuit filed in 1956 that gave him a co-writing credit)—and had the Penguins sing the song.

Around 1954, the Penguins signed with the local Los Angeles independent label Dootone Records. The group's first single was going to be

the uptempo "Hey Senorita", and the ballad "Earth Angel" was going to be the B-side.

Upon the release of the single in the latter half of 1954, Los Angeles radio stations were receiving more requests for "Earth Angel" than "Hey Senorita" and the song soon became the record's A-side. By the beginning of 1955, the single had scaled the national charts, spending three weeks at the top of the R&B charts and peaking at No. 8 on the pop charts.

For the next few years, the Penguins continued to record singles for Dootone Records. Shortly after the success of "Earth Angel," Tate left the group and Randolph Jones became their baritone vocalist. Around 1956, the Penguins left Dootone Records and signed with Mercury Records. After cutting some sides for Mercury, the group moved to Atlantic Records, where they had their second and final hit, "Pledge of Love," which climbed to No. 15 on the R&B charts in the summer of 1957. That same year, the group released their only album, *The Cool, Cool, Penguins*.

By 1959, the group had returned to their hometown of Los Angeles; shortly after their relocation, they broke up. Over the next four decades, Cleveland Duncan led various incarnations of the Penguins through reunion tours and re-recordings of their hits. In 1963, Duncan, Tisby, and two new members recorded "Memories of El Monte," a song future Mothers of Invention members Frank Zappa and Ray Collins wrote specifically for the group; the single failed to make any impact. Duncan went back to leading new incarnations of the Penguins, while Tisby briefly joined the Coasters. —*Stephen Thomas Erlewine*

Earth Angel / 1990 / Ace ✦✦✦
A 21-track anthology from the Dootone label, it's a deeper look at the group's '50s sides and style, built around the title track that sold five million copies worldwide. (Import) —*Hank Davis*

● **Authentic Golden Hits** / 1993 / Juke Box Treasures ✦✦✦✦
At long last, a well-thought-out compilation that gathers up all of the group's best sides for Dootone Records, including the original versions of the classics "Earth Angel" and "Hey, Senorita" in their original, unedited form. —*Cub Koda*

Best of the Mercury Years / Jul. 1996 / Polygram ✦✦✦✦
The Best of the Mercury Years isn't all that is appears to be. Instead of presenting all of the Penguins' hit singles, it only presents the group's Mercury recordings, which means that neither of the two versions of "Earth Angel" on the disc are not the original hit single versions, and that the remainder of their classic Dootone sides are missing. What is here is good, but not essential for anyone but hardcore doo wop collectors. —*Stephen Thomas Erlewine*

Michael Penn

b. Aug. 1, 1958, New York, NY
Guitar, Vocals / Singer-Songwriter, Pop-Rock
Michael Penn was one of the best singer-songwriters to emerge in the late '80s, capable of melding Beatlesque pop melodies with wordplay that rivals Elvis Costello. *March*, in 1989, was critically acclaimed and had a surprise hit single with "No Myth." Although his second album, 1992's *Free-for-All*, didn't have a hit on the size of "No Myth," it displayed his folk roots alongside his pop sensibilities. —*Stephen Thomas Erlewine*

● **March** / Sep. 1989 / RCA ✦✦✦✦
A solid debut album, it includes the hit "No Myth." —*Kenneth M. Cassidy*

Free-for-All / Sep. 15, 1992 / RCA ✦✦✦
Free-for-All, Michael Penn's second album, isn't as immediately accessible as *March*, but its cryptic lyrics and twisting melodies will work their way into your memory if given some time. —*Stephen Thomas Erlewine*

Resigned / Jun. 3, 1997 / 57 Records/Epic ✦✦✦✦
Backing away from the introspective inclinations of *Free-for-All*, Michael Penn delivers a concise and thoroughly infectious guitar-pop album with *Resigned*. Like most of Penn's music, the album relies heavily on *Revolver*-era Beatles, but his melodies are uniformly tighter and catchier than before, and producer Brendan O'Brien gives the record a crisp, attractive sound. None of the tracks initially stand out like "No Myth" or "Long Way Down," yet each song is well constructed and filled with hooks, making *Resigned* a terrific third album from Penn. —*Stephen Thomas Erlewine*

Pentangle

f. 1968, London, England
Folk, British Folk
Were Pentangle a folk group, a folk-rock group, or something that resists classification? They could hardly be called a rock 'n' roll act; they didn't use electric instruments often, and they were built around two virtuoso guitarists, Bert Jansch and John Renbourn, who were already well-established on the folk circuit before the group formed. Yet their hunger for

eclectic experimentation fit into the milieu of late-'60s progressive-rock and psychedelia well, and much of their audience came from the rock and pop worlds, rather than the folk crowd. With Jacqui McShee on vocals and a rhythm section of Danny Thompson (bass) and Terry Cox (drums), the group mastered a breathtaking repertoire that encompassed traditional ballads, blues, jazz, pop, and reworkings of rock oldies, often blending different genres in the same piece. Their prodigious individual talents perhaps ensured a brief lifespan, but at their peak they melded their distinct and immense skills to egg each other on to heights they couldn't have achieved on their own, in the manner of great rock combos like the Beatles and Buffalo Springfield.

When Pentangle formed around late 1966 or early 1967 (accounts vary), Jansch and Renbourn had already recorded one album together, (*Bert and John*), and done some solo recordings as well. Jansch was more inclined toward blues and contemporary songwriting than Renbourn, who was stronger in traditional British folk music. Jacqui McShee, whose bell-clear, high singing set the standard (along with Sandy Denny) for female British folk-rock vocals, began rehearsing with the pair. After a false start with a forgotten rhythm section, Thompson and Cox—who had been working with Alexis Korner—were brought in to complete the quintet.

Pentangle's first three albums—*The Pentangle* (1968), the double LP *Sweet Child* (1968), and *Basket of Light* (1969)—are not only their best efforts, but arguably their only truly essential ones. With Shel Talmy acting as producer, the band rarely took a misstep in its mastery of diverse styles and material. Thompson and Cox gave even the traditional folk ballads a jazz swing and verve; the guitar interplay of Jansch (who was also a capable singer) and Renbourn was downright thrilling, each complementing and enhancing the other without showing off or getting in each other's way. McShee's beautiful vocals, though not as emotionally resonant as her close counterpart Sandy Denny, were an underappreciated component to the band's success with the pop audience.

And Pentangle *were* very popular for a time, at least in England, where *Basket of Light* made No. 5, and "Light Flight" was a small hit single. They introduced some electric guitars on their early-'70s albums, which generally suffered from weaker material and a less unified group effort. The original lineup broke up in 1973; Jansch and Renbourn (who had never really abandoned their solo careers) continued to record often as soloists and remained top attractions on the folk circuit. Thompson joined John Martyn for a while and has remained active as a session musician, in addition to recording some work of his own for the Hannibal label. The original group reunited for the reasonably accomplished *Open the Door* album in the early '80s, and other versions of the group recorded and toured throughout the '80s and '90s, usually featuring McShee and Jansch as the sole remaining original members. —*Richie Unterberger*

Sweet Child / 1968 / Reprise ✦✦✦
A double album, one composed of studio recordings, the other of a 1968 concert. No other Pentangle LP covered as much ground as this one, which included original material, Scottish folk songs, jazz, and blues, as well as instrumentals and numbers that spotlighted McShee, Jansch, and Thompson as soloists. "In Time" is a sparkling guitar duel between Jansch and Renbourn that ranks as one of the highlights in both of their careers. —*Richie Unterberger*

The Pentangle / 1968 / Reprise ✦✦✦
A thrilling debut, which saw five virtuosos creating a progressive folk album that added up to more than the sum of its parts. Divided between traditional and original material, highlights included their arrangement of "Bruton Town" and the seven-minute instrumental "Pentangling." —*Richie Unterberger*

Basket of Light / 1969 / Edsel ✦✦✦✦
Although *Sweet Child* is usually cited as the group's high-water mark, *Basket of Light* finds them at their most progressive and exciting. Highlights of this album—which actually reached the Top Five in the UK—include the buzzing jazz dynamics of "Light Flight," their moving rendition of the traditional folk song "Once I Had a Sweetheart," their reinvention of the girl-group smash "Sally Go Round the Roses," and "Springtime Promises," one of their finest original tunes. —*Richie Unterberger*

● **Essential, Vol. 1** / 1986 / Transatlantic ✦✦✦✦
● **Essential, Vol. 2** / 1986 / Transatlantic ✦✦✦✦

A Maid That's Deep in Love / 1987 / Shanachie ✦✦✦✦
Currently, only this nine-track compilation is available to remind listeners of this British traditional folk-rock quintet, which provided Fairport Convention's main competition in the late '60s and early '70s. Much of it is lovely, notably McShee's haunting singing and Jansch's finger-picking. But a more complete picture is provided by the two volumes of *Essential* Pentangle on Transatlantic in the UK, which may be found in US record racks. —*William Ruhlmann*

Live at the BBC / Nov. 1995 / Band of Joy ✦✦✦
Taken from sessions and concerts held in 1969, 1970, and 1972, these 14 tracks aren't necessary supplements to their official releases from the same period—the arrangements are pretty close to the studio takes. But big Pentangle fans might like to have this, capturing the group playing live at its peak, with many songs from the *Sweet Child* and *Basket of Light* albums, a couple offered in two versions. All songs are Pentangle originals; the five from 1972, unsurprisingly, aren't in the same league as ones of earlier vintage. The group plays well, and the sound is excellent; the renditions of "Light Flight" and "In Time" are highlights. —*Richie Unterberger*

Pere Ubu

f. Sept. 1975, Cleveland, OH
Alternative Pop-Rock, Post-Punk
Named for the French absurdist play by Alfred Jarry, Pere Ubu is one of the most important and long-lived bands of the punk/new wave era. The group was organized in Cleveland in September 1975 by David Thomas (vocals) and fellow rock journalist Peter Laughner (guitar, bass) for the purpose of recording the apocalyptic single "30 Seconds over Tokyo." By the spring of 1976, Pere Ubu had recorded a second single, "Final Solution," and traveled to New York, where they gained exposure. The band was then reorganized, minus Laughner, who died the following year. Mercury/PolyGram Records signed Pere Ubu and issued their debut album, *The Modern Dance*, on its short-lived Blank Records label in February 1978. The album's combination of uncompromising rock, featuring odd noises, and Thomas' high-pitched singing, earned the group critical hosannas and commercial indifference beyond a loyal cult, a situation that would continue for the rest of their existence. That existence has been fitful. Pere Ubu was dropped by PolyGram and signed by Chrysalis, which released *Dub Housing* (1978) and *New Picnic Time* (1979), after which the group split again. But they were back to release *The Art of Walking* in 1980 on Rough Trade. *Song of the Bailing Man* (1981) was the last album before another lengthy split in 1982. Pere Ubu re-formed in 1987 with a lineup of Thomas, original member Allen Ravenstine (synthesizer), original member Scott Krauss (drums), Tony Maimone (bass), who had first joined in 1976, and two new members, Jim Jones (guitar) and Chris Cutler (drums). The group then released a series of slightly more commercially accessible albums: *The Tenement Year* (1987), *Cloudland* (1989), and *Worlds in Collision* (1991), reverting to its more abrasive style on *Story of My Life* (1993) and *Ray Gun Suitcase* (1995). As of 1995, Pere Ubu's lineup consisted of Thomas, Jones, Michele Temple, Robert Wheeler, and Scott Benedict. In 1996, Pere Ubu released a five-disc box set retrospective, *Datapanik in the Year Zero*. —*William Ruhlmann*

The Modern Dance / 1978 / Blank ✦✦✦✦
Aggressive punk rock, punctuated by found sounds and noises and topped by Thomas' remarkably affecting, near-falsetto shriek. It's not easy listening, but it's powerful and daring and has lost none of its impact since release. —*William Ruhlmann*

Dub Housing / 1979 / Rough Trade ✦✦✦✦
Relying increasingly on Allen Ravenstine's fascinating keyboard textures, *Dub Housing* is a visionary masterpiece; more impressionistic than *The Modern Dance*, David Thomas' obsessive songs and extraterrestrial vocals push the group further out on the ledge—"Navvy" and "I, Will Wait" are like pop songs transmitted from another dimension, while "Thriller!" and "Codex" are waking nightmares. —*Jason Ankeny*

New Picnic Time / 1979 / Rough Trade ✦✦✦✦
The addition of Mayo Thompson propels Pere Ubu into new realms of dadaism on *New Picnic Time*, the group's brightest and most surreal outing yet; David Thomas' songs, so heavily steeped in his devout spiritual faith, are even more disturbing when set against the almost whimsical backdrops of tracks like "The Fabulous Sequel." —*Jason Ankeny*

Art of Walking / 1980 / Rough Trade ✦✦✦
An early-'80s recording with guitarist Mayo Thompson, this is a buoyant and groovy accompaniment to Thomas' surrealism. —*Myles Boisen*

390 Degrees of Simulated Stereo (Live) / 1981 / Rough Trade ✦✦
This odds-and-ends sampler of early band activities (concerts, singles, and other crazy tidbits) is for collectors only. —*Myles Boisen*

Song of the Bailing Man / 1982 / Rough Trade ✦✦✦
David Thomas becomes more obtuse as the band heads toward breakup again. —*Myles Boisen*

★ **Terminal Tower** / 1985 / Twin/Tone ✦✦✦✦✦
The songs on *Terminal Tower—An Archival Collection*, many of them taken from Pere Ubu's first singles, demonstrate what helped make them one of the most original and challenging bands of the American new wave of the '70s. Be warned that songs like "30 Seconds over Tokyo" and "Final Solution" will have a polarizing effect on the listener: either this on-the-edge rock is just what you've been looking for, or it isn't. —*William Ruhlmann*

The Tenement Year / 1988 / Enigma ✦✦✦✦
Since the re-formed version of Pere Ubu reins in (slightly) the group's more extreme tendencies, this album, which nevertheless presents David Thomas' unique vision and the band's somewhat off-kilter approach to rock more or less intact, may be the place for neophytes to get their feet wet with a highly unusual group. This one should give you the idea—then you're on your own. — *William Ruhlmann*

One Man Drives / 1989 / Rough Trade ✦✦
A second live compilation, *One Man Drives While the Other Man Screams*, is more unified than *360 Degrees . . .*, with lots of their best material. —*Myles Boisen*

Cloudland / May 1989 / Fontana ✦✦✦✦
David Thomas returns to his favorite boyhood themes, with his new pop band in tow. —*Myles Boisen*

Worlds in Collision / May 21, 1991 / Fontana ✦✦✦
Their latest shows a definite commercial aspiration. It's still good, but lacks personality. —*Myles Boisen*

Story of My Life / Apr. 6, 1993 / Imago ✦✦✦
Although it is the most pop-oriented record Pere Ubu ever cut, *Story of My Life* didn't make much of a dent even in alternative radio. Nevertheless, there are many fine pop tunes here, occasionally spiked with some of their trademark experimentalism, although the music isn't as challenging as it was years before. — *Stephen Thomas Erlewine*

Ray Gun Suitcase / Aug. 22, 1995 / Cooking Vinyl ✦✦✦
Returned to indie label status for their tenth studio album, Pere Ubu again made music in the style familiar from their earliest recordings—staccato rhythms and noisy guitars backing David Thomas' disjointed singing of repeated, obscure lyrics. Typical was "Vacuum in My Head," which had some of the ominous tone of "30 Seconds over Tokyo," and in which Thomas spoke-sang, "Vacuum cleaner in my head / It sucks up everything I know." The playing often had more delicacy and precision than early on, and Thomas varied his effects from mutters to shrieks. An acoustic guitar rendition of the Beach Boys' "Surfer Girl" was a distinct change of pace, even if its author, Brian Wilson, might not have recognized it in Thomas' performance. But *Ray Gun Suitcase* was an album for the cult of fans who delighted in the band's offbeat lyrical viewpoint and musical cacophony, which was just as well, since the more conventional orientation attempted in the late 1980s and early '90s did not pay off in an expanded following. — *William Ruhlmann*

Hearpen Singles / Oct. 17, 1995 / Tim/Kerr ✦✦✦✦
Or, "Everything You Ever Wanted to Know About Ubu (But Were Afraid to Ask)." A computer-interactive CD-plus release, *Folly of Youth* goes way beyond the usual bonus cuts, band member bios, and photos that round out such multimedia releases, opting instead to include financial and business-related material on the band, including their tax returns. Also featured are two short films, "Story of Ubu" and "Ray Gun Suitcase" (the name of the album from which the single "Folly of Youth" is drawn), as well as lyrics, a discography, and bits of animation. By the way, there's music here too: the title track, a long jam called "Ball n' Chain," and a pair of demos, "Memphis" and "Down by the River II." —*Jason Ankeny*

Datapanik in the Year Zero [box] / Aug. 27, 1996 / DGC ✦✦✦✦
Pere Ubu's troubles with record companies are legendary within certain underground rock circles. In perhaps the most bizarre turn of events, the group's collected works of 1978-1982—after being out of print for nearly a decade—were reissued by Geffen as a five-disc box set, *Datapanik in the Year Zero*. Named after the group's 1978 EP, the set is arranged chronologically and occasionally substitutes live versions for studio tracks, but that hardly matters—nearly every song the band recorded during the five-year time span is included. In addition to the official Pere Ubu material, the box includes a disc of rare singles from early incarnations of Ubu and other Cleveland-area punk rockers like Rocket from the Tombs, 15-60-75, and Mirrors, which were released on David Thomas' independent record label. With this much material, it's safe to say that the set is a definitive retrospective, and its worth is increased because most of this material hasn't been widely available on compact disc, so collectors won't feel like they've paid a lot of money for a handful of rarities. However, if you're simply interested in Pere Ubu, consider the set carefully before investing. Pere Ubu was indeed one of the most innovative and challenging bands of their era, which means that their music is an acquired taste. However, those willing to invest will find a wealth of inventive, hard-edged avant-rock 'n' roll. —*Stephen Thomas Erlewine*

Carl Perkins (Carl Lee Perkins)

b. Apr. 9, 1932, Tiptonville, TN
Guitar, Vocals / Rock 'n' Roll, Traditional Country, Rockabilly
While some ill-informed revisionist writers of rock history would like to dismiss Carl Perkins as a rockabilly artist who became a one-hit wonder at the dawn of rock 'n' roll's early years, a deeper look at his music and

career reveals much more. A quick look at his songwriting portfolio shows that he has composed "Daddy Sang Bass" for Johnny Cash, "I Was So Wrong" for Patsy Cline, and "Let Me Tell You About Love" for the Judds, big hits and classics all. His influence as the quintessential rockabilly artist has played a big part in the development of every generation of rocker to come down the pike since, from the Beatles' George Harrison to the Stray Cats' Brian Setzer to a myriad of others in the country field as well. His guitar style is the other twin peak—along with that of Elvis' lead man Scotty Moore—of rockabilly's instrumental center, so pervasive that modern day players automatically gravitate toward it when called upon to deliver the style, not even realizing that they're playing Carl Perkins licks, sometimes note for note. As a singer, his interpretation of country ballads is every bit as fine as his better known rockers. And within the framework of the best of his music is a strong sense of family and roots, all of which trace straight back to Perkins' humble beginnings.

He was born to sharecroppers Buck and Louise Perkins (misspelled on his birth certificate as 'Perkings') and was soon out in the fields picking cotton and living in a shack with his parents, older brother, Jay, and his younger brother, Clayton. Working alongside Blacks in the field every day, it's not at all surprising that when Perkins was gifted with a second hand guitar, he went to a local sharecropper for lessons, learning firsthand the boogie rhythm that he would later build a career on. By his teens, Perkins was playing electric guitar and had recruited his brothers, Jay on rhythm guitar and Clayton on string bass, to become his first band. The Perkins Brothers Band, featuring both Carl and Jay on lead vocals, quickly established themselves as the hottest band in the get hot or go home, cutthroat, Jackson, TN, honky tonk circuit. It was here that Perkins started composing his first songs with an eye toward the future. Watching the dance floor at all times for a reaction, Perkins kept reshaping these loosely structured songs until he had a completed composition, which would then be finally put to paper. Perkins was already sending demos to New York record companies, who kept rejecting him, sometimes explaining that this strange new hybrid of country with a Black rhythm fit no current commercial trend. But once Perkins heard Elvis on the radio, he not only knew what to call it, but knew that there was a record company person who finally understood it and was also willing to gamble in promoting it. That man was Sam Phillips and the record company was Sun Records, and that's exactly where Perkins headed in 1954 to get an audition.

It was here at his first Sun audition that the structure of the Perkins Brothers Band changed forever. Phillips didn't show the least bit of interest in Jay's Ernest Tubb-styled vocals, but flipped over Carl's singing and guitar playing. A scant four months later, he had issued the first Carl Perkins record, "Movie Magg" and "Turn Around," both sides written by the artist. By his second session, he had added W.S. Holland—a friend of Clayton's—to the band playing drums, a relatively new innovation in country music at the time. Phillips was still channeling Perkins in a strictly hillbilly vein, feeling that two artists doing the same type of music (in this case, Elvis and rockabilly) would cancel each other out. But after selling Elvis' contract to RCA Victor in December, Perkins was encouraged to finally let his rocking soul come up for air at his next Sun session. And rock he did with a double whammy blast that proved to be his ticket to the bigs. The chance overhearing of a conversation at a dance one night between two teenagers coupled with a song idea suggestion from label mate Johnny Cash, the inspired Perkins approached Phillips with a new song he had written called "Blue Suede Shoes." After cutting two sides that Phillips planned on releasing as a single by the Perkins Brothers Band, Perkins laid down three takes each of "Blue Suede Shoes" and another rocker, "Honey Don't." A month later, Phillips decides to shelve the two country sides and go with the rockers as Perkins' next single. Three months later, "Blue Suede Shoes," a tune that borrowed stylistically from pop, country, and R&B music, is sitting at the top of all charts, the first record to accomplish such a feat, becoming Sun's first million-seller in the bargain.

Ready to cash in on a national basis, Perkins and the boys headed up to New York for the first time to appear on the *Perry Como Show*. While en route their car rammed the back of a poultry truck, putting Carl and his brother Jay in the hospital with a cracked skull and broken neck, respectively. While in traction, Perkins saw Presley performing his song on the *Dorsey Brother Stage Show*, his moment of fame and recognition snatched away from him. Perkins shrugged his shoulders and went back to the road and the Sun studios, trying to pick up where he left off.

The follow-ups to "Shoes" were, in many ways, superior to his initial hit, but each succeeding Sun single met diminishing sales, and it wasn't until the British Invasion and the subsequent rockabilly revival of the early '70s that the general public got to truly savor classics like "Boppin' the Blues," "Matchbox," "Everybody's Trying to Be My Baby," "Your True Love," "Dixie Fried," "Put Your Cat Clothes On," and "All Mama's Children." While labelmates Johnny Cash and Jerry Lee Lewis (who played piano on "Matchbox") were scoring hit after hit, Perkins was becoming disillusioned with his fate, fueled by his increasing dependence on alcohol and the death of brother Jay to cancer. He kept plugging along, and when Johnny Cash left Sun to go to Columbia in 1958, Perkins followed him over. The royalty rate was better, and Perkins had no shortage of great songs to record, but Columbia's Nashville watch-the-clock production methods killed any of the spontaneity that was the charm of the Sun records. By the early '60s, after being dropped by Columbia and moving over to Decca with little success, Perkins was back playing the honky tonks and contemplating getting out of the business altogether. A call from a booking agent in 1964 offering a tour of England changed all of that. Temporarily swearing off the bottle, Perkins was greeted in Britain as a conquering hero, playing to sold out audiences and being particularly lauded by a young beat group on the top of the charts named the Beatles. George Harrison had cut his musical teeth on Perkins' Sun recordings (as had most British guitarists) and the Fab Four ended up recording more tunes by him than by any other artist except themselves. The British tour not only rejuvenated his outlook, but suddenly made him realize that he had gone—through no maneuvering of his own—from has-been to legend in a country he had never played in before. Upon his return to the States, he hooked up with old friend and former labelmate Johnny Cash and was a regular fixture of his road show for the next ten years, bringing his battle with alcohol to an end. The '80s dawned with Perkins going on his own with a new band consisting of his sons backing him. His election to the Rock & Roll Hall of Fame in the mid-'80s was no less than his due. While battles with throat cancer and other ailments have curtailed his work load in the '90s, Carl Perkins continues to write, record and perform, still grateful to be a part of the music business, while being totally secure that his place in the history books is assured. —*Cub Koda*

Up Through the Years, 1954-1957 / 1986 / Bear Family ♦♦♦♦
An import collection of Perkins' groundbreaking Sun singles, *Up Through the Years* offers eight more tracks than Rhino's *Original Sun Greatest Hits;* both discs are definitive collections. —*Stephen Thomas Erlewine*

★ **Original Sun Greatest Hits** / 1986 / Rhino ♦♦♦♦♦
Original Sun Greatest Hits is exactly what it says it is—16 tracks of Carl Perkins' best sides for Sun, including all of the hits ("Blue Suede Shoes," "Boppin' the Blues," "Your True Love") and all of his most legendary songs ("Honey, Don't," "Everybody's Trying to Be My Baby," "Movie Magg," "All Mam's Children," "Matchbox," "Dixie Fried," "Lend Me Your Comb," "Glad All Over"). It's the essential compilation, providing everything you need to know about Carl Perkins and offering no filler. —*Stephen Thomas Erlewine*

Honky Tonk Gal / Apr. 1989 / Rounder ♦♦♦
Quirky, obscure, and offbeat, this is a much deeper look into Perkins' Sun period, with emphasis on hillbilly roots. —*Hank Davis*

The Classic / Feb. 1990 / Bear Family ♦♦♦♦
Simply the most comprehensive collection imaginable, included are all of his essential Sun tracks and alternate takes on five discs. All the 1958-1962 CBS sides are here, plus his 1963-1964 Decca sessions. It is indispensable for the serious fan and completist. —*Hank Davis*

The Jive After Five: Best of Carl Perkins (1958-1978) / Sep. 1990 / Rhino ♦♦♦♦
His later CBS work, much of it is excellent. —*Hank Davis*

Restless: The Columbia Recordings / May 12, 1992 / Columbia ♦♦♦
A strong collection of Perkins' singles for Columbia, concentrating on the late '50s and early '60s; some of his finest songs, including "Pink Pedal Pushers" and "Jive After Five," are included here. —*Stephen Thomas Erlewine*

Country Boy's Dream: the Dollie Masters / Jun. 1994 / Bear Family ♦♦♦
Upon signing to Dollie records in 1966, Carl Perkins decided to concentrate on country music. The result was two minor country hits, "Country Boy's Dream" and "Shine, Shine, Shine," that marked the first time he was on the charts since the late '50s. Though the Dollie recordings weren't blockbusters, they were solid, straightahead country and paved the way for Perkins' major label deal with Columbia, as well as a slot in Johnny Cash's band. *Country Boy's Dream: The Dollie Masters* contains all of Perkins' recordings for Dollie, including a handful of unreleased and rare tracks. Fans of Perkins' harder-edged, rocking sound won't find much to like on the compilation, yet it demonstrates that he was equally adept at country. Nevertheless, even fans of Carl's country records will find *Country Boy's Dream* a little tedious, since many of the songs on the album are simply unremarkable. —*Stephen Thomas Erlewine*

Go Cat Go / Oct. 15, 1996 / Dinosaur ♦♦♦
This album is a curious mixture; it isn't really a Carl Perkins album per se as it is an all-star tribute album with some of the big name guests actually getting to interface with their hero. Both John Lennon and Jimi Hendrix appear via the grave and the tape vaults, contributing their own versions of "Blue Suede Shoes" to the proceedings. And Carl works in

tandem with live guests Tom Petty, Johnny Cash, Bono, Ringo Starr, George Harrison, Paul McCartney, John Fogerty, and Paul Simon in right fine fashion. But the bottom line is that the real star of the show is Perkins himself, just playing and singing in a most masterful and rockin' way. If stars of this magnitude are tipping their hat, Carl shows on this waxing that their idolatry is well placed. —*Cub Koda*

The Persuaders

f. 1969, New York, NY
Soul, Quiet Storm
This group made a pair of marvelous heartache ballads in 1971 but have the unfortunate legacy of having their finest cuts turned into pop hits via covers. Lead singer Douglas Scott, whose nickname appropriately was "Smokey," Willie Holland, James Barnes, and Charles Stodghill formed in New York in 1969. They signed with Atlantic in the early '70s and had their lone R&B chart topper in 1971, the shattering classic "Thin Line Between Love & Hate." It was also their only gold single. The follow-up was nearly as strong; "Love's Gonna Pack Up (And Walk Out)" reached No. 8 on the R&B charts, but had no crossover appeal. They continued on Win & Lose until 1973; they then moved to Atco, where "Some Guys Have All the Luck" was a No. 7 R&B single in 1973. It was their final hit, though they kept recording until the late '70s, doing their last session for Calla. Besides the Pretenders redoing "Thin Line Between Love & Hate," Rod Stewart had a Top Ten pop hit with his version of "Some Guys Have All the Luck" in 1984. —*Ron Wynn*

● **Thin Line Between Love & Hate** / 1974 / Collectables ♦♦♦♦
A gritty soul unit, adept at tragic encounter tunes. The title song is a soul anthem. —*Ron Wynn*

Pet Shop Boys

f. Aug. 1981, London, England
Dance-Pop, House, Disco, Pop-Rock, Club-Dance, Alternative Dance
With their detached, intellectual, and often very funny lyrics and relentlessly hip, melodic, synth-driven disco, Neil Tennant and Chris Lowe were one of the most commercially successful groups in America and England in the late '80s, scoring a consistent string of hit singles through 1991. Through four albums and several singles, the Pet Shop Boys explored every dance trend from disco to house, creating beautifully lush, haunting soundscapes with their synthesizers and drum machines. By the time *Very* was released in 1993, the popular audience had shifted away from dance-pop and they had difficulty receiving mainstream airplay and MTV wouldn't air their videos. However, the duo continued to sell respectably while they continued to expand and redefine their music on releases like 1995's *Alternative* and 1996's *Bilingual*. —*Stephen Thomas Erlewine*

Please / 1986 / EMI America ♦♦♦
A collection of immaculately crafted and seamlessly produced synthesized dance-pop, the Pet Shop Boys' debut album, *Please*, sketches out the basic elements of the duo's sound. At first listen, most of the songs come off as mere excuses for the dance floor, driven by cold, melodic keyboard riffs and pulsing drum machines. However, the songcraft that the beats support is surprisingly strong, featuring catchy melodies that appear slight because of Neil Tennant's thin voice. Tennant's lyrics were still in their formative stages, with half of the record failing to transcend the formulaic constraints of dance-pop. The songs that do break free—the crass "Opportunities (Let's Make Lots of Money)," the lulling "Suburbia," and the hypnotic "West End Girls"—are not only classic dance singles, they're classic pop singles. —*Stephen Thomas Erlewine*

Disco / Oct. 1986 / EMI America ♦♦
Released at the height of dance-pop in 1986, the Pet Shop Boys' remix album *Disco* defiantly asserted the roots of the current trend with the title. And with its long remixes, *Disco* is designed to be pumped at a dance floor. As casual listening, it gets a bit tedious, but even at these extended lengths, the melodic craft of the Pet Shop Boys' material shines through. —*Stephen Thomas Erlewine*

Actually / Jun. 1987 / EMI America ♦♦♦♦
With their second album, *Actually*, the Pet Shop Boys perfected their melodic, detatched dance-pop. Where most of *Please* was dominated by the beats, the rhythms on *Actually* are part of a series of intricate arrangements that create a glamorous but disposable backdrop for Neil Tennant's tales of isolation, boredom, money, and loneliness. Not only are the arrangements more accomplished, but the songs themselves are more striking, incorporating a strong sense of melody, as evidenced by "What Have I Done to Deserve This?," a duet with Dusty Springfield. Tennant's lyrics are clever and direct, chronicling the lives and times of urban, lonely, and bored yuppies of the late '80s. And the fact that dance-pop is considered a disposable medium by most mainstream critics and listeners only increases the reserved emotional undercurrent of *Actually,* as well as its irony. —*Stephen Thomas Erlewine*

Introspective / Apr. 1988 / EMI America ✦✦✦
Featuring a mere six tracks, most of them well over six minutes in length, *Introspective* was a move back to the clubs for the Pet Shop Boys. Over the course of the album, they incorporated various dance techniques that were currently in vogue, including Latin rhythms and house textures. The title isn't entirely an arch joke, however. Like *Actually*, *Introspective* was an exploration of distant, disaffected yuppies, which naturally resulted in a good deal of self-analysis. Melodically, the essential song structures were as strong and multi-layered as the previous album, yet that was hard to hear beneath the varying rhythmic textures that composed the bulk of each track. Nevertheless, the mixes are more compelling than the remixes on *Disco*, and the songs include several of their best numbers, including "Left to My Own Devices" and "Domino Dancing," as well as the reconstruction of "Always on My Mind" and a cover of Blaze's club classic, "It's Alright." — *Stephen Thomas Erlewine*

Behavior / Oct. 1990 / EMI America ✦✦✦✦
Behavior was a retreat from the deep dance textures of *Introspective*, as it picked up on the carefully constructed pop of *Actually*. In fact, *Behavior* functions as the Pet Shop Boys' bid for mainstream credibility, as much of the album relies more on pop-craft than rhythmic variations. Although it's a subtle maneuver, it would have been rather disasterous if the results weren't so captivating. Tennant takes this approach seriously, singing the lyrics instead of speaking them. That doesn't necessarily give the album added emotional baggage—all of the distance and detachment in the duo's music is not a hinderance, it's part of the concept—but it does result in an ambitious and breathtaking pop album, which manages to include everything from the spiteful "How Can You Expect to Be Taken Seriously?" to the wistful "Being Boring." — *Stephen Thomas Erlewine*

★ **Discography: The Complete Singles Collection** / Nov. 5, 1991 / EMI America ✦✦✦✦
Most of the Pet Shop Boys' albums are well crafted and thoroughly intriguing in their own right, but dance-pop is a medium that is driven by hit singles. *Discography* collects all the duo's numerous hit singles, including a handful of non-album tracks, in their original seven-inch single mixes, which occasionally vary from the album versions, particularly in the case of the *Introspective* material. Presented chronologically, the singles not only demonstrate the band's increasing musical sophistication, they illustrate what fine songwriters Tennant and Lowe are. These 19 songs form one of the most consistent and innovative bodies of work of its era. Some of the production techniques have dated slightly, but the music has remained impressive. — *Stephen Thomas Erlewine*

Very / Oct. 5, 1993 / ERG ✦✦✦✦
Because they work in a field that isn't usually taken seriously, the Pet Shop Boys are often ignored in the rock world. But make no mistake—they are one of the most talented pop outfits working today, witty and melodic with a fine sense of flair. *Very* is one of their very best records, expertly weaving between the tongue-in-cheek humor of "I Wouldn't Normally Do This Kind of Thing," the quietly shocking "Can You Forgive Her?" and the bizarrely moving cover of the Village People's "Go West." Alternately happy and melancholy, *Very* is the Pet Shop Boys at their finest. — *Stephen Thomas Erlewine*

Disco 2 / Sep. 20, 1994 / Capitol ✦✦
The Pet Shop Boys' second remix record is more long-winded than their first, suffering not only from too many pointless remixes but from a surprising lack of cohesiveness, making it for devoted fans only. — *Stephen Thomas Erlewine*

Alternative / Aug. 29, 1995 / EMI ✦✦✦✦
Alternative is a double-disc set of the Pet Shop Boys' B-sides. Far from being a superfluous collection, the album contains a wealth of prime material, including several tracks that surpass those the duo put on their albums. Consequently, the set is worthwhile not only for hardcore fans, but for listeners with a passing interest in the group. — *Stephen Thomas Erlewine*

Bilingual / Sep. 1996 / Atlantic ✦✦✦
As a title, *Bilingual* is a double-edged sword. Disregard its sexual connotations and concentrate on its musical implications—*Bilingual* is a rich, diverse album that delves deeply into Latin rhythms. It's not a crass, simplistic fusion, where the polyphonic rhythms are simply grafted over synthesizers and a disco pulse. Instead, *Bilingual* is an enormously subtle album, with shifting rhythms and graceful, understated melodies. The music isn't the only thing subtle about the album—Neil Tennant's voice and lyrics are nuanced, suggesting more than they actually say. Furthermore, *Bilingual* consists of the most optimistic, happy set of songs the Pet Shop Boys have ever recorded. Whether it's the smooth disco of "Before" or the insistent rhythms of "Se a Vida e," *Bilingual* is filled with joyous, if subdued, sounds. If anything, it's further proof that even if the Pet Shop Boys aren't gracing the top of the charts as frequently as they did during the late '80s, they are crafting albums that are more adventurous and successful than they did when they were one of the top singles acts in pop music. — *Stephen Thomas Erlewine*

Peter & Gordon

f. 1963, London, England, db. 1968
British Invasion
In June 1964, Peter & Gordon became the very first British Invasion act after the Beatles to take the No. 1 spot on the American charts with "A World Without Love." That hit and their subsequent successes were due as much or more to their important connections as to their talent. Peter Asher was the older brother of Jane Asher, Paul McCartney's girlfriend for much of the 1960s. This no doubt gave Asher and Gordon Waller access to Lennon-McCartney compositions that were unrecorded by the Beatles, such as "A World Without Love" and three of their other biggest hits, "Nobody I Know," "I Don't Want to See You Again," and "Woman" (the last of which was written by McCartney under a pseudonym). But Peter & Gordon were significant talents in their own right, a sort of Everly Brothers-styled duo for the British Invasion that faintly prefigured the folk-rock of the mid-'60s. In fact, when Gene Clark first approached Jim McGuinn in 1964 about working together in a group that would eventually evolve into the Byrds, he suggested that they could form a Peter & Gordon-styled act.

Asher and Waller had been singing together since their days at Westminster School for Boys, a private school in London. "A World Without Love" was their biggest and best hit, one that sounded very much like the Beatles' more pop-oriented originals. Their other two 1964 hits, "Nobody I Know" and "I Don't Want to See You Again" were pleasant but less distinguished. Sounding like McCartney-dominated Beatle rejects (which, in fact, they were), the production employed a softer, more acoustic feel than the hits by the Beatles and other early British Invasion guitar bands. "I Don't Want to See You Again" used strings, as would several of the duo's subsequent hits, which became increasingly middle-of-the road in their pop orientation.

Some scattered folky B-sides showed that Asher and Waller may have been capable of developing into decent songwriters, but like many of the less talented British Invaders, their lack of songwriting acumen and ability to move with the times would eventually work against them. They did continue to hit the charts for a couple of years, with updates of the oldies "True Love Ways" (Buddy Holly) and "To Know You Is to Love You" (a variation of the Teddy Bears' "To Know Her Is to Love Her"). There was also a Top Ten cover of Del Shannon's "I Go to Pieces," and the brassy, McCartney-penned "Woman." The overtly cute and British novelty "Lady Godiva," though, became their last big hit in late 1966.

After Peter & Gordon broke up in 1968, Asher became an enormously successful producer, first as the director of A&R at the Beatles' Apple Records (where he worked on James Taylor's first album). Relocating to Los Angeles, in the 1970s he was one of the principal architects of mellow Californian rock, producing Taylor and Linda Ronstadt. — *Richie Unterberger*

Best of Peter & Gordon / Aug. 27, 1991 / Rhino ✦✦✦✦
This duo synthesized Beatles and Everly Brothers harmonies into a wonderfully seamless string of mid-'60s British Invasion lite-pop hits. The popular songs are all contained here, with great sound and well-rendered liner notes. — *Rick Clark*

● **Ep Collection** / Sep. 5, 1995 / See For Miles ✦✦✦✦
Although this 29-track compilation is ostensibly a roundup of songs that appeared on foreign EPs, it actually serves as a greatest-hits collection of sorts. The sequencing is unfortunately haphazard, jumping all over the place chronologically, but it does include all ten of their US Top 40 singles. In fact, it's a substantially better deal than the domestic best-of that appeared on Rhino a few years before this; it has more songs, presents some pretty good B-sides and non-45 tracks, and puts a greater weight on their original compositions. The inclusion of four French songs from a rare EP will please collectors, although for general listeners' purposes it would have been wiser to feature the English versions. — *Richie Unterberger*

Tom Petty

b. Oct. 20, 1953, Gainesville, FL
Rock 'n' Roll, Pop-Rock
Upon the release of their first album in the late '70s, Tom Petty & the Heartbreakers were shoehorned into the punk/new wave movement by some observers, who picked up on the tough, vibrant energy of the group's blend of Byrds riffs and Stonesy swagger. In a way, the categorization made sense. Compared to the heavy metal and art-rock that dominated mid-'70s guitar rock, the Heartbreakers' bracing return to roots was nearly as unexpected as the crashing chords of the Clash. As time progressed, it became clear that the band didn't break from tradition like their punk contemporaries. Instead, they celebrated it, culling the best parts of the British Invasion, American garage rock, and Dylanesque singer-songwriters to create a distinctively American

hybrid that recalled the past without being indebted to it. The Heartbreakers were a tight, muscular, and versatile backing band that provided the proper support for Petty's songs, which cataloged a series of middle-class losers and dreamers. While his slurred, nasal voice may have recalled Dylan and Roger McGuinn, Petty's songwriting was lean and direct, recalling the simple, unadorned style of Neil Young. Throughout their career, Petty & the Heartbreakers never departed from their signature rootsy sound, but they were able to expand it, bringing in psychedelic, Southern rock, and new wave influences; they were also some of the few traditionalist rock 'n' rollers who embraced music videos, filming some of the most inventive and popular videos in MTV history. His willingness to experiment with the boundaries of classic rock 'n' roll helped Petty sustain his popularity well into the '90s.

Born and raised in northern Florida, Tom Petty began playing music while he was still in high school. At the age of 17, he dropped out of school to join Mudcrutch, which also featured guitarist Mike Campbell and keyboardist Benmont Tench. By 1970, Mudcrutch had moved to Los Angeles with hopes of finding a record contract. The fledgling Shelter Records, founded by Leon Russel and Denny Cordell, offered the group a contract. However, Mudcrutch splintered apart shortly after relocating to L.A. Cordell was willing to record Petty as a solo act, but the singer's reception to the idea was tentative. Over the next few years, Petty drifted through bands, eventually hooking back up with Campbell and Tench in 1975. At the time, the duo were working with bassist Ron Blair and drummer Stan Lynch; soon, Petty became involved with the band, who were then named the Heartbreakers. Petty was still under contract to Shelter, and the group assumed his deal, releasing *Tom Petty & the Heartbreakers* in 1976.

Initially, the band's debut was ignored in the US, but when the group supported it in England with a tour opening for Nils Lofgren, the record began to take off. Within a few months, the band was headlining its own British tours and the album was in the UK Top 30. Prompted by the record's British success, Shelter pushed the album and the single "Breakdown" in the US, this time to success; "Breakdown" became a Top 40 hit and "American Girl" became an album-oriented radio staple. *You're Gonna Get It*, the Heartbreakers' second album, was released in 1978, and it became the group's first Amerian Top 40 record. Petty & the Heartbreakers were poised to break into the big time when they ran into severe record company problems. Shelter's parent company, ABC Records, was bought by MCA Records, and Petty attempted to renegotiate his contract with the label. MCA was unwilling to meet most of his demands, and halfway through 1979, he filed for bankruptcy. Soon afterward, he settled into an agreement with MCA, signing with their subsidiary Backstreet Records. Released late in 1979, *Damn the Torpedoes* was his first release on Backstreet.

Damn the Torpedoes was Petty's breakthrough release, earning uniformly excellent reviews, generating the Top Ten hit "Don't Do Me Like That" and the No. 15 "Refugee" and spending seven weeks at No. 2 on the US charts; it would eventually sell over two million copies. Though he was at a peak of popularity, Petty ran into record company trouble again when he and the Heartbreakers prepared to release *Hard Promises*, the 1981 follow-up to *Damn the Torpedoes*. MCA wanted to release the record at the list price of $9.98, which was a high price at the time. Petty refused to comply with their wishes, threatening to withhold the album from the label and organizing a fan protest, which forced the company to release the record at $8.98. *Hard Promises* became a Top Ten hit, going platinum and spawning the hit single "The Waiting." Later that year, Petty produced Del Shannon's comeback album *Drop Down and Get Me* and wrote "Stop Draggin' My Heart Around" as a duet for himself and Stevie Nicks. Featured on her album *Bella Donna*, which was recorded with the Heartbreakers' support, "Stop Draggin' My Heart Around" became a No. 3 hIt. Petty & the Heartbreakers returned late in 1982 with *Long After Dark*, which became their third Top Ten album in a row. Following its release, bassist Ron Blair left the band and was replaced by Howie Epstein, who previously played with John Hiatt.

Petty & the Heartbreakers spent nearly three years making *Southern Accents*, the follow-up to *Long After Dark*. Hiring Eurythmic Dave Stewart as a producer, the band attempted to branch out musically, reaching into new territories like soul, psychedelia, and new wave. However, the recording wasn't easy—at its worst, Petty punched a studio wall and broke his left hand, reportedly in frustration over the mixing. *Southern Accents* was finally released in the spring of 1985, preceded by the neo-psychedelic single "Don't Come Around Here No More," which featured a popular, pseudo-*Alice in Wonderland* video. *Southern Accents* was another hit record, peaking at No. 7 and going platinum. Following its release, Petty & the Heartbreakers spent 1986 on tour as Bob Dylan's backing band. Dylan contributed to the lead single, "Jammin' Me," from the Heartbreakers' next album *Let Me Up (I've Had Enough)*, which was released to mixed reviews in the spring of 1987. Just after the record's release, Petty's house and most of his belongings were destroyed by fire; he, his wife, and two daughters survived unscathed. During 1988, Petty became a member of the supergroup the Travelling

Wilburys, which also featured Dylan, George Harrison, Roy Orbison, and Jeff Lynne. The Wilburys released their first album at the end of 1988, and its sound became the blueprint for Petty's first solo effort, 1989's *Full Moon Fever*. Produced by Lynne and featuring the support of most of the Heartbreakers, *Full Moon Fever* became Petty's commercial pinnacle, reaching No. 3 on the US charts, going triple platinum, and generating the hit singles "I Won't Back Down," "Runnin' Down A Dream" and "Free Fallin'," which reached No. 7. In 1990, he contributed to the Travelling Wilburys second album, *Vol. 3*. Petty officially reunited with the Heartbreakers on *Into the Great Wide Open*, which was also produced by Jeff Lynne. Released in the spring of 1991, *Into the Great Wide Open* sustained the momentum of *Full Moon Fever*, earning strong reviews and going platinum.

Following the release of 1993's *Greatest Hits*, which featured two new tracks produced by Rick Rubin, including the Top 20 hit "Mary Jane's Last Dance," Petty left MCA for Warner Brothers; upon signing, it was revealed that he negotiated the $20 million deal in 1989. Drummer Stan Lynch left the Heartbreakers in 1994, while Petty was recording his second solo album with producer Rubin and many members of the Heartbreakers. Like *Full Moon Fever* before it, 1994's *Wildflowers* was greeted with enthusiastic reviews and sales, tying his previous solo album for his biggest-selling studio album. In addition to going triple platinum and peaking at No. 8, the album spawned the hit singles "You Don't Know How It Feels," "You Wreck Me," and "It's Good to Be King." Petty and the Heartbreakers reunited in 1996 to record the soundtrack for the Edward Burns film *She's the One*. The resulting soundtrack album was a moderate hit, peaking at No. 15 on the US charts and going gold.
—*Stephen Thomas Erlewine*

Tom Petty & the Heartbreakers / 1976 / Gone Gator ✦✦✦
Originally released on Denny Cordell's Shelter label, the 1976 self-titled debut was a real sleeper until the single "Breakdown" became Petty's first hit almost a year and a half later. This album's release coincided with the advent of the punk and new wave movements. The lean, edgy production and arrangements only enhanced that perception, in spite of the fact that the songs clearly drew inspiration from the Byrds and '60s Anglo rock. Among the highlights are the gritty riff-rocker "Strangered in the Night" (which features Dwight Twilley), "American Girl" (a song so shamelessly influenced by the Byrds that even Roger McGuinn covered it), "Hometown Blues" (later covered by Rosanne Cash), and "The Wild One, Forever." —*Rick Clark*

You're Gonna Get It! / 1978 / Gone Gator ✦✦✦
Not quite so strong as the debut, *You're Gonna Get It* exhibited a denser, Rickenbacker-heavy guitar sound. Petty's voice was practically buried in the mix, particularly on the rockers. Nevertheless, this album does have some great songs, particularly "I Need to Know" and "Listen to Her Heart." Each of the first two CDs clocks in at around 30 minutes of playing time. It would've been nice if Petty were true enough to his well-advertised principles (concerning gouging consumers value for their money) to fit these two albums on one disc when he re-released them on his own Gone Gator label. —*Rick Clark*

☆ **Damn the Torpedoes** / 1979 / MCA ✦✦✦✦✦
Petty switched producers to Jimmy Iovine, and together they created the masterful *Damn the Torpedoes*. For once, Petty's voice was up front in the mix, giving him much more character. The band never sounded so full or punchy before this. *Torpedoes* opens with a seamless string of great rockers, "Refugee," "Here Comes My Girl," and "Even the Losers." Other highlights include "Century City" and "Don't Do Me Like That." —*Rick Clark*

Hard Promises / 1981 / MCA ✦✦✦✦
Pre-album publicity made much of the fact that Petty was taking issue with his record label (MCA) over gouging his fans with a list-price increase on this album. Petty won, reinforcing the notion that he was a principled people's artist. The aptly titled *Hard Promises* became another platinum hit. Even though *Hard Promises* is a slight step down from its predecessor, there is plenty of strong material. "The Waiting," one of Petty's finest songs, is the stylistic epitome of his Byrds fixation. Other standouts include the rockers "Kings Road," "A Thing About You," and the darkly humorous "Something Big." —*Rick Clark*

Long After Dark / 1982 / MCA ✦✦
The highlights of this album, "Straight into Darkness," "Change of Heart," "Deliver Me," and "You Got Lucky," may be some of Petty's best, but much of *Long After Dark* suffers from weak melodies and flat-sounding production. —*Rick Clark*

Pack Up the Plantation: Live! / 1985 / MCA ✦✦
A solid-as-a-brick live set, featuring incredible symbiotic playing from all the Heartbreakers. —*Cub Koda*

Southern Accents / 1985 / MCA ✦✦✦
Produced by Dave Stewart, *Southern Accents* is an ambitious album, attempting to incorporate touches of psychedelia, soul, and country into a loose concept about the modern South. Occasionally, the songs work;

"Rebels" and "Spike" are fine rockers, and "Don't Come Around Here No More" and "Make It Better (Forget About Me)" expand the Heartbreakers' sound nicely. But too often, the record is weighed down by its own ambitions. —*Stephen Thomas Erlewine*

Let Me Up (I've Had Enough) / 1987 / MCA ✦✦✦

After the failed *Southern Accents*, Petty and company return to a fairly straightahead collection of rock 'n' roll. Except for a handful of strong tunes like the free-associating rocker (co-written with Dylan) "Jammin' Me," "Runaway Trains," and "My Life/Your World," much of this album feels like the product of an uninspired band. —*Rick Clark*

Full Moon Fever / 1989 / MCA ✦✦✦✦

Recorded as a casual side project, Petty's first solo album possessed more flashes of brilliance than most of his albums put together. It also produced four hits, with "Free Fallin'," "A Face in the Crowd," "Runnin' Down a Dream," and "I Won't Back Down." Another highlight was a great remake of the Byrds' "I'll Feel a Whole Lot Better." Petty ought to moonlight more often. —*Rick Clark*

Into the Great Wide Open / Jul. 2, 1991 / MCA ✦✦✦

This is Petty's first Heartbreakers album after his multi-platinum solo effort, *Full Moon Fever*. The band sounds a little more lively than on the previous two efforts, and the material is generally better than much of their previous two studio albums. However, *Full Moon Fever* is a stronger album, overall. —*Rick Clark*

★ Greatest Hits / Nov. 16, 1993 / MCA ✦✦✦✦✦

All of Petty's biggest hits collected, along with two new tracks—the excellent "Mary Jane's Last Dance" and a cover of Thunderclap Newman's "Something in the Air"—on one essential disc. Everything from "American Girl" to "Free Fallin'" is included, with 16 tracks proving that Petty is one of the best rockers of the past 15 years. —*Stephen Thomas Erlewine*

Wildflowers / Nov. 1, 1994 / Warner Brothers ✦✦✦✦

Under the guidance of producer Rick Rubin, Tom Petty turns in a stripped-down, subtle record with *Wildflowers*. Coming after two albums of Jeff Lynne-directed bombast, the very sound of the record is refreshing; Petty sounds relaxed and confident. Most of the songs are small gems, but a few are a little too laidback, almost reaching the point of carelessness. Nevertheless, the finest songs here ("Wildflowers," "You Don't Know How It Feels," "It's Good to Be King," and several others) match the quality of his best material, making *Wildflowers* one of Petty's most distinctive and best albums. —*Stephen Thomas Erlewine*

Playback / Nov. 20, 1995 / MCA ✦✦✦✦

The consequence of Tom Petty and the Heartbreakers' enduring affection for the music of the mid-'60s was that, in essence, they were a singles band, a fact driven home on the first three CDs of the six-disc set *Playback;* even when abbreviating each of their first nine studio albums to four to six cuts, the songs break down into the hits and the also-rans. To be fair, there are quite a few of the former, and some of the latter are could-have-beens; and since Petty is more a song maker (or, more precisely, a track cutter) than an album artist, his work is more amenable to compilation. Still, three discs are more than enough, and then come *three more discs* of rarities and outtakes. The first of these contains non-LP B-sides, most of which are pleasant throwaways (although "Trailer" suggests that the failed concept album *Southern Accents* could have been more of a success if it had been included). The last two discs present early and alternate histories of Petty, as his pre-Heartbreakers group, Mudcrutch, searches for a sound; later, he tries out different approaches that never made it onto his regular albums. Some of this material will be of interest to hardcore fans, but to justify the length and price of the box, there would have to be real lost treasures here. Not surprisingly, then, *Playback* is a box set that would have been twice as good at half the size. —*William Ruhlmann*

Songs and Music from 'She's the One' / Aug. 1996 / Warner Brothers ✦✦✦

Nominally a soundtrack to Ed Burns' film *She's the One*, Tom Petty's *Songs and Music from "She's the One"* plays like an entity of its own, standing up well without the movie itself. *She's the One* is one of Petty's most relaxed efforts—several of the songs feel like they were written and performed quickly, almost as if they were throwaways, but that ramshackle feeling actually works in the album's favor. With its loose ends, repeated songs, covers, brief instrumental bridges, and direct production, *She's the One* is a ragged listen, but it's a comfortable, engaging, and surprisingly eclectic one. Petty goes for a number of different moods, from the circular harmonies of "Walls (Circus)" (which features guest vocals from Lindsey Buckingham) and the hard-rocking "Zero from Outer Space" to the melancholy ruminations of "Grew Up Fast." Along the way, he tosses in two excellent covers of contemporary songwriters—Lucinda Williams' slyly sneering "Change the Locks" and Beck's stark, sad "Asshole"—which are performed with affection and vigor. In fact, that vigor is what makes *She's the One* so charming—Petty sounds like he's having a good time throughout the album. It's not a

major statement in his catalog, but it's all the more entertaining because of its simple, direct approach. —*Stephen Thomas Erlewine*

Pezband

f. 1975, Schaumburg, IL
Rock 'n' Roll, Power Pop

Hailing from the same state as Cheap Trick (Illinois), the Pezband were a mostly fine, occasionally wonderful, power-pop band that specialized in hook-filled hard rock with sweet multi-part harmonies. Led by the strong, blues-inflected singing of Mimi (a guy) Betinis and the rampaging, Jeff Beck-influenced guitar playing of Tommy Gawenda, the Pezzers' first LP (released in 1977) was not as hard and heavy as Cheap Trick, nor did it exhibit the berserk panache of their fellow Illini. But that all changed with their second LP, *Laughing in the Dark*, which contained a high quotient of good-to-great songs, excellent production by Jesse Hood Jackson, and a wonderful lack of the smugness and calculation that was slowly infiltrating every power-pop band in America. A huge public reaction, however, was not forthcoming. The band had its supporters (like most of the editorial staff of *Trouser Press*), but power-pop/hard rock from Illinois was dominated by Cheap Trick, and everybody else had to find a place in the pecking order. For bands like the Pezband, that meant far less coverage than they deserved. There was also another issue: the band didn't deliver another record as good as *Laughing*, nor could they recapture the excitement and messy mania of their live show (forever preserved on an excellent pair of EPs, *Too Old, Too Soon* and *Thirty Seconds Over Schaumburg*) in the studio. Hence, the rest of their recorded output is serviceable, but only hints at what the band was truly capable of doing. It's too bad, because they were such unpretentious, likable guys. By the early '80s, the Pezband had virtually vanished from the music scene, but a Chicago-based independent label (in 1994!) released some outtakes and other previously unreleased material, and the word is that Mimi Betinis is putting the band back together. Cautious optimism is suggested. —*John Dougan*

● Laughing in the Dark / 1978 / Radar ✦✦✦✦

Without a doubt, the best Pezband record available. Side one offers an especially strong trio of rock-pop songs ("Love Goes Underground," "I'm Leavin'," and "Stop! Wait a Minute"). Sadly, many other bands got more press, and this record was lost in the shuffle. The good news is that if you found it in a used record store (assuming there still are a few in your neighborhood), you could probably get it for $2. Some may dismiss it as formulaic, and that might be true, but no one ever said that formula couldn't be fun. —*John Dougan*

Too Old, Too Soon Live at Dingwalls / 1978 / Passport ✦✦✦

A great four-track live EP recorded at the much-missed club Dingwalls in London. Side one features rough-and-ready versions of "Stop! Wait a Minute" and "Lovesmith"; Side two features a manic "Not Fade Away" and a thoroughly great romp through the Swinging Blue Jeans' "Hippy Hippy Shake." Power pop with the accent on power. —*John Dougan*

Thirty Seconds over Schaumburg / 1978 / PVC ✦✦✦✦

The title is a tongue-in-cheek reference to the Chicago suburb from whence they came. The music is loud, ferocious, and wonderful. Tommy Gawenda is a little out of control here (too many multi-chorus solos), but after all is said and done, this record proves what a great live band the Pezband were. Extra point for a rippin' version of Jeff Beck's "Blue Wind" and its neat segue into the Yardbirds' "Stroll On." —*John Dougan*

PFM

f. Italy
Art-Rock/Progressive-Rock

Italy's leading progressive-rock outfit of the early '70s, PFM would've remained a purely Italian phenomenon had it not been for their being signed by Emerson, Lake & Palmer to the latter's Manticore label. Their sound was more distinctly rooted in the pre-classical era than that of their Germanic counterparts. In addition to electric keyboards (synthesizers, etc.), they also relied on violin and flute (recorder, actually) as major components of their music. Their name, by the way, was short for Premiata Forneria Marconi, the name of the bakery that originally sponsored them. —*Bruce Eder*

● Photos of Ghosts / 1973 / Great Expectations ✦✦✦✦

The group's phantasmagorical debut English-language album (sung phonetically), originally released on ELP's Manticore label, is filled with beautifully melodic, classically based songs; strong inclinations toward psychedelia; and a refreshingly open and airy sound, free from the thick, Germanic textures of competing classical rock bands. Additionally, PFM is not only unafraid of doing songs that change time signatures radically but revels and thrives in such unusual structures. The phonetically sung English lyrics take on a special eeriness on tracks such as "Promenade the Puzzle." The original Italian-language version of this album, with a couple of different tracks, is also available on CD. The CD of this mid-1970s progressive album makes up for lots of rotten vinyl pressings that

Americans had to contend with. Clean sound for the first time, especially on the quiet passages, and none of the fuzziness of the vinyl version of this record. —*Bruce Eder*

World Became the World / 1974 / Manticore ◆◆◆
A less interesting, second English-language album with fewer memorable melodies and less-distinctive songs, and lyrics that (except for the title track) seemed less provocative. It was missteps like this, being unable to match the worth of a solid debut album with a decent follow-up, that marred lots of art-rock bands. —*Bruce Eder*

Cook / 1975 / Manticore ◆◆◆
They didn't really, at least not at this live set, recorded at a concert in New York's Central Park. The material lacks the power and beauty of their best studio work, the performance lacks the power and energy needed to sustain a live album, and the recording itself seems distant. Completists may want it, however, as the only live document left behind by this most interesting progressive band. —*Bruce Eder*

Suonare Suonare / 1980 / Zoo ◆◆◆
Long after their contract with the Manticore label ended, PFM were still making records exclusively in their native Italy, which British RCA has seen fit to release on CD in England. By this time, the group had lightened up considerably from their early-'70s progressive-rock sound—Franco Mussida's guitars are the dominant instrument, Flavio Premoli is more likely to be playing piano than synthesizer, and Lucio Fabri is as likely to be sawing away with a country fiddle sound as bowing a concert violin. But their songs have a more easygoing character, without the attempted profundity of their *Photos of Ghosts/World Became the World* period. This version of the group relates to the earlier one the way later Genesis relates to earlier (i.e., *Lamb Lies Down on Broadway* and before) or the way ELP's *Love Beach* stood next to their earlier work. There is still some good music and playing: "Si Puo Fare" includes decent workouts on guitar, violin, and synthesizer, and it has a great beat; "Topolino" is a good showcase for Mussida's flashiest playing and has a nice melody; "Maestro Della Voce" has some pleasing moments, in which the players soar; and "Sogno Americano" has a catchy chorus. —*Bruce Eder*

Liz Phair

b. Apr. 17, 1967, New Haven, CT
Guitar, Vocals / Singer-Songwriter, Alternative Pop-Rock, Lo-Fi
Growing out of the American underground of the late '80s, Liz Phair fused lo-fi, indie-rock production techniques and styles with the sensibility and structure of classic singer-songwriters. *Exile in Guyville*, Phair's debut album, was enthusiastically praised upon its 1993 release, and it spawned a rash of imitators, particularly American female singer-songwriters, over the following years. For her part, Phair wasn't able to break into the mainstream, even with the support of the press and MTV. *Whip-Smart*, her second album, was heavily promoted upon its 1994 release, yet despite its relatively strong chart positions, it was viewed as a disappointment, and Phair's momentum declined steadily during the mid-'90s, as she took several years to record her third album.

Liz Phair (b. April 17, 1967) was born in New Haven, CT, and adopted by wealthy parents, who raised her in the Chicago suburb Winnetka. After high school, she studied art at Oberlin College in Ohio. At Oberlin, she became fascinated with underground indie-rock and eventually became friends with guitarist Chris Brokaw, who later joined Come. Following their college graduation, Phair and Brokaw moved to San Francisco, where she tried to become an artist.

Eventually, Brokaw moved out east and Phair moved back to Chicago, where she began writing songs. Soon, she began releasing homemade tapes of these songs under the name Girlysound. While she supported herself by selling her charcoal drawings on the streets of Wicker Park, she was becoming involved in various portions of the Chicago alternative-music scene; in particular, she became friends with Urge Overkill, a drummer named Brad Wood and John Henderson, the head of the Chicago-based indie label, Feel Good All Over. Henderson and Phair tried to re-record some of the Girlysound tapes with Wood, yet the pair had a falling out during the sessions, leaving Wood as Phair's only collaborator. Brokaw, who had by then joined Come, was still receiving Girlysound tapes, and he gave a copy to Gerard Cosley, the head of Come's record label, Matador. By the summer of 1992, Matador had signed Phair, and she began recording her debut album in earnest.

Adapting its title from an Urge Overkill song, *Exile in Guyville*, her debut album, was released to strong reviews in the summer of 1993. Many articles focused on Phair's claim that the double album was structured as a response to the Rolling Stones' classic *Exile on Main St.* Over the course of the year, the record slowly built a dedicated following in America, both among critics and alternative rock fans. At the end of the year, it topped many Best-of-the-Year critics' polls, including *The Village Voice* and *Spin*. With all the attention focused on Phair, many indie-rock figures—particularly members of the Chicago noise-rock scene, such as Steve Albini—were developing a resentment towards her and launching

an attack at the singer and the heavy media attention *Exile in Guyville* received. The criticism couldn't halt the progress of Phair and *Exile*, and in early 1994, she launched her first tour, which was plagued by her stage fright. Around the same time, MTV began airing "Never Said" and, as a result of all the hype, the album briefly appeared in the charts in February. By the spring of 1994, it had sold over 200,000 copies—a remarkable number for an independent release.

By that time, Phair had begun work on her follow-up record. Matador had signed a distribution deal with Atlantic Records in 1994, and her second album was going to be one of the first to be heavily promoted by the alliance. Indeed, *Whip-Smart* was released to a whirlwind of media attention—including Phair, dressed only in negligee, on the cover of *Rolling Stone*—that outweighed her celebrity. *Whip-Smart* debuted at No. 27 upon its fall 1994 release. "Supernova," the first single from the album, received heavy airplay on MTV and alternative rock radio, becoming a Top Ten modern rock hit. However, *Whip-Smart* received mediocre reviews and never developed into the hit that it was expected to be. Phair didn't tour to support the album and was slow to deliver a second single. By the time the title track was released as a single in the spring of 1995, the album had disappeared from the charts.

Phair quietly retreated from the spotlight during 1995, marrying Jim Staskausas, a Chicago-based film editor who had previously worked on Phair's videos. Later in the summer of 1995, she released the *Juvenilia* EP, which was essentially the "Jealousy" single amplified with the first official release of Girlysound material. During the summer of 1996, she released "Rocket Boy," a single pulled from the *Stealing Beauty* soundtrack that received little attention. For much of 1996, Phair worked on her third album with producer Scott Litt, yet by the fall, she decided to scrap the sessions, unsatisfied with their sound. Toward the end of 1996, Staskausas and Phair announced she was several months pregnant. On December 21, 1996, Phair gave birth to her first child, James Nicholas Staskausas. —*Stephen Thomas Erlewine*

★ Exile in Guyville / Jun. 22, 1993 / Matador ◆◆◆◆◆
Liz Phair's stunningly accomplished and ambitious debut album *Exile in Guyville* is loosely based on the Rolling Stones' classic *Exile on Main Street*, retelling that album's weary tales of love and sex from a female perspective. While there is some anger here ("Fuck and Run" and "6'1'"), there are also love songs ("Never Said"), lust songs ("Flower"), haunting character sketches ("Canary" and "Explain It to Me"), and exceptional narratives ("Divorce Song," "Stratford-on-Guy," and "Help Me Mary"). While her lyrics are literate without being pretentious, what makes the album so impressive is her musical diversity; from rock 'n' roll to folk, from experimental rock to just a piano and a voice, *Exile in Guyville* is an endlessly inventive album that only gets better with repeated plays. —*Stephen Thomas Erlewine*

Whip-Smart / Sep. 20, 1994 / Matador ◆◆◆
Expectations ran extremely high for Phair's follow-up to *Exile In Guyville*, one of the most critically acclaimed debut albums of all time. If there are flaws in this generally first-rate follow-up, they mostly arise in comparison with *Guyville*, a record of such unexpected impact that most anything Phair could have done may have been found lacking. She continues to explore sex and relationships with exhilarating frankness and celebration, employing her much-touted profanity to a conversational rather than a sensational effect. The sound is somewhat more produced, though still pretty basic, and the compositions are by and large tuneful and lyrically intriguing. It's not, after all is said and done, quite as striking as *Guyville;* like many sophomore efforts, it mines similar territory without making huge strides forward. Several songs are reprised from her widely circulated *Girly Sound* demo tapes, and in some instances the more heavily produced, self-consciously ingenious arrangements here suffer in comparison to their blueprints. The title track, one of the highlights of those tapes, comes off as particularly gimmicky in its new incarnation, with the addition of all manner of superfluous animal noises. There's no question that Phair is a major songwriter and artist, but this album is more a solidification of her talents than a breakthough statement. —*Richie Unterberger*

Pottymouth Girl [bootleg] / 1996 / Primadonna ◆◆◆
Good-sounding tape of a December 1, 1993, show in San Francisco, comprising an assortment of material from her first two albums. In accordance with her reputation as a live performer, the full-band arrangements can sound awkward and unpolished at times, and her vocals aren't as commanding as they are on record. It works best on the quietest, slowest numbers, like "Glory." There are also seven significant bonus tracks from a Portland show on April 11, 1995, also in good sound, performed solo on electric guitar, making for more of an interesting contrast with her albums. It includes two songs that (as of late 1996) she had yet to officially release, the eerie "Dream" and "See the Light," which is Phair at her gentlest. —*Richie Unterberger*

Girlysound [bootleg] / [Bootleg] ◆◆◆◆
Before signing to Matador Records, Phair recorded a wealth of home demos that were only circulated, primarily to acquaintances, on cassette.

In fact, it was a tape of this material that brought Phair to the attention of Matador in the first place. Featuring just Phair and her low-volume electric guitar, with layers of overdubs enabling Phair to harmonize with herself, this collection of over 20 lo-fi, intensely personal songs circulated among literally thousands of Phair fans, making this one of the most popular and sought-after alternative rock bootlegs of all time. A few of the tracks found their way onto her first couple of albums in drastically reworked versions, including "Stratford-on-Guy," "Flower," "Johnny Sunshine," "Whip-Smart," "Never Said," "Shane," and "Chopsticks." These stripped-down versions aren't necessarily better (although "Whip-Smart" sounds much less tongue-in-cheek and more effective in its original incarnation), but they are fascinating to hear in such bare-bones arrangements. The substantial majority of these have not been released by Phair, and while some are clearly tentative drafts or awkward, half-baked efforts, others are as tuneful and provoking as anything on her official albums. Phair is arguably a more powerful performer when stripped to her essentials of voice and guitar, and this tape is as vital to her legacy as her Matador discs. —Richie Unterberger

Sam Phillips

b. 1962
Vocals / Pop-Rock, Adult Alternative Pop-Rock
The acid-pop singer-songwriter born Leslie Phillips earned the nonsensical nickname "Sam" as a child; only when she was recording her debut album did she finally hear of the other, more renowned Sam Phillips and learn of his legacy as the founder of Sun Records, the label that launched the careers of Elvis Presley and Jerry Lee Lewis. In retrospect, however, her relative distance from the history and conventions of pop music may have been in her favor and accounted for the fresh perspective her work offered. A critic's darling, Phillips sold few records, but her songs won widespread praise not only from the press but also from her fellow performers.

Born in 1962, Phillips was raised in Glendale, CA. As a child she became fascinated by philosophy and religion, primarily fundamentalism; she began writing songs at the age of 14 as an outlet for exploring her Christian beliefs, as well as for coping with family strife. In 1984, under the name Leslie Phillips, she released her first LP, *Beyond Saturday Night*, on the Contemporary Christian label Word. Within the limited framework of the Christian rock community, Phillips became a star; her records, which also included 1984's *Dancing with Danger* and 1985's *Black and White in a Grey World*, regularly sold upwards of 200,000 copies, and she was a tremendous live draw while touring churches and coffeehouses.

With the aptly-titled *The Turning*, released in 1987, Phillips first teamed with producer T-Bone Burnett, a renowned pop producer who also helmed Bob Dylan's voyage into Christianity. After the album's release, she publicly denounced her label as a right-wing propaganda machine, and announced her retirement from CCM; disavowing all of her previous work, she adopted the name Sam on a permanent basis and, with Burnett's assistance, landed a contract with Virgin Records. With Burnett again in the producer's seat, she emerged in 1988 with her secular debut, *The Indescribable Wow*, which earned vast acclaim not only for her powerful vocals, penetrating lyrics, and gorgeous melodies but also for the record's lush, baroque production.

Phillips and Burnett married prior to the release of 1991's darker, more experimental *Cruel Inventions*, which featured a guest appearance from Elvis Costello. With 1994's Grammy-nominated *Martinis and Bikinis*, her sound flirted closely with Beatlesque popcraft; the album's finale, a cover of John Lennon's "Gimme Some Truth," further drove the comparisons home. After making her feature film debut in the 1995 blockbuster *Die Hard with a Vengeance*, Phillips returned with 1996's *Omnipop (It's Only a Flesh Wound Lambchop)*, another departure, which touched upon lounge pop and industrial sounds; on the song "Slapstick Heart," she even shared songwriting credits with the members of R.E.M. —Jason Ankeny

The Indescribable Wow / 1988 / Virgin ✦✦✦✦
Sam Phillips' aptly titled secular debut is a pop marvel, a bright, colorful collection produced with verve by T-Bone Burnett. At times, Phillips' sweet voice and bouncy songs conjure the spirit of prime girl-group-era pop, but her mature, pointed lyrics—largely devoted to sophisticated dissections of modern relationships—shrug off such easy comparisons. Similarly, Burnett's production straddles both the past and the present—for all the 1960s nods of the Beach Boys-like "I Can't Stop Crying" or the Beatlesque "Remorse," *The Indescribable Wow* never sounds dated or retro, just timeless. —Jason Ankeny

Cruel Inventions / May 28, 1991 / Virgin ✦✦✦
Darker and more idiosyncratic than *The Indescribable Wow*, Phillips' sophomore effort strips away the girl-group buoyancy of her debut to focus on a more understated sound. From the odd, metallic rhythms of the opener "Lying" onward, *Cruel Inventions* is tough minded and introspective, with many songs addressing issues of faith and spiritual-

ity; confident and distinctive, the record is less accessible than its predecessor, but remains a pure pop thrill nevertheless. —Jason Ankeny

● **Martinis & Bikinis** / Mar. 8, 1994 / Virgin ✦✦✦✦
With *Martinis & Bikinis*, Sam Phillips' music turns decidedly Beatlesque: edgier and more psychedelic than her previous work, songs like "Strawberry Road" and "Same Rain" springboard from John Lennon-inspired origins, while "Same Changes" brazenly borrows from "If I Needed Someone"—Van Dyke Parks' string arrangement for the stunning "Baby, I Can't Please You" even recalls "Tomorrow Never Knows." (To punctuate matters, the LP closes with a cover of Lennon's "Gimme Some Truth.") The difference between Phillips and the vast majority of her pop-revisionist contemporaries, however, is that she never coasts on the fumes of her influences, but turns them on their head and gives them new life—regardless of the approach, her impassioned, spiritually charged songs remain the product of a singular vision. —Jason Ankeny

Omnipop / Aug. 20, 1996 / Virgin ✦✦✦
Martinis & Bikinis was an edgy, catchy pop-rock album that expanded Sam Phillips' sonic palette without losing sight of her melodic, layered songwriting. With *Omnipop (It's Only a Fleshwound Lambchop)*, the follow-up to *Martinis & Bikinis*, Phillips concentrates on creating soundscapes that are vaguely experimental and layered with effects and synthesizers, sounding unlike much of her catalog. The problem is that the soundscapes hide a lack of substance within the songs themselves. Much of the lyrics are underdeveloped and cliched, while the music itself doesn't have the punch or hooks of her previous three albums. And that makes *Omnipop* a muddled, ineffective affair. A few songs sink in after repeated listens, but the album on the whole is a failed—but honorable—experiment. —Stephen Thomas Erlewine

Phish

f. 1983, Burlington, VT
Rock 'n' Roll, Fusion, Neo-Psychedelia
During the early '90s, Phish emerged as the heirs to the Grateful Dead's throne. Although their music is somewhat similar to the Dead's—it's an eclectic, free-form rock 'n' roll encompassing folk, jazz, country, bluegrass, and pop—the group adheres more to a jazz tradition than a folk tradition of improvisation and they have a looser, goofier attitude. After all, their drummer regularly plays a vacuum during their concerts.

Phish's main claim as the inheritors to the Dead's legacy is their approach to their musical career. The band didn't concentrate on albums, they dedicated themselves to live improvisation. Within a few years of their 1988 debut album, Phish had become an institution in certain sections of America, particularly college campuses. Their in-concert popularity didn't translate to record sales—by the middle of the '90s, Phish was able to pack stadiums, but none of their albums had gone gold.

Guitarist-vocalist Trey Anastasio, drummer Jon Fishman, and guitarist Jeff Holdsworth formed the band in late 1983 while attending the University of Vermont. After meeting and jamming in their dormitory, the trio posted flyers across campus, recruiting a bassist. Mike Gordon answered the advertisement, and he was soon added to the original lineup.

The group began practicing regularly, and they soon assembled a demo tape. In the fall of 1984, Phish began performing off-campus concerts. At this stage in their career, the band was augmented by percussionist Marc Daubert and, occasionally, by a vocalist called the Dude of Life. Soon, the group was playing concerts on nearby campuses, including Goddard College's Springfest in 1985. Page McConnell organized the Springfest at Goddard, and he became a fan of the band. Later in the year, McConnell convinced the group to add him as a keyboardist. Shortly after McConnell joined Phish, Holdsworth left the group. In the fall of 1986, Anastasio and Fishman transferred to Goddard College.

Early in 1988, Phish recorded *Junta*, which they sold at their shows as a cassette-only release. In 1989, the group played their first tour outside of New England, traveling through the Southeast. Phish also recorded their second album, *Lawn Boy*, in 1989, although the album wasn't released until the fall of 1990; the record was released on the independent record label Absolute A-Go-Go, a subsidiary of Rough Trade. Throughout early 1991, Phish toured America. During the summer, they recorded their third album, as well as a set of sessions with their old friend the Dude of Life.

Late in August, Rough Trade collapsed, taking Absolute A-Go-Go with it. Phish was left without a record contract, but they were soon signed by Elektra Records. In February of 1992, *A Picture of Nectar* was released by Elektra. After its release, the group embarked on an extensive national tour. In the summer of 1992, Phish played a handful of shows on the first H.O.R.D.E. tour. Also that summer, Elektra reissued *Lawn Boy* and *Junta*. *Rift*, the band's fourth album, and the first they recorded with a producer, appeared in February of 1993. During Phish's 1993 tour, the group sold tickets that were specifically designed for fans taping the concert. *Hoist*, the band's fifth album, was released in 1994.

"Down with Disease," one of the songs on *Hoist*, became the band's first video, and it received some airplay on MTV. *Hoist* sold better than the group's previous albums, which was an indication of how large the group's fan base had gotten. In the fall of 1994, *Crimes of the Mind*, the album Phish recorded with the Dude of Life in 1991, was released on Elektra Records.

In the summer of 1995, the band released the double live album, *A Live One*. In early 1996, Trey Anastasio released a free-form jazz side project called *Surrender to the Air*. In the fall of 1996, Phish released their sixth album, *Billy Breathes*, which was produced by Steve Lillywhite. —*Stephen Thomas Erlewine*

Junt / 1988 / Elektra ✦✦✦✦
Phish's debut album is a bit long-winded and unfocused, yet it establishes their dedication to musical exploration effectively. —*David Jehnzen*

Lawn Boy / 1991 / Elektra ✦✦✦
The Phish boys play real good in a variety of styles, writing amusing, surrealist lyrics full of non sequiturs, and they don't seem to take themselves too seriously. —*J. Poet*

A Picture of Nectar / Aug. 1991 / Elektra ✦✦✦✦
A wildly eclectic album in the vein of the Grateful Dead, *A Picture of Nectar* is the best studio example of Phish's genre-jumping good-time rock 'n' roll. —*David Jehnzen*

Rift / Feb. 2, 1993 / Elektra ✦✦
Rift, Phish's follow-up to their major-label breakthrough *A Picture of Nectar*, follows the same pattern as its predecessor, but doesn't live up to the surprising, adventurous music on *Nectar*. Instead, most of the album sounds like an uninspired retread, as the band tries to fashion their songs into a loose concept album. The concentration on thematic unity tends to rob Phish of the loose spontaneity that makes them unique and makes *Rift* a bland, tedious listen. —*Stephen Thomas Erlewine*

Hoist / Mar. 29, 1994 / Elektra ✦✦✦
Hoist is the most concise album Phish has recorded, but that's not necessarily a compliment. Phish's strength is not songcraft or hooks, it's their love of free-form song structures and extended jams. When the group's sound is reduced to its core, as it is on *Hoist*, it isn't quite as compelling. Nevertheless, the album is an improvement on the dismal *Rift*, and features several fine cuts. —*Stephen Thomas Erlewine*

Crimes of the Mind / Oct. 25, 1994 / Elektra ✦✦
Crimes of the Mind is a loopy, stoned excursion that winds through Dead-style rock and hippie folk-rock as interpreted by the Dude of Life. Throughout the record, the Dude is supported by his longtime friends Phish, who make the record somewhat interesting. While the Dude's vocals and lyrics are certainly an acquired taste, most Phish fans will appreciate the band's relaxed, sympathetic playing, which casually demonstrates their virtuosity. —*Stephen Thomas Erlewine*

A Live One / Jun. 27, 1995 / Elektra ✦✦✦✦
Phish's strength has always been its live shows, and *A Live One* shows why. Given the opportunity, they take their songs in every direction, winding through several different sounds within the course of a song. *A Live One* also features seven previously unreleased songs, making it worthwhile listening for even casual fans. Then again, most fans of Phish will want to hear everything the group has ever played. —*Stephen Thomas Erlewine*

Stash / 1996 / Elektra ✦✦✦✦
Stash is a Europe-only collection that was released to coincide with a 1996 tour. The compilation collects highlights from all of Phish's albums, from *Junta* and *Lawn Boy* to *Hoist* and *A Live One*. Though it doesn't work quite as well as their live performances, the album nevertheless contains many of their most popular songs and offers a good introduction to the band. —*Stephen Thomas Erlewine*

● **Billy Breathes** / Oct. 15, 1996 / Elektra ✦✦✦✦
Thanks to producer Steve Lillywhite, Phish finally delivered a concise pop album with *Billy Breathes*. Lillywhite had the band cut away their jams and accentuate their songwriting, resulting in a series of tightly written, melodic folk-rock and psychedelic pop songs. Phish still delve into the deeper waters with sweeping songs like "Theme from the Bottom," but what truly impresses about *Billy Breathes* is the group's seamless eclecticism and how they master all varieties of roots-rock and psychedelic styles. With the shorter songs, their musical depth and breadth is all the more apparent and impressive, making *Billy Breathes* the definitive Phish album the band has always strived to deliver. —*Stephen Thomas Erlewine*

Photek

b. Ipswich, England
Club-Dance, Jungle/Drum 'N Bass, Electronica
Ipswich native Rupert Parkes is the name behind noted experimental jungle outfit Photek, who was one of the first major-label signings of a

drum 'n' bass artist and, perhaps more surprisingly, has gained equal levels of success and influence in the underground as amongst more mainstream critics and fans. Parkes' start in music came as the result of a £2,000 federal loan, with which he set up a home studio in 1991 and began making the brand of hardcore techno and fast breakbeat from which jungle eventually mutated. Parkes' first several 12-inches on his own Photek imprint, as well as the Metalheadz and Good Looking labels, were enthusiastically rated for their hardcore edge and unflinching determination to take drum 'n' bass in new directions. That determination has since gelled into something of a recognizable sound, characterized by brittle, clangy snare-strikes, minimal instrumentation, and heavily syncopated polyrhythms. But for all its increasing familiarity, Parkes' style is uniquely his own, and subsequent releases have done anything but simply rest there. Sometimes painted as a practitioner of "intelligent" or "ambient" jungle, the category stretches only as far as the attention to detail and mood Parkes brings to his compositions. Usually dark and foreboding and laced with traces of fear and paranoia ("U.F.O.," "Hidden Camera"), Photek's work is anything but calm and quieting. Nonetheless, Virgin Records' experimental Science subsidiary (with whom Parkes signed a five-album nonexclusive contract) was willing to take a chance on him, and the visibility will likely do much for the genre's popularity (and Parkes' too). —*Sean Cooper*

● **The Hidden Camera Ep** / Jun. 11, 1996 / Science ✦✦✦✦
Photek's first release for the Virgin subsidiary is a nicely packaged double pack of tight, impeccably produced experimental drum 'n' bass not too dissimilar from the material released through Parkes' own label. The opener, "KJZ," is the EP's finest track, shuffling along on a fluid layer of crash -and-ride cymbals and a finely detailed, rubbery acoustic bassline. A pair of mixes of the title track bridge the gap between the two twelves, and the remaining track is a brief throwaway that could've used a bit more development. —*Sean Cooper*

Ni-Ten-Ichi-Ryu / Mar. 24, 1997 / Science ✦✦✦✦
Translated from the Japanese as "Two Swords Technique," Photek's second release for Science proves better than *The Hidden Camera* EP. Though there are only two tracks, the minimalistic paranoia of a kung-fu flick sword fight proves irresistible. —*John Bush*

Phranc

b. 1957, Los Angeles, CA
Guitar, Vocals / Singer-Songwriter, Folk-Rock, Contemporary Folk
Bursting onto the L.A. punk scene in 1985 like the proverbial breath of fresh air, self-proclaimed Jewish, lesbian folksinger Phranc has one of the most beautiful vocal instruments in the business. Born Susan Gottlieb in Los Angeles in 1957, Phranc began as a folksinger in the '70s before becoming a member of L.A. hardcore bands Catholic Discipline and Nervous Gender. Tiring of the genre's sexist and fascist leanings, she picked up her acoustic guitar again and debuted with *Folksinger* in 1985—a spare affair that tackled such topical and taboo subjects of the time as lesbianism, L.A. coroner Thomas Noguchi, and "Female Mudwrestling." Delivered in Phranc's unique, forthright, punk/folk style, the album received critical endorsement but never led to wider acceptance. Signed to Island by 1989, she enlisted the services of a band to play on the more fleshed-out *I Enjoy Being a Girl*, which included one of her trademark odes to a female sports figure in "Martina" (as in Navratilova). She followed it with 1991's *Positively Phranc*, a return to the spare style with which she made her mark. For the 1995 EP *Goofyfoot*, she paired up with Team Dresch's Donna Dresch and other Olympia, WA, underground female musicians for a collection of novelty songs. During the four-year period she didn't record, Phranc occasionally performed in drag as Neil Diamond. Though not extremely prolific, Phranc was and is an icon among alternative and lesbian musicians, as well as folksingers everywhere. —*Denise Sullivan*

Folksinger / 1985 / Island ✦✦✦✦
Jewish, lesbian folksinger Phranc took the punk world by surprise when she released her militant folk record in 1985. A former punk rocker herself, Phranc set topical songs like "Noguchi" and "Everywhere I Go (I Hear the Go Go's)," the anti-suicide "Lifelover," and the sing-along "Female Mudwrestling" beside her strict cover of Dylan's "The Lonesome Death of Hattie Carroll" to great effect. Acoustic folk music had yet to be embraced by the punk/new wave underground, making *Folksinger* a watershed album. —*Denise Sullivan*

● **I Enjoy Being a Girl** / May 1989 / Island ✦✦✦✦
Folksinger Phranc attempted to bust out of the solo acoustic mode for this record, produced by Violent Femme Victor DeLorenzo. Though some of the songs, like "Folksinger," "Take Off Your Swastika" and "Martina," work beautifully, others suffer from kitsch overkill (like her cover of "I Enjoy Being a Girl") and are not her strongest efforts. However, "Myriam and Esther," a traditional folk ballad with a distinctly female perspective, is the type of earnest song that only Phranc seems able to pull off in postmodern times. —*Denise Sullivan*

Positively Phranc / Mar. 19, 1991 / Island ✦✦✦

Positively Phranc isn't the L.A. native's best album, but even at her second best, the self-proclaimed "All-American Jewish lesbian folk singer" commands attention. Although "Billy Tipton," "Outta Here" (a lament for the victims of AIDS), and the defiant "Dress Code" pack a sociopolitical punch, the album generally isn't as political as one might expect. In fact, much of the material is rather lighthearted. Blessed with a fine sense of humor, Phranc has a lot of fun this time—especially on "Hitchcock" (an ode to actress Kim Novak), "'64 Ford," and a cover of the Beach Boys' "Surfer Girl." By Phranc's standards, "Gertrude Stein" and "'64 Ford" are unusually rockin' and surprisingly electric. Hardcore devotees will find much to admire on *Positively Phranc*, although novices would be better off starting out with *Folksinger*. *—Alex Henderson*

Goofyfoot [ep] / Aug. 18, 1995 / Kill Rock Stars ✦✦✦

After a few years off, Phranc returned to record this EP with Olympia, WA, musicians, including Donna Dresch from Team Dresch. Largely a collection of novelty songs, the EP includes covers of "Mrs. Brown You've Got a Lovely Daughter" and "Ode to Billie Joe," along with her "Bulldagger Swagger," a popular live favorite during her recording hiatus. It's a vital piece of the Phranc catalog after her long absence. *—Denise Sullivan*

Wilson Pickett

b. Mar. 18, 1941, Prattville, AL
Vocals / Soul, R&B

Of the major '60s soul stars, Wilson Pickett was one of the roughest and sweatiest, working up some of the decade's hottest dance floor grooves on hits like "In the Midnight Hour," "Land of 1000 Dances," "Mustang Sally," and "Funky Broadway." Although he tends to be held in somewhat lower esteem than more versatile talents like Otis Redding and Aretha Franklin, he is often a preferred alternative for fans who like their soul on the rawer side. He also did a good deal to establish the sound of Southern soul with his early hits, which were often written and recorded with the cream of the session musicians in Memphis and Muscle Shoals.

Before establishing himself as a solo artist, Pickett sang with the Falcons, who had a Top Ten R&B hit in 1962 with "I Found a Love." "If You Need Me" (covered by the Rolling Stones) and "It's Too Late" were R&B hits for the singer before he hooked up with Atlantic Records, which sent him to record at Stax in Memphis in 1965. One early result was "In the Midnight Hour," whose chugging horn line, loping, funky beats, and impassioned vocals combined into a key transitional performance that brought R&B into the soul age. It was an R&B chart topper, and a substantial pop hit (No. 21), though its influence was stronger than that respectable position might indicate: thousands of bands, Black and white, covered "In the Midnight Hour" on stage and on record in the 1960s.

Pickett had a flurry of other galvanizing soul hits over the next few years, including "634-5789," "Mustang Sally," and "Funky Broadway," all of which, like "In the Midnight Hour," were frequently adapted by other bands as a dance-ready number. The king of that hill, though, had to be "Land of 1000 Dances," Pickett's biggest pop hit (No. 6), a soul anthem of sorts with its roll call of popular dances, and it was covered by almost as many acts as "Midnight Hour" was.

Pickett didn't confine himself to the environs of Stax for long; soon he was also cutting tracks at Muscle Shoals. He recorded several early songs by Bobby Womack, and he used Duane Allman as a session guitarist on a hit cover of the Beatles' "Hey Jude." He cut some hits in Philadelphia with Gamble-Huff productions in the early '70s. He even did a hit version of the Archies' "Sugar, Sugar." The hits kept rolling through the early '70s, including "Don't Knock My Love" and "Get Me Back on Time, Engine Number 9."

One of the corollaries of '60s soul is that if a performer rose to fame with Motown or Atlantic, he or she would produce little of note after leaving the label. Pickett, unfortunately, did not prove an exception to the rule. His last big hit was "Fire and Water," in 1972. He continued to be active on the tour circuit. His most essential music, all from the 1960s and early '70s, was assembled for the superb Rhino double-CD anthology *A Man and a Half*. *—Richie Unterberger*

In the Midnight Hour / 1965 / Atlantic ✦✦✦

Wilson Pickett's first album, from 1965, was a bit of a hodgepodge, including singles from as far back as 1962. Three of these tracks were actually issued as singles by the Falcons (for whom Pickett sang lead) before he started his solo career; others were issued as singles before Pickett broke through as a national star with the title track. This 12-track album doesn't really suffer as a result, however. Besides the all-time classic "In the Midnight Hour," it includes the Mann/Weil-penned single "Come Home Baby," covered by several rock and soul artists; "Don't Fight It," which reached the R&B Top Ten in late 1965; "I'm Gonna Cry," a 1964 single Pickett wrote with fellow soul legend Don Covay; and "I Found a Love," the Falcons single that made the R&B Top Ten in 1962.

Working with several collaborators (including Steve Cropper), Pickett himself wrote most of the tunes on this album. The record also featured the first recordings he made with the Stax rhythm section in Memphis—a combination that would yield much fine soul music throughout the rest of the '60s. The 1993 CD reissue of this album features extensive liner notes and session details. *—Richie Unterberger*

The Exciting Wilson Pickett / 1966 / Atlantic ✦✦✦✦

Less of a hodgepodge than his debut *In the Midnight Hour* album, Pickett's second LP established—if there had been any doubt—his stature as a major '60s soul man. The 12 tracks include his monster hits "634-5789," "Ninety-Nine and a Half (Won't Do)," "In the Midnight Hour," and "Land Of 1000 Dances" (the last of which was his first Top Ten pop hit). Collectors will be more interested in the non-hit cuts, which are of nearly an equal level. These include covers of the R&B standards "Something You Got," "Mercy Mercy," and "Barefootin'"; several original tunes written in collaboration with Memphis soul greats Steve Cropper, Eddie Floyd, and David Porter; and Bobby Womack's "She's So Good to Me." It all adds up to one of the most consistent 1960s soul albums. The CD reissue of this 1966 record features detailed liner notes and session documentation. *—Richie Unterberger*

The Wicked Pickett / 1966 / Atlantic ✦✦✦✦

A fabulous album, done when Pickett was in the midst of his best period at Atlantic. It had everything—great songs, wonderful production and arrangements, and a hungry, galvanizing Wilson Pickett hollering, screaming, shouting, and soaring on anything he covered, from ballads to uptempo dance and midtempo wailers. It also has been deleted at present. *—Ron Wynn*

The Sound of Wilson Pickett / 1967 / Atlantic ✦✦✦✦

A masterpiece, perhaps his finest '60s album. This wasn't a hits collection but a batch of great singles. His version of "Funky Broadway" may still be the best; it was certainly the most swaggering and posturing, punctuated by his screams and jubilant cries. Pickett was all over the R&B charts in 1967, and this was one of three albums Atlantic issued on him that year. Each one was a classic. *—Ron Wynn*

I'm in Love / 1968 / Atlantic ✦✦✦

Bobby Womack's title track, which was a masterpiece of hurt and heartache, became in Wilson Pickett's hands a smashing, surging tale that managed to register the hurt Womack had in mind but also contained plenty of fire and energy as well. No one except James Brown could put as much crunching power behind a scream as Pickett, but he was also a first-rate soul vocalist who showed often that he could do more than just yell and bellow. *—Ron Wynn*

Midnight Mover / 1968 / Atlantic ✦✦✦

The title track was another of Pickett's smoking '60s soul singles; he rode the beat perfectly and then concluded the song with a series of bloodcurdling screams and triumphant exhortations. He turned in several other equally assertive, defiant, and excellent uptempo and ballad performances, continuing a run of great Atlantic albums. *—Ron Wynn*

Hey Jude / 1969 / Atlantic ✦✦✦

There were some in the soul world who scratched their heads when Wilson Pickett covered "Hey Jude" in 1969. They couldn't be found when the song became a Top 20 hit, one of five R&B smashes Pickett enjoyed that year. His cover was both outlandish and right on the button; the remainder of the album is just old-fashioned, urgent, gritty Southern soul. It's unfortunately out of print at present; hopefully, Rhino will put it back into circulation at some point. *—Ron Wynn*

Right On / 1970 / Atlantic ✦✦✦

Wilson Pickett encountered a momentary slump in 1970, as this album was his first for Atlantic in many years that stayed locked in the bottom rungs of the pop Top 200 albums. Pickett did get a fluke novelty hit with "Sugar, Sugar," maybe his worst soul smash ever. The album wasn't a total disaster, but everyone forgot about it quickly when Atlantic rushed out *Wilson Pickett in Philadelphia* later that year. *—Ron Wynn*

Wilson Pickett in Philadelphia / 1970 / Atlantic ✦✦✦✦

A landmark album, one of Pickett's all-time best and without question his finest '70s date. "Engine, Engine, Number 9" was a return to the great, funky days of the '60s. The edited single was a big radio and crossover hit, while the extended version was a club smash. It revived his career, although he was now feuding with Atlantic and would take almost a year and a half to follow this with any new material. *—Ron Wynn*

Don't Knock My Love / 1971 / Atlantic ✦✦✦

His final definitive Atlantic session. The title track was vintage Pickett—a driving, syncopated bass and surging horn arrangement punctuated by his aggressive, spiraling lead and concluding with a robust shout and defiant exhortation. That set the stage for some sharp ballads and a couple of other nice uptempo cuts. "Don't Knock My Love, Part 1" was Pickett's last No. 1 R&B hit and a Top 20 pop smash. He left Atlantic shortly after the album peaked on the charts, returning to RCA, and never enjoying similar success again. *—Ron Wynn*

A Man and a Half: The Best of Wilson Pickett / Apr. 21, 1992 / Rhino ✦✦✦✦

A Man and a Half—The Best of Wilson Pickett is a double-disc set that collects the absolute cream of Pickett's early sides with the Falcons and all the highlights of his successful alliance with the Atlantic label. With "Mustang Sally," "In the Midnight Hour," "Ninety Nine and a Half," "Hey Jude," "Land of a 1000 Dances," "You're So Fine," and "634-5789" all included, this excellent compilation should be one of the cornerstones of anybody's soul collection. —*Cub Koda*

★ **The Very Best of Wilson Pickett** / 1993 / Rhino ✦✦✦✦✦
Although the double-disc set *A Man and a Half* is necessary for serious soul fans, *The Very Best of Wilson Pickett* should satiate the needs of any casual fan. Featuring 16 of his biggest Atlantic hits—including "In the Midnight Hour," "634-5789 (Soulsville, USA.)," "Land of 1000 Dances," "Mustang Sally," "Funky Broadway," "She's Looking Good," and "I'm a Midnight Mover"—*The Very Best of Wilson Pickett* contains all of his truly essential items, making it both an excellent introduction and the closest thing possible to a definitive single-disc retrospective. —*Stephen Thomas Erlewine*

The Pink Fairies
....
f. 1970, West London, England, db. 1975
Rock 'n' Roll, Proto-Punk
The excessive, drug-fueled Pink Fairies grew out of the Deviants, a loose-knit band formed in 1967 by members of the West London hippie commune Ladbroke Grove. Initially dubbed the Social Deviants and consisting primarily of vocalist Mick Farren, guitarist Paul Rudolph, bassist Duncan Sanderson, and drummer Russell Hunter, the group also featured satellite members Marc Bolan, Steve Peregrine Took, and players from the band Group X, later rechristened Hawkwind. After three noisy, psychedelic albums and a US tour, Farren exited to become a music journalist; the remaining Deviants returned to London, where they recruited vocalist and former Pretty Things drummer Twink (born John Alder), who suggested the name Pink Fairies. Despite gaining a reputation for mythic debauchery, the group remained largely an underground sensation before signing to Polydor and issuing their 1971 debut *Never Never Land*, a manic, decadent album featuring the live staples "Do It" and "Uncle Harry's Last Freak Out."

Shortly after the record's release Twink departed, and the Pink Fairies continued on as a trio for 1972's *What a Bunch of Sweeties;* recorded with assistance from the Move's Trevor Burton, the album reached the Top 50 on the UK charts and was the group's most commercially successful effort. Soon, Rudolph exited to become a full-time member of Hawkwind and was replaced by UFO's Larry Wallis for 1973's hard-rock excursion *Kings of Oblivion.* Twink rejoined the Pink Fairies' ranks a short time later, but the group nonetheless disbanded before the end of the year.

In 1975, the *Kings of Oblivion*-era lineup reunited for a one-off London gig; an enthusiastic response led to the official re-formation of the nucleus of Rudolph, Sanderson, and Hunter, who added former Chilli Willi and Red Hot Peppers vocalist Martin Stone before again disbanding in 1977. A decade later, the original lineup—minus Rudolph, but including Wallis—reunited for the album *Kill 'Em and Eat 'Em* before calling it quits one more time. —*Jason Ankeny*

Never Never Land / 1971 / Polydor ✦✦✦
Peter Pan never imagined anything like this. —*John Dougan*

What a Bunch of Sweeties / 1972 / Polydor ✦✦✦
Slime, grunge, big guitars and "poetry." —*John Dougan*

● **Kings of Oblivion** / 1973 / Polydor ✦✦✦✦
Throbbing and nasty. Intellectual biker rock from hell! —*John Dougan*

Kill 'Em & Eat 'Em / 1987 / Skyclad ✦✦✦
The reunion LP. Surprisingly good and greasy! —*John Dougan*

Pink Floyd
....
f. 1965, London, England
Vocals / Art-Rock/Progressive-Rock, Psychedelic
Pink Floyd are the premier space-rock band. Since the mid-'60s, their music has relentlessly tinkered with electronics and all manner of special effects to push pop formats to their outer limits. At the same time, they have wrestled with lyrical themes and concepts of such massive scale that their music has taken on almost classical, operatic quality, in both sound and words. Despite their astral image, the group were brought down to earth in the 1980s by decidedly mundane power struggles over leadership and, ultimately, ownership of the band's very name. Since that time, they've been little more than a dinosaur act, capable of filling stadiums and topping the charts, but offering little more than a spectacular re-creation of their most successful formulas. Their latter-day staleness cannot disguise the fact that, for the first decade or so of

their existence, they were one of the most innovative groups around, in concert and (especially) in the studio.

While Pink Floyd are mostly known for their grandiose concept albums of the 1970s, they started as a very different sort of psychedelic band. Soon after they first began playing together in the mid-'60s, they fell firmly under the leadership of lead guitarist Syd Barrett, the gifted genius who would write and sing most of their early material. The Cambridge native shared the stage with Roger Waters (bass), Rick Wright (keyboards), and Nick Mason (drums). The name Pink Floyd, seemingly so far-out, was actually derived from the first names of two ancient bluesmen (Pink Anderson and Floyd Council). And at first, Pink Floyd were a much more conventional act than the act into which they would evolve, concentrating on the rock and R&B material that was so common to the repertoires of mid-'60s British bands.

Pink Floyd quickly began to experiment, however, stretching out songs with wild instrumental freak-out passages incorporating feedback, electronic screeches, and unusual, eerie sounds created by loud amplification, reverb, and such tricks as sliding ball bearings up and down guitar strings. In 1966, they began to pick up a following in the London underground; onstage, they began to incorporate light shows to add to the psychedelic effect. Most importantly, Syd Barrett began to compose pop-psychedelic gems that combined unusual psychedelic arrangements (particularly in the haunting guitar and celestial organ licks) with catchy melodies and incisive lyrics that viewed the world with a sense of poetic, childlike wonder.

The group landed a recording contract with EMI in early 1967 and made the Top 20 with a brilliant debut single, "Arnold Layne," a sympathetic, comic vignette about a transvestite. The follow-up, the kaleidoscopic "See Emily Play," made the Top Ten. The debut album, *The Piper at the Gates of Dawn*, also released in 1967, may have been the greatest British psychedelic album other than *Sgt. Pepper's*. Dominated almost wholly by Barrett's songs, the album was a charming funhouse of driving, mysterious rockers ("Lucifer Sam"), odd character sketches ("The Gnome"), childhood flashbacks ("Bike," "Matilda Mother"), and freakier pieces with lengthy instrumental passages ("Astronomy Domine," "Interstellar Overdrive," "Pow R Toch") that mapped out their fascination with space travel. The record was not only like no other at the time; it was like no other that Pink Floyd would make, colored as it was by a vision that was far more humorous, pop-friendly, and light-hearted than those of their subsequent epics.

The reason Pink Floyd never made a similar album was that *Piper* was the only one to be recorded under Barrett's leadership. Around mid-1967, the prodigy began showing increasingly alarming signs of mental instability. Syd would go catatonic on stage, playing music that had little to do with the material, or not playing at all. An American tour had to be cut short when he was barely able to function at all, let alone play the pop star game. Dependent upon Barrett for most of their vision and material, the rest of the group were nevertheless finding him impossible to work with, live or in the studio.

Around the beginning of 1968, guitarist Dave Gilmour, a friend of the band who was also from Cambridge, was brought in as a fifth member. The idea was that Gilmour would enable the Floyd to continue as a live outfit; Barrett would still be able to write and contribute to the records. That couldn't work either, and within a few months Barrett was out of the group. Pink Floyd's management, looking at the wreckage of a band that was now without its lead guitarist, lead singer, and primary songwriter, decided to abandon the group and manage Barrett as a solo act.

Such calamities would have proven insurmountable for 99 out of 100 bands in similar predicaments. Incredibly, Pink Floyd would regroup and not only maintain their popularity but eventually become even more successful. It was early in the game, after all; the first album had made the British Top Ten, but the group were still virtually unknown in America, where the loss of Syd Barrett meant nothing to the media. Gilmour was an excellent guitarist, and the band proved capable of writing enough original material to generate further ambitious albums, Waters eventually emerging as the dominant composer. The 1968 follow-up to *Piper at the Gates of Dawn, A Saucerful of Secrets*, made the British Top Ten using Barrett's vision as an obvious blueprint but taking a more formal, somber, and quasi-classical tone, especially in the long instrumental parts. Barrett, for his part, would go on to make a couple of interesting solo records before his mental problems instigated a retreat into oblivion (see separate entry on Syd Barrett for more details).

Over the next four years, Pink Floyd would continue to polish their brand of experimental rock, which married psychedelia with ever-grander arrangements on a Wagnerian operatic scale. Hidden underneath the pulsing, reverberant organs and guitars and insistently restated themes were subtle blues and pop influences that kept the material accessible to a wide audience. Abandoning the singles market, they concentrated on album-length works and built a huge following in the progressive-rock underground with constant touring in both Europe and North America. While LPs like *Ummagumma* (divided into live recordings and experimental outings by each member of the band), *Atom Heart Mother* (a collaboration with composer Ron Geesin), and *More* (a film soundtrack) were erratic, each contained some extremely effective music.

By the early '70s Syd Barrett was a fading or nonexistent memory for most of Pink Floyd's fans, although the group, one could argue, never did match the brilliance of that somewhat anomalous 1967 debut. *Meddle* (1971) sharpened the band's sprawling epics into something more accessible and polished the science-fiction ambience that the group had been exploring ever since 1968. Nothing, however, prepared Pink Floyd or their audience for the massive mainstream success of their 1973 album, *Dark Side of the Moon*, which made their brand of cosmic rock even more approachable with state-of-the-art production, more focused songwriting, an army of well-timed stereophonic sound effects, and touches of saxophone and soulful female backup vocals.

Dark Side of the Moon finally broke Pink Floyd as superstars in the US, where it made No. 1. More astonishingly, it made them one of the biggest-selling acts of all time. *Dark Side of the Moon* spent an incomprehensible 741 weeks on the *Billboard* album chart. Additionally, the primarily instrumental textures of the songs helped make *Dark Side of the Moon* easily translatable on an international level, and the record became (and still is) one of the most popular rock albums worldwide.

It was also an extremely hard act to follow, although the follow-up, *Wish You Were Here* (1975), also made No. 1, highlighted by a tribute of sorts to the long-departed Barrett, "Shine On You Crazy Diamond." *Dark Side of the Moon* had been dominated by lyrical themes of insecurity, fear, and the cold sterility of modern life; *Wish You Were Here* and *Animals* (1977) developed these morose themes even more explicitly. By this time Waters was taking a firm hand over Pink Floyd's lyrical and musical vision, which was consolidated by *The Wall* (1979).

The bleak, overambitious double concept album concerned itself with the material and emotional walls modern humans build around themselves for survival. *The Wall* was a huge success (even by Pink Floyd's standards), in part because the music was losing some of its heavy-duty electronic textures in favor of more approachable pop elements. Although Pink Floyd had rarely even released singles since the late '60s, one of the tracks, "Another Brick in the Wall," became a transatlantic No. 1. The band had been launching increasingly elaborate stage shows throughout the '70s, but the touring production of *The Wall*, featuring construction of an actual wall during the band's performance, was the most excessive yet.

In the 1980s, the group began to unravel. Each of the four had done some side and solo projects in the past; more troublingly, Waters was asserting control of the band's musical and lyrical identity. That wouldn't have been such a problem had *The Final Cut* (1983) not been such an unimpressive effort, with little of the electronic innovation so typical of their previous work. Shortly afterward, the band split up—for a while. In 1986, Waters was suing Gilmour and Mason to dissolve the group's partnership (Wright had lost full membership status entirely); Waters lost, leaving a Roger-less Pink Floyd to get a Top Five album with *Momentary Lapse of Reason* in 1987. In an irony that was nothing less than cosmic, about 20 years after Pink Floyd shed its original leader to resume its career with great commercial success, they would do the same again to his successor. Waters released ambitious solo albums to nothing more than moderate sales and attention, while he watched his former colleagues (with Wright back in tow) rescale the charts.

Pink Floyd still have a huge fan base, but there's little that's noteworthy about their post-Waters output. They know their formula, they can execute it on a grand scale, and they can count on millions of customers—many of them unborn when *Dark Side of the Moon* came out and unaware that Syd Barrett was ever a member—to buy their records and see their sporadic tours. *The Division Bell*, their first studio album in seven years, topped the charts in 1994 without making any impact on the current rock scene, except in a marketing sense. Ditto for the live *Pulse* album, recorded during a typically elaborately staged 1994 tour, which included a concert version of *The Dark Side of the Moon* in its entirety. Waters' solo career sputtered along, highlighted by a solo re-creation of *The Wall* performed at the site of the former Berlin Wall in 1990 and released as an album. Syd Barrett, it was reported in the summer of 1996, was lying ill in a Cambridge hospital, unable or unwilling to regulate his diabetic condition. —*Richie Unterberger*

☆ **The Piper at the Gates of Dawn** / Aug. 5, 1967 / Capitol ✦✦✦✦✦
The debut album combines long, group-written, largely instrumental compositions with shorter, whimsical, eclectic pop songs written by lead singer and guitarist Syd Barrett (his only full-length album appearance with the group). A wonderful evocation of the distinctly British take on '60s psychedelic music. (Note: Avoid the out-of-print LP version *Pink Floyd*, Tower 5093, which abridges the original UK album.) —*William Ruhlmann*

Tonite Let's All Make Love in London / 1968 / CBS ✦✦✦
Peter Whitehead's 1967 film *Tonight Let's All Make Love in London* was an attempt to document the mid-'60s swinging London pop scene at its

peak. The soundtrack was an instant collector's item, divided between interview snippets with such scene makers as Michael Caine, David Hockney, Julie Christie, and Mick Jagger, and marginal incidental music by unmemorable pop acts produced by Rolling Stones manager Andrew Loog Oldham (Vashti and Twice As Much). The Small Faces' contribution, "Here Comes the Nice," is easily available elsewhere. Allen Ginsberg (misspelled "Alan" on the original sleeve) reads the poem that gave the film its name. The chief attraction of this CD reissue is the addition of two lengthy, otherwise unavailable cuts by the original Pink Floyd lineup in 1967 (mere snippets had appeared on the original LP). Their 16-minute version of "Interstellar Overdrive" (re-recorded for their first LP) starts off scintillatingly, then degenerates into a rather aimless jam. The 12-minute "Nick's Boogie," not available in any other version, is a considerably more aimless, free-form instrumental piece dominated by scraping guitars. Even in its expanded CD reissue, this album will only appeal to hardcore collectors. —*Richie Unterberger*

A Saucerful of Secrets / Jun. 29, 1968 / Capitol ✦✦✦
A transitional album on which the band moved from Barrett's relatively concise and vivid songs to spacy, ethereal material with lengthy instrumental passages. Barrett's influence is still felt (he actually did manage to contribute one track, the jovial "Jugband Blues"), and much of the material retains a gentle, fairy-tale ambience. "Remember a Day" and "See Saw" are highlights; on "Set the Controls for the Heart of the Sun," "Let There Be More Light," and the lengthy instrumental title track, the band begin to map out the dark and repetitive pulses that would characterize their next few records. —*Richie Unterberger*

More / Jul. 1969 / Capitol ✦✦
Commissioned as a soundtrack to the seldom-seen French hippie movie of the same name, *More* was a Floyd album in its own right, reaching the Top Ten in Britain. The group's atmospheric music was a natural for movies, but when assembled for the record, these pieces were unavoidably a bit patchwork, ranging from folky ballads to fierce electronic instrumentals to incidental mood music. Several of the tracks are pleasantly inconsequential, but this record does include some strong compositions, especially "Cymbaline," "Green Is the Colour," and "The Nile Song." All of these developed into stronger pieces in live performances, and better, high-quality versions are available on numerous bootlegs. —*Richie Unterberger*

Ummagumma / Nov. 1969 / Capitol ✦✦✦
A double album, divided into live and studio discs. The live disc did a lot to put them on the map as figureheads of the international background, with precise, well-recorded versions of four of their most interesting, early lengthy opuses ("Astronomy Domine," "Careful with That Axe, Eugene," "Set the Controls for the Heart of the Sun," "A Saucerful of Secrets"). "Astronomy Domine," though performed minus its writer and original vocalist (Syd Barrett), could be said to surpass the original studio version (from *Piper at the Gates of Dawn*) in spookiness and drawn-out intensity. The studio disc allowed each of the four members one or two lengthy compositions, with variable results. The attempts at avant-garde experimentalism were unimpressive and have dated badly, but Roger Waters' "Grantchester Meadows," by contrast, is a lovely ballad and one of their best early songs. —*Richie Unterberger*

Atom Heart Mother / Oct. 1970 / Capitol ✦✦✦
Pink Floyd started to stretch out its long numbers here, with the orchestrated title track taking up an entire side of the album. Still not as focused as they would be, the group nevertheless was beginning to show the musical ambition that would lead to their later successes. —*William Ruhlmann*

Relics / May 1971 / Barclay ✦✦✦✦
A singles collection from the Syd Barrett era, containing the British hits "Arnold Layne" and "See Emily Play," among other psychedelic nuggets. —*William Ruhlmann*

Meddle / Oct. 30, 1971 / Capitol ✦✦✦✦
With *Meddle*, Pink Floyd instrumentally arrived at an airy ensemble sound, which would eventually find full flower on their 1973 classic *The Dark Side of the Moon*. This approach is particularly evident on "Echoes," a periodically languorous jam that takes up one half of the album. Nevertheless, there are enough sonic concepts and pleasant melodies at work on this album to make it worthwhile to the Floyd fan looking to dig deeper than *The Dark Side of the Moon* or *The Wall*. —*Rick Clark*

Obscured by Clouds / Jun. 1972 / Capitol ✦✦
Like *More*, *Obscured by Clouds* was a soundtrack album Pink Floyd threw together quickly for a film by Barbet Schroeder. Songs like "Free Four" show Roger Waters developing the songwriting skill that would catapult Pink Floyd to mass stardom with its next new release, *The Dark Side of the Moon*. —*William Ruhlmann*

★ **Dark Side of the Moon** / Mar. 24, 1973 / Capitol ✦✦✦✦✦
By condensing the sonic explorations of *Meddle* to actual songs and adding a lush, immaculate production to their trippiest instrumental sections, Pink Floyd inadvertently designed their commercial break-

through with *Dark Side of the Moon*. The primary revelation of *Dark Side of the Moon* is what a little focus does for the band. Roger Waters wrote a series of songs about mundane, everyday details which aren't that impressive by themselves, but when given the sonic backdrop of Floyd's slow, atmospheric soundscapes and carefully placed sound effects, they achieve an emotional resonance. But what gives the album true power is the subtly textured music, which evolves from ponderous, neo-psychedelic art-rock to jazz fusion and blues-rock before turning back to psychedelia. It's dense with detail, but leisurely paced, creating its own dark, haunting world. Pink Floyd may have better albums than *Dark Side of the Moon*, but no other record defines them quite as well as this one. — *Stephen Thomas Erlewine*

☆ **Wish You Were Here** / Sep. 12, 1975 / Columbia ✦✦✦✦✦
Pink Floyd followed the commercial breakthrough of *Dark Side of the Moon* with *Wish You Were Here*, a loose concept album about and dedicated to their founding member Syd Barrett. The record unfolds gradually, as the jazzy textures of "Shine On You Crazy Diamond" reveal its melodic motif, and in its leisurely pace, the album reveals itself to be a warmer record than its predecessor. Musically, it's arguably even more impressive, showcasing the group's interplay and David Gilmour's solos in particular. And while it's short on actual songs, the long, winding soundscapes are constantly enthralling. — *Stephen Thomas Erlewine*

Animals / Oct. 2, 1977 / Columbia ✦✦✦
Consisting of heavily reworked songs that had long been a part of Pink Floyd's live repertoire and were now given an Orwellian overview, *Animals* found Pink Floyd acting as the mouthpiece for Roger Waters' increasingly vitriolic takes on modern life. The result was one of its less successful later efforts. — *William Ruhlmann*

The Wall / Nov. 1979 / Columbia ✦✦✦✦
Roger Waters constructed *The Wall*, a narcissistic, double-album rock opera about an emotionally crippled rock star after spitting on an audience member who dared cheer during an acoustic song. Given its origins, it's little wonder that *The Wall* paints such an unsympathetic portrait of the rock star, cleverly named "Pink," who blames everyone—particularly women—for his neuroses. Such lyrical and thematic shortcomings may have been forgivable if the album had a killer batch of songs, but Waters took his operatic inclinations to heart, constructing the album as a series of fragments that are held together by larger numbers like "Comfortably Numb" and "Hey You." Generally, the fully developed songs are among the finest of Pink Floyd's later work, but *The Wall* is primarily a triumph of production: its seamless surface, blending melodic fragments and sound effects, makes the musical shortcomings and questionable lyrics easy to ignore. But if *The Wall* is examined in depth, it falls apart, since it doesn't offer enough great songs to support its ambition, and its self-serving message and shiny production seem like relics of the late-'70s Me Generation. — *Stephen Thomas Erlewine*

Collection of Great Dance Songs / Nov. 1981 / Columbia ✦✦
Anyone who knew anything about Pink Floyd knew that a dance band they were not, so this profit-taking, holiday-season compilation, courtesy of Columbia Records, was intended ironically. Arguably the quintessential album band, Pink Floyd is not well served by compilations, especially one on which the two parts of "Shine On You Crazy Diamond" are edited together and there's a re-recording of "Money." Stick to the full-length versions. — *William Ruhlmann*

Works / 1983 / Capitol ✦✦
Capitol Records gets into the Pink Floyd compilation game, but why bother when all you have in mind is the same old tired tracks, plus one previously unreleased song appropriately called "Embryo?" — *William Ruhlmann*

The Final Cut / Apr. 1983 / Columbia ✦✦✦
A Roger Waters solo album in all but name, containing the composer's response to Britain's Falklands War in the form of a massive condemnation of war and government. — *William Ruhlmann*

The Committee / 1985 / Funny Farm ✦✦
One of Pink Floyd's most interesting obscure projects was their soundtrack to a 1968 made-for-television film, *The Committee* (starring ex-Manfred Mann lead singer Paul Jones), that has rarely if ever been screened in the US. Side one of this bootleg has the bits of soundtrack that are graced by Floyd's presence. As enticing as it sounds, only hardcore fans will want this in their collections. The fidelity (sounding like it was taped from a television) is pretty bad, and the music is often obscured by dialogue. If the source tapes for the soundtrack still exist, their release might be pretty interesting; the group devised some pretty nifty instrumental licks, heavy on the haunting organs and slide guitar. Side two has three songs from a show at a club in Rome in May 1968, in execrable sound quality. In any case, this boot will be pretty hard to locate, as it was a limited edition of 300 copies. — *Richie Unterberger*

A Momentary Lapse of Reason / 1987 / Columbia ✦✦
A David Gilmour solo album in all but name, heavily featuring the kind of atmospheric instrumental music and Gilmour guitar sound typical of the Floyd before the now-departed Roger Waters took over but lacking Waters' unifying vision and lyrical ability. — *William Ruhlmann*

Delicate Sound of Thunder / Jan. 2, 1988 / Columbia ✦✦
This live album documents their 1987-1988 world tour. — *Rick Clark*

Shine On [Box Set] / Nov. 17, 1992 / Columbia ✦✦✦✦
A lavish and expensive nine-CD box set of Pink Floyd's greatest hits—which are all albums, naturally. Seven albums (*A Saucerful of Secrets*, *Meddle*, *The Dark Side of the Moon*, *Wish You Were Here*, *Animals*, *The Wall*, and *A Momentary Lapse of Reason*) have been digitally remastered; when the eight discs are set together on the shelf, their spines form the prism and rainbow from the cover of *The Dark Side of the Moon*. *Shine On* also includes an extra disc of early singles, housed in a digi-pak, and a hardcover book with plenty of pictures and text. Since there is no previously unreleased material included on the set, the only incentive for hardcore fans who already own the albums is the packaging and remastering, both of which are impressive. *Shine On* is certainly worth the investment for those who don't already own the music. — *Stephen Thomas Erlewine*

The Division Bell / Apr. 12, 1994 / Columbia ✦✦
The second post-Roger Waters Pink Floyd album is less forced and more of a group effort than *A Momentary Lapse of Reason*—keyboard player Rick Wright is back to full bandmember status and has co-writing credits on 5 of the 11 songs, even getting lead vocals on "Wearing the Inside Out." Some of David Gilmour's lyrics (co-written by Polly Samson and Nick Laird-Clowes of the Dream Academy) might be directed at Waters, notably "Lost for Words" and "A Great Day for Freedom," with its references to "the wall" coming down, although the more specific subject is the Berlin Wall and the fall of Communism. In any case, there is a vindictive, accusatory tone to songs such as "What Do You Want from Me" and "Poles Apart," and the overarching theme, from the album title to the graphics to the "I-you" pronouns in most of the lyrics, has to do with dichotomies and distinctions, with "I" always having the upper hand. Musically, Gilmour, Nick Mason, and Wright have largely turned the clock back to the pre-*Dark Side of the Moon* Floyd, with slow tempos, sustained keyboard chords, and guitar solos with a lot of echo. — *William Ruhlmann*

Pulse / Jun. 1995 / Columbia ✦✦
Pink Floyd claimed they had no intention of recording another live album when they began the *Division Bell* tour, but performing *The Dark Side of the Moon* in its entirety convinced the group to release another double live set, called *Pulse*. There's no question that the group is composed of talented musicians, including the number of studio professionals that augmented the trio on tour. Whether they're inspired musicians is up to debate. A large part of Pink Floyd's live show is based on the always impressive visuals; on the *Division Bell* tour, they closed each show with an unprecedented laser extravaganza. In order for the visuals and the music to coincide, the group needed to play the sets as tightly as possible, with little improvisation. Consequently, an audio version of this concert, separated from the visuals, is quite dull. Pink Floyd play the greatest hits and the new songs professionally, yet the versions differ only slightly from the original recordings, making *Pulse* a tepid experience. (The first edition of the album featured a blinking red light—a symbolic representation of the "pulse"—in the spine of the disc and cassette.) — *Stephen Thomas Erlewine*

Dark Side of the Moo / [Bootleg] ✦✦✦✦
Look at the title carefully; it's not the Floyd *meisterwerk*, but a wittily titled (and packaged, with *Atom Heart Mother*-like cows on the cover) bootleg of their rarest studio tracks. Presented in 99-100 percent of their original fidelity, these include some choice and necessary items that would cost you quite a bit to assemble piece by piece. From the Syd Barrett era, we have "Candy and a Currant Bun," the brilliant B-side to their debut "Arnold Layne" single, and "Apples and Oranges," the legendary flop single from late 1967. Other late-'60s (post-Syd) flop singles include the pleasant psychedelic ballads "It Would Be So Nice" and "Point Me at the Sky." A number of the other tracks, including their contributions to the *Zabriskie Point* soundtrack, the original studio version of "Astronomy Domine" (cut off the US version of the first LP), and the different "Interstellar Overdrive" that showed up on the *Tonite Let's All Make Love in London* soundtrack, have appeared on CD since the mid-'80s issue of this bootleg. If you're not inclined to spend an additional $50 or so tracking these down, it certainly makes sense to spring for this, if you can find it. — *Richie Unterberger*

Rhapsody in Pink (The Psychedelic Years: The Incredible BBC) / [Bootleg] ✦✦✦✦
Packaged under various titles, this is *the* collection of material to hunt for if you're looking for unreleased Floyd from the post-Barrett, pre-*Dark Side* era. Bootleg fidelity doesn't come any better than this; it's one of the very few occasions where you could argue that the sound may actually be *better* than most official releases. These BBC airshots from the late '60s and early '70s focus on rather obscure material: "Julia

Dream," "If," "Green Is the Colour," "Embryo," and the never-released "Murderistic Women" (a blueprint for "Careful with That Axe, Eugene"). There are also full-bore workouts of "Echoes" and "Atom Heart Mother Suite" that, depending on one's taste, could be argued to exceed the officially issued versions. The double LP, still findable, contains about 85 minutes of music and is a great value. —*Richie Unterberger*

Saucerful of Outtakes [bootleg] / [Bootleg] ✦✦✦

There is a huge demand for Syd Barrett material, and, alas, a very limited supply. This is probably the best compilation of unreleased Barrett-era Floyd, though the material and sound quality are erratic. "Lucy Leave" and "I'm a Kingbee" are the band's very first demos, showing a much more R&B-oriented outfit, and the live version of "Astronomy Domine" is pretty good. The BBC sessions contain a bunch of songs from the classic *Piper at the Gates of Dawn* album, in muffled, hissy fidelity that is nonetheless an improvement on many previous bootlegs. These include two of the most coveted Barrett-Floyd treasures, the unreleased songs "Vegetable Man" and "Scream Thy Last Scream," chaotic but fascinating pieces which illustrate Syd's descent into madness more vividly than anything else he recorded with the group. Be on the lookout, though, for much clearer studio outtakes of these two songs (perhaps recorded with Floyd, perhaps solo) that have appeared on bootlegs throughout the years. —*Richie Unterberger*

Gene Pitney

b. Feb. 17, 1941, Hartford, CT

Vocals / Pop, Pop-Rock, Teen Idol, Brill Building Pop

One of the most interesting and difficult-to-categorize singers in '60s pop, Gene Pitney had a long run of hits distinguished by his pained, one-of-a-kind, melodramatic wail. Pitney is sometimes characterized (or dismissed) as a shallow teen idol type prone to operatic ballads. It's true that some of his biggest hits—"Town Without Pity," "Only Love Can Break a Heart," "I'm Gonna Be Strong," "It Hurts to Be in Love," and "Twenty Four Hours from Tulsa"—are archetypes of adolescent or just-post-adolescent agony, characterized by longing and not a little self-pity.

But Pitney was not just an archetype of his style—he was one of the best at his style, and indeed one of the few (along with Roy Orbison) that could pull it off convincingly. Also (like Orbison), he had more range than he's generally given credit for, making forays into tough pop-rock, country, and even borderline rockabilly. Other than Dionne Warwick, he was the best interpreter of Bacharach-David's early compositions. Although he didn't pen much of his material, he was a composer of note, writing "He's a Rebel" for the Crystals and "Hello Mary Lou" for Rick Nelson. He was also something of a closet hipster—he was the first American artist to cover a Jagger-Richards song ("That Girl Belongs to Yesterday," which was a British hit before the Rolling Stones had ever entered the US Top 100), he contributed to an actual Rolling Stones session in early 1964 (during which they recorded "Not Fade Away"), he had a brief fling with a teenage Marianne Faithfull, and he recorded songs by Randy Newman and Al Kooper long before those musicians became famous.

Pitney broke into the music business as a songwriter in his late teens, getting his first taste of success when Rick Nelson had a hit with "Hello Mary Lou" in 1961. That same year, Pitney had a small hit with his first single, "(I Wanna Love My Life Away)," a self-penned demo on which he sang and played every instrument—an extraordinary feat for 1961. Another 1961 single, Goffin-King's "Every Breath I Take," was produced by Phil Spector and is one of the very first examples of his pull-out-the-stops Wall of Sound productions. Pitney didn't really find his metier, however, until late-1961's "Town Without Pity," which became his first Top 20 entry.

For the next four years, Pitney was one of the most successful, solo male vocalists in America, reeling off over a dozen more Top 40 hits. While lovelorn angst was his stock-in-trade, some of the singles were fairly innovative—"Half Heaven—Half Heartache" and "(The Man Who Shot) Liberty Valance" were crossover country-pop before that term existed, "Mecca" was one of the few big pop-rock hits to bear the influence of Middle Eastern music (albeit in a superficial fashion), and "Last Chance to Turn Around" was a hard-boiled, tough-luck tale worthy of a top-notch B-movie thriller.

Pitney withstood the initial onslaught of the British Invasion fairly well, scoring Top Ten hits in 1964 with "It Hurts to Be in Love" and "I'm Gonna Be Strong." By 1966, though, he was in serious trouble stateside. Ironically, by this time he was a much bigger star in Britain, making the UK Top Ten six times in 1965-66. He could also depend on a faithful international audience throughout Europe and frequently recorded in Italian and Spanish for overseas markets. In 1966, he became one of the first artists to reach success with Randy Newman compositions, taking "Nobody Needs Your Love" and "Just One Smile" into the British Top Ten. Pitney entered the US Top 20 one last time in 1968 with "She's a Heartbreaker," a rather forced updating of his trademark sound. That was basically it for his career as a significant recording artist, although

he remains a big concert draw on the overseas nostalgia circuit. In 1989, he made No. 1 in the UK again by duetting with Mark Almond on a remake of one of his '60s singles, "Something's Gotten Hold of My Heart." —*Richie Unterberger*

● **Anthology 1961-1968** / 1986 / Rhino ✦✦✦✦

The voice still sounds surreal, like no one else in pop music, and this collection of hits exudes class. Emotional, pained, stunning. Pitney is a master—rock's Caruso. —*Jeff Tamarkin*

More Greatest Hits / Apr. 11, 1995 / Varese Sarabande ✦✦✦✦

A very worthy supplement to *Anthology;* in fact, it's almost as good. Has a lot of minor hits, some of which ("I Must Be Seeing Things," "Backstage") rank among his best; "Nobody Needs Your Love," an early Randy Newman composition that was a No. 2 hit in England in 1966; Pitney's own versions of his compositions "Hello Mary Lou" and "Today's Teardrops," much better known via their interpretations by Rick Nelson and Roy Orbison, respectively; and interesting album tracks and flop singles. All cuts are from the '60s, except the 1989 version of "Something's Gotten Hold of My Heart," performed as a duet with Marc Almond. —*Richie Unterberger*

Pixies

f. 1986, Boston, MA, **db.** 1993

Alternative Pop-Rock

Combining jagged, roaring guitars and stop-start dynamics with melodic pop hooks, intertwining male-female harmonies, and evocative, cryptic lyrics, the Pixies were one of the most influential American alternative rock bands of the late '80s. The Pixies weren't accomplished musicians—Black Francis wailed and bashed out chords while Joey Santiago's lead guitar squealed out spirals of noise. But the band were inventive, rabid rock fans who turned conventions inside out, melding punk and indie guitar rock, classic pop, surf rock, and stadium-sized riffs with singer-guitarist Black Francis' bizarre, fragmented lyrics about space, religion, sex, mutilation, and pop culture. While the meaning of his lyrics may have been impenetrable, the music was direct and forceful. The Pixies' busy, brief songs, extreme dynamics, and subversion of pop song structures proved one of the touchstones of '90s alternative rock. From grunge to Brit-pop, the Pixies' shadow loomed large—it's hard to imagine Nirvana without the Pixies' signature stop-start dynamics and lurching, noisy guitar solos. While the Pixies were touted as the band to bring indie rock into the mainstream, they simply laid the groundwork for the alternative explosion of the early '90s. MTV was reluctant to play their videos, while even modern rock radio didn't put their singles into regular rotation. Furthermore, tensions between leader Black Francis and bassist-vocalist Kim Deal, who wanted to incorporate her songs into the band's repertoire, crippled the band's progress. By the time Nirvana broke the doors down for alternative rock in 1992, the Pixies were effectively broken up.

The Pixies were formed in Boston, MA, in 1986 by Charles Thompson and his roomate, Joey Santiago. Born in California, Thompson began playing music as a teenager before he moved to the East Coast during high school. Following graduation, he became an anthropology major at the University of Massachusetts. Halfway through his studies at the college, he went to Puerto Rico to study Spanish, and after six months he decided to move back to the US to form a band. Thompson dropped out of school and moved to Boston, managing to persuade Santiago to join him. Advertising in a music paper for a bassist who liked "Husker Du and Peter, Paul & Mary," the duo recruited Kim Deal (billed as Mrs. John Murphey on the group's first two records), who had previously played with her twin sister Kelly in the folk-rock garage band the Breeders in her hometown of Dayton, OH. On the advice of Deal, the group recruited drummer David Lovering. Inspired by Iggy Pop, Thompson picked the stage name Black Francis and the group named themselves the Pixies, after Santiago randomly flipped through the dictionary.

By the fall, the Pixies had played enough gigs to land a supporting slot for their fellow Boston band, Throwing Muses. At the Muses concert, Gary Smith, an artist manager and producer at Boston's Fort Apache studios, heard the group and offered to record them. In March 1987, the Pixies recorded 18 songs over the course of three days. The demo, dubbed *The Purple Tape*, was given to key players within the Boston musical community and the international alternative scene, including Ivo Watts, the head of England's 4AD Records. Impressed with the cassette, Watts signed the band and released eight of the demo's songs as the EP *Come On Pilgrim* in 1987.

The Pixies convened to record their first full-length album, *Surfer Rosa*, with producer Steve Albini, who had pioneered the thin, abrasive indie-guitar grind with Big Black. Albini gave the band a harder-edged, abrasive guitar sound, yet the group retained their melodic hooks. Released in the spring of 1988, *Surfer Rosa* earned enthusiastic reviews from the British weekly music press and became a college radio hit in America; in the UK, the album made inroads on the pop charts. By the end of the year, the buzz on the Pixies had become substantial, and the group signed to Elektra Records. At the end of 1988, the group re-entered the studio, this time with British producer Gil Norton. Released in the spring of 1989, *Doolittle* boasted a cleaner sound and received excellent reviews, which led to greater exposure in America. "Monkey Gone to Heaven" and "Here Comes Your Man" became Top Ten modern rock hits, clearing the way for *Doolittle* to peak at No. 98 on the US charts; in the UK, it entered the charts at No. 8. Throughout their career, the Pixies were more popular in Britain and Europe than America, as evidenced by the success of the "Sex and Death" tour. The band became notorious for Black Francis' motionless performances, which were offset by Deal's charmingly earthy sense of humor. The tour itself became infa-mous for the band's in-jokes, such as playing their entire set list in alphabetical order. By the completion of their second American tour for *Doolittle* at the end of 1989, the group had begun to tire of each other, and they decided to take a hiatus during the beginning of 1990.

During the hiatus, Black Francis went on a brief solo tour, and Kim Deal formed a group with Tanya Donelly from the Throwing Muses and bassist Josephine Wiggs of Perfect Disaster, naming it after her teen-age band, the Breeders. The Breeders recorded the Albini-produced *Pod*, which appeared on 4AD in early summer 1990, shortly after the Pixies reconvened to record their third album with Gil Norton. More atmo-spheric than its predecessors and relying heavily on Black's surf-rock obsession, *Bossanova* was released in the fall of 1990; unlike *Surfer Rosa* or *Doolittle*, it contained no songs by Deal. *Bossanova* was greeted with decidedly mixed reviews, but the record became a college hit, generating the modern rock hits "Velouria" and "Dig for Fire" in the US. In Europe, the record expanded the group's popularity, hitting No. 3 on the UK album charts and paving the way for their headlining appear-ance at the Reading Festival. Though the supporting tours for *Bossanova* were successful, tension continued to grow between Kim Deal and Black Francis—at the conclusion of their English tour, Deal announced from the stage of the Brixton Academy that the concert was "our last show."

While the Pixies did cancel their planned American tour, due to "exhaustion," the band reconvened in the spring of 1991 to record their fourth album, again with Gil Norton. Hiring former Captain Beefheart and Pere Ubu keyboardist Eric Drew Feldman as an auxiliary member, the band moved back toward loud rock, claiming to be inspired by the presence of Ozzy Osbourne in a neighboring studio. Upon its fall release, *Trompe le Monde* was hailed by some as a welcome return to the sound of *Surfer Rosa* and *Doolittle*, but closer inspection revealed that it relied heavily on sonic detail and featured very few vocals by Deal and none of her songs. The band embarked on another interna-tional tour, playing stadiums in Europe, but theaters in America. During the spring of 1992, the Pixies opened for U2 on the opening leg of the *Zoo TV* tour; it would be their last trek through the US. Upon conclu-sion of the *Zoo TV* tour, the Pixies went on hiatus, with Deal returning to the Breeders who released the EP *Safari* later that spring. Black Fran-cis began working on a solo album.

As he was preparing to release his solo debut, Black Francis gave an interview on BBC's Radio 5, announcing that the Pixies were disband-ing. He hadn't yet informed the other members; later that day, he faxed them his statement. Inverting his stage name to Frank Black, Black Francis released his eponymous debut that spring to mixed reviews; over the next few years, Frank Black's audience gradually shrunk to a small cult following. The Breeders released their second album, *Last Splash*, in the fall of 1993. The album became a surprise hit, going gold in the US and spawning the hit single "Cannonball." Santiago and Lov-ering formed the Martinis in 1995; as of 1997, the group had only appeared on the soundtrack to *Empire Records*. —*Stephen Thomas Erlewine*

Come on Pilgrim [EP] / 1987 / 4AD/Elektra ✦✦✦✦
The band's first mini-album is actually some of the demos that the group gave to 4AD. The label was so impressed by the group's potential that it released eight of the demos (paid for by Black Francis' dad). It's easy to see why they were impressed; *Come On Pilgrim* contains some of the group's best material, from the eerie opener "Caribou" to the pro-pulsive pop of the final track, "Levitate Me." Not one of the eight tracks on *Come On Pilgrim* is a ringer; "I've Been Tired," "Nimrod's Son," and "Ed Is Dead" also prove that the Pixies' debut is one of their finest efforts. —*Heather Phares*

☆ **Surfer Rosa** / 1988 / 4AD/Elektra ✦✦✦✦✦
Surfer Rosa is one of the seminal art-punk albums of the '80s. It mixes thrashy guitars, boy-girl harmonies, and strange lyrics in a way that still sounds fresh and innovative. Joey Santiago's prickly guitar work, Black Francis' psychotic shriek of a voice, Kim Deal's steady bass and lumi-nous vocals, and David Lovering's formidable drumming unite in nine blazing punk and unique pop. "Bone Machine," "Broken Face," "Oh My Golly!" and "Vamos" zip along at a fearsome rate, taking no prisoners. But the Pixies' beauty is just as apparent on *Surfer Rosa*. Tracks like Deal's "Gigantic" and Francis' "Where Is My Mind" provide refreshing

contrasts to the rest of the album's incandescent energy. —*Heather Phares*

★ **Doolittle** / 1989 / 4AD/Elektra ✦✦✦✦✦
The group's third album (and their first for Elektra) continues the Pixies' winning break. With Gil Norton producing, the band's raw edge is smoothed and streamlined into something too clever to be just punk but too edgy and neurotic to be simply pop. Driving surf tunes like "Debaser" and "Wave of Mutilation" coexist with raw, disturbing tracks like "Dead," "Tame," and "Gouge Away." But as always, the Pixies exhibit their schizophrenic pop sensibilities and also produce melodic and catchy tunes like "Here Comes Your Man" and "La La Love You." —*Heather Phares*

Bossanova / Aug. 1990 / 4AD/Elektra ✦✦✦✦
The Pixies' fourth album dives deeper into the group's twin fascinations of surf pop and science fiction. Much of the hyperkinetic punk energy of the first three albums is missing, resulting in a kinder, gentler, but no less iconoclastic band. "Is She Weird," "Rock Music," "Allison," and "All over the World" are some of the album's highlights, as well as "Havalina," which shows off Deal's glorious voice. —*Heather Phares*

Trompe le Monde / Oct. 8, 1991 / 4AD/Elektra ✦✦✦
The band's final album is not so much a return to their early, aggressive sound as it is a fusion of their raw energy and eccentricity. It's both arty and rousing, especially on fun tracks like "Subbacultcha," "Palace of the Brine," "D Equals RxT," and "U-Mass." Beautiful and offbeat songs like "Bird Dream of the Olympus Mons," "The Navajo Know," and "Letter to Memphis" confirm that the Pixies were and are one of the most individ-ual talents in alternative music. —*Heather Phares*

Pizzicato Five

f. Japan
Alternative Pop-Rock, Club-Dance
Truly an alternative '90s band for postmoderns, Japan's Pizzicato Five cuts up and deconstructs detritus from American pop with imagination and humor. Sound engineers Yashuaru Konishi and K-Taro Takanami compile, sample, and edit scraps from various critically ignored schools of pre-1980 pop, including disco, spy soundtracks, Bacharach-David pop, bossa nova, and easy listening; Maki Nomiya often lays her chanteuse English/Japanese vocals on top. After over a dozen albums in Japan, they were introduced to the US audience in 1994 via Matador's *Made in USA* compilation. Too kitschy for many listeners (both mainstream and alternative), there's no denying that Pizzicato Five go about their busi-ness with fun and intelligence on releases like 1995's *Sound of Music* and 1997's *Combinaison Spaciale* EP. —*Richie Unterberger*

● **Made in USA** / 1994 / Matador ✦✦✦✦
Although it's not billed as such, the group's stateside debut is actually a compilation of tracks from their 15 or so albums. You need a taste for irreverent sampling and ironic deconstruction of lightweight pop idioms to dig this. But within that narrow field, Pizzicato Five are as good as it gets. They devise fare that's both funky and funny, made more human than most such projects by Maki Nomiya's fetching vocals. —*Richie Unterberger*

The Sound of Music by Pizzicato Five / Oct. 31, 1995 / Atlantic ✦✦✦✦

Plainsong

f. 1972, London, England
Folk-Rock
A quartet formed by Ian Matthews in 1972 with Andy Roberts, Bob Ronga, and Dave Richards. They released the brilliant *In Search of Ame-lia Earhart* the same year to critical praise, but little commercial suc-cess. While working on their follow-up, the more country-oriented *Plainsong III*, Ronga quit, and Matthews and Richards were unable to agree on the direction the band would take musically. They disbanded before the album's completion. In 1993, a revived interest in the band inspired a new studio album, *Dark Side of the Room*, as well as a BBC recording of a promotional tour from 1972. In 1994, the band released *Voices Electric. Sister Flute* followed in 1996. In 1997, Clive Gregson (ex-Any Trouble, Gregson & Collister) joined the band. —*Chris Woodstra*

■ **In Search of Amelia Earhart** / 1972 / Elektra ✦✦✦✦
The theme of this album is loosely based on the disappearance of Ame-lia Earhart and features four tunes penned by Matthews including the spooky "For the Second Time" and "Call the Tune." Matthews also shows his ability to pick top-notch material by covering Paul Siebel's "Louise," the Jim & Jesse classic "Diesel on My Tail," and Rick Cunha's "Yo Yo Man" (a song Cunha attempted to chart with a year later). —*Jim Worbois*

On Air—Original Bbc Recordings / 1993 / Band of Joy ✦✦✦✦

Dark Side of The Room / Oct. 19, 1993 / Line ✦✦✦
Matthews and company regrouped for this 1993 album. Though the album lacks much of the charm of their first album, the songs have a

craftsmanlike precision and are certainly pleasant enough. The album is more closely connected to Matthews' later work than to its predecessor. —*Chris Woodstra*

Voices Electric / 1994 / Watermelon ✦✦

Sister Flute / Dec. 17, 1996 / Line ✦✦✦

Robert Plant

b. Aug. 20, 1948, Birmingham, England
Harmonica, Vocals / Hard Rock, Pop-Rock

British hard rock/heavy metal singer Robert Plant had released a couple of singles and worked with a number of bands before he hooked up with Jimmy Page's New Yardbirds, subsequently renamed Led Zeppelin, around the time of his 20th birthday in 1968. For the next 12 years, Plant was one of the biggest rock stars on the planet. He gradually developed as a singer, branching out into other styles within Zeppelin's hard rock framework, and he blossomed as a songwriter as well.

Plant launched a solo career in 1982 with the album *Pictures at Eleven*, a gold-selling hit. He did even better the following year with *The Principle of Moments*. It sold a million copies, included the Top 20 hit "Big Log" and led to his first post-Zeppelin concert tour. Surprisingly, Plant then organized a one-off mini-album, *The Honeydrippers—Vol. One*, recording some rock oldies with a superstar pickup band. He faced greater consumer resistance with his third solo album, *Shaken 'n' Stirred*, perhaps because joint appearances with Page led an audience to desire for a Zeppelin reunion. To an extent, Plant fed that desire with *Now and Zen*, which sampled Zeppelin tracks and featured Page. It was another million-seller. Plant's 1990 follow-up, *Manic Nirvana*, went gold. —*William Ruhlmann*

Pictures at Eleven / 1982 / Swan Song ✦✦✦✦

The directions in which Plant seemed to be heading in the later Zeppelin records—toward lighter, more melodic music, tempered with sometimes odd rhythms—are continued on his first solo album, which finds him singing less and screaming less. It wasn't Led Zeppelin, but then, that was the whole point. —*William Ruhlmann*

● **Principle of Moments** / 1983 / Es Paranza ✦✦✦✦

Plant reinvents rock and pop oldies in much the way Led Zeppelin did old blues songs. "Other Arms" recasts "Lay Down Your Arms," as Plant declares, "I'm not a prisoner of the big parade," while "In the Mood" retools an old pop theme. The playing is propulsive (thanks to guest drummer Phil Collins), and Plant's singing unusually supple. —*William Ruhlmann*

Shaken 'N' Stirred / 1985 / Es Paranza ✦✦✦

Robert Plant continued to expand the horizons of his music with his third album, *Shaken 'n' Stirred*, adding elements of worldbeat to his increasingly atmospheric and synth-driven pop-rock. Although the experimentation is admirable and occasionally successful, the most successful tracks on the album are straightforward numbers like "Little by Little." —*Stephen Thomas Erlewine*

Now & Zen / 1988 / Es Paranza ✦✦✦

Robert Plant hires a new band, prominently featuring keyboardist Phil Johnstone and also adds a backup singer for a fuller sound. At the same time, the appearance of Jimmy Page on "Tall Cool One," a Top 25 hit, casts a glance back at Plant's Led Zeppelin days. —*William Ruhlmann*

Manic Nirvana / Mar. 1990 / Es Paranza ✦✦

Manic Nirvana essentially continued the revitalized hard-rock crunch of *Now & Zen*. Unlike the previous record, *Manic Nirvana* played it a little closer to the vest, concentrating on a set of lean, driving riff-rockers instead of ponderous Led Zeppelin pomp. While the overall result is successful—especially on the frenzied "Hurting Kind," the technicolor stomp of "Tie Die on the Highway" and the affectionate rockabilly cover "Your Ma Said You Cried in Your Sleep Last Night"—the album sounds like a holding pattern instead of a step forward. —*Stephen Thomas Erlewine*

Fate of Nations / May 27, 1993 / Es Paranza ✦✦✦

At first, *Fate of Nations* seems so light and airy that it slips away through the layers of acoustic guitars, violins, and keyboards. Upon further listenings, more textures appear, and the album gains a calm sense of tension and reflectiveness. It's also Plant's most personal record ever; he addresses the death of his son in the beautiful "I Believe." Simultaneously, *Fate of Nations* is a political album—"Great Spirit" and "Network News" are two of the most socially conscious songs Plant has ever written. Yet, the album is never heavy-handed, and it doesn't fall into sermonizing or sentimentality. Plant has always had a folkie heart; on *Fate of Nations*, he wears it on his sleeve. —*Stephen Thomas Erlewine*

Plasmatics

f. 1979, New York, NY, **db.** 1983
Punk, New Wave

Although their "fame" lasted for a full 15 minutes, few bands entered rock 'n' roll with such a controversial reputation as did the Plasmatics. Founded by Rod Swenson (a porn film producer who fancied himself the next Malcolm McLaren), the Plasmatics were fronted by sex film "star" Wendy O. Williams, a muscular, raspy-voiced "singer" who generally wore little onstage. (Her most radical bit of fashion accessorizing consisted of covering her nipples with black electrical tape.) Almost as captivating was guitarist Richie Stotts, a tall, gangly geek who fancied garters and stockings and a blue mohawk; he also liked to smash his guitar against his head until he drew blood. Playing the New York punk circuit (i.e. CBGBs), the Plasmatics became notorious for their extreme stage shows, which, early on, culminated in Williams firing blanks from a sawed-off shotgun and taking a chainsaw to a human dummy filled with stage blood, sending a spray of fake gore throughout the club and anticipating the fake carnage of GWAR by nearly a decade. The music, however, was another story: mostly subliterate punk rock loaded with lots of quasi-sci-fi totalitarianism and consumer nightmares of Orwellian proportions that on record didn't work without the stage pyrotechnics, something I'm sure Swenson and the 'Matics understood completely as the stage shows quickly became more elaborate: cars were blown up, guitars were sawed in half (oddly, the dummy disappeared), equipment was set on fire—it was a Beavis and Butt-Head wet dream come to life.

None of this translated into significant record sales. While Williams became something of a demi-celebrity in punk circles, especially after she was busted (and brutalized by police) in Milwaukee for "public indecency," the Plasmatics were (gee, what a surprise) all show and no substance. Stotts, apparently on a quest for legitimacy, quit the band, and the focus became Williams rather than the bunch of unknowns backing her up, even though one of her backup musicians was future Ramones producer and one-shot, hard rock solo artist Jean Beauvoir. Williams eventually went solo, worked with Lemmy from Motorhead, and roped in Kiss' Gene Simmons to produce her totally useless album *W.O.W.* By the end of the '80s, she was recording rap tracks and acting in B-films. Her career since then is pretty much a mystery, one that's perhaps best left unsolved. —*John Dougan*

New Hope for the Wretched / 1980 / Stiff ✦✦

● **Beyond the Valley of 1984/Metal Priestess** / 1981 / PVC ✦✦✦✦

If you're interested in actually listening to the Plasmatics (though I'd guess watching a video of them performing would be infinitely more satisfying), this is the only recording worth getting. More of a heavy-metal than a punk record, it was reissued with their EP *Metal Priestess*, so you can get more bang (pun intended) for your buck. There are songs here worth playing more than once, and the outrage and vituperation seems real, even if it is a pose. Notable trivia: the drummer is ex-Alice Cooper tubman Neil Smith, a veteran of the *Killer* and *Billion Dollar Babies* Cooper era. —*John Dougan*

Metal Priestess / 1981 / PVC ✦✦✦✦

Coup D'Etat / 1982 / Capitol ✦✦✦

Plastic Bertrand

f. Belgium
New Wave

Plastic Bertrand was the alias of new wave prankster Roger Jouret, a native of Belgium who appropriated the sound and style of the new wave movement in order to give it a gently satirical poke in the ribs, while scoring several European hits in the process. Jouret began his musical career as a drummer for the Belgian punk trio Hubble Bubble, which recorded one unsuccessful album. When Jouret met producer-songwriter Lou Deprijck, the two struck up a recording partnership; Jouret emphasized his pretty-boy looks and punkish fashion sense. Their first effort, "Ca Plane pour Moi" ("This Life's for Me"), is widely regarded as a new wave classic for its gleefully deranged stupidity, with Jouret singing French nonsense lyrics in a cartoonish voice over basic three-chord rock 'n' roll complete with saxophones and a falsetto vocal hook straight out of the Beach Boys or Four Seasons. The song was a smash in Europe and became a cult favorite in America; Plastic Bertrand continued to release records in Europe, including a UK hit remake of the Small Faces' "Sha-La-La-La-Lee." Bertrand experimented with almost every new wave fashion, including spacy electronics, disco, bubblegum pop, reggae, and spoken-word raps, all with the same naggingly entertaining stupidity. He remained popular on the European continent and in Canada for several years, where audiences were more attuned to his largely French lyrics, but the novelty eventually wore off, and nothing was heard from Bertrand after 1982. Plastic Bertrand released several albums, all of which are difficult to find; a greatest-hits collection is also floating around. —*Steve Huey*

Plastic Bertrand AN1 / 1978 / Sire ✦✦✦✦

Ca Plane Pour Moi / 1978 / Sire ✦✦✦✦

J'te Fais Un Plan / 1979 / RKM ✦✦✦

L'album / 1980 / Attic ✦✦

Grand Succes/Greatest Hits / 1981 / Attic ✦✦✦

Plastiquez Vos Baffles / 1982 / Attic ✦✦✦

● **Plastic Hits** / 1995 / ✦✦✦✦

Apart from the gleefully deranged mini-masterpiece of absurdity "Ca Plane pour Moi" and the spacy "Major Tom," *Plastic Hits* consists of comical, frequently annoying, European regurgitations of new wave rock, which only occasionally place tongue in cheek. The sound is largely the same, and the simple choruses are usually repeated ad nauseum. That said, songs like "Hula Hoop," "Super Cool," and "C'est le Rock and Roll" (a ripoff of the Four Seasons' "Walk Like a Man") do have a certain dopey charm for those fascinated by trashy, formulaic imitations of American culture. —*Steve Huey*

Plastic People of the Universe

f. 1968, Prague, Czechoslovakia, **db.** 1984
Experimental
This band's debut may well have been one of the most amazing and radical records to be released during the punk era (or any era for that matter); it was recorded under the most extreme conditions in the years before punk rock was a reality (1973-74). Prague's Plastic People of the Universe, and the band they later became, Pulnoc, remain one of rock 'n' roll's great stories of triumph, showing how great music can be produced and survive even in the most hostile of environments. The band was founded in 1968 soon after 500,000 Soviet troops invaded Czechoslovakia. With the Kremlin not being particularly fond of Western-style rock that wasn't sanctioned by the state, the Plastic People, to paraphrase the Jefferson Airplane, quickly became outlaws in the eyes of Moscow (and the ruling Soviet government in Prague). From 1970 until the "Velvet Revolution" of 1989 that ended Soviet domination, the Plastic People lived a mostly illegal existence, with two of their members, Ivan Jirous and Jaroslav Vozniak, doing lengthy stretches in prison. Influenced by Zappa, English progressive rock/radical politicos Henry Cow, Captain Beefheart, and the Velvet Underground, the Plastic People appropriated the avant-garde leanings and anti-authoritarian outrage of these bands while working from their own sense of dread and desperation. Remember, according to Soviet law, they could not record, press and distribute albums, or play gigs; still, they did all three surreptitiously with the help of their numerous artist friends who made up an indefatigable support network known as the Invisible Organization.

Although all of their music remained unheard outside of Eastern Europe (or Czechoslovakia for that matter), their first record was released in the West in 1978. *Egon Bondy's Happy Hearts Club Banned* was not a proper record in the sense that the Plastic People entered a studio with the intent to record a "rock" record that would be placed into mass circulation. The reality was that these were grubby, low-fi demo recordings made by friends on primitive equipment and released without the band's knowledge. It also marked the first time the poetry of Czech dissident Egon Bondy was heard outside of Czechoslovakia. Bondy wrote lyrics that meshed perfectly with the Plastic People's cacophonous sound: harsh, dissonant soloing over repetitive, odd-metered rhythms. It remains dense, challenging music, totally oblivious to the state-approved pop music.

A ferocious government crackdown on the Plastic People and their supporters occurred in 1976. Many of them were jailed, their meager instruments and recording equipment confiscated or destroyed, all in the hope that this troublesome group of avant-garde, artistic, political radicals would finally be stopped. The problem was that Czech government officials didn't realize that the music of the Plastic People was being listened to in the West (thanks to favorable reviews of *Egon Bondy's* in the British music press and in America in the *Village Voice*) and that groups such as Amnesty International were now wondering why these musicians were being persecuted and jailed without trial. Although never reaching the fever pitch of, say, Nelson Mandela's incarceration, it wasn't long before the plight of the Plastic People became better known to an outraged Western pop community. After being released from prison, the band managed two more releases in the '80s that were (and still are) extremely difficult to find, unless you live in New York.

After 15 years of struggle, incarceration, harassment, and violence, the Plastic People quietly disbanded in 1984 but in no way stopped their antigovernment activities. Finally, in 1988, a year before the "Velvet Revolution" and the ascendancy of the poet Vaclav Havel (a longtime supporter and occasional lyricist for the Plastic People) to the presidency, the band was given government permission to perform under the name Pulnoc ("Midnight"). With three original Plastic People in the group (Milan Hlavsa, Josef Janicek, and Jiri Kabes), Pulnoc recorded an extraordinary debut for Arista in 1991 (*City of Hysteria*), and a difficult-to-find, live cassette was recorded at New York's vaunted experimental performance space PS 122. Unlike the radical, dissonant sounds of the Plastic People, Pulnoc had a more traditional, guitar-based rock sound and production polish, but its accessibility in no way detracts from its greatness

as a record. For reasons unknown to me, there has been little music from Pulnoc since *City of Hysteria*. But, whatever the case, this story had a much happier ending than anyone could have anticipated. Although much work is required in finding what little recorded work they made, the payoff is well worth the effort. —*John Dougan*

● **Egon Bondy's Happy Heart Club Banned** / 1978 / Invisible ✦✦✦✦

Sounding like a meeting between Zappa, Henry Cow, and Allen Ginsberg, this is a wild, politically charged chunk of avant-garde agit-prop. Bondy's poetry may not be the most lyrical you've ever heard, but his imagery is striking in its desperation and anger. Lots of honking saxes courtesy of Vratislav Brabenec, who is a big-time blower in the style of German free-jazz player Peter Brotzmann. For those whose love for late-'60s/early-'70s progressive-rock is boundless, this is absolutely essential. But, even if you're squeamish about anything labeled art-rock, don't pass this by; the raw emotions and intense idealism in the face of oppression, despite their being sung in a language you don't speak (there are English lyrics on the LP jacket), are very moving. —*John Dougan*

Leading Horses / 1983 / Bozi Mlyn ✦✦✦✦

I'll be honest, I've never heard either of these records. The only reviews of them I've ever read were by longtime Plastic People supporter Robert Christgau in his monthly *Village Voice Consumer Guide*. He gave *Passion Play* a B+ and *Leading Horses* an A-. That's all the info I need. If you find them before I do, please tell me where you purchased them. —*John Dougan*

Plastikman

b. 1970, London, England
Techno, Club-Dance, Electronica, Acid
His style formed with a minimal fusion of acid-house and Detroit techno, Richie Hawtin became a big name in techno during the early '90s due to his skill at DJing and his recorded output as Plastikman (for NovaMute) and FUSE (for Warp/TVT). Using the Roland 303 (a dinosaur in the techno field), Hawtin combines lean percussion and equally spare acid synth into haunting techno anthems that work just as well on the dance floor as in the living room.

While original Detroit technocrats like Derrick May and Juan Atkins were changing the face of electronic music, Richie Hawtin was growing up just across the river in Windsor, Canada. A native of England born in 1970, he moved to Canada with his family ten years later. Introduced to '70s electronic pioneers Kraftwerk and Tangerine Dream by his father (who worked in the auto industry), Hawtin began DJing at the age of 16 and soon landed gigs at Detroit hot spots like the Shelter and Music Institute. Though many of Motown's innovators were initially skeptical of the skinny, white Canadian, Richie Hawtin's formation of the Plus 8 label helped deflect much of the criticism.

Hawtin and co-founder John Acquaviva first began working together in 1990 to make a Derrick May megamix; instead, they emerged from the studio with "Elements of Tone." The duo issued the single that same year as the first release on Plus 8 Records (credited to States of Mind) and sat back while the techno world puzzled over who was responsible. Plus 8's later releases—by Kenny Larkin, Jochem Paap (aka Speedy J), and Mark Gage (aka Vapourspace), in addition to various Hawtin/Acquaviva projects—made the label famous for laboratory-precise techno. Demand grew at the same time for Hawtin's excellent DJing, which was obviously acid inspired but also reliant on slowly evolving and shifting tones reminiscent of the classic Motor City DJs.

The Plastikman project debuted in 1993 with releases for Plus 8: the single "Spastik" and an album, *Sheet One*. Hawtin's first wide release, however, came with the alter-ego FUSE (short for Further Underground Subsonic Experiments). A more varied and melodic project than Plastikman, FUSE released the album *Dimension Intrusion* for Warp/TVT in late 1993 as part of Warp's *Artificial Intelligence* series (also the wide-issue beginnings for Black Dog, B12, and Aphex Twin). Later, NovaMute signed Hawtin's Plastikman project and during 1994 re-released *Sheet One* plus the follow-up *Musik* and the retrospective *Recycled Musik*. All told, Hawtin was responsible for the issue of four albums in the span of just one year.

Hawtin's 1995 was much less busy. He spent time setting up the sub-labels Probe and Definition and continued to DJ around the world. Though he recorded singles for Plus 8 and related imprints, his only full-length release that year was the excellent *Mixmag Live!* album, taken from a DJ set recorded at the Building in Windsor. As mainstream techno began to unite around the fuller house sound of Orbital and Underworld, Richie Hawtin's minimalist acid remained popular with a shrinking audience of club kids that still called him the best in the business. —*John Bush*

● **Muzik** / Nov. 8, 1994 / Plus 8 ✦✦✦✦

Although limiting himself to tried-and-true boxes like the 909 and 303, Hawtin's creative use of potentially tired sounds is inspired. Not exactly for the casual listener, as development and dynamic are often a matter of subtlety and nuance, but still bright and involved enough to bear out repeat listenings. Hawtin's best overall. —*Sean Cooper*

Mixmag Live, Vol. 20: Plastikman / 1995 / Mixmag ✦✦✦✦
Richie Hawtin (aka Plastikman, F.U.S.E.) mixed this twentieth volume in *Mixmag*'s series of DJ compilations. —*John Bush*

The Platters

f. 1953, Los Angeles, CA
R&B, Pop, Doo Wop
The Platters started out as a Los Angeles-based, Black doo wop group with little identity of their own to make them stand out from the pack. They started out making their first records for Federal, a subsidiary of Cincinnati's King Records. These early sides don't sound *anything* like the better-known sides that would eventually emerge from this group, instead merely aping the current R&B trends and styles of the day. What changed their fortunes can be reduced down to one very important name—that of their mentor, manager, producer, songwriter, and vocal coach—Buck Ram. Ram took what many would say was a run-of-the-mill, R&B, doo wop vocal group and turned them into stars and into one of the most enduring and lucrative groups of all time. By 1954, Ram was already running a talent agency in Los Angeles, writing and arranging for publisher Mills Music, managing the Three Suns—a pop group with some success—and working with his protégés, the Penguins. The Platters seemed like a good addition to his stable.

After getting them out of their Federal contract, Ram placed them with the burgeoning, national independent label Mercury Records (at the same time he brought over the Penguins following their success with "Earth Angel"), automatically getting them into pop markets through the label's distribution contacts alone. Then Ram started honing in on the group's strengths and weaknesses. The first thing he did was put the lead vocal status squarely on the shoulders of lead tenor Tony Williams. Williams' emoting power was turned up full blast with the group (now augmented with Zola Taylor from Shirley Gunter and the Queens) working as very well structured vocal support framing his every note. With Ram's pop songwriting classics as its musical palette, the group quickly became a pop and R&B success, eventually earning the distinction of being the first Black act of the era to top the pop charts. Considered the most romantic of all the doo wop groups (i.e., the ultimate in "make out music"), hit after hit came tumbling forth in a seemingly effortless manner: "Only You," "The Great Pretender," "My Prayer," "Twilight Time," "Smoke Gets in Your Eyes," "Harbor Lights," all of them establishing the Platters as the classiest of all.

Williams struck out on his own in 1961, and by decade's end the group had disbanded with various members starting up their own versions of the Platters. This bit of franchising now extends into the present day with an estimated 125 sanctioned versions of "the original Platters" out on the oldies show circuit. —*Cub Koda*

The Very Best of the Platters / Oct. 22, 1991 / Mercury ✦✦✦✦
The Platters' 12 biggest hits are featured on this brief, but solid, collection; it's fine for those who don't want to spend the money on the double-disc set. —*Stephen Thomas Erlewine*

★ **The Magic Touch: An Anthology** / Oct. 22, 1991 / Mercury ✦✦✦✦✦
Double-disc set of all their best sides, including "The Great Pretender," "Smoke Gets in Your Eyes," "Only You," "Harbor Lights," and the title track. Great annotation and impeccable sound. All compilations should be done this well. —*Cub Koda*

The Plimsouls

f. 1978, Los Angeles, CA, **db.** 1983
Group / Rock 'n' Roll, New Wave, Power Pop
At a time when rock music was shifting gears, the Plimsouls threw British Invasion into the new wave mix and permanently altered the genre. Fun was the operative word, and bar bands everywhere joined the fray. But the Plimsouls were exceptional because they boasted the talents of singer-songwriter Peter Case.

The band formed in Los Angeles in 1978 and merged roots, retro, and guitar rock with a ramshackle punk aesthetic. Case had already collaborated with Jack Lee and Paul Collins in the Nerves, who had some success in 1976 with the single "Hangin' on the Telephone," later recorded by Blondie. In 1978, Case met L.A. locals guitarist Eddie Munoz, drummer Lou Ramirez, and bassist Dave Pahoa. After one EP, *Zero Hour* in 1980, and an album in 1981 that contained some stellar power-pop in songs like "Zero Hour" and "Hush, Hush," it looked like the band was a new wave one-off until a single from the soundtrack to *Valley Girl*, "A Million Miles Away," lifted them from new wave obscurity and cemented their reputation. The song remains a timeless classic. An album for Geffen, *Everywhere At Once*, followed in 1983 with a re-recorded version of the song, but ultimately, the liaison with the label was not a lasting one; the Plimsouls broke up shortly after the album's release. A testament to their strength as a live band was captured on

One Night in America and released in 1988. Case went on to record folk music for the label and remains a potent solo artist, while the rest of the band took on day jobs and various other musical projects. In 1995-96, the band, sans Ramirez, took a stab at re-forming and played a few reunion dates with former Blondie drummer Clem Burke, but after recording, plans to release new material were scrapped for the time being. —*Denise Sullivan*

● **The Plimsouls . . . Plus** / 1981 / Rhino ✦✦✦✦
The band's official debut boasts some of their greatest work, most of it culled from the *Zero Hour* EP, which is also included here. "Hush, Hush," "Zero Hour," and "How Long Will It Take?" stand as quintessential new wave gems. Singer Peter Case emerged as one of rock's great voices and songwriters, and the band speeds along in characteristic British Invasion/roots-rock fashion. —*Denise Sullivan*

Everywhere at Once / 1983 / Geffen ✦✦✦✦
An ill-fated stab at commercial acceptance, the Plimsouls broke up shortly after the release of their second album. "Oldest Story in the World" and "Inch by Inch" foretell the level singer-songwriter Peter Case might have gotten up to had the band stayed together, moving beyond their simple roots and attempting to take them into more mature rock territory. Re-recorded versions of "How Long Will It Take?" and the brilliant "A Million Miles Away" also make this long-hard-to-locate record worth seeking. —*Denise Sullivan*

One Night in America / 1988 / Fan Club ✦✦
Someone got the bright idea nearly six years after the band's breakup to release this live show from 1981 as a sort of official bootleg. It completely captures the group's essence in performance—tight but messy, retro but completely original. The signature tunes "Hush, Hush," "How Long Will It Take" and "A Million Miles Away" are here in all of their raw, live glory, but the band's cover of the Kinks' "Come On Now," also a standard in their live sets from the era, is what sells them. This is rock 'n' roll in its purest form that will appeal to the connoisseur as well as the most casual listener. —*Denise Sullivan*

PM Dawn

f. 1988, New Jersey
Hip Hop, Urban, Alternative Rap
Composed of brothers Prince B (Attrell Cordes) and DJ Minute Mix (Jarrett Cordes), the early-'90s group PM Dawn straddled the gap between hip-hop and smooth '70s-style soul, creating innovative urban R&B that owed as much to pop as it did to rhythm and blues. The brothers recorded their debut single, "Ode to a Forgetful Mind," in 1988. PM Dawn didn't release a full-length album until 1991. The record, *Of the Heart, of the Soul, of the Cross: The Utopian Experience*, was an immediate hit, thanks to the single "Set Adrift on Memory's Bliss," which sampled Spandau Ballet's new wave hit "True." Both the album and the single received glowing reviews, as did the 1993 follow-up, *The Bliss Album?*, which featured the hit singles "I'd Die Without You" and "Looking Through Patient Eyes." In 1995, PM Dawn returned with *Jesus Wept*, which received strong reviews but weak sales. —*Stephen Thomas Erlewine*

★ **Of the Heart, Of the Soul and Of the Cross . . .** / Aug. 6, 1991 / Gee Street ✦✦✦✦✦
Of the Heart, of the Soul and of the Cross: The Utopian Experience is a standout release, sandwiching psychedelic tinges, political/social discourse, and invigorating raps and production. Includes the hit "Set Adrift on Memory Bliss." —*Ron Wynn*

The Bliss Album? / Mar. 23, 1993 / Gee Street ✦✦✦✦
It's inaccurate to label PM Dawn a hip-hop band, since their sensibility lies with smooth ballads and mellow soul; they only use hip-hop to underscore their songs. In many ways, *The Bliss Album?* is a more focused album than their debut, containing such brilliant ballads as "I'd Die Without You" and "Looking Through Patient Eyes." When Prince Be tries to go harder, as on "Plastic," the results are well intentioned, but seriously flawed—they don't have the strength or power to pull off hardcore material. But when they stick to their pop-friendly R&B, PM Dawn is often quite remarkable; *The Bliss Album?* was the rare second album to expand on, rather than duplicate, the achievements of the debut. —*Stephen Thomas Erlewine*

Jesus Wept / Oct. 3, 1995 / Gee Street ✦✦✦✦
With their third album, *Jesus Wept*, PM Dawn doesn't necessarily make a great leap forward. Instead, they make some great refinements. Prince Be's lyrics are just as trippy and cryptic as ever, but they appear more focused, offering a poetic, spiritual worldview that is supported by the lovely, layered music. Using artists like Prince, Stevie Wonder, Marvin Gaye, and the Beatles as starting points, Prince Be creates a unique world assembled equally from soul, pop, hip-hop, and psychedelia. As individual pieces, the songs might not always make much sense, but taken as a whole, they create a singular world that is rich in lush melodies and sumptuous arrangements. Occasionally, PM Dawn's ambition

gets the best of them, and the results sound self-indulgent, not transcendent. However, those moments are few and far between on *Jesus Wept*, the group's best album. —*Stephen Thomas Erlewine*

Vibrations Of Love & Anger & The Ponderance of Life & Existence / 1996 / Island ✦✦✦

Poco

f. 1968, Los Angeles, CA
Group / Country-Rock, Soft Rock
One of the first and longest-lasting country-rock groups, Poco had its roots in the dying embers of the Buffalo Springfield. After co-founders Neil Young and Stephen Stills exited in the spring of 1968, only guitarist-singer Richie Furay and bassist Jim Messina remained to complete the group's swan song, *Last Time Around*. The final Springfield track, "Kind Woman," included only Furay and Messina, with a guest appearance on steel guitar by Rusty Young, formerly of Boenzee Cryque. He stuck with Furay and Messina, passing on a scheduled audition for a new group that Gram Parsons was putting together. Auditions followed before the fledgling group reached out to Young's ex-Boenzee Cryque bandmate George Grantham on drums and vocals and bassist-singer Randy Meisner. This lineup rehearsed for four months before making their debut at the L.A. Troubadour in November. A month later, they made their first appearance at the Fillmore West on a bill with the Steve Miller Band and Sly & The Family Stone.

At the time, they were using the name Pogo, but that didn't last. Walt Kelly, the creator of the comic strip *Pogo*, from which they'd freely admitted borrowing the name, didn't appreciate the group's choice and filed a lawsuit. Not wanting to lose all of the recognition and goodwill they'd built up locally over the previous five months, the result was a change of just one consonant, to Poco. Just one day after signing to Epic in early 1969, Randy Meisner suddenly left the band, apparently over personality clashes; he later joined the Eagles. Recorded as a four-piece, Poco's debut *Pickin' Up the Pieces* was released in June of 1969. The group was back to being a quintet in 1970 with the addition of bassist Timothy B. Schmit, whose arrival coincided with the recording of their second album, *Poco*. It wasn't long after that that Messina decided to leave, feeling that Furay had assumed too much control over the group's sound. Before departing, he secured the services of a capable replacement member—Paul Cotton, a onetime member of the Illinois Speed Press—and also played on and produced their subsequent album, *Deliverin'*, which rose to No. 26 and yielded the minor hit "C'mon." Their next album, 1971's *From the Inside*, was produced in Memphis by Booker T. and the M.G.'s guitarist Steve Cropper. The same lineup became the first Poco membership to last for more than one studio album. Their second album, *A Good Feelin' to Know*, was released in 1972, but by this time, even Furay had begun to lose heart over the band's lack of commercial success.

The band made one renewed effort, *Crazy Eyes*, their most accomplished studio album to date; released late in 1973, it became their most successful work. However, just as the LP was released, Furay left the group to hook up with Chris Hillman and John David Souther to form the Souther-Hillman-Furay Band. Still, Poco continued as a quartet. Their next album, *Seven*, released in the spring of 1974, failed to replicate the success of *Crazy Eyes*. The group was at a critical point in their history following the release of one more Epic album, *Cantamos*, which appeared in the fall of 1974 and got no higher than No. 76. After parting with Epic, in 1975 Poco signed with ABC Records. Their next album, *Head over Heels*, issued in mid-1975, surpassed expectations to fall just shy of the Top 40.

After the album *Rose of Cimarron*, the group came close to splitting up in 1976, with new member Al Garth exiting in the middle of the year. Finally, in the spring of 1977, *Indian Summer* was released. Four months later, Timothy Schmit exited the lineup to replace Meisner in the Eagles. Grantham followed him out of the band in January of 1978, eventually becoming Ricky Skaggs' drummer. The group re-formed with Charlie Harrison and Steve Chapman joining Young and Cotton. Kim Bullard, a Crosby, Stills & Nash alumnus, came in on keyboards in December of that year, and Poco was once again a quintet. All of these personnel changes seemed to have done the trick, because their next album, *Legend*, released late in 1978, became the best-selling LP in their history, earning a gold record in the course of rising to No. 14. The accompanying single "Crazy Love" reached No. 17, far and away their biggest seller to date. It was matched by Cotton's "Heart of the Night," which got to No. 20 during the summer of 1979.

However, their subsequent albums *Under the Gun, Blue and Gray*, and *Cowboys and Englishmen* did progressively worse. *Ghost Town*, issued late in 1982, peaked at an anemic No. 195. Furay rejoined the group briefly in mid-1984 along with Schmit, resulting in the *Inamorata* album, which scarcely made any impact. A five-year hiatus followed before the original quintet re-formed in the spring of 1989. Their comeback single, "Call It Love," hit the Top 20, accompanied by the

album *Legacy*, which made it to No. 40. Although the 1968 lineup didn't stay together, Poco was restored as a working band, touring periodically with Cotton and Young at its core. —*Bruce Eder*

Pickin' Up the Pieces / 1969 / Epic ✦✦✦✦
The group went into the studio with a sudden loss of one member (Randy Meisner), an engineer who didn't quite get what they were trying for, and a lot of pressure for a first album—and came up with this startlingly great record, as accomplished as any of the Buffalo Springfield and also reminiscent of the Beatles and the Byrds. *Pickin' Up the Pieces* is all the more amazing when one considers that Messina and Grantham were both covering for the departed Meisner in hastily learned capacities on bass and vocals, respectively. The title track is practically an anthem for the virtues of country-rock, with the kind of sweet harmonizing and tight interplay between the guitars that the Byrds, the Burritos, *et al* had to work a while to achieve. The mix of good-time songs ("Consequently So Long," "Calico Lady"), fast-paced instrumentals ("Grand Junction"), and overall good feelings makes this a great introduction to the band, as well as a landmark in country-rock only slightly less important (and more enjoyable than) *Sweetheart of the Rodeo*. —*Bruce Eder*

Poco / May 6, 1970 / Epic ✦✦✦
A slightly more laidback record, with a purer country feel to some of the songs ("Honky Tonk Downstairs"), and stronger playing. The quintet of Furay, Messina, Young, Grantham, and newly recruited bassist Timothy B. Schmit has a more assertive overall sound, especially their playing—Jim Messina's lead guitar is starting to move into Neil Young territory, and Grantham's drumming is about the best in country-rock. —*Bruce Eder*

From the Inside / 1971 / Epic ✦✦
Umm, crunchy guitars. *From the Inside* is the group's most unusual record, and one the band didn't like all that much, but a very good one anyway. Produced in Memphis by guitar legend Steve Cropper, *From the Inside* features a leaner, more stripped-down, somewhat bluesier sound. The harmonies are less radiant and the guitars (mostly acoustic) more radiant. The spirits are also a little more low-key than usual, but this is still a wonderful record, if a little offbeat. Grantham's drums and Schmit's bass are nice and up front in the mix, and the guitars have a really close presence. Highlights include "You Are the One," "Hoe Down," "Railroad Days" (maybe their hardest rocker) and "Ol' Forgiver." —*Bruce Eder*

Deliverin' / Jan. 13, 1971 / Epic ✦✦✦✦
Poco had originally made their name as a live act, and they'd always been at their best and most easygoing on stage. The result is this live album of all new material, featuring Jim Messina's swan song with the band and some of the tightest playing and best singing in their recorded history. Jewels include "C'mon," "Hear That Music," "Kind Woman," and "You'd Better Think Twice." About as perfect an album as they ever made and, not coincidentally, by far the biggest seller that the early group ever had. —*Bruce Eder*

A Good Feelin' to Know / Oct. 25, 1972 / Epic ✦✦✦
Good Feelin' to Know was Poco's big attempt to broaden their audience—the title track, one of their most popular concert numbers, was the group's push for a hit single, which didn't work. The album as a whole, however, features a louder, harder rocking sound a step or two removed from the country-rock they'd been known for, even on numbers like "Ride the Country," which has a more brittle sound than the group would've achieved on their earlier records. The guitars are all turned up really loud, and the harmonies are less sweet, overall making for a very heavy sound and one surprisingly similar to the Buffalo Springfield (one of their old numbers, "Go and Say Goodbye," is even included, in an arguably better version), making this a curious throwback/advance. This album's relative failure made Furay begin to lose faith in his own group's prospects. —*Bruce Eder*

Crazy Eyes / 1973 / Epic ✦✦✦✦
The third biggest selling album in the group's history, *Crazy Eyes* is also the group's most lively and bracing work and contains some of their most soulful music. In short, it is the fruition of everything they'd been working toward for four years. Curiously, it is also one of a handful of examples of their using outside help, including Chris Hillman on mandolin. The resulting sound is richer than anything found on any other Poco album, and the only tragedy is that the band reportedly cut enough tracks for two whole albums—one longs to hear the material that remained in the can. As it is, there's not a weak song or even a wasted note anywhere on this album, and most bands would kill for a closing track as perfect as "Let's Dance Tonight." The sound is excellent on this CD reissue, and only some historical notes would have improved it. —*Bruce Eder*

Seven / 1974 / Epic ✦✦✦
With strong, soaring harmonies, a healthy balance between acoustic country-rock and heavy rock 'n' roll, and some fairly strong songs, *Seven*

is a major surprise, given that this is the group's first post-Richie Furay album. George Grantham's drumming is a special highlight (check out his solo on "Drivin' Wheel"), but all of the playing is superb, and with one or two additional strong songs, this would be a highly recommended album, and as it is it is quite good. Unfortunately, not everything here is as strong as "Drivin' Wheel" or "Rocky Mountain Breakdown." —*Bruce Eder*

Cantamos / Dec. 1974 / Epic ✦✦✦
This album marks the emergence of Rusty Young as a composer of merit. Side one rocks out hard and fresh while the second side deals with lost love and broken-hearted romance. Much of the magic of their earlier albums has been recaptured. —*Jim Chrispell*

Head over Heels / Jul. 1975 / MCA ✦✦✦✦
Keeping the songs short and to the point, Poco lets loose with a fine batch of material. This time out, they even cover the Becker-Fagen song "Dallas" with great verve. There's less country but a lot more pop. —*Jim Chrispell*

The Very Best of Poco / Sep. 1975 / Epic ✦✦✦✦
A well-chosen, double LP compilation (now on one CD) chronicling Poco's Epic Records period, 1969-1974. —*William Ruhlmann*

Rose of Cimarron / 1976 / One Way ✦✦
Lushly produced pop-rock, *Rose of Cimmaron* hosts an array of sidemen, most notably Al Garth, formerly of Loggin & Messina, and keyboardist Steve Ferguson. The country influence is nearly abandoned except for the Rusty Young tune "Company's Comin'/Slow Poke." There are great tunes with great arrangements throughout. —*Jim Chrispell*

Live / Apr. 1976 / Epic ✦✦✦
The group's only full-length live recording (a concert track or two also turned up on at least one of those early-'70s festival albums), recorded along their winter 1974 tour. Without Richie Furay in the band, this isn't exactly the ideal showcase for the group, although they sound good, and they're certainly doing earlier material, including "Good Feelin' to Know." Worth tracking down as a companion to *Seven* and *Cantamos*. (Out-of-print) —*Bruce Eder*

Indian Summer / 1977 / MCA ✦✦✦
Although highly listenable, this album marks the slow descent of a band once at the forefront of the country-rock movement. High points include the title track and the mini-suite entitled "The Dance." Donald Fagen of Steely Dan adds synths here and there. —*Jim Chrispell*

Legend / Nov. 1978 / MCA ✦✦✦
The departure of Timothy B. Schmit to the Eagles should have signaled the end for Poco. However, they turned in a surprisingly tight set here and got their first Top 40 hit with "Crazy Love." —*Jim Chrispell*

Under the Gun / 1980 / MCA ✦✦
A deliberate follow-up to *Legend*, *Under the Gun* was a workmanlike but unremarkable effort. —*William Ruhlmann*

Blue and Gray / 1981 / One Way ✦✦
A concept album about the Civil War, not well executed. —*William Ruhlmann*

Cowboys & Englishmen / 1982 / One Way ✦
Poco's contractual obligation album to get off MCA Records (which had taken over ABC Records). A throwaway effort at a time when their career needed rejuvenation, not another wound. (Originally released on LP by MCA Records, *Cowboys & Englishmen* was licensed to One Way Records for CD reissue.) —*William Ruhlmann*

Backtracks / 1982 / MCA ✦✦✦✦
A nine-song compilation of Poco's tenure at ABC (later MCA) Records, 1975-1982, judiciously chosen. Later expanded for CD release and retitled *Crazy Loving: The Best of Poco 1975-1982*. —*William Ruhlmann*

Ghost Town / 1982 / Atlantic ✦✦✦
Surprise! Just when they had been written off by even the most loyal fans, Poco rebounds nicely here. Songs "Shoot for the Moon," "When Hearts Collide," and the title track are pleasant reminders of a band that once was. —*Jim Chrispell*

Inamorata / 1984 / Atlantic ✦✦
Poco was down to the duo of Rusty Young and Paul Cotton by this point, which may be why, having been visited in the studio by former members Richie Furay, Timothy Schmit, and George Grantham, they structured the credits in such a way that you might think the old group had reformed. Not so. Rather, this was a mediocre (and final) effort by an act long past its prime. —*William Ruhlmann*

Legacy / Aug. 1989 / RCA ✦✦
A reunion of the "Original Poco" could not stand up to the hype that surrounded its release. Jim Messina does his best on the hit "Call It Love," and Randy Meisner covers Richard Marx's tune "Nothin' to Hide." Other selections fall short of the mark. —*Jim Chrispell*

Crazy Loving: Best of Poco 1975-1982 / Oct. 1989 / MCA ✦✦✦✦
In the wake of Poco's success with *Legacy*, MCA Records resurrected their 1982 best of, *Backtracks*, added tracks to fill it out to respectable CD length, threw in some liner notes, and reissued it under a new title. It's not Poco's best period, but this is a good selection that will satisfy most casual listeners. —*William Ruhlmann*

● **The Forgotten Trail (1969-1974)** / Oct. 1990 / Epic ✦✦✦✦
This definitive two-CD collection is full of wonderful moments and great songs, so it is the obvious starting point. —*Bruce Eder*

The Pogues (Pogue Mahone)

f. 1982, Kings Cross, London, England, db. 1996
Alternative Pop-Rock, British Folk
By demonstrating that the spirit of punk could live in traditional Irish folk music, the Pogues were one of the most radical bands of the mid-'80s. Led by Shane MacGowan, whose slurred, incomprehensible vocal often disguised the sheer poetry of his songs, the Pogues were undeniably political—not only were many of their songs explicitly in favor of working-class liberalism but the wild, careening sound of their punk-injected folk was implicitly radical. While the band was clearly radical, they also had a wickedly warped sense of humor, which was abundantly clear on their biggest hit, the fractured Christmas carol "Fairy Tale of New York." The group's first three albums—*Red Roses for Me, Run Sodomy and the Lash, If I Should Fall from Grace from God*—were widely praised in both Britain and America, and by 1988 they had earned substantial cult followings in both countries. Yet MacGowan's darkly romantic, wasted lifestyle, which was so key to their spirit and success, ultimately proved to be their downfall. By the end of the decade, he had fallen deep into alcoholism and drug addiction, forcing the band to fire him if they wanted to survive. The Pogues carried on without him in the early '90s, playing to a slowly shrinking audience before finally disbanding in 1996.

Shane MacGowan, an Irish punk inspired by the Clash, formed the Pogues in 1982 after playing with the London-based punk band the Nipple Erectors, a group which was later called the Nips. MacGowan met Spider Stacy in a London tube station, where Stacy was playing a tin whistle. The two began working together, drafting former Nip Jim Fearnley to play guitar. Naming themselves Pogue Mahone—a Gaelic term meaning "kiss my ass"—the trio began playing traditional Irish tunes in London pubs and streets, eventually adding Jeremy Finer (banjo, guitar), Andrew David Ranken (drums), and Cait O'Riordan (bass) to make it a full band. As the group developed into a sextet, they added MacGowan's original songs to their repertoire and began earning a reputation as a wild, drunken, and exciting live act. Shortening their name to the Pogues, the group released an independent single, "Dark Streets of London," in early 1984 and supported the Clash on their summer tour. By the fall, they had signed with Stiff Records and had released their acclaimed debut, *Red Roses for Me*.

Red Roses for Me was a critical hit, establishing the Pogues as one of the most vital, and certainly one of the most political, bands in Britain. Early in 1985, they added guitarist Philip Chevron and recorded *Rum Sodomy and the Lash* with producer Elvis Costello. The album was an underground success and was widely praised, especially for MacGowan's songwriting—not only in the UK but also in the US, where they were becoming college radio staples. Instead of following *Rum Sodomy and the Lash* with a new album, the Pogues took nearly a full year hiatus from recording, releasing the *Poguetry in Motion* EP in 1986 and appearing in Alex Cox's film *Straight to Hell* in 1987. By 1988, O'Riordan had left the band to marry Costello, and she was replaced by Darryl Hunt; banjoist Terry Woods was also added to the band. Early in 1988, they signed to Island Records and released the Steve Lillywhite-produced *If I Should Fall from Grace with God* later that year. The album became the group's biggest hit, generating the No. 2 UK single "Fairytale of New York," which featured vocalist Kirsty MacColl.

Although the Pogues were peaking in popularity, Shane MacGowan's relentless drug and alcohol abuse was beginning to cripple the band. Although neither the 1989 hit single "Yeah Yeah Yeah Yeah" nor *Peace and Love* (also '89) were noticeably affected by his excesses, MacGowan missed the Pogues' prestigious opening dates in 1988 for Bob Dylan and stalked the stage like a madman during a pivotal *Saturday Night Live* performance. By 1990's *Hell's Ditch*, Spider Stacy and Jeremy Finer began singing the bulk of the Pogues' material. Despite positive reviews, *Hell's Ditch* was a flop, and the group wasn't able to support the record because of MacGowan's behavior. Consequently, he was asked to leave the band in 1991.Three years later, he returned with a new band, the Popes. For subsequent tours, the Clash's Joe Strummer filled in as lead vocalist, but by the time the band recorded their comeback *Waiting for Herb* in 1993, Stacy had become the permanent vocalist. *Waiting for Herb* was kindly reviewed, yet was also ignored, as was 1995's *Pogue Mahone*. In 1996, the Pogues decided to disband after 14 years in the business. —*Stephen Thomas Erlewine*

Red Roses for Me / 1984 / Enigma ✦✦✦

The Pogues' debut was hampered by an unfocused production, which lets the band run loose over the traditional numbers but gives Shane MacGowan's originals a careening power that belies the fact that he was still finding a distinctive voice. — *Stephen Thomas Erlewine*

Rum Sodomy & the Lash / 1985 / MCA ✦✦✦✦

A triumph, produced by Elvis Costello. Shane MacGowan has never sounded so intense, nor has the band played with such authority. A classic melding of punk-era-defined sensibilities and the magic of Celtic traditionalism. Features a stirring version of Eric Bogle's classic "And the Band Played Waltzing Matilda." — *John Dougan*

● **If I Should Fall from Grace with God** / 1987 / Island ✦✦✦✦

The Pogues' third album is another fiery, eclectic meld of traditional Celtic music and rock played with punk venom. The band can barely keep up with the breakneck pace of songs like "Bottle of Smoke," which is what makes the album so appealing. Overall, this album has more of a rock spirit than *Rum Sodomy & the Lash*, and MacGowan's songs show significant strides in quality. — *Stephen Thomas Erlewine*

Peace and Love / Jul. 1989 / Island ✦✦✦✦

Snarling with the anger and intensity of punk rock but always mindful of Irish and Celtic traditions, the Pogues ended the 1980s on a high note with the freewheeling *Peace and Love*. Influences ranging from the Clash to Bruce Springsteen (whose impact is most apparent on "USA Lorelei" and "Misty Morning, Albert Bridge") continue to inspire the distinctive Irish band, which wisely goes for rawness and gut feeling rather than precision. Lead singer Shane MacGowan's tragic drug and alcohol abuse was painfully obvious at that point, and at times, his vocals sound garbled—but even so, his passion and soulfulness come through. And on "Cotton Fields," "London, You're a Lady," and "Boat Train," MacGowan's songwriting is as inspired as ever. — *Alex Henderson*

Hell's Ditch / 1990 / Island ✦✦✦

From the beginning, the Clash had been one of the Pogues' primary influences. So it's most appropriate that Joe Strummer produced *Hell's Ditch*. The former Clash guitarist wisely and insightfully avoids smoothing out too many of the date's rough edges and seems to encourage rawness and go-for-broke passion (which generally serve the band well). This time, elements of Middle Eastern and Latin music are added to the Pogues' intriguing rock/Irish folk mix. It's hard to miss the effect that drugs and alcohol were having on the self-destructive Shane MacGowan, whose vocals are even more garbled than they were on *Peace and Love*. In fact, he sounds like he's in a drunken stupor most of the time. Nonetheless, his songwriting is often superb and brilliant on this risk-taking, if uneven, project. — *Alex Henderson*

Yeah Yeah Yeah Yeah Yeah / Sep. 1990 / Island ✦✦

A relentless, Motown-styled raveup, "Yeah Yeah Yeah Yeah Yeah" was one of the Pogues finest moments and one of their hardest rockers. It was a British hit in 1988, yet it took two years for an EP of the same name to appear. The EP is one of the group's most rock-oriented efforts—it even features a version of the Rolling Stones' "Honky Tonk Women"—but it's not entirely successful, with the noticeable exception of the title track. — *Stephen Thomas Erlewine*

The Essential Pogues / Nov. 19, 1991 / Island ✦✦✦✦

Essential Pogues doesn't cover *Red Roses for Me* or *Rum Sodomy & the Lash*, so it isn't a definitive collection. However, it does capture the majority of the highlights from their Island albums and functions as a good introduction to the band. One complaint: the tedious extended remix of "Yeah, Yeah, Yeah, Yeah, Yeah" was included instead of the punchy, energetic original single. — *Stephen Thomas Erlewine*

Waiting for Herb / Oct. 19, 1993 / Chameleon ✦✦

Without Shane McGowan, the Pogues are a competent Irish folk-rock band with several strong songs, yet they lack the fire of their earlier albums. For the diehard, *Waiting for Herb* will be necessary, even if it is a little disheartening. — *AMG*

The Pointer Sisters

f. 1971, East Oakland, CA
Soul, Urban, Pop-Rock

Versatile Ruth, Anita, June, and Bonnie Pointer regularly scored pop and soul hits throughout the '70s and '80s in a chameleonic variety of styles. Formed in Oakland, their first successes for Blue Thumb Records blended funky rhythms with a novel nostalgic attitude (beginning with their 1973 revival of Allen Toussaint's "Yes We Can Can"), leading up to their first No. 1 R&B item in 1975, "How Long (Betcha' Got a Chick on the Side)."

Bonnie signed with Motown in 1978 and kicked off her own string of R&B hits with "Free Me from My Freedom/Tie Me to a Tree (Handcuff Me)." (June and Anita also tried the solo route during the '80s, without leaving the fold.)

By 1979, when the remaining trio covered Bruce Springsteen's "Fire," the Pointers were headed in a more contemporary direction on the

Planet label, and "He's So Shy" (1980), "Slow Hand" (1981), "Automatic," and the anthemic "Jump (For My Love)" (the last two both 1984) were savvy ditties that blazed trails across the R&B and pop charts. However, the group's success declined during the late '80s, as their records began to sound more formulaic. The Pointer Sisters lost their major-label record contract in the early '90s, and the group began performing on oldies circuits occasionally. In 1995, the trio made a tenative return to the spotlight when they joined a revival performance of the Fats Waller musical *Ain't Misbehavin'*, yet the accompanying soundtrack album failed to gain much attention. — *Bill Dahl*

Steppin' / 1975 / Blue Thumb ✦✦✦✦

The second Pointer Sisters album didn't do as consistently well as its predecessor, although it earned them their second gold album and also won them a country Grammy for the song "Fairy Tale." They may have been the most unlikely country success story of all time, with their sassy attitudes and irreverent stage show, but they appeared all over the country landscape that year, even at the Grand Ole Opry. Regrettably, it was an indication of how wide the splits are musically and demographically that "Fairy Tale" didn't even chart on the R&B side. — *Ron Wynn*

So Excited / 1982 / Planet ✦✦✦✦

The Pointer Sisters put the title track on the charts twice; this was the original version, which peaked at No. 30 and was the cornerstone for this 1982 album. There was also the mild hit "American Music," which spoke to their eclecticism, and the less successful "If You Wanna Get Back Your Lady" and "Heart Beat." They were still carefully building their fan base, mixing soul-oriented cuts with lighter pop ones and not letting any single sister dominate the spotlight. — *Ron Wynn*

● **Greatest Hits** / 1982 / Planet ✦✦✦✦

A good anthology covering their '70s and '80s hits. There are now at least six Pointer Sisters anthologies, covering all of the Blue Thumb, Planet, and RCA material. This one was issued on vinyl and can't match the digital sound quality of some later Pointer Sisters releases, but it has more than enough hit material to satisfy even their hardcore fans. — *Ron Wynn*

Break Out / 1983 / Planet ✦✦✦✦

The Pointer Sisters landed the biggest album of their careers with this Richard Perry-produced, glossy pop package. The album eventually became a double-platinum success, while "Automatic," "Jump," and "Neutron Dance" were all pop and R&B hits. There was little surprise on these cuts, but the Pointer Sisters sang them with class and zest. — *Ron Wynn*

● **Jump: Best of the Pointer Sisters** / 1989 / RCA ✦✦✦✦

An excellent companion to their "Greatest Hits" collection, with the emphasis on their early work with Richard Perry's Planet label. The focal points, however, were the hits—"He's So Shy," "Slow Hand," "Fire," and the girl-groupish ditty "Should I Do It." — *John Lowe*

Very Best of the Pointer Sisters: Fire / Jun. 1996 / RCA ✦✦✦✦

Over the course of two CDs, *The Very Best of the Pointer Sisters: Fire* runs through every one of the group's biggest hits of the '70s, from their first hit "Yes We Can" through "Fire," and stopping just after their 1983-1984 peak of popularity with "Automatic," "Jump (For My Love)," "I'm So Excited," and "Neutron Dance." Two discs is too much material for anyone but devoted fans, but this is the most complete retrospective available about the Pointer Sisters, and it's hard to imagine that there will ever be another compilation quite so thorough. — *Stephen Thomas Erlewine*

Poison

f. 1983, Harrisburg, PA
Hard Rock, Pop-Rock, Heavy Metal, Hair Metal

A hard-rock quartet consisting of singer Bret Michaels, guitarist C.C. Deville, bassist Bobby Dall, and drummer Rikki Rockett, Poison was formed in Harrisburg, PA, in 1983, though the band members relocated to Los Angeles early on, where their highly visual approach (drummer Rockett was also a hairdresser who advised them on clothes, hair, and makeup) made them favorites in the city's glam-rock underground. C.C. Deville left the band in early 1992.

Deville's replacement, Richie Kotsen, appeared on 1993's *Native Tongue*, an attempt to become a grittier, serious rock band; he was fired during the subsequent tour. — *William Ruhlmann*

Look What the Cat Dragged in / 1986 / Capitol ✦✦✦

Glam-metal gets revived with the Los Angeles group, Poison, who turned many heads with their hook-filled songs as well as their looks. Although subsequent albums were more diverse, this one was loose and fun without a care for safety. Includes their first hit, "Talk Dirty to Me." — *John Book*

Open Up & Say . . . Ahh! / 1988 / Capitol ✦✦✦✦

This, the group's most popular album, presents its taste for straightforward hard rock ("Nothin' but a Good Time"), for acoustic ballads ("Every

Rose Has Its Thorn"), and for its roots in simple pop-rock ("Your Mama Don't Dance"). —*William Ruhlmann*

Flesh & Blood / Jun. 21, 1990 / Capitol ✦✦✦✦
On their third album, vocalist Bret Michaels puts in his best performance. "Unskinny Bop" and the anthemic "Something to Believe In" were both Top Ten hits. —*John Book*

Swallow This Live / Nov. 12, 1991 / Capitol ✦✦✦
A two-disc concert release that captures Poison in all its excess (six-and-a-half-minute drum solo, nine-and-a-half-minute guitar solo) and hard-rock glory, with live versions of the hits that are better produced and more impassioned than the original studio cuts. —*William Ruhlmann*

Native Tongue / Feb. 8, 1993 / Capitol ✦✦
Ditching most of their party anthems, as well as guitarist C.C. Deville because he allegedly wasn't up to par, Poison adds guitar whiz Richie Kotzen and makes a bid for respect. Leader Bret Michaels has decided to accentuate the populist strains of ballads like "Something to Believe In" throughout *Native Tongue*. It often falls short—Kotzen's playing is too proficient for the lite-metal hooks that the rest of the band have mastered—but Poison gets points for trying, and they do come up with some tracks, like the single "Stand," that could stand with some of their previous anthems. —*Stephen Thomas Erlewine*

● **Greatest Hits 1986-96** / Nov. 26, 1996 / Capitol ✦✦✦✦
Greatest Hits 1986-96 is as definitive as a Poison compilation could hope to be. Featuring a full 18 tracks, including all of their Top 50 hits ("Talk Dirty to Me," "I Want Action," "Nothin' but a Good Time," "Fallen Angel," "Every Rose Has Its Thorn," "Your Mama Don't Dance," "Unskinny Bop," Something to Belive In," "Stand," among others) plus two unreleased cuts ("Sexual Thing," "Lay Your Body Down"), the album boasts every worthwhile song the group ever recorded, augmented by Brett Michaels' track-by-track commentary. Though the album isn't sequenced in chronological order, it plays like an excellent mix tape, which actually makes the album more listenable. Even on a compilation, Poison wears a little thin—there are still dull moments among these 18 songs, mainly in the form of lesser-known album tracks and singles—but still, *Greatest Hits 1986-96* is the most entertaining album the band ever released. —*Stephen Thomas Erlewine*

The Police

f. 1977, London, England, db. 1985
New Wave, Pop-Rock

Nominally, the Police were punk rock, but that's only in the loosest sense of the term. The trio's nervous, reggae-injected pop-rock was punky, but it wasn't necessarily punk. All three members were considerably more technically proficient than the average punk or new wave band. Andy Summer had a precise guitar attack that created dense, interlocking waves of sounds and effects. Stewart Copeland could play polyrhythms effortlessly. And Sting, with his high, keening voice, was capable of constructing infectiously catchy pop songs. While they weren't punk, the Police certainly demonstrated that the punk spirit could have a future in pop music. As their career progressed, the Police grew considerably more adventurous, experimenting with jazz and various world musics. All the while, the band's tight delivery and mastery of the pop single kept their audience increasing, and by 1983 they were the most popular rock 'n' roll band in the world. Though they were at the height of their fame, internal tensions caused the band to splinter apart in 1984, with Sting picking up the majority of the band's audience to become an international superstar.

Stewart Copeland and Sting (born Gordon Sumner) formed the Police in 1977. Prior to the band's formation, Copeland, the son of a CIA agent, had attended college in California before he moved to England and joined the progressive-rock band Curved Air. Sting was a teacher and a ditch digger who played in jazz-rock bands, including Last Exit, on the side. The two musicians met at a local jazz club and decided to form a progressive-pop band with guitarist Henry Padovani. For the first few months, the group played local London pubs. Soon, they were hired to appear as a bleached-blond punk band in a chewing gum commercial. While the commercial provided exposure, it drew the scorn of genuine punkers. Late in 1977, the band released their first single, "Fall Out," on I.R.S., an independent label Stewart Copeland founded with his brother Miles, who was also the manager of the Police. The single was a sizable hit for an independent release, selling about 70,000 copies.

Padovani was replaced by Andy Summers, a veteran of the British Invasion, following the release of "Fall Out." Summers had previously played with Eric Burdon's second lineup of the Animals, the Zoot Money Big Roll Band, the Kevin Ayers Band, and Neil Sedaka. The Police signed with A&M by the spring of 1978, committing to a contract that gave the group a higher royalty rate in lieu of a large advance. A&M released "Roxanne" in the spring of 1978, but it failed to chart. The Police set out on a tour of America in the summer of 1978 without any record to support, traveling across the country in a rented van and playing with rented equipment. Released in the fall of 1978, *Outlandos d'Amour*

began a slow climb into the British Top Ten and American Top 30. Immediately after its release, the group began a UK tour supporting Alberto Y Lost Trios Paranoias and released the "So Lonely" single. By the spring of 1979, the re-released "Roxanne" had climbed to No. 12 on the UK charts, taking *Outlandos d'Amour* to No. 6. In the summer of 1979, Sting appeared in *Quadrophenia*, a British film based on the Who album of the same name; later that year, he acted in *Radio On*.

Preceded by the No. 1 British single "Message in a Bottle," *Regatta de Blanc* (fall 1979) established the group as stars in England and Europe, topping the UK charts for four weeks. Following its release, Miles Copeland had the band tour several countries that rarely received concerts from foreign performers, including Thailand, India, Mexico, Greece, and Egypt. *Zenyatta Mondatta*, released in the fall of 1980, became the Police's North American breakthrough, reaching the Top Ten in the US and Canada; in England, the album spent four weeks at No. 1. "Don't Stand So Close to Me," the album's first single, became the group's second No. 1 single in the UK; in America, the single became their second Top Ten hit in the spring of 1981, following the No. 10 placing of "De Do Do Do, De Da Da Da" in the winter. By the beginning of 1981, the Police were able to sell out Madison Square Garden. Capitalizing on their success, the band returned to the studio in the summer of 1981 to record their fourth album with producer Hugh Padgham. The sessions, which were filmed for a BBC documentary hosted by Jools Holland, were completed within a couple months, and the album, *Ghost in the Machine*, appeared in the fall of 1981. *Ghost in the Machine* became an instant hit, reaching No. 1 in the UK and No. 2 in the US, and "Every Little Thing She Does is Magic" became their biggest hit to date.

Following their whirlwind success of 1980 and 1981, in which they were named the Best British Group at the first Brit Awards and won three Grammys, the band took a break in 1982. Though they played their first arena concerts and headlined the US Festival, each member pursued side projects during the course of the year. Sting acted in *Brimstone and Treacle*, releasing a solo single, "Spread a Little Happiness," from the soundtrack; the song became a British hit. Copeland scored Francis Ford Coppola's *Rumble Fish*, as well as the San Francisco Ballet's *King Lear*, and released an album under the name Klark Kent; he also played on several sessions for Peter Gabriel. Summers recorded an instrumental album, *I Advance Masked*, with Robert Fripp. The Police returned in the summer of 1983 with *Synchronicity*, which entered the UK charts at No. 1 and quickly climbed to the same position in the US, where it would stay for 17 weeks. *Synchronicity* became a blockbuster success on the strength of the ballad "Every Breath You Take." Spending eight weeks at the top of the US charts, "Every Breath You Take" became one of the biggest American hits of all time; it spent four weeks at the top of the UK charts. "King of Pain" and "Wrapped Your Finger" became hits over the course of 1983, sending *Synchronicity* to multi-platinum status in America and Britain. The Police supported the album with a blockbuster, record-breaking world tour that set precedents for tours for the remainder of the '80s. Once the tour was completed, the band announced they were going on "sabbatical" in order to pursue outside interests.

The Police never returned from sabbatical. During the *Synchronicity* tour, personal and creative tensions between the band members had escalated greatly, and they had no desire to work together for a while. Sting began working on a jazz-tinged solo project immediately, releasing *The Dream of the Blue Turtles* in 1985. The album became an international hit, establishing him as a commercial force outside of the band. Copeland and Summers demonstrated no inclination to follow their bandmate's path. Copeland recorded the worldbeat exploration *The Rhythmatist* in 1985 and continued to compose scores for film and television; he later formed the progressive-rock band Animal Logic. With his solo career—which didn't officially begin until the release of 1987's *XYZ*—Summers continued his art-rock and jazz-fusion experiments; he also occasionally collaborated with Fripp and John Etheridge.

During 1986, the Police made a few attempts to reunite, playing an Amnesty International concert and attempting to record a handful of new tracks for a greatest hits album in the summer. As the studio session unraveled, it became apparent that Sting had no intention of giving the band his new songs to record, so the group re-recorded a couple of old songs, but even those were thrown off track after Copeland suffered a polo injury. Featuring a new version of "Don't Stand So Close to Me," the compilation *Every Breath You Take—The Singles* was released for the 1986 Christmas season, becoming the group's fifth straight British No. 1 and their fourth American Top Ten. Following its release, the group quietly disbanded, reuniting to play Sting's marriage in 1992. That same year, a *Greatest Hits* album was released in the UK. The following year, the box set *Message in a Box: The Complete Recordings* was released, followed in 1995 by the double album *Live*. —*Stephen Thomas Erlewine*

Outlandos d'Amour / Nov. 1978 / A&M ✦✦✦✦
The Police were always too cultured to be true punk rockers, or even new wavers, as their debut proves. Intercutting their terse pop with reg-

gae detours, the trio already displays a remarkable acumen for subtle, shaded instrumentation. However, they're not really trying for musical fusions at this stage of the game—they're trying to be punks, and, at their best, they pull it off with style. The speedy "Next to You" is a tight, invigorating rave-up, highlighted by unexpected harmonies on the chorus. "So Lonely," with its lithe reggae verses and poppy chorus, is equally terrific, as is the record's acknowledged classic, "Roxanne." Unfortunately, only a handful of other songs, most notably the punky "Born in the '50s," even come close to equaling that amazing triptych; the rest of the album is given over to engaging but inconsequential filler, highlighted by the bizarre "Be My Girl—Sally," a clever-clever love song to an inflatable doll. In that respect, the Police aren't that different from their new wave contemporaries—their debut is driven by a handful of great singles and padded out with filler. —*Stephen Thomas Erlewine*

Regatta de Blanc / 1979 / A&M ✦✦✦
While the Police sound tighter and more accomplished on their second album, *Regatta de Blanc*, the album itself isn't as consistent as their debut, *Outlandos d'Amour*. Since that album was plagued with filler, it's not a good sign that *Regatta de Blanc* also falls short on memorable songs, but the highlights are remarkable. The trippy reggae of "Walking on the Moon" is supple and textured, where that of "Message in a Bottle" is terse, nervy and infectious, and both "Bring On the Night" and "The Bed's Too Big Without You" indicate that Sting's popcraft is becoming subtle, unpredictable, and quite impressive. Evidently, he spent himself on those four songs, since the rest of the record lacks memorable tunes, and even the band's improved playing can't make them more memorable. —*Stephen Thomas Erlewine*

Zenyatta Mondatta / 1980 / A&M ✦✦✦✦
Zenyatta Mondatta was the Police's breakthrough record for a variety of reasons, chief among them Sting's considerable growth as a songwriter. Aiming for grander, more sophisticated territory than the punk-pop and reggae of the trio's first two records, Sting develops a signature style on *Zenyatta Mondatta*, one distinguished by textured yet undeniably catchy melodies and overly literate lyrics. The Police, in turn, bring these songs to life by returning to their jazz-rock roots, giving the music supple, textured rhythms. Not only is Stewart Copeland's drumming intricate and subtle, but Andy Summers' guitars shimmer with textures and unpredictable phrasings that skirt every conventional rule of pop-rock rhythm guitar. These innovations are so subtle that they aren't noticeable unless the Police choose to showcase them, as they do on two rather pointless instrumentals. Where they really shine is when they bring these sensibilities to Sting's catchy songs, which are the best set he ever composed for the Police. "Don't Stand So Close to Me" and "De Do Do Do, De Da Da Da" were hits, but almost every song on the record is nearly as good, from the skittering "Canary in a Coalmine" and the shimmering "Driven to Tears" to the pulsating "When the World is Running Down." The Police were never as pop oriented or as consistently engaging as they were on *Zenyatta Mondatta*. —*Stephen Thomas Erlewine*

Ghost in the Machine / 1981 / A&M ✦✦✦
As if he was uncomfortable with the pop success of *Zenyatta Mondatta*, Sting steers the Police toward self-consciously arty and important territory on *Ghost in the Machine*. Boasting layers of keyboards and saxophone (Sting just learned how to play the instrument), *Ghost in the Machine* is a denser album than any other Police record, and the songs tend to be serious minded; in other words, there's none of the humor that surfaced on the three previous records. Although the group occasionally sounds strong and muscular underneath the murky production, their actual attack isn't nearly as challenging as intended—it actually makes the group sound slick. And while Sting delivered a wonderful pop single with "Every Little Thing She Does Is Magic," the album is plagued with uneven material. There are a handful of fine songs—the terse, dissonant "Spirits in the Material World," the bluesy "Invisible Sun"—but the record on the whole is an unfocused, pretentious affair. —*Stephen Thomas Erlewine*

Synchronicity / 1983 / A&M ✦✦✦
Simultaneously more pop oriented and experimental than either *Ghost in the Machine* or *Zenyatta Mondatta*, *Synchronicity* made the Police superstars, generating no less than five hit singles. With the exception of "Synchronicity II," which sounds disarmingly like a crappy Billy Idol song, every one of those singles are classics. "Every Breath You Take" has a seductive, rolling beat masking its maliciousness, "King of Pain" and "Wrapped Around Your Finger" are devilishly infectious new wave singles, and "Tea in the Sahara" is hypnotic in its measured, melancholy choruses. But, like so many other Police albums, these songs are surrounded by utterly inconsequential filler. This time, the group relies heavily on jazzy textures for Sting's songs, which only work on the jumping, marimba-driven "Synchronicity I." Then, as if to prove that the Police were still a band, there's one song apiece from Stewart Copeland and Andy Summers, both of which are awful, as if they're trying to sabotage the album. Since they arrive on the first side, which is devoid of

singles, they do, making the album sound like two EPs: one filled with first-rate pop and one an exercise in self-indulgence. While the hits are among Sting's best, they also illustrate that he was ready to leave the Police behind for a solo career, which is exactly what he did. —*Stephen Thomas Erlewine*

Every Breath You Take: The Singles / 1986 / A&M ✦✦✦✦
A collection of singles from the five Police albums, this provides a consistent sampling of some of the Police's best work, from "Roxanne" to "Every Breath You Take." It's a good overview of the band's work and an excellent place to get an introduction to their music. This also includes a 1986 remake of "Don't Stand So Close to Me," featuring all three members of the band. —*Iotis Erlewine*

Message in a Box / Sep. 28, 1993 / A&M ✦✦✦✦
All of the studio recordings the trio made during their short career (except for a couple of foreign-language recordings, remixes, and live tracks) are collected together on the four-disc *Message in a Box*. There are enough rarities in this attractive, sonically impressive package to justify its purchase for hardcore fans; for anyone who doesn't own any Police, it is an easy way to have the entire collection at once, but casual fans will be more satisfied by *Every Breath You Take: The Singles*. —*Stephen Thomas Erlewine*

Live / Jun. 13, 1995 / A&M ✦✦
Featuring two complete concerts from two different stages in the band's career, the double disc *Live* is a comprehensive portrait of the Police's onstage prowess. Of the two shows, the first is rawer. Recorded on the *Zenyatta Mondatta* tour, the band still had enough spiky power to seem like a punk-new wave band, and they tear through their best songs, including a killer version of "So Lonely." At the time of the second disc, the group were one of the most popular acts in the world, playing arenas around the world. Somewhat predictably, the sound is slicker, yet it doesn't affect the impact of the music. When they were slick, the Police didn't seem manufactured, they seemed elegant. Neither of the concerts offers anything remarkably different than the studio versions, they just accentuate the underlying musical themes of the records. However, dedicated fans will not be disappointed by the overall quality of *Live*. —*Stephen Thomas Erlewine*

★ **Every Breath You Take: the Classics** / Sep. 12, 1995 / A&M ✦✦✦✦✦
Every Breath You Take: The Classics improves on the previous *Every Breath You Take: The Singles* by adding the original version of "Don't Stand So Close to Me," as well as a handful of other songs that aren't on its predecessor; the extra songs make *The Classics* the preferable collection. —*Stephen Thomas Erlewine*

The Pop Group

f. 1978, Bristol, England
New Wave, Post-Punk
Warning: this band's name is loaded with irony; there is little if anything "pop" about them. So if you happen across any of their albums and think you're getting something that sounds like a cross between the Raspberries and the Beatles, don't say you weren't warned. Emerging in the late-'70s, post-punk era, this militant gang of leftist, radical politicos from Bristol, England, specialized in a funk-driven cacophony of sound that was abrasive, strident, and ultimately very exciting. Railing against Margaret Thatcher's Tory government, the state of pop music, racism, sexism, and so forth, the Pop Group were not the easiest band of the early post-punk era to listen to, but those who made the effort were in for an interesting melange of primitive rhythms and avant-garde guitar racket. Led by the squalling "vocals" of Mark Stewart (which were little more than chanted political slogans), the Pop Group were unabashedly and stridently radical to the point of being hectoring. But, unlike others of their ilk, the music was so challenging, joyfully noisy, and downright weird that it was easy to cut them a little slack, even when their finger-pointing and ranting became a bit much. Never intending to make a serious run at the pop charts, the Pop Group imploded after three albums, the third being a collection of outtakes and assorted ephemera. They did, however, contribute some talented people to other bands, most notably Gareth Sanger, who formed the wild and woolly Rip Rig & Panic (named after a Rahsaan Roland Kirk LP), which also featured the lead vocals of a then-teenage Neneh Cherry; and the aforementioned Stewart, who went on to flourish in Adrian Sherwood's On-U stable of artists, recording with the Maffia and Tackhead. Despite its raw, inherent anti-commercialism, the Pop Group's dissonant agit-prop rock did influence a contemporary generation of political bands like Fugazi, Funda-Mental, and Rage Against the Machine. —*John Dougan*

● **The Pop Group** / 1979 / Radar ✦✦✦✦
Abrasive, but interesting, the Pop Group's debut is perhaps the most succinct summation of their angry and defiant approach to rock and roll. Although at times resembling the discordant funk of fellow post-punk radicals the Gang of Four, the Pop Group leave rhythm behind almost as quickly as they find it, and the result is a clattering din of sound

resembling an aural collage. I like it, but even I'll admit it's a bit meandering and overly experimental to take in one sitting. The longish, guitar-driven track "We Are Time" is the strongest cut, establishing a solid groove that won't let go. —*John Dougan*

Y / 1979 / Radar ✦✦✦

For How Much Longer Do We Tolerate Mass Murder? / 1980 / Rough Trade ✦✦✦

If the title doesn't tip you off as to what this record will probably sound like, then you're hopeless. More accusatory than their debut (only because the lyrics are more clearly recorded) and more funk-powered. Oddly, what hurts this is a lack of experimentation, but with the Pop Group, it's always too much of one thing and not enough of another. An interesting experiment that is as maddening as it is satisfying. —*John Dougan*

We Are Time / 1980 / Rough Trade ✦✦✦

Iggy Pop (James Newell Osterberg)

b. Apr. 21, 1947, Ypsilanti, MI
Vocals / Hard Rock, Proto-Punk
After the disbandment of the proto-punk group the Stooges, vocalist Iggy Pop (born James Osterberg) embarked on a solo career that flirted with the mainstream while keeping his fiery punk spirit alive. Pop laid low for a couple of years following the breakup of the Stooges, resurfacing in 1977 with two David Bowie-produced albums, *The Idiot* and *Lust for Life.*

These records expanded his trademark, full-throttle rock 'n' roll, incorporating a more pop-oriented approach that increased his audience. *The Idiot* remains his highest-charting album, peaking at No. 72 in America. However, Pop soon returned to straightforward, raging hard rock with the double punch of *TV Eye Live* (1978) and 1979's *New Values*, which was recorded with former Stooges guitarist James Williamson. Although he kept changing his backing band, both 1980's *Soldier* and 1981's *Party* followed the same blueprint as *New Values*. Released in 1982, the Chris Stein-produced *Zombie Birdhouse* (which appeared on Stein's label, Animal) was the most varied collection Pop had created since *Lust for Life.*

After the release of *Zombie Birdhouse*, Pop took some time off, reappearing four years later with the Bowie-produced *Blah-Blah-Blah;* the record became his highest-charting album since *The Idiot.* He followed it in 1989 with *Instinct*, another return to basic hard rock. Released the following year on Virgin Records, the Don Was-produced *Brick by Brick* was his most accessible and commercially successful album, producing his first Top 40 hit, "Candy." Pop began an acting career during the next few years, appearing in John Waters' *Cry Baby.* Pop's first album since *Brick by Brick* was *American Caesar* (1993), which was yet another return to punky hard rock. *American Caesar* sold relatively well, but it wasn't a hit. Neither was *Naughty Little Doggy*, which disappeared upon its spring 1996 release. —*Stephen Thomas Erlewine*

The Idiot / 1977 / Virgin ✦✦✦✦

Although it appears that producer David Bowie directed the proceedings a bit too carefully, remaking Iggy Pop entirely in his own image, *The Idiot* proves that Pop was equally responsible for the menacing electronic music. *The Idiot* was an effective reinvention on the part of Iggy Pop partially because it removed him completely from the primal heavy guitar grind of the Stooges. A different musical direction in itself would be meaningless if Pop and Bowie hadn't produced a set of songs that supported the new, synth-driven style. "Funtime" is essentially a sleazy, mid-tempo rocker that is re-energized by its context, but most of the album explores the various subtexts within the bleak, keyboard-dominated soundscapes. Pop's lyrics are some of his best, as he faithfully recreates the hedonistic underworld of jet-setting "Nightclubbing," with both humor and rage. Several of the songs—including "Funtime," "China Girl," and "Nightclubbing"—have become post-punk standards, but that doesn't remove the jarring, disturbing sound of the record. In its own quiet way, *The Idiot* is as discomforting as *Fun House.* —*Stephen Thomas Erlewine*

Lust for Life / 1977 / Virgin ✦✦✦✦

The pounding drums that open *Lust for Life* instantly signal that the album is a brighter, harder-rocking affair than *The Idiot.* While black humor is an undercurrent throughout *The Idiot*, it is brought to the front on *Lust for Life*, both musically and lyrically. Using the title track as a template, the record not only rocks, it swings and it swings hard. Bowie wrote most of the music for the record and it reflects his musical ambition, careening from the hard rock of the title track to the strutting piano of "The Passenger," the jaunty ironic sing-along of "Success," to the stylized R&B of "Tonight." While Iggy Pop spent most of the decade trying to escape the pop leanings of *Lust for Life*, he never made a better record. —*Stephen Thomas Erlewine*

TV Eye / 1978 / RCA ✦

A desultory live album recorded on a 1977 tour of America, *TV Eye* captures Iggy Pop at his most self-indulgent and his most uninspired. —*Stephen Thomas Erlewine*

New Values / 1979 / Arista ✦✦✦

On *New Values*, Iggy Pop teamed back up with Stooges guitarist James Williamson, creating a set of tough hard rock that was highlighted by the sly humor of "I'm Bored" and the driving title track. —*Stephen Thomas Erlewine*

Soldier / 1980 / Arista ✦✦✦

Recorded with an ad-hoc punk supergroup (Glen Matlock, Barry Andrews, Ivan Kral, Steve New, and Klaus Kruger), *Soldier* rages on with a lean precision, giving Pop's occasionally weak and bitter lyrics the extra kick they need. —*Stephen Thomas Erlewine*

Party / 1981 / Arista ✦✦

Party attempts to recapture the loose hard-rock professionalism of *Soldier*, even adding the Uptown Horns to the mix. However, the music winds up sounding stiff and like anything but a party, even when Pop tries to make the group unwind with the standards "Time Won't Let Me" and "Sea of Love." —*Stephen Thomas Erlewine*

Zombie Birdhouse / 1982 / IRS ✦✦

With the help of Chris Stein (Blondie), Iggy Pop attempts a self-consciously eclectic musical exploration with *Zombie Birdhouse.* By and large, the attempts are admirable, as Pop turns in a set of songs that range from social commentary and urban folk to bizarre poetry and philosophical ruminations. Instead of singing, Pop alternately raps and sings over sonic backdrops that have touches of hard rock, folk, and electronic music. It's an ambitious effort that never quite works and keeps listeners at a distance. —*Stephen Thomas Erlewine*

Choice Cuts / 1984 / RCA ✦✦✦✦

Following the success of David Bowie's version of "China Girl," RCA assembled *Choice Cuts*, a compilation of Iggy Pop's two albums for the label. Actually, "compilation" is a misleading word: Side one of *Choice Cuts* features side one of *The Idiot*, while side two features side one of *Lust for Life.* It effectively illustrates the differences between the records and includes most of the prime material from each collection, yet the two albums are necessary listens in their entirety, making *Choice Cuts* an engaging but useless compilation. —*Stephen Thomas Erlewine*

Blah Blah Blah / 1986 / A&M ✦✦✦

Iggy Pop reunited with producer David Bowie for *Blah Blah Blah.* While it adopts a number of different musical styles, the record isn't as cohesive or as ambitious as *The Idiot* or *Lust for Life.* Instead, it acts as an Pop sampler, offering a variety of material that is all competently performed but, with the notable exception of a cover of Johnny O'Keefe's "Real Wild Child (Wild One)," rarely compelling. —*Stephen Thomas Erlewine*

Instinct / 1988 / A&M ✦✦

After the pop-oriented smorgasbord of *Blah Blah Blah*, Iggy Pop teamed with producer Bill Laswell for the lackluster *Instinct*, a return to the pounding grind of his early '80s albums, not the classic grime of the Stooges. In fact, Laswell allows Pop's backing band, led by ex-Sex Pistols guitarist Steve Jones, to indulge their tendency to wallow in a heavy metallic thud, making *Instinct* his most tedious record. —*Stephen Thomas Erlewine*

Brick by Brick / Jun. 1990 / Virgin ✦✦✦✦

Instinct suggested that Iggy Pop had run out of ideas. *Brick By Brick* put an end to that speculation. While it's easily the most mainstream record Pop has ever recorded, it rivals his two Bowie-produced 1977 albums in terms of sheer accomplishment. Under the direction of producer Don Was, Pop twists through a number of styles, recorded with an ever-shifting assembly of studio musicians like David Lindley and Waddy Wachtel, members of Guns N' Roses, John Hiatt, John Mellencamp's drummer Kenny Aronoff, and the B-52's singer Kate Pierson. Pop's duet with Pierson on the pure pop of "Candy" is the highlight, yet the record also features Pop at his toughest ("Home," "Butt Town," "I Won't Crap Out," "Pussy Power") and his most sensitive ("Moonlight Lady"). Although there was potential for a slick, mainstream sellout with *Brick by Brick*, Was has helped Pop turn in a well-crafted and thoroughly enjoyable album. And with Pop, a consistent album is a rare occurence. —*Stephen Thomas Erlewine*

American Caesar / 1993 / Virgin ✦✦✦

Turning on themes of jealousy, hate, abuse, and corporate profits (it's not pretty, but then neither is Iggy Pop), *Caesar* marks his first album in decades backed by a permanent group. This likely explains why several songs echo the energy and sound of his legendary proto-punk band the Stooges. Unquestioned highlight is a disheveled and humorously political rendition of "Louie Louie." *American Caesar* is a raw, sometimes ugly, but ultimately very real album. —*Roch Parisien*

Naughty Little Doggie / Mar. 5, 1996 / Virgin ✦✦
After a while, Iggy Pop's albums all tend to blend together. There are slight lyrical variations on the same theme, and he rarely departs from a punky, heavy hard rock. *Naughty Little Doggie* is no exception. While there are some fine songs on the record, the majority of the album is undistinctive, lacking either the precision of *Brick by Brick*, the experimentalism of *The Idiot* and *Lust for Life*, or the raw fury of his Stooges material. On the whole, *Naughty Little Doggie* is a better, more focused album than the relative disaster of *American Caesar*, but it still isn't the vital slab of rock 'n' roll that it so desperately wants to be. —*Stephen Thomas Erlewine*

● **Nude & Rude: The Best of Iggy Pop** / Oct. 29, 1996 / Virgin ✦✦✦✦
Nude & Rude: The Best of Iggy Pop is an excellent 17-track overview of Pop's career, from the Stooges into the '90s. With the exception of *The Idiot, Lust for Life*, and *Brick by Brick*, Pop's solo career has been decidedly uneven, and many of his albums have been flat-out dull. *Nude & Rude* does a terrific job of selecting the best moments from these records, as well as many of the best Stooges tracks, thereby providing a nearly flawless introduction to Pop's music. With "I Wanna Be Your Dog," "No Fun," "Search & Destroy," "Gimme Danger," "I'm Sick of You," and "Kill City," representing the Stooges, a few of the band's essential items are missing, but all the essential solo tracks are here, including "Funtime," "Nightclubbing," "China Girl," "Lust for Life," "Real Wild Child," "Cold Metal," "Candy," and "Home." —*Stephen Thomas Erlewine*

Popol Vuh

f. 1969
Neo-Classical, Progressive Electronic, Ethnic Fusion
One of Germany's premier progressive electronic bands, Popol Vuh was founded in 1969 by keyboardist Florian Fricke. The band took its name from the Mayan Indian bible, and, in fact, the group's first album *Affenstunde* (*The Time of the Monkey King*) was a strong reflection of Fricke's interest in Mayan lore. Over the course of nearly 20 albums, Popol Vuh combined sacred musical traditions and instruments from around the world with classical, jazz, and rock elements. It also created quite a stir as one of the first bands to use the Moog synthesizer in the early '70s. As such, the band influenced several generations of electronic and contemplative artists. Popol Vuh also gained considerable attention for its scores to films by the celebrated German director Werner Herzog, including *Nosferatu* and *Aguirre, the Wrath of God*. —*Linda Kohanov*

In Den Garten Pharads / 1972 / Pilz ✦✦✦✦
"In Pharaoh's Garden" was the first real work of "Sacred Music" by Florian Fricke, guiding light of the mythical group Popol Vuh. Consisting of two extended works, his mixture of electronics and church organ with assorted winds and percussives, conjures up visions of the celestial light. Deeply emotional and filled with mysticism, this album marked the dawning of new age music and still today is a wonder to behold. —*Archie Patterson*

● **Tantric Songs** / 1991 / Celestial Harmonies ✦✦✦✦
Tantric Songs/Hosianna Mantra is new age, devotional rock chamber music that is spacey and spacious on this pairing of two early albums (from 1973 and 1978) on one CD. —*Michael P. Dawson*

For You & Me / Jan. 1991 / Milan ✦✦✦✦

Porno for Pyros

f. 1993, Los Angeles, CA
Alternative Pop-Rock
Perry Farrell's post-Jane's Addiction band, Porno for Pyros, followed the same path as his previous band, combining art-rock, punk, heavy metal, and funk into one shrieking whole. On their self-titled 1993 debut, Farrell's pretensions got out of hand at times, resulting in some ridiculously self-absorbed conceptual pieces sitting next to some straightforward rockers and pop songs; it sold well at first, but soon slipped down the charts. While he prepared new Porno material in 1994, Farrell returned to the organization of Lollapalooza—the traveling rock festival he conceived—for the first time since 1992. The band released *Good Gods Urge* in 1996. —*Stephen Thomas Erlewine*

Porno for Pyros / Apr. 27, 1993 / Warner Brothers ✦✦✦
Although Porno for Pyros was supposed to sound radically different than Jane's Addiction, Porno sounds like Jane's without the Zeppelinesque grandeur of David Navarro. Their self-titled debut should please Perry Farrell's fans, although it does shows signs of the limits of his vision. —*Stephen Thomas Erlewine*

● **Good Gods Urge** / Jun. 1996 / Warner Brothers ✦✦✦✦
Perry Farrell spent over two years writing and recording Porno for Pyros' second album, *Good God's Urge*, which doesn't sound overly labored—and that's part of the problem. The music on *Good God's Urge* is amorphous, floating through various sonic textures and rarely landing on a cohesive song structure. It's an album that builds on the experimental portions of the group's debut, and while its ambitions are admi-

rable, the execution is problematic. Ideas are brought to the surface, but never quite developed. Farrell hasn't abandoned grandiose hard rock, but he is exploring psychedelia with a passion he has never displayed before. Unfortunately, he sacrifices cohesive song structures for neo-psychedelia, and the result is an album that is intriguing but never quite compelling. —*Stephen Thomas Erlewine*

Portishead

f. 1991, Bristol, England
Alternative Pop-Rock, Trip-Hop, Adult Alternative Pop-Rock
Portishead may not have invented trip-hop, but they were among the first to popularize it, particularly in America. Taking their cue from the slow, elastic beats that dominated Massive Attack's *Blue Lines* and adding elements of cool jazz, acid house, and soundtrack music, Portishead created an atmospheric, alluringly dark sound. The group wasn't as avant-garde as Tricky, nor as tied to dance traditions as Massive Attack. Instead, the band wrote evocative, pseudo-cabaret pop songs that subverted their conventional structures with experimental productions and rhythms of trip-hop. As a result, Portishead appealed to a broad audience—not just electronic dance and alternative rock fans, but thirtysomethings who found techno, trip-hop, and dance as exotic as worldbeat. Before Portishead released their debut album *Dummy* in 1994, trip-hop's broad appeal wasn't apparent, but the record became an unexpected success in Britain, topping end critics polls and earning the prestigious Mercury Music Prize; in America, it also became an underground hit, selling over 150,000 copies before the group toured the US. Following the success of *Dummy*, legions of imitators appeared over the next two years, but Portishead remained quiet as they worked on their second album.

Named after the West Coast shipping town where Geoff Barrow grew up, Portishead formed in Bristol, England, in 1991. Prior to the group's formation, Barrow had worked as a tape operator at the Coach House studio, where he met Massive Attack. Through that group, he began working with Tricky, producing the rapper's track for the *Sickle Cell* charity album. Barrow also wrote songs for Neneh Cherry's *Home Brew*, though only "Somedays" appeared on the record. Around the time of Portishead's formation, he had begun to earn a reputation as a remix producer, working on tracks by Primal Scream, Paul Weller, Gabrielle, and Depeche Mode. Barrow met Beth Gibbons, who had been singing in pubs, in 1991 on a job scheme. Over the next few years, the pair began writing music, often with jazz guitarist Adrian Utley who had previously played with both Big John Patton and the Jazz Messengers.

Before releasing a recording, Portishead completed the short film *To Kill a Dead Man*, an homage to '60s spy movies. Barrow and Gibbons acted in the noirish film and provided the soundtrack, which earned the attention of Go! Records. By the fall, Portishead had signed with Go!, and their debut album, *Dummy*, was released shortly afterward. *Dummy* was recorded with engineer Dave MacDonald, who played drums and drum machines, and guitarist Utley, who rounded out Portishead's lineup.

Both Barrow and Gibbons were media-shy—the vocalist refused to participate in any interviews—which meant that the album received little attention outside of the weekly UK music press, which praised the album and its two singles, "Numb" and "Sour Times," heavily. Soon, Go! and Portishead had developed a clever marketing strategy based on the group's atmospheric videos that began to attract attention. *Melody Maker, Mixmag*, and *The Face* named *Dummy* as 1994's album of the year, and early in 1995, "Glory Box" debuted at No. 13 without any radio play. Around the same time, "Sour Times" entered regular rotation on MTV in America. Within a few weeks, *Dummy* and "Sour Times" were alternative rock hits in the US. Back in the UK, the album had crossed over into the mainstream, becoming a fixture in the British Top 40. In July, the record won the Mercury Music Prize for Album of the Year, beating highly touted competition from Blur, Suede, Oasis, and Pulp.

Following the Mercury Music Prize award, Barrow retreated to Coach House to begin work on Portishead's second album. The record is scheduled to appear in the fall of 1997. —*Stephen Thomas Erlewine*

● **Dummy** / Oct. 1994 / PolyGram ✦✦✦✦
Dummy plays like a romantic film noir, filled with reverb, sighing strings, dark, erotic arrangements, and the doomed, sighing vocals of Beth Gibbons. —*Stephen Thomas Erlewine*

The Posies

f. 1986, Seattle, WA
Alternative Pop-Rock, Power Pop
One of the major '90s power-pop revivalist groups, Seattle's Posies combine the genre's standard influences (Big Star, Raspberries, etc.) with Hollies-like harmonies, roaring guitars, and odd lyrics about mundane, everyday concerns. Their first record, 1988's *Failure*, featured founding guitarists/vocalists Jonathan Auer and sometime Sub Pop producer Ken Stringfellow and fit squarely into the "slacker" trend. Geffen Records

signed them, and they filled out the lineup with Dave Fox and Mike Musberger for *Dear 23*. 1993's Don Fleming-produced *Frosting on the Beater* (an allusion to masturbation) broke the band in the college radio market and was a critical success as well. 1996's *Amazing Disgrace* consolidated the Posies' position as critics' darlings with even wider acclaim. — *Steve Huey*

Failure / 1988 / Pop Llama ◆◆◆
Failure is worth looking up, not so much because it represents a mature work but because it's a nice diamond-in-the-rough portrait of a band with a deep creative resource and a strong sense of pop history. — *Rick Clark*

● **Dear 23** / Aug. 1990 / DGC ◆◆◆◆
From the Move-influenced "My Big Mouth" to the delicate, wistful "Everyone Moves Away," through tracks that would do Badfinger or Big Star proud, like "Apology," "Golden Blunders," and "Suddenly Mary," *Dear 23* is Anglo-pop-rock heaven. John Leckie's larger-than-life production might be a little overwhelming at times, but overall it highlights this band's gorgeous harmonies and arrangements to great effect. — *Rick Clark*

Frosting on the Beater / Apr. 27, 1993 / DGC ◆◆◆
The Posies turn up the rockets for their third album with an appealingly huge wall of guitars and bashola drumming. For the most part, the melodies and harmonies are still intact, but song for song, *Frosting on the Beater* doesn't hold up to *Dear 23*. Nevertheless, songs like "Different Door," "Solar Sister," and "Flavor of the Month" are wonderful. — *Rick Clark*

Amazing Disgrace / May 14, 1996 / DGC ◆◆
On their fourth album, the Posies sound like a bunch of high school kids desperately trying to fit into the in crowd, not realizing that the cool kids have already abandoned last year's fashions for something hipper. At the height of grunge, the Posies were stuck in power-pop territory. They began to move toward loud guitars on their second album, *Frosting on the Beater*, but they didn't embrace grunge until *Amazing Disgrace*, which appeared nearly four years after grunge peaked in popularity. That in itself wouldn't be so bad if the group didn't sound so wimpy. The Posies try to prove how hard they are by throwing the word "fuck" randomly into the lyrics. Furthermore, their ability to craft a sly, catchy hook has greatly diminished—the best songs here can't match the ones on their two previous albums. And to top it off, they offer a saccharine tribute to one of the great songwriters of the '80s, ex-Hüsker Dü drummer Grant Hart, without ever demonstrating an understanding of the man's music. It's clear from the bland textures of *Amazing Disgrace* that they never will, either. — *Stephen Thomas Erlewine*

Duffy Power

b. Sep. 9, 1941
Harmonica, Vocals / Blues-Rock, British Invasion
Power is a lost figure of the '60s who drifted into the inner circle of British blues after a middling career as a teen idol in the early '60s. He recorded one of the first Beatle covers (on an early 1963 single of "I Saw Her Standing There") and never experienced acclaim as a commercial pop singer or blues vocalist. But he recorded some fine, little-known blues-cum-R&B/rock sides in the '60s, some of which featured present and future members of the Graham Bond Organisation, Cream, and Pentangle. The pleasures of Power are subtle and not easily captured in print. He doesn't have the best voice and will never be mistaken for a Steve Winwood or Eric Burdon. But his original material is strong, his arrangements imaginative, and his performance sincere; he's grounded in the blues, but doesn't fall into shopworn clichés, bringing a lot of himself and the innovations of British '60s rock into the picture. — *Richie Unterberger*

Blues Power / 1992 / See For Miles ◆◆◆◆
Most of the recordings on *Blues Power* were originally released on Power's self-titled album on the tiny UK Spark label in 1969. Duffy says in the liner notes of this reissue that the album was never intended for release and that these sessions were acoustic demos for an LP that never got produced with the arrangements he had envisioned. That may be so, but it's still a worthy document of this underrated British bluesman at his most bare boned and haunting. With just his guitar and harmonica, Power runs through both moody originals and covers of R&B/blues standards (with the Beatles' "Fixing a Hole" thrown in) that are rearranged and drastically stripped down. This reissue includes the 15 tracks from the 1969 release, a couple more from the same sessions that were issued on the extremely obscure *Firepoint* compilation album, and three from the mid-'60s (also included on the *Little Boy Blue* reissue) that also explore acoustic moods, forming a picture of Power's most intimate work. — *Richie Unterberger*

● **Little Boy Blue** / 1992 / Edsel ◆◆◆◆
His best recordings, as noteworthy for the players on the album as for Power himself; they were laid down sometime in the mid-'60s. Power

(who sings and plays occasional guitar and harp) is backed by a rotating ensemble including, at various points, John McLaughlin and Jack Bruce (before they gained fame), as well as future Pentangle members Danny Thompson and Terry Cox. Neither as rock-oriented as the Stones nor as strictly revivalist as Alexis Korner (with whom Power played for a time), this is one of the best British blues recordings, cutting straight down the middle between gutbucket blues and soulful R&B. Divided equally between Power originals and R&B blues covers, the material and performances are spare, powerful, and as consistent as any '60s British blues album. Unfortunately, these sessions were unissued for several years, surfacing briefly under the title *Innovations* in 1970 on the British Transatlantic label. This reissue on another tiny British label is equally obscure, but should not be missed by fans of '60s British R&B. — *Richie Unterberger*

Just Say Blue / 1995 / Retro ◆◆◆◆
While not up to the level of the other vintage Power compilations available (*Little Boy Blue* and *Blues Power*), this is a worthwhile supplement to those CDs, featuring 21 tracks of rare and unreleased material cut by the singer from 1965 to 1971. The first half, focusing on his 1965-67 output, is the more interesting portion by a considerable margin, as much for the jazz-blues-R&B fusion of the arrangements (featuring contributions from Jack Bruce, John McLaughlin, Ginger Baker, and Pentangle's Danny Thompson and Terry Cox) as for Power's singing. The early-'70s songs that make up the remainder of the disc have a more pedestrian blues-rock feel, but there are some good, inspired moments, with cameos by Rod Argent, Thompson, Cox, and Alexis Korner. — *Richie Unterberger*

Prefab Sprout

f. 1982, Consett, Durham, England, **db.** 1990
Pop-Rock
Prefab Sprout, the vision of Newcastle singer-songwriter Paddy McAloon, garnered critical approval for its intelligent, quirky lyrics, jazzy pop often performed with synths and acoustic backing, and beautiful female harmony vocals. McAloon formed the band in 1982 with brother Martin on bass, plus drummer Neil Conti; early fan Wendy Smith joined on vocals and guitar following the recording of the "Lions in My Own Garden" single, which got the band signed to the Kitchenware label. Their debut, *Swoon*, was a showcase for Paddy's literate lyrics and found a fan in producer-synth whiz Thomas Dolby, who remixed a single and produced their next album, *Two Wheels Good* (titled *Steve McQueen* everywhere except in the US). 1988's *From Langley Park to Memphis* incorporated bits of lounge music and show tunes, with mixed results and featured appearances from Stevie Wonder and Pete Townshend. While the band took a bit of time to get its bearings, a collection of songs originally intended as the follow-up to *Two Wheels Good* called *Protest Songs* was released. Prefab Sprout returned in 1990 with *Jordan: The Comeback Album*, which explored McAloon's fascination with religion and American cultural icons such as Elvis Presley and was hailed as perhaps the band's greatest work. However, it failed to sell well, and Prefab Sprout has been silent since. — *Steve Huey*

Swoon / 1984 / Epic ◆◆◆
Their full-length album debut is rough around the edges, but shows the band reaching beyond the tried and clichéd. — *Scott Bultman*

Two Wheels Good / 1985 / Epic ◆◆◆◆
A strong album debut of atmospheric, breathy, and clever pop music, it features Thomas Dolby's tight production. Earthy and ethereal at the same time, the album was released overseas as *Steve McQueen* but was given a different name for the US version due to protests from the actor's estate. — *Scott Bultman*

From Langley Park to Memphis / 1988 / Epic ◆◆◆◆
A good but inconsistent record, it includes shining tracks like "The Golden Calf," "Cars and Girls," and "I Remember That." Paddy McAloon begins to explore his fixation with pop icons like Elvis and Springsteen. A must for fans. — *Scott Bultman*

Jordan: The Comeback / Sep. 1990 / Epic ◆◆◆◆
A stunning masterwork with 19 tracks (over 70 minutes) tied together by recurrent themes of God and Elvis, this one is stylistically all over the map—gospel, soul, rock, and pop. The pop songwriting has acknowledged influences from Jimmy Webb and Paul McCartney. — *Scott Bultman*

● **A Life of Surprises: The Best of Prefab Sprout** / Oct. 6, 1992 / Epic ◆◆◆◆
This hits package offers a well-chosen set and two previously unreleased tracks, "The Sound of Crying" and "If You Don't Love Me." The 16 tracks draw more selections from the *From Langley Park to Memphis* LP than the other albums, but this is a good single-disc introduction to Prefab Sprout's music. — *Scott Bultman*

Elvis Presley (Elvis Aron Presley)

b. Jan. 8, 1935, Tupelo, MS, **d.** Aug. 16, 1977, Memphis, TN
Guitar, Vocals / Rock 'n' Roll, Rockabilly, Pop, Pop-Rock

Elvis Presley may be the single most important figure in American 20th-century popular music. Not necessarily the *best* and certainly not the most consistent. But no one could argue that he was not the musician most responsible for popularizing rock 'n' roll on an international level. Viewed in cold sales figures, his impact was phenomenal. Dozens upon dozens of international smashes from the mid-'50s to the mid-'70s, as well as the steady sales of his catalog and reissues since his death in 1977, may make him the single highest-selling performer in history.

More important from a music lover's perspective, however, are his remarkable artistic achievements. Presley was not the very first white man to sing rhythm and blues; Bill Haley predated him in that regard, and there may have been others as well. Elvis was certainly the first, however, to assertively fuse country and blues music into the style known as rockabilly. While rockabilly arrangements were the foundations of his first (and possibly best) recordings, Presley could not have become a mainstream superstar without a much more varied palette that also incorporated pop, gospel, and even some bits of bluegrass and operatic schmaltz here and there. His 1950s recordings established the basic language of rock and roll; his explosive and sexual stage presence set standards for the music's visual image; his vocals were incredibly powerful and versatile.

Unfortunately, to much of the public, Elvis is more icon than artist. Innumerable bad Hollywood movies, increasingly caricatured records and mannerisms, and a personal life that became steadily more sheltered from real-world concerns (and steadily more bizarre) gave his story a somewhat mythic status. By the time of his death, he'd become more a symbol of gross Americana than of cultural innovation. The continued speculation about his incredible career has sustained interest in his life and supported a large tourist/entertainment industry that may last indefinitely, even if the fascination is fueled more by his celebrity than his music.

Born to a poor Mississippi family in the heart of Depression, Elvis had moved to Memphis by his teens, where he absorbed the vibrant melting pot of Southern popular music in the form of blues, country, bluegrass, and gospel. After graduating from high school, he became a truck driver, rarely if ever singing in public. Some 1953 and 1954 demos, recorded at the emerging Sun label in Memphis primarily for Elvis' own pleasure, helped stir interest on the part of Sun owner Sam Phillips. In mid-1954, Phillips, looking for a white singer with a Black feel, teamed Presley with guitarist Scotty Moore and bassist Bill Black. Almost by accident, apparently, the trio hit upon a version of an Arthur Crudup blues tune, "That's All Right Mama," that became Elvis' first single.

Elvis' five Sun singles pioneered the blend of R&B and C&W that would characterize rockabilly music. For quite a few scholars, they remain not only Elvis' best singles but the best rock and roll ever recorded. Claiming that Elvis made blues acceptable for the white market is not the whole picture; the singles usually teamed blues covers with country and pop ones, all made into rock and roll (at this point a term that barely existed) with a pulsing beat, slap-back echo, and Elvis' soaring, frenetic vocals. "That's All Right Mama," "Blue Moon of Kentucky," "Good Rockin' Tonight," "Baby Let's Play House," and "Mystery Train" remain core early-rock classics.

The singles sold well in the Memphis area immediately, and by 1955 were starting to sell well to country audiences throughout the South. Presley, Moore, and Black hit the road with a stage show that grew ever wilder and more provocative, Elvis' swiveling hips causing enormous controversy. The move to all-out rock was hastened by the addition of drums. The last Sun single, "I Forgot to Remember Forget"/"Mystery Train," hit No. 1 on the national country charts in late 1955. Presley was obviously a performer with superstar potential, attracting the interest of bigger labels and of Colonel Tom Parker, who became Elvis' manager. In need of capital to expand the Sun label, Sam Phillips sold Presley's contract to RCA in late 1955 for $35,000—a bargain, when viewed in hindsight, but an astronomical sum at the time.

This is the point where musical historians start to diverge in opinion. For many, the whole of his subsequent work for RCA—encompassing over 20 years—was a steady letdown, never recapturing the pure, primal energy that was harnessed so effectively on the handful of Sun singles. Elvis, however, was not a purist. What he wanted, more than anything, was to be successful. To do that, his material needed more of a pop feel; in any case, he'd never exactly been one to disparage the mainstream, naming Dean Martin as one of his chief heroes from the get go. At RCA, his rockabilly was leavened with enough pop flavor to make all of the charts, not just the country ones.

At the beginning, at least, the results were hardly any tamer than the Sun sessions. "Heartbreak Hotel," his first single, rose to No. 1 and, aided by some national television appearances, helped make Elvis an instant

superstar. "I Want You, I Need You, I Love You" was a No. 1 follow-up; the double-sided monster "Hound Dog"/"Don't Be Cruel" was one of the biggest-selling singles the industry had ever experienced up to that point. Albums and EPs were also chart toppers, not just in the US but throughout the world. The 1956 RCA recordings, while a bit more sophisticated in production and a bit less rootsy in orientation than his previous work, were still often magnificent, rating among the best and most influential recordings of early rock and roll.

Elvis' (and Colonel Parker's) aspirations were too big to be limited to records and live appearances. By late 1956, his first Hollywood movie, *Love Me Tender*, had been released; other screen vehicles would follow in the next few years, *Jailhouse Rock* being the best. The hits continued unabated, several of them ("Jailhouse Rock," "All Shook Up," "Too Much") excellent and often benefiting from the efforts of top early-rock songwriter Otis Blackwell, as well as the emerging team of Jerry Leiber-Mike Stoller. The Jordanaires added both pop and gospel elements with their smooth backup vocals.

Yet worrisome signs were creeping in. The Dean Martin influence began rearing its head in smoky, sentimental ballads such as "Loving You" and the vocal swoops became more exaggerated and stereotypical, although the overall quality of his output remained high. And although Moore and Black continued to back Elvis on his early RCA recordings, within a few years the musicians had gone their own ways.

Presley's recording and movie careers were interrupted by his induction into the Army in early 1958. There was enough material in the can to flood the charts throughout his two-year absence (during which he served largely in Germany). When he re-entered civilian life in 1960, his popularity, remarkably, was at just as high a level as when he left.

One couldn't, unfortunately, say the same for the quality of his music, which was not just becoming more sedate but was starting to either repeat itself or opt for operatic ballads that didn't have a whole lot to do with rock. Elvis' rebellious, wild image had been tamed to a large degree as well, as he and Parker began designing a career built around Hollywood films. Shortly after leaving the Army, in fact, Presley gave up live performing altogether for nearly a decade to concentrate on moviemaking. The films, in turn, would serve as vehicles to both promote his records and to generate maximum revenue with minimal effort. For the rest of the '60s, Presley ground out two or three movies a year that, while mostly profitable, had little going for them in the way of story, acting, or social value.

While there were some quality efforts on Presley's early '60s albums, his discography was soon dominated by forgettable soundtracks, mostly featuring material that was dispensable or downright ridiculous. In time he became largely disinterested in devoting much time to his craft in the studio. The soundtrack LPs themselves were sometimes filled out with outtakes that had been in the can for years (and these, sadly, were often the highlights of the albums). There were some good singles in the early '60s, like "Return to Sender"; once in a while there was even a flash of superb, tough rock, like "Little Sister" or "(Marie's the Name) His Latest Flame." But by 1963 or so, there was little to get excited about, although he continued to sell in large quantities.

The era spanning, roughly, 1962-67 has generated a school of Elvis apologists, eager to wrestle any kernel of quality that emerged from his recordings during this period. They also point out that Presley was assigned poor material and assert that Colonel Parker was largely responsible for Presley's emasculation. True to a point, but on the other hand it could be claimed, with some validity, that Presley himself was doing little to rouse himself from his artistic stupor, letting Parker destroy his artistic credibility without much apparent protest and holing up in his large mansion with a retinue of yes-men who protected their benefactor from much day-to-day contact with a fast-changing world.

The Beatles, all big Elvis fans, displaced Presley as the biggest rock act in the world in 1964. What's more, they did so by writing their own material and playing their own instruments—something Elvis had never been capable of, or particularly aspired to. The Beatles, and the British and American groups they influenced, were not shy about expressing their opinions, experimenting musically, and taking the reins of their artistic direction into their own hands. The net effect was to make Elvis Presley, who was still churning out movies in Hollywood while psychedelia and soul music became the rage, seem irrelevant, even as he managed to squeeze out an obscure Dylan cover ("Tomorrow is a Long Time") on a 1966 soundtrack album.

By 1967 and 1968, there were slight stirrings of an artistic reawakening by Elvis. Singles like "Guitar Man," "Big Boss Man," and "US Male," though hardly classics, were at least genuine rock and roll that sounded better than much of what he'd been turning out for years. A 1968 television special gave Presley the opportunity he needed to reinvent himself as an all-out, leather-coated rocker, still capable of magnetizing an audience and eager to revisit his blues and country roots.

The 1968 album *Elvis in Memphis* was the first LP in nearly a decade in which Presley seemed cognizant of current trends, as he updated his sounds with contemporary compositions and touches of soul to create some reasonably gutsy late-'60s pop-rock. This material and 1969 hits like "Suspicious Minds" and "In the Ghetto" returned him to the top of the charts. Arguably, it's been overrated by critics, who were so glad to have him singing rock again that they weren't about to carp about the slickness of some of the production or the mediocrity of some of the songwriting.

But Elvis' voice *did* sound good, and he returned to live performing in 1969, breaking in with weeks of shows in Las Vegas. This was followed by national tours that proved him to still be an excellent live entertainer, even if the exercises often reeked of show-biz extravaganza. (Elvis never did play outside of North America and Hawaii, possibly because Colonel Parker, it was later revealed, was an illegal alien who could have faced serious problems if he traveled abroad.) Hollywood was history, but studio and live albums were generated at a rapid pace, usually selling reasonably well, although Presley never had a Top Ten hit after 1972's "Burning Love."

Presley's 1970s recordings, like most of his '60s work, are the focus of divergent critical opinion. Some declare them to be, when Elvis was on, the equal of anything he did, especially in terms of artistic diversity. It's true that the material was pretty eclectic, running from country to blues to all-out rock to gospel (Presley periodically recorded gospel-only releases, going all the way back to 1957). At the same time, his vocal mannerisms were often stilted, and the material—though not nearly as awful as that '60s soundtrack filler—was sometimes substandard. Those who are not serious Elvis fans will usually find this late-period material to hold only a fraction of the interest of his '50s classics.

Elvis' final years have been the subject of a cottage industry of celebrity bios, tell-alls, and gossip screeds from those who knew him well or (more likely) purported to know him well. Those activities are really beyond the scope of a mini-bio such as this, but it's enough to note that his behavior was becoming increasingly instable. His weight fluctuated wildly, his marriage broke up, and he became dependent upon a variety of prescription drugs. Worst of all, he became isolated from the outside world except for professional purposes (he continued to tour until the end), rarely venturing outside of his Graceland mansion in Memphis. Colonel Parker's financial decisions on behalf of his client have also come in for much criticism.

On August 16, 1977, Presley was found dead in Graceland. The cause of death remains a subject of widespread speculation, although it seems likely that drugs played a part. An immediate cult (if cult is the way to describe millions of people) sprang up around his legacy, kept alive by the hundreds of thousands of visitors who make the pilgrimage to Graceland annually. Elvis memorabilia, much of it kitsch, is another industry in its own right. Dozens if not hundreds make a comfortable living by impersonating the King in live performance. And then there are all those Elvis sightings, reported in tabloids on a seemingly weekly basis.

Although Presley had recorded a mammoth quantity of both released and unreleased material for RCA, the label didn't show much interest in repackaging it with the respect due such a pioneer. Haphazard collections of outtakes and live performances were far rarer than budget reissues and countless repackagings of the big hits. In the CD age, RCA finally began to treat the catalog with some of the reverence it deserved, at long last assembling a box set containing nearly all of the 1950s recordings. Similar, although less exciting, box sets documented the 1960s, the 1970s, and his soundtrack performances. And exploitative reissues of Elvis material continue to appear constantly, often baited with one or two rare outtakes or alternates to entice the completists (of which there are many). In death, as in life, Presley continues to be one of RCA's most consistent earners. Fortunately, with a little discretion, a good Elvis library can be built with little duplication by sticking largely to the most highly recommended selections below. —*Richie Unterberger*

☆ Elvis Presley / Mar. 1956 / RCA ✦✦✦✦✦
While RCA had the material, they opted to play it safe and combine five Sun outtakes with seven new recordings and release the Hillbilly Cat's first album. This is a great way to begin a career! The best material here is on a par with the Sun singles. While "Blue Suede Shoes" is a cultural cornerstone of sorts, hearing Elvis' version of Clyde McPhatter's "Money Honey" is still, after four decades, revelatory. —*Neal Umphred*

☆ Elvis / Nov. 1956 / RCA ✦✦✦✦✦
Almost any rocker of the '50s could have claimed this as their best album. While there are some excellent rhythm numbers ("Rip It Up," "Paralyzed," and the too-country "When My Blue Moon Turns to Gold Again"), the album's standout is the panting "Love Me." —*Neal Umphred*

Loving You / Jul. 1957 / RCA ✦✦✦
Purporting to be the soundtrack to Elvis' second film, this album collects songs used in the film on one side with new material on the other. The weakness of a couple of the movie tunes and the fact that the new songs were leftovers from the sessions used to produce Elvis' first gospel EP and latest single add up to his weakest album offering, although any

album with "Got a Lot o' Living to Do" is alright. [The 1997 CD reissue adds 8 bonus tracks].—*Neal Umphred*

Loving You, Vol. 2 / Aug. 1957 / RCA ✦✦✦
The lesser four of the eight songs featured in Elvis Presley's second motion picture don't come close to the ones found on the first *Loving You* EP, but they're still not bad, especially "Mean Woman Blues" and "Got a Lot o' Livin' to Do." The other two songs are "Lonesome Cowboy" and "Hot Dog." —*William Ruhlmann*

Elvis' Golden Records, Vol. 1 / Mar. 1958 / RCA ✦✦✦✦
This is the greatest-hits album by which all greatest-hits albums need be measured. Fourteen sides sold umpteen bejillion records in the previous two years. The only discrepancy is the inclusion of "That's When Your Heartaches Begin," which failed to reach the Top 40 as the flip of "All Shook Up," at the expense of "I Was the One," "My Baby Left Me," and "Playing for Keeps," each much bigger hits. —*Neal Umphred*

King Creole / Aug. 1958 / RCA ✦✦✦
In which, backed by blaring horns, Elvis takes on New Orleans for the soundtrack to his fourth film. The arrangements work great on the uptempo numbers: "Hard Headed Woman" and "Trouble" are classics, "Dixieland Rock" and "New Orleans" should be, "Crawfish" is unlike anything Elvis would ever record again, and "King Creole" is probably the best title tune for a movie Elvis ever got. Had a couple more rockers been included, this could be more highly recommended. [The 1997 CD reissue adds 7 bonus tracks].—*Neal Umphred*

For LP Fans Only / Feb. 1959 / RCA Victor ✦✦✦✦
A compilation of four of the original Sun sides, five RCA single sides from 1956, and one song from the *Love Me Tender* EP, this was RCA's first effort at packaging the original Sun singles onto an LP (and, unfortunately, they allowed their engineers to "enhance" the tapes with boosted bass, added echo, etc.). As a package, this album and its companion, *A Date with Elvis*, is a disgrace, the songs treated as non-entities. There is not a trace of respect for the material or its history and the five songs per side was a rip-off. But the recordings themselves are great. —*Neal Umphred*

A Date with Elvis / Sep. 1959 / RCA Victor ✦✦✦✦
The companion volume to *For LP Fans Only*, this one collects five "enhanced" Sun sides (leaving the tenth side unavailable on album for almost 20 years), three from the *Jailhouse Rock* EP, and a *Love Me Tender* EP leftover. —*Neal Umphred*

50,000,000 Elvis Fans Can't Be Wrong: Elvis' Golden Records, Vol. 2 / 1960 / RCA ✦✦✦✦
The beginner is pointed toward the first two gold record sets, which contain the obvious hits that make up oldies fare and the not so well known, such as—in the case of this second volume—the smoldering "One Night" and the rousing "I Need Your Love Tonight." —*Neal Umphred*

Elvis Is Back! / Apr. 1960 / RCA ✦✦✦
The first album after the Army, *Elvis Is Back!* captures him at his secular best, which is nonetheless moved by gospel undertones. The sheer intensity of the performances from both Elvis on vocals and rhythm guitar, and the all-star band (which, aside from the regulars, includes Floyd Cramer, Hank Garland and Boots Randolph) overcomes any shortcomings the material might offer. "Make Me Know It," "Fever," "The Girl of My Best Friend" (a hit for soundalike Ral Donner here and for Elvis abroad) could have been chart toppers. "Dirty, Dirty Feeling," "Reconsider Baby," and "Such a Night" are among the very best—and "dirtiest"—numbers Elvis had ever cut. —*Neal Umphred*

G.I. Blues / Oct. 1960 / RCA ✦✦✦
Elvis was out of uniform in March and laying down vocals for his first big musical production in April. The confections that make up the soundtrack for *G.I. Blues* were the most trite collection of songs in his career, with the slight but affecting "Wooden Heart" the standout. Still, Elvis' enthusiasm makes even the puff listenable; one can't imagine even considering listening to this music had any other singer on the planet recorded it. [The 1997 CD reissue adds nine bonus tracks].—*Neal Umphred*

His Hand in Mine / Dec. 1960 / RCA Victor ✦✦✦✦
Presley cut several gospel albums over the course of his career, most of them overblown affairs. This one's easily his best; stripped down arrangements with Elvis passionately involved every note of the way. —*Cub Koda*

Something for Everybody / Jun. 1961 / RCA Victor ✦✦✦
Within a year, the emotional involvement and the sense of joie de vivre of both *Elvis Is Back!* and *His Hand in Mine* was replaced by the more stunted professionalism of *Something for Everybody*. While certainly not a compliment, the title was not meant as a total put-down. There are some excellent moments on this LP ("I Want You with Me" would have made a credible single) but, for the first time, it is the "rhythm numbers" that pull down the overall excellence, not the ballads. In the midst of

restraint, he cut "Feel So Bad," a scorcher that reached the upper reaches of the charts in 1961 and heated up the first side of *Golden Records, Vol. 3.* —*Neal Umphred*

Blue Hawaii / Oct. 1961 / RCA ✦✦✦
The soundtrack of what was to be Elvis' biggest movie called for an Hawaiianesque flavor, and, while Presley's vocals are excellent throughout, much of the material is of a throwaway caliber. Of course, any session that produces "Can't Help Falling in Love" is memorable, but said sessions also gave us "Rock-a-Hula Baby," which was a worldwide hit despite being as dumb as the title implies! Within a matter of months, critical fans would look back at *this* album as a high point. [The 1997 CD reissue adds 14 bonus tracks].—*Neal Umphred*

Pot Luck with Elvis / Jun. 1962 / RCA Victor ✦✦✦
This album continued the decline begun with *Something for Everybody:* While there are several excellent, continually underrated tracks ("Gonna Get Back Home Somehow," "Night Rider," "(Such an) Easy Question" and, of course, "Suspicion"), this album sounds like a collection of filler, the ballads especially tending toward the lugubrious. A good if unexceptional album. —*Neal Umphred*

Girls! Girls! Girls! / Nov. 1963 / RCA Victor ✦✦
An even lamer attempt at a Hawaiian backdrop produced a nice cover of the old Drifters number as the title tune and "Return to Sender," an excellent mid-tempo R&B-ish hit. The ballads are pleasant, though hardly memorable. Elvis is still singing well, especially considering the material and the arrangements. That would change shortly. While the movies Elvis made during the '60s and their accompanying soundtracks did produce a reliable source of income, they worked against Elvis in the long run. The initial enthusiasm that accompanied even the silliest of plots in 1960-62 was replaced by inevitable boredom. The Colonel's response to his boy's growing disillusionment was to find sillier scripts, reduce the budgets allotted for other actors and props, and accept songs the nonsense of which boggles the imagination. Still, during this time, especially those first few years when a movie meant having some fun, Elvis also cut a number of tracks for lesser, nonmusical films, including several affecting ballads for *Wild in the Country*. In 1963 Elvis teamed up with the luscious Ann-Margret, recording some of his most spirited singing in years for *Viva Las Vegas*. Had RCA Victor collected the best of these sessions, along with the standouts "Summer Kisses, Winter Tears," "King of the Whole Wide World," and "Follow That Dream," a surprisingly solid album could have been issued. Alas, these tracks were scattered to the winds, showing up on EPs, B-sides, and budget albums over a period of ten years. If one needs to delve into this period, an easy rule of thumb is that the further into the decade the soundtracks go, the less likely they are to please. —*Neal Umphred*

Elvis' Golden Records, Vol. 3 / Sep. 1964 / RCA ✦✦✦
This third package of gold captures most of the hits from 1960-1962 and is a marvelous album, a model in selection and programming. The songs are all excellent, Elvis was in a period that is always overlooked by fans, critics, and biographers, the band often cooked, and the production and engineering were flawless. Much of what Elvis achieved here on songs like "(Marie's the Name) His Latest Flame" and "Little Sister" has not been duplicated elsewhere in the field of rock 'n' roll, although the influences are sprouting up in contemporary country. —*Neal Umphred*

Elvis for Everyone / Jul. 1965 / RCA Victor ✦✦✦
To fill in the blank space between soundtracks (yes, it had come to that), RCA gathered a dozen leftovers stretching back to 1954(!) and assembled this album with a cover that lives up to the title. There is no attempt at programming a logical compilation, a set that might tell us something about Elvis. As usual, everything is treated as so much fodder for the unwashed masses. *And* this was his best album in two years! —*Neal Umphred*

How Great Thou Art / Mar. 1967 / RCA Victor ✦✦✦✦
Between 1966 and 1968, Elvis recorded just enough studio material to fill one complete secular album and *How Great Thou Art*, a far more polite (and slightly surreal) reading of traditional religious material than the previous outing, a half-dozen years earlier. The performances throughout are superb, the sound impeccable; this actually beat *Sgt. Pepper* as the Best Engineered Album of 1967 in the Grammys! This album is also much closer to mainstream gospel and may not be so immediately accessible to the unconverted; don't let that steer you away from an otherwise great record. —*Neal Umphred*

Elvis Gold Records, Vol. 4 / Feb. 1968 / RCA ✦✦✦
This is one of Elvis' most misunderstood albums. At the time of release the reviews almost without exception discussed how Elvis' gold was drained up and how he was reduced to filling up the fourth volume with B-sides. Actually there was more than enough gold for the set: "Wooden Heart," "Can't Help Falling in Love," and "Return to Sender" are the most obvious. "A Mess of Blues," "Witchcraft," and "Please Don't Drag That String Around" are fine uptempo numbers while "Love Letters"

and "It Hurts Me" are among the best ballads Elvis—or anyone else—recorded during the decade. —*Neal Umphred*

NBC TV Special / Dec. 1968 / RCA ✦✦✦✦
After years of making abysmal movies, Presley appeared before a live audience, scared to death. That he more than rose to the challenge is evidenced here, a masterly performance highlighted by the jam-session segment with DJ Fontana and Scotty Moore, where Presley plays electric guitar and knocks out drop-dead versions of "Baby, What You Want Me to Do" and "Tiger Man." —*Cub Koda*

☆ **From Elvis in Memphis** / May 1969 / RCA ✦✦✦✦✦
Presley returned to Memphis, recording 30-odd songs in Chips Moman's America Sound Studios in 1969, leading to his artistic and commercial resurgence ("In the Ghetto" and "Suspicious Minds") and what may be his single greatest album, *From Elvis in Memphis*. The first track opens with Elvis' hoarsely shouting "I had to leave town for a little while . . ." and then announces—in no uncertain terms—that he's back. A brilliant selection of material, Elvis sings like his life depended on it. (It didn't; his career did.) The musicians (all regulars from Chips Moman's American Sound Studios) cook, and the overdubbed horns and background vocals are among the most appropriate ever used on a white singer's record. —*Neal Umphred*

From Memphis to Vegas / From Vegas to Memphis / Nov. 1969 / RCA ✦✦✦✦
One half of the imponderably titled *From Memphis to Vegas / From Vegas to Memphis*, (later issued as a separate album, *Elvis in Person at the International Hotel*) captures Elvis from the summer of 1969 while the exhilaration of conquest was still evident. It's a nice compromise between mere entertainment and the revelatory. The first few songs are old hits to pull you in; the second side opens with a roaring medley of "Mystery Train" and Rufus Thomas' "Tiger Man" and leads to a staggering seven-minute "Suspicious Minds." The studio album, ten tracks from the previous Memphis sessions, are a letdown and, even at the time of release, the two-fer concept seemed ill conceived. Had the best of the rest of the Memphis material been collected on a single album and titled *Suspicious Minds*, it's possible this album could have leapt to No. 1 and outsold the first. —*Neal Umphred*

On Stage: February 1970 / Jun. 1970 / RCA Victor ✦✦
On Stage—February 1970 is a bit more tame than *Elvis in Person* but provides Elvis with a chance to cover a number of then-contemporary hits, which he carries with aplomb. Actually, two numbers, "Yesterday" and "Runaway," were recorded for the previous album in August past, so the title is only 80 percent accurate. As for the live albums that were to follow, you had to have been there. —*Neal Umphred*

Worldwide 50 Gold Award Hits, Vol. 1 / Aug. 1970 / RCA Victor ✦✦✦✦
A combination of the two four-LP *Worldwide* boxes, this two-CD set contains each of the 50 sides that RCA credits with accumulated worldwide sales in excess of 1,000,000 copies! And in chronological order of release in mono! One can either trace the obvious decline of the artist into entertainer or marvel at how good the bad stuff sounds in context. Million-selling B-sides and EPs that most assuredly had topped the seven-digit figure but were routinely ignored by most compilations are also included. If all you want in your collection from Elvis is the most obvious hits, this is the one to go with. —*Neal Umphred*

In Person at the International Hotel Las Vegas / Nov. 1970 / RCA Victor ✦✦✦✦
When Elvis and the Colonel decided it was time to start appearing live again, they assembled a crackerjack band (featuring guitarist James Burton) and took on Vegas full bore. Easily the King's best live album, the highlights on *In Person at the International Hotel Las Vegas* include "Johnny B. Goode," the "My Babe/Mystery Train/Tiger Man" medley, and "Suspicious Minds." —*Cub Koda*

Elvis Country / Jan. 1971 / RCA ✦✦✦✦
Elvis Country was the second album from the June 1970 sessions. It is Elvis' best single album from the '70s and one of his very best ever. Every performance has something to offer, from the pleading of "I Really Don't Want to Know" to the raving "(I Washed My Hands in) Muddy Water." Even "Snowbird" is sung with passion! —*Neal Umphred*

He Touched Me / Apr. 1972 / RCA Victor ✦✦✦✦
As if to make up for not recording in the studio for all those Hollywood years, Elvis took the first few years of his comeback deadly serious. As it stands, *He Touched Me* blends the earthiness of the 1960 gospel album with a bit of the preternatural churchiness of the 1966 recordings. This is a fine record, and you don't need to be a Christian to dig this music. —*Neal Umphred*

Elvis / Jul. 1973 / RCA Victor ✦✦✦
Ten tracks, all leftovers from previous projects, appeared in an ugly cover with nothing on the back except ads for other Presley product. Still, what was left off of Elvis' albums is more revealing than what went on. "It's Still Here" and "I Will Be True" are Elvis at the piano sans back-

ing, and they are glorious. Worth the price of the whole damn album. Period. —*Neal Umphred*

Raised on Rock / Oct. 1973 / RCA Victor ♦♦♦
In July 1973, Elvis returned to Memphis, this time to the source of Southern soul, Stax Studios. Apparently, the very idea of working with Elvis was intimidating, and the Stax musicians couldn't overcome their awe, so Elvis had to leave the building. In his absence, the rhythm tracks were laid down. He then returned to add his vocals, a practice only used during the last few years of the soundtracks, when he was too bored to show up and work. From all of this, five songs were attempted, one completed, and they're instantly forgettable. Elvis returned in December to Stax with a mix of his band and some Nashville cats, recording 18 tracks in a week. In between, he had tried a session at his Palm Springs home that didn't work, although three almost ponderously sincere ballads were completed. All in all, RCA had 30 new Elvis songs, enough quality material for two strong albums of 12 tracks each. Unfortunately, the material was issued as three cheesily packaged albums of a mere ten tracks each. *Raised on Rock, Good Times,* and *Promised Land* all have something to offer, but the lesser material dilutes the impact of the strong and the sound ranges from OK to atrocious, thus producing more evidence of Presley's growing mediocrity. —*Neal Umphred*

Recorded Live on Stage in Memphis / Jun. 1974 / RCA Victor ♦♦♦
This oft-ignored album, recorded in March 1974 at Memphis' Midsouth Coliseum (formerly the center of controversy when the proposed title, the Elvis Presley Coliseum, was poo-pooed), is easily the strongest live package of the '70s, the one worth having. Elvis is in exceptional vocal form and, between all the stuff that showed up on every other live album of the period, there is a great "Trying to Get to You" and strong versions of "My Baby Left Me" and "Lawdy, Miss Clawdy," material he otherwise left unnoticed. —*Neal Umphred*

Elvis Today / May 1975 / RCA ♦♦♦
Elvis Today is often cited by writers as Elvis' uncertain return to his Sun origins. There really isn't that much difference from the trio that resulted from 1973's Stax sessions, with the lesser tracks being a bit more substantial. The sound is better, but the packaging had become, at this point, practically offensive. One color close-up after another, almost all from the *Aloha from Hawaii* special (or that pre-bloated period), back covers with no noted or technical data, just ads for other Presley product. Still, an album with "Susan When She Tried," "T-R-O-U-B-L-E," and a hilariously appropriate reading of "I Can Help" is worth listening to any time. —*Neal Umphred*

From Elvis Presley Boulevard, Memphis, Tennessee / May 1976 / RCA ♦♦♦
By 1976 Elvis was recording at home in Graceland, cutting what would be the final recordings of his career. Filled with bathos and showing little rock 'n' roll vitality, these remain interesting nonetheless, as they implied his accepting his age somewhat and attempting to combine old-fashioned, melodramatic soul with contemporary country-pop. While the pain and decay are evident—especially in hindsight—Elvis could still sing. "Hurt" is excellent, one of his best, and, on "Danny Boy," Elvis reaches with an aching falsetto that closes the song, appropriately. Still, this is hardly the album to begin your collection with. —*Neal Umphred*

Moody Blue / Jul. 1977 / RCA ♦♦
For some reason, this album sold briskly on release, heading for the most respectable sales an Elvis album had had in years. Then, nothing. This is not one of his best, combining a few recently recorded tracks (October, back in his home studios), with leftovers from the February sessions, and a couple of live tracks, one of which had previously been released on the already deleted *Recorded Live on Stage in Memphis.* —*Neal Umphred*

Elvis Aron Presley / Aug. 1980 / RCA ♦♦♦
An eight-record boxed extravaganza, it promised so much and delivered so little. Averaging 12 minutes per side, this could have easily been a six album set with a considerably pared down retail price. The packaging is so ugly as to defy description, including inner sleeves that fell apart after sliding the albums in a couple of times. The programming of the discs by theme or concept was interesting but the box stands as a condemnation of the way that Presley was perceived by RCA. There is some good, previously unavailable material here; the side titled *Elvis at the Piano* contains four tracks of just that, including the complete take of "It's Still Here" from 1971 and the lovely but inexplicably never heard before "Beyond the Reef" from the *How Great Thou Art* sessions. —*Neal Umphred*

Elvis: The Beginning Years, 1954 to '56 / 1983 / Louisiana Hayride ♦♦♦
At the start of his career, Elvis played many engagements for the *Louisiana Hayride,* the most popular country radio show except for the *Grand Ole Opry.* Nine surviving airshots from those days are compiled on this album, including a few of his classic Sun singles, the otherwise unavailable covers "Tweedle Dee" and "Maybellene," and a very raw "Hound

Dog." The sound isn't bad considering the source; Elvis' vocals are always clear, the guitar sometimes bright and sometimes not, the bass all but inaudible. No one's buying this for high fidelity, though; what you want is a glimpse of the man at his peak before his live audience, and on that account, this comes through, with energetic performances that form a valuable historic document. —*Richie Unterberger*

The First Year (Elvis, Scotty and Bill) / 1983 / Sun/Charly ♦♦♦
The First Year chronicles an appearance by Elvis Presley, with his original backup musicians, Scotty Moore and Bill Black, at Eagle's Hall in Houston on March 19, 1955. Since the date was broadcast on local television, a primitive audio recording was made. This turns out to be low fidelity, though it still conveys the excitement apparent in one of Presley's earliest concerts. The five songs of the set are filled out to LP length by including interviews with Presley (recorded in 1956), Moore, and Houston disc jockey Diff Collie. (The Moore interview takes up the entire second side of the LP.) The result is a historical document that will interest fans. (Initially released as a bootleg in the US in November 1979 by Very Wonderful Golden Editions as King 31.) —*William Ruhlmann*

Elvis' Golden Records, Vol. 5 / 1984 / RCA ♦♦♦♦
The last volume in the Elvis Presley *Gold Records* compilation series had been released in February 1968, but Presley reissue producer Joan Deary (on her final project before turning over the reins to Gregg Geller) had the idea to revive it with a fifth volume in November 1984. It would have been a good idea in, say, 1978, since Presley had scored 14 gold or platinum singles since the last volume. It still wasn't that bad an idea in 1984 (leaving aside the redundancy factor), though the ten-track selection was skimpy, leaving out "Don't Cry Daddy," "The Wonder of You," "I've Lost You," "You Don't Have to Say You Love Me," "I Really Don't Want to Know," "Separate Ways," and "My Way," and idiosyncratic, including "If You Talk in Your Sleep" and "Moody Blue," which made the Top 40, but did not go gold, as well as "For the Heart," the B-side of the Top 40 hit "Hurt," an inclusion that is justifiable on aesthetic grounds (it's terrific) and for its influence—under the title "Had a Dream," it had been the Judds' first country hit earlier in the year. But the rest, from 1968's "If I Can Dream" to 1977's "Way Down," were Presley's most successful records of his final eight years and, in tunes like "Suspicious Minds" and "Burning Love," among his best recordings. —*William Ruhlmann*

Rocker / 1984 / RCA ♦♦♦♦
A&R director Gregg Geller took over stewardship of the Elvis Presley catalog at RCA in time to orchestrate a series of releases marking Presley's 50th birthday (January 8, 1985). This compilation put together 12 of Presley's hottest rock 'n' roll tracks from 1956-1957, including his versions of standards like Little Richard's "Long Tall Sally," Carl Perkins' "Blue Suede Shoes," and Big Mama Thornton's "Hound Dog" and numbers written for him, such as "Jailhouse Rock." Unlike the similar, but ill-fated *I Was the One,* which attempted to modernize '50s rock tracks with technology and overdubbing, this album was "digitally remastered from original monophonic master tapes," and it sounded great. —*William Ruhlmann*

☆ **Reconsider Baby** / 1985 / RCA ♦♦♦♦♦
A 12-song, budget-priced compilation of Elvis' most notable blues sides for the label. A good place to start digging Elvis' commitment to the music—always returning to it right up through the '70s like an old friend, whenever he needed a quick fix of the *real* thing—as he takes on everything from R&B slices like Tommy Tucker's "High Heel Sneakers" to Percy Mayfield's "Stranger in My Own Home Town." Major highlights on this collection are Elvis playing acoustic rhythm guitar and driving the band through a take of the Lowell Fulson title track, blistering versions of two Arthur Crudup songs, an unreleased Sun recording of Lonnie Johnson's "Tomorrow Night," and the R-rated take of Smiley Lewis' "One Night (of Sin)." —*Cub Koda*

Valentine Gift for You / Jan. 1985 / RCA ♦♦♦
Another release in the series of 50th birthday celebrations for Elvis Presley, *A Valentine Gift for You* was an album of Presley love songs, just right for that special someone in your life, and released in time for Valentine's Day. From "Are You Lonesome Tonight" to "Can't Help Falling in Love," Presley crooned his way through a collection of romantic ballads that ranged from the smoldering ("Fever") to the folkie ("Tomorrow Is a Long Time"). An imaginatively chosen and well-sequenced selection. (Pressed on red vinyl.) —*William Ruhlmann*

Always on My Mind / Jun. 1985 / RCA ♦♦♦
The other side of the romantic coin from *A Valentine Gift for You,* released five months earlier, *Always on My Mind* was a concept compilation album given over to breakup songs. Especially after his own divorce in 1972, Presley showed a real affection for maudlin, self-pitying material like "Don't Cry Daddy" (actually recorded in January 1969 and a Top Ten hit), "You Gave Me a Mountain" (recorded in February 1973), and, of course, the excuse-filled title track (recorded in March 1972, the month after he was legally separated from his wife). It's all here; put it

on, raise a glass, and cry in your beer. (Pressed on purple vinyl.) — *William Ruhlmann*

Return of the Rocker / Mar. 1986 / RCA ✦✦✦
A companion to the *Rocker* compilation, *Return of the Rocker* presented harder-edged material recorded by Elvis Presley in the early '60s. Presley was moderating his sound in this period, so even the rockier stuff wasn't as hard as what he had recorded in the 1950s. But songs like "Little Sister," "A Mess of Blues," and "Return to Sender" still maintained his standard for uptempo rock 'n' roll, and this is some of the best material Presley recorded in the decade. — *William Ruhlmann*

★ **Top Ten Hits** / 1987 / RCA ✦✦✦✦✦
The Top Ten Hits is exactly what it says it is—every Top Ten hit that Elvis Presley ever had during the course of his career, from "Heartbreak Hotel" in 1956 to "Burning Love" in 1972. Even though this double-disc set covers a lot of ground, there's a huge amount of terrific material that *isn't* included on the compilation. There's none of his Sun recordings, none of his gritty blues, none of his gospel, precious little of his country recordings, and many great singles for RCA aren't included. Still, the 38 songs on *The Top Ten Hits* are absolutely first-rate—there's no arguing with "I Want You, I Need You, I Love You," "Don't Be Cruel," "Hound Dog," "Love Me Tender," "Love Me," All Shook Up," "Jailhouse Rock," "One Night," "A Fool Such As I," "(Marie's the Name) His Latest Flame," "Can't Help Falling in Love," "Little Sister," "Return to Sender," "Suspicious Minds," and many, many others. It's the perfect way to start an Elvis collection and, for many casual fans, the only set to own. — *Stephen Thomas Erlewine*

The Number One Hits / 1987 / RCA ✦✦✦✦
Number One Hits contains 18 No. 1 records from the charts of *Billboard*, which somehow didn't rank "Crying in the Chapel," "In the Ghetto," "Burning Love," and "Way Down" as chart toppers, although other national surveys did. In fact, according to RCA, every copy of "Way Down" was sold out within days after Presley's death, not just here but all over the planet, and somehow, amazingly, it didn't even make the magazine's Top Ten! — *Neal Umphred*

☆ **The Memphis Record** / 1987 / RCA ✦✦✦✦✦
Coming hot off the heels of his breakthrough NBC special in 1968, Presley returned to Memphis to record for the first time in 12 years and laid down 20 tracks in the space of four days. He was hot, he was inspired, and it's all here. — *Cub Koda*

★ **The Complete Sun Sessions** / 1987 / RCA ✦✦✦✦✦
This is it, your perfect starting point to understanding how Elvis—as Howlin' Wolf so aptly put it—"made his *pull* from the blues." All the source points are there for the hearing: Arthur Crudup's "That's All Right (Mama)," Roy Brown's "Good Rockin' Tonight," Kokomo Arnold's "Milkcow Blues Boogie," Arthur Gunter's "Baby, Let's Play House," and Junior Parker's "Mystery Train." Modern day listeners coming to these recordings for the first time will want to reclassify this music into a million subgenres, with all the hyphens firmly in place. But what we ultimately have here is a young Elvis Presley, mixing elements of blues, gospel, and hillbilly music together and getting ready to unleash its end result—rock 'n' roll—on an unsuspecting world. — *Cub Koda*

The Essential Elvis: The First Movies / 1988 / RCA ✦✦✦✦
A great collection of movie-soundtrack alternates, it includes great, eye-opening versions of "Jailhouse Rock" and "Got a Lot of Livin' to Do." — *Hank Davis & Cub Koda*

Stereo '57: Essential Elvis, Vol. 2 / 1988 / RCA ✦✦✦
The second volume of *Essential Elvis* offers Elvis in binaural stereo from the January 1957 sessions that produced several hits. (RCA Victor generously filled the disc out with mono masters of the remaining songs to give the consumer a complete version of the sessions.) This is a lot of fun; the gaffes are numerous, obvious, and hilarious, and for ears raised on multi-track recording, it must be amazing to hear an entire record recorded live in the studio! — *Neal Umphred*

Alternate Aloha / May 1988 / RCA ✦✦✦
On January 14, 1973, Elvis Presley performed a concert at the Honolulu International Center Arena that was broadcast live on television in Europe and the Far East and taped for American broadcast on April 4. It produced a double-LP live album, *Aloha from Hawaii via Satellite*, which topped the charts and sold two million copies. As a backup against potential technical problems, Presley had performed a full dress rehearsal on January 12 that was filmed and recorded for backup. This album presents a 24-track, 64-minute version of that show. It has a running order similar to the earlier album, except that "Johnny B. Goode," "I Can't Stop Loving You," and a medley of "Long Tall Sally" and "Whole Lotta Shakin' Goin' On" have been omitted and three previously released Hawaiian-themed songs, "Blue Hawaii," "Hawaiian Wedding Song," and "K-U-U-I-P-O," actually performed on the 14th in a post-concert session and part of the US TV broadcast, but not released on the earlier album, have been added. The dress rehearsal has a less frantic, more relaxed feel than the broadcast performance, but it also has the

unmistakable air of a run-through. Still, it presents Presley at the peak of his 1970s live work and, if redundant by definition, on its own presents a worthwhile concert performance. — *William Ruhlmann*

☆ **Million Dollar Quartet** / Feb. 1990 / RCA ✦✦✦✦✦
For years available only as a poor-fidelity bootleg, this is Elvis jamming in the Sun studios with Carl Perkins, Jerry Lee Lewis, and others on a set of primarily gospel and hillbilly material. Loose as a goose, with a true jam-session spirit to it, it offers a fascinating glimpse of one of the few times Presley let his true musical soul come up for air with somebody (Sam Phillips) there to record it. — *Cub Koda*

Hits Like Never Before: Essential Elvis, Vol. 3 / Dec. 1990 / RCA ✦✦✦
A whopping 24 alternates of takes from his 1958 sessions. This has some substantially different versions of most of his big late-'50s hits—"I Got Stung," "A Fool Such As I," "I Need Your Love Tonight," "Wear My Ring Around Your Neck," and "A Big Hunk o' Love"—as well as alternates of songs from the *King Creole* film. Not exactly essential, but decent stuff. — *Richie Unterberger*

☆ **The King of Rock 'n' Roll: The Complete 50s Masters** / Jun. 23, 1992 / RCA ✦✦✦✦✦
A casual Elvis fan wanting to assemble a decent overview of the King's '50s sides could probably sweat it down to the *Sun Sessions* CD and Vol. 1 of the *Top Ten Hits* compilation. But for those of you who take your '50s Presley seriously, *The King of Rock 'n' Roll—The Complete 50s' Masters* is absolutely essential. For the hardcore Elvis fan, the booklet and CD graphics for this five-disc set provide incentive enough to justify its purchase. The liner notes by Presley expert Peter Guralnick are passionate, contagious in their enthusiasm, and filled with a real sense of history, time, and place. The treasure trove of unpublished photos, session information, and Elvis memorabilia accompanying the booklet text is no less inspiring. But it's the music (140 tracks in all) that's the real meat and potatoes of this set. Every studio track cut during the '50s—the seminal Sun sides, the early RCA hits, movie soundtracks, alternates, live performances, rarities (including both sides of the long-lost acetate he cut for his mother back in 1953)—it's all here in one gorgeous package. Soundwise, this box makes any of the previous issues of this material pale by comparison, the proper (non-reverbed) inclusion of the Sun masters being a particular treat. This is no mere rehash of what's been around a dozen times before—there's a lot of thought and care behind this package, and no serious fan of American rock 'n' roll should consider a collection complete without it. — *Cub Koda*

☆ **From Nashville to Memphis: The Essential 60's Masters** / Sep. 28, 1993 / RCA ✦✦✦✦
Continues the tradition of first-quality sound remastering and packaging. Much of Elvis' '60s work is arguably not as essential as the '50s stuff, but this meticulous five-disc, 130-track set makes an impressive case for the defense. A thick booklet contains riveting liner notes, full-color photos, complete discography, and session listings; a sheet of RCA album cover stamps tops off the set. — *Roch Parisien*

If Every Day Was Like Christmas / 1994 / RCA ✦✦✦
All of Elvis Presley's catalog Christmas material has been remastered and compiled on this single disc. RCA has taken the same masterful care with this 24-track collection as with the Elvis box sets. Sound quality is exceptional. Includes three unreleased alternate performances, solid liner notes, and a closing "Christmas Message from Elvis." — *Roch Parisien*

Amazing Grace: His Greatest Sacred Songs / Oct. 25, 1994 / RCA ✦✦✦
Elvis recorded quite a bit of gospel over the course of his career, and this two-CD, 55-song set has the bulk of it. Most of this is drawn from his three gospel LPs (*His Hand in Mine*, 1960; *How Great Thou Art*, 1967; *He Touched Me*, 1972), as well as a 1957 EP. Presley was undoubtedly heavily influenced by gospel (at times he indicated regret at not having chosen to become a gospel singer), and this material has played pretty well with critics. Elvis sings with skill and reasonable commitment, and the backing musicians include such Elvis/Nashville standbys as Scotty Moore, Hank Garland, Floyd Cramer, Charlie McCoy, Pete Drake, the Jordanaires, and James Burton. At the same time, let's have a reality check here. Rock—and pop-oriented fans are going to find this two-and-a-half hour set tough going, unless they have a taste for spirituals as well. Things get a little more accessible when the tempos brighten, but often it's on the sedate side. For both collectors and listeners, highlights of the collection are five previously unreleased tracks from 1972. Recorded with only Charlie Hodges on piano and J.D. Sumner & the Stamps on backing vocals, they present Presley's gospel at its sparsest and most spontaneous. — *Richie Unterberger*

The Great Elvis Presley Live / 1995 / Goldies ✦✦✦
The 14 cuts here are all from the *Louisiana Hayride* (with dates ranging from 1955 up until the early spring of 1956), the radio show on which Presley made his earliest major regional appearances in the South;

before he was a national phenomenon, he appeared on the program a total of 75 times. Although the emcee erroneously refers to the opening song as "Heartbreak Motel" and vocally steps on Elvis' opening line, the fidelity is a little shaky by today's standards, and some of the songs (especially "Hound Dog") were better represented elsewhere, this is still a priceless chance to hear some of the palpable excitement that Elvis generated at a time when he was not quite a national phenomenon, respected (or, at least, tolerated) by old-time country audiences, and not quite yet "the king of rock 'n' roll." The shouting of the kids is pretty daunting, and his covers of songs like "Long Tall Sally" and "Maybelline" aren't half-bad alongside his more familiar repertoire, which includes his early rockabilly numbers like "Blue Moon of Kentucky" and "Good Rockin' Tonight" as well as his earliest RCA sides. Scotty Moore and company could really cook during that first year, and it was all so fresh an experience they were throwing themselves into every performance. —*Bruce Eder*

Heart and Soul / Jan. 24, 1995 / RCA ♦♦
The concept that seems to be guiding this, one of the latest in a long line of rehash repackages, is a focus on romantic ballads. You get well-worn hits like "Love Me Tender," "Can't Help Falling in Love," and "Suspicious Minds," not-so-well-worn hits like "She's Not You," the original version of "The Girl of My Best Friend" (covered by Ral Donner for a big hit), and other odds and ends on this 22-track compilation. Not appealing for either the novice or serious fan, the rarities, if you could call them that, are a stereo version of "I've Lost You" and a version of "Bridge over Troubled Water" with the dubbed applause removed. Only regular pilgrims to Graceland need to get in line. —*Richie Unterberger*

Command Performances: The Essential '60s Masters II / Jul. 18, 1995 / RCA ♦♦♦
Elvis Presley's 1960s film soundtracks are renowned as the repository of his most frivolous (many would say ridiculous) material. This 62-song, double CD draws from no less than 26 of those screen vehicles to present the "best" of these performances; the idea is to complement the first volume of *Essential 60's Masters*, which focused on his non-soundtrack recordings from the decade, and doesn't include any of the cuts from this collection. The goal of this package may have been to boil away the dross (as big as this is, there's a LOT of stuff they left off). But if anything, it perhaps inadvertently demonstrates just how lousy most of those recordings were; even this selective, chronologically programmed set feels way too long and could have probably been cut in length to a single CD without too much loss. That's not to say that what's here is entirely negligible. There are some classic jokes ("Return to Sender," "Can't Help Falling in Love"), fair rockers ("What'd I Say," "Little Egypt"), and more than a few cuts that are transcendentally great/awful in their mindless silliness ("Rock-a-Hula Baby," "Viva Las Vegas," "Do the Clam"), songs which are archetypes, for better or worse, of the kitschiest facet of Presley's myth. But much of the rest is just unremarkable or even bad: stupid novelties ("Poison Ivy League"), drab ballads, and many mediocre rock tunes. This doesn't include such legendarily idiotic tunes as "No Room to Rhumba in a Sports Car," "Yoga Is As Yoga Does," and "Fort Lauderdale Chamber of Commerce"; you can find those on the original soundtracks or on a famous out-of-print bootleg, the aptly-titled *Elvis' Greatest Shit*. —*Richie Unterberger*

☆ **Walk a Mile in My Shoes: The Essential '70s Masters** / Oct. 10, 1995 / RCA ♦♦♦♦♦
In most conventional rock criticism, Elvis Presley's '70s records are considered his weakest, as they were recorded while he was falling deeper into drug addiction. However, as Dave Marsh argues in the liner notes of *Walk a Mile in My Shoes: The Essential '70s Masters*, the music on the five-CD box set is among the most personal and adventurous of Elvis' career, even if the individual albums don't always reflect that diversity. By cutting away all of the dross that accumulated over the decade and sequencing the songs in a logical, entertaining manner, *Walk a Mile in My Shoes* supports the argument. On the first two discs, all of the singles Presley released during the '70s are presented, and while there are couple of weak numbers, the music stands as an impressive continuation of his artistic rebirth of the late '60s. —*Stephen Thomas Erlewine*

Legend Begins / Jan. 15, 1996 / Magnum ♦♦♦
An absolutely astounding collection of early Elvis live performances, starting with his initial appearance on the *Louisiana Hayride* in 1954. Of particular note is the five-song performance from the Eagle's Hall in Houston, Texas (March of 1955), as well as the inclusion of *Hayride* performances of LaVern Baker's "Tweedlee Dee" and Chuck Berry's "Maybellene," two songs Presley never recorded commercially. Although this material has been around the block numerous times, its improved fidelity and legal issuance here makes this a true cornerstone for any '50s Presley collection. (British import) —*Cub Koda*

Elvis Presley '56 / Mar. 5, 1996 / RCA ♦♦♦♦
Sure the music on here's great. How could it not be? It has 22 of his hottest tracks from his first year at RCA, including not only the hits "Heartbreak Hotel," "Hound Dog," "Don't Be Cruel," and "Too Much" but such

noted early rockers as "My Baby Left Me," "Blue Suede Shoes," "Money Honey," and "So Glad You're Mine." From a collector's viewpoint, though, you have to wonder whether it was really necessary. The only previously unreleased item is a sparser, earlier take of "Heartbreak Hotel." Everything else has been widely available (even on CD) for years, and it's a good bet that many of the Elvis fans who buy this already have virtually all of the contents on the *King of Rock 'n' Roll* box set. —*Richie Unterberger*

The Essential Elvis, Vol. 4: 100 Years from Now / Jul. 1996 / RCA ♦♦♦♦
100 Years from Now is the fourth installment in RCA's *The Essential Elvis* series. The previous three volumes were all comprehensive box sets, but *100 Years from Now* is a single-disc collection that focuses on a very specific timeframe—namely, the sessions Elvis cut in Nashville during 1970 and 1971. With the addition of some between-song narration, the music from these sessions would later become the *Elvis: Country* album. All of the *Elvis: Country* record is presented on *100 Years from Now* in its original form—sans narration, without overdubs, and in full running time. There are also the standard rarities and previously unreleased songs, like a version of "The Lord's Prayer." Even with the newly discovered material, what is special about this set is the original *Elvis: Country* album, which represents his last great album, and it sounds even better in its original, uncut version. —*Stephen Thomas Erlewine*

Afternoon in the Garden / Mar. 25, 1997 / RCA ♦♦♦
Afternoon in the Garden is the first official release of Elvis Presley's afternoon concert at Madison Square Garden in June 1972. While highlights of the evening concerts were released weeks after the concert in 1972, the afternoon shows sat in the vaults until the 25th anniversary of the performance rolled around. Although the album is very similar to the previously released *Live at Madison Square Garden*, it is nevertheless quite entertaining, capturing Elvis at the height of his extravagant, Vegas-style hits revue. It may not offer any new insights, and it may not be necessary for anyone but hardcore fans, but the record is undeniably fun. —*Stephen Thomas Erlewine*

Billy Preston

b. Sep. 9, 1946, Houston, TX
Piano, Keyboards, Vocals / Soul, R&B
It's advantageous to get an early start on your chosen career, but Billy Preston took the concept to extremes. By age ten, he was playing keyboards with gospel diva Mahalia Jackson, and two years later, in 1958, he was featured in Hollywood's film bio of W.C. Handy, *St. Louis Blues*, as young Handy himself. Preston was a prodigy on organ and piano, recording during the early '60s for Vee-Jay and touring with Little Richard. He was a loose-limbed regular on the mid-'60s ABC-TV *Shindig* series, proving his talent as both vocalist and pianist, and he built an enviable reputation as a session musician, even backing the Beatles on their *Let It Be* album. That impressive Beatles connection led to Preston's big break as a solo artist with his own Apple album, but it was his early-'70s soul smashes "Outa-Space" and the high-flying vocal "Will It Go Round in Circles" for A&M that put Preston on the permanent musical map. Sporting a humongous Afro and an omnipresent gap-toothed grin, Preston showed that his enduring gospel roots were never far removed from his joyous approach, less so now than ever. —*Bill Dahl*

Most Exciting Organ Ever / 1965 / Vee-Jay ♦♦♦♦
The hyperbole of the title aside, Preston did produce some flamboyant organ solos and keyboard work throughout this album. His use of bass pedals, dazzling intervals, octave jumps, phrases, and chordal maneuvers were impressive. This hasn't been reissued by Vee Jay, and it certainly should be if the label hasn't lost the masters. It's another side of Preston, one that became lost as he gained more and more popularity in the '70s as a singer. —*Ron Wynn*

Wildest Organ in Town! / 1966 / Capitol ♦♦♦
A late '60s Capitol set with Preston displaying his jazz-blues side as an organist. Unfortunately, nothing on this album caught fire, even in the R&B community, and Preston would soon go on to work for Ray Charles and the Beatles. His early prowess as a flashy organ equivalent of Jimi Hendrix has been largely forgotten or overlooked, and the fact that this album hasn't been in print for many years hasn't helped. —*Ron Wynn*

That's the Way God Planned It / 1969 / Apple ♦♦♦♦
A great bit of gospel-soul in the title cut, and otherwise a fine record that didn't make Billy Preston a huge star but alerted everyone that he was more than just a talented keyboard player backing the Beatles. This was one of two albums Preston did on the Beatles' Apple label, and while nothing made the charts, it was a good introduction for those unaware of Preston's multiple skills. —*Ron Wynn*

● **The Best of Billy Preston** / 1988 / A&M ♦♦♦♦
It contains several fun pop hits, including "Will It Go Round in Circles" and "Outa-Space." —*Dan Heilman*

The Pretenders

f. 1978, London, England
Rock 'n' Roll, New Wave, Pop-Rock
Over the years, the Pretenders have become a vehicle for guitarist-vocalist Chrissie Hynde's songwriting, yet it was a full-fledged band when it was formed in the late '70s. With their initial records, the group crossed the bridge between punk-new wave and Top 40 pop more than any other band, recording a series of hard, spiky singles that were also melodic and immediately accessible. Hynde was an invigorating, sexy singer who bended the traditional male roles of rock 'n' roll to her own liking, while guitarist James Honeyman-Scott created a sonic palate filled with suspended chords, effects pedals, and syncopated rhythms that proved remarkably influential over the next two decades. After Honeyman-Scott's death, the Pretenders became a more straightforward rock band, yet Hynde's semi-autobiographical songwriting and bracing determination meant that the group never became just another rock band, even when their music became smoother and more pop-oriented.

Originally from Akron, OH, Hynde moved to England in the early '70s when she was in her 20s. British rock journalist Nick Kent helped her begin writing for the *New Musical Express;* she wrote for the newspaper during the mid-'70s. She also worked in Malcolm McLaren's Sex boutique before she began performing. After playing with Chris Spedding, she joined Jack Rabbit; she quickly left the band and formed the Berk Brothers.

In 1978, Hynde formed the Pretenders, which eventually consisted of Honeyman-Scott, bassist Pete Farndon, and drummer Martin Chambers.

Later in the year, they recorded a version of Ray Davies' "Stop Your Sobbing" produced by Nick Lowe. The single made it into the British Top 40 in early 1979. "Kid" and "Brass in Pocket," the group's next two singles, also were successful. Their self-titled debut album was released in early 1980 and eventually climbed to No. 1 in the UK. The Pretenders were nearly as successful in America, with the album reaching the Top Ten and "Brass in Pocket" reaching No. 14.

During an American tour in 1980, Hynde met Ray Davies and the two fell in love. Following a spring 1981 EP, *Extended Play,* the group released their second album, *Pretenders II.* Although it fared well on the charts, it repeated the musical ideas of their debut. In June of 1982, Pete Farndon was kicked out of the band, due to his drug abuse. A mere two days later on June 16, James Honeyman-Scott was found dead of an overdose of heroin and cocaine. Pregnant with Davies' child, Hynde went into seclusion following Honeyman-Scott's death. In 1983, two months after Hynde gave birth, Farndon also died of a drug overdose.

Hynde regrouped the Pretenders at the end of 1983, adding former Average White Band guitarist Robbie McIntosh and bassist Malcolm Foster; the reconstituted band released "2000 Miles" in time for Christmas. The new Pretenders released *Learning to Crawl* early in 1984 to positive reviews and commercial success. Hynde married Jim Kerr, the lead vocalist of Simple Minds, in May of 1984, effectively ending her romance with Ray Davies.

Apart from a performance at Live Aid, the only musical activity from the Pretenders during 1985 was Hynde's appearance on UB40's version of "I Got You Babe." Hynde assembled another version of the Pretenders for 1986's *Get Close.* Only McIntosh and she remained from *Learning to Crawl—the rest of the album was recorded with session musicians. Get Close* showed the Pretenders moving closer to MOR territory, with the bouncy single "Don't Get Me Wrong" making its way into the American Top Ten in 1987. Hynde recorded another duet with UB40 in 1988, a cover of Dusty Springfield's "Breakfast in Bed."

Hynde's marriage to Kerr fell apart in 1990, the same year the Pretenders released *packed!,* which failed to ignite the charts in either America or Britain. She was relatively quiet for the next few years, re-emerging in 1994 with *Last of the Independents,* which was hailed as a comeback by some quarters of the press. The album did return the Pretenders to the Top 40 with the ballad "I'll Stand by You." In the fall of 1995, the Pretenders released the live album, *Isle of View.* —*Stephen Thomas Erlewine*

★ **Pretenders** / 1980 / Sire ✦✦✦✦✦
Few rock 'n' roll records rock as hard or with as much originality as the Pretenders' eponymous first album. A sleek, stylish fusion of Stonesy rock 'n' roll, new wave pop, and pure punk aggression, *Pretenders* is teeming with sharp hooks and a viciously cool attitude. Although Chrissie Hynde establishes herself as a forceful and distinctively feminine songwriter, the record isn't a singer-songwriter's tour de force—it's a rock 'n' roll album, powered by a unique and aggressive band. Guitarist James Honeyman-Scott never plays conventional riffs or leads, and his phased, treated guitar gives new dimension to the pounding rhythms of "Precious," "Tattooed Love Boys," "Up the Neck," and "The Wait," as well as the more measured pop of "Kid," "Brass in Pocket," and "Mystery Achievement." He provides the perfect backing for Hynde and her tough, sexy swagger. Hynde doesn't fit into any conventional female rock stereotype, and neither do her songs, alternately displaying a steely exte-

rior or a disarming emotional vulnerability. It's a deep, rewarding record, whose primary virtue is its sheer energy. *Pretenders* moves faster and harder than most rock records, delivering an endless series of melody, hooks, and infectious rhythms in its 12 songs. Few albums, let alone debuts, are ever this astonishingly addictive. —*Stephen Thomas Erlewine*

Pretenders II / Aug. 1981 / Sire ✦✦✦✦
A fitting title, since *Pretenders II* essentially follows the same formula as the band's debut, only with lesser songs. Though a handful of songs could rival cuts from the debut—"Message of Love," "The Adultress," and "Talk of the Town" in particular—the songs aren't particularly distinctive, and the band sounds too tired to give them the energy they need to make the music work. It's a sad way for the original lineup of the Pretenders to bow out. —*Stephen Thomas Erlewine*

☆ **Learning to Crawl** / 1984 / Sire ✦✦✦✦✦
Chrissie Hynde and drummer Martin Chambers reassembled the Pretenders in 1982, following the death of James Honeyman-Scott and the departure of bassist Pete Farndon. *Learning to Crawl,* appropriately, is the sound of a band coming to grips with loss and the responsibilities that come with maturity. Even though the subject matter is undeniably serious, the Pretenders rock with a vigorous energy that was missing on *Pretenders II.* It helps that Hynde's songs are among her best, of course. "Middle of the Road" encapsulates the contradictions in the album's main themes, "Back on the Chain Gang" is a moving tribute to Scott, "My City Was Gone" is a vicious attack on Reagan-era economic devastation, and the beautiful, ringing "2000 Miles" is one of the few rock 'n' roll songs about Christmas to actually work. And while "Watching the Clothes" is a bit embarrassing, it isn't enough to stop *Learning to Crawl* from being one of the best rock 'n' roll records of the early '80s. —*Stephen Thomas Erlewine*

Get Close / 1986 / Sire ✦✦✦
By now, Hynde is writing songs to her child and taking on social issues. But the chiming guitars are gorgeous, and Hynde's caught-in-the-throat voice has never been more expressive. —*William Ruhlmann*

☆ **The Singles** / 1987 / Sire ✦✦✦✦✦
Although the singles-only format makes the Pretenders sound more pop oriented than they were, especially in the beginning, this album essentially addresses the legacy of punk in the ten years after its peak, tracing a heritage back to mid-'60s Merseybeat and forward to a more rock-based pop music. It also makes the case for Chrissie Hynde as a major artist. —*William Ruhlmann*

Packed! / May 1990 / Sire ✦✦
It may be true that Chrissie Hynde's songs on *Packed!* are the weakest in her career, but they are not the sole reason why the album is such a bland, uninspiring affair. In the hands of producer Mitchell Froom, Hynde's stylistic retreads become even more unfocused and lackluster. Froom's production lacks any edge, making the pleasant but pedestrian songs bland and featureless. Only a cover of Hendrix's "May This Be Love" and "When Will I See You," a collaboration with guitarist Johnny Marr, stand out amidst the number of undistinguished tracks on *Packed!* —*Stephen Thomas Erlewine*

Last of the Independents / May 10, 1994 / Sire ✦✦✦
Chrissie Hynde rebounded from the directionless *Packed!* with *Last of the Independents,* a tough album that proves she can mature without losing her edge. Most of the record crackles with the lean power of *Learning to Crawl,* occasionally stopping for lushly produced numbers recalling *Get Close.* Although the record goes on a little too long, and there are a couple of weak songs, particularly the anthemic "I'm a Mother," *Last of the Independents* re-established Hynde as a powerful and insightful rocker. —*Stephen Thomas Erlewine*

Isle of View / Oct. 24, 1995 / Warner Brothers ✦✦
An "unplugged" set without the MTV brand name, *The Isle of View* (say it fast a couple of times to catch the pun) presents songs by the Pretenders that already were the softest ones in their repertoire now played on acoustic guitars and backed by the Duke string quartet. Lead singer Chrissie Hynde's lyrics are slightly more discernible, and some of the songs are lovely. But they were to begin with, and Hynde and Co. have not really reimagined them for the acoustic format. Rather than deliberately picking ballads, Hynde might have tried rearranging some of her rockers to more interesting effect. Still, what's here is always pleasant and sometimes moving. —*William Ruhlmann*

Pretty Things

f. 1963, Dartford, Kent, England, **db.** 1976
Rock 'n' Roll, Art-Rock/Progressive-Rock, British Invasion
Of all the original British Invasion groups, perhaps none is as underappreciated in the US as the Pretty Things. Featuring the hoarse vocals of Mick Jagger-lookalike Phil May and the stinging leads of guitarist Dick Taylor (who actually played in early versions of the Rolling Stones with Jagger and Keith Richards), the Pretties recorded a clutch of raunchy

R&B rockers in the mid-'60s that offers a punkier, rawer version of the early Stones' sound. Their first two albums, as well as a brace of fine major and minor British hits (of which "Don't Bring Me Down" and "Honey I Need" were the biggest), feature first-rate original material and covers and remain the group's most exciting and influential recordings. Unfortunately, the band remained virtually unknown to American audiences, most of whom would first hear "Don't Bring Me Down" on David Bowie's *Pin Ups* album (which also included a version of the Pretties' "Rosalyn").

After their initial run of success, the group took a sharp left turn into psychedelia with the orchestrated album *Emotions* (1967), impressive singles that owed more to Pink Floyd than Bo Diddley, and, most significantly, *S.F. Sorrow* (1968). The first rock opera, *S.F. Sorrow* was a major influence upon Pete Townshend, who released his much more successful opera, *Tommy*, with the Who the following year. Founding member Taylor left shortly after *S.F. Sorrow*, and the group continued to record progressive-rock and hard rock with less impressive results through the mid-'70s, although *Parachute* (1970) was named by *Rolling Stone* as album of the year. The group reunites sporadically for occasional gigs and recordings in their early R&B vein. —*Richie Unterberger*

Pretty Things / 1965 / Fontana ✦✦✦✦
The Pretty Things' debut was one of the prime cuts of early British R&B, featuring such definitively raunchy exponents of the genre as "Roadrunner," "Big City," "Mama, Keep Your Big Mouth Shut," "Pretty Thing," and "Honey I Need." A couple of weak jams prevent the album from ranking as a true classic. It differs slightly from the US version of the record, which took off four tracks and substituted four others. Most of the songs from both versions of the LP are on the *Get a Buzz* compilation. —*Richie Unterberger*

The Pretty Things [U.S.] / 1965 / Fontana ✦✦✦✦
The Pretty Things' debut was one of the prime cuts of early British R&B, featuring such definitively raunchy exponents of the genre as "Roadrunner," "Big City," "Rosalyn," "Don't Bring Me Down," and "Honey I Need." A couple of weak jams prevent the album from ranking as a true classic. It differs slightly from the UK version of the record, which took off four tracks and substituted four others. Most of the songs from both versions of the LP are on the *Get a Buzz* compilation. —*Richie Unterberger*

Get the Picture? / Dec. 1965 / Fontana ✦✦✦
The group's second album wasn't quite as powerful as the first, and it showed them starting to shift their emphasis to more original material, with a more pronounced soul influence and tentative stabs at folk-rock. It's got plenty of good stuff, however, and "Can't Stand the Pain," "You'll Never Do It Babe," "I Want Your Love," and "London Town" are all among their best early songs. Most (but not all) of the better tracks appear on the *Get a Buzz* compilation; all of the LP's cuts have been reissued at one time or another. —*Richie Unterberger*

Emotions / 1967 / Fontana ✦✦✦
In accordance with their label's (and not the band's) wishes, the Pretties were teamed with a middle-aged orchestra directed by Reg Tilsley on this album, which saw the Phil May-Dick Taylor songwriting team making an effort to move beyond R&B knockoffs into more sophisticated territory. Sometimes the arrangements (dubbed onto tracks without much involvement from the group) worked; more often, they were an unnecessary hindrance. An interesting failure, it contained some genuinely top-rank originals that saw the group expanding their vision into social observation and tentative psychedelia, including "My Time," "The Sun," and especially the moody, folk-rock-ish "Death of a Socialite." —*Richie Unterberger*

S.F. Sorrow / 1968 / Chapter One ✦✦✦✦
No amount of scrutiny can disguise the fact that this rock opera—built around a short story by Phil May—is ultimately a bit of a confusing effort. Although it may have helped inspire *Tommy*, it is, simply, not nearly as good. That said, it was first, and has quite a few nifty ideas and production touches. —*Richie Unterberger*

Parachute / 1970 / Rare Earth ✦✦✦
The last Pretty Things album to explore interesting territory, this progressive-rock is grounded by some solid harmonies and riffs but is ultimately not nearly as compelling as its *Rolling Stone* Album of the Year award would suggest. —*Richie Unterberger*

The Singles A's & B's / 1977 / Harvest ✦✦✦
Thirteen tracks from their progressive/psychedelic era, 1967-71. Of special interest is the non-LP 1967 single "Defecting Grey," a brilliant cop of Syd Barrett-era Pink Floyd. Its B-side ("Mr. Evasion") and the follow-up single "Talkin' About the Good Times"/"Walking Through My Dreams" were also non-LP and also rank among the more coveted rarities of the early British psychedelic era. —*Richie Unterberger*

Electric Banana / 1991 / Repertoire ✦✦
As chart activity became slim for the Pretty Things around 1967, they started a sideline of recording songs specifically for film soundtracks. This compilation features their vocal contributions to these projects and

consists mostly of fairly pedestrian psychedelic-tinged rock of a lower standard than either their 1967-68 singles or the *S.F. Sorrow* album. Highlights are the driving, fuzzy rocker "Alexander" and an early version of the *S.F. Sorrow* track "I See You." —*Richie Unterberger*

● **Get a Buzz: The Best of the Fontana Years** / 1992 / Fontana ✦✦✦✦
It's missing a few good tracks, but this is a good retrospective of their British Invasion-era work, running through the 1967 *Emotions* LP. Includes all their major singles—"Rosalyn," "Don't Bring Me Down," "Honey I Need," "Midnight to Six Man," "Come See Me." —*Richie Unterberger*

On Air / 1992 / Band of Joy ✦✦
Fifteen BBC airshots of the Pretty Things, cut between 1964 and the early to mid-'70s (no dates are included in the liner notes). To this day, the Pretty Things are one of the most underappreciated British Invasion bands in the US. Failing to score a hit in this country, they emulated the best aspects of the early Rolling Stones in the UK, moving from raunchy rock-R&B to psychedelia and progressive-rock by the end of the '60s. The most exciting cuts on this disc are the six songs from the mid-'60s, which found them mining the line between rock and R&B. "Deflecting Grey," their Syd Barrett-esque single from 1967, is also heard in its live-in-the-studio version. That said, this compilation really is for fanatics only. These alternate versions have good fidelity, but don't differ notably from their official releases; if anything, they are a bit tamer. The last half of the disc, drawn from their progressive-hard rock days, is a bit of a waste and downright turgid in comparison with their early work. —*Richie Unterberger*

Pure and Pretty [bootleg] / [Bootleg] ✦✦
A most interesting document for Pretty Things fanatics, surely the most valuable selection of unreleased material that will ever emerge from their mid-'60s prime. The first seven tracks are undubbed versions of songs from their 1967 *Emotions* LP that are unencumbered by the overbearing, sometimes fatuous orchestration that was overlaid upon them without the band's input. Unsurprisingly, they are truer to the Pretty Things' spirit than the product that was eventually released, in the same manner that the oft-bootlegged stringless version of the Beatles' "The Long and Winding Road" makes the official one seem gloppy by comparison. Also included are some BBC radio, TV, and live recordings from 1965-70, which are rough in sound quality but appealing to aficionados. —*Richie Unterberger*

Alan Price

b. Apr. 19, 1941, Fatfield, Co. Durham, England
Piano, Vocals / Rock 'n' Roll, British Invasion
As the organist in the first Animals lineup, Alan Price was perhaps the most important instrumental contributor to their early run of hits. He left the group in 1965 after only a year or so of international success (he can be seen talking about his departure with Bob Dylan in the rockumentary *Don't Look Back*) to work on a solo career. Leading the Alan Price Set, he had a Top Ten British hit in 1966 with a terrific reworking of "I Put a Spell on You," complete with Animal-ish organ breaks and bluesy vocals. His subsequent run of British hits between 1966 and 1968—"Hi-Lili-Hi-Lo," "Simon Smith and His Dancing Bear," "The House that Jack Built," "Don't Stop the Carnival"—were in a much lighter vein, drawing from British music hall influences. "Simon Smith and His Dancing Bear," from 1967, was one of the first Randy Newman songs to gain international exposure, though Price's version—like all his British hits—went virtually unnoticed in the US. A versatile entertainer, Price collaborated with Georgie Fame, hosted TV shows, and scored plays in the years following the breakup of the Alan Price Set in 1968. His greatest achievement since the '60s is his score to Lindsay Anderson's *O Lucky Man!*, where his spare and droll songs served almost as a Greek chorus to the surreal, whimsical film (Price himself had a small role in the movie). His 1974 concept album *Between Today and Yesterday* was his most critically acclaimed work. —*Richie Unterberger*

● **Price Is Right** / 1968 / Parrot ✦✦✦✦
Though Price as a solo artist was unknown in the US in the '60s, he did issue one stateside album that collected most of his British hits, as well as a few other tracks. Besides "I Put a Spell on You" (head and shoulders his best early performance), it has all of his other late-'60s UK hits, with the exception of "Don't Stop the Carnival." There are also a couple of serviceable originals, a nice version of the little-known Goffin-King item "On This Side of Goodbye," and no less than five early Randy Newman songs in all. Price was surely Newman's biggest booster at the time, running what amounted to a Randy Newman appreciation society on disc. An uneven effort, running from solid bluesy pop-rock to mawkish, chipper quasi-vaudeville (the latter quality, unfortunately, is typical of the Newman tunes here). It's a better assortment, though, than *The World of Alan Price* (on Decca UK), which duplicates much of what's here. Both LPs, unfortunately, are pretty hard to find nowadays. —*Richie Unterberger*

The World of Alan Price / 1970 / Decca ✦✦✦
Best-of compilation of his '60s solo work, including all his hits. "I Put a Spell on You" is fabulous, one of the best British '60s hits that never made it big in the States. The rest is surprisingly disappointing good-timey pop, sometimes in a jazzy Georgie Fame mold, at times verging on vaudevillian. —*Richie Unterberger*

● **O Lucky Man** / 1973 / Warner Brothers ✦✦✦✦
Price's keyboard-dominated score to the Lindsay Anderson film works well on its own, with incisive tunes that dole out equal measures of cynicism and sympathy. The infectiously poignant "Poor People" is a highlight. —*Richie Unterberger*

Lloyd Price

b. Mar. 9, 1933, Kenner, LA, **d.** 1988
Vocals / R&B, Rock 'n' Roll, New Orleans R&B
Not entirely content with being a 1950s R&B star on the strength of his immortal New Orleans classic "Lawdy Miss Clawdy," singer Lloyd Price yearned for massive pop acceptance. He found it, too, with a storming rock 'n' roll reading of the ancient blues "Stagger Lee" and the unabashedly pop-slanted "Personality" and "I'm Gonna Get Married" (the latter pair sounding far removed indeed from his Crescent City beginnings).

Growing up in Kenner, a suburb of New Orleans, Price was exposed to seminal sides by Louis Jordan, the Liggins brothers, Roy Milton, and Amos Milburn through the jukebox in his mother's little fish-fry joint. Lloyd and his younger brother Leo (who later co-wrote Little Richard's "Send Me Some Lovin'") put together a band for local consumption while in their teens. Bandleader Dave Bartholomew was impressed enough to invite Specialty Records boss Art Rupe to see the young singer (this was apparently when Bartholomew was momentarily at odds with his longtime employers at rival Imperial).

At his very first Specialty date in 1952, Price sang his classic eight-bar blues "Lawdy Miss Clawdy" (its rolling piano intro courtesy of a moonlighting Fats Domino). It topped the R&B charts for an extended period, making Lloyd Price a legitimate star before he was old enough to vote. Four more Specialty smashes followed: "Oooh, Oooh, Oooh," "Restless Heart," "Tell Me Pretty Baby," and "Ain't It a Shame"—before Price was drafted into the Army and deposited most unhappily in Korea.

When he finally managed to break free of the military, Lloyd Price formed his own label, KRC Records, with partners Harold Logan and Bill Boskent and got back down to business. "Just Because," a plaintive ballad Price first cut for KRC, held enough promise to merit national release on ABC-Paramount in 1957 (his ex-valet, Larry Williams, covered it on Price's former label, Specialty).

"Stagger Lee," Price's adaptation of the old Crescent City lament "Stack-A-Lee," topped both the R&B and pop lists in 1958. By now, his sound was taking on more of a cosmopolitan bent, with massive horn sections and prominent pop background singers. Dick Clark insisted on toning down the violence inherent to the song's story line for the squeaky-clean *American Bandstand* audience, accounting for the two different versions of the song you're likely to encounter on various reissues.

After Lloyd Price hit with another solid rocker, "Where Were You (On Our Wedding Day)?," in 1959, the heavy brass-and-choir sound became his trademark at ABC-Paramount. "Personality," "I'm Gonna Get Married," and "Come into My Heart" all shot up the pop and R&B lists in 1959, and "Lady Luck" and "Question" followed suit in 1960.

Always a canny businessman, Price left ABC-Paramount in 1962 to form another firm of his own with Logan. Double L Records debuted Wilson Pickett as a solo artist and broke Price's Vegas lounge-like reading of "Misty" in 1963. Later, he ran yet another diskery, Turntable Records (its 45s bore his photo, whether on his own sizable 1969 hit "Bad Conditions" or when the single was by Howard Tate!), and operated a glitzy New York nightspot by the same name.

But the music business turned sour for Price when his partner, Logan, was murdered in 1969. He got as far away from it all as he possibly could, moving to Africa and investing in nonmusical pursuits. Perfect example: he linked up with electric-haired Don King to promote Muhammad Ali bouts in Zaire (against George Foreman) and in Manila (against Joe Frazier). He indulged in a few select oldies gigs (including an appearance on NBC-TV's *Midnight Special*), but overall, little was seen of Lloyd Price during the 1970s.

Returning to America in the early '80s, he largely resisted performing until a 1993 European tour with Jerry Lee Lewis, Little Richard, and Gary US Bonds convinced him there was still a market for his bouncy, upbeat oldies. Price's profile has been on the upswing ever since—he recently guested on a PBS-TV special with Huey Lewis & the News, and he regularly turns up to headline the Jazz & Heritage Festival in his old hometown. —*Bill Dahl*

Mr. Personality / 1959 / ABC ✦✦✦
Recorded in absolutely breathtaking stereo that greatly enhances the brass-heavy arrangements, this LP is worth grabbing any time you run

across it. Sure, Lloyd Price sounds off-key on the Tin Pan Alley chestnuts "I Only Have Eyes for You" and "Time After Time," but a forceful "I Want You to Know," the torchy "Dinner for One," and a rocking "Is It Really Love?" make up for the intrusions. —*Bill Dahl*

Mr. Personality Sings the Blues / 1960 / ABC ✦✦✦✦
Blues was no big stretch for the vocalist—his Crescent City output was solidly rooted in the idiom. On this LP, he does a fine job on Eddie Vinson's "Kidney Stew," Paul Perryman's "Just to Hold My Hand," and his own blasting "I've Got the Blues and the Blues Got Me." —*Bill Dahl*

Sings the Million Sellers / 1961 / ABC ✦✦✦
Lloyd Price sang the hits of the immediate time frame on this long out-of-print album, doing particular justice to "Ain't That Just like a Woman" (then a minor seller for Fats Domino), the Miracles' "Shop Around," the Midnighters' "The Hoochie Coochie Coo," and the Drifters' "I Count the Tears." Uptown soul arrangements by future Motown staffer Gil Askey give Price full-bodied support. —*Bill Dahl*

● **Greatest Hits [MCA]** / 1982 / MCA ✦✦✦✦
Price wasn't content with R&B fame; he yearned for pop acceptance too. He got plenty at ABC-Paramount from 1957 to 1960 (the time frame this 18-song retro addresses). Creating a brassy, accessible sound, Price hit huge with his rock 'n' roll rendition of "Stagger Lee" (here in two versions—original and *American Bandstand*-sanitized) and went all the way pop with the undeniably catchy "Personality." Innovative arrangements and Price's earnest vocals greatly distinguish "Have You Ever Had the Blues?," "Lady Luck," "Three Little Pigs," and "Where Were You (on Our Wedding Day)," and there's a previously unissued "That's Love" to further up the ante. —*Bill Dahl*

★ **Lawdy!** / Aug. 5, 1991 / Specialty ✦✦✦✦✦
Twenty-five stellar 1952-1956 examples of why Lloyd Price ranks with the greatest R&B performers ever to emerge from the Crescent City. Beginning with his debut smash "Lawdy Miss Clawdy," Price wails the rocking "Mailman Blues," "Where You At?," "Rock 'n' Roll Dance," and "Baby Please Come Home" in front of fat sax cushions, rolling pianos, and steamy rhythm sections. —*Bill Dahl*

Heavy Dreams, Vol. 2 / 1993 / Specialty ✦✦✦✦
No discernable artistic drop-off on Specialty's encore Price retrospective, distinguished by his classics "Oooh-Oooh-Oooh," "Tell Me Pretty Baby," "Ain't It a Shame?" (not Fats Domino's hit), "Country Boy Rock," and "Why" (he'd later recut the latter for ABC-Paramount). —*Bill Dahl*

● **Lloyd Price Sings His Big Ten** / Feb. 8, 1994 / Capitol/Curb ✦✦✦✦
Like all standard Curb anthologies, this is too skimpy, numbering ten tracks. It does, however, include all of Price's major hits—"Stagger Lee," "Personality," "I'm Gonna Get Married," "Where Were You on Our Wedding Day," "Lady Luck." And in its favor, it also includes the most famous of his pre-ABC hits, "Lawdy Miss Clawdy." —*Richie Unterberger*

Primal Scream

f. 1984, Glasgow, Scotland
House, Rock 'n' Roll, Alternative Pop-Rock, Club-Dance
Primal Scream's career could in many ways be read as a microcosm of British indie rock in the '80s and '90s. Bobby Gillespie formed the band in the mid-'80s while drumming for goth-tinged noise-rockers the Jesus & Mary Chain, who were the exact opposite of Primal Scream—the latter specialized in infectious, jangly pop on its early records.

After a brief detour to punky hard rock, the group reinvented themselves as a dance band in the early '90s, following through on the pop and acid-house fusions of the Stone Roses and Happy Mondays. With the assistance of producers Andrew Weatherall and Hugo Nicholson, Primal Scream created the ultimate indie-pop and dance fusion, *Screamadelica*, in 1991. *Screamadelica* broke down boundaries and changed the face of British pop music in the '90s, helping to make dance and techno acceptable to the rock mainstream. Instead of following through on the promise of the album, Primal Scream retreated to Stonesy boogie on their 1994 follow-up *Give Out But Don't Give Up*. When that record was greeted with indifference, they returned to dance-rock fusions with 1997's *Vanishing Point*, which re-established the group as a major force in British rock.

Bobby Gillespie (vocals) formed Primal Scream in 1984, while still drumming for the Jesus and Mary Chain. On its initial releases, Primal Scream was a group of '60s revivalists, crafting hooky, guitar-driven pop songs. The band signed to Creation Records in 1985, and over the next year, they released a pair of singles. However, Primal Scream didn't really take off until the middle of 1986, when Gillespie left the Mary Chain and guitarists Andrew Innes and Robert Young joined the band. "Velocity Girl," a rush of jangly guitars, was a B-side that wound up on *NME*s C86 cassette compilation, a collection of underground pop groups that defined the UK's mid-'80s indie-pop scene. The band's debut, *Sonic Flower Groove*, fit into the C86 sound. After the band rejected the initial version recorded with Stephen Street, they re-recorded the album with Mayo Thompson, and the record was finally released in 1987 on the Creation subsidiary, Elevation. The album was well received in the British indie community, as was its 1989 follow-up, *Primal Scream*, which demonstrated hard-rock influences from the Rolling Stones and New York Dolls to the Stooges and MC5.

As the '80s drew to a close, Britain's underground music scene became dominated by the burgeoning acid-house scene. Primal Scream became fascinated with the new dance music, and they asked a friend, a DJ named Andrew Weatherall, to remix a track from *Primal Scream*, "I'm Losing More Than I'll Ever Have." Weatherall completely reworked the song, adding a heavy bass groove echoing dub reggae, deleting most of the original instrumentation (even the layers of guitars), and interjecting layers of samples, including lines of Peter Fonda's dialogue from *The Wild Angels*. The new mix was retitled "Loaded," and it became a sensation, bringing rock 'n' roll to the dance floor and dance to rock 'n' rollers. "Come Together," the first single from their third album, was in much the same vein and was similarly praised.

For their third album *Screamadelica*, Primal Scream not only worked with Andrew Weatherall and Hugo Nicholson, the pair who essentially designed the sound of the album, but also the Orb and former Stones producer Jimmy Miller. The resulting album was a kaleidoscopic, neo-psychedelic fusion of dance, dub, techno, acid house, pop, and rock, and it was greeted with rapturous reviews in the UK. Released in the spring of 1991, *Screamadelica* also marked an important moment in British pop in the '90s, helping to bring techno and house into the mainstream. The album was a massive success, winning the first Mercury Music Prize in 1992.

In the wake of the groundbreaking *Screamadelica*, most observers wondered what Primal Scream would do next, yet few would have predicted their retreat to '70s hard rock for *Give Out But Don't Give Up*. Released in 1994, the album was eagerly awaited, but its Stonesy hard rock was not well received, and it was a relative commercial failure. More important, it hurt the group's reputation as innovators, a situation they reacted to with the title track to the hit 1996 film, *Trainspotting*. Primal Scream's contribution to the soundtrack was a return to the dance stylings of *Screamadelica*, only darker. The band continued to work on their next album, entitled *Vanishing Point*, over the course of 1996, finally releasing it to enthusiastic reviews in the summer of 1997. —*Stephen Thomas Erlewine*

Sonic Flower Groove / 1987 / Elevation ◆◆

Primal Scream's debut album draws from a variety of influences, pulling together strands of '60s pop with psychedelia, noisy proto-punk, and the detached cool of the Velvet Underground. However, most of the album is only impressive conceptually, as the group didn't write enough solid hooks to make their fusions memorable. —*Stephen Thomas Erlewine*

Primal Scream / 1989 / Mercenary ◆◆

On their self-titled second album, Primal Scream improves on their debut by turning in a handful of pop songs that manage to fulfill portions of their grand ambitions, yet the record remains a bit too unfocused to be memorable. —*Stephen Thomas Erlewine*

● Screamadelica / Oct. 8, 1991 / Sire ◆◆◆◆

Screamadelica is an impressive, innovative album that seamlessly combines classic rock with the throbbing beat of the dance club. While it doesn't contain any concise pop songs besides "Movin' On Up," the album is remarkably consistent and proved that it was possible to inject some true grit into the highly stylized world of techno, house, and rave. —*Stephen Thomas Erlewine*

Give Out but Don't Give Up / Sep. 1993 / Sire ◆◆◆

The rock undercurrents that ran throughout *Screamadelica* come to the forefront on the tired *Give Out but Don't Give Up*. While Primal Scream turn out a couple of good songs, "Jailbird" and "(I'm Gonna) Cry Myself Blind," the band sounds too mannered to be a truly successful ripoff of the Stones and Faces. And the colorful, reckless experimentation of their previous album is sorely missed. —*Stephen Thomas Erlewine*

Primus

f. 1986, San Francisco, CA
Alternative Pop-Rock, Funk Metal, Alternative Metal

Primus is all about Les Claypool; there isn't a moment on any of their records where his bass isn't the main focal point of the music, with his vocals acting as a bizarre side show. Which isn't to deny guitarist Larry LaLonde or drummer Tim "Herb" Alexander any credit—no drummer could weave in and around Claypool's convoluted patterns as effortlessly as Alexander, and few guitarists would as willingly push the spotlight away like LaLonde, so he can produce a never-ending spiral of avant-noise. All of this means that they are miles away from being another punk-funk combo like the Red Hot Chili Peppers; Claypool may slap and pop his bass, but there is little funk in the rhythm he and Alex-

ander lay down. Instead, they're a post-punk Rush spiked with the sensibility and humor of Frank Zappa. Primus doesn't want to make you dance, they want to play music; songs are secondary to showcasing their instrumental prowess.

Primus' music is willfully weird and experimental, yet it's not alienating; the band was able to turn their goofy weirdness into pop stardom. At first, the band was strictly an underground phenomenon, but in the years between their third and fourth albums, their cult grew rapidly. 1991's *Sailing the Seas of Cheese* went gold shortly before the release of *Pork Soda*. By the time of the album's 1993 release, Primus had enough devoted fans to make *Pork Soda* debut in the Top Ten. After touring for a year—including a headlining spot on 1993's Lollapalooza—Claypool revived his Prawn Song record label in 1994 and released a reunion record by Primus' original lineup under the name Sausage. In the summer of 1995, Primus released their fifth album, *Tales from the Punch Bowl*. It was another success, going gold before the end of the year. In the summer of 1996, Primus announced they were parting ways with their drummer, Tim Alexander. —*Stephen Thomas Erlewine*

Suck on This / Jan. 1990 / Caroline ◆◆◆

Originally released on their own Prawn Song label (a parody of Led Zeppelin's Swan Song Records), this is their debut, recorded live in a small club and featuring all of the greatness this trio has. It's hard, thrashy funk and punk with a sense of humor. The reissue on Caroline sounds a little muddy. Find the original vinyl pressing on Prawn, which sounds more like a CD than the CD. —*John Book*

Frizzle Fry / Feb. 1990 / Caroline ◆◆◆◆

Primus' eccentric, dissonant blend of avant-rock, funk, punk, and thrash has inspired comparisons to everyone from Frank Zappa to Devo to the Red Hot Chili Peppers. But whatever comparison is made, the fact is that this trio has created strikingly original music. *Frizzle Fry* is sometimes a bit too self-indulgent for its own good, but in general, Les Claypool's willingness to experiment and his risk-taking nature come through the most. "Too Many Puppies," "To Defy the Laws of Tradition," and "Mr. Knowitall" are among the nutty, weird treasures that helped establish Primus as alternative rock heroes and make *Frizzle Fry* the classic that it is. —*Alex Henderson*

● Sailing the Seas of Cheese / May 14, 1991 / Interscope ◆◆◆◆

Having acquired a passionate cult following, Primus switched from the small Caroline Records to a major label with *Sailing the Seas of Cheese*. But the trio didn't compromise its approach one iota, remaining as left of center and abstract as ever. What was true of *Frizzle Fry* is true of *Cheese*—Les Claypool can be highly self-indulgent, but his originality and imagination give the CD many more strong points than weaknesses. When *Cheese* was first released, few people in the music industry expected it to go gold. But with the rise of alternative rock in 1991 and 1992, *Cheese* was on its way to becoming the first Primus disc to reach sales of 500,000. —*Alex Henderson*

Miscellaneous Debris / Mar. 12, 1992 / Interscope ◆◆◆◆

What makes this five-song EP of covers Primus' best release is the material. For once, Les Claypool's crew plays actual songs instead of sketching out a few ideas as an excuse for jamming. As a result, *Miscellaneous Debris* isn't as weird and alienating as previous albums, and often their reinterpretations—from the clever ribbing of XTC's "Making Plans for Nigel" and Pink Floyd's "Have a Cigar" to the relatively respectful readings of the Meters, the Residents, and Peter Gabriel's "Intruder"—show flashes of brilliance, largely due to the loose yet focused musicianship. —*Stephen Thomas Erlewine*

Pork Soda / Apr. 20, 1993 / Interscope ◆◆◆◆

Apart from the bizarre murder tale "My Name Is Mud," few tracks on *Pork Soda* rival "Tommy the Cat" or "Jerry Was a Race Car Driver"; another troubling sign of a lack of songwriting ideas is that one track, "The Pressman," was originally released on *Suck on This*. However, the overall quality of the playing is so good that it almost doesn't matter that the songs are frequently simplistic and occasionally awful. Primus continue to improve as musicians, so *Pork Soda* is hardly a terrible album—in fact, it's their best, most consistent effort to date, even though it would benefit from some editing. —*Stephen Thomas Erlewine*

Tales from the Punch Bowl / May 23, 1995 / Interscope ◆◆

For most listeners, the differences between Primus albums are so small, they're not even noticeable. With each record, the group improves instrumentally, which isn't surprising since they're a musician's band. On *Tales from the Punchbowl*, the group consolidates the qualities that made them arena rock favorites, featuring the same novelty tunes ("Wynona's Big Brown Beaver") and instrumental workouts that have always appeared on Primus' albums. Nevertheless, there's not much to distinguish the record from previous performances—there's only so much the group has to say, after all. —*Stephen Thomas Erlewine*

Prince (Prince Rogers Nelson)

b. Jun. 7, 1958, Minneapolis, MN

Bass, Guitar, Drums, Keyboards, Vocals / Soul, Dance-Pop, Funk, Rock 'n' Roll, Urban, Pop-Rock, Club-Dance, Neo-Psychedelia

Few artists have created a body of work as rich and varied as Prince. During the '80s, he emerged as one of the most singular talents of the rock 'n' roll era, capable of seamlessly tying together pop, funk, folk, and rock. Not only did he release a series of groundbreaking albums, he toured frequently, produced albums, wrote songs for many other artists, and recorded hundreds of songs that still lie unreleased in his vaults. With each album he has released, Prince has shown remarkable stylistic growth and musical diversity, constantly experimenting with different sounds, textures, and genres. Occasionally, his music can be maddeningly inconsistent because of this eclecticism, but his experiments frequently succeed; no other contemporary artist can blend so many diverse styles into a cohesive whole.

Prince's first two albums were solid, if unremarkable, late '70s funk pop. With 1980's *Dirty Mind*, he recorded his first masterpiece, a one-man *tour de force* of sex and music; it was hard funk, catchy Beatlesque melodies, sweet soul ballads, and rocking guitar pop, all at once. The follow-up, *Controversy*, was more of the same, but *1999* was brilliant. The album was a monster hit, selling over three million copies, but it was nothing compared to 1984's *Purple Rain*.

Purple Rain made Prince a superstar; it eventually sold over ten million copies in the US and spent 24 weeks at No. 1. Partially recorded with his touring band the Revolution, the record featured the most pop-oriented music he has ever made. Instead of continuing in this accessible direction, he veered off into the bizarre psycho-psychedelia of *Around the World in a Day* (1985), which nevertheless sold over two million copies. In 1986, he released the even stranger *Parade*, which was in its own way as ambitious and intricate as any art-rock of the '60s; however, no art-rock was ever grounded with a hit as brilliant as the spare funk of "Kiss."

By 1987, Prince's ambitions were growing by leaps and bounds, resulting in the sprawling masterpiece *Sign o' the Times*. Prince was set to release the hard funk of *The Black Album* by the end of the year, yet he withdrew it just before its release, deciding it was too dark and immoral. Instead, he released the confused *Lovesexy* in 1988, which was a commercial disaster. With the soundtrack to 1989's *Batman* he returned to the top of the charts, even if the album was essentially a recap of everything he had done before. The following year he released *Graffiti Bridge*, the sequel to *Purple Rain*, which turned out to be a considerable commercial disappointment.

In 1991, Prince formed the New Power Generation, the most versatile and talented band he has ever assembled. With their first album, *Diamonds and Pearls*, Prince reasserted his mastery of contemporary R&B; it was his biggest hit since 1985. The following year, he released his twelfth album, which was titled with a cryptic symbol; in 1993, Prince legally changed his name to the symbol. In 1994, he independently released his "The Most Beautiful Girl in the World" single, which became his biggest hit in years. Late in the summer of 1994, he released *Come* under the name of Prince; the record was a moderate success, going gold.

After *Come*, Prince agreed to release *The Black Album* officially in November of 1994. In early 1995, he immersed himself in another legal battle with Warner, as the record company refused to release his new record, *The Gold Experience*. By the end of the summer, the disputes had been resolved, and the album was released in the fall. In the summer of 1996, Prince released *Chaos & Disorder*, which reportedly was his last album of original material for Warner Brothers Records. — *Stephen Thomas Erlewine*

For You / 1978 / Warner Brothers ♦♦

On his debut album *For You*, Prince shows exceptional skill for arranging and performing mainstream urban R&B and funk, but his songwriting remains conventional. Only on the mildly racy "Soft and Wet" does he demonstrate a personal touch, but the song is still more of a promise than a fulfillment. While *For You* isn't a bad record, it is merely a pleasant one, and it offers very little indication of his staggering talents. — *Stephen Thomas Erlewine*

Prince / 1979 / Warner Brothers ♦♦♦

Expanding the urban R&B and funk approach of his debut, *Prince* is a considerably more accomplished record than his first effort, featuring the first signs of his adventurous, sexy signature sound. Although the album is still rather uneven, a handful of songs rank as classics. "I Wanna Be Your Lover" is excellent lite-funk, and "Why You Wanna Treat Me So Bad?" is a wonderful, soulful plea, but "I Feel for You," a sexy slice of urban R&B with a strong pop melody, is the true masterpiece of *Prince*, indicating the major breakthroughs of his next album, *Dirty Mind*. — *Stephen Thomas Erlewine*

☆ Dirty Mind / 1980 / Warner Brothers ♦♦♦♦♦

Neither *For You* or *Prince* was adequate preparation for the full-blown masterpiece of Prince's third album, *Dirty Mind*. Recorded in his home studio, with Prince playing nearly every instrument, *Dirty Mind* is a stunning, audacious amalgam of funk, new wave pop, urban R&B, and pop, fueled by grinningly salacious sex and the desire to shock. Where other pop musicians suggested sex in lewd double entendres, Prince left nothing to hide—before its release, no other rock or funk record was ever quite as explicit as *Dirty Mind*, with its gleeful tales of oral sex, threesomes, and even incest. Certainly, it opened the doors for countless sexually explicit albums, but to reduce its impact to mere profanity is too reductive—the music of *Dirty Mind* is as shocking as its graphic language, bending styles and breaking rules with little regard for fixed genres. Basing the album on a harder, more rock-oriented beat than before, Prince tries everything—there's pure new wave pop ("When You Were Mine"), soulful crooning ("Gotta Broken Heart Again"), robotic funk ("Dirty Mind"), rock 'n' roll ("Sister"), sultry funk ("Head," "Do It All Night"), and relentless dance jams ("Uptown," "Partyup"), all in the space of half an hour. It's a breathtaking, visonary album, and its fusion of synthesizers, rock rhythms, and funk set the style for much of the urban soul and funk of the early '80s. — *Stephen Thomas Erlewine*

Controversy / 1981 / Warner Brothers ♦♦♦

Controversy continues in the same vein of new wave-tinged funk as *Dirty Mind*, emphasizing Prince's fascination with synthesizers and synthesizing disparate pop music genres. It is also more ambitious than its predecessor, attempting to tackle social protest ("Controversy," "Ronnie, Talk to Russia," "Annie Christian") along with sex songs ("Jack U Off," "Sexuality"), and it tries hard to bring funk to a rock audience and vice versa. Even with all of Prince's ambitions, the music on *Controversy* doesn't represent a significant breakthrough from *Dirty Mind*, and it is often considerably less catchy and memorable. Nevertheless, Prince's talents as musician make the record enjoyable, even if it isn't as compelling as most of his catalog. — *Stephen Thomas Erlewine*

☆ 1999 / 1982 / Warner Brothers ♦♦♦♦♦

With *Dirty Mind*, Prince had established a wild fusion of funk, rock, new wave, and soul that signaled he was an original, maverick talent, but it failed to win him a large audience. After delivering the soundalike album *Controversy*, Prince revamped his sound and delivered the double album *1999*. Where his earlier albums had been a fusion of organic and electronic sounds, *1999* was constructed almost entirely on synthesizers by Prince himself. Naturally, the effect was slightly more mechanical and robotic than his previous work and strongly recalled the electro-funk experiments of several underground funk and hip-hop artists at the time. Prince had also constructed an album dominated by computer-funk, but he didn't simply rely on the extended instrumental grooves to carry the album—he didn't have to when his songwriting was improving by leaps and bounds. The first side of the record contained all of the hit singles and, unsurprisingly, they were the ones that contained the least amount of electronics. "1999" parties to the apocalypse with a P-Funk groove much tighter than anything George Clinton ever did, "Little Red Corvette" is pure pop, and "Delirious" takes rockabilly riffs into the computer age. After that opening salvo, all the rules go out the window—"Let's Pretend We're Married" is a salacious extended lust letter, "Free" is an elegaic anthem, "All the Critics Love U in New York" is a vicious attack at hipsters, and "Lady Cab Driver," with its notorious bridge, is the culmination of all of his sexual fantasties. Sure, Prince stretches out a bit too much over the course of *1999*, but the result is a stunning display of raw talent, not wallowing indulgence. — *Stephen Thomas Erlewine*

☆ Purple Rain / 1984 / Warner Brothers ♦♦♦♦♦

Prince designed *Purple Rain* as the project that would make him a superstar, and, surprisingly, that is exactly what happened. Simultaneously more focused and ambitious than any of his previous records, *Purple Rain* finds Prince consolidating his funk and R&B roots while moving boldly into pop, rock, and heavy metal with nine superbly crafted songs. Even its best-known songs don't tread conventional territory. The bass-less "When Doves Cry" is an eerie, spare, neo-psychedelic masterpiece; "Let's Go Crazy" is a furious blend of metallic guitars, Stonesy riffs and a hard funk backbeat; the anthemic title track is a majestic ballad filled with brilliant guitar flourishes. Although Prince's songwriting is at a peak, the presence of the Revolution pulls the music into sharper focus, giving it a tougher, more aggressive edge. And, with the guidance of Wendy and Lisa, Prince pushed heavily into psychedelia, adding swirling strings to the dreamy "Take Me with U" and the hard rock of "Baby I'm a Star." Even with all of his new, but uncompromising, forays into pop, Prince hasn't abandoned funk, and the robotic jam of "Computer Blue" and the menacing grind of "Darling Nikki" are among his finest songs. Taken together, all of the stylistic experiments add up to a stunning statement of purpose that remains one of the most exciting rock 'n' roll albums ever recorded. — *Stephen Thomas Erlewine*

Around the World in a Day / 1985 / Paisley Park ✦✦✦
Purple Rain made Prince sound like he could do anything, but it still didn't prepare even his most fervent fans for the insular psychedelia of *Around the World in a Day*. Prince had made his interior world sound fascinating and utopian on *Purple Rain*, but *Around the World in a Day* is filled with cryptic religious imagery, bizarre mysticism, and confounding metaphors, which were drenched in heavily processed guitars, shimmering keyboards, grandiose strings, and layers of vocals. As an album, the record is a bit impenetrable, requiring great demands of the listener, but individual songs do shine through—"Raspberry Beret" is a brilliant piece of neo-psychedelia with an indelible chorus, "Pop Life" is a snide swipe at stardom that emphasizes Prince's outsider status, "Condition of the Heart" is a fine ballad, "America" is a good funk jam, "Paisley Park" is heavy and slightly frightening guitar psychedelia, while the title track is a sunny, kaleidoscopic pastiche of *Magical Mystery Tour*. The problem is, only a handful of the songs have much substance outside of their detailed production and intoxicating performances, and the album has a creepy sense of paranoia that is eventually its undoing. *—Stephen Thomas Erlewine*

Parade (Music from the Motion Picture "Under the Cherry Moon") / 1986 / Paisley Park ✦✦✦✦
Undaunted by the criticism *Around the World in a Day* received, Prince continued to pursue his psychedelic inclinations on *Parade*, which also functioned as the soundtrack to his second film, *Under the Cherry Moon*. Originally conceived as a double album, *Parade* has the sprawling feel of a double record, even if it clocks in at around 45 minutes. Prince and the Revolution shift musical moods and textures from song to song—witness how the fluttering psychedelia of "Christopher Tracy's Parade" gives way to the spare, jazzy funk of "New Position," which morphs into the druggy "I Wonder U"—and they're determined not to play it safe, even on the hard funk of "Girls and Boys" and "Mountains," as well as the stunning "Kiss," which hits hard with just a dry guitar, keyboard, drum machine, and layered vocals. All of the group's musical adventures, even the cabaret-pop of "Venus de Milo" and "Do U Lie?," do nothing to undercut the melodicism of the record, and the amount of ground they cover in 12 songs is truly remarkable. Even with all of its attributes, *Parade* is a little off-balance, stopping too quickly to give the haunting closer "Sometimes It Snows in April" the resonance it needs. For some tastes, it may also be a bit too lyrically cryptic, but Prince's weird religious and sexual metaphors are developing into a motif that actually gives the album weight. If it had been expanded to a double album, *Parade* would have equaled the subsequent *Sign o' the Times*, but as it stands, it's an astonishingly rewarding near-miss. *—Stephen Thomas Erlewine*

☆ **Sign o' the Times** / 1987 / Paisley Park ✦✦✦✦✦
Sprawling, eclectic, and messy, Prince's second double album, *Sign o' the Times*, falls into the tradition of great chaotic double albums like *The Beatles*, *Exile on Main St.*, and *London Calling* that are great because of their over-reaching, seemingly haphazard scope. In short, it's the album where Prince shows nearly all of his cards, from bare-bones electro-funk and smooth soul to pseudo-psychedelic pop and crunching hard rock. In between, he touches on gospel, blues, and folk, among many other stylistic flourishes. Originally intended as a triple-album set called *The Crystal Ball*, *Sign o' the Times* was the first album Prince recorded without the Revolution since 1982's *1999* (the band does appear on the in-concert rave-up, "It's Gonna Be a Beautiful Night"), and the effect on him is liberating—he is free to dive into all the styles he merely hinted at on *Around the World in a Day* and *Parade*. The music sounds open and, usually, inviting, even though many of these songs are the most cryptic, insular songs he's ever written. Most of these songs are leftovers from the aborted Camille project, an alter-ego Prince created that was personified with the use of sped-up vocals. Camille is the voice that sings "If I Was Your Girlfriend," the most disarming and bleak psycho-sexual song Prince ever wrote, as well as the equally chilling "Strange Relationship." The fraying relationships are weighted by the social chaos Prince hints at throughout the album with his apocalyptic imagery of drugs, bombs, empty sex, abandoned babies and mothers, and AIDS. But he also balances the despair with hope, whether it's God ("The Cross"), love ("Adore," "Forever in My Life"), or just having a good time ("Play in the Sunshine," "It's Gonna Be a Beautiful Night"). In its own roundabout way, *Sign o' the Times* is the sound of the late '80s—it's the sound of the good times collapsing and the natural reaction to retreat to your own world, so you can just dance all those problems away. It's an endlessly fascinating and provocative listen. The album was a hit, but not at the magnitude of his previous records. Nevertheless, *Sign o' the Times* was one of the last times an artist this diverse, perverse, and bloody eccentric could top the charts. *—Stephen Thomas Erlewine*

Black Album / 1987 / Warner Brothers ✦✦✦
Apart from the Beach Boys' *Smile*, few unreleased albums cultivated the myth of Prince's *Black Album*. Originally scheduled for release in

November of 1987—when it would have followed the double-album *Sign o' the Times* by just a matter of months—Prince pulled the album just weeks before its release. Several thousand copies, mostly on vinyl, had already been pressed and were immediately destroyed; rumors persisted for years that a handful of compact discs were also manufactured. Almost immediately, a legend grew around the album, that Prince refused to release it because he believed it was too bleak, that Warner Brothers didn't want to promote the album because of its explicit lyrical content. Bootleg copies of the album spread as quickly as the rumors, and by the end of 1988, it was arguably the most bootlegged album in history. In the fall of 1994—when Prince's commercial standing was in decline and after most diehard fans had obtained a copy of the record—*The Black Album* was suddenly released officially as a limited edition, most likely as a way for Prince to free himself from his record contract. And at that time, the general public learned what Prince fans had known for many years—*The Black Album* was fun, but not much more. With *The Black Album*, Prince recorded an album that was intended to silence all the critics who claimed he abandoned his funk and R&B roots. Every song on the brief eight-song collection is pure funk or R&B, from the slamming opener "Le Grind" to the smooth urban ballad "When 2 R in Love" (which happened to appear on *Lovesexy*, the album Prince released instead of *The Black Album*). Some of the tracks are genre exercises and nothing more. Occasionally, such as the lame attack on hardcore rappers "Dead on It," the music is flat-out embarrassing, but the best moments of *The Black Album* are when Prince indulges in his joyously perverse humor. On "Bob George," possibly the strangest song he ever recorded, Prince alters the tape so his voice sounds like a menacing baritone drawl, and he growls threats to his lover, who just had an affair with Prince—or, as Bob George calls him, "that skinny motherfucker with a high voice." "Cindy C" is a lascivious declaration of lust for supermodel Cindy Crawford, during which Prince claims he'll "pay the usual fee" to sleep with her. And "Superfunkyfragicalisexy" and "2 Nigs United 4 West Compton" burn with the best James Brown, George Clinton, and Sly Stone tracks. So, *The Black Album* might have salvaged his R&B reputation if it was released in 1987. Instead it became a legendary record that doesn't quite deserve its widespread reputation. It's a nice little gem that is primarily of interest to dedicated fans, but it doesn't quite hold the attention of casual fans. *—Stephen Thomas Erlewine*

Lovesexy / Feb. 1988 / Paisley Park ✦✦✦
It's nearly impossible to judge *Lovesexy* as anything but a hastily assembled substitute for the withdrawn *Black Album*, which does the record a disservice. An exactingly sequenced song cycle—the compact disc didn't have index markings to separate the individual tracks—*Lovesexy* is quite a different record than not only *The Black Album* but anything else Prince had recorded. Where *Dirty Mind* was single minded in its lust, *Lovesexy* connects the carnal with the spiritual, and the calmness of the music reflects this outlook. Even when the record dips into hard funk, such as on the title track or the single "Alphabet Street," there's a relaxed, casual quality to the music that is shocking after the dense paranoia of *Parade*, *Sign o' the Times*, and *Black Album*. Prince intends to enter a new phase of maturity with such considered music and ambitious lyrical themes, but neither his music nor his lyrics are consistently well stated over the course of the album. A handful of tracks are worthwhile—the sappy ballad "When 2 R in Love," the moving "I Wish U Heaven," the weird psychedelia of "Anna Stesia" and "Glam Slam," as well as the wonderful "Alphabet Street"—but it is his weakest album since *Controversy*. *—Stephen Thomas Erlewine*

Batman / Jun. 1989 / Paisley Park ✦✦✦
Prince had stumbled commercially with *Lovesexy*, which may be one of the reasons he decided to record the soundtrack for Tim Burton's dark, gothic interpretation of the DC comic *Batman*. Reportedly, the *Batman* album was recorded quickly, and it shows in the loose, offhand nature of the songs, which actually comes as some relief after the big ambitions of all of his records since *1999*. "The Future" and "Electric Chair" are fine, funky, one-man efforts, and "Vicki Waiting" is an excellent pure pop song, while "Arms of Orion" is embarrassingly enjoyable, sappy, mainstream balladry, and "Batdance" is a fun dance-club pastiche of the entire album. Even with these highlights, there are no true classics on the record, and it tends to evaporate in the memory after it's finished—there's no doubt it spent six weeks at the top of the charts because of the blockbuster film. Still, *Batman* sounds fine while it's playing. *—Stephen Thomas Erlewine*

Graffiti Bridge / Aug. 21, 1990 / Paisley Park ✦✦✦
Prince was shooting for the top of the charts with *Graffiti Bridge*, and he missed. The movie was a disaster, causing the soundtrack to sell very poorly. Despite its poor showing, *Graffiti Bridge* is not a bad album; in fact, it's often very good. Prince wrote all of the songs, but only performed a little over half the tracks, leaving the rest for the Time, Mavis Staples, and Tevin Campbell. With the exception of the Time's slamming "Release It" and Campbell's "Round and Round," the best songs are the

ones Prince performed himself. The George Clinton collaboration "We Can Funk," the psycho-blues of "The Question of U," the sinewy single "Thieves in the Temple," and the pop-rock of "Can't Stop This Feeling I Got," "Tick, Tick, Bang," and "Elephants & Flowers" make *Graffiti Bridge* a thoroughly enjoyable listen. — *Stephen Thomas Erlewine*

Diamonds and Pearls / Oct. 1991 / Paisley Park ✦✦✦
Prince spent the latter half of the '80s courting the pop audience, and by the time of *Graffiti Bridge*, he had lost much of his R&B fan base. As a response, he formed the New Power Generation and recorded *Diamonds and Pearls*, his first record to reconnect with the urban audience since *1999*, as well as his first to acknowledge the hip-hop revolution. Although he still has a problem with rap—"Jughead" is simply embarassing—he manages to skillfully reinvent himself as an urban soulman without sacrificing his musical innovation. The New Power Generation is a more skilled band than the Revolution, and they are able to make Prince's funk jazzier, particularly on "Willing and Able," the breezy "Strollin'," and "Walk Don't Walk." It's clear that these subtly textured songs are where his heart is at, but the songs designed to win back his audience—the slamming dance-floor rallying cry "Gett Off," the sexy T. Rex groove "Cream," the extraordinary Philly soul of the neglected masterpiece "Money Don't Matter 2 Night," and the drippy mainstream ballad "Diamonds and Pearls"—are all terrific pop singles. However, much of the rest of *Diamonds and Pearls* is composed of middling funk and R&B that sounds less like inspired workouts than stylistic exercises. Even with such weak moments, *Diamonds and Pearls* is a fine record, even though it's only marginally better than *Lovesexy* and *Graffiti Bridge*. — *Stephen Thomas Erlewine*

Love Symbol Album / Oct. 13, 1992 / Paisley Park ✦✦✦✦
The New Power Generation is the most talented and versatile band Prince has ever fronted, and they fulfill their potential on *Symbol*. Although the NPG factored heavily on *Diamonds and Pearls*, it still sounded like a solo Prince album. *Symbol* sounds like a band performing together, working off of each other's strengths and weaknesses. Opening with the dance smash "My Name Is Prince" and the deep funk of "Sexy M.F.," *Symbol* has Prince's best dance tracks since the *Black Album*. But Prince wasn't content; he decided to run the gamut of modern pop/R&B/dance, and the music is uniformly accomplished and excellent. Unfortunately, he also decided to make a "rock soap opera," so the music is saddled with ridiculous lyrics and annoying sound bridges by Kirstie Alley. However, *Symbol* has some of the finest, most inventive music of Prince's career. — *Stephen Thomas Erlewine*

★ **The Hits 1** / Sep. 14, 1993 / Paisley Park ✦✦✦✦✦
The primary fault with Prince's two-part *Hits* collection is that both volumes are missing some important singles and are sequenced incoherently, thereby failing to give an accurate impression of his astonishing musical growth. However, they do contain enough necessary items to illustrate why he was one of the most influential and gifted musicians of the '80s, as well as providing a reasonable introduction and compilation for casual fans. *Hits 1* contains a good cross-section of his biggest hits—"When Doves Cry" (presented in an edited version), "When You Were Mine," "Let's Go Crazy," "1999," "Sign o' the Times," "Alphabet Street," "Diamonds and Pearls," and "7"—plus new items like a "Pink Cashmere" and "Nothing Compares 2 U" (a Prince song that Sinead O'Connor took to No. 1), which are nearly as good as the familiar tracks. However, it provides an incomplete portrait, making *Hits 2* a necessary purchase. — *Stephen Thomas Erlewine*

★ **The Hits 2** / Sep. 14, 1993 / Paisley Park ✦✦✦✦✦
Like *Hits 1*, *Hits 2* presents an illogically sequenced cross-section of some of Prince's biggest hits and most notorious songs, including "Dirty Mind," "I Wanna Be Your Lover," "Head," "Delirious," "Little Red Corvette," "I Would Die 4 U," "Raspberry Beret," "Kiss," "U Got the Look," "Cream," and "Purple Rain." Two new tracks, "Peach" and "The Pope," are included among the 18 cuts, and while they don't match the rest of the songs (or the new cuts on *Hits 1*), they are nevertheless enjoyable. On the whole, *Hits 2* is a slightly stronger collection than its predecessor, but it still gives a rather incomplete portrait—if you buy *Hits 2*, you need to buy *Hits 1*. — *Stephen Thomas Erlewine*

The Hits / B-Sides / Sep. 14, 1993 / Paisley Park ✦✦✦✦
While it isn't a truly comprhensive set, Prince's singles collection does contain most of his biggest hits. The two volumes are available separately or packaged together with a third disc of B-sides; apart from the glorious "Erotic City," the flip sides are only of interest to devoted fans. — *Stephen Thomas Erlewine*

Come / Aug. 16, 1994 / Warner Brothers ✦✦
Released after Prince announced his retirement and his intention of never using the name "Prince" again, *Come* is something of a surprise: an album of reportedly all-new material, released by "Prince," not "The Artist Formerly Known As Prince." After listening to *Come*, its purpose becomes clear—it's a record fulfilling a contract, nothing more and nothing less. Some of the songs are good, but there's nothing on *Come* that Prince hasn't done before; he even sounds bored on certain tracks. On

top of that, the album has no obvious singles, making it a nightmare to sell. Not surprisingly, the album flopped. — *Stephen Thomas Erlewine*

Gold Experience / Oct. 1995 / Warner Brothers/NPG ✦✦✦✦
Prince changed his name to an unpronounceable symbol in 1993, but it wasn't until 1995 that he actually released a record credited to that symbol. During those two years, he released a greatest-hits collection, an official version of his much-bootlegged *Black Album*, and a final Prince album, the lackluster *Come*. Throughout 1994, he pressured Warner to release another album, *The Gold Experience*, but the company refused, and he staged a public protest in the media, calling himself a slave to the label. By the summer of 1995, the artist and the company had made amends and the record was released in the fall. In a way, *The Gold Experience* lives up to the manufactured hype created while it languished on the shelf. More of a creative rebirth than a change in direction, the record finds Prince and the New Power Generation running through a typically dazzling array of musical styles, subtly twisting new sounds out of familiar forms. Much like *The Love Symbol Album*, it follows a loose concept, interweaving a variety of pop, funk, rock, soul, and jazz styles into a vague story. Song for song, *The Gold Experience* is slightly stronger than its predecessor, as Prince's melodies are more immediate, especially on the Philly-soul tribute "The Most Beautiful Girl in the World" and the pure pop of "Dolphin." Also, the band's performance is lively and confident, bringing an effortless virtuosity to funk workouts ("P Control") and fuzzed-out rockers ("Endorphinmachine"), as well as ballads like "Eye Hate U." *The Gold Experience* is somewhat weighed down by interludes that attempt to further the story but wind up interrupting the flow of the music, yet that doesn't stop the album from being Prince's most satisfying effort since *Sign o' the Times*. — *Stephen Thomas Erlewine*

Chaos & Disorder / Jul. 1996 / Warner Brothers ✦✦✦
Like *Come* before it, *Chaos & Disorder* is a contractual obligation album for Prince, a way to get himself out of his contract with Warner Brothers. Unlike *Come*, *Chaos & Disorder* doesn't sound disjointed and pasted together—it's a fun, offhanded throwaway. For the first time since 1987's *Sign o' the Times*, Prince has made a pop-rock album, complete with squealing guitars and sighing melodies. None of the songs qualify as major songs in Prince's canon, but that's part of the record's charm—Prince sounds like he's having a good time, and he could really care less what anyone else has to say. Or, as he puts it in one of the album's best and most careening tracks, "I Rock, Therefore I Am." *Chaos & Disorder* sounds immediate, like the songs were recorded the same day they were written. While that might mean there's a handful of throwaways scattered throughout the album, there are wonderful moments like the stuttering jazz-funk of "Dig U Better Dead," the scathing "Had U," the pscyhedelic clashes of the title track, the heavy rock of "I Like It There" and the beautiful "Dinner with Delores," a rough gem that ranks as one of Prince's simplest and most charming singles of the '90s. So, *Chaos & Disorder* isn't Prince's best or most important work, but it is a really fun listen, especially if you're willing to accept it as what it is—a record that does nothing more than rock. — *Stephen Thomas Erlewine*

Emancipation / Nov. 19, 1996 / NPG/EMI ✦✦✦✦
Emancipation was a critical moment for Prince, one that he designed as an artistic rebirth and, optimistically, as a commercial comeback. In a typically perverse fashion, Prince decided to make the album a tripledisc set running exactly three hours, easily making it the longest album of all-new, original material ever released by a popular artist. As the first album he released since leaving Warner Brothers, *Emancipation* was supposed to dazzle, proving that he had not lost any of his creative skills or power. And it does dazzle, but it's hard to digest a full three discs of music, even if it is almost all of high quality. Fortunately, Prince made each disc into a distinct entity in its own right, with the first being the most pop, the second being a song cycle devoted to his new marriage, and the third being a dance-funk extravaganza. Throughout all three discs, Prince tries on a variety of styles, from jazz to R&B, but he doesn't break any new ground; instead, the album is simply a reaffirmation of his strengths as a composer and a musician. *Emancipation* doesn't have the bristling, colorful eclecticism of *Sign o' the Times* nor does it have the wildness of early one-man projects like *1999* or *Dirty Mind*, but with its gentle ballads and complex jams, it signals that Prince has evolved into middle age gracefully. It's a mature effort, to be certain, but in this case that doesn't mean that it's an album bankrupt of ideas—it means that Prince's craft continues to grow. — *Stephen Thomas Erlewine*

John Prine

b. Oct. 10, 1946, Maywood, IL
Guitar, Vocals / Singer-Songwriter, Contemporary Folk
An acclaimed singer-songwriter whose literate work flirted with everything from acoustic folk to rockabilly to straightahead country, John Prine was born October 10, 1946, in Maywood, IL. Raised by parents

firmly rooted in their rural Kentucky background, at age 14 Prine began learning to play the guitar from his older brother while taking inspiration from his grandfather, who had played with Merle Travis. After a two-year tenure in the US Army, Prine became a fixture on the Chicago folk music scene in the late 1960s, befriending another young performer named Steve Goodman.

Prine's compositions caught the ear of Kris Kristofferson, who was instrumental in helping him win a recording contract. In 1971, he went to Memphis to record his eponymously titled debut album; though not a commercial success, songs like "Sam Stone," the harsh tale of a drug-addled Vietnam veteran, won critical approval. Neither 1972's *Diamonds in the Rough* nor 1973's *Sweet Revenge* fared any better on the charts, but Prine's work won great renown among his fellow performers; the Everly Brothers covered his song "Paradise," while both Bette Midler and Joan Baez offered renditions of "Hello in There."

For 1975's *Common Sense*, Prine turned to producer Steve Cropper, the highly influential house guitarist for the Stax label; while the album's sound shocked the folk community with its reliance on husky vocals and booming drums, it served notice that Prine was not an artist whose work could be pigeonholed, and it was his only LP to reach the US Top 100. Steve Goodman took over the reins for 1978's folky *Bruised Orange*, but on 1979's *Pink Cadillac*, Prine took another left turn and recorded an electric rockabilly workout produced at Sun Studios by the label's legendary founder Sam Phillips and his son Knox.

Following 1980's *Storm Windows*, he formed his own label, Oh Boy Records, to release 1984's *Aimless Love*. Under his own imprint, Prine's music thrived. 1986's country-flavored *German Afternoons* earned a Grammy nomination in the Contemporary Folk category. After 1988's *John Prine Live*, he released 1991's Grammy-winning *The Missing Years*; his most successful outing to date, the album featured guest appearances from Bruce Springsteen, Bonnie Raitt, and Tom Petty. After making his film debut in 1992's John Mellencamp-directed *Falling from Grace*, Prine returned in 1995 with *Lost Dogs and Mixed Blessings*. —*Jason Ankeny*

☆ **John Prine** / 1971 / Atlantic ✦✦✦✦✦
A revelation upon its release, this album is now a collection of standards: "Illegal Smile," "Hello in There," "Sam Stone," "Donald and Lydia," and, of course, "Angel from Montgomery." Prine's music, a mixture of folk, rock, and country, is deceptively simple like his pointed lyrics, and his easy vocal style adds a humorous edge that makes otherwise funny jokes downright hilarious. —*William Ruhlmann*

Diamonds in the Rough / 1972 / Atlantic ✦✦✦
John Prine's second album was a cut below his first, only because the debut was a classic and the followup was merely terrific. "Sour Grapes" showed Prine's cracked sense of humor and "Souvenirs" his sentiment. Even if it was the second rank of his writing, *Diamonds in the Rough* demonstrated that Prine had an enduring talent that wasn't exhausted by one great album. —*William Ruhlmann*

Sweet Revenge / 1973 / Atlantic ✦✦✦✦
A bold and brilliant stab at (almost) straight country, it tempers Prine's cynical streak with the tone of a jaded humorist and social commentator. —*John Floyd*

Common Sense / 1975 / Atlantic ✦✦✦
A brash album, it's full of aggressive rock rhythms and morose tunes. Even the Chuck Berry cover, "You Never Can Tell," is shot full of melancholy. —*John Floyd*

Prime Prine / 1976 / Atlantic ✦✦✦✦
Atlantic Records' compilation of John Prine's first four albums was good for its time (and became his only gold record) but has been superseded by Rhino's *Great Days* anthology. —*William Ruhlmann*

Bruised Orange / 1978 / Asylum ✦✦✦✦
Despite some brilliant songs, Prine's follow-up albums to his stunning debut were uneven until this, his fifth, produced by his friend Steve Goodman. Here, Prine's always finely tuned sense of absurdity once again collides with his ability to depict pain sympathetically for a whole album, typified by "That's the Way That the World Goes 'Round," a neat statement of his philosophy, and "Sabu Visits the Twin Cities Alone," perhaps the best depiction ever written of life on the road in the entertainment business. —*William Ruhlmann*

Pink Cadillac / 1979 / Oh Boy ✦✦✦
John Prine went to Sam Phillips' studio in Memphis to make his sixth album, *Pink Cadillac*, and got some of the Sun Records sound of 1950s rockabilly on a record produced by Phillips' sons Knox and Jerry. (Sam produced two of the tracks himself.) Slap-back bass here, a Bo Diddley beat there, and an overall loose feel characterized music that may have been more fun to make than it is to listen to, even though it's quite entertaining. Prine wrote only five of the ten songs, however, and even though the covers were of high caliber—notably Roly Salley's "Killing the Blues" and Arthur Gunter's "Baby Let's Play House," a song Elvis

Presley did at Sun—*Pink Cadillac* was a good idea that went slightly awry in the execution. If Prine had had the songs as well as the studio, it would have been among his best. —*William Ruhlmann*

Storm Windows / 1980 / Oh Boy ✦✦✦
A relaxed effort, it's defined by straightforward love songs and subdued vocals. Modest but quite nice. —*John Floyd*

Aimless Love / 1984 / Oh Boy ✦✦✦
John Prine moved to his own independent label, Oh Boy, after stints at Atlantic and Asylum (later, he acquired his Asylum albums and reissued them on Oh Boy). On this label debut, he is under no commercial pressures, but that seems to make him more low-key, less striking. "The Oldest Baby in the World," "Somewhere Someone's Falling in Love," and "Unwed Fathers" are good examples of his new sweetness, which is as winning as, if less impressive than, his witty older songs. —*William Ruhlmann*

German Afternoons / 1986 / Oh Boy ✦✦✦
Another straight country set, but unlike *Sweet Revenge*, this is a sleepytown stroll, highlighted by some beautiful ballads and snappy accompaniment by the New Grass Revival. —*John Floyd*

Live / 1988 / Oh Boy ✦✦✦✦
With years of experience playing club dates, John Prine has evolved into a very entertaining live performer, and this album, originally a double LP and now a single CD, presents him at his intimate best, telling funny stories and performing his most impressive material in unadorned arrangements. —*William Ruhlmann*

The Missing Years / Sep. 1991 / Oh Boy ✦✦✦✦
Prine took five years between his ninth studio album and this, his tenth—enough time to gather his strongest body of material in more than a decade. From the caustic "All the Best" to the cliche compilation "It's a Big Old Goofy World," Prine's gifts for emotional revelation and off-the-wall humor are on display in abundance, and he's aided by excellent production (courtesy of Heartbreaker Howie Epstein) and strong backup musicians. *The Missing Years* won the 1991 Grammy Award for Best Contemporary Folk Album. —*William Ruhlmann*

★ **The Great Days: John Prine Anthology** / Aug. 17, 1993 / Rhino ✦✦✦✦✦
Prine's career has been rich but scattered, and *Great Days* gathers together almost all of his finest moments, providing a comprehensive introduction to one of the best songwriters of the past 20 years. —*Stephen Thomas Erlewine*

John Prine Christmas / 1994 / Oh Boy ✦✦✦
An eight-song EP of new and old works with a holiday theme. Knowing John Prine's sense of humor, you can expect that much of this is not to be taken straight, so when he sings of "Christmas in Prison" or in the live version of the romantic kiss-off "All the Best" you find you're in for a Christmas celebration unlike any other. —*William Ruhlmann*

Lost Dogs and Mixed Blessings / Apr. 4, 1995 / Oh Boy ✦✦✦
John Prine's follow-up to his comeback album, *The Missing Years*, is more of the same in terms of freeing up Prine's idiosyncratic muse and marrying the result to Howie Epstein's top-flight production sound. Fans of the early Prine may find the sound overproduced, but the songs never get lost, and with Prine's typically humorous, off-center view of the world (song titles include "Humidity Built the Snowman" and "He Forgot That It Was Sunday"), it's the songs that count. Actually, this is not quite as strong a collection of material as *The Missing Years*, but it has its moments, and Prine and Epstein show it off in its best possible light. —*William Ruhlmann*

Live on Tour / Apr. 8, 1997 / Oh Boy ✦✦✦

P.J. Proby (James Marcus Smith)

b. Nov. 6, 1938, Houston, TX
Vocals / British Invasion
Like the Walker Brothers, he wasn't British, he sang more ballads than rock 'n' roll, and he was far more successful in the UK than in the States. Texan P.J. Proby was pretty hot stuff in England for a time, as much—indeed, probably more—for his then-risqué stage act, which saw him incorporate split pants into his act after they (he claimed) accidentally ripped during a performance. Artistically, this is a case when the taste of the British listening public could be called into question. Proby sang in a pinched facsimile of Elvis and Gene Pitney that grew increasingly pained as it approached the upper register. A few of his hits were MOR ballads like "Somewhere" and "Maria," but he did manage an infectious Merseyish rocker on his first (and biggest) British smash, "Hold Me." In the US, he is most remembered for recording the Lennon-McCartney composition "That Means a Lot" in 1965 (which the Beatles themselves never released) and for his sole Top 40 US hit (from 1967), the Cajun-flavored "Nicki Hoeky." —*Richie Unterberger*

● **Legendary P.J. Proby at His Very Best: Vol. 2** / 1987 / See For Miles ✦✦✦✦

Oddly, this is a better compilation than Vol. 1, which focused more on his ballads; this is oriented towards his rock and soul recordings. Includes "Hold Me," "Nicki Hoeky," the 1964 British Top 20 single "Together," and "Just Call and I'll Be There" (also recorded by Francoise Hardy in French), where Proby sounds like the loser in a Gene Pitney soundalike contest. Spanning from 1964 to 1968, most of the rest consists of rock and soul covers that range from passable to horrid. —*Richie Unterberger*

I Am P.J. Proby / P.J. Proby / Mar. 19, 1996 / See For Miles ✦✦✦

P.J. Proby's first two albums, *I Am P.J. Proby* and *P.J. Proby*, are collected on this single disc. Before these records, he had primarily been known as a songwriter, and these were supposed to establish him as a performer. Although he had a number of hits in Britain, he didn't have much success in America, apart from the minor hits "Hold Me" and a cover of *West Side Story*'s "Somewhere." Both albums were post-British Invasion pop-rock, with lots of sugary melodies and ringing guitars. Though they have their moments, each one is riddled with filler, which is what makes the two-fer a bargain. The highlights of both discs combine to form one strong album. —*Stephen Thomas Erlewine*

In Town / Enigma / Mar. 19, 1996 / See For Miles ✦✦✦

In Town and *Enigma*, P.J. Proby's third and fourth albums, didn't have as many hits as his previous two albums (although, ironically, *Enigma* spawned his biggest American hit, "Nicki Hoeky"), partially because he was beginning to move toward a more middle-of-the-road sound, similar to Tom Jones. Though the albums are well produced and well crafted—they sound slick, stylish, and professional—they lack the spark of his first two records, even if the number of first-rate songs hasn't decreased. After *Enigma*, his career did begin to slide, but he was still a fun and popular pop-rock teen idol when he recorded these albums and that is what makes the disc an enjoyable period piece. —*Stephen Thomas Erlewine*

Procol Harum

f. 1967, London, England
Art-Rock/Progressive-Rock, Psychedelic

Procol Harum was arguably the most successful "accidental" group creation—that is, a band originally assembled in the studio—in the history of progressive rock. With "A Whiter Shade of Pale," a monster hit right out of the box, the band evolved from a studio ensemble into a successful live act, their music built around an eclectic mix of blues-based rock riffs and grand classical themes; at their most accessible, they were one of the most popular of progressive rock bands, their singles outselling all rivals.

Procol Harum's roots and origins are as convoluted as its success—especially between 1967 and 1973—was pronounced. Pianist Gary Brooker had formed a group at school called the Paramounts at age 14, with guitarist Robin Trower and bassist Chris Copping, singer Bob Scott and drummer Mick Brownlee. After achieving a certain degree of success at local youth clubs and dances, Brooker took over the vocalist spot from the departed Scott, and the group continued working after its members graduated. By 1962, they were doing formidable covers of American R&B, and got a residency at the Shades Club in Southend. Brownlee exited the band in early 1963 and was replaced by Barry J. (B. J.) Wilson; nine months later, Copping opted out as well, and was replaced by Diz Derrick. The following month, the Paramounts' demo record, consisting of covers of the Coasters' "Poison Ivy" and Bobby Bland's "Farther on Up the Road," got them an audition at EMI, and they soon signed to Parlophone.

The Paramounts' first single, "Poison Ivy," was released in January of 1964; the group also got an important endorsement from the Rolling Stones, with whom they'd worked on the television show *Thank Your Lucky Stars*, and who called the Paramounts their favorite British R&B band. Unfortunately, none of the group's subsequent Parlophone singles over the next 18 months found any chart success, and in September of 1966, they went their separate ways: Derrick left the business, and Trower and Wilson played gigs with other bands. Most fortuitously, Gary Brooker decided to develop his career as a songwriter, forging a partnership with lyricist Keith Reid. By the spring of 1967, they had a considerable body of songs prepared and began looking for a band to play them. An advertisement in *Melody Maker* led to the formation of a band initially called the Pinewoods, with Brooker as pianist/singer, Matthew Fisher on organ, Ray Royer on guitar, Dave Knights on bass, and Bobby Harrison on drums.

Their first recording was of a piece of surreal Reid poetry called "A Whiter Shade of Pale," which Brooker set to music loosely derived from Johann Sebastian Bach's "Air on a G String" from the *Suite No. 3 in D Major*. (By the time the recording was ready for release, the Pinewoods had been rechristened Procol Harum -- a name derived, as alternate stories tell it, either from Stevens' cat's birth certificate, Procol Harun, or the

Latin "procul" for "far from these things.") Producer Denny Cordell sent a copy of "A Whiter Shade of Pale" to Radio London, one of England's legendary offshore pirate radio stations, which played the record; not only was Radio London deluged with listener requests for more plays. Four days after Procol Harum made its concert debut in London opening for Jimi Hendrix on June 4, 1967, "A Whiter Shade of Pale" reached the top of the British charts for the first of a six-week run in the top spot, making Procol Harum only the sixth recording act in the history of British popular music to reach the No. 1 spot on its first release.

All of this seemed to bode well for the band, except for the fact that it had only a single song in its repertoire and no real stage act—literal one-hit wonders. The same month that the record peaked in the United States, Royer and Harrison were sacked and replaced by Brooker's former Paramounts bandmates Trower and Wilson; the "real" Procol Harum band was now in place, and a second single, "Homburg," was duly recorded. The group's debut album, entitled *Procol Harum*, soon followed. After subsequent singles failed to find an audience, by November a second album, *Shine on Brightly*—highlighted by the 18-minute epic "In Held 'Twas I"—was finished and in the stores. In March of 1969, Knights and Fisher exited the line-up shortly after finishing work on the group's new album, *A Salty Dog*, opening the way for bassist Chris Copping to join Procol Harum, thus recreating the line-up of the Paramounts.

Despite the group's moderate sales in England and America, they remained among the more popular progressive rock bands, capable of reaching listeners who didn't have the patience for Emerson, Lake & Palmer or King Crimson; Trower's flashy guitar playing made him the star of the group, and he was considered in the same league with Alvin Lee and any number of late-'60s/early-'70s British blues axemen. Ultimately, after releasing 1970's *Home*, Procol Harum began work on 1971's *Broken Barricades*, which proved to be Trower's swan song; the guitarist subsequently organized his own group, which had great success in America throughout the 1970s. His replacement was Dave Ball, and soon the line-up expanded by one with the addition of Alan Cartwright on bass, which freed Copping to concentrate full-time on the organ. It was this version of the band that performed on August 6, 1971 in a concert with the Edmonton Symphony Orchestra and the Da Camera Singers in Edmonton, Alberta, Canada which was released as an official live album in 1972.

Procol Harum's line-up again was thrown into turmoil in September when Ball left to join Long John Baldry's band. He was replaced by Mick Grabham, formerly of the bands Plastic Penny and Cochise, in time to record their next album, *Grand Hotel*. The group's next two albums, 1974's *Exotic Birds and Fruit* and the next year's *Ninth* (produced by rock & roll songsmiths Jerry Leiber and Mike Stoller), performed moderately well, and *Ninth*'s "Pandora's Box" became one of their bigger hits. July of 1976 saw a departure and a lateral shift in the group's line-up, as Cartwright left the band and Copping took over on bass, while Pete Solley joined as keyboard-player. By this time, the band's string had run out, as everyone seemed to know. A new album, *Something Magic*, barely scraped the charts in 1977, and the band split up following a final tour and a farewell concert at New York's Academy of Music on May 15, 1977.

Procol Harum had largely faded from the consciousness of the music world by the end of the 1980s. The death of B.J. Wilson in 1989 went largely unreported, to the chagrin of many fans, and it seemed as though the group was a closed book. Then, in August of 1991, Brooker reformed Procol Harum with Trower, Fisher, Reid, and drummer Mark Brzezicki. An album, *The Prodigal Stranger*, was recorded and released, and an 11-city tour of North America took place in September of 1991. Although this line-up didn't last—Trower and company, after all, were pushing 50 at the time—Brooker kept a new version of Procol Harum together, in the guise of himself, guitarist Geoffrey Whitehorn, keyboardman Don Snow, and Brzezicki on drums, which toured the United States in 1992. —*Bruce Eder*

Procul Harum / 1967 / Deram ✦✦✦✦

Their spectacular debut showed remarkable songwriting and became a late-'60s classic due to the immense popularity of "A Whiter Shade of Pale," which made their reputation. —*Cub Koda & Dan Heilman*

Shine On Brightly / 1968 / A&M ✦✦✦✦

Procol's ambitious sophomore effort expanded upon their symphonic-style rock, particularly the 18-plus-minute conceptual opus "In Held 'Twas I." The title track was another highlight. —*Rick Clark*

A Salty Dog / 1969 / A&M ✦✦✦✦

Procol's synthesis of blues and grand, classically inspired melodies reached an apex on their third album. The tasteful production featured sweeping orchestrations, subtle sound effects, and dynamic arrangements. *A Salty Dog* became one of Procol's signature numbers. —*Rick Clark*

Home / 1970 / A&M ✦✦✦
With Matthew Fisher gone, Procol embraced a harder, more rock-oriented approach best displayed on the herky-jerky riff-rocker "Whiskey Train," a Robin Trower showcase. —*Rick Clark*

Broken Barricades / 1971 / A&M ✦✦✦✦
Building on the more guitar-oriented sound of *Home*, *Broken Barricades* is Procol Harum's most mainstream rock album. Guitarist Robin Trower plays an unprecedented role in the album's sound, his last before leaving to form his own band; he contributes nearly as many songs as pianist Gary Brooker, including "Song for a Dreamer," which foreshadows the contemplative Hendrix-influenced style so prominent on his solo albums, and his guitar often dominates the material he didn't write. It was their best-sounding studio album to date, and showed each member of the band to their best advantage. With its generally single-length songs and strong guitar presence, *Broken Barricades* could have been the blueprint for a new sound for the band; with Trower's departure for a successful solo career, however, Procol Harum wound up falling back on the more ornate sound of their earlier albums. This would be Trower's last recording with the band for another 20 years, until the 1991 reunion album *Prodigal Stranger*. —*James A. Gardner*

Procol Harum Live: In Concert with the Edmonton Symphony Orchestra & The Da Camera Sin / 1972 / A&M ✦✦✦
With the help of the Edmonton Symphony Orchestra (Canada), Procol Harum does an impressive job re-creating their more stately numbers, complete with sound effects and a full choir. "Conquistador" became a No. 16 hit. —*Rick Clark*

The Best of Procol Harum / 1973 / A&M ✦✦✦✦
A fine wrap-up of the band's 1967-73 output, it documents their most creative era. —*Dan Heilman*

Exotic Birds & Fruit / 1974 / Chrysalis ✦✦✦
Now, this sounds more like a Procol Harum album than their previous efforts. From the opening comment by Gary Brooker, all the pistons are firing, producing some great music. While some of the lyrics deal in the stranger side of life (what Procol Harum doesn't), there are hooks galore to satisfy any listener's needs. The passing of years have only enhanced what lies here, sort of like fine wine. —*James Chrispell*

Procol's Ninth / 1975 / Chrysalis ✦✦✦
For their ninth album, Procol Harum turned to production by the veteran songwriting team of Leiber and Stoller, who had written the first single ("Poison Ivy") by Procol's predecessor band, the Paramounts. Though the band is in top form (especially drummer B.J. Wilson) and despite a strong start (with the exquisite "Pandora's Box," a UK hit), the album largely runs out of steam by side two. Too much of the Brooker and Reid material is competent rather than exciting. Likewise, Procol fails to render memorable versions of two cover songs, Leiber and Stoller's "I Keep Forgetting" or the Beatles' "Eight Days a Week." Most of this album's best material can be found on the *Chrysalis Years* collection. [*Grand Hotel* and *Procol's Ninth* were later re-released as *Cornerstone*, a budget double album.] —*James A. Gardner*

Something Magic / 1977 / Chrysalis ✦✦
Even fans call this one "Something Tragic." There are still hints of the tight ensemble playing that characterizes the best of Procol's Chrysalis albums, but most of the first side is dreary, uninspired stuff. While the title track captures some of the drama of early Procol, Brooker's distinctive voice is the sole link to their former glory on indifferent cuts like "Wizard Man." ["Strangers in Space" later appeared on the Brooker-produced *The Long Goodbye: The Symphonic Music of Procol Harum*.] "The Worm & the Tree" is a side-long extravagance, the first time the band had produced a work of this length since "In Held 'Twas I," on the 1968 release, *Shine On Brightly*. Unlike the whimsy and charm of that earlier suite, though, "The Worm & the Tree" lyrically evokes Emerson, Lake & Palmer at their most tedious (*Tarkus*). Seemingly out of steam, and out of step with the rising tide of punk music, Procol Harum packed it in, not to return until the '90s. —*James A. Gardner*

● **Classics, Vol. 17** / 1987 / A&M ✦✦✦✦
Classics, Vol. 17 is an adequate, 12-song retrospective of Procol Harum's biggest hits and best-known songs, featuring "A Whiter Shade of Pale," "Conquistador," "A Salty Dog," and "Homburg." Although the disc is hardly comprehensive, it nevertheless remains a good overview for casual fans. —*Stephen Thomas Erlewine*

Prodigal Stranger / Aug. 27, 1991 / Zoo ✦✦✦
After a 14-year break, Procol's principals reconvened for an album of new material. The disappointments presented by this album, though, are apparent with a glance at the personnel and the lyric sheet. Drummer B.J. Wilson, an important architect of the Procol sound, died before this reunion was realized. And a glance at song titles like "Holding On" and "One More Time" indicate that lyricist Keith Reid was writing in a mundane, conventional mode; one listen bears out this indication. No whaling stories or whiter shades of pale here. Brooker simply isn't given much to sing, despite being in top vocal form. The Brooker-Fisher-

Trower trio doesn't strike many sparks instrumentally, either. Far too often, especially with the frequent use of synthesizers in place of Hammond organ, this could be any competent AOR group. "(You Can't) Turn Back the Page" would later appear, more memorably, on the Brooker-produced *The Long Goodbye: The Symphonic Music of Procol Harum.* —*James A. Gardner*

The Long Goodbye / Jul. 18, 1995 / RCA Victor ✦✦
With its pop adaptations of Bach and its album with the Edmonton Symphony Orchestra, Procol Harum was an early advocate of a marriage between rock and classical music. So, this album of Procol Harum music recorded by the London Symphony Orchestra, the London Philharmonic Orchestra, and (on the title track) the Sinfonia of London, with former Procol Harum vocalist-pianist Gary Brooker singing on 7 of the 12 tracks and producing, and with former Procol Harum guitarist Robin Trower and organist Matthew Fisher appearing on a version of "Repent Walpurgis," would seem like a more comfortable combination than similar recent collections devoted to the Rolling Stones and Yes. But the effectiveness of the band's music lay in a balancing of styles, and here the symphonic approach dominates, making the music seem less stately than soporific. Brooker sounds bored, and the set only livens up vocally when guests Jerry Hadley ("Grand Hotel") and Tom Jones ("Simple Sister") step in. —*William Ruhlmann*

● **Greatest Hits** / May 7, 1996 / A&M ✦✦✦✦
Procul Harum's 1996 collection *Greatest Hits* features the same songs and sequencing as 1987's *Classics, Vol. 17*, except the music has been remastered. For most ears, the remastering isn't particularly noticeable, so if you already own *Classics*, *Greatest Hits* is completely unnecessary, yet the collection remains an adequate introduction for casual fans. —*Stephen Thomas Erlewine*

The Prodigy

f. 1990, London, England
Techno, Club-Dance, Rave, Electronica
The most successful holdover from the early-'90s rave/hardcore scene, the Prodigy initially scored with the 1991 UK hit "Charly" and became one of the decade's best-selling dance acts with a string of hit singles. Organized and fronted by Liam Howlett, the group also recorded acclaimed album works and toured the LPs with a stunning live show, which approximated the incendiary spirit of a rave better than any techno act.

Howlett (b. 1971), the prodigy behind the group's name, was classically trained on the piano while growing up in Braintree, Essex. Later, he began listening to rap and DJed with the hip-hop act Cut to Kill before moving on to acid house in the late '80s. His first production, the EP *What Evil Lurks*, became a major mover on the fledgling rave scene. After Howlett met up with dancers Keith Flint and Leeroy Thornhill (both Essex natives as well), the trio formed the Prodigy in late 1990. The group gained a contract with XL Records and re-released *What Evil Lurks* in February 1991.

Six months later, Howlett issued his second single "Charly," built around a sample from a children's public-service announcement. It hit No. 1 on the British dance charts and then crossed over to the pop charts, stalling only at No. 3. "Charly" also spawned the copycat craze that launched the Smart E's "Sesame Street," one of the first rave singles to chart in America. Two additional Prodigy singles, "Everybody in the Place" and "Fire/Jericho," charted in the UK during late 1991 and early 1992.

The Prodigy showed they were no one-anthem wonders in September 1992, when the group released one of the first LPs by a rave act. *The Prodigy Experience* appeared on XL in Great Britain and Elektra in America, fluidly mixing previous material with future singles ("Out of Space," "Wind It Up"); it proved a major hit. During 1993, Howlett added a ragga/hip-hop MC named Maxim Reality (Keeti Palmer) and occupied himself with remix work for Front 242, Jesus Jones, and Art of Noise. Howlett also released two white-label singles ("Earthbound, Vols. 1 & 2") to fool image-conscious DJs who had written off the Prodigy as hopelessly commercial. Late 1993 brought the new single "One Love" and, early the following year, "No Good (Start the Dance)."

The double album *Music for the Jilted Generation*, released in July 1994, was an us-against-them statement in opposition to the 1994 Criminal Justice Bill—the act that gave British police greater power to stop raves and prosecute their promoters and attenders. The album also continued the Prodigy's allegiance to breakbeat drum 'n bass; the style had only recently become commercially viable, but Howlett had incorporated it virtually from the beginning of his career. The non-album single "Firestarter," released in 1996, became the Prodigy's biggest hit in the US, and its video earned a spot on MTV's Buzz Bin. A second 1996 single, "Breathe," hit No.1 on half a dozen European countries' pop charts. —*John Bush*

Experience / Oct. 20, 1992 / Elektra ✦✦✦✦

● **Music for the Jilted Generation** / Feb. 28, 1995 / Mute ✦✦✦✦
With *Music for the Jilted Generation*, the Prodigy's sound was fully realized, as the duo created hard-edged, expressive sonic landscapes that were grounded in techno but exploded many of the limitations of the genre. It delivers all of the raw vitality and cutting-edge experimentalism of hardcore techno, but with enough musical panache and raw vitality to make it appeal to a wide audience. —*Daevid Jehnzen*

Professor Longhair (Henry Roeland Byrd)

b. Dec. 19, 1918, Bogalusa, LA, **d.** Jan. 30, 1980, New Orleans, LA
Piano, Vocals / Rock 'n' Roll, Piano Blues, New Orleans Blues, New Orleans R&B

Justly worshipped a decade and a half after his death as a founding father of New Orleans R&B, Roy "Professor Longhair" Byrd was nevertheless so down-and-out at one point in his long career that he was reduced to sweeping the floors in a record shop that once could have moved his platters by the boxful.

That Fess made such a marvelous comeback testifies to the resiliency of this late legend, whose Latin-tinged, rhumba-rocking piano style and croaking, yodeling vocals were as singular and spicy as the second-line beats that power his hometown's musical heartbeat. Byrd brought an irresistible Caribbean feel to his playing, full of rolling flourishes that every Crescent City ivories man had to learn inside out (Fats Domino, Huey Smith, and Allen Toussaint all paid homage early and often).

Roy Byrd grew up on the streets of the Big Easy, tap dancing for tips on Bourbon Street with his running partners. Local 88s aces Sullivan Rock, Kid Stormy Weather, and Tuts Washington all left their marks on the youngster, but Byrd brought his own conception to the stool. A natural-born card shark and gambler, Longhair began to take his playing seriously in 1948, earning a gig at the Caldonia Club. Owner Mike Tessitore bestowed Byrd with his professorial nickname (due to Byrd's shaggy coiffure).

Longhair debuted on wax in 1949, laying down four tracks (including the first version of his signature "Mardi Gras in New Orleans" complete with whistled intro) for the Dallas-based Star Talent label. His band was called the Shuffling Hungarians, for reasons lost to time! Union problems forced those sides off the market, but Longhair's next date for Mercury the same year was strictly on the up-and-up. It produced his first and only national R&B hit in 1950, the hilarious "Bald Head" (credited to Roy Byrd & His Blues Jumpers).

The pianist made great records for Atlantic in 1949, Federal in 1951, Wasco in 1952, and Atlantic again in 1953 (producing the immortal "Tipitina," a romping "In the Night," and the lyrically impenetrable boogie "Ball the Wall"). After recuperating from a minor stroke, Longhair came back on Lee Rupe's Ebb logo in 1957 with a storming "No Buts—No Maybes." He revived his "Go to the Mardi Gras" for Joe Ruffino's Ron imprint in 1959; this is the version that surfaces every year at Mardi Gras in New Orleans.

Other than the ambitiously arranged "Big Chief" in 1964 for Watch Records, the '60s held little charm for Longhair. He hit the skids, abandoning his piano playing until a booking at the fledgling 1971 Jazz & Heritage Festival put him on the comeback trail. He made a slew of albums in the last decade of his life, topped off by a terrific set for Alligator, *Crawfish Fiesta*. Longhair triumphantly appeared on the PBS-TV concert series *Soundstage* (with Dr. John, Earl King, and the Meters), co-starred in the documentary *Piano Players Rarely Ever Play Together* (which became a memorial tribute when Longhair died in the middle of its filming; funeral footage was included), and saw a group of his admirers buy a local watering hole in 1977 and rechristen it Tipitina's after his famous song. He played there regularly when he wasn't on the road; it remains a thriving operation.

Longhair went to bed on January 30, 1980, and never woke up. A heart attack in the night stilled one of New Orleans' seminal R&B stars, but his music is played in his hometown so often and so reverently, you'd swear he was still around. —*Bill Dahl*

★ **Fess: Professor Longhair Anthology** / Nov. 16, 1993 / Rhino ✦✦✦✦✦
The rhumba-rocking rhythms of Roy "Professor Longhair" Byrd live on throughout Rhino's 40-track retrospective of the New Orleans icon's amazing legacy. Most of the seminal stuff arrives early on. "Bald Head," the rollicking ode Byrd cut for Mercury in 1950, is followed by a raft of classics from his 1949 and 1953 Atlantic dates ("Tipitina," "Ball the Wall," "Who's Been Fooling You"), the storming 1957 "No Buts—No Maybes" and "Baby Let Me Hold Your Hand" for Ebb, and his beloved "Go to the Mardi Gras" as waxed for Ron in 1959. The second disc is a hodgepodge of material from his 1970s comeback, all of it wonderful in its own way but not as essential as the early work. —*Bill Dahl*

Chuck Prophet

b. California
Rock 'n' Roll, Country-Rock, Folk-Rock
Chuck Prophet is the least heralded guitar player of the '80s and '90s,

with songwriting skills to match his prodigious instrumental talent. Born in the mid-'60s in Southern California, Prophet first made his mark as the young guitarist in L.A.'s Green on Red, a forerunner of the Paisley Underground movement; however, Green on Red's attack was inspired more by American apple pie than psychedelics. After disbanding finally in 1992, Prophet began to focus all attention on the solo career he started with 1990's *Brother Aldo* (Fire). Prophet's devotion to roots music is for its sources, but he also sounds inspired by Bob Dylan's lyrics and Keith Richards' and Eric Clapton's guitars; his voice bears a resemblance to Tom Petty's. He followed with *Balinese Dancer* in 1993 and *Feast of Hearts* in 1995. Prophet earned positive critical attention on these shores, but his greatest success came overseas. Throughout his solo career, he's worked with legends and inspirations from Bob Neuwirth to Jim Dinkinson to Billy Swan and beat poet Hubert Huncke to most recently with Austin guitarist Calvin Russell. He maintained a friendship with legendary Memphis session man and songwriter Jim Dickinson, with whom Prophet collaborated on a live recording *A Thousand Footprints in the Sand*. The band he's used most consistently is Anders Rundblad (bass), Paul Revelli (drums), Max Butler (guitar), and Stephanie Finch (on keyboards). Finch is Prophet's partner, and they've worked together since *Brother Aldo*. In 1997, Prophet came through with *Homemade Blood* (Cooking Vinyl), a live-in-the-studio set that brings home the talents of a mature guitarist, songwriter, and singer. He has yet to be discovered by the masses, but when he's ultimately uncovered, fans will have a large catalog to mine. —*Denise Sullivan*

Brother Aldo / 1990 / Fire ✦✦✦
A homey slice of modern roots-rock, Prophet and his band slide through rockin' originals like "Look Both Ways" (penned with Steve Wynn and Chris Cacavas), the swampy "Say It Ain't So," and the dark folk of "Scarecrow." Aided by Stephanie Finch on vocals and accordion and Chris Isaak band member Roly Salley on bass, these city folk make authentic backporch blues and folk fused with rock. —*Denise Sullivan*

Balinese Dancer / May 11, 1993 / Dutch East India ✦✦✦✦
This ballad-oriented solo outing from former Green on Red guitarist Chuck Prophet offers up spare swamp rock, setting the singer's dusky voice against a backdrop of slide, steel, and finger-picked electric guitars. Opting for mood as much as content, the material is simple and homespun, adding touches of the blues and zydeco for an authentic backwoods feel. —*Jason Ankeny*

Feast of Hearts / 1995 / China ✦✦

● **Homemade Blood** / Mar. 18, 1997 / Cooking Vinyl ✦✦✦✦
The guitarist and singer-songwriter in Prophet become one on his finest achievement to date. The songs were inspired by a series of semi-autobiographical stories of growing up in suburbia only to enroll in the school of hard knocks and come out a fighter; it's simultaneously cynical and reverent. The band that backs his fiery guitar work is a roots-rock unit tightened up from ceaseless European touring, and this live-in-the-studio recording suits their no-prisoners delivery. This record ought to bring Prophet some well-deserved kudos. —*Denise Sullivan*

The Psychedelic Furs

f. 1977, London, England, **db.** 1991
Alternative Pop-Rock, New Wave
The Psychedelic Furs, whose name belies their punk-influenced music, were formed in England in 1977 by brothers Richard Butler (vocals) and Tim Butler (bass), along with saxophone player Duncan Kilburn and guitarist Roger Morris. By the time they released their self-titled debut album in 1980, the group had become a sextet, adding guitarist John Ashton and drummer Vince Ely. That album, featuring Butler's hoarse voice (the tone of which suggested John Lydon without the sneer), was a bigger hit in England, where it reached the Top 20, than in the US.

Talk Talk Talk (1981) did better, reaching the US Top 100 and producing two British singles-chart entries, one of which was "Pretty in Pink," later also a hit in the US when a new version was used as the title song of a film. *Forever Now* (1982) saw the band reduced to a quartet with the departure of Kilburn and Morris. The rest moved to the US, turned to producer Todd Rundgren, and scored a US Top 50 hit with "Love My Way." Ely then left, and the remaining trio of the two Butlers and Ashton made *Mirror Moves* (1984), the biggest Psychedelic Furs hit yet.

The film *Pretty in Pink* helped spread their name further before the release of their next album, *Midnight to Midnight* (1986), which consequently got to No. 12 in the UK and the Top 30 in the US and included the Top 30 US hit "Heartbreak Beat." *Book of Days* (1989) marked the return of Vince Ely but was a considerable commercial disappointment. *World Outside* (1991) also failed to find an audience. The Psychedelic Furs then folded up shop, and Richard Butler launched a new group, Love Spit Love. —*William Ruhlmann*

The Psychedelic Furs [1st LP] / 1980 / Columbia ✦✦✦✦
This auspicious debut finds the sextet turning out thick, noisy rock (especially in the saxophone-guitar combination) through which Rich-

ard Butler's voice cuts like a buzzsaw. Best track: "Imitation of Christ." (The UK version of *The Psychedelic Furs* (CBS 84084) differed from the US version and was released earlier, in February 1980.) —*William Ruhlmann*

Talk Talk Talk / Jun. 1981 / Columbia ✦✦✦✦
An even better follow-up makes explicit the Furs' connection to the Velvet Underground (their name comes from the Velvets' song "Venus in Furs"). Their strongest overall collection, this includes the original (superior) version of "Pretty in Pink," "Dumb Waiters," and the definitive Psychedelic Furs song, "Into You Like a Train." —*William Ruhlmann*

Forever Now / 1982 / Columbia ✦✦✦
Actually, Todd Rundgren's much-vaunted, clean, sharp production style has very little effect on the Furs' sound, which is still pretty noisy and still dominated by Butler's hoarse, slightly scornful voice on such songs as "Love My Way," "President Gas," and the title track. —*William Ruhlmann*

Mirror Moves / 1984 / Columbia ✦✦✦
On *Mirror Moves*, the Psychedelic Furs began to move toward a slicker, accessible pop-rock sound. By and large, the extra gloss works, as the group turns in a set of catchy rockers that manages to incorporate some mainstream concessions into their signature sound without losing their personality. It may not be as exciting as their first four records, but they pull off the streamlined pop on *Mirror Moves* with considerable panache. —*Stephen Thomas Erlewine*

Midnight to Midnight / 1987 / Columbia ✦✦✦
Midnight to Midnight continues the streamlining of the Psychedelic Furs. Unlike the previous *Mirror Moves*, *Midnight to Midnight* loses the essential character of the Furs' sound, as the production relies on a sleek, stylish pop production. Although the results don't have much to do with the group's early records, it's an entertaining record, filled with its share of pop thrills, including the single "Heartbreak Beat." —*Stephen Thomas Erlewine*

● **All of This and Nothing** / 1988 / Columbia ✦✦✦✦
Not a perfect Furs compilation, but this 12-track look back does contain the notable tracks from the albums *Mirror Moves* and *Midnight to Midnight*, plus some of the necessary ones from the albums listed above, and a good new song, "All That Money Wants." —*William Ruhlmann*

Book of Days / Oct. 1989 / Columbia ✦✦
The Psychedelic Furs seemed to close a chapter with the release of their 1988 compilation *All of This and Nothing*, ending a period when they used name producers and tried for a more commercial sound. With *Book of Days*, drummer Vince Ely rejoined for the first time since 1982, and the band returned to the sound of their first two albums (minus the saxophone), with songs in an uncompromising, droning style. Unfortunately, the result was uneven, with only "House" ranking among their better rockers, and those who had been attracted by their more accessible material didn't warm to the album, which started the group down the slippery slope of commercial decline. —*William Ruhlmann*

World Outside / Jul. 30, 1991 / Columbia ✦✦✦
Working with producer Stephen Street, the Psychedelic Furs made an album that echoed some of their best work. "In My Head" and "Better Days" had the pop propulsion of earlier songs like "Love My Way," while "Until She Comes," a college radio hit, showed a winning vulnerability to singer Richard Butler that hadn't been apparent previously. Other songs found the group branching out, especially in terms of more elaborate percussion. Unfortunately, their return to form came too late in their career: the album failed to chart, and the Furs broke up. —*William Ruhlmann*

B-Sides & Lost Grooves / Oct. 25, 1994 / Columbia/Legacy ✦✦✦
As the title suggests, *B-Sides & Lost Grooves* is a collection of Psychedelic Furs obscurities culled from throughout their career. Predictably, some of the tracks fall flat, but the great majority of the album is engaging, make the record a worthwhile complement to the group's first four albums. —*Stephen Thomas Erlewine*

Public Enemy

f. 1982, Long Island, NY
Hip Hop, East Coast Rap, Hardcore Rap
Public Enemy rewrote the rules of hip-hop, becoming the most influential and controversial rap group of the late '80s and, for many, the definitive rap group of all time. Building from Run-D.M.C.'s street-oriented beats and Boogie Down Productions' proto-gangsta rhyming, Public Enemy pioneered a variation of hardcore rap that was musically and politically revolutionary. With their powerful, authoritative baritone, lead rapper Chuck D rhymed about all kinds of social problems, particularly those plaguing the Black community, often condoning revolutionary tactics and social activism. In the process, he directed hip-hop toward an explicitly self-aware, pro-Black consciousness that became the culture's signature throughout the next decade. Musically, Public Enemy was just as revolutionary, as their production team, the Bomb Squad, created

dense soundscapes that relied on avant-garde cut-and-paste techniques, unrecognizable samples, piercing sirens, relentless beats, and deep funk. It was chaotic and invigorating music, made all the more intoxicating by Chuck D's forceful vocals and the absurdist raps of his comic foil Flavor Flav. With his comic sunglasses and an oversized clock hanging from his neck, Flav became the group's visual focal point, but he never obscured the music. While rap and rock critics embraced the group's late '80s and early '90s records, Public Enemy frequently ran into controversy with their militant stance and lyrics, especially after their 1988 album *It Takes a Nation of Millions to Hold Us Back* made them into celebrities. After all the controversy settled in the early '90s, once the group entered hiatus, it became clear that Public Enemy was the most influential and radical band of its time.

Chuck D (born Carlton Ridenhour, August 1, 1960) formed Public Enemy in 1982, while he was studying graphic design at Adelphi University on Long Island. He had been DJing at the student radio station WBAU, where he met Hank Shocklee and Bill Stepheny. All three shared a love of hip-hop and politics, which made them close friends. Shocklee had been assembling hip-hop demo tapes, and Ridenhour rapped over one song, "Public Enemy No. 1" around the same time he began appearing on Stepheny's radio show under the Chuckie D pseudonym. Def Jam cofounder and producer Rick Rubin heard a tape of "Public Enemy No. 1," and he immediately courted Ridenhour in hopes of signing him to his fledgling label. Chuck D initially was reluctant, but he eventually developed a concept of a literally revolutionary hip-hop group—one that would be driven by sonically extreme productions and socially revolutionary politics. Enlisting Shocklee as his chief producer and Stepheny as a publicist, Chuck D formed a crew with DJ Terminator X (born Norman Lee Rogers, August 25, 1966) and fellow Nation of Islam member Professor Griff (born Richard Griff) as the choreographer of the group's backup dancers, the Security of the First World, who performed homages to old Stax and Motown dancers with their martial moves and fake Uzis. He also asked his old friend William Drayton (born March 16, 1959) to join as a fellow rapper. Drayton developed an alter ego called Flavor Flav, who functioned as a court jester to Chuck D's booming voice and somber rhymes in Public Enemy.

Public Enemy's debut album, *Yo! Bum Rush the Show*, was released on Def Jam Records in 1987. Its spare beats and powerful rhetoric was acclaimed by hip-hop critics and aficionados, but the record was ignored by the rock and R&B mainstream. However, their second album *It Takes a Nation of Millions to Hold Us Back* was impossible to ignore. Under Schocklee's direction, PE's production team, the Bomb Squad, had developed a dense, chaotic mix that relied as much on found sounds and avant-garde noise as it did on old school funk. Similarly, Chuck D's rhetoric had gained focus, and Flavor Flav's raps were wilder and funnier. *A Nation of Millions* was hailed as revolutionary by both rap and rock critics, and it was—hip-hop had suddenly became a force for social change. As Public Enemy's profile was raised, they opened themselves up to controversy. In a notorious statement, Chuck D claimed that rap was "the Black CNN," relating what was happening in the inner city in a way that mainstream media could not project. Public Enemy's lyrics were naturally dissected in the wake of such a statement, and many critics were uncomfortable with the positive endorsement of Black Muslim leader Louis Farrakhan on "Bring the Noise." "Fight the Power," Public Enemy's theme for Spike Lee's controversial 1989 film, *Do the Right Thing*, also caused an uproar for its attacks on Elvis Presley and John Wayne, but that was considerably overshadowed by an interview Professor Griff gave the *Washington Times* that summer. Griff had previously said anti-Semitic remarks on stage, but his quotation that Jews were responsible for "the majority of the wickedness that goes on across the globe" was greeted with shock and outrage, especially by white critics who had previously embraced the group. Faced with a major crisis, Chuck D faltered. At first he fired Griff, then he brought him back to the group, and then he broke up the group. Griff gave one more interview where he attacked Chuck D and PE, which led to his permanent departure from the group.

Public Enemy spent the remainder of 1989 preparing their third album, releasing "Welcome to the Terrordome" as its first single in early 1990. Again, the hit single caused controversy; its lyrics "still they set me like Jesus" were labeled anti-Semitic by some quarters. Despite all the controversy, *Fear of a Black Planet* was released to enthusiastic reviews in the spring of 1990, and it shot into the pop Top Ten as the singles "911 Is a Joke," "Brothers Gonna Work It Out," and "Can't Do Nuttin' for Ya Man" became Top 40 R&B hits. For their next album, 1991's *Apocalypse 91... The Enemy Strikes Black*, the group re-recorded "Bring the Noize" with thrash metal band Anthrax, which was the first sign that the group was trying to consolidate its white audience. *Apocalypse 91* was greeted with overwhelmingly positive reviews upon its fall release, and it debuted at No. 4 on the pop charts, but the band began to lose momentum in 1992, as they toured with the second leg of U2's Zoo TV tour, and Flavor Flav was repeatedly in trouble with the law. In the fall of 1992, they released the remix collection *Greatest Misses* as an attempt to keep their name viable, but it was greeted with nasty reviews.

Public Enemy was on hiatus during 1993, as Flav attempted to wean himself of drugs, returning in the summer of 1994 with *Muse Sick-N-Hour Mess Age.* Prior to its release, it was subjected to exceedingly negative reviews in *Rolling Stone* and *The Source,* which affected the perception of the album considerably. *Muse Sick* debuted at No. 14, but it quickly fell off the charts because it failed to generate any singles. Chuck D retired Public Enemy from touring in 1995 as he severed ties with Def Jam, developed his own record label and publishing company, and attempted to rethink Public Enemy. In 1996, he released his debut album, *The Autobiography of Mista Chuck.* As it was released in the fall, he announced that he planned to record a new Public Enemy album the following year. —*Stephen Thomas Erlrewine*

Yo! Bum Rush the Show / 1987 / Def Jam ✦✦✦✦
When their debut was released in 1987, very few rap groups even approached Public Enemy's musical or political stance. Listening to the first album now, it's surprising how few of the songs are actually political—the sheer force of the sound fools the listener into thinking Chuck D is saying more than he actually is. Still, "Megablast," "Public Enemy No. 1," and "Miuzi Weighs a Ton" carry a small amount of political rhetoric. Much sparer than later releases, the album is carried over the top by Chuck D's bulldozer roar. —*Stephen Thomas Erlewine*

★ **It Takes a Nation of Millions to Hold Us Back** / 1988 / Def Jam ✦✦✦✦
Arguably the best hip-hop album ever made, *It Takes a Nation of Millions to Hold Us Back* was a huge leap forward not only for Public Enemy, but for all of hip-hop. PE's signature sound—a barrage of found sounds, densely woven samples, and noisy tape loops—was evident for the first time, courtesy of the Bomb Squad. Chuck D's lyrics, full of revolutionary rhetoric yet managing to avoid being hysterical, matched the aural onslaught. The group's political stance would be meaningless if the music didn't put it over the top throughout, and that does happen on "Black Steel in the Hour of Chaos," "Night of the Living Baseheads," "Rebel Without a Pause," "Don't Believe the Hype," and "Bring the Noise," in particular. There isn't a weak moment on the album. A landmark recording. —*Stephen Thomas Erlewine*

☆ **Fear of a Black Planet** / 1990 / Def Jam ✦✦✦✦✦
Public Enemy's artistic and commercial winning streak continued with its third album, *Fear of a Black Planet.* While other East Coast rappers were content to boast and boast about their prowess on the microphone, Public Enemy always had a lot to say. Though a few stinkers are included—the worst offender being the homophobic "Meet the G That Killed Me"—they are by far outnumbered by the gems. From "Burn Hollywood Burn" (a brutally honest attack on racism in the film industry) to the optimistic "Brothers Gonna Work It Out," the politically charged rappers have no problem maintaining the level of excellence they reached on *It Takes a Nation of Millions to Hold Us Back.* A gut-level attack on incompetence in the 911 system, "911 Is a Joke" illustrates just how on-target PE could be—in fact, it should be stressed that the song precedes by several years the incident in which 911 operators in Philadelphia came under attack for doing nothing to help a youth who was being beaten to death. And once again, PE's producers, the Bomb Squad, provide a collage of samples that is as imaginative as it is bombastic. —*Alex Henderson*

☆ **Apocalypse 91 . . . The Enemy Strikes Black** / Oct. 1, 1991 / Def Jam ✦✦✦✦✦
Although it falls short of the excellence of *Fear of a Black Planet* and *It Takes a Nation of Millions to Hold Us Back,* PE's fourth album proved that the Long Islanders could still be extremely stimulating—both lyrically and musically. This time, the obvious winners include "Shut Em Down" (a commentary on liquor stores profiting from human suffering in the Black commmunity), "By the Time I Get to Arizona" (an angry reflection on that state's refusal to celebrate Martin Luther King's birthday in the early '90s), and an invigorating rap-metal remake of "Bring the Noize" featuring thrash headbangers Anthrax. Although produced by the Imperial Grand Ministers of Funk instead of the Bomb Squad, the album boasts exactly the type of production one associates with PE—abrasive, hard, and dissonant. Unfortunately, PE's popularity would decline considerably after the album—and considerably less-talented N.W.A. clones would be selling a lot more albums. —*Alex Henderson*

Greatest Misses / Sep. 15, 1992 / Def Jam ✦✦
For the first time in their career, Public Enemy sounds unsure of the direction of their music. *Greatest Misses* is half original tracks and half remixes and consequently sounds muddled. Public Enemy sounds like it's treading water throughout the new songs; none of them are particularly bad, but unlike all of their previous material, none of it is groundbreaking. None of the remixes are awful, but they are neither revelatory nor insightful and often miss the original intent of the song. —*Stephen Thomas Erlewine*

Muse Sick-N-Hour Mess Age / Aug. 23, 1994 / Def Jam ✦✦
Public Enemy took a full three years between *Apocalypse 91* and *Muse Sick-N-Hour Mess-Age.* During that time, numerous hip-hop styles had come and gone, making Public Enemy seem hopelessly outdated by the time they actually released their fifth record. With the exception of the *Greatest Misses* compilation, *Muse Sick* didn't fare as well on the charts as the group's three previous albums, nor was it well received critically, receiving the poorest reviews of any of the group's efforts. And, again discounting *Greatest Misses, Muse Sick* is PE's weakest album. Conceptually, it's all over the place, as Chuck D strikes out at a number of his usual targets but without the focused, intelligent rage of *Nation of Millions* or *Fear of a Black Planet.* Similarly, the music careens out of control, as they try to incorporate recent hip-hop innovations to their signature sound. Nothing on the record sounds forced, but the album does sound directionless, which tends to cancel out the number of solid tracks on the album. Public Enemy doesn't necessarily seem outdated or musically bankrupt on *Muse Sick-N-Hour Mess-Age*—they just appear unsure of themselves. —*Stephen Thomas Erlewine*

Public Image Limited (PiL)

f. 1978, London, England, **db.** 1993
Alternative Pop-Rock, Experimental, Post-Punk
Public Image Ltd. (PiL) originally was a quartet led by singer John Lydon (formerly Johnny Rotten b. Jan. 31, 1956) and guitarist Keith Levene, who had been a member of the Clash in one of its early lineups. The band was filled out by bassist Jah Wobble (John Wordle) and drummer Jim Walker. It was formed in the wake of the 1978 breakup of Lydon's former group, the Sex Pistols. For the most part, it devoted itself to droning, slow-tempo, bass-heavy noise rock, overlaid by Lydon's distinctive, vituperative rant.

The group's debut single, "Public Image," was more of an uptempo pop-rock song, however, and it hit the UK Top Ten upon its release in October 1978. The group itself debuted on Christmas Day, shortly after the release of its first album, *Public Image.* Neither the single nor the album was released in the US.

Metal Box, the band's second UK album, came in the form of three 12-inch, 45-RPM discs in a film cannister. It was released in the US in 1980 as the double album *Second Edition.* (By this time, PiL was a trio consisting of Lydon, Levene, and Wobble.) The third album, not released in the US, was the live *Paris in the Spring* (1980). Lydon and Levene, plus hired musicians, made up the group by the time of *The Flowers of Romance* (1981), the much acclaimed fourth album, which reached No. 11 in the UK.

In 1983, PiL scored its biggest UK hit, when "This Is Not a Love Song" reached No. 5. By this time, however, Levene had left, and the name from here on would simply be a vehicle for John Lydon. A second live album, *Live in Tokyo,* appeared in England in 1983.

1984 saw the release of *This Is What You Want . . . This Is What You Get,* only PiL's third album to be released in the US, though it now had six albums out. It marked the start of Lydon's move toward a more accessible dance-rock style, a direction that would be pursued further in *Album* (1986) (also called *Cassette* or *Compact Disc,* depending on the format), notably on the hit "Rise," as well as on *Happy?* (1987) and *9* (1989). In 1990, PiL released the compilation album *The Greatest Hits, So Far,* and in 1991 came the new album, *That What Is Not.*

After completing his memoirs in late 1993, Lydon decided to put an end to PiL and pursue a solo career. —*William Ruhlmann*

Public Image Ltd / Dec. 1978 / Warner Brothers ✦✦✦
Public Image Ltd. finds the group trying to develop a musical identity, creating an album that falls halfway between defiant rock 'n' roll and self-consciously experimental musical explorations. Although the driving "Public Image" is the best moment on the record, the rest of the album is intriguing, if flawed. —*Stephen Thomas Erlewine*

Second Edition / Jul. 1980 / Warner Brothers ✦✦✦✦
A two-disc deconstruction of traditional rock music, its tempos steady but slow, its bass track mixed high as in a reggae dub album, and Lydon's droning voice, with its scornful lyrics, wafting in the back. It is what PiL called it at the time, "anti-rock 'n' roll," and it's fascinating. —*William Ruhlmann*

Flowers of Romance / 1981 / Warner Brothers ✦✦✦
The drums are loud and sharp, and Lydon wails like some sort of Middle Eastern street singer on this forbidding but rewarding album. —*William Ruhlmann*

This Is What You Want . . . This Is What You Get / 1984 / Virgin ✦✦✦✦
Lydon adds keyboards, horns, and even a violin, double-tracks his vocals, and writes shorter songs with faster tempos. *This Is What You Want . . . This Is What You Get* doesn't quite add up to a pop album, but you can dance to it. Contains the UK hit "This Is Not a Love Song." —*William Ruhlmann*

Album/Compact Disc/Cassette / 1986 / Elektra ✦✦✦✦
Hot guitars and 4/4 time signatures make this sound more like a hard-rock album than anything Lydon's done since the Sex Pistols. And the hit single "Rise" is actually a catchy number, believe it or not. — *William Ruhlmann*

Happy? / 1987 / Virgin ✦✦✦✦
Continuing with the deceptively pop-oriented studio sheen of *Album, Happy?* is a set of outwardly friendly material, which reveals its fractured melodies and concepts upon closer inspection. Song for song, *Happy?* isn't quite as strong as *Album*, but it continues its predecessor's sound to a fine effect. — *Stephen Thomas Erlewine*

9 / 1989 / Virgin ✦✦✦
Not only does *9* expand on the pop leanings of the two previous PiL albums, it adds elements of dance music and funk. At first, the record might seem a bit too slick, but it reveals more subtexts with each listen, although the music isn't quite as involving as the songs on *Album* and *Happy?*. — *Stephen Thomas Erlewine*

● **The Greatest Hits So Far** / 1990 / Virgin ✦✦✦✦
Fourteen tracks, recorded between 1978 and 1990, that trace PiL from the punk energy of the first single, "Public Image" (not previously released in the US), through the anti-rock of "Death Disco" and "Flowers of Romance" to the almost pop of "This Is Not a Love Song" and "Rise" and the best of the late-'80s material. — *William Ruhlmann*

That What Is Not / 1992 / Virgin ✦✦
Former Sex Pistol vocalist John Lydon has once again unleashed his Public Image Ltd. project, this time with a more basic, unrelenting rock 'n' roll attack than ever before. The audio assault of guitarist John McGeoch and bassist Allan Dias perfectly complements Lydon's frenzied, strangled bleating throughout. As usual, Lydon succeeds in being all of satirical and fatalistic, confrontational and self-deprecating. The album's opening words set the tone: "What does it mean, What does anything mean." It's spat out as a statement rather than a question. "Covered" unpredictably tosses sampled vocals, bluesy harmonica, and the Tower of Power horns into the mix. *That What Is Not* can be a difficult PiL to swallow, but the heady side-effects make the effort worthwhile. — *Roch Parisien*

Pulp

f. 1978, Sheffield, England
Alternative Pop-Rock, Brit-Pop, Post-Punk
Most bands hit the big time immediately and fade away, or they build a dedicated following and slowly climb their way to the top. Pulp didn't follow either route. For the first 12 years of their existence, Pulp languished in near total obscurity, releasing a handful of albums and singles in the '80s to barely any attention. At the turn of the decade, the group began to gain an audience, sparking a remarkable turn of events that made the band one of the most popular British groups of the '90s. By the time Pulp became famous, the band had gone through numerous different incarnations and changes in style, covering nearly every indie-rock touchstone from post-punk to dance. Pulp's signature sound is a fusion of David Bowie and Roxy Music's glam rock, disco, new wave, acid-house, Euro-pop, and British indie-rock. The group's cheap synthesizers and sweeping melodies reflect the lyrical obsessions of lead vocalist Jarvis Cocker, who alternates between sex and sharp, funny portraits of working-class misfits. Out of second-hand pop, Pulp fashioned a distinctive, stylish sound that made camp into something grand and glamourous that retained a palpable sense of gritty reality.

Jarvis Cocker formed Pulp in 1978, when he was 15 years old. Originally called Arabicus Pulp, the first lineup consisted of schoolmates of Cocker. After a year, the band's name was truncated to Pulp. While they were in school, Pulp performed a handful of gigs. The band recorded a demo sometime in 1980-81, giving the tape to John Peel at one of his traveling shows. Peel liked the tape and invited the band to appear on his show. Pulp had their first Peel session in November 1981. Instead of leading to record deals and pop stardom, Pulp's appearance on Peel led nowhere. Discouraged by the band's lack of success, every member but Cocker left the band in 1982 to go to university. The following year, Cocker assembled a new lineup that featured eight members, including keyboardist Simon Hinkler, who would later join the Mission. In this incarnation, Pulp had distinct folk overtones, as well as new wave underpinnings. The group landed their first record contract, releasing their debut album, *It*, in 1984. *It* didn't make much of an impact and the band fell apart again. After the second incarnation of Pulp disintegrated, Jarvis Cocker formed another version of the band, with guitarist-violinist Russell Senior, who became Cocker's first full-fledged collaborator. Cocker and Senior added drummer Magnus Doyle and bassist Peter Mansell to the group, as well as Tim Allcard, who did nothing but read poetry. Musically, Pulp backed away from the folky inclinations of *It*, adding keyboardist Candida Doyle in 1985, which led to a darker sound; shortly after her arrival, Allcard left the group. In 1985, Pulp released a series of singles on Fire Records. Just as their fortunes were looking up,

Jarvis was severely injured. As he was trying to impress a girl, he fell 30 feet out of a window, injuring his pelvis, foot, and wrist. For two months, he was confined to a wheelchair, but he performed concerts anyway.

Released in 1986, Pulp's second album *Freaks* was a dense, dark affair. Following its release, the band split during the filming of the video for "They Suffocate at Night." All of the members except Cocker and Senior left the group. For a year, the band was dormant, but Candida Doyle returned in 1987, with drummer Nick Banks and bassist Steven Havenhand joining shortly afterward. Havenhand was soon replaced by Anthony Genn, who was soon replaced by Steve Mackey. Although the group had a stable lineup, they weren't gaining much of a following. In 1988, Cocker moved to London with Mackey and began studying filmmaking at St. Martin's College. While he was studying, Pulp was offered the chance to record another album. The resulting album, *Separations*, was recorded in 1989 and reflected Cocker's newfound obsession with acid house, but it also boasted some full-fledged pop songs. *Separations* was released nearly three years after it was completed. Cocker was prepared to stake out a career in film when a single from the album, "My Legendary Girlfriend," was released. *NME* named the song Single of the Week in 1991, and Pulp's career suddenly took off.

In early 1992, Pulp left Fire Records for Gift and began releasing a series of singles that consolidated the success of "My Legendary Girlfriend." In particular, "Babies" earned the band a great deal of attention. "Babies" led to a contract with Island Records, their first major-label deal. Island released *PulpIntro*, a compilation of the Gift singles, as the band recorded its major-label debut, *His 'n' Hers*. Upon its spring 1994 release, *His 'n' Hers* earned positive reviews and became an unexpected success, reaching the British Top Ten; it was also nominated for the 1994 Mercury Award. For the rest of 1994 and the early part of 1995, Jarvis Cocker suddenly became omnipresent on British television. These suave, humourous television appearances became legendary, making Jarvis somewhat of a national hero, as well as a sex symbol.

No matter how popular Jarvis Cocker had become, the band didn't break into the big time until they released "Common People." The single became a massive hit upon its May 1995 debuting at No. 2 on the UK charts. In July, Pulp accepted a last-minute headlining slot at the Glastonbury festival when the Stone Roses had to cancel. Pulp's set was rapturously received, launching the band into superstar status in England and conveniently setting the stage for their forthcoming album, *Different Class*. During the recording of the album, guitarist Mark Webber—the president of Pulp's fan club—became a full-time member of the group. The first record to feature Webber was the double A-sided single, "Mis-shapes" and "Sorted for E's and Wizz," which was released in August, two months before *Different Class*. The single became a No. 2 hit, despite a major tabloid controversy over the lyrics to "Sorted."

Different Class arrived in late October to rave reviews throughout the British press. The album entered the charts at No. 1, going gold within its first week and platinum within the second. At the end of the year, the album topped many best-of-the-year lists. In February of 1996, *Different Class* was released in the United States to positive reviews. — *Stephen Thomas Erlewine*

It / 1983 / Red Rhino ✦✦
It is a gentle, mainly acoustic album that gives very few signs to the musical directions Pulp would later pursue. Lacking any hint of synthesizers or dance music, the album occasionally touches on the majestic, theatrical ballads of Scott Walker, as well as the stark, folky song poems of Leonard Cohen. However, at this stage, Jarvis Cocker is hardly the lyricist of either songwriter, and his singing is endearingly awkward—occasionally he misses notes, and he misses the tune every once in a while. Nevertheless, there are tunes throughout the album, whether it's the light opening single "My Lighthouse" or the silly, music hall stomp of "Love Love." *It* isn't a great album, but it has an effortless, amateurish charm that makes up for the unformed songs and the band's rudimentary musical skills. — *Stephen Thomas Erlewine*

Freaks / 1986 / Fire ✦✦
Freaks is so different than *It* that it nearly sounds like a different band. Granted, that is largely due to the fact that Pulp *was* a different band, apart from lead vocalist Jarvis Cocker. After the unsuccessful showing of *It*, the band broke up, leaving Cocker to assemble a new lineup. The most significant new member was Russell Senior, who brought a fascination with art, noise, and neo-gothic overtones to the band. But that change in sound isn't the only reason why *Freaks* is the darkest record Pulp ever made, or ever will make. Cocker's lyrics are neurotically gloomy and paranoid, obsessed with failures and outcasts. While this would become a signature theme for Pulp's songs, Cocker's outlook on *Freaks* is oppresively bleak—he finds no future for the mis-shapes and misfits in his songs. Not only are the songs hopeless, so is the production. The very sound of *Freaks* is muddy and impenetrable, making it difficult to find the occasional rewarding moment on the album, such as "Master of the Universe," "They Suffocate at Night," or Senior's "Anorexic Beauty." — *Stephen Thomas Erlewine*

Separations / 1992 / Razor & Tie ✦✦✦
Separations is the birth of the modern Pulp. Not only does the record feature the lineup that would eventually break through into the mainstream, it is the first album to contain the fusion of pop, dance, and rock that would take them to the top of the charts in the mid-'90s. More than anything, the influence of acid house and raves weighs heavily on *Separations*, as the band stretches out into the disco groove of "Countdown" and the long jam "This House Is Condemned." But what is especially noticeable about *Separations* is how Pulp is finally starting to write some fully realized songs. "My Legendary Girlfriend," the song that earned them their first Single of the Week in *NME*, is the leader of the pack with a brilliant, sly lyric and vocal from Cocker and an appropriately melodic and slightly dirty instrumental backdrop from the group. "Countdown," with its insistent beat, is nearly as good, as is the loping opener "Love Is Blind." Pulp isn't able to keep the pace throughout the album—there are several weak spots, particularly the awkward stab at house, "This House Is Condemned"—but *Separations* is the first album that illustrates their potential and exactly what the band could accomplish. —*Stephen Thomas Erlewine*

Pulpintro—The Gift Recordings / 1993 / Island ✦✦✦✦
All of the singles Pulp recorded for Gift Records, including both the A and B-sides, are collected on *PulpIntro—The Gift Recordings*. From the opening track, "Space," it's clear that Pulp's confidence and talents have grown considerably, even from the relatively accomplished *Separations*. Now, the band has created a signature sound that relies heavily on cheap, synthesized sounds as well as tight pop melodies and a theatrical attack that approximates the art-rock of Roxy Music and David Bowie. However, Pulp is too concerned with earthly pleasures to really recall Roxy or Bowie. Furthermore, the band's knack for creating terrific pop singles prevents them from being too pretentious, as the singles "O.U.," "Razzamatazz," and, particularly, "Babies," illustrates. And even though it's just a collection of singles, *PulpIntro* holds together as well as *Separations*, if not better. —*Stephen Thomas Erlewine*

Masters of the Universe / 1994 / Fire ✦✦
Masters of the Universe is a collection of singles that Pulp recorded for Fire Records in the mid-'80s, around the time of the *Freaks* album. During this time, the band was steeped in the morose obsessions of goth rock, like most of their British indie contemporaries, layering their music with droning synths and dissonant guitars. The group also had a noticeably arty attack—witness the performance art schlock of Russell Senior's rant "The Will to Power." While that preoccupation with goth and self-conscious art decreases the effectiveness of the music, *Masters of the Universe* does contain Pulp's first great leaps forward, "Little Girl (with Blue Eyes)" and "Dogs Are Everywhere," which demonstrate Jarvis Cocker's burgeoning lyrical skills and the band's increasing ability to paint evocative soundscapes. ("Silence" was the only non-album song of the era that wasn't included on the compilation.) —*Stephen Thomas Erlewine*

His 'n' Hers / Jun. 21, 1994 / Island ✦✦✦✦
Jarvis Cocker's update on Bryan Ferry's lounge lizard persona works because he recognizes the sleaziness beneath the style. Instead of chronicling the lives and times of jet-setting club hoppers, Cocker sneaks into the closet of his girlfriend to watch her sister have sex, reveals a fetish for pink gloves among other things, and remembers the first time. Pulp's fake, synthetic backdrop sounds like it was constructed on bargain Casio keyboards, adding an extra layer of seaminess to Cocker's songs. That sense of cheap, faux-glamour is essential to the success of *His 'n' Hers*, Pulp's commerical and artistic breakthrough. It's the sound of a poor man giving up everything he has so he can act out his expensive, elegant fantasies. He may never get there, but the approximation of glamour is more appealing and compelling than the reality, which is what gives *His 'n' Hers* a grand tragic romanticism. —*Stephen Thomas Erlewine*

● **Different Class** / Oct. 30, 1995 / Island ✦✦✦✦
After years of obscurity, Pulp shot to stardom in Britain with 1994's *His 'n' Hers*. By the time *Different Class* was released at the end of October 1995, the band, particularly lead singer Jarvis Cocker, were genuine British superstars, with two No. 2 singles and a triumphant last-minute performance at Glastonbury under their belts, as well as one tabloid scandal. On the heels of such excitement, anticipation for *Different Class* ran high, and not only does it deliver, it blows away all their previous albums, including the fine *His 'n' Hers*. Pulp doesn't stray from their signature formula at all—it's still grandly theatrical, synth-spiked pop with new wave and disco flourishes. Not only are the melodies and hooks significantly catchier and more immediate, the music explores more territory. From the faux-showtune romp of the anthemic opener "Mis-Shapes" and the glitzy, gaudy stomp of "Disco 2000" (complete with a nicked riff from Laura Branigan's "Gloria") to the aching ballad "Underwear" and the startling, sexual menace of "I Spy," Pulp construct a diverse, appealing album around the same basic sound. Similarly, Jarvis Cocker's lyrics take two themes, sex and social

class, and explore a number of different avenues in bitingly clever ways. As well as perfectly capturing the behavior of his characters, Cocker grasps the nuances of language, creating a dense portrait of suburban and working-class life. All of his sex songs are compassionate, while the subtle satire of "Sorted for E's & Wizz" is affectionate, but the best moment on the album is the hit single "Common People," about a rich girl who gets off by slumming with the lower class. Coming from Cocker, who made secondhand clothes and music glamourous, the song is undeniably affecting and exciting, much like *Different Class* itself. —*Stephen Thomas Erlewine*

Second Class / 1996 / Island ✦✦✦
Island repackaged Pulp's breakthrough album *Different Class* with a limited-edition bonus disc of B-sides titled *Second Class* in 1996. Although the compilation is haphazard—it leaves off the wonderful, Latin-tinged "His 'n' Hers," which is a stronger song than several that are included here, as well as the intriguing single mix of "Disco 2000"—it is extremely useful, since it collects the bulk of their best B-sides from *His 'n' Hers* and *Different Class*. The jaunty "Mile End," which was featured in *Trainspotting*, is a terrifically humorous slice of dead-end urban life that's disarmingly reminiscent of early Cure, while "Ansaphone" is an affecting theatrical ballad and "P.T.A. (Parent Teacher Association)" is a tongue-in-cheek portrait of perversion. The B-sides that are culled from *His 'n' Hers* are a little uneven, but "Your Sister's Clothes" is scarily sexy, and "Deep Fried in Kelvin" and "Street Lites" are two epic synth-pop numbers any Pulp devotee should hear. —*Stephen Thomas Erlewine*

Countdown [compilation] / Mar. 1996 / Nectar Masters/Fire ✦✦✦✦
A double-disc collection released to cash in on Pulp's massive success with *Different Class*, *Countdown* might be a rip-off compilation, but it does offer an effective introduction to Pulp's '80s catalog. Since their recordings on Fire were decidedly uneven, *Countdown* does distill all the highlights a casual fan could want to hear. Beginning with the latest track, the 1990 single "Countdown," and working its way backwards, the compilation's sequencing eases newer fans into both the band's more experimental and folkier work. Even though all of Pulp's best material from this era is included, they lacked the pop sense that they developed in the early '90s, which could make this rough sailing for some recent fans. For those that want to dig deeper, there is plenty of fascinating material here. —*Stephen Thomas Erlewine*

Pure Prairie League

f. 1971, Cincinnati, OH, **db.** 1983
Country-Rock
For a short time, Pure Prairie League was one of America's best country-rock bands, but personnel shifts ultimately destroyed its early promise. The group was formed in 1971 by vocalists-guitarists Craig Lee Fuller (the band's main songwriter) and George Powell, steel guitarist John Call, bassist Jim Lanham, and drummer Jim Caughlin, and they recorded their self-titled debut album just a year later. Its fusion of laid-back singer-songwriter-styled rock and country earned critical praise, but much of the group departed, leaving only Fuller, Powell, and several session musicians. Even so, *Bustin' Out* proved to be an unqualified success, featuring the innovative addition of string arrangements by David Bowie guitarist Mick Ronson. Unfortunately, Fuller left in 1975, leaving the group without a strong songwriter or leader. Powell carried on with guitarist Larry Goshorn, bassist Mike Reilly, and pianist Michael Connor for several albums, none of which were as commercially or artistically successful as *Bustin' Out*. The group did enjoy a brief resurgence in 1980 with the Top Ten single "Let Me Love You Tonight," featuring future country star Vince Gill on lead vocals but finally called it quits in 1983. Fuller has since joined Little Feat. —*Steve Huey*

Let Me Love You Tonight & Other Hits / 1971 / Polygram ✦✦✦

● **Bustin' Out** / 1972 / RCA ✦✦✦✦
Bustin' Out was this band's most distinctive album, featuring very bright, thin-sounding acoustic guitars and dramatic string arrangements, courtesy of David Bowie's lead player Mick Ronson. "Amie" became a standard of sorts for the college coffeehouse crowd. Other highlights include "Jazzman," "Early Morning Riser," "Boulder Skies," "Call Me Tell Me," and "Angel," a song originally recorded on J.D. Blackfoot's *The Ultimate Prophecy*. —*Rick Clark*

Pure Prairie League / 1972 / RCA ✦✦✦✦
For all those who think the Eagles are the be all and end all of country-rock, you owe it to yourself to search out this album. Any track here (or on the follow-up, *Bustin' Out*) holds up as well, if not better than, anything by the Eagles. This album also proves that Craig Fuller is a grossly underrated songwriter. A country-rock must! —*Jim Worbois*

Two Lane Highway / 1975 / RCA ✦✦✦
With the departure of Fuller, the face (and sound) of Prairie League changed considerably. Larry Goshorn (ex-Sacred Mushroom) has replaced Fuller as the main songwriter in the band. And, while the overall album isn't up to its predecessors, there are still some nice moments

including the title track, "Runner," and a humorous tribute to country music legend Merle Haggard. —*Jim Worbois*

If the Shoe Fits / 1976 / RCA ✦✦✦
PPL continues in the same vein as the last LP with only a couple of George Powell tunes bearing any resemblance to the sound of the first two records. Not a bad record, but it's becoming harder to find any traces of what made this band so special. —*Jim Worbois*

Dance / 1976 / RCA ✦✦
It's getting more difficult to find positive things to say about the band's records by this time. Aside from some fine playing by Andy Stein (ex-Lost Planet Airman), JD Call's superb pedal steel work, and the track "All the Way," there isn't much to recommend this album. —*Jim Worbois*

Live Takin' the Stage / 1977 / RCA ✦✦
Live, PPL fairly accurately re-created their studio sound. Which makes one wonder, why buy this record if you have all the previous albums? The band doesn't seem to feel they have anything to prove, so they walk through these tracks adding nothing. If you already like these songs, stick with the studio versions since nothing is added on this one. —*Jim Worbois*

Just Fly / 1978 / RCA ✦✦

Can't Hold Back / 1979 / RCA ✦✦
Another shake-up finds Goshorn and longtime steel player, JD Call gone. Goshorn has been replaced by future modern-country star, Vince Gill, as both main writer and leader of the group. By this time, they are PPL in name only as there is no resemblance between this and the original band. In fact, if you play "Rude Rude Awakening" next to the Eagles' "One of These Nights," it would be difficult to distinguish between the two bands. —*Jim Worbois*

Firin' Up / 1980 / Casablanca ✦
This last-gasp effort provided the band with their highest charting single, "Let Me Love You Tonight." By now, the band's sound was nearly indistinguishable from Firefall and many other bands of the period. A sad end to a band that had begun with such promise. Single aside, there is no reason to look for this album. —*Jim Worbois*

Amie & Other Hits / 1981 / RCA ✦✦✦
This best-of collection contains all the hits and most of the essential album cuts, including a healthy sampling from *Bustin' Out*. —*Rick Clark*

Home on the Range / 1983 / Pair ✦✦

Mementos 1971-1987 / 1987 / Rushmore ✦✦✦

● **Best of Pure Prairie League** / Aug. 8, 1995 / Mercury Nashville ✦✦✦✦
Containing most of their hits and key album tracks, *Best of Pure Prairie League* provides an effective introduction to the country-rock group. —*Sara Sytsma*

James and Bobby Purify

f. May 12, 1944, Pensacola, FL
Soul
James (b. May 12, 1944) and Bobby (b. Sep. 2, 1939) of this Southern soul duo were not actually brothers but cousins. James Purify and Robert Lee Dickey joined forces for some classic Southern soul duets during the mid-'60s. Producer Papa Don Schroeder brought the soulful Floridians to Muscle Shoals in 1966 to record at Rick Hall's Fame studios, and the result was the gorgeous mid-tempo "I'm Your Puppet." The Dan Penn-Spooner Oldham ballad proved their biggest hit for the Bell label, although "Let Love Come Between Us" and their revival of the Five Dutones' "Shake a Tail Feather" also made some major noise in 1967. When Bobby mutinied, James went it alone for a while before recruiting a new Bobby (Ben Moore), and they picked up right where the old duo left off. —*Bill Dahl*

● **Best of James Purify** / 1985 / Arista ✦✦✦✦
The Purify cousins made decent, occasionally excellent, confessional soul tunes for Bell from 1966 to 1968, the best of them being "I'm Your Puppet," "Shake a Tail Feather," and "Let Love Come Between Us." While some compared them to Sam & Dave, they were actually more like Mel & Tim, since they didn't have songs anywhere as transcendent as those Isaac Hayes and David Porter were giving Sam & Dave. —*Ron Wynn*

Pussy Galore

f. 1985, Washington, D.C., db. 1990
Alternative Pop-Rock, Indie Rock
You either loved them or loathed them (some did both), but it was difficult to ignore the bawling, intentionally crude, anti-musicianship coughed up by Pussy Galore. A bunch of scuzzy-looking juveniles from Washington, DC—their name coming from Honor Blackman's character in the James Bond film *Goldfinger*—and led by a young punk-rockin', bohemian, hipster wannabe named Jon Spencer, Pussy Galore created an unholy metallic ruckus that was part serious avant-garde noise wail,

part bullshit pose. Considering their limited skills, narcissistic tendencies, and drug-cult mythologizing, there is a sizable body of work from this band. The problem is that it's mostly hit-and-miss, which is a polite way of saying a little Pussy Galore goes a long way.

A serious discussion of Pussy Galore's musical attributes must thoroughly ignore technical ability; they have none. Spencer and guitarists (no bass) Julia Cafritz and Neil Hagerty locked horns in a badly played riff-fest, with ex-Sonic Youth drummer Bob Bert sounding as if he's dropping pots and pans on the floor. Surprisingly, with all of their hip attitude and condescending, arty indifference, Pussy Galore was capable of creating some great trash rock. However, I would argue that these moments were accidental, the by-product of doing something long enough and eventually getting it right.

Really the only difference between good Pussy Galore music and bad is that the latter is boring and the former is not—that is unless you have an extremely high tolerance for low-rent nihilism. At their noisiest and most frantic (e.g., the two fine EPs, *Groovy Hate Fuck* and *Sugarshit Sharp*) there is a messy ebullience to this muck that undercuts their normal snotty, calculatedly offensive shtick. And they did have a sense of humor as they proved on their 1986 cassette-only release, a track-by-track cover of the Rolling Stones' classic *Exile on Main Street*. This release is not recommended to Stones fans. Still, for a band that no one predicted would have a long life, Pussy Galore has turned out many interesting side projects and bands since their demise in 1990. Spencer went on to form Boss Hog and the more recent and much better Jon Spencer Blues Explosion, while also adding his distinctively smart-ass touch to recent recordings by the Gibson Bros. Neil Hagerty joined forces with Jennifer Herrema and formed Royal Trux. —*John Dougan*

Sugarshit Sharp / 1988 / Caroline ✦✦✦✦
Both of these records, *Groovy Hate Fuck* and *Sugarshit Sharp*, come highly recommended if only because, as EPs, filler is kept to a minimum. *Groovy Hate Fuck* lives up to its title; it's a mess of a record thrown together by a bunch of bored kids who want to be as offensive as possible. On that level it's a near total success. Don't be shocked by the song titles (e.g., "Cunt Tease," "You Look Like a Jew," "Dead Meat"), simply enjoy the violent, sonic chaos they whip up. It's very energetic. *Sugarshit Sharp* is even better. Side one is a cover of Einsturzende Neubauten's "Yu Gung," side two is more death-grunge rendered with a maximum of noise and minimum of panache. But at under 30 minutes, it's free of a lot of arty-farty jerking around. —*John Dougan*

● **Corpse Love: The First Year** / Feb. 14, 1992 / Caroline ✦✦✦✦
With the exception of *Corpse Love*, a pretty good career anthology, I recommend all of Pussy Galore's full-length records with this caveat: not a one of them is strong all the way through. All have their moments (especially *Right Now!*) but after a while (a short while), you'll be able to anticipate every one of their moves, and the cacophonous anti-rock thrash and bash becomes samey sounding. Freaks for this stuff will want all three records, but as trashy noise rock goes, there are better bands, and certainly plenty who are less patronizing to their audiences. —*John Dougan*

Pylon

f. 1978, Athens, GA, db. 1983
New Wave
This Athens, GA, band's approach was unique, if a little skewed, although they turned out to be one of the most enduring influences from the early-'80s scene there that also spawned the B-52's and R.E.M. Forming while students at the University of Georgia, Vanessa Briscoe's growly (never sweet) voice gave the band its edge, while the cracking rhythm section of Curtis Crowe (drums) and Michael Lachowski (bass) laid down miltaristic beats reminiscent of Gang of Four. Guitarist Randy Bewley was sprung from the same mold as the B-52's' Ricky Wilson. The mix was seductive and danceable. *Gyrate* for DB in 1980 had college radio buzzing and the dancefloors hopping with the song "Cool." A UK EP, *Pylon!*, followed. The double A-side single "Crazy" and "M-Train" widened their audience, and the album *Chomp* contained more signature tunes in "Beep" and "Yo-Yo." In 1988, five years after their breakup, DB released *Hits*, and the band found themselves opening dates of R.E.M.'s *Green* world tour. It was the fellow Athenians' way of saying thank you for the inspiration. The band also toured the cities where they were most beloved—Atlanta, New York, and San Francisco. They recorded *Chain* in 1990, but Pylon let the reunion idea go when it was decided amongst themselves that their time had passed. They appear in the documentary film *Athens, Georgia: Inside/Out*. —*Denise Sullivan*

Gyrate / Nov. 1980 / DB ✦✦✦

Chomp / 1983 / DB ✦✦✦✦
Like their Athens, GA, counterparts the B-52's, this band used dance beat music as the platform for its intriguingly eccentric style—but while the former group gleefully exploited the kitschy aspects of this

aesthetic, Pylon explored the spare, arty, new wave side of the genre. All the songs on this album are composed of short, static, obsessively repeated riffs propelled by dance mix drums, over which vocalist Vanessa Briscoe chant-sings surrealist lyrics. Within this seemingly narrow ambit, however, the group manages to find a fair bit of variety. "Italian Movie Theme" is an instrumental number featuring surf-derived guitar playing. "Gyrate" has a heavier, thumping, rock-oriented beat and a modest, funk-derived feel. "Yo-Yo" exhibits a Devo-like mechanical quality, while "K" shows the gloomy influence of Joy Division or early Siouxie and the Banshees. Hints of Go-Go's girl group touches are audible on "Crazy." The odd aural idea of R.E.M. as a dance mix group is suggested on one of the album's best tracks, "No Clocks." The group went on a lengthy hiatus after this platter and would not release another album for seven years. This odd record may take a few listens to reveal its merits, but it's worth the effort. *—David Cleary*

● Hits / 1989 / DB ✦✦✦✦
All the Pylon you'll ever need is here on one long disc, the best of their career culled from their albums *Gyrate* and *Chomp* and various singles. Vanessa Briscoe's lyrics take the form of admonishments and are set to the band's dance floor, militaristic beats. It's repetitive but enduring and helped launch a hundred bands, chiefly R.E.M., out of the small college town of Athens, GA, in the early '80s. "Crazy," the song R.E.M. chose to cover, is a fine pop song indeed, but the lesser-known rock blast "Feast on my Heart" absolutely kills. *—Denise Sullivan*

Chain / Oct. 1990 / Dog Gone ✦✦✦
The reformed Pylon acquit themselves nicely on *Chain* but never deliver a knockout blow. Stylistically speaking, there are no big changes here, but the exuberance and emotion carry even the most rote workouts. *—John Dougan*

The Pyramids

f. Long Beach, CA
Surf
In early 1964, the Pyramids made the Top 20 with "Penetration," the last big national instrumental surf hit and one of the best of its ilk. The Long Beach, CA, group achieved some notoriety for shaving their heads just as the British Invasion was attacking American shores. Their music wasn't all that special, though, aside from the majestically sleek, haunting groove of their big smash. They disbanded after recording one album and a few non-hit singles, divided between average surf instrumentals and clunky frat-rock vocal numbers; they also appeared in the quickie beach movie *Bikini Beach*. *—Richie Unterberger*

● **The Best of the Pyramids** / Jun. 26, 1995 / Sundazed ✦✦✦✦
Not just the best, but virtually *all* of the Pyramids, on this 20-track compilation: songs from their sole album, a few non-LP singles, and two previously unissued tracks from their appearance in the *Bikini Beach* film. "Penetration" is available on several surf compilations, and everyone but surf collectors should stick with those. *—Richie Unterberger*

Q

Suzi Quatro

b. Jun. 3, 1950, Detroit, MI
Bass, Vocals / Pop-Rock

It's pretty far-fetched, as some revisionists are now claiming, to view Suzi Quatro as a precursor to the "riot grrrls" of the '90s. Her brand of mid-'70s glam-pop was far more innocuous and, in any case, was often supplied by professional songwriters. What she did prove was that it was possible for a petite woman to play bass, sing, and wear leather with a reasonable degree of raunch and pride. That, along with enough musical hooks to draw in the teenage pop crowd, was enough to reel off a series of big British hit singles just before the advent of punk, although she remained virtually unknown in her native US.

To the British audience, it seemed as if Quatro emerged out of nowhere in 1973, but in fact she'd been playing professionally for nearly a decade. While still in her early teens, she joined the Pleasure Seekers, a Detroit band also featuring her sisters Arlene and Patti. One of the few all-girl garage bands who played their own instruments, they recorded a fine gritty single for the local Hideout label, "Never Thought You'd Leave Me"/"What a Way to Die." (Both sides were reissued in the 1980s on the *What a Way to Die* '60s garage compilation.) Another single followed for Mercury, and the group even toured Vietnam to entertain troops. In 1968, though, Arlene quit the band to raise her kids (one of whom is actress Sherilyn Fenn) and was replaced by yet another sister, Nancy.

The Pleasure Seekers became Cradle, which placed more emphasis on hard rock and original material. In the early '70s, British producer Mickie Most (the Animals, Lulu, Donovan, Herman's Hermits) happened to see Cradle while he was in Detroit to work on an album with Jeff Beck at Motown's studios. Most let Quatro know he was interested in working with her as a solo act; six months later, Cradle split up, and Quatro was on her way to London. (Patti joined the all-woman rock band Fanny in Los Angeles.)

After her first single flopped, Most hooked her up with songwriters Mike Chapman and Nicky Chinn, who were also supplying material to the Sweet. The Chapman-Chinn-penned "Can the Can" went to No. 1 in the UK in 1973, and over the next few years the same team would write about ten other British chart hits for her, including four Top Ten entries. Quatro fused glitter and bubblegum in much the same way as the Sweet did, though she was perhaps a tad raunchier (without ever getting downright scary). Quatro and her guitarist (and husband) Len Tuckey did write some of her material, though these efforts were usually confined to albums. In the US, though, she could barely get into the Top 100, though she did somehow get on the cover of *Rolling Stone* during a slow month.

Her American fortunes changed in the late '70s, when she had a short-lived, semi-regular stint on the sitcom *Happy Days* as the guitar-playing, sassy Leather Tuscadero. In 1979, she made the American Top Five with "Stumblin' In," although this was a duet with Chris Norman. Undoubtedly an influence on the Runaways and Joan Jett, and thus by extension a mild influence on a subsequent generation of female rockers, she's kept a low profile in the '80s and '90s, although she's done some television and theatrical work in Britain. —*Richie Unterberger*

● **The Wild One: Classic Quatro** / Apr. 1996 / Razor & Tie ◆◆◆◆
The definitive compilation—20 tracks, mostly from her mid-'70s prime, including all of her British and American hits and a few album tracks. —*Richie Unterberger*

Queen

f. 1971, London, England, **db.** 1995
Hard Rock, Art-Rock/Progressive-Rock, Pop-Rock

Few bands embodied the pure excess of the '70s like Queen. Embracing the exaggerated pomp of progressive-rock and heavy metal, as well as vaudevillian music hall, the British quartet delved deeply into camp and bombast, creating a huge, mock-operatic sound with layered guitars and overdubbed vocals.

Queen's music was a bizarre yet highly accessible fusion of the macho and the fey. For years, their albums boasted the motto "no synthesizers were used on this record," signaling their allegiance with the legions of post-Led Zeppelin hard-rock bands. But vocalist Freddie Mercury brought an extravagant sense of camp to the band, pushing them toward kitschy humor and pseudo-classical arrangements, as epitomized in their best-known song, "Bohemian Rhapsody." Mercury, it must be said, was a flamboyant homosexual, who managed to keep his sexuality in the closet until his death from AIDS in 1992. Nevertheless, his sexuality was apparent throughout Queen's music, from their very name to their veiled lyrics—it was truly bizarre to hear gay anthems like "We Are the Champions" turned into celebrations of sports victories. That would have been impossible without Mercury, one of the most dynamic and charismatic frontmen in rock history. Through his legendary theatrical performances, Queen became one of the most popular bands in the world in the mid-'70s. In England, they remain second only to the Beatles in popularity and collectibility in the '90s. Despite their enormous popularity, Queen were never taken seriously by rock critics—an infamous *Rolling Stone* review labeled their 1979 album *Jazz* as "fascist."

In spite of such harsh criticism, the band's popularity rarely waned; even in the late '80s, the group retained a fanatical following everywhere except in America. In the States, their popularity peaked in the early '80s, just as they finished nearly a decade's worth of extraordinarily popular records. And while those records were never praised, they sold in enormous numbers, and traces of Queen's music could be heard in several generations of hard rock and metal bands in the next two decades, from Metallica to Smashing Pumpkins.

The origins of Queen lay in the hard-rock psychedelic group Smile, which guitarist Brian May and drummer Roger Taylor joined in 1967. Following the departure of Smile's lead vocalist Tim Staffell in 1971, May and Taylor formed a group with Freddie Mercury, the former lead singer for Wreckage. Within a few months, bassist John Deacon joined them, and they began rehearsing. Over the next two years, as all four members completed college, they mainly rehearsed, playing just a handful of gigs. By 1973, they had begun to concentrate on their career, releasing the Roy Thomas Baker-produced *Queen* that year and setting out on their first tour. *Queen* was more or less a straight metal album, and it failed to receive much acclaim, but *Queen II* became an unexpected British breakthrough early in 1974. Before its release, the band played *Top of the Pops*, performing "Seven Seas of Rhye." Both the song and the performance were a smash success, and the single rocketed into the Top Ten, setting the stage for *Queen II* to reach No. 5. Following the album's release, the group embarked on their first American tour, supporting Mott the Hoople. On the strength of their campily dramatic performances, the album climbed to No. 43 in the states.

Queen released their third album, *Sheer Heart Attack*, before the end of 1974. The music hall-meets-Zeppelin "Killer Queen" climbed to No. 2 on the UK charts, taking the album to No. 2 as well. *Sheer Heart Attack* made some inroads in America as well, setting the stage for the breakthrough of 1975's *A Night At the Opera*. Queen labored long and hard over the record; according to many reports, it was the most expensive rock record ever made at the time of its release. The first single from the record, "Bohemian Rhapsody," became Queen's signature song, and with its bombastic, mock-operatic structure punctuated by heavy-metal riffing, it encapsulates their music. It also is the symbol for their musical excesses—the song took three weeks to record, and there were so many vocal overdubs on the record that it was possible to see through the tape at certain points. Queen shot one of the first conceptual music videos to support "Bohemian Rhapsody" and the gamble paid off, as the single spent nine weeks at No. 1 in the England, breaking the record for the longest run at No. 1. The song and *A Night At the Opera* were equally successful in America where the album climbed into the Top Ten and quickly went platinum.

Following *A Night At the Opera*, Queen were established as superstars, and they quickly took advantage of all their status had to offer. Their parties and indulgences quickly became legend in the rock world, yet the band continued to work at a rapid rate. In the summer of 1976, they performed a free concert at London's Hyde Park that broke attendance records, and they released the hit single "Somebody to Love" a few months later. It was followed by *A Day at the Races*, which was essentially a scaled-down version of *A Night at the Opera* that reached No. 1 in the UK and No. 5 in the US. They continued to pile up hit singles in both Britain and America over the next five years, as each of their albums went into the Top Ten, always going gold and usually platinum in the process. Because Queen embraced such mass success and adoration, they were scorned by the rock press, especially when they came to represent all of the worst tendencies of the old guard in the wake of punk. Nevertheless, the public continued to buy Queen records. Featuring the Top Five double-A-sided single "We Are the Champions" / "We Will Rock You," *News of the World* became a Top Ten hit in 1977. The following year, *Jazz* nearly replicated that success, with the single "Fat Bottomed Girls"/"Bicycle Race" becoming an international hit, despite the massive bad publicity surrounding their media stunt of staging a nude female bicycle race.

Queen were at the height of their popularity as they entered the '80s, releasing *The Game*, their most diverse album to date, in 1980. On the strength of two No. 1 singles—the campy, rockabilly "Crazy Little Thing Called Love" and the discofied "Another One Bites the Dust"—*The Game* became the group's first American No. 1 album. However, the bottom fell out of the group's popularity, particularly in the US, shortly afterward. Their largely instrumental soundtrack to *Flash Gordon* was coldly received later in 1980. With the help of David Bowie, Queen were able to successfully compete with new wave with 1981's hit single "Under Pressure"—their first UK No. 1 since "Bohemian Rhapsody"—which was included both on their 1981 *Greatest Hits* and 1982's *Hot Space*. Instead of proving the group's vitality, "Under Pressure" was a last gasp. *Hot Space* was only a moderate hit, and the more rock-oriented *The Works* (1984) was a minor hit, with only "Radio Ga Ga" receiving much attention. Shortly afterward, they left Elektra and signed with Capitol.

Faced with their decreased popularity in the US and waning popularity in Britain, Queen began touring foreign markets, cultivating a large, dedicated fan base in Latin America, Asia and Africa, continents that most rock groups ignored. In 1985, they returned to popularity in Britain in the wake of their show-stopping performance at Live Aid. The following year, they released *A Kind of Magic* to strong European sales, but they failed to make headway in the States. The same fate befell 1989's *The Miracle*, yet 1991's *Innuendo* was greeted more favorably, going gold and peaking at No. 30 in the US. Nevertheless, it still was a far bigger success in Europe, entering the UK charts at No. 1.

By 1991, Queen had drastically scaled back their activity, causing many rumors to circulate about Freddie Mercury's health. On November 22, he issued a statement confirming that he was stricken with AIDS; two days later, he died. The following spring, the remaining members of Queen held a memorial concert at Wembley Stadium, which was broadcast to an international audience of more than one billion. Featuring such guest artists as David Bowie, Elton John, Annie Lennox, Def Leppard and Guns N' Roses, the concert raised millions for the Mercury Phoenix Trust, which was established for AIDS awareness. The concert coincided with a revival of interest in "Bohemian Rhapsody," which climbed to No. 2 in the US and No. 1 in the UK in the wake of its appearance in the Mike Myers comedy *Wayne's World*. Following Mercury's death, the remaining members of Queen were fairly quiet. Brian May released his second solo album, *Back to the Light*, in 1993, ten years after the release of his first record. Roger Taylor cut a few records with the Cross, which he had been playing with since 1987, while John Deacon essentially retired. The three reunited in 1994 to record backing tapes for vocal tracks Mercury recorded on his death bed. The resulting album, *Made in Heaven*, was released in 1995 to mixed reviews and strong sales, particularly in Europe. — *Stephen Thomas Erlewine*

Queen / Sep. 1973 / Hollywood ✦✦✦
Queen had already staked out a distinct identity by the time of their debut album, led by Freddie Mercury's big-voiced flamboyance and Brian May's slabs of hard-rock guitar, all in the service of surprisingly poppy tunes. The most memorable track is the lead-off song, "Keep Yourself Alive." — *William Ruhlmann*

Queen II / Apr. 1974 / Hollywood ✦✦✦
Following Queen's debut album by only seven months, *Queen II* was the record that broke the group in its native country, where it hit No. 5 and spun off the No. 10 single "The Seven Seas of Rhye." It is a less impressive album than its predecessor, however, and today seems one of the weakest entries in Queen's catalog. — *William Ruhlmann*

Sheer Heart Attack / Nov. 1974 / Hollywood ✦✦✦✦
An effective demonstration of the range of Queen's musical tastes, from the guitar pyrotechnics of "Brighton Rock" to the vocal histrionics of "Killer Queen" and the on-the-road diary "Now I'm Here." — *William Ruhlmann*

☆ **A Night at the Opera** / Dec. 1975 / Hollywood ✦✦✦✦✦
Queen was straining at the boundaries of hard rock and heavy metal on *Sheer Heart Attack*, but they broke down all the barricades on *A Night at the Opera*, a self-consciously ridiculous and overblown hard-rock masterpiece. Using the multilayered guitars of its predecessor as a foundation, *A Night at the Opera* encompasses metal ("Death on Two Legs," "Sweet Lady"), pop (the lovely, shimmering "You're My Best Friend"), campy British music hall ("Lazing on a Sunday Afternoon," "Seaside Rendezvous") and mystical progressive-rock ("'39," "The Prophet's Song"), eventually bringing it all together on the pseudo-operatic "Bohemian Rhapsody." In short, it's a lot like Queen's own version of *Led Zeppelin IV*, but where Zep finds dark menace in their bombast, Queen celebrates its own pomposity. No one in the band takes anything too seriously, otherwise the arrangements wouldn't be as ludicrously exaggerated as they are. But the appeal—and the influence—of *A Night at the Opera* is in its detailed, meticulous productions. It's progressive-rock with a sense of humor as well as dynamics, and Queen never bettered their approach anywhere else. — *Stephen Thomas Erlewine*

A Day at the Races / Dec. 1976 / Hollywood ✦✦✦
A Day at the Races was the inevitable second-best follow-up to *A Night at the Opera*, the album that made Queen a superstar act. The group's patented brand of hard rock and melodic overstatement was in place on such songs as "Tie Your Mother Down" and "Somebody to Love" (the two hit singles), so that anyone who loved the previous album would at least like this one. — *William Ruhlmann*

News of the World / Nov. 1977 / Hollywood ✦✦✦
In the balance between Queen's operatic tendencies and its desire to rock out, the rock side once again gained an upper hand on this release. Not that the bombast lessened, but songs like "We Will Rock You" were actually dry runs for the stripped-down approach of *The Game*, and even "We Are the Champions" was a ballad. Well, almost. — *William Ruhlmann*

Jazz / Nov. 1978 / Hollywood ✦✦✦✦
Despite its commercial success, Queen's albums were hit-and-miss affairs, with every step forward (*News of the World*) seemingly followed by a misstep (*Jazz*). What they meant by the title has never been clear, and the single "Bicycle Race"/"Fat-Bottomed Girls," although it became a minor hit based on career momentum, is not among the group's more memorable efforts. After this, it was time for a new direction, and happily, Queen found it with *The Game*. — *William Ruhlmann*

Live Killers / Jun. 1979 / Hollywood ✦✦
At an artistic and commercial crossroads, Queen paused to release a two-LP live album chronicling their first five years of music making. Like most such efforts, it was basically redundant, although pleasant for fans. — *William Ruhlmann*

The Game / Jul. 1980 / Hollywood ✦✦✦✦
The basic elements of Queen's approach, from May's heavy guitar to Mercury's vocal army, were in attendance here, but the album owes its success to its novelties, especially "Another One Bites the Dust" and "Crazy Little Thing Called Love." — *William Ruhlmann*

Flash Gordon / Dec. 1980 / Hollywood ✦✦
This was a movie soundtrack, and it represented a relatively minor effort for Queen. — *William Ruhlmann*

★ **Greatest Hits [UK]** / Oct. 1981 / Elektra ✦✦✦✦✦
They may not have started out that way, but by 1981 Queen definitely was perceived as a singles act. This record gathers their biggest US/UK hits, 1973-1981, including the collaboration with David Bowie, "Under Pressure." Not to be confused with the 1992 Hollywood Records (61625) release also called *Greatest Hits*, which isn't as good but has the advantage of being in print in the US. — *William Ruhlmann*

Hot Space / May 1982 / Hollywood ✦✦✦
After turning out a movie soundtrack and a greatest-hits LP, Queen finally got around to following up its chart-topping 1980 album, *The Game*, with *Hot Space*. Taking a cue from the spare, rhythmic style of the previous album's hits, "Another One Bites the Dust" and "Crazy Little Thing Called Love," the band took an austere, beat-heavy dance-floor approach again, but without as much distinctiveness. The biggest American hit, "Body Language" (No. 11 US, No. 25 UK) was typical, with Fred-

die Mercury intoning "Give me your body" over and over. The album also contained the year-old single "Under Pressure," by Queen and David Bowie. — *William Ruhlmann*

The Works / Feb. 1984 / Hollywood ◆◆
Despite the presence of the hit singles "Radio Ga Ga" and "I Want to Break Free," *The Works* was Queen's weakest album to date, featuring a set of underdeveloped songs that lacked memorable hooks and melodies. — *Stephen Thomas Erlewine*

Live Magic / 1986 / Hollywood ◆◆◆
As their second live double-album, *Live Magic* might appear to be a bit unnecessary, but a closer look reveals that it's a better record than the previous *Live Killers*. Culled from a variety of dates from the 1986 *It's a Kind of Magic* tour but concentrating on the final show at Knebworth, *Live Magic* captures Queen, and Freddie Mercury in particular, at the height of their powers. While the set list might rely a bit too heavily on mediocre mid-'80s material for some tastes, the band is tight and professional, and Mercury has an undeniable hold over the crowd. It's to Queen's credit that the energy rarely dips over the course of the record. *Live Magic* may be designed for hardcore fans, but for those listeners it will provide a number of highlights, proving that the band's remarkable performance at Live Aid was no fluke. — *Stephen Thomas Erlewine*

A Kind of Magic / Jun. 1986 / Hollywood ◆◆
A Kind of Magic was a more diverse and ambitious collection than *The Works*, but it also suffered from a lack of memorable, fully developed songs. Again, it was a massive success in Britain, entering the charts at No. 1, but it failed to return Queen to superstar status in the US — *Stephen Thomas Erlewine*

The Miracle / May 1989 / Hollywood ◆◆
Queen had subsided to also-ran status in the US by the time of this, its next-to-last studio album, but with its return from disco to elaborate pop-rock it continued to reign in its native UK, where this album hit No. 1 and produced five Top 25 singles in "I Want It All," "Breakthru," "The Invisible Man," "Scandal," and "The Miracle." The approach is similar to that on Queen albums like *Sheer Heart Attack*, with overdubbed vocal choirs, elaborate arrangements, and Brian May's extended guitar runs. But as a re-creation of that style, it lacked freshness. — *William Ruhlmann*

Innuendo / Feb. 1991 / Hollywood ◆◆
Queen's final new studio album before the death of lead singer Freddie Mercury was its third straight UK chart topper, but a more modest success in the US, although "Headlong," "Innuendo," and "I Can't Live Without You" earned AOR radio play, and the album was Queen's first in seven years to go gold. *Innuendo* was very much in the tradition of Queen's slightly comic, operatic hard-rock style of the mid-'70s, with "Headlong" delivering heavy-handed guitar playing and hooks, and "I'm Going Slightly Mad" displaying Mercury's campier side. (As of this record, Queen's entire catalog dating back to 1973, previously on Elektra and Capitol, was acquired for US distribution by Hollywood Records, a subsidiary of Disney, which reissued its albums on CD.) — *William Ruhlmann*

Classic Queen / Mar. 10, 1992 / Hollywood ◆◆◆◆
Essentially, this 17-track album is a second-volume Queen's *Greatest Hits*, picking up the story from that album's 1981 release and taking it to the end of Queen's career. But the album also contains a few tracks—"Bohemian Rhapsody," "Keep Yourself Alive," and "Under Pressure"—that appeared on that first set, as well as a couple—"Stone Cold Crazy" and "Tie Your Mother Down"—from the same era. The remaining 12 tracks, culled from *The Works, A Kind of Magic, The Miracle,* and *Innuendo,* represent songs that were not big hits in the US. Nevertheless, with a resurgence of interest in Queen and the second coming of "Bohemian Rhapsody," courtesy of *Wayne's World,* this album returned Queen to platinum status and the US Top Five for the first time since the early '80s. — *William Ruhlmann*

● **Greatest Hits [US]** / Sep. 15, 1992 / Hollywood ◆◆◆◆
This is going to take a little explaining. In 1981, when it was contracted to Elektra Records in the US, Queen released an album called *Greatest Hits* (Elektra 564), which contained 14 songs that chronicled singles from 1973 to 1981. In 1990, Hollywood Records acquired CD rights to Queen's catalog, by which time the Elektra *Greatest Hits* had gone out of print on vinyl. Hollywood released *Classic Queen,* a compilation that covered Queen's hits from 1982 to its demise in 1991, with a few older songs thrown in. Then it released this album, its version of *Greatest Hits,* which is a 15-track album that deletes the songs from the first *Greatest Hits* that also appeared on *Classic Queen* (among them Queen's biggest hit, "Bohemian Rhapsody") and adds a few tracks from the 1973-1982 era that did not appear on the original release. The Elektra *Greatest Hits* LP had a superior selection, but it's gone now, so you're stuck with this. (New fans don't seem to have minded, as this new *Greatest Hits* sold better than the first one.) — *William Ruhlmann*

At the BBC / Mar. 7, 1995 / Hollywood ◆◆
A collection of early Queen material recorded for the British Broadcasting Corporation, *At the BBC* captures the band in their formative stages, as they were sketching out a cross between heavy metal and bombastically melodic pop. Several classic Queen songs, including "Killer Queen," are included and the performances are fascinating for hardcore fans, but there are only seven tracks on the album and it lists at full-price, which doesn't make it a bargain by any stretch of the imagination. — *Stephen Thomas Erlewine*

Made in Heaven / Nov. 7, 1995 / Hollywood ◆◆
During the 1980s, Queen ceased to be a big record seller in the US, but maintained its superstar status at home. In the '90s, following the death of Freddie Mercury, there was a brief resurgence of interest in America triggered by the inclusion of "Bohemian Rhapsody" in the movie *Wayne's World.* But in 1995, when the surviving members got around to releasing the final recordings done with Mercury in the form of *Made in Heaven,* the status quo had returned. The album topped the charts in Western Europe, with its single, "Heaven for Everyone," reaching the Top Ten, while in the US it was on and off the charts within weeks. Musically, *Made in Heaven* harked back to Queen's 1970s heyday with its strong melodies and hard-rock guitar playing, topped by Mercury's bravura singing and some of the massed choir effects familiar from "Bohemian Rhapsody." Even if one did not know that these songs were sung in the shadow of death, that subject would be obvious. The lyrics were imbued with life-and-death issues, from the titles—"Let Me Live," "My Life Has Been Saved," and "Too Much Love Will Kill You"—to lines like "It's hopeless—so hopeless to even try" ("It's a Beautiful Day"), "Waiting for possibilities / Don't see too many around" ("Made in Heaven"), and "I long for peace before I die" ("Mother Love"). The odd thing about this was that Mercury's over-the-top singing had always contained a hint of camp humor, and it continued to here, even when the sentiments clearly were as heartfelt as they were theatrically overstated. Maybe Freddie Mercury was determined to go out the same way he had come in, as a diva. If so, he succeeded. — *William Ruhlmann*

Queen Latifah

b. Mar. 18, 1970, Newark, NJ
Vocals / Hip Hop
Although Queen Latifah was certainly not the first female rapper, she was the first to bring a feminist consciousness to the genre's political agenda with her groundbreaking 1989 debut, *All Hail the Queen,* and its single "Ladies First." Latifah (an Arabic word translating as "delicate" or "sensitive") was born Dana Owens in Newark, NJ, and served a stint as a human beatbox in the group Ladies Fresh.

She recorded a single, "Wrath of My Madness," in 1988 and later released *All Hail the Queen* to strongly favorable reviews; the album showcased her versatility on material ranging from soul, dub reggae and dance to straight hip-hop and established a tough, no-nonsense, intelligent persona. *Nature of a Sista* expanded on that role with some more personal material, but *Black Reign* became her most popular album, probably boosted by Latifah's increased visibility as a cast member of the Fox sitcom *Living Single.* The album was dedicated to her late brother, who was killed in a motorcycle accident in 1992, and produced the hit single "U.N.I.T.Y.," which won a Grammy for Best Rap Solo Performance. In addition to *Living Single,* Latifah has also appeared in the films *Jungle Fever, Juice,* and *House Party 2.* — *Steve Huey*

● **All Hail the Queen** / Nov. 1989 / Tommy Boy ◆◆◆◆
As strong a buzz as Queen Latifah created with her debut single of 1988, "Wrath of My Madness" and its reggae-influenced B-side "Princess of the Posse," one would have expected the North Jersey rapper/actress' first album, *All Hail the Queen,* to be much stronger. Though not a bad album by any means, it doesn't live up to Latifah's enormous potential. The CD's strongest material includes "Evil that Men Do," a hard-hitting duet with KRS-One addressing Black-on-Black crime and other social ills; the infectious hip-house number "Come into My House"; the rap/reggae duet with Stetsasonic's Daddy-O "The Pros"; and the above-mentioned songs. Unfortunately, boasting numbers like "A King and Queen Creation" and "Queen of Royal Badness" aren't terribly memorable. Especially disappointing is "Mama Gave Birth to the Soul Children," a duet with De La Soul that surprisingly, is both musically and lyrically generic. To be sure, Latifah's rapping skills are top-notch—which is why *All Hail the Queen* should have been consistently excellent instead of merely good. — *Alex Henderson*

Nature of a Sista / Sep. 3, 1991 / Tommy Boy ◆◆◆
Nature of a Sista isn't the outstanding album Queen Latifah is quite capable of recording. But even so, it's a decent sophomore effort that has more strengths than weaknesses. The North Jersey native tends to spend too much time boasting about her microphone skills—something that can wear thin in a hurry—but there's no denying the fact that she has considerable technique. As on her first album, Latifah indicates that she

could hold her own in a battle with just about any rapper, male or female. And the positive image she projects is certainly commendable. But as likeable as much of this album is, it's obvious that she is capable of a lot more. Artistically, Latifah is selling herself short. —*Alex Henderson*

Black Reign / Nov. 16, 1993 / Motown ✦✦✦✦
Black Reign marked Latifah's move to Motown. It was also a return to the tough-talking, lyrically frank, frequently controversial material that established her as arguably the finest female rapper. "Coochie Bang" and "Weekend Love" were harsh and explicit attacks on would-be hit-and-run lovers, while "Just Another Day" and "I Can't Understand" examined the continuing inequities plaguing inner-city youth, and "Superstar" took a pointedly unglamorous view of her situation and the perils of hip-hop supremacy. —*Ron Wynn*

Queensryche

f. 1981, Bellevue, WA
Hard Rock, Art-Rock/Progressive-Rock, Heavy Metal, Progressive Metal
Although they were initially grouped in with the legions of pop/metal bands that dominated the American heavy metal scene of the '80s, Queensryche were one of the most distinctive bands of the era. Where their contemporaries built on the legacy of Van Halen, Aerosmith, and Kiss, Queensryche constructed a progressive form of heavy metal that drew equally from the guitar pyrotechnics of post-Van Halen metal and '70s art-rock, most notably Pink Floyd and Queen. After releasing a handful of ignored albums, the band began to break into the mainstream with the acclaimed 1988 album, *Operation: Mindcrime*. Its follow-up, *Empire*, was the group's biggest success, selling over two million copies due to the hit single, "Silent Lucidity." Queensryche never sustained that widespread popularity—like most late-'80s metal bands, their audience disappeared after the emergence of grunge. Nevertheless, they retained a large cult following well into the '90s.

Guitarists Chris DeGarmo and Michael Wilton formed Queensryche in 1981 in the Seattle, WA, suburb of Bellevue. Both guitarists had been playing in heavy-metal cover bands and had decided to form a group which would play original material. The duo recruited their high school friends Geoff Tate (vocals) and Eddie Jackson (bass), as well as drummer Scott Rockenfield. Instead of hitting the club circuit, the group rehearsed for two years, eventually recording and releasing a four-song demo tape. The cassette came to the attention of local record store owners Kim and Diana Harris, who offered to manage Queensryche. With the help of the Harrises, the tape circulated throughout the Northwest. In May of 1983, Queensryche released the EP *Queen of the Reich* on their own record label, 206 Records. *Queen of the Reich* sold 20,000 copies and in the process earned the band major-label attention. By the end of the year, the band signed to EMI, who released an expanded version of the EP as the *Queensryche* LP later in the year; the record peaked at No. 81.

At this stage, Queensryche sounded closer to the British heavy-metal bands like Iron Maiden and Judas Priest. Over the next few years, the group continued to refine their sound, as they opened for hard-rock acts as diverse as Bon Jovi and Metallica. Their next two albums—1984's *The Warning* and 1986's *Rage for Order*—each sold respectably, with the latter reaching No. 47 on the US charts. *Rage for Order* also demonstrated a flowering of progressive-rock influences, an idea which would reach its fruition with 1988's *Operation: Mindcrime*. Boasting orchestral arrangements from Michael Kamen, the album was Queensryche's most ambitious and focused effort to date, earning both positive reviews and strong sales. *Operation: Mindcrime* stayed on the American charts for a year, selling over a million copies during its chart run.

Queensryche returned in the fall of 1990 with the equally ambitious *Empire*. The album proved to be their commercial high watermark, peaking at No. 7 on the US charts and going double platinum in America; in the UK the album also cracked the Top Ten. *Empire*'s success was instigated by the stately art-rock ballad "Silent Lucidity," which received heavy airplay from MTV and album rock radio. All the exposure eventually sent "Silent Lucidity" to No. 5 on the US singles charts.

Following the long *Empire* tour—which included a spot on the 1991 Monsters of Rock tour—Queensryche released the live *Operation: Livecrime* in the fall of 1991. Recorded on the *Operation: Mindcrime* tour, the album replicated the group's live performance of the rock opera that comprised their 1988 artistic breakthrough; the package also included a video and a thick book. In the three years following the release of *Operation: Livecrime*, the band rested and leisurely worked on the follow-up to *Empire*. Occasionally, they contributed a song to a soundtrack, such as "Real World" for Arnold Schwarzenegger's 1993 movie *The Last Action Hero*.

Queensryche finally delivered their sixth studio album, *Promised Land*, in 1994. Though the heavy metal audience had changed drastically since *Empire*, with many fair-weather metal fans switching their allegiance to grunge and alternative rock, the group retained a strong

following, as evidenced by *Promised Land* debuting at No. 3 on the US charts. *Promised Land* would eventually go platinum and spawn two album rock hits, "I Am I" and "Bridge."

With 1997's *Hear in the New Frontier*, Queensryche stripped back their sound to the bare bones, leaving behind the progressive-rock influences that made them distinctive. Although the album debuted at No. 19, it received mixed reviews and quickly fell down the charts. —*Stephen Thomas Erlewine*

Queensryche / 1983 / EMI America ✦✦
Their first EP (released in 1983) would have been forgotten if it wasn't for the band's dedication. —*John Book*

The Warning / 1984 / EMI America ✦✦✦
This is good heavy metal with dominant synthesizer work. —*John Book*

Operation: Mindcrime / 1988 / EMI America ✦✦✦✦
Seattle's best-kept secret is let out of the box with a concept album that brought comparisons to Pink Floyd and the Who. Fantastic lyrics with a great story line, powerful playing by the band, and powerful vocals by Geoff Tate made them finally noticed by fans a year after this album's release. —*John Book*

● **Empire** / Aug. 1990 / EMI America ✦✦✦✦
One of the most praised metal albums of the late 1980s, *Operation: Mindcrime* was an extremely tough act to follow. But while *Empire* isn't quite on a par with that gem, it is certainly one of the most absorbing head-banger efforts of 1990. Highly conceptual and anything but redundant, *Empire* demonstrates beautifully just how imaginative Queensryche can be. If anyone has bridged the gap between the bombast of Iron Maiden and the artsiness of Pink Floyd, it is Queensryche. But as much as one may be reminded of Floyd's *The Wall* on pieces like "Anybody Listening?," "Silent Lucidity," and "Resistance," *Empire* leaves no doubt that Queensryche has a rich personality all its own. —*Alex Henderson*

Promised Land / Oct. 18, 1994 / EMI America ✦✦✦
Queensryche returned from a four-year absence with *Promised Land* only to find the hard-rock landscape very different than the one they left in 1990. But Queensryche did something smart. Instead of trying to adjust themselves to fit into the world that their Seattle brethren had created, they simply stayed the same. Not only was the record a commercial success—it went gold in four months—but it was also an engaging album. *Promised Land* lacks the conceptual unity and consistent songwriting of *Operation: Mindcrime*, but it makes it clear that the band hasn't run out of ideas yet. —*Stephen Thomas Erlewine*

Hear in the New Frontier / Mar. 25, 1997 / Capitol ✦✦✦
Another concept album in the tradition of *Operation: Mindcrime* and *Promised Land, Hear in the New Frontier* is a typically adventurous record from Queensryche, but not necessarily in the way you'd expect. By the late '90s, the band's concept albums and revitalized progressive-rock had begun to sound old-fashioned, so the group decided to strip back their sound and simply rock out. Still, they can't really abandon progressive-rock completely, and there are still grandiose ballads and sweeping guitar soundscapes—it's just not as orchestrated as their previous records. Even in such a spare, rock-oriented setting, there's no denying that the band continues to grow musically, which makes *Hear in the New Frontier* nearly as satisfying, if not as challenging, as their earlier albums. —*Stephen Thomas Erlewine*

? & the Mysterians

f. 1962, Flint, MI
Garage Rock, Rock 'n' Roll
Originally formed in Flint, MI, in 1962, this group took its name from the obscure science-fiction movie *The Mysterians*. They recorded the anthemic "96 Tears" for the local Spanish-music label Pa-Go-Go in 1966. It was immediately picked up for national consumption by Cameo-Parkway, going on to be one of the most covered garage-band classics of the '60s. Lead singer Question Mark (real name listed as both Rudy Martinez and Reeto Rodriguez) continues to front a version of the band on oldies package shows across the US —*Cub Koda*

● **96 Tears** / 1966 / Cameo ✦✦✦✦
A true garage band classic, featuring the title track and 11 others straight from the band's set list. —*Cub Koda*

Action / 1966 / Cameo ✦✦✦
96 Tears Forever / 1985 / ROIR ✦✦✦✦
This is a band that definitely got by on attitude, as this collection of lesser tracks shows. —*Dan Heilman*

Quicksilver Messenger Service

f. 1965, San Francisco, CA, **db.** 1973
Psychedelic, Acid Rock
The band that became Quicksilver Messenger Service originally was conceived as a rock vehicle for folk singer-songwriter Dino Valenti (b.

Nov. 7, 1943), author of "Get Together." Living in San Francisco, Valenti had found guitarist John Cipollina (b. Aug. 24, 1943, d. May 29, 1989) and singer Jim Murray. Valenti's friend David Freiberg (b. Aug. 24, 1938) joined on bass, and the group was completed by the addition of drummer Greg Elmore (b. Sep. 4, 1946) and guitarist Gary Duncan (b.Sep 4, 1946). As the band was being put together, Valenti was imprisoned on a drug charge, and he didn't rejoin Quicksilver until later.

They debuted at the end of 1965 and played around the Bay Area and then the West Coast for the next two years, building up a large following but resisting offers to record that had been taken up by such San Francisco acid-rock colleagues as Jefferson Airplane and the Grateful Dead. Quicksilver finally signed to Capitol toward the end of 1967 and recorded their self-titled debut album in 1968 (by this time, Murray had left). *Happy Trails*, the 1969 follow-up, was recorded live. After its release, Duncan left the band and was replaced for *Shady Grove* (1970) by British session pianist Nicky Hopkins. By the time of the album's release, however, Duncan had returned, along with Valenti, making the group a sextet.

This version of Quicksilver, prominently featuring Valenti's songs and lead vocals, lasted only a year, during which two albums, *Just for Love* and *What About Me*, were recorded. Cipollina, Freiberg, and Hopkins then left, and the remaining trio of Valenti, Duncan, and Elmore hired replacements and cut another couple of albums before disbanding. There was a reunion in 1975, resulting in a new album and a tour, and in 1986, Duncan revived the Quicksilver name for an album that also featured Freiberg on background vocals. — *William Ruhlmann*

Quicksilver Messenger Service / May 1968 / Capitol ✦✦✦✦
The band's debut effort was a little more restrained and folky than some listeners had expected, given their reputation for stretching out in concert. While some prefer the mostly live *Happy Trails*, this is inarguably their strongest set of studio material, with the accent on melodic folk-rockers. Highlights include their cover of folksinger Hamilton Camp's "Pride of Man," probably their best studio track; "Light Your Windows," probably the group's best original composition; and founding member Dino Valenti's "Dino's Song" (Valenti himself was in jail when the album was recorded). "Gold and Silver" is their best instrumental jam, and the 12-minute "The Fool" reflects some of the best and worst traits of the psychedelic era. — *Richie Unterberger*

Happy Trails / Mar. 1969 / Capitol ✦✦✦✦
Quicksilver was heard at its best on this partially live album, which contained a 25-minute version of Bo Diddley's "Who Do You Love." — *William Ruhlmann*

Shady Grove / Dec. 1969 / One Way ✦✦✦✦
Even though the opening title track featured all the elements that made Quicksilver one of the great Bay Area bands (particularly John Cipollina's vibrato-laden lead guitar), *Shady Grove* was a transitional album. The addition of pianist Nicky Hopkins (Rolling Stones, Steve Miller) gave the band more colors to work with. One of Quicksilver's better albums, *Shady Grove* shines brightest on tracks like "Joseph's Coat," the dazzling Hopkins keyboard instrumental showcase "Edward (The Mad Shirt Grinder)," and the title cut. The sound on this disc isn't particularly good. — *Rick Clark*

Just for Love / Aug. 1970 / One Way ✦✦✦
With the return of Gary Duncan and the recording debut of founder Dino Valenti, *Just for Love*, Quicksilver's fourth album, marked their debut as the band they were intended to be. The ironic thing about that is that, led by singer-songwriter Valenti, they were a much more pop-oriented band than their fans had come to expect. On *Just for Love*, Quicksilver finally was Valenti's backup group (he wrote all but one of the songs), and while this gave them greater coherence and accessibility, as well as their only Top 50 single in "Fresh Air," it also made them less the boogie band they had been. And it meant the band's days were numbered. — *William Ruhlmann*

What About Me / Dec. 1970 / One Way ✦✦✦
Recorded in part at the same 1970 sessions that produced *Just for Love*, *What About Me* was a similar effort, again dominated by Dino Valenti's songwriting and singing. It was also the swan song of the band, with guitarist John Cipollina, pianist Nicky Hopkins, and bassist David Freiberg dropping out after its completion. — *William Ruhlmann*

Anthology / Mar. 1973 / Capitol ✦✦✦✦
A two-record set chronicling Quicksilver's recorded history from 1967 to 1971 and including most of their best tracks. Now out of print, this collection has been superseded by the Rhino album *Sons of Mercury*. — *William Ruhlmann*

Solid Silver / Oct. 1975 / Capitol ✦✦
A one-off reunion album featuring the lineup of Dino Valenti, John Cipollina, David Freiberg, Greg Elmore, and Gary Duncan. Valenti again dominates, and the band is cohesive, but its creative spark is gone. — *William Ruhlmann*

Maiden of the Cancer Moon / 1983 / Psycho ✦✦✦
A double album of live material from 1968, this duplicates a lot of the material on *Happy Trails* and adds considerably more. This erratic collection reflects Quicksilver's best and worst qualities: the hard-driving blend of raga/folk/psychedelic rock is fine, the blues jams are fairly awful. Besides "Who Do You Love?" and "Mona" (two versions), this LP has covers of "Back Door Man," "Smokestack Lightning," Buffy St. Marie's "Codine," and versions of most of the songs from the first Quicksilver LP. The rendition of "The Fool" here eclipses the studio take, and the performance of "Gold and Silver" is fine except for the "Toad"-like drum solo. John Cippolina's slithery leads are consistently fine, and Quicksilver fans will find this worth the search. — *Richie Unterberger*

Peace by Piece / Jul. 1986 / Capitol ✦
A travesty. Guitarist Gary Duncan, apparently the owner of the Quicksilver name, rounds up David Freiberg for a few background vocals, along with some Bay Area regulars, and records an album that has nothing to do with Quicksilver Messenger Service and isn't any good. — *William Ruhlmann*

● **Sons of Mercury (1968-75)** / Jul. 2, 1991 / Rhino ✦✦✦✦
This thorough two-disc best-of contains Quicksilver's most familiar material from its various lineups, plus some rarities. The only thing keeping this from being essential is the exclusion of the complete live version of "Who Do You Love," over a single edited version. — *William Ruhlmann*

Quiet Riot

f. 1975, Los Angeles, CA, db. 1988
Hard Rock, Heavy Metal
In the early '80s, Quiet Riot became one of the first metal bands to hit the top of the pop charts with their remake of Slade's "Cum on Feel the Noize." By that time, Quiet Riot had been recording for a number of years, experiencing several changes. During the late '70s, the band was a straight-ahead metal group, distinguished only by the talented, young guitarist Randy Rhoads; he left in 1979 to join Ozzy Osbourne's band, causing Quiet Riot to change their sound slightly, adding more pop elements to their hard rock. It paid off with 1983's *Metal Health*, which hit No. 1. However, their following albums didn't have the same crossover appeal and started to slip down the charts. Throughout the '80s, the band was a solid concert attraction even if their albums didn't sell particularly well. In 1988, the band broke up; vocalist Kevin DuBrow assembled a new version of Quiet Riot in 1993 for a tour and an album. — *Stephen Thomas Erlewine*

● **Metal Health** / 1983 / Pasha ✦✦✦✦
On the strength of their gloriously stupid cover of Slade's "Cum on Feel the Noize," Quiet Riot shot to the top of the charts with *Metal Health*. While it was easily the best thing the band ever recorded, it is very inconsistent; but the album does contain some of the best dumb heavy metal of the early '80s. — *Stephen Thomas Erlewine*

Condition Critical / 1984 / Pasha ✦✦✦
Condition Critical, Quiet Riot's follow-up to their No. 1, multimillion-seller commercial breakthrough *Metal Health*, is nearly identical to its predecessor. Not only do they repeat the hard-driving pop-metal hybrid to the last detail, they even throw in another Slade cover. Like *Metal Health*, the Slade cover on *Condition Critical* ("Mama Weer All Crazee Now") is the finest moment on the record—it's the only time the riffs have a solid hook and the melody is memorable. However, the rest of the record is well-produced and sounds good, even if the quality of the songs is somewhat poor. — *Stephen Thomas Erlewine*

Randy Rhoads Years / Oct. 26, 1993 / Rhino ✦✦✦✦
A fine collection of Quiet Riot's earliest records, *The Randy Rhoads Years* captures the influential guitarist in his formative years. That alone would have made the disc essential for his fans, but it also includes some prime unreleased material, making it all the more desirable. — *Stephen Thomas Erlewine*

● **Best Of** / Feb. 20, 1996 / Sony ✦✦✦✦
For those interested in the genre, *Best Of* contains all of Quiet Riot's biggest hits, from "Cum on Feel the Noize" to a live version of "Metal Health." While some favorites such as "Winners Take All" are missing, the most enjoyable pop-metal songs produced by Quiet Riot through 1988 all made it to this compilation. — *Barry Weber*

R

Radio Birdman

f. 1975, Sydney, Australia, **db.** 1981
Punk

Although the best-known band of the early Australian punk scene of the late '70s was the Saints, the first band to wave the punk rock flag in the land down under was Radio Birdman. Formed by Australian emigre Deniz Tek (originally from Ann Arbor, Michigan) and Aussie surfer-turned-vocalist Rob Younger in 1975, Radio Birdman's approach to rock 'n' roll was rooted in the high-energy, apocalyptic guitar rant of the Stooges and MC5, sprinkled liberally with a little East Coast underground hard rock courtesy of Blue Oyster Cult. Their first EP, *Burn My Eye*, released in 1976, was a great record and, nearly 20 years later, still remains a seminal chunk of Aussie punk. Loud and snotty, with Younger bellowing his guts out and Tek on a search and destroy mission with his guitar, this was a great debut that set the stage for the impending deluge of Aussie punk bands waiting in the wings. After the release of their debut LP, *Radios Appear* (the title comes from a lyric in the Blue Oyster Cult song "Dominance and Submission"), a year later, Radio Birdman seemed poised to break Aussie punk worldwide. And although the American label Sire (then the home of the Ramones) was quick to sign them and distribute *Radios Appear* internationally, there was a gap of three years before they released a second album (*Living Eyes*). During that time, two things happened: dozens of other Aussie punk bands stole their thunder, and Radio Birdman split up almost immediately after *Living Eyes* was released. Sire never released the record outside of Australia, and Radio Birdman, who should have been the biggest band in Aussie punk, were now highly-regarded punk forefathers. After the band split in 1981, various members were busy forming other bands; space limitations prevent an exhaustive look at their post-Birdman careers. Tek formed the New Race with Younger, ex-Stooges guitarist Ron Asheton and ex-MC5 drummer Dennis Thompson, released a handful of solo singles and EPs, and became a surgeon (!); Younger started his own band, the New Christs, and produced records by the second generation of Aussie punk bands influenced by Radio Birdman, most notably the Celibate Rifles; other Radio Birdman alumni ended up in assorted Aussie bands such as the Lime Spiders, Hoodoo Gurus and Screaming Tribesmen. Now the grand old man of Aussie punk, Tek has formed an unnamed, part-time project with Celibate Rifles guitarist Kent Steedman that rocks with the same reckless abandon Radio Birdman did when they were changing the course of Australian rock forever. *—John Dougan*

Burn My Eye [EP] / 1976 / Trafalgar ✦✦✦
This is where Aussie punk got the kick in the pants it needed to become a worldwide phenomenon. Tough to locate the original, but it has been reissued more than once as an affordable import. The title track alone (later recorded by the Celibate Rifles) is worth the price of the record. *—John Dougan*

● **Radios Appear** / 1978 / Sire ✦✦✦✦
Starting off with a rip-snortin' cover of the Stooges' "T.V. Eye," this is primal (and prime) Birdman, with Tek and Younger firmly ensconced in the eye of this guitar-fueled hurricane. Tek's originals are pretty strong, especially the grimy tale of urban desolation "Murder City Nights" and the noisy freak-out "Descent Into the Maelstrom." One of Australia's great rock and roll bands in all of their glory. *—John Dougan*

Living Eyes / 1981 / WEA ✦✦✦

Under the Ashes / 1988 / WEA ✦✦✦
I've seen this box set exactly once (in Minneapolis to be exact), didn't pick it up and have regretted it almost daily ever since. If you've caught the fever of this band and are inclined to have their complete recorded

works—buy it! Also available as a multi-CD box. Well worth the investment. *—John Dougan*

Radiohead

f. 1989, Oxford, England
Alternative Pop-Rock, Brit-Pop

Radiohead was one of the few alternative bands of the early '90s to draw heavily from the grandiose arena rock that characterized U2's early albums. But the band internalized that epic sweep, turning it inside out to tell tortured, twisted tales of angst and alienation. Vocalist Thom Yorke's pained lyrics were brought to life by the group's three-guitar attack, which relied on texture—borrowing as much from My Bloody Valentine and Pink Floyd as R.E.M. and the Pixies—instead of virtuosity. It took Radiohead a while to formulate their signature sound. Their 1993 debut, *Pablo Honey*, only suggested their potential, and one of its songs, "Creep," became an unexpected international hit, its angst-ridden lyrics making it an alternative rock anthem. Many observers pigeon-holed Radiohead as a one-hit wonder, but the group's second album, *The Bends*, was released to terrific reviews in the band's native Britain in early 1995, and the group steadily promoted the album over the next year. It eventually won widespread acclaim from fellow musicians and critics, as well as strong sales, establishing the group as something more than a one-hit wonder.

Thom Yorke (vocals, guitar), Ed O'Brien (guitar, vocals), Jonny Greenwood (guitar), Colin Greenwood (bass), and Phil Selway (drums) formed Radiohead as students at Oxford University in 1988. Initially called On a Friday, the band began pursuing a musical career in earnest in the early '90s, releasing the *Drill* EP in 1992. Shortly afterward, the group signed to EMI/Capitol and released the single "Creep," a fusion of R.E.M. and Nirvana highlighted by a noisy burst of feedback prior to the chorus. "Creep" was a moderate hit, and their next two singles, "Anyone Can Play Guitar" and "Pop is Dead," built a small following, even as the British music press ignored the group. *Pablo Honey*, Radiohead's debut album, was released to mixed reviews in the spring of 1993. As the band launched a European supporting tour, "Creep" became a sudden smash hit in America, earning heavy airplay on modern rock radio and MTV. On the back of the single's success, Radiohead toured the US extensively, opening for Belly and Tears for Fears. All the exposure helped *Pablo Honey* go gold, and "Creep" was re-released in the UK at the end of 1993. This time, the single became a Top Ten hit, and the band spent the following summer touring the world.

Although "Creep" made Radiohead a success, it also led many observers to peg the band as one-hit wonders. Conscious of such thinking, the group entered the studio with producer John Leckie to record their second album, *The Bends*. Upon its spring 1995 release, *The Bends* was greeted with overwhelmingly enthusiastic reviews, all of which praised the group's deeper, more mature sound. Positive reviews didn't sell albums, however, as Radiohead struggled to be heard during the UK's summer of Brit-pop and as American radio programmers and MTV ignored the record. The band continued to tour as the opening act on R.E.M.'s prestigious *Monster* tour. By the end of the year, *The Bends* began to catch on, thanks not only to the band's constant touring, but also to the stark, startling video for "Just." The band many year-end Best of the Year lists in the UK, and early in 1996 the record re-entered the British Top Ten and climbed to gold status in the US. During the first half of 1996, Radiohead continued to tour before re-entering the studio that fall to record their third album, *OK Computer*, which was released in the summer of 1997. *—Stephen Thomas Erlewine*

Pablo Honey / Apr. 20, 1993 / Capitol ✦✦✦
Radiohead's debut album *Pablo Honey* is a promising collection that blends U2's anthemic rock with long, atmospheric instrumental pas-

sages and an enthralling triple-guitar attack that is alternately gentle and bracingly noisy. The group has difficulty writing a set of songs that are as compelling as their sound, but when they do hit the mark—such as on "Anyone Can Play Guitar," "Blow Out," and the self-loathing breakthrough single "Creep"—the band achieves a rare power that is both visceral and intelligent. —*Stephen Thomas Erlewine*

● **The Bends** / Apr. 4, 1995 / Capitol ✦✦✦✦
Pablo Honey in no way was adequate preparation for its epic, sprawling follow-up, *The Bends*. Building from the sweeping, three-guitar attack that punctuated the best moments of *Pablo Honey*, Radiohead create a grand and forceful sound that nevertheless resonates with anguish and despair—it's cerebral anthemic rock. Occasionally, the album displays its influences, whether it's U2, Pink Floyd, R.E.M. or the Pixies, but Radiohead turn cliches inside out, making each song sound bracingly fresh. Thom Yorke's tortured lyrics give the album a melancholy undercurrent, as does the surging, textured music. But what makes *The Bends* so remarkable is that it marries such ambitious, and often challenging, instrumental soundscapes to songs that are at their cores hauntingly melodic and accessible. It makes the record compelling upon first listen, but it reveals new details with each listen, and soon it becomes apparent that with *The Bends*, Radiohead have reinvented anthemic rock. —*Stephen Thomas Erlewine*

Rage Against the Machine

f. 1992, Los Angeles, CA
Alternative Pop-Rock, Alternative Metal, Rap-Metal
Rage Against the Machine earned acclaim from disenfranchised fans (and derision from critics) for their bombastic, fiercely polemical music, which brewed sloganeering leftist rants against corporate America, cultural imperialism and government oppression into a Molotov cocktail of punk, hip-hop and thrash. Rage formed in Los Angeles in the early '90s out of the wreckage of local groups: vocalist Zack de la Rocha (the son of Chicano political artist Beto) emerged from the bands Headstance, Farside, and Inside Out; guitarist Tom Morello (the nephew of Jomo Kenyatta, the first Kenyan president) originated in Lock Up; and drummer Brad Wilk played with future Pearl Jam frontman Eddie Vedder. Rounded out by bassist Tim Bob (a.k.a. Timmy C), a childhood friend of de la Rocha's, Rage debuted in 1992 with a self-released, self-titled 12-song cassette featuring the song "Bullet in the Head," which became a hit when reissued as a single later in the year. The tape won the band a deal with Epic, and their leap to the majors did not go unnoticed by detractors, who questioned the revolutionary integrity of Rage Against the Machine's decision to align itself with the label's parent company, media behemoth Sony. Undeterred, the quartet emerged in late 1992 with another eponymous release, which scored the hits "Killing in the Name" and "Bombtrack." After touring with Lollapalooza and declaring their support of groups like FAIR (Fairness and Accuracy in Reporting), Rock for Choice, and Refuse & Resist, Rage spent a reportedly tumultuous four years working on their follow-up; despite rumors of a breakup, they returned in 1996 with *Evil Empire*, which entered the US album charts at No. 1 and scored a hit single with "Bulls on Parade." —*Jason Ankeny*

● **Rage Against the Machine** / Nov. 3, 1992 / Epic ✦✦✦✦
Rage Against the Machine's debut album is overflowing with barely contained anger that comes across better in the scalding music than the half-baked, clichéd lyrics. —*Stephen Thomas Erlewine*

Evil Empire / Apr. 1996 / Epic ✦✦✦✦
Rage Against the Machine spent four years making their second album, *Evil Empire*. As the title suggests, their rage and contempt for the "fascist" capitalist system in America hasn't declined in the nearly half-decade they were away. Their musical approach didn't change, either. Lead vocalist Zach De La Rocha is caught halfway between the militant raps of Chuck D and the fanatical ravings of a street preacher, shouting out his simplistic, libertarian slogans over the sonically dense assault of the band. Since the band did not perform together much after 1993, there isn't a collective advance in their musicianship. Nevertheless, guitarist Tom Morello demonstrates an impressive palette of sound, creating new textures in heavy metal, which is quite difficult. Even with Morello's studied virtuosity, the band sounds leaden, lacking the dexterity to fully execute their metal/hip-hop fusion—they don't get into a groove, they simply pound. But that happens to fit the hysterical ravings of De La Rocha. Though his dedication to decidedly left-wing politics is admirable, his arhythmic phrasing and grating shouting cancel out any message he is trying to make. And that means *Evil Empire* succeeds only on the level of a sonic assault. —*Stephen Thomas Erlewine*

Rain Parade

f. 1981, Los Angeles, CA, **db.** 1987
Group / Alternative Pop-Rock, Power Pop, Paisley Underground, Neo-Psychedelia
Among the Los Angeles groups dubbed Paisley Underground (Dream

Syndicate, the Bangles, Three O'Clock), Rain Parade were the closest to being the real deal for their use of psychedelic flourishes throughout their first album. Formed in Los Angeles in the early '80s, the group consisted of David Roback (vocals, guitar), Steven Roback (vocals, bass), Matt Piucci (vocals, guitar), Will Glenn (keyboards), and Eddie Kalwa (drums). Their first single, "What She's Done to Your Mind," was a certifiable hit on college radio, and the band quickly followed with a full-length LP for Enigma in 1983, *Emergency Third Rail Power Trip*. For 1984's *Explosions in the Glass Palace* (Restless), the band lost David Roback to Opal, but John Thoman took over and Mark Marcum filled in for the departed Eddie Kalwa. The re-formed band recorded the live album *Beyond the Sunset* (1985, Restless) and *Crashing Dream* (Island, 1986) before disbanding. David Roback went on to finesse Opal into Mazzy Star, Steven Roback and Thoman worked as Viva Saturn, and Piucci recorded an album with Crazy Horse—yes, that Crazy Horse. —*Denise Sullivan*

● **Emergency 3rd Rail Power Trip** / 1983 / Restless ✦✦✦✦
Featuring the dreamy "What She's Done To Your Mind" and the Byrdsy "This Can't Be Today" (with the Dream Syndicate's Kendra Smith), Rain Parade fashioned traditional, gentle psychedelic pop. Clearly way ahead of their time, it would take years before sleepy music (a la founding Rain Parade member's David Roback's Mazzy Star) would catch on, and this record sounds no more made in the '80s than in the '60s or '90s. —*Denise Sullivan*

Explosions in the Glass Palace / 1984 / Enigma ✦✦✦

Beyond the Sunset / 1985 / Restless ✦✦✦

Crashing Dream / 1986 / Island ✦✦✦

Raincoats

f. 1978, London, England, **db.** 1984
Post-Punk
The Raincoats were one of the most experimental bands that immediately followed the initial burst of punk rock in the late '70s. With their minimalistic approach to guitar-driven folk-rock, the band developed a distinctive, jagged sound, punctuated by a shrill violin. The Raincoats were also one of the first all-female post-punk bands, which wasn't common in the late '70s and early '80s. When they were recording, the band gained a small cult following in their native England and an even smaller audience in America; they broke up in 1984. Nearly ten years later, the band became a hip name in alternative rock, thanks to Kurt Cobain's mention of the group in the liner notes to a Nirvana album. Geffen picked up the rights to the Raincoats' catalog and reissued their albums in late 1993 and 1994. The band reunited and toured with Nirvana in the UK before heading out on their own tour of the US in 1994. Two years later, the Raincoats released *Looking in the Shadows*, which was produced by Sonic Youth's Steve Shelley. —*Stephen Thomas Erlewine*

● **The Raincoats** / 1980 / DGC ✦✦✦✦
Picking the "best" Raincoats is more an intellectual exercise than it is a work of thoughtful criticism. So, to make it easy for the benighted, all three studio releases are absolutely essential. Their live cassette is wonderful, but I wouldn't start there. Better yet, start with their debut, a soaring, daring, avant-garde-influenced folk-punk record. Don't let the words "avant-garde" scare you off; the Raincoats are not harsh or unapproachable. In fact, this music, even at its most dissonant, is stunning and captivating. There's a great cover of the Kinks' "Lola" that's so skewed and obtuse, I'm sure Ray Davies never dreamed it could sound this way. Reissued by Geffen on CD with extra tracks in 1995. —*John Dougan*

Odyshape / 1981 / DGC ✦✦✦✦
It was the late Kurt Cobain (with some help from labelmates Sonic Youth) that initiated Geffen's reissue of the Raincoats' catalog. And listening to *Odyshape*, it's easy to see why Cobain loved them so. There's an emotional directness about these songs that hooks you from the start. Mostly you hear about emotions and situations, sometimes indirectly, almost as if you are eavesdropping on a conversation. Then it hits you: it's almost like you're talking to old friends. That's the way the Raincoats' music worked: it's deceptively simple, but extremely complicated. Also, as on this record, it makes demands of the listener. But songs like "Red Shoes" and "Dancing in My Head" say this far more eloquently. Reissued by Geffen with extra tracks in 1995. —*John Dougan*

Kitchen Tapes / 1983 / ROIR ✦✦✦✦
Rough, loose-limbed, warm, exciting, and everything you'd expect from the Raincoats onstage. Bolstered by the heavy percussion of Richard Dudanski and Derek Godard, this recording pulsates, while the band dances around the beat tossing in shards of guitar, vocals and violin. Excellent liner essay by Greil Marcus. —*John Dougan*

Moving / 1984 / DGC ✦✦✦✦
What a wonderful cacophony of sounds! The Raincoats' last record (until their reunion EP of 1995) is a triumph of excitement and intensity

equaling that of their previous studio work. Some of these songs are from the live tape and are in sharper (and I'd say better) form here. Yet another important record by one of the most important bands of the post-punk era. Reissued by Geffen with extra tracks in 1995. *—John Dougan*

Looking in the Shadows / May 14, 1996 / DGC ✦✦

Bonnie Raitt

b. Nov. 8, 1949, Cleveland, OH
Guitar, Vocals / Blues-Rock, Singer-Songwriter, Adult Contemporary, Pop-Rock
While some blues critics like to act as if *all* white practitioners of the music—especially those who achieve any kind of mainstream success—are little more than modern day carpetbaggers, few artists on the modern day charts have earned or come by their success more honestly or in a more hard won manner than Ms. Bonnie Raitt. Purists and naysayers will quickly point out that she's never made an album of just straight blues, but if it took Eric Clapton 30 plus years to get around to doing one, it's almost a certainty that the prolific redhead won't make blues lovers wait *quite* that long. As a vocalist, she's never been any less than soulful and as a guitarist—especially on slide, her specialty—she reduces the old macho saw of "she plays pretty for a girl" into the same antiquated thought processes as expecting all women to look and act like June Cleaver.

Born in 1949 into a show-business family (her dad is big-voiced Broadway star John Raitt), Bonnie started on guitar early on but really got the blues bug when she attended college in Cambridge, Massachusetts in the '60s. Learning the ropes firsthand from blues legends Son House, Mississippi Fred McDowell (her twin inspirations on slide), and classic blues woman vocalist Sippie Wallace, she started doing the local coffeehouse circuit (usually opening for John Hammond, Jr.), catching the eye of Dick Waterman, who managed all three artists and was soon managing her as well. She soon was appearing with all three performers, appearing on every folk and blues festival in existence, establishing herself as the little hippie girl who was undoubtedly the real deal. A recording contract with Warner Brothers soon followed, and her eponymously titled debut opus featured the talents of Chicago blues legends Junior Wells and A.C. Reed. But with eclectic tastes in abundance, Raitt was soon flexing her interpretive muscles on future outings, showing her love for the work of great modern songwriters of all genres. Dividing her time equally with more pop-oriented albums while playing smaller venues as a solo act, the years of trying to party hearty with the older bluesmen finally caught up with her and the mid-'80s found her overweight with an alcohol and drug problem to boot. To make matters even worse, Warner Brothers—her label of 15 years—unceremoniously dumped her. But her turnaround—both personally and professionally—couldn't have more dramatic if she had hired a Hollywood scriptwriter. With her booze and drug problems clearly behind her, she suddenly became the comeback kid with the 1989 Grammy-winning success of the aptly titled *Nick of Time.* She continued the run for the gold (or in this case, platinum) with the follow-ups *Luck of the Draw* and *Longing in Their Hearts.* But rather than kick back and hobnob with industry swells, her excellent contributions to John Lee Hooker's 1990 album *The Healer* and her tireless efforts on behalf of the Rhythm and Blues Foundation clearly illustrated that she hadn't left her blues roots in the trunk of the limo. No matter what eclectic path she follows from here on out, Bonnie Raitt remains one hell of a blues lady. *—Cub Koda*

Bonnie Raitt / 1971 / Warner Brothers ✦✦✦
By the time Raitt recorded this impressive self-titled debut, she had developed quite a set of blues chops playing with artists like Mississippi Fred McDowell, Howlin' Wolf, and other blues greats. In fact, she enlisted Chicago bluesmen Junior Wells and A.C. Reed to aid in the proceedings, which are relaxed and earthy. *—Rick Clark*

● **Give It Up** / Sep. 1972 / Warner Brothers ✦✦✦✦
Raitt's sophomore release is a classic. Of all the albums from her days with Warner, this is the one that put together her folky singer-songwriter sensitivities with her love for country-blues. *Give It Up,* which took 13 years to go gold, showcased an intelligent song selection, with tracks by Jackson Browne ("Under the Falling Sky"), Eric Kaz ("Love Has No Pride"), and Joel Zoss ("Been Too Long at the Fair"). Her self-penned "Love Me Like a Man" highlighted her impressive guitar technique. *—Rick Clark*

Takin' My Time / 1973 / Warner Brothers ✦✦✦✦
Raitt continued her streak of quality albums with *Takin' My Time.* Like her previous efforts, Raitt drew from the cream of the songwriting crop. Randy Newman's "Guilty" and Jackson Browne's "I Thought I Was a Child" are highlights. *—Rick Clark*

Streetlights / 1974 / Warner Brothers ✦✦✦
This album was undermined by slick production and unnecessary orchestration. At the time, Raitt seemed to be fighting the production by

Jerry Ragovoy. Versions of Joni Mitchell's "That Song About the Midway" and Allen Toussaint's "What Is Success?" are the main highlights of the album. *—Rick Clark*

Homeplate / 1975 / Warner Brothers ✦✦✦
On this return to form, Raitt shines with some great songs, particularly "Good Enough," "Your Sweet and Shiny Eyes," and "Run Like a Thief." *—Rick Clark*

Sweet Forgiveness / Apr. 1977 / Warner Brothers ✦✦
One of Raitt's lesser efforts, it includes her version of Del Shannon's "Runaway," a minor hit despite being pretty lifeless-sounding. Even though the production isn't quite as slick as *Streetlights,* the relatively weak selection of material is this album's failing. *—Rick Clark*

The Glow / 1979 / Warner Brothers ✦✦✦
With the success of "Runaway," Warner felt it was time to take Raitt all the way by pairing her up with hit-producer Peter Asher (Linda Ronstadt, James Taylor). Gone is the natural earthiness Raitt possessed on her first albums. In its place was an airbrushed slickness—from the cover photo all the way down to the grooves. A rendition of Isaac Hayes and David Porter's "Your Good Thing" and an original, "Standing by the Same Old Love," are among *The Glow's* few highlights. The single from this album was a Robert Palmer song, "You're Gonna Get What's Coming." *—Rick Clark*

Green Light / 1982 / Warner Brothers ✦✦✦✦
Raitt dumps the slick stuff and goes for the grit with this energetic set, featuring her band, which included keyboardist Ian MacLaglan (whose credits included the Stones and Faces). Raitt's sensitive electric slide-guitar work was finally up front in the mix. It's one of her very best albums. Raitt does spirited versions of NRBQ's "Green Light" and "Me and the Boys." Other standouts include the wreckless rockers "Willya Wontcha" and "I Can't Help Myself." "River of Tears" is a powerful track that Raitt has dedicated to the memory of Little Feat's Lowell George in shows over the years. *—Rick Clark*

Nine Lives / 1986 / Warner Brothers ✦✦✦
Bonnie Raitt's ninth and final album for Warner Bros. Records was a star-crossed affair that began in 1983 in a session with producer Rob Fraboni, which was a typical Raitt mixture of different genres and songwriters, from Jerry Williams ("Excited") and Eric Kaz ("Angel") to reggae star Toots Hibbert ("True Love Is Hard to Find") in a style similar to her 1982 LP *Green Light.* This record seems to have been rejected by Warner, but three years later Raitt returned to the studio with Bill Payne (Little Feat) and George Massenburgh and cut a group of commercial-sounding songs by the likes of Bryan Adams and Tom Snow. *Nine Lives* splits the difference between the two sessions, with four tracks rescued from 1983, and five added from 1986, plus the theme from a forgotten Farrah Fawcett movie ("Stand Up to the Night" from *Extremities*). The result is predictably scattered and strained, and it was Raitt's lowest-charting album since her debut. Not surprisingly, it was also the last straw in her relationship with Warner. *—William Ruhlmann*

● **Nick of Time** / Mar. 1989 / Capitol ✦✦✦✦
Few comebacks have been as celebrated as Raitt's multi-platinum hit *Nick of Time,* an album that included some of her strongest performances as a musician and singer. The determined "I Will Not Be Denied" seemed to say it all. Her poignant self-penned title cut revealed Raitt as a mature songwriter, on the level of the best writers whose work she had covered. She dug deep with some solid roadhouse R&B in "Love Letter," "Road's My Middle Name," and "Real Man." Her playful version of John Hiatt's "Thing Called Love" was another highlight. All in all, this is a very seamless album. Highly recommended. *—Rick Clark*

The Bonnie Raitt Collection / Jun. 28, 1990 / Warner Brothers ✦✦✦✦
A good (not great) sampler of Raitt's years at Warner, it's also a good starting place. *—Rick Clark*

Luck of the Draw / Jun. 1991 / Capitol ✦✦✦✦
Raitt followed *Nick of Time* with *Luck of the Draw,* another great album. Among the album's many highlights are "I Can't Make You Love Me" and a duet with Delbert McClinton on "Good Man, Good Woman." *—Rick Clark*

Longing in Their Hearts / Mar. 14, 1994 / Capitol ✦✦✦✦
On the follow-up to the follow-up (and another million-selling No.1 hit), Bonnie Raitt contributes more than her usual share of original songs, writing four songs herself and setting a lyric of her husband's to music for a fifth. Elsewhere, she draws on such strong writers as Richard Thompson and Paul Brady, all for a collection devoted to devotion. Song after song expresses passion, usually with happy results—this is not the album of a woman with the blues. Even when she's dressing down a parent in her own "Circle Dance," Raitt offers forgiveness and understanding. There, and in other songs, the object of her emotions rarely seems to be perfect, but she takes that in and loves him, anyway. Co-producer Don Was provides a detailed production in which single elements—an accordion, a harmony vocal by Levon Helm or David

Crosby—effectively color arrangements and complement Raitt's always soulful singing. — *William Ruhlmann*

Road Tested / Nov. 7, 1995 / Capitol ◆◆◆◆

In a 24-year recording career, Bonnie Raitt had not previously released a live album, so this concert set was overdue. Coming off three multi-platinum studio albums, Raitt and Capitol pulled out all the stops, compiling a 22-track, double-disc package from dates recorded in July 1995 in Portland and Oakland. Raitt ranged over her career, reaching back to her early folk-blues days and forward to the pop-rock songs that finally made her a big star in the late '80s and early '90s. She also shared the spotlight with such guests as Bruce Hornsby, Ruth Brown, Charles Brown, Kim Wilson of the Fabulous Thunderbirds, Bryan Adams, and Jackson Browne. But that didn't keep an artist who has spent the bulk of her career pleasing live audiences rather than cutting hits from displaying her personal warmth along with her singing and playing skills. She also introduced half a dozen songs new to her repertoire, including a surprising cover of Talking Heads' "Burning Down the House" and a few that had potential to help promote the album as singles, including "Never Make Your Move Too Soon" and "Shake a Little." Inexplicably, Capitol (which probably wished the album had been a more reasonably priced single-disc) failed to bring the record home to consumers. The company's choice for a single was the anonymous Adams rocker "Rock Steady," done as a duet with him—apparently, they were confusing Raitt with Tina Turner. As a result, the album stopped at gold, spending less than six months in the charts. Despite that commercial disappointment, it will be for many Bonnie Raitt fans an example of her at her best that effectively bridges the two parts of her career, and also a good sampler for first-time listeners. — *William Ruhlmann*

The Ramones

f. 1974, New York, NY, **db.** 1996
Punk

The Ramones are the first punk rock band. There were other bands, such as the Stooges and the New York Dolls, that came before them and set the stage and aesthetic for punk and bands that immediately followed, such as the Sex Pistols, that made the latent violence of the music more explicit, but the Ramones crystallized the musical ideals of the genre. By cutting rock 'n' roll down to its bare essentials—four chords, a simple, catchy melody, and irresistably inane lyrics—speeding up the tempo considerably, the Ramones created something that was rooted in early '60s, pre-Beatles rock 'n' roll and pop but sounded revolutionary. Since their breakthrough was theoretical as well as musical, they comfortably became the leaders of the emerging New York punk rock scene. While their peers such as Patti Smith, Television, Talking Heads and Richard Hell all were more intellectual and self-consciously artistic than the Ramones, they nevertheless appealed to the same mentality because of how they turned rock conventions inside out and celebrated kitschy pop culture with stylized stupidity. The band's first four albums set the blueprint for punk, especially American punk and hardcore, for the next two decades. And the Ramones themselves were major figures for the next two decades, playing essentially the same music without changing their style much at all. Although some punk diehards—including several of their peers—would have claimed the band's long career wound up undercutting the ideals the band originally stood for, the Ramones always celebrated not just the punk aesthetic, but the music itself.

Based in the Forest Hills section of Queens, New York, the Ramones formed in 1974. Originally, the band was a trio consisting of Joey Ramone (vocals, drums; born Jeffrey Hyman, May 19, 1952), Johnny Ramone (guitar; born John Cummings, Oct. 8, 1951), and Dee Dee Ramone (bass; born Douglas Colvin, Sept. 18, 1952), with Tommy Ramone (born Tom Erdelyi, Jan. 29, 1952) acting as the group's manager. All of the group's members adopted the last name "Ramone" and dressed in torn blue jeans and leather jackets, in homage to '50s greaser rockers. The group played their first concert on March 30, 1974, at New York's Performance Studio. Two months after the show, Joey switched to vocals and Tommy became the band's drummer. By the end of the summer, the Ramones earned a residency at CBGB's. For the next year, they played regularly at the nightclub, earning a dedicated cult following and inspiring several other artists to form bands with similar ideals. All of the Ramones sets clocked in at about 20 minutes, featuring an unrelenting barrage of short, barely two-minute songs. By the end of 1975, the Ramones secured a recording contract with Sire; discounting Patti Smith, they were the first New York punk band to sign a contract.

Early in 1976, the Ramones recorded their debut album for just over $6,000. The resulting album, *Ramones*, was released in the spring, gained some critical attention, and managed to climb to No.111 on the US album charts. On July 4, the band made their debut appearance in Britain, where their records were becoming a big influence on a new generation of bands. Throughout 1976, the Ramones toured constantly, inaugurating nearly 20 years of relentless touring. By the end of the year, the group released their second album, *Ramones Leave Home*.

While the album just scraped the US charts, *Leave Home* became a genuine hit in England in the spring of 1977, peaking at No. 48. By the summer of 1977, the Sex Pistols and the Ramones were seen as the two key bands in the punk rock revolution, but where the Pistols imploded, the Ramones kept on rolling. Following the UK Top 40 hit "Sheena Is a Punk Rocker," the Ramones released their third album, *Rocket to Russia*, in the fall of 1977.

Tommy Ramone left the band in the spring of 1977, although he produced the group's subsequent album. He was replaced by former Voidoid Marc Bee, who immediately changed his name to Marky Ramone. With their new drummer in place, the Ramones recorded their fourth album, *Road to Ruin*, which was released in the fall. *Road to Ruin* marked the band's first significant attempt to change their sound—not only were there stronger bubblegum, girl group, surf and '60s pop influences on the music, it was the first of their albums to run over a half hour. Although their sound was more accessible, it didn't gain the band a noticeably larger following. Neither did *Rock N' Roll High School*, the 1979 Roger Corman film in which the Ramones had a pivotal part. The soundtrack to *Rock N' Roll High School* and the UK-only live album *It's Alive* were the band's only releases of 1979. For most of the year, they were in the studio recording their fifth album with legendary '60s pop producer Phil Spector. The title song to the Corman movie was the first track released from the sessions, although the soundtrack album did feature a number of older Ramones songs remixed by Spector. *End of the Century*, the Spector-produced Ramones album, finally appeared in January of 1980 to mixed reviews. Despite the lukewarm reception to the album, the record's cover of the Ronettes' "Baby I Love You" became their only Top Ten British hit; in America, none of the singles made an impact, although the record became their biggest hit, peaking at No. 44.

The Ramones continued their attempts at crossover success with their sixth album, *Pleasant Dreams*, which was released in 1981. Featuring a production by former Hollies and 10cc member Graham Gouldman, the record was a commercial disappointment in both America and England. The band was relatively quiet during 1982, spending most of their time touring. In the spring of 1983, the band returned with *Subterranean Jungle*, which was produced by Ritchie Cordell and Glen Koltkin, the heads of the American indie label Beserkley Records. Not only did *Subterranean Jungle* fail to gain the band the larger audience they desired, it continued the erosion of the band's diehard fan base, as well as their decline in the eyes of many rock critics. Following the album's release, Marky Ramone left the band; he was replaced by Richard Beau, a former member of the Velveteens, who changed his name to Richie Ramone.

With 1984's *Too Tough to Die*, the Ramones delivered a belated response to America's burgeoning hardcore punk scene that was largely produced by Tommy Erdelyi. The album helped restore their artistic reputation, as did the 1985 single, "Bonzo Goes to Bitburg," an attack on President Ronald Reagan's 1985 visit to Germany. Instead of continuing with the sound of *Too Tough to Die*, the Ramones began pursuing a more streamlined, stylized, and conventional take on their songwriting formula with 1986's *Animal Boy*. This was a direction the group followed for the remaining ten years of their career. Following the release of 1987's *Halfway to Sanity*, Richie Ramone left the band and Marky Ramone rejoined the group. In 1988, the career retrospective *Ramones Mania* appeared. In 1989, the Ramones contributed the theme song to the Stephen King movie *Pet Sematary*, and the track was included on *Brain Drain*, which was released in the summer of that year. After its release, the group's bassist, Dee Dee Ramone, left the band to pursue a career as a rapper called Dee Dee King; after his debut rap recording failed miserably, he formed the band Chinese Dragons. Dee Dee was replaced by C.J. Ramone (born Christopher John Ward).

In the early '90s, the Ramones sobered up, with both Joey and Marky undergoing treatment for alcoholism. The band returned to recording in 1992, first releasing the live *Loco Live* and then *Mondo Bizarro*, their first studio album in three years. *Mondo Bizarro* turned out to be a commercial failure, as did their 1994 covers album, *Acid Eaters*.

Following the release of *Acid Eaters*, the mainstream guitar-rock audience in America finally embraced punk rock, in the form of young bands like Green Day and Offspring. Sensing that the climate may have been right for the crossover success they had desired for so many years, the Ramones immediately followed *Acid Eaters* with *Adios Amigos*, claiming that unless the new album sold in substantial numbers, the band would call it quits after a final farewell tour. *Adios Amigos* only spent two weeks in the charts. Nevertheless, the Ramones embarked on a long farewell tour that ran throughout the rest of 1995. The band was set to split in the beginning of 1996 when they were offered a slot on the sixth Lollapalooza festival. The Ramones toured with the festival that summer. Following the completion of the tour, the Ramones parted ways, 20 years after the release of their first album. — *Stephen Thomas Erlewine*

☆ **Ramones** / 1976 / Sire ✦✦✦✦✦

With the three-chord assault of "Blitzkrieg Bop," *The Ramones* begins at a blinding speed and never once over the course of its 14 songs does it let up. *The Ramones* is all about speed, hooks, stupidity and simplicity. The songs are imaginative reductions of early rock 'n' roll, girl group pop, and surf-rock. Not only is the music only boiled down to its essentials, but the Ramones offer a twisted, comical take on pop culture with their lyrics, whether it's the horror schlock of "I Don't Wanna Go Down to the Basement," the drug deals of "53rd and 3rd," the gleeful violence of "Beat on the Brat" or the maniacal stupidity of "Now I Wanna Sniff Some Glue." And the cover of Chris Montez's "Let's Dance" isn't a throwaway—with its single-minded beat and lyrics, it encapsulates everything the group loves about pre-Beatles rock 'n' roll. They don't alter the structure, or the intent, of the song, they simply make it louder and faster. And that's the key to all of the Ramones' music—it's simple rock 'n' roll, played simply, loud, and very, very fast. None of the songs clock in at any longer than two and half minutes and most are considerably shorter. In comparison to some of the music the album inspired, *The Ramones* sounds a little tame—it's a little too clean and compared to their insanely fast live albums, it even sounds slow—but there's no denying that it sounds fresh and intoxicatingly fun. —*Stephen Thomas Erlewine*

The Ramones Leave Home / 1977 / Sire ✦✦✦✦

Of course the Ramones' second album *Leave Home* is simply more of the same—14 songs, including one oldie ("California Sun"), delivered at breakneck speed and concluding in under a half hour. The Ramones have gotten slightly poppier, occasionally delivering songs like "I Remember You" that are cloaked neither in irony nor seedy rock 'n' roll chic. Still, the biggest impressions are made by the cuts that strongly recall the debut, whether it's the ersatz Beach Boys of "Sheena Is a Punk Rocker," the sing-along of "Pinhead" or the warped anthems "Gimme Gimme Shock Treatment" and "Commando." Song for song, it's slightly weaker than its predecessor, but the handful of mediocre cuts speed by so fast that you don't really notice its weaknesses until after it's all over. —*Stephen Thomas Erlewine*

☆ **Rocket to Russia** / Nov. 1977 / Sire ✦✦✦✦✦

The Ramones provided the blueprint and *Leave Home* duplicated it with lesser results, but the Ramones' third album, *Rocket to Russia*, perfected it. *Rocket to Russia* boasts a cleaner production than its predecessors, which only gives the Ramones' music more force. It helps that the group wrote its finest set of songs for the album. From the mindless, bopping opening of "Cretin Hop" and "Rockaway Beach" to the urban surf rock of "Sheena Is a Punk Rocker" and ridiculous anthem "Teenage Lobotomy," the songs are teeming with irresistibly catchy hooks; even their choice of covers, "Do You Want to Dance?" and "Surfin' Bird," provide more hooks than usual. The Ramones also branch out slightly, adding ballads to the mix. Even with these (relatively) slower songs, the speed of the album never decreases. However, the abundance of hooks and slight variety in tempos makes *Rocket to Russia* the Ramones' most listenable and enjoyable album—it doesn't have the revolutionary impact of *The Ramones*, but it's a better album and one of the finest records of the late '70s. —*Stephen Thomas Erlewine*

Road to Ruin / Jun. 1978 / Sire ✦✦✦✦

The loud-and-fast, campy-and-catchy formula began to wear thin by the time of the Ramones' fourth album, *Road to Ruin*. Following the exact same blueprint as its three predecessors, *Road to Ruin* simply doesn't yield the same results as the other records. In part, it's because the band sounds a little forced on the harder numbers, but the main problem lies with the undistinguished material. "I Wanna Be Sedated" is a classic, and "Questioningly" proves that the Ramones are just as effective when they slow the tempo down, yet much of the record sounds like the Ramones trying to give the people what they want. Since they were still in their prime, such nondescript material sounds good, but the record has neither the exuberant energy nor abundant hooks of *Ramones* and *Rocket to Russia*, and it's the first suggestion that the Ramones may have painted themselves into a corner. —*Stephen Thomas Erlewine*

It's Alive / 1979 / Sire ✦✦✦

A double-album live set that relies heavily on the Ramones' first three albums, *It's Alive* captures the whiplash frenzy of the group at their peak. —*Stephen Thomas Erlewine*

End of the Century / 1980 / Sire ✦✦✦✦

Road to Ruin found the Ramones stretching their signature sound to its limits; even though there were several fine moments, nearly all of them arrived when the group broke free from the suddenly restrictive loud-fast-hard formula of their first records. Considering that the Ramones did desire mainstream success and that they had a deep love for early-'60s pop-rock, it's not surprising that they decided to shake loose the constrictions of their style by making an unabashed pop album, yet it was odd that Phil Spector produced *End of the Century* because his painstaking working methods seemingly clashed with the Ramones' instinctual approach. However, the Ramones were always more clever than they appeared, so the matching actually worked better than it

could have. Spector's detailed production helped bring "Rock 'N' Roll High School" and "Do You Remember Rock & Roll Radio?" to life, yet it also kept some of the punkier numbers in check. Even so, *End of the Century* is more enjoyable than its predecessor, since the record has stronger material, and in retrospect, it's one of their better records of the '80s. —*Stephen Thomas Erlewine*

Pleasant Dreams / 1981 / Sire ✦✦✦

End of the Century didn't make the Ramones into the stars they so wanted to be, so they hooked up with another '60s icon, Graham Gouldman, for its follow-up, *Pleasant Dreams*. Oddly, Gouldman directs the band away from their bubblegum, British Invasion and surf fetishes towards acid rock and heavy metal. They still manage to squeak out a couple of irresistibly catchy songs, but the production is too clean to qualify as punk, and the music itself has lost sight of the infectious qualities that made their earlier records such fun. Yet those flaws seem endearing compared to the metallic meanderings of their late-'80s records. —*Stephen Thomas Erlewine*

Subterranean Jungle / 1983 / Sire ✦✦✦

Tentatively returning toward punk, or at least new wave, the Ramones turned in their most enjoyable record since *Rocket to Russia* with *Subterranean Jungle*. Producers Ritchie Cordell and Glen Kolotkin were the heads of the edgy power-pop and punk label Bomp!, so they steered the Ramones back toward the '60s pop infatuation that provided the foundation for their early records. It's a strategy that pays off well—for the most part, the group's originals are so punchy and catchy that they make the pair of covers superfluous. Comprised of a set of unabashedly hook-laden songs and driven by more subtle rhythms, *Subterranean Jungle* may not be a punk record in the strictest sense of the word, yet the Ramones haven't sounded quite as alive in a long, long while. —*Stephen Thomas Erlewine*

Too Tough to Die / 1984 / Sire ✦✦✦✦

With the Ramones' original drummer Tommy Erdelyi producing, the group returns to simple, scathing punk rock on *Too Tough to Die*. The group takes the big guitar riffs of *Subterranean Jungle* and makes them shorter and heavier. The Ramones rhythms are back up to jackhammer speed and the songs are down to short, terse statements. The results read like a reaction to hardcore punk, but the Ramones are more melodic than any hardcore band, as well as smarter than most. Apart from the occasional foray into pop, such as the surprisingly effective Dave Stewart-produced "Howling at the Moon," the album is a sterling set of lethal punk, the best the Ramones had made since the end of the '70s. It was also the last great record they would ever make. —*Stephen Thomas Erlewine*

Animal Boy / 1986 / Sire ✦✦✦

The Ramones get d-u-m-b again and score with a back-to-basics roaring set. —*Jeff Tamarkin*

Halfway to Sanity / 1987 / Sire ✦✦

Although *Halfway to Sanity* still bears remnants of the heavy guitar attack of *Animal Boy*, it's actually a much sharper record than its predecessor, since it doesn't ignore the band's trashy pop roots. There's still a noticeable lack of consistent material, yet cuts like "Go Lil' Camaro Go" and "I Know Better Now" have solid hooks, and a handful of other songs suggest that the Ramones could have handled their second decade a little more gracefully than they actually did. It may not be as strong as *Subterranean Jungle* or *Too Tough to Die*, but in many ways, *Halfway to Sanity* is the last time the Ramones still sounded like they mattered. —*Stephen Thomas Erlewine*

Ramones Mania / 1989 / Sire ✦✦✦✦

Ramones Mania is a relentless collection of 30 tracks from the Ramones' first ten albums, ranging from the classic *Ramones* to the less-than-classic *Halfway to Sanity*. Although not all of their great '70s songs are included, it boils down the highlights from the inconsistent '80s albums quite effectively, making it a useful summation of their peak period, even if the sequencing is not chronological. —*Stephen Thomas Erlewine*

Brain Drain / May 1989 / Sire ✦✦

It's the end, the end of the '80s and the Ramones have seemingly run out of new ideas. —*Jeff Tamarkin*

All the Stuff & More, Vol. 2 / 1990 / Sire ✦✦✦✦

The second volume of *All the Stuff & More* compiles the Ramones' third and fourth albums—*Rocket to Russia* and *Road to Ruin*—onto one compact disc, adding several live cuts, demos and B-sides as bonus tracks. Like its predecessor, *All the Stuff & More, Vol. 2* suffers slightly from its length, which happens to contradict the loud-fast nature of the band's songs and albums, yet the music isn't hurt by its presentation. *Rocket to Russia* is one of the classic rock 'n' roll albums, and while *Road to Ruin* isn't as consistent, it does have its moments, making *All the Stuff & More, Vol. 2* a good bargain. —*Stephen Thomas Erlewine*

★ **All the Stuff & More, Vol. 1** / May 1990 / Sire ✦✦✦✦✦

All the Stuff & More, Vol. 1 compiles the Ramones' first two albums—*Ramones* and *Leave Home*—onto one compact disc, adding a handful of B-sides, demos and live songs as bonus tracks as well. While the music on the disc is terrific and timeless, having both albums on one disc actually dilutes some of its impact, since the records were designed as a relentless rush of brief, speedy songs; in this form, the assault becomes a little tiring, and the distinctions between the two albums—and they are there—are lost. Still, these are minor flaws, especially considering that the music on *All the Stuff & More, Vol. 1* is essential for any rock 'n' roll library. —*Stephen Thomas Erlewine*

Loco Live / Oct. 1991 / Sire ◆◆
Ramones in the '90s, still kickin' ass. Still no guitar solos. Hope they never change. —*Jeff Tamarkin*

Mondo Bizarro / 1992 / Radioactive ◆◆
Although *Mondo Bizarro* is a serious attempt to revamp the Ramones, it doesn't work. Fond memories of the hard, fast punk band of the 1970s taint dull power ballads like "Poison Heart" and the by-the-book rock 'n' roll of the rest of the album. —*Stephen Thomas Erlewine*

Acid Eaters / 1994 / Radioactive ◆◆
Tearing through a bunch of psychedelic and garage-rock classics from the 1960s, the Ramones regain much of the fun and abandon of earlier records, making *Acid Eaters* easily their best record in a decade; the guest appearances of Pete Townshend ("Substitute") and ex-porn star Traci Lords ("Somebody to Love") help make the record a blast. —*Stephen Thomas Erlewine*

Adios Amigos / Jul. 18, 1995 / Radioactive ◆◆◆
The Ramones announced before the release of *Adios Amigos* that the record would likely be their last—unless it sold in massive quantities, that is. While it's hardly their best effort, *Adios Amigos* is an admirable way to bow out. The Ramones haven't progressed much since the mid-'80s, yet they have recaptured a bit of the inspiration that fueled their last great album, *Too Tough to Die*. Even with the extra kick of energy, there are moments on the album that veer too close to self-parody—even the grungy stomp through Tom Waits' "I Don't Wanna Grow Up," one of the record's best moments, seems forced. Still, the weakest moments of the record outshine the best songs on the stiff and over-produced *Brain Drain* and *Mondo Bizarro*. They might not have been on the top of their game, yet the Ramones knew that a record like *Adios Amigos* was the right way to call it a day—it rocks and it rolls, and it's not an embarrassment. —*Stephen Thomas Erlewine*

Greatest Hits Live / Jun. 18, 1996 / MCA ◆◆◆
Usually, *Greatest Hits Live* albums are the province of aging stars and reunited rock 'n' roll oldies group, well past their prime. They make no attempt to play new material or reinterpret their older material, they just churn it out to please the crowd. The Ramones' *Greatest Hits Live* is no exception to the rule. The world's first punk band acts like an oldies act, trotting out their classics ("Blitzkrieg Bop," "I Wanna Be Sedated," etc.) with an astonishing lack of interest or energy—they really sound like a *relic*, not a once-revolutionary force. The two new studio tracks—the masturbatory "R.A.M.O.N.E.S." and "Any Way You Want It" (which is disappointingly *not* a Journey cover)—confirm that the band threw in the towel a few years too late. —*Stephen Thomas Erlewine*

Willis Alan Ramsey

Guitar, Vocals / Singer-Songwriter
Willis Alan Ramsey was one of the bright lights of Austin's singer-songwriter movement of the '70s, and his laidback folky airs and sweet melodies impressed contemporaries. Indeed, his 1972 debut album featured songs later covered by Jimmy Buffett, America, Waylon Jennings, and Captain & Tennille, who took "Muskrat Love" to the Popular Top Five in 1976. His star shines less bright if only because he practically disappeared in the mid-'70s. A small cult of fans remained true, and their adoration was somewhat rewarded when Ramsey resurfaced, working with Lyle Lovett, who has also covered Ramsey in concert. —*John Bush*

Willis Alan Ramsey / 1972 / DCC ◆◆◆◆
One of the great (and sadly overlooked) albums of the '70s, Willis Alan Ramsey's self-titled debut had great impact among Austin's progressive country-folk songwriters. Although best known as the writer of "Muskrat Love," which Captain & Tennille took to the Top Ten, Ramsey's muse was rooted much deeper in American lore and folk music. Influences from Robert Johnson to Jimmie Rodgers to Woody Guthrie can be felt if not actually heard on these eleven highly original tracks. Unfortunately, Ramsey, a unique talent with a clear and idiosyncratic artistic vision, hasn't been heard from since. —*Tom Graves*

Rancid

f. 1991, San Francisco, CA
Alternative Pop-Rock, Alternative Metal, Punk Revival, Third Wave Ska-Revival
Drawing an enormous influence from the Clash, the Bay Area quartet Rancid followed the lead of fellow latter-day punks Green Day and the

Offspring to mainstream success. The group was led by singer/guitarist Tim Armstrong, a lifelong hardcore fan who first found underground success teamed with childhood friend and bassist Matt Freeman in the late-'80s ska-punk band Operation Ivy. After becoming fixtures at the legendary Gilman Street club, Op Ivy released a series of singles before issuing their debut LP *Energy* in 1989. Unable to deal with their growing popularity, however, the group disbanded shortly after the album's release, and Armstrong and Freeman briefly reteamed in the Dance Hall Crashers.

Freeman later served a stint in the band MDC, while Armstrong recorded with a series of other groups. Both were working a string of day jobs when Armstrong fell prey to alcoholism; Freeman helped him to get sober, and as part of his recovery they founded Rancid in 1991 with Gilman Street staple Brett Reed on drums. The trio issued their five-song debut in 1992, followed in 1993 by a self-titled full-length release on the prominent indie label Epitaph. After the addition of second guitarist Lars Frederiksen, formerly a member of the UK Subs, Rancid recorded its 1994 breakthrough album *Let's Go*, which sold close to a million copies on the strength of the single and video "Salvation." A major bidding war followed, but the band remained with Epitaph for 1995's *And Out Come the Wolves*, which featured the hits "Time Bomb" and "Ruby Soho." —*Jason Ankeny*

Rancid / May 10, 1993 / Epitaph ◆◆◆

Let's Go / Jun. 14, 1994 / Epitaph ◆◆◆◆
Whatever Rancid lacks in innovation, it makes up with sheer energy. The group rushes through *Let's Go* with an invigorating wrecklessness, sounding like a less-serious, party-ready version of the Clash. It's almost impossible to understand what vocalist Tim Armstrong sings at any given moment, yet there is no great meaning in what Rancid says—the message is in the buzzing guitars and speeding rhythms. It doesn't hurt that the band can throw out the occasional memorable hook or melody, like the single "Salvation," as well. —*Stephen Thomas Erlewine*

● **And Out Come the Wolves** / Oct. 1995 / Epitaph ◆◆◆◆
In the wake of the Offspring's success, Rancid became a hot band, earning a dedicated cult and sparking a major-label bidding war. After flirting with a handful of major labels, the band decided to stick with Epitaph and returned with *And Out Come the Wolves*. While the title is a veiled reference to the attention the band gained, the album doesn't mark an isolationist retreat into didactic, defiantly underground punk rock. Instead, Rancid develop their own identity on the record, which ironically makes them more accessible. Although they continue to draw heavily from the Clash and the Specials—and their roots in the ska-punk band Operation Ivy are quite clear throughout the record—the band plays with such energy and conviction, it's easy to forgive their derivativeness. On the whole, *And Out Come the Wolves* is a little too long to make a major impact, but individual tracks are classic moments of revivalist punk, including the skittering 2-Tone tribute "Time Bomb." —*Stephen Thomas Erlewine*

Rank & File

f. 1981, Los Angeles, CA, **db.** 1988
Rock 'n' Roll, Alternative Pop-Rock, New Wave
Formed by brothers Chip and Tony Kinman after they split up their hardcore punk band the Dils (who recorded the great Los Angeles punk single "Class War"), Rank & File were, at times, a dazzling roots-rock post-punk band that stumbled early in its career, only to flame out much too quickly and finally collapse with an embarrassing thud. Their debut record, *Sundown*, was a gem of tuneful, Byrdsian pop, with a healthy dollop of Gram Parsons and Merle Haggard to boot. The Kinmans' singing was distinctive; they weren't traditional harmony singers à la the Everly Brothers, but rather sang synchronized upper and lower octaves. The songwriting was wry, heartfelt and cliché-free; the band (which at the time featured the guitar of the immensely talented Alejandro Escovedo) rocked with gusto, but never bombastically, preferring nuance and subtlety over volume and simplicity. In fact, the Kinmans were so into cowpunk and so far from their hardcore punk beginnings that they even landed a spot on PBS's revered country music showcase *Austin City Limits*. The sophomore record *Long Gone Dead* was an excellent follow-up, but the self-titled third album (it's never a good sign when a band releases a self-titled record three records into a career), recorded three years after *Long Gone Dead*, was absolutely awful; the songs went nowhere, and the singing and playing, which had previously been so precise and artful, was now buried under a thicket of clichéd hard-rock-isms. After listening to side one, you knew these guys were done for. Sad, really. In a stunning repudiation of Rank & File's roots-rock style, the Kinmans' next project was the execrable Blackbird, an ill-conceived try at synth-pop that went a long way toward making them laughingstocks. Former guitarist Alejandro Escovedo formed the excellent (but also short-lived) True Believers with his brother Javier, and since their breakup has recorded a number of interesting solo records. —*John Dougan*

● **Sundown** / 1982 / Rough Trade ✦✦✦✦
This was the era of post-punk Los Angeles, and bands like X, the Blasters, and Rank & File made great records. *Sundown* is Rank & File's great contribution to this scene, and despite the bizarre and egregious career moves of the Kinman brothers over the past decade-plus, *Sundown* is as strong, tuneful, and compelling as the day it was released. With their voices locking together imperfectly and Alejandro Escovedo's guitar providing sharp counterpoint, this is a great chunk of cowpunk that would please even the most doctrinaire country traditionalist, as well as beat the hell out of nearly all of the new generation of country hacks. Not bad for a couple of punks from Los Angeles. —*John Dougan*

Long Gone Dead / 1984 / London ✦✦✦✦

Rank & File / 1987 / Rhino ✦✦✦

The Rascals

f. 1964, New York, NY, **db.** 1972
Pop-Rock, Blue-Eyed Soul
The Rascals, along with the Righteous Brothers, Mitch Ryder, and precious few others, were the pinnacle of '60s blue-eyed soul. The Rascals' talents, however, would have to rate above their rivals, if for nothing else than the simple fact that they, unlike many other blue-eyed soulsters, penned much of their own material. They also proved more adept at changing with the fast-moving times, drawing much of their inspiration from British Invasion bands, psychedelic rock, gospel, and even a bit of jazz and Latin music. They were at their best on classic singles like "Good Lovin'," "How Can I Be Sure," "Groovin'," and "People Got to Be Free." When they tried to stretch their talents beyond the impositions of the three-minute 45, they couldn't pull it off, a failure which—along with crucial personnel losses—effectively finished the band as a major force by the 1970s.

The roots of the Rascals were in New York-area twist and bar bands. Keyboardist/singer Felix Cavaliere, the guiding force of the group, had played with Joey Dee & the Starliters, where he met Canadian guitarist Gene Cornish and singer Eddie Brigati. Eddie would split the lead vocals with Cavaliere and also write much of the band's material with him. With the addition of drummer Dino Dinelli, they became the Rascals. Over their objections, manager Sid Bernstein (who had promoted the famous Beatles concerts at Carnegie Hall and Shea Stadium) dubbed them the Young Rascals, although the "Young" was permanently dropped from the billing in a couple of years.

After a small hit with "I Ain't Gonna Eat out My Heart Anymore" in 1965, the group hit No. 1 with "Good Lovin'," a cover of an R&B tune by the Olympics, in 1966. This was the model for the Rascals' early sound: a mixture of hard R&B and British Invasion energy, with tight harmony vocals and arrangements highlighting Cavaliere's Hammond organ. After several smaller hits in the same vein, the group began to mature at a rapid rate in 1967, particularly as songwriters. "Groovin'," "Beautiful Morning," "It's Wonderful," and "How Can I Be Sure?" married increasingly introspective and philosophical lyrics to increasingly sophisticated arrangements and production, without watering down the band's most soulful qualities. They were also big hits, providing some of the era's most satisfying blends of commercial and artistic appeal.

In 1968, almost as if to prove they could shake 'em down as hard as any soul revue, the Rascals made No. 1 with one of their best songs, "People Got to Be Free." An infectious summons to unity and tolerance in the midst of a very turbulent year for American society, it also reflected the Rascals' own integrationist goals. Not only did they blend white and Black in their music; they also, unlike many acts of the time, refused to tour on bills that weren't integrated as well.

"People Got to Be Free," surprisingly, was the group's last Top 20 hit, although they would have several other small chart entries over the next few years, often in a more explicitly gospel-influenced style. The problem wasn't bad timing or shifting commercial taste; the problem was the material itself, which wasn't up to the level of their best smashes. More worrisome were their increasingly ambitious albums, which found Cavaliere in particular trying to expand into jazz, instrumentals, and Eastern philosophy. Not that this *couldn't* have worked well, but it *didn't.* They had never been an album-oriented group, but unlike other some other giant mid-'60s bands, they were unable to satisfactorily expand their talents into full-length formats.

A more serious problem was the departure of Brigati, the band's primary lyricist, in 1970. Cornish was also gone a year later, although Cavaliere and Dinelli kept the Rascals going a little longer with other musicians. The band broke up in 1972, with none of the members going on to notable commercial or artistic success on their own, though Cavaliere remained the most active. —*Richie Unterberger*

Anthology (1965-1972) / Jul. 14, 1992 / Rhino ✦✦✦✦
Anthology is the most comprehensive overview of one of the greatest bands of the '60s. All 18 of their hits as well as important album cuts (including tracks from their Columbia releases) are here on this double-disc, 44-track set. —*Rick Clark*

● **The Very Best of the Rascals** / 1994 / Rhino/Atlantic ✦✦✦✦
Although Rhino issued a deluxe two-CD set covering the Rascals a few years ago, this single disc set contains enough essential songs for you to get the point. The Rascals, along with the Righteous Brothers, defined blue-eyed soul singing, making records that were as churchy, earthy, and convincing as anything that came out of the South or Motown in the '60s, backed by tight, anthemic arrangements and excellent combo playing. The 16 cuts include their first hit, "I Ain't Gonna Eat Out My Heart Anymore," and continues on into their flirtation with psychedelia in 1970. The only quibble is their failure to include "Look Around," a sociopolitical cut from the *Freedom Suite* album that's just a cut below "People Got to Be Free" or "A Ray of Hope." —*Ron Wynn*

The Raspberries

f. 1971, Mentor, OH, **db.** 1973
Power Pop, Pop-Rock
Led by Eric Carmen (b. Aug. 11, 1949), the Raspberries (from Cleveland, OH) brought out their exuberant Beatles-style Anglo-pop and matching outfits at a time in the early '70s when art rock, concept albums, and serious "statements" were being heralded. It was a time when pop for pop's sake was decidedly uncool. Capitol Records accentuated the band's teenybopper appeal by marketing their self-titled debut with a raspberry-scented scratch-and-sniff sticker on the cover. The band's dynamic first single, "Go All the Way" (No.5), was a huge hit.

Carmen's tenor had the range of Paul McCartney, and he had the goods to write a handful of truly great guitar-pop hits. Lead guitarist Wally Bryson, who filled out their sound with a Beatles-meets-Free crunch, also contributed some solid material. Unfortunately, the public increasingly cooled off on the band, unwilling to buy into harder-rocking single releases like "I'm a Rocker," "Ecstacy," and the truly amazing "Tonight."

Drummer Jim Bonfanti (b. Dec. 17, 1948) and bassist Dave Smalley (b. Jul. 10, 1949) left in 1973, frustrated over the group's image problems. They were replaced by drummer Michael McBride and bassist Scott McCarl.

The 1973 follow-up effort, *Starting Over,* documented the dreams and frustrations of wanting to be pop stars. The track "Overnight Sensation (Hit Record) went to No.18, but the album ended up being one of the great lost pop albums of the '70s. The group disbanded shortly afterward, and Eric Carmen went on to pursue a sporadically successful solo career that resembled Barry Manilow more than rock 'n' roll. —*Rick Clark*

Raspberries / 1972 / Capitol ✦✦✦✦
An excellent first effort, highlighted by "Go All the Way," "Don't Want to Say Goodbye," "I Saw the Light," and "Come Around and See Me." At the time, audiences thought they heard echoes of Paul McCartney's work with the Beatles, and they weren't far wrong, in terms of what the group was capable of. —*Bruce Eder*

Fresh / Dec. 1972 / Capitol ✦✦✦✦
The second best of the four albums issued by the band, with "I Wanna Be with You," "If You Change Your Mind," and "Drivin' Around" as highlights amid some overall incredibly superb rock craftsmanship. The band's sound overall is more confident, and more powerful. —*Bruce Eder*

Side Three / 1973 / Capitol ✦✦✦
One of the group's most accomplished album, almost Beatles-like in its richness, romanticism, cleverness, and even its packaging, which is one of the few "novelty" jacket designs (it's shaped like a basket of . . . you guessed it) that works. The band was at its peak and it showed in "Ecstacy" and "Last Dance," among numerous others. —*Bruce Eder*

Starting Over / 1974 / Capitol ✦✦✦
The band's last album is something of a disappointment, much louder and punchier than their previous work but lacking the elegance that characterized their overall sound. None of the songs is bad, and some are quite good, but they sound like they're going through the motions at this point, and they did break up soon after. —*Bruce Eder*

Overnight Sensation: the Best of the Raspberries / 1987 / Zap! ✦✦✦✦
A 15-song British compilation that was essentially rendered moot a few years later by the domestic Capitol anthology. In truth you're about as well off with either one. This album has a few songs that don't appear on the Capitol CD, includes all of the familiar hits, and features extensive liner notes by Brian Hogg. —*Richie Unterberger*

★ **Capitol Collectors Series** / Feb. 26, 1991 / Capitol ✦✦✦✦✦
Twenty songs covering an entire cross-section of the group's history, with more superb notes, and this time superb sound as well. Short of having the second and third albums, the best the group has to offer. —*Bruce Eder*

Greatest Hits / Aug. 1, 1995 / Capitol ✦✦✦✦
Although it isn't as comprehensive as *Capitol Collectors Series, Greatest Hits* is a terrific overview of the Raspberries' best songs, containing all of their hits—"Go All the Way," "I Wanna Be With You," "Let's Pretend," "Tonight," "Overnight Sensation (Hit Record)"—plus selected album tracks and lesser-known singles. Even though it does have less songs than its predecessor, it contains everything a casual fan will need.
—*Stephen Thomas Erlewine*

Power Pop, Vol. 2 / 1996 / RPM ✦✦✦✦
Featuring the hit singles "Tonight," "I'm a Rocker" and "Overnight Sensation (Hit Record)," *Power Pop, Vol. 2* combines the Raspberries' last two albums—*Side Three* and *Starting Over*—on one compact disc.
—*Stephen Thomas Erlewine*

Power Pop, Vol. 1 / 1996 / RPM ✦✦✦✦
Featuring the hit singles "Go All the Way," "Don't Want to Say Goodbye," "I Wanna Be with You," and "Let's Pretend," *Power Pop, Vol. 1* combines the Raspberries' first two albums—*Raspberries* and *Fresh Raspberries*—onto one compact disc. —*Stephen Thomas Erlewine*

Ratt

f. 1983, Los Angeles, CA, **db.** 1992
Hard Rock, Heavy Metal, Hair Metal
Ratt's brash, melodic heavy metal made the Los Angeles quintet one of the most popular rock acts of the mid-'80s. The group had its origins in the '70s group Mickey Ratt, which had evolved into Ratt by 1983; at that time the band featured vocalist Stephen Pearcy, guitarist Robbin Crosby, guitarist Warren D. Martini, bassist Juan Groucier, and drummer Bobby Blotzer. The band released their self-titled first album independently in 1983, which led to a major label contract with Atlantic Records. Their first album under this deal, 1984's *Out of the Cellar*, was a major success, reaching the American Top Ten and selling over three million copies. "Round and Round," the first single drawn from the album, hit No. 12, proving the band had pop crossover potential. While their second album, 1985's *Invasion of Your Privacy*, didn't match the multi-platinum figures of *Out of the Cellar*, it also reached the Top Ten and sold over a million copies. By that time, the band could sell out concerts across the country and were a staple on MTV and AOR radio. Both *Dancin' Undercover* (1986) and *Reach for the Sky* (1988) continued the band's platinum streak and their audience had only slipped slightly by the time of their final album, 1990's *Detonator*. In 1992, Pearcy left Ratt to form his own band; his departure effectively put an end to the group.
—*Stephen Thomas Erlewine*

Out of the Cellar / 1984 / Atlantic ✦✦✦✦
The first album by Los Angeles' Ratt brought them instant success and a number of memorable hits. The cover featured actress Tawny Kitaen.
—*John Book*

Invasion of Your Privacy / 1985 / Atlantic ✦✦✦✦
They may have been influenced by Aerosmith but at this stage Ratt were recording songs that were powerful as well as masterful hits. This album also showed they were a lot more than a hit-making machine.
—*John Book*

Dancin' Undercover / 1986 / Atlantic ✦✦✦
This is the band's last album before falling into a slump when their imitators got more attention. —*John Book*

● **Ratt & Roll 8191** / Sep. 1991 / Atlantic ✦✦✦✦
A terrific and comprehensive overview of Ratt's entire career, *Ratt & Roll 81-91* contains 19 tracks, including all of the group's hits ("Round and Round," "Wanted Man," "Lay It Down," "You're In Love," "Dance," "Way Cool Jr."), as well as all the best album tracks from their frequently uneven records. In other words, it's a definitive package, containing everything that anyone but hardcore fans could ever need. —*Stephen Thomas Erlewine*

Lou Rawls

b. Dec. 11, 1935, Chicago, IL
Vocals / Soul, R&B, Pop-Rock, Philly Soul
When Chicago-born Lou Rawls croons a soulful love song, his deep-hued pipes rumble with simmering passion. Rawls did the usual gospel apprenticeship before breaking out on a landmark jazz album with pianist Les McCann's trio for Capitol that launched his secular career. But it took Rawls a while to establish himself as a soul artist—perhaps he was perceived as a little too sophisticated and jazzy (although his uncredited responses on Sam Cooke's "Bring It on Home to Me" certainly proved he could wail). "Love Is a Hurtin' Thing" instantly changed that notion when it topped the R&B charts in 1966, and the unyielding "Dead End Street" and "Your Good Thing (Is About to End)" perpetuated his success.

After memorably delivering Bobby Hebb's powerful "A Natural Man" in 1971, Rawls joined forces with Philadelphia producers Kenny Gamble and Leon Huff in 1976, emerging with the silky "You'll Never Find

Another Love Like Mine," another gigantic R&B and pop smash tailor-made for nattily sweeping across the classiest disco dance floors. The disco era's long gone now, but Rawls maintains elegantly. He's still as cool as cool can be. —*Bill Dahl*

Lou Rawls Sings/Les McCann Plays Stormy Monday / 1962 / Capitol ✦✦✦✦
This reissue spotlights the Lou Rawls/Les McCann team, a highly popular soul-jazz duo in the '60s, in peak form. Rawls sang gritty blues and R&B, while McCann added funky keyboard solos and accompaniment. The album was an early indicator that McCann would be a steady, consistent seller working the same territory as Ramsey Lewis. The 1990 reissue included three bonus cuts. —*Ron Wynn*

● **Stormy Monday** / Feb. 5, 1962+Feb. 12, 1962 / Blue Note ✦✦✦✦
Lou Rawls has had a long and commercially successful career mostly singing soul, R&B, and pop music. Originally a gospel singer, Rawls' first album as a leader (reissued on CD) features him performing soulful standards backed by the Les McCann Trio. Few of the songs have exactly been under-recorded through the years, but they sound fresh and lively when sung by Rawls; highlights include "Stormy Monday," "In the Evening," and "I'd Rather Drink Muddy Water." Pianist McCann gets a generous amount of solo space and the reissue has three "bonus cuts" that were being released for the first time. This is still Lou Rawls' definitive recording in the jazz idiom, cut before he went on to more lucrative areas. —*Scott Yanow*

Black and Blue / 1963 / Capitol ✦✦✦
Super blues and jazzy soul by Lou Rawls from an early period on Capitol. He hadn't yet found the hit formula, but was cutting some superb singles. His voice had a resonance and strength developed for years on the gospel trail, and also during his work backing Sam Cooke. Even though he didn't get any hits, it's well worth the cost if you can find this album. —*Ron Wynn*

Tobacco Road / Jul. 29, 1963-Aug. 20, 1963 / Capitol ✦✦✦
His third album for Capitol had a good version of the title track, and tried to mix blues, soul, and R&B. Rawls sang in a strong, rousing manner, turning in both outstanding ballads and good uptempo tunes, but the company wasn't able to break any song enough for Rawls to even get on the charts. —*Ron Wynn*

For You My Love / Oct. 27, 1964-Nov. 27, 1968 / Capitol ✦✦
This reissue CD has highlights from two earlier albums. Singer Lou Rawls is featured in 1964 with a big band arranged by Benny Carter and in 1968 while backed by Benny Golson arrangements. It is a pity that neither Carter nor Golson were playing much at the time for their horns are very much missed. Rawls alternates superior standards with period soul/pop material such as "If I Had My Life to Live Over," "Whispering Grass," and "I Love You Yes I Do." Needless to say the earlier material (including "Gee Baby, Ain't I Good to You," "Just Squeeze Me" and a previously unissued "That's Your Red Wagon") is better but overall this set is a rather mixed bag, making one wish that Rawls had chosen to stick to jazz and blues. —*Scott Yanow*

Lou Rawls and Strings / May 5, 1965-Sep. 1965 / Capitol ✦✦✦✦
While the strings are overdone at times, Rawls fits his voice into the situation with verve and flair. He never tried to overpower or work against the support, moderated his voice, and paced each song to ensure that he would hit a vocal peak at the right point. The album still didn't generate much sales response, but it remains one of Rawls' most stunning works on any label. —*Ron Wynn*

Soulin' / 1966 / Capitol ✦✦✦✦
Lou Rawls began his roll onto the R&B and pop charts with this 1966 work. He was now doing soul material, songs where his gospel background and instincts took over, and he simply wailed, soared, and shouted, rather than interpreting or working with blues progressions. He scored a huge hit with "Love Is a Hurtin' Thing" and had finally found a successful formula. —*Ron Wynn*

Too Much / May 1967 / Capitol ✦✦✦
Lou Rawls was in the midst of a hot streak at Capitol, scoring smash singles and winning Grammy awards. This was one of three albums he released in 1967, all of which made the pop Top 40 albums chart. It was superbly produced and arranged by David Axelrod, with Rawls being bluesy, soulful, anguished, triumphant, and resigned. He displayed both a variety of moods and a vocal mastery at its peak. Unfortunately, this has also been deleted. —*Ron Wynn*

That's Lou / Aug. 1967 / Capitol ✦✦✦
Rawls topped his success of the previous year with an even bigger hit album. He won a Grammy for "Dead End Street" and got good notices for a follow-up cut about the joys and pains of being a celebrity. David Axelrod gave Rawls the production and arranging support he needed, keeping everything squarely in the background and letting Rawls' voice stay at the center and be the focus of the song. —*Ron Wynn*

You're Good for Me / 1968 / Capitol ✦✦✦
Things were beginning to cool a bit for Lou Rawls following the period when he topped the R&B charts, got great crossover exposure, and won a Grammy. This album didn't have the impact or sustained appeal of past works, although it was just as well produced and arranged, and Rawls sang with his usual vigor and impact. The songs were a bit below the normal standard, but it was otherwise a fine album—just not quite as potent. —*Ron Wynn*

Unmistakably Lou / 1977 / Philadelphia International ✦✦✦✦
Lou Rawls was riding another hot streak in the late '70s, his career rejuvenated by a string of fine albums and singles on the Philly International label. This was the follow-up to his huge hit LP *All Things in Time*. He only had one R&B chart song from the album, but in ways, his vocals are superior to those on the prior album. Where the Gamble/Huff production team's efforts on the preceding project rivaled Rawls' vocals, he took the spotlight this time, while their arrangements and productions were more on the subdued side. —*Ron Wynn*

At Last / Jun. 1989 / Blue Note ✦✦
He's never deserted either blues or jazz, but Lou Rawls hasn't always found a receptive audience for these styles at notoriously conservative major labels. That wasn't the case on this 1989 album, on which Rawls performed straightahead jazz and pre-rock pop or blues, and was backed by an all-star lineup including Ray Charles, Cornell Dupree, Steve Khan, Richard Tee and Dianne Reeves. His voice had an exuberance and fervor that spoke volumes about how happy he was in the setting. —*Ron Wynn*

It's Supposed to Be Fun / 1990 / Blue Note ✦✦
Alfred Lion would not have been pleased to have this CD on his Blue Note label. Lion rarely recorded vocalists (Sheila Jordan was one of the very few to lead her own session) and he would never have considered coming out with a soft soul-pop date like this 1990 session. The music is closer to lightweight country than to jazz and, although there are some notable cameos (by altoists Hank Crawford, Bobby Watts and Dick Oatts, the tenors of Eddie Harris, and Rick Margitza, trumpeter Jack Walrath and trombonist Steve Turre), Rawls' so-so vocals and the weak material dominate and sink the effort. —*Scott Yanow*

● **The Best of Lou Rawls** / Oct. 17, 1990 / Capitol ✦✦✦✦
A nice collection of Rawls' Capitol singles, which include his No. 1 hit "Love Is a Hurtin' Thing" and many other fine chart singles, all produced by David Axelrod. Rawls got in a groove during his Capitol years, singing songs that had a soul feel but a jazz and blues base. In some ways, he's never made better songs than his late-'60s and early-'70s stint at Capitol. —*Ron Wynn*

Portrait of the Blues / Apr. 13, 1992-Oct. 3, 1992 / Capitol ✦✦✦
The Las Vegas lounge act that Rawls has metamorphosized into over the last two decades may blemish some critics' view of him as a blues interpreter. However, this album holds the potential to put such thoughts to rest. From Willie Dixon's "I Just Want to Make Love to You" to Big Joe Turner's "Chains of Love," in his low baritone, Rawls gives the blues an authentically sophisticated turn. Joe Williams, Cornell Dupree, and other stellar roots musicians give their all on the set. A highlight is Rawls' calypso styled rendition of "A Lover's Question" with Phoebe Snow. However, for the most part, this is a polished set of blues standards, light enough to please Rawls' pop crowd, but genuine enough to attract some bluesers. —*Bil Carpenter*

Spotlight on Lou Rawls / Jan. 23, 1996 / Capitol ✦✦✦
This 18-track compilation isolates his most pop-oriented output for Capitol in the '60s, consisting largely of standards on the order of "St. James Infirmary," "Stormy Weather," and "Willow Weep for Me," often with orchestration. Includes one previously unreleased cut, "When It's Sleepy Time Down South." —*Richie Unterberger*

The Records

f. 1977, London, England, **db.** 1982
New Wave, Power Pop
The Records are probably best remembered for their cult classic and minor hit, "Starry Eyes"—a near-perfect song that defined British power pop in the '70s. And while they never quite matched the success of that record, their high-quality output from 1979 to 1982 has not only held up better than most of the era with its timeless appeal, but has also served as a blueprint for the various waves of British and American power-pop since then. Some have gone as far as to call them the "British Big Star," which is probably a fair comparison—within their genre, they're seen as giants, yet the general public has missed them for the most part.

The band was formed around 1977, when pub rockers Kursaal Flyers broke up. The drummer from the band, Will Birch, and vocalist/guitarist John Wicks, who had joined the Kursaals in the last stages, began writing together, inspired by the pure-pop tradition of the Raspberries, Badfinger, and Big Star. By 1978, they had completed the group by adding bassist Phil Brown and guitarist Huw Gower. After a series of live gigs,

they released their debut, "Starry Eyes," on the independent Record Company label in November the same year. They received some valuable early exposure on the Stiff label's "Be Stiff" tour which lead to their signing with Virgin Records.

Wicks and Birch continued to churn out should-have-been-hit pop classics over the next three years and three albums—1979's *Shades in Bed* (released in a slightly modified form as *The Records* in the US), 1980's *Crashes* (which found Jude Cole replacing Gower), and 1982's *Music on Both Sides* (which replaced Cole with Dave Whelan and added another vocalist, Chris Gent). Aside from a minor hit with "Starry Eyes" in the US, their efforts were criminally unrewarded. The band broke up in 1982, though they reformed temporarily in 1990 to contribute a track to a Brian Wilson tribute album. Birch went on to become a notable music critic and historian; he also compiled several compact disc reissues, including *Naughty Rhythms: The Best of Pub Rock*. Wicks began a solo career in the mid-'90s, appearing on the *Yellow Pills, Vol. 3* collection with a song co-written with Birch, "Her Stars Are My Stars"—a pop gem that picks up right where they left off. "Starry Eyes" continues to be a cult pop classic—still heavily requested on alternative radio retro shows. —*Chris Woodstra*

Shades in Bed / 1979 / Virgin ✦✦✦✦
The band's first UK LP is a pure pop masterpiece featuring the near-perfect singles "Starry Eyes" and "Teenarama." The album was retitled *The Records* and released in a modified form in America. The first pressings came with a bonus 12-inch entitled *High Heels*, which featured a collection of four covers. —*Chris Woodstra*

The Records / 1979 / Virgin ✦✦✦✦
Virtually every song here is a catchy guitar-driven pop song with sweet harmonies, from the single "Starry Eyes" through "Teenarama" and "Another Star." The album includes a bonus record containing the Records' versions of such oldies as the Kinks' "See My Friends" and Spirit's "1984." —*William Ruhlmann*

Crashes / 1980 / Virgin ✦✦✦
The Records' second American album is just as tuneful and nearly as catchy as its predecessor, though none of the songs have the punch of "Starry Eyes." "Girl in the Golden Disc" and "Hearts Will Be Broken" are the highlights. Unfortunately, the band's take on the brilliant "Hearts in Her Eyes" (a song written by Will Birch and John Wicks and covered more successfully by the reunited Searchers the previous year) is slightly lackluster and somewhat a letdown. —*Chris Woodstra*

Music on Both Sides / 1982 / Virgin ✦✦✦
With a tighter, harder-rocking five-man lineup, the Records returned with *Music on Both Sides*. Despite the usual strong material courtesy of the John Wicks/Will Birch partnership, the album failed to make an impact. This would be their last album. —*Chris Woodstra*

● **Smashes Crashes and Near Misses** / 1988 / Virgin ✦✦✦✦
The Records may not have been great innovators but they undeniably made some of the best singles of the era. *Smashes, Crashes and Near Misses*, a 20-track collection, is the definitive proof of the band's generally overlooked brilliance. Anyone interested in power-pop should start here. —*Chris Woodstra*

Paying for the Summer of Love / 1990 / Skyclad ✦✦
A collection of demos recorded prior to the first album, *Paying for the Summer of Love* provides an interesting look at the songs in their formative stages but only true fans need to seek this one out. —*Chris Woodstra*

The Red Hot Chili Peppers

f. 1983, Los Angeles, CA
Alternative Pop-Rock, Funk Metal
A quartet with varying personnel, anchored by lead singer Anthony Kiedis and bassist Flea (born Michael Balzary), the Red Hot Chili Peppers play a hybrid rock, incorporating punk, funk, rap, and metal. Though the mixture was ahead of its time when the group was first organized in the early '80s in Los Angeles, the music industry has since caught up to it, which earns the group the right to call itself the forerunner of an approach now adopted by such acts as Living Colour and Faith No More, and also means the Peppers themselves have finally hit the big time. In 1988, guitarist Hillel Slovak died of an overdose and the band reorganized, with John Frusciante on guitar and Chad Smith on drums. This lineup scored a commercial breakthrough with *Mother's Milk*, which went gold after its release in 1989. They ascended to real star status with the release of *Blood Sugar Sex Magik*, which sold two million copies and included the Top Ten hit "Under the Bridge." In mid-1992, Frusciante left the group and was replaced by Arik Marshall.

Marshall was replaced by Jesse Tobias in 1993. Tobias' tenure with the group was extremely brief; after a couple of months, he was replaced by ex-Jane's Addiction guitarist Dave Navarro. —*William Ruhlmann*

Red Hot Chili Peppers / 1984 / EMI America ✦✦✦✦
The Red Hot Chili Peppers' debut album sketched out their funk metal hybrid quite effectively, especially on the warped deep groove of "True Men Don't Kill Coyotes." Even though their fusion of heavy guitars and slapping bass was audacious, their first effort didn't quite gel into a cohesive album. — *Stephen Thomas Erlewine*

Freaky Styley / 1985 / EMI America ✦✦✦✦
Under the guiding hand of George Clinton, the Red Hot Chili Peppers turned in a nastier, funkier album their second time around with *Freaky Styley*. It also didn't hurt that it was the first album the group recorded with Hillel Slovak; he was performing with What Is This at the time the debut was recorded. Even though Slovak and Clinton help make the music more exciting, their contributions didn't necessarily mean that *Freaky Styley* was more coherent than the debut—it just meant that it was more compelling — *Stephen Thomas Erlewine*

The Uplift Mofo Party Plan / 1987 / EMI America ✦✦✦
If the Red Hot Chili Peppers' first two albums were incoherent, *The Uplift Mofo Party Plan* is a downright mess, with the band being torn between their metallic-punk instincts and their funk ambitions. Part of the album works, particularly the fierce "Fight Like a Brave," but most of the record reveals the group's tendency to wallow in shallow sexist chants, culminating in the sophomoric "Party on Your Pussy." — *Stephen Thomas Erlewine*

Mother's Milk / Aug. 1989 / EMI America ✦✦✦
While *Mother's Milk* is not their most adventurous or best release, it's a good album, which expanded the Chili Peppers' cult. Mainstream listeners were attracted to the band in large part because of their cover of Stevie Wonder's "Higher Ground," the best song on *Mother's Milk*. Other highlights include "Knock Me Down," "Taste the Pain," "Nobody Weird Like Me," and "Sexy Mexican Maid." — *Meredith Erlewine & Stephen Thomas Erlewine*

Blood Sugar Sex Magik / Sep. 1991 / Warner Brothers ✦✦✦✦
It isn't just that the world has finally come around to the Peppers' funk-rock mixture, it's that, with the help of producer Rick Rubin, they've found a focus and that, as musicians, they've reached a sufficient level of competence to execute their ideas. The result is their best album, containing the hit "Under the Bridge." — *William Ruhlmann*

● **What Hits!?** / Sep. 29, 1992 / EMI America ✦✦✦✦
A sampling of tracks from the band's ten-year career, it includes the hit "Under the Bridge," plus "Higher Ground" and "Fight Like a Brave." — *AMG*

Out in L.A. / Nov. 1, 1994 / EMI America ✦✦
A tepid collection of remixes and obscurities, *Out in L.A.* is only of interest to devoted Chili Peppers fans, and even they might have their patience tested by this overly long compilation. — *Stephen Thomas Erlewine*

One Hot Minute / Sep. 12, 1995 / Warner Brothers ✦✦✦
Following up *Blood Sugar Sex Magik* proved to be a difficult task for the Red Hot Chili Peppers. In 1993, two years after *Blood Sugar*, former Jane's Addiction gutiarist Dave Navarro joined up, but it was still another two years before *One Hot Minute* appeared, due to various personal problems. Navarro's metallic guitar shredding should have added some weight to the Chili Peppers' punk-inflected heavy-guitar funk, but tends to make it plodding. By emphasizing the metal, the funk is gradually phased out of the blend, as is melody; the grinding chant of "Warped" is hardly as twisted as anything on *Freaky Styley*, or even "Give It Away." The ballads "My Friends" and "Transcending" are blatant attempts to hold on to the mainstream audience gained by "Under the Bridge," but the melodies are weak and the lyrics are even more feeble. *One Hot Minute* is as musically ambitious as *Blood Sugar Sex Magik*, but is even more unfocused which means it provides the fewest thrills of any of the group's albums. — *Stephen Thomas Erlewine*

Red House Painters

f. 1989, San Francisco, CA
Alternative Pop-Rock, Folk-Rock
Red House Painters was primarily the vehicle of singer-songwriter Mark Kozelek, an evocative, compelling performer of rare emotional intensity. Like Mark Eitzel of American Music Club, to whose work the Painters were invariably compared and to whom their early success owed a tremendous debt, Kozelek laid his soul bare on record, conjuring harrowingly acute tales of pain, despair and loss; unlike Eitzel, Nick Drake, and other poets of decay, Kozelek's autobiographical songs walked the tightrope without a net—forsaking the safety offered by metaphor and allegory, he faced his demons in the first person, creating a singularly haunting body of work unparalleled in its vulnerability and honesty.

Kozelek was born and raised in the Midwest, and was addicted to drugs by the age of ten before entering rehab a few years later. Throughout his travails, he clung to music, and formed his first band, God Forbid, while in his teens. After relocating to Atlanta, Georgia, he struck up

a friendship with drummer Anthony Koutsos, and formed the first incarnation of Red House Painters. A move to San Francisco followed, where guitarist Gorden Mack and bassist Jerry Vessel rounded out the group's roster.

While performing on the Bay Area club circuit, the quartet came to the attention of American Music Club's Eitzel, who often named Red House Painters his favorite band. Through Eitzel, a demo tape of recordings cut in 1989 and 1990 made their way to the London offices of 4AD Records, which signed the group and in 1992 issued the unvarnished demos—a superb collection of spartan, atmospheric melodies lurking behind Kozelek's ghostly vocals—as the LP *Down Colorful Hill*.

In 1993, Red House Painters emerged from the studio with over two dozen new recordings, which they issued on back-to-back eponymously-titled albums. Taken in tandem, the LPs established Kozelek as a unique songwriter capable of conveying stunning emotional depths; compositions like "Grace Cathedral Park," "Katy Song," "Strawberry Hill," "Evil," and "Uncle Joe" expanded greatly upon the emotional palette evidenced on the first record, unflinchingly detailing Kozelek's erratic, abusive nature and troubled background.

A two-year layoff followed, during which time only an EP, *Shock Me*—a brief set built around a dramatic reading of an old Kiss song—appeared in 1994. Finally, the luminous *Ocean Beach*, a collection of pastoral, almost sunny performances, appeared in 1995, although not without controversy; initially, 4AD did not want to release the record, further straining already tenuous relations between the band and their label.

When Kozelek began work on a long-discussed solo album, 4AD threw in the towel; the album, a more rock-oriented work dubbed *Songs for a Blue Guitar*, appeared in 1996 on the Island imprint Supreme. Although Kozelek was the only band member to appear on the record, it was nonetheless issued under the Red House Painters name in order to give the group a push as it headed into the second phase of its career. — *Jason Ankeny*

Down Colorful Hill / Sep. 15, 1992 / 4AD ✦✦✦✦
Not a proper debut as such, *Down Colorful Hill* instead comprises the demo recordings which won Red House Painters their contract with the 4AD label, released here with minimal overdubbing. Regardless, the group has already reached full maturity; these lengthy, ponderous songs are remarkably evocative portraits of a distinctly tortured psyche—Mark Kozelek forgoes the camouflage of metaphor to lay his soul on the line, and the honesty of his craft is both beautiful and disturbing. — *Jason Ankeny*

Red House Painters / May 25, 1993 / 4AD ✦✦✦✦
The first of the group's two eponymously titled 1993 efforts is a sprawling, remarkable set distinguished by Mark Kozelek's continuing maturation as a songwriter; far removed from the uniform darkness of *Down Colorful Hill*, *Red House Painters* offers an expansion of both emotional and musical possibilities. Working outward from the cutting "Mistress"—included as both a spartan piano ballad and as a gauzy rock number—the record moves through a shifting, impressionistic backdrop of textures and sounds; from the luminous folk-pop of "Grace Cathedral Park" to the epic dissonance of the gut-wrenching "Strawberry Hill," the songs resonate with depth and poignancy, and rank as Kozelek's most fully realized collection of compositions. — *Jason Ankeny*

Red House Painters / Sep. 1993 / 4AD ✦✦✦
The second of two self-titled 1993 efforts, this *Red House Painters* collects the remaining tracks from the remarkably fruitful sessions which also launched the earlier, superior album. Far more experimental in nature, it opens with "Evil," an almost painfully slow and withdrawn song which acutely sets the album's haunting, dark tone. While not everything works—the electric version of "New Jersey" pales in comparison to the previous set's acoustic rendition, while the cover of Simon and Garfunkel's "I Am a Rock" is overripe—both the unrequited love song "Bubble" and the dysfunctional "Uncle Joe" rank among Mark Kozelek's most perfectly-realized compositions, and the closer, a marvelously downbeat reading of "The Star Spangled Banner," allows the group's often-unsung black humor to seep to the surface. — *Jason Ankeny*

● **Ocean Beach** / Mar. 28, 1995 / 4AD ✦✦✦✦
Red House Painters has always been Mark Kozelek's project, but *Ocean Beach* represents the first record that is almost entirely a solo project. Not that that distinction has made a great change in the music—*Ocean Beach* is a spare, gentle, nearly painfully introspective folk-rock album that draws more from Simon & Garfunkel than Bob Dylan. Kozelek reigns in the droning, experimental tendencies of the group's first full-length album, yet he is more generous with his melodies and arrangements than the band's second untitled record. While Red House Painters remains very arty and self-conscious, *Ocean Beach* shows the singer-songwriter breaking out of his shell ever so slightly, bringing more fully developed songs and melodies with him. — *Stephen Thomas Erlewine*

Songs for a Blue Guitar / Jul. 23, 1996 / Supreme ♦♦♦

Before *Songs for a Blue Guitar* could appear, the Red House Painters' singer-songwriter/guitarist Mark Kozelek had to leave his old label 4AD (allegedly over a Kozelek solo album 4AD rejected), split up the band, and find a new home for his music on Supreme Recordings. Fortunately for Kozelek and his audience, it's worth all the tumult. This is the solo album Kozelek wanted to make masquerading as a Red House Painters album; no other Painters are listed in the liner notes. The freedom from the group setting is evident in the songs on *Songs for a Blue Guitar*. They're a diverse group, including gently hypnotic folk like "Have You Forgotten" and "Trailways," country-rock both slow ("Song for a Blue Guitar") and fast ("Make Like Paper") as well as a diverse selection of covers. Mixed in with Kozelek's traditionally beautiful and sad material, Yes' "Long Distance Runaround," Paul McCartney's "Silly Love Songs," and the Cars' "All Mixed Up" bring light to the Red House Painters' typically shadowy songs. *Songs for a Blue Guitar's* deep beauty and eclecticism make it another artistic triumph for the Red House Painters. —*Heather Phares*

The Red Krayola

f. 1966, Houston, TX

Art-Rock/Progressive-Rock, Psychedelic, Experimental, Post-Punk

One of the longest-lived underground rock groups (if not *the* longest-lived), the Red Krayola lasted through the birth pangs of psychedelia past the death throes of post-punk. The one constant in its ever-shifting lineup was principal singer-songwriter/visionary Mayo Thompson, who seemed as concerned with deconstructing the language of "rock" music as with actually expressing himself within it. That made Red Krayola's catalog challenging, often difficult listening. Its saving grace was the quirky charm of Thompson's songs and vocals, with a whimsical humor and open-mindedness rather atypical of avant-rock.

The Red Krayola, initially spelled Red Crayola, were formed in Houston as a trio in 1966. The International Artists label, which was building a roster of Texas psychedelic bands, signed the group after watching one of their performances in a shopping mall, of all places. The company was convinced that if the musicians could entertain a crowd without anything in the way of conventional command of their instruments, they must be on to something. Early demos (now on the compilation *Epitaph for a Legend*) indicated a spacy folk-rock bent. But although some of the material was reprised on their debut, *The Parable of Arable Land*, by this time the group were taking a more confrontational, experimental approach in the studio. With "war sucks!" chants and layers of "free-form freakout" noise threatening to smother the songs underneath, it's been hailed as a precursor to the assault of industrial rock and made their International Artists labelmates, the 13th Floor Elevators, sound almost normal. Although the Krayola, like the Elevators, were able to attract a small cult following, it was a very small hardcore of devotees, centered around hip metropolises like San Francisco and New York.

An even more avant-garde follow-up, *Coconut Hotel*, was rejected for release by International Artists. A gentler, more song-based effort appeared in its place (*God Bless the Red Krayola and All Who Sail on Her*). But by the late '60s the Krayola had disbanded, partially due to disputes with their label. Thompson released a solo album in 1970 that was the very definition of "quirky," with an eclectic folk-rock base that bore some rough similarities to Syd Barrett's work. Red Krayola, however, was put in deep freeze as Thompson concentrated on non-musical media.

Red Krayola were unexpectedly resurrected in the late '70s, however. Thompson had moved to England, where he found that the old Red Krayola recordings enjoyed a cult among hip listeners. Thompson was never a champion of hippie ideals, and he was able to make the transition into the punk era effectively by forming new incarnations of the Red Krayola with such musicians as Gina Birch (the Raincoats), Epic Soundtracks (Swell Maps), and Lora Logic (X-Ray Spex). Red Krayola's releases on underground European labels like Rough Trade and Recommended presented an ensemble that dove into the heart of post-punk, with skronky guitars and horns, and disjointed, arty song structures.

Thompson joined Pere Ubu for a while in the early '80s. He always kept the Red Krayola going, however, although most of their releases went all but unheard in the US, as they were only available as obscure European indie imports. The situation changed to some degree in the mid-'90s, when the Krayola landed a US deal with Drag City and Thompson returned to the States after a long residency in Europe, even embarking on some modest American touring. Still resolutely uncommercial, the material was nonetheless more approachable for adventurous listeners who shied away from full-throttle avant-rock. Thompson's collaborators included members of Gastr Del Sol and Slovenly, as well as guitarist Jim O'Rourke. —*Richie Unterberger*

Parable of Arable Land / 1967 / Collectables ♦♦♦

The Red Krayola's debut remains their most celebrated and notorious effort. Although this was categorized as psychedelia when first released, it's more like futuristic avant-garde noise-rock. Thompson's flighty songs about hurricane fighter planes and transparent radiation are almost submerged by a cacophony of "free-form freakout" noise created on kazoos, flutes, harmonica, hammer, jugs, bottles, sticks, and more by a large ensemble of friends dubbed the Familiar Ugly. My minority opinion holds that the wistfulness of Thompson's tunes (the brittle "War Sucks" excepted) and voice may have been served better by less self-consciously far-out arrangements. (Several of the songs can be heard in more skeletal form on the *Epitaph for a Legend* compilation.) It's quite a daring statement for its day, however, with instrumental cameos by Roky Erickson on a couple of tracks. —*Richie Unterberger*

● **God Bless the Red Krayola & All Who Sail with It** / 1968 / Collectables ♦♦♦♦

A far gentler, though equally quirky, album as their maiden effort. The Krayola's second record was a series of odd miniatures that, though far more restrained than *Parable of Arable Land*, was a much more solid indication of the direction Mayo Thompson would explore over the next few decades. These are less "songs" than stream-of-consciousness fragments. Thompson's wavering, quizzical voice intones disjointed but evocative lyrics that may appear to be non sequiturs. Odd time meters and musical shifts do their best to defy conventional rock song structures. It's not very poppy, no, but if the description sounds foreboding, be assured that as experimental rock goes, it's far warmer and friendlier than the norm. —*Richie Unterberger*

The Red Krayola / Sep. 20, 1994 / Drag City ♦♦♦

Now working with such younger musicians as John McEntire (Tortoise), Jim O'Rourke, and David Grubbs, Mayo Thompson comfortably steers the Red Krayola into the mish-mash of '90s post-punkdom here. For Thompson, it's not so much a return to the scene (he had always kept recording, after all) as a continuation of his themes of musical eclecticism. It's heavy on the angular guitar lines and unusual lyrical construction/deconstruction, with occasional electronic flutters. It's not as highly recommended as his two subsequent Drag City releaes (*Amor and Language* and *Hazel*), which state the same thematic concerns with a tad more melodicism and warmth. —*Richie Unterberger*

Coconut Hotel / Apr. 1, 1995 / Drag City ♦♦

As strange as the Red Krayola's debut album was, their proposed follow-up, *Coconut Hotel*, was far stranger. This all-instrumental recording was more appropriately classified as twentieth-century avant-garde music than rock, and was rejected by International Artists for release in 1967, finally seeing the light of day on Drag City in 1995. All power to the Krayola for doing things their own way, but it's not hard to understand International Artists' reasoning. This has so little commercial potential that it makes Zappa's *Lumpy Gravy* sound like AM radio fodder. Dissonant exotic plucked strings, spooky organ clusters, 36 (yes, 36) "One-Second Pieces"—these are not tunes that you can hum, by any stretch of the imagination. Some acoustic guitar pieces bear the influence of John Fahey (with whom the Krayola recorded some unreleased material around this time). It's totally uncompromising, and rather wearisome, to be honest. It's like nothing else that nominally "rock" groups were doing in 1967, but it's not nearly as interesting as their official releases from the late '60s, which had at least a few loose ties to conventional song structures. —*Richie Unterberger*

Amor and Language / Jun. 15, 1995 / Drag City ♦♦♦

This is about as gentle as '90s experimental rock gets, and not without its pleasing riffs here and there. But the non-linear lyrics, odd electronic buzzes, and mild guitar dissonances effectively prohibit this from being viewed as a sellout of any sort. It's music for open-minded indie fans who don't necessarily want to be assaulted while they free-associate, and that can only be a good thing. —*Richie Unterberger*

Hazel / Nov. 19, 1996 / Drag City ♦♦♦

Mayo Thompson has expressed bemusement at the constant categorization of his work as "quirky." *Hazel*, however, will do nothing to stem the tide of that adjective showing up in reviews such as this one. The Red Krayola do not seem interested nearly as much in connecting disparate styles as jumbling them. So you'll hear a languid, Lou Reedish drone segue into a John Faheyish guitar pattern backed by weird female vocals, and then a light reggaeish thing about Christian soldiers marching onward. The lyrics are not constructed to make a point, but to reflect the rhythm and fragmented patterns of everyday thought and conversation. It's interesting, but too nonchalantly strange to evoke a passionate response. —*Richie Unterberger*

Leon Redbone

b. Canada

Guitar, Vocals / Ragtime, Folk

While his gravelly baritone and omnipresent fedora, dark glasses and Groucho Marx moustache made him one of the more distinct and recognizable characters in popular music, little is known about the neo-vaudeville crooner Leon Redbone. Throughout his career, he steadfastly refused to divulge any information about his background or personal life; according to legend, Redbone's desire to protect his privacy was so intense that when he was approached by the famed producer John Hammond, the contact number he gave was not his own phone, but that of a Dial-a-Joke service.

Because Redbone first emerged as a performer in Toronto during the 1970s, he was believed to be Canadian; his work, a revival of pre-World War II ragtime, jazz and blues sounds, recalled the work of performers ranging from Jelly Roll Morton and Bing Crosby to blackface star Emmett Miller. He made his recording debut in 1976 with *On the Track*, which featured legendary jazz violinist Joe Venuti as well as singer-songwriter Don McLean; his 1977 follow-up *Double Time* even reached the US Top 40 charts, largely on the strength of his frequent appearances on television's "Saturday Night Live."

After 1978's *Champagne Charlie*, Redbone began recording only sporadically; following 1981's *Branch to Branch*, he waited four years before re-entering the studio to cut *Red to Blue*. Invariably, his albums featured guest appearances from an eclectic cast of luminaries: while 1987's *Christmas Island* included a cameo by Dr. John, 1994's *Whistling in the Wind* included duets with Ringo Starr and Merle Haggard. Despite his low profile, Redbone also earned a certain measure of fame as a fixture in various television advertising campaigns. —*Jason Ankeny*

● On the Track / 1976 / Warner Brothers ✦✦✦✦
Debut album contains a typical collection of campy oldies ("Ain't Misbehavin'," "Lulu's Back in Town"), accompanied by a varied cast including folkie Don McLean and jazz stars Milt Hinton and Ralph McDonald. —*William Ruhlmann*

Leon Redbone Live / 1985 / Pair ✦✦✦✦
A live setting is just about ideal for a performer like Redbone, and he does not disappoint on this two-record set, which features "Diddy Wah Diddy," "Champagne Charlie," and other favorites. —*William Ruhlmann*

Red to Blue / 1985 / August ✦✦✦
Redbone's best overall album veers from country to jazz to folk to blues. Backup includes members of Vince Giordano's old-time jazz band, Dr. John, David Bromberg, and the Roches on songs ranging from "Lovesick Blues" to Bob Dylan's "Living the Blues," and with two Redbone originals, as well. —*William Ruhlmann*

Up a Lazy River / Feb. 25, 1992 / Private Music ✦✦✦

Redd Kross

f. 1980, Hawthorne, CA
Alternative Pop-Rock, Power Pop
Inspired as much by breakfast cereal and kiddie TV as by rock music, the punk-pop cult band Redd Kross was the brainchild of Steve and Jeff McDonald, brothers from the Los Angeles suburb of Hawthorne (also home of the Beach Boys) who began playing music together before either had hit puberty. Fueled by a series of dubious visits to famed area rock clubs like the Roxy and the Whiskey-a-Go-Go, they formed their first band, the Tourists, in 1978; Jeff, then 15, handled vocal duties while Steve, 11, took up the bass.

After rounding out the group with schoolmates Greg Hetson on guitar and Ron Reyes on drums, the Tourists played their first gig, opening for Black Flag. Following a name change to Red Cross, they issued their self-titled EP debut in 1980. After the departure of Hetson and Reyes (for the Circle Jerks and Black Flag, respectively), the McDonalds enlisted a revolving lineup of underground musicians for their full-length follow-up, 1981's *Born Innocent*, which found the group's pop-culture obsessions bubbling over on tributes like "Linda Blair" and "Charlie" (about Charles Manson, whose "Cease to Exist" they also covered).

Following the album's release, the band was threatened with a lawsuit from the real International Red Cross; as a result, they became Redd Kross, and returned in 1984 for *Teen Babes from Monsanto*, a collection of covers of artists ranging from David Bowie to the Rolling Stones and the Shangri-Las. That year, they also appeared in and composed the music for the no-budget film *Desperate Teenage Lovedolls*, which included their transcendent cover of the Brady Bunch's "(It's A) Sunshine Day."

Complete with new guitarist Robert Hecker and drummer Roy McDonald (no relation) 1987's *Neurotica*, with songs like "Frosted Flake," "The Ballad of Tatum O'Tot and the Fried Vegetables" and "Janus, Jeanie and George Harrison," appeared primed to push the band out of the underground; shortly after the album's release, however, their label Big Time folded, and legal hassles prevented Redd Kross from recording any new material under its own name for three years.

Instead, as the Tater Totz, the McDonald brothers corralled Three O'Clock member Michael Quercio and former Partridge Family kid Danny Bonaduce for 1989's *Alien Sleestaks From Brazil*, the title a nod to the Sid and Marty Krofft children's series *Land of the Lost*. A collection of satiric and surreal covers, the LP included renditions of "Give

Peace a Chance," "We Will Rock You," and Yoko Ono's "Don't Worry Kyoko." Prior to another Tater Totz effort, 1989's *Sgt. Shonen's Exploding Plastic Eastman Band Mono! Stereo* (recorded with ex-Runaway Cherie Currie and future Foo Fighter Pat Smear), the McDonalds detoured into another side project, Anarchy 6, for the 1988 mock punk tribute *Hardcore Lives!*

Finally, in 1990 Redd Kross landed a deal with Atlantic, issuing the surprisingly straighforward *Third Eye*. After an appearance (alongside David Crosby) in the kitschy 1991 film *Spirit of 76*, the band issued a handful of singles before 1993's *Phaseshifter*, augmented by guitarist Eddie Kurdziel, keyboardist Gere Fennelly, and drummer Brian Reitzell. Minus Fennelly, Redd Kross returned in 1997 with *Show World*. —*Jason Ankeny*

Teen Babes from Monsanto / 1984 / Enigma ✦✦✦✦
The title says it all. Speedy, sloppy pop loaded with fuzzed-up guitars and whiny vocals. Mostly covers (Stooges, Kiss, Bowie), it's a great little statement of purpose from these '70s hard-rock babes-turned-adults. —*John Dougan*

Born Innocent / 1986 / Frontier ✦✦✦
Red Cross' first full-length album celebrated pop culture icons from Linda Blair to Charles Manson, with a fuzzy, manic glee, but too much of the record sounds tossed off for it to be compelling. —*Stephen Thomas Erlewine*

● Neurotica / 1987 / Big Time ✦✦✦✦

Third Eye / Sep. 1990 / Atlantic ✦✦✦
Redd Kross reached its peak in the early 1980s, when the band made such humorous and clever contributions to punk rock as "Linda Blair." As the '80s progressed, Kross got away from punk and went for cleaner, less reckless alternative rock and power-pop. Those who play 1990's *Third Eye* next to Kross' early recordings will hear just how radically the band changed over the years. Whether rocking aggressively on "Shonen Knife," going for a very melodic "jangly guitar" approach on "Annie's Gone" and "I Don't Know How to Be Your Friend" or sounding positively Beatlesque on "Bubblegum Factory," Kross shows just how far it has come since the irreverent, freewheeling aggression of "Linda Blair." While some punk enthusiasts missed the old Kross, this decent though not outstanding CD proves that the band was still worthwhile at the dawn of the '90s. —*Alex Henderson*

Phaseshifter / Oct. 5, 1993 / This Way Up ✦✦✦✦
Fusion of several styles and decades; raving fuzz collides with bubblegum, jangly pop subverts arena-rock riffs. —*Roch Parisien*

Show World / Feb. 11, 1997 / Polygram ✦✦✦✦
Nearly four years after the release of *Phaseshifter*, Redd Kross delivered their follow-up, *Show World*. In between the two albums, the alternative punk-pop audience came and went, leaving Redd Kross slightly out of the loop, which meant *Show World* wasn't greeted to the kind of acclaim to might have received in 1994 or 1995. And that's too bad, because the record is one of the band's best albums, filled with tight, catchy hooks, memorably melodic songs and a bristling energy that makes it a compulsive listen. —*Stephen Thomas Erlewine*

Otis Redding

b. Sep. 9, 1941, Dawson, GA, d. Dec. 10, 1967, Madison, WI
Vocals / Soul
One of the most influential soul singers of the 1960s, Otis Redding exemplified to many listeners the power of Southern "Deep Soul"—hoarse, gritty vocals, brassy arrangements, and an emotional way with both party tunes and aching ballads. He was also the most consistent exponent of the Stax sound, cutting his records at the Memphis label/studios that did much to update rhythm and blues into modern soul. His death at the age of 26 was tragic not just because he seemed on the verge of breaking through to a wide pop audience (which he would indeed do with his posthumous No.1 single, "(Sittin' On) the Dock of the Bay"). It was also unfortunate because, as "Dock of the Bay" demonstrated, he was also at a point of artistic breakthrough in terms of the expression and sophistication of his songwriting and singing.

Although Redding at his peak was viewed as a consummate, versatile showman, he began his recording career in the early '60s as a Little Richard-styled shouter. The Georgian was working in the band of guitarist Johnny Jenkins at the time, and in 1962 he took advantage of an opportunity to record the ballad "These Arms of Mine" at a Jenkins session. When it became an R&B hit, Redding's solo career was truly on its way, though the hits didn't really start to fly until 1965 and 1966, when "Mr. Pitiful," "I've Been Loving You Too Long," "I Can't Turn You Loose," a cover of the Rolling Stones' "Satisfaction," and "Respect" (later turned into a huge pop smash by Aretha Franklin) were all big sellers.

Redding wrote much of his own material, sometimes with the assistance of Booker T. and the MG's guitarist Steve Cropper. Yet at the time, Redding's success was primarily confined to the soul market; his singles charted only mildly on the pop listings. He was nonetheless tremendously respected by many white groups, particularly the Rolling Stones, who covered Redding's "That's How Strong My Love Is" and "Pain in My Heart." (Redding also returned the favor with "Satisfaction.")

One of Redding's biggest hits was a duet with fellow Stax star Carla Thomas, "Tramp," in 1967. That was the same year he began to show signs of making major inroads into the white audience, particularly with a well-received performance at the Monterey Pop Festival (also issued on record). Redding's biggest triumph, however, came just days before his death, when he recorded the wistful "(Sittin' on) The Dock of the Bay," which represented a significant leap as far as examination of more intensely personal emotions. Also highlighted by crisp Cropper guitar leads and dignified horns, it rose to the top of the pop charts in early 1968.

Redding, however, had perished in a plane crash in Wisconsin on December 10, 1967, in an accident that also took the lives of four members from his backup band, the Bar-Kays. A few other singles became posthumous hits, and a good amount of other unreleased material was issued in the wake of his death. These releases weren't purely exploitative in nature, in fact containing some pretty interesting music, and little that could be considered embarrassing. What Redding might have achieved, or what directions he might have explored, are among the countless tantalizing "what if" questions in rock'n'roll history. As it is he did record a considerable wealth of music at Stax, which is now available on thoughtfully archived reissues. —*Richie Unterberger*

Pain in My Heart / 1964 / Atco ◆◆◆◆
Redding's first release. Includes the title track, a deep-soul gem, plus "These Arms of Mine" and "Security." —*Christine Ohlman*

The Great Otis Redding Sings Soul Ballads / 1965 / Atco ◆◆◆◆
Redding's second album includes "Mr. Pitiful," "That's How Strong My Love Is," "Chained and Bound." He moves out of the country-soul genre into his own stompin' thing. —*Christine Ohlman*

☆ **Otis Blue** / 1966 / Atco ◆◆◆◆◆
Pretty essential if you can only afford individual albums. Three Sam Cooke covers, including "Shake" and "A Change Is Gonna Come" are included, as well as "I've Been Loving You Too Long," "Satisfaction," and the original version of "Respect." —*Christine Ohlman*

☆ **The Dictionary of Soul** / 1966 / Atco ◆◆◆◆◆
If you can only afford one Redding album, start here. Includes "Try a Little Tenderness," "My Lover's Prayer," "Fa-Fa-Fa-Fa-Fa (Sad Song)." One of the best album covers ever! —*Christine Ohlman*

The Soul Album / 1966 / Atco ◆◆◆
Includes "Chain Gang," "Good to Me," and "Cigarettes and Coffee." —*Christine Ohlman*

King and Queen / 1967 / Atco ◆◆◆◆
Eleven duets by the undisputed ruler and his consort Carla Thomas. Includes "Tramp" and "Lovey Dovey." Sweet and soulful! —*Christine Ohlman*

Live in Europe / 1967 / Atco ◆◆◆
Ten of Redding's biggest hits, live before an ecstatic audience. Includes "Respect," "I Can't Turn You Loose," "Try a Little Tenderness," etc. Soul rave-up! —*Christine Ohlman*

In Person at the Whisky a Go Go / 1968 / Rhino ◆◆◆◆
Redding captured live in 1966, at the peak of his form! —*Christine Ohlman*

The Dock of the Bay / 1968 / Atco ◆◆◆◆
Includes the posthumously released classic title track plus the great "Ole Man Trouble." —*Christine Ohlman*

The Immortal Otis Redding / 1968 / Atco ◆◆◆
His later sides, including the wonderful "I've Got Dreams to Remember" and the super-funky "Hard to Handle." Produced by Steve Cropper. Redding on the border of a new soul frontier as a writer and performer, before his untimely death. —*Christine Ohlman*

Love Man / 1969 / Rhino ◆◆◆
Includes the heart-fixin' title track, plus "Free Me," "Look at That Girl," "Direct Me." —*Christine Ohlman*

Tell the Truth / 1970 / Rhino ◆◆◆
Another posthumously released collection, including "The Match Game" and "Tell the Truth." —*Christine Ohlman*

The Otis Redding Story / 1989 / Atlantic ◆◆◆◆
A few previously unissued tracks, plus *all* the hits, from "These Arms of Mine" (1962) through "Dock of the Bay" (1967). A magnificent tribute to a magnificent career. It's a little expensive but it'll completely rock your soul! —*Christine Ohlman*

Remember Me / 1992 / Stax ◆◆◆
Twenty-two previously unreleased tracks, finished and unfinished, from the Stax vaults. Includes outtakes, remakes, cover tunes, and some very tasty never-before-heard originals. A historically important release covering all of Redding's remaining studio material. —*Christine Ohlman*

★ **The Very Best of Otis Redding** / 1993 / Rhino ◆◆◆◆◆
For a single-disc collection, *The Very Best of Otis Redding* is unbeatable. All of his biggest hits are here—it's a dynamite album, essential for any lover of soul. —*Stephen Thomas Erlewine*

Good to Me: Live at the Whiskey A Go Go, Vol. 2 / Jan. 25, 1993 / Stax ◆◆◆
Despite the deluge of reissues and anthologies, there still remains some unreleased Otis Redding material. There are two pluses about this new release of vintage Redding cuts, four of them newly issued. The first is that it's live, and Redding was always worth hearing in that context. The second is that the bonus cuts are invigorating, frenetic workouts with Redding blazing through the verses and then reworking and reshaping them in fiery vocal improvisations. The only negative, if there is one, is that there are better versions of "Ole Man Trouble" and "Pain in My Heart" available on other Redding releases. —*Ron Wynn*

☆ **Otis! The Definitive Otis Redding** / Nov. 9, 1993 / Rhino ◆◆◆◆◆
Although it includes the same studio tracks, *Otis!* supplants the previous, excellent *Otis Redding Story* by adding improved liner notes and sound, as well as a fourth disc of prime live material gathered from various performances. —*Stephen Thomas Erlewine*

☆ **The Very Best of Otis Redding, Vol. 2** / Apr. 25, 1995 / Rhino ◆◆◆◆◆
The Very Best of Otis Redding did its job so well that its sequel is a little unsatisfactory. Although *The Very Best of Otis Redding, Vol. 2* has a couple of essential songs—"That's What My Heart Needs," "Security," "Chained and Bound," "Hard to Handle"—the bulk of this 16 track collection consists of solid, but unremarkable covers and strong album tracks. If you want to dig a little deeper than *The Very Best of Otis Redding*, skip this volume and head straight for the original albums or one of the box sets. —*Stephen Thomas Erlewine*

Lou Reed (Louis Firbank)

b. Mar. 2, 1942, Freeport, Long Island, NY
Guitar, Vocals / Rock 'n' Roll, Singer-Songwriter, Proto-Punk
The career of Lou Reed defies capsule summarization. Like David Bowie (whom Reed directly inspired in many ways), he has made over his image many times, mutating from theatrical glam-rocker to scary-looking junkie to avant-garde noiseman to straight rock 'n' roller to yer average guy. A firmer grasp of rock's earthier qualities has ensured a more consistent career path than Bowie's, particularly in his latter years. Yet his catalog is extremely inconsistent, in both quality and stylistic orientation. Liking one Lou Reed LP, or several, or all of the ones he did in a particular era, is no guarantee that you'll like all of them, or even most of them.

Few would deny Reed's immense importance and considerable achievements, however. As has often been written, he expanded the vocabulary of rock 'n' roll lyrics into the previously forbidden territory of kinky sex, drug use (and abuse), decadence, transvestites, homosexuality, and suicidal depression. As has been pointed out less often, he remained (and remains) committed to using rock 'n' roll as a forum for literary, mature expression well into middle age, without growing lyrically soft or musically complacent. By and large, he's taken on these challenging duties with uncompromising honesty and a high degree of realism. For these reasons, he's often cited as punk's most important ancestor. It's often overlooked, though, that he's equally skilled at celebrating romantic joy, and rock 'n' roll itself, as he is at depicting harrowing urban realities.

Although Reed achieved his greatest success as a solo artist, his most enduring accomplishments were as the leader of the Velvet Underground in the 1960s. If Reed had never made any solo records, his work as the principal lead singer and songwriter for the Velvets would have still ensured his stature as one of the greatest rock visionaries of all time. The Velvet Underground are discussed at great length in many other sources, but it's sufficient to note that the four studio albums they recorded with Reed at the helm are essential listening, as is much of their live and extraneous material. "Heroin," "Sister Ray," "Sweet Jane," "Rock and Roll," "Venus in Furs," "All Tomorrow's Parties," "What Goes On," and "Lisa Says" are just the most famous classics that Reed wrote and sang for the group. As innovative as the Velvets were at breaking lyrical and instrumental taboos with their crunching experimental rock, they were unappreciated in their lifetime. Five years of little commercial success was undoubtedly a factor in Reed leaving the group he had founded in August 1970, just before the release of their most accessible effort, *Loaded*.

Although Reed's songs and streetwise, sing-speak vocals dominated the Velvets, he was perhaps more reliant upon his talented collaborators than he realized, or is even willing to admit to this day. The most talented of these associates was John Cale, who was apparently fired by Reed in 1968, after the Velvets' second album (although the pair have worked together on various other projects since then). Reed has a reputation of being a difficult man to work with for an extended period, and that has made it difficult for his extensive solo oeuvre to compete with the standards of brilliance set by the Velvets. Nowhere was this more apparent than on his self-titled solo debut from 1971, recorded after he'd taken an extended hiatus from music, moving back to his parents' suburban Long Island home at one point. *Lou Reed* mostly consisted of flaccid versions of songs dating back to the Velvet days, and he could have really used the group to punch them up, as the many outtake versions of these tunes that he actually recorded with the Velvet Underground (some of which didn't surface until about 25 years later) prove.

Reed got a shot in the arm (no distasteful pun intended) when David Bowie and Mick Ronson produced his second album, *Transformer*. A more energetic set that betrayed the influence of glam rock, it also included his sole Top 20 hit, "Walk on the Wild Side," and other good songs like "Vicious" and "Satellite of Love." It also made him a star in Britain, which was quick to appreciate the influence Reed had exerted on Bowie and other glam rockers. Reed went into more serious territory on *Berlin* (1973), its sweet orchestral production coating lyrical messages of despair and suicide. In some ways Reed's most ambitious and impressive solo effort, it was accorded a vituperative reception by critics in no mood for a nonstop bummer (however elegantly executed). Unbelievably, in retrospect, it made the Top Ten in Britain, though it flopped stateside.

Having been given a cold shoulder for some of his most serious (if chilling) work, Reed apparently decided he was going to give the public what it wanted. He had guitarists Steve Hunter and Dick Wagner (who had already played on *Berlin*) give his music a pop-metal, more radio-friendly sheen. More disturbingly, he decided to play up to the cartoon junkie role that some of his audience seemed eager to assign to him. Onstage, that meant shocking bleached hair, painted fingernails, and simulated drug injections. On record, it led to some of his most careless performances. One of these, the 1974 album *Sally Can't Dance*, was also his most commercially successful, reaching the Top Ten, thus confirming both Reed's and the audience's worst instincts. As if to prove he could still be as uncompromising as anyone, he unleashed the double album *Metal Machine Music*, a nonstop assault of unlistenable electronic noise. Opinions remain divided as to whether it was an artistic statement, a contract quota-filler, or a slap at the face of the public.

While Reed has never behaved as outrageously (in public and in the studio) as he did in the mid-'70s, there's been plenty of excitement in the past two decades. When he decided to play it relatively straight, sincere, and hard-nosed, he could produce affecting work in the spirit of his best vintage material (parts of *Coney Island Baby* and *Street Hassle*). At other points, he seemed not to be putting too much effort into any aspect of his songs (*Rock & Roll Heart*). With 1978's *Take No Prisoners*, he delivered one of the weirdest concert albums of all time, more of a comedy monologue (which not too many people laughed hard at) than a musical document. Reed had always been an enigma, but no one questioned the serious intent of his work with the Velvet Underground. As a soloist, it was getting impossible to tell when he was serious, or whether he even wished to be taken seriously anymore.

At the end of the 1970s, *The Bells* set the tone for most of his future work. Reed would settle down; he would play it straight; he would address serious, adult concerns, including heterosexual romance, with sincerity. Not a bad idea, but though the albums that followed were much more consistent in tone, they remained erratic in quality and, worse, could occasionally be quite boring. The recruitment of Robert Quine as lead guitarist helped, and *The Blue Mask* (1982) and *New Sensations* (1984) were fairly successful, although in retrospect they didn't deserve the raves they received from some critics at the time. Quine, however, would also find Reed too difficult to work with for an extended period.

New York (1989) heralded both a commercial and critical renaissance for Reed, and in truth it was his best work in quite some time, although it didn't break any major stylistic ground. Reed works best when faced with a challenge, which arrived when he collaborated with former partner John Cale in 1990 on a song cycle for the recently deceased Andy Warhol. In both its recorded and stage incarnations, this was the most experimental work that Reed had devised in quite some time. *Magic and Loss* (1992) returned him to the more familiar straight rock territory of *New York*, again to critical raves. The reformation of the Velvet Underground for a 1993 European live tour could not be considered an unqualified success, however. European audiences were thrilled to see the legends in person, but critical reaction to the shows was mixed, and critical reaction to the live record was tepid. More distressingly, old conflicts reared their head within the band once again, and the reunion ended before it had a chance to get to America. Cale and Reed at this point seem determined never to work with each other again. (The death of Velvet Underground guitarist Sterling Morrison in 1995 seemed to permanently ice prospects of more VU projects.) Reed's solo work ultimately cannot stack up to his Velvets output, despite its many highlights. As distinctive as his street-talk vocals and basic rock melodies are, they've become more formulaic with time, and their limitations more apparent. Still, most would have to concede that with the exception of

Neil Young, no other star that rose to fame in the 1960s has continued to push himself so diligently into creating work that is meaningful and contemporary. If that means he relies on stock musical and lyrical ideas at times (as Young does), it also means he's proved that rock can remain relevant to listeners other than hormone-crazed teenagers. —*Richie Unterberger*

Lou Reed / 1972 / RCA ✦✦✦
Reed's first solo album, with "Walk It & Talk It," "Wild Child," and "Lisa Says" being particular standouts. —*Cub Koda*

Transformer / 1972 / RCA ✦✦✦✦
Produced by David Bowie and Mick Ronson, *Transformer* has a lushness and beauty to its production and arrangements that Reed's material had never before received. The hit single "Walk on the Wild Side" was a fluke brought about by the actions of one fill-in disc jockey at the BBC. The song chronicles several personages from Andy Warhol's Factory retinue, including speed-freaks and transvestites giving head; it is boggling to this day that it got by AM radio programmers. Other Reed classics such as "Vicious" and "Satellite of Love" get similar treatment. —*Rob Bowman*

Berlin / 1973 / RCA ✦✦✦
Relations between Bowie and Reed had been strained during the recording of *Transformer*, so for his third solo album, Reed hired Canadian studio whiz Bob Ezrin. Ezrin and Reed concocted a brilliant album-length concept loosely constructed around the song "Berlin," from Reed's first solo album. Reed, of course, wrote the basic songs (several stemming back to demos recorded but not released by the Velvet Underground), and Ezrin and Allan MacMillan wrote orchestral arrangements for each track. Recording in London, Ezrin assembled a dream band including Jack Bruce, Steve Winwood, Aynsley Dunbar, and two relatively unknown guitar heroes, Steve Hunter and Dick Wagner, while Reed's writing and singing have never been better. A number of reactionary writers thought that orchestration automatically meant somehow compromising one's authenticity, while others found the level of depression and vitriol in the story more than they wanted to bear. —*Rob Bowman*

Rock & Roll Animal / 1974 / RCA ✦✦✦
Retaining guitarists Hunter and Wagner from the *Berlin* sessions, Reed hired a rhythm section consisting of Prakash John on bass, Pentti Glan on drums, and Ray Colcord on keyboards. Two shows were recorded at New York's Academy of Music in 1973. Behind Reed, the band produced fierce near-heavy-metal twin-guitar apotheosis for 90 minutes. Just under half of the concert made it onto this album. An FM-radio staple at the time, *Rock 'n' Roll Animal* includes searing versions of the Velvet Underground classics "Sweet Jane," "Heroin," "White Light/White Heat," and "Rock 'n' Roll," plus "Lady Day" from *Berlin*. —*Rob Bowman*

Sally Can't Dance / 1974 / RCA ✦✦✦
Following the self-conscious artiness of *Berlin*, *Sally Can't Dance* was Lou Reed's blatant stab at commercial success, featuring beefed-up guitar riffs, horn charts, and the occasional slick melody. The move paid off—it was his only album to reach the Top Ten—but it's an inconsistent record, complete with lackluster material, terrific rockers ("Sally Can't Dance" and "Kill Your Sons"), and one of Reed's best ballads, "Billy." —*Stephen Thomas Erlewine*

Lou Reed Live / 1975 / RCA ✦✦✦
Most of the rest of the above-mentioned concert. Three songs from *Transformer*, two songs from *Berlin*, and the Velvet Underground's "I'm Waiting for the Man." Just a shade less visceral than *Rock 'n' Roll Animal*. —*Rob Bowman*

Metal Machine Music / 1975 / RCA Victor ✦
A double-record of galvanizing white noise, *Metal Machine Music* gained instant notoriety when it was released, inspiring reams of rock criticism speculating whether the album was a serious attempt at avant-garde music or not. Considering that the record was a relentless series of layered, overlapping loops of guitar feedback, it probably was intended as a mammoth "fuck you" not only to the fans he acquired with *Sally Can't Dance*, but to his dedicated followers, critics, and record company. Regardless of Reed's intentions, *Metal Machine Music* is the most uncompromising work he ever released, featuring no lyrics, no hooks, no songs, no melodic themes—there's nothing but endless layers of noise. It's not necessarily unlistenable—in the two decades since its release, the atonal guitar experiments of Sonic Youth and their offspring have made *Metal Machine Music* sound downright conventional. It is boring, however. There is no variation in the processed noise, making the record's four sides unbearably tedious. —*Stephen Thomas Erlewine*

Coney Island Baby / Feb. 1976 / RCA ✦✦✦✦
Coney Island Baby was an album of renewal for Reed. The year 1974 had witnessed one of his worst albums ever in *Sally Can't Dance*, and, early in 1975, in reaction to a career spinning out of control, he had released the lyricless sonic feedback assault of *Metal Machine Music*. *Coney Island Baby* was a return to peak songwriting form. The title

track reflected Reed's early love of doo wop. It is probably the grandest love song of his career. "Kicks" is a rather frightening internal study of a diseased mind that eventually turns to murder. As with most of Reed's writing in the '60s and '70s, he draws no conclusion; he simply paints a picture. — *Rob Bowman*

Rock & Roll Heart / Nov. 1976 / Arista ✦✦

Lou Reed continued the relaxed, R&B-inflected rock 'n' roll of *Coney Island Baby* with *Rock & Roll Heart*, released the same year as its predecessor. Reed's quick turnaround with *Rock & Roll Heart* is an indication of the inherent flaws of the album. Musically, it's appealing, but the record contains a set of lackluster songs that fail to match the gentle, humane songs that formed the core of *Coney Island Baby*. — *Stephen Thomas Erlewine*

Walk on the Wild Side: The Best of Lou Reed / 1977 / RCA ✦✦✦

Walk on the Wild Side: The Best of Lou Reed was the standard record company "hits" compilation surveying Reed's five-year, eight-album sojourn at RCA from 1972 to 1976. Its 11 songs included 2 from *Lou Reed*, 3 from *Transformer* (among them, of course, this album's title track, Reed's sole chart hit), 1 from *Berlin*, 2 from *Rock N' Roll Animal* (one of which is "Sweet Jane," minus the introductory fanfare), and the title tracks from *Sally Can't Dance* and *Coney Island Baby*, plus the previously non-LP B-side "Nowhere at All." It was a bullet-proof selection, as unimaginative as it was dependable, which oddly was why it worked so well. Reed's solo career had seen some extreme tangents, and this album caught them, from the Dylan-ish "Wild Child" to the glam-pop of the *Transformer* material, and from the heavy metal rearrangements of old Velvet Underground songs on *Rock N' Roll Animal* to the attempts at straightforward adult singer-songwriter rock on songs like "Coney Island Baby." The regular albums had been uneven, but here Reed came off as an accomplished dabbler in a variety of styles who really had something to say and said it, sometimes humorously, sometimes frantically, but always with conviction. Reed has been a prolific artist, and this album captures only a fraction of his catalog, but he is actually less eclectic as a rule than this collection makes him seem, so the result is an excellent introduction. — *William Ruhlmann*

Live: Take No Prisoners / 1978 / Arista ✦

Live: Take No Prisoners isn't so much a live album as it is a constant barrage of vicious, mean-spirited jokes by a third-rate, failed comedian. Throughout the double-album set, the songs take a back seat to Reed's rambling monologues, which include a number of personal attacks, including one on rock critic Robert Christgau. Instead of reinforcing Reed's clever wit, the record makes him seem rather pathetic, especially considering that this was recorded during the height of punk. And the music, performed by an anonymous pick-up band, is shockingly bland, providing no support for Reed's streetwise show-biz shtick. — *Stephen Thomas Erlewine*

Street Hassle / 1978 / Arista ✦✦✦

Reed's second album for Arista has a few weak spots, but most of it, including the 11-minute title song, is unmitigated brilliance. The sound is rather odd as Reed began experimenting with Manfred Schunke's binaural recording process. Some tracks on the album are part live and part studio while others are near totally live or totally studio. *Street Hassle* includes Reed's tongue-in-cheek take on racial stereotypes, "I Wanna Be Black," and a quite strange reinterpretation of the Velvet Underground's "Real Good Time Together." — *Rob Bowman*

The Bells / 1979 / RCA ✦✦✦

Like *Street Hassle*, *The Bells* is a conceptual tour de force, as Lou Reed delivers some of his most open and poetic material over a sonic backdrop that recalls rock 'n' roll, but owes more to streamlined jazz. It's one of his most intriguing records, as well as being one of his most giving and humane albums. — *Stephen Thomas Erlewine*

Growing Up in Public / 1980 / Arista ✦✦

As the title suggests, *Growing Up in Public* is a musical diary of Lou Reed entering middle age. Conceptually, the record is intriguing, and the lyrics are well-crafted on occasion, but the album is filled with too much mediocre, formulaic music to make it a compelling listen. — *Stephen Thomas Erlewine*

Rock & Roll Diary / 1980 / Arista ✦✦✦

An excellent wrap-up of his best work (1967-80), both with and without the Velvet Underground, this is the perfect place to start. — *Dan Heilman*

The Blue Mask / 1982 / RCA ✦✦✦

Reed took nearly two years off at the end of the '70s to dry out and clean up. When he did return to recording, it was with a vengeance. In an odd quirk of fate, Reed had re-signed with RCA and he had also gone back to a lineup of two guitars, a bass, and drums. *The Blue Mask* sounds immaculate. The guts of Reed's sound are still present in no uncertain terms, but there is also a richness to the finished mix that is striking. The bass player, Fernando Saunders, became Reed's right-hand man for the next several years, and guitarist Robert Quine was Reed's ideal foil for this and the subsequent *Legendary Hearts*. The result was Reed's best

album since *Berlin*. His songwriting had taken a quantum leap since his cleaning up. The maturity was inspiring, as was the breadth of the material. — *Rob Bowman*

Legendary Hearts / 1983 / RCA ✦✦✦✦

Continuing with Quine and Saunders, coupled with a different drummer in Fred Maher, Reed delivered his second superb album in a row. This was a more subdued affair than *The Blue Mask* but the writing was no less impressive. — *Rob Bowman*

Live in Italy / 1984 / RCA ✦✦✦✦

Lou Reed assembled one of his finest bands in the early '80s, consisting of Robert Quine on lead guitar, Fernando Saunders on bass, and Fred Maher on drums, and made some excellent albums with them, including *Legendary Hearts*, which was his current release when he toured Europe and recorded this live double LP in Verona and Rome in September 1983. Though never released in the US, the album, with its mixture of Velvet Underground tracks and Lou Reed solo songs, all effectively played in the band's direct, no-nonsense rock 'n' roll style, is the definitive Reed live record, outdistancing the heavy-metal reconstructions of *Rock N' Roll Animal/Lou Reed Live* and the comedy routines of *Take No Prisoners*. Some RCA executive should slip out a US CD reissue of this album (which, at a running time just over 74 minutes, could fit on one disc) and do Lou Reed fans a favor. — *William Ruhlmann*

New Sensations / 1984 / RCA ✦✦✦✦

After a few challenging (and critically acclaimed) albums, Reed dispensed with densely literate (and dissonant) excursions into the dark side of the human psyche and delivered a solid, upbeat (and at times humorous) collection of accessible rock 'n' roll. Reed celebrated love ("I Love You Suzanne"), poked fun at power-plays between the genders ("My Red Joystick"), and, as the title track suggested, generally looked forward with optimism. Reed's dirty-electric rhythm, Fernando Saunders' elastic bass work, and Fred Maher's forceful drumming provide a solid bed of ragged but tight ensemble work behind Reed's dry narratives. — *Rick Clark*

Mistrial / 1986 / RCA ✦✦✦

After three successive accomplished and mature albums, Lou Reed made an attempt to stay current with the stilted *Mistrial*. Six of the songs are driven by drum machines, which certainly gives the music a robotic feel. However, Reed doesn't help the situation any by turning in a set of songs that are stripped back to their bare rhythms, lacking memorable hooks and melodies. All of these spartan arrangements are designed to attract attention to the lyrics, which aren't among his finest efforts. Reed is in a social protest mode, particularly attacking violence, in both its domestic and global incarnations. Instead of personalizing the material, he relies on platitudes, which tend to make the processed chords and beats of the music even more grating. Nevertheless, he ends the album with two ballads that showcase many of his finer musical and lyrical skills. — *Stephen Thomas Erlewine*

New York / 1989 / Sire ✦✦✦✦

Reed's first album in three years hailed another peak in his recording career. In the past he had always painted pictures of any given social situation. Positive or negative, he had never stated a point of view. On *New York*, he rails. Sporting a new band, including bass virtuoso Rob Wasserman and Reed's brother-in-law, guitarist Mike Rathke, Reed indicts everyone from slum lords to polluters. *New York* contains, perhaps, his finest writing. — *Rob Bowman*

Songs for Drella / Jul. 1990 / Sire ✦✦✦✦

Reed and Cale's tribute to Andy Warhol brings out the best in both of them. It's a spare collection, the only instruments Reed's guitar and Cale's keyboards and viola. The songs trace Warhol's life in a witty, conversational way that evokes his spirit far better than any biographical work of the artist yet attempted. — *William Ruhlmann*

Magic and Loss / Jan. 14, 1992 / Sire ✦✦✦

Magic and Loss marks the third installment of a trilogy featuring mature, thematic works from Lou Reed, following 1989's *New York* (universal metaphor for urban decay) and 1990's collaboration with John Cale, *Songs for Drella* (a tribute to Andy Warhol). The disc is inspired by the loss of two of Reed's close friends to cancer in 1991, an experience that proved cathartic for the artist. The songs—a generous 14 tracks over 58 minutes—tend not to stand out as distinctive pieces, but work very much as an organic whole. An exception is "Power and Glory," featuring vocal backing from Little Jimmy Scott, startling in its contrast to Reed's understated monotone. The artist succeeds in making the project inspirational, a chronicle of how the magic of life transforms loss into something greater. — *Roch Parisien*

Between Thought and Expression: The Lou Reed Anthology / Apr. 14, 1992 / RCA ✦✦✦

Over the course of 45 songs on 3 CDs or cassettes, *Between Thought and Expression* chronicles the first 16 years of Lou Reed's solo work, from his debut, self-titled album that followed his 1970 departure from the Velvet Underground through the RCA and Arista years that culminated in 1986's *Mistrial*. On the way, the anthology delivers stellar moments from Reed's David Bowie-produced *Transformer* period, several pieces from the hauntingly doom-laden *Berlin*, and the '70s guitar anthem "Sweet Jane" from *Rock 'n' Roll Animal*. The set includes five previously unreleased tracks, one non-LP B-side, and two soundtrack-only numbers. The tracks were selected and remastered with Reed's participation, and the refurbished sound is a revelation, particularly on the early material. —*Roch Parisien*

Set the Twilight Reeling / Feb. 20, 1996 / Warner ♦♦

Set the Twilight Reeling is a welcome relief after the oppresively dark *Magic & Loss*, but while it sounds a bit more full-bodied than its skeletal predecessor, that doesn't necessarily make it a better album. Sounding like a more sonically varied *New York, Set the Twilight Reeling* doesn't break any new ground, nor does it offer that many new insights from Reed. At its best, the album deals with personal relationships, whether it's lust ("Hooky Wooky") or love ("Trade In"). At its worst, the album makes broad generalizations like "Sex With Your Parents" that come off as unbearably smug. As a whole, *Set the Twilight Reeling* ranks as one of the more listenable but least rewarding of Lou Reed's later works. —*Stephen Thomas Erlewine*

● Different Times: Lou Reed in the '70s / May 1996 / RCA ♦♦♦♦

Reed is very much an album-oriented artist, and those who think they may develop a serious interest in his work are better advised to seek individual titles than compilations. If you just want some of his best songs around the house, though, this is a well-chosen, economic 17-track survey of his best material from his best period as a solo act (the early to mid-'70s). Drawing most heavily from the *Transformer* and *Berlin* albums, this has his most famous/notorious early solo works ("Walk on the Wild Side," "Vicious," "Satellite of Love," "Caroline Says"); some inferior but notably different remakes of songs he recorded with the Velvet Underground ("Lisa Says," "I Can't Stand It," "Sweet Jane"); and other high points like "Kill Your Sons" and "Coney Island Baby." —*Richie Unterberger*

Sweet Jane / Oil Well [Bootleg] ♦♦♦♦

This recording of a 1972 radio show has been available in numerous guises for many years; the label listed is merely about the easiest to find as of the mid-'90s. This is inarguably among the finest of Reed's solo work, released or unreleased, split evenly between Velvet Undergroud classics and highlights from Reed's early solo albums, with a band featuring Dick Wagner and Steve Hunter on guitars. The sound is very good, Reed's singing is great, and the band plays in a raw and urgent manner that Lou should have employed on his solo albums, but didn't. The Velvets' songs are well done and considerably different from the originals, and the versions of solo classics like "Vicious," "Walk On The Wild Side," "I'm So Free," "Berlin," and "Satellite Of Love" slay the studio takes to shreds. Essential for Reed fanatics. —*Richie Unterberger*

R.E.M.

f. 1980, Athens, GA
Alternative Pop-Rock, Jangle-Pop

R.E.M. mark the point when post-punk turned into alternative rock. When their first single, "Radio Free Europe," was released in 1981 it sparked a back-to-the-garage movement in the American underground. While there were a number of hardcore and punk bands in the US during the early '80s, R.E.M. brought guitar-pop back into the underground lexicon. Combining ringing guitar hooks with mumbled, cryptic lyrics, and an D.I.Y. aesthetic borrowed from post-punk, the band simultaneously sounded traditional and modern. Though there were no overt innovations in their music, R.E.M. had an identity and sense of purpose that transformed the American underground. Throughout the '80s, they worked relentlessly, releasing records every year and touring constantly, playing both theaters and backwoods dives. Along the way, they inspired countless bands, from the legions of jangle-pop groups in the mid-'80s to scores of alternative-pop groups in the '90s, who admired their slow climb to stardom. It did take R.E.M. several years to break into the top of the charts, but they had a cult following from the release of their debut EP, *Chronic Town*, in 1982. *Chronic Town* established the haunting folk and garage rock that became the band's signature sound, and over the next five years, they continued to expand their music with a series of critically-acclaimed albums. By the late '80s, the group's fanbase had grown large enough to guarantee strong sales, but the Top Ten success in 1987 of *Document* and "The One I Love" was unexpected, especially since R.E.M. had only altered its sound slightly. Following *Document*, R.E.M. slowly became one of the world's most popular bands. After an exhaustive international tour supporting 1988's *Green*, the band retired from touring for six years and retreated into the studio to produce their most popular records, *Out of Time* (1991) and *Automatic for the People* (1992). By the time they returned to performing with the *Monster* tour in 1995, the band had been acknowledged by critics and musicians as one of the forefathers of the thriving alternative rock movement, and they were rewarded with the most lucrative tour of

their career. Toward the late '90s, R.E.M. was an institution, as its influence was felt in new generations of bands.

Though R.E.M. formed in Athens, Georgia in 1980, Mike Mills (b. December 17, 1958) and Bill Berry (b. July 31, 1958) were the only Southerners in the group. Both had attended high school together in Macon, playing in a number of bands during their teens. Michael Stipe (b. January 4, 1960) was a military brat, moving throughout the country during his childhood. By his teens, he had discovered punk rock through Patti Smith, Television, and Wire, and began playing in cover bands in St. Louis. By 1978, he had begun studying art at the University of Georgia in Athens, where he began frequenting the Wuxtry record store. Peter Buck (b. December 6, 1956), a native of California, was a clerk at Wuxtry. Buck had been a fanatical record collector, consuming everything from classic rock to punk and free jazz, and was just beginning to learn how to play guitar. Discovering they had similar tastes, Buck and Stipe began working together, eventually meeting Berry and Mills through a mutual friend. In April of 1980, the band formed to play a party for their friend, rehearsing a number of garage, psychedelic bubblegum and punk covers in a converted Episcopalian church. At the time, the group was playing under the name the Twisted Kites. By the summer, the band had settled on the name R.E.M. after flipping randomly through the dictionary, and had met Jefferson Holt, who became their manager after witnessing the group's first out-of-state concert in North Carolina.

Over the next year and a half, R.E.M. toured throughout the South, playing a variety of garage rock covers and folk-rock originals. At the time, the band was still learning how to play, as Buck began to develop his distinctive, arpeggiated jangle and Stipe ironed out his cryptic lyrics. During the summer of 1981, R.E.M. recorded its first single, "Radio Free Europe," at Mitch Easter's Drive-In Studios. Released on the local indie label Hib-Tone, "Radio Free Europe" was pressed in a run of only 1,000 copies, but most of the those singles fell into the right hands. Due to strong word-of-mouth, the single became a hit on college radio and topped the *Village Voice*'s year-end poll of Best Independent Singles. The single also earned the attention of larger independent labels, and by the beginning of 1982, the band had signed to I.R.S. Records, releasing the EP *Chronic Town* in the spring. Like the single, *Chronic Town* was well-received, paving the way for the group's full-length debut album, 1983's *Murmur*.

With its subdued, haunting atmosphere and understated production, *Murmur* was noticeably different than *Chronic Town* and it was welcomed with enthusiastic reviews upon its spring release; *Rolling Stone* named it the best album of 1983, beating out Michael Jackson's *Thriller* and the Police's *Synchronicity*. *Murmur* also expanded the group's cult significantly, breaking into the American Top 40. R.E.M. returned to a rougher-edged sound on 1984's *Reckoning*, which featured the college hit "So. Central Rain (I'm Sorry)." By the time the band hit the road to support *Reckoning*, they had become well-known in the American underground for their constant touring, aversion to videos, support of college radio, Stipe's mumbled vocals and detached stage presence, Buck's ringing guitar, and their purposely enigmatic artwork. Bands that imitated these very things ran rampant throughout the American underground, and R.E.M. threw their support towards these bands, having them open at shows and mentioning them in interviews. By 1985, the American underground was awash with R.E.M. soundalikes and bands like Game Theory and the Rain Parade, which shared similar aesthetics and sounds.

Just as the signature R.E.M. sound dominated the underground, the band entered darker territory with their third album, 1985's *Fables of the Reconstruction*. Recorded in London with producer Joe Boyd (Richard Thompson, Fairport Convention, Nick Drake), *Fables of the Reconstruction* was made at a difficult period in R.E.M.'s history, as the band was frought with tension produced by endless touring. The album reflected the group's dark moods, as well as its obsession with the rural South, and both of these fascinations popped up on the supporting tour. Stipe, whose on-stage behavior was always slightly strange, entered his most bizarre phase, as he put on weight, dyed his hair bleached blonde and wore countless layers of clothing. None of the new quirks in R.E.M.'s persona prevented *Fables of the Reconstruction* from becoming their most successful album to date, selling nearly 300,000 copies in the US. R.E.M. decided to record their next album with Don Gehman, who had previously worked with John Mellencamp. Gehman had the band clean up their sound and Stipe enunciate his vocals, making *Lifes Rich Pageant* their most accessible record to date. Upon its late summer release in 1986, *Lifes Rich Pageant* was greeted with the positive reviews that had become customary with each new R.E.M. album, and it outstripped the sales of its predecessor. Several months after *Lifes Rich Pageant*, the group released the B-sides and rarities collection, *Dead Letter Office*, in the spring of 1987.

R.E.M. had laid the groundwork for mainstream success, but they had never explicitly courted widespread success. Nevertheless, their audience had grown quite large, and it wasn't that surprising that the group's fifth album, *Document*, became a hit shortly after its fall 1987 release. Produced by Scott Litt—who would produce all of their records over the course of the next decade—*Document* climbed into the US Top Ten and went platinum on the strength of the single "The One I Love," which also went into the Top Ten; it also became their biggest UK hit to date, reaching the British Top 40. The following year, the band left I.R.S. Records, signing with Warner Bros. for a reported six million dollars. The first album under the new contract was *Green*, which was released on election day 1988. *Green* continued the success of *Document*, going double platinum and generating the Top Ten single "Stand." R.E.M. supported *Green* with an exhaustive international tour, in which they played their first stadium dates in the US. Though they had graduated to stadiums in America, the group continued to play clubs throughout Europe.

The *Green* tour proved to be draining for the group, and they took an extended rest upon its completion in 1989. During the break, each member pursued side projects, and *Hindu Love Gods*, an album Buck, Berry, and Mills recorded with Warren Zevon in 1986, was released. R.E.M. reconvened during 1990 to record their seventh album, *Out of Time*, which was released in the spring of 1991. Entering the US and UK charts at No. 1, *Out of Time* was a lush pop and folk album, boasting a wider array of sounds than the group's previous efforts; its lead single, "Losing My Religion," became the group's biggest single, reaching No. 4 in the US. Since the band was exhausted from the *Green* tour, they chose to stay off the road. Nevertheless, *Out of Time* became their biggest album, selling over four million copies in the US and spending two weeks at the top of the charts. R.E.M. released the dark, meditative *Automatic for the People* in the fall of 1992. Although the group had promised a rock album after the softer textures of *Out of Time*, *Automatic for the People* was slow, quiet and reflective, with many songs being graced by string arrangements by Led Zeppelin bassist John Paul Jones. Like its predecessor, *Automatic for the People* was a quadruple platinum success, generating the Top 40 hit singles "Drive," "Man on the Moon" and "Everybody Hurts."

After piecing together two albums in the studio, R.E.M. decided to return to being a rock band with 1994's *Monster*. Though the record was conceived as a back-to-basics album, the recording of *Monster* was difficult and plagued with tension. Nevertheless, the album was a huge hit upon its fall release, entering the US and UK charts at No. 1; furthermore, the album won praise from a number of old-school critics who had been reluctant to praise the band, since they didn't "rock" in conventional terms. Experiencing some of the strongest sales and reviews of their career, R.E.M. began their first tour since *Green* early in 1995. Two months into the tour, Bill Berry suffered a brain aneurysm while performing; he had surgery immediately and had fully recovered within a month. R.E.M. resumed their tour two months after Berry's aneurysm, but his illness was only the beginning of a series of problems that plagued the *Monster* tour. Mills had to undergo abdominal surgery to remove an intestinal tumor in July; a month later, Stipe had to have an emergency surgery to remove a hernia. Despite all the problems, the tour was an enormous financial success, and the group recorded the bulk of a new album. Before the record was released in the fall of 1996, R.E.M. parted ways with their longtime manager Jefferson Holt, allegedly due to sexual harrassment charges levied against Holt; the group's lawyer, Bertis Downs, assumed managerial duties. *New Adventures in Hi-Fi* was released in September 1996, just before it was announced that the band had re-signed with Warner Bros., reportedly for a record-breaking sum of eighty million dollars. In light of such a huge figure, the commercial failure of *New Adventures in Hi-Fi* was ironic. Though it received strong reviews and debuted at No. 2 in the US and No. 1 in the UK, the album failed to generate a hit single, and it only went platinum where its three predecessors went quadruple platinum. By early 1996, the album had already begun its descent down the charts. However, the members of R.E.M. were already pursuing new projects, as Stipe worked with his film company, Single Cell Pictures, and Buck co-wrote songs with Mark Eitzel and worked with a free-jazz group, Taturatura. *—Stephen Thomas Erlewine*

Chronic Town / 1982 / IRS ✦✦✦
Chronic Town established R.E.M.'s signature sound immediately, expanding the jangling riffs of their debut single "Radio Free Europe" into a full-fledged modus operandi. Recorded at Mitch Easter's Drive-In Studios, the EP has a endearingly ragged sound—it's a garage band playing jangling pop songs, and while the music is melodic and memorable, it has an underground mentality that keeps it from sounding conventional. Not only does the lo-fi production keep the music underground, but so do Pete Buck's ringing arpeggios, Michael Stipe's incomprehensible mumbled vocals and the band's amateurish enthusiasm. They might not be accomplished players, but already their songwriting is distinctive, with "Gardening at Night," "Wolves, Lower," and "Carnival of Sorts (Box Cars)" ranking as early classics. *—Stephen Thomas Erlewine*

☆ **Murmur** / 1983 / IRS ✦✦✦✦✦
Leaving behind the garagey jangle-pop of their first recordings, R.E.M. developed a strangely subdued variation of its trademark sound for its full-length debut album, *Murmur*. Heightening the enigmatic tendencies of *Chronic Town* by de-emphasizing the backbeat and accentuating the ambience of the ringing guitar, R.E.M. created a distinctive sound for the album—one that sounds eerily timeless. Even though it is firmly in the tradition of American folk-rock, post-punk and garage-rock, *Murmur* sounds as if it appeared out of nowhere, without any ties to the past, present or future. Part of the distinctiveness lies in the atmospheric production, which exudes a detached sense of mystery, but it also comes from the remarkably accomplished songwriting. The songs on *Murmur* sound if they've existed forever, yet they subvert folk and pop conventions by taking unpredictable twists and turns into melodic, evocative territory, whether it's the measured riffs of "Pilgrimage," the melancholic "Talk About the Passion" or the winding guitars and pianos of "Perfect Circle." R.E.M. may have made albums as good as *Murmur* in the years following its release, but they never again made anything that sounded quite like it. *—Stephen Thomas Erlewine*

☆ **Reckoning** / 1984 / IRS ✦✦✦✦✦
R.E.M. abandoned the enigmatic post-punk experiments of *Murmur* for their second album *Reckoning*, returning to their garage-pop origins instead. Opening with the ringing "Harborcoat," *Reckoning* runs through a set of ten jangle-pop songs that are different not only in sound but in style from the debut. Where *Murmur* was enigmatic in its sound, *Reckoning* is clear, which doesn't necessarily mean that the songs themselves are straightforward. Stipe continues to sing powerful melodies without enunciating, but the band has a propulsive kick that makes the music vital and alive. And, if anything, the songwriting is more direct and memorable than before—the interweaving melodies of "Pretty Persuasion" and the country-rocker "(Don't Go Back to) Rockville" are as affecting as the melancholic dirges of "Camera" and "Time After Time," while the ringing minor-key arpeggios of "So. Central Rain," the pulsating riffs of "7 Chinese Bros.," and the hard-rocking rhythms of "Little America" make the songs into classics. On the surface, *Reckoning* may not be as distinctive as *Murmur*, but the record's influence on underground American rock in the '80s is just as strong. *—Stephen Thomas Erlewine*

Fables of the Reconstruction / 1985 / IRS ✦✦✦✦
For their third album, R.E.M. made a conscious effort to break from the traditions *Murmur* and *Reckoning* established, electing to record in England with legendary folk-rock producer Joe Boyd. For a variety of reasons, the sessions were difficult, and that tension is apparent throughout *Fables of the Reconstruction*. A dark, moody rumination on American folk—not only the music, but its myths—*Fables* is creepy, rustic psychedelic folk, filled with eerie sonic textures. Some light breaks through occasionally, such as the ridiculous collegiate blue-eyed soul of "Can't Get There From Here," but the group's trademark ringing guitars and cryptic lyrics have grown sinister, giving even sing-alongs like "Driver 8" an ominous edge. *Fables* is more inconsistent than its two predecessors, but the group does demonstrate considerable musical growth, particularly in how perfectly it evokes the strange rural legends of the South. And many of the songs on the record—including "Feeling Gravity's Pull," "Maps and Legends," "Green Grow the Rushes," "Auctioneer (Another Engine)" and the previously mentioned pair—rank among the group's best. *—Stephen Thomas Erlewine*

Lifes Rich Pageant / 1986 / IRS ✦✦✦✦
Fables of the Reconstruction was intentionally murky, and *Lifes Rich Pageant* was constructed as its polar opposite. Teaming with producer Don Gehman, who previously worked with John Mellencamp, R.E.M. developed their most forceful record to date. Where previous records kept the rhythm section in the background, *Pageant* emphasizes the beat, and the band turns in its hardest rockers to date, including the anthemic "Begin the Begin" and the punky "Just a Touch." But the cleaner production also benefits the ballads and the mid-tempo janglers, particularly since it helps reveal Stipe's growing political obsessions, especially on the environmental anthems "Fall on Me" and "Cuyahoga." The group hasn't entirely left myths behind—witness the Civil War ballad "Swan Swan H"—but the band sounds more contemporary both musically and lyrically than they did on either *Fables* or *Murmur*, which helps gives the record an extra kick. And even with excellent songs like "I Believe," "Flowers of Guatemala," "These Days" and "What If We Give It Away," it's ironic that the most memorable moment comes from the garage rock obscurity "Superman," which is sung with glee by the wimpy Mike Mills. *—Stephen Thomas Erlewine*

Dead Letter Office / 1987 / IRS ✦✦✦
Arriving mere months before *Document* took the group into the Top Ten, the B-sides and rarities collection *Dead Letter Office* sums up all of the quirks and idiosyncrasies that made R.E.M. the leading underground guitar-pop band of the '80s. While only a handful of songs on *Dead Letter Office* rank among the group's best, the record is extremely enter-

taining, even for casual fans, particularly because it captures the wild spirit of R.E.M. that was evident at their concerts, but not always on their records. Among the gems scattered throughout the collection are the cheerily ridiculous "Band Wagon," "Voice of Harold" (which features Stipe singing the liner notes to a gospel album over the backing of "7 Chinese Brothers)", covers of the Velvet Underground, Pylon and Aerosmith, the ringing pop of "Burning Down" (which is later reworked as "Ages of You"), and "Walter's Theme," a drunken attempt at a commercial for a local restaurant that segues into a clueless cover of "King of the Road." The material may be slight, but it's fun—and R.E.M.'s albums aren't always fun. [The CD version of *Dead Letter Office* contains the group's debut EP, *Chronic Town*.] —*Stephen Thomas Erlewine*

☆ **Document** / 1987 / IRS ✦✦✦✦✦
R.E.M. began to move toward mainstream record production on *Lifes Rich Pageant*, but they didn't have a commercial breakthrough until the following year's *Document*. Ironically, *Document* is a stranger, more varied album than its predecessor, but co-producer Scott Litt—who would go on to produce every R.E.M. album in the following decade—is a better conduit for the band than Don Gehman, giving the group a clean sound without sacrificing their enigmatic tendencies. "Finest Worksong," the stream-of-conscious rant "It's the End of the World As We Know It (And I Feel Fine)" and the surprise Top Ten single "The One I Love" all crackle with muscular rhythms and guitar riffs, but the real surprise is how political the mid-tempo jangle-pop of "Welcome to the Occupation," "Disturbance At the Heron House" and "King of Birds" is. Where *Lifes Rich Pageant* sounded a bit like a party record, *Document* is a fiery statement, and its memorable melodies and riffs are made all the more indelible by its righteous anger. In other words, it's not only a commercial breakthrough, but a creative breakthrough as well, offering evidence of R.E.M.'s growing depth and maturity, and helping usher in the P.C. era in the process. —*Stephen Thomas Erlewine*

● **Eponymous** / 1988 / IRS ✦✦✦✦
Basically a singles collection from R.E.M.'s first five albums, *Eponymous* gives the listener a sense of R.E.M.'s change from a folk-rock band to a rock band. The songs are intelligently selected, distilling most of the best moments from their first five albums for I.R.S. Included is the original single of "Radio Free Europe," different mixes of "Gardening at Night" (where it's actually possible to hear the vocal) and "Finest Worksong," and the previously unreleased (and unspectacular) "Romance." (Note: An import collection, *The Best of R.E.M.*, doesn't have the rarities, but has 16 songs, including the remainder of *Eponymous*, plus many other important songs from their I.R.S. years. Worth the couple of extra dollars for the beginner.) —*Stephen Thomas Erlewine*

Green / 1988 / Warner Brothers ✦✦✦
As major-label debuts by underground bands go, *Green* is fairly uncompromising. While it displays a more powerful guitar sound on "Get Up," "Turn You Inside Out" and "Orange Crush," it also takes more detours than *Document*, whether it's the bizarrely affecting contemporary folk of "The Wrong Child" and "You Are the Everything," the bubblegum of "Stand" and "Pop Song 89" or the introspection of the lovely "Hairshirt" and "World Leader Pretend." But instead of presenting a portrait of a band with a rich, eclectic vision, *Green* is incoherent. While its best moments are flat-out great, the band has bitten off more than it can chew; many of the songs sound like failed experiments, and its arena-ready production now sounds slightly dated. Nevertheless, half of the record is brilliant, and it certainly indicates that R.E.M. is continuing to diversify its sound. —*Stephen Thomas Erlewine*

Out of Time / Mar. 12, 1991 / Warner Brothers ✦✦✦
The supporting tour for *Green* exhausted R.E.M., and they spent nearly a year recuperating before reconvening for *Out of Time*. Where previous R.E.M. records captured a stripped-down, live sound, *Out of Time* was lush with sonic detail, featuring string sections, keyboards, mandolins, and cameos from everyone from rapper KRS-1 to the B-52's' Kate Pierson. The scope of R.E.M.'s ambition is impressive, and the record sounds impeccable, its sunny array of pop and folk songs as refreshing as Michael Stipe's decision to abandon explicitly political lyrics for the personal. Several R.E.M. classics—including Mike Mills' Byrdsy "Near Wild Heaven," the haunting "Country Feedback," and the masterpiece "Losing My Religion"—are present, but the album is more notable for its production than its songwriting. Most of the songs are slight but pleasant, or are awkward experiments like "Radio Song"'s stab at funk, and while this sounds fine as the record is playing, there's not much substantive material to make the record worth returning to. —*Stephen Thomas Erlewine*

☆ **Automatic for the People** / Jul. 1992 / Warner Brothers ✦✦✦✦✦
Turning away from the sweet pop of *Out of Time*, R.E.M. created a haunting, melancholy masterpiece with *Automatic for the People*. At its core, the album is a collection of folk songs about aging, death and loss, but the music has a grand, epic sweep provided by layers of lush strings, interweaving acoustic instruments and shimmering keyboards. *Automatic for the People* captures the group at a crossroads, as they moved

from cult heroes to elder statesmen, and the album is a graceful transition into their new status. It is a reflective album, with frank discussions on mortality, but it is not a despairing record—"Nightswimming," "Everybody Hurts" and "Sweetness Follows" have a comforting melancholy, while "Find the River" provides a positive sense of closure. R.E.M. have never been as emotionally direct as they are on *Automatic for the People*, nor have they ever created music quite as rich and timeless, and while the record is not an easy listen, it is the most rewarding record in their oeuvre. —*Stephen Thomas Erlewine*

Monster / Sep. 27, 1994 / Warner Brothers ✦✦✦
Monster is indeed R.E.M.'s long-promised "rock" album; it just doesn't rock in the way one might expect. Instead of R.E.M.'s trademark anthemic bashers, *Monster* offers a set of murky sludge, powered by the heavily distorted and delayed guitar of Peter Buck. Stipe's vocals have been pushed to the back of the mix, along with Bill Berry's drums, which accentuates the muscular pulse of Buck's chords. From the androgynous sleaze of "Crush with Eyeliner" to the subtle, Eastern-tinged menace of "You," most of the album sounds dense, dirty and grimy, which makes the punchy guitars of "What's the Frequency, Kenneth?" and the warped soul of "Tongue" all the more distinctive. *Monster* doesn't have the conceptual unity or consistently brilliant songwriting of *Automatic*, but it does offer a wide range of sonic textures that have never been heard on an R.E.M. album before. —*Stephen Thomas Erlewine*

New Adventures in Hi-Fi / Sep. 10, 1996 / Warner Brothers ✦✦✦
Recorded during and immediately following their disaster-prone *Monster* tour, *New Adventures in Hi-Fi* feels like it was recorded on the road. Not only are all of Stipe's lyrics on the album about moving or travel, the sound is ragged and varied, pieced together from tapes recorded at shows, soundtracks, and studios, giving it a loose, careening charm. *New Adventures* has the same spirit of many of R.E.M.'s IRS records, which usually consisted of songs performed on the road initially, then recorded in the studio. However, don't take the title of *New Adventures in Hi-Fi* lightly—R.E.M. try different textures and different approaches to songs than they ever have before. "How the West Was Won and Where It Got Us" opens the album with a rolling, vaguely hip-hop drum beat and slowly adds on jazzily dissonant piano. "E-Bow the Letter" starts out as an updated version of "Country Feedback," then it turns in on itself with layers of moaning guitar effects and Patti Smith's haunting backing vocals. Clocking in at seven minutes, "Leave" is the longest track R.E.M. ever recorded and it's one of their strangest and best—an affecting minor-key dirge with a howling, siren-like feedback loop that runs throughout the entire song. Elsewhere, R.E.M. treads standard territory: "Electrolite" is a lovely piano-based ballad, "Departure" rocks like a *Document* outtake, the chiming opening riff of "Bittersweet Me" sounds like it was written in 1985, "New Test Leper" is gently winding folk-rock, "The Wake-Up Bomb" and "Undertow" rock like the *Monster* outtakes they are. On these more conventional songs, R.E.M. sounds invigorated; while on tour, they learned how to play as a band once again, which was a dynamic that was noticeably missing from *Monster*. *New Adventures in Hi-Fi* runs a little too long—it clocks in at 62 minutes, by far the longest album R.E.M. have ever released—but it remains convincing evidence that the band hasn't exhausted their creative possibilities yet. —*Stephen Thomas Erlewine*

The Rembrandts

f. Los Angeles, CA
Power Pop, Pop-Rock, Adult Alternative Pop-Rock
Even though they became best known for recording "I'll Be There for You," the theme song to the smash NBC sitcom *Friends*, the Rembrandts were actually rather successful back in 1991 with their self-titled debut album, which produced a Top 20 hit in "Just the Way It Is, Baby." The duo of songwriter Danny Wilde and Phil Solem, both originally in the Los Angeles band Great Buildings, forged a Beatle-tinged brand of pop-rock with ringing guitars and fresh harmonies that found favor with radio programmers across the country, as well as *Friends* co-producer Kevin Bright. The Rembrandts were invited to record a theme song for the show, which they completed in three days; after the show became a hit, radio demand for a full-length version was overwhelming, and one was added to 1995's *LP* at the last minute. While the song was an instant radio smash, topping *Billboard's* airplay chart for eight weeks, it wasn't released as a single until four months later in September, which makes its overall chart peak of No. 17 somewhat deceptive. *LP*, meanwhile, went platinum. —*Steve Huey*

● **The Rembrandts** / Aug. 1990 / Atco ✦✦✦✦
One of the more noteworthy "jangly guitar" acts of the 1990s, the Rembrandts were off to an enjoyable start with this debut album. Melodic and congenial but far from wimpy, such pop-rock as "If Not for Misery," "New King" and the small hit "Just The Way It Is, Baby" set the tone for the Los Angeles duo's career. A variety of influences from previous decades can be detected—everyone from the Beatles to the Byrds and Crosby, Stills & Nash to the Everly Brothers. And yet, this CD never

sounds dated, and has a definite freshness to it. With so many rap, metal, and industrial acts expressing deep pessimism in 1990, the optimistic, sociopolitical idealism of "Everyday People" (not to be confused with the Sly & the Family Stone classic) was a refreshing change. —*Alex Henderson*

Untitled / Sep. 15, 1992 / Atco ♦♦♦
Untitled didn't come close to the punch of *The Rembrandts*, as the duo moved away from the bright pop that shone on the previous effort in favor of a more subdued approach. And while the subject matter—mainly songs of yearning and lost love—hasn't changed much since the debut, the subtle string arrangements and minor-key melodies blend quite nicely, bringing out the themes more fully. Aside from the beautiful "Johnny Have You Seen Her," which is pleasantly reminiscent of Squeeze, the songs lack the instantly endearing quality of the debut but are no less rewarding with a little more effort. —*Chris Woodstra*

LP / May 23, 1995 / East West ♦♦♦
Most of the merits of the Rembrandts' third album, *LP*, were overshadowed by the massive success of "I'll Be There for You," the infectious theme from the hit Generation X sitcom "Friends." Included on *LP* at the last minute—the first pressings didn't list the song on the album cover—"I'll Be There for You" received saturation radio airplay, topping the adult contemporary charts, yet it was never released as a single, forcing fans of the song to buy the entire album to own the song. While the Monkees guitar riffs and layered harmonies are not entirely representative of the Rembrandts—it makes them out to be a bubblegum band—the record is filled with smart, hook-laden guitar pop that won't disappoint old Rembrandts fans or listeners attracted by the hit. —*Stephen Thomas Erlewine*

Renaissance

f. 1969, Surrey, England
Art-Rock/Progressive-Rock
The history of Renaissance is essentially the history of two separate groups, rather similar to the two phases of the Moody Blues or the Drifters. The original group was founded in 1969 by ex-Yardbirds members Keith Relf and Jim McCarty as a sort of progressive folk-rock band, who recorded two albums (of which only the first, self-titled LP came out in America, on Elektra Records) but never quite made it, despite some success on England's campus circuit.

The band went through several membership changes, with Relf and his sister Jane (who later fronted the very Renaissance-like Illusion) exiting and McCarty all but gone after 1971. The new lineup formed around the core of bassist Jon Camp, keyboardist John Tout, and drummer Terry Sullivan, with Annie Haslam, an aspiring singer with operatic training and a three-octave range.

Their first album in this incarnation, *Prologue*, released in 1972, was considerably more ambitious than the original band's work, with extended instrumental passages and soaring vocals by Haslam. Their breakthrough came with their next record, *Ashes Are Burning*, issued in 1973, which introduced guitarist Michael Dunford to the lineup and featured some searing electric licks by guest axeman Andy Powell. Their next record, *Turn of the Cards*, released by Sire Records, had a much more ornate songwriting style and was awash in lyrics that alternated between the topical and the mystical.

The group's ambitions, by now, were growing faster than its audience, which was concentrated on America's East Coast, especially in New York and Philadelphia—*Scheherazade* (1975) was built around a 20-minute extended suite for rock group and orchestra that dazzled the fans but made no new converts. A live album recorded at a New York concert date reprised their earlier material, including the "Scheherazade" suite, but covered little new ground and showed the group in a somewhat lethargic manner. The band's next two albums, *Novella* and *A Song for All Seasons*, failed to find new listeners, and as the 1970s closed out, the group was running headlong into the punk and new wave booms that made them seem increasingly anachronistic and doomed to cult status.

Their 1980s' albums were released with less than global or even national fanfare, and the group split up in the early '80s amid reported personality conflicts between members. During 1995, however, both Haslam and Dunford made attempts to revive the Renaissance name in different incarnations, and Jane Relf and the other surviving members of the original band were reportedly planning to launch their own "Renaissance" revival which, if nothing else, may keep the courts and some trademark attorneys busy for a little while. —*Bruce Eder*

Renaissance / 1969 / Elektra ♦♦♦
The original group's debut album was a then-groundbreaking meld of progressive rock with classical and jazz influences. The album is a little clunky by today's standards, and far druggier than the later group in its ambience (cofounders Keith Relf and Jim McCarty are the heavily psychedelic half of the final lineup of the Yardbirds, which made them anathema to Jimmy Page), but vocalist Jane Relf had a striking individ-

ual style and the classical influence was unique for its time. —*Bruce Eder*

Prologue / 1972 / One Way ♦♦♦♦
The debut of Renaissance, mark II, featuring Annie Haslam on lead vocals and John Tout on keyboards, is a solid meld of classical and rock, most of the material built around long, highly developed instrumental lines and Haslam's soaring three-octave range. Nineteenth-century European classical influences (especially Chopin) abound, in a mix of electric and acoustic rock. Reissued on CD by One Way Records in the '90s. —*Bruce Eder*

Ashes Are Burning / 1973 / One Way ♦♦♦
With electric guitarist Andy Powell sitting in on the title track, Renaissance delivered its best, and first fully formed album, mixing Russian, French, and Indian influences in musical settings that are both lively and elegant. The title track is one of the few lengthy progressive-rock pieces of the era that holds up, and the rest of the material runs the gamut from folk ("Carpet of the Sun") to Impressionist ("At the Harbor"), all of it hauntingly beautiful and enlivening. Reissued in 1993 by One Way Records, with excellent sound. —*Bruce Eder*

Turn of the Cards / 1974 / Sire ♦♦♦
An extension of *Ashes Are Burning*, even better produced and more unified thematically, but slightly lacking in the freshness and vibrancy of its predecessor; the classicism is the strongest element. Some of the material has an almost topical basis, which made it most unusual for progressive rock at the time. —*Bruce Eder*

Scheherazade & Other Stories / 1975 / Repertoire ♦♦♦♦
The group's most ambitious album is slightly disappointing because the material in the title track seems somewhat repetitive and the orchestra is mixed a little too far down. The rest of the material is livelier and, in some ways, more impressive and memorable. —*Bruce Eder*

Live at Carnegie Hall / 1976 / Sire ♦♦
Originally a double LP, this record showcased the group's live sound in full, including a performance of "Scheherazade" in concert with a 30-piece orchestra. All of the material (drawn from *Ashes Are Burning* onward) is stretched out from the studio originals, and not all of it really works on record. —*Bruce Eder*

Novella / 1977 / Sire ♦♦
By this time, the formula behind the group's sound was becoming predictable, as were many of the songs, although this record and its successor retained some interest for more than hard-core fans. —*Bruce Eder*

A Song for All Seasons / 1978 / Sire ♦♦
The last gasp for the group as anything resembling a band with an international following, this was their last record to get any serious exposure. The material lacks any of the life that resonated from the early-'70s releases, and even the classical pretensions now seem dullish if pretty. —*Bruce Eder*

In the Beginning / 1978 / Capitol ♦♦♦
This compilation of the *Prologue* and *Ashes Are Burning* albums should be great, but it isn't. The sound is flat and two major songs from *Ashes* were cut mercilessly. Good for a glimpse at the band. —*Bruce Eder*

● **Tales of 1001 Nights, Vol. 1** / 1990 / Sire ♦♦♦♦
An intelligently programmed collection of highlights from their Sire years. —*Bruce Eder*

Tales of 1001 Nights, Vol. 2 / Mar. 27, 1990 / Sire ♦♦♦♦
Less satisfying than the first volume with fewer memorable melodies, although it's worth a listen. —*Bruce Eder*

King Biscuit Flower Hour / Jan. 28, 1997 / King Biscuit ♦♦♦♦
An October 14, 1977 concert with the Royal Philharmonic Orchestra conducted by Harry Rabinowitz. The group had already done a live album with a 30-piece orchestra from Carnegie Hall, but this performance is, in some respects, better. The older songs are a curiosity when "Can You Understand" performed in a version more expansive (the horns of the RPO add a lot) but less taut than the original recording. "Carpet of the Sun" is similarly broadened from the studio original, but is lacking the bite of the original. But the "Song of Scheherazade" finally comes into its own here, in a performance superior to either the studio original or the Carnegie Hall version—the piece acquires some stature here, and is played and sung with more passion and feeling than any previously released rendition, though it also seems more pretentious and bombastic than ever as well, dating from a time when progressive rock's reach exceeded its grasp. —*Bruce Eder*

King Biscuit Flower Hour, Vol. 2 / Mar. 25, 1997 / King Biscuit ♦♦♦♦
The second part of this October 14, 1977 show is preferable to the first, showing the band in better form and doing songs that they seem to be playing and singing with greater enthusiasm and sympathy—and better songs. From "Running Hard" and "Mother Russia" to "Ashes Are Burning" (which turns into a 28-minute improvisation), they generally do credit to themselves and their repertory. The concert is rounded out with "Prologue" in a live performance from Asbury Park, N.J., and a previ-

ously unissued studio cut, "You (Pts. 1 & 2)." The recording captures the texture and nuance of Mick Dunford's acoustic guitar on "Midas Man" and "Ashes Are Burning" in exquisite detail—quite unexpected on a live album—and generally this record is more successful than its companion disc. —*Bruce Eder*

REO Speedwagon

f. Champaign, IL
Adult Contemporary, Soft Rock, Pop-Rock, Arena Rock
REO Speedwagon may not have been the most talented arena-rock band of the '70s, but they were almost certainly worked harder than any other group on the same circuit. In 1971, they released their first album of competent hard rock, but they didn't chart until 1974 with *Ridin' the Storm Out*. That album was recorded with temporary vocalist Michael Murphey, who would later have some solo success of his own; regular vocalist/rhythm guitarist Kevin Cronin rejoined the band in 1975. The first album released after Cronin rejoined REO was only moderately successful, but 1977's *REO Speedwagon Live/You Get What You Play For* began a string of gold and platinum albums, culminating with the 1980 album *Hi-Infidelity*, which sold over seven million copies in America. Although their style had shifted to a slick, mainstream AOR rock and they were known for power ballads, their hits didn't stop coming until 1990, when the band's support dropped off sharply; their 1991 album didn't even chart. However, the band remains a solid touring attraction, and they continue to release albums into the '90s. —*Stephen Thomas Erlewine*

R E O Speedwagon / 1971 / Epic ♦♦♦

R.E.O. 2 / 1972 / Epic ♦♦♦♦
An early album defining what was best about them in their opening-act days of the early '70s. —*Cub Koda*

Live: You Get What You Play For / 1977 / Epic ♦♦♦
REO Speedwagon built their audience through constant touring. Often, their live shows were more exciting than their records, which is what makes *You Get What You Play For*, a live run-through of their greatest hits, one of their better records of the era. —*Stephen Thomas Erlewine*

You Can Tune a Piano But You Can't Tuna Fish / 1978 / Epic ♦♦♦♦
You Can Tune a Piano, But You Can't Tuna Fish was REO Speedwagon's biggest hit of the '70s, featuring the singles "Roll with the Changes" and "Time for Me to Fly." —*AMG*

Decade of Rock & Roll '70-'80 / 1980 / Epic ♦♦♦♦
This is a well-chosen recap of REO's dues-paying years. —*Dan Heilman*

Hi-Infidelity / 1982 / Epic ♦♦♦♦
The band's breakthrough album with the masses. Heavy on the syrupy ballad formula that brought them success. —*Cub Koda*

Wheels Are Turnin' / 1984 / Epic ♦♦♦
Wheels Are Turnin' was REO Speedwagon's most popular post-*Hi-Infidelity* album, selling over two million copies and featuring the No. 1 single "Can't Fight This Feeling," as well as "I Do'wanna Know" and "One Lonely Night." —*AMG*

● **The Hits** / 1988 / Epic ♦♦♦♦
Hits does a fine job of collecting all of REO Speedwagon's biggest singles on 1 disc, featuring 14 of their best-known songs, including "Ridin' the Storm Out," "Roll With the Changes," "Time for Me to Fly," "Keep on Loving You," "Take It on the Run," "Don't Let Him Go," "Can't Fight This Feeling," "One Lonely Night," and "That Ain't Love," missing only the Top Ten "Keep the Fire Burnin'." —*Stephen Thomas Erlewine*

Second Decade of Rock & Roll / Sep. 24, 1991 / Epic ♦♦♦
Second Decade of Rock & Roll isn't as strong a compilation as *The Hits*, lacking the focused concentration of the previous compilation, but it does contain a fair amount of highlights from REO Speedwagon's '80s albums. —*AMG*

The Replacements

f. 1979, Minneapolis, MN, db. 1991
Rock 'n' Roll, Alternative Pop-Rock
The Replacements initially formed in 1979, when Paul Westerberg joined the garage-punk band formed by brothers Bob (guitar) and Tommy Stinson (bass) and drummer Chris Mars. Originally, the band was called the Impediments, but they changed their name to the Replacements after being banned from a local club for disorderly behavior. In their early days, they sounded quite similar to Hüsker Dü, the leaders of the Minneapolis punk scene. However, the Replacements were wilder and looser than the Hüskers and quickly became notorious for their drunken, chaotic gigs. After they built up a sizable local following, the Minneapolis label Twin/Tone signed them.

Sorry Ma, Forgot to Take Out the Trash, a sloppy hardcore collection, was released in 1981 but failed to make much of an impact on the national scene. It was followed the next year by the *Stink* EP, which followed the same pattern as the debut. It was the band's second album,

1983's *Hootenanny*, that first garnered the band attention and helped build their fan base. On *Hootenanny*, the group started playing around with other genres, adding elements of pop, straightforward rock 'n' roll, country and folk, although sometimes the eclecticism was ironic.

Hootenanny set the stage for *Let It Be*, the band's critical and artistic breakthrough. Released in 1984, *Let It Be* showed that the band had successfully expanded their musical reach and that Westerberg had grown considerably as a songwriter; he was now capable of pop like "I Will Dare," full-throttle rock 'n' roll, and introspective ballads like "Answering Machine." Critics and fellow musicians were quick to praise the band, and they developed a large underground following. The buzz was large enough to convince Sire to sign the band in 1985.

The Replacements' first major-label album, *Tim*, was scheduled to be produced by Westerberg's idol, Alex Chilton, but the sessions fell through; the album was produced by former Ramone Tommy Erdelyi. Upon its release in 1985, *Tim* garnered rave reviews that equalled those for *Let It Be*. Though the band was poised for a popular breakthrough, they were unsure about making the leap into the mainstream. As a result, they never let themselves live up to their full potential. The Replacements landed a spot on *Saturday Night Live*, but they were roaring drunk throughout their performances and Westerberg said "fuck" on the air. Their concerts had become notorious for such drunken, sloppy behavior. Frequently, the band was barely able to stand up, let alone play, and when they did play, they often didn't finish their songs. The Replacements also refused to make accessible videos—the video for "Bastards of Young" featured nothing but a stereo system, playing the song—thereby cutting themselves off from the mass exposure MTV could have granted them.

After the tour for *Tim*, Bob Stinson was fired from the band, allegedly for his drug and alcohol addictions. The Replacements recorded their next album as a trio in Memphis, TN, with former Big Star producer Jim Dickinson. The resulting album, *Pleased to Meet Me*, was more streamlined than their previous recordings. Again, the reviews were uniformly excellent upon its spring 1987 release, but the band didn't earn many new fans. During the tour for *Pleased to Meet Me*, guitarist Slim Dunlap filled the vacant lead-guitarist spot and he became a full-time member after the tour.

Two years later, the band returned in the spring of 1989 with *Don't Tell a Soul*, the Replacements' last bid for a mainstream audience. The band had cleaned up, admitting that their years of drug and alcohol abuse were behind them, and were now willing to play the promotional game. *Don't Tell a Soul* boasted a polished, radio-ready production and the group shot MTV-friendly videos, beginning with the single "I'll Be You." Initially, the approach worked—"I'll Be You" became a No. 1 album-rock track, crossing over to No. 51 on the pop charts. However, *Don't Tell a Soul* never really took off and failed to establish the band as a major commercial force.

Defeated from the lackluster performance of *Don't Tell a Soul*, Paul Westerberg planned on recording a solo album, but Sire rejected the idea. Consequently, the next Replacements album, *All Shook Down*, was a solo Westerberg record in all but name. Recorded with a cast of session musicians as well as the band, *All Shook Down* was a stripped-down, largely acoustic affair that hinted at the turmoil within the band. Chris Mars left shortly after its fall 1990 release, claiming that Westerberg had assumed control of the band; he would launch a solo career two years later. The Replacements toured in support of *All Shook Down*, with Steve Foley, formerly of the Minneapolis-based Things Fall Down, as their new drummer. Neither the tour nor the album were successful, and the Replacements disbanded in the summer of 1991. Tommy Stinson formed Bash & Pop the following year; in 1995, he formed a new band called Perfect. Dunlap released a solo album in 1993. Bob Stinson died February 15, 1995 from a drug overdose. Westerberg began a solo career slowly, releasing two songs on the *Singles* ("Dyslexic Heart," "Waiting for Somebody") soundtrack in 1992; he also scored the film. He released his debut solo album, *14 Songs*, in the summer of 1993 to mixed reviews. Paul Westerberg's second solo album, *Eventually*, was released in the spring of 1996. —*Stephen Thomas Erlewine*

Sorry Ma, Forgot to Take Out the Trash / 1981 / Twin/Tone ♦♦
Sorry Ma, Forgot to Take Out the Trash is a slight but enjoyable debut album from the Replacements, capturing the quartet halfway between the loud, fast punk rock of the Ramones and Hüsker Dü and the classic rock raunch of the Rolling Stones. Most of the record speeds by in a flurry of ragged guitars, rushed rhythms, and hoarse vocals—it's about the sound, not the songs. However, there are a handful of songs that indicate the Replacements are capable of depth, including the bluesy Johnny Thunder tribute "Johnny's Gonna Die," the tongue-in-cheek "I Hate Music," and the near-anthemic "Shiftless When Idle." —*Stephen Thomas Erlewine*

The Replacements Stink / 1982 / Twin/Tone ♦♦♦
Following quickly on the heels of the group's debut, the *Stink* EP takes the loud-hard-fast attitude of *Sorry Ma, Forgot to Take Out the Trash* to the extreme, mistakenly giving the impression that the Replacements

were a hardcore band. Even though the EP isn't much more than clamor, it's *better* clamor than before—the band doesn't sound tighter but their noise is more galvanizing and a handful of songs ("Kids Don't Follow," "Fuck School," "God Damn Job") suggest Paul Westerberg is improving as a songwriter. —*Stephen Thomas Erlewine*

Hootenanny / 1983 / Twin/Tone ✦✦✦
The Replacements came into their own with *Hootenanny*, a careening, drunken stumble through punk, rock 'n' roll, country, blues, and folk. The eclecticism of the album separated the Replacements from the post-punk hardcore pack, but it's also what makes the record a mess. Half of the record is devoted to ironic jokes, whether it's the Beatles pastiche of "Mr. Whirly," the tongue-in cheek title track or the silly closer "Treatment Bound." Not so coincidentally, those are songs where Westerberg branches out into other styles, and he found it easier to experiment under the guise of a joke. He does let his guard down on the extraordinary "Within Your Reach," a disarmingly open plea for love that he recorded entirely himself. It's the only truly vulnerable moment on the record, but the snide "Color Me Impressed" also comes close to true emotion. And it's fun to hear Westerberg act tough on "Take Me Down to the Hospital," "Run It," and "You Lose," especially considering how the group has improved. They're still sloppy, to be sure, but Bob Stinson's guitar stings and the rhythm section of Tommy Stinson and Chris Mars rocks with a loose abandon that makes even the filler—and there's a lot of filler—enjoyable garage-punk. —*Stephen Thomas Erlewine*

☆ **Let It Be** / 1984 / Twin/Tone ✦✦✦✦✦
The Replacements half-heartedly tried to expand their reach on *Hootenanny*, and they followed through on that album's promise on *Let It Be*. Kicking off with the country-rock shuffle of "I Will Dare," the record explodes into a series of pseudo-hardcore ravers before hitting Paul Westerberg's piano-driven rumination, "Androgynous," one of four major ballads that cuts to the core of Midwestern suburban alienation. "Sixteen Blue" is one of the definitive teenage anthems of the '80s, while "Unsatisfied" rages in despair and Westerberg rarely was more affecting than the solo performance of "Answering Machine." All four, along with "I Will Dare," form the core of Westerberg and the Replacements' canon, and are enough to make *Let It Be* a cornerstone post-punk album, even if the rest of the record pales next to the songs. All the remaining songs are convincing garage-rockers, even if they reveal the Replacements' former punk stance to be a bit of a pose—a cover of Kiss' "Black Diamond" comes off as a tribute, as does the co-opting of Ted Nugent's "Cat Scratch Fever" for "Gary's Got a Boner." Furthermore, the original numbers lean toward the Faces, leaving the Ramones behind and while everything except "Seen Your Video," which now sounds as dated as a "Disco Sucks" rant, are bracing rockers, they're a bit inconsequential and point the way towards the band's deadly fascination with classic rock. —*Stephen Thomas Erlewine*

★ **Tim** / 1985 / Sire ✦✦✦✦✦
Let it Be made the Replacements into college-radio and critical favorites, leading the group to a major-label contract with Sire. The band's major-label debut *Tim* does represent a bit of a compromise of the group's garage-punk sound. Producer Tommy Erdelyi (formerly of the Ramones) helped clean up the band's sound, primarily by harnessing the rhythm section to a click track—no longer does the band thrash all over the place, they keep a steady rocking beat. Similarly, Bob Stinson is kept in check, and his wildfire guitar bubbles the surface only on two cuts, "Dose of Thunder" and "Lay it Down Clown," which are both filler. Some of the rockers, even the anthemic "Bastards of Young," are gutted by the cleaner sound, but the overall effect of the record isn't hurt because Paul Westerberg turns in his finest overall set of songs, ranging from the charming love song "Kiss Me On the Bus" and the college-radio anthem "Left of the Dial" to the detailed chronicles of loneliness like "Here Comes a Regular," "Hold My Life," and "Swingin' Party." Westerberg's melodies and observations are sharper than ever, giving *Tim* an eloquent but edgy power that can't be diluted by the tame production. —*Stephen Thomas Erlewine*

The Shit Hits the Fans / 1985 / Twin/Tone ✦
Twin/Tone rush-released the cassette-only live album *The Shit Hits the Fans* before the Replacements left the label for Sire later in 1985. The album is an audience tape of an Oklahoma City concert from 1984 that a Replacements roadie confiscated from a patron that was bootlegging the show and it is presented unvarnished. Consequently, it is, as they like to say, a "warts-and-all" document of a standard Replacements show, capturing the group as they slaughter several of their best-known songs and run-through drunken covers of R.E.M., Thin Lizzy and the Rolling Stones. The tape sounds poor and the performances are, to be charitable, sloppy, but it's great fun for hardcore fans, especially those longing for the 'Mats alcohol-fueled live shows. —*Stephen Thomas Erlewine*

Pleased to Meet Me / 1987 / Sire ✦✦✦✦
Bob Stinson was kicked out of the band after *Tim*, allegedly because he

was unwilling to make the musical leap forward necessary for *Pleased to Meet Me*. With Stinson left the Replacements' hardcore roots, leaving behind the conflicting desires of Westerberg's wish to be a serious singer-songwriter and for the group to become either the Faces or Big Star. That conflict is played out throughout *Pleased to Meet Me*, and it isn't helped by the stultifyingly clean and detailed production by Jim Dickinson. Chris Mars and Tommy Stinson are reined in tighter than ever before, giving most of the songs a strangled, distanced feel which isn't helped by Dickinson's canned guitar sounds and the odd production flourishes, including the occasional sax and keyboard. The full-blown production works on the horn and string-drenched "Can't Hardly Wait," but it makes mindlessly rocking filler like "Shooting Dirty Pool" and "Red Red Wine" irritating. For the most part, Westerberg's songs make the clean sound tolerable, particularly on the Stonesy "I.O.U.," the suicide sketch of "The Ledge," the power-pop of "Never Mind" and "Valentine," and the lovely acoustic "Skyway." But the fan love-letter "Alex Chilton" reveals more than necessary—even though Westerberg is shooting for stardom, he has more affinity for the self-styled loser, which means he never wants to make the full leap to the mainstream. And that can only hurt a record like *Pleased to Meet Me*, which has stardom in its sights. —*Stephen Thomas Erlewine*

Don't Tell a Soul / 1989 / Sire ✦✦✦
All of the slick production of *Pleased to Meet Me* wasn't close to the glossy sound of *Don't Tell A Soul*, the Replacements' last-ditch attempt at mainstream success. Bathed with washes of synthesizers, shining guitars, backing vocals and a shimmering, AOR-oriented production, *Don't Tell a Soul* puts an end to the Replacements and begins Paul Westerberg's solo career. The bulk of the songs are self-consciously mature, as Westerberg looks back on his career (the autobiographical "Talent Show") and is haunted by the past ("Rock N Roll Ghost," "Darlin' One"), as he attempts to refashion himself as a craftsman. A few of these attempts work, particularly the country-rock ballad "Achin' to Be" and the arena-rock stab "I'll Be You," but the lite-funk workout "Asking Me Lies" and the stuttering "I Won't" are flat-out embarrassing. And the rest of the album suffers from Westerberg's determination to be adult. The songs are too self-consciously mature and the band is functions as a supporting act for the lyrics, which lack the unpretentious poetry of his best work. Ironically, Westerberg's desire to be an "adult" is the reason why radio ignored *Don't Tell a Soul*, because it meant that the record lacked both rockers or power-ballads which would have given them air-time. And most old fans found the production too heavy to make sorting through the album worthwhile. —*Stephen Thomas Erlewine*

All Shook Down / 1990 / Sire ✦✦✦✦
Though *Don't Tell A Soul* sounded like a Replacements record, it felt like a Paul Westerberg album. *All Shook Down* continues that trend—it's a Replacements record only in name. Recorded with a variety of session musicians and sporting no individual credits, *All Shook Down* emphasizes the songs, not the band, and it's a weary, beaten set of songs. Despite a handful of forced rockers—especially the downright embarrassing Johnette Napolitano duet "My Little Problem"—the album is a low-key and primarily acoustic set, finding Westerberg knowing that the band is over and wondering where it all went wrong. While *All Shook Down* doesn't have any nakedly emotional stunners like "Answering Machine" or "Skyway," it has a unified atmosphere and an off-the-cuff, unpretentious feel which comes as a relief after the weighty ambitions of *Don't Tell a Soul*. It also has a number of excellently crafted songs, ranging from the wistful "Sadly Beautiful" and the druggy "All Shook Down" to snappy pop-rockers like "Merry Go Round," "When It Began" and "Happy Town." As the loungey closer suggests, the record is meant to be "The Last,"and few bands ended their career in such a knowing, worn-out fashion. —*Stephen Thomas Erlewine*

The Residents

f. 1966, Shreveport, LA
Alternative Pop-Rock, Experimental, No Wave
Over the course of a recording career spanning several decades, the Residents remained a riddle of Sphinx-like proportions; cloaking their lives and music in a haze of willful obscurity, the band's members never identified themselves by name, always appearing in public in disguise—usually tuxedos, top hats and giant eyeball masks—and refusing to grant media interviews. Drawing inspiration from the likes of fellow innovators including Harry Partch, Sun Ra and Captain Beefheart, the Residents channelled the breadth of American music into their idiosyncratic, satiric vision, their mercurial blend of electronics, distortion, avant-jazz, classical symphonies, and gratingly nasal vocals reinterpreting everyone from John Philip Sousa to James Brown while simultaneously expanding the boundaries of theatrical performance and multimedia interaction.

It was commonly accepted that the four-member group emigrated to San Francisco, California from Shreveport, Louisiana at some point in the early '70s. According to longtime group spokesman Jay Clem—one member of the so-called Cryptic Corporation, the band's representative body—they received their name when Warner Bros. mailed back their anonymous demo tape, addressed simply "for the attention of residents." Finding no takers for their oddball sounds, the Residents founded their own label, Ralph Records, for the purposes of issuing their 1972 debut "Santa Dog," released in a pressing of 300 copies which were mailed out to luminaries from Frank Zappa to President Richard Nixon. Their full-length 1973 *Meet the Residents* reportedly sold fewer than 50 copies before the group was threatened with a lawsuit from Capitol Records over its cover, a twisted, dadaesque parody of the art to *Meet the Beatles*.

The follow-up, 1974's neo-classical excursion *Not Available*, was recorded with the intention of its music remaining unissued; locked in cold storage upon its completion, only a 1978 contractual obligation resulted in its eventual release. 1976's *Third Reich 'N' Roll* was the next official offering, a collection of pop oldies covers presented in a controversial jacket portraying Adolf Hitler clutching an enormous carrot. After a 1976 concert in Berkeley, California which cloaked the Residents behind an opaque screen, wrapped up like mummies—the most famous of only three live performances mounted during their first decade of existence—they issued an abrasive 1977 cover of the Rolling Stones' "Satisfaction," which became an underground hit on both sides of the Atlantic at the peak of the punk movement. As the decade drew to a close, the group released a flurry of recordings further building upon their growing cult following; among them were 1977's *Duck Stab/Buster & Glen*, 1979's *Eskimo* (purportedly a collection of native Arctic chants) and 1980's *Commercial Album*, a compilation of 40 one-minute mock advertising jingles.

In 1981 the Residents embarked upon their "Mole Trilogy," a prog-rock collection of albums—1981's *The Mark Of The Mole*, 1982's *The Tunes of Two Cities* and 1985's *The Big Bubble*—recounting an epic battle between a pair of tribes named the Moles and the Chebs; a lavish, multimedia tour, "The Mole Show," followed. In the interim, the group also mounted another ambitious project, the "American Composer" series, although only two of the projected titles—1984's *George and James* (a reinterpretation of songs by George Gershwin and James Brown) and 1986's *Stars and Hank Forever* (celebrating John Philip Sousa and Hank Williams)—ever appeared. Instead, in the wake of financial and corporate difficulties which resulted in the creation of a New Ralph label, the Residents issued the one-off *God in Three Persons* (a talking blues outing) and 1989's *The King and Eye* (a reinterpretation of Elvis Presley standards).

After losing control of the Ralph label as well as their back catalog, the Residents regained the rights to their music in 1990 and began reissuing long-out-of-print material as well as the new *Freak Show*, a meditation on circus sideshows and carnival dementia. Four years later, *Freak Show* was reissued as a CD-ROM, marking the group's first leap into the new digital interactive technology; *The Residents Have a Bad Day* followed in 1996, and included the soundtrack to the CD-ROM game "Bad Day on the Midway." In 1997, the band celebrated their silver anniversary with the release of the career-spanning overview *Our Tired, Our Poor, Our Huddled Masses.* —*Jason Ankeny*

Meet the Residents / 1974 / East Side Digital ✦✦✦
The Residents are true avant-garde crazies. Their earliest albums (of which this is the first) have precedents in Captain Beefheart's experimental albums, Frank Zappa's conceptual numbers from *Freak Out*, the work of Steve Reich and the compositions of chance music tonemeister John Cage—yet the Residents' work of this time really sounds like nothing else that exists. All of the music on this release consists of deconstructions of countless rock and non-rock styles, which are then grafted together to create chaotic, formless, seemingly haphazard numbers; the first six "songs" (including a fragment from the Nancy Sinatra hit "These Boots Are Made for Walkin'") are strung together to form a larger entity similar in concept to the following lengthier selections. The result is a series of unique, odd, challenging numbers that manage not to be entirely successful. The album cover is a fierce burlesque of the Beatles' first US Capitol label release, sporting puerilely doctored photographs of the Fab Four on the front and pictures of collarless-suited sea denizens on the back (identified as Paul McCrawfish, Ringo Starfish, and the like). This is an utterly bizarre platter that may appeal to very adventurous listeners. —*David Cleary*

Third Reich & Roll / 1975 / East Side Digital ✦✦✦✦

Eskimo / 1979 / East Side Digital ✦✦✦✦
A CD re-issue of the 1979 record. A wild vision of what original polar Eskimo life was like before government housing came along in the late '60s. Contains "The Walrus Hunt," "Birth," "Artic Hysteria," "The Angry Angakok," "A Spirit Steals A Child," "The Festival of Death." A totally engaging tone-poem, filled with humor, pathos, shamanism, and all the other great things, with skillful electronic sound-painting, and always the right touch. —*Blue* Gene Tyranny

The Commercial Album / Nov. 1980 / East Side Digital ✦✦✦✦
Forty brief stories, homilies, instrumentals, slices of life, each exactly 60 seconds long —"The Coming of the Crow," "Nice Old Man," "My Work Is So Behind," "Die in Terror," "Floyd," "Act of Being Polite," etc. . . . each unique in vocals and instrumentation, and each weirdly humorous, momentarily stunning. —*Blue* Gene Tyranny

★ **God in Three Persons** / 1988 / Rykodisc ✦✦✦✦✦
Employing the same stress scheme as Poe's "The Raven" throughout its 62 minutes, "God in Three Persons" is an extended work in talking-blues style for narrator, electronic instruments, and a chorus providing humorous comments not found in the libretto. As in all Residents pieces, the voices are modified electronically and the musical elements are deceptively minimal—most of its 14 episodes have only two chords, which still manage to instantly produce the correct atmosphere (Wagnerian thirds for mythic import, tonic-dominant in triplets for '50s teenage love story, etc.). There are only passing riffs, more like comments, and the only melody in the whole piece is a wheezy organ quote of the standard doxology hymn "Holy, Holy, Holy (God in Three Persons)." The subject matter is, in part, the derivation of religious and other symbolic images from the naturally erotic, but that's only part of it. Give this one a listen. —*Blue* Gene Tyranny

Paul Revere & the Raiders

f. 1960, Portland, OR
Rock 'n' Roll, Pop-Rock
With their Revolutionary War costumes and upbeat attitude, Paul Revere & the Raiders were one of the more entertaining rock 'n' roll bands of the mid-'60s. They began in the late '50s as a more hard-edged outfit, and after the mid-'70s, they evolved into a musical-comedy lounge act. The group was put together by keyboard player Paul Revere (b. Paul Revere Dick, Jan. 7, 1938, Harvard, NE) and singer/saxophonist Mark Lindsay (b. Mar. 9, 1942, Eugene, OR) in Caldwell, ID, and scored a Top 40 hit with the instrumental "Like, Long Hair" in 1961. They eventually based themselves in Portland, OR, where they competed in the lively Northwest circuit with acts like the Wailers and the Kingsmen and earned a recording contract with Columbia Records in 1963 on the strength of their recording of "Louie, Louie." (The Kingsmen, however, beat them out for a hit with the song.) But it wasn't until the summer of 1965, when they were chosen as the house band on the afternoon TV show "Where the Action Is," that Paul Revere & the Raiders really took off, with Lindsay becoming a teenage heartthrob. (Featuring Mark Lindsay" was added to their name.) In 1966 and 1967, they enjoyed four Top Ten hits—"Kicks," "Hungry," "Good Thing," and "Him or Me—What's It Gonna Be?"—and four Top Ten, gold-selling albums—*Just Like Us!*, *Midnight Ride*, *The Spirit of '67*, and *Greatest Hits*. Their good-time style became less fashionable in the late '60s, though they continued to reach the Top 40. After a temporary name change to simply "Raiders" in 1970, they scored their sole No. 1 hit with the gold single "Indian Reservation (The Lament of the Cherokee Reservation Indian)" in 1971. But in the early '70s, they made a transition to more of a Las Vegas-style live show and Revere's gags began to dominate the act. Lindsay left in early 1975, though he has occasionally reunited with the group onstage and on record. —*William Ruhlmann*

The Spirit of '67 / Nov. 1966 / Sundazed ✦✦✦
The Spirit of '67, Paul Revere and the Raiders' third gold-selling, Top Ten album to be released in 1966, marked the triumph of the group's in-house writing team of lead singer Mark Lindsay, Paul Revere, and producer Terry Melcher. "Hungry," the Top Ten follow-up to "Kicks," was written, like the earlier hit, by Barry Mann and Cynthia Weil, but Lindsay-Revere-Melcher then hit the Top 40 with "The Great Airplane Strike" and the Top Ten with "Good Thing." (Actually, Revere was not a writer on "Good Thing," as subsequent releases indicated.) Those hits anchored this collection, which was filled out by showcases for bassist Phil Volk and drummer Mark Smith (guitarist Drake Levin had been replaced by Jim Valley), plus some secondary material by the group's leaders. As usual, there were listening closely to their peers, and much of the material had the twangy guitar-rock sound common to 1966, though some of the experimental eclecticism that would lead to the elaborate productions of 1967's *Sgt. Pepper* psychedelic era was also apparent in songs like "Oh! To Be a Man" and "Undecided Man" (the latter a near-copy of the Beatles' "Eleanor Rigby"). This stylistic trend following did not bode well for the future, but for the moment Paul Revere and the Raiders were riding high. The CD reissue on Sundazed adds three bonus cuts, including the 45-single version of "The Great Airplane Strike," and an alternate version of "Hungry." —*William Ruhlmann*

Revolution! / 1967 / Sundazed ✦✦✦
Singer-songwriter Mark Lindsay and producer/songwriter Terry Melcher took an unprecedented nine months to craft their follow-up to *The Spirit of '67*, though they did come up with three singles in the interim. Two of those, the Rolling Stones-ish Top Ten hit "Him or Me—What's It Gonna Be?" and the whimsical Top 40 hit "I Had a

Dream," anchored this collection and defined its stylistic range. Competing in the eclectic, exploratory pop world of 1967, Lindsay and Melcher crafted an ambitious album that made extensive use of studio gimmickry (and mimicry). But there wasn't much substance to the experimentation, and the loss of the Raiders lineup of 1965-1967 robbed the music of the forcefulness of the group's initial hits. —*William Ruhlmann*

Something Happening / 1968 / Sundazed ✦✦✦
Following a couple of genre exercises in *A Christmas Present... And Past* and *Goin' to Memphis*, plus a couple of Top 40 singles, "Too Much Talk" and "Don't Take It So Hard" (both included here), *Something Happening* marked Terry Melcher's departure from the studio and singer-songwriter Mark Lindsay's debut as producer of Paul Revere and the Raiders. The group had embarked on a second TV series, *Happening*, and the album was tied into that, beginning and ending with the show's theme song. The LP also featured the two recent hits. Nevertheless, it failed to stem the Raiders' commercial decline, and no wonder. The challenge of an essentially imitative talent like Lindsay's is to keep up with trends, and in the fast-moving late '60s, that was almost impossible. Here, he was still copying the Beatles of 1966 ("Too Much Talk" was a rewrite of "Paperback Writer") and 1967 (much of the rest echoed *Sgt. Pepper*), while pop had moved back to a simpler, more direct approach. —*William Ruhlmann*

Legend of Paul Revere / Apr. 1990 / Columbia/Legacy ✦✦✦✦
This two-CD anthology, with 55 songs, may be a lot more Raiders than the average fan would want. But go for it and be amazed at how consistently this rocking band from the Great Northwest was. Includes all the hits. —*Jeff Tamarkin*

● **The Essential Ride '63-'67** / Jun. 6, 1995 / Columbia/Legacy ✦✦✦✦
A much more sensible buy than the double-CD *Legend of Paul Revere*, this 20-track compilation focuses on their toughest (and therefore best) early material. Has all the big early hits, and about half the songs weren't on *Legend*, most notably their fine pre-Monkees version of "Steppin' Stone." Note that the version of "Hungry" here is an alternate take, good or bad news depending on whether you have the original hit rendition already. —*Richie Unterberger*

Reverend Horton Heat

b. Corpus Christi, TX
Guitar, Vocals / Rockabilly, Alternative Pop-Rock, Rockabilly Revival
With his highly stylized, backwoods hick-preacher image, it would be easy to dismiss the Reverend Horton Heat as a poseur. But it would be wrong. Instead of treating rockabilly as a campy joke like the Cramps, the good Reverend rocks the hell out of his modern-day rockabilly, playing it as if it were the hardest of punk yet without any of the self-conscious trappings of either genre. Although his lyrics can be too silly, his music never is; it rocks harder than most of his punk and metal contemporaries, as evidenced by 1993's *Full Custom Gospel Sounds*, 1994's *Liquor in the Front* and 1996's *It's Martini Time*. —*Stephen Thomas Erlewine*

Smoke 'em If You Got 'em / 1992 / Sub Pop ✦✦✦✦
Reverend Horton Heat's first album is filled with tongue-in-cheek songs and killer riffs, made all the more exciting by the good Reverend's raw, gutsy, punk-injected rockabilly licks. —*Stephen Thomas Erlewine*

● **The Full Custom Gospel Sounds** / Apr. 26, 1993 / Sub Pop ✦✦✦✦
On Reverend Horton Heat's second album, the band sounds like it was having a race with the devil. All of their songs are played with a reckless abandon that makes their neo-rockabilly sound rawer and more vital than most punk or metal bands. —*Stephen Thomas Erlewine*

Liquor in the Front / Jul. 5, 1994 / Interscope ✦✦✦
Al Jourgensen's production makes Reverend Horton Heat sound more like a heavy metal band than they actually are, but that usually doesn't distract from the primal pleasures of the group's jacked-up rockabilly roar. —*Stephen Thomas Erlewine*

It's Martini Time / Jul. 1996 / Interscope ✦✦
As the photo on the back cover indicates, the Reverend Horton Heat spent the two years between *Liquor in the Front* and *It's Martini Time* living pretty hard. In addition to touring, the group has indulged in their boozy, campy ways a little too much, which is evident throughout *It's Martini Time*. Though the group sounds fine—by this point, they could probably play their overdriven rockabilly in their sleep— there is no spark to the record, it all sounds tired. Where the band had sounded intoxicatingly crazed in the past, songs like "Big Red Rocket of Love" and "Generation Why" have no energy, nor do they have any hooks. The Reverend Horton Heat simply sound burned out. Of course, most rockabilly bands—especially rockabillly revivalists—wind up sounding burned out or tired, but it's disheartening to hear the group sound so close to the end of the line so early in their career. —*Stephen Thomas Erlewine*

The Rezillos

f. 1976, Edinburgh, Scotland
Punk, New Wave
Although frequently aligned with the punk movement, the Rezillos' (later known as the Revillos) irreverent glam-rock image and affection for campy girl-group iconography set them distinctly apart from their peers. Formed in 1976 in Edinburgh, Scotland, the group was initially a fluid and highly informal collective centered around lead vocalists Eugene Reynolds (born Alan Forbes) and Fay Flfe (Sheila Hynde) and fleshed out by lead guitarist Luke Warm (Jo Callis), second guitarist Hi-Fi Harris (Mark Harris), Dr. D.K. Smythe on bass, drummer Angel Patterson (Alan Patterson), and backing vocalist Gale Warning.

The Rezillos' early repertoire contained material from the likes of Screaming Lord Sutch, the Dave Clark Five, and the Sweet. The success of their 1977 debut single "I Can't Stand My Baby" was unexpected, especially by the band members themselves, who never considered the group much more than a lark; as a result of the more serious pressures now exerted on the Rezillos, Harris, Smythe and Warning all departed, while bassist/saxophonist William Mysterious (born William Donaldson) signed on as a permanent member.

After signing to major label Sire, the quintet reached the UK Top 20 with a single titled, ironically enough, "Top of the Pops." After releasing their 1978 debut LP *Can't Stand the Rezillos*, Mysterious was replaced by Simon Templar, but internal problems continued to plague the group, and following a farewell tour, they disbanded in December 1978. Patterson, Warm and Templar continued on as Shake, while Reynolds and Fife, promised they could be released from their contract if they dropped the Rezillos name, formed the Revillos.

Rejoined by Harris as well as onetime Pork Dukes drummer Rocky Rhythm, bassist Felix and backing vocalists Babs and Cherie (a.k.a. the Revettes), the first incarnation of the Revillos recorded a pair of singles, "Where's the Boy for Me?" and "Motorbike Beat." In mid-1979, Harris left to become an architect, and was replaced by 17-year-old guitarist Kid Krupa in time to record 1980's *Rev Up*. Following the usual lineup fluctuations (Felix was replaced by Vince Spik, and Babs was replaced by singer Drax), the Revillos signed to the Superville label and issued the single "She's Fallen In Love With a Monster Man" and the 1983 LP *Attack!* After a pair of self-financed US tours, the band split in 1985; Reynolds formed Rockatomic and Planet Pop, while Fay joined Destroy All Men. The Revillos reformed in 1994 to play a series of concerts in Japan, ultimately recording the *Live and On Fire in Japan* album and the *Yeah Yeah* EP. In 1996, they issued a rarities compilation, *From the Freezer*, and played some live dates in Britain. —*Jason Ankeny*

● **Can't Stand the Rezillos** / 1978 / Sire ✦✦✦✦
Wild, untempered, poppish punk. One of the best outcomes of the new-wave era. —*David Szatmary*

Can't Stand the Rezillos: The (Almost) Complete Rezillos / 1993 / Sire/Warner Bros. ✦✦✦✦
All of *Can't Stand the Rezillos*, almost all of *Mission Accomplished... But the Beat Goes On*, and one single. This leaves a few tracks unaccounted for (including, surprisingly, "20,000 Rezillos Under the Sea"), but it's a dynamite package of demented power-pop all the same. The live set is a great addition, thanks to the wonderfully odd choices of songs to cover. —*Steven McDonald*

Emitt Rhodes

b. Feb. 1948, Hawthorne, CA
Keyboards, Vocals / Singer-Songwriter, Pop-Rock
Hawthorne, California, native Emitt Rhodes made his first mark in the music world in 1967 as the leader of the baroque-pop band the Merry-Go-Round. The band achieved some marginal success with the Rhodes-penned "Live," and "You're a Very Lovely Woman," recording one album of *Magical Mystery Tour*-inspired pop. When the band broke up in 1969, Rhodes set up a home studio in his parents' garage and began his solo career, engineering and playing all instruments himself. The strength of his initial demos, now showing a strong Paul McCartney influence, helped him get signed to ABC/Dunhill. His critically acclaimed, self-titled debut managed to break into the Top 40 in 1971, but pressure from his record company forced him to rush-release a follow-up, *Mirror*, the same year. *Mirror* was predictably a lesser effort, barely charting. By the time of the third album, 1973's *Farewell to Paradise*, Rhodes was running into legal problems with ABC, since he was unable to fulfill his contract, which demanded he deliver a new album every six months. Disillusioned, he retired from the performing side of the business, working instead as an engineer and studio operator for Elektra/Asylum. Though he hasn't released an album since *Farewell to Paradise*, he continues to write and demo new songs. —*Chris Woodstra*

Emitt Rhodes / 1970 / One Way ✦✦✦✦
Rhodes turns in a fine performance, much in the style of Paul McCartney's first solo album. Like McCartney, Rhodes wrote all the songs,

played all the instruments and recorded the album at home. There the comparison ends. Songs like "With My Face on the Floor" and "She's Such a Beauty" are the kinds of songs that pop into your head 20 years later and get you as excited as the first time you heard them. —*Jim Worbois*

The American Dream / 1971 / A&M ✦✦✦
If you wish to get an overview of the early career of Emitt Rhodes, this may be the place. Consisting of tracks recorded by his former band, Merry-Go-Round, as well as some "later" material on which he is backed by some of Los Angeles' finest, this record will only serve to whet your appetite. "You're a Very Lovely Woman" is strong inducement to look for further Merry-Go-Round material, while a song like "Pardon Me" points the way to Rhodes' first Dunhill album. —*Jim Worbois*

Mirror / 1972 / Dunhill ✦✦✦
Rhodes continues strolling down the same road as McCartney and has discovered some of the same potholes. Like McCartney, Rhodes is insulated from outside influences (especially peers), and the work isn't nearly as exciting or adventurous as the first time out. This is still a pleasant record but this is not the Emitt Rhodes album one would be inclined to grab first. —*Jim Worbois*

● **Listen, Listen: The Best of Emitt Rhodes** / Aug. 29, 1995 / Varese Sarabande ✦✦✦✦
Listen, Listen is an extensive, 21-track overview of Rhodes' commercially underappreciated career. A chronological collection, the disc begins with his work with the Merry-Go-Round (six tracks—nearly all of the band's finest moments), covers his solo years with highlights from the three albums as well as a rare single from 1972 ("Tame the Lion"), and ends with a track from a 1980 aborted solo album. —*Chris Woodstra*

The Rich Kids

f. 1977, London, England, **db.** 1978
New Wave
Following his 1977 firing from the Sex Pistols—reportedly for expressing an admiration for the Beatles—bassist Glen Matlock founded the Rich Kids, a more experimental pop-rock outfit rounded out by guitarist Steve New, drummer Rusty Egan and vocalist Midge Ure, formerly of the group Silk. Distancing themselves from the punk community, the Rich Kids recorded only one LP, 1978's *Ghosts of Princes in Towers*, before tension between Matlock and Ure resulted in the group's dissolution within a year of their formation. Ure and Egan later reunited in Visage, and Ure ultimately found success with Ultravox, while Matlock largely vanished from sight until publishing his autobiography *I Was a Teenage Sex Pistol* in the late 1980s. In 1996, he rejoined the Sex Pistols for their "Filthy Lucre" reunion tour. —*Jason Ankeny*

Ghosts of Princes in Towers / 1978 / EMI ✦✦✦
The single "Ghosts of Princes in Towers" was simply brilliant; unfortunately, the album that bore the same name failed to live up to the promise of the single, in most cases trading punky power-pop in favor of more dirge-like hard rock—muddy sound doesn't help matters either. Overall, the albums serves as a curiosity for the Sex Pistols completist or the Ultravox fan who wants a look at Midge Ure's formative years. [In 1993, Dojo Records reissued the album on CD with three B-sides added, "Empty Words," "Here Comes the Nice," and "Only Arsenic," making the complete recorded works of the band available on one disc.] —*Chris Woodstra*

Cliff Richard (Harry Webb)

b. Oct. 14, 1940, Lucknow, India
Rock 'n' Roll, Pop, Pop-Rock, Teen Idol
Britain's answer to Elvis Presley, Richard (born Harry Webb) dominated the pre-Beatles British pop scene in the late '50s and early '60s. An accomplished singer with a genuine feel for the music, Richard's artistic legacy is nonetheless meager, as he was quickly steered toward a middle-of-the-road pop direction. Several of his late-'50s recordings, however, were genuinely exciting Presley-esque rockers—especially his first hit, "Move It" (1958)—and gave British teenagers their first taste of genuine homegrown rock 'n' roll talent. Backed by the Shadows—clean-cut instrumental virtuosos who became legends of their own—Richard embarked on a truly awesome string of hit singles in Britain, scoring no less than 43 Top 20 hits between 1958 and 1969. One of these, although it was by no means one of the more successful, was an actual Mick Jagger/Keith Richards composition (the ballad "Blue Turns to Grey").

In his homeland, Richard's popularity was diminished only slightly by the rise of the Beatles, but in his prime, he had a much rougher time in the US, hitting the Top 40 only twice (with "Living Doll" in 1959 and "It's All in the Game" in 1963. Richard belatedly cracked the US Top Ten in 1976 with "Devil Woman," and racked up a few other hits ("We Don't Talk Anymore," "Dreaming," "A Little in Love") in a mainstream pop-rock style. He remains an institution in Britain, where he is one of the nation's most popular all-around entertainers of all time. —*Richie Unterberger*

● **20 Rock N'Roll Hits** / 1979 / EMI ✦✦✦✦
Concentrating mostly on his 1958-59 material, this has Richard's most untamed recordings (bearing in mind that they're still pretty polished compared to most US rockabilly). Includes his first brace of hits—"Move It," "High Class Baby," "Mean Streak," and "Never Mind"—along with the megasmash "Livin' Doll," which pointed the way toward the pop-ballad path he would follow in the '60s. —*Richie Unterberger*

Cliff Richard & the Shadows / 1984 / EMI ✦✦✦✦
Cliff Richard & the Shadows rock out like nobody's business on this classic live album (arguably rock's first authorized and professionally recorded concert album). Recorded in February 1959 at EMI in front of 500 screaming fans, the sound is raw and raunchy by British standards of the time. —*Bruce Eder*

Keith Richards

b. Dec. 18, 1943, Dartford, Kent, England
Guitar / Rock 'n' Roll
One of the few white guitarists with strong blues roots who has been able to take the form to new places, Richards' contribution to the vocabulary of rock guitar cannot be overestimated. His heavy reliance on Delta blues open tunings (mostly played on guitars with only five strings) has provided licks that are part and parcel for any player who wants to get the joint rocking and the dance floor packed. Though much has been made of his lifestyle, and time has reduced his voice to a sore-throated husk, it is as a guitarist and songwriter that Richards has ultimately established his reputation. —*Cub Koda*

● **Talk Is Cheap** / 1988 / Virgin ✦✦✦✦
Richards' first solo album includes "Take It So Hard," "Struggle," "I Could Have Stood You Up," and "Make No Mistake," with a classic Hi Rhythm Section groove and featuring great guest vocals by Sarah Dash. —*Cub Koda*

Live at the Hollywood Palladium (Dec. 15, 1988) / Dec. 1991 / Virgin ✦✦✦
A nicely ragged live album that captures Richards and the Winos at the top of their form. —*Stephen Thomas Erlewine*

Main Offender / Oct. 20, 1992 / Virgin ✦✦✦
Richards' second solo album is even more delightfully focused than his first. Highlights include "Wicked as It Seems," "Eileen," and the searing "999." New Rolling Stones albums should rock this hard. —*Cub Koda*

Lionel Richie

b. Jun. 20, 1949, Tuskegee, AL
Keyboards, Vocals / Urban, Pop, Pop-Rock
After he left the Commodores in 1981, Lionel Richie became one of the most successful solo artists of the early '80s, earning a string of thirteen Top Ten hits between 1981 and 1987, including five No. 1 singles ("Endless Love," "Truly," "All Night Long (All Night)," "Hello," "Say You, Say Me"). Between 1986 and 1992 he didn't release any new material, but in 1996 he re-emerged with a new album that sold well, although not up to the standards he set a decade earlier. —*Stephen Thomas Erlewine*

Lionel Richie / 1982 / Motown ✦✦✦✦
Lionel Richie was perhaps the dominant songwriter and performer of the early '80s. His overwhelmingly sentimental love tunes were massive crossover hits, and he turned awkwardness into an art form. This was his first big album, and it peaked at No.3 on the pop album chart, eventually selling over four million copies and staying on the charts for 140 weeks. —*Ron Wynn*

Can't Slow Down / 1983 / Motown ✦✦✦✦
The Lionel Richie gravy train was in full throttle on this second big hit album, which eventually sold over eight million copies. Richie earned the 1984 Grammy for Album of the Year, and such tunes as "Hello," "Running With the Night," "Stuck on You" and "Love Will Find a Way" were all over the R&B, pop, and even country airwaves. —*Ron Wynn*

Dancing on the Ceiling / 1986 / Motown ✦✦
Lionel Richie had a slump of sorts after the incredible success of *Can't Slow Down*. This record, which came some three years later, only sold four million instead of eight million copies, stayed atop the pop album charts for only one month instead of two, and only had a few pop hits in "Love Will Conquer All," "Say You, Say Me," "Se La" and "Deep River Woman." —*Ron Wynn*

● **Back to Front** / May 5, 1992 / Motown ✦✦✦✦
Back to Front is an ideal greatest-hits collection from Lionel Richie, featuring all of his biggest hits, including "All Night Long," "Truly," and "Say You, Say Me." It's the ideal place to start listening to Richie, as well as the most consistent, enjoyable record he ever released. —*Stephen Thomas Erlewine*

Louder Than Words / Apr. 1996 / Mercury ✦✦✦

After the greatest hits collection *Back to Front* disappeared without a trace in 1992, Lionel Richie spent four years making *Louder Than Words*, his first album for Mercury Records. Although there are some slight attempts to incorporate New Jack and hip-hop influences into Richie's sound, *Louder Than Words* relies on his trademark balladeering, which remains his forte. All of the weak moments on *Louder than Words* are ill-advised forays into rap—to put it bluntly, he can rap about as well as Snoop Doggy Dogg can sing. Although the ballads aren't as strong as his late-'70s and early-'80s standards, they are nevertheless pleasant, which makes the record a worthwhile purchase for fans. —*Stephen Thomas Erlewine*

Jonathan Richman

· ·

b. May 15, 1951, Boston, MA
Guitar, Vocals / Rock 'n' Roll, Pop-Rock, Proto-Punk
Jonathan Richman was one of rock's most eccentric and unpredictable cult figures, a performer whose eternally childlike public persona and seeming naivete—typified by songs like "Ice Cream Man," "Hey There Little Insect" and "I'm a Little Aeroplane"—tended to obscure the dexterity and craft of his music, which skirted from garage rock to country to Latin stylings and back. Born May 15, 1951 in Boston, Massachusetts, Richman began playing guitar at the age of 15, and within a year was making his first public appearances. In 1969 he relocated to New York, the home of the Velvet Underground (his central musical influence), and spent his first two weeks in the city sleeping on the Velvets' manager's couch.

While working a series of odd jobs, including a tenure as a foot messenger for *Esquire* magazine, Richman attempted to find a venue to perform his music, but his simple songs and adenoidal voice were roundly rejected; he ultimately moved back to Boston in 1970, where he formed the first incarnation of the influential proto-punk band the Modern Lovers with guitarist John Felice, drummer David Robinson, and bassist Rolfe Anderson. Within a few months, Anderson had been replaced by Ernie Brooks, and keyboardist Jerry Harrison stepped in for Felice; in 1972, the Modern Lovers recorded the demos which comprised their seminal self-titled debut, featuring long-standing Richman favorites like "Roadrunner," "Pablo Picasso," and "Hospital." Problems with their label, however, blocked the songs' release until 1976; at the same time, Richman wanted to quiet the group's minimalist, garagey sound, leading to their breakup in 1973.

Eventually, Richman formed a new, acoustic Modern Lovers with guitarist Leroy Radcliffe, Rubinoos bassist Greg "Curly" Keranen, and drummer D. Sharpe. In 1977, they debuted on *Jonathan Richman and the Modern Lovers*, which emphasized the doo wop flavor and wry pop melodies that remained hallmarks of his career. That same year, the group issued *Rock & Roll With the Modern Lovers*, and scored a major European hit with the instrumental "Egyptian Reggae." A year later, Richman went solo, and in 1979 issued *Back in Your Life*.

After a period of self-imposed exile, he resurfaced in 1983 with *Jonathan Sings!* A series of strong pop records followed, including 1985's *Rockin' and Romance*, 1986's *It's Time for Jonathan Richman and the Modern Lovers* (recorded with Andy Paley), and *Modern Lovers 88*. In 1990, he released the self-explanatory *Jonathan Goes Country*; later, he made another left turn with 1993's *Jonathan, Te Vas a Emocionar!*, a collection of Latin-influenced songs performed entirely in Spanish. No matter what path his music took, however, Richman's cult following remained fiercely loyal, and saw its ranks expand courtesy of his frequent appearances on the NBC program *Late Night with Conan O'Brien*. —*Jason Ankeny*

☆ **Modern Lovers** / 1976 / Rhino ✦✦✦✦✦

Compiled of demos the band recorded with John Cale in 1971, *The Modern Lovers* is one of the great proto-punk albums of all-time, capturing an angst-ridden adolescent geekiness which is married to a stripped-down, minimalistic rock 'n' roll derived from the art-punk of the Velvet Underground. While the sound is in debt to the primal three-chord pounding of early Velvet Underground, the attitude of Jonathan Richman and the Modern Lovers is a million miles away from Lou Reed's jaded urban nightmares. As he says in the classic two-chord anthem "Roadrunner," Richman is in love with the modern world and rock 'n' roll. He's still a teenager at heart, which means he's not only in love with girls he can't have, but also radios, suburbs, and fast food, and it also means he'll crack jokes like "Pablo Picasso was never called an asshole...not like you." "Pablo Picasso" is the classic sneer, but "She Cracked" and "I'm Straight" are just as nasty, made all the more edgy by the Modern Lovers' amateurish, minimalist drive. But beneath his adolescent posturing, Richman is also nakedly emotional, pleading for a lover on "Someone I Care About" and "Girl Friend," or romanticizing the future on "Dignified and Old." That combination of musical simplicity, driving rock 'n' roll, and gawky emotional confessions makes *The Modern Lovers* one of the most startling proto-punk records—it strips

rock 'n' roll to its core and establishes the rock tradition of the geeky, awkward social outcast venting his frustrations. More importantly, the music is just as raw and exciting now as when it was recorded in 1971, or when it was belatedly released in 1976. —*Stephen Thomas Erlewine*

Live / 1977 / Rhino ✦✦✦

This release catches Jonathan Richman at the height of his candyfloss novelty period. The music is warm and mild, almost all of it derived from 1950s and early-'60s models such as surf idioms and guitar instrumentals. The lyrics are sweet and charming, sure to appeal to fanciful youngsters with visions of ice cream men and little dinosaurs in their heads. The only bothersome misstep here is the repeated encore reprise of the chorus to "Ice Cream Man," which extends well past the point of honest enjoyment. Sound quality and instrumental balances are excellent, and performances are low-key and winsome. While not an essential album in the Modern Lovers' canon, this sunny little platter is a fetching listen. —*David Cleary*

Jonathan Richman & the Modern Lovers / Jan. 1977 / Beserkley ✦✦✦✦

Richman's second collection of Modern Lovers, over which he was billed (eventually, the group name would be dropped) had a lighter rock 'n' roll sound than the first. In fact, as often as not, Richman played acoustic guitar. And his lyrical concerns had similarly lightened up, to the point of childlike whimsy on such songs as "Hey There Little Insect" and "Here Come the Martian Martians." But the focus was still Richman's unabashed vocalizing (the word "sings" is put in quotes on the back cover), giving the whole album an amateurish charm. —*William Ruhlmann*

Rock 'N' Roll with the Modern Lovers / Feb. 1977 / Rhino ✦✦✦✦

Richman branches out to Japanese music, a "South American Folk Song," and even "Egyptian Reggae" (the last earning him a UK Top Five hit), but the real highlight on *Rock 'N' Roll with the Modern Lovers* is that ode to a totaled car, "Dodge Veg-O-Matic." —*William Ruhlmann*

Back in Your Life / 1979 / Beserkley ✦✦✦

Recorded with two different bands—the usual Modern Lovers crew and a vocals/string bass/glockenspiel combo—*Back in Your Life* ranks among the most eccentric albums in a career which is the very embodiment of quirkiness. Heavy on cover material, both the songs and performances are deliriously campy, closer to vaudeville than any recognizable strain of rock 'n' roll. —*Jason Ankeny*

The Jonathan Richman Songbook / 1980 / Beserkley ✦✦✦✦

The Jonathan Richman Songbook is a UK-only compilation of early material. —*Jason Ankeny*

The Original Modern Lovers / 1981 / Bomp! ✦✦✦✦

There's a good deal of confusion about when the demos on this album were recorded; the liner notes claim that they were made in 1972, before John Cale produced the tracks that eventually composed their official debut release (although it has been reported that the Cale sessions date from 1971). Anyway, the fidelity on these cuts (produced by Kim Fowley) is less than optimal, but the performances are probably the best that the original lineup managed to lay down during their haphazard existence, and the truest to the band's vision. Includes fiery takes of many of their best songs ("Roadrunner," "Astral Plane," "I'm Straight," "I Wanna Sleep"), and some Richman originals that are not to be found anywhere else. —*Richie Unterberger*

Jonathan Sings / 1983 / Rough Trade ✦✦✦

Richman emerges as an incurable romantic on *Jonathan Sings!*, an infectiously sunny effort which stands among his finest LPs. Recorded after a long layoff with a new Modern Lovers lineup, Richman sounds thoroughly recharged, even extolling the simple virtues of "This Kind of Music"; among his other enthusiasms are kids ("Not Yet Three") and travel ("Give Paris One More Chance"), but his primary focus here is romance—"You're the One for Me," "That Summer Feeling" and "Someone to Hold Me" are positively joyous in their lovestruck outlook. —*Jason Ankeny*

Having a Party with Jonathan Richman / 1983 / Rounder ✦✦✦

A hodgepodge of studio and live recordings, this *Party* is a rather quiet affair with just Jonathan and his guitar. Without a band to support him, Richman grows more pensive than usual; while interpersonal dynamics remain his primary focus, his thoughts turn to relatively serious examinations of adultery ("My Career as a Homewrecker") and commitment ("Just for Fun"). Similarly, the minutiae of romance is the concern of "The Girl Stands Up to Me Now," "When I Say Wife" (a fretful essay on nomenclature and possessiveness) and "She Doesn't Laugh at My Jokes." —*Jason Ankeny*

Rockin' & Romance / 1985 / Twin/Tone ✦✦✦✦

While it is generally true that many of Richman's post-1980 albums are all but interchangeable, with their earnest naive cheerfulness, this stands as one of the best, if you like his schtick and need to make a choice. The production is sparse, accentuating the acoustic guitar and the doo wop harmonies (both male and female), with light but purposeful drums. Jonathan covers his usual terrain here: juvenilia ("My Jeans," "The U.F.O. Man," "Chewing Gum Wrapper"), cultural heroes ("Vincent Van Gogh," "Walter Johnson"), and optimistic paeans to the simple pleasures of life ("The Beach"). Heart-warming and melodic stuff that might well sound insipid in the hands of others. —*Richie Unterberger*

It's Time for Jonathan Richman / 1986 / Upside ✦✦✦
Produced by Andy Paley, *It's Time for...* welcomes back to the fold former Modern Lovers guitarist Asa Brebner, resulting in a fuller and more lively sound than Richman has enjoyed in some time. Taking full advantage of Richman's sax blowing acumen, the record sports a wistful early rock 'n' roll feel: "Let's Take a Trip" and "Yo Jo Jo" are energetic rave-ups, "This Love of Mine" is a sweet doo wop ballad, and "It's You" is a joyous romantic romp. The highlight is "Corner Store," an impassioned plea against modernization. —*Jason Ankeny*

● **Beserkley Years** / 1987 / Rhino ✦✦✦✦
After the first Modern Lovers album, Richman's records were enjoyable but fairly spotty. Thankfully, *The Beserkley Years* collects the best moments from his '70s records, when his cutesiness was endearing, not irritating. With "Roadrunner," "Pablo Picasso," "Here Come the Martian Martians," "Important In Your Life," "Ice Cream Man," and "Dodge Veg-O-Matic" forming its core, this collection is a definitive portrait of his goofy, catchy, minimalist pop and rock. —*Stephen Thomas Erlewine*

Modern Lovers 88 / 1988 / Rounder ✦✦✦
One of his better '80s efforts, and certainly one of the most basic, performed in an acoustic trio format. It's nonetheless quite rocking, with heavy debts to doo wop and Bo Diddley rhythms, and a jolly (though not sappy) summertime campfire feel. Some of his best uptempo tunes are here, including "I Love Hot Nights," "California Desert Party," and "Gail Loves Me." —*Richie Unterberger*

Jonathan Richman / 1989 / Rounder ✦✦✦
As basic and bare-bones as its title, *Jonathan Richman* is a solo effort modeled after Richman's live show, spotlighting only his voice, guitar and percussive foot stomping. An eclectic mixture of originals and covers (occasionally sung in either French or Spanish), the record's simplicity is its charm; the high point, "I Eat With Gusto, Damn! You Bet," is a spoken-word paean to the joys of bad table manners. —*Jason Ankeny*

Jonathan Goes Country / 1990 / Rounder ✦✦✦
The Skeletons' Lou Whitney and D. Clinton Thompson, as well as a number of seasoned session vets, join Richman as he ventures into Nashville territory. The material consists of a batch of originals, a few covers, and a couple of old songs reworked from 1983's *Jonathan Sings!* The music's country affectations are entertaining without being gimmicky, and Richman sounds right at home in his twangy environs. —*Jason Ankeny*

I, Jonathan / Sep. 16, 1992 / Rounder ✦✦✦✦
A lo-fi effort cut in a California basement, *I, Jonathan* returns Richman to the full band setting and manic diversity which recent conceptual efforts have forsaken. Sloppy and wild, the album is a blast from start to finish; among its many concerns are skydiving ("Tandem Jump"), sea life (the surf instrumental "Grunion Run"), nightclubbing ("I Was Dancing in a Lesbian Bar,") and hero worship ("Velvet Underground"). —*Jason Ankeny*

Jonathan, Te Vas a Emocionar! / Feb. 28, 1994 / Rounder ✦✦✦
Although Richman's vocals have intermittently slipped into foreign tongues for years, *Jonathan, Te Vas a Emocionar!* is still a surprise: entirely sung in Spanish, the record is a charmer, transcending the language barrier with ease. Along with a few new originals and a handful of traditional Mexican tunes, the album primarily consists of loose Spanish reworkings of Richman favorites—*I, Jonathan's* "You Can't Talk to the Dude" becomes "No Te Oye," for example, while *Having a Party's* "Just for Fun" becomes "No Mas por Fun" and *Jonathan Goes Country's* "Reno" becomes, well, "Reno"; whatever the language, however, Richman remains his earnest, wistful self—none of his personality gets lost in the translation. —*Jason Ankeny*

Precise Modern Lovers Order / Aug. 2, 1994 / Rounder ✦✦✦
Live material recorded in various locations, circa 1971-1973 (the exact dates have become muddied with time). The fidelity and performances are fairly funky—this is essentially a high-quality bootleg—but the band (augmented by original guitarist John Felice on the earliest cuts) attacks the material with a fair amount of élan. Includes most of their best songs—"Roadrunner," "Girlfriend," "She Cracked," "I'm Straight," "Pablo Picasso"—as well as rarities like "The Mixer," "Womanhood," "Dance With Me," and a cover of the Velvet Underground obscurity "Foggy Notion." —*Richie Unterberger*

You Must Ask the Heart / Apr. 25, 1995 / Rounder ✦✦✦✦
The ambitious *You Must Ask the Heart* is Richman's most consistent effort in years; produced with clarity by Brennan Totten, the album is a neat summation of the singer's recent history, ranging in tone from the pensive ("To Hide a Little Thought") to the silly ("Vampire Girl") and spanning in style from country (the title track) to Spanish ("Amorcito

Corazon"). Offsetting his own material with a handful of superb covers—including Tom Waits' "The Heart of Saturday Night" and Sam Cooke's "Nothing Can Change This Love"—Richman sings with remarkable energy and honesty; even after dozens of records, his joyful spirit remains undimmed. —*Jason Ankeny*

Surrender to Jonathan / Sep. 10, 1996 / Vapor ✦✦✦
Surrender to Jonathan was Richman's return to a major label, and he constructed the album as a showcase of his finest, or at least most notorious, songs of the early '90s. "Egyptian Reggae" and "I Was Dancing in the Lesbian Bar" are hauled out of the woodwork and given moderately polished reworkings by Andy Paley. Even with the slicker sound, Jonathan remains Jonathan, and no amount of studio polish can erase the fact that his goofball, naive pop is better-suited for small clubs than records. There's a couple of worthy additions to his set-list, "Not Just A 'Plus One' on the Guest List Anymore" and "Surrender," but *Surrender to Jonathan* remains a marginal effort. —*Stephen Thomas Erlewine*

Ride

f. 1988, Oxford, England, db. Jan. 1996
Alternative Pop-Rock, Shoegazing, Dream-Pop
With their first records, Ride created a unique wall of sound that relied on massive, trembling distortion in the vein of My Bloody Valentine but with a simpler, more direct melodic approach. The shatteringly loud, droning neo-psychedelia the band performed was dubbed "shoegazing" by the British press, because they stared at the stage while they performed. Along with their initial influence, My Bloody Valentine, Ride stood apart from the shoegazing pack, primarily because of their keen sense of songcraft and dynamics. For a while, the band was proclaimed the last great hope of British rock but, they fell from the spotlight nearly as quickly as they entered it.

Ride was formed in Oxfordshire, England, in 1988 by guitarist/vocalist Andy Bell, vocalist/guitarist Mark Gardner, bassist Stephan Queralt, and drummer Loz Colbert when the group were still in their late teens. The band soon earned a dedicated following through their blisteringly loud, intense live shows. Creation Records signed the band in 1989 and the group released their self-titled debut EP later in the year. Not only did the British music critics praise *The Ride EP*, but the EP climbed into the lower reaches of the UK charts.

Play, Ride's second EP, appeared in the spring of 1990 and it surpassed the success of its predecessor, entering the Top 40 upon its release. Ride continued to gain new fans and quickly became darlings of the UK press. *Nowhere*, the group's first album, was released at the end of the year and became a significant hit in England, peaking at No. 14. The band's third EP, *Fall*, was released in the summer of 1991 and became a Top 20 hit in the UK. Ride released their second album, *Going Blank Again*, in the spring of 1992. *Going Blank Again* was successful, particularly in the UK where its first single, "Leave Them All Behind," went into the Top Ten, but didn't increase their audience dramatically.

That lack of a breakthrough success caused tensions within the band, especially between Bell and Gardner. After completing a frustrating American tour, the band decided to take an extended break. It would be two years before Ride re-emerged with their third album, *Carnival of Light*.

Carnival of Light represented a major shift toward conventional psychedelic rock and it turned out to be a commercial misstep. Not only did their diehard following dislike the record, but the band failed to pick up a new batch of fans with their stylistic makeover. Wounded from a lack of sales and critical respect, the band moved to the studio in the summer of 1995 to record their fourth album, *Tarantula*. Tensions between Bell and Gardner escalated throughout the recorded sessions. After *Tarantula* was completed in August 1995, Gardner left the band; Bell followed immediately afterward. Ride announced its disbandment in January of 1996. The album was released in March of 1996. — *Stephen Thomas Erlewine*

Smile / Jan. 1990 / Sire ✦✦✦✦
Their first two EPs from Britain's Creation label appear on one American collection. Sonically, it is muddier than *Nowhere* (if that can be possible), but the tuneful crash-and-burn of "Like a Daydream" is one of their best. —*Rick Clark*

● **Nowhere** / Dec. 1990 / Sire ✦✦✦✦
Rackety, reverberant, psychedelic drone-rock from Oxford, England. Fans of hypnotic detached singing against numbing waves of dissonance should find this somewhat interesting, particularly the throbbing "Polar Bear," the lumbering yet airy "Vapour Trail," the fairly accessible "Taste," and the reckless "Here and Now." The title cut is an effective fusing of early Pink Floyd sonic freakout and industrial noise sludge. —*Rick Clark*

Going Blank Again / Oct. 1991 / Sire ✦✦✦
Ride's second full-length album finds the band in a holding pattern. While the loud, atmospheric guitars and gorgeous melodies *sound* good, it isn't a big departure from *Nowhere*, and it doesn't point the

band in a new direction. Fortunately, they experienced a creative rebirth on their next album. —*Stephen Thomas Erlewine*

Carnival of Light / Jun. 28, 1994 / Sire ◆◆◆
A thoroughly impressive, assured set of swirling guitar psychedelia that recalls classic British pop without ever sounding dated. —*Stephen Thomas Erlewine*

Live Light / Oct. 24, 1995 / Elektra ◆◆◆
This ten-track live performance, recorded after *Carnival of Light*, has impressive sound quality and includes great versions of some of Ride's best songs, including "Chelsea Girl," "Leave Them All Behind," and "Magical Spring." On the down side, however, the crowd noise is filtered and sounds more doctored than a laugh track. —*John Bush*

Tarantula / Mar. 12, 1996 / Sire ◆◆◆
Tarantula certainly suggests that Ride was wise in calling it a day. Though the band doesn't sound like they're worn out, they do sound like they're reaching the end of the road, pulling each other in opposite directions. Ride sounds like they're straddling the line between their trademark shoegazing and classic '60s psychedelia. Instead of creating an effective fusion, guitarists Mark Gardner and Andy Bell simply pull each other in opposite directions. Consequently, *Tarantula* sounds muddy. Though there are some good tracks, it lacks the focus of *Nowhere* and *Carnival of Light*, and it doesn't have as many mild pleasures as *Going Blank Again*. The good moments can't hide the disheartening sound of a band falling apart. —*Stephen Thomas Erlewine*

The Righteous Brothers

f. 1962, California
Pop-Rock, Brill Building Pop, Blue-Eyed Soul
They weren't brothers, but Bill Medley and Bobby Hatfield (both born in 1941) were most definitely righteous, defining (and perhaps even inspiring) the term "blue-eyed soul" in the mid-'60s. The white, Southern California duo were an established journeyman doo wop/R&B act before an association with Phil Spector produced one of the most memorable hits of the 1960s, "You've Lost That Lovin' Feelin'." The collaboration soon fell apart, though, and while the singers had some other excellent hit singles in a similar style, they proved unable to sustain their momentum after just a year or two at the top.

When Medley and Hatfield combined forces in 1962, they emerged from regional groups the Paramours and the Variations; in fact, they kept the Paramours billing for their first single. By 1963, they were calling themselves the Righteous Brothers, Medley taking the low parts with his smoky baritone, Hatfield taking the higher tenor and falsetto lines. For the next couple of years they did quite a few energetic R&B tunes on the Moonglow label that bore similarity to the gospel/soul/rock style of Ray Charles, copping their greatest success with "Little Latin Lupe Lu," which became a garage band favorite covered by Mitch Ryder, the Kingsmen, and others.

Even on the Moonglow recordings, Bill Medley acted as producer and principal songwriter, but the duo wouldn't break out nationally until they put themselves at the services of Phil Spector. Spector gave the wall-of-sound treatment to "You've Lost That Lovin' Feelin'," a grandiose ballad penned by himself, Barry Mann, and Cynthia Weil. At nearly four minutes, the song was pushing the limits of what could be played on radio in the mid-'60s, and some listeners thought they were hearing a 45 single played at 33 rpm due to Medley's low, blurry lead vocal. No matter; the song had a power that couldn't be denied, and went all the way to No. 1.

The Righteous Brothers had three more big hits in 1965 on Spector's Philles label ("Just Once in My Life," "Unchained Melody," and "Ebb Tide"), all employing similar dense orchestral arrangements and swelling vocal crescendos. Yet the Righteous Brothers-Spector partnership wasn't a smooth one, and by 1966 the duo had left Philles for a lucrative deal with Verve. Medley, already an experienced hand in the producer's booth, reclaimed the producer's chair, and the Righteous Brothers had another No. 1 hit with their first Verve outing, "(You're My) Soul and Inspiration." Its success must have been a particularly bitter blow for Spector, given that Medley successfully emulated the wall-of-sound orchestral ambience of the Righteous Brothers' Philles singles down to the smallest detail, even employing the same Mann-Weil writing team that had contributed to "You've Lost That Lovin' Feelin'."

It's a bit of a mystery as to why the Righteous Brothers never came close to duplicating that success during the rest of their tenure at Verve. But they would only have a couple of other Top 40 hits in the 1960s ("He" and "Go Ahead and Cry," both in 1966), even with the aid of occasional compositions by the formidable Goffin-King team. In 1968 Medley left for a solo career; Hatfield, the less talented of the pair (at least from a songwriting and production standpoint), kept the Righteous Brothers going with Jimmy Walker (who had been in the Knickerbockers).

Medley had a couple of small hits in the late '60s as a solo act, but unsurprisingly neither "brother" was worth half as much as their own

as they were together. In 1974 they reunited and had a No. 3 hit with "Rock and Roll Heaven," a tribute to dead rock stars that some found tacky. A couple of smaller hits followed before Medley retired from performing for five years in 1976; they've toured the oldies circuit off and on in the 1980s and 1990s. —*Richie Unterberger*

★ **Anthology 1962-1974** / Jul. 1989 / Rhino ◆◆◆◆◆
For some listeners, a double-disc of the Righteous Brothers might seem like overkill, but *Anthology 1962-1974* should silence most skeptics. Over the course of the two discs, it becomes clear that the duo were the finest blue-eyed soul singers of their era. Not only do the hits ("Little Latin Lupe Lu," "You've Lost That Lovin' Feeling," "Unchained Melody," "Ebb Tide," "(You're My) Soul and Inspiration," "Rock and Roll Heaven") retain their power, there are numerous forgotten gems, like the harder-rocking "Justine" and an excellent version of "This Little Girl of Mine." For listeners who want to dig a little deeper into the Righteous Brothers' music than the hits, they'll be generously rewarded by *Anthology*. —*Stephen Thomas Erlewine*

Live 1967 / Live Gold ◆◆◆
This CD, a live performance from May of 1967, pretty much finds the boys at the top of their game in full cry on a hot night. The set list for the evening is a nice, evenly paced selection of Spector and Verve hits ("You've Lost That Lovin' Feelin'," "Soul & Inspiration" and "Unchained Melody" all present and accounted for), early Moonglow singles ("Little Latin Lupe Lu" and "My Babe") and crowd-pleasin' club staples (the "oldies" and "gospel" medleys, "That Lucky Old Sun," "Let the Good Times Roll" and "Ooh Poo Pah Doo") that they knew cold, inside out. They do not disappoint at any level; the band's tight and the boys are groovin'. The performance is the key to the success of this CD. The show itself comes from a performance at the Anaheim Stadium and if the sound is a mite overdriven in spots, so what? Just listen to these guys, they're singin' their asses off! This ain't no oldies show, 25 years down the road, when time has eroded some of the platinum off the old pipes, no sir. This is the real deal. —*Cub Koda*

Billy Lee Riley

b. 1933
Bass, Guitar, Harmonica, Drums, Vocals / Rockabilly
Billy Lee Riley is a rockabilly singer and multi-instrumentalist. An alumnus of Sun Records, he was one of the most crazed, unabashed rockers that label had to offer—in the company of Jerry Lee Lewis, Carl Perkins, and Sonny Burgess, that's saying a lot. Proficient at harmonica, guitar, bass, and drums, Riley contributed as a sideman to many a classic Sun session, and his combo the Little Green Men (most notably guitarist Roland Janes and drummer J.M. Van Eaton) in time became the Sun house band. Riley recorded for a number of labels in a variety of styles, especially effective with blues. Though never commercially successful, Riley's Sun recordings of "Flying Saucer Rock 'n' Roll" and "Red Hot" (both covered in wooden renditions by Robert Gordon) remain landmarks of the genre. —*Cub Koda*

● **Classic Recordings, 1956-1960** / Jul. 1990 / Bear Family ◆◆◆◆
All the classic Sun sides, plus later Memphis recordings in a brilliant two-CD set. Raw rockin' at its finest. —*Cub Koda*

Johnny Rivers (John Ramistella)

b. Nov. 7, 1942, New York, NY
Guitar, Vocals / Pop-Rock
Johnny Rivers, intent on getting a break in the music business, left his Baton Rouge home for New York and Nashville. DJ Alan Freed suggested the name change to Rivers, since he originated from the Delta South. After a series of movies and song cuts and a stint with Louie Prima, Rivers gained attention on the Los Angeles club scene, particularly at the Whiskey a Go-Go, where he recorded his debut, *Johnny Rivers at the Whiskey a Go-Go*, for Imperial Records. Versions of Chuck Berry's "Memphis" and "Maybellene" hit, launching a series of live hit singles that reflect his tendency to draw from the blues and old rock 'n' roll. Rivers scored with "Secret Agent Man," capitalizing on the then-current fascination with foreign espionage. After that, he increasingly turned his attentions to a lusher MOR formula with the No. 1 "Poor Side of Town," "Baby I Need Your Lovin'," "The Tracks of My Tears," and the haunting "Summer Rain." During the '70s, Rivers had a comeback with several remakes of old rock hits, as well as a hit with the romantic "Swayin' to the Music (Slow Dancin')." Besides his artistry, Rivers displayed good commercial instincts by discovering and signing the 5th Dimension and assisting the career of writer Jimmy Webb. Rivers continues to perform, sounding like he hasn't aged a day since his biggest hits. —*Rick Clark*

Last Boogie in Paris / 1974 / Atlantic ◆◆
Rivers delivered a set of well-known oldies for this 1973 concert, as well as his hit "Summer Rain" and a 10-minute tribute to "John Lee Hooker." Competent and uninspiring, the backing is provided by the session men

comprising his Los Angeles Boogie Band, who epitomize early-'70s slick professionalism. *—Richie Unterberger*

● **The Best of Johnny Rivers** / 1987 / EMI America ✦✦✦✦
A fine single-disc collection, *Best of Johnny Rivers* features most of his biggest hits, making it a good purchase for those who don't want the definitive double-disc set. *—Stephen Thomas Erlewine*

Anthology / Mar. 1991 / Rhino ✦✦✦✦
One of the great interpretive singers in rock 'n' roll. Rivers made every song his own, and this two-CD package is proof that he rarely faltered. *—Jeff Tamarkin*

Changes/Rewind / 1993 / Capitol ✦✦✦✦
Johnny Rivers took a dramatic step during the late '60s, embracing adult standards and recording several Jimmy Webb compositions. These were solemn, literate tales of woe, anguish, and turmoil requiring lyric interpretation and careful vocal pacing. They were also heavily produced numbers with string sections and background vocalists. The change didn't hurt Rivers' career; indeed, it won him new critical attention as a serious ballad stylist and landed him some hits. This single-disc collection covers 23 songs from 2 LPs, *Changes* and *Rewind*. Besides the hit covers "Tracks of My Tears" and "Baby, I Need Your Loving," there is arguably his greatest ballad, "Poor Side of Town." While not everything worked, this material showed another side of Johnny Rivers and expanded his popularity. *—Ron Wynn*

Meanwhile Back at the Whisky a Go-Go/Rocks the Folk / 1996 / RCA ✦✦✦
Johnny Rivers' two 1965 albums have been released together in a double-disc package. Though neither *Meanwhile Back At the Whisky A Go Go* or *Rockin' the Folk* were commercial disappointments, they weren't the singer's most popular records, either. Rivers' first album was also recorded live at the Whisky, so *Meanwhile* represents something of a homecoming. Since Rivers is essentially an interpretive singer, a live album suits his talents well—it features a set list that isn't plagued by filler and a tight, energetic backing band. Because of this, *Meanwhile* is the better record of the pair. *Rockin' the Folk* has its moments but many of these folk songs aren't as compelling as Rivers' rock and pop covers. It does have its moments—such as the minor hit "Where Have All the Flowers Gone"—but there are too many weak moments to make the record interesting for anyone but dedicated fans. Then again, only dedicated fans will have the need to purchase this double disc set. *—Stephen Thomas Erlewine*

The Rivieras

f. South Bend, IN
Rock 'n' Roll
A South Bend, IN, rock 'n' roll band, the Rivieras' one big hit was one of the last great gasps of pure American rock 'n' roll before the British Invasion took over the charts. Original members Otto Nuss (organ), Doug Gean (bass), Marty "Bo" Fortson (vocals and guitar), Joe Pennell (guitar), and Paul Dennert (drums) were local teen ballroom heroes. They recorded a supercharged version of the Joe Jones R&B semi-hit "California Sun" featuring a powerful drum intro and the now-famous signature guitar and organ riff. The song became a hit in the midst of the first flush of Beatlemania, only nudged out of the No.1 spot on the national charts by "I Want to Hold Your Hand." Although several equally fine 45s and two albums followed, the band's relatively young ages, coupled with numerous personnel changes caused by the draft and the changing musical climate, caused the band to break up by 1966. Nuss, Gean, and Fortson reunited the Rivieras in the mid-'80s, recording and doing local shows, sounding as great as ever. Though their time in the spotlight was brief, their one big hit continues to define for future generations everything that's pulsatingly great about American teen-band rock 'n' roll. *—Cub Koda*

● **California Sun** / 1964 / Sonet ✦✦✦✦
Import reissue of their first album. *—Cub Koda*

Campus Party / 1965 / Riviera ✦✦✦✦
Second album; classic frat-band sound. Out of print and impossibly rare but worth the search at any cost. *—Cub Koda*

The Rivingtons

f. 1962, Los Angeles, CA
R&B, Doo Wop
The Rivingtons were a West Coast vocal group featuring Al Frazier, Carl White, John "Sonny" Harris, and Turner "Rocky" Wilson, Jr. Though they are best known for their string of early-'60s novelties, the Rivingtons in reality had a rich tradition of doo wop in their background, going back to their original recordings for Federal as the Lamplighters in 1953. They did extensive backup group work throughout the '50s between their own stray releases under a number of different names (the Sharps (singing on the original "Little Bitty Pretty One" and "Over and Over" by Thurston Harris), the Tenderfoots, the Rebels (they do all the backups on

the Duane Eddy hits), the Four After Fives, the Crenshaws. They even sang backup on Paul Anka's first record, credited as the Jacks! In 1962 they became the Rivingtons and hit pay dirt with their first record, the self-penned "Pa Pa Ooh Mow Mow," one of the truly great rock 'n' roll songs to make a virtue of sheer gibberish. They hit the charts again a year later with "The Bird's the Word," capitalizing on a current West Coast dance fad that teenagers were doing to "Pa Pa Ooh Mow Mow." A landlocked surf-teen combo from Minnesota called the Trashmen combined the two songs, revved up the beat to warp factor nine, and scored a massive hit with "Surfin' Bird." Despite no further chart success, their place in rock 'n' roll history (both for the classic performances they recorded and for being the inspiration behind one of the great noise-rock anthems of all time) is assured. *—Cub Koda*

● **The Liberty Years** / Jun. 1991 / EMI America ✦✦✦✦
An excellent 23-track CD with detailed notes and great sound, featuring both sides of all their original-issue 45s (including the insane follow-up "Mama Ooh Mow Mow") plus all the tracks from their lone Liberty album, *Doin' the Bird*. *—Cub Koda*

Robbie Robertson

b. Jul. 5, 1943, Toronto, Ontario
Guitar / Singer-Songwriter, Pop-Rock
One of the premier songwriters of the rock era, Robbie Robertson was born July 5, 1943 in Toronto, Ontario. The son of a Jewish father and Mohawk mother, Jaime Robbie Robertson's first brush with live music came at the Six Nations Reservation, his mother's girlhood home; at the age of five, he also gained exposure to the country music of rural America. Not long after, he began taking guitar lessons from a cousin, and gradually began composing his first songs. As time wore on, his musical interests evolved from country to big band to rock, and he eventually dropped out of school to pursue a career as a performer. In 1958, he hooked up with rockabilly star Ronnie Hawkins' backing band the Hawks, joining fellow sidemen Levon Helm, Rick Danko, Garth Hudson, and Richard Manuel.

After remaining with Hawkins through 1963, the Hawks began working on their own; they soon came to the attention of Bob Dylan, and became the support unit on the singer's now-legendary 1965-1966 world tour. Continuing their affiliation with Dylan, the group, renamed simply the Band, went on to become one of rock's seminal acts; propelled by Robertson's acute, evocative examinations of American mythology and lore, they made a series of seminal LPs, including 1968's *Music From Big Pink* and the following year's self-titled masterpiece. The Band dissolved on Thanksgiving Day, 1976 following an all-star concert filmed by director Martin Scorsese and later released as *The Last Waltz*. The project marked the beginning of Robertson's long affiliation with Scorsese, as well as an interest in dramatic acting; in 1980, Robertson produced and starred in *Carny*, co-starring Jodie Foster and Gary Busey.

Also in 1980, he composed the score to Scorsese's brilliant *Raging Bull*, and continued to confine his musical activity to the film medium for the next several years, later working with Scorsese on the acerbic 1983 satire *The King of Comedy* and 1986's *The Color of Money*, the sequel to *The Hustler*. Finally, in 1987 Robertson released his self-titled solo debut, which included guest appearances from one-time Band mates Danko and Hudson as well as U2, Peter Gabriel, Daniel Lanois and Gil Evans. *Storyville*, a conceptual piece steeped in the sounds and imagery of a famed area of New Orleans, followed in 1990. In 1994, Robertson returned to his roots, teaming with the Native American group the Red Road Ensemble for *Music for The Native Americans*, a collection of songs composed for a television documentary series. *—Jason Ankeny*

● **Robbie Robertson** / 1987 / Geffen ✦✦✦✦
Robbie Robertson's first solo album, released 11 years after the Band called it quits at *The Last Waltz*, found the singer/guitarist mining radically new territory. Hiring Daniel Lanois as co-producer, Robertson crafted an album that owed very little to the Band's roots-Americana sound. Instead, Robertson opted for a quirky, enigmatic modern approach, using drum programs, the stick, and guest musicians such as U2, Peter Gabriel, and Bill Dillon. If the album had a weakness, it was in the vocal department. Robertson had only sung lead on a couple of songs with the Band. His reedy ghost of a voice can be quite effective but wears a bit thin over the course of a whole album. Ultimately that is a minor complaint, as the songwriting, arrangements, playing, and sound-painting are superb. Highlights: "Broken Arrow" and "Somewhere Down the Crazy River." *—Rob Bowman*

Storyville / Sep. 1991 / Geffen ✦✦✦
Robertson's second album was four years in the making. Once again he set out to explore an approach and sound markedly different from any of his previous work. The album is conceptual, roughing out a story over ten songs set in New Orleans' legendary turn-of-the-century Storyville red-light district. Co-produced by Robertson, Stephen Hague, and Gary

Gersh, the record was recorded in New Orleans with members of the Neville Brothers, Mardi Gras Indians, the Meters, and the Zion Harmonizers. Legendary New Orleans arranger Wardell Quezergue contributed stunning horn charts. More aggressive than Robertson's first solo release, *Storyville* is perhaps a little less mysterious and enigmatic. —*Rob Bowman*

Music for the Native Americans / Oct. 4, 1994 / Capitol ✦✦✦
With *Storyville*, Robbie Robertson's music began to directly incorporate more world-music influences; *Music for the Native Americans* makes that connection more explicit. Most of the album is quite evocative, recalling an American version of Peter Gabriel's Mediterranean exploration *Passion*. Robertson writes some fully formed songs, but most of the record is devoted to instrumental, incidental film music, and that's where he fully explores new musical territory. *Music for the Native Americans* is a soundtrack, yet contains some of Robertson's most challenging and complex music. —*Stephen Thomas Erlewine*

Smokey Robinson (William Robinson)

b. Feb. 19, 1940, Detroit, MI
Soul, R&B, Urban, Motown, Quiet Storm
If you're looking for the all-time No.1 purveyor of mainstream romantic soul, Smokey Robinson may well be the man, in the face of some towering competition. With the Miracles in the 1960s, he paced dozens of tuneful Motown hits with his beautiful high tenor. As a solo performer from the 1970s onwards, he's been one of the staples of urban contemporary music. But his singing gifts, as notable as they are, comprise only one of his hats: he's also one of pop's best and most prolific songwriters. As a songwriter and producer, he was the most important musical component to Motown's early success, not only on the hits by the Miracles, but for numerous other acts as well (especially Mary Wells and the Temptations).

Robinson first crossed paths with Motown founder Berry Gordy, Jr. in the late 1950s in Detroit. In retrospect, this may have been the most important meeting in both men's lives. Smokey needed a mentor and an outlet for his budding talents as a singer and songwriter; the ambitious Gordy needed someone with multi-faceted musical vision. Gordy encouraged and polished Robinson's songwriting in particular in the early days, in which the Miracles were one of many acts bridging the doo wop and early soul eras.

Before solidifying their relationship with the embryonic Motown operation, the Miracles issued a few singles on the End and Chess labels, the most successful of which was "Got a Job." There was no national action for the Miracles until "Shop Around" in late 1960. Gordy withdrew the original single in favor of a faster, more fully produced version of the song; it made No.2, doing much not only to establish the Miracles, but to establish the Motown label itself. The song also heralded many of the important elements of the Motown sound, with its gospelish interplay between lead and backup vocals, its rhythmic groove, and its blend of R&B and pop.

While Smokey Robinson is most often thought of as a romantic balladeer, the Miracles were also capable of grinding out some excellent uptempo party tunes, particularly in their early days. "Mickey's Monkey" (which the group gave an athletically electrifying performance of in the 1964 *T.A.M.I. Show* movie), a 1963 Top Ten hit, is the most famous of these; there was also "Going to a Go-Go" and smaller hits like "I Gotta Dance to Keep from Crying." The 1962 Top Ten hit "You've Really Got a Hold on Me," however, was the key cut in forming Robinson's romantic persona, with its pleading, soaring vocals, exquisite melody, and carefully crafted lyrics. Bob Dylan was impressed enough by Robinson's facility for imaginative wordplay to dub him "America's greatest living poet" (a phrase which has possibly become the most quoted example of one rock giant praising another).

Surveying Robinson's achievements during the 1960s, one wonders if the man ever slept. While the Miracles were never Motown's biggest act at any given time, they were one of its most consistent, entering the Top 40 25 times over the course of the decade. "I Second That Emotion," "The Love I Saw in You Was Just a Mirage," "The Tracks of My Tears," "Ooo Baby Baby," "Baby, Baby Don't Cry" were some of their biggest singles, and usually represented Motown at its most sophisticated and urbane. Robinson also was extremely active at Motown as a songwriter and producer for other acts. The No.1 singles "My Guy" (Mary Wells) and "My Girl" (Temptations) were each Robinson songs and productions (the latter with fellow Miracle Ronnie White), and Smokey also did some excellent work with the Marvelettes and Marvin Gaye. He also toured with the Miracles, and started a family with the Miracles' female singer, Claudette Rogers, whom he married in 1964. Rogers stopped touring with the group in the mid-'60s, although she continued to sing on their records.

Starting in 1967, the billing on Miracles releases was changed to Smokey Robinson & the Miracles, presaging Robinson's solo career. The group continued to spin out hits until the early '70s, however, get-

ting their only No.1 in 1970 with the upbeat "The Tears of a Clown" (which had actually been recorded back in 1966). Robinson left the group to go on his own in 1972; the Miracles continued without him with limited success, although they had a No.1 hit in 1976 with "Love Machine (Part 1)."

Robinson had been made a vice president at Motown near the beginning of his career in 1961. He recorded frequently as a solo artist for Motown in the '70s and '80s, in a considerably mellower vein than his Miracles work, in keeping with the general shift of Motown and soul towards urban contemporary. Smokey, in fact, provided that genre with one of its catch phrases with the title of his 1975 album, *A Quiet Storm.* "Cruisin'" (1979) and "Being with You" (1981) were his biggest solo hits, although artistically and commercially, his solo era wasn't nearly as successful as his music with the Miracles. —*Richie Unterberger*

Hi, We're the Miracles / 1961 / Motown ✦✦✦
The Miracles' first album is a magnificent debut, filled with impeccable vocal performances, inventive and occasionally brilliant songwriting, and an achingly romantic aura. "Shop Around" was the big hit on the record, but another highlight is the group's recut version (also available on the old Miracles' *Anthology* double-disc set) of their single "Way Over There" in a lusher, more beguiling arrangement, which anticipated Phil Spector's "pop symphony" productions with the Crystals, Darlene Love, the Ronettes, and Tina Turner. Smokey Robinson authored or co-authored (with Berry Gordy or fellow Miracle Ronnie White) all but one track here—all are winners, and songs like the ethereal Robinson-White "Heart Like Mine" are worth the price of the disc. They'd do classier, more elaborate work later on, but the youthful verve of Robinson, Claudette Rogers Robinson, Ronnie White, Bobby Rogers, Pete Moore, and Marv Tarplin on these tracks makes this an indispensable record, even for casual fans. —*Bruce Eder*

Cookin' with the Miracles / Nov. 1962 / Motown ✦✦✦
Their second album shows Smokey and Motown starting to "uptownize" with energetic strings, although it's still one of the Miracles' most uptempo and R&B-oriented efforts. A solid set, with virtually all the material coming from the pens of Robinson and Berry Gordy, although half of the tracks—comprising the best tunes, such as "That's The Way I Feel," "Ain't It Baby," and "Determination"—are available on the Smokey/Miracles box set. The CD reissue adds "Mighty Good Lovin'" as a bonus track. —*Richie Unterberger*

Going to a Go-Go / Nov. 1965 / Motown ✦✦✦✦
This was the first truly great Miracles album, and their first to crack the Top Ten on the LP chart. The title song was arguably Robinson's finest uptempo composition (along with "Get Ready"), and the album also contained the majestic ballads "Ooh Baby Baby" and "My Girl Has Gone," plus Robinson's signature tune, "Tracks Of My Tears." After those heavyweights, it didn't matter what else was there, but "In Case You Need Love" and "My Baby Changes Like The Weather" were the kind of afterthought gems Motown churned out with regularity during their prime. —*Ron Wynn*

Make It Happen / Aug. 1967 / Motown ✦✦✦
This album was re-released under the title *The Tears Of A Clown* after that song, which appears on the album, became a hit single in 1970. —*William Ruhlmann*

The Tears of a Clown / Aug. 1967 / Motown ✦✦✦
The title track revisited the arena of heartache and confessional soul that few have ever exploited more skillfully and memorably than Smokey Robinson. This album was actually an example of corporate greed at work; it was only grafting a new title onto an old album. Motown merely reissued *Greatest Hits, Vol. 2* with a fresh title to fill the gap as internal problems were preventing the completion of a new Miracles record. Of course, most of the songs were great, since "More Love" and "Love I Saw In You Was Just A Mirage" were among the many fine tunes on the album. But it was just an early example of the label's constant recycling of their hits, which is now standard operating procedure. —*Ron Wynn*

Time out For... / Jul. 1969 / Motown ✦✦✦
Smokey Robinson was in peak form on this 1969 album, even though he would end his involvement with the group three years later. His voice was still splendid, his delivery and soaring falsetto magical, and his writing and production skills keen. The album boasted "Doggone Right" and "Here I Go Again" as its prime hit material, and was done with the soulful charm and elegance that marked every Miracles record from the mid-'60s until Robinson went solo in 1972. —*Ron Wynn*

★ **Anthology** / 1973 / Motown ✦✦✦✦✦
Detroit vocal group the Miracles were a fixture at Motown from day one. Driven by Robinson's superior writing and smooth, silky falsetto, the Miracles placed a stunning 48 singles on the Billboard charts, 39 of those with Smokey in tow. Virtually all of them are included on this collection. Songs such as "Ooh Baby Baby," "The Tracks of My Tears," and "The Tears of a Clown" define much that was good about the '60s. The

1995 double-CD reissue is digitally remastered and includes virtually the same tracks, adding a couple previously unreleased songs and extensive liner notes. —*Rob Bowman*

Pure Smokey / Mar. 1974 / Tamla ✦✦✦✦
During his solo career, many of Smokey Robinson's best solo efforts are when he writes his own material, which is more personally involved and reflective than his earlier work with the Miracles and others. An exceptionally good, ballad-driven album, its highlight is the modest pop hit "Virgin Man," one of pop and soul music's first attempts to explore male sexual inexperience and insecurity. —*John Lowe*

A Quiet Storm / Mar. 1975 / Motown ✦✦✦✦
The landmark artistic release of Smokey Robinson's solo career. This album didn't equal the sales of his '80s LPs, but was extremely influential. Robinson linked the songs conceptually and produced the album with almost no breaks between selections. *A Quiet Storm* was as influential as Marvin Gaye's *What's Going On* or Isaac Hayes' *Hot Buttered Soul*. It also spawned the rise of a new sound—soul aimed at an adult audience. Many radio stations aired various unedited cuts from this LP late at night or after dark. Soon an entire format was developed that emphasized adult ballads and played album cuts as much as, if not more than, edited singles. This format was called "Quiet Storm." —*Ron Wynn*

Smokey's Family Robinson / Feb. 1976 / Motown ✦✦
Smokey Robinson sets up groove-based arrangements that take their tone from Sonny Burke's electric piano rhythms, but his own personal songwriting stamp often gives way to the percolating funk, notably on the single "Open" (No.10 R&B, No.81 Pop), which attempts to do what Marvin Gaye did the following year with "Got to Give It Up," but, with its prominent "backup" vocals, only succeeds in confusing the listener. The second side is more ballad-oriented, but there are no great songs even when the focus is on the singer. —*William Ruhlmann*

Where There's Smoke... / May 1979 / Motown ✦✦✦
This album was a considerable return to form, Smokey Robinson's most commercially successful solo LP up to this point (and highest-charting record in 11 years), entirely due to the single "Cruisin'" (No. 4 Pop and R&B), his biggest pop hit since "The Tears of a Clown." Motown doesn't **seem** to have recognized that track's potency, leading off with the flop "Get Ready" (a disco treatment of the old Temptations hit) before turning to "Cruisin'" as a second single several months after the LP's release. *Where There's Smoke...* then took off and peaked at No. 17 more than six months after first appearing. Although the LP is divided into "Smoke" and "Fire" sides, both sides start out with rhythmic songs and gradually slow down to near-ballad speed, with the sensuous "Cruisin'" the final "Fire" track. In retrospect, the album may be uneven and a touch too discoish in places, but in 1979-1980, *Where's There's Smoke...* brought Smokey Robinson back into the limelight. —*William Ruhlmann*

Warm Thoughts / Feb. 1980 / Motown ✦✦✦
On his follow-up to "Cruisin'," Smokey Robinson goes right back to that lazy, romantic style with "Let Me Be the Clock" (No.4 R&B, No.31 Pop), which leads off the aptly named *Warm Thoughts*. Robinson seems to have taken the success of "Cruisin'" as his opportunity to distance himself from disco and return to his more familiar ballad style, even injecting a touch of his old wordplay in "Into Each Rain Some Life Must Fall." Side two begins with the more uptempo "Melody Man," which was arranged, co-written, and co-produced by Stevie Wonder, but for the most part this is the bedroom Smokey Robinson, and that got him to No.14 on the LP chart, his highest solo peak yet. —*William Ruhlmann*

Being with You / Feb. 1981 / Motown ✦✦✦
Smokey Robinson landed his first big album of the 1980s with this release. The title track soared to the top of the R&B charts and stayed there, while it just missed topping the pop charts. Robinson's wonderful lead vocals, timing, dramatic delivery, and overall technique were as impressive as ever, and he got two more chart hits from the album. It eventually became his most successful LP ever from a commercial standpoint, although his artistic landmark as a solo artist remains *A Quiet Storm*. —*Ron Wynn*

Whatever Makes You Happy: More of the Best... / Feb. 16, 1993 / Rhino ✦✦✦✦
Solid compilation of 18 of the most interesting non-hits from Smokey's (and Motown's) golden era. Culled from 11 albums, this is an intelligent and consistent overview of Robinson's relatively unknown tunes. These cuts show the stylistic evolution of Motown as surely as any greatest hits collection, moving from bluesy, raucous R&B to assembly-line soul to songs reflecting the lyrical and instrumental innovations of the psychedelic era. Robinson's peerless soul songwriting and the Miracles' smooth harmonies remained constant no matter what the era, making this a much more fluid set than you might expect. Ultimately, the songs don't boast hooks quite as memorable as their classic hit singles, despite their similarities in structure and production. The early-'60s tracks are perhaps the record's most interesting, displaying a gritty, almost salacious

approach that had yet to be toned down by slicker production values. Dominated by Robinson originals, this collection also includes scattered covers of "Money" and hits by the Temptations and Supremes, as well as the original version of "From Head to Toe," later covered by Elvis Costello. —*Richie Unterberger*

☆ **Thirty-Fifth Anniversary Box** / Feb. 22, 1994 / Motown ✦✦✦✦✦
This four-CD boxed set covers every essential track that Smokey Robinson and the Miracles ever recorded, and then some—at least a dozen never previously anthologized tracks are included here, among them the original single versions of "Way Over There" (unavailable elsewhere) and "Shop Around" (which had already been released locally in Detriot when Berry Gordy decided one night to get a session together, punch up the rhythm, and lay down a new version, which became the hit). Even better is the remastering, which runs circles around any previous edition of the Miracles' work, and the annotation—including an essay by Claudette Robinson—that gives credit to all of the participants, including the backup musicians who were seldom if ever mentioned during Motown's heyday. The Smokey Robinson & the Miracles *Anthology* is a fine collection, but this set is the definitive history, and irreplaceable for anyone who genuinely loves the group. —*Bruce Eder*

Ultimate Collection / Mar. 25, 1997 / Motown ✦✦✦✦
While Robinson's solo work pales in comparison to his hits with the Miracles, this 17-track collection of Motown singles uncovers such minor gems as "Baby Come Close," "I Am I Am," "Cruisin'," "Let Me Be the Clock," "Tell Me Tomorrow," "I've Made Love to You a Thousand Times," "One Heartbeat," "Just to See Her," "Everything You Touch," "Baby That's Backatcha," "The Agony and the Ecstacy" and "Open." —*Jason Ankeny*

Tom Robinson

b. Jun. 1, 1950, Cambridge, England
Bass, Vocals / Rock 'n' Roll, New Wave
Although his career had pretty much flamed out by the start of the '80s, there were few punk-era major label performers as intensely controversial as Tom Robinson. Cutting his teeth with folk-rockers Cafe Society (who released a Ray Davies-produced record on the head Kinks' Konk label in 1975), Robinson roared into the spotlight in 1978 with a great single ("2-4-6-8 Motorway") and a much-ballyhooed contract with EMI. What was remarkable about this was that Robinson was the kind of politically conscious, confrontational performer that major labels generally ignored: he was openly gay and sang about it ("Glad to be Gay"), vociferous in his hatred for then-British Prime Minister Margaret Thatcher, helped form Rock Against Racism, and generally spoke in favor of any leftist political tract that would embarrass the ruling ultra-conservative Tory government. His debut album, 1978's *Power in the Darkness*, was an occasionally stunning piece of punk/hard rock agit-prop that, along with being ferociously direct, was politicized rock that focused more on songs than slogans.

However, by the release of the second album, the Todd Rundgren-produced *TRB Two*, the songs were getting weaker and Robinson began sounding like a boring idealogue. Similarly the band, even terrific guitarist Danny Kustow, sounds as if on automatic pilot. By the end of the '70s, Robinson had been dropped by EMI and signed to maverick major IRS as a solo act. In a wise move, he ditched the hard-rock polemics of the TRB for a more sophisticated pop-rock sound, but found his audience dwindling. A brief period of silence ended with him, somewhat surprisingly, signing with Geffen and releasing *Hope and Glory*, a politically tinged, but mostly mainstream rock record that featured a cover of that decidedly non-punk song, Steely Dan's "Rikki Don't Lose That Number," with Robinson deftly exploring the song's homoerotic subtext. Still, it wasn't enough to resuscitate his career and for the remainder of the decade Robinson released English-only albums that tried the patience of even longtime fans.

As to his current whereabouts, Robinson is rumored to be married to a woman (!) and raising a family in England. He's still writing songs and occasionally performing, but it can be safely assumed that whatever he's doing, it's light years away from the radical energy and excitement of *Power in the Darkness*. —*John Dougan*

● **Power in the Darkness** / 1978 / Razor & Tie ✦✦✦✦
This is angry British political punk at its best. —*David Szatmary*

TRB Two / 1979 / Razor & Tie ✦✦✦
A heartfelt record of political rock, Robinson made interesting albums after this one, but never again sounded as passionate, defiant, and full of himself. The band's secret weapon was guitarist Danny Kustow, whose playing makes even the most obvious and unsubtle moments enjoyable. Earnest and likeable, this is hands-down the best Tom Robinson record available (yes, even better than any of the TRB anthologies). The original American LP release included a bonus EP, with "Glad to Be Gay" (which doesn't hold up well) and the embarrassingly simplistic feminist ode "Right on Sister." *TRB Two* is only recommended to those who will appreciate a warmed-over version of *Power in the Darkness;* more slogans, less substance. —*John Dougan*

North by Northwest / 1982 / IRS ✦✦✦✦
Hope and Glory / 1984 / Geffen ✦✦✦
Robinson's only two interesting post-Power records. *North by Northwest* features collaborations by Peter Gabriel and a far less noisy pop-rock sound. It's an insinuating record, one that was dismissed cavalierly upon its release, but Robinson's songwriting is mostly good even when his singing (never much to write home about in the first place) is inadequate or just plain bad. *Hope and Glory* is good too, if only because it rocks a little harder and the simple, but emotional track "War Baby" is here. Neither of these records is the place to begin with Robinson, but the work is better than you'd expect. —*John Dougan*

Having It Both Ways / Jul. 2, 1996 / Cooking Vinyl ✦✦✦

Rocket From The Crypt

f. 1990, San Diego, CA
Alternative Pop-Rock, Indie Rock
Pledging to never play a venue with a stage, singer/guitarist John Reis formed San Diego's Rocket From The Crypt in the summer of 1990 after becoming disillusioned with the hardcore punk band he was in called Pitchfork. Joining with current Rocketeers bassist Petey X and guitarist ND, in addition to now departed drummer Sean and backing vocalist Elaina, Reis and company released *Paint as a Fragrance* in 1991.

Though the album caused a lot of people to take notice, a lineup change ensued; Atom became the drummer, and Apollo 9, a drinking buddy of Reis' who played sax in high school, joined as saxophonist. After the successful independent *Circa: Now!* was released on Cargo Records in 1992, a major-label bidding war resulted in Rocket From The Crypt signing with Interscope Records (in addition to Reis' other band, Drive Like Jehu, which features another former Pitchfork member, Rick Fork). Interscope then re-released *Circa: Now!* in 1993, and the single "Ditch Digger" spent some time in MTV's Buzz Bin. Eventually, a sixth member—JC 2000 on horn—was added in 1994, which preceded the release of a new ten-inch record, *The State of Art is on Fire*, in 1995. By the end of the year, the group released its most acclaimed album to date, *Scream, Dracula, Scream.* —*Matt Carlson*

Paint as a Fragrance / 1991 / Headhunter ✦✦✦
This record lurches through ten solid songs, which, though as aggressive as punk's roots, offer much more than your typical power-chord mosh pit anthems. John "Speedo" Reis stuns with his soulful, Sammy Davis, Jr.-meets-Eddie Cochran lead vocals, while backing vocalist Elaina adds rich harmony. In addition to more immediate punk scorchers, Rocket From The Crypt also explores other musical terrain; the band gears up with rockabilly-laden guitar riffs, which are then unleashed with some dissonant guitar harmonies and breakneck piano. —*Matt Carlson*

● **Circa: Now!** / 1993 / Headhunter ✦✦✦✦
Originally released on Cargo/Headhunter before the group was picked up by Interscope, *Circa: Now!* finds Speedo's army redirecting its sound slightly by adding saxophone and slowing the tempo down on some tracks. Of course, Rocket From The Crypt still imbues every second of these with unflinching power. The saxophone of Apollo 9, though sparsely decorated and subtly buried throughout the album, adds 1950s R&B flair on "Hairball Alley" and "March of Dimes." And though a majority of the songs pack a more direct wallop than *Paint as a Fragrance*, the record still finds room to settle down on the lush '60s pop of "Little Arm." —*Matt Carlson*

All Systems Go / 1994 / Headhunter ✦✦✦
This collection of Rocket From The Crypt's singles, issued for the first time on CD, captures the band in both of its incarnations—direct, no-nonsense punk maestros ("Live the Funk" and "Jumper K. Balls") and playful mood-swingers ("Lefty" and "Chantilly Face"). But *All Systems Go* makes its best excuse with "Pigeon Eater" and "The Paste That You Love," by far Rocket's best songs, released together as a Merge 45 in early 1994. —*Matt Carlson*

State of Art Is on Fire / 1995 / Sympathy for the Record Industry ✦✦✦✦
Certainly Rocket From The Crypt's most furious punk exploit to date, the ten-inch EP *The State of Art is on Fire* burns straight to the point. Rocket relinquishes its usual musical homage to rockabilly and R&B, and instead blazes through six explosive songs that don't slow down until the final track, "Human Spine." Reis' lyrics add more fuel to the fire, while Apollo 9 and JC 2000 blast their horns against the wall of sound. —*Matt Carlson*

Scream, Dracula, Scream / Oct. 10, 1995 / Atlantic ✦✦✦✦

Rockpile

f. 1976, London, England, **db.** 1981
Rock 'n' Roll, New Wave, Pop-Rock, Pub Rock
During the late '70s, Rockpile was the touring band for both Dave Edmunds and Nick Lowe. Like Edmunds, the band was passionate about traditional rock 'n' roll. Like Lowe, the band played with a reckless, trashy abandon. Driven by the powerful rhythm section of drummer Terry Williams and Lowe's bass, guitarists Billy Bremner and Edmunds were free to spit out crushing rock, blues, rockabilly, and country licks. With their fierce live energy and unpretentious rock 'n' roll, the band fit easily into the post-punk new wave at the end of the decade.

Although they only released one album as a group—1980's *Seconds of Pleasure*—the band provided support for most of the albums Lowe and Edmunds recorded in the late '70s. After the rushed release of *Seconds of Pleasure*, the band toured one last time before splitting apart, largely due to mismanagement. All of the members continued to occasionally collaborate with each other throughout the '80s. —*Stephen Thomas Erlewine*

Seconds of Pleasure / 1980 / Columbia ✦✦✦✦
Rockpile's only proper album is an inspired collection of old-fashioned rock 'n' roll, which sounds vital because of the band's unrelenting energy and Nick Lowe's consistently inventive songwriting. The CD includes the bonus EP of Everly Brothers covers that was included in the album's original pressing. —*Stephen Thomas Erlewine*

Tommy Roe

b. May 9, 1942, Atlanta, GA
Guitar, Vocals / Rock 'n' Roll, Pop-Rock, Bubblegum
Widely perceived as one of the archetypal bubblegum artists of the late '60s, Tommy Roe cut some pretty decent rockers along the way, especially early in his career—many displaying some pretty prominent Buddy Holly roots. In fact, Roe's initial pop smash, 1962's chart-topping "Sheila," was quite reminiscent of Holly's "Peggy Sue," utilizing a very similar throbbing drum beat and Roe's hiccuping vocal. The singer had previously cut the song for the smaller Judd label before remaking it in superior form for ABC-Paramount. The infectious "Everybody"—another hot item the next year—was waxed in Muscle Shoals at Rick Hall's Fame studios, normally an R&B-oriented facility (it's not widely known that Roe wrote songs for the Tams, a raw-edged soul group from his Atlanta hometown).

Once Roe veered off on his squeaky-clean bubblegum tangent, he stuck with it for the rest of the decade. His lighthearted "Sweet Pea" and "Hooray for Hazel" burned up the charts in 1966, and he was still at it three years later when he waxed his biggest hit, "Dizzy," and "Jam Up Jelly Tight." —*Bill Dahl*

● **Greatest Hits** / Sep. 28, 1993 / MCA ✦✦✦✦
Supplants previous anthologies as the best Roe collection available. Eighteen songs spanning 1962 to 1971, including all the big singles, with thorough liner notes. —*Richie Unterberger*

Greatest Hits / Jan. 25, 1994 / Curb ✦✦
There's an identically titled CD on MCA, issued around the same time. The Curb disc has many of the same songs, but considerably less in total (only ten in all). Since the MCA anthology also has much better liner notes, you'd be foolish to pick up this one instead. —*Richie Unterberger*

The Rolling Stones

f. Jan. 1963, London, England
Group / Rock 'n' Roll, Electric British Blues, Hard Rock, British Invasion, Pop-Rock, British Blues
By the time the Rolling Stones began calling themselves the World's Greatest Rock & Roll Band in the late '60s, they had already staked out an impressive claim on the title. As the self-consciously dangerous alternative to the bouncy Merseybeat of the Beatles in the British Invasion, the Stones had pioneered the gritty, hard-driving, blues-based rock 'n' roll that came to define hard rock. With his preening machismo and latent maliciousness, Mick Jagger became the prototypical rock frontman, tempering his macho showmanship with a detached, campy irony, while Keith Richards and Brian Jones wrote the blueprint for sinewy, interlocking rhythm guitars. Backed by the strong, yet subtly swinging rhythm section of bassist Bill Wyman and drummer Charlie Watts, the Stones became the breakout band of the British blues scene, eclipsing such contemporaries as the Animals and Them. Over the course of their career, the Stones never really abandoned blues, but as soon as they reached popularity in the UK, they began experimenting musically, incorporating the British pop of contemporaries like the Beatles, Kinks, and Who into their sound. After a brief dalliance with psychedelia, the Stones re-emerged in the late '60s as a jaded, blues-soaked, hard rock quintet. The Stones always flirted with the seedy side of rock 'n' roll, but as the hippie dream began to break apart, they exposed and reveled in the new rock culture. It wasn't without difficulty, of course. Shortly after he was fired from the group, Jones was found dead in a swimming pool; while at a 1969 free concert at Altamont, a concertgoer was brutally murdered during the Stones' show. But the Stones never stopped going. For the next 30 years, they continued to record and perform, and while

their records weren't always blockbusters, they were never less than the most visible band of their era—certainly, none of their British peers continued to be as popular or productive as the Stones. And no band since has proven to have such a broad fan base or far-reaching popularity, and it is impossible to hear any of the groups that followed them without detecting some sort of influence, whether it was musical or aesthetic.

Throughout their career, Mick Jagger (vocals) and Keith Richards (guitar, vocals) remained at the core of the Rolling Stones. The pair initially met as children at Dartford Maypole County Primary School. They drifted apart over the next ten years, eventually making each other's acquaintance again in 1960, when they met through a mutual friend, Dick Taylor, who was attending Sidcup Art School with Richards. At the time, Jagger was studying at the London School of Economics and playing with Taylor in the blues band Little Boy Blue and the Blue Boys. Shortly afterward, Richards joined the band. Within a year, they had met Brian Jones (guitar, vocals), a Cheltenham native who had dropped out of school to play saxophone and clarinet. By the time he became a fixture on the British blues scene, Jones had already had a wild life. He ran away to Scandinavia when he was 16; by that time, he had already fathered two illegitimate children. He returned to Cheltenham after a few months, where he began playing with the Ramrods. Shortly afterward, he moved to London. where he played in Alexis Korner's group, Blues Inc. Jones quickly decided he wanted to form his own group and advertised for members; among those he recruited was the heavyset blues pianist Ian Stewart.

As he played with his group, Jones also moonlighted under the name Elmo Jones at the Ealing Blues Club. At the pub, he became reacquainted with Blues, Inc., which now featured drummer Charlie Watts, and, on occasion, cameos by Jagger and Richards. Jones became friends with Jagger and Richards, and they soon began playing together with Dick Taylor and Ian Stewart; during this time, Mick was elevated to the status of Blues Inc's lead singer. With the assistance of drummer Tony Chapman, the fledgling band recorded a demo tape. After the tape was rejected by EMI, Taylor left the band to attend the Royal College of Art; he would later form the Pretty Things. Before Taylor's departure, the group named themselves the Rolling Stones, borrowing the moniker from a Muddy Waters song.

The Rolling Stones gave their first performance at the Marquee Club in London on July 12, 1962. At the time, the group consisted of Jagger, Richards, Jones, pianist Ian Stewart, drummer Mick Avory and Dick Taylor, who had briefly returned to the fold. Weeks after the concert, Taylor left again and was replaced by Bill Wyman, formerly of the Cliftons. Avory also left the group—he would later join the Kinks—and the Stones hired Tony Chapman, who proved to be unsatisfactory. After a few months of persuasion, the band recruited Charlie Watts, who had quit Blues Inc. to work at an advertising agency once the group's schedule became too hectic. By 1963, the band's lineup had been set, and the Stones began an eight-month residency at the Crawdaddy Club, which proved to substantially increase their fan base. It also attracted the attention of Andrew Loog Oldham, who became the Stones' manager, signing them from underneath Crawdaddy's Giorgio Gomelsky. Although Oldham didn't know much about music, he was gifted at promotion, and he latched upon the idea of fashioning the Stones as the bad-boy opposition to the clean-cut Beatles. At his insistence, the large yet meek Stewart was forced out of the group, since his appearance contrasted with the rest of the group. Stewart didn't disappear from the Stones; he became one of their key roadies and played on their albums and tours until his death in 1985.

With Oldham's help, the Rolling Stones signed with Decca Records, and that June, they released their debut single, a cover of Chuck Berry's "Come On." The single became a minor hit, reaching No. 21, and the group supported it with appearances on festivals and package tours. At the end of the year, they released a version of Lennon-McCartney's "I Wanna Be Your Man" which soared into the Top 15. Early in 1964, they released a cover of Buddy Holly's "Not Fade Away," which shot to No. 3. "Not Fade Away" became their first American hit, reaching No. 48 that spring. By that time, the Stones were notorious in their homeland. Considerably rougher and sexier than the Beatles, the Stones were the subject of numerous sensationalistic articles in the British press, culminating in a story about the band urinating in public. All of these stories cemented the Stones as a dangerous, rebellious band in the minds of the public, and had the effect of beginning a manufactured rivalry between them and the Beatles, which helped the group rocket to popularity in the US. In the spring of 1964, the Stones released their eponymous debut album, which was billed as "It's All Over Now," their first UK No. 1. That summer, they toured America to riotous crowds, recording the *Five By Five* EP at Chess Records in Chicago in the midst of the tour. By the time it was over, they had another No. 1 UK single with Howlin' Wolf's "Little Red Rooster," a song that was banned in America due to its suggestive lyrics.

Although the Stones had achieved massive popularity, Oldham decided to push Jagger and Richards into composing their own songs,

since they—and his publishing company—would receive more money that away. In June of 1964, the group released their first original single "Tell Me (You're Coming Back)," which became their first American Top 40 hit. Shortly afterward, a version of Irma Thomas' "Time Is On My Side" became their first US Top Ten. It was followed by "The Last Time" in early 1965, a No. 1 UK and Top Ten US hit that began a virtually uninterrupted string of Jagger-Richards hit singles. Still, it wasn't until the group released "(I Can't Get No) Satisfaction" in the summer of 1965 that they were elevated to superstars. Driven by a fuzz-guitar riff designed to replicate the sound of a horn section, "Satisfaction" signaled that Jagger and Richards had come into their own as songwriters, breaking away from their blues roots and developing a signature style of big, bluesy riffs and wry, sardonic lyrics. It stayed at No. 1 for four weeks and began a string of Top Ten singles that ran for the next two years, including such classics as "Get Off My Cloud," "19th Nervous Breakdown," "As Tears Go By" and "Have You Seen Your Mother, Baby, Standing in the Shadows?"

By 1966, the Stones had decided to respond to the Beatles' increasingly complex albums with their first album of all-original material, *Aftermath*. Due to Brian Jones' increasingly exotic musical tastes, the record boasted a wide range of influences, from the sitar-drenched "Paint It, Black" to the Eastern drones of " Going Home." These eclectic influences continued to blossom on *Between the Buttons*, (1967) the most pop-oriented album the group ever made. Ironically, the album's release was bookended by two of the most notorious incidents in the band's history. Before the record was released, the Stones performed the suggestive "Let's Spend the Night Together," the B-side to the medieval ballad "Ruby Tuesday," on *The Ed Sullivan Show*, which forced Jagger to alter the song's title to an incomprehensible mumble, or else face being banned. In February of 1967, Jagger and Richards were arrested for drug possession, and within three months, Jones was arrested on the same charge. All three were given suspended jail sentences, and the group backed away from the spotlight as the summer of love kicked into gear in 1967. Jagger, along with his then-girlfriend Marianne Faithfull, went with the Beatles to meet the Maharishi Mahesh Yogi; they were also prominent in the international broadcast of the Beatles' "All You Need Is Love." Appropriately, the Stones' next single, "Dandelion" / "We Love You," was a psychedelic pop effort, and it was followed by their response to *Sgt. Pepper*, *Their Satanic Majesties Request*, which was greeted with lukewarm reviews.

The Stones' infatuation with psychedelia was brief. By early 1968, they had fired Andrew Loog Oldham and hired Allen Klein as their manager. The move coincided with their return to driving rock 'n' roll, which happened to coincide with Richards' discovery of open tunings, a move that gave the Stones their distinctively fat, powerful sound. The revitalized Stones were showcased on the malevolent single "Jumpin' Jack Flash," which climbed to No. 3 in May 1968. Their next album, *Beggar's Banquet*, was finally released in the fall, after being delayed for five months due its controversial cover art of a dirty, graffiti-laden restroom. An edgy record filled with detours into straight blues and campy country, *Beggar's Banquet* was hailed as a masterpiece among the fledgling rock press. Although it was seen as a return to form, few realized that while it opened a new chapter of the Stones' history, it also was the closing of their time with Brian Jones. Throughout the recording of *Beggar's Banquet*, Jones was on the sidelines due to his deepening drug addiction and his resentment of the dominance of Jagger and Richards. Jones left the band on June 9, 1969, claiming to be suffering from artistic differences between himself and the rest of the band. On July 3, 1969—less than a month after his departure—Brian Jones was found dead in his swimming pool. The coroner ruled that it was "death by misadventure," yet his passing was the subject of countless rumors over the next two years.

By the time of his death, the Stones had already replaced Brian Jones with Mick Taylor, a former guitarist for John Mayall's Bluesbreakers. He wasn't featured on "Honky Tonk Women," a No. 1 single released days after Jones' funeral, and he contributed only a handful of leads on their next album, *Let It Bleed*. Released in the fall of 1969, *Let It Bleed* was comprised of sessions with Jones and Taylor, yet it continued the direction of *Beggar's Banquet*, signaling that a new era in the Stones' career had begun, one marked by ragged music and increasingly wasted sensibility. Following Jagger's filming of *Ned Kelly* in Australia during the first part of 1969, the group launched their first American tour in three years. Throughout the tour—the first where they were billed as the World's Greatest Rock & Roll Band—the group broke attendance records, but it was given a sour note when the group staged a free concert at Altamont Speedway. On the advice of the Grateful Dead, the Stones hired Hell's Angels as security, but that plan backfired tragically. The entire show was unorganized and in shambles, yet it turned tragic when the Angels murdered a young Black man, Meredith Hunter, during the Stones' performance. In the wake of the public outcry, the Stones again retreated from the spotlight and dropped "Sympathy for the

Devil," which some critics ignorantly claimed incited the violence, from their set.

As the group entered hiatus, they released the live *Get Yer Ya-Ya's Out* in the fall of 1970. It was their last album for Decca/London, and they formed Rolling Stones Records, which became a subsidiary of Atlantic Records. During 1970, Jagger starred in Nicolas Roeg's cult film *Performance*. He married Nicaraguan model Bianca Perez Morena de Macias, and the couple quickly entered high society. As Jagger was jet-setting, Richards was slumming, hanging out with country-rock pioneer Gram Parsons. Richards wound up having more musical influence on 1971's *Sticky Fingers*, the first album the Stones released though their new label. Following its release, the band retreated to Paris on tax exile, where they shared a house and recorded a double album, *Exile on Main St.* Upon its May 1972 release, *Exile on Main St.* was widely panned, but over time it came to be considered one of the group's defining moments.

Following *Exile*, the Stones began to splinter in two, as Jagger concentrated on being a celebrity and Richards sank into drug addiction. The band remained popular throughout the '70s, but their critical support waned. *Goats Head Soup*, released in 1973, reached No. 1, as did 1974's *It's Only Rock 'N' Roll*, but neither record was particularly well received. Taylor left the band after *It's Only Rock 'N' Roll*, and the group recorded their next album as they auditioned new lead guitarists, including Jeff Beck. They finally settled on Ron Wood, former lead guitarist for the Faces and Rod Stewart, in 1976, the same year they released *Black N' Blue*, which only featured Wood on a handful of cuts. During the mid- and late '70s, all the Stones pursued side projects, with both Wyman and Wood releasing solo albums with regularity. Richards was arrested in Canada in 1977 with his common-law wife Anita Pallenberg for heroin possession. After his arrest, he cleaned up and was given a suspended sentence the following year. The band reconvened in 1978 to record *Some Girls*, an energetic response to punk, new wave and disco. The record and its first single, the thumping disco-rocker "Miss You," both reached No. 1, and the album restored the group's image. However, the group squandered that goodwill with the follow-up *Emotional Rescue*, a No. 1 record that nevertheless received lukewarm reviews upon its 1980 release. *Tattoo You*, released the following year, fared better both critically and commercially, as the singles "Start Me Up" and "Waiting on a Friend" helped the album spend nine weeks at No. 1. The Stones supported *Tattoo You* with an extensive stadium tour captured in Hal Ashby's movie *Let's Spend the Night Together* and the 1982 live album *Still Life*.

Tattoo You proved to be the last time the Stones completely dominated the charts and the stadiums. Although the group continued to sell out concerts in the '80s and '90s, their records didn't sell well, partially because the albums suffered due to Jagger and Richards' notorious mid-'80s feud. Starting with 1983's *Undercover*, the duo conflicted about which way the band should go, with Jagger wanting the Stones to follow contemporary trends and Richards wanting them to stay true to their rock roots. As a result, *Undercover* was a mean-spirited, unfocused record that received relatively weak sales and mixed reviews. Released in 1986, *Dirty Work* suffered a worse fate, since Jagger was preoccupied with his fledgling solo career. Once Jagger decided that the Stones would not support *Dirty Work* with a tour, Richards decided to make his own solo record with 1988's *Talk Is Cheap*. Appearing a year after Jagger's failed second solo album, *Talk is Cheap* received good reviews and went gold, prompting Jagger and Richards to reunite late in 1988. The following year, the Stones released *Steel Wheels*, which was received with good reviews, but the record was overshadowed by its supporting tour, which grossed over $140 million dollars and broke many box office records. In 1991, the live album *Flashback*, which was culled from the *Steel Wheels* shows, was released.

Following the release of *Flashback*, Bill Wyman left the band; he published a memoir, *Stone Alone*, within a few years of leaving. The Stones didn't immediately replace Wyman, since they were all working on solo projects; this time, there was none of the animosity surrounding their mid-'80s projects. The group reconvened in 1994 with bassist Darryl Jones, who had previously played with Miles Davis and Sting, to record and release the Don Was-produced *Voodoo Lounge*. The album received the band's strongest reviews in years, and its accompanying tour was even more successful than the *Steel Wheels* tour. On top of being more successful than its predecessor, *Voodoo Lounge* also won the Stones their first Grammy for Best Rock Album. Upon the completion of the *Voodoo Lounge* tour, the Stones released the live, "unplugged" album *Stripped* in the fall of 1995. *—Stephen Thomas Erlewine*

The Rolling Stones (England's Newest Hitmakers) / May 30, 1964 / ABKCO ✦✦✦✦

The group's debut album was the most uncompromisingly blues/R&B-oriented full-length recording they would ever release. Mostly occupied with covers, this was as hard-core as British R&B ever got; it's raw and ready. But the Stones succeeded in establishing themselves as creative interpreters, putting '50s and early-'60s blues, rock, and soul classics (some quite obscure to white audiences) through a younger, more gui-

tar-oriented filter. The record's highlighted by blistering versions of "Route 66," "Carol," the hyper-tempoed "I Just Want to Make Love to You," "I'm a King Bee," and "Walking the Dog." Their Bo Diddleyized version of Buddy Holly's "Not Fade Away" gave them their first British Top Ten hit (and their first small American one). The acoustic ballad "Tell Me" was Jagger-Richards' first good original tune, but the other group-penned originals were little more than rehashed jams of blues cliches, keeping this album from reaching truly classic status. *—Richie Unterberger*

12 X 5 / Oct. 17, 1964 / ABKCO ✦✦✦✦

The evolution from blues to rock accelerated with the Stones' second American LP. They turned soul into guitar rock for the hits "It's All Over Now" and "Time Is on My Side" (the latter of which was their first American Top Ten single). "2120 South Michigan Avenue" is a great instrumental blues-rock jam; "Around and Around" is one of their best Chuck Berry covers; and "If You Need Me" reflects an increasing contemporary soul influence. On the other hand, the group originals (except for the propulsive "Empty Heart") are weak and derivative, indicating that the band still had a way to go before they could truly challenge the Beatles' throne. *—Richie Unterberger*

☆ **The Rolling Stones Now!** / Apr. 1965 / ABKCO ✦✦✦✦✦

Although their third American LP was patched together (in the usual British Invasion tradition) from a variety of sources, it's their best early R&B-oriented effort. Most of the Stones' early albums suffer from three or four very weak cuts; *Now!* is almost uniformly strong start-to-finish, the emphasis on some of their Blackest material. The covers of "Down Home Girl," Bo Diddley's vibrating "Mona," Otis Redding's "Pain in My Heart," and Barbara Lynn's "Oh Baby" are all among the group's best R&B interpretations. The best gem is "Little Red Rooster," a pure blues with wonderful slide guitar from Brian Jones (and a No.1 single in Britain, although it was only an album track in the US). As songwriters, Jagger and Richards are still struggling, but they come up with one of their first winners (and an American Top 20 hit) with the yearning, soulful "Heart of Stone." *—Richie Unterberger*

Out of Our Heads / Aug. 1965 / ABKCO ✦✦✦✦

In 1965, the Stones finally proved themselves capable of writing classic rock singles that mined their R&B/blues roots, but updated them into a more guitar-based, thoroughly contemporary context. The first enduring Jagger-Richards classics are here—"The Last Time," its menacing, folky B-side "Play with Fire," and the riff-driven "Satisfaction," which made them superstars in the States and defined their sound and rebellious attitude better than any other single song. On the rest of the album, they largely opted for mid-'60s soul covers, Marvin Gaye's "Hitch Hike," Otis Redding's "Cry to Me," and Sam Cooke's "Good Times" being particular standouts. "I'm All Right" (based on a Bo Diddley song) showed their '65 sound at its rawest, and there are a couple of fun, though derivative, bluesy originals in "The Spider and the Fly" and "The Under Assistant West Coast Promotion Man." *—Richie Unterberger*

December's Children / Dec. 1965 / ABKCO ✦✦✦✦

The last Stones album in which cover material accounted for 50% of the content was thrown together from a variety of singles, British LP tracks, outtakes, and a cut from an early '64 UK EP. Haphazard assembly aside, much of it's great, including the huge hit "Get Off of My Cloud" and the controversial, string-laden acoustic ballad "As Tears Go By" (a Top Ten item in America). Raiding the R&B closet for the last time, they also offered a breathless run-through of Larry Williams' "She Said Yeah," a sultry Chuck Berry cover ("Talkin' About You"), and exciting live versions of "Route 66" and Hank Snow's "I'm Moving On." More importantly, Jagger-Richards' songwriting partnership had now developed to the extent that several LP-only tracks were reasonably strong in their own right, such as "I'm Free" and "The Singer Not the Song." And the version of "You Better Move On" (which had featured on a British EP at the beginning of 1964) was one of their best and most tender soul covers. *—Richie Unterberger*

Big Hits High Tide and Green Grass / Mar. 1966 / ABKCO ✦✦✦✦

All of their American hits from "Not Fade Away" through "19th Nervous Breakdown," as well as a couple of B-sides. The music's great, of course, although several decades later, there are more wide-ranging compilations of their '60s classics available. *—Richie Unterberger*

☆ **Aftermath** / Jun. 1966 / ABKCO ✦✦✦✦✦

The Rolling Stones finally delivered a set of all-original material with this LP, which also did much to define the group as the bad boys of rock 'n' roll with their sneering attitude toward the world in general and the female sex in particular. The borderline misogyny could get a bit juvenile in tunes like "Stupid Girl." But on the other hand the group began incorporating the influences of psychedelia and Dylan into their material with classics like "Paint It Black," an eerily insistent No.1 hit graced by some of the best use of sitar (played by Brian Jones) on a rock record. Other classics included "Mother's Little Helper" (whose lyrics had extremely blatant and controversial drug references); Jones also added exotic accents with his vibes (on the jazzy "Under My Thumb") and dulcimer (the delicate Elizabethan ballad "Lady Jane"). Some of the material is fairly ho-hum, to be honest, as Jagger and Richards were still prone to inconsistent songwriting; "Going Home," a 11-minute blues jam, was remarkable more for its barrier-crashing length than its content. Look out for an obscure gem, however, in the brooding, meditative "I Am Waiting." —*Richie Unterberger*

Got Live If You Want It / Nov. 4, 1966 / ABKCO ♦♦

A live document of the Brian Jones-era Stones sounds enticing, but the actual product is a letdown. The sound is lousy, and for that matter not all of it's live; a couple of old studio R&B covers were augmented by screaming fans that had obviously been overdubbed. Partially recorded at a 1966 Royal Albert Hall performance (where the audience rioted at the opening of the concert), the performances and singing are on the sloppy side (and sometimes alarmingly out of tune), the sound balance is atrocious, and several of the songs are taken at a let's-get-this-over-with-and-off-the-stage-before-we-get-torn-apart pace. It's a fun souvenir in its own way; just don't expect top-notch value, even factoring in the primitive state of live rock recording technology in 1966. —*Richie Unterberger*

☆ Between the Buttons / Jan. 1967 / ABKCO ♦♦♦♦♦

The Rolling Stones' 1967 recordings are a matter of some controversy; many critics felt that they were compromising their raw, rootsy power with frothy emulations of the Beatles, Kinks, Dylan, and psychedelic music. Approach this album with an open mind, though, and you'll find it to be one of their strongest, most eclectic LPs, with many fine songs that remain unknown to all but Stones devotees. The lyrics are getting better (if more savage), and the arrangements more creative, on brooding near-classics like "All Sold Out," "My Obsession," and "Yesterday's Papers." "She Smiled Sweetly" shows their hidden romantic side at its best, while "Connection" is one of the record's few slabs of conventionally driving rock. But the best tracks were the two songs that gave the group a double-sided No.1 in early 1967: the lustful "Let's Spend the Night Together" and the beautiful, melancholy "Ruby Tuesday," which is as melodic as anything Jagger and Richards would ever write. —*Richie Unterberger*

Flowers / Jun. 1967 / ABKCO ♦♦♦♦

Dismissed as a ripoff of sorts by some critics, as it took the patchwork bastardization of British releases for the American audience to extremes, gathering stray tracks from the UK versions of *Aftermath* and *Between the Buttons*, 1966-67 singles (some of which had already been used on the US editions of *Aftermath* and *Between the Buttons*), and a few outtakes. Judged solely by the music, though, it's rather great. "Mother's Little Helper," "Lady Jane," "Ruby Tuesday," and "Let's Spend the Night Together" are all classics (although they had all been on LP before); the 1966 single "Have You Seen Your Mother, Baby, Standing in the Shadow" makes its first album appearance, and is the early Stones at their most surrealistic and angst-ridden. A lot of the rest of the cuts rate among their most outstanding 1966-67 work. "Out of Time" is hitworthy in its own right (and in fact topped the British charts in an inferior cover by Chris Farlowe); ; "Back Street Girl," with its European waltz flavor, is one of *the* great underrated Stones songs. The same goes for the psychedelic Bo Diddley of "Please Go Home," and the acoustic, pensively sardonic "Sittin' on a Fence," with its strong Appalachian flavor. Almost every track is strong, so if you're serious about your Stones, don't pass this by just because a bunch of people slag it as an exploitative marketing trick (which it is). There's some outstanding material you can't get anywhere else, and the album as a whole plays very well from end-to-end. —*Richie Unterberger*

Their Satanic Majesties Request / Nov. 1967 / ABKCO ♦♦♦

Without a doubt, no Rolling Stones album—and, indeed, very few rock albums from any era—split critical opinion as much as the Rolling Stones' psychedelic outing. Many dismiss the record as sub-*Sgt. Pepper* posturing; others confess, if only in private, to a fascination with the album's inventive arrangements, which incorporated some African rhythms, mellotrons, and full orchestration. Never before or since did the Stones take so many chances in the studio. This writer, at least, feels that the record has been unfairly undervalued, partly because purists expect the Stones to constantly champion a blues 'n' raunch worldview. About half the material is very strong, particularly the glorious "She's a Rainbow," with its beautiful harmonies, piano, and strings; the riff-driven "Citadel"; the hazy, dream-like "In Another Land," Bill Wyman's debut writing (and singing) credit on a Stones release; and the majestically dark and doomy cosmic rocker "2000 Light Years from Home," with some of the creepiest synthesizer effects (devised by Brian Jones) ever to grace a rock record. The downfall of the album was caused by some weak songwriting on the lesser tracks, particularly the interminable psychedelic jam "Sing This All Together (See What Happens)." It's a much better record than most people give it credit for being, though, with a strong current of creeping uneasiness that undercuts the gaudy psychedelic flourishes. In 1968, the Stones would go back to the basics,

and never wander down these paths again, making this all the more of a fascinating anomaly in the group's discography. —*Richie Unterberger*

☆ Beggars Banquet / Nov. 1968 / ABKCO ♦♦♦♦♦

The Stones forsook psychedelic experimentation to return to their blues roots on this celebrated album, which was immediately acclaimed as one of their landmark achievements. A strong acoustic Delta blues flavor colors much of the material, particularly "Salt of the Earth" and "No Expectations," which features some beautiful slide guitar work. Basic rock and roll was not forgotten, however: "Street Fighting Man," a reflection of the political turbulence of 1968, was one of their most innovative singles, and "Sympathy for the Devil," with its fire-dancing guitar licks, leering Jagger vocal, African rhythms, and explicitly satanic lyrics, was an image-defining epic. On "Stray Cat Blues," Jagger and buddies begin to explore the kind of decadent sexual sleaze that the group would take to the point of self-parody by the mid-1970s. At the time, though, the approach was still fresh, and the lyrical bite of most of the material ensured its place as one of the top blues-based rock records of all time. —*Richie Unterberger*

Through the Past Darkly (Big Hits, Vol. 2) / Sep. 1969 / ABKCO ♦♦♦♦

Their biggest '60s hits, from "Paint It Black" onward. Like *High Tide and Green Grass*, it's somewhat redundant these days, as all of the tracks appear on the more extensive *Hot Rocks* anthologies. What's in the grooves, though, is wall-to-wall classic, including "Ruby Tuesday," "Let's Spend the Night Together," "Jumpin' Jack Flash," "Honky Tonk Woman," "Have You Seen Your Mother, Baby, Standing in the Shadow," "She's a Rainbow," "Street Fighting Man," and more. —*Richie Unterberger*

☆ Let It Bleed / Nov. 28, 1969 / ABKCO ♦♦♦♦♦

Mostly recorded without Brian Jones, who died several months before its release (although he does play on two tracks), and was replaced by Mick Taylor (who also plays on just two songs). This extends the rock'n'blues feel of *Beggar's Banquet* into slightly harder-rocking, more demonically sexual territory. The Stones were never as consistent on album as their main rivals, the Beatles, and *Let It Bleed* suffers from some rather half-assed tracks, like "Monkey Man" and a countrified remake of the classic "Honky Tonk Woman" single (here titled "Country Honk"). Yet some of the songs are among their very best, especially "Gimme Shelter," with its shimmering guitar lines and apocalyptic lyrics; the harmonica-driven "Midnight Rambler"; the druggy party ambience of the title track; and the stunning "You Can't Always Get What You Want," which was the Stones' "Hey Jude" of sorts, with its epic structure, horns, philosophical lyrics, and swelling choral vocals. "You Got the Silver" (Keith Richards' first lead vocal) and Robert Johnson's "Love in Vain," by contrast, were as close to the roots of acoustic downhome blues as the Stones ever got. —*Richie Unterberger*

Get Yer Ya-Ya's Out / Sep. 4, 1970 / ABKCO ♦♦♦♦

Recorded during their American tour in late 1969, and centered around live versions of material from the *Beggars Banquet-Let It Bleed* era. Often acclaimed as one of the top live rock albums of all time, its appeal has dimmed a little today. The live versions are reasonably different from the studio ones, but ultimately not as good, a notable exception being the long workout of "Midnight Rambler," with extended harmonica solos and the unforgettable section where the pace slows to a bump-and-grind crawl. Some Stones aficionados, in fact, prefer a bootleg from the same tour (*Liver Than You'll Ever Be*, to which this LP was unleashed in response), or their amazing the-show-must-go-on performance in the jaws of hell at Altamont (preserved in the *Gimme Shelter*...film). Fans that are unconcerned with picky comparisons such as these will still find *Ya Ya's*...an outstanding album, and it's certainly the Stones' best official live recording. —*Richie Unterberger*

☆ Sticky Fingers / Apr. 23, 1971 / Virgin ♦♦♦♦♦

Pieced together from outtakes and much-labored over songs, *Sticky Fingers* manages to have a loose, ramshackle ambience that belies both its origins and the dark undercurrents of the songs. It's a weary, drug-laden album—well over half of the songs explicitly mention drug use, while the others merely allude to it either in subject matter or their tone—that never fades away, but it barely keeps afloat. Apart from the classic opener "Brown Sugar" (a gleeful tune about slavery, interracial sex, lost virginity and not in that order), the long workout "Can't You Hear Me Knocking" and the mean-spirited "Bitch," *Sticky Fingers* is a slow, bluesy affair, with a few country touches thrown in for good measure. The laid-back tone of the album gives ample room for new lead guitarist Mick Taylor to stretch out, particularly on the extended coda of "Can't You Hear Me Knocking." But the key to the album isn't the instrumental interplay, although that is terrific; it's the utter weariness of the songs. "Wild Horses" is their first non-ironic stab at a country song and it is a beautiful, heart-tugging masterpiece. Similarly, "I Got the Blues" is a ravished, late-night classic that ranks among their very best blues. "Sister Morphine" is a horrific overdose tale and "Moonlight Mile," with Paul Buckmaster's grandiose strings, is a perfect closure—sad, yearning, drug-addled and beautiful. With its off-handed mixture of decadence, roots music and outright malevolence, *Sticky Fingers* set the tone for the rest of the decade for the Stones. —*Stephen Thomas Erlewine*

● **Hot Rocks 1964-1971** / Jan. 1972 / ABKCO ✦✦✦✦
This import double-disc anthology contains their biggest hits on London, as well as many of their most popular album tracks. A stereo version of "Satisfaction" is the highlight, and worth the price, even though the US mono version is also pretty cool. —*Bruce Eder*

☆ **Exile on Main Street** / May 12, 1972 / Virgin ✦✦✦✦✦
Greeted with decidedly mixed reviews upon its original release, *Exile on Main Street* has become generally regarded as the Rolling Stones' finest album. Part of the reason why the record was initially greeted with hesitant reviews is that it takes a while to assimilate. A sprawling, weary double album encompassing rock 'n' roll, blues, soul, and country, *Exile* doesn't try anything new on the surface, but the substance is new. Taking the bleakness that underpinned *Let It Bleed* and *Sticky Fingers* to an extreme, *Exile* is a weary record, and not just lyrically. Jagger's vocals are buried in the mix, and the music is a series of dark, dense jams, with Keith Richards and Mick Taylor spinning off incredible riffs and solos. And the songs continue the breakthroughs of their three previous albums. No longer does their country sound forced or kitschy—it's lived-in and complex, just like the group's forays into soul and gospel. While the songs, including the masterpieces "Rocks Off," "Tumbling Dice," "Torn and Frayed," "Happy," "Let It Loose," and "Shine a Light," are all terrific, they blend together, with only certain lyrics and guitar lines emerging from the murk. It's the kind of record which is gripping upon the first listen, but each listen reveals something new—few other albums, let alone double albums, have been so rich and masterful as *Exile on Main Street*, and it stands as not only as one of the Stones' best records, but sets a remarkably high standard for all of hard rock. —*Stephen Thomas Erlewine*

● **More Hot Rocks (Big Hits and Fazed Cookies)** / Nov. 1972 / ABKCO ✦✦✦✦
Hot Rocks covers most of the monster hits from the Stones' first decade that remain in radio rotation in the 1990s. *More Hot Rocks* goes for the somewhat smaller hits, some of the better album tracks, and a whole LP side worth of rarities that hadn't yet been available in the US when this compilation was released in 1972. The material isn't as famous as what's on *Hot Rocks*, but the music is almost as excellent, including such vital cuts as "Not Fade Away," "It's All Over Now," "The Last Time," "Lady Jane," the psychedelic "Dandelion," "She's a Rainbow," "Have You Seen Your Mother, Baby, Standing in the Shadow?," "Out of Time," "Tell Me," and "We Love You." The eight rarities are pretty good as well, including their 1963 debut single "Come On," early R&B covers of "Fortune Teller" and "Bye Bye Johnnie," great slide guitar on Muddy Waters' "I Can't Be Satisfied," and the soulful 1966 UK B-side, "Long Long While." —*Richie Unterberger*

Goats Head Soup / Aug. 31, 1973 / Virgin ✦✦✦
Compared to the monumental *Exile on Main Street*, *Goats Head Soup* is bound to sound inferior, and it does. Nevertheless, the album doesn't deserve its bad reputation. It might be careless and decadent, but that excess is quite intoxicating, as the nasty rocker "Star Star" and the finely crafted ballad "Angie" prove. —*Stephen Thomas Erlewine*

It's Only Rock and Roll / Oct. 18, 1974 / Virgin ✦✦✦
It's uneven, but at times *It's Only Rock and Roll* catches fire. The songs and performances are stronger than those on *Goats Head Soup;* the tossed-off numbers sound effortless, not careless. Throughout, the Stones wear their title as the "World's Greatest Rock & Roll Band" with a defiant smirk, which makes the bitter cynicism of "If You Can't Rock Me" and the title track all the more striking, and the reggae experimentation of "Luxury," the aching beauty of "Time Waits for No One," and the agreeable filler of "Dance Little Sister" and "Short and Curlies" all the more enjoyable. —*Stephen Thomas Erlewine*

Metamorphosis / Jun. 1975 / ABKCO ✦✦
A motley assortment of 1960s outtakes, apparently compiled by the Stones' former managers to squeeze every last drop from the group's songwriting backlog. Most of the cuts are demos of weak Jagger/Richards songs that became flop singles for other artists; it's likely that some of the Stones don't even play on much of the album. The versions of "Out of Time" and "Heart of Stone" are abominable when compared to the more widely known original renditions. The late-'60s outtakes that make up most of side two (including a rare Bill Wyman original, "Downtown Suzie") probably do feature the actual group, but quite simply don't cut it. And did we mention the atrocious cover design? A couple exceptions make the LP worth picking up for Stones fanatics: a decent mid-'60s cover of Chuck Berry's "Don't Lie to Me," and "If You Let Me," a nice folk-rock outtake from *Between the Buttons*. Note: The British version contains two additional songs. —*Richie Unterberger*

Black & Blue / Apr. 20, 1976 / Virgin ✦✦✦
Ron Wood's first album with the Stones finds the band working through a number of reggae—and funk-tinged numbers, trying to expand their

sound. Consequently, songs are sacrificed for grooves; only the ballads "Memory Motel" and "Fool to Cry" are fully developed, but the grooves that dominate the album are strong enough to make the record successful. —*Stephen Thomas Erlewine*

Love You Live / Sep. 23, 1977 / Rolling Stones ✦✦
Recorded on the supporting tour for 1976's *Black & Blue*, the double-album set *Love You Live* is an adequate live album, capturing the Stones' transition from a lean, lethal rock 'n' roll band to accomplished show men. As show men, they aren't as compelling as they are when they're rockers, but the show-biz glitz of Mick Jagger's arena-rock schtick remains thoroughly entertaining, even when it robs the music of its power. —*Stephen Thomas Erlewine*

☆ **Some Girls** / Jun. 9, 1978 / Virgin ✦✦✦✦
During the mid-'70s, the Rolling Stones remained massively popular, but their records suffered from Jagger's fascination with celebrity and Keith's worsening drug addictions. By 1978, both punk and disco had swept the group off the front pages, and *Some Girls* is their fiery response to the younger generation. Opening with the disco-blues thump of "Miss You," *Some Girls* is a tough, focused and exciting record, full of more hooks and energy than any record since *Exile on Main Street*. Even though the Stones make disco into their own, they never quite take punk on their own ground. Instead, their rockers sound harder and nastier than they have in years. Taking "Star Star" as a starting point, the Stones run the through the seedy homosexual imagery of "When the Whip Comes Down" before landing on the bizarre, borderline misogynist vitriol of the title track, Keith's ultimate outlaw anthem "Before They Make Me Run," and the decadent closer, "Shattered." In between, they deconstruct the Temptations' "(Just My) Imagination," offer a devastating, snide country parody ("Far Away Eyes") and contribute "Beast of Burden," one of their very best ballads. *Some Girls* may not have the backstreet aggression of their '60s records, or the majestic, drugged-out murk of their early-'70s work, but in its glitzy, decadent hard rock, it offers a definitive Stones album. —*Stephen Thomas Erlewine*

Emotional Rescue / Jun. 23, 1980 / Virgin ✦✦✦
Coasting on the success of *Some Girls*, the Stones offered more of the same on *Emotional Rescue*. Comprised of leftovers from the previous album's sessions and hastily written new numbers, *Emotional Rescue* may consist mainly of filler, but it's expertly written and performed filler. The Stones toss off throwaways like the reggae-fueled, mail-order bride anthem "Send It to Me" or rockers like "Summer Romance" and "Where the Boys Go" with an authority that makes the record a guilty pleasure, even if it's clear that only two songs—the icy but sexy disco-rock of "Emotional Rescue" and the revamped Chuck Berry rocker "She's So Cold"—come close to being classic Stones. —*Stephen Thomas Erlewine*

Tattoo You / Aug. 30, 1981 / Virgin ✦✦✦✦
Like *Emotional Rescue* before it, *Tattoo You* was comprised primarily of leftovers, but unlike its predecessor, it never sounds that way. Instead, *Tattoo You* captures the Stones at their best as a professional stadium-rock band. Divided into a rock 'n' roll side and a ballad side, the album delivers its share of thrills on the tight, dynamic first side. "Start Me Up" became the record's definitive Stonesy rocker, but the frenzied doo wop of "Hang Fire," the reggae jam of "Slave," the sleazy Chuck Berry rockers "Little T&A" and "Neighbours," and the hard blues of "Black Limousine" are all terrific. The ballad side suffers in comparison, especially since "Heaven" and "No Use in Crying" are faceless. But "Worried About You" and "Tops" are effortless, excellent ballads, and "Waiting on a Friend," with its Sonny Rollins sax solo, is an absolute masterpiece, a moving lyric that captures Jagger in a shockingly reflective and affecting state of mind. "Waiting on a Friend" and the vigorous rock 'n' roll of the first side make *Tattoo You* an essential latter-day Stones album, ranking just a few notches below *Some Girls*. —*Stephen Thomas Erlewine*

Still Life / Jun. 1, 1982 / Rolling Stones ✦
Like *Love You Live* before it, *Still Life* showcases the Stones as pure entertainers, although the band adds enough rhythmic grit to keep the record from sinking into pure show-biz formula. Nevertheless, it isn't nearly enough grit to make it rock as hard as *Get Yer Ya-Ya's Out*. Or even *Love You Live*, depressingly enough. —*Stephen Thomas Erlewine*

Undercover / Nov. 7, 1983 / Virgin ✦✦✦
As their most ambitious album since *Some Girls*, *Undercover* is a weird, wild mix of hard rock, new wave pop, reggae, dub, and soul. Even with all the careening musical eclecticism, what distinguishes *Undercover* is its bleak, nihilistic attitude—it's teeming with sickness, with violence, kinky sex and loathing dripping from almost every song. "Undercover of the Night" slams with echoing guitars and rubbery bass lines, as Jagger gives a feverish litany of sex, corruption and suicide. It set the tone for the rest of the album, whether it's the runaway nymphomaniac of "She Was Hot" or the ridiculous slasher imagery of "Too Much Blood." Only Keith's "Wanna Hold You" offers a reprieve from the carnage, and its relentless bloodletting makes the album a singularly fascinating lis-

ten. For some observers, that mixture was nearly too difficult to stomach, but for others, it's a fascinating record, particularly since much of its nastiness feels as if the Stones, and Jagger and Richards in particular, are running out of patience with each other. — *Stephen Thomas Erlewine*

Dirty Work / 1986 / Virgin ✦✦✦
Reuniting after three years and one solo album from Mick Jagger, the Rolling Stones attempted to settle their differences and craft a comeback with *Dirty Work*, but the tensions remained too great for the group. Designed as a return to their rock 'n' roll roots after several years of vague dance experiments, *Dirty Work* is hampered by uneven songs and undistinguished performances, as well as a slick, lightly synthesized production that instantly dates the album to the mid-'80s. Jagger often sounds like he's saving his best work for his solo records, but a handful of songs have a spry, vigorous attack—"One Hit (To the Body)" is a classic, and "Winning Ugly" and "Had It With You" have a similar aggression. Still, most of *Dirty Work* sounds as forced as the cover of Bob & Earl's uptown soul obscurity "Harlem Shuffle," leaving the album as one of the group's most undistinguished efforts. — *Stephen Thomas Erlewine*

☆ Singles Collection: The London Years / 1989 / ABKCO ✦✦✦✦✦
The three-disc box set *Singles Collection: The London Years* contains every single the Rolling Stones released during the '60s, including both the A and B-sides. It is the first Stones compilation that tries to be comprehensive and logical—for all their attributes, the two *Hot Rocks* sets and the two *Big Hits* collections didn't present the singles in chronological order. In essence, the previous compilations were excellent samplers, where *Singles Collection* tells most of the story (certain albums, like *Aftermath*, *Beggars Banquet* and *Let It Bleed*, fill in the gaps left by the singles). The Rolling Stones made genuine albums—even their early R&B/blues albums were impeccably paced—but their singles had a power all their own, which is quite clearly illustrated by the *Singles Collection*. By presenting the singles in chronological order, the set takes on a relentless, exhilarating pace with each hit and neglected B-side piling on top of each other, adding a new dimension to the group; it has a power it wouldn't have had if it tried to sample from the albums. Although it cheats near the end, adding singles from the *Metamorphosis* outtakes collection and two singles from *Sticky Fingers*, this captures the essence of the '60s Stones as well as any compilation could. Casual fans might want to stick with the *Hot Rocks* sets, since they just have the hits, but for those that want a little bit more, the *Singles Collection* is absolutely essential. — *Stephen Thomas Erlewine*

Steel Wheels / Aug. 1989 / Virgin ✦✦✦
The band's best album of the '80s, embracing blues, classic rock, and even psychedelia ("Continental Drift"). — *Bruce Eder*

Flashpoint / Apr. 1991 / Rolling Stones ✦✦
The live follow-ups and a fond look back on 25 years of decadence. — *Bruce Eder*

Voodoo Lounge / Jul. 19, 1994 / Capitol ✦✦✦
While *Voodoo Lounge* sounds amazingly like the Stones' classic records from the early '70s, it's rather inconsistent and too long to make it one of their major works. Instead, it's simply another solid Stones record, with some fine tracks and typically strong playing. — *Stephen Thomas Erlewine*

Stripped / Nov. 14, 1995 / Virgin ✦✦✦
Despite the odds, the Rolling Stones' *Stripped* held out great promise. *Voodoo Lounge* was an energized return to studio form for the Borg of rock 'n' roll road shows. From that platform, the idea of taking it back to small clubs, live, lean and pared down without succumbing to the worn "unplugged" treadmill, seemed an inspired move. Patched together from an embroidery of tour rehearsals and live club dates in Paris and Amsterdam, the project was an extension of acoustic sets the group introduced on the North American leg of the *Voodoo Lounge* tour. The concept offered an invigorating opportunity to dust off some rough gems from the past that no longer felt at home on scoping stadium stages. Unfortunately, the cover photo depicting a lean, determined, leather-clad combo in spartan black and white proves to be misleading advertising. Within the brave packaging lies a listless, lethargic Dorian Gray bluff. Spongy keyboards gunk many of the tracks. The much-touted cover of Dylan's "Like a Rolling Stone" remains pointlessly devoted to the original. There are lazy, somnambulant versions of "I'm Free" and "Let It Bleed"; Keith Richards' painfully intoned "Slipping Away"; and there are dozens of lost songs that any fan would chose to have renovated before "Angie." — *Roch Parisien*

R.S.V.P. [bootleg] / 1996 / Cool Blokes Production ✦✦✦
A 78-minute disc of alternate mixes and outtakes from the *Beggars Banquet* session, in superb sound. This effectively acts as an alternate version of *Beggars Banquet* itself. There are different versions/mixes of every track from that album except "Street Fighting Man," along with five songs (some instrumental) never released by the Stones. It might read more exciting than it plays. Some of the alternates differ in such

subtle ways that they sound all but identical to the official versions, although trainspotters will appreciate differences like the prominent organ at the tag of "No Expectations." The otherwise unreleased tunes, which are loose, bluesy thangs with considerable funky charm, have already been found on various late-'60s Stones boots, although the sound quality here is unbeatable. Hardcore Stones scholars, though, will find the disc worth getting. — *Richie Unterberger*

Rolling Stones Rock & Roll Circus / Oct. 15, 1996 / ABKO ✦✦✦
The most interesting archival release of the Rolling Stones since *More Hot Rocks*, 20 years ago, and the first issue of truly unreleased material by the Stones from this period. And the Stones have some competition from the Who, Taj Mahal, and John Lennon on the same release. Filmed and recorded on December 10-11, 1968 at a North London studio, The *Rock And Roll Circus* has been, as much as the Beach Boys' *Smile*, "the one that got away" for most '60s music enthusiasts. The Jethro Tull sequence is the standard studio track, but the rest—except for the Stones' "Salt of the Earth"—is really live. The Who's portion has been out before, courtesy of various documentaries, but Taj Mahal playing some loud electric blues is new and great, the live Lennon rendition of "Yer Blues" is indispensable, and the Stones' set fills in lots of blanks in their history—"Jumpin' Jack Flash" in one of two live renditions it ever got with Brian Jones in the lineup, "Sympathy For the Devil" in an intense run-through, "Parachute Woman" as a lost live vehicle for the band, "You Can't Always Get What You Want" as a show-stopping rocker even without its extended ending (no Paul Buckmaster choir), and "No Expectations" as their first piece of great live blues since "Little Red Rooster." It's a must-own, period. — *Bruce Eder*

Bright Lights, Big City / [Bootleg] ✦✦✦✦
As you'd expect, there are a ton of Rolling Stones bootlegs, but there isn't a great deal of essential material from the '60s to be found on them. The exceptions are these outtakes from 1963 and 1964, which have popped up under quite a few guises, but most frequently under the *Bright Lights, Big City* title. The five early-1963 demos were cut shortly before they signed with Decca, and capture the band at their bluesiest and blackest; when Brian Jones was being frozen out of the Stones in the late '60s, it's said that he would play these for listeners as examples of the purity of the group's original vision. With clear fidelity, the standards of these performances are well up to official release; "Baby What's Wrong," "Road Runner," and "I Want to Be Loved" are downright electrifying. The four 1964 cuts were recorded at Chess Studios, and again (with the possible exception of the jam "Stewed And Keefed") are well up to release quality, with fine, spare readings of "Hi-Heel Sneakers," Howlin' Wolf's "Down In The Bottom," and Big Bill Broonzy's "Tell Me Baby." Essential for serious fans. — *Richie Unterberger*

BBC Sessions / [Bootleg] ✦✦✦
The Rolling Stones' BBC sessions haven't been accorded the same deluxe bootleg treatment as those of the Beatles, for two big reasons: they didn't record nearly as much for the Beeb as the Fab Four, and (unlike the Beatles) didn't record many tracks that they didn't release on record. Good fidelity tapes exist of a few dozen of their mid-'60s BBC airshots, and fans will find them worth picking up. Heavy on R&B covers (the Stones, like the Beatles, didn't record for the BBC after 1965), the tracks, as is par for the course on radio sessions, don't better or usually even equal the studio renditions, but have an interesting rougher live feel. They did manage to let rip on a half-dozen or so unreleased covers, and these tracks are naturally the most interesting, especially their takes on "Memphis, Tennessee" and their incendiary "Roll Over Beethoven," which is perhaps even better than the well-known Beatle version. — *Richie Unterberger*

Out of Time / [Bootleg] ✦✦✦✦
A great concept for an album that, no matter what Allen Klein might say, helps more people than it hurts: 16 songs assembled from the '60s B-sides, import-only singles, compilations, and soundtracks that have proven extremely hard to find in America. A few of the songs did finally show up on ABKCO's *Singles Collection*, but many remain unavailable. And some of these items are very good: a longer version of the smoking "2120 South Michigan Avenue" instrumental (only issued in Germany), the long, very different take of "Everybody Needs Somebody to Love" that was issued on their second British LP, "I've Been Loving You Too Long" minus the overdubbed screams on *Got Live If You Want It*, the Italian version of "As Tears Go By," Jagger's "Memo from Turner" (from the *Performance* soundtrack), and two early songs that only showed up on the British version of *Metamorphosis*. "I Want to Be Loved" and "I Wanna Be Your Man" (which were officially reissued on *Singles Collection*) are among their best early tracks. Good sound, topped off with a superb picture sleeve of the Stones in drag in 1966, add up to an LP that is essential for serious Stones fans, and indeed better than many of their "official" albums. — *Richie Unterberger*

Tricky Fingers & Sticky Ringers / [Bootleg] ✦✦✦
"Alternate versions" of entire albums are somewhat in vogue by rock bootleggers, who compile entire CDs of alternate/live takes of songs

from one specific full-length recording. This is one attempt at an alternate version of *Sticky Fingers*, and not bad, though not as successful as it may appear from a glance at the sleeve. There are indeed alternate studio takes of "Brown Sugar," "Wild Horses," "Sister Morphine," "You Gotta Move," and "Bitch." In fact, there are four different versions of "Brown Sugar" alone, including the famous one with a prominent slide guitar. The thing is, they really aren't *that* different; at a casual listen, they sound almost exactly like the album versions, sometimes amounting to nothing more drastic than different mixes. And it's uncertain whether the live versions of "Dead Flowers" and "Can't You Hear Me Knocking" actually come from 1969-1971, as the sleeve claims. A 14-minute performance of "Can't You Hear Me Knocking" sounds particularly enticing, but this fair-quality live recording (no source given) doesn't sound like it's from the *Sticky Fingers* period; indeed, it sounds suspiciously like it might be from a Jagger-less side project of Keith Richards or somebody. These reservations aside, hard-core Stones fans may find this worthwhile, with a 66-minute running time and the addition of a cover of Chuck Berry's "Let It Rock" (which was not included on *Sticky Fingers*). —*Richie Unterberger*

Henry Rollins

b. Feb. 13, 1961, Washington, D.C.
Vocals / Spoken Word, Alternative Pop-Rock
In the '90s, Henry Rollins emerged as a post-punk renaissance man, without the self-conscious trappings that plagued such '80s artists as David Byrne. Since Black Flag's breakup in 1986, Rollins has been relentlessly busy, recording albums with the Rollins Band, writing books and poetry, performing spoken-word tours, writing a magazine column in *Details*, acting in several movies, and, most surprisingly, appearing on MTV as an occasional VJ. All the while, he has kept his artistic integrity, becoming a kind of father figure for many alternative bands of the '90s on the strength of albums like 1992's *The End of Silence*, 1994's *Weight*, and 1997's *Come In and Burn*.

The Rollins Band's records are uncompromising, intense, cathartic fusions of hard rock, funk, post-punk noise, and jazz experimentalism, with Rollins shouting angry, biting self-examinations and accusations over the grind. On his spoken-word albums, he is remarkably more relaxed, showcasing a hilariously self-deprecating sense of humor that is often absent in his music. —*Stephen Thomas Erlewine*

Hot Animal Machine / 1987 / Texas Hotel ✦✦✦✦
A good solo effort, raw and powerful. This CD includes the EP *Drive by Shootings*. —*John Dougan*

Do It / 1988 / Texas Hotel ✦✦✦

Life Time / 1988 / Texas Hotel ✦✦✦

Sweatbox / 1989 / Quarterstick ✦✦✦✦

Hard Volume / 1989 / Texas Hotel ✦✦✦

Turned On / 1990 / Quarterstick ✦✦✦
A perfect example of the Rollins Band at work was recorded live in Vienna, Austria, in 1989 with some of his best songs from that era. Recorded digitally, but the CD treats the entire recording as one track. —*John Book*

Deep Throat / Feb. 1992 / Quarterstick ✦✦✦✦
All of Rollins' early spoken-word releases are gathered in the reasonably priced six-disc box set *Deep Throat*. As with each of his spoken albums, Rollins is incisive, moving, self-effacing, and very funny; it's worth the price of the discs. —*Stephen Thomas Erlewine*

● **The End of Silence** / Feb. 25, 1992 / Imago ✦✦✦✦
Intense is the only word that can describe Henry Rollins, and his band is the most intense unit recording today. *The End of Silence* is arguably the Rollins Band's best effort to date, full of angry, abrasive hardcore/jazz fusion, highlighted by the crushing "Low Self Opinion." —*Stephen Thomas Erlewine*

● **Rollins: The Boxed Life** / Jan. 26, 1993 / Imago ✦✦✦✦
Rollins' spoken-word records are comedy records, more like Lenny Bruce or Richard Pryor than Andrew Dice Clay or Eddie Murphy. Underneath all the laughter there are some serious themes; the humor is drawn from pain. But the main reason to hear *The Boxed Life* (or any of Rollins' spoken-word records) is that he's a superb storyteller with a wicked sense of humor. Some of the topics are squeamish (animal testing, safe sex, depression) and there is a generous helping of profanity, but it is genuinely funny and moving. —*Stephen Thomas Erlewine*

Weight / Apr. 12, 1994 / Imago ✦✦✦✦
On *Weight*, the Rollins Band is able to mix the musicians' love for jazz with a blindingly direct hard-rock assault, making a twisted form of metal-jazz. Rollins' lyrics have also begun to move away from his relentless self-examination, adding a touch of the self-effacing humor that distinguishes his spoken records. The new lyrical dimension adds depth to the band's music, making *Weight* the most impressive album they've released to date. —*Stephen Thomas Erlewine*

Everything / Jul. 1996 / Thirsty Ear ✦✦✦
Everything is a spoken-word recording of a chapter from Henry Rollins' book *Eye Scream*. Unlike most of his spoken-word albums, which are essentially long, rambling, and funny monologs, *Everything* is a recitation that intends to be somewhat important. Throughout the album, Rollins recites fairly awkward poetry over a minimalist, beatnik jazz backdrop provided by Charles Gayle and Rashied Ali. Rollins has a terrific sense of detail and humor, which is normally evident in his prose and monologs. In his poetry, he becomes clumsy and humorless—his clear, simple sentences don't have as much power when they're delivered in stanzas. Furthermore, the jazz bleatings in the background seep into the forefront too often, becoming a major annoyance by the time the album is halfway over. In a way, it's easy to admire Rollins' intentions with *Everything*, but the final result is ultimately too tedious and misdirected to take very seriously. —*Stephen Thomas Erlewine*

Come in & Burn / Mar. 25, 1997 / DreamWorks ✦✦✦
Weight found the perfect balance between Rollins' intense and funny spoken-word performances and his intense, fiery, and heavy music, and its success makes the stilted *Come In & Burn* all the more disappointing. In a sense, Rollins has painted himself into a corner—by his own admission he isn't much of a singer, and all he wants to do with his music is exorcise demons, so his records sound too similar. Still, the passion of his vocals and his band's volcanic rage made both *The End of Silence* and *Weight* captivating, but with this record, it all sounds tired. The band does try to venture into jazzier territory, but they're weighed down by a plodding backbeat. If Rollins had something new to say, the colorless music would be forgivable, yet he simply bellows out angst-ridden clichés, without the humor or insight that makes his books and spoken-word records so entertaining. *Come In & Burn* sounds like the Rollins Band has already reached the limits of what they can do. —*Stephen Thomas Erlewine*

Black Coffee Blues / Apr. 22, 1997 / Thirsty Ear ✦✦✦

The Romantics

f. 1977, Detroit, MI
Power Pop, Pop-Rock
In the early '80s, the Romantics were a terrific rock band, joyously tearing through loose, infectious power pop gems like the classic "What I Like About You." After two albums of energetic pop-rock, the band shifted its direction to a slicker, more radio-friendly pop; the change of style worked, resulting in the hit singles "Talking in Your Sleep" and "One in a Million" in 1983. Surprisingly, their drummer Jimmy Marinos left after their success; the band recorded one more album in 1985 before breaking up. In the early '90s, "What I Like About You" began appearing in television commercials, leading the band to reunite. They have recorded one EP and have toured several times since re-forming. —*Stephen Thomas Erlewine*

The Romantics / Feb. 1980 / Epic ✦✦✦✦
The cover, featuring the four members decked out in identical red leather outfits with the de rigeur skinny ties, leaves no doubt as to the album's content. This is your basic artifact of the era—lusty, girl-crazed, teen anthems sung to hard-driving, punchy power-pop. "What I Like About You" was the hit, but any of these songs could have been hits. It's easy to dismiss this band, but few albums provide this much guilty pleasure. —*Chris Woodstra*

National Breakout / Dec. 1980 / Epic ✦✦✦
Their sophomore effort follows much of the same formula of the debut. Unfortunately, none of the songs had the instantly endearing catchiness of "What I Like About You" and the album failed to live up to the optimistic title's promise. —*Chris Woodstra*

Strictly Personal / Oct. 1981 / Epic ✦✦✦
Strictly Personal, the Romantics' commercial breakthrough, loses much of the innocence (and fun) of the first two albums, with its slicker production. "Talking in Your Sleep" and "One in a Million" both broke the Top Ten, but the album offers little else. —*Chris Woodstra*

Rhythm Romance / 1985 / Nemperor ✦✦
Power-pop was very much of the moment; bands who held on as late as 1985 had to lose the silly ties and modify their sound or face ridicule. The Romantics certainly followed the rules with *Rhythm Romance*. This time the band is pictured on the cover dressed in *black* leather and bigger hair. They've become full-fledged arena rockers complete with a big ultraslick production . . . and an utterly forgettable batch of songs. —*Chris Woodstra*

● **What I Like About You (& Other Romantic Hits)** / Dec. 1990 / Nemperor ✦✦✦✦
What I Like About You (& Other Romantic Hits) is a ten-track best-of including the classic "What I Like About You," as well as some other fondly remembered hits like "Talking In Your Sleep" and "One in a Million." While this is a good distillation of the band's best moments (espe-

cially from the later albums), nothing matches the debut for consistent quality and power-packed catchiness. —*Chris Woodstra*

King Biscuit Flower Hour / Aug. 27, 1996 / King Biscuit ✦✦✦✦
Arguably the group's best album, and one of the best live albums ever released by anybody. This concert, recorded on Oct. 30, 1983 in San Antonio, at the peak of the group's popularity, captures them in a powerful, energetic performance, displaying their best garage punk attributes full force along with a surprisingly melodic sound that put them a few steps above bands like the Ramones. It's all here, including "Talking In Your Sleep" and climaxing with "What I Like About You," covering a big chunk of the band's history as well as some pre-history, like "Little Latin Lupe Lou." Along with Robyn Hitchcock & the Egyptians' *Gotta Let This Hen Out*, one of the great 1980s live albums, and only a step short of classics like *Live Kinks* and the Stones' *Got Live If You Want It*. Great sound, too, with some really cool crunchy guitars—a must-own collection. —*Bruce Eder*

Romeo Void

f. 1979, San Francisco, CA, **db.** 1984
New Wave
A post-punk quintet formed in San Francisco in 1979, consisting of singer Debora Iyall (b. 1956), bassist Frank Zincavage, guitarist Peter Woods, drummer Jay Derrah (replaced by John Stench and then Larry Carter), and saxophone player Ben Bossi. They released several albums on 415 Records (distributed by CBS) from 1981 to 1984. Iyall then left for a solo career. —*William Ruhlmann*

It's a Condition / Mar. 1981 / 415 ✦✦✦
Romeo Void ably represented the post-punk zeitgeist. Their simple, relentless beat and repetitive riffs complemented singer Debora Iyall's huffy posturing, in which the denial of emotion became an emotional statement in itself. In "White Sweater," Iyall obsessed on the clothing in which her sister committed suicide; she might demand, "Talk Dirty (To Me)," but never forgot that "Love Is an Illness," and one is best off keeping "Myself to Myself." Meanwhile, the band maintained a minimalist backing in which every note counted. If punk spoke of unmitigated rage, Romeo Void's music was no less angry, but far more resigned. —*William Ruhlmann*

Benefactor / 1982 / Columbia ✦✦✦
Those danceable beats, that tough-girl stance—maybe somebody at Columbia thought the label was getting its own Blondie by buying up 415 Records and its principal asset, Romeo Void. Certainly, *Benefactor* was a more commercial-sounding effort than the debut album, with the band even agreeing to eviscerate the four-letter word in "Never Say Never" and elsewhere playing uptempo dance-rock that almost, but not quite, overcame the disaffection of Debora Iyall's lyrics. But Romeo Void still was less a Blondie clone than an heir to X-Ray Spex or the Bush Tetras, playing bass-heavy, minimalist rock behind a pissed-off singer who, unlike Deborah Harry, wasn't kidding. "You don't get it?" asked Iyall. "Rain on you. And the world disappears." —*William Ruhlmann*

Instincts / 1984 / Columbia ✦✦✦
Perhaps in reaction against the more commercial sound of *Benefactor*, Romeo Void returned to producer David Kahne and the sound of their first album, *It's a Condition*, on their third, *Instincts*. Nevertheless, it proved to be their bestselling album. The group's instrumental attack continued to be spearheaded by saxophonist Benjamin Bossi, whose floating lines contrasted with the drive of the rhythm section and guitarist Peter Woods' Morse Code leads. Debora Iyall continued to pour out disappointed reflections on the romantic condition in songs with titles like "Your Life Is a Lie" and "Say No." One of them, "A Girl in Trouble (Is a Temporary Thing)," managed to be provocative and vague enough to inch into the Top 40, such that the album gained greater exposure and sales. But instead of marking a breakthrough for Romeo Void, *Instincts* marked their breakup, with Iyall going solo. —*William Ruhlmann*

● **Warm, In Your Coat** / May 2, 1992 / Columbia/Legacy ✦✦✦✦
Punk bands, of course, were not meant to last, and even if Romeo Void, with its dance beats and warm sax sound, as well as a distinctive lead singer with a gift for soundbite lyrics, seemed to have more commercial potential than most, its five-year, three-album existence was long enough to make some noise, make some compromises, and make it out alive. This 15-song, 65-minute compilation is notable not only for the signature songs—"White Sweater," "Myself to Myself," "A Girl in Trouble (Is a Temporary Thing)," and, especially, "Never Say Never"—but also for revealing the range of a band that seemed at the time mostly a backdrop for Debora Iyall. Romeo Void was a band, and from the evidence of this set, a good one, too. —*William Ruhlmann*

Chan Romero

b. Jul. 7, 1941, Billings, MT
Guitar, Vocals / Rock 'n' Roll
A somewhat obscure but quite interesting performer from the tail end of

the initial '50s rock 'n' roll explosion, Latino guitarist and singer Romero is most famous for writing and singing the original version of "Hippy Hippy Shake." Causing only a minor ripple in the US upon its 1959 release, it became a standard part of the repertoire for Liverpool bands in the early '60s. The Swinging Blue Jeans had a huge hit with it in 1964, reaching No. 2 in the UK (and the US Top 30). Although they never recorded it in the studio, the Beatles performed it often on the BBC; a superb 1963 version from this source, featuring a cord-shredding Paul McCartney vocal, was released on the group's *Live at the BBC* compilation.

Romero had more to offer than the typical one-song wonder, but didn't get much of a chance to prove it in the studio. Born to Mexican parents in Billings, MT, Romero began performing in the late '50s. The success of trailblazing Latino rocker Ritchie Valens impressed him deeply, spurring him to pen "The Hippy Hippy Shake," an uptempo rocker modeled on Valens. A tryout at Specialty lead to nothing, but in the wake of Valens' tragic death in February 1959, Romero's manager contacted the late singer's label, Del-Fi. Though perhaps opportunistic, the strategy was entirely appropriate; Romero's raw and enthusiastic high-pitched vocals and rockabilly-derived guitar playing was a pretty close approximation of Valens' style.

"Hippy Hippy Shake" did make No. 3 in Australia, leading to a 1960 tour there with Jerry Lee Lewis, but Chan's records didn't do much in the United States. Romero did record some other respectable sides for Del-Fi which, like Valens, saw him alternating raucous rockers with ballads. Del-Fi went as far as to have Romero record with the same musicians as Valens had, Rene Hall's Danelectro bass guitar (which was played as assertively as a lead instrument) being the most distinguishing feature of the arrangements. And Chan reminded Valens' mother of her late son so much that he stayed in her home for several months.

But Romero didn't stay at Del-Fi (or indeed record much there at all), leaving the label in the early '60s. Over the next few years he made some one-off singles for other companies, working on separate occasions with legendarily weird producers Kim Fowley and Shadow Morton. Eventually he concentrated on Christian-inspired music, founding his own Warrior label in the mid-'60s for that purpose. He remains an active performer, occasionally playing on the oldies circuit. —*Richie Unterberger*

● **Hippy Hippy Shake** / Aug. 8, 1995 / Del-Fi ✦✦✦✦
Romero's extremely slim legacy at Del-Fi is padded out to a full 15 tracks here: seven studio cuts from 1959, a 1965 single for Challenge, and seven songs of "Chan Unplugged" (solo home studio demos from 1959). As with many of Ritchie Valens' recordings, there's more promise than genius. Valens fans will certainly enjoy these high-spirited, driving sides, though. The title track is the predictable highlight, though it must be said that the Beatles' cover beats it by a mile: Chan's original sounds sweet and tame in comparison. The ballads are lukewarm, but Romero works up a good sweat on "My Little Ruby" and "Your Love." The two-track demos are more than mere curiosities, as Romero, accompanied only by his acoustic guitar, works through affecting, vocal reverb-heavy versions of "Hippy Hippy Shake," "La Bamba," and other songs. —*Richie Unterberger*

The Ronettes

f. 1959, New York, NY
Girl-Group
Before Phil Spector took them under his wing in the early '60s, the Ronettes had already recorded several singles and were regionally successful. But the Spector-produced records are what everyone remembers and for a good reason—they featured some of his biggest, best productions along with equally impressive songs. Beneath his monumental wall of sound, lead vocalist Ronnie Bennett, who would later marry Spector, sang songs of teenage love in a plain, girlish voice; "Be My Baby," the group's first and biggest hit, was the pinnacle of the group's talent, as well as being one of the producer's finest moments. None of their following singles (including "Baby, I Love You," "(The Best Part of) Breaking Up," and "Walking in the Rain") were quite as successful commercially, although they were nearly as strong artistically. While Spector was inactive in the mid-'60s, the Ronettes were also inactive; together they re-emerged in 1969, to a small commercial reception. After Ronnie divorced Spector in 1973, she formed a new version of the Ronettes that lasted for three years; after the group disbanded, she launched a solo career. —*Stephen Thomas Erlewine*

The Ronettes: The Early Years / 1965 / Rhino ✦✦✦✦
The early Ronettes songs weren't as immaculately produced or as evocative as Phil Spector's productions. Their sound was more generic and resembled other girl groups like the Shirelles or Chiffons. They recorded for Colpix and Dimension during 1961 and 1962, with Ronnie Bennett doing most of the leads, while her sister Estelle and cousin Nedra added soothing harmonies and backgrounds. At times, as on "My Guiding Angel" or "You Bet I Would," they came close to the appealing mix of

innocence and earnestness that characterized their later (and greatest) tracks. But despite getting material from such songwriters as Jackie DeShannon and Carole King, many of these cuts were more serviceable than classic. Still, this is the foundation for the sound that exploded in the mid-'60s. —*Ron Wynn*

The Greatest Hits, Vol. 2 / 1981 / Masters ✦✦✦
A good 16-track compilation of rare tracks and non-hit singles, highlighted by "I Can Hear Music," "Paradise," and "Is This What I Get for Loving You"; it also has three tracks that Ronnie Spector sang on, but which were credited to the Crystals. The most interesting material, however, is now available on the ABKCO CD. —*Richie Unterberger*

★ **The Best of the Ronettes** / Sep. 22, 1992 / ABKCO ✦✦✦✦✦
For a couple of years, the Ronettes made music that was as moving and unforgettable as any made during the rock era. Their voices merged sensuality, longing, anguish, and sentimentality, with Ronnie Spector's angelic leads framed by Phil Spector's sweeping production, and the lyrics of Ellie Greenwich, Jeff Barry, Barry Mann, Cynthia Weil, Spector, and others. While such songs as "Walking in the Rain," "Be My Baby," "Baby, I Love You," and "(The Best Part of) Breaking Up" may seem hopelessly naive and possibly sexist in today's cynical world, they're still classic love poems. Ronnie Spector's voice retains its allure and appeal, and the 18 tracks on this CD will never become dated. —*Ron Wynn*

Linda Ronstadt

b. Jul. 15, 1946, Tucson, AZ
Vocals / Country-Rock, Adult Contemporary, Pop, Soft Rock, Folk-Rock, Pop-Rock, Traditional Pop
With roots in the Los Angeles country and folk-rock scenes, Linda Ronstadt became one of the most popular interpretive singers of the '70s, earning a string of platinum-selling albums and Top 40 singles. Throughout the '70s, her laidback pop never lost sight of her folky roots, yet as she moved into the '80s, she began to change her sound with the times, adding new wave influences. After a brief flirtation with pre-rock pop, Ronstadt settled into a pattern of adult contemporary pop and Latin albums, sustaining her popularity in both fields.

While Ronstadt was a student at Arizona State University, she met guitarist Bob Kimmel. The duo moved to Los Angeles, where guitarist/ songwriter Kenny Edwards joined the pair. Calling themselves the Stone Poneys, the group became a leading attraction on California's folk circuit, recording their first album in 1967. The band's second album, *Evergreen, Vol. 2*, featured the Top 20 hit "Different Drum," which was written by Michael Nesmith. After recording one more album with the group, Ronstadt left for a solo career at the end of 1968.

Ronstadt's first two solo albums—*Hand Sown Home Grown* (1969) and *Silk Purse* (1970)—accentuated her country roots, featuring several honky tonk numbers. Released in 1971, her self-titled third album was a pivotal record in her career. Featuring a group of session musicians that would later form the Eagles, the album was a softer, more laidback variation of the country-rock she had been recording. With the inclusion of songs from singer-songwriters like Jackson Browne, Neil Young, and Eric Andersen, *Linda Ronstadt* had folk-rock connections as well. *Don't Cry Now*, released in 1973, followed the same formula to greater success, yet it was 1974's *Heart Like a Wheel* that perfected the sound, making Ronstadt a star. Featuring the hit covers "You're No Good," "When Will I Be Loved," and "It Doesn't Matter Anymore," *Heart Like a Wheel* reached No. 1 and sold over two million copies.

Released in the fall of 1975, *Prisoner in Disguise* followed the same pattern as *Heart Like a Wheel* and was nearly as successful. *Hasten Down the Wind*, released in 1976, suggested a holding pattern, even if it charted higher than *Prisoner in Disguise*. *Simple Dreams* (1977) expanded the formula by adding a more rock-oriented supporting band, which breathed life into the Rolling Stones' "Tumbling Dice" and Warren Zevon's "Poor Poor Pitiful Me." The record became the singer's biggest hit, staying on the top of the charts for five weeks and selling over three million copies. With *Living in the USA* (1978) Ronstadt began experimenting with new wave, recording Elvis Costello's "Alison"; the album was another No. 1 hit. On 1980's *Mad Love*, she made a full-fledged new wave record, recording three Costello songs and adopting a synth-laden sound. While the album was a commercial success, it signalled that her patented formula was beginning to run out of steam. That suspicion was confirmed with 1982's *Get Closer*, her first album since *Heart Like a Wheel* to fail to go platinum.

Sensing it was time to change direction, Ronstadt starred in the Broadway production of Gilbert & Sullivan's *Pirates of Penzance*, as well as the accompanying movie. *Pirates of Penzance* led the singer to a collaboration with Nelson Riddle, who arranged and conducted her 1983 collection of pop standards, *What's New*. While it received lukewarm reviews, it was a considerable hit, reaching No. 3 on the charts and selling over two million copies. Ronstadt's next two albums—*Lush Life* (1984) and *For Sentimental Reasons* (1986)—were also albums of pre-rock standards recorded with Riddle. At the end of 1986, Ronstadt

returned to contemporary pop, recording "Somewhere Out There," the theme to the animated *An American Tail*, with James Ingram; the single became a No. 2 hit. She also returned to her country roots in 1987, recording the *Trio* album with Dolly Parton and Emmylou Harris. That same year, Ronstadt recorded *Canciones de mi Padre*, a set of traditional Mexican songs that became a surprise hit. Two years later, she recorded *Cry Like a Rainstorm—Howl Like the Wind*—her first contemporary pop album since 1982's *Get Closer*. Featuring four duets with Aaron Neville, including the No. 2 hit "Don't Know Much," the album sold over two million copies. Ronstadt returned to traditional Mexican and Spanish material with *Mas Canciones* (1991) and *Frenesi* (1992). She returned to pop with 1994's *Winter Light*, which failed to generate a hit single, as did 1995's *Feels Like Home*. In 1996, she released the children's album *Dedicated to the One I Love*. —*Stephen Thomas Erlewine*

Hand Sown Home Grown / 1969 / Capitol ✦✦
Linda Ronstadt's debut album is a transitional effort, as the vocalist began to abandon the folk leanings of the Stone Poneys for a relaxed country-rock approach. Several of the songs are well performed, but the majority of the music is unfocused and Ronstadt occasionally sounds unsure of herself. —*Stephen Thomas Erlewine*

Silk Purse / 1970 / Capitol ✦✦✦
While it followed the same musical approach of the debut, *Silk Purse* was an improvement on *Hand Sown Home Grown*, featuring more confident vocals from Linda Ronstadt and a stronger selection of songs, including "Lovesick Blues" and "Long Long Time." —*Stephen Thomas Erlewine*

Linda Ronstadt / 1971 / Capitol ✦✦✦
Linda Ronstadt's self-titled third album captured the singer moving away from the rootsier charms of her first two albums, toward a more polished take on country-rock. Supported by the Eagles throughout the record, Ronstadt turns in a strong performance, aided by a fine selection of material, including "Rock Me on the Water," "Crazy Arms," "I Still Miss Someone," and "I Fall to Pieces." —*Stephen Thomas Erlewine*

Don't Cry Now / 1973 / Asylum ✦✦✦
Don't Cry Now expanded the pop-rock concessions of *Linda Ronstadt*, and the result was the singer's first genuine hit record, peaking at No. 45 on the charts. —*Stephen Thomas Erlewine*

Different Drum / 1974 / Capitol ✦✦✦✦
Different Drum collects the highlights of Linda Ronstadt's first three solo albums, adding five Stone Poneys tracks, including the hit "Different Drum," for good measure. It misses some fine tracks from her solo records, but the album remains a fine introduction to her early years. —*Stephen Thomas Erlewine*

☆ **Heart Like a Wheel** / 1974 / Capitol ✦✦✦✦✦
Following the same formula as her early records, *Heart Like a Wheel* doesn't appear to be a great breakthrough on the surface. However, Ronstadt comes into her own on this mix of oldies and contemporary classics. Backed by a fleet of Los Angeles musicians, Ronstadt sings with vigor and passion, helping bring the music alive. But what really makes *Heart Like a Wheel* a breakthrough is the inventive arrangements that producer Peter Asher, Ronstadt and the studio musicians have developed. Finding the right note for each song—whether it's the soulful reworking of "When Will I Be Loved," the hit "You're No Good," or the laidback folk-rock of "Willing"—the musicians help turn *Heart Like a Wheel* into a veritable catalog of Californian soft-rock, and it stands as a landmark of '70s mainstream pop-rock. —*Stephen Thomas Erlewine*

Prisoner in Disguise / 1975 / Asylum ✦✦✦✦
Linda Ronstadt followed the commercial and critical breakthrough success of *Heart Like a Wheel* with *Prisoner in Disguise*, a record that essentially repeated the formula of its predecessor. While it lacked the consistency of *Heart Like a Wheel*, it was thoroughly enjoyable, highlighted by sturdy remakes of the Motown classics "Tracks of My Tears" and "Heat Wave." —*Stephen Thomas Erlewine*

● **Greatest Hits, Vol. 1** / 1976 / Asylum ✦✦✦✦
Greatest Hits, Vol. 1 is good 12-track collection of Linda Ronstadt's biggest hits from the early '70s, beginning with the Stone Poneys' "Different Drum" and running through "Tracks of My Tears," from 1975's *Prisoner in Disguise*. In between, all of her best-known songs—"You're No Good," "When Will I Be Loved," "Heat Wave"—are included, plus selected minor hits, making it an excellent overview of her peak years. —*Stephen Thomas Erlewine*

Hasten Down the Wind / 1976 / Asylum ✦✦✦
Again, Linda Ronstadt repeats her slick, Californian pop/country-rock formula on *Hasten Down the Wind*. When the material is first-rate—such as "That'll Be the Day" or "Crazy"—Ronstadt's performances are terrific, but on the subpar songs—such as the three Karla Bonoff numbers—she's dragged down with her material. —*Stephen Thomas Erlewine*

A Retrospective / 1977 / Capitol ✦✦✦✦
A nice compilation of primarily country-influenced, pre-hit material.
—*Cub Koda*

Simple Dreams / 1977 / Asylum ✦✦✦✦
Featuring a broader array of styles than any previous Linda Ronstadt record, *Simple Dreams* reconfirms her substantial talents as an interpretive singer. Ronstadt sings Dolly Parton ("I Never Will Marry") with the same conviction as the Rolling Stones ("Tumbling Dice"), and she manages to update Roy Orbison ("Blue Bayou") and direct attention to the caustic, fledgling singer-songwriter Warren Zevon ("Poor Poor Pitiful Me" and "Carmelita"). The consistently adventurous material and Ronstadt's powerful performance makes the record rival *Heart Like a Wheel* in sheer overall quality. —*Stephen Thomas Erlewine*

Living in the U.S.A. / 1978 / Asylum ✦✦✦
On *Living in the USA*, Linda Ronstadt made the ill-advised move to incorporate some current musical trends, such as new wave, into her successful formula. While some of the record sounds good, the majority of the album is poorly executed, particularly her take on Elvis Costello's "Alison." —*Stephen Thomas Erlewine*

Greatest Hits, Vol. 2 / 1980 / Asylum ✦✦✦✦
Picking up where the first volume left off, *Greatest Hits, Vol. 2* contains Linda Ronstadt's biggest hits from the late '70s, including such songs as "It's So Easy," "Hurt So Bad," "Blue Bayou," "Back in the USA," "Poor Poor Pitiful Me," "Ooh Baby Baby," "How Do I Make You" and "Tumbling Dice." Since Ronstadt's late-'70s albums tended to be a little spotty, this is a very useful summation of their highlights. —*Stephen Thomas Erlewine*

Mad Love / 1980 / Asylum ✦✦
Linda Ronstadt made a full-fledged, new wave-influenced pop album with *Mad Love*. It's an unfocused, stilted effort that suggested her career at the top of the charts was coming to a close. —*Stephen Thomas Erlewine*

Get Closer / 1982 / Asylum ✦✦
Get Closer was another successful album for Ronstadt, even though it didn't perform up to her platinum standards. Part of the reason for the relative lack of success was the lackluster material, which again signals that Ronstadt had lost touch with the mainstream pop scene. —*Stephen Thomas Erlewine*

What's New / 1983 / Asylum ✦✦✦
Instead of trying to compete with a newer, fashion-conscious pop marketplace, Linda Ronstadt removed herself from the rat race, recording an album of traditional-pop standards with Nelson Riddle. Ronstadt's voice isn't always showcased to a fine effect on these songs, but the record is an interesting change of pace. And it would have been more interesting if she hadn't repeated its formula on her next two records. —*Stephen Thomas Erlewine*

Lush Life / 1984 / Asylum ✦✦
What's New illustrated that Linda Ronstadt was no longer interested in contemporary pop and since it was a surprise success, there was no reason not to repeat the formula on *Lush Life*. Working again with Nelson Riddle, Ronstadt runs through several pop standards—"When I Fall in Love," "Sophisticated Lady," "Falling in Love Again," "It Never Entered My Mind"—which are given lush, even syrupy, arrangements. Ronstadt's voice isn't entirely suited to this material, but she sings it professionally and *Lush Life* is just as effective as *What's New*, which means it's fine, but it's not as good as the real thing. —*Stephen Thomas Erlewine*

For Sentimental Reasons / Feb. 1986 / Asylum ✦✦
For Sentimental Reasons was the last traditional pop album Linda Ronstadt recorded with Nelson Riddle, and it is virtually indistinguishable from its two predecessors—it has the same sweeping arrangements, and her voice remains adequate, not spectacular. That said, *For Sentimental Reasons* is notable since it contains a high percentage of familiar—some might say overly-familiar—standards like "When You Wish Upon a Star," "Bewitched, Bothered and Bewildered," "My Funny Valentine," "Am I Blue" and "Round Midnight," which might make the album more appealing to casual fans who want to hear Ronstadt sing songs they know if they're going to hear her in this setting. —*Stephen Thomas Erlewine*

Round Midnight with Nelson Riddle and his Orchestra / 1986 / Asylum ✦✦✦
Round Midnight is a triple-disc box set that compiles all three of the traditional pop albums Linda Ronstadt recorded with Nelson Riddle (*What's New*, *Lush Life*, and *For Sentimental Reasons*). Only dedicated fans will need to own all three of the albums, and, for those listeners, this is a classy way to purchase them. —*Stephen Thomas Erlewine*

Canciones de Mi Padre / 1987 / Asylum ✦✦✦
Ronstadt's first all-Spanish album is a heartfelt tribute to her heritage. It also contains some of her finest performances of the '80s. —*AMG*

The Trio / 1987 / Warner Brothers ✦✦✦✦
Teaming up with Dolly Parton and Emmylou Harris, Linda Ronstadt recorded the country album *Trio* in 1987. It wasn't a great departure for Ronstadt, since her early records were almost all country-rock, yet it's still startling to hear how well she blends with Parton and Harris on this set of largely acoustic, neo-traditionalist country. It's a warm, charming, and thoroughly endearing album, and it's the best record Ronstadt has made in years. —*Stephen Thomas Erlewine*

Cry Like a Rainstorm—Howl Like the Wind / Sep. 1989 / Asylum ✦✦✦
On the strength of the hit duet with Aaron Neville, "Don't Know Much," *Cry Like a Rainstorm—Howl Like the Wind* returned Linda Ronstadt to the top of the charts. The album was a collection of well-constructed adult contemporary pop, which suits her voice better than the traditional pop she recorded during the mid-'80s. Musically, *Cry Like a Rainstorm* isn't as adventurous as *Canciones de Mi Padre*, nor is it as consistent as *Trio*, the album she recorded with Emmylou Harris and Dolly Parton, but it is her most satisfying mainstream pop album she has made since the late '70s. —*Stephen Thomas Erlewine*

Mas Canciones / 1990 / Asylum ✦✦✦
Mas Canciones is a thoroughly enjoyable collection of Spanish and Mexican songs that is arguably stronger than its predecessor, since Ronstadt sounds more comfortable with the material than ever before. —*Stephen Thomas Erlewine*

Frenesi / Aug. 25, 1992 / Asylum ✦✦
Frenesi is Linda Ronstadt's third in a series of Spanish-language releases. This one—inspired by her work on the soundtrack to the film *Mambo Kings*—tackles Afro-Cuban pop and jazz. While some tracks, especially "Entre Abismos," swing mightily, there's little that sounds street level or rootsy about these sessions. I can't help picturing a wind-up lounge band holding court at some tourist-trap Holiday Inn in Acapulco. —*Roch Parisien*

Winter Light / 1994 / Asylum ✦✦✦
Feels Like Home / Mar. 14, 1995 / Asylum ✦✦
Feels Like Home is a blandly professional collection of smooth, colorless adult-contemporary pop highlighted by an enjoyable, if slightly misguided, cover of Neil Young's "After the Gold Rush." —*Stephen Thomas Erlewine*

Dedicated to the One I Love / Jun. 1996 / Elektra ✦✦✦
Throughout her career, Linda Ronstadt has always interpreted rock and pop classics, but *Dedicated to the One I Love* is different from the rest of her albums—this time around, she reinterprets the oldies as children's lullabies. All of the songs are given lush, sweet, and soft arrangements, even when that approach is ludicrous; it might be a cute idea to deliver Queen's "We Will Rock You" as a rock-a-bye chant, but in practice it is simply ridiculous. Fortunately, most of the album relies on songs—"Be My Baby," "In My Room"—that can be sung as lullabies, and she sings them very well. Of course, the appeal of *Dedicated to the One I Love* is limited—only baby boomer parents will really find this interesting—but fans that find the concept intriguing won't be disappointed by the results. —*Stephen Thomas Erlewine*

The Roots

f. 1989, Philadelphia, PA
Hip Hop, Alternative Rap, Jazz-Rap
Though popular success has largely eluded the Roots, the Philadelphia group showed the way for live rap, building on Stetsasonic's "hip-hop band" philosophy of the mid-'80s by using strictly live instrumentation at their concerts and in the studio. Though their album works have been inconsistent affairs, more intent on building grooves than pushing songs, the Roots' live shows are among the best in the business.

The Roots' focus on live music began back in 1987 when rapper Black Thought (Tariq Trotter) and drummer ?uestlove (Ahmir Khalib Thompson) became friends at the Philadelphia High School for Creative Performing Arts. Since the duo had no money for the DJ essentials—two turntables and a microphone, plus a mixer and plenty of vinyl—they recreated classic hip-hop tracks with ?uestlove's drum kit backing Black Thought's rhymes. Playing around school, on the sidewalk and later at talent shows, the pair began to earn money and hooked up with bassist Hub (Leon Hubbard) and rapper Malik B. Moving from the street to local clubs, the Roots became a highly tipped underground act around Philadelphia and New York. When the group was invited to represent stateside hip-hop at a concert in Germany, they recorded an album to sell at shows; the result, *Organix*, was released in 1993 on Remedy Records. With a music-industry buzz surrounding their activities, the Roots entertained offers from several labels before signing with DGC that same year.

The Roots' first major-label album, *Do You Want More?!!!??!*, was released in January 1995; forsaking usual hip-hop protocol, the album was produced without any samples or previously recorded material. It peaked just outside the Top 100, but was mostly ignored by fans of hip-hop. Instead, *Do You Want More?!!!??!* made more tracks in alternative circles, partly due to the Roots playing the second stage at Lollapalooza that summer. The band also journeyed to the Montreux Jazz Festival in Switzerland. Two of the guests on the album who had toured around with the band, human beatbox Rahzel the Godfather of Noyze—previously a performer with Grandmaster Flash and LL Cool J—and Scott Storch (later Kamal) became permanent members of the group.

Early in 1996, the Roots released "Clones," the trailer single for their second album. It hit the Rap Top Five, and created a good buzz for the album. The following September, *Illadelph Halflife* appeared and made No. 21 on the album charts. Much like its predecessor, though, the Roots' second LP was a difficult listen. It made several very small concessions to mainstream rap—the band sampled material which they had recorded earlier at jam sessions—but failed to make a hit of their unique sound. *—John Bush*

Do You Want More?!!!??! / Jan. 1995 / DGC ✦✦✦✦
Because the Roots were pioneering a new style during the early '90s, the band was forced to draw its own blueprints for its major-label debut album. It's not surprising then, that *Do You Want More?!!!??!* sounds more like a document of old-school hip-hop than contemporary rap. The album is based on loose grooves and laidback improvisation, and where most hip-hoppers use samples to draw songs together and provide a chorus, the Roots just keep on jamming. The problem is that the Roots' jams begin to take the place of true songs, leaving most tracks with only that groove to speak for them. The notable exceptions—"Mellow My Man" and "Datskat," among others—use different strategies to command attention: the sounds of a human beatbox, the great keyboard work of Scott Storch, and contributions from several jazz players (trombonist Joshua Roseman, saxophonist Steve Coleman and vocalist Cassandra Wilson). By the close of the album, those tracks are what the listener remembers, not the lightweight grooves. *—John Bush*

● **Illadelph Halflife** / Sep. 24, 1996 / DGC ✦✦✦✦
The Roots always had ambition, which theoretically placed them ahead of many of their mid-'90s hip-hop contemporaries. Where many of their peers settled for gangsta cliches, tedious displays of lyrical skills, alternative hip-hop or half-hearted jazz-rap fusions, the Roots decided to take an entirely different route by merging streetlevel rhythms with jazz and old-school technique, and performing everything on live instruments. While their approach works well in theory, it doesn't always work in practice. Though it is decidedly tougher and more adventurous than the group's debut, *Illadelph Halflife* just misses the mark. Part of the problem with the record is the fact that it doesn't capture the relentless energy of their live show; without the reckless, rampaging momentum of their live show, the record is only sporadically engaging. Still, the best moments of *Illadelph Halflife* demonstrate the Roots are an exciting, inventive band that have great potential—they just haven't quite fulfilled it yet. *—Leo Stanley*

Diana Ross (Diane Earle)

b. Mar. 26, 1944, Detroit, MI
Vocals / Soul, Dance-Pop, Disco, Urban, Motown, Pop-Rock
As a solo artist, Diana Ross is one of the most successful female singers of the rock era. If you factor in her work as the lead singer of the Supremes in the 1960s, she may be *the* most successful.

With her friends Mary Wilson, Florence Ballard, and Barbara Martin, Ross formed the Primettes vocal quartet in 1959. In 1960, they were signed to local Motown Records, changing their name to the Supremes in 1961. Martin then left, and the group continued as a trio. Over the next eight years, the Supremes (renamed "Diana Ross and the Supremes" in 1967, when Cindy Birdsong replaced Ballard) scored 12 No. 1 pop hits. After the last one, "Someday We'll Be Together" (October 1969), Ross launched a solo career.

Motown initially paired her with writer/producers Nickolas Ashford and Valerie Simpson, who gave her four Top 40 pop hits, including the No. 1 "Ain't No Mountain High Enough" (July 1970).

Ross branched out into acting, starring in a film biography of Billie Holiday, *Lady Sings the Blues* (November 1972). The soundtrack went to No. 1, and Ross was nominated for an Academy Award.

She returned to record-making with the Top Ten album *Touch Me in the Morning* (June 1973) and its chart-topping title song. This was followed by a duet album with Marvin Gaye, *Diana & Marvin* (October 1973), that produced three chart hits. Ross acted in her second movie, *Mahogany* (October 1975), and it brought her another chart-topping single in the theme song, "Do You Know Where You're Going To." That and her next No. 1, the disco-oriented "Love Hangover" (March 1976), were featured on her second album to be titled simply *Diana Ross* (February 1976), which rose into the Top Ten.

Ross' third film role came in *The Wiz* (October 1978). *The Boss* (May 1979) was a gold-selling album, followed by the platinum-selling *Diana* (May 1980) (the second of her solo albums with that name, though the

other, a 1971 TV soundtrack, had an exclamation mark). It featured the No. 1 single "Upside Down" and the Top Ten hit "I'm Coming Out."

Ross scored a third Top Ten hit in 1980 singing the title theme from the movie *It's My Turn*. She then scored the biggest hit of her career with another movie theme, duetting with Lionel Richie on "Endless Love" (June 1981). It was her last big hit on Motown; after more than 20 years, she decamped for RCA. She was rewarded immediately with a million-selling album, titled after her remake of the old Frankie Lymon and the Teenagers hit, "Why Do Fools Fall in Love," which became her next Top Ten hit. The album also included the Top Ten hit "Mirror, Mirror."

Silk Electric (October 1982) was a gold-seller, featuring the Top Ten hit "Muscles," written and produced by Michael Jackson. *Swept Away* (September 1984) was another successful album, containing the hit "Missing You," but Ross had trouble selling records in the second half of the 1980s. By 1989, she had returned to Motown, and by 1993 was turning more to pop standards, notably on the concert album *Diana Ross Live: The Lady Sings . . . Jazz & Blues, Stolen Moments* (April 1993). Motown released a four-CD/cassette boxed set retrospective, *Forever Diana*, in October 1993, and the singer published her autobiography in 1994. *—William Ruhlmann*

Diana Ross / May 1970 / Motown ✦✦✦✦
This remains arguably her finest solo work at Motown and perhaps her best ever; it was certainly among her most stunning. Everyone who doubted whether Diana Ross could sustain a career outside the Supremes found out immediately that she would be a star. The single "Reach Out and Touch (Somebody's Hand)" remains a staple in her shows, and is still her finest message track. *—Ron Wynn*

Lady Sings the Blues / Dec. 1971 / Motown ✦✦✦
Her biggest album as a solo act, Diana Ross forever ended any association with the Supremes after this film. She not only got an Oscar nomination and more roles, she really did capture the spirit and flavor, if not the sound and timbre, of Billie Holiday's music; her performance was the film's only saving grace. *—Ron Wynn*

Diana / May 1980 / Motown ✦✦✦
Coming off four Top Ten hits in three years for their group Chic, producers Bernard Edwards and Nile Rodgers were *the* hot R&B/disco team of the day when they wrote and produced Diana Ross' second album, named simply *Diana*. (The first was her 1971 TV soundtrack, *Diana!*) The result was Ross' best selling album ever, paced by her biggest singles hit yet, "Upside Down," and its Top Ten follow-up, "I'm Coming Out." For the most part, disco productions tended to emphasize the beat over the voice, and it might be argued that, but for the billing, Ross had been reduced to guest vocalist on her own album. But it was exactly her struggle to retain an identity beyond the groove that made this music more compelling than Chic's records. *Diana* marked an important comeback for Ross, who had struggled in the late '70s after the early successes of her solo career. She celebrated by leaving Motown for a six-year, five-album sojourn at RCA. *—William Ruhlmann*

Diana: The Ultimate Collection / Oct. 1993 / EMI ✦✦✦
This compilation attempts to condense Diana Ross' most successful recordings into one 20-song, 71 1/2 minute disc. Well, there's good news and bad news. The good news is that Ross (who produced the album, which is to say picked the tracks) has included six of her Supremes recordings from the 1960s (one of them, "Someday We'll Be Together," in a new disco mix) and licensed a few songs from her stay at RCA in the 1980s, making this the most wide ranging of her compilations. The bad news is that she has jettisoned many possible hits (only ten of her 18 chart toppers are included) in the name of featuring four tracks from the 1990s that do not rank with her best, either aesthetically or in terms of popularity. In other words, Ross has constructed the album as she might a concert—a sprinkling of early Supremes hits, all her biggest solo hits, and what she considers the highlights of her current work. The result is a less than perfect, or "ultimate" portrait, since the selection implies erroneously that a forgettable piece of tripe like the 1991 Top 40 hit "When You Tell Me That You Love Me" is as much a milestone in the Ross catalog as "You Can't Hurry Love" or "Upside Down" (and that Ross remained as significant an artist in 1994 as she was in 1964 and 1974). But the album still makes a good sampler of Ross' entire 30+-year career for beginners. *—William Ruhlmann*

★ **Anthology** / Sep. 28, 1995 / Motown ✦✦✦✦✦
The double-disc set *Anthology* contains all of Diana Ross' solo hits for Motown Records, from "Ain't No Mountain High Enough" to "Endless Love." It's a comprehensive collection, featuring all of her biggest hits plus many important album tracks and smaller hit singles. Since it doesn't delve too deeply into obscurities and contains all of Ross' most popular songs, *Anthology* is the definitive career compilation for fans who want more than just the standard cuts but are unwilling to explore the original albums or invest in the box set. *—Stephen Thomas Erlewine*

Greatest Hits: RCA Years / Mar. 25, 1997 / RCA ✦✦✦✦
Diana Ross' glossy 1981-1987 tenure on RCA is the subject of this 18-track collection, which includes her hit tribute to the late Marvin Gaye, "Missing You." Other highlights include her cover of Frankie Lymon and the Teenagers' "Wht Do Fools Fall in Love," "Mirror, Mirror," "Swept Away" and a solo version of the chart-topping "Endless Love." —*Jason Ankeny*

Rotary Connection

f. 1966, Chicago, IL, **db.** 1974
Soul, Psychedelic, Pop-Rock, Acid Rock
The brainchild of Chess Records executive Marshall Chess, Rotary Connection represented the label's most successful attempt to expand into the rock/psychedelic market in the late '60s. Chess recruited three members of a white rock band, added a couple of female singers and Chess vocalist Sidney Barnes, and backed them up with star musicians from Chess' house band, including guitarist Pete Cosey and bassist Phil Upchurch. Arranger Charles Stepney co-wrote a lot of songs on their debut album, a desperately trendy effort that combined soul, folk-rock, psychedelic sitars, and quasi-classical themes and orchestration. Yet the band remains most noted for one of the female vocalists, Minnie Riperton, who graced many of the tracks with her impossibly high operatic sopranos. The self-titled debut album balanced original material with unlikely, even absurd, covers of contemporary rock hits by Dylan, the Rolling Stones, and the Beatles. "Amen" and "Lady Jane" were underground FM-radio favorites, and the record sold very well in Chicago and a few other Midwestern cities, though it didn't create much of a stir elsewhere. Rotary Connection hung on for five more albums, but it's the first record that listeners remember, if they recall the group at all. Riperton, her freaky five-octave range intact, went on to brief solo stardom in the 1970s. —*Richie Unterberger*

● **Rotary Connection** / 1967 / Chess ✦✦✦✦
Sure, this sort of throw-in-all-the-tricks sort of psychedelia is extremely dated. A psychedelic cover of "Soul Man," or a version of "Like a Rolling Stone" that wipes the lyrics off the verses to create a near-instrumental? Yet at the same time, this has the sort of headstrong risk-taking that, as indulgent as it was, makes the record quite an interesting curiosity, even if it's a period piece. Charles Stepney's fusion of psychedelic rock arrangements and baroque classical arrangements is most unusual, and occasionally graceful and beautiful. Minnie Riperton's ghostly trills, here used for background rather than lead, sound like nothing else. The Rotary Connection recorded half a dozen albums, but this debut is the one you want, and it's a lot easier to find after its CD reissue in 1996. —*Richie Unterberger*

David Lee Roth

b. Oct. 10, 1955, Bloomington, IN
Vocals / Hard Rock, Pop-Rock, Heavy Metal
With Van Halen, vocalist David Lee Roth raised the role of a heavy metal frontman to a performance art. After the band's commercial breakthrough with the *1984* album, Roth released *Crazy from the Heat*, a 1985 EP that displayed his blatant pop roots, covering everything from the Beach Boys to Louis Prima. With two hit singles, *Crazy from the Heat* confirmed Roth's solo commercial potential, prompting his decision to leave Van Halen in June of 1985.
For his first full-length album, 1986's *Eat 'em and Smile*, Roth hired guitarist Steve Vai and bassist Billy Sheehan for a grossly exaggerated take on heavy arena rock. It was a mammoth hit, as was the more pop-oriented follow-up, *Skyscraper*. After *Skyscraper*, Vai and Sheehan left to form their own bands (the Steve Vai Band and Mr. Big, respectively). Roth put together a new band for 1991's *A Little Ain't Enough*, which was his first album not to go platinum. Sensing that it was time for a change, he tried to refashion himself as a slick hard rock singer-songwriter with 1994's *Your Filthy Little Mouth*, but it resulted in his least successful album yet. —*Stephen Thomas Erlewine*

Crazy from the Heat / 1985 / Warner Brothers ✦✦✦✦
For his first solo effort, Roth stripped away the gonzo guitars that are Van Halen's trademark and accentuated his lounge-lizard-as-rock-star persona, resulting in an EP that succeeds because of that persona, not because the music is anything special. Certainly, he doesn't add anything to "California Girls" and "Just a Gigolo/I Ain't Got Nobody" other than his joking, over-the-top vocals. Then again, that's all he needs to do. —*Stephen Thomas Erlewine*

● **Eat 'em & Smile** / 1986 / Warner Brothers ✦✦✦✦
This flamboyant frontman is flanked by bassist Billy Sheehan and guitar-shredder Steve Vai, blazing the solo trail with these big and bawdy rockers, like "Goin' Crazy!" —*Donna DiChario*

Skyscraper / 1988 / Warner Brothers ✦✦✦
On his second full-length solo album, Roth turns down the guitars, adds more melody, and makes a more polished, but less interesting record,

highlighted by the soaring pop of "Just Like Paradise." —*Stephen Thomas Erlewine*

A Little Ain't Enough / Apr. 1991 / Warner Brothers ✦✦
Recorded with a new backing band, *A Little Ain't Enough* doesn't feature the gonzo instrumental kick of *Eat 'em and Smile*, nor is it a stab at pop-craft like *Skyscraper*. Instead, it's an attempt to regain the energy that fueled Van Halen's early albums, but Roth can't work up enough steam to make the driving riffs convincing or memorable. —*Stephen Thomas Erlewine*

Your Filthy Little Mouth / Mar. 8, 1994 / Warner Brothers ✦✦
Although the title wouldn't indicate it, *Your Filthy Little Mouth* was a retreat from the thundering hard rock of *A Little Ain't Enough*. David Lee Roth kept some of the pile-driving guitar riffs that always gave his records a foundation, but he added a smoother pop sensibility, along with self-consciously clever lyrics in an attempt to become a mature hard-rocker for all aging yuppies. It didn't work, either commercially or artistically, since most of the songs didn't have enough hooks to make them memorable. —*Stephen Thomas Erlewine*

The Roulettes

f. 1961, Liverpool, England
Group / British Invasion
An underrated British quartet made up of John Rogan (bass), Russ Ballard (lead guitar), Peter Thorpe (rhythm guitar), and Bob Henrit (drums), the Roulettes featured future Argent alumnus Russ Ballard on lead guitar. They were originally formed as a backing band for vocalist Adam Faith, who enjoyed a massively successful light rock 'n' roll career in the early '60s in England. Beginning in 1963 with the start of the rock 'n' roll explosion coming out of Liverpool, the group was somewhat reorganized, and their and Faith's work together became much more assertive; the result was Faith's last big hit, "The First Time," in August of 1963.
The group began recording on their own for EMI in late 1963 and revealed themselves as an above-average group, fully competitive on a musical level with acts like the Searchers and the Hollies. Their records, though fewer in number, display many of the same virtues found on the better-known work of the Beatles and the Searchers, including soaring harmonies behind strong lead vocals, crisp guitar playing, and a good ear for memorable hooks. Ballard and Henrit also appeared on "Concrete and Clay," a major hit for the acoustic rock outfit Unit Four Plus Two, but the Roulettes' own records stubbornly failed to make the charts. By 1965, they'd split with Adam Faith, but the concentration on their own careers didn't change the inexplicably lackluster performance of their records.
The group soldiered on through 1967 without any chart success, playing shows on the European continent, where any good British rock band could still earn a decent living. Finally, Ballard and Henrit joined Unit Four Plus Two, while Thorpe and Rogan left the music business. Following the breakup of Unit Four Plus Two in 1968, Ballard and Henrit hooked up with Rod Argent and Chris White, late of the Zombies, and formed Argent, a quartet that, for a brief time in the early 1970s, enjoyed some of the chart success that had eluded the Roulettes throughout their history. —*Bruce Eder*

Stakes & Chips / 1965 / BGO ✦✦✦✦
The definitive Roulettes collection, 22 songs covering the group's entire recorded history, with more highlights than one would expect to find. "Bad Time," "I'll Remember Tonight" (which is more familiar to Americans in its cover version by the Mugwumps), "Stubborn Kind of Fellow," and "I Hope He Breaks Your Heart" are priceless, and most of the rest isn't far behind. The sound is excellent, and the notes are entertaining and wonderfully detailed. —*Bruce Eder*

● **Russ, Bob, Pete and Mod** / 1983 / Edsel ✦✦✦✦
A superb collection of singles, B-Sides, and album tracks. All are enjoyable and memorable, especially the track "I'll Remember Tonight." (Import) —*Bruce Eder*

The Best of Adam Faith / 1989 / EMI ✦✦✦
Among the 26 songs here are four excellent numbers that the Roulettes cut backing Adam Faith, which belong in any complete collection of their work, as does that never-reissued *Faith Alive*. —*Bruce Eder*

Roxette

f. 1984, Halmstad, Sweden
Pop-Rock
It's tempting to write Roxette off as nothing more than a shallow pop-rock band, but their shameless hooks are precisely what makes them so enjoyable. Roxette has a knack for writing extremely catchy and simple hooks and melodies that are sweet but not saccharine; it's radio-friendly pop, but the hooks don't wear thin with repeated plays. The duo of guitarist Per Gessle and vocalist Marie Fredriksson released an album in 1986 that didn't display much of their talents, but the infectious follow-up, 1988's *Look Sharp!*, brought them to the top of the charts in America

and England; 1991's *Joyride* was almost equally successful. After a couple of years off, Roxette returned with a new album, *Crash! Boom! Bang!*, in 1994; *Baladas en Espanol* followed in 1997. *—Stephen Thomas Erlewine*

Look Sharp! / 1988 / EMI America ✦✦✦✦
A fun, dynamic debut, it features the hit singles "The Look," "Dressed for Success," "Listen to Your Heart," and "Dangerous." *—Dan Heilman*

Joyride / Mar. 1991 / EMI America ✦✦✦
Their second album, featuring infectious, solid song construction from Gessle and dynamite singing from Fredriksson. "Knock on Every Door," "Watercolours in the Rain," and the title track are among the highlights. *—Cub Koda*

Tourism (Songs from Studios, Stages, Hotelrooms & Other Strange Places) / 1992 / EMI America ✦✦✦
A completely live hits package from Roxette's first world tour (1991-1992), this features both concert and in-studio performances of some of their biggest hits, including "Joyride," "The Look," and "It Must Have Been Love." It was recorded in their native Stockholm, as well as in Zurich, Buenos Aires, and Sydney, Australia. *—AMG*

Crash! Boom! Bang! / Oct. 4, 1994 / EMI America ✦✦

● **Don't Bore Us . . . Get to the Chorus: Greatest Hits Vol. 1** / Nov. 1995 / EMI ✦✦✦✦
Roxette provided artificial pop thrills of the highest order, crafting a series of international hit singles that were as sweet as sugar and nearly as synthetic as plastic. However, that synthetic element is what made their hits so infectious—they were carefully crafted, as if by a machine, filled with catchy hooks and memorable melodies. As *Don't Bore Us . . . Get to the Chorus* proves, they didn't turn out winning singles at a rapid rate—there's a fair amount of dreck here—but when they were on, they produced some first-rate pop singles, particularly "The Look" and "Joyride." *—Stephen Thomas Erlewine*

Roxy Music

f. 1971, Newcastle, England, db. 1983
Art-Rock/Progressive-Rock, Glam Rock, Pop-Rock, Proto-Punk
Evolving from the late '60s art-rock movement, Roxy Music had a fascination with fashion, glamor, cinema, pop-art, and the avant-garde, that seperated the band from their contemporaries. Dressed in bizarre, stylish constumes, the group played a defiantly experimental variation of art-rock which vacillated between avant-rock and sleek pop hooks. During the early '70s, the group was driven by the creative tension between Bryan Ferry and Brian Eno, who each pulled in separate directions. Ferry had a fondness for American soul and Beatlesque art-pop, while Eno was intrigued with deconstructing rock with amateurish experimentalism inspired by the Velvet Underground. This incarnation of Roxy Music may have only recorded two albums, but it inspired a legion of imitators—not only the glam-rockers of the early '70s, but art-rockers and new wave pop groups of the late '70s. Following Eno's departure, Roxy Music continued with its arty inclinations for a few albums before gradually working in elements of disco and soul. Within a few years, the group had developed a sophisticated, seductive soul-pop that relied on Ferry's stylish crooning. By the early '80s, the group had developed into a vehicle for Ferry, so it was no surprise that he disbanded the group at the height of its commercial success in the early '80s to pursue a solo career.

The son of a coal miner, Bryan Ferry (vocals, keyboards) had studied art with Richard Hamilton at the University of Newcastle before forming Roxy Music in 1971. While at university, he sang in rock bands, joining the R&B group the Gas Board, which also featured bassist Graham Simpson. Ferry and Simpson decided to form their own band toward the end of 1970, eventually recruiting Andy Mackay (saxophone), who had previously played oboe with the London Symphony Orchestra. Through Mackay, Brian Eno joined the band. By the summer of 1971, the group—which was originally called Roxy, but a name change was necessary after the discovery of an American band called Roxy—had recruited classical percussionist Dexter Lloyd and guitarist Roger Bunn through an ad in *Melody Maker;* both musicians left within a month, but they did record the group's initial demos. Another ad was placed in *Melody Maker,* and this time the group landed drummer Paul Thompson and guitarist Davy O'List, who had previously played with the Nice. O'List left by the beginning of 1972 and was replaced by Phil Manzanera, a former member of Quiet Sun. Prior to recording their first album, Simpson left the band. Roxy Music never replaced him permanently; instead, they hired new bassists for each record and tour, beginning with Rik Kenton, who appeared on their eponymous debut for Island Records.

Produced by Peter Sinfield of King Crimson, *Roxy Music* climbed into the British Top Ten in the summer of 1972; shortly afterward, the non-LP single "Virginia Plain" rocketed into the British Top Ten, followed by the non-LP "Pyjamarama" in early 1973. While Roxy Music

had become a sensation in England and Europe, due to their clever amaglamation of high and kitsch culture, they had trouble getting a foothold in the United States. Both *Roxy Music* and the group's second album, 1973's *For Your Pleasure,* which was recorded with bassist John Porter, were greeted with enthusiasm in the UK, but virtually ignored in the US. Frustrated with Ferry's refusal to record his compositions, Eno left the band after the completion of *For Your Pleasure.* Before recording the third Roxy Music album, Ferry released a solo album, *These Foolish Things,* which was comprised of pop-rock covers.

Released in December of 1973, *Stranded* became the band's first No. 1 album in the UK. *Stranded* was recorded with new Roxy member Eddie Jobson, a multi-instrumentalist who previously played with Curved Air; it was also the first record to feature writing credits for Manzanera and Mackay. The album received a warmer reception in the US than its two predecessors, setting the stage for the breakthrough of *Country Life* in late 1974. Sporting a controversial cover of two models dressed in see-through lingerie, *Country Life* was banned in several stores, and it was eventually replaced with a photo of a forest in the US—*Country Life* was the first Roxy album to break the US Top 40 and became their fourth British Top Ten album. Following a tour with bassist John Wetton, the group recorded *Siren.* Featuring their first American Top 40 hit, the disco-flavored "Love is the Drug," *Siren* was another British Top Ten hit; in the US, it was moderate hit, peaking at No. 50. Following the tour for *Siren,* the band members began working on solo projects—Manzanera formed the prog-rock group 801, and Mackay, and Ferry both began recording solo albums—announcing in the summer of 1976 that they were temporarily breaking up. The live album, *Viva! Roxy Music* was released shortly after the announcement of the group's hiatus.

Roxy Music regrouped in the fall of 1978 after spending 18 months on solo projects. Ferry, Manzanera, Mackay and Thompson added former Ace keyboardist Paul Carrack to the band's lineup and hired Gary Tibbs, formerly of the Vibrators, and ex-Kokomo Alan Spenner as studio bassists; Jobson and Wetton, who were not asked to re-join the band, formed UK. Roxy Music's comeback effort, *Manifesto,* was released in the spring of 1979, and it boasted a sleek, disco-influenced soul-pop sound that was markedly different and more accessible than their earlier records. *Manifesto* confirmed their British popularity, reaching the Top Ten, became their highest-charting US record, peaking at No. 23 on the strength of the single "Dance Away." Roxy Music supported the album with an international tour that featured Carrack and Tibbs; prior to the tour's start, Thompson left the band after breaking his thumb in a motorcycle accident. *Flesh + Blood,* the followup to *Manifesto,* was recorded by just Ferry, Manzanera and Mackay, and a host of studio musicians. Released in the summer of 1980, *Flesh + Blood* became Roxy's second British No. 1 album on the strength of the Top Ten single "Over You"; in America, the album reached the American Top 40. In the spring of 1981, the band's non-LP cover of John Lennon's "Jealous Guy," recorded as a tribute to the slain singer, became the group's only British No. 1 single.

Nearly two years after the release of *Flesh + Blood,* Roxy Music returned in the summer of 1982 with *Avalon.* Marking a new level in the group's production and musical sophistication, *Avalon* became their biggest album, spending three weeks at the top of the British charts and reaching No. 27 on the US charts, generating the British hits "More Than This" and "Take a Chance With Me." The album became the group's only American gold album, and over the years, it worked its way to platinum status. Following a successful supporting tour for *Avalon,* the group released the live EP *Musique/The High Road* in the spring of 1983. The *Avalon* tour turned out to be Roxy Music's final activity as a group. Ferry began to concentrate on his solo career beginning with 1985's *Boys and Girls.* Manzanera and Mackay formed a band called the Explorers in 1985; the pair would record under a variety of guises, as well as pursue solo careers, over the next 15 years. The compilation *Street Life: 20 Great Hits,* which also featured Ferry solo hits, was released in 1989. A year later, *Heart Still Beating,* a live album documenting a 1982 concert, was released. *—Stephen Thomas Erlewine*

Roxy Music / 1972 / Reprise ✦✦✦
Falling halfway between musical primitivism and art-rock ambition, Roxy Music's eponymous debut remains a startling redefinition of rock's boundaries. Simultaneously embracing kitschy glamour and avant-pop, *Roxy Music* shimmers with seductive style and pulsates with disturbing synthetic textures. Although no musician demonstrates much technical skill at this point, they are driven by boundless imagination—Brian Eno's synthesized "treatments" exploit electronic instruments as electronics, instead of trying to shoehorn them into conventional acoustic patterns. Similarly, Bryan Ferry finds that his vampiric croon is at its most effective when it twists conventional melodies, and Phil Manzanera's guitar is terse and unpredictable, while Andy MacKay's saxophone subverts rock 'n' roll cliches by alternating R&B honking with atonal flourishes. But what makes *Roxy Music* such a confident, astonishing debut is how these primitive avant-garde tendencies are married to full-

fledged songs, whether it's the free-form, structure-bending "Remake/Remodel" or the sleek glam of "Virginia Plain," the debut single added to later editions of the album. That was the trick that elevated Roxy Music from an art-school project to the most adventurous rock band of the early '70s. — *Stephen Thomas Erlewine*

☆ **For Your Pleasure** / 1973 / Reprise ✦✦✦✦✦
On Roxy Music's debut, the tensions between Brian Eno and Bryan Ferry propelled their music to great, unexpected heights, and for most of the group's second album, *For Your Pleasure*, the band equals, if not surpasses, those expectations. However, there are a handful of moments where those tensions become unbearable, as when Eno wants to move towards texture and Ferry wants to stay in more conventional rock territory; the nine-minute "The Bogus Man" captures such creative tensions perfectly, and it's easy to see why Eno left the group after the album was completed. Still, those differences result in yet another extraordinary record from Roxy Music, one that demonstrates even more clearly than the debut how avant-garde ideas can flourish in a pop setting. This is especially evident in the driving singles "Do the Strand" and "Editions of You," which pulsate with raw energy and jarring melodic structures. Roxy also illuminates the slower numbers, such as the eerie "In Every Dream Home a Heartache," with atonal, shimmering synthesizers, textures that were unexpected and innovative at the time of its release. Similarly, all of *For Your Pleasure* walks the tightrope between the experimental and the accessible, creating a new vocabulary for rock bands, and one that was exploited heavily in the ensuing decade. — *Stephen Thomas Erlewine*

Stranded / 1973 / Reprise ✦✦✦✦
Without Brian Eno, Roxy Music immediately becomes less experimental, yet it remains adventurous, as *Stranded* illustrates. Under the direction of Bryan Ferry, Roxy moves toward relatively straightforward territory, adding greater layers of piano and heavy guitars. Even without the washes of Eno's synthesizers, Roxy's music remains unsettling on occasion, yet in this new incarnation, they favor more measured material, whether it's the reflective "A Song for Europe" or the shifting textures of "Psalm." Even the rockers, such as the surging "Street Life" and the segmented "Mother of Pearl," are distinguished by subtle songwriting that emphasizes both Ferry's tortured glamour and Roxy's increasingly impressive grasp of sonic detail. — *Stephen Thomas Erlewine*

★ **Country Life** / 1974 / Reprise ✦✦✦✦✦
Continuing with the stylistic developments of *Stranded*, *Country Life* finds Roxy Music at the peak of its powers, alternating between majestic, unsettling art-rock and glamorous, elegant pop-rock. At their best, Roxy combines these two extremes, like on the exhilarating opener "The Thrill of it All," but *Country Life* benefits considerably from the ebb and flow of the group's two extremes, since it showcases the group's deft instrumental execution and their textured, enthralling songwriting. And, in many ways, *Country Life* offers the greatest and most consistent set of Roxy Music songs, illustrating their startling depth. From the sleek rock of "All I Want is You" and "Prairie Rose" to the elegant, string-laced pop of "A Really Good Time," *Country Life* is filled with thrilling songs, and Roxy Music rarely sounded as invigorating as they do here. — *Stephen Thomas Erlewine*

☆ **Siren** / 1975 / Reprise ✦✦✦✦✦
Abandoning the intoxicating blend of art-rock and glam-pop that distinguished *Stranded* and *Country Life*, Roxy Music concentrates on Bryan Ferry's suave, charming crooner persona for the elegantly modern *Siren*. As the discofied opener "Love is the Drug" makes clear, Roxy embraces dance and unabashed pop on *Siren*, weaving them into their sleek, arty sound. It does come at the expense of their artier inclinations, which is part of what distinguished Roxy, but the end result is captivating. Lacking the consistently amazing songs of its predecessor, *Siren* has a thematic consistency that works in its favor, and helps elevate its best songs—"Sentimental Fool," "Both Ends Burning," "Just Another High"—as well as the album itself into the realm of classics. — *Stephen Thomas Erlewine*

Viva! / 1976 / Reprise ✦✦
As Roxy Music took an extended hiatus, the live album *Viva!* was released. Comprised of material recorded on tours from 1973, 1974 and 1975, *Viva!* is a tough, powerful document of Roxy at the peak of their live powers, featuring a fine cross-section of their best work. — *Stephen Thomas Erlewine*

Manifesto / 1979 / Reprise ✦✦✦
Returning to action after four years of solo projects, Roxy Music redefined its sound and agenda on *Manifesto*. More than ever, Roxy sounds like Bryan Ferry's backing band, as the group strips away their art-rock influences, edits out the instrumental interludes in favor of concise pop songs, and adds layers of stylish disco rhythms. Although the songwriting is distressingly inconsistent, there are a number of wonderful moments on the record, particularly in the sighing "Angel Eyes" and the heartbroken "Dance Away." Still, trading sonic adventure for lush, acces-

sible disco-pop isn't entirely satisfactory, even if it is momentarily seductive. — *Stephen Thomas Erlewine*

Flesh + Blood / 1980 / Reprise ✦✦
An even slicker record than *Manifesto*, *Flesh & Blood* precariously balances between alluringly seductive, sophisticated soul-pop and cloying, radio-ready disco-pop. At its best, the album is effortlessly suave and charming—"Over You" is one of their greatest singles, and "Oh Yeah" is nearly as persuasive—but much of the record is devoted to ill-formed, stylish lounge-pop. In particular, the reliance on reworked covers of "In the Midnight Hour" and "Eight Miles High" is distressing, not only because it signals a lack of imagination, but also because it suggests that *Flesh & Blood* is simply a lesser solo effort from Bryan Ferry. And even the handful of undeniably strong moments can't erase the feeling that Roxy Music was beginning to run out of ideas. — *Stephen Thomas Erlewine*

☆ **Avalon** / 1982 / Reprise ✦✦✦✦✦
Flesh & Blood suggested that Roxy Music was at the end of the line, but they regrouped and recorded the lovely *Avalon*, one of their finest albums. Certainly, the lush, elegant soundscapes of *Avalon* are far removed from the edgy avant-pop of their early records, yet it represents another landmark in their career. With its stylish, romantic washes of synthesizers and Ferry's elegant, seductive croon, *Avalon* simultaneously functioned as sophisticated make-out music for yuppies and as the maturation of synth-pop. Ferry was never this romantic or seductive, either with Roxy or as a solo artist, and *Avalon* shimmers with elegance in both its music and its lyrics. "More Than This," "Take a Chance With Me," "While My Heart is Still Beating" and the title track are immaculately crafted and subtle songs, where the shifting synthesizers and murmured vocals gradually reveal the melodies. It's a rich, textured album and a graceful way to end the band's career. — *Stephen Thomas Erlewine*

Atlantic Years (1973-1980) / 1983 / Atco ✦✦✦✦
Atlantic Years (1973-1980) provides the cream of *Flesh + Blood* and *Manifesto* (as well as a couple of key tracks from Roxy's earlier work on Reprise). Overall it lacks the substance of the original 1977 Atco *Greatest Hits* package, which was an essential showcase for their earlier work. — *Rick Clark*

Street Life: 20 Greatest Hits / 1986 / Reprise ✦✦✦✦
While the packaging and song selection leave something to be desired, *Street Life: 20 Greatest Hits* is a strong collection of Roxy Music and Bryan Ferry's crossover hits. Ignoring Roxy's art-rock inclinations, the collection concentrates on latter-day hits like "More Than This," "Over You," "Love Is the Drug," and "Jealous Guy," adding early singles like "Virginia Plain," "Do the Strand" and "Pyjamarama" for good measure. But a large portion of the record is devoted to Ferry's solo material, not only mid-'80s hits like "Slave to Love" but also '70s covers like "A Hard Rain's A-Gonna Fall," "These Foolish Things" and "Let's Stick Together." Consequently, *Street Life* is rather uneven, but it is an adequate collection for anyone that wants all the hits on one disc. — *Stephen Thomas Erlewine*

Thrill of It All / Nov. 20, 1995 / Virgin ✦✦✦✦
Album-rock artists like Roxy Music always make a difficult subject for comprehensive, multi-disc box sets. Frequently, their albums were designed as a cohesive whole and the idea of individual singles never really entered the picture at all. Roxy Music was slightly different than the average art/prog-rock band—not only did they make albums, they also made singles. And that is one of the reasons why the four-disc set *The Thrill of It All* is successful. Roxy's songs stand as individual works, and they make sense outside of their original context, even if they make more sense *within* their original context. Thankfully, the majority of each of their major albums are reproduced on the first three discs of this collection, leaving the fourth disc for non-LP singles, remixes, and B-sides. Most of this material has not been available on CD before, making *The Thrill of it All* essential for collectors. Nevertheless, it's a helpful guide to Roxy's career for casual fans—it contains all of the essential songs and shows why the group was one of the seminal bands of the '70s. — *Stephen Thomas Erlewine*

Royal Trux

f. 1985, New York City, NY
Alternative Pop-Rock, Indie Rock
From the noisy demise of underground kingpins Pussy Galore came two interesting bands. The first was Jon Spencer's blues deconstruction unit the Jon Spencer Blues Explosion; the second was Neil Hagerty and Jennifer Herrema's dissonant junkie nightmare known as Royal Trux. Interestingly, both bands started out as avant-noise combos playing little that resembled traditional rock 'n' roll. That doesn't mean the music they made was bad; it was rather a little difficult to figure out when they were really into it or simply pulling your chain. What was amazing is that after a protracted period of making harsh, nearly inaccessible

records, both bands, by the mid-'90s, were making records that sounded like '70s rock, only with gobs more attitude and noise. Early Royal Trux records (two self-titled records and *Twin Infinitives*) are, to say the least, extreme. Herrema and Hagerty play mostly beat-to-shit, thrift-store guitars, howl over the noise, and let a crappy little drum machine keep a beat. Both were raging junkies, and running the risk of turning this into a tabloid piece, the music sounds it. It's messy, self-indulgent, and on-the-nod, but's it's also jarring, exciting and full of potential. Both Herrema and Hagerty "play" like they couldn't care less about what they were doing (and they probably couldn't), but there's a spark here—maybe an accidental one, but a spark that makes these messy chunks of distortion more interesting than your average underground rant, although I can understand why people hate this stuff. It's not what you'd call friendly, inviting music. Most wouldn't consider it music.

Although their drug problems escalated (in a fit of Miles Davis-inspired bravado, Herrema and Hagerty allegedly spent a recording advance by their label Drag City on smack, only to ask the impoverished indie label for more money to make the record), they eventually got sober around the time of *Cats and Dogs*, their most lucid and last recording for Drag City. Now employing three other musicians and sounding like an honest-to-God rock band, Royal Trux was making music that sounded grimy and raunchy, the way the Stones did in the mid-'70s. It was an amazing and unexpected turnaround, but well worth the wait. After exhibiting a little stability, Royal Trux was gobbled up by Virgin as part of the post-Nirvana/Pearl Jam alternative-rock signing frenzy. While purists were hissing sellout (as they always do), Royal Trux hooked up with Neil Young producer David Briggs and cut *Thank You*, a great, greasy glob of lo-fi rock fueled by cigarettes and junk food. Hagerty's guitar playing still gleefully wanders into noiseland, but he's just as likely to cough up a '70s hard rock riff or two. Herrema actually sings now, but her voice still hasn't improved much beyond a one-octave catgrowl. Still, Royal Trux seems to have made it; and at the start of the decade, few people would have made that prediction. —*John Dougan*

Royal Trux [#1] / 1988 / Drag City ♦♦♦
Royal Trux's eponymous debut album is a virtually unlistenable collage of primitive guitar chords, clattering instrumentation, howled vocals and sheer white noise. Occasionally, the music showed signs of actual song-structure, as well as shards of Stonesy blues, but it generally sounded like an abrasive, self-conscious deconstruction of classic rock. Either that, or the band simply didn't have a clue how to play their instruments. —*Stephen Thomas Erlewine*

Twin Infinitives / 1990 / Drag City ♦♦♦
Noisier and harsher than the group's debut, *Twin Infinitives* is a polarizing record—you either understand Royal Trux's primal, atonal deconstructions of rock 'n' roll, or you think that it's self-indulgent, unlistenable crap. Either way, *Twin Infinitives* is noteworthy for stretching the amateurish trash-rock of *Royal Trux* to the extreme, creating a defiantly noisy and abrasive assault of gutted riffs, screams, tinny synthesizers and melodic fragments. It may not be particularly listenable, but it is some sort of achievement. —*Stephen Thomas Erlewine*

Royal Trux [#2] / Oct. 5, 1992 / Drag City ♦♦♦
With their untitled 1992 album, Royal Trux tentatively abandoned the noise aesthetic of their first two albums and began writing real songs. Surprisingly, they were strong songs, bristling with the group's love of rock sleaze and junkie culture, as well as riffs that are captivatingly tough and sloppy. And, Jennifer Herrema has never sounded as scarily sexy as she does throughout the album, slurring and snarling her bleak, disease-ridden lyrics with a compelling insolence. *Royal Trux* still is hampered by some meandering noise, but the emergence of real songs make them a primitive indie-rock band worth investigating. —*Stephen Thomas Erlewine*

Cats & Dogs / Jun. 14, 1993 / Drag City ♦♦♦♦
Recorded for America's No. 1 lo-fi underground label, *Cats and Dogs* was the first indication that Royal Trux could do more than whip up a tornado of distortion. A little more less focused than *Thank You*, it still has its moments of splendor, especially when it sounds as though it's going to fall apart and, suddenly, comes back together. —*John Dougan*

● **Thank You** / Apr. 1995 / Virgin ♦♦♦♦
I realize that this runs contrary to the beliefs of longtime Royal Trux fans, but the more Royal Trux resembles a standard rock band, the better they sound. If you want a little guitar skronk with your sci-fi surrealism (as in Herrema's lyrics), but like a little funky backbeat now and again, this is Royal Trux at their scuzzy best. It's still not for the weak, nor for those who like pretty melodies or great musicianship. But for the rest of us who like the occasional run through the jungle, songs like "The Sewers of Mars" and "You're Gonna Lose" are prime chunks of non-commercial alternative rock. It's a safe bet to assume that more '90s bands will continue to appropriate '70s rock stylings, but few will do it with the panache of Royal Trux. —*John Dougan*

Sweet Sixteen / Feb. 11, 1997 / Virgin ♦♦♦
Royal Trux always subverted classic rock by neglecting to learn how to

play their instruments and taking the junkie myths of Keith Richards and Johnny Thunders as fact. When they moved to a major label with 1995's *Thank You*, they cleaned up their sound and started writing actual songs, so it makes sense that its followup, *Sweet Sixteen*, is where they learn how to stretch out on their instruments. Opening up with a riff lifted from the Allman Brothers, *Sweet Sixteen* is a sloppy mess, filled with grime, sleaze and filth—just like the broken toilet that adorns the album's cover. While Royal Trux is now able to play these blues riffs, they don't have the desire to make them palatable. At heart, they still want to tap into what originally scared people about rock 'n' roll, and to a certain extent they do—they are a viciously anti-social band, snarling vocals and throwing riffs out carelessly. However, they are falling into a netherworld with music that is too slick for indie and too weird for the mainstream, which means *Sweet Sixteen* is unlikely to appeal outside of their cult. —*Stephen Thomas Erlewine*

The Royalettes

f. 1961, Baltimore, MD, **db.** 1969
Soul
This Baltimore quartet were something of a link between the girl group and "sweet soul" styles. Their harmonies were clearly grounded in the early-'60s girl-group approach. But they also benefited from pop-oriented, occasionally grandiose production at the MGM label, where they recorded their most successful work. If they sometimes sounded like a female version of Little Anthony & the Imperials' later recordings, it's no coincidence. Little Anthony's producer, Teddy Randazzo, also handled the Royalettes, and wrote much of their MGM material.

The Royalettes made some obscure singles for Chancellor and Warner Brothers before being signed to MGM in 1964. Their third single, the lush "It's Gonna Take a Miracle," was by far their most successful outing, stopping just shy of the Top 40. It was destined to be more identified, however, with singer-songwriter Laura Nyro, who made it the title track of her 1971 album of soul covers. In 1982, Deniece Williams took the song into the Top Ten with her own rendition.

The Royalettes did have another small hit in 1965 with "I Want to Meet Him," but never dented the charts again, although MGM spared no expense on their elaborate productions for the group's singles. A final MGM single, produced by Bill Medley of the Righteous Brothers, also failed to get anywhere, and the group broke up by the end of the 1960s, after a final 45 for Roulette. —*Richie Unterberger*

● **It's Gonna Take a Miracle: The MGM Sides** / Feb. 1996 / Soul Classics ♦♦♦♦
Eighteen songs from their MGM stint between 1964 and 1966, comprising both sides of their nine singles for the label (some of which were previously unavailable on LP). Though the Royalettes couldn't be considered a major group, their brand of pop-soul was certainly well-produced and competently performed, making this a pleasant listen for '60s soul fans. —*Richie Unterberger*

The Rubinoos

f. 1973, San Francisco, CA, **db.** 1983
New Wave, Power Pop
For a brief moment, San Francisco's the Rubinoos seemed to be the last hope for pure pop music, carrying on the tradition of the Raspberries with an engaging blend of innocent bubblegum and power pop. The band was formed in 1973 by teenage friends Jon Rubin (vocals, guitar) and Tommy Dunbar (guitar, keyboards, vocals) along with Royse Adler (bass) and Donn Spindt (drums) but it wasn't until 1977 that they made their recording debut for Beserkley Records. The single, a cover of Tommy James' "I Think We're Alone Now," made an appearance in the lower reaches of the US charts, giving the indie label their first hit. The same year, their self-titled LP received rave reviews all around but failed commercially. *Back to the Drawing Board* (1979), another solid collection of bouncy pop songs, again went ignored despite its classic single "I Wanna Be Your Boyfriend." The band effectively broke up the following year. Rubin and Dunbar returned in 1983, using the band name one more time for the Todd Rundgren-produced *Party of Two* EP. "If I Had You Back" from the EP saw some airplay on MTV but it failed to ignite enough interest for the band to go on. They reunited in the late '80s and have since issued collections of lost recordings from the early '80s, though new recordings have yet to be released. —*Chris Woodstra*

● **The Rubinoos** / 1977 / Beserkley ♦♦♦♦
This little gem is a celebration of pop music. There's no other way to describe this record. Catchy tunes with a touch of tongue-in-cheek, mixed with exuberance and joy, make this record as much fun as when it was first released. —*Jim Worbois*

Back to the Drawing Board / Jan. 1979 / Beserkley ♦♦♦
Overall, this is not quite as strong a record as the first one but still, not to be missed. There are some fine original tunes on this record and one

quite interesting cover, "Hold Me," taken from *Three Faces of Eve.* —*Jim Worbois*

Party of Two / 1983 / Warner Brothers ✦✦
New label, new look, new sound. Presumably, the label thought that teaming the band with Todd Rundgren would give them the exposure (and possibly, recognition) they deserved. Unfortunately, you get a record that sounds like another Todd Rundgren project. For instance, "Faded Dream" sounds more like a McCartney throwaway than a Rubinoos track. —*Jim Worbois*

Basement Tapes: Studio Demos Circa 1980-1981 / 1994 / One Way ✦✦✦
Basement Tapes is a collection of studio demos from 1980 to 1981 for an intended album that never happened. And while it lacks the polish of production, the material stands up against their released output. The track-by-track comments by the band members are a nice touch. —*Chris Woodstra*

Garage Sale / Jul. 29, 1994 / Big Deal ✦✦✦
A nice companion piece to One Way's *Basement Tapes*, *Garage Sale* collects previously unreleased demos, alternate takes, and other oddities ranging from their earliest recordings in 1973 (at age 15) through 1985—complete with track-by-track commentary. This provides an interesting look at a band with no shortage of great material. Essential for fans. —*Chris Woodstra*

Rufus

f. 1970, Chicago, IL, **db.** 1983
Soul, Funk, Quiet Storm
Rufus was one of the most commercially successful funk bands of the mid-'70s, primarily because lead vocalist Chaka Khan was a dynamic singer, capable of making even the band's pedestrian material seem interesting. Their self-titled debut album suffered from a lack of strong single material, but the follow-up featured Stevie Wonder's "Tell Me Something Good," which he wrote specifically for the band after hearing Khan sing; it became a No. 3 hit single. After that song, the hits kept coming until the end of the '70s. Chaka Khan began a solo career that eventually eclipsed Rufus' success in 1978, continuing to record with the band until 1983; the group fell apart shortly after her departure. —*Stephen Thomas Erlewine*

Rufusized / 1974 / MCA ✦✦✦✦
With the addition of guitarist/songwriter Tony Maiden, Rufus delivers one of their best albums. It features the hits "Once You Get Started" and "Please Pardon Me (You Remind Me of a Friend)." —*Rick Clark*

● **Rags to Rufus** / 1974 / MCA ✦✦✦✦
From the hard-funk opener of "You Got the Love" to the Stevie Wonder-penned "Tell Me Something Good," *Rags to Rufus* is a fine showcase for Chaka Khan's amazing vocals. —*Rick Clark*

Rufus Featuring Chaka Khan / 1975 / MCA ✦✦✦
Rufus continued their string of successful albums with this 1975 release, featuring the mellow soul of "Sweet Thing," a No. 5 million-seller, as well as jolting funk tunes like "Dance with Me." —*Bil Carpenter*

Ask Rufus / 1977 / MCA ✦✦✦
This solid album includes "Hollywood" and "At Midnight (My Love Will Lift You Up)." —*Rick Clark*

● **Very Best of Rufus & Chaka Khan** / Nov. 19, 1996 / MCA ✦✦✦✦
From 1974's *Rags To Rufus* to 1980's *Masterjam*, most of the albums that Chaka Khan recorded with Rufus are worth obtaining. But for those checking out their music for the first time, this 1996 CD is an OK, though not ideal, starting point. Most of the essential Rufus & Khan hits for ABC—everything from sweaty funk like "Dance With Me," "At Midnight," and the rock-influenced "Tell Me Something Good" to the sentimental "Please Pardon Me (You Remind Me Of Friend)" and the charming "Sweet Thing"—is included. But unfortunately, the LP-length CD isn't nearly long enough. MCA could have easily included another 20-25 minutes worth of five-star material, including such omissions as "Fool's Paradise" and "Everlasting Love." —*Alex Henderson*

The Rumour

f. 1975, London, England, **db.** 1980
Rock 'n' Roll, New Wave, Pub Rock
The Rumour are best known as Graham Parker's backing band during his heyday, but the band also took a stab at their own recording career. And even though they were overshadowed by their association with Parker and never received much attention for their efforts, they did manage to make three albums of really enjoyable music in the mold of a new wave-ish pub-rock band.

The Rumour consisted of pub-rock veterans Bob Andrews (keyboards) and Brinsley Schwarz (guitar/vocals) from the legendary Brinsley Schwarz, Martin Belmont (guitar/vocals) from Ducks Deluxe, and Stephen Goulding (drums/vocals) and Andrew Bodnar from Bontemps

Roulez. The group formed in 1975 as Graham Parker's backing band, recording and touring with him off and on through 1980. In 1977, they signed their own deal with Phonogram and released their debut album, *Max*, the same year. They followed with *Frogs Sprouts Clogs and Krauts* for Stiff in 1979 and *Purity of Essence* in 1980, and also worked extensively as one of Stiff's house bands, backing up Elvis Costello on "Watching the Detectives," as well as Carlene Carter, Rachel Sweet, Nick Lowe, and Dave Edmunds. By the end of 1980, lack of real success on their own led to their breakup. —*Chris Woodstra*

● **Max** / 1977 / Mercury ✦✦✦✦
On their debut, the Rumour play laidback pub-rock in a style (predictably) not too dissimilar to their work with Graham Parker, though it is looser and more in the style of later Brinsley Schwarz. *Max* is probably most noteworthy for the clear high point, the band's cover of Nick Lowe's "Mess With Love" (a song he wouldn't get around to recording himself until 1982's *Abominable Showman*), although the album is packed with some terrific music. —*Chris Woodstra*

Frogs Sprouts Clogs & Krauts / 1979 / Arista ✦✦✦
After signing to Stiff, the Rumour made a clear attempt to redefine themselves as a new wave band, incorporating quirky embellishments and more atmospheric keyboards. They're still a pub-rock band at heart, though, and the combination usually works quite well, at times making for some truly inspired moments like "Emotional Traffic," which sounds remarkably like a Nick Lowe song. —*Chris Woodstra*

Purity of Essence / 1980 / Hannibal ✦✦✦
Purity of Essence marked a successfully harder-rocking return to the pub, with a bunch of really good songs—mostly covers this time—that benefit from crisp new wave production, including the Bacharach/David tune "Little Red Book," Randy Newman's "Have You Seen My Baby," and Nick Lowe's "I Don't Want the Night to End." Unfortunately, the unremarkable, often half-hearted vocals fail to ignite the top-notch material for the most part. [*Purity of Essence* was issued in the US in a rearranged order, dropping three songs in favor of three others, the most notable being a Glenn Tilbrook (Squeeze) original, "Depression," which was never recorded by Squeeze. The UK CD retains the original tracks and adds "Name and Number" from the US edition. The US CD reissue in 1997 matches the UK edition.] —*Chris Woodstra*

Run-D.M.C.

f. 1982, Queens, NY
Hip Hop, East Coast Rap, Hardcore Rap
More than any other hip-hop group, Run-D.M.C. is responsible for the sound and style of the music. As the first hardcore rap outfit, the trio set the sound and style for the next decade of rap. With its spare beats and excursions into heavy metal samples, the trio was tougher and more menacing than its predecessors Grandmaster Flash and Whodini. In the process, it opened the door for both the politicized rap of Public Enemy and Boogie Down Productions, as well as the hedonistic gangsta fantasies of N.W.A. At the same time, Run-D.M.C. helped move rap from a singles-oriented genre to an album-oriented one—they were the first hip-hop artist to construct full-fledged albums, not just a collection with two singles and a bunch of filler. By the end of the '80s, Run-D.M.C. had been overtaken by the groups they had spawned, but they continued to perform to a dedicated following well into the '90s.

All three members of Run-D.M.C. were natives of the middle-class New York borough, Hollis, Queens. Run (born Joseph Simmons, November 14, 1964) was the brother of Russell Simmons, who formed the hip-hop management company Rush Productions in the early '80s; by the mid-'80s, Russell had formed the pioneering record label Def Jam with Rick Rubin. Russell encouraged his brother Joey and his friend, Darryl McDaniel (b. May 31, 1964) to form a rap duo. The pair of friends did just that, adopting the names Run and D.M.C. respectively. After they graduated from high school in 1982, the pair enlisted their friend, Jason Mizell (b. January 21, 1965), to scratch turntables; Mizell adopted the stage name Jam Master Jay.

In 1983, Run-D.M.C. released its first single, "It's Like That" / "Sucker M.C.'s," on Profile Records. The single sounded like no other rap at the time—it was spare, blunt and skillful, with hard beats and powerful, literate, daring vocals, where Run and D.M.C's vocals overlapped, as they finished each other's lines. It was the first "new school" hip-hop recording. "It's Like That" became a Top 20 R&B hit, as did the group's second single, "Hard Times" / "Jam Master Jay." Two other hit R&B singles followed in early 1984—"Rock Box" and "30 Days"—before the group's eponymous debut appeared.

By the time of their second album, 1985's *King of Rock*, Run-D.M.C. had become the most popular and influential rappers in America, already spawning a number of imitators. As the *King of Rock* title suggests, the group was breaking down the barriers between rock 'n' roll and rap, rapping over heavy metal records and thick, dense drum loops. Besides releasing the *King of Rock* album and scoring the R&B hits "King of Rock," "You Talk Too Much," and "Can You Rock It Like This" in

1985, the group also appeared in the rap movie *Krush Groove*, which also featured Kurtis Blow, the Beastie Boys, and the Fat Boys.

Run-D.M.C.'s fusion of rock and rap broke into the mainstream with their third album, 1986's *Raising Hell*. The album was preceded by the Top Ten R&B single "My Adidas," which set the stage for the group's biggest hit single, a cover of Aerosmith's "Walk This Way." Recorded with Aerosmith's Steven Tyler and Joe Perry, "Walk This Way" was the first hip-hop record to appeal to both rockers and rappers, as evidenced by its peak position of No. 4 on the pop charts. In the wake of the success of "Walk This Way," *Raising Hell* became the first rap album to reach No. 1 on the R&B charts, to chart in the pop Top Ten, and the first to go platinum, and Run-D.M.C. was the first rap act to received airplay on MTV—they were the first rappers to cross over into the pop mainstream. *Raising Hell* also spawned the hit singles "You Be Illin'" and "It's Tricky."

Run-D.M.C. spent most of 1987 recording *Tougher than Leather*, their follow-up to *Raising Hell*. *Tougher than Leather* was accompanied by a movie of the same name. Starring Run-D.M.C., the film was an affectionate parody of '70s Blaxploitation films. Although Run-D.M.C. had been at the height of their popularity when they were recording and filming *Tougher than Leather*, by the time the project was released, the rap world had changed. Most of the hip-hop audience wanted to hear hardcore political rappers like Public Enemy, not crossover artists like Run-D.M.C. Consequently, the film bombed and the album only went platinum, failing to spawn any significant hit singles.

Two years after *Tougher than Leather*, Run-D.M.C. returned with *Back from Hell*, which became their first album not to go platinum. Following its release, both Run and D.M.C. suffered personal problems as Daniels suffered a bout of alcoholism and Simmons was accused of rape. After Daniels sobered up and the charges against Simmons were dismissed, both of the rappers became born-again Christians, touting their religious conversion on the 1993 album, *Down with the King*. Featuring guest appearances and production assistance from artists as diverse as Public Enemy, EPMD, Naughty by Nature, A Tribe Called Quest, Neneh Cherry, Pete Rock, and KRS-1, *Down with the King* became the comeback Run-D.M.C. needed. The title track became a Top Ten R&B hit and the album went gold, peaking at No. 21. Although there were no longer hip-hop innovators, the success of *Down with the King* proved that Run-D.M.C. were still respected pioneers. —*Stephen Thomas Erlewine*

☆ **Run-D.M.C.** / 1984 / Profile ✦✦✦✦
Undeniably, *Run-D.M.C.* is among the most influential rap albums ever. Before Run-D.M.C.'s ascension in the mid-'80s, rap hits tended to be melodic and danceable. Whether the inspiration for their tracks was Chic, Ashford & Simpson or Kraftwerk, hip-hop recordings were generally more interested in grooving than rocking—that is, until Run-D.M.C. had so enormous an impact on rap with "Rock Box," and "Sucker Mcs" and other abrasive classics included on this landmark debut album. When these self-proclaimed "Kings from Queens" took off in the mid-'80s, it became fashionable for rappers to use the type of abrasive, amelodic tracks heard here—many of which consist of little more than a drum machine and the influential Jam Master Jay's cutting and scratching. When they do employ some type of melody on "Rock Box," it isn't a Chic groove—but a crunching, Black Sabbath-like guitar. Run-D.M.C.'s daring rap/metal fusion, in fact, influenced everyone from Whodini to Ice-T to the Beastie Boys. —*Alex Henderson*

King of Rock / 1985 / Profile ✦✦✦✦
Run-D.M.C.'s artistic winning streak continued with its superb second album, *King of Rock*. The fusion of rap and heavy metal the duo unveiled on "Rock Box" proved equally arresting on "You're Blind" and the title song, and the hip-hoppers' boasts were still among the finest in rap. Though boasting, rap's staple, can wear thin in a hurry, Run-D.M.C.'s boasts are consistently clever and often humorous. From the amusing "You Talk Too Much" to the insistent "Jam-Master Jammin'" to the inventive "Roots, Rap, Reggae," everything on *King of Rock* is a classic. By the end of the 1980s, fusing rap and reggae wasn't out of the ordinary—especially on the East Coast. But when Run-D.M.C. recorded "Roots, Rap, Reggae" in 1985, it was quite daring. —*Alex Henderson*

★ **Raising Hell** / 1986 / Profile ✦✦✦✦✦
Run-D.M.C. enjoyed its greatest triumph of all—both artistically and commercially—with its triple-platinum third album, *Raising Hell*. Much of the support that Run-D.M.C. enjoyed came from rock fans, and the MCs made their love of rock more than evident on "It's Tricky" (which samples the Knack's "My Sharona"), the forceful title song, and an inspired remake of Aerosmith's "Walk This Way" featuring Steve Tyler and Joe Perry themselves. Most of the other gems on *Raising Hell*—which range from the humorous "You Be Illin'" to the clever "My Adidas" to the uplifting "Proud to Be Black"—don't employ a screaming rock guitar. But even then, Run-D.M.C. is one of the loudest acts in hip-hop. —*Alex Henderson*

Tougher than Leather / 1988 / Profile ✦✦✦
At the end of 1986, *Raising Hell* was rap's best-selling album up to that

point, though it would soon be outsold by the Beastie Boys' *Licensed to Ill*. Profile Records hoped that Run-D.M.C.'s fourth album, *Tougher than Leather*, would exceed the Beastie Boys' quintuple-platinum status, but unfortunately, the group's popularity had decreased by 1988. One of Run-D.M.C.'s strong points—its love of rock 'n' roll—was also its undoing in hip-hop circles. Any type of crossover success tends to be viewed suspiciously in the hood, and hardcore hip-hoppers weren't overly receptive to "Miss Elaine," "Papa Crazy," "Mary, Mary" and other rap/rock delights found on the album. Thanks largely to rock fans, this album did go platinum for sales exceeding one million copies—which ironically, Profile considered a disappointment. But the fact is that while *Tougher than Leather* isn't quite as strong as Run-D.M.C.'s first three albums, it was one of 1988's best rap releases. —*Alex Henderson*

Back from Hell / 1990 / Profile ✦✦✦
Longevity isn't a realistic goal for most rappers, who are lucky if they aren't considered played out by their third or fourth album. By 1990, Run-D.M.C.'s popularity had decreased dramatically, and the Queens residents had lost a lot of ground to both West Coast gangster rappers like Ice Cube, Ice-T and Compton's Most Wanted. With its fifth album, *Back from Hell*, Run-D.M.C. set out to regain the support of the hardcore rap audience and pretty much abandoned rock-influenced material in favor of stripped-down, minimalist and consistently street-oriented sounds. Not outstanding but certainly enjoyable, such gritty reflections on urban life as "Livin' in the City," "The Ave." and "Faces" made it clear that Run-D.M.C. was still well worth hearing. —*Alex Henderson*

★ **Together Forever: Greatest Hits 1983-1991** / Nov. 6, 1991 / Profile ✦✦✦✦✦
For the most part, all of Run D.M.C.'s most important singles and biggest hits are included on *Together Forever: Greatest Hits 1983-1991*. That alone makes the compilation a necessary purchase. However, that doesn't mean that it is a perfectly assembled collection. Instead of presenting the singles in chronological order, the sequencing skips back and forth—for example, it opens with "Sucker M.C.'s," jumps ahead to "Walk This Way," jumps further ahead to "Together Forever," then slams back to "King of Rock." Still, *Together Forever* has 18 of the groundbreaking group's absolutely essential items, from "It's Like That" and "Hard Times" to "It's Tricky" and "Run's House," which makes it an ideal introduction and an enjoyable retrospective. It's just not the definitive collection it could have been. —*Stephen Thomas Erlewine*

Down with the King / May 4, 1993 / Profile ✦✦✦
After 1990's lackluster *Back From Hell*, most hip-hop fans thought that Run-D.M.C. was no longer capable of delivering a solid record. *Down With the King* proved those doubters wrong. Although it didn't burn up the charts like *Raising Hell* and wasn't as innovative as their first album, *Down With the King* showed that they remained strong and talented; it also didn't hurt that the production was provided by several of the 1990s' most talented artists, including Public Enemy, Pete Rock, Naughty by Nature, and Q-Tip. —*Stephen Thomas Erlewine*

The Runaways

f. 1975, Los Angeles, CA, **db.** 1980
Hard Rock, Heavy Metal
This rock 'n' roll band featured vocalist Cherie Currie and guitarists Joan Jett and Lita Ford. Organized by producer Kim Fowley in 1976, their raw, punkish style became a cult item in Japan and Europe, but unfortunately never connected with any kind of mainstream success stateside until Jett and Ford each went solo. —*Cub Koda*

The Runaways / 1976 / Touchwood ✦✦✦✦
Their debut album, produced by mentor Kim Fowley, loaded with excitement and featuring the classic "Cherry Bomb." —*Cub Koda*

Queens of Noise / 1977 / Touchwood ✦✦✦✦
Their definitive statement, with Joan Jett taking over lead-singing chores on six of the ten tracks. The title cut says it all. —*Cub Koda*

● **The Best of the Runaways** / 1987 / Mercury ✦✦✦✦
A good collection of the Runaways' finest moments, *Best of the Runaways* is the only consistently enjoyable disc from these trashy hardrockers. —*Stephen Thomas Erlewine*

Todd Rundgren

b. Jun. 22, 1948, Upper Darby, PA
Guitar, Keyboards, Vocals / Pop-Rock
Over the course of his lengthy career, Todd Rundgren (b. Jun. 22, 1948) has created some of popular music's finer moments, as well as some of its most frustrating. He has proved to be a master of great pop melodies (with influences from the Beatles to Philly Soul) and heartfelt lyrical sentiment, while also releasing albums of tedious prog-rock that only a diehard fan could care about. At times Rundgren's productions seemed to have existed independently of the music, rather than enhancing it; nevertheless, Rundgren is an influential Renaissance man in the history of rock. His first taste of success came with the psychedelic pop-rock

group the Nazz, in 1967. "Hello, It's Me" (No. 71/No. 66) charted twice, while the heavily phased riff-rocker "Open My Eyes" became a signature tune of sorts. Rundgren left the Nazz (future Cheap Trick guitarist Rick Nielson was his replacement) and pursued a solo career with the 1970 debut *Runt. Something/Anything,* Rundgren's third album, was his finest showcase as a songwriter. It was during this time that Rundgren began making a name for himself as an innovative producer. Over the years he has worked on projects for Badfinger, New York Dolls, Foghat, Patti Smith, Cheap Trick, XTC, Meat Loaf, and others. In 1974 Rundgren formed Utopia, a quartet that helped fulfill his prog-rock tendencies. By the late '70s, Rundgren was actively exploring the medium of rock video, opening his own computer video studio in Woodstock, NY. He continues to produce various artists and to release solo albums that enjoy a solid cult success. —*Rick Clark*

Runt / Sep. 1970 / Bearsville ◆◆◆◆
Runt, Todd Rundgren's debut, might have been a little uneven, but its homemade production, spirited arrangements, and great tunes, like "We Gotta Get You a Woman" and "I'm in the Clique," made this one of the most appealing albums of his career. —*Rick Clark*

Runt: Ballad of Todd Rundgren / Jun. 1971 / Rhino ◆◆◆
Rundgren's sophomore release didn't contain the flashes of brilliance found on *Runt,* but "Be Nice to Me," "Parole," and "Remember Me" are standouts on this relatively low-key effort. —*Rick Clark*

★ **Something/Anything?** / Feb. 1972 / Bearsville ◆◆◆◆◆
From beginning to end, *Something/Anything?* is Rundgren's best album, featuring the hit singles "I Saw the Light," and "Hello, It's Me." There are also a load of gems like "It Wouldn't Have Made Any Difference," "Wolfman Jack," and "Couldn't I Just Tell You?," one of the finest power-pop tracks ever cut. Rundgren plays every instrument and sings all the parts on three-fourths of this self-produced release. Even though Rundgren had flashes of brilliance after *Something/Anything?,* he never came up with an album with performances and material as consistently satisfying. —*Rick Clark*

A Wizard a True Star / Mar. 1973 / Bearsville ◆◆◆◆
Rundgren's keen sense for writing tight pop songs is almost nowhere to be found on this over-the-top production job. That's not to say that *A Wizard a True Star* doesn't have its virtues. Rundgren's take on *Peter Pan's* "Never Land" is otherworldly, and his Philly-soul medley is quite fine. "International Feel" and "Just One Victory" are other standout tracks. —*Rick Clark*

Initiation / May 1975 / Bearsville ◆◆◆
Todd Rundgren returned to solo billing here, although his studio musicians included current and future members of Utopia, and he remained interested in dense, extended compositions like "A Treatise on Cosmic Fire," which takes up all of side two. The most memorable track on the album, however, was "Real Man," which hit No.83 on the singles chart. —*William Ruhlmann*

Faithful / Apr. 1976 / Bearsville ◆◆◆
One-half of this outing features Rundgren delivering almost letter-perfect versions of '60s classics like "Good Vibrations" and "Rain," which are impressive in their attention to detail but sound strangely lifeless. On the other half of the album, he delivers some of his best work since *Something/Anything?,* particularly on "Black & White" and "When I Pray." —*Rick Clark*

Back to the Bars / 1978 / Bearsville ◆◆◆
A double live album, *Back to the Bars* presented Todd Rundgren at his most accessible, accompanied both by Utopia and by some of his other longtime sidemen, performing his most melodic pop-rock songs, from "Hello, It's Me" to "Love in Action," and even suggesting his roots in soul pop with covers of "Ooh Baby Baby" and "La La Means I Love You." —*William Ruhlmann*

Hermit of Mink Hollow / Apr. 1978 / Bearsville ◆◆◆◆
By the release of this album, Rundgren had ditched the homemade charm of *Something/Anything?* for a warbly hard rock/pop sound. Tracks like "Determination," "Out of Control," "You Cried Wolf," and "Fade Away" best exemplify that approach. "Can We Still Be Friends?" became a No. 29 hit. —*Rick Clark*

Healing / Feb. 1981 / Rhino ◆◆
Todd Rundgren's first solo studio album in nearly three years was one of his entirely self-contained efforts: he wrote, played, sang, produced, and engineered everything. It found him retreating from the hard-rock sound of recent efforts toward a more soulful, almost ambient approach. But though songs such as "Compassion" were in Rundgren's patented "Hello, It's Me" ballad style, there were no real classics this time around. (The original Bearsville Records LP package contained both a 12-inch record and a 7-inch, 33 1/3 rpm record with the tracks "Time Heals" and "Tiny Demons." The Rhino version, which contains those tracks, is a September 1987 CD reissue.) —*William Ruhlmann*

The Ever Popular Tortured Artist Effect / Jan. 1983 / Rhino ◆◆◆◆
This album, one of Rundgren's best do-it-yourself efforts of the '80s, contains his No. 63 hit "Bang the Drum All Day" and a swell remake of the Small Faces' "Tin Soldier." —*Rick Clark*

A Cappella / Sep. 1985 / Rhino ◆◆
Todd Rundgren was used to playing all the instruments on his albums himself. Here, he went one step further: all the sounds on this record come from Rundgren's voice, albeit sampled and filtered and edited to sound like instruments. Strip away the trickery, however, and you have a typical Rundgren pop collection, none of whose songs are among his best. —*William Ruhlmann*

● **Anthology (1968-1985)** / May 1989 / Rhino ◆◆◆◆
Anthology is a fairly comprehensive overview of Rundgren's entire career, starting with "Open My Eyes" by the Nazz, and including "Something to Fall Back On," from Rundgren's 1985 solo album *A Cappella.* All of his radio hits are included, as well as many important album tracks. Nevertheless, there are several key tracks missing, like "Wolfman Jack," "International Feel/Never Never Land," and the Nazz's "Forget All About It" and "Hang on Paul." Like all of Rundgren's reissues on Rhino, *Anthology* has been given a first-class remastering job. —*Rick Clark*

Nearly Human / May 1989 / Warner Brothers ◆◆◆
Included are strong songs and extraordinary recording. —*Jas Obrecht*

Second Wind / Jan. 1991 / Warner Brothers ◆◆
Todd Rundgren's last major-label album was recorded in July, 1990, at the Palace of Fine Arts Theatre in San Francisco before a live audience, although under recording studio conditions, with a backup band that included some local talent: Roger Powell of Utopia, Vince Welnick (who would join the Grateful Dead later in the year) and Prairie Prince of the Tubes, Ross Valory of Journey, and Jenni Muldaur. It's a mixed set, including three songs Rundgren wrote for the off-Broadway musical *Up Against It,* which was based on an unproduced screenplay British playwright Joe Orton wrote in the 1960s for the Beatles. Those songs have a Kurt Weill-ish tone, while songs like "Love Science" are uptempo R&B and the lead-off track "Change Myself" is in Rundgren's familiar pop-rock style. On the whole, though, there's nothing to get excited about here. —*William Ruhlmann*

No World Order / Jul. 6, 1993 / Forward ◆
Every Todd Rundgren album seems to have a gimmick, and on this one, the trick is that he recorded almost four hours of musical fragments of four to eight seconds each and put them on an interactive CD so that they could be combined in a nearly infinite number of ways. If you have a CD-I, that is. If you only have a regular old CD player, this noninteractive version presents ten songs and six variations on them. Rundgren has added rap to his arsenal, his lyrics are more political, and many of the tracks seem aimed at the dance floor. Rundgren fans will be put off, while the new jack swingers won't bother to listen. But the real problem is that it's just not very good. —*William Ruhlmann*

The Best of Todd Rundgren / Feb. 22, 1994 / Rhino ◆◆◆◆
The Best of Todd Rundgren is a budget-line collection of nine of his biggest hits—"We Gotta Get You a Woman," "I Saw the Light," "Hello It's Me," "Bang the Drum All Day"—that hardly functions as an adequate retrospective. —*Stephen Thomas Erlewine*

Rush

f. 1968, Toronto, Ontario
Hard Rock, Art-Rock/Progressive-Rock

Over the course of their decades-spanning career, the Canadian power trio Rush emerged as one of hard rock's most highly-regarded bands; although typically brushed aside by critics and rare recipients of mainstream pop radio airplay, the group nonetheless won an impressive and devoted fan following, while their virtuoso performance skills solidified their standing as musicians' musicians.

Rush formed in Toronto, Ontario in the autumn of 1968, and initially comprised guitarist Alex Lifeson (born Alexander Zivojinovich), vocalist/bassist Geddy Lee (born Gary Lee Weinrib) and drummer John Rutsey. In their primary incarnation, the trio drew a heavy influence from Cream, and honed their skills on the Toronto club circuit before issuing their debut single, a rendition of Buddy Holly's "Not Fade Away," in 1973. A self-titled LP followed in 1974, at which time Rutney exited; he was replaced by drummer Neil Peart, who also assumed the role of the band's primary songwriter, composing the cerebral lyrics (influenced by works of science fiction and fantasy) which gradually became a hallmark of the group's aesthetic.

With Peart firmly ensconced, Rush returned in 1975 with a pair of LPs, *Fly by Night* and *Caress of Steel.* Their next effort, 1976's *2112,* proved to be their breakthrough release: a futuristic concept album based on the writings of Ayn Rand, it fused the elements of the trio's sound—Lee's high-pitched vocals, Peart's epic-length compositions and Lifeson's complex guitar work—into a unified whole. Fans loved it—*2112* was the first in a long line of gold and platinum releases—while critics dismissed it as overblown and pretentious: either way, it established a formula from which the band rarely deviated throughout the duration of their career.

A Farewell to Kings followed in 1977, and reached the Top 40 in both the US and Britain. After 1978's *Hemispheres*, Rush achieved even greater popularity with 1980's *Permanent Waves*, a record marked by Peart's dramatic shift into shorter, less sprawling compositions; the single "The Spirit of Radio" even became a major hit. With 1981's *Moving Pictures*, the trio scored another hit of sorts with "Tom Sawyer," which garnered heavy exposure on album-oriented radio and became perhaps their best-known song.

As the 1980s continued, Rush grew into a phenomenally popular live draw, as albums like 1982's *Signals* (which generated the smash "New World Man"), 1984's *Grace Under Pressure* and 1985's *Power Windows* continued to sell millions of copies. As the decade drew to a close, the trio cut back on its touring schedule, while hardcore followers complained of a sameness afflicting slicker, synth-driven efforts like 1987's *Hold Your Fire* and 1989's *Presto*. At the dawn of the 1990s, however, Rush returned to the heavier sound of their early records and placed a renewed emphasis on Lifeson's guitar heroics; consequently, both 1991's *Roll the Bones* and 1993's *Counterparts* reached the Top Three on the US album charts. In 1996, the band issued *Test for Echo*. —*Jason Ankeny*

Rush / 1974 / Mercury ✦✦
Rush's eponymous debut album finds the group aping Cream and Led Zeppelin for most of the record, and while Alex Lifeson and Geddy Lee already demonstrate impressive technical skills, they're weighed down slightly by drummer John Rutsey, who isn't as imaginative as his successor, Neil Peart. Furthermore, most of the songs aren't particularly distinctive, wallowing in hard-rock clichés, with the notable exception of the group's breakthrough single, "Working Man." —*Stephen Thomas Erlewine*

Fly by Night / 1975 / Mercury ✦✦
The addition of drummer Neil Peart not only strengthens Rush's rhythmic attack, but also its lyrics, which helps elevate their second album, *Fly by Night*, above its predecessor somewhat. Nevertheless, the group still sounds a bit too much like a pedestrian hard-rock band, with very little of the musical complexities that distinguished their latter albums, but there's a handful of songs, like "In the End," that suggest that the band is improving. —*Stephen Thomas Erlewine*

Caress of Steel / 1975 / Mercury ✦✦
Caress of Steel finds Rush in a holding pattern, essentially repeating the hard-rock sounds of *Fly by Night*, even though the group tries to incorporate elements of prog-rock—note that there's not one but two multipart suites, "The Necromancer" and "The Fountain of Lamneth." Despite a couple of fine musical interludes, the record fails to capture the group's complex interplay that they were beginning on stage, and it's only interesting in retrospect. —*Stephen Thomas Erlewine*

2112 / 1976 / Mercury ✦✦✦✦
This is Rush's first successful stab at a concept album. Like many of Rush's albums during the '70s, this one deals with a futuristic scenario where an individual triumphs over an impersonalized high-tech society. —*Rick Clark*

All the World's a Stage / 1976 / Mercury ✦✦✦
The live album *All the World's a Stage* represents the culmination of Rush's early years as a metal band with prog inclinations, and it demonstrates that the band was more effective on stage than it was on record. Nearly every performance here outshines the studio counterpart, but the record can't help but demonstrate that the group's instrumental technique at this stage were far superior to their songwriting skills. —*Stephen Thomas Erlewine*

A Farewell to Kings / 1977 / Mercury ✦✦✦
Rush continues to explore their sci-fi fantasy themes and lofty concepts with this effort, which featured "Closer to the Heart," a substantial FM rock hit that also went No. 76 pop. —*Rick Clark*

Archives / 1978 / Mercury ✦✦✦
This is a good compilation of Rush's first three albums, including their first hits "Working Man," "Fly by Night," and "In the Mood." —*Rick Clark*

Hemispheres / 1978 / Mercury ✦✦✦
Included is the FM hit "The Trees," which can be found on *Chronicles*. Their extended pieces here aren't among their best, but the playing and dynamics of the arrangements keep things fairly interesting. —*Rick Clark*

Permanent Waves / 1980 / Mercury ✦✦✦✦
The cumulative effect of endless tours and obvious growth with each studio effort, Rush hit it big with this effort, delivering with their best material to date. "Spirit of the Radio," "Freewill," and "Entre Nous" were big FM rock hits. "Jacob's Ladder" was another highlight. —*Rick Clark*

● **Moving Pictures** / 1981 / Mercury ✦✦✦✦
On *Moving Pictures*, Rush's aggressive prog-rock hit a zenith, with challenging playing that never became formless or devoid of good melodic integrity. The trio's active ensemble work reached new levels of interplay. "Tom Sawyer," "Limelight," "Red Barchetta," and the instrumental "YYZ" are standouts. —*Rick Clark*

Exit Stage Left / 1981 / Mercury ✦✦✦✦
A good live collection, it's possibly the best of their three such releases. —*Rick Clark*

Signals / 1982 / Mercury ✦✦✦✦
This is the third in a trio of great albums. "Digital Man" and "Analog Kid" are powerful riff-rockers. "New World Man" was a No. 21 hit, and "Subdivisions" was an FM rock favorite. The soundstage lacks some of the ambience found on *Moving Pictures*, but the performances still pack quite a punch. —*Rick Clark*

Grace Under Pressure / 1984 / Mercury ✦✦
A loose concept album about the dangers of nuclear war, *Grace Under Pressure*—which was, after all, released several years after the "No Nukes" craze of the early '80s, so it may have been inspired by *The Day After*—finds Rush attempting to incorporate a few modern influences into their music, such as new wave synthesizers. By and large, the experiments fall flat, yet "Distant Early Warning" and "Red Sector A" make the record worthwhile. —*Stephen Thomas Erlewine*

Power Windows / 1985 / Mercury ✦✦✦
It's an improvement over the sterile techno of the 1984 release *Grace Under Pressure*. "Big Money" recalls the highlights of *Moving Pictures*, while "Manhattan Project" and "Territories" also shine. —*Rick Clark*

Hold Your Fire / 1987 / Mercury ✦✦✦
Even though the playing is typically exceptional, the clinical production keeps this album from really catching fire. "Time Stand Still," "Force Ten" and "Turn the Page" are among the highlights. —*Rick Clark*

A Show of Hands / Jan. 2, 1988 / Mercury ✦✦✦
A solid document of their live work, it concentrates on later albums. —*Rick Clark*

Presto / Nov. 1989 / Atlantic ✦✦✦✦
Presto, Rush's 13th album of new studio material, and their first for Atlantic, showed this Canadian trio coming out from under a succession of bloodless-sounding techno-excursions (*Grace Under Pressure*, *Hold Your Fire*) and going for a much more open, accessible sound. From beginning to end, the arrangements reflect more straightahead rock playing than on any of their other albums. *Presto* contains some of Neil Peart's best lyrics, and along with *Moving Pictures*, smartly presents many of Rush's virtues in their best light. —*Rick Clark*

Chronicles / Jul. 1, 1991 / Mercury ✦✦✦✦
Anyone wanting an essential overview of this Canadian band's prog-rock work should start here. All of their FM rock hits and most of the important album tracks are here. —*Rick Clark*

Roll the Bones / Jul. 1, 1991 / Atlantic ✦✦✦✦
Roll the Bones continues with the organic-sounding hard prog-rock spirit of *Presto*, and it's equally fine. After many years of albums and touring, it's obvious that Rush has maintained its edge as a musical unit. The playing and material are primo throughout. Highlights include "Neurotica," "Big Wheel," "Ghost of a Chance," and the title cut. —*Rick Clark*

Counterparts / Oct. 19, 1993 / Atlantic ✦✦
A solid collection of songs, it includes the AOR rock radio tracks "Stick it Out," "Animate," and "Nobody's Hero," the band's statement on the AIDS situation. The playing is typically top-notch, but the type of reverbs and equalization setting on this Peter Collins production make the band sound colder and more distant than usual. —*Rick Clark*

Test for Echo / Sep. 9, 1996 / Atlantic ✦✦✦
After flirting (albeit mildly) with alternative rock on *Counterparts*, Rush returns to classic progressive rock on *Test for Echo*. Cutting back many of the AOR production flourishes that hampered most of their late '80s and early '90s releases, the band concentrates on the sounds and styles that made albums like *Moving Pictures* huge successes in the late '70s and early '80s. *Test for Echo* is all instrumental gymnastics and convoluted song structures, all of which demonstrate each member's skills. And the key to the album is the individual performances, since each song isn't particularly memorable as a song, only as a way to showcase the solos. With Rush, such a tactic isn't necessarily a bad thing, since they have always been better at playing than writing, and they have rarely played better in the past ten years than they have on *Test for Echo*. —*Stephen Thomas Erlewine*

● **Retrospective, Vol. 1 (1974-80)** / May 5, 1997 / Polygram ✦✦✦✦
Retrospective, Vol. 1 (1974-80) was designed to replace the double-disc set *Chronicles*, and it is, in fact, a better compilation than its predecessor. By concentrating on Rush's earliest albums—from 1974's *Rush* to 1980's *Permanent Waves*—the album draws an excellent portrait of the group's

artiest work, leaving their hard-rock radio-rock hits for *Retrospective, Vol. 2* Meanwhile, *Vol. 1* contains nearly all of the highlights from their '70s albums, including "Closer to the Heart" and "Fly By Night," making it a near-flawless encapsulation of their early career. —*Stephen Thomas Erlewine*

Ed Rush

Club/Dance, Jungle/Drum 'N Bass, Electronica
Jungle producer Ed Rush's name has become almost synonymous with the word "dark." With a steady string of 12-inch releases dragging drum'n'bass to hell and back, forcing taut, kettle-sized snare snaps through ringing rides and thunderous, superdense basslines, Rush, together with oft collaborator Nico Sykes, has been almost singularly responsible for jungle's eventual (re)turn to the darkside. Recording most often for Nico-related labels No U-Turn and Nu Black, Rush has also more recently begun to cast his net farther out, bringing his brooding, dank-heavy brand of nightmare drum'n'bass to such labels as Prototype and Metalheadz. First introduced to jungle through late-period hardcore (tracks such as 2 Bad Mice's "Bombscare" and Doc Scott's "Here Come the Drums"), Rush began producing after hooking Nico (a for-hire producer who lived on Rush's block) on the sound. The pair released a few forgettable tracks before buckling down and working on putting together a new sound. Nico formed No U-Turn in 1993 as a vehicle for that sound, and the pair's first proper Ed Rush 12-inch, "Bloodclot Artattack," was released that same year.

Although he'd already been making tracks for a couple years, Rush's reputation began to grow in the wake of the 1996 backlash against the smooth, rolling atmospherics of ambient and heavily jazz-oriented jungle (Bukem, Alex Reece, Wax Doctor, PFM, etc.). With several tracks on the genre-coining compilation *Techsteppin'* (released by Emotif), and with darkness once again coming to the forefront among the DJs, Rush tracks such as "Guncheck," "Bloodclot Artattack," "Subway" (recorded with Dom of Dom & Roland), and "Check Me Out" began showing up in more and more (and more and more influential) DJ sets. Releases on Speed/Blue Note DJ Grooverider's Prototype label ("Kilimanjaro"), as well as twelves for Metalheadz ("Skylab") and Nico's No U-Turn offshoot, Nu Black ("Mad Different Methods," "Amtrak") further cemented Rush's rep at the forefront of a new style. Although he remains a free agent, demand for Rush tracks (as well as remixes) means he's been playing the field, releasing increasing quantities of material on a number of labels, both large and small. And while the over-the-top rumble of darkside techstep is bound to wane in popularity, Rush's most recent work has proven he's not reliant on the novelty of that sound. —*Sean Cooper*

● **Mad Different Methods** / 1996 / Nu Black ✦✦✦✦
The perfect blend of jump-up energy and darkside horrorcore atmospherics. The A-side's title track is on a more restrained hip-hop edge, with the flip given the overdrive treatment, all scissor hi-hats, noisy blasts, and polyrhythmic madness. As bold and efficient a statement of the Ed Rush/Nico sound as exists. —*Sean Cooper*

Skylab / Aug. 1996 / Metalheadz ✦✦✦
Far more restrained than his No U-Turn and Nu Black tracks, "Skylab" (Rush's debut for Goldie's Metalheadz label) is nonetheless a solid, satisfying release. The title cut is the keeper here, with a long ambient-ish intro preceding some tight, tech-leaning hardstep. —*Sean Cooper*

Leon Russell

b. Apr. 2, 1941, Lawton, OK
Piano, Vocals / Singer-Songwriter, Pop-Rock
Leon Russell has had a widely varied career as an artist, a songwriter, a record-label owner, a producer, and an in-demand session sideman. As part of Phil Spector's "Wall of Sound" wrecking crew, Russell played on hits by the Crystals. He also played on Herb Alpert's *Taste of Honey* and the Byrds' *Mr. Tambourine Man* and played and arranged tracks for Gary Lewis & the Playboys. Russell also toured with Delaney & Bonnie and briefly with Paul Revere & the Raiders when Revere was drafted. Russell organized Joe Cocker's Mad Dogs & Englishmen tour, which led him to tours with Bob Dylan, Eric Clapton, and the Rolling Stones, and a performance at George Harrison's Concert for Bangladesh.

In 1970 Russell formed Shelter Records with English producer Denny Cordell. The label eventually released albums by Willis Alan Ramsey, Dwight Twilley, and Phoebe Snow, among others. In October 1971, the Carpenters had a huge hit with Russell's "Superstar." (Years later, another composition, "This Masquerade," became a career-making hit for George Benson.)

All of this visibility set the stage for Russell's lucrative solo career, which fused gospel, blues, country, rock, and light jazz behind his quirky warble of a voice. Russell had seven Top 40 albums, with 1972's *Carney* peaking at No.2 for four weeks. "Tightrope" (No.11), "Lady Blue" (No.14), and a double-sided single remake of Hank Williams' "Roll in My Sweet Baby's Arms"/"I'm So Lonesome I Could Cry" (No.78) are a few of Rus-

sell's hits. In 1992, he released a comeback effort, *Anything Can Happen.* —*Rick Clark*

Leon Russell / 1970 / Capitol ✦✦✦✦
Russell's self-titled debut features his strongest set of songs and performances, with tracks like "A Song for You," "Dixie Lullaby," "Shoot Out at the Plantation," and "Delta Lady," which became one of Joe Cocker's early signature songs. The CD includes a brief version of Dylan's "Masters of War." —*Rick Clark*

And the Shelter People / 1971 / The Right Stuff ✦✦✦✦
Released hot on the heels of his Mad Dogs & Englishmen tour with Joe Cocker, Russell released this spirited outing, which included covers of tunes by George Harrison ("Beware of Darkness") and Dylan ("It's a Hard Rain Gonna Fall," "It Takes a Lot to Laugh, It Takes a Train to Cry") and some fine originals: "Alcatraz," "Home Sweet Oklahoma," "Stranger in a Strange Land" (an FM hit), and the title cut. The CD includes three bonus versions of Dylan tunes. —*Rick Clark*

Asylum Choir II / 1971 / Capitol ✦✦
Of all Russell's early work as an artist, this record is the weakest; in particular, songs like "Tryin' to Stay Live" and "When You Wish Upon a Fag" feel dated. Nevertheless, *Asylum Choir II* is still a pretty nice record. Especially noteworthy is Russell's own version of "Hello, Little Friend"; Joe Cocker would later record the definitive version of the song. (The 1995 CD reissue features five bonus tracks). —*Jim Worbois*

Carney / 1972 / Capitol ✦✦✦
Carney became Russell's highest charting album with the aid of the oddball No.11 hit "Tight Rope." Also included is "This Masquerade," a song that later became an international hit for George Benson. "If the Shoe Fits" is a great putdown of pop-star sycophants. Other highlights include "Manhattan Island Serenade" and "Cajun Love Song." —*Rick Clark*

Hank Wilson's Back / 1973 / Capitol ✦✦✦
A skewed but interesting Hank Williams tribute album, with capable country backing. —*Cub Koda*

Leon Live / 1973 / The Right Stuff ✦✦✦
A solid concert offering that showcases Russell's strengths (and weaknesses) as a live performer, with A-1 support throughout. —*Cub Koda*

● **Best of Leon Russell** / 1976 / DCC ✦✦✦✦
This is a straightforward hits and key-album-tracks collection, including "Lady Blue," "Tight Rope," "A Song for You," "This Masquerade," and "Stranger in a Strange Land," among others. —*Rick Clark*

Anything Can Happen / Sep. 1992 / Virgin ✦✦✦
Bruce Hornsby's active participation in Leon Russell's first recording in ten years is both a blessing and a curse. A blessing, because without Hornsby's encouragement, co-songwriting, production, and musical backing, the project would probably never have happened. A curse, because Hornsby imprints too much of his own personal style and mushy, middle-of-the-road keyboard washes on the sessions. Despite Russell's long layoff, the unique, drawling rasp that gave us "Tight Rope" and "Delta Lady" in the early '70s is still intact. However, the cloying instrumental backings to such tracks as "Angel Ways" and "Faces of the Children" have Hornsby engraved all over them. —*Roch Parisien*

● **Gimme Shelter** / Nov. 12, 1996 / EMI ✦✦✦✦
It's a little problematic to put together a compilation of such an album-oriented artist. But unless you're very deeply into the Russell catalog, this two-CD, 40-track best-of will serve as a retrospective of all that you need, largely covering his work from the first half of the '70s (a couple of songs from his 1992 Virgin album are also included), and featuring his best-known hits, big and small. It's a well-done tour through his blend of swamp rock, gospel, and bits of blues and country, with material from eight of his Shelter LPs, including the one he recorded in 1969 as part of the Asylum Choir. Interesting rarities include a 1974 single of "Wild Horses," a 1970 cover of Dylan's "She Belongs to Me" that only showed up on a compilation, and a folk-rockish 1965 single for Dot. —*Richie Unterberger*

The Rutles

Pop-Rock
Originally broadcast on network TV in 1978, ex-Monty Python member Eric Idle's satire of the Beatles legend was one of the very few successful rock parodies; only Spinal Tap, perhaps, has outdone it. One of the key elements of this mock "rockumentary" was the brilliantly executed "soundtrack" by Python associates and ex-Bonzo Dog Band member Neil Innes (he also played the character loosely based upon John Lennon in the film itself). As an actual peer of the group in the '60s the Bonzos even appeared in the *Magical Mystery Tour* film), Innes was well qualified to satirize the Fab Four phenomenon in song. With the exception of Idle, each of the four "Rutles" played their own instruments on the recording in addition to acting in the film. To complete the gag, the Rutles reconvened in 1996 to record a second album, *Archeology*, to coincide with the Beatles' *Anthology* projects. Masquerading as archival

material, most of *Archeology* was in fact newly recorded in the mid-'90s, and was as witty and well-executed as the soundtrack to their TV special nearly 20 years previously. —*Richie Unterberger*

● **The Rutles** / 1978 / Rhino ✦✦✦✦
Neil Innes delivered catchy, harmony-laden tunes that deftly and lovingly parody every phase of the moptops' career, from their Hamburg/Cavern Club days through "Get Back" (here retitled "Get Up and Go"). In between are fully realized send-ups of "If I Fell," "I Want to Hold Your Hand," "Penny Lane," "Lucy in the Sky," "I Am the Walrus," "All You Need Is Love," and more. "Ouch!," their hilarious mockery of "Help!," is perhaps the album's highlight. The 1990 CD reissue adds six very worthwhile "bonus tracks" that were used in the special but were unavailable on the original 1978 Warner album, making for 20 cuts in all. —*Richie Unterberger*

Archaeology / Oct. 29, 1996 / Virgin ✦✦✦✦
Since the Rutles never properly existed in the first place, they were free of the high expectations surrounding the "reunions" of groups with a higher profile (such as the prime targets of their satire, the Beatles). Although it was recorded 20 years after the first Rutles album, this is unexpectedly delightful continuation of that debut. Songwriter Neil Innes continues to masterfully lampoon the Beatles myth on this collection, billed as an archival release of unreleased material (in the mold of the Beatles' own *Anthology* series). The sound is extremely similar to the Rutles' earlier material, although most of the cuts here are spoofing the Beatles' work from *Sgt. Pepper* onwards, rather than striving for an equal balance between all Fab Four phases. Innes is a genius at weaving in musical and lyrical quotes/references from numerous Beatle tunes, with a subtle hilarity that takes several plays to fully unfold. —*Richie Unterberger*

Mitch Ryder (William Levise)

b. Feb. 26, 1945, Detroit, MI
Rock 'n' Roll
Mitch Ryder & the Detroit Wheels blended the Motown-soul sound with over-revved Midwestern rock 'n' roll. Mitch Ryder's (born William Levise) gutsy soul shouting and superhuman screams were some of the most electrifying sounds to charge AM radio in the mid-'60s, landing somewhere between the Rascals' Felix Cavaliere and Wilson Pickett. The Wheels sported two strong lead guitarists in Joe Cubert and Jim McCarty (later in Cactus and Detroit), and they were pushed along by one of the great unsung rock drummers of all time, John ("Johnny Bee") Badanjek.

It was producer Bob Crewe who signed the band to his New Voice label, releasing a string of high-octane raveups in "Jenny Take a Ride" (No.10), "Little Latin Lupe Lu" (No.17), "Devil with a Blue Dress On / Good Golly Miss Molly" (No.4), "Sock It to Me-Baby!" (No.6), and "Too Many Fish in the Sea" (No.24). In spite of all the hits and visibility, Mitch Ryder & the Detroit Wheels were victims of the era, making loads of money for Crewe and New Voice, but ending up broke. —*Rick Clark*

Take a Ride / 1966 / Sundazed ✦✦✦✦
The debut album of Ryder and the Wheels, fresh from the teenage ballroom circuit in Detroit, where they held court in earlier days as Billy Lee & the Rivieras. One of the defining moments in the history of Motor City music, *Take a Ride* is the sound of poor white kids claiming the music as theirs, too, while infusing it with the manic energy of the color-blind dreams of anybody who ever wanted to be somebody. Built entirely around their stage act, this album captures a band in full cry at the peak of their powers. This is what they mean when they say the words "high-energy Motor City rock 'n' roll." —*Cub Koda*

Breakout . . . !!! / 1966 / Sundazed ✦✦✦✦
Ryder & the Wheels' second album, featuring the classic "Devil with a Blue Dress On /Good Golly, Miss Molly" workout, continues the pattern of their debut; strong renditions of R&B classics, chopped and channeled and revved up to maximum torque. With the use of the original two-track master, the sound of it fairly sparkles. —*Cub Koda*

Sock It to Me / 1967 / Sundazed ✦✦✦✦
Ryder's last album with the Detroit Wheels before going solo finds the material reverting to producer Bob Crewe's readymades, no match for the authentic R&B found on the first two albums, but still strutted out with typical Detroit-like flair. Three bonus tracks and the use of the original stereo masters makes this a must have for serious Mitch Ryder collectors. —*Cub Koda*

Greatest Hits / 1981 / Roulette ✦✦✦
Eleven tracks that do cover his biggest hit singles and some good extras. But it's ridiculous to settle for this when the Rhino CD (with 20 songs) is so much more extensive. Only a couple of songs from this LP (covers of "Turn on Your Lovelight" and "I Got You") are missing from the Rhino best-of. —*Richie Unterberger*

● **Rev-Up: The Best of Mitch Ryder & the Detroit Wheels** / 1990 / Rhino ✦✦✦✦
Perhaps the most raucous white soul band of the '60s, Ryder and the Detroit Wheels scored hits in1966-1968, by souping up rock and R&B ravers to fever pitch. This is hard party music. —*William Ruhlmann*

● **All Hits** / 1997 / Sundazed ✦✦✦✦
Greatest-hits packages sometimes can rob an artist of their wider focus, only zeroing in on the hits and not giving the true big picture. But this is one time when the hits and the subsequent singles fills the bill in an absolutely perfect way. Although many of these songs turn up on other Mitch Ryder albums, many of the versions included here differ greatly, the most noticeable being the kickoff track, "Devil with a Blue Dress/ Good Golly Miss Molly." The reason is simple enough: these are the single mixes, the ones edited and compacted to fit on one side of a 45-rpm vinyl record. As a result, they aurally exude a brighter, more shimmering presence, and although not much else is done in the way of audio chicanery here (no speeded-up tracks, etc.), this one *does* have the sound. If you truly want to experience what a great kick-ass band the Detroit Wheels were in their prime and what a skunk-hot singer Mitch Ryder was in his young man days, this is the one you want to stick in the CD player and play over and over again. —*Cub Koda*

S
___

The Sabres of Paradise

f. 1992, London, England, **db.** 1995
Ambient, Techno, Electronica

Andrew Weatherall's Sabres of Paradise are one of the UK's most cele-brated experimental techno groups. A combined effort of Weatherall and collaborators Jagz Kooner and Gary Burns, the group has released a flood of singles and EPs, many of which have been collected on compila-tions released by Warp and Weatherall's other main focus: the Emissions label. Split into three imprints focusing on house, techno, and ambient/experimental, respectively, the Emissions stable includes such artists as Conemelt, Top, Bloodsugar, Bocca Juniors, Lords of Afford, Planet 4, Two Lone Swordsmen, and Blue. Born in Windsor, Berkshire, Weatherall con-siders himself a DJ first, and his exhausting schedule of deckwork has been arguably as influential as his records, inspiring scores of other DJs and anticipating trends in trance-techno, inelegant dance, and even trip-hop. Still, tracks such as "Smokebelch," "Theme," "Wilmott," and the expansive *Haunted Dancehall* have done much in helping to push post-techno beyond the often staid conventions of the dance floor. Weatherall has also gained visibility through remix and production work, working with Primal Scream and Scottish ambient-pop group One Dove, and reworking tracks for James, the Orb, Bjork, Therapy?, Happy Mondays, Future Sound of London, Bomb the Bass, Skylab, and the Moody Boys. His mixing skills can be sampled firsthand via the three-CD collection *Cut the Crap*, released by Six by 6 Records. After dissolving his Sabres of Paradise project and label, UK dance-don Andrew Weatherall set up the tripartite Emissions label group and launched his latest, perhaps most prodigious musical venture, Two Lone Swordsmen. A collaboration with Emissions engineer Keith Tenniswood, 2LS was formed in early 1996. The group speaks the same language of warped, downtempo grooves as much previous Sabres work (particularly "Smokebelch" and "Wilmott"), but opts instead for a syntax of minimal electronics and taut, brittle elec-tro-funk for structure and guidance. The group's first full-length release, 1996's *The Fifth Mission*, was a double-CD/triple-LP, both preceded and followed by additional EPs of new material ("Tenth Mission" and "Third Mission"). A few months later, the group issued two additional LP-length releases (both remix albums under the title *Swimming Not Skimming*, although the CD and LP versions sported different tracks), and by the end of 1996 had racked up no less than a half-dozen remixes (including Slab, Alter Ego, Sneaker Pimps, and David Holmes). — *Sean Cooper*

● **Sabresonic** / 1993 / Warp ✦✦✦✦
The Sabres' techno-oriented debut album includes crucial singles like "Smokebelch," "Wilmott" and previously unavailable items like "Still Fighting" and "Ano Electro." Also tacks on In the Nursery's beatless remix of "Smokebelch II." — *Sean Cooper*

Haunted Dancehall / 1994 / Warp ✦✦✦✦
The Sabres' second album is a conceptual manifesto of sorts, accompa-nied by a loose song-by-song narrative of descriptions written by the group. According to Weatherall, they initially hired Scottish novelist Irv-ine Welsh (*Trainspotting*) to pen the notes, but, unhappy with the results, threw together their own versions minutes before the record was shipped off to be pressed. Lots of thin, bubbly, minimalist ambient and mid-tempo breakbeat, with quirky, occasionally half-thought-out tracks aided by production assistance from Geoff Barrow (Portishead) and A. Carthy (Mr. Scruff). — *Sean Cooper*

Versus / 1995 / Warp ✦✦✦
Dirty, vigorous remixes from Depth Charge's J. Saul Kane and the Chem-ical Brothers. The CD includes extra versions, and a limited-edition vinyl triple-pack featured a ten-inch with LFO and Nightmares on Wax remixes and a one-sided seven-inch of "Haunted Dancehall" mixed by English post-classical group In the Nursery. — *Sean Cooper*

Sade (Helen Folsade Adu)

b. Jan. 16, 1959, Ibadan, Nigeria
Urban, Adult Contemporary, Pop

Sade's smooth, silky jazz-tinged pop-oriented R&B earned several hits and a large following in the mid-'80s. Borrowing the spirit, if not the sophisticated sound, of her idols Billie Holiday and Nina Simone, her music was lush and stylish, helped considerably by her talented support-ing band. After her 1988 album, *Stronger than Pride*, Sade disappeared for several years, reappearing in 1992 with *Love Deluxe*, which returned her to the spotlight, selling over a million copies in the first few months after it was released. — *Stephen Thomas Erlewine*

Diamond Life / 1984 / Portrait ✦✦✦✦
Former model Sade made an immediate and huge impact with her 1984 debut album. Her sound and approach were deliberately icy, her delivery and voice aloof, deadpan and cold, and yet she became an instant sensation through such songs as "Smooth Operator" and "Your Love Is King," where the slick production and quasi-jazz backing seemed to register with audiences thinking they were hearing a jazz vocalist. Sade won the Best New Grammy Award for 1985, and *Dia-mond Life* sold more than two million copies. — *Ron Wynn*

Promise / 1985 / Portrait ✦✦✦
Sade's second LP improved on the performance of her debut, as "Sweet-est Taboo" was a huge hit and "Never as Good as the First Time" landed in both the R&B and pop Top 20. She was once again the personification of cool, laidback singing, seldom extending or embellishing lyrics, regis-tering emotion or projecting her voice. This demeanor made her more desirable in the minds of many fans and was perhaps the ultimate mis-application of the notion of sophistication. But this album topped the pop-album charts and eventually went triple platinum. — *Ron Wynn*

Stronger than Pride / 1988 / Epic ✦✦✦
After two LPs with little or no energy, Sade demonstrated some intensity and fire on her third release. Whether that was just an attempt to change the pace a bit or a genuine new direction, she had more animation in her delivery on such songs as "Haunt Me," "Give It Up," and the hit "Par-adise." Not that she was suddenly singing in a soulful or bluesy manner; rather, Sade's dry and introspective tone now had a little more edge, and the lyrics were ironic as well as reflective. This was her third consecutive multi-platinum album, and it matched the two-million-plus sales level of her debut. — *Ron Wynn*

Love Deluxe / Oct. 20, 1992 / Epic ✦✦✦✦
Sade's fourth album included the hit "No Ordinary Love" and marked a return to the detached, cool jazz backing and even icier vocals that made her debut album a sensation. Although Sade's style is more suggestive than hypnotic, and her production and arrangements are in an urbane mode rather than a jazz one, she's maintained her popularity among the fusion and urban-contemporary audiences. This release also included "Mermaid," "Pearls," and "Feel No Pain." — *Ron Wynn*

● **Best of Sade** / 1994 / Epic ✦✦✦✦
It's easy to dismiss Sade as makeout music for Calvin Klein Obsession models, but the group created an impressive body of work over the course of a decade, a series of moody singles with cool jazz passion and the kick of good R&B. All the hits are here, of course, from "Smooth Operator" to "No Ordinary Love." — *Eddie Huffman*

St. Etienne

f. 1988, London, England
Alternative Pop-Rock, Club-Dance, Dream-Pop, Brit-Pop

Like most bands formed by former music journalists, St. Etienne was a highly conceptual group. The trio's concept was to fuse the British pop sounds of '60s London with the dance club rhythms and productions that defined the post-acid-house England of the early '90s. Led by songwriters Bob Stanley and Pete Wiggs, and fronted by vocalist Sarah Cracknell, the group managed to carry out their concept, and, in the process, they helped make indie-dance a viable genre within the UK. Throughout the early '90s, St. Etienne racked up a string of indie hit singles that were driven by deep club beats—encompassing anything from house and techno to hip-hop and disco—and layered with light melodies, detailed productions, clever lyrics and Cracknell's breathy vocals. They revived the sounds of swinging London, as well as the concept of the three-minute pop single being a catchy, ephemeral piece of ear candy, in post-acid house Britain, thereby setting the stage for Brit-pop. Though most Brit-pop bands rejected the dance inclinations of St. Etienne, they nevertheless adopted the trio's aesthetic, which celebrated the sound and style of classic '60s pop.

The origins of St. Etienne date back to the early '80s, when childhood friends Bob Stanley (b. December 25, 1964) and Pete Wiggs (b. May 15, 1966) began making party tapes together in their hometown of Croydon, Surrey, England. After completing school, the pair began worked various jobs—most notably, Stanley was a music journalist—before deciding to concentrate on a musical career in 1988. Adopting the name St. Etienne from the French football team of the same name, the duo moved to Camden, where they began recording. By the beginning of 1990, the group had signed a record contract with the indie label Heavenly. In the spring of 1990, St. Etienne released their first single, a house-tinged cover of Neil Young's "Only Love Can Break Your Heart," which featured lead vocals from Moira Lambert of the indie-pop band Faith Over Reason.

"Only Love Can Break Your Heart" became an underground hit, receiving a fair amount of airplay within nightclubs across England. Later in the year, St. Etienne released their second single, a cover of the indie-pop group Field Mice's "Kiss and Make Up," which was sung by Donna Savage of the New Zealand band Dead Famous People. "Kiss and Make Up" was also an underground hit, helping set the stage for "Nothing Can Stop Us." Released in the spring of 1991, "Nothing Can Stop Us" was the first St. Etienne single sung by Sarah Cracknell (b. April 12, 1967), whose girlish vocals became a signature of the group's sound. Cracknell was the main vocalist on the band's debut *Foxbase Alpha*, which was released in the fall of 1991. Following the release of *Foxbase Alpha*, Cracknell officially became a member of St. Etienne; she had previously sung in Prime Time.

"Only Love Can Break Your Heart" was re-released in conjunction with *Foxbase Alpha* and cracked the lower end of the British pop charts. St. Etienne was beginning to gain momentum, as the British press generally gave them positive reviews and their records were gaining a strong fan base not only in England, but throughout Europe. During 1992, the group released a series of singles—"Join Our Club," "People Get Real" and "Avenue"—which maintained their popularity. In addition to writing and recording music for St. Etienne, Stanley and Wiggs became active producers, songwriters, remixers and label heads as well. In 1989, Stanley had founded Caff Records, which issued limited-edition seven-inch singles of bands as diverse as Pulp and the Manic Street Preachers, as well as a number of other lesser-known bands like World of Twist. In 1992, Stanley and Wiggs founded Ice Rink, which intended to put out records by pop groups, not rock groups. The label released singles from several artists—including Oval, Sensurround, Elizabeth City Slate and Golden, which featured Stanley's girlfriend, Celina—none of which gained much attention.

Preceded by the single "You're in a Bad Way," St. Etienne's second album, *So Tough*, appeared in the spring of 1993 to generally positive reviews and increased sales. Over the course of 1993, the group released three more singles—"Who Do You Think You Are," "Hobart Paving," and "I Was Born on Christmas Day"—which all charted well. In 1994, the trio began to lose momentum, as their third album, *Tiger Bay*, was greeted with decidedly mixed reviews, even as singles like "Like a Motorway" continued to chart well. After completing a new track, "He's on the Phone," for their 1995 singles compilation, *Too Young to Die*, as well as a French-only single "Reserection," St. Etienne took an extended break during 1996. Sarah Cracknell pursued a solo project, releasing a single title "Anymore" in the fall of the year. Bob Stanley and Pete Wiggs began a record label for EMI Records, which had the intention of releasing music from young, developing bands. In the fall of 1996, St. Etienne released a remix album, *Casino Classics*. —*Stephen Thomas Erlewine*

Foxbase Alpha / Jan. 14, 1992 / Warner Brothers ✦✦✦
Despite a handful of classic pop singles, St. Etienne's debut album, *Foxbase Alpha*, is a tentative fusion of club culture and swinging '60s pop. Lead vocalist Sarah Cracknell hasn't been fully integrated into the band's lineup—she doesn't even sing on their astonishing Eurodisco cover of Neil Young's "Only Love Will Break Your Heart," which is not only cleverly ironic, but it also works—yet the filler remains thoroughly enjoyable, even if it rarely reaches the heights of the irresistible girl-group pop of "Kiss and Make Up." —*Stephen Thomas Erlewine*

So Tough / Mar. 9, 1993 / Warner Brothers ✦✦✦✦
St. Etienne's second album, *So Tough*, is a remarkable step forward from *Foxbase Alpha*, boasting a stronger set of songs and a sharper focus. Not only are the pop melodies catchier than before, the group's mastery of swinging '60s arrangements and Eurodisco rhythms is positively infectious, and Sarah Cracknell's light, airy vocals are alluringly dreamy, giving the record a wonderful, floating quality. The cool club beats, occasional sample and synthesized textures provide an inviting sonic backdrop for Bob Stanley and Pete Wiggs' infectious pop songs, and while the singles "You're in a Bad Way" and "Hobart Paving" stand out, there are several other tracks here that are nearly as good, making *So Tough* an irresistible set of danceable, well-constructed pop. —*Stephen Thomas Erlewine*

Tiger Bay / Jun. 28, 1994 / Warner Brothers ✦✦✦✦
Tiger Bay abandons the unassuming charm of *So Tough* for a grander sound. St. Etienne fill *Tiger Bay* with sonic details, from sampled bits of dialogue to musical references that give the record some depth, but occasionally those very sounds make the album feel over-labored. Still, the group frequently fulfills their ambitions, particularly on "Hug My Soul," "Like a Motorway" and the delightfully exuberant "I Was Born on Christmas Day," which features guest vocals by the Charlatans' Tim Burgess. Moments like these, plus St. Etienne's widening sonic palette, make *Tiger Bay* a thoroughly enjoyable affair, despite its handful of faults. —*Stephen Thomas Erlewine*

● **Too Young to Die** / Nov. 1995 / Heavenly ✦✦✦✦
Although their albums were considerably more consistent than most dance-pop acts, St. Etienne's high points were always their singles. Released prior to a quiet, lengthy hiatus, *Too Young to Die* collects all of their singles, from their debut disco cover of Neil Young's "Only Love Can Break Your Heart" to their last, "He's on the Phone," providing a thoroughly entertaining chronicle of the group's career. Much of the music sounds somewhat dated—which is always a problem with dance music—but St. Etienne was essentially a very good Euro-pop band, reveling in kitsch and style in equal measure. At their best—"Only Love Can Break Your Heart," "You're in a Bad Way," "Join Our Club," "Who Do You Think You Are," among others—they found the heart in nightclubbing. The quality of the music dips slightly in the latter half of the album, but there is prime pop throughout the disc. (Initial pressings came with a bonus disc of remixes, all of which are worthwhile for dedicated fans). —*Stephen Thomas Erlewine*

Casino Classics / Sep. 1996 / Heavenly ✦✦✦
The title makes a sly reference to a legendary Northern Soul club, which is appropriate, since *Casino Classics* is a collection of dance remixes. Comprised equally of classic 12-inch remixes and new offerings from the likes of the Aphex Twin and Chemical Brothers, the double-disc *Casino Classics* does have some wildly imaginative reinterpretations, but only dedicated St. Etienne collectors or dance-club devotees need to bother with the collection. —*Stephen Thomas Erlewine*

The Saints

f. 1977, Brisbane, Australia
Punk
Roaring out of Brisbane, Australia, in 1977 with the punk-era classic "(I'm) Stranded," the Saints, despite going through numerous incarnations, have been a part of rock 'n' roll for nearly 20 years, thanks mainly to their indefatigable leader (and founder) Chris Bailey. Although they haven't played anything that passes for punk rock since about 1978, and despite extended dormant periods, the Saints have never officially broken up (at least I'm unaware of it), and Bailey always seems to have another version of the band and record ready to release. Saints fans fall into two distinct camps: the punk-era fans (up to about 1980) and the mature pop fans, which for American audiences begins with the release of *All Fools Day* in 1987. I will here admit my biases and tell you that I am more of a fan of the punk era than of the mature pop era. This has nothing to do with the overall quality of the music; Bailey recorded two fine records with the late-'80s incarnation of the band. It's simply that the feral assault of their first three records (when co-founder Ed Kuepper was in the band) is more interesting and exciting. After Kuepper left in 1979 and the band became Bailey's show, the twists and turns he took them through (horns, folk/blues arrangements, as well his numerous solo excursions) produced some good music, but it was mostly too scattershot and lacked focus. It was simply too difficult to wade through the mediocre material.

Punk-era Saints was exactly what you'd expect: buzzsaw guitars, Bailey's pissed-off, nasal vocals, and locomotive rhythms supplied by bassist Kym Bradshaw and drummer Ivor Hay. After the LP *(I'm) Stranded* became a modest hit in England, the follow-up record, *Eternally Yours*, showed some changes (more varied tempos, acoustic guitars) that would set the stage for their third record, *Prehistoric Sounds*, which combined horn arrangements into a punkish sort of R&B. It was at this point that the Saints were beginning to change enough to not resemble the band they were just a scant two years earlier. Kuepper left to form the arty Laughing Clowns and eventually made a number of records as a solo act. Bailey, however, got to keep the name the Saints and soldiered on, taking time here and there to record his own solo records.

To most Americans, the Saints were a dead issue, if they were still an issue at all. (I'm) Stranded caught on with punk aficionados, but hardly anyone else; Eternally Yours came and went without a trace, and Prehistoric Sounds was never domestically released (neither were any of the post-Kuepper Saints records of the early '80s). So, by the time All Fools Day was released in 1987, there were many who thought the Saints were a brand new band—and they were right. Gone were the rapid-fire guitar sound and bellowing vocals, replaced by sophisticated pop arrangements and more technically accomplished singing. The music was strong, intelligent pop that was better than much of the late-'80s "new wave." The next LP, Prodigal Son, wasn't as good, but did nothing to hurt the reputation of the "new" Saints. Oddly enough, Kuepper has recently gotten together with Celibate Rifles guitarists Kent Steedman and Dave Morris and performed under the name the Aints. Gigging in Sydney, they generally play a set of (I'm) Stranded-era material, and have even recorded a couple of lo-fi live discs. It's all done for laughs, and I bet they're a hoot. As for Bailey, he's a credible performer who will continue to release interesting records, with or without the Saints. —John Dougan

● (I'm) Stranded / May 1977 / Sire ✦✦✦✦
Around the time Sire was scooping up every band under the sun that played like the Ramones, they had the smarts to sign the Saints, who were creating great punk rock. Along with the title track, there are rough and ready bits of speedburn, like "Erotic Neurotic," and very unpunk-like tracks in terms of song length, six minutes of "Messin' with the Kid" (not the Junior Wells song). Toss in a pisstake of Elvis' "Kissin' Cousins" and you've got the makings of a fine slice of history. I still think this is their best record for a lot of reasons, but primarily for its energy, high spirits, and smarts. —John Dougan

Eternally Yours / 1978 / Sire ✦✦✦✦
Retaining much of the raw punk raunch that fueled (I'm) Stranded, Eternally Yours adds horns to a couple of tracks as the Saints attempt to play a little high-speed R&B. This record doesn't have the recklessness of the first one, but there are plenty of strong songs, especially the music industry critique "Know Your Product." Recommended to those who want to repeat the buzz of the first LP, but need different songs. Incidentally, after the success of the first record, this was a major flop and doubtlessly precipitated Sire's decision to drop them. —John Dougan

All Fools Day / 1987 / TVT ✦✦✦✦
Call this the second coming of the Saints, but the only thing this record has in common with previous Saints recordings is Chris Bailey. Still, it's a sharp, tuneful, and (ahem) mature work that shows Bailey's increasing confidence as a singer and songwriter. One listen to songs as grabbing as "Celtic Ballad" or the great "Just like Fire Would" (which is kind of a neat pun) will convince you that despite the differences, the new Saints were a good band for completely different reasons than the old Saints. —John Dougan

Salt-N-Pepa

f. 1985, Queens, NY
Hip Hop, Urban
By the late '80s, hip-hop was on its way to becoming a male-dominated art form, which is what made the emergence of Salt-N-Pepa so significant. As the first all-female rap crew (even their DJs were women) of importance, the group broke down a number of doors for women in hip-hop. They were also one of the first rap artists to crossover into the pop mainstream, laying the groundwork for the music's widespread acceptance in the early '90s. Salt-N-Pepa were more pop-oriented than many of their contemporaries, since their songs were primarily party and love anthems, driven by big beats and interlaced with vaguely pro-feminist lyrics that seemed more powerful when delivered by the charismatic and sexy trio. While songs like "Push It" and "Shake Your Thang" made the group appear to be a one-hit pop group during the late '80s, Salt-N-Pepa defied expectations and became one of the few hip-hop artists to develop a long-term career. Along with LL Cool J, the trio had major hits in both the '80s and '90s, and, if anything, they hit the height of their popularity in 1994, when "Shoop" and "Whatta Man" drove their third album, Very Necessary, into the Top 10.

Cheryl "Salt" James and Sandy "Pepa" Denton were working at a Sears store in Queens, New York, when their co-worker, and Salt's boyfriend, Hurby "Luv Bug" Azor asked the duo to rap on a song he was producing for his audio production class at New York City's Center for Media Arts. The trio wrote an answer to Doug E. Fresh and Slick Rick's "The Show," entitling it "The Show Stopper." The song was released as a single under the name Super Nature in the summer of 1985, and it became an underground hit, peaking at No. 46 on the national R&B

charts. Based on its success, the duo, who were now named Salt-N-Pepa after a line in "The Show Stopper," signed with the national indie label Next Plateau. Azor, who had become their manager, produced their 1986 debut Hot, Cool & Vicious, which also featured DJ Pamela Green. He also took songwriting credit for the album, despite the duo's claims that they wrote many of its lyrics.

Three singles from Hot, Cool & Vicious–"My Mike Sounds Nice," "Tramp," "Chick on the Side"–became moderate hits in 1987 before Cameron Paul, a DJ at a San Francisco radio station, remixed "Push It," the B-side of "Tramp," and it became a local hit. "Push It" was soon released nationally and it became a massive hit, climbing to No. 19 on the pop charts; it became one of the first rap records to be nominated for a Grammy. Salt-N-Pepa jettisoned Green and added rapper and DJ Spinderella (b. Deidre "Dee Dee" Roper) before recording their second album, A Salt with a Deadly Pepa. Though the album featured the Top 10 R&B hit "Shake Your Thang," which was recorded with the go-go band E.U., it received mixed reviews and was only a minor hit.

The remix album A Blitz of Salt-N-Pepa Hits was released in 1989 as the group prepared their third album, Blacks' Magic. Upon its spring release, Blacks' Magic was greeted with strong reviews and sales. The album was embraced strongly by the hip-hop community, whose more strident members accused the band of trying too hard to cross over to the pop market. "Expression" spent eight weeks at the top of the rap charts, and went gold before it even cracked the pop charts, where it would later peak at 26. Another single from the album, "Let's Talk About Sex," became their biggest pop hit to date, climbing to No. 13. They later re-recorded the song as a safe-sex rap, "Let's Talk About AIDS."

Before they recorded their fourth album, Salt-N-Pepa separated from producer Hurby Azor, who had already stopped seeing Salt several years ago. Signing with London/Polygram, the group released Very Necessary in 1993. The album was catchy and sexy without being a sellout, and the group's new, sophisticated sound quickly became a monster hit. "Shoop" reached No. 4 on the pop charts, which led the album to the same position as well. "Whatta Man," a duet with the vocal group En Vogue, reached No. 3 on both the pop and R&B charts in 1994. A final single from the album, "None of Your Business," was a lesser hit, but it won the Grammy for Best Rap Performance in 1995. Since the release of Very Necessary, Salt N Pepa have been quiet, spending some time on beginning acting careers. Both had already appeared in the 1993 comedy Who's the Man? —Stephen Thomas Erlewine

Hot, Cool & Vicious / 1986 / London ✦✦✦✦
One of the earliest female rap groups, Salt-N-Pepa hit the big leagues with this debut that includes the pulsating "Push It" and the salacious "Tramp." —John Floyd

A Salt with a Deadly Pepa / 1988 / London ✦✦✦
A concept album musically, if not lyrically, this one fleshes out one terrific single, "Shake Your Thing," with a sharpening of the trio's sensibilities and talents. —John Floyd

A Blitz of Hits: The Hits Remixed / 1989 / London ✦✦
As remix albums go, Salt-N-Pepa's is fine, but their hit singles lose a bit of their magic in these extended forms. —Stephen Thomas Erlewine

● Blacks' Magic / Mar. 1990 / London ✦✦✦✦
Another concept album, this time the themes celebrate Black education and awareness, with some concise feminism included. —John Floyd

Very Necessary / Oct. 12, 1993 / PolyGram ✦✦✦✦
Driven by the ferociously sexy "Shoop," Salt-N-Pepa's latest album matches the drive of that hit as well as the best of their earlier classics, making it one of the best albums of their successful career. —AMG

Sam & Dave

f. 1961, Miami, FL
Soul
Perhaps no act epitomized soul music as the secularization of gospel more than Sam & Dave. The original pairing of Sam Moore and Dave Prater met in Florida in 1961, and they recorded unsuccessfully for several years before being signed to Atlantic Records in 1965. Atlantic persuaded their Memphis affiliate Stax Records to produce them, and in December that year the writing and production team of Isaac Hayes and David Porter delivered the crisply soulful "You Don't Know Like I Know." Hayes and Porter became the "eminences grises" behind Sam & Dave, much as Holland-Dozier-Holland pulled the strings behind the Supremes. They wrote, they produced—and the result was a string of hits, including "Soul Man," "Hold On, I'm Comin'" and "I Thank You," songs that survive as the very epitome of Southern soul. Certainly, Sam & Dave's hits are among the most soulful ever to crack the Hot 100. Their albums often bore the hallmarks of hasty execution, though. The dissolution of the partnership between Stax and Atlantic virtually sealed

the fate of Sam & Dave; there were a few more hits (and, later, a revival of interest thanks to the Blues Brothers), but the glory days were over.

Samuel Moore and David Prater were both raised in the South, where they sang in church as children. During the '50s, they performed in soul and R&B clubs before meeting each other in at the King of Hearts club in Miami in 1961. Moore was hosting an amateur-night contest where Prater was singing. Once Dave forgot the lyrics to Jackie Wilson's "Doggin' Around," Sam coached him through the song. Following that night, the singers became a duo and soon became a popular local Miami act and signed with Roulette Records, releasing a handful of singles. In 1965, they signed with Atlantic Records, but producer Jerry Wexler moved the duo to the label's Stax subsidiary.

Working with Stax's house band and songwriters/producers Isaac Hayes and David Porter, Sam & Dave created a body of sweaty, gritty soul that ranks among the finest and most popular produced in the late '60s. The duo's 1966 debut, "You Don't Know Like I Know," kicked off a series of Top Ten R&B hits that included "Hold On, I'm Comin'" (1966), "You Got Me Hummin'" (1966), "When Something Is Wrong with My Baby" (1967), "Soul Man" (1967), and "I Thank You" (1968). However, the duo's career began to unravel in 1968, when Stax's distribution deal with Atlantic ended. Since Sam & Dave were signed with Atlantic, not Stax, they no longer had access to the production team of Hayes and Porter or the house band of Booker T. & the MG's, and their recorded work took a slight dip in quality. Though the switch of labels was unfortunate, what really caused the duo's demise was their volatile relationship. While the duo had enormous creative energy, they frequently fought offstage. Nicknamed "Double Dynamite," Sam & Dave became famous for their energetic, infectious live performances during the late '60s, which complemented the overall high quality of their studio work. They may have communicated onstage, but behind the scenes it was reported that the duo could hardly stand each other's presence. The tension caused Sam & Dave to part ways in 1970, just a few years after their heyday.

During the '70s, Sam & Dave reunited several times to little attention. At the end of the decade, John Belushi and Dan Aykroyd's Blues Brothers routine—which borrowed heavily from Sam & Dave—sparked a resurgence of interest in the duo, and the pair performed a number of concerts during 1980. However, their personal animosity had not faded, and they separated after a performance on New Year's Eve 1981. For the next few years, Dave Prater toured as Sam & Dave with vocalist Sam Daniels. During the mid-'80s, Sam Moore revealed the sources of the duo's tensions in a series of interviews. Moore disclosed that he had been addicted to drugs during the '70s. Prater was arrested in 1987 for selling crack to an undercover policeman. A year later, he died in a car accident. Moore continued to perform sporadically, most notably on Bruce Springsteen's 1992 album *Human Touch* album. Sam & Dave were inducted into the Rock & Roll Hall of Fame that same year. —*Colin Escott & Stephen Thomas Erlewine*

Sam & Dave / 1962 / Roulette ✦✦✦
Sam Moore and Dave Prater cut one album for Roulette before coming to Stax, where they acheived soul superstardom. They displayed their potential on this set, although they didn't have the musical support, production greatness, or magnificent songs that they received at Stax. But Moore's earthy leads and Prater's gritty contrasts were already emerging, if in rough fashion. Since this was practically deleted the day after it was issued, forget about finding it unless you're willing to pay ripoff prices in a collector's auction or at a specialty store, or find someone who doesn't know what they're doing throwing it out one day in a garage sale. —*Ron Wynn*

Hold On, I'm Comin' / 1966 / Atlantic ✦✦✦✦
When the northern soulsters of Motown were employing strings and pop elements, Sam & Dave rejected pop wholesale and made sure they kept their Memphis soul simple and raw. Their albums never sounded heavily produced, and therein lies much of the appeal of *Hold On, I'm Comin'* (their first album for Atlantic). This wasn't a duo that believed in hiding behind lavish productions. Like the blues and gospel artists who paved the way for soul music, Sam & Dave knew how to seize the moment. From such major hits as "You Don't Know Like I Know" and the title song to solid album tracks like the riveting "It's a Wonder" and the tough yet vulnerable ballad "Just Me," this album epitomizes Memphis soul in all its unpretentious, down-home glory. A song-for-song reissue of the original LP, the CD version of *Hold On, I'm Comin'* that Atlantic put out in 1991 is rather skimpy by CD standards (as are the CD versions of *Soul Men* and *I Thank You*). Certainly Atlantic could have provided some bonus tracks. Nonetheless, this CD is well worth hearing. —*Alex Henderson*

Double Dynamite / 1967 / Atlantic ✦✦✦✦
This was the second Sam & Dave album to enjoy significant crossover appeal. The 1967 record included such hits as "Said I Wasn't Gonna Tell Nobody," "Soothe Me," and "When Something Is Wrong with My Baby." Isaac Hayes and David Porter were now rolling as songwriters, and even

though the record didn't attain big pop numbers, the singles clicked with both soul and pop audiences. More importantly, Sam & Dave's teamwork and vocal interaction were establishing them as major stars. —*Ron Wynn*

Soul Men / 1967 / Rhino ✦✦✦✦
Because R&B was such a singles-driven market in the 1960s, many albums released by Stax and Motown were big on filler. But that generally wasn't the case with Sam & Dave's albums, which boasted many gems that weren't released as singles and enjoyed little, if any, radio airplay. Listeners may be surprised to learn that as popular as this twosome was in 1967, *Soul Men* contains only one major single: the anthemic title song and its B-side, the charming "May I Baby." Among the first-class album tracks never released as singles were "Rich Kind of Poverty," the punchy "Hold It Baby," and the gospel-drenched ballads "Just Keep Holding On" and "I've Seen What Loneliness Can Do." For those with more than a casual interest in Memphis soul, *Soul Men* (reissued on CD in 1991) is highly recommended. —*Alex Henderson*

I Thank You / 1968 / Rhino ✦✦✦
Although not quite as strong as *Hold On, I'm Comin'* or *Soul Men*, *I Thank You* serves as a fine illustration of the splendor of Memphis soul. The best-known songs on this album (reissued on CD in 1992) are the title song and its infectious B-side, "Wrap It Up." Interestingly, this wasn't an album that contained a lot of major hits, but it does have a lot to admire, including "If I Didn't Have a Girl Like You" (a gem of a ballad), the driving "Ain't That a Lot of Love" and an inspired version of Otis Redding's "These Arms of Mine." As usual, Isaac Hayes' arranging and songwriting is a definite asset for the energetic duo, which really digs right into the material and spares no passion. —*Alex Henderson*

The Best of Sam & Dave / 1969 / Atlantic ✦✦✦✦
For many years this late-'60s Atlantic collection was the finest value available to soul fans who hadn't purchased the original albums. But Rhino's extensive 1993 two-volume set supplanted this collection, although it's still a nice set and is ideal for anyone who didn't want the B-sides and extra tracks from Rhino. Atlantic had the good sense to reissue it on CD in the mid-'80s, and it's still available. —*Ron Wynn*

Back at 'Cha! / 1976 / United Artists ✦✦✦
The great soul duo of Sam Moore and Dave Prater made a gallant attempt at a comeback with this mid-'70s release, but the times had changed dramatically, and there wasn't much demand on the urban contemporary horizon for an aging Southern soul duo. Their harmonies were still solid, although the leads and shared vocals were a little on the faded side. It was great to hear the two singing together again, but the combination of changed audience tastes and uneven material proved too much of an obstacle for Sam & Dave to get back in the spotlight. —*Ron Wynn*

☆ **Sweat 'n' Soul** / Jul. 20, 1993 / Rhino/Atlantic ✦✦✦✦✦
Sam Moore and Dave Prater were the ultimate soul duo; one a high-voiced wailer, the other a low-toned blaster. They came together in the mid-'60s to form a superb duo, singing tunes penned by soul's finest writing tandem, Isaac Hayes and David Porter. They made a host of great singles before ego battles broke them apart. This 50-cut, two-disc anthology not only has every song of significance, but plenty of obscure worthwhile items, like a "Stay in School" promo, some overlooked material done with the Dixie Flyers, and a couple of numbers cut by Moore as a solo act in the early '70s. The sound quality, annotation, and song sequencing are as outstanding as the songs themselves. —*Ron Wynn*

★ **The Very Best of Sam & Dave** / Feb. 28, 1995 / Rhino ✦✦✦✦✦
The Very Best of Sam & Dave contains all of Sam & Dave's Top 40 hits, including "You Don't Know Like I Know," "Hold On, I'm Comin'," "Said I Wasn't Gonna Tell Nobody," "You Got Me Hummin'," "When Something Is Wrong with My Baby," "Soothe Me," "Soul Man," and "I Thank You," plus a handful of essential album tracks and B-sides like "I Can't Stand Up for Falling Down." It's an expertly compiled, concise collection that contains everything you need to know. If you need to dig deeper, the double-disc *Sweat 'n' Soul* is essential, but most casual fans will be completely satisfied by *The Very Best of Sam & Dave*. —*Stephen Thomas Erlewine*

Santana (Devadip Carlos Santana)

f. 1966, San Francisco, CA
Guitar / Rock & Roll, Blues-Rock, Fusion, Psychedelic
Santana is the name of a band that has successfully married elements of blues, rock, and Latin music and enjoyed international acclaim for more than two decades. It is also the name of the guitarist, Carlos Santana, who has led that band and made other recordings over the same period of time. In its original manifestation, the Santana Blues Band was a group of equals, with Carlos named as leader only because of a musicians union requirement that such a designation be made. The group was formed in San Francisco in the mid-'60s and first gained recogni-

tion in the same dance halls that hosted the psychedelic rock groups of the era, although, with its Latin and African roots, Santana never quite fit in with the psychedelic sound. The group came under the direction of promoter Bill Graham and had already scored a contract with Columbia when it appeared at the Woodstock Festival in August 1969. Personnel at that time, in addition to Carlos, included Gregg Rolie (vocals and keyboards), Dave Brown (bass), Mike Shrieve (drums), Armando Peraza (percussion and vocals), and Mike Carabello and Jose Areas (percussion).

Santana, the debut album, was a massive success, including the No. 4 hit "Evil Ways." *Abraxas* (1970) did even better, topping the charts for six weeks and featuring the hits "Black Magic Woman" and "Oye Como Va." For *Santana III* (1971), the group expanded to a septet with the addition of guitarist Neal Schon, though an additional six sidemen were listed in the album credits. This album was No. 1 for five weeks.

Guitarist Santana released a live duet album with drummer and vocalist Buddy Miles (later a member of Santana) in 1972; then came the fourth Santana Band album, *Caravanserai*, on which different musician credits were listed for each track, none of them including bassist Dave Brown or percussionist Mike Carabello. The album was a Top Ten hit. Carlos released another duet album in 1973 with guitarist John McLaughlin (the two shared a guru), followed by *Welcome*, credited to "The New Santana Band," its only remaining original members being Santana, Mike Shrieve, Armando Peraza, and Jose Areas (Rolie and Schon had decamped to found Journey).

In subsequent years, "Santana" for the most part referred to Carlos and a band of hired musicians playing in the established Santana style, while the leader also made occasional solo albums that varied the style somewhat. In 1992, Santana ended his long association with Columbia and signed to Polydor, which set up a custom label for him, calling for him to sign his own new acts. *— William Ruhlmann*

Santana / Aug. 1969 / Columbia ✦✦✦✦
A brilliant combination of rock with Latin and African influences, prominently featuring the organ playing and husky vocals of Gregg Rolie; the energetic, precise drumming of Mike Shrieve; and, especially, the soaring, immediately identifiable guitar sound of Carlos Santana. Justifiably a massive hit and the prototype for an assembly line of similar records. Contains "Evil Ways" and "Soul Sacrifice." *— William Ruhlmann*

★ **Abraxas** / Sep. 1970 / Columbia ✦✦✦✦✦
The San Francisco Bay Area rock scene of the late '60s was one that encouraged radical experimentation and discouraged the type of mindless conformity that's often plagued corporate rock. When one considers just how different Santana, Jefferson Airplane, Moby Grape and the Grateful Dead sounded, it becomes obvious just how much it was encouraged. In the mid-'90s, an album as eclectic as *Abraxas* would be considered a marketing exec's worst nightmare. But at the dawn of the 1970s, this unorthodox mix of rock, jazz, salsa, and blues proved quite successful. Whether adding rock elements to salsa king Tito Puente's "Oye Como Va," embracing instrumental jazz-rock on "Incident at Neshabur" and "Samba Pa Ti" or tackling moody blues-rock on Fleetwood Mac's "Black Magic Woman," the band keeps things unpredictable yet cohesive. Many of the Santana albums that came out in the '70s are worth acquiring, but for novices, *Abraxas* is an excellent place to start. *— Alex Henderson*

Santana III / Sep. 1971 / Columbia ✦✦✦✦
Completes a trilogy of tightly constructed, exciting band albums filled with percolating, multirhythmic percussion and fiery guitar work. The last album that is the work of the Woodstock-era Santana band. *— William Ruhlmann*

Carlos Santana & Buddy Miles! Live! / Jun. 1972 / Columbia ✦✦
From December 1971 to April 1972, Carlos Santana and several other members of Santana toured with drummer/vocalist Buddy Miles, a former member of the Electric Flag and Jimi Hendrix's Band of Gypsys. The resulting live album contained both Santana hits ("Evil Ways") and Buddy Miles hits ("Changes"), plus a 25-minute, side-long jam. It was not, perhaps, the live album Santana fans had been waiting for, but at this point in its career, the band could do no wrong. The album went into the Top Ten and sold a million copies. (Reissued on CD on September 6, 1994.) *— William Ruhlmann*

Caravanserai / Oct. 1972 / Columbia ✦✦✦✦
Drawing on rock, salsa, and jazz, Santana recorded one imaginative, unpredictable gem after another in the 1970s. But *Caravanserai* is daring even by Santana's high standards. Carlos Santana was obviously very hip to jazz-fusion—something the innovative guitarist provides a generous dose of on the largely instrumental *Caravanserai*. Whether its approach is jazz-rock or simply rock, this album is consistently inspired and quite adventurous. Full of heartfelt, introspective guitar solos, it lacks the immediacy of *Santana* or *Abraxas*. Like the type of jazz that influenced it, this pearl (which marked the beginning of keyboardist/composer Tom Coster's highly beneficial membership in the band) requires a number of listenings in order to be absorbed and fully appre-

ciated. But make no mistake: this is one of Santana's finest accomplishments. *— Alex Henderson*

Love Devotion Surrender / 1973 / Columbia ✦✦✦
A duo album by John McLaughlin and Carlos Santana, this recording presents the two guitarists attempting jazz-fusion versions of the work of John Coltrane and McLaughlin compositions. Santana's fire is dampened somewhat by the solemn proceedings, but his commercial power held: this was the sixth straight Santana-related album to go gold, but the first to miss the Top Ten. *— William Ruhlmann*

Welcome / Nov. 1973 / Columbia ✦✦✦
On the group's fifth album, "The New Santana Band," as it was called, was an octet. Musically, the album was something of a companion piece to Carlos Santana's duet album with John McLaughlin, *Love Devotion Surrender*, even including a song by that title and, like the earlier record, containing compositions by McLaughlin and John Coltrane. In addition to the jazz influences, there was also a new blues sound courtesy of Leon Thomas, a smooth-voiced singer in the Joe Williams tradition. The record was musically adventurous, but as Santana continued to diverge from its Latin rock roots, its popularity eroded. *— William Ruhlmann*

Lotus / May 1974 / Columbia ✦✦✦✦
Recorded in Japan in July 1973, this massive live album, originally on three LPs and now on two compact discs, was available outside the United States in 1974, but held back from domestic release until long into the CD age. It features the same "New Santana Band" that recorded *Welcome* and combines that group's jazz and spiritual influences with performances of earlier Latin rock favorites like "Oye Como Va." *— William Ruhlmann*

● **Greatest Hits** / Jul. 1974 / Columbia ✦✦✦✦
This ten-song sampler presents the best of Santana, 1969-71, the period of its greatest popularity. The hits include "Black Magic Woman," "Evil Ways," "Everybody's Everything," and "Oye Como Va." But note that this is a bare minimum of prime Santana. Not only does the sampler choose from only Santana's first three albums, but it leaves out such seminal numbers as "Nobody to Depend On" and "Soul Sacrifice." Those looking for a more extensive overview should consider *Viva Santana!* *— William Ruhlmann*

Illuminations / Sep. 1974 / Columbia ✦✦
For his third duet album, Carlos Santana, who had been performing the works of John Coltrane, paired with Coltrane's widow, harpist/keyboardist Alice Coltrane, on this instrumental album. Side one includes several contemplative, string-filled numbers, while side two presents Santana's recreation of John Coltrane's late free-jazz style in "Angel of Sunlight." Columbia Records can't have been pleased at Santana's determined drift into esoteric jazz: *Illuminations* was the first of the nine Santana-related albums so far released in the US not to go gold. *— William Ruhlmann*

Borboletta / Oct. 1974 / Columbia ✦✦✦
Borboletta was the first new Santana band studio album in 11 months and the group's sixth overall. Once again, individual credits were listed for each song. The main problem was that the band seemed to be coasting; Carlos turned in the usual complement of high-pitched lead guitar work, and the percussionists pounded away, but the Santana sound had long since taken over from any individual composition, and the records were starting to sound alike. That, in turn, started to make them inessential; *Borboletta* spent less time in the charts than any previous Santana album. *— William Ruhlmann*

Amigos / Mar. 1976 / Columbia ✦✦✦✦
By the release of *Amigos*, the Santana band's seventh album, only Carlos Santana and David Brown remained from the band that conquered Woodstock, and only Carlos had been in the band continuously since. Meanwhile, the group had made some effort to arrest its commercial slide, hiring an outside producer, David Rubinson, and taking a tighter, more uptempo, and more vocal approach to its music. The overt jazz influences were replaced by strains of R&B/funk and Mexican folk music. The result was an album more dynamic than any since *Santana III* in 1971. "Let It Shine" (No. 77), an R&B-tinged tune, became the group's first chart single in four years, and the album returned Santana to Top Ten status. *— William Ruhlmann*

Festival / Jan. 1977 / Columbia ✦✦✦
Santana's follow-up to its comeback album, *Amigos*, was another David Rubinson-produced effort that moved back toward more of a Latin-rock feel, although it retained an essentially pop focus—"The River" was the first real vocal ballad on a Santana album. If any doubt still existed that the group was no longer a band of equals but a platform for its lead guitarist, the current lineup dispelled that; Carlos Santana was now the only original member of the band left. Although the album went gold, the lack of a hit single hurt the album's commercial standing; its No. 27 peak was the lowest yet for a Santana Band album. *— William Ruhlmann*

Moonflower / Oct. 1977 / Columbia ✦✦✦
Santana, which was renowned for its concert work dating back to Woodstock, did not release a live album in the US until this one, and it's only partially live, with studio tracks added, notably a cover of the Zombies' "She's Not There" (No. 27) that became Santana's first Top 40 hit in five years. The usual comings and goings in band membership had taken place since last time; the track listing was a good mixture of the old—"Black Magic Woman," "Soul Sacrifice"—and the recent, and with the added radio play of a hit single, *Moonflower* went Top Ten and sold a million copies, the first new Santana album to do that since 1972 and the last. —*William Ruhlmann*

Inner Secrets / Oct. 1978 / Columbia ✦✦
Since he had joined Santana in 1972, keyboard player Tom Coster had been Carlos Santana's right-hand man, playing, co-writing, co-producing, and generally taking the place of founding member Gregg Rolie. But Coster left the band in the spring of 1978, to be replaced by keyboardist/guitarist Chris Solberg and keyboardist Chris Ryne. Despite the change, the band soldiered on, and with *Inner Secrets* they scored three chart singles: the discoish "One Chain (Don't Make No Prison)" (No. 59), "Stormy" (No. 32), and a cover of Buddy Holly's "Well All Right" (No. 69), done in the Blind Faith arrangement. (There seems to be a Steve Winwood fixation here. The album also featured a cover of Traffic's "Dealer.") The singles kept the album on the charts longer than any Santana LP since 1971, but it was still a minor disappointment after *Moonflower*, and in retrospect seems like one of the band's more compromised efforts. —*William Ruhlmann*

Oneness: Silver Dreams Golden Realities / Mar. 1979 / Columbia ✦✦✦
This is the first Carlos Santana solo album. It features members of the Santana band as backup, however, so the difference between a group effort and a solo work seems to be primarily in the musical approach, which is more esoteric and more varied than on a regular band album. The record is mostly instrumental and given over largely to contemplative ballads, although there is also, for example, in the song "Silver Dreams Golden Smiles," a traditional pop ballad sung by Saunders King. —*William Ruhlmann*

Marathon / Sep. 1979 / Columbia ✦✦
Marathon marked the addition of keyboard player Alan Pasqua and singer Greg Walker's replacement by singer/guitarist Alex Ligertwood in the Santana lineup. Otherwise, the album was notable for consisting entirely of band-written material, although those songs were in the established R&B/rock style evolved on albums like *Amigos*, *Festival*, and *Inner Secrets*. The formula seemed to be wearing thin by now, however. Even with a Top 40 hit in "You Know That I Love You" (No. 35), *Marathon* became the first Santana album to fall below the 500,000-sales mark necessary for gold record certification. (It has since made the mark.) —*William Ruhlmann*

The Swing of Delight / Aug. 1980 / Columbia ✦✦
For his second "solo" album, Carlos Santana used Miles Davis' famed '60s group—Herbie Hancock, Wayne Shorter, Ron Carter, and Tony Williams—plus members of the current Santana band for a varied, jazz-oriented session that was one of his more pleasant excursions from the standard Santana sound. (Originally released as a double-LP, *The Swing of Delight* was reissued on a single CD.) —*William Ruhlmann*

Zebop! / Apr. 1981 / Columbia ✦✦
On *Zebop!*, a Santana band featuring newcomer Richard Baker on keyboards tried to preserve the better elements of the first and third trilogies of Santana albums—there was a heavy component of Latin-flavored percussion topped by Carlos' biting lead guitar work, and there were also three pop cover songs in Cat Stevens' "Changes," J.J. Cale's "The Sensitive Kind," and Russ Ballard's "Winning." The double strategy worked. "Winning" (No. 17) became Santana's first Top 20 single in a decade, "The Sensitive Kind" (No. 56) also charted, and the album was Santana's first Top Ten, gold-selling hit in four years. —*William Ruhlmann*

Shango / Aug. 1982 / Columbia ✦✦
Shango is notable for featuring the return, in the role of co-producer and co-songwriter, of original Santana keyboardist Gregg Rolie. The main producer, however, was Bill Szymczyk (James Gang, Eagles), who gave Santana an unusually sharp rock sound resulting in two more hit singles, "Hold On" (No. 15) and "Nowhere to Run" (No. 66), although the band once again slipped below Top Ten, gold-selling status, with the album peaking at only No. 22, and even this was the highest Santana would get from here on out. —*William Ruhlmann*

Havana Moon / Apr. 1983 / Columbia ✦✦✦
The third Carlos Santana solo album marks a surprising turn toward 1950s rock 'n' roll and Tex-Mex, with covers such as Bo Diddley's "Who Do You Love" and Chuck Berry's title song. Produced by veteran R&B producers Jerry Wexler and Barry Beckett, the album features an eclectic mix of sidemen, including Booker T. Jones of Booker T & the MG's,

Willie Nelson, and the Fabulous Thunderbirds. *Havana Moon* is a light effort, but it's one of Santana's most enjoyable albums, which may explain why it was also the best-selling Santana album outside the group releases in ten years. —*William Ruhlmann*

Beyond Appearances / Feb. 1985 / Columbia ✦✦
Seven months in the making, and appearing two and a half years after Santana's last album, *Beyond Appearances* was produced by Val ("Bette Davis Eyes") Garay in a hot 1980s style replete with prominent synthesizers and drum machines. In the interim, the band had undergone changes, with Alphonso Johnson replacing David Margen on bass, Chester D. Thompson and David Sancious replacing Richard Baker on keyboards, Chester Cortez Thompson replacing Graham Lear on drums, and singer Greg Walker rejoining. Garay co-wrote "Say It Again" (No. 46), Santana's final Hot 100 entry (a remake of Curtis Mayfield's "I'm the One Who Loves You" hit No. 102), but this latest pop interpretation of the Santana sound did not endear it to fans, and, at a peak of No. 50, *Beyond Appearances* was the lowest charting Santana album yet. —*William Ruhlmann*

Freedom / Feb. 1987 / Columbia ✦✦✦
Freedom marked several reunions in the Santana band, which was now a nonet. In addition to Carlos, the band consisted of percussionists Armando Pereza, Orestes Vilato, and Raul Rekow, returning drummer Graham Lear, bassist Alphonso Johnson, returning keyboardist Tom Coster, keyboardist Chester Thompson, and, on lead vocals, Buddy Miles, who had made a duet album with Santana 15 years before. Credited as an "additional musician" was keyboard player Gregg Rolie, an original member. The music also marked a return from the hyper-pop sound of Val Garay on *Beyond Appearances* to a more traditional Santana Latin rock style. Thus, *Freedom* was a literal return to form, but, unfortunately, not to the quality of early Santana albums. And the group's commercial decline continued, with the LP getting to only No. 95. —*William Ruhlmann*

Blues for Salvador / Oct. 1987 / Columbia ✦✦✦✦
On previous "solo" albums, Carlos Santana had made noticeable stylistic changes and worked with jazz, pop, and even country musicians. On this, his fourth Carlos Santana release, the line between a "solo" and a "group" project is blurred; this record is really a catchall of Santana band outtakes and stray tracks. For example, included are an instrumental version of "Deeper, Dig Deeper" from *Freedom* and an alternate take of "Hannibal" from *Zebop!*, as well as "Now That You Know" from the group's 1985 tour. Given the variety of material, the album is somewhat less focused than most Santana band albums, but there are individual tracks that are impressive, notably "Trane," which features Tony Williams on drums. (*Blues for Salvador* won the Grammy Award for Best Rock Instrumental Performance.) —*William Ruhlmann*

Viva Santana! / Aug. 1988 / Columbia ✦✦✦✦
A lovingly assembled two-disc retrospective set that collects the best of the Santana band, along with many interesting rarities. —*William Ruhlmann*

Spirits Dancing in the Flesh / Jun. 1990 / Columbia ✦✦✦
Following a 1989 20th-anniversary reunion tour to promote *Viva Santana!*, Carlos Santana reorganized the band as a sextet and recorded *Spirits Dancing in the Flesh*, Santana's 15th and final studio album for Columbia Records. It was an unusually eclectic collection, featuring songs by Curtis Mayfield ("Gypsy Woman"), the Isley Brothers ("Who's That Lady"), and Babatunde Olatunji ("Jin-Go-Lo-Ba"). For all those influences, it was more of a straightforward, guitar-heavy rock album than usual. Coming more than three years after Santana's last new album, *Freedom*, it sold to the band's core audience only, reaching No. 85. —*William Ruhlmann*

Milagro / May 5, 1992 / Polydor ✦✦✦
Santana signed to Polydor in 1991 after 22 years with Columbia Records. Their label debut has a somewhat elegiac tone, beginning with a stage introduction by the late promoter Bill Graham and featuring an excerpt from a speech by Dr. Martin Luther King, Jr., solos taken from Miles Davis and John Coltrane, and music written by Bob Marley, Coltrane, and Gil Evans. Despite the presence of all these heroic ghosts, however, *Milagro* is only an average Santana release, familiar-sounding but undistinguished, and it failed to arrest the band's commercial slide, becoming the first new Santana studio album not to crack the Top 100. —*William Ruhlmann*

Sacred Fire: Santana Live in South America / Oct. 19, 1993 / Polydor ✦✦
For its third live album, Santana introduced a new bass player, Myron Dove, and added guitarist Jorge Santana (Carlos Santana's brother) and singer Vorriece Cooper to bring the band up to nine members. Adopting the mantle of Bob Marley, the band played "Esperando," which borrowed Marley's characteristic audience chant. Much of the album, however, is given over to repeating Santana's earliest hits—"No One to Depend On," "Black Magic Woman," "Soul Sacrifice," etc.—which should

please the band's new record label (it's always good to have versions of the hits in your catalog), but which make the album inessential for fans. *Sacred Fire* spent one week at No.181 in the charts, the worst performance ever for a Santana album. — *William Ruhlmann*

Dance of the Rainbow Serpent / Aug. 8, 1995 / Columbia ✦✦✦
Guitarist Carlos Santana continues to record music but, when contemplating his body of work, it's difficult not to telescope to the "vintage" 1969-1975 period, from first albums *Santana* and *Abraxas* through to *Lotus*. Santana *Dance of the Rainbow Serpent* offers a well-rounded, three-disc overview of his career, but it remains the sultry Latin rhythms and stinging guitar of the early years—captured on disc one, subtitled *Heart*—that prove invigorating. The obvious hits like "Evil Ways" and "Black Magic Woman" are all included of course, although these are scorched by the speedy pyrotechnics of the likes of "Toussaint Overture" from *Lotus*. The second disc, mistitled *Soul*, covers material that is, to be kind, bland and overproduced. Without the Latin edge, there's nothing to distinguish the contents from a hundred other MOR performers. Third disc *Spirit* is more diverse, delving into the funkier examples of his later work, plus sessions with John Lee Hooker (including hit "The Healer") and previously unreleased material (including a workout with Living Color's Vernon Reid). In all, plenty here for fans of Santana's fluid, spiritual style—with one of three discs left to gather. — *Roch Parisien*

Live at Fillmore 1968 / Mar. 11, 1997 / Sony ✦✦✦
Two-CD package drawn from performances at the Fillmore West in December 1968, with an early lineup including Bob Livingston on drums and Marcus Malone on congas (both of whom would be gone by the time the group recorded their official debut in 1969). The band sound only a bit more tentative here than they would in their Woodstock-era incarnation, running through several of the highlights of their first album ("Jingo," "Persuasion," "Soul Sacrifice," and "Treat"). More interesting to collectors will be the five songs that have not previously appeared on any Santana recording, including covers of songs by jazzmen Chico Hamilton and Willie Bobo, and a half-hour original jam that concludes the set, "Freeway." The sound is excellent, and the arrangements a bit more improv-oriented than what ended up on the early studio records. Its appeal isn't solely limited to committed fans; on its own terms it's a fine release, highlighted by some burning organ-guitar interplay in particular. — *Richie Unterberger*

Joe Satriani

b. 1956, Long Island, NY
Guitar, Drums / Hard Rock, Fusion, Pop-Rock, Guitar Virtuoso
Joe Satriani was one of the best, most influential rock guitarists of the late '80s, equally capable of fast flights of blinding technique as well as sweet, lyrical passages. What also separates Satriani from most technically gifted guitar virtuosos is that he treats a song as a song, not as an excuse to shred. For these reasons, he appeals not only to guitarists but also to many rock fans who have never touched the instrument—his breakthrough 1987 album, *Surfing with the Alien*, was the first rock instrumental album in years to chart in the Top 30 on *Billboard*'s Top 200 Albums. Since then, he has added vocals to his records; while his voice can't compare to his guitar, it added another dimension to an artist that was already more versatile than the majority of contemporary musicians.

Before Satriani became a recording star, he taught guitar is San Francisco; several of his students became famous, influential guitarists in their own right, before he even recorded his first album in 1988. Metallica's Kirk Hammett was the first of his students to hit the big time, followed by Steve Vai and Larry LaLonde of Primus. — *Stephen Thomas Erlewine*

Not of This Earth / 1986 / Relativity ✦✦✦✦
Not of This Earth was the first studio release from guitar wizard Joe Satriani (not counting the hard-to-find *Joe Satriani EP*). This all-instrumental album was making ripples in the guitar-playing community not long after it was released, and it's easy to see why: superior compositions, a signature style, a unique tone and playing that's out of this world. Satriani shifts musical gears deftly, often layering multiple tracks together to make a complex soundscape. The fiery sound of "Not of This Earth" and "Hordes of Locusts" is tempered by the cool, dark tone of "Driving at Night," the far-out Eastern approach of "The Snake," and the quiet, thoughtful "Rubina." Satriani's fluid playing and wicked licks are enough to drop jaws and widen eyes. There isn't a weak track on this disc, even though the guitarist was still maturing when he released it. — *Phil Carter*

● **Surfing with the Alien** / 1987 / Relativity ✦✦✦✦
Not content to sit on his laurels, Satriani released this groundbreaking instrumental album in 1987, leaving guitarists and musicians everywhere stunned and amazed by the playing and musicianship displayed therein. Satriani defined his sound more sharply to further develop his distinct musical tone, and his playing continued to evolve to higher levels with each new panorama of notes he blazed out. Whether it was the

twisted, horizon-pushing "Ice 9," the churning "Surfing with the Alien," the bluesy rock shuffle of "Crushing Day," the straightahead, slamming "Satch Boogie," or the more subdued, soulful "Always with Me, Always with You," Satriani's style and songwriting were uniquely his own. Taking guitar playing and song composition to new levels, this is a remarkable recording. — *Phil Carter*

Dreaming #11 / 1988 / Relativity ✦✦✦
Dreaming No.11 is something of an oddity: a mini-disc released in 1988 with three live tracks and one new studio track. The live tracks, taken from the *Surfing with the Alien* tour and featuring the powerful duo of Stuart Hamm on bass and Jonathan Mover on drums, showcase Satriani's outstanding talents in a live atmosphere; however, they've been heard before ("Ice Nine" was on *Surfing with the Alien* and "Memories" and "Hordes of Locusts" came from *Not of This Earth*). The studio track, "The Crush of Love," immediately became a favorite of Satriani fans everywhere, mostly because of its catchy tune and its creative use of the wah-wah pedal to give the guitar an almost human voice. A recommended disc for musicians and fans, but not essential to the casual collector. — *Phil Carter*

Flying in a Blue Dream / Oct. 1989 / Relativity ✦✦✦✦
An hour-long disc filled with musical explorations and compositions that defy belief, *Flying in a Blue Dream* is unquestionably Satriani at his absolute best. Breaking his all-instrumental tradition for the first time, he croons on six of the disc's 18 tracks, including the weird "Strange," the bluesy, hard-rocking "Big Bad Moon," and the driving "Can't Slow Down." Satriani's voice isn't extraordinary, but it fits extremely well with the music he creates, especially on the acoustic-tinged, uplifting "I Believe." It's his playing that's the really impressive thing here, though; his unique tone and complex song structures are enhanced by his signature playing style and the incredible array of effects and tricks he wrestles out of his instrument. The disc closes with the high-flying, misty piece "Into the Light," leaving behind a feeling of real wonder. Soaring, powerful, and triumphant, this recording deserves a place in everyone's collection. — *Phil Carter*

The Extremist / Jul. 1992 / Relativity ✦✦✦✦
The Extremist lives up to its name, continuing Satriani's tradition of exploring new musical and compositional ground. A vastly different array of musicians assists him in creating the songs displayed on this all-instrumental disc, and as such the songs are different from even the usual Satriani fare. The chugging "Summer Song," the warm "Friends," the slamming "Motorcycle Driver," and the crunching "The Extremist" show Satriani's talents as a guitarist are undiminished, while the more traditional neo-folk approach to "Rubina's Blue Sky Happiness" and the bluesy "New Blues" are different from anything he has done before. So, too, is the droning rock of "War" and the plaintive, questioning funk-rock of "Why." — *Phil Carter*

Time Machine / Oct. 26, 1993 / Relativity ✦✦✦✦
Time Machine is an excellent double-CD set providing something for just about everyone who's interested in Satriani's music. Disc 1 reprints four tracks from the 1984 long-out-of-print *Joe Satriani EP*, while also showcasing nine new studio tracks and a loose jam session, and Disc 2 is a collection of 14 of Satriani's best live performances. Included among the new material is the booming "Time Machine," the straightforward but slamming "Mighty Turtle Head," and the hammering "Dweller on the Threshold," as well as "Banana Mango II," a new companion piece to the re-released "Banana Mango." Also of note is "Speed of Light," yet another of his trademark "surfing songs," and "Baroque," a beautiful acoustic piece. The 16-minute "Woodstock Jam" is interesting for a short time but tends to ramble; all the same, this set of recordings makes an excellent starting point for new fans and will give longtime fans something new as well. — *Phil Carter*

Joe Satriani / Oct. 1995 / Relativity ✦✦✦
The release of *Time Machine* essentially provided Joe Satriani a good place to musically reinvent himself with his fifth album, *Joe Satriani*. As the simple title implies, the music on the album is more direct than his previous efforts, largely due to the presence of producer Glyn Johns. Under Johns' direction, Satriani has stripped away the effects that have dominated his tone on previous albums, leaving his playing pure and unvarnished. The change in musical approach is emphasized by his supporting band. Featuring bassist Nathan East and guitarist Andy Fairweather-Low, both from Eric Clapton's band, and Peter Gabriel's drummer Manu Katche, the group provides the subtlest and most supportive music Satriani's playing has ever had. The result is one of his most impressive albums, showing that the guitarist is capable of more tricks than even his fans could have suspected. — *Stephen Thomas Erlewine*

Savage Republic

f. 1981, Los Angeles, CA, db. 1990
Post-Punk
Figures of considerable repute within the Los Angeles post-punk com-

munity of the 1980s, Savage Republic grafted tribal percussion, industrial drones, and raga-like guitar lines together to craft an idiosyncratically moody sound with flashes of both desolation and eloquent grandeur. Capable of both harsh dissonance and shimmering textures, the band's guiding force was guitarist Bruce Licher, a founder and constant presence in their shuffling lineups. Alternating between cyclic instrumentals and quasi-industrial assaults with gruff, chanted vocals, their records were unavoidably inconsistent, but most contain some enduring highlights.

Savage Republic were founded by former UCLA students Licher and drummer Mark Erkstine in the early '80s. Adding new members, the group originally called themselves Africa Corps, changing the name to Savage Republic just before releasing their first record in 1982. Exotic percussion would always play a big role in Savage Republic—even in the early days, they were using oil cans, metal pipes, and 55-gallon drums. Their early singles and their debut LP *Tragic Figures* (1982) show the group at their least accessible, though there are hints of the more mysterious and melodic elements to come.

After some personnel changes (some members went off to form 17 Pygmies), Savage Republic regrouped with a more guitar-oriented sound. On *Ceremonial* (1985), the band shifted their focus to mostly instrumental material, usually piloted by oddly tuned guitars (the group sometimes used guitars with six identically tuned strings). They'd never wholly abandon those droning, angst-driven chants, though. Combined with the fact that their instrumental material wouldn't break much new ground over the course of the decade, their studio albums were uneven listening. In any case, the band was best experienced live, where band members would burn trash cans of pampas leaves, play on Los Angeles' Skid Row, and use all sorts of unexpected objects for percussion in their quest to make each concert a unique event.

Savage Republic's albums, which were individually hand-letterpressed and numbered by Licher himself, received as much attention for their packaging as their music. Licher would perform the same services for other bands on his Independent Project label, even getting a Grammy nomination for his work on the first Camper Van Beethoven LP. Savage Republic was not destined to become nearly as big as Camper (not that this was ever their intent), and the group disbanded around 1990. After relocating to Arizona, Licher continues to run the Independent Project label and design sleeves (his most famous work in that department has been for an R.E.M. Christmas fan club single). Musically, he's recently resurfaced with the trio Scenic, which plays entirely instrumental material that blends the exotic flavor of Savage Republic with influences from Ennio Morricone and southwest border music. —*Richie Unterberger*

Tragic Figures / 1982 / Independent Project/Fundament ✦✦✦
This is really their most atypical full-length studio album, emphasizing harsh, grating vocals and instrumental drones to a greater degree than anything else in their catalogue. The throbbing percussion, though, would continue to be an element in everything they did, and quasi-Middle Eastern melodic motifs begin to assert themselves at times. Be aware that this, like all of Savage Republic's work, is not a collection of "songs" in the conventional rock sense, although many have vocals; it's more like a collection of "pieces" designed to establish moods and textures. The album is also distinguished by its exotic packaging, lettered entirely in Arabic script. The CD adds seven bonus tracks, including everything from their out-of-print seven-inch releases from 1983 and 1984. —*Richie Unterberger*

● **Ceremonial** / 1985 / Independent Project ✦✦✦✦
Their most accomplished and accessible work, largely jettisoning the harsher scrapings of the early records for expansive instrumentals featuring chiming guitars and occasional touches of ethereal trombone. Aiming for (and sometimes achieving) a hypnotic drone, at their best these have a melancholy beauty, bringing raga-rock into the post-punk age. The title track, unusually, features a female vocal from guest singer Louise Bialik, as well as (relatively) conventional lyrics. —*Richie Unterberger*

Live Trek / 1987 / Fundamental ✦✦✦
Seventy-five minutes of live material, much of which appears on their early studio recordings. A decent representation of their live presence, but the similarity of a lot of the riffs and arrangements make this hard to bear in such a big lump. For devoted fans of the group, it's a worthwhile document, with characteristically uneven material and sound quality (though the fidelity is on the whole fairly good). —*Richie Unterberger*

Jamahiriya / 1988 / Fundamental ✦✦✦
Considering that three years had passed since their previous full-length studio effort, little ground is broken here. The mood has turned more ominous and dour, though not to any great purpose. The Sturm-und-Drang, hoarsely screamed vocals also make something of a comeback, again not to any great purpose. However, their skills at crafting tribalistic instrumental rock remain intact, and "Pois Den Mila Yia Ti Lambri"

(with its martial accents) and "Lebanon 2000" (with its early Pink Floydish rumble) are among their better tracks. —*Richie Unterberger*

Customs / 1989 / Fundamental ✦✦
Savage Republic's originality had pretty much run its course by the time of their final studio album. Familiar instrumental motifs are repeated, but not expanded upon, though the Greek feel of "Song for Adonis" has a sweeter tone than they were usually inclined to employ. When they sing, half-formed lyrics and shouted vocals are still the order of the day (though "Mapia" probably includes their most conventional singing, aside from *Ceremonial*'s "Andalusia"). "Rapeman's 1st EP" is as difficult and grating as they ever got, though it's not effective as either art or satire (if that was an intention). —*Richie Unterberger*

Live in Europe 1988 / 1990 / Fundamental ✦✦
Like *Live Trek*, this is probably extraneous unless you're a big Savage Republic fan. If you want only one live Savage Republic record, *Live Trek*, featuring more extensive and wide-ranging material, is definitely a better investment than *Europe*, which is bit doomier and more plodding. —*Richie Unterberger*

Recordings from Live Performance, 1981-1983 / 1993 / Independent Project ✦✦
Savage Republic were probably more diligent about enshrining their live performances for posterity than they needed to be; there's almost as much live material available as there is from the studio. This set of two ten-inch records contains 14 tracks from the early days, including versions of songs from *Tragic Figures*, and some numbers that were never recorded in the studio. It tends toward the noisy side of their early evolution, so those who prefer the *Ceremonial* era will probably want to pass, although glimmers of surf-psychedelia can be found in "Exodus" and "Snakedance." The packaging, as usual, is damned impressive, with copious documentation and a five-color letterpress folder to enclose the vinyl. —*Richie Unterberger*

Savage Rose

f. 1966, Denmark
Art-Rock/Progressive-Rock
One of the most well-known rock groups from Continental Europe, Denmark's Savage Rose recorded a wealth of intriguing and eclectic progressive rock in the late '60s and '70s. In one of their early work, one hears faint echoes of the Airplane, Doors, Pink Floyd, and other psychedelic heavyweights, combined with classical jazz, and Danish-Euro folk elements. Their arrangements rely heavily on an incandescent, watery organ that sounds like nothing so much as psychedelic aquarium music. The most striking aspect of the band's sound, however, was the vocals of lead singer Annisette. Her childish wispy and sensual phrasing can suddenly break into jarring, almost histrionic wailing, like a Janis Joplin with Yoko Ono-isms, and eerily foreshadows Kate Bush's style.

Stars in their native land, Savage Rose also achieved a bit of underground success abroad, and several of their albums were released in North America. Between 1968 and 1978, the group released nine albums, moving from vaguely psychedelic rock and the heavily gospel-influenced *Refugee* to the nearly classical ballet score *Dodens Triumf* and the folky, nearly all-Danish *Sole Var Ogsa Din* (their first eight albums were sung entirely in English).

Always a radical band—the Black Panthers even invited the group to play at a benefit for Bobby Seale after hearing one of Savage Rose's records—they took the extremely radical step of withdrawing from the studio entirely by the end of 1970s to focus on using their music to support leftist political causes. Although they continued to make music and perform, they were often heard at benefits and free concerts, actually playing in Lebanese hospitals, schools, and refugee camps at the PLO's invitation. They eased back into recording in the early '80s with Danish-language efforts on small labels, eventually getting back into the mainstream music business with established distribution. Their mid-'90s album, *Black Angel*, was their first English-language recording in many years, and a substantial Danish hit. By this time the only remaining members from the original band were Thomas Koppel and Annisette (now his wife); Koppel also records and composes symphonic music as a solo artist. —*Richie Unterberger*

● **Savage Rose** / 1968 / Polydor ✦✦✦✦
Their debut is their lightest and most charming effort. Waltzing melodies give way to thunder-of-doom bass runs, and the storybookish lyrics have a forlorn, yearning quality. With its oddly hollow sound, one is never really sure whether the tone is supposed to be playful or ominous. —*Richie Unterberger*

In the Plain / 1969 / Polydor ✦✦✦
The band takes a more aggressive and soul-oriented approach on their second album, but the material isn't as strong, and much of the ethereal ambience that made their first LP special is lost. It does include the terrific, rollicking "Evening's Child," as well as the pre-

doom and gloom workout "A Trial in Our Native Town." —*Richie Unterberger*

Travelin' / 1969 / Polydor ✦✦✦
More excursions into soul-rock territory dominate one of their less distinguished albums. Highlights include the more serene and melodic cuts ("Travelin'," "Sailing Away") and the shockingly titled (for 1969) "My Family Was Gay," with its rather straightforward hints of incest. —*Richie Unterberger*

Your Daily Gift / 1970 / Gregar ✦✦✦
Their most well-known album, singled out for praise by critic Greil Marcus in his anthology *Stranded*. About half of this is fairly undistinguished heavy progressive-psychedelic rock, but the other half ranks among their most fragile and best material—the group was always better when they waxed reflective than when they tried to rock out. The lengthy, bittersweet, melancholy title track (complete with weepy European sidewalk cafe accordion) is one of their finest moments. —*Richie Unterberger*

Refugee / 1971 / Gregar ✦✦✦
Their most gospel and soul-influenced recording. Recalls Janis Joplin's more generic solo recordings, albeit with a more subdued feel. —*Richie Unterberger*

Dodens Triumf / 1972 / Polydor ✦✦✦✦
An unheralded landmark in art-rock, this features Savage Rose keyboardist Thomas Koppel's score for a ballet by Flemming Flindt (the title translates to "Triumph of Death"). Nearly entirely instrumental (one song features Annisette on vocals), this is one of the finest classically influenced rock records. Moody and melancholy, at times almost doomy, yet always melodic, this 40-minute selection of haunting pieces prominently features the group's unique underwater organ sound, and makes for compelling listening. —*Richie Unterberger*

Babylon / 1972 / Polydor ✦✦✦
With contributions by noted jazz saxophonist Ben Webster and the American gospel quintet the Stars of Faith, this is (along with *Refugee*) their most R&B-influenced recording, at times achieving a churchy, old-time New Orleans-like feel. —*Richie Unterberger*

Wild Child / 1973 / Polydor ✦✦✦
One of their better efforts. The R&B influence retreats in favor of a tender, melodic approach emphasizing the organ, piano, and accordions on a strong set that favors their European folk influences. —*Richie Unterberger*

Sole Var Ogsa Din / 1978 / Sonet ✦✦✦
A welcome return to their lightest and wispiest styles, with clear, shimmering instrumental textures that are almost like sonic waterfalls. Their enigmatic, moody song structures and melodies remain, with the most histrionic edges of Annisette's vocals toned down. As all but two of the songs are in their native Danish, this can perhaps be considered their most personal effort as well. —*Richie Unterberger*

25 / 1993 / Mega ✦✦✦
A double-CD compilation in commemoration of Savage Rose's 25th anniversary, drawing from most of the albums they recorded between the late 1960s and early 1990s. As an extremely eclectic and album-oriented group, Savage Rose isn't as well served by compilations as the average band. This is a decent enough way to get a rough feel for what the group has accomplished. But as an overview it's too diffuse, especially since the first disc only goes through 1973, and the second disc covers the decade 1982-1992 exclusively. There's nothing at all from one of their most celebrated albums (*Your Daily Gift*, 1970), or the Danish-language-dominated 1978 record, *Sole Var Ogsa Din*. In its favor, it does include several of their most outstanding early songs ("Wild Child," "A Girl I Knew," "A Trial in Our Native Town," "Dear Little Mother," "Evening's Child"). Also, the material from the 1980s and 1990s on disc two—which will be mostly unknown to US listeners—stacks up pretty well against (and is fairly similar to) their early recordings. —*Richie Unterberger*

Black Angel / 1995 / Mega ✦✦
Annisette and Thomas Koppel are the only original Savage Rose members left on this mid-'90s outing, on which they seem to be making a move toward the adult contemporary pop market. To say that's an ill-advised strategy is an understatement. It's a long way from the gothic classical-rock of *Dodens Triumf* to the shopping mall loudspeakers. But some of the material here, sadly, wouldn't sound terribly out of place in the background at K-Mart, although the arrangements are more sophisticated and conscientious, and Annisette's voice is still in top-notch shape. There's a slight R&B/soul feel, Mick Taylor makes a low-profile session appearance on guitar, and there are remakes of "Your Daily Gift" and "Sad Child Ballet" (from *Dodens Triumf*), as well as a cover of Pete Seeger's "Where Have All the Flowers Gone." But there's little that resembles the challenging progressive rock that characterized most of their career. —*Richie Unterberger*

Boz Scaggs (William Royce Scaggs)

b. Jun. 8, 1944, Ohio
Guitar, Vocals / Soft Rock, Pop-Rock, Blues-Rock
After first finding acclaim as a member of the Steve Miller Band, singer-songwriter Boz Scaggs went on to enjoy considerable solo success in the 1970s. Born William Royce Scaggs in Ohio on June 8, 1944, he was raised in Oklahoma and Texas, and while attending prep school in Dallas met guitarist Steve Miller. After joining Miller's group the Marksmen as a vocalist in 1959, the pair later attended the University of Wisconsin together, playing in blues bands like the Ardells and the Fabulous Knight Trains.

In 1963 Scaggs returned to Dallas alone, fronting an R&B unit dubbed the Wigs; after relocating to England, the group promptly disbanded, and two of its members—John Andrews and Bob Arthur—soon formed Mother Earth. Scaggs remained in Europe, singing on street corners; in Sweden he recorded a failed solo LP, 1965's *Boz*, before returning to the US two years later. Upon settling in San Francisco, he reunited with Miller, joining the fledgling Steve Miller Band; after recording two acclaimed albums with the group, *Children of the Future* and *Sailor*, Scaggs exited in 1968 to mount a solo career.

With the aid of *Rolling Stone* magazine publisher Jann Wenner, Scaggs secured a contract with Atlantic. Sporting a cameo from Duane Allman, 1968's soulful *Boz Scaggs* failed to find an audience despite winning critical favor; the track "Loan Me a Dime" later became the subject of a court battle when bluesman Fenton Robinson successfully sued for composer credit. After signing to Columbia, Scaggs teamed with producer Glyn Johns to record 1971's *Moments*, a skillful blend of rock and R&B that, like its predecessor, failed to make much of an impression on the charts.

Scaggs remained a critics' darling over the course of LPs like 1972's *My Time* and 1974's *Slow Dancer*, but he did not achieve a commercial breakthrough until 1976's *Silk Degrees*, which reached No. 2 on the album charts while spawning the Top Three single "Lowdown," as well as the smash "Lido Shuffle." 1977's *Down Two, Then Left* was also a success, and 1980's *Middle Man* reached the Top Ten on the strength of the singles "Breakdown Dead Ahead" and "Jo Jo."

However, Scaggs spent much of the 1980s in retirement, owning and operating the San Francisco nightclub Slim's and limiting his performances primarily to the club's annual black-tie New Year's Eve concerts. Finally, in 1988 he resurfaced with the album *Other Roads*, followed three years later by a tour with Donald Fagen's Rock and Soul Revue. The solo *Some Change* appeared in 1994, with *Come on Home* released in 1997. —*Jason Ankeny*

Boz Scaggs / 1969 / Atlantic ✦✦✦✦
Produced by Jann Wenner and featuring crack accompaniment by the Muscle Shoals house band, Scaggs' solo debut is a near-masterwork, mingling the pathos and heartbreak of vintage honky tonk with the celebration and release of Southern soul. The highlights of the album also flaunt its diversity: "Loan Me a Dime," an extended blues dirge, which features some of Duane Allman's finest work, and "Waiting on a Train," Scaggs' marvelous revamping of Jimmie Rodgers' classic hobo song. —*John Floyd*

Moments / 1971 / Columbia ✦✦✦
Scaggs' first album for Columbia is so low-key you barely notice the magic conjured on this set of introspective ballads. That is, until you really *listen*. —*John Floyd*

My Time / 1972 / Columbia ✦✦✦✦
Scaggs' last rock 'n' roll gasp, the ballads that would become his trademark are already surfacing, but you need this one for "Full-Lock Power Slide" and "Dinah Flo," two scorching rockers that give this album the muscle it needs. —*John Floyd*

Silk Degrees / Feb. 1976 / Columbia ✦✦✦✦
Both artistically and commercially, Boz Scaggs had his greatest success with *Silk Degrees*. The laidback singer hit the R&B charts in a big way with the addictive, sly "Lowdown" (which has been sampled by more than a few rappers, and remains a favorite among baby-boomer soul fans) and expressed his love of smooth soul music almost as well on the appealing "What Can I Say." But Scaggs was essentially a pop-rocker, and in that area, he has a considerable amount of fun on "Lido Shuffle" (another major hit single), "What Do You Want the Girl to Do" and "Jump Street." Meanwhile, "We're All Alone" and "Harbor Lights" became staples on adult contemporary radio. Though not remarkable, the ballads have more heart than most of the bland material dominating that format. —*Alex Henderson*

● **Hits!** / Nov. 1980 / Columbia ✦✦✦✦
In spite of the inclusion of "Dinah Flo," *Hits!* primarily focuses on Scaggs' '80s pop hits like "Lowdown," "Jojo," "Breakdown Dead Ahead" and "Look What You've Done to Me." —*Bil Carpenter*

Other Roads / 1988 / Columbia ♦♦

Boz Scaggs ended his retirement in 1988 and returned from running a restaurant to cut this session. It had its patented folk/soul mix and a few decent songs, but wasn't anywhere as ambitious or polished as any of his previous four platinum albums. Perhaps there really is truth to the old saying about going home again. His voice still had its introspective, bemused tone, but the production, arrangements, and compositions lacked conviction, power, or commercial appeal. He did get one hit with the single "Heart of Mine," but Toto's backing was more hindrance than help. —*Ron Wynn*

Some Change / Apr. 5, 1994 / Virgin ♦♦♦♦

This album has a nice organic feel to it that many of Scaggs' more commercially successful albums lacked. Scaggs plays a lot more guitar here and his singing has a relaxed soulfulness. This is one of his very best albums. —*Rick Clark*

Come on Home / Apr. 8, 1997 / Virgin ♦♦♦

Boz Scaggs' attempts to reclaim his soul and R&B roots on *Come on Home*, a collection of laidback, lightly grooving blue-eyed soul. Scaggs never was a gritty singer, but on *Come on Home* he's more laconic than ever, which doesn't save the frequently colorless songs and helps make the album a tedious exercise, even for longtime fans. —*Thom Owens*

Schnell Fenster

f. 1986, New Zealand, db. 1992
Alternative Pop-Rock

Schnell Fenster was an eclectic New Zealand-based band comprised of former Split Enz members Phil Judd (guitar/vocals/keyboards), Noel Crombie (drums), Nigel Griggs (bass) and Michael Den Elzen (guitar). The band formed in 1986 and released their first album, *Sound of Trees*, in 1988 in Australia. A warm reception in their homeland prompted an American contract with Atlantic Records the following year and a worldwide release for the album in 1990. Without a supporting tour outside of their homeland and poor promotion, the album quickly faded. The follow-up, 1991's *OK Alright a Huh Oh Yeah*, suffered the same fate, this time with a release limited to Australasia. While promoting the album, Crombie developed tinnitus, forcing them to postpone the tour. They eventually broke up, with the members playing a more active role behind the scenes in the music business. —*Chris Woodstra*

● **Sound of Trees** / 1988 / Atlantic ♦♦♦♦

The band's debut picks up where Split Enz left off in the mid-'80s, exploring some of the funkiness first heard on *Time and Tide* and the jazzy stylings of *Conflicting Emotions*. The always interesting Phil Judd turns in another quirky batch of lyrics as only he can sing, proving that his return was long overdue. —*Chris Woodstra*

OK Alright a Huh Oh Yeah / 1991 / WEA ♦♦♦

Though the songs aren't quite as strong as those on the debut, *OK Alright a Huh Oh Yeah* is still a solid, well-produced effort, worthwhile for longtime Split Enz fans. Released only in Australia, this would be their last album before disbanding. —*Chris Woodstra*

Klaus Schulze

b. , Germany
Synthesizer / Electronic, Kraut-Rock

One of the cornerstone figures in the German electronic scene, this pioneering synthesist has recorded nearly two dozen solo albums over the past 20 years. His music has grown and changed with the evolution of technology, but his concept of long-form, highly rhythmic sequencer music pulsing under soaring melodies has remained constant. Though he established his own identity years ago, Schulze was briefly a member of Tangerine Dream, appearing on one album, *Electronic Meditation*, in 1970. He did not, however, cave in to convention or engage in cheap pop-electronic exploits, as did his former TD colleagues in the mid-'80s and beyond. Still, Schulze's collaborations with former Santana drummer Michael Shrieve brought a new level of percussive intensity to his music, as well as a wider audience from the progressive-rock world. The availability of Schulze's music has always been inconsistent in the US, and many Americans have no idea how strong his influence has been on electronic music worldwide. (He was, for instance, the inspiration behind Kitaro's initial investigations of synthesizer music.) Schulze continues to perform throughout Europe and is tireless in releasing new recordings, some of which are better than others. When Schulze does hit the nail on the head, his music is immensely powerful. —*Linda Kohanov*

Cyborg / 1973 / A&M ♦♦♦♦

Cyborg was Schulze's second solo album. From the early days of electronic experimentation in the pop field, today it still stands as one of the most powerful examples of ambient pulse music ever conceived. The dense layers of rhythm and synthetic tone colors melt into a seamless, flowing soundscape of melody, motion, and spatial effects. It's a monumental double album of "cosmic music." —*Archie Patterson*

Timewind / 1975 / Blue Plate ♦♦♦♦

Two masterful sequencer essays make effective use of minimalistic patterns to suspend and ultimately erase all sense of objective "clock-time" experience. —*Linda Kohanov*

Mirage / 1977 / Island ♦♦♦

Mirage gives the listener impressionistic sequencer work depicting winter landscapes. —*Linda Kohanov*

X / 1978 / Gramavision ♦♦♦

Schulze's tenth solo release marks the peak of his most influential period of work. Presented with a classic sense of German drama, this double CD artfully combines the composer's synthesizers and sequencer patterns with live drums and full orchestra. Intense, driving, long-form pieces frame surreal, abstract sounds. Each of six pieces is named for a historical figure Schulze admires, beginning with a 24-minute selection titled "Friedrich Nietzsche." —*Linda Kohanov*

● **Beyond Recall** / Jul. 1991 / Venture ♦♦♦♦

Schulze is in a more sedate and reflective mood here, with acoustic guitar samples creating lyrical melodies. —*Linda Kohanov*

Dresden Performance / Jul. 12, 1991 / Venture ♦♦♦♦

● **Dome Event** / Apr. 23, 1993 / Plan 9/Caroline ♦♦♦♦

Scorn

f. 1991, Birmingham, England
Industrial, Experimental, Ambient Dub, Dark Ambient, Electronica

Closely allied with post-industrial dub terrorists such as Bill Laswell, Techno Animal, James Plotkin, Robert Musso, and Anton Fier, Birmingham-based artist Mick Harris is something of a study in extremes. A drummer with noted death metal outfit Napalm Death through the group's late-'80s/early-'90s heyday, Harris began experimenting with monochrome ambient and dub styles toward the tail end of his association with that group. Releasing material through Earache as Scorn (his ambient dub aegis) and through Sentrax as Lull, in addition to other sporadic projects, his genre-spanning activities have done much to jar the minds, expectations, and record collections of audiences previously kept aggressively opposed. To the present, Scorn and Lull, along with John Zorn's experimental jazz-dubcore outfit Painkiller, have remained Harris' primary ongoing projects, although one-off collaborations with the likes of James Plotkin, Nicholas Bullen, Bill Laswell, and Martyn Bates are common. Harris formed Scorn in 1991 in collaboration with bassist Nick Bullen, incorporating elements of ambient, industrial, dub, rock, and hip-hop. The group (though pared back to just Harris following *Evanescence*) has released a number of increasingly well received full-length recordings, including the remix LP *Ellipsis*, which features outbound reworkings by the likes of Coil, Autechre, Laswell, and Germ. Harris' solo work as Lull focuses on darker, more "isolationist" ambient soundscapes, some of which have been reissued domestically by Laswell's now-defunct Subharmonic imprint. —*Sean Cooper*

Evanescence / Aug. 23, 1994 / Earache ♦♦♦

A moderately successful, if somewhat obvious fusion of more traditional instrumentation with composed electronics and effects. Periodic vocals tend to distract from the shifting, exploratory nature of the music, but the instrumental tracks are well-crafted examples of dub-influenced experimental electronica. —*Sean Cooper*

Ellipsis / May 9, 1995 / Earache ♦♦♦

A barely recognizable recapitulation of *Evanescence*, thanks in no small part to some stunning remixes from Autechre, Meat Beat Manifesto, Bill Laswell, Scanner, Germ, and Coil. Also released on vinyl as a 5 x 12-inch box set. —*Sean Cooper*

● **Gyral** / Oct. 31, 1995 / Earache ♦♦♦♦

Harris' first Scorn release after the departure of bassist Nick Bullen is a refinement of previous concerns, with spare, repetitive rhythms and drum loops providing a tether for dark, brooding atmospherics and harsh, effects-heavy samples. Less immediately engaging perhaps than previous albums, *Gyral* works best as beat-oriented dark ambient, its strongest impact working at an almost subconscious or subliminal level. —*Sean Cooper*

Logghi Barogghi / Aug. 20, 1996 / Earache ♦♦♦♦

Logghi Barogghi is one of Scorn's most ambitious efforts to date, featuring a dark, menacing undercurrent of experimentation. Mick Harris doesn't really abandon the blueprint that distinguished the previous, acclaimed *Gyral*, but he does deepen the music by lessening the industrial influences and playing around with dub and techno. There are the occasional dull spots, but for the most part, *Logghi Barogghi* is a fascinating, disturbing listen. —*Stephen Thomas Erlewine*

Scorpions

f. 1969, Hanover, Germany
Heavy Metal

With a musical style similar to Iron Maiden or Judas Priest, the Scorpions have fully explored the world of rock 'n' roll time and time again. Known best for their 1984 anthem "Rock You Like a Hurricane" and the 1990 ballad "Wind of Change," the German rockers have sold well over 22 million records, making them one of the most successful rock bands ever.

Originally formed in 1969 by Rudolf Schenker, the initial lineup consisted of rhythm guitarist/vocalist Schenker, lead guitarist Karl-Heinz Follmer, bassist Lothar Heimberg, and drummer Wolfgang Dziony. In 1971, Schenker's younger brother Michael was brought along to play lead guitar, and good friend Klaus Meine became the new vocalist. The group recorded *Lonesome Crow* in 1972 and the release was used as a soundtrack to the German movie *Das Kalte Paradies*. Even though they failed to get into the public's eye, Michael Schenker was hired to play for UFO and left the band in 1973. Guitarist Uli Jon Roth replaced him, and under his guidance the group released four consecutive albums: *Fly to the Rainbow* (1974), *In Trance* (1975), *Virgin Killers* (1976) and *Taken by Force* (1977). Although these albums failed to attain any serious attention in the United States, they were all quite popular in Japan.

By the time *Taken by Force* was released, Roth made the decision to leave the band and form Electric Sun, feeling that his musical ideas would take the group in an entirely different direction. Because he was an alcoholic, Michael Schenker was kicked out of UFO and came back to play with the Scorpions in 1979. The group released *Lovedrive* that same year and played their first American tour, but *Lovedrive* failed to attract attention, being banned in the United States because of its sexually explicit cover. Still coping with his alcohol addiction, Michael missed tour dates repeatedly, and guitarist Matthias Jabs was hired to fill in for him on nights when he was absent. Michael eventually would leave the band a second time after realizing that he was failing to meet expectations.

Now with a lineup of Klaus Meine on vocals, Rudolf Schenker on rhythm guitar, Matthias Jabs on lead, Francis Bucholzon on bass, and Herman Rarebell on drums, the band released *Animal Magnetism* in 1980 and embarked on another world tour. Surprisingly, *Animal Magnetism* went gold in the United States, and the Scorpions immediately went back into the studio to record their next release. Problems arose, however, and the project was postponed because Meine had lost his voice and had to have surgery on his vocal chords. Many thought Meine had been fired from the band, and rumors spread that metal singer Don Dokken would replace him. The Scorpions proved these rumors untrue, however, when Meine returned for the 1982 release *Blackout*, which contained the hit "No One Like You." A major success worldwide, *Blackout* sold over one million copies in the US alone. But as popular as *Blackout* was, it was the band's powerful follow-up, *Love at First Sting*, that made them rock 'n' roll icons. Released in 1984, the album boasted the MTV single "Rock You Like a Hurricane" and would eventually achieve double-platinum status. The group kicked off their most successful world tour yet, boasting an outstanding stage show with high-energy performances.

After releasing *World Wide Live* in 1985, the band surprisingly remained uninvolved in the music industry for four years and continued to work on new music. The studio album *Savage Amusement* was finally released in 1988, and the hit ballad "Rhythm of Love" brought another major success. For their next project, the band participated in the Monsters of Rock tour in 1989 and performed in Russia for the first time, selling out seven shows in a row. Obtaining tremendous inspiration from their Russian tour, Meine wrote the song "Wind of Change," which was placed on the 1990 release *Crazy World*. The content of this album seemed perfect, and hit songs such as "Wind of Change" and "Tease Me, Please Me" contributed to making *Crazy World* the most popular Scorpions release ever.

Unfortunately, *Crazy World* was the last successful Scorpions release in the US. By the time their *Face the Heat* album hit the shelves in 1993, many longtime fans had already lost interest in the group and had begun to listen to alternative bands like Nirvana and Pearl Jam. *Face the Heat* did eventually go gold, and in 1995 the group released another live album, *Live Bites,* in an attempt to win back supporters. This album also didn't sell as many copies as they had hoped, but the band remained optimistic. With bassist Ralph Riekermann and drummer James Kottak, they released *Pure Instinct* in 1996, this time touring with shock-rock master Alice Cooper in hopes of attracting a bigger audience. This seemed to be a very smart move by the band, and since that time a larger group of fans have begun to show interest in them. Although they still do not have as much media attention as they did in the '80s, the Scorpions continue to perform to devoted audiences and "rock the world like a hurricane." *—Barry Weber*

Fly to the Rainbow / 1974 / RCA ✦✦✦

First US release features the title track, "Speedy's Coming," "Drifting Sun," and "They Need a Million." Early meisterwerk from these German hard rockers. *—Cub Koda*

In Trance / 1975 / RCA ✦✦✦✦

The Scorpions' third release continues to display their high-energy music that is impossible to ignore. With the eyebrow-lifting "Dark Lady" as the opening track, *In Trance* immediately captures the listener's attention and keeps it all the way until the end. The interesting title track is clearly the best song of the album, but singles such as the fast-paced "Robot Man" and the hard-rocking "Top of the Bill" also stand out as highlights. Excellent singing and powerful music make this the best Scorpions recording working with Uli Jon Roth. *—Barry Weber*

Virgin Killers / 1976 / RCA ✦✦✦✦

Features the title track, "Hell Cat," "Backstage Queen," "Polar Nights," and "Yellow Raven." *—Cub Koda*

Tokyo Tapes / 1978 / RCA ✦✦✦

Tokyo Tapes pulled this German band out of obscurity and into the spotlight. A quality sampling of their early material, *Tokyo Tapes* is a performance that is considered one of the band's best. Includes "All Night Long," "Back Stage Queen," and "Flight to the Rainbow." *—John Book*

Lovedrive / 1979 / Mercury ✦✦✦✦

Well-written songs and powerful singing from Klaus Meine are some of the reasons given for calling *Lovedrive* one of the best Scorpions ever. Rudolf Schenker and Matthias Jabs provide many of this album's highlights, with lots of great guitar. *—John Book*

Animal Magnetism / 1980 / Mercury ✦✦✦

Although this release contains such classic songs as "The Zoo" and "Make It Real," *Animal Magnetism* is somewhat disappointing when compared to its predecessor, *Lovedrive*. The well-written songs on this album end up saving it from total disaster, and it is obvious that the band wasn't sure what to exactly put on this record—many of the songs sound like the work of some other rock group and simply don't blend together as they should. Singer Klaus Meine, known for his excellent vocal performances, sounds bored and just plain overshadowed. Although far from bad, *Animal Magnetism* isn't a highlight of the Scorpions' career. *—Barry Weber*

Blackout / 1982 / Mercury ✦✦✦✦

The band experiments with pop smarts in a few of the songs, while retaining the solid hard-rock sound they have molded over the years. *Blackout* provided this German band with their first major hit, "No One Like You" (No. 65). *—John Book*

Love at First Sting / 1984 / Mercury ✦✦✦✦

Although the Scorpions had already achieved fame after 1982's *Blackout*, with *Love at First Sting* they gave the music industry a taste of rock 'n' roll that will never be forgotten. The hit single "Rock You Like a Hurricane" brought on even more US popularity, with some greatly underrated songs to back it up. *Love at First Sting* opens with the hair-raising "Bad Boys Running Wild" and continues with songs such as the richly entertaining "Big City Nights" and the half-ballad, half-powerhouse rocker "Coming Home." The album also contains what just may be the band's best ballad ever, the tear-jerking "Still Loving You." With such a great combination of outstanding music and talented vocals, *Love at First Sting* is clearly one of the best Scorpions recordings ever released. In fact, some have even called it one of the best rock recordings of the entire decade. *—Barry Weber*

World Wide Live / 1985 / Mercury ✦✦✦

This live album, originally released as a double-record set, succeeds in capturing the raw power and high energy that the group can actually attain performing live. Although a few songs were lost in the move from record to compact disc, the band's greatest hits are retained from their 1984-85 tour, from ballads such as "Holiday" to the rock anthem "Rock You Like a Hurricane." The album is never tedious, and all of the 14 songs on the recordings are captured with excellent authenticity. *World Wide Live* is one of the best Scorpions recording ever released, and is a must for fans of the genre. *—Barry Weber*

Savage Amusement / 1988 / Mercury ✦✦✦✦

This album, released in 1988, displays the most energy the Scorpions ever placed onto a studio album. From the moment the album opens with the rocking anthem "Don't Stop at the Top," *Savage Amusement* takes the listener on a nonstop ride of highly entertaining rock 'n' roll that meets the standards the band set on their previous releases. Although it may be a little polished when compared to their other releases, the album remains a fantastic display of stunning music and powerful singing. *—Barry Weber*

● The Best of Rockers 'n' Ballads / Oct. 1989 / Mercury ✦✦✦✦

Even though it's the official greatest-hits compilation of the Scorpions' '80s releases, *Best of Rockers 'n' Ballads* is actually missing some of their best rockers and ballads. Oh, it contains a lot of great music, but surely the Scorpions could have put a few more songs onto this release rather than the mere 12 listed. In fact, having the poor-quality song "Hey You" as one of the tracks is almost an insult when fans could been given "Is There Anybody There" or "Dynamite" instead. Still, what's here is good, and the album's brand-new track, "I Can't Explain," is very entertaining. Although it may not contain all the classics, *Best of Rockers 'n' Ballads* is a very enjoyable compilation. —*Barry Weber*

Crazy World / 1990 / Mercury ✦✦✦✦
Crazy World featured the Scorpions' biggest (and best) hit single, the reflective ballad "Wind of Change," which is the highlight on one of the band's most consistent, accomplished albums. —*Stephen Thomas Erlewine*

Face the Heat / May 1993 / Mercury ✦✦✦
Not even renowned metal producer Bruce Fairbairn could save this disappointing follow-up to the outstanding *Crazy World* album. Instead of concentrating on melodic tunes, *Face the Heat* seems to focus on noisy metal and glass-shattering screaming rather than the usual classic and emotional sounds that the Scorpions have put on their previous albums. Especially when compared to their previous recordings, *Face the Heat* is quite unsatisfactory. —*Barry Weber*

Hurricane Rock 74-88 / 1994 / Alex ✦✦✦✦
Imported from England, this 18-track disc is a compilation of the Scorpions' studio hits from *Fly to the Rainbow* through *Savage Amusement*. Many of the classics are here, but the album possesses one noticeable flaw—its lack of the Scorpions' ballads. Although the *Blackout* hit "When the Smoke Is Going Down" made it to the album, songs like "Still Loving You" and "Holiday" are surprisingly missing. But then again, maybe that is why the album is called *Hurricane Rock*, and in that aspect, it captures their anthems and rockers quite nicely. —*Barry Weber*

Live Bites 1988-95 / Apr. 18, 1995 / Mercury ✦✦
As the title suggests, *Live Bites 1988-95* is a collection of live tracks from the Scorpions, recorded at a time when they weren't at the top of their form, despite the hit single "Wind of Change." During this time, their audience was beginning to evaporate, partially because of changing tastes and partially because the band was losing its ability to rock out consistently. *Live Bites* documents this decay too effectively. There are occasional highlights, but too much of the disc contains half-hearted, tired perfomances to make it worthwhile for anyone but the most dedicated of fans. —*Stephen Thomas Erlewine*

Pure Instinct / May 21, 1996 / Atlantic ✦✦✦
On *Pure Instinct*, the Scorpions shoot for crossover success by concentrating on ballads—and that's not the power-ballad style, either. Though there are still distorted guitars, they're buried in the mix, which fulfills the intention of accentuating the melodies. Unfortunately, those melodies aren't particularly memorable, especially when placed in comparison with their previous mega-hit "Wind of Change." The handful of rockers don't do enough to vary the pace of *Pure Instinct;* the album, consequently, is a bore. —*Stephen Thomas Erlewine*

Gil Scott-Heron

b. Apr. 1, 1949, Chicago, IL
Piano / Fusion, Singer-Songwriter
Pianist, composer, and poet Gil Scott-Heron has had a prime influence on contemporary African-American popular music. He attended Lincoln and Johns Hopkins University, and wrote two novels, highly popular among Black college students, *The Vulture* and *The Nigger Factory*. He began working with musician Brian Jackson on putting music to his oral narratives and monologues. His 1972 release, *Small Talk at 125th and Lenox*, attracted underground attention, while the follow-up, *Pieces of a Man*, was a major hit. Throughout the '70s and early '80s, Heron's commentaries on racism, injustice, and inequality, with side trips on jazz, romance, and family life, were very popular among jazz fans with left-wing views as well as rock, R&B, and pop audiences. Although disputes with Arista over artistic direction and production control have resulted in very few Scott-Heron recordings in recent years, he continues to tour and give interviews. —*Ron Wynn*

Winter in America / Sep. 4, 1973+Oct. 11, 1973 / Strata East ✦✦✦
Gil Scott-Heron was at his most righteous and provocative on this album. The title cut was a moving, angry summation of the social injustices Scott-Heron felt had led the nation to a particularly dangerous period, while "The Bottle" was a great treatise on the dangers of alcohol abuse. He also offered his thoughts on Nixon's legacy with "The H2O Gate Blues," a classic oral narrative. Brian Jackson's capable keyboard, acoustic piano, and arranging talents helped make this a first-rate release, one of several the duo issued during the 1970s. —*Ron Wynn*

From South Africa to South Carolina / Jan. 1976 / Arista ✦✦✦
The Gil Scott-Heron/Brian Jackson collaboration was now a formal one, as they were issuing albums as a team. This was their second duo project to make the pop charts, and it included anti-nuclear and anti-apartheid themes, plus less political, more autobiographical/reflective material like "Summer of '42," "Beginnings (The First Minute of a New Day)" and "Fell Together." Scott-Heron was now a campus and movement hero, and Brian Jackson's production and arranging savvy helped

make his albums as arresting musically as they were lyrically. —*Ron Wynn*

● **The Best of Gil Scott-Heron** / 1984 / Arista ✦✦✦✦
An exemplary firebrand poet whose raps and lyrics influenced the entire hip-hop generation, yet who has said his own influence was jazz. —*Ron Wynn*

The Revolution Will Not Be Televised / 1988 / Bluebird ✦✦✦✦
The poem "The Revolution Will Not Be Televised" was perhaps Gil Scott-Heron's first major hit. It wasn't on any charts, but its searing message resounded on college campuses across the nation. This was the centerpiece for an album that also included several crackling protest pieces such as "Pieces of a Man," "Home Is Where the Hatred Is" and "Save the Children," plus the poignant "Lady Day and John Coltrane." The guest list of jazz participants included Ron Carter and Hubert Laws. —*Ron Wynn*

Jack Scott (Jack Scafone Jr)

b. Jan. 24, 1936, Windsor, Ontario, Canada
Guitar, Vocals / Rock & Roll, Traditional Country, Rockabilly
Jack Scott sounded tough, like someone you wouldn't want to meet in a dark alley unless he had a guitar in his hands. When he growled "The Way I Walk," wise men (and women) stepped aside. Despite his snarling rockabilly attitude, Scott hailed from Ontario, Canada, and grew up near Detroit, developing a love for hillbilly music along the way. His first sides for ABC-Paramount in 1957 exhibited a profound country-rock synthesis, and after moving to the Carlton label, Scott hit the charts the next year with the tremulous ballad "My True Love," backed by his vocal group, the Chantones. Flip it over, however, and you have the hauling rocker "Leroy," all about some wacked-out tough guy who's content to remain behind the bars of his local jail. Scott's pronounced emphasis on acoustic guitar distinguishes atmospheric rockers like "Goodbye Baby," "Go Wild Little Sadie," "Midgie," and "Geraldine." But his principal pop success came with tears-in-your-beer country-based ballads—"What in the World's Come Over You" and "Burning Bridges" were massive smashes on Top Rank in 1960, and he recorded an entire album's worth of Hank Williams covers for the firm the same year.

Born in Windsor, Ontario, Jack Scott (born Jack Scafone, Jr., January 28, 1936) moved to a town on the outskirts of Detroit, Michigan when he was ten years old. At the age of 18 he formed the Southern Drifters, and after leading the band for three years he signed to ABC as a solo artist in 1957. Over the next year, he released a handful of singles for the label, before moving to Carlton Records the following year. His double-A-sided debut for Carlton, "My True Love" / "Leroy," became a huge hit, with the first song peaking at No. 3 and that latter at No. 11; it also became a Top Ten hit in England. During the next two years, Scott had a number of minor hits for Carlton, highlighted by the No. 8 hit "Goodbye Baby" (fall 1958). On most of these tracks, the Chantones provided vocal support.

Late in 1959, he switched labels, signing with Top Rank. His first single for the label, "What in the World's Come Over You," became a No. 5 hit early in 1960. It was followed a few months later by another Top Ten hit, the No. 3 single "Burning Bridges." The pair of singles were his last major hits, and over the next two years his singles progressively charted at lower positions than their predecessors. Early in 1961, he signed with Capitol Records, but none of his three singles made the Top 40.

Scott continued to vacillate between cowboy crooner and roughedged rocker throughout the remainder of the '60s and '70s, recording for a variety of labels, including Groove and Dot. In 1974, he managed to have a minor country hit with his Dot single "You're Just Gettin' Better." During the '80s and '90s, Scott occasionally turned up on the oldies circuit, still looking and sounding like a man you seriously didn't want to mess with. —*Bill Dahl*

Scott on Groove / 1989 / Bear Family ✦✦✦✦
The music on *Scott on Groove* was recorded after Jack Scott's hit-making era on Capitol was finished. Scott recorded for Groove in the early '60s. During this time, he was trying to refashion his sound into a rock 'n' roll/rockabilly direction. Not all of the attempts were successful, but the set is interesting for dedicated fans, but they would probably rather acquire this material on *Classic Scott*, the more comprehensive box set. —*Stephen Thomas Erlewine*

● **Greatest Hits** / 1990 / Curb ✦✦✦✦
Curb's *Greatest Hits* was the only American Jack Scott compilation available in the mid-'90s, after Capitol pulled its *Collector's Series* from the market. Although *Greatest Hits* only has 11 tracks—including a recently recorded version of "Running Scared"—it has the essential big hits ("My True Love," "Goodbye Baby," "Burning Bridges," "Leroy," "The Way I Walk," "What in the World's Come Over You") and is a serviceable collection, even if it is frustratingly brief. —*Stephen Thomas Erlewine*

Capitol Collectors Series / Oct. 8, 1990 / Capitol ✦✦✦✦

Classic Scott / Jun. 27, 1994 / Bear Family ✦✦✦✦
Bear Family's *Classic Scott* is a four-disc, 138-track box set that contains all of Jack Scott's recordings for Capitol from the '50s, as well as a selection of material he recorded for smaller, independent labels like Groove in the early '60s. While the set is far too comprehensive for casual fans, it is ideal for collectors and worth their investment. — *Stephen Thomas Erlewine*

Peggy Scott & Jo Jo Benson

b. 1948
Soul, R&B
In the late '60s, this female-male duo made the pop Top 40 three times (charting much higher in the R&B section) with a clutch of good-natured southern-pop-soul tunes. Semi-legendary producer Huey Meaux, who had worked extensively with such soul and rock legends as Barbara Lynn and Doug Sahm, was responsible for putting the team together, and produced their first sessions in 1968 in Jackson, Mississippi. After "Lover's Holiday" and "Pickin' Wild Mountain Berries" yielded a couple quick hits, the producer's chair was turned over to Shelby Singleton, who cut a few sessions with the pair in Nashville. Some of these tracks were notable for their fusion of soul and country influences; a few featured top Nashville sessionmen Jerry Kennedy (on guitar) and, more unusually, Pete Drake, perhaps the first White country musician (and certainly one of the few) to play steel guitar on a soul record. Scott and Benson were competent talents, but ultimately would have to be classified as rather average performers who didn't establish a particularly distinguished or exciting style. The country influence and the odd sitarish guitar tone on several of their records were the most novel things they had going. Under Singleton's guidance, they landed their third hit within a year with perhaps their best track, "Soul Shake," but only managed one more minor hit, "I Want to Love You Baby," before leaving Singleton's SSS International label for Atco. Their relationship already strained, the duo's career petered out after a few obscure singles in the early '70s. — *Richie Unterberger*

● **The Best of Peggy Scott & Jo Jo Benson** / Jun. 27, 1995 / Ichiban/Soul Classics ✦✦✦✦
Twenty-track compilation has all their hit singles, a bunch of flops and B-sides, cuts from their two late-'60s LPs, and four songs from non-album 45s. — *Richie Unterberger*

Screaming Trees

f. 1983, Ellensburg, WA
Hard Rock, Alternative Pop-Rock, Psychedelic, Grunge
Where many of their Seattle-based contemporaries dealt in reconstructed Black Sabbath and Stooges riffs, the Screaming Trees fused '60s psychedelia and garage rock with '70s hard rock and '80s punk. Over the course of their career, their more abrasive punk roots eventually gave way to a hard-edged, rootsy psychedelia that drew from rock and folk equally. After releasing several albums on indie labels like SST and Sub Pop, the Screaming Trees moved to Epic Records in 1989. Though they were one of the first Seattle bands to sign with a major label, the group never attained the popularity of fellow Northwestern bands (and friends) like Nirvana and Soundgarden, largely due to their erratic work schedule. Throughout their career, the Trees were notorious for drinking and fighting, which caused them to break up briefly at several points in their career. Nevertheless, the band managed to cultivate a dedicated following, which included not only fans, but also fellow musicians.

Brothers Van Conner (bass) and Gary Lee Conner (guitar) formed the Screaming Trees with Mark Lanegan (vocals) in the mid-'80s. Lanegan and the Conners grew up in Ellensburg, Washington, a small college town some 90 miles from Seattle. The trio were the only people in their high school who listened to punk, garage rock, and independent music, so they eventually gravitated toward each other. After falling out with the Conners before either completed school, Lanegan contacted Van Conner several years later. By that point, Van had a band with a drummer named Mark Pickerel; the pair had recently kicked Lee Conner out of the band, so they invited Lanegan to sit in on drums. Eventually, Lee rejoined the group and they settled on a lineup that featured Lee on guitar, Van on bass, Lanegan on vocals, and Pickerel on drums.

Taking their name from a guitar distortion pedal, the Screaming Trees recorded their first demo tape in 1985, just a few months after their formation. Their producer, Steve Fisk, was able to convince the head of Velvetone Studios to release an album by the band. The result, *Clairvoyance*, appeared on Velvetone Records in 1986. With *Clairvoyance* in hand, Fisk was able to secure the Screaming Trees a contract with Greg Ginn's SST Records, who had already been releasing albums by Fisk. The band's first SST album, *Even If and Especially When*, was released in 1987 and the Trees began working the dying American indie circuit, playing shows across the country. The following year, SST reis-

sued the band's demo tape under the title *Other Worlds*, as well as their third album, *Invisible Lantern*.

Following the release of *Buzz Factory* in 1989, the group's contract with SST expired and they made the *Changes Come* EP for Sub Pop early the following year. By that time, tensions in the band had grown somewhat, and the group spent most of 1990 working on side projects. Mark Lanegan recorded a solo album, *The Winding Sheet*, which featured support from Nirvana's Kurt Cobain and Krist Novoselic; the album appeared on Sub Pop. Both of the Conners formed new bands and released albums on the SST subsidiary New Alliance. Van's band was called Solomon Grundy; Lee's was Purple Outside. By the end of 1990, the band had signed a major-label contract with Epic Records.

Screaming Trees reconvened to record their Epic debut, *Uncle Anesthesia*, with Chris Cornell of Soundgarden and Terry Date as producers. *Uncle Anesthesia* appeared in early 1991 and although it sold better than their previous efforts, the band remained a cult act. For much of the year, in fact, Van Conner was on hiatus from the band, choosing to tour as bassist with Dinosaur Jr. instead. Late in 1991, Nirvana's *Nevermind* became an unexpected commercial success, opening the gates for the rest of the Seattle scene. Where many of their peers were able to capitalize on that success, the Screaming Trees suffered more setbacks than the rest. Before they began work on their follow-up to *Uncle Anesthesia*, Pickerel left the group and was replaced by Barrett Martin.

Once Martin joined, the band finished "Nearly Lost You," their contribution to the *Singles* soundtrack, and their 1992 album *Sweet Oblivion*. "Nearly Lost You" became a MTV and alternative radio hit in the fall of 1992, thanks to the momentum of the *Singles* soundtrack. The single carried *Sweet Oblivion*—which had received more press attention than any previous Screaming Trees album—to the group's strongest sales, peaking at over 300,000 copies. The band supported *Sweet Oblivion* with a year-long tour, during which they fought frequently. After the tour was finished, the group decided to take an extended hiatus. During that time, Lanegan recorded his second solo album, *Whiskey for the Holy Ghost*, which was released in 1994. That same year, Martin drummed in the Layne Staley (Alice in Chains) and Mike McCready (Pearl Jam) side project Mad Season, which released its only album in the spring of 1995.

In early 1995, the Screaming Trees regrouped to begin work on their follow-up to *Sweet Oblivion*. Following one stillborn attempt at the album, the band hired George Drakoulias, who had previously worked with the Black Crowes and the Jayhawks, as producer. The resulting album, *Dust*, was released in the summer of 1996, nearly four years after its predecessor. *Dust* was greeted to positive reviews and its first single, "All I Know," became a moderate hit on modern rock radio. Still, the album didn't sell particularly well, even though the band supported the record by touring with 1996's Lollapalooza. Following the *Dust* tour, Screaming Trees took another hiatus, with Lanegan beginning work on his third solo album. — *Stephen Thomas Erlewine*

Clairvoyance / 1986 / Velvetone ✦✦✦

Even If and Especially When / 1987 / SST ✦✦✦✦
The Screaming Trees were still trying to define their style on their second album, *Even If and Especially When*, but that makes it one of their most intriguing and exciting efforts. — *Stephen Thomas Erlewine*

Invisible Lantern / 1988 / SST ✦✦✦
Solid neo-psychedelic pop. — *Robert Gordon*

Buzz Factory / 1989 / SST ✦✦✦

Uncle Anesthesia / Jan. 1991 / Epic ✦✦✦✦
Major-label bucks don't detract from their punch. — *Robert Gordon*

● **Anthology: SST Years** / 1991 / SST ✦✦✦✦
Anthology: SST Years is a terrific 21-track compilation of songs culled from the group's three albums for the label, hitting most of the highlights from all of the records and thereby providing an excellent summary of their early years. — *Stephen Thomas Erlewine*

Sweet Oblivion / Mar. 1992 / Epic ✦✦✦
The Screaming Trees' second album on Columbia is a step down from *Uncle Anesthesia*, but when the band kicks their '90s psychedelic hard rock into gear on "Dollar Bill" and the spectacular "Nearly Lost You," the shortcomings of the rest of the album are easy to ignore. — *Stephen Thomas Erlewine*

Dust / Jun. 25, 1996 / Epic ✦✦✦✦
In many ways, the Screaming Trees missed their opportunity. They released *Sweet Oblivion* just as grunge began to capture national attention and they didn't tour the album extensively, which meant nearly all of their fellow Seattle bands became superstars while they stood to the side. After four years, they returned with *Dust*, their second major label album, and by that point the band's sound was too idiosyncratic for alternative radio. Which is unfortunate because *Dust* is the band's strongest album. Sure, the rough edges that fueled albums like *Uncle Anesthesia* are gone, but in its place is a rustic hard-rock, equally informed by heavy metal and folk. The influence of Mark Lanegan's haunting solo

albums is apparent in both the sound and emotional tone of the record, but this is hardly a solo project—the rest of the band has added a gritty weight to Lanegan's spare prose. The Screaming Trees sound tighter than they ever have, and their melodies and hooks are stronger, more memorable, making *Dust* their most consistently impressive record. —*Stephen Thomas Erlewine*

Scritti Politti

f. 1977, Leeds, England
Dance-Pop, New Wave, Pop-Rock
The bouncy synth-pop outfit Scritti Politti began its existence as an avant-garde trio in Leeds, England, in 1977. An aggressively left-wing group that took its name from the Italian for "political writing," Scritti Politti was the vehicle of Green Gartside, a Welsh-born singer and one-time member of the Young Communist faction. After exiting the punk band the Against, Gartside enlisted fellow art students Matthew Kay on keyboards, Tom Morley on drums, and Nial Jinks on bass to provide support for his breathy vocals and dense lyrics; after relocating to North London, the group issued its debut single "Skank Bloc Bologna" in 1978, followed by opening spots for Joy Division and Gang of Four.

Prior to a 1980 concert, Gartside fell victim to psychosomatic paralysis and spent the next nine months in recovery in Wales; when Scritti Politti returned, Jinks had left the group, and Kay had moved into handling their business relations. The band's sound had also made a significant shift away from punk noise into smooth, soul-influenced pop territory; singles like "The Sweetest Girl" and the double A-sided "Asylums in Jerusalem"/"Jacques Derrida" (featuring guest Robert Wyatt) brought Scritti Politti's music to an entirely new audience. Following the release of their 1981 debut LP *Songs to Remember,* Morley exited the group, and Gartside headed for New York City in tandem with David Gamson, a former assistant sound engineer for the Rough Trade label.

In the United States, the duo hooked up with ex-Material drummer Fred Maher and plunged headlong into mainstream pop; 1984's "Wood Beez (Pray Like Aretha Franklin)," produced by Arif Mardin, was Scritti Politti's biggest hit to date. The LP *Cupid & Psyche 85* also fared well, even scoring a significant US hit with "Perfect Way." However, Gartside turned away from performing to write material for other singers, including Chaka Khan and Al Jarreau, and the group was silent for close to three years. After an appearance on the soundtrack to the 1987 Madonna flop *Who's That Girl,* Scritti Politti returned in 1988 with the single "Oh Patti (Don't Feel Sorry for Loverboy)" (which included a trumpet solo from Miles Davis) and the album *Provision.* The record was a commercial failure, however, and Gartside again fell ill; breaking with Gamson and Maher, he went into semi-retirement in Wales.

An appearance on the second volume of the British Electric Foundation's *Music of Quality and Distinction* series marked Gartside's initial return to music; when Scritti Politti itself returned in 1991, it was as a solo project immersed in reggae—covers of the Beatles' "She's a Woman" and Gladys Knight & the Pips' "Take Me in Your Arms and Love Me" featured guest appearances from, respectively, Shabba Ranks and Sweetie Irie. An LP's worth of material was reportedly recorded at the same sessions, but remains unreleased. —*Jason Ankeny*

Songs to Remember / 1982 / Rough Trade ✦✦✦
Scritti Politti's debut album was an infectious set of catchy, well-crafted pop songs that demonstrate Green Gartside's talent for deceptively simple hooks and melodies. —*Stephen Thomas Erlewine*

● **Cupid & Psyche 85** / 1985 / Warner Brothers ✦✦✦✦
On their second album, Scritti Politti essentially was Green Gartside, who directed drummer Fred Maher, keyboardist David Gamson, and a multitude of studio musicians through a state-of-the-art, immaculately constructed set of catchy, synth-pop on *Cupid & Psyche 85.* The results are as impressive as *Songs to Remember,* and produced the hit singles "Perfect Way" and "Wood Beez (Pray like Aretha Franklin)." —*Stephen Thomas Erlewine*

Provision / 1988 / Warner Brothers ✦✦
Provision expands the frothy, synthesized blue-eyed soul of *Cupid & Psyche 85* by emphasizing the bouncy, mechanical dance-pop rhythms and creating lush backing tracks with layers of keyboards. To be certain, it's a pleasant listen, and several tracks are pretty entertaining, but the music is so lightweight and Green Gartside's voice is so thin that the album virtually disappears into thin air, leaving behind no impression. That is, of course, with the exception of the unresolved question of why on earth did Miles Davis contribute a trumpet solo to "Oh Patti"? —*Stephen Thomas Erlewine*

The Sea and Cake

f. 1993, Chicago, IL
Alternative Pop-Rock, Post-Rock/Experimental, Indie Rock
The Sea and Cake was a post-rock supergroup of sorts comprised of luminaries from the Chicago independent scene. The band was led by

singer/guitarist Sam Prekop, who along with bassist Eric Claridge was an alumnus of the frequently brilliant Shrimp Boat. After that group's dissolution, Prekop and Claridge were offered the opportunity to embark on a new project, and hastily recruited ex-Coctails guitarist Archer Prewitt and Tortoise drummer John McEntire before entering the studio. Originally intended as a one-off project, the musicians decided to continue performing together, and after selecting the name the Sea and Cake—derived from McEntire's misinterpretation of the Gastr del Sol song "The C in Cake"—they issued their 1994 eponymous debut, an enigmatic collection highlighting Prekop's stream-of-consciousness wordplay and singular fusion of pop, jazz, blue-eyed soul, and Kraut-rock styles. In 1995, they returned with two more LPs, the intricate *Nassau* and the shimmering *The Biz. The Fawn* followed in 1997. —*Jason Ankeny*

● **The Sea and Cake** / 1994 / Thrill Jockey ✦✦✦✦
The Sea and Cake's buoyant debut is a breath of fresh air, an utterly distinctive and innovative work that expands the scope of frontman Sam Prekop's work in the great Shrimp Boat to incorporate a new fascination with Afro-Caribbean rhythms and textures. Recorded by Brad Wood, the album simply glows—Prekop's dry vocals and free-associative lyrics skip along a shimmering and lushly pastoral backdrop that nimbly fuses pop, soul, jazz, and even prog-rock; tracks like "Jacking the Ball," "Flat Lay the Water" and "Showboat Angel" are as seductive as they are elusive. —*Jason Ankeny*

Nassau / Jan. 1995 / Thrill Jockey ✦✦✦✦
Nassau, the Sea and Cake's sophomore album, is even more ambitious and eclectic than its predecessor. Opening with the bracing "Nature Boy," the group's most kinetically charged effort to date, the record quickly shifts gears to grow dark and subdued. The two instrumentals, "Earth Star" and the enigmatically titled "A Man Who Never Sees a Pretty Girl That He Doesn't Love Her a Little," spotlight the group's burgeoning jazz inclinations, while "The Cantina" is an abstract pop curveball; Sam Prekop's melodic gifts continue to blossom on the loping "Lamonts Lament" and the melancholy "Parasol," and the increased involvement of drummer/producer John McEntire pushes the group into new rhythmic and textural territory. Another winner. —*Jason Ankeny*

● **The Biz** / Oct. 1995 / Thrill Jockey ✦✦✦✦
The Sea and Cake's third album in a little over 12 months, *The Biz* nonetheless shows no signs of exhaustion. A less structured record than previous efforts, it's also the group's most restrained: songs like the title track, "Station in the Valley," and "Sending" are loose and languid, favoring a more jam-oriented and subconscious vibe over the taut dynamics of earlier work. As a result, *The Biz* lacks the immediacy of either the debut or *Nassau,* but is ultimately no less substantial—its subtle charms are not unlike buried treasures, and when they finally rise to the surface, the end result is immensely satisfying. —*Jason Ankeny*

The Fawn / Apr. 1, 1997 / Thrill Jockey ✦✦✦✦
The Fawn is the Sea and Cake's most experimental effort; the influence that the electronica movement exerts over the record is substantial—drum machines, sequencer tones, and synths are dominant throughout, and the group even dabbles in dub textures and sampling techniques, constructing "Bird and Flag" around an uncredited loop of Donald Byrd's "Lansana." As is again proven here, however, the group's greatest gift is their ability to assimilate the breadth of their inspirations, no matter how far afield, to emerge with something new and distinctive; *The Fawn* is seamless and sophisticated, impressive in scope and rich in detail. —*Jason Ankeny*

Seal

b. Feb. 19, 1963, Paddington, London, England
Vocals / Dance-Pop, Urban, Adult Contemporary, Pop-Rock, Club/Dance
Seal (born Sealhenry Samuel, February 19, 1963) emerged from England's house music scene in the early '90s to become the most popular British soul vocalist of the decade. Although his earliest material still showed signs of the acid house, by the mid-'90s he had created a distinctive fusion of soul, folk, pop, dance, and rock that brought him success on both sides of the Atlantic.

The son of Nigerian and Brazilian parents, Seal was raised in England. After graduating with an architectural degree, he took various jobs around London, including electrical engineering and designing leather clothing. After a while, he began singing in local clubs and bars. He joined an English funk band called Push, touring Japan with the band in the mid-'80s. When he was in Asia, he joined a Thailand-based blues band. After a short time with that group, he travelled throughout India on his own.

Upon returning to England, Seal met Adamski, a house and techno producer who had yet to make much of an impression within the UK. Seal provided the lyrics and vocals for Adamski's "Killer," which became a number one hit in 1990. After "Killer" became a hit, Seal signed a solo record contract. He recorded his eponymous debut album with Trevor Horn, who had previously worked with ABC, Frankie Goes to Hollywood, and the Buggles. The first single pulled from the album, "Crazy," became a No. 15 hit in the UK and reached No. 7 in America upon its release in 1991. Seal was also a success, reaching No. 24 in America and selling over three million copies around the world.

After the success of his debut, Seal took three years to complete his second album. In between the two records, he appeared on the Jimi Hendrix tribute album *Stone Free*, singing on Jeff Beck's version of "Manic Depression." In the summer of 1994, he released his second album, which was also titled *Seal*. Preceded by the American Top 40 hit "Prayer for the Dying," the album did well upon its release, peaking at No. 20 and selling a million copies by the spring of 1995, but it didn't really take off until a year after its release, when "Kiss from a Rose" was featured on the soundtrack to *Batman Forever*. "Kiss from a Rose" became a No. 1 pop single in America and spent a total of 12 weeks at the top of the adult contemporary charts; the single spent a total of 45 weeks on the adult contemporary charts. Its success sent its parent album, *Seal*, into multi-platinum status; two years after its original release, the album had sold over four million copies in the US alone. —*Stephen Thomas Erlewine*

Seal [91] / Jun. 11, 1991 / Sire ◆◆◆◆
This debut album features great dance music, some acoustic tunes, and moody ballads, highlighted by the hit singles "Crazy" and "Killer." —*John Book*

● **Seal [94]** / 1994 / Sire ◆◆◆◆
This self-titled second album continues Seal's richly produced style of dance-influenced pop with a soul. Themes of unconditional love, compassion, and spirituality prevail throughout. A fine album, it includes the hit "Prayer for the Dying." —*Rick Clark*

Seals & Crofts

f. 1969, Los Angeles, CA, **db.** 1980
Singer-Songwriter, Soft Rock, Pop-Rock
One of the 1970s' most successful soft-rock acts, the duo of Jim Seals and Dash Crofts met while playing with singer Dean Beard in 1958. That year, Beard was invited to join the Champs (of "Tequila" fame), and Seals and Crofts tagged along, remaining with the group until 1965. The two then bounced from the Mushrooms to the Dawnbreakers before deciding to strike out on their own as a duo in 1969. Seals played guitar, saxophone, and fiddle, while Crofts handled drums, mandolin, keyboards, and guitar. From 1972 to 1976, the duo had a string of five gold albums for Warner Brothers, with an additional greatest-hits compilation certified double platinum. Their hit singles from this period include "Summer Breeze," "Diamond Girl," "We May Never Pass This Way (Again)," and "Get Closer"; all except the third mentioned reached No. 6 on the *Billboard* charts. The group became embroiled in controversy in 1974 due to the title track of their *Unborn Child* album, an anti-abortion song written from the fetus' point of view; the album was a critical failure, while the single flopped and outraged abortion advocates, who held demonstrations at many of the group's shows.

By 1976, Seals & Crofts' appeal began to decline; their albums failed to sell as well, and they scored their last Top 40 hit in 1978 with "You're the Love." Warner dropped them shortly after their 1980 LP *The Longest Road*, but by this time both Seals and Crofts were more interested in devoting themselves fully to the Baha'i religion they had converted to back in 1969. The two have reunited occasionally at Baha'i gatherings, and for a short 1991-92 tour. Crofts has lived in several different countries, while Seals moved to a Costa Rican coffee farm in 1980. During the '80s, Seals' brother Dan became a prominent country singer after leaving the duo England Dan and John Ford Coley. —*Steve Huey*

Year of Sunday / 1972 / Warner Brothers ◆◆◆
With their pleasant folk-rock sound, Seals & Crofts deliver an album's worth of material that is pleasing enough to listen to, but unfortunately, nothing seems to stick. "Paper Airplanes," "Sudan Village" and the title cut are all well worth a spin, but one does come away from listening to *Year of Sunday* feeling as though they've just eaten cotton candy—sweet taste, but no substance. —*James Chrispell*

Summer Breeze / 1972 / Warner Brothers ◆◆◆◆
The title cut and "Hummingbird" are perfect for listening to on a summer's day. Breezy melodies and words that sound great even today help make *Summer Breeze* a worthy addition to anyone's music collection. And for a little melodrama, check out the cut "The Boy Down the Road." All around, this is a solid effort. —*James Chrispell*

Unborn Child / 1974 / Warner Brothers ◆◆
After a string of hits, *Unborn Child* was a mistake coming from the Seals & Crofts camp when it did. Blatantly anti-abortion, it did little to help their careers and nothing in the way of chart success. But one must consider that it does hold good music in its grooves, and with today's

attitudes changing, perhaps this isn't as harsh as it first appeared to be. —*James Chrispell*

● **Greatest Hits** / 1975 / Warner Brothers ◆◆◆◆
This album has all their hits, including "Summer Breeze," "Hummingbird," "We May Never Pass This Way (Again)," "Diamond Girl," and "When I Meet Them." —*Dan Heilman*

Seam

f. 1985, Chapel Hill, NC
Alternative Pop-Rock, Post-Rock/Experimental
Seam began as a trio out of Chapel Hill, North Carolina, with Sooyoung Park (guitars, vocals) and Lexi Mitchell (bass) of Bitch Magnet and Mac McCaughan of Superchunk (drums). Their first album, *Headsparks*, released in 1992, was filled with the slow, affecting melodies and vocals that would become their trademark. After the release of that record, McCaughan left the group to pursue Superchunk full-time, and the rest of Seam moved headquarters to Chicago. Bob Rising replaced McCaughan and Craig White joined on as an additional guitarist, turning Seam into a quartet. In 1993, *The Problem with Me* featured this new lineup and slightly more upbeat sounds. *Are You Driving Me Crazy?*, released in 1995, features an entirely new lineup except Park (the band currently consists of drummer Chris Manfrin, bassist William Shin, and guitarist Reg Shrader) but continues in the line of moody and challenging Seam releases, making their musical quality a constant in a constantly changing band. —*Heather Phares*

Headsparks / Mar. 11, 1992 / Homestead ◆◆◆
The group's debut album mixes plenty of droning guitars along with Park's plaintive vocals. "Shame" is one of the group's finest songs on the album; like the rest of the album, it's at times subtle and moving, and at other times bludgeoning and harsh. *Headsparks* is an appealing and impressive debut. —*Heather Phares*

● **The Problem with Me** / 1993 / Touch & Go ◆◆◆◆
Seam's first album for Touch and Go, *The Problem with Me*, further pushes the boundaries of slow-rock with sleepy, minimalist tracks like "Road to Madrid" and "Stage 2000," as well as noisier tracks like "Sweet Pea." —*Heather Phares*

Are You Driving Me Crazy? / Jun. 20, 1995 / Touch and Go ◆◆◆◆
The band's third album continues Seam's tradition of sleepy, droning, but beautiful and affecting music. The band's new lineup seems to work well with Park's musical sensibilities; *Are You Driving Me Crazy?* is as creative and moving as anything else the band has accomplished. —*Heather Phares*

The Searchers

f. 1957, Liverpool, England
British Invasion, Power Pop, Pop-Rock
Founded in 1957 by John McNally (guitar/vocals), the Searchers were originally one of thousands of skiffle groups formed in the wake of Lonnie Donegan's success with "Rock Island Line." The Searchers' immediate competitors included bands such as the Wreckers and the Confederates, both led by Michael Pender (guitar, vocals), and the Martinis, led by Tony Jackson (guitar/vocals). By 1959, McNally and Pender were working together as a duet; later in the year, Jackson joined as the lead vocalist. After drummer Norman McGarry left the Searchers he was replaced by Chris Crummy, who quickly renamed himself Chris Curtis. Other changes were in the works as Jackson built and learned to play a customized bass guitar. Learning his new job on the four-stringed instrument proved too difficult to permit him to continue singing lead, and McNally and Pender brought in a fifth member, Johnny Sandon (born Billy Beck). Johnny Sandon & the Searchers lasted from 1960 through February of 1962, and were extremely popular on the dance hall and club circuit in Liverpool. Sandon cut out for a career on his own, with another band called the Remo Four in early 1962.

Meanwhile, the Searchers, now a quartet with Jackson once again lead singer, became one of the top acts on the Liverpool band scene, playing textured renditions of American R&B, rock 'n' roll, country, soul, and rockabilly. The group was signed to Pye Records in mid-1963 and their first single, a cover of the Drifters' "Sweets for My Sweet," was released in August of 1963, hitting No. 1 on the British charts. While the Beatles quickly outdistanced all comers, the Searchers did, indeed, go to the top of the charts with two of their next three singles, "Needles and Pins" and "Don't Throw Your Love Away." Another record, "Sugar and Spice," written by their producer Tony Hatch under the pseudonym Fred Nightingale, stalled at the No. 2 spot. Over the next nine months, the band staked out a sound that was one of the most distinctive in a rock scene crawling with hundreds of bands. Their music was built around the sound of a crisply played 12-string guitar, coupled with strong lead vocals and carefully, sometimes exquisitely arranged harmonies, so that they could credibly cover American R&B standards like "Love Potion No. 9" or Phil Spector-based girl group pop like "Be My Baby." Their

1964 singles included a venture into folk-rock before the genre had been "invented" in the press, in the form of a cover of Malvina Reynolds' "What Have You Done to the Rain." Interestingly, their 12-string guitar sound would become a key ingredient in the success of the Byrds, who even took the riff from "Needles and Pins" and transformed it into the main riff of "Feel a Whole Lot Better."

In July of 1964, with the group riding the upper reaches of the British charts, and with their third album in nine months in release, it was announced that Tony Jackson was leaving the Searchers to form his own band. He would be replaced by Frank Allen, who had been playing bass with Cliff Bennett & the Rebel Rousers. The turning point for the band came in 1965, as the British and international fascination with the Liverpool sound faded away. The Searchers began casting their net wider for material to cover, in addition to coming up with one original hit, the Curtis/Pender-authored "He's Got No Love." By the beginning of 1966, the group's string of chart hits seemed to have run out, and Chris Curtis exited in early 1966, claiming to have become exhausted from the group's constant touring. The Searchers, with Johnny Blunt on drums, continued working and had their last hit, "Have You Ever Loved Somebody," which barely cracked the Top 50 in October of 1966. The group continued working, however, playing clubs and cabarets in England and Europe. Blunt exited at the end of the 1960s, but was replaced by Billy Adamson, and this lineup of the Searchers continued intact until the mid-1980s, working for 35 weeks a year throughout Europe with an occasional US visit. Although they played as part of Richard Nader's "Rock 'n Roll Revival" shows, they never became an "oldies" act, always adding new material, including originals and covers of work by songwriters such as Neil Young to their sets, and in 1972 the band cut an album for British RCA.

At the end of the 1970s, their recording fortunes were revived once again as Seymour Stein, the head of Sire Records, signed the Searchers for two albums. Those records, *The Searchers* and *Love's Melodies*, were the best work the group ever did, highlighted by achingly beautiful yet vibrant and forceful playing and singing, and an unerring array of memorable hooks and melodies. Those two albums were followed by a series of tracks recorded for their original label, Pye Records, in the early 1980s. The group held their audience well into the 1980s, playing before crowds of as large as 15,000 along one US tour. In 1985, after playing together for 26 years, Pender and McNally split up, with McNally continuing to lead the Searchers (with Adamson and Allen, with Spencer James added on second guitar and vocals), while Pender formed Mike Pender's Searchers, consisting of Chris Black (guitar, vocals), Barry Cowell (bass, vocals), and Steve Carlyle (drums, vocals). Both groups have toured extensively and the Searchers under McNally have recorded on occasion. *—Bruce Eder*

Sugar & Spice / 1963 / Castle ✦✦✦
The Searchers' 1963 debut LP was typical of most early British Invasion albums, built around one hit ("Sugar and Spice," a No. 1 hit in the UK) and 11 covers of American rock 'n' roll standards. This wasn't destined to be remembered as an artistic statement along the lines of *With the Beatles*, but it's better than the average period artifact, due to the group's always enjoyable harmonies and arrangements. Actually, nearly half of the tracks are first-rate. Their energetic rave-up of the Coasters' "Ain't That Just Like Me" was actually a minor US hit; "All My Sorrows" was an excellent arrangement of a Glenn Yarborough song that foreshadowed folk-rock; and "Hungry for Love" has the irresistibly saccharine appeal of Gerry & the Pacemakers' early hits. *—Richie Unterberger*

Meet the Searchers / 1963 / Castle ✦✦
The Searchers' second LP is arguably the most dispensable of their early albums now available on CD. "Sweets for My Sweet," the cover of the Drifters song, gave the band their second No. 1 single in Britain. That worthy cover version leads off the album, followed by their fine rendition of the obscure R&B song "Alright" (actually covered in turn by a number of garage bands) and "Love Potion No. 9," which would turn out to be their biggest US hit a year later, though it was never issued as a single in Britain. It's all downhill from then on, with routine covers of hits like "Money," "Stand by Me," "Da Doo Ron Ron," and "Twist and Shout," which aren't going to make anyone forget the originals, or for that matter the Beatles' own versions of "Money" and "Twist and Shout." Their neatly arranged covers of "Where Have All the Flowers Gone" and The Everly Brothers' "Since You Broke My Heart" are decent, if not earthshaking. *—Richie Unterberger*

It's the Searchers / 1964 / Castle ✦✦✦✦
Perhaps the best studio album by a band that is really best represented by greatest hit collections. This 1964 LP includes the classic hits "Needles and Pins" and "Don't Throw Your Love Away." It also features some of their best LP cuts, on which they applied their famed harmonies to American material that was both strong and obscure. The best of these covers are Bacharach/David's "This Empty Space" (originally by Dionne Warwick), the Jackie DeShannon-penned "Can't Help Forgiving You," the Drifters' "I Count the Tears," the folkish "Sea of Heartbreak," and

"Where Have You Been" (which was also part of the Beatles' repertoire during their Hamburg days). The harder-rocking songs don't lend themselves as well to the group's talents, which always (with some notable exceptions) lay more in the folk-rock and Merseybeat direction than R&B/rockabilly. *—Richie Unterberger*

Take Me for What I'm Worth / 1965 / PRT ✦✦
The Searchers were not only slipping in popularity by the time of this release, but were also slipping considerably behind the prevailing musical trends of the times. Maybe that's why they offered more original tunes (four) than usual. Still, the group sounded pretty much like they always did in the mid-'60s, though this is perhaps one of their weaker albums. Their interpretation of P.F. Sloan's anthemic protest folk-rock title track is good, and gave the group their final British Top 20 hit. But, as usual, their R&B covers (of Fats Domino and Marvin Gaye) are inoffensively second-rate and dated, and the originals equally inoffensive and unmemorable. Their cover of the Ronettes' "Be My Baby" is competent but ill-advised; nothing's going to compete with the original. The harmonies and arrangements are never less than pleasant and professional, but even big fans of the group will count this among their lesser relics. It does, however, include a couple of their better album tracks: a cover of the obscure Jackie DeShannon composition "Each Time" and, especially, a fine acoustic reading of Ian Tyson's "Four Strong Winds." *—Richie Unterberger*

The Searchers / 1979 / Castle ✦✦✦✦
Love Melodies / 1981 / Sire ✦✦✦✦
These two albums (*The Searchers* and *Love's Melodies*) represent the Searchers at their peak as a recording outfit, having maintained their original mid-'60s emphasis on excellent harmonies and crisply played guitars but also absorbed lessons from such '70s pub-rockers as Brinsley Schwarz and roots-rock expert Dave Edmunds. The material is some of the most beautifully recorded anytime in this era, and anyone lucky enough to spot a copy of either of these records—neither of which has yet shown up on compact disc—should grab them. *—Bruce Eder*

Silver Searchers / 1984 / PRT ✦✦
The best "best-of" on the band done up to the mid-'80s, with decent if not too extensive notes and sound. This collection was supplanted by Rhino's *Greatest Hits* and *The Searchers' 30th Anniversary Collection* in the early '90s. *—Bruce Eder*

● **Greatest Hits** / 1985 / Rhino ✦✦✦✦
The best American best-of on the band, and the most desirable for those on a budget, with superior sound to the *Silver Searchers* collection. *—Bruce Eder*

Play the System: Rarities, Oddities & Flipsides / 1987 / PRT ✦✦✦
Exactly what the title says: 18 tracks from 1963-67, including 14 non-LP B-sides, three non-LP A-sides, and the odd 1964 EP-only cut "The System," which was used in a 1964 film. The ten songs on side one are a pleasure for fans of the early Searchers sound, and also serve as a showcase for the group's songwriting talents, as all but one are originals. Rarely surfacing on albums, let alone on A-sides, it was only on B-sides that the band deigned to (or was allowed to) pen their own material. It's not like these are brilliant works on the level of Lennon-McCartney or Ray Davies, but they're very pleasant numbers highlighting the Searchers' strengths: melodies, harmonies, and clean arrangements. "It's All Been a Dream" and "Saturday Night Out" are good, energetic Merseybeat tunes; "This Feeling Inside" recalls the early Hollies; "Don't Hide It Away" is a good moody, downbeat tune; and "Till I Met You" is an exquisite ballad. Side two is a different story, showing the group trying to keep apace of '60s trends toward more sophisticated lyrics and arrangements with far less success than, say, the Hollies. It's not so much that the group wasn't up to the task as performers; it's simply that the material (all dating from 1966-67, except the closing track, "The System") is weak. The collection, with fine liner notes from Brian Hogg, can nonetheless be unreservedly recommended to Searchers fans on the strength of the first side alone. *—Richie Unterberger*

German, French & Rare Recordings / 1990 / Repertoire ✦✦
While this anthology does collectors a service by gathering many of the group's rarest recordings in one place, you've really got to be a hard-bitten fanatic to find this import worthwhile. This 24-song compilation includes the group's German versions of hits like "Sugar and Spice" and "Goodbye My Love," as well as their (poorly accented) French renditions of "Don't Throw Your Love Away" and "Sugar and Spice" (again). A half-dozen other German and French re-recordings of 1963-64 English B-sides and album tracks, some quite obscure even in their original English versions, are included as well. As you might expect, the group simply re-recorded their vocals over the original backing tracks for the Continental market, which most likely preferred the English versions anyway. The CD also includes drummer Chris Curtis' rare and forgettable 1966 single, as well as a clumsy medley of their greatest hits and ten dreadful, undocumented tunes that date from well after their mid-'60s heyday. Fans looking for decent rare Searchers should seek out the *Play the Sys-*

tem LP, which compiles '60s B-sides and rarities of considerably higher quality. —*Richie Unterberger*

30th Anniversary Collection / 1992 / Sequel ✦✦✦✦
Although it's missing one or two fairly strong tracks, this three-CD, 84-song set is a pretty definitive collection of the group's best '60s material, for those who want to go beyond the greatest hits. Besides including all of their key A—and B-sides, it has an entire disc of their best '60s album tracks. The rarities disc includes foreign-language versions, outtakes, mid-'60s BBC performances, and solo discs by Tony Jackson and Chris Curtis. Highlights here include an alternate take of "Someday We're Gonna Love Again," a BBC version of "Blowin' in the Wind," and the previously unreleased "Once Upon a Time" (recorded by Dusty Springfield). The package includes liner notes, discography, and a family tree. —*Richie Unterberger*

Live at the Star Club / 1994 / PolyGram ✦✦✦
Of all the British bands that recorded at the Star Club in 1962-63, the Searchers gave the best performance—polished, exciting, and utterly professional, lacking the finely honed 12-string guitar sound that their subsequent hits would display but still a fine testament to their early work and history. —*Bruce Eder*

Sebadoh
....
f. 1989, Northampton, MA
Alternative Pop-Rock, Lo-Fi, Indie Rock
As much a musician's collective as a band, Sebadoh was the quintessential lo-fi band of the '90s. Formed by singer-songwriter Lou Barlow while he was the bassist for Dinosaur Jr. in the late '80s, Sebadoh's music was a virtual catalog of '80s alternative rock and '90s indie rock, featuring everything from jangle-pop to noise-rock experimentalism. Upon being kicked out of Dinosaur Jr. in 1989, Barlow turned his attention toward Sebadoh, a home-recording project that he and drummer/songwriter Eric Gaffney developed into a backing band for both Barlow and Gaffney, as each submitted home-recorded tapes for release and toured behind the albums. Eventually adding drummer/songwriter Jason Loewenstein, the trio became an indie-rock sensation, as well known for the size and inconsistency of its output as the music itself. Often, Sebadoh sounded schizophrenic, flipping between Barlow's sensitive folk-rock and Gaffney's noise experiments without warning. This very diversity became the band's calling card, and by 1992 the band had earned a devoted following. As the media focused on Barlow—who also released a number of solo records under the name Sentridoh—Gaffney grew frustrated. Gaffney left in 1994, and with new drummer Bob Fay, Sebadoh produced its most accessible albums—*Bakesale* and *Harmacy*—which expanded its cult somewhat. Despite the group's flirtation with (relatively) polished production and the fluke success of Barlow's side-project Folk Implosion, Sebadoh remained a cult band, and became one the largest touchstones of '90s indie rock.

Sebadoh began as an outlet for Lou Barlow's frustration with J. Mascis, who refused to let Barlow contribute songs to any Dinosaur Jr. releases. In 1987, Barlow released *Weed Forestin',* a cassette of acoustic songs he had recorded at home on a four-track recorder, under the name Sentridoh. The cassette was sold at local Massachusetts record stores. Eric Gaffney contributed percussion to *Weed Forestin',* and when Barlow had a break from Dinosaur in 1988 the duo recorded *The Freed Man*, which consisted of songs by both songwriters. Also released as a homemade cassette, *The Freed Man* worked its way to Gerard Cosloy, the head of Homestead Records. Cosloy offered to release the cassette on his record label, and the tape was revised and expanded into a full-length album. Homestead released *The Freed Man* in 1989, and shortly after its appearance, Mascis kicked Barlow out of Dinosaur. and Barlow then turned his attentions towards Sebadoh. A revised and expanded *Weed Forestin'* was released in early 1990; the two records were combined on the CD *The Freed Weed* later that year.

By the end of 1989, Sebadoh added a full-time drummer, Jason Loewenstein, on the suggestion of Gaffney. Sebadoh began playing concerts regularly, concentrating on Gaffney's material and throwing in a few Barlow songs for good measure. Where their albums were acoustic-oriented, their concerts were noisy ventures into post-hardcore and Sonic Youth territory. Over the course of 1990, the group was active only sporadically, deciding whether they wanted to pursue a full-fledged career; a few seven-inch singles of primarily acoustic material appeared that year. As of early 1991, the band began recording electric material, as evidenced by the EP *Gimmie Indie Rock.* Released early in 1991, *Sebadoh III* was divided between Gaffney's electric songs and acoustic material by Barlow and Loewenstein. The band was prepared to embark on their first major tour when Gaffney abruptly left the band before its start. Barlow and Loewenstein carried on, initially performing shows as a duo, but soon hiring Bob Fay as a drummer. Upon the completion of the tour,

Gaffney returned to the band, but during his absence the direction of Sebadoh's music had shifted away from his songs and toward Barlow's.

Following a full-length national tour in the fall of 1991, Sebadoh recorded five of Barlow's songs as a demo tape, which served as its gateway to contracts with Sub Pop in the US and City Slang/20/20 in the UK. Gaffney left the band at the end of the year, and the group again hired Fay as a replacement. With Fay, Sebadoh toured America and Europe in early 1992, recording the British EPs *Rocking the Forest* and *Sebadoh vs. Helmet*, which were combined later that year on the Sub Pop album *Smash Your Head on the Punk Rock.* Gaffney again returned to the band after Sebadoh released these recordings, with Fay again leaving the band. Barlow and Loewenstein had begun to tire of Gaffney's constant sabbaticals, and Lou returned to his Sentridoh project, releasing a series of EPs, seven-inch singles and cassettes over the course of 1993 and 1994. Sebadoh released its fifth album, *Bubble and Scrape*, in the spring of 1993 and spent the remainder of the year touring behind the record, building their cult across America and Britain. Gaffney left for a final time in the fall of 1993 and Fay became his permanent replacement.

Before recording the sixth Sebadoh album, Barlow began a new band with John Davis called the Folk Implosion; the duo released three recordings over the course of 1994. Sebadoh returned with *Bakesale*, their first album without Eric Gaffney, in the summer of 1994. Boasting a somewhat more accessible sound, *Bakesale* became the group's most successful album to date, generating the near-modern rock hit "Rebound." The band took a break in 1995 and the Folk Implosion recorded the soundtrack to the controversial independent film *Kids.* Surprisingly, *Kids* spawned a genuine hit single with the haunting, hip-hop-tinged "Natural One," which climbed all the way into the Top 30 of the US pop charts. In light of the success of "Natural One," Sebadoh's next record, *Harmacy*, was expected to be a hit upon its fall 1996 release. Though it didn't match commercial expectations raised by "Natural One," *Harmacy* expanded the success of *Bakesale*, becoming the first Sebadoh album to chart in the US. —*Stephen Thomas Erlewine*

The Freed Weed / 1990 / Homestead ✦✦✦
The epitome of lo-fi, these 47 skeletal bits-of-songs were recorded by Lou Barlow and Eric Gaffney long before their Sebadoh days. Collects their first two self-released cassettes. Only for the curious or the collector. —*John Bush*

Weed Forestin' / 1990 / Homestead ✦✦
The press release to this LP boasted that it, unlike their debut, "was actually recorded with the knowledge that it would be released." Apparently Lou Barlow and Eric Gaffney had a pretty clear crystal ball; the music was taped in 1986 and 1987, but didn't actually come out on vinyl until 1990. Sebadoh's first LP, *The Freed Man*, boasts some of the most deliberately awful fidelity of all time (against some stiff competition); this is somewhat, but only somewhat, more hi-fi. Barlow's gifts are often in evidence: his appealing voice, sensitive wit, and knack for affected burned-out acid-folk. Alas, the merits are often buried beneath hiss and tomfoolery, as if he wasn't convinced his music was any good on its own terms, and so tried to pretend it was all a joke. The LP has since been reissued (along with most of *The Freed Man*) on the CD *The Freed Weed.* —*Richie Unterberger*

● **III** / 1991 / Homestead ✦✦✦✦
Far removed from the primitivism of the band's early work, *III* marks a pivotal moment in Sebadoh's creative evolution. The first full-length record to feature Jason Loewenstein, it's a radically diverse affair, offering vastly improved production and a newly discovered dedication to focused, controlled songcraft; though no two cuts sound even remotely similar, taken as a whole the album is a surprisingly cohesive affair. Among the highlights—and with 23 songs, there are many—are "The Freed Pig" (Lou Barlow's vicious swipe at former Dinosaur Jr. bandmate J. Mascis), Eric Gaffney's ominously jaunty "Violet Execution," and Barlow's tongue-in-cheek ode to sexual confusion, "Hassle." —*Jason Ankeny*

Smash Your Head on the Punk Rock / Nov. 6, 1992 / Sub Pop ✦✦✦
Sebadoh made its Sub Pop debut with *Smash Your Head on the Punk Rock*, which collects the highlights of the import compilations *Rockin' the Forest* and *Sebadoh vs. Helmet.* Lou Barlow's contributions are the gems here, especially the transcendent "Brand New Love," which first appeared in acoustic form on *Weed Forestin'* (and was later punked up by Superchunk); almost as good are "Vampire" and "Good Things," while an apt and poignant cover of David Crosby's "Everybody's Been Burned" underscores the emotional frailty that binds all of Barlow's work. —*Jason Ankeny*

Bubble and Scrape / Apr. 26, 1993 / Sub Pop ✦✦✦✦
Bubble and Scrape is the last Sebadoh record to feature Eric Gaffney, and accordingly, his contributions are not so much songs as tantrums; blistering rants like "Telecosmic Alchemy" and "Elixir Is Zog" offer much in the way of dissonant noise, but little in the way of substance. Still, the album has much to recommend it—not only does Jason Loewenstein emerge here as an increasingly adept songwriter, but Lou Barlow truly

hits his stride: both "Soul and Fire" and "Think (Let Tomorrow Bee)" are sterling additions to one of the most impressive catalogues of love songs on the planet, while "Cliche" stings with bitter intensity. —*Jason Ankeny*

In Tokyo / 1994 / Bolide ✦✦✦
The official bootleg *In Tokyo* documents a surprisingly tight July 1994 show that offers an intriguing mix of favorites ("Rebound," "Soul and Fire," "The Freed Pig"), new material ("Beauty of the Ride" and "On Fire," which appeared two years later on *Harmacy*), relative obscurities ("Plate O' Hatred," "Sing Something," "Soulmate"), and telling covers (Flipper's "No Tears," Pussy Galore's "Kill Yourself" and Husker Du's "What's Going On"). —*Jason Ankeny*

Bakesale / Sep. 1994 / Sub Pop ✦✦✦✦
With *Bakesale*, Sebadoh has trimmed down to Lou Barlow, Jason Loewenstein, and Bob Fay, with Barlow and Loewenstein taking on the lion's share of the songwriting. Maybe the change in personnel was needed, because *Bakesale* is their most accessible, concise work to date. Without the noise that usually envelops their records, the solid, unconventional pop songwriting of Barlow and Loewenstein shines through brightly. —*Stephen Thomas Erlewine*

Harmacy / Aug. 20, 1996 / Sub Pop ✦✦✦✦
Part of Sebadoh's charm is that their records are always rather inconsistent, flipping wildly between sonic extremes as well as musical genres. In a sense, *Harmacy* is no different than its predecessors, but there are some crucial differences that makes it their most accessible effort. Previously, that title was held by 1994's *Bakesale*, but in between that record and *Harmacy*, Lou Barlow had a genuine Top 40 hit with the Folk Implosion's "Natural One." Although nothing on *Harmacy* sounds much like the hip-hop hybrid of "Natural One," its success did have an effect on Barlow, leading him toward more straightforward song structures and cleaner productions—"Willing to Wait" even features strings. Instead of diluting the impact of Sebadoh's music, the clearer production actually strengthens it. Barlow's sighing melodies and jangling indie-rock become more resonant and affecting, and his batch of songs are among his best ever. Jason Loewenstein, Sebadoh's other main songwriter, suffers somewhat at the hands of cleaner production. Loewenstein tends to stick closer to the band's hardcore punk roots than Barlow, so his songs usually could use the extra layer of hiss and murk that cheap productions lend recordings. It also doesn't help that he tends to sink into rather faceless indie noise-rock. When Loewenstein takes a stab at pop melodies, such as "Can't Give Up," his songs are memorable but, on the whole, uneven and occasionally tedious. If it weren't for Loewenstein's erratic songwriting, *Harmacy* might rank as Sebadoh's masterpiece, but as it stands it's just another very fine and sometimes frustrating record from a band that produces nothing but very fine and sometimes frustrating records. —*Stephen Thomas Erlewine*

John Sebastian

b. Mar. 17, 1944, New York, NY
Harmonica, Vocals / Singer-Songwriter, Folk-Rock, Pop-Rock, Contemporary Folk
Born in New York City, the son of a classical harmonica player, John Sebastian grew up in the Greenwich Village coffeehouses and was a popular sideman to various folk artists prior to forming the folk-rock band the Lovin' Spoonful, for which he served as lead singer and songwriter in the mid-'60s. When the Spoonful broke up, Sebastian went solo, appearing at the Woodstock Festival in 1969 and releasing the Top 20 *John B. Sebastian* album in 1970. Subsequent efforts were less successful, but in 1976 Sebastian scored a No. 1 hit with "Welcome Back," the theme song from the TV series *Welcome Back, Kotter*. Sebastian continues to tour and play on occasional sessions; he released his first album since the '70s, *Tar Beach*, in 1993. —*William Ruhlmann*

John B. Sebastian / 1970 / MGM ✦✦✦✦
A strong debut solo album spotlighting Sebastian's warm voice and optimistic, melodic folk-pop songwriting. —*William Ruhlmann*

Cheapo Cheapo Production Presents / 1971 / Reprise ✦✦✦✦
Cheapo Cheapo Production Presents Real Live is an exuberant solo appearance in which Sebastian's humor and wit are at their apex. A wide variety of songs, from old folk-blues standards to Spoonful favorites. Makes you wish you'd been there. —*William Ruhlmann*

● **The Best of John Sebastian** / 1989 / Rhino ✦✦✦✦
A 16-track selection from Sebastian's solo albums from 1970 to 1976, including the hit "Welcome Back." —*William Ruhlmann*

Tar Beach / Feb. 10, 1993 / Shanachie ✦✦✦
A low-key comeback album from Sebastian, showing that his melodic folk-pop hasn't lost its charm in the 17 years since he recorded his last record. —*Stephen Thomas Erlewine*

I Want My Roots / Mar. 12, 1996 / MusicMasters ✦✦✦
John Sebastian's early group affiliations in the Even Dozen Jug Band and the Lovin' Spoonful rose out of the casual party jug-band music that enjoyed a brief period of popularity during the folk boom, mixing folk

elements with the more celebratory elements of country and blues with a touch of zany fun thrown in. Combining with guitarist Jimmy Vivino and drummer James Wormworth, Sebastian brought in original jug player Fritz Richmond from the Jim Kweskin Jug Band to form the J-Band, co-credited on this album, which updates jug music for the '90s. Sebastian opens the proceedings with the old Spoonful song "Mobile Line" for reference, and then things get really crazy. Sebastian and Vivino contribute four originals, but the heart of the album is material by the likes of Sleepy John Estes and Blind Willie McTell, and guest stars Paul Risell, Annie Raines, Rory Block, Yank Rachell, Richard Crooks, and John Simon are just as likely to be playing or singing as the nominal leader or his band, which can mean that Sebastian is frequently a sideman on his own album, especially during a three-song Rachell mini-set near the album's end. No matter. The result is like a particularly enjoyable club date in which friends keep stumbling onstage from the bar to sing a verse or play a lick. In other words, the spirit of jug band music has been brought back to life. —*William Ruhlmann*

King Biscuit Flower Hour / Aug. 27, 1996 / King Biscuit ✦✦✦
This Sept. 9, 1979, Long Island concert presents several sides of John Sebastian. Equally well versed in blues, folk, and rock, he manages to straddle all three superbly without making a lasting impression in any. The bluesy "Mobile Line" is followed by a stripped-down, reconsidered version of "Welcome Back," and a quartet of Lovin' Spoonful standards, "Nashville Cats," "Daydream," "Younger Generation," and "Darling Be Home Soon," all interspersed with a new song or two. He's in excellent voice—a little rougher than the late 1960s—and runs through blues and folk riffs with equal aplomb. —*Bruce Eder*

Jon Secada

b. , Cuba
Vocals / Dance-Pop, Urban, Latin Pop, Adult Contemporary, Pop
With only one album, Jon Secada became one of the biggest adult contemporary artist of the '90s, selling over six million albums worldwide. Secada's smooth mix of R&B, pop, and Latin music appealed to a number of different audiences. What separates him from the overly slick sound of most adult contemporary artists are his considerable songwriting skills; he's able to write sweet, affecting ballads that rarely seem contrived. As well as becoming a huge pop star, Secada is one of the hottest Latin artists recording in the '90s; his Spanish language album *Otro Dia Mas Sin Verte* was *Billboard*'s No. 1 Latin album in 1992 and won a Grammy for Best Latin Pop album. After 1995's *Amor*, he returned in 1997 with *Secada*. —*Stephen Thomas Erlewine*

● **Jon Secada** / 1992 / SBK ✦✦✦✦
Secada, formerly a backup singer for Gloria Estefan, provides an impressive mix of appealing Top Ten dance singles and powerful ballads in his English album debut. Notable cuts from this self-titled album include "Just Another Day" and "Angel," both of which have accompanying Spanish versions on the release, with Estefan and Secada collaborating on their lyrical content. Estefan also provides background vocals on "Otro Dia Mas Sin Verte," the Spanish version of "Just Another Day." If these titles are any indication of his future work, Secada will definitely be an important artist to watch in the coming years. —*Ashley S. Battel*

Heart, Soul & a Voice / May 24, 1994 / SBK ✦✦✦
While there aren't as many obvious singles on Jon Secada's second album, his voice sounds better than ever, making it a worthwhile sophomore effort. —*Stephen Thomas Erlewine*

Amor / Oct. 10, 1995 / EMI Latin/SBK ✦✦✦
Amor is a collection of Spanish love ballads, sung with grace by Jon Secada. The album is a more subdued and jazzy affair than Secada's previous efforts, proving that he is capable of many different styles as a vocalist. —*Stephen Thomas Erlewine*

Secada / Mar. 25, 1997 / Capitol ✦✦✦
Despite a couple of bland tracks and an overlong running time, *Secada* is a fine return to English-language adult-contemporary pop by Jon Secada. While the songs aren't always distinctive, Secada's voice is clear, pure, and lovely, making even the weakest songs tolerable. Only a handful of songs are first-rate—including the single "Too Late, Too Soon"—but the record is pleasant and makes for fine background music. —*Rodney Batdorf*

Secret Affair

f. 1978, London, England, **db.** 1982
New Wave, Power Pop, Mod-Revival
Secret Affair, consisting of Ian Page (vocals, trumpet, piano, organ), David Cairns (guitar, backing vocals), Dennis Smith (bass, backing vocals), and Seb Shelton (drums), formed in 1978. Taking their inspiration from the Jam, the group was quickly seen as one of the shining stars of the mod-revival movement of the late '70s. They received their most important early exposure by supporting the Jam on small-scale tours in England and followed with several mod package tours with bands such

as the Purple Hearts. Their first single, "Time for Action," was the perfect youth anthem for the time and certainly one the most memorable and successful of the movement. The band released its first album, *Glory Boys*, late in 1979 on their own label, I-Spy (distributed by Arista in the UK and Sire in the US). Both the album and their subsequent singles charted, but by the time 1980's *Behind Closed Doors* was released the revival was dissolving and they were too firmly rooted in the movement to change their arrogant stance. The band began to break up when drummer Seb Shelton left in 1980. They held on until 1982, releasing one more album, *Business as Usual*, to an uninterested public; the members went their separate ways shortly after its release. — *Chris Woodstra The*

Glory Boys / 1979 / Sire ++++
Glory Boys clearly placed Secret Affair at the top of the mod-revival's third wave. The songs are top-notch, building on rather than ripping off the Jam's sound—a refreshing change from the second—and third-rate soundalikes the revival usually produced. Ian Page's arrogant, self-important lyrics are a little too much in places, but overall, this was a promising debut. — *Chris Woodstra*

Behind Closed Doors / Nov. 1980 / I Spy +++
Unfortunately, Secret Affair couldn't match the bite of *Glory Boys* with the follow-up. They've gotten better with the formula sound but the songs really don't measure up this time out. — *Chris Woodstra*

Business As Usual / 1982 / Arista ++
The aptly titled third album shows a band that held on for too long without progressing. — *Chris Woodstra*

● **Glory Boys/Behind Closed Doors** / 1995 / Arista ++++
As far as mod-revival bands go, Secret Affair was probably the purest—a textbook example of all that was good (and bad) about the revival. They could write concise pop songs, but in the end their arrogance and inflexibility doomed them. *Glory Boys*, the band's first album, was one of the finest albums produced by the revival; the single "Time for Action" served as a perfect youth anthem. By 1980's *Behind Closed Doors* (the second album), the band seemed to place a little too much importance on the fad, staying in character even after it was clearly out of style—at the end of their career, they were verging on the point of parody. As an artifact, this two-fer is quite fun to revisit. As a portrait of the band, this is both the starting and the ending point. — *Chris Woodstra*

Neil Sedaka

b. Mar. 13, 1939, Brooklyn, NY
Piano, Vocals / Pop, Pop-Rock, Brill Building Pop
If Neil Sedaka had been born a bit earlier, he probably would have felt quite at home as a straight Tin Pan Alley tunesmith. Rock and roll had taken over by 1960, so he made a niche for himself as one of the Brill Building's most pop-oriented writers. Unlike most of the Brill Building heavyweights, he sang most of his hit records (which were composed in association with Howard Greenfield). And he had a lot of them in the late '50s and early '60s: "Oh Carol," "The Diary," "Stairway to Heaven," "Calendar Girl," "Next Door to an Angel," and "Happy Birthday, Sweet Sixteen." "Breaking Up Is Hard to Do," a No. 1 hit in 1962, is probably his best-known tune.

Sedaka was a promising pianist as a youngster, and was once selected by Arthur Rubinstein to play on New York City's classical radio station; he also studied at New York's prestigious Juilliard school. At the same time, he set down rock'n'roll and doo-wop roots by singing in an early version of the Tokens. After he had his first songwriting success with Connie Francis' "Stupid Cupid" in 1958, he got a deal with RCA in the late '50s as a solo artist. Sedaka's own hits were well crafted, but were probably the most innocuous, saccharine smashes to come out of the early Brill Building crowd. His rather thin, high vocals were boosted by multi-tracking, which was still a novel technique at the time.

The big hits stopped rolling in for Sedaka a good year or so before the Beatles became popular in America. He concentrated more on the songwriting end of the business for the next decade, continuing to write with Greenfield and scoring occasional successes. He made an unexpectedly successful comeback in England in the early '70s, where three of his albums were co-produced by Graham Gouldman of 10cc. By the mid-'70s he was recording for Elton John's Rocket label, and got a No. 1 hit with the ballad "Laughter in the Rain" in 1974. That and "Love Will Keep Us Together," which he and Greenfield wrote for the Captain and Tennille, did much to get MOR pop off the ground, and consequently make many wish that Sedaka had never re-emerged.

Sedaka got another No. 1 hit, "Bad Blood," in 1975, with Elton John helping out on background vocals. A slow remake of "Breaking Up Is Hard to Do" made the Top Ten the following year, and although he would never enter the Top 40 after 1980, he was well assured of a successful career as a perennial on the MOR circuit. — *Richie Unterberger*

● **All-Time Greatest Hits** / 1975 / RCA ++++
Includes "Calendar Girl," "Happy Birthday, Sweet Sixteen," "Breaking Up Is Hard to Do," and other sprightly pop numbers. — *Dan Heilman*

● **Laughter in the Rain: The Best of Neil Sedaka, 1974-1980** / Sep. 27, 1994 / Varese Sarabande ++++
His biggest and best work for MCA and Elektra are represented in this set, with "Laughter in the Rain," "Bad Blood," "Love in the Shadows," and his reconstruction of "Breaking Up Is Hard to Do" being the highlights. — *John Lowe*

Neil Sedaka / Circulate / RCA ++
Though Neil Sedaka earned his reputation as a pop-rock songwriter, very little of his early work was well developed. That is proved by this two-fer disc, which combines his early-'60s albums *Neil Sedaka* and *Circulate*. Both albums try to capitalize on then-current pop trends, with Sedaka trying his hand at bouncy pop, dance crazes, rock 'n' roll, and ballads. Apart from the hits "The Diary" and the frenzied "I Go Ape," most of the songs on the albums are simply dull, rendering the disc nothing more than an enjoyable, well-produced period piece. — *Stephen Thomas Erlewine*

The Seeds

f. 1965, Los Angeles, CA, **db.** 1972
Psychedelic, Garage Rock
Best known for the rock 'n' roll standard "Pushin' Too Hard," the Seeds combined the raw, Stonesy appeal of garage rock with a fondness for ragged, trashy psychedelia. And though they never quite matched the commercial peak of their first two singles, "Pushin' Too Hard" and "Can't Seem to Make You Mine," the band continued to record for the remainder of the '60s, eventually delving deep into post-*Sgt. Pepper* psychedelia and art-rock. None of their new musical directions resulted in another hit single, and the group disbanded at the turn of the decade.

Sky Saxon (born Richard Marsh; vocals) and guitarist Jan Savage formed the Seeds with keyboardist Daryl Hooper and drummer Rick Andridge in Los Angeles in 1965. By the end of 1966, they had secured a contract with GNP Crescendo, releasing "Pushin' Too Hard" as their first single. The song climbed into the Top 40 early in 1967, and the group immediately released two soundalike singles, "Mr. Farmer" and "Can't Seem to Make You Mine," in an attempt to replicate their success; the latter came the closest to being a hit, just missing the Top 40. While their singles were garage-punk, the Seeds attempted to branch out into improvisation blues-rock and psychedelia on their first two albums, *The Seeds* (1966) and *Web of Sound* (1966). With their third album, *Future* (1967), the band attempted a psychedelic conceept album in the vein of *Sgt. Pepper*. While the record reached the Top 100 and spawned the minor hit "A Thousand Shadows," it didn't become a hit. Two other albums-*Raw and Alive: Merlin's Music Box* (1968) and *A Full Spoon of Seedy Blues* (1969), which was credited to the Sky Saxon Blues Band—were released at the end of the decade, but both were ignored. The Seeds broke up shortly afterwards.

During the early '70s, Saxon led a number of bands before retreating from society and moving to Hawaii. Savage became a member of the Los Angeles Police Department. A collection of rarities and alternate takes, *Fallin' off the Edge*, was released in 1977. — *Stephen Thomas Erlewine*

Web of Sound / 1966 / GNP +++
A more ambitious but less successful venture into teenage rages and lusts. — *Bruce Eder*

The Seeds / 1966 / GNP ++++
Punk sneers, cheesy organ, and an attitude. A garage-band classic. — *Bruce Eder*

● **Evil Hoodoo** / 1988 / Bam Caruso ++++
The only serious attempt at a best-of Seeds retrospective features 16 songs culled from their half-dozen or so '60s albums. Besides "Pushin' Too Hard," it features their only other hit single of any magnitude ("Can't Seem to Make You Mine"), as well as other fairly well remembered cuts like "The Wind Blows Your Hair," "Tripmaker," "Falling Off the Edge of My Mind," "Mr. Farmer," and "Up in Her Room." Nonconverts to the Sky Saxon legend may be excused for wondering what all the fuss is about: even distilled to 16 cuts, the melodies and arrangements are almost interminably monotonous. Comes with an extensive group history by rock archivist Brian Hogg. — *Richie Unterberger*

Flower Punk / Nov. 19, 1996 / Demon ++++
The Seeds did write two garage rock classics with "Pushin' Too Hard" and "Can't Seem to Make You Mine," but that didn't mean their remaining records were as interesting as that pair of raw, vital rockers. *Flower Punk* acts otherwise, compiling all of the group's albums onto a triple-disc, book-bound collection. It's a beautifully packaged set and no song is overlooked, yet *Flower Punk* is only for serious garage rock and Seeds fetishists, since the band rarely ever hit the heights of "Pushin' Too Hard" and "Can't Seem to Make You Mine" again. Indeed, for many lis-

teners, a simple greatest hits collection can sound samey, but over the course of three CDs it becomes apparent that the Seeds and Sky Saxon were only capable of a few sounds, and you already have to be indoctrinated to find more than a handful of interesting cuts on *Flower Punk*. —*Stephen Thomas Erlewine*

Seefeel

f. 1992, London, England
Ambient Techno, Experimental, Dream-Pop, Electronica
London quartet Seefeel blends such influences as the Cocteau Twins and My Bloody Valentine with cut-and-paste studio techniques and a lack of traditional verse-chorus song structure to produce a brand of alternative rock/techno hybrid that strongly resembles ambient dance music but cannot be confined to any one genre. Led by singer/guitarist Sarah Peacock and guitarist Mark Clifford and supported by bassist Daren Seymour and percussionist Justin Fletcher, the group released its first EP, *More like Space*, in 1993; following another EP, its first full-length album, *Quique*, became available in the US in 1994.

Although both the EP and album explored more of the guitar-based post-rock territory of their most obvious influences, subsequent material would move increasingly toward the alien soundscapes and fidgety rhythmic textures of experimental ambient and techno groups such as Oval, Mouse on Mars, Locust, and Aphex Twin. Following some remix work and a smattering of stateside re-releases, that move came in 1995 in the form of the *Fracture* EP and *Succour* LP, both released on Warp and exhibiting the appropriate dabblings in edgy techno experimentation. In addition to pushing the group's own boundaries of genre confinement, the album helped bridge the gap between more indie-rock-oriented audiences and the increasingly complex output of the experimental bedroom-boffin set.

Seefeel went on temporary hiatus in 1995, with Clifford and Seymour recording solo material for Warp (as Disjecta and Woodenspoon, respectively). Seymour also combined with Locust's Mark Van Hoen as Aurobindo, releasing *Involution* in 1995, while the entire group collaborated with Van Hoen collectively as dark trip-hop outfit Scala. Seefeel reconvened in 1996 to release the *CH-VOX* LP through Rephlex. —*Sean Cooper*

Quique / 1993 / Too Pure ♦♦♦
Quique is the most obvious and derivative of Seefeel's releases, grabbing the warm six-string-and-stompbox textures of My Bloody Valentine and early Jesus and Mary Chain and expanding them into full, trance-inducing fuzzbox tone poems. —*Sean Cooper*

● **Polyfusia** / Jul. 22, 1994 / Astralwerks ♦♦♦♦
Combines the two previous *More Like Space* and *Pure, Impure* EPs, originally released on Too Pure in 1993. —*Sean Cooper*

Succour / 1995 / Warp ♦♦♦
Dark, bleepy, and somewhat abrasive, this is anything but the floaty guitar ambiance many have come to expect of Seefeel. The edge of melancholic beauty is still a primary feature, but the means have switched to the more clinical Warp style, with chromoly beats and sparse, austere melodies. A pretty accurate marker of new directions as subsequent solo splinterings (Disjecta, Aurobindo, Woodenspoon) have further explored this approach. —*Sean Cooper*

The Seekers

f. 1963, Australia, **db.** 1968
Pop-Rock, Folk-Rock
During the mid-'60s, Australia's Seekers scored several pop hits featuring their rich, folky harmonies and British Invasion leanings. The band was formed in 1963 and featured Athol Guy (standup bass), Bruce Woodley (vocals, guitar), Keith Potger (vocals, guitar), and Judith Durham (vocals), who replaced original vocalist Ken Ray before the group achieved popularity. After the Seekers appeared on television, producer and songwriter Tom Springfield offered his services. The Seekers broke through in the US and UK in 1965 with the hits "I'll Never Find Another You" and "A World of Our Own." Bruce Woodley formed a short songwriting partnership with Paul Simon, which produced the Cyrkle hit "Red Rubber Ball." In 1967, "Georgy Girl" was their biggest American hit, peaking at No. 2, but the group had little further success and broke up in 1990. Woodley became a television jingle writer, while Guy served in the Victoria parliament. Potger put together the New Seekers in 1970 with a completely different lineup and had some success, but a full-fledged Seekers reunion did not occur until Judith Durham was involved in a serious car accident in 1968. After recovering, she got the original group back together and toured Australia and New Zealand; they played several shows in the UK in 1994. —*Steve Huey*

Come the Day / 1966 / Columbia ♦♦♦♦
Their best album, with their biggest hit and the Simon-Woodley songs. Also includes a killer rendition of Tom Paxton's "The Last Thing on My Mind." US title is *Georgy Girl.* —*Bruce Eder*

● **Capitol Collectors Series** / Jul. 28, 1992 / Capitol ♦♦♦♦
The Seekers' rich folky harmonies, fronted by the clear alto of Judith Durham, are given an excellent presentation on this 23-song anthology. All of their Capitol hits are here, including "Georgy Girl," "A World of Our Own," "Come the Day," and "I'll Never Find Another You." Typical of *Capitol Collectors Series* reissues, this set contains ample annotation, track info, and photos. —*Rick Clark*

The Seekers / EMI ♦♦♦♦
A compilation featuring over one hour of hits and key album tracks on this British import. Completely comprehensive, with the best sound ever. —*Bruce Eder*

Bob Seger

b. May 6, 1945, Dearborn, MI
Guitar, Piano, Vocals / Rock & Roll, Pop-Rock
Originally a hard-driving rocker in the vein of fellow Michigan garage-rockers Mitch Ryder and the Rationals, Bob Seger developed into one of the most popular heartland rockers over the course of the '70s. Combining the driving charge of the Detroit Wheels with Stonesy garage rock and devotion to hard-edged soul and R&B, he crafted a distinctively American sound. While he never attained the critical respect of his contemporary Bruce Springsteen, Seger did develop a dedicated following through constant touring with his Silver Bullet Band. Following several years of missed chances and lost opportunities, Seger finally acheived a national audience in 1976 with the back-to-back release of *Live Bullet* and *Night Moves*. After the platinum success of those albums, Seger retained his popularity for the next two decades, releasing seven Top 10, platinum-selling albums in a row.

Seger began playing music in 1961 as the leader of the Detroit-based trio the Decibels; his future manager, Eddie "Punch" Andrews, was also a member of the band. Moving to Ann Arbor, he played with the Town Criers before he became the keyboardist and vocalist for Doug Brown & the Omens. Billing themselves as the Beach Bums, the band released "The Ballad of the Yellow Beret," a parody of the Sgt. Barry Sadler song "The Ballad of the Green Beret." The single was withdrawn shortly after its release after Sadler threatened a lawsuit. In 1966, Seger released his first solo single, "East Side Story," which became a regional hit. Several other local hit singles followed on Cameo Records, including "Persecution Smith" and "Heavy Music," before his label folded. In 1968, he formed the Bob Seger System and signed with Capitol Records, releasing his debut album *Ramblin' Gamblin' Man* in the spring of that year. The title track became a national hit, climbing to No. 17, but the group's follow-up, *Noah*, stiffed and Seger decided to quit the music business at the end of 1969 to attend college.

By the end of the summer, Seger had returned to rock 'n' roll with a new backing band, releasing *Mongrel* at the end of the year. For 1971's *Brand New Morning*, he disbanded his group and recorded a singer-songwriter effort. Following its release, he began performing with the duo Dave Teegarden and Skip "Van Winkle" Knape, and the duo provided support on 1972's *Smokin' OP's*, which was the first release on Palladium Records, a label he formed with Andrews. The album failed to sell, as did *Back in '72* (1973) and *Seven* (1974), and he moved back to Capitol Records for 1975's *Beautiful Loser*. For the recording of *Beautiful Loser*, Seger formed the Silver Bullet Band, which consisted of guitarist Drew Abbott, bassist Chris Campbell, keyboardist Robyn Robbins, saxophonist Alto Reed, and drummer Charlie Allen Martin. Seger supported *Beautiful Loser* with an extensive tour with the Silver Bullet Band, and while it didn't make the album a hit, it provided a widespread grassroots following across the country. The touring paid off in 1976, when *Live Bullet*, a double-album recorded in Detroit, became a hit, spending over three years on the US charts and going gold; the album would eventually go quadruple platinum.

The groundswell behind *Live Bullet* sent Seger's next studio album, *Night Moves* (1976), into the Top 10 early in 1977. *Night Moves* became a blockbuster, generating the hit singles "Night Moves," "Mainstreet" and "Rock & Roll Never Forgets." *Stranger in Town*, released in the summer 1978, was just as successful, featuring the hits "Still the Same," "Hollywood Nights," "We've Got Tonite," and "Old Time Rock & Roll." *Stranger in Town* confirmed his status as one of America's most popular rockers. Seger's next album, 1980's *Against the Wind*, became his first No. 1 album and all of its big hits—"Fire Lake," "Against the Wind," "You'll Accomp'ny Me"—were all ballads. The live album, *Nine Tonight*, continued his multi-platinum success in 1981, selling three million copies and peaking at No. 3.

Seger returned with *The Distance* in 1982. *The Distance* was the first album since *Seven* to be recorded with the addition of session musicians, which caused guitarist Abbott to quit the band in frustration. Over the course of the next decade, the membership of the Silver Bullet Band shifted constantly. While *The Distance* featured "Shame on the Moon," his biggest hit single to date, its sales plateaued at a million copies, suggesting that his popularity was beginning to level off. Seger also began to drastically reduce his recording and touring schedules—he only released one other album, 1986's *Like a Rock*, during the '80s. *Like a Rock* and its supporting tour were both successes, paving the way for "Shakedown," a song taken from the soundtrack to *Beverly Hills Cop II*, to become Seger's lone No. 1 hit, in 1987. Four years after its release, he returned with *The Fire Inside*. Although the album went platinum and reached the Top 10, it only appealed to Seger's devoted following, as did 1995's *It's a Mystery*, which became his first album since *Live Bullet* to fail to go platinum, levelling off at gold status. *—Stephen Thomas Erlewine*

66-67 / 1967 / KWR ✦✦✦✦
Unless you grew up in Michigan in the mid-'60s, you probably have no idea that Seger's roots extend further than his bar band/road band/singer-songwriter/arena star experiences. Way back before the '70s, he was one of many talented Michigan garage rockers, releasing several stomping singles in the style. Some were quite popular regionally, but none made it nationally; all were far raunchier in execution than anything he's done since. Perhaps he prefers to keep it in the closet, but these sides have proven very hard to come by; this compilation, almost certainly unauthorized, gathers together a dozen of them. And it's good stuff: the sub-"Subterranean Homesick Blues" of "Persecution Smith"; the local hit "East Side Story" (a mini-drama that sounds like Springsteen as a '60s punk); the satirical "Sock It to Me Santa" and "Ballad of the Yellow Beret"; the storming, twisting "Vagrant Winter"; and hints of the '70s singer-songwriter in "Heavy Music" and "Looking Back." Fans of tough '60s rock, indeed, will probably find this superior to most or all of his subsequent work, although fans of his more famous post-1970 recordings may feel a little lost. This LP is virtually impossible to locate these days; it's time for the official reissue of this material, as it can hold its head high next to top-flight Michigan rock of the time by Mitch Ryder, the Rationals, and others. *—Richie Unterberger*

Ramblin' Gamblin' Man / 1968 / Capitol ✦✦✦✦
The title track on Seger's Capitol debut is one of the all-time-great rock 'n' roll stompers with its bone-crunching two—and four-drum groove and gospel-choir backup. There's also the incredibly hard-rocking anti-war track "2 + 2 Equals ?," and "Down Home," a rude harmonica-driven rocker that sports an absolutely addled rhythm section. In spite of some cornball psychedelic-period mixes, *Ramblin' Gamblin' Man*, with its reckless over-the-top delivery, is Seger's hardest-rocking album. Throughout many of these tracks, Seger wails like a banshee. Seger's later rock hits sound absolutely tame next to this stuff. *—Rick Clark*

Mongrel / 1970 / Capitol ✦✦✦
Sounding retro but far from dated, the energetic *Mongrel* shows off a grittier side to Bob Seger than some are familiar with. The cover of "River Deep, Mountain High" and Seger's own "Song to Rufus" suggest a deep rhythm & blues base underneath the power-driven rock Seger is famous for. "Lucifer" rolls along like a stray cut from Creedence Clearwater Revival, and the surprising "Big River" contains some famous melodies in their infant state. *—James Chrispell*

Smokin' O.P.'s / 1973 / Capitol ✦✦✦
Smokin' O.P.'s was a fine showcase for Seger's workmanlike rock 'n' roll approach. "Heavy Music," an original, became a huge Detroit hit. Other highlights included Seger's versions of such standards as "Bo Diddley," "Let It Rock," and "Turn on Your Lovelight." *—Rick Clark*

Seven / 1974 / Capitol ✦✦✦✦
Recording with both Nashville musicians and the Silver Bullet Band, Bob Seger came up with an album he's subtitled "Contrasts." From the rollicking "School Teacher" to a forerunner of "Night Moves" in the track "20 Years from Now," there are many rewards on *Seven*. "UMC (Upper Middle Class)" would be a highlight on any other album, but here, that title goes to "Get Out of Denver," a great chunk of Chuck Berryish rock 'n' roll making it seem unbelievable that Seger had yet to break out nationally. *—James Chrispell*

Beautiful Loser / 1975 / Capitol ✦✦✦✦
After several years of relative obscurity, Seger emerged with this rather reflective effort. The hard-rocking "Katmandu," however, was a substantial hit in the Midwest. *—Rick Clark*

Live Bullet / 1976 / Capitol ✦✦✦✦
A blistering live show from Cobo Hall, containing raucous versions of early material like "Nutbush City Limits" and "Get Out of Denver" as highlights. *—Cub Koda*

★ **Night Moves** / 1976 / Capitol ✦✦✦✦✦
Seger's breakthrough album, a classic of blue-collar rock, features such standouts as the wistful "Mainstreet," the no-frills rock of "Rock and Roll Never Forgets," and the title track, a reflective coming-of-age masterpiece. Throughout, Seger believably details the characters in his songs with compassion. *—Rick Clark*

Stranger in Town / 1978 / Capitol ✦✦✦✦
It's not quite as strong as *Night Moves*, but *Stranger in Town* continues Seger's streak of great songwriting and performance. Highlights include the relentless rockers "Hollywood Nights" and "Feel like a Number." Seger's facility with the ballads "Still the Same" and "We've Got Tonight" produced substantial hits. *—Rick Clark*

Against the Wind / 1980 / Capitol ✦✦✦
Against the Wind became Seger's first No. 1 album, producing the hits and key album-rock-radio tracks, "Fire Lake," "You'll Accomp'ny Me," "The Horizontal Bop" and the No. 5 title cut. However, after two fine albums, Seger's lyrical abilities and melodic skills began to reveal a cookie-cutter sameness. His singing still had plenty of passion. *—Rick Clark*

Nine Tonight / 1981 / Capitol ✦✦✦
Features the title-track contribution to the *Urban Cowboy* movie soundtrack and an effective cover of "Trying to Live My Life Without You." *—Cub Koda*

The Distance / 1982 / Capitol ✦✦✦✦
The Distance was a strong rebound after the spotty *Against the Wind*, featuring his rocking Chuck Berry-like auto-worker's tribute, "Makin' Thunderbirds," the resolute rock anthem "Even Now," and a fine version of Rodney Crowell's "Shame on the Moon." *—Rick Clark*

Like a Rock / 1986 / Capitol ✦✦✦
At times sounding like a poor man's Springsteen, Bob Seger continued to mine the fields he'd plowed so well over previous efforts. There's the send-up of the USA. in "American Storm," the hard-rockin' "Sometimes," and the heartbreakingly beautiful "Somewhere Tonight." Oh yes, and the song used in those incessant commercials for American pickup trucks, "Like a Rock." A mature effort from a great American talent. *—James Chrispell*

● **Greatest Hits** / 1994 / Capitol ✦✦✦✦
For over 20 years, Bob Seger has been one of the best mainstream rock 'n' rollers in America, developing a distinctive body of honest, hard-rocking songs. More songs that can be put on this single-disc set, unfortunately. While many of Seger's trademarks are here—"Turn the Page," "Old Time Rock & Roll," "Night Moves"—there is no "Rock & Roll Never Forgets," "Katmandu," "Shame on the Moon," or any of his pulverizing early records, when he was as tough as fellow Michigan rockers the MC5 and the Stooges; this is one time when a double-disc set would have held enough quality material. Nevertheless, what is here is fine and contains enough first-rate material to satisfy most fans. *—Stephen Thomas Erlewine*

It's a Mystery / Oct. 24, 1995 / Capitol ✦✦✦
Since Bob Seger's midtempo, Middle American rock sound remains constant—the drums in the pocket, the guitars chugging along, the vocals husky and choked—it's the variables of performance and composition that separate his good albums from his great ones. On both counts, *It's a Mystery* is not great. Both as writer and performer, Seger seems tired and bitter. Always a reflective, backward-looking lyricist, Seger is full of regret in "Lock and Load" (one of four songs that contains references to firearms, including a cover to Tom Waits' "16 Shells from a 30-6"); and in "Rite of Passage," among other songs, he gives us a critical view of the state of the nation. The most personal of these complaints is "Revisionism Street," which criticizes the scandal mongerers who prey upon stars like himself. Though Seger assembles a revolving group of ace session players that includes keyboardist Roy Bittan of the E Street Band and members of Little Feat (the Silver Bullet Band has been a myth for a long time), the playing is formulaic. Though Seger had the usual four years to put this album together, he doesn't seem to have been ready to record, either in terms of coming up with enough quality material or getting his performing chops up. And he is at a point in his career when he can no longer coast: After ten straight million-selling albums in 20 years, *It's a Mystery* stopped at gold and became his first album since 1976 to miss the Top Ten, while his 1994 *Greatest Hits* album continued to rack up healthy sales, indicating that, as of 1995, Bob Seger was well on his way to becoming an oldies act. *—William Ruhlmann*

Selecter

f. 1978, Coventry, England
New Wave, Ska Revival
Despite being the band that got the least press during the ska revival of the early '80s, the Selecter, despite only recording one undeniably fine record, deserved better than they did. Hailing from Coventry, England, the same hometown as ska pals the Specials, the Selecter's secret weapon was lead singer Pauline Black, arguably the best lead singer of the ska revival, who gave the jumpy and jittery songs an edge that veered into haunting drama. Although they got off to a roaring start with their debut record, 1980's *Too Much Pressure*, the second record,

Celebrate the Bullet, was a strained follow-up that led to the band's rapid demise.

Black spent some time singing solo, and eventually rejoined guitarist Neol Davis in a Selecter reunion in the early '90s that has seen them become dance club favorites. According to those attending recent Selecter shows, the vibe is strong and the music great. However, don't expect a recording renaissance any time soon. —*John Dougan*

● **Too Much Pressure** / May 1980 / 2 Tone/Chrysalis ✦✦✦✦
At the time of its release, *Too Much Pressure* was relegated to second-class status behind the debut records by Madness and the Specials. Now it's easy to see that this record was the equal to the Specials record, and, (I realize I'm getting into trouble here) better than the first (and second) Madness records. Pauline Black is the key and she makes songs like "On My Radio" and the title track classic chunks of Caribbean-influenced pop rather than mere stylistic mimicry. Much better that the weak second record, *Celebrate the Bullet*, or the 1989 anthology, *Selected Selecter Selections*. —*John Dougan*

Celebrate the Bullet / Mar. 1981 / 2 Tone/Chrysalis ✦✦
Celebrate the Bullet failed to live up to the promise of the band's debut. It has its moments, but those can all be found on the collection *Selected Selecter Selections*. —*Chris Woodstra*

Selected Selecter Selections / 1989 / 2 Tone/Chrysalis ✦✦✦✦
Selected Selecter Selections is a no-frills, 14-track collection of the second-tier ska-revivalists' best moments. Predictably, most of the collection focuses on the often-inspired debut, but it also boils down the worthwhile tracks from the mediocre follow-up, making for an adequate career summary and a good introduction. When available, *Too Much Pressure* is still probably a better choice as a consistently enjoyable album containing all of the best-remembered tracks. —*Chris Woodstra*

Greatest Hits Live / 1997 / Emporio ✦✦
Greatest Hits Live captures a reunited Selecter running through their greatest hits at a Minneapolis club in 1991. Although they sound happy to be back on the stage, their performance lacks energy and spark, and it pales mightily to the original studio versions. —*Stephen Thomas Erlewine*

Selecterized: The Best of 1991-96 / 1997 / Dojo ✦✦
After spending nearly a decade apart, the Selecter re-formed in 1991 and released a handful of albums, most of which went ignored by anyone outside of the ska community. There was a reason for this—none of the records were particularly good. Nevertheless, *Selecterized—The Best of 1991-96* contains highlights from this best-forgotten era, and it's what any curious fan should check out, even though they'll inevitably be disappointed by the final result. —*Stephen Thomas Erlewine*

Sepultura

f. 1984, Belo Horizonte, Brazil, db. 1997
Thrash, Heavy Metal
Formed in Belo Horizonte, Brazil, in 1984, Sepultura includes Max Cavalera (guitar, vocals), Igor Cavalera (drums), Paulo Jr. (bass), and Andreas Kisser (guitar), who took over for Jairo T in 1987. Their name is the Portuguese word for grave. Their early work combined the compositional style of Metallica with the extreme sounds of the nascent death metal scene. Lyrically, they have been passionately preoccupied with the poor social and political conditions in Brazil, which makes them one of the few death metal bands with something to say. Their first recording, *Bestial Devastation*, was done with a Brazilian band called Overdose; it was badly recorded and badly circulated. A couple of albums, *Morbid Visions* and *Schizophrenia*, followed before the band signed with Roadrunner Records and came to international attention with *Beneath the Remains*. Their follow-up, *Arise*, proved to be their big breakthrough, becoming at that time the biggest-selling album in Roadrunner's history. In 1993, *Chaos A.D.* became their highest-charting album, entering *Billboard's* Top 40, and was hailed as arguably the best death-metal album thus far. The band returned with a follow-up album, *Roots*, in 1996. —*Steve Huey*

Morbid Visions / 1986 / Roadrunner ✦✦
This was America's first listen to what Brazil had to offer in the world of thrash. Before this, most bands were only known through trading tapes or demos in the underground. The sound quality isn't too good, though. —*John Book*

Schizophrenia / 1987 / Roadrunner ✦✦✦
There's a little experimentation on this album. —*John Book*

Beneath the Remains / May 1989 / Roadrunner ✦✦✦✦
Excellent thrash that immediately goes into the conciousness of the listener, this was the first metal band from Brazil to gain international acclaim. —*John Book*

Arise / Apr. 2, 1991 / Roadrunner ✦✦✦✦
Sepultura's breakthrough release still wears the band's Metallica influences proudly, featuring harmonized guitar lines and soft, non-distorted

passages to go with some Kirk Hammett-style solos and extremely powerful grooves. And, of course, there are some sections taken at death metal's typical high-velocity tempos. Nothing really innovative appears here, but the band is intense, passionate, and energetic, and the music is quite well done. —*Steve Huey*

● **Chaos A.D.** / 1993 / Epic ✦✦✦✦
Everything comes together for Sepultura on *Chaos A.D.* The band's strident political dissidence is more focused than ever. Death metal's standard thick, heavy guitars and hoarsely shouted vocals are here, but Sepultura draw on the influences of their native Brazil, audible in many of the rhythms and the acoustic instrumental "Kaiowas," to offer a much wider musical range than usual for the genre. The band's songwriting has become almost airtight, giving up the Metallica-esque passages and breakneck speed and concentrating instead on creating texture and dissonance. But it's the unbelievably powerful rhythmic base provided by Igor Cavalera that gives *Chaos A.D.* its knockout punch and helps make it one of the best metal albums ever, a remarkable achievement. —*Steve Huey*

Roots / Feb. 1996 / Roadrunner ✦✦✦✦
Listeners intrigued by the rhythmic innovations of *Chaos A.D.* will be quite pleased by Sepultura's sprawling, frequently brilliant follow-up. True to its title, *Roots* wholeheartedly embraces Sepultura's native Brazilian rhythms, augmenting their music with recordings of the Xavantes Indians, vocalist/percussionist Carlinhos Brown, and expanded percussion sections. The guitarists create an array of noisy, textural effects, so their technique and riff writing are not as impressive, but the emphasis is on the band's fluid yet powerful rhythms. The songs sacrifice the tight structure of *Chaos A.D.* for extended percussion jams, plus some acoustic instrumental work. At 72 minutes, *Roots* inevitably loses focus in spots, and the lyrics lack the intelligent political rage of *Chaos*, but when the music connects (and it does so often), it carries tremendous visceral impact. *Roots* consolidates Sepultura's position as perhaps the most distinctive, original heavy-metal band of the 1990s. —*Steve Huey*

The Sex Pistols

f. 1975, London, England, db. 1978
Punk
The Sex Pistols may have only been together for two years in the late '70s, but they changed the face of popular music. Through their raw, nihilistic singles and violent performances, the band revolutionized the idea of what rock 'n' roll could be. In England, the group was considered dangerous to the very fabric of society and was banned across the country; in America, they didn't have the same impact, but countless bands in both countries were inspired by the sheer sonic force of their music, while countless others were inspired by their independent, do-it-yourself ethics. Even if they didn't release any singles by themselves, there was an implicit independence in the way they played their music and handled their career. The band gave birth to the massive independent music underground in England and America that would soon include bands that didn't have a direct musical connection to the Sex Pistols' initial three-minute blasts of rage, but couldn't have existed without those singles.

Guitarist Steve Jones and drummer Paul Cook were regulars at a boutique owned by their manager, Malcolm McLaren; bassist Glen Matlock worked at the store. Vocalist John Lydon, who would later perform as Johnny Rotten, met the rest of the group at the shop and was asked to join the band. While the band played simple rock 'n' roll loudly and abrasively, Rotten arrogantly sang of anarchy, abortion, violence, fascism, and apathy; without Rotten, the band wouldn't have been threatening to England's government—he provided the band's conceptual direction, calculated to be as confrontational and threatening as possible. The publicity caused by their caustic first single "Anarchy in the UK" caused the band to be dropped by their record label, EMI. Matlock was fired before their next single "God Save the Queen," which was released on Virgin; it was banned by the BBC. Matlock's replacement was Sid Vicious, a street tough who, unlike the rest of the band, couldn't play his instrument.

After releasing one album in 1977, the band headed over to the US for a tour in January of 1978; it lasted 14 days. Rotten left the band after their show at San Francisco's Winterland Ballroom on January 14, heading back to New York; he would form Public Image Limited later that year. McLaren tried to continue the band but Cook and Jones soon turned against him. In the two decades following the Sex Pistols' implosion, an endless stream of outtakes, demos, repackagings, and live shows were released on a variety of labels, which only helped their cult grow.

In 1996, to celebrate their impending twentieth anniversary, the Sex Pistols reunited, with original bassist Glen Matlock taking the place of the deceased Sid Vicious. The band embarked on an international tour in June of 1996, releasing the *Filthy Lucre Live* album the following month. —*Stephen Thomas Erlewine*

★ **Never Mind the Bollocks** / Oct. 1977 / Warner Brothers ✦✦✦✦✦
While mostly accurate, dismissing *Never Mind the Bollocks* as merely a series of loud, ragged, mid-tempo rockers with a harsh, grating vocalist and not much melody would be a terrible error. Already anthemic songs are rendered positively transcendent by Johnny Rotten's rabid, foaming delivery. His bitterly sarcastic attacks on pretentious affectation and the very foundations of British society were all carried out in the most confrontational, impolite manner possible. Most imitators of the Pistols' angry nihilism missed the point: underneath the shock tactics and theatrical negativity were social critiques carefully designed for maximum impact. *Never Mind the Bollocks* perfectly articulated the frustration, rage, and dissatisfaction of the British working class with the establishment, a spirit quick to translate itself to strictly rock 'n' roll terms. The Pistols paved the way for countless other bands to make similarly rebellious statements, but arguably none were as daring or effective. It's easy to see how the band's roaring energy, overwhelmingly snotty attitude, and Rotten's furious ranting sparked a musical revolution, and those qualities haven't diminished one bit over time. *Never Mind the Bollocks* is simply one of the greatest, most inspiring rock records of all time. —*Steve Huey*

The Great Rock & Roll Swindle / 1979 / Warner Brothers ✦✦✦✦
A wildly inconsistent but often entertaining collection, the soundtrack to the Pistols' pseudo-documentary contains great music, wacked-out novelties, and flat-out tripe in approximately equal proportions. Some formative recordings are included—mostly covers like "(I'm Not Your) Stepping Stone," plus a demo of "Anarchy in the UK" that somehow manages to top the version on *Never Mind the Bollocks* in terms of raw rage and sheer power. "I Wanna Be Me" and a veiled chronicle of the band's breakup, "Silly Thing," are also necessary items. Devoted fans will enjoy the Black Arabs' disco medley of Pistols hits, a French version of "Anarchy in the UK" complete with accordion, two tracks sung by loony Edward Tudor-Pole (later of Tenpole Tudor), and Sid Vicious' awful but strangely appropriate reading of Frank Sinatra's "My Way." —*Steve Huey*

Flogging a Dead Horse / 1980 / Virgin ✦✦✦✦
This collects the band's seven British singles. There are some duplicates with *Never Mind the Bollocks*, but the B-sides can't be found elsewhere. —*John Floyd*

We Have Cum for Your Children/Wanted: The Goodman Tapes / 1988 / Skyclad ✦✦
Another of the entries in the mini-industry of Sex Pistols marginalia, assembled by the group's one-time soundman, Dave Goodman. The July 1976 demos (of "Submission," "Pretty Vacant," and "Suburban Kid" here are actually very good, from both fidelity and performance standpoints. Elsewhere the quality is much more variable—live songs, the famous Bill Grundy interview on British television, a "live in the studio" version of "Unlimited Supply," the "ultra-rare mystery track" "Revolution in the Classroom," and more. It's really not a bad historical document; it would rate higher except for the fact that the material is haphazardly assembled, and appears on other similar slapdash anthologies. And you *do* need a scorecard to keep such things straight by now: it's doubtful more than a few thousand listeners (if that) could tell you exactly what here has appeared elsewhere, and where. —*Richie Unterberger*

Chaos / Feb. 27, 1996 / Restless ✦✦
Is there anyone who's bothered to keep track of the numerous post-1980 compilations of Sex Pistols rarities? Such a person is the only one qualified to determine just which of these tracks (if any) were not previously released on one or more of those (mostly shoddy) productions. This 10-track disc, unfortunately, is no exception to the standard, with virtually nothing in the way of documentation and a ridiculously inappropriate and ugly cover. You get two songs from the April '76 "Spedding sessions"; five oldies covers (the sleeve says these have different mixes than the *R&R Swindle* versions, without making it clear what the differences are); and three marginal-fidelity live songs from an unspecified Swedish gig. The sound on the studio tracks is better, but still boxy and cardboardish. There *is* some interesting material here (though primarily from a historic viewpoint). But it's time for someone to construct a series of intelligently sequenced and annotated Sex Pistols oddity compilations; this just adds to the clutter. —*Richie Unterberger*

Filthy Lucre Live / Jul. 1996 / Virgin ✦✦✦
As the cliche says, the Sex Pistols were the last band anyone expected to see reunite. However, those observers were ignoring just how alluring the promise of easy money is to a band that never earned that much in the first place, so the Sex Pistols did what was previously unthinkable and reunited in 1996 for a summer-long tour of Europe and the United States. After playing two warm-up gigs, the band played their first official live concert at Finsbury Park in early June and the result is presented on *Filthy Lucre Live*, which was released just a matter of weeks after the concert. Two things about the reunited Pistols are clear from the outset—they can play their instruments, and they sound much heavier and less revolutionary than expected. In fact, the band doesn't

sound very *punk* at all—they sound like a professional hard rock band. But—and this is the most surprising thing—they sound fun. If you're a fan, it's hard to deny that it's fun to hear a live performance by the Pistols that doesn't degenerate into chaos and is recorded in clean audio. You can't call *Filthy Lucre Live* punk rock by any stretch of the imagination, but it is first-rate nostalgia, even if punk was about eliminating the need for records just like this one. —*Stephen Thomas Erlewine*

Ron Sexsmith

b. 1964, Canada
Guitar, Vocals / Singer-Songwriter
The earnest work of boyish Canadian singer-songwriter Ron Sexsmith won acclaim not only from critics but from fellow performers like Paul McCartney, Elvis Costello, and John Hiatt—some of the same artists, ironically enough, who initially inspired Sexsmith himself to become a musician. Born in 1964 and raised in the Niagara Falls area, he started his first band at the age of 14, and within a few years earned his first regular gig at an area club. Influenced by Pete Seeger, he began making the rounds on the folk circuit, but soon decided to focus his attentions on becoming a songwriter.

After moving to the Toronto area, Sexsmith formed the Uncool and began issuing his own material in 1985 with the cassette *Out of the Duff*, followed a year later by *There's a Way*. He continued performing while maintaining a day job as a courier, but did not release anything more until 1991's *Grand Opera Lane*, recorded by Blue Rodeo's Bob Wiseman. The collection of songs helped earn Sexsmith a songwriting contract, and eventually a recording deal, with Interscope Records; teamed with producer Mitchell Froom, he released his self-titled debut in 1995. A follow-up appeared two years later. —*Jason Ankeny*

Ron Sexsmith / May 16, 1995 / Interscope ✦✦✦✦
Ron Sexsmith is so anti-cool that this may actually be one the coolest albums you hear. The Toronto singer-songwriter's appearance matches his music perfectly—hair falling in tousled bangs over doe eyes and baby face; one of those guys who always got beat up in high school and couldn't string two words together in front of a real live girl without stammering. A wide-eyed innocent, Sexsmith's eponymous release marries the wonder of Jonathan Richman with the darker atmosphere of a Daniel Lanois. Superficially, the songs are so sparsely childlike that you're tempted to wonder if Sexsmith is either a master of affectation or some kind of idiot savant. —*Roch Parisien*

Phil Seymour

b. May 15, 1952, Tulsa, OK, **d.** 1993
New Wave, Power Pop
Phil Seymour is best remembered as one half of the creative force behind the Dwight Twilley Band, co-writing, with Dwight Twilley, some of the finest pop songs of the era, including the classic "I'm on Fire." After two albums (1976's *Sincerely* and 1978's *Twilley Don't Mind*), Seymour left to pursue a solo career. While waiting for a recording deal, he began recording solo sessions, as well as contributing session work for Tom Petty, 20/20, and Moon Martin. In 1980, he signed to Boardwalk Records after selling the label on a batch of demos recorded with fellow Tulsa natives 20/20. His self-titled debut was well received at the time (the single "Precious to Me" made it to No. 22 on the pop charts) and has become highly revered in power-pop circles as one of the landmark albums of the era. He followed in 1982 with *Phil Seymour 2*, a less satisfying album both creatively and commercially. Seymour was left without a label when Boardwalk president Neil Bogart died shortly after the record's release. In 1984, he joined Carla Olsen's Textones, drumming and singing on their *Midnight Mission* album for A&M. While supporting the album, Seymour was diagnosed with lymphoma. He returned to Tulsa, carrying on at a diminished pace and recording infrequently, until the disease took his life in August of 1993 while he was preparing a new album. —*Chris Woodstra*

Phil Seymour / 1980 / Boardwalk ✦✦✦✦

2 / 1982 / Boardwalk ✦✦✦

● **Precious to Me** / Jun. 25, 1996 / Right Stuff ✦✦✦✦
Precious to Me attempts to collect the many phases of Phil Seymour's all-too-brief career. The disc's 15 tracks cover his period as Dwight Twilley's partner, his solo work, a song he did with the Textones, and a handful of rarities and stray tracks. And while it is certainly a welcome compilation of his long-out-of-print work on to compact disc, this collection could have been better. Considering Seymour's small cult of obsessive fans, the Twilley tracks are redundant—anyone who buys this collection undoubtedly has the Dwight Twilley discs already—and the absence of any songs from Seymour's second solo album is simply a disservice. Any of Seymour's recordings are pure pop fun so *Precious to Me* is a good listen, and for the uninitiated this is a good enough starting point if only because so much of his work is unavailable. —*Chris Woodstra*

Shadows of Knight

f. 1964, Chicago, IL, db. 1969
Garage Rock

"The Stones, Animals, and Yardbirds took the Chicago Blues and gave it an English interpretation. We've taken the English version of the Blues and re-added a Chicago touch." The Shadows of Knight's self-description was fairly accurate. Although this mid-'60s garage band from the Windy City did not match the excellence of either their British or African-American idols, the teen energy of their recordings remains enjoyable, if not overwhelmingly original. The group took a tamer version of Them's classic "Gloria" into the American Top Ten in 1966, and also took a Yard-birdized version of Bo Diddley's "Oh Yeah" into the Top 40 the same year. Their patchy albums contained a few exciting R&B covers in the Yardbirds/Stones style and a few decent originals in the same vein. The group's original lineup splintered quickly, and the Shadows faded in the late '60s after briefly pursuing a more commercial pop sound. —*Richie Unterberger*

Gee-El-O-Are-I-Ay / 1985 / Edsel ✦✦✦✦
Boils the Shadows' legacy down to 16 essential tracks. Contains "Gloria," "Oh Yeah," and the flop singles "Bad Little Woman" and "I'm Gonna Make You Mine," as well as the better tracks from their first two LPs, including the impressive originals "Light Bulb Blues" and "Gospel Zone." —*Richie Unterberger*

Raw 'N Alive at the Cellar, Chicago 1966! / 1992 / Sundazed ✦✦✦
This is one of the very few live garage band tapes from the mid-'60s of relatively decent sound quality (considering the standards of the era). The song selection of this set should also please fans of one of the most famed '60s garage bands, captured here at a club in their home turf of Chicago in December 1966. The 13 songs include live versions of many of the tunes from their first (and best) album, as well as a six-minute workout of their lone national hit "Gloria" and a couple of Solomon Burke covers. However, it's not essential if you already have the original albums, or the fine best-of compilation released in the UK on Edsel, *Gee-El-O-Are-I-Ay*. These versions are very close in arrangement to the officially released ones, but the performance is less accomplished, as it were, and the sound quality worse. An interesting artifact that nevertheless has little appeal beyond '60s garage collector circles, although the very brief quotes from the Mothers of Invention's "Help I'm a Rock" are most curious and unexpected. —*Richie Unterberger*

Super K Kollection / Jun. 25, 1994 / Collectables ✦✦✦

● Dark Sides: The Best of Shadows of Knight / Aug. 16, 1994 / Rhino ✦✦✦✦
More easily available to North Americans than the British Edsel best-of, but not necessarily an improvement. Adds some tracks from both the original lineup and their unimpressive, more pop-oriented singles from the late '60s, and has more comprehensive liner notes, but also omits a few decent tracks that are on the UK compilation, particularly their smoking, over-the-top version of "I Just Want to Make Love to You." —*Richie Unterberger*

The Shaggs

f. 1969, Revere, MA
Alternative Pop-Rock

In 1969 the Shaggs, comprising three sisters—Dorothy, Betty, and Helen Wiggin—entered a Revere, MA, recording studio under the encouragement and financial support of their father, Austin Wiggin. The recording engineer, upon hearing the band, tactfully suggested that they weren't ready to be a recording unit, but their father insisted on catching the band on tape "while they were hot." The result of this session, their first album, was called *Philosophy of the World*. Their follow-up effort, the appropriately titled *Shaggs' Own Thing*, actually reflects some growth in the area of technical facility.

Depending on your point of view, this is the most hilarious-sounding mishmash of ineptitude ever committed to CD, or it's an unconscious musical realization of everything great naive American art desires to be, believably innocent. Either way, you'll either love them or hate them. —*Rick Clark*

● Philosophy of the World / 1969 / Rounder ✦✦✦✦
This release compiles the Wiggin sisters' (otherwise known as the Shaggs) two releases *Philosophy of the World* and *Shaggs' Own Thing*. Anyone with unconventional tastes interested in taking a harrowing trip into the twilight zone of naive Americana pop should check this out. —*Rick Clark*

Sham 69

f. 1977, London, England
Punk

I doubt there would be much disagreement with the assertion that of all the British punk bands of the late '70s, Sham 69 was the worst band to have a career lasting more than two records. Negligibly talented like their punk brethren the Cortinas and Eater, and specializing in simplistic political vituperation, shouted vocals and roaring guitars, Sham 69 was remotely interesting in the heady days of 1976-78, only to quickly descend to joke status (in America anyway) by the turn of the decade.

Led by vocalist and lyricist Jimmy Pursey, Sham's basic attack was "leftist" slogans chanted repeatedly over a wall of fast distorted guitars that exploded into shout-along choruses (all the better for their yob fans to participate). Unsurprisingly, this begat chart success (in England only) where the band released five, albeit indistinguishable, hit singles in their first year. Flushed with success, Pursey adopted the role of principal spokesman, erstwhile politico, and punk careerist, roles for which (except for the latter) he showed little talent. In 1980, shortly after the release of the album *The Game*, Pursey, in a move that indicated a tremendously inflated self-worth, broke up Sham 69 for a solo career; his four subsequent solo records exhibit a dearth of creativity and talent.

His solo career stalled, Pursey saw an opportunity to milk punk rock nostalgia for a few pounds and re-formed Sham 69. Exhibiting careerist proclivities and excessive crassness, the new Sham simply played like the old Sham, and Pursey fobbed the whole thing off as a retrenchment by an aging punk rocker to his "roots." Mostly it was pathetic, but based on Sham 69's history, totally unsurprising. —*John Dougan*

Tell Us the Truth / 1978 / Sire ✦✦✦✦
The first and only Sham 69 record released in America is the only one worth listening to, primarily because their fakery had not gotten in the way of their loud and proud shouting and bashing. And, given the rush of excitement that greeted most English punk rock records at the time, it was easy to get sucked in to this record's raffish, working-class charm. One side studio, one live side, it's intensely derivative, but dumb fun in a sophomorically liberating way. —*John Dougan*

That's Life / 1978 / Polydor ✦✦✦✦
A good follow-up to their debut *Tell Us the Truth*, this one includes "Hurry Up Harry." —*David Szatmary*

Hersham Boys / 1979 / Polydor ✦✦✦

First, The Best & The Last / 1980 / Polydor ✦✦✦

The Game / 1980 / Polydor ✦✦✦
This is a more experimental effort by these punkers. —*David Szatmary*

Live and Loud / 1987 / Link ✦✦✦✦
A blazing 1979 live set, it captures these Hersham punks at their best and includes many of their hit UK singles. —*David Szatmary*

● The Best Of / Jan. 1996 / Essential ✦✦✦✦

The Shangri-Las

f. 1963, Queens, NY, db. 1969
Girl Group, Brill Building Pop, Pop-Rock

Along with the Shirelles and the Ronettes, the Shangri-Las were one of the greatest girl groups; if judged solely on the basis of attitude, they were the greatest of them all. They combined an innocent adolescent charm with more than a hint of darkness, singing about dead bikers, teenage runaways, and doomed love affairs as well as ebullient high-school crushes. These could be delivered with either infectious, hand-clapping harmonies or melodramatic, almost operatic recitatives that were contrived but utterly effective. Tying it all together in the studio was Shadow Morton, a mad genius of a producer that may have been second in eccentric imagination only to Phil Spector in the mid-'60s.

Originally the Shangri-Las were comprised of two pairs of sisters from Queens, NY (identical twins Marge and Mary Ann Ganser and siblings Mary and Betty Weiss). They had already recorded a couple of obscure singles when they were hired by George "Shadow" Morton to demo a song he had recently written, "Remember (Walkin' in the Sand)." The haunting ballad, with its doomy "Moonlight Sonata"-like piano riffs, wailing lead vocal, and thunderous background harmonies seguing into an a cappella chorus backed by nothing except handclaps and seagull cries, made the Top Five in late 1964. It also began their association with Jerry Leiber and Mike Stoller's Red Bird label, which would handle the group for the bulk of their career.

The quality of Morton's work with the Shangri-Las on Red Bird (with assistance from Jeff Barry and Artie Butler) was remarkable considering that he had virtually no prior experience in the music business. The group's material, so over-the-top emotionally that it sometimes bordered on camp, was lightened by the first-class production, which embroidered the tracks with punchy brass, weeping strings, and plenty of imaginative sound effects. Nowhere was this more apparent than on "Leader of the Pack," with its periodic motorcycle roars and crescendo of crashing glass. The death-rock classic became the Shangri-Las' signature tune, reaching No. 1.

Several smaller hits followed in 1965 and 1966, many of them excellent. "Give Him a Great Big Kiss" proved they could easily handle more conventionally, bubbly girl-group fare; "I Can Never Go Home Anymore," a runaway tale that took their patented pathos to the extreme, would be their third and final Top Ten hit. These all show up on oldies collections, but lots of listeners remain unaware of the other fine singles in their catalog, like the moody "Out in the Streets," the dense orchestral swamp of "He Cried" (which cuts Jay & the Americans' original, "She Cried," to pieces), and another teen death tale, "Give Us Your Blessings." Some of their best songs, in fact, were B-sides; "Dressed in Black," yet another teen death drama, had a marvelously hushed and damned atmosphere, and "Paradise" was co-written by a young Harry Nilsson. Their most unusual single of all was "Past, Present, and Future," which didn't feature a single sung note, presenting a somber spoken monologue and occasional spoken background chants over a classical piano track reminiscent of "Remember (Walkin' in the Sand)." It was too unconventional to rise above the middle of the charts, especially given that the narrative could quite possibly be construed as recollections of an assault/rape victim.

Unlike some girl groups, the Shangri-Las were dynamic onstage performers, choreographing their dance steps to their lyrics, and wearing skin-tight leather pants and boots that were quite daring for the time. Their real lives, however, were not without elements of drama themselves. Their constant personnel changes baffle historians; sometimes they are pictured as a trio, and sometimes one of the members in the photos is clearly not one of the Weiss or Ganser sisters. Worse, the Red Bird label ran into serious organizational difficulties in the mid-'60s, and wound down its operations in 1966. The group moved to Mercury for a couple of dispirited singles, but had split by the end of the 1960s. Shadow Morton went on to an interesting, erratic career that included involvement with Janis Ian, the New York Dolls, and Mott the Hoople. Mary Ann Ganser died of encephalitis in 1971.

Even today, the Shangri-Las' history remains somewhat murky and mysterious; the original members have rarely reunited for oldies shows or talked to the press. The situation was exacerbated by frustratingly substandard reissues of their Red Bird work, which made it impossible to collect all of their fine sides without buying numerous packages, many of which had shockingly shoddy sound quality. Happily, the situation was rectified in the mid-'90s with excellent, comprehensive compilations of the Red Bird material in both the UK and US. *—Richie Unterberger*

Golden Hits of the Shangri-Las / 1984 / PolyGram ✦✦✦✦
It includes all the eerie three-minute melodramas from one of the all-time great girl groups: "Leader of the Pack," "Remember," "I Can Never Go Home Anymore," "Past, Present, and Future." *—George Bedard*

● **Myrmidons of Melodrama** / 1994 / RPM ✦✦✦✦
Until the release of this import, there had never been a truly satisfactory Shangri-Las anthology; in fact, the group had been subject to worse piecemeal mangling than almost any other significant act of the 1960s. This 33-track production finally sets the record straight, including all of the significant A-sides, B-sides, and album tracks they recorded for Red Bird between 1964 and 1966, as well as an earlier single for a different label, and four radio commercials. Includes every one of their hits, but anyone who likes those will be enchanted by quite a few of their more obscure numbers here; "Dressed In Black," "Paradise," "It's Easier To Cry," "Never Again," and "Heaven Knows" are all first-class (if sometimes mordant). Not everything is up to that level, but enough is to make a case for them as one of the very best girl groups, and the good sound and thorough liner notes are significant bonuses. It may be more extensive and expensive than some fans wish, but don't settle for the numerous skimpy/rip-off domestic compilations, most of which manage to leave off some key tunes; this is the definitive document. *—Richie Unterberger*

★ **Best of the Shangri-Las** / Jun. 18, 1996 / PolyGram ✦✦✦✦
This 25-song best-of actually covers most of their discography, containing all of the chart singles, and notable misses and B-sides like "Paradise" and "Dressed in Black." An excellent package, but the British *Myrmidons of Melodrama* (on RPM) is just a bit better, assembling a few more of their Red Bird tracks, including a couple of pretty notable ones ("It's Easier to Cry" and "The Boy") that this domestic anthology omits. This CD does have their rare (but unexceptional) final two singles, which don't appear on *Myrmidons of Melodrama*. *—Richie Unterberger*

Del Shannon (Charles Westover)

b. Dec. 30, 1934, Coopersville, MI, d. Feb. 8, 1990, Santa Clarita, CA
Guitar, Vocals / Rock & Roll, Teen Idol, Pop-Rock
One of the best and most original rockers of the early '60s, Del Shannon was also one of the least typical. Although classified at times as a teen idol, he favored brooding themes of abandonment, loss, and rejection. In some respects he looked forward to the British Invasion with his frequent use of minor chords and his ability to write most of his own material. In fact, Shannon was able to keep going strong for a year or two into the British Invasion, and never stopped trying to play original

music, though his commercial prospects pretty much died after the mid-'60s.

Born Charles Westover, Shannon happened upon a gripping series of minor chords while playing with his band in Battle Creek, MI. The chords would form the basis for his 1961 debut single, "Runaway," one of the greatest hits of the early '60s, with its unforgettable riffs, Shannon's amazing vocal range (which often glided off into a powerful falsetto), and the creepy, futuristic organ solo in the middle. It made No. 1, and the similar follow-up, "Hats off to Larry," also made the Top Ten.

Shannon had intermittent minor hits over the next couple of years ("Little Town Flirt" was the biggest), but was even more successful in England, where he was huge. On one of his European tours in 1963, he played some shows with the Beatles, who had just scored their first big British hits. Shannon, impressed by what he heard, would become the first American artist to cover a Beatles song when he recorded "From Me to You" for a 1963 single (although it would give him only a very small hit). Shannon's melodic style had some similarities with the burgeoning pop-rock wing of the British Invasion, and in 1965 Peter & Gordon would cover a Shannon composition, "I Go to Pieces," for a Top Ten hit.

Del got into the Top Ten with a late-1964 single, "Keep Searchin'," that was one of his best and hardest-rocking outings. But after the similar "Stranger in Town" (No. 30, 1965), he wouldn't enter the Top 40 again for nearly a couple of decades. A switch to a bigger label (Liberty) didn't bring the expected commercial results, although he was continuing to release quality singles. Part of the problem was that some of these were a bit too eager to recycle some of his stock minor-keyed riffs, as good as his prototype was. A brief association with producer Andrew Loog Oldham (also manager/producer of the Rolling Stones) found him continuing to evolve, developing a more baroque, orchestrated pop-rock sound, and employing British session musicians such as Nicky Hopkins. Much to Shannon's frustration, Liberty decided not to release the album that resulted from the collaboration (some of the material appeared on singles, and much of the rest of the sessions would eventually be issued for the collector market).

By the late '60s, Shannon was devoting much of his energy to producing other artists, most notably Smith and Brian Hyland. Shannon was a perennially popular artist on the oldies circuit (particularly in Europe, where he had an especially devoted audience), and was always up for a comeback attempt on record. Sessions with Jeff Lynne and Dave Edmunds in the '70s didn't amount to much, but an early-'80s album produced by Tom Petty (and featuring members of the Heartbreakers as backing musicians) got him into the Top 40 again with a cover of "Sea of Love." He was working on another comeback album with Jeff Lynne, and sometimes rumored as a replacement for Roy Orbison in the Traveling Wilburys, when he unexpectedly killed himself on February 8, 1990, while on anti-depressant drugs. *—Richie Unterberger*

Little Town Flirt / 1963 / Rhino ✦✦✦
Half of the songs on Shannon's second album—"Runaway," "Hats off to Larry," "Hey Little Girl," "Kelly," "Little Town Flirt," and "Two Kinds of Teardrops"—are on *Greatest Hits*. These are also the best and most popular songs on *Little Town Flirt*, which is filled out with competent but unremarkable covers of early-'60s hits like "Go Away, Little Girl," "Runaround Sue," and "Hey Baby." That means that everyone except Shannon collectors should head to *Greatest Hits* instead. *—Richie Unterberger*

Del Shannon Sings Hank Williams / 1965 / Rhino ✦✦✦✦
While tribute albums nowadays are commonplace, a quick examination of history 30 years ago shows us that it wasn't always thus. And when they *did* occur, it was usually a tip of the hat to some long-standing show-business icon like Al Jolson. Certainly departed country music stars like Hank Williams were considered outside the pale of such honors, which is only one of the reasons why this tribute album by rocker Del Shannon stands out as being something rarified and great. Shannon—like most aspiring rockers—grew up on Williams' songs and once success allowed him to show that side of his musical equation, he jumped at the opportunity. But rather than cutting a dozen tepid updates of Hank's best ("Kaw-Liga," "Your Cheatin' Heart," "I'm So Lonesome I Could Cry," "Hey Good Lookin'," etc.), awash in a sea of strings and female choruses, Shannon was smart enough to keep the music firmly in the style of Williams' backup band, the Drifting Cowboys. Although several Motown session players—including Dennis "Scorpio" Coffey on lead guitar—are on this session, the net result is heartfelt, understated country music with plenty of steel guitar to the fore, the kind you'd hear at the kinds of beer halls in Saginaw, MI, where Shannon honed his craft. Del sings the songs straight, minus any of his trademarked falsetto embellishments, and the result is one of the best straightforward country albums you'll ever hear. *—Cub Koda*

The Vintage Years / 1975 / Sire ✦✦✦✦
A very strong 28-track compilation of his best '60s work. Most fans will want to stick with *Greatest Hits*, but this more extensive (though out-of-

print) overview goes deeper without much filler. Major advantages are its inclusion of material from both the earlier and later part of the decade (with emphasis on pre-1966 sides), and extensive liner notes by Greg Shaw. —*Richie Unterberger*

Runaway Hits / 1986 / Bug ✦✦✦✦
Fine 16-track compilation of his best early—and mid-'60s hits, with good liner notes and discography. All but one of the songs, however, is included on Rhino's slightly more extensive *Greatest Hits*. —*Richie Unterberger*

I Go to Pieces / 1990 / Edsel ✦✦✦✦
A British import and an indispensable complement to the Rhino hits package. Sixteen important tracks, capturing Shannon's sound at its most achingly beautiful. —*Bruce Eder*

★ **Greatest Hits** / 1990 / Rhino ✦✦✦✦✦
Greatest Hits features 20 tracks from Del Shannon's early-'60s heyday, including all of the big hits—"Runaway," "Hats off to Larry," "Little Town Flirt," "Handy Man," "Keep Searchin' (We'll Follow the Sun)," "Stranger in Town"—plus a generous selection of lesser-known but equally fine singles and album tracks. Completists should fill in the gaps with his neglected gem *I Go to Pieces*, but *Greatest Hits* remains a definitive retrospective from one of the finest pre-Beatles rockers of the '60s. —*Stephen Thomas Erlewine*

The Liberty Years / Apr. 23, 1991 / EMI America ✦✦
Not the record to start with. An artist in search of a style, with some interesting attempts at finding one. —*Bruce Eder*

Sandie Shaw (Sandra Goodrich)

b. Feb. 26, 1947, Dagenham, Essex, England
Vocals / British Invasion, Girl Group
British singer Sandie Shaw had a string of girl group-styled singles in the mid-'60s before she retired in the early '70s. Shaw was discovered by pop singer Adam Faith in 1963, who led her to his manager, Eve Taylor; she released her debut single, "As Long As You're Happy," the following year. It didn't hit the charts, yet her next record, "(There's) Always Something There to Remind Me," hit No. 1 in the U.K.; the single hit No. 52 in the US, yet Shaw was never as big a star in the US as she was in the UK. For the next three years, she had a string of hits—many written by her producer, Chris Andrews—that kept her at the top of the charts. In 1967, Taylor began to move Shaw into cabaret territory; the approach proved a success when the Bill Martin/Phil Coulter song "Puppet on a String" hit No. 1. She recorded one more Coulter song, "Tonight in Tokyo," before returning to Chris Andrews. However, none of her further work with Andrews resulted in hit singles. Released in early 1969, her English version of the French "Monsieur Dupont" managed to crack the Top 20; it would turn out to be her last hit. In 1970, Shaw tried to become a family entertainer, yet those plans were scuttled by a failed marriage and scandalous rumors that circulated in the British newspapers. She subsequently retired for the rest of the '70s. Shaw returned to recording in the early '80s when BEF, a Heaven 17 side project, prompted her to record "Anyone Who Had a Heart," an old Cilla Black hit. the Smiths' lead singer, Morrissey, began championing her in interviews, as well, which led her to record a version of the band's "Hand in Glove" supported by the Smiths themselves; the single briefly appeared on the UK charts. Shaw recorded a version of Lloyd Cole's "Are You Ready to Be Heartbroken?" in 1986; like "Hand in Glove," it scraped the bottom of the pop charts. In 1988, she recorded an entire album, *Hello Angel;* although it featured songs by The Smiths and the Jesus and Mary Chain, it failed to make a large impression on the pop charts. —*Stephen Thomas Erlewine*

Sandie / 1965 / Pye ✦✦
Even if you're in the Sandie Shaw cult, you might be disappointed, even aghast, at the quality of her debut LP. From every standpoint, it betrayed hasty execution—wafer-thin production, shoddy original material (none of her early singles are included), lousy covers of American and British pop and rock hits, and one-dimensional vocalizing and interpretive skills from Sandie herself. The British public didn't care, sending it to No. 3 in the charts; in fact, it was her most successful album in the UK. The LP was reissued in its entirety as part of the 55-track *64/67 Complete Sandie Shaw*, where listeners can easily skip it or program its omission if they want to stick with the singles. —*Richie Unterberger*

Me / 1965 / Pye ✦✦✦
Shaw's second album was an improvement on her debut in every respect, though hardly a major effort. It helped that Chris Andrews (who wrote most of her hits) supplied a lot of the tunes, and Shaw herself contributed a fair effort with her first original composition, "Till the Night Begins to Die." "Down and Dismal Ways" is as down and dirty as Sandie ever got (which means that it's still pretty innocuous). Still, you can't help wondering how much better Lulu or Dusty Springfield would have done with the same material. No need to look for a rare, pricy copy of the original LP; all of the songs are included on the British double-CD compilation *64/67 Complete Sandie Shaw*. —*Richie Unterberger*

Love Me, Please Love Me / 1967 / RPM ✦✦
Fresh from her triumph at the 1967 Eurovision Song Contest, Shaw concentrated on determinedly MOR pop (not pop-rock) material on her third album. The program focused on songs by Jacques Brel, Antonio Carlos Jobim, Cole Porter, and the like, with only two contributions by her longtime songwriter Chris Andrews. She's no Barbra Streisand, to put it mildly, and the results held little charm either for her fan base or the larger adult market that she may have been trying to reach. The CD reissue is made more palatable by the addition of both sides of four 1967-68 singles, almost all of which were written by Andrews. These are more consistent with the pop-rock lite of her mid-'60s work, but are weaker than her biggest hits, although "Tonight in Tokyo," "You've Not Changed," and "Today" all made the UK Top 30; the Motown-influenced B-side "Stop" may be the highlight of the batch, although that's not saying much. —*Richie Unterberger*

The Sandie Shaw Supplement / 1968 / RPM ✦✦
Consisting of songs performed on her short-lived BBC television series, *The Sandie Shaw Supplement* was a very mixed bag, reflecting the repertoire of the all-around entertainer that she was apparently trying to become. The renditions of pop standards are okay, and the covers of pop-rock hits like "Satisfaction," "Homeward Bound," and "Route 66" are mediocre to embarrassing; there are also some tunes like "Change of Heart" that are reasonable continuations of her pure pop singles of the mid-'60s. It's a very uneven effort—selected tracks will be enjoyed by her fan club, but it will convert few new listeners to her cause. The CD reissue on RPM adds eight tracks from 1968-69 singles, mixing competent Chris Andrews-penned throwbacks to the vintage Shaw sound with some of her worst material (the vaudevillian "Show Me," an ill-conceived cover of "Those Were the Days"). But one of the singles, 1969's "Monsieur Dupont," would be her last big British hit. —*Richie Unterberger*

Reviewing the Situation / 1969 / RPM ✦✦✦
On her last album of the '60s, Shaw proved that she was hipper than a lot of people would have suspected. Moving away from the usual light pop and MOR, she chose a set of covers heavy on material by the likes of Bob Dylan, the Lovin' Spoonful, the Rolling Stones ("Sympathy for the Devil"!), Led Zeppelin's "Your Time Is Gonna Come" (double exclamation point!), Donovan, Dr. John, and the Bee Gees. That doesn't mean it's a great album. It's thoughtfully arranged and energetically delivered, but Shaw's slight, wispy voice is as ill-suited for some of the material as a nun is for the mosh pit. Hearing her attempt even the slightest hint of funky menace, as on "Sympathy for the Devil" and Dr. John's "Mama Roux," is apt to induce snickers, however heartelt the endeavor might have been. On the other hand, there's a nifty slinky, jazzy cover of the Beatles' "Love Me Do," and her version of the Spoonful's "Coconut Grove" is also good. The CD reissue adds ten bonus tracks from 1969-71 singles, most of which are far more akin to the straight pop of her earlier '60s work (a cover of Paul McCartney's "Maybe I'm Amazed" being an exception). None of the singles were especially memorable, and none of them were hits, closing the chapter on the first phase of her career. —*Richie Unterberger*

Collection / 1990 / Castle ✦✦✦✦
Collection is an effective overview of Sandie Shaw's entire career, from her early hits to her '80s collaborations with the Smiths. It covers more ground than the double-disc *Complete* but it doesn't have quite as much prime material. —*Stephen Thomas Erlewine*

● **64/67 Complete Sandie Shaw Set** / 1994 / Sequel ✦✦✦✦
A double-disc set that features all of her big hits as well as all of her minor ones, this provides the definitive portrait of the British girl group vocalist. —*Stephen Thomas Erlewine*

Nothing Less Than Brilliant: The Best Of / 1995 / Virgin ✦✦✦✦
Most of Sandie Shaw's biggest hits are included on *Nothing Less than Brilliant*, but the collection tries to balance her '60s hits with her '80s comeback, which makes the disc somewhat inconsistent. Nevertheless, it is a good career portrait, featuring many of her finest moments. —*Stephen Thomas Erlewine*

Sandie / Me / Jan. 30, 1996 / See For Miles ✦✦✦
Sandie Shaw's first two albums, *Sandie* and *Me*, are featured on this single disc. Both albums have their share of filler, but there's a high number of strong tracks on the records, and Shaw's joyful, girlish charisma carries many of the weak songs and covers. *Sandie* and *Me* were both included on the double-disc set *64/67 Complete Sandie Shaw*, which also featured all of her hit singles, which makes it preferable to this single-disc. —*Stephen Thomas Erlewine*

Jules Shear

b. Mar. 7, 1952, Pittsburgh, PA
Guitar, Vocals / Singer-Songwriter, Pop-Rock
Though he's never been able to record a hit of his own, singer-songwriter Jules Shear has recorded several albums of highly accessible, hit-

worthy material, and as a testament to his abilities, he's penned hits for others including "All Through the Night" for Cyndi Lauper and "If She Knew What She Wants" for the Bangles.

Born in Pittsburgh, Shear began writing songs as a teenager. He relocated to Los Angeles in the mid-'70s, joining his first band, a typically laidback combo called the Funky Kings. The band released one album for Arista in 1976. While "Slow Dancing" from the album (written by Jack Tempchin) would later be a hit for Johnny Rivers, the three Shear songs were clearly the highlights of the album. Shear left the following year to form his own group, Jules & the Polar Bears, who released two critically acclaimed, though commercially overlooked, albums for Columbia. When a third album was rejected by the label, Shear forged on as a solo artist.

Signing on to EMI-America, he released two solo albums, 1983's *Watch Dog* and 1985's *Eternal Return;* both received critical praise but few sales. Once again, he was dropped by his label and unable to secure another deal. Shear then formed the Reckless Sleepers with the Cars' Elliot Easton. In 1988, without Easton, the Reckless Sleepers released their sole album for IRS, *Big Boss Sounds;* it failed to make much impact though "If We Never Meet Again" from the album was later covered by Roger McGuinn. In contrast to the Reckless Sleepers' hard-rock tendencies, Shear teamed up with the Church's Marty Willson-Piper for an all-acoustic, Dylan-esque album, *The Third Party,* in 1989. The album ultimately led to a spot on MTV, hosting the first 13 episodes of *Unplugged*—he left when the show switched to the single-artist format. Since then, Shear has released the two strongest albums of his career, 1992's *The Great Puzzle* and 1994's *Healing Bones.* —*Chris Woodstra*

Watch Dog / 1983 / EMI ✦✦✦✦
His first solo album following the breakup of the Polar Bears, *Watch Dog* features a newfound maturity in songwriting with an eclectic mix of styles from ultra-smooth pop to R&B-inflected rockers. Shear sounds much more comfortable on his own, even under Todd Rundgren's heavy-handed production. Highlights includes "All Through the Night" (a hit for Cyndi Lauper), "Whispering Your Name," and the the more experimental, Brian Wilson-inspired "Longest Drink." Another unjustified commercial sleeper. —*Chris Woodstra*

Eternal Return / 1985 / EMI America ✦✦✦
Seemingly unfazed by *Watch Dog's* failure, Shear again produces a slick, pop delight in *Eternal Return.* Shear explores a more soulful side in songs like "Steady" and the yearning "You're Not Around" while perfecting his hook-laden melodies. Despite being perfectly in line with the mid-'80s sound, this one also slipped through the cracks. The Bangles would later find a hit in the leadoff track, "If She Knew What She Wants." —*Chris Woodstra*

Demo-Itis / 1987 / Enigma ✦✦
Of interest mainly to fans, this collection of demos shows Shear's true talent, free of the often smothering production that plagued his previous albums. In addition to early versions of old favorites, several songs that never made it on the LPs appear for the first time. —*Chris Woodstra*

The Third Party / 1989 / IRS ✦✦✦
Jules Shear joined up with the Church's Marty Willson-Piper in Sweden for *The Third Party,* a stark, bare-bones acoustic album. Stripped of all of the excessive production that sometimes marred earlier work, Shear's songs are allowed to come to the forefront, as they should. Shear's voice, phrasing, and the minimalistic, often folky arrangements led to Dylan comparisons, but the album really features Shear's own clever craftsmanship; the back-to-basics approach is certainly a welcome one (as are the guitar chords included in the booklet). Shear had proven long before his strong melodic sense, but with *The Third Party* his clever wordplay and interesting turns of phrase were allowed the proper platform. Though the album failed commercially, the approach undoubtedly led to Shear's hosting the first several *MTV Unplugged* episodes, which gave him more exposure than ever before. —*Chris Woodstra*

The Great Puzzle / Jan. 28, 1992 / Polydor ✦✦✦✦
Jules Shear left behind several albums worth of terrific music, from his earliest days with the Funky Kings to his work with Jules & the Polar Bears and on to a distinguished solo career. Even with tough competition, *The Great Puzzle* stands as Shear's high point, combining his never-failing gift of melody with tasteful, organic arrangements, highly personal yet universal lyrics, and probably his most consistent batch of songs to date. [Initial pressings of *The Great Puzzle* were packaged with a bonus disc, *Unplug This,* which had Shear reprise his best-known songs along with a couple from *The Great Puzzle* in a solo acoustic setting.] —*Chris Woodstra*

● **Horse of a Different Color (1976-1989)** / 1994 / Razor & Tie ✦✦✦✦
Horse of a Different Color collects tracks from all of the early phases of the sadly overlooked songwriter's career from 1976 to 1989, including "Nothing Was Exchanged" (a song that still stands as one of his finest moments) from the sole Funky Kings album, a couple of tracks each from the two released Jules & the Polar Bears albums, a handful from each of his proper solo albums up to 1989's *The Third Party* and the two

high points from the short-lived Reckless Sleepers project. Since so much of his early output is long out of print, this collection is a welcome addition, and as a career summary it's invaluable. Liner notes outlining Shear's ever-changing career would have been nice, but the sheer quality and consistency of music like this really speaks for itself. —*Chris Woodstra*

Healing Bones / Aug. 23, 1994 / PolyGram ✦✦✦
While Shear's albums are always packed with craftsmanlike songwriting, the production and arrangements often end up dating them. What sets *Healing Bones* apart from most of his back catalog is a certain timelessness of the sound. The songs are definitely among his finest. Includes a cover of the Walker Brothers' classic "The Sun Ain't Gonna Shine Anymore." —*Chris Woodstra*

Pete Shelley

b. Apr. 17, 1955, Leigh, Lancashire, England
Guitar / New Wave
Pete Shelley, the leader of the seminal punk band the Buzzcocks, actually had recorded a solo album in 1974, two years before the Buzzcocks had formed. Released in 1979, *Sky Yen* was a collection of electronic music that didn't sound much like his full-time band's blistering guitar-pop, yet it did contain the roots of his solo career. After the Buzzcocks disbanded in 1981, Shelley began a solo career that incorporated the electronic experimentations of *Sky Yen* with the pop sensibilities of his punk singles. Released in 1982, *Homosapien* showcased this musical merger and resulted in the UK hit single "Homosapien." The following year Shelley released *XL1,* which added more guitar to his dance-oriented synth-pop. Three years later he released his final solo album, *Heaven and the Sea,* which failed to capture an audience. Shelley then joined the short-lived band Zip; after its breakup, he rejoined the reunited Buzzcocks in 1988. —*Stephen Thomas Erlewine*

Sky Yen / 1979 / Groovy ✦✦
Pete Shelley's first solo album, *Sky Yen,* is comprised of solo electronic recordings that he made in 1974 but didn't release until 1979. In other words, it's a curiosity for devoted fans, especially since the primitive, droning electronics recall Krautrock, not punk rock. However, the timing of its release was quite curious, since within two years, Shelley would return to electronics for his official solo career. —*Stephen Thomas Erlewine*

● **Homosapien** / Dec. 1981 / Genetic/Arista ✦✦✦✦
Homosapien, for most intents and purposes, was Pete Shelley's first official solo album, and it's a pretty forceful break from the Buzzcocks' patented punk-pop rush. Shelley delved deep into synth-pop and dance rhythms, somewhat tempering those robotic influences with slight glam and gloomy psychedelic influences. While the songs might not be as consistent as his best Buzzcocks albums, there are a number of terse pop gems, much in the vein of the classic title track. —*Stephen Thomas Erlewine*

XL 1 / 1983 / Genetic/Arista ✦✦✦
With *XL1,* Pete Shelley integrates layers of guitar to the electronic synth-pop he essayed on his solo debut, *Homosapien.* While the result isn't quite as bracing as its predecessor, the music benefits from the guitar—it sounds edgier, making the record fairly captivating. There's still some weak material on the record, but "Telephone Operator" and "If You Ask Me (I Won't Say No)" are terrific, ranking among Shelley's best. —*Stephen Thomas Erlewine*

Heaven & the Sea / 1986 / Mercury ✦✦✦
Heaven and the Sea isn't quite as dance-oriented as Pete Shelley's first two albums, nor does it have the nervous pop energy that was a hallmark of those records and his work with the Buzzcocks. Instead, it's a layered and textured release, given a polished, mature production that ironically only emphasizes the lack of notable songs. There are a handful of relatively strong cuts on the record, but even they don't match the high points of its two predecessors. —*Stephen Thomas Erlewine*

The Shirelles

f. 1958, Passaic, NJ
Girl Group, Brill Building Pop
The Shirelles were instrumental in defining the girl group sound, and were one of the style's most successful acts between 1960 and 1963, when they placed six singles in the Top Ten. Bridging doo wop and uptown New York pop-soul, the group projected a beguiling mixture of tenderness and innocence that was grounded in R&B as much as pop-rock. Forming as high school classmates in New Jersey, the Shirelles came under the wing of manager Florence Goldberg, who also ran the Scepter label. Many of their classic early sides featured innovative, occasionally string-laden production by Luther Dixon, who also penned several of their greatest songs. Top Brill Building songwriters like Goffin-King, Bacharach-David, and Van McCoy also supplied the group with material. "Will You Love Me Tomorrow," "Baby It's You," "Foolish Little

Girl," "Soldier Boy," "Dedicated to the One I Love," and "Mama Said" were their biggest hits, but they also cut a number of delightful less famous sides, including "Boys," which (like "Baby It's You") was covered by the Beatles on their first LP. After mid-1963, the Shirelles were unable to dent the Top 40, although they recorded some excellent songs, including the original version of "Sha La La" (covered for a hit by Manfred Mann). The group recorded well into the '70s, updating their sound into a more soul-oriented mode that was lacking in comparison. *—Richie Unterberger*

Baby It's You / 1962 / Sundazed ✦✦✦
The best songs on here—the title track, "Big John," "A Thing of the Past," "Make the Night a Little Longer," "Soldier Boy," and "Putty in Your Hands"—are available on the Rhino best-of double album. Still, it's a pretty solid effort for its day, featuring state-of-the-art orchestral early-'60s New York girl group production and decent songwriting. *—Richie Unterberger*.

A Shirelles & King Curtis Give a Twist Party / 1962 / Sundazed ✦✦✦
A rather strange concept for an early-'60s album, pairing the Shirelles, then at the peak of their success, with R&B/soul sax great King Curtis. It's not so much a collaboration as an alternation; Curtis gets three instrumentals to himself, and sings "I Got a Woman" and another cut. King does a duet with the girls on "I Still Want You," and the Shirelles handle the rest of the material, mostly written by their chief producer/songwriter Luther Dixon, in a much more uptempo vein than their famous singles. No hits on this record, which is respectable but not terribly exciting, and a bit schizo in concept. *—Richie Unterberger*

★ **Anthology (1959-1967)** / 1988 / Rhino ✦✦✦✦✦
One of the most consistently creative and diverse of the '60s girl groups, the Shirelles were a hit-making machine. "Soldier Boy," "Dedicated to the One I Love," "Will You Still Love Me Tomorrow?," and 13 others can be found here. *—Jeff Tamarkin*

Lost & Found / Dec. 1, 1995 / Ace ✦✦
Twenty-nine songs from the Scepter vaults, most not released when the Shirelles were active (a few found their way onto flop singles, as well as the 1965 LP *Swing the Most*). Even Shirelles fans might find this album disappointing, though it's a long way from horrible. Much of the material was probably recorded after their 1960-63 prime (the source dates remain vague). This era often found them trying to emulate commercial pop-soul trends (particularly Motown) without much personality, and without the benefit of distinctive material. Goffin-King, Bacharach-David, David Gates, and Ashford-Simpson gave the group (little-known) compositions during this era. But while the results were competent, they were forgettable, despite the odd better-than-average track like the pleading "Remember Me," or the soulful "I'm Yours." *—Richie Unterberger*

Shirley & Lee

f. 1951, New Orleans, LA, **db.** 1963
R&B, New Orleans R&B
Shirley Goodman's (b. Jun 19, 1936) screechy vocals and Leonard Lee's (b. Jun 29, 1936–d. Oct 23, 1976) bluesy retorts added up to R&B gold during the '50s for the young Crescent City duo. The teenagers' debut on Aladdin, the Dave Bartholomew-produced "I'm Gone," was a major R&B hit in 1952. Shirley & Lee caught fire in 1955-56 with three rocking smashes: "Feel So Good," the R&B chart-topping "Let the Good Times Roll," and "I Feel Good," all written by Lee. The pair stayed on Aladdin into 1959 before moving to Warwick and re-doing "Let the Good Times Roll." The "Sweethearts of the Blues" broke up after a few 1962-63 singles for Imperial. In 1974 Goodman returned under the sobriquet of Shirley and Company with a No. 1 R&B smash, the disco-fied "Shame, Shame, Shame," for producer Sylvia Robinson on the Vibration logo. *—Bill Dahl*

● **Legendary Masters** / Mar. 16, 1990 / EMI America ✦✦✦✦
The "Sweethearts of the Blues" in all their glory, it includes "Let the Good Times Roll" and more. *—Dan Heilman*

Michelle Shocked

b. Feb. 24, 1962, Dallas, TX
Guitar, Vocals / Urban-Folk, Singer-Songwriter, Alternative Pop-Rock, Folk-Rock
According to her own, undoubtedly semi-fictional account, Michelle Shocked was born Michelle Johnston in Dallas, TX, in 1962, where she spent her early childhood travelling around army bases. In 1977, she ran away from her Mormon fundamentalist mother to live with her father, who introduced her to country bluesmen Big Bill Broonzy and Leadbelly as well as contemporary songwriters Guy Clark and Randy Newman. She spent the next several years exploring the folk underground, spending the early '80s in Austin, where she began honing her own songwriting skills. After dropping out of the University of Texas, she moved to San Francisco where she quickly embraced the city's punk

scene. When she returned home, her mother had her committed to a psychiatric hospital. She was released when her insurance ran out. Shocked left Texas in 1983, travelled throughout the US and became an activist in the squatters movement in New York. In 1984, she moved to Amsterdam.

In 1986, Shocked returned to the US. While volunteering at the Kerrville Folk Festival, Shocked impressed English producer Pete Lawrence with her campfire-side playing; he recorded her on his Sony Walkman. The recordings surfaced in the fall of that year as *The Texas Campfire Tapes* on Cooking Vinyl Records and became a surprise hit in England, eventually topping the independent charts. The success led to her signing with Mercury Records in 1988. *Short Sharp Shocked*, produced by Pete Anderson in 1988, displayed even more talent, combining the informal, tradition-rooted folkiness of *The Texas Campfire Tapes* with a strong post-modern feminist perspective and punk attitude. The album quickly earned her respect among the alternative community and critics. In an unexpected move, Shocked returned in 1989 with *Captain Swing*, a '40s-style big-band swing outing that shocked her fans initially but had no shortage of strong material. In 1992, she took something of a step back with *Arkansas Traveler*, a rootsy collection of songs based on the blackface minstrels that covered all forms of early American, home-grown music. In 1993, Mercury finally became fed up with her confusing style jumping and refused to release her proposed gospel album. She then left on a solo tour, selling her newly recorded, independently produced (with Tony Berg) *Kind Hearted Woman*. Late in 1995, Shocked began legal action against Mercury Records to break her contract.

By 1996, Shocked was released from Mercury and embarked on the First Annual Underground Test Site Tour, with Fianchna O'Braonain. Another independent release, *Artists Make Lousy Slaves*, was sold at the shows. *Kind Hearted Woman* was picked up for release by Private Music in 1996. *—Chris Woodstra*

The Texas Campfire Tapes / 1986 / Mercury ✦✦✦
Her debut, recorded live around a campfire on a Walkman, is a wildly overrated but interesting introduction to her talents. *—John Dougan*

★ **Short Sharp Shocked** / 1988 / Mercury ✦✦✦✦✦
Michelle Shocked is asked in the song "Anchorage," "What's It like to be a [New York City] skateboard punk rocker?" Perhaps it takes a flashback like *Short Sharp Shocked* to fully answer the more interesting question "How did you get there?" The album finds Shocked taking a semi-fond trip back to an East Texas childhood, and all of the defined roles, limited expectations, claustrophobia, and ultimate rebellion coming from that environment. Musically, she tackles the spectrum of rootsy folk in a warm way that shows not only a love for, but also a great deal of knowledge of the forms (producer Pete Anderson added a Nashville gloss to the recordings that shouldn't go unnoticed). The songs have a very personal, almost diary feel, but at the same time they speak a universal language—none so poignant as the album's centerpiece, "Anchorage," a touching letter from an old friend. The cover photo, which shows Shocked restrained by police officers during a protest, indicates little about the music found within (save for the uncredited album closer, the hardcore punk work-up of "Fog Town" featuring MDC), but the music certainly reveals much about the protestor. *—Chris Woodstra*

Captain Swing / Oct. 1989 / Mercury ✦✦✦
Shocked made a big jump from *The Texas Campfire Tapes* to *Short Sharp Shocked*, but no one expected the direction she would take for *Captain Swing*. Rather than continuing as the folky singer-songwriter, she opted instead to take on '40s swing and big band music complete with horn-heavy arrangements and bright orchestration. And though the cartoon image of her on the cover gives a smirk and a sly wink, the album is surprisingly devoid of irony. She treats the genre with affection and she's obviously having a good time swinging. *Captain Swing* may have confused fans of *Short Sharp Shocked* (and the material isn't nearly as consistently strong either), but the album has several great moments and, most of all, it offers a good time. *—Chris Woodstra*

Arkansas Traveler / Oct. 1991 / Mercury ✦✦✦✦
Part three of the trilogy that began with *Short Sharp Shocked*, *Arkansas Traveler* focuses this time on American roots music of the South, mainly rural-blues and country; according to her theory in the album's liner notes, all of these songs are based on the legacy of blackface minstrels. Recorded with a mobile studio at various nonconventional locations around the country, it features an amazing array of guest musicians including Pops Staples, Doc Watson, and Gatemouth Brown. Those who were put off by the unexpected direction of *Captain Swing* will certainly welcome this return to form—her best since *Short Sharp Shocked*. *—Chris Woodstra*

Kind Hearted Woman / 1994 / (no label) ✦✦✦
Shocked released *Kind Hearted Woman* on her own, selling it exclusively at live shows, when she ran into troubles with Mercury Records. Accompanied by only her own Stratocaster playing, she has produced her most touching, personal document to date even though the subject

matter is decidedly dark and bleak. Private Music reissued the album in 1996. —*Chris Woodstra*

Artists Make Lousy Slaves / 1996 / Independent ✦✦✦
Independently produced and sold during her First Annual Underground Test Site Tour in the Spring/Summer of 1996, *Artists Makes Lousy Slaves* is a collaboration with Hothouse Flowers' Fiachna O'Bra-onain—the two wrote most of the material together and appear as the sole musicians. The title refers to her long battle to free herself from her former label, Mercury Records. But while this album certainly gives the impression of relief, it fails to capture the raw energy and joy of the tour, which celebrates the dissolving of her contract—the songs are instead pleasantly reflective and low-key. It may not be groundbreaking or particularly representative, but *Artists Make Lousy Slaves* is a nice treat for those fans lucky enough to have witnessed the tour. —*Chris Woodstra*

● Mercury Poise: 1988-95 / Nov. 5, 1996 / Polygram ✦✦✦✦
With a title that plays on Graham Parker's corporate-venomous song and EP *Mercury Poisoning*, the disc skims a dozen layers of feminist-folk-punk cream from three eclectic albums (folk-rock, swing-jazz, and Southern roots music) recorded for the label between 1988 and 1991, plus tracks previously only available on soundtracks, compilations, and the 1994 indie release *Kind Hearted Woman*. —*Roch Parisien*

Shoes
f. 1975, Zion, IL
Power Pop
It may not have been the hip thing to do at the time, but Shoes carried on the pure pop traditions of the Beatles and the Raspberries during the late '70s and early '80s with a charming innocence and execution unmatched by the more derivative bands lumped into the category "power pop."

Shoes was formed by in Zion, IL, in 1975 by Jeff Murphy, John Murphy, Gary Klebe, and Skip Meyer—the Murphys and Klebe all sharing songwriting duties. After one self-made and extremely limited album (only 300 pressed), 1975's *Un Dans Versailles*, and the unreleased *Bazooka* (1976), Shoes recorded their true debut for national consumption, *Black Vinyl Shoes*, in Jeff Murphy's living room and released it on their own label, Black Vinyl Records. Though it was barely distributed, enough critics and key people heard the record to start a word-of-mouth buzz. Eventually, Greg Shaw, the head of Bomp! Records, heard the record and arranged for the band to release one single, the brilliant "Tommorrow Night"/"Okay," on his label. A contract with Elektra Records soon followed. Elektra released the group's next three textbook power-pop albums: *Present Tense* (1979), *Tongue Twister* (1981), and *Boomerang* (1982). Despite the instantly accessible, catchy quality of the songs, they were unable to achieve mainstream success—among specialists however, these albums, along with the debut, stand as the high points of the era.

Elektra dropped Shoes after the release of *Boomerang* and Meyer left the band. The remaining three retreated back to the home studio, returning with *Silhouette* in 1984, a more subtle, keyboard-oriented album released only in Europe. They disappeared for the next five years and popped up again in 1989 with *Stolen Wishes*, on their reactivated Black Vinyl Records. Since then Shoes have remained more or less active, releasing two new albums—*Propeller* (1994) and the live *Fret Buzz* (1995)—as well as producing other like-minded bands for release on Black Vinyl. The collective efforts of Shoes in the mid-'90s led to a power-pop revival in indie-rock circles in the US. —*Chris Woodstra*

Black Vinyl Shoes / 1977 / Black Vinyl ✦✦✦✦
A homemade demo that became their first national release, this is a dazzling collection of pop songs driven by thick sheets of guitar and warm, emotive singing. —*John Dougan*

Present Tense / 1979 / Elektra ✦✦✦✦
Their major-label debut suffers from a bit of overwhelming post-production, but there isn't enough interference to ruin this great collection of tunes. The CD version is a two-fer that combines *Present Tense* with *Tongue Twister*. —*John Dougan*

Tongue Twister / 1981 / Elektra ✦✦✦
After a short stint at Bomp! Records, the Shoes were snapped up by Elektra for their major label debut. The songs are good, the sound is right but something is missing. Maybe it's because they were saddled with a co-producer. Still, not to be missed. On the CD issue, *Tongue Twister* has been combined with *Present Tense*. —*Jim Worbois*

Boomerang/Shoes on Ice / May 1982 / Black Vinyl ✦✦✦✦
In an early interview, the Beatles were asked why they chose their name, to which Paul McCartney replied, "for all you know, we might have been called the Shoes." Fortunately, there *is* a band called the Shoes and this is one of the finest pop albums ever made. Back on their own territory and producing their own records, this is the album that *Tongue Twister* should have been. It stands as one of their best. [A live

EP, *Shoes on Ice*, which came with the initial pressing of the album, has now been added to the CD version.] —*Jim Worbois*

Silhouette / 1984 / Black Vinyl ✦✦✦
Now reduced to a three-piece (John Murphy, Jeff Murphy and Gary Klebe), the band recorded their fifth album independently in their home studio in Illinois. A pleasant, though unexceptional album, *Silhouette* is a softer, more keyboard-dominated effort. Without an American outlet (they left Elektra prior to recording), this album was only available in Europe until the band's own label, Black Vinyl Records, reissued it in the late '80s. —*Chris Woodstra*

● Shoes Best / 1987 / Black Vinyl ✦✦✦✦
A 22-song compilation, this is a wonderfully comprehensive overview of this wonderful band. Good liner notes by former *Trouser Press* head honcho Ira Robbins. —*John Dougan*

Stolen Wishes / 1989 / Black Vinyl ✦✦
The Shoes still sound good and they obviously still enjoy what they are doing, but the tunes on *Stolen Wishes* don't stand up to some of their earlier work. Still, the Shoes never released a bad album, so you won't be out anything if you take a chance on this one. —*Jim Worbois*

Propeller / 1994 / Black Vinyl ✦✦
Shoes returned in 1994 with *Propeller*, proving they're still vital with a harder-edged sound while managing to retain their classic melodies. —*Chris Woodstra*

Fret Buzz / May 2, 1995 / Black Vinyl ✦✦✦

As Is / 1996 / Black Vinyl ✦✦✦✦
The limited-edition, two-disc *As Is* is simply a delight for diehard Shoes fans. Boasting a disc of 27 demos and unreleased tracks as well as the ultra-rare *Bazooka* and *One in Versailles* albums in their entirety—both released before their official debut, *Black Vinyl Shoes*—and a detailed booklet, this collection works well not only as a rarities collection but also as a testament to the band's power-pop legacy. —*Chris Woodstra*

Shonen Knife
f. 1981, Osaka, Japan
Alternative Pop-Rock, Punk-Pop
At their best, the Japanese punk-pop band Shonen Knife is an irresistible delight, combining sweet Beatlesque pop with buzzing Ramones power chords, singing about the schlockiest things pop culture has churned out. At their worst, the band's cuteness seems contrived, as if they were using their fractured English and obsession about Barbie dolls, ice cream, and Hello Kitty as a deliberately cloying, cutesy marketing ploy. Even worse, at times it seems that their fans are not laughing with the band, they're laughing *at* their fascination with American kitsch culture and their bad English. Nevertheless, when taken on a strictly musical level, Shonen Knife's best records—including 1993's *Let's Knife* and 1997's *Brand New Knife*—are truly intoxicating, rocking hard with a melody you can hum for days. —*Stephen Thomas Erlewine*

Pretty Little Baka Guy / Live in Japan / 1986 / Rockville ✦✦✦✦
The CD reissue of this album adds eight live tracks (some that go as far back as 1982, when they were barely teens!) and makes this hands-down the best Shonen Knife record available. On *Baka Guy*, their pop culture obsessions are clearly and humorously articulated ("I Wanna Eat Choco Bars" and "Ice Cream City"), and the record includes the best song ever about public bath houses, "Public Bath." Too often, cute, condescending terminology is used to describe Shonen Knife as though they were candy-floss teddy bears instead of a rock band. So, let's get one thing straight: this is a great rock 'n' roll record by one of Japan's great rock 'n' roll bands. —*John Dougan*

Shonen Knife / 1990 / Positive ✦✦✦✦
A superb collection of material previously available only in Japan on the albums *Burning Farm* and *Yama No Attchan*, covering Shonen Knife's early career from 1983 to 1985. The purist in me has become increasingly disappointed with Shonen Knife's records, as they sound more and more like generic alternative rock. On these recordings there is a nearly palpable sense of joy that comes with the discovery that you've mastered four chords, can keep a steady beat, and are now considered a band. Also, this material is unforced, almost carefree and has little of the calculation that's creeping into their more recent work. Very simply, fabulous pop music. —*John Dougan*

712 / 1991 / Rockville ✦✦✦
"Good morning Shonen Knife freaks!" is the cry that opens *712*, Shonen Knife's last indisputably great record. The playing and songwriting has matured here, but not to the point where it begins to sound sterile or overly sophisticated. Of course, what would a Shonen Knife record be without a few goofy tributes to junk culture, as in "Fruit Loop Dreams" and "Expo '90"? There's a surprising cover of John Lennon's "Luck of the Irish" with vocal help from Redd Kross' Jeff McDonald. Note: the song "Blue Oyster Cult" is not a tribute to the band; it's about food poisoning from eating raw oysters. —*John Dougan*

● **Let's Knife** / Jan. 26, 1993 / Capitol ✦✦✦✦
Song titles "Twist Barbie," "Flying Jelly Attack," and "I Am a Cat" offer an accurate snapshot of this Japanese band . . . then there's the environmental anthem (?) "Bear Up Bison": "He has a right to live though he's ill ill ill-shaped/He's on the way to extinction/We only want what's best for him/Bear up bison never say die!" There's something fascinating about having Western culture thrown back at us in this quirky, unpretentious manner, and Shonen Knife are well on their way to becoming a cult favorite—for those who "get" it. —*Roch Parisien*

Rock Animals / Jan. 25, 1994 / Virgin ✦✦
Like Jonathan Richman, this group has carved out a niche that combines wide-eyed cuteness with unbridled rock 'n' roll. That's good and bad; like Richman, you can rely on Shonen Knife for consistent fun, but also like Richman, you shouldn't expect much variation or artistic growth from album to album. *Rock Animals* adds a somewhat harder edge to their sound without tempering their childlike innocence. Occasionally they branch out from their stock-in-trade mix of bubblegum and power punk. "Another Day" is an orchestrated piano ballad that recalls girl group dramas of the 1960s, and "Music Square" is a folkish tune featuring acoustic guitar and harmonica. The album features a guest appearance by Sonic Youth guitarist Thurston Moore on "Butterfly," and includes one track, "Quavers," that was not available on the import version of this CD. —*Richie Unterberger*

Birds & the B-Sides / Mar. 5, 1996 / Virgin ✦✦✦
Eighteen odds and ends from the Shonen Knife '90s catalog: single-only cuts, import-only songs or versions, four live performances from their first British gig, and contributions to tribute albums to the Carpenters, Beach Boys, and Nilsson. Shonen Knife have a devoted following for a cultish alternative act, and fanatics will appreciate the thoughtfully assembled, thoroughly annotated collection of these rarities, which would set you back a few hundred dollars or so if you tried to track them down via their original sources. If you're not devoted enough to become a fan club member, it's neither a place to start nor an essential addition. The covers (especially of "Heatwave" and the Beach Boys' "Don't Hurt My Little Sister") generally outpace the original material, which doesn't vary as much as it could or should. —*Richie Unterberger*

Brand New Knife / Mar. 11, 1997 / Big Deal ✦✦✦
Brand New Knife finds Shonen Knife returning to punk-pop after the metallic experiments of *Rock Animals*, both for better and for worse. While the record offers more thrills than its predecessors, it sounds more tired than their late-'80s and early-'90s records. For longtime fans, there's enough strong moments to make *Brand New Knife* fun, but there's enough filler to make it disheartening as well. [Seven bonus tracks, sung in Japanese, were added to the American CD edition.] —*Stephen Thomas Erlewine*

The Showmen

f. 1960, Norfolk, VA, **db.** 1968
New Orleans R&B, R&B
The Showmen were one of the R&B groups to bridge the gap between doo wop and soul in the early '60s, creating a buoyant, energetic fusion of harmonies and propulsive R&B beats. The group only had one hit, "It Will Stand," which charted both in 1961 and in 1964, but their lead singer, General Johnson, went on to greater success as the leader of the '70s soul group Chairmen of the Board.

Formed in Norfolk, VA, in the early '60s, the Showmen consisted of General Johnson (born Norman Johnson, May 23, 1943), Leslie Felton, Gene Wright, Dorsey Wright, and Milton Wells. In 1961, the group signed with Minit Records, which was based in New Orleans. Their first single was a rock 'n' roll anthem, "It Will Stand." Released in the fall of 1961, "It Will Stand" was a hit, particularly on the East Coast and in the New Orleans era, but it only peaked at No. 61 on the pop charts. Nevertheless, the song's popularity never decreased and it became a hit three years later, when re-released on the Imperial label. On its second release, the single peaked at No. 80 on both the R&B and pop charts.

Between the two chart appearances of "It Will Stand," the Showmen kept recording and performing. During this time they had no national hits, but "39-21-46" became a significant regional hit. In 1965, the group signed with Swan Records, but none of the ensuing singles became hits. In 1968, General Johnson left the band and moved to Detroit, where he formed the Chairmen of the Board, who would later have hits with "Give Me Just a Little More Time," "(You've Got Me) Dangling on a String," and "Everything's Tuesday" in the early '70s. In the three decades after the breakup of the Showmen, "It Will Stand" and "39-21-46" remained popular on the East Coast "beach music" scene and Johnson would later return to this area, carving out a living as a local performer. —*Stephen Thomas Erlewine*

● **It Will Stand** / Apr. 24, 1990 / Collectables ✦✦✦✦
A nice collection featuring the stuttering, sputtering vocals of General Johnson and company, otherwise known as the Showmen. The title track was one of the great pieces of rock and R&B testimony. They never

quite equaled it, although they produced some fine ballads and good uptempo tunes. "It Will Stand" wasn't a hit the first time out of the box; it didn't make it onto the R&B charts until 1964, three years after it had peaked at No. 61 on the pop charts, and then it only reached No. 80. —*Ron Wynn*

Shudder to Think

f. 1986, Washington, DC
Alternative Pop-Rock, Indie Rock
Shudder to Think's hardcore punk background (courtesy of DC's Dischord Records, also the home of Fugazi) isn't the best pointer toward their sound, since the group works in pop influences and a skewed sense of songwriting as well. Originally formed in 1986, the band's first lineup—vocalist/guitarist Craig Wedren, guitarist Chris Matthews, bassist Stuart Hill, and drummer Mike Russell—released two singles and one 1989 album (*Curse, Spells, Voodoo, Mooses*) before signing with the Dischord label. Shudder to Think released albums in 1990 (*Ten-Spot*), 1991 (*Funeral at the Movies*), and 1992 (*Get Your Goat*), and toured with Fugazi and the Smashing Pumpkins. Matthews and Russell had left by 1994, though; guitarist Nathan Larson and drummer Adam Wade replaced them, just in time for the band's first major-label contract. After signing with Epic, Shudder to Think released their fifth album, *Pony Express Record*, in 1994. Almost three years later, *50,000 B.C.* followed in early 1997. —*John Bush*

Ten Spot / 1990 / Dischord ✦✦✦

Funeral at the Movies / 1991 / Dischord ✦✦✦

Get Your Goat / 1992 / Dischord ✦✦✦✦

Funeral at the Movies / Ten Spot / 1993 / Dischord ✦✦✦✦

Hit Liquor / 1994 / Epic ✦✦✦

Your Choice Live Series / May 3, 1994 / Your Choice ✦✦✦

● **Pony Express Record** / Sep. 13, 1994 / Epic ✦✦✦✦

50,000 B.C. / Feb. 25, 1997 / Sony ✦✦✦✦
Pony Express Record might have been Shudder to Think's self-consciously difficult art-punk album, but *50,000 B.C.* is their move toward big-rock. Sporting a slick, polished guitar sound and anthemic harmonies, *50,000 B.C.* is more accessible than the rest of the group's catalog, at least on the surface. However, Craig Wedren's songs remain remarkably versatile and eclectic, ranging from Queen-style pomp-rock and power-pop to doo-wop and folk-rock. Shudder to Think can pull off these stylistic variations with aplomb, but the smooth production gives the music the illusion of being more accessible than it is; it is melodic, but the melodies follow twisted paths, and Wedren's high, vibrato-laden voice can be off-putting to some. This leaves Shudder to Think in an odd position. Their music is too odd for the mainstream, but it now sounds too slick for their old hardcore and indie-rock following, which means *50,000 B.C.* is the kind of eclectic post-punk that will primarily appeal to critics and record collectors. —*Stephen Thomas Erlewine*

Jane Siberry

b. Oct. 12, 1955, Toronto, Ontario
Vocals / Singer-Songwriter, Alternative Pop-Rock
The idiosyncratic Canadian art-pop chanteuse Jane Siberry was born in Toronto, Ontario, on October 12, 1955; after taking up the piano as a child, she began absorbing the classical and operatic inspirations that later distinguished her professional work. While earning a degree in microbiology, Siberry began performing at the local coffeehouse where she also worked as a waitress; ultimately, she used her tip money to fund her 1981 self-titled debut LP, a spartan offering spotlighting her ethereal vocal navigations through the eccentric rhythm changes and dramatic mood shifts that ornamented her abstract, atmospheric sound.

Three years later, Siberry resurfaced with *No Borders Here*, a more assured, cinematic collection highlighted by "Mimi on the Beach," an underground Canadian hit. The critical and commercial success of 1985's evocative *The Speckless Sky* brought her to the attention of Warner/Reprise for 1988's *The Walking*, a bold major label bow comprised of dense, epic-length soundscapes and subtle, intricate melodies. Despite considerable media acclaim, the album failed to dent the charts, and consequently Siberry's next record, 1989's *Bound by the Beauty*, reflected more commercial concerns, focusing on more direct production and succinct songwriting.

Siberry's next release was a 1992 career overview titled *Summer in the Yukon;* while comprised primarily of older material, one new cut—a drastic remix of *Bound by the Beauty*'s "The Life Is the Red Wagon"—proved revelatory, its painless transformation into a club-ready dance track revealing the true elasticity of the singer's music. As a result, 1993's *When I Was a Boy*, produced in part by Brian Eno and Michael Brook, emerged as her most eclectic and ambitious work yet, while 1995's *Maria* found the singer recording with a jazz quintet. After growing disenchanted with the compromises of remaining on a major label, in May 1996 Siberry formed her own record company, dubbed Sheeba; *Teenager*, her first self-released effort, followed a month later. —*Jason Ankeny*

Jane Siberry / 1981 / East Side Digital ✦✦
Siberry's first (low-budget) recording is her most conventional and folk-oriented, but already she is warning us that "Writers Are a Funny Breed" and is showing the offbeat perspective that will charm listeners later on. —*William Ruhlmann*

No Borders Here / 1983 / Open Air ✦✦✦✦
The sound has a new wave rock energy. The songs poke fun at "Extra Executives" as well as the artist, who muses that she'd probably be famous by now if she weren't such a good waitress. —*William Ruhlmann*

The Speckless Sky / 1985 / Open Air ✦✦✦

The Walking / Jul. 1988 / Reprise ✦✦✦

Bound by the Beauty / Aug. 1989 / Reprise ✦✦✦
Siberry has by now mastered an ability to make her unorthodox song forms (changing time signatures, surprising alterations of melody) work for her, and she's struck a balance between revealing too much and too little in her lyrics, so that such songs as "The Life Is the Red Wagon" really do reveal all the levels she's given it. And "Everything Reminds Me of My Dog" is one of the funniest and best songs of the year. —*William Ruhlmann*

When I Was a Boy / Aug. 3, 1993 / Reprise ✦✦✦✦
Considering the three-year delay since her last release (which reportedly saw one completed album scrapped altogether), Siberry has obviously gone through some intense soul searching to determine where her muse was to take her next. Judging by *When I Was A Boy*, she ended up retreating to some neutral ground that drew on several elements of her previous work without really taking things anywhere new. This is a very personal, introspective album, its intimate textures consistent with the ambient work that production collaborators Brian Eno and Michael Brook are well known for. Even average Siberry is still better than most of what gets foisted on the public as female vocalist pop these days. It's just that one has come to expect more from her—like surprises and wonder—rather than the sound of treading water. —*Roch Parisien*

● **A Collection 1984-1989** / 1994 / Duke/MCA ✦✦✦✦
This collection doesn't shy away from Jane Siberry's more extended, difficult, but ultimately rewarding work found on *The Walking*. Otherwise, this 14-track compilation gathers all the most accessible Duke Street-period material produced by a very unique vocalist—from "Mimi on the Beach" and "The Waitress" to "Bound by the Beauty." Missing in action: anything from her debut indie release or *When I Was a Boy*. —*Roch Parisien*

Maria / Aug. 29, 1995 / WEA ✦✦✦

Teenager / Oct. 15, 1996 / Koch International ✦✦✦
Appropriately, *Teenager* is comprised entirely of material Jane Siberry wrote as a teen and recorded as an adult. While the songs aren't quite as accomplished as her later work, it's nevertheless surprisingly engaging—it's quite melodic, and the songs often have a bright, innocent quality that is quite refreshing in light of the somberness of much of her later work. Still, these are subtle differences that only the most devoted fans will be able to hear, and those are the fans who will cherish *Teenager* the most. —*Thom Owens*

Silkworm

f. 1987, Seattle, WA
Indie Rock
The noisy, bracing Seattle-based post-punk unit Silkworm formed in their native Missoula, MT, in 1987. Originally comprised of vocalists/guitarists Andy Cohen and Joel Phelps, vocalist/bassist Tim Midgett, and drummer Ben Koostra, Silkworm rose from the ashes of the band Ein Heit; a prolific and eclectic group from their inception (everyone but Koostra, who exited in 1989, contributed to songwriting duties), they issued their debut cassette *Advantage* in 1988. After two more tapes, 1989's *Girl Harbrr* and its companion *Girl Harbrr Out-Takes* EP, the remaining trio moved to Seattle in the opening weeks of 1990, quickly recruiting drummer Michael Dahlquist to complete the lineup.
    Silkworm's "official" debut *L'ajre* followed in 1992, spotlighting the band's evolving, dissonant sound, anchored in Midgett's propulsive bass work. After the following year's *...his absence is a blessing* EP, the quartet signed to the C/Z label for 1994's *In the West*, recorded by fellow Montana native Steve Albini (who continued to oversee the majority of the group's work). After 1994's strong *Libertine*, Phelps left the band, resurfacing in 1996 under the name Joel R.L. Phelps with the solo effort *Warm Springs Night*. As a trio, Silkworm signed to Matador and in 1996 issued *Firewater*, a sprawling yet finely honed set that ranked as their finest record to date. *Developer* followed in 1997. —*Jason Ankeny*

In the West / Jan. 25, 1994 / C/Z ✦✦✦✦

Libertine / Aug. 26, 1994 / El Recordo ✦✦✦
● **Firewater** / Feb. 20, 1996 / Matador ✦✦✦✦
Developer / Apr. 8, 1997 / Matador ✦✦✦✦

The Silos

f. 1985, New York, NY
Alternative Pop-Rock, Roots-Rock, Folk-Rock
Guitarists/vocalists Walter Salas-Humara and Bob Rupe were active on the Florida music scene as members of the Vulgar Boatmen and the Bobs, respectively, but after moving to New York within several months of one another, they decided to form the Silos. The two added violinist Mary Rowell and used several session musicians to record the album *About Her Steps*, which they released and distributed themselves on their Record Collect label. Their raw, catchy, melodic brand of folk-rock drew favorable notices from critics and comparisions to R.E.M., the Velvet Underground, and the Byrds. After another self-released album, *Cuba*, the Silos were signed to RCA in 1989, after which Rowell left the group. *The Silos* came out the following year, but the group's A&R rep left the label and the album fizzled. Rupe departed in 1991, while Salas-Humara continued to record for small independent labels under the Silos name, occasionally with Rowell. He has also recorded a solo album (*Lagartija*) with the Setters. Rupe, meanwhile, appeared on Gutterball's 1993 debut and played bass for Cracker on their 1994 tour. —*Steve Huey*

About Her Steps / 1985 / Record Collect ✦✦✦
● **Cuba** / 1987 / Watermelon ✦✦✦✦
One of the great independent-label rock albums of the late '80s, it's decidedly American, anthemic, personal car music. —*Robert Gordon*

The Silos / Feb. 1990 / RCA ✦✦✦✦
Well-crafted and smooth, it lacks the punch of *Cuba*. —*Robert Gordon*

Hasta La Victoria! / 1993 / Watermelon ✦✦

Susan Across the Ocean / Mar. 15, 1994 / Watermelon ✦✦✦

Silver Apples

f. 1967, New York, NY
Psychedelic, Proto-Punk
Decades after their brief yet influential career, the Silver Apples remain one of pop music's true enigmas: a surreal, almost unprecedented duo. Their music explored interstellar drones and hums, pulsing rhythms, and electronically generated melodies years before similar ideas were adopted in the work of acolytes ranging from Suicide to Spacemen 3 to Laika. The Silver Apples formed in New York in 1967 and comprised percussionist Danny Taylor and lead vocalist Simeon, a bizarre figure who played an instrument also dubbed the Simeon, which (according to notes on the duo's self-titled 1968 debut LP) consisted of "nine audio oscillators and 86 manual controls... The lead and rhythm oscillators are played with the hands, elbows, and knees, and the bass oscillators are played with the feet." Although the utterly uncommercial record—an ingenious cacophony of beeps, buzzes, and beats—sold poorly, the Silver Apples resurfaced a year later with their sophomore effort, *Contact*, another delirious collection that fared no better than its predecessor. After the record's release, the duo seemingly vanished into thin air, perhaps returning to the alien world from whence they purportedly came; however, in 1996 the Silver Apples mysteriously resurfaced, as Simeon and new partner Xian Hawkins released the single "Fractal Flow." —*Jason Ankeny*

Silver Apples / 1968 / Kapp ✦✦✦✦
Contact / 1969 / Kapp ✦✦✦✦
● **Silver Apples/Contact** / 1994 / TRC ✦✦✦✦
As this two-fer collecting the duo's 1968 eponymous debut and 1969's *Contact* amply proves, the Silver Apples' music remains visionary—decades after their original release, these unprecedented panoramas of electronic melodies, alien drones, and surreal soundscapes are breathtakingly original and eerily prescient. —*Jason Ankeny*

The Silver Jews

f. 1992
Alternative Pop-Rock, Indie Rock
Not quite a side project but not quite a full band, the Silver Jews are a "sister band" of the wonderfully sprawling, beyond-diverse group Pavement. And what a sister! The Jews' leader, D.C. Berman, is joined by Pavement's guitarist/vocalist Stephen Malkmus and percussionist Bob Nastanovich, creating a sound that's definitely homespun, sometimes lighthearted, and other times emotional. Countrified ballads rest comfortably alongside experimental noise-fests on the group's two releases, 1993's *The Arizona Record* EP and 1994's *Starlite Walker*. Not surprisingly, *The Arizona Record* is a more rackety, unkempt affair than the

full-length *Starlite Walker*, which was recorded in an actual studio in Tennessee. *The Natural Bridge* followed in 1996. *—Heather Phares*

The Arizona Record [EP] / 1993 / Drag City ✦✦✦
D.C. Berman, Stephen Malkmus and Bob Nastanovich recorded this EP on a Walkman, and it sure shows. About as lo-fi, avant-garde and willfully experimental as you can get on a shoestring budget, it sounds like it was lots of fun to record. While it's not essential listening, it gives a sense of history to the group's other recordings. *—Heather Phares*

● **Starlite Walker** / Oct. 24, 1994 / Drag City ✦✦✦✦
Starlite Walker was recorded in an actual studio in Tennessee and contains lots of gorgeous pop songs penned by Berman and Malkmus. The album has an appealingly offhanded, laidback feel that gives simple but eloquent songs like "New Orleans," "Trains Across the Sea" and "Advice to the Graduate" an added intimacy and resonance. Aside from a couple of instrumentals, *Starlite Walker* is filled with enjoyable, folky-countrified pop that improves with each listen. *—Heather Phares*

The Natural Bridge / Oct. 1, 1996 / Drag City ✦✦✦

Silverchair

f. 1992, Newcastle, Australia
Alternative Pop-Rock, Post-Grunge
The Australian grunge band Silverchair quickly rose to international stardom in 1995 with their debut album, *Frogstomp*. Sounding like a bastard offspring of Nirvana and Pearl Jam, Silverchair gained more notoriety for their age than their music—at the time they released *Frogstomp*, they were 15 years old.

Originally called the Innocent Criminals, Silverchair was formed in 1992 in Newcastle, Australia, by three schoolmates—guitarist/vocalist Daniel Johns, bassist Chris Joannou, and drummer Ben Gillies. Two years later, their demo tape was chosen as the winner out of 800 entries in an Australian talent contest conducted by Nomad, an Australian music television show and a local radio station, 2JJJ-FM. Included in the prize was a day in the radio's recording studio, as well as a video for their winning song, "Tomorrow." 2JJJ-FM and Nomad began playing the video before the Innocent Criminals had signed a record contract, which helped the band earn a following of fans. It also began a bidding war among Australian record labels. By the end of the year they had a deal with Murmur, a subsidiary of Sony.

Before the release of their debut single "Tomorrow" in September of 1994, the group changed their name to Silverchair; the name was derived from Nirvana's "Sliver" (which was accidentally misspelled as "Silver") and You Am I's "Berlin Chair." "Tomorrow" became a major hit in Australia, reaching No. 1; it would eventually become the country's fourth biggest-selling single ever. In January 1995, Silverchair released a second single, "Pure Massacre," which also hit No. 1. That same month, the band recorded their debut album, *Frogstomp*, in just over a week. Upon its release, *Frogstomp* became the first album to enter the Australian charts at No. 1 and it went platinum within a week; it would soon go double platinum and spend six weeks in a row at No. 1.

Silverchair's success in the United States was nearly as quick. Released in America in the summer of 1995, *Frogstomp* began climbing the US charts quickly, thanks to heavy MTV exposure and modern rock airplay for "Tomorrow." Soon, the album went platinum in America as well, and by the end of 1995, "Pure Massacre" had become a radio/MTV hit in the US.

Silverchair toured throughout the first half of 1996, recording their second album in the second half. The band returned in early 1997 with *Freak Show*, a record that received better reviews than its predecessor, yet failed to match its sales. *—Stephen Thomas Erlewine*

● **Frogstomp** / Jun. 20, 1995 / Epic ✦✦✦
Silverchair's debut album, *Frogstomp*, faithfully follows the alternative rock tradition of Nirvana and Pearl Jam, which means that the group of Australian teenagers winds up sounding not like their idols, but like Stone Temple Pilots and Bush. For their age, their instrumental capabilities are quite impressive, as the guitars and vocals growl with the force of rockers in their early twenties. At the same time, their songwriting abilities aren't as strong, and they are never able to break away from the standard grunge formula. Nevertheless, the record does deliver a collection of songs replicating the thunder of "Tomorrow." *—Stephen Thomas Erlewine*

Freak Show / Feb. 4, 1997 / Sony ✦✦✦✦
Silverchair were slaves to their influences on their debut, *Frogstomp*, but on their second album, *Freak Show*, they're beginning to show signs of developing their own style. While they may still concentrate too heavily on Pearl Jam and Nirvana, they're beginning to fuse the elements together in a more interesting way, and are writing stronger hooks. *Freak Show* still has its share of mediocre moments, and Daniel Johns should try to sing instead of scream, but the album shows potential that *Frogstomp* never did. *—Stephen Thomas Erlewine*

Simon & Garfunkel

f. 1964, New York, NY, **db.** 1970
Folk-Rock
The most successful folk-rock duo of the 1960s, Paul Simon and Art Garfunkel crafted a series of memorable hit albums and singles featuring their choirboy harmonies, ringing acoustic and electric guitars, and Simon's acute, finely wrought songwriting. The pair always inhabited the more polished end of the folk-rock spectrum, and were sometimes criticized for a certain collegiate sterility. Many also feel that Simon, as both a singer and songwriter, didn't truly blossom until he began his own hugely successful solo career in the 1970s. But the best of S&G's work can stand among Simon's best material, and the duo did progress musically over the course of their five albums, moving from basic folkrock productions into Latin rhythms and gospel-influenced arrangements that foreshadowed Simon's eclecticism on his solo albums.

Simon and Garfunkel's recording history actually predated their first mid-'60s hit by almost a decade. Childhood friends while growing up together in Forest Hills, NY, they began making records in 1957, performing (and often writing their own material) in something of a juvenile Everly Brothers style. Calling themselves Tom and Jerry, their first single, "Hey Schoolgirl," actually made the Top 50, but a series of followups went nowhere. The duo split up, and Simon continued to struggle to make it in the music business as a songwriter and occasional performer, sometimes using the names of Jerry Landis or Tico & the Triumphs.

By the early '60s, both Simon and Garfunkel were coming under the influence of folk music. When they reteamed, it was as a folk duo, though Simon's pop roots would serve the act well in their material's synthesis of folk and pop influences. Signing to Columbia, they recorded an initially unsuccessful acoustic debut (as Simon and Garfunkel, not Tom and Jerry) in 1964, *Wednesday Morning 3 A.M.* They again went their separate ways, Simon moving to England, where he played the folk circuit and recorded an obscure solo album.

The Simon & Garfunkel story might have ended there, except for a brainstorm of their producer, Tom Wilson (who also produced several of Bob Dylan's early albums). Folk-rock was taking off in 1965, and Wilson, who had helped Dylan electrify his sound, took the strongest track from S&G's debut, "Sound of Silence," and embellished it with electric guitars, bass, and drums. It got to No. 1 in early 1966, giving the duo the impetus to reunite and make a serious go at a recording career, Simon returning from the UK to the US. In 1966 and 1967 they were regular visitors to the pop charts with some of the best folk-rock of the era, including "Homeward Bound," "I Am a Rock," and "A Hazy Shade of Winter."

Simon & Garfunkel's early albums were erratic, but they steadily improved as Simon sharpened his songwriting, and as the duo became more comfortable and adventurous in the studio. Their execution was so clean and tasteful that it cost them some hipness points during the psychedelic era, which was a bit silly. They were far from the raunchiest thing going, but managed to pull off the nifty feat of appealing to varying segments of the pop and rock audience—and various age groups, not just limited to adolescents—without compromising their music. *Parsley, Sage, Rosemary and Thyme* (late 1966) was their first really consistent album; *Bookends* (1968), which actually blended previously released singles with some new material, reflected their growing maturity. One of its songs, "Mrs. Robinson," became one of the biggest singles of the late '60s after it was prominently featured in one of the best films of the period, *The Graduate* (which also had other Simon & Garfunkel songs on the soundtrack).

It was unsurprising, in retrospect, that the duo's partnership began to weaken in the late '60s. They had known each other most of their lives, and been performing together for over a decade. Simon began to feel constrained by the limits of working with the same collaborator; Garfunkel, who wrote virtually none of the material, felt overshadowed by the songwriting talents of Simon, though Art's high tenor was crucial to their appeal. They started to record some of their contributions separately in the studio, and barely played live at all in 1969, as Garfunkel began to pursue an acting career.

Their final studio album, *Bridge over Troubled Waters*, was an enormous hit, topping the charts for ten weeks, and containing four hit singles (the title track, "The Boxer," "Cecilia," and "El Condor Pasa"). It was certainly their most musically ambitious, with "Bridge over Troubled Waters" and "The Boxer" employing thundering drums and tasteful orchestration, and "Cecilia" marking one of Simon's first forays into South American rhythms. It also caught the confused, reflective tenor of the times better than almost any other popular release of 1970.

That would be their last album of new material; although they didn't necessarily intend to break up at the time, the break from recording eventually became permanent, as Simon began a solo career that brought him as much success as the S&G outings, and Garfunkel pursued simultaneous acting and recording careers. They did reunite in 1975 for a Top Ten single, "My Little Town," and have periodically performed together since without ever coming close to generating albums of new material. A 1981 concert in New York's Central Park attracted half a million fans, and was commemorated with a live album; they also toured in the early '80s, but a planned studio album was canceled due to artistic differences. —*Richie Unterberger*

Wednesday Morning 3 A.M. / Oct. 1964 / Columbia ✦✦
This is something of a folk sampler, circa 1964. Only five of the 12 songs were written by Paul Simon, and they include the mournful "He Was My Brother," which Garfunkel, in his liner notes, accurately says is "cast in the Bob Dylan mold" and has "no subtlety." But "The Sounds of Silence," here in its original acoustic version, is the first Paul Simon song in the mature sense. And the album also contains such early—'60s folk standards as Ed McCurdy's "Last Night I Had the Strangest Dream" and Bob Gibson and Hamilton Camp's "You Can Tell the World," sung in S&G's trademark tenor harmonies. A promising beginning. — *William Ruhlmann*

The Sounds of Silence / Jan. 1966 / Columbia ✦✦✦
The sudden, if belated, success of the folk-rock version of "The Sounds of Silence" as a single called for an immediate accompanying album, so Simon & Garfunkel, who had more or less disbanded after the commercial failure of *Wednesday Morning 3 A.M.,* quickly reformed and recut many of the songs Simon had recorded in England for his *Paul Simon Songbook* solo album (issued only in the UK at the time). The album did not contain the follow-up hit to "The Sounds of Silence," "Homeward Bound," but it did contain the follow-up to that, "I Am a Rock," as well as Simon's musical rewrite of Edward Arlington Robinson's poem "Richard Cory" and other songs that aspired to poetry with an earnestness that made up for their preciousness. Still, this was a rushed album (S&G would never rush again), and it shows. — *William Ruhlmann*

Parsley, Sage, Rosemary & Thyme / Sep. 1966 / Columbia ✦✦✦✦
A far more considered album than the rushed *Sounds of Silence, Parsley, Sage, Rosemary & Thyme* features "Homeward Bound" and Simon & Garfunkel's fourth hit single, "The Dangling Conversation" (their first not to be a big hit), plus a slew of memorable album tracks: "Scarborough Fair/Canticle," which became a single in the wake of its appearance in the film *The Graduate;* "The 59th Street Bridge Song (Feelin' Groovy)," which became a hit for Harpers Bizarre; and "For Emily, Whenever I May Find Her," a showcase for Garfunkel's heavenly voice, among other songs. — *William Ruhlmann*

Bookends / Mar. 1968 / Columbia ✦✦✦✦
A conceptual album about friendship and old age, *Bookends* was one of the best and most ambitious records of the 1960s. Album tracks like "America" and "Old Friends" have become Simon & Garfunkel's standards, and the LP also contains four hit singles: "Mrs. Robinson," "A Hazy Shade of Winter," "Fakin' It," and "At the Zoo" (the last two redone from their single versions.) — *William Ruhlmann*

☆ **Bridge over Troubled Water** / Feb. 1970 / Columbia ✦✦✦✦✦
The massive commercial success of *Bridge over Troubled Water*—it topped the charts for 10 weeks, won the Grammy Award for Album of the Year, included four hit singles, and has sold more than five million copies in the US—tends to exaggerate its significance in the Simon & Garfunkel catalog. Actually, it's a step down from the masterpiece of *Bookends,* containing some filler, such as the comic if slight "Baby Driver" and the pleasant if inessential live cover of the Everly Brothers' "Bye Bye Love"; it also lacks the previous album's musical and thematic unity. Still, one is admittedly splitting hairs when talking about an album that contains such classics as the title song and "The Boxer," as well as such notable tunes as "Cecilia," "El Condor Pasa," and "So Long, Frank Lloyd Wright." This is Simon & Garfunkel's most popular album because it legitimately spoke to its audience, and much of it continues to set standards in thoughtful pop music decades later. — *William Ruhlmann*

● **Greatest Hits** / Jun. 1972 / Columbia ✦✦✦✦
Although it's hardly a definitive retrospective, Simon & Garfunkel's *Greatest Hits* is a useful compilation of the group's biggest hits, featuring all of their most familiar items—"Mrs. Robinson," "The 59th Street Bridge Song," "The Sound of Silence," "Scarborough Fair," "Homeward Bound," "Bridge over Troubled Water," "Cecilia" and "The Boxer," among many others. — *Stephen Thomas Erlewine*

☆ **Collected Works** / 1981 / Columbia ✦✦✦✦✦
The three-disc box set *Collected Works* contains all of Simon & Garfunkel's studio albums, from *Wednesday Morning 3 A.M.* to *Bridge over Troubled Water.* Though this is too much material for casual fans, any serious fan of Simon & Garfunkel or folk-rock will need to acquire the set, simply because it presents the albums in their best-ever sound. The duo did record a handful of tracks that didn't make the set—and if Columbia was assembling a true "collected works" compilation, they would have to be included—but the genuinely essential material is present, making it a good buy for the budget-conscious. — *Stephen Thomas Erlewine*

Concert in Central Park / Feb. 1982 / Warner Brothers ✦✦✦✦
Simon & Garfunkel reunited on September 19, 1981, to perform a free concert in Central Park, New York City. This two-record set presents some of the duo's biggest hits in a live context and also allows listeners a chance to hear what many Simon solo numbers could sound like in S&G mode. — *William Ruhlmann*

Carly Simon

b. Jun. 25, 1945, New York, NY
Guitar, Piano, Keyboards, Vocals / Singer-Songwriter, Adult Contemporary, Soft Rock, Pop-Rock
Carly Simon was one of the most popular of the confessional singer-songwriters who emerged in the early '70s. The youngest child in an upper-class New York family (her father, Richard Simon, co-founded the Simon and Schuster publishing company), Simon got her start in music as part of a duo with her sister Lucy (who later wrote the music for the Broadway show *The Secret Garden*). The Simon Sisters had a chart single with "Winkin' Blinkin' and Nod" in April 1964. But Simon's solo debut did not come until the release of her self-titled first album in February 1971. It contained her first solo hit, "That's the Way I've Always Heard It Should Be," an anti-marriage song co-written with Jacob Brackman that reached the Top Ten. Simon's second album, *Anticipation* (November 1971) (which went gold in two years), contained a Top 40 follow-up in the title song, and she won the 1971 Grammy Award for Best New Artist. Her third album, the gold No. 1 *No Secrets* (November 1972), was produced by Richard Perry and contained the gold No. 1 hit "You're So Vain," which aroused speculation about its subject. Mick Jagger, one of those suggested, sang backup on the recording. "The Right Thing to Do," a second single from the album, made the Top 40. Simon married fellow singer-songwriter James Taylor in November 1972. (They divorced in 1983.) Her fourth album, the Top Ten *Hotcakes* (January 1974), contained a gold Top Ten remake of the Inez and Charlie Foxx hit "Mockingbird" sung with Taylor and the Top Ten hit "Haven't Got Time for the Pain"; it became her third consecutive gold LP. *Playing Possum* (April 1975), containing the Top 40 hit "Attitude Dancing," was another Top Ten LP. Simon's sixth album, *Another Passenger* (June 1976) was a relative commercial disappointment. But in 1977, she sang "Nobody Does It Better," the theme song for the James Bond film *The Spy Who Loved Me,* resulting in a gold Top Ten hit. Her seventh album, *Boys in the Trees* (April 1978), was a million-selling success, buoyed by the Top Ten hit "You Belong to Me" and a Top 40 duet cover of "Devoted to You" with Taylor. Simon's eighth and ninth albums, *Spy* (June 1979) and *Come Upstairs* (June 1980), were less successful, though the latter contained the gold Top 40 hit "Jesse."
In October 1980, Simon collapsed of exhaustion onstage, after which her concert appearances became rare. Her next album, *Torch* (September 1981), was given over to pre- and non-rock covers. In 1982, Simon scored a Top Ten UK hit with "Why," a song produced by the disco group Chic from the movie *Soup for One.* In 1983, she returned to the UK Top 40 as the uncredited singer on the "Will Powers" (Lynn Goldsmith) satire "Kissing with Confidence." Simon's career in the US was in decline, however, as the albums *Hello Big Man* (September 1983) and *Spoiled Girl* (July 1985) were poor sellers. She returned to the Top 40 in 1986 with another movie theme, "Coming Around Again," from *Heartburn* (the *Coming Around Again* LP [March 1987] went platinum) and had yet another movie-related hit with the Grammy- and Oscar-winning "Let the River Run" from the film *Working Girl* in 1988. In 1990, Simon released both *My Romance* (March), another album of pop covers, and *Have You Seen Me Lately?* (September), an album of original songs. She scored the film *This Is My Life* in 1992. In 1993, Simon's "family opera," *Romulus Hunt,* premiered and was released on record. 1994 brought the release of a new album, *Letters Never Sent* (November), and a three-CD/cassette boxed set retrospective, *Clouds in My Coffee 1965-1995,* appeared in November 1995. — *William Ruhlmann*

Carly Simon / Feb. 1971 / Elektra ✦✦✦
"That's the Way I've Always Heard It Should Be," the leadoff track of Carly Simon's first album and a Top Ten hit, in which the singer expresses reservations about getting married, benefitted from a sense of role reversal—it's such a guy sentiment, but sung by a woman in 1971, it came across as a feminist statement, consistent with the overall disillusionment so prevalent then. Nothing on the rest of the album was quite as pointed, though the other songs maintained the same ambivalence toward romance. The one other standout track, "Dan, My Fling," in which the singer tries to rekindle a relationship with a man she has discarded, was, like the single, co-written by Jacob Brackman (in this case, with Fred Gardner, not Simon), suggesting that the real creative talent here was him and not her (especially since the writing credits also featured another four names). And since Simon, with her plaintive, proper, and relatively inexpensive voice, was such an unremarkable performer, her debut seemed less auspicious than the attention it attracted might have implied. — *William Ruhlmann*

Anticipation / Nov. 1971 / Elektra ✦✦✦
Carly Simon's second album found her extending the gutsy persona she had established on her debut album, notably on the title track, "Legend in Your Own Time" (both of them hit singles), and "I've Got to Have You." The last especially suggested a frankly passionate person whose vulnerability was a source of strength, not weakness, a valuable feminist trait and one Simon would pursue in her later work. — *William Ruhlmann*

No Secrets / Nov. 1972 / Elektra ✦✦✦✦
Carly Simon's best album was also her commercial breakthrough, topping the charts and going gold, along with its leadoff single, "You're So Vain." That song set the album's saucy tone, with its air of sexually frank autobiography ("You had me several years ago / When I was still quite naive") and its reflections on the jet-set lifestyle. But Simon's honesty meant that her lyrical knife was double-edged; now that she felt she had found true love ("The Right Thing To Do," another Top Ten hit, was her celebration of her relationship with James Taylor), she was as willing to acknowledge her own mistakes and regrets as she was to point fingers. But it wasn't only Simon's forthrightness that made the album work, it was also Richard Perry's simple, elegant pop-rock production, which gave Simon's music a buoyancy it previously lacked. And Perry paid particular attention to Simon's vocals in a way that made her more engaging (or at least less grating) to listen to. — *William Ruhlmann*

Hotcakes / Jan. 1974 / Elektra ✦✦
A glowing, pregnant Carly Simon smiles out from the cover of *Hotcakes*, one of her biggest selling albums, which featured the gold single "Mockingbird," a duet with her husband James Taylor that effectively remade the old Inez and Charlie Foxx hit and bested it on the charts. The album also included another hit, "Haven't Got Time for the Pain," as well as "Misfit," in which a wife implores her carousing husband to come home, and "Think I'm Gonna Have a Baby," which celebrated the joys of same. With such tracks, *Hotcakes* was an autobiographical concept album that defined domestic bliss at a time when Simon's listeners also were catching their breath and turning inward. — *William Ruhlmann*

Playing Possum / Apr. 1975 / Elektra ✦✦✦
Though it reached the Top Ten on career momentum, Carly Simon's fifth album, *Playing Possum*, marked a creative downturn. The burst of autobiographical songwriting that had taken her from her early twenties into married life seemed to have run out, as she sang generic love songs, while Richard Perry's production gave everything an anonymous pop veneer. "Attitude Dancing" made the Top 40, and "Waterfall" and "More and More" charted, but *Playing Possum* was the album of an artist treading water, unsure of her next step. — *William Ruhlmann*

● **The Best of Carly Simon** / Nov. 1975 / Elektra ✦✦✦✦
Good collection from Simon's most popular period, including "Anticipation," "That's the Way I've Always Heard It Should Be," and "You're So Vain." — *Cub Koda*

Another Passenger / Jun. 1976 / Elektra ✦✦✦
Carly Simon tried for a fresh start on her sixth studio album, *Another Passenger*, changing to producer Ted Templeton and employing his clients the Doobie Brothers as backup musicians, along with Little Feat and other notable West Coast session players. The result was an album full of tasty licks that sometimes didn't sound much like Carly Simon. Had Elektra released "Fairweather Father" (a sufficiently cutting song that Simon felt compelled to write a sleeve note saying it didn't refer to her husband, James Taylor) or "Dishonest Modesty," a finger-pointing song in the tradition of "You're So Vain," as singles, they might have better represented the album than they did by instead releasing Michael McDonald's "It Keeps You Runnin'," which had already appeared on the Doobie Brothers' *Takin' It to the Streets*, though it had not yet become a hit for the group. For Simon, it made the singles chart but didn't ignite her usual audience or round up a new one, and her commercial appeal continued to decline. — *William Ruhlmann*

Boys in the Trees / Apr. 1978 / Elektra ✦✦✦
Her career revitalized by the success of "Nobody Does It Better," the theme from *The Spy Who Loved Me*, Carly Simon returned to record-making with this classy Arif Mardin-produced session, backed by New York's best studio players (Steve Gadd, Eric Gale, Will Lee, Richard Tee, David Sanborn, the Brecker brothers, etc.). Simon reached the Top Ten with "You Belong to Me," a collaboration with Michael McDonald that showed both off at their best, and the album's other Top 40 single was another duet with husband James Taylor on the old Everly Brothers hit "Devoted to You." Taylor also turned up writing and singing elsewhere to good effect. But what really made the album a winner was that Simon had had a couple of years to write some strong songs in her unflinching, reflective style, and she continued to explore the loves and mores of her age and class movingly. — *William Ruhlmann*

Spy / Jun. 1979 / Elektra ✦✦✦
Carly Simon was on to something, naming her album after Anais Nin's book of erotic fiction, *A Spy in the House of Love*, and she used the con-

cept to come up with songs about maintaining the passion in a long-term relationship. But she didn't follow through completely, devoting two songs (including the singles chart entry "Vengeance") to attempts to remake "You're So Vain" and returning to producer Arif Mardin and his New York jazz-pop sessioners for an inappropriately slick and overdone sound. (Whoever expected a Carly Simon album with a drum solo on it?) Commercial considerations, in other words, marred what could have been an interesting concept album and still, despite the compromises, contained several good songs. And, of course, the commercial considerations were misplaced—the album became Simon's worst seller and prefaced her departure from Elektra Records. — *William Ruhlmann*

Come Upstairs / Jun. 1980 / Warner Brothers ✦✦✦
After two albums playing jazz-pop in the style of Paul Simon's *Still Crazy After All These Years* (and with the same musicians), Carly Simon acknowledged the new wave with *Come Upstairs*, turning out her version of a power-pop album. The title track was frisky and seductive, "Take Me as I Am" was an upbeat raver, and "Them" almost sounded like Devo. Of course, that was only part of the story. Other songs changed the pace, though Simon's emotions were unusually close to the surface throughout. "James" was a final plea to her soon-to-depart husband, and "In Pain" was the brutal cry of someone who sounded like she was. But the album's highlight was "Jesse," Simon's bestwritten pop-rock song since "You're So Vain" and a Top Ten hit to boot. So why wasn't this album a bigger hit? And why isn't it out on CD? — *William Ruhlmann*

Torch / 1981 / Warner Brothers ✦✦✦
Carly Simon slightly anticipated the trend toward contemporary pop singers turning to pop standards here, singing songs like "I Got It Bad and That Ain't Good" and "Body And Soul." The theme, of course, was romantic torment, and it was expressed no better than on the final track, a new song from Stephen Sondheim's then-upcoming musical *Merrily We Roll Along* called "Not a Day Goes By" that Simon delivered with heartbreaking conviction. — *William Ruhlmann*

Hello Big Man / Sep. 1983 / Warner Brothers ✦✦✦
Hello Big Man, Carly Simon's first new studio album of original material in more than three years, followed on from her 1981 album of standards, *Torch*, and the British Top Ten success of her collaboration with Chic, "Why." Both experiences (plus, perhaps, her 1980 hit "Jesse") seemed to have reinvigorated her taste in pop music, if *Hello Big Man* was any indication. The sound was a return to the style of *Anticipation* and *No Secrets* after years of following trends, while the songs were romantic, with the erotic edge that had charged much of Simon's best material. The album was typically uneven, what with its reggae material (including a redundant cover of Bob Marley's "Is This Love"), but also typically personal and compelling. The title track was a winning account of her parents' courting, complete with a happy-ever-after ending that didn't occur in real life. — *William Ruhlmann*

Spoiled Girl / 1985 / Epic ✦✦
Leaving Warner Bros. after the relative commercial failure of *Hello Big Man*, Carly Simon moved to the Epic label, which gave her the big-budget star treatment on the appropriately named *Spoiled Girl*. No less than eight producers labored over this, and they included such heavyweights as Don Was and Phil Ramone, although everyone from disco king Arthur Baker to the team of T-Bone Wolk and G.E. Smith, late of the Hall & Oates band, got a shot. Simon's sales continued to slide, with the album topping out at No. 88, and she and Epic parted company after only one release. — *William Ruhlmann*

Coming Around Again / Mar. 1987 / Arista ✦✦✦
After the debacle that was *Spoiled Girl*, Carly Simon moved to her fourth record label, Arista, and returned to soundtrack work. This time, she wrote "Coming Around Again" for *Heartburn*, and it hit No. 18 in early 1987, her biggest hit in more than six years. That set up Simon's comeback with this album, which became her biggest hit in a decade, producing two more chart singles, "Give Me All Night" (No. 61) and "All I Want Is You" (No. 54), and went platinum. Once again, a bevy of producers—nine this time—weighed in in an attempt to vary Simon's appeal. The big difference was that this time, Simon was willing to go to her strengths as a ballad singer rather than romping amid synthesized blips. Better to flirt with retro than disco, at least as far as Simon's audience is concerned. — *William Ruhlmann*

Greatest Hits Live / Aug. 1988 / Arista ✦✦✦✦
Okay, here's the problem: In 1975, Elektra released *The Best of Carly Simon*, which compiled her hits from 1971 to 1975. Simon then scored a couple more big hits for Elektra ("Nobody Does It Better," "You Belong to Me") before leaving the label in 1979, but not enough to justify another compilation. She had another hit on Warners ("Jesse"), where she spent the early '80s, crapped out on Epic, for whom she made one album in 1985, and revived her career on Arista starting with the Top 40 hit "Coming Around Again" in 1986. That means her catalog contained one obsolete best-of, while her other hits were strewn across several labels. The solution? A live album, of course. Except that Simon had

developed stage fright. Nevertheless, she was persuaded to do one show at her Martha's Vineyard summer home, which was filmed for the HBO special and home video *Carly in Concert—Coming Around Again* and taped for the album. The set list contained the most familiar of the early-'70s hits—"You're So Vain," "Anticipation," "The Right Thing to Do"—some of the later ones—"Nobody Does It Better," "You Belong to Me," "Coming Around Again"– and some recent material. The material was well-performed, and though these were re-recordings, the album's gold-selling commercial success confirmed that Simon's fans were looking for a good career retrospective and willing to settle. *— William Ruhlmann*

My Romance / Mar. 1990 / Arista ✦✦✦
On her second album of pop standards, Carly Simon was a little less interested in the lovelorn songs that had filled 1981's *Torch*, although she did soldier through "By Myself" and "When Your Lover Has Gone." For the most part, the theme was romantic, with classics like "My Funny Valentine" and "Bewitched" handled in Simon's sexy, plaintive style. Okay, she was no Peggy Lee, but she wasn't bad. *— William Ruhlmann*

Have You Seen Me Lately? / Sep. 1990 / Arista ✦✦✦
Have You Seen Me Lately? was Simon's first studio album of original material in three and a half years. Simon has always written songs for her age group; here, it's the fortysomethings of the 1990s. "I've been doing a lot of thinking/About growing older and moving on," she sings, and in her world that entails "protein shakes," "twelve-step groups," and stays in clinics. Some relief is provided in the single "Better Not Tell Her" and "Fisherman's Song," on which Simon duets with Judy Collins. But you can't help thinking that the ongoing life story portrayed in Simon's songs has become somewhat limited. At the end, "We Just Got Here" provides the summer's-end metaphor for middle age, and we are left with the impression that there's nothing ahead but cold weather. *— William Ruhlmann*

This Is My Life / Apr. 14, 1992 / Qwest ✦✦
Singing on soundtracks had been very good for Carly Simon, who scored four chart hits with movie themes between 1977 and 1989, so it's surprising she never did a full score until this, Nora Ephron's directorial debut about a single mother who becomes a standup comic. (Ephron had written the screenplay for *Heartburn*, which featured Simon's comeback hit, "Coming Around Again.") Simon contributed five light songs and some instrumentals in what for her was an unusually relaxed, playful style. In retrospect, maybe she wishes she'd waited and scored Ephron's second feature, the hit *Sleepless in Seattle*, the following year. ("Love of My Life" hit No. 16 on the Adult Contemporary chart, but the album itself did not chart.) *— William Ruhlmann*

Carly Simon's Romulus Hunt: A Family Opera / 1993 / Angel ✦✦
Fitting into that category also occupied by *Paul McCartney's Liverpool Oratorio*, *Carly Simon's Romulus Hunt: A Family Opera* is a 46-minute musical about a 12-year-old upper-class boy living in New York City who tries to effect a reconciliation between his divorced parents. The music is pop-classical, and the singing is done by a cast of five. Simon certainly knows the material, and it gives her a chance to stretch musically, but it might better have been rendered as an afterschool TV-movie than as an operetta. (Simon herself appears only at the end, singing one of the songs as a bonus track.) *— William Ruhlmann*

Letters Never Sent / Nov. 1, 1994 / Arista ✦✦✦
Like many singer-songwriters of her lineage, Carly Simon has learned to stretch out her albums of new songs while still maintaining a steady release schedule. She put out eight such albums in the 1970s and another four in the '80s. But in the three and a half years between 1987's *Coming Around Again* and 1990's *Have You Seen Me Lately?*, there was a live album and an album of standards. After that, Simon released a soundtrack and a "family opera" performed largely by others. *Letters Never Sent* is her first new studio album in more than four years and only her second of the '90s. In Simon's case, though, this is a good idea. In the '70s, she tended to record too frequently, before she'd written enough strong material, resulting in uneven albums. And with *Have You Seen Me Lately?*, which was freighted with the concerns of middle age, she seemed to have written herself into a corner. *Letters Never Sent* represents a fresh start, with little reference to aging, other than a song addressed to her late mother. Rather, Simon has returned to passion as her main subject matter, confessing, "I can never be in love, I can only be in heat." She gives off that heat in many of the album's songs, though she doesn't quite fulfill the promise of the title, which implies lots of secret revelations. Instead, there are mostly generalized songs of romance, delivered by Simon with a large cast of supporting players, including her children, a niece, and seemingly every musician who played on previous Simon albums. It's an unusually coquettish performance for a woman of 49, and practically weightless. *— William Ruhlmann*

Clouds in My Coffee 1966-1996 / Nov. 7, 1995 / Arista ✦✦✦
Rather than focusing on hits and other material most beloved by fans, retrospectives compiled by the artists themselves tend to reflect per-

sonal favorites, overbalanced with more recent material. By organizing this three-disc set into three different, non-chronological collections, Carly Simon partially defeats those tendencies. The first disc, "The Hits," performs the valuable function of bringing together most of her biggest singles, previously spread across many records on many labels. The second disc, "Miscellaneous & Unreleased," seems aimed at the collector. And the third, "Cry Yourself to Sleep," is the best-intentioned one of all—though perceived as a singles artist, Simon has written some of her best and most personal music on isolated album tracks. However, her choices frequently are not the best songs in her catalog; what is included is good stuff—it's just that a box set can offer the opportunity to provide an alternate view of an artist who may have been misjudged, as Carly Simon has, and that opportunity has been missed. *—William Ruhlmann*

Paul Simon (Paul Frederick Simon)
. . . .
b. Oct. 13, 1941, Newark, NJ
Guitar, Vocals / Singer-Songwriter, Adult Contemporary, World Beat, Soft Rock, Folk-Rock, Pop-Rock
In a career dating back to the 1950s, Paul Simon has established himself among the best and most popular songwriters of the rock era. Growing up in Queens, NY, Simon befriended schoolmate Art Garfunkel, who had an angelic tenor voice, and the two teamed up as Tom and Jerry, taking the names of the cartoon characters. In the winter of 1957-58, they scored a chart hit with "Hey Schoolgirl"; both were 16 years old.

Simon continued to try to score hits in the late '50s and early '60s, reaching the charts briefly in 1962 in the group Tico and the Triumphs with "Motorcycle" and under the name Jerry Landis in 1963 with "The Lone Teen Ranger." He and Garfunkel teamed up again as a folk duo in Greenwich Village, signed to Columbia Records, and released *Wednesday Morning 3 A.M.* (October 1964). The album flopped initially, but Simon, who had been spending a lot of time in England, was picked up as a solo artist by CBS [UK] and recorded *The Paul Simon Song Book*, released only in Great Britain in the spring of 1965.

In the wake of the folk-rock trend prevalent that year, producer Tom Wilson took the acoustic track "The Sounds of Silence" from the *Wednesday Morning* album, overdubbed electric guitar, bass, and drums, and released the result as a single in October 1965, a full year after the album's release. It took off and hit No. 1, establishing Simon and Garfunkel.

For the next five years, they were one of the most successful acts in pop music. Simon wrote the songs, and the two harmonized on a series of hit singles and albums. They split up in 1970, after the release of their most popular album, *Bridge over Troubled Water*.

Simon returned to solo work with *Paul Simon* (January 1972), which could not hope to match the success of *Bridge*, but which did sell a million copies and feature the reggae-tinged Top Ten single "Mother and Child Reunion." *There Goes Rhymin' Simon* (May 1973) was another million-seller, containing the hits "Kodachrome" and "Loves Me like a Rock." After a 1974 live album, Simon released *Still Crazy After All These Years* (October 1975), which topped the charts, won the Grammy for Album of the Year, and included the No. 1 hit "50 Ways to Leave Your Lover."

Simon took his time following this success, though he did release a greatest hits album featuring a new hit, "Slip Slidin' Away," and contributed to a remake of "What a Wonderful World" with Garfunkel and James Taylor. Moving to Warner Bros. Records, he wrote and starred in the film *One Trick Pony* (August 1980), the soundtrack of which contained the Top Ten hit "Late in the Evening."

Another three years passed before Simon returned with *Hearts and Bones* (October 1983), which did not match his usual level of commercial success. Simon experimented with songwriting styles and became interested in South African music, resulting in *Graceland* (August 1986), which became his biggest selling solo album and won him another Album of the Year Grammy. Four years later, he delivered *The Rhythm of the Saints* (October 1990), which did for Brazilian music what *Graceland* had done for South African music and was another multi-platinum seller. Simon played a free concert in Central Park in August 1991 (ten years after Simon and Garfunkel had done one) and released a live album from the show. In 1993, Warner Bros. released a boxed set retrospective on Simon's career, and he undertook a tour that featured Garfunkel on their old hits, as well as covering other aspects of his career. *— William Ruhlmann*

The Paul Simon Song Book / May 1965 / CBS ✦✦✦✦
After the initial commercial failure of Simon & Garfunkel's *Wednesday Morning 3 A.M.*, Paul Simon moved to England and cut his debut solo album, *The Paul Simon Song Book*. Containing 12 originals, the record not only established him as a major songwriting talent but also formed the core of Simon & Garfunkel's mid-'60s repertoire; "A Church Is Burning," a meditation on the racially motivated bombing of a Birmingham, Alabama church, was the only song not done, before or since, by the

duo. Of course, it is impossible to hear these versions without thinking of the later ones—"I Am a Rock," the leadoff track, may make more sense lyrically when sung alone, but somehow it sounds more stark and harsh without Garfunkel. Nevertheless, the solo versions are given much the same arrangements, and they confirm Simon's remarkable musical ability, suggesting a kind of alternative career path and demonstrating that he would have found an audience and given them much the same material anyway. — *William Ruhlmann*

☆ **Paul Simon** / Jan. 1972 / Warner Brothers ✦✦✦✦✦
If any musical justification were needed for the breakup of Simon and Garfunkel, it could be found on this striking collection, Paul Simon's post-split debut. From the opening cut, "Mother and Child Reunion" (a Top Ten hit), Simon, who had snuck several subtle musical explorations into the generally conservative S&G sound, broke free, heralding the rise of reggae with an exuberant track recorded in Jamaica for a song about death. From there, it was off to Paris for a track in South American style and a rambling story of a fisherman's son, "Duncan" (which made the singles chart). But most of the album had a low-key feel, with Simon on acoustic guitar backed by only a few trusted associates (among them Joe Osborn, Larry Knechtel, David Spinoza, Mike Manieri, Ron Carter, and Hal Blaine, along with such guests as Stefan Grossman, Airto Moreira, and Stephane Grappelli), singing a group of informal, intimate, funny, and closely observed songs (among them the lively Top 40 hit "Me and Julio Down by the Schoolyard"). It was miles removed from the big, stately ballad style of "Bridge over Troubled Water" and signaled that Simon was a versatile songwriter as well as an expressive singer with a much broader range of musical interests than he had previously demonstrated. You didn't miss Art Garfunkel on *Paul Simon*, not only because Simon didn't write Garfunkel-like showcases for himself, but because the songs he did write showed off his own, more varied musical strengths. — *William Ruhlmann*

There Goes Rhymin' Simon / May 1973 / Warner Brothers ✦✦✦✦
Retaining the buoyant musical feel of *Paul Simon*, but employing a more produced sound, *There Goes Rhymin' Simon* found Paul Simon writing and performing with assurance and venturing into soulful and R&B-oriented music. Simon returned to the kind of vocal pyrotechnics heard on the Simon and Garfunkel records by using gospel singers. On "Loves Me like a Rock" and "Tenderness" (which sounded as though it could have been written to Art Garfunkel), the Dixie Hummingbirds sang prominent backup vocals, and on "Take Me to the Mardi Gras," the Reverend Claude Jeter contributed a falsetto part that Garfunkel could have handled, though not as warmly. For several tracks, Simon traveled to the Muscle Shoals Sound Studios to play with its house band, getting a variety of styles, from the gospel of "Loves Me like a Rock" to the Dixieland of "Mardi Gras." Simon was so confident that he even included a major ballad statement of the kind he used to give Garfunkel to sing: "American Tune" was his musical State of the Union, circa 1973, but this time Simon was up to making his big statements in his own voice. Though that song spoke of "the age's most uncertain hour," *Rhymin' Simon* was mainly a collection of largely positive, optimistic songs of faith, romance, and commitment, concluding, appropriately, with a lullaby ("St. Judy's Comet") and a declaration of maternal love ("Loves Me like a Rock")—in other words, another mother and child reunion that made *Paul Simon* and *There Goes Rhymin' Simon* bookend masterpieces Simon would not improve upon (despite some valiant attempts) until *Graceland* in 1986. — *William Ruhlmann*

Live Rhymin' / Feb. 1974 / Warner Brothers ✦✦✦
One thing Simon and Garfunkel never did much of was tour, so a Paul Simon solo tour, following two commercially successful solo albums, was one more way for Simon to distance himself from the duo and, simultaneously, by performing songs like "The Boxer" and "Homeward Bound," to reclaim his songwriting catalog. Reflecting the musical explorations he had pursued since S&G, Simon brought along Brazilian group Urubamba and gospel group the Jessy Dixon Singers. The result wasn't perfect: Nobody needed to hear "Jesus Is the Answer" (a Dixons' spotlight number) on a Paul Simon album, and if it was inevitable that he would try his own version of "Bridge over Troubled Water," it was also predestined that he wouldn't come near to matching Garfunkel's original. Though the album was, like most live albums, artistically redundant (there was nothing new, and none of the live versions improved upon the studio ones), it served as a career statement and it had a marketing function, buying the relatively slow-working Simon time between new studio releases. (Simon completists should note that, as in all live performances of "The Boxer," Simon sings the extra verse [beginning "Now the years are rolling by me"] not included on the Simon and Garfunkel studio version.) — *William Ruhlmann*

Still Crazy After All These Years / Oct. 1975 / Warner Brothers ✦✦✦✦
Replacing the guitar with the piano as the primary instrument, Simon produced a quiet, introspective Grammy-winning album centering around lost love. Simon reunites with Garfunkel on "My Little Town," a track that sounds nothing like old S&G songs. *Still Crazy* doesn't really

resemble Simon's two previous albums; it is a serious, somber album with none of the light touches present on *Paul Simon* and *Rhymin' Simon*. — *Stephen Thomas Erlewine*

One Trick Pony [O.S.T.] / Aug. 1980 / Warner Brothers ✦✦✦
Though released to coincide with the film *One Trick Pony*, which Paul Simon wrote and starred in, the *One Trick Pony* album is not a soundtrack—at least, not exactly. If it were, it might contain the Simon song "Soft Parachutes" and other non-Simon music featured in the movie. Instead, this is a studio album containing many of the movie songs; the closest thing to a band album Simon ever made, it contains some of his most rhythmic and energetic singing. But it is also his most uneven album, simply because the songwriting, with the exception of the title song and the ballads "How the Heart Approaches What It Yearns" and "Nobody," is not up to his usual standard. Maybe he was too busy writing his screenplay to polish these songs to the usual gloss. In any case, though the album spawned a Top Ten hit in "Late in the Evening" and may have sold more copies than the film did tickets, it remained a disappointment in both artistic and commercial terms. — *William Ruhlmann*

Collected Works / 1981 / Columbia ✦✦✦✦
Like the identically titled Simon and Garfunkel boxed set released at the same time, Paul Simon's *Collected Works* was what it claimed to be: A five-LP set reissue containing *The Paul Simon Song Book* (in its first and only US release), *Paul Simon*, *There Goes Rhymin' Simon*, *Live Rhymin'/Paul Simon in Concert*, and *Still Crazy After All These Years*. The *Song Book*, containing solo Simon versions of songs that turned up on the first three Simon and Garfunkel albums, remained an interesting curiosity and *Live Rhymin'* remained an entertaining tour souvenir, but the heart of the matter was Simon's three 1970s studio albums, which constituted some of the most accomplished pop music of the period. By the time this set was released, Simon had decamped Columbia for Warner Brothers Records, and when the CD era dawned and his catalog followed him, *Collected Works* went out of print. — *William Ruhlmann*

Hearts and Bones / Oct. 1983 / Warner Brothers ✦✦✦✦
Hearts and Bones was a commercial disaster, the lowest-charting new studio album of Paul Simon's career. It is also his most personal collection of songs, one of his most ambitious, and one of his best. It retains a personal vision, one largely devoted to the challenges of middle-aged life, among them a renewed commitment to love; the title song is a notable testament to new romance, while "Train in the Distance" reflected on romantic discord. Elsewhere, "The Late Great Johnny Ace" was his meditation on John Lennon's murder and how it related to the mythology of pop music. Musically, Simon moved forward and backward simultaneously, taking off from the jazz fusion style of his last two albums into his old loves of doo wop and rock 'n' roll while also incorporating current sounds with such new collaborators as dance music producer Nile Rodgers and minimalist composer Philip Glass. The result was Simon's most impressive collection in a decade, and the most underrated album in Paul Simon's catalog. — *William Ruhlmann*

☆ **Graceland** / Aug. 1986 / Warner Brothers ✦✦✦✦✦
With *Graceland*, Paul Simon hit on the idea of combining his always perceptive songwriting with the little-heard mbaqanga music of South Africa, creating a fascinating hybrid that re-enchanted his old audience and earned him a new one. It is true that the South African angle (including its controversial aspect during the apartheid days) was a powerful marketing tool and that the catchy music succeeded in presenting listeners with that magical combination: something they'd never heard before that nevertheless sounded familiar. As eclectic as any record Simon had made, it also delved into zydeco and conjunto-flavored rock 'n' roll while marking a surprising new lyrical approach (presaged on some songs on *Hearts and Bones*); for the most part, Simon abandoned a linear, narrative approach to his words, instead drawing highly poetic ("Diamonds on the Soles of Her Shoes"), abstract ("The Boy in the Bubble"), and satiric ("I Know What I Know") portraits of modern life, often charged with striking images and turns of phrase torn from the headlines or overheard in contemporary speech. An enormously successful record, *Graceland* became the standard against which subsequent musical experiments by major artists were measured. — *William Ruhlmann*

● **Negotiations and Love Songs 1971-1986** / Oct. 1988 / Warner Brothers ✦✦✦✦
Paul Simon replaced his earlier compilation, *Greatest Hits, Etc.* (1977), with this new one, allowing *Hits* to go out of print. Fans may well wish that he had simply put together a *Greatest Hits, Etc., Volume II* instead, however, since this is a case of a 16-track album covering 15 years replacing a 14-track album covering five years while containing nine of the same songs. All the major hits have been retained (though "Mother and Child Reunion" and "Loves Me like a Rock" each have been shortened by 15 seconds), along with some of Simon's odd album track choices, such as "Have a Good Time." From the post-1977 period, we have the 1980 Top Ten hit "Late in the Evening," three selections from the underrated *Hearts and Bones*, and two from *Graceland*. (The origi-

nal double-LP version of *Negotiations and Love Songs* contained a third, the Grammy Record of the Year-winning title song, but the in-print CD and cassette versions do not.) The result is more sampler than compilation. An artist of Simon's calibre is difficult to condense, and most of the tracks here are worthy, but as a single-album career retrospective, this could have been better. — *William Ruhlmann*

The Rhythm of the Saints / Oct. 1990 / Warner Brothers ✦✦✦✦
Though he recorded the album's prominent percussion tracks in Brazil, Paul Simon fashioned *The Rhythm of the Saints* as a deliberate follow-up to the artistic breakthrough and commercial comeback that was South Africa-tinged *Graceland*. Several of the musicians who appeared previously were back, along with some of the New York session players who had worked with Simon in the 1970s, and the overall sound was familiar to fans of *Graceland*. Further, Simon's nonlinear lyrical approach was carried over: He continued to ruminate about love, aging, and the onslaught of modern life in disconnected phrases and images that created impressions rather than telling straightforward stories. But where *Graceland* had seamlessly merged its styles into an exuberant whole, *The Rhythm of the Saints* was less well-digested. Those drum tracks never seemed integrated effectively into what had been dubbed over them; at the same time, they tended to lock the songs into musical patterns that reined them in from the kind of excitement the South African music on *Graceland* generated and made the melodies harder to grasp. At the same time, Simon sang his lyrics in a less involved way, which sometimes made them seem like collections of random lines rather than the series of striking observations *Graceland* seemed to contain. No Paul Simon album could be lacking in craft or quality, and *The Rhythm of the Saints* was a typically tasteful effort. But this time around, Simon hadn't quite succeeded in bringing the wide-ranging elements together; the album sold about half as many copies as *Graceland* (that is to say, a none-too-shabby two million), and that's about right—where *Graceland* was an exotic adventure, *The Rhythm of the Saints* was more of an anthropology lesson. — *William Ruhlmann*

Paul Simon's Concert in the Park, August 15, 1991 / Nov. 1991 / Warner Brothers ✦✦✦✦
Ten years after playing a concert in Central Park with Art Garfunkel, Paul Simon returned, backed by the New York session musicians and the native musicians from South Africa and Brazil who had enlivened his solo work. The show was filmed and recorded, and the audio release was a 23-track double-disc set running nearly two hours. Half the selections came from his *Graceland* and *The Rhythm of the Saints* albums, but unlike the Graceland Tour of 1987, the Born at the Right Time Tour of 1991 made room for Simon's earlier solo work as well as a few Simon & Garfunkel songs. Simon made such stylistically various material work together by front-loading the set with the newer stuff and rearranging the older solo stuff, so that "Kodachrome," for example, was refitted with a guitar line courtesy of *Graceland* player Ray Phiri. (Wisely, except for a becalmed Africanization of "Cecilia," Simon didn't monkey with the S&G songs, most of which came at the end of the set.) But Simon also toned down the Brazilian percussion that had dominated the *Saints* material and sang it more convincingly, so that "Born at the Right Time," for example, was more effective than it had been in its studio version. On the whole *Concert in the Park* managed to be an enjoyable and cohesive career summary. — *William Ruhlmann*

1964-1993 / Sep. 28, 1993 / Warner Brothers ✦✦✦
Artist-designed boxed set retrospectives tend to be idiosyncratic, and this one is no exception. Take the title, which describes a 52-track, 200+-minute, three-disc set, the earliest recording from which actually was released in 1957 (that's Tom and Jerry's duet single, "Hey, Schoolgirl") and which contains no recordings from 1964 or from later than 1991. While Simon has included all of his biggest solo hits and most of those by Simon & Garfunkel (excepting "Homeward Bound" and "I Am a Rock"), and has grouped the songs into three roughly chronological sections (1957-1973, 1973-1983, and 1986-1991), within each section he has made song choices and sequencing decisions more reflective of his own taste than any historical or audience-based consideration. The music is so good it almost doesn't matter, but with only one previously unreleased song (a 1991 outtake from *The Rhythm of the Saints*), *Paul Simon 1964-1993* is little more than an abridged reshuffling of Simon's existing catalog, and one hopes for more from boxed sets than that. (Note also that Simon's tendency to edit his songs for use on compilations continues: "Loves Me like a Rock" is 13 seconds shorter than the version on *There Goes Rhymin' Simon*, while "50 Ways to Leave Your Lover" has lost 29 seconds from the *Still Crazy After All These Years* version.) — *William Ruhlmann*

Simple Minds

f. 1978, Glasgow, Scotland
Alternative Pop-Rock, Pop-Rock
Best known in the US for their 1985 No. 1 hit "Don't You (Forget About Me)" from the film *The Breakfast Club*, Scotland's Simple Minds have

evolved from a post-punk art-rock band influenced by Roxy Music into a grand, epic-sounding pop band along the lines of U2. The band grew out of a Glasgow punk group called Johnny and the Self-Abusers, which featured guitarist Charlie Burchill and lead singer Jim Kerr. The inaugural 1978 lineup of Simple Minds featured a rhythm section of Tony Donald on bass and Brian McGee on drums, plus keyboardist Mick McNeil; Donald was soon replaced by Derek Forbes. Their early albums leaped from one style to another, with *Life in a Day* consisting mostly of dense, arty pop songs; critical acclaim followed the darker, more experimental art-rock of *Real to Real Cacophony* and the Eurodisco of *Empires and Dance*. The group began a transition to a more accessible pop style with the albums *Sons and Fascination* and *Sister Feelings Call*, originally issued together and subsequently split up. *New Gold Dream (81-82-83-84)* became their first chart album in the US, and the tour-shy McGee quit, owing to burgeoning popularity, eventually being replaced by Mel Gaynor. Following the Steve Lillywhite-produced *Sparkle in the Rain*, Jim Kerr married Pretenders lead singer Chrissie Hynde (the two groups had toured together). After Bryan Ferry rejected the opportunity to sing "Don't You (Forget About Me)," Simple Minds almost did so as well; Kerr was dissatisfied with the song's lyrics, which he regarded as formulaic. His change of heart gave Simple Minds their only American chart-topper, and the song later became an international hit as well; however, Kerr's feelings about the song remained ambivalent, and it did not appear on the follow-up album, *Once Upon a Time*. This album went gold and reached the US Top Ten, in spite of criticism for its bombastic, over-the-top approach. A live album and the uncompromisingly political *Street Fighting Years* squandered Simple Minds' commercial momentum, however. By the time the group returned to more personal themes and its straightforward, anthemic rock on 1991's *Real Life*, personnel changes and audience loss left the group's future viability in doubt. As of 1996, Kerr and Burchill are the only remaining members. — *Steve Huey*

New Gold Dream (81-82-83-84) / Sep. 1982 / A&M ✦✦✦✦
New Gold Dream (81-82-83-84) was the first effort (after many spotty earlier releases) to exhibit a focused collection of strong songs. The material, overall, is a coolly elegant style of synth-rich dance-pop. Among the album's highlights are "Promised You a Miracle," "Glittering Prize," and the title song. — *Rick Clark*

Sparkle in the Rain / Feb. 1984 / A&M ✦✦✦✦
On *Sparkle in the Rain*, Simple Minds assembled the best songs of their career and brought in producer Steve Lillywhite (XTC, Psychedelic Furs, U2) to help articulate their vision. The result was the best album of their career, thus far. Lillywhite's sweeping cinematic soundscapes perfectly suited grand songs like "WaterFront," "Book of Brilliant Things," "Up on the Catwalk," "East of Easter," and a version of Lou Reed's "Street Hassle." "Kick Inside of Me" rocks harder than anything the band has ever done. Highly recommended! — *Rick Clark*

Once Upon a Time / Oct. 1985 / A&M ✦✦✦✦
On the wings of the popular 1985 *Breakfast Club* soundtrack hit, Simple Minds enlisted in-demand producers Jimmy Iovine and Bob Clearmountain and released the ready-made-for-American-FM-radio *Once Upon a Time*. In spite of the fact that this album generated three hits with "Alive & Kicking" (No. 3), "Sanctify Yourself" (No. 14), and "All the Things She Said" (No. 28), Simple Minds had lost the inspirational edge they had attained on *Sparkle in the Rain*. — *Rick Clark*

Live in the City of Light / May 1987 / A&M ✦✦✦
Simple Minds has a reputation as an excellent live unit, and this well-recorded 1986 set done in Paris is a testament to that fact. With the help of extra sidemen (background vocalists, computer programmer, and violinist), the band runs through a wide sampling of their best material. — *Rick Clark*

● **Glittering Prize—Simple Minds 81-92** / Oct. 1992 / A&M ✦✦✦✦
Glittering Prize falls short of being a true anthology of Simple Minds, eliminating many key tracks (not even "Glittering Prize," the song the album is named after, is included) and giving too much weight to the band's later years (an inexplicable three tracks from 1991's *Real Life* are included). Still, all the mid-'80s hits are here, including "(Don't You) Forget About Me," making its first appearance on a Simple Minds album, which will be enough for most casual fans. — *Stephen Thomas Erlewine*

Good News from the Next World / Feb. 7, 1995 / Virgin ✦✦
Appearing after the commercial failure of *Real Life*, *Good News from the Next World* managed to stir up some attention from both album and alternative rock stations. However, the record quickly faded and it's easy to see why—apart from the slick "She's a River," there is no strong single material. It's well-produced and performed, yet Simple Minds' songs just miss the mark. — *Stephen Thomas Erlewine*

Simply Red

f. 1984, Manchester, England
Dance-Pop, Adult Contemporary, Pop-Rock, Blue-Eyed Soul
The British soul-pop band Simply Red was formed in 1984 by singer

Mick "Red" Hucknall (born Michael James Hucknall, Jun. 8, 1960, Manchester, England) with three ex-members of Durutti Column, Tony Bowers (b. Oct. 31, 1952) (bass), Chris Joyce (b. Oct. 11, 1957, Manchester, England) (drums), and Tim Kellett (b. July 23, 1964, Knaresborough, England) (brass, keyboards), plus Sylvan Richardson (guitar) and Fritz McIntyre (b. Sep. 2, 1956, Birmingham, England) (keyboards). The group signed to Elektra Records and released *Picture Book* (October 1985), which featured "Money's Too Tight (to Mention)," a Top 40 cover of a 1982 R&B chart single by the Valentine Brothers, and "Holding Back the Years," a Hucknall original that topped the US charts, caused the album to go platinum, and made the group one of the major successes of 1986. *Men and Women* (March 1987), which featured two collaborations between Hucknall and soul songwriter Lamont Dozier, was less popular, though it generated the Top 40 hit "The Right Thing." (In the UK, "Infidelity" and a cover of Cole Porter's "Ev'ry Time We Say Goodbye" also made the Top 40.) Richardson left in 1987 and was replaced by guitarist Aziz Ibrahim, who was replaced by Heitor T.P. (b. Brazil). The third album, *A New Flame* (February 1989), went gold due to the cover of the 1972 Harold Melvin and the Blue Notes' hit "If You Don't Know Me By Now" that hit No. 1 and became a gold single. (In the UK, "It's Only Love" and "A New Flame" also made the Top 40.) By the time of the fourth album, *Stars* (September 1991), Bowers and Joyce had left, with Shaun Ward joining on bass and Gota on drums, and saxophonist Ian Kirkham had become a permanent member. *Stars* was a relative commercial disappointment in the US (though it spawned Top 40 hits in "Something Got Me Started" and "Stars" and eventually went gold), but it became a major success elsewhere, especially in the UK, where it was the best-selling album of 1991, topped the charts for 19 weeks, and spawned the Top Ten hits "Stars" and "For Your Babies" and the Top 40 hits "Something Got Me Started," "Thrill Me," and "Your Mirror." Worldwide, it had sold 8.5 million copies by the second quarter of 1993. Ward and Gota were gone by the release of Simply Red's fifth album, *Life* (October 1995), leaving a lineup of Hucknall, McIntyre, Heitor T.P., Kirkham, and backup singer Dee Johnson. The album again proved more of a success at home than in America, topping charts all over Europe, as did its leadoff single, "Fairground," while spending only three months in the US charts. — *William Ruhlmann*

Picture Book / 1985 / Elektra ✦✦✦✦
The band finds a steady R&B groove reminiscent of 60s Stax house band The MG's, and, as with The MG's, it's all in the service of a big-voiced soul singer, in this case a British redhead. Features the US No.1 "Holding Back the Years" and the UK Top 20 "Money's Too Tight (To Mention)." — *William Ruhlmann*

Men & Women / 1987 / Elektra ✦✦✦
After a monster debut, Simply Red's follow-up album simply didn't get the job done. It wasn't a half-hearted effort; Mick Hucknall's crackling vocals were just as exuberant, and the band's Stax/Volt-influenced lines were effectively played. The songs, however, were an uneven batch and lacked the kind of standout single Hucknall had enjoyed on the previous album with "Holding Back The Years." They did turn in an interesting version of "Ev'ry Time We Say Goodbye." — *Ron Wynn*

A New Flame / 1989 / Elektra ✦✦✦✦
Although Hucknall tries to resurrect soul in his own original songs, he's most successful at evoking the past, notably on Simply Red's second No.1, a remake of the Harold Melvin & The Blue Notes classic "If You Don't Know Me by Now." — *William Ruhlmann*

Stars / Sep. 30, 1991 / East West ✦✦✦✦
Although it didn't have a single as strong as "Holding Back the Years" or "If You Don't Know Me By Now," *Stars* was Simply Red's best album since its debut. It was smoother and more polished than their previous work, while Mick Hucknall was singing better than ever and his songwriting was improving. — *Stephen Thomas Erlewine*

Life / Oct. 24, 1995 / East West ✦✦✦
For *Life*, Simply Red retain the basic influences that fueled their earlier albums, especially American R&B of the early '70s, specifically the Marvin Gaye of *What's Going On* and Harold Melvin and the Blue Notes-era Teddy Pendergrass. Mick Hucknall's singing has calmed down and smoothed out on such songs as "You Make Me Believe" and "So Many People," but that only makes them sound more like the product of Philadelphia International Records. On "Fairground," he opts for a Latin-tinged sound that ends up evoking Herb Alpert more than Milton Nascimento; reggae turns up on "Out on the Range," and the big-time closer, "We're in This Together," is a South African-style anthem, complete with Hugh Masekela's fluegelhorn. Stripped of the international superstar trappings, *Life* is, of course, pretentious, but it does have a couple of promising songs, notably "So Beautiful" and "Remembering the First Time We Made Love." — *William Ruhlmann*

● **Best of Simply Red: Holding Back the Years 1985-1997** / Oct. 22, 1996 / East West ✦✦✦✦
Best of Simply Red: Holding Back the Years 1985-1997 contains all of Simply Red's biggest British and American hits, including "Holding

Back the Years," "If You Don't Know Me By Now," and "Something Got Me Started." In addition to the well-known singles, there are two new tracks added to the collection, including "Angel," a duet with the Fugees. Simply Red always worked better on singles than albums, making this single-disc compilation an excellent introduction. — *Stephen Thomas Erlewine*

Nancy Sinatra

f. Jun. 4, 1940, Jersey City, NJ
Vocals / Pop-Rock
A pop-rock performer who leaned very heavily toward the "pop" side of that designation, Frank Sinatra's daughter Nancy enjoyed a brief run of superstardom between 1966 and 1968. Not nearly the vocalist her father is, the family name didn't hurt her advances in the business, nor did the fact that she recorded for Frank's label, Reprise. Her first few singles met with little success, and Nancy was on the verge of being dropped when she hooked up with producer Lee Hazlewood and arranger Billy Strange. They urged her to lower her voice and toughen her delivery, and crafted material emphasizing growling bass lines and "go-go" tempos. One of their first efforts, the 1966 single "These Boots Are Made for Walkin'," topped the charts, inaugurating a series of hits over the next couple years, the biggest of which were "Sugar Town," "Lightning's Girl," "Love Eyes," and her No. 1 hit duet with her father, "Somethin' Stupid." No one could advance serious claims for Nancy as a significant artist, and her unabashedly pop output was certainly at odds with the innovations setting the worlds of rock and soul afire in the psychedelic era. But they were good fun, and her best singles are still good listening, capturing the most lightweight period charm of the Top 40 of her time.

Nancy's singles were as notable for their distinctive arrangements and the odd, brooding compositions of Lee Hazlewood, who wrote most of her hits, as her own sex-kitten vocals. Specializing in oddly disquieting songs with a sort of modern Western theme, Hazlewood teamed up with Sinatra for a few duets that presented the chalk'n'cheese combination of Nancy's thin voice with Lee's gravelly, almost spoken delivery, which recalled an off-kilter Johnny Cash. The team actually managed a few hits, some of which, especially "Some Velvet Morning," rank as some of the most bizarre MOR Top 40 pop hits of all time. Nancy didn't enter the Top 40, with or without Hazlewood, after early 1968. Sundazed has embarked upon an extensive Nancy Sinatra reissue series of her original albums, though all but completists should be satisfied by her greatest hits compilations. — *Richie Unterberger*

Boots / 1966 / Sundazed ✦✦✦✦
Unexceptional debut album, built around "These Boots Are Made for Walkin'" and covers of contemporary rock and pop hits, with a couple of other Lee Hazlewood songs. The CD reissue adds a few rare early single tracks (all penned by Hazlewood) as bonus cuts, as well as the mono single version of "Boots." — *Richie Unterberger*

How Does That Grab You? / 1966 / Sundazed ✦✦✦
Sinatra's sophomore effort sticks to her usual LP formula: a hit title track, a bunch of pop covers ("Bang Bang" is the best), and some unremarkable Lee Hazlewood songs, the exception being the classy Nancy & Lee duet "Sand." Four notable bonus tracks on the CD reissue from 45s: the fuzz-guitar-driven single "Lightning's Girl" (one of her very best songs), a cover of Buffy St. Marie's "Until It's Time for You to Go," the single "The Last of the Secret Agent," and the breezy California pop duet with her father, "Feelin' Kinda Sunday." — *Richie Unterberger*

Nancy in London / 1966 / Sundazed ✦✦✦
The change of locale for Nancy's third album didn't change her approach much: it's dominated by humdrum covers of contemporary pop and rock hits and pop standards, with some second-rank Lee Hazlewood country songs thrown in, though his compositions "Friday Child" and "Summer Wine" (the second of which is a Nancy/Lee duet) are strong, moody highlights. The four bonus tracks, taken from singles, outclass the original LP: "100 Years," "You Only Live Twice" (the single version), "Tony Rome," and her cringingly dated duet with her father, "Life's a Trippy Thing." — *Richie Unterberger*

Sugar / 1967 / Sundazed ✦✦
Even major Nancy fans may find their patience taxed by this album, on which she concentrates on non-rock popular standards by the likes of Irving Berlin, complete with weak vaudevillian MOR arrangements. Highlights are the Hazlewood-penned Top Ten hit "Sugar Town," and the two CD bonus tracks, taken from singles: "Somethin' Stupid" and the dramatic, almost menacing "Love Eyes." — *Richie Unterberger*

● **The Hit Years** / 1986 / Rhino ✦✦✦✦
Contains all the essential tracks: every hit, including those with her father and with Hazlewood, and a bunch of interesting misses, such as the theme song to the James Bond film *You Only Live Twice*. Focuses mostly on material penned by Hazlewood, and has comprehensive liner notes. An Australian best-of on the Raven label, *Lightning's Girl*, has a

few more songs, but this less expensive 18-track domestic compilation covers all the key bases. —*Richie Unterberger*

Fairy Tales & Fantasies: Best of Nancy Sinatra and Lee Hazelwood / 1989 / Rhino ◆◆◆
Basically a reissue of the 1968 album *Nancy and Lee*, with some bonus tracks. Has all of the duo's hits ("Summer Wine," "Jackson," "Sand," "Lady Bird," and "Some Velvet Morning"), which easily outclass the filler material. And those hits are about as inspired as middle-of-the-road pop gets, especially the eerie "Some Velvet Morning," one of the strangest songs ever to crack the Top 40. —*Richie Unterberger*

Siouxsie & the Banshees

f. 1976, London, England, **db.** 1996
Punk, Alternative Pop-Rock, Post-Punk
Siouxsie & the Banshees were among the longest-lived and most successful acts to emerge from the London punk community; over the course of a career that lasted two decades, they evolved from an abrasive, primitive art-punk band into a stylish, sophisticated unit that even notched a left-field Top 40 hit.

Throughout their numerous lineup changes and textural shifts, the group remained under the leadership of vocalist Siouxsie Sioux, born Susan Dallion on May 27, 1958. She and the Banshees' initial lineup emerged from the Bromley Contingent, a notorious group of rabid Sex Pistols fans; inspired by the growing punk movement, Dallion adopted the name Siouxsie and formed the Banshees in September 1976. In addition to bassist Steve Severin and guitarist Marco Perroni, the band included drummer John Simon Ritchie, who assumed the name Sid Vicious; they debuted later that year at the legendary Punk Festival held at London's 100 Club, where their entire set consisted of a savage, 20-minute rendition of "The Lord's Prayer."

Soon after, Vicious joined the Sex Pistols, while Perroni went on to join Adam and the Ants. The core duo of Sioux and Severin, along with new guitarist John McKay and drummer Kenny Morris, reached the UK Top Ten with their 1978 debut single, "Hong Kong Garden"; their grim, dissonant first LP, *The Scream*, followed later in the year. Two days into a tour for their 1979 follow-up *Join Hands*, both McKay and Morris abruptly departed, and guitarist Robert Smith of the Cure (the tour's opening act) and ex-Slits and Big in Japan drummer Budgie were enlisted to fill the void; although Smith returned to the Cure soon after, Budgie became a permanent member of the group, and remained with the Banshees' throughout the duration of their career.

With ex-Magazine guitarist John McGeoch on board, the band returned to the studio for 1980's *Kaleidoscope*, a more subtle and melodic effort than their prior records; on the strength of the UK Top 20 smash "Happy Hands," the album reached the Top Five. A year later, the Banshees released the psychedelic *Juju*, along with *Once Upon a Time*, a collection of singles; at the same time, Sioux and Budgie formed the Creatures, an ongoing side project. Following 1982's experimental *A Kiss in the Dreamhouse*, McGeoch fell ill, and Smith temporarily rejoined for the group's planned tour; a pair of 1983 performances at London's Royal Albert Hall were recorded and later issued as *Nocturne*. Also in 1983, Severin and Smith teamed as the one-off project the Glove for the LP *Blue Sunshine*.

After his recovery, McGeoch opted not to return, so the Banshees recruited former Clock DVA guitarist John Carruthers after Smith exited following the sessions for 1984's dark, atmospheric *Hyaena*. With 1986's *Tinderbox*, Siouxsie and the Banshees finally reached the US Top 100 album charts, largely on the strength of the excellent single "Cities in Dust." After 1987's all-covers collection *Through the Looking Glass*, Carruthers took his leave, and was replaced by ex-Specimen guitarist Jon Klein and keyboardist Martin McCarrick for 1988's *Peep Show*, a techno-inspired outing that gave the group their first US chart single with "Peek-a-Boo."

In 1991—the year in which Sioux and Budgie married—the Banshees performed on the inaugural Lollapalooza tour; their concurrent LP, *Superstition*, was their most commercially successful, spawning their lone US Top 40 hit with "Kiss Them for Me." Another singles collection, *Twice Upon a Time*, followed in 1992 before the group returned after a long absence with 1995's stylish *The Rapture*, produced in part by John Cale. A year later, the nostalgia surrounding the reunion of their former heroes the Sex Pistols prompted Siouxsie & the Banshees to finally call it quits; Siouxsie and Budgie turned to the Creatures as their primary project, while Severin composed the score for the controversial film *Visions of Ecstasy*. —*Jason Ankeny*

The Scream / 1978 / Geffen ◆◆◆◆
By waiting until punk essentially had blown over to sign a contract, the Banshees had a clear field for their harsh rock attack, and plenty of time to prepare it. The result is this fierce debut, which fulfills the promise of punk and suggests (unlike most of its progenitors) that it has a future. —*William Ruhlmann*

Join Hands / 1979 / Geffen ◆◆
Siouxsie and the Banshees have made some wonderful albums in their time, such as *Tinderbox, Hyaena*, and *Juju*. This early release is unfortunately not one of them. The songs on this platter are almost uniformly grim, with dragging tempos, bleak lyrics, long and wandering free-form structures, static and often unfocused harmony, and thick, colorless arrangements. Siouxsie Sioux is not in her best vocal form here; much of her singing lacks punch and fire. The best selection here is "Icons," which survives an unpromising beginning to open out into a faster main section with fuller vocal sound and gutsier guitar work. The notorious number "The Lords Prayer" [sic] is a major punk landmark, featuring stream-of-consciousness lyrics that digress in every imaginable direction from the basic devotional text; regrettably, the song isn't very interesting to listen to despite its energetic instrumental playing. Another failed experiment is essayed in "Mother/Oh Mein Papa"; Sioux sings a lopsided melodic line out of sync with a music box playing the latter song of this pairing. Some of these selections appear to strongly anticipate the work of Joy Division's second album, *Closer*, especially "Placebo Effect," whose guitar sound was a clear inspiration for that of the Manchester band's song "Colony." Sound quality here is drab and squelched. Despite the group's laudable attempts to take some risks here, I cannot recommend this release. —*David Cleary*

Kaleidoscope / 1980 / Geffen ◆◆◆◆
After *Join Hands*, guitarist John McKay and drummer Kenny Morris departed the Banshees, leaving the band at a crossroads. Siouxsie Sioux and Steven Severin elected to soldier on with ex-Slits drummer Budgie and two guitarists, ex-Sex Pistol Steve Jones and John McGeoch of Magazine, as guest Banshees. Despite the personnel upheaval, the result is a surprisingly strong record. While a number of the songs here are still dark-hued and feature bleak lyrics, they are made very palatable by extraordinarily imaginative production values featuring intricate synthesizer-flecked arrangements; psychedelic touches in "Christine," spaceship synthesizer swoops in "Tenant," and rhythmic camera clicks in "Red Light" all enliven their respective songs. Sound quality here is lighter and much clearer than on previous releases. Sioux's singing shows noticeable improvement here, still tuneless at times but also exhibiting more range and subtlety than previously. The song "Hybrid," a Joy Division-style number, shows her vocals running the gamut from primitive to inspired. Other highlights include the galloping, vibrant uptempo number "Skin," the spooky and atmospheric "Lunar Camel," the medium tempo rocker "Trophy," and the punky vocalise "Clockface." This was a make-or-break album for the band, and happily they came through strongly. —*David Cleary*

● **Once Upon a Time: The Singles** / 1981 / Geffen ◆◆◆◆
This compilation of UK singles (some appearing on an album for the first time) emphasizes the more pop sound of Siouxsie and the Banshees. Still not easy listening, though. —*William Ruhlmann*

Juju / Aug. 1981 / Geffen ◆◆◆
They're shifting gradually toward a more straightforward rock sound, but the Banshees also add Middle Eastern touches here. Contains the British hits "Spellbound" and "Arabian Knights." —*William Ruhlmann*

Kiss in the Dream House / 1982 / Geffen ◆◆◆
This release shows the band backpedaling a bit from its excellently forthright predecessor *Juju* to update the more avant-garde stylings of *Kaleidoscope*. This album is in fact the Banshees' crowning glory in this experimental vein. Production and arrangements are highly varied and accomplished, and Sioux's singing by now is excellent, capable of imaginative shadings and free of its former tunelessness. "Obsession" is scored for chimes, overdubbed breathing, swallowed synthesizer sounds, strings, and very occasional guitar touches; this all supports a fine vocal with lyrics about the speaker's fixation on her object of desire. "Green Finger" is a driving, uptempo number with Joy Division melodic bass, sparkling synthesizer touches, and wacky recorder tootlings. "Painted Bird" features a full helping of multitracked vocals propelled by a drumbeat that is alternately skittering and thumping; portions of this song suggest a nightmare version of Fleetwood Mac's "Go Your Own Way." "Cocoon" is best characterized as mutant bopping jazz with an often breathy, cooing vocal. "She's a Carnival" and "Slowdive" suggest eccentric stabs at mainstream acceptance, the former being a comparatively gutsy and forthright rocker, the latter a violin-colored dance beat number with hints of New Order or David Bowie that is a catchy melodic hook away from being the real thing. This fine platter is well worth purchasing. —*David Cleary*

Nocturne / 1983 / Geffen ◆◆◆
This is a top-notch live double album recorded in 1983 at the Royal Albert Hall. Sound quality is first-rate and the band performs excellently here. The songs given on this release run a wide chronological range, from early numbers like the Lennon/McCartney cover "Helter Skelter" (here given a fire-breathing performance) to their recent single of the time (another Beatles song), "Dear Prudence." Much of the material is culled from the group's recent releases *Juju, A Kiss in the Dreamhouse*,

and *Kaleidoscope*. This platter serves as an excellent, no-nonsense introduction to the band's music for neophytes, while fans of the group will appreciate the tight, gutsy, stripped-down performances. This album is strongly recommended. —*David Cleary*

Hyaena / 1984 / Geffen ✦✦✦
Siouxsie and the Banshees' first album to benefit from a major-label push in the US (and make the charts) finds them taking a more melodic, expressive approach and even covering the Beatles' "Dear Prudence." Old fans howled, but there were a lot of new fans. —*William Ruhlmann*

Tinderbox / 1986 / Geffen ✦✦✦✦
This is the most musically uptempo of all the Banshees' albums and the most stylistically consistent one since *The Scream* and *Join Hands*. Most of the selections here feature urgently rocking drumming, drivingly aggressive yet fully textured guitar playing, and masterful, gutsy singing. The songs here are intense and unfold slowly, some starting off less vigorously but becoming hard rockers further along. There is of course a fine line between consistency and lack of contrast, but this album stays firmly on the side of the former; in fact, there's a certain satisfying feel to the musically uniform wall of sound here. The arrangements are less complex than in immediately preceding albums, but there are still plenty of subtle, effective production touches to be found throughout, most notably in the song "Cannons." "Cities in the Dust," a dance-pop number with a bell-like synthesizer opening section, stretches the above-mentioned boundaries more than, though typically bleak lyrics keep this selection from any sense of vacuity. This excellent release is well worth purchasing. —*David Cleary*

Through the Looking Glass / 1987 / Geffen ✦✦✦
Well-selected album of rock and pop cover songs, including everything from Sparks' "This Town Ain't Big Enough for Both of Us" to "Strange Fruit." —*William Ruhlmann*

Peep Show / 1988 / Geffen ✦✦✦

● **Twice Upon a Time: The Singles** / Oct. 13, 1992 / Geffen ✦✦✦✦
A good collection of singles, *Twice Upon a Time* picks up where *Once Upon a Time* left off—1981 to 1993, their more mainstream period. The albums from this time span may be too ambitious for some, but the singles shouldn't be missed. This is probably the best introduction to the band. —*Chris Woodstra*

Rapture / Feb. 1995 / Geffen ✦✦✦

The Sir Douglas Quintet

f. 1964, San Antonio, TX, **db.** 1972
Rock & Roll, Tex-Mex

Texas had always had its own brand of rock 'n' roll—a little bit o' country, a little bit o' blues, with a heapin' helpin' o' hot sauce poured over the top. Doug Sahm was no stranger to the studio when he formed the Sir Douglas Quintet in 1964; he'd been at it since the age of six, and already possessed an encyclopedic knowledge and innate understanding of those local flavors when the band cut its first big hit, "She's About a Mover."

The ingredient that set the Quintet apart was Tex-Mex, that curious, joyous, irresistible, danceable, festive feast that married the jumpy Mexican *conjunto* to good ol' rock 'n' roll. With Augie Meyers on the organ and a rhythm section that couldn't stop cookin', Sir Doug Sahm let it be known that good-time music was alive and kickin' in San Antone.

After the Quintet itself dissolved, Sahm cut numerous solo albums and collaborations, spreading the Tex-Mex influence. In the late '80s he and Meyers teamed up with two of their mentors, Freddy Fender and Flaco Jimenez, to form The Texas Tornados, keeping that high and happy sound alive. —*Jeff Tamarkin*

● **Best of the Sir Douglas Quintet** / 1980 / Takoma ✦✦✦✦
Contains the hits "She's About a Mover" and "Mendocino." Not to be confused with the similarly titled albums on Tribe, Crazy Cajun, and Mercury. —*William Ruhlmann*

Sir Doug's Recording Trip: The Mercury Years / 1988 / Edsel ✦✦✦✦
An incredible 30-song sampling of his Quintet and solo years, it features most of the hits, some rare delicacies, and an educational set of notes by Ed Ward. —*John Floyd*

● **The Best of Doug Sahm & Sir Douglas Quintet** / 1990 / PolyGram ✦✦✦✦
This is not as thorough as *Sir Doug's Recording Trip*, but it's easier to find and gives you 22 essential tracks in sterling digital fidelity. —*John Floyd*

Sir Mix-A-Lot

b. Aug. 12, 1963, Seattle, WA
Vocals / Hip-Hop, West Coast Rap

Sir Mix-A-Lot put Seattle on the rap map in the late '80s with catchy, comedic dramas drenched in b-boy culture and punctuated by his whiny vocals. Sir Mix-A-Lot vaulted into the spotlight and into controversy

with the single "Baby Got Back." Not only was it an enormous pop and R&B hit, it triggered a backlash against what was widely viewed as both sexist and racist lyrics from Mix-A-Lot in his celebration of rear ends and putdown of women who lacked them. It helped make the *Mack Daddy* album one of 1992's biggest, although 1994's *Chief Booty Knocka* and 1996's *Return of the Bumpasaurus* failed to match its success. —*John Floyd*

Swass / 1988 / Def American ✦✦✦
Sir Mix-A-Lot is one of greatest ironies in the history of rap. His occasional sociopolitical statements show he can be every bit as intelligent a commentator as KRS-One or Chuck D.—the thing is that Mix's forte has always been the type of fun, escapist, even goofy fare that dominates his debut album, *Swass*. Though forceful and aggressive at times, the distinctive Seattle native never considered himself a hardcore rapper—and is quick to point out that his influences range from quirky new waver Gary Numan to metal bands to George Clinton. Ranging from aggressive rap/metal like "Hip-Hop Soldier" and his enjoyably silly impression of hillbillies on "Square Dance Rap" and "Buttermilk Biscuits," *Swass* set the tone for Mix's career by appealing to pop fans more than hardcore rap listeners. His strongest sociopolitical raps (including "Society's Creation" and "Jack Back") would come later. —*Alex Henderson*

● **Seminar** / Mar. 1988 / Def American ✦✦✦
With his second album, Sir Mix-A-Lot continued focusing primarily on the type of material that made his first reach gold status: escapist, lighthearted pop/rap that fared well among pop, R&B and dance-music circles, but generally wasn't well-received in "the hood." What few sociopolitical songs the CD does contain are first-rate, including "The (Peek-A-Boo) Game" (which uses Siouxsie & the Banshees as a reference point) and "National Anthem." An angry number addressing the Iran-Contra scandal, the drug plague, and the plight of Vietnam vets, the latter is as powerful as anything Public Enemy, KRS-One, or Ice-T has done. Nonetheless, what made *Seminar* a hit weren't those gems, but odes to cars, gold chains, and "fly girls." As enjoyable as such escapist fare as "My Hooptie" and "Beepers" is, Mix sells himself short by not including more message songs. —*Alex Henderson*

● **Mack Daddy** / Apr. 1991 / Def American ✦✦✦✦
Sir Mix-A-Lot scored a huge sleeper hit with his ridiculous paean to large buttocks, "Baby Got Back," in the summer of 1992. For those who want it, the rest of *Mack Daddy* offers more of the same—skeletal raps that verge on the point of parody. Sir Mix-A-Lot can barely rap, and his lyrics are full of posturing tales that never have a dose of reality. But this is the very element that makes *Mack Daddy* fun, because Sir Mix-A-Lot tries so hard and sounds so silly. —*Stephen Thomas Erlewine*

Chief Booty Knocka / Jul. 19, 1994 / Rhyme Cartel ✦✦✦

Return of the Bumpasaurus / Aug. 27, 1996 / Warner Brothers ✦✦✦
Having been quite visible in the R&B and pop markets thanks to such hits as "Baby Got Back," "Beepers" and the erotic "Put Em on the Glass," Sir Mix-A-Lot had his share of detractors in hardcore rap circles—which can be every bit as rigid and dogmatic as jazz purism. The Seattleite gives his detractors a vehement tongue-lashing on his fifth album, *Return of the Bumpasaurus*, which is essentially a fun and escapist party album despite all the anger it expresses. True to form, the distinctive Mix effectively combines the hard-hitting, the gritty, and the intense with healthy pop quirkiness. Once again, he makes a mistake by not including more social or political commentary—one of his strong points. But when it comes to party songs, he still delivers the goods. —*Alex Henderson*

Sister Double Happiness

f. 1986, San Francisco, CA, **db.** 1995
Group / Blues-Rock, Hard Rock, Alternative Pop-Rock

Sister Double Happiness formed in San Francisco in 1986 and immediately became the city's favorite concert draw before even releasing their first album of over-the-top, white blues-rock.

Gary Floyd and Lynn Perko, who'd played together in the punk group the Dicks, joined with Ben Cohen (from Pop-o-Pies and Polkacide) and Mikey Donaldson on bass. The foursome recorded a self-titled album of hard-driving songs for SST in 1988, the bulk penned by Floyd and Cohen. Owing much to Floyd's Texas roots as a blues/punk belter, the band played a fiery mix of blues-inflected hard rock and punk, the likes of which were incomparable. Subject matter was primarily confined to the human condition and spirituality in the face of AIDS and urban decay. The band's promise earned them a contract with Reprise in 1991 for *Heart and Mind*, but failed to find them a wider audience. That same year the band won a Bammie (Bay Area Music Award) for Outstanding Club Band, and Jeff Palmer replaced Donaldson on bass. A Sub Pop single and two albums for the label's German arm, 1993's *Uncut* and 1994's *Horsey Water*, followed. Danny Roman was added as a guitarist, and Miles Montalbano replaced Palmer on bass. The video release, *Greetings from Zurich*, is a lasting testament to their live prowess. The band also contributed to a number of tribute albums that were popular in the early '90s paying homage to artists as diverse as Roky Erickson, Dead Kennedys, and Frank Sinatra. The band broke up in 1995—none of their recorded work ever quite captured the heat they were capable of live. Floyd immediately formed the Gary Floyd Band and records and tours, mostly in Europe. Perko is in Imperial Teen with Faith No More's Roddy Bottum, and Cohen works as a guitarist, currently with El Destroyo. —*Denise Sullivan*

Sister Double Happiness / 1988 / SST ✦✦✦✦
A blazing debut of blues/punk originals distinctive for Gary Floyd's desperate growl, guitarist Ben Cohen's fiery work, and the band's urgency. "You Don't Know Me," "Sweet Talker" and "Freight Train" sound like rock standards upon first listen. The songwriting is strong and the band come closest to capturing their raw power as an exceptional live band here than on any of their later recordings. —*Denise Sullivan*

Heart & Mind / Apr. 1991 / Reprise ✦✦✦
Good songs like "Bobby Shannon" and the reprised "Sweet Talker and "You Don't Know Me" from the first album are overshadowed by a bungled production job. Nonetheless, Sister Double Happiness retain their spunk in the face of what could have been a complete diaster. —*Denise Sullivan*

Uncut / 1993 / Dutch East ✦✦✦
Reacting to their studio experience with the major label, Sister Double Happiness were keen to get across just how hot and nasty they could be. "The Whipping Song" opens with a screaming lead, the intensity of which wasn't allowed to rip on the previous recording, and "No Good for You" epitomizes the band's ferocity. As ever, Floyd's desperation cuts to the core. —*Denise Sullivan*

Horsey Water / 1994 / Sub Pop ✦✦✦
Finally the band gets wise and go for the live-in-the-studio sound in an attempt to recreate what they had mastered in the live setting. A softer side of the band ("Waiting for Anyone") rests side by side with howling blues like "Jack Freak" and "A&R Man." Never tame, the blues-rock of Sister Double Happiness is a far cry from Stevie Ray Vaughan, but no less heartfelt. —*Denise Sullivan*

Sister Sledge

f. 1971, North Philadelphia, PA, **db.** 1985
Soul, Disco
Sisters Debra, Joan, Kim, and Kathie began recording as Sisters Sledge for Money Back in 1971. They also did numerous sessions before dropping the "s" from their first name. They collaborated with Chic for some seminal dance/soul hits in the late '70s and early '80s. Sister Sledge enjoyed two No. 1 R&B hits and two other Top Ten singles from 1979 to 1981, as well as Top Ten pop hits. Both "He's the Greatest Dancer" and "We Are Family" were international smashes, with the Pittsburgh Pirates adopting "We Are Family" as their theme song during their world championship season in 1979. "Got to Love Somebody" and "All American Girls" were also major hits. The group began producing their own singles in 1981, but ran into tough sledding in the wake of the anti-disco backlash. They began on Atco in 1974, and remained on Cotillion from 1976 to 1983. They moved to Atlantic in 1985, but were unable to regain their former glory. Kathie Sledge issued her own LP on Epic, *Heart*, in 1992. —*Ron Wynn*

We Are Family / 1979 / Rhino ✦✦✦✦
The Sledge sisters floundered in search of a format for several years before Atlantic gave them, almost in desperation, to the Chic production team. This 1979 album ended eight years of frustration and was their greatest triumph. The title track became the theme song for the world champion Pittsburgh Pirates baseball team, while Nile Rodgers' splintering guitar and Bernard Edwards' steady bass, plus the duo's production genius, garnered two huge hits for Sister Sledge in "We Are Family" and "He's the Greatest Dancer." —*Ron Wynn*

● **The Best of Sister Sledge (1973-1985)** / Sep. 1, 1992 / Rhino ✦✦✦✦
Sister Sledge evolved quite a bit during the 12 years documented on this 1992 collection, which traces the Philadelphians' evolution from bubblegum soulsters to sexy but wholesome disco-era darlings to struggling urban-contemporary act. After early numbers like "Mama Never Told Me" and "Love Don't You Go Through No Changes on Me" (both recorded at a time when the sisters were still in their teens and came across as sort of a female Jackson 5), they dive head first into disco/soul with "Cream of the Crop" (an underrated, Philly-sounding pearl) and finally hit the big time with the Chic-produced mega-hits "We Are Family" and "He's the Greatest Dancer." One hears Sledge entering the '80s on a high note with "Got to Love Somebody," but by the middle of the decade sounding less inspired on the singles "Frankie" and "Dancing on the Jagged Edge." One of the collection's most disappointing tracks is the reggae remix of "He's Just a Runaway." While it's true that this is the ver-

sion that became a medium-size hit, the more rock-ish version found on *All American Girls* packs a much greater punch. But despite a few weak spots here and there, this is a gem-laden CD that paints a generally impressive picture of the group. —*Alex Henderson*

Sisters of Mercy

f. 1980, Leeds, England
Alternative Pop-Rock, Goth Rock
One of England's leading "goth" bands of the 1980s, the Sisters of Mercy play a slow, gloomy, ponderous hybrid of metal and psychedelia, often incorporating dance beats; the one constant in the band's career has been deep-voiced singer Andrew Eldritch. (There is some disagreement as to whether the group took its name from an order of Catholic nuns or from the Leonard Cohen song of the same name.) Eldritch originally formed the band in 1980 with guitarist Gary Marx and recorded its first single with a drum machine dubbed Doktor Avalanche. Guitarist Ben Gunn and bassist Craig Adams were added to make live gigs feasible, and the Sisters built a reputation through several singles and EPs. Gunn left the band in 1983 and was replaced by Wayne Hussey. The Sisters of Mercy recorded their first full-length album, *First and Last and Always*, in 1985, but two years later, internal dissent had split them apart; Marx left to form Ghost Dance, and Adams and Hussey departed shortly thereafter. A legal dispute ensued over the rights to the name Sisters of Mercy; Adams and Hussey attempted to use the name Sisterhood, but Eldritch released an EP under the name to prevent its usage, and the two finally settled on the Mission. Eldritch chiefly utilized a corps of temporary sidemen from this point on (although former Gun Club bassist Patricia Morrison was an official member of the group for a short time) and rebounded with his two biggest-selling American LPs, *Floodland* and *Vision Thing*. He is currently the group's only member. —*Steve Huey*

First & Last & Always / 1985 / Elektra ✦✦✦
Sisters of Mercy's first full-length album didn't quite have the powerful musical vision of their early EPs, but its gloom was more focused, making it an impressive debut album. —*Stephen Thomas Erlewine*

Floodland / 1987 / Elektra ✦✦✦✦
Sisters of Mercy's second album was a monolithic slab of goth-rock, featuring a more ambitious and accomplished musical scope than the debut, along with better lyrics. —*Stephen Thomas Erlewine*

Vision Thing / Nov. 1990 / Elektra ✦✦✦✦
Guitar-based pop fueled by the bright-sounding sensibilities of ex-Generation X axeman Tony James. —*David Szatmary*

● **Some Girls Wander by Mistake** / Oct. 20, 1992 / Elektra ✦✦✦✦
Collecting a number of their better singles, *Some Girls Wander by Mistake* offers a good introduction to the Sisters of Mercy. —*AMG*

The 6ths'

f. 1994, Boston, MA
Alternative Pop-Rock, Lo-Fi
The 6ths are a side project of the Magnetic Fields' Stephin Merritt, who produced and wrote all of the material on 1995's *Wasps' Nest*, as well as playing much of the music. He only sings one of the tracks, however, giving all of the remaining lead vocal slots to alternative rock faves like Barbara Manning, Dean Wareham (Luna), Georgia Hubley (Yo La Tengo), Chris Knox, Lou Barlow, Robert Scott (the Bats), Chris Knox, and Mary Timony (Helium). Brighter and poppier than his contemporaneous efforts with Magnetic Fields, it demonstrates (intentionally or inadvertently) that his principal talents are as a producer and composer, rather than a performer. —*Richie Unterberger*

Wasps' Nests / Mar. 21, 1995 / London ✦✦✦✦
A one-of-a-kind collaborative effort, masterminded by producer/songwriter Stephin Merritt, and sung well by various cult stars of the alternative rock scene. The results are unusually successful, if a bit towards the light and precious side, mixing indie attitude with melodicism and production finesse. —*Richie Unterberger*

Skee-Lo

b. , Poughkeepsie, NY
Vocals / Hip-Hop
Skee-Lo is an anomaly in the rap world of the '90s: instead of spinning violent gangsta tales or extolling the virtues of marijuana, Skee's songs are profanity-free, good-time stories with a self-deprecating sense of humor. Skee-Lo was born in Poughkeepsie, NY, and moved to Riverside, CA, at age nine. He was turned on to rap by Kurtis Blow records, admiring their down-to-earth quality. His "I Wish" single, with a video that parodied *Forrest Gump*, became a huge hit on radio and MTV during the summer of 1995, and his identically titled debut album was released shortly thereafter. —*Steve Huey*

● **I Wish** / Jun. 27, 1995 / Sunshine/Scotti Bros. ✦✦✦✦
"I Wish" was an irresistible piece of pop-rap, featuring a slinky, funky beat and a sunny hook that rang in your head for days. It's undeniably the highlight of Skee-Lo's debut album, but he has enough charm and self-deprecating wit to make the rest of the record enjoyable, even if none of the songs neither have beats, lyrics or hooks quite as intoxicating as the title track. *— Stephen Thomas Erlewine*

Skid Row

f. 1986, New Jersey
Hard Rock, Heavy Metal, Hair Metal
Before alternative music crossed over into the mainstream, Skid Row was one of the top heavy-metal bands of the '90s, pounding out a radio-friendly mix of Bon Jovi, Aerosmith, and Led Zeppelin. On the strength of the "18 and Life" and "I Remember You" singles, their 1989 debut album sold over three million copies. The 1991 follow-up, *Slave to the Grind*, sold a million copies and hit No. 1. Later that year, the band began a quick fall from the limelight, as Nirvana's success (who, ironically, were called Skid Row in an earlier incarnation) changed the rules of hard rock, making Skid Row seem irrelevant. In 1995, they released their third album, *Subhuman Race*. *— Stephen Thomas Erlewine*

Skid Row / 1989 / Atlantic ✦✦✦
With enough exposure, Skid Row became impossible to ignore. This is the beginning of a good band. *— John Book*

● **Slave to the Grind** / Jun. 11, 1991 / Atlantic ✦✦✦✦
Skid Row's impressive second album has some great rockers, a nice ballad or two, and even a heavy venture into thrash. It was one of the best metal albums of 1991. *— John Book*

B-Sides Ourselves / Sep. 22, 1992 / Atlantic ✦✦✦
B-Sides Ourselves was intended to be a stopgap EP, but it turned out to be Skid Row's last recording for three years. It wasn't a bad way to step away from the spotlight, actually. A collection of five covers, *B-Sides Ourselves* ranks among the best music Skid Row ever recorded, simply because it's so raw and seething with energy. Produced by the band, the EP careens through the songs—including selections by Kiss and the Sex Pistols—at a breakneck pace, creating a vicious rock 'n' roll that is more vital than their two previous albums. The band managed to harness that power and put it into their original material on their next album, 1995's *Subhuman Race*. *— Stephen Thomas Erlewine*

Subhuman Race / Mar. 28, 1995 / WEA ✦✦✦✦
Skid Row waited out the grunge storm and returned in 1995 with *Subhuman Race*, their strongest and most vicious record to date. Abandoning most of the pop-metal posturing of their early hit albums, Skid Row strips back their music to the basics—roaring guitars and Sebastian Bach's shriek. It wasn't a hit on the size of *Slave to the Grind*, yet it made an impressive showing, climbing into the Top 40. *— Stephen Thomas Erlewine*

The Skids

f. 1977, Dunfermline, Scotland, db. 1982
New Wave
The Scottish art-punk unit the Skids formed in Dunfermline in 1977. Comprised of the dramatic vocalist Richard Jobson, guitarist Stuart Adamson, bassist William Simpson, and drummer Tom Kellichan, the group issued the single "Reasons" on their own No Bad label before signing to Virgin. After two more singles, "Sweet Suburbia" and "The Saints Are Coming," they entered the UK Top 10 with "Into the Valley," included on their 1979 debut LP *Scared to Dance*, a fine document of the anthemic guitar riffs and chant-like vocals that typified the first phase of the group's music.

With their second effort, 1979's arty, overreaching *Days in Europa* (produced by Be-Bop Deluxe's Bill Nelson), the Skids scored a pair of Top 20 hits with "Masquerade" and "Working for the Yankee Dollar." Trouble loomed, however, as Jobson's increasingly grandiose plans for the group's music alienated not only their fans but also their own rhythm section, and both Simpson and Kellichan were long gone by the time of 1980's *The Absolute Game*, recorded with bassist Russell Webb and drummer Mike Baillie. By 1981's *Joy*, only Jobson remained from the Skids' original lineup; prior to recording the album, Adamson quit to form his own group, the internationally successful Big Country. After *Joy* failed commercially and critically, the Skids officially disbanded; Jobson soon returned as a solo artist before forming the Armoury Show and beginning a career as a broadcaster. *— Jason Ankeny*

● **Sweet Suburbia: the Best of the Skids** / Apr. 18, 1995 / Virgin ✦✦✦✦
Sweet Suburbia is a smartly assembled eighteen-track career overview of the Scottish punk/new wave outfit. Though the Skids' early albums had no shortage of fine material, in truth, *Sweet Suburbia* is probably the beginning and ending point for all but the completist, picking out most, if not all, of the high points. *— Chris Woodstra*

Skinny Puppy

f. 1982, Vancouver, B.C., Canada, **db.** 1996
Industrial, Alternative Pop-Rock
Drawing from the pioneering work of artists like Throbbing Gristle, Cabaret Voltaire, and Suicide, the dark avant-industrial group Skinny Puppy formed in 1982 in Vancouver, British Columbia. Originally a duo comprised of former Images in Vogue vocalist cEVIN Key (born Kevin Crompton) and Nivek Ogre (a.k.a. Kevin Ogilvie), Skinny Puppy followed their debut cassette *Back and Forth* with the EP *Remission*, the first of many recordings with producer David "Rave" Ogilvie, in 1984.

Keyboardist Wilhelm Schroeder joined the group for 1985's full-length debut *Bites*, but was replaced the next year by Dwayne Goettel, whose sampling and synth work proved significant in the development of the Skinny Puppy aesthetic from ominous dance music into a distinct fusion of industrial, goth, and electronic sounds. Subsequent releases like 1986's *Mind: The Perpetual Intercourse*, 1987's *Cleanse, Fold and Manipulate* and 1988's *VIVIsectVI* further honed the trio's style, as well as introducing the outspoken lyrical agenda that remained a thematic constant throughout much of the group's work.

In 1989, Ministry's Al Jourgensen added vocals, guitars, and production work to *Rabies;* later, he joined Ogre in the side project Pigface. Ultimately, the members' interest in pursuing similar outside projects began to unravel Skinny Puppy: in 1987, Key and Edward Ka-Spel of the Legendary Pink Dots recorded the album *Their Eyes Slowly Burning* under the name Tear Garden, and in 1990, he and friend Alan Nelson worked as Hilt. A major rift began splitting the band apart, and Key and Goettel often sided against Ogre, whom they felt was more interested in pursuing solo work than in keeping the trio intact; drugs had also become a serious problem, but Skinny Puppy nonetheless signed to American Recordings in 1993 and relocated to Los Angeles to begin production work.

The sessions for the album, titled *The Process*, proved disastrous; for the first time in nearly a decade, David Ogilvie did not oversee production duties, and the group went through several producers, including former Swan Roli Mosimann and Martin Atkins. Flooding and earthquakes further hampered the sessions, and Key was severely injured in a film shoot. After months of recording, Key and Goettel, dissatisfied with Atkins' work, absconded with the master tapes and returned to Vancouver in mid-1994 to finish production. Ogre remained in California, and later announced he was leaving Skinny Puppy to form W.E.L.T. A few months later, on August 23, 1995, Goettel was found dead of a heroin overdose in his parents' home; in his honor, Key and Ogilvie finally completed the album, and *The Process* was released in 1996. A multimedia history of the band, *Brap—Back and Forth Series 3 and 4*, followed a few months later, while Key returned to his new project, Download. *— Jason Ankeny*

Bites / 1985 / Nettwerk ✦✦✦
Skinny Puppy's first album recalls the gloomy throb of Cabaret Voltaire, but with a more pronounced beat; their debut EP, *Remission*, is included on the CD version of *Bites*. *— Stephen Thomas Erlewine*

Mind: The Perpetual Intercourse / 1986 / Nettwerk ✦✦
Skinny Puppy doesn't deviate from its dark vision on their second album; in fact, the record doesn't sound all that much different than the first. *— Stephen Thomas Erlewine*

Cleanse Fold & Manipulate / 1987 / Nettwerk ✦✦✦✦
While it doesn't deviate from their previous lyrical territory, the music is more intense and scary; for the first time, Skinny Puppy has made an album that actually *sounds* frightening. *— Stephen Thomas Erlewine*

Vivi Sect VI / Jul. 1988 / Nettwerk ✦✦✦✦
VIVIsectVI is the first explicitly political Skinny Puppy album, which adds some depth to their standard throbbing, gloomy industrial dance-rock. *— Stephen Thomas Erlewine*

Rabies / 1989 / Nettwerk ✦✦✦
Despite the presence of Ministry's Al Jourgensen and his brutal guitar riffs, Skinny Puppy sounds as if they're at a loss for ideas on their fifth album. *— Stephen Thomas Erlewine*

Too Dark Park / 1990 / Nettwerk ✦✦✦✦
When Ministry and the Revolting Cocks were offering what could be described as industrial noise for people who weren't industrial fans, Skinny Puppy continued to thrive on the extreme and remained far to the left of rock's center. Employing more bass than Puppy's previous albums, *Too Dark Park* has a bit of a funk element. But make no mistake: the industrial agitators (who had influenced Nine Inch Nails, Ministry, RevCo, Godflesh, and numerous others) were hardly going after rock's mainstream. Forceful and consistently abrasive, these twisted and disturbing collages of samples, electronics, distortion, and heavy guitars push the limits of rock and are about as hardcore as it gets. Those who have only a slight interest in industrial would probably be better off starting out with the more accessible Ministry, but this is a CD that the more seasoned industrial aficionados shouldn't miss. *— Alex Henderson*

● **12 Inch Anthology** / Jun. 1990 / Nettwerk ✦✦✦✦
Featuring both sides of four 12-inch singles from 1985 to1989, *12-Inch Anthology* offers a good introduction to Skinny Puppy's psycho-terrorist dance music. —*Stephen Thomas Erlewine*

The Process / Feb. 27, 1996 / Warner Brothers ✦✦

Brap / Apr. 30, 1996 / Nettwerk ✦✦

The Skyliners

f. , Pittsburgh, PA
Doo Wop
This Pittsburgh vocal group made a magnificent heartache ballad in 1959, "Since I Don't Have You." It remains among R&B's ultimate agonizing triumphs, and Chuck Jackson later did an equally gripping version. Jimmy Beaumont was the lead vocalist, with Janet Vogel, Wally Lester, Joe VerScharen, and Jackie Taylor. Beaumont, Taylor, and Lester had been in the Crescents, while Vogel and VerScharen were alumni of the El Rios. Their follow-up, "This I Swear," was a creditable effort that peaked at No. 20 on the R&B charts, but few remember it. Oddly, "Since I Don't Have You" only reached No. 3 on the R&B side and No. 12 on the pop charts. But it's certainly one song for whom the numbers really don't come close to telling the story. The Skyliners had two chart singles on Callico and then had one other song reach the R&B Top 40 in 1965, "The Loser," for Jubilee. —*Ron Wynn*

● **The Skyliners' Greatest Hits** / 1986 / Original Sound ✦✦✦✦
Since I Don't Have You / Ace ✦✦✦✦
The Skyliners were among the more dramatic, theatrical White doo wop groups. Their hit "Since I Don't Have You" has been covered by numerous performers, and it's among the 21 singles featured on this Ace anthology covering numbers recorded for Calico and Laurie. Jimmy Beaumont's tremendous leads distinguished "I Swear," "It Happened Today," and the title track, among others. It's no surprise that such flamboyant performers as Patti LaBelle and Chuck Jackson are big Skyliners fans. —*Ron Wynn*

Slade

f. 1966, Wolverhampton, England
Hard Rock, Glam Rock
One of the most successful British bands of the early '70s, Slade made it to the top of the charts after several years on the road. The band formed in 1966 in Wolverhampton as the N'Betweens. After taking on former Animals bassist Chas Chandler as their manager, they changed their name to Ambrose Slade, then shortened it to Slade.

Many of their records were a variations of upfront lead vocals, fat, loud, distorted guitar chords, a basic foot-stomping beat, and anthemic choruses. The simplicity of it all was played up even further by the deliberate misspelling of words in the song titles. At the turn of the '70s, "Get Down and Get with It" cracked the UK Top 20 and there was no turning back. Their next dozen singles were UK Top Five hits, six of them reaching No. 1. Their success wasn't limited to the singles charts, either; three of their albums also topped the charts during the same period. Their holiday song, "Merry Xmas Everybody," has entered the UK charts seven times, as well.

Despite their British success Slade barely cracked the US Hot 100. Even in England, the big hits stopped coming during the punk revolution in the late '70s. They enjoyed a brief revival in the early '80s when Quiet Riot covered "Cum on Feel the Noize" and took it to the top of the charts around the world. This revival even enabled Slade to chart in the American Top 40 with "Run Run Away" and "My Oh My." Slade recently celebrated its 25th anniversary and shows no sign of stopping. —*Jim Powers*

Slayed / 1972 / Polydor ✦✦✦✦
Slayed was Slade's best and most consistent original album, featuring "Mama Weer All Crazee Now." —*Stephen Thomas Erlewine*

● **Sladest** / 1973 / Reprise ✦✦✦✦
Sladest contains all of the British band's finest moments, including "Look Wot You Dun," "Mama Weer All Crazee Now," and "Cum on Feel the Noize." —*Stephen Thomas Erlewine*

Keep Your Hands off My Power Supply / 1984 / Epic ✦✦✦✦
An early-'80s album that managed to climb into the Top 40, thanks to the success of Quiet Riot's versions of "Cum on Feel the Noize" and "Mama Weer All Crazee Now." On *Keep Your Hands off My Power Supply*, Slade shows that they are still the masters of loud, trashy hard rock. —*Stephen Thomas Erlewine*

The Slade Collection: 81-87 / Oct. 19, 1993 / Castle ✦✦✦
For casual fans wishing to supplement the storming, sleazy fun of *Feel the Noize*, Castle's *The Slade Collection: '81-'87* contains all of the best latter-day tracks the group recorded, including "My Oh My" and "Run Run Away." Even in this condensed state, the material on '81-'87 isn't as compelling as it was between 1970 and 1975, but this compilation is cer-

tainly the best way to sample an inconsistent era. —*Stephen Thomas Erlewine*

● **Feel the Noize: the Very Best of Slade** / 1997 / Polydor ✦✦✦✦
The finest collection ever assembled on Slade's hit-making heyday, *Feel the Noize—The Very Best of...* contains all of the group's hit singles from the early '70s, from 1971's "Get Down and Get With It" to 1975's "Thanks for the Memory (Wham Bam Thank You Mam)". In between those two songs, all of the group's big, dumb, irresistible and misspelled hits—"Cuz I Luv You," "Take Me Bak 'Ome," "Mama Weer All Crazee Now," "Gudbuy T'Jane," "Cum on Feel the Noize," "Skweeze Me Pleeze Me"—are featured. Though it is missing latter-day hits like "My Oh My," Slade never got better than they did at their stomping glitter-rock peak, and *Feel the Noize* captures the essence of that era. —*Stephen Thomas Erlewine*

Slave

f. 1975, Dayton, OH
Funk, Disco
Arguably the hottest of the '70s Ohio funk bands, Slave had a great run in the late '70s and early '80s. Trumpeter Steve Washington formed the group in Dayton in 1975. Vocalist Floyd Miller teamed with Tom Lockett, Jr., Charles Bradley, Mark Adams, Mark Hicks, Danny Webster, Orion Wilhoite, and Tim Dozier. Vocalists Steve Arrington and Starleana Young came aboard in 1978, with Arrington ultimately becoming lead vocalist. Their first big hit was the thumping single "Slide" in 1977 for Cotillion, where they remained until 1984. Their best tracks were lyrically simple and at times silly, but the arrangements and rhythms were intense and hypnotic. Other Top Ten R&B hits were "Just a Touch of Love" in 1979, "Watching You" in 1980, and "Snap Shot" in 1981. Young, Washington, and Lockett departed to form Aurra in 1979. Arrington himself left in the early '80s. They added Charles C. Carter, Delburt Taylor, Sam Carter, Kevin Johnson, and Roger Parker as replacements and continued on, though much less successfully, into the late '80s. They moved to Atlantic for one LP in 1984, then switched to the Atlanta-based Ichiban in 1986 for singles and LPs that were just a shade of the former vibrant Slave sound. Their most recent release was *The Funk Strikes Back* in 1992. Rhino issued *Stellar Funk: The Best of Slave*, a first-rate anthology of their finest cuts, in 1994. —*Ron Wynn*

● **Stellar Funk: Best Of** / Feb. 22, 1994 / Rhino ✦✦✦✦
Slave's music was straight, simple funk: prominent bass lines, catchy phrases, and either comical or throwaway lyrics. This excellent 15-track anthology contains Slave's finest hits, each with a captivating, thudding bass riff: "Slide," "Just a Touch of Love," and "Watching You," among others. There are also five Steve Arrington numbers, among them his best dance cut ("Weak at the Knees") and topical tune ("Feel So Real"). Although not as acclaimed as Parliament/Funkadelic or Earth, Wind and Fire, this CD shows that Slave deserves recognition for its ability to keep the funk with style and verve. —*Ron Wynn*

Slayer

f. 1982, Huntington Beach, CA
Thrash, Heavy Metal, Speed Metal
Slayer was one of the most distinctive, influential, and extreme thrashmetal bands of the 1980s. Their graphic lyrics deal with everything from death and dismemberment to war and the horrors of hell. Their full-throttle velocity, wildly chaotic guitar solos, and powerful musical chops paint an effectively chilling sonic background for their obsessive chronicling of the dark side; this correspondence has helped Slayer's music hold up arguably better than the remaining Big Three '80s thrash outfits (Metallica, Megadeth, Anthrax). Naturally, Slayer has stirred up quite a bit of controversy over the years, with rumors flying about Satanism and Nazism that have only added to their mystique. Over the years, Slayer has put out some high-quality albums, one undisputed classic (*Reign in Blood*), and seen the numbers of naysayers and detractors shrinking as their impact on the growing death metal movement was gradually and respectfully acknowledged. Slayer has survived into the 1990s with arguably the most vitality and the least compromise of any pre-Nirvana metal band, and their intensity still inspires similar responses from their devoted fans.

Slayer was formed in 1982 in Huntington Beach, CA, by guitarists Kerry King and Jeff Hanneman; also recruited were bassist/vocalist Tom Araya and drummer Dave Lombardo. The band started out playing covers of Judas Priest and Iron Maiden songs, but quickly discovered that they could get attention (and fans) by exploiting threatening, Satanic imagery. The band was invited by Metal Blade's Brian Slagel to contribute a track to the *Metal Massacre III* compilation (a series that also saw the vinyl debuts of Metallica and Voivod); a contract and debut album, *Show No Mercy*, followed shortly thereafter. While Slayer's early approach was rather cartoonish, their breakneck speed and instrumental prowess were still highly evident. Two EPs, *Haunting the Chapel* and *Live Undead*, were released in 1984, but 1985's *Hell Awaits* refined their lyrical obsessions into a sort of concept album about damnation and torture and made an immediate sensation in heavy-metal circles, winning Slayer a rabid cult following. Def Jam's co-founder Rick Rubin took a liking to the band, signed them to his label, and contributed the first clear-sounding production heard on any Slayer album for the stripped-down *Reign in Blood.* Due to the graphic nature of the material, CBS refused to distribute the album, which garnered a great deal of publicity for the band; eventually, Geffen Records stepped in. Combining Slayer's trademark speed metal with the tempos and song lengths (if not structures) of hardcore, along with the band's most disturbing lyrics yet, *Reign in Blood* was an instant classic, breaking the band through to a wider audience, and was hailed by some as the greatest speed-metal album of all time (some give the nod to Metallica's *Master of Puppets*).

South of Heaven disappointed some of the band's hardcore followers, as Slayer successfully broke out of the potential stylistic straitjacket of their reputation as the world's fastest, most extreme band. Drummer Lombardo took some time off and was briefly replaced by Whiplash drummer Tony Scaglione, but soon returned to the fold. In 1990, *Seasons in the Abyss* was well received in all respects, incorporating more of the classic Slayer intensity into a more commercial—but no less uncompromising—sound. "War Ensemble" and the title track became favorites on MTV's *Headbanger's Ball,* and Slayer consolidated its position at the forefront of thrash, along with Metallica. Following the release of the double live album *Decade of Aggression,* Lombardo left the band for good due to personality conflicts with the other members and formed Grip Inc. Slayer remained quiet for a few years; the only new material released after 1990 was a duet with Ice-T recorded for the *Judgment Night* soundtrack on a medley of songs by the Exploited. After leaving his group the Forbidden, Paul Bostaph signed on as the new drummer for 1994's *Divine Intervention,* which was released to glowing reviews; thanks to the new death-metal movement, which drew upon Slayer and particularly *Reign in Blood* for its inspiration, Slayer were hailed as metal innovators. The album was a massive success, debuting at No. 8 on the *Billboard* album charts. Bostaph left the band to concentrate on a side project, the Truth About Seafood, and was replaced by ex-Testament drummer Jon Dette for *Undisputed Attitude,* an album consisting mostly of punk and hardcore covers. As of 1997, Bostaph is rumored to be rejoining the band for a forthcoming studio album of new material. —*Steve Huey*

Show No Mercy / 1984 / Metal Blade ✦✦
Slayer's debut came when the band wore makeup and were considered a joke in some circles. It was a big difference and a far cry from what they sound like now. —*John Book*

Hell Awaits / 1985 / Metal Blade ✦✦✦
Slayer's first relevant album is loosely tied together by the theme of eternal damnation. Some of the lyrics are pretty silly, and some of the songs could have been trimmed a bit, but it hints at the heights they would reach on their next release. It's also interesting to hear one of the genre's true innovators developing and honing their sound. —*Steve Huey*

★ **Reign in Blood** / 1986 / Def American ✦✦✦✦✦
Slayer's masterpiece opens and closes with two longer, now-standard tracks, "Angel of Death" and "Raining Blood." Sandwiched in between are eight short (all under three minutes), very fast bursts of aggression that change tempo or feel without warning, keeping the listener off balance and producing a very wild, disjointed, barely controlled effect. The short songs prevent the extreme graphic violence and paranoia in the lyrics from descending into self-parody. This is simply Slayer's best music, and it proved hugely influential in the evolution of the death-metal style. Along with Metallica's *Master of Puppets, Reign in Blood* is the pinnacle of thrash. —*Steve Huey*

South of Heaven / 1988 / Def American ✦✦
When it comes to death metal, no band is more convincing than Slayer. For other bands, focusing on death, Satanism, the supernatural, and the occult became a cliche; but Slayer's controversial reflections on evil always came across as honest and heartfelt. The group's sincerity is the thing that makes *South of Heaven* so disturbing and powerful—when the influential thrashers rip into such morbid fare as "Spill the Blood," "Mandatory Suicide" and "Ghosts of War," they are frighteningly convincing. With its fourth album, Slayer began to slow its tempos without sacrificing an iota of heaviness or incorporating any pop elements. *South of Heaven* would be Slayer's last album for Def Jam. When Rick Rubin and Russell Simmons (brother of Joseph "Run" Simmons of Run-D.M.C.) parted company, Slayer went to Rubin's new company Def American, while L.L. Cool J, Slick Rick, and other rappers recorded for Simmons at Def Jam. —*Alex Henderson*

Seasons in the Abyss / 1990 / Def American ✦✦✦
Slayer bounces back here, alternating between pounding speed and more mid-tempo grooves. Their music continues in a more refined direction, and it works better than on *South of Heaven.* The band doesn't turn to the supernatural quite as much for its subject matter, preferring to examine real topics like war, murder, and human weakness

from the traditional dark, dramatic Slayer viewpoint, but their music is so effective that the mood is much the same. This is probably their most accessible album, but it doesn't compromise a bit. —*Steve Huey*

Decade of Aggression: Live / Oct. 22, 1991 / Def American ✦✦✦
A double-length set, it has all of Slayer's great songs done in the only way the band should be experienced: in concert. This is the best-sounding live speed-metal album so far. —*John Book*

Divine Intervention / Sep. 27, 1994 / American ✦✦✦✦
The rock 'n' roll landscape changed dramatically between *Seasons in the Abyss* in 1991 and *Divine Intervention* in 1994. With the rise of alternative rock, many metal and hard rock bands that had been enormously successful at the dawn of the '90s were struggling by the middle of the decade. Instead of doing something calculated like emulating Nirvana or Pearl Jam—or for that matter, Nine Inch Nails or Ministry—Slayer wisely refused to sound like anyone but Slayer. Tom Araya & Co. responded to the new environment simply by striving to be the heaviest death-metal band it possibly could. Less accessible than *Seasons* but equally riveting, *Divine Intervention* marked drummer Paul Bostaph's studio debut with the band. Bostaph proved to be a positive, energizing influence on Slayer, which sounds better than ever on such dark triumphs as "Killing Fields," "Serenity in Murder" and "Circle of Beliefs." Characteristically grim and morbid, Slayer focuses on the violently repressive nature of governments and the lengths to which they will go to wield power. And true to form, Slayer's music is as disturbing as its lyrics. —*Alex Henderson*

Undisputed Attitude / Jun. 1996 / American ✦✦
Bizarrely following Guns N' Roses' lead, Slayer turns in a set of hardcore punk covers with *Undisputed Attitude.* While Slayer always played relentlessly fast, they never had any clear hardcore roots, which is confirmed by their approach to the album. Over the course of 14 tracks, the band drops in three originals, two songs from Minor Threat, three cuts from Verbal Abuse, two D.I. songs, and a track apiece from Dr. Know, D.R.I., T.S.O.L. and Iggy Pop. Out of this material, Slayer does touch on some classic hardcore bands—the genre is pretty much defined by Minor Threat, T.S.O.L., D.R.I.(and the absent Dead Kennedys—a few minor ones (Dr. Know, D.I.) and the completely obscure Verbal Abuse. Simply put, there's no sense of history here. Furthermore, Slayer's originals are lunkheaded—"DDAMM (Drunk Drivers Against Madd Mothers)" is indicative of their political leanings—and, surprisingly, relatively slow. *Undisputed Attitude* suffers under all this weight—instead of being a fun tear through some covers, it's humorless and, furthermore, a misguided history lesson. —*Stephen Thomas Erlewine*

Sleater-Kinney

f. 1994, Olympia, WA
Indie Rock, Riot Grrrl
The anthemic Olympia, Washington-based punk trio Sleater-Kinney formed from the ashes of Heavens to Betsy and Excuse 17, a pair of groups that rode the first wave of the riot grrrl movement. Singers/guitarists Corin Tucker and Carrie Brownstein first met in 1992, when Tucker was one half of the duo Heavens to Betsy; Brownstein, a classically trained pianist, was so inspired by Tucker and other grrrl musicians like Bikini Kill and Bratmobile (not coincidentally Tucker's own influences) that she formed her own band, Excuse 17, a year later.

Sleater-Kinney, which earned its name from a local freeway off-ramp, initially began as Tucker and Brownstein's side project; in late 1994, Australia-born Lora Macfarlane signed on as the group's first permanent drummer, and over the course of the following two weeks the trio recorded their self-titled 1995 debut for Team Dresch bassist Donna Dresch's Chainsaw label. Upon its release, the album earned widespread acclaim for its visceral intensity as well as the group's provocative, politically charged lyrics, passionate vocals, and intricate melodies. With 1996's brilliant *Call the Doctor,* Sleater-Kinney garnered even greater media exposure and critical applause on the strength of their incisive rants against gender inequity, consumerism, and indie rock's male-dominated hierarchy. *Dig Me Out,* recorded with new drummer Janet Weiss, followed in 1997. —*Jason Ankeny*

Sleater-Kinney / 1995 / Chainsaw ✦✦✦

● **Call the Doctor** / Mar. 25, 1996 / Chainsaw ✦✦✦✦
Sleater-Kinney's masterful sophomore effort *Call the Doctor* fulfills all the promise of the group's debut and more, forging taut melodicism and jaw-dropping sonic complexity out of barbed-wire emotional potency. The emergence of Carrie Brownstein as an equal shareholder in Corin Tucker's vision is the key—her four contributions (particularly "Stay Where You Are" and "I Wanna Be Your Joey Ramone") are stellar, while her harmonies complete Tucker's equally superb lead turns by reading between the lines to verbalize the naked aggression at the core of the songs' polemic power. Forget the riot grrrl implications inherent in the trio's music—*Call the Doctor* is pure, undiluted punk, and it's brilliant. —*Jason Ankeny*

Dig Me Out / Apr. 8, 1997 / Kill Rock Stars ✦✦✦✦
Having reinvented the girl-punk wheel with *Call the Doctor*, Sleater-Kinney continues to expand the boundaries of the form with the stunning *Dig Me Out*. Leaner and more intricate than its predecessor, the record is remarkably confident and mature; instead of succumbing to the pressures of "next big thing" status, the trio finds vindication in all of their critical adulation—the vocals are even more ferocious, the melodies are even more infectious, and the ideals are even more passionate. —*Jason Ankeny*

Percy Sledge

b. Nov. 25, 1941, Leighton, AL
Vocals / Soul
Percy Sledge will forever be associated with "When a Man Loves a Woman," a pleading, soulful ballad he sang with wrenching, convincing anguish and passion. Sledge sang all of his songs that way, delivering them in a powerful rush where he quickly changed from soulful belting to quavering, tearful pleas. It was a voice that made him one of the key figures of deep Southern Soul during the late '60s. Sledge recorded at Muscle Shoals studios in Alabama, where he frequently sang songs written by Spooner Oldham and Dan Penn. Not only did he sing deep soul, but Sledge was among the pioneers of country-soul, singing songs by Charlie Rich and Kris Kristofferson in a gritty, passionate style. During the '70s, his commercial success quickly faded away, but Sledge continued to tour and record into the '90s.

While he worked as a hospital nurse in the early '60s, Sledge began his professional music career as a member of the Southern soul vocal group the Esquires Combo. On the advice of local disc jockey Quin Ivy, he went solo in 1966. Ivy fancied himself a record producer and he agreed to help shape Sledge's song "When a Man Loves a Woman" into a full-fledged single, hiring Spooner Oldham to play a distinctive, legato organ phrase. Ivy released the single independently and quickly licensed it to Atlantic records, who quickly bought out Sledge's contract. "When a Man Loves a Woman" became a huge hit in the summer of 1966, topping both the pop and R&B charts. It was quickly followed that year by two Top 10 R&B hits, "Warm and Tender Love" and "It Tears Me Up," which were both in the vein of his first hit. Although few of his subsequent singles were hits—only "Take Time to Know Her" reached the R&B Top 10 in 1968—many of the songs, which were often written by Dan Penn and/or Spooner Oldham, were acknowledged as classics among soul aficionados.

Despite his strong reputation among deep soul fans, Sledge's sales had declined considerably by the early '70s, and he headed out on the club circuit in America and England. In 1974, he left Atlantic for Capricorn Records, where he surprisingly returned to the R&B Top 20 with "I'll Be Your Everything." Instead of reigniting his career, the single was a last gasp, as far as chart success was concerned. Over the next two decades he continued to tour, and in the late '80s, "When a Man Loves a Woman" experienced a resurgence in popularity due to its inclusion in movie soundtracks and in television commercials. Following its appearance in a 1987 Levi's commerical in the UK, the single was re-released and climbed to No. 2. Two years later, he won the Rhythm and Blues Foundation's Career Achievement Award. Sledge was able to turn this revived popularity into a successful career by touring constantly, playing over 100 shows a year into the '90s. In 1994, he released *Blue Night*, his first collection of new material in over a decade, to uniformly positive reviews. —*Stephen Thomas Erlrewine*

When a Man Loves a Woman / 1966 / Collectables ✦✦✦✦
A country/soul masterpiece. The title track remains among the most beloved, anthemic explanations of love's impact and travails ever written or performed. Had Sledge never made another song, he would still deserve kudos just for that one. But he continued to score with more simple, heartfelt, unsophisticated stories about disappointment, pain, rejection, and perseverance. —*Ron Wynn*

The Percy Sledge Way / 1967 / Atlantic ✦✦✦
This late-'60s album contains hard-hitting, memorable country/soul testimonies from Percy Sledge, who had hit his stride at Atlantic. His narratives were perfectly paced, written with irony and insight, and sung with the ideal mixture of crunching soul and country wit and wisdom. Hopefully, Rhino will one day reissue some of soul's archival sessions like this one, for it needs full exposure. —*Ron Wynn*

Take Time to Know Her / 1968 / Collectables ✦✦✦
The title track was another smashing Sledge gem, while the remainder of the album continues his evocative country/soul tales of woe and heartache. Sledge's late-'60s Atlantic singles and albums were landmarks in the genre; they should have been major country events just as Ray Charles' earlier cuts, but were simply too rooted in Black nuance to get any shot with the unimaginative types running country radio (although to be fair, there were also some great country songs in the period that should have been aired on soul stations). The songs were produced and arranged with the right amount of care and sensitivity,

never intruding or crowding Sledge as his stories unfolded. —*Ron Wynn*

I'll Be Your Everything / 1974 / Capricorn ✦✦✦
Some wonderful country/soul from Percy Sledge, whose throaty, energized, wonderfully Southern delivery hadn't lost either its earthiness or its zeal, but was so regional that it was losing its appeal to the cosmopolitan, urban types gaining hegemony in Black music circles. Sledge delivered several grainy, earnest country/soul weepers and wailers when he moved to Capricorn in the mid-'70s, but they didn't generate much attention anywhere beyond the South. —*Ron Wynn*

★ **It Tears Me Up** / Apr. 21, 1992 / Rhino ✦✦✦✦✦
This stunning compilation from the vaults of Atlantic Records spotlights the voice that gave us the original version of "When a Man Loves a Woman." Lesser-known hits like "It Tears Me Up," "Take Time to Know Her," and "Warm and Tender Love" are equally wonderful, and all are included in this must-have package. Great liner notes by Dave Marsh. Soul music just doesn't get any more heart-wrenching than this. Absolutely essential! —*Christine Ohlman*

Sleeper

f. 1993, London, England
Alternative Pop-Rock, Brit-Pop
Louise Wener (vocals, guitar); Jon Stewart (guitar); Andy Maclure (drums); Diid Osman (bass). Wener and Stewart met while studying politics at school in Manchester, England. Relocating to London, the two recruited Osman and Maclure and began playing Wener's original songs. The group made its debut in 1993, which led to a series of positive reviews in the British music weeklies. By November of 1993, the group had released an independent single ("Alice in Vain"). In February 1994, the band released "Swallow," which charted in the Top 100; the following May, "Delicious" was released and it became a No. 1 independent single. During May, Sleeper supported Blur on the London band's enormously successful *Parklife* tour. In February 1995, Sleeper released their debut album, *Smart*, which entered the UK album chart at No. 5 and the independent chart at No. 1; it would be certified a silver album in four months. *Smart* was released in the US in March to positive reviews, yet it failed to duplicate the band's British commercial success.

In the late spring of 1996, Sleeper released their second album, *The It Girl*. Again, the album was a major hit in the UK, yet it barely made an impact in the US. —*Stephen Thomas Erlewine*

Smart / Mar. 14, 1995 / Arista ✦✦✦✦
"Inbetweener" is an intoxicating single. Fuzz guitars, light harmonies, sing-song melodies, and hooks keep piling up until the whole thing collapses in a heap after three minutes. Unfortunately, there's nothing that matches it on *Smart*, Sleeper's debut album. Occasionally, Louise Wener comes up with a memorable hook, melody, or lyric, but never can quite pull them together into something as wellcrafted (and sexy) as "Inbetweener." Still, the flashes of inspiration scattered across *Smart* prove Sleeper has potential—which they have already fulfilled once, with the single. —*Stephen Thomas Erlewine*

● **The It Girl** / Jun. 18, 1996 / Arista ✦✦✦✦
Although it lacks a standout track on the level of *Smart*'s "Inbetweener," Sleeper's second album, *The It Girl*, is a stronger effort, suggesting that lead singer-songwriter Louise Wener could develop into a distinctive talent. Certainly, her melodies and hooks are uniformly better this time around, ranging from the bouncy "Sale of the Century" to the sighing melancholy of "What Do I Do Now?" Wener's lyrics continue to be underdeveloped and simplisitic, but her hooks usually make that tendency easy to ignore. What would have made *The It Girl* an even stronger album is a clearer, more focused production. Although the sound of the album changes subtly throughout the course of the record, the overall effect is numbingly similar. The rhythm section lacks drive and the guitars lack balls—they blend together into one dull grind. Out of all of Stephen Street's productions, this is the most undistinguished. Occasionally, the song is strong enough to compensate for the flat production, but Sleeper albums will not only improve according to the development of Louise Wener's songwriting, but also as the band finds the right producer. —*Stephen Thomas Erlewine*

Slick Rick

b. Jan. 14, 1965, London, England
Vocals / Hip-Hop, Hardcore Rap
Slick Rick foreshadowed and epitomized the pimpster attitude of many rappers during the late '80s and early '90s, with gold chains, his trademark eye-patch, and recordings that were no less misogynistic—"Treat Her like a Prostitute," for example, became an underground hit in 1988 though it was justly criticized for its view of women. His 1989 album, *The Great Adventures of Slick Rick*, was a certified-platinum classic, but before he could record a follow-up, Slick Rick was arrested for attempted murder. Out on bail thanks to Def Jam Records' label-head

Russell Simmons, Rick recorded *The Ruler's Back* in three weeks and released the album in 1991. After his release from prison two years later, he recorded *Behind Bars* for a 1994 release.

Born to Jamaican parents in South Wimbledon, London, on January 14, 1965, Ricky Walters was blinded by broken glass as an infant and took to wearing an eye-patch from an early age. He emigrated with his family to the Bronx in the late '70s and attended the La Guardia High School of Music & Art, where he became friends with future rapper Dana Dane. The two formed the Kangol Crew, and began performing in hip-hop battles around the city. At one 1984 battle in the Bronx, Rick met Doug E. Fresh, and began playing with his Get Fresh Crew (which also included Chill Will and Barry Bee). Fresh's No. 4 R&B hit "The Show" exploded just one year later, and MC Ricky D.—as Rick was then known—leaped to a solo contract two years later, after an acquaintance with Russell Simmons led to his signing to Def Jam Records, the biggest label in hip-hop at the time.

Slick Rick recorded his debut record, *The Great Adventures of Slick Rick*, and released the album in 1988. "Treat Her like a Prostitute" became a sensation on the streets, but R&B radio stations were understandably reluctant to play the track; instead, they pushed his duet with Al B. Sure!, "If I'm Not Your Lover," and it made No. 2 in 1989. "Children's Story" hit the R&B Top Five that same year, but early in 1990, Slick Rick was arrested after shooting at his cousin—who allegedly harassed Rick's mother—and leading police on a high-speed cruise. Before his sentencing, 21 songs were recorded and hastily released as *The Ruler's Back*. The album failed to move at all, though Rick's confession track "I Shouldn't Have Done It" scraped the R&B charts later in 1991. Featured in the rap documentary *The Show* (released in 1995)—in a segment where Russell Simmons actually visits the prison—Slick Rick was released on a work program in 1993, and his *Behind Bars* album appeared in 1994. —*John Bush*

★ **The Great Adventures of Slick Rick** / 1988 / Def Jam ✦✦✦✦✦
Slick Rick first gained an audience by rapping on Doug E. Fresh's "La-Di-Da-Di" and "The Show," two songs that immediately established him as a major talent upon their release in 1985. It may have taken him three years to deliver his full-length debut, but when *The Great Adventures of Slick Rick* arrived in 1988, it was an immediate classic. What makes *The Great Adventures of Slick Rick* such a stunning achievement isn't necessarily the music—in retrospect, it's strong, but unexceptional, street funk—but Rick's rhyming. His style was fluid, but filled with odd cadences and an idiosyncratic phrasing. Furthermore, his story-telling technique is unparalleled, full with detail and dramatic momentum; his skewed, slightly cartoonish viewpoint was nearly as influential. Unfortunately, his rampant misogyny and cool, amoralistic outlook became equally influential on '90s hip-hop. Even though Slick Rick released a series of fairly mediocre follow-ups and spent an extended stay in prison, his failure to live up to the potential of *The Great Adventures* doesn't dilute the impact of the album at all. Years after its release, it still sounds fresh. —*Stephen Thomas Erlewine*

The Ruler's Back / 1991 / Def Jam ✦✦✦✦
A fine follow-up from a troubled soul. —*Ron Wynn*

Behind Bars / Nov. 22, 1994 / Def Jam ✦✦

Slint

f. 1987, Louisville, KY, db. 1991
Instrumental Rock, Alternative Pop-Rock, Indie Rock
Though largely overlooked during their relatively brief lifespan, Slint grew to become one of the most influential and far-reaching bands to emerge from the American underground rock community of the 1980s; innovative and iconoclastic, the group's deft, extremist manipulations of volume, tempo, and structure cast them as clear progenitors of the post-rock movement that blossomed during the following decade.

Whatever the extent of Slint's own influence, the group grew out of Louisville, Kentucky's legendary Squirrel Bait, another seminal band that languished in relative obscurity during its own lifetime but ultimately spawned the likes of Gastr del Sol, Bitch Magnet, and Bastro. Guitarist/vocalist Brian McMahan formed his first group at the age of 12; within a few years, he teamed with drummer Britt Walford, and after the addition of vocalist Peter Searcy, guitarists David Pajo, and David Grubbs, and bassist Ethan Buckler, they founded Squirrel Bait in the mid-'80s. After two ferocious records, a self-titled 1985 effort and 1987's *Skag Heaven*, the group disbanded, leaving McMahan, Walford, Pajo and Buckler to continue on as Slint.

With producer Steve Albini, the quartet recorded 1989's *Tweez*, issued on their own Jennifer Hartman label; a collection of odd stylistic approaches, fractured rhythms, and strange lyrical fragments, the album owed debts to few (if any) historical precedents and steadfastly defied easy classification. Shortly after the record's completion, Buckler left to form King Kong, and was replaced by bassist Todd Brashear for 1991's *Spiderland*, an even more sophisticated and adventurous set.

With the exception of a posthumous 1994 EP (originally recorded

between the two full-length albums), *Spiderland* was Slint's swan song, although the individual members remained key figures in the independent scene. After attending art college, Pajo joined the ranks of Tortoise, while Walford (under the alias Shannon Doughton) played drums with the Breeders before rejoining Buckler in King Kong. McMahan and Brashear, meanwhile, aided Will Oldham in his ever-shifting Palace aggregate (which additionally housed Pajo and Walford at one point or another); McMahan and Pajo also briefly reunited as members of the For Carnation. —*Jason Ankeny*

● **Tweez** / 1989 / Plan 9/Caroline ✦✦✦✦
Tweez is a fine, if bizarre recording, often switching from bass-led rhythm to rhythm in the same song. The guitars are harsh, but not especially fast. Instead of singing, bits of dialogue, sound effects, and spoken lyrics are used. —*John Bush*

Spiderland / 1991 / Touch & Go ✦✦✦
Despite having only six tracks (though lengthy ones), Slint's first album is also their best. Unlike other releases, all but one of the songs have lyrics, either sung or spoken. —*John Bush*

The Slits

f. 1976, London, England, **db.** 1981
Punk, Post-Punk
Along with the Raincoats and Liliput, the Slits are one of the most significant female punk rock bands of the late '70s. Not only did they bravely (or foolishly, you be the judge) leap into the fray with little, if any, musical ability (on their debut tour with the Clash, Mick Jones used to tune their guitars for them), but through sheer emotion and desire created some great music, especially when they began working with veteran reggae producer Dennis Bovell, setting the stage for a future generation of riot grrrls. The Slits formed in 1976 when 14-year-old Ari Upp (sometimes Arri Up) ran into her friend Palmolive at a Patti Smith gig in London. The latter suggested the former consider becoming the lead singer for a new all-girl punk band. Upp agreed on the spot, and the Slits, with borrowed equipment and knowledge of two, maybe three chords, were a reality. They made some crude recordings (so crude that they make early Mekons recordings sound like 64-track by comparison) that were never widely circulated, and it wasn't until they nabbed the opening spot on the Clash's "White Riot" tour of England in 1977 that the Slits became a part of the punk pantheon. Despite this sudden notoriety, little was recorded by the Slits in the early days, save for a couple of sessions of John Peel's BBC radio show. These recordings place the Slits firmly in the punk rock aesthetic of blaring guitars and braying vocals. But it's not generic-sounding rant: Ari's voice bounces along, alternately hiccuping and bellowing to the stiff rhythms; the songs are meditations on alienation, but there is a satiric, tongue-in-cheek quality to the songs instead of strident preachiness.

It wasn't until 1979 that the Slits made their first proper record under the watchful, supportive eyes and ears of reggae vet Dennis Bovell. By the time *Cut* was released, the raging guitars were replaced by subtle reggae riddims, the band was now a trio (Palmolive had been replaced by new drummer Budgie, soon to join Siouxsie & the Banshees), and there was a stylistic suppleness that the Slits had heretofore never displayed. Ari's voice still warbled uncertain of the key, but for a band that had been playing their instruments for a little more than two years, this is a remarkably confident record. It was two years before a second record was released (*Return of the Giant Slits*), which was denser, darker, and full of surprises. But the Slits, due primarily to their interest in incorporating other forms of ethnic music into their mix, were leaping beyond what was commonly accepted as punk rock, and as a result, were no longer seen as a punk band. I'm sure this didn't distress them in the least, as they were more interested in expanding the barriers of punk rock rather than simply adhering to "rules" that claimed all punk bands must bash out simplistic guitar rant. By the close of 1981, Arri Up was singing in Adrian Sherwood's dub/funk aggregation the New Age Steppers, and the Slits had become both legendary and somewhat notorious. Though much derided in their short existence, what the Slits achieved and what they meant to succeeding generations of young female rockers cannot be underestimated. —*John Dougan*

● **Cut** / 1979 / Antilles ✦✦✦✦
Almost as well known for its cover (the three Slits are half-naked and covered in mud) as it was for the music, *Cut* is an ebullient piece of post-punk mastery that finds the Slits' interest in Caribbean and African rhythms smoothly incorporated into their harsher, punk rock stylings. Ari Upp's wandering voice (a touch like Yoko Ono) might be initially off-putting, but not so much so that it makes listening to the record difficult. Six tracks are revamped from earlier Peel sessions and sound better for the extra effort (especially "New Town" and "Love and Romance"). With its goofy charm, gleeful swing and sway, and subtle yet compelling libertarian feminism (get up and do it girls!), this is one of the best records of the era. —*John Dougan*

Return of the Giant Slits / 1981 / CBS ✦✦✦
Never released in America, the Slits' second and final record found them pushing the envelope rhythmically. Although designed to be more commercial than *Cut*, it's actually less so, sounding more like the innovative work a young Adrian Sherwood was doing with Creation Rebel. Fans of the early Slits, who were put off by the reggae of *Cut*, were no doubt further alienated by this record's comfortable use of Afro-pop tempos and style. Which was a shame, because this music was interesting, daring, and exciting. —*John Dougan*

The Peel Sessions / 1989 / Dutch East India ✦✦✦✦
This seven-track disc contains all of the material recorded at two sessions for John Peel's BBC radio show. It's vintage early Slits, lots of crashing and bashing, but with a touch of the sophistication and Caribbean influence that was to follow about a year later on *Cut*. Not just for completists, this is a valuable addition to any serious collection of the music of the punk era, and an interesting document of a young band's growth. —*John Dougan*

Sloan
f. 1991, Halifax, Nova Scotia, Canada
Alternative Pop-Rock, Power Pop
Sloan was one of the most successful Canadian bands of the '90s, which was both a blessing and a curse. While they were well known in their homeland, where their Beatlesque power pop became a radio staple, they had a difficult time breaking into the American market, especially after their label, DGC, decided not to market their hooky pop in the wake of grunge. After spending several years fighting the label, and nearly breaking up, Sloan re-emerged in 1996 with *One Chord to Another*, a record that became an instant success in Canada and a critical sensation in the US upon its American release in 1997, establishing the group as one of the leaders of the new wave of power-pop groups in the late '90s.

Andrew Scott (drums), Chris Murphy (bass, vocals), Patrick Pentland (guitar, vocals), and Jay Ferguson (guitar, vocals) formed Sloan in Halifax, Nova Scotia, Canada in 1991. Ferguson and Murphy had previously played in the local band Kearney Lake Rd, a group inspired by underground American bands like R.E.M. and the Minutemen. Scott and Pentland also played in various local bands, but the group didn't come together until Murphy and Scott met each other while studying at the Nova Scotia School of Art and Design. The group debuted in the spring of 1991, and within a few months, their feedback-laden live shows had gained a sizable audience. By the end of the year, their first recording, "Underwhelmed," appeared on the local Halifax compilation *Hear and Now*. Early in 1992, they released the *Peppermint* EP on their own Murderecords, and by the summer they had signed with DGC. Sloan's debut album, *Smeared*, a record where Sonic Youth met Beatlesque pop, appeared in October in Canada and in January 1993 in America, and it was greeted with positive reviews. While the band had a gold album in Canada, the good press didn't translate into sales in the US, even as the group supported the Lemonheads and fIREHOSE at several concerts. Nevertheless, the domestic success of *Smeared* sparked a brief period of interest in "the Halifax scene," with groups like Eric's Trip, Thrush Hermit, the Hardship Post, and Jale all benefitting from the exposure.

For their second album, 1994's *Twice Removed*, Sloan simplified their sound considerably, concentrating on melodic, hook-laden power pop. DGC wanted the album to be noisier, yet the band won its fight to keep it bright and melodic. Nevertheless, DGC failed to promote the album upon its release, especially in America, even in the wake of good reviews and strong Canadian sales. The band toured relentlessly to support *Twice Removed;* the record was named "The Best Canadian Album of All Time" in a poll by *Chart!* magazine and *Spin* called it one of the "Best Albums You Didn't Hear This Year," but DGC was not giving the band much support. By the end of the year, the group decided to cancel their remaining shows in the new year and decide whether they wanted to pursue a career.

Sloan re-emerged in the summer of 1995, playing a handful of concerts and releasing a single, "Same Old Flame," on Murderecords. During their hiatus, the members pursued various side projects, with Scott forming the Maker's Mark and playing in the Sadies, while Murphy drummed for the Super Friendz; Pentland wrote a handful of songs, and Ferguson worked at Murderecords and managed the Inbreds, as well as co-producing a record by the Local Rabbits. Toward late summer, Sloan decided they wanted to continue as a band, and that winter they recorded *One Chord to Another*, a record that expanded the power-pop approach of *Twice Removed* on a small budget. Although its origins were modest, the album was a huge Canadian hit upon its June 1996 release. After much negotiation, Sloan signed with the fledgling EMI subsidiary the Enclave in early 1997, and *One Chord to Another* was finally released in the US in the spring of 1997 to overwhelmingly positive reviews. —*Stephen Thomas Erlewine*

Smeared / Jan. 19, 1993 / Geffen ✦✦✦
Sloan's debut album *Smeared* is a bit of a mess, as the group tries to combine catchy pop melodies with punky rhythms and washes of dissonant feedback borrowed straight from Sonic Youth and My Bloody Valentine records. Those aren't the only two influences that are apparent on *Smeared*—references to all sorts of American indierock, from the Velvet Underground to Nirvana, are scattered throughout the record. Sloan, surprisingly, can harness these diverse influences into a winning combination of sighing melodies and swirling guitars, and while their songwriting is occasionally a little unfocused, the best songs—"Underwhelmed," "Two Seater," "I Am the Cancer," "What's There to Decide?"—are quite impressive. —*Stephen Thomas Erlewine*

Twice Removed / Aug. 30, 1994 / Enclave ✦✦✦✦
The difference between *Smeared* and Sloan's second album *Twice Removed* is quite remarkable. Stripping away most of their indie-rock influences, Sloan emerges as an astonishingly accomplished pure-pop band, one that evokes the sunny charm and effortless melodicism of the Beatles and Beach Boys without being beholden to preserving a tradition. Almost every song on *Twice Removed* sparkles with clear, graceful melodies, and the arrangements are dense with ideas. The album is a rarity—an unselfconscious power-pop album, one that is overflowing with fresh melodies and tough, energetic performances. —*Stephen Thomas Erlewine*

● **One Chord to Another** / 1996 / Enclave ✦✦✦✦
Following the bungled American release of *Twice Removed*, it seemed unlikely that Sloan would survive, let alone record an album as wonderful as *One Chord to Another*. On their previous album, Sloan had refashioned themselves as a power-pop band, often to terrific results, but on *One Chord to Another* their songwriting blossoms. Filled with catchy, jangling riffs and memorable melodies, the record is a tour de force of hooks and harmonies, filled with exceptionally strong songs and forceful performances, which give the record a firm, rocking foundation. Few power-pop records of the '90s are as infectious and memorable as *One Chord to Another*. [The initial American pressing of *One Chord to Another*, which appeared nearly a year after the original Canadian release, contained a bonus disc patterned after the Beach Boys' live-in-the-studio *Party*, which featured Sloan running through several of their best-known songs and a handful of covers, including a jaw-dropping medley of Canned Heat and Stereolab.] —*Stephen Thomas Erlewine*

P.F. Sloan
b. 1944, New York, NY
Guitar, Vocals / Singer-Songwriter, Folk-Rock
He was there at the dawn of surf music, he was crowned king of the West Coast protest folkies, and he created some of the finest American pop records of the '60s, yet today the name P.F. Sloan is scarcely remembered outside of a circle of collectors and other period enthusiasts. Teamed early with Steve Barri, Sloan had a lasting partner. The duo cashed in on the surf craze as the Fantastic Baggies, and Sloan has claimed to be involved with countless more surf productions. Sloan and Barri wrote and produced hits for the likes of the Turtles and Johnny Rivers, and may best be remembered for Barry McGuire's "Eve of Destruction." Sloan's own albums for Dunhill were based on the kind of material he had given McGuire, and despite being dismissed by the "serious" protest-folk community of the day, they stand as excellent on their own merits.

Sloan's attempt to shift away from the West Coast folk-rock he largely created was reflected with the R&B-tinged album *Measure for Pleasure*, and following another album in the early '70s, he was gone. In spite of the occasional live gig and rumors of a comeback, it appears that P.F. Sloan will remain forever connected with his '60s work, his behind-the-scenes efforts overshadowing the fine music under his own name. —*Steve Aldrich*

The Best of P.F. Sloan (1965-1966) / 1986 / Rhino ✦✦✦✦
While One Way's *Anthology* has a wider range, it may be that many listeners will prefer this 14-song collection, as it focuses exclusively on tracks from Sloan's first two LPs. This means you get nothing but sub-Dylanesque folk-rock, but after all, that's what most people value most by Sloan. The tracks are universally strong, including his most famous tunes ("Eve of Destruction," "The Sins of a Family," "Take Me for What I'm Worth") and lesser-known, equally worthy ones like "Lollipop Train," "From a Distance," "Here's Where You Belong," and "I Get out of Breath." —*Richie Unterberger*

P.F. Sloan/The Grass Roots / 1988 / Big Beat ✦✦✦
While this isn't as solid as the other P.F. Sloan collections, the concept is interesting, combining some of his most famous solo performances with five songs that were credited to the Grass Roots in the mid-'60s, but were for most intents and purposes Sloan performances. You can avoid this confusing approach by getting the Grass Roots' *Where Were You When I Needed You?* CD and Sloan's first two LPs. But those original

Sloan albums are pretty hard to come by these days, meaning that our choices are largely limited to relatively pathwork compilations such as these. —*Richie Unterberger*

● **Anthology** / Jul. 18, 1993 / One Way ✦✦✦✦
A well-compiled 18-track anthology featuring Sloan's overlooked recording career. This is essential folk-rock in the singer-songwriter tradition. Included is his wonderful version of "Eve of Destruction," which was written by Sloan and popularized by Barry McGuire. —*Chris Woodstra*

Sly & the Family Stone

f. 1967, San Francisco, CA, **db.** 1981
Soul, Funk, R&B, Pop-Rock

Sly & the Family Stone harnassed all of the disparate musical and social trends of the late '60s, creating a wild, brilliant fusion of soul, rock, R&B, psychedelia, and funk that broke boundaries down without a second thought. Led by Sly Stone, the Family Stone was comprised of men and women, and Blacks and Whites, making the band the first full integrated group in rock's history. That integration shone through the music, as well as the group's message. Before Stone, very few soul and R&B groups delved into political and social commentary; after him, it became a tradition in soul, funk, and hip-hop. And, along with James Brown, Stone brought hard funk into the mainstream. The Family Stone's arrangements were ingenious, filled with unexpected group vocals, syncopated rhythms, punchy horns, and pop melodies. Their music was joyous, but as the '60s ended so did the good times. Stone became disillusioned with the ideals he had been preaching in his music, becoming addicted to a variety of drugs in the process. His music gradually grew slower and darker, culminating in 1971's *There's a Riot Goin' On*, which set the pace for '70s funk with its elastic bass, slurred vocals, and militant Black power stance. Stone was able to turn out one more modern funk classic, 1973's *Fresh*, before slowly succumbing to his addictions, which gradually sapped him of his once prodigious talents. Nevertheless, his music continued to provide the basic template for urban soul, funk, and even hip-hop well into the '90s.

Sly Stone (b. Sylvester Stewart, March 15, 1944) and his family moved from his home state of Texas to San Francisco in the '50s. He had already begun to express an interest in music, and when he was 16 he had a regional hit with "Long Time Away." Stone studied music composition, theory, and trumpet at Vallejo Junior College in the early '60s; simultaneously, he began playing in several groups on the Bay Area scene, often with his brother Fred. Soon, he had become a disc jockey at the R&B station KSOL, later switching to KDIA. The radio appearances led to a job producing records for Autumn Records. While at Autumn, he worked with a number of San Franciscan garage and psychedelic bands, including the Beau Brummels, the Great Society, Bobby Freeman and the Mojo Men.

During 1966, Stone formed the Stoners, which featured trumpeter Cynthia Robinson. Though the Stoners didn't last long, he brought Robinson along as one of the core members of his next group, Sly & the Family Stone. Formed early in 1967, the Family Stone also featured Fred Stewart (guitar, vocal), Larry Graham, Jr. (bass, vocal), Greg Errico (drums), Jerry Martini (saxophone), and Rosie Stone (piano), who all were of different racial backgrounds. The group's eclectic music and multi-racial composition made them distinctive from the numerous flower-power bands in San Francisco, and their first single, "I Aint' Got Nobody," became a regional hit for the local label Loadstone. The band signed with Epic Records shortly afterward, releasing their debut album, *A Whole New Thing*, by the end of the year. The record stiffed, but the follow-up, *Dance to the Music*, generated a Top 10 pop and R&B hit with its title track early in 1968. *Life* followed later in 1968, but the record failed to capitalize on its predecessor's success. "Everyday People," released late in 1968, turned their fortunes back around, rocketing to the top of the pop and R&B charts and setting the stage for the breakthrough success of 1969's *Stand!*

Featuring "Everyday People," "Sing a Simply Song," "Stand," and "I Want to Take You Higher," *Stand!* became the Family Stone's first genuine hit album, climbing to No. 13 and spending over 100 weeks on the charts. *Stand!* also makred the emergence of the political bent in Stone's songwriting ("Don't Call Me Nigger, Whitey"), as well as the development of hard-edged, improvisational funk like "Sex Machine." The Family Stone quickly became known as one of the best live bands of the late '60s, and their performance at Woodstock was widely hailed as one of the festival's best. The non-LP singles "Hot Fun in the Summertime" and "Thank You (Falettinme Be Mice Elf Agin)" / "Everybody Is a Star" became hits, reaching No. 2 and No. 1 respectively in late 1969/early 1970. Both singles were included on *Greatest Hits*, which became a No. 2 record upon its fall 1970 release. While the group was at the height of its popularity, Sly Stone was beginning to unravel behind the scenes. Developing a debilitating addiction to narcotics, Stone soon became

notorious for arriving late for concerts, frequently missing the shows altogether.

Stone's growing personal problems, as well as his dismay with the slow death of the civil rights movement and other political causes, surfaced on *There's a Riot Goin' On*. Though the album shot to No. 1 upon its fall 1971 release, the record—including "Family Affair," his last No. 1 single—was dark, hazy and paranoid, and his audience began to shrink slightly. During 1972, several key members of the Family Stone, including Graham and Errico, left the band; they were replaced by Rusty Allen and Andy Newmark, respectively. The relatively lighter *Fresh* appeared in the summer of 1973, and it went into the Top 10 on the strength of the Top 10 R&B hit "If You Want Me to Stay." Released the following year, *Small Talk* was a moderate hit, reaching No. 15 on the charts and going gold, but it failed to generate a big hit single. *High on You*, released in late 1975 and credited only to Sly Stone, confirmed that his power and popularity had faded. "I Get High on You" reached the R&B Top 10, but the album made no lasting impact.

Disco had overtaken funk in terms of popularity, and even if Sly Stone wanted to compete with disco, he wasn't in shape to make music. He had become addicted to cocaine, his health was frequently poor, and he was often in trouble with the law. His recordings had slowed to a trickle and Epic decided to close out his contract in 1979 with *Ten Years Too Soon*, a compilation of previously released material that had the original funky rhythm tracks replaced with disco beats. Stone signed with Warner Brothers that same year, crafting the comeback effort *Back on the Right Track* with several original members of the Family Stone, but the record was critically panned and a commercial failure. In light of the album's lack of success, Stone retreated even further, eventually joining forces with George Clinton on Funkadelic's 1981 album *The Electric Spanking of War Babies*. Following the album's release, Stone toured with Clinton's P-Funk All-Stars, which led him to embark on his own tour, as well as a stint with Bobby Womack. The culmination of this burst of activity was 1983's *Ain't But the One Way*, an album that was ignored. Later that year, Stone was arrested for cocaine possession; the following year he entered rehab.

Stone appeared on Jesse Johnson's 1986 R&B hit "Crazay." The following year, he dueted with Martha Davis on "Love & Affection" for the *Soul Man* soundtrack; he also he recorded "Eek-a-Bo-Static," a single that didn't chart. Stone was arrested and imprisoned for cocaine possession by the end of 1987. He was never able to recover from the final arrest. Stone continued to battle his addiction, with varying degrees of success. By his 1993 induction to the Rock & Roll Hall of Fame, he had disappeared from public view. Following his appearance at the induction ceremony, he was found living in a sheltered-housing complex. Avenue Records gave Stone a recording contract in 1995, but as of 1997 his comeback album had not been recorded. —*Stephen Thomas Erlewine*

Whole New Thing / 1967 / Epic ✦✦✦
Their debut LP is more restrained and not nearly as funky or psychedelic as their subsequent efforts, owing far more to traditional soul arrangements. These aren't *that* traditional, though; Sly is already using goofier and/or more thoughtful lyrics than the soul norm, and taking some cues from rock in his adventurous and unexpected song construction. The Family Stone, similarly, aren't as innovative as they would shortly become, but are already a tight unit, particularly in the interplay between lead and backup vocals and the sharp horn riffs. The CD reissue adds a previously unissued track, "What Would I Do." —*Richie Unterberger*

Dance to the Music / 1968 / Epic ✦✦✦
Sly's second album reached the lower echelons of *Billboard*'s album charts due to the quintessential psychedelic soul single "Dance to the Music." The rest of the album is uneven, early, and tentative, with the full funk being a little further around the bend. —*Rob Bowman*

Life / 1968 / Epic ✦✦✦✦
The Family Stone's third album was a step forward with a harder drum sound, sharper horn lines, and more focused writing. Despite these developments, *Life* failed to yield a hit single ("Plastic Jim," "Life," and "M'Lady" were all fine candidates). —*Rob Bowman*

☆ **Stand!** / 1969 / Epic ✦✦✦✦✦
The album on which Sly's integrationist vision paid big dividends. Four of the record's seven songs, including "I Want to Take You Higher" and "Everyday People," charted as singles. The group contained Blacks and Whites, men and women; voices and instruments careened off one another in one apocalyptic vision of community. At the time, such an album seemed to be the clarion call of a new day. Brilliant. —*Rob Bowman*

★ **Greatest Hits** / 1970 / Epic ✦✦✦✦✦
This greatest-hits package was released as a stopgap while Sly was taking two years to record *There's a Riot Goin' On*. It's what you would expect from a greatest-hits package, with the addition of two newly recorded monster-hit singles, "Hot Fun in the Summertime" and "Thank You (Falettinme Be Mice Elf Agin)." —*Rob Bowman*

☆ **There's a Riot Goin' On** / 1971 / Epic ✦✦✦✦✦

Sly gets darker and funkier. By *Riot*, Sly was a bona fide superstar. His personal behavior became more erratic, and his songwriting became more eclectic and adventurous. There is no precedent for such a record; songs were conceived from the rhythm up, and often left in sparse, naked, seemingly semi-finished form. Sly's earlier hit, "Thank You (Falettinme Be Mice Elf Agin)" is slowed down, turned inside out, and retitled "Thank You for Talkin' to Me Africa." The result is an extremely personal stab at exorcism that takes the listener through the new reality of Black and White America in the early '70s. Mesmerizing. The album's most accessible songs, "Family Affair" and "Runnin' Away," were R&B and pop hit singles, the former reaching the No.1 spot on both charts. —*Rob Bowman*

☆ **Fresh** / 1973 / Epic ✦✦✦✦✦

Stripped down and funky, minus thumb-popping bass whiz Larry Graham (who had left to found Graham Central Station), Sly turned in a fine album. One Top Ten R&B hit resulted with "If You Want Me to Stay," while two other songs, "Frisky" and "If It Were Left up to Me," also received substantial airplay on Black radio. In the wake of Sly's politics on *Riot* and his increasingly erratic personal and concert behavior, most pop-radio programmers seemed to grow leery of the Family Stone. The first single, "If You Want Me to Stay," reached No.12 pop, but it was to be the last Sly Stone record to receive any significant pop success. —*Rob Bowman*

Small Talk / 1974 / Epic ✦✦

A new bass player and drummer signaled a toned-down Family Stone sound. Partially in keeping with changes in much of popular music in the early '70s, and maybe the result of marriage and a child, Sly became more introspective, quieter, and calmer, even employing a string section on various cuts. A less exhilarating album than earlier efforts, there is still much of merit here, including the Top Ten R&B hit "Time for Livin'." —*Rob Bowman*

★ **Anthology** / 1981 / Epic ✦✦✦✦✦

Anthology essentially replicates the previous collection *Greatest Hits* and adds singles from *There's a Riot Goin' On* and *Fresh* to the end of the album. Where *Greatest Hits* didn't follow chronological order, *Anthology* presents every single in the order they were released—and, with the exception of the latter-day singles and the inclusion of "Don't Call Me Nigger, Whitey," that is the major difference between the two collections. *Anthology* goes for a sweeping, definitive overview, while *Greatest Hits* is a brief blast of 12 of the finest singles of the rock 'n' roll era. Either compilation functions as an excellent introduction, but *Anthology* is more comprehensive, giving it the edge as a first purchase. —*Stephen Thomas Erlewine*

Family Affair / 1991 / Thunderbolt ✦✦

Beware of this deceptively titled, quasi-legal import. Sly Stone did indeed work with the Mojo Men, a minor San Francisco band, as a producer in the mid-'60s. No less than 11 of the 15 cuts here are not Sly, but mid-'60s Mojo Men tracks, available in much better fidelity on Sundazed's *Whys Ain't Supposed to Be* reissue (which has more songs to boot). This disc does end with three outtake-sounding Sly Stone tracks of obscure vintage (there are no liner notes). An educated guess would put them circa 1967, but they're not that interesting in any case. —*Richie Unterberger*

In the Still of the Night / 1991 / Thunderbolt ✦✦

The two years or so before Sly Stone signed to Epic saw him lay down a myriad of hazily documented official and unissued recordings. Now available on a variety of labels, *In the Still of the Night* has 17 of them, most seeming to date from his days as a producer at Autumn in the mid-'60s (the liner notes are of little help). These are mostly sketches, really, of primary interest to Sly historians: some soul covers, some instrumental R&B vamps, and tentative originals that show Stone approaching his singular rock/soul fusion. There's a good deal of duplication with other packages of early Sly material, and it's much less thoughtfully assembled than the best of those (Ace's *In the Studio with Sly Stone*). —*Richie Unterberger*

Dance to the Music / 1991 / Thunderbolt ✦✦

With the exception of Ace's *In the Studio with Sly Stone*, the import compilations of Sly's pre-1967 work seem determined to keep such trivial information as sources of material and dates secret. So we'll have to guess that most of the ten tracks on *Dance to the Music* come from the early '60s, even before Stone started working at Autumn Records (a couple, "Help Me with My Broken Heart"/"Long Time Alone," were definitely released as a solo single). Most of these have a late-period doo wop feel, and although the songs aren't that noteworthy, Sly sings well, and there's a nice pop/R&B feel to the production. It's a curiosity that fills out the puzzle of Sly's pre-Family history. A couple of tracks obviously date from his later, more sophisticated Autumn productions, like the female-sung "Honest," which has also appeared on other compilations. —*Richie Unterberger*

Sly Stone & The Mojo Men / 1993 / WPC ✦✦

A deceptively packaged collection of early work, most of which is not Sly himself but the Mojo Men, a minor San Francisco rock band that he worked with in the mid-'60s as a producer. It's the same as another dubious collection of early work (*Family Affair*), though it's missing one Sly track, "Seventh Son," which does appear on *Family Affair* and other murky reissues of early Sly material. —*Richie Unterberger*

Spotlight on Sly & The Family Stone / 1993 / Javelin ✦✦

One of several piecemeal compilations of pre-Epic Sly Stone floating around. Most or all of the 16 tracks here probably date from his mid-'60s demos (some performed by other singers) at Autumn Records. Much more straight R&B/soul-oriented than his late-'60s work, it's mostly of interest as an insight into his formative influences, although it offers some small pleasures. Ace's *In the Studio with Sly Stone* is the most comprehensive (and most professionally packaged) of these compilations by far. But if you're a completist, this does offer a few tracks that aren't frequently duplicated elsewhere, like the interesting soul/pop confection "Honest" (which has an unidentified woman on lead vocals). —*Richie Unterberger*

Remember Who You Are / May 1994 / Charly ✦✦

A reissue of his 1979 album *Back on the Right Track*, with the addition of a couple of previously unreleased outtakes that are more like jams than complete songs. —*Richie Unterberger*

Precious Stone: In the Studio / Sep. 13, 1994 / Ace ✦✦✦

Before forming the Family Stone, Sly Stone gained a lot of experience in the studio as the virtual in-house producer for the San Francisco-based Autumn label. The sessions he worked on during this era (performed by both himself and other artists) have appeared on numerous scattershot compilations. This 28-song anthology is the most comprehensive and intelligently assembled of these, including Sly solo performances, Sly collaborations with Billy Preston, and obscure soul-pop sides by Bobby Freeman, Gloria Scott, George & Teddy, and others. Over half of the cuts were previously unissued, and the lengthy liner notes provide an in-depth overview of his early accomplishments. Only serious collectors should seek this out, though. While Autumn afforded Stone the opportunity to experiment in the studio and devise various primitive collisions of soul and pop, his compositional, instrumental, and vocal skills were still in a very formative (if very promising) stage. Much of this is routinely pleasant, if lightly eccentric, period pop-soul, with occasional bursts of inspiration like Sly's wild scat vocals on "Scat Swim," the folk-rockish "As I Get Older," and a few songs that would be reworked for inclusion on the first couple of Family Stone albums. —*Richie Unterberger*

Slyest Freshest Funkiest Rarest / 1995 / Magicalmystery ✦✦

In 1967, before signing to Epic, Sly cut four tracks at Leo Kulka's Golden State Recorders studio—"Can't Turn You Loose," "I Ain't Got Nobody," "Take My Advice," and "Life of Fortune and Fame." All of those are here, plus 20—yes, 20—outtakes of instrumental backing tracks for those four tunes. So what you have here, basically, is the kind of thing that's better suited for a small-circulation bootleg for rabid fans than general release. The four primary tracks do have their interest: "Can't Turn You Loose" is direct evidence of Stone's soul roots, "Life of Fortune and Fame" shows his lyrical ambitions starting to flower, and "I Ain't Got Nobody" offers intriguing proof that Santana weren't the only San Francisco rock band around that devised rearrangements of that Latin-soul-jazz tune. The instrumental outtakes, most of which are pretty brief, are more suited for scholarly listening than entertainment, though Sly-heads may find the insight it affords into the young maestro's working methods interesting. If you can do without these outtakes, the four complete tracks are also available on such other shadowy reissues of early Sly material as *In the Still of the Night* and *Spotlight on Sly and the Family Stone*. —*Richie Unterberger*

The Small Faces

f. 1965, London, England, db. 1969
British Invasion, Pop-Rock, Mod

The Small Faces were the best English band never to hit it big in America. On this side of the Atlantic, all anybody remembers them for is their sole stateside hit, "Itchycoo Park"—but in England, the Small Faces were one of the most extraordinary and successful bands of the mid-'60s; their music remains some of the most valuable and enjoyable of the era.

Lead singer/guitarist Steve Marriott's formal background was on the stage; as a young teenager, he'd auditioned and won the part of The Artful Dodger in the Lionel Bart musical *Oliver!* Marriott was earning his living at a music shop when he made the acquaintance of Ronnie Lane (bass, backing vocals), who had formed a band called the Pioneers, which included drummer Kenney Jones. Lane invited Marriott to jam with the Pioneers at a show they were playing at a local club—the gig was a disaster, but out of that show the group decided to turn their talents toward American R&B. The band—with Marriott now installed permanently and Jimmy Winston recruited on organ—cast its lot with a faction of British youth known as the Mods, stylish posers who, among their other attributes, affected a dandified look and a fanatical love of American R&B. The quartet, now christened the Small Faces ("face" being a piece of Mod slang for a fashion leader), began making a name for themselves on stage, sparked by the group's no-holds-barred performance style.

The quartet was signed by manager Don Arden, and brought to Decca/London to record. The band's debut single, "What'cha Gonna Do About It," was released in August of 1965 and reached No. 14 on the charts; a second single, "I've Got Mine," failed to chart when released in November. Soon after its recording, Winston exited the lineup; he was replaced by Ian McLagan (organ/guitar/vocals). The group returned to the charts in February of 1966 with "Sha-La-La-La-Lee," which rose to No. 3 in England. Three months later, they were back at No. 10 with "Hey Girl," and heralded this new single release with their first album, *Small Faces*. "All or Nothing" marked their first chart-topping entry, and its follow-up, "My Mind's Eye," followed it nearly as high. On the surface, nothing could possibly have seemed wrong for the band. Keeping up the standard of songwriting and recording that they were maintaining was difficult, however, and they were increasingly unhappy with Arden. At the end of 1966, the band severed their ties with him and eventually moved under the wing of Rolling Stones manager/producer Andrew "Loog" Oldham. Oldham signed the group as clients; by the middle of the 1967 he had gotten them moved over to his new Immediate Records label.

With the shift in management and label, the group suddenly found themselves with a drastically reduced touring schedule and vastly increased time available in the studio. Their sound immediately became looser. They remained a top-flight R&B-driven band, but a much wider array of sounds and instruments began figuring in their music. Their first Immediate album, entitled *Small Faces* (known in the USA as *There Are but Four Small Faces*), was issued in mid-1967, and was an instant hit. In August of the year, they released "Itchycoo Park," a lilting, lyrical idyll to the Summer of Love that captured the hearts of listeners on both sides of the Atlantic. The band had bigger aspirations than doing more hit singles, and set to work across five months during 1968 in at least four different studios recording what proved to be their magnum opus, *Ogden's Nut Gone Flake*. The group's fortunes didn't equal the artistic success of the album. In June of 1968, to announce the release of the album, Immediate took out an ad in the music trade papers that included a parody of the Lord's Prayer that managed to offend several million people before an apology from the band was issued. And Immediate, over the objections of Marriott, chose to release the song "Lazy Sunday"—which he'd recorded as a joke—as a single, and its rise to No. 2 on the British charts did nothing to ease his unhappiness.

Already, the group was showing serious signs of strain. A tour of Australia ended with complaints from the authorities concerning the band's behavior, and there were reports of late arrivals (or no-shows) by the band at their English gigs. "The Universal," a single released in the summer of 1968, was to have been Marriott's most serious effort in that vein in over a year; it subsequently failed to crack the Top 20, and much of his interest in continuing with the band seemed to falter. The end came soon after, on New Year's Day, 1969, when Marriott suddenly left the stage while the band was jamming to "Lazy Sunday" during a show at the Alexandria Palace; he later called Peter Frampton, a guitarist from the Herd, and the two began mapping plans for a band of their own called Humble Pie.

The Small Faces did carry on into 1969, but it wasn't the same. With Marriott gone, they needed a replacement singer and lead guitarist, and found them in Rod Stewart and Ron Wood. They carried on under the name the Small Faces for one album, before dropping the "Small" and going on to greater glory as the Faces. During the mid-'70s the Small Faces reunited (without Ronnie Lane) for two albums, *Playmates* and *78 in the Shade*, that attracted a lot of press attention but nothing resembling the chart action of their earlier releases. Lane recorded with Pete Townshend, amongst others, before contracting multiple sclerosis, which ended his career as a musician (he later organized the A.R.M.S. benefit concerts to raise money for research into a cure for the disease). Jones subsequently joined the Who, replacing Keith Moon after the latter's sudden death in 1978, and did a couple of tours and a pair of albums with the band. Steve Marriott always seemed poised for a comeback, and in 1991 it looked as though he was going to finally pull it off—alas, he died in his sleep when fire swept his home in England, tragically just a couple of days after beginning work on a new album in America with his former bandmate Peter Frampton. —*Bruce Eder*

☆ **Small Faces** / 1966 / Deram ✦✦✦✦✦

This CD and the accompanying 1996 reissue of *From the Beginning* makes collecting the Small Faces' Decca sides complicated, containing as it does many tracks that are not on the anthology double-disc. The new remastering has turned this into a must-own disc for anyone who enjoys the early Rolling Stones or, especially, the early Who, and wants to hear a British Invasion band as good as they were that never quite

made it in the US, and which could have crossed swords with any garage band you care to name and carried the day. In those days, Steve Marriott had an even more soulful voice than Mick Jagger or Roger Daltrey; the main influences on the group were Sam Cooke and Marvin Gaye, and he was pretty formidable on guitar as well. The songs all have that really cool crunchy sound on the early Who records, except the sound is a little fuller and the tempos are better conceived, and there's even a pretty impressive bit of feedback throughout. The French EP tracks that comprise this disc's bonus songs are all distinctly different from the standard cuts, generally much more raw—like *real* American-style garage band stuff—including a feedback-laden opening to a completely different take of "What'cha Gonna Do About It" and totally different versions of "Shake" and "E to D." The sound on these cuts isn't quite up to the original album's 12 established tracks, as master tapes were impossible to find, but they—and the improved sound of the rest—make this a must-own CD, even more than *The Decca Anthology*. —*Bruce Eder*

From the Beginning / 1967 / Deram ✦✦✦✦

Another remastering of a classic piece of mid-1960s British rock 'n' soul, and as important and enjoyable a record as, say, the Beatles' *Rubber Soul* or the Stones' *Aftermath*, even if the album itself was slapped together by Decca in an effort to undercut the band's first new release for rival Immediate Records in 1967. Steve Marriott's cover of the Del Shannon classic "Runaway" almost makes up for the fact that neither Otis Redding nor Marvin Gaye ever got around to applying their respective talents to this jewel of a song—in his honest, agonized rendition, Marriott's performance also rips open a gaping hole in the soul of the listener that looks out on an eternity of loneliness, which is probably what Del had in mind when he wrote it in the first place. That's just the opening number, and there's some stuff even better than that here. There are some songs that overlap with the Immediate stuff, including some really spaced-out psychedelia ("Yesterday, Today, and Tomorrow"), cool dance numbers ("Have You Ever Seen Me," which must've kept them shimmying and shaking many a night at such swinging London locales as the UFO Club); some repeated tracks ("What'cha Gonna Do About It," "Sha-La-La-La-Lee") from the Decca *Small Faces* album (see above); killer Motown paeans ("You've Really Got a Hold on Me"—picture the early Who on a really, really good day covering this); and one original ("All or Nothing") that should be required listening for anyone who thinks they know the best music of the British invasion. And then there are the five bonus tracks, four from French-issued EPs that are completely different (and better) takes of "Baby Don't You Do It" et al, and a live BBC-recorded version of "What'cha Gonna Do About It." Marriott's playing on the latter is so loud and powerful, it could have melted the instruments of any American garage band this side of the Litter. At $11.99 list, this disc and its companion *Small Faces* reissue are the biggest British Invasion bargains going. —*Bruce Eder*

☆ **There Are But Four Small Faces** / 1968 / Sony ✦✦✦✦✦

The band's first album for Andrew "Loog" Oldham's Immediate label originally appeared in two different forms in England (where it was known as *Small Faces*) and America, and the two song lineups have been combined on an early-'90s American Sony Music reissue. The music here is much more fully developed and experimental than their preceding album, still largely R&B-based (apart from the delightfully trippy "Itchycoo Park," the band's sole American hit) but with lots of unusual sounds and recording techniques being attempted. —*Bruce Eder*

☆ **Ogden's Nut Gone Flake** / 1968 / Sony ✦✦✦✦✦

The best album the Small Faces ever released, and one of the great records of the late '60s, a kind of Cockney *Sgt. Pepper*, with tough, grinding rock numbers, blues shouts, and psychedelia all mixing together into one brilliant whole. A vital addition to any record or CD collection, and also a controversial one at the time—a promotional ad taken out in the British music trades at the time managed to blaspheme several religions at once. Alas, Steve Marriott decided to call it quits with the group less than six months after this record was released. —*Bruce Eder*

Autumn Stone / 1969 / Immediate ✦✦✦

An excellent collection of most of the band's most important songs from both their later Decca and their entire Immediate history, rounded out with their final single, "The Universal," and five live tracks taken from a 1968 concert. A decent set of liner notes would've been nice, though. —*Bruce Eder*

Playmates / 1977 / Atlantic ✦

78 in the Shade / 1978 / Atlantic ✦✦

Playmates and *78 in the Shade* are a pair of mid-'70s reunion albums that did little to advance the group's reputation. The recording on *Playmates*, in particular, seems flat and muted, and while *78 in the Shade* comes off better, it still wasn't going to make anyone forget the band's early history or revive its fortunes, either. —*Bruce Eder*

★ **25 Greatest Hits** / 1992 / Repertoire ✦✦✦✦✦
Featuring all of their big British hits from "What'cha Gonna Do About It" to "The Universal," as well as worthy obscurities like "Donkey Rides a Penny a Glass," *25 Greatest Hits* is the best Small Faces compilation available, even if the tracks aren't presented in chronological order. —*Stephen Thomas Erlewine*

All or Nothing / Jun. 30, 1992 / CBS ✦✦✦✦
The best collection to date of odd outtakes, obscure B-sides, and other rarities, remastered for superior sound and reconfigured so that, among other advantages, the live tracks from *Autumn Stone* are assembled together in sequence. Also contains lots of alternate takes, instrumental backing tracks, etc. —*Bruce Eder*

Singles A's & B's / Dec. 16, 1994 / See For Miles ✦✦✦✦

Decca Anthology 1965-1967 / 1996 / Decca ✦✦✦✦
This 36-song double-CD set covers most of the group's released songs from Decca, minus one song ("I Can't Make It") that they lost the rights to, and augmented with a handful of solo tracks by Steve Marriott and songs by Jimmy Winston's band. The sound is fair—none of the Decca songs by any band from this period seem to be in great shape—but not earth-shattering; what is earth-shattering is the performance of Marriott and company, especially on their earlier tracks. Despite being worked to death by the record company and their own touring schedule, and their rapidly growing disillusionment, they generated some incredibly passionate British Invasion-era R&B, embracing Stax and the more soulful sides of Motown with equal ease. The later material shows the first appearance of the druggy ambience and psychedelic haze that was to characterize their Immediate period, not surprising since they moved from Decca to Immediate in a matter of days, the moment they had enough material to satisfy (at least on paper) their Decca contract, with some songs ("E to D," etc.) shared in different versions between the two companies. The packaging is a bit unwieldy, however, and while the photos are great, Paolo Hewitt's well-intentioned notes seem driven more by enthusiasm than care or skill (not only is the connection between "You Need Loving" and Led Zeppelin's "Whole Lotta Love" debatable, but he gets the title of the Zeppelin song wrong, referring to it as "Whole Lotta Lovin'.") —*Bruce Eder*

● **The Immediate Years** / Jan. 1996 / Charly ✦✦✦✦
Okay, it's expensive as a four-CD set. And yeah, apart from "Itchycoo Park" and maybe "Lazy Sunday," not too much of what the Small Faces recorded ever made any lasting impression on American listeners. But there's a *lot* of good music here. The box opens up modestly enough with Steve Marriott's old band the Moments, covering the Kinks' "You Really Got Me" and doing one other song, "Money Money." A few of the band's Decca tracks that seem to float between Decca and Immediate follow, and then we plunge into the group's Immediate history. Andrew "Loog" Oldham's independent label wasn't much more organized than the typical blues label from Chicago in the 1950s, and the Small Faces' tape library is a mess. But the producers have included everything—every stereo and mono version of each song (where a different mix exists), the five official live tracks, the unfinished backing tracks, every known outtake. Anyone who thinks this is overkill doesn't know the Small Faces—they weren't much less prolific than the Rolling Stones, and were better than the Stones as both a soul band and a psychedelic band (the Stones never really made the jump into drug songs too comfortably); and based on the evidence, they could have cut the Who to shreds most nights. The sound varies, although it's all been nicely cleaned up (mildly CEDAR-ized, actually), and while three versions of "(Tell Me) Have You Ever Seen Me" may seem like overkill, it's all fascinating stuff, watching certain songs change and evolve. This is where it ends for the serious fan. —*Bruce Eder*

The Definitive Anthology of the Small Faces / Feb. 1996 / Repertoire ✦✦✦✦

Anthology: 1965-67 / Oct. 22, 1996 / Polygram ✦✦✦✦
The Small Faces' catalog is one of the most confusing in rock 'n' roll history, featuring multiple compilations bearing the same title but considerably different track listings, reworked original albums and haphazard retrospectives. The double-disc *Anthology: 1965-1967* goes a long way toward correcting those problems, yet it stops just short of being definitive. Containing all of the material the band recorded for Decca Records—including "What'cha Gonna Do About It?," "Sha-La-La-La-Lee," "Hey Girl," "All or Nothing" and "My Mind's Eye"—which means it cuts off just as the Small Faces were entering their most creative period. Still, the Small Faces were an excellent British R&B group and that phase is captured in all its glory on this set. —*Stephen Thomas Erlewine*

Deep Joy / [Bootleg] ✦✦
Spurred by the massive revival of interest in the group in the mid-'90s, bootlegs of the Small Faces are starting to appear, but they're really not a key to a wealth of worthy unavailable material. This is a lengthy (70-minute) pastiche of radio and TV broadcasts from throughout their career; most of the tracks are in substandard fidelity, and most of the

performances vary little from the official versions. Items of above-average interest include a 1968 BBC broadcast with an instrumental version of "Get Ready" and a long cover of "Every Little Bit Hurts," neither of which the band released. Serious Small Faces obsessives may find the broadcasts of "Itchycoo Park" and "Lazy Sunday" interesting, but even completists aren't missing much by passing this up. —*Richie Unterberger*

Smashing Pumpkins

f. 1989, Chicago, IL
Alternative Pop-Rock, Hard Rock
Of all the major alternative rock bands of the early '90s, Smashing Pumpkins were the group least influenced by traditional underground rock. Lead guitarist/songwriter Billy Corgan fashioned an amalgam of progressive rock, heavy metal, goth rock, psychedelia, and dream pop, creating a layered, powerful sound driven by swirling, distorted guitars. Corgan was wise enough to exploit his angst-ridden lyrics, yet he never shied away from rock-star posturing, even if he did cloak it in allegedly ironic gestures. In fact, the Smashing Pumpkins became the model for alternative rock success—Nirvana were too destructive, Pearl Jam shunned success. The Pumpkins, on the other hand, knew how to play the game—signing to a major-subsidized indie for underground credibility, moving to the major in time to make the group a multi-platinum act. And when the group did achieve mass success with 1993's *Siamese Dream*, they went a long way to legitimize heavy metal and orchestrated prog-rock, helping move alternative rock even closer to '70s AOR rock, especially in the eyes of radio programmers and mainstream audiences. And, unlike many of their contemporaries, the Pumpkins were able to withstand many internal problems and keep selling records, emerging as the longest-lasting and most successful alternative band of the early '90s.

The son of a jazz guitarist, Billy Corgan grew up in a Chicago suburb, leaving home at the age of 19 to move to Florida with his fledgling goth-metal band, the Marked. After the band failed down south, he returned to Chicago around 1988, where he began working at a used record store. At the shop he met James Iha (guitar), a graphic arts student at Loyola University, and the two began collaborating, performing, and recording songs with a drum machine. Corgan met D'Arcy Wretzky at a club show; after arguing about the merits of the Dan Reed Network, the two became friends, and she joined the group as a bassist. Soon, the band, who had named themselves Smashing Pumpkins, had gained a dedicated local following, including the head of a local club who booked them to open for Jane's Addiction. Before the pivotal concert, the band hired Jimmy Chamberlin, a former jazz musician, as the group's full-time drummer.

In 1990, the Smashing Pumpkins released their debut single "I Am One" on the local Chicago label Limited Potential. The single quickly sold out, and in December the band released "Tristessa" on Sub Pop. By this point, the Smashing Pumpkins had become the subject of a hot bidding war, and the group latched on to a clever way to move to a major label without losing indie credibility. They signed to Virgin Records, yet it was decided that the group's debut would be released on the Virgin subsidiary, Caroline; *then* the band would move to the majors. The strategy worked. *Gish*, a majestic mix of Black Sabbath and dream pop produced by Butch Vig, became a huge college and modern rock hit upon its spring 1991 release. While it earned a large audience, many indie-rock fans began to snipe at Smashing Pumpkins, accusing them of being careerists. Such criticism did the band no harm, and they embarked on an extensive supporting tour for *Gish*, which lasted over a year and included opening slots for Red Hot Chili Peppers and Pearl Jam.

During the *Gish* tour, tensions between the band members began to escalate, as Iha and D'Arcy, who had been lovers, went through a messy breakup, Chamberlin became addicted to drugs and alcohol, and Corgan entered a heavy depression. These tensions hadn't been resolved by the time the group entered the studio with Vig to record their second album. Towards the beginning of the sessions, the Pumpkins were given significant exposure through the inclusion of "Drown" on the *Singles* soundtrack in the summer of 1992. As the sessions progressed, Corgan relieved himself of his depression by working heavily—not only did he write a surplus of songs, he played nearly all of the guitars and bass on each recording, which meant that its release was delayed several times. The resulting album, *Siamese Dream*, was an immaculate production owing much to Queen, yet it was embraced by critics upon its July 1993 release. *Siamese Dream* became a blockbuster, debuting at No. 10 on the charts and establishing the group as stars. "Cherub Rock," the first single, was a modern rock hit, yet it was "Today" and the acoustic "Disarm" that sent the album into the stratosphere, as well as the group's relentless touring. Smashing Pumpkins became the headliners of 1994's Lollapalooza, and following the tour's completion the band went back into the studio to record a new album that Corgan had already claimed would be a double-disc set. To tide fans over until the new album, the

Pumpkins released the B-sides and rarities album *Pisces Iscariot* in October of 1994.

Working with producers Flood and Alan Moulder, Smashing Pumpkins recorded as a full band for their third album, which turned out to be, as Corgan predicted, a double-disc set called *Mellon Collie and the Infinite Sadness*. Although many observers were skeptical about whether a double-disc set, especially one so ridiculously named, would be a commercial success, *Mellon Collie* became an even bigger hit than *Siamese Dream*, debuting at No. 1 on the charts. On the strength of the singles "Bullet with Butterfly Wings," "1979," "Zero," and "Tonight, Tonight," it would sell over four million copies in the US, eventually being certified platinum over eight times (each disc in the set counted separately towards certification). The Pumpkins had graduated to stadium shows for the *Mellon Collie* tour, and the band was at the peak of its popularity when things began to go wrong again. On July 12, prior to two shows at Madison Square Garden, the group's touring keyboardist, Jonathan Melvoin, died from a heroin overdose; he was with Jimmy Chamberlin, who survived his overdose. In the wake of the tragedy, the remaining Pumpkins fired Chamberlin and spent two months on hiatus, as they recovered and searched for a new drummer. Early in August, they announced that Filter member Matt Walker would be their touring drummer, and Dennis Flemion, a member of the Frogs, would be their touring keyboardist for the remainder of the year. They returned to the stage at the end of August and spent the next five months on tour. During this time, Corgan contributed some music to Ron Howard's *Ransom*. Early in 1997, once the Pumpkins left the road, Iha and D'Arcy launched Scratchie Records, a subsidiary of Mercury Records. In the spring, the Smashing Pumpkins recorded two songs for the soundtrack of *Batman & Robin*. *— Stephen Thomas Erlewine*

Gish / May 1991 / Caroline ✦✦✦✦
Arriving several months before Nirvana's *Nevermind*, the Smashing Pumpkins' debut album *Gish*, which was also produced by Butch Vig, was the first shot of the alternative revolution that transformed the rock 'n' roll landscape of the '90s. While Nirvana was a punk band, the Smashing Pumpkins and guitarist/vocalist Billy Corgan are arena-rockers, co-opting their metallic riffs and epic art-rock song structures with self-absorbed lyrical confessions. Though Corgan's lyrics fall apart upon close analysis, there's no denying his gift for arrangements. Like Brian May and Jimmy Page, he knows how to layer guitars for maximum effect, whether it's on the pounding, sub-Sabbath rush of "I Am One" or the shimmering, psychedelic dream-pop surfaces of "Rhinoceros." Such musical moments like as, as well as the rushing "Siva" and the folky "Daydream," which features D'Arcy on lead vocals, demonstrate the Smashing Pumpkins' potential, but the rest of *Gish* falls prey to undistinguished songwriting and showy instrumentation. *— Stephen Thomas Erlewine*

Lull / 1992 / Caroline ✦✦✦
Lull is a four-song EP the Smashing Pumpkins released as they were preparing to enter the studio to record their second album, *Siamese Dream*. Essentially the "Rhinoceros" single and three B-sides, *Lull* is targeted toward diehard fans but the solo Billy Corgan acoustic ballad "Bye June" and the blistering "Slunk" illustrate that the sumptuous neo-psychedelic hard rock of *Gish* wasn't a fluke. *— Stephen Thomas Erlewine*

● **Siamese Dream** / Jul. 1993 / Virgin ✦✦✦✦
Dense with detail and texture, Smashing Pumpkins' breakthrough second album is a highly personal, ambitious record that unfolds after a few plays. *Siamese Dream* expands on all the promise of *Gish*, offering more pop melodies, heavy-metal riffs, bombastic progressive instrumental sections, and punk angst. Apart from the succinct "Today," the music is so dense and insular that it requires some patience for it to make sense, but given some time, *Siamese Dream* becomes addictive. *— Stephen Thomas Erlewine*

Pisces Iscariot / Oct. 1994 / Capitol ✦✦✦
Some bands can pull off a thoroughly entertaining compilation of B-sides and outtakes; Smashing Pumpkins cannot. While there are some gems in the tracks—the introspective acoustic lament "Soothe" and the full-blown "Plume" and "La Dolly Vita," in particular—*Pisces Iscariot* lacks the focus that made *Siamese Dream* so impressive. Hardcore fans will find several tracks of interest, but the album will wear on more casual listeners. *— Stephen Thomas Erlewine*

Mellon Collie and the Infinite Sadness / Oct. 24, 1995 / Virgin ✦✦✦✦
Smashing Pumpkins didn't shy away from making the follow-up to the grand, intricate *Siamese Dream*. With *Mellon Collie and the Infinite Sadness*, the band turns in one of the most ambitious and indulgent albums in rock history. Lasting over two hours and featuring 28 songs, the album is certainly a challenging listen. To Billy Corgan's credit, it's a rewarding and compelling one as well. Although the artistic scope of the album is immense, the Smashing Pumpkins flourish in such an overblown setting. Corgan's songwriting has never been limited by conventional notions of what a rock band can do, even if it is clear that he draws inspiration from scores of '70s heavy metal and art-rock bands.

Instead of copying the sounds of his favorite records, he expands on their ideas, making the gentle piano of the title track and the sighing "1979" sit comfortably against the volcanic rush of "Jellybelly" and "Zero." In between those two extremes lay an array of musical styles, drawing from rock, pop, folk, and classical. Some of the songs don't work as well as others, but *Mellon Collie* never seems to drag. Occasionally they fall flat on their face, but over the entire album the Smashing Pumpkins prove that they are one of the more creative and consistent bands of the '90s. *— Stephen Thomas Erlewine*

Aeroplane Flies High / Nov. 26, 1996 / Virgin ✦✦✦
The Aeroplane Flies High contains all five singles—"Bullet with Butterfly Wings," "1979," "Zero," "Tonight, Tonight," "Thirty-Three"—from *Mellon Collie and the Infinite Sadness* in a box set shaped like a 45-single carrying case from the '60s. Though the set contains all of the B-sides from the five singles, the running order isn't quite the same as the original releases—for example, in its original release, "Butterfly Wings" only had two B-sides, but it is augmented by four covers of new wave artists like the Cars, Blondie, and Missing Persons. In total, the box set has more songs than *Mellon Collie*, and, by and large, the quality of the music is quite strong. Occasionally, Billy Corgan's prolificness gets the better of him—there are a number of songs where his reach exceeds his grasp, and he doesn't quite come up with an engaging melody to match his detailed production. At other times, his musical experimentations catch hold, such as when he delves into jazz or orchestrated pop. Still, all of these pleasures are ones that are only of interest to dedicated Smashing Pumpkins fans who already know *Mellon Collie and the Infinite Sadness* inside and out. A casual fan will have a hard time sorting out the wheat from the chaff on *The Aeroplane Flies High*, but that work will be a pleasure for the diehards. *— Stephen Thomas Erlewine*

Huey "Piano" Smith

b. Jan. 26, 1934, New Orleans, LA
Piano / R&B, New Orleans R&B
At one time a madcap vocalist and underrated pianist, Huey "Piano" Smith was a star in New Orleans during the '50s. He sang with Earl King in the early '50s, then recorded with Guitar Slim from 1951 to 1954. He did several sessions and also led the Clowns, whose roster at one point included Bobby Marchan. Smith's biggest hit wasn't the song he's best known for, "Rocking Pneumonia and the Boogie Woogie Flu," but "Don't You Just Know It," which was his only Top Ten pop and R&B hit. It reached No. 4 R&B and No. 9 pop in 1958, a year after "Rocking Pneumonia" peaked at No. 5 R&B. Smith kept going until he became a Jehovah's Witness and left the music business. *— Ron Wynn*

● **Rock & Roll Revival** / Jan. 1991 / Ace ✦✦✦✦
A terrific 16-track collection of Huey "Piano" Smith & the Clowns' biggest hits and best material, including "Rocking Pneumonia" and "Don't You Just Know It," plus a couple of fine previously unreleased tracks. *— Stephen Thomas Erlewine*

Patti Smith

b. Dec. 30, 1946, Chicago, IL
Vocals / Rock & Roll, Proto-Punk
Patti Smith is a poet and rock singer who first gained notice when reading her poetry at gatherings in New York City in the early '70s. By 1974 Smith had edged toward music by reading with the backup of electric guitarist and rock critic Lenny Kaye, notably on her independent-label single "Piss Factory." By 1975 Smith had organized a band that was playing in such clubs as the punk birthplace in New York, CBGB's, and she earned a contract with Arista Records. This resulted in the release of *Horses*, a critically acclaimed album that featured her songs, sometimes melded to dramatic readings, and such rock oldies as "Land of 1,000 Dances." *Radio Ethiopia* was both mainstream-rock-oriented and more experimental, depending on which track you played. With 1978's *Easter*, Smith was definitely moving in a more commercial direction, especially by pairing with Bruce Springsteen for the hit single "Because the Night." That marked the high point of Smith's rock career. *Wave* (1979) found her waving goodbye; she married ex-MC5 guitarist Fred "Sonic" Smith and retired from the music business. Her return came with the promising 1988 album *Dream of Life*, but she was not back to full-time duty. Smith's husband died suddenly at the end of 1994. In 1995, she began making concert appearances again while preparing a new album due in 1996. In June 1996, Smith released *Gone Again*. *— William Ruhlmann*

★ **Horses** / Nov. 1975 / Arista ✦✦✦✦✦
It isn't hard to make the case for Patti Smith as a punk rock progenitor based on her debut album, which anticipated the new wave by a year or so: the simple, crudely played rock 'n' roll, featuring Lenny Kaye's rudimentary guitar work, the anarchic spirit of Smith's vocals and the emotional and imaginative nature of her lyrics all prefigure the coming movement as it evolved on both sides of the Atlantic. Smith is a rock critic's dream, a poet as steeped in '60s garage rock as she is in French

Symbolism; "Land" carries on from the Doors' "The End," marking her as a successor to Jim Morrison, while the borrowed choruses of "Gloria" and "Land of 1,000 Dances" are more in tune with the era of sampling than they were in the '70s. Producer John Cale respected Smith's primitivism in a way that later producers did not, and the loose, improvisatory song structures worked with her free verse to create something like a new spoken word/musical art form: *Horses* was a hybrid, the sound of a post-Beat poet, as she put it, "dancing around to the simple rock 'n' roll song." — *William Ruhlmann*

Radio Ethiopia / Oct. 1976 / Arista ✦✦✦

After the success of *Horses*, Patti Smith had something to prove to reviewers and to the industry, and *Radio Ethiopia* aimed at both. Producer Jack Douglas gave "the Patti Smith Group," as it was now billed, a hard rock sound, notably on the side-opening "Ask the Angels" and "Pumping (My Heart)," songs that seemed aimed at album-oriented rock radio. But the title track was a ten-minute guitar extravaganza that pushed the group's deliberate primitivism closer to amateurish thrashing. Elsewhere, Smith repeated the reggae excursions and vocal overlaying that had paced *Horses* on "Ain't It Strange" and "Poppies," but these efforts were less effective than they had been the first time around, perhaps because they were less inspired, perhaps because they were more familiar. It was a schizophrenic album in which the many elements that had worked so well together on *Horses* now seemed jarringly incompatible. With *Radio Ethiopia* Smith and her band encountered the same development problem the punks would—as they learned their craft, and competence set in, they lost some of the unself consciousness that had made their music so appealing. — *William Ruhlmann*

Easter / Mar. 1978 / Arista ✦✦✦✦

Patti Smith came back from the year-and-a-half break caused by her fall from a stage in January 1977 without having resolved the arts vs. commerce argument that had marred her second album, *Radio Ethiopia*. In fact, that argument was in some ways the theme of her third. *Easter*, produced by Bruce Springsteen associate Jimmy Iovine, was Smith's most commercial-sounding effort yet and, due to the inclusion of Springsteen's "Because the Night" (with Smith's revised lyrics), a Top Ten hit, it became her biggest seller, staying in the charts more than five months and getting into the Top 20 LPs. But Smith hadn't so much sold out as she had learned to use her poetic gifts within an album-rock context. Certainly, a song that proclaimed, "Love is an angel disguised as lust / Here in our bed until the morning comes," was pushing the limits of pop radio; and on "Babelogue," Smith returned to her days of declaiming poetry on New York's Lower East Side. That rant (significantly ending, "I have not sold my soul to God") led into the provocative "Rock N Roll Nigger," a charged rocker with a chorus that went, "Outside of society / Is where I want to be." Smith made the theme from the '60s British rock movie *Privilege* her own and even got into the UK charts with it. And on songs like "25th Floor," Iovine, Smith, and her group were able to accommodate both the urge to rock out and the need to expound. So, *Easter* turned out to be the best compromise Smith achieved between her artistic and commercial aspirations. — *William Ruhlmann*

Wave / May 1979 / Arista ✦✦✦

The Patti Smith Group's most conventional album, *Wave* was given a bright pop-rock sound by producer Todd Rundgren. It was the last album Smith made before marrying and retiring from record-making for nine years, and it can be heard as a farewell to the music business, from "Frederick," the love song to her husband-to-be, Fred "Sonic" Smith, that sets it off, to the version of "So You Want to Be (A Rock 'N' Roll Star)," among the most bitter accounts of fame on record. But Smith also achieves a sense of charm and sincerity on *Wave* that she hadn't even attempted on her earlier albums, even to the point of her imagined small-talk encounter with the late Pope John Paul I on the title track. Still, the overall mediocre quality of the material makes this the slightest of Smith's efforts. — *William Ruhlmann*

Dream of Life / Jun. 1988 / Arista ✦✦✦

The big difference between Patti Smith's four 1970s albums and this return to action after nine years lies in the choice of collaborator. Where Smith's main associate earlier had been Lenny Kaye, a deliberately simple guitarist, here her co-writer and co-producer (with Jimmy Iovine) was her husband, Fred "Sonic" Smith, formerly of the MC5, who played guitar with a conventional rock competence and who lent his talents to each of the tracks, giving them a mainstream flavor. In a sense, however, these polished love songs, lullabies, and political statements are not to be compared to the poetic ramblings of Smith's first decade of music making—she's so much . . . calmer this time out. But you can't help it. Where the Patti Smith of *Horses* inspired a generation of female rockers, the Patti Smith of *Dream of Life* sounds like she's been listening to later Pretenders albums and taking tips from Chrissie Hynde, one of her spiritual daughters. *Dream of Life* is the record of someone who is simply showing the flag, trying to keep her hand in, rather than announcing her

comeback. Not surprisingly, having made it, Smith retreated from the public eye again until the '90s. — *William Ruhlmann*

Gone Again / Jun. 18, 1996 / Arista ✦✦✦

After years of silence, Patti Smith returned to music with a series of concerts in late 1995. It had been years since she had performed live—for most of the '80s and '90s she concentrated on domestic life. Following the death of her husband, Fred "Sonic" Smith, in early 1995, Smith began playing music in public again and those concerts eventually led to the triumphant comeback *Gone Again*. Her husband wasn't the only loved one Smith lost between 1988's *Dream of Life* and 1996's *Gone Again*—her brother and her close friend Robert Mapplethorpe both died. Appropriately, grief and loss hang over *Gone Again*, but the overall effect is not one of indulgent melancholy. Instead, it's a sober but strengthening listen—this is healing optimistic music. Like most of Smith's best work, the songs on *Gone Again* aren't proper songs, they're song poems, with cascading music and dense, inspired lyrics. Smith sounds more mature than her earlier records—there are only a handful of out-and-out rockers, and most of the album is subtle and folky—which gives the album extra weight. *Gone Again* is more than a comeback, it's a revitalization—Patti Smith simply hasn't sounded so engaged and provocative since *Easter*. — *Stephen Thomas Erlewine*

Warren Smith

b. Feb. 7, 1933, d. Jan. 31, 1980
Vocals / Traditional Country, Rockabilly

For sheer, heartfelt vocalizing abilities, of all the folks who stood in front of the microphone at Sun studio, Warren Smith may have been the most talented. Equally adept at storming rockabilly and the most gut-wrenching of country ballads, Smith always sang it from the heart, without giving in to phony rasping or histrionics. Though typecast as strictly a rocker, Smith left Sun and achieved minor success in the '60s as a country singer, his first love. — *Cub Koda*

The Classic Recordings 1956-59 / 1992 / Bear Family ✦✦✦✦

Smith's entire output (31 tracks in all) for Sun Records. Includes the rockabilly classics "Rock n' Roll Ruby," "Ubangi Stomp," and "Miss Froggie," as well as heartfelt country performances on "The Darkest Cloud," "I'd Rather Be Safe than Sorry," and "Goodbye Mr. Love." No Sun collection can really be considered complete without adding this one to the list. — *Cub Koda*

● **Uranium Rock: Best Of** / May 23, 1995 / AVI ✦✦✦✦

Uranium Rock: The Best Of is a wonderful 24-track collection containing all of Warren Smith's essential Sun recordings, from "Rock 'n' Roll Ruby" and "Ubangi Stomp" to "Black Jack David," "Red Cadillac and a Black Moustache" and "Uranium Rock." It's a more concise and more effective compilation than Bear Family's *The Classic Recordings*, and therefore, it's arguably the definitive overview. — *Stephen Thomas Erlewine*

The Smithereens

f. 1980, Carteret, New Jersey
Rock & Roll

Dressed in leather, brandishing heavy guitars and an unabashed fetish for British Invasion pop, the Smithereens were an anomaly in the American college rock scene of the late '80s. Lead singer-songwriter Pat DiNizio stood out not only with his strange beatnik goatee, but also because his catchy hooks were haunting, not punchy, and because his lyrics were morose. As time wore on, the group became more straightforward, turning into an excellent bar band, one that attacked pop songs with the weight of AC/DC. A few hits followed, but the Smithereens seemed hopelessly out of date in the alternative rock explosion of the early '90s, and they quietly faded into a working cult band.

Of course, the Smithereens essentially started out as a working band. After playing in several cover bands, including a handful of prog-rock and metal groups, Pat DiNizio (vocals, guitar) was inspired to form his own band after listening to Buddy Holly. Placing an advertisement in a New York paper for musicians influenced by Holly, Nick Lowe, Elvis Costello, and the Clash, DiNizio eventually came into contact with New Jersey high school students Dennis Diken (drums), Jim Babjak (guitar), and Mike Mesaros (bass), who had all played together in school. By the end of 1980, they had independently released *Girls About Town*, an EP featuring four songs with "girl" in the title that was a moderate local success. For the next three years, the group played around New Jersey and New York, not releasing another record until 1983's *Beauty and Sadness*. While the EP earned some play on college radio and received a positive review in *Rolling Stone*, they still had trouble gaining an audience, so they began supporting traveling oldies groups like Otis Blackwell, with whom they recorded an album's worth of material, and the Beau Brummels.

By 1985, the Smithereens were growing frustrated by their lack of progress, as most of the demos they sent to labels were ignored. They did send a demo to Enigma, where Scott Vanderbilt, a former college DJ who was a fan of the band several years earlier, signed the group. In 1986, the band released their debut album, the Don Dixon-produced *Especially for You*, to positive reviews. On the strength of college airplay, as well as MTV's airing of "Blood and Roses"—a video financed by a film studio that included the song in the B-movie *Dangerously Close*—the album became a moderate hit, climbing to No. 51 on the charts and leading to a major-label contract with Capitol. The Smithereens supported the album with an extensive tour, and they recorded their second record weeks after they left the road.

Green Thoughts appeared early in 1988, and the first single, "Only a Memory," not only became a college and modern rock hit, but it crossed over to album-rock stations as well. The Smithereens made their attempt for big-time album-rock success with their third album, *11*. Hiring producer Ed Stasium brought a heavier guitar sound, which made "A Girl like You"—a song rejected as the theme for the comedy *Say Anything*—a Top 40 hit, sending *11* to gold status. "Too Much Passion," the first single from their fourth album *Blow Up*, indicated that the new record was more adventurous and produced, and the single did become a Top 40 hit, yet the album itself failed to replicate the success of its predecessor. *Blow Up* was their last album for Capitol, and they moved to RCA for 1994's *A Date with the Smithereens*, their first album since *Green Thoughts* to be produced by Don Dixon. By that time, the alternative and mainstream rock scenes had been heavily altered by grunge, which essentially left the band without an avenue for their records to be heard. The album bombed, but the group retained a sizable cult following that helped them tour successfully into the late '90s. In 1995, the band released a pair of compilations, the hits package *Blown to Smithereens* and the rarities collection *Attack of the Smithereens*. —*Stephen Thomas Erlewine*

Beauty & Sadness / 1983 / Enigma ✦✦✦
The Smithereens' second EP is an impressive collection of melodic guitar-driven power pop, particularly the title cut. Fans of the band should seek this out, but the uninitiated will get a better picture of the band with *Especially for You* and *Green Thoughts*. —*Rick Clark*

Especially for You / 1986 / Enigma ✦✦✦✦
On *Especially for You*, the Smithereens achieved a near-perfect blend of exuberant rockers and moody excursions. Don Dixon's production captured the band's exciting chemistry, while keeping lead singer Pat DiNizio up front in the mix, on this, their best album. "Behind the Wall of Sleep" and "Blood and Roses" were big college-music favorites, helping pave the way for greater success. Other highlights included "Strangers When We Meet," "Time and Time Again," "Groovy Tuesday," and "Alone at Midnight." —*Rick Clark*

Green Thoughts / 1988 / Capitol ✦✦✦✦
The follow-up to *Especially for You* was another impressive batch of power-pop rockers. "Only a Memory" and "House We Used to Live In" were FM rock hits. Again, Dixon's production demonstrated his empathy for the band's sound. Other highlights included "Something New," "Drown in My Own Tears," and the title track. —*Rick Clark*

11 / 1990 / Capitol ✦✦✦
On *11*, the Smithereens employed alternative hard rock producer Ed Stasium (Cavedogs, Living Colour) to beef up their sound. The result was a thick guitar-riff-heavy sound. The approach helped "A Girl like You" become a big rock and MTV hit but, taken as a whole, *11* lacked the dynamics and natural soundstage that made their earlier work so freshsounding. "Yesterday Girl," "Baby Be Good," and "A Girl like You" are highlights, though. —*Rick Clark*

Blow Up / Sep. 10, 1991 / Capitol ✦✦✦
An improvement over *11*, *Blow Up* displays Stasium's state-of-the-art power-rock production and a greater range of material. The soulful "Too Much Passion" was a hit, as was "Top of the Pops." —*Rick Clark*

Date with the Smithereens / Apr. 26, 1994 / RCA ✦✦✦
Producer Don Dixon returns to the helm, creating an album that synthesizes the jangly melodic appeal of *Green Thoughts* with the finesse of *11*. It includes the single "Miles from Nowhere." —*Rick Clark*

● **Blown to Smithereens: the Best of the Smithereens** / Apr. 4, 1995 / Capitol ✦✦✦✦
Collecting together all the hits and highlights from the Smithereens' Capitol albums, *Blown to Smithereens* contains all of their finest hard-rocking pop gems. —*Stephen Thomas Erlewine*

Attack of the Smithereens / Nov. 21, 1995 / Capitol ✦✦✦✦
At first glance, a Smithereens rarities compilation might seem like an odd release. After all, the band was never had more than one gold album and none of their singles cracked the Top 30. That doesn't mean the band didn't have fans, however, nor does it mean that their music was undistinctive, as *Attack of the Smithereens* proves. Filled with B-sides, demos, rare singles, and live tracks, the collection has a loose charm and freewheeling energy their proper albums occasionally lacked. Much of this material is as good as anything the group released,

making it a necessary purchase for most fans. Even casual fans will find something to cherish on *Attack of the Smithereens*. —*Stephen Thomas Erlewine*

The Smiths

f. 1982, Manchester, England, db. Aug. 1987
Alternative Pop-Rock
The Smiths were the definitive British indie-rock band of the '80s, marking the end of synth-driven New Wave and the beginning of the guitar rock that dominated English rock into the '90s. Sonically, the group was indebted to the British Invasion, crafting ringing, melodic three-minute pop singles, even for their album tracks. But their scope was far broader than that of a revivalist band. The group's core members, vocalist Morrissey and guitarist Johnny Marr, were obsessive rock fans inspired by the DIY ethics of punk, but they also had a fondness for girl groups, pop, and rockabilly. Morrissey and Marr also represented one of the strangest teams of collaborators in rock history. Marr was the rock traditionalist, looking like an elegant version of Keith Richards during the Smiths' heyday, and meticulously layering his guitar tracks in the studio. Morrissey, on the other hand, explicitly broke from rock tradition by singing in a keening, self-absorbed croon, embracing the forlorn, romantic poetry of Oscar Wilde, publicly declaring his celibacy, performing with a pocketful of gladiolas and a hearing aid, and making no secret of his disgust for most of his peers. While it eventually led to the Smiths' early demise, the friction between Morrissey and Marr resulted in a flurry of singles and albums over the course of three years that provided the blueprint for British guitar rock in the following decade.

Before forming the Smiths in 1982, Johnny Marr (b. John Maher, October 31, 1963; guitar) had played in a variety of Manchester-based rock 'n' roll bands, including Sister Ray, Freaky Part, White Dice, and Paris Valentinos. On occasion, Marr had come close to a record contract—one of his bands won a competition Stiff Records held to have Nick Lowe produce your band—but he never quite made the leap. Though Morrissey (b. Steven Patrick Morrissey, May 22, 1959; vocals) had sung for a few weeks with the Nosebleeds and auditioned for Slaughter & the Dogs, he had primarily contented himself to being a passionate, vocal fan of both music and film. During his teens, he wrote the *Melody Maker* frequently, often getting his letters published. He had written the biography/tribute *James Dean Isn't Dead*, which was published by the local Manchester publishing house Babylon Books in the late '70s, as well as another book on the New York Dolls; he was also the president of the English New York Dolls fan club. Morrissey met Marr, who was then looking for a lyricist, through mutual friends in the spring of 1982. The pair began writing songs, eventually recording some demos with the Fall's drummer Simon Wolstencroft. By the fall, the duo had settled on the name the Smiths and recruited Marr's schoolmate Andy Rourke as their bassist and Mike Joyce as their drummer.

The Smiths made their live debut late in 1982 and by the spring of 1983, the group had earned a small, but loyal, following in their hometown of Manchester and had begun to make inroads in London. Rejecting a record deal with the Mancunian Factory Records, the band signed with Rough Trade for a one-off single, "Hand in Glove." With its veiled references to homosexuality and its ringing riffs, "Hand in Glove" became an underground sensation in the UK, topping the independent charts and earning the praise of the UK music weeklies. Soon, Morrissey's performances became notorious, as he appeared on stage wearing a hearing aid and with gladiolas stuffed in his back pockets. His interviews were becoming famous for his forthright, often contrary opinions, which helped the band become media sensations. By the time of the group's second single, "This Charming Man," in late 1983, the Smiths had already been the subject of controversy over their songs "Reel Around the Fountain," a song that had been aired on a BBC radio session and was alleged to condone child abuse. It was the first time that Morrissey's detached, literary, and ironic lyrics were misinterpreted and it wouldn't be the last.

"This Charming Man" reached No. 25 on the British charts in December of 1983, setting the stage for the success of "What Difference Does It Make," which reached No. 12 in February. The Smiths' rise to the upper reaches of the British charts was swift, and the passion of their fans, as well as the UK music press, indicated that the group had put an end to the synth-powered New Wave that dominated Britain in the early '80s. After rejecting their initial stab at a first album, the Smiths released their eponymous debut in the spring of 1984, to strong reviews and sales—it peaked at No. 2. A few months later, the group backed '60s pop vocalist Sandie Shaw, who Morrissey had publicly praised in an article, on a version of "Hand in Glove" that reached the Top 40. "Heaven Knows I'm Miserable Now" reached No. 10, becoming their highest-charting single, amidst a storm of controversy about its B-side "Suffer Little Children," which was about the notorious Moors Murders. More controversy appeared when Morrissey denounced the hunger relief efforts of Band Aid, but the group's popularity was not affected. Though the Smiths had become the most popular new rock 'n' roll group in Britain, the group failed to make it outside of underground and college radio in the US, partially because they never launched a full-scale tour. At the end of the year, "William, It Was Really Nothing" became a Top 20 hit and *Hatful of Hollow*, a collection of B-sides, BBC sessions, and non-LP singles, went to the Top 10, followed shortly by "How Soon Is Now" peaking at No. 24.

Meat Is Murder, the band's second proper studio album, entered the British charts at No. 1 in February of 1985, despite some criticism that it was weaker than *The Smiths*. Around the time of the release of *Meat Is Murder*, Morrissey's interviews were becoming increasingly political, as he trashed the Thatcher administration and campaigned for vegetarianism; he even claimed that the Smiths were all vegetarians, and he forbid the remaining members to be photographed eating meat, even though they were still carnivores. Marr, for his part, was delving deeply into the rock 'n' roll lifestyle, and looked increasingly like a cross between Keith Richards and Brian Jones. By the time the non-LP "Shakespeare's Sister" reached No. 26 in the spring of 1985, the Smiths had spawned a rash of soundalike bands, including James, who opened for the group on their spring 1985 tour, most of which Morrissey supported. However, all of the media attention on the Smiths launched a mild backlash later in 1985, when "That Joke Isn't Funny Anymore" was pulled from *Meat Is Murder* and failed to reach the Top 40.

"The Boy with the Thorn in His Side" revived the band's fortunes in the fall of 1985, and their third album, *The Queen Is Dead*, confirmed their popularity upon its release in the spring of 1986. Greeted with enthusiastic reviews and peaking at No. 2 on the UK charts, *The Queen Is Dead* also expanded their cult in the US, cracking the Top 100. Shortly before the album was completed, former Aztec Camera guitarist Craig Gannon became the band's rhythm guitarist, and he played with the band throughout their 1986 international tour, including a botched American tour. The non-LP "Panic," which was criticized as racist by some observers for its repeated refrain of "Burn down the disco . . . Hang the DJ," reached No. 11 late in the summer. A few months after its release, Marr was seriously injured in a car crash. During his recuperation, Gannon was fired from the band, as was Rourke, who was suffering from heroin addiction. Though Rourke was later reinstated, Gannon was never replaced.

The Smiths may have been at the height of their popularity in early 1987, with the non-LP singles "Shoplifters of the World" and "Sheila Take a Bow" reaching No. 11 and 10 respectively, and the singles and B-sides compilation *The World Won't Listen* (revamped for US release as *Louder Than Bombs* later in 1987) debuting at No. 2, but Marr was growing increasingly disenchanted with the band and the music industry. Over the course of the year, Morrissey and Marr became increasingly irritated with each other. The singer wished that Marr would stop playing with other artists like Bryan Ferry and Billy Bragg, while the guitarist was frustrated with Morrissey's devotion to '60s pop and hesitancy to explore new musical directions. A few weeks before the fall release of *Strangeways, Here We Come*, Marr announced that he was leaving the Smiths. Morrissey disbanded the group shortly afterward and began a solo career, signing with Parlophone in the UK and staying with the Smiths' US label, Reprise. Marr played as a sideman with a variety of artists, eventually forming Electronic with New Order frontman Bernard Sumner. Rourke retired from recording and Joyce became a member of the reunited Buzzcocks in 1991.

Rank, a live album recorded on the *Queen Is Dead* tour, was released in the fall of 1988. It debuted at No. 2 in the UK. A widely criticized, two-part *Best Of* compilation was released in 1992; the praised *Singles* compilation was released in 1995. Joyce and Rourke sued Morrissey and Marr in 1991, claiming they received only 10 percent of the group's earnings while the songwriters received 40 percent. Rourke eventually settled out of court, but Joyce won his case in late 1996. An appeal was scheduled. —*Stephen Thomas Erlewine*

☆ The Smiths / 1984 / Sire ✦✦✦✦✦

Arriving in an era dominated by synth-pop and gloomy post-punk, the Smiths' eponymous debut was the bracing beginning of a new era. On the surface, the Smiths' sound wasn't radically different from traditional British guitar pop—Johnny Marr's ringing layered guitars were catchy and melodic—but it was actually an astonishing subversion of the form, turning the structure inside out. Very few of the songs followed conventional verse-chorus structure, yet they were quite melodic within their own right. Marr's inventive songwriting was made all the more original and innovative by Morrissey's crooning and lyrics. Writing about unconventional topics, from homosexuality ("Hand in Glove") to child molestation and murder, Morrissey had a distinctively ironic, witty, and literate viewpoint whose strangeness was accentuated by his off-kilter voice, which would move from a croon to a yelp in a matter of seconds. While the production of *The Smiths* is a little pristine, the songs are vital and alive, developing a new, unique voice within pop music. Though the Smiths continued to improve over the course of their career, their debut remains startling and exciting. —*Stephen Thomas Erlewine*

☆ Hatful of Hollow / 1984 / Sire ✦✦✦✦✦

Several months after releasing their first album, the Smiths issued the singles and rarities collection *Hatful of Hollow*, establishing a tradition of repackaging their material as many times and as quickly as possible. While several cuts on *Hatful of Hollow* are BBC versions of songs from *The Smiths*, the versions on the compilation are nervy and raw—and they're also not the selling point of the record. the Smiths treated singles as individual entities, not just ways to promote an album, and many of their finest songs were never issued on their studio albums. *Hatful of Hollow* contains many of these singles, including the sweet rush of "William, It Was Really Nothing," the sardonic "Heaven Knows I'm Miserable Now," the tongue-in-cheek lament of "Please, Please, Please Let Me Get What I Want," the wistful "Back to the Old House," "Girl Afraid," and the pulsating, tremolo-laced masterpiece "How Soon Is Now?" With such strong material forming the core of the album, it's little wonder that *Hatful of Hollow* is as consistent as *The Smiths*, and arguably captures the excitement surrounding the band even better. —*Stephen Thomas Erlewine*

Meat Is Murder / 1985 / Sire ✦✦✦

With their second proper album, *Meat Is Murder*, the Smiths begin to branch out and diversify, while refining the jangling guitar-pop of their debut. In other words, it catches the group at a crossroads, unsure quite how to proceed. Taking the epic, layered "How Soon Is Now?" as a starting point (the single, which is darker and more dance-oriented than the remainder of the album, was haphazardly inserted into the middle of the album for its American release), the group crafts more sweeping, midtempo numbers, whether it's the melancholy "That Joke Isn't Funny Anymore" or the failed, self-absorbed protest of the title track. While the production is more detailed than before, the Smiths are at their best when they stick to their strengths—"The Headmaster Ritual" and "I Want the One I Can't Have" are fine elaborations of the formula they laid out on the debut, while "Rusholme Ruffians" is an infectious stab at rockabilly. However, the rest of *Meat Is Murder* is muddled, repeating lyrical and musical ideas of before without significantly expanding them or offering enough hooks or melodies to make it the equal of *The Smiths* or *Hatful of Hollow*. —*Stephen Thomas Erlewine*

☆ The Queen Is Dead / 1986 / Sire ✦✦✦✦✦

Meat Is Murder may have been a holding pattern, but *The Queen Is Dead* is the Smiths' great leap forward, taking the band to new musical and lyrical heights. Opening with the storming title track, *The Queen Is Dead* is a harder-rocking record than anything the Smiths had attempted before, but that's only on a relative scale—although the backbeat is more pronounced, the group certainly doesn't rock in a conventional sense. Instead, Johnny Marr has created a dense web of guitars, alternating from the minor-key rush of "Bigmouth Strikes Again" and the faux-rockabilly of "Vicar in a Tutu" to the bouncy acoustic pop of "Cemetry Gates" and "The Boy with the Thorn in His Side," as well as the lovely melancholy of "I Know It's Over" and "There Is a Light That Never Goes Out." And the rich musical bed provides Morrissey with the support for his finest set of lyrics. Shattering the myth that he is a self-pitying sap, Morrissey delivers a devastating set of clever, witty satires of British social mores, intellectualism, class, and even himself. He also crafts some of his finest, most affecting songs, particularly in the wistful "The Boy with the Thorn in His Side" and the epic "There Is a Light That Never Goes Out," two masterpieces that provide the foundation for a remarkable album. —*Stephen Thomas Erlewine*

Louder than Bombs / 1987 / Sire ✦✦✦✦

,A compilation of singles, B-sides, album tracks and BBC sessions assembled for the American market, *Louder Than Bombs* is an overlong and unfocused collection that nevertheless boasts a wealth of brilliant material. Since *Hatful of Hollow* was unavailable in the US at the time of the release of *Louder Than Bombs*, the record contains large chunks of that album, as well as several cuts from *The Smiths*, which makes the record a little redundant for most Smiths fans. Also, the album contains some of the worst material the group ever recorded, including the bland instrumentals "Oscillate Wildly" and "Rubber Ring" and a cover of Twinkle's "Golden Light." Excluding all of this material, the remainder of the record is brilliant. The singles "Shakespeare's Sister," "Panic," "Ask," "Shoplifters of the World Unite" and "Sheila Take a Bow" are all definitive, as are the elegiac "Unloveable," "Asleep," "Stretch Out and Wait," and "Half a Person," which are all unavailable anywhere else (excluding the British counterpart to *Louder Than Bombs*, *The World Won't Listen*). Furthermore, the sneering, bouncing pop of "You Just Haven't Earned It Yet, Baby" and the bizarre travelogue of "Is It Really So Strange?" are two other essential songs not available anywhere else. Though *The World Won't Listen* is a more concise collection, *Louder Than Bombs* is a necessary purchase for any Smiths fan. —*Stephen Thomas Erlewine*

Strangeways Here We Come / 1987 / Sire ✦✦✦✦

Recorded as the relationship between Morrissey and Marr was beginning to splinter, *Strangeways, Here We Come* is the most carefully considered and elaborately produced album in the group's catalog. Though it aspires greatly to better *The Queen Is Dead*, it falls just short of its goals. With producer Stephen Street, the Smiths created a subtly shaded and skilled album, one boasting a fuller production than before. Morrissey and Marr also labored hard over the songs, working to expand the Smiths' sound within their very real boundaries. For the most part, they succeed. "I Started Something I Couldn't Finish," "Girlfriend in a Coma," "Stop Me If You Think You've Heard This One Before," and "I Won't Share You" are classics, while "A Rush and a Push and the Land Is Ours," "Death of a Disco Dancer," and "Last Night I Dreamt That Somebody Loved Me" aren't far behind. However, the songs also have a tendency to be glib and forced, particularly on "Unhappy Birthday" and the anti-record company "Paint a Vulgar Picture," which has grown increasingly ironic in the wake of the Smiths' and Morrissey's love of repackaging the same material in new compilations. Still, *Strangeways* is a graceful way to bow out. While it doesn't match *The Queen Is Dead* or *The Smiths*, it is far from embarrassing and offers a summation of the group's considerable strengths. —*Stephen Thomas Erlewine*

Rank / 1988 / Sire ♦♦
A solid but unexceptional live album recorded on *TheQueen Is Dead* tour. —*Stephen Thomas Erlewine*

★ **Singles** / May 23, 1995 / Reprise ♦♦♦♦♦
The *Best of the Smiths* collections didn't work since they didn't have a sense of history and distorted the underlying sense of urgency that helped make the Smiths important. *Singles* simply collects all of the singles from one of the greatest singles bands since the Beatles. It's essential and influential guitar-pop, presented in a way that makes sense and is endlessly listenable. —*Stephen Thomas Erlewine*

Smog

Alternative Pop-Rock, Lo-Fi, Indie Rock, Singer-Songwriter
An underrecognized pioneer of the lo-fi revolution, Smog was essentially the alias of one Bill Callahan, an enigmatic singer-songwriter whose odd, fractured music neatly epitomized the tenets and excesses of the home-recording boom. Melancholy, poignant, and self-obsessed, Callahan's four-track output offered a peep-show view into an insular world of alienation and inner turmoil, his painfully intimate songs ping-ponging wildly through a scrapbook of childhood recollections, failed relationships, bizarre fetishes, and dashed hopes.
Smog debuted in 1988 with the spare, primitive *Macrame Gunplay*, a cassette-only release issued on Callahan's own Disaster label. *Cow* followed in 1989, while three more tapes—*A Table Setting, Tired Tape Machine*, and *Sewn to the Sky*—were issued a year later. With 1991's *Floating* EP, Smog signed to the Chicago-based indie label Drag City, and with the move began an advancement towards more traditional songcraft; the subsequent full-length *Forgotten Foundation* was his most well-rounded effort yet, employing a stronger sense of melody while remaining true to the trademark bare-bones atmosphere.
1993's superb *Julius Caesar* raised the stakes considerably: recorded with collaborators Cynthia Dall and Jim O'Rourke, the album expanded the Smog palette to include touches of cello, violin, and even banjo. At the same time, Callahan's songs were his best yet: highlighted by the touching "Chosen One" and the menacing "Your Wedding," *Julius Caesar* also featured "I Am Star Wars!," a hilarious rant built around a tape loop of the intro to the Stones' "Honky Tonk Women." The six-track *Burning Kingdom* EP appeared the following year.
1995's *Wild Love* continued Smog's approach towards relative sonic grandeur; led off by the remarkable "Bathysphere" (its title a fitting metaphor for Callahan's self-absorption) and climaxed by the epic "Prince Alone in the Studio" (a virtual theme song for a solitary creative existence), the LP reflected his bitter obsessions with stunning clarity, emerging as a triumph of abject failure. After 1996's *Kicking a Couple Around* EP, Smog resurfaced later in the year with *The Doctor Came at Dawn; Red Apple Falls* followed in 1997. —*Jason Ankeny*

Julius Caesar / 1993 / Drag City ♦♦♦
The second album from Bill Callahan, Cynthia Dall, and company is rife with downbeat and occasionally poignant indie pop that mixes clangy guitars with strings and synthesizers for a unique, evocative sound. One of the standout tracks is "Your Wedding," as bitter and complex a jealousy song as you're likely to hear. —*Heather Phares*

Burning Kingdom / Sep. 20, 1994 / Drag City ♦♦♦
Four vignettes of concentrated sadness, *Burning Kingdom* has to be one of the darkest-sounding EPs released in recent memory. Particularly effective is the haunting "Reneé Died," which pits Dall's frail voice against brittle acoustic guitars. —*Heather Phares*

● **Wild Love** / Mar. 27, 1995 / Drag City ♦♦♦♦
The group's third full-length album is slightly less melancholy than *Burning Kingdom*, and even manages some pitch-black humor in tracks like "Prince Alone in the Studio," "Be Hit" and "Sweet Smog Children." But some of the most poignant songs Callahan has written appear on

Wild Love, including "Bathysphere," "The Candle," "Limited Capacity," and the luminous, empathetic "It's Rough." "Goldfish Bowl" is one of the catchiest numbers on Wild Side which is Smog's finest work to date. —*Heather Phares*

Sewn to the Sky / Nov. 29, 1995 / Drag City ♦♦♦♦

Kicking a Couple Around [ep] / Apr. 1996 / Drag City ♦♦♦♦
This four-song EP contains some of Smog's finest, most heartbreaking songs—"Your New Friend," a tale of how claustrophobic relationships can get when they're ending, "Back in School," "The Orange Glow of a Stranger's Living Room," and the moving "I Break Horses," which likens love affairs to taming horses. *Kicking a Couple Around* is perhaps Smog's most intimate-sounding release, featuring singer-songwriter Bill Callahan on guitar backed with some understated percussion. This restrained, minimal sound is a perfect foil for Callahan's warm, empathetic voice and eloquent lyrics: "I'm trying to learn your language / It's like a fly learning how to bark," from "Back in School," and "Just a few well-placed words / And their wandering hearts are gone" from "I Break Horses" tell sad stories in a short time. *Kicking a Couple Around* is Smog's most affecting, accessible release yet, and a must for both fans and those curious about the band. —*Heather Phares*

Doctor Came at Dawn / Sep. 10, 1996 / Drag City ♦♦♦♦

Red Apple Falls / May 20, 1997 / Drag City ♦♦♦♦

The Smoke

f. , London, England
British Invasion, Psychedelic, Garage Rock, Mod
More than any other band, the Smoke epitomized the groove of Swinging London. Their sound fell somewhere between mod and the Beatles—their instrumental attack was somewhat Who/Small Faces-like, yet they delighted in cheerful vocals and infectious harmonies and melodies. Only slightly popular on their home turf, and unknown in the US, their biggest success was in Germany (oddly enough, for such a British-sounding group). *It's Smoke Time*, their only album, was issued in Germany in 1967, and is one of the most cheerful records ever made, though not at all wimpy. "My Friend Jack," with its crushing reverb feedback, was a big hit in Germany, and on its way to becoming a hit in the UK when it was banned by British radio for supposed drug references. The Smoke issued several rare singles, some of them quite good, after the album before disbanding. —*Richie Unterberger*

My Friend Jack [1974 Reissue] / 1974 / Gull ♦♦♦
A retitled reissue of the *It's Smoke Time* LP. For a long time it was the only Smoke record available. But now you're much better off with the Repertoire CD of *It's Smoke Time*, which doubles its length and then some with 14 bonus tracks. —*Richie Unterberger*

My Friend Jack [1988 Compilation] / 1988 / Morgan Blue Town ♦♦♦
Unsatisfyingly skimpy 12-song compilation of the group's work, presenting seven of the 12 cuts from the *It's Smoke Time* album, and adding some non-LP tracks, including a 1965 version of the band). All of the songs but one appear on Repertoire's far more extensive *It's Smoke Time* compilation. The one that doesn't, "Like a Good Man Should" (origin undocumented in the sleeve notes), is not so remarkable that this LP is worth tracking down on that count alone. —*Richie Unterberger*

● **It's Smoke Time** / 1994 / Repertoire ♦♦♦♦
Besides "My Friend Jack," other highlights of the group's only album (all but one of whose tracks were group originals) include the beautiful mid-tempo ballad "Waterfall" and the bee-humming guitars and lilting backup vocals on "You Can't Catch Me." The German CD reissue adds 14 additional cuts, including non-LP singles, a single issued in 1965 by the Shots (an earlier version of the group), a single puzzlingly issued under the alias the Chords Five, and an interesting alternate take of "My Friend Jack." A lot of these tracks pale in comparison to the12 from the original album, but "Have Some More Tea" is a great Who-ish number, and "Sydney Gill" is a good stab at a more progressive mood. —*Richie Unterberger*

Sneaker Pimps

f. 1995, Reading, England
Trip-Hop, Electronica
Sneaker Pimps are a trip-hop trio that formed in Reading, England, in 1995, following the success of Portishead's *Dummy* and Tricky's *Maxinquaye*. Borrowing heavily from Portishead and Massive Attack, Sneaker Pimps have a trancey but edgy sound, highlighted by Kelli Dayton's soulful vocals. While Dayton is the focal point, Chris Corner (guitar) and Liam Howe (keyboards) are the band's leaders, writing all of the songs and producing the records. Howe and Corner had been playing in bands since the early '90s, to no success. After seeing Dayton sing with a pub band in 1995, they convinced her to join the fledgling Sneaker Pimps,

who had taken their name from an article the Beastie Boys published in *Grand Royal* about a man they hired to track down classic sneakers.

Sneaker Pimps released their first single, "Tesko Suicide," in May of 1996 and it was greeted with positive reviews in the UK music press. *Becoming X*, the group's debut, was released in August and it was a critical success, with *Q* magazine naming the album one of the best albums of the year. However, the band failed to make an impact on the pop charts in the UK. *Becoming X* was released in the United States in February 1997, preceded by the single "6 Underground." — *Stephen Thomas Erlewine*

● **Becoming X** / Feb. 25, 1997 / Virgin ◆◆◆◆
Becoming X is one of the most engaging by-products of post-Portishead trip-hop. While the Sneaker Pimps don't have the doomed romanticism of Portishead, or the nasty experimental tendencies of Tricky, they have a cool sense of pop hooks and an edgier guitar attack than their predecessors. "Tesko Suicide" moves along with jagged guitars and rhythms, while "6 Underground" is cooly detached post modern soul. *Becoming X* creates an airy, urban atmosphere, and while the record begins to unravel towards the end, it is an exciting, entrancing listen. — *Stephen Thomas Erlewine*

The Sneakers

f. 1975, Chapel Hill, NC, **db.** 1978
Power Pop
While the Sneakers never made much of an impact when they were together, the band marks the first appearance of several seminal figures of the alternative pop scene of the early '80s. Chris Stamey, Mitch Easter, and Will Rigby formed the core of the Sneakers, writing well-crafted, guitar-driven pop rockers; their self-titled debut EP was engineered by Don Dixon, who went on to be a successful producer, as well as a solo artist. After one excellent full-length album, the Sneakers broke up. Stamey and Rigby went on to form the dB's, one of the '80s best American guitar-pop bands; Easter led Let's Active, as well as becoming a record producer (including R.E.M.'s first two albums). However, the Sneakers are more than historical curiosity; although they didn't record very much, their album and EP contain some of the finest power pop of the late '70s. — *Stephen Thomas Erlewine*

In the Red / 1978 / Car ◆◆◆
● **Racket** / Nov. 27, 1992 / East Side Digital ◆◆◆◆
This disc contains selections from the Sneakers' unfinished third record, *Wig Cleaner*, as well as all the original compositions from *In the Red* and the band's first release, *Carnivorous No.1*. While all of the songs were written in the late '70s, some of the recordings were done as recently as 1992. Songs like "Some Kinda Fool" and "Story of a Girl" exude an effortless sophistication of chord structure and melody. Lovers of quirky guitar pop-rock (read: early dB's fans) should have this one. — *Rick Clark*

Snoop Doggy Dogg

b. Oct. 20, 1972, Long Beach, CA
Vocals / Hip-Hop, G-Funk, West Coast Rap
As the embodiment of '90s gangsta rap, Snoop Doggy Dogg blurred the lines between reality and fiction. Introduced to the world through Dr. Dre's *The Chronic*, Snoop Dogg quickly became the most famous star in rap, partially because of his drawled, laconic rhyming and partially because the violence that his lyrics implied seemed real, especially after he was arrested on charges of being a murder accomplice. The arrest certainly strengthened his myth, and it helped his debut album, 1993's *Doggystyle*, become the first debut album to enter the charts at No. 1, but in the long run it hurt his career. Snoop had to fight charges throughout 1994 and 1995, and while he was eventually cleared, it hurt his momentum. *The Doggfather*, his second album, wasn't released until November 1996, and by that time, pop and hip-hop had burned itself out on gangsta-rap. *The Doggfather* sold half as well as its predecessor, which meant that Snoop remained a star, but he no longer had the influence he had just two years before.

Nicknamed Snoop by his mother because of his appearance, Calvin Broadus (b. October 20, 1972) was raised in Long Beach, California, where he frequently ran into trouble with the law. Not long after his high school graduation, he was arrested for possession of cocaine, beginning a period of three years where he was often imprisoned. He found escape from a life of crime through music. Snoop Dogg began recording homemade tapes with his friend Warren G, who happened to be the stepbrother of N.W.A.'s Dr. Dre. Warren G gave a tape to Dre, who was considerably impressed with Snoop's style and began collaborating with the rapper.

When Dre decided to make his tentative first stab at a solo career in 1992 with the theme song for the film *Deep Cover*, he had Snoop rap with him. "Deep Cover" started a buzz about Snoop Dogg that escalated into full-fledged mania when Dre released his debut album, *The*

Chronic, on Death Row Records late in 1992. Snoop Dogg rapped on *The Chronic* as much as Dre, and his drawled vocals were as important to the record's success as its P-Funk bass grooves. Dre's singles "Nuthin' but a 'G' Thang" and "Dre Day," which prominently featured Snoop, became Top 10 pop crossover hits in the spring of 1993, setting the stage for Snoop Doggy Dogg's much-anticipated debut album, *Doggystyle*. While he was recording the album with producer Dr. Dre in August, Snoop was arrested in connection with the drive-by-shooting death of Phillip Woldermarian. According to the charges, the rapper's bodyguard, McKinley Lee, shot Woldermarian as Snoop drove the vehicle; the rapper claimed it was self-defense, alleging that the victim was stalking Snoop. Following a performance at the MTV Music Awards in September 1993, he turned himself in to authorities.

After many delays, *Doggystyle* was finally released on Death Row in November of 1993, and it became the first debut album to enter the charts at No. 1. Despite reviews that claimed the album was a carbon copy of *The Chronic*, the Top 10 singles "What's My Name?" and "Gin & Juice" kept *Doggystyle* at the top of the charts during early 1994, as did the considerable controversy over Snoop's arrest and his lyrics, which were accused of being exceedingly violent and sexist. During an English tour in the spring of 1994, tabloids and a Tory minister pleaded for the government to kick the rapper out of the country, largely based on his arrest. Snoop exploited his impending trial by shooting a short film based on the *Doggystyle* song "Murder Was the Case," and releasing an accompanying soundtrack that debuted at No. 1 in 1994. By that time, *Doggystyle* had gone quadruple platinum.

Snoop Dogg spent much of 1995 preparing for the case, which finally went to trial in late 1995. In February of 1996, he was cleared of all charges and he began working on his second album, this time without Dre as producer. Nevertheless, when *The Doggfather* was finally released in November 1996, it bore all the evidence of a Dre-produced, G-funk record. The album was greeted with mixed reviews, and it initially sold well, but it failed to produce a hit along the lines of "What's My Name?" and "Gin & Juice." Part of the reason of the moderate success of *The Doggfather* was the decline of gangsta rap. Tupac Shakur, who had become a friend of Snoop Dogg during 1996, died weeks before the release of *The Doggfather*, and Dre had left Death Row to his partner Suge Knight, who was indicted on racketeering charges by the end of 1996. Consequently, Snoop's second album got lost in the shuffle, stalling at sales of two million, which was disappointing for a superstar. Perhaps sensing something was wrong, Snoop began to revamp his public image, moving away from his gangsta roots towards a calmer lyrical aesthetic. He also began making gestures toward the rock community, signing up to tour with Lollapalooza 1997 and talking about two separate collaborations with Beck and Marilyn Manson. — *Stephen Thomas Erlewine*

● **Doggystyle** / Nov. 23, 1993 / Interscope ◆◆◆◆
Snoop Doggy Dogg's debut entered the charts at No.1, and it has proven popular even though there's little departure musically or production-wise from Dr. Dre's release. *Doggystyle* features more of Dogg's part-drawl, part-spoken word narratives, but expresses a vision more paranoid than confident. Throughout the disc, Snoop has nightmares about being killed, and spends most of his time either defaming women or getting out of conflicts. The single "Who Am I (What's My Name)?" uses nearly the same samples and basslines as "Dre Day," as only Snoop's lean, almost casual sneers and rejoinders differentiate it from Dre's prior recording. He also throws a few darts at Eazy-E, but otherwise, this is prototype gangsta rap with Snoop's signature style as its major hook. — *Ron Wynn*

Doggfather / Nov. 12, 1996 / Death Row/Interscope ◆◆◆
A lot happened to Snoop Doggy Dogg between his debut *Doggystyle* and his second album, *The Doggfather*. During those three years, he became the most notorious figure in hip-hop through a much-publicized murder trial, where he was found not guilty, and he also became a father. Musically, the most important thing to happen to Snoop was the parting of ways between his mentor Dr. Dre and his record label, Death Row. Dre's departure from Death Row meant that Snoop had to handle the production duties on *The Doggfather* himself, and the differences between the two records are immediately apparent. Though it works the same G-funk territory, the bass is less elastic and there is considerably less sonic detail. In essence, all of the music on *The Doggfather* reworks the funk and soul of the late '70s and early '80s, without updating it too much—there's not that much difference between "Snoop's Upside Ya Head" and "Oops Up Side Your Head." Though the music isn't original, and the lyrics break no new territory, the execution is strong—Snoop's rapping and rhyming continue to improve, while the bass-heavy funk is often intoxicating. At over 70 minutes, *The Doggfather* runs too long to not have several filler tracks, but if you ignore those cuts, the album is a fine follow-up to one of the most successful hip-hop albums in history. — *Stephen Thomas Erlewine*

Phoebe Snow (Phoebe Laub)

b. Jul. 17, 1952, New York, NY

Guitar, Vocals / Singer-Songwriter, Pop, Contemporary Folk

Renowned for her elastic contralto and jazz-scat vocal gymnastics, singer Phoebe Snow was born Phoebe Laub on July 17, 1952, in New York City. During her childhood in Teaneck, New Jersey, she initially studied piano, but switched to the guitar in her teens, writing poetry that gradually mutated into her first songs. Overcoming her stage fright, Snow began playing Greenwich Village clubs in the early 1970s, honing an eclectic set that spotlighted both folk and pop sounds as well as jazz, blues, and even torch songs.

After signing to Leon Russell's Shelter label, Snow issued her self-titled debut LP in 1974; on the strength of her Top Five smash "Poetry Man," the album itself rose to the No. 4 position. A tour with Paul Simon followed, along with an appearance on his hit "Gone at Last"; after returning to the studio, Snow emerged in 1976 with *Second Childhood*, another highly successful effort that, like its predecessor, achieved gold-selling status.

The record appeared in the wake of personal tragedy, however: in 1975, the singer's newborn daughter Valerie was diagnosed with profound autism, and against the wishes of doctors, Snow—a single mother—decided to raise the child at home by herself. As a consequence, her career as a performer became dwarfed by her parental duties; despite a flurry of records throughout the latter half of the decade, including 1976's *It Looks Like Snow*, 1977's *Never Letting Go*, and 1978's *Against the Grain*, Snow receded from view as the 1980s dawned, and following the release of 1981's *Rock Away*, she did not record again for eight years.

Upon signing to Elektra, Snow resurfaced in 1989 with *Something Real*, followed by a series of New York club appearances as a member of ex-Steely Dan frontman Donald Fagen's all-star Rock and Soul Revue. Apart from lending her voice to a number of radio and television advertisements, Snow again fell silent in subsequent years, although in 1994 she appeared at Woodstock with a gospel group additionally comprised of Mavis Staples, CeCe Peniston, and Thelma Houston. —*Jason Ankeny*

● **Phoebe Snow** / Jul. 1974 / DCC ✦✦✦✦
A wondrous folk, pop, and jazz album of Snow's original songs and some well-chosen covers, all showcasing her one-of-a-kind voice. Includes the Top Five hit "Poetry Man." —*William Ruhlmann*

Second Childhood / Jan. 1976 / Columbia ✦✦✦
Although it lacked a hit single to match "Poetry Man," Phoebe Snow's second album was another folk-pop-jazz confection that effectively showcased her one-of-a-kind voice in musical settings featuring the cream of New York's session musicians, produced by Phil Ramone. It was a classy job on which Snow contributed seven originals and displayed her versatility on covers ranging from Motown to Gershwin. —*William Ruhlmann*

It Looks Like Snow / Feb. 1976 / Columbia ✦✦✦✦
The cover songs start to overwhelm the originals, but when Snow is able to bring such powerful interpretations to "Don't Let Me Down," "Shakey Ground," and "Teach Me Tonight," who could complain? —*William Ruhlmann*

Never Letting Go / Oct. 1977 / Columbia ✦✦✦
Phoebe Snow made it onto the soul chart with her version of Barbara Acklin's 1968 hit "Love Makes a Woman" (No.87), which served as the lead-off track on her fourth album. But the record marked a fall-off in both her commercial success and her artistic accomplishment. The tasty studio musicians and Phil Ramone's pop-jazz production were still in place, and Snow remained a remarkable singer, but her synthesis of styles was beginning to seem not so much inspired as muddled. —*William Ruhlmann*

Against the Grain / Oct. 1978 / Columbia ✦✦✦
Phoebe Snow should have, could have had hits with her covers of Paul McCartney's "Every Night" and the Roches' "The Married Men," but by her fourth Columbia album and fifth release overall, the company seems to have been content to let her records find their audience without pushing them. (Actually, "Every Night" did hit No.79 in the UK.) Maybe they'd given up trying to figure out whether she was a folksinger, a pop singer, a soul singer, or a jazz singer, and forgot that she was a great singer. The decision to add Barry Beckett as co-producer with Phil Ramone helped add an R&B depth and fervor, but *Against the Grain* was just a more impassioned effort than its predecessor. That didn't keep Columbia from dropping Phoebe Snow when it didn't hit, though. —*William Ruhlmann*

● **The Best of Phoebe Snow** / 1981 / Columbia ✦✦✦✦

Rock Away / Mar. 1981 / Atlantic ✦✦
Phoebe Snow a rock singer? Well, she certainly had the pipes, and producers Greg Ladanyi and Richie Cannata surrounded her with Billy Joel's backup band for a standard New York rock sound. With Snow con-

tributing only three original tunes, the song selection was odd—Rod Stewart's "Gasoline Alley," the Buckinghams/Cannonball Adderley hit "Mercy, Mercy, Mercy," Bob Dylan's "I Believe in You." *Rock Away* sold better than her last two albums and produced two chart singles, "Games" (No.46) and "Mercy, Mercy, Mercy" (No.52). But anyone who had heard her first two albums knew that this was not the whole story by a long shot. —*William Ruhlmann*

Something Real / Feb. 1989 / Elektra ✦✦✦
"This time when I reach out, it may be my last try," warns Phoebe Snow on the title track to her seventh album, which is her first in eight years. Perhaps with that in mind, it's a well-considered effort, and one that brought moderate success, including two Adult Contemporary chart hits in "If I Can Just Get Through the Night" (No.13) and "Something Real" (No.29). Snow takes a slightly more relaxed approach to the rock style of her last album, *Rock Away*. She sticks to contemporary songs for the most part (there's a dance music cover of the Emotions' "Best of My Love"), and writes half of them herself. She tends to de-emphasize the more unusual aspects of her voice, although not so much that you'd confuse it with anybody else's. The result is a sturdy, respectable set, although not one likely to launch a major comeback. —*William Ruhlmann*

Social Distortion

f. 1978, Los Angeles, CA

Rock & Roll, Alternative Pop-Rock

The enduring L.A. punk band Social Distortion has overcome numerous personnel shifts, the demise of the Los Angeles hardcore scene that spawned them, and the heroin addiction of singer/guitarist/bandleader Mike Ness to achieve a measure of mainstream acceptance for their rootsy, hard-hitting punk without compromise. Inspired by the fertile L.A. punk scene, Ness formed the group in 1978 with drummer Casey Royer and brothers Frank (bass) and Rikk Agnew (guitar). When the Agnews left to join the Adolescents, Ness' schoolmate Dennis Danell joined on bass; the next few years saw a revolving-door membership. When the group finally recorded its debut album, *Mommy's Little Monster*, in 1983, the band consisted of Ness, Danell (now on guitar), bassist Brent Liles, and drummer Derek O'Brien. Their music was often described as a punk version of the Rolling Stones, and "Another State of Mind" was one of the few punk videos to air on MTV in 1984. However, the band took four years to record a follow-up, as Ness descended into heroin addiction and self-consciously rebellious behavior. Liles and O'Brien left, and Ness finally regrouped after straightening himself out in 1988 with John Maurer on bass and Chris Reece on drums. This lineup recorded *Prison Bound*, a mature album broadening Social Distortion's roots-rock influences with a country feel. Their self-titled 1990 effort included a cover of Johnny Cash's "Ring of Fire" and returned the group to MTV via "Ball and Chain." *Somewhere Between Heaven and Hell* became their most popular album to date, producing a minor radio hit in "Bad Luck" and keeping with their now-established blend of punk, blues, country, and rockabilly.

Social Distortion took an extended hiatus following the release of *Somewhere Between Heaven and Hell*, returning in 1996 with *White Light, White Heat, White Trash*, which proved to be a moderate hit on MTV and modern-rock radio. —*Steve Huey*

Mommy's Little Monster / 1983 / Time Bomb ✦✦✦✦
Their debut is full of wailing guitars, sharp lyrics, tugging melodies, and snarling vocals. —*John Floyd*

Prison Bound / 1988 / Time Bomb ✦✦✦
The release of this album brought acoustic guitars, ballads, and a cautious step toward the rock mainstream that makes their music of use for more than just hardcore nihilists. —*John Floyd*

Social Distortion / Mar. 1990 / Epic ✦✦✦✦
Their major-label debut repeated the winning formula of *Prison Bound*—Ramones meet The Blasters meet Johnny Thunders—but with better production. —*John Floyd*

● **Somewhere between Heaven and Hell** / 1991 / Epic ✦✦✦✦
Social Distortion wallows in rock 'n' roll rebellion and fatalism. The combination of urgent lyrics and unbeatable riffs make this their best album. —*John Floyd*

Mainliner (Wreckage of the Past) / Jul. 18, 1995 / Time Bomb ✦✦✦

White Light, White Heat, White Trash / Sep. 1996 / 550 Music/Epic ✦✦✦
With *White Light, White Heat, White Trash*, Social Distortion made a conscious attempt to cash in on the alternative "revolution" of the early '90s. Underneath the layers of glossy hard rock production, the band still holds fast to some of their punk roots, but too often they sound like a heavy hard rock band. Of course, that commercial sheen is intentional—it's the only way they could appeal to the legions of post-grunge alternative fans that appeared since Social Distortion released *Somewhere Between Heaven and Hell* in 1991. The problem is, the band

doesn't deliver enough songs to justify the production. Mike Ness still wails away and growls out confessional lyrics, but too often they are ham-fisted and cliched, much like the music that supports them. The band sounds tight and muscular, but the songs have no hooks to make them memorable. In trying to appeal to a wider audience, Social Distortion has lost their identity on *White Light, White Heat, White Trash.* If it does win the band new fans, they will be listeners that only have a vague idea about what the group is about. *—Stephen Thomas Erlewine*

The Soft Boys

f. 1976, Cambridge, England, **db.** 1981
Alternative Pop-Rock, New Wave, Post-Punk
The Soft Boys have turned out to be one of the most influential bands in shaping contemporary alternative music, though few are completely familiar with the quirky band's legacy. Formed in Cambridge, England, in 1976 on the heels of the punk revolution, the Soft Boys eschewed the three-chord nihilism of punk and opted for a crude version of psychedelic/folk-rock that was well on its way out of fashion, but oddly, just on the cusp of a resurgence.

Robyn Hitchcock recruited Cambridge musicians Morris Windsor on drums, Andy Metcalfe on bass, and guitarist Alan Davies, and recorded *Give It to the Soft Boys* in Hitchcock's living room in 1976. Davies was soon replaced by guitarist Kimberley Rew. The band released a single, "(I Want to Be an) Anglepoise Lamp," followed by the *A Can of Bees* album in 1979.

While recording the follow-up, Metcalfe left the band and was replaced by Matthew Seligman. The new lineup started fresh and recorded *Underwater Moonlight,* the album that found the band trading psychedelic jams for a more straightahead jangle-guitar-rock sound. The LP has become extremely influential in the guitar rock canon—the Replacements, R.E.M., and the L.A. Paisley Underground scene all claimed it as a prime influence. The album launched a thousand bands, but it turned out to be the Soft Boys' swan song. Two more recordings were released posthumously: the *Two Halves for the Price of One* EP in 1981, and some early sessions compiled on *Invisible Hits* in 1983. The first EP was re-released in 1984 as *Wading Through a Ventilator.*

Windsor and Metcalfe began to collaborate with Hitchcock again in 1984 as the Egyptians, while Seligman became an in-demand session musician and Rew went on to form Katrina and the Waves. Hitchcock has had a prolific post-Soft Boys recording career, sticking to the unusual style he's forged and finessed since 1976, with 15 albums to his credit. *—Denise Sullivan*

A Can of Bees / 1979 / Rykodisc ✦✦✦✦
One of the band's earliest recordings, featuring their signature tune "Give It to the Soft Boys," *A Can of Bees* includes a lot of the zaniness principal member Robyn Hitchcock would become known for in his later work, but the band had not yet jelled and found them still in search of their ultimate sound, an amalgam of new wave and psychedelia. However, the record is essential to any Soft Boys collection, as it demonstrates the band flying in the face of what was happening musically at the time and creating their own unique style. *—Denise Sullivan*

★ **Underwater Moonlight** / 1980 / Rykodisc ✦✦✦✦✦
A watershed guitar rock album—the one that launched a thousand bands, including the Replacements and R.E.M., and a quintessential cult favorite. Beautiful harmonies and Byrdsian guitar dominate this set of songs, the standouts being the punk-pop of "I Wanna Destroy You," "Positive Vibrations," and the chiming "Queen of Eyes." Robyn Hitchcock found his voice on this record, singing his mostly nonsensical lyrics with unusual conviction, and guitarist Kimberley Rew played with a tidiness rarely heard on most underground recordings from the era. *—Denise Sullivan*

Invisible Hits / 1983 / Rykodisc ✦✦✦✦
A collection of lost recordings and previously unreleased tracks, a number of this album's cuts feature Soft Boys classics, like "Rock 'n' Roll Toilet," "Wey Wey Hep Uh Hole," "Have a Heart Betty (I'm Not Fireproof)," and "He's a Reptile." Most of the songs were recorded in 1978-79 during the sessions prior to *A Can of Bees* and *Underwater Moonlight,* and though it isn't as strong as the latter, it is essential to the Soft Boys collector—their recorded output is so spare that every last detail is crucial. *—Denise Sullivan*

1976-81 / Aug. 10, 1993 / Rykodisc ✦✦✦✦
This double-CD set compiles unreleased material, select cuts from *Give It to the Soft Boys, A Can of Bees, Invisible Hits* and *Underwater Moonlight,* as well as two tracks from the live bootleg *At the Portland Arms* and "Only the Stones Remain" from the *Two Halves for the Price of One* EP. Although it may appear to be a good introduction to the Soft Boys oeuvre, the inclusion of rarities and alternate takes makes it ideal for diehard Soft Boys fans and inappropriate for the novice. *—Denise Sullivan*

Soft Cell

f. 1980, Leeds, England, **db.** 1984
Dance-Pop, New Wave, New Romantic
A synth-pop duo famed for its uniquely sleazy electronic sound, art students Marc Almond and David Ball formed Soft Cell in Leeds, England, in 1980. Originally, vocalist Almond and synth player Ball teamed to compose music for theatrical productions, and as Soft Cell, their live performances continued to draw heavily on the pair's background in drama and the visual arts. A self-financed EP titled *Mutant Moments* brought the duo to the attention of Some Bizarre label head Stevo, who enlisted Daniel Miller to produce their underground hit single "Memorabilia" the following year.

It was the next Soft Cell effort, 1981's "Tainted Love," that brought the duo to international prominence; written by the Four Preps' Ed Cobb and already a cult favorite thanks to Gloria Jones' soulful reading, the song was reinvented as a hypnotic electronic dirge that became the year's bestselling British single, as well as a major hit abroad. The group's debut LP, *Non-Stop Erotic Cabaret,* was also enormously successful, and was followed by the 1982 remix collection *Non-Stop Ecstatic Dancing.*

While 1983's *The Art of Falling Apart* proved as popular as its predecessors, the LP's title broadly hinted at the internal problems plaguing the duo; prior to the release of 1984's *The Last Night in Sodom,* Soft Cell had already broken up. Almond immediately formed the electro-soul unit Marc and the Mambas; another group, Marc Almond and the Willing Sinners, followed before the singer finally embarked on a solo career in the late '80s. After a number of years of relative inactivity, Ball later resurfaced in the techno outfit the Grid. *—Jason Ankeny*

● **Memorabilia: Singles** / Oct. 8, 1991 / Mercury ✦✦✦✦
Although it doesn't contain a couple of key tracks, including the 12-inch version of "Tainted Love/Where Did Our Love Go," *Memorabilia* is the best Soft Cell collection available. *—Stephen Thomas Erlewine*

The Soft Machine

f. 1966, Canterbury, England, **db.** 1976
Art-Rock/Progressive-Rock, Psychedelic, Early Jazz-Rock
The Soft Machine were never a commercial enterprise, and indeed still remain unknown even to many listeners that came of age during the late '60s, when the group was at their peak. In their own way, however, they were one of the more influential bands of their era, and certainly one of the *most* influential underground ones. One of the original British psychedelic groups, they were also instrumental in the birth of both progressive-rock and jazz-rock. They were also the central foundation of the family tree of the "Canterbury school" of British progressive-rock acts, a movement that also included Caravan, Gong, Matching Mole, and National Health, not to mention the distinguished solo careers of founding members Robert Wyatt and Kevin Ayers.

Considering their well-known experimental and avant-garde leanings, the roots of the Soft Machine were in some respects surprisingly conventional. In the mid-'60s, Wyatt sang and drummed with the Wilde Flowers, a Canterbury group that played more or less conventional pop and soul covers of the day. Future Soft Machine members Ayers and Hugh Hopper would also pass through the Wilde Flowers, whose original material began to reflect an odd sensibility, cultivated by their highly educated backgrounds and a passion for improvised jazz. In 1966, Wyatt teamed up with bassist/singer Ayers, keyboardist Mike Ratledge, and Australian guitarist Daevid Allen to form the first lineup of the Soft Machine. This incarnation of the group, along with Pink Floyd and Tomorrow, were the very first underground psychedelic bands in Britain, and quickly became well loved in the burgeoning London psychedelic underground. Their first recordings (many of which only surfaced years later on compilations of 1967 demos) were by far their most pop-oriented, which doesn't mean they weren't exciting, or devoid of experimental elements. Surreal wordplay and unusually (for rock) complex instrumental interplay gave an innovative edge to their ebullient early psychedelic outings. They only managed to cut one (very good) single, though, which flopped. Allen, the weirdest of a colorful group of characters, had to leave the band when he was refused re-entry into the UK after a stint in France, due to the expiration of his visa.

The remaining trio recorded their first proper album in 1968. The considerable melodic elements and vocal harmonies of their 1967 recordings were now giving way to more challenging, artier postures that sought—sometimes successfully, sometimes not—to meld the energy of psychedelic rock with the improvisational pulse of jazz. The Softs were taken on by Jimi Hendrix's management, leading to grueling stints supporting the Jimi Hendrix Experience on their 1968 American tours. Because of this, the group at this point were probably more well known in the US than their homeland. In fact, their debut LP was only issued, oddly, in the States. For a couple of months in 1968, strangely enough, the Soft Machine became a quartet again with the addition of future Police guitarist Andy Summers, although that didn't work out, and they soon reverted to a trio. The punishing tours took their toll on the group, and Ayers had left by the end of 1968, to be replaced by Wyatt's old chum Hugh Hopper.

Their second album, *Vol. 2* (1969), further submerged the band's pop elements in favor of extended jazzy compositions, with an increasingly lesser reliance on lyrics and vocals. Ratledge's fuzzy, buzzy organ, and Wyatt's pummeling, imaginative drumming and scat vocals, paced the band on material that became increasingly whimsical and surrealistic, if increasingly inaccessible to the pop-rock audience. For their third album, they went even further in these directions, expanding to a seven-piece by adding a horn section. This record virtually dispensed with vocals and conventional rock songs entirely, and is considered a landmark by both progressive-rock and jazz-rock aficionados, though it was too oblique for many rock listeners. The Soft Machine couldn't afford to continue to support a seven-member lineup, and scaled back to a quartet for their fourth album, retaining Elton Dean on sax. Wyatt had left by the end of 1971, briefly leading the similar Matching Mole, and then establishing a long-running solo career. In doing so he was following the path of Kevin Ayers, who already had several solo albums to his credit by the early '70s; Daevid Allen had become a principal of Gong, one of the most prominent and enigmatic '70s progressive-rock bands.

For most intents and purposes, Wyatt's departure spelled the end of the Soft Machine's reign as an important band. Although the Soft Machine were always a collaborative effort, Wyatt's humor, humanism, and soulful raspy vocals could not be replaced. Ratledge and Hopper kept the group going with other musicians, though by now they were an instrumental fusion group with little vestiges of their former playfulness. Hopper left in 1973, and Ratledge, the last original member, was gone by 1976. Other lineups continued to play under the Soft Machine name, amazingly, until the 1990s, but these were the Soft Machine in name only. *—Richie Unterberger*

Live at the Proms 1970 / 1988 / Reckless ♦♦♦
Initially recorded for the BBC in August 1970, this is a good document of the group in concert shortly after the release of *Third*, stripped down to the quartet of Wyatt, Ratledge, Hopper, and saxophonist Elton Dean. Most of the material comes from their second and third albums, and Wyatt, disappointingly, barely sings at all. These versions aren't much different from the ones found on the official releases, though they're perhaps a bit more spontaneous, so this is primarily recommended for hardcore fans. *—Richie Unterberger*

● **Vols. 1 & 2** / Sep. 1989 / Big Beat ♦♦♦♦
A combination of their first two studio albums onto one CD. Their first (originally titled *The Soft Machine*, from 1968), recorded with the trio of Wyatt, Ratledge, and Ayers, combines goofy humor, psychedelia, and some free jazz into an erratic but invigorating brew that was comparable to little else in the late-'60s rock world. Ayers had left to be replaced by Hugh Hopper for 1969's *Volume Two*, which took a definite spin toward jazz and increasingly surrealistic material, stringing together whimsical bits and pieces for side-long suites. Not as pop-oriented as their initial 1967 recordings or as jazz-oriented as their final albums with Wyatt, the material compiled here is perhaps the best representation of the Soft Machine's accomplishments. *—Richie Unterberger*

Jet-Propelled Photograph / Sep. 13, 1994 / Charly ♦♦♦♦
The latest available CD version of a title which has been repackaged and retitled several times over the last 20 years. Recorded in London in April 1967 and produced by the legendary Giorgio Gomelsky, these nine demos feature the original Soft Machine lineup of Robert Wyatt, Kevin Ayers, Mike Ratledge, and Daevid Allen. Although not intended for release, these rough but accomplished performances show the band at their most pop—and song-oriented. Not far removed from Syd Barrett-era Pink Floyd, the jazzy chord changes, unpredictable bursts of scat singing, glib free-association lyrics, ominous buzzing organ, and Robert Wyatt's soulful rasp convey the freewheeling abandon and giddy high spirits that characterized the best early British psychedelia. For similar but more elaborately produced relics from the Daevid Allen lineup, check for the three tracks on the hard-to-find triple LP *Triple Echo*. *—Richie Unterberger*

Live at the Paradiso 1969 / 1995 / Voiceprint ♦♦♦
Previously available as a bootleg, this is a sanctioned release of a 1969 concert in Amsterdam, with excellent sound (particularly by late-'60s standards). The group runs through most of their second LP on this set, without much difference from what you'll hear on the official record (though the pungency of the organ and thick bass comes through well). It's only recommended to serious fans of the group, but that constituency will probably find it a worthwhile purchase. *—Richie Unterberger*

Son Volt

f. 1994, Belleville, IL
Alternative Country-Rock
Following the acrimonious dissolution of the influential alternative country trio Uncle Tupelo, the group's singer/guitarist Jay Farrar formed the roots-rock unit Son Volt. Joined by onetime Tupelo drummer Mike Heidorn along with brothers Jim (bass, vocals) and Dave Boquist (guitar, banjo, fiddle, lap steel), Farrar set about authoring the group's 1995 debut record, *Trace*, an edgy, stark affair that earned virtually unanimous praise from the critical community as well as scoring a minor hit with its first single, "Drown." Son Volt returned in the spring of 1997 with the album *Straightaways*. *—Jason Ankeny*

● **Trace** / Sep. 19, 1995 / Warner Brothers ♦♦♦♦
Jay Farrar always provided the darkest, grittiest moments in Uncle Tupelo, so it comes as no surprise that Son Volt is a rawer record than *A.M.*, the first album by Wilco, a band led by his former partner Jeff Tweedy. Throughout Son Volt's debut *Trace*, the group reworks classic honky tonk and rock 'n' roll, adding a disparate, determined edge to their performances. Even when they rock out, there is a palpable sense of melancholy to Farrar's voice, which lends a poignancy to the music. *Trace* isn't a great step forward from Tupelo's last album, the lovely *Anodyne*, but it is a fine continuation of the ideas Farrar has pursued over the course of his career. *—Stephen Thomas Erlewine*

Straightaways / Apr. 22, 1997 / Warner Brothers ♦♦♦♦
Although none of the songs on *Straightaways* immediately jump off the grooves, as was the case with the band's brilliant debut *Trace*, repeated spins reveal a strong effort nonetheless. Whereas former Uncle Tupelo partner Jeff Tweedy and his band Wilco used its sophomore release to explore new territory, Son Volt leader and songwriter Jay Farrar keeps his band mining the same country-folk vein that Uncle Tupelo quarried. There are plenty of threads to connect *Straightaways* to *Trace*, such as the expressive playing of multi-instrumentalist Dave Boquist on guitars, fiddle, banjo, and lap steel, and Farrar's forlorn vocal delivery, which could give even the weakest song emotional power. On *Straightaways*, his songs live on the same late-night backwoods rural highways that "Trace" inhabited, with song titles like "Creosote" and "Cemetery Savior" conjuring up dark imagery. The album contains plenty of high points: the aforementioned songs, as well as the lonesome "Back into Your World" and "Last Minute Shakedown." And the only place it comes up short is the lyrics—unlike *Trace*, whose songs "Windfall" and "Tear Stained Eye" stood by themselves and provided a universal feel and emotion that was easily grasped, much of the lyrical content of *Straightaways* seems open-ended and fragmented, with the intensity building on the haunting instrumental arrangements and Farrar's affecting vocal phrasing. *—Jack Leaver*

Sonic Youth

f. 1981, New York, NY
Alternative Pop-Rock, Experimental, Indie Rock
Sonic Youth was one of the most unlikely success stories of underground American rock in the '80s. Where contemporaries R.E.M. and Hüsker Dü were fairly conventional in terms of song-structure and melody, Sonic Youth began their career by abandoning any pretense of traditional rock 'n' roll conventions. Borrowing heavily from the free-form noise experimentalism of the Velvet Underground and the Stooges, and melding it with a performance-art aesthetic borrowed from the New York post-punk avant-garde, Sonic Youth redefined what noise meant within rock 'n' roll. Sonic Youth rarely rocked, though they were inspired directly by hardcore punk, post-punk, and no wave. Instead, their dissonance, feedback, and alternate tunings created a new sonic landscape, one that redefined what rock guitar could do. Their trio of independent late-'80s records—*EVOL*, *Sister*, *Daydream Nation*—became touchstones for a generation of indie rockers, who either replicated the noise or reinterpreted it in a more palatable setting. As their career progressed, Sonic Youth grew more palatable, as well, as their more free-form songs began to feel like compositions and their shorter works began to rock harder. During the '90s, most American indie bands, and many British underground bands, displayed a heavy debt to Sonic Youth, and the band themselves had become a popular cult band, with each of their albums charting in the Top 100.

Such success was unthinkable when guitarists Thurston Moore and Lee Ranaldo formed Sonic Youth with bassist Kim Gordon in 1981. Moore had spent his childhood in Bethel, Connecticut; Ranaldo was from Long Island. Both guitarists arrived in Manhattan during the height of the New York-based post-punk movement No Wave, and began performing with the avant-garde composer Glenn Branca, whose dissonant, guitar-based music provided the basis for much of Sonic Youth's early music. Moore's girlfriend Gordon had been active in the avant and No Wave scenes for some time, and the pair helped stage the "Noise Festival" in which the band made their live debut during the summer of 1981. At the time, Sonic Youth also featured keyboardist Ann DeMarinis and drummer Richard Edson. DeMarinis left the band shortly afterward, and the quartet recorded their eponymous debut EP, which was released on Branca's Neutral Records the following year. During 1983, Edson left the band to pursue an acting career and he was replaced by Bob Bert, who drummed on the group's debut album, *Con-*

fusion Is Sex (1983). The band supported the album with their first European tour. Later that year, the group released the EP *Kill Your Idols* on the German label Zensor.

Early in 1984, Moore attempted to land the band a contract with the British indie label Doublevision, but the label rejected the demos. Paul Smith, one of the owners of Doublevision, decided to form Blast First Records in order to release Sonic Youth records. Soon, he received a distribution deal from the hip UK indie label Rough Trade, and the band had its first label with strong distribution. During all these record label negotiations in 1984, the cassette-only live album *Sonic Death: Sonic Youth Live* was released on Ecstatic Peace. *Bad Moon Rising*, the group's first album for Blast First, was released in 1985 to strong reviews throughout the underground music press. The album was markedly different from their earlier releases—it was the first record they made that incorporated their dissonant, feedback-drenched experimentations to a relatively straightforward pop song structure. Following the release of the *Death Valley 69* EP, Bert was replaced by Steve Shelley, who became the group's permanent drummer.

Bad Moon Rising had attracted significant attention throughout the American underground, including some offers from major labels. Sonic Youth decided to sign with SST, home of Hüsker Dü and Black Flag, instead, releasing *EVOL* in 1986. With *EVOL*, the group became fixtures on college radio, and their status grew significantly with 1987's *Sister*, which was heavily praised by mainstream publications like *Rolling Stone*. The group's profile increased further with their 1988 *Ciccone Youth* side-project *The Whitey Album*, which was a tongue-in-cheek tribute to Madonna and other parts of mainstream pop culture. The band's true breakthrough was the double-album *Daydream Nation*. Released on Enigma Records, *Daydream Nation* was a tour de force that was hailed as a masterpiece upon its fall 1988 release, and it generated a college radio hit with "Teenage Riot." Though the album was widely praised, Enigma suffered from poor distribution and, eventually, bankruptcy, which meant the album occasionally wasn't in stores. These factors contributed heavily in the band's decision to move to the major label DGC in 1990.

Signing a contract that gave them complete creative control, as well as letting them function as pseudo-A&R reps for the label, Sonic Youth established a precedent for alternative bands moving to majors during the '90s, proving that it was possible to preserve indie credibility on a major label. Released in the fall of 1990, *Goo*, the band's first major-label album, boasted a more focused sound, yet it didn't abandon the group's noise aesthetics. The result was a college radio hit, and the group's first album to crack the Top 100. Neil Young invited the band to open for him on his arena tour for *Ragged Glory*, and though they failed to win over much of the rocker's audience, it represented their first major incursion into the mainstream; it also helped make Young a cult figure within the alternative circles during the '90s. For their second major-label album *Dirty*, Sonic Youth attempted to replicate the sloppy, straightforward sound of grunge rockers Mudhoney and Nirvana. The band had been supporting these two Seattle-based groups for several years—they had released a split single with Mudhoney and brought Nirvana to DGC Records—and while the songs on *Dirty* were hardly grunge, it was more pop-oriented and accessible than their earlier records. Produced by Butch Vig, who also produced Nirvana's *Nevermind*, *Dirty* became an alternative hit upon its summer 1992 release, generating the modern rock hits "100%," "Youth Against Fascism," and "Sugar Kane." Sonic Youth quickly became hailed as one of the godfathers of the alternative rock that had become the most popular form of rock music in the US, and *Dirty* became a hit along with the exposure, eventually going gold.

Sonic Youth again worked with Vig for 1994's *Experimental Jet Set, Trash and No Star*, which entered the US charts at No. 34 and the UK charts at No. 10, making it their highest-charting album ever. The high chart position was proof of their popularity during the previous two years, as it received decidedly mixed reviews and quickly fell down the charts. Later in 1994, Moore and Gordon—who had married several years before—had their first child, a daughter named Coco Haley. Sonic Youth agreed to headline 1995's American Lollapalooza package tour, using the earnings to build a new studio. Following the completion of the tour, Sonic Youth released *Washing Machine*, which received their strongest reviews since *Daydream Nation*. —*Stephen Thomas Erlewine*

Sonic Youth / 1982 / SST ✦✦

Kill Your Idols / 1983 / Zensor ✦✦

Confusion is Sex / 1983 / SST ✦✦

Out of all their early recordings, *Confusion Is Sex* is Sonic Youth's most listenable record, but that doesn't mean it's an easy listen, by any means. Dense with ideas and noisy guitars, the record only works in fits and spurts, but it reveals the band's potential, even if most of the record is exceedingly difficult and under developed. —*Stephen Thomas Erlewine*

Sonic Death / 1984 / SST ✦✦

Bad Moon Rising / 1985 / DGC ✦✦✦

On *Bad Moon Rising*, the songs gained a focus so that moods and styles that formerly had spread scross several releases could be accomplished in one album. —*Robert Gordon*

EVOL / 1986 / SST ✦✦✦✦

Sonic Youth made its first moves toward rock with *EVOL*, a stunningly fluent mixture of avant-garde instrumentation and subversions of rock 'n' roll. The band benefits greatly from the addition of structure, which gives their aural experiments a firm grounding, but the addition of drummer Steve Shelley is essential to the group's new, dangerous edge. With the added propulsion, the fearless rush of "Expressway to Yr Skull" (a.k.a. "Madonna, Sean and Me") and the near-pop of "Green Light" are undeniably powerful, as are the eerie textures of "Shadow of a Doubt." —*Stephen Thomas Erlewine*

☆ **Sister** / 1987 / SST ✦✦✦✦✦

EVOL was a major leap forward for Sonic Youth, but *Sister* is a masterpiece, demonstrating the group's rapidly evolving musicality. More than ever before, Sonic Youth's songs sound like actual songs, and their collages of noise, distortion, and alternate tunings are now used to provide texture and depth to the music, which is original, complex, and rewarding. Not only is there the full-throttle roar of "Tuff Gnarl," but there are shimmering layers of ambient harmonics and dissonance which are as haunting and challenging as any of their barrages of feedback. Furthermore, *Sister* has a warm sound, which lures the listeners into music that's defiantly arty but never indulgent. It's one of the singular art-rock records of the '80s, surpassed only by Sonic Youth's next album, *Daydream Nation*. —*Stephen Thomas Erlewine*

★ **Daydream Nation** / 1988 / DGC ✦✦✦✦✦

By refining the song-oriented breakthroughs of *Sister* and developing their fascination with noise and alternate tunings, Sonic Youth created a masterpiece of post-punk art-rock with the double album *Daydream Nation*. Though the self-conscious sprawl of the album might appear self-indulgent on the surface, *Daydream Nation* is powered by a sustained vision, one that encapsulates all of the group's quirks and strengths. Alternating between tense, hypnotic instrumental passages and furious noise explosions, the music demonstrates a range of emotions and textures and, in many ways, it's hard not to listen to the record as one long piece of shifting dynamics. But the songs themselves are remarkable, from the anti-anthem of "Teenage Riot" and the punky "Silver Rocket" to the hazy drug dreams of "Providence" and the rolling waves of "Eric's Trip." *Daydream Nation* demonstrates the extent to which noise and self-conscious avant-art can be incorporated into rock, and the results are nothing short of stunning. —*Stephen Thomas Erlewine*

Goo / Jun. 1990 / DGC ✦✦✦

Though *Goo* is not a sellout, it didn't advance the band in the leaps their previous few albums had. Mostly it sounds like *Daydream Nation* rehashed. Included are "Tunic," "Dirty Boots," and "Kool Thing." —*Robert Gordon*

Dirty / Jul. 21, 1992 / DGC ✦✦✦✦

Sonic Youth could never sell out, no matter how hard they tried. Their sound—a jarring barrage of distorted guitars and feedback—is entirely too singular and avant-garde to ever completely cross over. However, *Dirty* is the closest Sonic Youth has ever come to the mainstream, and it is their most accessible album to date. "100%" is nearly a pop single, complete with hooks and an identifiable song structure. But Sonic Youth hasn't lost their edge, as Kim Gordon's tracks prove in particular . —*Stephen Thomas Erlewine*

Experimental Jet Set, Trash & No Star / May 3, 1994 / DGC ✦✦

Opening with their first acoustic number ever, *Experimental Jet Set, Trash and No Star* is Sonic Youth's calmest record to date. While the band's sound is different, their ideas aren't—they're essentially repeating *Sister*. There are a couple of interesting tracks, but most of the album is surprisingly boring. —*Stephen Thomas Erlewine*

Made in USA / Feb. 28, 1995 / Rhino ✦✦

A soundtrack to an obscure 1986 movie, *Made in USA* captures Sonic Youth trying to fit their expansive ideas into the brief space allotted to incidental film music. Keeping the atmospherics but scaling back the noise, the band manages to evoke different textures than their albums, textures that are drier and less overtly avant-garde. Nevertheless, *Made in USA* doesn't rank among their finest work but not because i'ts on a smaller scale, but because it all sounds tossed-off; there's not much thought to any of this music. Even so, the disc is still quite listenable, which shows how good the band was in 1985 and 1986. —*Stephen Thomas Erlewine*

Screaming Fields of Sonic Love / Apr. 25, 1995 / DGC ✦✦✦

Sonic Youth isn't really a singles band, nor a band that works best taken as individual songs, so the idea of a compilation seems a little half-hearted. And, *Screaming Fields of Sonic Love* is a bit haphazard. —*Stephen Thomas Erlewine*

Washing Machine / Oct. 1995 / DGC ✦✦✦✦

After the regressive, low-key *Experimental Jet Set, Trash and No Star,* Sonic Youth appeared to be floundering somewhat, but *Washing Machine* erased any notion that the band had run out of things to say. Easily their most adventurous, challenging, and best record since *Daydream Nation,* the album finds Sonic Youth returning to the fearless exploration of their SST records, but the group has found a way to work that into tighter song structures. Not only are the songs more immediate than most of the material on their earlier records, the sound here is warm and open, making *Washing Machine* their most mature and welcoming record to date. It's not a commercial record, nor is it a pop record, but *Washing Machine* encompasses everything that made Sonic Youth innovators and shows that they can continue to grow, finding new paths inside their signature sound. —*Stephen Thomas Erlewine*

The Sonics

f. , Tacoma, WA
Rock & Roll, Garage Rock
A rock 'n' roll band from Tacoma, Washington, the Sonics' original members were Gerry Roslie (lead singer and piano/organ), Andy Parypa (guitar), Larry Parypa (bass), Bob Bennett (drums), and Rob Lind (saxophone). Forming in the wake of the early-'60s success of local favorites the Kingsmen and the Wailers (whose Etiquette label they recorded for), the Sonics combined the classic Northwest-area teen-dance raunch with early English band grit (particularly influenced by the Kinks), relentless rhythmic drive, and unabashed '50s-style blues-shouting for a combination that still makes their brand of rock 'n' roll perhaps the raunchiest ever captured on wax. Lead singer Gerry Roslie was no less than a White Little Richard, whose harrowing soul-screams were startling even to the Northwest teen audience, who liked their music powerful and driving with little regard to commercial subtleties. With hit after hit on the local charts (and influencing every local band that ever took the stage), the band inexplicably was never able to break out nationally, leaving their sound largely undiluted for mass consumption. Breaking up in the late '60s (after one ill-fated album attempt to water down their style for national attention), the Sonics continue today to be revered by '60s collectors the world over for their unique brand of rock 'n' roll raunch. —*Cub Koda*

Here Are the Sonics!!! / 1965 / Etiquette ✦✦✦
Debut album, featuring early hits "The Witch" and "Psycho." —*Cub Koda*

The Sonics Boom / 1966 / Etiquette ✦✦✦
Second album, featuring unusual take on "Louie Louie." —*Cub Koda*

● **Here Are the Ultimate Sonics** / 1991 / Etiquette ✦✦✦✦
Combining all the tracks from their first two Etiquette albums, three tracks from the label's Christmas album, live tracks, and an alternate take of "The Witch," this compilation more than lives up to its title. The definitive overview. —*Cub Koda*

Sonny & Cher

f. 1964, Los Angeles, CA, **db.** 1974
Folk-Rock, Pop-Rock
Sonny & Cher proved one of the magical musical combinations of the '60s, with their wisecracking repartee providing counterpoint to a series of adoring hit duets. Sonny Bono (b. Feb 16, 1935) started out at Los Angeles-based Specialty Records as a songwriter in the late '50s. While working sessions with legendary producer Phil Spector, Bono met and married background singer Cher (born Cherilyn Lapierre, May 20, 1946) and formed a duet with his new wife. Neither was blessed with an outstanding vocal range, but no matter—they went gold in 1965 with the pop chart-topper "I Got You Babe" on Atco and did well with "Baby Don't Go" on Reprise. At the same time, both enjoyed success separately—Sonny with "Laugh at Me" for Atco, Cher with "All I Really Want to Do" and "Bang Bang (My Baby Shot Me Down)" on Imperial. "The Beat Goes On" in 1967 and "All I Ever Need Is You" four years later presaged the pair's anointment as popular TV variety-hour hosts from 1971 to 1974 (the year they were divorced). Since then, Cher has gone on to mega-stardom on record and on the silver screen. Sonny, meanwhile, was elected mayor of Palm Springs, CA. —*Bill Dahl*

● **The Beat Goes On: The Best of Sonny & Cher** / 1975 / Atco ✦✦✦✦
They were the ultimate "hip luv" couple of the '60s and their many hits are still fun to listen to. "I Got You Babe," "Laugh at Me," and the title track are three of the 21 original recordings included on this definitive collection. —*Jeff Tamarkin*

All I Ever Need: the Kapp/Mca Anthology / Jan. 1996 / MCA ✦✦✦✦

The Sorrows

f. 1963, Coventry, England, **db.** 1969
British Invasion
One of the most overlooked bands of the British Invasion, the Sorrows offered a tough brand of R&B-infused rock that recalled the Pretty Things (though not as R&B-oriented) and the Kinks (though not as pop-oriented). Their biggest British hit, "Take a Heart," stopped just outside the UK Top 20; several other fine mid-'60s singles met with either slim or a total lack of success. With the rich, gritty vocals of Don Fardon, taut raunchy guitars, and good material (both self-penned and from outside writers), they rank as one of the better British bands of their era, and certainly among the very best never to achieve success of any kind in the US. After their sole LP (also titled "Take a Heart"), they issued a couple impressive singles with psychedelic and Dylanesque overtones, and had somehow relocated to Italy in the late '60s, where they played out their string with material in a much more progressive (and less distinctive) vein. Don Fardon had a Top 20 hit in America with a pre-Raiders version of "Indian Reservation" in 1968. —*Richie Unterberger*

● **Take a Heart** / 1965 / Repertoire ✦✦✦✦
A reissue of their mid-'60s album, with eight bonus tracks, including the fine non-LP singles by the original lineup and foreign-language versions of some tunes. One of the best obscure British Invasion records. —*Richie Unterberger*

Take a Heart [Australian Compilation] / 1982 / Raven ✦✦✦✦
There are four or five reissues of the Sorrows' mid-'60s material; this Australian LP was the first of the batch. The others are more comprehensive, especially Sequel's *The Sorrows,* with 20 tracks (including all 14 of the ones on this Australian comp). You really don't lose much, however, if you choose to stick with this one. It has the very best stuff and it's sequenced better than some of the other reissues, although it doesn't have any historical liner notes. —*Richie Unterberger*

In Italy / 1983 / Eva ✦✦✦
With an altered lineup, the Sorrows cut these tracks in a much more progressive vein in the late '60s, heavily influenced by Traffic, Family, and the Small Faces (five of the fourteen songs here are covers of compositions by those groups). Not nearly as impressive as their beat material. —*Richie Unterberger*

● **The Sorrows** / 1991 / Sequel ✦✦✦✦
The best reissue of the *Take a Heart* album (which has also been reissued in other configurations). Includes all the tracks from the LP, all the important non-LP singles, a couple unissued tracks, and Don Fardon's version of "Indian Reservation." —*Richie Unterberger*

Soul Asylum

f. 1983, Minneapolis, MN
Group / Rock & Roll, Alternative Pop-Rock, Pop-Rock
Soul Asylum is the quintessential little band that could; it only took ten years to turn them from a teenage garage band into multiplatinum-selling rock stars. Guitarist Dan Murphy, bassist Karl Mueller, and drummer Dave Pirner formed in 1981 as Loud Fast Rules in Minneapolis, MN. When the shambolic, no longer teenage band burst on to the scene in 1984, they'd added Grant Young on drums and switched Pirner to rhythm guitar and vocals for the loud and fast Twin Tone album, *Say What You Will Clarence... Karl Sold the Truck.* Sadly, the record was overshadowed by the current releases by fellow Twin Cities denizens the Replacements and Hüsker Dü; Soul Asylum have gone on record stating they were dubbed "the B-teamers" by the Replacements, which created bad feelings between the bands for years. Still, the band forged their way on college radio and countless US club tours, which gained them a devoted following. The "hell-on" rock band, in guitarist Murphy's words, released *Made to Be Broken* (1986) and followed with the similar *While You Were Out* (1986), but Pirner's songwriting always far outshone the form.

The band signed to A&M Records in 1989 as part of a distribution pact between Twin Tone and A&M for the harder rock-sounding *Hang Time,* produced by Lenny Kaye. The record garnered some college radio attention, but by 1990's *And the Horse They Rode In On,* Soul Asylum had fallen out of favor with the indie-rock set and were left languishing in limbo, having almost entirely forsaken their post-punk indie roots. Pirner and Murphy spent the time regrouping, working out songs as the acoustic duo Murphy and Pirfinkle, touring the Midwest. The songs found their way to Columbia Records and onto *Grave Dancers Union* in 1992, which ultimately earned the band a multiplatinum record after a slow start. The magical third single, "Runaway Train," propelled by a public service announcement-style video for missing children, helped push the single to No. 5 and the album to No. 11 and turned the band into a household name. They performed at the Clinton Inaugural in 1992.

Shortly after the release of *Grave Dancers,* drummer Young left the band and was replaced by Sterling Campbell for the recording of *Let Your Dim Light Shine* in 1995. Though it charted at No. 6 and a single, "Misery," hit the Top 20, the band never reached the dizzying heights nor masses they touched with "Runaway Train." Murphy records and tours with the Minneapolis "supergroup" Golden Smog, while Pirner also contributed vocals to their 1996 recording, *On Golden Smog.* Pirner's well-publicized romance with actress Winona Ryder since 1994 has left skeptics predicting the band would break up, but as of 1997, the band hadn't packed it in. Needless to say, the little band's fame ultimately eclipsed those other guys from Minneapolis. —*Denise Sullivan*

Say What You Will / 1984 / Twin/Tone ✦✦✦
Produced by Hüsker Dü's Bob Mould, it's unsurprising that Soul Asylum's debut record shares the same tendencies as the Hüskers to loud, fast punk rock. Compared to the more structured songs he writes today, Dave Pirner was jumpy with nervous energy, and the songs reflect this frantic need to communicate and make some noise. Fans of post-stardom Soul Asylum might find this a bit too much to handle, but it remains expressive speed-rock that will leave you breathless. —*John Dougan*

While You Were Out / 1986 / Twin/Tone ✦✦✦
Producer and ex-Suicide Commando Chris Osgood was an excellent choice to produce this first attempt at a breakthrough record. And, despite a few songs simply sounding like retreads, this is a pretty snappy collection, with Pirner's songwriting showing a depth and nuance that had previously been lost amid the roaring. The LP closer, "Passing Sad Daydream," is even a country-tinged wallow that, despite being too long, was an indication that this band was developing a style that would allow them to make the transition out of speed-rock's obsession with, well, speed. —*John Dougan*

Made to Be Broken / 1986 / Twin/Tone ✦✦
If *Say What You Will*'s inchoate, raunchy blur is a bit much, then album number two, again produced by Mould, straightens things out a bit and lets riffs emerge from the walls of distortion. The record's first single, "Tied to the Tracks," is a rip-snorting bull ride of volume and power, but then again, so is much of the record. Although they were derisively written off by some wags as Hüsker Jr., that was a critical view offered by the short-sighted. They may have shared the same sound, but were very different bands. —*John Dougan*

Time's Incinerator / 1986 / Twin/Tone ✦✦✦
A cassette-only release, this is a collection of outtakes and live tracks covering the period from 1981to1986 when the band was metamorphosing from their former selves as Loud Fast Rules into Soul Asylum. Obviously, when you give your band a name like Loud Fast Rules, you're not going to be playing folk-rock, but despite the insistence on speed and volume, there are some surprises here, most notably a live cover of James Brown's "Hot Pants." An interesting document of a band growing up and becoming more comfortable with getting better, whether they wanted to or not. —*John Dougan*

Clam Dip and Other Delights / Jan. 1988 / Twin/Tone ✦✦✦✦
A great EP with a hysterical cover parody of Herb Alpert's sexy *Whipped Cream and Other Delights* album cover, this shows Soul Asylum growing up but not growing old. Starting with the huge thudding riff of "Just Plain Evil," this adds the triumphantly poppy "Chains" and the funky "Take It to the Root," which originally appeared on *Time's Incinerator*. Oddly, what was originally intended as a minor release turned out to be a major work in Soul Asylum's early career. —*John Dougan*

● **Hang Time** / Feb. 1988 / A&M ✦✦✦✦
More riff-heavy than usual, with considerable help from producer Lenny Kaye, *Hang Time* turned out to be the best of Soul Asylum's early records. The guitars of Pirner and Dan Murphy synchronize into a sonic wad of incredible power, while the songs (especially "Cartoon," "Some Time to Return," and "Beggars and Choosers") showed that Pirner had become a first rate songwriter. Clever without being glib, and heartfelt without resorting to cliches, Pirner was doing something that eluded many of his peers: dealing with the transition from youth to adulthood and all the inherent conflicts that arise during this time. They would become superstars later, but this record should have done the trick. —*John Dougan*

And the Horse They Rode on / 1990 / A&M ✦✦✦
The band had already begun to trade in the loud and fast sound for something a little more roots-based, as found on "We 3," while other songs dabbled in heavy metal ("All the King's Friends"). On alternate tracks, the experiment didn't really work, and it left old fans confused and cold while arriving a little too early to cash in on the alt-rock explosion. Consequently, this otherwise fine record was left unheralded. It stands as one of the last pre-grunge alternative rock records, but had it not been perceived to fail so miserably, the band's success with its following album wouldn't have been nearly as sweet. —*Denise Sullivan*

Grave Dancers Union / May 1992 / Columbia ✦✦✦✦
The band's breakthrough, million-selling album yielded the mega-hit "Runaway Train" and put Soul Asylum in a whole new league; longtime fans were predictably disappointed with the slick results. This is a solid alternative rock record with singer-songwriter/vocalist Dave Pirner up front, a role he was built for but always seemed to resist until the clear do-or-die moment for the band. They did; however, they've never matched the success or consistency of this album. Tracks like "Home

Sick" and "New World" bear the roots of the country-rock revival later forged by Son Volt and Wilco, while the angst-ridden "Somebody to Shove" is pure joy Soul Asylum style. —*Denise Sullivan*

Let Your Dim Light Shine / Jun. 6, 1995 / Columbia ✦✦
Following the same pattern and approach as *Grave Dancer's Union*, *Let Your Dim Light Shine* firmly positions Soul Asylum as a mainstream rock 'n' roll band. Gone are the breakneck punk rockers, replaced with searching, introspective ballads and socially conscious mid-tempo rockers. In itself, that wouldn't be a problem, but Dave Pirner has taken the weight of the world upon his shoulders, which becomes apparent from the lyrics. Pirner's lyrics are so overwrought that they not only approach self-parody, they go completely beyond it. Every lyric is weighted with such self-importance, making it easy to overlook the relative merits of the music, which isn't quite as impressive as their previous records. —*Stephen Thomas Erlewine*

Soul II Soul

f. 1989, London, England
Soul, House, Urban, Club-Dance

Led by producer/vocalist/songwriter DJ Jazzie B, Soul II Soul were one of the most innovative dance/R&B outfits of the late '80s, creating a seductive, deep R&B that borrowed from Philly soul, disco, reggae, and '80s hip-hop. Originally featuring Jazzie B, producer/arranger Nellee Hooper, and instrumentalist Philip "Daddae" Harvey, the musical collective came together in the late '80s. The group had a residency at the Africa Centre in London's Covent Garden, which led to a record contract with 10, a subsidiary of Virgin. Two singles, "Fairplay" and "Feel Free," began to attract attention both in clubs and in the press.

Featuring the vocals of Caron Wheeler, Soul II Soul's third single, "Keep on Movin'," reached the UK Top Five in March of 1989. Released in the summer of 1989, "Back to Life" also featured Wheeler and became another Top Ten hit. Soul II Soul released their debut album, *Club Classics Volume One*, shortly afterward. The album was released in America under the title *Keep on Movin'*; both "Keep on Movin'" and "Get a Life" became substantial hits, propelling the album to double platinum status.

Wheeler left the group before the recording of the group's second album, *Vol. II: 1990—A New Decade*. The album debuted at No. 1 in the UK, yet it caught the group in a holding pattern. Hooper soon left the collective, leaving Jazzie B. to soldier on alone. Hooper went on to work with several of the most influential and popular acts of the early '90s, including Massive Attack (*Blue Lines*), Bjork (*Debut* and *Post*), Madonna (*Bedtime Stories*), and U2 ("Hold Me, Thrill Me, Kiss Me, Kill Me"). In 1992, Soul II Soul released *Vol. 3: Just Right*, to both lukewarm reviews and sales. The group's fourth album of original material was scheduled for release in the fall of 1995. —*Stephen Thomas Erlewine*

● **Keep on Movin'** / Jun. 1989 / Virgin ✦✦✦✦
When American urban-contemporary radio was bombarding its listeners with one Guy clone after another in the late '80s and early '90s, British neo-soulsters like Soul II Soul, Lisa Stansfield and the Chimes offered highly creative and gutsy alternatives. With influences ranging from Chic to hip-hop to African music, Soul II Soul's debut album, *Keep on Movin'*, was among the most rewarding R&B releases of 1989. Soul II Soul leader/producer/composer Jazzie B takes one risk after another—all of which pay off. The group enjoyed major hits with the Chic-influenced gems "Keep on Movin'" and "Back to Life" (both of which feature the gifted Caron Wheeler), and equally superb are the African-influenced reflections of "Dance" and "Holdin' On," the soulful grit and intensity of "Feel Free" and the hypnotic house music of "Happiness." Though Wheeler was Soul II Soul's best-known singer and went on to enjoy a career as a solo artist, Rose Windross and Do'Reen (both expressive soul divas) also do their part to make *Movin'* the artistic triumph that it is. —*Alex Henderson*

Vol. 2: 1990: A New Decade / May 1990 / Virgin ✦✦✦✦
A better album but a deceptive one: even the best songs here don't intoxicate as thoroughly as "Keep on Movin'," but within the context of the album, each plays a vital part. In other words, this is a genuine *album*, and not a pastiche of singles. —*John Floyd*

Vol. 3 Just Right / Apr. 28, 1992 / Virgin ✦✦

Vol. 5: Believe / Sep. 26, 1995 / Virgin ✦✦✦
Six years after they revolutionized R&B and soul with their debut album *Keep on Movin'*, Soul II Soul returned with *Volume 5: Believe*. Since their debut, the soul collective had been struggling to regain their position as musical innovators; in the process, they turned out two confused albums that had their moments, but nothing quite as stirring as their initial singles, which were collected on the British-only *Volume 6: The Classic Singles*. *Believe*, their fourth album of original material, doesn't necessarily make a case for Soul II Soul as pioneers in the mid-'90s, but it does represent something of a comeback. Where their two previous albums were muddled affairs, *Believe* is clear and confident, filled with

fully formed songs. It helps that Jazzie B, the leader of the group, has persuaded former members Caron Wheeler and Penny Ford to make appearances on the album and has recruited some genuine new talent that helps spark him into recording his best music since the group's debut. Granted, it doesn't push down many boundaries, but *Believe* fits comfortably into the laidback, jazz-saturated grooves of '90s R&B.
—*Stephen Thomas Erlewine*

Soundgarden

f. 1985, Seattle, WA, **db**. Apr. 9, 1997
Alternative Pop-Rock, Heavy Metal, Grunge
Soundgarden made a place for heavy metal in alternative rock. Their fellow Seattle rockers Green River may have spearheaded the grunge sound, but they relied on noise-rock in the vein of the Stooges. Similarly, Jane's Addiction was too fascinated with prog-rock and performance art to appeal to a wide array of metal fans. Soundgarden, however, developed directly out of the grandiose blues-rock of Led Zeppelin and the sludgy, slow riffs of Black Sabbath. Which isn't to say they were a straightahead metal band. Soundgarden borrowed the DIY aesthetics of punk, melding their guitar-driven sound with an intelligence and ironic sense of humor that was indebted to the American underground of the mid-'80s. Furthermore, the band rarely limited themselves to simple, pounding riffs, often making detours into psychedelia. But the group's key sonic signatures—the gutsy wail of vocalist Chris Cornell and the winding riffs of guitarist Kim Thayil—were what brought the band out of the underground. Not only were they one of the first groups to record for the legendary Seattle indie Sub Pop, but they were the first grunge band to sign to a major label. In fact, most critics expected Soundgarden to be the band that broke down the doors for alternative rock, not Nirvana. However, the group didn't experience an across-the-boards success until 1994, when *Superunknown* became a No. 1 hit.

For a band so heavily identified with the Seattle scene, it's ironic that two of its founding members were from the Midwest. Kim Thayil (guitar), Hiro Yamamoto (bass), and Bruce Pavitt were all friends in Illinois who decided to head to Olympia, Washington, to attend college after high school graduation in 1981. Though none of the three completed college, all of them became involved in the Washington underground music scene. Pavitt was the only one that didn't play—he founded a fanzine that later became the Sub Pop record label. Yamamoto played in several cover bands before forming a band in 1984 with his roommate Chris Cornell (vocals), a Seattle native who had previously played drums in several bands. Thayil soon joined the duo and the group named themselves Soundgarden after a local Seattle sculpture. Scott Sundquist originally was the band's drummer, but he was replaced by Matt Cameron in 1986. Over the next two years, Soundgarden gradually built up a devoted cult following through their club performances.

Pavitt signed Soundgarden to his fledgling Sub Pop label in the summer of 1987, releasing the single "Hunted Down" before the EP *Screaming Life* appeared later in the year. *Screaming Life* and the group's second EP, 1988's *FOPP*, became underground hits, and earned the attention of several major labels. The band decided to sign to SST instead of a major, releasing *Ultramega OK* by the end of 1988. *Ultramega OK* received strong reviews among alternative and metal publications, and the group decided to make the leap to a major for their next album, 1989's *Louder Than Love*. Released on A&M Records, *Louder Than Love* became a word-of-mouth hit, earning positive reviews from mainstream publications, peaking at No. 108 on the charts and earning a Grammy nomination. Following the album's fall 1989 release, Yamamoto left the band to return to school. Jason Everman, a former guitarist for Nirvana, briefly played with the band before Ben Shepard joined in early 1990.

Soundgarden's third album, 1991's *Badmotorfinger*, was heavily anticipated by many industry observers as a potential breakout hit. Though it was a significant hit, reaching No. 39 on the album charts, its success was overshadowed by the surprise success of Nirvana's *Nevermind*, which was released the same month as *Badmotorfinger*. Prior to *Nevermind*, Soundgarden had been marketed by A&M as a metal band, and the group had agreed to support Guns N Roses on the fall 1991 "Lose Your Illusion" tour. While the tour did help sales, Soundgarden benefited primarily from the grunge explosion, whose media attention helped turn the band into stars. The band was also helped by the Top 10 success of *Temple of the Dog*, a tribute to deceased Mother Love Bone singer Andrew Wood Cornell and Cameron recorded with members of Pearl Jam. By the spring release of 1994's *Superunknown*, Soundgarden's following had grown considerably, which meant that the album debuted at No. 1 upon its release. (A year before its release, Shepherd and Cameron released an eponymous album by their side project, Hater.) *Superunknown* became one of the most popular records of 1994, generating a genuine crossover hit with "Black Hole Sun," selling over three million copies and earning two Grammies. Soundgarden returned in 1996 with *Down on the Upside*, which entered the charts at No. 2. Despite the record's strong initial sales, it failed to generate a big

hit, and was hurt by grunge's fading popularity. Soundgarden retained a sizable audience—the album did go platinum, and they were co-headliners on the sixth Lollapalooza—but they didn't replicate the blockbuster success of *Superunknown*.

After completing an American tour following Lollapalooza that was plagued by rumors of internal fighting, Soundgarden announced that they were breaking up on April 9, 1997, to pursue other interests.
—*Stephen Thomas Erlewine*

Ultramega OK / 1988 / SST ✦✦✦✦
A noticeable improvement from their EPs, Soundgarden's first full-length release is an impressive mixture of slow Zeppelin/Sabbath-style riffs updated for a new generation with even more murkiness. Cornell's vocals can be irritatingly overblown, and the band can be unfocused (as on their cover of Howlin' Wolf's "Smokestack Lightning"), but the whole thing sounds fresh. —*Stephen Thomas Erlewine*

Louder than Love / 1990 / A&M ✦✦✦
The first major-label release from Soundgarden is a step down from the independent *Ultramega OK*, as Thayil's guitar drowns in the murkiness of the production that Cornell tries to bellow through. It's uneven, but there are some staple Soundgarden songs that are among their best, including "Full on Kevin's Mom," "Hands All Over," "Ugly Truth," and the extraordinarily stupid "Big Dumb Sex." —*Stephen Thomas Erlewine*

Screaming Life / **Fopp** / Jun. 1990 / Sub Pop ✦✦✦
Soundgarden's first two EPs for Sub Pop weren't particularly impressive at first listen, since they wallowed a bit too heavily in sub-Sabbath and Zeppelin riffery, but in retrospect, the record offers a good indication of where the band would go. Still, they aren't as sonically powerful as they would later become, nor are their songs particularly compelling, making this only interesting as a historical recording. —*Stephen Thomas Erlewine*

Badmotorfinger / 1991 / A&M ✦✦✦✦
The presence of new bassist Ben Shepherd gives *Badmotorfinger* a stronger, tougher rhythm section than earlier Soundgarden albums, but what really makes the record a breakthrough is the songwriting. A monolithic collection of heavy rockers that turn metal inside out with complex riffs and cryptic, self-consciously ambitious lyrics, *Badmotorfinger* is cerebral metal that packs a gut-level force. Soundgarden layers each song with subtly shifting sonic textures that add depth to Chris Cornell's songs, whether it's the mock-hardcore rush of "Jesus Christ Pose" or the slow, stalking "Outshined." —*Stephen Thomas Erlewine*

● **Superunknown** / Mar. 8, 1994 / A&M ✦✦✦✦
Superunknown expands on the bottomless heavy metal of *Badmotorfinger* by adding touches of psychedelia and pop to Soundgarden's signature sludge. The result is the band's best album, full of powerful, expertly crafted hard rock that improves with repeated listens. —*Stephen Thomas Erlewine*

Down on the Upside / May 21, 1996 / A&M ✦✦✦
Superunknown was a breakthrough in many ways. Not only did the album bring Soundgarden a new audience, it dramatically expanded their vision, as well as their accomplishments. If *Down on the Upside* initially seems a retreat from the grand, layered textures of *Superunknown*, let it sink in. The sound of *Down on the Upside* is certainly more immediate, but the band hasn't returned to the monstrous, unfocused wailing of *Louder Than Love*. Instead, they've retained their ambitious song structures, neo-psychedelic guitar textures, and winding melodies but haven't dressed them up with detailed production. Consequently, *Down on the Upside* is visceral as well as cerebral—"Rhinosaur" goes for the gut, while "Pretty Noose" is updated, muscular prog-rock. *Down on the Upside* is a deceptive album—it might seem like nothing more than heavy metal, but a closer listen reveals that Soundgarden hasn't tempered their ambitions at all. —*Stephen Thomas Erlewine*

Epic Soundtracks

b., London, England
Alternative Pop-Rock, Singer-Songwriter
In the '70s, Epic Soundtracks formed Swell Maps, with his brother, Nikki Sudden; the band influenced many groups, from Sonic Youth to the Lemonheads. Considering his past, it may seem strange that Epic returned in the early '90s after a long hiatus to write moving piano ballads. His first solo LP, *Rise Above*, featured J Mascis and Kim Gordon, among others. He returned two years later with a second album, *Sleeping Star; Change My Life* followed in 1996. —*John Bush*

● **Rise Above** / 1993 / Bar/None ✦✦✦✦
Epic Soundtracks writes affecting piano ballads and midtempo pieces with an ease that belies how good these songs are. Though J Mascis (drums on two tracks) and Kim Gordon (voice on "Big Apple Graveyard") do contribute, this is Epic's show; he provides most of the music and all the magic. Many songs have a traditional feel and sound strangely familiar. —*John Bush*

Sleeping Star / Oct. 19, 1994 / Bar/None ✦✦✦
Sleeping Star is not exactly identical to Epic's first album, but little has changed. The songs still have that traditional ballad feel; witness "Tonight's The Night (Rock 'N' Roll Lullabye)," a song that borrows heavily from the long history of ballad procedure. Not that any of this is bad. "Emily May" has a rolling piano line and uptempo rhythm that makes it the highlight of the disc. Most of the songs, however, are a bit too traditional to provoke any reaction by the listener. —*John Bush*

Change My Life / Apr. 23, 1996 / Bar/None ✦✦✦
It's basically more of the same from Mr. Soundtracks on his third album, which isn't necessarily a bad thing. He doesn't solely stick to the loungish piano ballads that have been his trademark, occasionally jangling things up a bit. Considering his background, though, his best assets are turning out to be the surprisingly conventional ones of tuneful, affecting slow pieces. These should appeal to fans of John Cale, David Bowie, Alex Chilton, and Brian Wilson, to name a few reference points. When he tries to rock harder, the results are strained and awkward, as his voice isn't strong enough to carry raucous material. —*Richie Unterberger*

Source Direct

f. 1994, St. Albans, England
Club-Dance, Jungle/Drum 'N Bass, Electronica
St. Albans-based duo Source Direct are renowned for the ambient-leaning progressive drum 'n' bass they've released on the Metalheadz, Basement, Certificate 18, and Street Beats labels, as well as on their own self-titled imprint. Often compared with such rolling, relaxed junglists as LTJ Bukem, Peshay, and Goldie, Source Direct actually figure closer to the taut, brooding complexity of Photek and edgier PFM, wrapping sweeping minor-key melodies around sharp, splintered breaks and deep basslines far more oppositional than the sweet retreat of much of the LGR and Metalheadz stables. Claiming close affinity with '70s soul, jazz, and funk groups such as Grover Washington, Bob James, and Average White Band, SD's Jim Baker and Phil Aslett began making music together when they were just 14. Renting out midnight studio time at Hackney's Panic Studio, they assembled demo cassettes of (still unreleased) material while setting their DJ skills in order and organizing and hosting underground (usually illegal) hardcore parties. They soon pieced together their own studio in their St. Albans home (near Ipswich, home to Rupert "Photek" Parkes), and began releasing a string of highly acclaimed 12-inches by the ages of 17. The pair record under a variety of pseudonyms for various labels, including Intensity (Basement), Sounds of Life (Certificate 18), and Oblivion (Street Beats), but have released most of their material as Source Direct (primarily on Odyssey, Metalheadz, Looking Good, and their own label). Source Direct tracks have been featured on Looking Good and Metalheadz label compilations, and the pair have completed remixes for the likes of the Shamen, Code of Practice, and Medicine Man. —*Sean Cooper*

● **Two Masks / Black Domina** / 1997 / Science ✦✦✦✦
After much speculation about whether or not they'd make the jump, Source Direct's major label debut finally arrived in the form of *Two Masks*, the pair's darkest, most accomplished material to date. A bit of a distance from earlier releases for Metalheadz, Certificate 18, and their own SD label, *Two Masks* (which also marks the first SD release available on CD) is chilling, cavernous stuff, with complex beat patterns, hand-fashioned breaks, and eerie, echoing atmospheres reaching deep into colleague Rupert "Photek" Parkes territory. Excellent. —*Sean Cooper*

Joe South

b. Feb. 28, 1940, Atlanta, GA
Guitar, Vocals / Singer-Songwriter, Pop-Rock
Singer-songwriter Joe South (born Joe Souter) began his career as a country musician, performing on an Atlanta radio station and joining Pete Drake's band in 1957. The following year, he recorded a novelty single, "The Purple People Eater Meets the Witch Doctor," and became a session musician in Nashville and at Muscle Shoals. South appeared on records by Marty Robbins, Eddy Arnold, Aretha Franklin, Wilson Pickett, Bob Dylan (*Blonde on Blonde*), and Simon & Garfunkel ("The Sounds of Silence"). During the '60s, South began working on his songwriting, crafting hits for Deep Purple ("Hush") and several for Billy Joe Royal, including "Down in the Boondocks." South began recording his own material in 1968, scoring a hit with the Grammy-winning "Games People Play" (Song of the Year) the following year. While South produced hits like "Don't It Make You Want to Go Home" and "Walk a Mile in My Shoes," Lynn Anderson had a smash country and pop hit in 1971 with South's "(I Never Promised You a) Rose Garden."

South took several years off after his brother's suicide in 1971, moving to Maui and living in the jungles. He had proven a rather prickly character, recording a song entitled "I'm a Star"; he was also busted for drugs and, never entirely comfortable performing, was known for an antagonistic stance in concert (he once suggested that audience mem-

bers start dancing around the concert hall and kiss his ass as they approached the stage). South briefly returned in 1975 with the *Midnight Rainbows* LP, but retired from recording and performing soon afterwards. South returned in 1994 in a London concert showcasing American Southern performers and has since re-entered the music publishing industry. —*Steve Huey*

● **The Best of Joe South** / Jul. 1990 / Rhino ✦✦✦✦
This is an essential collection featuring South's brand of Southern-style pop idealism. Classic hits like "Games People Play," "Walk a Mile in My Shoes," "Don't It Make You Want to Go Home," and "Birds of a Feather," as well as notable South originals like "Down in the Boondocks," "Rose Garden," "I Knew You When," and "Hush" are here, too. Good liner notes and sound round out this package. —*Rick Clark*

Southside Johnny

b. Dec. 4, 1948, New Jersey
Rock & Roll
Southside Johnny and the Asbury Jukes were the second band after Bruce Springsteen and the E Street Band to emerge from the New Jersey shore scene, and though they carried over a significant influence (and some key personnel) from their predecessors, they were a more generic White R&B horn band in the Memphis Stax Records tradition. The group was organized in 1974 by singer John Lyon (b. Dec. 4, 1948, Neptune, NJ) and guitarist/songwriter "Miami" Steve Van Zandt (b. Nov. 22, 1950, Boston). Van Zandt decamped for the E Street Band in 1975, but he continued to direct the Jukes, managing them, writing their songs, and producing their records. The original Jukes lineup was: Billy Rush (b. Aug. 26, 1952) (guitar); Kevin Kavanaugh (b. Aug. 27, 1951) (keyboards); Al Berger (b. Nov. 8, 1949) (bass); Kenny Pentifallo (b. Dec. 30, 1940) (drums); Carlo Novi (b. Aug. 7, 1949, Mexico City) (tenor sax); Eddie Manion (b. Feb. 28, 1952) (baritone sax); Tony Palligrosi (b. May 9, 1954) (trumpet); Ricky Gazda (b. Jun 18, 1952) (trumpet); and Richie "La Bamba" Rosenberg (trombone). The group signed to Epic Records and released *I Don't Want to Go Home* (1976), which featured songwriting by Springsteen and cameos by Ronnie Spector and Lee Dorsey. *This Time It's for Real* (1977) contained more Springsteen tunes and appearances by the Coasters, the Drifters, and the Five Satins. Critical consensus said that their third album, *Hearts of Stone* (1978), was the Jukes' peak, but they failed to break through to mass success and were dropped by Epic. Moving to Mercury, they made *The Jukes* (1979), on which all songwriting was handled by Lyon and Rush, and followed with *Love Is a Sacrifice* (1980) and the live double-LP *Reach Up and Touch the Sky* (1981). Moving to the Atlantic Records subsidiary Mirage, they worked with producer Nile Rodgers on the uncharacteristic *Trash It Up!* (1983), then returned to form on *In the Heat* (1984). The group had suffered personnel shifts all along, but the departure of Billy Rush left Lyon to write much of *At Least We Got Shoes* (1986), after which he made a "solo" album, *Slow Dance* (1988). Southside and the Jukes reunited with Springsteen and Van Zandt for *Better Days* (1991). —*William Ruhlmann*

I Don't Want to Go Home / 1976 / Epic ✦✦✦✦
The Jukes' debut is an R&B revivalist's delight, capped by splendid duets with Lee Dorsey ("How Come You Treat Me So Bad?") and Ronnie Spector ("You Mean So Much to Me"). —*Kit Kiefer*

This Time It's for Real / 1977 / Epic ✦✦✦✦
Southside Johnny's sophomore release was another strong collection of early-'60s R&B—and doo wop-influenced pop-rock. To underscore those elements, *This Time It's for Real* features guest appearances by the Drifters, the Coasters, and the Five Satins. Highlights include "Without Love," "Love on the Wrong Side of Town," and the title track. —*Rick Clark*

Hearts of Stone / 1978 / Epic ✦✦✦✦
This is the most successful merger of old R&B with modern songwriting and sensibilities in the Jukes' catalog. "Hearts of Stone" features more great Van Zandt originals ("Got to Be a Better Way Home," "This Time Baby's Gone for Good") and Springsteen's knockout title tune. —*Kit Kiefer*

Havin' a Party with Southside Johnny / 1979 / Epic ✦✦✦✦
The highlights of this New Jersey band's first few albums are included, plus a fine remake of Sam Cooke's "Having a Party." It's a great starting place for the uninitiated. —*Rick Clark*

The Jukes / 1979 / Mercury ✦✦✦
After none of the Jukes' first three records got higher than No.85 in the charts, Epic Records dropped the band. The feeling was that Southside was too closely identified with Springsteen and Van Zandt, and needed to establish a separate identity. So, the band dumped its producer and songwriter and moved to Mercury Records for its fourth album, on which Jukes guitarist Billy Rush took over the songwriting. Given that, however, the result is not half bad. Southside and Rush collaborate on the excellent leadoff track, "All I Want Is Everything," and Rush contrib-

utes "I'm So Anxious," "Living in the Real World," and several other respectable numbers. The glory days were over, and the band really wouldn't make a big success on its own, but they remained workmen making the best of a bad situation. — *William Ruhlmann*

Love Is a Sacrifice / 1980 / Mercury ✦✦
The title track is the best of the Jukes' second album under the writing aegis of Billy Rush and Southside Johnny. It seems to have been determined that covers were out, so the band generates soul retreads in search of something that will catch fire with listeners. — *William Ruhlmann*

Reach Up & Touch the Sky: Live / 1981 / Mercury ✦✦✦
Southside Johnny and the Asbury Jukes' first commercially released live album, a two-LP set, was recorded in June and July 1980 and allowed the band to mine its catalog for songs previously heard on the excellent Epic albums as well as re-opening the door on covers (there's a fine Sam Cooke medley). They may have been at an artistic impasse, but they were a fun band to see live. — *William Ruhlmann*

Trash It Up / 1983 / Mirage ✦✦
For their first studio album in three years, the Jukes moved to their third record label, the Mirage subsidiary of Atlantic, dropped the "Asbury" from their name, and hired hot producer Nile Rodgers to give them a dance-rock sheen like the one he'd given to David Bowie on *Let's Dance*. It didn't work. — *William Ruhlmann*

In the Heat / 1984 / Atco ✦✦✦
Atlantic (Atco) let Southside Johnny and Billy Rush produce themselves after things didn't work out with Nile Rodgers and *Trash It Up*. They tried a few covers in addition to Rush's well-meant but not classic originals, including Smokey Robinson's "Don't Look Back" and Tom Waits' "New Coat of Paint." These gave diversity to the proceedings, but on the whole this still wasn't great Jukes. — *William Ruhlmann*

At Least We Got Shoes / 1986 / Atlantic ✦✦✦
Billy Rush had decamped by the time the Jukes reconvened to record their third and final Atlantic album. Southside Johnny's originals were only okay, although the selection of covers—"Walk Away Renee" and "I Only Want to Be with You"—was stellar as usual. Still, this was something of a swan song for the band, who did not record again for five years. — *William Ruhlmann*

Better Days / Oct. 1991 / Impact ✦✦✦✦
A comeback album that by all rights shouldn't be this good, *Better Days* reunites Southside Johnny with his old cohorts Springsteen and Van Zandt and some special guests (Jon Bon Jovi, Flo and Eddie) for 11 bittersweet originals capped by the gorgeous soul ballad "It's Been a Long Time." — *Kit Kiefer*

● **The Best of Southside Johnny & the Asbury Jukes** / Aug. 11, 1992 / Columbia/Legacy ✦✦✦✦
Concentrating on the highlights from Southside Johnny & the Asbury Jukes' late-'70s albums, *Best of Southside Johnny* offers a good introduction to the hard R&B-influenced rock of the New Jersey band. — *Stephen Thomas Erlewine*

● **All I Want Is Everything** / 1993 / Rhino ✦✦✦✦
The companion to Epic's *Best Of* (52733), this 14-song compilation traces The Jukes' career through their stints on Mercury/Polygram, Mirage/Atlantic, and Impact/MCA. These were not their best years, but on each album they managed a few worthy cuts, and this set chooses the best of the period, making for a collection that nearly matches the Epic years. — *William Ruhlmann*

Spittin' Fire / 1997 / Grapevine Musidisc ✦✦
Spittin' Fire is a surprisingly lackluster live double-disc collection from Southside Johnny. Although he runs through all of his best-known songs, the setting—it was recorded at Chesterfield Cafe in Paris—and the faceless backing band don't inspire him to new heights. In fact, without vigorous support from the ace bar band the Jukes, Johnny sounds tired, which makes his songs appear tired and resigned, and they've never sounded that way before. — *Thom Owens*

Spacemen 3

f. 1982, Rugby, England, **db.** 1991
Alternative Pop-Rock, Neo-Psychedelia, Space Rock
Spacemen 3 were psychedelic in the loosest sense of the word; their guitar explorations were mind-altering, but not in the sense of the acid rock of the '60s. Instead, the band developed its own minimalistic psychedelia, relying on heavily distorted guitars to clash and produce their own harmonic overtones; frequently, they would lead up to walls of distortion with over-amplified acoustic guitars and synths. Often the band would jam on one chord or play a series of songs, all in the same tempo and key. Though this approach was challenging, often approching avant-garde, Spacemen 3 nevertheless gained a dedicated cult following. After releasing several albums in the late '80s, the band fell apart in 1991.
In 1982, Sonic Boom (guitar, organ, vocals; born Pete Kember on Nov.

19, 1965) and Jason Pierce (guitar, organ, vocals; also born Nov. 19, 1965) formed Spacemen 3 in Rugby, Warwickshire, England. Sonic Boom and Pierce added a rhythm section comprised of Pete Baines and Rosco, and spent the next four years rehearsing and jamming. In 1986, the group released their debut album, *Sound of Confusion*, on Glass Records. At first the band sounded a bit like a punked-up garage rock band, but their music quickly evolved into their signature trance-like neo-psychedelia. Spacemen 3's second album, 1987's *The Perfect Prescription*, was the first to capture the group's distinctive style.
Following 1989's *Playing with Fire*, Baines and Rosco left the group to form their own band, the Darkside. They were replaced by Will Carruthers and John Mattock. Despite the addition of new blood to the group's lineup, the band was beginning to fray because of in-fighting between Sonic Boom and Pierce, as well as the former's increasing drug dependency. The new lineup struggled through a final album, 1991's *Recurring*, which featured Boom's songs on side one and Pierce's on side two. By the time of the release of *Recurring*, Pierce was performing with Carruthers and Mattock in a new band called Spirtualized. Shortly after the release of *Recurring*, Spacemen 3 split, and Spirtualized became Pierce's full-time band, eventually earning a cult following of their own. —*Stephen Thomas Erlewine*

Sound of Confusion / 1986 / Glass ✦✦✦
Spacemen 3's debut captures the band's drone-rock aesthetic in its earliest stages of development: louder and more abrasive than their later work, the album quickly establishes its mood and then maintains it, with only minor fluctuations of rhythm and tempo—its songs, a combination of statement-of-purpose originals ("Losing Touch with My Mind," "O.D. Catastrophe") and odd covers (the Stooges' "Little Doll," the 13th Floor Elevators' "Rollercoaster," and Glen Campbell's "Mary Anne"), fuse together to forge an enveloping sonic haze. A mesmerizing, primal immersion in noise. —*Jason Ankeny*

Perfect Prescription / 1987 / Glass ✦✦✦✦
A record mirroring the evolution of drug-induced euphoria from its inception (the blistering "Take Me to the Other Side") to its peak ("Feel So Good") to, finally, the inevitable crash ("Call the Doctor"), Spacemen 3's brilliant sophomore effort greatly expands the parameters of the narcotic drone-rock of *Sound of Confusion* to forge a rapturous and intensely visceral sonic experience. Recorded with a minimal use of percussion and a maximum use of spatial atmosphere, tracks like "Walkin' with Jesus" and a glistening symphonic cover of the Red Crayola's "Transparent Radiation" are masterpieces of texture, evocative and darkly beautiful; a representation of the band's unique vision at its most unified, *The Perfect Prescription* travels beyond the corporeal into new realms of consciousness and bliss. —*Jason Ankeny*

Performance / 1988 / Genius ✦✦✦✦
Recorded in Amsterdam in 1988, the live *Performance* documents a set from the *Perfect Prescription* tour; the emphasis here is on the group's loud, noisy origins—only the closing "Feel So Good" hints at the more subdued atmospheres and textures that emerged as Spacemen 3's primary focus as they approached *Playing with Fire*. Among the highlights: "Take Me to the Other Side," "Walkin' with Jesus" and "Come Together." —*Jason Ankeny*

Playing with Fire / 1989 / Fire ✦✦✦✦
A transitional effort bridging the dark, droning riffs of *The Perfect Prescription* with the ethereal atmospherics of *Recurring*, *Playing with Fire* ties together the disparate threads of the Spacemen 3 sound into an integrated whole. Apart from the incendiary single "Revolution" and the throbbing tribute "Suicide," the record is delicate and spare, a carefully modulated and expressive collection of elliptical melodies and pulsing backdrops tempered by an increasing fascination with minimalism and repetition. Although cohesive and organic, the album underscores the growing dichotomy separating Jason Pierce and Sonic Boom—while the former's songs are yearning and spiritual, the latter's are obsessive and ominous; not surprisingly, the follow-up, *Recurring*, was to be a Spacemen 3 LP in name only. —*Jason Ankeny*

Taking Drugs to Make Music to Take Drugs To / 1990 / Father Yod Productions ✦✦✦
The sonic manifesto *Taking Drugs to Make Music to Take Drugs To* compiles a number of circa-1986 demos, offering rough sketches of *Sound of Confusion*. —*Jason Ankeny*

Dreamweapon / 1990 / Fierce ✦✦✦✦
Taking off from the ideals that form the core of LaMonte Young's concept of Dream Music, the heart of *Dreamweapon* is "An Evening of Contemporary Sitar Music," a transfixing 40-minute-plus document of a landmark Spacemen 3 performance recorded at Waterman's Art Centre in Hammersmith on August 19, 1988. Perhaps the purest expression of the Spacemen aesthetic, the piece is an unbroken tapestry of hypnotic drones, throbbing tones and repetitive phrases, dappled here and there by evaporating fragments of the melodies that later resurfaced on *Playing with Fire*. The cumulative effect is one of utter disorientation—all

notions of time and space quickly give way to complete conscious immersion in the music's narcotic tug. A pair of epic rarities, Sonic Boom's feedback sculpture "Ecstasy in Slow Motion" and "Spacemen Jam," round out the package. —*Jason Ankeny*

● **Recurring** / Mar. 1991 / Dedicated ◆◆◆◆
In essence, *Recurring* is as much the final Spacemen 3 studio effort as it is the joint debut of Spectrum and Spiritualized, the two pivotal groups to emerge from the band's ashes. Split evenly between solo music from Pete "Sonic Boom" Kember and Jason Pierce, the record diverges from the shared mind-set of earlier releases to paint a portrait of a band at the breaking point: while Pierce's tracks—recorded with the same battery of musicians with whom he formed Spiritualized—are minimalist symphonies, Sonic's are more pop-oriented, even employing sequencers on the ten-minute opener "Big City (Everybody I Know Can Be Found Here)." Still, the record is surprisingly cohesive; even when moving in opposite directions, Sonic and Pierce retain the same point of departure and the same objectives—throughout, *Recurring* is beautiful and transcendent, a fitting farewell. —*Jason Ankeny*

Translucent Flashbacks / 1995 / Fire ◆◆◆◆
Translucent Flashbacks fills in some of the gaps in the early chapters of the Spacemen 3 story, compiling singles, B-sides, and rarities issued primarily in conjunction with the *Sound of Confusion* and *The Perfect Prescription* albums. Among the essentials: the complete "Ecstasy Symphony" (a fragment of which leads into *Prescription's* "Transparent Radiation"), the early single version of "Walkin' with Jesus," and the full-on 17-minute "Rollercoaster." —*Jason Ankeny*

Spacemen Are Go! / Apr. 23, 1995 / Bomp! ◆◆

For All Fucked up Children of This World We Give / Apr. 28, 1995 / Sympathy For the Record Industry ◆◆◆
For All the Fucked-Up Children of This World, We Give You Spacemen 3 contains the group's first-ever recordings; never again were their garage-punk influences clearly as evident as on these embryonic stabs at "Walkin' with Jesus" and "Things Will Never Be the Same." —*Jason Ankeny*

Spacetime Continuum

f. , London, England
Ambient Techno, Club-Dance, Electronica
Ambient techno innovator Jonah Sharp has recorded several albums and EPs as Spacetime Continuum and played an important role in consolidating the San Francisco experimental ambient and techno scenes through his Reflective imprint. A London native and an acid jazz drummer before embarking on his career in electronic music, Sharp was an in-demand session drummer until the rigors of the club scene and the mawkish obsolescence of the genre had him experimenting with other styles. Glomming onto ambient and techno as a DJ, Sharp was a founding member of the periodic Spacetime parties, held in a hologram factory in London and host to such early new ambient luminaries as Mixmaster Morris, David Moufang, and Dr. Atmo. Sharp left London for America in the early '90s, settling in San Francisco, where he established his Reflective label and recorded the bulk of his work to date. Although that work has been split over a number of different project headings (Emit Ecaps, Alien Community, Reagenz, Electro Harmonix, and others), his most consistently visible work has been as Spacetime Continuum. Sharp signed a nonexclusive multi-album deal with Astralwerks in 1992 and released his first full-length work—a live recording of a collaboration with author Terrence McKenna and didgeridoo player Stephen Kent—the following year. The largely ambient *Sea Biscuit* followed in 1994, and was released through the Fax label in Europe (Sharp has recorded a number of collaborative projects for Fax). *Emit Ecaps*, released in early 1996, returned to Sharp's dance-floor roots, incorporating elements of house, techno, and jungle. It also spawned a remix album, *Remit Recaps*, featuring work by Autechre, Plaid, and others. In addition to a smattering of Sharp-related releases (including the collectible *Flurescence EP*), the Reflective label has issued albums by Subtropic, Velocette, Kid Spatula (aka Mike Paradinas), and Single Cell Orchestra, as well as a stream of 12-inches. —*Sean Cooper*

Flurescence Ep / 1993 / Reflective ◆◆◆◆
A satisfying first statement, released on the now-influential Reflective label. Hailed by Mixmaster Morris as among the best things he'd ever heard at the time of release, the album's tricky balance of dance-floor groove and chill room ambiance has been much copied. Reissued in 1994 on the Source label. —*Sean Cooper*

Alien Dreamtime / Sep. 1993 / Astralwerks ◆◆◆
The ambient-groove soundtrack of *Alien Dreamtime* is a vivid accompaniment to McKenna's live spoken-word performance. —*John Bush*

Sea Biscuit / Sep. 23, 1994 / Astralwerks ◆◆◆
Sharp's first album-length solo work is full of expansive, fluffy environments, a bit sugary at times and with a tendency to go nowhere in particular. Still, some nice hand-built sounds and interesting, engulfing

arrangements place this near the top of the new ambient heap. Also released on the Fax label. —*Sean Cooper*

● **Remit Recaps** / Feb. 1996 / Astralwerks ◆◆◆◆
In which some of the biggest names in dance-based electronic music—both experimental and straightahead—are given the midi files to Spacetime's *Emit Ecaps* and entreated to go nuts. Remixers include Carl Craig, Autechre, Higher Intelligence Agency, Subtropic, Matthew Herbert, David Moufang (as Move D), and Spacetime's own Jonah Sharp. The stealers are up for grabs, but the spicier cuts include Subtropic's jungled-up take on "Kairo," Herbert's deep house fry of "Movement No.2," and HIA's dense electro mix of "Funkyar." Also released on Reflective as two separate 12-inches. —*Sean Cooper*

Spandau Ballet

f. Nov. 1979, London, England, **db.** 1990
New Wave, Pop-Rock, New Romantic
As one of the leading New Romantic bands, Spandau Ballet racked up a number of British hits—as well as one Top Ten American hit, "True"—during the early '80s, becoming one of the most successful groups to emerge during new wave. The only other new romantic band to enjoy greater commercial success was Duran Duran, yet Spandau Ballet was there first, scoring three Top Ten hit singles during 1981 with their synthesized dance-pop. By 1983, the London-based quintet had shed its Roxy Music-inspired robotic art-disco and picked up on Bryan Ferry's latter-day crooner persona, revamping themselves as a slick, stylish White soul act. It was in this incarnation that Spandau Ballet experienced its greatest success, as "True" reached No. 1 in Britain and No. 4 in America. However, their time in the spotlight was short-lived. Though they had a few more hits in Britain, none of them were particularly big, and in America they disappeared at the end of 1984. By the end of the decade, the group had split, with their core members, brothers Gary and Martin Kemp, launching acting careers with the 1990 film *The Krays*.
The Kemps—who played guitar and bass—founded Spandau Ballet in 1979 with Tony Hadley (vocals), Steve Norman (rhythm guitar, saxophone, percussion), and John Keeble (drums). The group hired their schoolfriend Steve Dagger as manager. Spandau Ballet began playing nightclubs in London that had responded to punk by embracing exaggeratedly fashionable clothes and makeup. Soon, the band was one of the most popular on this scene, which was subsequently dubbed by the British press as "New Romantic." Chris Blackwell, the head of Island Records, saw the group at a London party and offered them a contract on the spot. They rejected his offer, choosing to set up their own label, Reformation. Early in 1980, the group licensed Reformation to Chrysalis, giving their label the distribution power of a major label.
"To Cut a Long Story Short," Spandau Ballet's first single, shot to No. 5 in Britain upon its fall 1980 release. It was quickly followed by the No. 17 hit "The Freeze" in early 1981, and "Musclebound," which reached No. 10 in the spring. The singles made their way over to America, where they received play in dance clubs. By the spring, their debut album, *Journey to Glory*, had been released. In the summer, they released a new, non-LP single, "Chant No. 1 (I Don't Need This Pressure On)," which boasted a funkier beat and soulful flourishes. The group continued to pursue this direction on their subsequent singles, including the gold-selling Top Ten UK hits "Instinction" and "Lifeline," as well as their 1982 album *Diamond*, but it didn't reach fruition until the 1983 album *True*.
True was a full-fledged White-soul album, much like the sophisticated pop of late-'70s Roxy Music albums. The title ballad reached No. 1 in Britain during the spring and a few months later, the single and album became a hit in America, peaking at No. 4 and 19 respectively. Spandau Ballet managed to hit the Top Ten once more in the UK with "Gold," which peaked at No. 2; in the US, it reached 29. "Communication," a third American single from *True*, fizzled in the spring of 1984. Its failure was the beginning of the band's commercial downfall. "Only When You Leave," the first single from 1984's *Parade*, was a No. 3 hit in the UK, yet it only reached 34 in the US; furthermore, it was their last American hit ever. *Parade* was a success in Britain, yet it wasn't as big as its predecessor. In 1985, Spandau Ballet sued Chrysalis, claiming that the label wasn't providing enough promotional support for the band, especially in the US, and thereby harming its career. The suit was settled in 1986, and the group jumped ship for CBS/Columbia (Epic in the US), where they released *Through the Barricades* that same year. The title track was a Top Ten hit, but its follow-up, "How Many Lies?," became the group's last Top 40 hit ever. Following the release of *Heart like a Sky* in 1989, the group quietly disbanded the following year.
Gary and Martin Kemp played the notorious British mobsters the Krays in a 1990 film of the same title. Gary Kemp pursued acting as his vocation during the '90s, appearing in *The Bodyguard* with Whitney Houston, HBO's *The Larry Sanders Show*, and *Embrace of the Vampire* with Alyssa Milano. Tony Hadley released a solo album, *State of Play*, in 1993. —*Stephen Thomas Erlewine*

● **The Singles Collection** / 1985 / Chrysalis ◆◆◆◆
Traces the group's development from the melodramatic, "new-romantic"
dance-pop style of "To Cut a Long Story Short" to the lush ballad "True."
Spandau Ballet always went in for big effects, but they became more
subtle as they went along. — *William Ruhlmann*

The Sparkletones

f. 1955, Spartanburg, SC, **db.** 1958
Group / Rockabilly
Chances are, unless you're a hardcore rockabilly buff or you come from
Spartanburg, South Carolina, you don't remember the Sparkletones.
Equally likely, though, you may remember their biggest hit, "Black
Slacks," either in its original version or the 1970s cover by rockabilly
revivalist Robert Gordon.
The Sparkletones were Joe Bennett (lead vocals, lead guitar), Howard
"Sparky" Childress (rhythm guitar, vocals), Wayne Arthur (bass, vocals),
and Jimmy Denton (drums), who got together in 1955 when their ages
ranged from 12 to 16 years old. They played some of the hottest roacka-
billy this side of Memphis, and they sang well, too. They were discovered
by a talent manager from CBS the following year and got some bookings on local television in Spartanburg and the surrounding area. That
led to a national tour and an audition at ABC-Paramount Records in
New York City. The same day they passed the audition, the quartet went
into the studio to cut the Bennett-Denton original "Black Slacks," a
breezy little number in two-part harmony with some vocal gimmicks
coached by producer Don Costa. It sold a million copies in 1956, and the
Sparkletones went on to appear on *American Bandstand* and *The Ed
Sullivan Show*, and were booked on Alan Freed's rock 'n' roll shows.
The group cut a total of eight more sides in 1956, none of which hit
and only four of which were ever released. By 1958, their one hit long
behind them, the Sparkletones called it quits and decided to finish their
respective educations. Joe Bennett remained a songwriter, however, and
as of the early 1980s he was still active as a composer. — *Bruce Eder*

Black Slacks / MCA ◆◆◆◆
The Sparkletones never released an LP in their own time, but 25 years
after they split up, MCA Records (which inherited the ABC-Paramount
library) put together this brilliant ten-song album, made up of "Black
Slacks," five other released songs, and four numbers that weren't
released until 1983. Apart from the title track, one of the greatest rockabilly originals, the album's numerous highlights include Bennett's previously unreleased "Rocket" and "Let's Go Rock 'n Roll," and the collectively authored "Maybe Baby" (no connection with the Buddy Holly
song). One European pirate label issued a longer Sparkletones collection
later in the 1980s, but the sound quality on some of those cuts was relatively poor. And the fact that MCA hasn't reissued this on CD is a crime.
(Out of print) — *Bruce Eder*

Sparks

f. 1970, Los Angeles, CA
New Wave, Pop-Rock, Club-Dance
Sparks was a vehicle for the skewed pop smarts and wiseguy wordplay
of brothers Ron and Russell Mael, Los Angeles natives who spent their
childhood modeling young men's apparel for mail-order catalogues.
While attending UCLA in 1970, the Maels formed their first group,
Halfnelson, which featured songwriter Ron on keyboards and Russell as
lead vocalist; the band was rounded out by another pair of brothers, guitarist Earle and bassist Jim Mankey, and drummer Harley Feinstein.
Halfnelson soon came to the attention of Todd Rundgren, who helped
land the group a contract with Bearsville and produced their self-titled
1971 debut. Their quirky, tongue-in-cheek art-pop failed to find an audience, however, and their manager successfully convinced the Maels to
change the group's name; after becoming Sparks, they almost equaled
the Hot 100 with the single "Wonder Girl." In 1972, the sublimely bizarre
A Woofer in Tweeter's Clothing cemented the band's cult status, and
scored another near-hit with "Girl from Germany."
While touring the UK, Sparks was warmly received by the British
music press, and ultimately, the Mael brothers relocated to London,
leaving the rest of the band behind; Earle Mankey subsequently became
a noted producer, while Jim later joined Concrete Blonde. In need of a
new support unit, the Maels placed an advertisement in *Melody Maker*,
and with guitarist Adrian Fisher, bassist Matt Gordon, and drummer
Norman "Dinky" Diamond firmly in place they recorded 1974's glam-
bubblegum opus *Kimono My House*, which reached the Top Five of the
UK album charts and spawned two major British hits, "This Town Ain't
Big Enough for the Both of Us" and "Amateur Hour."
With new guitarist Trevor White and bassist Ian Hampton, Sparks
returned later that year with *Propaganda*, another UK smash that
scored with the hits "Never Turn Your Back on Mother Earth" and
"Something for the Girl with Everything." Overblown production from
Tony Visconti derailed 1975's *Indiscreet*, however, and when the record
fared less successfully than its predecessors, the Maels returned to the

US, where they recruited Tuff Darts guitarist Jeff Salen, former Milk 'n'
Cookies bassist Sal Maida, and drummer Hilly Michaels for 1976's *Big
Beat*.
By 1977's ironic *Introducing Sparks*, recorded with a series of Los
Angeles session players, the Mael brothers were treading water, so they
enlisted disco producer Giorgio Moroder to helm 1979's synth-powered
dance-pop confection *Number One in Heaven*, which spurred the group
to renewed success in England on the strength of the hit singles "The
Number One Song in Heaven," "Beat the Clock" and "Tryouts for the
Human Race." Moroder's sidekick Harold Faltermeyer took the produc-
tion reins for the immediate follow-up *Terminal Jive*, which scored a
massive French hit with "When I'm with You."
Sparks left disco in the dust with 1981's *Whomp That Sucker*,
recorded in Munich with a new supporting band comprised of guitarist
Bob Haag, bassist Lesile Boehm, and drummer David Kendrick (who
also played together as the Gleaming Spires). After 1982's *Angst in My
Pants*, they recorded 1983's *Sparks in Outer Space*; the wonderful "Cool
Places," a duet with the Go-Go's Jane Wiedlin, nearly reached the US Top
40, and was the band's biggest hit.
In 1984, the disastrous *Pulling Rabbits Out of a Hat* derailed any
chart momentum the band had gathered at home, however. After 1986's
self-explanatory *Music That You Can Dance To*, Sparks—again reduced
to the core duo of Ron and Russell—recorded 1988's *Interior Design*,
which was followed by a long hiatus. Outside of composing the music
for a film by Hong Kong action maestro Tsui Hark, Sparks remained
silent until *Gratuitous Sax and Senseless Violins*, released in 1994.
— *Jason Ankeny*

Kimono My House / 1974 / Island ◆◆◆◆
Sparks specializes in keyboard-based pop songs with clever, ironic lyrics
(by Ron Mael), sung in a near-falsetto by Russell Mael. Examples include
"Here in Heaven" (in which a disappointed, dead Romeo sings to a still-
living Juliet who "broke our little pact"), "Thank God It's Not Christmas,"
and the UK hits "This Town Ain't Big Enough for Both of Us" and "Amateur Hour." — *William Ruhlmann*

Propaganda / 1974 / Island ◆◆◆◆
More of Ron's wit ("Don't Leave Me Alone with Her," "Who Don't Like
Kids") and Russell's operatic singing with catchy rock backings, though
it's hard to get the jokes without the lyric sheet. — *William Ruhlmann*

Number One in Heaven / 1979 / Elektra ◆◆◆
After flirting with hard rock, Sparks turned to disco producer Giorgio
Moroder and scored three UK hits, "Tryouts for the Human Race," "Beat
the Clock," and "The Number One Song in Heaven," all in an aggressive
electro-dance rock style. — *William Ruhlmann*

Angst in My Pants / 1982 / Atlantic ◆◆◆
Sparks turns to power pop and scores their first US singles chart entry
with the hilarious "I Predict" on an album that also includes such novelties as "Eaten by the Monster of Love." — *William Ruhlmann*

Sparks in Outer Space / 1983 / Teldec ◆◆◆
"Cool Places," an uptempo duet with ex-Go-Go Jane Wiedlin (and No.49
hit) paces this collection, perhaps Sparks' biggest US seller. — *William
Ruhlmann*

Mael Intuition: the Best of Sparks 1974-1976 / 1990 / Island ◆◆◆◆
A well-chosen, 20-track compilation derived from the group's three best
albums (*Kimono My House*, *Propaganda*, and *Indiscreet*), released during their brief, productive tenure with Island Records. Producers Muff
Winwood (for the first two, harder rocking albums) and Tony Visconti
(the more varied and elaborately arranged *Indiscreet*) both provide the
Mael brothers with solid, sympathetic settings for their witty, rapid-fire
lyrics and manic delivery. Songs range from the aggressive riff of "At
Home, At Work, At Play" (a precursor to the heavier sound of the 1976
album, *Big Beat*) to the uncanny Andrews Sisters evocation, "Looks,
Looks, Looks." Russell Mael's quavery falsetto is an acquired taste, and
his vocal affectations can try the listener's nerves on prolonged exposure. Also, their tendency to deliver a few hundred lyrics in as many seconds makes interpretation a challenge, but their perverse humor
rewards the effort. This is probably all the Sparks the casual fan needs.
— *James A. Gardner*

● **Profile: Ultimate Collection** / Apr. 1991 / Rhino ◆◆◆◆
Unfortunately, Sparks never enjoyed more than a small, though
devoted, cult following. But it certainly wasn't for a lack of effective
hooks and clever, insanely funny lyrics. While a few of the L.A. pop-rockers' albums were disappointing, many others were exceptional. For
those seeking an introductory overview of Sparks' legacy, this two-CD
set is highly recommended. From "Achoo" to "Tips for Teens" to "This
Town Ain't Big Enough For the Both of Us," *Profile* makes it clear just
how delightfully goofy Sparks could be. Often willing to experiment, the
group embraces everything from hard rock on "Big Boy" to Euro-disco
on Giorgio Moroder-produced songs like "The Number One Song in
Heaven" and "Beat the Clock." Despite the inclusion of a few throwaways—such as the disappointing *Music You Can Dance To's* title

song—*Profile* paints an impressive picture of a wrongly neglected band. —*Alex Henderson*

The Specials

f. 1977, Coventry, England, **db.** 1985
New Wave, Ska Revival
True innovators of the punk era, the Specials began the British ska-revival craze, combining the highly danceable ska and rocksteady beat with punk's energy and attitude, and taking on a more focused and informed political and social stance than their predecessors and peers.

The band was originally formed in Coventry in 1977 as the Coventry Automatics and later the Special A.K.A. by songwriter/keyboardist Jerry Dammers with Terry Hall (vocals), Lynval Golding (guitar, vocals), Neville Staples (vocals, percussion), Roddy Radiation (guitar), Sir Horace Gentleman (bass), and John Bradbury (drums). An opening slot for the Clash stirred up interest with the major labels, but Dammers instead opted to start his own 2-Tone label, named for its multiracial agenda and after the two-tone tonic suits favored by the like-minded mods of the '60s. The Dammers-designed logos, based in '60s pop art with black and white checks, gave the label an instantly identifiable look. Dammers' eye for detail and authenticity also led to the band adopting '60s-period rude-boy outfits (porkpie hats, tonic and mohair suits, and loafers). The band released the "Gangsters" single, which reached the UK Top Ten. Soon after, hordes of bands and fans followed in the same tradition and the movement was in full swing. Over the next several months, 2-Tone enjoyed hits by similar-sounding bands, such as Madness, the (English) Beat, and the Selecter. Late in 1979, the band released its landmark self-titled debut album, produced by Elvis Costello. They followed with several 2-Tone package tours and a live EP, *Too Much Too Young* (confusingly credited to Special A.K.A.). The title track, a pro-contraception song, was banned by the BBC but reached the No. 1 spot in the UK. At this time, the band switched musical directions, releasing album number two, *More Specials*, with a new neo-lounge persona. Signs indicated that the movement was fading and 2-Tone began to experience financial troubles. The Specials released the timely "Ghost Town" single in 1981 amid race-related unemployment riots in Brixton and Liverpool. The single jumped to No. 1, but the band was falling apart. Hall, Staples, and Golding left to form Fun Boy Three, leaving the band without its trademark voice. Dammers held on, reverting back to the old name, Special A.K.A. and enlisting a new vocalist, Stan Campbell. After several years in the studio, they returned with *In the Studio* in 1984. The album managed a few hits with "Racist Friend" and "Free Nelson Mandela" but the album stiffed. Dammers dissolved the unit, pursuing political causes such as Artists Against Apartheid.

In 1996, in response to a third wave of ska revival, a Dammers-less version of the band reappeared with a shameful cash-in album, *Today's Specials*. —*Chris Woodstra*

★ **The Specials** / Nov. 1979 / 2 Tone/Chrysalis ✦✦✦✦✦
The Specials' self-titled debut sparked the Two-Tone movement in the late '70s. With well-chosen ska classics and Prince Buster-inspired originals, the band mixed political and social activism and blended punk's intensity with an infectious dance beat. *The Specials* is a landmark recording that, while very much a product of its time, hasn't really dated at all. Produced by Elvis Costello. —*Chris Woodstra*

More Specials / Oct. 1980 / 2 Tone/Chrysalis ✦✦✦✦
Branching away from their ska roots, the band moves somewhat directionlessly into a neo-lounge act. Still in full force is the biting social commentary only in a slightly skewed environment. While this can be seen as a slight disappointment after the brilliant debut, with time *More Specials* can be nearly as rewarding—many of the songs are just as strong. —*Chris Woodstra*

In the Studio / 1984 / 2 Tone/Chrysalis ✦✦✦
When Hall, Staples, and Golding left to become Fun Boy Three, Jerry Dammers decided to continue with the addition of vocalist Stan Campbell. Nearly three years in the making, *In the Studio* lacks any hint of ska and Campbell's vocals, while good, lack the tension needed for the overtly political direction of the band. The highpoints, "Racist Friend" and the anthem "Free Nelson Mandela," can be found on the *Singles Collection* so only completists need to bother. —*Chris Woodstra*

☆ **The Singles Collection** / Sep. 1991 / 2 Tone/Chrysalis ✦✦✦✦✦
All of the essential singles from their three albums are present on this 15-track collection. Not only the perfect starting point for the curious, the inclusion of B-sides and rarities, like an inspired cover of Dylan's "Maggie's Farm," makes this essential for fans. —*Chris Woodstra*

Coventry Automatics aka the Specials: Dawning of a New Era / Mar. 1994 / Receiver ✦✦
The first incarnation of the Specials, a six-piece band called the Automatics, recorded a batch of demos in London in 1978, hoping to obtain a major recording deal; *Dawning of a New Era* presents them for the first time. As is the case with most demos, these recordings have a limited

audience, but diehard fans will thrill to the early, rawer versions of their favorites along with songs that never made it to actual albums. —*Chris Woodstra*

Today's Specials / May 1996 / Virgin ✦
Without Jerry Dammers or Terry Hall onboard, the Specials' reunion feels half hearted and sounds even worse. Abandoning all of the cross-cultural tendencies of their original work, the remaining Specials decide to become UB40. They turn '60s pop classics into "reggae" numbers, reaching a nadir with "A Little Bit Me, a Little Bit You" and Ewan MacColl's British folk classic "Dirty Old Town." And they cover reggae classics—"Pressure Drop," "Somebody Got Murdered," "Simmer Down"—that don't need to be recorded again, especially in versions as slick and lifeless as these. Certainly, the band never received the money they deserved when they were recording in the early '80s, but that is no reason to make a cash-in effort as tacky as *Today's Specials*. —*Stephen Thomas Erlewine*

Phil Spector

b. Dec. 26, 1940, Bronx, NY
Rock & Roll, Pop-Rock, Brill Building Pop
Strictly speaking, Phil Spector doesn't belong in this section—he's a musician, yes, but he very rarely released records under his name. However, as a producer—and, to a significant extent, songwriter, label owner, and session player—he's influenced the course of rock 'n' roll more than all but a handful of performers. The "Wall of Sound" that he perfected in the early '60s opened unlimited possibilities for arrangements and sound construction in rock and pop, and his brilliant talents imprinted the discs that he produced with an artistic vision that was much more attributable to him than the talented performers with whom he worked.

Spector entered the record business in 1958 as songwriter, guitarist, and backup singer for the L.A. group the Teddy Bears, who landed a left-field No. 1 with their first release, "To Know Him Is to Love Him." The Teddy Bears couldn't follow their hit up and soon disbanded, but Spector almost immediately moved to New York and became a songwriter and producer. After producing a few hits, he founded his own label, Philles, and ran off a series of brilliant smashes, primarily with girl groups the Crystals and the Ronettes.

To an extent that had never been imagined in rock 'n' roll, Spector pumped his records full of orchestration—strings, horns, rattling percussion—that coalesced into teenage symphonies, never overwhelming the material or the passionate vocals. Often called a mad genius because of his eccentric and temperamental behavior, Spector's idiosyncrasies were almost always validated by the artistic and commercial results of his sessions, which combined dozens of instruments and innovative production techniques into end products that only he could combine into works of art. His influence was immense, not only in the dozens of imitation Wall of Sound productions (some very accurate and worthy, it must be added) that flooded the market between 1962 and 1965, but as an inspiration to Brian Wilson of the Beach Boys, Rolling Stones producer Andrew Loog Oldham, and others.

Spector was hip to the British Invasion before it had even reached the US, befriending the Beatles and Rolling Stones, but had nearly as much trouble as the rest of the industry in maintaining his success. Self-contained bands were writing more adventurous material and finding more adventurous sounds, and Spector's teen operas were becoming out of fashion, although he enjoyed a lot of success with blue-eyed soul duo the Righteous Brothers in the mid-'60s. After the failure of Ike & Tina Turner's 1966 single "River Deep, Mountain High"—which he always considered among his greatest achievements, blaming a vengeful US music industry for its poor sales (although it was a big hit in Britain)—he retired to his L.A. mansion, marrying Ronnie Spector, lead singer of the Ronettes.

Spector re-emerged in the late '60s, and was hired by the Beatles to do post-production on their controversial *Let It Be* album; critics and Paul McCartney himself found Spector's work faulty, although it must be pointed out that the material he was given to work with didn't rank among the Beatles' best work. He then produced George Harrison and John Lennon's first solo albums; though these were artistic triumphs, they were hardly Spector productions in the classic sense, owing much more of their success to the talents of the performers than the producer. For the past couple of decades, he's been active only sporadically, producing isolated albums by Dion, Leonard Cohen, and the Ramones. Today he's one of rock's most legendary recluses, rarely appearing in public, but his accomplishments cast a shadow over all performers and producers who aspire to create works of art in the studio. —*Richie Unterberger*

Early Productions 1958-1961 / 1983 / Rhino ✦✦✦
A sampling of Spector's earliest work, generally more pop-oriented, sappy, and far less distinguished than his early-and mid-'60s classics. The Teddy Bears' "To Know Him Is to Love Him," Gene Pitney's "Every Breath I Take," the Paris Sisters' "I Love How You Love Me," and Curtis

Lee's "Pretty Little Angel Eyes" are fine hits that reveal much of the talent that would fully blossom on his Philles singles. The other tracks, including rarities by the Ducanes, Kell Osborne, and Spector's Three, suffer from weak songwriting, and would be downright dispensable if not for their historical significance. —*Richie Unterberger*

★ **Back to Mono (1958-1969)** / Nov. 12, 1991 / ABKCO ✦✦✦✦✦
If you look hard enough, you can find decent one-album samplers of Phil Spector's greatest recordings, but this four-disc boxed set (three sets of singles and the entire *A Christmas Gift for You* on the fourth) is the jewel of Spector's legacy. Aside from his sporadic '70s productions, *Back to Mono* contains everything you'd ever want by rock's supreme romantic: early productions with Curtis Lee, Ben E. King, and Gene Pitney; the girl group effervescence of the Ronettes, the Crystals, and Darlene Love; the soul innovations of the Righteous Brothers and the Checkmates; and his notorious sessions with Ike and Tina Turner. Throughout the set, Spector's artistic vision (which has influenced dozens of producers and hundreds of performers) shines like the smile on a lover's lips. This is one of the greatest and most fully realized boxed sets ever issued. —*John Floyd*

Benny Spellman

b. Dec. 11, 1931, Pensacola, FL
Vocals / New Orleans R&B, R&B
New Orleans R&B vocalist. His deep bass voice booms through loud and clear on many early-'60s Allen Toussaint productions, but Benny Spellman enjoyed a major hit of his own in 1962, "Lipstick Traces (On a Cigarette)." Spellman spent some time with Huey "Piano" Smith and the Clowns before signing with Minit, where Toussaint utilized his deep pipes to full advantage as a backing vocalist behind Ernie K-Doe on "Mother-in-Law" and countless others. The Rolling Stones covered "Fortune Teller," the flip-side of this hit. Spellman recorded through much of the '60s, his "Word Game" turning up on Atlantic in 1965, before he took a day gig as a beer salesman. —*Bill Dahl*

Fortune Teller / 1988 / Collectables ✦✦✦✦
Infectious and influential early-'60s New Orleans R&B. Spellman's low-pitched vocals are perfectly produced by pianist Allen Toussaint. —*Bill Dahl*

Skip Spence

b. Apr. 18, 1946, Windsor, Ontario, Canada
Guitar, Drums, Vocals / Singer-Songwriter, Psychedelic, Folk-Rock
Like a rough, more obscure American counterpart to Syd Barrett, Skip Spence was one of the late-'60s' most colorful acid casualties. The original Jefferson Airplane drummer (although he was a guitarist who had never played drums before joining the group), Spence left after their first album to join Moby Grape. Like every member of that legendary band, he was a strong presence on their first album, playing guitar, singing, and writing "Omaha," one of the LP's best songs. The group ran into rough times in 1968, and Spence had the roughest, flipping out and (according to varying accounts) running amok in a record studio with a fire axe, ending up committed to New York's Bellevue Hospital. Upon his release, Spence cut an acid-charred classic, *Oar*, which came out in 1969. Though released on a major label (Columbia), this was reportedly one of the lowest-selling items in its catalog, and is hence one of the most valued psychedelic collector items. Much rawer and more homespun than the early Grape records, it features Spence on all (mostly acoustic) guitars, percussion, and vocals. With an overriding blues influence and doses of country, gospel, and acid freakout thrown in, this sounds something like Mississippi Fred McDowell imbued with the spirit of Haight-Ashbury 1967. It also featured great cryptic, punning lyrics and wonderful wraithlike vocals that range from a low Fred Neil with gravel hoarseness to a barely heard high wisp. Sadly, it was his only solo recording; more sadly, mental illness continues to prevent Spence from reaching a fully functional state to this day, although he periodically plays music, sometimes with former members of the Grape. —*Richie Unterberger*

● **Oar*** / 1969 / Sony ✦✦✦✦
The tight, charging S.F. rock of The Grape in no way prepares the listener for the spaced-out, rural ambience here. Drug-addled, yes, but also inspirational, warm, and haunting, like a charred but charming survivor of the Summer of Love. The CD reissue of this premier acid folk album adds a few previously unreleased loose jams. —*Richie Unterberger*

Jon Spencer Blues Explosion

f. 1990, New York, NY
Guitar, Vocals / Alternative Pop-Rock, Indie Rock, Blues-Rock
After a long and semi-successful tenure as leader of scuzz-rock heroes Pussy Galore, Jon Spencer took his anti-rock vision and hooked up with guitarist Judah Bauer and drummer Russell Simins to create the scuzz-blues trio the Jon Spencer Blues Explosion. Postmodern to the core, this is an ironic name; little of what this band plays resembles standard

blues. There is, however, a blues feel to what they play, meaning that in many instances they appropriate aspects of the blues (very often cliches) and incorporate them into their anarchic, noisy sound. Not part of alternative rock's commercial establishment, Spencer has also managed to sharply divide critics who tend to see him as either inspired showman or mendacious con man (frankly, he's both). He is, however, gaining popularity and critical respect, and, as of this writing, seems poised for greater success.

As with Royal Trux, the other band to emerge after the breakup of Pussy Galore, the Blues Explosion's earliest recordings are virtually incomprehensible (and impossible to find). The bass-less mix is awash in distorted guitars, precious little backbeat and howled vocals. In its favor is the music's exciting, improvisatory feel; also true is that it's frequently incoherent and careless and doesn't hold up well to repeated listenings. It was with the band's 1992 self-titled release that the band began to write semi-coherent songs; Spencer adopted an imitation blues vocal style, and the band riffed wildly and crashed around him in a bluesy sort of way. It was mostly fun, but it also seemed like a bit of a put-on, and more than a little smug.

The Blues Explosion's "breakthrough" came (as it did for Royal Trux) when they began to sound like a '70s rock band. With the release of *Extra Width* in 1993, Spencer and Co. actually got some air time on MTV's alternative rock show *120 Minutes* with the video for the song "Afro." The most noticeable change was the new emphasis on tight songs, funky backbeats, and loads of catchy riffs and hooks. As for Spencer, he was now singing like a grade-Z Elvis impersonator, but in turn lost some of the condescending attitude. Live, the band was (and remains) quite a show, generating the kind of sweat and excitement that became anathema to many punk and post-punk bands. *Orange*, which is even more accessible than *Extra Width*, netted the band even more fans upon its release in 1994. Still, there is a compelling argument to be made that despite his hip credentials, Spencer is more style than substance. Love him or loathe him (and it's easy to do both), he's a force to reckoned with. —*John Dougan*

Jon Spencer Blues Explosion / Apr. 24, 1992 / Caroline ✦✦✦
Produced by underground rock's most notorious producer, Steve Albini, this is as close as you're going to get to the Blues Explosion's primal, industrial strength noise-rock. From the cacophonous start of "Write a Song," it's clear that this is not going to be your average blues album. Still, it's contagious in a demented kind of way, and the sloppiness, intentional crudeness, and semicoherence are punk rock to the core (the furious, psychobilly track "Rachel"). Not recommended as a place to start with Spencer, and definitely not recommended to those who think they're going to hear Muddy Waters songs. —*John Dougan*

Extra Width / Nov. 1, 1993 / Matador ✦✦✦✦
Much more accessible than the aforementioned record, but in no way does its accessibility detract from the record's adventurousness. *Extra Width* is a crankin' piece of bluesoid ranting, with Spencer working up one hysterical performance after another. "Afro" is as funky as all get-out and sounds like an old Curtis Mayfield track. Similarly, "Soul Letter" is a hefty chunk of riff-muck, as is the noisy bliss of "Soul Typecast." The playing is energetic and unhinged, and Spencer drives the engine with his whoopin' and hollerin'. Plenty of noticeably '70s production techniques add to the atmosphere, contributing significantly to what may be Spencer's best record. —*John Dougan*

Orange / Oct. 1994 / Matador ✦✦✦✦
By this juncture, you either love Spencer enough to listen to every record, or you've heard plenty and are decidedly uninterested. Still, *Orange* mines the same territory as *Extra Width*, and that may not be enough. At times, even during *Orange*'s best tracks ("Bell Bottoms"), the thin, retro-'70s worshiping sounds phoned-in and lacking in real emotional commitment. But, as with a lot of junk-rock, sometimes it can be appreciated for simply being junk, and that's fine. But I'm willing to bet that Spencer's core fans like the idea of the blues more than the reality. In other words, they don't mind the pose, nor do they mind the facade. In Jon Spencer's world, image is everything. —*John Dougan*

● **Now I Got Worry** / Oct. 15, 1996 / Capitol ✦✦✦✦
Where *Orange* had some awkward attempts at funk, *Now I Got Worry* is a raw bloozy workout, full of harsh guitars and barked vocals. The sound of the Blues Explosion is so fiery and alive that it overshadows Spencer's habit for campy posturing, and that's what keeps *Now I Got Worry* afloat. Once it's finished, it becomes hard not to second-guess Spencer's intentions, but the album is the closest the Blues Explosion has come to capturing their wild, intense live show on record. —*Stephen Thomas Erlewine*

Spice Girls

f. 1993, London, England
Dance-Pop, Euro-pop, Euro-dance
The Spice Girls were the first major British pop music phenomenon of the mid-'90s to not have a debt to independent pop-rock. Instead, the all-

female quintet derived from the dance-pop tradition that made Take That the most popular British group of the early '90s, but there was one crucial difference. The Spice Girls used dance-pop as a musical base, but they infused the music with a fiercely independent, feminist stance that was equal parts Madonna, post-riot-grrrl alternative-rock feminism, and a co-opting of the good-times-all-the-time stance of England's new lad culture. Their proud, all-girl image and catchy dance-pop appealed to younger listeners, while their colorful, sexy personalities and sense of humor appealed to older music fans, making the Spice Girls a cross-generational success. The group also became chart-toppers throughout Europe in 1996, before concentrating on America in early 1997.

Every member of the Spice Girls was given a specific identity by the British press from the outset, and each label was as much an extension of their own personality as it was a marketing tool, since each name derived from their debut single and video, "Wannabe." Geri Estelle Halliwell was the "sexy Spice"; Melanine Janine Brown was the "scary Spice"; Victoria Addams was "the posh Spice"; Melanie Jayne Chisholm was "the sporty Spice"; Emma Lee Bunton was "the shy Spice." Each one of these personas were exploited in the group's press articles and videos, which helped send "Wannabe" to the top of the charts upon its summer release in 1996. If all of the invented personalities makes the Spice Girls seem manufactured, that's because they are to a certain extent. Every member of the group was active in England's theatrical, film, and modeling circuit, and they all responded to an advertisement requesting five "lively girls" for a musical group in the summer of 1993. The manager who placed the ad chose all five members of the Spice Girls, yet the women rejected his plans for their career and set out on their own two months after forming. For the next two years, the Girls fought to get a record contract, since most record labels insisted that the band pick one member as a clear leader, which is something the group refused.

Eventually, the Spice Girls signed a contract to Virgin Records, but they were without a manager, which made recording a debut album nearly impossible. All five members moved into a house and went on the dole as they searched for a manager. By the end of 1995, the group had signed with Annie Lennox's manager Simon Fuller, and began writing songs with Elliot Kennedy. "Wannabe," the Spice Girls' first single, was released in the summer of 1996, and it became the first debut single by an all-female band to enter the charts at No. 1 in England. It remained at No. 1 for seven weeks, and by the end of the year, "Wannabe" had hit No. 1 in 21 other countries. Immediately following the success of "Wannabe," the Spice Girls became media icons in Britain, as stories of their encounters with other celebrities became fodder for numerous tabloids, as did nude photos of Geri that she posed for earlier in her career. All of this added to the group's momentum, and their second single, "Say You'll Be There," entered the charts at No. 1 in the fall, selling 200,000 copies a week. *Spice*, their debut album, was released at the end of the year, accompanied by their first ballad, "2 Become 1." Both the album and single went directly to No. 1, staying there for several weeks; both records were at No. 1 over the Christmas week, making the Spice Girls one of three other artists to achieve that feat.

Having topped the charts in virtually every other country in the Western world, the Spice Girls concentrated on America in early 1997, releasing "Wannabe" in January and *Spice* in February. — *Stephen Thomas Erlewine*

Spice / 1996 / Virgin ✦✦✦✦
Spice doesn't need to be original to be entertaining, nor do the Spice Girls need to be good singers. It just has to be executed well, and the innocuous dance-pop of *Spice* is infectious. None of the Girls have great voices, but they do exude personality and charisma, which is what drives bouncy dance-pop like "Wannabe," with its ridiculous "zig-a-zig-ahhh" hook, into pure pop guilty pleasure. What is surprising is how the sultry soul of "Say You'll Be There" is more than just a guilty pleasure, and how ballads like "2 Become 1" are perfect adult contemporary confections. The rest of the album isn't quite as catchy as those first three singles, but it is still an irresistible, immaculately crafted pop that gets by on the skills of the producer and the charisma of the five Spices. Sure, the last half of the album is forgettable, but it sounds good while it's on, which is the key to a good dance-pop record. — *Stephen Thomas Erlewine*

Spin Doctors

f. 1988, New York
Pop-Rock
There were many pseudo-hippie, jam-oriented blues-rockers in New York during the early '90s, but only the Spin Doctors made it big. And they made it big because not only could they immerse themselves in a groove, but they also had concise pop skills. "Little Miss Can't Be Wrong" and "Two Princes" were cleverly written singles, full of clean, blues-inflected licks and ingratiating pop melodies. *Pocket Full of Kryptonite* had been around for nearly a year when MTV and radio began playing "Little Miss Can't Be Wrong," but once they started playing it, they

couldn't stop. The Spin Doctors became an overnight sensation, selling millions of albums around the world.

Their second album, 1994's *Turn It Upside Down*, didn't sell very well when it was released, largely because the first single, "Cleopatra's Cat," was a failed experiment in funk. But the second single, "You Let Your Heart Go Too Fast," was in the vein of "Two Princes," and the album began to sell after the song was released. In the summer of 1996 the Spin Doctors released *You've Got to Believe in Something*. After the album failed to make an impression on the charts, the Spin Doctors were dropped from Epic in the fall of the year. — *Stephen Thomas Erlewine*

● **Pocket Full of Kryptonite** / Aug. 1991 / Epic ✦✦✦✦
This sleeper album took a while to catch on, but when it did, the Spin Doctors' slightly jazzy style of funky groove rock went multi-platinum. The first single, "Little Miss Can't Be Wrong," is a likeable, lightweight bit of pop that sounds like something Steve Miller could've done. "Two Princes" was another huge hit. Other highlights include "Jimmy Olsen's Blues," "What Time Is It?" and "Forty or Fifty." — *Rick Clark*

Turn It Upside Down / Jun. 14, 1994 / Epic ✦✦
A weaker album than *Kryptonite*, *Turn It Upside Down* suffers from weaker material and lifeless production. Nevertheless, the first single, "Cleopatra's Cat," is an appealing slice of bop funk-rock. A few steps down there's "Big Fat Funky Booty," "Biscuit Head," and "You Let Your Heart Go Too Fast." — *Rick Clark*

You've Got to Believe in Something / May 1996 / Epic ✦✦✦
With their second album, *Turn It Upside Down*, the Spin Doctors lost nearly all of the audience they had gained with their debut, *Pocket Full of Kryptonite*. On *Turn It Upside Down*, the band attempted to explore elastic, groove-oriented territory and left behind the simple, catchy songs that made the debut a hit. Perhaps because the result was a commerical disaster, the band has returned to pop songs for their third album, *You've Got to Believe in Something*. Although it doesn't have the ingratiating charm of *Pocket Full of Kryptonite*—after all, those songs were in the band's set list for years before they actually recorded them— *You've Got to Believe in Something* does have its fair share of catchy moments. The first single, "She Used to Be Mine," is a blatant return to the goofy Steve Miller boogie of "Little Miss Can't Be Wrong," but it works. Furthermore, that is what the band does well—when they stretch out, like on the bonus cover of KC and the Sunshine Band's "That's the Way (I Like It)" recorded with Biz Markie, the band falls flat on its face. They don't stretch out too much on *You've Got to Believe in Something* to make it the son of *Turn It Upside Down*, but they also don't come up with enough hooks to rival *Pocket Full of Kryptonite*. It just falls somewhere in the middle, which makes it a return to form, of sorts. — *Stephen Thomas Erlewine*

The Spinanes

f. 1991, Olympia, WA
Alternative Pop-Rock, Indie Rock
In alternative rock, as in any other genre, it's hard to stand out from a crowded field. When the Spinanes emerged in the early '90s, they got a couple legs up on the competition in the drive to be different. Taking the power trio format one stage further, they created a full-bodied rock sound with just two members, guitarist/singer Rebecca Gates and drummer Scott Plouf. They also were one of the first Sub Pop bands that did *not* subscribe to a grungy metallic sound, although they rocked pretty hard.

Beyond these striking characteristics, however, the Spinanes' music isn't far off the beaten path of standard college-radio alternative fare, with its droning guitar textures, occasional harmonies, and measured vocals that avoid both slickness and extreme emotion. They're wise enough to realize the limits of their format, and their second album, *Strand* (1996), expands their instrumental, production, and songwriting ranges in enough interesting ways to make the group worth keeping an eye on. — *Richie Unterberger*

Manos / Oct. 26, 1993 / Sub Pop ✦✦✦
While singer/guitarist Rebecca Gates and drummer Scott Plouf are the only musicians on their debut album, the approach isn't minimalist a la Mecca Normal or some such band. They're a full-bodied rock group that happens to only have two members. That oddity factor aside, this is accomplished but fairly standard alternative pop-rock, a bit on the downbeat side at times, and not diverse enough to keep the interest level from dragging over the course of a full-length record. — *Richie Unterberger*

● **Strand** / Feb. 27, 1996 / Sub Pop ✦✦✦✦
Although Gates and Plouf still play almost everything on their second outing, they make things more interesting by fooling around with a greater variety of instruments (adding more keyboards particularly) and getting outside guest vocalists to harmonize on a few songs. The songwriting (now handled by Gates exclusively) gets more penetrating as

well, and the production is more imaginative (but does not approach slickness). At their most morose they recall "sadcore" groups like Low and Spain, but the Spinanes have more diversity than those acts. —*Richie Unterberger*

The Spinners

f. 1961, Detroit, MI
Soul, Philly Soul, Quiet Storm
The Spinners were the greatest soul group of the early '70s, creating a body of work that defined the lush, seductive sound of Philly Soul. Ironically, the band's roots lay in Detroit, where they formed as a doo wop group during the late '50s. Throughout the '60s, the Spinners tried to land a hit by adapting to the shifting fashions of R&B and pop. By the mid-'60s, they had signed with Motown Records, but the label never gave the group much consideration. "It's a Shame" became a hit in 1970, but the label continued to ignore the group, and dropped the band two years later. Unsigned and featuring new lead singer Phillipe Wynne, the Spinners seemed destined to never break into the big leagues, but they managed to sign with Atlantic Records, where they began working with producer Thom Bell. With his assistance, the Spinners developed a distinctive sound, one that relied on Wynne's breathtaking falsetto and the group's intricate vocal harmonies. Bell provided the group with an appropriately detailed production, creating a detailed web of horns, strings, backing vocals, and lightly funky rhythms. Between 1972 and 1977, the Spinners and Thom Bell recorded a number of soul classics, including "I'll Be Around," "Could It Be I'm Falling in Love," "Mighty Love," "Ghetto Child," "Then Came You," "Games People Play" and "The Rubberband Man." Wynne left in 1977 and the Spinners had hits for a few years after his departure, but the group will always be remembered for its classic mid-'70s work.

Originally, called the Domingoes, the Spinners formed when the quintet were high school students in the Detroit suburb of Ferndale in 1957. At the time, the group featured Bobbie Smith, Pervis Jackson, George W. Dixon, Billy Henderson, and Henry Fambrough. Four years later, they came to the attention of producer Harvey Fuqua, who began recording the group—who were now called the Spinners—for his Tri-Phi Records. The band's first single, "That's What Girls Are Made For," became a Top 10 R&B hit upon its 1961 release and featured Smith on vocals. Following its release, Dixon was replaced by Edgar "Chico" Edwards. Over the next few years, the group released a series of failed singles, and when Tri-Phi was bought out by Motown in the mid-'60s, the Spinners became part of the larger company's roster. By that time, Edwards had been replaced by G.C. Cameron.

Though the Spinners had some R&B hits at Motown during the late '60s, including "I'll Always Love You" and "Truly Yours," they didn't have a genuine crossover success until 1970, when Stevie Wonder gave the group "It's a Shame." Motown never concentrated on the Spinners, and they let the group go in 1972. Before the band signed with Atlantic Records, Phillipe Wynne replaced Cameron as the group's lead vocalist. Wynne had previously sung with Catfish and Bootsy Collins.

At Atlantic Records, the Spinners worked with producer Thom Bell, who gave the group a lush, seductive sound, complete with sighing strings, a tight rhythm section, sultry horns, and a slight funk underpinning. Wynne quickly emerged as a first-rate soul singer, and the combination of the group's harmonies, Wynne's soaring leads, and Bell's meticulous production made the Spinners the most popular soul group of the '70s. Once the group signed with Atlantic, they became a veritable hit machine, topping the R&B and pop charts with songs like "I'll Be Around," "Could It Be I'm Falling in Love," "One of a Kind (Love Affair)," "Ghetto Child," "Rubberband Man" and "You're Throwing a Good Love Away." Not only were their singles hits, but their albums constantly went gold and charted in the Top 20.

Phillip Wynne left the band to pursue a solo career in 1977; he was replaced by John Edwards. Though none of Wynne's solo records were big hits, his tours with Parliament-Funkadelic were well received, as were his solo concerts. In October 1984, he died of a heart attack during a concert in Oakland, California. The Spinners, meanwhile, had a number of minor hits in the late '70s, highlighted by their disco covers of "Working My Way Back to You" and the medley "Cupid/I've Loved You for a Long Time." During the early '80s, they had several minor hits before fading away from the charts and entering the oldies circuit. —*Stephen Thomas Erlewine*

Party: My Pad After Surfin' / 1963 / Time ✦✦✦
Their debut for Tri-Phi put the Spinners on the R&B map quickly with the single "That's What Girls Are Made For." Of course, confusion quickly reigned when it turned out that Harvey Fuqua had sung the lead and wasn't even in the group. Chico Edwards replaced George Dixon when the band was signed to Motown, but they wouldn't enjoy another huge hit until they left Motown for Atlantic. If you find this album, grab it immediately. It's been deleted forever. —*Ron Wynn*

The Second Time Around / 1970 / VIP ✦✦✦
The Spinners began making some soul noise in 1970, when Stevie Wonder produced a pair of hit singles for them. "It's a Shame" was their first Top 10 R&B song since 1965, and was the swan song for G.C. Cameron as lead vocalist. Phillipe Wynne stepped in and shortly after made everyone forget (who remembered) that Cameron was ever in the band. The follow-up tune, "We'll Have It Made," wasn't bad either. —*Ron Wynn*

Mighty Love / Jan. 1974 / Atlantic ✦✦✦✦
Phillippe Wynne's twisting, soulful, frequently captivating voice was at its finest on this 1974 album. The title track was a smash in edited single form, and the extended album version contains marvelous Wynne ad-libs and exchanges nicely contrasted by the group's harmonizing. The album contains many other fine songs, like "Ain't No Price on Happiness" and "I'm Coming Home," and was their second Atlantic release. It equaled the gold-selling pace of its predecessor and cemented the Spinners' status as R&B stars. —*Ron Wynn*

New & Improved / Feb. 1974 / Atlantic ✦✦✦

Live / 1975 / Atlantic ✦✦
A nice concert album that did much better than anticipated. It featured extended versions, concert ambience, and exuberant harmonies and treatments of familiar numbers. Like most live dates, it had its padding and filler, but as a portrait of an R&B institution doing its thing before the faithful, it was well worth the cost of a double album. —*Ron Wynn*

Pick of the Litter / 1975 / Atlantic ✦✦✦✦
The Spinners were rolling in the 1970s, and this proved to be their biggest album ever. It peaked in the pop Top 10 at No. 8, and they racked up four consecutive R&B Top 10 singles, including the chart topper "They Just Can't Stop It (The Games People Play)." Phillipe Wynne sang with an amazing mix of class and fire, sophistication and earthiness, that hadn't been heard in soul circles for years. Of course, this is now out of print. —*Ron Wynn*

Happiness Is Being with the Spinners / 1976 / Atlantic ✦✦✦

Spinners / 1977 / Atlantic ✦✦✦✦
A superb album, arguably their finest, though not their biggest, crossover work. The Spinners teamed with Thom Bell and made Motown look stupid with this album of glorious anthems. "I'll Be Around" and "Could It Be I'm Falling in Love" ended any discussions, mentions, or even thoughts of their former lead singer G.C. Cameron, as Phillipe Wynne was emerging as the king of immaculate, sophisticated soul. They had three R&B chart toppers from this album and were now dominating the Motown acts they once idolized. —*Ron Wynn*

Yesterday Today & Tomorrow / 1977 / Atlantic ✦✦✦

The Best of the Spinners / 1978 / Atlantic ✦✦✦✦
The Spinners lost lead singer Philipe Wynne in 1977, as he left to join Parliament/Funkadelic. While they were getting replacement John Edwards acclimated, Atlantic issued this greatest-hits LP containing all the gems with Wynne as their lead singer. Until the Atlantic two-CD set was issued, this was a definitive work, and it's still as complete a single album package as available. It includes "Could It Be I'm Falling in Love," "How Could I Let You Get Away," "Mighty Love," "Rubberband Man" and "One of a Kind (Love Affair)," among others. —*Ron Wynn*

Dancin' and Lovin' / 1979 / Rhino ✦✦✦
While soul purists recoiled in horror, the Spinners climbed off the ropes and soared back into the spotlight by recasting themselves as a modified dance/crossover band with soul/R&B influences. It worked in the short run, as their remake of the Four Seasons' "Working My Way Back to You," mixed with their own wailer, "Forgive Me Girl," made a nice sandwich at No. 2 pop and No. 6 R&B. It took nearly a year, but they were revived. While they wore the formula out with a similar follow-up, it gave them a fresh start and the necessary credibility to eventually return to their customary sophisticated soul. —*Ron Wynn*

From Here to Eternally / 1979 / Atlantic ✦✦✦
The Spinners began the slow climb back to respectability with this album. Phillipe Wynne's second tenure had ended due to poor health (he eventually suffered a fatal heart attack), and they started a resurgence with a new lead singer, John Edwards. Edwards had been tearing up Southern soul clubs for years, but many wondered if he could adjust to being in a group rather than being the whole show. He quickly proved that he could, and the Spinners were on their way back. —*Ron Wynn*

Love Trippin' / 1980 / Atlantic ✦✦✦

Labor of Love / 1981 / Atlantic ✦✦✦
The Spinners began to slide again with this release, following two consecutive big albums. The problem was that they had established an identity that had crossover and pop types thinking they were just a cover band. When they returned to the ebullient soul ballads and uptempo tunes that had been their forte since the 1960s, the trendy types moved on to the next fashionable thing. Meanwhile, the R&B landscape was shifting, and they were caught in the move. They also went to the

medley well one more time with "Yesterday Once More/Nothing Remains the Same." —*Ron Wynn*

Superstar Series, Vol. 9 / 1981 / Motown ✦✦✦
They weren't really superstars either at Motown, but this anthology does collect their best material. It shows that the Spinners had the potential to achieve at Motown what they did at Atlantic, but weren't given the horses until the end. G.C. Cameron never made much noise on his own, but on "It's a Shame" he achieved greatness. —*Ron Wynn*

Grand Slam / 1982 / Atlantic ✦✦
This wasn't quite a disaster, but it was too close for comfort. The confidence and renewed vigor that the Spinners had shown in the 1980s seemed shaken, although the lightweight ballads and uninspired uptempo material they received for this date may have had something to do with that. The album didn't flop as quickly as its predecessor, but it didn't last long on the charts either. —*Ron Wynn*

Lovin' Feelings / 1985 / Mirage ✦✦
Nothing worked from start to finish on this mid-'80s number, both a commercial and artistic flop. John Edwards couldn't generate any energy or fire, while the usually splendid harmonies were both feeble and often flat, and the production, arrangements, and compositions weren't able to retain any interest. —*Ron Wynn*

The Best of the Spinners / 1988 / Motown ✦✦✦
Yet another Motown collection (that makes at least three for a group that only had four hits from 1965 to 1971) of Spinners singles. It's not as extensive as the anthology, so if you only want hits, they're available. Otherwise, take your pick between it and the others. —*Ron Wynn*

Down to Business / Sep. 1989 / Volt ✦✦✦
The Spinners made a bid for renewed stardom on a soul independent when they signed with the revived Volt in 1989. Unfortunately, they also found out quickly that being on Volt didn't mean in the late '80s what it meant in the '60s and '70s. Despite a representative effort, with some excellent harmonizing and fine, soulful leads from John Edwards, they couldn't even get a nibble from urban contemporary radio. They're still working the nostalgia/oldies circuit, but this one was a shocker all around. —*Ron Wynn*

Can't Shake This Feeling / 1990 / Atlantic ✦✦✦
The Spinners revival was waning when this album was released, and it didn't stop the downward slide. They had run out of entertaining medleys and uptempo tunes, and the ballads were uninspired as well. Not even the usually dynamic John Edwards could do much with this collection of halfhearted tracks, disjointed production, and leaden arrangements. —*Ron Wynn*

☆ **One of a Kind Love Affair** / Nov. 5, 1991 / Atlantic ✦✦✦✦✦
Spanning from their first single, 1961's "That's What Girls Are Made For," to their last charting single more than 20 years later, *One of a Kind Love Affair—The Anthology* is the definitive Spinners collection. The bulk of the two-CD compilation is the group's work with Thom Bell during the mid-'70s, easily the best work they ever recorded and arguably the finest Philly soul singles. All of the Spinners' major hits are here, as are excellent, informative liner notes (including complete personnel and discography). —*Stephen Thomas Erlewine*

★ **The Very Best of the Spinners** / Apr. 20, 1993 / Rhino ✦✦✦✦✦
The Very Best of the Spinners contains all of the group's essential hits, from "It's a Shame" and "I'll Be Around" to "The Rubberband Man" and "Working My Way Back to You/Forgive Me, Girl." A few hits are missing, but the serious fan can find those on the double—disc set *One of a Kind Love Affair*. For the casual fan, who only wants the biggest hits, *The Very Best of the Spinners* is a necessary purchase. In a concise 16 tracks, it makes a convincing case that the group was the greatest soul vocal group of the '70s. —*Stephen Thomas Erlewine*

The Very Best of the Spinners, Vol. 2 / May 27, 1997 / Rhino ✦✦✦✦
The Very Best of the Spinners, Vol. 2 rounds up the lesser-known hits that didn't make the first volume, plus selected album tracks, including "Heaven on Earth," "You're Throwing a Good Love Away," "Love or Leave," "Wake Up Susan" and "Easy Come, Easy Go." —*Stephen Thomas Erlewine*

Spirit

f. 1967, Los Angeles, CA
Art-Rock/Progressive-Rock, Psychedelic
California's eclectic Spirit blended hard rock and jazz with elements of blues, country, and folk to produce a series of acclaimed albums during the late '60s and early '70s. The group was formed in 1967 by guitarist Randy California (born Randy Wolfe) and his shaven-headed stepfather, percussionist Ed "Mr. Skin" Cassidy. Cassidy had played with such legendary jazz artists as Thelonious Monk, Cannonball Adderley, Art Pepper, and Gerry Mulligan, and had also joined Ry Cooder and Taj Mahal in Rising Sons. California was given his nickname by Jimi Hendrix, whom he had played with in the Blue Flames. The two first played

together in a band called the Red Roosters in 1965, which also featured future Spirit members Jay Ferguson (vocals) and Mark Andes (bass). Cassidy and California moved to New York and played with several bands in 1966 and formed Spirit upon their return to Los Angeles. Keyboardist John Locke, an acquaintance of several members, was the first to join Cassidy and California, and the group christened itself Spirits Rebellious, after a book by Kahlil Gibran; the name was shortened to Spirit when Ferguson and Andes signed on. The group's unique style, Cassidy's visual distinctiveness, and the idea of a stepfather/stepson combo quickly attracted attention, and Spirit recorded two well-received albums in 1968 (*Spirit* and *The Family That Plays Together*). The latter produced their only hit, "I Got a Line on You." 1970's *The Twelve Dreams of Dr. Sardonicus* was hailed as their finest album, and ultimately proved to be their biggest seller as well. However, Ferguson and Andes left the band in 1971 to form Jo Jo Gunne; Andes would later join Firefall and Heart. Brothers Christian and Al Staehely were brought in on guitar and bass, respectively, but California and Cassidy themselves left after the *Feedback* album.

California moved to England and played with Peter Hammill, but a concussion sustained in a fall from a horse and a nervous breakdown interrupted his career. He returned in 1972 with a spotty solo LP, *Kaptain Kopter and the (Fabulous) Twirlybirds*. Spirit reformed for the first of several times in 1974 with California, Cassidy, and bassist Barry Keene. Their ensuing LPs sold rather poorly, leading to periodic break-ups and reunions. California continued to lead various Spirit lineups, usually with Cassidy, until his accidental drowning death in January 1997. —*Steve Huey*

Spirit / 1968 / Epic ✦✦✦✦
Spirit's debut unveiled a band that seemed determine to out-eclecticize everybody else on the California psychedelic scene, with its melange of rock, jazz, blues, folk-rock, and even a bit of classical and Indian music. Teenaged Randy California immediately established a signature sound with his humming, sustain-heavy tone; middle-aged drummer Ed Cassidy gave the group unusual versatility; and the songs tackled unusual lyrical themes, like "Fresh Garbage" and "Mechanical World." As is often the case in such hybrids, the sum fell somewhat short of the parts; they could play more styles than almost any other group, but couldn't play (or, more crucially, write) as well as the top acts in any given one of those styles. There's some interesting stuff here, nonetheless; "Uncle Jack" shows some solid psych-pop instincts, and it sounds like Led Zeppelin lifted the opening guitar lines of "Taurus" for their own much more famous "Stairway to Heaven." The 1996 CD reissue has four previously unissued bonus tracks cut during the same time as the *Spirit* sessions, including an alternate take of the lengthy, jazzy "Elijah." —*Richie Unterberger*

Clear / 1969 / Edsel ✦✦✦✦
Previous to the recording of this album, Spirit had been working on music for a soundtrack for the movie *The Model Shop*. *Clear* reflected that effort with an odd blend of off-the-wall (occasionally goofy-sounding) rock-influenced songs and strangely sparse instrumentals (with titles like "Ice" and "Clear"). Highlights include "Dark Eyed Woman" (No. 118), "Policeman's Ball," "Give a Life, Take a Life," and "New Dope in Town." The 1996 CD reissue adds four bonus tracks, one of which, the 1969 single "1984," is especially key, as it was one of their most popular songs. The disc also has the B-side of that single ("Sweet Stella Baby") and two previously unissued songs. —*Rick Clark*

Family That Plays Together / 1969 / Edsel ✦✦✦✦
Lou Adler's unusual production, coupled with Marty Paich's ethereal orchestrations, on songs like "Aren't You Glad?," "It Shall Be," "Poor Richard," and "Silky Sam," gave Spirit's music a quality of icy distance. The only other band that comes to mind who employed such otherworldly arrangements was Love, with their masterful *Forever Changes*. This is a wonderful album worth getting. The 1996 CD reissue adds five songs that were recorded at the same sessions, three of which were previously unissued, two of which had only been available on the *Time Circle* compilation. —*Rick Clark*

The Twelve Dreams of Dr. Sardonicus / 1970 / Epic ✦✦✦✦
Although this has the reputation of being their most far-out album, it actually contains the most disciplined songwriting and playing of the original lineup, cutting back on some of the drifting and offering some of their more melodic tunes. The lilting "Nature's Way" was the most enduring FM standard on the album, which also included some of Spirit's best songs in "Animal Zoo" and "Mr. Skin." The 1996 CD reissue has four bonus tracks, though these are on the inessential side: mono versions of "Animal Zoo" and "Morning Will Come," the 1970 single "Red Light Roll On," and the previously unissued "Rougher Road." —*Richie Unterberger*

Feedback / 1972 / Epic ✦✦

Spirit of '76 / 1975 / Mercury ✦✦

• **Time Circle** / Jul. 23, 1991 / Epic ✦✦✦✦
A generous helping of practically everything Spirit accomplished in their years on Lou Adler's Ode Records and Epic Records, this collection is sonically satisfactory and there are generous, informative liner notes. —*Rick Clark*

Mercury Years / Mar. 25, 1997 / Polygram ✦✦✦
The double-disc set *The Mercury Years* is a comprehensive overview of Spirit's late-'70s recordings for Mercury Records, containing nearly all of their 1975 album *Spirit of '76*, plus highlights from *Farther Along* (1976), *Son of Spirit* (1976) and *Future Games* (1977). Though this music isn't among the band's best, it's occasionally intriguing, and for dedicated fans of Spirit's '60s albums, this compilation is the best way to appreciate their late '70s work. —*Stephen Thomas Erlewine*

Spiritualized

f. 1989, Rugby, England
Alternative Pop-Rock, Post-Rock/Experimental, Indie Rock, Neo-Psychedelia, Space Rock, Dream Pop
Formed from the ashes of the trance-rockers Spacemen 3, singer/guitarist Jason Pierce's group Spiritualized did not break away from his prior band's trademark hypnotic minimalism; instead, they perfected it. Drawing on the continued influence of the Velvet Underground, LaMonte Young, and Steve Reich, Spiritualized staked out a common ground between minimalism and lush symphonics—while powered by simple, repetitious motifs, their songs simultaneously blossomed into rich, shimmering sonic panoramas inspired by the majestic studio wizardry of Phil Spector and Brian Wilson. Such seeming contradictions were essential to the group's alchemy: while the infamous Spacemen 3 tag of "taking drugs to make music to take drugs to" remained a cornerstone of their craft, at the same time Spiritualized's very name acknowledged the existence of other forces, further reflected in their heavy debt to gospel and soul music as well as an affinity for mantras and devotional hymns.

Although Spiritualized fully emerged after the acrimonious breakup of Spacemen 3, in truth the band's roots extended back to the band's final LP, 1990's *Recurring*. A Spacemen 3 album in name only, *Recurring* was split evenly between independently recorded work from Pierce and estranged partner Pete "Sonic Boom" Kember; as a result, while Kember's side presaged his eventual work with Spectrum, Pierce's half, recorded with most of the musicians who would later comprise Spiritualized (including guitarist Mark Refoy, bassist Willie B. Carruthers, and drummer Jon Mattock), predated the orchestral drones that became the band's hallmark. The first true Spiritualized single, a dramatic reading of the Troggs' "Anyway That You Want Me," was the final nail in the coffin—reportedly, Kember was so incensed by the Spacemen 3 logo that appeared on the disc's jacket that he disbanded the group for good.

In 1991, Spiritualized returned with a string of EPs—*Feel So Sad*, *Run/I Want You* and *Smile/Sway*—before their long-awaited debut *Lazer-Guided Melodies* finally appeared the following year. The masterful, blissed-out result of Pierce's obsessive studio fine-tuning and endless remixing, the album was promoted by the band's slot on the high-profile "Rollercoaster" tour, where they appeared with the Jesus and Mary Chain and Curve. An excellent limited-edition live document, *Fucked Up Inside*, followed in 1993, trailed by another EP, *Electric Mainline*, later in the year.

In 1995, Spiritualized—now a trio consisting of Pierce, keyboardist/guitarist Kate Radley, and bassist Sean Cook—issued *Pure Phase*, a heady, dense production that boasted separate mixes from each stereo channel. With 1997's *Ladies and Gentlemen, We Are Floating in Space*, Pierce deliberately jettisoned many of the band's usual points of departure, including drones, tremolos, and phase tones; recorded with new drummer Damon Reece and guitarist Mike Moony, it featured a cameo appearance from legendary New Orleans pianist Dr. John on one track, while Memphis studio legend Jim Dinkinson appeared on another. Other guests included the Belanescu Quartet (also featured on *Pure Phase*), the Greater London Gospel Community Choir, and Spring Heel Jack. —*Jason Ankeny*

Lazer Guided Melodies / 1992 / Dedicated ✦✦✦✦
The group's seminal debut album is aptly titled: The melodies shimmer and drone and hum like otherworldly pop tunes, and Radley and Pierce's vocals hover gently in the mix. One of the premier dream-pop albums, *Lazer-Guided Melodies* is both beautiful and innovative. —*Heather Phares*

Pure Phase / Mar. 28, 1995 / Dedicated ✦✦✦
Spiritualized's eagerly-awaited second album continues the group's ethereal tradition, this time with a loopier, more symphonic sound. Many of the songs swell past the six-minute mark, ebbing and flowing majestically. "Medication," "Electric Phase," "Lay Back in the Sun" and "Spread Your Wings" typify the dreamy grandeur of most of the album. —*Heather Phares*

Split Enz

f. 1972, Auckland, New Zealand, db. 1985
New Wave
Best known for their early-'80s new wave pop hits, particularly "I Got You," Split Enz—after surviving a dizzying array of image and personnel changes and a full decade without any recognition outside of their homeland—became the first New Zealand band to achieve worldwide success. Although they never reached superstar status outside of Australia and New Zealand, the band developed a strong international cult following that continued to thrive over a decade after their breakup. Split Enz's output always seemed slightly outside of the times and often frustratingly obscure, but in the end they left behind a body of work that was always interesting and often reached pure pop brilliance.

The group was founded in 1972 in Auckland, New Zealand, by Brian Timothy Finn and Phil Judd. Initially, the band was a light acoustic combo called Split Ends consisting of Judd (guitar, vocals), Finn (vocals, piano), Miles Golding (violin), Mike Howard (flute), and Mike Chunn (bass). Finn and Judd were the main songwriting force of the band's early years. Judd drew his inspiration from a wild variety of often nonmusical sources while Finn's tastes leaned toward the British pop of the Beatles, the Kinks, and the Move. In a creative rush that lasted several months, the two bashed out songs on acoustic guitars—Judd working out the basic song with lyrics and Finn providing the melodies. Miles Golding came from a classical background and pushed the band into complex, neoclassical structures and arrangements. The result was an eclectic mix of styles that was quite original though not very commercial. After months of rehearsals, the group went into the studio to record their first single, "For You"/"Split Ends," in February of 1973. After the single was released, the band launched a small tour; upon its completion, Golding left the group to study in London. At Chunn's urging, the band went for a new, electric sound, adding Geoff Chunn on drums, Wally Wilkinson on guitar, and saxophonist Rob Gillies, who was only a part-time member. After the new lineup was in place, Judd refused to tour, claiming their music was too complex for stage presentation; he stayed behind to write and record new material while the rest of the band toured, although he would later re-join the live lineup. The group made an appearance on the televised New Zealand talent contest, *New Faces*—though they finished second to last, it gave them some crucial early exposure. In 1974, keyboardist Tony (Eddie) Rayner was added to the band and they changed their name to Split Enz. Following the name change, the group embarked on a series of radio-sponsored "Buck-A-Head" shows—rather than play the more traditional pub circuit, they played theaters, which seemed more suited to the band's style. The group's shows took on a theatrical tone, as the band members wore wild, colorful costumes and sported a variety of odd hairdos. Finn acted as master of ceremonies, giving odd spoken soliloquies. Judd made the occasional appearanceas as did costume designer and spoons soloist Noel Crombie. By the fall of 1974, Crombie was added as a full-time member on percussion. Before the tour was completed, Geoff Chunn was replaced by Paul Crowther and Rob Gillies left the group.

In March of 1975, the group traveled to Australia—at this time, all members except Judd switched to using their middle names. Mistakenly billed as "New Zealand's raunchiest rock 'n' roll band," the band struggled for nine months but they eventually earned a small cult following and secured a contract with Mushroom Records. Their debut album, *Mental Notes*, was recorded in two weeks. While their inexperience in the studio combined with an unsympathetic producer led to a less than satisfying result in the band's eyes, the album encapsulated the band at its artiest and most ambitious. The album made a brief appearance on both the Australian and New Zealand charts. By November of 1975 Wilkinson was fired and Gillies rejoined.

Split Enz had caught the attention of Roxy Music's Phil Manzanera, who offered to help the band with their next album; they arranged to meet him in England to redo *Mental Notes*. Before leaving, they recorded a new single, "Late Last Night." Despite the complex songstructure, the single showed the band moving toward a pop direction; nevertheless, it failed to have much impact. "Late Last Night" was accompanied by a video clip, which was an uncommon practice in 1976; the band would continue to make conceptual clips from that point on. In April of 1976, Split Enz joined up with Manzanera in England and signed to Chrysalis for worldwide distribution. While the recordings went well, they found it impossible to secure live work in Britain without an agent. The band rehearsed constantly, although the songwriting partnership of Judd and Finn had dried up and no new songs were being written. *Second Thoughts*, essentially a reworked *Mental Notes*, was released toward the end of 1976 (it was released internationally as *Mental Notes*). Before the band supported the album with a US tour in early 1977, Crowther was replaced on drums by Mal Green. Judd, fed up with uninterested audiences and the demands of promotion, left the band during the tour and Chunn left two months later. The band returned to England to regroup—they replaced Judd with Tim's younger brother Neil and recruited bassist Nigel Griggs.

Tim Finn assumed leadership of the new incarnation of Split Enz and the group began to move away from its arty, theatrical tendencies on their next LP, 1977's *Dizrhythmia*. In Australia, the album went gold and the single "My Mistake" became their first Top 20 hit. In England, the group fared far worse. In the wake of the punk explosion, Split Enz seemed slightly out of touch. Though their odd looks and new, leaner material wasn't so far removed from post-punk styles, their earlier reputation seemed more in line with the progressive rock the punks sought to destroy. However, they did manage to keep a small cult following within the UK.

By early 1978, Split Enz had been dropped by Chrysalis and, unable to get gigs, they were forced to go on the dole. They continued writing new material at a feverish pace and rehearsing constantly. Gillies was fired and Judd rejoined, but he found himself unable to fit into the new direction of the band and left the group shortly thereafter; he later found limited success as the leader of the Swingers and as a solo artist. The New Zealand Arts Council came to the band's aid with a five-thousand-dollar grant. A studio in Luton was booked and the band knocked off 28 songs in under five days. These sessions, known as the "Rootin' Tootin' Luton Tapes," displayed a newfound edge and considerable commercial potential. Around the same time, they recorded a new single with producer David Tickle—a straightahead rocker called "I See Red"—which charted respectably in Australia. Split Enz returned to Australia to make their next album, 1978's *Frenzy*, re-recording many songs from the Luton tapes. However, the final product paled in comparison to the demos—the high energy of the original tapes simply wasn't captured and many of the best songs were left on the demos. Many of the Luton recordings would later resurface on the A&M version of *Frenzy*, released in North America in 1981.

The band teamed up again with David Tickle for their next album, *True Colours*, in 1979. The album lacked the excesses of their previous albums and showcased their new pure pop direction. With Neil Finn's seductive "I Got You," the band finally broke through—the single and album hit No. 1 in Australia and New Zealand, eventually selling 200,000 albums in Australia, the equivalent of one in every 10 homes in that country. The success led to an international deal with A&M Records. *True Colours* performed well in the UK and the US and went platinum in Canada. The band quickly recorded a follow-up during a mid-year break in touring. The result—called *Corroboree* in Australia and *Waiata* internationally—was released in April of 1981. The record was somewhat disappointing, seeming to follow the same formula as its predecessor but with decidedly lesser material. The album failed to match the success of *True Colours*, but it did manage two hit singles, "One Step Ahead" and "History Never Repeats." On their subsequent North American tour, Split Enz were billed equally with Tom Petty & the Heartbreakers, which stands as a testament to the band's growing popularity. Mal Green left the band to work on solo projects and Crombie took over on drums.

By late 1981, after many months of intensive touring, the band retreated to the studio to record their most personal and creatively satisfying album to date, *Time & Tide*. Released in 1982, it immediately topped the Australian and New Zealand charts. The advent of MTV and the channel's commitment to new wave acts helped the band's growing cult status in America—both "Dirty Creature" and "Six Months in a Leaky Boat" (as well as earlier videos) saw heavy airplay on the channel—but the album failed to see much chart action.

Early in 1983, Tim took a break from Split Enz to work on a solo album, *Escapade*. The album was a big success in Australasia, spawning several hit singles including the Top Ten "Fraction Too Much Friction." For all of its success, though, the album distracted Tim, delaying the follow-up to *Time & Tide* and effectively ending the momentum Split Enz had built over the previous three albums. *Conflicting Emotions* was finally finished by the fall of 1983. Prior to this album, Tim had been the primary contributor, but for this effort he was overshadowed by brother Neil who had written a considerable majority of songs for the first time. The album, while predictably successful in Australia/New Zealand, saw a delayed release in the States and failed to make much impact. A new drummer, Paul Hester, was added, demoting Crombie to percussion. Before work was begun on the next album, Tim announced that he was leaving the band. With Neil Finn as the leader, the band carried on for one more album—1984's *See Ya Round*, an uneven album that was released only in Australia, New Zealand, and Canada. Neil decided to fold the band following a farewell tour, *Enz with a Bang!*, for which Tim rejoined the group.

Neil and Paul Hester went on to form the internationally successful Crowded House, and Tim continued a sporadic solo career, joining Crowded House for the *Woodface* album in 1991. Nigel Griggs, Noel Crombie, and Phil Judd formed Schnell Fenster, releasing two albums before disbanding, and Eddie Rayner has done session work and formed his own combo—the Makers. Tim and Neil Finn reunited for a

Finn Brothers album in 1995. Split Enz remains an institution in their homeland, frequently re-forming for one-off reunion gigs. In 1996, the New Zealand Symphony Orchestra performed a symphonic tribute to Split Enz under the direction of Eddie Rayner with contributions from both Tim and Neil Finn as well as other New Zealand artists including Dave Dobbyn—the resulting album, *ENZSO*, spent several weeks in the Australian and New Zealand Top Ten. —*Chris Woodstra*

Mental Notes [Mushroom] / 1975 / Mushroom ✦✦✦✦
The first proper Enz album features the band at it's eccentric best. *Mental Notes* is completely non commercial art-rock filled with ambitious arrangements and slightly disturbing themes courtesy of the Phil Judd and Tim Finn songwriting partnership. Finn's bittersweet crooning perfectly compliments Judd's madman persona on tracks like "Stranger than Fiction." Although the album would be repackaged, renamed, and re-recorded in years to come, the band would never again produce anything like it. —*Chris Woodstra*

Second Thoughts / 1976 / Mushroom ✦✦✦
After *Mental Notes* failed commercially, the band left for England to rework the tracks with Roxy Music's Phil Manzanera producing. *Second Thoughts* is an eccentric album filled with the theatrics that gained the band its early notoriety. Mainly new versions of old songs, the album adds some new tracks such as the brilliant "Late Last Night" and "Woman Who Loves You." Released in America and the UK as *Mental Notes* with a modified cover. —*Chris Woodstra*

Dizrhythmia / Oct. 1977 / Mushroom ✦✦✦✦
Dizrhythmia marks a change not only in personnel (half of the band had been replaced) but also musically and lyrically. With Tim Finn taking over the band, gone almost entirely are the neo-classical arrangements and abstract imagery in favor of a more direct approach that draws heavily from British Invasion-era pop as well as incorporating British music hall and straight ahead rock 'n' roll. And though the band is still hiding behind hair, colorful costumes, and the occasional swirl of carnival sounds, beneath it all Finn makes his most personal statements to date, showing his optimism and determination for the band's future while also revealing his uncertainty and fears. Most of the songs deal with relationships and, more specifically, his parting-of-ways with former collaborator and close friend Phil Judd. —*Chris Woodstra*

Frenzy [Australian] / 1978 / Mushroom ✦✦✦
Although often thought of as a transitional album, *Frenzy* shows the band in top form. Produced in England on a diminished budget, the album showcases pure pop with a hungry edge. "I See Red," added after the initial pressing, became a moderate hit in Australia and New Zealand, allowing the band the financial freedom to follow up with the blockbuster *True Colours* in 1980. Stripped down of the earlier excesses, the album hints at the direction the band would take in the '80s while capturing a rare, rougher side to their music. [The album was reissued in the US in 1981, dropping half of the tracks and adding songs from the legendary "Rootin' Tootin' Luton Tapes" recorded in 1978.] —*Chris Woodstra*

True Colours / 1979 / Mushroom ✦✦✦✦
Split Enz found their place in new wave with *True Colours*, shedding the eccentricities and excesses of their past in favor of bright, highly memorable, Beatlesque pop. The album also marked Neil Finn's emergence as a great songcraftsman—his infectious "I Got You" helped to push the album and the band to international success. Both the single and the album stand as high points of the new wave era. As part of its marketing, the album was released in several different-colored covers with laser-etched vinyl. —*Chris Woodstra*

Beginning of the Ends / 1979 / Mushroom ✦✦✦✦
A compilation of demos from 1972 to1975. This Australian-only release shows the band in its eccentric formative years before a recording contract. Light acoustic arrangements of songs appearing on later albums coupled with long-forgotten gems make this a favorite among diehard fans. Not the most representative picture of the band, but an interesting one. —*Chris Woodstra*

Beginning of the Enz / 1980 / Chrysalis ✦✦
Not to be confused with the Australian *Beginning of the Ends*, this British release compiles early Enz tracks from 1975 to1977 (mainly from 1976's *Second Thoughts* and 1977's *Dizrhythmia*). A nice introduction to the band's earlier work but the albums should really be heard in their entirety. The inclusion of the non-LP track "Another Great Divide" made this essential for collectors/completists but it has since been made completely redundant. —*Chris Woodstra*

Waiata (Corroboree) / May 1981 / Mushroom ✦✦✦
Because of the hurried schedule of newfound international success, the follow-up to *True Colours* suffered. *Waiata* follows much of the same formula of its predecessor, though in a slightly darker form that often lacks the punch that made *True Colours* great. Despite a couple of classic singles—"One Step Ahead" and "History Never Repeats"—and a handful of other inspired tracks, the album marks the band's first lateral

move. Waiata is the Maori word for party (the album was given the Aboriginal party title, *Corroboree*, in Australia). Following in the trend of *True Colours*, A&M issued three-different colored covers for the worldwide release. — *Chris Woodstra*

Time & Tide / 1982 / Mushroom ✦✦✦✦
Time & Tide stands as the band's creative peak and most fully realized effort. On previous albums, Split Enz remained distant and removed, only revealing what little they did between the lines; for *Time & Tide*, Tim and Neil Finn, while still clearly standing as outsiders, opened up, giving a rare glimpse at their feelings and thought processes. Tim exorcised demons and fears in the funky workout of "Dirty Creature," experienced a joyful communion with nature in "Never Ceases to Amaze Me," outlined a global view in "Small World" and explored ancient folk music with "Six Months in a Leaky Boat" and "Haul Away," an autobiographical sea shanty. Neil, on the other hand, gave darkly evocative yet slightly more abstract accounts in "Giant Heartbeat," "Take a Walk," and the claustrophobic "Log Cabin Fever" while still producing an infectious rocker in "Hello Sandy Allen." In addition to the peaks in songwriting, the Enz never sounded tighter as a band, with lean, tasteful arrangements. The result is a timeless, thoroughly consistent album and the high point of the Enz catalog. — *Chris Woodstra*

Conflicting Emotions / 1983 / Mushroom ✦✦✦
The distraction of a Tim Finn solo project (1983's *Escapade*) may have robbed Split Enz of the creative momentum produced by *Time & Tide;* Tim obviously spent much of his energy on that project, leaving him with a minority of songwriting credits for the first time since taking leadership of the band. So, despite a strong batch of songs from Neil—which includes the achingly beautiful love song "Message to My Girl" and the contemplative "Our Day," which intimates the thoughts of the soon-to-be father—the album suffers from a general lack of focus. A misguided overreliance on drum machines and generally heavy-handed production are the real downfall, though, ultimately dating a solid though unexceptional album. The telling title track, as well as the album closer, "Bon Voyage," hinted at Tim Finn's imminent departure from the band. Initial pressings of the album in New Zealand included a bonus 12" of "Kia Kaha" and "Parasite"—songs unavailable elsewhere until the release of the box sets. — *Chris Woodstra*

Enz of an Era / 1983 / Mushroom ✦✦✦✦
A solid collection of the singles from *Second Thoughts* (1976) to *Time and Tide* (1982). Although not all of the singles are present, all of the hits from that period are covered. *Enz of an Era* was originally most notable for inclusion of the rare "Another Great Divide" but it has been superseded by more current (and more easily found) collections. — *Chris Woodstra*

See Ya Round / 1984 / Mushroom ✦✦
With Tim Finn departing for a solo career, Neil Finn takes charge of the aging band for their final studio album. While not living up to the band's previous brilliance, songs such as "Years Go By," "One Mouth Is Fed" and an early version of "I Walk Away" are delightful Finn compositions. Side two features songs written by each of the remaining members. Released only in Australia, New Zealand, and Canada. — *Chris Woodstra*

Living Enz / 1985 / Mushroom ✦✦✦
A double live album with tracks from the farewell *Enz with a Bang* tour and a few from the 1982 *Time & Tide* tour. Rather than just focusing on the hit singles, the album revives old album favorites with new live arrangements. Mainly a gift for the fans, this album is a showcase for the band at its crowd-pleasing best. — *Chris Woodstra*

● **History Never Repeats: The Best of Split Enz** / 1987 / A&M ✦✦✦✦
Split Enz are probably best remembered in the US for their new wave-era singles; *History Never Repeats: The Best of Split Enz* collects all of the major singles from the band's A&M albums in a single disc package. For the casual fan, there is no better starting point. The Australian issue is far superior as a career overview however, as it covers their pre-hit period beginning in the mid-'70s and adds a rare mix of "Late Last Night." — *Chris Woodstra*

History Never Repeats [Aus] / 1987 / Mushroom ✦✦✦✦
The Australian version of *History Never Repeats: The Best of Split Enz* offers a better picture of the band through a wider range (all of the albums are represented on this one) and better song selection. Although it may be hard to find, collectors will find this essential if only for the alternate mix of "Late Last Night," not available elsewhere. — *Chris Woodstra*

1973-1979: Oddz & Enz / 1993 / Mushroom ✦✦✦
This Australian-only box set covers the band's more experimental beginnings (1973-1979). From the light acoustic demos of *Beginning of the Enz* and the art-rock of *Mental Notes*, to the edgy pop of *Frenzy*, the listener gets a strong sense of the band's pre-popularity evolution. With over an hour of non-LP tracks on the bonus disc and improved sound quality, this is essential for fans. — *Chris Woodstra*

1980-1984: Rear Enz / 1993 / Mushroom ✦✦✦
This Australian-only box set covers the period of the band's peak in popularity (1980-1984). Beginning with *True Colours* and ending with their swansong, *See Ya Round*, it shows the band in perfect pop form. While this is too ambitious for the casual fan, the devoted will find this essential for considerably improved sound and the bonus disc of previously unreleased tracks. — *Chris Woodstra*

Anniversary / 1994 / Fuel ✦✦
Recorded live during the band's 20th Anniversary tour of New Zealand in March 1993, *Anniversary* serves mainly as a souvenir for longtime fans. There are some interesting song choices, such as the never-before-released "Best Friend" and the rarely-heard first single, "Split Ends," but the band seems to lack the energy that the enthusiastic audience deserved. Fans will delight in this release but *Living Enz* is still a better representation of the band's live shows. [In 1997, Fuel Records issued the album in the US with different cover art.] — *Chris Woodstra*

● **Best of Split Enz** / Jun. 28, 1994 / Chrysalis ✦✦✦✦
Chrysalis Records handled the band's non-Australia/New Zealand releases from 1976 to 1977—an extremely low point in terms of sales. Not surprisingly, *Best of Split Enz* focuses a little too heavily on this early period to truly give the casual listener a representative collection of the band's better-known period. The big A&M/newwave-era hits ("I Got You," "One Step Ahead") are covered adequately, but this was clearly an attempt to cash in on Crowded House's success in Europe the year before. — *Chris Woodstra*

The Spongetones
....
f. 1980, Charlotte, NC
Power Pop
One of the most underrated power-pop bands of the '80s, the Spongetones released several albums of effortlessly catchy guitar pop that captured the feel of '60s British Invasion pop with remarkable accuracy and innocent charm. While they never received much critical or commercial attention, their music has aged much better than most power pop of the era (late 70s/early 80s), and among specialists they're highly revered not only for their studio prowess but also for their spirited live shows. They are one of the few bands to carry on past the "skinny tie" fad into the '90s gracefully—not as strict revivalists but as something unique. The band, comprised of Steve Stockel (vocals, bass), Pat Walters (vocals, guitar), Jamie Hoover (vocals, guitar), and Rob Thorne (drums), began as a covers band in Charlotte, North Carolina, in the early '80s. They signed to the Ripete label in 1982 and released their first full length, *Beat Music*, the same year, following with the *Torn Apart* EP in 1984—the latter featuring esteemed guests Don Dixon, Mitch Easter, and R.E.M. on hand claps. Stockel temporarily left the band, returning in 1991. By 1987, it seemed the Spongetones wanted to distance themselves from their revivalist reputation, leaving Ripete in favor of the independent Triapore and recording probably their most experimental and most un-Spongetones album, *Where-Ever Land*. The album, produced by Don Dixon, flirted with garage rock, psychedelia, and the more fashionable jangle-pop—all in all it marked a more muscular and harder-edged approach. The experiment failed for the most part and was short-lived. The band signed to Vinyl records (owned by power-pop icons Shoes) and found a true home in 1991. There they created, in the mold of their first two releases, possibly their most focused Mersey pastiche, *Oh Yeah!. Textural Drone Thing* followed in 1995. In addition to regular band activities, Jamie Hoover released a solo album, *Coupons, Questions and Comments*, for Triapore in 1990 and formed the Van Delecki's with Bryan Shumate, releasing *Letters from the Desk of Count S. Van Delecki* on Permanent Press in 1996. — *Chris Woodstra*

Beat Music / 1982 / Ripete ✦✦✦✦
Beat Music, the Spongetones' debut album, features some of their finest music, drawing heavily on the Beatles, Dave Clark Five, and the Hollies without shame. And while this is certainly derivative stuff, rarely is a nostalgia trip so well executed and so enjoyable. *Beat Music* and its follow-up, *Torn Apart*, have been combined on a single disc, *Beat & Torn*, released on Black Vinyl Records. — *Chris Woodstra*

Torn Apart / 1984 / Ripete ✦✦✦

Where-Ever Land / 1987 / Triapore ✦✦
Not their strongest effort, *Where-Ever Land* shows a slight move from their trademark Mersey-inspired pop in favor of slightly harder material with a touch of radio-ready gloss. Fortunately, this deviation was short-lived. — *Chris Woodstra*

● **Oh Yeah!** / 1991 / Black Vinyl ✦✦✦✦
The Spongetones return after a long absence with 1991's *Oh Yeah* They effectively pick up where they left off in the '80s with their infectious Beatlesque power pop. Easily their best songwriting and a good place to get acquainted with the band. — *Chris Woodstra*

Beat & Torn / Jun. 30, 1994 / Black Vinyl ✦✦✦✦
Now combined on one CD, *Beat Music* and *Torn Apart* represent the band's earliest recordings and some of their finest. These two albums are simply power-pop at its best and this package is essential for fans of pure pop. —*Chris Woodstra*

Textural Drone Thing / Feb. 21, 1995 / Black Vinyl ✦✦✦
Textural Drone Thing may not reach the heights of its predecessor, *Oh Yeah!*, but that's tough competition. The approach is considerably more subtle and it lacks the band's usual immediacy, but with melodies like these, it's well worth the effort. —*Chris Woodstra*

Dusty Springfield (Mary O'Brien)
b. Apr. 16, 1959, Hampstead, London, England
Vocals / Soul, Pop-Rock, Girl Group
Born Mary O'Brien before changing her name professionally, Dusty Springfield first emerged during the early '60s as one-third of the British folk-pop trio the Springfields, which also included her brother Tom. They had several hits, including "Island of Dreams" and "Silver Thread and Golden Needles," and the latter made the US Top 20 a year before the Beatles first records.

In 1963, the Springfields split up, with Tom going off to produce the Seekers. Dusty made herself over vocally, evolving from a folk alto into a powerful White soul singer, capable of credibly covering Motown material (she duetted with Martha Reeves on television's *Ready, Steady, Go* without embarrassing herself at all) and belting out British pop numbers with seismic intensity. "I Only Want to Be with You," "Stay Awhile," "Wishin' and Hopin'," and "24 Hours from Tulsa" were just a few of her successes, and all were heavily played in either England or America. In 1969, Springfield recorded *Dusty in Memphis*, a landmark White soul album done at Stax studios, which received critical raves and is something of a legendary record.

Since the early '70s, Springfield has recorded and made infrequent appearances, but none of her work since the Memphis album has been taken up by the public. She remains a respected and much-loved figure from British rock's heyday, however, even 30 years on. —*Bruce Eder*

Dusty / 1964 / Philips ✦✦✦
Not quite as good as her first American LP, but a good mix of soul/R&B covers and orchestrated pop-rock in the manner of early Dionne Warwick. Standouts include the cover of Bacharach-David's "I Just Don't Know What to Do with Myself" (a British hit), "All Cried Out," and the epic ballad "Summer Is Over," which foreshadows the style she'd use on her later hit "You Don't Have to Say You Love Me." —*Richie Unterberger*

Stay Awhile/I Only Want to Be with You / 1964 / Philips ✦✦✦✦
Her most rock 'n' roll-oriented album, and one of the finest solo rock albums of the mid-'60s. Besides the two hit title tracks, Dusty covers various American soul and pop tunes that usually rank at least equal to the originals, in some cases totally outclassing them. In particular, she improves upon "24 Hours from Tulsa," "Anyone Who Had a Heart," "You Don't Own Me," and "When the Lovelight Starts Shining Through His Eyes." The production is the most credible approximation of the Phil Spector wall of sound ever managed in the UK, with full brass and strings, soulful female backup choruses, and pounding piano and drums. Also includes a first-rate Springfield original, "Somethin' Special." —*Richie Unterberger*

Oooooooweeee!!! / 1965 / Philips ✦✦✦
No hits here (though "Losing You" made the British Top 10), and a couple of pointless repeats from the first album. Still, it's another solid set of exuberant, soulful girl group-style British Invasion pop. "Losing You," "Once Upon a Time," and "He's Got Something" remain some of her most unjustly overlooked performances. —*Richie Unterberger*

Ev'rything's Coming up Dusty / 1965 / Beat Goes On ✦✦✦
Dusty started to lean in a somewhat less R&B and somewhat more pop direction on this album, with covers of "La Bamba" and Anthony Newley's "Who Can I Turn To?" Still, it has good interpretations of songs by Goffin/King, Jerry Ragovoy, Randy Newman, Bacharach-David, and the Zombies' Rod Argent, highlighted by "Oh No! Not My Baby" and Newman's "I've Been Wrong Before." —*Richie Unterberger*

Golden Hits / 1966 / Philips ✦✦✦✦
A fair representation of her mid-'60s hits, with major gaps. The imported CDs are preferable. —*Bruce Eder*

★ **Dusty in Memphis** / 1969 / Rhino ✦✦✦✦✦
Sometimes memories distort or inflate the quality of recordings deemed legendary, but in the case of *Dusty in Memphis*, the years have only strengthened its reputation. The idea of taking England's reigning female soul queen to the home of the music she had mastered was an inspired one. The Jerry Wexler/Tom Dowd/Arif Mardin production and engineering team picked mostly perfect songs, and those that weren't so great were salvaged by Springfield's marvelous delivery and technique. This set has definitive numbers in "So Much Love," "Son of a Preacher Man," "Breakfast in Bed," "Just One Smile," "I Don't Want to Hear About

It Anymore" and "Just a Little Lovin'," and offers exquisite mastering, informative notes, and an unreleased version of "What Do You Do When Love Dies." It's truly a disc deserving of its classic status. —*Ron Wynn*

A Brand New Me / 1970 / Rhino ✦✦✦✦
While it's not quite as uniformally excellent as *Dusty in Memphis*, *A Brand New Me* comes close to recapturing its predecessor's magic and is easily one of Springfield's best albums. —*Stephen Thomas Erlewine*

● **The Silver Collection** / Jan. 1988 / Philips ✦✦✦✦
Twenty-four songs, encompassing her British and American chart history for the '60s. Superb sound. —*Bruce Eder*

Sounds of the 60's / 1989 / Pickwick ✦✦✦
Intelligently assembled Springfield compilations have proven to be a surprisingly elusive concept, if you want to go beyond the big hits. There's lots of good stuff on this 24-track survey of her 1960s work: some (not all) of her big early hits, and some superb mid-'60s LP-only covers like "Oh No! Not My Baby" and "Anyone Who Had a Heart." These are interspersed with less-impressive items from later in the decade, and chronologically and stylistically it jumps all over the place. So it's not bad, but doesn't really satisfy either the collector or the listener who just wants the greatest hits. —*Richie Unterberger*

Something Special / 1996 / Mercury ✦✦✦✦
A 48-song, double-CD set of rarities and album tracks, including eight previously unreleased cuts and plenty of songs that had rarely or never been on album before. Sure, this is primarily for Springfield fans, and not the first (or second) anthology recommended to casual listeners. But quite a bit of this is on par, or nearly on par, with her best work. What's more, the bulk of it dates from her '60s prime, although there are about a dozen mediocre numbers from the late '70s/early '80s on which her voice still cuts it, but the material and production don't. Big Dusty Springfield fans will already have some or all of the songs taken from albums, but about half of this is very hard or impossible to find elsewhere, and much of it is very good. Highlights include the title track (one of her best girl group-style numbers); a 1965 Italian-language single in the "You Don't Have to Say You Love Me" ballad style; soulful mid-'60s B-sides like "I'm Gonna Leave You" and "I'll Love You for a While"; and the strange 1968 outtake "Don't Speak of Love," based on a classical piece by Wagner. —*Richie Unterberger*

Stay Awhile—I Only Want to Be with You/Dusty / Feb. 11, 1997 / Taragon ✦✦✦✦
This CD combines the 24 songs off of Dusty Springfield's first two US-released albums, which comprises a ton of great material, all remastered from what sure sound like first-generation tapes. The sound is vivid and, at times, shattering, in the best Phil Spector sense of that word, as Springfield's bigger than life voice fills every corner of the room and your soul. At least as worthwhile as any hits collection that exists on her. —*Bruce Eder*

Rick Springfield
b. Aug. 23, 1949, Sydney, Australia
Guitar, Keyboards, Vocals / Power Pop, Pop-Rock
Before he became a soap star, Rick Springfield was a rock star in his native Australia. After scoring several hits with his band Zoot in the early '70s, he went solo and tried to make the big time in America. Springfield released several power-pop albums to no success; he then decided to become a television actor, landing a role on *General Hospital*. While he was acting on the soap opera, he gained a strong following, which led him to revive his singing career in the early '80s. This time, his records were more successful—"Jessie's Girl," his first single since returning to music, hit No. 1. Several other Top Ten hits followed, before his career started to slip in the mid-'80s; despite his diminished sales, he continued recording and acting through the rest of the decade. —*Stephen Thomas Erlewine*

Beginnings / 1972 / Capitol ✦✦
"Come on Everybody" aside, this is a different side of Springfield of which fans of his work in the '80s may not be aware. This is the work of an artist trying to fit into the sensitive singer-songwriter mold. While not a bad record, it's most interesting for "Speak to the Sky," his first American hit, and as a clue to the roots of the work for which he is best known. —*Jim Worbois*

Comic Book Heroes / 1974 / Columbia ✦✦✦
Springfield grew considerably as a writer between his first record and *Comic Book Heroes*. Although he is still doing some sensitive singer-songwriter material, it no longer sounds as awkward. In fact, a couple tracks, like "Weep No More," are very memorable. On the other hand, "Misty Water Woman" sounds like an overly melodramatic attempt at being Elton John. Still, the good stuff makes it worth owning. —*Jim Worbois*

Wait for Night / 1976 / Chelsea ✦✦
While there is nothing that really jumps off *Wait for Night* that makes it stick in your mind, it is still quite a nice record. Of course, the addition of

Elton John's rhythm section and Jimmy Haskell's string work contributes to the album's overall quality. —*Jim Worbois*

● **Working Class Dog** / 1981 / RCA ✦✦✦✦
Forget that Rick Springfield was a soap star for a moment and listen to his music, because he made some of the finest guitar-driven mainstream pop-rock of the early '80s. *Working Class Dog* is his finest moment, filled with expertly crafted pop songs, highlighted by the massive hit "Jessie's Girl." —*Stephen Thomas Erlewine*

Success Hasn't Spoiled Me Yet / 1982 / RCA ✦✦✦✦
Rick Springfield's follow-up to his commercial breakthrough *Working Class Dog* wasn't quite as consistent, but it contained a number of solid power-pop tracks, including "Calling All Girls," "What Kind of Fool Am I," "How Do You Talk to Girls," "The American Girl," and the Top Ten hit "Don't Talk to Strangers." —*Stephen Thomas Erlewine*

Living in Oz / 1983 / RCA ✦✦✦
Although the singles "Affair of the Heart" and "Human Touch" were Rick Springfield classics, the rest of *Living in Oz* contained too much filler to make it rank with *Working Class Dog* and *Success Hasn't Spoiled Me Yet* as one of his best albums. —*Stephen Thomas Erlewine*

Hard to Hold / 1984 / RCA ✦✦
The soundtrack to Rick Springfield's movie features the powerful rocker "Love Somebody," but the rest of the album comprises filler instrumentals, lukewarm power-pop tracks from Springfield and bland tracks from Graham Parker, Nona Hendryx, and Peter Gabriel. —*Stephen Thomas Erlewine*

Tao / 1985 / RCA ✦✦✦
Rock of Life / 1988 / RCA ✦✦

Greatest Hits / Aug. 1989 / RCA ✦✦✦✦
Greatest Hits contains 12 of Rick Springfields biggest hits from the early '80s, including "Jessie's Girl," "I've Done Everything for You," "Love Is Alright Tonight," "Don't Talk to Strangers," "Affair of the Heart," and "Love Somebody." Every one of his major hits is included, making it a perfect collection for casual fans, even though *Working Class Dog* is a fine record in its own right. —*Stephen Thomas Erlewine*

Bruce Springsteen

b. Sep. 23, 1949, Freehold, NJ
Guitar, Vocals / Rock & Roll, Singer-Songwriter, Pop-Rock
When Bruce Springsteen finally broke through to national recognition in the fall of 1975, after a decade of trying, critics hailed him as the savior of rock 'n' roll, the single artist who brought together all the exuberance of '50s rock and the thoughtfulness of '60s rock, molded into a '70s style. He rocked as hard as Jerry Lee Lewis, his lyrics were as complicated as Bob Dylan's, and his concerts were near-religious celebrations of all that was best in the music. One critic became so enamored that he quit reviewing to become Springsteen's manager.

But the hosannas, when piped through the publicity machine of a major record company, were perceived as hype by a significant part of the public as well as the mainstream media—Springsteen landed on the covers of *Time* and *Newsweek*, but both magazines were covering the phenomenon, not the music. Springsteen's album, *Born to Run*, became a hit, and he jumped to arena status as a live act, but as many people were turned off by the press campaign as turned on by the records and shows.

Two decades later, however, Springsteen remained an established star who could look back on a career that had produced one of the best-selling albums of all time, sold-out stadium shows, Grammy Awards and an Oscar, and a group of imitators who constituted their own subgenre of popular music. If he no longer seemed divine, he remained popular enough for his *Greatest Hits* album to enter the charts at No. 1, and he had won over many of those skeptics from 1975.

Growing up in southern New Jersey, Springsteen turned to rock 'n' roll as a teenager and played in a series of bands from the mid-'60s on, varying in style from garage rock to power trio blues-rock. By the early '70s, he was trying his hand at being a folkie singer-songwriter in Greenwich Village. But when he was signed to Columbia Records in 1972, he brought into the studio many of the New Jersey-based musicians with whom he'd played over the years.

The result was *Greetings from Asbury Park, N.J.* (January 1973), which went unnoticed upon initial release, though Manfred Mann's Earth Band would turn its leadoff track, "Blinded by the Light," into a No. 1 hit four years later. *The Wild, the Innocent and the E Street Shuffle* (September 1973) also failed to sell, despite some rave reviews. (Both albums have since gone platinum.)

The following year, Springsteen revised his backup group—dubbed "The E Street Band"—settling on a lineup that included saxophone player Clarence Clemons, second guitarist "Miami" Steve Van Zandt, organist Danny Federici, pianist Roy Bittan, bassist Gary Tallent, and drummer Max Weinberg. With this unit he barnstormed the country while working on his third and last chance with Columbia. By the time

Born to Run (August 1975) was released, the critics and a significant cult audience were with him, and the title song became a Top 40 hit while the album reached the Top Ten.

What Springsteen needed to do in the wake of the hype, of course, was to play and record more to consolidate his position. He was prevented at least from the latter by a former manager, who kept him in court during the next couple of years. Meanwhile, the musical world changed. Part of the reason critics had welcomed Springsteen so enthusiastically in 1975 was that he seemed a return to basic rock 'n' roll values in a world of soft rock, heavy metal, and art-rock.

By the time Springsteen returned with his fourth album, *Darkness at the Edge of Town* (June 1978), however, the punk/new wave movement had outflanked him, pushing him from the vanguard to the mainstream. Similar-sounding heartland rockers such as Bob Seger had appeared, so that Springsteen sounded less like an innovator than a member of an established genre.

Nevertheless, he set about winning fans with an album that found the lost children of his early albums stuck in factory jobs, still longing for some escape. The album was a hit, though it did not match the success of *Born to Run*. Springsteen returned with the double album *The River* (October 1980), which topped the charts and featured his first Top Ten hit, "Hungry Heart."

Nobody was calling him a hype anymore, but Springsteen retreated from his expanding success, next recording the low-key album *Nebraska* (September 1982), a virtual demo tape-on-vinyl. (Springsteen did not tour to promote the album, and in the interim E Street Band guitarist Van Zandt amicably left the group for a solo career, to be replaced by Nils Lofgren.)

But then came *Born in the USA* (June 1984) and a two-year international tour. The album threw off seven hit singles and sold over ten million copies, putting Springsteen in the pop heavens with Michael Jackson and Prince. After touring for more than a year, he released a five-LP/three-CD concert album, *Bruce Springsteen & the E Street Band/Live 1975-85* (November 1986), which topped the charts.

Characteristically, Springsteen returned with a more introverted effort, *Tunnel of Love* (October 1987), which presaged his divorce from his first wife. (He married a second time to singer Patti Scialfa, who had joined the E Street Band.)

After another marathon tour, Springsteen gave the E Street Band notice in November 1989, breaking up a celebrated unit that had stayed together 15 years. In March 1992, he simultaneously released *Human Touch* and *Lucky Town*, and though the albums premiered near the top of the charts, they were less successful with fans than previous albums. In the fall, Springsteen taped an *MTV Unplugged* segment (though he plugged in after one song), and the performance was released as an album in Europe in 1993.

Springsteen continued to tour until July 1993. In the fall, he wrote and recorded "Streets of Philadelphia" for the soundtrack to the film *Philadelphia*, which concerned a lawyer dying of AIDS. The song became a Top Ten hit in 1994, winning the Academy Award for Best Song and cleaning up in the Grammys the following year. At the same time, Springsteen had readied his *Greatest Hits* album (February 1995), reassembling the E Street Band to record a few new tracks. The album was an immediate bestseller. Springsteen followed it with *The Ghost of Tom Joad* (November 1995), another low-key, downcast, near-acoustic effort, and embarked upon a brief "solo" tour. At the start of 1996, he was said to be planning to record his first album with the E Street Band since *Born in the USA*, to be followed by their first tour in a decade. —*William Ruhlmann*

Greetings from Asbury Park NJ / Jan. 5, 1973 / Columbia ✦✦✦✦
Bruce Springsteen's debut album found him squarely in the tradition of Bob Dylan: folk-based tunes arranged for an electric band featuring piano and organ (plus, in Springsteen's case, 1950s-style rock 'n' roll tenor saxophone breaks), topped by acoustic guitar and a husky voice singing lyrics full of elaborate, even exaggerated imagery. But where Dylan had taken a world-weary, cynical tone, Springsteen was exuberant. His street scenes could be haunted and tragic, as they were in "Lost in the Flood," but they were still imbued with romanticism and a youthful energy. *Asbury Park* painted a portrait of teenagers cocksure of themselves, yet bowled over by their discovery of the world. It was saved from pretentiousness (if not preciousness) by its sense of humor and by the careful eye for detail that kept even the most high-flown language rooted. Like the lyrics, the arrangements were busy, but the melodies were well developed and the rhythms, pushed by drummer Vincent Lopez, were breakneck. —*William Ruhlmann*

☆ **The Wild, the Innocent and the E Street Shuffle** / Sep. 11, 1973 / Columbia ✦✦✦✦✦
Bruce Springsteen expanded the folk-rock approach of *Greetings from Asbury Park, N.J.*, to strains of jazz, among other styles, on its ambitious follow-up. His chief musical lieutenant was keyboard player David Sancious, whose piano work was the backbone of tracks like "Incident on 57th Street" and "New York City Serenade"; with his help, Springsteen

created a street-life mosaic of suburban society that owed much in its outlook to Van Morrison's romanticization of Belfast in *Astral Weeks*. Though Springsteen expressed endless affection and much nostalgia, his message was clear: this was a goodbye to all that from a man who was moving on. *The Wild, the Innocent & the E Street Shuffle* represented an astonishing advance even from the remarkable promise of *Greetings:* musically and lyrically, Springsteen had brought an unruly muse under control to make a mature statement that synthesized popular musical styles into complicated, well-executed arrangements and absorbing suites. Its songs contain the best realization of Springsteen's poetic vision, which soon enough would be tarnished by disillusionment. Later, he would make different albums, but he never made a better one. — *William Ruhlmann*

☆ **Born to Run** / Aug. 25, 1975 / Columbia ✦✦✦✦✦
Layers of guitar, layers of echo on the vocals, lots of keyboards, thunderous drums—*Born to Run* had a big sound, and Bruce Springsteen wrote big songs to match it. The overall theme of the album was similar to that of *The Wild, the Innocent & the E Street Shuffle:* Springsteen was describing, and saying farewell to, a romanticized teenage street life. But what had been affectionate, even humorous before, was now becoming increasingly bitter—"Backstreets" was a howl of betrayal, while "Born to Run" suggested Springsteen's heroes ("tramps like us") were just roaring around, however heroically they might be depicted. If Springsteen had celebrated his dead-end kids on his first album and viewed them nostalgically on his second, on his third he seemed to despise their failure; he now felt removed, composing an updated *West Side Story* with spectacular music that owed more to Bernstein than to Berry and idealized (or demonized) characters. To call *Born to Run* overblown is to miss the point; Springsteen's precise intention is to blow things up, both in the sense of expanding them to gargantuan size and of exploding them. An intentional masterpiece, it declared its own greatness with songs and a sound that lived up to Springsteen's promise. — *William Ruhlmann*

Darkness on the Edge of Town / Jun. 2, 1978 / Columbia ✦✦✦✦
Coming three years and one extended court battle after *Born to Run*, *Darkness on the Edge of Town* was highly anticipated. Some attributed the album's embattled tone to Springsteen's legal troubles, but it carried on from *Born to Run*, in which Springsteen had first begun to view his colorful cast of characters as "losers." On *Darkness*, he began to see them as the working class: his characters, some of whom he inhabited and sang for in the first person, had little and were in danger of losing even that. Their only hope for redemption lay in working harder, and their only escape lay in driving. Springsteen presented these hard truths in hard-rock settings, the tracks paced by powerful drumming and searing guitar solos. Though not as heavily produced as *Born to Run*, *Darkness* was given a full-bodied sound; Springsteen's stories were becoming less heroic, but his musical style remained grand—the sound, and the conviction in his singing, added weight to songs like "Racing in the Street" and the title track, transforming the pathetic into the tragic. But despite the lack of 'n roll fervor, *Darkness* was no easy listen, and it served notice that Springsteen was already willing to risk his popularity for his principles. — *William Ruhlmann*

☆ **The River** / Oct. 10, 1980 / Columbia ✦✦✦✦✦
Imbedded within the double-disc running time of *The River* is a single-disc album that follows up on the themes and sound of *Darkness on the Edge of Town*—wide-screen, mid-tempo rock and stories of the disillusionment of working-class life and the conflicts within families. In these songs, which include the title track, "Independence Day," and "Point Blank," Springsteen's worldview is just as dire as it had become on *Darkness*, but less judgmental. "Independence Day," for example, is a father-and-son ballad that has little of the anger of its hard rock counterpart on *Darkness*, "Adam Raised a Cain." Springsteen's heroes again seek to overcome their crushing troubles through defiance and by driving around, and though "The River" repeats the soured love theme of "Racing in the Street," he also posits romance as a possible escape, sometimes combining it with one of the other solutions, as on the eight-plus-minute "Drive All Night." But there is also another album lurking within *The River*, and it is a more light-hearted pop-rock collection of short, sometimes humorous songs like "Sherry Darling" and "I'm a Rocker." At times Springsteen combines elements of the two, as on "Out in the Street," perhaps the album's quintessential song, a catchy, upt-empo number that sounds like something from the early '60s and echoes the theme of the Vogues' 1966 hit "Five O' Clock World." "Hungry Heart," which became Springsteen's first Top Ten hit, combines a rollicking musical track with a more sober lyrical theme that emphasizes longing over disappointment. But a better guide to Springsteen's development are the songs "Stolen Car" and the album-closing "Wreck on the Highway," gentle, moody ballads imbued with a sense of hopelessness that anticipate his next record, *Nebraska*. — *William Ruhlmann*

☆ **Nebraska** / Sep. 20, 1982 / Columbia ✦✦✦✦✦
There is an adage in the record business that a recording artist's demos of new songs often come off better than the more polished versions later

worked up in a studio. But Bruce Springsteen was the first person to act on that theory, when he opted to release the demo versions of his latest songs, recorded with only acoustic or electric guitar, harmonica, and vocals, as his sixth album, *Nebraska*. It was really the content that dictated the approach, however. *Nebraska's* ten songs marked a departure for Springsteen, even as they took him farther down a road he had been traveling previously. Gradually, his songs had become darker and more pessimistic, and those on *Nebraska* marked a new low. They also found him branching out into better-developed stories. The title track was a first-person account of the killing spree of mass murderer Charlie Starkweather. (It can't have been coincidental that the same story was told in director Terrence Malick's 1973 film *Badlands*, also used as a Springsteen song title.) That song set the tone for a series of portraits of small-time criminals, desperate people, and those who loved them. Just as the recordings were unpolished, the songs themselves didn't seem quite finished; sometimes the same line turned up in two songs. But that only served to unify the album. Within the difficult times, however, there was hope, especially as the album went on. "Open All Night" was a Chuck Berry-style rocker, and the album closed with "Reason to Believe," a song whose hard-luck verses were belied by the chorus—even if the singer couldn't understand what it was, "people find some reason to believe." Still, *Nebraska* was one of the most challenging albums ever released by a major star on a major record label. — *William Ruhlmann*

★ **Born in the U.S.A.** / Jun. 4, 1984 / Columbia ✦✦✦✦✦
Bruce Springsteen had become increasingly downcast during his recording career, and his pessimism bottomed out with *Nebraska*. *Born in the USA.*, his popular triumph, trafficked in much the same struggle, albeit set to galloping rhythms and set off by chiming guitars. That the Reagan regime attempted to co-opt the title track as an election-year campaign song wasn't so surprising: the verses described the disenfranchisement of a lower-class Vietnam vet, and the angry chorus came off as anthemic. Too, Springsteen had softened his message with nostalgia and sentimentality: "Glory Days" employed his trademark disaffection, yet it came across as a couch potato's drunken lament. More than anything else, the album marked the first time that Springsteen's characters really seemed to relish the fight and had something to fight for; they were not defeated ("No Surrender"), and they had friendship ("Bobby Jean") and family ("My Hometown") to defend—the restless hero of "Dancing in the Dark" even pledged himself in the face of futility. The "romantic young boys" of his early work, chastened by "the working life" and despair on subsequent efforts, were still alive here, with their sense of humor and their determination intact: *Born in the USA.* was their apotheosis, the place where they renewed their commitment and where Springsteen remembered that he was a rock 'n' roll star. — *William Ruhlmann*

Live 1975-1985 / Nov. 10, 1986 / Columbia ✦✦✦✦
Long before he sold substantial numbers of records, Bruce Springsteen began to earn a reputation as the best live act in rock 'n' roll. Fans had been clamoring for a live album for a long time, and with *Live 1975-1985* they got what they wanted, at least in terms of bulk. His concerts were marathons, and this box set, including 40 tracks and running over three and a half hours, was about the average length of a show. In his brief liner notes, Springsteen spoke of the emergence of the album's "story" as he reviewed live tapes, and that story seems nothing less than a history of his life, his concerns, and his career. The first cuts present the Springsteen of the early to mid-'70s; these performances, most of them drawn from a July 1978 show at the Roxy in Los Angeles, give us the romantic, hopeful, earnest Springsteen of "4th of July, Asbury Park (Sandy)" and "Thunder Road." The second section begins with his first Top Ten hit, "Hungry Heart"—this is the Springsteen of the late '70s and early '80s, an arena-rock star with working-class concerns. After an acoustic mini-set given largely to material from *Nebraska*—songs of economic desperation and crime—comes a reshuffling of *Born in the USA*, songs in which Springsteen and his characters start to fight back and rock out. Finally, he brings it all back home to New Jersey, starting with the unofficial state anthem, "Born to Run," and including "Tenth Avenue Freeze-Out" and "Jersey Girl." Fans could rejoice that it found room for seven previously unreleased songs, including "Because the Night," but it wasn't as funny, as moving, or as exhilarating as a Springsteen show could be. Maybe no single album, however long, could have been, but where Springsteen impressed in concert because he tried so hard, here he seemed to have tried a little too hard to make a live album carry the freight of everything he had to say. — *William Ruhlmann*

☆ **Tunnel of Love** / Oct. 9, 1987 / Columbia ✦✦✦✦✦
Bruce Springsteen followed the most popular album of his career, *Born in the USA.*, with the low-key, anguished *Tunnel of Love*. As its title suggested, it was an album of romantic exploration: in song after song, Springsteen questioned the trust and honesty on both sides in a romantic relationship, specifically a married relationship. Since he sounded more autobiographical than ever before ("Ain't Got You" referred to his popular success, while "Walk Like a Man" seemed another explicit mes-

sage to his father), it was hard not to wonder about the state of his own two-and-a-half-year-old marriage, and it wasn't surprising when that marriage collapsed the following year. And although *Tunnel of Love* was a commercial success, Springsteen was as much at a crossroads with his audience as he seemed to be in his work and in his personal life.— *William Ruhlman*

Human Touch / Mar. 31, 1992 / Columbia ♦♦
Bruce Springsteen has always been steeped in mainstream pop-rock music, using it as a vocabulary for what he wanted to say about weightier matters. He has always written generic pop as well, but *Human Touch* was the first album to consist entirely of this kind of minor genre material, which he seems capable of turning out endlessly and effortlessly. Having largely jettisoned the E Street Band, Springsteen enlisted some sturdy minor talent to play and sing, among them ace studio drummer Jeff Porcaro, Sam Moore of Sam and Dave, and Bobby Hatfield of the Righteous Brothers. It's pleasant enough stuff, and easy to listen to, but it is not the kind of record Springsteen had conditioned his audience to expect, and its release brought considerable disappointment. Though at nearly 59 minutes it was the longest single-disc album of his career, and though it contained several songs that could have been big hits—the "Tunnel of Love" soundalike title track, which actually made the Top 40 "Roll of the Dice," an AOR radio favorite and "Man's Job"—*Human Touch* was an uninspired Springsteen album, his first that didn't at least aspire to greatness. — *William Ruhlmann*

Lucky Town / Mar. 31, 1992 / Columbia ♦♦♦
Reportedly, Bruce Springsteen recorded most of *Human Touch* in 1990, but left it unreleased. He returned to work in the fall of 1991, intending to add a song, but ended up recording a whole new album, *Lucky Town*, and then decided to release both records at the same time in the spring of 1992. He might have been better off pulling a couple of the stronger songs from the earlier album, adding them to the later one (which runs less than 40 minutes), and shelving the rest. While *Human Touch* was a disappointing album of second-rate material, *Lucky Town* was an ambitious collection addressing many of Springsteen's major concerns and moving them forward. Here was the rage and the humor, the sense of compassion, the loyalty and commitment that had been the stuff of Springsteen's best music from the beginning. Songs like "Better Days" and "Local Hero" commented on and deflated the commercial success with which Springsteen clearly felt uncomfortable; "If I Should Fall Behind" and "Book of Dreams" expressed romantic fidelity and generosity; "Souls of the Departed" contained scathing social commentary; and "My Beautiful Reward" was a meditative epilogue. The lyrics were better, the arrangements tighter, the performances more powerful than those on the companion release. If *Lucky Town*, like *Tunnel of Love* and *Human Touch* before it, sounded a little underproduced, it nevertheless had the mark of the major artist Springsteen is, and if he had released it alone it might have had a more significant impact. — *William Ruhlmann*

Greatest Hits / Feb. 28, 1995 / Columbia ♦♦♦
Compiling a "Greatest Hits" of Bruce Springsteen should be an easy task, yet *Greatest Hits* manages to miss the mark. Nothing from his first two albums is included and the set includes such non-hits like "Atlantic City" and "The River" instead of hits like "Cover Me," "Tunnel of Love," and "Fade Away." In fact, a good portion of his hits are missing, as are important album tracks like "Backstreets," "Rosalita," and "Candy's Room," making this neither a straight hits collection nor a compilation of his best tracks. What's left is some of his biggest hits and best songs ("Born to Run," "Glory Days," "The River"), but not all of them, as well as four new tracks, the best of which is an outtake from the *Born in the USA.* sessions ("Murder Inc.") Aside from "Murder Inc.," the new tracks follow the synth-laden adult contemporary direction Springsteen began pursuing with "Streets of Philadelphia," only without the lyricism or melody. So, it's a mixed bag, drawing an incomplete portrait of one of the prime rockers of the '70s and '80s. Casual fans would be better served by *Born in the USA.* which encompasses all of Springsteen's sides. — *Stephen Thomas Erlewine*

Ghost of Tom Joad / Nov. 21, 1995 / Columbia ♦♦
The Son of Nebraska is what this collection could just as easily be called, given its spare instrumentation and restrained singing, as well as its focus on story songs about drifters, itinerant workers, and small-time criminals. But where *Nebraska* focused on the Upper Midwest, *Tom Joad* follows the trail of John Steinbeck's character from *The Grapes of Wrath* through the Southwest to California. Several songs touch on immigration issues, as undocumented aliens interact with border guards. Death and despair haunt the material, but Springsteen's treatment of his characters is so gentle and understanding, so personal, that it barely touches on the political overtones implicit in the stories. Nor does he leaven the tone with humor, as Woody Guthrie, who also wrote a "Tom Joad" song, did. Springsteen doesn't offer his heroes, or his listeners, any out. If you're looking for another "Born to Run," this is not

the place to find it, but if you found "Streets of Philadelphia" compelling, prepare to be enthralled. — *William Ruhlmann*

Squarepusher

Club-Dance, Jungle/Drum 'N Bass, Electronica
Tom "Squarepusher" Jenkinson makes manic, schizoid experimental drum 'n' bass with a heavy progressive jazz influence and a lean toward pushing the cliches off the genre out the proverbial window. Rising from near-total obscurity to drum 'n' bass cause célèbre in the space of a couple of months, Jenkinson released only a pair of EPs and a DJ Food remix for the latter's *Refried Food* series before securing EP and LP release plans with three different labels. His first full-length work, *Feed Me Weird Things* (on Richard "Aphex Twin" James' Rephlex label), is a dizzying, quixotic blend of superfast jungle breaks with Aphex-style synth textures, goofy, offbeat melodies, and instrumental arrangments (Jenkinson samples his own playing for his tracks) that recall vaguely jazz fuston pioneers such as Mahavishnu Orchestra and Weather Report. A skilled bassist and multi-instrumentalist, Jenkinson's fretless accompaniment is a staple of his music and one of the more obvious affiliations with jazz (although his formal arrangements are often as jazz-derived as his playing).

Barely into his twenties, Jenkinson grew up listening to jazz and dub greats like Miles Davis, Augustus Pablo, Charlie Parker, and Art Blakey. The son of a jazz drummer, Jenkinson followed in his father's footsteps, playing bass and drums in high school. Introduced to electronic music through experimental electro-techno groups such as LFO and Carl Craig, Jenkinson soon began assembling the rolls of disparate influence into amalgams of breakbeat techno and post-bop avant-garde and progressive jazz. Claiming a closer affinity with jazz than jungle (although he draws from both equally in his music), Jenkinson's EPs as Squarepusher and the Duke of Harringay (Jenkinson moved to Harringay from his Chelmsford birthplace) were initially disregarded as misplaced perversions of jungle's more obvious compositional principles, but found a ready audience in fans of post-acid house experimental listening music. He inked a deal with Warp in 1995, releasing the *Port Rhombus* EP and three others through a variety of different labels. — *Sean Cooper*

Bubble and Squeak / 1996 / Worm Interface ♦♦♦♦
Jenkinson's early blast on the Warp-like Worm Interface label is probably the most varied and least derivative of his work to date. The jazz influence is strong but also finds a less gimmicky place in the mix. — *Sean Cooper*

Feed Me Weird Things / 1996 / Rephlex ♦♦♦
Fractured beats, frenetic bass licks, and alternately silly and moving melodies tie together Squarepusher's first full-length effort. Much of the material—with its lo-fi synth damage and often tongue-in-cheek feel—places Jenkinson closer to Aphex territory than traditional drum 'n' bass, but the distinctions begin breaking down from word go. Flawed but promising. — *Sean Cooper*

Port Rhombus Ep / 1996 / Warp ♦♦♦
More polished and restrained than some of his Rephlex work, with the proggy bass masturbation toned down to a more manageable level. — *Sean Cooper*

● **Hard Normal Daddy** / 1997 / Warp ♦♦♦♦
Tom Jenkinson's jazz roots come through louder and clearer on his full-length Warp debut. Although, like the preceding EP "Port Rhombus," this LP sounds substantially cleaner and more thought out than previous releases for Spymania and Rephlex, it also far surpasses those releases in terms of musicality and track development, not simply relying on the shock value of "tripping-over-myself" drum programming and light-speed fretless bass noodling. Jenkinson's bass accompaniment also sounds far less prog-rock-influenced here, making *Hard Normal Daddy* his overall most listenable work to date. — *Sean Cooper*

Squeeze

f. 1974, South London, England
New Wave, Pop-Rock
As one of the most traditional pop bands of the New Wave, Squeeze provided one of the links between classic British guitar pop and post-punk. Inspired heavily by the Beatles and the Kinks, Squeeze was the vehicle for the songwriting of Chris Difford and Glenn Tilbrook, who were hailed as the heirs to Lennon and McCartney's throne during their heyday in the early '80s. Unlike Lennon and McCartney, the partnership betweeen Difford and Tilbrook was a genuine collaboration, with the former providing the music and the latter writing the lyrics. Squeeze never came close to matching the popularity of the Beatles, but the reason for that is part of their charm. Difford and Tilbrook were wry, subtle songwriters that subscribed to traditional pop songwriting values, but subverted them with literate lyrics and clever musical references. While their native Britain warmed to Squeeze immediately, sending singles like "Take Me I'm Yours" and "Up the Junction" into the Top 10, the band

had a difficult time gaining a foothold in the States; they didn't have a Top 40 hit until 1987, nearly a decade after their debut album. Even if the group never had a hit in the US, Squeeze built a dedicated following that stayed with them into the late '90s, and many of their songs—"Another Nail in My Heart," "Pulling Mussels (from the Shell)," "Tempted," "Black Coffee in Bed"—became pop classics of the New Wave era, as the platinum status of their compilation *Singles—45's and Under* indicates.

Chris Difford (b. April 11, 1954; guitar, vocals) and Glenn Tilbrook (b. August 31, 1957; vocals, guitar) formed Squeeze in 1974. Tilbrook answered an advertisement Difford had placed in a store window, and the pair began writing songs. By the spring of 1974, the duo had recruited pianist Jools Holland (b. Julian Holland, January 24, 1958) and drummer Paul Gunn, and had named themselves Squeeze, after the disowned Velvet Underground album that featured none of the group's original members. Squeeze began playing the thriving pub rock circuit, although their songs were quirkier and more pop-oriented than many of their peers. By 1976, the band had added bassist Harry Kakoulli and replaced Gunn with Gilson Lavis (b. June 27, 1951), a former tour manager and drummer for Chuck Berry. They had also signed a contract with Miles Copeland's burgeoning BTM record label and management company. Squeeze had already recorded several tracks for RCA, including two cuts with Muff Winwood, that the label rejected. BTM went bankrupt before it could release the band's debut single, "Take Me I'm Yours," in early 1977, but Squeeze was able to work with John Cale on their debut EP, due to a contract Copeland had arranged with Cale.

Squeeze released their debut EP, *Packet of Three*, on Deptford Fun City Records, in the summer of 1977 and soon arranged an international contract with A&M Records, becoming the label's first New Wave act since their disastrous signing of the Sex Pistols. The band entered the studio with producer Cale later that year to work on their debut album, provisionally titled *Gay Guys* by the group's producer. Cale had the group throw out most of their standard material, forcing them to write new material; consequently, the record wasn't necessarily a good representation of the band's early sound. By the time the album was released in the spring of 1978, the group and A&M had abandoned the record's working title, and it was released as *Squeeze*. In America, the band and album had to change their name to US Squeeze, in order to avoid confusion with an American band called Tight Squeeze; by the end of the year, they had reverted back to Squeeze in the US. Preceded by the hit single "Take Me I'm Yours," the album became a moderate success, but the group's true British breakthrough arrived in 1979, when they released their second album, *Cool for Cats*. More representative of the band's sound than its debut, *Cool for Cats* generated two No. 2 singles in its title track and "Up the Junction." Later in 1978, the EP *Six Squeeze Songs Crammed into One Ten-Inch Record* EP was released. Squeeze tried for a seasonal hit that year with "Christmas Day," but the single failed to chart. Kakoulli was fired from the band after the release of *Cool for Cats* and was replaced by John Bentley.

Released in the spring of 1980, *Argybargy* received the strongest reviews of any Squeeze album to date, and produced moderate UK hits with "Another Nail in My Heart" and "Pulling Mussells (from the Shell)." Both songs, plus "If I Didn't Love You," became hits on college radio and New Wave clubs in America, increasing the band's profile considerably; it was the first Squeeze album to chart in America, reaching No. 71. Jools Holland, whose fascination with boogie-woogie piano was beginning to sit uncomfortably with Difford and Tilbrook's increasingly sophisticated compositions, left the band in late 1980 to form the Millionaires; he was replaced by Paul Carrack, formerly of the pub-rock band Ace. Following *Argybargy*, critics in both the UK and US were calling Difford and Tillbrook "the new Lennon and McCartney," and in order to consolidate their growing reputation Squeeze made an attempt at their own *Sgt. Pepper* with 1981's *East Side Story*. Initially, the album was to be produced by Dave Edmunds, but the group scrapped those sessions to work with Elvis Costello and Roger Bechirian. Upon its summer release, *East Side Story* was hailed with excellent reviews, but it didn't become a huge hit as expected. Nevertheless, it found an audience, peaking at No. 19 in the UK and No. 44 on the US charts. The soulful, Carrack-sung "Tempted" failed to reach the UK Top 40, but it did become the group's first charting US single, reaching the Top 50. The country-tinged "Labelled with Love" became the group's third, and last, British Top 10 hit that fall. Carrack left at the end of 1981 to join Carlene Carter's backing band; he was replaced with Don Snow, a classically trained pianist who formerly played with the Sinceros.

Ever since the release of their debut, Squeeze had been touring and recording without break, and signs of weariness were evident on *Sweets from a Stranger*. Though it was the group's highest-charting US album, reaching No. 32 shortly after its spring release, *Sweets from a Stranger* was uneven. In the UK, it was a considerable disappointment, reaching No. 37, with its single "Black Coffee in Bed" stalling at No. 51. Nevertheless, the band had earned a considerable fan base, and were able to play Madison Square Garden that summer. Tired of touring and its frustrat-

ing commercial fortunes, Difford and Tilbrook decided to disband Squeeze late in 1982, releasing the compilation *Singles—45's and Under*, shortly after its announcement. Ironically, *Singles* peaked at No. 3 on the British charts; it would later go platinum in the US.

Though they had disbanded Squeeze, Difford and Tilbrook had no intention of ending their collaboration—they simply wanted to pursue other projects. In particular, they saw themselves as songwriters in the classic tradition of Tin Pan Alley or the Brill Building, and began writing for Helen Shapiro, Paul Young, Billy Bremmer, and Jools Holland. They also worked on *Labelled with Love*, a musical based on their songs, which played briefly in Deptford, England, early in 1983. The duo released an eponymous album in the summer of 1984, showcasing a sophisticated new sound, as well as long, flowing haircuts and coats. The record was a moderate success, but the duo already were thinking of re-forming Squeeze. Early in 1985, the band reunited to play a charity gig, which prompted Difford, Tilbrook, Holland, and Lavis (who had been driving a cab) to permanently re-form, adding bassist Keith Wilkinson. *Cosi Fan Tutti Frutti* was released in the fall of 1985 to positive reviews and moderately successful sales. During 1986, Andy Metcalfe, a member of Robyn Hitchcock's Egyptians, joined the band as a second keyboardist. *Babylon and On* followed in the fall of 1987, and the album became a surprise hit, reaching No. 14 in the UK and generating their biggest American hits—"Hourglass," which reached No. 15 on the strength of MTV's heavy rotation of the song's inventive video, and the Top 40 "853-5937." After completing an international tour, which featured another concert at Madison Square Garden and a headlining spot at the Reading Festival, Metcalfe left the band; he was not replaced.

Babylon and On may have been a hit, but Squeeze's renewed success wasn't long-lasting. The group's next album, *Frank*, was released in the fall of 1989 and it wasn't given much promotional push by A&M. Consequently, it flopped in both the US and the UK. During the supporting tour for *Frank*, A&M dropped Squeeze, leaving the band in the cold. Following the tour, Holland left the band to concentrate on his career as a recording artist, as well as a television host for the BBC. Squeeze released a live album, *A Round and a Bout*, on IRS in the spring of 1990. Early in 1991, the band signed with Reprise Records and began recording a new album, hiring Steve Nieve, Bruce Hornsby, and Matt Irving as session keyboardists. The resulting album, *Play*, was released in the fall of 1991 to little attention, partially because it received no support from the label. During the *Play* tour, the band hired Don Snow and Carol Isaacs as keyboardists. Over the course of 1992, Difford and Tilbrook began to play the occasional acoustic concert, as Squeeze revamped its touring lineup again, hiring Steve Nieve as their touring keyboardist. Longtime drummer Gilson Lavis left the band later that year to play in Jools Holland's Big Band; he was replaced by Pete Thomas who, like Nieve, was a member of the Attractions.

Squeeze resigned with A&M Records in early 1993 and recorded their new album, *Some Fantastic Place*, with Thomas on drums and Paul Carrack on keyboards. Released in the September of 1993, the album became a moderate British hit, debuting at No. 26; it was ignored in the US. During 1994, Thomas left the band to join the reunited Attractions; by the end of the year, the group had replaced him with Andy Newmark. Prior to the recording of 1995's *Ridiculous*, Kevin Wilkinson—no relation to bassist Keith Wilkinson—became the group's drummer. Released in the UK in the fall of 1995, *Ridiculous* became a moderate hit, generating the hits "This Summer" and "Electric Trains." The album was released in America in the spring of 1996 on IRS Records. Under the name John Savannah, Don Snow contributed keyboards on *Ridiculous* and the album's supporting tour.

During 1996, Squeeze released two compilations, the single-disc *Piccadilly Collection* in the US and the double-disc *Excess Moderation* in the UK. The compilations were their final releases for A&M Records. —*Stephen Thomas Erlewine*

U.K. Squeeze / Mar. 1978 / A&M ✦✦
The band's debut, credited (in the US) to UK Squeeze to avoid confusion with a similarly named band, is quite unlike anything that would follow and nearly seems like the work of another band. Much of the reason for this comes from producer John Cale's somewhat warped vision of the band. Cale threw out all of the songs the band came to the studio with and demanded that they write new ones on the spot (he also proposed calling the album *Gay Guys*, and undoubtedly had something to do with the hot pink bodybuilder cover and the shirtless photo of the band on the back). The rough and ragged songs that resulted from the studio writing range from raw, inspired rockers like "Sex Master," "Strong in Reason," and "Get Smart" to the utterly bizarre, near-funk instrumental "Wild Sewerage Tickles Brazil," which features wild shrieks throughout. The band-produced "Take Me I'm Yours" is a fondly remembered hit, but the album in general remains an oddity of the Squeeze catalog. —*Chris Woodstra*

Cool for Cats / Apr. 1979 / A&M ✦✦✦✦
After the false start of the debut, Squeeze recast themselves as a quintessentially British band, packing the songs with exaggerated accents and

British slang, and incorporating a nearly cinematic narrative style to make incisive observations on British working-class life with a sly, skewed wit and a sex-obsessed thematic undercurrent. Musically, the band often rocks harder than they did on the debut, this time adding synth-driven arrangements while retaining a working-class pub-rock sensibility. *Cool for Cats* stands as the band's first truly great album and boasts arguably their finest song-story in "Up the Junction," a timeless gem, as well as the unforgettable Difford-sung hit title track. —*Chris Woodstra*

☆ **Argybargy** / Mar. 1980 / A&M ✦✦✦✦✦
Where *Cool for Cats* marked a great leap over the debut, *ArgyBargy* improved at least that far over its own predecessor. Still a distinctly British band, Squeeze compensated with an incredibly catchy batch of songs that, despite the subject matter, spoke the universal language of bright, bouncy, instantly endearing pop. The acute observations of the British working class were even more vivid—none so poignant as the classic "Pulling Mussels (from the Shell)," which offers a series of detailed snapshots of the different walks of life on a seaside holiday, or the often-overlooked courting-to-breakup story-song "Vicky Verky," which nearly matched of "Up the Junction" brilliance. *ArgyBargy* is simply packed with perfect, timeless pop that stands not only as the band's crowning achievement, but also as a landmark recording of the era. —*Chris Woodstra*

East Side Story / May 1981 / A&M ✦✦✦✦
East Side Story was originally planned as a double album with each side produced by a different "hot" producer—Elvis Costello, Nick Lowe, Dave Edmunds, and Paul McCartney were the proposed lineup. And while only Elvis Costello (along with Roger Bechirian) ended up doing the job, save for one track by Edmunds, Costello's push for decidedly un-Squeeze-like material and sympathetic production style resulted in not only the band's most diverse but also their most creatively rewarding album to date. *East Side Story* is definitely packed with the band's trademark bouncy Brit-pop numbers like "In Quintessence," "Piccadilly," "Is That Love" and "Mumbo Jumbo," but the standouts come from the unexpected turns—the country lament of "Labeled with Love," the trippy near-psychedelia of "There's No Tomorrow," the lush and delicate "Woman Work" and "Vanity Fair," and the soulful groove of "Tempted" (the song the band is probably best known for, sung by newly added member Paul Carrack). —*Chris Woodstra*

★ **Singles 45's & Under** / 1982 / A&M ✦✦✦✦✦
Above all, Squeeze were a great singles act—among the finest of the era—and *Singles 45's and Under* offers proof of that fact, giving a chronological survey of their biggest hits from their early, pre-breakup period. Most of the songs can be found on the actual albums, aside from the slightly different single version of "Goodbye Girl" and the new "Annie Get Your Gun," but with a perfect collection like this, even those with the albums should purchase this one as well. —*Chris Woodstra*

Sweets from a Stranger / May 1982 / A&M ✦✦
Perhaps the accolades from *East Side Story* and the constant Lennon/McCartney comparisons went to their head, or maybe the strain of constant touring sapped a lot of their energy and better judgment. Whatever the case, *Sweets from a Stranger* suffers from self-conscious sophistication, overambition, and general lack of direction. And though the album is certainly flawed, an average Squeeze album is still pretty good, and when it hits—as in "I've Returned," "His House Her Home" and the favorite "Black Coffee in Bed"—it really hits. With previous albums, Difford and Tilbrook were able to make incisive observations on British life; the same holds true here, but the alcohol-soaked imagery and chaos between the lines of songs also reveals much about the internal problems of the band. Not surprisingly, the group disbanded shortly after the release. —*Chris Woodstra*

Cosi Fan Tutti Frutti / Aug. 1985 / A&M ✦✦✦
Cosi Fan Tutti Frutti marked not only a re-formation of the band but also a reunion with Jools Holland. And while history and a dated production style hasn't been particularly kind to the album, it is not without its merits. True, it is marred by much of the overblown ambition that undercut *Sweets from a Stranger* and the *Difford and Tilbrook* album, but several of the songs—especially the often overlooked "King George Street"—are real gems in the classic Squeeze tradition, and the move toward "sophistication" is more fully realized and effective. A flawed but certainly worthwhile album, *Cosi Fan Tutti Frutti* deserves reassessment. —*Chris Woodstra*

Babylon and on / Sep. 1987 / A&M ✦✦
Following a brief period of arty, self-conscious indulgence, Squeeze decided to return to the more straight ahead pop of their classic period. *Babylon and On* strips back a bit and, although the return is a welcomed one, much of the material misses the mark, and the move seems a little forced. Flaws aside, there are some moments of inspiration, and the near-novelty of "Hourglass," unfortunately not one of those moments, became the band's biggest Stateside hit. —*Chris Woodstra*

Frank / Sep. 1989 / A&M ✦✦
Though *Babylon and On* was hailed as a return to form, the unfairly overlooked follow-up, *Frank*, comes much closer to the sound of classic Squeeze. While irresistible songs like "If It's Love" and "She Doesn't Have to Shave" more than make up for the blandness of the previous album, much of the material unfortunately misses the mark. —*Chris Woodstra*

A Round & A Bout (Live) / May 1990 / IRS ✦✦
Recorded on 1990's *Frank* tour in England, this live album finds the band still having fun playing their nearly ten-year-old classics. A nice companion to their greatest hits. —*Chris Woodstra*

Play / Aug. 1991 / Reprise ✦✦✦
This unfortunately overlooked album finds the songwriting team of Difford and Tilbrook still in strong form through a 12-track song cycle. Now a four-piece band, there is less dependence on keyboards and a focus on more acoustic arrangements. A considerably more subdued mood but no less rewarding on repeated listening. —*Chris Woodstra*

Some Fantastic Place / Sep. 14, 1993 / A&M ✦✦✦
The band's tenth proper album reunites the core of Glen Tilbrook and Chris Difford with former member Paul Carrack and adds drummer Pete Thomas (Elvis Costello & the Attractions). Their classic sound is still there through the melodic power-pop of "Third Rail" to the blue-eyed soul of "Loving You Tonight" (nearly a rewrite of "Tempted"). Another in a series of commercial sleepers, but definately worth a listen. —*Chris Woodstra*

Ridiculous / Nov. 1995 / A&M ✦✦✦
After nearly 20 years of recording, it would be easy to write Squeeze off as spent creative force—certainly their most recent albums have seemed like somewhat forced attempts to recapture the glory days of *Cool for Cats, Argybargy*, and *East Side Story*. With *Ridiculous*, Difford and Tilbrook (the only original members left and still the band's primary songwriters) seem content to have passed the Brit-pop torch on, and, as a result, this effortless album is also one of their most enjoyable in recent years. *Ridiculous* isn't an embarrassing attempt to rewrite previous hits, but rather, a natural progression executed with a dignified maturity rather than resignation. "This Summer" and "Electric Trains," though not candidates for the top of the charts at this point, certainly rank among their finest singles. —*Chris Woodstra*

Piccadilly Collection / Aug. 20, 1996 / A&M ✦✦✦
It bills itself as a greatest hits compilation, but *Piccadilly Collection* doesn't quite fit that description. Granted, the 18-track disc features some of Squeeze's biggest hits —including "Tempted," "Black Coffee in Bed," "Pulling Mussels (from a Shell)," and "Hourglass"—but the majority of the album consists of songs that will be totally unfamiliar to casual fans. Aside from that handful of hits, *Piccadilly Collection* alternates between album tracks from latter-day Squeeze albums like *Frank* and *Some Fantastic Place*, and B-sides that have never before appeared on compact disc. Certainly, dedicated fans will be delighted to have the B-sides on CD, but they would have been better served by a full-fledged rarities collection. Similarly, casual fans would have been better served by a straight singles collection, or a more thorough retrospective—even though this features 18 tracks, it short-changes all of the group's early records, including such classic new wave albums as *Cool for Cats, Argybargy*, and *East Side Story*, in favor of the interminable medley "Squabs on Forty Fab." So, that leaves the question of, just who is *Piccadilly Collection* for? It's not for casual fans, it's not for diehards—it's just a wasted opportunity, despite the inclusion of many wonderful songs. —*Stephen Thomas Erlewine*

Excess Moderation / Nov. 1996 / A&M ✦✦✦✦
Excess Moderation one-ups its American counterpart, *The Piccadilly Collection*, by offering two discs worth of mainly rarities and B-sides along with the stray missed album track, complete with track-by-track comments from Chris Difford and Glenn Tillbrook. While, even in combination with *The Piccadilly Collection*, there are still many B-sides left unavailable on disc, this is certainly a welcome addition for any fan. —*Chris Woodstra*

Squire

f. 1977, Guildford, England, **db.** 1985
New Wave, Power Pop, Mod-Revival
Though they never received the recognition they deserved, Squire was one of the earliest and finest mod-revival bands of the late '70s. Like the founders of the revival, the Jam, Squire were able to transcend the limits of the genre with their high-quality blend of pop smarts and songcraft that drew equal parts from punk spirit and '60s sensibilities.

The band formed in Guildford, England, around 1977 as a covers band consisting of Enzo Esposito (vocals/bass), Steve Baker (guitar), and Ross Di'Landa (drums). In June 1978, songwriter/guitarist Anthony Meynell joined just prior to a high-profile gig opening for the Jam. The addition of Meynell changed the band's focus to producing original material, and by 1979 they had released their first single for ROK Records, "Get Ready to Go." While the single gained them some airplay, their biggest break came with the newly termed mod-revival movement and their appearance on the legendary *Mods Mayday* album that featured two new songs by the band. Ian Page of Secret Affair (one of Squire's mod peers) had just started his own I-Spy label and signed the band on the merits of their appearance on *Mods Mayday*. The signing led to some personnel changes. First, Di'Landa was replaced by Kevin Meynell, then Baker quit without replacement. In 1979, Squire released two wonderful singles for I-Spy: "Walking Down the Kings Road" and "The Face of Youth Today." Out of the two singles, only "Walking Down the Kings Road" charted. In 1980, Squire switched record labels, signing with another independent, Stage One Records. The band's first release on Stage One was "My Mind Goes Round in Circles," which, like its predecessors, barely made an impact on the charts. Frustrated by a lack of success, the band essentially dissolved when the last original member, Esposito, left.

Anthony Meynell decided to give it another try when he started his own label, Hi-Lo, in 1981. The first release was *Hits from 3000 Years Ago*, a collection of demos and leftovers from the original Squire lineup. He reactivated the band, adding Jon Bicknell on bass, and releasing a new single, "No Time for Tomorrow," in 1982. Though they were still virtually unknown in their homeland, America had begun picking up on *Hits from 3000 Years Ago*. Delayed by a short promotional tour in the States, their first proper album, *Get Smart*, was finally released late in 1983. They never made the breakthrough into the mainstream, but the album and its follow-up EP, *September Gurls* (the title track was a cover of the Big Star classic), in 1984 became cult classics in American power-pop circles. Squire began preparation for their next album, *Smash*, but decided to call it quits before its completion. —*Chris Woodstra*

Hits from 3000 Years Ago / 1981 / Hi-Lo ◆◆◆
After several years of wallowing in obscurity, Squire leader Anthony Meynell started his own label, Hi-Lo, with hopes of taking matters into his own hands. With *Hits from 3000 Years Ago* he emptied the Squire vaults, releasing the remainder of the band's recordings—mainly demos. England ignored it but American power-pop fans stumbled on to it and as word spread, it sold respectably—and deservedly so, the music here is pure pop, hook-filled, melodic and instantly endearing. —*Chris Woodstra*

● **Big Smashes** / 1992 / Tangerine ◆◆◆◆
Big Smashes is a 24-track Best Of that compiles the band's mod-revival singles from the '70s and the more power-pop-oriented material from their Hi-Lo albums. As an introduction to this unfairly overlooked band, there is no better place to begin. These are truly lost classics that deserve discovery. —*Chris Woodstra*

Get Ready to Go! / 1995 / Tangerine ◆◆◆
A nice companion to the *Big Smashes* collection, *Get Ready to Go!*, focuses on the early work of the original lineup from their mod days. This release supplants *Hits from 3000 Years Ago* by picking the highlights (most of the album) and combining their first single, the brilliant "Get Ready Go," with B-sides, previously unreleased material, a track from the *Odd Bods, Mods and Sods* compilation, and a track from a fan club release. —*Chris Woodstra*

SRC

f. , Detroit, MI
Hard Rock, Psychedelic, Acid Rock
Along with the Stooges, MC5, and the Amboy Dukes, SRC were local heroes of the Michigan rock scene in the late '60s and early '70s, although in terms of national success they were relegated to the second division populated by such bands as the Frost and the Rationals. Led by the Quackenbush brothers Gary and Glenn, the Ann Arbor group evolved out of the Fugitives, adding lead singer Scott Richardson from fellow garage band the Chosen Few. SRC recorded three erratic albums for Capitol that blended Motor City crunch with sustain-laden psychedelic guitar, pompous bursts of organ, spacy lyrics, and unexpectedly wispy, vulnerable vocals, throwing in some pretty ballads and harmonies to temper the hard rock excess. —*Richie Unterberger*

Milestones / 1969 / One Way ◆◆◆
Their second album, although rather erratic, proved to be SRC's most popular. Containing their version of Grieg's "In the Hall of the Mountain King" and Ravel's "Bolero," it's easy to see why they were such a draw in the psychedelic ballrooms across the Midwest in the late '60s. —*James Chrispell*

Traveller's Tale / 1970 / Capitol ◆◆◆
SRC's final album was recorded after the departure of guitarists Gary Quackenbush and Steve Lyman, Ray Goodman assuming all the guitar chores. Despite the shakeup, the sound hardly changed at all, perhaps becoming a bit more progressive-minded. The organ-guitar duels and alternation of concise hard rock with lengthy progressive passages also

remained intact. If this album came out today, you'd swear it was a satire of the progressive rock era, some of it is so prototypical. But these guys were serious about what they did, and impressive in their own way. The CD reissue includes a non-LP B-side from the same era, "My Fortune's Coming True." —*Richie Unterberger*

● **The Revenge of the Quackenbush Brothers** / 1987 / Bam Caruso ◆◆◆◆
Good selection of key cuts from all three albums; "Daystar," "Marionette," and "Black Sheep" are first-rate hard psychedelia. One Way has reissued all of the original albums, as well as some unissued material, but this is the best and most judicious selection. Comes with detailed group history. —*Richie Unterberger*

Chris Stamey

b. Dec. 6, 1954, Chapel Hill, NC
Bass, Guitar, Vocals / Power Pop, Experimental, Jangle-Pop
Chris Stamey might not be a household name, but among the cult of melodic guitar pop-rock fans, he's a major player. Stamey played with seminal the North Carolina '70s pop band the Sneakers and was a founding member of the dB's. After the dB's fell apart, Chris Stamey recorded an album with his fellow dB Peter Holsapple; after that album, Stamey released his first solo record. —*Rick Clark*

Instant Excitement / 1984 / Coyote ◆◆◆

It's Alright / 1987 / A&M ◆◆◆◆
With the help of Alex Chilton, Richard Lloyd, Mitch Easter, Marshall Crenshaw, and others, Stamey presented a cohesive body of fine pop-rock songs, most notably "Cara Lee," "Incredible Happiness," "27 Years in a Single Day," and "The Seduction." —*Rick Clark*

● **Fireworks** / Oct. 22, 1991 / Rhino/RNA ◆◆◆◆
Fireworks, the album that A&M allegedly rejected, surfaced on Rhino's new artist imprint RNA. While it is arguably his best solo album, the overly reverberant production and thin sounds steal the thunder from this album. Another problem comes in the lyric department. Stamey's earnest lyrics are often too airy, while failing to communicate any real enhancing art. Nevertheless, Stamey delivers some beautiful melodies and songs like "The Company of Light," "Something Came over Me," "Glorious Delusion," and "On the Radio (For Ray Davies)" are wonderful listens. —*Rick Clark*

Wonderful Life / Nov. 27, 1992 / East Side Digital ◆◆◆
This playful disc includes Stamey's 1982 solo effort, *It's a Wonderful Life* and 1984's *Instant Excitement*. Stamey experiments with percussion triggering other types of instrumental sounds—something he calls the Groovegate System. All in all this disc feels like an idea scrapbook more than a polished release. —*Rick Clark*

Robust Beauty / Apr. 4, 1995 / East Side Digital ◆◆
Be warned: this is not the typical, power-pop release from Chris Stamey. For *Improper Linear Models in Decision Making* Stamey teams up with Kirk Ross for his most experimental outing to date—essentially free improvisation combined with more complex compositions for guitar. As a theoretical exercise, this may be interesting to some, but Stamey fans will most likely be confused and put off by this deviation. —*Chris Woodstra*

The Standells

f. 1962, Los Angeles, CA, **db.** 1972
Garage Rock, Pop-Rock
The Standells made No. 11 in 1966 with "Dirty Water," an archetypal garage rock hit with its Stonesish riff, lecherous vocal, and combination of raunchy guitar and organ. While they never again reached the Top Forty, they cut a number of strong, similar tunes in the 1966-67 era that have belated been recognized as '60s punk classics. "Garage rock" may not have been a really accurate term for them in the first place, as the production on their best material was full and polished, with some imaginative touches of period psychedelia and pop.

The Los Angeles band were actually hardly typical of the young suburban outfits across America who took their raw garage sound onto obscure singles recorded in small studios. They'd been playing L.A. clubs since the early '60s, with a repertoire that mostly consisted of covers of pre-Beatle rock hits. Drummer (and eventual lead singer) Dick Dodd had been a Mouseketeer on television, organist Larry Tamblyn was the brother of noted film actor Russ Tamblyn, and Tony Valentino was a recent immigrant from Italy. Gary Leeds (later to join the Walker Brothers) was an early member (though he was replaced by Dodd).

The Standells' pre-"Dirty Water" history is a little vague and confusing; they recorded some ordinary albums and singles for Liberty, MGM, and Vee Jay, appeared in the movie *Get Yourself a College Girl*, and did a lot of television work (most notably a well-remembered guest appearance on *The Munsters*, where they did a woeful version of "I Want to Hold Your Hand"). There were flashes of gritty inspiration on early cuts like "Big Boss Man" and "Someday You'll Cry," but the group didn't really hit their stride until teaming up with producer Ed Cobb, formerly of the clean-cut vocal group the Four Preps. It was Cobb who wrote "Dirty Water," which marked quite a change of direction from their previous clean-cut image. In fact, the group didn't even like the song, which took about six months to break into a hit.

Their image now considerably toughened, the group churned out four albums in 1966 and 1967, as well as appearing in (and contributing the theme song to) the psychedelic exploitation movie *Riot on Sunset Strip*. Cobb, in addition to writing "Dirty Water," also penned their other most enduring singles, including "Sometimes Good Guys Don't Wear White," "Why Pick on Me," and "Try It" (the last of which was widely banned for its suggestive delivery). The group did write some decent material of their own, such as the tense "Riot on Sunset Strip," and the psychedelic "All Fall Down," which bears an interesting similarity to some of Pink Floyd's early work. Their albums were quite inconsistent—in fact, one of them, consisting of covers of big mid-'60s hits, was altogether dispensable—which makes it advisable for all but the truly committed to look for greatest hits compilations that selectively weed out the best stuff.

The Standells never had a stable lineup; bass players were constantly leaving (John Fleck, aka John Fleckenstein, who was briefly in an early version of Love, held the spot for a while), and Dick Dodd went solo in 1968, the year they released their last single. Tower, as was the case with most of its artists, didn't apply intelligent long-range planning to the band's career, issuing too many albums at once. The group didn't help their own cause by issuing an awful vaudeville-rock single, "Don't Tell Me What to Do," under the transparent pseudonym of the Sllednats. They didn't record after 1968, though the group dragged on in one form or another until the early '70s (Lowell George was even a member briefly). —*Richie Unterberger*

Dirty Water / 1966 / Sundazed ✦✦✦
Along with *Why Pick on Me*, this was the group's strongest album, although you're always better off with a greatest hits collection. "There Is a Storm Comin'" and "Pride and Devotion" are a couple of strong numbers that don't make it onto compilations, and "Rari," the moody B-side of "Dirty Water," is one of their best little-known tracks. The CD reissue takes off one cut (the easily found "Sometimes Good Guys Don't Wear White") and adds six bonus tracks of only mild interest, including a version of "Batman." Add points for finding a longer version of "Rari," though. —*Richie Unterberger*

Why Pick on Me / 1966 / Sundazed ✦✦✦
This pop-punk relic isn't bad, but as the best of these songs—"Why Pick on Me," "Sometimes Good Guys Don't Wear White," "Mainline"—have been issued on whatever best-of Standells compilation you might pick up, its appeal is really limited to big fans. Of the more obscure tracks, "Black Hearted Woman" is a decent slow, menacing number, "Mr. Nobody" a decent punky cut, and "The Girl and the Moon" one of their best pop-oriented compositions. This CD reissue adds five tracks that were previously unissued in the US, which are okay but nothing too special. —*Richie Unterberger*

Hot Ones / 1966 / Sundazed ✦✦
Having the Standells do an album of 1966 Top 40 covers—in 1966—was a boneheaded idea to begin with, and hardly worthy of revisitation. This CD reissue eliminates a couple of the ten songs (which are available on other Standells reissues on Sundazed), and adds seven rare tracks of mild interest, most of which were previously unissued, or previously unavailable in the US. These include the early 1965 cut "You Were the One," a vaguely Beatleish number; a couple of outtakes from their 1966 *Try It* album, including a reasonably nifty 11-minute instrumental jam, their unreleased version of "Misty Lane," which was done better by the Chocolate Watch Band; a rendition of the Graham Gouldman song "School Girl,"; and the awful, vaudevillian-flavored single they issued under the name the Sllednats. —*Richie Unterberger*

Try It / 1967 / Sundazed ✦✦
The Standells' final studio album is a mixed effort, despite the outstanding title track. The early Pink Floyd-like "All Fall Down," "Barracuda," and especially "Riot on Sunset Strip" are top-notch pop-punk, but the record is weighed down by some ill-chosen soul covers and some weak pop material. The CD reissue adds five rare but unremarkable bonus tracks, including outtakes and a non-LP single. —*Richie Unterberger*

Anthology of Legendary Recordings, Vol. 1 / 1981 / AVI ✦✦✦✦
There have been various best-of compilations since this vinyl-only one came out in the early '80s, the one on Rhino being the easiest to acquire. There's nothing particularly wrong with this one, though; the 16 tracks include all of the big hits, and some good LP tracks like "All Fall Down" and "Trip to Paradise," as well as good liner notes. —*Richie Unterberger*

● **The Best of the Standells** / 1984 / Rhino ✦✦✦✦
Most '60s punk bands could barely fill an album side with decent material. This 18-song compilation is a tribute to the vitality of the Standells' raunch-and-roll attack, including not only their one hit ("Dirty Water")

but salacious essentials ranging from the swaggering "Sometimes Good Guys Don't Wear White" to the horny wail of "Barracuda." —*John Floyd*

The Staple Singers

f. 1951, Chicago, IL
Soul, Gospel, Country-Soul
The Staples story goes all the way back to Winona, MS, in 1915. It was then and there that patriarch Roebuck Staples entered the world. A contemporary and familiar of Charley Patton, Roebuck quickly became adept as a solo blues guitarist, entertaining at local dances and picnics. Gradually drawn to the church, by 1937 he was singing and playing guitar with a spiritual group based out of Drew, MS., the Golden Trumpets. Moving to Chicago four years later, he continued playing gospel music with the Windy City's Trumpet Jubilees. A decade later Pops Staples (as he had become known) presented two of his daughters, Cleotha and Mavis, and his one son, Pervis, in front of a church audience, and the Staple Singers were born.

The Staples recorded in an older, slightly archaic, deeply Southern spiritual style first for United and then for Vee-Jay. Pops and Mavis Staples shared lead vocal chores, with most records underpinned by Pops' heavily reverbed Mississippi cottonpatch guitar. In 1960 the Staples signed with Riverside, a label that specialized in jazz and folk. With Riverside and later Epic, the Staples attempted to move into the then-burgeoning White folk boom. Two Epic releases, "Why (Am I Treated So Bad)" and a cover of Stephen Stills' "For What It's Worth," briefly graced the pop charts in 1967.

In 1968 the Staples signed with Memphis-based Stax. The first two albums, *Soul Folk in Action* and *We'll Get Over*, were produced by Steve Cropper and backed by Booker T and the MG's. The Staples were now singing entirely contemporary "message" songs such as "Long Walk to D.C." and "When Will We Be Paid." In 1970 Pervis Staples left, and was replaced by sister Yvonne Staples. Even more significantly, Al Bell took over production chores. Bell took them down the road to Muscle Shoals, and things got decidedly funky.

Starting with "Heavy Makes You Happy (Sha-Na-Boom Boom)" and "I'll Take You There," the Staples counted 12 chart hits at Stax. When Stax encountered financial problems, Curtis Mayfield signed the Staples to his Curtom label and produced a No. 1 hit in "Let's Do It Again." The Staples went on to continued chart success, albeit less spectacularly, with Warner, through 1979. One more album followed on 20th Century-Fox in 1981. After a three-year hiatus, they signed a two-album deal with Private I and hit the R&B charts five more times, once with an unlikely cover of Talking Heads' "Slippery People."

The Staple Singers found a new audience in 1994 when they teamed with Marty Stuart to perform "The Weight" on the *Rhythm, Country and Blues* LP for MCA. —*Rob Bowman*

Uncloudy Day/Will The Circle Be Unbroken / 1955-1960 / Vee-Jay ✦✦✦✦
The Staple Singers brilliantly fused gospel, folk, blues, and soul into a cohesive, commercially potent sound in the '50s and '60s. They perfected this approach during their tenure at Vee-Jay, the first label that allowed the twangy, expert guitar licks of Roebuck "Pop" Staples to be heard in the group's mix and fully presented their harmonies. This single disc contains two pivotal Staples albums; *Uncloudy Day* includes such gospel favorites as "I Know I Got Religion" and "Let Me Ride," while *Will the Circle Be Unbroken* offers the splendid title track, plus masterpieces like "Pray On" and "Come Up in Glory." —*Ron Wynn*

Great Day / 1963 / Milestone ✦✦✦
This two-album Fantasy reissue is an anthology of the material the Staples recorded for Riverside between 1960 and 1963. For Riverside, the Staples recorded mostly gospel but the shouting was toned down a bit. A few modern-day "message" songs make their way into their repertoire as well, including Bob Dylan's "Masters of War." Not quite as cataclysmic as their Vee-Jay material but still essential. —*Rob Bowman*

Make You Happy / 1964 / Epic ✦✦✦
From Riverside, the Staples moved on to Columbia subsidiary Epic in 1964. With Epic, they delved further into the secular realm, hitting the pop charts twice with Pops Staples' plaintive "Why (Am I Treated So Bad)?" and a cover of Stephen Stills' "For What It's Worth." Both are included on this two-disc anthology, as is a stunning side of live performance. Great stuff. —*Rob Bowman*

Freedom Highway / 1965 / CBS ✦✦✦
A reissue of their first great Riverside collection, with "Daddy" Roebuck and the legendary Mavis Staples as leads. The Staples once again mix a positive political message with a dash of religion. —*Kip Lornell*

Soul Folk in Action / 1968 / Stax ✦✦✦
The Staples' debut Stax release included covers of Otis Redding's "(Sittin' on) the Dock of the Bay" and the Band's "The Weight." Steve Cropper produced and the Stax songwriting staff concocted a number of socially

conscious lyrics, the most notable being "Long Walk to D.C." —*Rob Bowman*

Pray on / 1968 / Hob ✦✦✦✦
The Staple Singers recorded ten 78s over a four-year period for Chicago's Vee-Jay. These have been reissued countless times in various forms. The Charly CD is simply the most recent. For Vee-Jay the Staples recorded a number of Pops Staples originals as well as radical rearrangements of standards. Pops Staples and Mavis Staples shared the lead singing chores, with Pervis and Cleotha Staples moaning in the background. Superb gospel shouting. —*Rob Bowman*

We'll Get Over / 1970 / Stax ✦✦✦
Their second Stax release was similar to *Soul Folk in Action.* The album's highlight is Randall Stewart's "When Will We Be Paid?" —*Rob Bowman*

The Staple Swingers / 1971 / Stax ✦✦✦
The Staples' first album produced by Al Bell and recorded in Muscle Shoals hit the winning formula. Other changes saw Pervis Staples departing just before the album was recorded and being replaced by sister Yvonne Staples. Everything was in place for the Staples' golden years. Three songs, "Heavy Makes You Happy," "Love Is Plentiful," and "You've Got to Earn It," all charted. —*Rob Bowman*

Be Altitude: Respect Yourself / 1972 / Stax ✦✦✦
The Staples' finest single album, containing three Top Ten R&B hits, "Respect Yourself," "I'll Take You There," and "This World." The first two also were pop Top 20s, "I'll Take You There" going all the way to No.1. —*Rob Bowman*

Be What You Are / 1973 / Stax ✦✦✦
Continuing in the same vein, *Be What You Are* contained three chart hits, the title song, "If You're Ready (Come Go with Me)," and "Touch a Hand, Make a Friend." The Stax songwriters, combined with Mavis Staples' unbelievably seductive vocals, were on a roll. —*Rob Bowman*

City in the Sky / 1974 / Stax ✦✦✦
Stax was teetering on its last legs, but the label still managed to squeeze two final chart hits out of the Staple Singers in the title cut and "My Main Man." A cut below the previous three albums. —*Rob Bowman*

Best of the Staple Singers [Stax] / 1975 / Buddah ✦✦✦
Exactly what the title implies—seven monster soul hits plus three judiciously chosen album cuts. One chart hit, "Oh La De Dah," makes its only album appearance here. This disc is nearly too rich for one sitting. Early-'70s soul simply does not get better. —*Rob Bowman*

Let's Do It Again / 1975 / Curtom ✦✦✦
As Stax neared bankruptcy, the Staples signed with Curtis Mayfield's Curtom label for this soundtrack album. The title track was a No.1 hit and "New Orleans" reached No.70, returning the Staples to the upper echelons of the charts for the last time. —*Rob Bowman*

● **Chronicle** / 1979 / Stax ✦✦✦✦

★ **Best Of** / Oct. 17, 1990 / Stax ✦✦✦✦✦

Edwin Starr

b. Jan. 21, 1942, Nashville, TN
Vocals / Soul, Motown
One of the best soul-shouters to come from the Motown stable, Starr's style was closer to James Brown than to any of the other male Motown artists. Best known for his 1970 hit "War," he made a brief comeback during the disco craze, but he now tours Europe and plays the oldies circuit. Detroit vocalist Edwin Starr returned to the vocal wars in 1984 when he recorded a tribute album to Marvin Gaye for England's Streetwave label. He had relocated to Britain and moved to Warwickshire. Starr signed with Hippodrome and issued a pair of singles on that label in 1985 and 1986. He then recorded briefly for Virgin, being produced by the Stock/Aitken/Waterman trio, and then recorded for Motorcity in England and WEA in Germany. Starr also had some songs featured on the Walt Disney release *Mousersize.* —*Rick A. Bueche*

Soulmaster / 1968 / Motown ✦✦✦✦
Edwin Starr was never able to hit a groove while at Motown. He made some good and a few great tracks, but just couldn't get the steady stream of great material and hit records that made many others at Motown household names. This was arguably his best album; it included both Gordy and Ric Tic singles like "Agent Double-O-Soul." It shows that at times Starr could be as riveting and exciting as any male singer on the soul circuit; he was simply unable to consistently maintain that level. —*Ron Wynn*

War & Peace / 1970 / Motown ✦✦✦✦
Edwin Starr went from run-of-the-mill second-level act to hitmaker with this 1970 album, without question his finest. Norman Whitfield gave Starr the chance to cut a song that had been intended for The Temptations. They later did a version of "War," but Starr completely vaporized their rendition to the extent that most people today think he wrote it.

Starr was now a celebrity and briefly in Motown's top echelon. The fact that everything else on the album is only fair to average didn't even matter in the scope of things. —*Ron Wynn*

Hell up in Harlem / 1970 / Motown ✦✦✦
Edwin Starr got both creative control and topical material on this soundtrack, turning in strong, confident vocals on this soundtrack. Starr was so thrilled at getting room to express himself and call the shots that he soon bolted Motown and signed with 20th Century. Like many 1970s "blaxploitation" flicks, Starr's songs and music were superior to the film. —*Ron Wynn*

Involved / 1971 / Motown ✦✦✦
Although he didn't repeat the enormous successes of 1970, Starr continued to make his presence felt on the soul trail. But the album lacked any strong lead single, and almost dissipated the momentum Starr had built with his previous smash hits. —*Ron Wynn*

Edwin Starr / 1977 / GTO ✦✦
Edwin Starr marked time with this late-'70s release. He hadn't become acclimated to disco, and wasn't really getting first-rate soul and R&B songs either, so he tried to slip between the cracks and revamp himself into a modified supper-club and light soul vocalist. It wasn't fully successful, but wasn't a travesty either. He landed a low chart single, and the album had a few good ballads. It's now history, but at the time it kept Starr afloat in a tenuous era for soul and R&B vocalists. —*Ron Wynn*

Clean / 1978 / 20th Century ✦✦✦
In the late '70s, Edwin Starr was adjusting to the disco era, like many other soul and R&B vocalists. He hadn't gotten fully comfortable with bustling dance tracks, but this album helped ease the transition. It laid the groundwork for Starr's next LP, in which he returned to prominence and found a way to accomodate the demands of the dance floor without sacrificing his own integrity. —*Ron Wynn*

● **Motown Superstar Series, Vol. 3** / 1980 / Motown ✦✦✦✦
Not every vocalist enjoyed consistent success on Motown. Edwin Starr, despite having a bombastic style and striking voice, only enjoyed a few hits during his Motown tenure. But they were definitive ones, notably "25 Miles" and the landmark "War." Although the Temptations also cut the single, Starr's shattering, angular version was unforgettable. Those and other lesser-known Starr tracks are included on this anthology. It's an interesting release showing that sometimes Starr didn't get first-rate material, and at other times, his own performances weren't that grabbing. —*Ron Wynn*

The Best of Edwin Starr / 1981 / 20th Century ✦✦✦
Starr's best Motown singles were jubilant, energetic, and emancipating in their power and vocal brilliance. He didn't make enough to justify a greatest hits collection or anthology, but if you don't have the singles and want to get them, as well as some decent follow-up singles and album cuts, this will be worth the purchase. —*Ron Wynn*

25 Miles/War and Peace / Motown ✦✦✦✦
Edwin Starr was never a great album artist, but he could sure pack a punch on the right single. Both of these albums are loaded with filler, but their title cuts are triumphant. Starr managed to obliterate the Temptations' version of "War," his greatest single ever. He was almost that good on "25 Miles," helped by a great arrangement darting in and out at the perfect times, allowing his booming voice to re-enter and punch the lyrics home. Those songs make this a good two-in-one CD, especially if you're a Starr fan. —*Ron Wynn*

Ringo Starr (Richard Starkey)

b. Jul. 7, 1940, Dingle, Liverpool, England
Drums, Vocals / Pop-Rock
Ringo Starr, born Richard Starkey, was the drummer in the Beatles from 1962 to 1970 and thus one of the most famous musicians of the '60s. Though the least-prominent member of the quartet, he distinguished himself as an occasional singer of good-natured material and as an actor. Upon the group's split, Starr went solo with two novelty projects: the first, an album called *Sentimental Journey,* found him covering pre-rock standards, and the second, *Beaucoups of Blues,* was a country music collection.

Starr then scored Top Ten hits with two non-album singles, "It Don't Come Easy" in 1971 and "Back off Boogaloo" in 1972. In 1973 he paired with producer Richard Perry and, with assistance from the three other ex-Beatles, made *Ringo,* which featured two No. 1 hits, "Photograph" and "You're Sixteen." "Oh My My," a Top Ten hit, was also included. Almost as successful was the 1974 follow-up, *Goodnight Vienna,* which featured the hits "Only You" and "No No Song."

Starr continued to release albums through 1981, though with diminishing success. His 1983 album *Old Wave* did not find a US distributor. Starr was also suffering from the excesses of his lifestyle, but by the late '80s he had cleaned up, and in 1989 he toured with his "All-Starr Band." In 1992, he signed to Private Music and released a new studio album, *Time Takes Time.* —*William Ruhlmann*

Sentimental Journey / Mar. 27, 1970 / Capitol ✦✦✦
Ringo actually started recording his first solo album in late 1969, before the Beatles had officially split. Partially to please his parents, he set out to record an album not of rock 'n' roll, but of standards from the 1930s and 1940s, with help from a bellyful of top arrangers (Richard Perry, Chico O'Farrill, Maurice Gibb, Klaus Voorman, George Martin, Quincy Jones, Elmer Bernstein, Oliver Nelson, and Paul McCartney). Savaged by some critics, it's really not all that bad. But it ain't rock 'n' roll, it's not what Ringo does best, and it's not an essential part of anyone's collection, Beatle fan or otherwise, though it rose into the UK Top Ten and US Top 30 when it was released, largely on the strength of Starr's then-fresh association with the Beatles. Reissued on CD in 1995. —*Richie Unterberger*

Beaucoups of Blues / Sep. 28, 1970 / Capitol ✦✦✦✦
Ringo Starr had a demonstrated affinity for country music, as heard on such Beatles recordings as "Act Naturally," and he sounded as modestly comfortable on this Nashville-recorded session as in any other musical context. The cream of the city's session players backed up the former Beatle on a set of newly written songs, and the result was a typical country effort, pleasant as long as you didn't expect too much. Of course, this was the second straight genre exercise for Starr, following his pop standards album *Sentimental Journey*, and now he had tackled two styles that depend on vocal stylists for much of their appeal. On both, Ringo was Ringo. But with the Beatles fading into history, his suddenly frontburner solo career was starting to look like a series of dabblings rather than a coherent follow-up to the group's success. What could be next, an album of Motown songs? Wisely, he returned to Beatles-style pop-rock in subsequent releases. (*Beaucoups of Blues* was reissued on August 1, 1995, by Capitol with two bonus tracks, "Coochy Coochy," which had been released as the B-side of the single "Beaucoups of Blues," and the six-and-a-half-minute impromptu instrumental "Nashville Jam," which was previously unreleased.) —*William Ruhlmann*

● **Ringo** / Nov. 2, 1973 / Capitol ✦✦✦✦
With *Ringo*, Ringo Starr finally put his solo career in gear in 1973, after serving notice with back-to-back Top Ten singles in 1971 and 1972 that he had more to offer than his eccentric first two solo albums. *Ringo* was a big-budget pop album produced by Richard Perry and featuring Ringo's former Beatles bandmates as songwriters, singers, and instrumentalists. On no single track did all four appear, though George Harrison played the guitars on the John Lennon-penned lead off track, "I'm the Greatest," with Lennon playing piano and singing harmony. But it wasn't only the guests who made *Ringo* a success: Ringo advanced his own cause by co-writing two of the album's Top Ten singles, the No. 1 "Photograph" and "Oh My My." The album's biggest hit was a second chart-topper, Ringo's cover of the old Johnny Burnette hit "You're Sixteen." Songs like "Have You Seen My Baby," a Randy Newman song with guitar by Marc Bolan, and Ringo and Vini Poncia's "Devil Woman" were just as good as the hits. Ringo's best and most consistent new studio album, *Ringo* represented both the drummer/singer's most dramatic comeback and his commercial peak. The original ten-track 1973 album (Apple 3413) got even better in 1991 as a 13-track CD reissue (Capitol 95637), the bonus tracks including the 1971 gold single "It Don't Come Easy" and its B-side, "Early 1970," a telling depiction of Ringo's perspective on the Beatles breakup. —*William Ruhlmann*

Goodnight Vienna / Nov. 18, 1974 / Capitol ✦✦✦
Goodnight Vienna was very much a follow-up to *Ringo*, on which Ringo Starr called upon his bevy of musical buddies, most prominent among them John Lennon, who again wrote the lead off track, "(It's All Da-Da-Down to) Goodnight Vienna," and played on three songs, and also including Elton John, who wrote and played on "Snookeroo," Dr. John, Billy Preston, Robbie Robertson, and Harry Nilsson. Richard Perry again produced, bringing his strong pop sensibility to the diverse material. The only real fall-off was in the songwriting—the album's Top Ten hits were "No Only You," the old Platters song, and Hoyt Axton's novelty number "No No Song," which winked at intoxicants, but little else on the set stood out. *Goodnight Vienna* was another enjoyable Ringo record, but it lacked the star power and consistency of its predecessor. Still, compared to the rest of his '70s albums, it was a masterpiece. —*William Ruhlmann*

● **Blast from Your Past** / Nov. 20, 1975 / Capitol ✦✦✦✦
Capitol Records marked Ringo Starr's impending departure from the label with this ten-song compilation drawn from three of his solo albums, along with the previously non-LP hits "It Don't Come Easy" and "Back off Boogaloo" and the B-side "Early 1970." As it happened, the set was perfectly timed, since Ringo never threatened the Top Ten again and he was caught here at his 1971-1975 commercial peak, with all seven of his Top Ten hits accounted for, including the gold-selling chart-toppers "Photograph" and "You're Sixteen." —*William Ruhlmann*

Ringo's Rotogravure / Sep. 27, 1976 / Atlantic ✦✦✦
The formula that had worked for *Ringo* and *Good Night Vienna* was followed again on Ringo Starr's Atlantic Records debut. Arif Mardin

replaced Richard Perry in the producer's chair, but he hewed to the bouncy, eclectic pop style Perry had pioneered for *Ringo*, and the drummer called in such name help as Peter Frampton, Dr. John, Melissa Manchester, the Brecker brothers, Paul McCartney, John Lennon, and Eric Clapton. The last three all contributed songs, too, as did George Harrison. As usual, there was an oldie, Bruce Channel's "Hey Baby," which came out as a single, as did the lead off track, "A Dose of Rock 'N' Roll." The latter was the only Top 40 hit, as the times seemed to be passing Ringo's happy-go-lucky style by. Or maybe it was just time for a new formula. —*William Ruhlmann*

Ringo the 4th / Sep. 26, 1977 / Atlantic ✦✦
On his previous three albums, Ringo Starr had depended on superstar friends, a few oldies, and a light hearted attitude to get him through. The commercial disappointment of *Rotogravure* seemed to dictate a change of approach, and *Ringo the 4th* attempted to be a slick '70s soul-pop effort with hints of disco. Ringo was accompanied by New York studio pros, and he wrote most of the songs with Vini Poncia. The result marked the difference between disappointment and disaster, as the record flopped commercially and Atlantic bounced him. —*William Ruhlmann*

Bad Boy / Apr. 21, 1978 / Portrait ✦✦
Leaving Atlantic Records after the sales disaster of *Ringo the 4th*, Ringo Starr signed to CBS's Portrait label and returned to the record racks after only seven months with *Bad Boy*. Working again with Vini Poncia and with a largely pseudonymous band (lead guitar by "Push-alone," bass by "Diesel"), Ringo turned out a competent effort with a few interesting song choices, notably the old Benny Spellman song "Lipstick Traces (on a Cigarette)" (bet it was a favorite back in Liverpool) and Gallagher & Lyle's "Heart on My Sleeve," and some that were beyond him, such as the Supremes' "Where Did Our Love Go." But Ringo needed more than competence to reverse his career decline, and *Bad Boy* sold only to the same hardcore of Beatle collectors who had pushed *Ringo the 4th* into the lower reaches of the charts for half a dozen weeks. —*William Ruhlmann*

Stop & Smell the Roses / Oct. 27, 1981 / The Right Stuff/Capitol ✦✦✦
The idea, back in 1980, was to resurrect Ringo Starr's recording career by the same method that it had been launched with the *Ringo* album in 1973—by having his fellow Beatles and other well-known friends help out. John Lennon was working on a song called "Nobody Told Me," and George Harrison had one ready to go. Then Lennon was murdered in December. His Ringo song languished (his own version would be released in 1984), while Harrison took his tune back and rewrote the lyrics for what became his own hit, "All Those Years Ago." Then Ringo's label, Portrait, lacked enthusiasm for the album and he moved on to Boardwalk. Finally released as Boardwalk 33246, *Stop and Smell the Roses* was Ringo's strongest and most effervescent album since *Goodnight Vienna*, containing two good songs by Paul McCartney and one by George Harrison—"Wrack My Brain," which became Ringo's final Top 40 hit—along with music by Harry Nilsson, Ron Wood, and Stephen Stills. Long out of print, *Stop and Smell the Roses* reappeared on Capitol's the Right Stuff reissue label on September 6, 1994, with six bonus tracks, reflecting the changes made in the album from its original, unreleased version, that increased the album's length by nearly 70 percent and demonstrated that the later song selection was better. —*William Ruhlmann*

Old Wave / Jun. 8, 1983 / Right Stuff/Capitol ✦✦
Produced by Joe Walsh, *Old Wave* was a well-put-together collection of good pop-rock songs that was all wrong for Ringo Starr. The songs required interpretive abilities simply not found in a singer of Ringo's pleasant but limited voice and phrasing. "She's About a Mover" and "I Keep Forgettin'" were appropriate covers, but Ringo was out of his depth on reflective songs like "Picture Show Life" and "As Far As We Can Go." There was also a throwaway instrument, "Everybody's in a Hurry but Me," featuring Eric Clapton and John Entwistle. Neil Bogart, the head of Boardwalk, Ringo's record label, died during the making of this album, and the closest it got to an American release was on RCA Canada, which was just as well. (Originally released in Canada on June 8, 1983, as RCA 3233, as well as in Japan, South America, and Germany, *Old Wave* was finally released in the US by the Right Stuff/Capitol on September 6, 1994, with one extra bonus track, an orchestral version of "As Far As We Can Go.") —*William Ruhlmann*

Starr Struck: Best of, Vol. 2 / 1989 / Rhino ✦✦✦
A follow-up compilation to *Blast from Your Past*, *Starr Struck* gathered together the better tracks from Ringo Starr's less successful albums originally released between 1976 and 1983. "A Dose of Rock 'N' Roll" and "Wrack My Brain" were Top 40 singles, and the album contained specially written songs by Ringo's Beatle colleagues. The album also marked the first US release for four songs from Ringo's 1983 album *Old Wave*. The result was a good substitute for five Ringo albums that were out of print when it was released, but no match for the hit-filled *Blast from Your Past*. —*William Ruhlmann*

All-Starr Band / Oct. 1990 / Rykodisc ✦✦✦
Ringo Starr went back to work in the summer of 1989 fronting a tour of rock stars who, like him, had become golden oldies. Ringo sang hits like "It Don't Come Easy" and "Photograph," Dr. John sang "Iko Iko," Levon Helm of the Band sang "The Weight," his bandmate Rick Danko sang "Raining in My Heart," an old Buddy Holly tune, Billy Preston sang "Will It Go Round in Circles," and Joe Walsh sang the Eagles' "Life in the Fast Lane." (Less interesting were E Street Band members Nils Lofgren, who sang a non-hit, and Clarence Clemons, who did a rap version of "Quarter to Three.") Ringo had always depended on his friends to support his solo career, but this extended the concept to one in which he served as a sort of master of ceremonies. The tour was a success; it guaranteed a night of good and varied music, and it was fun. As a record, of course, it was redundant, but still fun. — *William Ruhlmann*

Time Takes Time / May 1992 / Private Music ✦✦✦✦
On his first new studio album to released in the US in 11 years, Ringo Starr made a neo-'60s-sounding record that, if it didn't feature his Beatle-mates, certainly evoked them. Don Was, the king of creative retro, produced half the album, bringing in bands like Jellyfish and the Posies who devote their careers to trying to sound like the Beatles of 1965-66. Here, with a real Beatle on drums and vocals, they came much closer. Of course, it's always a little weird when a veteran star makes what is essentially clone music meant to resemble the sound of his glory days. But Ringo remains a distinctive drummer and an engaging singer, so even when he was singing something called "Golden Blunders," it was hard to blame him. Besides, there are worse things to copy than the Beatles. — *William Ruhlmann*

Live from Montreux, Vol. 2 / 1994 / Rykodisc ✦✦✦
As on his previous All-Starr Band outing, Ringo Starr performs several of his better-known songs, among them the Beatles chestnuts "Yellow Submarine" and "With a Little Help from My Friends," and then acts as M.C. as various bandmembers perform some of their own better-known songs. Returnee Joe Walsh once again sings an Eagles song he did not sing when it was a hit, "Desperado," while his bandmate Timothy B. Schmit delivers the Eagles' "I Can't Tell You Why." The band is top-heavy with guitarists: Dave Edmunds does "Girl Talk," and Todd Rundgren brings "Bang on the Drum," while keyboardist Burton Cummings relives the Guess Who with "American Woman." There are fewer All-Starrs and more tracks, so many get second chances. But the show, recorded June 13, 1992, at the Montreux Jazz Festival, is less impressive than the first one; even Ringo sounds a little less enthusiastic. — *William Ruhlmann*

Status Quo

f. 1967, London, England
Hard Rock, Psychedelic, Boogie Rock, Rock & Roll
Status Quo is one of Britain's longest-lived bands, staying together for over 30 years. During much of that time, the band was only successful in the UK, where they racked up a string of Top Ten singles that ran into the '90s. In America, the group was ignored after they abandoned psychedelia for heavy boogie rock in the early '70s. Before that, the Quo managed to reach No. 12 in the US with the psychedelic classic "Pictures of Matchstick Men" (a Top Ten hit in the UK). Following that single, the band suffered a lean period for the next few years, before deciding to refashion themselves as a hard-rock boogie band in 1970 with their *Ma Kelly's Greasy Spoon* album. Over the next 25 years, the Quo basically recycled the same simple boogie on each successive album and single, yet their popularity never waned in Britain. If anything, their very predictability ensured the group a large following.

The origins of Status Quo lie in a London-based beat group called the Spectres. Francis Rossi (vocals, guitar) and Alan Lancaster (bass) were the core members of the Spectres from their inception; within a few years, the band had added drummer John Coughlan and organist Roy Lynes. The Spectres released three unsuccessful singles before changing their style to psychedelia and adopting the name Traffic Jam and releasing the unsuccessful single "Almost but Not Quite There." After it flopped, the group added Rick Harrison (guitar, vocals), formerly of the cabaret band the Highlights. When Harrison joined the band in August 1967, the group again changed their name, this time to Status Quo.

At first, Status Quo backed British solo artists, including Tommy Quickly, while working on their own material. "Pictures of Matchstick Men," the group's debut single, was released toward the end of the year and quickly shot to No. 7 on the UK charts; within a few months, it was a No. 12 in the US as well. The immediate follow-up single, "Black Veils of Melancholy," was a flop, but "Ice in the Sun," written by former British pop star Marty Wilde, became Status Quo's second Top Ten hit in the fall of 1968. Over in America, the single barely registered, squeaking to No. 70; it was the last time the group would ever chart in the US.

For the next year, Status Quo tried to replicate the success of their first two singles with similar psychedelic material, but they had little luck. Finally, they revamped their sound—and jettisoned organist

Lynes—in the summer of 1970, debuting their new heavy, bluesy boogie rock with the single "Down the Dustpipe." The single reached No. 12, yet the full-fledged hard-rock album *Ma Kelly's Greasy Spoon* didn't gain much attention. Status Quo began playing concerts regularly across England, slowly building up a strong following in England. Following well-received sets at 1972's Reading and Great Western festivals, the band became a hot property. The group signed with Vertigo Records and their first single for the label, "Paper Plane," cracked the Top Ten in early 1973, while their first album for Vertigo, *Piledriver*, reached No. 5. Later that year, *Hello* entered the charts at No. 1, while its accompanying single "Caroline" reached No. 5. Also in 1973, keyboardist Andy Bown, formerly of the Herd and Judas Jump, became the band's unofficial keyboardist.

Throughout the '70s, each album Status Quo released went into the Top Five, while their singles—including the No. 1 "Down Down" (1974), "Roll over Lay Down" (1975), "Rain" (1976), "Wild Side of Life" (1976), and a cover of John Fogerty's "Rockin' All over the World" (1977)—consistently hit the Top Ten and frequently went gold. Since they were experiencing a great deal of success, they didn't change their sound at all, they just kept churning out the same heavy boogie. America basically ignored Status Quo, yet their eponymous album managed to chart at 148 in 1976. Nevertheless, they were an English phenomenon, and England continued to support them even when pop music was undergoing drastic changes in the late '70s.

Following the release of 1980's *Just Supposin'*, drummer John Coughlan left the band in 1981 to form his own group, Diesel. Former Original Mirrors drummer Pete Kircher replaced him; his first appearance with the group was 1982's *Never to Late*. During the early '80s, tensions escalated between bassist Lancaster and guitarists Rossi and Parfitt, who were the group's main songwriters. Lancaster left the band after performing with them for a final time at Live Aid. He subsequently took Rossi and Parfitt to court to prevent them from using the name "Status Quo." Lancaster lost his battle, and the name became the property of the guitarists.

Once the lawsuit was settled, Rossi and Parfitt assembled a new band, hiring bassist John Edwards, drummer Jeff Rich, and keyboardist Andy Bown, who officially became a member of the group. The new lineup continued Status Quo's remarkable success, as they racked up a number of new Top Ten singles and hit albums, as well as consistently selling out concerts across England and Europe. In 1994, the group had its second No. 1 hit of its career, with the football anthem "Come on You Reds"; the single was recorded with the football champions, Manchester United. By the mid-'90s, Status Quo had scored 50 British hit singles, which was a greater number than any other band in rock 'n' roll's history. — *Stephen Thomas Erlewine*

● **Collection** / 1985 / Pickwick ✦✦✦✦
Featuring everything from their early psychedelic days to the years when they were the kings of simple, heavy guitar boogie, *Collection: Status Quo* is the definitive single-disc collection of this popular British band. — *Stephen Thomas Erlewine*

Steely Dan

f. 1972, Los Angeles, CA, **db.** 1981
Pop-Rock, Jazz-Rock, Soft Rock
Most rock 'n' roll bands are a tightly wound unit that developed their music through years of playing in garages and clubs around their hometown. Steely Dan never subscribed to that aesthetic. As the vehicle for the songwriting of Walter Becker and Donald Fagen, Steely Dan defied all rock 'n' roll conventions. Becker and Fagen never truly enjoyed rock—with their ironic humor and cryptic lyrics, their eclectic body of work shows some debt to Bob Dylan—preferring jazz, traditional pop, blues and R&B. Steely Dan created a sophisticated, distinctive sound with accessible melodic hooks, complex harmonies and time signatures, and a devotion to the recording studio. With producer Gary Katz, Becker and Fagen gradually changed Steely Dan from a performing band to a studio project, hiring professional musicians to record their compositions. Though the band didn't perform live after 1974, Steely Dan's popularity continued to grow throughout the decade, as their albums became critical favorites and their singles became staples of AOR and pop radio stations. Even after the group disbanded in the early '80s, their records retained a cult following, as proven by the massive success of their unlikely return to the stage in the early '90s.

Walter Becker (bass) and Donald Fagen (vocals, keyboards) were the core members of Steely Dan throughout its variety of incarnations. The two met at Bard College in New York in 1967 and began playing in bands together shortly afterward. The duo played in a number of groups—including the Bad Rock Group, which featured future comedic actor Chevy Chase on drums—which ranged from jazz to progressive rock. Eventually, Becker and Fagen began composing songs together, hoping to become professional songwriters in the tradition of the Brill Building. In 1970, the pair joined Jay & the Americans' backing band, performing under pseudonyms; Becker chose Gustav Mahler, while Fagen used Tristan Fabriani. They stayed with Jay & the Americans until halfway through 1971, when they recorded the soundtrack for the low-budget film *You Gotta Walk It Like You Talk It*, which was produced by the Americans' Kenny Vance. Following the recording of the soundtrack, Becker and Fagen attempted to start a band with Denny Dias, but the venture was unsuccessful. The pair then moved to New York City with hopes of becoming professional songwriters. Though Barbara Streisand recorded "I Mean to Shine," the duo was unsuccessful. During their stint in New York, they did meet producer Gary Katz, who hired them as staff songwriters for ABC/Dunhill in Los Angeles, where he had just become a staff producer. Katz suggested that Becker and Fagen form a band as a way to record their songs, and Steely Dan—who took their name from a dildo in William Burroughs' *Naked Lunch*—was formed shortly afterward.

Recruiting guitarists Denny Dias and Skunk Baxter, drummer Jim Hodder, and keyboardist/vocalist David Palmer, Becker and Fagen officially formed Steely Dan in 1972, releasing their debut *Can't Buy a Thrill* shortly afterward. Palmer and Fagen shared lead vocals on the album, but the record's two hit singles—the Top 10 "Do It Again" and "Reeling in the Years"—were sung by Fagen. *Can't Buy a Thrill* was a critical and commercial success, but its supporting tour was a disaster, hampered by an under-rehearsed band and unappreciative audiences. Palmer left the band following the tour. *Countdown to Ecstasy*, released in 1973, was a critical hit, but it failed to generate a hit single, even though the band supported it with a tour.

Steely Dan replaced Hodder with Jeff Pocaro and added keyboardist/backup vocalist Michael McDonald prior to recording their third album, *Pretzel Logic*. Released in the spring of 1974, *Pretzel Logic* returned Steely Dan to the Top 10 on the strength of the single "Rikki Don't Lose That Number." After completing the supporting tour for *Pretzel Logic*, Becker and Fagen decided to retire from live performances, and make Steely Dan a studio-based band. For their next album, 1975's *Katy Lied*, the duo hired a variety of studio musicians—including Dias, Pocaro, guitarist Elliot Randall, saxophonists Phil Woods, bassist Wilton Felder, percussionist Victor Feldman, keyboardist Michael Omartian, and guitarist Larry Carlton—as supporting musicians. *Katy Lied* was another hit, as was 1976's *The Royal Scam*, which continued in the vein of its predecessor. On 1977's *Aja*, Steely Dan's sound became more polished and jazzy, as they hired jazz-fusion artists like Wayne Shorter, Lee Ritenour and the Crusaders as support. *Aja* became their biggest hit, reaching the Top Five within three weeks of release and becoming one of the first albums to be certified platinum. *Aja* also gained the respect of many jazz musicians, as evidenced by Woody Herman recording an album of Becker/Fagen songs in 1978.

Following the release of *Aja*, ABC was bought out by MCA Records, resulting in a contractual dispute with the label that delayed the release of their follow-up album until 1980. During the interim, the group had a hit with the theme song for *FM* in 1978. Steely Dan finally released *Gaucho*, the follow-up to *Aja* in late 1980, and it became another Top 10 hit for the group. During the summer of 1981, Becker and Fagen announced that they were parting ways. The following year, Fagen released his solo debut, *The Nightfly*, which became a critical and commercial hit.

Fagen didn't record another album until 1993, when he reunited with Becker, who produced *Kamakiriad*. The album was promoted by the first Steely Dan tour in nearly 20 years, and while the record failed to sell, the concerts were very popular. In 1994, Becker released his solo debut, *11 Tracks of Whack*, which was produced by Fagen. The following year, Steely Dan mounted another reunion tour. —*Stephen Thomas Erlewine*

You Gotta Walk It Like You Talk It (Or You'll Lose That Beat) / 1971 / Visa ♦♦

This is an eight-track, 31-1/2 minute soundtrack to a low-budget 1970 film that features an embryonic version of Steely Dan—Donald Fagen on keyboards, Walter Becker on bass and guitar, and Denny Dias on guitar and percussion, plus John Discepolo on drums. There are only four actual songs, plus three instrumentals and a reprise of the title track. Yet the playing is suggestive of the sinuous sound that Becker and Fagen would cook up a couple of years hence in the Dan. Nevertheless, it should be sought out by the hard core fans only; there are no gems here, only some baubles. —*William Ruhlmann*

Can't Buy a Thrill / 1972 / MCA ♦♦♦

Walter Becker and Donald Fagen were remarkable craftsmen from the start, as Steely Dan's debut *Can't Buy a Thrill* illustrates. Each song is tightly constructed, with interlocking chords and gracefully interwoven melodies, buoyed by clever, cryptic lyrics. All of these are hallmarks of Steely Dan's signature sound, but what is most remarkable about the record is how it differs from their later albums. Of course, one of the most notable differences is the presence of vocalist David Palmer, a professional blue-eyed soul vocalist who oversings the handful of tracks where he takes the lead. Palmer's very presence signals the one major

flaw with the album—in an attempt to appeal to a wide audience, Becker and Fagen tempered their wildest impulses with mainstream pop techniques. Consequently, there are very few of the jazz flourishes that came to distinguish their albums—the breakthrough single "Do It Again" does work an impressively tight latin-jazz beat, and "Reelin' in the Years" has jazzy guitar solos and harmonies—and the production is overly polished, conforming with all the conventions of early-'70s radio. Of course, that gives these decidedly twisted songs a subversive edge, but compositionally these aren't as innovative as their later work. Even so, the best moments ("Dirty Work," "Kings," "Midnite Cruiser," "Turn That Heartbeat over Again") are wonderful pop songs that subvert traditional pop conventions, and more than foreshadow what paths Steely Dan would later take. —*Stephen Thomas Erlewine*

☆ **Countdown to Ecstasy** / 1973 / MCA ♦♦♦♦♦

Can't Buy a Thrill became an unexpected hit, and as a response, Donald Fagen became the group's full-time lead vocalist and he and Walter Becker acted like Steely Dan was a rock 'n' roll band for the group's second album, *Countdown to Ecstasy*. The loud guitars and pronounced backbeat of "Bodhisattva," "Show Biz Kids" and "My Old School" camouflage the fact that *Countdown* is a riskier album, musically speaking, than its predecessor. Each of its eight songs have sophisticated, jazz-inflected interludes and apart from the bluesy vamps "Bodhisattva" and "Show Biz Kids," which sound like they were written for the stage, the songs are subtlety textured. "Razor Boy," with its murmuring marimbas, and the hard-bop tribute "Your Gold Teeth" reveal Becker and Fagen's jazz roots, while the country-flavored "Pearl of the Quarter" and the ominous, skittering "King of the World" are both overlooked gems. *Countdown to Ecstasy* is the only time Steely Dan played it relatively straight, and its eight songs are either rich with musical or lyrical detail that their album-rock or art-rock contemporaries couldn't hope to match. —*Stephen Thomas Erlewine*

☆ **Pretzel Logic** / 1974 / MCA ♦♦♦♦♦

Countdown to Ecstasy wasn't half the hit that *Can't Buy a Thrill* was, and Steely Dan responded by trimming the lengthy instrumental jams that were scattered across *Countdown* and concentrating on concise songs for *Pretzel Logic*. While the shorter songs usually indicate a tendency toward pop conventions, that's not the case with *Pretzel Logic*. Instead of relying on easy hooks, Becker and Fagen assembled their most complex and cynical set of songs to date. Dense with harmonics and counter-melodies and bop phrasing, *Pretzel Logic* is vibrant with unpredictable musical juxtapositions and snide, but very funny, wordplay. Listen to how the album's hit single, "Rikki Don't Lose That Number," opens with a syncopated piano line that evolves into a graceful pop melody, or how the title track winds from a blues to a jazzy chorus—Becker and Fagen's craft has become seamless while remaining idiosyncratic and thrillingly accessible. Since the songs are now paramount, it makes sense that *Pretzel Logic* is less of a band-oriented album than *Countdown to Ecstasy*, yet it is the richest album in their catalog, one where the backhanded Dylan tribute "Barrytown" can sit comfortably next to the gorgeous "Any Major Dude Will Tell You." Steely Dan made more accomplished albums than *Pretzel Logic*, but they never made a better one. —*Stephen Thomas Erlewine*

☆ **Katy Lied** / 1975 / MCA ♦♦♦♦♦

Building from the jazz-fusion foundation of *Pretzel Logic*, Steely Dan created an alluringly sophisticated album of jazzy pop with *Katy Lied*. With this record, Becker and Fagen began relying solely on studio musicians, which is evident from the immaculate sound of the album. Usually, such a studied recording method would drain the life out of each song, but that's not the case with *Katy Lied*, which actually benefits from the duo's perfectionist tendencies. Each song is given a glossy sheen, one that accentuates not only the stronger pop hooks, but also the precise technical skill of the professional musicians drafted in to play the solos. Essentially, *Katy Lied* is a smoother version of *Pretzel Logic*, featuring the same cross-section of jazz-pop and blues-rock. The lack of innovations doesn't hurt the record, since the songs are uniformly brilliant. Less overtly cynical than previous Dan albums, the album still has its share of lyrical stingers, but what really is notable is the melodies, from the seductive jazzy soul of "Doctor Wu" to the lazy blues of "Chain Lightning" to the terse "Black Friday" and mock-calypso of "Everyone's Gone to the Movies." It's another excellent record in one of the most distinguished rock 'n' roll catalogs of the '70s. —*Stephen Thomas Erlewine*

The Royal Scam / 1976 / MCA ♦♦♦

The Royal Scam is the first Steely Dan record that didn't exhibit significant musical progress from its predecessor, but that doesn't mean that the album is any less interesting. The cynicism that was suppressed on *Katy Lied* comes roaring to the surface on *The Royal Scam*—not only are the lyrics bitter and snide, but the music is terse, broken, and weary. Not so coincidentally, the album is comprised of Becker and Fagen's weakest set of songs since *Can't Buy a Thrill*. Alternating between mean-spirited bluesy vamps like "Green Earrings" and "The Fez," and jazzy soft-rock numbers like "The Caves of Altamira," there's nothing particularly bad on the album, yet there are fewer standouts than before. Nevertheless, the best songs on *The Royal Scam*, like the sneering "Kid Charlemagne" and the gorgeous ballad "Sign in Stranger," rank as genuine Steely Dan classics. —*Stephen Thomas Erlewine*

Aja / 1977 / MCA ✦✦✦✦
Steely Dan hadn't been a real working band since *Pretzel Logic*, but with *Aja*, Becker and Fagen's obsession with sonic detail and fascination with composition reached new heights. A coolly textured and immaculately produced collection of sophisticated jazz-rock, *Aja* has none of the overt cynicism or self-consciously challenging music that distinguished previous Steely Dan records. Instead, it's a measured and textured album, filled with subtle melodies and accomplished, jazzy solos that blend easily into the lush instrumental backdrops. But *Aja* isn't just about texture, since Becker and Fagen's songs are their most complex and musically rich set of songs—even the simplest song, the sunny pop of "Peg," has layers of jazzy vocal harmonies. In fact, Steely Dan ignores rock on *Aja*, preferring to fuse cool jazz, blues, and pop together in a seamless, seductive fashion. It's complex music delivered with ease, and although the duo's preoccupation with clean sound and self-consciously sophisticated arrangements would eventually lead to a dead end, *Aja* is a shining example of jazz-rock at its finest. —*Stephen Thomas Erlewine*

Gaucho / 1980 / MCA ✦✦✦
Aja was cool, relaxed, and controlled; it sounded deceptively easy. Its follow-up, *Gaucho*, while sonically similar, was its polar opposite: a precise and studied record, where all of the seams were showing. *Gaucho* essentially replicates the smooth jazz-pop of *Aja*, but with none of that record's dark, seductive romance or elegant aura. Instead, it's meticulous and exacting; each performance has been rehearsed so many times that they no longer have any emotional resonance. Furthermore, Becker and Fagen's songs are generally labored, only occasionally reaching their past heights, like on the suave "Babylon Sisters," "Time Out of Mind" and "Hey Nineteen." Still, those three songs are barely enough to make the remainder of the album's glossy, meandering fusion worthwhile. —*Stephen Thomas Erlewine*

Gold / 1982 / MCA ✦✦✦✦
Now expanded past its original length, this companion to *Decade* features newly remastered versions of tracks like "FM (No Static at All)," Donald Fagen's "Century's End," and previously unreleased live work. —*Rick Clark*

★ **A Decade of Steely Dan** / 1985 / MCA ✦✦✦✦✦
A Decade of Steely Dan was one of the first compilations designed for CD, so it was intended to showcase digital sound as much as the music itself. Consequently, it's balanced to showcase at least one song from each of the band's albums, leaving such minor hits as "Pretzel Logic," "The Fez" and "Josie" off the compilation. Nevertheless, the songs here—including "Do It Again," "Reeling in the Years," "My Old School," "Rikki Don't Lose That Number," "My Old School," "Kid Charlemagne," "Peg," "Deacon Blues," "Hey Nineteen" and the non-LP "FM (No Static at All)"—provide a good overview of Steely Dan's career, making the disc a fine introduction to the innovative jazz-rock group. —*Stephen Thomas Erlewine*

Citizen Steely Dan / Dec. 14, 1993 / MCA ✦✦✦
Collecting all of Steely Dan's albums in chronological order, plus all of their two or three B-sides and one demo in a four-CD box, *Citizen Steely Dan* is only worthwhile for the fan replacing their old records. The remastering on the box is exactly the same as the newly upgraded CDs, and everything but the demo is available on other discs. —*Stephen Thomas Erlewine*

Alive in America / Oct. 17, 1995 / Giant ✦✦
When Donald Fagen and Walter Becker re-formed Steely Dan in 1994, they didn't put out a new album, they undertook a tour of sports arenas, their first tour since the days of *Countdown to Ecstasy*. Since Steely Dan became stars after they retired from performing, many of their dedicated fans never got a chance to see the group in concert. Given those circumstances, maybe the uniformly positive reviews of the tour were predictable. But as *Alive in America* proves, the shows weren't earthshaking. Certainly they were fun—there's no denying it's a thrill to hear these songs in a live setting, both for fans and for Becker and Fagen themselves—but essentially they were exercises in nostalgia. *Alive in America* is enjoyable, but it offers no new insight into Steely Dan as performers, or Becker and Fagen as songwriters. It's a gas while it lasts, but it doesn't leave any lasting memories. —*Stephen Thomas Erlewine*

Steppenwolf

f. 1967, Los Angeles, CA, **db.** 1972
Hard Rock, Psychedelic, Acid Rock
Led by John Kay (born Joachim Krauledat, April 12, 1944), Steppenwolf's blazing biker anthem "Born to Be Wild" roared out of speakers everywhere in the fiery summer of 1968, John Kay's threatening rasp sounding a mesmerizing call to arms to the counterculture movement rapidly sprouting up nationwide. German immigrant Kay got his professional start in a bluesy Toronto band called Sparrow, recording for Columbia in 1966. After Sparrow disbanded, Kay relocated to the West Coast and formed Steppenwolf, named after the Herman Hesse novel. "Born to Be Wild," their third single on ABC-Dunhill, was immortalized on the soundtrack of Dennis Hopper's underground film classic *Easy Rider*. The song's reference to "heavy metal thunder" finally gave an assignable name to an emerging genre. Steppenwolf's second monster hit that year, the psychedelic "Magic Carpet Ride," and the follow-ups "Rock Me," "Move Over," and "Hey Lawdy Mama" further established the band's credibility on the hard-rock circuit. By the early '70s, Steppenwolf ran out of steam and disbanded. Kay continued to record solo, as other members put together ersatz versions of the band for touring purposes. During the mid-'80s Kay re-formed his own version of Steppenwolf, grinding out his hits (and some new songs) at oldies shows. Nevertheless, they'll be remembered for generations to come for creating one of the ultimate gas 'n' go rock anthems of all time. —*Bill Dahl & Cub Koda*

Early Steppenwolf / 1969 / MCA ✦✦✦
Early live recordings made when the band was still called "Sparrow," working more out of a blues-band mold; features a surprisingly great version of Junior Wells' "Messin' with the Kid." —*Cub Koda*

● **16 Greatest Hits** / 1973 / MCA ✦✦✦✦
Just what the name implies; "Born to Be Wild," "Magic Carpet Ride," "The Pusher," and "Rock Me" are just some of the highlights. Everything you're going to want to hear in one neat little package. —*Cub Koda*

Born to Be Wild: A Retrospective / Nov. 5, 1991 / MCA ✦✦✦✦
A double-disc collection of Steppenwolf's lengthy career, *Born to Be Wild: A Retrospective* includes more music than anyone but hardcore fans need, but the song selection and packaging are superb, making it essential for those devoted fans. —*Stephen Thomas Erlewine*

Stereo MCs'

f. 1985, London, England
Hip-Hop, House, Acid Jazz, Club-Dance
One of the most successful hip-hop acts to emerge from Great Britain, the Stereo MC's formed in London in 1985 when rapper Rob B. (born Rob Birch) and DJ/producer the Head (Nick Hallam) formed the Gee Street label as a means of promoting their music. Gee Street soon signed a distribution deal with the New York-based 4th and Broadway label, and a series of singles followed before the Stereo MC's' debut album, *33-45-78*, surfaced in 1989.

After the departure of founding member Cesare, the group—now consisting of Rob B., the Head, drummer Owen If (born Owen Rossiter), and vocalist Cath Coffey—issued the 1990 single "Elevate My Mind," which became the first British rap single ever to reach the US pop charts. Following the release of the album *Supernatural*, the Stereo MC's toured with the Happy Mondays and EMF before returning to the studio to record their 1992 breakthrough *Connected*, a sample-free album recorded completely with live instruments that spawned such major hits as "Step It Up," "Creation," and "Ground Level." After more than five years of production and remix work, the group's long-awaited (and oft-delayed) follow-up was scheduled for release in the late autumn of 1997; that May, Coffey also issued her debut solo single, "Wild World." —*Jason Ankeny*

Supernatural / 1990 / 4th & Broadway ✦✦✦✦
The only thing that separates *Supernatural* and its hit follow-up *Connected* is that *Connected* had a hit. Otherwise, the albums are nearly identical and are equally enjoyable. —*AMG*

● **Connected** / 1992 / PolyGram ✦✦✦✦
Stereo MCs' American breakthrough is an energetic, club-oriented collection of colorful, funky dance tracks—the raps almost seem like an afterthought, yet that doesn't distract from the sheer pleasure of their sound. —*AMG*

Stereolab

f. 1991, London, England
Alternative Pop-Rock, Experimental, Post-Rock/Experimental, Indie Rock
Combining an inclination for melodic '60s pop with an art-rock aesthetic borrowed from Kraut-rock bands like Faust and Neu!, Stereolab were one of the most influential alternative bands of the '90s. Led by Tim Gane and Laetitia Sadier, Stereolab legitimized forms of music that were either on the fringe of rock, or brought attention to a strand of pop music—bossa nova, lounge-pop, movie soundtracks—that were traditionally banished from the rock lineage. The group's trademark sound—a droning, hypnotic rhythm track overlaid with melodic, mesmerizing sing-song vocals, often sung in French and often promoting revolutionary, Marxist politics—was deceptively simple, providing the basis for a wide array of stylistic experiments over the course of their

prolific career. Throughout it all, Stereolab relied heavily on forgotten methods of recording, whether it was analog synthesizers and electronics or a fondness for hi-fi test records, without ever sinking to the level of kitsch.

Tim Gane (b. July 12, 1964; guitar, keyboards) was the leader of McCarthy, a London-based band from the late '80s that functioned as a prototype for Stereolab's sound. Gane met Laetitia Sadier (b. May 6, 1968; vocals, keyboards), a French-born vocalist, at one of McCarthy's concerts. The pair began a romantic relationship that became a musical collaboration after McCarthy disbanded in 1990; Sadier did sing on the final McCarthy album. The duo began releasing mail-order singles under the name Stereolab, borrowing their name from a form of record mastering from the late '50s. At that point, the group was working with Th Faith Healers' drummer Joe Dilworth and former Chills bassist Martin Kean; Gina Morris occasionally provided backup vocals. All three singles by this incarnation of Stereolab released were compiled on *Switched On*, an album released on Too Pure Records in 1992. *Switched On* was released at the same time as the band's official debut album, *Peng!*. Both albums featured a variation on a maniacally grinning cartoon, which was their only visual trademark at the time.

Switched On and *Peng!*, along with the 1992 *Lo-Fi* EP and a series of limited edition singles like "John Cage Bubblegum"—which, coincidentally, was the first Stereolab recording to feature keyboardist/vocalist Mary Hansen and drummer Andy Ramsay, who became two of the group's core members—Stereolab carved out a cult following, particularly in the UK underground. Released in early 1993, *The Groop Played "Space Age Batchelor Pad Music"* featured the core group of Gane, Sadier, Hansen, and Ramsay, along with ex-Microdisney guitarist Sean O'Hagen and bassist Duncan Brown. One of the first '90s alternative records to explicitly draw from the "Space Age" lounge-pop music of the '50s, *The Groop* became an underground sensation, paving the way towards Stereolab's first American record contract with Elektra Records. But before the band made their major-label debut, they released the split 10-inch EP *Crumb Duck* with Nurse With Wound in the summer of 1993 and formed their own UK label, Duophonic.

Stereolab's next album, and their first American release, was *Transient Random Noise Bursts with Announcements*. Released in the fall of 1993, *Transient* became an underground and college hit throughout the US and UK, and Stereolab soon became a hip name to drop for many musicians, including Sonic Youth, Pavement, and Blur, who had Laetitia Sadier provide guest vocals on their 1994 hit single, "To the End." Where *Transient* was dominated by a lo-fi experimentalism, the group's sound became lusher and more layered with *Mars Audiac Quintet*, which was released in the fall of 1994. O'Hagan moved from a full-member to a part-time guest during the recording of the album—he was busy forming his own band, the High Llamas—and the band added keyboardist Katherine Gifford.

By the time of *Mars Audiac Quintet*'s release, the Stereolab sound had become prominent throughout the underground, and the group began to make efforts to change their sound, as the limited-edition 1995 EP *Music for the Amorphous Body Centre* indicated. Created for an interactive art exhibit by Charles Long, the EP boasted detailed, intricate string and vocal arrangements that were more sophisticated than the group's previous releases. That fall, the band rounded up a bunch of singles and B-sides for the second *Switched On* compilation, *Refried Ectoplasm*, which was released on Drag City in the US. Before the band recorded a new album, Gifford was replaced by Morgane Lhote. *Emperor Tomato Ketchup*, released in the spring of 1996, was a break from the drone-rock of its two predecessors, demonstrating a heavy hip-hop, jazz, and dance influence. The album was the greatest success to date, earning positive reviews in both the US and UK and becoming a significant college hit in the process. After the recording of *Emperor Tomato Ketchup*, bassist Duncan Brown was replaced by Richard Harrison. At the end of 1996, Stereolab released the limited-edition, horn-driven *Fluorescences* EP. —*Stephen Thomas Erlewine*

Switched On / 1992 / Slumberland ✦✦✦
Stereolab's musical vision was nearly full-formed on their debut album, *Switched On*. Driven by calm vocals, light pop melodies, and droning keyboards and guitars, the simple production keeps the record edgy. —*Stephen Thomas Erlewine*

Peng! / 1992 / Too Pure/American ✦✦✦
Peng! is the band's debut full-length album, on which Stereolab continue to develop their unique approach to experimental pop music. "Super Falling Star," "Peng! 33," "K-Stars," "The Seeming and the Meaning" and "Surrealchemist" are just some of the album's standout tracks, combining dreamy harmonies and swirling keyboards with dissonant guitars and Marxist lyrics. —*Heather Phares*

The Groop Played "Space Age Batchelor Pad Music" / 1993 / Too Pure/American ✦✦✦
This EP consists of eight tracks that suggest a more experimental direction for the band, especially the burbling "Space Age Bachelor Pad

Music (Mellow)," the driving "We're Not Adult Orientated" and "U.H.F.-MFP." As usual, Sadier's and Hansen's vocals and the heavy keyboards come together in a distinctively Stereolab way. —*Heather Phares*

Transient Random Noise Bursts with Announcements / Aug. 1993 / Elektra ✦✦✦✦
Stereolab's major-label debut is also one of their finest and most experimental releases. More emphasis is placed on instrumentals and instrumental breaks on *Transient Random Noise Bursts*. The 15-minute "Jenny Ondioline" and noisy cuts like "Our Trinitone Blast" and "Analogue Rock" showcase Stereolab's experimental tendencies, while tracks like "Tone Burst," "Pack Yr Romantic Mind," and "Lock Group Lullaby" show that the group is just as capable of creating beautiful, if offbeat pop songs as it is adept at bringing the noise. The group's most varied and characteristic recording. —*Heather Phares*

Mars Audiac Quintet / Aug. 9, 1994 / Elektra ✦✦✦✦
The band's fourth album tones down their avant-garde edge, concentrating instead on Sadier's and Hansen's vocal interplay, as well as song structures. A beautiful, if less challenging album, *Mars Audiac Quintet* features plenty of bouncy, dreamy tunes like "Three-Dee Melodie," "Des Étoiles Électroniques," "Ping Pong," "Seven Longers Later," and "Fiery Yellow." *Mars Audiac Quintet* is a good starting point for Stereolab novices, as it gives an appealing but accurate introduction to the group's distinct and innovative sound. —*Heather Phares*

Refried Ectoplasm (Switched On, Vol. 2) / 1995 / Duophonic/Drag City ✦✦✦✦
Refried Ectoplasm (Switched On, Vol. 2) collects 13 singles and rarities Stereolab released between 1992 and 1995, and it is far more than a mere oddities collection. More than any other album, *Refried Ectoplasm* charts Stereolab's astonishing musical growth between those three years, and offers several definitive songs—including "Lo Boob Oscillator," "French Disko" and "John Cage Bubblegum"—not available on any album. While such items are essential for collectors, the quality and accessiblity of the music is very strong, showcasing Stereolab's complexity and providing an excellent introduction to the group. —*Stephen Thomas Erlewine*

Music for the Amorphous Body Center / Apr. 1995 / Duophonic ✦✦✦✦
Recorded especially for an art exhibit, *Music for the Amorphous Body Center* expands on Stereolab's trademark guitar-and-organ drone by adding strings. With the subtle, lush strings as support, the group's easy-listening and '60s-pop inclinations become more pronounced, making the overlapping textures of "Pop Quiz" swirl magnificently. Such small adjustments make the EP quite wonderful; it proves that there are hidden variations in Stereolab's music that don't quite come to the forefront immediately. —*Stephen Thomas Erlewine*

● **Emperor Tomato Ketchup** / Apr. 1996 / Elektra ✦✦✦✦
Stereolab was poised for a breakthrough release with *Emperor Tomato Ketchup*, their fourth full-length album. Not only was their influence becoming apparent throughout alternative rock, but *Mars Audiac Quintet* and *Music for the Amorphous Body Center* indicated they were moving closer to distinct pop melodies. The group certainly hasn't backed away from pop melodies on *Emperor Tomato Ketchup*, but just as their hooks are becoming catchier, they bring in more avant-garde and experimental influences, as well. Consequently, the album is Stereolab's most complex, multi layered record. It lacks the raw, amateurish textures of their early singles, but the music is far more ambitious, melding electronic drones and sing-song melodies with string sections, slight hip-hop and dub influences, and scores of interweaving counter melodies. Even when Stereolab appears to be creating a one-chord trance, there is a lot going on beneath the surface. Furthermore, the group's love for easy listening and pop melodies means that the music never feels cold or inaccessible. In fact, pop singles like "Cybele's Reverie" and "The Noise of Carpet" help ease listeners into the group's more experimental tendencies. Because of all its textures, *Emperor Tomato Ketchup* isn't as immediately accessible as *Mars Audiac Quintet*, but it is a rich, rewarding listen. —*Stephen Thomas Erlewine*

Stetsasonic

f. 1981, Brookly, NY, **db.** 1992
Hip-Hop
One of the first rap groups to use a live band, Brooklyn's Stetsasonic formed in 1981 and were also among the first to promote a positive black consciousness that found its ultimate expression in the so-called daisy-age sounds of De La Soul and the Jungle Brothers. The group consisted of DJs "Prince Paul" Huston and Leonard "Wise" Roman, keyboardist/drummer/DJ Marvin "DBC" Nemley, and rappers Glenn "Daddy-O" Bolton, Martin "Delite" Wright, and Bobby "Fruitkwan" Simmons. Daddy-O and Delite founded the group as the Stetson Brothers, after the hat company, and began performing in New York hip-hop clubs, picking up other members along the way. Their debut, *On Fire,*

was released in 1986, but it was the follow-up, *In Full Gear*, that brought them critical acclaim and an R&B hit, "Sally." In 1991, *Blood, Sweat and No Tears* was considered by many to be their best and most diverse album, but Daddy-O decided that they had run out of ideas and broke up the band. He went on to work with Mary J. Blige, Queen Latifah, Big Daddy Kane, and the Red Hot Chili Peppers as a producer and remixer. Meanwhile, Prince Paul had already established himself as a producer for his work with De La Soul and Fine Young Cannibals, and later worked with Fruitkwan in the Gravediggaz. — *Steve Huey*

On Fire / 1986 / Tommy Boy ✦✦✦
There weren't many bands utilizing a hip-hop format in the mid-'80s, making Stetasonic quite unique on the pop front in 1986. While their subject matter was invariably light and their raps now hopelessly tame and effete, they were ground breaking at the time and retain a certain charm. — *Ron Wynn*

● **In Full Gear** / 1988 / Tommy Boy ✦✦✦✦
They're not "the world's only hip-hop band" anymore, but this seven-piece group (real drums even!) paved the way. Their second disc documents their innovative best, culminating in the anthemic "Talkin' All That Jazz." — *John Floyd*

Blood, Sweat & No Tears / 1991 / Tommy Boy ✦✦✦

Cat Stevens (Steve Georgiou)

b. Jul. 21, 1947, London, England
Synthesizer, Guitar, Piano, Keyboards, Vocals / Singer-Songwriter, Soft Rock, Pop-Rock
Cat Stevens (born Steve Georgiou in London) was the son of a Greek father and a Swedish mother. Stevens became interested in folk and rock 'n' roll in his teens and scored his first UK hit, "I Love My Dog," before he turned 20. Stevens reached the singles charts four more times, getting to No. 2 with "Matthew & Son" and releasing the similarly titled Top Ten album before he contracted tuberculosis in 1968 and was forced to retire from music. He re-emerged with a new, mature style in 1970 with the album *Mona Bone Jakon* and hit the UK Top Ten with "Lady D'Arbanville." But it was his late-1970 follow-up, *Tea for the Tillerman*, that made him an international success. The album hit the Top Ten and went gold in the US, producing the hit "Wild World." *Teaser and the Firecat*, released in 1971, did even better, including the hits "Peace Train" and "Morning Has Broken." Stevens became so successful as an albums artist that, even though his next couple of albums did not generate big hit singles, they were still big sellers: *Catch Bull at Four* (1972) went to No. 1 and *Foreigner* (1973) reached No. 3. Stevens' 1974 album *Buddha and the Chocolate Box*, which included the No. 10 hit "Oh Very Young," reached No. 2. Stevens' records were gradually less successful during the second half of the '70s. In 1979, he became a Muslim, adopted the name Yusef Islam, and retired from music. He was not heard from for another ten years, until he shocked admirers at the end of the '80s by supporting the death sentence ordered by the Ayatollah Khomeini against novelist Salman Rushdie for writing the book *The Satanic Verses*. Some "classic rock" radio stations discontinued playing him as a result, though his music remains popular. — *William Ruhlmann*

Matthew & Son / 1967 / Deram ✦✦✦
Released in the late winter of 1967, 19-year-old Cat Stevens' debut album, *Matthew & Son*, contained his breakthrough UK hits "I Love My Dog" (No.28) and the title song (No.2), and spawned a third, "I'm Gonna Get Me a Gun" (No.6). (The Tremeloes took a cover of the album's "Here Comes My Baby" to UK No.4.) While it is a precocious effort (Stevens wrote all the songs) and the material is undeniably catchy, it's also wildly overproduced, with gimmicky arrangements typical of the mid-'60s British pop sound around the time of *Sgt. Pepper*. This is especially noticeable, heard in the context of Stevens' later, less-produced, more meaningful efforts. — *William Ruhlmann*

New Masters / 1967 / Deram ✦✦
Cat Stevens' first career proved short-lived as this, his second album, failed to chart in the UK when it was released at the end of 1967. The album contained Stevens' fifth—and lowest—charting single, "Kitty" (No.47), but in retrospect is best remembered for "The First Cut Is the Deepest," a No.18 UK hit for P.P. Arnold prior to the album's release and since then a hit for Rod Stewart. — *William Ruhlmann*

Mona Bone Jakon / Jul. 1970 / A&M ✦✦✦
Mona Bone Jakon was Stevens' first effort for A&M Records, unveiling him as a sensitive singer-songwriter, with gentle tracks like "Trouble," "Katmandu," "Lady D'Arbanville," "Lily White," and "I Wish I Wish." Fans of *Teaser and the Firecat* or *Tea for the Tillerman* should check this one out. — *Rick Clark*

☆ **Tea for the Tillerman** / Nov. 1970 / A&M ✦✦✦✦✦
Tea for the Tillerman is like a musical collection of children's tales by Stevens. The delicacy of the arrangements, Paul Samwell-Smith's brilliant otherworldly production, and Stevens' entrancing melodies and images easily make this his best work. "Wild World" was a huge hit, but

emotive tracks like "Father and Son," "Where Do the Children Play?," and the haunting "Into White" and "Sad Lisa" make this a must-own for fans of singer-songwriter pop. — *Rick Clark*

Teaser & the Firecat / Oct. 1971 / A&M ✦✦✦✦
The follow-up to *Tea for the Tillerman* was almost as impressive. Sonically, less energy was put into creating empty real soundscapes, with more emphasis on tighter song constructions and immediacy. The result paid off with three international hits, "Peace Train," "Moonshadow," and "Morning Has Broken." Other highlights included "Tuesday's Dead," "The Wind," "Bitter Blue," and "Ruby Love." After *Tea for the Tillerman*, this is the one to get. — *Rick Clark*

Catch Bull at Four / Oct. 1972 / A&M ✦✦✦✦
Catch Bull at Four was Stevens' commercial peak, holding the No.1 spot for three weeks. Much of the reason for this was probably public anticipation that this would be as smoothly appealing as his previous two outings. With this album, Stevens' melodies became more ornate and his delivery became a little gruffer. Overall, it is one of his better albums with "Eighteenth Avenue," "Sitting," and "Can't Keep It In" as highlights. — *Rick Clark*

Buddha & the Chocolate Box / Apr. 1974 / A&M ✦✦✦
At the time of its release, this was heralded as Stevens' best effort since *Tea*.... It wasn't. It did have a few good tunes, particularly "Oh Very Young" and "Ready," both hits. — *Rick Clark*

● **Greatest Hits** / Jun. 1975 / A&M ✦✦✦✦
This is the most popular best-of collection. It has his biggest hits and a couple of important album tracks. The CD version is just a straight reissue of the original LP release, therefore utilizing only about half of the time available on disc. — *Rick Clark*

Footsteps in the Dark: Greatest Hits, Vol. 2 / Nov. 1984 / A&M ✦✦✦✦
Cat Stevens' greatest hits were contained on the album of that title released in June 1975, though that set did not include the minor Top 40 entry "The Hurt" and though Stevens made the singles chart four more times between 1976 and 1979, with "Banapple Gas," the Top 40 "(Remember the Days of the) Old Schoolyard," "Was Dog a Doughnut," and "Bad Brakes." One might expect that an album subtitled *Greatest Hits, Vol. 2* would contain all those tracks, but if so, one would be disappointed. The only chart single on the 14-track *Footsteps in the Dark* is "The Hurt." Actually, the album is a non-hits compilation of good album tracks drawn from seven of Stevens' nine A&M albums originally released between 1970 and 1978, plus a non-LP B-side and two songs that previously had only appeared in the 1972 film *Harold and Maude*. It leans heavily to the earlier, folkier period, with ten songs drawn from 1970 to 1972, and thus emphasizes the vulnerable, seeking singer-songwriter of *Tea for the Tillerman* over the more pop-oriented and musically ambitious artist who made albums like *Izitso*. The material is sometimes dated ("I'd like to live on a commune and / People can call me a hippie"), and, in the wake of Stevens' conversion to Islam, one inevitably hears lines like "Where I'll end up well I think, / Only God really knows" in a different light. But Stevens' songwriting still impresses, his childlike wonder and earnestness are still endearing, and such political statements as "Where Do the Children Play?" remain timely. Though Stevens' best albums, *Tea for the Tillerman* and *Teaser and the Firecat*, work best as albums, *Footsteps in the Dark* confirmed that, a decade on from their initial appearance, his songs had maintained their quality. — *William Ruhlmann*

Classics, Vol. 24 / 1987 / A&M ✦✦✦✦
After several collections, there has yet to be a definitive representation of Stevens' work. Half of his Top 40 hits (like "Wild World," "Another Saturday Night," "Two Fine People," "The Hurt," and "Ready") are missing. On the plus side, some nice album cuts like "The Wind" and "18th Avenue" and highlights from the movie *Harold & Maude* are here. — *Rick Clark*

Al Stewart

b. Sep. 5, 1945, Glasgow, Scotland
Guitar, Keyboards, Vocals / Singer-Songwriter, Art-Rock/Progressive-Rock, Folk-Rock
Glasgow native Al Stewart began his career playing guitar in Tony Blackburn's band the Sabres, and moved from there to the London folk club scene. After an unsuccessful single on Decca, "The Elf" (which featured Jimmy Page on guitar), Stewart signed with CBS and released a series of albums largely consisting of introspective, confessional love songs beginning in 1967. *Love Chronicles* was the only one to be released in the US, and the autobiographical title track, which detailed Stewart's romantic involvements, attracted a bit of attention for the singer's use of the word "fucking" in a song with supposed artistic credibility. On 1973's *Past, Present and Future*, Stewart switched gears, exploring his fascination with historical tales, and was rewarded with his first US chart album. *Modern Times* was even more successful, and

Year of the Cat was an unqualified hit, selling over a million copies and spawning the Top Ten title single. *Time Passages* duplicated both feats, but Stewart's creativity dried up soon afterwards, and difficulties over his contract and change of labels prevented him from releasing any new material until 1984. *Russians and Americans* was highly political, but sales were disappointing. Even so, Stewart has recorded and toured sporadically in the late '80s and '90s while devoting time to his hobby of wine collecting. —*Steve Huey*

Bedsitter Images / 1967 / Epic ✦✦
Al Stewart's debut album was an intriguing but hesitant effort, filled with searching acoustic love songs laced with strings. —*Daevid Jehnzen*

Love Chronicles / 1969 / Epic ✦✦✦
It's notable for the 18-minute coming-of-age title cut, which caused a stir at the time for its use of the word "fucking." Jimmy Page is featured on guitar. —*Rick Clark*

Zero She Flies / 1970 / Epic ✦✦✦
On his third album, *Zero She Flies*, Al Stewart continued in a familiar gentle, folk-based singer-songwriter vein. The album's key track was "Manuscript," one of Stewart's first historical songs. —*Daevid Jehnzen*

Orange / 1972 / Beat Goes On ✦✦✦
Orange was the last album Al Stewart recorded where the love songs were prominent, and it was one of his most lovely records. —*Daevid Jehnzen*

Past, Present & Future / 1973 / Arista ✦✦✦
On *Past, Present and Future*, Al Stewart began to reach his artistic fruition, as he crafted a lush, winding song cycle about the writings of Nostradamus, highlighted by the majestic "Nostradamus." —*Daevid Jehnzen*

Modern Times / 1975 / Rhino ✦✦✦✦
Stewart's airy (sometimes sentimental) obsessions with the passage of time take on a special resonance on this outing. Highlights include "Carol," "Apple Cider Re-Constitution," "Dark and Rolling Sea," and "The Modern Times." —*Rick Clark*

Year of the Cat / 1976 / Arista ✦✦✦✦
Stewart's calm delivery gives his songs a reserved, tasteful sense of understatement, especially on the title track, one of those "mysterious woman" songs, which captivated listeners and turned the album into a million-seller. —*William Ruhlmann*

Time Passages / 1978 / Arista ✦✦✦✦
A return to Stewart's historical themes lyrically, though it's still the overall smoothness of his music that connected with another million listeners. —*William Ruhlmann*

24 Carrots / 1980 / Razor & Tie ✦✦✦
One of his most underrated albums, *24 Carrots* features some of Al Stewart's finest songs about historical events, all set to a lush sonic backdrop. —*Daevid Jehnzen*

Live Indian Summer / 1981 / Arista ✦✦
Comprised of a professional but uninspiring live set and a handful of new studio albums, *Live Indian Summer* is one of his lesser efforts. —*Daevid Jehnzen*

Russians & Americans / 1984 / Passport ✦✦
Out of all his grandly ambitious albums, *Russians and Americans* is among the most problematic, since he takes an actual political position, which tends to hurt the flow of the music. —*Daevid Jehnzen*

● **The Best of Al Stewart** / 1988 / Arista ✦✦✦✦
All of Al Stewart's stateside hits are available here, as well as most of the best cuts from the hit albums *Year of the Cat* and *Time Passages*. Not a comprehensive overview of his career, it's still the best sampler available. —*Rick Clark*

Last Days of the Century / 1988 / Enigma ✦✦
Stewart was prevented from releasing new music for four years in the mid-'80s, and when he did return, it was with the muddled *Last Days of the Century*, which failed to capture the excitement of his earlier work. —*Daevid Jehnzen*

Rhymes in Rooms / Feb. 25, 1992 / Mesa Blue Moon ✦✦✦
A pleasant unplugged set featuring most of Al Stewart's greatest hits, *Rhymes in Rooms* is a delight for devoted fans. —*Daevid Jehnzen*

Billy Stewart

b. Mar. 24, 1937, Washington, DC, d. Jan. 17, 1970
Piano, Vocals / Soul
Billy Stewart was one of the most distinctive vocal stylists of the '60s. His stuttering, word-doubling attack owed more to jazz scat singing than to the gospel influences of many of his peers. A jovial, rotund piano player who toured with Bo Diddley and, through him, gained entry to Chess Records, Stewart scored biggest in 1966 with a smash Top Ten version of George Gershwin and Dubose Heyward's "Summertime," an atypically (for Chess) big-band arrangement (featuring Earth, Wind &

Fire's Maurice White on drums) with Stewart in a vocal tour de force, masterfully scatting around, stuttering through, and generally turning the melody inside out. It was not your typical '60s soul music, but Stewart's success opened the door for other jazz-influenced singers like Georgie Fame to gain a place on radio playlists of the day. Stewart died tragically at age 32 in a 1970 auto accident. —*Christine Ohlman*

I Do Love You / 1965 / Chess ✦✦✦✦
Billy Stewart's greatest album and song were both contained on this fine LP from the mid-'60s. "I Do Love You" was that rare anguished testimonial that never became vapid, sappy, or overly sentimental, and was compelling and captivating throughout Stewart's marvelous leads and the piercing harmonies. The album also contained other gems like "Fat Boy," "Reap What You Sow," and "Sitting in the Park." Maybe someday this album will be reissued intact, after Stewart's hits have finally been recycled to death. —*Ron Wynn*

Unbelievable / 1966 / Chess ✦✦✦✦
The second legitimate Billy Stewart album that wasn't a later rehash or repackaged collection. It was issued in 1966 and contained some magnificent numbers, among them the great "Summertime," "Foggy Day," "Moon River," and "Misty." Chess kept priming the pump after Stewart's tragic death, repeatedly putting these songs onto different anthologies and collections. They were sung with beauty, dignity, and passion, and should be heard in the manner they were released. —*Ron Wynn*

● **One More Time: the Chess Years** / Oct. 1990 / Chess ✦✦✦✦
Although a minor soul star of the '60s, Stewart possessed one of the most unique and sweetest styles. His hits "Summertime," "I Do Love You," and "Sitting in the Park" are classics of the era. —*Jeff Tamarkin*

David A. Stewart

b. Sep. 9, 1952, Sunderland, Tyne and Wear, Englan
Piano / Pop-Rock
Dave Stewart was the musical mastermind of Eurythmics, but on his solo recordings with the Spiritual Cowboys he made more atmospheric, guitar-based albums that became minor hits in the UK in the early '90s. Stewart also has written several soundtracks and produced many artists, including Bob Dylan and Mick Jagger. —*Stephen Thomas Erlewine*

Lily Was Here / 1989 / Anxious ✦✦✦
The soundtrack to a fairly unknown film, *Lily Was Here* was Dave Stewart's first solo effort. It's an atmospheric, subdued effort, highlighted by a revamped "Here Comes the Rain Again," with Annie Lennox on lead vocals, and a handful of tracks featuring saxophonist Candy Dulfer. —*Sara Sytsma*

● **Dave Stewart & Spiritual Cowboys** / Aug. 1990 / Arista ✦✦✦✦
Dave Stewart's first album with the Spiritual Cowboys is a fine collection of atmospheric pop-rock. —*AMG*

Honest / 1991 / Arista ✦✦✦✦
Dave Stewart's second album with the Spiritual Cowboys expanded the musical ideas of their debut, although it was slightly less focused and pop-oriented than its predecessor. —*Sara Sytsma*

Greetings from the Gutter / Feb. 28, 1995 / East West ✦✦✦
Greetings from the Gutter is Dave Stewart's first official solo album and it's his most mainstream album to date, featuring several concise pop songs, as well as a handful of more complex, involved pieces. —*Sara Sytsma*

Rod Stewart

b. Jan. 10, 1945, London, England
Vocals / Rock & Roll, Adult Contemporary, Pop-Rock
Rod Stewart may have began his career as a respected singer, yet that respect eroded as he got older, as he became more concerned with stardom than music. While he has recorded some terrible albums—and he would admit that freely—Stewart was once rock 'n' roll's best interpretive singer, as well as an accomplished songwriter, creating a raw combination of folk, rock, blues, and country that sounded like no other folk-rock or country-rock. Instead of finding the folk in rock, he found how folk-rocked like hell on its own. After he became successful, he began to lose the rootsier elements of his music, yet he remained a superb singer, even as Stewart abandoned his own artistic path in favor of following pop trends.

Stewart began his musical career after spending some time as an apprentice with the Brentford Football Club, touring Europe with folksinger Wizz Jones in the early '60s; during this time he was deported from Spain for vagrancy. When he returned to England in 1963, he joined the Birmingham-based R&B group Jimmy Powell & the Five Dimensions, as a vocalist and harmonica player. The band toured the UK and recorded one single for Pye Records, which featured Stewart on blues harp. After moving back to London, he joined Long John Baldry's band, the Hoochie Coochie Men. The group recorded a single in 1964,

"Good Morning Little Schoolgirl," which failed to chart and soon afterward the group evolved into Steampacket.

During the summer of 1965, the group supported the Rolling Stones and the Walker Brothers on a UK tour, as well as recording an album that remained unreleased until 1970. Early in 1966, Steampacket disbanded and Stewart became a member of the blues-rock combo Shotgun Express, which released one single that fall before splitting. Rod Stewart then joined the Jeff Beck Group at the end of 1966.

With the Jeff Beck Group, Rod Stewart began his climb to stardom. Stewart and the former Yardbird guitarist pioneered the heavy bluesrock team of a virtuoso guitarist and a dynamic, sexy lead vocalist that became the standard blueprint for heavy metal. *Truth*, the band's debut album, was released in the fall of 1968, becoming a hit in both America and Britain. The Jeff Beck Group toured both countries several times in 1968 and 1969, gaining a dedicated following. In the summer of 1969, they released their second album, *Beck-Ola*, which became another hit record in both the US and UK. However, the group fell apart in the fall.

After rejecting an offer to join the American rock group Cactus, Stewart and Jeff Beck Group bassist Ron Wood joined the Small Faces, replacing the departed vocalist/guitarist Steve Marriott. With Wood switching over to guitar, the group shortened their name to The Faces and recorded their debut album, *First Step*. During this time, Stewart had also signed a solo contract, releasing his first album, *An Old Raincoat Won't Let You Down* (re-titled *The Rod Stewart Album* for its American release), at the end of 1969; the record failed to chart in the UK, yet it made it to No. 139 on the US charts. On the album, Stewart's folk roots meshed with his R&B and rock influences, creating a distinctive, stripped-down acoustic-based rock 'n' roll that signalled he was a creative force in his own right.

The Faces released *First Step* in the spring of 1970. The album was a departure both from the R&B/pop direction of the Small Faces and the heavy blues of the Jeff Beck Group; instead, the group became a boisterous, boozy, and sloppy Stones-inspired rock 'n' roll band. The album fared better in the UK than it did in the US, yet the group built a devoted following on both continents with their reckless, messy live shows. Stewart released his second solo album, *Gasoline Alley*, in the fall of 1970, supporting it with an American tour.

The following year proved to be pivotal in Stewart's career. At the beginning of 1971, the Faces released their second album, *Long Player*, which became a bigger hit than *First Step*, yet his third solo album, *Every Picture Tells a Story*, made Rod Stewart a household name, reaching No. 1 in both America and Britain. "Reason to Believe" was the first single from the album, becoming a minor hit in both the countries, but when DJs began playing the B-side, "Maggie May," the single became a No. 1 hit in both the UK and US for five weeks in September. The Faces released their third album, *A Nod Is As Good As a Wink... to a Blind Horse*, a couple of months later. Thanks to the success of *Every Picture Tells a Story*, the album was a Top Ten hit in both countries; it also launched the single "Stay with Me," which became the band's only Top 40 hit in the US.

The following year, the Faces began a lengthy spring tour. During the tour, tensions grew within the band as Stewart's solo career increased in popularity. That summer, Stewart released his fourth solo album, *Never a Dull Moment*, which nearly replicated the success of *Every Picture Tells a Story*, peaking at No. 2 in the US and No. 1 in the UK. In the spring of 1973, the Faces released their final album, *Ooh La La*. Stewart expressed his disdain for the record in the press, yet it hit No. 1 in the UK and No. 21 in the US. After releasing the "Pool Hall Richard" single in the beginning of 1974, the band went on tour; it would prove to be their last. Stewart released *Smiler* in the fall of 1975. *Smiler* followed the same formula as his previous four albums—and it also became a hit—yet it showed signs that the formula was wearing thin. In March of 1975, he began a love affair with Swedish actress Britt Ekland; the romance, along with a bitter fight with UK tax collectors, prompted him to apply for US citizenship. *Atlantic Crossing*, released in the summer of 1975, made the singer's relocation explicit. Recorded with producer Tom Dowd and the Muscle Shoals rhythm section, the album removed much of the singer's folk roots and accentuated his pop appeal. At the end of the year, Stewart left the Faces and the band finally called it quits.

Recorded in Los Angeles with a group of studio musicians, 1976's *A Night on the Town* continued Stewart's move to slicker pop territory and proved quite successful, becoming his first platinum album; it featured the hit single "Tonight's the Night," which was No. 1 in the US for eight weeks. *Foot Loose and Fancy Free*, released the following year, followed the same artistic pattern as *A Night on the Town* while surpassing its commercial performance, selling over three million copies. Stewart incorporated some disco to his musical formula for 1978's *Blondes Have More Fun*. Supported by the No. 1 single "Da Ya Think I'm Sexy?," the record became Stewart's first No. 1 album since *Every Picture Tells a Story*, selling over four million records. By this time, Stewart was notori-

ous for his jet-set lifestyle, particularly the series of actresses and models he dated.

With 1981's *Tonight I'm Yours*, Stewart began adding elements of new wave and synth-pop to his formula, resulting in another platinum album. Soon afterward, his career hit a slump—his next four albums sounded forced and he only scored three Top Ten hits between 1982 and 1988; out of those four albums, only 1983's *Camouflage* went gold. Stewart rebounded with 1988's *Out of Order*, recorded with Duran Duran's Andy Taylor and Chic's Bernard Edwards. His version of Tom Waits' "Downtown Train," taken from the 1989 four-disc box set *Storyteller*, became his biggest hit since "Da Ya Think I'm Sexy?" *Vagabond Heart* (1991) reflected a more mature and reflective Rod Stewart and continued his comeback streak.

Stewart reunited with Ron Wood to record an *MTV Unplugged* concert in 1993; the accompanying album launched the Top Ten hit single, "Have I Told You Lately." *Unplugged* also returned Stewart to a more acoustic-based sound. On his 1995 album, *A Spanner in the Works*, the singer explored a more polished version of this sound, scoring another hit with Tom Petty's "Leave Virginia Alone." The following year, he released *If We Fall in Love Tonight*, which was comprised of both previously released and new material. *—Stephen Thomas Erlewine*

The Rod Stewart Album / 1969 / Mercury ✦✦✦✦

On his debut album (titled *An Old Raincoat Won't Ever Let You Down* in Britain, and *The Rod Stewart Album* in America, presumably because its original title was "too English" or cryptic for US audiences), Rod Stewart essays a startlingly original blend of folk, blues, and rock 'n' roll. The opening cover of the Stones' "Street Fighting Man" encapsulates his approach. Turning the driving acoustic guitars of the original inside out, the song works a laidback, acoustic groove, bringing a whole new meaning to the song before escalating into a full-on rock 'n' roll attack—without any distorted guitars, just bashing acoustics and thundering drums. Through this approach, Stewart establishes that rock can sound as rich and timeless as folk, and that folk can be as vigorous as rock. And he does this not only as an interpreter, breathing new life into Ewan MacColl's "Dirty Old Town" and defining Mike D'Abo's "Handbags & Gladrags," but also as a songwriter, writing songs as remarkable as "Man of Constant Sorrow," "An Old Raincoat Won't Ever Let You Down," and "Cindy's Lament." The music and the songs are so vivid and rich with detail that they reflect a whole way of life, and while Stewart would later flesh out this blueprint, it remains a stunningly original vision. *—Stephen Thomas Erlewine*

☆ Gasoline Alley / 1970 / Mercury ✦✦✦✦✦

Gasoline Alley follows the same formula of Rod Stewart's first album, intercutting contemporary covers, with slightly older rock 'n' roll and folk classics and originals written in the same vein. The difference is in execution. Stewart sounds more confident, claiming Elton John's "Country Comfort," the Small Faces' "My Way of Giving," and the Rolling Stones' version of "It's All Over Now" with a ragged, laddish charm. Like its predecessor, nearly all of *Gasoline Alley* is played on acoustic instruments—Stewart treats rock 'n' roll songs like folk songs, reinterpreting them in individual, unpredictable ways. For instance, "It's All Over Now" becomes a shambling, loose-limbed ramble instead of a tight R&B/blues groove, and "Cut Across Shorty" is based around a howling, mideastern violin instead of a rockabilly riff. Of course, being a rocker at heart, Stewart doesn't let these songs become limp acoustic numbers—these rock harder than any fuzz-guitar workout. The drums crash and bang, the acoustic guitars are pounded with a vengance—it's a wild, careening sound that is positively joyous with its abandon. And on the slow songs, Stewart is nuanced and affecting—his interpretation of Bob Dylan's "Only a Hobo" is one of the finest Dylan covers, while the original title track is a vivid, loving tribute to his adolescence. And that spirit is carried throughout *Gasoline Alley*. It's an album that celebrates tradition while moving it into the present and never once does it disown the past. *—Stephen Thomas Erlewine*

★ Every Picture Tells a Story / 1971 / Mercury ✦✦✦✦✦

Without greatly altering his approach, Rod Stewart perfected his blend of hard rock, folk, and blues on his masterpiece, *Every Picture Tells a Story*. Marginally a harder-rocking album than *Gasoline Alley*—the Faces blister on the Temptations cover "(I Know I'm) Losing You," and the acoustic title track goes into hyperdrive with Mick Waller's primitive drumming—the great triumph of *Every Picture Tells a Story* lies in its content. Every song on the album, whether it's a cover or original, is a gem, combining to form a romantic, earthy portrait of a young man joyously celebrating his young life. Of course, "Maggie May"—the ornate, ringing ode about a seduction from an older woman—is the centerpiece, but each song, whether it's the devilishly witty title track or the unbearably poignant "Mandolin Wind," has the same appeal. And the covers, including definitive readings of Dylan's "Tomorrow Is Such a Long Time" and Tim Hardin's "Reason to Believe," as well as a rollicking "That's All Right," are equally terrific, bringing new dimension to the songs. It's a beautiful album, one that has the timeless qualities of the best folk, yet one that rocks harder than most pop music—few rock albums are quite this powerful or this rich. —*Stephen Thomas Erlewine*

☆ **Never a Dull Moment** / 1972 / Mercury ✦✦✦✦✦
Essentially a harder-rocking reprise of *Every Picture Tells a Story, Never a Dull Moment* never quite reaches the heights of its predecessor, but it's a wonderful, multi faceted record in its own right. Opening with the touching, autobiographical rocker "True Blue," which finds Rod trying to come to grips with his newfound stardom but concluding that he'd "rather be back home," the record is the last of Stewart's series of epic fusions of hard rock and folk. It's possible to hear Stewart go for super-stardom with the hard-rocking kick and fat electric guitars of the album, but the songs still cut to the core. "You Wear It Well" is a "Maggie May" rewrite on the surface, but it develops into a touching song about being emotionally inarticulate. Similarly, "Lost Paraguayos" is funny, driving folk-rock, and it's hard not to be swept away when the Stonesy hard-rocker "Italian Girls" soars into a mandolin-driven coda. The covers—whether a soulful reading of Jimi Hendrix's "Angel," an empathetic version of Dylan's "Mama You Been on My Mind," or a stunning inter-pretation of Etta James' "I'd Rather Go Blind"—are equally effective, making *Never a Dull Moment* a masterful record. He never got quite this good ever again. —*Stephen Thomas Erlewine*

Smiler / 1974 / Mercury ✦✦
Rod Stewart's classic formula ran out of gas on *Smiler*, his fifth solo album. The failure of *Smiler* wasn't a matter of weak songs, nor was it a matter of Stewart being in poor voice. Instead, the album failed because everything, from the choice of songs to the production, sounded too pat and predictable. The predictability held "Sweet Little Rock 'N Roller" from truly rocking and it made the reworking of "(You Make Me Feel Like) A Natural Man" unbearably smug. Apart from the free-wheeling take on Elton John's "Let Me Be Your Car" and the inspired version of Dylan's "Girl from the North Country," *Smiler* is an utter waste of time. —*Stephen Thomas Erlewine*

Atlantic Crossing / 1975 / Warner Brothers ✦✦✦✦
Atlantic Crossing wasn't simply the moment when Rod Stewart left Britain for the greener pasture of America, it was the moment when he accepted his role as a full-fledged, jet-setting superstar. Stewart aban-doned the formula of his first five solo records, as well as most of his folk-rock and hard rock undercurrents, trading them for a professionally polished, rock and soul-inflected pop, courtesy of Muscle Shoals' musi-cians and producer Tom Dowd. The glossy production doesn't obscure or trivialize Stewart's talents—coming after the tired *Smiler*, the slick-ness actually accentuated his strength as an interpretive singer. "The fast half" suffers from a couple of weak tracks, but "Three Time Loser" and "Stone Cold Sober" catch fire, and "the slow half" is generally excellent, but Stewart's heart-wrenching rendition of Danny Whitten's "I Don't Want to Talk About It" ranks as one of his finest performances. —*Stephen Thomas Erlewine*

A Night on the Town / 1976 / Warner Brothers ✦✦✦✦
After bouncing back to life with *Atlantic Crossing,* Rod Stewart crafted his most self-consciously ambitious record with *A Night on the Town.* The centerpiece of the album, "The Killing of Georgie (Part I and II)," was a long, winding Dylan-esque tale of the murder of one of Stewart's gay friends and was one of his better songs of the mid-'70s. Even if "The Killing of Georgie" was the conscious artistic focal point of *A Night on the Town,* the true masterpiece of the album was an eloquent rendition of Cat Stevens' "The First Cut Is the Deepest." Apart from the flawed political platitudes of "Trade Winds," the rest of the album was filled with competent, professional pop-rock, highlighted by the No. 1 hit "Tonight's the Night (Gonna Be Alright)," a ballad where the gallant Rod relieves a teenager of her virginity. And, again, the "Slow Half" was more convincing than the frequently perfunctory "Fast Half." —*Stephen Thomas Erlewine*

Foot Loose & Fancy Free / 1977 / Warner Brothers ✦✦
Following the same formula as *Atlantic Crossing* and *A Night on the Town,* but not explicitly breaking the record into fast and slow sides, *Foot Loose & Fancy Free* was a limp effort from an increasingly compla-cent Rod Stewart. With the exception of the dumb, sleazy "Hot Legs," none of the rockers are discernable from each other, and this time he doesn't have a strong set of ballads to save him. The affectionately sappy acoustic ballad "You're in My Heart" was the big hit, but Stewart sounds completely convincing only on "I Was Only Joking." Coming at the end of the album, the song seems like a justification for the uninspired, by-the-book record that preceded it. —*Stephen Thomas Erlewine*

Blondes Have More Fun / 1978 / Warner Brothers ✦✦✦
In its simplest terms, *Blondes Have More Fun* is Rod Stewart's disco album, filled with pulsating rhythms and slick, synthesized textures. It's also his trashiest, most disposable album, filled with cheap come-ons and bad double entendres. Of course, that makes *Blondes Have More Fun* one of his most enjoyable records, even if all the pleasures are guilty. With its swirling strings and nagging chorus, "Da Ya Think I'm Sexy?" was the reason the record hit No. 1 and, two decades later, the

song stands as one of the best rock-disco fusions. The rest of the record isn't as engaging, but he throws out a handful of winning tracks in the same mould, including "Ain't Love a Bitch," "Attractive Female Wanted," and the title track. —*Stephen Thomas Erlewine*

Greatest Hits / 1979 / Warner Brothers ✦✦✦✦
Even though it has a couple of flaws—particularly the appearance of "Maggie May," which doesn't quite fit in with the rest of the material ——*Greatest Hits* is an enjoyable sampler of Rod Stewart's first four Warner albums, including most of the hits but not necessarily all of his greatest performances. —*Stephen Thomas Erlewine*

Foolish Behaviour / 1980 / Warner Brothers ✦✦
Rod Stewart followed the faux-disco trash of *Blondes Have More Fun* with *Foolish Behaviour,* which sanded out most of the character of the previous album. The result was a bland but professional—even at their worst, Rod and his band are always professionals—collection, mainly comprised of dance-oriented, lightly synthesized pop-rock. The passion-less "Passion" was the hit but the only worthwhile song was the gor-geous "Oh God, I Wish I Was Home Tonight," which has the clever wit and self-deprecating melancholy of his finest work. —*Stephen Thomas Erlewine*

Tonight I'm Yours / 1981 / Warner Brothers ✦✦✦✦
Though it lacks a truly great selection of songs, *Tonight I'm Yours* is a fine latter-day effort from Rod Stewart, and one of the last records that makes Rod sound like he's hip. Sporting a shiny new wave production, *Tonight I'm Yours* has a sleek, professional sound that can make even mindless rave-ups like "Tora, Tora, Tora (Out with the Boys)" a guilty pleasure. But the key to the album lays in songs like "Tonight I'm Yours" and the haunting "Young Turks," where Rod sounds totally at ease with a synth-pop beat. They are some of the best examples of mainstream rock co-opting the nervy, quirky appeal of new wave, and they make *Tonight I'm Yours* an enjoyable, if lightweight, listen. —*Stephen Thomas Erlewine*

Absolutely Live / 1982 / Warner Brothers ✦

Body Wishes / 1983 / Warner Brothers ✦✦
Two of the songs are first-rate synth-laden, disposable pop-rock filler—"Baby Jane" and "What Am I Gonna Do (I'm So in Love with You)"—but when those songs sound *substantial* next to dreck like "Ready Now" and "Sweet Surrender," it's clear that *Body Wishes* is one of Rod Stewart's worst efforts. —*Stephen Thomas Erlewine*

Camouflage / 1984 / Warner Brothers ✦✦
Camouflage is better than the disastrous *Body Wishes,* but that's only a relative term. Jeff Beck adds the occasional rock guitar flourish, but that doesn't save the faceless material. Again, the two singles—"Infatuation" and "Some Guys Have All the Luck"—are fine, ready-made pop hits, but they wear thin after a few plays, and they're the best things on the record. —*Stephen Thomas Erlewine*

Rod Stewart / 1986 / Warner Brothers ✦
Featuring a set of amazingly vapid material—led by the empty Top Ten hit "Love Touch"—and an embalmed, mechanical production, *Rod Stewart* is the worst album the singer recorded. After a series of faceless albums, it's not surprising that the record was uninspired; what was surprising was the utter lack of convincing pop-craft. The highlights of the album, "Love Touch" and "Every Beat of My Heart," were the singles but they lacked the well-constructed precision of "Some Guys Have All the Luck," "Infatuation," and "Baby Jane," which leaves *Rod Stewart* a soulless, and ultimately depressing, album. —*Stephen Thomas Erlewine*

Out of Order / 1988 / Warner Brothers ✦✦✦
With the support of the Power Station's guitarist Andy Taylor and drummer Bernard Edwards, Rod Stewart rebounds from his previous career nadir of "Love Touch" with *Out of Order.* Alternating between professional, driving rock 'n' roll like "Lost in You" and ballads like "My Heart Can't Tell You No," *Out of Order* is a well-constructed set of mainstream pop-rock and his best album since *Tonight I'm Yours,* even if none of the songs rank among his best work. —*Stephen Tho-mas Erlewine*

Storyteller: Complete Anthology / Oct. 1989 / Warner Brothers ✦✦✦✦
Storyteller: The Complete Anthology is a flawed but effective four-disc box set covering Rod Stewart's entire career. Although most of Stewart's biggest hits and best-known songs are on *Storyteller,* the collection is poorly paced, containing too much hesitant early mate-rial and not enough Jeff Beck Group or Faces selections. Nevertheless, the box traces his evolution from a working-class singer to Rod the Mod to superstar, featuring most of his essential songs—including whole sides of *Every Picture Tells a Story* and *Never a Dull Moment*—along the way. For casual fans looking for an in-depth over-view, it's an essential purchase, but more serious fans should stick with individual albums, especially his classic early-'70s albums. —*Stephen Thomas Erlewine*

Downtown Train (Selections from the Storyteller Anthology) / Mar. 6, 1990 / Warner Brothers ♦♦♦
Downtown Train (Selections from the Storyteller Anthology) is a 12-track distillation of Rod Stewart's four-disc box set, but instead of containing early hits, it concentrates on '80s singles like "Passion," "Young Turks," "Infatuation," "People Get Ready," and "Forever Young," adding a few '70s songs ("Stay with Me," "Tonight's the Night," "Killing of Georgie," "I Don't Want to Talk About It") and the new hit single "Downtown Train" for good measure. Although none of the material on the disc is bad, the compilation lacks focus or cohesion, making it no more than a good sampler for casual fans. —*Stephen Thomas Erlewine*

Vagabond Heart / Mar. 26, 1991 / Warner Brothers ♦♦♦
Rod Stewart continued to regain his strength with *Vagabond Heart*, the follow-up to his comeback album, *Out of Order*. *Vagabond Heart* is a stronger, more diverse album than its predecessor, featuring a more consistent set of songs, including Robbie Robertson's "Broken Arrow" and the hit "Motown Song," as well as a convincing, impassioned performance by Stewart. —*Stephen Thomas Erlewine*

The Mercury Anthology / Sep. 22, 1992 / Mercury ♦♦♦♦
A two-disc anthology of Rod Stewart's early Mercury recordings, which, in conjunction with the albums he recorded with the Faces, are inarguably his finest (nothing from the Faces records is included). Most of the highlights of his terrific first four albums are here—"Maggie May," "You Wear It Well," "Handbags and Gladrags," "Gasoline Alley"—as well as selections from the lukewarm *Smiler*, a live album recorded with the Faces, and a couple of rare B-sides. —*Stephen Thomas Erlewine*

Unplugged . . . And Seated / May 25, 1993 / Warner Brothers ♦♦♦
The inherent problem with Rod Stewart's *Unplugged* album is that it seems like a supremely calculated attempt to revive his career exactly as Eric Clapton did. Stewart returns to the acoustic rock 'n' roll and folk that marked his greatest recordings; Ron Wood's supporting guitar is a nice bonus recalling the glory days. Naturally, *Unplugged* can't hope to match *Gasoline Alley* or *Every Picture Tells a Story*, but the amazing thing is how close it comes at times. He sounds fine, if a little bit ragged at first, but as the album progresses, his performances become more genuine and heartfelt, culminating in yet another sublime Tom Waits cover with "Tom Traubert's Blues (Waltzing Matilda)," as well as a hit single with Van Morrison's "Have I Told You Lately?" —*Stephen Thomas Erlewine*

Spanner in the Works / Jun. 6, 1995 / Warner Brothers ♦♦♦
Following the success of *Unplugged . . . and Seated*, Rod Stewart had shrewdly repositioned himself as a mature, middle-aged man who still had a slight streak of his wilder days in him. Unsurprisingly, the music both recalled his past glories in instrumentation, yet the attack was different—the acoustics rocked, but it wasn't bracing; it was like a backporch jam session. Stewart expanded that approach on *A Spanner in the Works*, his first album since *Unplugged*. The acoustics are still there, but they're strummed a little more gently and set in a bed of unobtrusive synths. More importantly, Stewart tackles his most ambitious and varied set of material since *A Night on the Town*. From the pop-rock of Tom Petty's "Leave Virginia Alone" and the reflective take on Dylan's "Sweetheart like You" through the R&B tribute of "Muddy, Sam and Otis" and the rocking "Delicious" to the British folk of "Purple Heather," the songs recall his classic early albums in ambition and musical diversity. *A Spanner in the Works* isn't quite as successful as *Gasoline Alley* or *Every Picture Tells a Story*—it's a content album, not a probing one, which is appropriate for a middle-aged singer—yet it is the most inspired and ambitious record Stewart has released in nearly 20 years. —*Stephen Thomas Erlewine*

If We Fall in Love Tonight / Nov. 12, 1996 / Warner Brothers ♦♦♦
Taking its cue from Madonna's ballad collection *Something to Remember*, Rod Stewart's *If We Fall in Love Tonight* combines several of his biggest ballads with three new songs. *If We Fall in Love Tonight* is targeted directly toward an older, adult-contemporary audience who no longer wants to hear Stewart's harder-edged material. Which means that not only is "Maggie May" not included, but neither is "This Old Heart of Mine," since both are a bit too uptempo for this collection. Instead, the album is nothing but ballads, going back as far as "Tonight's the Night," "The First Cut Is the Deepest," "I Don't Want to Talk About It" and "You're in My Heart," but concentrating on '80s and '90s hits like "Downtown Train," "All for Love," "My Heart Can't Tell You No," "Have I Told You Lately" and "Broken Arrow." The compilation also contains rarities like the Sting and Bryan Adams collaboration "All for Love" and the Carole King cover "So Far Away," a new version of "Forever Young," a cover of Leo Sayer's "When I Need You, the James Newton Howard song "For the First Time" and the Jimmy Jam & Terry Lewis collaboration "If We Fall in Love Tonight." The new songs are good adult-contemporary radio fodder, yet they pale next to his classic '70s cuts. Nevertheless, *If We Fall in Love Tonight* is a very enjoyable soft-rock collection. It may not draw an accurate portrait of Stewart's career, but it does offer a good overview of his soft-rock hits. —*Stephen Thomas Erlewine*

Stiff Little Fingers

f. 1977, Belfast, Ireland, **db.** 1982
Punk
A taut, explosive Belfast-based punk band, Stiff Little Fingers (named after a Vibrators song) had the dubious distinction of being referred to as "The Irish Clash." What must have seemed like a compliment at the time did little to help their career, only because it made comparisons between the two bands inevitable. Granted, there were many similarities: both bands debuted playing revved-up late-'70s punk rock, both were politically inclined, featured pissed-off lead singers, a love for reggae, and a near-palpable sense of isolation and desperation. But as we all know, the Clash offered complexity, panache, and a consistently breathtaking body of work. Stiff Little Fingers, on the other hand, were simply a very good punk rock band. With sandpaper-throated frontman Jake Burns leading the way, SLF did release an auspicious, if badly produced, debut album, *Inflammable Material*, that featured the band's two best songs, "Alternative Ulster" and "Suspect Device." Both were passionate, ferocious songs dealing with the harsh, deadly realities of growing up in the middle of two decades of Northern Ireland's violence. These songs thrust SLF into the limelight and got them loads of enthusiastic press, which led to a contract with the decidedly anti-punk Chrysalis label in 1980. After that, SLF released a handful of pretty good records (including a terrific live album, *Hanx*), but their unregenerate fast and loud punk style started to sound stale. In 1982, the band released their most non-punk record (*Now Then . . .*), which was greeted by general apathy. In a musical rut, dogged by the facile Clash comparisons, and with punk rock running out of steam, Burns pulled the plug on SLF.
Sadly, the band's breakup lasted only five years. After a string of forgettable solo singles and a stint as a BBC Radio producer, Burns, hoping to cash in on punk nostalgia, reformed SLF (with another aging punk rocker, ex-Jam bassist Bruce Foxton) in 1987 and released a bunch of lousy (mostly live) records for the rest of the decade. —*John Dougan*

● **Inflammable Materials** / 1979 / Restless ♦♦♦♦
With "Alternative Ulster" and "Suspect Device" leading the way, this is a compelling, raging record that derives most of its style from the Sex Pistols and simply cranks up the personal political issues a notch or two. There is a so-so version of Bob Marley's "Johnny Was" (call it the obligatory reggae cover), but that doesn't hamper the enjoyment, nor does it detract from the record's overwhelming power. Issued on CD by Restless Retro in 1990. —*John Dougan*

Hanx / 1980 / Restless ♦♦♦
The other SLF studio recordings all contain some fine songs, but are recommended only to hardcore fans. *Hanx*, however, is a live recording that brilliantly serves two purposes: first, as proof of what incendiary live shows SLF was capable of; second, as a greatest hits record. Unsurprisingly, the tempos here are much faster than the studio recordings, but that simply adds to the excitement. Overlooked upon its release, *Hanx* is a raging, non-stop hunk of punk rock that sounds great even after all these years. Issued on CD by Restless Retro in 1990. —*John Dougan*

Nobody's Hero / Jan. 1980 / Restless ♦♦♦♦

Go for It / May 1981 / Restless ♦♦♦

Now Then / 1982 / Chrysalis ♦♦♦

All the Best / 1983 / One Way ♦♦♦♦
The best anthology of SLF available. A 30-track chronological overview that's as articulate an argument for SLF's greatness as anything else they released. A perfect way to hear their development from the early punk days to their more "mature" punk-pop period just prior to their breakup: Jake Burns goes from shouter to singer, hooks and riffs replace simple walls of distorted guitars, the reggae influence becomes stronger and is played with greater dexterity; all and all, you simply can't go wrong here. —*John Dougan*

Stephen Stills

b. Jan. 3, 1945, Dallas, TX
Guitar, Vocals / Singer-Songwriter, Pop-Rock
Famed for his work in Buffalo Springfield and Crosby, Stills & Nash, two of pop music's most successful and enduring groups, Stephen Stills was born in Dallas, Texas, on January 3, 1945. He became fascinated by music at a young age, and by the age of 15 was playing professionally. He eventually dropped out of college to move to New York City to try his hand as a folk performer before signing on as a guitar player with the Au Go Go Singers, where he befriended a fellow bandmate named Richie Furay.
After a tour of Canada (during which they headlined a bill with the Squires, which featured guitarist Neil Young), Stills left the Au Go Go's in 1965 for Los Angeles, where he became enmeshed in the city's burgeoning folk-rock community. After a series of session gigs and auditions (including one for the TV series *The Monkees*), in the spring of

1966 Stills enlisted Young, Furay, bassist Bruce Palmer, and drummer Dewey Martin to form the Herd, later dubbed the Buffalo Springfield. A year later, the group issued their eponymous debut; its Stills-penned single "For What It's Worth," made them stars. Internal problems, ego clashes and drugs were already tearing the band apart, however, and by the release of 1968's *Last Time Around*, the Springfield had already dissolved.

Stills quickly resurfaced with 1968's *Super Session*, recorded with fellow guitarists Mike Bloomfield and Al Kooper. A jam session with ex-Byrd David Crosby and former Hollies member Graham Nash led to the formation of the vocal harmony supergroup Crosby, Stills & Nash; released in 1969, their self-titled debut was hugely successful, propelled by the single "Suite: Judy Blue Eyes," written by Stills for folk singer Judy Collins. Later that year, Neil Young joined the loose-knit group, and in 1970, as Crosby, Stills, Nash & Young, they issued *Deja Vu*, another major hit.

From its inception, CSNY was designed to allow the individual performers great latitude for their solo work, and following the recording of the group's live LP *Four Way Street*, in late 1970 Stills released his self-titled solo debut. Sparked the success of the hit single "Love the One You're With," the album, which featured cameos from Jimi Hendrix and Eric Clapton, was another smash, as was his 1971 follow-up *Stephen Stills 2*. In 1972, Stills began performing with a new backing unit, Manassas, which featured ex-Byrd and Flying Burrito Brother Chris Hillman; both their eponymous debut and 1973's *Down the Road* continued Stills' long string of chart successes.

In 1975, he celebrated his signing to Columbia with *Stills*, followed a year later by *Illegal Stills*. In the summer of 1976, he planned to tour with Neil Young; however, Young was hampered with throat problems, so Stills took to the road alone, although he and Young did team for the LP *Long May You Run*. In 1977, Stills reunited with Crosby and Nash for *CSN*, which sold over four million copies; the following summer the trio mounted an acoustic tour, and Stills issued the solo record *Thoroughfare Gap*. CSN continued their reunion throughout the early years of the next decade, teaming in 1980 for *Replay* and in 1982 for *Daylight Again*, which featured the hits "Southern Cross" and "Wasted on the Way."

Following 1983's live CSN effort *Allies*, Stills again went solo for 1984's *Right by You*. In 1985, Crosby was sent to prison on drug possession charges, and Stills spent much of the late 1980s out of the public eye. Following Crosby's release, in 1988 the reconstituted Crosby, Stills, Nash & Young recorded *American Dream*, followed in 1990 by the CSN release *Live It Up*. In 1991, Stills issued the solo LP *Stills Alone*, while CSN's *After the Storm* appeared in 1994. —*Jason Ankeny*

● **Stephen Stills** / 1970 / Atlantic ✦✦✦✦
Stephen Stills' self-titled debut started out his solo career with much promise. The opening cut, "Love the One You're With," was a huge hit. His warm, husky voice is used to great effect on most of these tracks, and the album features a cast of 1970 all-stars like Jimi Hendrix, Eric Clapton, David Crosby, Graham Nash, John Sebastian, and Rita Coolidge. Hendrix's lead contribution is occasionally buried by Stills' overbearing organ work, and Clapton's guitar tone is too thin and brittle, but the hit "Sit Yourself Down," with its powerful piano introduction, is flawless in production and performance. —*Rick Clark*

Stephen Stills 2 / 1971 / Atlantic ✦✦✦
Manassas / 1972 / Atlantic ✦✦✦✦
After the uneven 1971 release *Stephen Stills 2*, Stills formed a band around him of some solid players (Chris Hillman, Joe Lala, Al Perkins, Fuzzy Samuels, Dallas Taylor, etc.) and called it Manassas. Their first of two albums was a self-titled double-record set. Many consider *Manassas* to be Stills' finest effort; it would have made a grand single album. Atlantic has managed to fit the whole thing on a single CD. —*Rick Clark*

Down the Road / 1973 / Atlantic ✦✦
Stills / 1975 / Columbia ✦✦
A new label brought about this lackluster attempt at reviving Stills' career. MOR arrangements capsize such potentially good tunes as "My Favorite Changes," "First Things First" and a cover of Neil Young's "New Mama." Includes a Crosby, Stills & Nash track "As I Come of Age" that should have been a hit. Unfortunately, it's the only bright spot on a rather dull release. —*James Chrispell*

Illegal Stills / 1976 / Columbia ✦✦
More coherent than his last effort, *Illegal Stills* still is mostly filler. Much of it co-written with Donnie Dacus, it finds Stephen Stills trying to recover after too many flops. Includes a curious cover of Neil Young's "The Loner," which Stills apparently always wanted to cover. Young's beats this version hands down. —*James Chrispell*

Long May You Run / 1976 / Reprise ✦✦✦
The Best of Stephen Stills / 1977 / Atlantic ✦✦✦✦
This is a decent sampling of his solo work up to this point. It includes "Change Partners" from *Stephen Stills 2*, as well as main tracks from

the debut. —*Rick Clark*

Thoroughfare Gap / 1978 / Columbia ✦✦
A rather poor attempt of Stephen Stills' to adapt to the disco/dance craze. Includes lame covers of Buddy Holly ("Not Fade Away") and Gregg Allman ("Midnight Rider") along with the semi-hit title track. —*James Chrispell*

Live / 1979 / Atlantic ✦✦
Right by You / 1984 / Atlantic ✦✦
See the racing boat taking off into outer space on the front cover. Flip the jacket over, and see Stephen Stills apparently co-piloting just such a ship, and you'll understand why the title of this album is so right. It's "Right by You" in so many ways, although it does contain a good bluegrass tune "No Hiding Place" and lead guitar by one Jimmy Page on several cuts. Maybe this was where Stills thought of sailing off into the sunset. This album didn't help his career. —*James Chrispell*

Stills Alone / Sep. 11, 1991 / Vision ✦✦✦

Sting (Gordon Sumner)

b. Oct. 2, 1951, Wallsend, England
Bass, Guitar, Vocals / Adult Contemporary, Pop-Rock, Jazz-Rock
After disbanding the Police at the peak of their popularity in 1984, Sting quickly established himself as a viable solo artist, one obsessed with expanding the boundaries of pop music. Sting incorporated heavy elements of jazz, classical, and worldbeat into his music, writing lyrics that were literate and self-consciously meaningful, and he was never afraid to emphasize this fact in the press. For such unabashed ambition, he was equally loved and reviled, with supporters believing that he was at the forefront of literate, intelligent rock and his critics finding his entire body of work pompous. Either way, Sting remained one of pop's biggest superstars for the first ten years of his solo career, before his record sales began to slip.

Before the Police were officially disbanded, Sting began work on his first solo album late in 1984, rounding up a group of jazz musicians as a supporting band. Moving from bass to guitar, he recorded his solo debut, 1985's *The Dream of the Blue Turtles*, with Branford Marsalis, Kenny Kirkland, and Omar Hakim. The move wasn't entirely unexpected, since Sting had played with jazz and progressive rock bands in his youth, but the result was considerably more mature and diverse than any Police record. The album became a hit, with "If You Love Somebody Set Them Free," "Love Is the Seventh Wave," and "Fortress Around Your Heart" reaching the American Top Ten. Sting brought the band out on an extensive tour, which was captured on a documentary called *Bring on the Night*, which appeared in 1986, along with a live double album of the same name. That year, Sting participated in a halfhearted Police reunion that resulted in only one new song, a re-recorded version of "Don't Stand So Close to Me."

Following the aborted Police reunion, Sting began working on the ambitious *Nothing Like the Sun*, which was dedicated to his recently deceased mother. Working from a jazz foundation, and again collaborating with Marsalis, Sting worked with a number of different musicians on the album, including Gil Evans and former Police guitarist Andy Summers. The album received generally positive reviews upon its release in late 1987, and it generated hit singles with "We'll Be Together" and "They Dance Alone." Following its release, Sting began actively campaigning for Amnesty International and environmentalism, establishing the Rainforest Foundation, which was designed to raise awareness about preserving the Brazilian rainforest. An abridged Spanish version of *Nothing Like the Sun, Nada Como el Sol*, was released in 1988.

Sting took several years to deliver the follow-up to *Nothing Like the Sun*, during which time he appeared in a failed Broadway revival of *The Threepenny Opera* in 1989. His father also died, which inspired 1991's *The Soul Cages*, a dense, dark, and complex album. Although the album peaked at No. 2 and spawned the Top Ten hit "All This Time," the record was less successful than its predecessor. Two years later, he delivered *Ten Summoner's Tales*, a light, pop-oriented record that became a hit on the strength of two Top 20 singles, "If I Ever Lose My Faith in You" and "Fields of Gold." At the end of 1993, "All for Love," a song he recorded with Rod Stewart and Bryan Adams for *The Three Musketeers*, became a No. 1 hit. The single confirmed that Sting's audience had shifted from new wave/college rock fans to adult contemporary, and the 1994 compilation *Fields of Gold: The Best of Sting* played to that audience.

Three years after *Ten Summoner's Tales*, Sting released *Mercury Falling* in the spring of 1996. Although the album debuted high, it quickly fell down the charts, stalling at platinum sales and failing to generate a hit single. While the album failed, Sting remained a popular concert attraction, confirming his immense popularity. —*Stephen Thomas Erlewine*

The Dream of the Blue Turtles / 1985 / A&M ✦✦✦✦
Sting's early jazz experience was very evident on his solo debut album. Kenny Kirkland (piano), Omar Hakim (drums), Darryl Jones (bass), and

Branford Marsalis (sax) contributed greatly to the jazz "feel" of the songs. This captures some of the energy and exuberance of the early Police, like *Regatta de Blanc*, but also maintains some of the somber, serious tone of *Synchronicity*. Sting's first album is his most impressive, boasting such songs as "Love Is the Seventh Wave," "Fortress Around Your Heart," "Children's Crusade," and "Moon over Bourbon Steet." —*Iotis Erlewine*

Bring on the Night / 1986 / A&M ♦♦♦
A terrific live-concert album, this contains songs dating back to Sting's years with the Police, as well as works from his first solo album, *Dream of the Blue Turtles*. In addition to performances of well-known songs, Sting performs the haunting "I Burn for You," a song written for the film *Brimstone and Treacle* (in which Sting had a role) but not included on any of Sting's own albums. This two-CD set features Branford Marsalis (sax), Omar Hakim (drums), Darryl Jones (bass), Kenny Kirkland (keyboards), and Janie Pendarvis and Dolette McDonald (vocals). —*Iotis Erlewine*

Nothing Like the Sun / 1987 / A&M ♦♦♦♦
This album is more somber than *Dream of the Blue Turtles* and light on the jazz influences, focusing more on Brazilian and Hispanic rhythms. Not as lively and concise as *Dream* due to the heavy, political lyrics (on such songs as "They Dance Alone" and "Fragile"), this is a good album, nevertheless. Along with Sting's own songs, the album includes a cover of Hendrix's "Little Wing." This album includes guests Mark Knopfler, Eric Clapton, the Gil Evans Band, former Police bandmember Andy Summers (who plays on "Lazarus Heart"), and, once again, Branford Marsalis featured on sax. —*Iotis Erlewine*

The Soul Cages / Jan. 17, 1991 / A&M ♦♦♦
This long-awaited album followed the death of Sting's father, which may explain the melancholy, pained tone of these songs. The focus here is very much on death and dying, making the album a bit of a downer and hard to listen to in a single sitting. Although the material may not be as good overall as Sting's previous work, the song "All This Time" is definitely one of his best. —*Iotis Erlewine*

● **Ten Summoner's Tales** / Mar. 9, 1993 / A&M ♦♦♦♦
Ten Summoner's Tales is the most song-oriented, lighthearted collection Sting has delivered since his solo debut. Sting's songs remain densely literate, although the melodies aren't; they are devoid of the jazz pretensions of *Nothing Like the Sun* and the oppressive seriousness of *The Soul Cages*. When he doesn't get carried away by his own cleverness, Sting can deliver the goods with some terrific pop songs ("If I Ever Lose My Faith in You," "It's Probably Me," "Epilogue [Nothin' 'Bout Me]," and "Seven Days"). Those songs help make *Ten Summoner's Tales* one of his strongest solo releases. —*Stephen Thomas Erlewine*

Fields of Gold: Best of Sting 1984-1994 / Nov. 8, 1994 / A&M ♦♦♦
This collection eliminates a lot of the more pretentiously "sophisticated" album tracks. The legion of Sting fans who consider the previous sentence heresy already own 12 out of 14 tracks; two new songs are included: "When We Dance" and "This Cowboy Song." —*Roch Parisien*

Mercury Falling / Mar. 12, 1996 / A&M ♦♦♦
Falling somewhere between the pop sensibilities of *Ten Summoner's Tales* and the searching ambition of *The Soul Cages*, *Mercury Falling* is one of Sting's tighter records, even if it fails to compel as much as his previous solo albums. Though he doesn't flaunt his jazz aspirations as he did in the mid-'80s, *Mercury Falling* feels more serious than *The Dream of the Blue Turtles*, primarily because of its reserved, high-class production and execution. Building from surprisingly simple, memorable melodies, Sting creates multi layered, vaguely soul-influenced arrangements that carry all of the hallmarks of someone who has studied a music, not lived it. Of course, there are many pleasures in the record—for all of his pretensions, Sting remains an engaging melodicist, as well as a clever lyricist. There just happens to be a distinct lack of energy, stemming from the suffocating layers of synthesizers. *Mercury Falling* is a record of modest pleasures; it's just not an infectious, compulsive listen. —*Stephen Thomas Erlewine*

Stone Poneys

f. 1964, Los Angeles, CA, db. 1968
Folk-Rock, Pop-Rock
Before becoming a solo act, Linda Ronstadt was the lead singer of the Stone Poneys, an L.A.-based trio with an acoustic, folkish sound and strong original material. The band's focal point and greatest asset was Ronstadt's clear, powerful vocals. Originally recording in a coffeehouse folk style not far removed from Peter, Paul & Mary, the group rocked up their sound slightly and scored a Top 20 hit with "Different Drum," written by Mike Nesmith of the Monkees, in 1967. —*Richie Unterberger*

● **Stone Poneys Featuring Linda Ronstadt** / 1967 / Capitol ♦♦♦♦
It doesn't have "Different Drum," but the first Stone Poneys album is their folkiest and best, dominated by close harmonies and strong origi-

nal material by the group's guitarists, Bob Kimmel and Ken Edwards. —*Richie Unterberger*

Evergreen, Vol. 2 / 1967 / Capitol ♦♦♦
Evergreen, Vol. 2 wasn't as strong as their debut album, but it did contain their only hit, "Different Drum," as well as several other pleasant songs in a similar vein. —*Stephen Thomas Erlewine*

Stone Poneys & Friends, Vol. 3 / 1968 / Capitol ♦♦♦
The Stone Poneys broke up during the recording of their final album, leaving Ronstadt to finish the work with various sessionmen (hence the billing "Stone Poneys & Friends"). It's a solid effort, though, of decent if muted Californian folk-rock, with a laid back (but not offensively so), carefully produced feel. Certainly the material is varied, with selections from the Stone Poneys, Mike Nesmith, and Laura Nyro, and occasional intimations of the country-rock direction that Ronstadt would frequently pursue during the '70s. The inclusion of three Tim Buckley songs serves as evidence that Ronstadt was hipper than some of her detractors have made her out to be. —*Richie Unterberger*

The Stone Roses

f. 1985, Manchester, England, **db.** Oct. 1996
Alternative Pop-Rock, Brit-Pop, Alternative Dance
Meshing '60s-styled guitar pop with an understated '80s dance beat, the Stone Roses defined the British guitar-pop scene of the late '80s and early '90s. After their eponymous 1989 debut album became an English sensation, countless other groups in the same vein became popular, including the Charlatans (UK), Inspiral Carpets, and Happy Mondays. However, the band was never able to capitalize on the promise of their first album, waiting five years before they released their second record and slowly disintegrating in the year and half after its release.

The Stone Roses emerged from the remains of English Rose, a Manchester-based band formed by schoolmates John Squire (guitar) and Ian Brown (vocals). In 1985, the Stone Roses officially formed, as Squire and Brown added drummer Reni (b. Alan John Wren), guitarist Andy Couzens, and bassist Pete Garner. The group began playing warehouses around Manchester, cultivating a dedicated following rather quickly. Around this time, the group was a cross between classic British '60s guitar pop and heavy metal, with touches of goth rock. Couzens left the group in 1987, followed shortly afterward by Garner. Garner was replaced by Mani (b. Gary Mounfield) and the group recorded their first single, "So Young," which was released to little attention by Thin Line Records. At the end of 1987, the Stone Roses released their second single, "Sally Cinnamon," which pointed the way toward the band's hook-laden, ringing guitar-pop. By the fall of 1988, the band secured a contract with Silvertone Records and released "Elephant Stone," a single that set the band's catchy neo-psychedelic guitar-pop in stone.

Shortly after the release of "Elephant Stone," the Stone Roses' bandwagon took off in earnest. In early 1989, the group was playing sold-out gigs across Manchester and London. In May, the Stone Roses released their eponymous debut album, which demonstrated not only a predilection for '60s guitar hooks, but also a contemporary acid-house rhythmic sensibility. *The Stone Roses* received rave reviews and soon, a crop of similar-sounding bands appeared in the UK. By the end of the summer, the Stone Roses were perceived as leading a wave of bands that fused rock 'n' roll and acid house culture. "She Bangs the Drums," the third single pulled from the debut, became the group's first Top 40 single at the end of the summer. In November, the group had their first Top Ten hit when "Fool's Gold" climbed to No. 8. By the end of the year, the band had moved from selling out clubs to selling out large theaters in the UK.

For the first half of 1990, re-releases of the band's earlier singles clogged the charts. The group returned in July 1990 with the single "One Love," which entered the charts at No. 4. Prior to the release of "One Love," the Stone Roses organized their own festival at Spike Island in Widnes. The concert drew over 30,000 people and would prove to be their last concert in England for five years. After Spike Island, the Stone Roses became embroiled in a vicious legal battle with Silvertone Records.

The group wanted to leave the label but Silvertone took out a court injunction against the group, preventing them from releasing any new material. For the next two years, the band fought Silvertone Records while they allegedly prepared the follow-up to their debut album. However, the Stone Roses did next to nothing as the court case rolled on. In the meantime, several major record labels began negotiating with the band in secret. In March of 1991, the lawsuit went to court. Two months later, the Stone Roses won their case against Silvertone and signed a multi-million deal with Geffen Records.

For the next three years, the Stone Roses worked sporadically on their second album, leaving behind scores of uncompleted tapes. During these years, the group kept a low profile in the press but that wasn't to preserve the mystique—they simply weren't doing much of anything besides watching football. Finally, in the spring of 1994, Geffen demanded that the group finish the album and the band complied, completing the record, titled *Second Coming*, in the fall. "Love Spreads," the Stone Roses' comeback single, was debuted on Radio One in early November. The single received a lukewarm reaction and entered the charts at No. 2, not the expected No. 1. *Second Coming* received mixed reviews and only spent a few weeks in the Top Ten. The Stone Roses planned an international tour in early 1995 to support the album, but the plans kept unraveling at the last minute. Before they could set out on tour, Reni left the band, leaving the group without a drummer. He was replaced by Robbie Maddix, who had previously played in Rebel MC. After Maddix joined the band, they embarked on a short American tour at the conclusion of which John Squire broke his collar bone in a bike accident. Squire's accident forced them to cancel a headlining spot at the 25th Glastonbury Festival, which would have been their first concert in the UK in five years. As Squire recuperated, the Stone Roses continued to sink in popularity and respect—even as their peers, the Charlatans and former Happy Mondays vocalist Shaun Ryder, made unexpectedly triumphant comebacks.

The Stone Roses added a keyboardist to the lineup prior to their UK tour at the end of 1995—it was the first British tour since 1990. In the spring of 1996, John Squire announced that he was leaving the band he founded in order to form a new, more active band. The Stone Roses announced their intention to carry on with a new guitarist. —*Stephen Thomas Erlewine*

★ **The Stone Roses** / Jul. 1989 / Silvertone ✦✦✦✦✦
Since the Stone Roses were the nominal leaders of Britain's "Madchester" scene—an indie-rock phenomenon that fused guitar pop with drug-fueled rave and dance culture—it's rather ironic that their eponymous debut only hints at dance music. What made the Stone Roses important was how they welcomed dance and pop together, treating it as if it were the same beast. Equally important was the Roses' cool, detached arrogance that was personified by Ian Brown's nonchalant vocals. Brown's effortless malevolence is brought to life with songs that equal both his sentiments and his voice—"I Wanna Be Adored," with its creeping bass line and waves of cool guitar hooks, doesn't demand adoration it just *expects* it. Similarly, Brown can claim "I Am the Resurrection" and lay back, as if there were no room for debate. But the key to *The Stone Roses* is John Squire's layers of simple, exceedingly catchy hooks and how the rhythm section of Reni and Mani always imply dance rhythms without overtly going into the disco. On "She Bangs the Drums" and "Elephant Stone" the hooks wind into the rhythm inseparably—the '60s hooks and the rolling beats manage to convey the colorful, neo-psychedelic world of acid house. Squire's riffs are bright and catchy, recalling the British Invasion while suggesting the future with their phased, echoey effects. *The Stone Roses* was a two-fold revolution—it brought dance music to an audience that was previously obsessed with droning guitars, while it revived the concept of classic pop songwriting, and the repercussions of its achievement could be heard throughout the '90s, even if the Stone Roses could never achieve this level of achievement ever again. —*Stephen Thomas Erlewine*

Turns Into Stone / Oct. 27, 1992 / Silvertone ✦✦✦
Not a new Stone Roses album, it's another collection of European B-sides and selected songs from their debut album. If they don't already own the singles, hardcore fans will want to purchase this despite the heavy repetition of tracks; most listeners will be content with the debut. —*AMG*

Second Coming / Dec. 1994 / Geffen ✦✦✦
There's no denying that *Second Coming* is a bit of a letdown. None of the songs are quite as strong as the best on their debut, but there is plenty of good music on the band's much-delayed second record. The Stone Roses create a dense tapestry of interweaving guitars and pulsing bass grooves. Ian Brown growls a little more than before, but he isn't the center of the music; John Squire's endlessly colorful riffs are. It's clear that Squire has been listening to a bit of hard rock, particularly Led Zeppelin. While the songs occasionally take a back seat to the grooves, several tracks—"Ten Storey Love Song," "Begging You," "Tightrope," "How Do You Sleep," and "Love Spreads"—rank as true classics. It might not be the long-awaited masterpiece it was rumored to be, but *Second Coming* is a fine sophomore effort. —*Stephen Thomas Erlewine*

The Complete Stone Roses / Jun. 27, 1995 / Silvertone ✦✦✦✦
The title's a bit of a misnomer. *The Complete Stone Roses* concentrates on the band's first album, compiling the A—and B-sides of the group's hits from "Elephant Stone" to "One Love." In addition to the familiar material, the disc includes rare, early singles like "So Young" and "Sally Cinnamon" for the first time on compact disc, giving their classic material some context. The loud guitars of "So Young" are clearly the work of a hesitant band, while "Sally Cinnamon" is the first indication of John Squire's gift for ringing, melodic guitar hooks. However, their inclusion—as well as the appearance of the B-sides, which lack the consistent brilliance of "I Wanna Be Adored," "She Bangs the Drums," "Elephant Stone," "Waterfall," etc.—make *The Complete Stone Roses* a flawed introduction to the band. Nevertheless, there's a fair amount of classic

pop here and the rarities are necessary for dedicated fans. —*Stephen Thomas Erlewine*

Stone Temple Pilots

f. 1992, San Diego, CA
Hard Rock, Alternative Pop-Rock, Grunge
Stone Temple Pilots were able to make alternative rock into stadium rock; naturally, they became the most critically despised band of their era. Accused by many critics of being nothing more than rip-off artists, pilfering from Pearl Jam, Soundgarden, and Alice in Chains, the band nevertheless became major stars in 1993. And the influences of those bands *are* apparent in their music, but Stone Temple Pilots do manage to change things around a bit. STP are more concerned with tight song structure and riffs than punk rage. Their closest antecedents are not the Sex Pistols or Hüsker Dü; instead the band resembles arena rock acts from the '70s—it's popular hard rock that sounds good on the radio and in concert. No matter what the critics might say, Stone Temple Pilots have undeniably catchy riffs and production; there's a reason why over three million people bought their debut album, *Core*, and why their second album, *Purple*, shot to No. 1 when it was released.

Following the success of *Purple* and its accompanying tour, the band took some time off, during which the group's lead singer, Scott Weiland, developed a heroin addiction. In the spring of 1995, he was arrested for possession of heroin and cocaine, and he was sentenced to a rehabilitation program. Following his completion of the program, Stone Temple Pilots recorded their third album. Released in the spring of 1996, *Tiny Music... Songs from the Vatican Gift Shop* entered the charts at No. 4. Shortly after its release, Stone Temple Pilots announced that Weiland had relapsed and had entered a drug rehabilitation facility, thereby canceling the group's plans for a summer tour. Weiland's drug problems and the group's inability to support *Tiny Music* with a tour meant that the album couldn't replicate the success of its predecessors—by the end of the summer, it had fallen out the Top 50 and had stalled at platinum, which was considerably less than what the group's two previous albums achieved. —*Stephen Thomas Erlewine*

Core / Sep. 29, 1992 / Atlantic ✦✦✦✦
While the Stone Temple Pilots may not be sincere alternative rockers, they do know how to write a killer riff, which is why their debut album sold nearly as many copies as Pearl Jam. Admittedly, STP can sound like either Pearl Jam ("Plush"), Alice in Chains ("Sex Type Thing" and "Wicked Garden"), Soundgarden ("Dead & Bloated"), or even R.E.M. ("Creep"), depending on their mood, but their hooks are undeniably catchy, making the songs much better than they have any right to be. In fact, Stone Temple Pilots appear to be the hard-rock arena act for the 1990s, and that's a compliment. —*Stephen Thomas Erlewine*

● **Purple** / May 31, 1994 / Atlantic ✦✦✦✦
Stone Temple Pilots may have topped the charts with *Core*, yet it was with *Purple* that they established their across-the-board popularity. Trimming back the excesses of their debut, *Purple* is a lean, throttling piece of post-alternative hard rock. STP doesn't rely simply on riffs, although there is a fair share of killer hooks; the band writes songs, where the melodies and chords intertwine, becoming inseparable. From the brooding ballad "The Big Empty" to the simple, pounding, fuzzy riffs of "Vasoline," the group has improved in every facet—their songs are stronger and their playing is more convincing and powerful. Best of all is "Interstate Love Song." Clocking in at under three minutes, the record became one of the biggest album rock hits ever, spending 15 weeks at the top of the charts, and deservedly so—with its carefully measured dynamics and memorable melody, it's a showcase for everything that's good about hard rock. —*Stephen Thomas Erlewine*

Tiny Music... Songs from the Vatican Gift Shop / Mar. 26, 1996 / Atlantic ✦✦✦✦
Purple established that Stone Temple Pilots were not one-album wonders but *Tiny Music... Songs from the Vatican Gift Shop* illustrates that the band isn't content with resting on the laurels. Without abandoning their trademark hard rock, STP have added a new array of sounds that adds depth to their immediately accessible hooks. Dean DeLeo layers his guitar tracks to create distinctive, multi-textured sounds that make his riffs more powerful. Though there are hints of grunge scattered throughout the album, what makes *Tiny Music* impressive is how the band brings in elements of psychedelia, trancy shoegazing, jangle-pop, and other forms of melodic alternative guitar-pop. By accentuating their pop tendencies in both their riffs and melodies, they are able to slip in a number of creative arrangements that manage to expand their musical repertoire significantly. Although the lyrics are nearly as ambitious as the music, they simply don't have the same weight. But with a band like Stone Temple Pilots, the music is what matters and *Tiny Music* showcases the band at their most tuneful and creative. —*Stephen Thomas Erlewine*

The Stooges

f. 1967, Ann Arbor, MI, db. 1973
Hard Rock, Proto-Punk

During the psychedelic haze of the late '60s, the grimy, noisy, and relentlessly bleak rock 'n' roll of the Stooges was conspicuously out of time. Like the Velvet Underground, the Stooges revealed the underside of sex, drugs, and rock 'n' roll, showing all of the grime beneath the myth. The Stooges, however, weren't nearly as cerebral as the Velvets. Taking their cue from the over-amplified pounding of British blues, the primal raunch of American garage rock, and the psychedelic rock (as well as the audience-baiting) of the Doors, the Stooges were raw, immediate, and vulgar. Iggy Pop became notorious for performing smeared in blood or peanut butter, diving into the audience. Ron and Scott Asheton formed a ridiculously primitive rhythm section, pounding out chords with no finesse—in essence, the Stooges were the first rock 'n' roll band completely stripped of the swinging beat that epitomized R&B and early rock 'n' roll. During the late '60s and early '70s, the group was an underground sensation, yet the band was too weird, too dangerous to break into the mainstream. Following three albums, the Stooges disbanded, but the group's legacy grew over the next two decades, as legions of underground bands used their sludgy grind as a foundation for a variety of indie-rock styles, and as Iggy Pop became a pop cultural icon.

After playing in several local bands in Ann Arbor, Michigan, including the blues band the Prime Movers and the Iguanas, Iggy Pop (b. James Osterberg) formed the Stooges in 1967 after witnessing a Doors concert in Chicago. Adopting the name Iggy Stooge, he rounded up brothers Ron and Scott Asheton (guitar and drums, respectively) and bassist Dave Alexander, and the group debuted at a Halloween concert at the University of Michigan student union in 1967. For the next year, the group played the Midwest relentlessly, earning a reputation for their wild, primitive performances, which were largely reviled. In particular, Iggy gained attention for his bizarre onstage behavior. Performing shirtless, he would smear steaks and peanut butter on his body, cut himself with glass and dive into the audience. The Stooges were infamous, not famous—while they had a rabidly devoted core audience, even more people detested their shock tactics. Nevertheless, the group lucked into a major-label record contract in 1968 when an Elektra talent scout went to Detroit to see the MC5 and wound up signing their opening act, the Stooges, as well.

Produced by John Cale, the Stooges' primitive eponymous debut was released in 1969, and while it generated some attention in the underground press, it barely sold any copies. As the band prepared to record their second album, every member sank deeper into substance abuse, and their excess eventually surfaced in their concerts, not only through Iggy's antics, but also in the fact that the band could barely keep a simple, two-chord riff afloat. *Fun House*, an atonal barrage of avant-noise, appeared in 1970 and, if it was even noticed, it earned generally negative reviews and sold even fewer copies than the debut. Following the release of *Fun House*, the Stooges essentially disintegrated, as Iggy sank into heroin addiction. At first, he did try to keep the Stooges afloat. Dave Alexander left the band and Ron Asheton moved to bass as James Williamson joined as guitarist, but this incarnation wasn't able to land a record deal, despite recording a handful of demos. For the next two years, the band was in limbo, as Iggy weaned himself off heroin and worked various odd jobs. Early in 1972, Pop happened to run into David Bowie, then at the height of his Ziggy Stardust popularity. Bowie made it his mission to resuscitate Iggy and the Stooges, as the band was now billed. With Bowie's help, the Stooges landed a management deal and a contract with Columbia, and he took control of the production of the group's third album, *Raw Power*.

Released in 1973 to surprisingly strong reviews, *Raw Power* had a weird, thin mix due to various technical problems. Although this would be the cause of much controversy later on—many Stooges purists blamed Bowie for the brittle mix—its razor-thin sound helped kickstart the punk revolution. At the time, however, *Raw Power* flopped, essentially bringing the Stooges' career to a halt. Iggy stuck with Bowie, who helped him shake heroin and establish a solo career with the 1977 albums *The Idiot* and *Lust for Life*.

The Ashetons formed New Order, which quickly fell apart, leaving Ron to join Destroy All Monsters. Toward the late '70s, when Pop separated from Bowie, James Williamson began working with the vocalist, playing on a number of records and tours. By the mid-'80s, a decade after the group's demise, the Stooges were hailed as one of the first punk rock bands, and there were legions of underground groups replicating their sound, as well as several others—such as Sonic Youth and Mudhoney—who expanded and updated that sound, making it one of the cornerstones of alternative rock. Meanwhile, the Stooges lived on in countless semi-legal releases and repackagings of live shows, demos and outtakes, all of which were consumed avidly by a still-devoted cult.
—Stephen Thomas Erlewine

The Stooges / 1969 / Elektra ✦✦✦✦
The Stooges' eponymous debut album suffers from John Cale's flat production, which turns much of the record into a numbing grind, but "I Wanna Be Your Dog" and "1969" suggest the punky fury that would explode on *Fun House*. *—Stephen Thomas Erlewine*

☆ **Fun House** / 1970 / Elektra ✦✦✦✦✦
Fun House is the quintessential Stooges album, the one where the music constantly sounds as if it was falling apart. Most of the songs on *Fun House* essentially recycle the same riff, but the key to the record isn't the songs, it's the sound. Where John Cale gave *The Stooges* a sound that was a bit too clean, *Fun House* sounds completely unproduced. Instruments bleed all over the place, Ron Asheton bangs out impossibly primitive riffs, Scott Asheton and Dave Alexander pound out brutal, simple rhythms and Iggy Pop screams incoherent babble. *Fun House* only has seven songs, but it plays as one long piece—the violent swagger of "Down on the Street" morphs into the open wound of "T.V. Eye" and the dark dirge of "Dirt" before it all comes crashing down in the atonal climax of "L.A. Blues." At the time of its release, no other record sounded quite so raw, amateurish and noisy—the Velvet Underground may have explored the avant-garde with the white noise experiments on their first two albums, but the Stooges sound as if they are leaving any artistic pretensions behind and are simply celebrating the sound of feedback, shouts, and crashing drums. *—Stephen Thomas Erlewine*

★ **Raw Power** / 1973 / Columbia ✦✦✦✦✦
The Stooges broke up after Elektra Records dropped them following the release of *Fun House*. Upon the urging of David Bowie, the group reformed with a new guitarist, James Williamson, and proceeded to record *Raw Power*. Many Stooges fans have continually debated the merits of the group's third and final album, claiming that Bowie diluted the sound of the record by mixing the bass almost entirely out of the final version and not giving the guitars enough power. Even though there is some truth to these allegations, *Raw Power* remains a definitive Stooges album—the group positively seethes with energy. The cleaner production and performances don't hurt the band. Instead, they give Iggy Pop a clearer, more direct platform for his scary posturing. Being able to hear everything on the record gives it a lethal force, though fans of *Fun House* will miss the murk. Nevertheless, *Raw Power* is the group's most accessible effort and many of the Stooges imitators that followed in the '80s and '90s basically reworked the sound of this album, making it just slightly grungier. *—Stephen Thomas Erlewine*

Metallic K.O. / 1976 / Skydog ✦✦✦✦
The last Stooges live show;, scary as hell. Bootleg import. Worth the search. *—Cub Koda*

Kill City / 1978 / Bomp! ✦✦✦✦

I Got a Right / 1987 / Revenge ✦✦✦
When Iggy and the newly reformed Stooges were starting work on what would eventually their final album, *Raw Power*, their initial efforts shocked their management and were summarily rejected, only to surface on numerous vinyl bootlegs over the next couple of decades. One of the more famous couplings was released as a single, the flame-throwing "I Got a Right" and the equally wild "Gimme Some Skin." This collection rounds up every existing take of those two titles with a live version of the title cut to round things out. This is Iggy and the Stooges at arguably their peak and well worth seeking out as the sound is appreciably better than the original 45 issue. *—Cub Koda*

Rough Power / Jan. 30, 1995 / Bomp! ✦✦✦
The final mix by David Bowie of the Stooges' final studio album has been a subject of open debate since the day of its release in 1973. Some see it as a total botch job, with the vocals and guitar overdubs set so far out front of the bass and drums (collapsed into mono, stripped of its high frequencies, then echoed to death) as to appear comical. Others see it as a mix every bit as anarchic as the music itself. That debate is fueled even further by the first legal appearances of these alternate mixes done by Iggy and the Stooges prior to Bowie's intervention. On tracks like "I Need Somebody" and "Gimme Danger," the focus is much sharper than the released version, while on others ("Hard to Beat," "Raw Power," "Search and Destroy") Iggy's vocal is obscured by liberal doses of too much echo. An aircheck from early 1973 gives us grainy, abrasive speeded up alternates of seven more tracks and the compilation closes with three more from late in 1972, clearly showing that the boys had theories on mixing that were every bit as off the wall as Bowie's finals. Final score: not necessarily better, but very different. *—Cub Koda*

Year of the Iguana / Feb. 27, 1997 / Bomp! ✦✦✦
There's little doubt that in the decades since their demise, Iggy and the Stooges have achieved legendary status as the seminal and defining influence on the late-'70s punk rock movement; without them, there would have been no Sex Pistols, etc. In those intervening years, they have been exhaustively documented, with seemingly every scrap of magnetic tape bearing their imprint reissued at one time or another. This is an interesting collection primarily culled from other Bomp CD

collections and ten-inch vinyl LPs, and includes alternate mixes ("Death Trip"), raw rehearsal tapes ("Rubber Legs," "Head On," "Till the End of the Night" and an extended "Raw Power"), and "suppressed masters" from the original *Raw Power* sessions ("I Got a Right," "Gimme Some Skin," and "Scene of the Crime"). For the new fan who's just discovered the chaotic magic that was the Stooges—and has heard the rumors that there's material far more incendiary than their three studio albums—this compilation sifts through the unending maze of unissued material to make a single-disc package that hits all the right spots. —*Cub Koda*

Stories

f. 1972, New York, NY
Pop-Rock
After the demise of the Left Banke, classically trained keyboardist and songwriter Michael Brown (b. Apr 25, 1949) formed Stories in 1972 with singer Ian Lloyd. Their first two albums, *Stories* and (particularly) *About Us*, featured a brilliant collection of ultra-melodic pop-rock songs that were less baroque than those of Left Banke and (at times) harder-hitting than those of fellow pop-rockers like Badfinger.

Neither of these albums achieved any real success, and Stories would have (more than likely) sadly sunk without a trace had fate not intervened with the totally left-field hit (about an interracial encounter) titled "Brother Louie" (No. 1), written by Errol Brown of the British group Hot Chocolate. Their label, Kama Sutra, jammed the tune on *About Us*, and the album ended up charting at No. 29.

Brown left the group, and they released the spotty *Travelling Underground*, which produced the "Brother Louie"-carbon-copy "Mammy Blue" (No. 50) and "If It Feels Good, Do It" (No. 88). Stories broke up shortly thereafter. —*Rick Clark*

Stories / 1972 / Kama Sutra ◆◆◆◆
Travelling Underground / 1973 / Kama Sutra ◆◆◆
● About Us / 1973 / Pair ◆◆◆◆
The second Stories album melded ornate Anglo-pop with ever-so-slight art-pop tendencies. Loaded with great melodies and smart arrangements. Fans of Badfinger and Beatles-style pop-rock should love this outing. It was a commercial sleeper until the band's version of Hot Chocolate's "Brother Louie" became a No. 1 hit. Unfortunately, the song didn't resemble anything else on the album. Highlights include "Darling," "Hey France," "Please Please," "What Comes After," and "Top of the City." This disc may be hard to find, since their reissue label has historically done little to promote reissue product. —*Rick Clark*

Straitjacket Fits

f. 1985, Auckland, New Zealand
Alternative Pop-Rock
Auckland, New Zealand's Straitjacket Fits are cast in much the same mold as other bands on the Flying Nun label, playing hooky guitar pop with the usual mood of longing. However, the band distinguishes itself by injecting some guitar muscle every now and then and bringing more attitude than many of their contemporaries. The band is led by vocalists/guitarists Shayne Carter and Andrew Brough. —*Steve Huey*
● Hail / 1990 / Rough Trade ◆◆◆◆
Dissonant, dreamy, and hypnotic garage rock with an aggressive edge from this New Zealand band. Highlights include "She Speeds" and "All That That Brings." The import CD contains additional tracks. —*Scott Bultman*
Melt / Jun. 25, 1991 / Arista ◆◆◆
Not as soaring as their first US album, their musicianship and dark hypnotic energy make it worthwhile. —*Scott Bultman*
Blow / May 25, 1993 / Arista ◆◆

The Strangeloves

f. 1964, Brooklyn, NY, db. 1968
Rock & Roll
While the Strangeloves managed to produce one garage band classic, their story is probably more interesting than their actual music. Bob Feldman, Jerry Goldstein, and Richard Gottehrer were a trio of Brooklyn songwriter-producers who landed a No. 1 girl group hit with the Angels' "My Boyfriend's Back." When the British Invasion crested in the mid-'60s, they decided to get in on the act by recording as a group, billing themselves as an Australian outfit to cash in on the mystique being attached to foreign groups.

"I Want Candy," with its crunching Bo Diddley beat, joyous chorus, and rambling lead guitar, was their great moment, reaching No. 11 in 1965. Forced to put together a live act to support their disc, they made outrageous claims to hail from the nonexistent town of Armstrong, Australia, where they had made a fortune as sheepherders who had developed a cross-breed. They also made the Top 40 with a couple fairly gutsy

follow-ups, "Cara-Lin" and "Night Time," both of which were built around crunching claps, stomps, and drums. Also recording an album and several non-hit singles, most of their material unashamedly plagiarized the Bo Diddley beats of "I Want Candy," with forgettable results. They withdrew from performing and recording to concentrate on writing and producing for the McCoys, although Strangeloves releases continued to appear until 1968. Goldstein went on to produce records for War in the 1970s, and Gottehrer produced efforts by Blondie, the Go-Go's, and others. —*Richie Unterberger*

● I Want Candy: the Best of The Strangeloves / 1995 / Epic/Legacy ◆◆◆◆
Twenty tracks from the mid-'60s, including all the hits, a lot of stuff from their sole LP, non-hit singles, rare 45s they recorded for Swan (in 1964) and Sire (in 1968), and an item they put out under the pseudonym of the Beach-Nuts. But it's really not deserving of such thoughtful archiving; beyond "I Want Candy," "Cara-Lin," and "Night Time," only hardcore collectors will be interested. —*Richie Unterberger*

The Stranglers

f. 1975, Chiddington, Surrey, England, db. 1993
Rock & Roll, Punk
As were their contemporaries the Vibrators, the Stranglers were fauxpunks; grimy, slightly arty rockers that found the notoriety surrounding punk bands too irresistible to ignore. So armed with short haircuts and reticent about revealing their true ages (drummer Jet Black was a certifiable old fart when the band formed in 1975), the Stranglers became stars of Brit punk's class of 1976-77, garnering headlines for their sexist posturing, drug use, occasional arrests, and oh yeah, their music too.

Truth be told, the Stranglers became a far less interesting band immediately after they stopped acting like a punk band. At least on the first two albums (*Rattus Norvegicus* and *No More Heroes*) there were plenty of taut, guitar-driven songs, rife with urban doom, gloom, and paranoia. With the nasty vocals and slashing guitar of Hugh Cornwell setting the pace, bassist Jean-Jacques Burnel added his distorted grumbling to a mix that also featured Dave Greenfield's cheesy organ fills. Usually dressed in black, always unsmiling, and rude to their audiences (listen to Cornwell's between-song badinage on the LP *Live (X-Cert)*) the Stranglers worked very hard at being difficult and unlikable. They also made no bones about the fact that women were good for sex and little else, making their feeling clear on such transparently chauvinistic doggerel as "London Lady" and "Bring on the Nubiles."

Rock critics at the time were suspicious of the Stranglers' motives: although they ran in "proper" punk circles, and gigged at "proper" punk clubs, they always seemed slightly out-of-place musically with the London-based punk scene dominated by the Sex Pistols, the Damned, and Clash. The Stranglers offered no sense of outrage (despite being outrageous) or unpredictability, every moved seemed calculated, as if it were an approximation of a punk aesthetic. Consequently, with each passing record, the Stranglers seemed more and more intent upon distancing themselves from the movement that had provided them their initial career momentum.

After 1978's *Black and White* failed to generate interest beyond their somewhat rabid fan base (more so in Europe than in America), A&M dropped them, but unlike many bands of the time that became trivia questions, the Stranglers soldiered on and focused their attention on their devoted Euro-fans, a wise move considering their records were no longer consistently released in America. In 1982, the band signed with Epic and began a lengthy relationship that lasted through the decade and into the '90s. The music, never really compelling in the first place, suffered greatly during this time. Prisoners of their own careerist impulses, the Stranglers turned to covering older rock classics in a desperate attempt to win American ears. Trying twice, first with the Kinks' "All Day and All of the Night" and then ? and the Mysterians' "96 Tears," the Stranglers sounded as if flogging a dead horse was the best they could do. Gone also was their characteristic gritty and grimy sound, replaced by a pop sheen that smelled of adult, new wave marketability (eventually Queen producer Roy Thomas Baker was brought in to help). There were plenty of mostly lousy solo records by everyone but Jet Black, and some fairly good compilations, but the saga of the Stranglers ends with them hanging around far too long. —*John Dougan*

Rattus Norvegicus / Apr. 1977 / A&M ◆◆◆
Like the Vibrators, the Stranglers were an older band that managed to gain visibility and success through association with Britain's punk movement. Musically, the group is much more polished than some of their rawer brethren such as the Adverts and Siouxsie and the Banshees. The Stranglers' early work is most properly described as stripped-down pop played with a hardcore sensibility; fairly lengthy songs with frequent solo breaks, prominent keyboard usage, and occasional employment of vocal harmony set them apart from their peers. But snarling lead singing that puts forth macho/critical/distasteful lyrics predominates here, clearly showing the group's punk affinity. Most of the songs

on this album fit the description of hardcore pop to a tee, but there are a few deviations from this model. "Princess of the Streets" is a slow-tempo selection with blueslike echoes. The ambitious "Down in the Sewer" crosses the concept of episodic numbers like the Who's "A Quick One" with early 1960s instrumentals. And the energetic "London Lady" is almost a true punk song—or at least as close as the band gets to one. While not the equal of their best album, *No More Heroes*, this release is solid and worthwhile, a rewarding listen. —*David Cleary*

No More Heroes / Oct. 1977 / A&M ✦✦✦✦

Rattus is hardly a punk rock classic but still is a pretty good chunk of art-punk. Hugh Cornwell's testosterone level is very high here and the macho preening gets a bit much, but it's still an enjoyable bit of noise that holds up better than I'm sure anyone would have guessed at the time. Still, it's odd to think of this as a part of the punk rock era; with the exception of the fast and sloppy production by Martin Rushent, and the short songs, there's not much that's overtly punk about it. *Heroes* on the other hand is faster, nastier, and better. At this point the Stranglers were on top of their game and the ferocity and anger that suffuses these records would never be repeated. —*John Dougan*

Black & White / 1978 / A&M ✦✦✦

Live (X Cert) / 1979 / IRS ✦✦✦

Recorded at various gigs in 1977-78, *Live (X Cert)* is worthy if only to hear Hugh Cornwell bait and insult the audience (very punk!). Plus the band sounds pretty good, loads of aggression and volume add to the fun. Not essential but a very interesting snapshot of an era. —*John Dougan*

The Raven / 1979 / United Artists ✦✦✦

By the time this album was released, the group had branched out a bit from their punk-influenced pop music stylings and grouchy personal-relationship-based lyrics. Half the songs on this album (among them "Dead Loss Angeles," [sic] "Nuclear Device," "Shah Shah a Gogo," [sic] and "Genetix" [sic] spout verses critical of social or political issues. Only the first of these four numbers, with its clipped vocal delivery and stripped-down, bass-heavy arrangement, shows significant Brit-punk influence. Certain songs here exhibit strong mainstream tendencies with no hardcore sensibilities whatsoever, such as "Duchess" (a tuneful power pop number with clear chart-oriented influences) and "Don't Bring Harry" (a slow-tempo, piano-dominated selection). Still other influences can be seen in "Meninblack," a Devo-derived number featuring a synthesized clipped beat/electronic pulse texture, chilly and sanitized-sounding organ, lockstep drums, and Alvin and the Chipmunks-style sped-up vocals. The intriguing "Ice" boasts interesting production touches and an inventively dubious tonal focus. The songs are lengthy, with at times prolix instrumental openings and interludes. Sound quality on the EMI America re-release is uneven at times, with occasional distortion in the drums and percussive low synthesizer. This is a generally good album worth hearing. Original pressings of this release have a 3-D picture on the front cover. Approximately half the songs on this album would be reissued one year later on the US label release *IV*. —*David Cleary*

Stranglers IV / 1980 / IRS ✦✦

The Meninblack / 1981 / Liberty ✦✦

La Folie / 1981 / Liberty ✦✦✦✦

La Folie is a welcome album in the group's oeuvre, mainly a collection of tight, punchy songs that often suggest the forthright approach of American new wave bands. With one exception, the songs are shorter and more pointed, hearkening back to the comparative conciseness of some of the tunes on the band's first two albums, *Rattus Norvegicus* and *No More Heroes*, though acidic lyrics still predominate. "Non-Stop" is a typical example, featuring a half-spoken vocal that suggests Lou Reed, a Cars-influenced organ sound, and a bouncy, dance-derived drum beat; this particular song is atypical, however, because it employs a blues-oriented progression. An interesting excursion is encountered in the song "Golden Brown," a subdued, jazz-influenced number with purring vocals, a coolly executed synthesizer/harpsichord backing texture, and a periodically stumbling beat. Only the plushly understated title track suggests the sprawl typical of the group's immediately preceding releases. This fine album is well worth purchasing. —*David Cleary*

Feline / 1983 / Epic ✦✦✦

Aural Sculpture / 1984 / Epic ✦✦✦

Dreamtime / 1987 / Epic ✦✦

● Greatest Hits 1977-1990 / 1990 / Epic ✦✦✦✦

Despite its rather cheeky title, this is a good place to sample the entire Stranglers output. From the squalor of the late-'70s material, to the smoothed out gloom pop of songs like "Skin Deep" and other mid-to late-'80s neo-Goth rock, this is a solid anthology that values substance over style and exhaustive track selection. Trust me, a well-edited Stranglers anthology is the only way to enjoy them, they recorded way too much dross to spend time searching out all of their plentiful, marginal records. —*John Dougan*

10 / May 1990 / Epic ✦✦✦

Early Years 1974-76 / Oct. 14, 1994 / Castle ✦✦✦

About Time / 1995 / When? ✦✦

About Time is a competent but unexceptional record from the latter-day Stranglers, featuring a couple of tough, catchy songs that recall the group's heyday ("Lies and Deception," "Golden Boy"), but it is largely bogged down by tepid songwriting and undistinguished performances. —*Stephen Thomas Erlewine*

Saturday Night Sunday Morning / Mar. 10, 1996 / Castle ✦✦

Written in Red / 1997 / When ✦✦

The Stranglers, now without Hugh Cornwell, return to the synth-spiked territory of their latter-day records with the Andy Gill-produced *Written in Red*. Though the group sounds tight and professional, the record lacks strong songs, making *Written in Red* an utterly undistinguished album. —*Stephen Thomas Erlewine*

The Hit Men / Feb. 1997 / EMI ✦✦✦✦

The Stranglers worked better as a singles band than they did as album artists, but that doesn't mean that the double-disc, 43-track retrospective *The Hit Men: The Complete Singles 1977-1991* is consistently engaging. Considerably older than their punk peers, the Stranglers nevertheless knocked out several terrific songs in their first records, including "(Get a) Grip (on Yourself)" and "Hanging Around," but by the mid-'80s they had become a little bland and predictable, as evidenced by covers of "96 Tears" and "All Day and All of the Night." That decline is charted on *The Hit Men*, as it runs through all of the group's EMI and Epic singles, as well as selected album tracks. All of the group's best moments are here, but there's also an abundance of mediocre tracks making this of interest primarily to completists. Casual fans will be content with the single-disc *Greatest Hits 1977-1990*. —*Stephen Thomas Erlewine*

Syd Straw

b. , Los Angeles, CA
Vocals / Alternative Pop-Rock, Jangle-Pop
Vocalist, singer-songwriter, and guitarist Syd Straw first made a name for herself as part of the Golden Palominos, a band led by Anton Fier that enjoyed a cult following in the 1980s. Her Capricorn Records debut, *War and Peace*, was released in 1996, and since then her unique blend of folk-rock and blues-rock have found a home with Triple A (adult album alternative) radio stations and their audiences around the country. Straw has only one other solo album, *Surprise*, released in 1990 to good reviews. That recording chronicled Straw's emergence as a songwriter, as she had thought of herself primarily as a song interpreter before that. On *Surprise*, Straw was joined by Michael Stipe (R.E.M.), John Doe (X), Ry Cooder, Daniel Lanois, Don Was, Richard Thompson, and Marshall Crenshaw.

Straw was raised in Los Angeles, the daughter of Hollywood film and TV actor Jack Straw, best known for his starring role in *The Pajama Game*. She was drawn to a life as a performer, and after high school she headed straight for Manhattan, arriving in New York in 1978. Shortly after that, she landed her first job singing harmonies for Pat Benatar, and later joined the Golden Palominos' ever-changing lineup, which also included Michael Stipe and Matthew Sweet. Straw can be heard on the Palominos' *Visions of Excess* and *Blast of Silence* albums. She also toured the US and Europe with the band, performing at the Montreaux Jazz Festival one year.

In the midst of promoting and touring for *War and Peace*, Straw has kept up her profile as a scenemaker, sitting in at clubs and lending her gifted musical sensibilities to records by Vic Chesnutt, Wilco, Rickie Lee Jones, David Sanborn, and Evan Dando. Her song "Howl" served as the title cut for a film by Eric Stolz, *Sleep with Me*. Straw was the first female singer signed by Capricorn, a roots-rock and blues label now based in Nashville. On *War and Peace*, she's accompanied by a gifted bar band from Missouri, Lou Whitney and the Skeletons, and she recorded the album without a lot of extras at their studio off Route 66 in Springfield, MO. On the album, Straw addresses themes including love and the lack of it on a track by the same name, "Love and the Lack of It," as well as loneliness, as on "All Things Change."

Although Straw may only have two albums out, she's an enormously gifted vocalist and songwriter who has her own distinct musical vision, as evidenced on her self-produced *War and Peace*. That vision is a rootsy one, with lots of country and blues influences. Her 14 originals on the record prove it. Although she didn't set out to, she also plays rhythm guitar on many of the tracks on the album. Straw says with the biography accompanying *War and Peace* that she doesn't see the album as a "comeback" at all, "because things have been constantly busy and changing for me since *Surprise* came out. But I really threw myself into the new record in a way that I haven't been inspired to do for a long time." Great records and a wider following are in the offing for this unique, multi-genre vocalist and songwriter. —*Richard Skelly*

● **Surprise** / Jun. 1989 / Virgin ✦✦✦✦

War and Peace / May 7, 1996 / Capricorn ✦✦✦

Emerging out of the Golden Palominos, Syd Straw made 1989's *Surprise*, one of those big-budget, name-producer, multiple-recording-studio star-making extravaganzas, and good as it was, it didn't get noticed. It took her seven years to mount a second try, and to do so she just tooled down to Springfield, Missouri, and cut a quick record with the semi-legendary Skeletons backing her up. The result is a jangly-guitar, singer-songwriter folk-rock feast and a glimpse into an apparently tortured soul. Straw sings of liquor and love gone wrong; there is a vague story line here, what with the references to Spain and recurrent self-debasement. But there is also a deadpan humor, plenty of tuneful music and an intriguing, if wounded, persona who comes under unyielding self-examination. *— William Ruhlmann*

War and Peace / May 7, 1996 / Capricorn ✦✦✦

Emerging out of the Golden Palominos, Syd Straw made 1989's *Surprise*, one of those big-budget, name-producer, multiple-recording-studio star-making extravaganzas, and good as it was, it didn't get noticed. It took her seven years to mount a second try, and to do so she just tooled down to Springfield, Missouri, and cut a quick record with the semi-legendary Skeletons backing her up. The result is a jangly-guitar, singer-songwriter folk-rock feast and a glimpse into an apparently tortured soul. Straw sings of liquor and love gone wrong; there is a vague story line here, what with the references to Spain and recurrent self-debasement. But there is also a deadpan humor, plenty of tuneful music, and an intriguing, if wounded, persona who comes under unyielding self-examination. *— William Ruhlmann*

Strawberry Alarm Clock

f. 1966, Los Angeles, CA, **db.** 1971
Psychedelic, Pop-Rock

Strawberry Alarm Clock was a psychedelic bubblegum band of the mid-'60s, reaching the top of the charts with "Incense and Peppermints" at the height of the flower power era. Originally called the Sixpence, the Californian group consisted of Ed King (lead guitar), Lee Freeman (rhythm guitar), Gary Lovetro (bass), Mark Weitz (organ), and Randy Seol (drums). On the band's debut single, "Incense and Peppermints," lead vocals were sung by Greg Munford, a 16-year-old friend of the band. Before recording their full-length debut album, the band added George Bunnell, who also played bass; more importantly, Bunnell became the group's main songwriter.

In the summer of 1967, the Strawberry Alarm Clock contributed music to the film *Psych-Out*, as well as appearing in it. Gary Lovetro left the band before they recorded their second album, *Wake Up It's Tomorrow*, which also appeared in 1967. Between 1968's *The World in a Seashell* and 1969's *Good Morning Starshine* the band went through a number of lineup changes; as of *Good Morning Starshine* the band featured King on bass, Weitz, guitarist Jimmy Pitman, and drummer Gene Gunnels. By this time, the Strawberry Alarm Clock had lost much of its audience. They managed to keep performing until 1971, when the band finally broke up. Ed King went on to join Lynyrd Skynyrd; several of the former members of Strawberry Alarm Clock reunited in the '80s to perform on oldies tours. *— Stephen Thomas Erlewine*

● **Strawberries Mean Love** / 1992 / Big Beat ✦✦✦✦

For a little more money, this 21-track CD compilation is a better deal than its American counterpart (One Way's *Anthology*), offering a slightly more extensive selection and extensive liner notes, and including almost all of the cuts contained on *Anthology*. Drawn from their four albums (with the accent, properly, on the first two), it also has a clutch of non-LP singles. "Incense and Peppermints" and the small follow-up hit "Tomorrow" are by far the best things on here; much of the rest is trendy period pop/psychedelia, sounding at various times like a much bigger league Doors, or a *really* spaced out Association, with a bit of garage raunch tossed in on the B-side of "Incense" ("The Birdman of Alkatrash"). The two hits were included on Rhino's *Nuggets* compilations, which might be a better context in which to appreciate the group's fairly minimal contributions to psychedelia. *— Richie Unterberger*

● **Anthology** / Jun. 30, 1993 / One Way ✦✦✦✦

For most fans, the 16-track *Anthology* will simply be too much Strawberry Alarm Clock to digest, since the band rarely hit the heights of "Incense and Peppermints." Most of the rest of the album consists of period pieces like "Sit with the Guru," "Rainy Day Mushroom Pillow," "They Saw the Fat One Coming," "The Birdman of Alkatrash" and the three-part suite "Black Butter," which are entertaining as artifacts, but aren't particularly good songs. Nevertheless, it's hard to imagine anyone assembling a more comprehensive overview than *Anthology*, even if it is lacking any cuts from the *Beyond the Valley of the Dolls* soundtrack. It's a near-definitive retrospective. *— Stephen Thomas Erlewine*

The Strawbs

f. 1968, London, England
Art-Rock/Progressive-Rock, Folk-Rock, British Folk

One of the better British progressive bands of the early '70s, the Strawbs differed from their more successful compatriots—the Moody Blues, King Crimson, Pink Floyd—principally in that their sound originated in English folk music, rather than rock. Founded in 1967 as a bluegrass-based trio called the Strawberry Hill Boys by singer/guitarist Dave Cousins, the group at that time consisted of Cousins, guitarist/singer Tony Hooper, and mandolinist Arthur Philips, who was replaced in 1968 by Ron Chesterman on bass. That same year, the group—now rechristened the Strawbs, and doing repertory well beyond the bounds of bluegrass music—briefly became a quartet with the temporary addition of Sandy Denny, who stayed long enough to record a relative handful of tracks with the group on the Hallmark label before joining Fairport Convention.

In 1969, the Strawbs were signed to A&M Records and cut their first album, the acoustic-textured *Strawbs*, that same year. For their second album, *Dragonfly*, recorded and released the following year, the group broadened their sound with the presence of a group of session musicians, including piano/organist Rick Wakeman. Soon after the release of this record, the group became a full-fledged band with the addition not only of Wakeman but also Richard Hudson and John Ford, on drums and bass, respectively. These changes, coupled with Cousins' increasing dexterity on electric guitar, gave the Strawbs a much more powerful sound that was showcased on their next album.

The live *Just a Collection of Antiques and Curios* (1970) sold well, and was followed the next year with *From the Witchwood*. In 1971, Wakeman left the Strawbs in order to join Yes; he was replaced by Blue Weaver formerly of the Amen Corner. *Grave New World* (1972) showed the band entering its strongest period, with Cousins' songwriting augmented by the new prowess of the composing team of Hudson and Ford. The record became their bestselling album to date. Unfortunately, its release also heralded the exit of Tony Hooper. He was replaced by Dave Lambert, a more aggressive, rock-oriented guitarist, and his addition brought the group into its peak period. The Strawbs' 1973 album, *Bursting at the Seams*, featured two Top Ten UK hits, "Lay Down" and "Part of the Union," and one album track, "Down by the Sea," racked up substantial airplay on American FM radio.

It was all too good to last, and it didn't. Blue Weaver left after one more tour, while Hudson and Ford exited to form Hudson-Ford, also signed to A&M. The Strawbs regrouped in 1974 with *Hero and Heroine*, recorded with a new lineup consisting of Cousins, Lambert, keyboardist John Hawken, bassist Chas Cronk, and drummer Rod Coombes. The new album was a critical and commercial failure in England, but proved popular in America. Their next two albums, *Ghosts* (1975) and *Nomadness* (1976), both did better in the US than they did in the UK. None of this was enough to sustain the group, however, which continued to lose members and also left A&M Records. Two more albums on the Oyster label were poorly distributed and received, and one album for Arista, *Deadlines* (1978), was a failure, while a second record for the label was never released. The group ceased to exist at the end of the 1970s, and Cousins embarked on some solo projects in association with guitarist Brian Willoughby that attracted the interest of diehard fans but few others. That might have been the end of the group's history, if it hadn't been for an invitation to play the 1983 Cambridge Folk Festival. The Strawbs responded, in the guise of Cousins, Hooper, Hudson, Ford, Weaver, and Willoughby, and the response was so favorable that a tour was scheduled, which, in turn, led to their return to America in the mid-'80s. The group followed this up with two new studio albums released in Canada, and still plays whenever other commitments allow Cousins and company (with Rod Demick on bass and Chris Parren on keyboards) to get together. In 1993, they released their own retrospective concert album *Greatest Hits Live!*, which summed up many of the high points of their history. *— Bruce Eder*

Sandy Denny & the Strawbs / 1968 / Hannibal ✦✦✦✦

Acoustic folk and bluegrass. Mostly a showcase for Denny, plus a few clues to the group's future evolution. *— Bruce Eder*

Strawbs / 1969 / A&M ✦✦✦

Still an acoustic sound but with a much more expansive song structure and growing seriousness. *— Bruce Eder*

Dragonfly / 1970 / A&M ✦✦✦

A transitional record, profound in some of its intent, but lacking muscle and excitement. *— Bruce Eder*

Just a Collection of Antiques and Curios / 1970 / A&M ✦✦✦

For some American fans, this was the first album by the Strawbs they ever heard, the first to be released over here, and a strange one in the sense that it was recorded live in concert at London's Queen Elizabeth Hall (a top venue for chamber groups and small orchestras). Although the group by now had drums, electric bass, and organ in its instrumental lineup, the textures of the music (especially the guitars) were still largely acoustic, making for a very interesting sound. They paint a broad canvas in a series of intense performances, and some long jams (most notably the 10-minute-plus epic "Where Is That Dream of Your Youth," which started life as a three-minute piece on an earlier album), with one important new topical number ("Martin Luther King's Dream"). Wakeman's acoustic piano solo didn't really fit the rest of the album, though it did anticipate his later solo spot on *Yessongs* as well as his solo album debut, *The Six Wives of Henry VIII*, and his playing added a vast range to the group's sound. —*Bruce Eder*

From the Witchwood / 1971 / A&M ✦✦✦
Another transitional album at a different stage—where *Dragonfly* bridged the gap from folk and bluegrass to folk-rock, *From the Witchwood* tries with limited success to ford the space between traditional and modern sensibilities, featuring longer and more complex story-songs sparked by Rick Wakeman's rippling keyboards. The group was now at the outer limit of where their devotion to folk themes could take them on acoustic instruments—"Witchwood" would be among the last of their acoustic-textured, traditional folk-like songs, and constitutes a gorgeous farewell of sorts to that era; "The Hangman and the Papist," by contrast, was a peculiar topical song and a daring political allegory (with personal overtones for composer Dave Cousins) about religious war set in some past time but clearly meant to refer to the strife in Northern Ireland. Not all of the rest was as strong, apart from "The Shepherd's Song," but there was no turning back from this point, as the group plunged into progressive rock. —*Bruce Eder*

Grave New World / 1972 / A&M ✦✦✦✦
Fulfillment! Singer-songwriter Dave Cousins finds a space somewhere between Bob Dylan and John Bunyan, Hudson and Ford come up with some superb hooks, and the electric sound is powerful and majestic. Powerful and sincere, if a little too serious and downbeat. —*Bruce Eder*

Bursting at the Seams / 1973 / A&M ✦✦✦✦
A magnum opus: romantic, mystical, electrifying, and it rocks with a defiant smile. "Down by the Sea" is as fine a piece of progressive rock as was ever produced. —*Bruce Eder*

Strawbs by Choice / 1974 / A&M ✦✦✦
A concise retrospective of some of the better moments from the first four A&M albums. —*Bruce Eder*

Hero and Heroine / 1974 / A&M ✦✦✦
The group's last great album, filled with mysticism and sexuality but lacking melodic subtlety. Loud, but with less richness of expression. —*Bruce Eder*

Ghosts / 1975 / A&M ✦✦
Deteriorated sound and material, with beautiful and profound moments, but too much forgettable material around them. —*Bruce Eder*

Best of Strawbs / 1978 / A&M ✦✦✦
A double-album retrospective that misses the mark with too little of the best material from their best albums. Too much dross, and somehow flat-sounding. —*Bruce Eder*

Preserves Uncanned / 1991 / Road Goes On Forever ✦✦✦✦
A double CD of 38 previously unreleased songs (one is unlisted on the sleeve) dating from 1966 to 1968, prior to the recording of their proper debut album. Most of these are demos, and many would surface (sometimes in altered form) on future Strawbs and Dave Cousins albums, although quite a few were never officially rerecorded. Its appeal isn't just limited to Strawbs specialists—it's good, versatile (if slightly derivative) late-'60s British folk-rock, recalling Fairport Convention and (to a lesser degree) Pentangle in its eclecticism, though the Strawbs were no match for the Fairports in the vocal department. Most of the songs are Cousins originals, including tuneful, almost poppy harmony numbers and wordy tracts that take their lyrical cues from Bob Dylan and Ray Davies; the traditional folk tunes and bluegrass instrumentals, though indicative of the group's multifaceted talents, are less interesting. Self-penned compositions like "October to May," "Martin Luther King's Dream," "Where Is the Dream of Your Youth," and "The Man Who Called Himself Jesus" are among the best (not to mention lyrically ambitious) songs Cousins has ever done; "All I Need Is You" and the Beatles-ish "And You Need Me" are among the poppiest. Good sound quality, and detailed liner notes by Cousins himself. —*Richie Unterberger*

● **A Choice Selection of Strawbs** / 1993 / A&M ✦✦✦✦
Very few of the UK group's albums have been released in CD format, and this comprehensive, 74-minute collection goes a long way to sating the resultant thirst. While there are elements of The Strawbs' mellotron-based sound that make *A Choice Selection* sound dated at times, the material survives better than many of the group's "progressive-minded" contemporaries. The Strawbs' roots went back to folk and bluegrass, and leader David Cousins never let instrumental virtuosity get in the way of a good song and well-turned lyric. —*Roch Parisien*

Halcyon Days / 1997 / A&M ✦✦✦✦
In the course of nine years, the Strawbs evolved from an obscure, quirky British bluegrass group into one of the most beloved progressive-rock bands in the world. This 150-minute collection covers most of that history, encompassing most (but not all) of the key songs from their nine A&M albums, as well as lost B-sides, songs by ex-members Richard Hudson and John Ford, and a pair of tracks off of Dave Cousins' 1972 solo album *Two Weeks Last Summer.* The selection of material is inspired, juxtaposing rarities with a good deal of important music from the core of their output. The programming straddles the collectable and the historical/musical significance of the material, so we get early 1970s FM hits such as "The River" and "Down by the Sea" sharing space with material such as "Martin Luther King's Dream" and subsequent extended progressive material like "Ghosts." The range of styles is daunting, from Dylan-esque acoustic folk-style numbers to extended songs in which Mellotrons, synthesizers and loud, complex electric guitar runs are the dominant presences. —*Bruce Eder*

Stray Cats

f. 1979, Long Island, NY, **db.** 1984
New Wave, Rockabilly Revival
This US rock trio consists of Brian Setzer (b. 1960), standup bass slapper Lee Rock (born Lee Drucher), and drummer Slim Jim Phantom (born James McDonnell). It was formed in 1979 in the midst of the punk/new wave scene, playing retro-rockabilly style. Emigrating to England shortly thereafter, they caught on quickly with a music scene that was always interested in the "next big thing," and their top-notch production by Dave Edmunds quickly moved them into the charts. Visual image and European success augered well for their return to the US just in time to mine the early motherlode of MTV video-land. By the mid-'80s, after much success, the gimmick had worn off, and the band broke up by late 1984. They regrouped in the '90s after various solo projects had fizzled, with their style relatively unchanged, but again disbanded after 1994's *Choo Choo Hot Fish.* —*Cub Koda*

Built for Speed / Jun. 1982 / EMI America ✦✦✦✦
The best tracks from the Stray Cats' two UK albums, the best produced by Dave Edmunds, as the group updates rockabilly and Brian Setzer comes on like a rock star. Infectious. —*William Ruhlmann*

Rant N' Rave with the Stray Cats / 1983 / EMI America ✦✦✦✦
Rant N' Rave, the Stray Cats' second album, sounded identical to *Built for Speed,* and—thanks to the hits "(She's) Sexy + 17" and the ballad "I Won't Stand in Your Way"—it was equally as strong. —*Stephen Thomas Erlewine*

Rock Therapy / 1986 / EMI America ✦✦✦
Rock Therapy wasn't as consistently engaging as *Built for Speed* and *Rant N' Rave,* but it was a spirited, inspired effort that continued their trademark sound to a fine effect. —*Stephen Thomas Erlewine*

Blast Off / 1989 / EMI America ✦✦
Featuring a set of pleasant, but unexciting, songs, *Blast Off* indicated that the Stray Cats' revved-up rockabilly ran out of gas quickly. —*David Jehnzen*

● **The Best of Stray Cats: Rock This Town** / Oct. 1990 / EMI America ✦✦✦✦
The Best of the Stray Cats is a brief but effective 10-song compilation featuring all of the rockabilly revivalists' biggest American hits, including "Stray Cat Strut," "Rock This Town," "(She's) Sexy & 17," "I Won't Stand in Your Way," "Bring It Back Again," and "Look at That Cadillac." Although other compilations offer a larger selection, *Rock This Town* contains all of the necessary items, making it a good choice for most casual fans. —*Stephen Thomas Erlewine*

● **Runaway Boys: A Retrospective '81–'92** / Jan. 14, 1997 / EMI ✦✦✦✦
An exemplary best-of, this has 25 tracks from throughout their career, leaning heavily on the earliest and best material. It also contains a few tunes that were previously unreleased in the US, the B-side cover of the Supremes' "You Can't Hurry Love," and all three non-album songs from their 1983 double 45 "(She's) Sexy + 17." Those that prize authenticity might continue to scorn this rockabilly revivalism. But now that the debate over whether the group were poseurs or not has become irrelevant, it's a surprisingly solid guilty pleasure, even if it's more or less reheated Gene Vincent. —*Richie Unterberger*

Barbra Streisand

b. Apr. 24, 1942, Brooklyn, NY
Vocals / Adult Contemporary, Pop, Soft Rock, Show Tunes
Barbra Streisand's status as one of the most successful singers of her generation is all the more remarkable not only because her popularity has been achieved in the face of a dominant musical trend—rock 'n' roll—which she did not follow, but also because, despite an amazing singing voice that has enthralled practically anyone who has heard it,

she has always used singing as a mere stepping-stone to other careers, as a stage and film actress and as a film director.

Streisand struggled briefly as an actress and nightclub singer in New York in the early 1960s before landing her first part in a Broadway show, *I Can Get It for You Wholesale*, in 1962. The cast album for that show and a subsequent appearance on a studio revival of *Pins and Needles* were her first recordings. Signed to Columbia Records, she released her first album, *The Barbra Streisand Album*, in 1963. It became a Top Ten, gold-selling record, turning Streisand into one of the bestselling recording artists of the early 1960s. But despite three successful albums by early 1964, Streisand turned her back on potentially lucrative concert bookings in favor of a starring role in the Broadway show *Funny Girl*, in which she appeared for more than two years. "People" from that show became her first Top Ten single, and the *People* album her first chart-topping LP. She turned to television in 1965 with *My Name Is Barbra*, the first of five network specials. In 1967, Streisand went to Hollywood to film *Funny Girl*, for which she would win an Academy Award. But by 1970, with her second and third films flops and her recording career flagging in the face of rock, she seemed consigned to Las Vegas before turning 30. Instead, she returned to hit-making with a Top Ten cover of Laura Nyro's "Stoney End" and a successful non-singing performance in the comedy *The Owl and the Pussycat*.

In the 1970s, Streisand successfully married her musical and film acting interests, first in *The Way We Were*, a hit film with a theme song that became her first No. 1 single, and then with *A Star Is Born*, which featured her second No. 1 single "Evergreen," a song she co-wrote. From that point on, every album she released sold at least a million copies. In the late '70s, she found recording success in collaboration: Her duet with Neil Diamond, "You Don't Bring Me Flowers," hit No. 1, as did "No More Tears (Enough Is Enough)," a dance record sung with Donna Summer. She had her biggest selling album in 1980 with *Guilty*, which was written and produced by Barry Gibb of the Bee Gees and which contained the No. 1 hit "Woman in Love." In 1983, Streisand's first directorial effort, *Yentl*, became a successful film with a Top Ten soundtrack album. In 1985, *The Broadway Album* returned her to the top of the charts. The year 1991 saw the release of *Just for the Record…*, a boxed set retrospective, and her second film as a director, *The Prince of Tides*. Streisand returned to the concert stage in 1994, resulting in the Top Ten, million-selling album *The Concert*. In 1996, she directed her third film, *The Mirror Has Two Faces*. — *William Ruhlmann*

Pins and Needles [O.S.T.] / 1962 / Columbia ✦✦✦

☆ **The Barbra Streisand Album** / Feb. 25, 1963 / Columbia ✦✦✦✦✦
Of course, the first thing that strikes you listening to the first Barbra Streisand album, recorded and released before the singer's 21st birthday, is *that great voice*. And it isn't just the sheer quality of the voice, its purity and its strength throughout its register, it's also the mastery of vocal effects that produce dramatic readings of the lyrics—each song is like a one-act musical. Streisand opens with Julie London's signature torch song, "Cry Me a River," and she doesn't only surpass London, she sets off a thermonuclear explosion. From there, versatility and novelty are emphasized—a breakneck version of "Who's Afraid of the Big Bad Wolf?," a slow, emotion-drenched performance of "Happy Days Are Here Again." But Streisand's debut, inventively arranged and conducted by Peter Matz, is notable as much for the surprising omissions as the surprising selections. Arriving in 1963, ten years into the revival of sophisticated interwar theater songs led by Frank Sinatra and followed by all other adult pop singers, Streisand virtually ignores the modern masters like Gershwin and Berlin. When she does do Rodgers and Hart or Cole Porter, she picks obscure songs; her idea of a good 1930s number is Fats Waller and Andy Razaf's "Keepin' Out of Mischief Now." She is much more comfortable with recent theater material, choosing two songs from *The Fantasticks* (1960) and the title song from the stage play *A Taste of Honey* (1962). *The Barbra Streisand Album* is an essential recording in the field of pop vocals because it redefines that genre in contemporary terms. (*The Barbra Streisand Album* won Grammy Awards for Album of the Year, Best Female Vocal Performance, and Best Album Cover.) — *William Ruhlmann*

The Second Album / Oct. 1963 / Columbia ✦✦✦

People / 1964 / Columbia ✦✦✦✦

The Third Album / Feb. 1964 / Columbia ✦✦✦

My Name Is Barbra / 1965 / Columbia ✦✦✦✦

My Name Is Barbra 2 / Oct. 1965 / Columbia ✦✦✦

Color Me Barbra / 1966 / Columbia ✦✦✦

Je M'appelle Barbra / Nov. 1966 / Columbia ✦✦✦

Simply Streisand / Oct. 1967 / Columbia ✦✦✦

A Happening in Central Park / 1968 / Columbia ✦✦✦

What About Today? / 1969 / Columbia ✦✦

The Owl and the Pussycat / 1970 / Columbia ✦

● **Greatest Hits** / 1970 / Columbia ✦✦✦✦
At a time when Barbra Streisand's career was in decline, what turned out to be only her first greatest hits album seemed to serve as both a summing up and a kiss-off of her 1960s recordings. Streisand was not primarily a singles artist; between 1964 and 1969, she enjoyed nine chart singles, of which only one, "People," made the Top Ten, with only one other, "Second Hand Rose," reaching the Top 40. But in that time, she scored seven gold-selling, Top Ten albums. This hits collection contained seven of her chart singles, plus her non-charting early single, "My Coloring Book," "Happy Days Are Here Again," which was one of the highlights of her debut album (heard here in the live version from *A Happening in Central Park*), and "Don't Rain on My Parade" from the *Funny Girl* soundtrack. For casual fans, that made for a good sampling of Streisand's most prominent '60s work, and if at the time it seemed likely that this was all the hits there would be, instead the '60s proved to be only the first chapter in Streisand's career. — *William Ruhlmann*

On a Clear Day You Can See Forever / Jul. 1970 / Sony ✦✦✦

Barbra Joan Streisand / 1971 / Columbia ✦✦✦✦
On her follow-up to the comeback album *Stoney End*, Barbra Streisand tried to do for (or to) Carole King what she had done the last time around with Laura Nyro, i.e., redo her material in a similar manner and essentially hijack it (while providing a big jump in songwriter royalties, of course). This was not so easy to do in the case of "Beautiful," "Where You Lead," and "You've Got a Friend," however, since, unlike the Nyro songs, by the time Streisand got to these tunes, they were already on King's own chart-topping album *Tapestry*. Nevertheless, Steisand, who after all is a much more powerful singer than King, did them well and even eked out a Top 40 single on "Where You Lead." And the album contained other gems, such as a delicate reading of John Lennon's "Love" (a take on his "Mother" was far less successful) and the only recording of "I Mean to Shine," written by Donald Fagen and Walter Becker, soon to launch Steely Dan. Streisand was not able to make the final transition into the pop-rock realm for the simple reason that she wasn't a writer, but she had spent a career making other people's songs her own, and she was as effective doing that here as she had been on very different material in the '60s. — *William Ruhlmann*

Stoney End / Feb. 1971 / Columbia ✦✦✦✦
Barbra Streisand scored her second Top Ten hit in early 1971 by treating Laura Nyro's recording of her song "Stoney End" as a demo and copying it practically note for note. "Mama, let me start all over," she sang, and her wish was granted. The follow-up album of the same title was in its way as surprising as Streisand's debut album eight years earlier. Where that record had redefined the role of the traditional pop singer in contemporary terms for the early '60s, *Stoney End* redefined Streisand as an effective pop-rock singer, which her last outing, *What About Today?*, had failed to do. Maybe she listened as closely to Nyro and Joni Mitchell as she had to Ethel Merman and Judy Garland a decade earlier, but somehow she reoriented her approach to music, adapting herself to vocal demands that were very different in terms of dynamics, expressiveness, and especially rhythm from the traditional pop and theater music she had sung previously. Producer Richard Perry may have eased the transition by using session men like Randy Newman, who played piano on two of his own compositions, and who bridged the worlds of show music and rock. But Streisand herself found something to identify with in songs like Gordon Lightfoot's "If You Could Read My Mind" (maybe that passage about the movie queen) and Mitchell's "I Don't Know Where I Stand." *Stoney End* was not a perfect album—the reliance on minor Brill Building material and two more Nyro copies kept it from classic status—but it was so far removed from what Streisand's fans and her detractors thought her capable of that it stands as one of her major triumphs. It was also her biggest seller in four years and launched the comeback that saw her through the '70s. — *William Ruhlmann*

Live Concert at the Forum / Oct. 1972 / Columbia ✦✦✦

Barbra Streisand…and Other Musical Instruments / Nov. 1973 / Columbia ✦✦

The Way We Were / Jan. 1974 / Columbia ✦✦✦
Though usually referred to as *The Way We Were*, the unwieldy full title of this album is *Barbra Streisand Featuring the Hit Single The Way We Were and All in Love Is Fair*, an important distinction because it was released almost simultaneously with the original soundtrack album for the film *The Way We Were* (Columbia 32830), which also contained a Streisand recording of the title song, along with the film score composed by Marvin Hamlisch. This album was thrown together quickly after that song took off as a single (in a recording different from the one in the film) in the wake of the success of the movie. In addition to the single and the Stevie Wonder song that also features in its title, the album contained a grab bag of stray tracks dating back as far as seven years and coming from Streisand's fourth TV special, *The Belle of 14th Street*, and an unfinished album project called *The Singer* largely made up of ballads written by Alan and Marilyn Bergman and Michel Legrand. The result was not one of Streisand's more impressive collections, but the com-

bined commercial impact of the film and the single propelled this album to the top of the charts. — *William Ruhlmann*

ButterFly / Oct. 1974 / Columbia ✦✦✦

Barbra Streisand's first album of newly recorded, non-soundtrack studio material in three years, *ButterFly* was ridiculed at the time of its release because its credited producer was her boyfriend, Jon Peters, whose musical credentials were nonexistent. In retrospect, the real power on the album was arranger Tom Scott, a reed player who had perfected a light jazz-pop style in his work on Joni Mitchell's *Court and Spark* earlier in the year. *ButterFly* backed off from the pop-rock style of its predecessors, *Stoney End* and *Barbra Joan Streisand*, but it still found Streisand essaying contemporary material by such writers as Bob Marley, Graham Nash, and David Bowie. Unlike Richard Perry, who had produced those albums, Scott adapted the songs to Streisand's powerful and individual vocal style rather than having her ape existing versions of the songs. The result was more of a compromise with contemporary pop that, while it sold only to Streisand's existing fan base, nevertheless had its charms. — *William Ruhlmann*

Lazy Afternoon / 1975 / Columbia ✦✦✦

Lazy Afternoon was Barbra Streisand's Rupert Holmes album. Holmes, later known for his No. 1 hit "Escape (The Pina Colada Song)," arranged, conducted, and co-produced the album and wrote or co-wrote four songs. He helped Streisand to continue her evolution into a kind of post-rock contemporary pop artist. This was achieved largely through the sympathetic ballad arrangements, which surrounded Streisand's voice with delicately played individual instruments while focusing on her calm vocals. The exception was a cover of the Four Tops' "Shake Me, Wake Me," which was given a disco treatment. For the most part, *Lazy Afternoon* was true to its title, a collection of relaxed performances that was pleasant without being particularly impressive. — *William Ruhlmann*

Funny Lady / 1975 / Bay Cities ✦✦

Classical Barbra / Feb. 1976 / Columbia ✦✦✦

A Star Is Born / Nov. 1976 / Columbia ✦✦

Though it is credited to Barbra Streisand and Kris Kristofferson, *A Star Is Born* is in effect the soundtrack album to the motion picture of the same name, a rock-oriented retelling of the story that had been filmed three times before. That it is not billed as a soundtrack only indicates that the album contains the songs featured in the film, but not the score. Of course, the main drawing card here is "Love Theme from 'A Star Is Born'" (Evergreen)," the No. 1 hit. But the rest of the album is slight. Streisand isn't much of a rock singer, and these aren't much as rock songs (the songwriters include Paul Williams and Rupert Holmes). For his part, Kristofferson sounds even more gravelly than usual, and he isn't even growling his own compositions, which doubtless would have been superior to what he's been given to sing. Nevertheless, spurred by the hit single and the box office success of the film, *A Star Is Born* was the best-selling album of Barbra Streisand's career up to this point. ("Evergreen," co-written by Streisand and Williams, won Grammy Awards for Song of the Year and Best Female Pop Vocal.) — *William Ruhlmann*

Streisand Superman / 1977 / Columbia ✦✦✦

Appearing only seven months after *A Star Is Born*, *Streisand Superman* seemed to continue much of its rock-oriented feel, even including several songs that had been intended for the film. It was unusual in featuring all recently written songs, many first recorded here. Streisand co-wrote the rockish "Don't Believe What You Read," an attack on her negative press coverage, while Alan Gordon contributed both the discoish "I Found You Love" and the album's Top Ten single ballad "My Heart Belongs to Me." *Streisand Superman* seemed to be an unusually personal album for the singer, reflecting her feelings and viewpoints. That did not make it one of her best, however. — *William Ruhlmann*

★ **Barbra Streisand's Greatest Hits, Vol. 2** / 1978 / Columbia ✦✦✦✦✦

Between the release of Barbra Streisand's first hits collection in 1970 and her second in 1978, she essentially became a different kind of recording artist. In the 1960s, she made a series of consistent albums devoted largely to show music material, but she scored precious few singles hits, with only one, "People," reaching the Top Ten. But in the 1970s, she shifted to contemporary soft-rock and released a series of highly successful ballad singles, while her albums became largely inconsistent. For that reason, the hit quotient of her second hits album was much higher—"The Way We Were," "Love Theme from 'A Star Is Born'" (Evergreen)," and the duet version of "You Don't Bring Me Flowers," sung with songwriter Neil Diamond and released on album here for the first time, all were No. 1 hits, while "Stoney End" and "My Heart Belongs to Me" were Top Tens and "Sweet Inspiration/Where You Lead," "Songbird," and "Love Theme from 'Laura Mars' (Prisoner)" reached the Top 40. That was enough material to make *Volume 2* Streisand's definitive hits collection, so much so that later compilations like *Memories* and *A Collection/ Greatest Hits . . . and More* would be forced to cannibalize it. It was also a genre-defining album in terms of the emergence of a

post-'60s contemporary pop music that drew upon the rock revolution to redefine classic pop for a new generation. — *William Ruhlmann*

Songbird / 1978 / Columbia ✦✦✦

Songbird was a competent, professional effort from Barbra Streisand, typical of the soft-rock style of her '70s work, but unexceptional. Gary Klein, who had produced *Streisand Superman*, guided a middle course between bombast and balladry, resulting in, for example, perhaps the least objectionable version possible of the frankly awful "Tomorrow" from the Broadway musical *Annie* and a good reading of Neil Diamond's "You Don't Bring Me Flowers" that would help inspire the hit duet version a year later. But though Streisand now seemed to have access to the efforts of a raft of good songwriters, most of the material here was not memorable. The intended hit, obviously, was the title song, which was patterned after Streisand's recent string of hit ballads. But it was not as effective as its predecessors and didn't perform as well as they had in the charts, only breaking into the Top 40. — *William Ruhlmann*

Wet / 1979 / Columbia ✦✦✦

A concept album of sorts in the sense that each of the songs has something to do with water, *Wet* was the third of a trilogy of albums produced by Gary Klein in a soft-rock vein increasingly set in the synth-pop style of the late '70s and early '80s. The concept allowed for a range of material, from old favorite Harold Arlen's "Come Rain or Come Shine" to an updated version of the old Bobby Darin hit "Splish Splash." The album's No. 1 was "No More Tears (Enough Is Enough)," a disco duet with Donna Summer. But most of the songs were newly written ballads attempting to recreate the "Evergreen"/"The Way We Were" style of Streisand's recent hits. "Kiss Me in The Rain" grazed the Top 40, but most of that material was substandard. Yet there was enough variety on the album to make it an average Streisand outing. — *William Ruhlmann*

The Main Event / Jun. 1979 / Columbia ✦✦

Barbra Streisand performs long, short, and ballad versions of the discoish title track, and the album is filled out by some rock 'n' roll oldies and more disco tracks. Upon release, this record (like the film) was at least timely, and both were successful. Neither has worn well, and today this is a very minor entry in the Streisand catalog. — *William Ruhlmann*

Guilty / 1980 / Columbia ✦✦✦✦

The biggest selling album of Barbra Streisand's career is also one of her least characteristic. The album was written and produced by Barry Gibb in association with his brothers and the producers of the Bee Gees, and in essence it sounds like a post-*Saturday Night Fever* Bee Gees album with vocals by Streisand. Gibb adapted his usual style somewhat, especially in slowing the tempos and leaving more room for the vocal, but his melodic style and the backup vocals, even when they are not sung by the Bee Gees, are typical of them. Still, the record was more hybrid than compromise, and the chart-topping single "Woman in Love" has a sinuous feel that is both right for Streisand and new for her. Other hits were the title song and "What Kind of Fool," both duets with Gibb. (The song "Guilty" won a Grammy Award for Best Pop Vocal by Duo or Group.) — *William Ruhlmann*

Memories / Nov. 1981 / Columbia ✦✦✦

As albums go, *Memories* made a great single. A compilation, but not exactly a hits collection, it contained two newly recorded songs, "Memory" from the musical *Cats* and the Top 40 hit "Comin' in and out of Your Life," plus a re-recorded version of "Lost Inside of You," a song previously done as a duet with Kris Kristofferson in *A Star Is Born*, and seven tracks from the previous eight years, three of which were making their third or fourth appearance on record. In other words, *Memories* was a blatant consumer rip-off, highly unusual for an artist who usually gave value for money. That said, the album contained some of Streisand's biggest hits—"You Don't Bring Me Flowers," "No More Tears (Enough Is Enough)," "Evergreen," and "The Way We Were," as well as some excellent performances, such as Streisand's take on Billy Joel's "New York State of Mind." Thus, it was a good collection thought of independently (which may help explain why it became one of Streisand's biggest sellers), even if in the context of her overall catalog it was an album of reruns baited with a couple of new songs. (In the UK, the album was released with four additional tracks—"Kiss Me in the Rain," "I Don't Break Easily," "Wet," and "A Man I Loved"—under the title *Love Songs* [CBS 10031].) — *William Ruhlmann*

Yentl / 1983 / Columbia ✦✦✦

Emotion / Oct. 1984 / Columbia ✦✦✦

Barbra Streisand's first album of contemporary material in four years was a typical '80s "Adult Contemporary" superstar release, each track written and produced as a potential "power ballad" single by an extensive team of other performers, in this case including Richard Perry, Kim Carnes, Maurice White of Earth, Wind and Fire, Jim Steinman, Albhy Galuten (the Bee Gees' producer), Richard Baskin, Diane Warren, John Mellencamp, and Streisand herself. Streisand proved capable of handling everything from White's space-age R&B to Steinman's melodramatic overproduction. (He was the man who brought you Meat Loaf.) But as usually happens with such big budget efforts, the album lacked consistency, and as Columbia tried to pull several singles off it without notable success it sold only to Streisand's million-member base audience. — *William Ruhlmann*

☆ **The Broadway Album** / 1985 / Columbia ✦✦✦✦✦
Barbra Streisand's abandonment of Broadway was the worst thing that happened to the theater in the '60s. Her retreat from theater music on record was less of a loss, if only because she had tended to focus on second-rank composers and obscure songs by first-rate ones, while practically ignoring, for example, Stephen Sondheim, who, as of the early '70s, became the pre-eminent Broadway songwriter. When she returned to show songs in 1985, she reversed these failings. Now, the singer who had never done much with Rodgers and Hammerstein, Frank Loesser, George Gershwin, or Jerome Kern finally felt confident enough to take on "If I Loved You" from *Carousel*, "Adelaide's Lament" from *Guys and Dolls*, "Can't Help Lovin' That Man" from *Showboat*, and a medley from *Porgy and Bess*, and she did them well. Even better, on seven tracks with Sondheim's name on them, she proved the perfect intepreter of the most contemporary and intellectual of Broadway's writers, whether singing his lyrics over the music of Leonard Bernstein (another composer she'd largely neglected) from *West Side Story* or making the most of material drawn from shows like *Company, A Little Night Music, Sweeney Todd,* and *Sunday in the Park with George.* Sondheim collaborated with Streisand, penning special lyrics for songs like "Putting It Together" and even his standard, "Send in the Clowns." Also on board was Streisand's arranger from the early and mid-'60s, Peter Matz. The result was an album that repositioned some of Broadway's best in a pop context (doubtless many people heard these great songs for the first time) and showed that Streisand was still at her best when presenting the dramatically satisfying story songs of the theater. Apparently, many longtime fans agreed: At sales over three million, *The Broadway Album* was Streisand's most commercially successful album in five years. (*The Broadway Album* won a Grammy Award for Best Female Pop Vocal.) — *William Ruhlmann*

One Voice / Apr. 1987 / Columbia ✦✦✦

Till I Loved You / Oct. 1988 / Columbia ✦✦✦

Greatest Hits … and More / Sep. 1989 / Columbia ✦✦✦
Like *Memories, A Collection/Greatest Hits … and More* was an odd compilation, not quite a hits set, though it gathered up the big hits not heard on the earlier record—"The Main Event/Fight," "Woman in Love," "Guilty," "What Kind of Fool"—since it also seemed to be a grab bag, including a few stray album tracks, recycling the two new songs from *Memories* (!), "Comin' in and out of Your Life" and "Memory," and adding a couple of new recordings, "We're Not Makin' Love Anymore" (by Diane Warren and Michael Bolton) and "Someone That I Used to Love." The selection made no apparent sense, but then neither had *Memories*, and that album sold several million copies. This one wasn't so fortunate, though many Streisand fans must have received it as a present for Christmas 1989, which probably was the idea. — *William Ruhlmann*

Just for the Record … / Sep. 24, 1991 / Columbia ✦✦✦✦
As they evolved in the 1980s, boxed set retrospectives tended to contain a full complement of an artist's essential recordings, plus enough rarities to suggest the artist's inspirations and ambitions. Not all boxed sets conformed to this outline, however. Barbra Streisand was unusual, in that she had a large base of devoted fans interested in the minutiae of her career, and in that her entire recorded catalog, including four compilation albums, remained in print. She had also worked with the same record company for her entire career and maintained her status as a frontline artist, so she had complete creative control over this retrospective. The result was a four-disc, 77-track, four plus-hour box devoted almost entirely to rare, previously unreleased material. Here and there, Streisand tossed in one of her most familiar recordings, such as the hit version of "People." But the overwhelming bulk of *Just for the Record …* was given over to homemade demonstration tapes, live recordings, television appearances, and outtakes from unfinished album projects, not to mention tributes to her by composers, a roast by Don Rickles, her acceptance speeches at awards shows, and other special material. The album was not so much a comprehensive career overview as an aural scrapbook. To Streisand's army of fans, that made it a delight, but practically by definition, that did not make it a great Barbra Streisand album unto itself. Unlike most boxed sets, this was not a one-stop shopping item that gave you the best and the rest of Barbra Streisand. It was the bits and pieces of a great career, intended for those who already had everything else. That is not to say that there weren't some fascinating and terrific performances included. Especially notable was a set of eight songs recorded at a nightclub in 1962 and originally intended for Streisand's debut album. It was clear listening that that album was scrapped because she changed her idea of what her initial introduction to the record-buying public should be, not because there was anything wrong with the performance or the sound quality. A duet

with Judy Garland from her TV show and a rendering of "In the Wee Small Hours of the Morning" from a Las Vegas show were equally impressive. Other recordings, such as excerpts from the final Broadway stage performance of *Funny Girl* and the rough demo of Streisand's Oscar-winning composition "Evergreen," had historical interest. Nevertheless, *Just for the Record …* was an album to buy in addition to her hits collections and landmark albums, not in place of them. — *William Ruhlmann*

Prince of Tides / Nov. 12, 1991 / Columbia ✦✦✦

Back to Broadway / Jun. 29, 1993 / Columbia ✦✦✦

Barbra: The Concert / Sep. 1994 / Sony ✦✦✦✦
Barbra Streisand's fourth live album was the only one to be drawn from a concert tour and not a one-time occasion, but it is no less special for that. For her first tour in 28 years, Streisand didn't just come out and sing her greatest hits for an hour and a half. Instead, she wove a selection of her best-known songs together with what she considered career highlights and added new and special material, starting with the customized lyrics of "As If We Never Said Goodbye" and "I'm Still Here" and including "Ordinary Miracles," by her conductor, Marvin Hamlisch, and her house lyricists, Alan and Marilyn Bergman. The show was a musical autobiography crafted (as her 1991 boxed set *Just for the Record …* had been) for fans who would catch the references and agree with the artist on her viewpoints about her life, her career, the entertainment business, and politics. (And it was an abridged resume—rockers like "Stoney End" and disco hits like "Enough Is Enough" were omitted.) There was no denying that the 52-year-old singer, backed by a large orchestra and singing the songs that had kept her at the forefront of popular music for 30 years, was an impressive concert performer. But Streisand insisted that her listeners also encounter everything from her film directing ambitions to her psychoanalyst, which made this an idiosyncratic performance from an artist determined to make public art out of her private story. As a result, *The Concert* may not be the place for neophytes to be introduced to her, though for fans it was the culmination of decades of wishing. — *William Ruhlmann*

The Concert—Highlights / May 2, 1995 / Columbia ✦✦✦✦

The Mirror Has Two Faces [original Soundtrack] / Nov. 12, 1996 / Sony ✦✦

Barrett Strong

b. Feb. 5, 1941, Westpoint, MS
Vocals / Soul, R&B, Motown
A pivotal figure in Motown's formative years, singer/composer Barrett Strong was a key associate and friend of Berry Gordy. It was his hit "Money (That's What I Want)" for Anna Records in 1960 that provided vital capital for Gordy to expand his operation. The song gave Strong his only major hit as a vocalist, reaching No. 2 on the R&B charts and barely missing the pop Top 20. During the late '60s and early '70s, Strong collaborated with Norman Whitfield on some historic songs that included Marvin Gaye's "I Heard It Through the Grapevine" and "Too Busy Thinking About My Baby," the Temptations' "Papa Was a Rolling Stone" and "Ball of Confusion," Edwin Starr's "War," and "Take Me in Your Arms and Love Me" for Gladys Knight and the Pips, which he also co-wrote. Strong left Motown when they moved to Los Angeles in 1972, and he signed with Epic. After one failed single, Strong moved to Capitol, where he had the LP *Stronghold* released in 1975 and later *Live & Love* in 1976. Though it wasn't a hit, his song "Man up in the Sky" was a '70s soul gem. Johnny Bristol later re-recorded it. Strong continued into the '80s, recording "Rock It Easy" for an independent label and writing and arranging "You Can Depend on Me," which was included on the Dells' *The Second Time* LP in 1988. —*Ron Wynn*

● **Stronghold** / 1975 / Capitol ✦✦✦✦

Live & Love / 1976 / Capitol ✦✦

Nolan Strong

f. 1950, Detroit, MI, **db.** 1977
R&B
This early Detroit R&B vocal group formed in 1950, originally featuring Nolan Strong, Juan Guiterriec, Willie Hunter, Quentin Eubanks, and Bob "Chico" Edwards on guitar. Strong was blessed with a beautiful high tenor voice (and even higher falsetto) and writing and arranging skills far surpassing those of most doo wop groups of the era. What makes his recordings (with and without the Diablos) so special is that we're hearing the Motown sound in its embryonic form. Nolan was the original Smokey Robinson, the original Michael Jackson, years before either of them stood before a microphone at Motown. Recording his entire career for the tiny independent Fortune (Detroit's first Black R&B label), Strong's influence on Smokey and the early Motown stable of talent was unmistakable. As late as the early '60s, Berry Gordy tried to buy Nolan's contract from Fortune and install him as head arranger and producer

but to no avail. (The job went instead to Robinson.) Incredibly handsome with a strong stage presence, Strong came close to the big time on several occasions (when his "Mind over Matter" started to break nationally, Gordy recruited the Temptations to cover it under the name the Pirates, the only time in the history of Motown that this was done), but his erratic temperament and lifestyle ensured that it was not to be. The genius of one of the greatest and yet most underappreciated artists in the history of pop music lives on in the 20-odd years of recordings Strong did in a tiny, crudely equipped studio situated in the back of a record shop. The original sound of the Motor City, indeed. —*Cub Koda*

● **Fortune of Hits, Vol. 1** / 1961 / Fortune ✦✦✦✦
All the early hits, and the perfect place to start. —*Cub Koda*

Fortune of Hits, Vol. 2 / 1962 / Fortune ✦✦✦✦
The companion piece to *Fortune of Hits—Vol. 1.* —*Cub Koda*

Daddy Rock / 1963 / Fortune ✦✦✦
A great batch of rare and unreleased sides. —*Cub Koda*

The Style Council

f. 1983, London, England, db. 1990
Pop-Rock, New Wave

Guitarist/vocalist Paul Weller broke up the Jam, the most popular British band of the early '80s, at the height of their success in 1982 because he was dissatisfied with their musical direction. Weller wanted to incorporate more elements of soul, R&B, and jazz into his songwriting, which is something he felt his punk-oriented bandmates were incapable of performing. In order to pursue this musical direction, he teamed up in 1983 with keyboardist Mick Talbot, a former member of the mod revival band the Merton Parkas. Together, Weller and Talbot became the Style Council—other musicians were added according to what kind of music the duo were performing. With the Style Council, the underlying intellectual pretensions that ran throughout Weller's music came to the forefront.

Although the music was rooted in American R&B, it was performed slickly—complete with layers of synthesizers and drum machines—and filtered through European styles and attitudes. Weller's lyrics were typically earnest, yet his leftist political leanings became more pronounced. His scathing criticisms of racism, unemployment, Margaret Thatcher, and sexism sat uneasily beside his burgeoning obsession with high culture. As his pretensions increased, the number of hits the Style Council had decreased; by the end of the decade, the group was barely able to crack the British Top 40 and Weller had turned from a hero into a has-been.

Released in March of 1983, the Style Council's first single "Speak like a Child" became an immediate hit, reaching No. 4 on the British charts. Three months later, "The Money-Go-Round" peaked at No. 11 on the charts as the group was recording an EP, *Paris*, which appeared in August; the EP reached No. 3. "Solid Bond in Your Heart" became another hit in November, peaking at No. 11.

The Style Council released their first full-length album, *Cafe Bleu*, in March of 1984; two months later, a resequenced version of the record, re-titled *My Ever Changing Moods*, was released in America. *Cafe Bleu* was Weller's most stylistically ambitious album to date, drawing from jazz, soul, rap, and pop. While it was musically all over the map, it was their most successful album, peaking at No. 5 in the UK and No. 56 in the US. "My Ever Changing Moods" became their first US hit, peaking at No. 29. In the summer of 1985, the Style Council had another UK Top Ten hit with "The Walls Come Tumbling Down." The single was taken from *Our Favorite Shops*, which reached No. 1 on the UK charts; the record was released as *Internationalists* in the US. The live album, *Home and Abroad*, was released in the spring of 1986; it peaked at No. 8.

The Style Council had its last Top Ten single with "It Didn't Matter" in January of 1987. *The Cost of Loving*, an album that featured a heavy emphasis on jazz-inspired soul, followed in February. Although it received unfavorable reviews, the record peaked at No. 2 in the UK. That spring, "Waiting" became the group's first single not to crack the British Top 40, signaling that their popularity was rapidly declining. In July of 1988, the Style Council released their last album, *Confessions of a Pop Group*, which featured Weller's most self-important and pompous music—the second side featured a ten-minute orchestral suite called "The Gardener of Eden." The record charted fairly well, reaching No. 15 in the UK, but it received terrible reviews. In March of 1989, the Style Council released a compilation, *The Singular Adventures of the Style Council*, which reached No. 3 on the charts. Later that year, Weller delivered a new Style Council album, which reflected his infatuation with house and club music, to the band's record label Polydor. Polydor rejected the album and dropped both the Style Council and Weller from the label.

Paul Weller and Mick Talbot officially broke up the Style Council in 1990. In 1991, Weller launched a solo career that would return him to popular and critical favor in the mid-'90s, while Talbot continued to

play, both with Weller and as a solo musician. —*Stephen Thomas Erlewine*

Introducing the Style Council / 1983 / Polydor ✦✦✦✦
A solid EP collection of the band's initial British singles, it includes the ersatz soul of "Long Hot Summer," the bubbling pop of "Speak like a Child," and "Money-Go-Round," a fine British-funk manifesto. —*John Floyd*

Cafe Bleu / 1984 / Polydor ✦✦✦✦
Style Council's first proper album, *Cafe Bleu*, was one of their better efforts, but it indicated the group's fatal flaw—a tendency to be too eclectic and overambitious. Amidst the lazy jazz instrumentals, many of them courtesy of Mick Talbot, Paul Weller inserted several solid soul-tinged pop songs, including "My Ever Changing Moods," "Headstart for Happiness," "You're the Best Thing," and "Here's One that Got Away." However, that doesn't excuse the rap experiment, "A Gospel." The album was later released with a slightly different running order as *My Ever Changing Moods* in the US; the American edition included the UK hit "A Solid Bond in Your Heart." —*Stephen Thomas Erlewine*

Our Favourite Shop / 1985 / Polydor ✦✦✦✦
Our Favourite Shop, the Style Council's second proper album, was still quite eclectic, but it didn't seem as schizophrenically diverse as *Cafe Bleu*. Weller had been able to incorporate his soul and jazz experiments into his songwriting, writing the fine "Walls Come Tumbling Down," "Come to Milton Keys," "Boy Who Cried Wolf," and "Down in the Seine," which were some of his best songs for the Style Council. The occasional misguided experiment remained—the stiff funk of "The Internationalists" and the self-righteous "The Stand Up Comic's Instructions" were particularly embarrassing—but the record was more cohesive and stronger than the debut. In America, the album was released without "Our Favourite Shop" and retitled *Internationalists*. —*Stephen Thomas Erlewine*

Home & Abroad / 1986 / Geffen ✦✦
Home & Abroad is a slick and earnest live set, but it's only of interest to diehard Paul Weller fans. —*Stephen Thomas Erlewine*

The Cost of Loving / 1987 / Polydor ✦✦
A full-fledged soul album, *The Cost of Loving* illustrated why Paul Weller's star was rapidly declining in the late '80s. Filled with bland, professional soul-pop, few of the songs have memorable melodies and the band tends to meander through the slick arrangments. Weller's lyrics were self-important and under-developed, with only the hit single "It Didn't Matter" making a lasting impression among the undistinguished songs that comprised the majority of the album. —*Stephen Thomas Erlewine*

Confessions of a Pop Group / 1988 / Polydor ✦
If *The Cost of Loving* was a thoroughly mediocre affair, *Confessions of a Pop Group* was flat-out bad, without a single like "It Didn't Matter" to redeem its indulgences. Throughout the album, Weller engages in some of his most pretentious and mean-spirited lyrics, but they are no match for the music he's written, which ranges from self-important jazz-pop fusions to an orchestral suite that finishes the album. The result was bad enough to leave him without a record contract in the UK, where he was considered a god just eight years earlier. —*Stephen Thomas Erlewine*

● **The Singular Adventures of the Style Council** / Jun. 1989 / Polydor ✦✦✦✦
The Style Council's albums were always weighed down by their far-reaching musical ambitions, which meant that their ideas were usually best heard on their singles. And while this period of Paul Weller's career has been criticized heavily, he wrote several excellent songs during the Style Council, most of which are featured on the fine compilation *The Singular Adventures of the Style Council*. Not all of the 16 songs are first-rate, as it begins to lose steam toward the end of the band's life, but "My Ever Changing Moods," "You're the Best Thing," "Long Hot Summer," "Shout to the Top!," "A Solid Bond in Your Heart," "Money Go Round," "Walls Come Tumbling Down," and "Speak like a Child" are terrific, and make the collection worthwhile for fans of the Jam and Weller's solo career, as well as fans of New Romantic New Wave and jazzy sophisti-pop. —*Stephen Thomas Erlewine*

Here's Some That Got Away / Feb. 22, 1994 / Polydor ✦✦✦
Since the Style Council's albums were either inconsistent or downright boring, the idea of a B-sides and rarities collection isn't exactly enticing. However, *Here's Some That Got Away* is surprisingly enjoyable, proving that Paul Weller was at his best when he wasn't trying to make serious, self-important music. —*Stephen Thomas Erlewine*

The Style Council Collection / Mar. 1996 / Polydor ✦✦✦✦
Not a strict greatest hits, *The Style Council Collection* balances some of the group's biggest singles with some relatively obscure album tracks. Like the band itself, the album loses steam towards the end but the best songs here—"My Ever Changing Moods," in particular—prove that, contrary to popular belief, the Style Council wasn't a complete waste of Paul

Weller's time and that he did explore some new territory with the group. —*Stephen Thomas Erlewine*

The Stylistics

f. 1968, Philadelphia, PA
Soul, Quiet Storm
After the Spinners and the O'Jays, the Stylistics were the leading Philly soul group produced by Thom Bell. During the early '70s, the band had 12 straight Top 10 hits, including "You Are Everything," "Betcha by Golly, Wow," "I'm Stone in Love With You," "Break Up to Make Up" and "You Make Me Feel Brand New." Of all their peers, the Stylistics were one of the smoothest and sweetest soul groups of their era. All of their hits were ballads, graced by the soaring falsetto of Russell Thompkins, Jr., and the lush, yet graceful productions of Thom Bell, which helped make the Stylistics one of the most successful soul groups of the first half of the '70s.

The Stylistics formed in 1968, when members of the Philadelphia soul groups the Monarchs and the Percussions joined forces after their respective band dissolved. Russel Thompkins, Jr., James Smith, and Airrion Love hailed from the Monarchs; James Dunn and Herbie Murrell were from the Percussions. In 1970, the group recorded "You're a Big Girl Now," a song their road manager Marty Bryant co-wrote with Robert Douglas, a member of their backing band Slim and the Boys, and the single became a regional hit for Sebring Records. The larger Avco Records soon signed the Stylistics, and single eventually climbed to No. 7 in early 1971.

Once they were on Avco, the Stylistics began working with producer/ songwriter Thom Bell, who had previously worked with the Delfonics. The Stylistics became Bell's pet project and with lyricist Linda Creed, he crafted a series of hit singles that relied as much on the intricately arranged and lush production as they did on Thompkins' falsetto. Every single that Bell produced for the Stylistics was a Top 10 R&B hit, and several—"You Are Everything," "Betcha By Golly, Wow," "I'm Stone in Love with You," "Break Up to Make Up," and "You Make Me Feel Brand New"—were also Top 10 pop hits.

Following "You Make Me Feel Brand New" in the spring of 1974, the Stylistics broke away from Thom Bell and began working with Van McCoy, who helped move the group towards a softer, easy listening style. In 1976, they left Avco and signed with H&L. The group's American record sales declined, yet they remained popular in Europe, particularly in Great Britain, where "Sing Baby Sing" (1975) "Na Na Is the Saddest Word" (1975), "Can't Give You Anything" (1975) and "Can't Help Falling in Love" (1976) were all Top Five hits. The Stylistics continued to tour and record throughout the latter half of the '70s, as their popularity steadily declined. In 1980, Dunn left the group because of poor health, and he was followed later that year by Smith. The remaining Stylistics continued performing as a trio on oldies shows into the '90s. —*Stephen Thomas Erlewine*

The Stylistics / 1971 / Avco Embassy ✦✦✦
The brilliant album that got everything started. Heads turned, people snapped to attention (women especially), and the "sweet" soul fraternity was turned on its head when this five-member group featuring the sugary, sweeping falsetto of Russell Tompkins, Jr., hit the scene with such singles as "Betcha By Golly, Wow," "People Make the World Go Round," and "Stop, Look and Listen to Your Heart." His delivery, shimmering style, and brilliant pacing and control temporarily rendered almost every other "sweet" soul vocalist and group speechless; pretty soon, the Delfonics, Blue Magic, Moments, and others would fight back, but in 1972, everyone was playing catchup to the Stylistics. —*Ron Wynn*

Round 2 / 1972 / Amherst ✦✦✦✦
The Russell Tompkins, Jr., legend began to grow in the early '70s with this superb album. His version of "You'll Never Get to Heaven If You Break My Heart" inspired fantasies from women that probably surpassed what Dionne Warwick generated in men, while "Break Up to Make Up" and "I'm Stone in Love with You" were instant anthems and are still among the great 1970s love ballads. —*Ron Wynn*

Love Hits / 1974 / Amherst ✦✦✦✦
Another anthology, this one covering the beautiful love songs and romantic ballads that were the Stylistics' specialty. These are all magnificent, some of the finest sentimental soul that's ever been recorded. But it's also been issued before, and Amherst's mastering isn't anything to write home about, especially the way they tend to wash out Russell Tompkins, Jr.'s high notes. —*Ron Wynn*

Let's Put It All Together / 1974 / Avco Embassy ✦✦✦
Their finest album, the Stylistics climbed the "sweet" soul mountain in 1974. "You Make Me Feel Brand New" and the title cut were among the year's premiere love/romance numbers, and Russell Tompkins, Jr., had nudged past Blue Magic's Ted Mills and the Delfonics' Hart brothers as the falsetto voice of choice among female fans. Their run on Avco, with Thom Bell at the production helm, was one of the greatest in modern soul annals. —*Ron Wynn*

Heavy / 1974 / Avco Embassy ✦✦✦
The magical union between the Stylistics and producer/writer Thom Bell ended with this album, but the legacy had included a string of fabulous hit singles and arguably the greatest "sweet" soul productions of all time. Russell Tompkins, Jr., was in his prime as a lead vocalist, and while this album didn't have any blockbusters like its predecessors, it still had plenty of exquisitely sung, nicely harmonized ballads and love tunes. —*Ron Wynn*

● **The Best of the Stylistics** / 1975 / Amherst ✦✦✦✦
Any of their collections are good, but this one features their biggest and best hits, including "I'm Stone in Love with You," "Rockin' Roll Baby," "Betcha by Golly, Wow," and "You Make Me Feel Brand New." —*Cub Koda*

● **Very Best of the Stylistics** / 1983 / H&L ✦✦✦✦
This is one of many collections that gather their hit singles; "Make Up to Break Up," "You Are Everything," "Rock and Roll Baby" and many others are landmark numbers, even if thematic variety and stylistic diversity weren't Stylistics traits. —*Ron Wynn*

Styx

f. 1970, Chicago, IL
Hard Rock, Art-Rock/Progressive-Rock, Pop-Rock, Arena Rock
Styx were one of the biggest art-rock bands of the late '70s, capable of producing monster hits with their stadium rock, power ballads, and concept albums. More than any other art-rock band, Styx was able to cross over into the pop charts, scoring hits with "Babe," "Lady," "Come Sail Away," "Too Much Time on My Hands," and "Don't Let It End." Never one for subtlety, their ballads featured sweeping, over-arranged guitars and keyboards while their rockers were long and detailed, with several different sections and gargantuan guitar solos. When MTV rolled around in the early '80s, the hits stopped coming; they broke up in 1984. Six years later, they reunited and released *Edge of the Century;* the record featured "Show Me the Way," which became popular as a Gulf War anthem. The band went on hiatus a couple of years after the album's release. —*Stephen Thomas Erlewine*

The Serpent Is Rising / 1973 / RCA ✦✦
Styx's third album, *The Serpent Is Rising,* has hints of the group's signature blend of art-rock and arena rock, but at this stage, the band neither has the compositional nor the instrumental skills to execute their ideas accurately. —*Stephen Thomas Erlewine*

Styx II / 1973 / RCA ✦✦✦
Styx's second album was a belated success, scoring a Top Ten hit with "Lady," two years after its release. In retrospect, it is easy to see why *Styx II* was ignored upon its release. Apart from "Lady" and "You Need Love," most of the album is bland. However, it's the best of the group's first three records. —*Stephen Thomas Erlewine*

Man of Miracles / 1974 / RCA ✦✦✦
Man of Miracles lacks a song as strong as "Lady," but the record demonstrates that Styx's fusion of bombastic arena rock and pompous prog-rock is beginning to gel. —*Stephen Thomas Erlewine*

Equinox / 1975 / A&M ✦✦✦
Equinox benefitted from the belated success of *Styx II* and its single, "Lady," spending 50 weeks on the charts. The record was actually stronger than the earlier set, featuring a more consistent set of songs including the Top 40 hit "Lorelei." —*Stephen Thomas Erlewine*

Crystal Ball / 1976 / A&M ✦✦✦
Crystal Ball wasn't as successful as *Equinox,* but it was a better album, showcasing Styx's increased skill for crafting simple, catchy pop hooks out of their bombastic sound. —*Daevid Jehnzen*

The Grand Illusion / 1977 / A&M ✦✦✦✦
With *The Grand Illusion,* Styx catapulted to Top Ten and multi-platinum status, thanks to the hit single, "Come Sail Away." Although the group's sound was still based in art-rock, the best moments on the record occur when they fit majestic pomp into the constraints of a pop song like "Fooling Yourself (The Angry Young Man)" or "Come Sail Away." —*Stephen Thomas Erlewine*

Pieces of Eight / 1978 / A&M ✦✦✦✦
Pieces of Eight continued Styx's winning streak, selling over three million copies over the years. Styx was savvy enough to make their art-rock appear like arena rock, as the "Blue Collar Man (Long Nights)" single indicates, as well as the hit "Renegade." —*Stephen Thomas Erlewine*

Cornerstone / 1979 / A&M ✦✦✦✦
"Babe" became Styx's first No. 1 single and its accompanying album, *Cornerstone,* saw the band expanding their pop accessibility without dispensing the art-rock traditions that made them famous. —*Stephen Thomas Erlewine*

Paradise Theater / 1980 / A&M ✦✦✦✦
Paradise Theater was Styx's masterpiece, filled with conceptually ambitious songs as well as concise pop singles, like the driving hard rocker

"Too Much Time on My Hands" and the power ballad "The Best of Times." It perfectly encapsulates both the band's progressive side and their catchy, hard rock leanings. —*Daevid Jehnzen*

Kilroy Was Here / 1983 / A&M ✦✦✦
An ambitious—and, to be frank, pretty silly—concept album about an Orwellian future controlled by a fascist dictator who has outlawed rock 'n' roll and the rebellion led by an exiled rocker, *Kilroy Was Here* was a pretty odd way for the original lineup of Styx to end their recording career. Some of the album is quite listenable—the ballad "Don't Let It End" is powerful, while "Mr. Roboto" is an infectious pomp-rocker—but the album is hampered by a lack of memorable melodies. —*Stephen Thomas Erlewine*

Caught in the Act / 1984 / A&M ✦✦
A live set recorded during their 1983 tour, *Caught in the Act* is a lackluster record. —*Daevid Jehnzen*

Classics, Vol. 15 / 1987 / A&M ✦✦✦✦
This best-of collection amply covers this group's primary radio hits and key album cuts. Included are "Babe," "Best of Times," "Too Much Time on My Hands," "Mr. Roboto," "Don't Let It End," "Blue Collar Man (Long Nights)," "Come Sail Away," "Crystal Ball," and "Grand Illusion." —*Rick Clark*

Edge of the Century / 1990 / A&M ✦✦
Melodic hard pop and power ballads, obviously cut from the same cloth as Journey, but with a nod to modern metal. "I've Got a Lot to Learn About Love," the song that sounds the most like classic Journey, was an AOR hit. —*Brian Mansfield*

● **Greatest Hits** / Aug. 22, 1995 / A&M ✦✦✦✦
Replacing the band's volume in A&M's *Classics* series, *Greatest Hits* collects all Styx's major chart and radio hits, from "Lady" to "Show Me the Way." Although they were a definitive album rock band, creating records that were meant to be listened to as a whole, their finest moments were always their singles, making *Greatest Hits* the only Styx disc many fans will need to own. —*Stephen Thomas Erlewine*

Greatest Hits Part II / Jun. 1996 / A&M ✦✦✦
Greatest Hits, Part II collects all of Styx's radio hits that weren't featured on the first collection, as well as a a handful of newly-recorded tracks. While there are some fine songs on *Part II*, the overall quality isn't as high as that of the first volume, which did have all of the hits. Still, for fans wanting to fill in the holes left by *Greatest Hits* and don't have the desire to dig deep into their back catalog, *Greatest Hits Part II* is a good purchase. —*Stephen Thomas Erlewine*

Return to Paradise / May 5, 1997 / CMC International ✦✦
The classic Styx lineup of Dennis DeYoung, Tommy Shaw, James Young, and Chuck Panozzo, augmented by a new drummer, reunited to record 1997's double-disc *Return to Paradise*. The title alludes to the band's biggest hit, *Paradise Theater*, and the music indeed is an attempt to replicate their past glories. On the first half, Styx runs through new songs, all of which are familiar in style, yet none of them quite hits the heights of their earlier work, which becomes painfully clear on the second half of the album, which consists entirely of new live versions of hits like "Come Sail Away," "Lady," and "Too Much Time on My Hands." The live disc is competent and not in league with the originals, yet it sounds much more forceful than the new material, which suffers from being bland and undistinguished. It is better than some of their late-'80s recordings, simply because the band sounds more professional, yet *Return to Paradise* is on the whole a halfhearted return to form. —*Stephen Thomas Erlewine*

Sublime

f. 1988, Long Beach, CA, **db.** 1996
Funk Metal, Punk Revival, Third Wave Ska-Revival, Ska-Metal
Formed in Long Beach, CA, in 1988 as a garage-punk band, Sublime grew to fame in the mid-'90s on the back of the Cali punk explosion engendered by Green Day and the Offspring, though Sublime mixed up their punk rage with reggae and ska influences. The band released just two albums during its first seven years, finally finding a hit with the self-titled third. It was Sublime's last, however, as lead singer Brad Nowell died in May 1996, just two months before the album's release.

The trio that comprised Sublime—vocalist/guitarist Nowell, bassist Eric Wilson, and drummer Bud Gaugh—played their first gig on the 4th of July 1988 at a small Long Beach club (a show that sparked the infamous Peninsula Riot). The group began aggressively touring around the area with an increasingly substantial following, especially among the surf/skate beach crowd. After four years of concentrating strictly on live shows, Sublime's first album (*40 Oz. to Freedom*) was recorded in 1992. The LP was released on Skunk Records—the label formed by Nowell with Sublime manager Miguel—and sold at shows, but really started to break when KROQ began playing the single "Date Rape" two years after

its initial release.

Mostly due to the radio exposure, Sublime signed to MCA for 1994's *Robbin' the Hood*, which revealed an experimental ethic more in keeping with cut-and-paste dub than with the well-tuned rage of the Cali punk revival. The album performed well at college radio, and set the stage for the breakout success of their self-titled third album. On May 25, 1996, however, Brad Nowell was found in a San Francisco hotel room, dead of a heroin overdose. The band collapsed, but *Sublime* was still slated for a July release. On the strength of the alternative radio hit "What I Got," the album was certified gold by the end of 1996. —*John Bush*

40 Oz. to Freedom / 1992 / Skunk ✦✦✦
With their debut *40 Oz. to Freedom*, Sublime attempts to have it both ways. The group wants to appeal to alterna-punks, but they want to cut a little deeper and make some sort of social statement, both with their lyrics and their self-consciously eclectic music. Since the group has a knack for combining dancehall reggae with hardcore punk, the music can be nervy and invigorating, but their joyous blend of cultures falls apart at the lyrical level. No matter how you look at it, "Date Rape" isn't a bold, ironic satire on macho mores—it's frat-rock that's bound to be misinterpreted, especially with its homophobic "I don't feel too sorry for his kind/now that he gets it in the behind" conclusion. Lyrics like that prevent *40 Oz. to Freedom* from being the cracking, skanking skate-punk record that it had the potential to be. —*Stephen Thomas Erlewine*

Robbin' the Hood / 1994 / MCA ✦✦✦✦
Pieced together rather quickly, *Robbin' the Hood* wasn't really intended to be the follow-up to Sublime's debut *40 Oz. to Freedom*, but what is shocking is how much better the record is than its predecessor. Boasting a wider range of influences—including elements of reggae and old-school hip-hop—the record is a loose, infectious blend of styles that rides along on its own sense of energy. Brad Nowell's songwriting might still be at a rudimentary level, but the group sounds more muscular and musical than before, demonstrating that the breakthrough of its sole major-label record, *Sublime*, wasn't an accident. —*Stephen Thomas Erlewine*

● **Sublime** / 1996 / MCA ✦✦✦✦
Sublime's eponymous major-label debut arrived a few months after the band's leader Brad Nowell died tragically of a heroin overdose. As a show of sympathy, the album tended to be slightly overrated in some critical quarters, who claimed that Nowell was an exceptionally gifted lyricist and musical hybridist, but *Sublime* doesn't quite suppport those claims. The trio does have a surprising grace in its unabashedly traditionalist fusion of Californian hardcore punk, light hip-hop and reggae. Switching between bracing hardcore and slow, sexy reggae numbers, Sublime displays supple, muscular versatility and, on occasion, a gift for ingratiatingly catchy hooks, as on the hit single "What I Got." What they don't have is the vision—either lyrical or musical— to maintain interest throughout the course of the entire album. *Sublime* sags when the band delves too deeply into their dub aspirations or when their lyrics slide into smirking humor. The low moments don't arrive that often—by and large, the album is quite engaging—but they happen frequently enough to make the record a demonstration of the band's blossoming ability, but not the fulfillment of their full potential. Of course, Nowell's death gives the record a certain pathos, but that doesn't make the album any stronger. —*Stephen Thomas Erlewine*

Suede

f. 1989, London, England
Alternative Pop-Rock, Brit-Pop
Suede kick-started the Brit-pop revolution of the '90s, bringing English indie-rock pop music away from the swirling layers of shoegazing and dance-pop fusions of Madchester, and reinstating such conventions of British pop as mystique and the three-minute single. Before the band had even released a single, the UK weekly music press was proclaiming them as the "Best New Band in Britain," but Suede managed to survive their heavy hype due to the songwriting team of vocalist Brett Anderson and guitarist Bernard Butler. Equally inspired by the glam crunch of David Bowie and the romantic bed-sit pop of the Smiths, Anderson and Butler developed a sweeping, guitar-heavy sound that was darkly sensual, sexually ambiguous, melodic and unabashedly ambitious. At the time of the release of their first single, "The Drowners," in 1992, few of their contemporaries—whether it was British shoegazers or American grunge rockers—had any ambitions to be old-fashioned, self-consciously controversial pop stars and the British press and public fell hard for Suede, making their 1993 debut the fastest-selling first album in UK history. Though they had rocketed to the top in the UK, Suede was plagued with problems, the least of which was an inability to get themselves heard in America. Anderson and Butler's relationship became antagonistic during the recording of their second album, *Dog Man Star*, and the guitarist left the band before its fall release, which inevitably hurt its sales. Instead of breaking up, the band soldiered on, adding new guitar-

ist Richard Oakes and a keyboardist before returning in 1996 with *Coming Up,* an album that returned them to the top of the British charts.

Through all of Suede's incarnations, vocalist/lyricist Brett Anderson and bassist Mat Osman remained at the band's core. The son of a cab driver, Anderson formed the Smiths-inspired Geoff in 1985 with his schoolmate Osman and drummer Danny Wilder. Anderson was the group's guitarist; Gareth Perry was the band's vocalist. Geoff recorded two demos before splitting up in 1986, as Anderson and Osman left to attend university in London. A few years later, the pair formed Suave & Elegant, which lasted only a few months. By the end of 1989, the pair had placed an advertisement in *New Musical Express,* asking for a "non-muso" guitarist. Bernard Butler responded, and the trio began recording songs, primarily written by Anderson and Butler, with the support of a drum machine. Taking the name Suede after Morrissey's "Suedehead" single, the trio sent a demo tape, *Specially Suede,* to compete in "Demo Clash," a radio show on GLR run by DJ Gary Crowley. "Wonderful Sometimes" won the "Demo Clash" for five Sundays in a row during 1990, leading to a record contract with the Brighton-based indie label RML. By the time the band signed with RML, Anderson's girlfriend Justine Frischmann had joined as a second guitarist.

Suede placed an advertisement for a drummer and former Smiths member Mike Joyce responded. Joyce appeared on the group's debut single for RML, "Be My God" / "Art." Scheduled to be released on a 12-inch in the fall of 1990, the single was scrapped shortly before its release, due to a fight between the band and the label. Throughout 1991, the group rehearsed and recorded demos, eventually adding drummer Simon Gilbert. Frischmann left Suede in early 1992 to form Elastica; she was not replaced. A few months later, Suede signed a two-single deal with the indie label Nude Records. Shortly afterward, the band appeared on the cover of *Melody Maker,* without having released any material. The weekly newspaper declared them the Best New Band in Britain.

"The Drowners," the band's first single, appeared shortly after the *Melody Maker,* and it became a moderate hit, debuting at No. 49 due to strong reviews and word-of-mouth. "Metal Mickey," released in the fall, became their breakthrough hit, reaching No. 17 on the UK charts after a suggestive, controversial performance on *Top of the Pops.* Anderson soon became notorious for causing controversy, and his infamous comment that he was "a bisexual man who never had a homosexual appearance" was indicative of how the group both courted controversy and a sexually ambiguous, alienated audience.

A short tour before the spring release of their eponymous debut album was very successful, setting the stage for "Animal Nitrate" debuting at No. 7. Shortly afterward, *Suede* entered the charts at No. 1, registering the biggest initial sales of a debut since Frankie Goes to Hollywood's *Welcome to the Pleasuredome.* By the summer, Suede had become the most popular band in Britain—winning the prestigious Mercury Music Prize for Best Album that fall—and they attempted to make headway into the United States. Their progress was halted when Butler's father died in the fall, forcing the cancellation of their second tour; they had already begun to be upstaged by their opening act, the Cranberries, who received the support from MTV that Suede lacked. Shortly afterward, the band was forced to change its name to the London Suede in America, due to a lawsuit from an obscure lounge singer performing under the name Suede.

Tensions had begun to develop between Bernard Butler and the rest of the band during the group's 1993 tours, and they peaked when they re-entered the studio to record a new single in late 1993. Butler conceived the song "Stay Together" as a sweeping epic, partially in tribute to his father, and while it was a success upon its February 1994 release, debuting at No. 3, the recording was not easy. As they were working on Suede's second album, Anderson and Butler began to fight frequently, with the guitarist claiming in a rare interview that the singer worked too slowly and that his partner was too concerned with rock stardom, often at the expense of the music. Butler left the band toward the end of the sessions for the second album, and the group finished the record with Anderson playing guitar. Bernard's departure launched a flurry of speculation about Suede's future and *Dog Man Star* didn't answer any of those questions. A grandiose, ambitious, and heavily orchestrated double-album, *Dog Man Star* was greeted with enthusiastic reviews, but muted commercial response. As Suede was working on their second album, their remarkable commercial success was eclipsed by that of Blur and Oasis, whose lighter, more accessible music brought the groups' blockbuster success in the wake of Suede.

While *Dog Man Star* sold nearly as much as *Suede,* the impression in the press was the group was rapidly falling apart, and the band didn't help matters when they replaced Butler with Richard Oakes, a 17-year-old amateur guitarist, in September. Suede embarked on a long, grueling international tour during late 1994 and the spring of 1995, before disappearing to work on their third album. During the interim, Butler had a Top 10 single with vocalist David McAlmont, and Gilbert, the only homosexual member of Suede, was attacked in a hate crime in the fall. At a fanclub gig in January of 1996, the group debuted several new

songs, as well as their new keyboardist Neil Codling, the cousin of Gilbert. Suede returned as a five-piece in September of 1996 with *Coming Up.* A lighter, band-oriented affair than either of the group's two previous albums, *Coming Up* was an unexpected hit, entering the charts at No. 1 and generating three Top 10 hits—"Trash," "Beautiful Ones" and "Saturday Night." *Coming Up* was a hit throughout Europe, Canada, and Asia, but it wasn't released in the US until the spring of 1997. *—Stephen Thomas Erlewine*

● **Suede** / Apr. 1993 / Nude/Columbia ✦✦✦✦
Borrowing heavily from David Bowie and the Smiths, Suede forged a distinctively seductive sound on their eponymous album. Guitarist Bernard Butler has a talent for crafting effortlessly catchy, crunching glam hooks like the controlled rush of "Metal Mickey" and the slow, sexy grind of "The Drowners," but he also can construct grand, darkly romantic soundscapes like the sighing "Sleeping Pills" and the tortured "Pantomime Horse." What brings these elegant sounds to life is Brett Anderson, who invests them with bed-sit angst and seamy sex. Anderson's voice is calculatedly affected and theatrical, but it fits the grand emotion of his self-consciously poetic lyrics. Suede are working-class lads that strive for glamour, and they achieve it by piecing together remnants of the past with pieces of the present, and never forgetting the value of a strong hook in the process. And while the sound of *Suede* frequently recalls the peak of glam-rock, its punk-influenced passion and self-conscious appropriation of the past makes it thoroughly post-modern. Coincidentally, its embrace of trashy pop helped usher in an era of Brit-pop, but few bands captured the theatrical melancholy that gave *Suede* such resonance. *—Stephen Thomas Erlewine*

Dog Man Star / Oct. 25, 1994 / Nude/Columbia ✦✦✦✦
Instead of following though on the Bowie-esque glam stomps of their debut, Suede concentrated on their darker, melodramatic tendencies on their ambitious second album, *Dog Man Star.* By all accounts, the recording of *Dog Man Star* was plagued with difficulties—Brett Anderson wrote the lyrics in a druggy haze while sequestered in a secluded Victorian mansion, while Bernard Butler left before the album was completed—which makes its singular vision all the more remarkable. Lacking any rocker on the level of "The Drowners" or "Metal Mickey"—only the crunching "This Hollywood Life" comes close—*Dog Man Star* is a self-indulgent and pretentious album of dark, string-drenched epics. But Suede are one of the few bands that wear pretensions well and, after a few listens, the album becomes thoroughly compelling. Nearly every song on the record is hazy, feverish, and heart-broken, and even the rockers have an insular, paranoid tenor that heightens the album's melancholy. The whole record would have collapsed underneath its own intentions if Butler's compositional skills weren't so subtly nuanced and if Anderson's grandiose poetry weren't so strangely affecting. As it stands, *Dog Man Star* is a strangely seductive record, filled with remarkable musical peaks, from the Bowie-esque stomp of "New Generation" to the stately ballads "The Wild Ones" and "Still Life," which are both reminiscent of Scott Walker. And while Suede may choose to wear their influences on their sleeve, they synthesize them in a totally original way, making *Dog Man Star* a singularly tragic and romantic album. *—Stephen Thomas Erlewine*

Coming Up / Sep. 2, 1996 / Nude Columbia ✦✦✦✦
After Bernard Butler left Suede in the final sessions for *Dog Man Star,* most observers speculated that the group couldn't survive without his contributions. However, Brett Anderson carried on, adding a teenage guitarist and restructuring the intent of Suede, if not the sound. By the time they recorded their third album, *Coming Up,* Suede was not only a different band, physically—in addition to guitarist Richard Oakes, they added keyboardist Neil Godling—they were a different sonically. The first thing you notice about *Coming Up* is the simplicity. Gone are the grand, sweeping gestures of both *Suede* and *Dog Man Star* and what is left is the glammiest elements of Suede's music, spiked with an invigorating of sense of self-belief—Brett Anderson is out to prove that he's a survivor, and he does give a damn whether you believe he is or not. So *Coming Up* is all about getting dressed up and going out; there's none of the lush, melancholy and, ultimately, paranoid overtones of *Dog Man Star.* It's about celebrating being young, taking drugs, having sex, and living life. What makes the songs a more than hedonistic celebration are the wistful undertones in Anderson's voice—this is a man that's nearly 30, talking about the new youth, those "Shaved heads" that are "psycho for sex and glue." And it sounds just like it reads—Richard Oakes pounds out fizzy, fuzzy guitar riffs while the rhythm section lays back with dirty, sexy grooves and new keyboardist Neil Godling exudes a sultry, unattainable cool. But it is Anderson, who can never disguise his working-class roots, that gives *Coming Up* a center, particularly on its ballads, "By the Sea" and "Picnic by the Motorway." Even on these wistful numbers, there's none of the enveloping melancholy that consumed *Dog Man Star*—they're as optimistic as the buoyant, melodic rockers that comprise the rest of the album. As a statement of purpose, *Coming Up* is unimpeachable. Though it doesn't break any new ground for the

band—unless you count the newfound sense of optimism—it's a remarkable consolidation and crystallization of Suede's talents and all the evidence anyone needs that Brett Anderson was always the guiding force behind the band. —*Stephen Thomas Erlewine*

Sugar

f. 1992, Minneapolis, MN, **db.** 1995
Alternative Pop-Rock

After two solo albums, ex-Hüsker Dü guitarist/vocalist Bob Mould formed Sugar in 1992, with bassist David Barbe and drummer Malcolm Travis; the band signed with Rykodisc in the US, Creation in the UK.

Sugar's first album, *Copper Blue*, was released in the fall of 1992 to enthusiastic reviews and it became Mould's most successful project to date. *Copper Blue* nearly went gold and spawned several alternative radio and MTV hits, including "Helpless" and "If I Can't Change Your Mind." In the spring of 1993, Sugar released the mini-LP *Beaster*, a more abrasive collection than *Copper Blue* that was recorded at the same sessions.

Around the time of the release of *Beaster*, Mould was forced out of the closet by various gay publications, with hopes that he would embrace their political cause; he rejected their requests.

Mould wrote the material for the second Sugar album during 1993. The band began recording in the spring of 1994, but the sessions ground to a halt and the tapes were erased. Mould decided to give the album one more try and it was recorded quickly late that spring. The album, *File Under: Easy Listening*, appeared in the fall of 1994. Although it received good reviews and was moderately successful commercially, it didn't match the performance of *Copper Blue*.

In the spring of 1995, it was announced that Sugar was on hiatus. *Besides*, a collection of rarities and B-sides, was released that summer. By the fall, Mould had broken up the band and begun to work on a third album entirely by himself. Mould played all of the instruments on his self-titled third album, which was released in the spring of 1995. —*Stephen Thomas Erlewine*

● **Copper Blue** / Sep. 4, 1992 / Rykodisc ✦✦✦✦
Featuring some of Mould's best songwriting, Sugar's debut album is a stunning piece of hook-laden punk-pop, highlighted by the '60s-style "If I Can't Change Your Mind," the loud, beautiful guitars of "Man on the Moon," and "Helpless," and the tongue-in-cheek Pixies tribute "A Good Idea." —*Stephen Thomas Erlewine*

Beaster / Apr. 6, 1993 / Rykodisc ✦✦✦
Recorded at the same time as *Copper Blue*, *Beaster* is a darker, more intense record than Sugar's debut, but it's never as black as Mould's *Black Sheets of Rain*. The fusion of pop melodies with a punk roar, which made *Copper Blue* so magnificent, is here, but the guitars are harsher and the loose crucifixion concept provides a downbeat atmosphere, provided you can hear the lyrics. Mould's vocals are mixed beneath all the other instruments, contributing to the claustrophobic, oppressive atmosphere. But *Beaster* is not nihilistic. In fact, Mould ends the EP optimistically, albeit cautiously, with the gorgeously circular organ-based "Walking Away." —*Stephen Thomas Erlewine*

File Under: Easy Listening / Sep. 6, 1994 / Rykodisc ✦✦✦✦
Given Bob Mould's reputation for searing electric rock 'n' roll, it may be easy to think that the title is ironic, and it is to a certain extent. But beneath the loud guitars lay the friendliest, most relaxed pop songs Mould has ever written. "Your Favorite Thing" and "Can't Help You Anymore" are two of Mould's most direct, pop-oriented songs, driven by instantly memorable melodies and hooks; they are also the most conventional songs on the record. The best moments come when Sugar push the boundaries a bit, whether it's on the country-rock of "Believe What You're Saying," the swirling "What You Want It to Be" and "Company Book," the searching ballad "Panama City Motel," or "Explode and Make Up," which bristles even at its most delicate moments. Mould throws in one classic spite-fueled rocker, "Granny Cool," but the record's finest moment is "Gee Angel," a powerhouse melodic scorcher. —*Stephen Thomas Erlewine*

Besides / Jul. 25, 1995 / Rykodisc ✦✦✦
The strength of *Besides* is not only a measure of the quality of Bob Mould's songwriting, it's a measure of how good a band Sugar is. Collecting all of the B-sides and rare tracks left over from the group's three albums, *Besides* isn't filled with sub-par material. Frequently, Mould would leave fine songs off the album because it didn't fit the mood, such as the scorching rocker "Needle Hits E." That consistent quality means the record is a thoroughly engaging experience, even during live and alternate versions of "Explode and Make Up" and "If I Can't Change Your Mind." The first 25,000 copies included a bonus disc, featuring a complete Sugar concert; it's a typically mesmerizing, galvanizing show. —*Stephen Thomas Erlewine*

Sugarcubes

f. 1986, Reykjavik, Iceland, **db.** 1992
Alternative Pop-Rock

The Sugarcubes were the biggest group ever to emerge from Iceland, which helps explain their off-kilter sense of melody. Their 1988 debut, *Life's Too Good*, attracted terrific reviews and became a college radio hit, but they never were able to recapture that sense of excitement.

According to group legend, the Sugarcubes formed on June 8, 1986, the day that vocalist Björk (b. Björk Gundmundsdottir) gave birth to her son. Prior to that day, the members of the group had been a variety of Icelandic bands. Björk had the longest career out of any of the members. When she was 11 years old, the vocalist had recorded a children's album. In her late teens, she joined the Icelandic post-punk band Tappi Tikarrass, who released two albums before splitting in 1983. Drummer Siggi Baldursson (born Sigtryggur Baldursson, October 2, 1962) was a member of Theyer, whose most prominent international moment came in 1982, when they recorded with Youth and Jaz Coleman of Killing Joke. At the same time Theyer was popular within Iceland, Einar Benediktsson and Bragi Olafsson formed a punk band called Purrkur Pillnikk, who released records on Benediktsson's own label, Gramm.

By 1984, Björk, Einar Benediktsson, and Siggi Baldursson had joined forces, forming KUKL with keyboardist Einar Mellax. KUKL—which means witch in Icelandic—was a noisy, artsy post-punk band that released several singles on the independent British record label Crass. In 1986, KUKL evolved into the Sugarcubes, adding Björk's then-husband Thor Jonson on guitar and Bragi Olafsson on bass.

In late 1987, the band signed to One Little Indian in the UK, Elektra Records in the US. The Sugarcubes released their debut album, *Life's Too Good*, in 1988 to critical acclaim in both the UK and the US. "Birthday," the first single from the album, became an indie hit in Britain and a college radio hit in America. In particular, Björk received a heap of praise, which began tensions between her and Einar Benediktsson. By the time the group recorded their second album, Thor had divorced Björk and married Magga Ornolfsdottir, who became the group's keyboardist after Einar Mellax left. Furthermore, Bragi Olaffson divorced his wife—who happened to be the twin sister of Siggi Baldursson's wife—and married Benediktsson, making their union the first openly gay marriage in pop music.

Here Today, Tomorrow, Next Week!, the Sugarcubes' second album, was released in 1989. The album featured a greater vocal contribution by Einar, which was criticized in many of the record's reviews, which were noticeably weaker than those for *Life's Too Good*. After the release of *Here Today, Tomorrow, Next Week!*, the band embarked on a lengthy international tour. At the conclusion of the tour in late 1990, the band members pursued their own individual interests. *Stick Around for Joy*, the band's third album, was released in 1992; before the record appeared, a collection of remixes called *It's It* was released in Europe. *Stick Around for Joy* received better reviews than *Life's Too Good*, but the album failed to yield a hit single. Following its release, the Sugarcubes disbanded. In 1993, Björk launched a critically acclaimed and commercially successful solo career that was based in dance music. —*Stephen Thomas Erlewine*

● **Life's Too Good** / 1988 / Elektra ✦✦✦✦
With strong songs built around Bjork Gudmundsdottir's piercing, striking voice, this record lived up to all the advance hype. With songs like "Birthday" and "Motorcrash," this is the perfect introduction to the 'Cubes. —*John Dougan*

Here Today, Tomorrow, Next Week! / Sep. 1989 / Elektra ✦✦✦
A slip from the first album, but not so much that it's without merit. —*John Dougan*

Stick Around for Joy / Feb. 18, 1992 / Elektra ✦✦✦
While it's a bit better than their second record, the Sugarcubes' final album isn't as exciting as their debut, even if it shows more musical range. Too often, it slips into a self-conscious goofiness, and even Bjork's fine vocals can't save the music from its smirking, self-involved in-jokes. —*Stephen Thomas Erlewine*

The Sugarhill Gang

f. 1979, New York, NY, **db.** 1985
Hip-Hop, Electro-Funk, Old School Rap

The Sugarhill Gang inaugurated the history of recorded hip-hop with their single "Rapper's Delight," a multi-platinum seller and radio hit in 1979. The Sugarhill Gang were cooked up to cash in on a supposed novelty item; music-industry producer and label-owner Sylvia Robinson had become aware of the massive hip-hop block parties occurring around the New York area during the late '70s, so she gathered three local rappers (Master Gee, Wonder Mike and Big Bank Hank) to record a single. Infectious and catchy, "Rapper's Delight" borrowed the break from Chic's "Good Times" and became a worldwide hit, eventually selling over eight million copies. Most industry people figured rap for a short-lived trend, and though they were dead wrong, the Sugarhill Gang certainly didn't carry the torch; despite several modest hits ("8th Wonder," "Apache") the trio faded quickly and were gone by the mid-'80s. —*John Bush*

Rapper's Delight: Hip Hop Remix / 1980 / Sugar Hill ✦✦✦✦
The Sugarhill Gang's 1979 hit "Rapper's Delight" is arguably the first true rap song to gain widespread recognition and, as such, the progenitor of one of the major musical genres of the '80s. No wonder it doesn't sound dated yet. —*William Ruhlmann*

The Sugarhill Gang / 1980 / Sugar Hill ✦✦✦✦

8th Wonder / 1992 / Sugar Hill ✦✦✦
The Sugarhill Gang enjoyed its final moments in the spotlight with this 1982 LP. They scored two moderate hits with the title cut and "Apache," while continuing the old-school approach that initially gained mainstream attention and exposure for rap. —*Ron Wynn*

● **Best of Sugarhill Gang** / Jul. 1996 / Rhino ✦✦✦✦
The Sugarhill Gang's biggest hits are collected on this single-disc compilation. In addition to "Rapper's Delight"—the first rap single to reach the pop Top Ten—the group's seven other R&B hits are included on the disc, plus three other singles that never made the charts. All of the songs are presented in their original 12-inch versions. Not all of the material is first-rate—in retrospect, the group's old-school groove tended to be a little simplistic, monotonous, and too polished, while their rhymes are frequently stilted and sometimes just outright silly—but this music, especially "Rapper's Delight," is important historically. Most casual fans of old-school hip-hop will be content with purchasing "Rapper's Delight" on a various artists collection, but for those wanting to dig deeper into the trio's history, *The Best of Sugarhill Gang* is a definitive retrospective. —*Stephen Thomas Erlewine*

Suicidal Tendencies

f. 1982, Venice, CA
Hardcore Punk, Heavy Metal, Speed Metal, Thrash
Suicidal Tendencies were formed in Venice, CA, as a punk/hardcore band and virtually came to define the phrase "skate-punk." Vocalist/bandleader Mike Muir has earned a reputation for addressing various political and personal topics with focused rage and thoughtfulness, and also for his keen sense of humor, which helps set the band apart from its competition. During the '80s, the group was frequently banned in the Los Angeles area, as their gigs often turned into out-of-control melees. Over the years, the band has mixed speed metal, more relaxed alternative rock, and touches of funk into its sound. Muir and bass virtuoso Robert Trujillo led the metal/funk party band Infectious Grooves as a side project for Muir's nonpolitical side. —*Steve Huey*

● **Suicidal Tendencies** / 1983 / Epitaph ✦✦✦✦
The album that started it for this band; it's not heavy metal but hardcore punk. A lot of aggression, with some fun, it includes the classic song "Institutionalized." —*John Book*

Join the Army / 1987 / Caroline ✦✦✦
The band incorporates a little more metal influences on this one and includes "Possessed to Skate." —*John Book*

How Will I Laugh Tomorrow When I Can't Even Smile Today / 1988 / Epic ✦✦✦✦
The band is a bit more metal-oriented but still as aggressive as in their punk days. *How Will I Laugh Tomorrow When I Can't Even Smile Today* has lots of great songs, including "Trip to the Brain" and the title track. —*John Book*

Lights . . . Camera . . . Revolution! / Jun. 1990 / Epic ✦✦✦
Their strongest album since the debut has great songs like "Send Me Your Money" and "You Can't Bring Me Down." —*John Book*

The Art of Rebellion / Jun. 1992 / Epic ✦✦
On the group's earliest albums, vocalist Mike Muir specialized in intense, angst-ridden rants, harrowing but one-dimensional. He has since developed into a rock-solid vocalist, his voice a powerful and fluid instrument. Muir still delivers emotionally ferocious spoken-word segments on "Nobody Hears" and "I Wasn't Meant to Hear This," but the trademark is woven into good songs rather than being an end onto itself. A clenched fist in a velvet glove—or is it an open hand in chain mail?—whichever, *The Art of Rebellion* packs a punch that should win over new devotees while maintaining the group's hardcore following. —*Roch Parisien*

Suicide

f. 1971, New York, NY, **db.** 1982
Electronic, Punk, Post-Punk
Although they barely receive credit, Suicide (singer Alan Vega and keyboardist Martin Rev) is the source point for virtually every synth-pop duo that glutted the pop marketplace (especially in England) in the early '80s. Without the trailblazing Rev and Vega, there would have been no

Soft Cell, Erasure, Bronski Beat, Yaz, you name 'em, and while many would tell you that that's nothing to crow about, the synth-poppers merely appropriated Suicide's keyboards/singer look and none of Rev and Vega's extremely confrontational performance style and love of dissonance. The few who did (Throbbing Gristle, Cabaret Voltaire) were considered too extreme for most tastes. Suicide had been a part of the performing arts scene in New York City's Lower East Side in the early/mid-'70s New York Dolls era. Their approach to music was simple: Rev would create minimalistic, spooky, hypnotic washes of dissonant keyboards and synthesizers, while Vega sang, ranted, and spat neo-Beat lyrics in a jumpy, disjointed fashion. Onstage, Vega became confrontational, often baiting the crowd into a riotous frenzy that occasionally led to full-blown violence, usually with the crowd attacking Vega. With their reputation as controversial performers solidified, what was lost was that Suicide recorded amazingly seductive and terrifying music. A relationship with Cars mastermind Ric Ocasek proved successful, bringing their music to a wider audience and developing unlikely fans (Bruce Springsteen went on record as loving Suicide's Vietnam-vet saga "Frankie Teardrop"), but after numerous breakups and reconciliations, Rev and Vega settled for being more influential than commercially successful. Ironically, the '90s proved to be a decade of vindication for Suicide with the rise of industrial dance music, Chicago's Wax Trax label, and the bands associated with it (Revolting Cocks, Ministry, 1000 Homo DJs, etc.). Although not a big part of the scene anymore, the influence of Suicide on a generation of younger bands is readily apparent. —*John Dougan*

● **Suicide** / 1977 / Restless ✦✦✦✦
Suicide's debut is extreme, noisy, confrontational, and everything you'd want them to be. A slap in the face of the guitar-oriented punk rock that was coming out of New York and England at this time, Rev and Vega prove they were ahead of their time, even if audiences hated them for it. What doesn't hurt this record is the presence of some of their best material, "Rocket USA" and the deathless "Frankie Teardrop." —*John Dougan*

Half Alive / 1981 / ROIR ✦✦✦✦
Nasty live stuff. Singer Alan Vega is especially obnoxious. —*John Dougan*

Ghost Riders / 1986 / ROIR ✦✦✦
Originally a cassette-only release, this live recording at Walker Arts Center in Minneapolis marked Rev and Vega's 10th anniversary. And while not as deliberately offensive as some of their earlier live gigs (the impossible-to-locate *24 Minutes over Brussels*), this is a compelling, interesting document of their ever-evolving stage show. Not as transcendent as their debut album, but well worth the effort. Reissued on CD by the French Danceteria label in 1990. —*John Dougan*

The Way of Life / 1988 / Wax Trax! ✦✦✦
The unwitting godfathers of industrial noise-squall return after a long absence to reclaim their throne on *A Way of Life*. Produced by Ric Ocasek, Suicide's Alan Vega and Martin Rev pick up exactly where they left off, crafting beautifully ominous drone-rock founded on pulsing sequences, dramatic vocals, and dense atmospherics. —*Jason Ankeny*

Sukia

f. 1995, Los Angeles, CA
Electronica, Indie Rock, Experimental
Taking their name from a Mexican lesbian vampire comic book heroine, the avant-lounge quartet Sukia emerged from Los Angeles' famed Silverlake scene (the same musical community home to Beck, the Beastie Boys, and the Dust Brothers). Comprised of multi-instrumentalists Sasha Fuentes, Ross Harris, Grace Marks, and Craig Borrell, Sukia combined Moog-driven grooves laced with found samples and space-age pop aesthetics on their 1996 debut *Contacto Especial con el Tercer Sexo*, produced by the Dust Brothers and issued on their Nickel Bag label. —*Jason Ankeny*

● **Contacto Especial con el Tercer Sexo** / Oct. 1996 / Nickel Bag ✦✦✦✦
An ominous, free-floating collage of found sounds, drum machines, cheap keyboards and samples, Sukia's debut album *Contacto Especial con el Tercer Sexo* flirts with exotica and the avant-garde without committing to either. And it's the better for it. Sukia's instrumentals are alternatingly mesmerizing and disturbing, fueled by pseudo-bossa nova rhythms, jazzy chords and sheets of noise. It's not necessarily an alienating record, but anyone well versed in the cut-paste productions of the Dust Brothers, who also helmed this record, will be more inclined towards meeting the album halfway, since the music isn't strictly lounge-revival, avant-pop, or electronic music. It's a fascinating, darkly humorous melange of all three, and it's endlessly fascinating. —*Stephen Thomas Erlewine*

Donna Summer

b. Dec. 31, 1948, Boston, MA
Vocals / Dance-Pop, Disco, Urban, Pop-Rock, Club-Dance
Born Donna Gaines to a churchgoing family in the Mission Hill section

of Boston, Summer took her name from Helmut Sommer, whom she married while living in Munich, Germany, as a member of a travelling cast of *Hair.* Italian electro-pop arranger Giorgio Moroder met her, and in 1975 they recorded "Love to Love You Baby," a 16-minute, riff-driven update of Jane Birkin and Serge Gainsbourg's version of "Je t'aime . . . moi non plus." But Summer, as it turned out, had a sturdiness quite different from Birkin's short bursts of this and that, and a flair for kitschy show tunes and overproduced slickness, both of which ideally complimented the transparent impersonality of Moroder's electronic rhythms. She and Moroder created entire sub-genres of disco, and there was no stopping them until Summer stopped herself.

Beginning with 1980's *The Wanderer* (except for the title song) she began to sing exactly the kind of pop-rock material her daring impressionism had fought against. She tried to become a pop singer; and when, as in *She Works Hard for the Money,* she drew upon gospel styles, she was listened to. But during the '70s, she wasn't merely listened to, she was a leader. Today Summer tries to catch up, sadly, with a generation whose greatest aesthetic achievement was to catch up with her. —*Michael Freedberg*

Love to Love You Baby / Sep. 1975 / Casablanca ✦✦✦✦
"Love to Love You Baby"'s 16:50 of arousal and refill—ticklishly sensitive rhythm and fusion—threw disco into a tizzy overnight, but the tonally starved blues-of-isolation on the B-side isn't to be missed, either: the broken promises Summer bemoans in "Full of Emptiness"; "Need-A-Man Blues," with its unrequitedly sexy guitar rhythm as out of range of Summer's voice as she of satisfaction; the imaginary seaside hold-me in "Whispering Waves"; and "Pandora's Box," where Summer and guitar scream icily at one another as they turn their backs on each other's body music. Hunger without recourse: essential disco. —*Michael Freedberg*

Love Trilogy / Mar. 1976 / Casablanca ✦✦✦
Summer's quizzical "Try Me," "I Know," and "We Can Make It" wings her nervous little falsetto from risk to dare and from dare to mad hope, and her rhythm section gropes from testy touch beats to tightrope-walkers' guitar figures and safety-net harmonies. The second side substitutes dance with imaginary lovers for the debut album's love starvation blues. Don't dismiss its subtle mood poems the way fans of "Love to Love You" sped right past the B-side of Summer's debut; the flightier Summer plays a rhythm, the dicier her resolution. —*Michael Freedberg*

Four Seasons of Love / Oct. 1976 / Casablanca ✦✦✦
One's inclined to resist this package of self-conscious stardom concepts—the LP sports its own 1977 calendar featuring La Summer dressed up as winter, spring, summer, and Marilyn Monroe vamping on the subway grating (fall, I guess), and the four "seasonal" dancey suites promise more and say less than Summer's intimate touch-me's deliver without any hype. Fortunately the music has a mind of its own. The rhythms push and go poof as delicately as ever, the horn section mutes and jazzes the melody, the beats stop, run, and stop again whenever they damn please, and Summer falsettoes in private rapture as she smooches oohs and aahs onto the mix like lipstick traces. —*Michael Freedberg*

I Remember Yesterday / May 1977 / Casablanca ✦✦✦
Donna Summer continued her climb to superstardom with this late-'70s album, her first since the attention-grabbing *Love to Love You Baby* album in 1975 to crack the pop Top 20. The single "I Feel Love" was her second Top 10 R&B and pop hit, and paved the way for Summer to emerge shortly after as disco's reigning queen. —*Ron Wynn*

Once upon a Time / Nov. 1977 / Casablanca ✦✦✦
Summer and her liberators have created one audience and redefined another, and this record's four sides of dreamworlds without end sometimes manipulate each audience. The candy-girl music of "Fairy Tale High," "Queen for a Day," and "If You Got It, Flaunt It" explicitly recognizes her newly created gay audience, a daring acknowledgement coming from a mainstream pop star. As for her redefined audience of naive young things who live in the suburbs and dream of romance, adventure, and sex while they search for identity, Summer works her music into a true-to-life Cinderella story staged as four acts of impatient pulse, delirious space noise, wish-upon-a-star voice monologues, and motion. —*Michael Freedberg*

Live & More / Sep. 1978 / Casablanca ✦✦
Live at the Universal Amphitheater, she sings her hits up to the time plus a medley of standards featuring "The Man I Love" and "I Got It Bad and That Ain't Good." Also included is one side of studio music with "Heaven Knows" and "MacArthur Park." —*Bil Carpenter*

Bad Girls / May 1979 / Casablanca ✦✦✦✦
Summer defined "feminine" for an age in love with femininity and made the disco experience an adventure, even for those who had trouble learning how to fantasize. Now, on her third two-record set in two years, she has altered her outlook on femininity and changed her mind about the adventure. The disco queen becomes a streetwalker ready to sell her voice to any guy (read: producer) for a dime ("Bad Girls," "Hot

Stuff") or anyone at all blindly searching for a lover they'll never find ("Sunset People"). —*Michael Freedberg*

Walk Away: The Best of Donna Summer (1977-1980) / 1980 / Casablanca ✦✦✦✦
A collection of later Donna Summer material, including such songs as "Winter Melody," "I Feel Love," and "Bad Girls." Although disco was beginning to peak, Summer was riding high, dominating the R&B and pop charts. In some ways, these songs were more varied than her pre-'77 cuts, because only "Love to Love You Baby," from her Oasis material, was a major hit. —*Ron Wynn*

The Wanderer / Oct. 1980 / Geffen ✦✦✦✦
This first post-Casablanca set has a hard-rock edge that shines best on the title cut, "Cold Love," and "Night Life." —*Bil Carpenter*

Donna Summer / Jul. 1982 / Geffen ✦✦✦
The follow-up to Donna Summer's first big Geffen album did reasonably well and proved to be the lull before the storm. "State of Independence" just missed being a hit, and "Woman in Me" cracked the pop and R&B Top 40, although it wasn't a smash. But the album mostly reaffirmed that Summer was back in stride and hadn't merely scored a fluke with her previous release. —*Ron Wynn*

She Works Hard for the Money / Jun. 1983 / Casablanca ✦✦✦✦
Summer's brassy, matter-of-fact mezzo does not play the sexy sanctified diva, and her musicians' crisp loud beats don't evoke rapture or delirium. Instead, she and her rhythm men live up to the title of "She Works Hard for the Money." Here's praise for a waitress' 12-hour workday that sums up Summer's own post-dance queen job status as well as disco fans' own spotlighted lives and maintains the pressure from the steel-and-synth riffs of "Stop, Look & Listen" to the impatient tenderness of "People, People." No one writes about love with as mesmeric a sense of wonder as Summer confesses in "Love Has a Mind of Its Own," "Unconditional Love," and "I Do Believe (I Fell in Love)." —*Michael Freedberg*

Cats without Claws / 1984 / Warner Brothers ✦✦
Although it's now widely perceived as a flop, in truth Donna Summer made the Top 40 with this album, and the song "There Goes My Baby" reached the Top 30 on both the R&B and pop charts, while "Supernatural Love" also made both surveys. But it wasn't as lofty a triumph as Summer had routinely enjoyed, and there were danger signs lurking in her relationship with Geffen. Still, as her 1980s output goes, this was far superior to the reviews it received and the reputation it carries. —*Ron Wynn*

● **The Donna Summer Anthology (Chronicles Series)** / Sep. 21, 1993 / Casablanca ✦✦✦✦
A double-disc set that collects all of Summer's biggest hits and finest moments, it's the definitive anthology. —*AMG*

★ **Endless Summer: The Very Best Of** / 1995 / Casablanca ✦✦✦✦✦
A condensed, more concise collection than *Anthology, Endless Summer: The Very Best of Donna Summer* has greater historical depth than previous compilations and all the major hits, from "Love to Love You Baby" to "She Works Hard for the Money," are represented here. —*John Lowe*

I'm a Rainbow / Aug. 20, 1996 / Polygram ✦✦✦✦
Originally scheduled for release in 1981, the double-album *I'm a Rainbow* was shelved at the last minute. In the prooes, it became legendary among Donna Summer fanatics. In 1996, *I'm a Rainbow* was finally released as a single compact disc. Like most of Summer's recordings from the late '70s and early '80s, it was produced by Giorgio Moroder and Pete Bellotte, who give the stylish disco a sleek, sexy sheen. The difference between *I'm a Rainbow* and its predecessors—and, indeed, its sequels—is the subject matter. Throughout *I'm a Rainbow,* Summer turns in some of her most personal, introspective lyrics and singing, which gives the album an emotional force her albums sometimes lacked. In fact, given the quality of the music, it's hard to see why this was shelved at the time because it is stronger than the majority of her official studio albums. —*Leo Stanley*

The Sundays

f. 1987, Camden, London
Alternative Pop-Rock, Dream Pop
Building on the jangly guitar pop of the Smiths and the trance-like dream pop of bands like the Cocteau Twins, the Sundays cultivated a dedicated following in indie-rock circles, both in their native England and in America, in the early '90s. Although the sales of their first two albums were strong, the band never crossed over into the mainstream, as so many observers and critics predicted they would.

The Sundays formed in the summer of 1987 in London, England. Originally, the group consisted of vocalist Harriet Wheeler, who had previously sung with a band called Jim Jiminee, and guitarist David Gavurin. After the duo had written several songs, they added a rhythm section, featuring bassist Paul Brindley and drummer Patrick Hannan. In August of 1988, the Sundays performed their first concert, playing at the Falcoln "Vertigo Club" in Camden, London. The concert generated good word-of-mouth within the industry and the group were the target of a record-label bidding war. By the end of the year, the band had signed to Rough Trade; they would sign a deal with DGC Records for American distribution within a year.

"Can't Be Sure," the Sundays' first single, appeared in January of 1989 and entered the UK charts at No. 45. The group took a year to record their first album, *Reading, Writing, Arithmetic.* The debut was released in early 1990 to very positive critical notices and unexpectedly entered the UK charts at No. 4. Upon its American release later in the year, the album became a modern rock hit, peaking at No. 39. Its success in the US was largely due to heavy radio and MTV airplay for the single "Here's Where the Story Ends." The single wound up topping the modern rock charts in America. The Sundays spent the rest of 1990 successfully touring America, Europe, and Japan.

During 1991, Rough Trade collapsed due to financial mismanagement. After the label went out of business, the Sundays signed a deal with Parlophone Records in the UK; *Reading, Writing & Arithmetic* went out of print in England and it would not go back in print until 1996. Even considering the setback of Rough Trade's implosion, the Sundays took a long time to write and record their second album. They finally delivered the follow-up to *Reading, Writing & Arithmetic* in the fall of 1992. The resulting album, entitled *Blind,* was greeted with mixed reviews but it was an immediate hit in the US and UK. In America, "Love" became a No. 2 modern rock hit and "Goodbye" peaked at No. 11. Although *Blind* was initially successful, it didn't have they staying power of the debut and dropped out of the charts by the summer of 1993. The Sundays supported the album with an international tour.

After the release of *Blind,* the Sundays were quiet for the next several years. The only sign of the band was the use of their cover of the Rolling Stones' "Wild Horses" in an American television commercial in 1994. —*Stephen Thomas Erlewine*

● **Reading, Writing & Arithmetic** / Apr. 1990 / DGC ✦✦✦✦
The Sundays' debut album built on the layered, ringing guitar hooks and unconventional pop melodies of the Smiths, adding more ethereal vocals and a stronger backbeat. As evidenced by the lilting, melancholy single "Here's Where the Story Ends," it was a winning combination, making *Reading, Writing & Arithmetic* a thoroughly engaging debut. —*Stephen Thomas Erlewine*

Blind / Oct. 20, 1992 / DGC ✦✦✦
Featuring gentle, folk-based guitars and pop melodies, The Sundays' second album isn't much of a sonic departure from their first album. While it does have several fine numbers, it doesn't have as many outstanding songs as *Reading, Writing & Arithmetic;* nevertheless, *Blind* will please most fans of the group. —*Stephen Thomas Erlewine*

Super Furry Animals

f. 1993, Cardiff, Wales
Alternative Pop-Rock, Brit-Pop, Neo-Psychedelia
Super Furry Animals were one of the first post-alternative bands, fusing together a number of disperate musical genres—including power pop, punk rock, techno, and progressive rock—creating a shimmering, melodic, irreverent and willfully artsy rock 'n' roll. As one of the leading bands of the mid-'90s Welsh movement, they were already tagged as outsiders by their tendency to sing entire songs in their native tongue, but their very approach was unique, fully of both whimsy and left-wing political activism. What set them apart from their fellow Welsh bands was their infectious melodic sensibilities and their wildly irreverent attitude, which peers like Gorky's Zygotic Mynci, 60 Foot Dolls, and Catatonia lacked. Super Furry Animals' 1996 debut album, *Fuzzy Logic,* became a major English hit, charting in the Top 40 and placing in the Top 10 of many year-end critic's polls.

Formed in Cardiff, Wales, in 1993, Super Furry Animals was comprised of Gruff Rhys (lead vocals, guitar), Huw "Bunf" Bunford (guitar, vocals), Guto Pryce (bass), Cian Ciaran (keyboards, electronics), and Dafydd Ieuan (drums). All five members had played in bands throughout their teens prior to forming the group, most notably Rhys, who had previously played in a jangle-pop band named Emily, which were briefly signed to Creation, as well as a Welsh noise-rock band called Ffa Coffi Pawb. Following the dissolution of Ffa Coffi Pawb, Rhys played in a trio with Pryce and Ieuan, which eventually evolved into Super Furry Animals. Initially, the group was a techno outfit, yet they quickly evolved into a neo-psychedelic and progressive-pop outfit. After two years of writing and touring, the band signed with the Cardiff-based independent label Ankst and released their debut EP, *Lianfairpwllgywgyllgoger Chwymdrobwlltysiliogoygoyocynygofod (In Space),* which was sung entirely in Welsh. It was followed within a few months by another EP, *Moog Droog,* which was also sung in Welsh. Both EPs were produced by Gorwel Owen.

By the end of 1995, Super Furry Animals had gained a strong, cross-generational fan base in Wales, while gathering a strong cult following in Britain, which led to a six-album record contract with Creation

Records. Prior to signing with Creation, the band had decided to sing the majority of their songs in English, in order to reach a wider audience. Super Furry Animals and Owen produced the group's debut album, which was preceded by two singles in the spring of 1996—"Hometown Unicorn" and "God! Show Me Magic"—which became moderate hits. *Fuzzy Logic,* the band's debut album, was released in the UK in June of 1996 to uniformly excellent reviews. Within a few months, SFA had become one of the hippest bands in British independent music, and several of the group's lyrical touchstones—most notably the notorious Welsh dope smuggler Howard Marks, who appeared on the cover of *Fuzzy Logic*—had become pop-culture refrences. Super Furry Animals also became infamous during the summer of 1996 for attending all of the pop music festivals in a gigantic tank.

"Something 4 the Weekend" and "If You Don't Want Me To Destroy You" became hit singles in the summer and fall of 1996. The latter single was scheduled to have a B-side called "The Man Don't Give a Fuck," which was built on a sample of Steely Dan's "Showbiz Kids," but Donald Fagen refused to give the group permission to use the recording. By November, he relented and "The Man Don't Give a Fuck" was released as a limited-edition single in early December, and it reached No. 22 on the UK charts.

Super Furry Animals entered the studios in January of 1997 to record their second album, which was scheduled for release in August of 1997. —*Stephen Thomas Erlewine*

● **Fuzzy Logic** / May 1996 / Creation ✦✦✦✦
Super Furry Animals are eclectic, to say the least. Fusing together pop melodies, psychedelia, and art-rock with an impish, punky fury, the band covers more ground on their debut album, *Fuzzy Logic,* than most indie bands do in their entire career. However, the album works better as a series of moments than as a collection, mainly due to their overreaching ambition. Each song floats by on irresistible, catchy vocal harmonies, while the music alternates between glitzy overdriven guitars and sighing, sweeping keyboard, guitar and string backdrops. Over these lush sonic beds, lead vocalist Gruff sings lyrics that are either mystical, nonsensical, or bizarrely funny—none of the songs make much literal sense, but that doesn't quite matter when the music is as free-spirited as this. The songs may start conventionally, but they'll be undercut by wild synthesizers and careening guitar solos, or off-kilter vocal melodies. Taken as individual moments—as the singles "God! Show Me Magic" (relatively straighthead punk-pop), "Hometown Unicorn" (gorgeous psychedelia), and "Something for the Weekend" (which finds the middle ground between the first two singles) prove—the music of Super Furry Animals is quite intoxicating, but when assembled together, they don't sustain momentum. However, the individual pleasures of each song become more apparent with each listen and *Fuzzy Logic* suggests that the group could blossom into something quite distinctive and utterly unique within a few albums. —*Stephen Thomas Erlewine*

Superchunk

f. 1989, Chapel Hill, NC
Alternative Pop-Rock, Indie Rock
In the big-business world of '90s alternative rock, Superchunk remains a staunchly independent guitar rock band. When their record label, Matador, signed a major-label distribution deal, the band refused to be a part of the deal; with their next record, they switched labels to their privately owned Merge label. All the while, the band continues to gain more fans. Superchunk's stripped-down, speedy punk rock is proudly low-fidelity, yet their songs are well-written, packed with hooks and raw, energetic rocking. Although their singles and albums show little stylistic variation, they rock so hard the similiarity hardly matters. —*Stephen Thomas Erlewine*

No Pocky for Kitty / 1992 / Matador ✦✦✦✦
After a series of blistering singles, Superchunk released *No Pocky for Kitty,* which confirmed their status as one of the best and most diverse punk rock groups of the early '90s. —*Stephen Thomas Erlewine*

● **Tossing Seeds (Singles 89-91)** / 1992 / Merge ✦✦✦✦
Featuring the classic '90s anti-anthem "Slack Motherfucker," *Tossing Seeds (Singles 89-91)* is a superb collection of early non-LP singles by one of the best indie guitar bands of the early '90s. —*Stephen Thomas Erlewine*

On The Mouth / 1993 / Matador ✦✦✦✦
On the Mouth is one of Superchunk's best albums, not because it offers anything different from their previous work, but because the band's songwriting is at a peak, which makes songs like "The Question Is How Fast" sound fresh and exciting, not empty exercises in punk nostalgia. —*Stephen Thomas Erlewine*

Foolish / Dec. 1993 / Merge ✦✦✦
Foolish may not be as consistent as *On the Mouth,* but it makes up for that with musical ambition and strong songwriting. —*Stephen Thomas Erlewine*

Incidental Music / Jun. 20, 1995 / Merge ++++
Singles are the most effective forum for Superchunk's music, which makes *Incidental Music (singles 92-94)* one of their most consistent records. It might not have a single song as definitive as "Slack Mother-fucker," but this collection of non-LP singles is filled with some of their finest moments. —*Stephen Thomas Erlewine*

Here's Where the Strings Come In / Sep. 19, 1995 / Merge +++
Without changing their tensely wound, post-Husker Du punk-pop style at all, Superchunk sounds completely weary on *Here's Where the Strings Come In.* No longer do their their nervous, amateurish songs sound energetic—they sound tired and broken. This actually results in some really interesting music, as Mac McCaughan tries to reconcile his broken spirits with his passion for punk. These songs tend to have more resonance than by-the-books rave-ups like "Hyper Enough," no matter how well those are written, and they suggest that Superchunk may be better off if they decide to revamp their signature sound completely. —*Stephen Thomas Erlewine*

Supergrass

f. 1993, Oxford, England
Alternative Pop-Rock, Brit-Pop
Like many other British bands of the '90s, Supergrass' musical roots lie in the infectiously catchy punk-pop of the Buzzcocks and the Jam, as well as the post-punk pop of Madness and the traditional British pop of the Kinks and Small Faces. Perhaps because of their age—two of the trio were still in their teens when they recorded their debut single—the band also brings in elements of decidedly un-hip groups like Elton John, as well as classic rockers like David Bowie, the Beatles and the Rolling Stones. With an exuberant, youthful enthusiasm, Supergrass tied all of their influences together in new surprising ways, where a Buzzcocks riff could slam into three-part harmonies out of "Crocodile Rock," or have a galloping music hall rhythm stutter like the best moments of the Who.

Consisting of guitarist/vocalist Gaz Coombes, bassist Mickey Quinn, and drummer Danny Goffey, Supergrass released their first single, the semi-autobiographical "Caught by the Fuzz," in the summer of 1994 on the indie label Backbeat; Parlophone signed the band and reissued the single in the fall of the year. "Caught by the Fuzz" generated a significant amount of buzz, including praise from Blur and Elastica. "Mansize Rooster," the group's second single, was released in the spring of 1995; it made it into the pop charts, as did "Lenny," which was released right before their debut album, *I Should Coco.*

Released in May, 1995, *I Should Coco* received glowing reviews in the UK press and debuted in the Top Ten. The band's popularity continued to grow, leading to the number two double-A-sided single, "Alright"/"Time." Staying in the top three for nearly a month, the single pushed the album to No. 1. *I Should Coco* was released in the US three months later and a buzz began to build there, as "Caught by the Fuzz" began receiving MTV and radio play. —*Stephen Thomas Erlewine*

● **I Should Coco** / Jul. 18, 1995 / Parlophone ++++
Tearing by at a breakneck speed, *I Should Coco* is a spectacularly eclectic debut by Supergrass, a trio barely out of their teens. Sure, the unbridled energy of the album illustrates that the band is young, yet what really illustrates how young the band is is how they borrow from their predecessors. Supergrass treat the Buzzcocks, the Beatles, Elton John, David Bowie, Blur, and Madness as if they were all the same thing—they don't make any distinction between what is cool and what isn't, they just throw everything together. Consequently, the jittery "Caught by the Fuzz" slams next to the music-hall rave-up "Mansize Rooster" and the trippy psychedelia of "Sofa of My Lethargy," or the heavy stomp of "Lenny" or the bona fide teen anthem "Alright." *I Should Coco* is the sound of adolescence, but performed with a surprising musical versatility that makes the record's exuberant energy all the more infectious. —*Stephen Thomas Erlewine*

In It for the Money / May 5, 1997 / Capitol ++++
Supergrass' debut album *I Should Coco* rushed by at such a blinding speed that some listeners didn't notice the melodic complexity of its best songs. On their second album, the cleverly-titled *In It for the Money,* Supergrass brought the songs to their forefront, slowing the tempos considerably and constructing a varied, textured album that makes their ambition and skill abundantly clear. From the droning mantra of the opening title track, it's clear that the band has delved deeply into psychedelia and hints of *Magical Mystery Tour* are evident throughout the album, from swirling organs and gurgling wah-wahs to punchy horn charts and human-beat-boxes. In fact, Supergrass has substituted the punky rush of *I Should Coco* for such sonic details, and while that means they only occasionally touch upon the breakneck pace of the debut (the hard-driving "Richard III"), they also deepen its joyful exuberance with subtle songs and remarkably accomplished musicianship. There might not be a "Caught by the Fuzz" or "Alright" on *In It for the Money,* but that's not a problem, since the bright explosion of "Sun Hits the Sky" and the nervy "Tonight" are just as energetic, and the album

features introspective numbers like the gorgeous "Late in the Day" and "It's Not Me" that give the album substantial weight. And even with all this musical maturity, they haven't sacrificed their good-natured humor, as the detailed production and the bizarre closer "Sometimes I Make You Sad" makes abundantly clear. Sometimes, maturity turns out to be everything it's supposed to be. [The initial American editions of *In It for the Money* were released with a bonus disc that collected nearly all of the B-sides from the *I Should Coco* singles, plus selected B-sides from the "Richard III" and "Goin' Out" singles. The B-sides disc is more than just a curiosity, since it contains several gems—including the Kinks-meets-*Revolver* stomp of "Melanie Davis," the hilarious country parody "Sex?," the trancy "Nothing More's Gonna Get in My Way" and the gentle "Wait for the Sun"—that deserve to be in any comprehensive Supergrass library. And it only leaves off three B-sides: a cover of the First Edition's "Condition," a live version of "Strange Ones" and the beat-box blooper reel "Sometimes We're Very Sad," which are all of negligible worth. In other words, it's a an excellent bargain.] —*Stephen Thomas Erlewine*

Supertramp

f. 1969, London, England
Art-Rock/Progressive-Rock, Pop-Rock
Once upon a time in 1969, a young Dutch millionaire by the name of Stanley August Miesegaes gave his acquaintance, vocalist and keyboardist Roger Davies a "genuine opportunity" to form his own band; he could form the band of his dreams and Miesegaes would pay for it. After placing an ad in *Melody Maker,* Davies assembled Supertramp. Supertramp released two long-winded progressive-rock albums before Miesegaes withdrew his support. With no money or fan base to speak of, the band was forced to redesign their sound. Coming up with a more pop-oriented form of progressive rock, the band had a hit with their third album, *Crime of the Century.* Throughout the decade, Supertramp had a number of bestselling albums, culminating in their 1979 masterpiece, *Breakfast in America. Breakfast in America* marked their first album that tipped the scale completely in the favor of pop songs; on the strength of the hit singles "Goodbye Stranger," "Logical Song," and "Take the Long Way Home" it sold over 18 million copies worldwide. After that album, Supertramp continued to develop a more R&B-flavored style; the change in direction was successful on 1982's *Famous Last Words,* but they soon ran out of hits. The band continued to sporadically record and tour into the '90s. —*Stephen Thomas Erlewine*

Supertramp / 1970 / A&M ++
Supertramp's debut album was by and large an undistinguished progressive-rock affair, filled with long, ponderous instrumental solos. —*Stephen Thomas Erlewine*

Indelibly Stamped / 1971 / A&M ++
Indelibly Stamped, Supertramp's second album, was an improvement on their debut, although the group did have a tendency to indulge themselves in long-winded instrumental sections. —*Stephen Thomas Erlewine*

Crime of the Century / 1974 / A&M ++++
With *Crime of the Century,* Supertramp established themselves as one of the handful of progressive-rock acts that could sell albums and have hit singles. Stripping away the long-winded excesses of their first two albums, *Crime of the Century* featured tighter, more melodic songs, as evidenced by the singles "Bloody Well Right" and "Dreamer." —*Stephen Thomas Erlewine*

Crisis? What Crisis? / 1975 / A&M +++
Crisis? What Crisis? wasn't quite as fully developed as its predecessor, *Crime of the Century,* lacking any instant standouts like "Dreamer" or "Bloody Well Right." Nevertheless, it had a handful of fine songs that signalled that Supertramp was continuing to refine and expand their sound. —*Stephen Thomas Erlewine*

Even in the Quietest Moments / 1977 / A&M ++++
Like *Crisis? What Crisis?, Even in the Quietest Moments* is a jumbled affair, alternating between long, unfocused sections and relatively concise pop songs, like the hit "Give a Little Bit." —*Stephen Thomas Erlewine*

● **Breakfast in America** / 1979 / A&M ++++
With *Breakfast in America,* Supertramp had a genuine blockbuster hit, topping the charts for four weeks in the US and selling millions of copies worldwide; by the 1990s, the album had sold over 18 million units across the world. Although their previous records had some popular success, they never even hinted at the massive sales of *Breakfast in America.* Then again, Supertramp's earlier records weren't as pop-oriented as *Breakfast.* The majority of the album consisted of tightly written, catchy, well-constructed pop songs, like the hits "The Logical Song," "Take the Long Way Home," and "Goodbye Stranger." Supertramp still had a tendency to indulge themselves occasionally, but *Breakfast in*

America had very few weak moments. It was clearly their high-water mark. *—Stephen Thomas Erlewine*

Paris / 1980 / A&M ♦♦

Recorded in the wake of the global success of *Breakfast in America*, *Paris* is a competent but ultimately unnecessary live album that fails to live up to the standards of their studio material. *—Stephen Thomas Erlewine*

...famous last words... / 1982 / A&M ♦♦♦

Even though ... famous last words..., Supertramp's follow-up to *Breakfast in America*, was slicker and more pop-oriented than its predecessor, it wasn't quite as successful. Where the singles on *Breakfast* still had a progressive-rock edge, most of ... famous last words... was light, synthesized pop, with the shimmering "It's Raining Again" being the only song melodic enough to support the lush, layered sound. *—Stephen Thomas Erlewine*

Brother Where You Bound / 1985 / A&M ♦♦

On *Brother Where You Bound*, Supertramp appeared to be floundering in an attempt to keep their trademark sound current without losing their dedicated fan base. The band managed to score a hit with "Cannonball," but most of the album was too ponderous for pop success and too simple to qualify as good progressive rock. Not surprisingly, the group's lead vocalist, Roger Hodgson, left after the record's release. *—Stephen Thomas Erlewine*

Free as a Bird / 1987 / A&M ♦♦

Lacking the pop sensibilities of *Breakfast in America* and ...famous last words, as well as the jazzy fusions of *Brother Where You Bound*, *Free as a Bird* is a colorless and tuneless collection of prog-rock meandering that is only distinguished by the fact that future Crowded House guitarist Mark Hart was featured on the recording. *—Stephen Thomas Erlewine*

● **Classics, Vol. 9** / 1987 / A&M ♦♦♦♦

This is a fairly good sampler of this band's bigger radio tracks as well as key album numbers. Included are "Bloody Well Right," "Ain't Nobody but Me," "The Logical Song," "Give a Little Bit," "It's Raining Again," "Goodbye Stranger," "Take the Long Way Home," and "Dreamer." Unfortunately, "Even in the Quietest Moments" is curiously omitted. *—AMG*

Some Things Never Change / Jun. 3, 1997 / Chrysalis ♦♦

Rick Davies, Bob Siebenberg, Mark Hart, and John Helliwell re-formed Supertramp with a number of anonymous studio musicians in 1997 to record and release *Some Things Never Change*, their first album in ten years. And the title is correct—nothing much has changed within Supertramp's world; they're simply churning out the same sophisticated jazzy, lite-funk-inflected pop as they did in the mid-'80s. The only thing that is different is that the group can no longer write ingratiatingly catchy melodies as they did when they called it quits in the '80s, but hardcore fans will still find the instrumental interplay a joy to hear. *—Stephen Thomas Erlewine*

The Supremes

f. 1961, Detroit, MI
Soul, Motown, Girl Group

The most successful Black performers of the 1960s, the Supremes for a time rivaled even the Beatles in terms of red-hot commercial appeal, reeling off five No. 1 singles in a row at one point. Critical revisionism has tended to undervalue the Supremes' accomplishments, categorizing their work as more lightweight than the best soul stars' (or even the best Motown stars'), and viewing them as a tool for Berry Gordy's crossover aspirations. There's no question that there was about as much pop as soul in the Supremes' hits, that even some of their biggest hits could sound formulaic, and that they were probably the Black performers who were most successful at infiltrating the tastes and televisions of middle America. This shouldn't diminish either their extraordinary achievements or their fine music, the best of which renders the pop vs. soul question moot with its excellence.

The Supremes were not an overnight success story, although it might have seemed that way when they began topping the charts with surefire regularity. The trio that would become famous as the Supremes—Diana Ross, Mary Wilson, and Florence Ballard—met in the late '50s in Detroit's Brewster housing project. Originally known as the Primettes, they were a quartet (Barbara Martin was the fourth member) when they made their first single for the Lupine label in 1960. By the time they debuted for Motown in 1961, they had been renamed the Supremes; Barbara Martin reduced them to a trio when she left after their first single.

The Supremes' first Motown recordings were much more girl-group-oriented than their later hits. Additionally, not all of them featured Diana Ross on lead vocals; Flo Ballard, considered to have as good or better a voice, also sang lead. Through a lengthy series of flops, Berry Gordy remained confident that the group would eventually prove to be one of Motown's biggest. By the time they finally did get their first Top

40 hit, "When the Lovelight Starts Shining Through His Eyes," in late 1963, Ross had taken over the lead singing for good.

Ross was not the most talented female singer at Motown; Martha Reeves and Gladys Knight in particular had superior talents. What she did have, however, was the most purely pop appeal. Gordy's patience and attention paid off in mid-1964, when "Where Did Our Love Go" went to No. 1. Written by Holland-Dozier-Holland, it established the prototype for their run of five consecutive No. 1 hits in 1964-65 (also including "Baby Love," "Stop! In the Name of Love," "Come See About Me," and "Back in My Arms Again"). Ross' cooing vocals would front the Supremes' decorative backup vocals, put over on television and live performance with highly stylized choreography and visual style. Holland-Dozier-Holland would write and produce all of the Supremes' hits through the end of 1967.

Not all of the Supremes' singles went to No. 1 after 1965, but they usually did awfully well, and were written and produced with enough variety (but enough of a characteristic sound) to ensure continual interest. The chart-topping (and uncharacteristically tough) "You Keep Me Hangin' On" was the best of their mid-period hits. Behind the scenes, there were some problems brewing, although these only came to light long after the event. Other Motown stars (most notably Martha Reeves) resented what they perceived as the inordinate attention lavished upon Ross by Gordy, at the expense of other artists on the label. The other Supremes themselves felt increasingly pushed to the background. In mid-1967, as a result of what was deemed increasingly unprofessional behavior, Ballard was replaced by Cindy Birdsong (from Patti LaBelle and the Bluebelles). Ballard become one of rock's greatest tragedies, eventually ending up on welfare, and dying in 1976.

After Ballard's exit, the group would be billed as Diana Ross & the Supremes, fueling speculation that Ross was being groomed for a solo career. The Supremes had a big year in 1967, even incorporating some mild psychedelic influences into "Reflections." Holland-Dozier-Holland, however, left Motown around this time, and the quality of the Supremes' records suffered accordingly (as did the Motown organization as a whole). The Supremes were still superstars, but as a unit, they were disintegrating; it's been reported that Wilson and Birdsong didn't even sing on their final hits, a couple of which ("Love Child" and "Someday We'll Be Together") were among their best.

In November 1969, Ross' imminent departure for a solo career was announced, although she played a few more dates with them, the last in Las Vegas in January 1970. Jean Terrell replaced Ross, and the group continued through 1977, with some more personnel changes (although Mary Wilson was always involved). Some of the early Ross-less singles were fine records, particularly "Stoned Love," "Nathan Jones," and the Supremes-Four Tops duet "River Deep—Mountain High." Few groups have been able to rise to the occasion after the loss of their figurehead, though, and the Supremes proved no exception, rarely making the charts after 1972. It is the Diana Ross-led era of the 1960s for which they'll be remembered. *—Richie Unterberger*

★ **Diana Ross and the Supremes Greatest Hits** / Aug. 1967 / Motown ♦♦♦♦♦

Although all of these 20 songs were credited to the Supremes when they were released between 1963 and 1967, this album marked the first LP on which the group was billed as "Diana Ross and the Supremes." However you credit it, this out-of-print double-LP contains the bulk of the best of the Supremes, no less than 10 No. 1 hits from "Where Did Our Love Go" to "The Happening," and thus some of the most popular music of the 1960s. Ross and the Supremes, together and separately, continued to score afterwards, but this was their peak. *—William Ruhlmann*

★ **Anthology** / May 1974 / Motown ♦♦♦♦♦

When it was released in 1974, Motown's Diana Ross and the Supremes *Anthology* was the most comprehensive compilation yet issued on one of the 1960s' most popular groups. A 35-track triple-LP, it superseded the 1967 double-LP *Greatest Hits*, including 17 of that album's 20 tracks, as well as the 1969 *Greatest Hits, Volume 3*, all of which was repeated. All 27 of the Supremes' R&B hits between 1962 and 1969 were featured, as well as 28 of their 30 pop chart entries. That represented a formidable chunk of the decade's biggest hits, among them the chart toppers "Where Did Our Love Go," "Baby Love," "Come See About Me," "Stop! In the Name of Love," "I Hear a Symphony," "You Can't Hurry Love," "You Keep Me Hangin' On," "Love Is Here and Now You're Gone," "The Happening," "Love Child," and "Someday We'll Be Together." The lengthy album also found space for some of the group's musical experiments devoting a five-song side, dubbed "Versatile Stylists," to material culled from the albums *A Bit of Liverpool, The Supremes Sing Country Western & Pop, We Remember Sam Cooke, The Supremes Sing Rodgers & Hart*, and *Diana Ross and the Supremes Sing and Perform "Funny Girl".* They made for an interesting interlude, but the heart of the matter remained the Supremes' brilliant interpretations of the Holland-Dozier-Holland hits of the mid-'60s, which were all here. (The Diana Ross and the Supremes *Anthology* [Motown 794] was released as a triple-LP containing 35 songs in May 1974. In August 1986,

Motown issued a 50-song double-CD under the same title [Motown 6198]. Nine years later, the label again revamped the *Anthology* idea for a 52-track double-CD [Motown 0511] released on September 28, 1995.) —*William Ruhlmann*

70's Greatest Hits & Rare Classics / Motown ✦✦✦
An interesting anthology, one of the few that don't merely recycle shopworn hits. This collection covers the Supremes in the post-Diana Ross era, with tracks that featured both the group and solo tracks from Jean Terrell and Scherrie Payne, plus the few hits they had when Mary Wilson shared the leads with Terrell. It also contains some rare Supremes album tracks. Overall, it's more valuable than the umpteenth repackaged Diana Ross album. —*Ron Wynn*

The Surfaris

f. 1963, Glendora, CA
Surf
Glendora, CA, surf group remembered for "Wipe Out," the No. 2 1963 hit that ranks as one of the great rock instrumentals, featuring a classic up-and-down guitar riff and a classic solo drum roll break, both of which were emulated by millions (the number is no exaggeration) of beginning rock 'n' rollers. They recorded an astonishing number of albums (about half a dozen) and singles in the mid-'60s; the "Wipe Out" follow-up "Point Panic" was the only one to struggle up to the middle of the charts. The Surfaris were not extraordinary, but they were more talented than the typical one-shot surf group; drummer Ron Wilson was praised by session stickman extraordinaire Hal Blaine, and his uninhibited splashing style sounds like a direct ancestor to Keith Moon. He also took the lead vocals on the group's occasional passable Beach Boy imitations. —*Richie Unterberger*

● **Wipe Out! The Best of the Surfaris** / Jul. 5, 1994 / Varese Sarabande ✦✦✦✦
Decent 18-track distillation of their 1962-65 work, including several album tracks and non-LP singles. "Wipe Out" is by far the best cut, of course, but the instrumentals, packed with reverbed guitars, honking saxes, and high-end drums aplenty, usually have an admirably sleek power. Two of the vocal surf tunes were co-written by Gary Usher, who also worked with the Beach Boys during this time. —*Richie Unterberger*

Surfaris Stomp / Jul. 4, 1995 / Varese Saraband ✦✦✦✦
Aside from the significant drawback of missing "Wipe Out," this second anthology of the Surfaris' best work is just as good as the other Varese Sarabande compilation, *The Best of the Surfaris* (which doesn't duplicate any of the tracks here). Largely taken from rare singles and albums that the group recorded for Decca between 1963 and 1965, it also has a few previously unreleased cuts, some dating from their initial session (the same one that produced "Wipe Out"). If you like *The Best of the Surfaris*, you can't go wrong by adding this one to your collection as well—it's packed with haunting reverb, Ron Wilson's nonstop drum fills rank among the best stickwork of the pre-Keith Moon era, and one of the three vocal cuts is one of the most obscure Brian Wilson compositions ever released ("My Buddy Seat," co-written with Gary Usher). —*Richie Unterberger*

Screaming Lord Sutch

b. Nov. 10, 1940, Middlesex, England
Vocals / Rock & Roll
He couldn't properly be considered part of the British Invasion—he never had a hit in the US or the UK—but Screaming Lord Sutch laid some unheralded groundwork for the phenomenon. With a rock 'n' horror act based to a large degree on Screamin' Jay Hawkins, David "Lord" Sutch was one of the first genuine rock 'n' roll longhairs, and his bands employed such sterling instrumentalists as Jimmy Page, Jeff Beck, Ritchie Blackmore, Nicky Hopkins, and Mitch Mitchell before they became famous. His early-'60s singles—mostly over-the-top Halloween novelties or covers of early rock and R&B standards—aren't brilliant, but they are genuinely energetic and fun performances that rank among the few out-and-out raunchy rock 'n' roll records waxed in Britain before the ascension of the Beatles. Twiddling the knobs on his first five singles was the legendarily eccentric Joe Meek, who embellished Sutch's modest talents with his usual grab bag of treated instruments, compression, and odd effects. While he holds a position of undeniable importance in the history of British rock, Sutch was not a talented singer or musician, and the records he made after the mid-'60s were pretty lame, despite the presence of some stars who remembered him fondly (and had even sometimes played in his band in the old days). A well-known public figure in Britain, he ran for Parliament several times in the '60s representing the "national teenage party," and founded the pirate radio station Radio Sutch in 1964. He published his autobiography in the early '90s. —*Richie Unterberger*

● **Story** / (no label) ✦✦✦✦
Except for one B-side, this has both sides of his first seven singles

(released 1961-66), most produced by Joe Meek between 1961 and 1965, some featuring sterling guitar work by Mssrs. Page, Beck, and Blackmore. Divided into a "horror" and a "rock" side, this is fun if silly stuff; tracks like "She's Fallen in Love with the Monsterman," "Monster in Black Tights," and "Dracula's Daughter" are great for Halloween parties. No record label name is given for this reissue, but it's easy enough to locate through specialty mail-order outfits. —*Richie Unterberger*

SVT

Group / Rock & Roll, New Wave
The most mainstream of the San Francisco club bands from the late '70s and early '80s, SVT made two records, notable because Jack Casady was their bass player. Singer Brian Marnell hailed from Sacramento, and upon moving to San Francisco started the band with Casady on bass (formerly of Jefferson Airplane and still with Hot Tuna) and drummer Paul Zahl. They were an unlikely combo, similar in musical attack to the Clash with their anthemic pop songs. Zahl and Casady were an unfailing, powerhouse rhythm section, and Marnell the quintessential frontman. They debuted with the single "Heart of Stone," which was a hit on local FM station KSAN, a fairly unprecedented feat for an unsigned local band, but a handful did earn the distinction due to new wave advocate Howie Klein's involvement. Before recording an EP, *Extended Play*, for 415 Records, the band added Nick Buck on keyboards. Another album for a small Bay Area label disappeared before it was released. Marnell's death in a car crash ensured the end of the band, but by that point they had started to fall out of favor with the art crowd that comprised San Francisco's punk scene for being strict rock 'n' roll traditionalists. Casady, of course, continues to play with Hot Tuna, and Zahl performed briefly with Tuxedomoon before dropping out of sight entirely. —*Denise Sullivan*

● **Extended Play** / 1980 / 415 ✦✦✦✦
A spartanly produced and played effort, it's notable as Jack Casady's stint with a bona fide new wave band. Brian Marnell's songs, "Always Come Back for More" and "Price of Sex," are the standouts, as they bear some relation to the songs of Mick Jones and Joe Strummer, if only in form (surely not content). I'm hard pressed to recommend this as anything but an artifact from the era, and probably only those who remember Marnell's electricity as a live performer will appreciate it. —*Denise Sullivan*

No Regrets / 1981 / MSI ✦✦✦

Swamp Dogg

b. Jul. 1942, Portsmouth, VA
Piano, Keyboards, Vocals / Soul, R&B, Blues-Rock
One of the great characters in rock and soul music is Jerry Williams, better known as the eccentric, idiosyncratic, and always entertaining Swamp Dogg (no relation to Snoop Doggy Dogg). A Virginia native, Williams invented his own legend by claiming that he had little proper schooling, only to wake up one day and find himself a musical genius (his words). Actually, Williams is very talented, and an early association with Jerry Wexler and Phil Walden led to him working for a number of years as a producer, engineer, and occasional songwriter with Atlantic in the '60s. At decade's end, however, he decided that the time was right to unleash Swamp Dogg's singular view of the world on an unsuspecting public. The initial result was one of the most gloriously gonzo soul recordings of all time, *Total Destruction to Your Mind*. Along with living up to its title, it was a renegade chunk of not-quite-commercial music, with an unforgettable (though fuzzy) cover shot of the portly Dogg in his underwear. Although undeniably great, *Total Destruction to Your Mind* is one of the most obscure soul records ever made. That, however, has nothing to do with the music, which rocks in a way reminiscent of Solomon Burke or Wilson Pickett. It may have to do with Dogg's worldview, part libertarian politics, part Zappa-style critiques of commerciality and capitalism, and part horny male, the latter defining for better and worse his view of women. Although he spent years working in the industry, Dogg was simply not the standard-issue soul type. And that was good. Dogg has continued to make records, albeit infrequently, since 1969, some good, a few great, and most all extremely difficult to find. With contemporary soul (Boyz II Men, En Vogue, Mary J. Blige) sounding increasingly mannered and sterile, Dogg's yelling, screaming, and general craziness is missed. Thankfully, he hasn't disappeared for good, although he only makes records when he feels like it. His last release, *Surfin' in Harlem*, came out in 1991. And as is often the case with quirky "legends," what he's up to at any given time is the source of wild speculation. It would be wise to not count him out; just when you think this Dogg is down and out, he sneaks up and bites you. —*John Dougan*

● **Total Destruction to Your Mind** / 1970 / Canyon ✦✦✦✦
Easily on my Top Ten list of long-out-of-print records that deserve a CD reissue. The title track is a slam-bangin' chunk of rock and funk that's pushed by a great session band including guitarist Jesse Carr and drum-

mer Johnny Sandlin, and is easily Dogg's finest moment on record. But the rest of this is great too, ranging from the consumer nightmare "Synthetic World" to the paternity blues of "Mama's Baby, Daddy's Maybe." Plus, Dogg is a great singer, and his dizzying range gets a workout on these songs. Good luck finding a copy. —*John Dougan*

Rat On / 1971 / Elektra ✦✦✦✦

The cover of this LP—Swamp Dogg riding a white rat, hands raised and fists clenched in triumph—lets you know that you're not in for any ol' R&B record, even before the needle hits the grooves. It's a satisfying continuation of the eclectic soul-singer-songwriter mix of his debut. Vocally, Swamp Dogg sounds like a cross between General Johnson (of Chairmen of the Board) and Van Morrison; as a songwriter, he's his own man. With the exception of Sly Stone, no other soul men of the period were investigating controversial topics with such infectious musicality and good humor. He takes on promiscuity with unbridled frankness in cuts like "Predicament No. 2," bemoans the eternal delay of American justice for minorities in "Remember I Said Tomorrow," and twists Irving Berlin's "God Bless America" into a protest song (and also, bizarrely, covers the Bee Gees' "Got to Get a Message to You"). None of this endeared him to industry insiders, and Swamp Dogg was dropped by Elektra after the album's release. It's long been out of print, but in the UK Charly has reissued it on CD on a two-fer with *Total Destruction of Your Mind*. —*Richie Unterberger*

Cuffed, Collared and Tagged / 1972 / Cream ✦✦✦✦

This UK import, part of a two-fer, features a great band with dynamite lyrics. —*Richard Pack*

Gag a Maggot / 1973 / Stonedogg ✦✦✦✦

Another great album title, another tiny label, another great record long forgotten. Not as consistently manic as *Destruction*, *Maggot* is as ferocious sounding and does have a good cover of Wilson Pickett's "In the Midnight Hour." Never one to let a love lyric go by without a sarcastic twist, Dogg's love song here is called "I Couldn't Pay for What I Got Last Night." —*John Dougan*

I'm Not Selling Out, I'm Buying In / 1981 / Takoma ✦✦✦✦

After years of keeping a low profile, Dogg emerged from out of nowhere with this fine record. Instead of streamlined hard soul, this record carries a rock 'n' roll clout that keeps even its most banal moments ("Wine, Women and Rock 'n' Roll") from terminal tedium. Song title highlight: Dogg's duet with Esther Phillips, "The Love We Got Ain't Worth Two Dead Flies." Kind of says it all, doesn't it. —*John Dougan*

● Total Destruction to Your Mind/Rat On / 1991 / Charly ✦✦✦✦

These two early Swamp Dogg albums were unheralded landmarks of early-'70s soul; Charly has now combined both of them onto a single-disc CD reissue. The liner notes seem to have been written by someone who speaks English as a third language, but that minor gripe aside, this probably contains the singer's most significant work. —*Richie Unterberger*

Surfin' in Harlem / Oct. 31, 1991 / Volt ✦✦

Come the 1990s, Swamp Dogg's voice still sounds fine, and he's still singing about racism and promiscuity with some wit. He's still a soul iconoclast, and for some longtime fans, that in itself might be enough to recommend this album. It couldn't be classified among his better releases, though, chiefly because the updated soul backing is sort of leaden. "I've Never Been to Africa (And It's Your Fault)," however, was a strong contender for Song Title of the Month award. —*Richie Unterberger*

● Best of 25 Years of Swamp Dogg . . . or F**k the Bomb, Stop the Drugs / Mar. 5, 1996 / Pointblank/Virgin ✦✦✦✦

The 18-track retrospective *Best of 25 Years of Swamp Dogg* collects many of the highlights from his scattershot career. Concentrating on his '80s output, the compilation doesn't provide a definitive portrait of the warped blues and soul man, but it does offer enough of his best material to make it an excellent introduction. —*Stephen Thomas Erlewine*

Billy Swan

b. May 12, 1942, Cape Giradeau, MS
Guitar, Keyboards, Vocals / Rock & Roll, Country-Rock

One of rock's more interesting fringe characters, Billy Swan had been in the music business for more than a decade before he landed a surprise No. 1 neo-rockabilly hit in 1974 with "I Can Help." His composition "Lover Please" was a hit for Clyde McPhatter in the early '60s, and he spent the rest of the decade as a combination roadie, engineer's assistant, and songwriter, penning material for Conway Twitty, Waylon Jennings, and Mel Tillis. He played with Kris Kristofferson, Kinky Friedman, and Billy Joe Shaver in the '70s before the success of "I Can Help," whose swirling organ and classic '50s rockabilly arrangement anchored one of the best hit singles of the mid-'70s. Swan recorded a few albums as a solo act that were well received by critics, but he never hit the Top 40 again. Too eclectic to be characterized as a '50s revivalist, he actually mixed country, soul, and pop into his sound more frequently than out-

and-out rockabilly. After a few years, Swan returned to Kristofferson's band, where he stayed until 1992. —*Richie Unterberger*

● Billy Swan's Best / Aug. 31, 1993 / Red Baron ✦✦✦✦

Listeners expecting tuneful updated rockabilly along the lines of "I Can Help" (which leads off this collection) may be disappointed by this CD. There's nothing as instantly compelling as the big hit (only "Vanessa" approaches its energy), much of the material lies closer to country than rock, and there are a few tame covers of '50s oldies. Nonetheless, Swan ranks among the more interesting country-pop-rock hybrids, as you could guess from the song title "(You Just) Woman Handled My Mind," and his thin, wavering voice is oddly memorable. Most of the material on this best-of is written by Swan, with occasional assistance from notables Guy Clark, Buddy Emmons, and Kris Kristofferson. —*Richie Unterberger*

Sweet

f. 1968, London, England, **db.** 1982
Rock & Roll, Glam Rock, Pop-Rock, Bubblegum

In some ways, Sweet epitomized all the tacky hubris and garish silliness of the early '70s. Fusing bubblegum melodies with crunching, fuzzy guitars, the band looked a heavy metal band, but were as tame as any pop group. It was a dichotomy that served them well, as they racked up a number of hits in both the UK and the US. Most of those hits were written by Nicky Chinn and Mike Chapman, a pair of British songwriters that had a way with silly, simple and catchy hooks. Chinn and Chapman and Sweet were smart enough to latch on to the British glam-rock fad, building a safer, radio-friendly, and teen-oriented version of Queen, T. Rex, and Gary Glitter. By the end of the '70s, the group's time at the top of the charts had expired, but their hit singles lived on not only as cultural artifacts but also as the predecessors for the pop/metal of the '80s.

Originally, Sweet were called the Sweetshop and consisted of Brian Connolly (vocals), Mick Tucker (vocals, drums), Frank Torpey (guitar), and Steve Priest (bass). In 1970, the group truncated their name to Sweet and signed a record contract with Fontana/EMI, releasing four unsuccessful singles. Following the failure of the four singles, Torpey left the group and was replaced by Andy Scott. The new lineup of Sweet signed to RCA Records in 1971, where they were placed under the direction of songwriters Nicky Chinn and Mike Chapman. Chinn and Chapman wrote a number of light bubblegum pop songs for the group, the first of which, "Funny Funny," reached No. 13 on the UK charts. Following "Funny Funny," the duo wrote five more Top 40 hits for the group—including "Little Willy" and "Wig-Wam Bam"—which were all lightweight bubblegum numbers loaded with double entendres. During this time, Sweet were writing their own B-sides and album tracks. All of the group's compositions were harder than Chinn and Chapman's songs, featuring crunching hard-rock guitars. Consequently, the duo decided to write tougher songs for the group. "Blockbuster," the first result of Chinn and Chapman's neo-glam rock approach, was the biggest hit Sweet ever had in the UK, reaching No. 1 on the charts in early 1973 and eventually going platinum. For the next two years, Sweet continued to chart with Chinn and Chapman compositions, including the Top Ten hits "Hell Raiser," "Ballroom Blitz," "Teenage Rampage," and "The Six Teens."

By the summer of 1974, the members of Sweet had grown tired of the control Chinn and Chapman exerted over their career and decided to record without the duo. The resulting album, *Sweet Fanny Adams*, reached No. 27 in the UK, but it yielded no hits. In the spring of 1975, Sweet had their first self-penned hit with "Fox on the Run," which reached the Top Ten in both the UK and the US. "Fox on the Run" appeared on the collection *Desolation Boulevard;* in America, its release helped "Ballroom Blitz" reach the Top Ten in the summer of 1975. *Strung Up*, released in the fall of 1975, continued the group's move toward album-oriented rock. For the rest of the decade, the group continued to churn out albums, which were all less successful than their predecessor. Sweet bounced back into the charts in 1978 with "Love Is like Oxygen," but the single proved to be their last gasp—they never reached the Top Ten again, neither in the US nor the UK.

Connolly left the band after "Love Is like Oxygen" and the group replaced him with keyboardist Gary Moberley. The group carried on for three more years, releasing three more albums that all achieved little success. After several years of little success or attention, Sweet broke up in 1982. In the decade following their breakup, Sweet reunited on various occasions. In 1985, a dance club medley of their hits called "It's the Sweet Mix" became a British Top 50 hit and following the single's success, the group re-formed for a tour that proved to be less anticipated than expected. Later in the decade, Scott toured as part of the group Paddy Goes to Holyhead. In 1989, Scott and Tucker re-formed Sweet to record a live album at London's Marquee Club. —*Stephen Thomas Erlewine*

Desolation Boulevard / 1974 / Capitol ✦✦✦✦

Sweet hit the peak of their powers on *Desolation Boulevard*, a wonderfully lightweight collection of fizzy melodies and big, dumb hooks. Essentially, the album consists of three dynamic singles buoyed by a bunch of filler, but those singles—"Ballroom Blitz," "The Six Teens" and "Fox on the Run"—are addictive slices of bubblegum glam-rock. And the filler is ridiculously silly and enjoyable, with "Sweet F.A.," "I Wanna Be Committed," and "No You Don't" sounding a kind of bizarre prototype for the Ramones' punky bubblegum. Only without the irony, of course. Although the filler is relatively strong, there's a number of weak patches on *Desolation Boulevard*, but it remains an intoxicatingly fun record and one that sounds surprisingly fresh, even with all of its kitschy '70s production techniques. —*Stephen Thomas Erlewine*

Live at the Marquee / 1989 / Maze/Kraze ✦✦✦
Although Sweet had long since passed its creative and commercial peak by the time the small Maze label released *Live at the Marquee* in 1990, the band (which had undergone some personnel changes) continued playing to enthusiastic audiences. Certainly, Sweet remained quite influential, and that influence was especially strong on such pop/metal outfits as Motley Crue, Warrant, and Poison. Indiana hair rockers Sweet FA, in fact, took their name from a Sweet song. Not breathtaking but certainly enjoyable, performances of such '70s classics as "Fox on the Run," "Ballroom Blitz," and "Love Is like Oxygen" demonstrate that Sweet could still pack a punch onstage. For diehard Sweet devotees, the album is well worth hearing, although more casual listeners would be better off with *The Best of Sweet* or *Desolation Boulevard*. —*Alex Henderson*

● **The Best of Sweet** / Mar. 1, 1993 / Capitol ✦✦✦✦
Nobody played rock 'n' roll trashier or dumber than Sweet, and their best moments shine on this terrific 16-track compilation. Every one of their hits were powered by an irresistibly stupid melody, big dumb guitars, and, on occasion, a whining synthesizer. It was glitter-rock for teens at its best, without the dark sensuality of T. Rex. Even today, Sweet's best songs—"Ballroom Blitz," "Little Willy," "Blockbuster," "Teenage Rampage," and the nearly perfect "Fox on the Run"—still sound gloriously trashy. —*Stephen Thomas Erlewine*

The Sweet Inspirations

f. 1967, New York, NY
Soul
If you were cutting a soul, R&B, pop, rock, or girl group record in New York in the 1960s and needed female backup vocals, chances are you'd try to get the Sweet Inspirations first. The group found their way onto numerous recordings, including hits by the Drifters, Van Morrison, Wilson Pickett, Solomon Burke, Garnett Mimms, and most famously, Aretha Franklin (with whom they sometimes toured).

The group evolved from the '50s gospel group the Drinkard Singers. At various points, soul singers Doris Troy, Judy Clay, Dionne Warwick, and sister Dee Dee Warwick were members. By the time they began to record on their own in 1967, their leader was Cissy Houston (mother of Whitney), and the women were renamed the Sweet Inspirations.

As an Atlantic recording act, the group cut some fine sides that rank among the clearest illustrations of the close links between soul music and gospel harmony. Usually sticking to material by famed soul and pop songwriters, they had about half a dozen moderate R&B hits in the late '60s; the biggest, "Sweet Inspiration," was a Top 20 pop single. Houston left the group at the end of the '60s, and the Inspirations left Atlantic in the early '70s, sometimes working with Elvis Presley, and recording an album for Stax in 1973. —*Richie Unterberger*

Estell, Myrna and Sylvia / 1973 / Stax ✦✦✦✦
Though Cissy Houston was long gone from the group by the time they made this album, it's a fine set of gospel-pop-soul, with arrangements that manage to be sophisticated without getting slick. Co-produced by David Porter and Ronnie Williams, who as a pair also wrote most of the material; the songs are good and varied, the vocals and harmonies emotive and ebullient. The CD reissue adds two hits that they recorded for Atlantic in 1967 with Houston in the lineup ("Why [Am I Treated So Bad]" and "Sweet Inspiration"). —*Richie Unterberger*

● **Best of the Sweet Inspirations** / Nov. 22, 1994 / Ichiban/Soul Classics ✦✦✦✦
Solid retrospective of their Atlantic years (1967-71), including all the hits and several misses. A lot of the songs were cut at Muscle Shoals, Memphis, or Atlantic Studios, and accordingly the arrangements have a deep soul flavor characteristic of Atlantic's late-'60s releases (although they worked briefly in Philadelphia in 1969 for a Gamble-Huff-flavored sound). Includes covers of songs by Isaac Hayes, Roebuck Staples, Dan Penn, and Gamble/Huff, all of which they make their own with lovely harmonies and imaginative interpretations. —*Richie Unterberger*

Matthew Sweet

b. 1964, Lincoln, NE
Guitar / Alternative Pop-Rock, Power Pop
After spending the '80s as an unappreciated jangle-pop guitarist with

Oh-OK and Lloyd Cole, as well as a solo artist, Matthew Sweet emerged in 1991 as the leading figure of the American power-pop revival. Like his British counterparts Teenage Fanclub, Sweet adhered to traditional songcraft, yet subverted the form by adding noisy post-punk guitar and flourishes of country-rock, resulting in an amalgam of the Beatles, Big Star, R.E.M. and Neil Young. Recorded with guitarists Richard Lloyd and Robert Quine, Sweet's third album, *Girlfriend* (1991), became a word-of-mouth critical and commercial hit over the course of 1992, with its title track reaching the Top Five on the Modern Rock charts. For the next five years, as alternative rock was the dominant commercial force in rock 'n' roll, Sweet was a popular concert attraction, and his reputation as an alternative-pop singer-songwriter was at its peak—his next two records, *Altered Beast* (1993) and *100% Fun* (1995), were both critically acclaimed and relatively successful albums, with the latter reaching gold status and making many year-end "Best Of" lists. Beginning with 1997's *Blue Sky on Mars*, Sweet settled into cult status, and while he wasn't enjoying the success of his previous records, most power-pop records of the latter half of the '90s were indebted to *Girlfriend*.

Matthew Sweet began playing music while he was a high school student in his native Lincoln, Nebraska. Upon his graduation in 1983, he decided to attend the University of Georgia in Athens because of its burgeoning underground music scene. Once he arrived at college, he met Lynda Stipe and joined her band, Oh-OK, in time to play on their second EP, the Mitch Easter-produced *Furthermore What*, which was released late in 1983. The following year, he and Oh-OK drummer David Pierce formed Buzz of Delight, releasing *Sound Castles* later that year. Over the course of 1984 and 1985, Sweet cut a demo tape with producer Don Dixon. Columbia Records heard the Buzz of Delight record and the demo and offered him a contract in 1985. Upon signing with Columbia, he relocated to New York and recorded his debut, *Inside*. Released in 1986, *Inside* featured Sweet playing nearly all of the instruments on the record, supported by a drum machine; the album also featured several cameos, including Chris Stamey, Fred Maher, Anton Fier, and Aimee Mann. That same year, Sweet guested on *Blast of Silence*, an album by Fier's band, the Golden Palominos.

Despite positive reviews, *Inside* was ignored upon its release and Columbia dropped Sweet. During 1988, he signed with A&M Records and recorded his second album, *Earth*. Produced by Fred Maher and released in 1989, *Earth* again featured Sweet as a one-man band, augmented by guitarists Robert Quine (Lou Reed, Richard Hell) and Richard Lloyd (Television). The album failed to make any impact, and A&M dropped Sweet as he was working on his third album in 1990. Over the next year, he earned money by touring as Lloyd Cole's guitarist while shopping a demo of his album to various labels, with little success. Eventually, the president of Zoo signed him upon overhearing the demo in an office. *Girlfriend*, an album largely inspired by the dissolution of his marriage, was the first album Sweet recorded with a live band, and its sound—which was powered by Lloyd and Quine—was considerably more immediate and raw than its predecessors. Upon its late-1991 release, *Girlfriend* earned strong reviews and "Divine Intervention" became a moderate hit, but it wasn't until the spring of 1992, when the title track took off, that the album became a genuine hit. By the end of the year, *Girlfriend* had gone gold and Sweet had moved to Los Angeles.

Sweet recorded the follow-up to *Girlfriend* with producer Richard Dashut, who had previously been best known for his work with Fleetwood Mac and Lindsey Buckingham. Again featuring Quine and Lloyd, the resulting *Altered Beast* was messier than *Girlfriend* and consequently received mixed reviews upon release in early 1993, yet it became a sizable college radio hit on the strength of the modern rock and MTV hits "The Ugly Truth" and "Time Capsule." After releasing the stopgap EP *Son of Altered Beast* in the spring of 1994, Sweet recorded his fifth album, this time with a more commercial producer—Brendan O'Brien, who had previously worked with Pearl Jam and Stone Temple Pilots. Released in the spring of 1995, *100% Fun* received Sweet's strongest reviews to date and went gold on the strength of "Sick of Myself," his first single to scrape the bottom reaches of the pop charts. Following *100% Fun*, Sweet parted ways with Richard Lloyd and Robert Quine, but retained O'Brien for 1997's *Blue Sky on Mars*. Despite the strong initial placing for its lead single "Where You Get Love," *Blue Sky on Mars* received mixed reviews upon its spring release, and it failed to match the success of its immediate predecessor. —*Stephen Thomas Erlewine*

Inside / 1986 / Columbia ✦✦
Matthew Sweet's debut solo album was a tentative effort, featuring a handful of good songs, but it was weighed down by too many guest artists (everyone from Valerie Simpson and the Heartbreakers' Mike Campbell to Chris Stamey, Bernie Worrell, and Anton Fier) and a glossy, synth-heavy production. —*Stephen Thomas Erlewine*

Earth / 1989 / A&M ✦✦✦
Despite the presence of guitarists Richard Lloyd and Robert Quine, Matthew Sweet's second album, *Earth*, remains a spotty affair. Like *Inside* before it, *Earth* has an overly glossy production, as well as a set of songs that are, by and large, forgettable—in fact, the songs on the second

album are even more undistinguished than the ones on the previous record. —*Stephen Thomas Erlewine*

● **Girlfriend** / Oct. 22, 1991 / Zoo ✦✦✦✦
Matthew Sweet's third album is a remarkable artistic breakthrough. Grounded in the guitar-pop of the Beatles, Big Star, Byrds, R.E.M., and Neil Young, *Girlfriend* melds all of Sweet's influences into one majestic, wrenching sound that encompasses both the gentle country-rock of "Winona" and the winding guitars of the title track and "Divine Intervention." Sweet's music might have recognizable roots, but *Girlfriend* never sounds derivative; thanks to his exceptional songwriting, the album is a fresh, original interpretation of a classic sound. —*Stephen Thomas Erlewine*

Altered Beast / Jul. 13, 1993 / Zoo ✦✦✦✦
Compared to the concise songwriting of *Girlfriend*, *Altered Beast* is all over the place, both emotionally and musically. Ranging from piercing guitar rave-ups ("Dinosaur Act") to gorgeous country-rock ("Time Capsule"), the album not only covers all sides of Sweet's musical personality, but pastes them together haphazardly. Consequently, it takes a bit of time for all of it to make sense, but after a few listens, it falls together, and its best moments equal *Girlfriend*. —*Stephen Thomas Erlewine*

Son of Altered Beast / Mar. 15, 1994 / Zoo ✦✦✦
Collecting several B-sides and outtakes, *Son of Altered Beast* is actually more consistent and enjoyable than the full-length *Altered Beast*. —*Stephen Thomas Erlewine*

100% Fun / Mar. 14, 1995 / Zoo ✦✦✦✦
Clocking in at 45 minutes, Matthew Sweet's third record of guitar-dominated, hook-laden power pop runs through its 12 songs at a classic speed, piling up songs that lovingly conform to the three-minute pop tradition. Richard Lloyd's gnarled guitars save Sweet's melodies and harmonies from being saccharine or sappy. Behind Sweet's bright hooks lies something darker—the self-loathing of "Sick of Myself" and the mental manipulation of "We're the Same" aren't evident from the sound of the record, which obliterates any hidden meanings with its chiming guitars and driving rhythms. It might not have the consistent barrage of great songs like *Girlfriend*, yet it tames the wilder impulses of *Altered Beast* into an album that rocks its worries away without ever getting rid of them. —*Stephen Thomas Erlewine*

Blue Sky on Mars / Mar. 25, 1997 / Zoo ✦✦✦
On Matthew Sweet's early-'90s power-pop trilogy of *Girlfriend*, *Altered Beast* and *100% Fun*, Richard Lloyd's angular, unpredictable lead guitar functioned as a gritty counterpoint to Sweet's pretty melodies and tales of lost love, giving the music an unexpected depth. Sweet parted ways with Lloyd before he made *Blue Sky on Mars*, and his departure greatly effects the music. Without Lloyd, the songs are more predictable and the band, even with Brendan O'Brien's warm production, sounds rather canned. However, the music isn't the only thing hurting *Blue Sky on Mars*—the songs themselves are considerably more uneven than before, lacking the effortless hooks of its three predecessors. Sweet manages to turn out a handful of good songs—the swirling "Where Do You Get Love" has an infectious chorus, and "Come to California" has a sunny, Californian feel—but the simple problem is that most of the songs are colorless, and that comes as a major disappointment after the inspired songcraft since *Girlfriend*. —*Stephen Thomas Erlewine*

Rachel Sweet

b. 1963, Akron, OH
Vocals / New Wave, Pop-Rock
At Stiff Records, nothing was sacred; often the label's slogans and unorthodox promotion were as memorable as the truly inspired music they released. With teenage Rachel Sweet, whom they marketed as a "jailbait" country singer (and later as a leather-clad child abductor), it would seem that their perverse humor had finally gone too far. One listen to her albums, however, and all questionable images and in-jokes fall into the background; the "little girl with the big voice" made some terrific music, holding her own on a roster that had no shortage of talent.

Akron-born Rachel Sweet began her singing career at age six, doing everything from singing commercial jingles to touring with Mickey Rooney and opening for Bill Cosby's Las Vegas act. By her teens she had recorded a couple of failed country singles and a handful of demos for songwriter Liam Sternberg, who shopped them to Stiff Records. Stiff signed the young singer and debuted her on the *Akron Compilation*. She recorded her first album, *Fool Around*, with backing from the Rumour in 1978. She promoted the album on the Stiff package tour—the "Be Stiff Tour"—using the Records as her band. The album didn't sell particularly well, but it did receive a fair amount of critical praise. The attention was short-lived, though, and *Protect the Innocent*, released through Stiff/Columbia, went virtually ignored the following year. She switched to Columbia in 1981 for *...And Then He Kissed Me*, an uneven album that nevertheless featured the Top 40 hit "Everlasting Love," a duet with Rex Smith. After one more album, 1982's *Blame It on*

Love, Sweet retired from the music business to pursue an education, returning sporadically, most notably to sing the title track to John Waters' *Hairspray*, as well as *Cry Baby*. Her focus has since turned to acting. —*Chris Woodstra*

Fool Around / Oct. 6, 1978 / Stiff ✦✦✦✦
Protect the Innocent / 1980 / Rhino ✦✦✦
Sweet's second and most perfectly realized album features "Take Good Care of Me" and a slam-bang version of "Baby, Let's Play House." Out of print, but it's worth the search. —*Cub Koda*

And Then He Kissed Me / Aug. 1981 / Columbia ✦✦✦
Blame It on Love / 1982 / Columbia ✦✦

● **Fool Around: The Best of Rachel Sweet** / Mar. 24, 1992 / Rhino ✦✦✦✦
Fool Around: The Best of Rachel Sweet compiles the finest moments of the singer's career with the first album represented in its entirety (including the US version additions), the rare "I'll Watch the News" and "Be Stiff" from Stiff Records samplers, a couple each from her two lesser albums, and the title track from the *Hairspray* soundtrack. A strong collection, this is probably the only Rachel Sweet disc to own for all but the obsessive completist. —*Chris Woodstra*

Swell Maps

f. 1972, London, England, **db.** 1980
Alternative Pop-Rock, Post-Punk
Noisy and experimental, Britain's Swell Maps experienced little commercial success during the course of their chaotic career, but in hindsight they stand as one of the pivotal acts of the New Wave: not only was the group an acknowledged inspiration to the likes of Sonic Youth and Pavement, but their alumni—most notably brothers Nikki Sudden and Epic Soundtracks—continued on as key players in the underground music community.

Although Sudden (vocals/guitar) and Soundtracks (piano/drums) formed the first incarnation of the Swell Maps (named after the charts used by surfers to gauge wave intensities) as far back as 1972, the group did not begin to truly take shape until 1976, when the siblings enlisted bassist Jowe Head and guitarist Richard Earl. In the spirit of punk's "do-it-yourself" mentality, they formed their own label, Rather Records, and issued their debut single—the brief, jarring "Read About Seymour"—in the early weeks of 1978. Local media support soon won the group a distribution pact with Rough Trade, but they did not resurface until over a year later with the single "Dresden Style." In mid-1979, the Swell Maps released their full-length debut *A Trip to Marineville*, a crazy-quilt of punk energy and Kraut-rock-influenced clatter. After the release of the speaker-shredding single "Let's Build a Car," the group recorded one final studio LP, *The Swell Maps in "Jane from Occupied Europe"*, before breaking up. A series of outtakes and singles collections—1981's *Whatever Happens Next...*, 1982's *Collision Time*, and 1987's *Train out of It*—followed, while the members followed their own career paths: Sudden formed the Jacobites, Soundtracks joined Crime and the City Solution, and Head played with the Television Personalities. All later enjoyed solo careers as well. —*Jason Ankeny*

Trip to Marineville / 1979 / Mute ✦✦✦✦
Swell Maps' debut album was a scattershot affair, ranging from blistering three-chord punk to free-form noise experiments, that was intriguing, yet frequently incoherent. —*Stephen Thomas Erlewine*

In "Jane from Occupied Europe" / 1980 / Mute ✦✦✦✦
Swell Maps displayed even more ambition and confidence than on their debut, which was a plus. Even though their music was still somewhat fragmented, *Jane from Occupied Europe* was more focused and compelling than their debut. —*Stephen Thomas Erlewine*

Whatever Happens Next / 1981 / Mute ✦✦
Featuring two albums of homemade demos, some of them dating back to the early '70s, *Whatever Happens Next* contains a fair number of fine songs, but the overall quality of the album is too inconsistent to make *Whatever Happens Next...* worthwhile for anyone besides dedicated fans. —*Stephen Thomas Erlewine*

Train out of It / 1987 / Mute ✦✦✦✦
Compiling a number of outtakes and singles, *Train out of It* features more quality material than their similar rarities collection, *Whatever Happens Next...* —*Stephen Thomas Erlewine*

● **Collision Time Revisited** / 1989 / Mute ✦✦✦✦
A good intro, this 27-track album collects tracks from the band's four LPs, along with B-sides and unreleased tracks. —*John Bush*

Swingers

f. Nov. 1978, New Zealand, **db.** May 1982
New Wave
Phil Judd was a founding member and major creative force behind the

early incarnation of Split Enz. Judd left the band in February of 1977, rejoining a year later only to leave shortly after finding himself unable to fit into the new direction of the band. In June of 1978, he joined the New Zealand punk band Suburban Reptiles as a part-time member. When the band broke up a couple of months later, he had a short stint with the legendary Enemy (who later became Toy Love).

Obviously inspired by the punk movement, Judd left behind all of the art excesses he had become known for in Split Enz and formed Swingers in late 1978, a no-frills, no image, straightforward power trio, with Dwayne "Bones" Hillman (bass) and Buster Stiggs (drums)—both formerly of Suburban Reptiles. After five months of constant rehearsals without gigs, the band made their live debut with an opening spot for Split Enz. Afterwards, they switched to smaller venues as headliners, where they built a strong following throughout 1979. In April of 1980, they recorded a single for Ripper Records, "One Good Reason"—the single eventually broke the NZ Top 20. The band set off for Australia on an opening slot for the Sports. While in Australia, they teamed up with David Tickle (who had just finished working with Split Enz) to re-record "One Good Reason" as well as the infectious "Counting the Beat." Judd and Stiggs had a falling out when Judd decided to take a stronger leadership of the band (previously the band was a democracy with all songwriting credited to Swingers). Stiggs left to join the Models in December of 1980 and was replaced by Ian "Killjoy" Gillroy. The new recording of "Counting the Beat" was an instant smash in Australia, hitting No. 1 in February of 1981. The follow-up, "It Ain't What You Dance," failed to chart though. In July, the band recorded several songs for the soundtrack to the film *Starstruck* (Judd would also write additional incidental music and the band made several appearances in the film). The following month, their full-length debut, *Practical Jokers*, was released by Mushroom Records. Resequenced and edited, the album saw an American release under the title *Counting the Beat* in 1982 on Backstreet Records. The title track, "It Ain't What You Dance," and the newly added single, "One Good Reason (Gimme Love)," seemed to fit perfectly into the new wave and found a fair amount of exposure on the then-infant MTV. *Starstruck* also found a cult following in the US, giving the band a real chance for a breakthough in the States, but momentum was running out for the band. Their Australian following was dwindling and, in response, they added a new frontman, Andrew McLennan, formerly of Pop Mechanix. The new lineup released one single, the wonderfully catchy "Punch and Judy," in early 1982. The single failed and Judd dissolved the unit in May the same year to pursue a solo career.

Hillman later found success as a member of Midnight Oil. Judd released one poorly received solo album (1983's *Private Lives*) and two more with ex-Split Enz bandmates as Schnell Fenster; he now keeps a low profile, dividing his time between artistic pursuits and composing music for films. —*Chris Woodstra*

● **Practical Jokers** / 1979 / Mushroom ✦✦✦✦

For *Practical Jokers*, his first post-Enz project, Judd left his arty leanings behind in favor of a tight blend of mid-'60s pop, punk and new wave, resulting in a fine collection of fractured, eccentric pop songs that were surprisingly accessible. With the exception of "Ayatollah," which instantly dates the album, much of it remains fresh with a timeless appeal. The quirky "Counting the Beat," became a hit single in Australia/New Zealand. [A resequenced, slightly modified version of the album with the single "One Good Reason (Gimme Love)" added was issued in the US as *Counting the Beat* in 1982.] —*Chris Woodstra*

Counting the Beat / 1982 / Backstreet ✦✦✦✦

In an attempt to capitalize on US interest in the band generated by their appearance in the cult film *Starstruck*, Backstreet Records resequenced the *Practical Jokers* album, dropped a couple of songs and added the "One Good Reason (Gimme Love)" from the film. Unfortunately, it failed to make much of an impact in the States and was quickly deleted. —*Chris Woodstra*

Swinging Blue Jeans

f. 1960, Liverpool, England
British Invasion
Although they're only remembered today for their 1964 hit "Hippy Hippy Shake," the Swinging Blue Jeans were actually one of the strongest of the Liverpool bands from the '60s British Invasion. "Hippy Hippy Shake"—a cover of an obscure '50s rocker that was actually done much better by the Beatles on tapes of their BBC performances—was their only Top 30 entry in the US. But the band enjoyed some other major and minor hits in the UK, including a topnotch Merseyization of Betty Everett's (and later Linda Ronstadt's) "You're No Good," which they took into the British Top Five in 1964. They also wrote some catchy and energetic, if slightly sappy, originals in the purest Merseybeat style. While it doesn't add up to an enduring legacy, there's a lot to be said for the naive energy of the best of their early tunes. —*Richie Unterberger*

Blue Jeans a Swinging / 1964 / EMI ✦✦

The only album the Swinging Blue Jeans released in their native UK during the 1960s (a couple of other collections appeared in North America). It's a thin if reasonably energetic affair, filled to the gills with Merseyized covers of classic rock and R&B tunes that don't display a lot of imagination in either approach or selection ("Long Tall Sally," "Lawdy Miss Clawdy," "Tutti Frutti," "Save the Last Dance for Me"). It does have an okay, hard-to-find harmony ballad, "All I Want Is You," which was a single by fellow Liverpool group the Escorts. The Japanese CD adds 11 bonus cuts, all of which are available on the domestic EMI compilation, so even fans of the group will probably find this unnecessary. —*Richie Unterberger*

The Best of the EMI Years / 1992 / EMI ✦✦✦

Weighing in at a hefty 34 tracks, this is the most exhaustive Swinging Blue Jeans anthology available. Do not mistake this, however, for the best collection of these cheery Liverpool British Invaders. That honor belongs to the American *Hippy Hippy Shake* collection, which is nearly as comprehensive (at 26 tracks) but much more well-chosen. All their UK hits—half a dozen, more or less—are included here, as well as many B-sides, flop singles, and eight previously unreleased tracks (most of which bear the writing credits "unknown," even the relatively well-known Little Richard song "Ready Teddy"). At their best, the Blue Jeans were one of the better British Invasion pop-rockers, and they did manage a fair number of good tracks, but a great deal of the selections here are uneventful or downright difficult to bear in their dated quaintness, fallow MOR pop, or lame rehashing of '50s rock. The small bonus is that the version of their 1968 single "Now That You've Got Me (You Don't Seem to Want Me)," written by Clint Ballard (also responsible for "You're No Good" and other great '60s tunes), is, for some reason, much better than the one on *Hippy Hippy Shake*. That's hardly worth the fairly hefty price of this import—stick with the US compilation. —*Richie Unterberger*

● **Hippy Hippy Shake: The Definitive Collection** / May 4, 1993 / Capitol ✦✦✦✦

All of their UK and US hits are included on this compilation. Highlights are "You're No Good," "Hippy Hippy Shake," and their fine (pre-Who) cover of Johnny Kidd's "Shakin' All Over," though even for the Anglophile, about half of this CD is forgettable, especially the dreary post-1966 stuff. This anthology includes several non-LP/rare singles and unreleased songs. —*Richie Unterberger*

The Swirlies

f. 1990, Cambridge, MA
Lo-Fi, Shoegazing, Indie Rock, Dream-Pop
Formed in 1990 as a Go-Go's cover band, the Swirlies quickly evolved beyond their humble beginnings, ultimately honing a far-ranging, fascinating sound that drew primarily from shoegazing dream pop, lo-fi tape manipulations and shimmering jangle-pop. A product of the Boston/Cambridge "chimp rock" scene that also gave rise to Kudgel and Fat Day, the Swirlies initially comprised singers/guitarists Damon Tutunjian and Seana Carmody, bassist Andy Bernick and drummer Ben Drucker; in 1991, they debuted with the six-song EP *Swirlies Number One*, followed by a series of singles and *Fish Dreams Red*, a split release with Kudgel.

After signing to the Taang! label, the band issued 1992's *What to Do About Them*, which collected a number of earlier recordings along with a handful of new sides. With 1993's *Blonder Tongue Audio Baton*, the Swirlies greatly expanded on their sound, wrapping their songs in dense sheets of feedback, Moogs, Mellotrons, and white noise. Following the release of 1993's *Brokedick Car* EP, the group went through several tumultous years of personnel changes; by 1996's mini-album *Sneaky Flutes*, only Tutunjian and Bernick remained from the original lineup, which now included vocalist Christina Files and drummer Anthony DeLuca. After the release of *They Spent Their Wild Youthful Days in the Glittering World of the Salons*—an album owing a clear debt to the work of Stereolab—both Files and DeLuca exited, paving the way for the addition of drummer Adam Pierce. —*Jason Ankeny*

What to Do About Them / Oct. 2, 1992 / Taang! ✦✦✦

● **Blonder Tongue Audio Baton** / Mar. 26, 1993 / Taang! ✦✦✦✦

The Swirlies do sound a bit like My Bloody Valentine, only their songs tend to be less atmospheric and more structured. Despite their obvious dedication to My Bloody Valentine, the Swirlies' *Blonder Tongue Audio Baton* is a swell album that is both noisy and tuneful. —*AMG*

They Spent Their Wild Youthful Days in the Glittering World of the Salons / Apr. 1996 / Taang! ✦✦✦

On their long-awaited second full-length album *They Spent Their Wild Youthful Days in the Glittering World of the Salons*, the Swirlies show once again why they're so aptly named. From "In Her Money New Found Freedom" to "The Vehicle Is Invisible," the band's songs float, hover, threaten to fall apart, and yes, swirl. Though the Swirlies have undergone several lineup changes since their excellent 1992 debut album, *Blonder Tongue Audio Baton*, their trademark mix of samples, sweet vocals and noisy drums and guitars remains pretty much intact. Songs like "Sounds of Sebring," "San Cristobal de las Casas" and "Two Girls Kissing" present the more focused, accessible side of their dreamy music, while "No Identifier," "You Can't Be Told It, You Must Behold It," and "Boys, Protect Yourselves from Aliens" use plenty of buzzing noises and Speak 'n' Spells to make more experimental noise. A noisy, sonically interesting album, *They Spent Their Wild Youthful Days in the Glittering World of the Salons* may not be the most straightforward album, but the eddies and dips in the Swirlies' sound are more than worth a listen. —*Heather Phares*

SWV

f. 1990, New York, NY
Hip Hop, Dance-Pop, Urban
With their Teddy Riley-produced 1992 debut *It's About Time*, the all-female new jack swing trio SWV scored a string of Top 10 R&B hits that established them as one of the most popular urban R&B groups of the '90s.

SWV—their name is an acronym for Sisters With Voices—is comprised of three school friends: Coko (born Cheryl Gamble), Taj (born Tamara Johnson), and Lelee (born Leanne Lyons). All three vocalists sang in church as children, which is where they learned how to harmonize. A demo tape the group assembled caught the attention of producer Teddy Riley, a former member of Guy and arguably the father of New Jack Swing. Prior to SWV, Riley helped establish the careers of Jodeci and Mary J. Blige. Riley's luck didn't wear out with SWV—he helped the group craft their debut *It's About Time*, which went double platinum within its first year of release.

The release of *It's About Time* was preceded by "Right Here" in the fall of 1992. The single reached No. 13 on the R&B charts, but it was the No. 2 hit "I'm So Into You" that established the trio as a commercial force early in 1993. It was followed by two No. 1 R&B singles in a row—"Weak" and "Right Here / Human Nature," a remix of their first single that featured samples of Michael Jackson's hit, "Human Nature." "Weak" also hit No. 1 on the pop charts; "Right Here / Human Nature" reached No. 2 on the pop charts. One other Top 10 R&B hits from *It's About Time*—"Always on My Mind"—followed late in 1993. "Anything," SWV's contribution to the soundtrack of *Above the Rim*, became a Top 10 R&B hit in the spring of 1994. Also in the spring of 1994, SWV released *The Remixes*, which went gold by the end of the year. In the summer of 1995, the trio lent vocal harmonies to BLACKstreet's Top 40 R&B hit, "Tonight's the Night."

In 1996, SWV returned with *New Beginning*, which was preceded by the No. 1 R&B hit, "You're the One." —*Stephen Thomas Erlewine*

● **It's About Time** / Oct. 27, 1992 / RCA ◆◆◆◆
SWV (Sisters With Voices) electrified the urban contemporary world with *It's About Time*. Their deep, sensual harmonies, sometimes naughty lyrics and aggressive style immediately struck a responsive chord, particularly among male fans. Their CD shows their versatility, as they handled New Jack tunes, romantic ballads like "It's About Time," and sassy, innuendo-laden fare such as "Blak Pudd'n" and "That's What I Need." Their hits "Weak" and "Right Here" had the same blend of heat and vulnerability that underscore the best En Vogue material, and even though this CD was padded by remixes and repeats, it was still among the finest debuts issued in 1992. —*Ron Wynn*

New Beginning / Apr. 1996 / RCA ◆◆◆◆
As a title, *New Beginning* may be something of an overstatement—after all, it is only SWV's second album. Nevertheless, the group does take a different approach on *New Beginning*, backing away from the New Jack grooves that dominated their debut and exploring a more direct, organic R&B vibe. They haven't left hip-hop behind, but they've added a new array of sonic textures that gives their music added depth. But the true strength of *New Beginning* is the vocal capabilities of SWV—they can handle smooth soul like "Don't Waste Your Time" as easily as the funk of "Whatcha Need." There may be a couple of weak spots on the album, but the trio's considerable talents make those moments easy to forgive. —*Stephen Thomas Erlewine*

Sylvia

b. May 29, 1936, New York, NY
Vocals / Rap, Soul, Disco
Going strictly by the chart book, Sylvia was a one-hit wonder, hitting No. 3 pop (and No. 1 R&B) with her 1973 single "Pillow Talk," a slice of proto-disco bedroom funk. Few other one-hit wonders, however, had a career as multidimensional as Sylvia Robinson's. For one thing, she was actually no stranger to the hit parade when "Pillow Talk" started to catch on. In the 1950s, she'd been one-half of the rock 'n' roll duo Mickey & Sylvia, remembered for eternity for their classic "Love Is Strange." As a one-named solo artist 15 years later, Sylvia would help lay the ground

for disco, urban contemporary, and even rap with her cooing whispers and orgasmic sighs. Murmuring about romantic love with a seductive come-on that was pretty bawdy by early-'70s standards, she was the yin to Barry White's yang, if you will, offering a kinder, gentler brand of between-the-sheets soul from a feminine viewpoint. Unlike many of the singers who would follow a similar path, Sylvia was no producer's tool: she played guitar and co-wrote and co-produced most of her material, which was released on a record company run by her and her husband Joe. In the late '70s and early '80s, she would play a crucial role in the birth of rap as the co-founder of Sugar Hill Records.

"Pillow Talk" began life as a song that Sylvia hoped to pitch to Al Green. After nothing came of that plan, she issued it herself on the Vibration label, an imprint of the All Platinum company that she had founded with her husband in the late '60s in New Jersey. It would be her only major pop crossover hit, but she did have a handful of small R&B hits in the mid-'70s in a similar vein, her hushed sexy whispers backed by laconic funk-cum-disco grooves and occasional strings. Not nearly as risque as Millie Jackson, this was nonetheless fairly forthright stuff for its era; when she pushed it to the limit, it could have passed for some of the milder routines on phone sex lines. In this sense, she could be considered as a precursor not only to rap, but to R&B performers like Prince who would make plainly stated lust a centerpiece of their compositions. While her Sugar Hill activities took most of her time by the 1980s, she still found some time for recording, making the middle of the R&B charts again with a rap tune, "It's Good to Be the Queen." —*Richie Unterberger*

● **Pillow Talk: the Sensuous Sounds of Sylvia** / Aug. 20, 1996 / Rhino ◆◆◆◆
Twenty-track compilation drawn primarily from her mid-'70s albums, adding four songs from non-LP singles of the era, and a couple of cuts from 1982 Sugar Hill singles. It can get a little gooey over the course of its 79 minutes, not to mention a bit comically unsubtle at times. Her cover of Marvin Gaye's "You Sure Love to Ball," to take one example, would be raunchy enough to ruin the day of many a Republican delegate even 20 years later, when such sexual come-ons are far more commonplace on the radio. It's not all candlelight-on-the-way-to-the-bedroom stuff, though. "My Thing" (the flip of "Pillow Talk") proves she could sing fairly straight soul when given the inclination, and "Sunday" and "Not on the Outside" are sparsely produced ballads, sung with great tenderness. They make one wish that Sylvia had pursued a somewhat more versatile direction during the '70s, but there's no question that the "Pillow Talk" was bringing in the bacon, and this compilation supplies it in droves. —*Richie Unterberger*

David Sylvian

b. Feb. 23, 1958, Lewisham, London, England
Guitar, Keyboards, Vocals / Art-Rock/Progressive-Rock
Following the 1982 dissolution of Japan, the group's onetime frontman David Sylvian staked out a far-ranging and esoteric career that encompassed not only solo projects but also a series of fascinating collaborative efforts and forays into filmmaking, photography and modern art. Born David Batt in Kent, England, on February 23, 1958, Sylvian formed Japan in 1974, and served as their primary singer-songwriter throughout the group's eight-year existence. Just prior to Japan's breakup, Sylvian began working with composer Ryuichi Sakamoto, with whom he released the single "Bamboo Houses" in 1982, marking the beginning of a long-standing musical relationship.

After 1983's "Forbidden Colours," another joint effort with Sakamoto composed for the film *Merry Christmas, Mr. Lawrence*, Sylvian released his 1984 solo debut, *Brilliant Trees*. The first step in his music's evolution from Japan's post-glam synth-pop into richly-textured, poetic ambience, the album featured contributions from Sakamoto as well as Jon Hassell and Can alumnus Holger Czukay. That year, Sylvian also published his first book of photographs, *Perspectives: Polaroids 82/84;* in 1985, he released *Preparations for the Journey*, a documentary filmed in and around Tokyo, as well as the EP *Words with the Shaman*.

Gone to Earth, an ambitious double-LP recorded with assistance from Robert Fripp and Bill Nelson, followed in 1986, while 1987 marked the release not only of the beautiful *Secrets of the Beehive* album but also the book collection *Trophies: The Lyrics of David Sylvian*. At the same time, he began composing the score for modern dancer Gaby Abis' *Kin*, which premiered at London's Almeida Theater that September; another collaboration with Abis, *Don't Trash My Altar, Don't Alter My Trash*, bowed in November 1988.

Also in 1988, Sylvian reunited with Holger Czukay for the instrumental LP *Plight and Premonition;* the duo reteamed in 1989 for *Flux + Mutability. Ember Glance: the permanence of memory*, an installation of sculpture, sound, and light created by Sylvian and Russell Mills, was staged in Tokyo Bay, Shinagawa, in 1990; a year later, he and the other members of Japan, who had briefly reunited under the name Rain Tree Crow, issued a self-titled album. In 1994, Sylvian emerged in tandem with Robert Fripp for both an album, *The First Day,* and *Redemption,* another sound-and-image installation exhibited in Japan. —*Jason Ankeny*

Gone to Earth / 1986 / Virgin ♦♦♦

Sylvian is joined by guitarists Robert Fripp and Bill Nelson on this 68-minute CD, which features tracks of Sylvian's trademark vocals and instrumentals. These dreamy, atmospheric works have nice musical support from Steve Nye, Kenny Wheeler, and Mel Collins. —*Scott Bultman*

● Secrets of the Beehive / 1987 / Virgin ♦♦♦♦

A consistent mood is sustained throughout this one. Sylvian is joined by Ryuichi Sakamoto, David Torn, Mark Isham, ex-Japan drummer Steve Jansen, and others. It includes a vocal version of the Sylvian/Sakamoto cut "Forbidden Colours" from the *Merry Christmas, Mr. Lawrence* soundtrack. —*Scott Bultman*

Plight & Premonition / 1988 / Venture ♦♦♦♦

This is a collaboration between David Sylvian, frontman for Japan, and Holger Czukay, the bassist for Can. —*Michael P. Dawson*

Flux and Mutability / 1989 / Venture ♦♦♦

A follow-up to *Plight and Premonition,* it features Holger Czukay and consists of two lengthy, dreamlike pieces. —*Michael P. Dawson*

The Syndicate of Sound

f. 1964, San Jose, CA, **db.** 1970
Garage Rock, Pop-Rock

Formed in San Jose, CA, in 1964, the Syndicate of Sound was one of the premier garage bands and forerunners of psychedelic rock, establishing a national following based on one massive 1966 hit, "Little Girl." Comprised of vocalist/guitarist Don Baskin, guitarist/keyboardist John Sharkey, lead guitarist Jim Sawyers, bassist Bob Gonzalez, and drummer John Duckworth, the predecessors to the Syndicate of Sound were groups called the Pharoahs and Lenny Lee and the Knightmen. After recording an unsuccessful single for the Scarlet label, on January 9, 1966, the Syndicate of Sound recorded "Little Girl" at a studio in San Francisco for Hush Records; it became a regional hit in California after San Jose radio stations latched onto it, attracting the attention of executives at Bell Records in New York, who later asked the group to record an album.

"Little Girl" began to break nationally first in Oklahoma City, and the record entered *Billboard* magazine's Top 40; just before the single broke, original guitarist Larry Ray was pushed out of the band, and the group hired Jim Sawyers instead. When they flew to New York that summer, it was with Sawyers, and since Bell Records was anxious to get their group on the road, the Syndicate of Sound toured constantly for the latter half of 1966, taking time off to tape TV shows like *American Bandstand* and *Where the Action Is;* James Brown, who appeared with them on one of the TV shows, was so impressed that he invited them to open his theater show in San Francisco. After drummer Duckworth was drafted at the height of the Vietnam conflict, the band went through sev-

eral other changes from its original lineup and recorded three singles at the end of 1969, "You're Lookin' Fine" (a Kinks cover), "Brown Paper Bag," and "Mexico." After Baskin moved to Los Angeles in 1970, he and Gonzalez—the only other remaining original member of the band—mounted an unsuccessful attempt at recording another album for Capitol Records in 1970, and then disbanded. —*Richard Skelly*

Little Girl / 1966 / Sundazed ♦♦♦

The teen band pride of San Jose, California, the Syndicate of Sound scaled the heights of the rock 'n' roll world for a very brief moment in the summer of 1966 with their Top Ten hit, "Little Girl." With a catchy and jangly electric 12-string guitar riff, a solid beat, a macho teen vocal and a chord progression heavily influenced by myriad versions of "Hey Joe," the tune perfectly mirrored the sound of the times and was a can't-miss hit, a British sound played with American garage band enthusiasm. But the success ride was a short one for the band; within a year or two, their ranks were decimated from the draft, touring exhaustion, and the musically changing times. This reissue will serve as their lasting legacy, combining the original 12-song album package with four additional bonus tracks. Kicking off with a pair of souped-up R&B covers (Jimmy Reed's "Big Boss Man" and Chuck Berry's "Almost Grown"), the album casts a pretty wide net musically, with half of the dozen tunes penned by various band members. Of the self-penned numbers, the ballads "You" and "So Alone" sit alongside rockers like "Lookin' for the Good Times (The Robot)" and "Rumors" (complete with Yardbirds-style fuzz guitar rave-up in the middle), while the Kinks-style "That Kind of Man" heads even further into the terrain of imaginative British-sound knockoffs. The outside material included here, however, is where the band shows their true chameleon-like strength as a teen combo. Covers of the Hollies' "I'm Alive," Louis Jordan's "Is You Is or Is You Ain't My Baby" (via Buster Brown's version), the Sonics' "The Witch," and Roy Orbison's "Dream Baby" show a band that could either play a song "just like the record"—or damn close to it—or bring their own little twist to the proceedings. The four CD bonus tracks appended to the original album ("The Upper Hand," "Mary," "Keep It Up," and "Good Time Music") likewise demonstrate that the group had no shortage of original material, but unfortunately nothing compiled here has the hit sound of "Little Girl," an easy explanation as to why the group ended up with one-hit wonder status. This 16-track collection captures their brief moment in the sun. —*Cub Koda*

● Little Girl—the History of the Syndicate of Sound / Nov. 1, 1995 / Performance ♦♦♦♦

"Little Girl" is a rock 'n' roll classic. With its sneering vocals, vague threats, crude chords and rhythms, it's a menacing, swagger masterpiece of garage rock. It's also the only good thing The Syndicate of Sound ever recorded. *Little Girl—The History of the Syndicate of Sound* compiles nearly everything the group recorded, yet none of it comes close to matching the power of their hit single; it's a mess of weak originals and limp covers. The patience of even the most-dedicated garage rock fan will be tested by the disc.—*Stephen Thomas Erlewine*

T

T.Power

f. 1994

Club/Dance, Jungle/Drum 'N Bass, Electronica

TPower's Mark Royal first came to prominence working with hardcore techno group Bass Selective, whose 1991 hit "Blow Out Part II" was an influential proto-jungle track. He's since risen to new acclaim as a solo artist with TPower's experimental blend of lush ambience and often over-the-top rhythmic complexity. His 12-inch "Horny Mutant Jazz," as well as the follow-up full-length *The Self-Evident Truth of an Intuitive Mind* (both for the Sound of the Underground label) are widely considered early masterpieces of ambient-jungle, and did much conceptual trailblazing where jungle's absorption of jazz and other more measured, relaxed compositional elements are concerned. Although subsequent work has strayed from jungle's rhythmic syncopation into more traditional techno and even entirely beatless ambient, drum'n'bass remains the core element of much of TPower's music. Royal's roots are, not surprisingly, in hip-hop, in which he immersed himself during its UK heyday in the early to mid-'80s. Burning out on hip-hop early, Royal's affection for breaks and hard-hitting rhythms followed him into his explorations of the music of David Sylvian, Ryuichi Sakamoto, and Pat Metheny, and those two components—complex breaks and a keen sense of melody—inform much of his solo work to the present day. —*Sean Cooper*

The Self-Evident Truth of an Intuitive Mind / 1995 / S.O.U.R. ✦✦✦✦

TPower's *Self-Evident Truth* was one of the first full-length releases in jungle, and at that one of its first concept albums. Split into two records—one each chronicling emotion and intellect—TPower's tight, raucous blend of jungle's twisting, mutating percussion with ambient-style melodic themes is best stated here. It's a bit sugar-coated at times, with long, syrupy melodic passages often taking the place of more creative song development, but the album's rhythmic tweak is often so severe you hardly notice. —*Sean Cooper*

• **Waveform** / 1996 / Anti-Static/S.O.U.R. ✦✦✦✦

Balking at the influence of his debut, *The Self-Evident Truth Of An Intuitive Mind*, TPower's Mark Royal takes the admirable route with his follow-up of forgetting everything he's known. While elements of drum'n'bass are in evidence on a number of tracks, Royal opts instead to dissolve jungle's sweeping, low-bass moans and skittery rhythms in a vat of paranoid, abstract electronics. The result is a far less predictable, ultimately more enjoyable collection of post-dance, beat-oriented electronica seamlessly blending ambient, jungle, electro (lots, in fact), and avant-garde-leaning electro-acoustic. Masterful. —*Sean Cooper*

The Tages

f. Sweden

Pop-Rock, Rock 'n' Roll

Without a doubt, the best Swedish band of the '60s, and one of the best '60s rock acts of any sort from a non-English-speaking country. Although the group's first recordings were pretty weak Merseybeat derivations, in the mid-'60s they developed a tough, mod-influenced sound which echoed the Who and the Kinks, and recorded quite a few good originals, making the Swedish Top Ten a dozen times in all. More than any other Continental group, the Tages could have passed for a genuine British band, following the UK acts that served as their obvious inspirations into hard rock, baroque pop, and blue-eyed soul. Big throughout Scandinavia, the group actually made a determined effort to crack the English market in 1968, playing quite a few UK shows and releasing records there; they failed, and disbanded at the end of the year. The Tages evolved into Blond in the late '60s, a pop-oriented group which had an album released in the United States. —*Richie Unterberger*

• **1964-68!** / 1983 / EMI ✦✦✦✦

Definitive double-album anthology, including all of their hit singles and many other tracks. "The One for You," "Crazy 'Bout My Baby," "The Man You'll Be Looking For," and "Miss McBaren," especially, are accomplished mod rockers on par with some of the best material of the sort being produced in Britain in the mid-'60s. —*Richie Unterberger*

Talk Talk

f. 1981, London, England, **db.** 1991

Synth-pop, New Wave, New Romantic

Talk Talk began their career as a synth-pop new wave band, but as the years moved on, the group refashioned themselves as an art-rock outfit, recording albums that flirted with the ambient, textural experimentations of Brian Eno. Formed in England in 1981, Talk Talk comprised Mark Hollis (vocals), Simon Brenner (keyboards), Paul Webb (bass), and Lee Harris (drums). They were quickly signed to EMI, Duran Duran's record label. Like Duran Duran, Talk Talk looked pretty and sounded slick, enabling them to fit in with the "new romantic" pop movement of the early '80s. After scoring a couple of hits—"Talk Talk" and "Today"—and touring with Duran Duran, the group took a year off to regroup. Hollis reorganized the lineup during the recording of the group's second album, 1984's *It's My Life*. While it was slightly more experimental than their previous album, it still followed pop structures. *The Colour of Spring*, released two years later, completed the group's transition to an art-rock group. Appearing in 1988, *Spirit of Eden* was Talk Talk's most experimental record, which proved to be a commercial disaster. EMI's release of a remix collection in 1991, *History Revisited*, without the band's consent or involvement, led to a legal dispute and eventually the band and label parted ways. Talk Talk then signed with Polydor Records, releasing *Laughing Stock* in 1991. Lee Harris and Paul Web went on to form O'rang. —*Stephen Thomas Erlewine*

The Party's Over / 1982 / EMI America ✦✦✦

Talk Talk began life as a slavishly derivative, Duran Duran-styled, new romantic synth-pop band, as their debut, *The Party's Over*, clearly shows. Much of the album seems to attempt to recreate Duran Duran's debut, but even with their most blatant ripoffs, like the single "Talk Talk," they do it with a naive charm that makes for some really enjoyable music, even if it isn't particularly innovative or groundbreaking. —*Chris Woodstra*

It's My Life / 1984 / EMI America ✦✦✦✦

After an unremarkable debut, Talk Talk regrouped and refashioned themselves more in the style of sophisto-era Roxy Music while developing their own voice. *It's My Life* shows a great leap in songwriting, the band making highly personal statements with a sexy, seductive groove and a diversity that transcends the synth-pop tag. Synthesizers still play a dominant role, but the music is made far more interesting by mixing "real" instruments and challenging world music rhythms seamlessly with the technology. Still capable of pulling off the catchy single (like "Dum Dum Girl" and the title track, as well as the simply sublime "Does Caroline Know?"), with *It's My Life*, Talk Talk also proved themselves capable of achieving a cohesive album—a rare feat for the time and an unexpected surprise from a band that seemed to be simply a bandwagon-jumper. —*Chris Woodstra*

The Colour of Spring / 1986 / EMI America ✦✦✦✦

With *It's My Life*, Talk Talk proved that they could pull off an entire album of strong material. With *Colour of Spring*, they took it one step further, moving to a near-concept song cycle, following the emotional ups and downs of relationships and pondering life in general. Musically, they built on the experimental direction of the previous album with interesting rhythms, sweeping orchestration, complex arrangements, and even a children's chorus to create an evocative, hypnotic groove. Though the songs were catchier on the earlier efforts and the ambient experimentation was more fully achieved later on, *Colour of Spring* succeeded in marrying the two ideas into one unique sound for their most thoroughly satisfying album. —*Chris Woodstra*

Spirit of Eden / 1988 / EMI America ✦✦✦

Moody and atmospheric, *Spirit Of Eden* was a 360-degree turn away from Talk Talk's predecessor *Colour Of Spring*. Once dismissed as free-form ramblings, *Spirit Of Eden* could now be considered something of a forerunner to the mid-'90s ambient movement. While the songs tend to flow into and out of one another, the album's dark, emotional ride becomes more rewarding with repeated listenings. Throughout the album, lyrics deal with dark passions, addiction, and desire, while the music ebbs and flows in an oft-times reassuring manner. Difficult, but well worth the effort. —*James Chrispell*

● Natural History: The Very Best of Talk Talk / Oct. 1990 / EMI America ✦✦✦✦

During the band's hiatus following *Spirit of Eden*, EMI issued a hits collection, compiling the singles from the first four albums as well as the non-LP "My Foolish Friend," a couple of live tracks, and an edit of "Desire." *Natural History* serves as a nice introduction to the band, showing them as an effective singles act despite their more recent album-concept experiments, and the added rarities make the package a necessary addition for fans as well. —*Chris Woodstra*

History Revisited / Feb. 1991 / EMI America ✦✦✦

Released as a companion piece to the hits collection *Natural History*, *History Revisited* compiles mainly new remixes of the band's best-known, pre-experimental output. Only the dub mix of "Happiness Is Easy" had been released before—the rest were done without the band's involvement, and the band reportedly tried to block the album's release. Talk Talk's brand of synth-pop lends itself to this sort of treatment, so the collection works quite well, although there aren't many surprises. A nice companion piece for fans, but probably the least essential of their catalog. —*Chris Woodstra*

Laughing Stock / Nov. 19, 1991 / Polydor ✦✦✦✦

Virtually ignored upon its initial release, *Laughing Stock* continues to grow in stature and influence by leaps and bounds. Picking up where *Spirit of Eden* left off, the album operates outside of the accepted sphere of rock to create music that is both delicate and intense; recorded with a large classical ensemble, it defies easy categorization, conforming to very few structural precedents—while the gently hypnotic "Myrrhman" flirts with ambient textures, the percussive "Ascension Day" drifts towards jazz before the two sensibilities converge to create something entirely new and different on "New Grass." The epic "After the Flood," on the other hand, is an atmospheric whirlpool laced with jackhammer guitar feedback and Mark Hollis' remarkably plaintive vocals; it flows into "Taphead," perhaps the most evocative, spacious and understated piece on the record. A work of staggering complexity and immense beauty, *Laughing Stock* remains an underrecognized masterpiece, and its echoes can be heard throughout much of the finest experimental music issued in its wake. —*Jason Ankeny*

● The Very Best of Talk Talk [UK] / Jan. 27, 1997 / EMI ✦✦✦✦

The Very Best of Talk Talk is the most comprehensive retrospective assembled on the synth group to date, following the band from its new wave origins to its latter-day atmospheric new age recordings. Although the compilation features nothing from 1991's *Laughing Stock* and all of the songs from 1988's *Spirit of Eden* are presented in edited versions, the disc remains a good overview of the band's evolution and features all of their big hits, including "Talk Talk" and "Today." —*Stephen Thomas Erlewine*

Talking Heads

f. 1974, New York, NY, **db.** 1991
New Wave, Pop-Rock, Post-Punk, Alternative Pop-Rock

At the start of their career, Talking Heads were all nervous energy, detached emotion, and subdued minimalism. When they released their last album about 12 years later, the band had recorded everything from art-funk to polyrhythmic worldbeat explorations and simple, melodic guitar-pop. Between their first album in 1977 and their last in 1988, Talking Heads became one of the most critically acclaimed bands of the '80s, while managing to earn several pop hits. While some of their music can seem too self-consciously experimental, clever, and intellectual for its own good, at their best, Talking Heads represents everything good about art-school punks.

And they were literally art-school punks. Guitarist/vocalist David Byrne, drummer Chris Franz, and bassist Tina Weymouth met at the Rhode Island School of Design in the early '70s; they decided to move to New York in 1974 to concentrate on making music. The next year, the band won a spot opening for the Ramones at the seminal New York punk club, CBGB's. In 1976, keyboardist Jerry Harrison, a former mem-

ber of Jonathan Richman's Modern Lovers, was added to the lineup. By 1977, the band had signed to Sire Records and released their first album, *Talking Heads '77*. It received a considerable amount of acclaim for its stripped-down rock 'n' roll, particularly Byrne's geeky, overly intellectual lyrics and uncomfortable, jerky vocals.

For their next album, 1978's *More Songs About Buildings and Food*, the band worked with producer Brian Eno, recording a set of carefully constructed, arty pop songs, distinguished by extensive experimenting with combined acoustic and electronic instruments, as well as touches of surprisingly credible funk. On their next album, the Eno-produced *Fear of Music*, Talking Heads began to rely heavily on their rhythm section, adding flourishes of African-styled polyrhythms. This approach came to a full fruition with 1980's *Remain in Light*, which was again produced by Eno. Talking Heads added several sidemen, including a horn section, leaving them free to explore their dense amalgam of African percussion, funk bass and keyboards, pop songs, and electronics.

After a long tour, the band concentrated on solo projects for a couple of years. By the time of 1983's *Speaking in Tongues*, the band had severed their ties with Brian Eno; the result was an album that still relied on the rhythmic innovations of *Remain in Light*, except within a more rigid pop-song structure. After its release, Talking Heads embarked on another extensive tour, which would turn out to be their last; it's captured on the Jonathan Demme-directed concert film, *Stop Making Sense*. After releasing the straightforward pop album *Little Creatures* in 1985, Byrne directed his first movie, *True Stories*, the following year; the band's next album featured songs from the film. Two years later, Talking Heads released *Naked*, which marked a return to their worldbeat explorations, although it sometimes suffered from Byrne's lyrical pretensions.

After its release, Talking Heads were put on "hiatus;" Byrne pursued some solo projects, as did Harrison; Franz and Weymouth continued with their side project, the Tom Tom Club. In 1991, the band issued an announcement that they had broken up. —*Stephen Thomas Erlewine*

☆ Talking Heads '77 / Sep. 16, 1977 / Sire ✦✦✦✦

The most highly touted of the new wave bands to emerge from the CBGB's scene in New York of the mid-'70s, it was not clear at first whether Talking Heads' Lower East Side art-rock approach could make the subway ride to the midtown pop mainstream successfully. All pretenses of normality were abandoned by "New Feeling," the second track of their landmark debut *Talking Heads '77*, as the group started to sound on record they way they did downtown: the staggered rhythms and sudden tempo changes, the odd guitar tunings and rhythmic, single-note patterns, the non-rhyming, non-linear, non-narrative lyrics full of aphoristic soundbites that came across like odd remarks overheard from a psychiatrist's couch, and that voice, singing above its normal range, leaping into falsetto and from there into strangled cries like a madman trying desperately to sound normal. Undeniably catchy, even at its most ominous—especially on "Psycho Killer," frontman David Byrne's supreme statement of demented purpose—Talking Heads used existing elements in unusual combinations to create something new that still managed to be oddly familiar. —*William Ruhlmann*

☆ More Songs About Buildings and Food / Jul. 14, 1978 / Sire ✦✦✦✦✦

New co-producer Brian Eno brought a musical unity which tied Talking Heads' sophomore effort *More Songs About Buildings and Food* together, especially in terms of the rhythm section, the sequencing, the pacing, and the mixing. Where Talking Heads had previously been about David Byrne's voice and words, Eno moved the emphasis to the bass-and-drums team of Tina Weymouth and Chris Frantz; all the songs were danceable, and there were only short breaks between them. Byrne held his own, however, and he continued to explore the eccentric persona first heard on *77*, most notably on "The Big Country," a country-tinged reflection on flying over middle America that crystallized his artist-vs-ordinary people perspective in unusually direct and dismissive terms, turning the old Chuck Berry patriotic travelogue theme of rock 'n' roll on its head and employing a great hook in the process. —*William Ruhlmann*

Fear of Music / Aug. 3, 1979 / Sire ✦✦✦✦

By titling their third album *Fear of Music* and opening it with the African rhythmic experiment "I Zimbra," complete with nonsense lyrics by poet Hugo Ball, Talking Heads made the record seem more of a departure than it was. Though *Fear of Music* was musically distinct from its predecessors, mostly because of the use of minor keys that gave the music a more ominous sound. Previously, David Byrne's offbeat observations had been set off by an overtly humorous tone; on *Fear of Music*, he was still odd, but no longer so funny. At the same time, however, the music had become even more compelling. Worked up from jams (though Byrne received sole songwriter's credit), the music was becoming denser and more driving, notably on the album's standout track, "Life During Wartime," with lyrics that matched the music's power. "This ain't no party," declared Byrne, "this ain't no disco, this ain't no fooling around." The other key song, "Heaven," extended the dismissal Byrne had expressed for the US in "The Big Country" to paradise itself:

"Heaven is a place where nothing ever happens." It was also the album's most melodic song. Those were the highlights. What kept *Fear of Music* from being as impressive an album as Talking Heads' first two was that much of it seemed to repeat those earlier efforts, while the few newer elements seemed so risky and exciting. It was an uneven, transitional album, though its better songs were as good as any Talking Heads ever did. — *William Ruhlmann*

☆ **Remain in Light** / Oct. 8, 1980 / Sire ✦✦✦✦✦

The musical transition that seemed to have just begun with *Fear of Music* came to fruition on Talking Heads' fourth album, *Remain in Light.* "I Zimbra" and "Life During Wartime" from the earlier album served as the blueprints for a disc on which the group explored African polyrhythms on a series of driving groove tracks, over which David Byrne chanted and sang his typically disconnected lyrics. *Remain in Light* had more words than any previous Heads record, but they counted for less than ever in the sweep of the music. The album's single, "Once in a Lifetime," flopped upon release, but over the years became an audience favorite due to a striking video, its inclusion in the band's 1984 concert film *Stop Making Sense,* and its second single release (in the live version) because of its use in the 1986 movie *Down and Out in Beverly Hills,* when it became a minor chart entry. Byrne sounded typically uncomfortable in the verses ("And you may find yourself in a beautiful house, with a beautiful wife / And you may ask yourself—Well . . . how did I get here?"), which were undercut by the reassuring chorus ("Letting the days go by"). Even without a single, *Remain in Light* was a hit, indicating that Talking Heads were connecting with an audience ready to follow their musical evolution, and the album was so inventive and influential, it was no wonder. As it turned out, however, it marked the end of one aspect of the group's development and their last new music for three years. — *William Ruhlmann*

The Name of This Band Is Talking Heads / Mar. 24, 1982 / Sire ✦✦✦

For their first live album, Talking Heads devised a thorough retrospective, drawing material for the two-disc set from shows played between 1977 and 1981. The first disc chronicled the original quartet and its quirky new wave songs, including the previously unreleased "A Clean Break" and the previously single-only "Building on Fire." The album title was drawn from David Byrne's unadorned stage introductions ("The name of this band is Talking Heads. The name of this song is . . . "). On the second disc, the expanded '80s version of Talking Heads explored African rhythms and complex musical patterns, with each of the instruments doubled—Adrian Belew was on guitar, Bernie Worrell on keyboards, Busta Jones on bass, and Steve Scales on percussion, while Dolette McDonald and Nona Hendryx helped out on vocals. More than the typical live album, *The Name of This Band Is Talking Heads* was an intelligently programmed live history, but like nearly all live albums, it wasn't really essential. — *William Ruhlmann*

Speaking in Tongues / Jun. 1, 1983 / Sire ✦✦✦✦

Talking Heads found a way to open up the dense textures of the music they had developed with Brian Eno on their two previous studio albums for *Speaking in Tongues,* and were rewarded with their most popular album yet. Ten backup singers and musicians accompanied the original quartet, but somehow the sound was more spacious, and the music admitted aspects of gospel, notably in the call-and-response of "Slippery People," and John Lee Hooker-style blues, on "Swamp." As usual, David Byrne determinedly sang and chanted impressionistic, nonlinear lyrics, sometimes by mix-and-matching clichés ("No visible means of support and you have not seen nuthin' yet," he declared on "Burning Down the House," the Heads' first Top Ten hit), and the songs' very lack of clear meaning was itself a lyrical subject. "Still don't make no sense," Byrne admitted in "Making Flippy Floppy," but by the next song, "Girlfriend Is Better," that had become an order : "Stop making sense," he chanted over and over. Some of his charming goofiness had returned since the overly serious *Remain in Light* and *Fear of Music,* however, and the accompanying music, filled with odd percussive and synthesizer sounds, could be unusually light and bouncy. The album closer, "This Must Be the Place (Naive Melody)," even sounded hopeful. Well, sort of. Despite their formal power, Talking Heads' last two albums seemed to have painted them into a corner, which may be why it took them three years to craft a follow-up, but on *Speaking in Tongues,* they found an open window and flew out of it. — *William Ruhlmann*

Stop Making Sense / 1984 / Sire ✦✦✦

Like *The Name of This Band Is Talking Heads,* the soundtrack to their concert film *Stop Making Sense* captures the group at the peak of their live powers. Even though it duplicates three numbers from the previous live album, the performances on *Stop Making Sense* are so energetic that the album never sounds like a retread. — *Stephen Thomas Erlewine*

Little Creatures / Jun. 10, 1985 / Sire ✦✦✦✦

Talking Heads' most immediately accessible album, *Little Creatures* eschewed the pattern of recent Heads albums, in which instrumental tracks had been worked up from riffs and grooves, after which David Byrne improvised melodies and lyrics. The songs on *Little Creatures,*

most of which were credited to Byrne alone (with the band credited only with arrangements) sounded like they'd been written as songs. Perhaps as one result, the band had been streamlined, with extra musicians used only for specific effects rather than playing along as an ensemble. Byrne, who was singing in his natural range for once, frequently was augmented with backup singers. The overall result: ear candy. *Little Creatures* was a pop album, and an accomplished one, by a band that knew what it was doing. True, Byrne's lyrics were still intriguingly quirky, but even his subject matter was becoming more mature. "I've seen sex and I think it's okay," he sang on "Creatures of Love," and suddenly the geek had become a man. Where he had once pondered the hopes of boys and girls, he was now making observations about children. And even if his impulses remained strange—"I wanna make him stay up all night," he declared about a baby (presumably not his own) in "Stay Up Late"—he retained his charm and inventiveness. *Little Creatures* was, in a sense, Talking Heads lite. It was hard to think of this as the same band that produced "Psycho Killer." But for the band's expanding audience, who made this their second platinum album, that was okay. And their popularity was being accomplished with no diminution in their creativity. — *William Ruhlmann*

True Stories / 1986 / Sire ✦✦

Featuring songs written for David Byrne's film of the same name, *True Stories* is even more pop-oriented than *Little Creatures,* full of simple, catchy melodies and guitar hooks. Unfortunately, Byrne thinks pop should not only be simple, but simplistic; too often, his genuinely engaging songs are weighed down by his trite lyrics and condescending attitude. Fortunately, with their exceptional musical versatility, the rest of the band keeps the album from being a complete failure. — *Stephen Thomas Erlewine*

Naked / Mar. 1988 / Fly ✦✦

On what turned out to be their final new album, Talking Heads, recording in Paris with co-producer Steve Lillywhite, returned to an expanded format that was heavy on African talking drums and other percussion, plus horns on a couple of tracks. It made for a burbling, rhythmic sound that de-emphasized the melodies and lyrics, making the songs less memorable. But then, lyricist/singer David Byrne seemed to have less to say, his words as scattered as ever but seeming not so much surprising as random. The most coherent lyric also made for the best song, "(Nothing But) Flowers," a fanciful vision of reverse-urbanization in which discount stores turned into cornfields. But even that sounded familiar—for Byrne. *Naked* was one of Talking Heads' more pleasant efforts, but also one of its least substantial. — *William Ruhlmann*

● **Popular Favorites, 1984-1992: Sand in the Vaseline** / Oct. 13, 1992 / Sire ✦✦✦✦

Featuring material from every Talking Heads album except the live *The Name of This Band Is Talking Heads, Sand in the Vaseline* is a terrific double-disc retrospective of the band's long and varied career. Featuring all of their hit singles and trademark songs ("Psycho Killer," "Take Me to the River," "Burning Down the House," "And She Was," "Once In a Lifetime," "Swamp," "Memories Can't Wait," "Crosseyed and Painless," "Road to Nowhere," "(Nothing But) Flowers," "Life During Wartime"), the set also includes five previously unreleased tracks. — *Stephen Thomas Erlewine*

Tall Dwarfs

f. 1979, Dunedin, New Zealand, db. 1988
Alternative Pop-Rock

Formed in the early '80s by ex-Toy Love members Alex Bathgate and Chris Knox, the Tall Dwarfs were one of the most influential bands to emerge from New Zealand's independent scene of the '80s. Arguably the first lo-fi band in indie-rock, the Tall Dwarves' albums were made at home on a four-track tape recorder. While the group's songs were highly melodic, the fidelity of their recordings—as well as the fact they frequently employed non-conventional instruments—always twisted their most accessible material into something otherworldly.

The group's first record, the *Three Songs* EP, was released in 1981; two years later, the group released its first full-length album, *Canned Music.* Since they were all recorded with the same equipment, their recordings are more or less interchangeable; surprisingly, the quality of their material was remarkably high as well. The Tall Dwarfs stopped recording around 1988 when Chris Knox began a solo career. Even in New Zealand their original recordings are rare; *Hello Cruel World* collects the highlights of their career on one disc. — *Stephen Thomas Erlewine*

Canned Music / 1983 / Flying Nun ✦✦✦✦

That's the Short and Long of It / 1985 / Flying Nun ✦✦✦

It's true, to a certain degree, that there isn't a great deal of variation in Tall Dwarfs' approach from record to record. It's also true, to a greater degree, that you can always count on a great deal of variation within any given record itself. That's the case with this hybrid LP-EP, which showed the group capable of expanding their template from their earliest releases. Side one, which plays at 45 rpm, has two related pieces, "Nothings Going to Happen" and "Nothings Going to Stop It," which sound sort of like a garage *Sgt. Pepper* with their lo-fi wall of orchestral psychedelia. It's back to 33 rpm for the ten songs on side two, a salad bar with samplings of pretty acoustic guitar, a bit of surf influence, some blasts of garage organ, nods to both Lennon and McCartney ("Woman" sounds like primal scream-era Lennon backed by a sloppy San Francisco psychedelic act), and more. —*Richie Unterberger*

Throw a Sickie / 1986 / Flying Nun ✦✦✦
Although this 12-inch release has nine songs, it might be more properly classified as an EP due to its brief running time. It's one of their most marginal releases, both because of the relatively short slice of material, and because some of the tracks show the group's brand of lo-fi/psych at its most grating. Committed fans won't be disappointed, but non-completists would be far better off with one or some of their full-length discs. —*Richie Unterberger*

● **Hello Cruel World** / 1987 / Positive ✦✦✦✦
The band's US debut, *Hello Cruel World*, collects their legendary and most influential early recordings from 1981 to 1984—with selections from the ultra-rare *Three Songs* EP (1981), *Louis Loves His Daily Dip* EP (1982), *Canned Music* (1983), and *Slugbucket Hairybreath Monster* EP (1984). An excellent introduction to a truly unique and innovative band. —*Chris Woodstra*

Weeville / 1990 / Flying Nun ✦✦✦
As the liner notes proclaim, this is "the first straightforward LP by Tall Dwarfs . . . in terms of having the same number of tracks on each side—both of which play at the same speed and which ain't a compilation." If Tall Dwarfs had only done one or two albums, this would have seemed like a more impressive document. But new ground isn't broken here—it's more of the same eclectic melange of homespun latter-day psychedelia. The converted will have no complaints. But for my money it's much better when it abandons the arty noise for acoustic-guitar-driven, airy melodies, as it does here on a number of occasions. —*Richie Unterberger*

Fork Songs / 1992 / Flying Nun ✦✦✦
The group's second proper album, though they had ten years of active recording under their belt by this time. It might be a little more subdued and serious than much of their previous output, as is often the case when manic rock experimentalists get older and more experienced. For the Tall Dwarfs, that's a good thing, since personal wistfulness generally dates better than throwing things in the kitchen sink. They haven't lost their capacity to exasperate, though, as evidenced by the endless headache-inducing fuzz riffs of "Boys." The CD tacks on all six tracks from their 1988 EP *Dogma*. —*Richie Unterberger*

3 Eps / 1994 / Flying Nun ✦✦✦✦
The *Hello Cruel World* compilation is the best way to get acquainted with Tall Dwarfs, but if you want just one of their other albums, this is probably the best choice. Recorded in 1992 and 1993, it has just as much variety as any other disc (compilation or otherwise) by the group, but doesn't wear out its welcome as much over the course of the merry-go-round. Some of their most spaced-out stuff is here: the fogged-over hurdy-gurdy waltz of "Bob's Yer Uncle," the stoner psychedelia of "Two Dozen Lousy Hours" (complete with warp-simulation sound effects), the white blues satire (how long has it been since you heard one of those?) "Postmodern Deconstructivist Blues." They can't resist succumbing to numbing repetitive lo-fi fuzz riffs from time to time (as on "Self-Deluded Dreamboy (In a Mess)"), but after a dozen years it seems unreasonable to expect that they'll grow up in this regard. —*Richie Unterberger*

Stumpy: the Album / Feb. 11, 1997 / Flying Nun ✦✦✦

Tams
....
f. 1959, Atlanta, GA
Soul
A "beach" music favorite, Atlanta's Tams were among the more popular uptempo soul groups of the '60s, although they were never able to break Motown's pop stranglehold. Joseph Pope's gravelly-voiced leads were their selling point. He was joined by his brother Charles, Robert Smith, Floyd Ashton, and Horace Key. They began on Swan in 1960, then landed their first hit with "Untie Me" for Arlen in 1962. It peaked at No. 12 on the R&B charts (No. 11 pop). They moved to ABC-Paramount the next year, where they remained until 1968. They scored their biggest hit in 1963 with "What Kind of Fool (Do You Think I Am)." But many soul fans regard 1968's "Be Young, Be Foolish, Be Happy" as their ultimate hit, although it only reached No. 26 on the R&B charts. —*Ron Wynn*

● **Best Of** / 1995 / BGO ✦✦✦✦
Fourteen songs from singles that they recorded for ABC-Paramount between 1963 and 1969, their most productive era. Includes "What Kind of Fool (Do You Think I Am)," "Be Young, Be Foolish, Be Happy," and a few late-'60s songs by Joe South. Decent, somewhat retro-flavored (even

for the time) soul with heavy pop and doo wop influences, sounding at times like a very unschooled variation of the early Impressions. Unfortunately, this doesn't include their early-'60s hit "Untie Me," which was recorded before the group joined ABC-Paramount. —*Richie Unterberger*

Tangerine Dream
....
f. 1967, Berlin, Germany
Electronic, Art-Rock/Progressive-Rock, Kraut-Rock
Formed as a rock group in 1967 by Edgar Froese, Tangerine Dream is one of the most important entities to shape contemporary instrumental music over the last 20 years. The turbulent '60s, Froese's association with surrealist painter Salvador Dali, and the arrival of the Moog synthesizer were just a few of the forces that helped to fuel this German electronic group through a barrage of constant change in style and personnel. Core members over the years have included Froese and Chris Franke as well as Peter Baumann, who went on to start the Private Music label. Curiously enough, the band's most recent addition is Jerome Froese, Edgar's son, whose enigmatic photos as a baby can be found in the artwork to TD's early albums. Over the past 25 years or so, the TD sound has moved from the droning nightmares of *Zeit*, to the mesmerizing sequencer-based masterpieces of *Rubycon* and *Ricochet* in the '70s, to the sparkling high-tech rock of the '80s. A cult phenomenon for decades, Tangerine Dream gained wider recognition when the group's highly evocative music attracted the interest of William Friedkin. This resulted in the score to the film *Sorcerer* and the beginning of a large number of soundtracks. (TD's music for the Tom Cruise scorcher, *Risky Business*, probably attracted the most attention.) In recent years, Tangerine Dream has moved toward shorter, song-based pieces that seem superficial and predictable compared to the group's pioneering work, yet Froese and company must be admired for TD's continuous output and place in electronic-music history. —*Linda Kohanov*

Zeit / 1972 / Relativity ✦✦✦
T.D.'s purest expression of "space music," this double album ebbs and flows effortlessly from one tone cluster to another. Almost classical in construction, the music is structured so as to evolve in sections as one theme literally melts into the next. Florian Fricke (of Popol Vuh) played the big Moog on this album, and the overall texture of the electronics is warm and shimmering. —*Archie Patterson*

Phaedra / 1974 / Virgin ✦✦✦✦
Tangerine Dream was sailing into uncharted waters back in 1973 when they recorded *Phaedra*. Full of eerie Moog and Mellotron sequences, selections whooshed and whooped along through the galaxy with hints of loneliness that could only come from deep space. —*James Chrispell*

Rubycon / 1975 / Virgin ✦✦✦
Classic, uncompromising Tangerine Dream, is a must for any serious collector of electronic music. —*Linda Kohanov*

Ricochet / 1975 / Virgin ✦✦✦
Recorded live in France and Great Britain in the autumn of 1975, *Ricochet* consists of the title track, parts one and two, and is a souvenir of what it's like to be at a Tangerine Dream concert, circa mid-70's. —*James Chrispell*

Stratosfear / 1976 / Virgin ✦✦✦
Expanding their style to now include six—and 12-string guitar, mouth organ, grand piano, and percussion, Tangerine Dream's *Stratosfear* unleashes many a different soundscape for listeners to visit. Highlights include the title track and the bluesy "3 a.m. at the Border of the Marsh from Okefenokee," a track you have to hear to believe. —*James Chrispell*

Cyclone / 1978 / Virgin ✦✦✦
Many changes came to pass for Tangerine Dream by the time they recorded *Cyclone* in 1978. Although still full of the spacey whoosh of the past, *Cyclone* found them adding lyrics (i.e., vocals) to the mix with mixed results. Things like "Bent Cold Sidewalk" and "Risingrunner Missed by Endless Sender" were hard enough to describe with music, let alone words, so get ready for a much different–sounding excursion this time out. Incidentally, although this was recorded in 1978, it wasn't released until 1988, so unsure was the record company about this change in direction. Now one wonders what all the fuss was about. —*James Chrispell*

Logos / 1982 / Virgin ✦✦✦✦
This live recording captures The Dream at a high point that occurred midway through the band's career. Longer, more intricate pieces are present, yet the action takes place at a brisk pace, moving through many of the trademark TD motifs and soundscapes. The recording's studio quality and engrossing performances are clearly inspired. —*Linda Kohanov*

Le Parc / 1985 / Relativity ✦✦✦✦
A selection of different moods, all of a consistently high quality, each track takes its name and inspiration from a different park in the world, Central or Yellowstone, for example. —*Vladimir Bogdanov*

Legend / 1986 / MCA ✦✦

Tangerine Dream's soundtrack to Ridley Scott's *Legend* is a vaguely interesting set of atmospheric, electronic soundscapes, but it doesn't quite match the splendor of their earlier work. Furthermore, their music is interrupted by mediocre songs by Bryan Adams and Jon Anderson, making *Legend* a less than fulfilling effort. —*Daevid Jehnzen*

Tyger / 1987 / Relativity ✦✦✦

Tyger sees Tangerine Dream set the poetry of William Blake to music. While the combination of styles will inevitably be off-putting to some—particularly stuffy Blake fans—the results are surprisingly evocative and listenable. *Tyger* might not be one of the most accessible albums within Tangerine Dream's catalog, but for those wishing to explore their more adventurous side, it's a worthwhile listen. —*Stephen Thomas Erlewine*

Canyon Dreams / 1987 / Miramar ✦✦✦✦

TD received its first Grammy nomination with this album. The music was originally composed for a scenic video on the Grand Canyon, released under the same title. The style is a rather ingenious combination of the group's progressive style and current commercial leanings, and, as such, is Tangerine Dream's finest album of recent years. —*Linda Kohanov*

Melrose / Sep. 1990 / Private Music ✦✦✦

Quite a contrast from *Logos*, this album is one of the better examples of the band's recent immersion in adult-alternative electronic pop. —*Linda Kohanov*

Rockoon / Feb. 12, 1992 / Miramar ✦✦✦

Though the music has its moments, TD's most recent album is listed mostly as a reference. —*Linda Kohanov*

Dream Roots Collection / Nov. 6, 1996 / Castle ✦✦✦

The Dream Roots Collection is a five-disc retrospective of Tangerine Dream's career, including one disc of previously unreleased material. All of the material on the collection has been remixed and reworked by Edgar Froese and his son Jerome, and while these remixes might not be historically accurate, they nevertheless retain the essence of the original versions, making the box an intriguing journey through the group's past. While the set is too extensive for casual fans, hardcore fans will find the new mixes and rarities fascinating, making the set a worthwhile addition to their collection. —*Stephen Thomas Erlewine*

Brick: Grammy Nominated Albums / Feb. 25, 1997 / Miramar ✦✦✦✦

Grammy Nominated Albums contains all five of Tangerine Dream's five Grammy-nominated albums—*Canyon Dreams, 220 Volt Live, Rockoon, Turn of the Tides, Tyranny of Beauty*—complete and unedited in one box set. —*Stephen Thomas Erlewine*

Tarnation

f. 1992, San Francisco, CA

Alternative Country-Rock, Dream-Pop

The country art band Tarnation was essentially a vehicle for Paula Frazer, a talented singer and songwriter who returned to roots music only after a successful foray into 1980s post-punk. Frazer was born and raised in Sautee Nacoochee, Georgia, a tiny community located in the foothills of the Smoky Mountains, where as a child she sang in her father's church choir, developing a remarkably adept soprano. When she was 14, the Frazers moved to Arkansas, where she began performing with local jazz groups.

After graduating high school, Frazer relocated to San Francisco, where she followed a stint in a Bulgarian women's choir with tenures in a number of area punk groups, most notably the all-female Frightwig. In 1992, she formed Tarnation with former SF Seals members Lincoln Allen and Michelle Cernuto, along with steel guitarist Matt Sullivan. Setting their dark ballads and love songs against a stark, ominous backdrop dominated by reverb-soaked guitars, Tarnation debuted in 1993 with *I'll Give You Something to Cry About*. In 1995, they issued *Gentle Creatures*, their first LP for the arty British label 4AD. Shortly after the record's release, Allen, Cernuto, and Sullivan left the group, and were replaced by guitarist Alex Oropeza, drummer Joe Byrnes, and bassist/lap steel player Bill Cuevas. —*Jason Ankeny*

● **Gentle Creatures** / Aug. 22, 1995 / 4AD ✦✦✦✦

Given that Tarnation's frontwoman Paula Frazer is best known for her work with the Los Angeles post-punk band Frightwig—and since *Gentle Creatures* is, after all, a product of the arty 4AD label—the absolute-torch-and-twang authenticity that defines the record is a wonderful surprise; ethereal yet earthy, the album's strength derives from all of its seeming contradictions. Powered by Frazer's deft songwriting and smoky vocals, *Gentle Creatures* is melancholy and gorgeous, its love songs and ballads cloaked in reverb and gothic imagery. What Tarnation shares with its 4AD stablemates is an uncanny knack to build and maintain a rich, dense atmosphere; the record is dusky and otherworldly, haunted by the spirits of failed relationships, late-night radio transmissions, and other ghostly presences. —*Jason Ankeny*

Mirador / Apr. 8, 1997 / Reprise ✦✦✦✦

With *Mirador*, Tarnation became, for all intents and purposes, the Paula Frazer Band, both for better and for worse. Frazer certainly dominated *Gentle Creatures*, and Matt Sullivan is not missed anywhere on *Mirador*, but the second album doesn't have the brilliant highs of the debut. That said, it is a more consistent record, and her new developments are quite intriguing. Frazer has created a dark, neo-Spanish feel that owes as much to spaghetti Westerns as it does to traditional country, and while her songwriting has improved, it's distressing that the cover of the Nightcrawlers' "Little Black Egg" stands out on the initial listen. Subsequent plays reveal the depth and subtlety of her songs, which her rich, powerful voice makes all the more effective. If *Mirador* is a stumble, it's only a slight one—Tarnation are still one of the most provocative bands dream-pop and alt-country has yet produced. —*Stephen Thomas Erlewine*

Howard Tate

b. 1938, Macon, GA

Vocals / Soul

Highly regarded by soul music cultists, and virtually unknown by anybody else, Howard Tate had some minor success with the Verve label in the late '60s. The singer brought a lot of blues and gospel to his phrasing, but what made him palatable to the modern R&B (and, to a lesser degree, pop) audience was the Northeast soul production of Jerry Ragovoy, who also wrote much of Tate's material. Howard made the R&B Top 20 three times in the late '60s (with "Ain't Nobody Home," "Stop," and "Look at Granny Run Run"). However, he's most famous to rock audiences as the original performer of "Get It While You Can," which became one of Janis Joplin's signature tunes.

Before establishing himself as a solo performer, Tate sang with the Gainors, a North Philadelphia doo wop group that also included future soul star Garnet Mimms. In the early '60s, he was the vocal frontman for Bill Doggett, the organist famous for the instrumental hit "Honky Tonk." Jerry Ragovoy was urged to check out Tate by a member of the Enchanters, Garnet Mimms' backup singers. He recorded about ten singles with Tate between 1966 and 1969, the first for the small Utopia label, the rest for Verve.

Tate moved on to Lloyd Price's Turntable label, for which he recorded a few singles in the late '60s and early '70s. From there he chalked up a short stint with Atlantic, which saw a few other 45s and a critically well-received album, but again little commercial success. A 1974 single for Epic was his swan song. Always somewhat of a mysterious figure, he hasn't been seen since the early '80s. His music has received its greatest exposure via cover versions: Jimi Hendrix and Hugh Masekela did "Stop," Ry Cooder covered "Look at Granny Run Run," B.B. King recorded "Ain't Nobody Home,"and rappers Brand Nubian sampled "Look at Granny Run Run." And of course Joplin (who also raided the Ragavoy catalog for "Try (Just a Little Bit Harder)," "Cry Baby," and "My Baby") did "Get It While You Can" in a manner closely derived from Tate's interpretation. —*Richie Unterberger*

● **Get It While You Can: Legendary Sessions** / Jun. 20, 1995 / Mercury ✦✦✦✦

Tate's entire Verve output, condensed into a tidy 17-track compilation, including all of his late '60s singles for the label and one previously unreleased track. Solid period soul with a slight eclectic bent for the blues, gospel, and some pop influences. —*Richie Unterberger*

James Taylor

b. Mar. 12, 1948, Boston, MA

Guitar, Vocals / Singer-Songwriter, Adult Contemporary, Soft Rock

When people use the term "singer-songwriter" (often modified by the word "sensitive"), in praise or in criticism, it's James Taylor that they're thinking of. Yet in a career now extending three decades, Taylor's biggest hits have come with his cover versions of other people's songs. Go figure. Taylor grew up in Massachusetts and North Carolina, forming the Flying Machine with guitarist Danny Kortchmar in 1967. He was signed as a solo artist by the Beatles' Apple label in 1968 and released his debut album, *James Taylor*. But it was his 1970 Warner Brothers LP, the triple-platinum *Sweet Baby James*, with its understated, autobiographical Top Ten hit "Fire and Rain," that was his commercial breakthrough. *Mud Slide Slim and the Blue Horizon* (1971) was another million-seller and contained the No. 1 single "You've Got a Friend," written by Carole King. Taylor married Carly Simon in 1972, around the time that the gold *One Man Dog* was released. *Walking Man* (1974) was less successful, but Taylor scored a gold Top Ten single the same year by covering the old Inez and Charlie Foxx hit "Mockingbird" in a duet with his wife. *Gorilla* (1975) did better, spurred by Taylor's Top Ten remake of Marvin Gaye's "How Sweet It Is (To Be Loved by You)." *In the Pocket* (1976) was Taylor's last album for Warner Brothers; he moved to Columbia Records for *JT* (1977), a double-platinum comeback that featured a Top Ten cover of Jimmy Jones' "Handy Man." *Flag* (1979) and *Dad Loves His Work* (1981) were Top Ten gold albums. In 1983, Taylor and Simon divorced (Taylor remarried in 1985). *That's Why I'm Here* (1985), released after a gap of four and a half years, was only modestly successful, but *Never Die Young* (1988) and *New Moon Shine* (1991) were gold-sellers. Responding to the success of his annual tours, Taylor released the double-disc (*Live*) (1993), which went platinum. — *William Ruhlmann*

James Taylor / Dec. 6, 1968 / Capitol ✦✦✦✦

On this self-titled debut album, James Taylor's reflective lyrics, containing his melancholic observations on life and love, were leavened by his attractive folk melodies, his acoustic guitar fingerpicking, and his warm, rich voice, which was unconsciously reminiscent of the calm crooning school of Bing Crosby and Perry Como. To these, producer Peter Asher added the accomplished but subdued string and brass arrangements, using a few pieces per track, with musical "links" between songs, building up to a full orchestra on the last two songs. The result was an amazingly distinctive effort, all in the service of Taylor's songs, which included "Knocking 'Round the Zoo" (a comic, bluesy reminiscence on life in a mental institution), "Something in the Way She Moves," "Rainy Day Man," and "Carolina in My Mind" (with Paul McCartney on bass), songs that have been concert favorites for decades. However personal Taylor's young angst may have been, it connected strongly with his generation's, and remains among his better efforts. — *William Ruhlmann*

☆ Sweet Baby James / Feb. 1970 / Warner Brothers ✦✦✦✦✦

The heart of James Taylor's appeal is that you can take him two ways. On the one hand, his music, including that warm voice, is soothing; its minor-key melodies and restrained playing draw in the listener. On the other hand, his world view, especially on such songs as "Fire and Rain," reflects the pessimism and desperation of the 1960s hangover that was the early '70s. That may not be intentional: "Fire and Rain" was about the suicide of a fellow inmate of Taylor's at a mental institution, not national malaise. But Taylor's sense of wounded hopelessness—"I'm all in pieces, you can have your own choice," he sings in "Country Road"—struck a chord with music fans, especially because of its attractive mixture of folk, country, gospel, and blues elements, all of them carefully understated and distanced. Taylor didn't break your heart, he understood that it was already broken, as was his own, and he offered comfort. As a result, *Sweet Baby James* sold millions of copies, spawned a Top Ten hit in "Fire and Rain" and a Top 40 hit in "Country Road," and launched not only Taylor's career as a pop superstar but also the entire singer-songwriter movement of the early '70s that included Joni Mitchell, Carole King, Jackson Browne, Cat Stevens, and others. A second legacy became clear two decades later, when country stars like Garth Brooks began to cite Taylor, with his use of steel guitar, references to Jesus, and rural and Western imagery on *Sweet Baby James*, as a major influence. — *William Ruhlmann*

Mud Slide Slim and the Blue Horizon / Apr. 1971 / Warner Brothers ✦✦✦✦

James Taylor's commercial breakthrough in 1970 was predicated on the relationship between the private concerns expressed in his songs and the larger philosophical mood of his audience. He was going through depression, heartbreak, and addiction; they were recovering from the political and cultural storms of the '60s. On his follow-up to the landmark *Sweet Baby James*, Taylor brought his listeners up to date, wisely trying to step beyond the cultural, if not the personal, markers he had established. Despite affirming romance in songs like "Love Has Brought Me Around" and the moving "You Can Close Your Eyes" as well as companionship in "You've Got a Friend," the record still came as a defense against the world, not an embrace of it; Taylor was unable to forget the past or trust the present. The songs were full of references to the road and the highway, and he was uncomfortable with his new role as spokesman. The confessional songwriter was now, necessarily, writing about what it was like to be a confessional songwriter: *Mud Slide Slim and the Blue Horizon* served the valuable function of beginning to move James Taylor away from the genre he had defined, which ultimately would give him a more long-lasting appeal. — *William Ruhlmann*

One Man Dog / Nov. 1972 / Warner Brothers ✦✦✦

A lot was riding on this album, James Taylor's follow-up to his two big hits, *Sweet Baby James* and *Mud Slide Slim and The Blue Horizon;* this was released 21 months after the latter, a long time between records in those days. And what a letdown. *One Man Dog* contained 18 tracks, some of them instrumentals, many of them running less than two minutes. A lot of it was sketchy and seemingly unfinished, and none of it had the impact of the best songs on the last two albums. *One Man Dog* spawned a Top 20 hit in "Don't Let Me Be Lonely Tonight," and it made the Top Ten and went gold itself largely on the momentum of Taylor's career. But it disappointed fans, and in the 19 months it took him to record another album, Taylor was bypassed by the singer-songwriter movement. — *William Ruhlmann*

Walking Man / Jun. 1974 / Warner Brothers ✦✦✦

One Man Dog drastically lowered expectations for a new James Taylor album, and those expectations were almost met by *Walking Man*, a more considered effort than its predecessor that managed to be just as trivial but even less interesting. As a result, it became the worst-selling album of Taylor's career. Somehow, a songwriter who had seemed in 1970 to have as precise an idea of the national mood as Bob Dylan had had in 1965 now seemed to be a man without a country. Instead, *Walking Man*, which began with Taylor asking, "Who is this walking man?" and ended with his commenting, "It's really not so bad to be fading away," sounded like the statement of a songwriter who either had nothing to say or didn't know how to say it. — *William Ruhlmann*

Gorilla / May 1975 / Warner Brothers ✦✦✦

Gorilla served notice to anyone expecting James Taylor to continue on in the personal, confessional vein of his first few albums that he did not intend to do so. Recording in Burbank with Warners staff producers Lenny Waronker and Russ Titelman, Taylor used a stellar backup band augmented by such guests as Graham Nash and David Crosby (who harmonized on the chart single "Mexico"), his wife Carly Simon, mandolinist David Grisman, saxophone player David Sanborn, Randy Newman on "hornorgan," and Little Feat slide guitarist Lowell George. This team worked on a set of light, pleasant songs that bordered on the generic—one was called "Music," another "Love Songs"—but were performed and sung with taste and care. Taylor was relentlessly upbeat; even "Angry Blues," which confessed, "I can't help it if I don't feel so good," didn't seem like things were that bad. But then, these songs didn't seem to be about Taylor, or if they were, in the extended metaphor of the title track, the connection was so oblique that it was hard to say what the point was. Still, one could glide on Taylor's easy vocals and the band's competence, and *Gorilla* was an enjoyable listening experience. "How Sweet It Is (To Be Loved by You)," the first of a series of bleached R&B covers, became a Top Ten hit, and the album restored Taylor's commercial fortunes, setting him on the steady path he would follow for decades after. But who would have thought only a few years before that the king of the confessional song poets would turn into such a lightweight? — *William Ruhlmann*

In the Pocket / Jun. 1976 / Warner Brothers ✦✦✦

James Taylor's seventh album and last new recording for Warner Bros. is notable for producing his biggest self-written hit in four years, "Shower The People" (No. 22 pop, No. 1 easy listening). Bobby Womack's "Woman's Gotta Have It" was the album's only cover, and elsewhere Taylor took on a surprisingly rough set of issues in his typically gentle style, including "A Junkie's Lament" and "Money Machine." There were also reflections on being a "Family Man" even if, due to his peripatetic touring life, "Daddy's All Gone." Guest stars included Art Garfunkel, who harmonized on "Captain Jim's Drunken Dream," and Stevie Wonder, who co-wrote and played harmonica on "Don't Be Sad 'Cause Your Sun Is Down." On the whole, a respectable effort for an artist who was evolving into more of a craftsman than a virtuoso. — *William Ruhlmann*

● Greatest Hits / Nov. 1976 / Warner Brothers ✦✦✦✦

James Taylor had scored eight Top 40 hits by the fall of 1976 when Warner Brothers marked the end of his contract with this compilation. One of those hits, the Top Ten gold single "Mockingbird," a duet with his wife Carly Simon, was on Elektra Records, part of the Warners family of labels and presumably available, but it was left off. "Long Ago and Far Away," a lesser hit (though it made the Top Ten on the Easy Listening charts), wasn't used either. In addition to the six hits—"Fire and Rain," "Country Road," "You've Got a Friend," "Don't Let Me Be Lonely Tonight," "How Sweet It Is (To Be Loved by You)," and "Shower the People"—that were included, the album featured a couple of less successful singles, "Mexico" and "Walking Man," the album track "Sweet Baby James," and three previously unreleased recordings—a live version of "Steamroller" and newly recorded versions of "Something in the Way She Moves" and "Carolina in My Mind," songs featured on Taylor's 1968 debut album, recorded for Apple/Capitol. The result was a reasonable collection for an artist who wasn't particularly well-defined by his singles. One got little sense of Taylor's evolution from the dour, confessional songs of his first two albums to the more conventional pop songs of his sixth and seventh ones. But one did hear isolated examples of Taylor's undeniable warmth and facility for folk/country-tinged pop. By the next summer, Taylor was back in the Top Ten on Columbia, and *Greatest Hits* was out of date. But it remains a good sampler of Taylor's more popular early work. And, decades later, it remained the only Taylor compilation in print in the US. — *William Ruhlmann*

JT / Jun. 1977 / Columbia ✦✦✦✦

On his last couple of Warner Brothers albums, *Gorilla* and *In the Pocket*, James Taylor seemed to be converting himself from the shrinking violet, too-sensitive-to-live "rainy-day man" of his early records into a mainstream, easy-listening crooner with a sunny outlook. *JT*, his debut album for Columbia Records, was something of a defense of this conversion. Returning to the autobiographical, Taylor declared his love for

Carly Simon ("There We Are"), but expressed some surprise at his domestic bliss. "Isn't it amazing a man like me can feel this way?" he sang in the opening song, "Your Smiling Face" (a Top 40 hit). At the same time, domesticity could have its temporary depressions ("Another Grey Morning"). The key track was "Secret O' Life," which Taylor revealed as "enjoying the passage of time." Working with his long-time backup band of Danny Kortchmar, Leland Sklar, and Russell Kunkel, and with Peter Asher back in the producer's chair, Taylor also enjoyed the playing of music, mixing his patented acoustic-guitar-based folk sound with elements of rock, blues, and country. He even made the Country charts briefly with "Bartender's Blues," a genre exercise complete with steel guitar and references to "honky tonk angels" that he would later re-record with George Jones. JT was James Taylor's winning remake of Jimmy Jones' "Handy Man," which replaced the grit of the original with his characteristic warmth. JT was James Taylor's best album since Mud Slide Slim and the Blue Horizon because it acknowledged the darkness of his earlier work while explaining the deliberate lightness of his current viewpoint, and because it was his most consistent collection in years. Fans responded: JT sold better than any Taylor album since Sweet Baby James. — William Ruhlmann

Flag / May 1979 / Columbia ✦✦✦✦
James Taylor followed his double-platinum Columbia Records label debut JT with this hodgepodge of a record. There are pointless covers of the Beatles' "Day Tripper" and the Drifters' "Up on the Roof" (No.7 Adult Contemporary, No.28 Pop), a remake of Taylor's own "Rainy Day Man," songs written for the failed Broadway musical Working, and a few inconsequential new Taylor compositions. The usual brain trust (producer Peter Asher) and the usual backup team (Danny Kortchmar, Dan Grolnick, Leland Sklar, Russ Kunkel) were on board, but the cruise was a snooze. — William Ruhlmann

Dad Loves His Work / Mar. 1981 / Columbia ✦✦✦
James Taylor bounced back from the spotty Flag with this all-original album led by his collaboration with J.D. Souther on "Her Town Too" (No.11 Pop, No.5 Adult Contemporary), his biggest pop hit since "Handy Man" and biggest non-cover hit since his first, "Fire And Rain," in 1970. Also included were "Hard Times" (No.72 Pop, No.23 Adult Contemporary) and "Summer's Here" (No.25 Adult Contemporary), not to mention the unusually impassioned "Stand and Fight." After simmering this long, there wasn't much hope Taylor would ever come to a boil, but that track indicated he could at least heat up now and then. — William Ruhlmann

That's Why I'm Here / Oct. 1985 / Columbia ✦✦✦
Taylor took four and a half years off from record-making in the early 1980s, returning with That's Why I'm Here, which suggested he had found his long-term niche with Baby Boomer fans now permanently tuned to soft-rock radio. This was Taylor's first record to spawn three Top Ten adult contemporary hits, with the title track, "Only One," and a cover of Buddy Holly's "Everyday." But those boomers just don't go to the record store as often as their children, and the album failed to go gold and was his lowest-charting effort since his debut. If, in the title song, he had reconciled himself to the notion that he was here to sing "Fire And Rain" at summer concerts, that also meant he was settling for a complacent position in which his new material was virtually irrelevant, and that being the case, why should people buy it? — William Ruhlmann

Never Die Young / Jan. 1988 / Columbia ✦✦
While his aging contemporaries took a variety of tacks to keep up with changing fashions, from adopting more synthesized, percussive production styles to assembling an orchestra and singing standards, James Taylor just kept playing a summer concert tour each year and periodically putting out another collection of similar-sounding songs. Never Die Young was unusual only in that there was no big oldies cover from the '50s or '60s—every song was written or co-written by Taylor—but otherwise it addressed the same audience in much the same terms as he always had. The title song and "Baby Boom Baby" (both adult contemporary hits) referred to the passage of time, and the rest floated on a sea of yuppie contentment. "I work hard to see that you remember my name," he sang, and that work seemed to consist of reminding his listeners why they had liked him in the first place. — William Ruhlmann

• **Classic Songs** / 1990 / CBS ✦✦✦✦
Classic Songs is the only compilation to feature the original versions of all of James Taylors' classics from his debut up through 1985's That's Why I'm Here. Unfortunately, it's only available in Europe, yet it remains the best, most comprehensive collection of his work to date. — Chris Woodstra

New Moon Shine / Sep. 24, 1991 / Columbia ✦✦✦
James Taylor produced a typical collection of familiar-sounding songs on New Moon Shine, his concerns ranging from romance to the life of the working man to political issues like war and civil rights, on which he took the expected liberal positions. The album was written, played, and sung with typical craft and care, and was a worthy addition to Taylor's catalog. Taylor's reliability means that his records do not disappoint

his faithful audience, but neither do they provide any revelations. New Moon Shine provided four Adult Contemporary chart entries in "Copperline," "(I've Got To) Stop Thinkin' 'Bout That," a cover of Sam Cooke's "Everybody Loves to Cha Cha Cha," and "Like Everyone She Knows," and the album went gold, staying in the charts more than nine months, a good showing for a record that essentially repeated previous efforts. — William Ruhlmann

Live / Aug. 10, 1993 / Columbia ✦✦✦
"A live James Taylor album has been suggested, demanded, and contemplated for many years," writes Taylor's manager/producer Peter Asher in this album's liner notes, and the reasons are not hard to find. For one thing, Taylor has been a successful concert attraction for more than 20 years. For another, an artist who has scored in excess of 30 chart records (on four different labels) over those years is a natural for a 20-year-old hits compilation. The 30-track, two-hour (Live), drawn from a tour staged specifically to record it, is an attempt to address those points. Fronting a typically top-notch band, Taylor ranges across his repertoire, back to 1968 for "Something in the Way She Moves" and "Carolina in My Mind," and up to 1991 for "Copperline," among other songs drawn from New Moon Shine. In between come most of his hits. (The most notable exception is "Her Town, Too," and there is a general paucity of later recordings like "That's Why I'm Here" and "Never Die Young.") Taylor treats the material in his relaxed, assured style, making occasional ironic or self-deprecatory remarks between songs and charming his audience even more. The effect of presenting the songs in a uniform manner is to imply an equality between them, as though the deeper material were less significant and the slighter songs more substantial. But that doesn't keep the set from being a consistently enjoyable listening experience. Taylor remains sorely in need of a retrospective that would bring his work into concise coherence, but this one at least presents most of his best-known material in effective performances. — William Ruhlmann

Original Flying Machine 1967 / Oct. 8, 1996 / Gadfly ✦✦
Original Flying Machine 1967 is comprised of recordings James Taylor made with his band the Flying Machine a year before he signed to Apple Records. At this stage, Taylor was still trying to find his voice, yet that is the very reason why these recordings are of interest to fans. Most of the material on Original Flying Machine 1967 re-appeared on Taylor's eponymous debut album for Apple, while these originals stayed in the can. These arrangements are a bit more full-bodied, featuring the support of a full band, led by guitarist Danny Kortchmar. Though these are a bit more fleshed out, they aren't quite as strong as the later versions. Nevertheless, the album makes for a fascinating one-time listen for most fans. (The 1996 CD reissue features six of the original album's seven songs, adding the unreleased "Kootch's Song" as the seventh song.) — Stephen Thomas Erlewine

Hour Glass / May 20, 1997 / Sony ✦✦✦
James Taylor stopped pushing himself into new musical and lyrical territories in the late '70s, so it doesn't come as a great surprise that Hour Glass, his first studio album in six years, doesn't offer anything new—it's a collection of pleasant, melodic simple songs about love, family, and social activism. That's not necessarily a bad thing, since Taylor has a gift for such material, and on Hour Glass, he sounds as good as ever. The music, in many ways, has greater depth than previous records, since it features cameos from such heavy hitters as Stevie Wonder, Yo-Yo Ma, Shawn Colvin, Michael Brecker, Mark O'Connor, and Branford Marsalis. There are a few songs that fall a little flat, failing to make much of an impression one way or the other, but on the whole Hour Glass is a nice addition to his catalog. — Stephen Thomas Erlewine

Johnnie Taylor

b. May 5, 1938, Crawfordsville, AR
Vocals / Soul, Disco, Soul Blues, Quiet Storm
Aptly dubbed the "Philosopher of Soul" by the Stax publicity department, Johnnie Taylor set the ladies' hearts aflutter during the early '70s with his tender brand of Memphis soul. Taylor wasn't always the sincere crooner he developed into. A Sam Cooke protégé who took over with the Soul Stirrers when Cooke went secular, and who retained a hint of his mentor's mellifluous delivery, Taylor took the same pop route via Cooke's SAR label in 1961. Once he got on the Stax label in 1966, the vocalist forged a sublime blues/soul synthesis with a series of absolutely gorgeous efforts. But there was nothing subtle about Taylor's first No. 1 in 1968: "Who's Making Love," an uncompromising treatise on cheating lovers, with storming brass and slashing guitar. The follow-ups "Take Care of Your Homework" and "Jody's Got Your Girl and Gone" pounded the same message home from different angles. As the decade turned, though, Taylor perceptibly mellowed, turning increasingly to ballads for inspiration—"I Believe in You (You Believe in Me)," "We're Getting Careless with Our Love." By the time he went platinum with the horribly repetitive "Disco Lady" in 1976, the rough edges that made his early work so absorbing were smoothed away, although his recent Mal-

aco output sometimes manages to suggest Taylor's glory years. —*Bill Dahl*

● **The Johnnie Taylor Chronicle** / 1977 / Stax ✦✦✦✦
The definitive Johnnie Taylor retrospective/anthology package. It contains every major Stax hit, some album cuts, and an extensive set of liner notes from Robert Palmer. While the soul hardcore had already purchased it in vinyl, anyone who missed it that time around should immediately rush and get the CD. If you love soul, you can't be without it. —*Ron Wynn*

● **The Best of Johnnie Taylor: Rated X-Traordinaire** / Mar. 12, 1996 / Columbia/Legacy ✦✦✦✦
The 16-track *Rated X-Traordinaire* sets out to rescue the reputation of the Johnnie Taylor of 1976-1980, the period that began with his biggest smash, "Disco Lady," but that found him, so the conventional wisdom goes, a Southern soul man set adrift on the disco wave. Annotator Kalamu ya Salaam argues that "Disco Lady" is not a disco song, and backs this up by noting that the track actually was played by members of Parliament-Funkadelic. True enough, though that only applies to Taylor's debut Columbia album, *Eargasm*. Elsewhere, Taylor did drift, from Muscle Shoals tracks that updated his Stax Memphis sound to tracks that sounded like Marvin Gaye. The early years, 1976 and 1977, were more accomplished than the later ones, and that's where compilation producer Leo Sacks focuses, with 12 of the 16 tracks coming from then. In so doing, he ignores R&B chart singles like "Keep on Dancing" and "Ever Ready," but he satisfies the "best of" title. —*William Ruhlmann*

Bram Tchaikovsky

f. Nov. 10, 1950, Lincolnshire, England
Rock 'n' Roll, New Wave, Power Pop
Bram Tchaikovsky (born Peter Bramall) began playing in local pub-rock bands in Lincolnshire, England, in the late '60s. He joined the Motors in 1977 and was relegated to mere sideman status by the nucleus of the band, songwriters Andy McMaster and Nick Garvey. While waiting on pre-production work for the second Motors album, Tchaikovsky took the opportunity to do some recording of his own. The resulting single, "Sarah Smiles," drew enough interest for him to leave the Motors and form his own band. In addition to its leader, the band Bram Tchaikovsky consisted of Mike Broadbent (bass, keyboards) and Keith Boyce (drums). They signed to the new Radar label in 1978 along with Stiff expatriates Nick Lowe and Elvis Costello. The band showed a great deal of promise with their first album, *Strange Man Changed Man*, fitting in nicely with the growing power-pop movement. The unforgettable "Girl of My Dreams," a true high point of the time, became a minor hit on both sides of the Atlantic. Tchaikovsky continued on through rapid personnel changes for two more albums, *The Russians Are Coming* (released in the US as *Pressure*) in 1980 and *Funland* in 1981. A considerable drop in sales prompted Tchaikovsky to dissolve the band and retire from the music business. —*Chris Woodstra*

● **Strange Man, Changed Man** / 1979 / Polydor ✦✦✦✦
Strange Man Changed Man, remains Bram Tchaikovsky's finest moment. Produced by his former Motors bandmate Nick Garvey on a shoestring buget, the resulting thin sound only serves to enhance the songs, which owe as much to '60s pop as they do to pub/punk rock. The pure pop of "Girl of My Dreams" (a minor hit in the US) perfectly encapsulates late-'70s Brit-pop and stands as one of the classic singles of the era. —*Chris Woodstra*

Pressure / 1980 / Polydor ✦✦✦
Pressure, released in the US as *The Russians Are Coming*, is not quite as strong as the first album but still worthwhile. —*Chris Woodstra*

Funland / May 1981 / Arista ✦✦✦
By the time of the difficult third album, constant personnel changes and general lack of inspiration on the part of the band's leader had taken its toll. The deceptively titled *Funland* is a lackluster effort that effectively ended the band's career. —*Chris Woodstra*

The Teardrop Explodes

f. 1978, Liverpool, England, db. 1983
New Wave, Post-Punk
One of the pivotal groups to emerge from the Liverpool neo-psychedelia community during the late '70s, the Teardrop Explodes was a showcase for Julian Cope, a notoriously eccentric figure whose unfashionable love of Krautrock and hallucinogenic drugs set him distinctly apart from the prevailing punk mentality of the era. Cope formed the band in 1978 after a tenure in the Crucial Three (also comprised of Echo and the Bunnymen's Ian McCulloch and Wah!'s Pete Wylie); taking their name from a panel in a Marvel comic book, the premiere lineup of the Teardrop Explodes also featured guitarist Mick Finkler and drummer Gary Dwyer as well as keyboardist Paul Simpson, with whom Cope previously played in the short-lived A Shallow Madness. Upon signing to Bill Drummond and David Balfe's fledgling Zoo label, the quartet issued

their 1979 debut single "Sleeping Gas," a surreal electro-pop effort distinguished by its swirling keyboard washes; Simpson exited the Teardrop Explodes' ranks in the wake of the record's release, allowing Balfe to assume keyboard and production duties for the bizarre follow-up "Bouncing Babies." After touring with Echo and the Bunnymen, the group concentrated on steamlining the more excessive elements of its sound: the result, the buoyant "Treason (It's Just a Story)," nearly reached the pop charts.

After Finkler was replaced by former Dalek I Love You guitarist Alan Gill, the Teardrop Explodes issued 1980's infectious "When I Dream," which hit the UK Top 50 and even garnered some airplay in the US. Finally, in October the band's debut LP *Kilimanjaro* appeared to rave reviews and respectable sales; early in 1981, the single "Reward" hit the Top Ten, and a subsequent reissue of "Treason (It's Just a Story)" surged into the Top 20. Still, the Teardrop Explodes' roster continued to fluctuate wildly, and soon Gill exited to make room for guitarist Troy Tate in time to record 1981's ambitious *Wilder*, highlighted by the smash "Passionate Friend."

A tour of the States followed, with disastrous results; Tate quickly broke ranks to join Fashion, leaving the remaining trio to begin work on a planned third LP, to be dubbed *Everybody Wants to Shag the Teardrop Explodes*. In the midst of recording, however, Cope dissolved the band; only a 1983 EP dubbed *You Disappear from View* appeared on schedule, although the unfinished sessions were finally released in full in 1990 under their projected title. In the wake of the Teardrop Explodes' breakup, Balfe later re-emerged as the founder of the Food Records label, while Cope embarked on a successful and occasionally brilliant solo career. —*Jason Ankeny*

● **Kilimanjaro** / 1980 / Skyclad ✦✦✦✦
The Teardrop Explodes' debut album was a surprisingly accomplished set of lush, layered psychedelic pop that creates a consistent, dream-like mood. The album was released in different editions in the UK and the US, but the essential qualities of the music remained the same in both versions. —*Stephen Thomas Erlewine*

Wilder / 1981 / Skyclad ✦✦✦
Although the individual songs on the Teardrop Explodes' second album, *Wilder*, were more concise than the ones on their debut, the record wasn't quite as focused or mesmerizing as the debut. Nevertheless, it features a number of fine, compelling moments. —*Stephen Thomas Erlewine*

Piano / 1990 / Document ✦✦
Piano collects the Teardrop Explodes' early recordings, featuring three singles and three tracks recorded for compilations. The songs make it clear the band was still trying to figure out their musical direction, but *Piano* is fascinating listening for dedicated fans of the group. —*Stephen Thomas Erlewine*

Everybody Wants to Shag the Teardrop Explodes / May 1990 / Fontana ✦✦✦✦
Released eight years after their dissolution, *Everybody Wants to Shag the Teardrop Explodes* reconstructs the band's aborted third album, gathering seven outtakes with the four-track *You Disappear from View* EP. Although it isn't as polished as their two official studio albums, *Everybody* is filled with adventurous music and is frequently more exciting than *Wilder*. —*Stephen Thomas Erlewine*

Tears for Fears

f. 1981, Bath, England
New Wave, Pop-Rock, Synth-Pop
Tears for Fears were always more ambitious than the average synth-pop group. From the beginning, the duo of Roland Orzabal and Curt Smith were tackling big subjects—their very name derived from Arthur Janov's primal scream therapy, and his theories were evident throughout their debut, *The Hurting*. Driven by catchy, infectious synth-pop, *The Hurting* became a big hit in their native England, setting the stage for international stardom with their second album, 1985's *Songs from the Big Chair*. On the strength of the singles "Everybody Wants To Rule the World" and "Shout," the record became a major hit, establishing the duo as one of the leading acts of the second generation of MTV stars. Instead of quickly recording a follow-up, Tears for Fears labored over their third album, the psychedelic and jazz-rock-tinged *The Seeds of Love*. While the album was a big hit, it was the end of an era instead of a new beginning. Smith left the group early in the '90s, and Orzabal continued with Tears for Fears, pursuing more sophisticated and pretentious directions to a smaller audience.

Roland Orzabal and Curt Smith met as children in Bath, England. Both boys came from broken homes, and Smith was leaning toward juvenile delinquence. Orzabal, however, turned towards books, eventually discovering Arthur Janov's primal scream therapy, a way of confronting childhood fears that John Lennon embraced after the Beatles disbanded. Orzabal turned Smith on to Janov, but before the duo explored this theory further, they formed the ska-revival band Graduate in the late '70s. After releasing a handful of singles, including "Elvis Should Play Ska," Graduate dissolved in the early '80s, and the duo went on to form Tears for Fears, a synth-pop outfit directly inspired by Janov's writings.

Riding in on the tail end of new wave and new romantic, Tears for Fears—which featured musical contributions from former Graduate keyboardist Ian Stanley on early albums—landed a record contract with Polygram in 1982. The following year, the band released their debut *The Hurting*, which became a major hit in Britain, generating no less than three Top Five hit singles. Two years later, the group released *Songs from the Big Chair*, which demonstrated a more streamlined and soul-influenced sound. *Songs from the Big Chair* became a huge hit in America, rocketing to the top of the charts on the strength of the singles "Everybody Wants to Rule the World" and "Shout," which both hit No. 1, and the No. 3 "Head Over Heels," which were all supported by clever, stylish videos that received heavy MTV airplay.

Instead of quickly following *Songs from the Big Chair* with a new record, Tears for Fears labored over their new record, eventually delivering the layered, beatlesque *The Seeds of Love* in 1989. Featuring soulful vocals from Oleta Adams, who dominated the hit "Woman in Chains," the album became a hit, reaching No. 8, while the single "Sowing the Seeds of Love" reached No. 2 in the US. Again, Tears for Fears spent several years working on the follow-up to *Seeds of Love*, during which time they released the collection *Tears Roll Down (Greatest Hits '82-'92)*. Smith and Orzabal began to quarrel heavily, and Smith left the group in 1992, making Tears for Fears' 1993 comeback *Elemental* essentially a solo record from Orzabal. On the strength of the adult contemporary hit "Break it Down Again," *Elemental* became a modest hit, reaching gold status in the US, yet was hardly up to the group's previous levels. Smith, meanwhile, released a solo album in 1993, *Soul on Board*, which went ignored. Orzabal returned with another Tears for Fears album, *Raoul and the Kings of Spain*, in 1995, which failed to make much of an impact. In late 1996, the group released a rarities collection. —*Stephen Thomas Erlewine*

The Hurting / 1983 / Mercury ✦✦✦✦
Roland Orzabal and Curt Smith's debut featured the morose synth-pop hits "Pale Shelter" and "Mad World." —*Scott Bultman*

Songs from the Big Chair / 1985 / Mercury ✦✦✦✦
Their best album is a good mix of synthesizers and traditional instruments. It includes the hits "Shout," "Head over Heels," and "Everybody Wants to Rule the World." —*Kenneth M. Cassidy*

The Seeds of Love / Sep. 1989 / Fontana ✦✦✦
Their third album was an overreaching effort that (in spite of itself) produced a couple of gems, particularly "Sowing the Seeds of Love" and "Woman in Chains." Oleta Adams' soulful voice added life to the proceedings. —*Rick Clark*

● **Tears Fall Down (The Hits 1982-1992)** / Mar. 17, 1992 / Fontana ✦✦✦✦
All of this duo's hits (plus some other key tracks) are included from throughout their career. It's a perfect overview and (essentially) the only disc to have. This anthology includes "Pale Shelter," "Shout," "Everybody Wants to Rule the World," "Head over Heels," and "Sowing the Seeds of Love," among others. —*Rick Clark*

Elemental / Jun. 22, 1993 / Mercury ✦✦
On *Elemental*, Tears for Fears *is* Roland Orzabal, and he backs away from the cinematic production of *The Seeds of Love*, preferring a more direct and soulful style of pop music that appealed to both adult contemporary and adult alternative radio audiences. While some of the material was a little weak, the record was easily as good as its immediate predecessor. —*Stephen Thomas Erlewine*

Raoul & The King of Spain / Oct. 10, 1995 / Epic ✦✦

Saturnine Martial & Lunatic / Aug. 1996 / Polygram ✦✦✦
Spanning the group's prime period of 1983 to 1993, *Saturnine Martial & Lunatic* is an odd, incomplete collection of B-sides and rarities from Tears For Fears. Although this material is valuable for hardcore fans, it only scratches the surface of the group's B-sides. Nevertheless, several prime tracks—including the non-LP UK hit single "The Way You Are" and a cover of David Bowie's "Ashes to Ashes"—are featured, which makes it worthwhile for dedicated fans, even though its incompleteness (especially since it comes at the expense of several weaker latter-day cuts) will make *Saturnine Martial & Lunatic* a frustrating listen. —*Stephen Thomas Erlewine*

Teenage Fanclub

f. 1989, Glasgow, Scotland
Group / Rock 'n' Roll, Alternative Pop-Rock, Power Pop, Pop-Rock
Teenage Fanclub are three singer-songwriters from Glasgow and a drummer who make unearthly pop music but remain underappreciated. So what else is new? Teenage Fanclub formed in the late '80s in the Glasgow suburb of Bellshill. Songwriter and guitarist Norman

Blake, formerly of the BMX Bandits, met songwriter/guitarist Raymond McGinley in the Glasgow clubs. Initially known as the Boy Hairdressers, the Fanclub was soon joined by songwriter and bassist Gerard Love and drummer Brendan O'Hare . Though Mersey Beat is at the core of their shimmering pop tunes, unlike the Beatles, it's often difficult to distinguish the voices of Norman, Gerry, and Raymond as their songs serve the band entity as one very pleasing whole. But like the Beatles, they sing with American accents.

Even before their Matador debut, *A Catholic Education*, the indie sensation of 1989, the band had already made a splash as the pick to click in their native UK's trendy music press. It was their second album, *Bandwagonesque* for Geffen, that put the Scots on the pop music map. Long before the record was released, insiders talked of how this album was going to blow some minds. Indeed it did, and ended up on most critics' ten-best lists for the year. But not because it was a continuation of the dark and slow indie-trend formula they created for Matador; rather it sounded like a lost Big Star album. The Fanclub made no secret about their love for the obscure American pop band and it was a sound that stuck over the course of their next two albums, *Thirteen* and *Grand Prix*, both for Geffen. Paul Quinn replaced O'Hare for the latter recording. Often relegated to opening-band status, the band didn't even tour their 1995 album in the US save for some dates opening for Weezer. Their awaited fifth album, *Songs from Northern Britain*, is tipped to be a pop masterpiece. So what else is new? —*Denise Sullivan*

Catholic Education / 1990 / Matador ✦✦✦
A very displeasing record, unless grinding guitars and indistinguishable lyrics and vocals are what you're after. Released on the cusp of the grunge explosion, the band were in the pocket trendwise, but ironically, they dumped the sound no sooner had they cast the mold for the next five years of indie-rock. Only the single "Everything Flows" is of interest. —*Denise Sullivan*

● **Bandwagonesque** / Nov. 19, 1991 / DGC ✦✦✦✦
Might as well be subtitled "Big Star Four" for its resemblance to the obscure Memphis pop band. "What You Do to Me" is an insta-pop classic, as are "December" and "Star Sign." But for all it's attention to the power-pop form, this record could never have been made in the '70s for all its shrewd, indie-rock touches. "The Concept" sports the controversial line, "She don't do drugs but she does the pill," that had humorless rock critics and indie-fans inflamed. They're joking. Geddit? —*Denise Sullivan*

Thirteen / Nov. 9, 1993 / DGC ✦✦✦✦
A reaction to having been the victim of hype and their diminished expectations as the next great pop hope, the Fanclub took their time with this overworked and overwrought collection of songs that take turns at stabbing the music industry, in title and lyrics: "Radio," "120 Minutes," and "Commercial Alternative" to name but a few highlights, and the George Harrison-esque "The Cabbage" is one of their greatest songs ever. Previously underrated by critics and fans alike. —*Denise Sullivan*

Deep Fried Fanclub / 1995 / Paperhouse/Fire ✦✦
An odds-and-sods collection of outtakes and B-sides, *Deep Fried Fanclub* is woefully short on memorable material, making it worthwhile only for the most devoted fans of the group. —*Stephen Thomas Erlewine*

Teenage Fanclub Have Lost It / 1995 / Creation ✦✦✦✦
The band took to a living room to record some off-the-cuff acoustic versions of songs from each of their albums; "Don't Look Back," "Everything Flows," "Starsign," and "120 Mins." It works, but the between—song noodling is annoying and makes it difficult for radio DJs and home tapers to segue. —*Denise Sullivan*

Grand Prix / Jul. 3, 1995 / DGC ✦✦✦✦
The band wisely trade in the oh-so-trendy wall of guitar sound they so studiously employed for a lighter touch, so it's the songwriting that sings through this time out. Guitars and harmonies ring out in "About You"; the same riff is slowed down for "Don't Look Back"; "Neil Jung" is a twin-guitar gem and "I'll Make It Clear" chimes. It's astonishing that this band hasn't become permanently embedded in the hearts of rock fans everywhere. —*Denise Sullivan*

Television

f. 1973, New York, NY, **db.** 1978
Punk, Proto-Punk
Television were one of the most creative bands to emerge from New York's punk scene of the mid-'70s, creating an influential new guitar vocabulary. While guitarists Tom Verlaine and Richard Lloyd liked to jam, they didn't follow the accepted rock structures for improvisation—they removed the blues while retaining the raw energy of garage rock, adding complex, lyrical solo lines that recalled both jazz and rock. With its angular rhythms and fluid leads, Television's music always went in unconventional directions, laying the groundwork for many of the

guitar-based post-punk pop groups of the late '70s and '80s.

In the early '70s, Television began as the Neon Boys, a group featuring guitarist/vocalist Tom Verlaine, drummer Billy Ficca, and bassist Richard Hell. At the end of 1973, the group reunited under the name Television, adding rhythm guitarist Richard Lloyd. The following year, the band made its live debut at New York's Townhouse theater and began to build up an underground following. Soon, their fan base was large enough that Verlaine was able to persuade CBGB's to begin featuring live bands on a regular basis; the club would become an important venue for punk and new wave bands. That year, Verlaine played guitar on Patti Smith's first single, "Hey Joe"/"Piss Factory," as well as writing a book of poetry with the singer.

Television recorded a demo tape for Island Records with Brian Eno in 1975, yet the label decided not to sign the band. Hell left the band after the recording of the demo tape, forming the Heartbreakers with former New York Doll guitarist Johnny Thunders; the following year, he began a solo career supported by the Voivods, releasing a debut album, *Blank Generation*, in 1977. Hell was replaced by ex-Blondie bassist Fred Smith, and Television recorded "Little Johnny Jewel," releasing it on their own Ork record label. "Little Johnny Jewel" became an underground hit, attracting the attention of major record labels. In 1976, the band released a British EP on Stiff Records, which expanded their reputation. They signed with Elektra Records and began recording their debut album.

Marquee Moon, the group's first album, was released in early 1977 to great critical acclaim, yet it failed to attract a wide audience in America; in the UK, it reached No. 28 on the charts, launching the Top 40 singles "Prove It" and "Foxhole." Television supported Blondie on the group's 1977 tour, but the shows didn't increase the group's following significantly.

Television released its second album, *Adventure*, in the spring of 1978. While its American sales were better than those of *Marquee Moon*, the record didn't make the charts; in Britain, it became a Top Ten hit. Months later, the group suddenly broke up, largely due to tensions between the two guitarists. Smith rejoined Blondie, while Verlaine and Lloyd both pursued solo careers; Lloyd also played on John Doe's first solo album, as well as joining Matthew Sweet's supporting band with the 1991 album, *Girlfriend*.

Nearly 14 years after their breakup, Television re-formed in late 1991, recording a new album for Capitol Records. The reunited band began their comeback with a performance at England's Glastonbury summer festival in 1992, releasing *Television* a couple months later. The album received good reviews, as did the tour that followed, yet the reunion was short-lived—the group disbanded again in early 1993. *—Stephen Thomas Erlewine*

★ **Marquee Moon** / 1977 / Elektra ✦✦✦✦✦
Marquee Moon is a revolutionary album, but it's a subtle, understated revolution. Without question, it is a guitar rock album—it's astonishing to hear the interplay between Tom Verlaine and Richard Lloyd—but it is a guitar rock album unlike any other. Where their predecessors in the New York punk scene, most notably the Velvet Underground, had fused blues structures with avant-garde flourishes, Television completely strips away any sense of swing or groove, even when they are playing standard three-chord changes. *Marquee Moon* is comprised entirely of tense garage rockers that spiral into heady intellectual territory, which is achieved through the group's long, interweaving instrumental sections, not through Tom Verlaine's words. That alone made *Marquee Moon* a trailblazing album—it's impossible to imagine post-punk soundscapes without it. Of course, it wouldn't have had such an impact if Verlaine hadn't written an excellent set of songs that conveyed a fractured urban mythology unlike any of his contemporaries. From the nervy opener "See No Evil" to the majestic title track, there is simply not a bad song on the entire record. And what has kept *Marquee Moon* fresh over the years is how Television fleshes out Verlaine's poetry into sweeping sonic epics. *—Stephen Thomas Erlewine*

Adventure / 1978 / Elektra ✦✦✦✦
This is a subdued set in both sound and content, but the songs sport stronger melodies, and "Glory" anticipates R.E.M.'s sound. *—John Floyd*

Blow Up / 1982 / ROIR ✦✦✦
Crappy fidelity mars this live set, but Verlaine and Lloyd conjure some scarifying and beautiful six-string magic. *—John Floyd*

Television / Sep. 28, 1992 / Capitol ✦✦✦
It's been 13 years since New York avant-rockers Television split after releasing the seminal/influential *Marquee Moon* and its follow-up *Adventure*. Now that the rest of the music universe has caught up with the group's sparse but progressive sensibilities, the four original members have reunited for the new *Television*. Once again, guitarist and nerve center Tom Verlaine's dry, '50s-instrumental, murder-mystery style entwines masterfully with Richard Lloyd's more emotive, pealing riffs. The performances range from hypnotically atonal to ragingly cascading, the mood from paranoid to blissful. *Television's* highlights

include the blistering ecstasy of "Call Mr. Lee," and the trance and dance of "Shane, She Wrote This." *—Roch Parisien*

Television Personalities

f. 1977, London, England
Alternative Pop-Rock, New Wave, Post-Punk
Britain's Television Personalities enjoyed one of the new wave era's longest, most erratic, and most far-reaching careers: over the course of a musical evolution which led them from wide-eyed, shambling pop to the outer reaches of psychedelia and back, the group directly influenced virtually every major pop uprising of the period, with artists as diverse as feedback virtuosos the Jesus and Mary Chain, twee-pop titans the Pastels, and lo-fi kingpins Pavement readily acknowledging the TVPs' inspiration.

The Television Personalities were the brainchild of singer-songwriter Dan Treacy, who grew so inspired by the nascent punk movement that he recorded a 1977 single, "14th Floor," with his friends in the group O Level. The BBC's John Peel became a vocal supporter of the group—soon dubbed the Television Personalities—and a year later they issued an EP, *Where's Bill Grundy Now?*, which featured their lone hit, "Part-Time Punks."

Always a loose-knit group, the first relatively stable TVP line-up consisted of Treacy, organist/vocalist Ed Ball and guitarist Joe Foster, who recorded the band's 1980 debut ...And Don't the Kids Just Love It, a step into psychedelic pop typified by songs like "I Know Where Syd Barrett Lives." Treacy and Ball soon founded their own label, Whaam! (later renamed Dreamworld after threats from George Michael's attorneys), to issue 1981's *Mummy You're Not Watching Me*, which made the Personalities one of the figureheads of a London psychedelia revival.

Ball exited around the time of the release of 1982's *They Could Have Been Bigger than the Beatles*, a collection of re-recordings along with renditions of the Creation's "Making Time" and "Painter Man." 1984's dark, moody *The Painted Word* was followed by the 1985 live set *Chocolat-Art*, by which point the TVPs were in dire straits; broke and without a label, the group could do little but infrequently perform live for several years, and were forced to watch the C-86/anorak pop groundswell—a movement they directly presaged—from the sidelines.

Comprised of Treacy, ex-Swell Map Jowe Head, and drummer Jeffrey Bloom, the band finally won a contract with Fire Records in 1989, and resurfaced later that year with the EP *Salvador Dali's Garden Party*, followed in 1990 by the mod-flavored *Privilege*. After a handful of singles and EPs, the Television Personalities issued the 1992 double-LP *Closer to God*; despite critical approval, the album failed to find an audience, and Treacy reportedly fell prey to depression and drug problems. After several more years of occasional singles, they issued the harrowing *I Was a Mod Before You Was a Mod*, followed in 1996 by *Top Gear* and *Made in Japan*. *—Jason Ankeny*

Bill Grundy / 1979 / Rough Trade ✦✦✦

...And Don't the Kids Just Love It / 1980 / Razor & Tie ✦✦✦✦
The cover of ...And Don't the Kids Just Love It—a collage bringing together supermodel Twiggy and *The Avengers'* John Steed—is a strong indication of where the Television Personalities are coming from: their debut is a loving ode to '60s-era pop and pop culture, referencing movies ("Look Back in Anger"), Kinks-like class commentary ("Geoffrey Ingram") and psychedelic casualties ("I Know Where Syd Barrett Lives"). *—Jason Ankeny*

Mummy You're Not Watching Me / 1981 / Whaam! ✦✦✦✦
Where the TVPs merely tested the waters of psychedelia on their debut releases, they take the full plunge on the lo-fi *Mummy You're Not Watching Me*, which replaces the pop-culture references of the debut ...And Don't the Kids Just Love It for the high culture of acid-pop excursions including "Lichtenstein Painting," "David Hockney's Diaries" and "Painting by Numbers." *—Jason Ankeny*

They Could Have Been Bigger than the Beatles / 1982 / Whaam! ✦✦✦

The Painted Word / 1984 / Whaam! ✦✦✦
A more cleanly-produced TVPs record than most of their previous efforts, *The Painted Word* is also a more serious album, less whimsical but no less charming; favoring a subtle, droning pop sound, tracks like the politically-charged "Back to Vietnam" and the lovely "Someone to Share My Life With" are heartfelt and resonant, foreshadowing the more dramatic twists taken by Dan Treacy's songwriting following the band's long late-1980s layoff. *—Jason Ankeny*

Chocolat-Art / 1985 / Pastell ✦✦✦

● **Privilege** / 1989 / Fire ✦✦✦✦
Given that the crisp *Privilege* is the Television Personalities' first studio LP in four years, Dan Treacy has every right to be in a less-than-sunny mood—songs like "All My Dreams Are Dead," "This Time There's No Happy Ending" and "Sad Mona Lisa" are to be expected when a fertile songwriting talent finds himself without means of recording and releas-

ing new material. The end result is one of the group's most personal and dark records, although the wonderful "Salvador Dali's Art Party"—which runs down all of the luminaries on the guest list—is a return to the psychedelic name-dropping of the group's formative years. —*Jason Ankeny*

Camping in France / 1991 / Overground ✦✦✦
Closer to God / 1992 / Seed ✦✦✦✦
The TVPs' most musically accessible album to date, *Closer to God* is also their most gloomy (although it's a ray of sunshine when compared to its follow-up, *I Was a Mod Before You Was a Mod*). Embellished by bright arrangements, strings and horns, tracks like "This Heart's Not Made of Stone" and "Coming Home Soon" are white lies, upbeat productions masking downbeat songs; more honest are "My First Nervous Breakdown" and "Very Dark Today," which make no bones about the depths of Dan Treacy's despair. —*Jason Ankeny*

Yes Darling, But is It Art? (Early Singles & Rarities) / Feb. 14, 1995 / Fire ✦✦✦✦
A superb, generous introduction to the Television Personalites' early years, *Yes Darling, But Is It Art?* assembles rarities and obscurities from singles, EPs, and various artists' collections dating back to the group's debut "14th Floor" and including their lone hit "Part-Time Punks." —*Jason Ankeny*

I Was a Mod Before You Was a Mod / Oct. 1995 / Overground ✦✦✦
Virtually a Dan Treacy solo record, *I Was a Mod Before You Was a Mod* strips away all remaining vestiges of the buoyancy long associated with the Television Personalities, leaving behind a harrowing portrait of alienation, desperation and self-loathing; "A Stranger to Myself," "Haunted," "Evan Doesn't Ring Me Anymore," "A Long Time Gone," and "I Can See My Whole World Crashing Down" are frighteningly bleak and painfully affecting. —*Jason Ankeny*

Temple of the Dog

f. 1990, Seattle, WA, **db.** 1990
Hard Rock, Alternative Pop-Rock, Grunge
Temple of the Dog was a one-album project conceived in 1990. The purpose of Temple of the Dog was to pay tribute to the late Andrew Wood, the lead singer of Mother Love Bone, who died of a heroin overdose in 1990. Following his death, Mother Love Bone broke up, but Wood's bandmates Jeff Ament (bass) and Stone Gossard (guitar) decided to continue working together. Before Ament and Gossard formed a new band, they assembled Temple of the Dog, recruiting Chris Cornell (vocals) and Matt Cameron (drums) from Soundgarden to form the core of the group. Temple of the Dog also featured contributions from the then-unknown vocalist Eddie Vedder and guitarist Mike McCready.

Temple of the Dog recorded their eponymous album in 1990, releasing it the following year on A&M Records. The album received positive reviews upon its release, but it didn't chart until the summer of 1992, when Pearl Jam—a band Ament, Gossard, Vedder, McCready and drummer Dave Krusen formed in late 1990 after the completion of the Temple of the Dog album—had a Top Ten album with their debut record, *Ten*. Following the success of *Ten*, A&M re-released "Hunger Strike"—a duet between Vedder and Cornell—as a video and single, and the album quickly scaled the charts, reaching the Top Ten and going platinum before the end of 1992. —*Stephen Thomas Erlewine*

Temple of the Dog / Dec. 1990 / A&M ✦✦✦✦
While it doesn't sound all that different from either Soundgarden or Pearl Jam, *Temple of the Dog* does feature some of the finest music that members of either band have ever made. Chris Cornell displays a better grasp of melody and song structure than he ever had on any previous Soundgarden album, and Eddie Vedder shows signs of developing into a distinctive, original vocalist. But the real power of the album is in the guitars of Stone Gossard and the rhythm section of Jeff Ament and Matt Cameron; together, they make the occasionally clichéd tributes to the late Andrew Wood into a genuinely moving, heartfelt elegy for their departed friend. —*Stephen Thomas Erlewine*

The Temptations

f. 1960, Detroit, MI
Soul, R&B, Motown
Thanks to their fine-tuned choreography—and even finer harmonies—the Temptations became the definitive male vocal group of the 1960s; one of Motown's most elastic acts, they tackled both lush pop and politically-charged funk with equal flair, and weathered a steady stream of changes in personnel and consumer tastes with rare dignity and grace.

The Temptations' initial five-man lineup formed in Detroit in 1961 as a merger of two local vocal groups, the Primes and the Distants. Baritone Otis Williams, Elbridge (aka El, or Al) Bryant and bass vocalist Melvin Franklin were longtime veterans of the Detroit music scene when they joined together as the Distants, who in 1959 recorded the sin-

gle "Come On" for the local Northern label. Around the same time, the Primes, a trio comprised of tenor Eddie Kendricks, Paul Williams (no relation to Otis), and Kell Osborne, relocated to the Motor City from their native Alabama; they quickly found success locally, and their manager even put together a girl group counterpart dubbed the Primettes. (Later, three of the Primettes—Diana Ross, Mary Wilson, and Florence Ballard—formed the Supremes.)

In 1961, the Primes disbanded, but not before Otis Williams saw them perform live, where he was impressed both by Kendricks' vocal prowess and Paul Williams' choreography skills. Soon, Otis Williams, Paul Williams, Bryant, Franklin, and Kendricks joined together as the Elgins; after a name change to the Temptations, they signed to the Motown subsidiary Miracle, where they released a handful of singles over the ensuing months. Only one, the 1962 effort "Dream Come True," achieved any commercial success, however, and in 1963, Bryant either resigned or was fired after physically attacking Paul Williams.

The Tempts' fortunes changed dramatically in 1964 when they recruited tenor David Ruffin to replace Bryant; after entering the studio with writer/producer Smokey Robinson, they emerged with the pop smash "The Way You Do the Things You Do," the first in a series of 37 career Top Ten hits. With Robinson again at the helm, they returned in 1965 with their signature song, "My Girl," a No. 1 pop and R&B hit; other Top 20 hits that year included "It's Growing," "Since I Lost My Baby," "Don't Look Back," and "My Baby."

In 1966, the Tempts recorded another Robinson hit, "Get Ready," before forgoing his smooth popcraft for the harder-edged soul of producers Norman Whitfield and Brian Holland. After spotlighting Kendricks on the smash "Ain't Too Proud to Beg," the group allowed Ruffin to take control over a string of hits including "Beauty's Only Skin Deep" and "(I Know) I'm Losing You." Beginning around 1967, Whitfield assumed full production control, and their records became ever rougher and more muscular, as typified by the 1968 success "I Wish It Would Rain."

After Ruffin failed to appear at a 1968 live performance, the other four Tempts fired him; he was replaced by ex-Contour Dennis Edwards, whose less polished voice adapted perfectly to the psychedelic-influenced soul period the group entered following the success of the single "Cloud Nine." As the times changed, so did the group, and as the 1960s drew to a close, the Temptations' music became overtly political; in the wake of "Cloud Nine"—its title a thinly-veiled drug allegory—came records like "Run Away Child, Running Wild," "Psychedelic Shack," and "Ball of Confusion (That's What the World Is Today)."

After the chart-topping success of the gossamer ballad "Just My Imagination (Running Away with Me)" in 1971, Kendricks exited for a solo career. Soon, Paul Williams left the group as well; long plagued by alcoholism and other personal demons, he was eventually discovered dead from a self-inflicted gunshot on August 17, 1973 at the age of 34. In their stead the remaining trio recruited tenors Damon Harris and Richard Street; after the 1971 hit "Superstar (Remember How You Got Where You Are)," they returned in 1972 with the brilliant No. 1 single "Papa Was a Rolling Stone."

While the Tempts hit the charts regularly throughout 1973 with "Masterpiece," "Let Your Hair Down," and "The Plastic Man," their success as a pop act gradually dwindled as the 1970s wore on. After Harris exited in 1975 (replaced by tenor Glenn Leonard), the group cut 1976's *The Temptations Do the Temptations*, their final album for Motown. With Louis Price taking over for Dennis Edwards, they signed to Atlantic, and attempted to reach the disco market with the LPs *Bare Back* and *Hear to Tempt You*. After Edwards returned to the fold (resulting in Price's hasty exit), they re-entered the Motown stable, and scored a 1980 hit with "Power. "In 1982, Ruffin and Kendricks returned for *Reunion*, which also included all five of the current Tempts; a tour followed, but problems with Motown, as well as personal differences, cut Ruffin and Kendricks' tenures short.

In the years that followed, the Temptations continued touring and recording, although by the 1990s they were essentially an oldies act; only Otis Williams, who published his autobiography in 1988, remained from the original lineup. The intervening years were marked by tragedy: after touring in the late '80s with Eddie Kendricks and Dennis Edwards as a member of the "Tribute to the Temptations" package tour, David Ruffin died on June 1, 1991 after overdosing on cocaine; he was 50 years old. On October 5, 1992, Kendricks died at the age of 52 of lung cancer, and on February 23, 1995, 52-year-old Melvin Franklin passed away after suffering a brain seizure. —*Jason Ankeny*

★ **Anthology** / Feb. 1973 / Motown ✦✦✦✦✦
The double-disc/triple-LP set *Anthology* is a comprehensive collection that features all of the Temptations' major hit singles, as well as the best of the group's lesser-known hit singles and album tracks. For fans wanting a more extensive compilation than the single-disc greatest hits collection, but unwilling to invest in the multi-disc box set *Emperors of Soul*, *Anthology* is the ideal purchase. —*Stephen Thomas Erlewine*

● **All the Million-Sellers** / 1982 / Motown ✦✦✦✦
An excellent anthology, even though the Temptations had many great tunes that weren't big sellers. But it does contain almost every major hit, and they're well-mastered versions. The original Temptations anthology is probably still preferable, but this ranks as one of their better specialty reissues. —*Ron Wynn*

25th Anniversary / 1986 / Motown ✦✦✦
Motown celebrated the Temptations' 25th anniversary by issuing a retrospective/anthology album complete with an eight-page booklet that offered more details about the group's accomplishments than the three-record *Anthology* had years earlier. It was also interesting as to what songs they included ("Cloud Nine," "Don't Look Back," "Papa Was a Rolling Stone," "Power," "My Girl" and "Since I Lost My Baby," among others) and excluded ("Girl Why You Wanna Make Me Blue," "Ball Of Confusion (That's What the World Is Today)," and "Way You Do the Things You Do"). They fleshed the set out with previously unreleased tracks, none of them surpassing prior Temptations hits. —*Ron Wynn*

Hum Along and Dance: More of the Best (1963-1974) / Feb. 16, 1993 / Rhino ✦✦✦
This 18-track compilation contains Temptations B-sides, non-hit cuts and obscure sides recorded from 1963-1974. It includes such sumptuous ballads as "What Love Has Joined Together" and "Gonna Keep On Trying Till I Win Your Love," plus uptempo wailers and an occasional dud ("Stop the War Now"). The early tracks show the group evolving from its doo wop roots into soul's premier group. While the cuts on this disc aren't the ones that made the Temptations popular music institutions, they're still a vital part of their legacy. —*Ron Wynn*

Emperors of Soul / Sep. 20, 1994 / Motown ✦✦✦✦
The Temptations were unquestionably one of Motown's greatest groups, recording a large number of classic singles. They were also one of the handful of Motown groups that were able to successfully make the transition from the '60s to the '70s, giving them a sizable amount of quality material from both decades. *Emperors of Soul*, a lavishly produced five-CD box set, draws from the Temptations' entire career, treating all aspects of it with equal respect. For the dedicated fan, the box set is a treasure—the sound is great and there are numerous rarities. However, for most listeners, it is simply too much music, featuring too many unfamiliar songs. —*Stephen Thomas Erlewine*

☆ **Anthology [1995]** / May 23, 1995 / Motown ✦✦✦✦✦
There were three versions of this collection (first released in 1973) that provided a comprehensive overview of their career at Motown. The second (1986) collection was an update that featured digitally remastered sound and later hits that were not featured in the earlier incarnation, like "Shakey Ground" (1975), "Power" (1980), and the excellent "Treat Her like a Lady" (1983). Unfortunately, the updated 1995 collection (like the previously two incarnations) omits many fine tracks recorded and released before their 1964 breakthrough, like "I Want a Love I Can See" (1962) and "Check Yourself" (1963). Even so, *Anthology* is a more concise, less expensive alternative to the box-set *Emperors of Soul*. —*John Lowe*

One by One: Best of Their Solo Years / Mar. 19, 1996 / Motown ✦✦✦
An interesting concept for a compilation, devoted to the most significant solo tracks by Temptations vocalists David Ruffin, Eddie Kendricks, Dennis Edwards, and Paul Williams. In other words, this two-CD, 35-track compilation isn't really a Temptations CD at all, although it's more appropriate to list it under their entry than anywhere else. The ex-Temps' solo outings had their high points, like David Ruffin's Top Ten hit "My Whole World Ended (The Moment You Left Me)," and Eddie Kendricks' "Keep on Truckin'." But overall, this isn't as anything special, with a pleasantly generic late-period Motown sound that sometimes begs the inevitable unfavorable comparisons with the Temptations' own work, from the perspectives of both material and execution. Kendricks comes off best here, but Motown fans will be interested in the chance to track down many obscure minor hits and flops by the singers, and even a few unreleased cuts. It's too late to do anything about it, but the best of these solo hits would have been far more appropriate selections for the *Emperors of Soul* box than most of the group-performed post-"Papa Was a Rolling Stone" material that made the cut. —*Richie Unterberger*

Ultimate Collection / Mar. 25, 1997 / Motown ✦✦✦✦
The Ultimate Collection is just that, a superb introduction to the Tempts' greatest hits. Included are 16 of the group's Top Ten smashes, among them "My Girl," "Get Ready," "Ain't Too Proud to Beg," "(I Know) I'm Losing You," "You're My Everything," "I Wish It Would Rain," "I Can't Get Next to You," "Ball of Confusion," "Just My Imagination," and "Papa Was a Rolling Stone." —*Jason Ankeny*

10cc

f. 1972, Manchester, England
Art-Rock/Progressive-Rock, Soft Rock, Pop-Rock

Deriving their name from the metric total of semen ejaculated by the average male, the tongue-in-cheek British art-pop band 10cc comprised an all-star roster of Manchester-based musicians: vocalist/guitarist Graham Gouldman was a former member of the Mockingbirds and the author of hits for the Yardbirds, the Hollies, Herman's Hermits and Jeff Beck; singer/guitarist Eric Stewart was an alum of Wayne Fontana and the Mindbenders; and vocalists/multi-instrumentalists Kevin Godley and Lol Creme were both highly regarded studio players. Formed in 1970, 10cc began as a session unit dubbed Hotlegs; after establishing residence at Stewart's Strawberry Studios, Hotlegs scored a surprise UK smash with the single "Neanderthal Man," subsequently issuing an LP, *Thinks: School Times* and touring with the Moody Blues.

After signing to Jonathan King's UK label and rechristening themselves 10cc (a name suggested by King himself), the group backed Neil Sedaka before recording 1972's "Donna," a sly satire of late-1950s doo wop. The single reached the No. 2 position on the British charts, establishing not only a long-running string of major hits but also the quartet's fondness for ironic and affectionate reclamations of musty pop styles. The follow-up, "Rubber Bullets," topped the charts in 1973, and both the subsequent single "The Dean and I" (a nostalgic look at academia recalling Jerry Lee Lewis' "High School Confidential") and an eponymously titled debut LP further solidified 10cc as a major force in British pop.

While 1974's *Sheet Music* and singles including the Brian Wilson-esque "Wall Street Shuffle," "Silly Love," and "Life Is a Minestrone" continued 10cc's dominance of the UK charts, they found the American market virtually impenetrable prior to the release of 1975's "I'm Not in Love," which topped the charts at home and climbed as high as No. 2 in the States. After 1975's *The Original Soundtrack* and the next year's *How Dare You!*, Godley and Creme exited to focus on video production as well as developing the Gizmo, a guitar-modification device the duo invented. In the wake of their departure, Gouldman and Stewart continued on alone, enlisting the aid of session men to record 1977's *Deceptive Bends*, highlighted by the perennial "The Things We Do for Love." After recruiting guitarist Rick Fenn, keyboardist Tony O'Malley and drummer Stuart Tosh as full-time members, 10cc returned in 1978 with *Bloody Tourists*, which yielded the No. 1 reggae nod "Dreadlock Holiday." Following unsuccessful efforts, including 1980's *Look Hear?*, 1981's *10 Out of 10*, and 1983's *Window in the Jungle*, the group disbanded; while Stewart produced Sad Cafe and worked with Paul McCartney, Gouldman supervised recordings from the Ramones and Gilbert O'Sullivan before joining Andrew Gold in the duo Wax. In 1992, the original lineup of 10cc reunited for the LP *Meanwhile*, while only Gouldman and Stewart remained for 1993's *Mirror Mirror*. —*Jason Ankeny*

● **10 CC/Sheet Music** / 1973 / DCC ✦✦✦✦
This includes both of 10cc's first two albums on a single disc. The self-titled debut featured material that spoofed lightweight late-'50s/early-'60s pop, with songs like "Donna" (which became a No. 2 UK hit) and "Johnny Don't Do It." "Rubber Bullets," off that album, became a No. 1 UK hit, reaching No. 73 stateside. On *Sheet Music*, 10cc took a more sophisticated arty direction. With that album, they became favorites of college-radio programmers, who liked the band's clever pretensions. Highlights on *Sheet Music* include "Wall Street Shuffle" and "The Worst Band in the World." Even though none of the band's major hits are here, this is probably the best starting place for the uninitiated. —*Rick Clark*

The Original Soundtrack / 1975 / Mercury ✦✦✦
There are some very nice-*sounding* songs here. The atmospheric "I'm Not in Love" was a worldwide hit. "Brand New Day" and "Second Sitting for the Last Supper" are highlights, but extended pieces like "Une Nuit À Paris" come off like art-pop for the terminally cute. —*Rick Clark*

How Dare You? / 1976 / Mercury ✦✦✦
"Lazy Days" and the title cut are nice, and fans of the band champion tracks like "I'm Mandy, Fly Me," "Art for Art's Sake," and "I Want to Rule the World" as evidence of 10cc's smarts, but the end result is a little too smug at times. In terms of production, 10cc's ultra-clean production sound is impressive. —*Rick Clark*

Deceptive Bends / 1977 / Mercury ✦✦✦
After *How Dare You*, Lol Creme and Kevin Godley left Eric Stewart and Graham Gouldman to work on their own devices. The result was *Deceptive Bends*, a poppier, at times McCartneyish album, which produced three hits: "People in Love," "Good Morning Judge," and the internationally successful "The Things We Do for Love." —*Rick Clark*

● **The Best of 10cc [uk]** / 1997 / Mercury ✦✦✦✦
The Best of 10cc contains the bulk of the group's hits, including "Neanderthal Man," "Donna," "Rubber Bullets," "The Dean & I," "I'm Not in Love," and "The Things We Do for Love," making it a fine introduction and distillation for casual fans. —*Stephen Thomas Erlewine*

10,000 Maniacs

f. 1981, Jamestown, NY
Alternative Pop-Rock, Folk-Rock

10,000 Maniacs (named after the low-budget horror movie *2,000 Mani-*

acs) was formed in Jamestown, NY, in 1981 by singer Natalie Merchant and guitarist John Lombardo. Other members of the sextet were Robert Buck (guitar), Steven Gustafson (bass), Dennis Drew (keyboards), and Jerry Ausugstyniak (drums). The group gigged extensively and recorded independently before signing with Elektra and making *The Wishing Chair* in 1985. Cofounder Lombardo left the band in 1986, and they continued as a quintet, releasing the second album, *In My Tribe*, in 1987. This album broke into the charts, where it stayed 77 weeks, peaking at No. 37. *Blind Man's Zoo*, the 1989 follow-up, hit No. 13 and went gold.

After 1992's *Our Time in Eden* had finished its run on the charts, Natalie Merchant announced that she was leaving for a solo career. *MTV Unplugged* was released a few months after her departure. The remaining 10,000 Maniacs decided to continue performing, adding the folk-rock duo John & Mary. Merchant released her first solo album, *Tiger Lily*, in the summer of 1995. — *William Ruhlmann*

Human Conflict Number Five / 1982 / Mark ♦♦

Secrets of the I Ching / 1983 / Christian Burial Music ♦♦

The Wishing Chair / 1985 / Elektra ♦♦♦
Put simply, 10,000 Maniacs sound a lot like Fairport Convention with Sandy Denny, so it's appropriate that Fairport's original producer, Joe Boyd, was brought in to handle their major-label debut. The result is a gentle folk/rock record that highlights the haunting voice of Natalie Merchant. — *William Ruhlmann*

● **In My Tribe** / 1987 / Elektra ♦♦♦♦
The band's breakthrough album and creative high point, *In My Tribe* offers a survey in social concerns including child abuse ("What's the Matter Here"), illiteracy ("Cherry Tree"), war ("Gun Shy") and the environment ("Campfire Song")—all tackled subtly and tastefully without too much preaching or pretension and in believable, real-life situations. Producer Peter Asher, whose credits include James Taylor and Linda Ronstadt, provides the perfect sheen—the group's pleasant folk-pop lends itself nicely to the '70s-styled singer-songwriter production. In the end, the album proves powerful not for the ideas (they've been covered before) but rather for the graceful execution and pure listenability. *In My Tribe* has served as one of the soundtracks for P.C. living and was required listening on college campuses in the late '80s. — *Chris Woodstra*

Blind Man's Zoo / May 1989 / Elektra ♦♦♦
After the success of *In My Tribe*, it would be expected that hordes of bands would take a stab at the market with their own second-rate versions of the album—it's disappointing that 10,000 Maniacs would be one of them, churning out not only *In My Tribe, Pt. 2*, but an inferior copy at that. It's not that the album is bad—certainly they've perfected their sound and in many cases, the songs are catchier this time out—but in handling the issues (there's no shortage of them), Merchant has become more direct and obvious. For all of its earnestness and good-intentioned teachings, *Blind Man's Zoo* ultimately fails in its heavy-handed and generally uninteresting approach. — *Chris Woodstra*

Hope Chest: The Fredonia Recordings 1982-1983 / Oct. 1990 / Elektra ♦♦♦
Hope Chest collects the ultra-rare early recordings of the band—the *Human Conflict Number 5* EP from 1982 and *Secrets of the I Ching* from 1983—remastered and resequenced presumably for easier listening. While the songs are predictably unfocused and full of underdeveloped (though ambitious) ideas, these recordings give an interesting picture of the band's formative years. — *Chris Woodstra*

Our Time in Eden / Sep. 29, 1992 / Elektra ♦♦♦♦
On their last album, *Our Time In Eden*, 10,000 Maniacs experiment with their trademark sound without ever losing sight of the gentle, melodic folk-rock that has gained them legions of fans. They wind up with their best album since *In My Tribe*, highlighted by the rolling "These Are Days" and the horn-spiked "Candy Everybody Wants." — *Stephen Thomas Erlewine*

MTV Unplugged / Oct. 26, 1993 / Elektra ♦♦
When it was recorded, nobody knew that *MTV Unplugged* would be 10,000 Maniacs' last album with Natalie Merchant. As it stands, it's a quiet, gentle way for her to bow out, offering no new revelations but several solid versions of the group's signature songs (mainly concentrating on *Our Time in Eden*) and a cover of Patti Smith's "Because the Night." It's nothing new, but for fans it's a graceful way to say goodbye. — *Stephen Thomas Erlewine*

Ten Years After

f. 1967, Nottingham, England, db. 1975
Electric British Blues, Blues-Rock, British Blues
Ten Years After is a British blues-rock quartet consisting of Alvin Lee (b.Dec 19, 1944), guitar and vocals; Chick Churchill (b.Jan 2, 1949), keyboards; Leo Lyons (b.Nov 30, 1944) bass; and Ric Lee (b.Oct 20, 1945), drums. The group was formed in 1967 and signed to Decca in England. Its first album was not a success, but its second, the live *Undead* (1968)

containing "I'm Going Home," a six-minute blues workout by the fleet-fingered Alvin, hit the charts on both sides of the Atlantic. *Stonedhenge* (1969) hit the UK Top Ten in early 1969. Ten Years After's US break-through came as a result of its appearance at Woodstock, at which it played a nine-minute version of "I'm Going Home." Its next album, *Ssssh*, reached the US Top 20, and *Cricklewood Green*, containing the hit single "Love Like a Man," reached No. 14. *Watt* completed the group's Decca contract, after which it signed with Columbia and moved in a more mainstream pop direction, typified by the gold-selling 1971 album *A Space in Time* and its Top 40 single "I'd Love to Change the World." Subsequent efforts in that direction were less successful, however, and Ten Years After split up after the release of *Positive Vibrations* in 1974. They reunited in 1988 for concerts in Europe and recorded their first new album in 15 years, *About Time*, in 1989. — *William Ruhlmann*

Undead / 1968 / Deram ♦♦♦♦
A live album from a group best experienced live, including some amazing guitar playing at phenomenal speeds from Alvin Lee. — *William Ruhlmann*

Greatest Hits / 1977 / Deram ♦♦♦♦
The group's 1968-1970 best, including the hit "Love like a Man" and the Woodstock version of "I'm Going Home." — *William Ruhlmann*

● **Essential** / 1991 / Chrysalis ♦♦♦♦
While it doesn't include all of their prime material, *Essential* features enough of their best songs to make it a fine introduction. — *AMG*

Tenpole Tudor

f. 1974, London, England, db. 1982
New Wave, Pub Rock
Tenpole Tudor was one the strangest and silliest groups on Stiff Records, a label that was known for its oddballs. Led by Eddie Tudor (born Edward Tudor-Pole), a former actor that could barely carry a tune, the group played a mixture of punk, roots-rock, pop and British dance-hall music, developing a thoroughly entertaining and ridiculous style. Tudor formed the band in 1974 with guitarist Bob Kingston, bassist Dick Crippen, and drummer Gary Long. Before recording the band's first album, Tudor appeared in the Sex Pistols' movie *The Great Rock 'N' Roll Swindle*, singing "Who Killed Bambi." After releasing a single on Korova records, the group joined the Stiff roster, releasing "Three Bells in a Row." Tenpole Tudor released their debut album, *Eddie, Old Bob, Dick and Gary* in 1981; it sold well, launching two minor singles in addition to "Three Bells in a Row"—"Wunderbar" and "Swords of a Thousand Men." That same year, the group released their second album, *Let the Four Winds Blow*, which also performed well. The following year, Eddie Tudor broke up Tenpole Tudor; while he led a Cajun-inspired version of Tenpole Tudor, the rest of the band became the Tudors. After the new incarnation of Tenpole Tudor failed, Tudor left Stiff Records and began performing in jazz and swing bands, as well as returning to acting; he has since concentrated on acting, although he has assembled new versions of Tenpole Tudor since. — *Stephen Thomas Erlewine*

● **Eddie, Old Bob, Dick & Gary** / 1981 / Stiff ♦♦♦♦
Tenpole Tudor's music is so defiantly silly and raucous that it would be easy to dismiss if it wasn't qutie so fun. Taking the punk aesthetic to an extreme, no one in Tenpole Tudor, particularly lead vocalist Eddie Tudor, can sing *at all*, so each song turns into a drunken, noisy sing-along. And most of these songs are sing-alongs, filled with rousing choruses, big hooks, and clattering chords that are messy and infectious. What's surprising about the group's debut album *Eddie, Old Bob, Dick & Gary* is how many flat-out excellent songs are on the record. Combining ridiculous swords-and-sorcery imagery with laddish party anthems, nearly half of the record is invigorating, noisy rock 'n' roll, with the boozy "Swords of a Thousand Men," "Wunderbar," "Three Bells in a Row," "I Wish," and "There Are The Boys" standing out among the clatter. The rest of the album isn't quite as good, but it has reckless charm that makes *Eddie, Old Bob, Dick & Gary* a thrillingly primitive rock 'n' roll record. — *Stephen Thomas Erlewine*

Let the Four Winds Blow / 1981 / Stiff ♦♦♦
Tenpole Tudor falters somewhat on their second album, *Let the Four Winds Blow*, partially in a wish to expand their musical reach. Instead of relying on the boozy, punky pub-rock that dominated their debut, the band attempts to claim funk, music-hall, pop and country as their own, with mixed results. The record starts off with a great one-two punk of the title track and the ridiculous "Throwing My Baby Out with the Bathwater" before it quickly runs out of steam, making clear that the real problem with the record isn't patchy songwriting—the debut had that flaw as well—but a tamer performance, and when they play it calm, Tenpole Tudor isn't quite as endearing as when they rock out. Still, there are just enough good tracks to make the record necessary for the devoted, but without the relentlessly goofy and catchy appeal of *Eddie, Old Bob, Dick & Gary*, *Let the Four Winds Blow* simply won't be able to convert the uninitiated. — *Stephen Thomas Erlewine*

Wunderbar: Best of Tenpole Tudor / Oct. 26, 1994 / Castle ◆◆◆◆

Tesla

f. 1985, Sacramento, CA
Hard Rock, Heavy Metal
With their first album, *Mechanical Resonance*, Tesla quickly established themselves as one of the better hard rock/heavy metal bands of the late '80s. Although they weren't utterly original, the band was tight and showed an ability for crafting melodic, driving riffs. What made Tesla different from other metal bands with pop inclinations was the fact that their music was grounded in gritty, bluesy hard rock instead of slick arena rock.

Although their debut climbed all the way to No. 32 on the *Billboard* charts, their second album, 1989's *The Great Radio Controversy*, was an even greater success, scoring a Top Ten hit with the ballad "Love Song." Their follow-up album, *Five Man Acoustical Jam*, showed that the band didn't need overdriven amplifiers in order to play; it also showed that they had a fondness for sentimental hippie oldies, as their hit version of "Signs" proved. The record also turned out to be their biggest hit, reaching No. 12 on the charts. While its follow-up, *Psychotic Supper*, wasn't as commercially successful, it captured Tesla branching into new musical territories; it proved that the band hadn't lost its creative spark. —*Stephen Thomas Erlewine*

Mechanical Resonance / 1986 / Geffen ◆◆◆◆
Tesla's debut is one of their stronger albums. —*John Book*

The Great Radio Controversy / 1989 / Geffen ◆◆◆◆
More use of acoustic instruments make this a treat. It features the Top Ten hit "Love Song," as well as "The Way It Is" and "Heaven's Trail (No Way Out)." —*John Book*

Five Man Acoustical Jam / Dec. 1990 / Geffen ◆◆◆
With the advent of *MTV Unplugged*, it became popular for all types of groups to prove that they didn't have to rely on walls of amps and outboard gear to get their music across. *Five Man Acoustical Jam* was one of the most successful outings of that type, featuring versions of the Five Man Electrical Band's "Signs," Creedence's "Lodi," and a smattering of originals. —*Rick Clark*

Psychotic Supper / Aug. 30, 1991 / Geffen ◆◆◆
This is one of the few heavy metal bands who can release albums with more than ten songs and still end up with quality product. —*John Book*

Bust a Nut / Aug. 23, 1994 / Geffen ◆◆

● **Time's Makin Changes: the Best of Tesla** / Nov. 1995 / Geffen ◆◆◆◆
Tesla's greatest hits and most popular album rock cuts are collected on *Time's Makin' Changes: The Best of Tesla*. In addition to hits like "Signs," "The Way It Is," and "Love Song," the compilation includes a new song, "Steppin' Over," which isn't particularly distinctive. Nevertheless, the record remains the one to get for casual fans—it has all the hits, in one place, after all. —*Stephen Thomas Erlewine*

Joe Tex (Joe Arrington, Jr.)

b. Aug. 8, 1933, Rogers, TX, **d.** Aug. 13, 1982, Navasota, TX
Vocals / Soul, Funk
Often pausing in the middle of a ballad for a brief but sincere secular sermon on the inherent value of true love or the hazards of cheating, Joe Tex was one of the Southern soul genre's most enduring performers—and one of its most versatile. With a stage surname reflecting his home state, Tex first entered a recording studio in 1955 for King, singing some potent R&B before trying his luck in New Orleans with Ace. Tex joined forces with Nashville producer Buddy Killen (who formed the Dial logo to market the singer's output) and finally scaled the soul playlists in 1965 with his smash "Hold What You've Got." The intense gospel-tinged ballad proved the prototypical Tex track, loaded with sound advice and downhome homilies.

That's not to say that Tex didn't record some hard-driving uptempo soul during the mid-'60s—"A Sweet Woman like You," "S.Y.S.L.J.F.M. (The Letter Song)," and "Show Me" all sizzle, while the hilarious "Skinny Legs and All," another major R&B and pop hit, accurately testifies to Tex's live charisma. With his microphone-stand acrobatics a longtime trademark, Tex's winning streak endured into the next decade with the grunting "I Gotcha," his biggest crossover success in 1972. He eked out another smash in the midst of disco fever with "Ain't Gonna Bump No More (With No Big Fat Woman)," his ebullient sense of humor still intact. Tex died in 1982. —*Bill Dahl*

I Believe I'm Gonna Make It / 1988 / Rhino ◆◆◆◆
First-rate country/soul, sung with the just the right blend of whimsy, worry, and relief. Joe Tex was routinely turning out excellent cuts throughout the mid-'60s, but it wasn't until his novelty/disco tunes of the mid-'70s that he finally attained any widespread recognition. Sadly, none of his great Dial albums are currently in print. —*Ron Wynn*

Show Me: The Hits . . . & More / Oct. 12, 1992 / Ichiban ◆◆◆◆
While he could spin a mean yarn, Tex was also a mournful, moving vocalist whose convincing delivery on country/soul ballads was sorely underrated. This 18-track collection includes some of Tex's biggest hits, fine covers of "Dark End Of The Street" and "You're Right," plus several Tex originals such as "I Want to Do Everything for You," "Same Old Soup," and "King Thaddeus." While there are some notable and surprising exclusions, it's a representative Tex collection, but isn't as complete as Rhino's single-disc anthology from 1988. —*Ron Wynn*

● **The Very Best of Joe Tex** / 1996 / Rhino ◆◆◆◆
Excellent 16-track survey of Tex's best material, from the mid-'60s to the mid-'70s. It favors his country/soul period rather than the disco one, with all but three tracks originating from the '60s, but it does include his biggest '70s hits, "I Gotcha" and "Ain't Gonna Bump No More (With No Big Fat Woman)." —*Richie Unterberger*

Terre Thaemlitz

f. 1992, New York, NY
Ambient Techno, Electronica
New York-based composer Terre Thaemlitz is one of only a handful of significant American artists working in the new ambient vein. He's released the bulk of his material through the Instinct Ambient label, but has also issued tracks (under his own name and as Chugga) on his own Comatonse label and through others. Although Thaemlitz' entree into electronic came in a somewhat traditional fashion—as a house DJ—his explorations in electronic abstraction have been anything but, focusing on themes of abjection, alienation, fracture, and contradiction in his music. Thaemlitz' recorded work, collected on albums such as *Tranquilizer* and *Soil*, is closer in tone to ambient-leaning industrialists such as B. Lustmord, Carl Stone, and (some) Merzbow, as well as "deep listening" composers such as Pauline Oliveros and Robert Rich. He's also recorded with Bill Laswell, releasing *Web* in 1995, and done remix work for Interpieces Organization and the Golden Palaminos, among others.

Born in Minnesota and raised in Missouri, Thaemlitz moved to New York in the mid-'80s to pursue art scholarship at Cooper Union. Soon distracted by the growing New York house scene, he began DJing at drag balls and benefits, leading to an Underground Grammy for best DJ in 1991. Although Thaemlitz is primarily a dance-floor DJ, his insistence upon integrating house music's more simplistic monotony with challenging, complicated breaks and references earned him an uneasy relationship with club promoters looking for DJs whose only commitment was the 4/4 beat. Retiring from club DJing in the early '90s (although he continues to spin experimental electronic music at art galleries, one-offs, and in other marginal contexts), Thaemlitz began making his own tracks, beginning with house but quickly moving into genre-defying fusions of funk, soul, disco, and musique concrete, and eventually settling into experimental ambient. One of his earliest works, "Raw From A Straw," in addition to limited release through his own Comatonse label, appeared on an early ambient compilation on Instinct, and earned him an almost instant reputation. He's since fortified that with a pair of full-length releases remarkably free of many of the cliched conventions of club-driven ambient. He continues to support new talent through Comatonse. —*Sean Cooper*

Soil / Jul. 25, 1995 / Instinct ◆◆◆◆
A flowing, shifting, almost timeless statement incorporating equal parts confusion and calm across six tracks of entirely beatless ambient. Thaemlitz' ability to infuse elements of immediacy and physicality into a measured, slowly evolving style traditionally bogged down by either disinterested elitism or faux collectivist spirituality figures him as one of America's most important contemporary composers, and a singular voice in new ambient. —*Sean Cooper*

Die Roboter Roboto / Mar. 11, 1997 / Mille Plateaux ◆◆◆◆
Electro-acoustician Thaemlitz takes the long road around expectation for his Mille Plateaux debut, opting for a set of solo piano extrapolations of songs by German electro innovators Kraftwerk. Built on a high-clearing deck of post-industrial cultural analysis over the course of its seven-plus pages of liner notes, the music on the disc requires little in the way of explanation; Thaemlitz' sparse, inventive interpretations are pleasing enough on their own. Although the themes of classics such as "The Robots," "Space Lab," and "Computer World" are sometimes so obtusely stated as to elude recognition, Thaemlitz' inspired performances make it hardly a problem. —*Sean Cooper*

that dog.

f. 1991, Los Angeles, CA
Alternative Pop-Rock
The lineup of the Los Angeles-based indie-pop quartet that dog. represented the flowering of a second generation of musical luminaries: singer/guitarist Anna Waronker was the daughter of famed producer and Warner Bros. head Lenny Waronker, while bassist Rachel Haden

and her violinist sister Petra were two of the triplet daughters born to jazz titan Charlie Haden. Friends since high school, the trio first began playing music together in Waronker's bedroom in the early '90s. Joined by drummer Tony Maxwell in 1992, that dog. issued their debut double seven-inch on the tiny Magnatone Records, quickly becoming a staple of the Los Angeles club circuit; a flurry of label interest followed, and the group signed with DGC in 1993. that dog's self-titled debut LP appeared in 1994; an energetic and quirky punk-pop effort highlighted by sunny harmonies and the intriguing use of violin and cello, the record became a college radio hit, and the lighthearted video for the lead single "Old Timer" even garnered some MTV airplay. The follow-up, *Totally Crushed Out!*, was issued a year later; a concept album wittily exploring the teen angst of unrequited love (packaged to recall a *Sweet Valley High* romance novel), the record marked a significant maturity in Waronker's songwriting, evidenced by tracks like "Ms. Wrong" and "He's Kissing Christian." A planned Waronker solo project was scheduled to follow, but instead her more pop-oriented material became the basis for the third that dog. record; co-produced by Brad Wood, the stellar *Retreat From the Sun* appeared in 1997. —*Jason Ankeny*

That Dog. / Mar. 1994 / DGC ✦✦✦
The group's debut is uneven but exciting. The mix of sweet harmonies, crunchy guitars and scratchy violins makes it an entertaining listen, especially on songs like "Raina" and "Punk Rock Girl." —*Heather Phares*

● **Totally Crushed Out!** / Jul. 18, 1995 / DGC ✦✦✦✦
An appealing concept album about crushes and puppy love, *Totally Crushed Out!* is full of tight punk-pop and pretty ballads. Tracks like "Ms. Wrong," "Silently," and "One Summer Night" capture the giddiness of first love with their three-part harmonies and sweet melodies. *Totally Crushed Out!* is cute and clever without being too cutesy or precious, and almost as memorable as a first crush. —*Heather Phares*

Retreat from the Sun / Apr. 8, 1997 / DGC ✦✦✦✦
Retreat from the Sun began its life as Anna Waronker's first solo album, and if you listen intently, those origins are apparent, particularly in the tenor of the songs themselves. that dog. previously veered towards cute-pop, and while there are remnants of that throughout the album, Waronker's songs are considerably more personal than before, which adds emotional depth to the record. Just as important, her songs are tighter and more melodic, demonstrating considerable growth in songcraft. Producer Brad Wood helps form these songs into shiny alterna-pop nuggets, making *Retreat from the Sun* into the best album Liz Phair never made. It comes at the expense of the raw, ragged and surprisingly hooky post-punk of *Totally Crushed Out*, which was quite charming in its own right, but with maturity do come greater rewards, as *Retreat from the Sun* proves. —*Stephen Thomas Erlewine*

That Petrol Emotion

f. 1984, Derry, Northern Ireland, **db.** Apr. 1994
Alternative Pop-Rock
After the Undertones broke up, brothers Sean (formerly known as John) and Damian O'Neill formed That Petrol Emotion. While they were more politically oriented and noisier than the Undertones, they managed to keep their former band's energetic, melodic kick. With their first album, *Manic Pop Thrill*, That Petrol Emotion became critics' favorites, as well as earning a respectable following in the UK. Over the years, their music remained endlessly diverse, incorporating elements of every style of independent guitar rock. Occasionally, their albums would be wildly uncohesive because of this, yet they managed to turn in several excellent songs on each record. Sean left the band after their third album, *End of the Millennium Psychosis Blues*. The album showed signs that That Petrol Emotion's exuberant diversity was beginning to wear thin; their next albums proved that they were running out of things to say. After eight years, That Petrol Emotion broke up in 1994. —*Stephen Thomas Erlewine*

Manic Pop Thrill / 1986 / Demon ✦✦
● **Babble** / 1987 / Polydor ✦✦✦✦
On their second album, That Petrol Emotion's electrifying mix of spiky guitar hooks, direct melodies, and righteous, socially conscious lyrics solidifies into a distinctive sound that's a little messy but completely invigorating. Although they released several records in the next seven years, the band were never able to replicate the sheer power and solid hooks of *Babble*. —*Stephen Thomas Erlewine*

End of the Millennium Psychosis Blues / 1988 / Virgin ✦✦✦
Chemicrazy / Mar. 1990 / Virgin ✦✦✦
Fireproof / Feb. 15, 1994 / Rykodisc ✦✦

The The

f. 1979, Derbyshire, England
Alternative Pop-Rock, Alternative Dance
The The was the guise of Matt Johnson, a mercurial singer-songwriter

whose music ran the gamut from dance-pop to country. Born August 15, 1961 in London, Johnson was raised in the flat above his father's pub, the Two Puddings, a haven for well-known celebrities and criminals; he also became exposed to music at the nightclubs and dancehalls owned by his uncle, where he saw performers like Howlin' Wolf, the Kinks, and Muddy Waters. Johnson formed his first band, Roadstar, when he was 11; at the age of 15, he was hired as a tea boy for the DeWolfe music publishing company, and within three years, he was working in their recording studio as an assistant engineer.

After the demise of the duo the Marble Index in 1979, Johnson formed the first incarnation of The The with synth player Keith Laws; after playing their debut gig opening for Scritti Politti, the group issued its first single, "Controversial Subject," on the 4AD label in 1980. A year later, contractual obligations forced Johnson to issue the LP *Burning Blue Soul* under his own name; that year, he also recorded as a guitarist with the band the Gadgets, and The The contributed a track to the *Some Bizzare Album* compilation.

In 1982, The The—now essentially a Johnson solo project, backed by a revolving coterie of musicians—recorded the album *The Pornography of Despair*, which a dissatisfied Johnson chose not to release; a 1983 single recorded with Orange Juice's Zeke Manyika, "This Is the Day," formed the centerpiece of The The's proper debut, 1984's *Soul Mining*, an excursion into dance-flavored pop. Illness sidelined Johnson for much of the following year, and The The did not return until 1986's *Infected*, an eclectic commentary on the state of Britain in the modern world. Recorded with the aid of talents like Neneh Cherry, Art of Noise's Anne Dudley and Swans' Roli Mosimann, *Infected* was also accompanied by an ambitious album-length video.

When The The returned with the dissonant *Mind Bomb* in 1989, they were once again a true band, with Johnson joined by ex-Smiths guitarist Johnny Marr as well as bassist James Eller and former ABC drummer Dave Palmer. The same lineup remained for 1993's pared-down *Dusk*, but 1995's *Hanky Panky* marked yet another new direction when Johnson was joined by guitarist Eric Schermerhorn, keyboardist D.C. Collard, harmonica player Jim Fitting and drummer Brian MacLeod. The first in a series of occasional albums celebrating the work of legendary performers, *Hanky Panky* was a brooding covers collection honoring the music of country great Hank Williams. —*Jason Ankeny*

Burning Blue Soul / 1981 / 4AD ✦✦✦✦
Matt Johnson's work thrives on the tension between accessible pop and dissonant experimentation; between joyful wonder and despairing bleakness. *Burning Blue Soul* was a more disjointed solo album Johnson released under his own name in 1981 before these tensions were fully integrated. This reissue is a valuable sketchbook for The The fans interested in dissecting the early inner workings of Johnson's art, but the meandering tape-collages that serve as framework will leave most others cold. —*Roch Parisien*

Soul Mining / 1983 / Epic ✦✦✦
On The The's first album, Matt Johnson crafted a pleasant but unengaging set of dance-pop just barely hinting at the experimentalism he would develop on later records like *Infected* or *Mind Bomb*. —*Stephen Thomas Erlewine*

Infected / 1986 / Epic ✦✦✦✦
Infected is such a leap forward from *Soul Mining* that the album hardly seems like the work of the same band. Instead of the light, agreeable dance-pop of the previous album, *Infected* draws a dense, dark sonic landscape that accurately conveys the alienation and despair Matt Johnson sings about. —*Stephen Thomas Erlewine*

● **Mind Bomb** / Jun. 1989 / Epic ✦✦✦✦
With the addition of former Smiths guitarist Johnny Marr, The The attempted their most ambitious album yet with *Mind Bomb*. Instead of the darkly polished dance-pop stylings of *Infected*, *Mind Bomb* opens up the music to reveal a slow, winding textured world of sound that celebrates its rough edges instead of hiding them. It's serious, dance-influenced rock of the highest order. —*Stephen Thomas Erlewine*

Dusk / Jan. 5, 1993 / Epic ✦✦✦✦
Sixth album *Dusk*—with its themes of desire, fall, redemption, and death—creates both a familiar and dislocating atmosphere, like a well-known film-noir plot for a movie produced on some other planet. Several songs have echoed, phased vocals—as if they were alien transmissions being randomly captured by this life-cycle soundtrack. The mutant blues of "Dogs of Lust" is an especially effective example of this unsettling terrain. Even when Johnson gets more conventional, there is no lack of depth. Dusk never looked so convergingly bright—and dark—as on *Dusk*. —*Roch Parisien*

Hanky Panky / Feb. 14, 1995 / 550 Music/Epic ✦✦
It is true that Matt Johnson offers some startingly original interpretations of Hank Williams songs on *Hanky Panky*—he makes them sound like The The songs. That doesn't necessarily mean he's tapped into the essence of Williams' music, it means that he is a gifted arranger. Most of the song pulse to an electronic beat and the atmosphere is thick with

forboding doom. Strangely enough, it works better than several The The records, since Hank Williams is a better songwriter than Matt Johnson. —*Stephen Thomas Erlewine*

Thee Midniters

f. 1964, Los Angeles, CA, **db.** 1972
Rock 'n' Roll, Garage Rock
Indisputably the greatest Latino rock band of the '60s, Thee Midniters took their inspiration from both the British Invasion sound of the Rolling Stones and the more traditional R&B that they were weaned on in their native Los Angeles. Hugely popular in east Los Angeles, the group, featuring both guitars and horns, had a local hit (and a small national one) with their storming version of "Land of a Thousand Dances" in 1965. Much of their repertoire featured driving, slightly punkish rock/R&B, yet lead singer Willie Garcia also had a heartbreaking delivery on slow and steamy ballads. In the manner of other local phenomenons like the Rationals (from Detroit), they were equally talented at whipping up a storm with uptempo numbers and offering smoldering, romantic soul tunes. After a few albums and an interesting detour into social consciousness with the single "Chicano Power," the group split in the early '70s, though their legacy is felt in later popular Latino Los Angeles rock acts like Los Lobos. —*Richie Unterberger*

Unlimited / 1967 / Whittier ♦♦♦
Except for the greatest-hits compilation, this is the group's most interesting album, as eight of the twelve songs were group originals. They favor a more straightforward blue-eyed soul approach than they do on many of their singles over the course of this LP, which also includes the unusually punky (for them) number "Never Knew I Had It So Bad." —*Richie Unterberger*

● **Best of Thee Midniters** / 1983 / Rhino ♦♦♦♦
An excellent compilation of 14 of their best songs, including "Land of a Thousand Dances" and "Chicano Power." They make a fair Latino Rolling Stones on "Empty Heart," "Everybody Needs Somebody," and "Whittier Blvd." (a thinly disguised reworking of the Stones' "2120 South Michigan Ave."); "That's All," "Dreaming Casually," and "Sad Girl" are exceptional slow R&B ballads; and "Jump, Jive and Harmonize" is a tough garage-punk original. —*Richie Unterberger*

Thelonious Monster

f. 1986, Los Angeles, CA
Group / Alternative Pop-Rock, Indie Rock
A sort of all-star collection of L.A. scenesters and musicians, Thelonious Monster formed in 1986 and specialized in what would best be described as drunk-rock in the tradition of the Replacements. Ramshackle, loose live performances—one was never sure if the band would actually turn up or finish out—seemed to be their hallmark, yet at times lead vocalist and lyricist Bob Forrest was capable of brilliance. No matter the lyrical scenario, nothing was ever good enough for him. The band began with a messy, four-guitar record, *Baby....You're Bumming My Life Out in a Supreme Fashion* in 1986 with Pete Weiss, drums; Jon Huck, bass; K.K., guitar; Bill Stobaugh, guitar; Chris Handsome, guitar; and Dix Denney, guitar. They followed it with *Next Saturday Afternoon,* a more coherent effort. The John Doe-produced *Stormy Weather* in 1989 was a step up, as the band had since been taken under the wing of X and the Red Hot Chili Peppers, serving as a support act and getting some informal studio help from Doe and Flea on occasion. The lineup revolved, but in the end, Weiss, Denney, and Handsome remained true to Forrest. *Beautiful Mess,* an uneven, all-star gala (appearances by Tom Waits, Al Kooper, and Soul Asylum) came out three years later. Forrest occasionally appears as a solo acoustic act, and the band tours sporadically. —*Denise Sullivan*

Baby, You're Bummin' My Life out in a Supreme Fashion / 1986 / Epitaph ♦♦
Given the band's moniker and tracks like "Psychofuckindelic" and "Union Street," one might be led to believe this is a loose, jazz-loving combo. Instead, the record is an amalgam of punk, funk and roots music that veers from the brilliant ("Try") to the completely wretched. Mercifully, they would soon find their way, but this album doesn't nearly capture the unwieldy charm the band would become capable of later on disc and in the live setting. —*Denise Sullivan*

Next Saturday Afternoon / 1987 / Combat ♦♦♦

Stormy Weather/Next Saturday Afternoon / 1989 / Combat ♦♦♦♦
Collected on one long CD, the band's second and third albums make for nice companion pieces, as this was a band at the height of its strength and (limited) live popularity. "Next Saturday Afternoon," "Swan Song," and "Lookin' to the West" reveal the band's weakness for '70s rock, and they celebrate slacker lifestyle ("Michael Jordan") before "Gen-X" had been identified. The title track of *Stormy Weather* expands the band's folkish/country roots with the aid of punk/traditionalist producer John Doe. A reading of Tracy Chapman's "For My Lover" works well, as does

a piano ballad, "My Boy," because of Bob Forrest's convincing, severely tormented vocals. "Sammy Hagar Weekend" encapsulates the band's perverse humor and rock fandom, and "See That My Grave Is Kept Clean" rates alongside the best versions of the Blind Lemon Jefferson blues standard. —*Denise Sullivan*

Stormy Weather / 1989 / Relativity ♦♦♦♦

Beautiful Mess / Oct. 12, 1992 / Capitol ♦♦♦
The most impressive part of this album is the list of names that contributed. Dave Pirner and Dan Murphy from Soul Asylum sing on "Blood Is Thicker than Water," Benmont Tench plays the organ, and Michael Penn sings on "Body and Soul?" Joe Hardy produced along with Pete Anderson and Al Kooper, the latter of whom oversaw "Adios Lounge," a duet between singer Bob Forrest and Tom Waits. Oddly, the all-male Caucasian rock band chose another African-American female for inspiration (they cover Joan Armatrading's "Weakness In Me") after paying homage to Lena Horne and Tracy Chapman on the previous record. Even this star-studded lineup couldn't save the band, who were their own worst enemies and basically fell off the musical map after this release. —*Denise Sullivan*

Them

f. 1963, Belfast, Northern Ireland, **db.** 1971
Rock 'n' Roll, British Invasion, British Blues
Not strictly a British group, but packaged as part of the British Invasion, Them forged their hard-nosed R&B sound in Belfast, Ireland, moving to England in 1964 after landing a deal with Decca Records. The band's simmering sound was dominated by boiling organ riffs, lean guitars, and the tough vocals of lead singer Van Morrison, whose recordings with Them rank among the very best performances of the British Invasion. Morrison also wrote top-notch original material for the outfit, whose lineup changed numerous times over the course of their brief existence. As a hit-making act, their résumé was brief—"Here Comes the Night" and "Baby Please Don't Go" were Top Ten hits in England, "Mystic Eyes" and "Here Comes the Night" made the Top 40 in the US—but their influence was considerable, reaching bands like the Doors, who Them played with during a residency in Los Angeles just before Van Morrison quit the band in 1966. Their most influential song of all, the classic three-chord stormer "Gloria," was actually a B-side, although the Shadows of Knight had a hit in the US with a faithful, tamer cover version.

Morrison has recalled his days with Them with some bitterness, noting that the heart of the original group was torn out by image-conscious record company politics, and that session men (including Jimmy Page, who played a scorching solo on "Baby Please Don't Go") often replaced members on recordings. That may be, but whether the records are faithful to the original Them sound or not, they were usually great—in addition to hits, Them released a couple fine albums and several flop singles that mixed fine Morrison compositions with hot R&B and soul covers, as well as a few songs written for them by producers like Bert Berns (who penned "Here Comes the Night"). After Morrison left the group, Them splintered into the Belfast Gypsies, who released a decent album that (except for the vocals) approximated Them's early records, and a psychedelic outfit that kept the name Them, releasing four fairly weak LPs with little resemblance to the tough sounds of their mid-'60s heyday.

Them's legacy is disgracefully underrepresented on CD; no major British Invasion act has been worse served by reissues in the digital age. Almost everything they recorded under Morrison's leadership is worth hearing, and a double CD compiling all several dozen of their songs from 1964 to 1966 would have little filler. For the time being, their output is scattered among some skimpy CD collections and various out-of-print LPs. —*Richie Unterberger*

Them [Parrot] / 1965 / Parrot ♦♦♦♦
The debut album by the group, also known as *The Angry Young Them,* and half its tracks make it a dead-on rival to the Stones' debut album. This reissue features the album's original British configuration ("Just a Little Bit," "I Gave My Love a Diamond," "Bright Lights, Big City," and "My Little Baby" are here, "One Two Brown Eyes" and "Here Comes the Night" are absent); "My Little Baby" was no huge loss, being a pale imitation of "Here Comes the Night," but the omitted "Just a Little Bit" features a Howlin' Wolf/"Spoonful"-style performance by Van Morrison that would have incinerated a lot of American teens. On the other hand, Morrison's soul-shouting performance on the deleted "I Gave My Love a Diamond," appropriated by Bert Berns from the public domain "Cherry Song," would have shocked any folkie familiar with the original. Morrison's "You Just Can't Win" isn't nearly as impressive, but even as a time-filler it isn't half bad. And then there's "Gloria," rock's ultimate '60s sex anthem, and one of the handful of white-authored songs that can just about hold its own against any blues standard you'd care to name. —*Bruce Eder*

Them Again / Apr. 1966 / Parrot ✦✦✦

The group's second and, for all intents and purposes, last full album was recorded while Them was in a state of imminent collapse. To this day, nobody knows who played on the album, other than Van Morrison and bassist Alan Henderson, though it is probable that Jimmy Page was seldom very far away when Them was recording. The 17 songs here are a little less focused than the first LP. The material was cut under siege conditions, with a constantly shifting lineup and a grueling tour schedule; essentially, there was no "group" to provide focus to the sound, only Morrison's voice, so the material bounces from a surprisingly restrained "I Put a Spell on You" to the garage-punkoid "I Can Only Give You Everything." Folk-rock rears its head not only on the moody cover of Dylan's "It's All Over Now, Baby Blue" but also the Morrison-authored "My Lonely Sad Eyes," but the main thrust is soul, which Morrison oozes everywhere—while there's some filler, his is a voice that could easily have knocked Mick Jagger or Eric Burdon off their respective perches. —*Bruce Eder*

Backtrackin' / 1974 / London ✦✦✦

This collection of ten tracks from all phases of their career is haphazard, but the material is mostly excellent. Highlights include their blistering raveup of "Baby Please Don't Go" with Jimmy Page on guitar, a Top Ten hit in Britain; the angry cover of Paul Simon's "Richard Cory," their breakneck version of Slim Harpo's "Don't Start Crying Now," which was their first single in 1964; the great obscure, bluesy Morrison-penned B-side, "All for Myself," and the vicious cover of the R&B standard "Just a Little Bit." —*Richie Unterberger*

Story of Them / 1977 / London ✦✦✦

Another ragtag compilation of material that somehow hadn't found its way to an American album, this uneven but worthy collection is divided between R&B covers (Jimmy Reed's "Bright Lights, Big City" and Jimmy Witherspoon's "Times Gettin' Tougher Than Tough" are the best) and some good Morrison originals. Of those, the folk-tinged "Philosphy" and "Friday's Child" point to his more expressive solo work, and "The Story of Them" is a rambling, seven-and-a-half-minute autobiographical talking blues about the group's early days. —*Richie Unterberger*

20 Super Hits by Them / 1980 / Decca ✦✦✦✦

Awful sleeve art, to be sure. But the paucity of Them material on CD forces us to look hard for alternatives, and this is one of the best compilations (in content if not packaging) should you come across it. It has the well-known singles and many of the best album tracks, including a few that are pretty hard to find on anthologies, like "I'm Gonna Dress in Black." —*Richie Unterberger*

● **Them Featuring Van Morrison [CD]** / 1987 / London ✦✦✦✦

Not to be confused with the identically titled Parrot Records release, which is an out-of-print 20-track double-LP set, this is a 13-track single CD set and a US reissue of the Decca UK LP from 1982. It would have been less confusing if they had called it *Them's Greatest Hits*, since it is primarily a singles compilation. But then, only four of Them's singles were hits, either in the UK or the US—"Baby, Please Don't Go," "Gloria," "Here Comes the Night," and "Mystic Eyes," all included here. Also featured are such non-charting singles as "Don't Start Crying Now," "One More Time," "(It Won't Hurt) Half as Much," and "Richard Cory." This is not the ideal Them compilation, but this is the one in print on CD and that contains Them's most familiar material, so it will stand as the pick among their releases unless PolyGram, which owns the catalog, decides to do the kind of thorough retrospective the group deserves. —*William Ruhlmann*

Collection / Oct. 19, 1993 / Castle ✦✦✦

They Might Be Giants

f. 1983, Boston, MA
Alternative Pop-Rock

Combining a knack for infectious melodies with a quirky, bizarre sense of humor and a vaguely avant-garde aesthetic borrowed from the New York post-punk underground, They Might Be Giants became one of the most unlikely alternative success stories of the late '80s and early '90s. Musically, the duo of John Flansburg and John Linell borrowed from everywhere, but their free-wheeling eclecticism was enhanced by their arcane, geeky sense of humor. They would reference everything from British Invasion to Tin Pan Alley, while making allusion to pulp fiction and President Polk. Through their string of indie releases and constant touring as a duo, They Might Be Giants built up a huge following on college campuses during the late '80s, switching to a major label in the early '90s. With support from MTV, 1990's *Flood* became a gold album, and with it, the band began to reap commercial rewards, elevating them into the status of one of the most popular alternative bands before grunge. However, the group's whimsical outlook became buried in the avalanche of post-grunge groups that dominated MTV and modern rock radio in the mid-'90s, and the group retreated to its cult following. Flansburg and Linnell met when they were children in Lincoln, Massachu-

setts. During high school, they began writing songs together, yet they never officially formed a band. Both Johns went to college after high school, with Linnell playing in the Mundanes, a New Wave group from Rhode Island. By 1981, the pair had reunited, deciding to move to Brooklyn to pursue a musical career. Taking their name from a George C. Scott film and performing their original material with a drum machine, They Might Be Giants soon became fixtures on the Manhattan underground. Although the duo was building a cult following, they had a hard time getting a record deal, so they set up Dial-A-Song—a phone line that played songs on an answering machine—as a way to get their songs heard. The gimmick worked. Not only did it lead to a deal with the indie label Bar/None, but over the years it was a successful venture; at one point, the service was receiving hundreds of calls a day.

They Might Be Giants released their eponymous debut in 1986, and the album became a college radio hit; it also made waves on MTV, due to the inventive video for "Don't Let's Start." Two years later, the band released *Lincoln*, which expanded their following considerably. Featuring the college hit "Ana Ng," *Lincoln* climbed to No. 89 on the charts, earning the attention of major labels. They Might Be Giants decided to sign with Elektra Records in 1990, releasing *Flood* later that year. *Flood* worked its way to gold status, thanks to the singles "Birdhouse in Your Soul" and "Istanbul (Not Constantinople)," both of which had popular videos directed by Flansburg. In the wake of the group's success, Restless/Bar/None released the B-sides and rarities compilation *Misc. T.* in 1991.

Apollo 18, released in 1992, wasn't quite as successful as *Flood*, yet it consolidated the group's cult. For the album's supporting tour, They Might Be Giants performed with a full backing band for the first time, hiring former Pere Ubu bassist Tony Maimone and drummer Brian Doherty. The shift towards a full band coincided with the dominance of grunge rock in alternative rock. Though they were strengthened by the powerful sound of a full band, They Might Be Giants failed to receive much attention from MTV, mainstream modern rock radio, or college radio when they released *John Henry* in the fall of 1994. Recorded with their full band, *John Henry* lost the group several fans, yet the group's concerts remained popular attractions, especially on American college campuses. Still, the band's next album, 1996's *Factory Showroom*, was virtually ignored by the press, MTV, and radio. —*Stephen Thomas Erlewine*

They Might Be Giants / 1986 / Restless ✦✦✦✦

They Might Be Giants' eponymous debut album is a wild fusion of new wave pop and arty post-punk experiments borrowed from the New York underground. It runs through a head-spinning 19 songs in just over 45 minutes, running the gamut from the performance-art schtick of "Chess Piece Face" and "Youth Culture Killed My Dog" to the pure pop of "Don't Let's Start" and "Everything Right Is Wrong Again." While there are a lot of geeky jokes and barely developed ideas scattered throughout the album, the sheer kaleidoscopic array of styles is intoxicating, and it helps the best songs—the Costello-esque "Put Your Hand Inside the Puppet Head," the sighing "Hide Away Folk Family," the stomping "(She Was A) Hotel Detective," and the gorgeous "She's an Angel"—stand out in sharp relief. —*Stephen Thomas Erlewine*

● **Lincoln** / 1989 / Restless ✦✦✦✦

Cutting away some of the artier aspects of their debut, They Might Be Giants craft another wildly eclectic and geekily fun collection of alterna-pop with *Lincoln*. In general, the album displays greater musical ambition than its predecessor, especially since the duo have trimmed many of the weirder excesses of the debut. Without such arty trappings, their gift for irresistible pop hooks becomes all the more clear, with "Ana Ng," "Purple Toupee," the Latin shuffle of "The World's Address," "Santa's Beard," the surprisingly affecting "They'll Need a Crane," and the lounge jazz of "Kiss Me, Son of God" standing out among the 18 songs. And when They Might Be Giants don't go for the hooks, as on "Pencil Rain" or "Cage & Aquarium," they prove to be expert musical satirists, which means that *Lincoln* is every bit as infectious as the debut. —*Stephen Thomas Erlewine*

Flood / Jan. 1990 / Elektra ✦✦✦

On their major-label debut *Flood*, They Might Be Giants exchange quirky artiness for unabashed geekiness and a more varied and polished musical attack. Although the album contains two of the group's finest singles in "Birdhouse in Your Soul" and "Istanbul (Not Constantinople)," the overall record is uneven, since the group's hooks aren't quite as sharp as before and the humor is either too geeky or leavened with awkward social statements like "Your Racist Friend." Even with its faults, *Flood* has a number of first-rate songs, and it's a strong addition to their catalog, even if it isn't as weirdly intoxicating as its predecessors. —*Stephen Thomas Erlewine*

Miscellaneous T / Jul. 1991 / Bar/None ✦✦✦

Several of They Might Be Giants' finest songs were buried on B-sides, which makes the rarities compilation such a welcome addition to their catalog. While several of these songs are nothing but endearing jokes

("Mr. Klaw," "Lady is a Tramp," "For Science"), there are just as many gems. "We're the Replacements" is a fun homage to the Minneapolis legends, "The Famous Polk" is silly and infectious, "It's Not My Birthday" has a great hook, as does "Nightgown of the Sullen Moon," while "Hey Mr. DJ, I Thought You Said We Had a Deal" is a fun satire. Songs like these often capture the irreverent sense of humor that the group lost when they signed to a major label. —*Stephen Thomas Erlewine*

Apollo 18 / Mar. 24, 1992 / Elektra ✦✦✦
Although it lacks a standout single like "Birdhouse in Your Soul," *Apollo 18* is a more consistent album than *Flood*, overflowing with ideas and pop hooks. The most noteworthy idea may have been "Fingertips," a "suite" of 21 song fragments designed to make each random play a new experience, but the meat of the album lies in pop songs like "I Palindrome I," "My Evil Twin," "She's Actual Size," and "Which Describes How You're Feeling." The album has a slightly darker feeling than its predecessors, but that just gives the album a resonance that was missing on *Flood*. —*Stephen Thomas Erlewine*

John Henry / Sep. 13, 1994 / Elektra ✦✦
They Might Be Giants recorded with a full band for the first time in their career on *John Henry*. Instead of relying on their quirky charm, the album is direct and obvious, lacking the infectious melodies and cleverly geeky lyrics that characterize the best of their work. —*Stephen Thomas Erlewine*

Factory Showroom / Oct. 8, 1996 / Elektra ✦✦
Factory Showroom, They Might Be Giants' second effort with a full band, is a stronger album than its predecessor *John Henry*, boasting a more natural sound and a more diverse selection of material. However, Flansburgh and Linnell are still suffering from a slight creative block—they even recycle an old B-side, "James K. Polk"—as evidenced by the lack of memorable hooks and forced jokes. —*Stephen Thomas Erlewine*

Then: the Earlier Years / Mar. 25, 1997 / Restless ✦✦✦✦
Then: The Earlier Years is a double-disc set containing all of They Might Be Giants' original, independent records—the two albums *They Might Be Giants* and *Lincoln*, plus all of the B-sides and EP tracks that were compiled on *Misc. T*—adding nearly 20 previously unreleased tracks. While the bonus tracks are of varying quality—only "Now That I Have Anything" and demos of "Don't Let's Start," "Which Describes How You're Feeling," and "Hope That I Get Old Before I Die" are of interest to anyone but hardcore collectors—the official releases remain surprisingly fresh, a combination of melodic skills, inventive arrangements, self-consciously clever lyrics, and bizarre, geeky humor. For most listeners, *Then* is the definitive They Might Be Giants, encapsulating all of their charm and quirkiness and capturing them at the height of their career. —*Stephen Thomas Erlewine*

Thin Lizzy

f. 1970, Dublin, Ireland, **db.** 1983
Hard Rock, Heavy Metal
Despite a huge hit single in the mid-'70s ("The Boys Are Back in Town") and becoming a popular act with hard rock/heavy metal fans, Thin Lizzy are still, in the pantheon of '70s rock bands, underappreciated. Formed in the late '60s by Irish singer-songwriter/bassist Phil Lynott, Lizzy, though not the first band to do so, combined romanticized working-class sentiments with their ferocious, twin-lead guitar attack. As the band's creative force, Lynott was a more insightful and intelligent writer than many of his ilk, preferring slice-of-life working-class dramas of love and hate influenced by Bob Dylan, Bruce Springsteen, and virtually all of the Irish literary tradition. Also, as a Black man, Lynott was an anomaly in the nearly all-white world of hard rock, and as such imbued much of his work with a sense of alienation; he was the outsider, the romantic guy from the other side of the tracks, a self-styled poet of the lovelorn and downtrodden. His sweeping vision and writerly impulses at times gave way to pretentious songs aspiring to clichéd notions of literary significance, but Lynott's limitless charisma made even the most misguided moments worth hearing.

After a few early records that hinted at the band's potential, Lizzy released *Fighting* in 1975, and the band (Lynott, guitarists Brian Robertson and Scott Gorham, and drummer Brian Downey) had molded itself into a pretty tight recording and performing unit. Lynott's thick, soulful vocals were the perfect vehicle for his tightly written melodic lines. Gorham and Robertson generally played lead lines in harmonic tandem, while Downey (a great drummer who had equal amounts of power and style) drove the engine. Lizzy's big break came with their next album, *Jailbreak*, and the record's first single, "The Boys Are Back in Town." A paean to the joys of working-class guys letting loose, the song resembled similar odes by Bruce Springsteen, with the exception of the Who-like power chords in the chorus. With the support of radio and every frat boy in America, "Boys" became a huge hit, enough of a hit as

to ensure record contracts and media attention for the next decade ("Boys" is now used in beer advertising).

Never the toast of critics (the majority writing in the '70s hated hard rock and heavy metal), Lizzy toured relentlessly, building an unassailable reputation as a terrific live band, despite the lead guitar spot becoming a revolving door (Eric Bell, Gary Moore, Brian Robertson, Snowy White, and John Sykes all stood next to Scott Gorham). The records came fast and furious, and despite attempts to repeat the formula that worked like a charm with "Boys," Lynott began writing more ambitious songs and wrapping them up in vaguely articulated concept albums. The large fan base the band had built as a result of "Boys" turned into a smaller, yet still enthusiastic bunch of hard rockers. Adding insult to injury was the rise of punk rock, which Lynott vigorously supported, but it made Lizzy look too traditional and too much like tired old rock stars.

By the mid-'80s, resembling the dinosaur that punk rock wanted to annihilate, Thin Lizzy called it a career. Lynott recorded solo records that more explicitly examined issues of class and race, published a now-out-of-print book of poetry, and sadly, became a victim of his longtime abuse of heroin, cocaine, and alcohol, dying in 1986 at age 35. As the mega-popular alternative rock bands of the mid-'90s appropriate numerous musical messages from their '70s forebears, it's hoped that the work of Phil Lynott and Thin Lizzy will been seen for the influential rock 'n' roll it is. —*John Dougan*

Jailbreak / 1976 / Mercury ✦✦✦✦
Purely and simply a great rock and roll record. "Boys" is here in all its rabble-rousing glory, but better yet is the title track. Robertson and Gorham sound inspired, and Lynott's solid singing is made better by the sharp melodies he's written. Perhaps a greatest hits compilation is a better place for the uninitiated to start, but *Jailbreak* is a keeper. —*John Dougan*

Johnny the Fox / 1976 / Mercury ✦✦✦
Hot on the heels of *Jailbreak* came *Johnny the Fox*, which was a thematically linked group of songs that (fortunately) worked individually or as a concept record. The band sounds looser and funkier here (Lynott was sucker for a James Brown-style rhythmic kick), and that pays off big time. Not essential, but by no means a waste of time. —*John Dougan*

Bad Reputation / 1977 / Mercury ✦✦✦
Although this record had an obvious attempt at a hit single ("Dancing in the Moonlight"), it also had the relentlessly propulsive title track and a half-dozen or so great songs that showed a band hitting its stride, comfortable with its place in the world and not losing one bit of power. Lizzy's third great record in a row. —*John Dougan*

Live & Dangerous / 1978 / Warner Brothers ✦✦✦✦
Some prefer the 1983 set *Life* (and it's very good), but I like this (albeit studio-enhanced) live record, which has as strong a selection of Lizzy fare in one place as one is likely to find. Along with the live standards ("Boys," "Cowboy Song," "Jailbreak," and "Dancing in the Moonlight"), there are some great semi-obscurities (Bob Seger's "Rosalie" and the macho "The Rocker"). Loud, proud and chock full of dazzling guitar solos, this is a hard rock dream come true. Proof positive that in the arena rock sweepstakes, few bands were better onstage than Thin Lizzy. —*John Dougan*

● **Dedication: The Very Best of Thin Lizzy** / Apr. 2, 1991 / Mercury ✦✦✦✦
A good, if somewhat brief, look at all the high spots, featuring great guitar from fretmeisters Gary Moore, Eric Bell, John Sykes, and others. —*Cub Koda*

Peel Sessions / 1995 / Strange Fruit ✦✦✦✦
Better than the too-short, but still OK, *Dedication* greatest hits compilation released by Mercury in 1991, *The Peel Sessions* features raw and wild versions of great Lizzy songs that provide a great historical overview of the band's development. For what it's worth, this is the only Peel session release with liner notes written by John Peel himself. —*John Dougan*

Thinking Fellers Union Local #282

f. 1987, San Francisco, CA
Alternative Pop-Rock, Experimental, Indie Rock
With such a longwinded moniker, it's almost a given that this group could be nothing but a bunch of pretentious art-school rejects. Fortunately, that's pretty far from the truth. Thinking Fellers Union Local No.282 formed in 1987 in San Francisco and released their first album *Wormed By Leonard* on their own label, Thwart, a year later. In 1991, the group made the jump to the Matador label, where nearly all of their material has been released since, from 1991's critically acclaimed *Lovelyville* to 1994's *Strangers from the Universe*. Their sound is based on noodling on organs, electric banjos and mandolins, and heavy, fuzzed-out guitar blasts. A hybrid of art-rock and punk rock, Thinking Fellers Union Local No.282 is worth joining. —*Heather Phares*

Wormed, by Leonard / 1988 / Thwart Productions ✦✦
The group's difficult-to-find, cassette-only debut album finds the group performing some of their most avant-garde, inaccessible lunacy. —*Heather Phares*

Tangle / 1989 / Thwart Productions ✦✦✦
Tangle, the group's second album, contains more melodic but no less bizarre material than their debut. Both these albums are released on the group's own aptly-named Thwart Productions record label. —*Heather Phares*

Lovelyville / 1991 / Matador ✦✦✦✦
The group's first album for Matador is also one of their more accessible ones, with the group's penchant for willful eccentricity colliding with some hummable melodies. However, this release also contains plenty of what TFUL No.282 fans lovingly call "Feller-filler," i.e., noise-pieces that have no real beginning, or ending, or point for that matter. —*Heather Phares*

Mother of All Saints / 1992 / Matador ✦✦✦
Mother of All Saints is The Fellers' magnum opus. At 23 songs, it might be longer than most people's attention spans, but inside it lurks some of their finest moments, such as "Tell Me," "Hive," "Hummingbird in a Cube of Ice," and "Infection." True, there is plenty of "Feller-filler" on *Mother of All Saints* (an inspired piece called "Tuning Notes" attests to that) but the group's melodic sensibilities prevail on the actual songs on this album. —*Heather Phares*

● **Strangers of the Universe** / Sep. 12, 1994 / Matador ✦✦✦✦
The group's most subdued and melodic album yet, *Strangers* is ironically the Fellers' least strange album. It's also their most diverse; the goofy "My Pal the Tortoise" shares space with the genuinely disturbing "The Operation" and the genuinely catchy weirdo-pop of "Socket," and "The Piston and the Shaft," "Noble Experiment," "February," and "Cup of Dreams" explore the group's rare sentimental side, and the result is the group's most complete and listenable album. —*Heather Phares*

Funeral Pudding / Jan. 1, 1995 / Ajax ✦✦✦

3rd Bass

f. 1987, Queens, NY, **db.** 1992
Hip Hop, East Coast Rap
Along with the Beastie Boys, 3rd Bass stand as the rare white hip-hop act that's actually won respect and credibility among the rap hardcore. Pete Nice, one-time English major at Columbia whose radio program "Top of the Hip-hop" was unceremoniously cancelled by the purportedly progressive WKCR-FM, teamed with MC Serch to offer devastating put-downs of the hip-hop lifestyle and worldview. They have since disbanded, but their two albums were definitive, if at times uneven. —*Ron Wynn*

● **The Cactus Album** / 1989 / Def Jam ✦✦✦✦
With their first album, 3rd Bass turned in a surrealistically funky record of uproarious jokes, cutting social criticism, and eclectic music, drawing from Stax and Blood, Sweat and Tears. —*Stephen Thomas Erlewine*

Derelicts of Dialect / 1991 / Def Jam ✦✦✦
Although 3rd Bass didn't fully realize their tremendous potential, the Brooklyn rappers offered enjoyable, if uneven, albums. Like the group's 1989 debut, their second and final album, *Derelicts of Dialect*, makes it clear that the MCs weren't aiming for the pop charts—and were loyal only to the hip-hop hardcore. When MC Serch and Pete Nice tear into such aggressive and forceful declarations as "Pop Goes the Weasel" (an inflammatory attack on Vanilla Ice), "Portrait of the Artist as a Hood," and "Ace in the Hole," it's clear why they were among the few white MCs who were successful in the young Black community—someone who heard their rapping without seeing their picture could easily assume they were Black. Although the goofy "Herbalz in Your Mouth" shows some De La Soul and Tribe Called Quest influence, 3rd Bass doesn't allow itself to be nearly as light hearted, and keeps things hardcore and intense. —*Alex Henderson*

13th Floor Elevators

f. 1965, Austin, TX, **db.** 1968
Psychedelic, Garage Rock
Featuring the yelping vocals and visionary, occasionally demented lyrics of Roky Erickson, the 13th Floor Elevators were one of the original acid-rock bands. Formed in Texas in the mid-'60s, the Elevators started as a garage rock outfit, scoring their one and only modest national hit with "You're Gonna Miss Me." While Erickson's loopy persona, along with Tommy Hall's odd "jug" percussion, was the band's most distinguishing feature, several members of the group's original lineup contributed strong material to their albums. Although these inconsistent efforts sometimes wander off into a cloudy haze, they also include sturdy folk-rock tunes and driving psychedelic rockers. Trips to San Francisco established the group as up-and-coming underground favorites, but Erick-

son's drug problems led to the singer's commission to a state mental hospital in the late '60s, an ordeal from which he has never fully recovered. The band was really only at full power for a couple of albums, although all of their releases for the legendary International Artists label—produced by, of all people, Kenny Rogers' brother Leland—are revered among psychedelic collectors. Live recordings and outtakes of the Elevators continue to surface, though a cogent domestic compilation of the best of these erratic pioneers' work remains overdue. —*Richie Unterberger*

● **13th Floor Elevators** / 1966 / International Artists ✦✦✦✦
Their first album is their best, although their second (*Easter Everywhere*) also had some good material. Besides "You're Gonna Miss Me," includes "Fire Engine," "Tried to Hide," "Roller Coaster," and Erickson's best composition, the gentle folk-rocker "Splash 1." —*Richie Unterberger*

Easter Everywhere / 1967 / Collectables ✦✦✦
Basically an extension of the sound of their first album, but more overtly trippy, with material that is not quite as strong. "She Lives (In a Time of Her Own)" is probably the best cut; the rustic folk mood on "Dust" and "I Had to Tell You" is a good change of pace. —*Richie Unterberger*

Bull of the Woods / 1968 / Collectables ✦✦✦
Guitarist Stacy Sutherland wrote most of the songs on the band's final studio album, as Roky was largely absent due to drugs and problems with the law. Decent psychedelic rock—pretty straightahead and disciplined for the genre, actually—that doesn't match the inspired heights of their previous material. The closing "May the Circle Be Unbroken," with its wads and wads of reverb, may be the strangest thing the band ever cut. —*Richie Unterberger*

Live at the Avalon, 1966 / 1978 / Lysergic ✦✦✦
This quasi-legal production has shown up in other packages (and titles) since its original issue. It's a fair-quality tape of a 1966 concert that's a decent document for fans. The versions don't differ a heck of a lot from the ones on the records, though "Splash I," given a more forceful and full-bodied folk-rock arrangement, is a notable exception. There are also a few somewhat unexpected covers, like "Roll Over Beethoven," "You Really Got Me," Buddy Holly's "I'm Gonna Love You Too," and the Beatles' "The Word." —*Richie Unterberger*

Fire in My Bones / 1985 / Texas Archive ✦✦✦
The best collection of previously unreleased Elevators. Side one has six songs from an early 1966 live Dallas TV broadcast, including "You're Gonna Miss Me" and "Fire Engine," as well as covers of hits by the Kinks, Them, and Chuck Berry. Side two has alternate versions of four songs from the first LP that are more uninhibited in spots than the official versions, as well as the previously unreleased song "Fire in My Bones" and a live jam. —*Richie Unterberger*

Elevator Tracks / 1987 / Texas Archive ✦✦✦
More unreleased tracks. Side one has a previously unreleased acetate of "I Don't Ever Want to Come Down," and six alternate takes of officially released tunes (circa 1966) that are pretty close to the records, including "You're Gonna Miss Me," "Tried to Hide," and "Splash One." Side two is a fair-quality recording of a live summer 1966 gig in Houston, including covers of "Satisfaction," the Beatles' "I'm Down," and James Brown's "I Feel Good." Decent, but for completists. —*Richie Unterberger*

Original Sound of / 1988 / 13th Hour - ✦✦
The outtake barrel starts to run thin on yet another collection of unreleased material. Side one has different (not too different) studio versions of songs from the first LP, and side two is a fair-quality tape of five songs from a club gig in Austin in 1966. —*Richie Unterberger*

● **Best of the 13th Floor Elevators** / 1994 / Eva ✦✦✦✦
Finally, a best-of compilation for one of the most popular cult psychedelic groups of all time. The 22 tracks draw most heavily upon the first LP, with choice bits from the second and third, as well as some material Roky Erickson cut with his pre-Elevators group the Spades. —*Richie Unterberger*

.38 Special

f. 1975, Jacksonville, FL
Southern Rock, Hard Rock, Arena Rock
Initially, .38 Special was one of many Southern rock bands in the vein of the Allman Brothers and Lynyrd Skynyrd; in fact, the band was led by Donnie Van Zant, the brother of Skynyrd's leader, Ronnie Van Zant. After releasing a couple of albums of straight-ahead Southern boogie, the band revamped their sound to fall halfway between country-fried blues-rock and driving, arena-ready hard rock. The result was a string of hit albums and singles in the early '80s, highlighted by "Caught Up in You," "If I'd Been the One," "Back Where You Belong," and "Like No Other Night." .38 Special's popularity dipped in the late '80s, as MTV-sponsored pop and heavy metal cut into their audience. Though the band had their biggest hit in 1989 with the ballad "Second Chance," it

proved to be their last gasp—they faded away in the early '90s, retiring to the oldies circuit.

Donnie Van Zant (vocals) formed the Jacksonville, Florida-based .38 Special in 1975 with Jeff Carlisi (guitar), Don Barnes (guitar, vocals), Ken Lyons (bass), Jack Grondin (drums), and Steve Brookins (drums). Two years later, the band signed with A&M Records and released their eponymous debut. Neither .38 Special nor its followup, *Special Delivery*, received much attention, but the group began to build up a following through their constant touring. Bassist Lyons left before the recording of 1979's *Rockin' into the Night*, the album that demonstrated a more melodic, driving sound; he was replaced by Larry Junstrom. *Rockin' into the Night* became a moderate hit, but 1981's *Wild-Eyed Southern Boys* was a genuine hit, going platinum and generating the Top 40 "Hold On Loosely." *Special Forces*, released in 1982, was even more popular, spawning the Top Ten single "Caught Up In You" and "If I'd Been the One." *Tour De Force* (1983) and *Strength in Numbers* (1986) were both successes, and the band continued to be a popular turning outfit. Barnes and Brookins left in 1987 and were replaced by Danny Chauncey and Max Carl, respectively.

While *Strength in Numbers* had been popular, it didn't stay on the charts as long as its predecessors. *Flashback*, the 1987 greatest hits album, was moderately successful, but the band took precautions to retain their audience by recording the polished *Rock & Roll Strategy*. Released in 1989, the album slowly became a hit on the strength of "Second Chance," an adult-contemporary-oriented ballad that reached the Top Ten.

Rock & Roll Strategy became the band's final big hit. Barnes returned to the band in 1991 and the group replaced drummer Carl with Scott Hoffman and added keyboardist Bobby Capps. Even with the extensive retooling and the support of a new label, Charisma, 1991's *Bone Against Steel* failed to gain much attention. .38 Special didn't release another album for six years. In the summer of 1997, they released a comeback effort titled *Resolution* on Razor & Tie Records. *—Stephen Thomas Erlewine*

● **Flashback: Best of .38 Special** / 1987 / A&M ✦✦✦✦
Flashback: Best of .38 Special is a terrific compilation of the Southern rock's group's biggest hits, including "Caught Up In You," "If I'd Been the One," "Back Where You Belong," "Wild-Eyed Southern Boys," and the non-LP soundtrack contribution, "Teacher Teacher." Since *Flashback* was released in 1987, it doesn't contain their biggest hit, 1989's syrupy ballad "Second Chance," but it remains a comprehensive overview of their best moments, and makes a convincing case that they were the last great Southern rock singles band. *—Stephen Thomas Erlewine*

This Mortal Coil

f. 1983, London, England, **db.** 1991
Alternative Pop-Rock, Dream-Pop
This Mortal Coil is the brainchild of 4AD's president, Ivo Watts. It's not really a band, it's a way for Watts to explore different musical territory and cover his favorite artists, including Syd Barrett, Alex Chilton, Talking Heads, Tim Buckley, and Gene Clark. Over the years, the lineup has featured various stars from the record label's roster including Kim Deal, Tanya Donelly, Heidi Berry, and Robin Guthrie and Elizabeth Fraser from the Cocteau Twins. Like most 4AD bands, This Mortal Coil is atmospheric, sometimes dreamy, other times haunting. Watts has said that 1991's *Blood* is the last album the outfit will release. *—Stephen Thomas Erlewine*

It'll End in Tears / 1984 / 4AD ✦✦✦
Features the Cocteau Twins' Elizabeth Fraser singing Tim Buckley's "Song to the Siren," Gordon Sharp singing Rema-Rema's "Fond Affections," and Howard Devoto singing Alex Chilton's "Holocaust." Lisa Gerrard and Brendan Perry of Dead Can Dance are also included on this first collection of covers from 4AD. *—Heather Phares*

Filigree & Shadow / 1986 / 4AD ✦✦✦✦
The second album of This Mortal Coil interpretations includes the vocalist, Jean, doing a version of Van Morrison's "Come Here My Love," and Deirdre and Louise Rutkowski singing Tim Buckley's "Morning Glory." Other songs include David Byrne's "Drugs" and Gene Clark's "Strength of Strings." *—Heather Phares*

● **Blood** / May 13, 1991 / 4AD ✦✦✦✦
The final This Mortal Coil album includes some of the project's finest moments, including a cover of The Byrds' "I Come and Stand at Every Door" by Louise and Deidre Rutkowski, Syd Barrett's "Late Night," sung by Caroline Crawley of Shellyan Orphan, a cover of Gene Clark's "With Tomorrow," and a standout performance of Chris Bell's "You and Your Sister" by The Breeders' Kim Deal and Belly's Tanya Donelly. *—Heather Phares*

1983-1991 / Mar. 30, 1993 / 4AD ✦✦✦
All three of This Mortal Coil's albums packaged in an expensive slipcase, along with a disc of the original versions of the songs they covered. Fans

of 4AD bands like Throwing Muses, the Cocteau Twins, and Dead Can Dance will thoroughly enjoy This Mortal Coil's lush, haunting music; some members of these bands play on various tracks on the box, including a standout duet between Kim Deal and Tanya Donelly on Chris Bell's "You and Your Sister." Although the packaging is beautiful, there are no liner notes. *—Stephen Thomas Erlewine*

Carla Thomas

b. Dec. 21, 1942, Memphis, TN
Vocals / Soul
In the glorious decade and a half of sound that was Stax in the '60s and early '70s, Carla Thomas was the Queen of Memphis Soul. She was born in Memphis in 1942, and 18 years later she recorded a duet with her father Rufus Thomas, giving the fledgling Satellite label its first taste of success with the regional hit "Cause I Love You." As her 18th birthday drew nigh, she cut her first solo single, the teen ballad "Gee Whiz (Look at His Eyes)." Written a few years earlier and rejected by Vee-Jay in Chicago, it gave Satellite its first national hit, breaking the Top Ten mark on both the R&B and pop charts. Shortly thereafter Satellite became Stax, and Carla proceeded to claw her way onto the national charts another 22 times with such immortal slices of soul as her answer song to Sam Cooke, "I'll Bring It on Home to You," as well as "Let Me Be Good to You," "B-A-B-Y," "Tramp" (with Otis Redding), and "I Like What You're Doing to Me." Carla released six solo albums and, with Otis Redding, one duet album on Stax between 1961 and 1971. *—Rob Bowman*

Gee Whiz / 1961 / Atlantic ✦✦✦
Carla Thomas' first album was typical fare for the R&B market of the time, combining two chart entries (the title song and "A Love of My Own") with covers of recent chart hits (the Drifters' "Fools Fall in Love" and "Dance with Me," the Five Satins' "To the Aisle"), standards ("The Masquerade Is Over"), and a handful of originals. This was the first album produced by the then-fledgling Stax label and the unique Stax sound was not yet manifest. *—Rob Bowman*

Carla / 1966 / Atlantic ✦✦✦✦
Paired with Stax writing whiz-kids Isaac Hayes and David Porter, Thomas had her greatest chart run, beginning with the hit "B-A-B-Y" and continuing with "Let Me Be Good to You." Both of those appear here, alongside evocative slabs of country-soul in covers of Hank Williams' "I'm So Lonesome I Could Cry" and Patsy Cline's "I Fall to Pieces." For good measure, Thomas also tries her hand at the blues with covers of Howlin' Wolf's "Little Red Rooster" and Jimmy Reed's "Baby What You Want Me to Do?" *—Rob Bowman*

Comfort Me / 1966 / Atlantic ✦✦✦✦
A collection of 12 tracks recorded over a year and a half, *Comfort Me* showcases Thomas in the midst of the developed Stax sound. Backed by Booker T. and the MG's and the Mar-Key horns, Thomas turns in fine covers of Baby Washington's "Move on Drifter," the Marvelettes' "Forever," the Shirelles' "Will You Love Me Tomorrow?," the Everly Brothers' "Let It Be Me," Jackie DeShannon's "What the World Needs Now," the Toys' "Lover's Concerto," and Barbara Mason's "Yes I'm Ready," coupled with a number of efforts by Thomas herself, Steve Cropper, and Eddie Floyd. The highlight is the Cropper-Floyd title cut, with utterly gorgeous backing by Gladys Knight and the Pips. *—Rob Bowman*

Hidden Gems / 1992 / Stax ✦✦✦
Twenty outtakes recorded for Stax between 1960 and 1968, a number of which are gems. In fact, it is really surprising just how good the unreleased Stax stuff was in the '60s. "Loneliness," "Sweet Sensation," and "It Ain't No Easy Thing" all could have been superb singles. *—Rob Bowman*

● **Gee Whiz: the Best of Carla Thomas** / Jul. 19, 1994 / Rhino ✦✦✦✦
Gee Whiz: The Best of Carla Thomas is a wonderful 22-track collection of her seminal recordings for Atlantic and Stax, featuring all of her biggest hits—"Gee Whiz," "I'll Bring It Home to You," "B-A-B-Y," "Tramp," "I Like What You're Doing (To Me)"—as well as a terrific selection of lesser-known singles and album tracks. *—Stephen Thomas Erlewine*

Sugar / Sep. 30, 1994 / Stax ✦✦✦
A collection of odds and ends from the late '60s and early '70s, including some obscure Stax singles, duets with Pervis Staples and Johnnie Taylor, and three live numbers from the *Wattstax* soundtrack. It's not the first (or second) Carla Thomas collection you should pick up, but it's solid material. Donny Hathaway and Chips Moman each produced a couple of the singles spotlighted here (A-sides and B-sides are included), adding moderately ambitious variations on the standard Stax sound. *—Richie Unterberger*

Irma Thomas

b. Feb. 18, 1941, Ponchatoula, LA
Vocals / Soul, Classic Female Blues, New Orleans R&B
Radiating an outgoing joy that's inevitably at the heart of her infectious vocal delivery, Irma Thomas has no rivals as the Soul Queen of New

Orleans. Working at a Crescent City nightery as a waitress in 1959, Thomas sat in one night with Tommy Ridgely's band and made such a favorable impression that the veteran bandleader hustled her into the studio shortly thereafter to wax her first hit for the Ron label, the driving "Don't Mess with My Man." She joined forces with producer Allen Toussaint to make some of her most moving outings for Minit Records during the early '60s, notably "It's Raining," "Ruler of My Heart," and "Cry On," before venturing to the West Coast, where she cut both her biggest seller, the lushly produced "Wish Someone Would Care," and her best-known song, the original "Time Is on My Side"—and she's still bitter enough about the Rolling Stones' cover stealing her thunder to discourage requests for the tune.

The highly adaptable chanteuse also made some sizzling soul at Rich Hall's Muscle Shoals studio for Chess in the summer of 1967 before cooling off for a while during the '70s. But she's back now, as radiant as ever—and for convincing proof, listen to her buoyant 1990 concert performance on Rounder, *Live! Simply the Best*. Now that's truth in packaging!

Irma Thomas finally fulfilled a lifelong ambition in 1993 by recording her first gospel release. *Walk Around Heaven* was as magnificently sung and emotionally convincing as any of her classic New Orleans soul cuts. Thomas followed the album in 1997 with *The Story of My Life*, which featured several songs written by Dan Penn. —*Bill Dahl*

Time is on My Side [Kent] / 1983 / Kent ◆◆◆◆
Solid 16-song compilation of material from the mid-'60s. Most of this is duplicated by the more extensive CD compilations of the same era on EMI and Razor & Tie. But it's not entirely superfluous; five of the songs don't appear on either of the other collections. Those tracks are worth hearing, particularly the gutsy soul-pop concoction "Baby Don't Look Down," one of Randy Newman's earliest compositions. —*Richie Unterberger*

Ruler of Hearts / 1989 / Charly ◆◆◆
Sides from her early-'60s Minit sessions. The most New Orleans R&B-influenced of Thomas' early work, it includes "Cry On," "It's Raining," and "Ruler of My Heart," as well as lesser-known but equally moving cuts like "Two Winters Long" and "It's Too Soon to Know." —*Richie Unterberger*

★ **Time Is on My Side (The Best of Irma Thomas), Vol. 1 / Apr. 21, 1992 / EMI America ◆◆◆◆◆**
Twenty-three sides representing the cream of Irma Thomas' brilliant Minit/Liberty years (1961-1966), when her reputation as "The Soul Queen of New Orleans" was built. Virtually all her best-known tunes are here—"Wish Someone Would Care," "Ruler of My Heart," "It's Raining," and "Time Is on My Side" (covered note for note by the Stones). Beautiful singing from one of the first ladies of soul music. Essential. —*Christine Ohlman*

Sweet Soul Queen of New Orleans: the Irma Thomas Collection / Feb. 20, 1996 / Razor & Tie ◆◆◆◆
Twenty-three-track collection of early and mid-'60s sides largely duplicates the material on EMI's *Time Is on My Side* collection, with some additions and subtractions. The EMI set has a very slight edge, though for most listeners either compilation will do the job. It's too bad somebody doesn't take the plunge and issue an 80-minute CD documenting this era; as it is, serious Irma fans will need to get each best-of, as each contains tracks not on the others. —*Richie Unterberger*

Story of My Life / Feb. 11, 1997 / Rounder ◆◆◆
The Story of My Life stands out among latter-day Irma Thomas albums not only because she gives a consistently excellent performance, but because the record boasts three new songs from Dan Penn, who wrote some of the greatest soul songs of the '60s. While his new songs ("Hold Me While I Cry," "I Count the Teardrops," "I Won't Cry for You") aren't quite as strong as his best, they are nevertheless wonderful contemporary soul numbers, and they help make the record, the remainder of which is comprised of covers and slightly weaker new numbers, one of Thomas' best latter-day albums. —*Stephen Thomas Erlewine*

Rufus Thomas

b. Mar. 26, 1917, Cayce, MS
Vocals / Soul, R&B, Electric Memphis Blues
Few of rock 'n' roll's founding figures are as likable as Rufus Thomas. From the 1940s onward, he has personified Memphis music; his small but witty cameo role in Jim Jarmusch's *Mystery Train*, a film which satirizes and enshrines the city's role in popular culture, was entirely appropriate. As a recording artist, he wasn't a major innovator, but he could always be depended upon for some good, silly, and/or outrageous fun with his soul dance tunes. He was one of the few rock or soul stars to reach his commercial and artistic peak in middle age, and was a crucial mentor to many important Memphis blues, rock, and soul musicians.

Thomas was already a professional entertainer in the mid-'30s, when he was a comedian with the Rabbit Foot Minstrels. He recorded music as early as 1941, but really made his mark on the Memphis music scene as a deejay on WDIA, one of the few Black-owned stations of the era (his broadcasts could be heard from the '40s through the mid-'70s). He also ran talent shows on Memphis' famous Beale Street that helped showcase the emerging skills of such influential figures as B.B. King, Bobby Bland, Junior Parker, Ike Turner, and Roscoe Gordon.

Thomas had his first success as a recording artist in 1953 with "Bear Cat," a funny answer record to Big Mama Thornton's "Hound Dog." It made No. 3 on the R&B charts, giving Sun Records its first national hit, though some of the sweetness went out of the triumph after Sun owner Sam Phillips lost a lawsuit for plagiarizing the original Jerry Leiber/Mike Stoller tune. Thomas, strangely, would make only one other record for Sun, and recorded only sporadically throughout the rest of the 1950s.

Thomas and his daughter Carla would become the first stars for the Stax label, for whom they recorded a duet in 1959, "'Cause I Love You" (when the company was still known as Satellite). In the '60s, Carla would become one of Stax's biggest stars. On his own, Rufus wasn't as successful as his daughter, but issued a steady stream of decent dance/novelty singles.

These were not deep or emotional statements, or meant to be. Vaguely prefiguring elements of funk, the accent was on the stripped-down groove and Rufus' good-time vocals, which didn't take himself or anything seriously. The biggest by far was "Walking the Dog," which made the Top Ten in 1963, and was covered by the Rolling Stones on their first album.

Thomas hit his commercial peak in the early '70s, when "Do the Funky Chicken," "(Do The) Push and Pull," and "The Breakdown" all made the R&B Top Five. As the song titles themselves make clear, funk was now driving his sound rather than blues or soul. Thomas drew upon his vaudeville background to put them over onstage with fancy footwork that displayed remarkable agility for a man well into his 50s. The collapse of the Stax label in the mid-'70s meant the end of his career, basically, as it did for many other artists with the company. —*Richie Unterberger*

● **Do the Funky Somethin': Best Of / Apr. 1996 / Rhino ◆◆◆◆**
Overdue career-spanning collection of his best material, centering around his Stax hits from the '60s and early '70s. The whole "dog" series of novelty dance songs from 1963-64 is here, as well as the hit "Jump Back" and a clutch of Stax singles that weren't hits, but became pretty well-known anyway, like "Sister's Got a Boyfriend" and "Sophisticated Sissy." There are also the early-'70s funk dance hits "Do the Funky Chicken," "(Do the) Push and Pull," "The Breakdown," and "Do the Funky Penguin," a couple of '60s duets with his daughter Carla, and his 1953 blues single "Bear Cat (The Answer to Hound Dog)," the first hit on Sun Records. A few other compilations have gone into specific phases of his career in greater depth, but this is certainly the best overview of a man who offered some of the funkiest and funniest Memphis soul around. —*Richie Unterberger*

The Thompson Twins

f. 1977, Cheshire, England, db. 1993
Dance-Pop, Synth-pop, New Wave, Pop-Rock
The Thompson Twins—who were neither a duo nor related, but simply named after the *Tin Tin* cartoon—were one of the more popular synth-pop groups of the early MTV era, scoring a handful of hits before fading away into lite-funk obscurity. While many of their contemporaries indulged in stylish variations on Roxy Music or robotic electronic funk, the Thompson Twins were more pop-oriented, even when they strayed into dance-pop. Despite their success—"Hold Me Now," "Lay Your Hands on Me," and "King for a Day" all reached the US Top Ten—the group was unable to successfully expand their synth-pop sound and, consequently, their audience had virtually disappeared by the late '80s.

Founding member Tom Bailey was attending a teacher's college in Cheshire, England and harboring dreams of becoming a classical pianist when he met Joe Leeway, a fledgling actor, in 1977. The pair hit it off, yet Leeway wasn't part of the original incarnation of the Thompson Twins, which featured Bailey (vocals, keyboards), guitarist Pete Dodd, guitarist John Roog, and drummer Chris Bell. During the late '70s and early '80s, the band released a handful of independent singles and became fixtures on the burgeoning New Romantic scene in London before signing with Arista Records in 1981. That year, they released their debut album, *A Product Of . . .*, to little attention.

Not long after the release of *A Product Of . . .*, Bailey added his girlfriend Alannah Currie (percussion, saxophone, vocals), Joe Leeway (percussion, vocals) and former Soft Boys bassist Matthew Seligman to the group. The Thompson Twins recorded one album in this seven-piece incarnation, 1982's *Set*, which was released in America as *In the Name of Love*. The record was a bomb, and following its release, the group was trimmed to a trio—Bailey, Currie, and Leeway. The revamped Thompson Twins released *Quick Step and Side Kick* in 1983, and the album became a major hit in the UK, climbing all the way to No. 2, as the singles "Love on Your Side" and "We Are Detective" reached the Top Ten. In America, the record was released under the truncated title *Side Kicks* and earned a cult following.

The Thompson Twins had their American commercial breakthrough in 1984 with *Into the Gap*. "Hold Me Now," the first single from the album, became a bigger hit in the US than it did in the UK, peaking at No. 3; it reached No. 4 in England. *Into the Gap* also featured the hits "Doctor Doctor" and "You Take Me Up," and the Thompson Twins quickly followed the record in 1985 with *Here's to Future Days*. "Lay Your Hands On Me" became an American Top Ten hit, as did "King for a Day," but none of the singles from the record became major hits in the UK, signaling that the group's popularity was beginning to decline. Leeway left the group in 1986, and the Thompson Twins remained a duo, releasing *Close to the Bone* the following year. Bailey and Currie made their romance public in 1988, when the couple had a child. That same year, they released the remix album *The Best of Thompson Twins: Greatest Mixes*, which was generally ignored.

By the late '80s, the Thompson Twins' audience had decreased substantially. *Big Trash*, their 1989 debut for Warner, produced the minor US hit "Sugar Daddy," but it was overlooked in England. In 1991, they released *Queer*, which was ignored in both the US and the UK. In 1994, Bailey and Currie decided to form a new band, Babble, in order to explore newer electronic musics such as ambient. Working with programmer Keith Fernley, Babble released *The Stone* in 1994 on Reprise to little notice. — *Stephen Thomas Erlewine*

Side Kicks / 1983 / Arista ✦✦✦
Side Kicks is the American version of the Thompson Twins' third album, *Quick Step & Side Kick*, featuring the same songs in a different sequencing. The record was the first group as a trio and, not coincidentally, it finds the group discovering their signature dance-inflected synth-pop sound. The singles "Love on Your Side" and "In the Name of Love" are the high points, but it's surprising how many of the remaining songs are enjoyable, cleverly-crafted and catchy synth-pop gems. — *Stephen Thomas Erlewine*

Into the Gap / 1984 / Arista ✦✦✦✦
Their American breakthrough album featured the hits "Doctor Doctor" and "Hold Me Now." This is the best single album. — *Kenneth M. Cassidy*

Here's to Future Days / 1985 / Arista ✦✦✦✦
On their follow-up to the commercial breakthrough *Into the Gap*, the Thompson Twins attempt to toughen up their sound, but the results are only partially successful. In fact, the most infectious number, "Lay Your Hands on Me," sounds like it could have been an outtake from the previous album. — *Stephen Thomas Erlewine*

Close to the Bone / 1987 / Arista ✦✦
By the time the Thompson Twins recorded *Close to the Bone*, they were reduced to the duo of Tom Bailey and Alannah Currie, and they had abandoned new wave synth-pop for lite funk-inflected dance-pop. Most of *Close to the Bone* is too sterile and predictable to be truly enjoyable, yet there are a handful of tracks that serve as a reminder that the group can turn out well-constructed and catchy pop songs when they choose. — *Stephen Thomas Erlewine*

Big Trash / Mar. 1989 / Red Eye ✦✦✦
Big Trash was a successful attempt to add a stronger rhythmic sensibility to The Thompson Twins' sound, but the album failed to produce any hit bigger than the No. 28 "Sugar Daddy," although there were several other strong numbers on the record. — *Stephen Thomas Erlewine*

Queer / Oct. 1991 / Warner Brothers ✦✦
With *Queer*, the Thompson Twins began incorporating current dance trends, particularly the dense, psychedelic Manchester sound of the Happy Mondays. It is an ambitious effort, but it isn't entirely successful—the group doesn't work the groove as effectively as the Madchester groups, nor do they come up with a catchy dance-pop tune. Instead, you can hear the group work to re-establish themselves as artists. *Queer* is an an admirable attempt, but that doesn't make it a good listen. — *Stephen Thomas Erlewine*

● **Love Lies & Other Strange Things: Greatest Hits** / Oct. 1, 1996 / Arista ✦✦✦✦
Love Lies & Other Strange Things is the first American compilation of the Thompson Twins' career and it is a definitive collection, containing all of their Top 40 hits—including "Lies," "Hold Me Now," "Doctor Doctor," "Lay Your Hands on Me," "King for a Day"—plus selected highlights from the group's albums. — *Stephen Thomas Erlewine*

Mayo Thompson

Art-Rock/Progressive-Rock, Psychedelic, Experimental
Thompson is primarily known as the leader (and only constant member) of the Red Krayola, the long-running underground band that initially made their mark on the '60s psychedelic scene, and went on to become noted players in the post-punk era. In 1970, he released a little-known album under his own name, *Corky's Debt to His Father*, for the

small Texas Revolution label. By and large it's as unclassifiably oddball as his Red Krayola stuff. But on the whole it's more accessible and, in a way, rather charming, its off-kilter, folk-rock sensibility bearing some similarities to the work of Syd Barrett. It was reissued on CD in the 1990s by the Drag City label. — *Richie Unterberger*

Corky's Debt to His Father / 1970 / Texas Revolution ✦✦✦✦
Although this, to put it mildly, is not a record for mainstream tastes, it nevertheless may be more palatable to pop ears than any of Thompson's numerous Red Krayola records. With a folkier bent than his group projects, Thompson projects himself as a lovable oddball of sorts, stringing together free-associative, non-sequitur lyrics against chord progressions and time signatures that, as is his wont, refuse to adhere to accepted norms. Much of it's rather catchy (if not hummable), though, with a whimsical sense of fun that makes it impossible to dismiss as pretentious artsiness. — *Richie Unterberger*

Richard Thompson

b. Apr. 3, 1949, London, England
Dulcimer, Guitar, Mandolin, Vocals / Singer-Songwriter, Folk-Rock, British Folk, Contemporary Folk
Richard Thompson is among the most admired guitarists and songwriters in folk-rock music, and in the 1980s and '90s, he moved from a fervent cult following to broader exposure while maintaining critical accolades for his biting guitar work and sardonic songs. He was a founding member of Fairport Convention, the most important British folk-rock group to emerge in the 1960s, and he recorded five albums with them—*Fairport Convention* (June 1968), *What We Did on Our Holidays* (January 1969), *Unhalfbricking* (July 1969), *Liege and Lief* (December 1969), and *Full House* (July 1970). Quitting the group in January 1971, he made his debut solo album, *Henry the Human Fly* (June 1972), before forming a duo with his wife Linda. The Thompsons released six albums—*I Want to See the Bright Lights Tonight* (April 1974), *Hokey Pokey* (March 1975), *Pour Down like Silver* (November 1975), *First Light* (November 1978), *Sunnyvista* (1979), and *Shoot Out the Lights* (1982)—before breaking up personally and professionally. In 1981, Thompson had made a second solo album of instrumentals, *Strict Tempo!*; with 1983's *Hand of Kindness*, his first charting album, he relaunched his solo career. (Five years later, Jo-el Sonnier took "Tear-Stained Letter," from the album, into the Country Top Ten.) Thompson followed with an acoustic live album, *Small Town Romance* (1984). He had recorded primarily for Island Records or his friend and producer Joe Boyd's Hannibal/Carthage labels, and his albums had been distributed inconsistently in the US. With *Across a Crowded Room* (February 1985), he moved to Polydor, a major. The album spent more than three months in the US charts. Polydor seems to have expected better sales than that, however, and after *Daring Adventures* (October 1986), Thompson left for Capitol Records, for which he has made *Amnesia* (October 1988), *Rumor and Sigh* (May 1991), *Mirror Blue* (February 1994), and *You? Me? Us?* (April 1996). Thompson's earlier work has been reissued extensively by Hannibal Records through Rykodisc, including a three-disc retrospective, *Watching the Dark* (April 1993). *Beat the Retreat* (October 1994), a tribute album featuring Thompson's songs performed by R.E.M., Bob Mould, Bonnie Raitt, Los Lobos, and David Byrne, among others, offered further testimony to the high regard in which Thompson is held. — *William Ruhlmann*

Henry the Human Fly / 1972 / Hannibal ✦✦✦✦
Supposedly the worst-selling album in the history of Warner Bros. Records (now available through Hannibal), this was Richard Thompson's debut solo album after a couple of years of playing sessions that followed his departure from Fairport Convention in 1970. It's a dry run for his six duet albums with his wife Linda, who is credited here under her maiden name, Linda Peters, and features some terrific folk songs, notably "Nobody's Wedding." — *William Ruhlmann*

Hokey Pokey / 1974 / Hannibal ✦✦✦
Richard and Linda Thompson's second album was a somewhat lighter one than their debut, *I Want to See the Bright Lights Tonight*, from earlier in 1974, but with tracks like "The Sun Never Shines on the Poor," not much. "I'll Regret It All in the Morning" and especially "A Heart Needs a Home" were classics. — *William Ruhlmann*

☆ **I Want to See the Bright Lights Tonight** / Apr. 1974 / Hannibal ✦✦✦✦✦
The debut album by the duo of Richard and Linda Thompson picked up from where Richard had left off in Fairport Convention. Casting his wife in the role of Sandy Denny (a part she carried off beautifully), Richard mixed rock and blues elements with traditional British folk music to striking effect. But where Fairport had employed some actual traditional songs and used the dark tone of some folk music sparingly, Richard plunged in on his original songs, painting portraits of drunks and beggars for whom religion provides the salvation to be found in death. Linda's moving voice made songs like "Withered and Died" and "The Great Valerio" as compelling as they were mournful, but Richard could

be terrifying: He began the devil's lullaby "The End of the Rainbow" with "I feel for you, you little horror," and went on to inform the infant, "There's nothing to grow up for anymore." The album was uncompromising and riveting. It seemed like a set of songs unearthed from the Dark Ages, and argued that those times had never really left. (Originally released in the UK in April 1974 as Island 9266, *I Want to See the Bright Lights Tonight* was released in the US in 1976 as one of the two LPs that made up *Richard Thompson Live! (More or Less)*. It was reissued in 1983 as Carthage 4407 and in 1991 as Hannibal/Rykodisc 4407.) — *William Ruhlmann*

Pour Down Like Silver / 1975 / Hannibal ✦✦✦✦
The third Richard and Linda Thompson album (and the first to be released in the US) features "For Shame of Doing Wrong," "Beat the Retreat," and "Dimming of the Day/Dargai," all doomy Richard Thompson songs, the last with an extensive guitar coda. But there's also the rollicking "Jet Plane in a Rocking Chair." The couple appeared on the album cover in mufti, indicative of their dedication to the Sufi sect of Islam, which would consume their attention for the next few years, such that they didn't release another new album until 1978. — *William Ruhlmann*

Richard Thompson Live ! (More or Less) / 1976 / Island ✦✦
With Richard and Linda Thompson in temporary religious retirement, Island Records, their label at the time, issued differing compilation albums on each side of the Atlantic. In the US, there was this double-record set, which consists of the Thompsons' debut album, *I Want to See the Bright Lights Tonight*, not previously released in America, and a second album compiling various outtakes and live performances by Fairport Convention, Richard solo, and Richard and Linda. This second disc was an abbreviation of the set Island issued in England, *Guitar, Vocal*. Subsequently, that album and *Bright Lights* were released in the US on Hannibal, and this album, now redundant, went out of print. — *William Ruhlmann*

Guitar & Vocal 1967-1976 / May 1976 / Hannibal ✦✦✦✦
A superb 68-minute collection of obscure and unreleased tracks from Thompson's career, covering late 1967 until April 1976. The album's first six tracks are devoted to Thompson's career with Fairport Convention—highlights include "Throwaway Street Puzzle" (the B-side of the single "Meet on the Ledge"), the BBC recording of "Mr. Lacey," the *Liege and Lief* session outtake "The Ballad of Easy Rider," the *Full House* session outtake "Poor Will and The Jolly Hangman," and "Sweet Little Rock 'N' Roller" from the L.A. Troubadour (*House Full*) concert tapes. Thompson plays some sizzling guitar on these cuts, though "Ballad of Easy Rider"—played here the way Dylan might've covered it on *John Wesley Harding*—is more representative of Sandy Denny than Thompson. The post-Fairport material includes an alternate arrangement of "A Heart Needs a Home" from *Hokey Pokey;* a beautifully sung live rendition of "The Dark End of the Street" (featuring one of Linda Thompson's best performances); their hard-rocking live rendition of Jack Clement's "It'll Be Me"; the exquisite solo acoustic guitar instrumental "Flee As a Bird"; and two epics, "Night Comes In" and "Calvary Cross," featuring Thompson and his band stretching out on stage. Despite the existence of the triple-CD career retrospective, this disc still has enough prime rarities to rate as a must-own, even for casual fans. — *Bruce Eder*

First Light / 1978 / Hannibal ✦✦✦
Richard and Linda Thompson returned to action with this, their fourth duo album, after three years away from music. It was not one of their best albums, although it did include the impressive "Don't Let a Thief Steal into Your Heart" and the title track. — *William Ruhlmann*

Sunnyvista / 1979 / Hannibal ✦✦✦
Richard and Linda Thompson's fifth album was more of a pop record than previous releases (although Chrysalis, their label, didn't see fit to release it in the US after *First Light* failed to sell, and it didn't appear domestically until it was picked up by Hannibal in 1983). Many Fairport Conventioneers guested, but the songwriting was not up to Richard Thompson's usual standard. — *William Ruhlmann*

Strict Tempo! / 1981 / Hannibal ✦✦
"Traditional & Modern Tunes for All Occasions!!" proclaims the album cover of this acoustic instrumental record on which Richard Thompson plays a series of reels, polkas, and jigs on a variety of stringed instruments. It's an effervescent set of traditional music that reveals some of Thompson's musical roots; not to be confused with a full-fledged Thompson vocal album, but enjoyable nevertheless. (Originally released in the UK in 1981 on Richard Thompson's own Elixir label, *Strict Tempo!* was released in the US in 1983.) — *William Ruhlmann*

★ **Shoot out the Lights** / 1982 / Hannibal ✦✦✦✦✦
Recorded as Richard and Linda Thompson's marriage was breaking up, *Shoot Out the Lights* is a stark emotional masterpiece, overflowing with brilliant songs and remarkably empathetic performances. Writing with a focus he occasionally lacked in the late '70s, Richard assembled eight of his finest songs for the album, and while the record is not strictly

autobiographical, it's informed with the pain of a disintegrating relationship. That pain shines through on haunting ballads like "Walking on a Wire," "Just the Motion," and "Did She Jump," all of which Linda sings with grace, which makes the strained relationships and emotions of the songs all the more resonant. With the exception of the dark, imploding title track, the songs Richard sings are lighter on the surface, but the subtext of "Don't Renege on Our Love" and the desperate "Man in Need" are just as stark as the ballads. And while it is occasionally harrowing, *Shoot Out the Lights* is not nearly as bleak as *I Want to See the Bright Lights Tonight*, especially since it's levied with the bounce of "Back Street Slide" and the closer "Wall of Death," a gentle resolution to begin again which gives the album a sense of optimism after the despair and heartbreak. — *Stephen Thomas Erlewine*

Hand of Kindness / Jul. 1983 / Hannibal ✦✦✦✦
It was too big a coincidence for most listeners that Richard Thompson's first solo album after his breakup with his wife and musical partner Linda Thompson was full of painful, sometimes venomous songs about romance gone wrong; the assumption (denied by Thompson) was that this was his divorce album. Whether or not that was the case, heartache gave Thompson a focus for some of the most accomplished songwriting of his career, beginning with "Tear-Stained Letter" ("And just when I thought I could learn to forget her / Right through the door came a Tear-Stained Letter"), covered by Jo-el Sonnier for a Top Ten Country single in 1988, and continuing with the heart-wrenching "How I Wanted To" and "A Poisoned Heart and a Twisted Memory." With his typically authoritative six-string work driving the folk-rock music (played by a band anchored by members of Fairport Convention), which could be surprisingly jaunty given the subject matter, Thompson turned in his finest solo effort and, in the estimation of many critics including this one, one of the best rock albums of 1983. — *William Ruhlmann*

Small Town Romance / 1984 / Hannibal ✦✦✦
This is a live album taken from club appearances made by a solo, acoustic Richard Thompson in January and September 1982. It provides an opportunity to hear songs from throughout his career (plus previously unreleased ones) in a bare setting, and many are all the better for that. Nevertheless, Thompson has expressed antipathy for the album, and Hannibal has obediently let it go out of print. — *William Ruhlmann*

Across a Crowded Room / Feb. 1985 / Polydor ✦✦✦✦
After *Hand of Kindness* earned critical kudos and broke into the charts on the tiny Hannibal label, Polydor signed Richard Thompson with hopes of a commercial breakthrough. His first major-label solo album, *Across a Crowded Room*, was very much in the style of *Hand of Kindness*. He was not through expressing anger about love gone wrong; the lead-off track, "When the Spell Is Broken," plunged right back in, with Thompson intoning, "Can't cry if you don't know how." In "You Don't Say," backup singers Christine Collister and Clive Gregson filled the verses with criticisms made by a woman scorned. "Do you mean she still cares?" asked Thompson in the chorus. And so it went, as love was equated with spying ("Love in a Faithless Country") and violence ("She Twists the Knife Again"). Thompson's worldview had always been dire, and so it remained ("Walking Through a Wasted Land"). But his romantic venom gave his disdain energy, and the musical combination of blues-rock and Scots-Irish folk was compelling on its own. *Across a Crowded Room* was a worthy successor to *Hand of Kindness* and even threatened to make the Top 100 bestsellers list, though that turned out to be an aberration. — *William Ruhlmann*

Doom and Gloom from the Tomb, Vol. 1 / 1985 / Flypaper ✦✦✦
A fan-club follow-up to the *(guitar, vocal)* rarities compilation, *Doom and Gloom from the Tomb, Vol. 1* was a cassette-only release made available to subscribers of the Richard Thompson fanzine *Flypaper*. Compiled with the help of Richard and Linda Thompson, it contained 18 tracks dating back to the original 1968 lineup of Fairport Convention, though half of it came from demos and live recordings made by Richard and Linda between 1977 and 1982. There were interesting cover tunes, songs with different lyrics from the released versions, previously unreleased songs, and bravura live performances. And the later material sounded just as good as the early stuff—a live version of "Tear-Stained Letter" from Richard's 1983 "Big Band" tour was an amazing workout, and the unreleased "Jenny, My Love," written for but not included on *Across a Crowded Room*, was as moving a song as any Richard had ever written. By definition, *Doom and Gloom* was an album for the converted, but that didn't mean it was without some real gems. — *William Ruhlmann*

Daring Adventures / Mar. 1986 / Polydor ✦✦✦
Richard Thompson's second Polydor album contained some terrific and varied songs, from the raucous "A Bone Through Her Nose" to the mournful "Missie How You Let Me Down" and "Al Bowlly's In Heaven." Good as it was, it didn't establish Thompson as a big seller, and Polydor dropped him. — *William Ruhlmann*

Amnesia / 1988 / Capitol ◆◆◆◆
Here Thompson has really redefined himself, taking the more pop
sound of *Dangerous Adventures* further. Again produced by Mitchell
Froom, this record smokes with the concert favorite "Turning of the
Tide," "The Reckless Kind," and the bittersweet "Waltzing for Dreamers."
—Richard Meyer

Rumor and Sigh / May 1991 / Capitol ◆◆◆◆
Richard Thompson's second Capitol Records outing and second collaboration with producer Mitchell Froom was a lengthy 14-track opus that
gave a thorough airing to his usual concerns—twisted love, crime, death,
drinking. Somehow, all of this had come to seem a little less and a little
more derivative, both of earlier Thompson and of Bob Dylan. Compare
a lyric like "I ask you what's wrong, and you say, / I'm all yours / I ask
who your friend is, / And you say, Santa Claus" (Thompson's "I Plead"),
for example, with "Well, I go to pet your monkey / I get a face full of
claws / I ask who's in the fireplace / And you tell me Santa Claus"
(Dylan's "On the Road Again"). "Psycho Street," meanwhile, sounds like
the kind of weird recitals John Cale used to cook up for the Velvet
Underground. The trio of songs that open the album, "Read About
Love," "I Feel So Good," and "I Misunderstood," are worthy additions to
Thompson's repertoire of witty doomed love songs, and "1952 Vincent
Black Lightning" is a timeless death ballad, but not all of the album
reaches that standard, and with a running time over an hour, it just goes
on too long. Froom abets Thompson's more extreme tendencies rather
than reining them in, so it's no surprise *Rumor and Sigh* became his
first major-label solo album to miss the charts. *—William Ruhlmann*

Doom and Gloom II (Over My Dead Body) / 1991 / Flypaper ◆◆◆
Another interesting collection of rarities produced by the Richard
Thompson fanzine *Flypaper, Doom and Gloom II* contains 15 tracks,
more of them given over to Thompson's solo career of the 1980s and
'90s, though there are also recordings dating back to Fairport Convention and the duo of Richard and Linda Thompson. Highlights include a
cover of Hank Williams' "Mind Your Own Business" with vocals shared
by Thompson, Clive Gregson, and Christine Collister; "Bad News Is All
the Wind Can Carry," from Thompson's first early-'70s solo demo tape
(Thompson said the song could be used for this album "over my dead
body." "He relented," writes compiler Frank Kornelussen, "we got the
song and our title."); and the first Fairport Convention performance of
"Who Knows Where the Time Goes." The *Flypaper* releases are intended
for fans: The sound quality is sometimes only passable, and the songs
are often familiar ones made distinctive by their rarity. (The tape even
includes a notation asking that it not be reviewed, a request we might
honor if it were being given away free.) Casual fans don't care to bother,
but hardcore fans do. Write to *Flypaper*, P.O. Box 516, Middle Village, NY
11379. *—William Ruhlmann*

Watching the Dark / May 11, 1993 / Hannibal ◆◆◆◆
A sprawling three-disc compilation tracing Richard Thompson's career
from his beginnings with Fairport Convention, through his days with
his ex-wife Linda, to his recent solo recordings, *Watching the Dark* is a
treasure for longtime fans as well as those who want an introduction to
his distinctive English folk-rock. Instead of being assembled chronologically, each disc contains three separate eras, which helps illustrate how
consistently rich his music has been through the years. Nearly half of
the tracks are rare or unreleased; instead of betraying Thompson's gifts,
the song selection helps convey the breadth and scope of his talents.
Although the material might be skewed towards hardcore fans, anyone
unfamiliar with Thompson will realize why he is one of the most
revered (and, unfortunately, unknown) songwriters and guitarists of his
era by listening to *Watching the Dark*. *—Stephen Thomas Erlewine*

Mirror Blue / Feb. 8, 1994 / Capitol ◆◆
In many ways, *Mirror Blue* is Thompson's pop record, with shorter
songs and a crisp, slick production. While that may put some fans off,
the songs prove to be another set of rich, detailed stories; even the supposed toss-offs are bright, catchy, and memorable. In fact, the best
moments of *Mirror Blue* equal the best of *Rumor and Sigh*—it's hard to
equal the subtle power of "Mingus Eyes" or "Mascara Tears," and the
closing song, "Taking My Business Elsewhere," is one of the best things
he has ever written. *—Stephen Thomas Erlewine*

Live at Crawley 1993 / 1995 / Flypaper ◆◆◆
Accompanied by acoustic bassist Danny Thompson, acoustic guitarist
Richard Thompson presents stripped-down versions of some of the
songs featured on his recent albums. Thompson is an engaging performer whose nuances and improvisations can be appreciated well in
this intimate format. The album is a fan-club recording and "is part of
our recent policy to regularly release live recordings . . . in an effort to
stop inferior bootleg versions . . . ," Thompson writes in the liner notes.
Of course, hardcore fans will buy both, but it's nice to see Thompson
joining the Grateful Dead in finding a way outside the usual record-
company structure to address his fans' desires. Write to *Flypaper*, P.O.
Box 516, Middle Village, NY 11379. *—William Ruhlmann*

You? Me? Us? / Apr. 16, 1996 / Capitol ◆◆◆
On the surface, *You? Me? Us?* appears to be a major statement from
Richard Thompson. Spread out over two discs, the budget-priced album
features 19 tracks, separated into an electric ("Voltage Enhanced") disc
and an acoustic ("Nude") disc, which each run around 40 minutes;
"Razor Dance" and "Hide It Away" appear on both discs. Despite its
appearance, *you? me? us?* isn't one of Thompson's major works. What
sinks the album isn't the songs—as always, Thompson has written a
handful of gems—but Mitchell Froom's production. Froom's gauzy,
pseudo-experimental approach masks the songs in an impenetrable
haze, which neither Thompson's guitar nor voice can cut through. There
is no texture to the album's sound—it is mushy and colorless, which cuts
away at the heart of Thompson's direct, emotional songs. If the songs on
you? me? us? were given the simple, direct production they deserve, it
would have been a completely different, more compelling experience.
As it stands, it's a wildly uneven and unengaging listen, like the great
majority of the Froom-produced Richard Thompson records. *—Stephen
Thomas Erlewine*

George Thorogood

f. Dec. 31, 1952, Wilmington, DE
Guitar, Vocals / Rock 'n' Roll, Blues-Rock, Boogie Rock
A blues-rock guitarist who draws his inspiration from Elmore James,
Hound Dog Taylor, and Chuck Berry, George Thorogood never earned
much respect from blues purists, but he became a popular favorite in
the early '80s through repeated exposure on FM radio and the arena
rock circuit. Thorogood's music was always loud, simple, and direct—his
riffs and licks were taken straight out of '50s Chicago blues and rock 'n'
roll—but his formulaic approach helped him gain a rather large audience in the '80s, when his albums regularly went gold.
   Originally, Thorogood was a minor-league baseball player, but
decided to become a musician in 1970 after seeing John Paul Hammond
in concert. Three years later, he assembled the Destroyers in his home
state of Delaware; in addition to Thorogood, the band featured bassist
Michael Lenn, second guitarist Ron Smith, and drummer Jeff Simon.
Shortly after the group was formed, he moved them to Boston, where
they became regulars on the blues club circuit. In 1974, they cut a batch
of demos that were later released in 1979 as the *Better than the Rest*
album.
   Within a year of recording the demos, the Destroyers were discovered
by John Forward, who helped them secure a contract with Rounder
Records. Before they made their first album, Lenn was replaced by Billy
Blough. Thorogood and the Destroyers' eponymous debut was released
in early 1977. The group's second album, *Move It on Over*, was released
in 1978. The title track, a cover of Hank Williams' classic, was pulled as a
single and it received heavy FM airplay, helping the album enter the
American Top 40 and go gold. Its success led to MCA's release of *Better
than the Rest*, which the band disdained. In 1980, Ron Smith left the
band and the group added a saxophonist, Hank Carter, and released
their third album, *More George Thorogood and the Destroyers*.
   Following the release of *More George Thorogood*, the guitarist signed
with EMI Records, releasing his major-label debut *Bad to the Bone* in
1982. The title track of the album became his first major crossover hit,
thanks to MTV's saturation airplay of the song's video. The album went
gold and spent nearly a full year on the charts. Thorogood's next three
albums after *Bad to the Bone* all went gold. Between *Bad to the Bone*
and Thorogood's next album, 1985's *Maverick*, the Destroyers added a
second guitarist, Steve Chrismar.
   By the beginning of the '90s, Thorogood's audience began to decrease.
None of the albums he released went gold, even though the title track
from 1993's *Haircut* was a No. 2 album rock hit. Despite his declining
record sales, Thorogood continued to tour blues and rock clubs, and he
usually drew large crowds. *—Stephen Thomas Erlewine*

George Thorogood & the Destroyers / 1977 / Rounder ◆◆◆◆
Contains Thorogood's crowd-pleasing rendition of John Lee Hooker's
"One Bourbon, One Scotch, One Beer." Its basic approach—heavy on
Thorogood's bluesy guitar playing—serves as the prototype for every
Destroyers record that followed. *—William Ruhlmann*

Move It on Over / 1978 / Rounder ◆◆◆
In 1978, George Thorogood was just beginning to make some noise on
the blues-rock circuit. This was his second album, and what's now
almost a cliche then sounded fresh and vital. Thorogood's energy, rousing vocals and driving guitar playing came roaring through on inspired
covers of Elmore James' "The Sky Is Crying," Bo Diddley's "Who Do You
Love," and Chuck Berry's "It Wasn't Me." He even did a credible Piedmont blues on Brownie McGhee's "So Much Trouble." While Thorogood
went on to make more commercially succesful albums, the spirit and
innocence in his early releases has seldom been duplicated. This
Rounder CD reissue returns him to a simpler, and in some ways superior, period. *—Ron Wynn*

More George Thorogood and the Destroyers / 1980 / Rounder ✦✦
George Thorogood was honing his focus and getting the Destroyers concept down pat on this 1986 album. He hadn't yet become so established and comfortable that his rocking blues licks and vocals were more show business than intensity and energy. Thorogood's playing and singing on such tracks as "House of Blue Lights," "Night Time," and "I'm Wanted" was earnest enough to make the treatments convincing, and retain interest. While this wasn't quite as memorable as his earlier dates, George Thorogood still had the hunger that fueled his breakout sessions. —*Ron Wynn*

Bad to the Bone / 1982 / EMI America ✦✦✦✦
Though songs such as "Back to Wentzville" are credited to G. Thorogood, he'd be the first to admit that they are proudly disciples of Chuck Berry and his other mentors. The title track, another Thorogood copyright, has become ubiquitous in *Terminator 2* and the *Problem Child* movies and elsewhere, but it's still terrific. —*William Ruhlmann*

● **The Baddest of George Thorogood and the Destroyers** / Jul. 28, 1992 / EMI America ✦✦✦✦
The aptly-titled *The Baddest of George Thorogood and the Destroyers* offers a dozen tracks that cleanse the church of rock'n'roll of all but its most basic elements: guitar, bass, drums, and a pile of Chuck Berry, Bo Diddley and Rolling Stone licks. Delaware's George Thorogood has never quite captured his wildman live presence in the studio, but having all his best material gathered on one disc—including "Bad to the Bone," "Move It on Over," and "One Bourbon, One Scotch, One Beer"—makes for a great party. Steve Morse's liner notes are brief but, like the songs, get right to the point . . . cut to the bone, you might say. —*Roch Parisien*

Haircut / Jul. 27, 1993 / EMI America ✦✦
You wouldn't expect any changes from George Thorogood, whose piledriving rocking-blues and boogie have maintained their appeal despite the emergence of numerous similar-sounding ensembles. Thorogood's rough-hewn singing and always tantalizing playing are on target through the usual mix of originals and covers (this time including Bo Diddley and Willie Dixon). Besides the bonus of major label engineering and production, Thorogood's work has never lost its edge because he avoids becoming indulgent or a parody, and continues to sound genuinely interested in and a fan of the tunes he's doing. —*Ron Wynn*

Rockin' My Life Away / Mar. 25, 1997 / Capitol ✦✦
As the title says, George Thorogood has been rockin' his life away, churning out a series of heavy blues-rock records, all of them stylistically identical to each other. *Rockin' My Life Away* is no exception to the rule, and while it is marginally better than the tepid *Haircut*, it sounds so damned similar to all of his other records that even fans have to wonder what the point is anymore. There are some differences, most notably that the selection of material is more interesting than before—out of the ten covers, there are songs by John Hiatt ("The Usual"), Jerry Lee Lewis, Frank Zappa, and Chuck Willis—and while he's losing energy as he ages, it actually adds some subtlety to his music. Still, if *Rockin' My Life Away* is anything, it's bloozy boogie and it's predictable, and for longtime fans, the lack of spark may cancel out the strength of the material. —*Stephen Thomas Erlewine*

Three Dog Night

f. 1968, Los Angeles, CA
Pop-Rock
Three Dog Night scored a succession of 21 hit singles, including 11 Top Tens and 12 consecutive gold albums from 1969 to 1975, thanks to the slick, sometimes soulful vocal harmonies of singers Danny Hutton, Chuck Negron, and Cory Wells and an excellent ear for quality material. While often criticized as commercial, the band was noted for its creative arrangements and interpretations, and their cover choices gave exposure (and royalties) to several talented songwriters: Nilsson ("One"), Laura Nyro ("Eli's Coming"), Randy Newman ("Mama Told Me [Not to Come]"), Hoyt Axton ("Joy to the World"), Argent's Russ Ballard ("Liar"), and Leo Sayer ("The Show Must Go On"). Wells and Hutton met in the '60s while the former was the lead singer of the Enemies and the latter, a former cartoon voice who had recorded several flop singles, served as producer. In 1967, Hutton conceived the idea of a three-vocalist group, and he and Wells enlisted mutual friend Negron. They took their name from an Australian expression describing low nocturnal temperatures in the Outback (the colder the night, the more dogs needed to keep warm while sleeping). The three cut a few unsuccessful singles and decided to expand their range by hiring backing musicians, who included guitarist Mike Allsup, keyboardist Jimmy Greenspoon, bassist Joe Schermie, and drummer Floyd Sneed. "One" became the band's first Top Ten hit in 1969, while "Mama Told Me (Not to Come)" hit No. 1 a year later. "Joy to the World" became the group's biggest hit in 1971, spending six weeks on top of the *Billboard* charts, and their streak continued with their final No. 1, 1972's "Black and White" (a UK reggae hit for Greyhound), and their final Top Ten, 1974's "The Show Must Go On." By 1976, internal dissent arose in the group, as the original concept of

three equal singers had given way to Negron taking the leads on most of their songs. Dissatisfied, Hutton finally left the group, and Three Dog Night officially disbanded a year later. There was a brief reunion in the early '80s, and Hutton and Wells have since taken a version of Three Dog Night out on the oldies circuit. —*Steve Huey*

● **The Best of Three Dog Night** / 1983 / MCA ✦✦✦✦
This collection contains all of Three Dog Night's hits, plus a few key album tracks. Among the tracks included are "One," "Easy to Be Hard," "Eli's Coming," "Mama Told Me Not to Come," "Joy to the World," "Black & White," "Shambala," "An Old-Fashioned Love Song," "Never Been to Spain," and "Celebrate." —*Rick Clark*

Celebrate: The Three Dog Night Story, 1965-1975 / Dec. 7, 1993 / MCA ✦✦✦✦
A comprehensive double-disc anthology, *Celebrate* is necessary for devoted fans of Three Dog Night, but most listeners will be content with *The Best of Three Dog Night*, which features all of the hits on a single disc. —*AMG*

Three O'Clock

f. 1980, Los Angeles, CA, **db.** 1988
Alternative Pop-Rock, Psychedelic, Paisley Underground
The Three O'Clock were the quintessential L.A. Paisley Underground band. Lead singer and bassist Michael Quercio in fact coined the term to describe the set of bands, including the Dream Syndicate, Rain Parade, Green On Red, and the Bangles, who incorporated the chiming guitars of the Byrds and the Beatles into their pop songs with a psychedelic bent, and the clothes to match. Beginning as the Salvation Army in 1982 as a three-piece and forsaking the name due to a conflict with the actual organization, the Three O'Clock originally included Quercio and guitarist Louis (formerly Gregg) Gutierrez. The band plied a garagey sound on their self-titled debut in 1982. When ex-Weirdos drummer Danny Benair and keyboardist Mickey Mariano joined for the follow-up EP *Baroque Hoedown* and the LP *Sixteen Tambourines* in 1983, the band found a more polished, perfect pop sound. In 1985 they released *Arrive Without Travelling* for IRS, followed by *Ever After* (IRS). Gutierrez departed in 1986. For their Warner Brothers/Paisley Park debut (Prince was a fan), *Vermillion*, Jason Faulkner was added on guitar. Sadly, it proved to be their undoing, as they never really fulfilled the label's expectations and Quercio refused to be pigeonholed as a pretty-boy pop star or spokesperson for the premature retro revival. Quercio continues to play in Los Angeles pop bands, while Gutierrez became a principal member of Mary's Danish, and Faulkner a solo recording artist. —*Denise Sullivan*

Salvation Army / 1982 / Frontier ✦✦✦
A rough but engaging debut for this three-piece garage rock band with a '60s bent. Punk in spirit but filled in with near-psychedelic guitar swirls and pop vocals, the band forged the foundation of the Paisley Underground movement, a sound that incorporated the best of the '60s from the Beatles to the Byrds to the Velvet Underground. "She Turns to Flowers" and "While We Were In Your Room Talking to Your Wall," if only in their titles, send a clear message of where the band was coming from. —*Denise Sullivan*

Baroque Hoedown / 1982 / Frontier ✦✦
The band found its sound on this essential EP from Los Angeles' influential paisley underground scene. "With a Cantaloupe Girlfriend" and "I Go Wild" capture the essence of the swirling psych-pop sound the band had naively mastered by this time, and their cover of the Easybeats' "Sorry" is worth the price of admission alone. Lead singer Michael Quercio's high, almost creepy voice could at times recall Syd Barrett, but was a unique instrument in its own right. —*Denise Sullivan*

16 Tambourines / 1983 / Frontier ✦✦✦
As the band matured, they naturally got better technically, but in this case it wasn't necessarily a good thing. No longer a loose garage outfit, keen production by Los Angeles pop whiz Earle Mankey put the keyboards up front, and next to vocalist Michael Quercio's unusually high voice, the band ended up sounding a little twee. Still, "When Lightning Starts" is irresistibly cute, and their choice of cover material was always inspiring; the version of the Bee Gees' "In My Own Time" included here is a perfect fit. —*Denise Sullivan*

Arrive without Travelling / 1985 / IRS ✦✦✦✦

Befour Three O'clock / 1985 / Frontier ✦✦

Ever After / 1986 / IRS ✦✦✦
Another solid neo-psychedelic pop album. Though it fails to distinguish itself from previous releases, *Ever After* is still an interesting venture. —*Chris Woodstra*

● **Vermillion** / 1988 / Paisley Park ✦✦✦✦
The band's final album is also their strongest. No longer restricted to their paisley underground roots, they stretch out stylistically with rewarding results. Includes the wonderful "Neon Telephone" (written by Prince). —*Chris Woodstra*

Throbbing Gristle

f. Sep. 1975, London, England, db. 1981
Industrial, Experimental

Abrasive, aggressive, and antagonistic, Britain's Throbbing Gristle pioneered industrial music; exploring death, mutilation, fascism, and degradation amidst a thunderous cacophony of mechanical noise, tape loops, extremist anti-melodies, and bludgeoning beats, the group's cultural terrorism—the "wreckers of civilization," one tabloid called them—raised the stakes of artistic confrontation to new heights, combating all notions of commerciality and good taste with a maniacal fervor.

Formed in London in the autumn of 1975, Throbbing Gristle consisted of vocalist/ringleader Genesis P-Orridge, his then-lover, guitarist Cosey Fanni Tutti, tape manipulator Peter "Sleazy" Christopherson, and keyboardist Chris Carter. A performance art troupe as much as a band, their early live shows—each starting with a punch clock and running exactly 60 minutes before the power to the stage was cut—threatened obscenity laws; during their notorious premiere gig, P-Orridge even mounted an art exhibit consisting entirely of used tampons and soiled diapers.

Upon forming their own label, Industrial, the group issued their introductory release, *The Best of Throbbing Gristle Vol. 2*, in 1976. A full-length debut, *2nd Annual Report*, followed in 1977, in a pressing of only 500 copies; bowing to fan demand, the record was later reissued—cut from a master tape played backwards. The 1977 underground hit "United" marked a tiny step towards accessibility, thanks to the inclusion of a discernible rhythm. Typically, when the track reappeared on 1978's *D.O.A.: The Third and Final Report*, it was sped up to last all of 17 seconds; no less provocative was "Hamburger Lady" (inspired by the story of a burn-unit victim) or "Death Threats" (a compilation of murderous messages left on the group's answering machine).

20 Jazz Funk Greats, a harsh electro-pop outing, followed a year later, and after 1980's live-in-the-studio *Heathen Earth*, Throbbing Gristle called it quits: while P-Orridge and Christopherson soon formed Psychic TV, the remaining duo continued on as Chris and Cosey. As Throbbing Gristle's influence swelled, a seemingly endless series of posthumous releases followed, most of them taken from live dates; among the more notable were 1981's *24 Hours* (later reissued as *36 Hours*), 1983's *Once Upon a Time (Live at the Lyceum)* and 1986's *TG CD1*. —*Jason Ankeny*

2nd Annual Report / 1977 / Mute ✦✦✦
Actually their first album, it has singles and different live versions of two early pieces. —*Myles Boisen*

D.O.A. / Dec. 1978 / Mute ✦✦✦
A dark lyrical content dominates these 15 tracks. —*Myles Boisen*

20 Jazz Funk Greats / 1979 / Mute ✦✦✦✦
This is as close as they got to the industrial-dance style of their many imitators; it's fairly accessible. —*Myles Boisen*

Heathen Earth / 1979 / Mute ✦✦✦
Live in the studio, this combines the best of both harrowing worlds. —*Myles Boisen*

Mission of Dead Souls / 1981 / Mute ✦✦✦
Their final and perhaps most extreme musical assault was recorded live in San Francisco. —*Myles Boisen*

● **Greatest Hits** / 1984 / Mute ✦✦✦✦
Like the title says (with irony), it's an industrial primer with song sensibility. —*Myles Boisen*

TG CD 1 / 1986 / Resonance ✦✦✦
A very raw studio session. —*Myles Boisen*

Throwing Muses

f. 1983, Boston, MA, db. 1997
Alternative Pop-Rock, Singer-Songwriter

One of the quietly great college bands from the 1980s, Throwing Muses was formed in 1983 by guitarist/vocalist Kristin Hersh and her half-sister, guitarist/vocalist Tanya Donelly (now of Belly) with a few friends from high school. In 1986 the group's debut album was put out by the prestigious British label 4AD; Throwing Muses were the first American band to be released on that label. Throwing Muses' angular, anguished, mercurial sound had much to do with Hersh's mental illness (she suffered from a form of bipolarity that caused her to hallucinate), especially on the early albums like *House Tornado*. 1991's *The Real Ramona* marked a break from the heaviness of the previous albums, with lots of shimmery pop gems penned both by Hersh and Donelly, who contributed at least one song an album throughout her stay in the band. Creative tensions between the two songwriters rose until Donelly left in 1992 to play with the Breeders and ultimately form Belly. That year Hersh reformed the Muses with drummer David Narcizo and released the band's fourth album, *Red Heaven*. After that, Hersh released a solo album and toured extensively, leaving fans to wonder about the status of the Muses. In 1995, however, Hersh and the rest of the Muses (Narcizo

and bassist Bernard Georges) released *University*, one of the band's most cohesive and accessible efforts; *University* was followed by *Limbo* in 1996. Though Throwing Muses have had little commercial success throughout their career, they have released some of the most challenging and genuine music of recent years — and hopefully will continue to do so. —*Heather Phares*

Throwing Muses / 1986 / 4AD ✦✦✦✦
The band's eponymous first album is a startling, uncompromising collection of musings from Hersh and Donelly. Songs like "Hate My Way, " "Call Me," and "Vicky's Box" feature mercurial dynamic and meter shifts. Hersh's guitar playing and voice are particularly dramatic; both swing from delicate melodicism to shrill atonality, especially on "Rabbits Dying" and "Delicate Cutters." Tanya Donelly contributes an ethereally beautiful love song in "Green." While this is not the most accessible album in the Muses' repertoire, it is an emotionally powerful and genuine one. —*Heather Phares*

Chains Changed [ep] / 1987 / 4AD ✦✦✦
This four-song EP is difficult to find, but is nevetheless worth the search. It contains some of Hersh's finest songs, including the rockabilly-tinged "Cry Baby Cry," the tumultuous "Finished," and "Snailhead." *Chain's Changed* combines the group's fiery intensity and moodiness with the pop prowess the band gradually developed. —*Heather Phares*

The Fat Skier [EP] / 1988 / 4AD/Sire ✦✦✦
Like the *Chains Changed* EP, this release is hard to find on its own, but is included on the import version of *House Tornado*. Some of their most commanding music is included, like the mesmerizing "A Feeling" and Donelly's "Pools in Eyes." The punky "Garaux Des Larmes" and wrenching "A She Wolf After the War" make this a concise but accurate sample of the Muses' variety. —*Heather Phares*

House Tornado / 1988 / 4AD/Sire ✦✦✦
House Tornado is a more melodic take on Throwing Muses' challenging style: Hersh's vocals are commanding and varied, especially on "Colder" and "Saving Grace." But the Muses' pop side surfaces more on this album than on their previous work, particularly on tracks like "Juno," "Run Letter," and on Donelly's "Giant." Like their debut, this album is an acquired taste, but an ultimately rewarding one. —*Heather Phares*

Hunkpapa / Oct. 1990 / 4AD/Sire ✦✦
On the group's third full-length album and their second for Sire, Throwing Muses display a rare creative lull. Many of the songs are just not as powerful as their prior material, but the album is not a total loss. The wild, desolate "Bea" and explosive "Mania" are two of Hersh's finest songs, and Donelly's "Dragonhead" and "Angel" show her growing prowess as a songwriter. —*Heather Phares*

● **The Real Ramona** / Mar. 12, 1991 / 4AD/Sire ✦✦✦✦
The Real Ramona is the Muses' finest pop moment. Hersh's material is some of her most melodic and accessible, yet it retains her unflinching honesty and emotional pull. "Counting Backwards," "Ellen West," "Hook in Her Head," and "Red Shoes" are both catchy and riveting works of songwriting. "Graffiti" and "Two-Step" are two of Hersh's most appealing pop snippets, and Donelly contributes two of the best songs she's ever written, the gleeful and giddy "Not Too Soon" and "Honeychain." Simply put, *The Real Ramona* is a great starting point for new Muses fans. —*Heather Phares*

Red Heaven / Aug. 11, 1992 / 4AD/Sire ✦✦✦
The Muses' fourth album is their first as a trio, with Tanya Donelly exiting and original bassist Leslie Langston replacing Fred Abong. The material is more rock-oriented than on the Muses' lighter and more abstract material, especially on "Furious," "Firepile," and "Dio," on which Hersh duets with Bob Mould. "Summer St." is one of Hersh's most endearing songs, and tunes like "Carnival Wig" and "Earl" maintain her reputation as an inventive and thoughtful songwriter. —*Heather Phares*

University / Jan. 17, 1995 / Sire/Reprise ✦✦✦✦
University, the group's most recent album, sees Hersh, drummer David Narcizo and new bassist Bernard Georges grow into writing and playing material for a trio. The result is some of the group's most buoyant punk-pop music, with "Bright Yellow Gun," "Start," and "Shimmer" being the chief examples. The delicate melodies of "That's All You Wanted" and "Crabtown" and the intensity of "Fever Few" show that Hersh has not lost her creative edge. Another good introduction to the Muses' work, especially their post-Donelly material. —*Heather Phares*

Limbo / Aug. 13, 1996 / Rykodisc ✦✦✦✦
Throwing Muses' album *Limbo* is their first on their self-owned record label, Throwing Music. Though it should be a celebration of the band's liberation from a major label that was a major disappointment, it's a strangely anticlimactic record. While a solid, well-written affair, it lacks the shimmery spark of the group's best material. The opening three songs—"Buzz," "Ruthie's Knocking" and "Freeloader"—get *Limbo* off to a propulsive start. But on the whole, the album suffers from similar rhythms and progressions on each song. *Limbo* is also poorly sequenced, with most of the louder songs on the first half, and the

slower, quieter songs sinking to the end of the album. The result isn't so much limbo as it is dejá vu—it's ironic that a band that started out as wildly mercurial is now edging towards predictability. There are moments worthy of vintage Throwing Muses on *Limbo*, however. "Tango" and "Serene" are subtly edgy, "Night Driving" is a dreamy ballad and "Shark" closes the album on a malevolent note. *Limbo* is a Throwing Muses album, after all. But for that to mean something so predictably peculiar is somewhat disappointing. —*Heather Phares*

Johnny Thunders

b. Jul. 15, 1952, Leesburg, FL, d. Apr. 23, 1991
Guitar / Rock 'n' Roll, Punk
Following in the footsteps of his idol Keith Richards, Johnny Thunders (born John Anthony Genzale, Jr.) lived the ultimate rock 'n' roll life, spending most of his days wasted and churning out tough, sloppy three-chord rock 'n' roll. He made his greatest impact as a member of the New York Dolls, the proto-punk glam rockers of the early '70s. During the late '70s, he was a familiar figure on the New York punk scene, both with the Heartbreakers and as a solo artist. Thunders kept performing and recording until his death in 1991, turning out a series of records that inadvertently documented his descent into heroin addiction.

Under the name Johnny Volume, Genzale began performing in high school with Johnny and the Jaywalkers; after leaving that band, he joined Actress, which featured future Dolls Arthur Kane and Billy Murcia. Actress became the New York Dolls in 1971 and Genzale renamed himself Johnny Thunders. After recording two acclaimed but unsuccessful albums, the Dolls broke up. In 1975, Thunders and the group's drummer Jerry Nolan formed the Heartbreakers with former Television bassist Richard Hell and guitarist Walter Lure. Hell left the group shortly afterward to form the Voidoid and was replaced by Billy Rath. With Thunders leading the band, the Heartbreakers toured America and Britain, releasing one official album, *L.A.M.F.*, in 1977. The group relocated to the UK, where their popularity was significantly greater, particularly among punk bands, than it was in the US. Thunders earned a reputation for incoherent, sloppy, drunken performances, as well as appearing on stage, unannounced, with other artists. After several months, the group returned to America, where they played a series of farewell gigs in New York.

Thunders went solo in 1978, recording *So Alone* with various rock and punk celebrities, including the Sex Pistols' Steve Jones and Paul Cook, Steve Marriott (Small Faces, Humble Pie), Peter Perrett (Only Ones), Paul Gray (Eddie And The Hot Rods, the Damned), and Thin Lizzy's Phil Lynott. After its release, Thunders and Sex Pistols bassist Sid Vicious played in the Living Dead for a short time. During the early '80s, Thunders re-formed the Heartbreakers for various tours; the group recorded their final album in 1984.

For most of the '80s, the only Johnny Thunders product available was haphazard compilations of live tracks and demos. In 1985, he released *Que Sera Sera*, a collection of new songs that showed he could still perform convincingly. Three years later, the guitarist recorded an album of rock and R&B covers with vocalist Patti Palladin, *Copy Cats*. Late in the decade, Thunders formed a group with ex-MC5 guitarist Wayne Kramer called Gang War; they released one album in 1990.

After years of abuse, Johnny Thunders was found dead in a New Orleans hotel room in April of 1991. While the autopsy didn't disclose the cause of death, most later reports claimed the guitarist died of a heroin overdose. Although it was a sad ending, it was appropriate—no other rock 'n' roller ever lived as hard as Johnny Thunders. —*Stephen Thomas Erlewine*

● **So Alone** / 1978 / Real Music ✦✦✦✦
Thunders' first solo shot enlisted members of the Sex Pistols, the Hot Rods, and the Only Ones, featuring a variety of material that showcased both his mangy vocals and his strangling guitar attack. —*John Floyd*

New Too Much Junkie Business / 1983 / Combat ✦✦✦
The best of Thunders' live and outtake documents is for diehards only. —*John Floyd*

'Til Tuesday

f. 1983, Boston, MA, db. 1989
New Wave, Pop-Rock
Remembered for their lone hit single "Voices Carry," 'Til Tuesday gradually evolved from a new wave pop band into a vehicle for the songwriting of Aimee Mann. Emerging at the tail end of new wave, 'Til Tuesday's commercial fortunes were helped dramatically by a stylish video for "Voices Carry," which quickly became an MTV favorite. However, the group wasn't able to follow up the single with another hit; furthermore, their albums weren't just ignored by the public, they received little media attention as well. By their third album, *Everything's Different Now*, the band had no chance at reaching the charts, but Mann's songs had gained a cult following, including musicians like Elvis Costello.

Once the album stiffed, the stage was set for Mann to pursue a solo career.

After studying at the Berklee School of Music in Boston, Aimee Mann (vocals, bass) became involved the in the city's punk scene, singing with the Young Snakes and an early incarnation of Ministry. By 1983, she had formed 'Til Tuesday with her boyfriend Michael Hausman (drums), Joey Pesce (keyboards), and Robert Holmes (guitar). 'Til Tuesday played around the Boston area during the next year, eventually winning a battle-of-the-bands contest at a local radio station. Shortly after the contest, the band signed with Epic Records. By the time the group recorded their 1985 debut *Voices Carry*, Mann and Hausman had separated and their failed romance provided the basis for many of the songs on their album. *Voices Carry* became a hit a few months after its release, as the title track climbed into the Top Ten; the record peaked in the Top 20. By the time of the album's release, Mann had become involved in a well-publicized romance with songwriter Jules Shear.

'Til Tuesday quickly re-entered the studio to record their second album, *Welcome Home*. Released in the fall of 1986, *Welcome Home* failed to produce any big hits, with "What About Love" and "Coming Up Close" both failing to make the Top 40. Pesce left the band after the release of the album and was replaced by Michael Montes; the band also added guitarists Jon Brion and Clayton Scobel. Around the time of the release of *Welcome Home*, Mann's relationship with Shear dissolved, and she entered a writer's block, which was relieved by a collaboration with Elvis Costello. Costello co-wrote one song on 'Til Tuesday's third and final album, *Everything's Different Now*. Released in 1988, the album was largely inspired by Mann's breakup with Shear. Though it sold even worse than *Welcome Home*, the album received strong reviews that cited the growth of her songwriting.

'Til Tuesday broke up after *Everything's Different Now*. Aimee Mann became embroiled in legal problems with Epic, which meant she couldn't begin her solo career until 1993, when she released *Whatever*. Mann's solo debut received strong critical reviews, and she enjoyed a successful cult following throughout the '90s. —*Stephen Thomas Erlewine*

Voices Carry / 1985 / Epic ✦✦✦
'Til Tuesday showed a lot of promise with this debut album, which focused on Aimee Mann's emotive singing, notably on the title track. —*William Ruhlmann*

Welcome Home / 1986 / Epic ✦✦✦
Everything's Different Now / 1988 / Epic ✦✦✦✦
As commercially successful as 'Til Tuesday's debut album was, the Boston band could have easily slipped into formula and continued making infectious, synth-soaked pop-rock. But instead, Tuesday continued to challenge itself and grow with each album. *Everything's Different Now*, the group's third and final album, lacks the immediacy of *Voices Carry* and is even more intimate than *Welcome Home*, but is every bit as rewarding. An often poignant and moving singer/composer, Aimee Mann leaves no doubt that she's coming from the heart on such introspective and personal gems as "Long Gone (Buddy)," "Why Must I," and "(Believed You Were) Lucky." Comparing something as slick as "No More Crying" to much more organic and understated offerings like "Rip in Heaven" and "J for Jules," it becomes obvious just how much Tuesday evolved in the course of three albums. —*Alex Henderson*

● **Coming up Close: Retrospective** / Sep. 24, 1996 / Sony ✦✦✦✦
Coming Up Close: A Retrospective is a comprehensive overview of 'Til Tuesday's career, selecting highlights from all three of the group's albums, including the singles "Voices Carry," "What About Love," "Coming Up Close," and "(Believed You Were) Lucky," as well as the previously unreleased "Do It Again." Though *Everything's Different Now* is an excellent album in its own right, *Coming Up Close* salvages the finest tracks from the group's uneven first two records, making it an excellent introduction to the group. —*Stephen Thomas Erlewine*

The Time

f. 1981, Minneapolis, MN, db. 1984
Funk, Urban
From their origins as Prince's first pet project to their self-produced funk-rock oeuvre, the Time has been a fascinating and outrageous congregation. Vocalist Morris Day infused his cocky, swaggering personality into dance hits that would make Rufus Thomas envious and, unlike most of the competition, the band managed to do something unique with Prince's genre-busting innovations. The Time broke up in the late '80s, with Day going on to a somewhat disastrous solo career, Jesse Johnson crafting two dazzling solo albums, and Jimmy Jam and Terry Lewis becoming one of the most successful production teams this side of Gamble-Huff, working with everyone from Full Force and Janet Jackson to the S.O.S. Band and Human League. The group re-formed in 1990 and released the excellent *Pandemonium*. —*John Floyd*

The Time / 1981 / Warner Brothers ◆◆◆
These Prince proteges became stars in their own right in the early '80s. Their debut album had a smart combination of funk, rock, pop, and punk, with Morris Day the erstwhile lead singer and a cast also including Terry Lewis, Jimmy "Jam" Harris, Jesse Johnson, and Jellybean Johnson. Their early singles "Get It Up" and "Cool" were surly, suggestive, and just as energetic and electric as Prince's. —*Ron Wynn*

● **What Time Is It?** / 1982 / Warner Brothers ◆◆◆◆
After a tentative debut, the Time bounced back with one of 1982's best dance albums, full of hilarious stompers and braggadocio ballads. —*John Floyd*

Ice Cream Castle / 1984 / Warner Brothers ◆◆◆◆
Ice Cream Castle finds the band stepping out of Prince's purple shadow and discovering their own personality. The relentless "Jungle Love" is their best song. —*John Floyd*

Pandemonium / Jun. 1990 / Paisley Park ◆◆
Jam and Lewis bring their groundbreaking production techniques to a set that alternately demonstrates just how timeless the Time's boogie can be and just what the band members picked up during their sabbatical. —*John Floyd*

Tindersticks

f. 1992, Nottingham, England
Alternative Pop-Rock
Tindersticks were one of the most original and distinctive British acts of the '90s, standing apart from both the British indie scene and the rash of Brit-pop guitar combos that dominated the UK charts. Where their contemporaries were often direct and to-the-point, Tindersticks were obtuse and leisurely, crafting dense, difficult songs layered with literary lyrics, intertwining melodies, mumbling vocals and gently melancholy orchestrations. Essentially, the group filtered the dark romanticism of Leonard Cohen, Ian Curtis and Scott Walker as filtered through the bizarre pop songcraft of Lee Hazlewood and the aesthetics of indie-rock. Though their music was far from casual listening, Tindersticks gained a dedicated cult following in the mid-'90s, beginning with their eponymous 1993 debut album, which was named Album of the Year by the *Melody Maker*.

The origins of Tindersticks lay in Asphalt Ribbons, a Nottingham-based indie-rock band that featured vocalist Stuart Staples, keyboardist David Boulter, and violinist Dickon Hinchcliffe. All three members formed Tindersticks in 1992; the remaining members included guitarist Neil Fraser, bassist Mark Cornwill, and drummer Al McCauley. In November of 1992, the band released their first single, "Patchwork," on their own label, Tippy Toe. "Marbles" followed early in 1993, as did "A Marriage Made in Heaven," a collaboration with Huggy Bear's Niki Sin that appeared on Rough Trade's Singles' Club. Following the release of the *Unwired* EP on Tippy Toe, the fledgling This Way Up signed the band.

Tindersticks' eponymous debut appeared halfway through 1993, earning rave reviews from most sections of the British press. By the end of the year, the group and the album had won over most of the UK critics, and *Tindersticks* was named Album of the Year by the *Melody Maker*. Tindersticks spent a quiet year in 1994, releasing a single of John Barry's James Bond theme "We Have All the Time in the World" (from *On Her Majesty's Secret Service*), a live album entitled *Amsterdam 1994*, and a cover of Pavement's "Here." Also that year, *Tindersticks* was released on Bar/None in the US. In the spring of 1995, the group released their untitled second album, which featured cameos from Gallon Drunk's Terry Edwards and the Walkabouts' Carla Torgerson. Like its predecessor, it received rave reviews and appeared on nearly every British Top Ten list of the Best of 1995. In November of 1995, the group released another live album, *Bloomsbury Theatre, 12.3.95*.

Tindersticks were quiet for most of 1996, releasing the soundtrack to the Claire Denis film, *Nénette et Boni*, in the fall of the year. The album was comprised of old songs, new songs, and rearranged older material. A new version of "A Marriage Made in Heaven," featuring vocals from actress Isabella Rosselini, was released a few months after *Nénette et Boni*. —*Stephen Thomas Erlewine*

Tindersticks [debut] / 1994 / Bar/None ◆◆◆◆
A thrilling, revelatory debut, *Tindersticks* is a chamber-pop masterpiece of romantic elegance and gutter debauchery. Within the framework of a remarkably consistent and mesmerizingly dank atmosphere, the group covers a stunning amount of ground: "Her" is a crashing flamenco number, "The Walt Blues" is a tipsy organ instrumental, and "Paco de Renaldo's Dream" is an impenetrable cinematic monologue punctuated by subdued guitars, pianos, and strings. Stuart Staples' bacchanalian songs are obsessed with fluids, both bodily ("Blood," "Jism") and otherwise ("Nectar," "Whiskey and Water," "Raindrops"); no topic is too personal or too disturbing. "Piano Song" is frightening in its callousness, while "City Sickness" is an unflinching examination of emotional and physical desperation. Fascinatingly constructed and strikingly ambi-

tious, *Tindersticks* is insidiously labyrinthine: the music speaks softly but carries tremendous weight, and its hold grows more and more unbreakable with each listen. —*Jason Ankeny*

● **Tindersticks [second Album]** / Mar. 1995 / This Way Up/London ◆◆◆◆
Tindersticks' second consecutive eponymously titled double-LP set refines the approach of their debut; while every bit as ambitious and adventuresome, it achieves an even greater musical balance, stretching into luxuriously long compositional structures and more intricate arrangements. While Stuart Staples' songs remain as obsessive and haunted as before, he wards off his demons with fits of pitch-black humor (the narrative "My Sister") and a more tender perspective; similarly, while his funereal vocals remain the focus, there's a new reliance on extended instrumental passages, and even a pair of duets (the centerpiece, "Travelling Light"—a gorgeous collaboration with the Walkabouts' Carla Torgeson—is akin to a Lee Hazlewood & Nancy Sinatra record trapped in emotional purgatory). Another awesome triumph of mood and atmosphere. —*Jason Ankeny*

This Way Up / Oct. 1995 / London ◆◆◆

The Bloomsbury Theatre, 12.3.95 / Nov. 1995 / This Way Up ◆◆◆
Early in 1995, Tindersticks launched the release of their second album with a lavish concert at the Bloomsbury Theatre, performed with a full orchestra. In November, they released a limited-edition disc of the show. The grand, sweeping arrangements perfectly complement the lush, aching melancholy of their songs and, at times, even improve on the original album versions. —*Stephen Thomas Erlewine*

Nenette Et Boni Original Soundtrack / 1996 / This Way Up ◆◆◆◆

TLC

f. 1991, Atlanta, GA
Hip Hop, Dance-Pop, Urban
Comprised of Tionne "T-Boz" Watkins, Rozonda "Chilli" Thomas, and Lisa "Left Eye" Lopes, the Atlanta, Georgia-based hip-hop trio TLC released their first album, *Ooooooooh... On the TLC Tip*, in early 1992 to immediate success. Masterminded by the successful R&B producer/singer Pebbles, the group had three consecutive Top Ten hits in 1992, including "Ain't 2 Proud 2 Beg," "What About Your Friends," and "Baby-Baby-Baby." Shortly before the release of their second album, Lopes was arrested for burning down the house of her boyfriend, Andre Rison, a member of the Atlanta Falcons. Lopes' arrest didn't affect the sales of their second album, 1994's *Crazysexycool*, which featured three No. 1 singles and sold over four million copies. —*Stephen Thomas Erlewine*

Oooooooohhh... On the TLC Tip / Feb. 25, 1992 / La Face ◆◆◆
TLC's debut album was a well-produced but inconsistent effort, with the three hit singles—"Ain't 2 Proud 2 Beg," "Baby-Baby-Baby," and "What About Your Friends"—being the catchiest and most memorable songs on the album. —*Sara Sytsma*

● **Crazysexycool** / 1994 / LaFace ◆◆◆◆
On their second album, TLC downplays their overt rap connections, recording a smooth, seductive collection of contemporary soul reminiscent of both Philly soul and Prince, powered by new jack and hip-hop beats. Lisa Lopes contributes the occasional rap, but the majority of *CrazySexyCool* belongs to Tionne Watkins and Rozonda Thomas. While they're not the most accomplished vocalists—they have a tendency to be just slightly off-key—the material they sing is consistently strong. As the cover of Prince's "If I Was Your Girlfriend" indicates, TLC favors erotic, mid-tempo funk. Yet the group removes any of the psychosexual complexities of Prince's material, leaving a batch of sexy material that just sounds good, especially the hit singles. Both "Creep" and "Red Light Special" have a deep groove that accentuates the slinky hooks, but it's "Waterfalls," with its gently insistent horns and guitar lines and instantly memorable chorus, that ranks as one of the classic R&B songs of the '90s. —*Stephen Thomas Erlewine*

Toad the Wet Sprocket

f. 1988, Santa Barbara, CA
Folk-Rock, Pop-Rock, Adult Alternative Pop-Rock
Toad the Wet Sprocket's second-generation, R.E.M.-derived guitar-pop made them stars in 1992, with the gentle, highly melodic *Fear*. Although they released two albums before their commercial breakthrough, they hadn't yet developed a signature style; with *Fear* the band's songwriting improved and their sound developed into a graceful folk-rock that incorporated the band's influences instead of mimicking them. Both radio and MTV played the singles "All I Want" and "Walk on the Ocean" constantly, making the album a hit. In 1994, the band released *Dulcinea*, which was a hit upon its release, thanks to the single, "Fall Down." —*Sara Sytsma*

Bread & Circus / Jul. 1989 / Columbia ◆◆◆

Pale / Jan. 1990 / Columbia ✦✦✦✦
Pale improved on the formula Toad The Wet Sprocket sketched out on their debut, *Bread and Circus*, since the band contributed a set of stronger songs with catchier melodies. —*Sara Sytsma*

● **Fear** / Aug. 27, 1991 / Columbia ✦✦✦✦
Since their first release, *Bread and Circus*, Toad has grown dramatically as players and songcrafters. *Fear* is the pleasant result of these developments. It contains the Top 40/alternative hit single "All I Want"; the opening track, "Walk on the Ocean," is another highlight. —*Rick Clark*

Dulcinea / May 24, 1994 / Columbia ✦✦✦
Over two years in the making, *Dulcinea* builds upon the sound laid down in *Fear*. "Fall Down" was the first hit, while "Fly from Heaven" and "Inside" have the same potential for both alternative and mainstream pop-rock appeal. —*Rick Clark*

In Light Syrup / Oct. 24, 1995 / Columbia ✦✦✦
Toad The Wet Sprocket's rarities and B-sides collection *In Light Syrup* works surprisingly well. Instead of sounding like a motley assortment of leftovers, the record forms a cohesive whole and highlights the group's considerable melodic talents. There aren't many departures from their gentle, R.E.M.-derived folk-rock, but that is the band's strongest point. No fan of Toad will be disappointed by *In Light Syrup*. —*Stephen Thomas Erlewine*

Coil / May 20, 1997 / Sony ✦✦✦
Toad the Wet Sprocket illustrate that their ability to craft gentle, alternative folk-rock in the vein of R.E.M. continues to grow on *Coil*, a marginally darker record than the previous *Dulcinea*. Although the album is a little more somber, it is far from haunting, since Toad's talent is for a pleasant, lightly melodic acoustic-pop, and *Coil* is no different from the rest of their catalog in that respect. In fact, it offers little new, but Toad is more reliable than predictable, since the record is quite well-crafted. While it won't win the group any new fans, it's a solid effort that will certainly please fans. —*Stephen Thomas Erlewine*

Tommy Tutone

f. 1978, **db.** 1984
New Wave, Power Pop, Pop-Rock
Tommy Tutone were an early-'80s power-pop band led by vocalist Tommy Heath and guitarist Jim Keller. The group's first single, 1980's "Angel Say No," scraped the bottom of the American Top 40, yet it was 1981's "867-5309/Jenny" that sent the group to the top of the charts. Peaking in early 1982, the single hit No. 4 and went gold. Tommy Tutone was never able to duplicate that success, and the band broke up after the release of their third album, 1983's *National Emotion*.
In 1994, Heath returned using the name Tommy Tutone for a new release, *Nervous Love*, a collection of various post-Tommy Tutone recordings. —*Stephen Thomas Erlewine*

Tommy Tutone / 1980 / Columbia ✦✦✦✦
Main songwriters Jim Keller and Tom Heath show a rare talent for writing catchy hooks and memorable melodies on this fine debut. Despite a considerable promotional push from Columbia and no shortage of quality material, this record lacked the extra something needed to distinguish it from the masses of similar-sounding bands of the time. The single "Angel Say No" was a minor US hit. —*Chris Woodstra*

● **Tommy Tutone 2** / 1981 / Columbia ✦✦✦✦
The band's breakthrough features the unforgettable "867-5309/Jenny" and its lesser follow-up, "Which Man Are You" along with a batch of similar sounding originals. *Tommy Tutone 2* is consistently fun, hard-driving, working-class power-pop that was unfortunately overshadowed by the smash hit single. —*Chris Woodstra*

National Emotion / 1983 / Columbia ✦✦✦
Nothing could follow up "867-5309/Jenny," and it seems the band realized that. *National Emotion* finds the band going through the motions, half-heartedly repeating the formula of *Tommy Tutone 2*, rocking harder in places but generally lacking inspiration. —*Chris Woodstra*

Nervous Love / 1994 / Appaloosa ✦✦
Though it's credited as a Tommy Tutone record, *Nervous Love* is actually the work of Tommy Heath after the band's demise. There's nothing as instantly endearing as "867-5309/Jenny " or "Angel Say No," but this is a fine collection of mainly working-class/bar-band rock 'n' roll crossed with power-pop that isn't too dissimilar to Tommy Tutone's heyday. —*Chris Woodstra*

Tomorrow

f. 1965, London, England, **db.** 1968
Psychedelic
In the early days of British psychedelia, three bands were consistently cited as first-generation figureheads of the London-based underground sound: Pink Floyd, the Soft Machine, and Tomorrow. Pink Floyd became superstars, and the Soft Machine influential cult legends, but Tomorrow

is mostly remembered (if at all) for featuring Steve Howe as their lead guitarist in his pre-Yes days. That's a pity, as Tomorrow were nearly the equal of the two more celebrated outfits. With the early Floyd and Softs, they shared a propensity for flower-power whimsy. Though they were less recklessly innovative and imaginative, their songwriting was accomplished, with adroit harmonies, psychedelic guitar work, and adventurous structures and tempo changes. They never succumbed to mindless indulgence or jamming; indeed, their tracks were rather short and tightly woven in comparison with most psychedelic bands. A couple singles (especially "My White Bicycle") were underground favorites, but the group only managed to record one album before breaking up in 1968. Lead singer Keith West, even before the breakup, had a No. 2 British hit with "Excerpt from a Teenage Opera," which helped inspire Pete Townshend's *Tommy*. Drummer Twink joined the Pretty Things and, later, the Pink Fairies. —*Richie Unterberger*

● **Tomorrow** / 1968 / Decal ✦✦✦✦
Tomorrow's sole album was a solid effort, with quite a few first-rate tracks. "My White Bicycle" was one of the first songs to prominently feature backwards guitar phasing, "Real Life Permanent Dream" has engaging English harmonies and sitar riffs, "Revolution" is an infectious hippie anthem, and "Now Your Time Has Come" features intricate riffing from Steve Howe. "Hallucinations," with its irresistible melody, gentle harmonies, and affectingly trippy lyrics, was perhaps their best track. The more self-conscious English whimsy—populated by jolly little dwarfs, Auntie Mary's dress shop, colonels, and the like—is less successful, although the band's craftsmanship is strong enough to avoid embarrassment. The 1986 reissue of this album features detailed liner notes and the worthy B-side "Claremont Lake," though unfortunately West's sappy but influential "Excerpt From A Teenage Opera" was deleted. —*Richie Unterberger*

Tone-Loc

b. Los Angeles, CA
Vocals / Hip Hop, Crossover Rap
Tone-Loc (born Tony Smith) soared from obscurity into pop stardom in 1989 when his hoarse voice and unmistakable delivery made the song "Wild Thing" (using a sample from Van Halen's "Jamie's Cryin'") a massive hit. The song was co-written by Marvin Young, better known as Young MC, as was the second single smash "Funky Cold Medina." The album *Loc-ed After Dark* became the second rap release to top the pop charts.
Tone-Loc expanded his horizons into acting in 1992 and 1993, appearing a few times on the FOX sitcom *Roc*. He was also in the films *Posse* and *Ace Ventura: Pet Detective*. —*Ron Wynn*

● **Loc-ed After Dark** / 1989 / Delicious Vinyl ✦✦✦✦
A pop hit—however inventive—can be the kiss of death in hip-hop circles. When Tone Loc's incredibly infectious and highly original rap/rock hits "Wild Thing" and "Funky Cold Medina" took the pop world by storm, his reputation suffered considerably among b-boys. The Angelino maintained that those singles were the exception, not the rule—and that he was a hardcore rapper first and foremost. Indeed, most of *Loc-ed After Dark* bears that out. While this striking debut album does contain the above-mentioned hits, hardcore rap like "Next Episode," "Don't Get Close," and "Cheeba Cheeba" is in fact dominant. When "Cheeba Cheeba" was first released in 1987, the song took its share of criticism for promoting marijuana at a time when numerous rappers were vehemently protesting drug use. (Unfortunately, pro-drug songs would later become the norm in rap.) Deadpan and relaxed, the distinctive Loc isn't a rapper with much technique—though he certainly has a lot of personality. —*Alex Henderson*

Cool Hand Loc / 1991 / Delicious Vinyl ✦✦✦
Aiming for credibility among hardcore hip-hoppers, Delicious Vinyl was careful not to include a lot of pop-influenced material on Tone-Loc's second album, *Cool Hand Loc*. But sadly, the inventiveness he displayed on "Wild Thing" continued working against Loc among b-boys and hip-hop's hardcore, who still resented the success he'd enjoyed in the pop market. Though not quite as strong as the triple platinum *Loc-ed After Dark*—either commercially or artistically—the album is a respectable and satisfying effort. The former Los Angeles gang member tends to overdo it with boasting lyrics—a problem he shares with quite a few other rappers—but his boasts are often quite clever. Sadly, Tone-Loc didn't have much longevity; after *Cool Hand Loc*, little was heard about him. —*Alex Henderson*

Tony! Toni! Toné!

f. 1987, Oakland, CA
Hip Hop, Soul, Urban
Brothers Dwayne and Raphael Wiggins and cousin Timothy Christian have proven themselves durable guardians of the soul and funk tradition, while also infusing their music with enough contemporary devices

to remain popular. This Oakland trio scored a No. 1 R&B hit right out of the box in 1988 with "Little Walter," a song that generated some criticism from gospel audiences for its use of the melody from "Wade in the Water." But they've since been able to keep things going on their own, as their LPs, *The Revival* in 1990 and *Sons of Soul* in 1993, have also been enormously successful.

Tony! Toni! Toné! released their fourth album, *House of Music*, in the fall of 1996. —*Ron Wynn*

Who? / Jan. 1988 / Wing ✦✦✦

Dwayne and Raphael Wiggins, along with cousin Timothy Christian, made a quick and lasting impact with their 1988 debut album. The lead single, "Little Walter," used the melody from "Wade in the Water" and laid out in vivid detail the rise and fall of a comrade who lacked control and direction. It proved a huge R&B hit and got moderate pop attention, but it helped establish the trio and their creative mix of vintage soul and contemporary hip-hop and New Jack production. "Baby Doll" and "For the Love of You" also got sizable pop attention, and Tony! Toni! Toné! were on their way. —*Ron Wynn*

The Revival / Apr. 1990 / Wing ✦✦✦✦

The trio followed their fine debut album with an even more polished and better-produced second effort. "Feels Good" was an uptempo, hook-laden hit, while "It Never Rains in Southern California" was a nicely sung, elegantly arranged, and tightly performed ballad, and a sign that they were real craftsmen rather than trendy followers. "The Blues" expressed their love for vintage music, while "Whatever You Want" was another love tune that displayed genuine style and compositional depth. —*Ron Wynn*

● **Sons of Soul** / Jun. 22, 1993 / PolyGram ✦✦✦✦

With their third album, Tony! Toni! Toné! received their greatest chart success without compromising their music; it was still the finely crafted, highly eclectic, and funky pop-soul that distinguished their first two albums, while the band's songwriting and playing had improved. The result was the band's most successful album yet, both commercially and successfully. —*Stephen Thomas Erlewine*

House of Music / Nov. 19, 1996 / Mercury ✦✦✦✦

When Tony! Toni! Toné! finally delivered *House of Music*, the follow-up to their 1993 breakthrough *Sons of Soul*, their influence was beginning to be apparent, as younger soul singer-songwriters like Tony Rich and Maxwell began reaching the R&B charts. Like Tony! Toni! Toné!, Rich and Maxwell relied on traditional soul and R&B values of songwriting and live performances, discarding the synth-heavy productions of the late '80s and early '90s. But, as *House of Music* makes clear, the difference between the Tonies and their successors is that they know how to seamlessly incorporate hip-hop and new jack swingbeat into their essentially traditional sound. Embellishing soul and funk with slamming '90s beats, Tony! Toni! Toné! sounds modern, and they can successfully accomplish their fusion of the traditional and contemporary. More importantly, they can do this within the framework of memorable, catchy songs, whether it's the party funk of "Let's Get Down" or the balladry of "Let Me Know." In short, *House of Music* continues the Tonies' tradition of excellence and demonstrates that the group is getting stronger and better all the time. —*Leo Stanley*

Too $hort

f. Apr. 28, 1966, Los Angeles, CA
West Coast Rap, Gangsta Rap, Hip-Hop
Born in Los Angeles but an Oakland resident by the age of 14, Too $hort was the first West Coast rap star, recording four albums on his own before he made his major-label debut with 1986's gold album *Born to Mack;* his next four all went platinum. Anticipating much of the later gangsta phenomenon, he restricted his lyrical themes to tales of sexual prowess and physical violence, with the occasional social-message track to mix things up. After the release of *Gettin' It (Album Number Ten)* in 1996, Too $hort decided to retire, his status assured as one of the most successful solo rappers of the 1980s and early '90s.

Born Todd Shaw on April 28, 1966, $hort grew up in Los Angeles' South Central; soon after his family moved to Oakland in the early '80s, he began selling tapes out of the back of his car. Signed to the local label 75 Girls, he released his first proper album in 1983, *Don't Stop Rappin'.* Three albums followed in the next two years, after which Too $hort formed his own Dangerous Music label with friend Freddy B. He recorded *Born to Mack* in 1986, and sold over 50,000 copies just by riding around the region. New York's Jive Records picked up on the buzz from across the country, and provided a national deal for the album one year later. With virtually no radio airplay, *Born to Mack* went gold and its follow-up *Life Is . . . Too $hort* achieved platinum sales by 1989.

The immense success of Too $hort during 1988-89 made him much more viable for radio airplay, and "The Ghetto"—from 1990's *Short Dog's in the House*— made No. 12 on the R&B charts, even enjoying a brief stay just outside the pop Top 40. He continued his hit track record with 1992's *Shorty the Pimp* and 1993's *Get in Where You Fit In*, both of

which went platinum. By the time of 1995's *Cocktails*, however, Too $hort began to be drowned out by a glut of similar-sounding West Coasters, and though *Gettin' It (Album Number Ten)* became his fifth platinum by late 1996, he decided to retire. —*John Bush*

Born to Mack / 1988 / Jive ✦✦✦
A breakout release. —*Ron Wynn*

● **Life Is . . . Too $hort** / 1988 / Jive ✦✦✦✦

Too $hort never had the skills or technique of LL Cool J or Big Daddy Kane, but what the Oakland rapper lacks in technique, he's always more than made up for with irresistible, '70s-inspired funk grooves that simply won't quit. When Short—after enjoying a small cult following for a few years in Northern California—joined a major label with *Life Is . . . Too $hort's* predecessor, *Born to Mack*, too many East Coast MCs were inundating hip-hop with clichéd tracks consisting of only James Brown samples and a drum machine. Too Short, however, presented an attractive alternative with highly melodic, danceable tracks that made no secret of his love of '70s funk heroes like Parliament, the Ohio Players and Cameo. This CD's X-rated, sexually explicit lyrics received their share of vehement criticism, and the MC responded that Too $hort is an outrageous character who shouldn't be taken too seriously. Be that as it may, his commanding reflection on the drug plague, "City of Dope," underscores the fact that he's cheating himself artistically by not devoting more time to social commentary and less time to exploiting sex. —*Alex Henderson*

● **Short Dog's in the House** / Aug. 1990 / Jive ✦✦✦✦

With *Short Dog's in the House*, Oakland's most sexually explicit MC gave his followers more of what he was known for: X-rated lyrics, a relaxed style of rapping and addictive, melodic tracks recalling the splendor of '70s funk. R&B fans who complained that rap on the whole wasn't sufficiently melodic couldn't make that complaint about the distinctive Too Short. When his raunchy lyrics continued to come under fire, he maintained that he was simply portraying a character—and that he wasn't really the ghetto pimp he portrayed. As entertaining as his albums are, Short's inspired interpretation of Donny Hathaway's "The Ghetto" makes it crystal clear that he would do well to be more lyrically challenging more often. —*Alex Henderson*

Get in Where You Fit In / 1993 / Jive ✦✦

Although he tries to cop part of the current P-Funk inspired gangsta rap, Too $hort sounds lost and dated on his latest album, the overlong, sample-reliant, grotesquely misogynist, and musically muddled *Get in Where You Fit In.* —*AMG*

Greatest Hits, Vol. 1: The Player Years, 1983-1988 / Nov. 10, 1993 / In-A-Minute ✦✦✦✦

If you've never read the collected works of Chester Himes or Iceberg Slim, simply run through this Too $hort anthology and you'll have the general idea. Although never an inventive rapper or clever composer of rhymes, Too $hort was smart enough to find his niche and stick to it. Most people who continually mined the pimp arena quickly become merely tedious; Too $hort became both tedious and profitable. —*Ron Wynn*

Gettin' It (Album Number Ten) / Jun. 18, 1996 / Dangerous ✦✦✦

At the time of its release, Too $hort claimed that *Gettin' It* was his retirement album. If that is indeed the case, he picked the perfect moment to drop out of the hip-hop business—as the album shows, he's already beginning to border on self-parody. There are some good moments on the album, particularly the singles "Buy You Some" and "Gettin' It," which feature Erick Sermon and Parliament/Funkadelic, respectively. But too much of the album consists of tired boasts and worn-out beats. Furthermore, the album is padded with filler, making it more difficult to dig out the gems buried next to the dreck. Too $hort may not have worn out his welcome with *Gettin' It*, but a string of albums similar to it would prove to be too much for even his dedicated fans. After *Gettin' It*, he either needs to make good on his promise of retiring, or he needs to find a new sound. —*Stephen Thomas Erlewine*

The Tornadoes

f. 1962, Redlands, CA
Instrumental Rock, Surf
Not to be confused with the British studio group that gave the world the Joe Meek-produced instrumental "Telstar," or the Midwest group that recorded "Scalping Party" on Cuca, *or* the Kennewick, Washington combo of the same name, this group of Tornadoes burst onto the national scene with one of the very first surf instrumentals, "Bustin' Surfboards," in 1962. A family band, their lineup consisted of two brothers (Gerald and Norman Sanders), their cousin Jesse Sanders and a friend, Leonard Delaney. They started out as instrumental group from San Bernardino, California called the Vaqueros. After adding sax man George White to the lineup, they changed their name to the Tornadoes. Their lone national chart entry was nonetheless an important one, with "Bustin' Surfboards" in 1962 making the playlists in cities that were far

removed from any kind of surfing activity and signaling the beginnings of surf music as a national craze. Although using an off-brand echo unit in place of the Fender reverb unit (which hadn't been invented yet), the record had the prerequisite sound of this fledgling genre, utilizing a solid surfer's stomp drum beat and crashing wave sound effects throughout. More recordings followed, with a name change to the Hollywood Tornadoes for their next two singles in deference to their British namesakes, who had charted higher with "Telstar." Their fourth single, "Shootin' Beavers," was banned from radio play because of the so-called suggestive title. No more hits were forthcoming from the band, although they did release one excellent album that stands as one of the earliest—and best—examples of the genre. —Cub Koda

Bustin' Surfboards / 1993 / Sundazed ✦✦✦✦
The Tornadoes' biggest hit became the title track of this, their only album, which also includes acknowledged surf classics like "Shootin' Beavers" and "The Gremmie." The inclusion of three bonus tracks (including the previously unreleased "Charge of the Tornadoes") make this a must-own for fans of the surfin' sound. —Cub Koda

The Tornados

f. 1961, London, England, db. 1964
Instrumental Rock
A fascinating footnote in '60s rock, the Tornados topped the charts in both Britain and the US in 1962 with their instrumental classic "Telstar." Inspired by the American satellite, this haunting, other-worldly tune—with its inimitable piercing clavioline, harp-like glissandos, outer-space sound effects, and mysterious wordless chanting near the end—was probably Joe Meek's finest production. It was also the first British rock 'n' roll record to top the charts in the US, beating the Beatles by a full year.

The Tornados were actually a group of British sessionmen that Meek had been using on his independently produced recordings. Quite a few Meek-produced singles followed in the next few years, all employing piercing organ and mysterious percolating percussion, sounding like nothing so much as pre-psychedelic roller rink music. None of them came close to matching the majestic "Telstar"; in fact, they were usually pretty thin and gimmicky, although tracks like "Ridin' the Wind," "Love and Fury," and "Blue, Blue, Blue Beat" fascinate with their spectral, shimmering organs. The Tornados never entered the US Top 40 again, though they had more Top 20 hits at home in 1963 with "Globetrotter," "Ice Cream Man," and "Robot." Bassist Heinz Burt departed in 1963 for brief stardom as a Meek-produced solo vocalist. —Richie Unterberger

Away from It All / 1963 / Castle ✦✦
The only album recorded by the original lineup. Even if your interest in the Tornados extends beyond "Telstar," you may find this effort a humdrum affair, with weak material that can't overcome their trademark outer-space roller-rink organ and Meek's usual, at times clichéd bag-of-tricks production. Has no overlap with their greatest hits CD on Music Club, if that is a concern. —Richie Unterberger

Yesterday's Pop Scene / 1972 / Decca ✦✦✦
When Tornados compilations were extremely scarce, this was one of the best bets around if you were determined to find *something* by the band. All of the 12 songs, though, were reissued on CD in the 1990s on Music Club's *Telstar* anthology in the UK. —Richie Unterberger

● **Telstar: the Original Sixties Hits of the Tornados** / 1994 / Music Club ✦✦✦✦
All you could possibly want to hear: both sides of the nine singles they cut for Decca between 1962 and 1964, along with the small US hit "Ridin' the Wind" and a cut from a soundtrack LP. A fun, if slight, document of one of the most distinctive instrumental rock groups of the early '60s, with thorough liner notes. —Richie Unterberger

Tortoise

f. 1990, Chicago, IL
Experimental, Post-Rock/Experimental
With only two proper albums to its credit, Tortoise has revolutionized indie-rock by dabbling in and incorporating a variety of experimental genres from the past 20 years, including ambience, prog-rock, Krautrock, dub, and '90s techno/trip-hop. The group gained fame for their second album, especially the 21-minute track "Djed," a pastiche incorporating all of the above genres except trip-hop. Tortoise kept all their bases covered, however, by recruiting the cream of European electronica to remix the album on a series of 12-inch singles.

First formed in Chicago in 1990, Tortoise began when Doug McCombs (bass; formerly of Eleventh Dream Day) and John Herndon (drums, keyboards, vibes; formerly with the Poster Children) began experimenting with production techniques. The duo intended to record on their own as well as provide an instant rhythm section for needy bands—receiving inspiration from the reggae duo Sly & Robbie. Next aboard was producer/drummer/vibes-player John McEntire (formerly of

Bastro and Shrimp Boat), guitarist Bundy K. Brown (who had played with Gastr del Sol) and multi-instrumentalist Dan Bitney.

The five-piece recorded seven-inch singles for both David Wm. Sims' Torsion label and Thrill Jockey, and then released their eponymous debut full-length on Thrill Jockey in 1994. The album's sound—restrained indie-rock with subtle jazz influences and a debt to prog-rock—was pleasant but not quite revolutionary. Several tracks took a more slanted course, though, sounding like a reaction to England's ambient/techno scene filtered through the '70s experimentalism of Can and Faust. The LP became an underground classic and spawned the remix work *Rhythms, Resolutions and Clusters*. With help from Jim O'Rourke, Steve Albini, and Brad Wood, the album steadily segued from techno and found-sound environment recordings to feedback ambience and hip-hop—complete with samples of A Tribe Called Quest and Minnie Riperton. Later in 1994, the group released a 12-inch single on Stereolab's Duophonic label.

Tortoise added guitarist David Pajo—formerly of Slint and also a member of the For Carnation—for second album *Millions Now Living Will Never Die*, released in early 1996. Much of the album was similar to the debut, but the British weeklies and American music magazines championed the strength of "Djed," the album-opener, which blends a rumbling bassline, scratchy ambience, and dub technology. During the rest of 1995, Tortoise toured with Stereolab in England and headlined a US tour with 5iveStyle and the Sea & Cake. John McEntire also remained busy with production, working on Stereolab's *Empire Tomato Ketchup* and eponymous debut LPs from 5iveStyle, Trans Am, and Rome.

Instead of a remix album to accompany *Millions Now Living Will Never Die*, Tortoise optioned tracks out to several techno/experimental contemporaries during 1996. Mo' Wax heroes U.N.K.L.E. recorded a remix of "Djed" on the first of what became a four-volume series, with later interpretations coming from Oval, Jim O'Rourke & Bedouin Ascent, Spring Heel Jack, and Luke Vibert, among others. —John Bush

Tortoise / 1994 / Thrill Jockey ✦✦✦✦
This debut is a highly original album; although Tortoise take their guitar inspiration from indie rock bands like Slint, the sound is more laidback and encompasses a wider idiom, including jazz and a twisted form of lo-fi techno (contradictory as it sounds). Most tracks have no vocals, but the band has no trouble keeping ears busy. With the great vibes of jazz and the cool chill of good ambience, this album never grows old. —John Bush

Rhythms, Resolutions & Clusters / 1995 / Thrill Jockey ✦✦✦✦
Tortoise invited several people (including Steve Albini and Liz Phair's producer Brad Wood) to dissect the band's debut album. The result, a 30-minute continuous mix, includes a great hip-hop remix (with A Tribe Called Quest and Minnie Riperton samples), though most of the disc is on the experimental side. Beginners should buy the debut album first. —John Bush

● **Millions Now Living Will Never Die** / Jan. 30, 1996 / Thrill Jockey ✦✦✦✦
Tortoise's second album, *Millions Now Living Will Never Die*, continues their sonic explorations, using instruments and silence as a way of creating a musical sculpture. All of the band's instrumental pieces—and they can't be called songs, since there are hardly any structured songs on the record—are slow, almost maddeningly obscure. It isn't music that is designed for casual listening, yet intense listening doesn't quite yield rewards since the music is so repetitive, cryptic, and cerebal. —Stephen Thomas Erlewine

Toto

f. 1978, Los Angeles, CA
Soft Rock, Pop-Rock
Toto was formed in Los Angeles in 1978 by David Paich (b. Jun. 21, 1954, Los Angeles) (keyboards, vocals), Steve Lukather (b. Oct. 21, 1957, Los Angeles) (guitar, vocals), Bobby Kimball (born Robert Toteaux, Mar. 29, 1947, Vinton, LA) (vocals), Steve Porcaro (b. Sep. 2, 1957, Connecticut) (keyboards), David Hungate (b. Texas) (bass), and Jeff Porcaro (b. Apr. 1, 1954, Hartford, CT-d. Aug. 5, 1992, Holden Hills, CA) (drums). Paich was the son of arranger Marty Paich; the Porcaros were the sons of percussionist Joe Porcaro. The band members had met in high school and at studio sessions in the 1970s, when they became some of the busiest session musicians in the music business. Paich, Hungate, and Jeff Porcaro wrote songs for and performed on *Silk Degrees*, the multi-million-selling 1976 album that combined pop, rock, and disco elements into a slick combination that heavily influenced mainstream pop music. Toto released its self-titled debut album in September 1978, and it hit the Top Ten, sold two million copies, and spawned the gold Top Ten single "Hold the Line." The gold-selling *Hydra* (October 1979) and *Turn Back* (January 1981) were less successful, but *Toto IV* (April 1982) was a multi-platinum Top Ten hit, featuring the No. 1 hit "Africa" and the Top Tens "Rosanna" (about Lukather's girlfriend, movie star Rosanna Arquette)

and "I Won't Hold You Back." At the 1982 Grammys, "Rosanna" won awards for Record of the Year, Best Pop Vocal Performance, and Best Instrumental Arrangement with Vocal, and *Toto IV* won awards for Album of the Year, Best Engineered Recording, and Best Producer (the group). In 1984, a third Porcaro brother, Mike (b. May 29, 1955), joined the group on bass, replacing Hungate. Then lead singer Kimball quit and was replaced by Dennis "Fergie" Frederiksen (b. May 15, 1951, Wyoming, MI). Toto's fifth album, *Isolation* (November 1984), went gold, but was a commercial disappointment. Frederiksen was replaced by Joseph Williams (b. Santa Monica), the son of the conductor/composer John Williams, for *Fahrenheit* (August 1986). Steve Porcaro quit in 1988, prior to the release of *The Seventh One*. In 1990, Jean-Michel Byron replaced Williams for the new recordings on *Past to Present 1977-1990*, then left, as Lukather became the group's lead singer. Jeff Porcaro died of a heart attack in 1992, but was featured on the group's next album, *Kingdom of Desire*. By this time, Toto was far more popular in Japan and Europe than at home. The group added British drummer Simon Phillips. *Tambu*, released in Europe in the late fall of 1995, appeared in the US in June 1996. The group members continued to do session work during the band's tenure, contributing significantly to the sound of mainstream pop-rock in the 1970s, '80s, and '90s. — *William Ruhlmann*

Toto / Oct. 1978 / Columbia ✦✦✦✦
It's as easy to see why radio listeners loved Toto as it is to see why critics hated them. Toto's sessionman rock-studio chops allowed them to play any current pop style at the drop of a hi-hat: one minute prog-rock, the next hard rock, the next funky R&B. It all sounded great, but it also implied that music-making took craft rather than inspiration and that the musical barriers critics like to erect were arbitrary. Then, too, Toto's timing couldn't have been much worse. They rode in in the middle of the punk/new wave with its D.I.Y. aesthetic, and their competence was an affront. There's always been an alternate history of popular music not available to rock critics (it's written in record stores and concert halls and on the radio), and in that story, Toto was a smash. Singles like "I'll Supply the Love" and "Georgy Porgy" (featuring Cheryl Lynn) made the charts, and "Hold the Line" hit the Top Ten and went gold. The members of Toto had already influenced the course of '70s popular music by playing on half the albums that came out of Los Angeles. All they were doing with this album was going public. — *William Ruhlmann*

Hydra / Oct. 1979 / Columbia ✦✦✦
If Toto's musical advantage was that, since its members continued to play on many of the successful records made in Los Angeles, its own music was popular almost by definition, its disadvantage was that it made little attempt to seek an individual musical signature—a particular style, say, or a distinctive singer (Bobby Kimball was not it) who could make its records immediately identifiable. "Hold the Line" had been a big hit, but who did it? Boston? Foreigner? As a result, Toto was less well positioned than most to come off a big debut album with the follow-up, and *Hydra* was unusually dependent on its lead-off single, "99." Maybe it was a tribute to the female lead on the old *Get Smart* TV show, but many listeners didn't get a song with a chorus that went, "Oh, 99, I love you," and the single stalled in the bottom half of the Top 40. The album went gold on momentum, but the songs, however well played, simply were not distinctive enough to consolidate the success Toto had achieved with its debut album. — *William Ruhlmann*

Turn Back / Jan. 1981 / Columbia ✦✦✦
Toto went from disappointment to disaster with its third album, the generic *Turn Back*. The group's ability to turn out highly competent studio rock was not translating into an individual sound, and since *Turn Back* had no memorable songs on it, one was left with nothing more than those famous chops that Toto possessed in abundance. The group would rally from this retreat, but for the moment a better title would have been *Fall Back*, as in the studio jobs the band members had to fall back on. — *William Ruhlmann*

Toto IV / Apr. 1982 / Columbia ✦✦✦✦
It was do or die for Toto on the group's fourth album, and they rose to the challenge. Largely dispensing with the anonymous studio rock that had characterized their first three releases, the band worked harder on its melodies, made sure its simple lyrics treated romantic subjects, augmented Bobby Kimball's vocals by having other group members sing, brought in ringers like Timothy B. Schmit, and slowed down the tempo to what came to be known as "power ballad" pace. Most of all, they wrote some hit songs: "Rosanna," the old story of a lovelorn lyric matched to a bouncy beat, was the gold, Top Ten comeback single accompanying the album release; "Make Believe" made the Top 30; and then, surprisingly, "Africa" hit No. 1 ten months after the album's release. The members of Toto may have more relatives who are NARAS voters than any other group, but that still doesn't explain the sweep they achieved at the Grammys, winning six, including Album of the Year and Record of the Year (for "Rosanna"). Predictably, rock critics howled, but the Grammys helped set up the fourth single, "I Won't Hold You Back," another soft-rock smash and Top Ten hit. As a result, *Toto IV* was both

the group's comeback and its peak; it remains a definitive album of slick Los Angeles pop for the early '80s, and Toto's best and most consistent record. Having made it, the members happily went back to sessions, where they helped write and record Michael Jackson's *Thriller*. — *William Ruhlmann*

Isolation / Nov. 1984 / Columbia ✦✦✦
Having traded in lead singer Bobby Kimball for Fergie Frederiksen, a smooth tenor wailer in the tradition of Journey's Steve Perry, Toto proceeded to follow its power-ballad smash *Toto IV* with a Journey clone album, minus the aching ballads that had made Journey such a success. A workout for drummer Jeff Porcaro, keyboardist David Paich, and guitarist Steve Lukather, *Isolation* was anything but the kind of record those millions who had loved "Rosanna" were waiting for. It seemed intended to restore the band members' heady studio reputations as hard rock technicians, which it did by dispensing with the elements that finally had made the band a big success in 1982. — *William Ruhlmann*

Fahrenheit / Aug. 1986 / Columbia ✦✦
After the ballad-deprived *Isolation* failed to meet the marketplace like its predecessor, *Toto IV*, Toto returned to making lush, midtempo tunes of romantic despair on *Fahrenheit*, enlisting their third lead singer, Joseph Williams, and calling in chips all over Los Angeles to score cameos from the likes of Michael McDonald, Don Henley, David Sanborn, and even Miles Davis, who had the closing track, "Don't Stop Me Now," pretty much to himslf. Williams was a slightly grittier and more identifiable vocalist than Bobby Kimball or Fergie Frederiksen. But while the return to power ballads had the intended effect on the pop and adult contemporary charts (both "I'll Be over You" and "Without Your Love" scored), the album had a relatively low chart peak and failed to go gold. That kind of disconnection always indicates that the radio audience is failing to identify the songs with the group that made them, and it always means a career in trouble. — *William Ruhlmann*

The Seventh One / Mar. 1988 / Columbia ✦✦
Toto attempted to satisfy commercial considerations by loading up the first half of its seventh album with the kind of power ballads that had given it recognition before, especially songs named after women whose names end in "A" like "Pamela" and "Anna." But these thinly veiled rewrites of "Rosanna" earned only modest radio play, and the rest of the album, which rocked harder as it went on—while it may have been truer to the band's musical aspirations—continued to sound too anonymous to earn any response beyond the band's fan base, especially its international one (which it seemed to be acknowledging by printing some of the sleeve notes in Japanese). — *William Ruhlmann*

● **Past to Present 1977-1990** / Sep. 1990 / Columbia ✦✦✦✦
Toto's compilation is to be recommended in that it contains all four of the group's Top Ten hit singles—"Hold the Line," "Rosanna," "Africa," and "I Won't Hold You Back." It also contains four more of Toto's 14 pop chart singles—"Georgy Porgy," "99," "I'll Be over You," and "Pamela." But that means it leaves out six chart entries, including the Top 40 hits "Make Believe," "Stranger in Town," and "Without Your Love." In their place are an album track from the most recent album, *The Seventh One*, and four newly recorded songs co-written and sung by the group's fourth lead vocalist, Jean-Michel Byron, who is more soulful than his predecessors, but no more memorable. As such, this is not the ideal Toto best-of and earns its "pick" designation over *Toto IV* only by virtue of its inclusion of the group's first hit, "Hold the Line." — *William Ruhlmann*

Tambu / May 1995 / Legacy ✦✦
Toto waxed philosophical on its first album to be recorded since the death of founding member Jeff Porcaro and his replacement by drummer Simon Phillips. The song lyrics were full of abstractions—apathy, dignity, faith, freedom, hope, hopelessness, hypocrisy, rage, trust (those are all from just the first song, "Gift of Faith")—which seemed to indicate that the band members were reflecting seriously, if not too specifically, on weighty issues in an angry, questioning manner. Some of the lyrics couched these internal struggles in romantic terms, but more often they seemed to refer to more general anguish. The group came up with a more focused, harder, bluesier musical style to carry the weight, and Steve Lukather sang expressively, making you wonder why they bothered so long with those cookie-cutter vocalists. Like a patient new to psychoanalysis, Toto went on at length (the album runs over 70 minutes), and without much coherence, about "the pain of my lifetime" and "a world of blind ambition," among other things. You couldn't call the result accomplished, but *Tambu* suggested that Toto was embarked on a personal and musical journey that might lead in an interesting direction. (Released in Europe in the late fall of 1995, *Tambu* was released in the US as Legacy 64957 on June 4, 1996.) — *William Ruhlmann*

Allen Toussaint

b. 1938, New Orleans, LA
Piano, Vocals / R&B, Electric Louisiana Blues, New Orleans R&B
His inherently funky piano work heavily influenced by his Crescent City

forefathers—Professor Longhair, Huey "Piano" Smith, and Fats Domino—and with a heavy dose of Ray Charles, a young visionary named Allen Toussaint almost singlehandedly fashioned a fresh, vital New Orleans R&B sound for the early '60s. Earning a vaunted reputation as a session pianist, Toussaint debuted on vinyl in 1958 with an obscure RCA album whimsically billed as "A. Tousan." When Joe Banashak inaugurated his Minit label in 1960, Toussaint joined the firm as A&R man and quickly proved himself the ultimate behind-the-scenes wizard on the New Orleans scene. During the early to mid-'60s, Toussaint tirelessly wrote, arranged, produced, and played on hits by Ernie K-Doe, Irma Thomas, Jessie Hill, Chris Kenner, Barbara George, Lee Dorsey, Benny Spellman, the Showmen, and many more, his rolling keyboards vital to the charm of virtually all of them.

After unleashing the Meters on the world, Toussaint finally began to step out as a front man in 1970, although his low-key vocals have never achieved quite the same level of success as his previous productions for others. His brilliant compositions have been covered by everyone from Herb Alpert & the Tijuana Brass to Robert Palmer and Bonnie Raitt. Allen Toussaint's stature as a New Orleans musical legend endures.

Allen Toussaint found a new audience in 1994 when he joined country legend Chet Atkins for an updated rendition of "Southern Nights" on the CD *Rhythm, Country and Blues*. —*Bill Dahl*

The Wild Sound of New Orleans / 1958 / RCA Victor ◆◆◆◆
His debut album, featuring a killer band, storming second-line instrumentals, and Toussaint's rolling 88s. —*Bill Dahl*

Toussaint / 1971 / Scepter ◆◆◆
New Orleans production and performing wizard Allen Toussaint launched his solo career with this early-'70s release. But for some strange reason, the same performer who's written and produced marvelous material for Irma Thomas, Lee Dorsey, Chocolate Milk, and General Johnson, among others, was never able to score the same success working as a lead act. There was nothing on this album even in the same arena as his classic R&B tunes, and throughout Toussaint's run of solo releases, only the song "Southern Nights," which Glen Campbell made a hit, could be even mentioned in the same sentence with Toussaint classics like "Ride Your Pony" or "It Will Stand." —*Ron Wynn*

Motion / Aug. 1978 / Reprise ◆◆◆
A nicely produced, competently performed, but disappointing album by New Orleans giant Allen Toussaint. He seemed unable to find a groove or a sound, dabbling in pop, light R&B, rock, and mild funk, but never coming close to duplicating prior magical productions or compositions. This was perhaps Toussaint's least impressive material, and was especially surprising in light of the artistic success of his prior Warner Bros. album *Homage*. —*Ron Wynn*

● **Allen Toussaint Collection** / Apr. 30, 1991 / Reprise ◆◆◆◆
A representative cross-section of the legendary New Orleans piano man's solo output—uneven but interesting. —*Bill Dahl*

The Complete "Tousan" Sessions / 1992 / Bear Family ◆◆◆◆
A compilation of instrumentals from 1958 and 1959 featuring Toussaint at the top of his form, *The Complete "Tousan" Sessions* is a wonderful portrait of the seminal New Orleans pianist; it's also the first time this material has ever been available on CD. —*Stephen Thomas Erlewine*

Pete Townshend

b. May 19, 1945, Chiswick, London, England
Guitar, Vocals, Keyboards / Rock 'n' Roll, Singer-Songwriter
Pete Townshend was the guitarist and songwriter for the Who from 1964 to 1982. Best known for his conceptual works, he wrote *Tommy* and *Quadrophenia* for the group. Townshend made his first, tentative solo album, *Who Came First*, in 1972. Dedicated to his guru, Meher Baba, the album continued themes pursued in the previous Who album, *Who's Next*, and contained material from an abortive conceptual work, *Lifehouse*. The album sold modestly. In 1976, Townshend made a duo album, *Rough Mix*, with Ronnie Lane, formerly the bassist in the Small Faces.

Townshend's first full-fledged solo effort, however, was *Empty Glass* (1980), which sold half a million copies, reached the Top Five, and featured the Top Ten hit "Let My Love Open the Door," as well as the minor hits "A Little Is Enough" and "Rough Boys." Townshend followed this in 1982 with *All the Best Cowboys Have Chinese Eyes*.

Following the demise of the Who, Townshend released *Scoop*, a two-disc collection of demos, in 1983 (a second volume appeared in 1987). In 1985 he returned to thematic efforts with the album *White City—A Novel*, which included the Top 30 single "Face the Face." In the same year, Townshend published a book of short stories, *Horse's Neck*. As part of the *White City* project, Townshend appeared in an accompanying film, for which he organized a band called Pete Townshend's Deep End. The unit played only a few gigs, but one was videotaped and recorded, resulting in the 1986 album *Pete Townshend's Deep End Live!* In 1989, Townshend released an album based on Ted Hughes' children's story,

The Iron Man. The record featured guest vocals by John Lee Hooker and Nina Simone, as well as two tracks featuring the three surviving members of the Who. Simultaneous with the album's release, Townshend embarked on a reunion tour with the Who.

Although the reunion tour was successful, it didn't help *The Iron Man* at all. Four years later, Townshend delivered *Psychoderelict* to mixed reviews and lukewarm sales. By that time, he had successfully reinvented himself as a Broadway tunesmith—the Broadway production of *The Who's Tommy* had become a runaway hit, earning Townshend a Tony and prompting him to pursue more stage musicals. —*William Ruhlmann*

Who Came First / 1972 / Rykodisc ◆◆◆◆
Pete Townshend's first solo album was a homespun, charming forum for low-key, personal songs that weren't deemed suitable for the Who, as well as spiritual paeans (direct and indirect) to his spiritual guru Meher Baba. Who fans will be immediately attracted by the presence of a couple of songs from the aborted Who concept album *Lifehouse* (much of which ended up on *Who's Next*), "Pure & Easy," and "Let's See Action." The Who did eventually release their own versions of both those songs. But Townshend's own versions aren't the highlights of this record, which shows a folkier and gentler side to the Who's chief muse than his albums with the group. "Sheraton Gibson" is a neat tune about rock 'n' roll road life, and "Time Is Passing" takes very subtle inspiration from Baba. Most of the rest of the album contains some of the most unusual pieces Townshend has released: his acoustic cover of Jim Reeves' "There's a Heartache Following Me" (recorded because it was one of Baba's favorite tunes), "Evolution" (which is actually pretty much a solo track by his buddy Ronnie Lane of the Faces), "Parvardigar" (adapted from Baba's Universal Prayer), and "Content" (a philosophical poem by Maud Kennedy that Townshend put to music). The 1993 reissue of this LP for compact disc fleshes out the program considerably with six previously unreleased tracks, including Townshend's demo of the Who single "The Seeker." The other bonus cuts are by no means filler; meditative and melancholy originals, they're just as strong as the tracks on the original release. —*Richie Unterberger*

Rough Mix / 1977 / Atco ◆◆◆◆
Pete Townshend and Ronnie Lane rock it up, with some good melodies thrown in. Tops among Townshend's non-Who projects. —*Bruce Eder*

★ **Empty Glass** / 1980 / Atco ◆◆◆◆◆
Townshend may have recorded two solo records before *Empty Glass*, but they were idiosyncratic, personal albums—with *Empty Glass*, he's aiming right for the Who's prime audience with songs that could have fit musically onto a Who album. Beneath the surface, however, the songs reveal themselves as intensely personal, autobiographical affairs, documenting a mid-life crisis, and it's hard to imagine Roger Daltrey investing the songs with the necessary vulnerability. Townshend's thin, trembling voice opens the songs up, whether it's the sweet, synth-fueled pop of "Let My Love Open the Door" and "A Little Is Enough," the stark "And I Moved," or even the faux-toughness of "Rough Boys." Supported by a tight, professional backing band, Townshend brings some of his finest songs since the early '70s to vibrant life. And while the operatic flourishes of "Jools and Jim" and "Keep On Working" wear a little thin, *Empty Glass* remains a stunning fusion of pop songcraft and confessional songwriting. —*Stephen Thomas Erlewine*

All the Best Cowboys Have Chinese Eyes / 1982 / Atco ◆◆◆
Pete Townshend followed his pop breakthrough *Empty Glass* with *All the Best Cowboys Have Chinese Eyes*, his most ambitious and difficult album. Abandoning conventional pop structures, Townshend creates long, twisting soundscapes with intricate, synth-based arrangements and dense poetry. For some, the self-conscious poetry and obtuse, winding melody lines are nearly impenetrable, but the album features some of his most intriguing and beautiful work, including the cascading "The Sea Refuses No River" and "Uniforms." —*Stephen Thomas Erlewine*

Scoop / 1983 / Atco ◆◆◆◆
Pete Townshend's demos had grown legendary among Who collectors well before the official release of the double-album *Scoop* in 1983. On each demo, Townshend worked out full arrangements, which the Who would often follow exactly. He also recorded a wealth of songs and instrumental pieces that never made it to record. Over the course of two albums, *Scoop* features 25 of these demos, including both classic Who songs ("So Sad About Us," "Bargain," "Behind Blue Eyes," "Magic Bus," "Love Reign O'er Me") and unreleased gems ("Politician," "Melancholia," "To Barney Kessell," "Mary"). Occasionally, the songs sound better in their demo versions, particularly on latter-day Who songs, which were overwrought in their official incarnations. But what makes *Scoop* so fascinating is its revelation of the depth and detail of Townshend's imagination, and how he refined his ideas. But even casual fans will find the sheer musicality of the record worthwhile—it's one of the most focused and impressive albums he has ever released. —*Stephen Thomas Erlewine*

White City: A Novel / 1985 / Atco ✦✦✦
After the experimental *All the Best Cowboys Have Chinese Eyes*, Pete Townshend returned to a more traditional form of concept album with *White City*. Built around a loose narrative concerning urban despair, the album doesn't work very well conceptually, yet a handful of the individual songs are among his finest solo work, including the punchy "Face the Face" and the anthemic "Give Blood." —*Stephen Thomas Erlewine*

Pete Townshend's Deep End Live! / 1986 / Atco ✦✦✦
An energetic live album featuring a handful of R&B classics (including "Barefootin'"), a few Who chestnuts, and some of his best solo work, *Pete Townshend's Deep End Live!* is the tightest rock 'n' roll record he released as a solo artist. —*Stephen Thomas Erlewine*

Another Scoop / 1987 / Atco ✦✦✦✦
Like its predecessor, *Another Scoop* is a collection of 27 demos Pete Townshend recorded for the Who and, if anything, it surpasses the first volume in terms of quality. *Another Scoop* has a greater percentage of familiar Who classics—including "You Better You Bet," "Pinball Wizard," "Happy Jack," "Substitute," "Long Live Rock," "Pictures of Lily" and "The Kids Are Alright"—and the outtakes are uniformly excellent, ranging from his takes on "Driftin' Blues" and "Begin the Beguine" to neglected gems "Girl In a Suitcase," "Holly Like Ivy," and "Ask Yourself," and even weird experiments like "Football Fugue." For any Townshend fan, *Another Scoop* is necessary listening, containing some of his best and most adventurous work. —*Stephen Thomas Erlewine*

The Iron Man: a Musical / Jun. 1989 / Atlantic ✦✦
Pete Townshend adapted "The Iron Man," a children's fable written by the British poet Ted Hughes, for his sixth studio solo album, *Iron Man: A Musical*. Casting himself, Roger Daltrey, Nina Simone, and John Lee Hooker in leading roles, the album doesn't suffer from a lack of talent—it suffers from a lack of songs. Townshend has failed to come up with a set of compelling melodies for Hughes' poems, and the arrangements are obvious and overblown, making *Iron Man* an overwrought, ambitious failure. —*Stephen Thomas Erlewine*

Psychoderelict / Jun. 15, 1993 / Atlantic ✦✦
In the past, Townsend has let his lyrics tell the story from within the music, and that has allowed much of his work to stand timeless both as individual songs and entire concept pieces. On *Psychoderelict*, songs and music fight the spoken word "drama" throughout. Some individual songs are interesting; many are forgettable. Townsend shoots for hip, self-deprecating irony with numbers like "Let's Get Pretentious" and "Outlive the Dinosaur," but the strategy is transparent. Throw in the added static of instrumental passages paying tribute to Townsend's spiritual mentor Meher Baba, and the overall effect is disjointed and most unsatisfying. —*Roch Parisien*

Coolwalkingsmoothtalkingstraightsmokingfirestoking: Best of Pete Townshend / Apr. 1996 / Atlantic ✦✦✦✦
Despite some unnecessary problems, *Coolwalkingsmoothtalkingstraightsmokingfirestoking: The Best of Pete Townshend* is a good sampling of Townshend's biggest solo hits, as well as some of the songwriter's personal favorites. One of the major problems of the collection is Townshend's inability to use the original mixes alone—for instance, there are two versions of "Let My Love Open the Door," and neither of them is the original version. Furthermore, some tracks have longer mixes, others are shorter, and occasionally the mixes are significantly different from those on the album. Even with these problems, the album provides a good idea of the arc of Townshend's solo career, making it an adequate starting point for neophytes. For dedicated fans, it's a very frustrating release: not only is it baited with the unreleased *Psychoderelict* outtake "Uneasy Street" and the "E. Cola mix" of "Let My Love Open the Door," but the remixes and edits are awkward for those intimately familiar with the tracks. Which means *The Best of Pete Townshend* is best as a sampler, not as a definitive retrospective. —*Stephen Thomas Erlewine*

Toy Love

f. 1979, Dunedin, New Zealand, db. 1980
New Wave
Toy Love were a New Zealand new wave band that grew out of the country's first punk band of note, the Enemy. And while their small number of recordings are pretty much by-the-numbers new wave pop with a few moments of inspiration, Toy Love (and especially their founding member, Chris Knox) proved to be an important starting point for New Zealand's alternative rock scene of the '80s.

The Enemy was formed in 1977 in Dunedin by singer-songwriter Chris Knox (who also attempted bass for a short time), guitarist Alex Bathgate, drummer Mike Dooley, and guitarist Chris Pendergast. Pendergast was replaced shortly by a friend and former collaborator of Knox's, Mick Dawson. The band built a cult following, playing gigs throughout 1978 in Dunedin and Christchurch; Knox's reputation for wild onstage antics (such as self-mutilation) drew much attention. Dawson left the band by year's end and was replaced for a short time by Phil

Judd (ex-Split Enz), but the band decided to call it quits by January of 1979.

Remaining members Knox, Bathgate, and Dooley recruited keyboardist Jane Walker and bassist Paul Kean to complete the lineup for their new band, Toy Love. WEA New Zealand signed the band for a single, "Rebel"/"Squeeze," in July 1979. The single received a lot of critical attention in New Zealand and probably stands as their finest recorded moment. In 1980, they recorded another single, "Don't Ask Me," for the independent Deluxe. The band were received well in their homeland, but an attempt to break into Australia failed, and constant touring took its toll on the band. They recorded one self-titled album before internal disputes forced the band to break up in late 1980. Though an artistic failure for the most part, the album and the single, "Bride of Frankenstein," saw some moderate success in New Zealand. The band broke up shortly after the release. Knox went on to a successful solo career and (along with Bathgate) formed Tall Dwarves, Flying Nun Records' first recording act. Kean later joined the Bats.

Very few of the band's recordings are available (the band's sole LP is a long-out-of-print collectible), but a couple of their tracks have been made available on various CD compilations: "Rebel" can be found on *Bigger Than Both of US*, and radio session versions of "Squeeze" and "Frogs" were released on *AK79*. —*Chris Woodstra*

Toy Love / 1980 / WEA ✦✦
Toy Love's sole album was recorded at a low point for the band during a hectic touring schedule and a failed attempt to break out of New Zealand into Australia. Predictably, the album lacked much of the live energy for which the band had come to be known, turning out instead to be pretty standard new wave fare. Though it didn't properly showcase what the band was capable of, it did hint at Knox's potential as a songwriter, and it proved to be influential to the emerging alternative scene in New Zealand, providing the blueprint for much of that scene's unique sound: fractured, off-kilter garage-pop owing as much to the '60s as it does to punk. —*Chris Woodstra*

Traffic

f. 1967, Midlands, England, **db.** 1975
Art-Rock/Progressive-Rock, Psychedelic, Pop-Rock
Among all the bands to emerge from England in the '60s, Traffic is one of the few who have aged gracefully.

At the time of Traffic's inception in 1967, former Spencer Davis bandmate Stevie Winwood (b. May 12, 1948) was its most noted member, but with the release of their debut, *Mr. Fantasy*, it became clear that this was truly a band of four equally creative multi-instrumentalists. Their initial efforts fused an ecumenical range of musical genres through a fairly psychedelic sensibility, most of it among the best examples of that approach to late-'60s pop-rock. Guitarist and vocalist Dave Mason (b. May 10, 1947) penned some particularly strong material on those first Traffic albums, especially "Feelin' Alright," a song that was later popularized by Joe Cocker, Three Dog Night, and many others.

After many instances of quitting the band over creative differences (the remaining three were resistant to his obvious pop tendencies), Mason left for good after 1971's *Welcome to the Canteen* (No. 26), a live album. By then, he had already earned a gold album for his 1970 debut, *Alone Together* (No. 22).

After their second self-titled album, Traffic parted ways when Winwood joined the short-lived supergroup, Blind Faith. After Blind Faith's demise, Winwood began a solo effort, tentatively titled *Mad Shadows*. As the project developed, Winwood increasingly sought the input of Chris Wood and Jim Capaldi. The result was the funkier, earthier *John Barleycorn Must Die* (No. 5).

Traffic's studio follow-up, *The Low Spark of High Heeled Boys* (No. 7), incorporated a spacier improvisational sound. The title cut became an FM rock-radio standard. Several more albums followed, and the band parted ways in 1974.

Wood died on July 12, 1983, of liver failure. Capaldi and Dave Mason have experienced sporadically successful solo careers. Winwood, on the other hand, has had a long and profitable string of releases.

When Winwood's solo career began to sag in 1994, he re-formed Traffic with Capaldi; Mason didn't participate, choosing to stay in Fleetwood Mac. While the album proved a commercial disappointment, the reunited Traffic tour was successful, although neither proved exciting. —*Rick Clark*

☆ **Mr. Fantasy** / Jan. 1967 / Island ✦✦✦✦✦
Produced by Jimmy Miller (Rolling Stones, Spooky Tooth, Blind Faith), *Mr. Fantasy* is sonically decked out in *Sgt. Pepper* -period psychedelic splendor. Although much of the period sounds quite dated, *Mr. Fantasy* and the self-titled follow-up have aged gracefully. This is in no small part due to Dave Mason's refined pop sensibilities. Even though he occasionally gets lost in a sea of sitars ("Utterly Simple"), Mason gives the material much of the form and restraint that latter-period Traffic, at times, desperately needed. Even Winwood turns in some of the tightest

pop-song constructions in his career, thanks to Jim Capaldi and Chris Wood's co-writing input. The band's almost whimsical approach to integrating its eclectic influences keeps the material sounding fresh too. Traffic's hodgepodge of psychedelia always sounds like the product of a band that really plays together rather than existing as a studio concoction. Check out "Coloured Rain" or the title cut for an example. —*Rick Clark*

★ **Traffic** / Feb. 1968 / Island ✦✦✦✦✦
It's songs like "Feelin' Alright," "Pearly Queen," "You Can All Join In," "Vagabond Virgin," and "40,000 Headmen" that make Traffic's second effort a classic. Although not quite as trippy as their debut, most of the sonic observations mentioned for *Mr. Fantasy* apply here. —*Rick Clark*

Last Exit / Jan. 1969 / Island ✦✦✦
This collection of leftover studio tracks and live recordings from their 1968 tour was thrown together after Winwood jumped ship to go play with Blind Faith. It's a little spotty, but "Shanghai Noodle Factory" and the funky "Medicated Goo" are among their best early recorded work. —*Rick Clark*

John Barleycorn Must Die / Jan. 1970 / Island ✦✦✦✦
Upon the demise of the short-lived supergroup project Blind Faith, Stevie Winwood began work on a solo album entitled *Mad Shadows*. As the project developed, it evolved into a Traffic reunion of sorts, as Winwood brought in Wood and Capaldi. The result, *John Barleycorn Must Die*, became an instant success, with its lengthy funky, R&B, jazz, and folk explorations. The playing is top-notch throughout, with Wood blowing some inspired sax, Capaldi laying down his trademark fluid percussion grooves, and Winwood's Hammond B3 and piano work in peak form. "Glad," "Freedom Rider," "Empty Pages," and the title cut are the highlights. —*Rick Clark*

The Low Spark of High Heeled Boys / Jan. 1971 / Island ✦✦✦
Opening with the pastoral "Hidden Treasure," *Low Spark* flows effortlessly, almost lazily, to the last song, "Rainmaker." The band does shake things up a little with "Rock & Roll Stew" and "Light Up or Leave Me Alone." The title cut, at over 12 minutes of spacey jamming, is one of Traffic's most well-known FM hits. —*Rick Clark*

Welcome to the Canteen / Feb. 1971 / Island ✦✦✦
This fine live effort revealed Traffic as a seven-man touring unit, a precursor to their upcoming studio directions. On board for this outing were percussionist Reebop Kwaku Baah, drummer Jim Gordon, bassist Rick Grech, and Dave Mason, who briefly rejoined Winwood, Capaldi, and Wood for the tour. A revamped version of the Spencer Davis classic "Gimmie Some Lovin' (Part One)" became a moderate hit. —*Rick Clark*

Shoot Out at the Fantasy Factory / 1973 / Island ✦✦✦
The title cut has its moments, but the augmentation of Muscle Shoals studio heavies Barry Beckett, Roger Hawkins, and David Hood ultimately turned down most of the remaining sparks in search of the eternal groove. —*Rick Clark*

When the Eagle Flies / 1974 / Island ✦✦
Pared down to a quartet again and moving back to the English countryside should have re-kindled the magic of past glories. Unfortunately, the songs Traffic chose to release were too long in the tooth and meandered on without ever going anywhere. True, there are some fine moments here, but on the whole this is a rather uninspired set. Good, but not one of their best. —*James Chrispell*

Smiling Phases / Nov. 19, 1991 / Island ✦✦✦✦
Island remastered the tracks included in this double-disc anthology, and the difference is remarkable. Except for a few curious omissions, this is absolutely essential. —*Rick Clark*

Far from Home / May 3, 1994 / Virgin America ✦✦
In terms of capturing the spirit of playful creativity found on Traffic's best early work, this polished 1994 reunion album is indeed *Far from Home*. Traffic lovers may be disappointed, but fans of Winwood's later solo work will probably like this. Essentially, it's an extension of the sound he's created for the last ten years, with more instrumental stretching out—a nod to the band esthetic of '70s-era Traffic. —*Rick Clark*

Perfumed Garden / [Bootleg] ✦✦✦
If you're looking for unreleased early Traffic, this is certainly the collection to get, with 15 BBC tracks from 1967-68 and six marginally different alternate studio takes from 1967. Contains different versions of most of the songs from their first two albums and early singles; sound quality is variable, but usually quite good, and never less than listenable. In the manner of many BBC sessions, the differences between the studio and live versions are slight, but interesting for serious fans. —*Richie Unterberger*

The Trampps

f. 1973, Philadelphia, PA
Soul, Disco
Disco's most soulful vocal group began in the '60s as the Volcanos, and

were also called the Moods. Gene Faith was the original lead vocalist, with Earl Young, Jimmy Ellis, guitarist Dennis Harris, keyboardist Ron Kersey, organist John Hart, bassist Stanley Wade, and drummer Michael Thomas. But by the time they'd gone through various identities and emerged as the Trammps in the mid-'70s, the lineup featured lead vocalist Ellis, Harold and Stanley Wade, Robert Upchurch, and Young. A snappy revival of Judy Garland's '40s tune "Zing Went the Strings of My Heart" was their first chart single, reaching No. 17 on the R&B list in 1972. Despite their well-deserved reputation and boisterous, jubilant harmonies and sound, the Trammps were never huge commercial successes even during disco's heyday. Indeed, they had only three R&B Top Ten hits from 1972 through 1978, and such wonderful records as "Soul Bones," "Ninety-Nine and a Half," and "I Feel Like I've Been Livin' (On the Dark Side of the Moon)" stiffed on the charts though they were beloved by club audiences and R&B fans alike. Their only huge hit was "Disco Inferno" in 1977, which was a No. 9 R&B single in 1977 and was also featured in the movie *Saturday Night Fever*. Yet it missed the pop Top Ten, peaking at No. 11. But the Trammps' prowess can't be measured by chart popularity; Jimmy Ellis' booming, joyous vocals brilliantly championed the celebratory fervor and atmosphere that made disco both beloved and hated among music fans. —*Ron Wynn*

● **The Best of the Trammps** / 1978 / Atlantic ✦✦✦✦
A good collection of the band's best tracks, including the monolithic "Disco Inferno" and "Disco Party." —*Stephen Thomas Erlewine*

Translator

f. 1979, Los Angeles, CA, **db.** 1986
Group / Rock, New Wave
Inspired by the Beatles, the four-piece Translator featured the talents of two singer-songwriters, Steve Barton (guitar) and Bob Darlington (guitar), and a sound that spanned Merseybeat to psychedelia. Larry Dekker on bass and Dave Scheff on drums completed the lineup, which remained constant during the band's seven-year stay.

Formed in Los Angeles in 1979, the band relocated to San Francisco and were swiftly signed to Howie Klein's independent label, 415 Records, on the strength of their demo version of "Everywhere That I'm Not," the song that would remain the band's signature tune.

Heartbeats and Triggers (415/Columbia 1982), produced by David Kahne, was a college-radio hit. The second album, 1983's *No Time Like Now*, didn't fare as well, and Kahne's production didn't do much to enhance the sound. The band was struggling to break away from the tight new wave formula and started to on their lush, third album from 1985, simply titled *Translator*. As the decade wore on, the band became increasingly interested in exploring psychedelia, and their live shows were often three-hour affairs that included lots of jamming. Their final album, *Evening of the Harvest* (1986), was both the sound of a band that had matured and their most realized statement. *Everywhere That I'm Not—A Retrospective* was released by Columbia in 1986. Two more CD retrospectives were released on the band, *Translation* on Oglio and *Everywhere That We Were—The Best of Translator* by Columbia Legacy, in 1995 and 1996, respectively. The band took a stab at reuniting in 1993 and 1995, but not for long. In 1996, they were paid the highest compliment when voracious Beatles fans alerted the world via Internet and fanzines that the Fab Three had re-recorded a version of the Beatles instrumental "Cry For a Shadow" during the *Anthology* sessions. The tape was later found to be an old Translator B-side. All members of the band continue to play music in some form; Scheff immediately joined Winter Hours for a brief spell, and Barton was working as a solo artist but has yet to release anything. —*Denise Sullivan*

Heartbeats and Triggers / 1982 / 415 ✦✦✦
The band's signature song, "Everywhere That I'm Not," a sweet slice of new wave guitar pop mourning the loss of John Lennon, is included here, along with nine other tracks that simultaneously celebrate love and alienation; naturally, it was critically embraced during the post-punk era. The recording is a completely apt portrayal of the San Francisco guitar-band sound from the era—shrouded in darkness and masked with a perky new wave drum sound. —*Denise Sullivan*

No Time Like Now / 1983 / CBS ✦✦✦
Translator took the new wave formula too far on this one, though "No Time Like Now" and "Un-Alone" ring through with the sound of chiming guitars, inspired by the Byrds, Beatles, and the young R.E.M. —*Denise Sullivan*

Translator / 1985 / 415/Columbia ✦✦✦
Translator got the essential ingredients (solid songwriting, impeccable musicianship) back together on this one. "Fall Forever" and "Heaven by a String" are simply beautiful; "Another American Night" proves the guys can rock while taking on topical subjects, and "O Lazarus" became a fan favorite. Although it is unable to pass the blindfold test as to whether it was recorded in the '80s (clearly it was!), Ed Stasium's crisp production was a step in the right direction. —*Denise Sullivan*

● **Evening of the Harvest** / 1986 / 415/Columbia ✦✦✦
Psychedelia, blues, folk, and pop come home to roost on Translator's swan song. Finally finding their strength as a live band with supreme musicianship, this record comes closest to capturing what Translator really were: a great rock band that would have been recognized for the ages had their heyday not been during the early to mid-'80s. Sadly, because their three previous recordings were mostly unheralded, the band's demise was imminent upon this release. —*Denise Sullivan*

Translation / Aug. 15, 1995 / Oglio ✦✦✦
The adequate career compilation *Translation* includes beauties like the cover of the Jefferson Airplane's "Today" and the original "These Old Days," both culled from the brilliant *Evening of the Harvest* album. —*Denise Sullivan*

● **Everywhere That We Were: The Best of Translator** / Mar. 26, 1996 / Columbia/Legacy ✦✦✦✦
The Legacy collection in preferable to the *Translation* retrospective since it contains four more songs for the money, including the rare B-side and Beatles instrumental, "Cry for a Shadow," and the strident "When I Am With You" from *Heartbeats and Triggers*. Seek out *Evening of the Harvest* in addition to *Everywhere That We Were* and you'll have a fairly complete translation. —*Denise Sullivan*

The Trashmen

f. 1962, Minneapolis, MN, db. 1968
Rock 'n' Roll, Surf, Garage Rock
A Minneapolis rock 'n' roll band, the Trashmen evolved from Jim Thaxter & the Travelers, recording one single under that name ("Sally Jo"/"Cyclone"). The group comprises Tony Andreason (lead guitar), Dan Winslow (guitar/vocals), Bob Reed (bass), and Steve Wahrer (drums/vocals). Unfairly depicted as a novelty act, the Trashmen were in actuality a top-notch rock 'n' roll combo, enormously popular on the teen-club circuit, playing primarily surf music to a landlocked Minnesota audience. Drummer Steve Wahrer combined two songs by the Rivingtons ("The Bird's the Word" and "Pa Pa Ooh Mow Mow"), added freakish vocal effects and a pounding rhythm to the mix, and, by early 1964, the group was in the Top Ten nationwide with "Surfin' Bird." Though the group continued to release great follow-up singles and an excellent album, their moment in the sun had come and gone; they disbanded by late 1967/early 1968. They re-formed in the mid-'80s and continued to play locally until Wahrer's death. The Trashmen are revered by '60s collectors as one of the great American teen-band combos of all time, their lone hit exemplifying wild, unabashed rock 'n' roll at its most demented. bare-bones-basic, lone-E-chord finest. —*Cub Koda*

Surfin' Bird / 1964 / Sundazed ✦✦✦✦
The only album released by the group during their lifetime actually outstrips most of the Southern California-based competition, due to the ferocious grit of the playing and a vaguely demented, go-for-broke recklessness. A good mix of instrumentals and vocals, though nothing else is on the level of the title cut; the CD reissue adds demos of "Surfin' Bird" and "Bird Dance Beat," and a couple rare singles. —*Richie Unterberger*

Live Bird '65-'67 / 1990 / Sundazed ✦✦✦
Storming unreleased live recordings. —*Cub Koda*

● **Best of the Trashmen** / 1992 / Sundazed ✦✦✦✦
The original *Surfin' Bird* album, plus all the original Garrett singles from that period. The perfect primer set. —*Cub Koda*

The Great Lost Trashmen Album! / Oct. 21, 1994 / Sundazed ✦✦✦✦
The Great Lost Trashmen Album! features some fine unreleased studio recordings. —*Cub Koda*

Comic Book Collector / NPR ✦✦✦
This 11-song collection marks the final recording session of the original group, about a year before the untimely death of drummer/lead singer Steve Wahrer in 1989. While the recuts of their classics "Surfin' Bird" and "King of the Surf" don't hold a candle to the manic energy of the originals, their set list takes on "House of the Rising Sun," "Summertime Blues," "Believe What You Say," and "Love's Made a Fool of You" reveal a band that never lost its touch. The other three remaining tracks feature the current lineup with the drumming talent of Mark Andreason (brother of lead guitarist Tony) standing in for Steve, keeping the tradition alive and the heart of rock 'n' roll still beating with a shot of fresh blood. This includes the title cut, a strong indication that this band still has a lot of gas left in the tank. —*Cub Koda*

On Tour / Sundazed ✦✦✦

The Traveling Wilburys

f. 1988
Pop-Rock
Reversing the usual process by which groups break up and give way to solo careers, the Traveling Wilburys are a group made up of solo stars. The group was organized by former Beatle George Harrison (b.Feb 25,

1943), former Electric Light Orchestra leader Jeff Lynne (b.Dec 30, 1947), Bob Dylan (b.May 24, 1941), Tom Petty (b.Oct 20, 1953), and Roy Orbison (b.Apr 23, 1936–d.Dec 6, 1988), thus representing three generations of rock stars. In 1988, the five (who had known each other for years) came together to record a Harrison B-side single and ended up writing and recording an album on which they shared lead vocals. It turned out to be a way to transcend the high expectations made of any of them as individuals, and a delighted public sent the album to No. 3, with two singles, "Handle with Care" and "End of the Line," hitting the charts. Unfortunately, Orbison died of a heart attack only a few weeks after the album's release.
Two years later, the remaining quartet released a second album, inexplicably titled *Vol. 3*. It was another million-selling hit. —*William Ruhlmann*

● **The Traveling Wilburys** / 1988 / Wilbury ✦✦✦✦
The idea of Dylan, Orbison, Harrison, Lynne, Petty, and session drummer Jim Keltner getting together on a single album was pretty bizarre, inspiring curiosity and a little dread. Instead of trying to create something on a grand scale, these guys achieved much more by tossing together a refreshingly playful and unpretentious collection of homey pop-rock tunes. "Handle with Care" and "End of the Line" were minor hits from this release. —*Rick Clark*

Traveling Wilburys, Vol. 3 / Oct. 19, 1990 / Wilbury ✦✦✦
Skipping over *Volume 2*, the Wilburys managed a more unified and harder-rocking sound. Party rave-ups like "Wilbury Twist" and "She's My Baby" indicate that these guys seem to enjoy how their fabricated identities have allowed them to ditch their living-legends status and possibly become more themselves in the process. —*Rick Clark*

The Tremeloes

f. 1959, Dagenham, Essex, England
British Invasion, Pop-Rock
Quartet most famous for being picked for a contract by England's Decca Records in early 1962 in place of the Beatles. They actually started long before the Beatles, but it wasn't until after the Liverpool quartet hit that they saw any success in England or America. Their biggest British success was a version of the Contours' "Do You Love Me," but the hottest number on their first album was a searing (by British standards) rendition of "I Want Candy," later popularized by the Strangeloves, whose Bo Diddley-based beat Bob Porter and company handled with admirable style. Poole later faded into obscurity, while the Tremeloes achieved success on their own. —*Bruce Eder*

Here Come the Tremeloes / 1967 / CBS ✦✦✦✦
A pleasant, upbeat collection with a jovial mood, but nothing as impressive as their Brian Poole-era "I Want Candy." —*Bruce Eder*

● **The Best of the Tremeloes** / Feb. 25, 1992 / Rhino ✦✦✦✦
A generous twenty-track collection of the band's finest moments, it includes all of their US hits. —*AMG*

The Treniers

f. Mobile, AL
R&B, Jump Blues
Featuring twin brothers Cliff and Claude Trenier, the Treniers helped link swing music to rock 'n' roll with their brand of hot jump blues in the late '40s and early '50s. To the latter-day listener, their early-'50s singles can sound closer to swing than rock; indeed, Cliff and Claude had once sung with the Jimmie Lunceford Orchestra. The group did anticipate some crucial elements of rock 'n' roll, though, with their solid, thumping beats, their squealing saxophone solos, and their song titles, such as "Rocking on Sunday Night," "Rockin' Is Our Business," and "It Rocks! It Rolls! It Swings!" The Treniers' brand of swing-cum-R&B was undoubtedly an influence on Bill Haley, who saw them when both acts were playing summer shows at Wildwood, NJ. Their best work was recorded for OKeh in the early '50s; by the middle of the decade, their sound was more R&B-oriented. Like many early R&B pioneers, they were unable to find success in the rock 'n' roll era, though they appeared in a few of the first rock 'n' roll films. —*Richie Unterberger*

● **They Rock! They Roll! They Swing!: the Best of the Treniers** / Feb. 28, 1995 / Legacy/Epic ✦✦✦✦
This 20-track compilation has all of their key early—and mid-'50s Okeh singles (only one of which, "Go! Go! Go!," was actually an R&B hit), five previously unreleased songs, and their 1953 version of Bill Haley's "Rock-A-Beatin' Boogie," which must rank as one of the first covers of a white rock song by a Black artist. —*Richie Unterberger*

T. Rex

f. 1967, London, England, db. 1977
Rock 'n' Roll, Glam Rock, Proto-Punk
Initially a British folk-rock combo called Tyrannosaurus Rex, T. Rex was

the primary force in glam rock, thanks to the creative direction of guitarist/vocalist Marc Bolan (b. Marc Feld). Bolan created a deliberately trashy form of rock 'n' roll that was proud of its own disposability. T. Rex's music borrowed the underlying sexuality of early rock 'n' roll, adding dirty, simple grooves and fat, distorted guitars, as well as an overarching folkie/hippie spirituality that always came through most clearly on ballads. While most of his peers concentrated on making cohesive albums, Bolan kept the idea of a three-minute pop single alive in the early '70s. In Britain, he became a superstar, sparking a period of "T. Rextacy" among the pop audience with a series of Top Ten hits, including four No. 1 singles. Over in America, the group only had one major hit—the Top Ten "Bang a Gong (Get It On)"—before disappearing from the charts in 1973. T. Rex's popularity in the UK didn't begin to waver until 1975, yet they retained a devoted following until Marc Bolan's death in 1977. Over the next two decades, Bolan emerged as a cult figure, and the music of T. Rex has proven quite influential on hard rock, punk, new wave, and alternative rock.

Following a career as a teenage model, Marc Bolan began performing music professionally in 1965, releasing his first single, "The Wizard," on Decca Records. Bolan joined the psychedelic folk-rock combo John's Children in 1967, appearing on three unsuccessful singles before the group disbanded later that year. Following the breakup, he formed the folk duo Tyrannosaurus Rex with percussionist Steve Peregrine Took. The duo landed a record deal with a subsidiary of EMI in February 1968, recording their debut album with producer Tony Visconti. "Debora," the group's first single, peaked at No. 34 in May of that year, and their debut album, *My People Were Fair and Had Sky in Their Hair, But Now They're Content to Wear Stars on Their Brow*, reached No. 15 shortly afterward. The duo released their second album, *Prophets, Seers and Sages, the Angels of the Ages*, in November of 1968.

By this time, Tyrannosaurus Rex was building a sizable underground following, which helped Bolan's book of poetry, *The Warlock of Love*, enter the British best-seller charts. In the summer of 1969, the duo released their third album, *Unicorn*, as well as the single "King of the Rumbling Spires," the first Tyrannosaurus Rex song to feature an electric guitar. Following an unsuccessful American tour that fall, Took left the band and was replaced by Mickey Finn. The new duo's first single did not chart, yet their first album, 1970's *A Beard of Stars*, reached No. 21.

The turning point in Bolan's career came in October of 1970, when he shortened the group's name to T. Rex and released "Ride a White Swan," a fuzz-drenched single driven by a rolling backbeat. "Ride a White Swan" became a major hit in the UK, climbing all the way to No.2. The band's next album, *T. Rex*, peaked at No. 13 and stayed on the charts for six months. Encouraged by the results, Bolan expanded T. Rex to a full band, adding bassist Steve Currie and drummer Bill Legend (b. Bill Fifield). The new lineup recorded "Hot Love," which spent six weeks at No. 1 in early 1971. That summer, T. Rex released "Get It On" [retitled "Bang a Gong (Get It On)" in the US], which became their second straight UK No. 1; the single would go on to be their biggest international hit, reaching No. 10 in the US in 1972. *Electric Warrior*, the first album recorded by the full band, was released in the fall of 1971; it was No. 1 for six weeks in Britain and cracked America's Top 40.

By now, "T. Rextacy" was in full swing in England, as the band had captured the imaginations of both teenagers and the media with its sequined, heavily made-up appearance; the image of Marc Bolan in a top hat, feather boa, and platform shoes, performing "Get It On" on the BBC became as famous as his music. At the beginning of 1972, T. Rex signed with EMI, setting up a distribution deal for Bolan's own T. Rex Wax Co. record label. "Telegram Sam," the group's first EMI single, became their third No. 1 single.

"Metal Guru" also hit No. 1, spending four weeks at the top of the chart. *The Slider*, released in the summer of 1972, shot to No. 1 upon its release, allegedly selling 100,000 copies in four days; the album was also T. Rex's most successful American release, reaching No. 17. Appearing in the spring of 1973, *Tanx* was another Top Five hit for T. Rex; the singles "20th Century Boy" and "The Groover" soon followed it to the upper ranks of the charts. However, those singles would prove to be the band's last two Top Ten hits. In the summer of 1973, rhythm guitarist Jack Green joined the band, as did three backup vocalists, including the American soul singer Gloria Jones, who would soon become Bolan's girlfriend. At the beginning of 1974, drummer Bill Legend left the group and was replaced by Davy Lutton, as Jones became the group's keyboardist.

In early 1974, the single "Teenage Dream" was the first record to be released under the name Marc Bolan and T. Rex. The following album, *Zinc Alloy and the Hidden Riders of Tomorrow*, was the last Bolan recorded with Tony Visconti. Throughout the year, T. Rex's popularity rapidly declined: by the time "Zip Gun Boogie" was released in November, it could only reach No. 41. Finn and Green left the group at the end of the year, while keyboardist Dino Dins joined. The decline of T. Rex's popularity was confirmed when 1975's *Bolan's Zip Gun* failed to chart.

Bolan took the rest of the year off, returning in the spring of 1976 with *Futuristic Dragon*, which peaked at No. 50. Released in the summer of 1976, "I Love to Boogie," a disco-flavored, three-chord thumper, became Bolan's last Top 20 hit.

Bolan released *Dandy in the Underworld* in the spring of 1977; it was a modest hit, peaking at No. 26. While "The Soul of My Suit" reached No. 42 on the charts, T. Rex's next two singles failed to chart. Sensing it was time for a change of direction, Bolan began expanding his horizons in August. In addition to contributing a weekly column for *Record Mirror*, he hosted his own variety television show, *Marc*. Featuring guest appearances by artists like David Bowie and Generation X, *Marc* helped restore Bolan's hip image. Signing with RCA Records, the guitarist formed a new band with bassist Herbie Flowers and drummer Tony Newman, yet he never was able to record with the group. While driving home from a London club with Bolan, Gloria Jones lost control of her car, smashing into a tree. Marc Bolan, riding in the passenger's seat of the car, was killed instantly.

While T. Rex's music was intended to be disposable, it has proven surprisingly influential over the years. Hard rock and heavy metal bands borrowed the group's image, as well as the pounding insistence of their guitars. Punk bands may have discarded the high heels, feather boas, and top hats, yet they adhered to the simple three-chord structures and pop aesthetics that made the band popular. —*Stephen Thomas Erlewine*

T. Rex / 1970 / Fly ✦✦✦

T. Rex's self-titled first album was still heavily indebted to Marc Bolan's folk roots, even featuring a revamped version of "One Inch Rock," but it showed that hints of the trashy rock and pop synthesis that would come to fruition on T. Rex's next album, *Electric Warrior*. —*Stephen Thomas Erlewine*

★ **Electric Warrior / 1971 / Reprise ✦✦✦✦✦**

Kicking off with the fat guitars of "Mambo Sun," *Electric Warrior* winds through all of Marc Bolan's obsessions, from sleazy teenage rock 'n' roll to spacy mysticism. "Bang a Gong (Get It On)" was the well-deserved hit, full of lust and flamboyance, but it's by no means the only good thing here. With the trashy blues stomps of "Jeepster" and "Lean Woman Blues" sitting next to the space-age rock of "Monolith" and "Planet Queen," *Electric Warrior* has nothing but teenage kicks; it's glam rock at its absolute best. Without question, the definitive, classic T. Rex. —*Stephen Thomas Erlewine*

☆ **The Slider / Jan. 1972 / Polygram ✦✦✦✦✦**

The Slider was the peak of T. Rex-mania, both in Britain, where "Telegram Sam" and "Metal Guru" were No. 1 hits, and in America, where it was the group's highest-charting album record, without the benefit of a Top 40 hit. It's easy to see why the album was such a success. Although it doesn't offer anything new—it's still the same trashy glam-rock and pseudo-mystical folk of *Electric Warrior* —the songs were at a consistent high quality, with each cut offering a killer riff or hook. "Baby Strange," "Buick Mackane," and "Ballroom of Mars rank among Marc Bolan's classics, but even sillier filler like "Baby Boomerang," and "Chariot Choogle" are performed with so much style that he doesn't come across as a fool. *The Slider*, in many ways, is the peak of Bolan's career, and he rarely came close to matching his achievements here ever again. —*Stephen Thomas Erlewine*

Tanx / Feb. 1973 / Polygram ✦✦✦✦

Although the songs are not quite as well-constructed as those on *Electric Warrior*, *Tanx* still finds Bolan and T. Rex in top form, storming through a set of songs that kick hard, like "Country Honey"; swing, like "Mad Donna"; and sigh, like "Brokenhearted Blues." It's prime T. Rex and a terrific record. —*Stephen Thomas Erlewine*

Zinc Alloy & the Hidden Riders of Tomorrow / 1974 / Combat ✦✦

Coming after a series of well-constructed and best-selling albums, *Zinc Alloy and the Hidden Riders of Tomorrow* was a bit of a disappointment, with a good majority of the material seeming forced and incomplete, but the swaggering "Venus Loon" and "Teenage Dream" make up for the weaker moments. —*Stephen Thomas Erlewine*

Bolan's Zip Gun / 1975 / Relativity ✦✦

Bolan's Zip Gun was an improvement over the stilted, over-produced *Zinc Alloy*, featuring a relatively stripped-back production and a number of tight rockers, including "Light of Love" and "Token of My Love." —*Stephen Thomas Erlewine*

Futuristic Dragon / 1976 / Relativity ✦✦✦

Marc Bolan tried to make T. Rex's sound more contemporary on *Futuristic Dragon*, adding elements of disco and soul. Nevertheless, his simple, swaggering rock 'n' roll was the dominant musical approach on the album, which featured his most consistent set of songs since *Tanx*. —*Stephen Thomas Erlewine*

Dandy in the Underworld / 1977 / Relativity ✦✦✦

Dandy in the Underworld abandoned the disco experiments of *Futuristic Dragon* for a more direct rock 'n' roll approach that recalled the early T. Rex albums. The material wasn't quite as strong as *Tanx* or even *Zip*

Gun, but there were a handful of stomping rockers that ranked with the best of his work. —*Stephen Thomas Erlewine*

20th Century Boy / 1985 / Relativity ✦✦✦
20th Century Boy is a solid compilation that features most of his hits, but not necessarily all of his best material. A serviceable introduction, but nothing more. —*Stephen Thomas Erlewine*

The Essential Collection / 1991 / Relativity ✦✦
T. Rex is worthy of a great box set, but *The Essential Collection* isn't it. Bypassing all of Bolan's earlier folk work, the set has no cohesion—it's just a bunch of tracks piled together haphazardly. "Jeepster," not "Bang a Gong (Get It On)," is the only track from *Electric Warrior* to make the box, leaving its best record woefully underrepresented; instead, the box concentrates on the spottier records from the mid-'70s. Ultimately, *The Essential Collection* does a disservice to T. Rex. —*Stephen Thomas Erlewine*

Rabbit Fighter (The Alternate Slider) / 1994 / Edsel ✦✦
When Edsel Records reissued the T. Rex catalog with bonus tracks in 1994, they also began releasing alternate versions of each of T. Rex's albums, compiled from alternate takes and demos of the finished records, as well as adding alternate versions of the B-sides. *Rabbit Fighter: The Alternate Slider* was the first in this series and it reveals the depths of Marc Bolan's musical vision, as all of the arrangements of the final album were already sketched out on the demo tapes. Casual fans might find *Rabbit Fighter* tedious, but it's a goldmine for dedicated followers. —*Stephen Thomas Erlewine*

Definitive Tyrannosaurus Rex / Oct. 25, 1994 / Sequel ✦✦✦✦
Featuring over 20 tracks of prime Tyrannosaurus Rex material, *The Definitive Tyrannosaurus Rex* is indeed the definitive portrait of Marc Bolan's early years. —*Stephen Thomas Erlewine*

Great Hits 1972-77, Vol. 1: A-Sides / Nov. 8, 1994 / Edsel ✦✦✦✦
Great Hits 1972-77, Vol. 1: A-Sides is a wonderful collection of T. Rex's post-*Electric Warrior* singles, featuring such timeless pop songs as "Telegram Sam," "Metal Guru," "Children of the Revolution," "20th Century Boy" and "The Groover." Even though it lacks some of Marc Bolan's best-known songs—most notably "Bang a Gong (Get It On)," "Jeepster," and "Ride a White Swan"—it remains a terrific compilation, especially since it features a handful of songs that weren't included on T. Rex's official albums. —*Stephen Thomas Erlewine*

Great Hits 1972-77, Vol. 2: B-Sides / Nov. 8, 1994 / Edsel ✦✦✦
Frequently, T. Rex's B-sides were just as good as their album tracks, since Marc Bolan really didn't have any sense of quality control. Consequently, a lot of great songs slipped out on these flip-sides, which makes *Great Hits 1972-77, Vol. 2: B-Sides* a useful compilation. Most of these cuts wound up on bonus tracks on reissues of his post-*Electric Warrior* albums, but it's nice to have these collected in one place. —*Stephen Thomas Erlewine*

Unchained / 1995 / Demon ✦✦
As part of their T. Rex reissue series, Edsel Records began releasing a series of discs that compiled all of Marc Bolan's outtakes and demos on a year-by-year basis. *T. Rex Unchained: Unreleased Recordings* is certainly designed with the fan in mind—several of the songs are unfinished and the liner notes are lovingly detailed—but the discs prove that Bolan was holding back material that was the equal of what he released, so they may be of interest even to casual fans. —*Stephen Thomas Erlewine*

Left Hand Luke / Jun. 20, 1995 / Demon ✦✦
Left Hand Luke: The Alternate Tanx is quite similar to *Rabbit Fighter* in its presentation and content, presenting a fascinating working version of *Tanx.* Again, the album is primarily of interest to dedicated fans, but it is a compelling listen. —*Stephen Thomas Erlewine*

A Wizard, a True Star / Nov. 5, 1996 / Demon ✦✦✦✦
Compiling the highlights of the six-volume rarities series *Unchained,* the three-disc, 92-track box set *A Wizard, a True Star: Marc Bolan & T. Rex 1972-1977* is the best way for moderately dedicated Bolan fans—the ones who don't need every note he ever recorded—to catch up with the highlights Bolan left in the vaults. Not everything he left behind was terrific, but there were enough highly enjoyable variations on his bluesy glam-rock style to fill out a box set. Unfortunately, *A Wizard, A True Star* isn't quite it. There are many fine moments on the set, to be sure, from standard T. Rex boogies to surprisingly soulful variations on the sound, as well as fascinating home demos, but there are an abundance of minutely different alternate takes and interviews that clutter the album (however, hearing Bolan trying to apologize for inadvertently insulting Roy Wood while they were collaborating is priceless). Furthermore, there are a couple of cuts on the set that aren't anywhere else, making it necessary for completists that already own the bulk of this material. Then again, anyone who buys *A Wizard, A True Star* is a completist to a certain extent, because the pleasures these rarities offer are only evident to listeners who know the official catalog so well that they can hear a different lick or lyric on album tracks from *Zip Gun.* For

those listeners, the set is necessary, no matter how much duplication with other releases it offers. —*Stephen Thomas Erlewine*

A Tribe Called Quest

f. 1988, New York, NY
Hip Hop, Alternative Rap, East Coast Rap, Jazz-Rap

Without question the most intelligent, artistic rap group during the '90s, A Tribe Called Quest jump-started and perfected the hip-hop alternative to hardcore and gangsta-rap. In essence, they abandoned the macho posturing that rap music had been constructed upon, and focused instead on abstract philosophy and message tracks. The "sucka MC" theme had never been completely ignored in hip-hop, but Tribe confronted numerous black issues—date rape, use of the word nigger, the trials and tribulations of the rap industry—all of which overpowered the occasional game of the dozens. Just as powerful musically, Quest built upon De La Soul's jazz-rap revolution, basing tracks around laidback samples instead of the played-out James Brown-fests that many rappers had made a cottage industry by the late '80s. Comprised of Q-Tip, Ali Shaheed Muhammad, and Phife, A Tribe Called Quest debuted in 1989 and released their debut album one year later. Second album *The Low End Theory* was, quite simply, the most consistent and flowing hip-hop album ever recorded, though the trio moved closer to their harder contemporaries on 1993's *Midnight Marauders.* A spot on the 1993 Lollapalooza Tour showed their influence with the alternative crowd—always a bedrock of A Tribe Called Quest's support—but the group kept it real on 1996's *Beats, Rhymes and Life,* a dedication to the streets and the hip-hop underground.

A Tribe Called Quest was formed in 1988, though both Q-Tip (b. Jonathan Davis) and Phife (b. Malik Taylor) had grown up together in Queens. Q-Tip met DJ Ali Shaheed Muhammad while at high school and, after being named by the Jungle Brothers (who attended the same school), the trio began performing. A Tribe Called Quest's recording debut came in August 1989, when their single "Description of a Fool" appeared on a tiny area label (though Q-Tip had previously guested on several tracks from De La Soul's *3 Feet High and Rising* and later appeared on Deee-Lite's "Groove Is in the Heart").

Signed to Jive Records by 1989, A Tribe Called Quest released their first album, *People's Instinctive Travels and the Paths of Rhythm,* one year later. Much like De La Soul, Tribe looked more to jazz as well as '70s rock for their sample base: "Can I Kick It?" plundered Lou Reed's classic "Walk on the Wild Side" and made it viable in a hip-hop context. No matter how solid their debut was, second album *The Low End Theory* outdid all expectations and has held up as perhaps the best hip-hop LP of all time.

The Low End Theory had included several tracks with props to hip-hop friends, and A Tribe Called Quest cemented their support of the rap community with 1993's *Midnight Marauders.* The album cover and booklet insert included the faces of over 50 rappers—including obvious choices such as De La Soul and the Jungle Brothers as well as mild surprises like the Beastie Boys, Ice-T, and Heavy D. Though impossible to trump *Low End's* brilliance, the LP offered several classics (including Tribe's most infectious single to date, "Award Tour") and a harder sound than the first two albums. During the summer of 1994, A Tribe Called Quest toured as the obligatory rap act on the Lollapalooza Festival lineup, and spent a quiet 1995, marked only by several production jobs for Q-Tip. Returning in 1996 with their fourth LP, *Beats, Rhymes and Life,* Tribe showed signs of wear; it was a good album, but proved less striking than *The Low End Theory* or *Midnight Marauders.* —*John Bush*

People's Instinctive Travels and the Paths of Rhythm / Mar. 1990 / Jive ✦✦✦
With its superb debut album, A Tribe Called Quest established itself as leader of alternative rap—a term also applied to De La Soul, Digable Planets, and the Pharcyde. Though De La had a strong influence on Quest, the experimental New York group projected a highly appealing personality of its own. Quirky, abstract, and cerebral, the album lacks the immediacy of more hardcore rap and wasn't as big a seller as many of the gangster rap CDs released in 1990. In fact, much of its support came from alternative rock aficionados, who were drawn to its complexity. Jazz is a strong influence here, and like many jazz recordings, this is an album that necessitates several listenings in order to be fully appreciated and absorbed. —*Alex Henderson*

★ **The Low End Theory** / Sep. 24, 1991 / Jive ✦✦✦✦✦
A Tribe Called Quest came into their own with their second album, *The Low End Theory.* Where their debut only hinted at the group's musical depths, *The Low End Theory* explodes all expectations—it's the first album that successfully fuses jazz and hip-hop together. Not only does the music ebb and flow like the best soul-jazz and hard bop (partially due the presence of bassist Ron Carter), so do the rhymes of Q-Tip and Phife, as evidenced by such hit singles as "Check the Rhime" and "Award Tour." Furthermore, the album doesn't feel forced or pretentious—it

flows naturally, as the rhythms and rhymes play off of each other. Others tried to replicate its sound and Tribe tried desperately to duplicate its magic, but *The Low End Theory* stands not only as the group's finest moment, but the pinnacle of the jazz/hip-hop fusion. —*Stephen Thomas Erlewine*

Midnight Marauders / Nov. 9, 1993 / Jive ✦✦✦✦
Midnight Marauders was an intriguing and smartly paced collection that ranged from descriptive verbal essays on city life to confrontational taunts, comic expositions, denunciations, and even quasi-religious theorizing. While their celebrated hip-hop/jazz roots were often evident, the group also utilized fusion, urban contemporary, Afro-Latin, and funk samples, while Q-Tip's rap style could be cool and deadpan, reflective, analytical, satirical, or disgusted and angry. There was precious little "gangsta" posturing or sexist rhetoric, and such numbers as "Sucka Nigga," "God Lives Through," "Electric Relaxation," and "Award Tour" were cleverly delivered and brilliantly composed. —*Ron Wynn*

Beats, Rhymes and Life / Aug. 1996 / Jive ✦✦✦✦
With their fourth album, *Beats, Rhymes and Life*, A Tribe Called Quest manages to be one of the few hip-hop acts to successfully age by pushing both their music and their lyrics into new directions. Stylistically, the record is closest to its immediate predecessor, *Midnight Marauders*, in the sense that the group's jazz-rap fusion is downplayed and the beat stays surprisingly hard throughout the album. What distinguishes *Beats, Rhymes and Life* from *Marauders* is a deeper sense not only of eclecticism, but of spirtuality and maturity. Shortly before the album was written and recorded, Q-Tip converted to Islam; the religion's ideals are an undercurrent in nearly every track on the album. But what really stands out is Tip's unease with the transience of the youth-oriented hip-hop scene and his own urges to settle down. Unlike most rappers, he confronts these feelings in the music, by writing lyrics and helping to create music that illustrates the contradictions of growing old with hip-hop. And by tackling the issue head-on, A Tribe Called Quest sound fresh and suggest that it is possible to sustain a career in rap as you approach a full decade of recording, after all. —*Leo Stanley*

Tricky

b. 1964, Bristol, England
Vocals / Alternative Pop-Rock, Trip-Hop
Originally, Tricky was a member of the Wild Bunch, a Bristol-based rap troupe that eventually metamorphosed into Massive Attack during the early '90s. Tricky provided pivotal raps on Massive Attack's groundbreaking 1992 album *Blue Lines*. The following year, he released his debut single, "Aftermath." Before he recorded "Aftermath," he met a teenage vocalist named Martina, who would become his full-time musical collaborator; all albums released under Tricky's name feature her contributions.

Tricky signed a contract with 4th & Broadway in 1994. The contract contained a clause that allowed him to release side projects under different names, in addition to regular Tricky releases. "Ponderosa" and "Overcome" were released over the course of 1994; that same year, he made a cameo on Massive Attack's second album, *Protection*. Tricky's debut album, *Maxinquaye*, appeared in the spring of 1995. Not only did the album receive overwhelmingly positive reviews when it was released, but it entered in the UK charts at No. 2, despite the total lack of daytime radio airplay. Throughout 1995, Tricky was omnipresent in the UK, collaborating with and remixing for a wide variety of artists, including Bjork, Luscious Jackson, and Whale. In the fall of 1995, he released *Tricky Vs. the Gravediggaz*, a collaboration with the American hardcore rap group, as well as a single called "I Be the Prophet," which was released under the name Starving Souls. At the end of the year, *Maxinquaye* topped many year-end polls in Britain, including the *Melody Maker* and *NME*.

In February of 1996, *Nearly God*—an album featuring Tricky's collaborations with artists as diverse as Terry Hall, Bjork, Alison Moyet, and Neneh Cherry—was released, again to strong reviews; the album was released in the US six months later. After completing the second full-fledged Tricky album, he relocated to New York City early in 1996, where he began working with underground rappers. An EP called *Grassroots* was released in the US in September. Two months later, Tricky's official second album, *Pre-Millenium Tension*, was released. Again, Tricky received positive reviews, though there were a few dissenting opinions.

In addition to his three releases of 1996, he remixed artists as diverse as Elvis Costello, Garbage, Yoko Ono and Bush. —*Stephen Thomas Erlewine*

★ **Maxinquaye** / Apr. 18, 1995 / 4th & Broadway ✦✦✦✦✦
Though he hates the label of trip-hop, Tricky's debut album *Maxinquaye* is one of the finest that the genre has to offer. "Ponderosa," "Suffocated Love," and "Pumpkin" are disturbing and beautiful, with ominous background noises and Martina's soaring vocals, while tracks like the group's cover of "Black Steel" show off their harder side. A striking

debut, Tricky's *Maxinquaye* is only the beginning for this innovative artist. —*Heather Phares*

Nearly God / Apr. 29, 1996 / Fourth & Broadway/Durban Poison ✦✦✦✦
Nearly God is Tricky's unofficial second album—he calls it a collection of brilliant, incomplete demos. When Tricky signed his contract with Island, it allowed him to release an album a year under a different name, and *Nearly God* is the first of these efforts. Tricky recorded the record with a diverse cast of collaborators—in addition to his partner Martina, there's Terry Hall, Bjork, Neneh Cherry, Cath Coffey, Dedi Madden, and Alison Moyet (Damon Albarn pulled his track just before the album's release). Building on the ghostly, dark soundscapes of Tricky's debut, *Maxinquaye*, *Nearly God* narrows the focus of his first record by making the music slower, hazier, and more disturbing. It's not as coherent as *Maxinquaye*, but that's part of its appeal. *Nearly God* is a haunting, fractured, surreal nightmare that doesn't always make sense, but never fails to make an impact. Certain collaborators work better than others—Tricky understands the eeriness of Terry Hall's voice, but he does nothing to tame Alison Moyet's inappropriate bluesy shrieking—but the overall effect of the album is quietly devastating. It gets under your skin and stays there. It's a brilliantly evocative nightmare. —*Stephen Thomas Erlewine*

Grassroots EP / Aug. 1996 / ffrr ✦✦✦
Perhaps in an effort to establish himself in the American hip-hop market—which largely ignored his groundbreaking debut, *Maxinquaye*—Tricky released the *Grassroots* EP in the summer of 1996. Recorded in early 1996, *Grassroots* consists primarily of one-off collaborations with a variety of underground and relatively undistinctive New York rappers and musicians, whose music is given weight by Tricky's menacing, hazy production. Tricky appears in the background of each song, murmuring indecipherably, but it's only when he takes the forefront on "Tricky Kid" that the EP matches the tense, psychotic soundscapes of *Maxinquaye* and *Nearly God*. The remaining four tracks have their moments—Drunkenstein's backing vocals are evocative, and "Devils Helper" is entrancing—but for the most part, *Grassroots* consists of experiments that never quite reach their full potential. —*Stephen Thomas Erlewine*

Pre-Millennium Tension / Nov. 19, 1996 / Polygram ✦✦✦✦
Maxinquaye was an unexpected hit in England, launching a wave of similar-sounding artists who incorporated Tricky's innovations into safer pop territory. Tricky responded by travelling to Jamaica to record *Pre-Millennium Tension*, a nervy, claustrophobic record that thrives on its own paranoia. Scaling back the clattering hooks of *Maxinquaye* and slowing the beat down, Tricky has created a hallucinatory soundscape, where the rhythms, samples, and guitars intertwine into a crawling processions of menacing sounds and disembodied lyrical threats. Its tone is set by the backward guitar loops of "Vent," and continued through the shifting "Christiansands" and the tense, lyrically dense "Tricky Kid," easily Tricky's best straight rap to date. Occasionally, the gloom is broken, such as when the shimmering piano chords of "Makes Me Want to Die" ring out, but nearly as often, it becomes bogged down in its own murk, as in the long ragga rant "Ghetto Youth." While the lyrics are often quite effective in conveying dope-addled paranoia, what ties the album together are its layered rhythms and soundscapes. Though it might not sound that way immediately, *Pre-Millennium Tension* is as much Tricky reaching back to his hardcore rap roots as it is a sonic exploration. As such, it stands as a transition record for Tricky, but its overall effect is only slightly less powerful than *Maxinquaye* or *Nearly God*. —*Stephen Thomas Erlewine*

The Troggs

f. 1964, Andover, Hampshire, England
British Invasion, Rock 'n' Roll, Pop-Rock, Garage Rock, Psychedelia
Remembered chiefly as proto-punkers who reached the top of the charts with the "caveman rock" of "Wild Thing" (1966), the Troggs were also adept at crafting power-pop and ballads. Hearkening back to a somewhat simpler, more basic British Invasion approach as psychedelia began to explode in the late '60s, the group also reached the Top Five with their flower-power ballad "Love Is All Around" in 1968. While more popular in their native England than the US, the band also fashioned memorable, insistently riffing hit singles like "With a Girl like You," "Night of the Long Grass," and the notoriously salacious "I Can't Control Myself" between 1966 and 1968. Paced by Reg Presley's lusting vocals, the group—which composed most of their own material—could crunch with the best of them, but were also capable of quite a bit more range and melodic invention than they've been given credit for.

Hailing from the relatively unknown British town of Andover, the Troggs hooked up with manager/producer Larry Page (who was involved in the Kinks' early affairs) in the mid-'60s. After a flop debut single, they were fortunate enough to come across a demo of Chip Taylor's "Wild Thing" (which had already been unsuccessfully recorded by the Wild Ones). In the hands of the Troggs, "Wild Thing"—with its grungy chords and off-the-wall ocarina solo—became a primeval three-chord monster, famous not only in its original hit Troggs version, but in its psychedelic revamping by Jimi Hendrix, who used it to close his famous set at the 1967 Monterey Pop Festival.

"Wild Thing" made No. 1 in the States, but the Troggs' momentum there was impeded by a strange legal dispute that saw their early records simultaneously released on two different labels. Nor did it help that the band didn't tour the US for a couple of years. As a consequence, the fine follow-up singles "With a Girl like You" and "I Can't Control Myself" didn't do as well as they might have. In Britain, it was a different story—they were smashes, but "I Can't Control Myself" had such an open-hearted lust that it encountered resistance from conservative radio programmers all over the globe.

The Troggs tempered their image on subsequent ballads, which utilized a sort of pre-"power ballad" approach. These weren't bad, and a few of them were British hits, but they weren't as fine as the initial blast of singles that established the band's image. "Love Is All Around," which restored them to the American Top Ten in 1968, was their finest effort in this vein. It was also their final big hit on either side of the Atlantic.

But the Troggs would keep going for a long, long time. In a sense they were handicapped by their image—they were not intellectuals, certainly, but they weren't dumb, either. They wrote most of their songs, and their albums were reasonably accomplished, if hardly up to the level of the Kinks or Traffic, containing some nifty surprises like the gothic ballad "Cousin Jane," or the tongue-in-cheek psychedelia of "Maybe the Madman." By 1970, though, they were struggling. They continued to release a stream of singles, most of which had a straightforward simplicity that was out of step with the progressive rock of the time, all of which flopped, though some were fairly good.

The Troggs' image as lunkheads couldn't have been helped by the notorious *Troggs Tapes,* a 12-minute studio argument that was captured on tape while the band were unawares. The *Spinal Tap* -like dialog helped keep their cult alive, though, and as punk gained momentum in the mid-'70s, they gained belated appreciation as an important influence on bands like the Ramones and (earlier) the MC5. They found enough live work (sometimes on the punk/new wave circuit) to keep going, although their intermittent records generally came to naught. In 1992, they rose to their highest profile in ages when three members of R.E.M., which had covered "Love Is All Around," backed the Troggs on the comeback album *Athens Andover.* —*Richie Unterberger*

● **The Best of the Troggs** / 1988 / PolyGram ✦✦✦✦
Polygram's *Best of the Troggs* is a basic primer, containing all of the group's best-known songs ("Wild Thing," "With a Girl Like You," "I Can't Control Myself," "Love Is All Around"), as well as a smattering of some of their better obscurities, making it a fine introduction to the primitive British Invasion band. —*Stephen Thomas Erlewine*

Athens Andover / 1992 / Rhino ✦✦✦
Most comeback albums never work; *Athens Andover* is the rare exception that does. Backed by members of R.E.M. and the dB's, the Troggs make some of their best pop ever, full of ringing guitars and chiming melodies. (*Athens Andover* was reissued in 1996 by the Music Club label as *Athens, Georgia & Beyond* with additional tracks.) —*Stephen Thomas Erlewine*

Archeology (1967-1977) / Sep. 22, 1992 / Fontana ✦✦✦✦
A double-CD, 52-track box set that proves there was a lot more to the Troggs than "Wild Thing" and "Love Is All Around." This archetypally primitive British Invasion quartet scored many hits in the UK that barely dented the charts in the US, like "With a Girl Like You," "Night of the Long Grass," and the notoriously racy "I Can't Control Myself." They're all here, along with notable album cuts, B-sides, and worldwide post-1968 flops. Primitive they may have been, but the Troggs—who wrote most of their own material—did not lack a flair for hard pop hooks, and could display a surprising delicacy in their ballads. Several of their obscure singles and album tracks are equal in worth to their hits, like the gothic but pretty "Cousin Jane," and the witty light psychedelia of "Maybe the Madman" and "Purple Shades." Some of the '70s hard rockers and glammish novelties are unimpressive, and 52 songs are arguably excessive. But there are a fair number of obscure gems to be found on this well-annotated package. —*Richie Unterberger*

Doris Troy

b. Jan. 16, 1937, New York, NY
Vocals / Soul
Surely one of the most talented one-hit wonders of the rock era, Doris Troy hit the Top Ten with "Just One Look" in 1963, but also recorded many other fine pop-soul sides for Atlantic between 1963 and 1965. Unlike many soul performers of the time, Troy wrote most of her own material (under the pseudonym Payne), and had already written for other artists, and sung backup with Dionne and Dee Dee Warwick and Cissy Houston on New York soul records, before striking out on her own.

More melodically ambitious and stylistically eclectic than many of her peers, her Atlantic sides blend elements of gospel, girl group, blues, and pop into a rich New York soul sound. Troy never reached the charts again after "Just One Look," but was more appreciated in England, where she toured occasionally, and where the Hollies covered her "What'cha Gonna Do About It" on their first album. Moving to Britain, she recorded an album for Apple in 1970 with assistance from George Harrison and Billy Preston. In the early '70s, she sang backup vocals for British rock groups, as well as recording a couple more albums. In the '80s, she starred in *Mama I Want to Sing,* a musical based on her life story. —*Richie Unterberger*

Doris Troy / 1970 / Capitol ✦✦✦
An all-star cast supported Troy on her lone Apple effort: George Harrison, Billy Preston, Peter Frampton, Stephen Stills, Klaus Voormann, Jackie Lomax, Eric Clapton, Leon Russell, and Delaney & Bonnie all contributed, and Harrison, Stills, Lomax, Preston, Voormann, and Ringo Starr pitched in on the songwriting, though Troy wrote or co-wrote most of the songs. Well-received by some critics, it really doesn't add up to the sum of its parts. Troy is in great voice, but much of the material is pedestrian, and the heavy rock/soul arrangements often have an over-beefy, early-'70s supersession feel. It works best when Troy puts the brakes on the hard rock to deliver emotional, slower soul tunes. The CD reissue adds five interesting cuts from non-LP singles and outtakes. —*Richie Unterberger*

● **Just One Look: the Best of Doris Troy** / Aug. 23, 1994 / Ichiban Soul Classics ✦✦✦✦
This 21-track anthology of her 1963-65 Atlantic sides is as comprehensive as one could ask for. It includes all of her singles, her rare album, three cuts only issued on British singles, and her rare 1965 single for the Calla label, "I'll Do Anything (He Wants Me To Do)." Besides "Just One Look," there are quite a few other downright excellent lost gems here: "What'cha Gonna Do About It," the bluesy "Draw Me Closer," the driving "You'd Better Stop" (with a fierce guitar break that sounds like a young Jimmy Page), and the soulful wall of sound on "I'll Do Anything." "How My Heart Aches" is a special standout that ranks among the very finest wrenching, melancholy soul ever waxed. Much more than a collector's item, this proves Troy to be a genuinely overlooked major talent. —*Richie Unterberger*

True West

f. 1980, Davis, CA, **db.** 1987
Group / Alternative Pop-Rock, Paisley Underground
Out of the same mold as Los Angeles' Paisley Underground bands, True West didn't fit because they were from Davis, CA (operating out of the nearby nexus for guitar bands, San Francisco) and a little darker and less dreamy than the others. They debuted with *True West,* an EP in 1983 on Bring Out Your Dead Records. It was produced by the band's Russ Tolman and the Dream Syndicate's Steve Wynn. *Hollywood Holiday,* released by France's then-very hip New Rose label that same year, contained the debut EP as well as some new tracks. By 1984, the band signed a deal with US indie label PVC for *Drifters.* Guitarist Josef Becker left to join the similar, though darker California-centric roots band Thin White Rope, and after recording, so too did Tolman. 1986's *Hand of Fate* for CD Presents features guitar work by the Rain Parade's Matt Piucci and Green on Red's Chuck Prophet in place of Tolman. Shortly after, the band called it quits. *West Side Story* (Skyclad, 1989) is an odds-and-sods collection, *Best Western* (Skyclad, 1990) a compilation of old demos, and *TV Western* (Skyclad, 1990) adds some live tracks to the demo sessions. Singer Gavin Blair and guitarist Richard McGrath worked as Fool Killers after the breakup, and Tolman is a prolific singer-songwriter. Becker went on to play with Game Theory. The group's bassist was Kevin Staydohar. —*Denise Sullivan*

True West EP / 1983 / Bring Out Your Dead ✦✦✦✦

Hollywood Holiday / 1983 / PVC ✦✦✦
Singer Gavin Blair's Barrett-like voice and Russ Tolman's insistent, psychedelic guitar leanings made the band the perfect candidate to cover the Floyd, and they did on a fine rendition of "Lucifer Sam." "Hollywood Holiday" was a sort of signature tune for True West, encapsulating the band's lowdown, California aesthetic. A fine intro to the band, as it includes their debut EP, *True West,* produced by Tolman and the Dream Syndicate's Steve Wynn. —*Denise Sullivan*

● **The Drifters** / 1984 / PVC ✦✦✦✦

Hand of Fate / 1986 / CD Presents ✦✦

West Side Story / 1989 / Skyclad ✦✦

TV Western EP / 1990 / Skyclad ✦✦✦

Two True / 1992 / Skyclad ✦✦

Tsunami

f. 1990, Arlington, VA
Alternative Pop-Rock, Indie Rock
Tsunami are a punk-pop band from Arlington, Virginia. Guitarist/vocalist Jenny Toomey (also of Grenadine and Licorice) and Kristin Thomson (bass) run their own record label, Simple Machines, on which they release their own material and works from like-minded artists (such as Scrawl). Like many indie bands, Tsunami have appeared on a plethora of singles and EPs since their 1990 inception. They released their first full-length album, *Deep End*, in 1993 and followed it up with *The Heart's Tremolo* in 1994. A much-needed singles compilation was released in 1995. Their mix of politics, melodiscism, and heavy guitars make them a strong and respected voice in the alternative community. —*Heather Phares*

Deep End / May 31, 1993 / Simple Machines ✦✦✦✦
The group's melodic, witty debut manages to be both heavy and catchy. Toomey and Thompson's vocal and guitar interplay make this an interesting listen. —*Heather Phares*

● **The Heart's Tremolo** / 1994 / Simple Machines ✦✦✦✦
The 11 songs on *The Heart's Tremolo* are more polished, complex, and accomplished than those of their debut. Toomey's torchy vocals and the group's trademark droning guitars make this album even better than *Deep End*. —*Heather Phares*

B-Sides Compilation / 1995 / Simple Machines ✦✦✦✦
This B-side compilation collects the group's plethora of singles in one place. These singles capture the bouncier, poppier side of Tsunami's sound, and this collection could be the starting point for the average listener. —*Heather Phares*

World Tour & Other Destinations / Apr. 16, 1995 / Simple Machines ✦✦✦

The Tubes

f. 1972, San Francisco, CA, **db.** 1986
Pop-Rock, Arena Rock
The Tubes were arch satirists of popular culture whose outrageous performance-art concepts—which swung wildly from soft-core pornography to suit-and-tie conservatism—frequently eclipsed their elusive musical identity. The Tubes formed in Phoenix, Arizona in 1972 under the name Radar Men From Uranus, which incorporated refugees from a pair of local bands, the Red, White & Blues and the Beans. Originally comprised of guitarists Roger Steen and Bill Spooner, keyboardist Vince Welnick, bassist Rick Anderson and drummer Prairie Prince, the Radar Men became the Tubes following a move to San Francisco and the addition of Michael Cotten on keyboards and former roadie Fee Waybill on lead vocals. Over the course of the next few years, the Tubes earned a devoted cult following on the strength of Spooner's parodic songs and the group's surreal live shows, which featured Waybill adopting a variety of personas including the "crippled Nazi" Dr. Strangekiss, country singer Hugh Heifer and Quay Lewd, a drug-addled British pop star. After signing to A&M in 1975, they released their self-titled debut, followed a year later by *Young and Rich;* while both failed to transfer the manic energy and theatrical complexity of their live set onto record, the single "White Punks on Dope" became a minor hit and a radio staple.

After 1977's failed concept record *The Tubes Now*, the group toured England, where a series of banned performances made them a media sensation. However, during the recording of the concert LP *What Do You Want From Live?* Waybill broke his leg onstage while acting out his punk character Johnny Bugger; the remainder of the tour was cancelled, and with it died the band's chart momentum. After returning to the US, they recruited producer Todd Rundgren and recorded 1979's *Remote Control*, a concept album exploring the influence of television; when it met a similar commercial fate as its predecessors, the Tubes were dropped by A&M.

After signing to Capitol, they recorded 1981's *Completion Backwards Principle*, an album based on an actual sales training instruction manual; both "Talk to You Later" and "Don't Want to Wait Anymore" earned significant radio play, and the LP became the Tubes' first Top 40 hit. Thanks to its provocative video, the single "She's a Beauty" reached the Top Ten, and pushed the 1983 LP *Outside/Inside* into the Top 20 Albums chart; after 1986's *Love Bomb* stiffed, however, the Tubes disbanded, and Welnick later joined the Grateful Dead. In 1993, the Tubes reunited; consisting of Waybill, Steen, Anderson, Prince, and new keyboardist Gary Cambra, they toured the US and Europe before releasing a new LP, *Genius of America*, in 1996. Spooner also issued his own solo record, *Mall to Mars*. —*Jason Ankeny*

The Tubes / 1975 / A&M ✦✦✦
The debut album for The Tubes, featuring the anthem "White Punks on Dope." —*Cub Koda*

Young & Rich / 1976 / A&M ✦✦✦✦
Their breakthrough album and the best representation of the band's early days. —*Cub Koda*

Now / 1977 / A&M ✦✦✦

What Do You Want from Life / 1978 / A&M ✦✦✦
A great live album, featuring a good sampling from their mind-boggling '70s stage act. —*Cub Koda*

Remote Control / 1979 / A&M ✦✦

T.R.A.S.H. (Tubes Rarities & Smash Hits) / 1981 / A&M ✦✦✦✦

The Completion Backward Principle / 1981 / Capitol ✦✦✦✦

Outside/Inside / 1983 / Capitol ✦✦

Love Bomb / 1985 / Capitol ✦✦

● **The Best of the Tubes** / Nov. 9, 1992 / Capitol ✦✦✦✦
The Best of the Tubes is the best Tubes disc available, containing all of their hits and trademark songs. —*AMG*

Genius of America / Oct. 15, 1996 / Popular/Critique ✦✦

Maureen Tucker

Drums / Alternative Pop-Rock
When the Velvet Underground was America's most admired avant-garde rock band, it was easy to imagine solo success for principal songwriter Lou Reed and enigmatic Welsh multi-instrumentalist John Cale, but no one could have predicted that some of the best solo recordings from a former member of this seminal band would come from drummer Maureen (Moe) Tucker. After the demise of the Velvets, Tucker lived in relative obscurity in Douglas, Georgia, raising her children and working for minimum wage at a Wal-Mart—salient points that form the thematic basis of her solo career. No longer strictly a drummer, Tucker switched to guitar, and with the help of a new generation of avant-rock players (Half Japanese's Jad and David Fair, Daniel Johnston, Sonic Youth) and longtime pals (Lou Reed) began recording terse, guitar-driven songs about single motherhood, working hard for minimum wage, and hating the corporatization of rock 'n' roll. These were proud, no-bullshit, pissed-off songs that found a home on the wonderfully idiosyncratic indie label 50 Skidillion Watts, principally owned by Velvets fan Penn Jillette (of the comedy/magic duo Penn and Teller), who gave Tucker a regular outlet for her music. Occasionally, Tucker has had to return to the underpaying world of 9-5 to supplement her rock 'n' roll income, but as she released more records, her popularity in alternative-rock circles has grown (especially in Europe) to the point where she can make a living as a full-time musician. Good news indeed! —*John Dougan*

● **Playin' Possum** / 1981 / Trash ✦✦✦✦
Moe is the whole show on her 1981 debut, singing and playing drums, guitars, bass, and a variety of other instruments. Consisting mostly of raw and primitive covers of rock 'n' roll oldies by Bo Diddley, Little Richard, and Chuck Berry, she also throws in a version of "Heroin" and covers of Dylan's "I'll Be Your Baby Tonight" and Vivaldi's "Concerto In D Major," as well as the "original" "Ellas," which is a six-minute extrapolation of the basic Bo Diddley beat. This inspired lesson in rock 'n' roll auteurism is probably her best effort. —*Richie Unterberger*

Moejadkatebarry / 1987 / 50 Skidillion Watts ✦✦✦

Life in Exile After Abdication / 1989 / 50 Skidillion Watts ✦✦✦✦
Fantastic. Wonderfully dry, witty and sarcastic songs about everyday life, *Life in Exile* features help from Lou Reed and Sonic Youth and terrific songs like the Andy Warhol eulogy "Andy" and a great cover of the Velvets' "Pale Blue Eyes." Best of all, though, is the working-class lament "Spam Again," which, more than most songs about stretching paychecks, connects with equal amounts of anger and humor. —*John Dougan*

I Spent a Week There the Other Night / 1991 / Young God ✦✦✦✦
With more help from her indie-rock bigshot pals (Don Fleming, Brian Ritchie), *Week* also featured the first (sort of) Velvet Underground reunion, with Cale, Reed, and Sterling Morrison guesting on separate tracks. Covering "And Then He Kissed Me" was inspired, as is the inclusion of the accusatory (and appropriately titled) "Fired Up." From start to finish, it rocks like crazy. —*John Dougan*

Dogs Under Street / Jul. 19, 1994 / Sky ✦✦✦

Big Joe Turner

b. May 18, 1911, Kansas City, MO, d. Nov. 24, 1985, Inglewood, CA
Vocals / R&B, Rock 'n' Roll, Blues, Swing, Jump Blues
The premier blues shouter of the postwar era, Big Joe Turner's roar could rattle the very foundation of any gin joint he sang within—and that's without a microphone. Turner was a resilient figure in the history of blues—he effortlessly spanned boogie-woogie, jump blues, even the first wave of rock 'n' roll, enjoying great success in each genre. Turner,

whose powerful physique certainly matched his vocal might, was a product of the swinging, wide-open Kansas City scene. Even in his teens, the big-boned Turner looked entirely mature enough to gain entry to various K.C. niteries. He ended up simultaneously tending bar and singing the blues before hooking up with boogie piano master Pete Johnson during the early '30s. Theirs was a partnership that would endure for 13 years.

The pair initially traveled to New York at John Hammond's behest in 1936. On December 23, 1938, they appeared on the fabled Spirituals to Swing concert at Carnegie Hall on a bill with Big Bill Broonzy, Sonny Terry, the Golden Gate Quartet, and Count Basie. Big Joe and Johnson performed "Low Down Dog" and "It's All Right, Baby" on the historic show, kicking off a boogie-woogie craze that landed them a long-running slot at the Cafe Society (along with piano giants Meade Lux Lewis and Albert Ammons).

As 1938 came to a close, Turner and Johnson waxed the thundering "Roll 'Em Pete" for Vocalion. It was a thrilling up-tempo number anchored by Johnson's crashing 88s, and Turner would re-record it many times over the decades. Turner and Johnson waxed their seminal blues "Cherry Red" the next year for Vocalion with trumpeter Hot Lips Page and a full combo in support. In 1940, the massive shouter moved over to Decca and cut "Piney Brown Blues" with Johnson rippling the ivories. But not all of Turner's Decca sides teamed him with Johnson; Willie "The Lion" Smith accompanied him on the mournful "Careless Love," while Freddie Slack's Trio provided backing for "Rocks in My Bed" in 1941.

Turner ventured out to the West Coast during the war years, building quite a following while ensconced on the Los Angeles circuit. In 1945, he signed on with National Records and cut some fine small combo platters under Herb Abramson's supervision. Turner remained with National through 1947, belting an exuberant "My Gal's a Jockey" that became his first national R&B smash. Contracts didn't stop him from waxing an incredibly risqué two-part "Around the Clock" for the aptly named Stag imprint (as Big Vernon!) in 1947. There were also solid sessions for Aladdin that year that included a wild vocal duel with one of Turner's principal rivals, Wynonie Harris, on the ribald two-part "Battle of the Blues."

Few West Coast indie labels of the late '40s didn't boast at least one or two Turner titles in their catalogs. The shouter bounced from RPM to Down Beat/Swing Time to MGM (all those dates were anchored by Johnson's piano) to Texas-based Freedom (which moved some of their masters to Specialty) to Imperial in 1950 (his New Orleans backing crew there included a young Fats Domino on piano). But apart from the 1950 Freedom 78, "Still in the Dark," none of Big Joe's records were selling particularly well. When Atlantic Records bosses Abramson and Ahmet Ertegun fortuitously dropped by the Apollo Theater to check out Count Basie's band one day, they discovered that Turner had temporarily replaced Jimmy Rushing as the Basie band's front man, and he was having a tough go of it. Atlantic picked up his spirits by picking up his recording contract, and Big Joe Turner's heyday was about to commence.

At Turner's first Atlantic date in April of 1951, he imparted a gorgeously world-weary reading to the moving blues ballad "Chains of Love" (co-penned by Ertegun and pianist Harry Van Walls) that restored him to the uppermost reaches of the R&B charts. From there, the hits came in droves: "Chill Is On," "Sweet Sixteen" (yeah, the same downbeat blues B.B. King's usually associated with; Turner did it first), and "Don't You Cry" were all done in New York, and all hit big.

Big Joe Turner had no problem whatsoever adapting his prodigious pipes to whatever regional setting he was in. In 1953, he cut his first R&B chart-topper, the storming rocker "Honey Hush" (later covered by Johnny Burnette and Jerry Lee Lewis), in New Orleans, with trombonist Pluma Davis and tenor saxman Lee Allen in rip-roaring support. Before the year was through, he stopped off in Chicago to record with slide guitarist Elmore James' considerably rougher-edged combo and hit again with the salacious "T.V. Mama."

Prolific Atlantic house writer Jesse Stone was the source of Turner's biggest smash of all, "Shake, Rattle and Roll," which proved his second chart-topper in 1954. With the Atlantic braintrust reportedly chiming in on the chorus behind Turner's rumbling lead, the song sported enough pop possibilities to merit a considerably cleaned-up cover by Bill Haley & the Comets (and a subsequent version by Elvis Presley that came a lot closer to the original leering intent).

Suddenly, at the age of 43, Big Joe Turner was a rock star. His jumping follow-ups—"Well All Right," "Flip Flop and Fly," "Hide and Seek," "Morning, Noon and Night," "The Chicken and the Hawk"—all mined the same goodtime groove as "Shake, Rattle and Roll," with crisp backing from New York's top session aces and typically superb production by Ertegun and Jerry Wexler.

Turner turned up on a couple episodes of the groundbreaking TV program *Showtime at the Apollo* during the mid-'50s, commanding center stage with a joyous rendition of "Shake, Rattle and Roll" in front of saxman Paul "Hucklebuck" Williams' band. Nor was the silver screen

immune to his considerable charms: Turner mimed a couple of numbers in the 1957 film *Shake Rattle & Rock* (Fats Domino and Mike "Mannix" Connors also starred in the flick).

Updating the pre-war number "Corrine Corrina" was an inspired notion that provided Turner with another massive seller in 1956. But after the two-sided hit "Rock a While"/"Lipstick Powder and Paint" later that year, his Atlantic output swiftly faded from commercial acceptance. Atlantic's recording strategy wisely involved recording Turner in a jazzier setting for the adult-oriented album market; to that end, a Kansas City-styled set (with his former partner Johnson at the piano stool) was laid down in 1956 and remains a linchpin of his legacy.

Turner stayed on at Atlantic into 1959, but nobody bought his violin-enriched remake of "Chains of Love" (on the other hand, a revival of "Honey Hush" with King Curtis blowing a scorching sax break from the same session was a gem in its own right). The '60s didn't produce too much of lasting substance for the shouter—he actually cut an album with longtime admirer Haley and his latest batch of Comets in Mexico City in 1966!

But by the tail end of the decade, Big Joe Turner's essential contributions to blues history were beginning to receive proper recognition; he cut LPs for BluesWay and Blues Time. During the '70s and '80s, Turner recorded prolifically for Norman Granz's jazz-oriented Pablo label. These were super-relaxed impromptu sessions that often paired the allegedly illiterate shouter with various jazz luminaries in what amounted to loosely-run jam sessions. Turner contentedly roared the familiar lyrics of one or another of his hits, then sat back while somebody took a lengthy solo. Other notable album projects included a 1983 collaboration with Roomful of Blues, *Blues Train*, for Muse. Although health problems and the size of his humongous frame forced him to sit down during his latter-day performances, Turner continued to tour until shortly before his death in 1985. They called him the Boss of the Blues, and the appellation was truly a fitting one: when Big Joe Turner shouted a lyric, you were definitely at his beck and call. —*Bill Dahl*

★ **Big, Bad & Blue: The Big Joe Turner Anthology** / Dec. 30, 1938-Jan. 26, 1983 / Rhino ✦✦✦✦

Rhino has done a stellar job of cross-licensing to present an exhaustive three-disc, 62-track compilation that traces the booming jump blues belter's recording career from its Kansas City-bred beginnings with pianist Pete Johnson in 1938 through the postwar years with the National, Aladdin, Down Beat, and Freedom labels and on into his R&B heyday on Atlantic from 1951 to 1959. Of course, all the great prototypical rockers are aboard—"Honey Hush," "Shake, Rattle and Roll," "Flip Flop and Fly," "Corrine Corrina"—and the set closes with three far more recent entries that are the weakest tracks on the entire anthology. The sheer power of Big Joe's pipes was overwhelming, his combos cooked mercilessly, and this set is one to get. —*Bill Dahl*

Tell Me Pretty Baby / Nov. 1947-1949 / Arhoolie ✦✦✦✦

Lusty, romping jump blues and boogies from 1947-1949 that teams Big Joe Turner with his longtime piano partner Pete Johnson and a coterie of solid L.A. sessioneers. The two dozen entries include party rockers like "Wine-O-Baby Boogie," "Christmas Date Boogie," "I Don't Dig It," and an incredibly raunchy two-part "Around the Clock Blues" (where Turner spends his time in a by-the-hour sexual tryst). —*Bill Dahl*

★ **Big Joe Turner's Greatest Hits** / Apr. 19, 1951-Jan. 22, 1958 / Atlantic ✦✦✦✦

The best single-disc collection available of Turner's seminal 1950s Atlantic sides (21 sides in all). Most of the essential stuff is here—the world-weary blues ballads "Chains of Love" and "Sweet Sixteen," the rockers "Shake, Rattle and Roll," "Flip Flop and Fly," and "Boogie Woogie Country Girl," and a lusty "Well All Right" that rates with Turner's best jump blues outings ever. —*Bill Dahl*

Ike Turner

b. Nov. 5, 1931, Clarksdale, MS
Guitar, Piano, Vocals / Soul, R&B, Soul Blues, Electric Memphis Blues
It is arguably true that Ike Turner would have never amounted to more than a footnote of rock history if he hadn't joined forces with Tina Turner in 1960. But as a solo artist, he's an important footnote. In 1951, he made a lasting contribution to the music by playing piano on Jackie Brenston's "Rocket 88," which is often cited as one of the very first rock 'n' roll records. That session was one of the first blues/R&B/rock 'n' roll dates produced at Sun Studios in Memphis; Turner learned guitar shortly afterwards, and backed up other R&B artists at Sun in the early '50s. Throughout the decade, the guitarist and piano player was a prolific session player, contributing to records by blues legends Elmore James, Howlin' Wolf, and Otis Rush.

Ike also backed a host of obscure R&B artists in his early years, occasionally issuing discs under his name. Not much of a singer, both his own records and the ones he contributed to and/or produced often showcased his stinging, bluesy licks, and the best of his solo outings tended to be his instrumentals. He continued to put out the occasional solo session and work with other artists after he hooked up with Tina, sometimes under the name Ike Turner's Kings of Rhythm. His career has lurched along in obscurity since he broke up with Tina in the mid-'70s, though he remains active. —*Richie Unterberger*

1958-1959 / May 13, 1993 / Paula ✦✦✦✦
Ever the hustler, Ike Turner found himself picking up some extra money on a road trip through Chicago recording for Cobra Records both as a bandleader and sideman. After contributing the sparkle to several Otis Rush classics (an alternate of one of them, "Keep On Loving Me Baby" is found here) and some early Buddy Guy sides, Turner also recorded a handful of sides, scant few of them seeing release until now. This CD collects them all up, including surviving alternate versions, and is a delightful fly-on-the-wall invite to a 1950s Chicago blues session. —*Cub Koda*

● **I Like Ike! the Best of Ike Turner** / Nov. 15, 1994 / Rhino ✦✦✦✦
Eighteen songs spotlighting Turner's work as a bandleader, guitarist, and solo artist from 1951 to 1972, concentrating heavily on his work in the 1950s and early '60s. Leading off with Jackie Brenston's classic "Rocket 88," it includes rare singles featuring Turner by Dennis Binder, the Sly Fox, Willie King, and others, along with rare Turner solo recordings, some under the pseudonym Icky Renrut, and a 1958 45 with Tina, then known as Annie Mae Bullock, on backing vocals. These singers are usually journeymen, frankly, and the material is rather standard-issue R&B; better are the instrumentals, which give Ike a chance to really strut his distinctive tone. —*Richie Unterberger*

Rhythm Rockin' Blues / Nov. 1995 / Ace ✦✦✦
While Ike Turner's prodigious talents as a musician, producer, and hustler have been dealt the short end of the stick, his music and vibe should be enshrined as some of the best of early rock 'n' roll. Recording for one company after another, Turner produced a body of pre-Tina work utterly overwhelming in its scope. The major highlight here is "All the Blues, All the Time" from *Ike Turner Rocks the Blues* (one of the great unsung budget albums of all time), where Turner's wild-ass guitar playing takes on B.B. King, Elmore James, Little Son Jackson, John Lee Hooker, and Floyd Murphy. Turner was also a great boogie-woogie/rock 'n' roll piano man, too, and the ghost of Fats Domino and Guitar Slim's hit "The Things You Used to Do" looms large on a lot of tracks here as Turner was chasing after the hit sounds of the day. Johnny Wright's "The World Is Yours" and Turner's own "The Way You Used to Treat Me" come close to Guitar Slim, while tracks like Dennis "Long Man" Binder's "I Miss You So" plow Fats' sax romp territory. Bottom line is, here's a collection of 1954 Ike Turner tracks that gives a much bigger picture of a man with prodigious talents and a short bank roll playing his way out of Clarksdale, Mississippi. —*Cub Koda*

Ike and Tina Turner

f. 1959, **db.** 1976
Soul, R&B
There was a time when the Ike and Tina Turner Revue was one of the hottest, most durable, and potentially most explosive of all R&B ensembles. Fronted by Tina, with one of the rawest, most sensual, and impossibly dynamic voices in Black music, the Ike and Tina Revue was an ensemble that dripped musical discipline while manifesting nearly unbearable tension, eventually giving way to wave upon wave of catharsis.

Their story is a long and convoluted one. Ike was born in 1931 in Clarksdale, MS; Tina was born Annie Mae Bullock in 1938 in Nutbush, TN. They met in 1959 in East St. Louis, where Ike's Kings of Rhythm were the reigning patriarchs of the local R&B scene. Up to that point, Ike had been a DJ on WROX in Clarksdale, a talent scout and producer for Modern Records (waxing sides for the likes of B.B. King, Rosco Gordon, Elmore James, and Junior Parker), and a recording artist, his Kings of Rhythm appearing in one guise or another on Chess, Modern, King, Cobra, Artistic, and Stevens. Their most famous record, "Rocket 88," appeared under the moniker "Jackie Brenston with his Delta Cats" in 1951. It played an integral part in jump-starting the rock 'n' roll revolution.

Once Tina joined the Kings of Rhythm, life changed for all concerned. They recorded a demo of "A Fool in Love" in late 1959; by the autumn of 1960 the record was a No. 2 R&B hit on Sue Records. "I Idolize You," "It's Gonna Work Out Fine," "Poor Fool," and "Tra La La La La" all quickly followed, giving the Revue five Top Ten R&B hits in two and a half years. All told, from 1960 to 1975 Ike and Tina Turner placed 25 records on the R&B charts for nine separate record companies. Their most successful pop recording was a reworking of Creedence Clearwater Revival's "Proud Mary" in 1971. —*Rob Bowman*

River Deep & Mountain High / 1966 / A&M ✦✦✦✦
These sessions, recorded in 1966, were produced by Phil Spector. Spector's production chops and Tina's voice were a match made in heaven. Tina possesses one of the strongest voices ever committed to wax; Spector envelops it in the grandest version of his Wall of Sound that he ever

conceived. Besides the title track, Spector cut the Turners redoing their first three chart hits, "A Fool in Love," "I Idolize You," and "It's Gonna Work Out Fine." Although it's a sacrilege to say so, these versions are better than the originals. Finally, Turner's performance of the obscure Holland-Dozier-Holland ditty "A Love like Yours" bowls me over with every listen. —*Rob Bowman*

Workin' Together / 1970 / Liberty ✦✦✦
The most successful album ever issued by Ike and Tina Turner, this contains their best message song in the title selection, plus arguably their best-known song in their version of "Proud Mary" and a good cover of "Ooh Poo Pah Doo." Things went plunging downhill from here, as Tina Turner's autobiography vividly detailed years later. —*Ron Wynn*

Nutbush City Limits / 1973 / United Artists ✦✦✦✦
The album that marked the end of the Ike and Tina Turner alliance, although it wasn't their last album. But the turmoil that they were undergoing offstage would soon shatter their personal and professional union. They scored a major international hit with the title cut, and also told their life story, although it turned out that this tale was a fantasy. Here's one of the few Ike and Tina Turner albums that deserves to be back in print. —*Ron Wynn*

● **Proud Mary: The Best of Ike & Tina Turner** / Mar. 18, 1991 / EMI America ✦✦✦✦
Proud Mary: The Best of Ike and Tina Turner is a fine 23-track collection that looks at the Turners' career at the beginning and the end. Their early-'60s hits on Juggy Murray's Sue label are included, as are their early- and mid-'70s successes on Liberty and United Artists. The mid- and late-'60s recordings for Kent, Loma, Modern, Innis, Blue Thumb, and Minit are not here, unfortunately. Superior liner notes round out a fine package. —*Rob Bowman*

Tina Turner (Annie Mae Bullock)

b. Nov. 26, 1938, Nutbush, TN
Vocals / Soul, R&B, Pop-Rock
The most dynamic female soul singer in the history of the music, Tina Turner oozed sexuality from every pore in a performing career that began the moment she stepped onstage as lead singer of the Ike & Tina Turner Revue in the late '50s. Her gritty and growling performances beat down doors everywhere and looked back to the double-barrelled attack of gospel fervor and sexual abandon that had originally formed soul in the early '50s. Divorced from Ike in the mid-'70s, she recorded only occasionally later in the decade but resurfaced in the mid-'80s with a series of hit singles and movie appearances; her high-profile status was assured well into the '90s.

Born Annie Mae Bullock near Brownsville, Tennessee, she began singing as a teen, and joined Ike Turner's touring show as an 18-year-old backup vocalist. Just two years later, Tina was the star of the show, the attention-grabbing focal point for an incredibly smooth-running soul revue headed by Ike and his Kings of Rhythm. The couple began hitting the charts in 1960 with "A Fool in Love," and notched charting singles throughout the '60s, though the disappointing position of "River Deep, Mountain High"—cited by Phil Spector as one of his best productions—was very hard to take. All expectations were filled in 1971 with "Proud Mary," a No. 4 hit that became the capstone of Ike & Tina's Revue. Frustrated by Ike's increasingly irrational behavior, though, Tina walked out just three years later.

She celebrated her new-found freedom in 1975 with a role in the film version of the Who's *Tommy*. Playing the Acid Queen, she delivered an outrageous, all-too-brief performance in an otherwise forgettable mistake of a movie. Several albums were recorded for United Artists during the late '70s, but she appeared to be washed up by the turn of the decade. Surprisingly, Tina returned in 1983, first teaming with a Heaven 17 project named BEF on a remake of the Temptations' "Ball of Confusion." Tina's vocal was understandably apocalyptic, and she gained a solo deal with Capitol that same year. Her first single, a cover of Al Green's "Let's Stay Together," hit the Top 30 early in 1984. Second single "What's Love Got to Do with It" became one of the year's biggest hits, spending three weeks at No. 1. Her album *Private Dancer* included two more Top Ten singles, the title track, and "Better Be Good to Me." With another movie role in 1985 (*Mad Max: Beyond Thunderdome*), she found a No. 2 hit with its theme, "We Don't Need Another Hero." Her next big hit followed in 1986 ("Typical Male"), after which Tina began to decline, still charting occasionally and selling respectably with each album. —*John Bush*

● **Private Dancer** / Nov. 16, 1984 / Capitol ✦✦✦✦
In 1984, a 45-year-old Tina Turner made one of the most amazing comebacks in the history of American popular music. A few years earlier, it was hard to imagine the veteran soul/rock belter reinventing herself and returning to the top of the pop charts, but she did exactly that with the outstanding *Private Dancer*. And Turner did so without sacrificing her musical integrity. To be sure, this pop-rock/R&B pearl is decidedly slicker than such raw, earthy, hard-edged Ike & Tina classics as "Proud

Mary," "Sexy Ida," and "I Wanna Take You Higher." But she still has a tough, throaty, passionate delivery that serves her beautifully on everything from the melancholy, reggae-influenced "What's Love Got to Do with It" to the gutsy "Better Be Good to Me" to heartfelt remakes of the Beatles' "Help," Al Green's "Let's Stay Together" and David Bowie's "1984." A reflection on the emptiness of a stripper's life, the dusky title song is as poignant as it is depressing. Without question, this was Turner's finest hour as a solo artist. — *Alex Henderson*

Break Every Rule / 1986 / Capitol ✦✦✦
Because it contains its share of memorable and inspired material—and even a few gems—it seems inappropriate to call *Break Every Rule* a disappointment. But because *Private Dancer* was so incredible a comeback, one greeted this anxiously awaited follow-up with such high expectations that anything less than outstanding would have been disappointing. And the album isn't outstanding—generally quite enjoyable and far from weak, but not outstanding. Be that as it may, there's a lot to savor here. "Two People" is forgettable, but Turner definitely has some gems in the power ballad "I'll Be Thunder," the driving rocker "Back Where You Started," and the haunting David Bowie piece "Girls." While *Private Dancer* would be a much better introduction to Turner's work as a solo artist, this has more pluses than minuses. — *Alex Henderson*

Foreign Affair / Sep. 13, 1989 / Capitol ✦✦✦
Turner's last studio album for Capitol was produced by the late Dan Hartman of "Instant Replay" disco fame; however, this was not a retro '70s-style album. This set was comprised of 12 mature, middle—range, adult rock and pop songs. Turner tackled rock on "Steamy Windows" and "The Best"—the latter a universal hit. She created fine club tracks such as "Falling Like Rain," "I Don't Wanna Lose You," and "Look Me In The Heart." Still, she cooled down long enough for a couple of gutbucket ballads in "Be Tender With Me Baby" and "Ask Me How I Feel." The most interesting cut was the scorching return to Turner's Delta roots on the flawless "Undercover Agent for the Blues"—one of the finest pop-blues performances since B.B. King's "The Thrill Is Gone." Despite the slight musical style variations, the whole project was wrapped in an enticing pop style that gave it buoyancy and synthesis. — *Bill Carpenter*

Simply the Best / 1991 / Capitol ✦✦✦✦
A solid greatest-hits collection culled from her solo Capitol albums. Includes "Typical Male," "Steamy Windows" (written and produced by Tony Joe White), "I Can't Stand the Rain," and a duet with Rod Stewart on "It Takes Two." — *Cub Koda*

What's Love Got to Do with It / Jun. 15, 1993 / Capitol ✦✦✦
This is the soundtrack for the Tina Turner film that got Angela Bassett and Lawrence Fishburne Oscar nominations. There's little here that you couldn't get elsewhere in better versions, but if you only want a hint of the music Tina Turner made in various contexts, with and without Ike, this would be a serviceable purchase. Otherwise, get the film and hear the music in the correct setting. — *Ron Wynn*

Collected Recordings—Sixties to Nineties / Nov. 15, 1994 / Capitol ✦✦✦
Over the course of three discs, *Collected Recordings—Sixties to Nineties* runs through most of Tina Turner's biggest hits, both with and without Ike Turner. However, the third disc comprises nothing but obscurities, making the collection a bit too much for anyone but the most devoted fans. — *Stephen Thomas Erlewine*

The Turtles

f. 1963, Los Angeles, CA, db. 1970
Folk-Rock, Pop-Rock
The Turtles were a pop-rock quintet 1963-69, with varying personnel, though always featuring lead singer Howard Kaylan (b. Jun 22, 1945) and backup/harmony singer Mark Volman (b. Apr 19, 1944). Other original members were guitarists Al Nichol (b. Mar 31, 1945) and Jim Tucker, and bassist Chuck Portz (b. Nov 8, 1945). They began life as a surf band called the Crossfires, but by the time of their debut album on White Whale Records, they'd become a folk-rock group singing Bob Dylan songs including their first hit, "It Ain't Me Babe." More characteristic of their style, however, was the sweet pop hit "You Baby" of 1966. The Turtles topped the charts with "Happy Together" in 1967 and scored several more romantic pop hits before they split up at the end of the '60s, after which Kaylan and Volman hooked up with Frank Zappa in the Mothers, then performed on their own as Flo and Eddie. Today, they continue to perform under that name and as the Turtles. — *William Ruhlmann*

It Ain't Me Babe / 1965 / Rhino ✦✦✦✦
The Turtles' first album presents them as a folk-rock group covering a lot of Dylan and P. F. Sloan material. They also found "It Was a Very Good Year" on a Kingston Trio album and cut it. Frank Sinatra heard their version and had one of his bigger hits with it, but their version is good too. — *William Ruhlmann*

You Baby / 1966 / Sundazed ✦✦✦
On their second album, the Turtles stuck to the same brand of sunny, commercial folk-rock as their debut. It's pleasant fare, but hardly in the same league as the Byrds, Lovin' Spoonful, or the Mamas & the Papas, and the group's original material is spotty and sometimes awkward. The best cuts are the ones penned by the Barri/Sloan songwriting team, including the hits "You Baby" and "Can I Get to Know You Better." — *Richie Unterberger*

Happy Together / 1967 / Rhino ✦✦✦✦
The Turtles' best studio album includes the title hit, "She'd Rather Be with Me," "Guide for the Married Man," and then-unknown Warren Zevon's "Like the Seasons," among other songs. — *William Ruhlmann*

Wooden Head / 1970 / Sundazed ✦✦✦
In 1970, both White Whale Records and the Turtles, their biggest act, were on the verge of ending. This assortment of unreleased odds and ends from their early years was hastily assembled as a posthumous collection, although several of the tracks hadn't been properly finished. Surprisingly, it survives as one of their stronger albums, focusing almost exclusively on their early pop/folk-rock sound. Arguably, it's better than either of their first two official LPs, perhaps because they weren't able to sweeten the tracks with superfluous overdubs. Besides several strong originals, it features interesting compositions by P.F. Sloan, David Gates, and Peter & Gordon. The album, confusingly, has been reissued at various points by Rhino, Repertoire, and Sundazed, all with different bonus tracks. The Rhino configuration (out of print, and only on LP), which adds the nice folk-rocker "Is It Any Wonder?" and the odd, mordant, psychedelic-tinged 1966 flop single "Grim Reaper of Love," is a bit preferable to the Sundazed one. The Sundazed edition, however, is available on CD, and much easier to find as of 1997. — *Richie Unterberger*

● **20 Greatest Hits** / 1983 / Rhino ✦✦✦✦
A witty and underrated band, the Turtles compiled this fine set themselves. — *Dan Heilman*

20/20

f. 1976, Tulsa, OK
Power Pop
20/20 was formed in Tulsa, Oklahoma, by high school friends Steve Allen (guitar, vocals) and Ron Flynt (bass, vocals). They relocated to Los Angeles in 1977, adding Mike Gallo on drums, and began playing local clubs. Greg Shaw, the head of Bomp!, was impressed with their highly charged power-pop and signed them to his label in 1978. The resulting single, "Under the Freeway," created enough interest in the band to secure a deal with Portrait Records. They added keyboardist Chris Sylgali and recorded their first LP, *20/20*. "Cheri" from the album saw some minor regional success but the album was virtually ignored apart from critical acclaim. The follow-up, *Look Out!* (1981), was equally strong but again failed. The band was dropped by Portrait in 1982 and effectively disbanded. They returned in 1983 with the independently released *Sex Trap*, but by this time, their sound was out of style and the band finally called it quits. A revived interest in the genre in the '90s inspired the band to reunite, contributing a few new songs to Big Deal's *Yellow Pills* compilations and recording a new album, *House Tornado*, for the fall of 1995. — *Chris Woodstra*

● **20/20** / 1979 / Portrait ✦✦✦✦
Released during the initial power-pop craze of the late '70s, the band's self-titled debut quickly stood out among the masses with its consistent quality, strict adherence to the melodic three-minute form, and tight, driving rhythm. Though the sales didn't reflect the strength of the album, songs like "Cheri" and "Yellow Pills" are considered classics of the period, the latter becoming the title for the premier power-pop fanzine, still in existence today. — *Chris Woodstra*

Look Out! / Jun. 1981 / Portrait ✦✦✦✦
An equally strong follow-up, *Look Out!* is a pure pop artifact with its teen anthems discussing the "nuclear boys in the nuclear world," obsessing over girls (the haunting "Girl like You"), and telling the tale of a bizarre alien love affair (the silly "Alien"). *Look Out!* and *20/20* have been reissued as a two-fer CD on Oglio in 1995—an essential part of any power-pop collection. — *Chris Woodstra*

Sex Trap / 1982 / Teldec ✦✦
The mid-'80s were not kind to "skinny tie" bands like 20/20. By 1984, Portrait had dropped the band, forcing them to go independent with *Sex Trap*. As the title indicates, they shifted to a raunchier, harder rocking band, with all of the gloss of the previous efforts removed. A sad misstep and the least essential of their catalog. — *Chris Woodstra*

4 Day Tornado / Sep. 19, 1995 / Oglio ✦✦✦
During their brief existence in the early '80s, 20/20 represented all that was great about power-pop with their youthful exuberance and endlessly catchy melodies. *4 Day Tornado* marks the band's long—awaited return, picking up right where they left off more than a decade earlier. The album serves as a gift to loyal fans rather than attempting to break

new ground or increase the band's small following. Those who loved the first two albums won't be disappointed with this one either. —*Chris Woodstra*

Dwight Twilley

b. Jun. 6, 1951, Tulsa, OK
Keyboards, Vocals / Power Pop

Though the Dwight Twilley Band only had one hit (Twilley had another on his own), Twilley and partner Phil Seymour created an enduring and highly memorable brand of power-pop that blended Beatlesque pop and Sun rockabilly "slapback" echo. Only a fraction of the band's early output was made available at the time, but these records are highly revered by power-pop aficionados.

According to the legend, Dwight Twilley met Phil Seymour in 1967 at a theater where they had gone to see the Beatles' *A Hard Day's Night.* After the film they immediately went to Twilley's house to start writing and recording. The two continued the partnership over the next several years, calling themselves Oister and recruiting another part-time member, Bill Pitcock, on lead guitar. After developing their sound in their homemade studio, "The Shop," they decided to take a stab at professional recording and headed out to Nashville, though they ended up stopping first at the legendary Sun Studios. Jerry Philips (Sam's son) was impressed enough to team them up with former Sun artist Ray Harris, who introduced them to the "Sun Sound," roughing up their Beatles-obsessed style a bit and creating a unique and endearing sound.

The two signed to Shelter Records in 1974. Their first single, "I'm on Fire," became a national hit in 1975, peaking at No. 16, with relatively no promotion. During an appearance on *American Bandstand,* the band previewed what was to be the follow-up single, "Shark," an equally infectious, hit-worthy rocker. The success of the film *Jaws* caused the label to reject the single, however, to keep them from becoming perceived as a cash-in novelty act. This was just the beginning of bad luck that would plague the group from that point on. Their follow-up single and completed album went unreleased for 18 months due to label problems, and a second album recorded in England was left unreleased altogether, creating a myth around the band in some circles while the general public quickly lost interest. The belated follow-up single, "You Were So Warm," ended up failing due to distribution problems. Predictably, when the album *Sincerely* was finally released, it failed as well. Seymour and Twilley befriended the like-minded Tom Petty and contributed backing vocals on several tracks. Petty repaid the favor for their second album, *Twilley Don't Mind,* for Arista in 1977. Despite the once again unquestionably high quality of songs, the album stiffed as well. Seymour left the band the following year, pursuing a brief solo career before lymphoma cut his life short in 1993.

Twilley carried on as a solo act, releasing *Twilley* for Arista in 1979 and *Scuba Divers* for EMI in 1982, and found success again with *Jungle* in 1984, when he scored his second hit with "Girls." His final album, *Wild Dogs,* went unnoticed on its 1986 release. In addition, he recorded an album in 1980, *Blueprint,* that remains unreleased and contributed one track to the *Wayne's World* soundtrack, "Why You Want to Break My Heart." Two newly recorded songs appeared on the "best of" collection *XXI* and he is reportedly working on a new album entitled *The Luck. The Great Lost Twilley Album* collects a fraction of the "hundreds" of unreleased songs Twilley and Seymour recorded in the early, ill-fated days. —*Chris Woodstra*

Sincerely / 1976 / The Right Stuff ✦✦✦✦

From the opening Anglo-pop-rock-meets-rockabilly blast of the Top 20 hit single "I'm on Fire," through breezy jangle-rock numbers like "You're So Warm," "Just like the Sun," and "England," to the dirge-like psychedelia of the title song, *Sincerely* is Twilley's finest album. It's a must-own for fans of guitar pop-rock. (The CD includes four bonus tracks.) —*Rick Clark*

Twilley Don't Mind / 1977 / The Right Stuff ✦✦✦✦

Twilley drops the ball slightly on this second album, in spite of good tracks like "Looking for the Magic," "Here She Come," "Sleeping," and the title cut. —*Rick Clark*

Twilley / 1979 / Arista ✦✦✦✦

This self-titled third album rivals Twilley's debut as best album with super tracks like "Alone in My Room," "It Takes a Lot of Love," "Darlin'," and "I Want to Make Love to You." As of this printing, this fine pop-rock album has yet to see a CD release. If you like Twilley's other albums, then this is worth the search. —*Rick Clark*

Scuba Divers / 1982 / EMI ✦✦✦

1982's *Scuba Divers* continues the band's fine pop tradition, though the material is not quite up to the standards of its predecessors. —*AMG*

Jungle / 1984 / EMI ✦✦✦

Twilley makes an unexpected return to the charts with the Top 20 hit single "Girls." The rest of *Jungle* is as enjoyable as that single. —*AMG*

Wild Dogs / 1986 / CBS ✦✦

The Great Lost Twilley Album / Apr. 1993 / Shelter ✦✦✦✦

The rumor had always been that the original Dwight Twilley Band had completed four albums between 1974 and 1978 that were never released due to problems with their label, Shelter Records; the few writers and personal friends who heard the albums claimed the material was superior to much of their released work. *The Great Lost Twilley Album* collects the best "lost" tracks from this era, as well as prime material from the unreleased *Blueprint* album from 1980; true to the myth, the songs are easily as good as the band's classic early albums. The band especially shines on the proposed follow-up to the hit "I'm on Fire," "Shark," an infectious rocker that stands as one of the great "should have been hits." —*Chris Woodstra*

● **XXI** / Mar. 19, 1996 / The Right Stuff ✦✦✦✦

Despite critical raves at the time and the undeniable high quality of the songs, the Dwight Twilley Band never quite achieved the success they so sorely deserved. *XXI* collects the finer moments of the band's brief recording career, which only ran from 1976 to 1978, as well as highlights from Twilley's solo work, spanning from 1979 to late 1995. This 21-track compilation offers a good sampling of album favorites, the hits ("I'm on Fire" and "Girls"—both peaked at No. 16), some lost should-have-been hits ("Shark" and "Somebody to Love"), a never-before-released song from an aborted 1994 album, and a newly recorded track, "That Thing You Do." For fans, the rarities and song-by-song commentary by Twilley make *XXI* an essential addition. For those unfamiliar with Twilley and company's perfect pop, there is no better place to start. —*Chris Woodstra*

Rock Yourself / Del Rack ✦✦✦

Rock Yourself is a budget-line ten-track Twilley collection focussing on the band's prime '70s period. The odd song selection that omits their biggest hit, "I'm on Fire," makes this largely unnecessary despite the strength of the material that is included. Completists should note, however, that the version of "Shark" included is actually different from the one released on *The Great Lost Twilley Album* and on the *XXI* collection. —*Chris Woodstra*

Twisted Sister

f. 1973, Long Island, NY, db. 1987
Hard Rock, Heavy Metal

Long Island metal band featuring lead singer Dee Snider, with guitarists Jay French and Eddie Ojeda, bassist Mark "The Animal" Mendoza (formerly of the Dictators), and drummer A.J. Pero. Their original purpose was to be the antithesis of disco, creating a bizarre, outrageous look for themselves with frizzy hair and heavy makeup. Musically, they played simple, melodic metal with consciously provocative lyrics and oft-repeated choruses. The group got a major push from MTV in 1984, as their image attracted the attention of teenage boys throughout the country. Their adolescent anthems "We're Not Gonna Take It" and "I Wanna Rock" pushed *Stay Hungry's* sales into the double-platinum range. This proved to be the peak of their success, and they disbanded in 1987 when their label decided they had run out of ideas. Snider then formed Desperado. —*Steve Huey*

You Can't Stop Rock 'n' Roll / 1983 / Atlantic ✦✦✦

Stay Hungry / 1984 / Atlantic ✦✦✦✦

Hard-hitting aggressively progressive metal, this set includes "The Price," "I Wanna Rock," and "We're Not Gonna Take It." —*Bil Carpenter*

Come Out & Play / 1985 / Atlantic ✦✦✦

● **Big Hits and Nasty Cuts: Best of Twisted Sister** / Mar. 17, 1992 / Atlantic ✦✦✦✦

Big Hits and Nasty Cuts: Best of Twisted Sister rounds up ten of the metal band's best-known songs, including "We're Not Gonna Take It" and "I Wanna Rock," adding five live tracks as an enticement for hardcore Sister collectors. Even though the live tracks are of questionable quality, the disc remains an excellent summation of the group's career. —*Stephen Thomas Erlewine*

2 Live Crew

f. 1986, Miami, FL
Bass Music, Old School Rap, Southern Rap, Hip-Hop

This Florida rap band was organized, supervised, and conceived by Luther Campbell, a promoter, record-label owner, and rapper, as an updated version of oldtime X-rated party performers. Campbell's production consists of heavy doses of booming synthesized bass, scratching effects, samples, and explicit sex raps and leers. From their beginnings in 1986, the notoriety of Campbell and the group grew in direct proportion to the lewdness of the material. As their songs attained more national prominence, Campbell became part of a national controversy involving censorship and lyrics. He's issued two solo records. 2 Live Crew hasn't found the going quite as smooth in the '90s. They've continued recording for Luke Records, but haven't scored as much success with such releases as *Move Somethin'* and *Sports Weekend.* Founder Luther Campbell issued both clean and dirty versions in an effort to defuse criticism, but 2 Live Crew's detractors have moved on to gangsta-rap, and the group's most recent releases have been almost ignored. They resurfaced in 1994 as the New 2 Live Crew, releasing *Back at Your Ass for the Nine 4*. Campbell also announced plans to start a men's magazine in either 1994 or 1995.

Back at Your Ass for the Nine 4 did well briefly, peaking at No. 9 on the R&B chart. But their brand of X-rated humor seemed almost tame compared to the mix of explicit sex and violence available on more hardcore gangsta-rap sessions, while the Jamaican toasters like Shabba Ranks or the Mad Cobra outdistanced them in creative lewdness. Nevertheless, 2 Live Crew continued to tour and record, following *Back at Your Ass* with 1996's *Shake a Lil' Something*, which failed to gain much attention. —*Ron Wynn*

2 Live Crew Is What We Are / 1986 / Luke ✦✦✦
The record that launched the whole phenomenon. If the puerile language and vulgarity had been allowed to run its course without censorship attempts, this lunacy might have ended right here. The production does provide good examples of Miami "bass" music. —*Ron Wynn*

Move Somethin' / 1987 / Luke ✦✦✦✦
Luther Campbell hits on the ingenious idea of issuing clean and dirty versions simultaneously in an ill-fated attempt to take censorship heat off. The clean version lacks guts; the dirty version lacks taste. —*Ron Wynn*

As Nasty As They Wanna Be / 1989 / Luke ✦✦✦✦
Not only did it cause all the legal controversies, but *As They Wanna Be* is the quintessential 2 Live Crew album, showing all of their tasteless, bass-driven glory. —*AMG*

Banned in the USA / Jul. 1990 / Atlantic ✦✦✦
When Florida attorney Jack Thompson did everything he could to have the X-rated music of the 2 Live Crew outlawed, his assault on the First Amendment led many free-speech advocates to take up the group's cause. Thompson's actions inspired quite a bit of anger from both white liberals and African-American rappers, who saw something obscene about a prosperous lawyer declaring war on a young Black entrepreneur who had avoided the pitfalls of Miami's Liberty City ghetto. Luke was under attack for doing the very thing Republicans consistently advocate—using free enterprise to pull himself up by the bootstraps. Ironically, many of those who defended his First Amendment rights had little or no use for his lyrics. *Banned in the USA*, the Crew's first album for a major label and its first after the battle with Thompson, is for many a guilty pleasure. Say what you will about Luke's high-school locker-room lyrics; the Crew's Miami bass rap can be quite catchy, infectious, and amusing. Many New York hip-hoppers were quick to critcize the fast tempos employed by Miami rappers like Luke, but the fact that they did it their own way instead of emulating Northeastern MCs is something to admire instead of lambaste. —*Alex Henderson*

Sports Weekend: As Nasty as They Wanna Be, Pt. 2 / Oct. 8, 1991 / Luke ✦✦✦

● **2 Live Crew's Greatest Hits** / Sep. 29, 1992 / Luke ✦✦✦✦
Full of the low-minded humor that made this Miami outfit notorious throughout the country, *Greatest Hits* does contain the best material 2 Live Crew ever recorded; it is all The 2 Live Crew most will ever need to hear. —*Stephen Thomas Erlewine*

Back at Your Ass for the Nine-4 / Feb. 8, 1994 / Luke ✦✦

Shake a Lil' Somethin' . . . / Aug. 6, 1996 / Lil'Joe✦✦✦

2 Pac

b. Jun. 16, 1971, New York, NY, d. Sep. 13, 1996
Gangsta Rap, G-Funk, West Coast Rap
Tupac Shakur became the unlikely martyr of gangsta rap, becoming the tragic symbol of hardcore rap. At the outset of his career, it didn't appear that he would emerge as one of the definitive rappers of the '90s, especially since he was a second-string rapper for Digital Underground, joining after they had their biggest hit. But in 1992, he delivered an acclaimed debut album, *2Pacalypse Now*, which quickly followed with a star-making performance in the urban drama, *Juice*. Over the course of one year his profile rose substantially, as he became as well-known for his run-ins with the law as he was for his music. By 1994, 2 Pac was rivalling Snoop Doggy Dogg as the most controversial figure in rap, as he was spending as much time in prison as he was in the recording studio. His burgeoning outlaw mythology helped his 1995 album *Me Against the World* enter the charts at No. 1, and it also opened himself up to charges of exploitation. Yet, as the single "Dear Mama" illustrated, he was capable of sensitivity as well as violence. Unfortunately, the gangsta lifestyle he captured in his music soon overtook his own life. Signing with Death Row Records in late 1995, Shakur released the double-album *All Eyez on Me* in the spring of 1996, and the record, as well as its hit single, "California Love," confirmed his superstar status. While his celebrity was at its peak, he was publicly fighting with his rival the Notorious B.I.G., and there were tensions brewing at Death Row. Even

with such conflicts, 2 Pac's drive-by-shooting in September 1996 was unexpected. On September 13, six days after the shooting, Shakur passed away, leaving behind a legacy that was based as much on his lifestyle as his music.

The son of two Black Panther members, Tupac Amaru Shakur was born in New York City. His parents had separated before he was born, and his mother moved him and his sister around the country for much of their childhood. Frequently, the family was at the poverty level, but Shakur managed to gain acceptance to the prestigious Baltimore School of the Arts as a teenager. While he was at the school, his creative side flourished, as he began writing raps and acting. Before he could graduate, his family moved to Marin City, California, when he was 17 years old. Over the next few years, he lived on the streets and began hustling. Eventually, he met Shock-G, the leader of Digital Underground. The Oakland-based crew decided to hire him as a dancer and roadie, and as he toured with the group, he worked on his own material. 2 Pac made his first recorded appearance on the group's spring 1991 record, *This is an E.P. Release*, and he also appeared on their second album, *Sons of the P*. The following year, he released his own debut, *2Pacalypse Now*. The album became a word-of-mouth hit, as "Brenda's Got a Baby" reached the R&B Top 30 and the record went gold. However, its blunt and explicit lyrics earned criticisms from moral watchdogs, and Vice President Dan Quayle attacked the album while he was campaigning for re-election that year.

Shakur's profile was raised considerably by his acclaimed role in the Ernest Dickerson film, *Juice*, which lead to a lead role in John Singleton's *Poetic Justice* the following year. By the time the film hit theaters, 2 Pac had reased his second album, *Strictly 4 My N.I.G.G.A.Z.*, which became a platinum album, peaking at No. 4 on the R&B charts and launching the Top Ten R&B hit singles "I Get Around" and "Keep Ya Head Up," which peaked at Nos. 11 and 12,respectively, on the pop charts. Late in 1993, he acted in the basketball movie *Above the Rim*. Although Shakur was selling records and earning praise for his music and acting, he began having serious altercations with the law; prior to becoming a recording artist, he had no police record. He was arrested in 1992 after he was involved in a fight that culminated with a stray bullet killing a six-year-old bystander; the charges were later dismissed. 2 Pac was filming *Menace II Society* in the summer of 1993 when he assaulted director Allen Hughes; he was sentenced to 15 days in jail in early 1994. The sentence arrived after two other high-profile incidents. In October of 1993, he was charged with shooting two off-duty police officers in Atlanta. The charges were dismissed, but the following month he and two members of his entourage were charged with sexually abusing a female fan. In 1994, he was found guilty of sexual assault. The day after the verdict was announced, he was shot by a pair of muggers while he was in the lobby of a New York City recording studio. Shakur was sentenced to four and a half years in prison on February 7, 1995.

Later that month, Tupac Shakur began serving his sentence. He was in jail when his third album, *Me Against the World*, was released in March. The record entered the charts at No. 1, making 2 Pac the first artist to enjoy a No. 1 record while serving a prison sentence. While he was in prison, he accused the Notorious B.I.G., Puffy Combs, Andre Harrell, and his own close friend Randy "Stretch" Walker of orchestrating his New York shooting. Shakur only served eight months of his sentence, as Suge Knight, the president of Death Row Records, arranged for parole and posted a $1.4 million bond for the rapper. By the end of the year, 2 Pac was out of prison and working on his debut for Death Row. On November 30, 1995—the one-year anniversary of the New York shooting—Walker was killed in a gangland-style murder in Queens.

2 Pac's Death Row debut, *All Eyez on Me*, was the first double-disc of original material in hip-hop history. It debuted at No. 1 upon its February release, and would be certified quintuple platinum by the fall. Although he had a hit record and, with the Dr. Dre duet "California Love," a massive single on his hands, Shakur was beginning to tire of hip-hop and started to concentrate on acting. During the summer of 1996, he completed two films, the thriller *Bullet* and the black comedy *Gridlock'd*, which also starred Tim Roth. He also made some recordings for Death Row, which was quickly disintegrating without Dr. Dre as the house producer, and as Knight became heavily involved in illegal activities.

At the time of his murder in September 1996, there were indications that Shakur was considering leaving Death Row, and maybe even rap, behind. None of those theories can ever be confirmed, just as the reasons behind his shooting remain mysterious. Shakur was shot on the Las Vegas strip as he was riding in the passenger seat of Knight's car. They had just seen the Mike Tyson-Bruce Seldon fight at the MGM Grand, and as they were leaving the hotel, 2 Pac got into a fight with an unnamed young Black man. It has been suggested that this was the cause of the drive-by shooting; it has also been suggested that Knight's ties to the mob and to gangs were the reason behind the shooting; another theory is that the Notorious B.I.G. arranged the shooting as retaliation for 2 Pac's comments that he slept with Biggie's wife, Faith

Evans. Either way, Shakur was shot four times and admitted to University of Nevada Medical Center. Six days later, he died from his wounds.

Hundreds of mourners appeared at the hospital upon news of his death, and the entire entertainment industry mourned his passing, especially since there were no leads to his killer. Many believed his death would end the much-hyped East Coast-West Coast rivalry and decrease Black-on-Black violence. Sadly, six months after his death, his rival the Notorious B.I.G. was murdered in similar circumstances. —*Stephen Thomas Erlewine*

2Pacalypse Now / 1992 / Interscope ✦✦✦
Few expected former Digital Underground member Tupac Amaru Shakur to become hip-hop enemy No. 1 when he made his solo debut with this 1992 album. Songs like "Crooked Ass Nigga" and "Tha' Lunatic" might have hinted that storm clouds were on the horizon, but there were also excellent advocacy numbers like "Words Of Wisdom" and "Young Black Male." This didn't make him a celebrity, but it put Tupac Shakur on the road to stardom. —*Ron Wynn*

Strictly 4 My N.I.G.G.A.Z. / Feb. 16, 1993 / Atlantic ✦✦✦✦
Tupac Shakur not only became a crossover acting and singing success with this release, but found himself on police blotters coast to coast and the designated demon of anti-rap forces nationwide. This disc yielded a couple of hits, with the fiery message track "Keep Your Head Up" particularly outstanding. Unfortunately, several ugly personal incidents, among them a public physical fight with film directors the Hughes brothers, allegations of violent attacks on an off-duty police officer, and sexual misconduct threatened to derail a promising multi-media career. —*Ron Wynn*

● **Me Against the World** / Mar. 14, 1995 / Interscope ✦✦✦✦
Released just after 2 Pac began serving a jail sentence for sexual assault, *Me Against the World* became a No. 1 hit, and it's fairly easy to see why—the record is impeccably produced, with rumbling, funky bass and rhythms that flow throughout the entire album. 2 Pac's rhymes are so considered and graceful that it's hard to believe the same man was imprisoned. —*David Jehnzen*

All Eyez on Me / Feb. 13, 1996 / Death Row ✦✦✦✦
As the first double-disc collection of original rap material released, 2 Pac's first post-prison album, *All Eyez On Me*, would have been notable, even if the rapper didn't deliver the musical goods. However, he has made a messy, sprawling album that illustrates his talents quite effectively. Certainly, the album could have been trimmed down to one disc, but his ambition is admirable at a time when even the big hip-hop artists play it safe. Even with the abundance of mediocre and unfinished material, there are enough prime tracks—from the G-Funk update of the Dr. Dre duet "California Love" to his smooth soul experiments—to make the record an engaging, fascinating listen, even if it doesn't have the consistency of *Me Against the World*. —*Stephen Thomas Erlewine*

Don Killuminati: the 7 Day Theory / Nov. 5, 1996 / Death Row/Interscope ✦✦
Everything about *The Don Killuminati: The 7 Day Theory* smacks of exploitation. Released only eight weeks after Tupac Shakur died from gunshot wounds, Death Row released this posthumous album under the name of Makaveli, a pseudonym derived from the Italian politician Niccolo Machiavelli, who faked his own death and reappeared seven days later to take revenge on his enemies. Naturally, the appearance of *The Don Killuminati* so shortly after Tupac's death led many conspiracy theorists to surmise the rapper was still alive, but it was all part of a calculated marketing strategy by Death Row—the label needed something to sustain interest in the album, since the music on the album is so shoddy. *All Eyez on Me* proved that Tupac was continuing to grow as a musician and a human being, but *The Don Killuminati* erases that image by concentrating on nothing but tired G-funk beats and tiring, back-biting East Coast/West Coast rivalries. Tupac himself sounds uninterested in the music, which makes the conventional, unimaginative music all the more listless. If he had survived to complete *The Don Killuminati*, it is possible that the record could have become something worthwhile, but the overall quality of the material suggests that the album would have been a disappointment no matter what circumstances it appeared under. —*Stephen Thomas Erlewine*

U

U2

f. 1976, Dublin, Ireland

Alternative Pop-Rock, Pop-Rock, Post-Punk

Through a combination of zealous righteousness and post-punk experimentalism, U2 became one of the most popular rock 'n' roll bands of the '80s. Equally known for their sweeping sound as for their grandiose statement about politics and religion, U2 were rock 'n' roll crusaders during an era of synthesized pop and heavy metal. The Edge provided the group with a signature sound by creating sweeping sonic landscapes with his heavily processed, echoed guitars. Though the Edge's style wasn't conventional, the rhythm section of Adam Clayton and Larry Mullen, Jr., played the songs as driving hard rock, giving the band a forceful, powerful edge that was designed for arena rock. And their lead singer, Bono, was a frontman who had a knack of grand gestures that played better in arenas than small clubs. It's no accident that footage of Bono parading with a white flag with "Sunday Bloody Sunday" blaring in the background became the defining moment of U2's early career—there rarely was a band that believed so deeply in rock's potential for revolution as U2, and there rarely was a band that didn't care if they appeared foolish in the process. During the course of the early '80s, the group quickly built up a dedicated following through constant touring and a string of acclaimed records. By 1987, the band's following had grown large enough to propel them to the level of international superstars with the release of *The Joshua Tree.* Unlike many of their contemporaries, U2 was able to sustain their popularity in the '90s by reinventing themselves as a post-modern, self-consciously ironic, dance-inflected pop-rock act, owing equally to the experimentalism of late-'70s Bowie and '90s electronic dance and techno. By performing such a successful reinvention, the band confirmed its status as one of the most popular bands in rock history, in addition to earning additional critical respect.

With its textured guitars, U2's sound was undeniably indebted to post-punk, so it's slightly ironic that the band formed in 1976, before punk had reached their hometown of Dublin, Ireland. Larry Mullen Jr. (b. October 31, 1961; drums) posted a notice on a high school bulletin board asking for fellow musicians to form a band. Bono (born Paul Hewson, May 10, 1960; vocals, guitar), the Edge (born David Evans, August 8, 1961; guitar, keyboards, vocal), Adam Clayton (bass), and Dick Evans responded to the ad, and the group formed as a Beatles and Stones cover band called the Feedback, before changing their name to the Hype in 1977. Shortly afterward, Dick Evans left the band to form the Virgin Prunes. Following his departure, the group changed their name to U2.

U2's first big break arrived in 1978, when they won a talent contest sponsored by Guinness; the band were in their final year of high school at the time. By the end of the year, the Stranglers' manager Paul McGuinness saw the band play and offered to manage the group. Even with a powerful manager in their corner, the band had trouble making much headway—they failed an audition with CBS Records at the end of the year. In the fall of 1979, U2 released their debut EP *U2:3.* The EP was available only in Ireland and it topped the national charts. Shortly afterward, they began to play in England, but they failed to gain much attention.

U2 had one other chart-topping single, "Another Day," in early 1980 before Island Records offered the group a contract. Later that year, the band's debut, *Boy,* was released. Produced by Steve Lillywhite, the record's sweeping, atmospheric but edgy sound was unlike most of its post-punk contemporaries, and the band earned further attention for its public embrace of Christianity; only Clayton was not a practicing Christian. Through constant touring, including opening gigs for Talking Heads and wet T-shirt contests, U2 was able to take *Boy* into the American Top 70 in early 1981. *October,* also produced by Lillywhite, followed

in the fall, and it became their British breakthrough, reaching No. 11 on the charts. By early 1983, *Boy*'s "I Will Follow" and *October*'s "Gloria" had become staples on MTV, which, along with their touring, gave the group a formidable cult following in the US.

Released in the spring of 1983, the Lillywhite-produced *War* was U2's breakthrough release, entering the UK charts at No. 1 and elevating them into arenas in the United States, where the album peaked at No. 12. *War* had a stronger political message than its predecessors, as evidenced by the UK, college radio, and MTV hits "Sunday Bloody Sunday" and "New Year's Day." During the supporting tour, the band filmed their concert at Colorado's Red Rocks Amphitheater, releasing the show as an EP and video titled *Under A Blood Red Sky.* The EP entered the UK charts at No. 2, becoming the most successful live recording in British history. U2 had become one of the most popular bands in the world, and their righteous political stance soon became replicated by many other bands, providing the impetus for the Band Aid and Live Aid projects in 1984 and 1985, respectively. For the follow-up to *War,* U2 entered the studios with coproducers Brian Eno and Daniel Lanois, who helped give the resulting album an experimental, atmospheric tone. Released in the fall of 1984, *The Unforgettable Fire* replicated the chart status of *War,* entering the UK charts at No. 1 and reaching No. 12 in the US. The album also generated the group's first Top 40 hit in America with the Martin Luther King, Jr. tribute "(Pride) In The Name of Love." U2 supported the album with a successful international tour, highlighted by a show-stealing performance at Live Aid. Following the tour, the band released the live EP, *Wide Awake in America* in 1985.

While U2 had become one of the most successful rock bands of the '80s, they didn't truly become superstars until the spring 1987 release of *The Joshua Tree.* Greeted with enthusiastic reviews, many of which proclaimed the album a masterpiece, *The Joshua Tree* became the band's first American No. 1 hit and its third straight album to enter the UK charts at No. 1; in England, it set a record by going platinum within 28 hours. Generating the US No. 1 hits "With or Without You" and "I Still Haven't Found What I'm Looking For," *The Joshua Tree* and the group's supporting tour became the biggest success of 1987, earning the group the cover of respected publications like *Time* magazine. U2 decided to film a documentary about their American tour, recording new material along the way. The project became *Rattle & Hum,* a film that was supported by a double-album soundtrack that was divided between live tracks and new material. While the album *Rattle & Hum* was a hit, the record and film received the weakest reviews of U2's career, with many critics taking issue with the group's fascination with American roots music like blues, soul, country, and folk. Following the release of *Rattle & Hum,* the band took an extended hiatus.

U2 reconvened in Berlin 1990 to record a new album with Eno and Lanois. While the sessions for the album were difficult, the resulting record, *Achtung Baby,* represented a successful reinvention of the band's trademark sound. Where they had been inspired by post-punk in the early career and American music during their mid-career, U2 delved into electronic and dance music with *Achtung Baby.* Inspired equally by late-'70s Bowie and the Madchester scene in the UK, *Achtung Baby* was sonically more eclectic and adventurous than U2's earlier work, and it didn't alienate their core audience. The album debuted at No. 1 throughout the world and spawned Top Ten hits with "Mysterious Ways" and "One." Early in 1992, the group launched an elaborate tour to support *Achtung Baby.* Dubbed Zoo TV, the tour was an innovative blend of multimedia electronics, featuring a stage filled with televisions, suspended cars and cellular phone calls. Bono devised an alter ego called "the Fly", which was a knowing send-up of rock stardom. Even under the ironic guise of the Fly and Zoo TV, it was evident that U2 was looser and more fun than ever before, even though they had not abandoned their trademark righteous political anger.

Following the completion of the American Zoo TV tour and before the launch of the European leg of the tour, U2 entered the studio to complete an EP of new material that became the full-length *Zooropa*. Released in the summer of 1993 to coincide with the tour of the same name, *Zooropa* demonstrated a heavier techno and dance influence than *Achtung Baby* and it received strong reviews. Nevertheless, the album stalled at sales of two million and failed to generate a big hit single. During the Zooropa tour, the Fly metamorphosed into the demonic "MacPhisto," which dominated the remainder of the tour. Upon the completion of the Zooropa tour in late 1993, the band took an extended break. During 1995, U2 re-emerged with "Hold Me, Thrill Me, Kiss Me, Kill Me," a glam rock theme to *Batman Forever* that was produced by Nellee Hooper (Bjork, Soul II Soul). Later that year, they recorded the collaborative album *Original Soundtracks, Vol. 1* with Brian Eno, releasing the album under the name the Passengers in 1995. It was greeted with a muted reception, both critically and commercially.

Many hardcore U2 fans, including drummer Larry Mullen, Jr., were unhappy with the Passengers project, and U2 promised their next album, to be released in the fall of 1996, would be a rock 'n' roll record. The album took longer to complete than usual, being pushed back to the spring of 1997. During its delay, a few tracks, including the forthcoming first single "Discotheque," were leaked, and it became clear that the new album was going to be heavily influenced by techno, dance, and electronic music. When it was finally released, *Pop* did indeed bear a heavier dance influence, but it was greeted with strong initial sales, as well as some of the strongest reviews of U2's career. — *Stephen Thomas Erlewine*

Boy / 1980 / Island ✦✦✦✦
From the outset, U2 went for the big message—every song on their debut album *Boy* sounds huge, with oceans of processed guitars cascading around Bono's impassioned wail. It was an inspired combination of large, stadium-rock beats and post-punk textures. Without the Edge's echoed, ringing guitar, U2 would have sounded like a traditional hard rock band, since the rhythm section and Bono treat each song as an anthem. Of course, that's the charm of *Boy:* all of its emotions are on the surface, delivered with optimistic, youthful self-belief, yet the unusual, distinctive guitar textures give it an unexpected tension that makes it an exhilarating debut. The songs may occasionally show some weakness—the driving "I Will Follow," the dark "An Cat Dubh" and the shimmering "The Ocean" stand out among the sonic textures—yet the band's musical and lyrical vision keep *Boy* compelling until the finish. — *Stephen Thomas Erlewine*

October / 1981 / Island ✦✦✦
U2 sounded so confident and assured on their debut that perhaps it was inevitable they would stumble slightly on its follow-up, *October*. The record isn't weaker than its predecessor because it repeats the formula of *Boy*. It's because the band tries too hard to move forward. Bono, in particular, tries too hard to make big political, emotional, and religious statements, but the remainder of the band isn't innocent. In general, the music is too pompous, with the sound overwhelming the actual songs. But when U2 do marry the message, melody, and sound together, as on "Gloria," "I Threw a Brick Through a Window" and "I Fall Down," the results are thoroughly impressive. — *Stephen Thomas Erlewine*

☆ **War** / 1983 / Island ✦✦✦✦✦
Opening with the ominous, fiery protest of "Sunday Bloody Sunday," *War* immediately announces itself as U2's most focused and hardest-rocking album to date. Blowing away the fuzzy, sonic indulgences of *October* with propulsive, martial rhythms and shards of guitar, *War* bristles with anger, despair and, above all, passion. Previously, Bono's attempts at messages came across as grandstanding, but his vision became remarkably clear on this record, as his anthems ("New Year's Day," "40," "Seconds") are balanced by effective, surprisingly emotional love songs ("Two Hearts Beat As One"), which are just as desperate and pleading as his protests. He performs the difficult task of making the universal sound personal, and the band helps him out by bringing the songs crashing home with muscular, forceful performances that reveal their varied, expressive textures upon repeated listens. U2 always aimed at greatness, but *War* was the first time they achieved it. — *Stephen Thomas Erlewine*

Under a Blood Red Sky / 1983 / Island ✦✦✦
War turned U2 into arena-rock stars, and the EP *Under a Blood Red Sky* captures the band on its supporting tour as they adjusted to their larger audiences. Unsurprisingly for a band that always favored the grand statement, the group flourished in such a setting, as this mini-EP attests. Comprised of material recorded in America and Germany, *Under a Blood Red Sky* draws equally from the band's first three albums, and these live versions, while less textured, are considerably tougher than their studio counterparts and illustrate quite effectively why U2 were

considered one of the best, most exhilarating live bands of the '80s. — *Stephen Thomas Erlewine*

The Unforgettable Fire / 1984 / Island ✦✦✦
In many ways, U2 took their fondness for sonic bombast as far as it could go on *War*, so it isn't a complete surprise that they chose to explore the intricacies of the Edge's layered, effects-laden guitar on the follow-up, *The Unforgettable Fire*. Working with producers Brian Eno and Daniel Lanois, U2 created a dark, near-hallucinatory series of inter-locking soundscapes which are occasionally punctuated by recognizable songs and melodies. In such a setting, the band both flourishes and flounders, creating some of their greatest music, as well as some of their worst. "Elvis Presley and America" may well be Bono's most embarrassing attempt at poetry, yet it is redeemed by the chilling and wonderful "Bad," a two-chord elegy for an addict that is stunning in its control and mastery. Similarly, the wet, shimmering textures of the title track, the charging "A Sort of Homecoming" and the surging Martin Luther King, Jr., tribute "Pride (In the Name of Love)" are all remarkable, ranking among their very best music, making the missteps that clutter the remainder of the album somewhat forgivable. — *Stephen Thomas Erlewine*

Wide Awake in America / 1985 / Island ✦✦
As the band were completing the supporting tour for *The Unforgettable Fire*, they released the four-track EP *Wide Awake in America*. Comprised of two outtakes ("Three Sunrises," "Love Comes Tumbling") and two live cuts (including "Bad"), the record may be aimed at the hardcore collector, but most U2 fans will find it necessary, since the two rejects are actually stronger than about half of *The Unforgettable Fire*, and the live cuts again demonstrate U2's undeniable talent for captivating concerts. — *Stephen Thomas Erlewine*

★ **The Joshua Tree** / 1987 / Island ✦✦✦✦✦
Using the textured sonics of *The Unforgettable Fire* as a basis, U2 expanded those innovations by scaling back the songs to a personal setting and adding a grittier attack for its follow-up, *The Joshua Tree*. It's a move that returns them to the sweeping, anthemic rock of *War*, but if *War* was an exploding political bomb, *The Joshua Tree* is a journey through its aftermath, trying to find sense and hope in the desperation. That means that even the anthems—the epic opener "Where the Streets Have No Name," the yearning "I Still Haven't Found What I'm Looking For"—have seeds of doubt within their soaring choruses, and those fears take root throughout the album, whether it's in the mournful sliding acoustic guitars of "Running to Stand Still," the surging "One Tree Hill" or the hypnotic elegy "Mothers of the Disappeared." So it might seem a little ironic that U2 became superstars on the back of such a dark record, but their focus has never been clearer, nor has their music been catchier, than on *The Joshua Tree*. Unexpectedly, U2 have also tempered their textural post-punk with American influences. Not only are Bono's lyrics obsessed with America, but country and blues influences are heard throughout the record, and instead of using these as roots, they're used as ways to add texture to the music. With the uniformly excellent songs—only the clumsy, heavy rock and portentous lyrics of "Bullet the Blue Sky" fall flat—the result is a powerful, uncompromising record that became a hit due to its vision and its melody. Never before have their big messages sounded so direct and personal. — *Stephen Thomas Erlewine*

Rattle & Hum / 1988 / Island ✦✦✦
Evidently, the massive success of *The Joshua Tree* left U2 a little confused, if its half-live, half-studio, double-album follow-up *Rattle & Hum* is any indicator. Functioning as both the soundtrack to the group's disastrous feature-film documentary and as a tentative follow-up to their career-making blockbuster, *Rattle & Hum* is all over the place. The live cuts lack the revelatory power of *Under a Blood Red Sky* and are undercut by heavy-handed performances and Bono's embarrassing stage patter; prefacing a leaden cover of "Helter Skelter" with "This is a song Charles Manson stole from the Beatles, and now we're stealing it back," is bad enough, but even that pales next to Bono's exhortation "OK, Edge, play the blues!" on the otherwise worthy and decidedly unbluesy "Silver and Gold." Both comments actually reveal more than they intend—throughout the album, U2 are paralyzed by the idea that they have now inherited the mantle of "rock's most important artist" by predecessors like Bob Dylan, Jimi Hendrix, the Rolling Stones, and the Beatles. In an apparent attempt to boost their credibility, they have decided to embrace American roots-rock, something they ignored before. Occasionally, these experiments work: "Desire" has an intoxicating Bo Diddley beat, "Angel of Harlem" is a punchy, sunny Stax-soul tribute, "When Loves Come to Town" is an endearingly awkward blues duet with B.B. King, and the Dylan collaboration "Love Rescue Me" is an overlooked minor bluesy gem. However, these get swallowed up in the bluster of the live tracks, the misguided gospel interpretation of "I Still Haven't Found What I'm Looking For" and the embarassing answer to John Lennon's searing confession "God," "God Part II." A couple of affecting laments—the cascading "All I Want Is You" and "Heartland,"

which sounds like a *Joshua Tree* outtake—do slip out underneath the posturing, but *Rattle & Hum* is by far the least focused record U2 ever made, and it's little wonder that they retreated for three years after its release to rethink their whole approach. —*Stephen Thomas Erlewine*

☆ **Achtung Baby** / Nov. 19, 1991 / Island ◆◆◆◆◆
Reinventions rarely come as thorough and effective as *Achtung Baby*, an album that completely changed U2's sound and style. The crashing, unrecognizable distorted guitars that open "Zoo Station" are a clear signal that U2 have traded their Americana pretensions for post-modern, contemporary European music. Drawing equally from Bowie's electronic, avant-garde explorations of the late '70s and the neo-psychedelic sounds of the thriving rave and Madchester club scenes of early-'90s England, *Achtung Baby* sounds vibrant and endlessly inventive. Unlike their inspirations, U2 rarely experiment with song structures over the course of the album. Instead, they use the thick dance beats, swirling guitars, layers of effects, and found sounds to break traditional songs out of their constraints, revealing the tortured emotional core of their songs with the hyper-loaded arrangements. In such a dense musical setting, it isn't surprising that U2 have abandoned the political for the personal on *Achtung Baby*, since the music, even with its inviting rhythms, is more introspective than anthemic. Bono has never been as emotionally naked as he is on *Achtung Baby*, creating a feverish nightmare of broken hearts and desperate loneliness; unlike other U2 albums, it's filled with sexual imagery, much of it quite disturbing, and it ends on a disquieting note. Few bands as far into their career as U2 have recorded an album as adventurous or fulfilled their ambitions quite as successfully as they do on *Achtung Baby*, and the result is arguably their best album. —*Stephen Thomas Erlewine*

Zooropa / May 1993 / Island ◆◆◆◆
U2 planned to record a new EP before launching the European leg of their ambitious Zoo TV tour in 1993, but the EP quickly turned into the full-length album *Zooropa*. Picking up where *Achtung Baby* left off, *Zooropa* delves heavily into U2's newfound affection for experimental music and dance clubs. While the title track marries those inclinations to the anthems of *The Joshua Tree*, most of the record is far more daring than its predecessor. While that occasionally means it's unfocused and meandering, it also results in a number of wonderful moments, like the quiet menace of "Daddy's Gonna Pay for Your Crashed Car," the space-age German disco of "Lemon," Edge's droning mantra "Numb," and the gentle, heartbroken "Stay (Faraway, So Close!)," one of U2's very best love songs. As the album winds to a close, it drifts off track, yet the best moments of *Zooropa* rank among U2's most inspired and rewarding music. —*Stephen Thomas Erlewine*

Pop / Mar. 1997 / Island ◆◆◆◆
No matter which way you look at it, *Pop* doesn't have the same shock of the new that *Achtung Baby* delivered on its first listen. Less experimental and more song-oriented than *Zooropa*, *Pop* attempts to sell the glitzy, electronic rush of techno to an audience weaned on arena rock. And that audience includes U2 themselves. While they never sound like they don't believe in what they're doing, they still remove most of the radical elements of electronic dance, which is evident to anyone with just a passing knowledge of the Chemical Brothers and Underworld. To a new listener, however, *Pop* has flashes of surprise—particularly on the rampaging "Mofo"—but underneath the surface, U2 relies on anthemic rockers and ballads. "Discotheque" might be a little clumsy, but "Staring at the Sun" shimmers with synthesizers borrowed from Massive Attack and a chorus Noel Gallagher will think he has written. Similarly, "Do You Feel Loved" and "If You Wear That Velvet Dress" fuse old-fashioned U2 dynamicism with a keen sense of the cool eroticism that makes trip-hop so alluring. Problems arise when the group tries to go for the conventional rock song, not only in "Last Night on Earth," but also on "Miami," which rides a menacing groove that becomes deflated once the guitars come crashing down. "Miami" also is symptomatic of the return of U2's crusade for salvation. *Pop* is inflicted with the desire for a higher power to come save the world for its jaded spiral of decay and immorality, which is why the group's embrace of dance music never seems joyous—instead of providing an intoxicating rush of gloss and glamour, it functions as a backdrop for a plea of salvation. *Achtung Baby* also was a comment on the numbing isolation of modern culture, but it made sweeping statements through personal observations; *Pop* makes sweeping statements through sweeping observations. The difference is what makes *Pop* an easy record to admire, but a hard one to love. —*Stephen Thomas Erlewine*

UB40

f. 1978, Birmingham, England
Reggae, Adult Contemporary, Pop-Rock
Named after a British unemployment benefit form, pop-reggae band UB40 was formed in a welfare line in 1978, and its multiracial lineup reflected the working-class community its members came from. The band consolidated its street credibility with political topics appealing to

dissatisfied youth and got a boost from fans of the waning 2-Tone ska revival movement. Brothers Robin (lead guitar) and Ali Campbell (guitar, lead vocals) formed the centerpiece of the group, which also included bassist Earl Falconer, keyboardist Mickey Virtue, saxophonist Brian Travers, drummer Jim Brown, percussionist Norman Hassan, and toaster Terence "Astro" Wilson. The band purchased its first instruments with compensation money Ali Campbell received after a bar fight, even though few of the members knew how to play them. But by the end of the year, the group was invited to tour with the Pretenders. Their "Food For Thought" single reached the UK Top Ten in 1980, beginning a long streak of chart appearances. *Signing Off* and *Present Arms* were big sellers in Britain, if not America, and addressed the political issues of the day in songs like "One in Ten," a Top Ten hit blasting Margaret Thatcher for the country's unemployment rate. 1983's *Labour of Love*, an album of reggae cover songs, gave the group its first chart album in America and first No. 1 UK hit with Neil Diamond's "Red Red Wine." Several albums of original material sold well in the UK, but only respectably in the US, where the group's biggest hit was a Top 30 cover of Sonny and Cher's "I Got You Babe" featuring the Pretenders' Chrissie Hynde.

In 1988, the group performed "Red Red Wine" at a Nelson Mandela tribute concert, and a Phoenix radio station trotted the single out for a second go-round. Listener response was far more enthusiastic, and "Red Red Wine" re-entered the charts and went all the way to the top. Finally having hit on a way to conquer the lucrative American market, UB40 responded with another covers album, *Labour of Love II*, which produced Top Ten singles with versions of the Temptations' "The Way You Do the Things You Do" and Al Green's "Here I Am (Come and Take Me)." The group scored a huge hit in America with Elvis Presley's "Can't Help Falling In Love," which was initially featured in the Sharon Stone film *Sliver* and spent seven weeks at No. 1. By this time, UB40 had largely abandoned its trademark left-wing politics and was concentrating more on perfecting its reggae oldies covers than its original material; however, the gimmick has thus far resulted in huge sales figures in both the US and UK, with *Promises and Lies* reaching No. 6 and No. 1, respectively. —*Steve Huey*

Signing Off / Nov. 1980 / Graduate ◆◆◆

Present Arms / Jun. 1981 / Virgin ◆◆◆

Present Arms in Dub / Oct. 1981 / Virgin ◆◆

Best of UB40 (1980-1983) / 1983 / A&M ◆◆◆
This US compilation gathers the best of the early days of the UK's top White reggae band, displaying their love of dub and some of their best songs of the period, such as the caustic "One in Ten." —*William Ruhlmann*

● **Labour of Love** / Sep. 1983 / A&M ◆◆◆◆
Long stars in England, UB40 finally found Stateside success (and that belatedly) by recording an album of their favorite Jamaican cover tunes. One of these, "Red Red Wine," finally took off in the US in 1988 and went to No. 1. —*William Ruhlmann*

Geffery Morgan / 1984 / A&M ◆◆◆◆
UB40 was faced with following up the surprisingly successful covers album *Labour Of Love* (which had topped the UK chart and become their US chart debut) with this album of original material. Their own songs were good, but no match for what then seemed a one-of-a-kind collection. "If It Happens Again," which went to No. 9 in Britain, sounded like a song by the English Beat, while the second single, "Riddle Me" (No. 59), was a deeper reggae groove tune. It was a good set, but without a classic like "Red, Red Wine" suffered from a certain anonymity, especially in the US. —*William Ruhlmann*

Baggariddim / 1985 / DEP Int'l ◆◆◆
Baggariddim combines a thoroughly appealing three-song EP, highlighted by the catchy "Don't Break My Heart" and a duet with Chrissie Hynde on Sonny & Cher's "I Got You, Babe," with dub mixes of cuts from *Labour of Love* and *Geffery Morgan*, which feature guest toasters on almost every song. The dubs are among the strongest the band have ever released, emphasizing their reggae roots, and the new material is melodic and engaging, making *Baggariddim* a strong follow-up to two of their finest albums. [*Baggariddim* was trimmed to the three originals and two dub mixes for its initial US release, *Little Baggariddim*. In 1997, the full album was released in America for the first time.] —*Stephen Thomas Erlewine*

Little Baggaridim / 1985 / A&M ◆◆◆
UB40 scored their first Top 30 hit in the US with a cover of Sonny and Cher's "I Got You, Babe," set to a reggae beat and sung with the Pretenders' Chrissie Hynde, heard on this mini-album. —*William Ruhlmann*

Rat in the Kitchen / 1986 / A&M ◆◆◆◆
In the UK, UB40 were major stars, and this album was their sixth Top Ten hit, featuring the singles "Sing Your Own Song" (No. 5), "All I Want To Do" (No. 41), and "Rat In Me Kitchen" (No. 12). In the US, the group remained a developing act with a modest following, only able to score a hit by covering a previous hit like "I Got You, Babe." *Rat In The Kitchen*

did nothing to change that, although it was, as usual, a tuneful collection of reggae. — *William Ruhlmann*

UB40 CCCP: Live in Moscow / 1987 / A&M ✦✦
It's hard to imagine what A&M had in mind releasing a live album by a group that hadn't really broken in the US yet. Nevertheless, the record actually spent eight weeks in the charts, but it sold only to diehards, and although it's an appealing enough set, featuring covers like "Cherry Oh Baby" and "I Got You, Babe" (minus Chrissie Hynde) and such British hits as "If It Happens Again" and "Sing Our Song," it's hard to imagine it doing any better. — *William Ruhlmann*

UB40 / 1988 / A&M ✦✦✦✦
UB40 was the first indication that the band was abandoning the political inclinations of their earlier work and concentrating solely on pop-reggae. Of course, pop informed all of their albums since *Labour of Love*, but on *UB40*, the group concentrates solely on the grooves, from the instrumental "Dance With the Devil" to a sultry cover of "Breakfast in Bed," featuring Chrissie Hynde on vocals. Even though the album and all of its mellow grooves are thoroughly enjoyable, it's hard not to long for something a little deeper, whether it's the tributes of *Labour of Love* or the edgy *Rat in the Kitchen*. — *Stephen Thomas Erlewine*

Labour of Love II / Nov. 1989 / Virgin ✦✦
UB40 repeats their formula for even more success, with reggae versions of "Here I Am (Come and Take Me)" and "The Way You Do the Things You Do." — *William Ruhlmann*

Promises and Lies / Jul. 27, 1993 / Virgin ✦✦
Carried by the hit "I Can't Help Falling in Love with You," *Promises and Lies* finishes UB40's transition from a reggae band to an adult-contemporary band that plays pop-reggae. Fans of the single will be satisfied by *Promises and Lies*, but older fans will find the whole affair rather dismaying. — *AMG*

The Best of UB40, Vol. 2 / Oct. 1995 / Virgin ✦✦✦
UB40's tepid reggae-pop crossover had enough edge in its early years to justify an initial compilation, but *The Best of Volume Two* stretches the concept considerably. A paltry ten tracks in which the group confuses rhythmic reworkings of "The Way You Do the Things You Do," "Superstition," and "Can't Help Falling in Love" with originality. — *Roch Parisien*

The Best of UB40, Vol. 1 / Nov. 14, 1995 / Virgin ✦✦✦✦

UK

f. 1977, db. 1979
Art-Rock, Progressive-Rock
Featuring members of Yes, King Crimson, Roxy Music, and Soft Machine, UK was one of the most prominent progressive-rock supergroups of the late '70s. Various members of UK—guitarist Allan Holdsworth, keyboardist and violinist Eddie Jobson, bassist and vocalist John Wetton, and drummer Bill Bruford—had played together in their previous bands, but when the group formed in 1977, it was the first time all of the musicians had played together. Although the lineup was unstable—Holdsworth and Bruford left after one album, with former Frank Zappa drummer Terry Bozzio replacing Bruford—and the group was short-lived, the band maintained a dedicated cult following years after their early-'80s breakup. Prior to the formation of UK, Bill Bruford and John Wetton had recently played together in King Crimson and Allan Holdsworth had played guitar on Bruford's debut album, 1978's *Feels Good to Me*. Shortly after the recording of *Feels Good to Me*, Bruford, Holdsworth, and Wetton formed UK, adding former Roxy Music member Eddie Jobson to the lineup. UK released their eponymous debut in 1978 and the album captured the attention of progressive-rock and jazz-fusion fans, as did the record's supporting tour. At the conclusion of the tour, Holdsworth and Bruford left the group to form Bruford, leaving keyboardist Jobson as the band's leader. UK didn't hire another guitarist, but they did have Terry Bozzio replace Bruford. The new lineup of UK released *Danger Money* in 1979 and followed the album with a tour. Once the tour was completed, the group broke up. The posthumous live album *Night After Night* was released shortly afterward. Following the disbandment of UK, Eddie Jobson became a member of Jethro Tull, Terry Bozzio formed Missing Persons, and John Wetton formed Asia with fellow progressive-rock stars Steve Howe, Carl Palmer, and Geoffrey Downes. — *Stephen Thomas Erlewine*

● **UK** / 1978 / EG ✦✦✦✦
An impressive debut album, it features Allan Holdsworth, John Wetton, Bill Bruford, and Eddie Jobson. — *Paul Kohler*

Danger Money / 1979 / EG ✦✦✦
The follow-up album has Terry Bozzio taking over the drumming. It features exceptional synth work by Eddie Jobson and bass and vocals from John Wetton. — *Paul Kohler*

Night After Night / 1979 / EG ✦✦✦
A great live album, it includes the *Danger Money* lineup and songs from

both studio recordings. — *Paul Kohler*

Tracey Ullman

b. Dec. 30, 1959, Buckinghamshire, England
Vocals / New Wave, Pop-Rock
Before she became a famous TV comedienne, Tracy Ullman recorded two albums in the early '80s that effortlessly recalled the classic girl-group sound of the '60s. Ullman covered everything from Doris Day's ("Move over Darling") to Blondie's ("(I'm Always Touched by Your) Presence, Dear"), finding the underlying connections between classic pop songs of all eras. *You Broke My Heart in 17 Places*, her debut album, was a hit in the UK and she even managed to have a Top Ten hit in America with a version of Kirsty MacColl's "They Don't Know." Although it had some fine numbers, the follow-up *You Caught Me Out* wasn't as successful, prompting Ullman to return to television. By the end of the '80s, her comedy show, *The Tracy Ullman Show*, was one of the most critically acclaimed television shows in America; she hasn't recorded any music since. — *Stephen Thomas Erlewine*

You Broke My Heart in 17 Places / 1983 / Stiff/Repertoire ✦✦✦✦
Ullman's first album, recorded in the middle of the new wave and synth-pop movements, provided a refreshing break with its retro girl group sound. Includes her only US hit, "They Don't Know" (written by Kirsty MacColl) as well as carefully chosen oldies. One of the great lost classics of the new wave era. — *Chris Woodstra*

You Caught Me Out / 1984 / Repertoire ✦✦✦
The second album follows the same formula as the first—a well-chosen collection of covers from obscure oldies to contemporary favorites (Madness' "My Girl"—retitled here as "My Guy") and even another stab at a Kirsty MacColl song ("Terry")—all done in the classic '60s-girl-group sound. Though it failed to produce the smash hits of the debut, "My Guy" and "Sunglasses" were minor hits in the UK, and the album is nearly as much fun. Repertoire has released a CD version with six bonus tracks. — *Chris Woodstra*

● **The Best of Tracey Ullman** / 1991 / Rhino ✦✦✦✦
This 20-track compilation provides an extensive look at the nearly forgotten singing career of this now famous actress. Combining the entire first LP, *You Broke My Heart in 17 Places*, the highlights from her second effort *You Caught Me Out*, and well chosen B-sides, it more than lives up to its name. Although this material was recorded in the early '80s, lovers of the classic '60s-girl-group sound will find these retro-gems a familiar delight. — *Chris Woodstra*

Ultramagnetic MC's

f. 1984, Bronx, NY, db. 1993
Hip Hop, Old School Rap
Arising from the Boogie Down Bronx in the mid '80s as a far-flung hip-hop trio with a heap of new ideas to try out, Ultramagnetic's Kool Keith, Ced Gee, and DJ Moe Love occupy something of a singular place in the old school pantheon. Combining funk-heavy tracks with jeep-rocking beats and obscure lyrical references, the UMCs have a list of firsts to their credit: the first group to employ a sampler as an instrument, the first to feature extensive use of live instrumentation . . . the first to feature a former psychiatric patient (Keith) on the mic. Early singles like "Something Else" and "Space Groove" were block-party staples and created waves in the underground, eventually landing the group on the disco-dominated Next Plateau label, where they released their underappreciated debut album. The following years found the group shuffling from label to label, releasing albums on Mercury and Wild Pitch before splitting to pursue various projects. A reunion project is in the works. — *Sean Cooper*

● **Critical Beatdown** / 1988 / Next Plateau ✦✦✦✦
Another one for the unfortunately crowded "waaaay too far ahead of its time to be commercially successful" file, the UMCs' debut was loaded with deep, crushing breakbeats and musical ideas only recently being excavated by hip-hop. Keith's rhymes are a wonderfully confused lot, and DJ Moe Love's turntable niceties round out an all-time classic. — *Sean Cooper*

Funk Your Head Up / Mar. 17, 1992 / Mercury ✦✦✦
Four years in the making, the follow-up was somewhat easy to ignore, overly crowded with half-thought ideas and water-treading glances back. Produced the radio hit "Poppa Large." — *Sean Cooper*

The Four Horsemen / Aug. 10, 1993 / Wild Pitch ✦✦✦✦
Back on track and on yet another label. The last album by the group before Keith would head off on his solo Doctor Octagon tangent. — *Sean Cooper*

● **Basement Tapes: 1984-1990** / May 17, 1995 / Tuff City ✦✦✦✦
Basement Tapes: 1984-1990 compiles a selection of the Ultramagnetic MC's outtakes, rarities and demos. Considerably rougher than their official studio records, *Basement Tapes* has raw street vibe, and although

it's clear why some of these tracks were never widely released, it's an exciting record, proving that the Ultramagnetic MC's were sorely neglected while they were active. — *Stephen Thomas Erlewine*

Ultravox

f. 1974, London, England, db. 1987
New Wave, Pop-Rock

Ultravox (or Ultravox!—as it was called at first) had two separate identities and styles of music during its existence. Formed in London in 1974, it was originally intended as a platform for singer John Foxx (born Dennis Leigh) and included guitarist Stevie Shears, keyboardist and violinist Billy Currie, bassist Chris Cross, and drummer Warren Cann. With this lineup, the group recorded its debut album, *Ultravox!* (1977), produced by Brian Eno and Steve Lillywhite during the height of the punk and new wave movement. A second album, *Ha! Ha! Ha!* (1977), was released only in the UK. A third, *Systems of Romance* (1978), marked the last appearance of Foxx, who went solo, and of guitarist Robin Simon, who had replaced Shears. The remaining trio enlisted singer and guitarist Midge Ure, formerly of the teenybop band Slik, and recorded *Vienna* (1980), which marked a sharp turn toward synthesizer pop and helped give birth to the British "new romantic" movement of the early '80s. The album was Ultravox's first to chart; the title track went to No. 2 and "All Stood Still" reached the Top Ten. There followed a series of successful albums in the UK: *Rage in Eden* (1981), *Quartet* (1982), *Monument—The Soundtrack* (1983), *Lament* (1984), and *U-Vox* (1986). *The Collection* (1984) was a hits album. Of these, only *Quartet* made any significant inroads in the US Ultravox split in mid-1987, when Ure decided to turn his full attention to his solo career. — *William Ruhlmann*

Ultravox / 1977 / Island ✦✦✦
John Foxx proves to have an odd, Bowie-influenced vision, here aided and abetted by Brian Eno (then a Bowie crony) and Steve Lillywhite. "My Sex" and "I Want to Be a Machine" are standouts. — *William Ruhlmann*

Ha Ha Ha / 1977 / Island ✦✦✦

Systems of Romance / Dec. 1978 / Island ✦✦✦

Vienna / 1980 / Chrysalis ✦✦✦✦
The new Ultravox, under Midge Ure, has a dreamy, ethereal sound heard at its best on its debut album, which features the title song, "All Stood Still," "Passing Strangers," and "Sleepwalk," all UK hits. — *William Ruhlmann*

Rage in Eden / 1981 / Chrysalis ✦✦✦

Quartet / 1982 / Chrysalis ✦✦✦

Lament / 1984 / Chrysalis ✦✦✦✦

● **The Collection** / 1984 / Chrysalis ✦✦✦✦
Ultravox's UK hit singles during the Midge Ure era. — *William Ruhlmann*

U-Vox / 1986 / Chrysalis ✦✦

Rare, Vol. 1 / 1994 / Chrysalis ✦✦
Compiles in chronological order 17 rare single B-side tracks which the British electro-pop group released between 1980 and 1983. For hardcore fans only. — *Roch Parisien*

Dancing with Tears in My Ears / 1997 / EMI ✦✦✦✦
Dancing with Tears in My Ears is a 15-track overview of Ultravox's early-'80s commercial peak, hitting most, but not all, of their biggest hits, including "Sleepwalk," "Vienna," "All Stood Still," and "Reap the Wild Wind." It's not a bad collection, but if it had included hits like "The Thin Wall," it could have been a definitive retrospective. — *Stephen Thomas Erlewine*

Uncle Tupelo

f. 1987, Belleville, IL, db. 1994
Alternative Pop-Rock, Indie Rock, Alternative Country-Rock

With the release of their 1990 debut LP *No Depression*, the Belleville, Illinois trio Uncle Tupelo launched more than their own career—by fusing the simplicity and honesty of country music with the bracing fury of punk, they kick-started a revolution which reverberated throughout the American underground. Thanks to a successful on-line site and subsequent fanzine which adopted the album's name, the tag "No Depression" became a catchall for the like-minded artists who, along with Tupelo, signalled alternative rock's return to its country roots—at much the same time, ironically enough, that Nashville was itself embracing the slick gloss associated with mainstream rock and pop.

Uncle Tupelo was led by singer-songwriters Jay Farrar and Jeff Tweedy, lifelong friends born in the same Belleville hospital in 1967. During high school, the pair formed a punk cover band called the Primitives along with drummer Mike Heidorn and Farrar's older brother, Wade. After Wade enlisted in the Army, the Primitives broke up. But in

1987, the remaining trio reunited, changed their name to Uncle Tupelo, and began incorporating elements of country into their music as well as writing original material. Touring constantly throughout the Midwest, the band members eventually quit school as their music became more and more successful, and in 1989 they signed a contract with the small independent label Rockville.

Taking its name from the A.P. Carter gospel song covered therein, *No Depression* reflected the band's disparate influences, ranging from Hank Williams to bluesman Leadbelly through to the famed post-punk trio Husker Du. The most rock-centric of Uncle Tupelo's releases, its songs were meditations on small-town, small-time life—candid snapshots of days spent working thankless jobs, and nights spent in an alcoholic fog. After the release of "I Got Drunk," a brilliant single backed with a cover of the Flying Burrito Brothers' "Sin City," 1991's *Still Feel Gone* struck a finer balance between their rock and country aims. While Farrar's contributions—sung in his reedy, Neil Young-like voice—were often informed by a rootsy, scorched-earth mentality, Tweedy's, with their grittier vocals, delved deeper into the trio's punk origins, as typified by the song "D. Boon," a tribute to the late frontman of the legendary Minutemen.

A year later, Uncle Tupelo released *March 16-20, 1992,* an acoustic record which saw the group plunging fully into country and folk. Recorded live in the studio with producer Peter Buck (of the band R.E.M.), the album drew heavily on painstakingly authentic covers of standards like "Moonshiner" and "Satan, Your Kingdom Must Come Down," along with a fitting rendition of the Louvin Brothers' "The Great Atomic Power", and Farrar and Tweedy's originals, which maintained the record's spare, haunting ambience. Shortly after its release, Mike Heidorn left the group to devote time to his family, and was replaced by drummer Ken Coomer, formerly of the group Clockhammer. Multi-instrumentalists Max Johnston and John Stirratt also signed on as part-time members.

In 1992, Uncle Tupelo signed to major label Sire/Reprise, and in 1993 issued the LP *Anodyne*. Widely regarded as the group's definitive statement, it was a true country-rock hybrid which accented the power of both musical forms; the album even featured a cover of the song "Give Back the Key to My Heart" sung with its writer, roots-rock pioneer Doug Sahm. After a tour in support of the album, however, the long-standing relationship between Farrar and Tweedy dissolved in bitter acrimony, and Uncle Tupelo disbanded; shortly thereafter, Tweedy recruited Coomer, Johnston, and Stirratt to form the band Wilco, while Farrar reunited with Heidhorn in Son Volt. — *Jason Ankeny*

No Depression / 1990 / Rockville ✦✦✦✦
Uncle Tupelo's landmark opening salvo is the group's most rock-oriented album, steeped more in breakneck speed, punk crunch, and guitar dissonance than any of their subsequent efforts. Indeed, despite the presence of mandolins, fiddles, and banjos—as well as inclusion of the title track, a faithful cover of the A.P. Carter classic—the trio's vaunted country leanings are less musical than thematic on *No Depression*, thanks in large part to singer-songwriters Jay Farrar and Jeff Tweedy's acute depictions of rural, blue-collar life. Like the Replacements—never more obvious an influence than on this LP—Uncle Tupelo's songs paint grim, unrelenting portraits of aimless Midwestern existence, split between days working on the opening cut's "Factory Belt" and nights spent blurry-eyed and wasted ("Whiskey Bottle," "Before I Break"). Still, for all of the record's doleful cynicism—virtually every cut nods towards dashed hopes, broken promises, and paralyzing fear—there's an undeniable electricity afoot as well; by channeling the mournful clarity of country into the crackling fury of punk, *No Depression* brings new life to both musical camps. — *Jason Ankeny*

Still Feel Gone / Sep. 17, 1991 / Rockville ✦✦✦
Still Feel Gone is Tupelo's transitional record; while it goes far in fusing the band's rock origins with their country aspirations, the alliance is often an uneasy, even schizophrenic, one. Writers Jay Farrar and Jeff Tweedy are rarely in synch; while the former's contributions embrace roots music wholeheartedly, Tweedy's songs journey more deeply into rock than ever before—his opening track, "Gun," is the most straightforward pop number the trio ever recorded, while "D. Boon," a tribute to the fallen leader of the legendary post-punk trio the Minutemen, borders on thrash. Still, while *Still Feel Gone* lacks the consistency of its predecessor *No Depression*, it's a more wide-ranging record, deeper in maturity, subtlety and texture—all clear evidence of things to come. — *Jason Ankeny*

March 16-20, 1992 / Aug. 3, 1992 / Rockville ✦✦✦✦
Produced by R.E.M.'s Peter Buck, *March 16-20, 1992* represents Uncle Tupelo's full evolution into a true country unit; with the exception of the eerie squalls of guitar feedback which haunt Jeff Tweedy's composition "Wait Up," there's virtually no evidence of the trio's punk heritage. Instead, the all-acoustic album—a combination of Tupelo originals and well-chosen traditional songs—taps into the very essence of backwoods culture, its music rooted in the darkest corners of Appalachian life. An

inescapable sense of dread grips this collection, from the large-scale threat depicted in the stunning rendition of the Louvin Brothers' "The Great Atomic Power" to the fatalism of the worker anthems "Grindstone" and "Coalminers"; even the character studies, including a revelatory "Moonshiner," are relentlessly grim. A vivid glimpse at the harsh realities of rural existence, *March 16-20, 1992* is a brilliant resurrection of a bygone era of American folk artistry. —*Jason Ankeny*

● **Anodyne** / May 1993 / Sire ✦✦✦✦
Uncle Tupelo never struck a finer balance between rock and country than on *Anodyne*, their major-label debut and parting shot. For all of the ill will undoubtedly simmering throughout these sessions, Jay Farrar and Jeff Tweedy have never before been more attuned to each other musically; where earlier records often found the band's twin forces moving in opposing directions, *Anodyne* bears the full fruits of their shared vision. Recorded live in the studio, the LP encompasses and reinterprets not only country-rock (evidenced by the group's pairing with Doug Sahm on his "Give Back the Key to My Heart") but also traditional country (the tribute to the songwriting legacy of "Acuff-Rose"), rock (the churning "The Long Cut," "Chickamauga") and folk ("New Madrid," "Steal the Crumbs"), the band's reach never once exceeding its grasp. —*Jason Ankeny*

The Undertones

f. 1976, Derry, Northern Ireland, **db.** 1983
Punk, New Wave
There are those who would disagree vehemently, but in my estimation the Undertones were Ireland's best rock band—ever. Roaring out of the Northern Ireland city of Derry in 1976, the Undertones fused speedy, loud, Ramones-inspired walls of guitar racket with irresistible '60s pop hooks, with just a touch of mid-'70s glam rock for good measure. With the singular tenor vocals of frontman Feargal Sharkey making them instantaneously recognizable, Undertones' songs tended to eschew punk vitriol for songs about teenage love, girls, snotty cousins, and summertime—life's simple joys (and pains). No more succinct a summation of their style, wit, and power can be found than on their out-of-print debut EP *Teenage Kicks*, released in 1978 on the Belfast indie label Good Vibrations. A record of startling ebullience, the songs (many of which showed up on their eponymous debut album) sound as exhilarating today as they did nearly 20 years ago. However, the Undertones did not go into creative stasis with their winning punk-pop and simply replicate a proven formula over and over. As they grew as musicians, so did their albums change, incorporating some of the Tamla/Motown soul music they loved as kids. As a live band, they were tremendous; just ask anyone who saw them opening for the Clash in the late '70s. Sadly, the Undertones' story ended far too quickly. Growing up meant too much change too fast, and by the time they released their mediocre fourth album, restlessness and "musical differences" were splitting them apart. Sharkey went off to a short-lived solo career, while the guitar-playing O'Neill brothers put together the politically charged That Petrol Emotion. In the late '80s, there were whispers of a reunion that didn't occur, much to the relief of those who preferred the Undertones' legacy to remain unsullied. —*John Dougan*

★ **The Undertones** / 1979 / Rykodisc ✦✦✦✦✦
An absolutely essential purchase. One of the best albums of the punk era, or any era. Song after song is infused with a liberating joy and intensity that only a handful of rock records at the time equalled. A crucial record, the 'Tones' debut shows how influential '70s commercial pop was on the growing punk community, who embraced it and then tore it all to hell. A record that hasn't lost its luster after hundreds of plays and nearly two decades. Reissued on CD with seven bonus tracks by Rykodisc in 1994. —*John Dougan*

Hypnotised / 1980 / Rykodisc ✦✦✦✦
It's ridiculous to not encourage you to purchase the first three Undertones records, because they are such wonderful distillations of all that makes rock 'n' roll great. *Hypnotised* picks up where the debut leaves off, but adds a slightly more sarcastic touch to some of the songs, especially the witty "My Perfect Cousin" and the goofy "More Songs About Chocolate and Girls" (a not-so-subtle parody of the title of Talking Heads' second LP *More Songs About Buildings and Food*). Reissued on CD with five bonus tracks by Rykodisc in 1994. —*John Dougan*

Positive Touch / 1981 / Rykodisc ✦✦✦
By this time, The Undertones had switched labels and made a challenging, slightly arty record that didn't sound much like their first two, and showed an amazing artistic development. There are musical elements not on the previous recordings (horns, Paul Carrack's keyboards); still, the band's creativity, intelligence and personality make this a tremendously rewarding record. Not where one unfamiliar with the 'Tones should start (get that guitar rush first), but once under their spell, *Positive Touch* will become almost as important as the first two albums. Reissued on CD with four bonus tracks by Rykodisc in 1994. —*John Dougan*

The Very Best of the Undertones / Oct. 25, 1994 / Rykodisc ✦✦✦✦
The Very Best Of The Undertones collects the cream of the catalogue. The group's earliest high-energy teenage anthems (themes of doubt, deceit, yearning, and infatuation) give way, over the course of 25 songs, to the sublime intimacy of "Wednesday Week" and "Julie Ocean," and then the sophisticated, Tamla/Motown layering of "Soul Seven." Group members discuss each track in the informative liner notes. Start here, fall in love, then go find the individual albums! —*Roch Parisien*

Underworld

f. 1988, Romford, Essex, England
House, Techno, Club-Dance, Electronica
One of the most popular intelligent techno acts to emerge during the genre's ascendence during the '90s, Underworld began life in the late '80s as a funk-rock group including vocalist Karl Hyde and guitarist Richard Smith. The duo left after two albums, but resurfaced several years later with a new member—DJ Darren Emerson—and a sound much closer to straightahead techno and trance, though much more rock-oriented than its electronic contemporaries—especially early on. First album *DubNoBass WithMyHeadMan* appeared in 1994, and the trio gained a US deal with TVT the following year. *Second Toughest in the Infants* was released in early 1996 to outstanding acclaim; the LP also sold well, thanks in part to the nonalbum single "Born Slippy," which was featured on the soundtrack to the seminal *Trainspotting* film.

Karl Hyde first played with Richard Smith back in the early '80s; the two had formed the new wave band Freur and released *Doot-Doot* in 1983. *Get Us Out of Here* followed two years later, but Freur then disintegrated. During the '80s, Hyde worked on projects for Debbie Harry and Prince, among others, but again joined with Smith to form Underworld in 1988. The group earned an American contract with Sire and released albums in 1988 and 1989, though with little attention. By the end of the decade, Underworld had disappeared.

As they had several years earlier, Hyde and Smith shed their skin yet again in 1992, recruiting hotshot DJ Darren Emerson and renaming themselves Lemon Interrupt. Two singles were released on the Junior Boy's Own label that year, "Dirty/Minneapolis" and "Bigmouth/Eclipse." The trio's first two singles as Underworld, 1993's "Rez" and "MMM...Skyscraper I Love You," caused a sensation upon release; the album *Dub No Bass with My Head Man* followed later that same year. Instead of adding small elements of techno to a basically rock formula, Underworld treated techno as a dominant force, with only occasional guitar parts and soft-spoken vocals providing a focus. Hyde, Smith, and Emerson impressed many at their concert dates as well; the group apparently relished playing live and received a large ovation for their appearance at the Glastonbury Festival.

Dub No Bass with My Head Man was released in the US in 1995 after TVT Records licensed the album. During the rest of the year, Underworld worked on their second album but did release one single, "Born Slippy." The group's sophomore effort, *Second Toughest in the Infants*, was released in early 1996 to much praise. Underworld came to major attention later in the year when "Born Slippy" was featured on the *Trainspotting* soundtrack, a controversial film that connected with many youths. Underworld work as remixers as well, altering tracks by Depeche Mode, Bjork, Simply Red, Orbital, Leftfield and the Chemical Brothers; also, Emerson continues to DJ occasional club-nights. —*John Bush*

Dubnobasswithmyheadman / Feb. 1994 / Wax Trax! ✦✦✦✦
A great record; Hyde's sultry songwriting meshes with Emerson's beat-driven instrumentation, and Smith provides occasional guitar work. The tracks are long, and are closer to techno with vocals than normal songs with techno backing. Underworld are truly a multi-genre group in a decade awash with fusion. —*John Bush*

● **Second Toughest in the Infants** / Mar. 12, 1996 / Wax Trax! ✦✦✦✦
On their second album, Underworld continues to explore the fringes of dub, dance, and techno, creating a seamless, eclectic fusion of various dance genres. *Second Toughest in the Infants* carries the same knockout punch of their debut, *Dubnobasswithmyheadman*, but it's subtler and more varied, offering proof that the outfit is one of the leading dance collectives of the mid-'90s. —*Stephen Thomas Erlewine*

The Undisputed Truth

f. 1970, Detroit, MI
Soul, Funk
It's not exactly fair to peg the Undisputed Truth as a one-hit wonder, because they did have a few hits for Motown in the first half of the 1970s (albeit only one big one), as well as making half a dozen albums for the label. Still, it's not that far from the truth. Nothing else they did matched the strength of "Smiling Faces Sometimes," which made No.3 in 1971. Crafted by Norman Whitfield, Motown's most adventurous producer of the time, it employed the funk-psychedelic guitars and ominous,

socially-aware lyrics that were also characteristic of his work with the Temptations during the period.

The Undisputed Truth came into being after Bobby Taylor brought Billie Rae Calvin and Brenda Joyce to Motown as part of the Delicates. When the Delicates broke up, the pair kept busy doing background vocals for the Four Tops, Diana Ross, and Edwin Starr. Whitfield teamed them up with Joe Harris of the Preps, laying the groundwork for the male-female vocal interplay that would typify their Motown sessions.

It's fair to say that the Undisputed Truth were little more than a mouthpiece for Whitfield. He wrote most of their material (sometimes in association with Barrett Strong), and used their sessions as a laboratory to devise funk rhythms and psychedelic guitar effects. He was doing the same thing with the Temptations, and the Undisputed Truth's records couldn't help but suffer in comparison. As vocalists they weren't in the same league as the Temps, and Whitfield was most likely reserving his real killer songs for the more famous group.

The group never approached the success of "Smiling Faces Sometimes" again, although they racked up a series of modest R&B hits through the mid '70s. The best of these were "You Make Your Own Heaven and Hell Right Here on Earth" (which perhaps recalled "Smiling Faces" a little too closely) and the original version of "Papa Was a Rollin' Stone," which Whitfield would quickly redo with the Temptations for a much more definitive (and massively successful) version. Little else in the Undisputed Truth discography demands attention, though Motown scholars will find their work worth a listen to investigate some of the ideas rattling around Whitfield's head in the 1970s. —*Richie Unterberger*

The Best of the Undisputed Truth / Apr. 30, 1991 / Motown ✦✦✦✦
"Smiling Faces Sometimes" is among the hits included on this album. —*Rick A. Bueche*

● **Milestones** / Aug. 8, 1995 / Motown ✦✦✦✦
Milestones collects all of the Undisputed Truth's hit singles, as well as a significant number of their album tracks. Although the album is certainly definitive, it may be a bit too much for anyone but devoted fans. —*Stephen Thomas Erlewine*

The United States of America

f. 1967, Los Angeles, CA, **db.** 1969
Psychedelic
Formed at the University of California at Los Angeles, the United States of America released a self-titled album in 1968 that blended an avant-garde sensibility (leader and founder Joseph Byrd was a respected contemporary composer) with eerie, piercing instrumentation and coolly foreboding lyrics. Musically it's quite advanced for its era, with an eclectic array of then-futuristic electronic instruments augmenting the standard rock lineup. But what saves the music from coming off as too calculated are Dorothy Moskowitz's lovely vocals, which bring to mind a somewhat icier Grace Slick. The group dissolved quickly, breaking up after just one LP. Joe Byrd released a similar, less impressive album as the leader of Joe Byrd & the Field Hippies; Moskowitz briefly joined Country Joe & the Fish in the early '70s. —*Richie Unterberger*

United States of America / 1992 / Sony ✦✦✦
Originally released on Columbia in 1968, this is one of the legendary pure psychedelic space records. Some of the harder-rocking tunes have a funhouse recklessness that recall aspects of early Pink Floyd and the Velvet Underground at their freakiest; the sedate, exquisitely orchestrated ballads, especially "Cloud Song" and the wonderfully titled "Love Song for the Dead Che," are among the best relics of dreamy psychedelia. Occasionally things get too excessive and self-conscious, and the attempts at comedy are a bit flat, but otherwise this is a near classic. The CD reissue adds two previously unreleased outtakes. —*Richie Unterberger*

Unrest

f. 1981, Washington, D.C., **db.** 1994
Alternative Pop-Rock, Indie Rock
Unrest formed in the early '80s and was originally conceived as an artsy hardcore act. In this incarnation, the Washington, DC group released many singles and seven-inches, but did not gain their definitive, ultra-melodic and catchy sound until bassist-songwriter-vocalist Bridget Cross joined in 1990. In 1992 the band released their first full-length album, *Imperial f.f.r.r.* which featured the closely intertwined, harmonic playing of Cross and guitarist-songwriter-vocalist Mark Robinson. More singles and EPs followed, culminating in the release of 1993's more experimental *Perfect Teeth*. After a few more singles, the group broke up in early 1994, with Robinson and Cross forming the group Air Miami after the split. —*Heather Phares*

Imperial f.f.r.r. / Jul. 14, 1992 / TeenBeat/No. 6 ✦✦✦✦
Imperial is Unrest's full-length debut. It fleshes out the pop promise of their early singles, and expands on their pop and experimental background as well. " I Do Believe You Are Blushing," "Cherry Cream On,"

"Suki," "Isabel," and "June" are still some of the band's best songs, mixing high-energy guitars and subjects like girls and death to infectious effect. A near-perfect album of indie-pop. —*Heather Phares*

Isabel Bishop [EP] / 1993 / 4AD/TeenBeat ✦✦✦✦
This mini-album is Unrest's debut on 4AD. A re-recorded, lusher "Isabel" starts off this small but great collection, which includes "Teenage Suicide," "Yes She Is My Skinhead Girl," and "Like to Know." —*Heather Phares*

● **Perfect Teeth** / Aug. 24, 1993 / 4AD/TeenBeat ✦✦✦✦
The band's final and best album is both jangly and lush, and covers many styles of pop music, "Angel, I'll Walk You Home" is filled with pristine vocal harmonies, while "Cath Carroll" is flashy, thrashy punk-pop. "Light Brigade" is both wistful and triumphant. "Breather x.o.x.o" is majestically melancholy, and "West Coast Love Affair" is breezy and tongue-in-cheek. Unrest's experimental and pop leanings come together with terrific success on *Perfect Teeth*, making it a high point in the band's too-brief recording career. —*Heather Phares*

Fuck Pussy Galore and All Her Friends / 1994 / Matador ✦✦✦
This aptly-titled album is a collection of the group's B-sides. If anything, it shows just how important bassist Bridget Cross was in shaping the group's sound. While it's a welcome addition to the Unrest fan's collection, not much here is absolutely vital. —*Heather Phares*

Midge Ure

b. Nov. 10, 1953, Glasgow, Scotland
Guitar, Vocals / Pop-Rock
One of the key members of the new wave band Ultravox, guitarist-vocalist Midge Ure began his professional music career with Salvation, a Glasgow-based group that became the bubblegum band Slik in 1974. Upset in the change of direction, Ure left the band to join the Rich Kids, a punk-pop group led by former Sex Pistol bassist Glen Matlock. The Rich Kids only released one album, 1978's *Ghosts of Princes in Towers*, before breaking up later that same year. Ure spent a brief time with the Misfits (not the American hardcore band) before forming Visage with drummer Rusty Egan and vocalist Steve Strange; he left the group to replace Gary Moore in Thin Lizzy, who left in the middle of an American tour. After the tour was finished, he fulfilled an agreement to join Ultravox.

Once he joined the band in 1980, Ure helped make Ultravox a mainstream success; during this time he also worked as a producer, making records with Steve Harley and Modern Man. In 1982, Ure released a solo single, a cover of the Walker Brothers' hit "No Regrets;" it climbed into the UK Top Ten. Ure and Bob Geldof formed Band Aid, a special project to aid famine relief efforts in Ethiopia. In 1984. The two wrote the song "Do They Know It's Christmas?" and assembled an all-star band of British musicians to record the single; it sold millions of copies over the 1984 holiday season and prompted Geldof to organize the benefit concert Live Aid in 1985.

In 1985, Ultravox was put on hiatus and Ure began to pursue a full-time solo career. Recorded entirely by Ure, his 1985 solo debut *The Gift* launched the No. 1 single "If I Was," as well as the minor hits "That Certain Smile" and "Call of the Wild." The following year, he recorded the final Ultravox album; in 1987, the band broke up and he began recording his second solo album. The resulting record, 1988's *Answers to Nothing*, was less successful than *The Gift* in the UK, yet it charted in the US, which is something Ure's previous album failed to do. Three years later, Ure released his third album, *Pure;* while it didn't do any business in America, the album featured the Top 20 British hit "Cold, Cold Heart." He attempted a comeback in 1996 with *Breathe*, which went ignored by both the American and British markets. —*Stephen Thomas Erlewine*

The Gift / 1985 / Chrysalis ✦✦✦

Answers to Nothing / 1988 / Chrysalis ✦✦✦✦

Pure / Sep. 24, 1991 / RCA ✦✦

● **If I Was: The Very Best of Midge Ure & Ultravox** / 1993 / Chrysalis ✦✦✦✦
All of Midge Ure and Ultravox's best tracks are here (including "Dear God," "Reap the Wild Wind," and Band Aid's "Do They Know It's Christmas?," which was co-written by Midge Ure), collected on one definitive 17-track CD. —*AMG*

Breathe / Jun. 18, 1996 / RCA ✦✦✦
With *Breathe*, Midge Ure attempted to make a comeback to the pop mainstream in the mid-'90s by targeting the adult alternative market. Consequently, *Breathe* is atmospheric and lush, with airy melodies and interweaving keyboards. The new approach might have been a success if Ure had written songs as memorably melodic as his earlier solo hits—not to mention his singles with Ultravox—but he has opted for texture over songcraft, which makes *Breathe* a pleasant, but unengaging listen. —*Stephen Thomas Erlewine*

Urge Overkill

f. 1985, Chicago, IL
Rock & Roll, Alternative Pop-Rock
Few bands ever lusted after rock stardom quite as blatantly as Chicago's Urge Overkill. Although they draped their quest for stardom in a cloak of ironic detachment, it quite clear that the trio expected that if they acted like stars, they would become stars. For a while, their stylish retro-'70s outfits, matching medallions, and heavy Cheap Trick homages earned the group a popular following in alternative rock circles. The *SuperSonic Storybook* and the *Stull* EP were both underground hits in the early '90s, before alternative rock became big business. Once alternative rock entered the big leagues, it seemed likely that Urge Overkill, with their exceptionally accessible combination of arena rock, power-pop and underground punk, would follow Nirvana to the top of the charts, but mainstream America never quite understood their ironic outlook, embracing the group only after their cover of Neil Diamond's "Girl, You'll Be A Woman Soon" was used in a key scene in *Pulp Fiction*. Instead of breaking down the doors to the stardom, the song proved to be a breaking point. *Exit the Dragon*, the first album released after the hit single, was a bomb, receiving little radio or MTV support, and the band soon fell prey to their widely-documented excesses.

Of course, Urge Overkill were always unlikely candidates for rock stardom. The group's core members, Nash Kato (born Nathan Katruud; occasionally billed as National Kato) and Eddie "King" Roeser were Midwest suburbanites who met at college in Chicago. Taking their name from a Parliament song, the duo formed Urge Overkill in 1985 with drummer Jack Watt (billed as "The Jaguar") and recorded their debut EP, *Strange, I . . .* with Kato's roommate Steve Albini the following year. Neither *Strange, I* nor its full-length follow-up, the Albini-produced *Jesus Urge Superstar*, gained much attention, primarily because the group was attempting to replicate the noise-rock aesthetic of so many other Chicago-based acts on Touch & Go Records. However, the Butch Vig-produced *Americruiser* (1990), featured an improved sound and sense of style, highlighted on the near-college hit, "Ticket to LA."

Drummer Black Onassis (born Johnny Rowan) was added to the band prior to recording their third album. With Onassis in the band, the group landed on their Stonesy fusion of arena rock and punk, as well as their idea to act like stars. The new Urge Overkill was debuted on 1991's *The SuperSonic Storybook*, which became an underground hit thanks to strong reviews and a slot opening for Nirvana on the American *Nevermind* tour. Urge hired Kramer to produce the 1992 *Stull* EP, which featured both "Girl, You'll Be A Woman Soon" and "Goodbye to Guyville," a kiss-off to the Chicago indie-rock scene that the band had alienated; Liz Phair would later borrow the term "guyville" for her acclaimed debut album, *Exile in Guyville*.

Urge Overkill signed to DGC Records in 1992, although they were still contracted to record another record for Touch & Go. Their jump to the majors angered all of Touch & Go, particularly their former producer Albini, who publicly attacked the band in several interviews. Still, the band's 1993 major-label debut, *Saturation*, was greeted with strong reviews upon its summer release. Produced by the Butcher Brothers (Cypress Hill), the album sounded like a sure-fire alternative crossover hit, but only "Sister Havana" earned much airplay. Furthermore, the band began to alienate certain members of the alternative rock community with its constant preening, and a few anti-Urge campaigns were launched in the American indie-rock underground.

As the band was preparing to record its follow-up to *Saturation*, Quentin Tarantino picked the group's cover of "Girl, You'll Be A Woman Soon" for the soundtrack to his unexpected hit, *Pulp Fiction*. On the strength of the movie's success, the song became a hit, seemingly setting the stage for a breakthrough success with 1995's *Exit the Dragon*. The success never happened. Scheduled for early summer of 1995, the album didn't appear until the fall, when it was greeted with mixed reviews. The lead single from the album, "The Break," was rather uncommercial, and received little airplay. The group began a tour that fall which quickly turned disastrous, with opening act Guided By Voices being kicked off the tour amidst much controversy a few weeks into the tour. A few weeks later, the remaining concerts were cancelled altogether; they were never rescheduled. Toward the end of the year, Blackie Onassis was picked up for heroin possession. No charges were pressed and the incident was kept quiet, but the album was already pronounced dead in the water by the media and DGC. Urge Overkill spent 1996 in seclusion as they attempted to regroup. By the end of the year, tensions between Nash Kato and Eddie "King" Roeser had escalated, resulting in Roeser's departure from the band. Kato and Onassis continued on as a duo, leaving DGC for 550 Music in early 1997. As the band were preparing their first album for 550 Music, Roeser was replaced with guitarist Nils St. Cyr. *— Stephen Thomas Erlewine*

Jesus Urge Superstar / 1989 / Touch & Go ✦✦

Americruiser / 1990 / Touch & Go ✦✦✦

Americruiser/Jesus Urge Superstar / Oct. 1990 / Touch & Go ✦✦✦
Urge's first two albums were recorded at a time when their visions eclipsed their talents—while there is a lot of good indie-guitar bluster here, there aren't that many memorable songs. With its flat Steve Albini production, *Jesus Urge Superstar* is the weaker of the records. *Americruiser*, with production courtesy of Butch Vig, not only has a fuller sound, but also some real songs. "Ticket to LA." is a classic rocker, with a locomotive riff and great lyrics. It was a sign of things to come. (The CD also includes their gonzo cover of Jimmy Webb's "Wichita Lineman.") *— Stephen Thomas Erlewine*

The Supersonic Storybook / 1991 / Touch & Go ✦✦✦✦
With the addition of drummer Blackie Onassis, Urge Overkill shapes up into a killer rock 'n' roll combo. It also doesn't hurt that the songs are the finest they have written to date. Although the production is a little flat, there's no denying the force of the best tracks. "The Candidate" boasts a huge, stadium-size riff, "The Kids Are Insane" is a frenzied, frenetic rocker, "Today Is Blackie's Birthday" is gleefully stupid, and the band is surprisingly sexy on the old soul song "Emmaline." Things bog down a bit on the second side, but Urge is starting to sound like the rock stars they always knew they were. *— Stephen Thomas Erlewine*

Stull [EP] / Aug. 10, 1992 / Touch & Go ✦✦✦✦
It's not the full-throttle rock masterpiece that *Supersonic Storybook* suggested, but the *Stull* EP is almost as remarkable. Opening with a straight cover of Neil Diamond's "Girl, You'll Be a Woman Soon" (which fits Urge Overkill's image perfectly), the EP is an atmospheric guitar workout. While "Stitches" is a salute to their punk roots, the most impressive moments come during the stylish kiss-off to indie-rock "Goodbye to Guyville" and "Stull," with its sly, laidback groove. As the richness of *Stull* proves, Urge's vision was too large for the independents, and it was time to move on. *— Stephen Thomas Erlewine*

● **Saturation** / Jun. 8, 1993 / DGC ✦✦✦✦
When they hit the major labels, Urge Overkill followed through on their promise with the blistering *Saturation*. It's stadium rock by clever post-punkers who are smart enough to not let their carefully crafted image interfere with the music. Every one of the 12 songs is a killer, from the outlandish menace of "Stalker" to the moving ballad "Back On Me," as well as the tongue-in-cheek "Woman 2 Woman" and the radio hit "Sister Havana." *— Stephen Thomas Erlewine*

Exit the Dragon / Oct. 1995 / DGC ✦✦✦✦
Sonically falling somewhere between *Supersonic Storybook* and *Stull*, *Exit the Dragon* is a dark, lean album, the flipside of *Saturation*'s glossy celebration of '70s rock 'n' roll excess and easily Urge Overkill's most haunting collection of songs. It kicks off with "Jaywalking," a terse, powerful rocker lamenting "all the evil in this world," which sets the album's tone. *Exit the Dragon* is dominated by Eddie "King" Roeser, with Nash Kato on only six of the 14 songs. As usual, Roeser's songs are more claustrophobic than Kato's, particularly the clenched riffs of "The Break" and the slow crawl of "Tin Foil." Although Kato contributes the flat-out rocker "Need Some Air," many of his songs are nearly as dark as Roeser's, whether it's the acoustic "View of the Rain" (previously released as "Take a Walk" on the *No Alternative* compilation), the skipping pop of "Somebody Else's Body," the power-pop of "Monopoly," or the soaring closer "Digital Black Epilogue," a duet with an uncredited female soul singer. But the heart of the record is Blackie Onassis' "The Mistake," an eerie tale of a drug overdose which helps *Exit the Dragon* take the form of a loose concept album about a rock 'n' roll band beset by troubles on the road. While the subject is ripe for parody, Urge Overkill performs *Exit the Dragon* without much irony at all. Instead of being a fatal misstep, this choice proves that Urge is a tight, powerful rock 'n' roll band blessed with first-rate songwriters, capable of more emotions than many listeners might have expected. *— Stephen Thomas Erlewine*

Uriah Heep

f. 1970, London, England
Hard Rock, Art-Rock/Progressive-Rock, Heavy Metal
Uriah Heep's by-the-books progressive heavy metal made the British band one of the most popular hard rock groups of the early '70s. Formed by vocalist David Byron and guitarist Mick Box in the late '60s, the group went through an astonishing number of members over the next two decades—nearly 30 different musicians passed through the band over the years. Byron and Box were members of the mid-'60s rock band called The Stalkers; once that band broke up, the duo formed another group called Spice. Spice would eventually turn into Uriah Heep in the late '60s, once Ken Hensley (guitar, keyboards, vocals) and bassist Paul Newton joined the pair. Former Spice drummer Alex Napier was the band's drummer for a brief time; he was quickly replaced by Nigel Olsson.

Uriah Heep released their debut album *Very 'eavy, Very 'umble* (called *Uriah Heep* in the US) in 1970. After its release, Keith Baker became the group's drummer; he recorded *Salisbury*, the group's second album, before deciding he couldn't keep up with the band's extensive touring and was replaced by Ian Clarke. Featuring a 16-minute title track recorded with a 26-piece orchestra, *Salisbury* showcased the band's more progressive tendencies. Later that year, Ian Clarke was replaced by Lee Kerslake and Mark Clarke replaced Newton; Mark Clarke quickly left the band and Gary Thain became the group's bassist. This lineup of Uriah Heep was its most stable and popular; beginning with 1972's *Demons and Wizards*, they released five albums between 1972 and 1975.

After 1975, the band's popularity began to slip. Byron left the band in 1977 and was replaced by John Lawton, yet the group's fortunes kept declining right into the early '80s. However, Uriah Heep soldiers on, continuing to release albums in the '90s. — *Stephen Thomas Erlewine*

Very 'umble Very 'eavy / 1970 / Mercury ✦✦✦
It may not have approached the musical complexity of their mid-'70s work, but Uriah Heep's debut album was a heavy, stomp-rock delight. —*Daevid Jehnzen*

Salisbury / 1971 / Mercury ✦✦✦
No, not the steak, but Uriah Heep does raise the stakes on their second album, *Salisbury*. Instead of relying on the throbbing boogie of *Very 'eavy, Very 'umble*, it weaves a complex instrumental web imbedded with twisting, winding solos. The album achieves its summit with the epic, 16-minute title track, recorded with a lush, 26-piece orchestra. It exposes just how grand Uriah Heep's ambitions are. —*Daevid Jehnzen*

Look at Yourself / 1971 / Mercury ✦✦✦✦
Look at Yourself was the beginning of Uriah Heep's commercial fortunes, as it became the first of their albums to hit the UK charts. Musically, it compromised the boogie of their debut with the sweeping ambitions of *Salisbury*. —*Daevid Jehnzen*

Demons & Wizards / Jan. 1972 / Mercury ✦✦✦✦
As the fanciful title suggests, Uriah Heep began to delve deeper and deeper into mystical lyricism on their fourth album, which was supported by their spacy but earthy guitar rock. —*Daevid Jehnzen*

Magician's Birthday / Feb. 1972 / Mercury ✦✦✦✦
Magician's Birthday continued to expand the mystical concerns of *Demons & Wizards*, and it was nearly as successful, thanks to the group's knack for heavy guitars. —*Daevid Jehnzen*

Uriah Heep Live / 1973 / Mercury ✦✦
Uriah Heep may have been a popular concert attraction, but that didn't necessarily mean their concerts were always entertaining, as the dull *Uriah Heep Live* proves. —*Daevid Jehnzen*

Sweet Freedom / 1973 / Roadrunner ✦✦✦✦
Sweet Freedom continued Uriah Heep's mid-'70s winning streak. —*Daevid Jehnzen*

Wonderworld / 1974 / Roadrunner ✦✦✦
Wonderworld is indeed a wondrous world of heavy rock and spacy rock. Sadly, it was their last big hit album in the US. Sometimes, people just don't realize what they've got until it's gone. Fortunately, Uriah Heep stuck around for another 20 years to remind them of what they were missing. —*Daevid Jehnzen*

Return to Fantasy / 1975 / Castle ✦✦✦
The lads never really *left* fantasy behind, but the intent is appreciated all the same. Fans hoped the record would be a *Return to Magic* with the addition of ex-Roxy Music John Wetton, but it was nothing more than another fine Uriah Heep album. And, sometimes, that's enough, but a little magic every once in a while would be nice, too. —*Daevid Jehnzen*

● **The Best of Uriah Heep** / 1976 / Mercury ✦✦✦✦
Collecting the best moments of their sometimes inconsistent albums, *Best of Uriah Heep* is an effective introduction to the band. —*Daevid Jehnzen*

High and Mighty / 1976 / Bronze ✦✦
Well, they better not be getting *High and Mighty* if this is the kind of lukewarm product they're going to be pawning off on fans. The beginning of the decline is right here, folks. —*Daevid Jehnzen*

Firefly / 1977 / Castle ✦✦
Featuring a new singer in John Lawton, Uriah Heep still couldn't pull themselves up by the bootstraps with *Firefly*. —*Daevid Jehnzen*

Innocent Victim / 1977 / Castle ✦
Innocent Victim? Well, one guesses they're talking about their fans, since there's no way they were asking for this kind of faceless, plodding heavy rock. Again, you have to ask, where is the magic? —*Daevid Jehnzen*

Fallen Angel / 1978 / Castle ✦
Evidently the boys are speaking about themselves, since nothing illustrates Uriah Heep's fall from grace better than the bland boogie rock of *Fallen Angel*. —*Daevid Jehnzen*

A Time of Revelation / Aug. 5, 1996 / Essential ✦✦✦✦
A Time of Revelation is a four-disc box set spanning Uriah Heep's entire career. The bulk of the set draws from the Heep's '70s heyday, including

album tracks, live cuts, and previously unavailable-on-disc rarities. For the diehard collector, the set is a must-have for its obscure items, but the set is too much for casual fans, even those that want more than a simple greatest hits collection. After all, Uriah Heep were an album rock band that tailored individual albums, which means their songs often make more sense in the context of their original albums, not on compilations like these. —*Stephen Thomas Erlewine*

Us3

f. 1991, London, England
Jazz-Rap, Hip Hop
Jazz and hip-hop fusion collective Us3 scored a major hit in 1994 with "Cantaloop (Flip Fantasia)," a song which displayed the group's fondness for sampling classic recordings on the Blue Note label (in this case, Herbie Hancock's "Cantaloupe Island"). The group was founded in London in 1991 when concert promoter and jazz writer Geoff Wilkinson met Mel Simpson, who was writing music for television shows and ad jingles and had once played keyboards with John Mayall. The two produced an independent single, "Where Will We Be in the 21st Century?," which sold less than 250 copies. In 1992, their song "The Band That Played the Boogie" attracted the attention of Blue Note owner Capitol Records, which gave Simpson and Wilkinson free rein to sample anything from the catalog. The two immediately went to work, hiring several musicians and rappers Kobie Powell and Rahsaan Kelly, with Tukka Yoot joining later. The sessions resulted in the hit "Cantaloop" and the album *Hand on the Torch*. The group toured Japan and Europe, gradually weaning itself away from using samples in a live setting, and played a well-received show at the 1993 Montreux Jazz Festival. *Hand on the Torch* was ignored by most jazz publications, but was chosen Album of the Year by Japan's *Swing Journal*, and the group were named Jazz Musicians of the Year by Britain's *Independent*. After a nearly three-year delay, Us3 returned in 1997 with *Broadway & 52nd*, an album which received positive reviews but failed to generate a hit. —*Steve Huey*

● **Hand on the Torch** / Nov. 16, 1993 / Blue Note ✦✦✦✦
Hip-hop/jazzers Us3 have forged the most elaborate union between the styles since the early days of Gang Starr and A Tribe Called Quest. Blue Note's vast catalog gives them a huge advantage over several similar groups in terms of source material, and classic sounds by Art Blakey, Horace Silver and Herbie Hancock provide zest and fiber to their narratives. Indeed, when things falter, it's because the raps aren't always that creative. They are serviceable and sometimes catchy, but too often delivered without the snazzy touches or distinctive skills that make Quest and Gang Starr's material top-notch. But when words and music mesh, as on "Cantaloop" or "The Darkside," Us3 show how effectively hip-hop and jazz can blend. —*Ron Wynn*

Broadway & 52nd / Apr. 8, 1997 / Capitol ✦✦✦✦
Though Us3's second album *Broadway & 52nd* lacks a single song as infectious as "Cantaloop (Flip Fantasia)," it holds up better as an album. Geoff Wilkinson is better able to fuse his samples and hip-hop rhythms with jazz sensibilities, and while the rappers weigh the record down with inane rhymes, the production is quite intoxicating. —*Stephen Thomas Erlewine*

King Uszniewicz & His Uszniewicztones

f. 1969, Detroit, MI, db. 1979
Novelty, Rock & Roll
A hilariously inept Detroit bowling-alley lounge band fronted by Ernie "King" Uszniewicz (b.1945) from 1969 to 1979. The crudest tenor saxophonist in the history of rock 'n' roll, King Uszniewicz (pronounced "yousnev-vitch") & the U-Tones had only one single, issued on a local label during the '70s. Dubbed by one critic as "the worst oldies band I ever heard in my life," they played with a bludgeoning energy, oblivious to the fact that they were woefully shy in the talent department. However, when the group's first album showed up on several college-radio playlists in 1989, they earned a minor cult following among both record collectors and young alternative music fans. —*Stephen Thomas Erlewine*

Teenage Dance Party / Norton ✦✦✦
Their first album, featuring both sides of their original and lone 45 ("Surfin' School"/"Cry on My Shoulder") and insane versions of "Papa Ooh Mow Mow," "Little Latin Lupe Lu," and "This Should Go On Forever." Raw, crude, tuneless and wonderful. —*Stephen Thomas Erlewine*

● **Twistin' and Bowlin'** / Norton ✦✦✦✦
Subtitled "just when you thought it was safe to go back into the bowling alley," and more than living up to all that implies. Drunken, out-of-control versions of "Way Down Yonder in New Orleans," "Peppermint Twist," and Johnny Mathis' "Chances Are" are among the numerous highlights. Scary. —*Stephen Thomas Erlewine*

Doin' the Woo-Hoo / Norton ✦✦✦✦
More oldies-band mayhem. "At the Hop," "G.T.O.," "Love Letters in the Sand," the title cut, and King Uszniewicz's wife Arlene belting out "It's

My Party" are just a few of the standout tracks. Extremely potent stuff. —*Stephen Thomas Erlewine*

Utopia

f. 1976, New York, NY, **db.** 1986
Art-Rock/Progressive-Rock, Power Pop, Pop-Rock

Utopia is a rock quartet that theoretically features equal participation by its members, although singer and guitarist Todd Rundgren (b.Jun 22, 1948), who formed the band, is a recognized solo star and frequently dominates the group. The first two albums found them billed as Todd Rundgren's Utopia, a six-piece unit. But as of the third album, *Ra*, Utopia was a four-piece unit, including Rundgren, Roger Powell, John Wilcox, and Kasim Sulton, and that lineup was still in place as of 1986, which is the last time they released new material. —*William Ruhlmann*

Todd Rundgren's Utopia / Oct. 1974 / Bearsville ✦✦
After five solo albums released between 1970 and 1974, Todd Rundgren organized the band Utopia, although he also maintained a solo career. At this point, the group, a sextet featuring Kevin Ellman on percussion, Moogy Klingman and Ralph Schukett on keyboards, M. Frog Labat on synthesizers, and John Siegler on bass and cello, had little independent existence, as indicated by its billing, but later it would be a more equal unit. On this debut album, TR's U plays extended compositions—three of the four tracks run over 10 minutes each, with "The Ikon" clocking in over half an hour—in a hard rock/heavy metal/progressive rock mode with little of Rundgren's usual melodic appeal. —*William Ruhlmann*

Another Live / Oct. 1975 / Bearsville ✦✦
By the time of its second album, Todd Rundgren's Utopia had altered its personnel, with M. Frog Labat replaced by Roger Powell on synthesizers and John "Willie" Wilcox taking over the drum chair in the sextet. It remained a vehicle for Rundgren's harder-rocking tendencies, although this album, recorded live, was more kinetic, featuring group versions of such Rundgren favorites as "Heavy Metal Kids" and his signature song, "Just One Victory," plus a cover of the Move/ELO oldie "Do Ya." —*William Ruhlmann*

RA / Feb. 1977 / Bearsville ✦✦✦
By the time of its third album, Utopia had become an independent band, without the possessive "Todd Rundgren's" attached to it, and it was stripped down to a quartet of Rundgren, Roger Powell (keyboards), Kasim Sulton (bass), and John (Willie) Wilcox (drums). Rundgren shared writing and lead vocal chores with his bandmates. Ironically, the result sounded more like Rundgren's solo work than Utopia's first two albums, mixing Bernard Herrmann movie music with the show-music approach of "Magic Dragon Theatre" and a typically Rundgrenesque ballad style on "Eternal Love," which was written by Powell and Sulton and sung by Sulton. All of that was on side one, however, with side two largely given over to "Singing and the Glass Guitar," the kind of extended, progressive rock compositions that must have helped inspire *This Is Spinal Tap*. —*William Ruhlmann*

Oops! Wrong Planet / Sep. 1977 / Bearsville ✦✦✦
Utopia's fourth album (and second to be released in 1977) found the quartet moving in a much more pop-rock direction, with Todd Rundgren especially contributing catchy songs like "Love in Action" and "Love Is the Answer." —*William Ruhlmann*

Adventures in Utopia / Jan. 1980 / Bearsville ✦✦✦
At this point in Todd Rundgren's career, he seems to have juggled a schedule of alternating one year's solo work, during which he'd record two albums, with a year's work with Utopia, during which he'd also record two albums. Thus, in January, 1980, Utopia returned for the first of two albums, *Adventures in Utopia*. Having moved Utopia in more of a pop direction with *Oops! Wrong Planet*, Rundgren & Co. went even further this time and were rewarded with two hit singles, "Set Me Free" (No.27) and "The Very Last Time" (No.76), while the album, reaching No.32, was Utopia's highest-charting ever and bettered any Rundgren solo release except *Something/Anything?* Anyone who enjoyed the pop sound of Rundgren's early work would feel comfortable here. —*William Ruhlmann*

Deface the Music / Oct. 1980 / Bearsville ✦✦✦
On his solo album *Faithful*, Todd Rundgren had devoted a side of the LP to remaking elaborate studio recordings like the Beach Boys' "Good Vibrations" exactly. On Utopia's sixth album, it took a slightly different tack on the same notion, recording original songs in the style of the Beatles, as the Beatles evolved from "I Want to Hold Your Hand" to their

more psychedelic efforts. The result is not unlike Eric Idle's parody album *The Rutles*. —*William Ruhlmann*

Swing to the Right / Mar. 1982 / Bearsville ✦✦
After Todd Rundgren's 1981 solo year with *Healing*, Utopia returned to action with two 1982 albums, the first of which was this R&B-flavored effort, a far cry from the band's progressive rock beginnings, which even featured a cover of "For the Love of Money." Maybe because things at Bearsville were winding down (this was the last Rundgren or Utopia album on the label), *Swing to the Right* missed cracking the Top 100 on the LP chart, but songs like "Lysistrata," a Rundgren pop tune based on the Greek antiwar play, showed the group was still in good form on occasion. —*William Ruhlmann*

Utopia / Sep. 1982 / Rhino ✦✦
For its second album of 1982, Utopia moved from the Bearsville subsidiary of Warner Bros. Records, a division of Warner Communications, to the Network subsidiary of Elektra/Asylum Records, another division of Warner Communications. Sounds like corporate shuffling, but it's the difference between being in print (the Bearsville recordings were reissued by Rhino in 1987) and being out of print. That's a shame, since this self-titled album-and-a-half (it was issued as two LPs, the second of which had Side Three pressed on both sides) is one of Utopia's better efforts, featuring their third and final hit single, "Feet Don't Fail Me Now" (No.82), as well as the excellent "Hammer In My Heart" and "Princess Of The Universe," one of the group's best rockers, sung by drummer Willie Wilcox. —*William Ruhlmann*

POV / Jan. 1985 / Food For Thought ✦✦
Utopia's last album of new material, *POV* is not one of its more impressive efforts. Its best track is "Mated," a characteristically emotional Todd Rundgren ballad, but otherwise the songs don't live up to Utopia's usual standards. —*William Ruhlmann*

Trivia / Jun. 1986 / Passport ✦✦
Trivia is a compilation album of Utopia tracks from 1982-1986, including such favorites as "Hammer In My Heart," "Feet Don't Fail Me Now," "Princess Of The Universe," "Crybaby," and "Mated." It's a good selection, but it was superseded by the more complete *Anthology (1974-1985)* in 1989 and is, in any case, out of print. —*William Ruhlmann*

● **Anthology** / May 1989 / Rhino ✦✦✦✦
Annotator Bud Scoppa calls this "the definitive Utopia album," which is fair enough. Utopia's ten albums tended to be uneven affairs, with the first three, *Todd Rundgren's Utopia*, *Another Live*, and *RA*, very much in a fusion/progressive style that could be somewhat opaque. *Deface The Music* was an overt pastiche of the Beatles, but the other six albums also bore the influence of pop's master group, as the four band members shared songwriting and lead vocal duties in a series of commercial-sounding ballads and rockers, only three of which became charting singles. *Anthology* rescues those tracks and several others from *Oblivion* (one of their ironic album titles) and even gives a taste of the band's early space-rock tendencies. A good companion to the Todd Rundgren *Anthology* released simultaneously by Rhino. —*William Ruhlmann*

Oblivion Pov & Some Trivia / Apr. 9, 1996 / Rhino ✦✦✦✦
Utopia lasted for a decade or so, originally to air out some of Todd Rundgren's more experimental musical ideas and later settling down into a quartet format that veered comfortably between power-pop and an interesting set of rock variations. Unfortunately, the one thing that seemed to elude the band was serious commercial success—Utopia developed a strong fan following, but somehow never managed to achieve the huge sales that conventional wisdom suggested should be theirs. With the 1983 release of *Oblivion*, the band had signed with Passport Records and the future seemed to be full of possibilities for success. Unfortunately, internal tensions were beginning to splinter the band, making the recording of *POV* a difficult process. Two tracks were recorded for *Trivia*, a compilation, and that was it for the band—and for their label, Passport, which sank along with JEM Records, a major independent distributor, with the consequence that this is the first major CD release for these cuts. Altogether a pity, because Utopia consistently made excellent music. Rundgren's influence was felt throughout, of course, but the input from Willie Wilcox, Kasim Sulton, and Roger Powell effectively redirected Rundgren and provided Utopia with its own musical identity. In some respects it could be said that Utopia's downfall was due to its members' insistence on intelligence—there is a great deal of clever material here. This Rhino two-disc compilation is an excellent place to start investigating the Utopia catalog—and an excellent place to conclude. —*Steven McDonald*

V

Steve Vai

b. Jun. 6, 1960, Long Island, NY
Hard Rock, Fusion, Heavy Metal, Guitar Virtuoso
Vai was a pupil of Joe Satriani as a teenager and studied at The Berklee School of Music before moving to Los Angeles at age 19. He was a huge fan of Frank Zappa's and joined Zappa's band after proving that he knew most of the repertoire and could transcribe orchestral pieces by ear. Zappa credited him on albums as the "stunt guitarist." He released the self-produced *Flex-Able* in 1984, combining his Zappa and Satriani influences, and went on to play with Alcatrazz, David Lee Roth, and Whitesnake. Vai released his finest solo effort, the varied *Passion and Warfare*, in 1990. He then formed a backing group called VAI featuring vocalist Devin Townsend for *Sex & Religion* before recording the solo *Alien Love Secrets; Fire Garden* followed in 1996. Vai is considered to be one of rock's top instrumentalists. — *Steve Huey*

Flex-able / 1984 / Akashic ♦♦♦♦
The self-released solo album from this former Zappa guitarist, featuring Zappa-influenced vocals, was recorded by Vai at home on an eight-track machine. The CD offers extra material from the *Flex-able* sessions originally released as a ten-inch EP. — *Paul Kohler*

● **Passion & Warfare** / Sep. 1990 / Relativity ♦♦♦♦
One of the most creative, musical, and mystical guitar albums ever made, it is a must-have. — *Paul Kohler*

Sex & Religion / Jul. 27, 1993 / Relativity ♦♦
Steve Vai formed a new straight-ahead heavy metal combo for the follow-up to his instrumental masterpiece, *Passion & Warfare*. In this context, the imaginative guitarist is saddled down by a pedestrian band and an overwrought vocalist, which limits Vai's ability to stretch out. Consequently, the record is the most predictable and conventional—not to mention boring—of Vai's usually remarkable career. — *Stephen Thomas Erlewine*

Alien Love Secrets / Mar. 21, 1995 / Relativity ♦♦♦
After the disastrous full-band heavy metal project of *Sex & Religion*, Steve Vai returned to recording solo with *Alien Love Secrets*, a moodier, more atmospheric collection than his masterpiece *Passion and Warfare*, which makes it slightly revelatory. With the new sonic textures, the guitarist again demonstrates his fluid technique, which manages to never become completely mechanical. — *Stephen Thomas Erlewine*

Fire Garden / Sep. 17, 1996 / Epic ♦♦♦♦
Steve Vai offers the following words of advice about *Fire Garden*, his fifth solo album: "This is essentially a double CD packed onto one. In this package there are over 74 minutes of music. Phase I (for the most part) is all instrumental music, and Phase II (for the most part) is all vocal selections, with the exception of 'Warm Regards.' ... Being as dense as it is, this CD may best be experienced by devouring it in pieces, but those with a strong constitution may dare to consume it whole as it is." Seldom has an artist provided more telling liner notes for their own album. *Fire Garden* is indeed a dense album, filled with a never-ending arrray of sonic textures and guitar tones. Unlike most guitar heroes, Vai doesn't treat music as a way to demonstrate his technical skill. Instead, he channels his astonishing technical skill into creating soundscapes that will showcase his virtuosity as often as not. The result is a guitar album that is enjoyable for non-guitar freaks, as well. Vai's vocals still have a way to go before they are as expressive as his instrumental work, but this subtle and dense concept album is the closest he's ever gotten to integrating the two sides of his musical personality together. An impressive effort from a musician that continues to grow and stretch himself with each new release. — *Stephen Thomas Erlewine*

Ritchie Valens

b. May 13, 1941, Pacoima, CA, **d.** Feb. 3, 1959, Clear Lake, IA
Guitar, Vocals / Rock 'n' Roll
Valens will forever be known primarily as one of the two rock stars (along with the Big Bopper) who perished with Buddy Holly when their private plane crashed in the midst of a Midwest tour in 1959. At the time, Valens had just established himself as one of the most promising young talents in rock 'n' roll, just missing the top of the charts with his ballad "Donna," and recording a pioneering blend of rock and Latin music with its almost equally popular flipside, "La Bamba." More than almost any other rock star who died prematurely, it's difficult to assess his unrealized potential; he was only 17 at the time of his death, and had just barely begun to make records.

The first Hispanic rock star, Valens grew up in Los Angeles suburbs, and was playing guitar by the time he was in junior high school. Inspired by Little Richard and rockabilly performers, he was discovered by producer Bob Keane in 1958. Keane signed the guitarist to his Del-Fi label, and they soon had a sizable hit with the brash "Come on Let's Go," which made No. 42. It was the pensive, almost awkward "Donna" that got him to No. 2 in early 1959. More innovative was the flipside, "La Bamba," sung entirely in Spanish, and featuring some fierce guitar work, as well as the thick sound of the Danelectro bass, which gave the instrument more electric presence than it had ever previously enjoyed on a rock 'n' roll disc.

Valens only had about two albums worth of material in the can, as well as some lo-fi live tapes of a gig at a local junior high, before his death; undoubtedly some or many of these were demos or unfinished tracks. A few other singers emulated Valens' Mexican-American brand of rock in the following years, most notably Chan Romero (originator of "Hippy Hippy Shake," who also recorded for Del-Fi and used some of the same musicians that had backed Valens) and Chris Montez. In the 1980s and 1990s, Los Angeles Latino rock band Los Lobos were often cited for reflecting Valens' influence. The 1987 film *La Bamba* (whose soundtrack featured Los Lobos) gave his story the Hollywood treatment, exposing his legacy to millions even as it introduced the usual distortions and factual errors in its dramatization of his brief life. — *Richie Unterberger*

In Concert at Pacoima Jr. High / 1960 / Rhino ♦♦♦
A bizarre piece of work: a home-made tape of a high school concert. Possibly rock's earliest "official" live album, padded with narration and unfinished studio tracks. In shaky sound, but unique. — *Bruce Eder*

The Best of Ritchie Valens / 1986 / Rhino ♦♦♦♦
The virtually complete recording legacy of an all-too-brief career. — *Bruce Eder*

The Ritchie Valens Story / Jun. 15, 1993 / Del Fi ♦♦
While this compilation features the official versions of Ritchie's three biggest songs ("La Bamba," "Donna," and "Come on, Let's Go"), the bulk of it is turned over to recently unearthed rehearsal takes and demos of his better-known sides. Not the place to start your Valens collection, but a real good place to go after you've absorbed the hits. — *Cub Koda*

● **Rockin' All Night: The Very Best of Ritchie Valens** / 1995 / Del-Fi ♦♦♦♦
This supplants all previously available Valens best-of packages, at least until Del-Fi releases the inevitable multi-CD box set. With 22 tracks compiled here, this single-disc compilation covers almost everything the average fan will want to hear and then some. Hardliners will possibly decry the absence of anything from *In Concert at Pacoima Jr. High*, but will rejoice with the inclusion of the previously unreleased "stereo mix" (actually two mono mixes synched up, giving Ritchie's guitar intro a phased out sound that's almost psychedelic) of "La Bamba." With no

maddening alternate takes or studio fluff aboard, this is the first stop you make in absorbing the genius of this pioneering Chicano artist, whose absence as a member of the Rock'n'Roll Hall Of Fame becomes more ponderous with each passing year. —*Cub Koda*

Ritchie Valens: The Lost Tapes / Nov. 6, 1995 / Del-Fi ✦✦✦
The first major release of Ritchie Valens demos reveals his creative process in fragmentary form, with multiple outtakes of songs like "La Bamba" and "Cry Cry Cry," among others. The sound is somewhat shaky at times (none of this material was intended to be heard in public) but the variations on familiar songs show Valens' evolution as a musician and composer, as well as the contribution of session players and arrangers like Rene Hall (who also played on Sam Cooke's "You Send Me") and Carol Kaye. —*Bruce Eder*

Van Der Graaf Generator

f. 1967, Manchester, England, **db.** 1978
Art-Rock/Progressive-Rock
An eye-opening trip to San Francisco's Haight-Ashbury district during the summer of 1967 inspired British-born drummer Chris Judge-Smith to compose a list of possible names for the rock group he wished to form. Upon his return to Manchester University, he began performing with singer-songwriter Peter Hammill and keyboardist Nick Peame; employing one of the names from Judge-Smith's list, the band dubbed itself Van Der Graaf Generator (after a machine which creates static electricity), eventually earning an intense cult following as one of the era's preeminent art rock groups.

Despite the early involvement of Judge-Smith and Eames, the group found true success as a vehicle for Hammill, whose dark, existentialist lyrics made him the focus of considerable attention. After the release of the 1968 single "People You Were Going To," Judge-Smith left Van Der Graaf Generator, which by then consisted of Hammill, keyboardist Hugh Banton, bassist Keith Ellis, and drummer Guy Evans. The group soon split, and in 1968 Hammill entered the studio, ostensibly to record a solo album; however, he ultimately called in his ex-bandmates for assistance, and when *The Aerosol Grey Machine* appeared, it did so under the Van Der Graaf Generator name. Although Ellis was replaced by Nic Potter and woodwind player David Jackson, the reconstituted group continued on for 1969's *The Least We Can Do Is Wave to Each Other*. After 1970's *H to He Who Am the Only One*, Potter departed; the Generator recorded one more LP, 1971's *Pawn Hearts*, before Hammill left for a solo career, putting an end to the group.

After five solo efforts, however, Hammill again reformed Van Der Graaf Generator in 1975 for *Godbluff*. Following a pair of 1976 albums, *Still Life* and *World Record*, Banton and Jackson exited; as simply Van Der Graaf, the band recorded *The Quiet Zone* with new violinist Graham Smith. After a 1978 live set, *Vital*, the group officially disbanded, although most members made appearances on Hammill's subsequent solo records. Twice during the 1990's, Van Der Graaf also reunited for one-off gigs. —*Jason Ankeny*

The Least We Can Do Is Wave to Each Other / Feb. 1969 / Blue Plate ✦✦✦
On their ambitious second album, bandleader Peter Hammill was already writing enduring songs. —*Michael P. Dawson*

● **H to He, Who Am the Only One** / Jan. 1970 / Blue Plate ✦✦✦✦
A superb album, it includes the heavy metal-ish "Killer" and a guest appearance by guitarist Robert Fripp. —*Michael P. Dawson*

Pawn Hearts / 1971 / Blue Plate ✦✦✦✦
Lengthy progressive-rock epics mix with Peter Hammill's intensely emotional lyrics. Robert Fripp guests on guitar. —*Michael P. Dawson*

Godbluff / 1975 / Blue Plate ✦✦✦
The start of a mid-'70s comeback, after a long hiatus, was stark, doomy, and richly musical. —*Michael P. Dawson*

World Record / 1976 / Blue Plate ✦✦✦✦
The last album by the "classic" Van Der Graaf lineup was released in 1976. —*Michael P. Dawson*

Still Life / 1976 / Blue Plate ✦✦✦✦
The second and best of the mid-'70s comeback albums, it's highlighted by the incredible title track. —*Michael P. Dawson*

The Quiet Zone / 1977 / Blue Plate ✦✦✦
This recording debuted a new VDGG lineup, with violin and bass taking the place of sax and organ—a somewhat rawer sound. —*Michael P. Dawson*

Vital / 1978 / Blue Plate ✦✦
The last Van Der Graaf release was a 1978 live double-LP on a single CD. —*Michael P. Dawson*

Maida Vale / 1995 / Strange Fruit ✦✦✦

Van Halen

f. 1974, Pasadena, CA
Hard Rock, Pop-Rock, Heavy Metal
With their 1978 eponymous debut, Van Halen simultaneously re-wrote the rules for rock guitar and hard rock in general. Guitarist Eddie Van Halen redefined what electric guitar could do, developing a blindingly fast technique with a variety of self-taught two-handed tapping, hammer-ons, pull-offs, and effects that mimicked the sound of machines and animals. It was wildly inventive and over-the-top, equaled only by vocalist David Lee Roth, who brought the role of a metal singer to near performance art standards. Roth wasn't blessed with great technique, unlike Eddie, but he had a flair for showmanship, derived as much from lounge performers as from Robert Plant. Together, they made Van Halen into the most popular American rock 'n' roll band of the late '70s and early '80s, and, in the process, set the template for hard rock and heavy metal for the '80s. Throughout the '80s, it was impossible not to hear Van Halen's instrumental technique on records that ranged from the heaviest metal to soft-pop. Furthermore, Roth's irony-drenched antics were copied by singers who took everything literally. Once of those was Sammy Hagar, an arena-rock veteran from the '70s who replaced Roth after the vocalist had a falling out with Van Halen in 1985. Hagar stayed with the band longer than Roth, helping the group stay at the top of the charts through the late '80s and early '90s. However, the group's sales began to slide in the mid-'90s, just as tensions between Hagar and Eddie began to arise. In one of the most disastrous publicity stunts in rock history, Hagar was fired (or quit) and Roth was brought back on, seemingly as a permanent member, but only for two songs on a greatest hits album. He was subsequently replaced by Gary Cherone, a former member of Extreme.

Through all the upheaval over lead vocalists, Eddie Van Halen and his prodigious talent remained at the core of Van Halen. The son of a Dutch bandleader, Eddie and his family moved from the Netherlands to Pasadena, California in 1967, when he was 12 years old and his older brother Alex was 14. As their father supported the family by playing in wedding bands, Eddie and Alex continued their classical piano training. Soon, both boys were enraptured by rock 'n' roll. Eddie learned how to play drums and Alex took up the guitar, eventually switching instruments. The brothers began a hard-rock called Mammoth and began playing around Pasadena, eventually meeting David Lee Roth. At the time, Roth, who had been raised in a wealthy Californian family, was singing in Redball Jet. Impressed by the Van Halen brothers, he joined forces with the group. Shortly afterward, bassist Michael Anthony, who was singing with Snake, became a member of Mammoth.

After discovering another band had the rights to the name Mammoth, the group decided to call themselves Van Halen in 1974, rejecting the proposed Rat Salade. For the next three years, Van Halen played throughout Pasadena, Santa Barbara, and Los Angles, playing both clubs and hotel bars. The band's repertoire covered everything from pop and rock to disco, but they eventually worked in their own original material. Within a few years, they had become the most popular local band in Los Angeles, and Eddie became well-known for his groundbreaking technique. In 1977, Kiss' Gene Simmons financed a demo recording session for Van Halen after seeing them at the Starwood club. On the strength of Simmons' recommendation, Mo Ostin and Ted Templeman signed Van Halen to Warner Bros., releasing the band's debut the following year. *Van Halen* became a hit due to strong word-of-mouth, constant touring and support from AOR radio. Within three months, the album had gone gold and five months later, it went platinum. It would eventually sell over six million copies, thanks to the album-rock staples "You Really Got Me," "Jamie's Cryin'," and "Runnin' With the Devil."

Van Halen II, released in 1979, continued the band's success, as "Dance the Night Away" became their first Top 20 single. *Women and Children First* (1980) didn't have any charting singles, but it was a success on the album charts, reaching No. 6. The band supported the album with their first headlining, international arena tour, and the group was quickly on its way to being superstars. Released in 1981, *Fair Warning* wasn't quite as popular as their previous records, yet it still peaked at No. 6. *Diver Down*, released in 1982, was a huge hit, spawning a No. 12 cover of Roy Orbison's "(Oh) Pretty Woman" and reaching No. 3.

While all of their previous albums were successful, Van Halen didn't become superstars until 1984, when their album *1984* became an across-the-boards smash. Released on New Year's Day, *1984* rocketed to No. 2 on the strength of the No. 1 single "Jump." Like many songs on the album, "Jump" was driven by Eddie's new synthesizer, and while Roth was intially reluctant to use electronics, the expansion of the group's sound was widely praised. Throughout 1984, Van Halen gained steam, as "I'll Wait" and "Panama" became Top 15 singles, and "Hot for Teacher" became a radio and MTV staple. Despite the band's breakthrough success, things were not well within the band. During their *1984* tour, each member played separate solo sets, and were physically separated on the stage. Roth was unhappy with Eddie's appearance on Michael Jackson's 1983 hit "Beat It," and Van Halen grew tired of the comic antics of Diamond Dave. In 1985, Roth released a solo EP, *Crazy from the Heat*, which spawned hit covers of "California Girls" and "Just A Gigolo / I Ain't Got Nobody." When Roth delayed the recording of Van Halen's followup to *1984*, he was fired from the band.

Most observers were taken by surprise when Van Halen named Sammy Hagar as Roth's replacement. The former lead singer of Montrose, Hagar's solo career had been sporadically successful, highlighted by such arena-metal hits as "Three-Lock Box" and "I Can't Drive 55." Though many critics suspected Hagar wouldn't be able to sustain Van Halen's remarkable success, his first album with the band, 1986's *5150*, was a huge hit, reaching No. 1 and spawning the hit singles "Why Can't This Be Love," "Dreams," and "Love Walks In." Released in 1988, *OU812* was just as successful, earning stronger reviews than its predecessor and generating the hits "When It's Love" and "Finish What You Started." For *Unlawful Carnal Knowledge*, released in 1991, was another No. 1 hit, partially due to the MTV hit "Right Now." Van Halen followed the album with its first live record, the double-album *Van Halen Live: Right Here, Right Now* in 1993.

By the spring 1995 release of *Balance*, tensions between Eddie Van Halen and Sammy Hagar had grown considerably. Van Halen had recently undergone well-publicized treatment for alcoholism, and Hagar was notorious for his party-hearty ways, even writing a paean to Amsterdam's hash bars with "Amsterdam" on *Balance*. Furthermore, the band had become subject to criticism that it simply repeated a formula. While *Balance* was successful, entering the charts at No. 1 and selling two million copies shortly after its release, it stalled quickly afterward. The band wanted to release a greatest hits collection, but Hagar balked at the idea, escalating the tensions even further. Following a skirmish in 1996 over the recording of a song for the *Twister* soundtrack, Eddie decided to make a change by switching singers. Van Halen began recording new material with Roth without informing Hagar, who went ballistic upon learning of the group's reunion. According to Hagar, Eddie fired him shortly afterward; Van Halen claimed Sammy quit. Roth proceeded to record two new songs for Van Halen's *Best of... Vol. 1*, and once the reunion became public, the rock media reacted positively to the news; MTV began airing a "welcome back" commercial days after the announcement. However, the "reunion" was not to be. Following an appearance at the MTV Music Awards, Van Halen fired Roth from the band, claiming that he was only on board to record two new songs. Dave said that he was duped into recording the songs, believing that reunion was permanent. Former Extreme vocalist Gary Cherone was announced as the band's new lead singer. Though the resulting *Best Of... Vol.1* was a success, Eddie Van Halen's reputation as a nice guy was tarnished over the entire affair. Van Halen's next album was scheduled for the fall of 1997. — *Stephen Thomas Erlewine*

★ **Van Halen** / 1978 / Warner Brothers ✦✦✦✦✦
Van Halen's eponymous debut was an epochal album in the history of hard rock and heavy metal, providing the template for hard rock bands for the next decade and a half. What's even more remarkable is how they redefined the rules for hard-rock without changing the instrumentation or structure at all—they simply took it to the extreme. Everything about *Van Halen* is over-the-top, from David Lee Roth's grandstanding vocals and Eddie Van Halen's exaggerated riffing to the rhythm section's absurd eighth-note pulse. Eddie dominates the record, firing off hooks and solos with a liquid grace, thereby providing a cover for Roth, who can't really sing, but provides enough charisma to make him an excellent frontman. And the songs, which have been culled from years of playing clubs and hotels, are all first-rate hard-rockers and many of them—"Runnin' With the Devil," "Ain't Talkin' 'Bout Love," "Jamie's Cryin'," "Ice Cream Man," "I'm the One," "Atomic Punk," the Kinks cover "You Really Got Me" and Eddie's showcase "Eruption"—became hard rock classics. Decades after the album's release, echoes of the big, dumb riffs, complex soloing and simple, sing-along melodies could be heard throughout mainstream rock, but *Van Halen* retained its energy, simply because no one else could do it better. — *Stephen Thomas Erlewine*

Van Halen II / 1979 / Warner Brothers ✦✦✦✦
Van Halen's second album sounded identical to their debut, yet it lacked the consistent songwriting of the first album. "Dance the Night Away" was a Top 20 hit and "Beautiful Girls" became one of their AOR staples, but most of the album sounded rushed and incomplete. — *Stephen Thomas Erlewine*

Women & Children First / 1980 / Warner Brothers ✦✦✦✦
Women and Children First expanded the musical range of Van Halen, as Eddie Van Halen increased his bag of tricks, flipping out bizarre noises and lightning-fast licks as mere asides. David Lee Roth used Eddie's aural jokes as a platform for lyrical jokes. In a whirlwind performance, Roth acted more like a comedian than a lead singer, and

while that may be annoying on occasion, it certainly kept the record interesting. — *Stephen Thomas Erlewine*

Fair Warning / 1981 / Warner Brothers ✦✦✦
Perhaps as a reaction to David Lee Roth's unhinged performance on *Women & Children First, Fair Warning* was dominated by Eddie Van Halen, who has rarely played better than he has here, filling the record with imaginative sonic textures. However, sonic textures don't necessarily make for great songs, and that's the main problem with *Fair Warning*. Eddie's guitar has as much personality as Diamond Dave's strutting vocals, and given the right context could carry an album as effectively as Roth did with *Women & Children First*, but the songs do not provide a consistently strong support for his playing. Still, few guitarists match his power or his grace, and his performance is quite compelling. — *Stephen Thomas Erlewine*

Diver Down / 1982 / Warner Brothers ✦✦✦
Although it went platinum, *Fair Warning* didn't match the multi-platinum standards of Van Halen's first three records, so the group revamped their sound slightly for the follow-up, *Diver Down*. Adding the slightest hints of synthesizers and streamlining both the guitar indulgences of Eddie Van Halen and the vocal excesses of David Lee Roth, the album contained some of the group's most pop-oriented performances—and they were all in the guise of covers. "(Oh) Pretty Woman" and "Dancing in the Street" had the traditional mechanical Van Halen rhythmic pulse, as well as concise solos from Eddie and restrained vocals from Diamond Dave, which helped them become the hits they were designed to be. If they were offset by more original material like "Hang 'Em High," the concessions would have been acceptable, but the rest of *Diver Down* is filled with covers, including "Big Bad Bill," "Where Have All the Good Times Gone," and a closing "Happy Trails." All of the songs are professionally performed, and the music features more ideas than most previous Van Halen albums, but the lack of strong original material makes *Diver Down* less of an accomplishment than it appears. — *Stephen Thomas Erlewine*

☆ **1984** / 1984 / Warner Brothers ✦✦✦✦✦
Designed as a showcase for Eddie's burgeoning infatuation with synthesizers, *1984* brought heavy metal storming into the '80s—it was the first hard rock record to acknowledge and incorporate the technological advances of new wave. And it wasn't just in the synthesizers that Van Halen changed. *1984* contains more pop songs than ever before, highlighted by the classic "Jump." Despite his initial reservations with the material, David Lee Roth rises to the occasion throughout the record, elevating his Diamond Dave persona to ridiculous heights on the stylish hard-rocker "Panama," the tongue-in-cheek "Hot for Teacher," and "I'll Wait," where he falls in love with a centerfold. A few songs are simple hard rock workouts, but what sticks around are all of the aforementioned songs. Each has huge guitar hooks and catchy melodies, and are kept in check by Eddie Van Halen, who uses his solos as a way to further the song instead of designing the song to showcase his playing. While the synth riffs, particularly the instrumental opener, sound incredibly dated, the best songs retain their vitality and illustrate why Van Halen was the leading American metal band of their era. — *Stephen Thomas Erlewine*

5150 / 1986 / Warner Brothers ✦✦✦
Van Halen proves it can survive in the post-Roth era, as Eddie continues to burn up the fretboard and Sammy Hagar turns out to fit into the group's style just fine. Includes "Why Can't This Be Love," "Dreams," and "Love Walks In." — *William Ruhlmann*

OU812 / 1988 / Warner Brothers ✦✦✦
Van Halen broke open the pop innovations of *5150* with *OU812*, their second album with Sammy Hagar. On *OU812*, Hagar's direct approach is fully incorporated into the group, as the band churns out straightahead heavy rockers like "Black and Blue" and pulsing power ballads like "Feels So Good." Under Eddie's direction, the group adds a couple of stylistic quirks—from the chicken-picking of "Finish What You Started" and the Hawaiian flourishes of "Cabo Wabo" to the driving, jazz-inflected metallic "Mine All Mine"—which make *OU812* one of the band's most intriguing and rewarding albums. — *Stephen Thomas Erlewine*

For Unlawful Carnal Knowledge / Jun. 17, 1991 / Warner Brothers ✦✦
The smirking title indicates the true nature of *For Unlawful Carnal Knowledge*, Van Halen's third album with Sammy Hagar. Backing away from the diversity of *OU812*, the band turns in some of the most basic, straightforward rock 'n' roll of their career. At times, *F.U.C.K.* recalls the sleek hard rock of Hagar's early-'80s albums, and it's undeniable that his limited vocal power had a great deal to do with the obvious nature of most of this music. While the band is still tight and professional—and Eddie's guitar work remains impressive—the songwriting is, by and large, undistinguished, with the anthemic "Right Now" standing out as the most memorable song of the batch, mainly because of its incessant chorus. — *Stephen Thomas Erlewine*

Van Halen Live: Right Here, Right Now / Feb. 23, 1993 / Warner Brothers ♦♦
Van Halen assembled its first live album, the two-CD *Live: Right Here Right Now*, from a collection of tapes dating from 1985, when Sammy Hagar replaced David Lee Roth, to the present. Only a few songs recall Roth's days, and too many songs from *For Unlawful Carnal Knowledge* are featured (10 of its 11). With the exception of the consistently impressive Eddie Van Halen, the album slows to a halt during the solo passages. Most of the time, the performances aren't all that different from the original studio recordings. Despite the moments of tedium, *Live: Right Here Right Now* deserves to be in any real Van Halen fan's collection; those who aren't devoted to the band would be advised to stick with the original albums. — *Stephen Thomas Erlewine*

Balance / 1995 / Warner Brothers ♦♦
Balance tries to open up the Van Hagar formula somewhat. Eddie Van Halen sincerely attempts to improve the group musically, by adding more subtle and assured ballads and more fearless rockers. No matter how hard he tries, he's weighed down by the most predictable rhythm section in all of rock 'n' roll, which gives each number the same unvarying deadlocked pulse, completely obliterating Eddie's increased musical sensitivity. Of course, he isn't helped by Hagar, either. Hagar also tries to follow the social conscience that served him so well on "Right Now," on the first single "(Don't Tell Me What) Love Can Do." Unfortunately, he can't help himself and slips back to the raucous partying of "Amsterdam"—you know, the place where they're allowed to smoke pot and stuff. — *Stephen Thomas Erlewine*

● **Best of Van Halen, Vol. 1** / Oct. 22, 1996 / Warner Brothers ♦♦♦♦
In theory, a Van Halen greatest-hits collection should be easy to assemble, but *The Best of Van Halen, Vol. 1* proves that isn't the case. By trying to give the David Lee Roth and Sammy Hagar eras equal space, they wind up not representing either particularly well. The first eight songs run through several of Diamond Dave's biggest songs—"Ain't Talkin' 'Bout Love," "Runnin' with the Devil," "And the Cradle Will Rock," "Jump," and "Panama." It's hard to argue with any of the choices, yet significant songs like "You Really Got Me," "Beautiful Girls," "(Oh) Pretty Woman," "I'll Wait," and "Hot for Teacher" are missing. Similarly, the Sammy era has many big hits—"Why Can't This Be Love," "Dreams," "When It's Love," and "Right Now"—but skips over hits like "Love Walks In," "Black and Blue," and "Finish What Ya Started." Clearly, the collection would have been better served if it had been assembled as a double-disc set, with Dave and Sammy getting a disc apiece. Furthermore, the much-hyped reunion tracks with Roth, "Can't Get This Stuff No More" and "Me Wise Magic," are a slight disappointment; the band sounds good, but neither track contains a memorable hook. Also, the presence of "Humans Being," one of Van Halen's worst tracks, is an insult, considering how many great songs are missing. Nevertheless, *Best Of, Vol. 1* remains a good single-disc encapsulation of Van Halen's career, even if it isn't a definitive retrospective. — *Stephen Thomas Erlewine*

Luther Vandross

b. 1951, Bronx, NY
Vocals / Soul, Dance-Pop, Urban, Quiet Storm
In R&B music, Luther Vandross ranked with Prince, Stevie Wonder, and Michael Jackson as one of the most successful singer-songwriters and producers of the '80s. Amazingly, unlike those peers, Vandross for the most part did not cross over to widespread pop appeal, a situation that finally began to change at the end of the '80s and the start of the '90s. Born in New York City, Vandross has an elastic tenor that made him a natural for backup singing and commercial work in the '70s, when he became a top session vocalist. In 1975, Vandross worked with David Bowie on the latter's *Young Americans* album, even co-writing (with Bowie and John Lennon) the No. 1 hit "Fame." In the second half of the '70s, he recorded under a variety of guises, cutting two albums for Cotillion under the name "Luther," recording with the session groups Roundtree and Change, and singing on hits by Chic.
In 1981, Vandross signed with Epic and released his debut album *Never Too Much*, which topped the R&B chart and sold a million copies. The title track was also an R&B No. 1 hit single and reached the pop Top 40. Vandross went on to produce albums for Aretha Franklin and other female singers, while maintaining his own career through the '80s. His albums *Forever, for Always, for Love* (1982), *Busy Body* (1983), *The Night I Fell in Love* (1985), *Give Me the Reason* (1986), and *Any Love* (1988) were all million-sellers that spawned major R&B hits, but Vandross' pop success was spotty until 1989, when Epic released *The Best of Luther Vandross . . . The Best of Love*, a double-pocket greatest-hits album containing the new track "Here and Now," which became Vandross' first Top Ten pop hit. That proved his breakthrough, and Vandross' next album, *Power of Love* (1991), another million-seller, featured two pop hits, "Power of Love/Love Power" and "Don't Want to Be a Fool." Things basically went smoothly for Luther Vandross on the commercial

front in the early '90s, though not so smoothly behind the scenes. He toured with Anita Baker in 1990 and En Vogue in 1993, and on both tours there were disputes that eventually went public. Vandross issued *Never Let Me Go* in 1993, and while it did well, it wasn't quite the commercial powerhouse of his past releases. Vandross bounced back with 1994's all-covers *Songs*, which went double platinum, and 1996's *Your Secret Love*. — *William Ruhlmann*

Never Too Much / 1981 / Epic ♦♦♦♦
The auspicious debut, demonstrating Vandross' gorgeous vocal arrangements and his lush, romantic singing on the No.1 R&B smash "Never Too Much" and the Top Ten "Don't You Know That?," plus the tour de force version of "A House Is Not a Home." — *William Ruhlmann*

Forever for Always for Love / 1982 / Epic ♦♦♦
Luther Vandross scored his first platinum album and cemented his status as the new heartthrob king of the 1980s with this fine second release. Strangely, his sublime version of "Since I Lost My Baby" wasn't issued as a single, but the combination hit "Bad Boy/Having A Party" was an R&B sensation and helped secure the album's crossover success. — *Ron Wynn*

Busy Body / 1983 / Epic ♦♦♦
An accurate title for a man who seemed to be producing all the divas in the business at this time, including Dionne Warwick, who turns up for a duet on "How Many More Times Can We Say Goodbye." It's one of three R&B Top Ten hits here, the others being "I'll Let You Slide" and the brilliant medley "Superstar/Until You Come Back to Me (That's What I'm Gonna Do)." — *William Ruhlmann*

The Night I Fell in Love / 1985 / Epic ♦♦♦♦
A wonderful version of Stevie Wonder's "Creepin'" almost gets lost on another hit-filled collection, which includes the Top Five R&B smashes "Til My Baby Comes Home" and "It's Over Now." — *William Ruhlmann*

Give Me the Reason / 1986 / Epic ♦♦♦
Luther Vandross was riding high in the 1980s, dominating the R&B charts and slowly, but steadily, increasing his pop exposure. This was his fourth consecutive platinum smash and second straight double-platinum winner, but beyond that was a superbly sung, expressive triumph. "Stop To Love" and "Give Me The Reason" were beautifully produced, arranged, and performed numbers and huge R&B hits (the latter a chart topper), and deserved a better pop fate. — *Ron Wynn*

Any Love / 1988 / Epic ♦♦♦♦
There were some who felt that Vandross suffered a slight slump when this album only reached the platinum level after two consecutive double-platinum winners. But "Here And Now" was a huge smash, and by now the pop crowd was fully aware of Vandross' vocal charms and allure. "She Won't Talk To Me" was a bit on the posturing side, but still managed to do decently, while there were also fine album cuts like "I Wonder" and "Are You Gonna Love Me." — *Ron Wynn*

★ **The Best of Luther Vandross** / Sep. 1989 / Epic ♦♦♦♦♦
By the time this way-overdue double-record hits collection came out, Vandross had done many more R&B singles than could fit on it, so *The Best of Luther Vandross . . . The Best of Love* is inadequate to encompass him. It does, however, contain "Here and Now," which broke Vandross through to the pop Top Ten long after most people had given up hope that he'd ever cross over. — *William Ruhlmann*

Power of Love / Apr. 23, 1991 / Epic ♦♦♦
Power of Love finds Luther Vandross at his peak, crafting immaculate urban R&B hits that are seductive and soulful. The singles "Power of Love / Love Power," "Don't Want to Be a Fool," "The Rush" and "Sometimes It's Only Love" are the highpoints, but the album is filled with songs that are nearly as powerful, including a wonderful cover of Ben E. King's "I (Who Have Nothing)." — *Stephen Thomas Erlewine*

Never Let Me Go / Jun. 1, 1993 / Epic ♦♦
Luther Vandross may have fallen a bit from his lofty perch among R&B stars, but it wasn't due to any dip in skills. This release contains more examples of his supple, fluid vocals, expert delivery, and sophisticated yet soulful style. Indeed, Vandross hasn't made many better overall albums from a strict singing standpoint; his voice is full and impressive in every register, and there's no sign of strain when he reaches to the top of an arrangement or extends notes and phrases. Perhaps there are signs of creative wear and tear; there's no real blockbuster single, and the final medley, which blends classics from the Spinners and Bee Gees, sounds thrown together. A retooling might be in order. — *Ron Wynn*

Songs / Sep. 27, 1994 / Sony ♦♦
Luther Vandross could sing almost anything convincingly, which is one of the reasons *Songs* is so entertaining. A collection of personal favorites, *Songs* suffers from the common flaws of covers albums—it isn't consistent, it sounds slightly canned, and seems like a way to buy time between "real" albums. Nevertheless, Vandross is a truly fine singer, which is what makes *Songs* worthwhile. — *Stephen Thomas Erlewine*

Greatest Hits 1981-1995 / Jan. 1996 / Epic ◆◆◆◆
Greatest Hits 1981-1995 is an adequate single-disc overview of Luther Vandross' biggest hits for Epic Records, but the double-disc *The Best Of* is a richer collection that makes a stronger case for his talent as a smooth soul vocalist and a songwriter. —*Stephen Thomas Erlewine*

Your Secret Love / Oct. 1, 1996 / Epic ◆◆◆
Your Secret Love is a typically seductive and romantic record from Luther Vandross. As usual, his performance is stellar throughout the album, yet the material is slightly uneven, but the singles—including the sublime title track—make it worthwhile for fans. —*Leo Stanley*

The Vapors

f. 1978, Guildford, Surrey, England, **db.** 1981
New Wave, Power Pop, Mod-Revival
Led by vocalist/guitarist Dave Fenton, the Vapors were a short-lived new wave guitar group that is best known for the spiky pop single "Turning Japanese." Fenton formed the first version of the Vapors in 1978, yet he was the only member to survive that lineup; in 1979, former Ellery Bops members Ed Bazalgette (lead guitar) and Howard Smith (drums) joined the band and bassist Steve Smith came aboard shortly afterward. One of the band's first concerts was seen by the Jam's Bruce Foxton, who asked them to perform on his group's *Setting Sons* tour. Before long, the Vapors were managed by Foxton and John Weller, the manager of the Jam, as well as the father of the group's leader, Paul Weller.
The Vapors signed to United Artists, releasing their first single, "Prisoners," at the end of 1979; it failed to chart. "Turning Japanese," the band's second single, became a major hit, reaching No. 3 on the UK charts in March of 1980. *New Clear Days*, the band's debut album, was released two months later, but didn't sell as well as the single. In 1981, the Vapors released the more ambitious *Magnets*, yet it received lukewarm reviews and poor sales; the group disbanded shortly after its release. —*Stephen Thomas Erlewine*

New Clear Days / Jun. 1980 / United Artists ◆◆◆◆
It's easy to dismiss this band as a one-hit wonder—surely the album has nothing quite as infectious as the single, "Turning Japanese." *New Clear Days* is, however, a fine example of punchy Brit-pop in the vein of the Jam that holds up better than most albums from the period. —*Chris Woodstra*

Magnets / 1981 / Liberty ◆◆◆
David Fenton was obviously growing tired of being written off as lightweight after "Turning Japanese" and responded with the more ambitious and mature *Magnets*. Here he explores the darker side of life, discussing the Kennedy assasination ("Magnets"), police harrassment ("Civic Hall") and even cult leader/mass murderer Rev. Jim Jones ("Jimmy Jones," the failed single). Musically the band is more sophisticated, taking the occasional misstep in the arrangements by adding an annoying sythesizer in songs like "Spiders." Virtually ignored by both critics and the buying public, this is a strong follow-up that deserved a better fate. —*Chris Woodstra*

● **Anthology** / May 30, 1995 / One Way ◆◆◆◆
A somewhat misleading title, *Anthology* is a straight reissue of *New Clear Days* with four songs from *Magnets* tacked on to the end. Since the band only made two albums it would have been nice to release both as a two-fer—or at least add some rare tracks to the anthology. Minor complaints aside, this is probably all the Vapors most people will ever need. —*Chris Woodstra*

● **Turning Japanese: the Best of the Vapors** / 1996 / EMI ◆◆◆◆
A far better collection than its American counterpart, *The Best of the Vapors* offers a bit more for the fans, combining all of the singles, five rare B-sides, and most of the best album tracks (though the *Magnets* album is still woefully underrepresented). As an introduction, there is no better place to start. For collectors, it's indispensable. —*Chris Woodstra*

The Vaselines

f. 1986, Bellshill, Lanarkshire, Scotland, **db.** 1990
Alternative Pop-Rock
Eugene Kelly and Frances McKee were bored with their town, so they decided to form a band; they were called the Vaselines. Adding drummer Charles Kelly and bassist James Seenan, the Scottish quartet began rehearsing in their basements; soon they began recording their rough, simple and highly melodic pop songs in studios in Glasgow and Edinburgh. They recorded about 20 raw, pure pop gems that were barely heard by anyone. The Vaselines would likely have faded away into obscurity if it wasn't for Nirvana, who recorded two of their songs (both appear on the *Incesticide* compilation); Kurt Cobain was very vocal about his admiration for the band and Eugene Kelly in particular. By this time, the Vaselines had broken up and Kelly had formed Captain America, which later became Eugenius; soon, Eugenius became a hip band in alternative circles and the Vaselines' music was reissued. —*Stephen Thomas Erlewine*

● **The Way of the Vaselines** / Jul. 31, 1992 / Sub Pop ◆◆◆◆
The Way of the Vaselines collects everything the Vaselines ever recorded; it's a rough gem of raw pop. —*Stephen Thomas Erlewine*

Stevie Ray Vaughan

b. Oct. 3, 1954, Dallas, TX, **d.** Aug. 27, 1990, East Troy, WI
Guitar / Modern Electric Blues, Blues-Rock
With his astonishingly accomplished guitar playing, Stevie Ray Vaughan ignited the blues revival of the '80s. Vaughan drew equally from bluesmen like Albert King, Otis Rush, and Muddy Waters and rock 'n' roll players like Jimi Hendrix and Lonnie Mack, as well as the stray jazz guitarist like Kenny Burrell, developing a uniquely eclectic and fiery style that sounded like no other guitarist, regardless of genre. Vaughan bridged the gap between blues and rock like no other artist had since the late '60s. For the next seven years, Stevie Ray was the leading light in American blues, consistently selling out concerts while his albums regularly went gold. His tragic death in 1990 only emphasized his influence in blues and American rock 'n' roll.
Born and raised in Dallas, Stevie Ray Vaughan began playing guitar as a child, inspired by older brother Jimmie. When he was in junior high school, he began playing in a number of garage bands, which occasionally landed gigs in local nightclubs. By the time he was 17, he had dropped out of high school to concentrate on playing music. Vaughan's first real band was the Cobras, who played clubs and bars in Austin during the mid-'70s. Following that group's demise, he formed Triple Threat in 1975. Triple Threat also featured bassist Jackie Newhouse, drummer Chris Layton, and vocalist Lou Ann Barton. After a few years of playing Texas bars and clubs, Barton left the band in 1978. The group decided to continue performing under the name Double Trouble, which was inspired by the Otis Rush song of the same name; Stevie Ray became the band's lead singer.
For the next few years, Stevie Ray Vaughan and Double Trouble played the Austin area, becoming one of the most popular bands in Texas. In 1982, the band played the Montreux Festival and their performance caught the attention of David Bowie and Jackson Browne. After Double Trouble's performance, Bowie asked Vaughan to play on his forthcoming album, while Browne offered the group free recording time at his Los Angeles studio, Downtown; both offers were accepted. Stevie Ray laid down the lead guitar tracks for what became Bowie's *Let's Dance* album in late 1982. Shortly afterward, John Hammond, Sr. landed Vaughan and Double Trouble a record contract with Epic and the band recorded their debut album in less than a week at Downtown.
Vaughan's debut album, *Texas Flood*, was released in the summer of 1983, a few months after Bowie's *Let's Dance* appeared. On its own, *Let's Dance* earned Vaughan quite a bit of attention, but *Texas Flood* was a blockbuster blues success, receiving positive reviews in both blues and rock publications, reaching No. 38 on the charts, and crossing over to album-rock radio stations. Bowie offered Vaughan the lead guitarist role for his 1983 stadium tour, but Stevie Ray turned him down, preferring to play with Double Trouble. Stevie Ray and Double Trouble set off on a successful tour and quickly recorded their second album, *Couldn't Stand the Weather*, which was released in May of 1984. The album was more successful than its predecessor, reaching No. 31 on the charts; by the end of 1985, the album went gold. Double Trouble added keyboardist Reese Wynans in 1985, before they recorded their third album, *Soul To Soul*. The record was released in August, 1985 and was also quite successful, reaching No. 34 on the charts.
Although his professional career was soaring, Vaughan was sinking deep into alcoholism and drug addiction. Despite his declining health, Stevie Ray continued to push himself, releasing the double live album *Live Alive* in October of 1986 and launching an extensive American tour in early 1987. Following the tour, Vaughan checked into a rehabilitation clinic. The guitarist's time in rehab was kept fairly quiet and for the next year, Stevie Ray and Double Trouble were fairly inactive. Vaughan performed a number of concerts in 1988, including a headlining gig at the New Orleans Jazz & Heritage Festival, and wrote his fourth album. The resulting record, *In Step*, appeared in June of 1989 and became his most successful album, peaking at No. 33 on the charts, earning a Grammy for Best Contemporary Blues Recording, and going gold just over six months after its release.
In the spring of 1990, Stevie Ray recorded an album with his brother Jimmie, which was scheduled for release in the fall of the year. In the late summer of 1990, Vaughan and Double Trouble set out on an American headlining tour. On August 26, 1990, their East Troy, WI gig concluded with an encore jam featuring guitaritsts Eric Clapton, Buddy Guy, Jimmie Vaughan, and Robert Cray. After the concert, Stevie Ray Vaughan boarded a helicopter bound for Chicago. Minutes after its 12:30 AM takeoff, the helicopter crashed, killing Vaughan and the other four passengers. Vaughan was only 35 years old.
Family Style, Stevie Ray's duet album with Jimmie Vaughan, appeared in October and entered the charts at No. 7. *Family Style* began a series of posthumous releases that were as popular as the albums

Stevie Ray released during his lifetime. *The Sky is Crying*, a collection of studio outtakes compiled by Jimmie Vaughan, was released in October of 1991; it entered the charts at No. 10 and went platinum three months after its release. *In the Beginning*, a recording of a Double Trouble concert in 1980, was released in the fall of 1992 and the compilation *Greatest Hits* was released in 1995. —*Stephen Thomas Erlewine*

Texas Flood / 1983 / Epic ✦✦✦
A late-arriving star, Vaughan did not make his first album until the age of 28. By that time he had become a seasoned player. This doesn't really sound like a debut album; rather, it sounds like a blues guitar master at the top of his form. Highlights include "Pride & Joy," "Love Struck Baby," "Lenny," and the hard blues title cut. —*William Ruhlmann*

Couldn't Stand the Weather / 1984 / Epic ✦✦✦✦
Vaughan does not ease up on this second set, even taking on Jimi Hendrix in a rendttion of "Voodoo Chile (Slight Return)," and handling it beautifully. —*William Ruhlmann*

Soul to Soul / 1985 / Epic ✦✦✦✦
Soul to Soul shows that Vaughan is a great guitarist, but everybody already knew that. What makes this album different from his two previous efforts is the inspired backing of Double Trouble—who finally sound like they aren't intimdated by their leader—and Vaughan's considerably more soulful and assertive vocals. —*Stephen Thomas Erlewine*

Live Alive / Jul. 1986 / Epic ✦✦✦
Live Alive not only covers many of Vaughan's most popular album tracks, but it also showcases a version of Stevie Wonder's "Superstition." Other standout tracks include "Look at Little Sister," "Willie the Wimp," and "Cold Shot." —*Rick Clark*

In Step / Jun. 1989 / Epic ✦✦✦✦
Vaughan sounds just as fierce sober as he did before, and he is beginning to bloom as a songwriter, a fact most notable on the driving "The House Is Rockin'" and the confessional "Wall of Denial." —*William Ruhlmann*

The Sky Is Crying / Nov. 5, 1991 / Epic ✦✦✦✦
The posthumously released *The Sky Is Crying*, assembled out of tracks recorded between 1984 and 1989, is a lovingly assembled tribute to Vaughan's brilliance as a guitarist. Arguably this is Vaughan's finest album. The first-rate playing is unforced and natural in execution. On the songs, from his impeccable version of Hendrix's "Little Wing" to the hard blues shuffle of "Empty Arms," Vaughan's execution is unforced and his phrasing is relaxed. The release contains great liner notes and track information. Fans of hard blues-rock should check this one out. —*Rick Clark*

In the Beginning / Oct. 6, 1992 / Epic ✦✦
Although this is a very rough early concert from 1980, this album captures an energetic Stevie Ray Vaughan still developing his signature style, which makes it essential for fans. —*Stephen Thomas Erlewine*

★ **Greatest Hits** / Nov. 21, 1995 / Epic ✦✦✦✦✦
Stevie Ray Vaughan was a great guitarist, but he had trouble making consistent albums. *Greatest Hits* rectifies that problem by collecting all of his best-known tracks, from "Pride and Joy" to "Crossfire." Not only is it a terrific introduction, it's his most consistent album, demonstrating exactly why he was one of the most important guitarists of the '80s. —*Stephen Thomas Erlewine*

Bobby Vee

b. Apr. 30, 1943, Fargo, ND
Vocals / Pop-Rock, Teen Idol, Brill Building Pop
Bobby Vee enjoyed his greatest success in the early '60s, with five Top Ten singles, including the classic, "Take Good Care of My Baby." Vee's vocal style was similar to that of his hero, Buddy Holly. Ironically, Vee's break came when he filled in for Holly the day after his death in a plane crash. Like those of many of his contemporaries, his career went into a tailspin with the arrival of the British Invasion in 1964. He did score one more Top Ten single in 1967 with "Come Back When You Grow Up." —*Kenneth M. Cassidy*

Bobby Vee Meets the Crickets / 1962 / EMI America ✦✦✦
The reissue of this enjoyable album includes *ten* bonus tracks, including alternate takes, unreleased songs, and the "Buddy Holly Medley," a recent recording by Vee and the Crickets. —*Stephen Thomas Erlewine*

I Remember Buddy Holly / 1963 / EMI America ✦✦✦
Vee's fun tribute to Buddy Holly has been beefed up on its CD reissue. Ten bonus tracks have been included, and any songs that overlap with the *Meets the Crickets* album have been replaced with alternate versions. —*Stephen Thomas Erlewine*

● **Legendary Masters** / 1990 / EMI America ✦✦✦✦
The most complete collection of Vee's recordings includes "Take Good Care of My Baby," "Rubber Ball," and "The Night Has a Thousand Eyes." —*Kenneth M. Cassidy*

Greatest Hits / Mar. 8, 1994 / Curb ✦✦✦
Ten of his biggest hits, including "Take Good Care of My Baby," "Run to Him," and "Come Back When You Grow Up," for those of you who are in a rush and have no time for nuances like liner notes and low-charting singles. These *are* all original recordings, though the minimal packaging and liner notes on Curb's *Greatest Hits* series might lead you to suspect otherwise. —*Richie Unterberger*

Suzanne Vega

b. Aug. 12, 1959, New York, NY
Guitar, Vocals / Singer-Songwriter, Adult Alternative Pop-Rock, Contemporary Folk
Vega was born in Santa Monica, CA, and moved to New York City at age two. She attended the High School of Performing Arts, then Barnard College. Vega was still at Barnard when she began attracting attention at Greenwich Village folk clubs and was featured on several issues of the songwriters' magazine/record album *The CooP* (later *The Fast Folk Musical Magazine*) in 1982. She was signed to A&M Records in 1984 and released her first album, *Suzanne Vega* in 1985. It was a critical success and a moderate seller. Vega's second album, *Solitude Standing*, featured "Luka," a song about child abuse that became a surprise hit single in 1987. The album itself went gold. Vega took three years to release the follow-up, *Days of Open Hand* (1990), which was a commercial disappointment, though a few months later a couple of British DJs, under the name D.N.A., put out a dance version of her a cappella song "Tom's Diner" from the album *Solitude Standing*, and it became a hit.
On her next album, 1992's *99.9° F*, Vega experimented with the dance rhythms that made "Tom's Diner" a hit; although the result was interesting, it didn't give her any hits. Vega's fifth album was scheduled for release in the spring of 1996. —*William Ruhlmann*

Suzanne Vega / May 1985 / A&M ✦✦✦✦
Though early comparisons were made to Joni Mitchell, Suzanne Vega's true antecedents were Janis Ian and Leonard Cohen. Like Ian, she sang with a precise, frequently half-spoken phrasing that gave her lyrics an intensity that seemed to suggest an unsteady control consciously held over emotional chaos. Like Cohen, Vega observed the world in poetic metaphor, her cold urban landscapes reflecting a troubled sense of love and loss. The key track was "Small Blue Thing," in which the singer pictured herself as an object "Like a marble / or an eye," "made of china / made of glass," "lost inside your pocket" and "turning in your hand." The sharply picked acoustic guitar and other isolated musical elements echoed the closely observed scenes—everything seemed to be in tight closeup and sharp focus. Often, the singer seemed to be using the songs to measure an emotional distance; sometimes, as in "Marlene on the Wall," she observed her own actions from a remove. In "Freeze Tag," she had told a companion, "I will be Dietrich / and you can be Dean"; in "Marlene," a poster of the aloof movie star "watches from the wall" observing the singer's succession of lovers, and she tries to emulate her heroine's persona, telling the current one, "Even if I am in love with you / All this to say, what's it to you?" The ten songs on *Suzanne Vega* constituted the self-analysis of a young woman who desired possession without offering commitment; no wonder that, upon its release, it was taken to heart by young women across the country and in Europe. —*William Ruhlmann*

● **Solitude Standing** / Apr. 1987 / A&M ✦✦✦✦
The songs on *Solitude Standing*, Suzanne Vega's second album, had years listed beside them on the lyric sheet, so you could see that some of them dated back to 1978. But that bold admission heralded the album's triumph—its diversity was what made it so good. Partially, that was because the old songs were the equal of anything on the first album—tunes like the a cappella slice-of-life "Tom's Diner" and the warmly romantic "Gypsy" simply wouldn't have fit thematically on the debut. On *Solitude Standing*, however, they became part of an album of story songs set in a variety of musical contexts; many had band arrangements, and in fact, members of Vega's touring band often were credited as co-writers. Additionally, Vega had developed more as a singer without losing the focused intonation that had made her debut—one of many compelling elements which helped make "Luka," a character song about domestic abuse, a fluke hit. —*William Ruhlmann*

Days of Open Hand / Apr. 1990 / A&M ✦✦
Suzanne Vega is a beautiful example of an artist excelling despite her limitations. While the singer-songwriter doesn't have much of a voice, she has no problem being incredibly expressive. Subtlety is the quality that defines *Days of Open Hand*, an album every bit as compelling as the superb *Solitude Standing*. Vega doesn't need to shout or preach in order to get her points across. On "Men in a War," the folk-pop-rock explorer examines the plight of disabled veterans without expressing the type of anger that Bruce Cockburn would when addressing such a subject. Restrained and understated, treasures like "Those Whole Girls (Run in Grace)," "Rusted Pipe" and "Room Off the Street" and the unsettling "Institution Green" show that for all their delicacy, Vega's songs can

be quite meaty and give listeners a great deal to think about. *—Alex Henderson*

99.9° F. / Sep. 8, 1992 / A&M ✦✦✦
While this is not the techno album that Suzanne Vega was rumored to be making, *99.9° F.* does offer a significant departure from her previous contemporary folk albums. Vega uses more synthesizers and drum machines, often evoking a bizarre carnival-esque atmosphere on the album. Still, *99.9° F.* is a folk album at heart; every song is steeped in traditional song form, and Vega's writing is strong. Fans of Vega's previous work might be taken aback, but those willing to listen to the album will find that Vega has produced one of her strongest records yet. *—Stephen Thomas Erlewine*

Nine Objects of Desire / Sep. 10, 1996 / A&M ✦✦✦
Under the guidance of producer Mitchell Froom, who produced *99.9° F.* and married her shortly after that album was completed, Suzanne Vega continues to explore more textured and vaguely experimental musical territory on *Nine Objects of Desire*. While it is less bold on the surface than its predecessor—most notably, there are no pseudo-industrial rhythms—*Nine Objects of Desire* still bears all the trademarks of a Mitchell Froom production. There is cheap, garage-yard percussion scattered throughout the record, layered keyboards, and overly mannered, arty arrangements. It's not as extreme as Froom's work for Los Lobos, for instance, but it is still more self-consciously pretentious than any of Vega's albums, besides *99.9° F.* Vega's songs manage to cut through the murky production more often than not and while the album doesn't boast her most consistent set of songs, they are on the whole stronger than the ones on her previous record. The songs on *Nine Objects of Desire* are more classically structured and inviting than the ones on its predecessor—it is only the production that keeps the listener at a distance. And that's ironic, since half of these songs rank among Vega's most personal work. *—Stephen Thomas Erlewine*

The Vejtables

f. 1964, San Francisco, CA, **db.** 1966
Psychedelic, Garage Rock, Folk-Rock
A footnote of the dawn of San Francisco rock, the Vejtables scraped the bottom of the charts in 1965 with "I Still Love You," a pleasant, poppy folk-rocker. Their pair of singles for the San Francisco-based Autumn label strongly recalled a much poppier Beau Brummels, with their 12-string guitars, folky harmonies, and sparse harmonica. The similarity was quite understandable: the Beau Brummels were not only also from San Francisco, but also on the same label. The Vejtables' chief distinguishing mark and asset was one of the very few female drummers in a mid-'60s rock group, Jan Errico, who also sang and wrote much of their material (including "I Still Love You").

For a group with such a brief lifespan, the Vejtables' history was pretty tangled and twisting. Their tenure at Autumn was rudely interrupted when the label went bust. Errico, who had recorded a bit of solo material at Autumn (under, confusingly, the name of Jan Ashton), joined fellow embryonic S.F. band the Mojo Men, who had also had small hits on Autumn. To make matters more confusing, the Mojo Men continued to call themselves the Mojo Men after adding Errico, who (as she had in the Vejtables) sang and wrote many of their songs. The Mojo Men-with-Errico, now under contract to Warner Brothers, recorded some pleasant pop-folk-rock in 1966 and 1967, making the Top 40 with a cover of Buffalo Springfield's "Sit Down, I Think I Love You." In April of 1966 the Vejtables' guitarist, Jim Sawyers, joined the Syndicate of Sound, who had just hit it big with "Little Girl."

Vejtable vocalist Bob Bailey kept the band going in 1966, however, with constantly shifting lineups (future Moby Grape bassist Bob Mosley was very briefly a member, although he didn't record with the group). A couple more singles appeared on the Uptown and Tower labels in 1966, finding the band probing a much more aggressive and psychedelic vein, sounding like an entirely different outfit from the "I Still Love You" lineup. "Feel the Music" (which appeared on a *Pebbles* compilation) was a legitimately outstanding effort from this time, even though it ripped off the Who's "Out in the Streets." But the band lacked either the songwriting depth or the instrumental finesse of the best acts on the now-burgeoning San Francisco psychedelic scene. The Vejtables finally withered on the vine around the end of 1966. *—Richie Unterberger*

Feel . . . The Vejtables / 1995 / Sundazed ✦✦✦
Although the Vejtables only released a few (very rare) singles in 1965 and 1966, this career retrospective has been fleshed out to album length with the addition of several unissued tracks. The 17 songs span both the folk-rock and psychedelic eras, switching abruptly from their soothing Autumn sides to slashing garage psychedelia. The folk-rock certainly outshines the psychedelic material, which (aside from "Feel the Music") are usually dirge-like and thinly written, the players trying to compensate for the weak songwriting with some too-feverish guitar meandering. Other than a few strong tracks, the Vejtables were really not a terribly interesting group; unless you're a heavy collector of the folk-

psychedelic-garage style, the tracks that have surfaced on compilations (such as *Nuggets Vol. 7: Early San Francisco*) should be enough. *—Richie Unterberger*

Velocity Girl

f. 1990, Washington, D.C., **db.** 1996
Alternative Pop-Rock, Indie Rock
After all their grunge bands left for the majors, Sub Pop's most popular band was, surprisingly, Velocity Girl. Velocity Girl is the exact opposite of grunge; their guitars may be a little dirty, but their music is pure pop, with shiny melodies and Beach Boys harmonies. Their hooks are sharp enough to make the band one of the few college-radio favorites that don't wear thin with repeated listens. *—Stephen Thomas Erlewine*

Velocity Girl / 1992 / Slumberland ✦✦✦
Velocity Girl's eponymous debut EP compiles six highlights from a series of singles and contributions to various artists collections from the early '90s. Half of the record is weighed down by waves of hazy guitars, but the other half is engaging indie-pop, highlighted by "Always," "I Don't Care If You Go," and the wonderful "Forgotten Favorite," which combines a sunny melody with layers of feedback reminiscent of My Bloody Valentine. *—Stephen Thomas Erlewine*

● **Copacetic** / Mar. 26, 1993 / Sub Pop ✦✦✦✦
An enjoyable collection of alternative pop, in the vein of R.E.M. and the Velvet Underground, is highlighted by Sarah Shannon's thin, girlish voice which is showcased to its best effect on "Audrey's Eyes." *—AMG*

Simpatico / 1994 / Sub Pop ✦✦✦✦
On their second album *Simpatico*, Velocity Girl ironed out most of their indie-rock influences, revamping themselves as a jangle-pop band. When the group has a strong song, such as the irresistible "Sorry Again," the results are positively infectious, but the clearer sound also works against them, since it reveals that their songwriting is wildly uneven. Also, part of *Copacetic*'s appeal was how it walked the thin line between white noise and pure pop, since that resulted in some unusual, appealing sounds that indicated that Velocity Girl could develop a signature sound. On *Simpatico*, they simply sound like another jangly indie-pop band, one that's competent but not particularly exciting. *—Stephen Thomas Erlewine*

Gilded Stars and Zealous Hearts / Mar. 12, 1996 / Sub Pop ✦✦
Buried beneath the loud guitars and pseudo-grungy riffs of *Gilded Stars and Zealous Hearts*, there are hints of the effortless pop sensibilities that made Velocity Girl's first two albums so charming. However, it takes a lot of digging to find those hints. Vocalist Sarah Shannon sounds completely lost admist the carefully considered bombast of the guitars. When she does make herself heard, it's usually at the expense of her melodic skills. Velocity Girl has been *both* melodic and loud before—check out the intoxicating rush of "My Forgotten Favorite"—but throughout *Gilded Stars and Zealous Hearts* they sound too concerned with proving that they can rock and are not just a cute, little pop band. In the process, they forgot to write melodies for either the vocals or the guitars. *—Stephen Thomas Erlewine*

Velvet Crush

f. 1989, Rhode Island
Alternative Country-Rock, Power Pop
A classic power-pop band in the tradition of the Raspberries and Big Star, Velvet Crush formed in Rhode Island in 1989, although their roots actually extended west to Champagne, Illinois, where vocalist/bassist Paul Chastain and drummer Ric Menck first met and began performing together. There Menck founded his own small label, Picture Book, on which he and Chastain recorded solo material as well as singles under various group names like the Springfields, Choo Choo Train, the Paint Set and Bag O'Shells. Picture Book also released records by the Milwaukee-based White Sisters, led by guitarist Paul Borchardt, with whom Menck struck up a friendship.

When Borchardt eventually moved to Providence, Rhode Island in 1988, he encouraged Menck and Chastain to follow; they did, and Velvet Crush soon began performing their first shows. In 1991, longtime friend Matthew Sweet produced their debut, *In the Presence of Greatness;* a hit with the British music press, the record earned the group a deal with the influential UK label Creation. For 1994's *Teenage Symphonies to God* (the title taken from Brian Wilson's description of the music intended for the Beach Boys' legendary *Smile* LP), Velvet Crush enlisted producer Mitch Easter, known for his work with R.E.M. and as the leader of Let's Active. The members of the group also continued working on solo projects; Borchardt led the superb pop group Honeybunch, while Menck issued his solo debut *The Ballad of Ric Menck* in 1996. *—Jason Ankeny*

In the Presence of / Oct. 18, 1991 / Ringers Lactate ✦✦✦
Velvet Crush's debut album had a couple of fine cuts, yet it was a rather unfocused effort, saved by the band's infectious energy. *—Sara Sytsma*

● **Teenage Symphonies to God** / Jul. 5, 1994 / Epic ✦✦✦✦

Velvet Crush's second album is an old-fashioned pop record: 12 songs in 40 minutes, filled with ultra-melodic guitar hooks and simple, memorable melodies. While it's traditional in form, the music on *Teenage Symphonies to God* isn't retro. Velvet Crush manage to inject a real enthusiasm and freshness in the standard three-minute pop song, whether they're playing originals that sound like forgotten classics ("Time Wraps Around You," "This Life is Killing Me," "My Blank Pages," "Hold Me Up") or forgotten classics themselves (Gene Clark's "Why Not Your Baby" and Matthew Sweet's "Something's Gotta Give"). With a crisp, warm production from Mitch Easter, *Teenage Symphonies to God* is one record that deserves to take its title from Brian Wilson. —*Stephen Thomas Erlewine*

The Velvet Underground

f. 1964, New York, NY, **db.** 1973
Rock 'n' Roll, Proto-Punk

Few rock groups can claim to have broken so much new territory, and maintain such consistent brilliance on record, as the Velvet Underground during their brief lifespan. It was the group's lot to be ahead of, or at least out of step with, their time. The mid-to-late '60s was an era of explosive growth and experimentation in rock, but the Velvets' innovations—which blended the energy of rock with the sonic adventurism of the avant-garde, and introduced a new degree of social realism and sexual kinkiness into rock lyrics—were too abrasive for the mainstream to handle. During their time, the group experienced little commercial success; though they were hugely appreciated by a cult audience and some critics, the larger public treated them with indifference or, occasionally, scorn. The Velvets' music was too important to languish in obscurity, though; their cult only grew larger and larger in the years following their demise, and continues to mushroom today. By the 1980s, they were acknowledged not just as one of the most important rock bands of the '60s, but one of the best of all time, and one whose immense significance cannot be measured by their relatively modest sales.

Historians often hail the group for their incalculable influence upon the punk and new wave of subsequent years, and while the Velvets were undoubtedly a key touchstone of the movements, to focus upon these elements of their vision is to only get part of the story. The group were uncompromising in their music and lyrics, to be sure, sometimes espousing a bleakness and primitivism that would inspire alienated singers and songwriters of future generations. But their colorful and oft-grim soundscapes were firmly grounded in strong, well-constructed songs that could be as humanistic and compassionate as they were outrageous and confrontational. The member most responsible for these qualities was guitarist/singer-songwriter Lou Reed, whose sing-speak vocals and gripping narratives have come to define street-savvy rock 'n' roll.

Reed loved rock 'n' roll from an early age, and even recorded a doo wop type single as a Long Island teenager in the late '50s (as a member of the Shades). By the early '60s, he was also getting into avant-garde jazz and serious poetry, coming under the influence of author Delmore Schwartz while studying at Syracuse University. After graduation, he set his sights considerably lower, churning out tunes for exploitation rock albums as a staff songwriter for Pickwick Records in New York City. Reed did learn some useful things about production at Pickwick, and it was while working there that he met John Cale, a classically-trained Welshman who had moved to America to study and perform "serious" music. Cale, who had performed with John Cage and LaMonte Young, found himself increasingly attracted to rock 'n' roll; Reed, for his part, was interested in the avant-garde as well as pop. Reed and Cale were both interested in fusing the avant-garde with rock 'n' roll, and had found the ideal partners for making the vision (a very radical one for the mid-'60s) work; their synergy would be the crucial axis of the Velvet Underground's early work.

Reed and Cale (who would play bass, viola, and organ) would need to assemble a full band, making tentative steps along this direction by performing together in the Primitives (which also included experimental filmmaker Tony Conrad and avant-garde sculptor Walter DeMaria) to promote a bizarre Reed-penned Pickwick single ("The Ostrich"). By 1965, the group was a quartet called the Velvet Underground, including Reed, Cale, guitarist Sterling Morrison (an old friend of Reed's), and drummer Angus MacLise. MacLise quit before the band's first paying gig, claiming that accepting money for art was a sellout; the Velvets quickly recruited drummer Maureen Tucker, a sister of one of Morrison's friends.

Even at this point, the Velvets were well on their way to developing something quite different. Their original material, principally penned and sung by Reed, dealt with the hard urban realities of Manhattan, describing drug use, sadomasochism, and decadence in cool, unapologetic detail in "Heroin," "I'm Waiting for the Man," "Venus in Furs," and "All Tomorrow's Parties." These were wedded to basic, hard-nosed rock riffs, toughened by Tucker's metronome beats, the oddly tuned, rumbling guitars, and Cale's occasional viola scrapes. It was an uncommer-

cial blend to say the least, but the Velvets got an unexpected benefactor when artist and all-around pop-art icon Andy Warhol caught the band at a club around the end of 1965. Warhol quickly assumed management of the group, incorporating them into his mixed-media/performance art ensemble, the Exploding Plastic Inevitable. By spring 1966, Warhol was producing their debut album.

Warhol was also responsible for embellishing the quartet with Nico, a mysterious European model/chanteuse with a deep voice whom the band accepted rather reluctantly, viewing her spectral presence as rather ornamental. Reed remained the principal lead vocalist, but Nico did sing three of the best songs on the group's debut, often known as "the banana album" because of its distinctive Warhol-designed cover. Recognized today as one of the core classic albums of rock, it featured an extraordinarily strong set of songs, highlighted by "Heroin," "All Tomorrow's Parties," "Venus in Furs," "I'll Be Your Mirror," "Femme Fatale," "Black Angel's Death Song," and "Sunday Morning." The sensational drug-and-sex items (especially "Heroin") got most of the ink, but the more conventional numbers showed Reed to be a songwriter capable of considerable melodicism, sensitivity, and almost naked introspection.

The album's release was not without complications, though. First, it wasn't issued until nearly a year after it was finished, due to record-company politics and other factors. The group's association with Warhol and the Exploding Plastic Inevitable had already assured them of a high (if notorious media) profile, but the music was simply too daring to fit onto commercial radio; "underground" rock radio was barely getting started at this point, and in any case may well have overlooked the record at a time when psychedelic music was approaching its peak. The album only reached No. 171 in the charts, and that's as high as any of their LPs would get upon original release. Those who heard it, however, were often mightily impressed; Brian Eno once said that even though hardly anyone bought the Velvets records at the time they appeared, almost everyone who did formed their own bands.

A cult reputation wasn't enough to guarantee a stable livelihood for a band in the '60s, and by 1967 the Velvets were fighting problems within their own ranks. Nico, never considered an essential member by the rest of the band, left or was fired sometime during the year, going on to a fascinating career of her own. The association with Warhol weakened, as the artist was unable to devote as much attention to the band as he had the previous year. Embittered by the lukewarm reception of their album in their native New York, the Velvets concentrated on touring cities throughout the rest of the country. Amidst this tense atmosphere, the second album, *White Light/White Heat*, was recorded in late 1967.

Each of the albums the group released while Reed led the band was an unexpected departure from all of their other LPs. *White Light/White Heat* was probably the most radical, focusing almost exclusively on their noisiest arrangements, overamped guitars, and most willfully abrasive songs. The 17-minute "Sister Ray" was their most extreme (and successful) effort in this vein. Unsurprisingly, the album failed to catch on commercially, topping out at No. 199.

By the summer of 1968, the band had a much graver problem on its hands than commercial success (or the lack of it). A rift developed between Reed and Cale, the most creative forces in the band and, as one could expect, two temperamental egos. Reed presented the rest of the band with an ultimatum, declaring that he would leave the group unless Cale was sacked. Morrison and Tucker reluctantly sided with Lou, and Doug Yule was recruited to take Cale's place.

The group's self-titled third album (1969) was an even more radical left turn than *White Light/White Heat*. The volume and violence had nearly vanished; the record featured far more conventional rock arrangements that were sometimes so restrained it seems as though they were making an almost deliberate attempt to avoid waking the neighbors. Yet the sound was nonetheless effective for that; the record contains some of Reed's most personal and striking compositions, numbers like "Pale Blue Eyes" and "Candy Says" ranking among his most romantic, although cuts like "What Goes On" proved they could still rock out convincingly (though in a less experimental fashion than they had with Cale). The approach may have confused listeners and critics, but by this time their label (MGM/Verve) was putting little promotional resources behind the band anyway.

Even in the absence of Cale, the Velvets were still capable of generating compelling heat onstage, as *Live 1969* (not released until the mid-'70s) confirms. MGM was by now in the midst of an infamous "purge" of its supposedly drug-related rock acts, and the Velvets were setting their sights elsewhere. Nevertheless, they recorded about an album's worth of additional material for the label after the third LP, although it remains unclear whether this was intended for a fourth album or not. Many of the songs, though, were excellent, serving as a bridge between *The Velvet Underground* and 1970's *Loaded;* a lot of it was officially released in the 1980s and 1990s.

The beginning of the 1970s seemed to herald considerable promise for the group, as they signed to Atlantic, but at this point the personnel problems that had always dogged them finally became overwhelming.

Tucker had to sit out *Loaded* due to pregnancy, replaced by Yule's brother Billy. Doug Yule, according to some accounts, began angling for more power in the band. Unexpectedly, after a lengthy residency at New York's famous Max's Kansas City club, Reed quit the band near the end of the summer of 1970, moving back to his parents' Long Island home for several months before beginning his solo career, just before the release of *Loaded*, his final studio album with the Velvets.

Loaded was by far the group's most conventional rock album, and the most accessible one for mainstream listeners. "Rock and Roll" and "Sweet Jane" in particular were two of Reed's most anthemic, jubilant tunes, and ones that became rock standards in the '70s. But the group's power was somewhat diluted by the absence of Tucker, and by the decision to have Doug Yule handle some of the lead vocals. Due to Reed's departure, though, the group couldn't capitalize on any momentum it might have generated. Unwisely, the band decided to continue, though Morrison and Tucker left shortly afterwards. That left Doug Yule at the helm of an act that was the Velvet Underground in name only, and the 1973 album that was billed to the group (*Squeeze*) is best forgotten, not considered as a true Velvets release.

With Reed, Cale, and Nico establishing important solo careers of their own, and such important figures as David Bowie, Brian Eno, and Patti Smith making no bones about their debts to the band, the Velvet Underground simply became more and more popular as the years passed. In the 1980s, the original albums were reissued, along with a couple of important collections of outtakes. Hoping to rewrite the rules one last time, Reed, Cale, Morrison, and Tucker attempted to defy the odds against successful rock reunions by re-forming in the early '90s (Nico had died in 1988). A European tour and a live album were completed in 1993, to mixed reviews; before a planned American jaunt could start, Reed and Cale (who have feuded constantly over the past few decades) fell out yet again, bringing the reunion to a sad close. Sterling Morrison's death from illness in 1995 seems to have permanently iced any prospect of more projects under the Velvet Underground name, although a few of the surviving members played together when they were inducted into the Rock and Roll Hall of Fame. By that time, an impressive five-CD box set (containing all four of the studio albums issued when Reed was in the band, as well as a lot of other material) was available to enshrine the group's legacy for the ages. —*Richie Unterberger*

☆ **The Velvet Underground & Nico** / Jan. 1967 / Verve ✦✦✦✦✦
Nominally produced by Andy Warhol, *The Velvet Underground and Nico* is one of the most important and influential albums of all time. The only record the group recorded with Nico, the disc includes the seminal "Heroin," "I'm Waiting for the Man," and "Venus in Furs." As with the finest films and books, each song provides a window into a world that most will otherwise not have experienced. "Heroin" is probably the finest example of this, with the rush and subsequent down of the drug masterfully conveyed via Tucker's unorthodox drum style (simply involving padded beaters on a bass drum turned on its side), continuous changes in tempo, different musicians playing in different tempos at the same time, and Cale's shrieking viola-induced feedback at the end. In terms of sound the whole album is wide ranging, moving from the melodic beauty of "Femme Fatale" to the intense cacophony of "European Son." —*Rob Bowman*

☆ **White Light/White Heat** / 1967 / Verve ✦✦✦✦✦
By the time of *White Light/White Heat*, Nico had departed to embark upon a solo career. The Velvets, now also minus Warhol, concocted an extraordinarily abrasive, tension-filled album, full of mind-numbing feedback and incessant drones. The playing and production on this album herald a punk aesthetic eight years ahead of the fact. Standout tracks include the sidelong improvisatory "Sister Ray" and the John Cale-narrated, Lou Reed-written "The Gift." —*Rob Bowman*

☆ **The Velvet Underground** / 1969 / Verve ✦✦✦✦✦
In an unexpected, abrupt departure from the ferocity of their first two albums, The Velvets' third album is a muted, folk-rockish, even warm affair. The impression is almost of a band deliberately turning down to create a restrained, haunting ambience, but it suffers not in the least for the loss of volume: "Pale Blue Eyes," "I'm Set Free," and "Candy Says" are some of Reed's greatest songs, "Some Kinda Love" will satisfy those looking for the requisite Velvet kinkiness, and "Beginning To See The Light" and "What Goes On" prove that the group can handle straightforward, charging rockers masterfully. —*Richie Unterberger*

☆ **Loaded** / 1970 / Warner Brothers ✦✦✦✦✦
Recorded in the summer of 1970 while the band was playing a summerlong residency at Max's Kansas City in New York. Feeling increasingly disaffected, Reed walked out after the last gig at Max's, never to return. The album was remixed and edited without him, much to his later chagrin. Whatever imperfections may have consequently occurred, *Loaded* remains an absolute must. The Velvets were now playing stripped-down rock 'n' roll and Reed was writing such enduring classics as "Sweet Jane" and "Rock & Roll," as well as the underrated "New Age," "Train Round the Bend," and "Oh! Sweet Nuthin'." —*Rob Bowman*

Live at Max's Kansas City / 1972 / Cotillion ✦✦✦
Literally recorded the last night Lou Reed ever played with the Velvet Underground, at New York's Max's Kansas City, we have this album due to the foresight of Warhol acolyte and employee Brigid Polk, who happened to bring her cassette recorder to document that evening. The sound is a little one-dimensional, and you can hear Jim Carroll ask for Tylenol and others order drinks over the course of the record, but the recording is nonetheless fascinating. Brigid's tape was about an hour and a half long. Cotillion released just under half of it. The sound of the group is a little different, because Doug Yule's brother Billy was temporarily replacing drummer Maureen Tucker, since the latter was pregnant with her first child. —*Rob Bowman*

Squeeze / 1973 / Polydor ✦
After Lou Reed left the Velvet Underground, bassist Doug Yule took control of the group. Retaining the name "The Velvet Underground," Yule assembled several new lineups of the band and toured the US. By the time Yule's VU recorded their first album, the band featured Boston-based vocalist Willie Alexander and was playing a set of conventional pop-rock songs. *Squeeze*, the only album recorded with a bastardized version of the Velvet Underground, was released in 1973 to uniformly terrible reviews; Yule broke up the band shortly after its release. Over the years, *Squeeze* has not only become increasingly rare—after all, not many copies of the record were pressed—it has disappeared from the official Velvet Underground discography and Yule's attempt to prolong the band's career has virtually been forgotten. —*Stephen Thomas Erlewine*

☆ **1969: Velvet Underground Live** / 1974 / Mercury ✦✦✦✦✦
Originally a double album and released in two volumes with added songs on CD, *1969: Velvet Underground Live* is a stunning document of the Reed, Yule, Morrison, Tucker edition of the Velvets at their pinnacle. Recorded privately in Texas and San Francisco, the Velvets play extended, intensely driven, out-and-out versions of songs from their first three albums as well as then-unreleased material such as "Ocean," "Real Good Time Together," and "Sweet Bonnie Brown." —*Rob Bowman*

☆ **VU** / 1985 / Verve ✦✦✦✦✦
Composed principally of songs that would have appeared on the Velvets' unreleased fourth MGM album, this is only slightly less impressive than their first three LPs, striking a balance between the searing pre-punk of their first two efforts and the calm eloquence of the third. "Lisa Says," "Ocean," and "Stephanie Says" are some of Reed's greatest ballads; "I Can't Stand It" is one of the Velvets' toughest and best conventional hard rock songs. Some of the other tunes are slight (if engaging) in comparison with the Velvets' prime work. Many of the tracks were re-recorded by Reed on his early solo albums, and in every instance, the Velvets' versions are better. —*Richie Unterberger*

Another View / 1986 / Verve ✦✦✦
Polygram finally started to scrape the bottom of the barrel with this grab bag of outtakes from 1967 to 1969, most of which don't approach the magnificence of most of the Velvets' studio output. It's never less than interesting, though, and certainly worth perusal by Velvets fans. Especially noteworthy are a gloriously tough version of "We're Gonna Have a Good Time Together" (one of their best simple rock tunes), the grinding instrumental "Guess I'm Falling In Love," and an early version of "Rock And Roll." —*Richie Unterberger*

● **Best of the Velvet Underground** / Sep. 1989 / Verve ✦✦✦✦
The Best of the Velvet Underground: Words and Music of Lou Reed is a 15-track summary of the Velvets' career, borrowing heavily from the debut (six tracks) and featuring "Sweet Jane" and "Rock & Roll," licensed from Atlantic. —*William Ruhlmann*

What Goes On? / Aug. 9, 1993 / Raven ✦✦✦
An Australian box set covering their enormously influential career, *What Goes On?* covers nearly all of their most famous songs ("The Gift" is missing), but its real strength is in its rarities. Hardcore fans will adore the radio commercials for the band, as well the original mono mixes from *The Velvet Underground & Nico* and the alternate, "closet" mixes of the third album. Because of these tracks, diehard fans will need this box. —*Stephen Thomas Erlewine*

Live MCMXCIII / Oct. 26, 1993 / Warner Brothers ✦✦
The four original Velvets chose to put decades-old differences aside and reunite for a series of European concerts. Recorded at L'Olympia Theatre in Paris over three nights, *Live MCMXCIII* is available as either a two-disc set containing the whole show, or as an abridged single-disc set. There's a real cutting edge to this concert recording that screams rejuvenation. The dour Velvets are actually having fun. Vocals are right up front in the mix not a consistent advantage, as Reed sometimes comes unglued here. In a daring move, Cale takes effective vocal turns on "All Tomorrow's Parties" and "Femme Fatale." But it's the often overlooked Tucker and Morrison who construct a flawless percussive and rhythmic backbone that give the event its real cohesion and structure. —*Roch Parisien*

☆ **Peel Slowly and See** / Sep. 26, 1995 / Polydor ✦✦✦✦✦

Does this five-CD box set feature an abundance of essential material? Certainly. It has all four of the studio albums released by the Lou Reed-led lineup, and a wealth of previously unreleased goodies. Is it an essential purchase? That depends on your level of fanaticism. Most serious Velvets fans have all four of the core studio albums already (although the third, self-titled LP is presented in its muffled, so-called "closet" mix), and will be most interested in the previously unavailable recordings, which do hold considerable fascination. The entire first disc is devoted to a drummer-less 1965 rehearsal tape in John Cale's loft, with radically different, almost folky run-throughs of some of the most important songs from their classic debut ("Venus in Furs," "I'm Waiting for the Man," "All Tomorrow's Parties," "Heroin"), as well as a song that only made it onto Nico's first LP ("Wrap Your Troubles in Dreams"), and one which makes its first appearance anywhere (the Dylanesque "Prominent Men"). "Venus in Furs" (with Cale on vocals) and "All Tomorrow's Parties" sound particularly different here, almost like English folk ballads. Other big bonuses include no less than seven outtakes from *Loaded,* featuring excellent, high-spirited versions of "Ocean," "Satellite of Love," and other songs re-done by Reed on his early solo albums, though the versions here are considerably better. Then there are several early 1967 demos (in lo-fi but listenable quality) of songs that never got recorded by the Velvets otherwise, some very good. And there are sundry other unreleased live and studio items, highlighted by a scorching live 1967 "Guess I'm Falling in Love" and the 1969 demo "Countess from Hong Kong." There are also highlights from *VU* and *Another View,* longer versions of *Loaded's* "Sweet Jane" and "New Age" that restore fragments edited out in the final mix, and an 80-page booklet. The thing is, though, that virtually everyone who's interested in this material has already bought the four studio albums, sometimes several times over. A separate release of the two discs or so of truly new material would have been welcomed by the many fans who aren't interested in paying for a five-CD box of stuff when they already have well over half of it. But as a friend of mine is fond of saying, that eats into profit margins real fast. —*Richie Unterberger*

Loaded: Fully Loaded Edition / Feb. 18, 1997 / Rhino ✦✦✦✦

This does include the original *Loaded* album, with full-length versions of "Sweet Jane," "Rock & Roll," and "New Age" replacing the earlier edited ones. But that's less than half of the package; the rest of the two-disc, 33-track set is comprised of alternate mixes, alternate takes, and demos of the ten *Loaded* songs, as well as some songs that the group recorded during the *Loaded* era that didn't make it onto that LP. Some of this rare extraneous material surfaced on the *Peel Slowly and See* box, but a good half of this (17 tracks) was previously unreleased anywhere. Basically, it presents an entirely alternate version of the album, plus more where that came from. Those who aren't serious fans may well want to stick with the regular album release; many of the alternate takes and mixes are only subtly different. There are some real goodies here, though: a Dylanish demo of "I Found a Reason," a clumsy early version of "Sweet Jane," a previously unavailable outtake of "I'm Sticking with You," a more basic demo version of "Rock & Roll," a previously unissued spooky take of "Ocean," and "Love Makes You Feel Ten Feet Tall," the one song on this set that has been previously unreleased by the Velvets in any way, shape, or form (although Reed would do it on his first album as "Love Makes You Feel"). With a lengthy essay by David Fricke, it's fascinating history, and pretty good listening on its own terms. —*Richie Unterberger*

The Ventures

f. 1959, Tacoma, WA
Rock 'n' Roll, Instrumental Rock, Surf
From Tacoma, Washington, the Ventures were formed in 1959 originally named the Versatones. The early lineup consisted of Don Wilson (b. 1937), rhythm guitar; Bob Bogle (b. 1937), lead guitar; Nokie Edwards (b. 1939), bass; and Howie Johnson (b.?), drums. They pressed a twangy, rocked-up version of Johnny Smith's "Walk Don't Run" on their own Blue Horizon label, which was later picked up by Dolton Records. It became a No. 2 hit in 1960. Bogle and Edwards switched instruments and Mel Taylor replaced Johnson on drums in 1962. More hit singles featuring their cleanly played but rockin' style followed, but the band wisely entered the album market early on, and it was there they found their true format, placing 37 chart entries and recording more than 50 albums between 1960 and the mid '70s.

The Ventures are the biggest-selling instrumental group of all time, but their influence extends far beyond mere record sales. With their solid-body Fender guitars (later switching to Mosrite Ventures models) and matching suits, their album covers defined what a rock 'n' roll combo should look like. Likewise, their sound was so popular that they released several successful instructional albums in the *Play with the Ventures* series that many later rock stars cut their teeth on. Because they played instrumentals, they were among the first American bands to

break big in Japan (no language barrier), eventually honored as the first foreign members of that country's Conservatory of Music for selling over 40 million records. Edwards left and was replaced for a while by Jerry McGee, but he returned in 1972, restoring the early '60s lineup, which has endured to the present day. They continued to tour and record, sounding better than ever, their place in rock 'n' roll guitar history assured. —*Cub Koda*

The Ventures Play Telstar— The Lonely Bull and Others / 1962 / Liberty ✦✦

A Top Ten album for the group in early 1963, it really doesn't hold up today. Like many of their LPs, it demonstrates their versatility on faithful covers of a number of contemporary hits, ranging from rock to soul to easy listening. In every case, you're better off with the original versions. The CD reissue combines this album and their 1963 LP *The Ventures in Space.* —*Richie Unterberger*

Ventures in Space / 1963 / Dolton ✦✦✦

Few listeners need to dig deeper than a greatest hits collection for the Ventures, but this early effort is an arguable exception. The group embellished their trademark sleek guitar instrumentals with creepy, then-futuristic production effects, sounding at times like a mix of surf music and the incidental music to *Star Trek.* The ghostly, theremin-like sounds on several tracks are actually produced by top session player Red Rhodes on steel guitar. The British instrumental group the Tornados (of "Telstar" fame) did this kind of stuff better, if you're looking for this kind of thing. The CD reissue combines this album and the 1962 LP *The Ventures Play Telstar—The Lonely Bull and Others.* —*Richie Unterberger*

The Ventures on Stage / 1965 / Dolton ✦✦✦✦

Explosive live recordings from Japan, England, and the US, with a hot greatest-hits medley and a wild "Driving Guitars" being among the highlights. *The Ventures on Stage Around the World* is out of print but worth any search. —*Cub Koda*

★ **Walk, Don't Run: The Best of the Ventures** / 1990 / EMI America ✦✦✦✦✦

A perfect 29-track CD compilation, with great notes and superlative sound. All the hits, from "Walk Don't Run" to "Hawaii Five-O." Important album sides, plus interviews and radio spots. A perfect introduction. —*Cub Koda*

Live in Japan '65 / May 30, 1995 / Capitol ✦✦✦✦

Originally released in Japan as a double album, this live set was unavailable in the US until 1995. So cleanly recorded (the drums are especially crisp) that one is tempted to believe these tracks might have actually been laid down in the studios, it has a speedy, frenetic, well-executed edge that makes this worth checking out by Ventures fans. 78 minutes of material, including most of their big '60s hits, covers of then-contemporary surf and British Invasion tunes, and surprises like "The Pink Panther Theme" and a 10-minute version of Duke Ellington's "Caravan." —*Richie Unterberger*

Tele-Ventures / Nov. 12, 1996 / EMI ✦✦

The Ventures recorded a lot of instrumental versions of TV themes in the 1960s and 1970s, whether it was actually used as the theme (as with their hit "Hawaii Five-O") or, as was usually the case, was just a cover. It sounds like it might be a neat idea, but buyers beware: about half of the CD dates from 1976, and has discofied renditions of not-too-fondly remembered themes to the likes of *Charlie's Angels* and *Starsky & Hutch.* More in keeping with the classic lean Ventures sound are the 1960s cuts, which include versions of "Batman," "Secret Agent Man," "The Twilight Zone," and (maybe best of all) "The Man From U.N.C.L.E." Most of this really isn't too imaginative; only fan club members, for either the Ventures or the TV shows in question, should feel compelled to investigate. —*Richie Unterberger*

The Verlaines

f. 1982, New Zealand
Alternative Pop-Rock
A New Zealand guitar-pop group, the Verlaines released their first record in 1984. Led by singer-songwriter/guitarist Graeme Downes, the group has gone through several lineup changes throughout their career; by 1993, he was the only original member left in the group. —*Stephen Thomas Erlewine*

Hallelujah All the Way Home / 1985 / Homestead ✦✦✦

Hallelujah All the Way Home finds the band looking for a style, somewhat aimlessly. Through epic-length complex compositions, the band sometimes loses its way, but in a few cases (such as "It Was Raining") a glimpse of potential is revealed. Not a great album, but a few very good songs. —*Chris Woodstra*

● **Bird Dog** / 1987 / Homestead ✦✦✦✦

The strongest of their early albums and probably the defining Verlaines work, *Bird Dog* is the band's first great album and serves as the blueprint for much of their later work with its ambitious arrangements, unorthodox song structures and a mood that rapidly shifts from manic to melancholy . —*Chris Woodstra*

Juvenilia / 1987 / Homestead ✦✦✦✦
A collection of singles from the band's early career which provides an adequate introduction to the Verlaines' unique style. —*Chris Woodstra*

Some Disenchanted Evening / 1990 / Homestead ✦✦✦
Some Disenchanted Evening returns with an approximation of its predecessor's brilliance. This time the band is more effective on the more traditional straightahead rock than on the experiments. While it's not as cohesive an effort, "Jesus What a Jerk" is probably their best pop song to date. —*Chris Woodstra*

Ready to Fly / Jul. 1991 / Slash ✦✦
Ready to Fly marked the band's major label debut and (predictably) an increased mainstream pop awareness—the album sounds sort of like Verlaines-lite. Though it lacks the punch of *Bird Dog*, it is not without good points—Graeme Downes' songwriting is interesting as usual. —*Chris Woodstra*

Way out Where / Sep. 14, 1993 / Slash ✦✦
Now the only original member remaining in the band, songwriter Graeme Downes seems to have lost interest in his pet project. The songs are craftsmanlike pop but uninspired. Its commercial failure made the band decide to call it quits. —*Chris Woodstra*

Versus

f. 1992, New York, NY
Indie Rock
New York City's Versus evolved from the remnants of Flower, a band led by singer/guitarist Richard Baluyut. In the final months of Flower's existence, the group was joined by vocalist/guitarist Fontaine Toups, who remained with Baluyut in the short-lived Saturnine before the duo formed Versus (borrowing the name from an LP by Mission of Burma) with Baluyut's brother, Ed. After playing their first shows with a lineup comprising three guitars and a drum machine, Ed Baluyut relocated to the Phillipines, and Toups switched over to bass; upon Ed's return, he assumed drumming duties, and Versus issued its 1992 debut single, "Insomnia." In 1993, the trio issued the stellar EP *Let's Electrify!*, a taut, melodic collection spotlighting their intricate, dissonant guitar work and odd harmonies. After signing to the Teenbeat, Versus issued their 1994 full-length debut, *The Stars Are Insane* (originally titled *Meat, Sports and Rock*, three subjects the band ardently supported, much to the dismay of the prevailing indie-scene mentality of the moment). A collection of singles, compilation tracks, and demos titled *Dead Leaves* appeared in 1995, followed in early 1996 by the EP *Deep Red*. Another Baluyut brother, James, signed on for the 1996 LP *Secret Swingers*. —*Jason Ankeny*

Let's Electrify! / 1993 / Remora ✦✦✦✦
Issued on Richard Baluyut's own Remora label, Versus' six-cut opening salvo is the group's most viscerally exciting work; although the sameness of the production prompts the record to wear out its welcome by the closing "Sea Girl," much of *Let's Electrify!* is tense and wonderful—in particular, both the slow-burning "Noogie" and the dive-bombing title track rank among the trio's very best work. An auspicious debut. —*Jason Ankeny*

The Stars Are Insane / 1994 / TeenBeat ✦✦✦
Versus' full-length debut offers a more accomplished and textured sound than the trio's early singles or the *Let's Electrify!* EP. Opening with the atmospheric "Thera," the album is slow and seductive, relying on minimalist songwriting and an increased emphasis on the wonderfully off-kilter harmonies of Richard Baluyut and Fontaine Toups (most notably on the brilliant centerpiece "River"). —*Jason Ankeny*

Dead Leaves / Apr. 25, 1995 / TeenBeat ✦✦✦
Dead Leaves is a collection of singles, outtakes, and demos featuring Versus' debut offerings "Insomnia" and "Bright Light" as well as "Tin Foil Star," their stunning contribution to the Simple Machines label's *Working Holiday* series. Energetic but erratic, it's by no means the best introduction to the group, but the abundance of obscure material makes it essential for fans. —*Jason Ankeny*

Deep Red [EP] / 1996 / TeenBeat ✦✦✦
Issued as a stopgap between full-length releases, the beautifully packaged five-song EP *Deep Red* typifies Versus at their most tedious and uninspired. From "Dead City" (a dull rewrite of the brilliant "Let's Electrify!") to the lackluster noise blast "Linus" and the overwrought title cut, *Deep Red* is lifeless and muddy; still, as a test drive with just-added second guitarist James Baluyut, the record serves its purpose, getting the kinks out of the group's new, more complex sound in advance of the stellar *Secret Swingers*. —*Jason Ankeny*

● **Secret Swingers** / Jul. 30, 1996 / Caroline ✦✦✦✦
The addition of second guitarist James Baluyut brings a new, more intricate dimension to the Versus sound on *Secret Swingers*, a superbly tex-tured set more consistent and eclectic than anything else the band has done to date. While the *Deep Red* EP suggested that Versus had painted itself into a songwriting corner, each track here—from the taut "Glitter of Love" to the shimmering "Jealous"—sounds fresh and invigorated. Additionally, the group has learned the value of subtlety: the ethereal "One Million" is lovely, while "Ghost Story" achieves the haunting atmosphere promised by its title. Better still is the majestic "Angels Rush In," in which the point/counterpoint vocals of Richard Baluyut and Fontaine Toups stand firm against a slow-building but ultimately monolithic sound. —*Jason Ankeny*

Veruca Salt

f. 1993, Chicago, IL
Alternative Pop-Rock, Hard Rock
Veruca Salt reshaped the jagged, abrasive punk-pop of the Pixies and Breeders into a more accessible, riff-driven power-pop formula that also borrowed from hard pop-rockers like Cheap Trick. It was a successful formula, both musically and commercially, yet it didn't ensure them indie-rock credibility; in fact, they became one of the most harshly criticized bands of the post-Nirvana alternative rock era.

Led by guitarist/vocalist Louise Post and Nina Gordon, Veruca Salt released their debut single, "Seether"/"All Hail Me," in 1994 on a Chicago-based independent label, Minty Fresh. Produced by Brad Wood (Liz Phair), the record became a word-of-mouth sensation, working its way to alternative and college radio stations. While supporting Hole on their fall tour, Veruca Salt released their debut album, *American Thighs*, on Minty Fresh, yet they soon cut a deal with Geffen, who re-released the album. "Seether" became an MTV hit as well, and soon the single was an across-the-board success. However, the group received scathing criticism from magazines and fanzines, claiming the band were nothing but rip-off artists, using Minty Fresh as a way to gain credibility. Nevertheless, the group's popularity didn't suffer and *American Thighs* went gold, even though their next two singles—"Number One Blind" and "All Hail Me"—didn't attract half the attention of "Seether."

After releasing the stopgap, Steve Albini-produced EP *Blow It Out Your Ass It's Veruca Salt* in 1996, the band returned in early 1997 with *Eight Arms to Hold You*, which found the band moving toward hard rock and heavy metal. —*Stephen Thomas Erlewine*

● **American Thighs** / Oct. 25, 1994 / Minty Fresh ✦✦✦✦
With their thin, sing-song vocals and fuzzed-out guitars, Veruca Salt may sound like the Breeders and the Pixies, but lack either band's talent for inverting pop conventions, or taste for the bizarre. What Veruca Salt has instead is a raw talent for simple, infectious pop songs; the result is a surprisingly fresh fusion of alternative pop and bubblegum. Louise Gordon and Nina Post try hard to inject meaning into the sweet, distorted rush of "Seether," but all that sticks is the infectious melody and crushing guitars. That also applies to the slower songs, from the enchanting lust of "Spiderman '79" to "Forsythia," which is too close to the Breeders' *Pod* for comfort. But musically, *American Thighs* is surprisingly satisfying; it's a pure pop album masquerading as the next big thing. —*Stephen Thomas Erlewine*

Blow It out Your Ass It's Veruca Salt / Apr. 1996 / Minty Fresh/DGC ✦✦✦
Blow It Out Your Ass It's Veruca Salt is Veruca Salt's belated attempt for indie credibility. Recorded with Steve Albini, the four-song EP is a noisy, shrieking slice of indie guitar rock, featuring two songs apiece from Nina Gordon and Louise Post. Both of the songwriters contribute one pop song and one dirge-like grind; in both cases, the pop song is the superior song. However, the pop songs (Gordon's "Shimmer Like a Girl" and Post's "I'm Taking Europe with Me") are masked in shards of noise and screams that tend to obscure the melodies. But that was the intent of the EP—to prove that Veruca Salt isn't a simpering, little pop band. Unfortunately they are at their best when they have strong, catchy hooks—something "New York Mining Disaster 1996" and "Disinherit" completely lack—and when they try to be nothing but a noise-rock band, they just aren't as powerful. —*Stephen Thomas Erlewine*

Eight Arms to Hold You / Feb. 11, 1997 / Outpost ✦✦✦
In case the AC/DC allusion in the title of *American Thighs* didn't clue you in, the balls-to-the-wall crunch of *Eight Arms to Hold You* makes it clear that Veruca Salt were always closet metal fans. Sure, the album's title was the working title for *Help!* and there's an endearing love-note to David Bowie on the record, but the album couldn't sound further from the British Invasion or gender-bending art-rock if it had been recorded by the Prodigy. Thanks to producer Bob Rock, every song on the record is powered by fully-rounded heavy guitars and big, big drums—a sound that went out of style in 1990. Beneath it all, Nina Gordon and Louise Post still have a knack for charming, sing-song melodies, but only occasionally do these songs call for bombastic production. Those that do, like the infectious "Seether" re-write "Volcano Girls," qualify as guilty pleasures, but too often, the songs are buried by heavy guitars, since

Veruca Salt sounds awkward when they try to rock out. —*Stephen Thomas Erlewine*

The Verve

f. 1989, Wigan, England
Alternative Pop-Rock, Shoegazing, Dream-Pop
Crossing the crushingly loud, shimmering guitar textures of shoegazing with a sense of song structure derived from late-'60s psychedelia, the Verve earned a dedicated cult following in their native Britain during the early '90s. Though they never truly crossed over into the mainstream, their two albums received positive reviews and the praise of a number of their contemporaries, most notably Oasis' Noel Gallagher.

Originally called Verve, the band formed in 1989 in Wigan, England, comprised of vocalist Richard Ashcroft (b. September 11, 1971), guitarist Nick McCabe (b. July 14, 1971), bassist Simon Jones (b. July 29, 1972), and drummer Peter Salisbury (b. September 24, 1971). Verve gave their first concert in the fall of 1989, signing with the Virgin subsidiary Hut Records the following year. For the next few years, the band released a string of acclaimed singles, such as "(She's a Superstar)" and "Blue," which did well on the indie charts. *Storm in Heaven*, the group's debut album, was released in June of 1993.

Storm in Heaven received positive reviews in both Britain and America. In the UK, Verve became a hot band, as the music press began touting the band as one of the "next big things." It was a different situation in the US, where the record label Verve prevented the band from performing or releasing albums under the name "Verve." After a protracted legal battle, the band compromised and rechristened themselves the Verve.

In 1994, the Verve released the singles and B-sides compilation *No Come Down* and toured the US, performing on Lollapalooza's second stage. They also toured the UK, co-headlining with Oasis, who quickly befriended the Verve and eclipsed them in terms of success. The Verve hooked up with Oasis' producer Owen Morris to make their second album, *A Northern Soul.*

A Northern Soul was released in the summer of 1995 to overwhelmingly positive reviews from the British press, yet it was virtually ignored in America. Nevertheless, it performed well on the British charts, climbing into the Top 20. Despite the strong performance of the album, the Verve suddenly split during the fall of 1995 because of a creative and personal rift between Ashcroft and McCabe. Ashcroft performed a couple of solo acoustic shows, opening for Oasis toward the end of 1995. In the spring of 1996, Ashcroft, Jones, and Salisbury re-formed under a different band name and began working on demos; McCabe began working on his own solo project. —*Stephen Thomas Erlewine*

A Storm in Heaven / Jun. 1993 / Vernon Yard ✦✦✦✦
The Verve's debut album is a collection of cascading guitars and meandering melodies made memorable by the band's elliptical sense of songwriting. —*Stephen Thomas Erlewine*

No Come Down / May 17, 1994 / Vernon Yard ✦✦✦
No Come Down collects various singles, B-sides, and rarities; it's for devoted fans only. —*Stephen Thomas Erlewine*

● **A Northern Soul** / Jul. 1995 / Vernon Yard ✦✦✦✦
As the Verve's first album arrived amidst a torrent of good reviews and high commercial expectations, English guitar rock was just being revived with the glam-stop of Suede. By the time *A Northern Soul,* their second full-length album, was released, a lot had changed. Oasis and Blur had changed the scene of British guitar rock, bringing it away from the long, trance-inducing meditations of My Bloody Valentine and to a harder, more pop-oriented rock 'n' roll. With *A Northern Soul,* the band tried to rein in their psychedelic flourishes, working with Oasis' producer Owen Morris, bringing a pronounced backbeat to their sound. Nevertheless, their songs drag on a little too long to capitalize on their sheer sonic power—instead of seeming epic, the songs just seem ponderous. —*Stephen Thomas Erlewine*

The Verve Pipe

f. 1992, East Lansing, MI
Alternative Pop-Rock, Post-Grunge
The Verve Pipe were formed in Lansing, Michigan in 1992 by Brian Vander Ark (vocals, guitar), Donny Brown (drums, backup vocals), Brad Vander Ark (bass, backup vocals), and Brian Stout (guitar, backup vocals). The Vander Arks had played previously in Johnny with an Eye, and Brown and Stout had played in Water 4 the Pool—both bands had been local favorites throughout Michigan. They released their first independent album in the fall of 1992, *I've Suffered a Head Injury.* Stout was dropped in 1993 and was replaced by A.J. Dunning. The same year, they released their second independent album, *Pop Smear.* Through constant touring, they developed a strong reputation and rabid following in their home state, selling out larger venues and eventually selling a combined total of more than 40,000 copies of their first two albums.

In 1995, the Verve Pipe signed to RCA Records, releasing their major label debut, *Villains,* the following year. The album spent 15 weeks on *Billboard's* Heatseekers chart and the single, "Photograph," saw respectable airplay on alternative radio and MTV. Keyboardist Doug Corella was added as a full-time member the same year.

After spending a full year touring and promoting *Villains,* including an opening spot for Kiss on the European leg of their much-hyped reunion tour, the Verve Pipe finally began to make some headway in early 1997, when a re-recorded version of "The Freshman"—originally on the group's debut, *I've Suffered a Head Injury*—was released as a single. By the spring, "The Freshman" had become a No. 1 modern rock hit and a Top Ten pop hit, sending the album into the Top 40 and into gold status as well. —*Chris Woodstra*

I've Suffered a Head Injury / 1992 / Transom ✦✦✦
I've Suffered a Head Injury, released only months after the band formed, collects some of the stronger material from the members' previous bands (Johnny With An Eye and Water 4 the Pool) with each member contributing songs. While it's clearly a flawed debut, there is no shortage of great songs and the album shows a great deal of promise, incorporating a competent blend of quirky pop reminiscent of XTC crossed with the rocking side of R.E.M. and a brooding introspection obviously influenced by Bob Mould. [Upon signing to RCA, the album was reissued in a slightly modified form, dropping three songs including "The Freshman," the stark, emotional closer and easily the highpoint of the album. A re-recorded version of "The Freshman" would later appear on the RCA debut. The song was re-recorded again for the single release and became the band's first national hit.] —*Chris Woodstra*

Pop Smear / 1993 / LMNO Pop! ✦✦✦✦
With their second album, the addition of A.J. Dunning to the mix gives them a more agressive guitar sound. At the same time, they show a more adventurous side, exploring a broad definition of pop music from delicate love songs and 3/4 ballads to edgy, bitter rockers, even taking on the occasional Latin rhythm—each song takes on a different character, but all are tied together by pop smarts, clever songwriting, and lush four-part harmonies. —*Chris Woodstra*

● **Villains** / Mar. 26, 1996 / RCA ✦✦✦✦
The Verve Pipe made their major-label debut under the direction of producer Jerry Harrison with *Villains,* recasting themselves in the inauspicious mold of a post-grunge act. On an initial listen, the album does little to distinguish itself from the masses, though patient revisiting reveals a band of more depth, with Brian Vander Ark's songwriting improving vastly over previous albums and more subtle aspects, like the tasteful organic keyboard arrangements, actually adding texture and dimension to the sound. The band seemed to acknowledge the misstep by re-recording (yet again) "The Freshmen" for single release and subsequent pressings, which ultimately earned them their first national hit. —*Chris Woodstra*

The Vibrators

f. 1976, London, England
Punk
One of the great myths in rock 'n' roll is that only serious, dedicated musicians can make great records; a philosophical tract dictating that great rock 'n' roll is not the province of bandwagon jumpers, poseurs, fakes, and commercially minded trend groupies. The reality is that great rock 'n' roll can be made by anyone, even accidentally. Case in point, the Vibrators. If you saw a photograph of this "punk" band a few months before they signed a label deal with Columbia in 1976, you would have seen long hair, and bell-bottom trousers—they were bloody hippies! But, by the time they released their debut LP, *Pure Mania,* they had short hair, fake leopard skin pants, safety pins, cheap sunglasses, all the accoutrements a good born-again punk band needed. Did that make them inherently bad? Not really, a tad disingenuous perhaps, but no worse than a punk band (e.g., Generation X) that professed to being real punks all the while secretly harboring the desire of being as commercially viable as the dinosaur bands they purportedly loathed.

Although the existence of *Pure Mania* is a good illustration of accidental inspiration, it also proves that moments like this can happen once in a cross-filled career. Such was the case with the Vibrators who went on to record nearly a dozen records over a 15-year period, none of them worth mentioning. *Pure Mania,* on the other hand, remains as good now as it did when it was released. This is due to the fact that the band simply adapted a formula that eschewed the rage and ranch of the Sex Pistols and Clash for the relative accessibility of the Ramones and the Damned. So, while the Pistols sang "No Future," *Pure Mania* is jumpstarted by a track called "Into the Future." Even the songs about emotional desolation ("No Heart") are more catchy than frightening or ominous. Sure, *Pure Mania* is a fake through and through, but hating it for that reason alone makes you the boring old fart. Besides, the speedy guitars, irresistible hooks, and snappy songs are infectious. —*John Dougan*

Pure Mania / 1977 / Columbia ✦✦✦✦

Don't be fooled into thinking that, based on *Pure Mania*, the Vibrators released anything else of merit. They didn't. But this is a fine, funny fake of a record from the squalling "Into the Future . . ." to the softcore fantasy "Whips and Furs" to the tongue-in-cheek sexism of "I Need a Slave." Punky pop not punk rage. Not inspirational, but what did you expect from a bunch of poseurs? —*John Dougan*

● **The Power of Money: The Best of the Vibrators** / Dec. 1991 / Continuum ✦✦✦✦

By taking the best moments from the Vibrators' debut *Pure Mania*, as well as their inconsistent follow-ups, *Power of Money* winds up as a fine collection of their energetically melodic punk rock. —*Stephen Thomas Erlewine*

The Village People

f. 1977, New York, NY
Disco

Part clever concept, part exaggerated camp act, the Village People were worldwide sensations during disco's heyday and keep reviving like the phoenix. Producer Jacques Morali in 1977 assembled a group designed to attract gay audiences while parodying (some claimed exploiting) that same constituency's stereotypes. He landed a deal with Casablanca, then carefully recruited an appropriate cast of characters. These included go-go dancer Felipe Rose, who was dressed in Native American headdress when first spotted, Alexander Briley, Randy Jones, David Hodo, Glenn Hughes, and Victor Willis, the one group member with some genuine vocal skills. Songwriters Phil Hurtt and Peter Whitehead were tabbed to compose songs with gay underpinnings, and other roles and costumes were carefully selected; among them were a cowboy, biker, soldier, policeman, and construction worker complete with hard hat. The group clicked first in England with the single "San Francisco (You Got Me)" in 1977, then reaped stateside honors with "Macho Man" in 1978. "Y.M.C.A." and "In the Navy" were worldwide smashes, both peaking at number two on the pop charts. Neither song did as well on the R&B/soul side, with "In the Navy" doing best at number 30. Though a disco band rather than an R&B, soul, or funk unit, the Village People's ranks included at one time or another three solid singers in original lead vocalist Willis, his replacement Ray Simpson, and later Miles Jaye, who took Simpson's place. After two more successful singles, "Go West" and "Can't Stop the Music," the group's fortunes plummeted, in large part due to their participation in the ill-fated film also titled *Can't Stop the Music*. They tried a comeback with updated dance-rock material, but flopped. They've resurfaced in the '90s with more new cuts, though they haven't rekindled past success. Jaye became a major figure in Urban Contemporary circles in 1987, and continues recording and performing as a solo vocalist. —*Ron Wynn*

● **Greatest Hits** / 1988 / Rhino ✦✦✦✦

Rhino's *Greatest Hits* is a comprehensive overview of the Village People's biggest-hits, featuring 13 of their best-known songs, plus two bonus "disco mixes" of "Y.M.C.A." and "In the Navy." Not only are crossover hits like "Macho Man," "Go West," "Ready for the 80's" and "Can't Stop the Music" included, but so are key club hits like "Sodom and Gomorrah," "San Francisco (You've Got Me)," "My Roomate" and "Hot Cop," making it a near-definitive collection. —*Stephen Thomas Erlewine*

The Best of the Village People / Mar. 22, 1994 / Casablanca ✦✦✦✦

Casablanca's *The Best of the Village People* is nearly identical to Rhino's *Greatest Hits*, since it contains all of the big hits, plus a similar selection of club hits. This 14-track collection contains only one remix ("Y.M.C.A.," which is also present in its original single version), substitutes "Key West" for "Sodom and Gomorrah," and also includes "In Hollywood (Everybody Is a Star)." These are such slight differences that the collection will be just as appealing as Rhino's to most fans, and both are first-rate retrospectives. —*Stephen Thomas Erlewine*

Gene Vincent (Vincent Eugene Craddock)

b. Feb. 11, 1935, Norfolk, VA, d. Oct. 12, 1971, Los Angeles, CA
Vocals / Rock 'n' Roll, Rockabilly

Gene Vincent only had one really big hit, "Be Bop A Lula," which epitomized rockabilly at its prime in 1956 with its sharp guitar breaks, spare snare drums, fluttering echo, and Vincent's breathless, sexy vocals. Yet his place as one of the great early rock and roll singers is secure, backed by a wealth of fine smaller hits and non-hits that rate among the best rockabilly of all time. The leather-clad, limping, greasy-haired singer was also one of rock's original bad boys, lionized by romanticists of past and present generations attracted to his primitive, sometimes savage style and indomitable spirit.

Vincent was bucking the odds by entering professional music in the first place. As a 20-year-old in the Navy, he suffered a severe motorcycle accident that almost resulted in the amputation of his leg, and left him with a permanent limp and considerable chronic pain for the rest of his life. After the accident he began to concentrate on building a musical career, playing with country bands around the Norfolk, Virginia area. Demos cut at a local radio station, fronting a band assembled around Gene by his management, landed Gene Vincent and the Blue Caps a contract at Capitol, which hoped they'd found competition for Elvis Presley.

Indeed it had, as by this time Vincent had plunged into all-out rockabilly, capable of both fast-paced exuberance and whispery, almost sensitive ballads. The Blue Caps were one of the greatest rock bands of the '50s, anchored at first by the stunning silvery, faster-than-light guitar leads of Cliff Gallup. The slap-back echo of "Be-Bop-A-Lula," combined with Gene's swooping vocals, led many to mistake the singer for Elvis when the record first hit the airwaves in mid-1956, on its way to the Top Ten. The Elvis comparison wasn't entirely fair—Vincent had a gentler, less melodramatic style, capable of both whipping up a storm or winding down to a hush.

Brilliant follow-ups like "Race with the Devil," "Bluejean Bop," and "B-I-Bickey, Bi, Bo-Bo-Go" failed to click in nearly as big a way, although these too are emblematic of rockabilly at its most exuberant and powerful. By the end of 1956, the Blue Caps were beginning to undergo the first of constant personnel changes that would continue throughout the '50s, the most crucial being the departure of Gallup. The 35 or so tracks he cut with the band—many of which showed up only on albums or B-sides—were unquestionably Vincent's greatest work, as his subsequent recordings would never again capture their pristine clarity and uninhibited spontaneity.

Vincent had his second and final Top 20 hit in 1957 with "Lotta Lovin'," which reflected his increasingly tamer approach to production and vocals, the wildness and live atmosphere toned down in favor of poppier material, more subdued guitars, and conventional-sounding backup singers. He recorded often for Capitol throughout the rest of the '50s, and it's unfair to dismiss those sides out of hand; they were respectable, occasionally exciting rockabilly, only a marked disappointment in comparison with his earliest work. His act was captured for posterity in one of the best scenes of one of the first Hollywood films to feature rock and roll stars, *The Girl Can't Help It*.

Live Vincent continued to rock the house with reckless intensity and showmanship, and he became particularly popular overseas. A 1960 tour of Britain, though, brought tragedy when his friend Eddie Cochran, who shared the bill on Gene's UK shows, died in a car accident that Gene was also involved in, though Vincent survived. By the early '60s, his recordings had become much more sporadic and lower in quality, and his chief audience was in Europe, particularly in England (where he lived for a while) and France.

His Capitol contract expired in 1963, and he spent the rest of his life recording for several other labels, none of which got him close to that comeback hit. Vincent never stopped trying to resurrect his career, appearing at a 1969 Toronto rock festival on the same bill as John Lennon, though his medical, drinking, and marital problems were making his life a mess, and diminishing his stage presence as well. He died at the age of 36 from a ruptured stomach ulcer, one of rock's first mythic figures. —*Richie Unterberger*

● **Bop That Just Won't Stop** / 1974 / Capitol ✦✦✦✦

A good distillation of 12 of Vincent's best early tracks. Subsequent compilations have included this material and much more. But this is one of the most consistent of the lot, eliminating a lot of the average stuff and focusing exclusively on tracks cut with the band's first and best lineup (with guitarist Cliff Gallup). Beware of later editions of the LP that, inexcusably, eliminated a couple of the better songs. —*Richie Unterberger*

The Capitol Years 1956-63 / 1987 / Charly ✦✦✦✦

While Vincent recorded a fair number of overlooked gems during his prime, he also cut a greater number of uninspired tracks. This lavishly packaged and exhaustively annotated ten-album set inadvertently charts the rapidly plummeting quality of his recordings, even as it unearths worthy obscurities. It does manage to gather all of his classic 1956 sessions with guitarist Cliff Gallup in the same place, but Gene's subsequent efforts could have easily been boiled down to a supplementary disc or two. —*Richie Unterberger*

★ **Capitol Collectors Series** / 1990 / Capitol ✦✦✦✦✦

Breathless, unintelligible, and spirited rockabilly at its non-Sun best, this 21-track compilation covers Vincent's Capitol recordings (including "Be-Bop-A-Lula," "Race with the Devil," and "Lotta Lovin'") in admirable form. —*Hank Davis & Stephen Thomas Erlewine*

Greatest Hits / 1993 / Curb ✦✦

The bare bones of Vincent's best work, with ten tracks including "Be-Bop-A-Lula," "Lotta Lovin'," "Bluejean Bop," and "Race with the Devil." It gets a comparably low rating not for the quality of the music (which is good), but its brevity. There's a much more thorough, slightly more expensive Gene Vincent best-of available (on Capitol) that can be found with a minimum of effort. —*Richie Unterberger*

Gene Vincent Box Set / 1994 / EMI ✦✦✦✦
Six CDs containing the complete Capitol and EMI-Columbia recordings by Vincent, from 1956 through 1964. The 151 tracks may seem excessive, but the sound glitters, and since most of the post-1962 material was never issued in the United States, this stuff could be revelatory to serious fans. And the booklet is filled with detailed notes, sessionographies, and great photos. —*Bruce Eder*

★ **The Screaming End: Best of Gene Vincent** / Jan. 21, 1997 / Razor & Tie ✦✦✦✦
The Screaming End: The Best Of Gene Vincent & His Blue Caps contains 20 of Gene Vincent's very best songs, including all of his hit singles ("Be Bop A Lula," "Race With the Devil," "Lotta Lovin'," "Wear My Ring," "Dance to the Bop") and several lesser-known but equally exciting singles and album tracks ("Bluejean Bop," "Crazy Legs," "Cruisin'," "Cat Man," "Who Slapped John," "Jump Back, Honey, Jump Back," "B-I-Bickey Bi, Bo-Bo Go," "Red Blue Jeans & a Ponytail"). *The Screaming End* may have one less song than *Capitol Collectors Series*, but it contains a stronger selection of material and the original mixes, plus a more infectious, listenable sequence, making it the defintive single-disc overview of this rock 'n' roll pioneer. —*Stephen Thomas Erlewine*

Violent Femmes

f. 1982, Milwaukee, WI
Alternative Pop-Rock, New Wave
The textbook American cult band of the 1980s, the Violent Femmes captured the essence of teen angst with remarkable precision; raw and jittery, the trio's music found little commercial success but nonetheless emerged as the soundtrack for the lives of troubled adolescents the world over.

The Violent Femmes formed in Milwaukee, Wisconsin in the early '80s, and comprised singer/guitarist Gordon Gano, bassist Brian Ritchie and percussionist Victor DeLorenzo; Ritchie originated the band's oxymoronic name, adopting the word "femme" from the Milwaukee area's slang for wimps. After being discovered by the Pretenders' James Honeyman-Scott, the trio signed to Slash and issued their self-titled 1983 debut, a melodic folk-punk collection which struck an obvious chord with young listeners who felt a strong connection to bitter, frustrated songs like "Blister in the Sun," "Kiss Off" and "Add It Up." Though never a chart hit, the album remained a rite of passage for succeeding generations of teen outsiders, and after close to a decade in release it achieved platinum status. With 1984's *Hallowed Ground*, Gano's lyrics began to reflect his devout Baptist upbringing, while the group's music approached more traditional folk and country structures. Produced by the Talking Heads' Jerry Harrison, 1986's *The Blind Leading the Naked* advanced towards a more mainstream sound; a cover of the T. Rex chestnut "Children of the Revolution" even became a minor hit. After the record's release, the Femmes temporarily disbanded: Gano recorded a self-titled 1987 album with his gospel side project the Mercy Seat, while Ritchie issued a pair of solo LPs, 1987's *The Blend* and 1989's *Sonic Temple & Court of Babylon* for SST and *I See a Noise* for Dali Records in 1990.

In 1989, the group resurfaced with *3*, and followed in 1991 with *Why Do Birds Sing?*, which featured the Femmes' deconstructionist cover of Culture Club's "Do You Really Want to Hurt Me?" Following the release of the 1993 compilation *Add It Up (1981-1993)*, DeLorenzo exited to resume the solo career he began two years prior with the release of *Peter Corey Sent Me*; his sophomore effort, *Pancake Day*, appeared in 1996. Onetime Oil Tasters and BoDeans drummer Guy Hoffman was tapped as DeLorenzo's replacement in time to record 1994's *New Times* for Elektra Records. They left the label the following year. *Rock!!!!!* was released in 1995 on Mushroom Records only in Australia.—*Jason Ankeny*

★ **Violent Femmes** / 1983 / Slash ✦✦✦✦✦
One of the most distinctive records of the early alternative movement and an enduring cult classic, *Violent Femmes* weds the geeky, child-man persona of Jonathan Richman to the tense, jittery, hyperactive feel of new wave, plus the band's own raw, amateurish acoustic folk-rock. The music also owes something to the Modern Lovers' minimalism, but powered by Brian Ritchie's busy acoustic bass riffing and the urgency and wild abandon of punk rock, the Femmes forged a sound all their own. But the main reason *Violent Femmes* became the preferred soundtrack for the lives of many an angst-ridden teenager is lead singer and songwriter Gordon Gano. Naive and childish one minute, bitterly

frustrated and rebellious the next, Gano's vocals perfectly captured the contradictions of adolescence and the difficulties of making the transition to adulthood. Clever lyrical flourishes didn't hurt either; while "Blister In the Sun" has deservedly become a standard, songs like "Kiss Off," with its "count-up" section, "Add It Up," with its pleading "Why can't I get just one . . ." series of couplets, and "Gimme the Car"'s use of a guitar bend in place of the word "fuck," ensured that Gano's intensely vulnerable confessions of despair and maladjustment came off as catchy and humorous as well. Even if the songwriting slips a bit on occasion, Gano's personality keeps the music engaging and compelling without overindulging in his seemingly willful naivete. For the remainder of their career, the group would only approach this level in isolated moments. —*Steve Huey*

Hallowed Ground / 1985 / Slash ✦✦✦
Though mistaken for a parody when it was released, *Hallowed Ground* features Gordon Gano's serious Christian convictions. The teenage angst is pushed aside on this more mature effort based, for the most part, in traditional American folk—of course, it's slightly skewed. —*Chris Woodstra*

Blind Leading the Naked / 1986 / Slash ✦✦✦✦
A more mainstream effort courtesy of producer Jerry Harrison (Talking Heads). Gano returns to his troubled teen persona and the band rocks harder than on the previous two releases. A nice cover of the T-Rex classic "Children of the Revolution" and the yearning "I Held Her in My Arms," complete with a horn section, are highlights. —*Chris Woodstra*

3 / 1989 / Slash ✦✦
The fourth album finds the band in somewhat of a rut creatively. Fans of the band's early days will appreciate the slightly stripped-back acoustic production but, without much energy and less focus on teen angst, the album falls flat in most places. Only the single "Nightmares," and the confessional "See My Ships" leave any lasting impression. —*Chris Woodstra*

Debacle: The First Decade / 1991 / Slash ✦✦✦✦
This album is a compilation of all of their best recordings. Even though it contains a variety of the Femmes' changes in style, it doesn't live up to the standards of their first release. Still, enough highlights are covered to make this album the only other Violent Femmes album you'll need. —*Meredith Erlewine*

Why Do Birds Sing? / Apr. 30, 1991 / Reprise ✦✦✦
After a several-year absence, the Femmes make a comeback of sorts with the charming *Why Do Birds Sing?* Returning to their street-busking roots, the band plays stripped-back acoustic songs as a three piece. Though they can't fight the fact that they have grown up, the songs show that they can still have fun. —*Chris Woodstra*

Add It Up (1981-1993) / Sep. 14, 1993 / Warner Brothers ✦✦✦✦
Although it isn't as comprehensive as it seems, *Add It Up* is a good collection of most of the Violent Femmes' best tracks. —*AMG*

New Times / May 17, 1994 / Elektra ✦✦
This quirky release shows the band casting far afield stylistically after the comparatively consistent (and excellent) platter *Why Do Birds Sing?* Only the catchy "4 Seasons" and the guitar-vocal-only "I'm Nothing" are in the jittery busking style of their previous album. There are a modest number of harder-rocking selections here, such as "Key of 2," "Don't Start Me on the Liquor," and the title track. The rest of the songs on this release are highly eccentric, showing wide stylistic variation. "Mirror Mirror" is an ethnic-flavored ditty that would fit right alongside the numbers in the Broadway musical *Fiddler on the Roof;* oddly, the song ends with an avant-garde jazz improvisation section. "Jesus of Rio" alternates between slow waltz and fast polka sections. "Breakin' Up," with lyrics that reference Neil Sedaka's "Breaking Up Is Hard to Do," is a dour, menacing slow-tempo number that features growling, low-register singing. Also threatening in manner is "This Island Life," a moderate-speed song with a girl-group-derived thumping beat, a more upfront chorus, and a psychedelic closing section. Most unusual of all is "Machine"; derived from synthesizer techno-dance-beat music, this selection also slows the tempo considerably from other examples in that genre, mechanizes the musical delivery, and features electronically altered vocals. Lyrics are intelligent and effective; two selections, "Agamemnon" and the title cut, have verses derived from Walter Mehring's *Einfach Klassisch*. Sound quality and production are good. This at times bewildering album is worth a listen, especially for those with eclectic taste. —*David Cleary*

W

Wagon Christy

f. 1991, Falmouth, Cornwall, England
Trip-Hop, Club/Dance, Electronica
Luke Vibert is one of a new breed of European club music experimentalists whose work spans several genres simultaneously, and is one of a very few of that set to make any headway into US audiences. A native of Cornwall, Vibert's work has been compared with other West Country bedroom denizens like Aphex Twin and mu-Ziq, although his output over the past few years has been far more eclectic than that connection would seem to imply. Beginning with tweaky post-techno and moving through ambient and experimental hip-hop as Wagon Christ and, most recently, experimental drum'n'bass as Plug, Vibert has explored the outer reaches of post-techno electronica without sounding hasty or swank. Although Vibert's first musical experience was in a Beastie Boys knockoff band called the Hate Brothers, he quickly moved into the low-cost environment of solo bedroom composition. Although he had no intention of ever releasing any of the work, his reputation as a creative young voice in stylistic cross-pollination has created an increasing demand for his pioneering, often left-field work.

Vibert became involved in electronic music through his passion for hip-hop (he has commented that hip-hop is the only music style he really keeps up with), as well as the environment of bedroom experimentalism associated with the swelling late-'80s UK dance scene. He released an album through the Rephlex label (a solo album nonetheless billed as *Vibert and Simmons*) before coming to the attention of Caspar Pound's Rising High label. As a result of the growing exchange value of the style, RH commissioned an ambient album from Vibert, who, despite never having heard much ambient, delivered the well-received *Phat Lab Nightmare* under the Wagon Christ name in 1993. Silent (but for the quickie EP, *At Atmos*) for nearly two years following its release, Vibert came back in early 1995 with *Throbbing Pouch*, a collection of minimal, funky, off-kilter hip-hop that had fans familiar with his earlier work scratching their heads. Though lumped in with the so-called "trip-hop" movement attributed to Portishead, Tricky, Massive Attack, and the Mo'Wax label, the album's upbeat, cheeky edge was anything but stoney and laidback. Following up with a number of remixes and a Mo'Wax EP under his own name, Vibert embarked on his next major mutation with his Plug project, releasing a trio of sample-laden, epileptic jungle EPs, as well as the *Drum and Bass for Papa* LP in 1996. — *Sean Cooper*

Phat Lab Nightmare / 1993 / Rising High ✦✦✦
Twittering, at times noodly experimental ambient. Vibert's lack of familiarity with the genre's more formal properties is probably what makes this a worthwhile release. — *Sean Cooper*

Risalecki EP / 1994 / Rising High ✦✦✦✦
A portent of things to come, this EP was released the week before *Throbbing Pouch*, and indicated an adjustment in focus. Thumping breakbeats and minimal, scratchy electronics far closer to hip-hop or funky breaks than his first album. — *Sean Cooper*

Redone EP / 1995 / Rising High ✦✦✦
This EP includes a laidback version of "Reedin'" (from the *Throbbing Pouch* album), and one very experimental remix each from Aphex Twin and Voafose & Boymerang. — *John Bush*

● **Throbbing Pouch** / Sep. 5, 1995 / Rising High (UK) ✦✦✦✦
Scattered with dime-store samples and goofy melodies, this is eazy-listening instrumental hip-hop like Jay-Z or Premier would do it. Though the material is heavily sequenced, Vibert's arranging skills are in rare form, reordering elements and dropping tracks in and out with liquid, barely noticeable aplomb. Reissued by the short-lived Rising High USA. — *Sean Cooper*

The Wailers

f. 1958, Tacoma, WA, **db.** 1968
Rock 'n' Roll, Instrumental Rock, Garage Rock
The historical importance of the Wailers is undeniable. They were one of the very first, if not the first, of the American garage bands. Backing Rockin' Robin Roberts, they revamped an obscure R&B song called "Louie Louie" into a 1961 local hit (included here) that served as the prototype for the countless subsequent versions of the most popular garage song of the '60s. And their stomping, hard-nosed R&B/rock fusion inspired the Sonics, who took the Wailers' raunch to unimaginable extremes. While they anticipated the British Invasion bands with their brash, self-contained sound, their inability to write first-rate original material, as well as their rather outdated sax and organ-driven frat rock, put them in a distinctly lower echelon. As the decade progressed, the group did absorb mild folk-rock and psychedelic influences without great effect, either commercially or on their sound itself. — *Richie Unterberger*

● **Fabulous Wailers, The Boys From Tacoma: Anthology 1961-1969** / 1993 / Etiquette ✦✦✦✦
A 27-song anthology drawn from their many singles and albums. Whether backing other singers, playing instrumentals, or performing their own material, the group rarely escaped the classic three-chord progression. What must have been a revelation in the teen ballrooms of the early '60s is a rather flat and repetitious listening experience. This is a fun compilation, but it should not be mistaken for a work of major significance. — *Richie Unterberger*

John Waite

b. 1955, Lancashire, England
Bass, Vocals / Soft Rock, Pop-Rock, Arena Rock
As a solo artist and as the lead singer of the Babys and Bad English, John Waite was a fixture on album-oriented rock radio stations during the '70s and '80s. Waite had a talent for power ballads and driving arena-rock, occasionally touching on new wave-styled power-pop, as well. Though he didn't consistently have hits, several of his songs—including "Missing You," the Babys' "Isn't It Time," and Bad English's "When I See You Smile"—became radio staples.

John Waite formed the Babys in London, England in 1976 with Wally Stocker (guitar), Mike Corby (vocals, keyboards), and Tony Brock (drums). Initially conceived as a teen-pop band, the group earned a record contract based on the strength of a video demo they constructed with producer Mike Mansfield. Chrysalis pushed the band heavily, resulting in "Isn't It Time" becoming a hit in the US and UK in 1977. As their career progressed, the group began to experiment with synthesized, new wave-inspired power pop, which resulted in a handful of minor hits. Jonathan Cain became the band's keyboardist in 1978, and he and Waite developed a close relationship. When Cain left the Babys to join Journey in 1981, the group disbanded.

Waite began his solo career the following year, releasing *Ignition* on Chrysalis. While the album generated the minor hit "Change," his second album, 1984's *No Brakes*, became a genuine Top Ten hit on the strength of the No. 1 single "Missing You." While "Missing You" was an international smash, eventually becoming one of the best-remembered songs of the early MTV era, *No Brakes* produced only one other hit, the Top 40 "Every Step of the Way." Its failure to produce another blockbuster was indicative of how Waite's solo career would proceed. Neither *Mask of Smiles* (1985) nor *Rover's Return* (1987) produced any hits, bringing Waite's career to a standstill.

With his career stalled, Waite formed the supergroup Bad English with former Babys Jonathan Cain and Ricky Phillips (bass), ex-Journey guitarist Neal Schon, and drummer Deen Castronovo. The group's eponymous debut, released in 1989 on Epic Records, became a platinum success after the power ballad "When I See You Smile" became a No. 1 hit. "Price of Love" was a Top Ten hit in the wake of "When I See You Smile," but their 1991 followup *Backlash* suffered from one. Bad English broke up shortly after the album's release. Waite resumed his solo career in 1995, releasing *Temple Bar* on Imago. — *Stephen Thomas Erlewine*

● **Falling Backwards: the Complete John Waite** / Nov. 12, 1996 / EMI ✦✦✦✦

A 17-track career retrospective that not only spans the mid-'70s to the mid-'90s, but also encompasses solo cuts and songs that he recorded with the Babys in the '70s, and Bad English in the '80s. For all that, it's remarkably inconsequential right-of-center mainstream commercial rock, whether he's playing guitar-based pop-rock with the Babys, or doing the power ballad thing with Bad English. Includes his 1984 No.1 solo single "Missing You," the Bad English smashes "When I See You Smile" and "Price of Love," and several smaller hits. — *Richie Unterberger*

The Waitresses

f. 1981, New York, NY, **db.** 1983
New Wave
The Waitresses existed for the purpose of performing the witty, often female-oriented songs of guitarist Chris Butler, who had previously led a series of new wave bands in Cleveland. The personnel of the band as of its 1982 debut album, *Wasn't Tomorrow Wonderful*, was, in addition to Butler, singer Patty Donahue, backup singer Ariel Warner, reed player Mars Williams, bassist David Horstra, drummer Billy Ficca (a once and future member of Television), and keyboardist Dan Klayman. The group recorded two albums and a mini-LP in the early '80s, stirring critical acclaim and international interest before both Donahue and Butler left. Ficca fronted the band for a while, then they broke up. Donahue died of cancer in 1996. — *William Ruhlmann*

Wasn't Tomorrow Wonderful? / 1982 / Polydor ✦✦✦✦
"No Guilt," in which Donahue's matter-of-fact voice details what a spurned lover has found out since the breakup ("I learned the reason for a three-pronged outlet"), and "I Know What Boys Like" are the standouts among these clever songs, but the whole album has an attitude that won't quit. — *William Ruhlmann*

Bruiseology / 1983 / Polydor ✦✦
By 1983, the band had all but fallen apart and *Bruiseology* reflects much of the inner turmoil with a generally lackluster batch of songs—obviously the novelty hadn't held up well for the band and the fun had worn off. Nothing on the album approached "I Know What Boys Like" or even "Square Pegs," released slightly before the album. — *Chris Woodstra*

● **The Best of the Waitresses** / Oct. 1990 / Polydor ✦✦✦✦
Best of the Waitresses gives a good career overview of the band, collecting the bulk of the highpoints from their two albums, of course including the unforgettable "I Know What Boys Like" as well as some fun non-LP cuts like "Square Pegs" (the theme from the "valley girl" TV show *Square Pegs*) and the fun holiday rap, "Christmas Wrapping." *Best of the Waitresses* offers ample proof that the band deserved more than "one-hit wonder" status though this collection is probably all that most people need. The more ambitious should add the *King Biscuit Flower Hour* disc for a sampling of the band's truly inspired live shows. — *Chris Woodstra*

King Biscuit Flower Hour / Mar. 25, 1997 / King Biscuit ✦✦✦✦
Recorded live at My Father's Place in Roslyn, Long Island, New York, at the time of the release of their first album, this concert catches the Waitresses at the outset of their all-too-brief national career. Captured live for posterity are "I Know What Boys Like," "No Guilt," "Christmas Wrapping," and eight other songs, all jewels in the output of Chris Butler and catching the late Patty Donahue at her early peak—when she does the telephone monologue bit on "No Guilt" ("I'm just a busy girl . . .") or the spoken/sung part on "Wise Up," she shows herself a better actress than Madonna. Mars Williams' stuttering sax is also a treat. The only thing missing is the title theme they did to the TV series *Square Pegs*. Better than their Polygram best-of. God bless King Biscuit for putting this out. — *Bruce Eder*

Tom Waits

b. Dec. 7, 1949, Pomona, CA
Organ, Guitar, Piano, Harmonium, Vocals / Singer-Songwriter, Experimental
In the 1970s, Tom Waits combined a lyrical focus on desperate, lowlife characters with a persona that seemed to embody the same lifestyle, which he sang about in a raspy, gravelly voice. From the '80s on, his work became increasingly theatrical as he moved into acting and composing. Growing up in Southern California, Waits attracted the attention of manager Herb Cohen, who also handled Frank Zappa, and was

signed by him at the beginning of the 1970s, resulting in the material later released as *The Early Years* and *The Early Years, Vol. 2*. His formal recording debut came with *Closing Time* (1973) on Asylum Records, an album that contained "Ol' 55," which was covered by labelmates the Eagles on their *On the Border* album. Waits attracted critical approbrium and a cult audience for his subsequent albums, *The Heart of Saturday Night* (1974), the two-LP live set *Nighthawks at the Diner* (1975), *Small Change* (1976), *Foreign Affairs* (1977), *Blue Valentine* (1978), and *Heart Attack and Vine* (1980). His music and persona proved highly cinematic, and starting in 1978 he launched parallel careers as an actor and as a composer of movie music. He wrote songs for and appeared in *Paradise Alley* (1978), wrote the title song for *On the Nickel* (1980), and was hired by director Francis Coppola to write the music for *One from the Heart* (1982), which earned him an Academy Award nomination. While working on that project, Waits met and married playwright Kathleen Brennan, with whom he later collaborated. Moving to Island Records, Waits made *Swordfishtrombones* (1983), which found him experimenting with horns and percussion and using unusual recording techniques. The same year, he appeared in Coppola's *Rumble Fish* and *The Outsiders*, and in 1984, he appeared in the director's *The Cotton Club*. In 1985, he released *Rain Dogs*. In 1986, he appeared in *Down by Law* and made his theatrical debut with Chicago's Steppenwolf Theatre in *Frank's Wild Years*, a musical play he had written with Brennan. An album based on the play was released in 1987, the same year Waits appeared in the films *Candy Mountain* and *Ironweed*. In 1988, he released a film and soundtrack album depicting one of his concerts, *Big Time*. In 1989, he appeared in the films *Bearskin: An Urban Fairytale*, *Cold Feet*, and *Wait Until Spring*. In 1991, he appeared in the films *Quee's Logic*, *The Fisher King*, and *At Play in the Fields of the Lord*. In 1992, he scored the film *Night on Earth*, released the album *Bone Machine*, which won a Grammy Award for Best Alternative Music Album, and appeared in the films *Deadfall* and *Bram Stoker's Dracula*. In 1993, he released *The Black Rider*, the recording of a musical he had co-written with Beat novelist William Burroughs for opera director Robert Wilson in 1990, and appeared in the film *Short Cuts*. — *William Ruhlmann*

● **Closing Time** / 1973 / Asylum ✦✦✦✦
Tom Waits' debut album was a minor-key masterpiece filled with songs of late-night loneliness. Within the apparently narrow range of the cocktail bar pianistics and muttered vocals, Waits and producer Jerry Yester managed a surprisingly broad collection of styles, from the jazzy "Virginia Avenue" to the uptempo funk of "Ice Cream Man" and from the acoustic guitar folkiness of "I Hope that I Don't Fall in Love with You" to the saloon song "Midnight Lullaby," which would have been a perfect addition to the repertoires of Frank Sinatra or Tony Bennett. Waits' entire musical approach was stylized, of course, and at times derivative—"Lonely" borrowed a little too much from Randy Newman's "I Think It's Going to Rain Today"—and his lovelorn lyrics could be sentimental without being penetrating. But he also had a gift for gently rolling pop melodies, and he could come up with striking, original scenarios, as on the best songs, "Ol' 55" and "Martha," which Yester discreetly augmented with strings. *Closing Time* announced the arrival of a talented songwriter whose self-conscious melancholy could be surprisingly moving. — *William Ruhlmann*

The Heart of Saturday Night / 1974 / Asylum ✦✦✦
If *Closing Time*, Tom Waits' debut album, consisted of love songs set in a late-night world of bars and neon signs, its follow-up, *The Heart of Saturday Night*, largely dispensed with the romance in favor of poetic depictions of the same setting. On "Diamonds on My Windshield" and "The Ghosts of Saturday Night," Waits didn't even sing, instead reciting his verse rhythmically against bass and drums like a Beat hipster. Musically, the album contained the same mixture of folk, blues, and jazz as its predecessor, with producer Bones Howe occasionally bringing in an orchestra to underscore the loping melodies. Waits' songs were sometimes sketchier in addition to being more impersonal, but "(Looking For) The Heart of Saturday Night" and "Semi Suite" were the equal of anything on *Closing Time*. Still, with lines such as " . . . the clouds are like headlines / Upon a new front page sky" and references to "a 24-hour moon" and "champagne stars," Waits' imagery was beginning to get florid, and in material this stylized, the danger of self-parody was always present. — *William Ruhlmann*

Nighthawks at the Diner / Oct. 1975 / Asylum ✦✦✦
For his third album, Tom Waits set up a nightclub in the studio, invited an audience, and cut a 70-minute, two-LP set of new songs. It was an appropriate format for compositions that dealt even more graphically and, for the first time, humorously, with Waits' late-night world of bars and diners. The love lyrics of his debut album had long since given way to a comic lonely guy stance glimpsed in "Emotional Weather Report" and "Better off Without a Wife." But what really mattered was the elaborate scene-setting of songs like the six-and-a-half-minute "Spare Parts," the seven-and-a-half-minute "Putnam County," and especially the

eleven-minute "Nighthawk Postcards" that were essentially poetry recitations with jazz backing. Waits was a colorful tour guide of midnight Los Angeles, raving over a swinging rhythm section of Jim Hughart (bass) and Bill Goodwin (drums), with Pete Christlieb wailing away on tenor sax between paragraphs and Mike Melvoin trading off with Waits on piano runs. You could call it overdone, but then, this kind of material made its impact through an accumulation of miscellaneous detail, and who was to say how much was too much? — *William Ruhlmann*

Small Change / Oct. 1976 / Asylum ✦✦✦✦
The fourth release in Tom Waits' series of skid-row travelogues, *Small Change* proved to be the archetypal album of his '70s work. A jazz trio comprising tenor sax player Lew Tabackin, bassist Jim Hughart, and drummer Shelly Manne, plus an occasional string section, backed Waits and his piano on songs steeped in whiskey and atmosphere in which he alternately sang in his broken-beaned drunk's voice (now deeper and overtly influenced by Louis Armstrong) and recited jazzy poetry. It was as if Waits was determined to combine the Humphrey Bogart and Dooley Wilson characters from *Casablanca* with a dash of *On the Road's* Dean Moriarty to illuminate a dark world of bars and all-night diners. Of course, he'd been in that world before, but in songs like "The Piano Has Been Drinking" and "Bad Liver and a Broken Heart," Waits gave it its clearest expression. *Small Change* is not Tom Waits' best album. It is, like most of the albums he made in the '70s, uneven, probably because he was putting out one a year and didn't have time to come up with enough first-rate material. But it is the most obvious and characteristic of his albums for Asylum Records. If you like it, you also will like the ones before and after it; otherwise, you're not Tom Waits' kind of listener. — *William Ruhlmann*

Foreign Affairs / Sep. 1977 / Asylum ✦✦✦
Tom Waits gave one side of his fifth album to his more structured, bluesy ballads and the other to his jazz raps. On side one, you got his duet with Bette Midler on the singles-bar dialogue "I Never Talk to Strangers" and his take on his Beat predecessors, Jack Kerouac and Neal Cassidy on "Jack Neal." On side two, you found the extended observations of "Potter's Field" and "Burma Shave." Waits' voice was becoming ever more gravelly, but his basic musical approach remained the same, and he had attracted a steady cult audience that enjoyed his verbal flights and boozy philosopher persona, even as critics began to complain that he was repeating himself. By the way, that's Waits' then-girlfriend, the then-unknown Rickie Lee Jones, on the cover with him. — *William Ruhlmann*

Blue Valentine / Oct. 1978 / Asylum ✦✦✦
Two welcome changes in style made *Blue Valentine* a fresh listening experience for Tom Waits fans. First, Waits had altered the instrumentation, bringing in electric guitar and keyboards and largely dispensing with the strings for a more blues-oriented, hard-edged sound. Second, though his worldview remained fixed on the lowlifes of the late night, he had expanded beyond the musings of the barstool philosopher who previously had acted as the first-person character of most of his songs. When Waits did use the "I," it was to write a "Christmas Card from a Hooker in Minneapolis," not the figure most listeners had associated with the singer himself. The result was a broadening of subject matter, a narrative discipline that made most of the tunes story songs, and a coherent framing for Waits' typically colorful and intriguing imagery. These were not radical reinventions, but Waits had followed such a rigidly stylized approach on his previous albums that for anyone who had followed him so far, the course correction was big news. — *William Ruhlmann*

Heartattack and Vine / Sep. 1980 / Asylum ✦✦✦
Heartattack and Vine, Tom Waits' first album in two years and his last of seven for Asylum Records, was a transitional album, with tracks like the rhythm-heavy title song and "'Til the Money Runs Out" foreshadowing the sonic experiments of the Island albums, while piano-with-orchestra tracks like "Saving All My Love for You" and "On the Nickel" (written as a motion-picture title tune) harked back to Waits' Randy Newman-influenced early days. It was just as well that Waits never entirely gave up on the ballad material; "Jersey Girl," a Drifters-style song, was a winner, and it was appropriated by Bruce Springsteen on his 1981 tour. Also, at least at this point, the rougher tunes all tended to sound the same. — *William Ruhlmann*

☆ **Swordfishtrombones** / Sep. 1983 / Island ✦✦✦✦
Between the release of *Heartattack and Vine* in 1980 and *Swordfishtrombones* in 1983, Tom Waits got rid of his manager, his producer, and his record company. And he drastically altered a musical approach that had become as dependable as it was unexciting. *Swordfishtrombones* had none of the strings and much less of the piano work that Waits' previous albums had employed; instead, the dominant sounds on the record were low-pitched horns, bass instruments, and percussion, set in spare, close-miked arrangements (most of them by Waits) that sometimes were better described as "soundscapes." Lyrically, Waits' tales of the drunken and the lovelorn had been replaced by surreal accounts of

people who burned down their homes and of Australian towns bypassed by the railroad—a world (not just a neighborhood) of misfits now had his attention. The music could be primitive, moving to odd time signatures, while Waits alternately howled and wheezed in his gravelly bass voice. He seemed to have moved on from Hoagy Carmichael and Louis Armstrong to Kurt Weill and Howlin' Wolf (as impersonated by Captain Beefheart). Waits seems to have had trouble interesting a record label in the album, which was cut 13 months before it was released, but when it appeared rock critics predictably raved: After all, it sounded weird and it didn't have a chance of selling. Actually, it did make the bottom of the bestseller charts, like most of Waits' albums, and, now that he was with a label based in Europe, even charted there. Artistically, *Swordfishtrombones* marked an evolution of which Waits had not seemed capable (though there were hints of this sound on his last two Asylum albums), and in career terms it re-invented him. — *William Ruhlmann*

★ **Rain Dogs** / Aug. 1985 / Island ✦✦✦✦✦
From the New York streets to the Orient ("Singapore") and back, Waits continues his colorful survey, alternately challenging the listener (especially in Marc Ribot's guitar playing) and returning to the melodic style of the past ("Downtown Train"). Keith Richards guests on gritty "Big Black Mariah," while "Time" is one of his best ballads. — *William Ruhlmann*

The Asylum Years / Oct. 1986 / Asylum ✦✦✦✦
The second British Tom Waits compilation was a more extensive look at the 1973-1980 Asylum Records catalog than the first, *Bounced Checks* from 1981 (fourteen tracks vs. ten), but it was another idiosyncratic selection. Waits' stellar first two albums were better represented, with three strong tracks drawn from *The Heart of Saturday Night* and two from *Closing Time*, but "Ol' 55" was ignored again, and nothing was included from the third album, *Nighthawks at the Diner*, which is the favorite of many Waits fans. Three tracks were repeated from *Bounced Checks* —"Burma Shave," "I Never Talk to Strangers," a duet with Bette Midler, and "Tom Traubert's Blues"—and they were worthy, but where was "Jersey Girl"? The choices from the later albums were spotty: Why use Waits' questionable cover of "Somewhere" from *West Side Story* and leave out a brilliant story song like "Romeo Is Bleeding"? The overall unevenness of the Asylum albums cries out for a well-chosen compilation. After three attempts in the US and UK, it still hasn't been assembled. — *William Ruhlmann*

Franks Wild Years / Aug. 1987 / Island ✦✦✦✦
Tom Waits wrote a song called "Franks Wild Years" for his 1983 *Swordfishtrombones* album, then used the title (minus its apostrophe) for a musical play he wrote with his wife, Kathleen Brennan, and toured with in 1986. The *Franks Wild Years* album, drawn from the show, is subtitled, "un operachi romantico in two acts," though the songs themselves do not carry the plot. Rather, this is just the third installment in Waits' eccentric series of Island Records albums in which he seems most inspired by German art song and carnival music, presenting songs in spare, stripped-down arrangements using instruments like marimba, baritone horn, and pump organ and singing in a strained voice that has been artificially compressed and distorted. The songs themselves often are conventional romantic vignettes, or would be, minus the oddities of instrumentation, arrangement, and performance. For example, "Innocent When You Dream," a song of disappointment in love and friendship, has a winning melody, but it is played in a seesaw arrangement of pump organ, bass, violin, and piano, and Waits sings it like an enraged drunk. (He points up the arbitrary nature of the arrangements by repeating "Straight to the Top," done as a demented rhumba in Act I, as a Vegas-style Frank Sinatra swing tune in Act II.) The result on record may not be theatrical, exactly, but it certainly is affected. It also has the quality of an inside joke that listeners are not being let in on. — *William Ruhlmann*

Big Time / Sep. 1988 / Island ✦✦✦
Big Time is an 18-track live album running nearly 68 minutes, its material drawn mostly from Tom Waits' trio of recent studio albums, *Swordfishtrombones*, *Rain Dogs*, and *Franks Wild Years*. (One track, "Falling Down," is a previously unissued studio recording. The performance of "Strange Weather" marks Waits' first recording of a song he and his wife, Kathleen Brennan, wrote for Marianne Faithull.) It's challenging music, made somewhat more accessible in a live context. Waits' performances tended to be somewhat over the top on the studio versions of these songs, but before a live audience his theatrics seem more appropriate, and he even includes a mini-set of piano ballads. Still, it takes him until the seventh tune, "Way Down in the Hole," to bring the audience to life, and he rarely speaks, in marked contrast to the earlier live-in-the-studio album *Nighthawks at the Diner*. But *Big Time* makes a useful sampler of Waits' later work that might enable a listener to determine whether to invest in the studio recordings. — *William Ruhlmann*

The Early Years / Jul. 1991 / Bizarre/Straight ✦✦✦✦
This is an album of early demos recorded by a 21-year-old Tom Waits in 1971, two years before the release of his first album, *Closing Time*, and issued on the record label owned by his ex-manager. Waits accompanies himself on piano or guitar and sings in an unaffected nasal tenor. (One track, "Ice Cream Man," is given a full-band treatment.) Several of these songs, notably "Ice Cream Man," "Virginia Ave.," "Midnight Lullaby," and "Little Trip to Heaven," turned up on his later albums, but the overall level of writing and performance is well below Waits' usual standard. Clearly, his better early material was chosen for his Asylum albums. Hardcore fans will want to hear this album, of course, but others need not bother. — *William Ruhlmann*

Night on Earth / Apr. 1992 / Island ✦✦
Tom Waits brings an appropriately international flavor to his mostly instrumental score for Jim Jarmusch's globetrotting taxicab movie. As in all his music of the past ten years, Waits' chief influence is Kurt Weill, and using horns and accordion among other instruments, he recreates Weill's creepy, catchy style in 16 short tracks running almost 53 minutes. He and Kathleen Brennan contribute three songs with lyrics, which Waits performs in a calmer, more melodic way than those on some of his recent albums. Still, this soundtrack is very much in the style of Waits' *Swordfishtrombones*, *Rain Dogs*, and *Franks Wild Years* albums. — *William Ruhlmann*

☆ **Bone Machine** / Aug. 1992 / Island ✦✦✦✦✦
A set of dark, stripped-down songs, Bone Machine is a bleak, melancholy song cycle of decay and despair. It's also his best album, full of wonderfully evocative songs and haunting, primitive sounds. — *Stephen Thomas Erlewine*

The Early Years, Vol. 2 / Feb. 1993 / Bizarre/Straight ✦✦✦✦
Like its predecessor, *The Early Years, Vol. 2* consists of demos recorded by Tom Waits in 1971, two years before he released his debut album, *Closing Time*. "Hope I Don't Fall in Love with You," "Ol' 55," "Grapefruit Moon," and "Old Shoes" later turned up on that album, while "Shiver Me Timbers," "Diamonds on My Windshield," and "Please Call Me Baby" appeared on Waits' second album, *The Heart of Saturday Night*, in 1974. The release of the two *Early Years* albums demonstrates that Waits' better early material made it onto his regular releases—the previously unreleased stuff, while interesting, is not as good. And since Waits' albums were not overproduced, the main difference between these versions and the familiar ones is that the familiar ones are better. Still, Waits fans will enjoy hearing, for example, "Ol' 55" performed in a higher key and with an acoustic guitar backing. — *William Ruhlmann*

The Black Rider / Nov. 2, 1993 / Island ✦✦
Written with William S. Burroughs and Robert Wilson, Tom Waits' version of their operetta is an intriguing mess that tends to be too scattered to be truly effective. — *Stephen Thomas Erlewine*

Rick Wakeman

b. May 18, 1949, London, England
Keyboards / Art-Rock/Progressive-Rock
Born in Perivale, Middlesex, England, Rick Wakeman's interest in music manifested itself very early, and from the age of seven on he studied classical piano. At the age of 14, he joined a local band, Atlantic Blues, the same year he left school to enroll in the Royal College of Music. He had his eye on a career as a concert pianist, but Wakeman was dismissed from the college after it became clear that he preferred playing in clubs to studying technique.

By his late teens, he was an established session man, playing on records by such diverse acts as Black Sabbath, Brotherhood of Man, and Edison Lighthouse. At the end of the 1960s, his name also began appearing on the credits of albums by such artists as Al Stewart and David Bowie, and one set of sessions with a folk-rock band called the Strawbs led to his joining the group in 1970. After two albums with the Strawbs, Wakeman joined Yes, a post-psychedelic hard rock band that had attracted considerable attention with their first three albums. Wakeman played a key role in the final shape of the group's fourth record, *Fragile*, creating a fierce, swirling sound on an array of synthesizers, Mellotrons, electric and acoustic pianos. *Fragile* was a hit, driven by the chart success of the single "Roundabout," and Wakeman was suddenly elevated to star status.

Yes' next album, *Close to the Edge*, expanded his audience and his appeal, for his instruments were heard almost continually on the record. During the making of *Close to the Edge* in 1972, Wakeman also recorded his first solo album, an instrumental work entitled *The Six Wives of Henry VIII*, which consisted of his musical interpretations of the lives and personalities of the said six royal spouses. Released early in 1973 on A&M Records, it performed respectably on the charts. Public reception of Yes' 1974 album, *Tales from Topographic Oceans*, was mixed, and the critics were merciless in their attacks upon the record. Wakeman exited the group before the album's supporting tour. His new solo album, *Journey to the Center of the Earth*, adapted from the writings of Jules Verne, and featuring a rock band, narrator (David Hemmings), and full orchestral and choral accompaniment, was released to tremendous public response in both America and England, where it topped the charts. In 1975, his next album, *The Myths and Legends of King Arthur and the Knights of the Round Table*, was given a grand-scale premiere at Wembley's Empire Pool, although it also cost Wakeman a fortune to stage the event on ice. During this same period, Wakeman began working on film scores with the music for Ken Russell's *Lisztomania*, which was a modest hit.

In 1977, Wakeman returned to Yes, with which he has continued recording and touring. His solo career continued on A&M into the end of the 1970s, with *Criminal Record* and *Rhapsodies*, which were modestly successful. Wakeman's biggest media splash during this period, however, came through his alleged role in getting the Sex Pistols dropped by A&M Records soon after being signed. None of this bothered his fans, which rapidly expanded to encompass those he picked up through his work with lyricist Tim Rice on a musical adaptation of George Orwell's *1984*, and his burgeoning film work, which included the music to movies about the 1976 Winter Olympics and the 1982 soccer World Cup competition. Additionally, he became a regular on Britain's Channel 4. Wakeman's audience and reputation survived the 1980s better than almost any progressive rock star of his era, as he continued releasing albums on his own label. He was also remained associated with Yes into the '90s. — *Bruce Eder*

● **The Six Wives of Henry the VIII** / 1973 / A&M ✦✦✦✦
Wakeman's first solo album is also his least pretentious work and, in many respects, his most effective. Essentially a selection of six electronic tone paintings done on a multitude of synthesizers, Mellotrons, and other keyboard instruments, all of the material here is beautifully melodic and excitingly played and arranged, based on the lives and perceived personalities of Henry VIII's six spouses. Some of the music comes off as trite 19th-century Romantic meanderings, but the running times are held in check, and besides, that seems to be exactly what Wakeman was aiming for. — *Bruce Eder*

Journey to the Center of the Earth / Jan. 1974 / A&M ✦✦✦✦
Wakeman's chart-topping album (in England) paints a broader musical canvas than its predecessor, with orchestra, chorus, narrator, and rock band surrounding his dozen or so swirling keyboard instruments. The mass of sounds is nowhere near as neat or concise as Wakeman's first album, but it evidently satisfied people looking for a post-psychedelic thrill as well as the more majestic side of progressive rock, and in its own pretentious way, is very effective. — *Bruce Eder*

Lisztomania / 1975 / A&M ✦✦
The soundtrack to Ken Russell's movie provided Wakeman with a canvas upon which to work his magic (or do his damage—it depends upon one's attitude) upon the music of Franz Liszt and, to a lesser degree, Richard Wagner. Actually, much of what is here is more substantial than the material on *Journey* or *Myths and Legends*, which can be attributed largely to the composers' contributions. — *Bruce Eder*

Myths and Legends of King Arthur & the Knights of the Round Table / 1975 / A&M ✦✦
Just as ambitious as *Journey to the Center of the Earth*, this album treads little new ground. Essentially more of the same, with a little less freshness this time out since it is the second album of its kind. — *Bruce Eder*

● **Voyage: The Very Best of Rick Wakeman** / 1997 / A&M ✦✦✦✦
Voyage: The Very Best of Rick Wakeman culls the highlights from the prog-rocker's frequently ponderous early-'70s solo albums, and while it is incongruous to treat Wakeman as a singles artist, the compilation is a good sampler for the curious and casual fans. — *Stephen Thomas Erlewine*

The Walkabouts

f. 1984, Seattle, WA
Alternative Pop-Rock, Alternative Country-Rock
Despite their background (punk), geography (Seattle), and label affiliation (Sub Pop), the Walkabouts were anything but a grunge band; dark, haunting and elegaic, their work instead sprung forth from the storytelling traditions of American roots music and the kinetic excitement of rock 'n' roll. The Walkabouts were formed in 1984 by Chris Eckman and his brothers Curt and Grant, all of whom had previously played together in a number of punk/pop outfits, along with singer Carla Torgerson, a veteran of folk and street singing. The group's lineup proved fluid, although Chris Eckman and Torgerson remained the Walkabouts' driving forces; a later roster including bassist Michael Wells, multi-instrumentalist Glenn Slater, and drummer Terri Moeller did hang together for a number of years.

After issuing a self-titled cassette in 1984, the Walkabouts released the EP *22 Disasters* a year later. A full-length LP, *Weights and Rivers*, was planned for 1987, but the record was never released—a harbinger of music industry problems to come. Instead, the group offered *See Beautiful Rattlesnake Garden* in 1988, which not only marked the continued maturity of Eckman's and Torgerson's songwriting but also earned the Walkabouts a contract with the fledgling Sub Pop label. The deal resulted in upgraded production values, as evidenced by 1989's *Cataract* and its follow-up, the next year's six-song EP *Rag & Bone*, which featured the keyboard work of the newly-added Slater.

1991's *Scavenger* proved to be the last Walkabouts record issued in their native land for some time, however; while the deal with Sub Pop's American division went sour, the label's European division Glitterhouse hung on to the band, where their following had been steadily growing. Between 1993 and 1995, the Walkabouts issued a staggering seven full-length records in Europe—three by the full band, a limited-edition live collection, and three more released by the duo of Chris & Carla. Finally, in 1995 the three aforementioned Walkabouts albums—the double LP set *New West Motel*, the all-covers *Satisfied Mind*, and the more rock-oriented *Setting the Woods on Fire*—all appeared domestically. A year later, the band issued two more albums, the all-new *Devil's Road* (recorded with the Warsaw Philharmonic Orchestra) and *Death Valley Days: Lost Songs and Rarities, 1985-1995*, a collection of odds and ends. In November 1996, Wells left the Walkabouts to devote himself to his side project, Pluto Boy; he was replaced by bassist Baker Saunders. —*Jason Ankeny*

See Beautiful Rattlesnake Gardens / 1987 / Pop Llama ✦✦✦
On the Walkabouts' debut, the band's sound is still in its embryonic stages; the focus is on jangly, electric folk-rock, with few traces of the country, blues, and roots music from which their later work would draw. Still, the songwriting of Chris Eckman and Carla Torgerson is already strong, and Torgerson's vocals are lovely. —*Jason Ankeny*

Cataract / 1989 / Sub Pop ✦✦✦
The band's first Sub Pop LP is a diverse affair sewn together from an ever-expanding array of influences and passions, highlighted by such haunting roots meditations as "Hell's Soup Kitchen," "Long Black Veil" (an original composition, and not the standard), and "Whiskey XXX." —*Jason Ankeny*

Rag & Bone / 1990 / Sub Pop ✦✦✦
The addition of keyboardist Glenn Slater fleshes out the Walkabouts' sound on the six-song *Rag & Bone* EP, texturing typically strong efforts like the honky-tonk rave-up "The Anvil Song" and the gentle "Medicine Hat" with even greater color and dimension. —*Jason Ankeny*

Scavenger / Oct. 1990 / Sub Pop ✦✦✦
Like its predecessors, *Cataract* refines the Walkabouts' sound even as the band's scope broadens—the further afield their fascination with music's backroads takes them, the more remarkably assured they grow. —*Jason Ankeny*

● **Satisfied Mind** / 1993 / Creative Man ✦✦✦✦
Like Yo La Tengo's *Fakebook*, the Walkabouts' *Satisfied Mind* is a definitive artistic statement masquerading as a loose-knit collection of acoustic covers. Sometimes a group's selection of cover material, combined with their ability to make the songs their own, winds up revealing as much about their craft as their original music, and such is the case here; mining the work of diverse artists like the Carter Family, Gene Clark, Mary Margaret O'Hara, John Cale, and Nick Cave, *Satisfied Mind* represents the purest evocation to date of the Walkabouts' aesthetic and its standing at the crossroads of country, rock, folk, and punk. By casting well-known songs in an entirely new light—Patti Smith's "Free Money" becomes an ominous waltz, while Charlie Rich's "Feel like Going Home" is renewed as an epic dirge—the album makes explicit all of the implicit connections in the Walkabouts' work. By extension, it underlines the connections binding the spectrum of roots music as well; *Satisfied Mind* doesn't simply suggest that diverse sounds can co-exist together—it proves that they always have. —*Jason Ankeny*

New West Motel / 1993 / Glitterhouse ✦✦✦✦
The double-album *New West Motel* bears more than a passing similarity to the work of Neil Young (whose "Like a Hurricane" gets covered here), thanks to its edgy juxtaposition of blistering guitar workouts and plaintive acoustic cuts. —*Jason Ankeny*

Setting the Woods on Fire / 1994 / Cargo ✦✦✦✦
Despite taking its title from a Hank Williams song, *Setting the Woods on Fire* ranks among the Walkabouts' most rock-based efforts. A sweeping, stately record, it owes a great deal to the Stones' *Exile on Main St.*, particularly on the boogie shuffle "Old Crow" and the horn-powered, R&B-flavored "Hole in the Mountain." —*Jason Ankeny*

Devil's Road / 1996 / Virgin Schallplatten ✦✦✦✦
Half of the tracks comprising *Devil's Road* feature the string arrangements of the Warsaw Philharmonic Orchestra, giving greater depth to a sound that's already impossibly rich. Recorded in Berlin, the album is dark and soulful, the work of a band at the peak of its powers. —*Jason Ankeny*

Death Valley Days: Lost Songs and Rarities, 1985-1995 / Nov. 1996 / Glitterhouse ✦✦✦
Death Valley Days is a fragmentary collection reining in scattered tracks drawn from demos, B-sides, unreleased albums, compilations and tribute records, along with a few covers left off the domestic reissue of *New West Motel*. —*Jason Ankeny*

The Walker Brothers

f. 1964, Los Angeles, CA, db. 1967
Pop, British Invasion, Soft Rock, Pop-Rock
They weren't British, they weren't brothers, and their real names weren't Walker, but Californians Scott Engel, John Maus, and Gary Leeds were briefly huge stars in England (and small ones in their native land) at the peak of the British Invasion. Engel and Maus were playing together in Hollywood when drummer Leeds suggested they form a trio and try to make it in England. And they did—with surprising swiftness, they hit the top of the British charts with "Make It Easy on Yourself" in 1965. "The Sun Ain't Gonna Shine Any More" repeated the feat the following year, and the group also had UK hits with "My Ship Is Coming In," "(Baby) You Don't Have to Tell Me," "Another Tear Falls," and others. For a few months they experienced frenzied adulation almost on the level of the Beatles and Stones, though in the US (where they rarely performed), only "Make It Easy on Yourself" and "The Sun Ain't Gonna Shine Any More" entered the Top 20.

While the Walkers looked the part of British Invaders with their shaggy moptops, in fact they were far more pop than rock. Nor did they play on most of their records. With producer Johnny Franz and veteran British arrangers like Ivor Raymonde (who also worked with Dusty Springfield) and Reg Guest, they favored orchestrated ballads that were a studied attempt to emulate the success of another brother act who weren't really brothers—the Righteous Brothers. Not as soulful as the Righteous Brothers, lead singer Scott Walker's deep croon wasn't chopped liver by any means, although it betrayed strong debts to non-rock vocalists like Tony Bennett and Frank Sinatra. While their biggest hits were covers of songs by American pop songwriting teams like Bacharach-David and Mann-Weill, Scott (and occasionally John Walker) could write strong brooding originals in a more personal, less overblown style when given the chance.

In the intensely competitive days of 1967, the Walkers' brand of pop suddenly became passé, and the group disbanded in the face of diminishing success and Scott's increasingly fruitful solo career. Scott ran off a series of Top Ten British solo albums in the late '60s, which have attracted a sizable cult with their idiosyncratic marriage of Scott's brooding, insular songs and ornate orchestral arrangements. Gary Walker released a few singles and an album with his group the Rain, in a much harder rocking guitar-oriented format. The Walkers reunited for a while in the mid-'70s, which produced a final British hit ("No Regrets") but disappointing music. Much of the Walkers' story is retold in the biography *Scott Walker: A Deep Shade of Blue*, published only in Britain. —*Richie Unterberger*

Introducing the Walker Brothers / 1965 / Smash ✦✦✦
Their debut album was an erratic affair; they hit their trademark balladeering groove with the hits "Make It Easy On Yourself" and "My Ship Is Comin' In," but sound stiff on uptempo R&B numbers like "Land of 1,000 Dances" and "Dancing in the Street." It does include some interesting tracks which haven't been reissued, most notably the obscure early Randy Newman composition "I Don't Want to Hear It Any More" and the Scott Engel original "You're All Around Me," both of which are the kind of pop-rock ballads which were the Walkers' strongest suit. —*Richie Unterberger*

No Regrets / 1975 / GTO ✦✦✦
The Walker Brothers reunited in 1975 to record *No Regrets*, a collection of well-produced pop, soul, and folk covers. Although both Scott Walker and John Maus are in fine voice, the majority of the album is overly slick and fails to make much of an impression. Nevertheless, the title track is a masterpiece, featuring an achingly gorgeous vocal from Scott that ranks among the band's finest performances. —*Stephen Thomas Erlewine*

Lines / 1977 / GTO ✦✦
No Regrets found the Walker Brothers returning as an accomplished mainstream pop act, capable of turning out appealingly professional covers of folk, soul, and pop songs. Its follow-up, *Lines*, took that glossy veneer a little too far, as the group spent more time on production and not enough on substance. There are some good songs here—Jimmy Cliff's "Many Rivers to Cross," Randy Newman's "Have You Seen My Baby," Jesse Winchester's "Brand New Tennessee Waltz"—but even those are given dull arrangements and blandly sung, making *Lines* a thoroughly uninvolving record. —*Stephen Thomas Erlewine*

Nite Flights / 1978 / GTO ✦✦✦
The difference between the numbing *Lines* and *Nite Flights* is startling. Between the two records, Scott Walker decided to begin writing again,

and his new songs ignored all the conventional song structures of pop-rock. With "Shutout," "Fat Mama Kick," "Nite Flight" and the chilling "The Electrician," Walker created a quartet of haunting songs that had eerie, electronic arrangements and cryptic, evocative lyrics. It was a far cry from the bland MOR of the Walker Brothers' two reunion albums, and John Maus and Gary Leeds sensed this, so they tried to write songs that were just as disturbing as Scott's, but they had no idea how to make titles like "Disciples of Death," "The Fury and the Fire," "Den Haague" and "Child of Flames" into real songs or to venture into new sonic territory; they simply made their signature folk-pop a little darker. As a result, *Nite Flights* isn't as good as it could have been, suffering from a full side of bad material, but Scott Walker's songs are essential and represent a remarkable artistic comeback. —*Stephen Thomas Erlewine*

● **After the Lights Go Out: The Best of 1965-1967** / 1990 / Fontana ◆◆◆◆
Twenty of their best songs, including all of their hit singles. On original compositions like "Mrs. Murphy," "Archangel," "Orpheus," and "Deadlier Than The Male," Scott Walker unveils the disturbed visions that would characterize his solo work, and John Walker's "Saddest Night In The World" and "I Can't Let It Happen To You" display a solid writing talent that he was sadly unable to develop into a solo career of his own. —*Richie Unterberger*

Anthology / Aug. 8, 1995 / One Way ◆◆◆◆
Although it contains the Walker Brothers' big hits from the '60s, *Anthology* is basically a resequenced version of the group's first album, adding a couple of bonus tracks. Nevertheless, it's a serviceable introduction to the group. —*Stephen Thomas Erlewine*

Junior Walker

b. 1942, Blytheville, AR
Saxophone, Vocals / Soul, Motown
Of all the great musicians who played on scores of Motown records, none of them got label credit, much less a chance to bask in the spotlight. The lone exception was Junior Walker (born Audrey Dewalt), whose tenor sax wailings were made up of equal parts Illinois Jacquet high-note shrieks, Coleman Hawkins growls, and pure Midwest soul. Never much of a vocalist, Walker nonetheless scored hits with his rough-grained chops, though the sax solos remained the definite focal point. Highly influential on the Tom Scott/David Sanborn crowd, Walker should be close to the top of any list of rock 'n' roll's great tenor saxophonists. —*Cub Koda*

Home Cookin' / 1969 / Motown ◆◆◆
Solid, mostly uptempo album, featuring some of his biggest late-'60s hits: "What Does It Take (To Win Your Love)," "Come See About Me," and "Hip City." Among the other tracks, the bittersweet instrumental "Sweet Soul" is a highlight. As with many Motown albums, the most noteworthy tracks are featured on best-of compilations. —*Richie Unterberger*

● **Greatest Hits** / 1982 / Motown ◆◆◆◆
All the hits, including "Shotgun," "What Does It Take to Win Your Love," and "Roadrunner." The definitive package. —*Cub Koda*

Nothing But Soul: the Singles / 1994 / Motown ◆◆◆◆
This 40-song double CD includes virtually every Walker track of significance, and then some. Walker is a great player and hits a great groove, but that groove can get tiring over the course of several dozen tracks, especially the similar-sounding early instrumental cuts. Also, the post-'60s selections that take up much of disc two are hampered by material that is inferior to the best output of his '60s heyday. Excellent package and liner notes, but most listeners should be satisfied with the single-disc *Greatest Hits*, leaving this one for the collectors and specialists. —*Richie Unterberger*

Scott Walker (Noel Scott Engel)

b. Jan. 9, 1943, Hamilton, OH
Vocals / Pop, Soft Rock, Pop-Rock, Experimental
One of the most enigmatic figures in rock history, Scott Walker was known as Scotty Engel when he cut obscure, flop records in the late '50s and early '60s in the teen idol vein. He then hooked up with John Maus and Gary Leeds to form the Walker Brothers. They weren't named Walker, they weren't brothers, and they weren't English, but they nevertheless became a part of the British Invasion after moving to the UK in 1965. They enjoyed a couple years of massive success there (and a couple hits in the US) in a Righteous Brothers vein. As their full-throated lead singer and principal songwriter, Scott was the dominant artistic force in the group, which split in 1967.

While remaining virtually unknown in his homeland, Scott launched a hugely successful solo career in Britain with a unique blend of orchestrated, almost MOR arrangements with idiosyncratic and morose lyrics. At the height of psychedelia, Walker openly looked to crooners like Sinatra, Jack Jones, and Tony Bennett for inspiration, and to Jacques Brel

for much of his material. None of those balladeers, however, would have sung about the oddball subjects—prostitutes, transvestites, suicidal brooders, plagues, and Joseph Stalin—that populated Walker's songs. His first four albums hit the Top Ten in the UK—his second, in fact, reached No. 1 in 1968, in the midst of the hippie era. By the time of 1969's *Scott 4*, the singer was writing all of his material. Although this was perhaps his finest album, it was a commercial disappointment, and unfortunately discouraged him from relying entirely upon his own material on subsequent releases.

The 1970s were a frustrating period for Walker, pocked with increasingly sporadic releases and a largely unsuccessful reunion with his "brothers" in the middle of the decade. His work on the Walkers' final album in 1978 prompted admiration from David Bowie and Brian Eno. After a long period of hibernation, he emerged with an album in 1984, *Climate of Hunter*, which drew critical raves for a minimalistic, trance-like ambience that showed him keeping abreast of cutting-edge '80s rock trends. This notoriously reclusive figure, who has rarely been interviewed or even seen in public since his days of stardom, emerged from hibernation in 1995 with a new album, *Tilt*. He was a substantial, if largely overlooked, influence upon the vocal style of David Bowie and Bryan Ferry. A biography, *Scott Walker: A Deep Shade of Blue*, was published by Virgin in the UK in 1994. —*Richie Unterberger*

Scott / 1967 / Fontana ◆◆◆◆
Scott Walker's success as a teen idol singer of Spectorish ballads with the Walker Brothers in no way prepared listeners for the mordant, despairing lyrics of his solo debut. To compound the surprise, he does his best to imitate the vocal girth of Tony Bennett and Frank Sinatra on this mix of original tunes and covers, which also features sweeping, bloated orchestral arrangements. It was hardly rock, and pop of a most oddball sort, but it found a surprisingly large audience—in Britain, anyway, where it reached the Top Three in 1967. Poke behind the velvet curtain of the languid MOR arrangements, and one finds a surprisingly literate existentialist at the helm of these proceedings. His lyrical nuances were probably lost on his audience of predominantly teenage girls, though they've earned him a small cult audience that endures to this day. Besides presenting three of his own compositions, Walker covers tunes by Weil/Mann, Tim Hardin, and Andre & Dory Previn on this album, as well as three songs by his favorite writer, Jacques Brel. Highlights include his exquisitely anguished rendition of Brel's classic "Amsterdam" and his dramatic cover of the early-'60s Toni Fisher pop ballad "The Big Hurt." —*Richie Unterberger*

Scott 2 / 1968 / Fontana ◆◆◆◆
Although Walker's second album was his biggest commercial success, actually reaching No.1 in Britain, it was not his greatest artistic triumph. His taste remains eclectic, encompassing Bacharach/David, Tim Hardin, and of course his main man Jacques Brel (who is covered three times on this album). And his own songwriting efforts hold their own in this esteemed company. "The Girls From the Streets" and "Plastic Palace People" show an uncommonly ambitious lyricist cloaked behind the over-the-top, schmaltzy orchestral arrangements, one more interested in examining the seamy underside of glamour and romance than celebrating its glitter. The Brel tune "Next" must have lifted a few teenage mums' eyebrows with its not-so-hidden hints of homosexuality and abuse. Another Brel tune, "The Girl And The Dogs," is less controversial, but hardly less nasty in its jaded view of romance. Some of the material is not nearly as memorable, however, and the over-the-top show ballad production can get overbearing. The album included his first Top 20 UK hit, "Jackie." —*Richie Unterberger*

Scott 3 / 1969 / Fontana ◆◆◆
Scott Walker's final British Top Ten album was the first to be dominated by his own songwriting. Ten of the thirteen tunes on this 1969 LP are originals; the remaining three, naturally, were written by one of his chief inspirations, Jacques Brel. There are some interesting moments here. "Big Louise" talks about a hefty prostitute with shocking explicitness for a pop star album of the era. "Copenhagen" (like much of Walker's '60s work) foreshadows David Bowie. "Funeral Tango" is a particularly vicious Brel song. "30 Century Man" is an uncommonly folkish and focused tune for Walker. "We Came Through" is an oddball cavalry charge featuring one of his occasional forays into Ennio Morricone spaghetti Western-like production. The tension between Walker's dense, foreboding lyrics and orchestral production is unusual, to say the least. But too often, it's too difficult to penetrate Walker's insights through Wally Scott's string-drenched production. It shrouds the lyrics in a fog that's often too syrupy to justify the effort needed to fight through it. —*Richie Unterberger*

Scott 4 / 1969 / Fontana ◆◆◆◆
Walker dropped out of the British Top Ten with his fourth album, but the result was probably his finest '60s LP. While the tension between the bloated production and his introspective, ambitious lyrics remains, much of the over-the-top bombast of the orchestral arrangements has been reined in, leaving a relatively stripped-down approach that com-

plements his songs rather than smothering them. This is the first Walker album to feature entirely original material, and his songwriting is more lucid and cutting. Several of the tracks stand among his finest. "The Seventh Seal," based upon the classic film by Ingmar Bergman, features remarkably ambitious (and relatively successful) lyrics set against a haunting Ennio Morricone-style arrangement. "The Old Man's Back Again" also echoes Morricone, and tackles no less ambitious a lyrical palette; "dedicated to the neo-Stalinist regime," the "old man" of this song was supposedly Josef Stalin. "Hero Of The War" is also one of Walker's better vignettes, serenading his war hero with a cryptic mix of tribute and irony. Other songs show engaging folk, country, and soul influences that were largely buried on his previous solo albums. —*Richie Unterberger*

Til the Band Comes In / 1970 / BGO ✦✦✦
Walker's sixth album was really the last of his prime eccentric pop crooner era, and in comparison to his previous solo output, it was a bit inconsistent. For one thing, Walker wrote the original material with his manager of the time, Ady Semel; more puzzlingly, after ten original tracks, the album concluded with five covers of pop standards along the lines of "Stormy" and material by Henry Mancini and Michel Legrand. Strangest of all, one of the original cuts was sung not by Walker, but by Esther Ofarim. There's a goodly amount of fine stuff, though, that's characteristic of Walker's unique mix of lounge crooning with morose psychodrama. "Time Operator," a verite monologue of a lonely man's conversation with a telephone operator, may be his most devastating deadpan lyric; "Joe" is Walker in his best pseudo-Tony Bennett voice; and "The War Is Over" and "Little Things" also have a fetching candy-coated melancholy. Even the covers aren't a total loss, featuring as they do some of his trademark masterful balladeering. —*Richie Unterberger*

The Moviegoer / 1972 / Philips ✦✦
Following the disappointing performance of *Til Band Comes In,* Scott Walker returned to middle-of-the-road pop with *The Moviegoer.* Assembling a set of songs from his favorite films, including compositions from Michel Legrand and Henry Mancini, Walker essentially created a harmless mainstream pop album and delivered it without much care. The record did boast some nice arrangements by Johnny Franz, but the music was seldom noteworthy. —*Stephen Thomas Erlewine*

Stretch / 1973 / CBS ✦✦
Stretch, Scott Walker's first album for CBS, purports to be a detour into country music, but it is a sideroad that Walker decided not to pursue thoroughly. Only a handful of songs, like Tom T. Hall's "That's How I Got to Memphis" and Mike Newbury's "Sunshine," are genuine country songs, and the remainder of the album consists of mainstream pop and folk-rock songs that are quite similar to his latter-day Phillips albums. The difference is that Walker sounds more committed on this record, singing with a greater passion than on any record since *Til the Band Comes In,* but that still doesn't save *Stretch* from being anything more than a curiosity for dedicated fans. —*Stephen Thomas Erlewine*

We Had It All / 1974 / CBS ✦✦
We Had It All follows the same pattern as the previous *Stretch,* but it leans a little heavier toward country, as the centerpiece of four Billy Joe Shaver songs indicates. Although the album is still a little musically tentative, and while it is a disappointment to hear no new original material from Walker, *We Had It All* is his strongest record in years, since the country leanings are a welcome change of pace and he sings with authority throughout the record. —*Stephen Thomas Erlewine*

Climate of Hunter / 1984 / Virgin ✦✦✦
Walker's only album of the 1980s was both a blow for artistic credibility, and a blow against most of his old fans. The voice of the balladeer was still intact, and still even crooned sometimes. But the arrangements backed brow-furrowingly obtuse lyrics with '80s-oriented rock that incorporated some quasi-classical structures. Walker was seemingly more interested in painting abstracts in which the textures counted more than the content. This made for an album which may have been a hell of a lot more interesting than '80s efforts by other '60s pop stars, but at the same time it was rather impenetrable, and one's attention tended to drift off over the course of the set. Yet it was not half as radical as the avant-garde direction he would stake out with his next album ten years later, *Tilt.* —*Richie Unterberger*

● **Boy Child: Best of 1967-1970** / 1992 / Fontana ✦✦✦✦
This collection of "Scott's best self-composed songs" features 20 Walker originals from his 1967-70 heyday. While he covered some interesting material on his albums during this period, paying tribute to Jacques Brel with special devotion and frequency, his original compositions are his most enduring achievements. Besides such highlights as "Big Louise," "We Came Through," "The Seventh Seal," "Plastic Palace People," and "The Old Man's Back Again," it includes half a dozen songs that were not included on the four other solo albums that Fontana UK has reissued on CD. Some of those cuts are very strong, especially "The Rope And The Colt," a dramatic Western ballad with an arrangement that would do Ennio Morricone proud; the positively eloquent despair of

the ennui-ridden "Time Operator"; and "The Plague," a representative sampling of Walker's taste for the disquieting and bizarre. This is a recommended starting point for those interested in checking out this singularly strange '60s phenomenon, who was a relatively unacknowledged and undetected, but nonetheless substantial, influence on David Bowie and other fashionably decadent British singers. —*Richie Unterberger*

No Regrets: Best of Scott Walker & Walker Brothers / 1992 / Fontana ✦✦✦✦
Including both of the Walker Brothers' big hits ("The Sun Ain't Gonna Shine Any More," "Make It Easy on Yourself") and highlights from Scott Walker's first four solo albums, *No Regrets: The Best of the Walker Brothers* is a fine overview of Walker's more pop-oriented music, containing the majority of his best-known songs including "Joanna," "Lights of Cincinnati," "Boy Child," "Montague Terrace in Blue," "Jackie," and "If You Go Away," plus the best songs from the Walkers' '70s reunion ("No Regrets"). —*Stephen Thomas Erlewine*

Tilt / 1995 / Fontana ✦✦
Tilt, Scott Walker's first album in eleven years, is a dense, impenetrable record, bleak in its outlook and approach. Walker has dispensed with conventional pop songwriting—actually, he's dispensed with pop altogether. *Tilt* is nearly operatic, with long, twisting melody lines, no verses, and no choruses. Lyrically, the record is just as inaccessible, with obscure literary references and winding, oblique prose. There's no escaping that the record is some sort of an accomplishment—very few pop musicians have ever attempted a record of this scope, one that is free-form in structure but with carefully considered arrangements. Nevertheless, it's hard to like the album because very little of it ever sinks in, and it's hard to appreciate it because it takes its pretensions so seriously. It's arguably the most inaccessible, difficult album ever recorded. —*Stephen Thomas Erlewine*

Looking Back with Scott Walker / 1996 / Repertoire ✦✦
When he was still in high school, Walker made his first ventures into the record business as a teen idol-type singer (under the name Scott Engel) for several small labels. All them sank without a trace at the time, although some were reissued (along with tracks that hadn't previously seen the light of day) in the latter half of the 1960s, after Scott had reached stardom with the Walker Brothers. This has 27 cuts from the late '50s and early '60s, and the music betrays not a shred of the one-of-a-kind talent that would generate his avid cult following. It's putrid stuff that would hold no interest whatsoever for latter-day listeners if Walker had not developed into something else entirely. He does sing well for a teenager (in a much higher voice than he would employ in the '60s), but the material (none penned by Scott) is of strictly hold-your-nose stuff. Much of it, in fact, isn't really rock at all, but son-of-Eddie-Fisher-type pap, arranged with an oh-so-slight eye for the teen rock audience; some of it makes Paul Anka sound gritty by comparison. If you're a completist, it should be said, it's a well-assembled package, gathering most of his excruciatingly rare (and just plain excruciating) early sides in one place. Just beware that the relationship between this Scott Walker and the one that sang morose, complex ballads years later is nil. —*Richie Unterberger*

It's Raining Today: The Scott Walker Story (1967-70) / Oct. 15, 1996 / Razor & Tie ✦✦✦
As the first Scott Walker album to be released in the US, *It's Raining Today: The Scott Walker Story* is an adequate 17-song overview of his solo career, containing many of the highlights from his first five albums ("Jackie," "Montague Terrace (In Blue)," "The Seventh Seal," "The Old Man's Back Again (Dedicated to the Neo-Stalinist Regime)," "Big Louise," "Lights of Cincinnati," "Joanna"), while overlooking some minor gems, including "Matilda" and the B-side "The Plague." Nevertheless, it remains a terrific introduction to Walker's music. —*Stephen Thomas Erlewine*

The Wallflowers

f. 1990, New York, NY
Adult Alternative Pop-Rock
As part of the mid-'90s revival of roots-rock, the Wallflowers held a special connection to one of the original inspirations: vocalist/songwriter/guitarist Jakob Dylan. Though he is the son of a legend, Jakob's similarities to his father are occasional—in fact, the Wallflowers are more influenced by Tom Petty & the Heartbreakers than original '60s folk-rock, though lyrically Jakob remains a close companion to the original Dylan.
Born in 1970, Jakob Dylan was raised in Los Angeles by his mother, Sara Lowndes, after his parents' divorce in 1977. He studied at private schools in Los Angeles and New York, and decided to follow in his father's footsteps by the late '80s. He formed the Wallflowers with guitarist Tobi Miller, keyboardist Rami Jaffee, bassist Barrie Maguire, and drummer Peter Yanowitz, and signed to Virgin. Released in August 1992, the Wallflowers' self-titled debut album sold poorly, and Virgin soon dropped their contract. Undaunted, Dylan assembled a new Wallflowers—guitarist Michael Ward, bassist Greg Richling, and drummer

Mario Calire—keeping only Jaffee. The group signed to Interscope and recorded its second album with producer T-Bone Burnett, a long-time friend of the Dylan family. *Bringing Down the Horse* was released in May 1996, producing the alternative radio hit "6th Avenue Breakdown." Late in 1996, the single "One Headlight" was released, and by the spring of 1997, it had become a Top Ten hit, pushing *Bringing Down the Horse* into the upper reaches of the charts, as well. —*John Bush*

The Wallflowers / Aug. 25, 1992 / Virgin ◆◆◆

The Wallflowers' eponymous debut album is a little too studied and underwritten to make much of an impression, yet there are enough promising moments to suggest that the group was capable of the lean, contemporary folk-rock that made *Bringing Down the Horse* such a winning record. —*Stephen Thomas Erlewine*

● **Bringing Down the Horse** / May 21, 1996 / Interscope ◆◆◆◆

No sophomore jinx here. Of course, there are only two Wallflowers left from their finest release, so this could be called a whole new band. No matter, because the music here is assured and contemporary with just enough of the past showing through to catch one's eye. Jakob Dylan has been polishing his compositional chops and it really shows on such cuts as "Invisible City," the hit "6th Avenue Heartache" and especially "One Headlight." A fine effort indeed. —*James Chrispell*

Joe Walsh

b. Nov. 20, 1947, Wichita, KS

Guitar / Rock 'n' Roll, Boogie Rock, Arena Rock

After coming to national fame as the leader of the James Gang, Walsh's skewed humor and bluesy guitar chops have forged a nice solo career for him. Walsh's solo debut *Barnstorm* displayed him as not only an innovative guitarist but a competent keyboardist and a songwriter with much scope. Walsh's second solo effort, *The Smoker You Drink, the Player You Get*, perfectly suited the tastes of FM-rock programmers and firmly established his career. "Rocky Mountain Way" and "Meadows" are hits off that album. Walsh also produced some outside projects, including Dan Fogelberg's first hit album, *Souvenirs*.

The Eagles enlisted Walsh as a replacement for Bernie Leadon in December of 1975. Their next studio album, *Hotel California*, heavily featured Walsh's playing, particularly on "Life in the Fast Lane" and "Hotel California." Walsh played on their live album and *The Long Run*, the band's swan song.

All along, Walsh has continued his solo efforts, scoring big in 1978 with *But Seriously Folks...*, an album that brings his goofy humor to the forefront, with the hit "Life's Been Good." "All Night Long," a track from the *Urban Cowboy* soundtrack, continued Walsh's string of success. During the '80s, Walsh has had sporadic success.

In addition to Dan Fogelberg, Walsh has produced other artists, including Spirit's Jay Ferguson, and Ringo Starr (working as bandleader on Starr's late-'80s tours). In 1994, Walsh joined the reunited Eagles for their *Hell Freezes Over* tour. —*Cub Koda and Rick Clark*

Barnstorm / 1972 / Mobile Fidelity ◆◆◆◆

Even though he had developed quite a rep as the lead guitarist for the James Gang, Joe Walsh's debut (under the band moniker Barnstorm) was an impressive showcase for his songwriting and arranging. Produced by Bill Szymczyk, *Barnstorm* exudes a thick, textured sound. Some of Walsh's most distinctive guitar sounds are found here. Sonically, *Barnstorm* is shown to fine effect on this Mobile Fidelity reissue. (Currently, there isn't a regular domestic disc available.) Highlights include "Here We Go," "Mother Says," and "Turn to Stone." —*Rick Clark*

The Smoker You Drink, the Player You Get / 1973 / MCA ◆◆◆◆

On Walsh's second outing, he fused the dynamics and textures of *Barnstorm*, mixed in a few well-crafted tunes, perfect for FM radio, and scored his highest charting album. *Smoker*'s centerpiece was the plodding "Rocky Mountain Way," a perfect vehicle for his soaring slidework and squirrelly tenor strangle. "Meadows" was also a substantial FM hit. Other highlights are "Days Gone By" and "Happy Ways." —*Rick Clark*

So What / 1975 / MCA ◆◆◆

You Can't Argue with a Sick Mind / 1976 / MCA ◆◆

The Best of Joe Walsh / 1978 / MCA ◆◆◆

The Best of Joe Walsh is a concise, nine-track collection that is split between James Gang hits like "Funk No.49" and early solo hits like "Rocky Mountain Way." Since this lacks his best song, "Life's Been Good," as well as any of his '80s album-rock hits, this is not even close to a comprehensive collection, but it's not a bad sampler for extremely casual fans. —*Stephen Thomas Erlewine*

But Seriously Folks / 1978 / Asylum ◆◆◆◆

This is his biggest solo success, featuring the hit "Life's Been Good." —*Cub Koda*

There Goes the Neighborhood / 1981 / Asylum ◆◆◆

You Bought It: You Name It / 1983 / Warner Brothers ◆◆

Joe Walsh attempts and nearly makes the free throw that wins the game. Great songs like "I Can Play That Rock & Roll" and "Space Age Whiz Kids" show he hasn't lost his edge. But the big claim to fame on this record is his "I.L.B.T.s" or "I Love Big Tits." Rather retro in feel, like the title, it harkens back to a wackier time. Good, but flawed. —*James Chrispell*

The Confessor / 1985 / Full Moon ◆◆

Joe Walsh just hasn't been able to produce a complete album of great material, and *The Confessor* is no exception. Side one is drek, with such titles as "I Broke My Leg" and "Bubbles." Turn the record over, and we find one of Walsh's masterpieces. The title tune is great! Over seven minutes of pure Joe Walsh rock with cryptic lyrics and a socko arrangement. Side two also includes a cover of Michael Stanley's "Rosewood Bitters" which Walsh played on long ago. Worthwhile for the title track alone. —*James Chrispell*

Got Any Gum? / 1987 / Full Moon ◆◆

There's nothing sadder than seeing a talented artist come up with a real bummer, but that's just what this record is. Joe Walsh heads to Memphis to record but comes up way short of anything rockish. Perhaps this is one of those contractual obligation albums you hear so much about. In any event, the back picture of Walsh blowing a big bubble kind of says it all. —*James Chrispell*

Ordinary Average Guy / Jan. 1991 / Epic ◆◆◆

Songs for a Dying Planet / May 1992 / Epic ◆◆

Night Riding / Jun. 30, 1992 / Castle ◆◆

Future to This Life / 1995 / Pyramid/Rhino ◆◆

● **Look What I Did!: The Joe Walsh Anthology** / May 23, 1995 / MCA ◆◆◆◆

A double-disc set that draws from all of the phases of Joe Walsh's career, with the notable exception of the Eagles, *Look What I Did!* features almost every worthwhile song the guitarist ever recorded, even though it does contain pure dreck like "I.L.B.T.s," which is also known as "I Love Big Tits." —*David Jehnzen*

Travis Wammack

b. 1946, Memphis, TN

Guitar, Vocals / Rock 'n' Roll

A guitarist, singer, and young instrumental genius from Memphis who cut his first record at the tender age of twelve, Travis Wammack is one of the great unheralded guitarists of rock 'n' roll. A contemporary of Lonnie Mack, Wammack was simply the fastest guitar player in a town bursting at the seams with great guitarists. By the time he was 17, he appeared on the national charts with "Scratchy," a speed-burner instrumental featuring incredible distortion and dazzling technique. Several incredible singles followed, but none charted. By the late '60s, Wammack had moved into session work at the FAME Studios in Muscle Shoals, AL, playing on countless hits. He continues recording and touring to the present day (recently working as musical director for Little Richard), his hot and speedy guitar chops intact. —*Cub Koda*

● **That Scratchy Guitar from Memphis** / 1987 / Bear Family ◆◆◆◆

Wammack's best instrumental and vocal sides, 1964-1967. Simply incredible. —*Cub Koda*

Wang Chung

f. 1979, London, England, db. 1991

Dance-Pop, New Wave, Pop-Rock

The London-based new wave group Wang Chung had a handful of hits in the mid-'80s, achieving their greatest popularity in the US. Originally called Huang Chung, the band consisted of vocalist/guitarist Jack Hues, bassist Nick Feldman, and drummer Darren Costin. The band recorded four tracks for 101 Records in the late '70s, all of which appeared on a pair of compilation albums. Huang Chung released their first single, "Isn't It About Time We Were on Television?," in 1980; the record led to a contract with Arista Records. The group released their first album, *Huang Chung*, in 1982. By the time they recorded 1984's *Points on a Curve*, the band had changed their name to Wang Chung. "Dance Hall Days" was a small hit in Britain, yet the band hit the Top 40 twice in America—"Don't Let Go" made it to No. 36, while "Dance Hall Days" reached No. 16. From this point on, Wang Chung ignored the UK market, choosing to concentrate on the US. "To Live and Die in L.A.," the theme song from William Friedkin's thriller, just missed making the Top 40 in 1985. That same year, Wang Chung switched from Geffen Records to A&M and Costin left the band. Hues and Feldman continued as a duo and released *Mosaic* in 1986. The album was their biggest hit, launching the No. 2 hit "Everybody Have Fun Tonight" and the Top Ten "Let's Go!"

Wang Chung returned in 1989 with *The Warmer Side of Cool*, which spent a mere six weeks on the charts, spawning the minor hit, "Praying to a New God." After the relative disappointment of the album, the group quietly stopped touring and recording. *—Stephen Thomas Erlewine*

Huang Chung / 1982 / One Way ++
Wang Chung's eponymous debut—released when they were still called Huang Chung—is a misguided collection of lite New Romantic pop that relies less on drum machines and stylized keyboards than their contemporaries. The group also fails to write any convincing hooks, which makes *Huang Chung* little more than a vaguely interesting new wave artifact. *—Stephen Thomas Erlewine*

Points on the Curve / 1984 / Geffen ++++
Wang Chung's second album became a moderate hit thanks to the hit singles "Dance Hall Days" and "Don't Let Go." While there was some pleasant new wave-influenced pop-rock on the rest of the album, none of the songs matched the inspired pop craft of the hits. *—Stephen Thomas Erlewine*

To Live and Die in L.A. / 1985 / Geffen +++
Wang Chung provided the score for William Friedkin's thriller *To Live and Die in L.A.*, contributing a set of atmospheric, moody synth-pop, highlighted by the hit single "To Live and Die in L.A." *—Stephen Thomas Erlewine*

Mosaic / 1986 / Geffen +++
The incessantly catchy pop-funk number "Everybody Have Fun Tonight" illustrates the change in musical direction Wang Chung undertook on *Mosaic.* Backing away from the synth-laced pop-rock that characterized their earlier albums, the duo concentrated on dance-pop. Apart from the singles "Everybody Have Fun Tonight," "Let's Go!," and "Hypnotize Me," the band had trouble coming up with well-constructed pop songs, making *Mosaic* a checkered affair. *—Stephen Thomas Erlewine*

The Warmer Side of Cool / 1989 / Geffen ++
With *The Warmer Side of Cool,* Wang Chung continued the dance-pop direction of *Mosaic,* yet they failed to come up with enough memorable material to produce a successful follow-up. *—Stephen Thomas Erlewine*

● **Everybody Wang Chung Tonight: Greatest Hits** / Mar. 25, 1997 / Geffen ++++
In addition to the hit "Everybody Have Fun Tonight" (from which the title of the collection takes its name), this overview of Wang Chung's career includes demos, remixes (including a revamped version of the smash "Dance Hall Days") and even a new track, "Space Junk." *—Jason Ankeny*

War

f. 1969, Long Beach, CA
Soul, Funk, Pop-Rock
Freewheeling War mixed rock, jazz, and soul influences into a spicy stew throughout the '70s, resulting in a series of R&B and pop hits sporting funky melodies and politically aware messages. Born in Long Beach in 1969, the large combo initially served as rocker Eric Burdon's group, backing the ex-Animal on his 1970 million-seller "Spill the Wine." Bidding Burdon adieu, the band signed with United Artists in 1971 and enjoyed its first smash the next year with "Slippin' into Darkness." Tapping into a sizzling, horn-fueled rock/soul synthesis, "The World Is a Ghetto," "The Cisco Kid," and "Why Can't We Be Friends?" all went gold during the mid-'70s. Despite numerous personnel and label changes, War remained eminent throughout the '80s.

In the early '90s, War experienced a revival, partially due to the fact that all of their albums were reissued. But the group was also acknowledged as a primary influence on contemporary R&B and hip-hop. War returned to recording in 1994 capitalize on their new-found popularity. While 94's *War* wasn't a blockbuster, it was a moderate success, enabling the group to continue recording into the late '90s. *—Bill Dahl*

Eric Burdon Declares War / 1970 / Rhino +++
The debut effort by Eric Burdon & War was an erratic effort that hinted at more potential than it actually delivered. Three of the five tunes are meandering blues-jazz-psychedelic jams, two of which, "Tobacco Road" and "Blues For Memphis Slim," chug along for nearly 15 minutes. These showcase the then-unknown War's funky fusion and Burdon's still-impressive vocals, but suffer from a lack of focus and substance. "Spill The Wine," on the other hand, is inarguably the greatest moment of the Burdon-fronted lineup. Not only was this goofy funk shaggy-dog story one of the most truly inspired off-the-wall hit singles of all time, it was War's first smash—and Eric Burdon's last. The odd closing track, a short piece of avant-garde sentimentality called "You're No Stranger," was deleted from re-releases of this album for years due to legal complications, but was restored for its CD reissue. *—Richie Unterberger*

The Black-Man's Burdon / 1970 / Rhino ++++
Burdon's second and final album with War was a double set that could have benefited from quite a bit of judicious editing. Composed mostly of sprawling psychedelic funk jams, it does find War mapping out much of the jazz/Latin/soul grooves that, cut down to much more economical

song structures, would shortly bring them success on their own. Highlights include the soulful vamps "Pretty Colors" and "They Can't Take Away Our Music"; the 13-minute "Paint It Black" medley is the height of their eccentricity, and not one, but two covers of "Nights In White Satin" are absurd low points. *—Richie Unterberger*

War / Jan. 1971 / Rhino ++
War laid the groundwork for future developments on their debut album without Eric Burdon. The intriguing "Sun Oh Son," with its nice vocal arrangement, and "Lonely Feeling" were close-but-no-cigar singles. Still, they did what they had to do: establish an identity without Burdon and begin to blend their diverse elements. *—Ron Wynn*

All Day Music / Feb. 1971 / Rhino ++++
A great War album, the first where all their influences meshed. They blended gospel-tinged soul, funk, Afro-Latin, and light jazz, with enthusiastic group vocals and interplay, plus just the right amount of instrumental support and occasional solos by Lee Oskar on harmonica, Lonnie Jordan on keyboards, and Charles Miller on saxophones and flute. It also contained the fantastic "Slippin' Into Darkness," one of their best-arranged and performed numbers. *—Ron Wynn*

The World Is a Ghetto / 1972 / Rhino ++++
War hit its peak with this 1972 album, the only one they ever released that topped the pop charts. The title track was a triumphant blend of great exchanges and unison vocals, plus concise and spirited musical contributions all around. It also contained the delightful "Cisco Kid" and elaborate "City, Country, City," plus the curious "Beetles in the Bog." Harmonica player Lee Oskar and percussionist Papa Dee Allen were at their best, as were keyboardist Lonnie Jordan and saxophonist/flutist Charles Miller. *—Ron Wynn*

Deliver the Word / 1973 / Rhino +++
War began to slide a bit from their early-'70s peak with this release. The best selection, "Gypsy Man," had to be edited for radio, and thus Lee Oskar's roaring harmonica solo wasn't heard by anyone who didn't purchase the album. "Me and Baby Brother" was another of their mock-humorous hits, but overall, this wasn't nearly as sharp or effective an album as the ones they had been making. *—Ron Wynn*

War Live / 1973 / Rhino ++
Live albums are usually throwaways issued to fill the gap between sessions, or to keep an act's name in public for a label they've left. But War was at its peak when this live date was issued, although they were having a few internal problems. It served its purpose, giving its fans concert versions of "All Day Music," "Cisco Kid," and "Slipping Into Darkness," while the new track "Ballero" even became a hit. *—Ron Wynn*

Why Can't We Be Friends / 1975 / Rhino ++++
War returned with a vengeance and new material in the mid-'70s, as the title hit was both a pop and R&B Top Ten smash and "Low Rider" did even better, topping the soul surveys and peaking at No. 7 pop. More importantly, they were once more a carefree, loose, jamming band. Unfortunately, it was the last definitive War album, as ego and production battles would soon undermine their success. *—Ron Wynn*

★ **Greatest Hits** / 1976 / United Artists +++++
If you can find this collection (only available on vinyl), get it. *Greatest Hits* truly lives up to the title, with tracks like "Summer," "All Day Music," "Cisco Kid," "Slippin' into Darkness," "The World Is a Ghetto," and more. *—Rick Clark*

Love Is All Around / 1976 / ABC/Paramount +++
When War debuted as Eric Burdon's backing band in the late '60s, they were on ABC-Paramount. The group was still hot in 1976, and ABC reissued vault material from their early days in a deceptive package trying to coast on the band's hitmaker status. The album deservedly flopped, and ABC's clumsy attempt failed. *—Ron Wynn*

Platinum Jazz / 1977 / MCA ++
War became a superstar funk unit in the '70s by seamlessly fusing several elements: R&B vocals, Afro-Latin rhythms, rock theatrics, and even occasional jazz strains. This 12-track reissue presents instrumentals featured on War albums, songs that were generally longer than their hit singles and didn't get much attention in original issue. They show that while the band members weren't great soloists, they had an energy and improvisational elan that kept their extended jams from dragging. *—Ron Wynn*

Galaxy / 1977 / Rhino +++
War had been on cruise control for over two years due to internal and record company troubles when they resurfaced in the late '70s on MCA. This album was a pleasant surprise, even though it had more disco production than their funk fans wanted. But they got a hit out of the title track, and the better tracks retained the old War grit and eclectic fire. *—Ron Wynn*

Youngblood / 1978 / United Artists ++
War got decent mileage from the soundtrack for this B-movie, which premiered near the end of the first blaxploitation era. They ended with

two R&B hits, and while they were perturbed that United Artists, the label they had left, reaped the benefits, it at least kept them active and in the R&B hunt. —*Ron Wynn*

★ **The Best of War & More** / 1991 / Rhino/Avenue ✦✦✦✦✦
It's not a perfect compilation by any means—there's no "The World is a Ghetto" and a bad remix of "Low Rider," for starters—but *Best of War & More* is the only compilation available from this influential band, so it's the pick by default. But search for that original vinyl, because it was definitive. —*Stephen Thomas Erlewine*

● **Anthology** / Oct. 18, 1994 / Rhino/Avenue ✦✦✦✦
A two-disc set collecting the highlights from War's long, prolific career, *Anthology (1970-94)* is the definitive retrospective of the seminal funk band, containing all of their hits as well as most of their best album tracks. —*Stephen Thomas Erlewine*

The Best of War & More, Vol. 2 / Sep. 3, 1996 / Rhino ✦✦✦✦
Since Avenue botched War's *The Best of . . . and More* by neglecting to put on hit singles like "The World is A Ghetto" and "Gypsy Man"—although there was plenty of room for both songs, among others—the company needed to assemble a second compilation to take care of all the leftover singles and songs that didn't make the first volume. But, they managed to botch *The Best of War . . . And More, Vol. 2* as well. Sure, "The World Is a Ghetto," "Gypsy Man," "L.A. Sunshine," "Good, Good Feelin'," and several other R&B hit singles made the cut this time around, but the album is baited by an unnecessary remix of "Spill the Wine" by Junior Vasquez, plus selections from their latter-day albums (such as "Peace Sign") that could have been replaced by more first-rate album tracks in the vein of the killer "Don't Let No One Get You Down." Still, if you want to supplement the first *Best of* collection, *Vol. 2* is necessary. However, if you're going to spring for just two discs of War, you might as well go with the comprehensive double-disc collection, *Anthology.* —*Stephen Thomas Erlewine*

Billy Ward

b. Sep. 19, 1921, Los Angeles, CA
Piano / R&B
The ultra-strict disciplinarian and bandleader of a seminal R&B group, Billy Ward ruled over the Dominoes in a tight-fisted manner. He attempted to regulate everything from onstage harmonies to offstage lifestyles. The group's ranks at one time included Clyde McPhatter and Jackie Wilson, but Ward's insistence on dictatorial control resulted in both of them soon bolting for solo status. The group remained active until the early '60s and scored ten Top Ten R&B hits and two colossal No. 1 singles during its heyday from 1951 to 1957. "Sixty Minute Man" in 1951 was the ultimate innuendo hit, while "Have Mercy Baby" was a landmark uptempo stomper. Each topped the R&B charts for more than two months. All their hits were on either Federal or King, except for their final one, a cover of "Star Dust" in 1957 for Liberty that reached No. 5 R&B and No. 12 pop. —*Ron Wynn*

★ **Sixty Minute Men: The Best of Billy Ward & His Dominoes** / Nov. 16, 1993 / Rhino ✦✦✦✦✦
Billy Ward was neither a flamboyant vocalist nor a great instrumentalist; his success came directly from his ability to spot and nurture talent. Unfortunately, Ward was also a taskmaster and couldn't hold onto singers very long after discovering and recruiting them for his groups. But for a short period in the 1950s, Ward and the Dominoes ruled R&B by featuring two of its premier vocalists, Clyde McPhatter and Jackie Wilson. Neither stayed long, but were in the band enough time to make some seminal hits, included in this 20-cut anthology. Ironically, the song the group is remembered the most for featured bass vocalist Bill Brown doing the lead on the title track. —*Ron Wynn*

Jennifer Warnes

b. Mar. 3, 1947, Seattle, WA
Keyboards, Vocals / Country-Rock, Adult Contemporary, Pop
Jennifer Warnes has succeeded in a number of nearly unrelated areas of popular music—as a contemporary pop singer, as a country singer, as a singer of movie themes, and as an interpreter of the work of Leonard Cohen. She first came to public notice when she became a regular on the television show *The Smothers Brothers Comedy Hour* in 1967, under the name Jennifer Warren or simply Jennifer. In 1968, she was part of the original cast of the Los Angeles production of the musical *Hair*, and she signed to the Parrot Records subsidiary of London Records, which released her debut album, *I Can Remember Everything*. Her second album, *See Me, Feel Me, Touch Me, Heal Me!*, appeared in 1969. Neither album was a commercial success, and she moved on to the Reprise division of Warner Bros. Records, which released *Jennifer*, produced by John Cale, in 1972. When that album also flopped, Warnes signed on as a backup singer with Leonard Cohen. She joined Arista Records in 1976 and finally registered in the charts in 1977 with "Right Time of the Night," a Top Ten pop hit that reached No. 1 in the Easy Listening charts

and also made the Top 40 in the Country charts. It was drawn from her Arista debut album, *Jennifer Warnes*. The follow-up, *Shot Through the Heart* (1979), featured "I Know a Heartache When I See One," a Top Ten Country and Top 40 Pop and Easy Listening hit. Warnes' next album was an Arista hits compilation, *Best of Jennifer Warnes* (1982). In July 1982, Island Records released "Up Where We Belong," the love theme from the movie *An Officer and a Gentleman*, a duet between Warnes and Joe Cocker. She had sung movie themes before, but never with such success: "Up Where We Belong" hit No. 1 and went platinum. Not surprisingly, moviemakers sought her out, and in 1983 she had chart entries with "Nights Are Forever" (from *Twilight Zone—The Movie*) and the title theme from *All the Right Moves*, a duet with Chris Thompson. In 1986, she became the first signee to the short-lived Cypress Records label, which released her acclaimed *Famous Blue Raincoat*, an album of Leonard Cohen songs, at the start of 1987. In July of that year, RCA Records released "(I've Had) The Time of My Life," the love theme from the film *Dirty Dancing*, a duet between Warnes and Bill Medley of the Righteous Brothers. It topped the charts and went gold. Warnes spent five years crafting a follow-up to *Famous Blue Raincoat*, releasing *The Hunter*, which featured songs by various writers, herself included, in 1992. Note that Warnes' many label affiliations preclude any compilation from adequately covering her career and that, amazingly enough, neither of her biggest hits is available on a Jennifer Warnes album. —*William Ruhlmann*

I Can Remember / 1968 / Parrot ✦✦
I Can Remember Everything, the debut album by 21-year-old Jennifer (as she is billed) is a product of the eclectic pop trend of the late '60s, fostered by the Beatles' dabblings in music-hall whimsy and classical music on albums like *Revolver* and *Sgt. Pepper's Lonely Hearts Club Band*. Producer Martin Cooper favors arrangements beginning with isolated acoustic instruments—a bass or a conga drum or a harpsichord—to underly Jennifer's alto, with strings or other instruments joining in as the song goes on. The selections include one each from the Bee Gees, Joni Mitchell, the Beatles, and the Rolling Stones, along with a clutch of mediocrities written by Cooper or published by Martin Cooper Music. Actually, though, Jennifer is less interesting on familiar tunes like "Chelsea Morning" and "Here, There and Everywhere," which she tends to oversing in an affected way. On the forgettable stuff, she is more at ease, and the album demonstrates that she can be an effective, emotive interpreter, sometimes suggesting Janis Ian, sometimes Petula Clark. —*William Ruhlmann*

See Me / 1969 / Parrot ✦✦✦
By the time of the release of her second album, Jennifer (still going by only her first name), in addition to her appearances with the Smothers Brothers, had taken over a prominent role in the Los Angeles production of *Hair*, which Parrot Records played up by having her lead off the record with "Let the Sunshine In" (which, unlike the 5th Dimension, who scored a hit with it, she sang with the apocalyptic verses intact) and "Easy to Be Hard" from the musical. Guitarist/comedian Mason Williams, who had jumped to fame on the Smothers Brothers show with his instrumental hit "Classical Gas" (and featured Jennifer on his 1968 LP *The Mason Williams Ear Show*), turned up here to accompany her on his "Saturday Night at the World" and, of all things, an excerpt from Donizetti's *Don Pascale*. Otherwise, producer Al Capps followed the first album formula of having Jennifer cover contemporary material, including songs by the Rolling Stones, Bob Dylan, Jacques Brel, and, as the title indicated, the finale from the Who's new rock opera *Tommy*. This time, though, the filler that marred the first album was gone, and Jennifer had grown as a singer primarily by learning not to oversing. By toning down the histrionics, she sounded more involved emotionally, and with arrangements that had more of a rock edge, she even got to do some belting, which demonstrated the power of her voice. Like her first album, her second was not a popular success; unlike her first, it deserved to be. —*William Ruhlmann*

Jennifer / 1972 / Reprise ✦✦✦

Jennifer Warnes / Jan. 1977 / Arista ✦✦✦
Jennifer Warnes' fourth album was her Arista Records debut and the first LP on which she was billed under her full name. While eight of its ten tracks were produced by horn player Jim Price, the other two, "Right Time of the Night" and "I'm Dreaming," were produced by country producer Jim Ed Norman, and released as singles. Both became hits, but while they were the most accessible tracks on the album, they were also the least impressive; "Right Time," with its coy sexuality, was embarrassingly awkward. On the other hand, the bulk of the album consisted of well-sung Los Angeles pop material, the highlights being covers of "Love Hurts" and the Rolling Stones' "Shine a Light." As her previous albums had demonstrated, Warnes had a warm, inviting voice and a strong sense of phrasing, but she suffered from the basic disadvantage all interpretive singers faced in the 1970s: the paucity of good available songs. —*William Ruhlmann*

Shot through the Heart / May 1979 / Arista ✦✦✦✦
Having compromised on her Arista debut and gotten a hit single for her
trouble, Jennifer Warnes took charge of the recording of her second
Arista album, co-producing it and writing three songs, including the title
track. It was hard to miss the point when Warnes covered Dionne Warwick's 1963 hit "Don't Make Me Over" (written by Burt Bacharach and
Hal David) that she was finished with having people tell her what to do.
On her own, her taste was impeccable, her song choices including the
work of Jesse Winchester, Bob Dylan, and Stephen Foster, and her own
songwriting was good, too. She also managed to satisfy the commercial
expectations aroused by her previous album, with "I Know a Heartache
When I See One" rising into the Country Top Ten and the pop and Adult
Contemporary Top 40. (She also made it into all three charts with "Don't
Make Me Over" and into the pop and AC charts with "When the Feeling
Comes Around.") She proved an adept producer, achieving a smooth
pop-rock sound. All that was wrong with it was that, with session stars
like Andrew Gold aboard, Warnes succeeded in making what sounded
like the great lost Linda Ronstadt album. Granted, she handled strong
material like Dylan's "Sign on the Window" better than Ronstadt could,
but Ronstadt had originated this kind of '70s Los Angeles country/pop-
rock style, and it was impossible to do it without sounding like you were
copying her. Maybe that was why, despite three chart singles, the album
wasn't a big commercial success. In turn, the disappointing sales may
have injured Warnes' relationship with Arista. Instead of releasing
another new album, Arista followed with a best-of, and Warnes didn't
release another new album until 1987. — *William Ruhlmann*

The Best of Jennifer Warnes / 1982 / Arista ✦✦✦✦
Incomplete and premature, this ten-track compilation appeared at a
time when Jennifer Warnes had released only two albums on Arista,
resulting in five pop singles chart entries, including the Top Ten hit
"Right Time of the Night" and the Top 40 hit "I Know a Heartache When
I See One." This album contained four of the five, plus "Could It Be Love"
and "Come to Me," which subsequently charted, a third newly recorded
song, "Run to Her," two LP tracks composed by Warnes, and "It Goes
like It Goes," the theme from the movie *Norma Rae,* which had won an
Academy Award. Skimpy when released, the album has since become
potentially deceptive, since it is easy for consumers to pick it up assuming it contains later Warnes hits like "Up Where We Belong" and "(I've
Had) The Time of My Life." In fact, since Warnes has been on many
labels and several of her hits are one-off movie themes, there is no reliable compilation of her work. — *William Ruhlmann*

● **Famous Blue Raincoat** / Jan. 1987 / Private Music ✦✦✦✦
Jennifer Warnes was familiar with Leonard Cohen from a tour of duty as
one of his backup singers in the early '70s, but this collection of Cohen's
songs must have shocked her AM radio fans who knew her from her
'70s country-pop hits and her movie themes, if they were even able to
connect the woman who sang, "It's the right time of the night for makin'
love" with the one who declared, "First we take Manhattan, then we take
Berlin" over stinging guitar work by Stevie Ray Vaughan on the opening
track here. As that pairing suggests, Warnes wisely took a tougher, more
contemporary approach to the arrangements than such past Cohen
interpreters as Judy Collins used to. Where other singers tended to geld
Cohen's often disturbingly revealing poetry, Warnes, working with the
composer himself and introducing a couple of great new songs ("First
We Take Manhattan" and "Song of Bernadette," which she co-wrote),
matched his own versions. The high point may have been the Warnes-
Cohen duet on "Joan of Arc," but the album was consistently impressive.
And it went a long way toward re-establishing Cohen, whose reputation
was in a minor eclipse in the mid-'80s. A year later, with the way paved
for him, he released his brilliant comeback album, *I'm Your Man.* For
Warnes, the album meant her first taste of real critical approbrium: Suddenly a singer who had seemed like a second-rate Linda Ronstadt now
appeared to be a first-class interpretative artist. — *William Ruhlmann*

Just Jennifer / Mar. 1992 / Deram ✦✦✦
This 63-minute, 22-track UK-only disc combines Jennifer Warnes' first
two albums, *I Can Remember Everything* and *See Me, Feel Me, Touch
Me, Heal Me!,* originally released in the late '60s when she was just
known as Jennifer. Covering material by Bob Dylan, the Beatles, and the
Rolling Stones, Warnes shows considerable promise, even though the
arrangements, especially on the first half, are gimmicky and she is not
as assured an interpreter as she would become. — *William Ruhlmann*

The Hunter / Jun. 9, 1992 / Private Music ✦✦✦
It took Jennifer Warnes five years to construct a follow-up to *Famous
Blue Raincoat,* and she still wasn't able to come up with a unifying con-
cept as simple and workable as recording a set of songs by Leonard
Cohen. She did find some excellent covers, including Todd Rundgren's
"Pretending To Care" and the Waterboys' "The Whole Of The Moon,"
that may have been new to her listeners, and got a song from Donald
Fagen ("Big Noise, New York"). She also did some of her own writing
and got participation from Cohen on "Way Down Deep." All of which is
to say that there are some worthy selections on *The Hunter,* but on the

whole the record doesn't match its illustrious predecessor. — *William
Ruhlmann*

Dee Dee Warwick

b. 1945, East Orange, NJ
Vocals / Soul, R&B
Like Darlene Love and Cissy Houston, Dee Dee Warwick's considerable
gifts as a soul singer were mostly confined to session work. And like
Aretha Franklin's sisters, Dee Dee had to struggle with the shadow of a
superstar sibling, Dionne Warwick. Certainly she had the talent to compete as an artist in her own right, but she only had a sporadic run of
small hits in the 1960s and early '70s, and benefited from neither frequent recording opportunities nor substantial promotion from her
labels.
Dee Dee began singing with her older sister Dionne as a teenager in
the 1950s. They formed the Gospelaires, who sometimes sang with the
Drinkard Singers, a long-running gospel outfit that their mother Lee
had helped found, and that also featured their aunt, Cissy Houston. Like
many gospel singers, Dee Dee moved into secular soul in the early '60s.
Along with Dionne, Cissy, Doris Troy, and the Sweet Inspirations, she
was one of New York's most in-demand session vocalists during the era,
contributing to numerous pop/soul records by the likes of the Drifters,
Chuck Jackson, Garnet Mimms, Aretha Franklin, Nina Simone, and Wilson Pickett.
During her early career, Dee Dee was content to make a comfortable
living as a backup singer. She began making her own records in 1963,
however, cutting the original version of "You're No Good," which Betty
Everett covered for a hit (and which Linda Ronstadt took to No. 1 in
1975). It was produced by Jerry Leiber and Mike Stoller, who tried one
more time with her in 1964 on "Standing By"; a single for the small
Hurd label also flopped. She began treating her solo career more seriously in the second half of the 1960s, during which she released almost
a dozen singles for Mercury, as well as a couple of albums.
Dee Dee's 1960s recordings, while much less successful than
Dionne's, were good New York pop/soul with a more pronounced R&B
influence than her sister's. Some of these were actually substantial R&B
hits; "I Want to Be with You," "Foolish Fool," and "I'm Gonna Make You
Love Me" all made the R&B Top 20. The Supremes and the Temptations,
however, would steal some of Dee Dee's thunder when their duet cover
of "I'm Gonna Make You Love Me" made No. 2 on the pop charts.
Warwick signed to Atco at the beginning of the 1970s, getting a Top
Ten R&B single right off the bat with "She Didn't Know (She Kept on
Talking)." Over the next couple of years she'd make several other singles
and an album, all of which comprised her earthiest work to date, sometimes with help from the Dixie Flyers rhythm section and backup vocals
by the Sweet Inspirations. Only "Cold Night in Georgia" made a little
commercial noise, however, and she returned to Mercury in 1973 (she
has since claimed that Atlantic was throwing most of its promotional
weight for female soul singers behind Aretha Franklin and Roberta
Flack). She continued to record for various labels in the 1970s, but only
"Get out of My Life" (1975) dented the R&B charts. During the last couple of decades, she has done backup vocals for Dionne Warwick, and
recorded sporadically on her own. A collection of her 1960s work is long
overdue, although Soul Classics compiled her best Atco recordings for
compact-disc reissue in 1996. — *Richie Unterberger*

● **I Want to Be with You** / 1967 / Mercury ✦✦✦✦
Not too easy to find, but a strong album that features the original versions of "I'm Gonna Make You Love Me" (which would reach No. 2 as a
duet between the Supremes and the Temptations), "Gotta Get a Hold of
Myself" (covered by the Zombies), and the Latin-tinged "House of Gold,"
which sounds like a super-soulful cover of a Jay & The Americans tune.
— *Richie Unterberger*

She Didn't Know: The Atco Sessions / Feb. 1996 / Soul Classics
✦✦✦✦
In the early '70s, Warwick recorded for Atco with limited success, reaching the R&B Top Ten with "She Didn't Know (She Kept on Talking)," and
gaining a couple of smaller R&B hits with "Cold Night in Georgia" and a
cover of "Suspicious Minds." She did quite a bit of recording for Atco
between 1970 and 1972 in a fairly down-home vein, sometimes with
backing by the esteemed Dixie Flyers rhythm section, and backup
vocals by the Sweet Inspirations, Cissy Houston, and Judy Clay. These
sessions sounded something like a poppier variation on the Stax sound,
though none of the songs had the arresting qualities necessary to break
her to the pop audience. This 22-track compilation of her Atco work is a
typically high-class Soul Classics production, including all the hits, non-
LP singles, tracks from her 1970 LP *Turning Around,* and seven unreleased songs that are just as impressive as her official performances
from the era. Dee Dee, incidentally, sounds nothing like her famed sister
Dionne here, favoring far gutsier vocals, material, and arrangements. It's
good late-period vintage soul, and more evidence that Warwick was one

of the more unjustly neglected soul performers of her time. —*Richie Unterberger*

Dionne Warwick

b. Dec. 12, 1940, East Orange, NJ
Vocals / Soul, Pop, Brill Building Pop, Pop-Rock
The magically melodic voice of Dionne Warwick and the sophisticated pop compositions of Burt Bacharach and Hal David were the proverbial match made in heaven. Warwick proved the prolific songwriting team's favorite interpreter, scaling the pop and soul charts time and again with her soaring renditions of their memorable songs.

Warwick hailed from a musical brood with a strong gospel heritage, and her sister Dee Dee scored a few hits of her own. Dionne's sultry pipes stood out, even on the highly competitive background vocal scene in New York, and she got a chance to step out front in 1963, hitting big on Scepter with the uptown soul classic "Don't Make Over."

Under the expert tutelage of Bacharach and David, who doubled as her producers, Warwick's sound soon became smoother and more accessible to pop programming—a formula that resulted in the massive acceptance of her "Walk On By," "I Say a Little Prayer," "This Girl's in Love with You," and a slew of others.

Strangely, Warwick never made it to the top of the pop charts until she broke away from her mentors, traveling to Philadelphia to record the R&B-oriented "Then Came You" with the Spinners in 1974. As elegant and tasteful as ever, Dionne Warwick's breathy vocals still haven't gone out of style—she's managed to remain contemporary while never jeopardizing her appeal. —*Bill Dahl*

★ **The Dionne Warwick Collection: Her All-time Greatest Hits** / 1989 / Rhino ✦✦✦✦✦
The finest collection of Warwick material compiled by anyone, this excellent set gathered every Warwick gem and smartly remastered them. It's a definitive CD, containing several landmark releases featuring the collaborative compositions of Burt Bacharach and Hal David. These songs underscored Warwick's ability to embody her pop tunes with a soulful, but also light and innocent, quality. It also has excellent liner notes and intelligent sequencing. This is by far the set to get if you want a comprehensive presentation of Warwick's pop/soul greatness. —*Ron Wynn*

Greatest Hits 79-90 / Oct. 1989 / Arista ✦✦✦
This collection gathered the great hits from Dionne Warwick's rebirth on Arista. Barry Manilow wisely recast her doing sophisticated pop, moving her into adult contemporary love ballads and away from straight soul and R&B. It was an inspired move, and returned her to the top of the charts frequently in the late '70s and '80s. But while the songs were good, the collection didn't fare so well on the charts. —*Ron Wynn*

Hidden Gems: Best of Dionne Warwick, Vol. 2 / Mar. 24, 1992 / Rhino ✦✦✦✦
A fine collection of rarities and forgotten singles from Warwick's heyday with Bacharach/David; it's a good supplement to Rhino's *Dionne Warwick Collection.* —*Stephen Thomas Erlewine*

Presenting Dionne Warwick/Anyone Who Had a Heart / 1995 / Sequel ✦✦✦✦
Her first two albums, combined onto one disc for CD reissue. While many of the songs are available on domestic reissue compilations, it's a superb package of early work that qualifies among her best and most soulful, enhanced by tasteful digital New York orchestral pop-rock production. Includes her earliest hits ("Don't Make Over," "Anyone Who Had a Heart") and lesser-known but excellent songs by Bacharach-David and other composers. —*Richie Unterberger*

From the Vaults / Oct. 1995 / Soul Classics ✦✦✦
An anthology of 24 fairly obscure tracks, drawn from Warwick's 1963-66 albums and B-sides. Although it has the look of something that would appeal primarily to serious fans and collectors, this is hardly any less satisfying than the album's collections covering the same era. It's also just as good as Rhino's *Hidden Gems,* another anthology of little-known Warwick recordings from the '60s; what's more, it doesn't repeat any selections from that previous compilation. The first half of the CD (covering 1962-64) shows Dionne at her most girl groupish and soulful, with arrangements that often recall those of her labelmates, the Shirelles (who in fact recorded their own versions of a few of these songs). "It's Love That Really Counts" and "Get Rid of Him" are highlights; "Mr. Heartbreak" is a wrenching, stately ballad, easily up to the standard of her hits of the period. The last half of the program covers material from 1965 and 1966, all of which (like most of the songs she sang in the late '60s) was penned by Bacharach-David. These show her going in a smoother, adult pop-oriented direction, and while I prefer the somewhat gutsier earlier sides, there are some good tunes that are impossible to come by otherwise, except on long-out-of-print LPs. —*Richie Unterberger*

Was (Not Was)

f. 1980, Detroit, MI, **db.** 1993
Urban, Alternative Pop-Rock, Pop-Rock
Was (Not Was) plays contemporary R&B dance music, with lyrics that range from the satiric to the bizarre. The group is led by Detroit-natives David Weiss (David Was), who plays flute and writes those lyrics, and Don Fagenson (Don Was), who plays bass and writes music, but the group is fronted by singers Harry Bowens and Sweet Pea Atkinson. Was (Not Was) first gained notice for a dance single called "Wheel Me Out" in 1980. Their first album, *Was (Not Was)* (1981), did not reach the charts, but its follow-up, *Born to Laugh at Tornados* (1983), did. Then little was heard from the group for five years. They returned in 1988 with *What Up, Dog?,* which featured the No.16 hit "Spy in the House of Love" and the No. 7 hit "Walk the Dinosaur." (During this period, Don Was had become a prominent record producer, handling the board for Bonnie Raitt's Grammy-winning *Nick of Time,* among many other mainstream pop records.) The fourth Was (Not Was) album, *Are You Okay?,* appeared in 1990.

Are You Okay? wasn't as commercially successful as the previous *What Up, Dog?* After the album's release, Don Was continued to pursue his production career, which began to increase tensions between him and David. In 1993, Was (Not Was) officially parted ways. —*William Ruhlmann*

Was (Not Was) / Aug. 1981 / Island ✦✦
Born to Laugh at Tornados / 1983 / Geffen ✦✦✦
The Was brothers provide a strange bunch of songs with irresistible dance beats, plus an array of guest singers that is, well, unusual to say the least: Mitch Ryder, Doug Fieger (of the Knack), Ozzy Osbourne, and, on the ballad "Zaz Turned Blue," Mel Tormé. —*William Ruhlmann*

● **What Up, Dog?** / 1988 / Chrysalis ✦✦✦✦
The guests are fewer (though Frank Sinatra, Jr., sings one song), but the oddities go on, with "11 MPH," a review of the JFK assassination, and "Dad I'm in Jail," a proud rant by David Was. Also included: the hits "Spy in the House of Love" and "Walk the Dinosaur." —*William Ruhlmann*

Are You Okay? / Jul. 1990 / Chrysalis ✦✦✦
The "hit" is a remake of "Papa Was a Rollin' Stone," but the album is more memorable for typically oddball tunes like "I Blew Up the United States" and "Elvis' Rolls Royce," which features a droll vocal by Leonard Cohen. —*William Ruhlmann*

The Waterboys

f. 1981, London, England, **db.** 1993
Alternative Pop-Rock, Folk-Rock
Led by the literate singer-songwriter Mike Scott, the group's sole constant member, the mercurial Waterboys formed in London in 1981. Born December 14, 1958 in Edinburgh, Scotland, Scott first became involved in music as the creator of the fanzine *Jungleland,* and later played in a series of local punk outfits. After college, where he studied English and philosophy, Scott and his band, Another Pretty Face, moved to London; following the group's breakup, he formed the Waterboys, so named after a line in the Lou Reed song "The Kids" but wholly appropriate given Scott's recurring lyrical fascination with sea imagery.

A newspaper advertisement calling for musicians led to a response from multi-instrumentalist Anthony Thistlethwaite; along with drummer Kevin Wilkinson, the Waterboys issued their self-titled debut in 1983. Keyboardist Karl Wallinger and trumpeter Roddy Lorimer joined for the 1984 follow-up *A Pagan Place,* which expanded the group's rich, dramatic sound while further exploring Scott's interest in spirituality. With 1985's *This Is the Sea,* the Waterboys reached an early peak; a majestic, ambitious record, it earned the group a significant hit with the single "The Whole of the Moon."

However, after the album's release, Wallinger departed to form World Party, which prompted Scott and Thistlethwaite to relocate to Ireland and begin with a clean slate. When the Waterboys returned in 1988 with the acclaimed *Fisherman's Blues,* they were joined by traditional Irish players like fiddler Steve Wickham, drummer Dave Ruffy, keyboardist Guy Chambers, and bassist Marco Weissman, resulting in a stripped-down, folky sound that was continued on 1990's *Room to Roam.*

In 1991, Scott moved to New York without Thistlethwaite or any other band members; the release of 1993's *Dream Harder,* cut with session musicans, marked a return to an electric, more rock-oriented sound. Soon Scott moved back to Scotland, where he began a lengthy stay at a spiritual commune; there he recorded the folk-tinged *Bring 'Em All In* under his own name, apparently putting the Waterboys to rest for good. —*Jason Ankeny*

The Waterboys / 1983 / Ensign ✦✦✦✦
The Waterboys' eponymous debut album finds Mike Scott essaying his vision of big music. Part Van Morrison, part U2, it was sweeping and romantic, with nearly every song stretched out to epic length. At this

point, Scott's vision far exceeds his grasp, yet it's fascinating to hear him try to reconcile the two extremes. — *Stephen Thomas Erlewine*

A Pagan Place / 1984 / Chrysalis ✦✦✦
On their second album, *A Pagan Place*, the Waterboys turn Celtic folk-rock into a monumental fusion of Van Morrison's poetry, arena rock and Phil Spector's monolithic wall of sound. Mike Scott's ideas are simply too grand to be executed properly, yet *A Pagan Place* has enough thrilling moments to make his embarrassing missteps forgivable. — *Stephen Thomas Erlewine*

This Is the Sea / 1985 / Chrysalis ✦✦✦✦
Expanding the epic, multi-layered sound of *A Pagan Place*, *This is the Sea* is a more ambitious yet a more successful record, since it finds Mike Scott at his melodic peak. Consequently, the album has enough strong, accessible moments to make his indulgences forgivable. — *Stephen Thomas Erlewine*

Fisherman's Blues / 1988 / Ensign ✦✦✦✦
Mike Scott had been pursuing his grandiose "big music" since he founded the Waterboys, so it came as a shock when he scaled back the group's sound for the Irish and English folk of *Fisherman's Blues*. Although the arena-rock influences have been toned down, Scott's vision is no less sweeping or romantic, making even the simplest songs on *Fisherman's Blues* feel like epics. Nevertheless, the album is the Waterboys' warmest and most rewarding record, boasting a handful of fine songs ("And a Bang on the Ear," the ominous "We Will Not Be Lovers," "Has Anybody Here Seen Hank?," and the title track), as well as a surprisingly successful cover of Van Morrison's breathtaking "Sweet Thing." — *Stephen Thomas Erlewine*

Room to Roam / 1990 / Ensign ✦✦✦
With *Room to Roam*, Mike Scott essentially expands the traditional folk of *Fisherman's Blues* by relying heavily on his Celtic leanings, but the record isn't quite as successful, since the record lacks the memorable songs that made its predecessor a surprising success. — *Stephen Thomas Erlewine*

● **The Best of the Waterboys (1981-1990)** / 1991 / Ensign ✦✦✦✦
Although it omits some fine tracks, *The Best of the Waterboys '81-'90* is useful overview of the Waterboys' career, selecting highlights from the group's first five albums and accurately tracing their evolution from U2 and Van Morrison fanatics to neo-traditionalist folk-rockers. — *Stephen Thomas Erlewine*

Dream Harder / May 25, 1993 / Geffen ✦✦
After two albums of neo-traditional Irish music, Mike Scott brings The Waterboys back to the big rock sound of earlier albums like *This is the Sea*. Coming after the remarkably accomplished *Fishermen's Blues* and *Room to Roam*, *Dream Harder* is a bit of a disappointment. Its best material doesn't carry the same weight as compositions from *Blues*—compare the simple beauty of *Fishermen's Blues'* "Has Anyone Hear Seen Hank" to *Dream Harder's* overblown "The Return of Jimi Hendrix". Scott can still bang out some good songs, but on *Dream Harder* there aren't as many as on previous efforts. — *Stephen Thomas Erlewine*

The Secret Life of the Waterboys 81-85 / 1994 / Chrysalis ✦✦
The Secret Life of the Waterboys 81-85 collects 14 outtakes, live tracks and demos from the time when Mike Scott was fervently pursuing his concept of "Big Music." These alternate versions and unreleased songs are generally a little more modest than the released takes, which, of course, makes *The Secret Life* very interesting for diehard fans, but there are not enough revelations to make it worthwhile for the curious. — *Stephen Thomas Erlewine*

Roger Waters

b. Sep. 6, 1944, Great Bookham, Cambridge, England
Bass / Art-Rock/Progressive-Rock, Pop-Rock
Roger Waters was the bassist for Pink Floyd from 1965 to 1983. Waters assumed an increasingly dominant position in the band, writing all lyrics in addition to some of the music as of *The Dark Side of the Moon* (1973) and singing most of the lead vocals on *The Wall* (1979). Waters issued his debut solo album, *The Pros and Cons of Hitch Hiking*, in 1984. In the mid-'80s, he engaged in a protracted legal battle, arguing that the other members of Pink Floyd could not continue using the name without him in the band; he lost. In 1987, Waters released his second album, *Radio K.A.O.S.*, and in 1990 he staged a concert version of *The Wall* in Berlin. In 1992 he released his third album, *Amused to Death*. — *William Ruhlmann*

Music from "The Body" / 1970 / Restless ✦✦✦
This soundtrack album, credited to Ron Geesin and Roger Waters, contains various sound effects and musical fragments, plus a few folkish songs on which Waters accompanies himself on acoustic guitar and sings. The result is a precursor to some of Waters' and Pink Floyd's later work ("Breathe," for example, is suggestive of *The Dark Side Of The Moon*), but in an embryonic form. — *William Ruhlmann*

The Pros & Cons of Hitch-Hiking / 1984 / Columbia ✦✦✦✦
The loose framing device of this album is a series of daydreams experienced while waking up. Eric Clapton contributes guitar, but he can't provide enough musical interest to sustain Roger Waters' lyric-heavy ruminations. — *William Ruhlmann*

Radio K.A.O.S. / 1987 / Columbia ✦✦✦✦
There's more story than can be effectively told on this concept album dealing with radio, computers, and the threat of nuclear war, but many of the songs are up to Waters' Pink Floyd standard, and some rock out more than his former band ever did. — *William Ruhlmann*

The Wall in Berlin 1990 / Aug. 1990 / Mercury ✦✦✦
This is a gala two-disc live rendition of the Pink Floyd concept album, employing a raft of guest stars including Van Morrison, Sinéad O'Connor, Joni Mitchell, the Scorpions, and others. — *William Ruhlmann*

● **Amused to Death** / Sep. 1, 1992 / Columbia ✦✦✦✦
Yet another installment in Waters' lectures about the horrors of war and man's inhumanity to man, *Amused to Death* is helped considerably by the presence of Jeff Beck, who contributes some brilliant, free-form guitar to the meandering songs. Waters himself is in fine form, spitting out bitter, sarcastic lyrics over his slow, grandiose instrumental backdrops. While he could have fleshed out the melodies a little bit more, his execution is what matters, and his performance on *Amused to Death* is the liveliest of any of his solo records. — *Stephen Thomas Erlewine*

Jimmy Webb

b. Aug. 15, 1946, Elk City, OK
Piano, Keyboards, Vocals, Singer / Singer-Songwriter, Pop-Rock, Adult Alternative Pop-Rock
Jimmy Webb was that rarity in rock music, a professional songwriter; he was also a singer, but his performing career never eclipsed his success as a composer and producer. Between 1966 and 1969 alone, he was responsible for such platinum-selling classics as "By the Time I Get to Phoenix," "Wichita Lineman," "Up Up and Away," "MacArthur Park," and "Didn't We," indeed, Webb may well have kept the craft of the songwriter in popular music alive and kicking in a new generation, saving the profession from being ghettoized onto the Broadway stage and the world of the commercial jingle.

Jimmy Webb was born the son of a Baptist minister in Elk City, Oklahoma on August 15, 1946. An avid music enthusiast as a boy, he made his first public appearance as a "performer" playing the organ at his father's church, and even then, he improvised and re-arranged and reharmonized the hymns. In his teens he began his composing career with religious songs, and later led his own rock 'n roll band. His interest in music intersected with his love of literature and writing, and even in his teens, Webb was able to dissect the popular songs around him, and began turning his attention to writing informal "follow-up" efforts. He quickly realized that his songs were sometimes superior to the originals, and set his sights on a career as a songwriter.

Webb soon took off for Los Angeles, where his first job in music was transcribing other people's songs. During this period, as he made the rounds of publishing houses, he wrote a bittersweet romantic ballad entitled "By the Time I Get to Phoenix," which languished for two years. Finally, in 1966, Johnny Rivers recorded the song, which became a modest hit; Glen Campbell later cut it as well, and scored a gold record. Meanwhile, Webb was put in charge of the songs for their first album for a fledgling pop group called the Fifth Dimension; the result was a chart-topping million-selling single, "Up Up and Away." Between them, "By the Time I Get to Phoenix" and "Up Up and Away" won eight Grammy Awards the following year, and turned Jimmy Webb into the most prominent songwriter of his generation.

Like many of his peers, Webb had begun thinking of longer compositions and more coherent bodies of songs, and soon wrote "MacArthur Park," which fit into the new spirit of the era—the lyrics, although not remotely "psychedelic," were as rich and ornate as anything the Beatles or the Beach Boys were experimenting with, and the arrangement was as a vast sonic canvas, filled with the combined sounds of a rock combo and a full orchestra and choir. He offered the song to the Association, who rejected it, prompting Webb decided to record the piece on his own. It was finally placed with his friend, the actor Richard Harris; after Webb recorded the orchestral part in Los Angeles, Harris' voice was added on at a studio in Dublin.

Webb tried selling "MacArthur Park" to several major labels, and was rejected—nobody felt that a seven-minute-plus single by an actor scarcely known as a singer had any chance of being played, much less becoming a hit. Luckily, Lou Adler's Dunhill Records felt differently, and bought the single and the accompanying album, *A Tramp Shining*. "MacArthur Park" climbed to No. 2 on the American pop charts over a period of 13 weeks, and in the process shattered every preconception of air-time restrictions on AM radio. *A Tramp Shining* also became a hit, rising as high as No. 4 in July of 1968. Webb and Harris' second album together, *The Yard Went on Forever*, was an even better work, with Harris in better voice and Webb writing some of the most haunting lyrics and melodies of his career.

In the meantime, Glen Campbell's version of Webb's "Wichita Lineman" became a gold record and one of the biggest singles of his career; other Webb-penned hits that followed included "Galveston," "The Worst That Could Happen," "Carpet Man," and "Paper Cup." He also wrote and arranged Thelma Houston's 1969 album *Sunshower,* and in 1970 wrote his first feature film score, *Tell Them Willie Boy Is Here.* When a number of projected theatrical projects failed to happen, Webb decided to use the unexpected hiatus to his advantage to mount a solo career. His first ventures into public performance were conducted almost as an underground effort, without much publicity or fanfare; his fans did attend and enjoy, but his club performances were an acquired taste, marred by his somewhat ragged singing and piano playing. Webb was perhaps closer in spirit to a Leonard Cohen (or, perhaps, Bob Dylan back in his folk club days), presenting his hit songs as much more personal expressions.

An elaborately produced and recorded 1970 debut, *Words and Music,* was followed a year later by the more basic, stripped down *And So: On,* which included a contribution from jazz guitarist Larry Coryell. 1972's *Letters* was highlighted by Webb's own rendition of "Galveston," as well as his Righteous Brothers homage "Just One Time," and featured a cameo appearance by Joni Mitchell, who returned for 1974's *Land's End.* Webb continued to write and produce throughout the decade, including 1973's *The Supremes Produced and Arranged by Jimmy Webb* and Glen Campbell's 1974 *Reunion;* 1975's *Earthbound* put him back with the Fifth Dimension, and he also wrote and produced for Joan Baez, Joe Cocker, and Frank Sinatra. Art Garfunkel's 1978 *Watermark*—in large part, a Webb songwriting showcase—was another huge success.

Webb's own 1977 album *El Mirage,* produced by George Martin, included a new song called "The Highwayman," which was later turned into a hit by a quartet of Johnny Cash, Kris Kristofferson, Willie Nelson, and Waylon Jennings. In 1983, Webb ventured into a new field of music, writing the cantata *The Animals' Christmas,* a telling of the Christmas story from the point of view of animals, which had its premiere at New York's Cathedral of St. John the Divine, conducted by the composer and featuring Garfunkel in its cast of performers. In 1988, Webb returned to doing live concerts, accompanied by Coryell, and in 1996, he released the solo recording, *Ten Easy Pieces,* featuring new interpretations of some of his best-known songs. —*Bruce Eder*

Jim Webb Sings Jim Webb / 1968 / Epic ♦♦
A set of early demo recordings, redubbed and reorchestrated by the record company without Webb's participation or consent. None of his known hits or better songs are here, and the sound isn't terribly impressive either. Webb reportedly hated this release, which tried for the same effect as those early Randy Newman albums on Warner Bros. with far less success, artistic or commercial. Of purely historical interest. —*Bruce Eder*

Words & Music / Feb. 1970 / Reprise ♦♦♦
Words and Music marked Webb's official debut as a singer of his own songs. Though the second side's experiments (a suite in three movements and a song cycle/medley linking "Let It Be Me," "Never My Love," and "I Wanna Be Free") are a little too ambitious for comfort, side one features the concise, well-crafted pop (such as "P.F. Sloan" and "Love Song") that would feature heavily on later releases. —*Chris Woodstra*

And So On / 1971 / Reprise ♦♦♦
Webb's second album stripped down the excesses of its predecessor for a more consistently enjoyable set, featuring the haunting "Met Her on a Plane" (later covered by Ian Matthews) as well as the equally powerful "If Ships Were Made to Sail," "One Lady" and "All My Love's Laughter." —*Chris Woodstra*

Letters / 1972 / Reprise ♦♦♦

Lands End / 1974 / Asylum ♦♦♦

El Mirage / 1977 / Atlantic ♦♦♦♦
Produced by George Martin, *El Mirage* is one of Webb's strongest albums. As always, the songs are perfectly constructed but this time sung with more confidence than ever before. Highlights include "If You See Me Getting Smaller" and "Christian No." —*Chris Woodstra*

Angel Heart / 1982 / Sony ♦♦
Even though Webb delivers another solid batch of songs on this 1982 album, the MOR-schlock arrangements are far too over-the-top, making this the weakest of his catalog. —*Chris Woodstra*

● **Archive** / 1993 / WEA ♦♦♦♦
Archive is an excellent 20-track (UK import only) overview of Webb's criminally overlooked career as a performer from 1970 to 1977, his most productive period. While he is best remembered as the composer of hits for others, this collection offers proof that he was equally adept at interpreting his own songs—often times bringing more emotion to them. —*Chris Woodstra*

Suspending Disbelief / Sep. 7, 1993 / Elektra ♦♦♦
After a several-year absence, Webb returns with one of his most polished efforts to date. His hook-filled melodies are instantly endearing, while he sings a love song to his sports car and remembers a meeting with Elvis. His voice, never one of his strong points in the past, has aged particularly well. —*Chris Woodstra*

10 Easy Pieces / Oct. 15, 1996 / Guardian ♦♦♦♦
The idea of releasing a collection of Jimmy Webb's best known songs sung by the author himself may seem like a no-brainer, but it's taken 20+ years for it to happen, apparently mostly because Webb needed to put some distance between himself and most of these numbers, in order to approach them in a fresh manner that makes this disc more than a mere exploitation effort. The result is the best and most accessible of all Webb's albums, featuring his 1990s takes on "Galveston," "By The Time I Get To Phoenix," "Didn't We," "MacArthur Park," "The Moon Is A Harsh Mistress," "Wichita Lineman," and "All I Know," amongst others. His voice is more expressive than ever, and the performances are generally grittier, with more raw emotion than the better known hit versions display. The arrangements are generally very simple and straightforward, with Webb's piano the primary instrument, and several of the songs are performed in a deeply personal manner, more akin to home recording for Webb's own pleasure than to a commercial release—"Wichita Lineman," in particular, sounds here like the most personal and private of performances, filled with wrenching loneliness at which the Glen Campbell version only hints. The notes are very personal and revealing as well. —*Bruce Eder*

The Wedding Present

f. 1985, Leeds, England
Alternative Pop-Rock, Indie Rock
Emerging in the wake of the Smiths' demise as the UK's most successful indie-pop band during the late '80s, the Wedding Present were founded in Leeds, England in 1985. Formed from the ashes of the short-lived Lost Pandas, the Weddoes (as they were affectionately dubbed by fans) were essentially the vehicle of singer-songwriter David Gedge, the only constant member throughout the group's tumultuous history; initially rounded out by guitarist Peter Salowka, bassist Keith Gregory, and drummer Shaun Charman, the fledgling band quickly won a loyal following among university students, as well as the patronage of influential DJ John Peel, for whom they cut their first radio session in February 1986.

Named in honor of the popular soccer star, *George Best,* the Wedding Present's remarkable debut LP appeared on their own Reception label in 1987. The group became the darlings of the British press overnight, winning acclaim for their distinct guitar-pop frenzy as well as Gedge's idiosyncratic vocal style and wittily lovelorn, conversation-like lyrics. After the album established a foothold on the UK indie charts, *Tommy*—a hastily compiled overview of early singles, covers and radio broadcasts—followed in 1988.

The Wedding Present's next effort came completely out of left field: titled *Ukrainski Vistupi v Johna Peel,* the collection brought together Peel session dates with a sampler of traditional Ukrainian folk tunes inspired by Salowka's father. Additionally, it marked the recording debut of new drummer Simon Smith, recruited after Charman exited to form the Popguns. After reaching the Top 40 with the primal single "Kennedy," the Weddoes in 1989 with *Bizarro,* a more conventional effort highlighted by the single "Brassneck," produced by Steve Albini. 1991's aggressive *Seamonsters* returned Albini to the producer's seat and marked the departure of Salowka, who continued to explore his roots in the Ukrainians; guitarist Paul Dorrington was tapped as his replacement.

Instead of recording a new studio LP, the Wedding Present spent the entirety of 1992 issuing a single on the first Monday of each month. Later compiled as the two-volume *Hit Parade* set, the singles featured original material on their A-sides and cover songs on the flipsides, among them interpretations of the Monkees' "Pleasant Valley Sunday," Neil Young's "Don't Cry No Tears," Isaac Hayes' "Theme from Shaft," and Julee Cruise's "Falling" (better known as the theme to *Twin Peaks*).

After the departure of Gregory (to found Cha Cha Cohen) left Gedge the group's last original member, the Weddoes resurfaced with new bassist Darren Belk for 1994's *Watusi,* a nod towards the Amer-indie love-rock scene produced by Olympia, Washington-based producer Steve Fisk, complete with vocal assistance from Beat Happening's Heather Lewis. Following a rather uneventful 1995, the group returned in 1996 with a flurry of new material; first up was the auto-obsessed *Mini* EP, later reissued with bonus tracks as *Mini Plus.* The full-length *Saturnalia* appeared at the end of the year, followed early in 1997 by the single "Montreal." —*Jason Ankeny*

Tommy / Jul. 1988 / Reception ♦♦♦
Just one year after releasing their debut album *George Best,* the Wedding Present compiled several early, hard-to-find singles and EPs onto

Tommy. Not quite the best-of it should be, the album still is necessary for those interested in the band's complete discography. —*John Bush*

Bizarro / Oct. 1989 / RCA ✦✦✦✦
Two years on from their debut album, the Wedding Present delivered a proper sophomore effort, one quite distanced from the jangle-punk days of 1987's *George Best*. Though David Gedge's obsession with the love-lorn had by no means disappeared, the band finally found a way to frame his lyrics properly, resulting in a darker album with more emotional weight where needed. "Brassneck," the Weddoes' first collaboration with engineer Steve Albini, became their biggest hit yet, peaking at No. 24 on the British charts. —*John Bush*

Seamonsters / May 1991 / First Warning ✦✦✦✦
Steve Albini's production gives *Seamonsters* a noisy, discordant feel in some spots, but David Gedge's superb songwriting lies just under the surface. He manipulates his limited vocal range into a rich, wistful voice just about to crack. The Wedding Present work best on this album when Gedge's plaintive love songs explode into a distorted fury, as on "Dalliance," and "Suck." —*John Bush*

The Hit Parade 1 / Jun. 1992 / First Warning ✦✦✦✦

● **Watusi** / Sep. 1994 / PolyGram ✦✦✦✦
A year and a half after *Hit Parade*, the band released their Island debut. On *Watusi*, the noisy rhythms of *Seamonsters* are gone. Steve Fisk's production gives the LP a more varied musical feel; he lends his piano and organ skills over the crackling and popping of a turntable on the beautiful "Spangle." The first track, "So Long, Baby," begins as a normal, uptempo number, but then completely changes rhythm and melody for the chorus, a surprising and enjoyable move. "Yeah Yeah Yeah Yeah Yeah" is a high-powered, infectious sing-along. Although *Seamonsters* has more beautiful songs, *Watusi's* diversity gives it an added edge. —*John Bush*

Saturnalia / Sep. 24, 1996 / Cooking Vinyl ✦✦✦

Ween

f. 1984, New Hope, PA
Alternative Pop-Rock, Indie Rock, Comedy Rock
Ween was the ultimate cosmic goof of the alternative rock era, a prodigiously talented and deliriously odd duo whose work travelled far beyond the constraints of parody and novelty into the hallucinatory heart of surrealist ecstasy. Despite a mastery for seemingly every mutation of the musical spectrum, the group refused to play it straight; in essence, Ween were bratty deconstructionists, kicking dirt on the pop world around them with demented glee. Along with the occasional frat-boy lapses into misogyny, racism, and homophobia, the band's razor-sharp satire cut to the inherently silly heart of rock 'n' roll with hilariously acute savagery; fueled by psilocybin mushrooms and an all-consuming craving for hot meals, Ween created its own self-contained universe, a parallel dimension where the only sacred cow was their own demon god, the Boognish.

The duo formed in suburban New Hope, Pennsylvania in 1984, when 14-year-olds Mickey Melchiondo and Aaron Freeman adopted their respective fraternal aliases Dean and Gene Ween and cut the first of literally thousands of home recordings. At about the same time Freeman—working under the name Synthetic Socks—issued an eponymous 1987 solo cassette on the fledgling TeenBeat label, Ween released its own debut tape, *The Crucial Squeegie Lip*, on their own Bird O' Pray imprint. After a pair of 1988 self-releases, titled *Axis: Bold as Boognish* and *The Live Brain Wedgie/WAD LP*, Ween signed to the Minneapolis-based independent-label Twin/Tone, which in 1990 issued the double album *God Ween Satan—The Oneness*, a sprawling, often brilliant release which careened from the headlong hardcore rush of the opening "You Fucked Up" to the helium-pop of "Don't Laugh I Love You" to the Prince-xeroxed funk of "L.M.L.Y.P."

A move to the Shimmy Disc label followed prior to the release of 1991's *The Pod*, another masterpiece of dementia recorded on four-track under the influence of inhaled Scotchgard; darker and more deranged than its predecessor, *The Pod* expanded the Ween palette to include Beatlesque pop (the sublime "Pork Roll Egg and Cheese"), oddball folk ("Oh My Dear [Falling in Love]") and mystic hard rock ("Captain Fantasy"). Against all odds, the record won the Weens a deal with major-label Elektra; against even greater odds, the leap to the big leagues did nothing to alter the duo's mindset—1992's *Pure Guava*, their Elektra debut, was their most consistently weird and wonderful outing to date. Highlighted by the disturbingly infectious single "Push th' Little Daisies" (a Top Ten hit in Australia), *Pure Guava* found the group as snarky as ever on self-explanatory workouts like "Reggaejunkiejew," "Hey Fat Boy (Asshole)" and "Flies on My Dick"; "Springtheme" mocked love songs at their queasiest, while the climactic "Don't Get 2 Close (2 My Fantasy)" distilled the overblown excesses of Queen's "Bohemian Rhapsody" and

Queensryche's "Silent Lucidity" into an epic art-rock portrait of child molestation.

Dedicated to the late comedic actor John Candy, 1994's *Chocolate and Cheese*—its title a perfect summation of the duo's blend of R&B and schlock—upped the ante yet again. Widening the net to ensnare cowboy songs ("Drifter in the Dark"), Philly soul ("Freedom of '76"), Afro-Caribbean funk ("Voodoo Lady") and Sergio Leone-inspired spaghetti western epics ("Buenas Tardes Amigo"), *Chocolate and Cheese* also featured "Spinal Meningitis (Got Me Down)" and "Mister Would You Please Help My Pony," two of the creepiest tales of childhood trauma ever committed to vinyl. Having taken their anything-goes aesthetic to its logical extreme, Ween took a sharp left turn for 1996's *12 Golden Country Greats*, a ten-track concept album recorded in Nashville with Music City session luminaries including the Jordanaires, Bobby Ogdin, Russ Hicks, Hargus "Pig" Robbins, and Charlie McCoy. While the song titles alone—among them "Japanese Cowboy," "Mister Richard Smoker" and "Help Me Scrape the Mucus Off My Brain"—served notice that the group's lyrical attitude had not altered one whit, the music was remarkably evocative of Nashville's golden era, and performed with skill and affection. A tour with Ogdin and a backing unit dubbed the Shit Creek Boys followed prior to the release of 1997's *The Mollusk.* —*Jason Ankeny*

GodWeenSatan: The Oneness / 1990 / Twin/Tone ✦✦✦✦
A crank phone call of epic proportions, this 20-plus song strong debut is filled with plenty of inanity, insanity, and obscenity. Stylistically, the group veers off in all directions. The helium-laced pop of "Don't Laugh, I Love You," the stomp of "Old Queen Cole" and the delicate ballad "Squelch the Little Weasel" make this a crazy, unfocused collection of gross fun. —*Heather Phares*

The Pod / 1991 / Shimmy Disc ✦✦✦
The Pod continues the wackiness and effrontery that the Ween brothers started on *GodWeenSatan.* However, the tone of the album is more sluggish and off-kilter, perhaps from the severe case of mononucleosis the group had when they recorded this. "Dr. Rock" and "Pollo Asado" are two standouts on this bizarre and somewhat inaccessible album. —*Heather Phares*

Pure Guava / Nov. 10, 1992 / Elektra ✦✦✦✦
The band's third album finds them moving in a more pop direction. Tunes like "Push the Little Daisies," "Springtheme" and "Don't Get 2 Close (2 My Fantasy)," though certainly bizarre, are catchy and fun to listen to. However, the Ween boys don't forget to be disgusting, as song titles like "Reggaejunkiejew" and "Flies on My Dick" subtly hint. —*Heather Phares*

● **Chocolate & Cheese** / Sep. 27, 1994 / Elektra ✦✦✦✦
Chocolate and Cheese is the group's fourth and most accomplished album yet, focusing their gonzo sensibilities into a collection of hummable tunes. "Take Me Away" and " Tear for Eddie" are clever parodies of classic rock, while "Roses Are Free" and "Freedom of '76" pay homage to Prince and '70s soul respectively. The touching Mexican ballad "Buenos Tardes Amigo" and the downright creepy "Spinal Meningitis Got Me Down" show that Ween's smirks are still firmly on their faces, even if they are creating increasingly memorable tunes. *Chocolate and Cheese* is a good beginning point for novices to the crazy world of Dean and Gene Ween. —*Heather Phares*

12 Golden Country Greats / Jul. 1996 / Elektra ✦✦✦
Throughout their career, Ween have relentlessly taken the piss out of nearly every genre of music, often cramming in a ridiculous array of style into one music. What has saved them from appearing irredeemingly smug and cynical is their talent for crafting catchy songs and how nothing escapes their vicious satirization. And the problem with *12 Golden Country Greats* (which only contains ten songs, by the way) is that it's their first album to concentrate on a single music genre, namely country music, so it gives them the appearance of being above the genre. But that isn't entirely the case. Ween recorded *12 Golden Country Greats* in Nashville with numerous legendary musicians, including the Jordanaires, Buddy Spicher, Charlie McCoy, Hargus "Pig" Robbins, and Russ Hicks. The presence of these musicians gives the music a very authentic feeling, even though the songs stick to '60s trends like country-pop, country-folk, and polished honky tonk. Some of Ween's songs fit this style perfectly, such as the rolling "You Were the Fool," "I'm Holding You," "Japanese Cowboy," "Fluffy," "Help Me Scrape the Mucus Off My Brain," and "Pretty Girl." Even the vulgar honky tonk of "Piss up a Rope" works. The duo runs into trouble on the homophobic "Mister Richard Smoker," as well as with some of the vaguely elitist views that underpin the songs—occasionally, such as on "I Don't Wanna Leave You on the Farm," they sound like suburban youth making fun of a culture they don't know anything about. Still, Ween's gift for songcraft and the talents of the Nashville musicians save the album from being a smirking disaster. In its own way, it's as gutsy an album as any Ween have ever released—after all, no country fan will want to hear this record and most of their fans are deathly afraid of country music. And, even with the

faults of *12 Golden Country Greats*, that is sort of an admirable move.
—*Stephen Thomas Erlewine*

Weezer

f. 1993, Los Angeles, CA
Alternative Pop-Rock, Punk-Pop

As one of the most popular groups to emerge in the post-grunge alternative rock aftermath, Weezer received equal amounts of criticism and praise for their hook-heavy guitar-pop. Drawing from the heavy power-pop of arena rockers like Cheap Trick and the angular guitar leads of the Pixies, Weezer leavened their melodies with doses of '70s metal learned from bands like Kiss. But what set the band apart was their geekiness. None of the members of Weezer, especially leader Rivers Cuomo, were conventional rockers—they were kids that holed up in their garage, playing along with their favorite records when they weren't studying or watching TV. As a result, their music was infused with a quirky sense of humor and an endearing awkwardness that made songs like "Undone (The Sweater Song)," "Buddy Holly" and "Say It Ain't So" into big modern rock hits during 1994 and 1995. All the singles were helped immeasurably by clever videos, which may have made the songs into hits, but they also made many critics believe that the band were one-hit wonders. Perversely, Cuomo began to feel the same way, and decided that the band would not rely on any visual gimmicks for the second album, 1996's *Pinkerton*. Simultaneously, Cuomo took control of the band, making it into a vehicle for his songwriting. While the album didn't sell as well as their 1994 eponymous debut, it did earn stronger reviews than its predecessor.

Cuomo's assumption of the leadership of Weezer wasn't entirely a surprise, since he had been the band's primary songwriter since its inception in 1993. Raised in Massachusetts, Cuomo moved out to Los Angeles to go to college in the late '80s. During high school, he had played with a number of metal bands, but once he arrived in college, he became interested in alternative and post-punk music. By 1993, he had formed Weezer with bassist Matt Sharp and drummer Patrick Wilson. Over the course of the next year, they played in the competitive Los Angeles club scene, eventually landing a deal with DGC during the post-Nirvana alternative signing boom. Three days before the band began recording their debut with producer Ric Ocasek, they added guitarist Brian Bell.

Upon completing the record, Weezer went on hiatus temporarily—Cuomo was studying at Harvard when their eponymous debut record came out. With the support of DGC and a striking, Spike Jonze-directed video, "Undone (The Sweater Song)" became a modern rock hit in the fall of 1994, but what made *Weezer* a crossover hit was "Buddy Holly." Jonze created an innovative video that spliced the group into old footage from the sitcom *Happy Days*, and the single quickly became a hit, making the album a multi-platinum hit as well. By the time the album's final single, "Say It Ain't So," was released in the summer of 1995, the group had gone on hiatus, with Cuomo returning to Harvard. During the time off, Sharp and Wilson formed the new wave revival band the Rentals, which had a hit later that year with "Friends of P."

During the hiatus, Cuomo became a recluse, disappearing at Harvard and suffering writer's block. When Weezer reconvened in the spring of 1996 to record their second album, he had written a loose concept album which featured far more introspective material than their debut. Ironically, the band sounded tighter on the resulting album, *Pinkerton*. Released in the fall to generally strong reviews, the album failed to become a hit, partially because Cuomo did not want to the band to record another series of clever videos. Grudgingly, the remainder of the band contented themselves to be a supporting group for Cuomo, largely because each member had their own solo project scheduled for release within the next year. DGC, however, had the band make one last chance at a hit with "The Good Life," but by the time the single was released, MTV and modern rock radio had withdrawn their support not only to Weezer, but its style of guitar-driven punk-pop in general. —*Stephen Thomas Erlewine*

● **Weezer** / May 10, 1994 / DGC ✦✦✦✦
Falling between the warped pop of the Pixies and the straightahead thump of arena rock, Weezer's debut album offers embarrassingly pleasurable pop thrills. Weezer is unabashedly pop. Songs like "Buddy Holly," "Undone—The Sweater Song," "In the Garage," "The World Has Turned and Left Me Here," and "Surf Wax America" are filled with strong, simple guitar hooks and relentlessly catchy melodies. What makes the band so enjoyable is their charming geekiness; instead of singing about despair, they sing about love, which is kind of refreshing in the gloom-drenched world of '90s guitar-pop. —*Stephen Thomas Erlewine*

Pinkerton / Sep. 24, 1996 / Geffen ✦✦✦✦
From the pounding, primal assault of the opening track "Tired of Having Sex," it's clear from the outset that *Pinkerton* is a different record than the sunny, heavy guitar-pop of Weezer's eponymous debut. The first

noticeable difference is the darker, messier sound—the guitars rage and squeal, the beats are brutal and visceral, the vocals are mixed to the front, filled with overlapping, off-the-cuff backing vocals. In short, it sounds like the work of a live band, which makes it all the more ironic that *Pinkerton*, at its core, is a singer-songwriter record, representing Rivers Cuomo's bid for respectability. Since he hasn't changed Weezer's blend of power-pop and heavy metal (only the closing song, "Butterfly," is performed acoustically), many critics and much of the band's casual audience didn't notice Cuomo's signficant growth as a songwriter. Loosely structured as a concept album based on *Madame Butterfly*, each song works as an individual entity, driven by powerful, melodic hooks, a self-deprecating sense of humor ("Pink Triangle" is about a crush on a lesbian) and a touching vulnerability ("Across the Sea," "Why Bother?"). Weezer can still turn out catchy, offbeat singles—"The Good Life" has a chorus that is more memorable than "Buddy Holly," "El Scorcho" twists Pavement's punk-culture references in on itself, "Falling for You" is the most propulsive thing they've yet recorded—but their endearing geekiness isn't as cutesy as before, which means the album wasn't as successful on the charts. But, it's the better album, full of crunching power-pop with a surprisingly strong emotional undercurrent that becomes all the more resonant with each play. —*Stephen Thomas Erlewine*

Paul Weller

b. May 25, 1958, Woking, Surrey, England
Guitar, Vocals / Pop-Rock, Singer-Songwriter, Rock 'n' Roll

As the leader of the Jam, Paul Weller fronted the most popular British band of the punk era, influencing legions of English rockers that ranged from his mod-revival contemporaries to the Smiths in the '80s and Oasis in the '90s. During the final days of the Jam, he developed a fascination with Motown and soul, which led him to form the sophisti-pop group the Style Council in 1983. As the Style Council's career progressed, Weller's interest in soul developed into an infatuation with jazz-pop and house music, which eventually led to gradual erosion of his audience—by 1990, he couldn't get a record contract in the UK, where he had previously been worshipped as a demi-god. As a solo artist, Weller returned to soul music as an inspiration, cutting it with the progressive, hippie tendencies of Traffic. Weller's solo records were more organic and rootsier than the Style Council, which helped him regain his popularity within Britain. By the mid-'90s, he had released three successful albums which were both critically-acclaimed and massively popular in England, where contemporary bands like Ocean Colour Scene were citing him as an influence. Just as importantly, many observers, while occasionally criticizing the trad-rock nature of his music, acknowledged that Weller was one of the few rock veterans that had managed to stay vital within the second decade of his career.

Weller's climb back to the top of the charts was not easy. After Polydor rejected the Style Council's fifth, house-influenced album in 1989, Weller broke up the group and lost both his record contract and his publishing deal. Over the next two years, he was in seclusion as he revamped his music. In 1991, he formed the Paul Weller Movement and released "Into Tomorrow" on his own independent label, Freedom High Records. A soulful, gritty neo-psychedelic song that represented a clear break from the Style Council, "Into Tomorrow" reached the UK Top 40 that spring, and he supported the single with an international tour, where he worked out the material that comprised his eponymous 1992 solo debut. Recorded with producer Brendan Lynch, *Paul Weller* was a joyous, soulful return to form that was recorded with several members of the Young Disciples, former Blow Monkey Dr. Robert, and Weller's then-wife, Dee C. Lee. The album debuted at No. 8 on the UK charts, and was received with positive reviews.

Wild Wood, Weller's second solo album, confirmed that the success of his solo debut was no fluke. Recorded with Ocean Colour Scene guitarist Steve Craddock, *Wild Wood* was a more eclectic and ambitious effort than its predecessor. Greeted with enthusiastic reviews, it entered the charts at No. 2 upon its fall 1993 release. The album would win the Ivor Novello Award for "Outstanding Contemporary Song Collection" the following year. Weller supported the album with an extensive tour, which featured Craddock as the group's leader; the guitarist's exposure on *Wild Wood* helped him successfully relaunch Ocean Colour Scene in 1995. At the end of the tour, Weller released the live album, *Live Wood*, late in 1994.

Preceded by "The Changingman," which became his 17th Top Ten hit, 1995's *Stanley Road* was his most successful album since the Jam, entering the charts at No. 1 and eventually selling nearly a million copies in the UK. By this point, Weller decided to stop attempting to break into the United States and cancelled his North American tour. Of course, he was doing so well in England he didn't need to set his sights outside of the UK. *Stanley Road* may have been greeted with mixed reviews, but Weller had been re-elevated to his status as an idol, with the press claiming that he was the father of the thriving Brit-pop movement, and artists like Noel Gallagher of Oasis singing his praises. In fact, while neither artist released a new album in 1996, Weller and Gallagher's influence was felt throughout the British music scene, as roots-oriented, '60s bands like Ocean Colour Scene, Cast, and Kula Shaker became the most popular groups in the UK. Weller was scheduled to release a new album in 1997. —*Stephen Thomas Erlewine*

Paul Weller / Oct. 6, 1992 / London ✦✦✦✦
Weller's voice has matured into a deep, soulful, resonant instrument, in keeping with his new inward-looking material. He's obviously come to terms with being an effective chronicler of his own feelings rather than being the spokesperson of a generation. His ease with this role makes *Paul Weller* a comfortable—if not groundbreaking—listening experience all around. —*Roch Parisien*

● **Wildwood** / 1993 / PolyGram ✦✦✦✦
Paul Weller signalled that the songwriter had returned to form, but *Wildwood* is the album that re-established him as a British superstar. And for good reason, too. Expanding the tight, stripped-down soul and R&B-inflected pop of his debut, Weller adds a relaxed, laidback approach that recalls the better moments of Traffic. Throughout the record, Weller's songwriting is concise and soulful, giving the musicians a solid foundation for their instrumental excursions, which never become boring and indulgent. —*Stephen Thomas Erlewine*

Paul Weller Live Wood / 1994 / Go! Discs ✦✦✦
Weller's career was revitalized with *Wild Wood*, which sparked an equally successful world tour captured on the energetic *Live Wood*. The songs remain just as impressive, but what makes the live record worthwhile is the wonderful interplay of the band. They frequently launch into tight jams that never seem bloated, which is the mark of a good live album. —*Stephen Thomas Erlewine*

Stanley Road / Jun. 7, 1995 / Go! Discs ✦✦✦
In many ways, *Stanley Road* is *Wild Wood—Part Two*, a continuation of the laidback, soul-inflected rock that dominated his previous albums. Named after the street where he grew up, *Stanley Road* could be seen as a return to Paul Weller's roots, yet his roots were in the Who and the Kinks, not in Traffic. (At this point, the sound of the Jam matters little in what his music sounds like.) Weller's music has always had R&B roots—the major difference with both *Wild Wood* and *Stanley Road* is how much he and his band stretch out. *Stanley Road*, in particular, features more jamming than any of his previous work. That doesn't mean he has neglected his songwriting—a handful of Weller classics are scattered throughout the album. Unfortunately, too much of it is spent on drawn-out grooves that are self-conscious about their own authenticity. Still, he has the good sense to revive Dr. John's "I Walk on Gilded Splinters" and invite his disciple Noel Gallagher (Oasis) along to jam. —*Stephen Thomas Erlewine*

Mary Wells

b. May 13, 1943, Detroit, MI, d. Jul. 26, 1992
Vocals / Soul, Motown, Girl-Group
Time and legions of other soul superstars have obscured the fact that for a brief moment, Mary Wells was Motown's biggest star. She came to the attention of Berry Gordy as a 17-year-old, hawking a song she'd written for Jackie Wilson; that song, "Bye Bye Baby," became her first Motown hit in 1961. The full-throated approach of that single was quickly toned down in favor of a pop-soul sound. Few other soul singers managed to be as shy and sexy at the same time as Wells (Barbara Lewis is the only other that springs to mind), and the soft-voiced singer found a perfect match with the emerging Motown production team, especially Smokey Robinson. Smokey wrote and produced her biggest Motown hits—"Two Lovers," "You Beat Me to the Punch," and "The One Who Really Loves You" all made the Top Ten in the early '60s, and "My Guy" hit the No. 1 spot in mid-1964, at the very height of Beatlemania.

Mary turned 21 years old as "My Guy" was rising to the top of the charts, and left Motown almost immediately afterwards for a reported advance of several hundred thousand dollars from 20th Century Fox. The circumstances remain cloudy thirty years later, but Wells and her husband-manager felt Motown wasn't coming through with enough money for its new superstar; she was also lured by the prospect of movie roles through 20th Century Fox (which never materialized). It's been rumored that Wells was being groomed for the sort of plans that were subsequently lavished upon Diana Ross; more nefariously, it's also been rumored that Motown quietly discouraged radio stations from playing Wells' subsequent releases. What is certain is that Wells never remotely approached the success of her Motown years, entering the pop Top 40 only once (although she had some R&B hits). Motown, for its part, took care throughout the rest of the '60s not to lose its big stars to larger labels.

Wells' departure from Motown was so dramatic and unsuccessful that it's tended to overshadow the quality of her later work, which has almost always been dismissed as trivial by critics. True, it didn't match the quality of her Motown recordings—Smokey Robinson could not be replaced, but her '60s singles for 20th Century Fox (whom she ended up leaving

after only a year), Atco, and Jubilee were solid pop-soul on which her vocal talents remained undiminished. She wrote and produced a lot of her late-'60s and early-'70s sessions with her second husband, guitarist Cecil Womack (brother of Bobby), and these found her exploring a somewhat earthier groove than her more widely known pop efforts. She had trouble landing recording deals in the '70s and '80s, and succumbed to throat cancer in 1992. —*Richie Unterberger*

Greatest Hits / Apr. 15, 1964 / Motown ✦✦✦✦
Since Mary Wells left Motown in 1964, this 12-song compilation, released at the time, contains all her successful singles for the label, from "Bye Bye Baby" to "My Guy," with the exception of "I Don't Want To Take A Chance." As such, it is just about all the Mary Wells anyone reasonably needs. —*William Ruhlmann*

Complete Jubilee Sessions / 1993 / Sequel ✦✦✦✦
More proof that Wells still had what it took after leaving Motown. This 26-song collection assembles everything she recorded for the Jubilee label in the late '60s and early '70s: her 1968 LP *Servin' Up Some Soul*, a couple non-LP B-sides, and the entirety of a scrapped follow-up album (although some of the songs from that unreleased LP appeared on singles, seven were unreleased before this reissue). This is Wells' gutsiest period, with the majority of the material penned by her and husband Cecil Womack, who provides some excellent bluesy guitar licks. Wells is in top voice on both the fairly strong originals and a variety of well-done covers. The earlier *Servin' Up Some Soul* sessions have the edge over the later, slicker tracks, but almost all of it is well worth hearing. —*Richie Unterberger*

★ **Looking Back 1961-1964** / Sep. 7, 1993 / Motown ✦✦✦✦✦
This two-CD, 43-track box set is the most comprehensive retrospective of Motown's biggest female star before Diana Ross. Although her first hit, "Bye Bye Baby," presented Wells as a blues belter, she quickly settled into a sly and sassy groove. Subsequent hits like "You Beat Me To The Punch," "Two Lovers," and "My Guy" (all included here) made the most of her shy, seductive voice by teaming her with some great songs and production by Smokey Robinson. Though many of these tunes were relegated to B-sides, album tracks, or even the can (11 were previously unreleased), the material—written by Motown stalwarts like Berry Gordy, Holland-Dozier-Holland, and Mickey Stevenson when Smokey was unavailable—is not far below the hits in quality. This is as much a testimony to Motown's overflow of prolific talent as Wells, but doesn't detract from the consistency of this set, which includes her duets with Marvin Gaye (as well as a previously unreleased duet with Smokey Robinson). Includes a comprehensive essay in the photo-packed booklet, although the mysterious absence of the excellent "Was It Worth It" is a notable loss. —*Richie Unterberger*

Ain't It the Truth: The Best of Mary Wells 1964-1982 / Aug. 30, 1994 / Varese Sarabande ✦✦✦
It doesn't have anything from her 1965-67 years with Atco (those tracks are compiled on a separate collection), but otherwise this does a good job of assembling the highlights of her post-Motown career. The focus is on her handful of minor mid-'60s hits for 20th Century Fox (which were conscious or half-conscious attempts to emulate her mid-Motown sound) and her grittier 1968-70 recordings for Jubilee (which she co-wrote and co-produced with guitarist and husband/producer Cecil Womack). A couple of unimpressive tracks from her 1981 Epic album round out the collection; Wells is in fine form throughout. —*Richie Unterberger*

Dear Lover: The Atco Sessions / Jan. 1995 / Ichiban Soul Classics ✦✦✦
In his autobiography, Jerry Wexler characterized Wells' tenure with Atlantic from 1965-67 as a failure for all parties concerned, but he's being too harsh. Commercially, it was certainly a fallow period; only the title track (a Top Ten R&B hit) paid off. But actually, her Atco singles were solid mid-'60s soul, usually recorded in Chicago and bearing the influence of that city's noted soul producer, Carl Davis (who produced some of these tracks). This collection includes both sides of all four of her Atco singles, five covers from her sole Atco LP, and a couple of decent previously unreleased tracks. —*Richie Unterberger*

Never, Never Leave Me: The 20th Century Sides / Feb. 1996 / Soul Classics ✦✦✦
If Wells' brief stint with 20th Century had been a total misdirected failure, it would be easier to dismiss. It wasn't, though. Wells continued to deliver pop-flavored soul in just as good a voice as ever, and in fact had a few small hits. The problem is not so much approach as quality. Her material, though not bad, lacked the special magic of her best Motown classics; the production was somewhat thinner as well. This 18-track anthology assembles her best 20th Century performances, including her singles (some of them previously unavailable on album), songs from her first 20th Century LP, and three previously unreleased songs. Though it's principally of interest to Wells fans, it's better than you might expect, worth hearing for the pleasure of Wells' voice if not the average material. —*Richie Unterberger*

The West Coast Pop Art Experimental Band

f. Los Angeles, CA
Psychedelic

If a band could ever be called the "average" psychedelic group, the West Coast Pop Art Experimental Band fit the bill. This somewhat mysterious collection of Los Angeles players issued several albums in the late '60s that plugged into the era's standard folk-rock, freakouts, and trippy lyrics without establishing a solid identity of their own. But, because the currents they were riding were themselves so inspired, "average" in this case doesn't necessarily mean bad. In fact, they cut a fair number of pretty strong tracks, moving without rhyme or reason from straightforward Byrds and Kinks cops to zany orchestrated self-absorbed psychedelic pop to self-conscious exercises in hippy outrageousness (including, of all things, a cover of the Mothers' "Help I'm a Rock"). Though their legacy reeks of determined trendiness, the best of their output holds up reasonably well. —*Richie Unterberger*

● **Transparent Day** / 1986 / Edsel ◆◆◆◆
Well-chosen collection of 16 tracks from their first two albums. "Transparent Day" is a ringing folk-rocker, the throbbing "I Won't Hurt You" a soundtrack to the beginning of an acid trip; "Shifting Sands" and the string-laden "Will You Walk With Me" are tremulous tunes with an odd undercurrent of fear and uncertainty. Other highlights are the early Kinks copy "If You Want This Love" and the P.F. Sloan cover "Here's Where You Belong." —*Richie Unterberger*

Paul Westerberg

b. Dec. 31, 1960
Guitar, Piano, Vocals / Rock 'n' Roll, Alternative Pop-Rock, Singer-Songwriter

After disbanding the Replacements in 1991, singer-songwriter Paul Westerberg resurfaced the following year with two songs on the *Singles* soundtrack. A year later, Westerberg released his first solo album, *14 Songs*, in the summer of 1993. Although the record received generally positive reviews and spawned the modern rock hit, "World Class Fad," the album failed to break the songwriter into the mainstream. Three years later, Westerberg released his second solo album, *Eventually*. Like *14 Songs* and the entire Replacements catalog before it, *Eventually* received good reviews but failed to become a commercial success. —*Stephen Thomas Erlewine*

● **14 Songs** / Jun. 15, 1993 / Sire ◆◆◆◆
Westerberg's first solo album since the breakup of the Replacements is a strong yet incoherent collection of songs from one of the most influential songwriters of the 1980s. Falling somewhere between the sound of *All Shook Down* and the songwriting of *Tim*, *14 Songs* is a more mature effort from Westerberg, sounding like the optimistic brother of the last Replacements album. It's not as raw as *Let it Be* or *Tim* or as consistent as *Pleased to Meet Me*, but it is a solid collection of expertly crafted rock and pop songs. —*Stephen Thomas Erlewine*

Eventually / Apr. 1996 / Reprise ◆◆◆
Paul Westerberg's second solo album, *Eventually*, delivered a full three years after his debut *14 Songs*, illustrates that he has problems telling the difference between maturity and stodginess. *Eventually* follows the same pattern as *14 Songs*, as he balances uptempo, Stonesy rockers with introspective, folky ballads. Generally, his slower numbers cut the deepest, as the affectionate Bob Stinson tribute, "Good Day," and the heart-tugging "MamaDaddyDid." When Westerberg rocks out, he sounds tired and mannered; neither his riffs nor his performance have the energy of vintage Replacements, or '70s and '80s Stones, for that matter. And the rockers demonstrate the major flaw of *Eventually*—its carefully-considered production. Though the production is clean and professional, its very slickness emphasizes the uneven quality of Westerberg's songwriting. Of course, there are some gems here—in fact, there are even more this time around than *14 Songs*—but Westerberg still sounds uncertain of what direction he wants to pursue and how to grow old gracefully. —*Stephen Thomas Erlewine*

Wham!

f. 1981, London, England, **db.** 1986
Pop-Rock

Wham! was a UK pop-dance duo formed in 1981 by George Michael (born Yorgos Panayiotou, Jun 26, 1963) and Andrew Ridgeley (b.Jun 25, 1963). Combining light soul music with slow, romantic ballads, they first hit the UK charts in the fall of 1982 with "Young Guns (Go for It)." It hit No. 3, the first of ten UK Top Ten hits for the duo. The first Wham! album, *Fantastic*, topped the UK charts in 1983. The group broke through in the US the following year with "Wake Me Up Before You Go-Go," the first of three straight No. 1 hits. The second of those chart-toppers was "Careless Whisper," billed as "featuring George Michael," the first sign that Michael, who sang lead and wrote the songs, was emerging as a solo entity. Nevertheless, Wham! continued through 1986, fin-

ishing their career at Wembley Stadium in England, after which Michael went on to a successful solo career. —*William Ruhlmann*

Fantastic! / 1983 / Columbia ◆◆
● **Make It Big** / 1984 / Columbia ◆◆◆◆
George Michael demonstrates a thorough knowledge of danceable pop, from the '60s-ish "Wake Me up Before You Go-Go" to the tear-jerking ballad "Careless Whisper." Also includes "Everything She Wants" and "Freedom." —*William Ruhlmann*

Music from the Edge of Heaven / 1986 / Columbia ◆◆◆
More of a hodgepodge of tracks than a coherent album, this still includes the Top Ten hits "I'm Your Man," "A Different Corner," and "The Edge of Heaven." —*William Ruhlmann*

Ian Whitcomb

b. Jul. 10, 1941, Woking, Surrey, England
Vocals / British Invasion, British Music-Hall

An odd footnote of the British Invasion, English singer and pianist Ian Whitcomb formed his R&B group, Bluesville, in Dublin, Ireland, never had a hit in the UK, and wasn't all that wild about rock 'n' roll in the first place, preferring traditional forms of blues, ragtime, and Tin Pan Alley. But "You Turn Me On"—a tongue-in-cheek three-chord knockoff at the end of a session, with exaggerated falsetto vocals and an unforgettable orgasmic vocal hook—hit No. 8 in America in 1965, and Whitcomb was briefly a star. The bluesy follow-up, "N-N-Nervous," was a small hit, and that was the end of Whitcomb's hitmaking days. Not much of a rock 'n' roll singer, Whitcomb quickly turned to vaudevillian, British-music-hall styled material on his subsequent releases (which continue to this day), with meager commercial (and artistic) results. A dedicated archivist, Whitcomb's book *After the Ball* is a thorough history of pre-rock popular music forms, the most entertaining part being his autobiographical account of his fleeting rock 'n' roll stardom. —*Richie Unterberger*

● **Best of Ian Whitcomb** / 1985 / Rhino ◆◆◆◆
Fifteen songs from 1965-67, including "You Turn Me On," the small hits "This Sporting Life" and "N-N-Nervous," and the protest song "Too Many Cars On The Road." The rockers are okay, but the post-1965 vaudevillian tunes that compose the bulk of this compilation are lame indeed, sounding almost unbearably quaint and stilted nearly 30 years later. Session players supporting Ian on these tracks (most recorded in Hollywood) include James Burton, Delaney Bramlett, Gerry Roslie of the Sonics, and Mitch Mitchell. Includes exhaustive liner notes by Whitcomb himself. —*Richie Unterberger*

White Zombie

f. 1985, New York, NY
Hard Rock, Alternative Pop-Rock, Heavy Metal

All garish colors and trashy noise, White Zombie brought some sleazy fun back to heavy metal, celebrating the sheer schlock of cheap sex and bad horror movies. Although they gathered a cult following with a series of independent albums in the late '80s, it wasn't until their video for "Thunder Kiss '65" was aired on MTV's *Beavis & Butt-head* in 1993 that the band crossed over to a large audience. And they were the rare metal band that could appeal to jaded, post-modern hipsters; with their campy lyrics and theatrics, it was clear that the band didn't take themselves seriously.

White Zombie consolidated their success in 1995 with *Astro Creep: 2000—Songs of Love, Destruction*, which sold over two million copies. In the summer of 1996, the group released a collection of remixes from *Astro Creep* called *Supersexy Swingin' Sounds*. —*Stephen Thomas Erlewine*

● **La Sexorcisto: Devil Music, Vol. 1** / Mar. 17, 1992 / Geffen ◆◆◆◆
White Zombie carves out a unique identity for itself in the grunge/thrash genre with this one. The prerequisite loud guitars and shouting vocalist are here, but this album shows an obsession with '60s trash culture, particularly fast cars and grade-B horror movies. The subject matter of Rob Zombie's lyrics, along with frequent movie samples, help this group stand out from their more generic, disaffected brethren. —*Steve Huey*

Astro Creep: 2000—Songs of Love, Destruction / Apr. 11, 1995 / Geffen ◆◆◆◆
Following the belated surprise success of *La Sexorcisto, Astro-Creep: 2000—Songs of Love, Destruction and Other Synthetic Delusions of the Electric Head* carried the weight of high expectations, something that White Zombie was never familiar with before. Unsurprisingly, White Zombie plays it safe on *Astro-Creep*, never straying from their white-trash-on-acid metal. While it's undeniably campy, the band genuinely loves the trash they sing about, so they fit right into the tradition of tongue-in-cheek heavy metal bands from Alice Cooper to Kiss. Where those bands relied on songcraft beneath their schtick, White Zombie relies on a full-throttle roar. Borrowing such techniques as distorted vocals and drilling riffs from pseudo-industrial metal like Ministry, the

band beefs up their basic sound, making it powerful enough to disguise the lack of solid song structures and memorable riffs. Sonically, *Astro Creep* delivers the initial goods, yet it never develops into trash as substantial as "Thunder Kiss '65." —*Stephen Thomas Erlewine*

Supersexy Swingin' Sounds / Aug. 1996 / Geffen ✦✦✦
With *Supersexy Swingin' Sounds*, White Zombie offer a collection of ten remixes of songs from *Astro-Creep 2000*, plus a new mix of their cover of KC & the Sunshine Band's "I'm Your Boogie Man" (which was originally on *The Crow II* soundtrack). Not quite as experimental or dance-oriented as they would like to be, the band has always flirted with industrial and disco, but at their core they are a metal band. Granted, they're a metal band that reconfigures the kitschy pleasures of pop culture much in the vein of the Cramps and the B-52's. However, with *Supersexy Swingin' Sounds* the weaknesses in their approach becomes clear. Despite the presence of remixers like the Dust Brothers, P.M. Dawn, and Charlie Closer (among several others), there simply isn't enough interesting original material to make the reconfigured versions compelling. Furthermore the album artwork—featuring pseudo-exotica design and an array of scantly-clad or naked pin-ups, all dressed like '60s pin-up models—seems like the band is hopping on the bandwagon, instead of carving out new camp territory of their own. It's not a bad listen, but it is a surprisingly unengaging one. —*Stephen Thomas Erlewine*

Barry White

b. Sep. 12, 1944, Galveston, TX
Keyboards, Vocals / Soul, Disco, Urban
Barry White has been involved in the popular music industry since age 11, when he played piano on Jesse Belvin's hit single "Goodnight My Love." He recorded with the Upfronts for Lumntone in 1960, then as a lead vocalist for Atlantic in 1964 and for Downey and Veep in 1965 under the name of Barry Lee. He was an A&R man for Mustang/Bronco Records in 1966 and 1967. White formed the female trio Love Unlimited in 1969, and also became leader of the 40-piece Love Unlimited Orchestra. His solo career was revitalized in the early '70s as his formidable, deep, captivating bass, coupled with pseudo-sophisticated strings and elaborate productions, helped him rack up five No. 1 hits and seven other Top Ten R&B hits from 1973 until 1978 for 20th Century Records. He also scored five Top Ten pop singles and one No. 1 in that same stretch. "I'm Gonna Love You a Little More Baby" started the string in 1973, and his final Top Ten R&B single was "Your Sweetness Is My Weakness," which peaked at No. 2 in 1978. White continued recording for United Gold, 20th Century again, United Gold, and A&M. He scored a mild comeback by being one of the featured vocalists on Quincy Jones' single "The Garden" in 1989 and continues recording for A&M in the '90s. *The Icon Is Love* (1994) marked White's return as a potent commercial force. —*Ron Wynn*

Greatest Hits, Vol. 1 / 1975 / Casablanca ✦✦✦✦
Before a definitive multi-disc boxed set was issued in the 1990s, there were two single-album volumes of Barry White hits released by Casablanca in the 1970s. The first edition was the best, with sweeping versions of such disco classics as "Can't Get Enough of Your Love, Babe" and "You're the First, The Last, My Everything." White's productions and arrangements were never as intricate as they seemed, but his booming baritone and romantic dialogue sounded convincing when underscored by the lush backgrounds. If you only want a little Barry White, this is the album to grab. —*Ron Wynn*

Greatest Hits, Vol. 2 / 1981 / Casablanca ✦✦✦✦
This second set of Barry White hits isn't quite as impressive or essential as its predecessor. White's arrangements and compositions grew stale as the 1970s wore on, and he recycled the romantic dialogue and exploited the robust baritone until he became a caricature of himself. Put this one in the "for fans only" category. —*Ron Wynn*

Just for You / Nov. 17, 1992 / Casablanca ✦✦✦✦
A three-disc box set containing more music than anyone but the most devoted fan could want. —*Stephen Thomas Erlewine*

★ **All Time Greatest Hits** / 1995 / Mercury ✦✦✦✦✦
Condensing the best moments from the two *Greatest Hits* collections onto one disc, *All Time Greatest Hits* contains all of Barry White's biggest hits, including "I'm Gonna Love You Just A Little More Baby," "Never, Never Gonna Give Ya Up," "Can't Get Enough of Your Love, Babe," "You're the First, the Last, My Everything," and "It's Ecstasy When You Lay Down Next to Me." *All Time Greatest Hits* is the definitive collection of Barry White's '70s heyday, containing all of his truly essential songs. —*Stephen Thomas Erlewine*

Tony Joe White

b. Jul. 23, 1943, Oak Grove, LA
Guitar, Vocals / Rock 'n' Roll, Country-Rock, Country-Pop, Pop-Rock
Tony Joe White has parlayed his songwriting talent into a modestly successful country and rock career in Europe as well as America. July 23,

1943, in Goodwill, LA, White was born into a part-Cherokee family. He began working clubs in Texas during the mid-'60s, and moved to Nashville by 1968. White's Top Ten pop hit "Polk Salad Annie" and another charting single, "Roosevelt and Ira Lee (Night of the Moccasin)." That same year, Dusty Springfield reached the charts with his "Willie and Laura Mae Jones." Brook Benton recorded a version of White's "Rainy Night in Georgia" that hit No. 4 early in 1970; the song has since become a near-standard with over 100 credits. Tony Joe White's own "Groupie Girl" began his European success with a short stay on the British charts in 1970.

White moved to Warner Brothers in 1971, but success eluded him on his three albums—*Tony Joe White, The Train I'm On* and *Homemade Ice Cream*. Other stars, however, continued to keep his name on the charts during the '70s: Elvis charted with "For Ol' Times Sake" and "I've Got a Thing About You Baby" (Top Five on the Country charts), and Hank Williams, Jr. took "A Rainy Night in Georgia" to No. 13 Country. White himself recorded *Eyes* for 20th Century Fox in 1976, but then disappeared for four years. He signed to Casablanca for 1980's *The Real Thang* but moved to Columbia in 1983 for *Dangerous*, which included the modest country hits "The Lady in My Life" and "We Belong Together."

Tony Joe White was inactive through much of the '80s, but worked with Tina Turner on her 1989 *Foreign Affair* album, writing four songs and playing guitar and harmonica. He released *Closer to the Truth* a year later for his own Swamp label, and toured with Eric Clapton and Joe Cocker to very receptive French crowds. (*Closer to the Truth* has sold 100,000 copies in that country alone.) His 1993 album *Path of a Decent Groove* was released only in France, though Warner's *The Best of Tony Joe White* earned an American release the same year. —*John Bush*

● **Polk Salad Annie: The Best of Tony Joe White** / 1994 / Warner Archive ✦✦✦✦
Warner Archive's *Polk Salad Annie: The Best of Tony Joe White* contains all of his most familiar and best tracks from his time at Warner, making it a definitive single-disc retrospective of the songwriter's work. —*Thom Owens*

Whitesnake

f. 1977, London, England, **db.** 1990
Hard Rock, Heavy Metal, Hair Metal
After recording two solo albums, former Deep Purple vocalist David Coverdale formed Whitesnake around 1977. In the glut of hard rock and heavy metal bands of the late '70s, their first albums got somewhat lost in the shuffle, although they were fairly popular in Europe in Japan. During 1982, Coverdale took some time off, so he could take care of his sick daughter. When he re-emerged with a new version of Whitesnake in 1984, the band sounded revitalized and energetic. *Slide It In* may have relied on Led Zeppelin and Deep Purple's old tricks, but the band had a knack for writing hooks; the record became their first platinum album. Three years later, Whitesnake released an eponymous album which was even better. Portions of the album were blatantly derivative—"Still of the Night" was a dead ringer for early Zeppelin—but the group could write powerful, heavy rockers like "Here I Go Again" that were driven as much by melody as riffs, as well as hit power ballads like "Is This Love." *Whitesnake* was an enormous international success, selling over six million copies in the US alone.

Before they recorded their follow-up, 1989's *Slip of the Tongue*, Coverdale again assembled a completely new version of the band, featuring guitar virtuoso Steve Vai. Although the record went platinum, it was a considerable disappointment after the across-the-boards success of *Whitesnake*. Coverdale put Whitesnake on hiatus after that album. In 1993, he released a collaboration with former Led Zeppelin guitarist Jimmy Page that was surprisingly lackluster. The following year, Whitesnake released a greatest hits album and it seemed likely that Coverdale was going to form a new version of the band. —*Stephen Thomas Erlewine*

Slide It In / 1984 / Geffen ✦✦✦✦
With its combination of stadium-sized hard-rock riffing and solid commercial melodies, *Slide It In* laid the groundwork for the blockbuster follow-up *Whitesnake*. Nevertheless, the album is rawer and cruder than their subsequent pop hit and is more representative of the band's metal roots. —*Stephen Thomas Erlewine*

Whitesnake / 1987 / Geffen ✦✦✦✦
After slugging it out in the British hard rock market for almost ten years, Whitesnake achieved platinum success with this highly crafted mainstream AOR. It includes the No.1 "Here I Go Again," "Is This Love?" (No.2), and the Led Zeppelin rip "Still of the Night." —*AMG*

● **Whitesnake's Greatest Hits** / Jul. 19, 1994 / Geffen ✦✦✦✦
All of the best moments from Whitesnake's late-'80s glory days collected on one disc. —*Stephen Thomas Erlewine*

The Who

f. 1964, London, England, db. 1983
Rock 'n' Roll, Hard Rock, British Invasion, Pop-Rock

Few bands in the history of rock 'n' roll were riddled with as many contradictions as the Who. All four members had wildly different personalities, as their notoriously intense live performances demonstrated. The group was a whirlwind of activity, as the wild Keith Moon fell over his drum kit and Pete Townshend leaped into the air with his guitar, spinning his right hand in exaggerated windmills. Vocalist Roger Daltrey strutted across the stage with a thuggish menace, as bassist John Entwistle stood silent, functioning as the eye of the hurricane. These divergent personalities frequently clashed, but these frictions also resulted in a decade's worth of remarkable music.

As one of the key figures of the British Invasion and the mod movement of the mid-'60s, the Who were a dynamic and undeniably powerful sonic force. They often sounded like they were exploding conventional rock and R&B structures with Townshend's furious guitar chords, Entwistle's hyperactive bass lines, and Moon's vigorous, chaotic drumming. Unlike most rock bands, the Who based their rhythm on Townshend's guitar, letting Moon and Entwistle improvise wildly over his foundation, while Daltrey belted out his vocals. This was the sound the Who thrived on in concert, but on record they were a different proposition, as Townshend pushed the group toward new sonic territory. He soon became regarded as one of the finest British songwriters of his era, as songs like "The Kids Are Alright" and "My Generation" became teenage anthems, and his rock opera *Tommy* earned him respect from mainstream music critics.

Townshend continually pushed the band toward more ambitious territory, incorporating white noise, pop art, and conceptual extended musical pieces into the group's style. The remainder of the Who, especially Entwistle and Daltrey, weren't always eager to follow him in his musical explorations, especially after the success of his first rock opera, *Tommy*. Instead, they wanted to stick to their hard-rock roots, playing brutally loud, macho music instead of Townshend's textured song suites and vulnerable pop songs. Eventually, this resulted in the group abandoning their adventurous spirit in the mid-'70s, as they settled into their role as arena-rockers. The Who continued on this path even after the death of Keith Moon in 1978, and even after they disbanded in the early '80s, as they reunited numerous times in the late '80s and '90s to tour America. The group's relentless pursuit of the dollar was largely due to Entwistle and Daltrey, who never found successful solo careers, but it had the unfortunate side effect of tarnishing their reputation for many longtime fans. However, there's little argument that at their peak, the Who were one of the most innovative and powerful bands in rock history.

Pete Townshend and John Entwistle met while attending high school in the Shepherd's Bush area of London. In their early teens, they played in a Dixieland band together, with Entwistle playing trumpet and Townshend playing banjo. By the early '60s, the pair had formed a rock 'n' roll band, but Entwistle departed in 1962 to play in the Detours, a hard-edged rock band featuring a sheet-metal worker named Roger Daltrey. By the end of the year, Townshend had joined as a rhythm guitarist, and in 1963, Daltrey became the group's lead vocalist once Colin Dawson left the band. Within a few months, drummer Doug Sandom had parted ways with the Detours, and the group added Keith Moon, who had previously drummed in a surf-rock band called the Beachcombers. The Detours changed their name to the Who in early 1964.

As the group struggled to get a break, Pete Townshend attended art school, while the remaining three worked odd jobs. Soon, the band became regulars at the Marquee club in London, which is where Townshend first smashed one of his guitars out of frustration with the sound system; the destruction would become one of his performing signatures. Soon, the group cultivated a small following, which led to the interest of manager Pete Meaden. Under the direction of Meaden, the Who changed their name to the High Numbers and began dressing in sharp suits in order to appeal to the style and R&B-obsessed mod audience. The High Numbers released one single, "I'm the Face" / "Zoot Suit," which was comprised of two songs written by Meaden. After the single bombed, the group ditched him and began working with Kit Lambert and Chris Stamp, two fledgling music business entrepreneurs who had previously failed as film directors. Instead of moving the band away from mod, Lambert and Stamp encouraged them to embrace the movement, offering them advice on both what to play and what to wear, including pushing the target T-shirt that became a key visual signature. The group reclaimed the Who name and began playing a set that consisted entirely of soul, R&B and Motown—or, as their posters said, "Maximum R&B." By late 1964, they had developed an enthusiastic mod following. At the end of 1964, the Who signed with Decca on the strength of Townshend's "You Really Got Me" knockoff, "I Can't Explain." The group entered the studio with producer Shel Talmy, who previously

worked with the Kinks, and the single was released to little attention in January 1965. Once the Who appeared on the television program *Ready, Steady, Go*, the single shot up the charts, since the group's incendiary performance, featuring Townshend and Moon destroying their instruments, became a sensation. "I Can't Explain" reached the British Top Ten, followed that summer by "Anyway, Anyhow, Anywhere." That fall, "My Generation" climbed all the way to No. 2 on the charts, confirming the band's status as British pop phenomenons. An album of the same name followed at the end of the year, and early in 1966, "Subsitute" became their fourth British Top Ten hit.

Following "Substitute," the Who acrimoniously left Talmy, and Lambert became the group's producer. Lambert and Stamp decided that every member of the Who should contribute songs to the group's second album in order to generate more revenue. Although the ploy meant *A Quick One* was uneven, Lambert's presence allowed Townshend to write the title track as a 10-minute mini-opera, an idea he would expand over the next few years. Upon its 1966 release, *A Quick One* became another British hit. In America, the group was ignored until *A Quick One* was retitled *Happy Jack* and its title track reached the Top 40 in 1967. By that time, the group had already eclipsed *A Quick One* with *The Who Sell Out*, a concept album constructed as a mock-pirate radio broadcast. The album featured "I Can See for Miles," which became the group's first Top Ten hit in America. That year, the group also appeared at the Monterey Pop Festival.

During 1968, the Who delivered their final mod single with the bizarre "Dogs." By that time, the mod audience had declined considerably, and the single bombed, sending Townshend into seclusion to write a rock opera about a deaf, dumb and blind boy with a gift for pinball. As he worked on the record, the compilation *Magic Bus—The Who on Tour* was released in America.

The Who returned in 1969 with the double concept album *Tommy*, which was acclaimed as the first successful rock opera. The album became a huge hit, earning positive reviews from mainstream publications as well as underground rock magazines. *Tommy* climbed into the American Top Ten as the group supported the album with an extensive tour, where they played the opera in its entirety, including dates at the London Coliseum and the Metropolitan Opera House in New York. In some respects, *Tommy* became too successful, since it soon overshadowed the Who themselves; it was performed as a play across the world and would eventually be filmed by Ken Russell in 1975 (the movie starred Roger Daltrey)—plus, in 1993, Townshend turned it into a Broadway musical with director Des McAnuff.

While the legacy of *Tommy* would prove formidable, in 1970 Townshend was stumped about how to follow it up. As he worked on new material, the group released *Live at Leeds* in 1970, as well as the single "The Seeker." The following year a singles collection called *Meaty, Beaty, Big and Bouncy* was released. Eventually, he settled on a sci-fi rock opera called *Lifehouse*, which he intended to be strongly influenced by the teachings of his guru, Meher Baba. Townshend also intended to incorporate electronics and synthesizers on the album, pushing the group into new sonic territory. The remainder of the Who wasn't particularly enthralled with *Lifehouse*, claiming not to understand its plot, and their reluctance contributed to Townshend suffering a nervous breakdown. Once he recovered, the group picked up the pieces of the now-abandoned *Lifehouse* project and recorded *Who's Next* with producer Glyn Johns. Boasting a harder, heavier sound, *Who's Next* became a major hit, and many of its tracks—including "Baba O'Riley," "Bargain," "Behind Blue Eyes," "Won't Get Fooled Again" and Entwistle's "My Wife"—became cornerstones of album-oriented FM radio in the '70s.

The success of *Who's Next* prompted Townshend to attempt another opera. This time, he abandoned fantasy in order to sketch a portrait of a '60s mod with *Quadrophenia*. As he wrote the album in 1972, he released *Who Came First*, a collection of private recordings and demos he made for Meher Baba. Around that time, Entwistle, frustrated at his lack of songwriting input in the Who, began his own solo career, pursuing his with more dedication than Townshend. *Quadrophenia* was released as a double album in 1973, and although the band attempted to play the music on tour, technical difficulties prevented them from doing so.

The Who began to fragment after the release of *Quadrophenia*, as Townshend began to publicly fret over his role as a rock spokesman; in private, he began sinking into alcohol abuse. Entwistle concentrated heavily on his solo career, including recordings with his side projects Ox and Rigor Mortis, as Daltrey alternately pursued an acting career and solo recordings. Moon, meanwhile, continued to party, celebrating his substance abuse and eventually releasing the solo album *Two Sides of the Moon*, which was studded with star cameos. During this hiatus, the group released the rarities collection *Odds and Sods*. Meanwhile, Townshend continued to work on songs for the Who, resulting in the disarmingly personal *The Who By Numbers* in 1975. The record and its accompanying tour became a hit, but following the tour's completion, they officially took an extended hiatus. The Who reconvened in 1978 to release *Who Are You*. Instead of responding to the insurgent punk movement, which labeled the Who as has-beens, the album represented the group's heaviest flirtation with prog-rock since *Quadrophenia*. The album became a huge hit, peaking at No. 2 in the American charts and reaching platinum. Instead of being a triumphant comeback, though, *Who Are You* became a symbol of tragedy, since Keith Moon died of a drug overdose on September 7, 1978, mere weeks after the record's release. Since Moon was such an integral part of the Who's sound and image, the band had to debate whether continuing on was a wise move. Eventually, they decided to continue performing, but all three surviving members would later claim that they felt the Who ended with Moon's death.

Hiring Kenny Jones, a former member of the Small Faces, as Moon's replacement, as well as keyboardist John "Rabbit" Bundrick to round out the lineup, the Who began working on new material in 1979. Before they released a new record, they released the live documentary *The Kids Are Alright* and contributed music to Franc Roddam's cinematic adaptation of *Quadrophenia*, which starred Phil Daniels. The Who began touring later in 1979, but the tour's momentum was crushed when 11 attendees at the group's December 3, 1979 concert at Cincinnati's Riverfront Coliseum were trampled to death in a rush for choice festival seating. The band wasn't informed of the incident until after the concert was finished, and the tragedy deflated whatever good will they had.

Following the Cincinnati concert, the Who slowly fell apart. Townshend became addicted to cocaine, heroin, tranquilizers, and alcohol, suffering a near-fatal overdose in 1981. Meanwhile, Entwistle and Daltrey soldiered on in their solo careers. The band reconvened in 1981 to record and release *Face Dances*, their first album since Moon's death. The album was a hit but received mixed reviews. The following year, they released *It's Hard* and embarked on a supporting tour billed as their farewell to fans. The live *Who's Last* was released in 1984 as a commemoration of the tour.

The farewell tour didn't turn out to be the final goodbye from the Who. While Entwistle and Daltrey slowly faded away, Townshend continued recording to relative success. However, the Who still haunted him. The group reunited to play Live Aid in 1985, and three years later, they played a British music awards program. In 1989, Townshend agreed to reunite the band, with Jones being replaced by session drummer Simon Phillips, for a 25th anniversary tour of America. Whatever goodwill the Who had with many fans and critics was squandered on that tour, which was perceived as simply a way to make a lot of money. The Who reunited again in 1994 for two concerts to celebrate Roger Daltrey's 50th birthday. Following the success of his Broadway adaptation of *Tommy*, Townshend decided to revive *Quadrophenia* in 1996, reuniting the Who to perform the piece at the Prince's Trust concert in Hyde Park that summer. The Who followed it with an American tour in the fall, which proved to be a failure. The following summer, the Who launched an oldies tour of America which was ignored by the press. *—Stephen Thomas Erlewine*

The Who Sings My Generation / 1965 / MCA ✦✦✦✦
An explosive debut, and the hardest mod pop recorded by anyone. At the time of its release, it also had the most ferociously powerful guitars and drums yet captured on a rock record. Townshend's exhilarating chord crunches and guitar distortions threaten to leap off the grooves on "My Generation" and "Out in the Street"; Keith Moon attacks the drums with a lightning, ruthness finesse throughout. Some "Maximum R&B" influence lingered in the two James Brown covers, but much of Townshend's original material fused Beatlesque hooks and power chords with anthemic mod lyrics, with "The Good's Gone," "Much Too Much," "La La La Lies," and especially "The Kids Are Alright" being highlights. "A Legal Matter" hinted at more ambitious lyrical concerns, and "The Ox" was instrumental mayhem that pushed the envelope of 1965 amplification with its guitar feedback and nonstop crashing drumrolls. While the execution was sometimes crude, and the songwriting not as sophisticated as it would shortly become, the Who never surpassed the pure energy level of this record. *—Richie Unterberger*

A Quick One (Happy Jack) / 1966 / MCA ✦✦✦✦
The group's second album is a less impressive outing than their debut, primarily because, at the urging of their managers, all four members penned original material (though Townshend wrote more than anyone else). The pure adrenaline of *My Generation* also subsided somewhat, as the band began to grapple with more complex melodic and lyrical themes, especially on the erratic mini-opera, "A Quick One While He's Away." Still, there's some great madness on Moon's instrumental "Cobwebs and Strange," and Townshend delivered some solid mod pop with "Run Run Run" and "So Sad About Us." John Entwistle was also revealed to be a writer of considerable talent (and a morbid bent) on "Whiskey Man" and "Boris the Spider." The 1995 CD reissue adds ten bonus tracks: some 1966-67 B-sides, their UK-only 1966 *Ready Steady Who!* EP, an acoustic version of "Happy Jack," and a previously unreleased cover of the Everly Brothers' "Man with the Money." *—Richie Unterberger*

☆ **The Who Sell Out** / 1967 / MCA ✦✦✦✦✦
Townshend originally planned this as a concept album of sorts that would simultaneously mock and pay tribute to pirate radio stations, complete with fake jingles and commercials linking the tracks. For reasons that remain somewhat ill-defined, the concept wasn't quite driven to completion, breaking down around the middle of side two (on the original vinyl configuration). Nonetheless, on strictly musical merits, it's a terrific set of songs that ultimately stands as one of the group's greatest achievements. "I Can See For Miles" (a Top Ten hit) is the Who at their most thunderous; tinges of psychedelia add a rush to "Armenia, City in the Sky" and "Relax"; "I Can't Reach You" finds Townshend beginning to stretch himself into quasi-spiritual territory; and "Tattoo" and the acoustic "Sunrise" show introspective, vulnerable sides to the singer-songwriter that had previously been hidden. "Rael" was another mini-opera, with musical motifs that reappeared in *Tommy*. The album is as perfect a balance between melodic mod pop and powerful instrumentation as the Who (or any other group) would achieve; psychedelic pop was never as jubilant, not to say funny (the fake commercials and jingles interspersed between the songs are a hoot). The 1995 CD reissue has over half a dozen interesting outtakes from the time of the sessions, as well as unused commercials, the B-side "Someone's Coming," and an alternate version of "Mary Anne with the Shaky Hand." *—Richie Unterberger*

Magic Bus / 1968 / MCA ✦✦✦
A ripoff of sorts even upon its original release, with a few senseless repeats of tracks from *Quick One* and *Sell Out*, as well as a sleeve that erroneously implied a live recording. This mish-mash of singles, B-sides, and stray tracks from past British releases did have some fine moments, particularly the singles "Call Me Lightning" and the Bo Diddley-influenced "Magic Bus," which became one of their most popular concert numbers. Other highlights are the fine 1966 pop-art tune "Disguises" and Entwistle's hysterical "Doctor, Doctor," but these (and a few of the other cuts) are now available as bonus tracks on the *Quick One* and *Sell Out* reissues. Completists should know that one song, Entwistle's typically black-humored "Dr. Jekyll & Mr. Hyde," is unavailable on any other US release, so it's not time to throw away your copy of *Magic Bus* just yet. *—Richie Unterberger*

Tommy / 1969 / MCA ✦✦✦✦
The full-blown rock opera about a deaf, dumb, and blind boy that launched the band to international superstardom, written almost entirely by Townshend. Hailed as a breakthrough upon its release, its critical standing has diminished somewhat in the ensuing decades, because of the occasional pretensions of the concept, and the insubstantial nature of some of the songs that functioned as little more than devices to advance the rather sketchy plot. Nonetheless, the double album has many excellent songs, including "I'm Free," "Pinball Wizard," "Sensation," "Christmas," "We're Not Gonna Take It," and the dramatic ten-minute instrumental, "Underture." Though the album was slightly flawed, Townshend's ability to construct a lengthy conceptual narrative brought new possibilities to rock music. Despite the complexity of the project, he and the Who never lost sight of solid pop melodies, harmonies, and forceful instrumentation, imbuing the material with a suitably powerful grace. *—Richie Unterberger*

☆ **Live at Leeds** / 1970 / MCA ✦✦✦✦✦
A loud, raunchy concert showcase for the group, with surprisingly little material from *Tommy*. The group's R&B roots are showcased here far better than on their post-*My Generation* studio albums, and the only problem for some listeners is the lack of the sophisticated studio sound they'd developed on previous releases. The 1995 CD reissue doubles the length of the original LP, with plenty of additional material from the same performance, including versions of some more of their early singles and unexpected items like "Tattoo" and the R&B standard "Fortune Teller." *—Bruce Eder*

★ **Meaty, Beaty, Big & Bouncy** / 1971 / MCA ✦✦✦✦✦
The first halfway-decent retrospective on the group, covering their American singles as of 1972, including "I Can See for Miles," "My Generation," "The Magic Bus," "The Seeker," and a lot of other material that subsequently became staples of FM radio. *—Bruce Eder*

★ **Who's Next** / 1971 / MCA ✦✦✦✦✦
The group's magnum opus, a rich, expressive, loud piece of hard rock that summed up the first six years of the band's history. "Won't Get Fooled Again" became a major radio anthem and "Behind Blue Eyes" unexpectedly became a favorite Pete Townshend number as well. Roger Daltrey never sang better, and John Entwistle's bass achieved new heights of prominence, while Keith Moon turned in an explosive performance on drums. *—Bruce Eder*

Quadrophenia / 1973 / MCA ✦✦✦✦
Pete Townshend revisited the rock opera concept with another double-album opus, this time built around the story of a young mod's struggle to come of age in the mid-'60s. If anything, this was a more ambitious project than *Tommy*, given added weight by the fact that the Who weren't devising some fantasy, but were re-examining the roots of their

own birth in mod culture. In the end, there may have been *too* much weight, as Townshend tried to combine the story of a mixed-up mod named Jimmy with the examination of a four-way split personality (hence the title *Quadrophenia*), in turn meant to reflect the four conflicting personas at work within the Who themselves. The concept might have ultimately been too obscure and confusing for a mass audience. But there's plenty of great music anyway, especially on "The Real Me," "The Punk Meets the Godfather," "I'm One," "Bell Boy," and "Love, Reign O'er Me." Some of Townshend's most direct, heartfelt writing is contained here, and production-wise it's a tour de force, with some of the most imaginative use of synthesizers on a rock record. Various members of the band griped endlessly about flaws in the mix, but really these will bug very few listeners, who in general will find this to be one of the Who's most powerful statements. *—Richie Unterberger*

Odds & Sods / 1974 / MCA ✦✦✦
This compilation of outtakes and rarities from the Who's first decade was a rather jumpy listen that harbored few songs that could be termed top-of-the-line. Also, since its 1974 release, several of the tracks have been issued on other compilations, or as bonus tracks to CD reissues of legitimate Who albums. Setting your expectations at the appropriate level, you'll find much of this worthwhile. "Pure and Easy," "Naked Eye," and "Long Live Rock" were all concert favorites of the group in the 1970s; "Glow Girl" introduced some riffs that would resurface in *Tommy*; "Postcard," Entwistle's tale of rock life on the road, was one of his better compositions. This also has their very first single, "I'm the Face," recorded in 1964 when the group were known as the High Numbers. *—Richie Unterberger*

The Who By Numbers / 1975 / MCA ✦✦✦
The Who by Numbers functions as Pete Townshend's confessional singer-songwriter album, as he chronicles his problems with alcohol ("However Much I Booze"), women ("Dreaming from the Waist" and "They Are All in Love"), and life in general. However, his introspective musings are rendered ineffective by Roger Daltrey's bluster and the cloying, lightweight filler of "Squeeze Box." In addition, Townshend's songs tend to be under-developed, relying on verbosity instead of melodicism, with only the simple power of "Slip Kid," the grace of "Blue Red and Grey," and John Entwistle's heavy rocker "Success Story" making much of an impact. The 1996 CD reissue adds three live tracks from a 1976 concert. *—Stephen Thomas Erlewine*

Who Are You / 1978 / MCA ✦✦✦
On the band's final album with Moon, their trademark honest power started to get diluted by fatigue and a sense that the group's collective vision was beginning to fade. As instrumentalists, their skills were intact. More problematic was the erratic quality of the material, which seemed torn between blustery attempts at contemporary relevance ("Sister Disco," "New Song," "Music Must Change") and bittersweet insecurity ("Love Is Coming Down"). Most problematic of all were the arrangements, heavy on the symphonic synthesizers and strings, which make the record sound cluttered and over-anxious. Daltrey's operatic tough-guy braggadacio in particular was beginning to sound annoying on several cuts. Yet Townshend's better tunes—"Music Must Change," "Love Is Coming Down," and the anthemic title track—continued to explore the contradictions of aging rockers in interesting, effective ways. Whether due to Moon's death or not, it was the last reasonably interesting Who record. The 1996 CD reissue adds five previously unreleased alternate takes and demos. *—Richie Unterberger*

The Kids Are Alright / 1979 / MCA ✦✦✦
This double-album soundtrack to the film documentary of the Who featured live material from the '60s and '70s, recorded at various TV shows, festivals, and concerts, and included many of their most famous songs. It's not the definitive live compilation that it might have been. Some of the performances are memorable, like the version of "My Generation" from the Smothers Brothers TV show, the performance of "A Quick One" for *The Rolling Stones Rock and Roll Circus,* and the excerpts from Woodstock. Others are barely different from the studio versions, and some of the more bombastic renditions drag. *—Richie Unterberger*

Face Dances / 1981 / MCA ✦✦✦
Without Keith Moon, the Who may have lacked the restless firepower that distinguished their earlier albums, but *Face Dances* was some of Pete Townshend's best, most incisive compositions since *Quadrophenia.* "Don't Let Go the Coat" was one of his better odes to the Meher Baba, "You Better You Bet" was a driving rocker, as was the rueful "Cache Cache," while "How Can You Do It Alone" was a solid ballad. While Townshend's songs were graceful and introspective, Roger Daltrey delivered them without any subtlety, rendering their power impotent. *—Stephen Thomas Erlewine*

It's Hard / 1982 / MCA ✦✦
Driven by Pete Townshend's arching musical ambitions, *It's Hard* was an undistinguished final effort from the Who. Featuring layers of synthesizers and long-winded, twisting song structures, the album featured few memorable melodies and little energy, with only the anthemic "Ath-

ena" and the terse "Eminence Front" making a lasting impression. *—Stephen Thomas Erlewine*

Who's Missing / 1985 / MCA ✦✦✦
A dozen B-sides, UK-only singles, and other oddities from the 1960s and early '70s. Some of these are really good: the raucous 1965 cover of James Brown's "Shout and Shimmy," "Heaven and Hell" (one of John Entwistle's better tunes), the 45 version of "Mary Anne with the Shaky Hand," the obscure Roger Daltrey tune "Here for More." Other cuts are pretty peripheral, like the lame '65 R&B of "Lubie (Come Back Home)," or the live version of "Bargain." Also, a few of these have since been tacked onto CD reissues of proper Who albums as bonus tracks. It's not bad, but it's really only for fans of the band. *—Richie Unterberger*

Two's Missing / 1987 / MCA ✦✦✦
Like *Who's Missing,* this is an assortment of B-sides, UK-only tracks, outtakes, and live cuts from the 1960s and early '70s. Again, there's some notable, even terrific, material here: the fiery 1967 covers of the Rolling Stones' "The Last Time" and "Under My Thumb," the strange 1968 UK single "Dogs," the heavy R&B of the 1965 British B-side "Daddy Rolling Stone." Yet much of the rest of the album is extraneous to all but die-hards, like a sluggish 1965 cover of Martha & the Vandellas' "Motoring," Keith Moon's novelty B-side "Wasp Man," or the 1969 instrumental "Dogs, Part 2" (which *does* have some slick guitar runs and manic drumming). The record's haphazardly sequenced as well. Also, *Who's Missing* and *Two's Missing* still manage to miss a couple '60s B-sides that Who fanatics might want (Entwistle's "I've Been Away" and Keith Moon's "In the City"), although those two cuts are now available on the CD reissue of *A Quick One.* In fact, the well-known bootleg *Who's Zoo* does a much better job of assembling most of the group's early rarities into two albums. *—Richie Unterberger*

Who's Better Who's Best / Nov. 14, 1988 / MCA ✦✦✦✦
Who's Better Who's Best is an adequate compilation of the Who's best-known songs, containing all of the familiar items—"I Can't Explain," "I Can See for Miles," "Pinball Wizard," "Won't Get Fooled Again," "Who Are You," "You Better You Bet"—but presented without much care or logic. Nevertheless, it's a solid career overview and is useful for both casual fans and neophytes. *—Stephen Thomas Erlewine*

Quadrophenia Demos / 1994 / [Bootleg] ✦✦✦
Though the sleeve only credits Pete Townshend—and although Townshend may well be the only musician involved on this material—it's more properly classified as a Who bootleg, as most of the songs were used for the group's *Quadrophenia* album. If you have the official *Scoop* collections, you know what to expect from Townshend's demos: well thought-out prototypes of what the Who ended up recording, with boxier sound and, of course, Pete's vocals in place of Roger Daltrey's. This actually only has eight tracks that ended up on *Quadrophenia,* meaning that less than half of the album's songs are contained here. It's a decent investment for big Who fans, however, as it gives us a chance to hear working versions of key cuts like "The Real Me" and "Drowned"; "Bell Boy" is a particular highlight. The sound is imperfect, not so much from the clarity standpoint, but because on most tracks the bass and drums are annoyingly overmodulated. Being that this isn't an official release, though, it's kind of hard to complain about the production values of music that, as the RIAA reminds us, we have no legal or moral right to hear. This has come out in several different configurations; the Black Dog version adds five significant non-*Quadrophenia* related cuts, including a 1968 demo of "Dogs," a couple of decent unreleased 1975 tunes, a "Who Are You" demo, and a ten-minute instrumental version of "Baba O'Riley." *—Richie Unterberger*

Thirty Years of Maximum R&B / Jul. 5, 1994 / MCA ✦✦✦
One of the more overblown recent box sets, this four-CD collection does include all of their big hits and the lion's share of their key album tracks. Previously unreleased rarities include some interesting selections (the '60s outtakes "Early Morning Cold Taxi" and "Melancholia"), but these bits and pieces, which include some live versions, commercials, Keith Moon sketches, and the like, are mostly inessential. The post-Keith Moon cuts that bring us up to the present are out of the league of the body of the Who's work. As most of the Who's '60s and '70s albums are very strong, cohesive works in and of themselves, this can't be recommended as either a starting point or a necessary addition. *—Richie Unterberger*

● **My Generation: The Very Best of the Who** / Aug. 27, 1996 / MCA ✦✦✦✦
The Who have issued more greatest hits collections than any other major artist, releasing a vast array of compilations while they were together and in the years following their breakup. Released in 1996, *My Generation: The Very Best of the Who* was intended to be the definitive single-disc collection, replacing all the others that preceded it. While it is a very good collection, it just misses being a definitive sampler. Essentially, *My Generation* is a replica of *Who's Better, Who's Best* that adds four tracks that were missing from the previous compilation, including the seminal post-*Tommy* single "The Seeker" and the original single mix

of "Magic Bus." *My Generation* isn't strictly a singles collection, since it contains such album rock staples as "Baba O'Riley" and the full-length version of "Won't Get Fooled Again." It also spans the group's entire career, so it has a bit of a scattershot feel to it—"You Better You Bet" sounds a little odd next to tense early singles like "Substitute" and "I Can See For Miles." The career-spanning approach doesn't make for as cohesive a collection as *Meaty, Beaty, Big and Bouncy,* but it does mean that *My Generation* is an excellent—even necessary—introduction. There's a lot more in the Who's catalog that needs to be heard, but *My Generation* does boil down the most essential items (even though the abominable "Squeeze Box" is included) to a fine single-disc set. —*Stephen Thomas Erlewine*

Live at the Isle of Wight Festival 1970 / Oct. 29, 1996 / Castle ✦✦✦✦
This double CD is pretty similar in sound and content to the expanded *Live at Leeds* album, except there's much more from *Tommy,* and a few semi-obscure numers like "I Don't Even Know Myself," "Water," and "Naked Eye." Hardcore Who fanatics seem to prefer *Live at Leeds,* which was recorded only a few months before this material. That viewpoint is understandable: the performances are sharper on *Leeds,* and if you're not a big-league fan, that single-disc set is a more economical survey of the band in concert during this era. If you *do* like the Who a lot, though, *Isle of Wight* is worth having. The sound and performances are decent, although be aware that the band's onstage version of *Tommy* omits some decent songs from the opera, such as "Sensation" and "Underture." —*Richie Unterberger*

Maximum BBC / Red Robin ✦✦✦
A most worthwhile find for the serious Who fan, comprising 27 tracks that the group recorded for the BBC between 1965 and 1970, the accent falling heavily on the 1965-67 period. Decent though not pristine sound and good performances, which usually don't deviate a great deal from the record, but are occasionally substantially different: Entwistle's bass, in particular, comes through much more strongly on some of the 1966-67 material. It also includes some unusual covers that never made their way onto official releases: "Just You And Me" (James Brown), "Man With Money" (the Everly Brothers), and "Dancing In The Streets." The 1970 version of "Shakin' All Over" may be the best take of this concert staple ever taped by the band. —*Richie Unterberger*

Live at the Fillmore East, 4/5/68 / [Bootleg] ✦✦✦
Recorded during their early 1968 American tour, this was considered as an official release, but rejected by the group. The only really satisfactory quality live Who tape from the '60s that has surfaced, it has good performances and an interesting song selection, including quite a few numbers that weren't included on Who releases of the time: "Little Billy," "Fortune Teller," and Eddie Cochran's "My Way" (here credited as "Easy Goin' Guy"). There's also a much heavier and elongated version of "Relax" (which unfortunately cuts off in the instrumental break), as well as standbys like "Can't Explain," "Happy Jack," and "Shakin' All Over." It's recommended for those who want the firepower of *Live at Leeds* without as much of the heavy guitar bombast. —*Richie Unterberger*

Tommy Demos / Yellow Dog ✦✦✦
Superb quality demos for the famous rock opera, including working versions of almost all of the songs that ended up on the album. Townshend takes lead vocals on a lot of these, which are, more often than not, extremely similar in arrangement and delivery to the versions that ended up on the finished product; one assumes that most of these may be Pete's own recordings, on which he played most or all of the instruments. It's low on extraordinary revelations, but it's an interesting document of the creative process for this hugely influential album. —*Richie Unterberger*

Who's Zoo / [Bootleg] ✦✦✦✦
One of the "classic" early bootlegs, this double-LP did collectors a tremendous favor by assembling almost all of the Who's rare studio recordings—from non-LP B-sides and UK-only singles and EPs—into one convenient place, in excellent sound, although most or all of it was probably dubbed from vinyl. And it's not extraneous stuff—much of it, like "Daddy Rolling Stone," "Shout and Shimmy," "The Last Time," "Dogs," and "Heaven and Hell," is great. Just about everything has subsequently appeared on official reissues (although the 1966 instrumental B-side "Waltz for a Pig," which is actually Graham Bond and not the Who, has not). Although MCA would not appreciate the observation, the fact remains that this is the best and most well-sequenced Who rarity compilation, with sound that is not significantly different from legitimate releases. And there's the significant bonus of side four, which has incendiary live performances (in fair-to-good quality) from various mid-'60s TV programs. —*Richie Unterberger*

Whodini

f. 1981, Brooklyn, NY
Hip Hop, Old School Rap
Coming out of the fertile early-'80s New York rap scene, Whodini was

one of the first rap groups to add a straight R&B twist to their music, thus laying the groundwork for the new jack swing movement. The group consisted of rappers Jalil Hutchins and John "Ecstasy" Fletcher, adding legendary DJ Drew "Grandmaster Dee" Carter, known for being able to scratch records with nearly every part of his body, in 1986. Whodini made its name with good-humored songs like "Magic's Wand" (the first rap song to feature an accompanying video), "The Haunted House of Rock" (a rewrite of "Monster Mash"), and "Freaks Come Out at Night," and their live shows were the first rap concerts to feature official dancers (U.T.F.O. members Dr. Ice and Kangol Kid). Following 1987's *Open Sesame,* Whodini went on hiatus due to problems with their record company, as well as to concentrate on new families. The group attempted a comeback in 1991 with *Bag-A-Trix* without much success, despite receiving their due as rap innovators. Five years later, Whodini returned with their sixth album, appropriately titled *Six.* The album disappeared shortly after its release. —*Steve Huey*

Whodini / 1983 / Jive ✦✦✦
More singers than straight rappers, Jali Hutchins and Ecstasty made a successful conversion to hip-hop, scoring two hits on their debut with "Rap Attack" and "The Haunted House of Funk," a reworking of "The Monster Mash." —*Ron Wynn*

Escape / 1984 / Jive ✦✦✦✦
Their best release, containing "Friends," "Freaks Come out at Night," and "Big Mouth." Memorable tunes and state-of-the-art (for that time) production. —*Ron Wynn*

Back in Black / 1986 / Jive ✦✦✦
Signs of stagnation and decay are evident, though the cut "Funky Beat" forestalled the decline for a short while. —*Ron Wynn*

Open Sesame / 1987 / Jive ✦✦
Millie Jackson made a wonderful guest appearance on "Be Yourself," but not only was the handwriting on the wall, it was soon readable by everyone. —*Ron Wynn*

★ **Greatest Hits** / Jun. 1990 / Jive ✦✦✦✦✦
When funksters and soulsters who reached adulthood in the 1960s and '70s criticize rap, their No.1 complaint is usually that too much of it isn't melodic enough. But they seldom make that complaint about Whodini, which in the mid-'80s enjoyed a lot more support from R&B fans than the more forceful and abrasive sounds of Run-D.M.C. or LL Cool J. While those artists rocked hard, Whodini grooved. Many of Whodini's early albums are well worth acquiring—including *Escape* and *Back in Black*—but for the more casual listener, *Greatest Hits* serves as a fine introduction. From the poignant rap ballad "One Love" to such addictive and highly danceable grooves as "Five Minutes of Funk" and "Freaks Come Out at Night," *Greatest Hits* makes it clear why Whodini was so successful in the mid-'80s. —*Alex Henderson*

Bag-A-Trix / Mar. 19, 1991 / MCA ✦✦
Whodini's popularity had decreased considerably by the 1990s, when the Brooklyn rappers left their longtime home of Jive/Arista Records for MCA. Though a decent effort, Whodini's first MCA release, *Bag-A-Trix,* wasn't strong enough to help Whodini return to the top of the charts. the group's approach—very danceable and melodic compared to a lot of rap, and drawing heavily on '70s soul and funk—hadn't changed much since the early '80s, and remained quite recognizable. While nothing on *Bag-A-Trik* is in a class with "Freaks Come Out at Night," "Five Minutes of Funk" or "One Love," this CD definitely has its strong points—including the invigorating "The Party Don't Start," the erotic "Taste of Love" and an inspired remake of the Undisputed Truth's soul classic "Smiling Faces Sometimes." A better introduction to Whodini would be *Escape,* but for the most devoted fans, this is worth hearing. —*Alex Henderson*

● **Jive Collection Series, Vol. 1** / Jun. 27, 1995 / Jive ✦✦✦✦
Whodini's installment of the *Jive Collection Series* contains all of the group's groundbreaking singles from the early '80s, plus a selection of lesser-known album tracks and singles, making it an ideal introduction to the group. —*Stephen Thomas Erlewine*

Six / Sep. 17, 1996 / Sony ✦✦✦

Wilco

f. 1994, Belleville, IL
Alternative Pop-Rock, Alternative Country-Rock
The alternative country band Wilco rose from the ashes of the seminal roots-rockers Uncle Tupelo, who disbanded in 1994. While Jay Farrar, one of the group's two singer-songwriters, went on to form the band Son Volt, his ex-partner Jeff Tweedy established Wilco along with the remaining members of Tupelo's final incarnation, which included drummer Ken Coomer as well as part-time bandmates John Stirratt (bass) and Max Johnston (mandolin, banjo, fiddle and lap steel). Guitarist Jay Bennett rounded out the group, which in 1995 issued their debut album, *A.M.,* a collection of spry country-rock tunes that followed the course established in Tweedy's earlier work. Wilco's sophomore effort, 1996's two-disc set *Being There,* marked a radical transformation in the group's

sound; while remaining steeped in the style that earned Tweedy his reputation, the songs took unexpected detours into psychedelia, power-pop
and soul, complete with orchestral touches and R&B horn flourishes.
Shortly after the release of *Being There*, which most critics judged to be
among the year's best releases, Johnston left the group to play with his
sister, singer Michelle Shocked, and was replaced by guitarist Bob Egan
of the band Freakwater. At the same time, while remaining full-time
members of Wilco, Stiratt, Bennett and Coomer also began performing
together in the pop side project Courtesy Move. *—Jason Ankeny*

A.M. / Mar. 28, 1995 / Sire/Reprise ◆◆◆
Not surprisingly, Wilco's debut album, *A.M.*, isn't a great departure from
Uncle Tupelo. Wilco's music rocks in a more conventional way than
Uncle Tupelo, rolling along with a loping beat that swings more than it
rocks. "Casino Queen" is a shambling, bluesy honky-tonk number that's
boozier than anything Tupelo recorded, which is indicative of the major
difference between the bands. Wilco wears its heart on its sleeve, writing
songs that fit into the conventions of country-rock, not ones that rework
the rules. "Box Full of Letters" doesn't deviate from the standard mid-
tempo country-rock number, yet it's done so well, it doesn't matter. Still,
the opener, "I Must Be High"—a clever love song that subtly tweaks both
lyrical and musical cliches, as well as featuring a killer melody—casts a
shadow over *A.M.*, offering the knowledge that Wilco can subvert the
genre without losing its accessibility. In its light, all the very good songs
that follow seem somewhat disappointing. *—Stephen Thomas Erlewine*

● **Being There** / Oct. 29, 1996 / Sire/Reprise ◆◆◆◆
While Wilco's debut *A.M.* spread its wings in an expectedly country-rock
fashion, their sophomore effort *Being There* is the group's great leap forward, a masterful, wildly eclectic collection shot through with ambitions
and ideas. Although a few songs remain rooted in their signature sound,
here Jeff Tweedy and band are as fascinated by their music's possibilities
as its origins, and they push the songs which make up this sprawling
two-disc set down consistently surprising paths and byways. For starters,
the opener "Misunderstood" is majestic psychedelia, built on studio
trickery and string flourishes, while "I Got You (At the End of the Century)" is virtual power-pop, right down to the handclaps. The lovely
"Someone Else's Song" borrows heavily from the Beatles' "Norwegian
Wood," while the R&B-influenced boogie of "Monday" wouldn't sound
at all out of place on *Exile on Main St.;* and on and on. The remarkable
thing is how fresh all of these seeming cliches sound when re-imagined
with so much love and conviction; even the most traditional songs take
unexpected twists and turns, never once sinking into mere imitation.
"Music is my savior/I was named by rock 'n' roll/I was maimed by rock
'n' roll/I was tamed by rock 'n' roll/I got my name from rock 'n' roll,"
Tweedy sings on "Sunken Treasure," the opener of the second disc, and
throughout the course of these 19 songs he explores rock as though he
were tracing his family genealogy, fervently seeking to discover not only
where he came from but also where he's going. With *Being There*, he
finds what he's been looking for. *—Jason Ankeny*

The Wilde Flowers

f. 1963, Canterbury, England, **db.** 1969
British Invasion, Psychedelic
The Wilde Flowers never released a record during their existence, but
their influence exceeds that of many groups with lengthy discographies.
The band served as the wellspring of the so-called "Canterbury sound":
future Soft Machine members Robert Wyatt, Kevin Ayers, and Hugh
Hopper all played with the Wilde Flowers before the Softs were
founded, and Pye Hastings, David Sinclair, Richard Sinclair, and Richard
Coughlan played in the group at various points before forming Caravan.
The musicians who wandered through the Wilde Flowers (which went
through several lineups between 1963 and 1969) came from a far more
intellectual, jazz-oriented, and artistic background than was the norm
for pop musicians in the mid-'60s. Thus, although the group played
"beat" fare much like thousands of other British combos in their formative days, when they began to write their own material, it betrayed the
bemused whimsy—replete with odd jazzy flourishes, droll obtuse lyrics,
and adventurous chord changes—that would come to characterize the
Canterbury bands, and prove influential on the development of psychedelia and progressive rock. At long last, a wealth of Wilde Flowers
demos and unreleased recordings was released in 1994. *—Richie Unterberger*

● **Tales of Canterbury: The Wilde Flowers Story** / Dec. 8, 1994 / Voiceprint ◆◆◆◆
Twenty-two tracks, recorded between 1965 and 1969 by various aggregations of the band. Some of the fidelity is primitive, and the performances are much more tentative and less virtuosic than what the musicians would tender on their Soft Machine and Caravan records. But the
songs are playful and melodic, pushing the boundaries of the British
Invasion pop they began with towards something more idiosyncratic
and adventurous. Several of the songs, like "Memories" (three versions,
considerably different from each other, are included here), ended up in

the Soft Machine's early repertoire. Indeed, it's a shame that the Softs
didn't record more of them; the chief flaw of these tracks is that the
arrangements and instrumental proficiency are underdeveloped, and
the Soft Machine could have transformed them into prime stuff. A few
of the cuts were recorded in late 1969, and could have easily slotted in
on the Wyatt-era Soft Machine albums. Wyatt and Hugh Hopper appear
on most of the 22 tracks; to a lesser extent, Kevin Ayers, Pye Hastings,
and even Mike Ratledge also pop up. Comes with an excellent booklet
of photos and an extensive history by Wilde Flowers guitarist Brian
Hopper, brother of Hugh. *—Richie Unterberger*

The Wilde Knights

f. 1964, Seattle, WA, **db.** 1965
Rock 'n' Roll, Garage Rock
A regional '60s garage band with a tangled history, the Wilde Knights
were nevertheless in their brief lifespan responsible for two of the all-
time garage classics. "Beaver Patrol," featured on *Pebbles, Vol. 1*, was
perhaps the lewdest '60s garage single. They also recorded the original
version of "Just like Me," which Paul Revere bought from group member and co-songwriter Rick Dey for a few thousand dollars; Revere &
the Raiders covered the tune in 1965 for their first really big smash.
　　The Wilde Knights themselves only issued a couple of singles, both in
1965. Prior to that, they had played under the names of the Furys and
Pipers IV, releasing a couple of decent Northwest frat rock singles in
1962-63. After the Wilde Knights days, the lineup evolved into Genesis,
King Biscuit Entertainers, and American Cheese, all of whom put out
generic singles on various tiny labels in the late '60s. The best tracks
from the whole menagerie of Wilde Knights-family bands were assembled on a reissue LP in the mid-'80s. *—Richie Unterberger*

Beaver Patrol / 1984 / Voxx ◆◆◆
Only three of the 13 songs on this compilation were actually released
under the Wilde Knights name (including "Beaver Patrol" and the original "Just like Me," which is tamer than the famous Paul Revere version).
Side one was recorded by earlier versions of the band under the Furys
and Pipers IV monikers; this is fairly tough Northwest frat rock, sometimes instrumental, with a prominent organ and R&B influence. Side
two, after the Wilde Knights cuts, is filled out with a couple of pop-rock
tunes by Genesis, and a bad hard rock thing by King Biscuit Entertainers. Certainly this is more of a document of a typical ensemble of the
times than anything exciting or significant. But garage collectors will
find some decent things here, although the two standout items ("Beaver
Patrol" and "Just like Me") have been available on garage compilations.
Includes extensive history by garage scholar Greg Shaw. *—Richie
Unterberger*

Kim Wilde

b. Nov. 18, 1960, Chiswick, England
Vocals / New Wave, Club/Dance
The daughter of '50s British pop singer Marty Wilde, Kim Wilde had several pop hits during the '80s. Initially, her synth-driven pop fit in with
the new wave movement, but as the decade progressed, it became clear
that her strength was mainstream pop.
　　In 1980, Kim Wilde signed with producer Mickie Most's Rak Records,
releasing her first single, "Kids in America" early in 1981. "Kids in
America" climbed to No. 2 on the British charts that spring, while her
second single, "Chequered Love" made it into the Top Ten; her self-titled
debut album performed as well as her singles. The following year, "Kids
in America" became a Top 40 hit in America, while *Select* kept her in
the British charts. However, Wilde wasn't able to keep her momentum
going and it wasn't until late 1986 that she had another hit with a dance
cover of the Supremes' "You Keep Me Hangin' On," which charted in the
Top Ten on both sides of the Atlantic. Wilde never had another hit in
America, yet she was back in the charts in the summer of 1987 with
"Another Step (Closer to You)," a duet with Junior Giscombe. After the
single's success, she began changing her image, becoming sexier. The
approach didn't entirely pay off, though she had a handful of hit singles
from her 1988 album, *Close*, including "You Came," "Never Trust a
Stranger" and "Four Letter Word." Wilde has continued to record in the
'90s, scoring the occasional hit, either in the dance or adult contemporary field. *—Stephen Thomas Erlewine*

● **The Singles Collection 1981-1993** / Nov. 9, 1993 / MCA ◆◆◆◆
A 16-track collection featuring all of her greatest hits, *The Singles Collection 1981-1993* is not only an effective introduction to Kim Wilde's
music, it's the finest moment of her career. *—Stephen Thomas Erlewine*

Andre Williams

b. 1936, Chicago, IL
Vocals / R&B
Singer-songwriter, arranger, producer, and one of the mightiest talents
to emerge from Detroit's pre-Motown era, Andre Williams started

recording in 1957 for the tiny Fortune label, with his group, the Five Dollars (aka the Don Juans), and as a solo artist. Employing his stop-time "wavy gravy" beat and hitting the charts with oddball spoken-word numbers like "Bacon Fat," "The Greasy Chicken," and "Jail Bait," Williams was the original rapper before there was ever a name for it. Moving to Chicago in the early '60s, he wrote "Shake a Tail Feather" for the 5 Du-Tones and "Twine Time" for Alvin Cash, produced albums for Bobby Blue Bland, and scored national hits of his own for Chess with "Cadillac Jack," "Girdle Up," and "Humpin', Bumpin' & Thumpin'." He continues to record and produce other artists sporadically, still keeping abreast of the times, still "Mr. Rhythm," the original rappin' man. —*Cub Koda*

● **Jail Bait** / Fortune ✦✦✦✦
Good (though not complete) overview of Andre's Fortune period. —*Cub Koda*

Fat Back & Corn Liquor / St. George ✦✦✦
Andre Williams, the man who was rappin' three decades before they had a name for it, is back after a much too long sabbatical, with the kind of comeback album that would do any R&B legend proud. With a tight little band and the El Dorados providing crackerjack support, producer George Paulus has managed to restoke some of the fires that burned so brightly on a spate of brilliant, creative singles for Fortune and Checker in the '50s and '60s. The big plus here is that Williams can still deliver that dead-pan bad-ass turn of the phrase better than anybody. Although I personally find the recuts here of his old Fortune classics like "Jail Bait" ill-advised (to quote Rocky, the Flying Squirrel, "That trick never works!"), there's just so much great stuff on this biscuit that it's a minor niggling point at best. By far and away, my favorite track on here is one simply titled "Gin." Recalling one of his legendary Fortune sides, "Please Pass the Biscuits," without xeroxing it, this is four minutes plus of Williams at his nutzo best. A winner. —*Cub Koda*

Larry Williams

b. May 10, 1935, New Orleans, LA, d. Jan. 7, 1980
Piano, Vocals / R&B, Rock 'n' Roll
A rough, rowdy rock 'n' roll singer, Larry Williams had several hits in the late '50s, several of which—"Bony Maroney," "Dizzy, Miss Lizzy," "Short Fat Fannie," "Bad Boy," "She Said Yeah"—became genuine rock 'n' roll classics and were recorded by British Invasion groups; John Lennon, in particular, was a fan of Williams, recording several of his songs over the course of his career.

As a child in New Orleans, Williams learned how to play piano. When he was a teenager, he and his family moved to Oakland, CA, where he joined a local R&B group called the Lemon Drops. In 1954, when he was 19 years old, Williams went back to New Orleans for a visit. During his trip, he met Lloyd Price, who was recording for Specialty Records. Price hired the teenager as his valet and introduced him to Robert "Bumps" Blackwell, the label's head producer. Soon, the label's owner, Art Rupe, signed Williams to a solo recording contract.

Just after Specialty signed Larry Williams, Specialty lost Little Richard, who had been their biggest star and guaranteed hitmaker. Little Richard decided to abandon rock 'n' roll for the ministry shortly after Williams cut his first single, a cover of Price's "Just Because," with Richard's backing band; "Just Because" peaked at No. 11 on the R&B charts in the spring of 1957. After Richard left the label, the label put all of its energy into making Williams a star, giving him an image makeover and a set of material—ranging from hard R&B, rock 'n' roll, to ballads—that were quite similar to Richard's hits.

Williams' first post-Little Richard single was the raucous "Short Fat Fannie," which shot to No. 1 on the R&B charts and No. 5 on the pop charts in the summer of 1957. It was followed in the fall by "Bony Maronie," which hit No. 4 on the R&B charts and No. 14 on the pop charts. Williams wasn't able to maintain that momentum, however. "You Bug Me, Baby" and "Dizzy Miss Lizzy," his next two singles, missed the R&B charts but became minor pop hits in late 1957 and early 1958. Despite the relative failure of these singles, Williams' records became popular import items in Britain; the Beatles would cover both sides of the "Dizzy Miss Lizzy" single (the B-side was "Slow Down") in the mid-'60s. However, Williams' commercial fortunes in America continued to decline, despite Specialty's release of a constant stream of singles and one full-length album.

In 1959, Williams was arrested for selling narcotics, which caused Specialty to drop him from the record label. He drifted through a number of labels in the early '60s, recording songs for Chess, Mercury, Island, and Decca. By the mid-'60s, he had hooked up with Johnny "Guitar" Watson and the duo cut several sides for OKeh Records in the mid- and late '60s, including the Top 40 R&B hits "Mercy, Mercy, Mercy" (spring 1967) and "Nobody," which was recorded with Kaleidoscope (early 1968). Williams also became a house producer for OKeh Records in 1966, although very few of his productions became hits.

Between 1968 and 1978, Williams was inactive, recording nothing and performing very little. In 1978, he released a funk album, *That's*

Larry Williams, for Fantasy Records that sold poorly and received bad reviews. In 1980, Larry Williams was found dead in his Los Angeles home; he died of a gunshot wound to his head. The medical examiners called the death a suicide, but rumors persisted for years after his death that he was murdered because of his involvement in drugs, crime and—allegedly—prostitution.

A compilation of Larry Williams' biggest hits and best-known songs entitled *Bad Boy* was released on Specialty records in 1989. —*Stephen Thomas Erlewine*

Unreleased Larry Williams / 1986 / Specialty ✦✦✦
This deeper look into the obscure and alternate takes of Williams' work is mostly for collectors. —*Hank Davis*

★ **Bad Boy** / 1989 / Specialty ✦✦✦✦✦
Bad Boy compiles 23 tracks Larry Williams recorded between 1957 and 1958. The core of the collection are his hit singles—"Bony Maronie," "She Said Yeah," "Lawdy Miss Clawdy," "Just Because," "Dizzy Miss Lizzy," "Short Fat Fannie," "Bad Boy," "Slow Down"—many of which became standards. —*Stephen Thomas Erlewine*

Lucinda Williams

b. Jan. 26, 1953, Lake Charles, LA
Guitar, Vocals / Singer-Songwriter, Folk-Rock, Alternative Country-Rock, Contemporary Folk, Americana
Lucinda Williams isn't the kind of artist who caves in easily. Faced with label executives and producers who want to shape her music into clean-cut, radio-friendly rock or country numbers—no doubt with someone like Bonnie Raitt in mind—Williams has time and again proven herself to be as stubborn (and most certainly for her own good) as she is talented. She's released a mere four albums (and one EP) since her debut on Folkways in 1979 partly because she's had such a hard time finding a label whose demands don't get in the way of the music as she hears it.

Raised under the intellectual nurture of her father—poet, critic, and English lit professor Miller Williams (a buddy of Tom T. Hall)—Lucinda spent her youth on the ramble from one college burg to another in the American South, as well as Mexico City and Santiago, Chile. She was already singing and playing by the time she was 12, when Dylan's *Highway 61 Revisited* had seeped into her psyche, and later found inspiration in the raw Delta blues of singers like Skip James, Bukka White, and Robert Johnson. By the early '70s she was playing shows of her own, mixing folk-inspired originals and traditional material. She traveled a bit before landing in Austin in 1974 at the height of the cosmic cowboy era. Next she tried Houston and became part of a folk scene there that also included Nanci Griffith, Lyle Lovett, and Townes Van Zandt.

In 1978 she spent an afternoon in the Jackson, MS R&B studio Malaco, and the result was her 1979 debut for Folkways, *Ramblin' on My Mind*, a collection of traditional blues and country standards. A year later she recorded "Happy Woman Blues" in Houston. This time all the songs were originals, and they featured a full band of acoustic guitar, fiddle, pedal steel, bass, and drums. Both albums have since been reissued on Smithsonian/Folkways.

It was eight years, however, until Williams' third album, *Lucinda Williams*, was recorded for the indie-rock label Rough Trade. In the meantime she had moved back and forth between Houston and Austin before moving to Los Angeles in 1984. She's been courted by several labels, but always held out for creative control. In the end she won it, and her Rough Trade album immediately stood out for its integration of traditional folk, country, and blues influences into a rock and roll format. The album featured such stellar songs as "The Night's Too Long," "Passionate Kisses," and "Changed the Locks," and marked a new, more rock-oriented direction for Williams. Her guitarist and co-producer on that album, Gurf Morlix, has also become a vital part of her music, recording and touring with her ever since. In 1989 Rough Trade released the EP *Passionate Kisses*, which included four additional songs, three of which were live radio broadcasts.

An ill-fated association with RCA followed, but again Williams was unhappy with the results, and left the label before releasing anything. Her next album, *Sweet Old World*, didn't emerge until 1992, and again it was on an indie label, Chameleon. Well worth the wait, it was again rich with Williams' hearty, twangy voice and solid, Southern-inflected rock 'n' roll originals. Once again, too, critics and fans found it irresistible, and practically thanked God that Williams had chosen to keep her artistic integrity intact, no matter how long it had taken.

Since then Williams has switched labels again, this time to American Recordings. A new album has been scheduled and rescheduled several times already, and it's expected to finally see the light in late 1996. —*Kurt Wolff*

Ramblin' / Mar. 1978 / Folkways ✦✦
A collection of blues and country standards by Robert Johnson, Memphis Minnie, Hank Williams, and others. Williams is accompanied only by guitarist John Grimaudo. Re-released by Smithsonian/Folkways in 1991 as *Ramblin'*. —*Kurt Wolff*

● **Happy Woman Blues** / 1980 / Folkways ✦✦✦✦
Williams' first collection of original material—recorded with a full band—is stunning for its mixture of blues, folk, and country traditions with her captivating, complex, and visceral approach to writing and singing. Songs like "Lafayette," "King of Hearts," and "Sharp Cutting Wings" are classics: structurally solid and emotionally intense. A gutsy, refreshingly rootsy album. Re-released by Smithsonian/Folkways in 1990. —*Kurt Wolff*

Lucinda Williams / 1988 / Rough Trade ✦✦✦✦
Williams shows her rock and roll colors here, mixing her rootsy Southern twang with big, burly production and arrangements and a full-on electric band that includes guitarist Gurf Morlix, who's collaborated with her ever since. Williams' writing skills continue to strengthen, the result being such indelible gems as "The Night's Too Long," "Side of the Road," and "Changed the Locks." This album revived Williams' career and cemented her reputation. —*Kurt Wolff*

Passionate Kisses / 1989 / Rough Trade ✦✦✦
The title track of this EP comes from Williams' 1988 album. Also included are four live acoustic cuts—"Side of the Road" and three blues covers. —*Kurt Wolff*

● **Sweet Old World** / Aug. 25, 1992 / Chameleon ✦✦✦✦
A bright, lively, rock and roll album that picks up where "Lucinda Williams" left off. The arrangements mix fiddle and dobro with the electric guitars, and while the production is big, the songs speak on a personal level and are wholly down to earth. The album contains a new slate of Williams classics, including "He Never Got Enough Love," "Little Angel, Little Brother," and the knockout "Pineola." —*Kurt Wolff*

Maurice Williams

f. 1955, Lancaster, NC
R&B, Doo Wop
Although Maurice Williams & the Zodiacs only had one big hit, the song became one of the classic singles in the history of rock 'n' roll and R&B. The song, "Stay," was a No. 1 hit upon its release in 1960. Williams and the Zodiacs' career didn't prove to be as popular as the song itself. They only had two more minor pop hits before they disappeared from the charts, but over the course of the next three decades, "Stay" remained one of the most popular songs of the era and it was played constantly on oldies radio stations. "Stay" was covered by numerous other artists and has enjoyed a few revivals in mass popularity, most notably when it was featured in the hit 1987 film, *Dirty Dancing*.

Before he formed the Zodiacs, Maurice Williams sang with a number of different doo wop and R&B vocal groups, beginning with the Royal Charms in the early '50s. In 1955, he formed the Gladiolas with Earl Gainey, Willie Jones, William Massey, and Norman Wade. The Gladiolas signed to Excello and recorded "Little Darlin'," which reached No. 11 on the R&B charts, No. 41 pop in the spring of 1957. The single's acension on the pop charts was undercut by a cover of the song by the White Canadian vocal group, the Diamonds. After a financial dispute, Williams lost the rights to the name the Gladiolas in 1959.

Maurice Williams formed the Zodiacs in 1960, recruiting Wiley Bennett, Albert Hill, Henry Gaston, Little Willie Morrow, and Charley Thomas. The group released their first single, "Stay," on Herald records in the summer of 1960. The song worked its way up the charts, peaking at No. 3 on the R&B charts and No. 1 on the pop charts. After the single charted nationally, the Zodiacs constantly toured America, playing revues with artists like James Brown. The group released a follow-up single titled "I Remember" at the end of the year, but it didn't make it past 86 on the pop charts and didn't appear on the R&B charts at all. Neither did "Come Along," which was released in the spring of 1961 and only climbed to No. 83 on the pop charts.

Maurice Williams and the Zodiacs continued to release singles until the late '60s, but none of the records received any attention. Throughout the '70s and '80s, Williams led various incarnations of the Zodiacs on oldies tours, primarily on the Beach Music circuit on the US East Coast. —*Stephen Thomas Erlewine*

● **Best of Maurice & the Zodiacs** / 1989 / Relic ✦✦✦✦
Not much thought went into this set, but it'll do. —*Dan Heilman*

Vanessa Williams

b. Mar. 18, 1963, Tarrytown, NY
Vocals / Dance-Pop, Urban, Adult Contemporary
When Vanessa Williams lost her Miss America crown in 1984, it seemed like her career was over. Actually, the truth was quite different. Four years later, she re-emerged as an urban R&B vocalist with *The Right Stuff*, which featured the Top Ten hit "Dreamin'." Her next album was an even bigger success, thanks to the smash hit "Saving the Best for Last"; it confirmed her status as one of urban R&B's most popular vocalists. *The Sweetest Days* followed in 1995. —*Stephen Thomas Erlewine*

The Right Stuff / Feb. 1988 / Wing ✦✦✦✦
The disc is evenly divided between dance-floor fodder and AOR fluff, and it ain't half bad. Despite the fact that Williams works with six producers and eight songwriters, the disc has a consistent feel, and while Vanessa doesn't have a voice suited to belting out raunchy R&B, she's smart enough to stay within her limitations and let her personality take up the slack. —*J. Poet*

● **The Comfort Zone** / Aug. 20, 1991 / Wing ✦✦✦✦
Typically, Vanessa Williams' albums are mixed bags. She's at her most exciting when taking chances and coming from the heart, and at her worst when recording frightfully dull material that is designed strictly for commercial radio airplay. This is certainly true of her sophomore effort, *The Comfort Zone*. Williams is at her best on the sexy, alluring title song and a striking remake of the Isley Brothers' "Work to Do," and at her worst on the hit adult contemporary ballad "Save the Best For Last." The song isn't genuinely romantic, only corny and insipid. One wishes Williams would stick to songs that are worthy of her, but when artists are under pressure from labels to sell as many albums as possible, artistic considerations easily fall by the wayside. —*Alex Henderson*

Sweetest Days / 1995 / Wing ✦✦✦
More diverse than Vanessa Williams' two previous albums, *The Sweetest Days* finds the singer exploring jazz-influenced songs without giving up the type of boring, radio-minded fluff that had enabled her to sell millions of albums. The CD's standout track is "Ellamental," an irresistible R&B/jazz/hip-hop tribute to Ella Fitzgerald. (Much to her credit, Williams was insightful enough to praise the jazz legend while she was still alive instead of waiting until after her death). She's almost as appealing on "Sister Moon" (a torchy Sting gem) and the Babyface contributions "You Can't Run" (which has a Sade-ish quality) and the haunting "Betcha Never." But sadly, Williams doesn't hesitate to waste her talent on such contrived, hopelessly dull "adult contemporary" fluff as the title song—a song that's every bit as cliched and insipid as "Save the Best For Last." —*Alex Henderson*

Star Bright / Nov. 5, 1996 / Polygram ✦✦✦
Star Bright is a collection of holiday and Christmas songs as sung by Vanessa Williams. Boasting a polished yet warm production, *Star Bright* works best as pleasant background music, but it is good background music—Williams has an engaging voice and the music is familiar, making it a nice seasonal album. —*Rodney Batdorf*

Victoria Williams

b. Shreveport, LA
Guitar, Vocals / Singer-Songwriter, Folk-Rock, Alternative Country-Rock, Contemporary Folk
Despite a successful career as a idiosyncratic country-folk performer, Victoria Williams was perhaps best known as a songwriter—thanks, ironically enough, to a tribute album recorded in her honor. Born in Louisiana in 1959, Williams taught herself to play the guitar while still in her teens, and soon began composing songs. In college, she joined her first band, the G.W. Korners. After spending some time on the road, she ended up in California in 1979, where she was a regular at Los Angeles' famed Troubadour Club's "Hoot Nights." After first returning to Louisiana with the intent of forming a band, she moved back to Los Angeles, where she performed on Venice Beach and ultimately signed a recording contract which proved fruitless.

Soon after, Williams met musician Peter Case, formerly of the Plimsouls. Not only did they form an act together—a jugband-like trio named the Incredibly Strung Out Band—but the couple also married. Finally, Williams made her solo recording debut in 1987 with *Happy Come Home*, a collection showcasing her vivid songcraft as well as her off-kilter, squeaky vocal style. After the record was released, Williams starred in a documentary by the filmmaker D.A. Pennebaker. In 1989, she and Case divorced; a follow-up record, *Swing the Statue!*, appeared in 1990.

In 1992, while opening for Neil Young, Williams began experiencing a numb feeling in her hands which made it increasingly difficult to play her guitar. Upon visiting a doctor, she was diagnosed with the degenerative neurological disorder multiple sclerosis. The medical bills quickly piled up, and like many musicians, she was not covered by health insurance. In response, her manager began assembling friends and fans to record Williams' songs for a benefit album; the result, 1993 *Sweet Relief: A Benefit for Victoria Williams*, featured the likes of Pearl Jam, Lou Reed, Matthew Sweet, the Jayhawks and Soul Asylum, whose rendition of "Summer of Drugs" was the record's first single. Due to its all-star lineup, *Sweet Relief* far outsold any of Williams' own efforts, raising not only funds for her medical treatment but her visibility within the musical community as well. Additionally, the record's success enabled Williams to establish the Sweet Relief Fund, created to assist other musicians with health problems; in 1996, a second tribute record, honoring the paralyzed singer-songwriter Vic Chestnutt, was released. In 1994 Williams issued *Loose*, a varied collection featuring duets with Soul

Asylum's Dave Pirner and the Jayhawks' Mark Olson, Williams' second husband. A year later, she and her Loose Band released *This Moment in Toronto,* a live career overview which also offered a handful of standards ("Smoke Gets in Your Eyes," "Imagination") as well as one new song, "Graveyard." —*Jason Ankeny*

Happy Come Home / 1987 / Geffen ✦✦✦
This debut LP by Victoria Williams is as wonderful as it is eclectic. Van Dyke Parks' arrangements give the collection a carnival feel, while Anton Fier's pop productions never let this become anything close to an ordinary singer-songwriter album. But how could it, with Williams' elastic vocals and trippy lyrics? This is a great record to play when anyone says that all Los Angeles pop albums are slick and sanitized. —*Richard Meyer*

● **Swing the Statue** / 1990 / Mammoth ✦✦✦✦
Victoria Williams' second album was her most accomplished set of folk-rock, featuring the remarkable "Summer of Drugs." —*Stephen Thomas Erlewine*

Loose / 1994 / Mammoth ✦✦✦✦
What a great collection. Victoria Williams has put together a fine-tuned tight but loose band, as expressed in the title. Her folk-rock Carol Channing voice is perfectly suited to the arrangements, some of which were written by Van Dyke Parks, and include players such as Greg Cohen, Peter Buck, and Don Heffinton. Her originals are quirky and beautiful. WIlliams' choice of covers is also refreshing. She does a heartbreaking take on "What a Wonderful World" and revives the psychedelic chestnut "Nature's Way," making it her own. *Loose* is a wonderful album, full of life. —*Richard Meyer*

This Moment: Live in Toronto / Nov. 7, 1995 / Atlantic ✦✦✦
Recorded on the *Loose* tour, Victoria Williams' live album *This Moment: Live in Toronto* demonstrates the depths of her songwriting talents. Performing with a sympathetic folk-rock supporting band, Williams runs through her catalog, playing nearly all of her fans' favorite songs. She is in fine voice, turning in an impassioned performance, but the best thing about the record is how all of the songs play off each other. Unlike her other records, there is no filler on *This Moment,* which makes the album a perfect introduction to her rich talents. —*Stephen Thomas Erlewine*

Chuck Willis

b. Jan. 31, 1928, Atlanta, GA, **d.** Apr. 10, 1958, Atlanta, GA
Vocals / R&B
There were two distinct sides to Chuck Willis. In addition to being a convincing blues shouter, the Atlanta-born Willis harbored a vulnerable blues balladeer side. In addition, he was a masterful songwriter who penned some of the most distinctive R&B numbers of the 1950s. We can't grant him principal credit for his 1957 smash adaptation of "C.C. Rider," an irresistible update of a classic folk-blues, but Willis did write such gems as "I Feel So Bad" (later covered by Elvis Presley, Little Milton, and Otis Rush), the anguished ballads "Don't Deceive Me (Please Don't Go,)" "It's Too Late" (the latter attracting covers by Buddy Holly, Charlie Rich, and Otis Redding,) and his swan song, "Hang Up My Rock and Roll Shoes."

Harold Willis (he adopted Chuck as a stage handle) received his early training singing at YMCA-sponsored "Teenage Canteens" in Atlanta and fronting the combos of local bandleaders Roy Mays and Red McAllister. Powerful DJ Zenas "Daddy" Sears took an interest in the young vocalist's career, hooking him up with Columbia Records in 1951. After a solitary single for the major firm, Willis was shuttled over to its recently reactivated OKeh R&B subsidiary.

In 1952, he crashed the national R&B lists for OKeh with a typically plaintive ballad, "My Story," swiftly encoring on the hit parade with a gentle cover of Fats Domino's "Goin' to the River" and his own "Don't Deceive Me" the next year and "You're Still My Baby" and the surging Latin-beat "I Feel So Bad" in 1954. Willis also penned a heart-tugging chart-topper for Ruth Brown that year, "Oh What a Dream."

Willis moved over to Atlantic Records in 1956 and immediately enjoyed another round of hits with "It's Too Late" and "Juanita." Atlantic strove mightily to cross Willis over into pop territory, inserting an exotic steel guitar at one session and chirpy choirs on several more. The strategy eventually worked when his 1957 revival of the ancient "C.C. Rider" proved the perfect number to do the "Stroll" to; *American Bandstand* gave the track a big push, and Willis had his first R&B No. 1 hit as well as a huge pop seller (Gene "Daddy G" Barge's magnificent sax solo likely aided its ascent).

Barge returned for Willis' similar follow-up, "Betty and Dupree," which also did well for him. But the turban-wearing crooner's time was growing short—he had long suffered from ulcers prior to his 1958 death from peritonitis. Much has been made of the ironic title of his last hit, the touching "What Am I Living For," but it was no more a clue to his impending demise than its flip, the joyous "Hang Up My Rock and Roll Shoes." Both tracks became massive hits upon the singer's death, and his posthumous roll continued with "My Life" and a powerful "Keep A-Driv-

ing" later that year. Willis' cousin, Robert "Chick" Willis, who began his career as a backup singer for Chuck, remains active nationally. —*Bill Dahl*

My Story / 1980 / Columbia ✦✦✦✦
Not as exhaustive as Legacy's subsequent look at Willis' early-to-mid-'50s hitmaking stint at OKeh, but this 14-tracker still gets the job done with the smooth ballads "Going to the River," "Don't Deceive Me," "My Story," and Willis' surging, Latin-tempoed original "I Feel So Bad." —*Bill Dahl*

Let's Jump Tonight! The Best of Chuck Willis 1951-56 / 1994 / Epic/ Legacy ✦✦✦✦
Before his brief turn as a rock 'n' roll star with Atlantic, Willis cut a lot of material for OKeh in much more of an R&B/jump blues vein. This 26-cut collection includes all of his early and mid-'50s R&B hits—"My Story," "Goin' To The River," "Don't Deceive Me," "You're Still My Baby," and his most famous number from this period, "I Feel So Bad" (revived by Elvis Presley, among others). The influence of Joe Turner, Charles Brown, early Lloyd Price, and similar performers is strongly felt; Willis could shout competently, but was much better on the emotional R&B ballads. Not as strong or distinctive as his Atlantic material, this includes several cuts that were previously unreleased or previously unavailable in the US. —*Richie Unterberger*

★ **Stroll On: The Chuck Willis Collection** / Oct. 19, 1994 / Razor & Tie ✦✦✦✦✦
All 25 of the versatile Atlanta-bred singer's Atlantic Records sides, presented beautifully (every R&B reissue on CD should be packaged so well, with plenty of brilliant stereo). Willis really hit his stride at Atlantic, doing the Stroll with his easy-going "C.C. Rider" and "Betty and Dupree" (both boasting darting sax breaks from Gene Barge), baring his tender soul on a devotional "What Am I Living For," and taking R&B into fresh directions with a jumping "Kansas City Woman," the relentless "Keep A-Drivin'," and a buoyant "Hang Up My Rock and Roll Shoes." —*Bill Dahl*

Jackie WIlson

b. Jun. 9, 1934, Detroit, MI, **d.** Jan. 21, 1984, Mount Holly, NJ
Vocals / Soul, R&B
Jackie Wilson was one of the most important agents of Black pop's transition from R&B into soul. In terms of vocal power (especially in the upper register), few could outdo him; he was also an electrifying onstage showman. He was a consistent hitmaker from the mid-1950s through the early 1970s, although never a crossover superstar. His reputation isn't quite on par with Ray Charles, James Brown, or Sam Cooke, however, because his records did not always reflect his artistic genius. Indeed, there is a consensus of sorts among critics that Wilson was something of an underachiever in the studio, due to the sometimes inappropriately pop-based material and arrangements that he used.

Wilson was well-known on the R&B scene before he went solo in the late '50s. In 1953 he replaced Clyde McPhatter in Billy Ward & the Dominoes, one of the top R&B vocal groups of the '50s. Although McPhatter was himself a big star, Wilson was as good as or better than the man whose shoes he filled. Commercially, however, things took a downturn for the Dominoes in the Wilson years, although they did manage a Top 20 hit with "St. Therese of the Roses" in 1956. Elvis Presley was one of those who was mightily impressed by Wilson in the mid-'50s; he can be heard praising Jackie's onstage cover of "Don't Be Cruel" in between-song banter during the *Million Dollar Quartet* session in late 1956.

Wilson would score his first big R&B (and small pop) hit in late 1956 with the brassy, stuttering "Reet Petite," which was co-written by an emerging Detroit songwriter named Berry Gordy, Jr. Gordy would also help write a few other hits for Jackie in the late '50s, "To Be Loved," "Lonely Teardrops," "That's Why (I Love You So)," and "I'll Be Satisfied"; they also crossed over to the pop charts, "Lonely Teardrops" making the Top Ten. Most of these were upbeat, creatively arranged marriages of pop and R&B that, in retrospect, helped set the stage both for '60s soul, and for Gordy's own huge pop success at Motown. The early Gordy-Wilson association has led some historians to speculate how much differently (and better) Jackie's career might have turned out had he been on Motown's roster instead of the Brunswick label.

In the early '60s, Wilson maintained his pop stardom with regular hit singles that often used horn arrangements and female choruses that have dated somewhat badly, especially in comparison with the more creative work by peers such as Charles and Brown from this era. Wilson also sometimes went into out-and-out operatic pop, as on "Danny Boy" and one of his biggest hits, "Night" (1960). At the same time, he remained capable of unleashing a sweaty, uptempo, gospel-soaked number: "Baby Workout," which fit that description to a T, was a No.5 hit for him in 1963. It's true that you have to be pretty selective in targeting the worthwhile Wilson records from this era; 1962's *At the Copa,* for instance, has Jackie trying to combine soul and all-around entertainment, and not wholly succeeding with either strategy. Yet some of his early Brunswick material is also fine uptown soul; not quite as earthy as some of his fans would have liked him to sound, no doubt, but worth hearing.

Wilson was shot and seriously wounded by a female fan in 1961, though he made a recovery. His career was more seriously endangered by his inability to keep up with changing soul and rock trends. Not everything he did in the mid-'60s is totally dismissable; "No Pity (In the Naked City)," for instance, is something like *West Side Story* done uptown soul style. In 1966, his career was briefly revived when he teamed up with Chicago soul producer Carl Davis, who had been instrumental in the success of Windy City performers like Gene Chandler, Major Lance, and Jerry Butler. Davis successfully updated Wilson's sound with horn-heavy arrangements, getting near the Top Ten with "Whispers," and then making No.6 in 1967 with "Higher and Higher." And that was really the close of Wilson's career as either a significant artist or commercial force, although he had some minor chart entries through the early '70s.

While playing a Dick Clark oldies show at the Latin Casino in New Jersey in September 1975, Wilson suffered an onstage heart attack while singing "Lonely Teardrops." He lapsed into a coma, suffering major brain damage, and was hospitalized until his death in early 1984. —*Richie Unterberger*

Mr. Excitement / Nov. 10, 1992 / Rhino ✦✦✦✦
A three-CD box from the experts of reissue at Rhino, *Mr. Excitement* takes Wilson's career from his first sides with Billy Ward and the Dominoes in 1956 through his final recordings in the early '70s. The former Detroit boxer hit either the R&B or pop chart over 50 times, making him the 26th most successful R&B artist, in chart terms at least. Every one of those recordings is contained in this set, including such classics as "Reet Petite," "Lonely Teardrops," and "(Your Love Keeps Lifting Me) Higher and Higher." Wilson had an explosive falsetto and a downright weird sense of phrasing that made him utterly unique. Some of his productions were a little overwrought but even in the most extreme cases, that voice was a gift from God. Seminal. —*Rob Bowman*

★ **Very Best of Jackie Wilson** / Feb. 4, 1993 / Ace ✦✦✦✦✦
Similar to the US greatest-hits collection of the same name (on Rhino), but with substantially more tracks. This 24-song anthology has all the familiar big singles on the Rhino compilation, but goes into his late-'60s to early-'70s material in greater depth. His best stuff was recorded before that, though, so you're not much (if at all) worse off by sticking to the cheaper, more easily available domestic collection. —*Richie Unterberger*

★ **Very Best of Jackie Wilson** / Jan. 18, 1994 / Rhino ✦✦✦✦✦
The Very Best of Jackie Wilson is a terrific single-disc collection, containing all of Wilson's biggest hits, including "Reet Petite," "Lonely Teardrops," "Doggin' Around," "Higher and Higher," and "Baby Work Out," among others. —*Stephen Thomas Erlewine*

Wimple Winch

f. 1963, Liverpool, England, **db.** 1969
British Invasion, Psychedelic
Despite the silly name and their near-total lack of commercial success, Wimple Winch were an interesting British '60s group, weaving soul, intricate harmonies, and unusual whimsical lyrics into their original material. Starting out as Just Four Men, the Liverpool-area outfit were initially just one of the dozens of Mersey groups riding the Beatles' coattails, although they cut a couple of fair singles. Changing their name to Wimple Winch, they released three much more progressive singles that were popular locally, including the explosive raver "Save My Soul" and the dramatic story-song "Rumble on Mersey Square South." Arguably the most creative group to work from Liverpool after the Merseybeat boom dried up, they broke up in the late '60s, leaving a wealth of unreleased material. Much of that material, as well as their rare singles, eventually appeared on compilations of British Invasion and British psychedelic rarities in the 1980s. —*Richie Unterberger*

The Wimple Story 1963-1968 / 1992 / Bam Caruso ✦✦✦
The definitive document, including all the Just Four Men and Wimple Winch singles, as well as a wealth of unreleased music recorded by both incarnations of the band—28 songs and 78 minutes in all. Despite the group's meager legacy, the material (almost all self-penned) is generally quite strong. The psychedelic-era songs in particular are intriguing blends of crunching mod pop, psychedelia, and soul, with unexpected tempo shifts, superb harmonies, strong melodies, and unusual lyrics, although they sometimes get a little airy-fairy. —*Richie Unterberger*

Jesse Winchester

b. May 17, 1944, Shreveport, LA
Guitar, Keyboards, Vocals / Singer-Songwriter, Contemporary Folk
Jesse Winchester was the music world's most prominent Vietnam War draft-evader, though his renown came from a body of wry, closely observed songs. After growing up in Memphis, Winchester received his draft notice in 1967 and moved to Montreal, Canada, rather than serve

in the military. In 1969, he met Robbie Robertson of the Band, who helped launch his recording career. In the same way that James Taylor's history of mental instability and drug abuse served as a subtext for his early music, Winchester's exile lent real-life poignancy to songs like "Yankee Lady," which appeared on his debut album, *Jesse Winchester* (1970). He became a Canadian citizen in 1973. Despite critical acclaim, his inability to tour in the US prevented him from taking his place among the major singer-songwriters of the early '70s, but he made a series of impressive albums—*Third Down, 110 to Go* (August 1972), *Learn to Love It* (August 1974), *Let the Rough Side Drag* (June 1976), and *Nothing but a Breeze* (March 1977)—before President Jimmy Carter instituted an amnesty that finally allowed him to play in his homeland. By that time, the singer-songwriter boom had passed, though Winchester continued to record (*A Touch on the Rainy Side* [July 1978], *Talk Memphis* [February 1981], *Humour Me* [1988]) and even scored a Top 40 hit with "Say What" in 1981. His most prominently covered songs include "Yankee Lady" (Brewer & Shipley), "The Brand New Tennessee Waltz" (Joan Baez, Ian Matthews), "Biloxi" (Tom Rush, Jimmy Buffett), "Mississippi, You're on My Mind" (Jerry Jeff Walker, Stoney Edwards [for a Top 40 country hit]), "Defying Gravity" (Jimmy Buffett, Emmylou Harris), "Rhumba Girl" (Nicolette Larson [for a pop chart entry]), "Well-A-Wiggy" (the Weather Girls [for an R&B chart entry]), and "I'm Gonna Miss You, Girl" (Michael Martin Murphey [for a Top Ten country hit]). —*William Ruhlmann*

Jesse Winchester / 1970 / Rhino ✦✦✦✦
Jesse Winchester first gained notice as a protégé of the Band's Robbie Robertson, who produced and played guitar on his debut album and brought along bandmate Levon Helm to play drums and mandolin. The album had much of the rustic Southern charm and rollicking country-rock of the Band. Winchester's other immediate appeal was a certain sense of mystery. A Southern American expatriate living in Canada, he was unable to appear in the US to promote the album, which was released in a fold-out LP jacket that featured the same sepia-toned portrait (which looked like one of those austere Matthew Brady photos from the Civil War era) on each of its four sides. Winchester emphasized the dichotomy between his southern origins and his northern exile in songs like "Snow" (which Robertson co-wrote), "The Brand New Tennessee Waltz" ("I've a sadness too sad to be true"), and "Yankee Lady." *Jesse Winchester* was timely: It spoke to a disaffected American generation that sympathized with Winchester's pacifism. But it was also timeless: The songs revealed a powerful writing talent (recognized by the numerous artists who covered them), and Winchester's gentle vocals made a wonderful vehicle for delivering them. (Originally released by Ampex in 1970, *Jesse Winchester* was reissued by Bearsville Records in 1976 and again in 1988 by Rhino/ Bearsville.) —*William Ruhlmann*

Third Down, 110 to Go / 1972 / Bearsville ✦✦✦✦
If Jesse Winchester's debut album was an auspicious introduction to a powerful new songwriting talent, his two-and-a-half-years-in-the-making follow-up was in some ways even more impressive. Without the influence of Robbie Robertson, Winchester, who produced most of the album himself (three tracks were handled by Todd Rundgren), gave it a homemade feel, using small collections of acoustic instruments, an appropriate setting for a group of short, intimate songs that expressed a deliberately positive worldview set against an acknowledgement of desperate times. Winchester found hope in religion and domesticity, but the key to his stance was a kind of good-humored accommodation. "If the wheel is fixed," he sang, "I would still take a chance. If we're skating on thin ice, then we might as well dance." The album was littered with such examples of aphoristic folk wisdom, adding up to a portrait of a man, cut off from his very deep roots and yet determined to maintain his dignity with grace and even occasionally a goofy sense of humor. —*William Ruhlmann*

Learn to Love It / 1974 / Stony Plain ✦✦✦
As the title suggests, making a virtue of necessity had always been a goal of Jesse Winchester's, and by the time of the release of his third album, the American expatriate had gone ahead and assumed Canadian citizenship. This seemed to free him to comment explicitly on his anti-war exile in "Pharaoh's Army" and especially a version of the old campaign song "Tell Me Why You Like Roosevelt" updated with new lyrics: "In the year of 1967, as a somewhat younger man, the call to bloody glory came, and I would not raise my hand." Elsewhere, Winchester continued to write love songs to his lost South ("L'Air De La Louisiane," "Mississippi, You're on My Mind") and, to a lesser extent, to pursue the wistful philosophizing found on *Third Down, 110 to Go* ("Defying Gravity"). The sense that he was repeating himself was inescapable, however, and with one-third of the album written by others and two of the originals in French Canadian, it was also obvious that Winchester was straining to come up with material. Interestingly, the two Russell Smith songs included "Third Rate Romance" (which Smith sang uncredited) and "The End Is Not in Sight," which went on to become Top 40 Country hits for Smith's group, the Amazing Rhythm Aces, in the next

two years. Stoney Edwards took "Mississippi, You're on My Mind" into the Country Top 40 in 1975. — *William Ruhlmann*

Let the Rough Side Drag / 1976 / Stony Plain ◆◆◆

At his best, Jesse Winchester is an inspired songwriter with a unique worldview. But even at less than his best, he is a craftsman, capable of turning out an album's worth of well-written songs like these that, now and then, suggest his personal viewpoint. The title track, another of Winchester's reflections on the importance of persevering under difficult circumstances, and "Damned If You Do," which suggests that you might as well follow your heart because you're in trouble either way, are up to his usual standard. But even slight songs like "Everybody Knows But Me" are clever and enjoyable, and overall, *Let the Rough Side Drag*, with its accomplished mixture of country and R&B, was Winchester's most accessible album so far, even if it was his least ambitious. — *William Ruhlmann*

Nothing But a Breeze / 1977 / Stony Plain ◆◆◆

Jesse Winchester regularly took two years between record releases, but he brought in his fifth album, *Nothing but a Breeze*, a mere nine months after its predecessor, *Let the Rough Side Drag*. The impetus for such speed seems to have been the potential commercial bonanza to be gained by Winchester's first US appearances since he moved to Canada to avoid the draft in 1967, due to President Jimmy Carter's amnesty program. Winchester also used a real producer, Brian Ahern (known for his work with Emmylou Harris), for the first time, and augmented his usual backup band with session stars such as Ricky Skaggs and James Burton, plus supporting vocalists like Harris and Anne Murray. The result was an Ahern-style country-pop album, but, perhaps predictably, a rather light effort for Winchester, who performed three covers among the ten tracks and included among the originals such comic trifles as "Twigs and Seeds" and "Rhumba Man." The title track, which became his first singles-chart entry, and "My Songbird," which Harris later covered, were effective songs, but the significance of *Nothing but a Breeze*, which enjoyed a media buzz and became Winchester's highest charting album (which isn't saying much), was in inverse proportion to the attention it received. — *William Ruhlmann*

A Touch on the Rainy Side / 1978 / Stony Plain ◆◆◆

With American recording studios open to him for the first time, Jesse Winchester traveled to Nashville and enlisted producer Norbert Putnam, who assembled the elements of the Nashville Sound, with its strings and horns and backup choruses, to make an album that moved him more toward lush country and especially R&B. Winchester's flexible voice, capable of gliding into a sweet falsetto, made the latter more successful than might have been expected. What kept the album from being one of his better collections was not the slick production, it was the material. A year after a media blitz had failed to make him a star, Winchester was starting to show signs of strain. He led the album off with the title track, an explicit expression of devotion to his wife, who he mentioned by name. This was followed by a sour on-the-road song, "A Showman's Life," and later on there were tributes to driving and drinking. In fact, the most heartfelt song was "Little Glass of Wine," an alcoholic's love song. None of this was up to his songwriting standard. — *William Ruhlmann*

Talk Memphis / 1981 / Stony Plain ◆◆◆

Having rushed to make *Nothing but a Breeze* and *A Touch on the Rainy Side* and getting his two least impressive albums for his trouble, Jesse Winchester spent two and a half years woodshedding before returning to the record racks with *Talk Memphis*. For the album, he returned to his hometown and worked with producer Willie Mitchell, best known for his Al Green records. It wasn't as unlikely a matching as might be imagined; Winchester had always had a soulful, flexible voice as ready as Green's to take off into the upper registers to express emotion. And Memphis-style R&B had always been an element, along with country, folk, pop, and gospel, in Winchester's sound. On his early albums, his lighthearted style had been in the service of an embattled vision, but gradually that darkness gave way, to the point that he began to seem lightweight. *Talk Memphis* put his effervescence and musicality to good use, resulting in his first Top 40 hit, the catchy "Say What," and the rest of the album was just as easy on the ears, with the title track providing a suitably gritty Memphis-soul sendoff. But that wasn't enough to break the album beyond the bottom rungs of the charts, and after 7 albums in 11 years, Winchester left the world of major-label record-making. — *William Ruhlmann*

Humour Me / 1988 / Sugar Hill ◆◆◆

After seven years, Jesse Winchester returned to record stores with a well-crafted pop album made up of new originals in his familiar, winning style. He mixed elements of folk, rock, country, R&B, and gospel on the songs, employing a first-rate backup group featuring New Grass stars Sam Bush, Jerry Douglas, Bela Fleck, Edgar Meyer, and Mark O'Connor, plus saxophonist Jim Horn. These pros were able match Winchester's forays into light gospel ("Let's Make a Baby King") and R&B ("Well-A-Wiggy," which had been a hit for the Weather Girls), as well as the

straightforward romantic pop songs that made up the bulk of the record. *Humour Me* lacked the depth of Winchester's best work, but it was easily on a par with his substantial body of craftsmanlike music of the mid-'70s. His voice remained warm and supple, so that his own versions of the songs were effective, and the album also served as a demo for other singers in search of good pop material. — *William Ruhlmann*

● The Best of Jesse Winchester / 1989 / Rhino ◆◆◆◆

Jesse Winchester wrote and recorded more than enough great songs for Bearsville to fill a single-disc compilation, which means that some of them were bound to be left off. The trick was to balance the material from the brilliant first two albums with a careful selection from the subsequent five albums, each of which had its virtues. This 14-track album chooses four from *Jesse Winchester*, including the essential "Yankee Lady," "Biloxi," and "The Brand New Tennessee Waltz," and three from its follow-up, *Third Down, 110 to Go*. There are three from *Learn to Love It*, one each from *Nothing but a Breeze* and *A Touch on the Rainy Side*, and two from *Talk Memphis*. Lesser material such as "Tell Me Why You Like Roosevelt" and "Rhumba Man" could have been excised in favor of more from *Third Down*, but the selection is good enough to give a reasonable representation of Winchester's seven Bearsville albums, which contain some of the most impressive songwriting of the 1970s. — *William Ruhlmann*

The Windbreakers

f. 1981, Mississippi
Alternative Pop-Rock, Jangle-Pop

The Mississippi-based power-pop group, the Windbreakers primarily comprised the duo of singer/guitarists Tim Lee and Bobby Sutliff. After debuting in 1982 with *Meet the Windbreakers*, a seven-inch EP issued on their own Big Monkey label, the band enlisted the aid of producer Mitch Easter for the follow-up, 1983's *Any Monkey With a Typewriter*, which featured an appearance by the Bongos' Richard Barone. Two years later, the Windbreakers released their full-length debut *Terminal*; among the guests were the Rain Parade, who produced and played on a cover of Television's "Glory." (In 1986, Lee and Rain Parade member Matt Piucci also teamed in the side project Gone Fishin'.) After Lee and Sutliff reconvened in 1986 for *Run*, recorded with Easter and long-standing associate Randy Everett, the Windbreakers disbanded, although the following year's *A Different Sort...*, essentially a Lee solo project, appeared under the band's name. After a handful of solo projects, the Windbreakers reunited in 1989 for the self-produced *At Home With Bobby and Tim*, followed in 1991 by *Electric Landlady*. —*Jason Ankeny*

Terminal / 1985 / Homestead ◆◆◆

This album, the group's first full-length release after two EPs, puts forth Bobby Sutliff and Tim Lee as New South style songwriters to be watched. Sutliff's songs are especially memorable; "Off and On" exhibits a wonderfully audacious set of chord progressions, "Can't Go on This Way" is delightfully tuneful and winsome, and "New Red Shoes" boasts a buoyant accompaniment that is irresistible. His excellent "Stupid Idea" would later appear in fuller arrangement on his solo outing *Only Ghosts Remain*. Lee's work is less strong here, though the guitar hook on his "All That Stuff" is naggingly memorable. "Running Out of Time" (a co-authored song) hints clearly at the energetic excellence to come in the group's late-'80s albums. And an agreeably rustic cover, complete with ragged fiddle and rough-hewn vocals, of the television song "Glory" (given here in conjunction with the group Rain Parade) is a standout. While this record doesn't have the panache, polish, and drive of later releases (the vocals in particular lack a certain oomph), *Terminal* possesses a craggy forthrightness that makes it well worth hearing. —*David Cleary*

Run / 1986 / DB ◆◆◆◆

This release is generally a leap forward over the group's prior albums. Songwriting here is mostly top-notch, with Tim Lee's work in particular showing strong improvement over previous outings. Lee's songs range widely here, from the hard-rocking fuzz guitar and organ number "This Time—She Said," the odd and lumbering psychedelic-oriented song "You Don't Know" which sports a filtered vocal and unusual chord progressions, the classic jangle-pop cut "I'll Be Back" that features an unusual growled vocal and twangy sitar, and the wonderfully gutsy and driving title track. Bobby Sutliff's songs here are all jangle-pop-oriented and a bit less consistent, but he has some standout tracks, such as "Ghost Town" (an atypically sad, weary song in this genre), "Don't Say No" (with an especially lithe, arching melodic line), and "Visa Cards and Antique Mirrors" (which features unusually strong lyrics—not always a Sutliff virtue). A few of the songs are not so successful; Sutliff's "Voices in My Head" sets verses about mental illness to inappropriately untroubled-sounding music, while Lee's "Nation of Two" is a long, draggy, and unmemorable song. Sound quality at times is badly distorted, most noticeably in "Visa Cards and Antique Mirrors." But despite its few shortcomings, this is a fine album well worth hearing. —*David Cleary*

- **A Different Sort** / 1987 / DB ✦✦✦✦
- **At Home With Bobby & Tim** / 1989 / DB ✦✦✦✦

On this release, Bobby Sutliff rejoins Tim Lee after a one-album hiatus from the Windbreakers. Here, the pair turn out a brace of capable songs, some of which refine old styles and others of which explore new ground. Lee's atypical "Closer to Home" is a sparely arranged, acoustic-guitar-dominated, country-influenced song with a direct, homespun melody. More typical of his older output are "Just Fine," an uptempo rocking song that borrows its chorus from the Eagles' "Already Gone," and "Ill at Ease," a slow-speed number with a definite R.E.M. sound. R.E.M. debts are evident in some of Sutliff's work as well, especially in "Cold, Cold Rain" (which is marred by an overwrought guitar solo) and "I Thought You Knew" (a number that somehow manages to be simultaneously uptempo and anguished). "On the Wire" is a slow-tempo track (rare for Sutliff) that has cut-to-the-chase lyrics such as "For all I care/You can go/Straight to hell." At times, Sutliff strains noticeably to get high notes in the manner of Neil Young on this release, a less-welcome new feature. The album also contains a cover of a decent tune by former True West guitarist Russ Tolman. Sound quality is good if not utterly polished at times. This solid album is worth hearing, especially for fans of this fine band. —*David Cleary*

- **Electric Landlady** / 1991 / DB ✦✦✦✦
- **I'll Be Back** / DB ✦✦✦

This brief EP primarily serves as a showcase for the title track; "I'll Be Back" originally appeared on the album *Run* and is a strong number to select in representation of this release. The song's twangy, gritty tunefulness is very engaging. Side two contains a faithfully earnest cover of a Katrina and the Waves song "Don't Take Her Out of My World" and a yearningly attractive tune by Howard Wuelfing. It's all worth a listen. —*David Cleary*

Johnny Winter

b. Feb. 23, 1944, Leland, MS
Guitar, Vocals / Blues-Rock

Blues guitarist Johnny Winter became a major star in the late '60s and early '70s. Since that time he's confirmed his reputation in the blues by working with Muddy Waters and continuing to play in the style, despite musical fashion. Born in Leland, MS, Winter formed his first band at 14 with his brother Edgar in Beaumont, TX, and spent his youth in recording studios cutting regional singles and in bars playing the blues. His discovery on a national level came via an article in *Rolling Stone* in 1968, which led to a management contract with New York club owner Steve Paul and a record deal with Columbia. His debut album (there are numerous albums of juvenilia), *Johnny Winter*, reached the charts in 1969. Starting out with a trio, Winter later formed a band with former members of the McCoys, including second guitarist Rick Derringer. It was called Johnny Winter And. He achieved a sales peak in 1971 with the gold-selling *Live/Johnny Winter And*. He returned in 1973 with *Still Alive and Well*, his highest-charting album. His albums became more overtly blues-oriented in the late '70s and he also produced several albums for Muddy Waters. In the '80s he switched to the blues label Alligator for three albums, and has since recorded for the labels MCA and Pointblank/Virgin. —*William Ruhlmann*

Johnny Winter / 1969 / Columbia ✦✦✦✦
Winter's stunning debut features his fiery blues playing in both electric and acoustic settings, with backup that includes Willie Dixon. —*William Ruhlmann*

- **Second Winter** / 1969 / Columbia ✦✦✦✦

Winter leans more toward mainstream rock 'n' roll, though the guitar playing remains fierce. Originally a three-sided LP, this now makes a long CD. —*William Ruhlmann*

Johnny Winter and . . . / 1970 / Columbia ✦✦✦✦
Winter puts together a new band and takes on the assistance of Rick Derringer, who co-produces and provides such great songs as "Rock and Roll, Hoochie Koo." —*William Ruhlmann*

Johnny Winter and . . . Live / 1971 / Columbia ✦✦✦
Winter and his new band turn out hard-rock versions of "Jumpin' Jack Flash," "Johnny B. Goode," and other rock 'n' roll favorites. —*William Ruhlmann*

Saints & Sinners / 1974 / Columbia ✦✦✦
Johnny Winter's sixth Columbia album was also his second since his comeback from drug addiction. Its predecessor, *Still Alive and Well*, had been his highest charting effort. *Saints & Sinners* was just as energetically played, but its mixture of material, including 1950s rock 'n' roll oldies like Chuck Berry's "Thirty Days," Larry Williams' "Bony Moronie," and Leiber and Stoller's "Riot in Cell Block No.9," recent covers like the Rolling Stones' "Stray Cat Blues," and a couple of originals, was more eclectic than inspired. (Van Morrison completists should note that the album also contains Winter's cover of Morrison's "Feedback on Highway 101," a typical bluesy groove song that Morrison recorded for his 1973

Hardnose the Highway album but dropped. Winter's is the only released recording of the song.) Abetted by the members of the old Johnny Winter And band, Rick Derringer, Randy Hobbs, and Richard Hughes, plus his brother Edgar and Dan Hartman, Winter produced forceful hard rock focused on his searing lead guitar runs and rough-edged voice. It was the less-impressive choice of material that kept this collection from matching its predecessor. (Originally released in February 1974, *Saints & Sinners* was reissued on February 27, 1996 with the previously unreleased song "Dirty," a Winter original, added. The slide-guitar and flute track is not consistent with the rest of the album, but it is interesting to hear. (Wonder who played the flute?) —*William Ruhlmann*

Nothin' but the Blues / 1977 / Blue Sky ✦✦✦✦
After a long period making rock records, Winter fronts the Muddy Waters band (with Waters singing) on this Chicago blues workout. He sounds happier than ever before. —*William Ruhlmann*

Guitar Slinger / 1984 / Alligator ✦✦✦✦
The first of three blues albums recorded after a four-year studio hiatus finds Winter as fleet-fingered as before and sounding more vocally involved than in some of the later Columbia material. —*William Ruhlmann*

Birds Can't Row Boats / 1988 / Relix ✦✦✦✦
Aside from "Ice Cube" (a 1959 instrumental), these tracks date from 1965-68. Many are previously unissued or only available on rare 45s. Those accustomed to his more famous recordings are in for a jolt, as this shows Johnny in several unexpected settings: grinding Texas psych-punk, the British Invasion-cum-folk-rock garage single "Gone for Bad," blue-eyed R&B/soul, an Everly Brothers cover, a *Highway 61*-era Dylan imitation, and even a shit-kickin' C&W tune. There are also some straight, predominantly acoustic blues numbers. —*Richie Unterberger*

Let Me In / Aug. 1991 / Point Blank ✦✦✦✦
Let Me In is a star-studded all-blues set from Johnny Winter, featuring cameos from Dr. John, Albert Collins, and several others. Though the set focuses on blues material, Winters can never leave his rock roots behind—the sheer volume and pile-driving energy of his performances ensures that. For most of the record, his enthusiasm is contagious, but there are a couple of bland, generic exercises that fail to work up a head of steam. But there is a lovely acoustic number called "Blue Mood," which shows Winter trying to stretch a bit by playing jazzy licks. It's a refreshing change of pace. —*Thom Owens*

Scorchin' Blues / Jun. 16, 1992 / Epic ✦✦
Scorchin' Blues marries tracks from Johnny Winter's early Columbia albums—including the classic National steel-driven "Dallas" from his 1969 debut—with material from his return-to-roots Blue Sky-period in the late '70s. The aggressive playing and raunchy vocals will appeal to both blues and rock fans, and Ben Sandmel crams an authoritative biography into seven pages, complete with interesting Winter quotes. The one downside: a miserly 10 tracks spread over only 45 minutes of playing time. —*Roch Parisien*

Collection / Jun. 30, 1992 / Castle ✦✦✦

Hey, Where's Your Brother? / Jul. 1992 / Point Blank ✦✦✦
On the classic, 1972 live album *Roadwork*, Edgar Winter immortalized the words, when introducing brother Johnny: "Everybody asks me . . . where's your brother?" It's a question that fans have besieged both Winters with for over two decades, and now Johnny gets a chance to return the tribute with his latest. Edgar does in fact guest on the sessions, blowing sax and tinkling keys on a few tracks, and dueting with big bro on a superb, seasonal rendition of "Please Come Home for Christmas." —*Roch Parisien*

A Rock N' Roll Collection / 1994 / Columbia/Legacy ✦✦✦✦
A two-CD survey of Winter's recordings for Columbia between 1969 and 1979, the era of his greatest commercial success. This collects many of his most popular tracks, though it doesn't do much to argue a case for artistic diversity. Includes two otherwise unavailable songs: an alternate take of "30 Days," and a previously unreleased 1973 cover of Robert Johnson's "Come on in My Kitchen." —*Richie Unterberger*

Relix Records Best of Blues, Vol. 2 / Apr. 15, 1997 / Relix ✦✦✦

Steve Winwood

b. May 12, 1948, Birmingham, England
Guitar, Keyboards, Vocals / Pop-Rock, Adult Contemporary

Singer-songwriter, keyboardist, and guitarist Steve Winwood was a well-known musician long before he finally embarked on a solo career in the second half of the '70s. Born in Birmingham, England, Winwood joined the Spencer Davis Group with his older brother Muff when he was only 15 years old. His was the soulful, Ray Charles-like voice on such hits as "Gimme Some Lovin'" and "I'm a Man," songs he also co-wrote. In 1967 he formed Traffic, which he led, with time off for the supergroup Blind Faith in 1969, until 1974. Winwood finally released his first solo album in 1977 and, in 1981 had his first million-seller with his second album, *Arc of a Diver. Talking Back to the Night* (1982) was not as much of a success, and Winwood spent four years preparing *Back in the High Life* (1986), which sold three million copies. *Roll with It* (1988) went to No. 1, but *Refugees of the Heart* (1990) was not up to his usual standard. After the relative failure of *Refugees of the Heart*, Winwood and Jim Capaldi re-formed Traffic in 1994; although their record and tour were well-received, the reunion wasn't as successful as expected, and Winwood began work on a solo album in 1995. Winwood was scheduled to return with his first solo album in seven years during the summer of 1997. — *William Ruhlmann*

Steve Winwood / Jun. 1977 / Mobile Fidelity ✦✦✦
Rock fans had been waiting for a Steve Winwood solo album for more than a decade, as he made his way through such bands as the Spencer Davis Group and Traffic. When Winwood finally delivered with this LP, just about everybody was disappointed. Traffic had finally petered out three years before, but Winwood, using such former members as Jim Capaldi and Reebop Kwaku Baah, failed to project a strong individual identity outside the group. That great voice was singing the songs, that talented guitarist/keyboardist was playing them, and that excellent songwriter had composed them, but nothing here was memorable, and the long-awaited debut proved a bust. — *William Ruhlmann*

Arc of a Diver / Jan. 1981 / Island ✦✦✦✦
Utterly unencumbered by the baggage of his long years in the music business, Winwood reinvents himself as a completely contemporary artist on this outstanding album, leading off with his best solo song, "While You See a Chance." Winwood also plays all the instruments. — *William Ruhlmann*

Talking Back to the Night / Aug. 1982 / Island ✦✦✦
Okay, so after missing with his first solo album, Steve Winwood had hit the jackpot with his second, *Arc of a Diver*, finally fulfilling his enormous promise. What did he do next? He returned to the record racks only a year and a half later with this retread, which attempted to turn the "While You See a Chance" sound into a formula and to a large extent succeeded, unfortunately. "Valerie" (No. 70 US, No. 51 UK), the lead-off track, had that same keyboard sound and tempo, and Winwood kept it up for much of the rest of the record, including the album's biggest US single, "Still in the Game" (No. 47). Fans were dismayed, and *Talking Back to the Night* had an even lower chart peak than *Steve Winwood*. — *William Ruhlmann*

● **Back in the High Life** / Jun. 1986 / Island ✦✦✦✦
Turning to involved percussion tracks and horns, Winwood turns another musical corner on this sophisticated album, which contains echoes of everything from gospel to Caribbean music. Contains the No. 1 hit "Higher Love." — *William Ruhlmann*

Chronicles / Nov. 1987 / Island ✦✦✦✦
This isn't an adequate compilation of the years 1977-1986, but it does manage to gather some of the better songs. — *William Ruhlmann*

Roll with It / Jun. 1988 / Virgin ✦✦✦
Winwood manages to reintroduce some of the R&B elements of the Spencer Davis Group and some of the psychedelic effects of early Traffic here, though this is also an effective follow-up to the directions indicated on *Back in the High Life*. Contains the No. 1 title track and "Don't You Know What the Night Can Do?" — *William Ruhlmann*

Refugees of the Heart / Nov. 1990 / Virgin ✦✦✦
The key to Steve Winwood's solo career is inconsistency; *Refugees Of The Heart* was a letdown. The distinction between a great Winwood album and one that's only okay is dangerously small—it has more to do with performance than composition—and on *Refugees of the Heart*, as on *Talking Back to the Night*, Winwood was unable to invest Will Jennings' pedestrian lyrics with the soulful feeling of which he's capable. The album's standout is a collaboration with ex-Traffic partner Jim Capaldi, "One and Only Man," which topped *Billboard*'s Album Rock Tracks chart. Perhaps noting this exception, Winwood next teamed with Capaldi in a 1994 reunion of Traffic. — *William Ruhlmann*

The Finer Things / Mar. 21, 1995 / Island ✦✦✦✦
Steve Winwood has led a long and varied career, recording everything from straight R&B and jazz-flavored rock to folk and pop. Over the course of four discs, *The Finer Things* chronicles the entirety of his career, beginning with the Spencer Davis Group, through Traffic and Blind Faith, right until his successful solo career. It includes all of the hits and many of his finest album tracks, yet the overall approach is rather exhausting—the rarities are rarely illuminating, they're just there for the sake of being there. Nevertheless, it is a worthwhile purchase for anyone wanting a comprehensive picture of Winwood in all of his various guises. — *Stephen Thomas Erlewine*

Wire

f. 1976, London, England, db. 1991
Punk, Alternative Pop-Rock, Post-Punk
Wire's brief, fractured songs and minimalistic sound made the band the

artiest of all punk bands, as well as one of the most influential. Unlike most other punk bands, their stripped-down approach was not an attempt to get back to rock's roots; it was cutting the music to its raw nerve, so nothing extraneous was left. On their 1977 debut, *Pink Flag*, Wire managed to tear through 21 songs in under 40 minutes. While the two followups to *Pink Flag*, *Chairs Missing* and *154*, weren't as visionary as the band's debut, they refined and expanded the group's sound, earning great critical praise in the process. Just as the group's cult following was growing, Wire suddenly broke up in late 1979. After spending several years pursuing various solo projects, the band members reunited in 1986. For the next five years, Wire released a series of experimental pop records which generally received popular reviews. However, their cult was slowly shrinking, and the group disbanded for good in 1991.

Art students Colin Newman (guitar, vocals), Bruce Gilbert (guitar), Graham Lewis (bass, vocals), and Robert Gotobed (b. Mark Field; drums) formed Wire in 1976 after becoming infatuated with the fledgling punk scene. At the time, none of the members knew how to play their instruments, which is one of the reasons why their music had a raw, vital experimental quality. Wire had lone cut on a live punk compilation before signing with Harvest Records in September of 1977. Harvest was known for their prog-rock bands, and in a sense Wire wasn't too far removed from that aesthetic. Though they had a nervy, dissonant avant-pop sound, they approached their music as an art experiment, not as a rock 'n' roll group. As a result, their 1977 debut, *Pink Flag*, was a revolutionary album, a collection of 21 brief songs that displayed a blinding array of ideas. *Pink Flag* was acclaimed by many critics, as was the band's 1978 follow-up, *Chairs Missing*. Produced by Mike Thorne, *Chairs Missing* was a more measured, detailed record that was just as well-received. Boasting a dense, layered production, *154* followed in 1979. Following its release, Wire disbanded, claiming they had exhausted their ideas.

Over the next six years, the band released several live albums and solo projects. In 1986, they decided to re-form, releasing *The Ideal Copy* in 1987. Initially, the reunited Wire was greeted with positive reviews, but the good will gradually eroded away, and the band was left with a small, devoted cult following by the early '90s. Frustrated with his bandmates' continued experimentations with technology, Gotobed left Wire in 1991 after the release of *The Drill* EP. The group dropped the "e" from their name and released *The First Letter* as Wir later that year. Following its release, the group quietly disbanded, with Newman, Gilbert, and Lewis all pursuing solo projects.

In 1995, Wire experienced a brief revival, as Elastica sampled "Three Girl Rhumba" for their hit single "Connection" and Menswear revamped the band's angular riffs into bubblegum. No member of Wire publicly supported either group, though Newman and Elastica's Justine Frischmann later collaborated on a one-off project in 1997. — *Stephen Thomas Erlewine*

☆ **Pink Flag** / Dec. 1977 / Restless ✦✦✦✦✦
Wire's debut effort, *Pink Flag*, was one of the strongest releases of the late-'70s British punk scene, mixing the aggressive punch of the Sex Pistols with the humor and brevity of the Ramones. *Pink Flag* packed 21 tracks into the space of 37 minutes; 12 of the tracks were under a minute and a half. ("Field Day for the Sundays" clocked in at just 28 seconds.) Somehow none of these tracks felt short; Wire merely made their point and moved on to the next idea. — *Rick Clark*

Chairs Missing / Aug. 1978 / Restless ✦✦✦✦
In *Chair's Missing*, Wire stretched out into longer pieces and artier production. Not as impressive as *Pink Flag*, the album does contain some standout tracks with "Outdoor Miner," "French Film Blurred," "I Am the Fly," and "Question of Degree." — *Rick Clark*

154 / 1979 / Restless ✦✦✦✦
154 integrated more keyboards and slowed the pace down a bit, but Wire didn't lose any of the eccentric edge. They just kept getting stranger. If *Ummagumma*-period Pink Floyd, early King Crimson, and the Moody Blues at their musically most cosmic, were filtered through the punk movement, you'd get an idea what a peculiar album *154* is. Call it psychedelic punk. Among the highlights are "Two People in a Room," "The 15th," "Map Ref. 41ø N 93ø W," "The Other Window," "Single K.O.," and "40 Versions." — *Rick Clark*

Document & Eyewitness / 1981 / Mute ✦✦

Snakedrill / 1986 / Enigma ✦✦✦

The Ideal Copy / 1987 / Enigma ✦✦✦
Wire's first new full-length effort in eight years is a stunning comeback picking up where *154* left off while also reflecting the strides made by the members' solo work. Finding its footing in dark, edgy dance rhythms and ominous digital textures, *The Ideal Copy* is experimental and forward-thinking, spanning from the buzzing melodies of "Ahead" and "Ambitious" to the taut minimalism of "Feed Me"; the record has its flaws, but its restless creative spirit and refusal to rest on past glories

make it one of the few reunion efforts which actually matters. —*Jason Ankeny*

A Bell Is a Cup . . . Until It Is Struck / 1988 / Enigma ✦✦✦
Like *The Ideal Copy, A Bell Is a Cup Until It Is Struck* continues to push Wire into avant-dance territory, tempering the music's digital rhythms with an increasingly strong sense of melodic ingenuity. More inviting and accessible than the previous LP (or, for that matter, the vast majority of the group's prior work), the album relies heavily on textured guitar patterns to create a warm, dreamy sound; the songs follow suit, spinning surreal, densely free-associative narratives which further enhance the record's abstract allure. —*Jason Ankeny*

● **On Returning (1977-1979)** / 1989 / Restless ✦✦✦✦
This magnificent 31-song overview collects highlights from *Pink Flag,* and many of the best songs from the two follow-ups, plus some interesting rarities. —*John Floyd*

It's Beginning to & Back Again / May 1989 / Enigma ✦✦✦
Begun as a collection of live recordings cut in Chicago and Portugal, the songs which comprise *IBTABA* were subsequently reconstructed in the studio to the point of becoming virtually unrecognizable. The material largely reprises tracks from *A Bell Is a Cup . . .* along with a number of new cuts, highlighted by the single "Eardrum Buzz"; while the record is respectable on its own terms, it's impossible to discern its relevance—neither a true live album nor a remix collection, its original intentions remain lost in the translation. —*Jason Ankeny*

Manscape / May 1990 / Restless ✦✦
Wire's gradual move towards dance music and techno becomes complete on *Manscape.* Syncopated beats, synths and sequencer riffs are the dominant musical motifs, with Graham Lewis taking a larger share of the vocal turns. Still, what the group has gained in technical acumen over time has been lost in tension and interpersonal dynamics; taken for what it is, *Manscape* is edgy, brainy dance music, but taken as part of the largely brilliant Wire oeuvre, it's a disappointment. —*Jason Ankeny*

The First Letter / Oct. 29, 1991 / Mute ✦✦
With *The First Letter* Wire re-named itself Wir and continued its move toward more detailed soundscapes. Like the previous *Manscape,* the vocals mean considerably less than the musical textures—it's all about the sound, not the song. Some of the soundscapes are quite interesting, but much of the music fails to be compelling. Nevertheless, the concentration on sonic textures made it no surprise that Colin Newman began pursuing a career as a techno label owner after the album's release. —*Stephen Thomas Erlewine*

A List / May 18, 1993 / Elektra ✦✦

Behind the Curtain / 1995 / EMI ✦✦✦
Behind the Curtain collects live tracks and demos from *Pink Flag, Chairs Missing* and *154.* —*John Bush*

Turns & Strokes / Apr. 1996 / WMO ✦✦✦

Wire Train

f. Apr. 1983, San Francisco, CA, **db.** 1993
New Wave
Wire Train was formed as the Renegades in April 1983 in San Francisco by San Francisco State University students and guitarists Kevin Hunter and Kurt Herr with the rhythm section of Anders Rundblad (bass) and Frederico Gil-Sola (drums). The group signed to the local 415 label, also home to acts like Romeo Void and Translator, all of which found themselves with national distribution when 415 entered into a deal with Columbia Records. Wire Train's first album, *In a Chamber,* made the national charts in 1984, but the group began to suffer personnel changes. Gil-Sola was replaced by Brian Macleod for the second album, *Between Two Words,* after which Herr left, to be replaced by Jeffrey Trott. A third album, *Ten Women,* charted in 1987. The group's last two albums, *Wire Train* (1990) and *No Soul No Strain* (1992), appeared on MCA. —*William Ruhlmann*

In a Chamber/Between Two Words / Jan. 31, 1995 / Oglio ✦✦✦✦

● **Last Perfect Thing: A Retrospective** / Mar. 26, 1996 / Columbia/Legacy ✦✦✦✦
Wire Train's musical style reflected the cross-breeding between post-new wave power-pop and post-disco dance music that characterized the early '80s. The guitars jangled and there were hooks and catchy choruses with harmony vocals, just like the mid-'60s (not to mention covers of Bob Dylan and Buffalo Springfield), but the tempos were unusually quick and the drummer even pushed the beat, while touches of keyboard sometimes shimmered on the edges of the sound picture. More popular bands such as U2 and R.E.M. were doing roughly the same thing at the same time, if with a bit more distinction. But Wire Train frontman Kevin Hunter had an ear for a good melody and an adequate voice to express his pop sentiments, so there's no real answer to the question, why didn't Wire Train make it? This hour-long, 16-track compilation selects the highlights from the group's three Columbia albums

(but not its two MCA albums), along with a few rarities. (Amazingly, early copies mistakenly substituted the B-side "Half a Lifetime" for the title song. The problem was to be corrected, but meanwhile an interesting collector's item had been created.) —*William Ruhlmann*

Wishbone Ash

f. 1966, Devon, England
Group / Rock 'n' Roll, Hard Rock, Art-Rock/Progressive-Rock
During the early and middle 1970's, Wishbone Ash were among England's most popular hard rock acts.

The group's roots dated to the summer of 1966, when drummer Steve Upton formed a band called Empty Vessels with bassist/vocalist Martin Turner and guitarist Glen Turner. Empty Vessels soon changed their name to Tanglewood and moved to London; during a gig at the Country Club in Hampstead, they were seen by would-be rock manager Miles Copeland, who was impressed with the jazz and progressive rock influences within the band and offered to be their manager.

Glen Turner left the band at that point, and an advertisement for a guitarist resulted in the addition of both David Alan "Ted" Turner and Andy Powell, who provided the basis for the sound of the new lineup with intertwining riffs and phrases drawn from both soul and blues, coupled with Martin Turner's melodic bass sound and Upton's jazz-influenced drumming. A new name was called for, after several suggestions by Copeland that proved unacceptable. "Wishbone Ash" was chosen from two lists of words. The group rehearsed for weeks at Copeland's home, working out an entirely new repertoire, and played their first gig opening for Aynsley Dunbar's Retaliation. It wasn't too long before they were opening for Deep Purple, where a sound check jam between Powell and Ritchie Blackmore led to a recording contract with the American Decca label.

Their self-titled first album appeared in 1970; *Pilgrimage* and *Argus* followed over the next two years, and each showed a major advance in the band's sound. The release of 1973's *Wishbone Four* reflected a greater maturity to the group, and was their first fully developed album, with songwriting that didn't hide behind a progressive pose but luxuriated in the members' folk music inclinations, without compromising the harder edge of their music. The album also saw the departure of Ted Turner, who was replaced by Laurie Wisefield.

Locked In and *New England* followed; Martin Turner departed after 1979's *Just Testing,* to be replaced by ex-King Crimson bassist/singer John Wetton. Wishbone Ash soldiered on through the 1980s, and in 1986 even got back with Copeland, by now a major player in the recording industry by virtue of his management of the Police and his founding of I.R.S. Records. Wishbone Ash's history came full circle with the reunion of Powell, Upton, Ted Turner, and Martin Turner, and the recording of three albums for I.R.S. They remained a working band into the 1990's, led by Andy Powell and Ted Turner and touring and recording regularly. —*Bruce Eder*

Wishbone Ash / 1970 / MCA ✦✦
A relatively straightforward blues-based metal album, with lots of heavy riffing between Powell and Ted Turner, the stuff that teenagers of the era used to listen to for hours at a time (usually when they should've been studying), and some folk elements that were probably lost on most fans at the time, although it helped make the music that much more attractive. The 11-minute long "Handy" probably served as backdrop to lots of pot parties at the time. The stuff played much better in concert, but this was a good sample of what the band could do, even if Led Zeppelin's outtakes had more punch and inventiveness. —*Bruce Eder*

Pilgrimage / 1971 / MCA ✦✦✦
A somewhat more progressive sounding effort, built on better songs and playing that is less showy for its own sake. —*Bruce Eder*

Argus / 1972 / MCA ✦✦✦
The group's magnum opus, *Argus* is also the album from which Wishbone Ash's reputation as a progressive band stems—not only is the playing and the songwriting about as studied and elegant as they ever achieved, but for the first time, the melodies and the development of the songs matches the seriousness of the group's approach. Of course, much of what is here would only be considered "progressive" by the same people who got off on the progressive side of Uriah Heep, but it sounded real good. —*Bruce Eder*

Wishbone Four / 1973 / MCA ✦✦✦✦
The progressive aspirations were put aside for this, the group's most solid rocking album, though the folk-based element is still there, more solid than ever. "Ballad of the Beacon" is a genuinely beautiful song, and might've come from any number of electric folk-rock bands—the fact that it came from Wishbone Ash indicates just how serious they were in wanting to explore some of these sounds. Their most mature and successful album. —*Bruce Eder*

Live Dates / 1973 / MCA ✦✦✦✦
No surprise—in concert was the best way to hear Wishbone Ash,

because the studio was just too sterile an environment, at least for their hardest rocking stuff to take off. Anyone really into the group should own this record. —*Bruce Eder*

There's the Rub / 1974 / MCA ✦✦✦
With producer Bill Szymczyk running the sessions, the group finally gets a studio sound as solid as their concert sound. Most impressive all the way through. —*Bruce Eder*

Locked in / 1976 / Atlantic ✦✦

Classic Ash / 1977 / Barclay ✦✦✦

Front Page News / 1977 / MCA ✦✦✦
Another very enjoyable recording, with their folk inclinations rising to the fore again on several tracks. —*Bruce Eder*

No Smoke without Fire / 1978 / MCA ✦✦✦

Just Testing / 1980 / MCA ✦✦

Live Dates II / 1981 / MCA ✦✦

Number the Brave / 1981 / MCA ✦✦

Hot Ash / 1981 / MCA ✦✦

Nouveau Calls / 1989 / IRS ✦✦

● **Time Was: Wishbone Ash Collection** / 1993 / MCA ✦✦✦✦
A two-disc snapshot of this band's more vital work, from the meat-and-potatoes rock of their eponymous 1970 debut, the thematic, progressive-minded peak of *Pilgrimage* and *Argus*, and a return to more basic structures for *Wishbone 4*. Mercifully, their less "enduring" albums from the later '70s and early '80s are touched on only sporadically. The set includes a pair of previously unreleased tracks and a good booklet with interviews; somehow the digital remastering has left the sound a little thin. —*Roch Parisien*

Raw to the Bone / Oct. 19, 1993 / Castle ✦✦✦

There's the Rub/Locked In / 1995 / MCA ✦✦✦

BBC Radio One Live / Oct. 1995 / Griffin ✦✦✦

Live / Dec. 19, 1995 / Griffin Music ✦✦

Live at Geneva / Mar. 18, 1997 / Pavement ✦✦✦

Live in Concert / ROIR ✦✦

Time Was: Wishbone Ash Collection / MCA ✦✦✦✦

Bill Withers

b. Jul. 4, 1938, Slab Fork, WV
Vocals / Soul, Urban
It was a chance 1970 meeting with the legendary Booker T. Jones (of Stax's Booker T. & the MG's) that opened the door for Bill Withers into the world of pop success. At the time of their meeting, Withers was working in a factory that built toilet seats for jet airplanes. Jones, impressed with Withers' demos, helped secure a deal with Sussex Records. Withers' Jones-produced debut, *Just As I Am*, was a classic of folky acoustic-guitar-driven soul, complemented by Withers' earthy vocal delivery and largely autobiographical tales. His next few albums capitalized on that sound, but as the late '70s came around, Withers gravitated toward a sophisticated urban R&B sound, sometimes collaborating with groups like the Crusaders. —*Rick Clark*

● **Lean on Me: The Best of Bill Withers** / Aug. 9, 1994 / Sony ✦✦✦✦
18 tracks, from the early '70s to the mid-'80s, including his early Top Ten singles, but also minor hits like "Grandma's Hands," "Kissing My Love," and "Lovely Day." Those who admire songs like "Lean on Me" and "Ain't No Sunshine" are advised to approach this best-of with caution; from the mid-'70s onward, Withers forsook his folky singer-songwriter soul for more anonymous, slick MOR soul and urban contemporary. His early sound was far more distinctive, and his early-'70s Sussex albums are recommended alternatives to this compilation. —*Richie Unterberger*

Wolfgang Press

f. 1983, London, England
Alternative Pop-Rock, Alternative Dance
Enigmatic, moody, and challenging, Britain's Wolfgang Press were one of the most mercurial talents of the post-punk era, restlessly moving from Gothic noise to dark balladry to eccentric funk; paradoxically, the group was also the 4AD label's longest tenured artist—even their stylish album packages were all the product of the same designer, Alberto Ricci.

Formed in London in 1983, the Wolfgang Press comprised vocalist Michael Allen, guitarist Andrew Gray and keyboardist Mark Cox. Allen and Cox first teamed in the group Rema Rema, which also featured Adam and the Ants alum Marco Perroni; after reuniting in the short-lived quartet Mass, the duo recruited Gray, and the Wolfgang Press issued their cacophonous, gloomy debut LP *The Burden of Mules* in 1983. An EP trilogy co-produced by Cocteau Twin Robin Guthrie followed in quick succession: while 1984's *Scarecrow* was a lighter, more

streamlined affair, 1985's *Water* spotlighted ominously sparse torch songs, and the same year's *Sweatbox* explored deconstructionist pop.

The Wolfgang Press' second full-length effort, 1986's *Standing Up Straight*, incorporated industrial and orchestral influences into the mix, while the *Big Sex* EP's "God's Number" offered a soulful backing chorus, a harbinger of things to come. Indeed, after 1988's hypnotic *Bird Wood Cage* and its leadoff single "King of Soul" introduced strong elements of dub, reggae, and R&B, the trio took the full plunge into the dance arena with 1991's *Queer*, an idiosyncratic outing admittedly inspired by De La Soul's landmark *Three Feet High and Rising*; the first single, a surreal cover of the Randy Newman-penned "Mama Told Me Not to Come," was a minor hit. 1995's *Funky Little Demons* completed the Wolfgang Press' transition into white funk; prior to its release, however, Cox exited the group's ranks. —*Jason Ankeny*

The Burdon of Mules / 1983 / 4AD ✦✦
Dark, noisy and intense, the Wolfgang Press' debut *The Burden of Mules* remains among the group's most impenetrable efforts; tracks like "Lisa (The Passion)," "Prostitute" (in two parts) and "Compleate and Utter" are so morose and vehement as to verge on self-parody. —*Jason Ankeny*

● **Legendary Wolfgang Press & Others** / 1985 / Nesak ✦✦✦✦
The Legendary Wolfgang Press and Other Tall Stories compiles the EPs *Scarecrow*, *Water* and *Sweatbox*, three strong, eclectic efforts produced by the Cocteau Twins' Robin Guthrie. Displaying marked leaps in sophistication and textural variety over their earliest work, the set establishes the trio as witty and incisive pop deconstructionists: a tongue-in-cheek cover of Otis Redding's "Respect" reveals a newfound sense of humor, while Neil Young's "Heart of Gold" undergoes such a radical transformation that it even receives a new title, "Heart of Stone." —*Jason Ankeny*

Standing up Straight / 1986 / Nesak ✦✦✦✦
The ambitious *Standing Up Straight* builds on the eclecticism of the EPs collected on *The Legendary Wolfgang Press*, further broadening the trio's horizons by layering their dark, unforgiving sound with elements of industrial and classical music. While "Hammer the Halo" and "Rotten Fodder" in particular stand out as two of the group's most aggressive efforts, the intensity level remains high throughout—a challenging, even punishing album, but a rewarding one as well. —*Jason Ankeny*

Bird Wood Cage / 1988 / 4AD ✦✦✦✦
Bird Wood Cage remains one of the most pivotal records in the Wolfgang Press catalog; here, the trio begins to incorporate the dance and funk elements which would ultimately emerge as the dominant facet of their work. The lead single "King of Soul," with its female backing chorus, is the first tip-off, while the Talking Heads-like "Kansas" adopts a wah-wah guitar line; a bit of dub even underscores "Hang on Me (For Papa)." Michael Allen's forbidding vocals are also warmer and more soulful, and while the group's trademark gloom hangs over the proceedings, a significant transformation in both musical and emotional outlook is clearly afoot, leaving *Bird Wood Cage* as the bridge from the Wolfgang Press' past to their future. —*Jason Ankeny*

Queer / Jun. 1991 / 4AD ✦✦✦
Recorded with the aid of ex-Throwing Muses bassist Leslie Langston, *Queer* is the Wolfgang Press' leap into the world of dance music. The cover of Randy Newman's "Mama Told Me (Not to Come)" underscores the record's stranger-in-a-strange-land vibe as Michael Allen's dramatic vocals and arcane obsessions collide head-on with the ecstatic physicality and immediacy of the dancefloor; cold and remote, the result is alien funk, a collection of idiosyncratic rhythms, dark textures, and ominous grooves. —*Jason Ankeny*

Funky Little Demons / Jan. 24, 1995 / 4AD ✦✦✦
Wolfgang Press continues its trademark kitsch-dance with *Funky Little Demons*, an album that boasts a more focused production than many previous records without sacrificing any of their style. —*Stephen Thomas Erlewine*

Bobby Womack

b. Mar. 4, 1944, Cleveland, OH
Guitar, Vocals / Soul, R&B, Quiet Storm
Few careers in American popular music have been as consistently productive and influential as that of singer-songwriter and guitarist Bobby Womack. Sam Cooke, for whom Womack played guitar, financed his first recordings in the early '60s. With his brothers as the Valentinos, he cut two R&B classics, "It's All Over Now" (later a hit for the Stones) and "Lookin' for a Love" (a mega-hit for J. Geils). The Valentinos' combination of shouting lead vocals and blues/gospel harmonies predated late-'60s soul music.

Womack knew and championed Jimi Hendrix early on, befriending him during a 1962 soul package tour. Womack's lean, groundbreaking guitar work, so similar in flavor to that of his contemporary Curtis Mayfield, influenced Hendrix. Later, Hendrix would return the favor by popularizing the wah-wah—an effect Womack would use to chilling effect on Sly Stone's *There's a Riot Goin' On* album and its smash single, "Family Affair" (he doubled here on bass). That's also Womack's guitar on Wilson Pickett's "Funky Broadway" and on Aretha Franklin's *Lady Soul* album.

In fact, Womack himself was one of the legendary "wild" soul men, friend and partying companion of Wilson Pickett, for whom he wrote "Midnight Mover" and "I'm in Love." He even scored a movie, *Across 110th Street*, which came out at the same time as the landmark blaxploitation film *Shaft*.

Womack's singing career resumed in the '70s; James Taylor covered his No. 1 R&B hit, "Woman's Got to Have It." He made a stunning 1981 comeback with the No. 1 R&B album *The Poet* and reunited with old Memphis studio friends and producer Chips Moman on 1986's *Womagic*.

Although he wasn't recording frequently during the '90s, Bobby Womack continued to perform, both as a solo artist and with other musicians. —*Christine Ohlman*

Greatest Hits / 1974 / Liberty ✦✦✦✦
Includes his great remake of the Valentinos hit "Lookin' for a Love," as well as his other chart hits—"That's the Way I Fell About Cha," "Harry Hippy," and "Nobody Wants You When You're Down and Out." —*Christine Ohlman*

● **Midnight Mover** / Feb. 1993 / EMI ✦✦✦✦
Spanning the length of his influential career, *Midnight Mover* features two discs of one of the major figures of contemporary soul and R&B, covering all of his hits and best moments. It is essential for any R&B collection. —*AMG*

Only Survivor: The MCA Years / Mar. 26, 1996 / MCA ✦✦✦

Soul Of / Oct. 29, 1996 / EMI ✦✦✦✦
This solid collection of his best early and mid-'70s work is some of the better (and rootsier) soul music that emerged from the era just prior to disco. Besides the hits "Lookin' For a Love," "Nobody Wants You When You're Down and Out," "Harry Hippie," "You're Welcome, Stop on By," "Daylight," and "That's the Way I Feel About Cha," it adds a few album tracks, minor singles, and an interesting previously unreleased demo of "Across 110th Street." —*Richie Unterberger*

Stevie Wonder (Steveland Morris)

b. May 13, 1950, Saginaw, MI
Piano, Vocals / Soul, Funk, Urban, Motown, Pop-Rock
When Stevie Wonder began recording in 1963, he was only 13 years old. Even then, his talent was evident, although there was no sign of how deep it was. After all, the music was the work of a startlingly gifted child; it was all exuberant flash, with few complexities. Soon, Wonder would go far beyond the infectious energy of "Fingertips (Part 2)." In two years, he became one of Motown's finest artists, recording a series of brilliant singles for a solid nine years, the overwhelming majority of which he wrote himself. During this time, his albums were like other Motown albums—a combination of killer singles and pleasant filler, only Wonder was allowed to record the occasional number that reflected his increasing social consciousness, like his hit version of Bob Dylan's "Blowin' in the Wind." By the end of the '60s, he was not only hitting the charts with his own records, but writing material for many other Motown artists, including the Spinners' "It's a Shame" and co-writing "The Tears of a Clown" with Smokey Robinson.

With his creativity growing by leaps and bounds, Wonder soon felt limited by Motown's strict production and publishing contracts. When his record contract expired in 1971, Wonder recorded two full albums by himself and used them as a bargaining tool during contract negotiations with Motown. The record label gave him total artistic control of his albums, as well as the rights to his own songs. Soon afterwards, the two albums—*Where I'm Coming From* and *Music of My Mind*—were released.

Music of My Mind, especially, helped usher in a new era of soul/R&B. Along with Sly Stone and Marvin Gaye, Wonder was responsible for making soul and R&B albums not just collections of singles, but cohesive artistic statements, where artists could extend their music beyond the confines of a three-minute hit single. With his next two albums, *Talking Book* and *Innervisions*, Wonder's music became richly complex and inventive; in addition to his musical innovations, Wonder's lyrics addressed social and racial issues as eloquently and incisively as any other pop songwriter. Wonder sustained his creative peak through 1974's *Fulfillingness' First Finale* and 1976's *Songs in the Key of Life*.

Three years later, he released the ambitious and bewildering *Journey Through the Secret Life of Plants*, which received terrible reviews upon its release. Wonder released the more straightforward *Hotter than July* in 1980; the album received substantially better reviews and became his first platinum album. However, he wasn't able to sustain that momentum for the rest of the decade. Although his records sold well and he scored the occasional hit—including the smash hit ballad "I Just Called to Say I Love You"—his albums weren't as focused as they were a decade

earlier. By the '90s, he was still an immensely respected musician, but his music was no longer on the cutting edge. —*Stephen Thomas Erlewine*

The 12 Year Old Genius / May 31, 1963 / Motown ✦✦✦
Recorded live, this includes the full seven-minute version of his No. 1 hit "Fingertips." The rest of the album shows him as a young prodigy fixated on Ray Charles; indeed, the final three songs are covers of the early Charles tunes "Hallelujah I Love Her So," "Drown In My Own Tears," and "Don't You Know." A couple jams and a cover of "(I'm Afraid) The Masquerade Is Over" fill out this seven-song LP. —*Richie Unterberger*

Greatest Hits / Mar. 1968 / Motown ✦✦✦✦
When it was released, Stevie Wonder's first hits collection, a 12-track disc tracing his work from 1963 to 1967, served a common function of compilations: it gathered together stray, disparate pieces, from "Fingertip—Pt. 2" to "I Was Made to Love Her," and focused attention on the artist. Wonder had a spotty singles record: five Top Ten hits, but only two of them in succession, over the four and a half years, but *Greatest Hits* made him seem like a consistent hitmaker with an astounding range, from those early harmonica instrumentals to soulful wailers like "Uptight (Everything's Alright)" and even oddball ballads like "A Place in the Sun." By now this set has long since been eclipsed, notably by the *Looking Back* album, but as a demonstration of Wonder's early promise, it is notable. —*William Ruhlmann*

Signed, Sealed & Delivered / Aug. 7, 1970 / Motown ✦✦✦
Stevie Wonder was beginning to rebel against the Motown hit factory mentality in the early '70s. While he certainly hadn't lost his commercial touch, Wonder was anxious to address social concerns, experiment with electronics and not be restricted by radio and marketplace considerations. Still, he gave the label another definitive smash with the title track, while sneaking in a cover of the Beatles' "We Can Work It Out" and penning more intriguing tunes like "I Can't Let My Heaven Walk Away" and "Never Had A Dream Come True." —*Ron Wynn*

Where I'm Coming From / Apr. 12, 1971 / Motown ✦✦✦✦
Released one month before Stevie Wonder's 21st birthday, *Where I'm Coming From* is really his first adult album, and although it was not a massive hit, it anticipated the musical approach of his commercial breakthrough, *Talking Book*, by a year and a half. The lovely "Never Dreamed You'd Leave In Summer," as the B-side to a cover of the Beatles' "We Can Work It Out," has become a Wonder standard, and the album's real hit, "If You Really Love Me" (No.8 pop, No.4 R&B), marked the first rewards of his alliance with then-wife Syreeta Wright. Elsewhere, Wonder, who produced and composed all the tracks, introduced the funky keyboard style that would take him through the next few years, as well as the social concerns that would absorb him later on. This album was a shot across the bow, fair warning that a major, nearly mature talent had arrived. —*William Ruhlmann*

Greatest Hits, Vol. 2 / Oct. 1971 / Motown ✦✦✦
Stevie Wonder's second hits collection, gathering together his singles from 1968 to 1971, traces his development into a virtuoso talent, from upbeat Motown numbers like "For Once In My Life" to the emergence of Wonder's own style in songs like "Never Dreamed You'd Leave In Summer" and "If You Really Love Me." Along the way, he demonstrates an amazingly broad pop sensibility that allows him to handle soul, pop-rock, and ballads, all with equal ease. And, of course, the remarkable thing is that this set was obsolete the day it came out, the summing up of what turned out to be only the first phase of Wonder's remarkable career. This LP has been superseded by the *Looking Back* compilation. —*William Ruhlmann*

Music of My Mind / Mar. 1972 / Motown ✦✦✦✦
When Wonder turned 21 he renegotiated his Motown contract; the key issue was control. Stevie Wonder had a vision that veered far away from that of the Motown hit-making machine. Influenced by the work of Isaac Hayes in 1969 and 1970 and labelmate Marvin Gaye in 1971, Wonder was no longer content with putting out albums that were a collection of two or three hit singles plus filler; he wanted to record full-length albums that had an integrity unto themselves. *Music of My Mind* was the first such effort. Wonder produced, wrote the songs, and played the majority of the instruments. At the time it was a revelation. Compared with Wonder's subsequent efforts, it pales just slightly. —*Rob Bowman*

☆ **Talking Book** / Nov. 1972 / Motown ✦✦✦✦✦
Talking Book is the album that crystallized Wonder as the self-contained singer-songwriter. "Superstition" and "You Are the Sunshine of My Life" were both No.1 singles. The rest of the album maintains an equally torrid level. —*Rob Bowman*

☆ **Innervisions** / Aug. 1973 / Motown ✦✦✦✦✦
For my money, Stevie Wonder's finest moment. Three massive hits, "Higher Ground," "Living for the City," and "Don't You Worry 'Bout a Thing," were drawn from the album. "Golden Lady" and "He's Misstra Know-It-All" could have been equally successful. From the titles alone, one can see that Wonder had developed a social concience and, as many

other singer-songwriters of the time were doing, he politicized his music. Intelligent lyrics that one can boogie to—what more could one want from popular music? —*Rob Bowman*

Fulfillingness' First Finale / Jul. 1974 / Motown ✦✦✦✦
The funky "Boogie on, Reggae Woman" and "You Haven't Done Nothin'" are the high points of this record. Much of the rest of the album is centered around the electric piano, a sound ubiquitous in Black music in the early '70s. Wonder occasionally gets a little syrupy on the non-hit material, although his phrasing is so fine that one tends to be forgiving. —*Rob Bowman*

Songs in the Key of Life / Sep. 1976 / Motown ✦✦✦✦
Wonder the auteur began to get out of hand with this sprawling double album plus four-song-EP set. Much is maudlin, cloying, and pretentious; yet great songs, such as "Sir Duke," rear their heads at various junctures throughout the set. —*Rob Bowman*

★ **Looking Back** / Dec. 1977 / Motown ✦✦✦✦✦
Between 1963 and the end of 1971, Little Stevie Wonder placed 25 songs on *Billboard*'s charts. Twenty-four of those, including such radio staples as "Fingertips—Pt. 2," "Uptight (Everything's Alright)," "I Was Made to Love Her," "For Once in My Life," "My Cherie Amour," and "Signed, Sealed, Delivered, I'm Yours" appear on *Looking Back*. Wonder's recordings in the '60s stand apart from most Motown acts partially because he was paired with producers and writers who very rarely worked with the Temptations, Supremes, et al. In the beginning Wonder was often produced by Clarence Paul and/or William Stevenson; during the golden years Henry Cosby was usually manning the controls. Then in 1970 Wonder started producing himself, beginning with "Signed, Sealed, Delivered." Most of Wonder's singles were written by Wonder himself in tandem with a variety of others, or by Ron Miller. The hits alternated between stomping barnburners and mid-tempo, understated ballads. —*Rob Bowman*

Journey through the Secret Life of Plants / Oct. 1979 / Motown ✦✦✦
Perhaps the most curious album in Stevie Wonder's career, this was ostensibly a soundtrack for a film few people saw (if indeed it was ever released). These were mostly instrumentals, plus a few oddball vocals, but most observers didn't know what to make of it at the time. Wonder was so hot that the record peaked at No. 4 on the pop albums chart, despite the lack of any real singles and confounding almost everyone who heard it. "Outside My Window" was the lone tune to scrape the middle regions of the pop charts, while the R&B community ignored the entire album. —*Ron Wynn*

Hotter Than July / Sep. 1980 / Motown ✦✦✦✦
Hotter Than July was Wonder's real follow-up to *Songs In The Key Of Life*, even if it took him the then-unconscionably long four years to release it. Wonder had been perhaps the most accomplished and successful pop artist of the years 1972-1977, but his absence had cooled him off commercially, and this album demonstrated that, artistically, he was also past his peak. Individual moments suggested his earlier triumphs, and Wonder remained a remarkably facile singer/player/composer, but he had lost his ability to amaze his listeners. The album's biggest single was "Master Blaster (Jammin')" (No.5 pop, No.1 R&B), an adequate but unremarkable reggae number, but the standout track was "Happy Birthday," the theme song for the ultimately successful campaign to make Dr. Martin Luther King, Jr's birthday a national holiday. —*William Ruhlmann*

★ **Original Musiquarium I** / May 1982 / Motown ✦✦✦✦✦
Most of Wonder's chart hits from 1972 through 1982 (although why "You Haven't Done Nothin'" is not here I will never know) are included on *Stevie Wonder's Original Musiquarium I*, plus three newly written and recorded tunes. Simply put, some of the finest Black music made in the '70s. Essential. —*Rob Bowman*

In Square Circle / 1985 / Motown ✦✦✦
Although it went platinum, nothing stands as better evidence of how cyclical the pop experience is than the response to *In Square Circle*. Wonder actually wrote some superb songs, and several, like "Overjoyed" and "I Love You Too Much," were superior to the hit single "Part-Time Lover." But that one zoomed to the top spot and became the album's definitive tune in the minds of many. —*Ron Wynn*

Characters / Nov. 1987 / Motown ✦✦✦
Wonder shocked fans by taking only two years to release his next new non-soundtrack studio album, *Characters*. Unfortunately, it had long since become clear that Wonder was willing to settle for good pop music without challenging himself to make great pop music. And by now, a big chunk of his formerly mass audience had gotten the message: this was Wonder's first new album to miss the pop Top Five in 15 years. (The Black music audience, however, responded far more favorably, as the album topped the R&B charts for seven weeks.) The biggest single was the "Superstition"-like dance track "Skeletons" (No.19 Pop, No.1 R&B), and Wonder also charted with the pretty "You Will Know" and an uptempo duet with Michael Jackson, "Get It." —*William Ruhlmann*

Jungle Fever / May 28, 1991 / Motown ✦✦✦
Despite all of the hype surrounding it, the soundtrack to *Jungle Fever* is Stevie Wonder's best work in years. Although it can't compare to Wonder's glory days, *Jungle Fever* is a considerable improvement from his bland late-'80s albums. Wonder still borders on saccharine on his ballads, although even the sappiest of them ("These Three Words") is never as sickening as "I Just Called to Say I Love You." While the keyboard funk of "Chemical Love," "Gotta Have You" and "Queen in the Black" doesn't sound new, it does sound alive, which is better than Wonder has sounded in years. —*Stephen Thomas Erlewine*

Conversation Peace / Mar. 21, 1995 / Motown ✦✦✦
Stevie Wonder's albums have not caught the public's attention since the mid-'80s and *Conversation Peace* did not change that, although it wasn't for lack of trying. Wonder's gift for melody is still in place and he incorporates understated hip-hop rhythms into his music well, yet he isn't able to make music that fits into the rigid playlists of '90s urban contemporary radio. —*Stephen Thomas Erlewine*

Natural Wonder / Nov. 21, 1995 / Motown ✦✦✦
Following the relative commercial failure of *Conversation Peace*, Stevie Wonder rushed out this double-disc live album drawn from an international tour during which he was backed by different symphony orchestras, his older songs featuring string parts in place of the synthesizer lines. He introduced several new songs—"Dancing to the Rhythm," the instrumental "Stevie Ray Blues," "Stay Gold," and "Ms. & Mr. Little Ones"—which demonstrated that his melodic muse was still with him and that he remained an awkward lyricist when he was more interested in the political stance than the poetical scansion. But for most of the running time, he acted as a human jukebox, pumping out his hits with enthusiasm and humor before an audibly enthralled audience. That made *Natural Wonder* entertaining, but inessential. —*William Ruhlmann*

★ **Song Review: Greatest Hits** / Dec. 10, 1996 / Motown ✦✦✦✦✦
While it's not quite the definitive compilation it could have been, the double-disc *Song Review: Greatest Hits* is still a good overview of Stevie Wonder's long, prolific career. Skipping over "Fingertips, Pt. 2" and picking up with "Uptight (Everything's Alright)" and "I Was Made to Love Her," *Song Review* runs through the next three decades, hitting most of his biggest hits along the way, including "Signed, Sealed, Delivered I'm Yours," "Superstition," "You Are the Sunshine of My Life," "Higher Ground," "Living for the City," "You Haven't Done Nothin'," "I Wish," "Master Blaster (Jammin')," "Ebony and Ivory," "I Just Called to Say I Love You," and "Part-Time Lover." Unfortunately, none of the songs are presented in chronological order. It begins in the '80s, switches to the '70s, and hits the '80s again before going back to the '60s—in other words, it's not really coherent. Nevertheless, it is a good cross-section of his very best songs, making *Song Review* a fine, but not perfect, introduction to his career. —*Stephen Thomas Erlewine*

Brenton Wood

b. Jun. 26, 1941, Shreveport, LA
Vocals / Soul
Brenton Wood's charmingly unpredictable phrasing and his infectious sense of good times made the smooth uptown soul of "The Oogum Boogum Song" and "Gimme Little Sign" into hits in 1967. Despite his skill as a pop-soul vocalist, Wood was never able to match such heights again, yet those two songs became genuine R&B classics of their era.

Born Alfred Jesse Smith in Shreveport, Louisiana, Brenton Wood moved west to San Pedro, California as a child. After learning how to play piano, he began forming vocal groups, inspired by Sam Cooke and Jesse Belvin. One of these groups, Little Freddie and the Rockets, recorded a single in 1958. While he was studying at Compton College, he assumed the name Brenton Wood, naming himself after his home county. Wood formed the Quotations during college, but soon after graduation he became a solo act. Signing with Double Shot Records, Wood had a hit single in the spring of 1967 with "The Oogum Boogum Song," which reached No. 19 on the R&B charts and No. 34 pop. It was quickly followed by "Gimme Little Sign," which climbed to No. 9 pop and matched its predecessor's R&B position. It was a promising start to a career, but Wood wasn't able to follow it thorugh. "Baby You Got It" stalled in the bottom reaches of the pop and R&B Top 40 in early 1968 and "Some Got It, Some Don't" failed to make the pop charts later that year. Wood continued to perform and even recorded a duet with Shirley Goodman, but he wasn't able to reach the charts again until 1977, when "Come Softly to Me" registered in the lower reaches of the R&B Top 100. Following its release, Wood faded away, becoming part of the oldies soul circuit. —*Stephen Thomas Erlewine*

● **Brenton Wood's 18 Best** / 1991 / Original Sound ✦✦✦✦
Probably the best collection of Brenton Wood, one of the few voices that rival Sam Cooke's in both quality and content. This collection of 18 songs includes all the hits and shows what a great singer this underappreciated artist is. Songs like "Gimme Little Sign,""Oogum Boogum,"

and "Baby You Got It" most of us know. But lesser known songs like "I'm the One Who Knows," "Catch You on the Rebound," and "Two Time Loser" make for some great listening. — *Michael Erlewine*

Ron Wood

b. Jun. 1, 1947, Hillingdon, London
Guitar / Rock 'n' Roll
UK guitarist Ron Wood has spent most of his career in groups—the Creation, the Jeff Beck Group, Faces, and, since 1976, the Rolling Stones—but he's found time to make a variety of non-group albums, including duet albums with Ronnie Lane and with Bo Diddley, and even a few solo albums that serve as assemblages of his friends. — *William Ruhlmann*

I've Got My Own Album to Do / 1974 / Warner Brothers ✦✦✦✦
For his first album, Ron Wood enlisted Keith Richards and the Faces' pianist Ian McLagan as support and turned in a loose, good-humored album that catches fire on the swaggering "Take a Look at the Guy," the earnest cover of "If You Gotta Make a Fool of Somebody," and the grinding R&B workout "Crotch Music." — *Stephen Thomas Erlewine*

Now Look / 1975 / Warner Brothers ✦✦✦✦
Now Look, Ron Wood's second solo album, was a tighter affair than his debut, yet it lost none of its predecessor's off-the-cuff charm, thanks to convincing, ragged covers of Ann Peeble's "I Can't Stand the Rain" and "I Got Lost When I Found You," which was written by the album's producer, Bobby Womack. — *Stephen Thomas Erlewine*

Mahoney's Last Stand / 1976 / Atco ✦✦✦
● **Gimme Some Neck** / 1979 / Columbia ✦✦✦✦
Wood leads a pickup band that includes, on various cuts, fellow Rolling Stones Charlie Watts, Mick Jagger, and Keith Richards, plus Mick Fleetwood, Dave Mason, and other notables. The highlight is a then-unreleased Bob Dylan song called "Seven Days," where the rough-voiced Wood sounds uncannily like Mr. D himself. — *William Ruhlmann*

1234 / 1981 / CBS ✦✦

Slide on This / Sep. 1992 / Continuum ✦✦✦
Ron Wood's first solo album in over ten years is a relaxed, rocking, star-studded affair, including appearances by Charlie Watts, Hothouse Flowers, Joe Elliott from Def Leppard, and the Edge. Nothing here is earth-shaking, but the quality of "Knock Yer Teeth Out," "Show Me," and a cover of the Parliaments' "Testify" makes *Slide on This* Wood's best solo album. — *AMG*

Slide on Live / 1994 / Continuum ✦✦
A document of an energetic live show, *Live at the Ritz* is an enjoyable but inconsequential record. — *Stephen Thomas Erlewine*

Roy Wood

b. Nov. 8, 1946, Birmingham, England
Bass, Guitar, Horn, Keyboards, Vocals, Wind, Multi Instruments / Art-Rock/Progressive-Rock, Pop-Rock
Roy Wood, born Ulysses Adrian Wood in Birmingham, England, has long been regarded as one of the most important, if eccentric, rock musicians to have come out of that city, primarily for his role as the leader/cofounder of both the Move and the Electric Light Orchestra.

Wood took up the guitar in his early teens and the first "successful" band of which he was a member was Gerry Levene and the Avengers, which actually got to record a single. They broke up in mid-1964, and Wood joined Mike Sheridan and the Nightriders. During this period, Wood attended the Moseley College of Art, from which he was expelled in 1964. That same year, he organized the Move, with Bev Bevan (drums), Carl Wayne (lead vocals), Ace Kefford (bass), and Trevor Burton (guitar). The band was fortunate enough to land a residency at London's Marquee Club, where they began to build an enthusiastic following.

Wood contributed most of the songs and eventually many of the vocals to the Move. Their single "Night of Fear" rose to No. 2 on the UK charts in early 1967. The group evolved over the ensuing three years, eventually becoming a quartet. Later, the group added guitarist Jeff Lynne and passed through psychedelic, progressive, and heavy metal phases. Albums such as *Shazam*, *Message from the Country*, and *Looking On* were popular in England but virtually unknown in America. Their sound not only embraced old time rock 'n' roll, including Duane Eddy and even some doo wop influences, but also displayed Beatles-style harmonies and lyrical complexity.

By 1971, Wood had developed ideas and ambitions that were too wide to be embraced by any one band, and proposed the formation of an off-shoot of the Move called the Electric Light Orchestra. The group's eponymous debut was released on the Harvest label in England to strong critical approval and decent sales—indeed, the new band seemed to attract more serious attention than the Move had been getting. Originally ELO and the Move were to have existed side-by-side, but ELO supplanted the Move, and the latter ceased to exist. Wood exited soon after,

leaving ELO in the hands of Lynne and Bevan, while Wood went off to form Wizzard.

Wizzard's first single, "Ballpark Incident," combined the Move's hard rock with a texture reminiscent of Phil Spector's "wall of sound" productions, and rose to No. 6 on the British charts. In April of 1973, Wizzard reached No. 1 with "See My Baby Jive." Unfortunately, the band's first album, *Wizzard's Brew*, didn't fare nearly as well, being a highly experimental body of work. The group's fortunes, even as a singles band, faltered after this, partly because of Wood's decision to continue recording and releasing records under his own name in addition to his work with Wizzard. His Phil Spector-ish "I Wish It Could Be Christmas Everyday" reached No. 4 in England in 1973, and "Forever" made it to No. 8 the same year. The Wizzard albums *See My Baby Jive* and *Eddie & the Falcons* were both critical and commercial failures, and the unsuccessful release of the latter led to the demise of the group. Meanwhile, Wood's own solo albums, *Boulders* (1970) and *Mustard* (1975), were too idiosyncratic to achieve major followings.

The Roy Wood Story (Harvest), released in 1976, summed up his career with EMI Records, and performed well as a best-of. His subsequent records, *On the Road* (1979) and *Starting Up* (1987) failed to achieve anything like the success of his early-'70s work, and since then Wood has become one of the more elusive active musicians of his generation, although he has continued to record into the 1990s. — *Bruce Eder*

Boulders / 1973 / BGO ✦✦✦✦
Wood's solo albums are a mixed lot, mostly thanks to the sheer diversity of sound that he's comfortable dealing with. *Boulders* is his best solo work to date, a strangely offbeat, hard-rocking yet progressive, lush yet minimalist-sounding work that encompasses all of Wood's influences, from Duane Eddy to the Beatles to classical music's late-19th-century Romanticism. — *Bruce Eder*

16 Greats from '70s / Feb. 6, 1996 / Griffin Music ✦✦✦✦

Through the Years: The Best of Roy Wood / 1997 / EMI ✦✦✦✦

● **The Roy Wood Years 1971-73 You Can Dance the Rock 'n Roll** / EMI/Harvest ✦✦✦✦
The finest compilation of Wood's work to date, drawing on his closing years with the Move, his sole album with ELO, the biggest hits of Wizzard, and Wood's official solo albums and singles. — *Bruce Eder*

The Woodentops

f. 1983, Northhampton, England, db. 1992
Alternative Pop-Rock
Taking punk's D.I.Y. ideals and applying it to stripped-down acoustic pop, the Woodentops achieved a great deal of critical success in the short time they were together. Formed in the early '80s in Northhampton, England, the group consisted of Rolo McGinty (vocals, guitar), Frank de Freitas (bass), Simon Mawby (guitar), Benny Staples (drums), and Alice Thompson (keyboards). The band released their debut single "Plenty" on Food Records; the record led to a contract with Rough Trade. Throughout 1985, the Woodentops released a series of singles, all written by McGinty, that began to attract an audience in the UK. The group released their acclaimed debut album, *Giant*, in 1986. The following year, the band began experimenting with their sound, adding tougher guitars and electronics. These changes were particularly evident in their live show, as shown by their 1987 live recording, *Hypno-Beat*. Featuring the contributions of professional studio musicians Bernie Worrell and Doug Wimbish among others, 1988's *Wooden Foot Cops on the Highway* continued the group's experimentations with rhythmic and sonic textures.

While the band managed to keep creative, they weren't able to gain much of an audience anywhere outside Japan. In 1991 and 1992, they toured the world without ever becoming any bigger than a cult band. Soon after, the Woodentops broke up. — *Stephen Thomas Erlewine*

Well Well Well: The Unabridged Singles Collection / 1986 / Upside ✦✦✦✦
While the Woodentops' music obliquely shows influences as diverse as Devo, Talking Heads, and 1950s rockabilly (this last sped up to double, even triple time), they are primarily a pure pop band—perhaps the most manic one ever. This album, a collection of early singles and B-sides, is their most diverse. "Move Me," "Get It On," and the title cut are all itchy, frantic, and wonderful pop tunes with more raw energy than a roomful of hyperactive toddlers. "It Will Come" exhibits a broader-breathed line than the other selections of this type, while "Do It Anyway" ratchets the tempo even faster to a truly dizzying speed. The other three numbers (all B-sides) are totally unlike anything else in the band's oeuvre. All are highly experimental pop-derived numbers with definite psychedelic touches, imaginatively produced and quite lengthy. The standout track of these three is "Steady Steady," a chilling, reverb-drenched song about terminal illness with ominous bass/low synthesizer underpinnings and imaginatively tasteful use of guitar feedback that sounds like screaming. This is an excellent release well worth hearing. — *David Cleary*

● **Giant** / 1986 / Columbia ✦✦✦✦
This album, the group's best, explores a wide range of variations on the band's signature manic pop style, here adding occasional marimba, trumpet, accordion, and strings to the mix. The nervous single "Get It On" is presented in an intricately redone version, an improvement over its appearance on *Well Well Well*. Other great jittery numbers here include the frantic "Love Train" and "Travelling Man," as well as the stun-level manic "Shout" and "Hear Me James." The mid-tempo numbers here are generally excellent, especially the warmly expressive "Good Thing" and the lovely, loping "Give It Time." "Last Time" is a sadly yearning number with some odd touches that nearly undermine its mood, while "So Good Today" is a breezy, accordion-dominated selection that shamelessly flirts with wimpiness and only partially escapes. "Everything Breaks" manages to combine martial drums, funk guitar touches, a ringing arrangement, and production-number aspirations into one very effective package. There are also two songs that are just plain wacky fun, the nerdy Devo-inspired number "History" and the hiccuping fiddle-flecked song "Love Affair with Everyday Living." Production values here are utterly inspired. If you like pure, bouncy pop, you'll love this release. —*David Cleary*

Hypno Beat Live / 1987 / Virgin ✦✦
This release catches the group in live performance at Los Angeles' Palace Theatre in November 1986. Most of the material given here consists of tracks from the album *Giant* and some early singles. Recording quality is good, though the group's onstage sound mix is rather opaque, obscuring some of the band's subtle touches; backing vocals, keyboards, and acoustic guitars in particular tend to get swallowed up on this recording at times. Many of the songs are given at an unbelievable breakneck speed, even faster than on corresponding studio releases. On rare occasions, such mania results in garbled lead vocals or finger-tied keyboard playing, but by and large, the sheer visceral sweep of these performances proves to be bracing. Most interesting here is the arrangement of "Everyday Living"; this buoyantly frothy album track from *Giant*, when performed at a faster tempo and without violin, becomes a surprisingly primitive and driven number. This platter is an intriguing listen, recommended especially to fans of this unusual band. Note that different review sources give slightly different titles to this album—to this reviewer, it appears most correctly to be *Live Hypno Beat Live*. —*David Cleary*

Wooden Foot Cops on the Highway / 1988 / Columbia ✦✦
The Woodentops' last album to date shows the group experimenting with different styles in their own eccentrically nervous way. "They Can Say What They Want" is best described as infectiously nerdy funk, while "Wheels Turning" is a lengthy song that's as close to a danceable number as the group ever produced. "In a Dream" is a manic, poppish, rap-tinged number, while "You Make Me Feel" is a capable selection that exhibits discreet country influences. Other experiments are less successful. "Heaven" is a slow, synthesizer-dominated number with gospel touches that is marred by a haphazardly jumbled text setting. "Tuesday Wednesday" is a bizarre folkish number with mild Latin coloration and odd beeping interjections. "What You Give Out" is a barely disguised ripoff of the Talking Heads song "The Great Curve"—listenable, to be sure, but unbelievably derivative. For those hoping to find attractively manic, pure pop numbers like those on prior releases, there are two excellent examples here, "Maybe It Won't Last" and "Stop the Car." Production values are again intricate and often clever, though at times they seem at cross purposes with the musical mood the band is trying to create. This album is not bad, though not on a par with previous releases. —*David Cleary*

World Party

f. 1986, London, England
Alternative Pop-Rock, Pop-Rock
World Party began as an outlet for the pop infatuations of vocalist and multi-instrumentalist Karl Wallinger, previously best known for his tenure with the Waterboys. Born October 19, 1957 in Prestatyn, Wales, Wallinger grew up enamored not only of the Beatles but also of the Motown and Merseybeat sounds, and made his professional debut in 1976 as a member of the group Quasimodo. (Years later, after Wallinger had exited to move to London to work as a clerk for ATV/Northern Songs, Quasimodo evolved into the Alarm.)

Following a tenure as the musical director of a West End performance of *The Rocky Horror Picture Show*, Wallinger joined a funk band dubbed the Out before signing on with Mike Scott's Waterboys in 1984 to record the LP *A Pagan Place*. After 1985's superb *This Is the Sea*, Wallinger amicably departed to form World Party, a one-man project heavily indebted to *Revolver*-era Beatlesque pop; recorded in Wallinger's home studio, the 1987 debut *Private Revolution* scored a Top 40 hit with the infectious lead single "Ship of Fools."

After a long layoff (during which time Wallinger aided Sinead O'Connor in recording her 1988 debut *The Lion and the Cobra*), World Party

returned in 1990 with *Goodbye Jumbo*, another successful collection offering the minor hits "Way Down Now" and "Put the Message in the Box." After the 1991 stop gap EP *Thank You World* (including a cover of the Beatles' "Happiness Is a Warm Gun"), Wallinger recruited guitarist Dave Caitlin-Birch and drummer Chris Sharrock as full-fledged members for 1993's *Bang!*, which reached the No. 2 position on the British album charts. —*Jason Ankeny*

Private Revolution / Mar. 1987 / Ensign ✦✦✦✦
This debut album from World Party is a solid release, even if it is a bit heavy on the synthesized sounds (what can you expect from a one-man band?). Wallinger's insightful songs deal primarily with the responsibility of the individual to recognize and cope with the problems of the world. Features mainly original songs like "Private Revolution," "World Party," and "It's All Mine," as well as a cover of Dylan's "All I Really Want to Do," which remains surprisingly true to the original version. —*Iotis Erlewine*

● **Goodbye Jumbo** / Apr. 1990 / Ensign ✦✦✦✦
This excellent follow-up album from World Party is much tighter than the debut. Dealing with issues from the environment ("Take It Up," "Put the Message in the Box") to relationship woes ("And I Fell Back Alone"), these tracks manage to maintain a hopeful, positive mood without becoming trivial. In these songs, Wallinger has developed his own distinct style. A great album, worth checking out just for the uptempo groove of "Way Down Now." —*Iotis Erlewine*

Bang! / Apr. 20, 1993 / Capitol ✦✦✦
On his previous releases, Wallinger has displayed a social conscience, but never has it taken prominence like it does on *Bang!*, World Party's third album. *Bang!* does contain some glorious music that equals his masterpiece *Goodbye Jumbo*, but the album slows down when he tries to say too much (as in the quasi-operatic "And God Said"). Even then, Wallinger's preaching doesn't obliterate the considerable pleasures of the music. Wallinger has often been accused of recycling the Beatles, but the truth is that he can combine the Beatles, Beach Boys, Sly Stone, Dylan, and Prince into a musical style that is distinctive and unique yet familiar. *Bang!*, for all of its shortcomings, is as strong an album as any Wallinger has released. —*Stephen Thomas Erlewine*

Link Wray

b. 1930, Dunn, NC
Guitar / Rock 'n' Roll, Instrumental Rock
Link Wray may never get into the Rock & Roll Hall of Fame, but his contribution to the language of rockin' guitar would still be a major one, even if he had never walked into another studio after cutting "Rumble." Quite simply, Link Wray invented the power chord, the major modus operandi of modern rock guitarists. Listen to any of the tracks he recorded between that landmark instrumental in 1958 through his Swan recordings in the early 1960s and you'll hear the blueprints for heavy metal, thrash, you name it. Though rock historians always like to draw a nice, clean line between the distorted electric guitar work that fuels early blues records to the late-'60s Hendrix-Clapton-Beck-Page-Townshend mob, with no stops in between, a quick spin of any of the sides Link recorded during *his* golden decade punches holes in that theory right quick. If a direct line from a black blues musician crankin' up his amp and playing with a ton of violence and aggression can be traced to a young, White guy doing a mutated form of same, the line points straight to Link Wray, no contest. Pete Townshend summed it up for more guitarists than he probably realized when he said, "He is the king; if it hadn't been for Link Wray and 'Rumble,' I would have never picked up a guitar." Everything that was handed down to today's current crop of headbangers from the likes of Led Zeppelin and the Who can be traced back to the guy from Dunn, North Carolina, who started out in 1955 recording for Starday as a member of Lucky Wray and the Palomino Ranch Hands. You see, back in the early '50s, it was a different ballgame altogether. Rock 'n' roll hadn't become a national event yet, and if you were young and White and wanted to be in the music business, you had two avenues for possible career moves. You could be a pop-mush crooner like Perry Como or a hillbilly singer like the late Hank Williams, and that was about it. With country music all around him as a youth in North Carolina, the choice was obvious; Wray joined forces with his brothers Vernon and Doug, forming Lucky Wray and the Lazy Pine Wranglers, later changing it to the spiffier-sounding Palomino Ranch Hands. By the end of 1955, they had relocated outside of Washington, D.C. and added Shorty Horton on bass. With Link, Horton, and brothers Doug and Vernon ("Lucky," named after his gambling fortunes) handling drums and lead vocals respectively, they fell in with some local songwriters, and the results made it to vinyl as an EP on the local Kay label, with the rest of the sides being leased to Starday Records down in Texas.

But by 1958, the music had changed, and so had Wray's life. With a lung missing from a bout with tuberculosis during his stint in the Korean War, the doctor had advised him to let brother Vernon do all the vocalizing. So Link started stretching out more and more on the guitar, coming up with one instrumental after another. By this time, the band had sweated down to a trio, and changed its name to the Ray-Men. After a brief flirtation as a teen idol—changing his name to Ray Vernon—the third Wray brother became the group's producer/manager.

Armed with a 1953 Gibson Les Paul, a dinky Premier amp, an Elvis sneer and a black leather jacket, Link started playing the local record hops around the D.C. area with disc jockey Milt Grant, who became his de facto manager. One night during a typical set, says Link, "They wanted me to play a stroll. I didn't know any, so I made one up. I made up 'Rumble.'"

Originally issued on Archie Bleyer's Cadence label back in 1958, Bleyer was ready to pass on it when his daughter expressed excitement for the primitive instrumental, saying how it reminded her of the rumble scenes in *West Side Story*. Bleyer renamed it (what its original title was back then, if any, is now lost to the mists of time), and "Rumble" jumped to No.16 on the national charts, despite the fact that it was banned from the radio in several markets (including New York City), becoming Link's signature tune to this day. But despite the success and notoriety of "Rumble," it turned out to be Link's only release on Cadence. Bleyer, under attack for putting out a record that was "promoting teenage gang warfare," wanted to clean Link and the boys up a bit, sending them down to Nashville to cut their next session with the Everly Brothers' production team calling the shots. The Wrays didn't see it that way, so they immediately struck a deal with Epic Records. Link's followup to "Rumble" was the pounding, uptempo "Rawhide." The Les Paul had been swapped for a Danelectro Longhorn model (with the longest neck ever manufactured on a production line guitar), its "lipstick tube" pickups making every note of Link's power chords sound like he was strumming with a tin can lid for a pick. The beat and sheer blister of it all was enough to get it up to No.23 on the national charts, and every kid who wore a black leather jacket and owned a hot rod had to have it.

But a pattern was emerging that would continue throughout much of Link's early career; the powers that be figured that if they could tone him down and dress him up, they'd sell way more records in the bargain. What all these producers and record execs failed to realize was the simplest of truths: if Duane Eddy twanged away for white, teenage America, Link Wray played for juvenile delinquent hoods, plain and simple. By the end of 1960, Wray found himself in the mucho-confining position of recording with full orchestras, doing dreck like "Danny Boy" and "Claire De Lune." But when these gems failed to chart as well, relations with Epic came to a close, and by year's end, Link and Vern formed their own label, Rumble Records.

Rumble's three lone issues included the original version of Wray's next big hit, "Jack the Ripper." If "Rumble" sounded like gang warfare, then "Jack the Ripper" sounded like a high-speed car chase, which is exactly what it became in the movie soundtrack for the Richard Gere version of *Breathless*. Link's amp was recorded at the end of a hotel staircase for maximum echo effect, while he pumped riffs through it that would become the seeds of a million metal songs. After kicking up noise locally for a couple of years, it was going through another period of disc jockey spins when Swan Records of Philadelphia picked it up and got it nationwide attention. Certainly Wray was at his most prolific during his tenure with Swan, and label president Bernie Binnick gave Link and Vernon pretty much free reign to do what they wanted. Turning the family chicken coop into a crude, three-track studio, the Wray family spent the next decade recording, experimenting with sounds and styles. At least now they could succeed—or fail—on their own terms. Most of these sides were leased out as one-shot deals to a zillion microscopic labels under a variety of names like the Moon Men, the Spiders, the Fender Benders, etc. What fueled this period of maximum creativity is open to debate. A lot of it had to do with the fact that Link and the boys honed their particular brand of rockin' mayhem working some of the grimiest joints on the face of the planet when these tracks were cut. When Swan label chief Bernie Binnick was questioned as to how he could issue such wild-ass material, he would smile, throw his hands up in the air and say, "What can you do with an animal like that?"

As the new decade dawned, Link's sound and image was updated for the hippie marketplace. Link's career fortunes waxed and waned throughout the '70s, a muddle of albums in a laidback style doing little to enhance his reputation. After a stint backing '70s rockabilly Robert Gordon, Link went solo again, taking most of Gordon's band (including drummer Anton Fig) with him. But if the studio sides were a bit uneven, (Wray recorded several albums in the '80s backed by nothing more than a clumsy drum machine), he still could pack a wallop live, and his rare forays on the stages of the world spread the message that rock 'n' roll's original wild guitar man still had plenty of gas left in the tank. These days Link lives in Denmark, recording the stray album for the foreign market, still capable of strapping on a guitar and making it sound nastier than anyone in their 60s has a right to. Too old to rock and roll? The evidence indicates otherwise. —*Cub Koda*

Missing Links, Vol. 1: Hillbilly Wolf / 1990 / Norton ✦✦✦✦
Unlike many early cult rock 'n' roll greats, Link Wray recorded dozens upon dozens of sides that are good (and diverse) enough to make the search for his rarities worthwhile. This is the first volume of a three-part series of way-obscure sides from his early days, some previously unreleased. Some, indeed, aren't credited to Link himself, though he plays a prominent role on the tracks here credited to Lucky Wray (actually Link's brother Vern), Ray Vernon, the Wraymen, and Marvin Rainwater. Much of this is as unhoned as early rockabilly and instrumental rock got, the mid-'50s exposing Wray's hillbilly roots like raw nerve endings. It's a fine collection, worth getting if you have enough interest in Link to fish beyond a best-of compilation. —*Richie Unterberger*

Missing Links, Vol. 2: Big City After Dark / 1990 / Norton ✦✦✦
A mix of super-rare cuts, a couple of unissued outtakes, and live material, all from the 1960s. It's rawer than Link's norm (which is durned raw indeed), but not necessarily any less exciting than all but the best of his material in wide circulation. "Big City After Dark" and "Rawhide '63," for instance, have some of the best Wray string-bending you're likely to hear; "Hold It" is pre-Beatle garage rock at its most ferocious. This compilation gets a slightly lower rating than its companion volumes in the *Missing Links* series because the live material that takes up most of side two is of a somewhat lower standard than the other rarities, in both musical quality and audio fidelity. —*Richie Unterberger*

Missing Links, Vol. 3: Some Kinda Nut / 1990 / Norton ✦✦✦✦
Another great grab bag of hideously rare Link, all from the 1960s on this volume, including tracks that Wray issued under his own name, and side projects that he lent his guitar to (by the Fender Benders, Moon Men, and Bunker Hill). "Baby Doll" and "Please Please Me" are surprisingly cool fusions of Wray raunch with Merseybeat; the primitive late-'60s recordings from the rare *Yesterday and Today* LP were some of his most menacing cuts ever. On the lighter side are the hot rod-flavored instros by the Fender Benders, and the wild R&B/rock outings of Bunker Hill, a singer that Link backed who made Little Richard sound like Ricky Nelson. —*Richie Unterberger*

Walkin' with Link / Apr. 1992 / Epic ✦✦✦✦
After cutting the anthemic instrumental "Rumble" for Cadence Records, Link took his followup "Rawhide" over to Epic Records and this 20-track compilation is the most excellent distillation of his tenure at the label. Although the honchos at Columbia were trying their level best to tame Link down for mass consumption (Duane Eddy twanged for White teenage America; Link Wray played for hoods). Fortunately here we're spared having to hear "seemed like a good idea at the time" atrocities like "Trail Of The Lonesome Pine" and "Clare De Lune" in favor of 20 tracks of solid rockin' mayhem. Casual fans who only think of Wray as a wild-ass guitarist (his tone on the title track is pure, de-tuned, hacking filth) will be very surprised to find that rebel nature also applies to his vocal cords on such raucous outings as Jimmy Reed's "Ain't That Lovin' You Baby" (in two different takes here), Ray Charles' "Mary Anne," and the previously unissued rocker "Oh Babe Be Mine." This compilation may lack some of the big hits that a best-of collection would have to offer (thus denying it first-purchase status), but as another essential piece in building the perfect Link Wray (or rock 'n' roll guitar gods) collection, one would be very hard pressed to imagine it *not* residing in the pile. Link at his best, and that's just about as wild and crazy as original rock 'n' roll guitar gets. —*Cub Koda*

★ **Rumble! The Best of Link Wray** / May 18, 1993 / Rhino ✦✦✦✦✦
Finally, a multi-label Link Wray collection spanning his lengthy career is available. Starting, appropriately enough, with "Rumble," *Rumble! The Best of Link Wray* illustrates through its 20 tracks (15 on cassette) that Wray was indeed one of the pioneering guitarists of rock 'n' roll, expanding the sonic possibilites of the instrument with a variety of effects. All of the tracks feature some truly warped, genius-caliber fretboard work from Wray, and a few also feature his equally demented vocals. *Rumble! The Best of Link Wray* is the definitive Wray collection. —*Stephen Thomas Erlewine*

Mr. Guitar / Jun. 20, 1995 / Norton ✦✦✦✦
While Link cut some great records in the late '50s and early '60s, he really reached his peak during his stay with the Swan label in the early and mid-'60s. This double-CD, 63-song set documents this period with as much thoroughness as anyone is likely to attempt, including great singles like "Jack The Ripper," "Mr. Guitar," "Ace Of Spades," and "The Fat Back," where Link let loose with his dirtiest and most groundbreaking fuzz tones. Including quite a few rarities and tracks that were never previously released in the US, as well as a good number of vocal performances (which were never Wray's forte), this is perhaps too exhaustive for the average fan. A single-disc distillation of his best Swan sides would be absolutely killer, but this is still one of the greatest collections of instrumental rock out there, despite its unevenness. —*Richie Unterberger*

Guitar Preacher: The Polydor Years / Aug. 22, 1995 / Polydor ✦✦✦
Wray's image as leather-clad, fuzz-drenched cowpunk is so indelibly etched into the minds of most fans that it's been convenient to overlook the fact that in the early '70s, he eschewed grungy instrumentals for laidback, homespun roots-rock. He wrote lyrics and sang on these albums as well, some of which were recorded in a three-track studio built in a converted chicken coop on his family farm. Reflecting the pastoral, rural influence of the Band and other groups of the day, Link also largely abandoned his electric guitars for acoustic ones on some of the albums, though he returned to harder-rocking electric sounds by the middle of the 1970s. This double-CD box set collects 37 songs from 5 albums spanning 1971 to 1974. One of these LPs only surfaced in England (*Beans and Fatback*), and another was an odd effort by one Mordecai Jones on which Link played most of the instruments and wrote most of the material. The anthology rightfully emphasizes his self-titled 1971 comeback album, the best of these recordings, which has an enigmatic backwoods ambience and spiritual lyrics, and contains a couple tunes later covered by the Nevilles ("Fire and Brimstone" and "Fallin' Rain"). The later albums, some of which featured high-profile guests like Jerry Garcia and Tower of Power, had a more generic early '70s AOR rock feel; not so on the Mordecai Jones tracks, though, on which rustic arrangements back Jones' vocals, which sound like a more subdued Robert Plant. As a whole, the work assembled here isn't nearly as important as Wray's instrumental recordings from the '50s and '60s—and Wray's wracked, tense vocals are something of an acquired taste—but it's rather intriguing stuff with little relationship to the rest of his catalog. —*Richie Unterberger*

Missing Links, Vol. 4: Streets of Chicago / 1997 / Norton ✦✦✦
Considering Norton had already issued no less than three previous Link Wray rarities volumes (in addition to a 63-song CD with entirely different material from the 1960s), it's a bit of a miracle that they even managed to assemble enough material for a fourth installment. Only one of these songs (a version of "Lillian" from the *Great Guitar Hits* LP) has been released before. As you would expect, at this point the well is starting to run a little dry, though this 17-track compilation of stray items from the early and mid-'60s has its moments. The studio outtakes are mostly original, with detours into covers of Gene Vincent and Elvis; they're typical Wray guitar-grinders, with occasional vocals, but not as compelling as his greatest material. There are also half a dozen live recordings, including more Elvis covers and versions of classics like "Rumble" and "Ace of Spades"; the performances on these are suitably energetic, though the fidelity is average at best, and rather poor at worst. The best track is probably "Bluebeard," an early demo of a growling instrumental that ended up being retitled "Mustang" for its official release. For those of us who love the Linkster, this is a worthwhile disc, but even more than the previous *Missing Links* volumes, its appeal is limited to aficionados. —*Richie Unterberger*

Wreckless Eric

b. Newhaven, Sussex, England
Guitar, Vocals / Rock 'n' Roll, New Wave, Pub Rock
Wreckless Eric gained notoriety as part of Stiff Records' highly eccentric roster of punk and new wave artists during the late '70s. With his whiny, slurred cockney voice, Eric couldn't carry a tune, but that didn't prevent him from being an enjoyable, if limited, rock 'n' roller. With his early Stiff singles "Whole Wide World," "Semaphore Signals," and "Take the Cash (K.A.S.H.)," Eric bashed out a series of ragged, chaotic, three-chord punk-pop singles driven by his pent-up energy and a knack for melodic pop hooks. Wreckless Eric never had a big pop hit, but his engaging sense of humor and fondness for simple rock 'n' roll helped make him a cult figure that continued to have a following into the '90s.

Born Eric Goulden in Newhaven, Sussex, England, Wreckless Eric became interested in music through the pub-rock scene of the mid-'70s. Once punk emerged in the late '70s, he became attracted to its amateurish sense of freedom, and his music soon reflected his fascination with the music. Stiff Records signed him in 1977, and had Nick Lowe produce Eric's debut single, "Whole Wide World" / "Semaphore Singles." In addition to producing the record, Lowe played most of the instruments on the single. "Whole Wide World" received positive reviews and became a moderate hit in the punk underground, but what made Wreckless Eric infamous were his performances on the *Live Stiffs* package tours. On both of the *Live Stiff* tours, Eric earned headlines in the UK press for his ridiculous drunken antics, which occurred as frequently onstage as they did behind the scenes. His 1978 eponymous debut had the same boozy sense of charm, but his second album, *The Wonderful World of Wreckless Eric* (1979), demonstrated a previously unknown musical versatility. However, the album didn't receive much attention after its release, primarily because Stiff was concentrating their efforts on Ian Dury and Madness, as well as a variety of half-baked marketing schemes. Wreckless Eric fashioned his third album, *Big Smash*, as a commercial break-

through, but the record was poorly-received and neglected by Stiff, prompting him to quit the music industry in the early '80s.

After spending several years in retirement, Wreckless Eric returned to music in 1985 with Captains of Industry, a group he formed with several former members of Ian Dury's Blockheads. The group released a record called *A Roomful of Monkeys* on Go! Discs before disbanding. The following year, Eric formed the Len Bright Combo with bassist Russ Wilikins and drummer Bruce Brand, who had both played with the Milkshakes. The Len Bright Combo released two albums in 1986 before disbanding. Shortly after the group's breakup, Eric moved to France, where he reelased *Le Beat Group Electrique* in 1989. By the early '90s, Wreckless Eric had developed a more subdued pop direction which was often compared to that of Jonathan Richman. Throughout the '90s, he released records and performed in France, occasionally venturing to England and other parts of Europe. —*Stephen Thomas Erlewine*

Wreckless Eric / 1978 / Stiff/Repertoire ✦✦✦
Wreckless Eric's eponymous debut is a ragged, endearing collection of crude rock 'n' roll. In a way, crude doesn't even begin to describe Eric's music. A muddle of scratchy guitars, pounding drumming and snarled, indecipherable vocals, the record is pure, primal garage rock in the oldfashioned sense. Although Wreckless Eric has the demeanor of a punk, his music is straight out rock 'n' roll in the old-fashioned sense—there are even saxophones and organs popping out of the mix. What makes *Wreckless Eric* such fun is its combination of catchy hooks, spirited playing, and downright rudeness. Only a handful of songs are fully-formed, and those—"Whole Wide World" and Ian Dury's "Rough Kids"—are punk-inflected pub-rock classics, pure pop songs in every sense of the term. The remainder are off-kilter, idiosyncratic pop songs—about everything from "Personal Hygiene" and "Waxworks" to "Telephoning Home" and "Brain Thieves"—performed with sloppy, drunken abandon. Too punk for pub-rockers, too straightforward for punk and too weird for everybody else, Wreckless Eric's debut album is one of the small gems of the punk era. —*Stephen Thomas Erlewine*

Tge The Wonderful World of Wreckless Eric / Nov. 1978 / Stiff ✦✦✦✦
Wreckless Eric had already begun to tire of Stiff's promotion of him as a drunken rebellious lout by the time of his second album, *The Wonderful World of Wreckless Eric*. He hadn't grown strong enough to break free of Stiff's hold, but he was able to clean up his sound enough for *The Wonderful World* to make his music slightly more accessible—which means it just doesn't sound as messy as his debut. Wreckless Eric still has an odd, idiosyncratic point of view, but the sound is streamlined enough to make his snarls and growls palatable. Also, his hooks are getting stronger overall, and while only "Take the Cash" is on the level of "Whole Wide World," the rest of the record is comprised of rockers (and two pointless covers of Tommy Roe and Buddy Holly) that are quite enjoyable. —*Stephen Thomas Erlewine*

● **The Whole Wide World** / 1979 / Stiff ✦✦✦✦
The Whole Wide World was an American-only collection of Wreckless Eric singles that provided an excellent distillation of his best moments, from "Whole Wide World" to "Semaphore Signals" and "Take the Cash (K.A.S.H.)." The album was added as a bonus LP to the original pressings of Eric's third album, *Big Smash!* —*Stephen Thomas Erlewine*

Big Smash / 1980 / Stiff/Repertoire ✦✦✦
Big Smash was Wreckless Eric's big crossover attempt, designed to bring him closer to the mainstream. However, the polished production and tempered performances remove much of his charm. While the music may be more accessible, Eric simply doesn't have a voice suited for careful productions, and that undercuts even the best songs on the record. And that's a shame, because it's clear that he is continuing to grow as a songwriter, finding more and better hooks, as well as sharp clever lyrics. But without the rough ragged music that made his first two records so exciting, *Big Smash* is a disappointment. The songs are there, but the record is not as fun as his first pair of albums. —*Stephen Thomas Erlewine*

Le Beat Group Electrique / 1989 / New Rose ✦✦✦✦
This overlooked comeback effort was an unheralded triumph for Eric, on which he fronted a guitar-bass-drums trio (he also plays his usual cheesy organ) on a stripped-down set of strong songs with a live production feel. With his strangled, yearning vocals, basic melodic hooks, and songs about messed-up relationships, Wreckless recalls some of Lou Reed and Syd Barrett's better solo work, as he makes his confusion a cause for infectious celebration instead of gloomy moping. —*Richie Unterberger*

Betty Wright

b. Dec. 21, 1953, Miami, FL
Vocals / Soul, Quiet Storm
A consistently strong presence on the Miami music scene throughout the '70s and '80s, Betty Wright was just 15 when she cut the Top 40 "Girls Can't Do What the Guys Do." A child gospel star who switched to

R&B at age 13, she put the Miami scene on the map in 1971 with the No.6 hit "Clean Up Woman," notable for its prominent guitar riff and Wright's swaggering lead vocal. She won a Grammy in 1974 for "Where Is the Love?" (not to be confused with the Roberta Flack/Donny Hathaway tune of the same name). She collaborated with Stevie Wonder in 1981 on the Epic hit "What Are You Gonna Do with It?" Betty continues to live and work in the Miami area. —*Christine Ohlman*

● **The Best of Betty Wright** / Sep. 29, 1992 / Rhino ✦✦✦✦
An excellent collection, covering the years between 1968 and 1978; it's 20 tracks of Betty Wright at her best. —*Stephen Thomas Erlewine*

Charles Wright

b. 1942, Los Angeles, CA
Guitar, Vocals / Soul, Funk
Charles Wright headed one of the late-'60s and early-'70s great funk groups, the Watts 103rd Street Band. Wright, who was born in Clarksdale, MS, was a singer, pianist, guitarist, and leader of the eight-member band, recruited from Watts in Los Angeles. They were originally known as the Soul Runners. Bill Cosby helped get the band off the ground by giving them appearances at his gigs. They began recording for Keyman in 1967, then moved to Warner Bros. in 1969. While "Do Your Thing" and "Till You Get Enough" were Top 20 R&B hits, their finest selection was "Express Yourself," a song that expressed the urge for freedom as adroitly as the Isley Brothers' "It's Your Thing" had in the '60s. It has also been among the most sampled funk tracks for hip-hop and rap groups. "Your Love (Means Everything to Me)" was their final R&B hit in 1971, peaking at No. 9 R&B and No. 12 pop. The group's best ballad, "Love Land," did better pop-wise than among R&B fans, many of whom saw it as a bit soft. They continued recording for Dunhill in 1973 before disbanding. Drummer James Gadson and guitarist Al McKay, who later joined Earth, Wind & Fire, were among the instrumental corps of the Watts 103rd Street Rhythm Band. —*Ron Wynn*

● **Express Yourself: The Best of Charles Wright** / 1993 / Warner Brothers ✦✦✦✦
A definitive, 16-track collection of Charles Wright's best material. —*Stephen Thomas Erlewine*

In the Jungle Babe/Express Yourself / Apr. 8, 1997 / Warner Brothers ✦✦✦✦
Released in 1997, this two-fer collects Charles Wright and the Watts 103rd Street Rhythm Band's third and fourth records, 1969's *In the Jungle, Babe* and the following year's *Express Yourself.* A transitional work, *In the Jungle, Babe* captures a group struggling to find its own identity; for every superb workout like the shimmering "Love Land" or the propulsive "I'm a Midnight Mover," there's a redundant cover of the Doors' "Light My Fire" or Sly and the Family Stone's "Everyday People" which falls flat on its face. *Express Yourself,* on the other hand, is the group's masterpiece, a remarkable fusion of funk attitude and soul conviction. Highlighted by the classic title hit—one of the most powerful declarations of independence in the canon, as well as one of the most sampled records of all time—*Express Yourself* is a whirlwind tour through the spectrum of R&B; from the poignance of the Otis Redding-worthy ballad "Tell Me What You Want Me to Do" (arguably Wright's best vocal turn ever) to the supple funk-jazz jam session "High as Apple Pie—Slice I and II," the record is assured and muscular, a primal blast of soul power. —*Jason Ankeny*

O.V. Wright

b. Oct. 9, 1939, Memphis, TN, d. Nov. 16, 1980
Vocals / Soul
A truly incendiary deep-soul performer. O.V. Wright's melismatic vocals and Willie Mitchell's vaunted Hi Rhythm Section combined to make classic Memphis soul during the early '70s. Overton Vertis Wright learned his trade on the gospel circuit with the Sunset Travelers before going secular in 1964 with the passionate ballad "That's How Strong My Love Is" for Goldwax in Memphis. Otis Redding liked the song so much that he covered it, killing any chance of Wright's version hitting. Since Wright was already under contract to Houston-based Peacock as a gospel act, owner Don Robey demanded his return, and from then on, Wright appeared on Robey's Back Beat subsidiary. Wright's sanctified sound oozes sweet soul on the spine-chilling "You're Gonna Make Me Cry," a 1965 smash, but it took Memphis producer Willie Mitchell to wring the best consistently from Wright. Utilizing Mitchell's surging house rhythm section, Wright's early-'70s Back Beat singles "Ace of Spades," "A Nickel and a Nail," and "I Can't Take It" rank among the very best Southern soul of their era. No disco bandwagon for O.V. Wright—he kept right on pouring out his emotions through the '70s, convincing his faithful that "I'd Rather Be (Blind, Crippled & Crazy)," that he was "Into Something (Can't Shake Loose)." Unfortunately, he apparently was—drugs have often been cited as causing Wright's downfall; the soul great died at only 41 years of age in 1980. —*Bill Dahl*

● **The Soul of O.V. Wright** / Dec. 22, 1992 / MCA ✦✦✦✦
O.V. Wright epitomized gospel-based soul singing. He screamed, roared, belted, hollered, and wailed, proclaiming his need for love. His songs were simple; they were often anguished remembrances of lost loves or pleas that this time things might be different. Occasionally, he did an uptempo dance or novelty number, but Wright was at his best on slow burners. This collection of 1960s and '70s material for Don Robey's Back Beat label includes evocative ballads, lightweight but enjoyable numbers, and songs which returned him to his gospel days. While several foreign anthologies spotlighting Wright have been issued, this 18-track CD stands as the most complete domestic reissue package currently available. —*Ron Wynn*

Wu-Tang Clan

f. 1992, Staten Island, NY
Hip Hop, East Coast Rap, Hardcore Rap
Emerging in 1993, when Dr. Dre's G-funk had overtaken the hip-hop world, the Staten Island, New York-based Wu-Tang Clan proved to be the most revolutionary rap group of the mid-'90s and only partially because of their music. Turning the standard concept of a hip-hop crew inside out, the Wu-Tang Clan was assembled as a loose congregation of nine MCs almost as a support group. Instead of releasing one album after another, the Clan was designed to overtake the record industry in as profitable a fashion as possible—the idea was to establish the Wu-Tang as a force with their debut album, and then spin off into as many side projects as possible. In the process, the members would all became individual stars, as well as receive individual royalty checks.

Surprisingly, the plan worked. All of the various Wu-Tang solo projects elaborate on the theme the group laid out on their 1993 debut, the spare, menacing *Enter the Wu-Tang: 36 Chambers.* Taking their group name from an powerful, mythical kung fu sword wielded by an invincible congregation of warriors, the crew is a loose collective of nine MCs. All nine members work under a number of psuedonyms, but they are best known as: the RZA (formerly Prince Rakeem, as well as the Rzarecta, Chief Abbot, and Bobby Steels; born Robert Diggs), Genius/GZA (a.k.a. Justice, Maxi Million; born Greg Grice), Ol' Dirty Bastard (aka Unique Ason, Joe Bannanas, Dirt McGirt; born Russell Jones, circa 1969), Method Man (aka Johnny Blaze, Ticallion Stallion, Shakwon, Methical, the MZA; born Clifford Smith), Raekwon the Chef (aka Shallah Raekwon, Lou Diamonds; born Corey Woods), Ghost Faced Killa (aka Tony Starks, Sun God; born Dennis Coles), U-God (aka Golden Arms, Lucky Hands, Baby U, 4-Bar Killer; born Lamont Hawkins), Inspecta Deck (aka Rebel INS, Rollie Fingers; born Jason Hunter), and Masta Killa (aka Noodles; born E. Turner).

Although he wasn't one of the two founding members—Genius/GZA and Ol' Dirty Bastard were the first—the vision of the Wu-Tang Clan is undoubtedly due to the musical sklls of the RZA. Under his direction, the group—through its own efforts and the solo projects, all of which he produced or co-produced—he created a hazy, surreal and menacing soundscape out of hardcore beats, eerie piano riffs, minimal samples. Over these surrealistic backing tracks, the MCs rapped hard, updating the old school attack with vicious violence, martial arts imagery, and a welcome warped humor. By 1995, the sound was one of the most instantly recognizable in hip-hop. It wasn't always that way. Like most rappers, they began their careers trying to get ahead whatever way they could. For the RZA, that meant releasing a silly single, "Ooh, I Love You Rakeem," on Tommy Boy Records in 1991. On the advice of his label and producers, he cut the humorous, lover-man single that went absolutely nowhere. Neither did the follow-up single, "My Deadly Venom." The experience strengthed his resolve to subvert and attack record industry conventions. He found partners in Genius and Ol' Dirty Bastard. Genius had also released a record in 1991, the full-length *Words from the Genius* on Cold Chillin', which was preceded by the single "Come Do Me." Both records were unsuccessful. After the failure of his album, Genius teamed with an old friend, Ol' Dirty Bastard, to form the crew that would evolve into the Wu-Tang Clan within a year.

The RZA quickly became part of the crew, as did several other local MCs, including Method Man, Ghost Faced Killa, Raekwon, U-God, Inspecta Deck, and Masta Killa, who rarely raps. The nine rappers made a pact to a form an artistic and financial community—the Wu-Tang Clan wouldn't merely be a group, it would be its own industry. In order to do this, they decided to establish themselves through a group effort and then begin to spread the word through solo projects, picking up additional collaborators along the way and, in the process, becoming stronger and more influential.

The first Wu-Tang Clan single, the hard-hitting "Protect Ya Neck," appeared on their own, independent label and became an underground hit. Soon, the record labels were offering them lucrative contracts. The group held out until they landed a deal that would allow each member to record solo albums for whatever label they chose—in essence, each rapper was a free agent. Loud/RCA agreed to the deal and the band's debut album, *Enter the Wu-Tang: 36 Chambers,* appeared in November of 1993. *Enter the Wu-Tang: 36 Chambers* was both critically acclaimed and commercially successful, although its financial success wasn't immediate, but the result of a slow build. "C.R.E.A.M.," released in early 1994, was the single that put them over the top and won them a devoted following. The group wasted no time in pursuing other projects, as a total of five of the members—Genius, RZA, Raekwon, Method Man, and Ol' Dirty Bastard—landed solo contracts as a result of the success of "C.R.E.A.M." RZA was the first to re-enter the studio, this time as a member of the Gravediggaz, a group he founded; in addition to RZA, who was rechristened the Rzarecta, the group included De La Soul's producer Prince Paul, Stetsasonic's Fruitkwan, and Brothers Grimm's Poetic. The Gravediggaz's album, *6 Feet Deep*, appeared in August 1994; it eventually would go gold. Labelled "horrorcore" by the group, it was an ultra-violent but comical tour de force that demonstrated the RZA's production prowess. Shortly after its release, Raekwon released his first single, "Heaven and Hell" on the *Fresh* soundtrack; the song was produced by RZA and featured Ghost Face Killa.

The first Wu-Tang member to become a major solo star was Method Man. In November 1994, he released *Tical*, the first official Wu-Tang solo album. Again, the RZA produced the album, creating a dense, dirty sonic collage. *Tical* became a big hit in early 1995, as did Method's duet with Mary J. Blige, "You're All I Need (To Get By)." Ol' Dirty Bastard followed Method's breakthrough success with *Return to the 36 Chambers: The Dirty Version*, which appeared in March, 1995 on Elektra Records. Thanks to the hits "Brooklyn Zoo" and "Shimmy Shimmy Ya," the record became a gold success. Out of all the solo albums, it was the one that sounded the most like *Enter the Wu-Tang*, although it did have a more pronounced comic bent, due to Ol' Dirty's maniacal vocals. Around this time, Ol' Dirty Bastard became instrumental in the formation of the Zoo, a group of Wu-Tang proteges. *Tales from the Hood*, a movie soundtrack featuring Inspecta Deck's first solo track appeared in May.

Later in 1995, the two most critically-acclaimed Wu-Tang records appeared—Raekwon's *Only Built 4 Cuban Linx* and Genius' *Liquid Swords*. In August, 1995 Raekwon released his solo album on Loud/ RCA; most of the record featured extensive contributions—a total of 12 songs—from Ghostface Killa. Genius' second solo album was released by Geffen Records in November 1995. In February of 1996, Ghost Face Killa's first solo track, "Winter Warz," appeared on the *Don't Be a Menace to South Central While You're Drinking Your Juice in the Hood* soundtrack. The Wu-Tang Clan finally returned with their second album, *Wu-Tang Forever*, in June of 1997. — *Stephen Thomas Erlewine*

★ **Enter the Wu-Tang (36 Chambers)** / Nov. 1993 / Loud ✦✦✦✦✦
The Wu-Tang Clan's debut album *Enter the Wu-Tang (36 Chambers)* wasn't an across-the-boards blockbuster like Dr. Dre's *The Chronic*, the other seminal hip-hop record of the early '90s, but its impact was just as widespread. Where Dr. Dre was loose, hedonistic and funky, the Wu-Tang was tense, scary and funny. *Enter the Wu-Tang* is a series of intense, surrealistic soundscapes that draws equally from pop culture, martial arts, and gangsta traditions. Other hardcore gangstas simply boasted about their hardness—the Wu-Tang clan boasted, but they supported their inventive rhymes with stripped-down samples and lean, menacing beats that evoked their gritty, urban surroundings more effectively than their words. And that's what makes *Enter the Wu-Tang* so effective—the group's unique lyrical obsessions and the distinctive, innovative production techniques of Prince Rakeem. After releasing this pioneering debut, all the members pursued solo careers that explored various elements of *Enter the Wu-Tang* in more depth—and, occasionally, with more different results—but this contains the roots of everything that followed. — *Stephen Thomas Erlewine*

Wu-Tang Forever / Jun. 3, 1997 / Loud/RCA ✦✦✦✦
The Wu-Tang Clan's long-awaited second album *Wu-Tang Forever* arrived to great anticipation and the double-disc set does not disappoint. Where contemporaries like 2-Pac and the Notorious B.I.G. issued double-discs that were cluttered with filler, *Wu-Tang Forever* is purposeful and surprisingly lean, illustrating the immense depth of producer RZA and the entire nine-piece crew. Each rapper has a different lyrical style, from Ol' Dirty Bastard's bizarre rants to Raekwon's story sketches, and RZA subtely shifts his trademark style for each song, creating an album of cinematic proportions. There's no great musical innovations on the album, since the Wu-Tang's signature blend of skeletal beats, scratchy samples, eerie pianos and spectral strings remains intact. Yet the music is more nuanced and focused than ever before, balanced equally between scary soundscapes and darkly soulful tracks. The result is an intoxicating display of musical and lyrical virtuosity, one that reveals how bereft of imagination the Wu-Tang's contemporaries are. — *Stephen Thomas Erlewine*

Robert Wyatt

b. Jan. 28, 1945, Bristol, England
Drums, Vocals / Art-Rock/Progressive-Rock
An enduring figure who came to prominence in the early days of the

English art-rock scene, Robert Wyatt has produced a significant body of work, both as the original drummer for art-rockers the Soft Machine and as a radical political singer-songwriter. Born in Bristol, England, Wyatt came to the Soft Machine during the exciting slightly post-psychedelic Canterbury scene of the mid-'60s that produced bands like Gong. Unlike many of the art-rock bands that would come later (Jethro Tull, Yes, King Crimson), Soft Machine eschewed bloated theatrical excess, preferring a standard rock format that interpolated jazz riffing, extended soloing, and some forays into experimental noise. Wyatt, then Soft Machine's drummer, left the band during its initial wave of popularity for a solo career that was built less around his abilities as a percussionist and more around his frail tenor voice, capable of breaking your heart with its falsetto range.

It was not long after his first solo release, *End of an Ear*, that Wyatt fell from an open window during a party, fracturing his back and permanently paralyzing him from the waist down. After months of painful recuperation, Wyatt re-emerged with the harrowing *Rock Bottom* (1974) and the bizarre *Ruth Is Stranger Than Richard* (1975), the former dealing explicitly with his post-accident life, the latter a series of surreal fables. And while the music on these records is trance-like and experimental, Wyatt shockingly recorded a straight version of the Monkees "I'm a Believer" in 1974 that became a big British hit. Controversy ensued when the BBC's long-running weekly pop music program *Top of the Pops* refused to allow Wyatt to perform the song in his wheelchair. After a significant protest played out in the music trade papers, Wyatt did perform.

Despite his success, Wyatt remained quiet for much of the rest of the decade, breaking his silence during the punk era with a handful of singles recorded for the great English indie label Rough Trade. Again, going against audience expectations, he recorded a beautiful version of Chic's "At Last I Am Free," which signalled the start of a full-fledged career renaissance that included numerous albums and artists such as Elvis Costello writing songs for him. His albums were lush, at times almost meditative, and Wyatt's voice—clear, emotionally charged and always on the verge of breaking—brought great depth and soul to songs that, if recorded by a lesser artist, would have sounded terse and tired.

Always on the political left, Wyatt's radicalism increased exponentially during Margaret Thatcher's years as Prime Minister, as he maintained an unwavering support of Communism even as *glasnost* was nigh. The resulting music he recorded during this period reflects his strong, bordering on strident political beliefs. Lately, Wyatt has comfortably worked in and out of the music business. He records when he feels like it, paints, writes, devotes time to political work and continues to show no interest in the machinations of the music industry. But, despite his occasionally strident political posture, he has recorded some stunning music, full of wonder, possibility and pure emotion that remains undiscovered by many. — *John Dougan*

Rock Bottom / 1974 / Blue Plate ✦✦✦✦
A progressive rock-era masterpiece, it features brilliantly simple songs, poems, and textures, with all-star support. — *Myles Boisen*

Ruth Is Stranger Than Richard / 1975 / Blue Plate ✦✦✦✦
Another enduring collaboration with Brian Eno, Fred Frith, and other '70s luminaries, it's on a par with *Rock Bottom*. — *Myles Boisen*

● **Rock Bottom/Ruth Is Stranger** / 1981 / Virgin ✦✦✦✦
The CD era makes these two hard-to-find recordings available on one disc. Of the two, *Rock Bottom* is the most intense, and perhaps the most odd—the songs are repetitive, meditative and spacy in a way that anticipates the ambient music of Brian Eno and the more contemporary Orb and Moby. Two different versions of the same song show up here ("Little Red Riding Hood Hit the Road"), but that's not a criticism as much as a statement of fact. The backing musicians are a classy bunch of veteran English avant-garde, art-rock types (Hugh Hopper, Richard Sinclair, Fred Frith) who play with great skill and style. The music tends to be melancholy, but is not self-pitying or lachrymose. This is prime Wyatt in the early part of his post-accident career. That they are both on one disc makes for rewarding, if difficult, listening. — *John Dougan*

Old Rottenhat / 1985 / Gramavision ✦✦✦
Wyatt has been quoted as declaring that this record was "a conscious attempt to make un-misuable music," i.e. music that couldn't be appropriated by the Right or broadcast on Voice of America. VOA doesn't broadcast uncommercial music such as this in any case, but Wyatt did succeed in stating some of his political concerns—imperialism, the carnage in East Timor, the flaws of rigid political ideology—in an understated manner. He went back to writing his own material for this album, after having focused on eclectic "covers" in the early '80s, with fair success. It's perhaps an even moodier outing than usual for Wyatt; his melancholy is amplified by the foggy, spooky keyboards. It was reissued on CD in 1990 as half of *Compilation*, which also includes the entirety of *Nothing Can Stop Us Now*. — *Richie Unterberger*

Compilation / Apr. 1990 / Gramavision ✦✦✦✦
Somewhat erroneously titled, this is not a collection of Wyatt's work but rather 1981's *Nothing Can Stop Us Now* and 1985's *Old Rottenhat* on one CD. A bit strident politically and a tad cynical, these are, however, wonderful records built upon righteous indignation that is never cruel or simplistic. As with much of Wyatt's work, these recordings are emotionally complex, somewhat ambiguous, and always rewarding. —*John Dougan*

Dondestan / 1991 / Gramavision ✦✦✦✦
For half of these songs, Wyatt put music to the poetry of his wife Alfreda Benge; he wrote both words and music for the remainder (with the exception of "Lisp Service," whose music was written by ex-Soft Machine bassist Hugh Hopper). Roughly speaking, the collaborations with Benge are more abstract, and the other compositions more politically oriented, dealing with concerns such as Palestine, privatization, and the Communist Party (the wittily titled "CP Jeebies"). If you're worried that this is agit-prop, don't fret; it's all delivered with Wyatt's typical understated melancholy, subtle humor, and trademark eerie keyboards. Indeed, the mix of jazz, pop, and progressive rock—owing, as ever, little to contemporary trends—is appealing enough that it may take a while for the subversive lyrical ideas to make themselves apparent. —*Richie Unterberger*

Floatsam Jetsam / 1994 / Rough Trade ✦✦✦
Not for the neophytes, this is a spectacular collection of unreleased oddities that span the years 1968-1990. Included are Wyatt's work with Jimi Hendrix (Soft Machine toured America as Hendrix's opening act in 1968) and his work with veteran avant-gardists Lol Coxhill and Dagmar Krause. Nothing here matches Wyatt's most important work, but for those so inclined, this is a unique opportunity to explore some of the hidden nooks and crannies of an always-interesting artist's career. Caveat emptor: as with *Going Back a Bit*, this is an expensive English import. —*John Dougan*

● **Going Back a Bit: A Little History of Robert Wyatt** / 1994 / Virgin ✦✦✦✦
A wonderfully compiled 28-track, two-CD set that includes some of Wyatt's work with Soft Machine and his short-lived band of radical politicos Matching Mole (who, frankly, are not very interesting). Also, this generous set includes some outtakes and unreleased material. As for a basic overview of Wyatt's career that doesn't skimp on the strong stuff and provides a sense of chronology, you can't do much better. The lone drawback is that the set is only available as a pricy English import. But if you've got the time and money, it's well worth the investment. —*John Dougan*

Short Break / Oct. 8, 1996 / Resurgent ✦✦✦

Steve Wynn
....

b. Feb. 21, 1960, Los Angeles, CA
Singer-Songwriter, Alternative Pop-Rock, Pop-Rock, Paisley Underground
Born February 21, 1960 and raised in Los Angeles, Steve Wynn, as founder of the Dream Syndicate in the early '80s, almost singlehandedly made college-age rock fans open their eyes to two decades' worth of the guitar-drenched rock that inspired him.
After graduating from the University of California in Davis and a stint with his new wave band, Suspects, Wynn took a cross-country trip in search of Alex Chilton, one of his spiritual mentors, who had been sorely missed on the music scene since his days with the seminal pop band Big Star. When he returned to California, almost simultaneously the underground rock scene was experiencing a guitar-rock revival, aided by fellow Chilton devotees R.E.M. and the Replacements. Wynn

abruptly did an about face and embraced the feedback-flooded sounds of the Velvet Underground for his new band Dream Syndicate. Heralded as the leaders of the Paisley Underground, a neo-'60s scene out of Los Angeles that included the Bangles and the Three O'Clock, Dream Syndicate were by far the most "outside" band in the bunch, often challenging their audiences to three-hour sets built around endless jams and feedback sessions. After four albums on four labels and a change in direction (Wynn traded in his Lou Reed fixation for Neil Young), the Syndicate called it quits and Wynn embarked on his solo career. Out of the gate with *Kerosene Man* (Rhino, 1990) and followed by *Dazzling Display* (Rhino 1992), Wynn relied on his keen songwriting skill, unique vocal style, and a bunch of friends (including Peter Buck) for the recordings. 1994's *Fluorescent* (Mute) took Wynn even further out of the spotlight due to the difficulty of finding the record in shops and his subtle stylistic variance from rocker to semi-folkie. With Gutterball, his side project with the House of Freaks and Bob Rupe of the Silos, Wynn used the opportunity to cut loose and unleash his most drunken rambler material in the context of a very unserious rock 'n' roll band. —*Denise Sullivan*

Kerosene Man / Apr. 1990 / Rhino ✦✦✦
Wynn's solo debut is a logical extension of his work with the now-legendary Dream Syndicate. "Tears Won't Help," "Carolyn" and "Killing Time" are fairly straightforward pop. "Something to Remember Me By" and "Kerosene Man" is in more familiar Wynn territory—a mean-spirited character and his professional persona respectively spit out some handy lyrics set to neo-roots music. —*Denise Sullivan*

Dazzling Display / 1991 / Rhino ✦✦✦
For those who wondered what Wynn would sound like orchestrated, everything including the kitchen sink went into the making of this record. Peter Buck co-wrote "A Dazzling Display," and there's a Serge Gainsbourg cover and a hymn by Wynn's granddad. John Wesley Harding's harmonica was left uncredited on the over-the-top "Tuesday," on which Flo & Eddie and Susan Cowsill also sing while violins, cello and Buck's 12-string ring out like the bells of Rhymney. Johnette Napolitano, Russ Tolman, and Chris Cacavas also guest. —*Denise Sullivan*

Kerosene Man [EP] / 1991 / RNA ✦✦✦✦
For those that never made it to the end of Wynn's solo debut to hear the nifty title cut, this disc sticks it up front. Followed by the Jim Thompson-esque "Something to Remember Me By," the reason to own this EP is for the covers: Sonic Youth's "Kool Thing" and Paul Simon's "Boy in the Bubble" reveal Wynn's love of all music and his ability to share his wealth of enthusiasm. —*Denise Sullivan*

Take Your Flunky and Dangle / 1993 / Return to Sender ✦✦✦
Hard to explain this one other than a bunch of his cronies got together and fooled around in the studio. Wynn likes to record quick and it's a sure bet that this collection of spare, unused songs written between 1987-1993 took the time it takes to play the CD to lay down. Still, it cuts to the heart of Wynn's love of pure indigenous music. —*Denise Sullivan*

● **Fluorescent** / Mar. 29, 1994 / Mute ✦✦✦✦
No longer does Wynn allow his various bands to crash and burn or his producers to drown out his fire. With some subtle shifts in instrumentation, Wynn takes on Dylan's *Nashville Skyline* voice (a tone that suits him) and turns out pop, folk ("That's Why I Wear Black") and even Victoria Williams on "Layer by Layer." —*Denise Sullivan*

Melting in the Dark / Jul. 29, 1996 / Zero Hour ✦✦✦
With mixed results, Wynn returns to the Velvet Underground-inspired, feedback-heavy style of his halcyon days in the Dream Syndicate on this self-produced solo effort, on which he's backed by members of the band Come. —*Jason Ankeny*

X

X

f. 1977, Los Angeles, CA
Group / Rock, Punk, Alternative Pop-Rock

X were the quintessential Los Angeles punk rockers before they grew into a world-class rock 'n' roll band and live band; however, enthusiasm for their unique, intelligent, and humorous work never quite reached critical mass.

Formed in 1977 after songwriter and bassist John Doe (b. Feb. 24, 1956) met (and later married) Exene Cervenka (b. Feb. 1, 1956) at a Venice poetry workshop, with rockabilly veteran Billy Zoom (b. Feb. 20, 194?) on guitar and D.J. Bonebrake (b. Dec. 8, 1955) on drums, the band garnered an immediate following. "Discovered" by ex-Doors keyboardist Ray Manzarek, he took the band into the studio for the recording of *Los Angeles* in 1980. It was curious, at a time when punks were supposed to hate hippies, that X's merging with an ex-Door was not only tolerated, but earned them stature as California's preeminent punk band when the record earned across-the-board raves. 1981 saw the release of the similarly punked-up *Wild Gift*, while their 1982 album, *Under the Big Black Sun*, began what would be a long career in merging hard rock, country, and folk into their fiery mix. The band successfully began to mix in their populist politics with an eye toward matters of the heart.

As the band began to reach wider audiences, both Doe and Cervenka enjoyed outside careers in the arts—he as an actor in films like *Great Balls of Fire* and *Roadside Prophets*, and she as a poet and spoken-word artist, collaborating with Lydia Lunch and Wanda Coleman.

In 1983, the rootsy songs on *More Fun In the New World* lent themselves to acoustic performances which the band had taken to trying live. They took it one step further on their side project, the Knitters (with Dave Alvin) which yielded one Slash album, *Poor Little Critter in the Road*, in 1985. *Ain't Love Grand* was a harder rock album in 1986 and was followed by Zoom's departure. He was momentarily replaced by Alvin, but for recording purposes, the band recruited Tony Gilkyson (formerly of Lone Justice) for *See How We Are*, the band's most decidedly hard rock record in the catalog. Gilkyson stayed for the recording *Live at the Whisky A Go-Go* in 1988 before the band took some much-needed time off, although they never broke up. In the interim, Doe and Cervenka had since divorced, and the pair continued to work as solo artists, releasing Cervenka's *Old Wives Tales* (Rhino, 1989) and *Running Sacred* (1990) and Doe's *Meet John Doe* for Geffen in 1990.

By 1993, the band got together for the recording of *Hey Zeus!*, a collection of new songs, but the response was underwhelming, and it was back to solo work. Doe released *Kissingsohard* for Rhino in 1995. Exene also released *Surface to Air Serpents* for the 2.13.61 label, as well as a reading of the *Unabomber Manifesto*, after changing her name to Cervenkova. During their frequent hiatuses, X would occasionally appear in Los Angeles and San Francisco and during one stay, recorded a live album in San Francisco in 1995, *Unclogged*, and self-released it. Cervenkova's latest project is Auntie Christ with Bonebrake and Matt Freeman of Rancid. Gilkyson also works as a solo artist. X also appeared in three films: Penelope Spheeris' punk documentary *The Decline of Western Civilization*, *Urgh! A Music War*, and a documentary of their lives and times, *The Unheard Music*. *—Denise Sullivan*

Los Angeles / 1980 / Slash ✦✦✦✦
Although classified as punk because of their simple hard rock sound and caustic lyrics ("The World's a Mess; It's in My Kiss"), X always had more of a rockabilly edge, courtesy of former Gene Vincent guitarist Billy Zoom, and were always funnier than the punk label implies, which may be why they were a cut above their competition. *—William Ruhlmann*

Wild Gift / May 1981 / Slash ✦✦✦✦
As with many groups, X had more good songs in their repertoire than could fit on their debut, and their second album presents the rest. Appropriately, the two albums have been packaged together on a single CD. *—William Ruhlmann*

Under the Big Black Sun / Jul. 1982 / Elektra ✦✦✦✦
The first album in their new deal with Elektra, X suddenly sounded professional, but it was not to their detriment as a punk band. The cushier contract allowed them to stretch out and incorporate the roots music they loved, and they came up with what have come to be known as X classics: "The Hungry Wolf," "Riding With Mary," "Because I Do," "Blue Spark," and "The Have Nots." *—Denise Sullivan*

More Fun in the New World / 1983 / Elektra ✦✦✦✦
By this time, X were at the height of their powers as a live act and as lyricists; "The New World" and "I Must Not Think Bad Thoughts" take on the zeitgeist of the desperate Reagan era. X captured the little people's anger in the lyrics and seething delivery. As usual, there's fun in their cover of "Breathless" recorded for a remake of the Godard film with the same title. A better *sounding* record than the first two, it was becoming clear that it was make or break time for the band, and in a perfect world, they would have broken through with this fine collection of songs. *—Denise Sullivan*

Ain't Love Grand! / 1985 / Elektra ✦✦✦✦
Some called this X's hard rock album, perhaps because they chose to work with a new producer, Michael Wagener, primarily known for his work in the metal arena. But there's nothing wrong with this roster of songs, worthy of a roll call: "Burning House of Love," "Love Shack," "My Soul Cries Your Name," "My Goodness," "What's Wrong With Me," and "I'll Stand Up For You" are all stone-cold X classics. "Watch the Sun Go Down" is uncharacteristically straight-ahead chart-type pop (probably the closest X came to a soul send-up with Zoom on sax)), but it works beautifully. *—Denise Sullivan*

See How We Are / 1987 / Elektra ✦✦✦
"I'm Lost" is classic bash and punk X; Exene puts on her best Debbie Harry voice for "You," and Dave Alvin's fine "4th of July" is among X's finest recorded minutes. Save for the title cut, this album never lets the band shine to the best of their considerable abilities, though critically it was a favorite—perhaps owing to the Alvin cut, which sounds as if the distinctly Los Angeles scenario was written exclusively for this decidedly Los Angeles band. *—Denise Sullivan*

Live at the Whiskey a Go-Go / 1988 / Elektra ✦✦✦
A ferocious live set featuring 6 new songs and 18 classic X tracks, *Live at the Whiskey A Go-Go on the Fabulous Sunset Strip* is seething with energy and eclipses their previous two albums in terms of sheer power. After showing signs of life with this set, the band called it quits shortly after its release; they reunited three years later. *—Stephen Thomas Erlewine*

★ **Los Angeles/Wild Gift** / Sep. 20, 1988 / Slash ✦✦✦✦✦
The first two records come packaged as one long CD. X's debut is an enduring testament to Los Angeles punk rock. Produced by Ray Manzarek and augmented by his creepy organ, the band delve into the underbelly of Los Angeles subculture, chiefly heroin use. A distant kin to England's and New York's brand of punk, John Doe's and Exene Cervenka's literary bent and unique harmonies alongside Billy Zoom's rockabilly guitar put X's music in a class of its own. It was critically acclaimed across the board. The follow-up *Wild Gift* is more of the same, but curiously a little rougher, due to the absence of Manzarek's keys, however, he's still at the board. It contains some of the band's most important work: the punk anthem "We're Desperate," the catchy "Adult

Books," the political "White Girl" and the domestic drama in which X excelled, "In This House That I Call Home." —*Denise Sullivan*

Hey Zeus! / Jun. 8, 1993 / Big Life ✦✦✦
From the opening notes of the record, one would be hard pressed to guess this was an X album. Perhaps giving to the six years between studio recordings, contemporary music had changed and X, always at the forefront, were in the unenviable position of having to play catch-up. It's not that the songs are bad, they're simply tainted by production maestros Tony Berg and Tchad Blake and the lack of focus drawn from a band who'd ceased to continue working as a family unit. "Big Blue House" is as close to the real John and Exene as it gets. —*Denise Sullivan*

Unclogged / Jun. 13, 1995 / Infidelity/Sunset Boulevard ✦✦✦✦
Perhaps referring to the staid forum known as contemporary "unplugged music," or their own aging arteries, *Unclogged* successfully reprises X's finest work in an electro-acoustic live set. No worse for the wear, John Doe and Exene Cervenka are in perfect voice, while Tony Gilkyson and D.J. Bonebrake play the songs they played a million times with the renewed spirit of a band that can finally relax and rest on its laurels. If there was ever anything to prove—that X was a supreme live band and that Doe and Cervenka were two of the most talented songwriters to come out of punk—this is the evidence. —*Denise Sullivan*

X-Ray Spex

f. 1976, London, England
Punk
One of the great English punk bands of the late '70s, there is only one thing wrong with the careers of X-Ray Spex and lead singer Poly Styrene—they didn't record enough music. Formed in 1976 by school friends Marion Elliott (Styrene) and Susan Whitby (saxophonist Lora Logic), X-Ray Spex exploded onto the punk scene with one of the era's great singles, the feminist punk rallying cry "Oh Bondage, Up Yours." With Logic's sax laying down the melody semi-tunefully and Jak Airport's guitar laying down a wash of distorted chords, Styrene's vocal, especially on the chorus, is a marvel. Along with the early Sex Pistols and Clash singles, this was one of punk rock's great moments.

So, too, was X-Ray Spex's debut LP *Germ Free Adolescents*, which was great in spite of "Oh Bondage" not being on it (a situation that would be rectified with the 1993 CD reissue). Lora Logic was gone (to form Essential Logic), but her replacement Rudi Thompson played in as rudimentary a fashion, but stayed in tune a little more. The songs were guitar-driven punk-pop that combined outrage and aggression with a sense of alienation and disenfranchisement about rampant commerciality and an increasingly sterile and artificial world. Styrene's songs were more likely to be about drowning in a sea of corporate-designed consumer fantasies than straight-out attacks against the government. This didn't mean the songs were any less political; they simply attacked the zeitgeist from a different vantage point.

Tragically, there was no second X-Ray Spex record. But there was Poly Styrene's only full-length solo record, *Translucence*. Abandoning completely the loud guitars of X-Ray Spex, *Translucence* is quiet and jazzy in a way that anticipates the work of Ben Watt and Tracey Thorn in *Everything But the Girl*. It's a bit of a shock coming after *Germ Free Adolescents*, but it's a beautiful album, and her singing, though not as exciting and unhinged, is frequently stunning. Consistent with her career up to this point, Poly Styrene dropped out of music entirely shortly after the release of *Translucence* and joined a London-based Hare Krishna sect. She emerged from "retirement" in 1986 with a wonderful EP titled *Gods and Goddesses*. Although rumored to be preparing another LP, she's been pretty quiet for the last decade. —*John Dougan*

● **Germ Free Adolescents** / Nov. 1978 / Blue Plate ✦✦✦✦
The CD adds "Oh Bondage, Up Yours," making this one of the five best punk records made. The excitement here is contagious, the songs smart and captivating, the playing energetic if occasionally sloppy. In other words, brilliant. Buy it today. —*John Dougan*

Conscious Consumer / Oct. 24, 1995 / Receiver ✦✦✦
When the original X-Ray Spex disbanded and Poly Styrene joined the Hare Krishnas, rather wild speculation ensued among some fans that she'd gone off the deep end. She's still in the Hare Krishna sect, but this unexpected comeback effort demonstrates that her worldview hasn't changed all that much since the punk era, though the music (much of which was written over ten years before this was recorded) has mellowed somewhat. She's still examining the crassness of consumer culture on cuts like "Cigarettes" and "Junk Food Junkie," but her experiences as an adult are reflected in more subdued cuts like "India" and "Prayer for Peace." Original group members Lora Logic and Paul Dean are still on board for this outing, which finds Styrene in just as good a voice as the old days, though the brash exuberance has been toned down. It might not be all that old-school punk fans would wish for, but

it's worth checking out, and the languid "Crystal Clear" may be the catchiest tune she's ever laid down. —*Richie Unterberger*

XTC

f. 1976, Swindon, Wiltshire, England
Alternative Pop-Rock, New Wave, Pop-Rock
XTC was one of the smartest—and catchiest—British pop bands to emerge from the punk and new wave explosion of the late '70s. From the tense, jerky riffs of their early singles to the lushly arranged, meticulous pop of their later albums, XTC's music has always been driven by the hook-laden songwriting of guitarist Andy Partridge and bassist Colin Moulding. While popular success has eluded them in both Britain and America, the group has developed a devoted cult following in both countries that remains loyal nearly 20 years after their first records.

Partridge, Moulding, and drummer Terry Chambers formed the first version of the band around 1976, calling themselves Star Park. As punk rock took off in 1977, the group changed their name to Helium Kidz and added former King Crimson keyboardist Barry Andrews. After being turned down by CBS Records, the band changed their name to XTC and secured a record contract with Virgin; they released their first EP, *3-D*, in October of 1977. *White Music*, the band's first full-length album, was recorded in a week and released by the end of the year. Critics praised the angular yet melodic pop, and the album reached No. 38 in the UK charts. However, none of the singles released from the album charted (including "This Is Pop"), nor did "Are You Receiving Me?," the teaser single for their second album, *Go 2* (1978).

After returning from a brief US tour, Andrews quit the band; he would eventually form the League of Gentlemen with Robert Fripp, as well as pursue a solo career. Guitarist David Gregory was added to the lineup after Andrews' departure and the group recorded their first charting single, "Life Begins at the Hop." XTC released their third album, the calmer, more pop-oriented *Drums and Wires*, that summer; the record climbed to No. 37 on the charts, thanks to the hit single "Making Plans for Nigel." While *Drums and Wires* began to climb the US charts, Partridge released his first solo album early in 1980; outside of the band's devoted fans, the record appeared without much fanfare.

XTC continued to smooth out their edges on 1980's *Black Sea*, bringing in elements of mid-'60s Beatles and Kinks to their guitar-driven pop; thanks to the singles "Generals and Majors" and "Towers of London," the album was the group's most successful American album, peaking at No. 41 while reaching No. 16 on the British charts. Released the following year, *English Settlement* featured more complex arrangements, as well as more intellectual lyrics, particularly from Andy Partridge. Nevertheless, the album was XTC's biggest success in the UK, reaching No. 5 on the album charts and launching the Top Ten single, "Senses Working Overtime."

While on tour in March of 1982, Partridge collapsed while on stage, suffering from exhaustion. Less than a month later, he collapsed again with a stomach ulcer. The band cancelled the tour shortly after his second collapse, prompting Chambers to leave the group. In November, Partridge announced that XTC would never play live again, concentrating on recording instead; he also blamed his collapses on intense stage fright. As the band completed their new album, a compilation called *Waxworks—Some Singles (1977-1982)* was released at the end of the year.

Mummer, the first album the studio-bound XTC recorded, appeared in the summer of 1983; former Glitter Band member Pete Phipps recorded the drum tracks for the record. XTC refused to tour for the record, which caused some tension between the band and Virgin, and was presumably the reason why "Love on a Farmboy's Wages" didn't make it past No. 50 on the charts. Recording under the name the Three Wise Men, the group released the holiday single "Thanks for Christmas" at the end of the year.

Released in the fall of 1984, *The Big Express* essentially followed the same pattern as *Mummer*, yet it charted higher in the UK. XTC released a psychedelic parody album, *25 O'Clock*, under the name the Dukes of Stratosphear in 1985. After a difficult recording session with producer Todd Rundgren, the pastoral *Skylarking* appeared in the fall of 1986. Upon its release the album was hailed as a masterwork by critics, even though the band were claiming they were unsatisfied with the production. *Skylarking* was a bigger hit in the US than it was in the UK, spending over six months on the charts and peaking at No. 70.

XTC recorded another Dukes of Stratosphear album, *Psonic Psunspot*, in 1987; the two Stratosphear albums were collected on one disc the following year. *Oranges and Lemons* (1989) reworked the psychedelia of the Stratosphear side project, leaving out much of the loopy humor and replacing it with a Ray Davies-inspired nostalgia. The album was a minor hit in both Britain and America, reaching No. 28 and No. 44, respectively; "Mayor of Simpleton" became XTC's only charting US single, reaching No. 72 while peaking at No. 46 on the British charts. Three years later, the group released *Nonsuch*, an album that recalled both *Pet Sounds* and *Revolver*. Like every XTC record, its critical acclaim was greater than its sales—the album dropped out of the British charts after two weeks. In America, *Nonsuch* was more successful, reaching No. 97 and staying on the charts for 11 weeks.

XTC's lack of commercial success isn't because their music isn't accessible—their bright, occasionally melancholy, melodies flow with more grace than most bands—it has more to do with the group constantly being out of step with the times. However, the band has left behind a remarkably rich and varied series of albums that make a convincing argument that XTC is the great lost pop band. —*Stephen Thomas Erlewine*

White Music / Jan. 20, 1978 / Geffen ✦✦✦
XTC's first full album shows the band going full throttle in true punk spirit. More dissonant than their latter period, the young band shines with directionless energy and a good sense of humor. Highlights include the catchy singles, "This Is Pop" and "Radios in Motion," as well as a jumpy version of "All Along the Watchtower." Their first release, the EP *3-D*, has been appended to the CD version. —*Chris Woodstra*

Go 2 / Oct. 13, 1978 / Geffen ✦✦
Recorded in a rush, less than a year after *White Music*, *Go 2* predictably suffered. The album, while slightly more melodic, reprises much of the quirky, high-energy playing of *White Music*, but the material is considerably weaker this time out. Aside from a couple of standout tracks like "Mechanic Dancing," *Go 2* is probably most memorable for its witty, word-heavy cover art. —*Chris Woodstra*

Drums & Wires / Aug. 17, 1979 / Geffen ✦✦✦✦
Following *Go 2*, keyboardist Barry Andrews left the band and, rather than finding a replacement keyboard player, the band opted to recruit another guitarist (who could also play keyboards), Dave Gregory. The album that followed the lineup change, *Drums and Wires*, marked a turning point for the band, with a more subdued set of songs that reflected an increasing songwriting proficiency. The aimless energy of the first two albums was focused into a cohesive statement with a distinctive voice that retained their clever humor, quirky wordplay, and decidedly British flavor. Musically, *Drums and Wires*, titled to reflect the big drum sound they developed for the album, is certainly driven by the powerful rhythms and angular, mainly minimalistic arrangements, but the addition of a second guitarist also allowed for some inventive and interesting guitar work (the "wires") that made up for the lack of Andrews' odd flourishes—the tension between the two sounds creates some truly inspired, nervy pop. Colin Moulding also came into his own as a songwriter, penning their first substantial hit, the new wave classic "Making Plans for Nigel." [The CD reissue contains tracks from the bonus single originally included with the LP—"Limelight" and "Chain of Command"—as well as "Life Begins at the Hop."] —*Chris Woodstra*

Black Sea / Sep. 12, 1980 / Geffen ✦✦✦✦
XTC continued on with the big drum sound of *Drums and Wires*, adding more polish and an even heavier-hitting approach for *Black Sea*—their arrangements are fuller and they rock harder than ever before. Where *Drums and Wires* implied social commentary, *Black Sea* more directly addressed sociopolitical concerns, handling them not strictly in a theoretical sense, but rather showing a human response to the circumstances. Of course, the band's skewed outlook and mid-'60s pop sense keeps things from becoming too heavy—included are some of their finest songs, like "Respectable Street," "Generals and Majors," and "Towers of London," as well as the thoroughly enjoyable pop fluff throwaway, "Sgt. Rock (Is Going to Help Me)," to keep the mood light. All in all, there isn't a bad song in the bunch—*Black Sea* was their most consistent album up to that point—and although XTC always operated on the fringes, the album is their most commercial-sounding, fitting in perfectly with the new wave of the late '70s/early '80s. [The CD reissue adds three tracks—"Smokeless Zone," "Don't Lose Your Temper," and "The Somnambulist"—to the middle of the album. And while the extras are welcomed (especially "Don't Lose Your Temper"), they really should have been tacked on to the end rather than disrupting the original.] —*Chris Woodstra*

English Settlement / Feb. 12, 1982 / Geffen ✦✦✦✦
Andy Partridge's discovery of the 12-string guitar set the tone for *English Settlement*, an album which moved away from the pop gloss of *Black Sea* in favor of lighter, though still rhythmically heavy, acoustic numbers with more complex and intricate instrumentation. There are plenty of pop gems—"Senses Working Overtime" stands as one of their finest songs—but the main focus seems to be the more expansive sound; most of the songs are drawn out to near-epic length, ultimately taking some of the impact of the songs away. Despite several terrific tracks, *English Settlement* seems more a transitional album than anything else, although the textural sound of the album is quite remarkable, indicating the direction they would take in their post-touring incarnation. —*Chris Woodstra*

● **Waxworks: Some Singles 1977-1982** / Nov. 1982 / Geffen ✦✦✦✦
Though it has been since supplanted by more comprehensive collections—the most notable being *Fossil Fuel*, which repeats all of the *Wax-*

works tracks plus the later singles—*Waxworks—Some Singles 1977-1982* remains the classic compilation of the band's first, pre-studio-bound period. Originally, the album was packaged with a second record, *Beeswax—Some B-Sides 1977-1982*, later made available separately. —*Chris Woodstra*

Beeswax: Some B-Sides 1977-1982 / Nov. 1982 / Virgin ✦✦✦
A nice companion to *Waxworks, Beeswax* does a fine job of collecting the B-sides to the singles up to 1982. While these songs were often as engaging as the A-sides, their addition to the CDs as bonus tracks now makes this collection redundant. —*Chris Woodstra*

Mummer / Aug. 30, 1983 / Geffen ✦✦✦
Mummer, the first album to follow Andy Partridge's mental breakdown which led to the band's retirement from touring, is very much the work of an eccentric in isolation. The album is a collection that builds on the groundwork of *English Settlement* with gentle, acoustic songs that evoke pastoral images and peaceful times. There are moments of real inspiration, resulting in some of their finest songs to date—"Love on a Farmboy's Wages," "Great Fire," and "Lady Bird"—and the sound sets a pleasingly consistent mood, although the sameness tends to work against the lesser material. Only the out-of-place afterthought of "Funk Pop A Roll," a tirade against the music industry, breaks things up, recapturing the abrasive Partridge of past. [When *Mummer* was reissued on CD, six tracks were added to the middle of the album. While "Jump," "Toys" and "Desert Island" are welcome additions of pop confection, the atmospheric instrumentals "Frost Circus" and "Processions Toward the Learning Land," from the simply bizarre *Homo Safari Series*, serve to disrupt the album's flow.] —*Chris Woodstra*

The Big Express / Oct. 15, 1984 / Geffen ✦✦✦
XTC took full advantage of their studio-bound status with *Big Express*, creating their most painstakingly detailed, multi-layered, sonically dynamic album to date. The more upbeat material and brighter sound recall some of the band's earlier moments, but most of all, *Big Express* signals a turning point for the band, setting the blueprint for their later approach—a combination of studio perfection matched with impeccable songcraft that results in a thoroughly consistent and enjoyable album beginning to end. *Skylarking*, the album that followed, gets much more glory, and certainly its impact was greater (this one was virtually ignored), but really, *Big Express* covers much of the same territory and is just as strong an album in many ways. [Three songs were added to the middle of the CD reissue—"Red Brick Dream," "Washaway," and "Blue Overall"—but they fit seamlessly into the complete picture.] —*Chris Woodstra*

★ **Skylarking** / Oct. 27, 1986 / Geffen ✦✦✦✦✦
Working with producer Todd Rundgren didn't necessarily bring XTC a sense of sonic cohesion—after all every record since *English Settlement*, *Mummer*, and *The Big Express* followed their own interior logic—but it did help the group sharpen their focus, making *Skylarking* their tightest record since *Drums and Wires*. Ironically, *Skylarking* had little to do with new wave and everything to do with the lush, post-psychedelic pop of the Beatles and Beach Boys. Combining the charming pastoral feel of *Mummer* with the classicist English pop of *The Big Express*, XTC expands their signature sound by enhancing their intelligently melodic pop with graceful, lyrical arrangements and sweeping, detailed instrumentation. Rundgren may have devised the sequencing, helping the record feel like a song cycle even if it doesn't play like one, but what really impresses is the consistency and depth of Andy Partridge's and Colin Moulding's songs. Each song is a small gem, marrying sweet, catchy melodies to decidedly adult lyrical themes, from celebrations of love ("Grass") and marriage ("Big Day") to skepticism about maturation ("Earn Enough for Us") and religion ("Dear God"). Moulding's songs complement Partridge's songs better than before, and each writer is at a melodic and lyrical peak, which Rundgren helps convey with his supple production. The result is a pop masterpiece—an album that has great ambitions and fulfills them with ease. [The initial release of *Skylarking* didn't feature "Dear God," which was originally the B-side of "Grass." After "Dear God" became an unexpected hit, "Mermaid Smile" was pulled from the album so the hit single could be added to the record.] —*Stephen Thomas Erlewine*

Compact XTC: The Singles 1978-85 / 1987 / Virgin ✦✦✦✦
Taking the *Waxworks* collection one step further, this 18-track disc collects all of the pre-*Skylarking* singles. Not a bad place for beginners to start though the two-disc *Fossil Fuel* offers a more complete picture of the band. —*Chris Woodstra*

Oranges & Lemons / Feb. 27, 1989 / Geffen ✦✦✦✦
Skylarking was an ambitious yet concise record, one that recalled such graceful concept albums as *Pet Sounds* and *Sgt. Pepper*, so it wasn't entirely a surprise that XTC embraced psychedelia on its double-album follow-up *Oranges and Lemons*, especially if their celebrated side-project Dukes of Stratosphear was taken into consideration as well. *Oranges and Lemons* lacks the singular focus of *Skylarking*, but at its best, it's just as impressive as its predecessor. Instead of revelling in the

form of psychedelic pop, as they did with the Dukes, XTC bring the genre's sensibility to the mature pop of *Skylarking*, spiking it with a wry, occasionally absurd, sense of humor that was missing from its predecessor. The result is a record that's exploding with detail, not the least of which are backward guitars, sound effects and head-spinningly eclectic arrangements. It's sonically rich and filled with immaculately-crafted songs, but *Oranges and Lemons* falls just short of being a tour de force, since each song feels like an island—they work well as individual tracks, but they don't form a cohesive statement. However, that's a minor complaint, because Colin Moulding and Andy Partridge in particular are in peak form, contributing some of their very finest songs with "Garden of Earthly Delights," "The Loving," "One of the Millions," "Merely A Man," "Pink Thing" and the elegaic "Chalkhills and Children." Such songs make the relative weakness of the album well worth enduring. —*Stephen Thomas Erlewine*

Explode Together (The Dub Experiments '78-'80) / Aug. 1990 / Virgin ++
Between 1978 and 1980, Andy Partridge experimented with the power of the studio—the results were the puzzling releases of *Go+* (an EP of dub remixes of the *Go 2* album) and *Take Away/Lure of the Salvage* (an electronic collage based on the *Drums and Wires* album and credited under the name Mr. Partridge). *Explode Together* combines the two unusual projects. This is purely experimental music for the curious completists only. —*Chris Woodstra*

Rag 'N' Bone Buffet / Sep. 24, 1990 / Geffen +++
Rag 'N' Bone Buffet collects 24 rarities, B-sides, and side projects including "Too Many Cooks in the Kitchen" (released under the pseudonym the Colonel), "Thanks for Christmas" (by the Three Wise Men), "Mermaid Smiled," the song dropped from *Skylarking* to make room for "Dear God," "Take This Town," from the film *Times Square*, and a handful of BBC sessions. Finding the complete recorded works of XTC is a collector's nightmare and *Rag 'N' Bone Buffet* really only scratches the surface of what's out there, but it is a start. Even though these songs were thrown away by the band, there is really some terrific music to be found here—the collection is just as essential as the proper albums. —*Chris Woodstra*

Nonsuch / Mar. 30, 1992 / Geffen ++++
Since *Skylarking*, each XTC album was carefully composed and crafted, and *Nonsuch* is no different. Working with producer Gus Dudgeon (Elton John), XTC crafted their most immaculate album to date with *Nonsuch*. A measured and reflective record, recalling the Beach Boys more than the Beatles, the album retains some of their late '80s psyche-

delic flourishes, but those have been integrated into an elaborate, lush pop setting that falls somewhere between *Skylarking* and *Oranges and Lemons*. While it lacks the thematic unity of *Skylarking*, as well as the grand-standing eclecticism of *Oranges and Lemons*, *Nonsuch* is in many ways more consistent musically, presenting a set of 17 wonderfully detailed and immediate catchy pop, ranging from the relatively rocking "The Ballad of Peter Pumpkinhead" to the sweet "Holly up on Poppy." Occasionally, the album dips slightly lyrically—Moulding's "The Smartest Monkeys" and "War Dance" are a little too preachy)—but never musically, making *Nonsuch* a modest, minor masterpiece. —*Stephen Thomas Erlewine*

Drums and Wireless: BBC Live / 1994 / Virgin +++
Drums and Wireless does a good job of collecting the bulk of the band's BBC appearances from 1977 to 1989—many of which have previously been available only on inferior bootlegs. While many band's BBC sessions differ only slightly from the studio recordings, XTC was able to stretch out on their sessions for significantly different interpretations. This is a necessary addition to any fan's collection. —*Chris Woodstra*

★ **Fossil Fuel: The XTC Singles 1977-1992 / 1996 / Virgin/EMI +++++**
Fossil Fuel: The XTC Singles 1977-92 is a splendid double-disc set that runs through every one one of the group's 31 A-sides, from the nervy "Science Friction" to the lush, sighing "Wrapped In Grey." Between those two songs, XTC's craftsmanship grows remarkably fast—based on the edgy pop of their new wave singles "Statue of Liberty," "This is Pop," "Are You Receiving Me?" and "Life Begins at the Hop," it's hard to believe that they would later write the subtle, near-pastoral Beatles, Kinks, and Beach Boys pastiches of "Love on a Farmboy's Wages," "Great Fire," and "Grass." And those songs just scratch the surface of the terrific pop singles that are available on *Fossil Fuel*—"Making Plans for Nigel," "Ten Feet Tall," "Generals and Majors," "Towers of London," "Respectable Street," "Senses Working Overtime," "This World Over," "Dear God," "The Mayor of Simpleton," "King for a Day," and "The Ballad of Peter Pumpkinhead" are wonderful songs and forgotten classics. Although XTC continually made carefully constructed albums, they were a dynamite singles band, releasing songs that were tightly constructed and impossibly catchy. They never had hits, because their unabashed pop was never in fashion and Andy Partridge's voice was too pinched and his lyrics frequently too cerebral, but XTC's music stands as some of the best and most influential pop music of their era, and nowhere is that more evident than on *Fossil Fuel*. —*Stephen Thomas Erlewine*

Y

Yachts

f. 1978, Liverpool, England, db. 1981
Rock 'n' Roll, New Wave, Power Pop
Power-pop/new wave group the Yachts was formed in 1978 by Liverpool art-schoolmates Henry Priestman (vocals, keyboards), Martin Watson (guitar, vocals), Martin Dempsey (bass, vocals), Bob Bellis (drums, vocals), and J.J. Campbell (vocals). They signed to Stiff Records after a supporting spot for Elvis Costello in 1977, releasing the endlessly catchy "Suffice to Say" single (produced by Will Birch) before following Costello to Radar Records. They released two power-pop classics, *Yachts* (1979) and *Yachts Without Radar* (1980), before disbanding in the early '80s when power-pop fell from favor. —*Chris Woodstra*

● Yachts / 1979 / Radar ◆◆◆◆
On the Yachts' self-titled debut (also known as *S.O.S* due to the misleading cover art), the former art-school students couldn't completely leave behind their arty pretentions, but power-pop eventually prevails. Frontman Henry Priestman's tacky organ flourishes surprisingly compliment the typical power-pop arrangements. Includes "Suffice to Say," the striking debut single, as well as the infectious "Yachting Type" and "Look Back in Love." —*Chris Woodstra*

Yachts Without Radar / 1980 / Radar ◆◆
The second album, titled to reflect their parting of ways with their British label (Radar), is a mediocre follow-up and the band's parting shot. —*Chris Woodstra*

The Yardbirds

f. 1963, Surrey, England, db. Jul. 1968
Group / Rock 'n' Roll, Electric British Blues, Blues-Rock, British Invasion, Psychedelic, British Blues
The Yardbirds are mostly known to the casual rock fan as the starting point for three of the greatest British rock guitarists—Eric Clapton, Jeff Beck, and Jimmy Page. Undoubtedly these three figures did much to shape the group's sound, but throughout their career, the Yardbirds were very much a unit, albeit a rather unstable one. And they were truly one of the great rock bands—one whose contributions went far beyond the scope of their half dozen or so mid-'60s hits ("For Your Love," "Heart Full of Soul," "Shapes of Things," "I'm a Man," "Over Under Sideways Down," "Happenings Ten Years Time Ago"). Not content to limit themselves to the R&B and blues covers they concentrated upon initially, they quickly branched out into moody, increasingly experimental pop-rock. The innnovations of Clapton, Beck, and Page redefined the role of the guitar in rock music, breaking immense ground in the use of feedback, distortion, and amplification with finesse and breathtaking virtuosity. With the arguable exception of the Byrds, they did more than any other outfit to pioneer psychedelia, with an eclectic, risk-taking approach that laid the groundwork for much of the hard rock and progressive rock from the late '60s to the present.

No one could have predicted the band's metamorphosis from their humble beginnings in the early '60s in the London suburbs as the Metropolis Blues Quartet. By 1963, they were calling themselves the Yardbirds, with a lineup featuring Keith Relf (vocals), Paul Samwell-Smith (bass), Chris Dreja (rhythm guitar), Jim McCarty (drums), and Anthony "Top" Topham (lead guitar). The 16-year-old Topham was only to last for a very short time, pressured to leave by his family. His replacement was an art-college classmate of Relf's, Eric Clapton, nicknamed "Slowhand." The Yardbirds quickly made a name for themselves in London's rapidly exploding R&B circuit, taking over the Rolling Stones' residency at the famed Crawdaddy club. The band took a similar guitar-based, frenetic approach to classic blues/R&B as the Stones, and for their first few years they were managed by Giorgio Gomelsky, a colorful figure who had acted as a mentor and infomal manager for the Rolling Stones in that band's early days.

The Yardbirds made their first recordings as a backup band for Chicago blues great Sonny Boy Williamson, and little of their future greatness is evident in these sides, in which they were still developing their basic chops. (Some tapes of these live shows were issued after the group had become international stars; the material has been reissued ad infinitum since then.) But they really didn't find their footing until 1964, when they stretched out from straight R&B rehash into extended, frantic guitar-harmonica instrumental passages. Calling these ad hoc jams "rave ups," the Yardbirds were basically making the blues their own by applying a fiercer, heavily amplified electric base. Taking some cues from improvisational jazz by inserting their own impassioned solos, they would turn their source material inside out and sideways, heightening the restless tension by building the tempo and heated exchange of instrumental riffs to a feverish climax, adroitly cooling off and switching to a lower gear just at the point where the energy seemed uncontrollable. The live 1964 album *Five Live Yardbirds* is the best document of their early years, consisting entirely of reckless interpretations of US R&B/blues numbers, and displaying the increasing confidence and imagination of Clapton's guitar work.

As much they might have preferred to stay close to the American blues and R&B that had inspired them (at least at first), the Yardbirds made efforts to crack the pop market from the beginning. A couple of fine studio singles of R&B covers were recorded with Clapton that gave the band's sound a slight polish without sacrificing its power. The commercial impact was modest in the UK and non-existent in the States, however, and the group decided to change direction radically on their third single. Turning away from their blues roots entirely, "For Your Love" was penned by British pop-rock songwriter Graham Gouldman, and introduced many of the traits that would characterize the Yardbirds' work over the next two years. The melodies were strange (by pop standards) combinations of minor chords; the tempos slowed, speeded up, or ground to a halt unpredictably; the harmonies were droning, almost Gregorian; the arrangements were, by the standards of the time, downright weird, though retaining enough pop appeal to generate chart action. "For Your Love" featured a harpsichord, bongos, and a menacing Keith Relf vocal; it would reach No. 2 in Britain, and No. 6 in the States.

For all its brilliance, "For Your Love" precipitated a major crisis in the band. Eric Clapton wanted to stick close to the blues, and for that matter didn't like "For Your Love," barely playing on the record. Shortly afterwards, around the beginning of 1965, he left the band, opting to join John Mayall's Bluesbreakers a bit later in order to keep playing blues guitar. Clapton's spot was first offered to Jimmy Page, then one of the hottest session players in Britain; Page turned it down, figuring he could make a lot more money by staying where he was. He did, however, recommend another guitarist, Jeff Beck, then playing with an obscure band called the Tridents, as well as having worked a few sessions himself.

While Beck's stint with the band lasted only about 18 months, in this period he did more to influence the sound of '60s rock guitar than anyone except Jimi Hendrix. Clapton saw the group's decision to record adventurous pop like "For Your Love" as a sellout of their purist blues ethic. Beck, on the other hand, saw such material as a challenge that offered room for unprecedented experimentation. Not that he wasn't a capable R&B player as well—on tracks like "The Train Kept A-Rollin'" and "I'm Not Talking," he coaxed a sinister sustain from his instrument by bending the notes and using fuzz and other types of distorted amplification. The Middle Eastern influence extended to his work on all of their material, including his first single with the band, "Heart Full of Soul," which (like "For Your Love") was written by Gouldman. After initial attempts to record the song with a sitar had failed, Beck saved the day by emulating the instrument's exotic twang with fuzz riffs of his own. It became their second transatlantic Top Ten hit; the similar "Evil-Hearted You," again penned by Gouldman, gave them another big British hit later in 1965.

The chief criticism that could be levied against the band at this point was their shortage of quality original material, a gap addressed by "Still I'm Sad," a haunting group composition based around a Gregorian chant and Beck's sinewy, wicked guitar riffs. In the United States, it was coupled with "I'm a Man," a rehaul of the Bo Diddley classic that built to an almost avant-garde climax, Beck scraping the strings of the guitar for a purely percussive effect; it became a Top 20 hit in the United States in early 1966. Beck's guitar pyrotechnics came to fruition with "Shapes of Things," which (along with the Byrds' "Eight Miles High") can justifiably be classified as the first psychedelic rock classic. The group had already moved into social comment with a superb album track, "Mr. You're a Better Man than I"; on "Shapes of Things" they did so more succinctly, with Beck's explosively warped solo and feedback propelling the single near the US Top Ten. At this point the group were as innovative as any in rock 'n' roll, building their résumé with the similar hit follow-up to "Shapes of Things," "Over Under Sideways Down."

But the Yardbirds could not claim to be nearly as consistent as peers like the Beatles, Rolling Stones, and Kinks. 1966's *Roger the Engineer* was their first (and, in fact, only) studio album comprised entirely of original material, and highlighted the group's erratic quality, bouncing between derivative blues-rockers and numbers incorporating monks-of-doom chants, Oriental dance rhythms, and good old guitar raveups, sometimes in the same track. Its highlights, however, were truly thrilling; even when the experiments weren't wholly successful, they served as proof that the band were second to none in their appetite for taking risks previously unheard of within rock.

Yet at the same time, the group's cohesiveness began to unravel when bassist Samwell-Smith—who had shouldered most of the production responsibilities as well—left the band in mid-1966. Jimmy Page, by this time fed up with session work, eagerly joined on bass. It quickly became apparent that Page had more to offer, and the group unexpectedly reorganized, Dreja switching from rhythm guitar to bass, and Page assuming dual lead guitar duties with Beck.

It was a dream lineup that was, like the best dreams, too good to be true, or at least to last long. Only one single was recorded with the Beck/Page lineup, "Happenings Ten Years Time Ago," which—with its astral guitar leads, muffled explosions, eerie harmonies, and enigmatic lyrics—was psychedelia at its pinnacle. But not at its most commercial—in comparison with previous Yardbirds singles, it fared poorly on the charts, reaching only No. 30 in the States. Around this time, the group (Page and Beck in tow) made a memorable appearance in Michaelangelo Antonioni's film classic *Blow Up*, playing a reworked version of "The Train Kept-A-Rollin'" (retitled "Stroll On"). But in late 1966, Beck—who had become increasingly unreliable, not turning up for some shows and suffering from nervous exhaustion—left the band, emerging the following year as the leader of the Jeff Beck Group.

The remaining Yardbirds were determined to continue as a quartet, but in hindsight it was Beck's departure that began to burn out a band that had already survived the loss of a couple important original members. Also to blame was their mysterious failure to summon original material on the order of their classic 1965-66 tracks. More to blame than anyone, however, was Mickey Most (Donovan, Herman's Hermits, Lulu, the Animals), who assumed the producer's chair in 1967, and matched the group with inappropriately lightweight pop tunes. The band's unbridled experimentalism would simmer in isolated moments on some B-sides and album tracks, like "Puzzles," the psychedelic U.F.O. instrumental "Glimpses," and the acoustic "White Summer," which would serve as a blueprint for Page's acoustic excursions with Led Zeppelin. "Little Games," "Ha Ha Said the Clown," and "Ten Little Indians" were all low-charting singles from 1967, but were travesties compared to the magnificence of their previous hits, trading in fury and invention for sappy sing-along pop. The 1967 *Little Games* album (issued in the US only) was little better, suffering from both hasty, anemic production and weak material.

The Yardbirds continued to be an exciting concert act, concentrating most of their energies upon the United States, having been virtually left for dead in their native Britain. The B-side of their final single, the Page-penned "Think About It," was the best track of the entire Jimmy Page era, showing they were still capable of delivering intriguing, energetic psychedelia. It was too little too late—the group were truly on the wane by 1968, as an artistic rift developed within the ranks. To overgeneralize somewhat, Relf and McCarty wanted to pursue more acoustic, melodic music; Page especially wanted to rock hard and loud. A live album was recorded in New York in early 1968, but scrapped; overdubbed with unbelievably cheesy crowd noises, it was briefly released in 1971 after Page had become a superstar in Led Zeppelin, but was withdrawn in a matter of days (it has since been heavily bootlegged). By this time the group was going through the motions, leaving Page holding the bag

after a final show in mid-1968. Relf and McCarty formed the first incarnation of Renaissance. Page fulfilled existing contracts by assembling a "New Yardbirds" that, as many know, would soon change their name to Led Zeppelin.

It took years for the rock community to truly comprehend the Yardbirds' significance; younger listeners were led to the recordings in search of the roots of Clapton, Beck, and Page, each of whom had become a superstar by the end of the 1960s. Their wonderful catalog, however, has been subject to more exploitation than any other group of the '60s; dozens, if not hundreds, of cheesy packages of early material are generated throughout the world on a seemingly monthly basis. Fortunately, the best of the reissues cited below (on Rhino, Sony, Edsel and EMI) are packaged with great intelligence, enabling both collectors and new listeners to acquire all of their classic output with a minimum of fuss and repetition. *—Richie Unterberger*

Five Live Yardbirds / Dec. 1964 / Rhino ✦✦✦✦
Recorded live at London's Marquee Club, *Five Live Yardbirds* is the best document of Eric Clapton's work with the band. Tracks like "Too Much Monkey Business," "Got Love If You Want It," and "Smokestack Lightning" were good representations of The Yardbirds' "rave-ups," which were open-ended improvisations that helped lay the groundwork for groups like Cream and the Jimi Hendrix Experience. *—Rick Clark*

Roger the Engineer / 1966 / Edsel ✦✦✦✦
Roger the Engineer is a classic Yardbirds studio album, thanks to tracks like "Lost Woman," "Over Under Sideways Down," "What Do You Want?," "Psycho Daisies," and "Ever Since the World Began." Not available in the States, this British import (on Edsel) is the best-sounding Yardbirds CD by a long shot and a must-own for fans of this band. *—Rick Clark*

★ Greatest Hits, Vol. 1: 1964-1966 / 1986 / Rhino ✦✦✦✦✦
Sonically, these tracks fail to match the brilliance and warmth of the original vinyl pressings, but *Greatest Hits* has more punch. "For Your Love" is an exception, with the record version sounding extremely compressed. Of the various Yardbird collections that exist, this is still the most intelligently chosen, even though it lacks key tracks from *Roger the Engineer*. *—Rick Clark*

On Air / 1991 / Band of Joy ✦✦✦
Like most of the major British Invasion bands, the Yardbirds recorded many sessions for the BBC during their heyday. *On Air* contains 27 of these, recorded between 1965 and 1968; 21 of them feature Jeff Beck, the rest Jimmy Page (Eric Clapton is not featured on any). The BBC sessions offered listeners the opportunity to hear groups in a relatively live setting with relatively good sound quality, and that's basically what you get here. Most of their major hits—"For Your Love," "Heart Full of Soul," "Shapes of Things," "Over Under Sideways Down," "Still I'm Sad"—are included. By and large, these versions don't differ enormously from the studio cuts, with slightly different arrangements and guitar solos. One could argue, of course, that with a band so responsible for pushing rock guitar to the stratosphere, different guitar solos are a tasty discovery. And they are interesting, but they don't outdo the stellar studio renditions. Of most interest, if not highest quality, are a few covers never waxed by the group on their official releases: "Dust My Blues," "The Sun Is Shining," Garnett Mimms' "My Baby," and Dylan's "Most Likely You'll Go Your Way." On cuts like "I'm Not Talking" and "Too Much Monkey Business," Beck's pyrotechnics are truly breathtaking. But generally this release is more for Yardbirds fans than novices. *—Richie Unterberger*

Vol. 1: Smokestack Lightning / Oct. 1, 1991 / Sony ✦✦✦✦
This double-disc set focuses on tracks from *For Your Love* and *Having a Rave-Up with the Yardbirds*. Included are live tracks recorded at the Crawdaddy Club while touring with Sonny Boy Willamson. Most of these tracks on *Smokestack Lightning* (as well as *Blues, Backtracks*) were mastered off of safety tapes, as opposed to the original masters, since EMI England has possession of them. Considering that EMI won't release the masters to anyone, this is a respectable sound—though not as good as the first vinyl pressings. *—Rick Clark*

Vol. 2: Blues, Backtracks and Shapes of Things / Oct. 1, 1991 / Sony ✦✦✦✦
Another double-disc set, this covers some later hits (including the classic future-rock of "Shapes of Things"), *Roger the Engineer* outtakes, and various other oddities. The sound on some of the outtakes is pretty respectable, considering some of them were taken from the original acetates. *—Rick Clark*

The Yardbirds Little Games Sessions & More / Aug. 25, 1992 / EMI America ✦✦✦
This digitally remastered 32-track, double-disc set covers Jimmy Page's tenure with The Yardbirds. This period didn't contain the band's best work, mainly because Mickie Most's poppish production reined in the band's experimental strengths. Nevertheless, tracks like "Little Games," "Puzzles," "Smile on Me," "Drinking Muddy Water," and a wonderful acoustic version of Jimmy Page's "White Summer" make this a good

overview of the Yardbird's final stretch as a band. This set includes extensive liner notes and discography—a real treat for fans. —*Rick Clark*

Little Games [1996 Expanded] / Nov. 12, 1996 / EMI ✦✦✦
A curious release that basically condenses 1992's *Little Games Sessions & More* 32-track double CD into a 26-song, single-disc package. Six of the less essential cuts from the expanded version were dropped, with all of the group's principal 1967-68 material (from the *Little Games* LP and a few non-LP singles) remaining, along with a few alternates and outtakes. You don't lose that much in the transition, but it's annoying because anybody who bothers to track down this stuff in the first place is probably a collector who would prefer the double CD with everything, rather than a slightly abridged version. —*Richie Unterberger*

Yaz

f. 1981, Basildon, Essex, England, **db.** 1983
Dance-Pop, Synth-pop, New Wave
Yaz was the American name taken by Yazoo, a British duo made up of former Depeche Mode synthesizer player Vince Clarke and singer Alison Moyet (b.Jun 18, 1961). The two stayed together only about a year and a half (1982-1983), but that was long enough to score four British hit singles and two top-selling albums. Moyet then went solo and Clarke eventually formed another successful duo, Erasure. —*William Ruhlmann*

Upstairs at Eric's / 1982 / Sire ✦✦✦✦
Yaz's music is spare, striking electronic backup contrasted with full-throated, emotional singing, but one shouldn't discount some remarkable songwriting, especially the hits "Don't Go," "Only You," and "Situation." —*William Ruhlmann*

● **You & Me Both** / 1983 / Sire ✦✦✦✦
Perhaps a more consistent collection overall than the first album, this one demonstrates that the duo was anything but played out. While both have gone on to successful careers, you can't help regretting that this is the end of Yaz. —*William Ruhlmann*

Yello

f. 1979, Zurich, Switzerland
Art-Rock/Progressive-Rock, Club/Dance
The ambitious Swiss electronic duo Yello comprised vocalist/conceptualist Dieter Maier—a millionaire industrialist, professional gambler and member of Switzerland's national golf team—and composer/arranger Boris Blank. Meier, a former solo artist who also spent time with the group Fresh Colour, began collaborating with Blank in 1979, and the duo bowed with the single "I.T. Splash." After signing with the Residents' label Ralph Records, Yello issued their 1980 debut LP, *Solid Pleasure*, which spawned the dance hit "Bostitch."
With 1981's *Claro Que Si,* Yello made its first forays into music video; their clip for the single "Pinball Cha Cha," directed by Maier, garnered considerable acclaim and in 1985 was selected as one of 32 works included in the Museum of Modern Art's Music Video Exhibition. Visual accompaniment remained a pivotal component of the duo's work after they signed to Elektra in 1983 for the LP *You Gotta Say Yes to Another Excess,* as the videos for "I Love You" and "Lost and Found" received heavy airplay on MTV.
1985's *Stella* proved to be Yello's commercial breakthrough: while the singles and videos "Desire" and "Vicious Games" found success upon their initial release, the duo enjoyed a delayed hit with the album track "Oh Yeah," which reached the US singles chart after being prominently featured in the films *Ferris Bueller's Day Off* and *The Secret of My Success.* After the remix project *1980-1985: The New Mix in Go,* Yello recruited diva Shirley Bassey and ex-Associate Billy McKenzie for 1987's *One Second.*
Despite the success of 1988's *Flag,* which contained the international hit "The Race," over the course of the next several years Yello grew increasingly involved with film projects: after scoring the comedy *Nuns on the Run,* Maier directed his own feature, 1990's *Snowball.* In 1991, the duo resurfaced with *Baby,* followed three years later by *Zebra.* 1995's *Hands on Yello* compiled reinterpretations of the group's songs by the likes of Moby, the Orb and the Grid, while *Pocket Universe,* a collection of new material, appeared in 1997. —*Jason Ankeny*

Solid Pleasure / 1980 / Mercury ✦✦✦
Yello's debut *Solid Pleaure* is a darkly ambitious combination of avant-garde electronics, disco rhythms and European pop that is surprisingly challenging and often quite rewarding. —*Stephen Thomas Erlewine*

Claro Que Se / 1981 / Ralph ✦✦✦
Claro Que Si is an impressive fusion of European dance rhythms, synth-pop and avant-garde electronics that subverts both new wave and dance club conventions. —*Stephen Thomas Erlewine*

You Gotta Say Yes to Another Excess / 1983 / Mercury ✦✦✦✦
You Gotta Say Yes to Another Excess finds the perfect ground between accessible dance music and relatively cutting-edge electronics, resulting in one their very finest albums. —*Stephen Thomas Erlewine*

Stella / 1985 / Mercury ✦✦✦✦
On *Stella,* Yello begains to abandons their more challenging electronic elements to pursue a Euro-disco sound, typified by the cult favorite, "Oh Yeah." —*Stephen Thomas Erlewine*

Yello 1980-1985: The New Mix in One Go / 1986 / American Gramaphone ✦✦✦
The New Mix in One Go: 80-'85 is a double-record set that is comprised of remixes and re-recordings of older songs, plus a handful of new material designed to entice collectors. —*Stephen Thomas Erlewine*

One Second / 1987 / Mercury ✦✦✦
One Second expands the Euro-disco approach of *Stella,* and while it's considerably less adventurous than Yello's earlier works, it's engaging dance music, highlighted by some clever uses of Latin rhythms and vocal cameos from Billy Mackenzie and Shirley Bassey. —*Stephen Thomas Erlewine*

Flag / 1988 / Mercury ✦✦✦✦
This is Yello's most dynamic album, with excellent composition. Picking highlights would be difficult, since the songs segue, and the album just begs to be listened to as a whole. —*Vladimir Bogdanov*

● **Essential** / 1992 / Smash ✦✦✦✦
Essential is a fine 16 compilation that features all of Yello's best-known Euro-dance hits including, of course, their signature song, "Oh Yeah." —*Stephen Thomas Erlewine*

Yes

f. 1968, Birmingham, England
Art-Rock/Progressive-Rock, Pop-Rock
Far and away the longest-lasting and the most popular of the 1970s' progressive rock groups, Yes proved one of the lingering success stories from that musical genre. The band, founded in 1968, overcame a generational shift in its audience and the departure of its most visible members at key points in its history to reach the end of the century as the definitive progressive rock band. Where rivals such as Emerson, Lake & Palmer withered away commercially after the mid-'70s, and Genesis and King Crimson altered their sounds so radically as to become unrecognizable to their original fans, {Yes} consistently retained the same sound, a mix of daunting virtuosity, cosmic (often mystical) lyrics, complex musical textures, and powerful yet delicate lead vocals. Lead singer Jon Anderson started out during the British beat boom as a member of the Warriors, and later was in the band Gun before going solo in 1967. He was making a meager living cleaning up at a London club called La Chasse in June of 1968, and was thinking of starting up a new band. One day at the bar, he chanced to meet bassist/vocalist Chris Squire, a former member of the Syn. The two learned that they shared several musical interests, and within a matter of days were trying to write songs together. They began developing the beginnings of a sound that incorporated harmonies with a solid rock backing, rooted in Squire's very precise approach to the bass. {Anderson} and {Squire} saw the groups around them as having either strong vocals and weak instrumental backup, or powerful backup and weak lead vocals, and they sought to combine the best of both. They recruited Tony Kaye, formerly of the Federals, on keyboards; Peter Banks, also previously a member of the Syn, on guitar; and drummer Bill Bruford, who had joined the blues band Savoy Brown just a few weeks earlier. The name Yes was chosen for the band as something short, direct, and memorable.
The British music scene at this time was in a state of flux. The pop/psychedelic era was drawing to a close, replaced by the heavier sounds of groups like Cream. Progressive rock, with a heavy dose of late-19th-century classical music, was also starting to make noise, in the guise of acts such as the Nice and the original Deep Purple. Yes' break came in October of 1968 when they played a gig at the Speakeasy Club in London, filling in for an absent Sly & the Family Stone. The group was later selected to open for Cream's November 26, 1968 farewell concert at Royal Albert Hall, leading to a residency at London's Marquee Club and their first radio appearance, on John Peel's *Top Gear* show. Yes subsequently opened for Janis Joplin at her Royal Albert Hall concert in April 1969, and were soon signed to Atlantic Records. Their first album, *Yes,* was released in November of 1969, and displayed the basic sound that would characterize the band's subsequent records, including impeccable high harmonies, clearly defined, emphatic playing, and an approach to music that derived from folk and classical far more than the R&B from which most rock music sprung. Also present was a hint of the "space rock" sound (on "Beyond and Before") in which they would later come to specialize.
By the time the second Yes album *Time and a Word* was released in June of 1970, Banks had left the lineup, to be replaced by guitarist Steve

Howe, a former member of the Syndicats, the In Crowd, Tomorrow and Bodast. Howe played his first show with the group at Queen Elizabeth Hall on March 21, 1970, but Banks actually played *Time and a Word;* far more sophisticated than its predecessor, it even included an overdubbed orchestra on some songs, the only time that Yes would rely on outside musicians to augment their sound. The group's fame in England continued to rise as they became an increasingly popular concert attraction, and it was with the release of the Top Ten hit *The Yes Album* in April of 1971 that the public began to glimpse the group's full potential. That record, made up entirely of original compositions, was filled with complex, multi-part harmonies, loud, heavily layered guitar and bass parts, beautiful and melodic drum parts, and surging organ passages bridging them all. *The Yes Album* opened a new phase in the group's history and its approach to music—none of it was pop music in the "Top 40" sense of the term; instead, it was built on compositions which resembled sound paintings rather than songs.

Early in 1971, Yes made their first U.S. tour opening for Jethro Tull and were back late in the year sharing billing with Ten Years After and the J. Geils Band. The band began work on their next album, but were interrupted when Kaye quit in August of 1971, to join Peter Banks in the group Flash. He was replaced by former Strawbs keyboard player Rick Wakeman, a far more flamboyant musician than Kaye not only in his approach to playing but the number of instruments that he used and the way he played them. The group completed their next album, *Fragile,* in less than two months, partly out of a need to get a new album out to help pay for all of Wakeman's equipment. And partly due to this haste, the new album featured only four tracks by the group as a whole—"Roundabout," "The South Side of the Sky," "Heart of the Sunrise," and "Long Distance Runaround" (although, significantly, all except "Long Distance Runaround" ran between seven and thirteen minutes)—and was rounded out by five pieces showcasing each member of the band individually.

Fragile, released in December of 1971, reached No. 7 in England and No. 4 in America. The album's success was enhanced by the release of an edited single of "Roundabout," the group's first (and, for over a decade, only) major hit, which reached No. 13 on the U.S. charts. For millions of listeners, "Roundabout" -- with its crisp interwoven acoustic and electric guitar parts and very vivid bass textures, exquisite vocals, swirling keyboard passages, and brisk beat -- proved an ideal introduction to the Yes sound; even the album's jacket, designed by artist Roger Dean, featured distinctive, surreal landscape graphics, evoking images seemingly related to the music inside. These paintings would become part-and-parcel with the audience's impression of Yes' music, and later tours by the group would feature stage sets designed by Dean as an integral part of their shows.

Close to the Edge, recorded in the late spring of 1972 and released in September of that year, showed just where Yes was headed, consisting of only three long tracks in which the overall sound and musical textures mattered more than the lyrics or any specific melody, harmonization, or solo—"Siberian Khatru" was almost a rock adaptation of Stravinsky's *Rite of Spring.* By the time of the record's release, however, Bruford had left the band to join King Crimson, and was replaced by Alan White, a session drummer who was previously best known for having played with John Lennon and Yoko Ono's Plastic Ono Band. With White installed at the drum kit, the group went on tour behind the new album; as an added bonus for fans, Wakeman had completed his first solo LP, the instrumental concept album *The Six Wives of Henry VIII,* which was released in early 1973. A large part of the *Close to the Edge* tour was recorded, and a three-LP set entitled *Yessongs,* released in May of 1973, was assembled from the best performances. *Yessongs* became a model for progressive rock live albums - at over 120 minutes, it included the band's entire stage repertoire, all of it uncut and all of it well-played. The live album reached No. 7 in England and No. 12 in the United States.

Yes spent the second half of 1973 trying to come up with a follow-up to four successive hit albums. The resulting record, a double LP entitled *Tales from Topographic Oceans,* was released in January of 1974 with such high expectations that it earned a gold record from its advanced orders. It broke all previous boundaries, consisting of four long tracks each taking up the full side of an LP, with titles like "The Revealing Science of God (Dance of the Dawn)." Originally inspired by Jon Anderson's reaction to a set of Shastric scriptures, the album displayed a sublime beauty in many parts, and immense, mesmerizing stretches of high-energy virtuosity for most of its length. The group toured behind *Topographic Oceans* early in 1974, performing most of the album on stage. Following this tour, plans were announced for each member of the group to release a solo album of his own. At this point, the group faced another major lineup change as Wakeman—whose second solo album, *Journey to the Center of the Earth,* appeared in 1974—announced that he was leaving Yes' lineup in June to pursue a solo career. His decision created a major problem for the band, for the keyboard player had become a star within their ranks, and was the group's most well-known individ-

ual member. In August of 1974, it was announced that Patrick Moraz, formerly of the progressive rock trio Refugee, had replaced Wakeman. Three months later, Yes' new album, *Relayer,* was released, reaching the British No. 4 spot and the American No. 5 position; Moraz proved an adequate replacement for {Wakeman,} but lacked his predecessor's gift for showmanship and extravagance. The group toured in the wake of *Relayer*'s release in November of 1974, but didn't record together again for two and a half years. In November of 1975, Chris Squire's solo effort *Fish Out of Water* and Steve Howe's *Beginnings* were both released, followed in March of 1976 by Alan White's *Ramshackled* and Moraz's self-titled venture. Finally, in July of 1976 Jon Anderson's *Olias of Sunhillow* appeared. Amid all of these solo projects, the group's lineup changed once again, as Wakeman announced his return to the fold in late 1976, while Moraz exited. Wakeman's original plan was to assist the group in the studio on their new album, but the sessions proved so productive that he made the decision to return to Yes lineup permanently. Their new album, *Going for the One,* released in August of 1977, represented a much more austere, basic style of rock music, built around shorter songs.

Tormato, released nearly a year later (heralded by the single "Don't Kill the Whale"), made the Top Ten in both England and America. Once again, after finishing the tour behind the album, the group members began working on solo projects. The year 1979 saw the release of *The Steve Howe Album,* while early in 1980 Anderson hooked up with Greek-born keyboard player Vangelis, and the two released *Short Stories.* (Jon & Vangelis, as the team became known, went on to cut several more records together.) In March of 1980, Yes' lineup began to collapse, as Wakeman and then Anderson walked out after an unsuccessful attempt to start work on a new album. Two months later, vocalist/guitarist Trevor Horn and keyboardist Geoff Downes (keyboards), formerly of the Buggles, joined the Yes lineup of Steve Howe, Chris Squire, and Alan White. This configuration recorded a new album, *Drama,* which was released in August of 1980; the hybrid lineup lasted for a year, but the old Yes incarnation remained much closer to the hearts of fans, and in January of 1981 Atlantic Record released *Yesshows,* a double live album made up of stage performances dating from 1976 through 1978.

Finally, in April of 1981, the breakup of Yes was announced. Downes formed Asia with Squire (after the latter tried hooking up with Robert Plant and Jimmy Page), which went on to some considerable if short-lived success in the early '80s, and the rest of the band scattered to different projects. For a year-and-a-half, the group seemed a dead issue, until Squire and White announced the formation of a new group called Cinema, with original Yes keyboard player Tony Kaye and South African guitarist Trevor Rabin. This band proved unsatisfactory, and Squire invited Anderson to join. It was just about then that everyone realized that they'd reformed virtually the core of the Yes lineup, and that they should simply revive the name. In late 1983, this Yes lineup, with Trevor Horn serving as producer, released an unexpected chart-topping hit (No. 1 in the U.S. in January of 1984) single in "Owner of a Lonely Heart," displaying a stripped-down modern dance-rock sound unlike anything the group had ever produced before. The remaining group released a successful dance-rock style album, *90125,* under Horn's guidance, which sold well but also proved a dead-end, with no follow-up, when Horn chose not to remain with the group.

Yes was invisible for nearly two years after that, until the late 1987 release of *The Big Generator,* which performed only moderately well. The proliferation of ex-Yes members gathering together in various combinations led to an ongoing legal dispute over who owned the group name, which came to a head in 1989. Luckily for four of them, the name "Anderson Bruford Wakeman Howe" was recognizable enough to reach the fans, which sent the resulting album into the US Top 30 and the British Top 20, more or less handing them a victory by acclamation (later supported by the settlement) in their dispute over the name. By touring with "An Evening of Yes Music," they presented their classic music to sell-out houses all over the country. The legal squabbles had all been settled by the spring of 1991, at which time a composite "mega Yes" group consisting of Anderson, Howe, Wakeman, Squire, Kaye, White, Rabin, and Bruford embarked on a blow-out world tour. The accompanying reunion album, *Union,* debuted on the British charts at No. 7. —*Bruce Eder*

Yes / Oct. 15, 1969 / Atlantic ✦✦✦
Early pop/folk-rock. Their first, and it should be taken as such. —*Bruce Eder*

Time and a Word / Nov. 2, 1970 / Atlantic ✦✦✦
A more ambitious second album, in search of a style. —*Bruce Eder*

The Yes Album / Mar. 19, 1971 / Atlantic ✦✦✦✦
The album that first gave shape to the established Yes sound, build around science-fiction concepts, folk melodies, and soaring organ, guitar, and vocal showpieces. "Your Move" actually made the US charts as a single, and "Starship Trooper," "Perpetual Change," and "Yours Is No Disgrace" became much-loved parts of the band's concert repertory for

many tours to come. Remastered in 1995 with significantly improved sound. —*Bruce Eder*

★ **Fragile** / Jan. 4, 1972 / Atlantic ✦✦✦✦✦
The band's breakthrough album, dominated by science-fiction and fantasy elements and new member Rick Wakeman, whose organ, synthesizers, Mellotrons, and other keyboard exotica added a larger-than-element to the proceedings. Ironically, the album was a patchwork job, hastily assembled in order to cover the cost of Wakeman's array of instruments. But the group built effectively on the groundwork left by *The Yes Album*, and the group had an AM-radio sucker-punch, aimed at all of those other progressive bands who eschewed the notion of hit singles, in the form of "Roundabout," the edited version (sort of "highlights" of the album version) of which pulled in millions of young kids who'd never heard them before. The single clicked, most album-buyers liked the long version and all of the rest of what they found, and the band was made. Remastered with much improved sound and graphics in 1995 with a reference to "digital remastering" across the top back of the jewel case. —*Bruce Eder*

☆ **Close to the Edge** / Sep. 13, 1972 / Atlantic ✦✦✦✦✦
For most fans, this album represents the peak of Yes' work. Side-length suites allowed Jon Anderson even more opportunity for vocal acrobatics and Rick Wakeman an even bigger canvas on which to paint his electronic synthesizer swirls, organ arpeggios, and great swathes of Mellotron-generated color. Steve Howe's playing took on a particularly urgent quality here, but never lost sight of its lyricism, while Chris Squire's bass is practically another lead instrument, and Bill Bruford—in his then seeming swansong with the band—contributed some of his most elegant drumming. The 1995 remastering, referred to on the top back of the jewel box, was especially welcome on this album, the new CD version being many steps superior to the old one in terms of sound. —*Bruce Eder*

Yessongs / May 4, 1973 / Atlantic ✦✦✦✦
The best live album to emerge from the entire early-'70s art-rock scene, a compendium of blazing performances covering the previous three studio albums by the group and the accompanying solo career of Rick Wakeman. Some of the performances are superior to their studio originals, most notably "Siberian Khatru," although "And You and I" is something of a disappointment next to the version on *Close to the Edge*. Virtually a live "best-of" album. The 1995 remastered version, in the narrow double jewel box with the label stating that it is the remastered version on the top of the back of the jewel box, is the version to own, being far superior to the old edition. —*Bruce Eder*

Tales from Topographic Oceans / Jan. 9, 1974 / Atlantic ✦✦✦✦
Either the finest record or the most overblown album in Yes' output. When it was released, critics and fans raved over its 20-minute-long tracks, each taking up one side of a double album, and it sold very well. By the 1980s, it was being derided by critics as one of the worst examples of progressive rock's over-indulgent nature. Jon Anderson's fascination with Eastern religions never manifested itself more clearly or broadly, but one needn't understand any of that to appreciate the many sublimely beautiful moments on this album, some of the most gorgeous passages ever recorded by the band. The newly remastered version, in the narrow double jewel box, with a reference to the remastering on the top back of the jewel case, is the version to own, with crisp textures, vivid sound, and excellent reproductions of the original art. —*Bruce Eder*

Relayer / Dec. 5, 1974 / Atlantic ✦✦✦
Yes had fallen out of critical favor with *Tales from Topographic Oceans*, a two-record set of four songs that reviewers found indulgent. But they had not fallen out of the Top Ten, and so they had little incentive to curb their musical ambitiousness. *Relayer*, released 11 months after *Tales*, was a single-disc, two-song album, its music organized into suites that alternated abrasive, rhythmically dense instrumental sections featuring solos for the various instruments with delicate vocal and choral sections featuring poetic lyrics devoted to spiritual imagery. Such compositions seemed intended to provide an interesting musical landscape over which the listener might travel, and enough Yes fans did that to make *Relayer* a Top Ten, gold-selling hit, though critics continued to complain about the lack of concise, coherent song structures. —*William Ruhlmann*

Yesterdays / Feb. 27, 1975 / Atlantic ✦✦✦
A slightly disappointing compendium of odd early tracks. For true fanatics. Supplanted, in part, by *Yesyears*. —*Bruce Eder*

Going for the One / Jul. 7, 1977 / Atlantic ✦✦✦
Going For the One is perhaps the most overlooked item in the Yes catalog. It marked Rick Wakeman's return to the band after a three-year absence, and also a return to shorter song forms after the experimentalism of *Close to the Edge, Tales from Topographic Oceans* and *Relayer*. In many ways, this disc could be seen as the follow-up to *Fragile*. Its five tracks still retain mystical, abstract lyrical images, and the music is

grand and melodic, the vocal harmonies perfectly balanced by the stinging guitar work of Howe, Wakeman's keyboards, and the solid rhythms of White and Squire. The title track features Howe on steel guitar (he's the only prog-rocker who bothers with the instrument). "Turn of the Century" and the album's single, "Wonderous Stories," are lovely ballads the way only Yes can do them. "Parallels" is the album's big, pompous song, so well done that in later years the band opened concerts with it. Wakeman's stately church organ, recorded at St. Martin's Church, Vevey, Switzerland, sets the tone for this "Roundabout"-ish track. The concluding "Awaken" is the album's nod to the extended suite. Again, the lyrics are spacy in the extreme, but Anderson and Squire are dead-on vocally, and the addition of Anderson's harp and White's tuned percussion round out this evocative track. —*Ross Boissoneau*

Tormato / Sep. 20, 1978 / Atlantic ✦✦
Drama / Aug. 18, 1980 / Atlantic ✦✦✦
Yesshows / Nov. 24, 1980 / Atlantic ✦✦✦
Not *Yessongs* in terms of comprehensiveness of the material, and at just under 80 minutes this could've been put on one CD. But this budget-priced double-disc set, newly remastered for its first CD release in the US, does feature key elements of the group's mid—and late-'70s repertory, including an excellent performance of "The Gates of Delirium," along with "Parallels," "Don't Kill the Whale," "Ritual," and "Wonderous Stories," and their live reconsideration of "Time and a Word." Rick Wakeman is mostly featured, with a few Moraz tracks. The group is a good deal noisier on this record than they were on *Yessongs*, but the performances are reasonably urgent, and the sound is considerably improved over the old imported version from Japan. Only flaw is the indexing on disc two, which doesn't match the label. —*Bruce Eder*

Classic Yes / Nov. 30, 1981 / Atlantic ✦✦✦✦
Classic Yes collects the group's biggest radio hits, which were frequently their most accessible and catchy songs. Nevertheless, Yes made albums, not singles, in the '70s, so these songs make more sense in their original context than they do on this compilation. —*Stephen Thomas Erlewine*

90125 / Nov. 7, 1983 / Atlantic ✦✦✦✦
A ridiculously successful "comeback" album with a slightly different membership. For completists. —*Bruce Eder*

Big Generator / Sep. 17, 1987 / Atlantic ✦✦
The four-years-in-the-making follow-up to Yes' comeback album, *90125*, *Big Generator* was also a million-selling hit, although not as successful as its predecessor, probably because the singles "Love Will Find a Way" (No. 30) and "Rhythm of Love" (No. 40) couldn't match "Owner of a Lonely Heart" from the previous LP, even if they were favorites on AOR radio at the time. Actually, it was the title track that was a carbon-copy of "Owner," so maybe that was the problem. More likely, though, "Owner" was a one-shot (courtesy of producer Trevor Horn), and as Yes asserted itself more here, they reverted more to their old style, making for some confusion. Nevertheless, this album was the group's last major hit. —*William Ruhlmann*

Union / Apr. 30, 1991 / Arista ✦✦
The various Yes members settled their differences by putting together a mega-version of the band, featuring eight members from various eras, and recorded this compromise effort, on which they attempted to recapture the early '70s sound of Yes. AOR radio was willing, and the single "Lift Me Up" topped Billboard's Album Rock Tracks chart for six weeks, with two other cuts also making the list. But the single limped to No. 86 on the Hot 100, and although the album shot to No. 15 and went gold, this was a serious fall-off from previous sales, appropriate to an album that was one of those (increasingly frequent) corporate attempts to clone a band's old style. —*William Ruhlmann*

Yesyears / Aug. 6, 1991 / Atlantic ✦✦✦✦
This four-CD set is sonically so far superior to the individual CDs by the group that on this basis alone it is worth owning. Unfortunately, there are important songs that didn't get the remastering treatment, and they are missed. —*Bruce Eder*

● **The Very Best of Yes** / Sep. 21, 1993 / Atlantic ✦✦✦✦
The very best of Yes is hard to stick on merely one disc; this set includes tracks from each era of the band. Not essential, it's still a decent sampler. —*Rick Clark*

Talk / Mar. 22, 1994 / Victory ✦✦
The opening song, "The Calling," is solid later-era sounding Yes. Overall, it's an album hardcore fans will accept, but not one of their best. —*Rick Clark*

Keys to Ascension / Oct. 29, 1996 / CMC International ✦✦✦✦
Yes, this time consisting of Jon Anderson, Chris Squire, Steve Howe, Rick Wakeman, and Alan White got together for three nights in March of 1996 at San Luis Obispo, California to cut this, the group's fourth live album in 28 years, which is rounded out with two new studio creations. Four of the seven live tracks are covers of songs that the band originally recorded between 1970 and 1974. The group has aged well, and *Keys To*

Ascension is a more satisfying album than 1980's *Yesshows*. "Siberian Khatru" has less intensity, but more lyricism than it did 23 years ago, making it slightly less dramatic—the ending lacks some necessary attack, replacing it instead with more articulate guitar. *Tales From Topographic Oceans* is represented by "The Revealing Science of God," which shows off some superb ensemble playing on a 20-minute piece that is most difficult to bring off on stage, with Rick Wakeman the standout among the instrumentalists. Jon Anderson's falsetto has lowered slightly with age, and lost a bit of its power in the process as well, but the ensemble carries the piece successfully to its conclusion. Nearly as surprising is the presence of Paul Simon's "America," a song they cut back in the early 1970s, which comes off as a lot more engaging here than it did back when. "Onward" and "Awaken," from the late 1970's, are well represented, in beautiful live covers. The new songs featured as studio recordings on the second disc are superior to anything on the recent *Union* "mega-Yes" album, with soaring harmonies and very spacious song construction. —*Bruce Eder*

Yo La Tengo

f. 1984, Hoboken, NJ
Alternative Pop-Rock, Indie Rock
Yo La Tengo was in many respects the quintessential critic's band: in addition to their adventurous eclecticism, defiant independence, and restless creative ambition—three qualities which virtually guarantee music press acclaim—the group's frontman, Ira Kaplan, even tenured as a rock scribe prior to finding success as a performer. So frequently compared to the Velvet Underground that they even portrayed the legendary group in the 1996 film *I Shot Andy Warhol*, the Hoboken, New Jersey-based unit explored the extremes of feedback-driven noise-rock and sweetly melodic pop, shading their work with equal parts scholarly composure and fannish enthusiasm; prolific and mercurial, Yo La Tengo ultimately transcended its myriad influences to ensconce itself as a beloved institution of the indie community.

The core of Yo La Tengo (Spanish for the outfielder's cry of "I've got it!") comprised singer/guitarist Kaplan and his wife, drummer/vocalist Georgia Hubley; after forming the band in 1984, they placed an advertisement seeking other musicians to round out the lineup, requesting applicants who shared their fondness for the Soft Boys, Mission of Burma and Arthur Lee's Love. A number of bassists and lead guitarists passed through the band's roster during their formative years, but after bowing in late 1985 with the single "The River of Water," backed by a cover of Love's "A House Is Not a Motel," Yo La Tengo's membership appeared to stabilize with the additions of guitarist Dave Schramm and bassist Mike Lewis prior to the sessions for 1986's full-length roots-pop debut *Ride the Tiger*, produced by former Mission of Burma bassist Clint Conley.

However, both Schramm and Lewis exited in the wake of the record's release, leaving Kaplan to assume lead guitar duties. Bassist Stephen Wichnewski signed on for 1987's *New Wave Hot Dogs*, a more assured outing which brought to the fore the group's Velvet Underground obsession via a cover of the early VU composition "It's Alright (The Way That You Live)"; not only did Kaplan's introverted, half-spoken vocals and buzzing guitar work closely recall Lou Reed, but Hubley's rock-steady drumming and breathy backing turns simultaneously conjured memories of vintage Maureen Tucker. Even better was 1989's *President Yo La Tengo*, recorded with producer and guest bassist Gene Holder; opening with the droning squalls of the stunning "Barnaby, Hardly Working," the record spotlighted the group's sonic schizophrenia by including two Jekyll-and-Hyde versions of the track "The Evil That Men Do"—one a gorgeous instrumental, the other a blistering feedback freakout.

Schramm returned to the fold for 1990's *Fakebook*, a remarkable acoustic folk-pop journey through Kaplan's record collection and a virtual family tree of Yo La Tengo reference points. A wonderfully low-key collection of covers ranging from forgotten nuggets (the Kinks' "Oklahoma USA," the Flamin' Groovies' "You Tore Me Down," Gene Clark's "Tried So Hard") to absolute obscurities (Rex Garvin and the Mighty Cravers' "Emulsified," the Escorts' "The One to Cry," the Scene Is Now's "Yellow Sarong"), *Fakebook* also included a handful of outstanding new originals as well as luminous retakes of the previous record's "Barnaby, Hardly Working" and *New Wave Hot Dogs'* "Did I Tell You?" The superb *That Is Yo La Tengo* EP previewed 1992's *May I Sing With Me*, the first effort to feature permanent bassist James McNew (formerly of Christmas); a return to noise typified by the hotwired nine-minute feedback saga "Mushroom Cloud of Hiss," the record balanced out its extemist tendencies with the occasional sidestep into melodic beauty ("Detouring America With Horns") and infectious indie-pop ("Upside-Down").

A move to the Matador label predated the release of 1993's *Painful*, another winner informed by the atmospherics of shoegazer drones and dream-pop; bookended by radically opposed renditions of the track "Big Day Coming"—the first an organ-driven mood piece, the other an edgy guitar outing—the record pushed Yo La Tengo in a multitude of new directions, significantly expanding the trio's palette of sounds and tex-

tures. 1995's *Electr-o-Pura* continued the progression, zig-zagging from dead-on British Invasion recreations (the sparkling "Tom Courtenay") to shimmering folk (the Hubley-sung "Pablo and Andrea") to bracing sonic experimentation ("Decora"). After 1996's *Genius + Love Equals Yo La Tengo*, a two-disc compendium of B-sides, compilation tracks, rare singles, and unreleased material, the trio resurfaced in the spring of 1997 with the *Autumn Sweater* EP, a collection of title-track remixes from the likes of Tortoise and My Bloody Valentine's Kevin Shields; the full-length *I Can Hear the Heart Beating As One*, recorded in Nashville, followed a few weeks later. —*Jason Ankeny*

Ride the Tiger / 1986 / Coyote/Twintone ♦♦♦♦
A fine debut that shows off this band's smarts and style. Not as aggressive in the noise department as some later releases, this is still a confident and assured record. As usual, Kaplan comes up with a cool, if fairly obscure cover or two (here it's Ray Davies' "Big Sky") as well as loading up the record with some fine originals. The presence of ex-Mission of Burma bassist Clint Conley as producer adds a touch of professionalism that doesn't detract from the album's cheery and insistent low-fi charm. —*John Dougan*

● **President Yo La Tengo/New Wave Hot Dogs** / 1989 / Twin/Tone ♦♦♦♦
Two records now available as a single CD, these really show off Yo La Tengo's ability to create musical extremes. *New Wave Hot Dogs* has the firm pop sense and strong songwriting of the debut, but *President Yo La Tengo* offers up a little more free-form skronk in the ten-minute live version of "The Evil That Men Do," a gloriously squalling, over-the-top crash and bash session which proves how liberating and fun sonic dissonance can be. Just in case you don't like that sort of thing, "Evil" also shows up as a straightahead folk-rock track. This is a great collection of material that, as well as anything else they have recorded, gets to the heart of what makes this band tick. —*John Dougan*

Fakebook / 1990 / Bar/None ♦♦♦♦
Recommending *Fakebook* as the best place to begin a relationship with Yo La Tengo is slightly disingenuous, mainly because Yo La Tengo has never made another record like it, and perhaps never will. So, as completely wonderful as this record is (and believe me, it is), it's an accurate representation of one side of Yo La Tengo, and assuming that everything sounds like *Fakebook* might be disappointing. A collection of cover songs that lean towards the idiosyncratic (e.g., Peter Stampfel, Daniel Johnston, Jad Fair), *Fakebook* is warm, low-key and lovely, with heartfelt singing and playing that never flags after hundreds of replays. It's impossible to imagine playing this record and not smiling and singing along. A big bonus is a great version of the Flamin' Groovies' "You Tore Me Down." —*John Dougan*

May I Sing with Me / Feb. 28, 1992 / Alias ♦♦♦
With song titles like "Mushroom Cloud of Hiss" and "Five-Cornered Drone (Crispy Duck)," *May I* is classic Yo La Tengo merging pop and noise in an awesome aural display. Songs start with Kaplan's repetitive (and very simple) chord changes, as Hubley and (at this juncture) regular bassist James McNew add layer after layer of supportive sound. During the noisier tracks (especially the aforementioned "Mushroom Cloud of Hiss"), the song explodes in paroxysms of feedback and drops the rhythmic pulse altogether, eventually returning the backbeat after a few minutes of white noise. That may not be everybody's cup of tea, but for those who like this adventurousness and recklessness, it's a lot of fun. —*John Dougan*

Upside Down / Apr. 1992 / Alias ♦♦♦

Painful / Oct. 5, 1993 / Matador ♦♦♦♦
Yo La Tengo has released several fine albums before, but only *Painful* encapsulates their folky guitar experimentalism perfectly. Alternating between dreamy Velvet Underground-style ballads and raving, Sonic Youth guitar squalls, *Painful* also finds the group improving their songwriting skills immeasurably. Before, they relied on soundscapes; now, the sound fleshes out their songs, from the trance-like "Nowhere Near" to the dense "From A Motel 6" and the two versions of "Big Day Coming," which cover both ends of the spectrum. A subtly addicting album. —*Stephen Thomas Erlewine*

Electr-O-Pura / May 2, 1995 / Matador ♦♦♦
Electr-O-Pura is somewhat of a departure for the band. Gone is much of the soft, dreamy quality that characterized *Painful*. There are slower songs, but they don't work as well as on their previous release. Yo La Tengo instead emphasizes its American indie roots on "Tom Courtenay," "False Alarm," and "Decora." —*John Bush*

Genius + Love " Yo La Tengo / Sep. 10, 1996 / Matador ♦♦♦
A double-disc compilation of rarities and outtakes, featuring one disc of vocals and one disc of instrumentals, *Genius + Love Yo La Tengo* is far from being consistent—there's a reason why half of these songs were never released—but the album offers enough neglected gems to make it worthwhile for dedicated fans. —*Stephen Thomas Erlewine*

I Can Hear the Heart Beating as One / Apr. 22, 1997 / Matador ✦✦✦✦
Functioning as a virtual catalog of mid-'90s indie-rock trends, *I Can Hear the Heart Beating as One* is an astonishing tour de force from Yo La Tengo, establishing their deep talents as songwriters and musicians. Although the album may run a little long for some tastes, there are very few throwaways on the record—even the shoegazer cover of the Beach Boys' "Little Honda" is a revelatory gem. But what truly impresses is how the songs, ranging from hypnotically droning instrumentals to tightly written and catchy pop songs, hold together to form what is arguably Yo La Tengo's finest and most coherent album to date. *—Stephen Thomas Erlewine*

Young Marble Giants

f. 1978, Cardiff, Wales, **db.** 1981
Alternative Pop-Rock, New Wave, Post-Punk
One of the quirkiest and most idiosyncratic groups to emerge from the early British new wave indie scene, Young Marble Giants (from Cardiff, Wales) were not so much new wave in sound as in strategy. They subverted conventional pop-rock methods by stripping both song construction and instrumentation to its essence. A reverberant funky bass, a shrill organ, short choppy bursts of guitar chords, a softly clicking drum machine—that was all the trio needed. The hauntingly spacious sound was made both more intimate and foreboding by Alison Statton's coolly intoned, almost neutral vocals. The words were more important for their mood than their content. Pop minimalism of the first order, it now stands as one of the first fully formed expressions of the sub-genre that would be called post-punk.

Needless to say, it was also quite resistant to widespread commercial success, although it quickly attracted a cult following. Almost the whole of their output is contained on their debut and, as it turned out, only album, *Colossal Youth* (1980). After an EP in 1981, the group broke up. Alison Statton went into a more jazz-lounge-pop direction with Weekend and solo recordings. YMG guitarist and principal YMG songwriter Stuart Moxham formed the Gist, and in the 1990s, after a series of personal setbacks, began regularly releasing solo products with fuller and more traditional rock arrangements than those identified with the Young Marble Giants. *—Richie Unterberger*

● **Colossal Youth** / 1980 / Crepuscule ✦✦✦✦
Young Marble Giants' one album is a collection of sparse, evocative tunes emphasizing Statton's floating vocals and minimal guitar/organ/bass/drum machine arrangements. Comparable to little else from its time or since, this is rock music at its most austere. The original album had 15 songs; a subsequent CD added a few more. But the 1994 edition on Crepuscule is the one to get, pushing the total to 24 tracks with additions from the *Testcard* EP, the 1979 "Final Day" single, and a compilation cut—everything they ever did, in fact. *—Richie Unterberger*

Young MC

b. May 10, 1967, London, England
Hip Hop, Crossover Rap
Intelligent and middle-class, rapper Marvin Young earned a degree in economics from USC, where he met Michael Ross and Matt Dike, cofounders of the fledgling Delicious Vinyl rap label. He made his debut as Young MC on the single "I Let 'Em Know." In 1989, Young collaborated with Tone Loc on "Wild Thing," the first Top Ten pop hit for a Black rapper, and the follow-up smash "Funky Cold Medina." Young MC stepped out on his own later in the year with the Top Ten smash "Bust a Move," a good-natured examination of romantic successes and failures spiced by his sense of humor and quick-tongued rapping. The song won a Grammy for Best Rap Performance, and its strong pop appeal helped the attendant album *Stone Cold Rhymin'* go platinum. The follow-up, "Principal's Office," was a humorous, everyday high school tale resembling a Chuck Berry plot and also climbed into the Top 40.

Following Young MC's success, he split acrimoniously from Delicious Vinyl, citing restrictions on his work and unwanted tinkering with his album; the label sued him for breach of contract and eventually settled out of court. Young signed with Capitol and released *Brainstorm* in 1991, expanding into message tracks promoting personal responsibility. The album didn't fare as well, and by 1993, audience tastes had shifted towards harder-edged hip-hop, rendering *What's the Flavor?* a flop. *—Steve Huey*

Brainstorm / 1989 / Capitol ✦✦✦
In hardcore hip-hop circles, more commercial rappers generally aren't thought of as having a lot of technique—the consensus is that they're getting over on their pop or R&B appeal rather than their rapping skills. After "Bust a Move" became a major hit in the R&B market, Young MC was viewed suspiciously by b-boys. But make no mistake: the clean-cut Los Angeles rapper has considerable technique and could no doubt hold his own in a microphone battle. While his second album wasn't the hit that *Stone Cold Rhymin'* was, it's a decent, enjoyable effort with strong hooks and dancefloor appeal. Such congenial, R&B-ish fare as

"That's the Way Love Goes," "Listen to the Beat of the Music" and "After School" obviously wasn't aimed at hardcore rap audiences, but leaves no doubt that Young MC could flow with the best. *—Alex Henderson*

● **Stone Cold Rhymin'** / 1989 / Delicious Vinyl ✦✦✦✦
Young MC's first album was a major hit, featuring pop-rap crossover classics like "Bust a Move" and "Principal's Office." With his friendly, clever rhyming and a warm, funky production dominating the album, *Stone Cold Rhymin'* was not only Young MC's most popular album, but also his best. *—Stephen Thomas Erlewine*

What's the Flavor? / Jun. 7, 1993 / Capitol ✦✦✦
On his third album, Young MC was trying to recapture his audience, adding elements of jazz-rap—thanks to the production of A Tribe Called Quest's Ali Shaheed—to his pop-oriented style. While it didn't rocket him back to the top of the charts, the results were agreeable and likeable, with only a couple of embarrassing tracks. *—Stephen Thomas Erlewine*

Neil Young

b. Nov. 12, 1945, Toronto, Ontario
Guitar, Piano, Ukulele, Vocals / Rock 'n' Roll, Country-Rock, Singer-Songwriter, Hard Rock, Folk-Rock
After Neil Young left the Californian folk-rock band Buffalo Springfield in 1968, he slowly established himself as one of the most influential and idiosyncratic American singer-songwriters of his generation. Young's body of work ranks second only to Bob Dylan in terms of depth, and he was able to sustain his critical reputation, as well as record sales, for a longer period of time than Dylan, partially because of his willfully perverse work ethic. From the beginning of his solo career in the late '60s until the late '90s, he never stopped writing, recording and performing; his official catalog only represented a portion of his work, since he kept countless tapes of unreleased songs in his vaults. Just as importantly, Young continually explored new musical territory, from rockabilly and the blues to electronic music. But these stylistic exercises only gained depth when compared to his two primary styles—gentle folk and country-rock, and crushingly loud electric guitar rock, which he frequently recorded with the Californian garage band Crazy Horse. Throughout his career, Young alternated between these two extremes, and both proved equally influential; there were just as many simpy singer-songwriters as there were grunge and country-rock bands claiming to be influenced by Neil Young. Despite his enormous catalog and influence, Young continued to move forward, writing new songs and exploring new music in his fourth decade as a performing artist. That restless spirit ensured that he was one of the few rock veterans as vital in his old age as he was in his youth.

Born in Toronto, Canada, Neil Young moved to Winnipeg with his mother following her divorce from his sports-journalist father. Young began playing music in high school. Not only did he play in garage-rock outfits like the Esquires, but he also played in local folk clubs and coffeehouses, where he eventually met Joni Mitchell and Stephen Stills. During the mid-'60s, he returned to Toronto, where he played as a solo folk act. By 1966, he joined the Mynah Birds, which also featured bassist Bruce Palmer and Rick James. The group recorded material for Motown that was not released. Frustrated by his lack of success, Young moved to Los Angeles in his Pontiac hearse, taking Palmer along as support. Shortly after they arrived in Los Angeles, they happened to meet Stills, and they formed Buffalo Springfield, who quickly became one of the leaders of the Californian folk-rock scene. Despite the success of Buffalo Springfield, the group was plagued with tension, and Young quit the band several times before finally leaving to become a solo artist in May of 1968. Hiring Elliot Roberts as his manager, Young signed with Reprise Records and released his eponymous debut album in early 1969. By the time the album was released, he had begun playing with a local band called the Rockets, which featured guitarist Danny Whitten, bassist Billy Talbot and drummer Ralph Molina. Young renamed the group Crazy Horse and had them support him on his second album, *Everybody Knows This Is Nowhere*, which was recorded in just two weeks. Featuring such Young staples as "Cinnamon Girl" and "Down By the River," the album went gold. Following the completion of the record, he began jamming with Crosby, Stills and Nash, eventually joining the group for their spring 1970 album, *Deja Vu*. Although he was now part of Crosby, Stills and Nash, Young continued to record as a solo artist, releasing *After the Gold Rush* at the end of the year. *After the Gold Rush*, with its accompanying single "Only Love Can Break Your Heart," established Young as a solo star, and fame only increased through his association with CSN&Y.

Although Crosby, Stills, Nash and Young were a very successful act, they were also volatile, and they had split by the spring 1971 release of the live *Four Way Street*. The following year, Young had his first No. 1 album with the mellow country-rock of *Harvest*, which also featured his first (and only) No. 1 single, "Heart of Gold." Instead of embracing his success, he spurned it, following it with the noisy, bleak live film *Journey*

Through the Past. Both the movie and the soundtrack received terrible reviews, as did the live album *Time Fades Away,* a record recorded with the Stray Gators that was released in 1973.

Both *Journey through the Past* and *Time Fades Away* signaled that Young was entering a dark period in his life, but they only scratched the surface of his anguish. Inspired by the overdose deaths of Danny Whitten in 1972 and his roadie Bruce Berry the following year, Young wrote and recorded the bleak, druggy *Tonight's the Night* late in 1973, but declined to release it at the time. Instead, he released *On the Beach,* which was nearly as harrowing, in 1974; *Tonight's the Night* finally appeared in the spring of 1975. By the time of its release, Young had recovered, as indicated by the record's hard-rocking follow-up *Zuma,* an album recorded with Crazy Horse and released later that year.

Young's focus began to wander in 1976, as he recorded the duet album *Long May You Run* with Stephen Stills and then abandoned his partner midway through the supporting tour. The following year he recorded the country-rock-oriented *American Stars 'n Bars,* which featured vocals by Nicolette Larson, who was also prominent on 1978's *Comes a Time.* Prior to the release of *Comes a Time,* Young scrapped the country-rock album *Homegrown* and assembled the triple-album retrospective *Decade.* At the end of 1978, he embarked on an arena tour called Rust Never Sleeps, which was designed as a showcase for new songs. Half of the concert featured Young solo, the other half featured him with Crazy Horse. That was the pattern that *Rust Never Sleeps,* released in the summer of 1979, followed. The record was hailed as a comeback, proving that Young was one of the few rock veterans who attacked punk rock head-on. That fall he released the double album *Live Rust* and the live movie *Rust Never Sleeps.*

Rust Never Sleeps had restored Young to his past glory, but he perversely decided to trash his goodwill in 1980 with *Hawks & Doves,* a collection of acoustic songs that bore the influence of conservative, right-wing politics. In 1981, Young released the heavy rock album *Re*Ac*tor,* which received poor reviews. Following its release, he left Reprise for the fledgling Geffen Records, where he was promised lots of money and artistic freedom. Young decided to push his Geffen contract to the limit, releasing the electronic *Trans,* where his voice was recorded through a computerized vocoder, later that year. The album and its accompanying, technology-dependent tour were received with bewildered, negative reviews. The rockabilly of *Everybody's Rockin'* (1983) was equally scorned, and Young soon settled into a cult audience for the mid-'80s.

Over the course of the mid-'80s, Young released three albums that were all stylistic exercises. In 1985, he released the straight country *Old Ways,* which was followed by the new wave-tinged *Landing on Water* the following year. He returned to Crazy Horse for 1987's *Life,* but by that time, he and Geffen had grown sick of each other, and he returned to Reprise in 1988. His first album for Reprise was the bluesy, horn-driven *This Note's for You,* which was supported by an acclaimed video that satirized rock stars endorsing commercial products. At the end of the year, he recorded a reunion album with Crosby, Stills and Nash called *American Dream,* which was greeted with savagely negative reviews.

American Dream didn't prepare any observer for the critical and commercial success of 1989's *Freedom,* which found Young following the half-acoustic/half-electric blueprint of *Rust Never Sleeps* to fine results. Around the time of its release, Young became a hip name to drop in indie rock circles, and he was the subject of a tribute record titled *The Bridge* in 1989. The following year, Young reunited with Crazy Horse for *Ragged Glory,* a loud, feedback-drenched album that received his strongest reviews since the '70s. For the supporting tour, Young hired the avant-rock band Sonic Youth as his opening group, providing them with needed exposure while earning him hip credibility within alternative rock scenes. On the advice of Sonic Youth, Young added the noise collage EP *Arc* as a bonus to his 1991 live album, *Weld.*

Weld and the Sonic Youth tour helped position Neil Young as an alternative and grunge rock forefather, but he decided to abandon loud music for its 1992 followup, *Harvest Moon.* An explicit sequel to his 1972 breakthrough, *Harvest Moon* became Young's biggest hit in years, and he supported the record with an appearance on *MTV Unplugged,* which was released the following year as an album. Also in 1993, Geffen released the rarities collection *Lucky Thirteen.* The following year, he released *Sleeps with Angels,* which was hailed as a masterpiece in some quarters. Following its release, Young began jamming with Pearl Jam, eventually recording an album with the Seattle band in early 1995. The resulting record, *Mirror Ball,* was released to positive reviews in the summer of 1995, but it wasn't the commercial blockbuster it was expected to be; due to legal reasons, Pearl Jam's name was not allowed to be featured on the cover. In the summer of 1996, he reunited with Crazy Horse for *Broken Arrow* and supported it with a brief tour. That tour was documented in Jim Jarmusch's 1997 film *The Year of the Horse,* which was accompanied by a double-disc live album. — *Stephen Thomas Erlewine*

Neil Young / Jan. 1969 / Reprise ✦✦✦
Young's debut, one of his most low-key efforts, went almost unnoticed at the time, but did introduce many of the traits that would characterize much of his work: countryish ballads, medium-tempo rockers with searing lead guitar lines, tasteful strings and female backing vocals, and gentle but disquieting romantic ruminations. The material isn't strong enough to qualify this as one of his better albums, but it has a touching grace, embellished by Jack Nitzsche's elaborate production on a few tracks. The nine-and-a-half-minute closer, "The Last Trip To Tulsa," is Young's most long-winded and Dylanesque surrealist epic. — *Richie Unterberger*

☆ **Everybody Knows This Is Nowhere** / May 1969 / Reprise ✦✦✦✦✦
Young's breakthrough album is also the first one to feature the backup of Crazy Horse for a seminal rock session that produced the Young favorites "Cinnamon Girl," "Down by the River," and "Cowgirl in the Sand." — *William Ruhlmann*

☆ **After the Gold Rush** / Aug. 1970 / Reprise ✦✦✦✦✦
The years have only been kind to what sounded like Young's best album when it was released. It's a mixture of his folkie ("Tell Me Why"), country ("Oh, Lonesome Me"), and hard-rocking ("Southern Man") selves, and there's also that mystical title track, which remains Neil Young's definitive statement of purpose. — *William Ruhlmann*

Harvest / Feb. 1972 / Reprise ✦✦✦✦
Uneven, yes, perhaps due to the overambitiousness of the orchestral pieces, but this album, Young's biggest seller, still contains "Heart of Gold," the rocker "Alabama," and such telling ballads as "Old Man." — *William Ruhlmann*

Journey through the Past / Nov. 1972 / Reprise ✦✦
Neil Young's unexpected followup to the million-selling *Harvest* was this two-LP soundtrack to his rarely seen film. It contains performances by Buffalo Springfield and Crosby, Stills, Nash and Young, plus Young himself, all previously familiar, except for one minor new Young song, "Soldier." — *William Ruhlmann*

Time Fades Away / Oct. 1973 / Reprise ✦✦✦
The beginning of Young's mid-70s descent into decadence, this is part of a trilogy including *Tonight's the Night* and *On the Beach* that explores drug addiction, desperation, and determination, and the subject matter isn't only expressed in the lyrics, it's in the roughly played music and the strained vocals. The most gripping music of Young's career. — *William Ruhlmann*

☆ **On the Beach** / Jul. 1974 / Reprise ✦✦✦✦✦
Following the 1973 *Time Fades Away* tour, Neil Young wrote and recorded an Irish wake of a record called *Tonight's the Night* and went on the road drunkenly playing its songs to uncomprehending listeners and hostile reviewers. Reprise rejected the record, and Young went right back and made *On the Beach,* which shares some of the ragged style of its two predecessors. But where *Time* was embattled and *Tonight* mournful, *On the Beach* was savage and, ultimately, triumphant. "I'm a vampire, babe," Young sang, and he proceeded to take bites out of various subjects: threatening the lives of the stars who lived in Los Angeles' Laurel Canyon ("Revolution Blues"); answering back to Lynyrd Skynyrd, whose "Sweet Home Alabama" had taken him to task for his criticisms of the South in "Southern Man" and "Alabama" ("Walk On"); and rejecting the critics ("Ambulance Blues"). But the barbs were mixed with humor and even affection, as Young seemed to be emerging from the grief and self-abuse that had plagued him for two years. But the album was so spare and underproduced, its lyrics so harrowing, that it was easy to miss Young's conclusion: he was saying goodbye to despair, not being overwhelmed by it. — *William Ruhlmann*

☆ **Tonight's the Night** / Jun. 1975 / Reprise ✦✦✦✦✦
Written and recorded in 1973 shortly after the death of roadie Bruce Berry, *Tonight's the Night* was Young's musical expression of grief, combined with his rejection of the stardom he had achieved in the late '60s and early '70s. The title track, performed twice, was a direct narrative about Berry, while the late Crazy Horse guitarist Danny Whitten was heard singing "Come on Baby Let's Go Downtown," a live track recorded years earlier. Performing with the remains of Crazy Horse, bassist Billy Talbot and drummer Ralph Molina, along with Nils Lofgren and Ben Keith, Young performed in the ragged manner familiar from *Time Fades Away*—his voice was often hoarse and he strained to reach high notes, while the playing was loose, with mistakes and shifting tempos. But the style worked perfectly for the material, emphasizing the emotional tone of Young's mourning; it was the work of a man trying to turn his torment into art and doing so unflinchingly. — *William Ruhlmann*

Zuma / Nov. 1975 / Reprise ✦✦✦✦
Having apparently exorcised his demons by releasing the cathartic *Tonight's the Night,* Neil Young returned to his commercial strengths with *Zuma* (named after Zuma Beach in Los Angeles, where he now owned a house). Seven of the album's nine songs were recorded with the

reunited Crazy Horse, in which rhythm guitarist Frank Sampedro had replaced the late Danny Whitten, but there were also nods to other popular Young styles in "Pardon My Heart," an acoustic song that would have fit on *Harvest*, his most popular album, and "Through My Sails," retrieved from one of Crosby, Stills, Nash & Young's abortive recording sessions. Young had abandoned the ragged, first-take approach of his previous three albums, but Crazy Horse would never be a polished act, and the music had a lively sound well-suited to the songs, which were some of the most melodic, pop-oriented tunes Young had crafted in years, though they were played with an electric-guitar-drenched rock intensity. The overall theme concerned romantic conflict, with lyrics that lamented lost love and sometimes longed for a return ("Pardon My Heart" even found Young singing, "I don't believe this song"), though the overall conclusion, notably in such catchy songs as "Don't Cry No Tears" and "Lookin' for a Love," was to move on to the next relationship. But the album's standout track (apparently the only holdover from an early intention to present songs with historical subjects) was the seven-and-a-half-minute epic "Cortez the Killer," a commentary on the Spanish conqueror of Latin America that served as a platform for Young's most extensive guitar soloing since his work on *Everybody Knows This Is Nowhere*. — *William Ruhlmann*

Long May You Run / Sep. 1976 / Reprise ✦✦
Long May You Run is not a Neil Young solo album. It is credited to "The Stills-Young Band," which is to say, Stephen Stills and his band with Young added, and the two divide up the songwriting and lead vocals, five for Young, four for Stills. The pairing, though it proved short-lived and had, in fact, ended before this album was released, must have seemed commercially logical. Like Young, Stills had seen his record sales decline after a successful period following the 1970 breakup of CSNY. So had erstwhile partners David Crosby and Graham Nash, but they had returned to Top Ten, gold-selling status in the fall of 1975 with their *Wind on the Water* duo album. Why couldn't Stills and Young do the same thing? Maybe they could have (and, actually, this was the first gold album for either in two years) if they had made a better record together. Young's songs were pleasant newly written throwaways with the exception of the title track, a trunk song he had written as a tribute to an old car. Stills' compositions seemed more seriously intended, but still were not substantial. The playing, largely handled by the professional sessionman-types in Stills' band, was far smoother than what one was accustomed to in a Young album. The result was a listenable record, but not a compelling one, and thus well below Young's usual standard and Stills' best. (As of mid-1996, *Long May You Run* had not been released in the US on CD.) — *William Ruhlmann*

American Stars 'N Bars / Jun. 1977 / Reprise ✦✦✦
Neil Young made a point of listing the recording dates of the songs on *American Stars 'N Bars;* the dates even appeared on the LP labels. They revealed that the songs had been cut at four different sessions dating back to 1974. But even without such documentation, it would have been easy to tell that the album was a stylistic hodge-padge, its first side consisting of country-tinged material featuring steel guitar and fiddle, plus backup vocals from Linda Ronstadt and the then-unknown Nicolette Larson, while the four songs on the second side varied from acoustic solo numbers like "Will to Love" to raging rockers such as "Like a Hurricane." Just as apparent was the album's unevenness: side one consisted of lightweight compositions, while side two had more ambitious ones, with "Will to Love," for example, extending the romantic metaphor of a salmon swimming upsteam across seven minutes. The album's saving grace was "Like a Hurricane," one of Young's classic hard rock songs and guitar workouts, a perennial concert favorite. Without it, *American Stars 'N Bars* would have been one of Young's least memorable albums, and since it turned up the following year on the compilation *Decade*, the LP was rendered inessential. (As of mid-1996, *American Stars 'N Bars* had not been released on CD in the US.) — *William Ruhlmann*

★ **Decade** / Nov. 1977 / Reprise ✦✦✦✦✦
Given the quirkiness of Neil Young's recording career, with its frequent cancellations of releases and last-minute rearrangements of material, it is a relief to report that this two-disc compilation is so conventional and so satisfying. A 35-track selection of the best of Young's work between 1966 and 1976, it includes songs performed by Buffalo Springfield, Crosby, Stills, Nash & Young, and the Stills/Young Band, as well as solo work. In addition to five unreleased songs, *Decade* offers such key tracks as the Springfield's "Mr. Soul," "Broken Arrow," and "I Am a Child"; "Sugar Mountain," a song that had appeared only as a single before; "Cinnamon Girl," "Down by the River," and "Cowgirl in the Sand" from *Everybody Knows This Is Nowhere;* "Southern Man" and the title track from *After the Gold Rush;* and "Old Man" and the chart-topping "Heart of Gold" from *Harvest*. This is the material that built Young's reputation between 1966 and 1972, although he is more idiosyncratic with the later material, including the blockbusters "Like a Hurricane" and "Cortez the Killer" but mixing in more unreleased recordings as the set draws to a close. He seems intent on making the album a

listenable one that will appeal to a broad base of fans, and he succeeds despite the exclusion of much of the harrowing work of 1973-1975. Nevertheless, the album is an ideal sampler for new listeners, and since there is no one-disc Young compilation covering any significant portion of his career, this lengthy chronicle is the place to start. — *William Ruhlmann*

Comes a Time / Oct. 1978 / Reprise ✦✦✦✦
Six and a half years later, *Comes a Time* finally was the Neil Young album for the millions of fans who had loved *Harvest*, an acoustic-based record with country overtones and romantic, autobiographical lyrics, and many of those fans returned to the fold, enough to make *Comes a Time* Young's first Top Ten album since *Harvest*. He signaled the album's direction with the lead-off track, "Goin' Back," its retrospective theme augmented with an orchestral backup and the deliberate beat familiar from his No. 1 hit "Heart of Gold." Of course, Young remained sly about this retrenchment. "I feel like goin' back," he sang, but added, "Back where there's nowhere to stay." Doubtless he had no intention of staying with this style, but, for the length of the album, melodies, love lyrics, lush arrangements, and steel guitar solos dominated, and Young's vocals were made more accessible by being paired with Nicolette Larson's harmonies. Larson's own version of Young's "Lotta Love," released shortly after the one heard here, became a Top Ten hit single. Other highlights included the reflective "Already One," which treats the unusual subject of the nature of a divorced family, the ironic "Field of Opportunity," and a cover of Ian Tyson's folk standard "Four Strong Winds" (a Country Top Ten hit for Bobby Bare in 1965). — *William Ruhlmann*

☆ **Rust Never Sleeps** / Jul. 1979 / Reprise ✦✦✦✦✦
Rust Never Sleeps, its aphoristic title drawn from an intended advertising slogan, was an album of new songs, some of them recorded on Neil Young's 1978 concert tour. His strongest collection since *Tonight's the Night*, its obvious antecedent was Bob Dylan's *Bringing It All Back Home*, and, as Dylan did, Young divided his record into acoustic and electric sides while filling his songs with wildly imaginative imagery. The lead-off track, "My My, Hey Hey (Out of the Blue)" (repeated in an electric version at album's end as "Hey Hey, My My [Into the Black]" with slightly altered lyrics), is the most concise and knowing description of the entertainment industry ever written; it was followed by "Thrasher," which describes Young's parallel artistic quest in an extended metaphor that also reflected the album's overall theme—the inevitability of deterioration and the challenge of overcoming it. Young then spent the rest of the album demonstrating that his chief weapons against rusting were his imagination and his daring, creating an archetypal album that encapsulated his many styles on a single disc with great songs—in particular the remarkable "Powderfinger"—unlike any he had written before. — *William Ruhlmann*

Live Rust / Nov. 1979 / Reprise ✦✦✦✦
All the kudos Neil Young earned for *Rust Never Sleeps* he lost for *Live Rust*, the double-LP live album released four months later. *Live Rust* was the soundtrack to Young's concert film, *Rust Never Sleeps* (he had wanted to give it that title, but Reprise vetoed the idea, fearing confusion with the earlier album), and like it was recorded Oct. 22, 1978, at the Cow Palace in San Francisco. But much of the *Rust Never Sleeps* album had been recorded on the same tour and *Live Rust* repeated four songs from that disc, and since Young had released the career retrospective *Decade* in 1977, critics felt he was unfairly recycling his older material and repeating his new material. In retrospect, however, *Live Rust*, now a single 74-minute CD, comes off as an excellent Neil Young live album and career summary, starting with the early song "Sugar Mountain" and running through then-new songs like "My My, Hey Hey (Out of the Blue)" and "Powderfinger." Young is effective in both his acoustic folksinger and hard-rocking Crazy Horse bandleader modes. The various distractions of the concert itself and the film, such as the pretentious props and cowled roadies, are absent, and what's left is a terrific Neil Young concert recording. — *William Ruhlmann*

Hawks & Doves / Nov. 1980 / Reprise ✦✦✦
Following the triumph of *Rust Never Sleeps*, *Hawks & Doves* benefited from the enormous critical goodwill Neil Young had amassed, though fans and critics nevertheless were baffled by its set of obscure acoustic and country-tinged songs. The seven-plus-minute "The Old Homestead" (copyright 1974) was interpreted by some as an allegory for Young's relationship to CSNY, perhaps because that was the only way to make any sense of the most mysterious Young lyric since "The Last Trip To Tulsa." In retrospect, now that we know Young was distracted by domestic medical concerns while working on the album, its theme of perseverance in the face of adversity, both in a personal context of family commitment ("Stayin' Power," "Coastline"), and in a national context of hard work and patriotism ("Union Man," "Comin' Apart At Every Nail," "Hawks & Doves") seems more apparent, as does the sense that Young may have been trying to fulfill his recording contract (even with the inclusion of trunk songs like "The Old Homestead," the album runs less than half an

hour) while devoting a bare minimum of his time and attention to the effort. The result is correspondingly slight. (As of October 1996, *Hawks & Doves* still had not been issued on CD in the US). — *William Ruhlmann*

Re-ac-tor / Nov. 1981 / Reprise ♦♦
Neil Young employs Crazy Horse to help him bash out a guitar-drenched hard rock set made up of thrown-together material. The group plays fiercely, as usual, but the lyrics are sketchy, seemingly improvised the nadir is the nine-minute "T-Bone," which consists of the lines "Got mashed potato / Ain't got no t-bone" repeated over and over), and frequently cranky, as in "Motor City," which finds Young criticizing Japanese cars, and "Rapid Transit," which takes a belated swipe at new wave music while sounding like second-rate Talking Heads. For the second album in a row, Young seems to be just fulfilling his one-album-a-year record contract. The exception is the album-closing "Shots" (written by 1978), a more substantive and threatening song given a riveting performance. Later, it would be revealed that Young was finding time for his music while giving most of his attention to caring for his disabled son. Still, he might have been better advised to have suspended record-making for a few years instead of turning out half-baked efforts like this one. — *William Ruhlmann*

Trans / Jan. 1983 / Geffen ♦♦
When it was released, *Trans* was Neil Young's most baffling album. He had employed a Vocoder to synthesize his voice on five of the album's nine tracks, resulting in disembodied singing, the lyrics nearly impossible to decipher without the lyric sheet. And even when you read the words, "Computer Age," "We R In Control," "Transformer Man," "Computer Cowboy," and "Sample and Hold" seemed like a vague mishmash of hi-tech jargon. Later, Young would reveal that some of the songs expressed a theme of attempted communication with his disabled son, and in that context, lines like "I stand by you" and "So many things still left to do / But we haven't made it yet" seemed clearer. But the Vocoder, which robbed Young's voice of its dynamics and phrasing, still kept the songs from being as moving as they were intended to be. And despite the crisp dance beats and synthesizers, the music sounded less like new Kraftwerk than like old Devo. A few more conventional Young songs (left over from an earlier rejected album) seemed out of place. *Trans* had a few good songs, notably "Sample And Hold" (which seemed to be about a computer dating service for robots), a remake of "Mr. Soul," and "Like An Inca" (an intended cross between "Like A Hurricane" and "Cortez The Killer"?), but on the whole it was an idea that just didn't work. (*Trans* has been released in the US on CD. The European CD release replaces the original 5:09 take of "Sample And Hold" with the 8:04 alternate take later used on the *Lucky Thirteen* compilation.) — *William Ruhlmann*

Everybody's Rockin' / Aug. 1983 / Geffen ♦♦
By following the hi-tech *Trans* after only seven months with a rockabilly album, Neil Young baffled his audience. Just as he had followed the sales peak of *Harvest* in 1972 with a series of challenging, uncommercial albums, Young had now dissipated the commercial and critical acceptance he had enjoyed with 1979's *Rust Never Sleeps* with a series of mediocre albums and inexplicable genre exercises. *Everybody's Rockin'*, credited to "Neil and the Shocking Pinks," represented the nadir of his attempted career suicide. Running less than 25 minutes, it found Young covering early rock evergreens like "Betty Lou's Got A New Pair Of Shoes" and writing a few songs in the same vein ("Kinda Fonda Wanda"). If he had presented this as a mini-album at a discount price, it would have been easier to enjoy the joke Young seemed to intend. As it was, fans who already had their doubts about Young dropped off the radar screen; *Everybody's Rocking* was his lowest charting album since his 1969 solo debut, and he didn't release another album for two years (his longest break ever between records). *Everybody's Rockin'* has not been released on CD in the US, though it has appeared in other countries, including Canada. — *William Ruhlmann*

Old Ways / Aug. 1985 / Geffen ♦♦♦
In 1984, Geffen Records sued Neil Young on the grounds that he had submitted uncharacteristic, uncommercial records to the label. By the time a settlement had been reached, Young had been on the road with a country band called the International Harvesters for over a year and recorded a revamped version of *Old Ways*, a 1982 LP originally rejected by Geffen which was cut in the style of *Harvest* and *Comes a Time*, but with a stronger country leaning. Young depends heavily on friends, especially for vocals—Waylon Jennings sings harmony on six out of the ten tracks, and one of the others is a duet with Willie Nelson. Though populated by cowboys and country references, Young's take on the genre is typically idiosyncratic, including a reworked version of his autobiography in "Get Back to the Country," a cover of the 1956 Gogi Grant hit "Wayward Wind," and the uncategorizable "Misfits," which portrays astronauts watching Muhammad Ali fights on television in space. *Old Ways* is not a great Neil Young album and at the time of its

release served to alienate him even further from his audience, but it has its moments. — *William Ruhlmann*

Landing on Water / Jul. 1986 / Geffen ♦♦
Backed only by co-producer Danny Kortchmar on guitar and Steve Jordan on drums, with all three playing synthesizers, Neil Young turns in an album that attempts to mix the raunchy rock thrust of his Crazy Horse-style music with contemporary trends in pop, especially the tendency to turn the drums way up in the mix. It's an uneasy combination in which Jordan's forceful drumming dominates the tracks, with Young's vocals nearly buried. But that only means that the production has ruined a group of songs few of which were any good anyway. The only one that offers the promise of being one of Young's better efforts is "Hippie Dream," a sober criticism of what became of '60s idealism in general and Young's erstwhile bandmate David Crosby in particular. But if *Landing On Water* was not a good album, at least it seemed to point Young away from the stylistic dabbling of his last three albums and back toward the kind of rock he did best, and at least some of his fans returned as a result, giving him a slight uptick in sales. — *William Ruhlmann*

Life / Jul. 1987 / Geffen ♦♦♦
Life, Young's first album with Crazy Horse since 1981's *Re-ac-tor*, was not one of his best albums. It was, however, better than most of the other albums he made in the 1980s, and the first really interesting record he'd made in a long time. Despite the return to Crazy Horse, Young continued to use some of the production techniques from *Landing on Water*, especially the loud drums and synthesizers. But he mixed things up, including acoustic-based songs such as "Long Walk Home" and "Inca Queen." It could be argued that Young was repeating himself on much of this material and that the album was typically uneven, but *Life* was an encouraging step back to the tried and true for an exploratory artist who finally seemed to have realized that he had experimented too much for his own good. — *William Ruhlmann*

This Note's for You / Apr. 1988 / Reprise ♦♦♦
This Note's for You was another installment in Neil Young's '80s tour of genres, recorded with a ten-piece, horn-driven blues band. In terms of style, it was merely another genre exercise, but the songs on the album were his strongest in several years, particularly the haunting "Coupe Deville," and began his late '80s return to form. — *Stephen Thomas Erlewine*

Eldorado / 1989 / Reprise ♦♦♦
When this five-song, 25-minute EP was released in Japan in 1989, it served notice that Neil Young was capable of writing powerful songs and playing fierce rock 'n' roll again, a fact confirmed by the subsequent release of the *Freedom* album. Three of the songs on *Eldorado* turned up on that record ("Don't Cry" in a different version), but "Cocaine Eyes" and "Heavy Love" did not, making this disc a necessary purchase for Young completists. — *William Ruhlmann*

Freedom / Oct. 1989 / Reprise ♦♦♦♦
Neil Young is famous for scrapping completed albums and substituting hastily recorded ones in radically different styles; *Freedom*, a major critical and commercial comeback, seemed to be a selection of the best tracks from several different unissued projects. First and foremost was a hard rock album like the material heard on Young's recent EP *Eldorado* (released only in the Far East), several of whose tracks were repeated on *Freedom*. On these songs—especially "Don't Cry" and a cover of the Drifters' "On Broadway"—Young played distorted electric guitar over a rhythm section in an even more raucous fashion than on his Crazy Horse records. Second was a follow-up to *This Note's For You*, which featured a six-piece horn section; they were back on the lengthy "Crime in the City" and "Someday," each of which contained a series of seemingly unrelated, mood-setting verses. Third, there were tracks that harked back to acoustic-based, country-tinged albums like *Harvest* and *Comes a Time*, including "Hangin' on a Limb" and "The Ways of Love." What made it all work was that Young had once again written a great bunch of songs, bookended by acoustic and electric versions of one of Young's greatest anthems, "Rockin' in the Free World." — *William Ruhlmann*

☆ **Ragged Glory** / Oct. 11, 1990 / Reprise ♦♦♦♦♦
Having re-established his reputation with the musically varied, lyrically enraged *Freedom*, Neil Young returned to being the lead guitarist of Crazy Horse for the musically homogenous, lyrically hopeful *Ragged Glory*. The album's dominant sound was made by Young's noisy guitar, which bordered on and sometimes slipped over into distortion, while Crazy Horse kept up the songs' bright tempos. Despite the volume, the tunes were catchy, with strong melodies and good choruses, and they were given over to love, humor, and warm reminiscence. They were also platforms for often extended guitar excursions: "Love To Burn" and "Love And Only Love" ran over ten minutes each, and the album as a whole lasted nearly 63 minutes with only ten songs. Much about the record had a retrospective feel—the first two tracks, "Country Home" and "White Line," were newly recorded versions of songs Young had

played with Crazy Horse but never released in the '70s; "Mansion On The Hill," the album's most accessible track, celebrated a place where "psychedelic music fills the air" and "peace and love live there still"; there was a cover of the Premiers' garage rock oldie "Farmer John"; and "Days That Used To Be," in addition to its backward-looking theme, borrowed the melody from Bob Dylan's "My Back Pages" (by way of the Byrds' arrangement), while "Mother Earth (Natural Anthem)" was the folk standard "The Water Is Wide" with new, environmentally aware lyrics. Young was not generally known as an artist who evoked the past this much, but if he could extend his creative rebirth with music this exhilarating, no one was likely to complain. — *William Ruhlmann*

Weld / Oct. 1991 / Reprise ✦✦✦✦
Weld, Neil Young's two-hour-plus double-CD chronicle of his 1991 Ragged Glory/Smell the Horse Tour with Crazy Horse, was received with only mild enthusiasm from Young's fans and rock critics, perhaps because it seemed redundant. Such warhorses as "Like A Hurricane" and "Cortez The Killer" were making their fourth appearances on a Young album, and the five songs from the *Ragged Glory* album were basically unchanged from their studio versions. Containing only 16 tracks, the album's songs averaged over seven and a half minutes in length, and that length was given over to extended guitar improvisations, which often were filled with feedback and distortion. Where Young's previous double live album, *Live Rust*, which bore some similarities to this one, was a career retrospective including some acoustic numbers, *Weld* was all electric rock with Crazy Horse. The one previously unreleased song was a Gulf War-era cover of Bob Dylan's "Blowin' In The Wind," complete with gunshots and exploding bombs. In retrospect, *Weld* seems like an excellent expression of one part of Young's musical persona, putting some of his best hard rock material onto one album. (Initially, *Weld* was released in a 25,000 copy limited edition called *Arc Weld* [Reprise 26746] containing a third disc made up of guitar feedback and called *Arc.*) — *William Ruhlmann*

Harvest Moon / Oct. 27, 1992 / Reprise ✦✦✦
After 20 years, Neil Young finally decided to release the sequel to *Harvest*, his most commercially successful album. *Harvest Moon* is a better album, lacking the orchestral bombast that stifled some of the songs on the first album and boasting a stronger overall selection of songs. *Harvest Moon* manages to be sentimental without being sappy, wistful without being nostalgic. The lovely "Unknown Legend," "From Hank To Hendrix" and the beautiful "Harvest Moon" are among Young's best songs. Only the overlong (11 minutes) and oversimplified "Natural Beauty" hurts a beautiful album that proudly displays scars, heartaches, and love. — *Stephen Thomas Erlewine*

Lucky Thirteen / Jan. 5, 1993 / Geffen ✦✦✦
Geffen Records seems to have intended a straightforward "best-of" compilation containing the singles released from Neil Young's five albums with the label between 1982 and 1987. Then Young himself became involved, and his version of a Geffen sampler naturally turned out to be more unusual. There were four songs never before released on a Young album—"Depression Blues," "Get Gone" and the bluesy "Don't Take Your Love Away From Me" (live recordings with the Shocking Pinks) and "Ain't It the Truth" (a live track cut with the Bluenotes). There were also an alternate version of *Trans'* "Sample and Hold"and a live take of "This Note's for You," the title song from Young's 1988 return to Reprise Records. None of these were revelatory, and Young's choices from his Geffen era failed to represent his best work; given that he veered wildly from synth-pop to rockabilly to country to rock during this period, assembling a coherent compilation was something of a challenge, and Young didn't even try, just picking his favorites and sequencing them chronologically. There were some interesting songs here to be sure, notably "Hippie Dream" and "Mideast Vacation," but this summing up of Young's least impressive, most bizarre era, instead of rehabilitating that era, was itself bizarre and unimpressive, too. — *William Ruhlmann*

Unplugged / Jun. 15, 1993 / Reprise ✦✦✦✦
Like Paul McCartney's, Neil Young's *Unplugged* seems to be an attempt to thwart bootleggers by releasing the material before they get a chance. Young's album doesn't offer any revelations—it's just a solid, thoroughly enjoyable concert. Acoustic performances of "Mr. Soul," "World On a String," "Like a Hurricane," and especially the synthesized "Transformer Man" are essential for the serious Young collector. Fans of *Harvest, After the Gold Rush, Comes A Time*, and *Harvest Moon* will find that *this* is the live Neil Young they need in their collection; hardcore fans will realize that this is the acoustic equivalent of the stunning *Weld*. — *Stephen Thomas Erlewine*

Sleeps with Angels / Aug. 16, 1994 / Reprise ✦✦✦✦
Reportedly spurred by the death of Kurt Cobain (who quoted Young's line, "It's better to burn out than to fade away," in his suicide note), Young turns in an unusually low-key, elegiac effort, its songs worrying about depression, lack of communication, and drive-by shootings, its music (despite the presence of Crazy Horse) slow and meditative (except for the funny change-of-pace rocker "Piece Of Crap"). The result is not as

gloomy as *Tonight's The Night* (in which Young seemed past the point of caring and even managed a certain gallows humor), but extremely mournful, with only glimmers of hope. — *William Ruhlmann*

Mirror Ball / Jun. 27, 1995 / Reprise ✦✦✦
Knocked out in about two weeks, Neil Young's collaboration with Pearl Jam is considerably different than *Sleeps with Angels;* the record sounds like a spiritual rebirth after its bleaker predecessor. Playing with the Seattle band has reinvigorated Young. In fact, it has reinvigorated him so much that he hasn't spent much time on the songs, preferring to let the music carry the record. Pearl Jam's grooves are more elastic than Crazy Horse, yet new drummer Jack Irons reigns in the group's tendency to meander. As does Young himself, who dominates the proceedings with his jerky, wailing guitar. A couple of stray, minute-long organ-and-voice fragments from the *Sleeps with Angels* album punctuate the second side, yet the album isn't contemplative—it barrels ahead. — *Stephen Thomas Erlewine*

Dead Man / Feb. 27, 1996 / Vapor ✦✦
Even within the unpredictable Neil Young discography, this qualifies as one of his most unpredictable efforts. This soundtrack to the Jim Jarmusch film *Dead Man* is entirely instrumental, with the exception of some poetry read by Johnny Depp (who stars in the film) and a bit of dialogue. What's more, these untitled instrumental passages are dominated by subterranean guitar rumbles that manage to sound both grungy and subdued. Young also takes care to vary his approach a bit, switching occasionally to pump organ, detuned piano, and acoustic guitar. The results not only evoke the hostile, desolate landscapes of the film's Old West, but work on their own terms as ambient mood music for the non-new age crowd, creating an atmosphere of restless disturbance with subtlety and grace. It's not necessarily for the typical Neil Young fan (whoever that might be), but it's certainly one of his most successful experimental efforts. — *Richie Unterberger*

Broken Arrow / Jul. 2, 1996 / Reprise ✦✦✦
In many ways, *Broken Arrow* follows the same path as Neil Young's other '90s albums with Crazy Horse. *Broken Arrow* floats on waves of lumbering guitars and cascading feedback, ebbing and flowing with winding solos and drifting melodies. In a typical display of artistic perversion, Young has front-loaded the album with three epics with a combined running time of just over 25 minutes. Following the three epiclength songs come four concise tunes that range from the country-rock stomp of "Changing Highways" to the reflective "Music Arcade." Like the three songs that preceded them, these songs are uneven, with hazy melodies and under-developed lyrics. Finally, a long live workout of Jimmy Reed's "Baby What You Want Me To Do"—which sounds like it was taken from audience recordings—is tacked on to the end of the album. Although the song is a standout, it raises the question of: What is the purpose of *Broken Arrow?* The album floats from song to song, with the guitars drowning out the sound of Young's voice. There are some fine songs buried admist the long jams but the album is directionless, and that lack of direction never manages to develop a consistent emotional tone. — *Stephen Thomas Erlewine*

Paul Young

b. Jan. 17, 1956, Luton, Bedfordshire, England
Vocals / New Wave, Pop-Rock
A soulful UK interpretive singer who gained fame in his native country in 1983 with a cover of Marvin Gaye's "Wherever I Lay My Hat (That's My Home)" and in the US with Daryl Hall's "Everytime You Go Away" in 1985. Young found less success writing his own songs, then returned to the US Top Ten with a cover of the Chi-Lites' "Oh Girl" in 1990. In 1992, he left Columbia and moved to MCA. — *William Ruhlmann*

No Parlez / 1983 / Columbia ✦✦✦✦
Paul Young's debut album was a strong set of soulful covers of forgotten classics ("Love of the Common People," "Wherever I Lay My Hat (That's My Home") and contemporary classics ("Love Will Tear Us Apart"), as well as the occasional made-to-order original, like the hit "Come Back and Stay." — *Stephen Thomas Erlewine*

The Secret of Association / 1985 / Columbia ✦✦✦✦
The Secret of Association continued the formula of *No Parlez* to a fine effect and, thanks to a No. 1 version of Hall & Oates' "Everytime You Go Away" that bettered the original, it was a bigger hit. — *Stephen Thomas Erlewine*

Between Two Fires / 1986 / Columbia ✦✦
Paul Young's third album, *Between Two Fires*, suffered from a lack of strong material and an overly slick production, with only the minor hit single "Some People" to recommend it. — *Stephen Thomas Erlewine*

Other Voices / Jun. 1990 / Columbia ✦✦✦
Other Voices marked a comeback from the tepid *Between Two Fires*, featuring a set of lush, soulful covers (the Top Ten hit "Oh Girl") and several harder rocking numbers, including a cover of Free's "A Little Bit of Love." — *Stephen Thomas Erlewine*

● **From Time to Time: The Singles Collection** / Nov. 1991 / Columbia ✦✦✦✦

All Young's UK and US hits, among them "Everytime You Go Away," "Come Back and Stay," "I'm Gonna Tear Your Playhouse Down," "Love of the Common People," "Wherever I Lay My Hat (That's My Home)," and "Oh Girl." — *William Ruhlmann*

Reflections / 1995 / Vision Music ✦✦✦

Young-Holt Unlimited

f. 1966, Chicago, IL, **db.** 1974
Soul, Soul Jazz
In the mid-'60s, bassist Eldee Young and drummer Isaac "Red" Holt, who had done time for about a dozen years as Ramsey Lewis' rhythm section, split to form their own act. As the Young Holt Trio they had a quick Top 20 R&B hit with the infectiously silly "Wack Wack," after which they changed their name to Young- Holt Unlimited. On most of their material, they cut an invigorating soul-jazz groove that explored the territory between Jimmy Smith and Junior Walker, with dour bass, Ray Charles-inspired keyboards, faint scat vocals, and a live party ambience. When they tightened up and added some funky rhythms, they had a left-field smash with the instrumental "Soulful Strut," which went to No. 3 in 1969. — *Richie Unterberger*

● **Wack Wack** / 1986 / Kent ✦✦✦✦
Sixteen late-'60s tracks, taken from various LPs and singles. An enjoyable if minor collection of this forgotten group, whose excursions into jazz-soul work much better than their attempts to milk the "Soulful Strut" groove on lesser followups. Includes "Wack Wack," "Soulful Strut," and a surprisingly successful reworking of Donovan's "Mellow Yellow" into a cool jazz-funk jive number. — *Richie Unterberger*

The Best of Young Holt Unlimited / Jun. 6, 1995 / Brunswick ✦✦✦✦
Twelve of their most famous cuts, including the hits "Soulful Strut" and "Wack Wack," a live medley, and some neat obscurities (like "Give It Up" and the propulsive "Dig Her Walk"). It's not quite as comprehensive, however, as the 16-track British import *Wack Wack* (on Kent), which is still the better collection to pick up if you can find it. The only song here that's not on *Wack Wack* is their version of "Light My Fire." — *Richie Unterberger*

The Youngbloods

f. 1965, New York, NY, **db.** 1972
Folk-Rock
The Youngbloods could not be considered a major '60s band, but they were capable of offering some mighty pleasurable folk-rock in the late '60s, and produced a few great tunes along the way. One of the better groups to emerge from the East Coast in the mid-'60s, they would temper their blues and jugband influences with gentle California psychedelia, particularly after they moved to the San Francisco Bay area. For most listeners, they're identified almost exclusively with their Top Ten hit "Get Together," but they managed several respectable albums as well, all under the leadership of singer-songwriter Jesse Colin Young.

Young got his start on the folk circuits of Boston and New York, and had already cut a couple of solo albums before forming the Youngbloods. John Sebastian was one of the supporting musicians on Young's second LP, and comparisons between the two—and between the Youngbloods and the Lovin' Spoonful—are inevitable. Both groups offered good-timey folk-rock with much stronger jugband influences than West Coast rivals like the Byrds, though the Youngbloods made greater use of electric keyboards than the Spoonful, courtesy of the enigmatically named Lowell "Banana" Levinger. The Youngbloods didn't craft nearly as many brilliant singles as the Lovin' Spoonful, but (unlike the Spoonful) endured well into the hippie/psychedelic era.

While Young was always the focal point of the band, their first two albums also had songwriting contributions from guitarist Jerry Corbitt. Produced by Felix Pappalardi (who also worked with Cream), these records (*The Youngbloods* and *Earth Music*) were engaging and mature, if inconsistent, folk-rock. Corbitt's "Grizzly Bear" was a small hit, as was "Get Together," a Dino Valenti song that had previously been recorded by the Jefferson Airplane. The Youngbloods' slow, soulful interpretation of "Get Together" was definitive, but it wouldn't reach the Top Ten until it was re-released in 1969, after the song had been used in a television public service ad.

By that time, Corbitt had left, and the Youngbloods, reduced to a trio, were living in Marin County, CA. 1969's *Elephant Mountain* was produced by, of all people, Charlie Daniels. Reflecting the mellowing influence of San Francisco psychedelia, it was their best effort, featuring some of Young's best songs. They released a few more albums in the early '70s (some live), but on these the mellow California rock sound that had served them well on *Elephant Mountain* had begun to turn limpid and wimpy. The group broke up in 1972, and Jesse Colin Young

had a long and moderately successful career as a solo singer-songwriter. — *Richie Unterberger*

The Youngbloods / 1967 / Edsel ✦✦✦✦
The New York quartet come off as a mini-Lovin' Spoonful on their engaging debut, with a deeper touch of melancholy and more prominent electric keyboards. As with the Spoonful, they would have been better off leaving the blues alone, but the rest of the material is good, highlighted by "Get Together" and the achingly tuneful "All Over The World (La-La)." — *Richie Unterberger*

Earth Music / 1967 / Edsel ✦✦✦
Similar but a bit inferior to their debut, with the same division between accomplished folk-rock, good-timey ragtime-influenced romps, and pedestrian blues-rock. Includes one of the best versions of Tim Hardin's oft-covered standard "Reason to Believe." — *Richie Unterberger*

Elephant Mountain / 1969 / RCA ✦✦✦✦
By the time they made this album, the group had relocated to Northern California from New York and guitarist Jerry Corbitt had departed, leaving the songwriting chores almost exclusively in the hands of Jesse Colin Young. The mellower, more psychedelic sound reflected the group's new surroundings, and despite some weak moments, it remains their strongest and most cohesive LP. Young's acoustic love song "Sunlight" is his best original composition, and the Youngbloods' best track besides "Get Together"; "Darkness, Darkness" and "Smug" are also outstanding. — *Richie Unterberger*

● **The Best of the Youngbloods** / 1970 / RCA ✦✦✦✦
It's a bit short at ten songs, but this collection offers a nice overview of this '60s band's growth from good-time ragtimers to laidback jammers. — *Jeff Tamarkin*

Timi Yuro

b. Aug. 4, 1941, Chicago, IL
Vocals / Pop, Pop-Rock, Brill Building Pop
Known as "the little girl with the big voice," Timi Yuro's booming, resonant vocals were sometimes mistaken for being Black, being a man's, or both. Her voice was indeed mammoth, and her delivery astonishingly mature, on her debut single, "Hurt." This 1961 version of the pop standard reached No. 4, and was followed by a brief period of stardom in the early '60s. Too pop in orientation to be called a rock singer, too conscious of rock and soul trends to be pigeonholed into what was then called the "adult" market, Yuro's undoubted talents never fully jibed with her material. While there was soul in her voice, it was of the Dinah Washington or Nancy Wilson sort, with perhaps more of a bent for straight pop than pop-rock. Over the course of the few years following "Hurt," she actually found her greatest success on the easy listening charts, but also dabbled in girl group pop, R&B, Gene Pitney-like ballads, and Patsy Cline-like country. She scored several minor hits during this time, the biggest of which was the most soulful, "What's a Matter Baby (Is It Hurting You)"; reaching No. 12 in the US, it was covered by the Small Faces a few years later as the B-side of their first single. Continuing to record throughout the '60s and into the '70s, she experienced little success after leaving the Liberty label in 1964. — *Richie Unterberger*

● **The Best of Timi Yuro: Hurt** / 1992 / EMI America ✦✦✦✦
Twenty-five-song compilation of her Liberty work, all but one dating from her commercial and artistic peak in 1961-64. Includes all of her chart singles, and some of her more memorable LP tracks, as well as an informative history by Dawn Eden. A jumpy document of an impressive talent whose material was not always up to her skills, with early-'60s arrangements ranging from effective to dated. — *Richie Unterberger*

The Lost Voice of Soul / 1993 / RPM ✦✦✦✦
Twenty-six-track British import best of is perhaps a shade less MOR-oriented than the American EMI *Best of Timi Yuro* compilation. Both have the biggest hits, but *The Lost Voice of Soul* isn't a redundant purchase if you're a serious Yuro fan, as about half the songs don't appear on the EMI anthology. It's difficult to make an argument over which disc's track selection is better; what you prefer, if you want just one, will depend very much on your taste, although North American listeners will have an easier time locating the US anthology. — *Richie Unterberger*

The Voice That Got Away / 1996 / RPM ✦✦✦✦
If you want more Yuro that what you can find on the greatest hits collections, this 26-track compilation is the next stop. Drawn primarily from her Liberty material (from both the early and late '60s), it also has a few obscure '70s sides that hold up much better than expected. B-sides, non-hit singles, and album tracks abound, and the songs are of nearly equal quality to her more celebrated performances. It also showcases her remarkable versatility, which may have been both an asset and a hindrance, as listeners found it difficult to match a solid musical identity with that magnificent voice. She does blue-eyed soul, orchestral pop ballads, pop-rock, and country with assurance, but rarely latches onto a classic bit of material. — *Richie Unterberger*

Z

Zakary Thaks

f. , Corpus Christi, TX
Garage Rock

One of the best garage bands of the '60s, and one of the best teenage rock groups of all time, Zakary Thaks released a half-dozen regionally distributed singles in 1966 and 1967; some were hits in their hometown of Corpus Christi, TX, but none were heard elsewhere until they achieved renown among '60s collectors. Heavily indebted (as were so many bands) to R&B-influenced British heavyweights like the Stones, Kinks, and Yardbirds, the group added a thick dollop of Texas raunch with their fuzzy, distorted guitars and hell-bent energy. Most importantly, they were first-rate songwriters, with the breakneck "Bad Girl" (later compiled on *Pebbles, Vol. 2*), "Won't Come Back," the smoking "Face to Face," "Can't You Hear Your Daddy's Footsteps," and the folk-rock/Mersey hybrid "Please" ranking among the top echelon of American '60s garage rock. Their 1967 singles found the group moving into psychedelic territory; some songs betrayed a Moby Grape influence, and some good melodic numbers were diluted by poppy arrangements that recalled the Buckinghams and Grass Roots. Lead singer Chris Gerniottis, only 15 when Zakary Thaks began making records, joined another interesting Corpus Christi garage-psychedelic group, the Liberty Bell. —*Richie Unterberger*

● **Texas Band** / 1980 / Moxie ♦♦♦♦
Both sides of all six of their singles, marred only by some subpar sound quality (the tracks were mastered from rare singles). —*Richie Unterberger*

Texas Reverberations / 1982 / Texas Archive ♦♦♦
Side one has a couple of alternate takes (an instrumental version of "Daddy's Footsteps," a longer cut of "Face To Face") and some songs by the Liberty Bell. Side Two is a subpar fidelity live recording (though the performances are rabble-rousing) of cover versions the band performed in a promotional film. For collectors only. —*Richie Unterberger*

J-Beck Story 2 / 1984 / Eva ♦♦♦
All 12 of their officially released songs, plus a couple rarities. Remastered from tape, this would displace *Texas Band* as the definitive Zakary Thaks collection, except that the remixes have actually diluted the punch of several of the tracks. —*Richie Unterberger*

Frank Zappa (Frank Vincent Zappa)

f. Dec. 21, 1940, Baltimore, MD, **db**. Dec. 4, 1993
Guitar, Vocals, Keyboards / Hard Rock, Fusion, Art-Rock/Progressive-Rock, Jazz-Rock, Experimental, Psychedelic

Frank Zappa was one of the most accomplished composers of the rock era; his music combines an understanding of and appreciation for such contemporary classical figures as Stravinsky, Stockhausen, and Varese with an affection for late-'50s doo wop rock 'n' roll and a facility for the guitar-heavy rock that dominated pop in the '70s. But Zappa was also a satirist whose reserves of scorn seemed bottomless and whose wicked sense of humor and absurdity have delighted his fans, even when his lyrics crossed over the broadest bounds of taste. Finally, Zappa was perhaps the most prolific record-maker of his time, turning out massive amounts of music on his own Barking Pumpkin label and through distribution deals with Rykodisc and Rhino after long, unhappy associations with giants like Warner Brothers and the now-defunct MGM.

Zappa became interested in music early and pursued his studies in school, up through a six-month stint at Chaffey College in Alta Loma, CA. He scored a couple of low-budget films and used the money to buy a low-budget recording studio. In 1964, he joined a local band called the Soul Giants, which, over the course of the next two years, evolved into the Mothers, who played songs written by Zappa. The band was signed to the Verve division of MGM by producer Tom Wilson in 1966 and recorded its first album, a two-LP set called *Freak Out!*, which introduced Zappa's interests in both serious music and pop as well as his scathing wit. (Verve insisted on adding "of Invention" to the band's name.) Subsequent albums extended the musical and lyrical themes of the debut, and they came frequently. Three albums, for example, hit the charts in 1968: *We're Only in It for the Money*, a Mothers album that made fun of hippies and *Sgt. Pepper*; *Lumpy Gravy*, a Zappa solo album recorded with an orchestra; and *Cruising with Ruben & the Jets*, on which the Mothers played neo-doo wop. Toward the end of the '60s, Zappa expanded the Mothers lineup, turning more toward instrumental jazz-rock, much of which displayed his technically accomplished guitar playing. But by the end of the decade, he had broken up the band.

In 1970, however, Zappa reassembled a new edition of the Mothers, featuring former Turtles lead singers Mark Volman and Howard Kaylan as frontmen. The lineup moved the group the direction of X-rated comedy, notably on the album *Fillmore East June 1971*, but it was short-lived: during a performance at the Rainbow Theatre in London, Zappa was pushed from the stage by a demented fan and seriously injured.

While he recovered, Zappa released several albums, then he reformed the Mothers with himself as lead singer and made pop-rock albums, such as *Over-nite Sensation*, which were among his best-selling records ever. By the end of the '70s, Zappa was recording on his own labels, distributed in some cases by the majors, and he had attracted a consistent cult following for both his humor and his complex music. (Zappa's band, in fact, became a training ground for high-quality rock musicians, much as Miles Davis' was for jazz players.)

In the '80s, Zappa gained the rights to his old albums and began to reissue them, at first on his own and then through the pioneering Rykodisc CD label. He wrote his autobiography and embarked on a world tour in 1988. That was the end of his live performing, except for such isolated appearances as one in Czechoslovakia at the invitation of its post-Communist president, Zappa fan Vaclav Havel.

In late 1991, it was confirmed that Zappa was seriously ill with cancer. Nevertheless, his schedule of album releases continued to be rapid. Zappa died in December of 1993. —*William Ruhlmann*

Freak Out / Jul. 1966 / Rykodisc ♦♦♦♦
This seminal double concept album foreshadowed both art-rock and punk. Its first half consists of melodic, satirical pop-rock songs influenced by R&B and doo-wop, with topics ranging from paranoia and militant nonconformity to emotional alienation and insults addressed to the audience. Zappa also suggests that music can encompass more than the cretin simplicity of teenage love songs, and posits new directions on the album's exploratory second half. Following the perceptive Watts riot protest "Trouble Every Day," Zappa exchanges song structure for experiments with musique concrète, amelodic dissonance, rhythm, and vocal effects. The album articulates Zappa's political agenda of acceptance of difference and free individual expression, as well as his project of synthesizing popular and avant-garde music; as such, it is essential listening and provides an accessible (if incomplete) introduction. —*Steve Huey*

Absolutely Free / May 26, 1967 / Rykodisc ♦♦♦♦
The Mothers' second album finds Zappa experimenting with tape manipulation, abrupt editing, expanded instrumentation, and even an orchestrated mini-rock opera ("Brown Shoes Don't Make It") whose musical style shifts every few lines. Zappa's abundant influences give the record a freewheeling, almost schizophrenic quality, encompassing everything from complex mutations of "Louie, Louie" to jazz improvisations and quotes from Stravinsky's *Rite of Spring*. The lyrics become more absurd and bizarre, as Zappa rants against such byproducts of commercialism as artificiality, corruption, and conformity, while con-

tinuing to mock teenage shallowness. It may be more difficult to make sense of than *Freak Out!*, but *Absolutely Free* is every bit as essential. —*Steve Huey*

★ **We're Only in It for the Money** / Jan. 1968 / Rykodisc +++++
Zappa's masterpiece simultaneously skewers the hippies and the straights, mocking the hollow superficiality of the former while viciously attacking the narrow-mindedness of the latter, which he fears might lead to authoritarian violence (eerily predicting the Kent State killings). There is an odd, whimsical feel to the music, which belies the darkness of some subject matter; some of the instruments and most of the vocals have been manipulated to produce odd textures and cartoonish voices. Most songs are abbreviated, segue into others through edited snippets of music and dialogue, or are broken into fragments by more snippets, consistently interrupting the album's continuity. However, once the listener is accustomed to it, Zappa's melodies reveal themselves as some of his best, and his politics and satirical instinct have rarely been so focused and relevant. —*Steve Huey*

Lumpy Gravy / Mar. 1968 / Rykodisc ++++
Initially commissioned by Capitol Records when the Mothers of Invention were signed to Verve, *Lumpy Gravy* was Frank Zappa's first solo album, one on which be continued his tape experiments and employed an orchestra along with members of the Mothers. Snatches of conversation and sound collages make up the bulk of it, so that it is the most exploratory (but not the most accomplished) album Zappa made in the 1960s. —*William Ruhlmann*

Cruising with Ruben and the Jets / Oct. 1968 / Rykodisc +++
The music of Frank Zappa and the Mothers of Invention always retained roots in soul and doo wop, even at its most satirical. On this, the Mothers' fourth album (and their final release for Verve, now available as a Rykodisc CD reissue), they tried playing it straight, making an affectionate genre album for the low-riding Los Angeles pachucos, although the result is still tongue-in-cheek, as the cover blurb, "Is this the Mothers of Invention recording under a different name in a last ditch attempt to get their cruddy music on the radio?," makes clear. When Zappa prepared the album for reissue in the 1980s, he re-recorded the rhythm tracks, which mars the original. It is this version that is the only one currently available, however. —*William Ruhlmann*

Uncle Meat / Apr. 1969 / Rykodisc ++++
The Mothers' second double album began as the largely instrumental soundtrack to an unfinished film; it places the focus on Zappa's wry melodic sense and compositional dexterity and the Mothers' emerging virtuosity. What few lyrics there are, Zappa says in the notes, are in-jokes relevant only to the band. As before, there are abrupt changes of style and few pauses between songs; *Uncle Meat* also scatters variations on previous musical themes throughout. Some of Zappa's catchiest and most enduring compositions are here, including "Uncle Meat," "Dog Breath, In the Year of the Plague," "A Pound for a Brown on the Bus," and the rhythmically kinetic blowing vehicle "King Kong." —*Steve Huey*

Burnt Weenie Sandwich / Jun. 1969 / Barking Pumpkin ++++
Burnt Weenie Sandwich was the first of two albums by Frank Zappa and the "original" Mothers of Invention (1965-1969) compiled by Zappa from live and studio recordings after he disbanded the group. (The second was *Weasels Ripped My Flesh.*) It is bookended by doo wop songs in the style of *Cruising With Ruben & The Jets*, and in between are extended instrumental passages with solos by pianists Ian Underwood and Don Preston and violinist Sugar Cane Harris. —*William Ruhlmann*

Hot Rats / Oct. 10, 1969 / Rykodisc ++++
Zappa's first solo album finds him collaborating with ex-Mother Ian Underwood on a series of straightforward, focused compositions effectively fusing the musical sophistication of jazz with rock's down and dirty attitude. The album features shorter compositions like the stately "Peaches en Regalia," but the emphasis is on extended, virtuosic jams like "The Gumbo Variations" and "Willie the Pimp" (the latter, based on a greasy blues riff, features Captain Beefheart on vocals). *Hot Rats* never sounds boring, mellow, or uptight, and its rock energy and excitement never waver. It stands as one of the best early jazz-rock fusion efforts, and one of Zappa's most influential recordings. —*Steve Huey*

Weasels Ripped My Flesh / Aug. 1970 / Rykodisc ++++
Live material recorded from 1967 to 1969 and featuring an expanded lineup with horn section. Highlights include Sugar Cane Harris' violin work on Little Richard's "Directly from My Heart to You" and Zappa's vocal on "My Guitar Wants to Kill Your Mama." —*William Ruhlmann*

Fillmore East: June 1971 / Aug. 1971 / Rykodisc +++
A new Mothers lineup led by ex-Turtles singers Mark Volman and Howard Kaylan makes for a virtual comedy act based on the theme of life on the road. Very funny, and some of the playing is amazing too. —*William Ruhlmann*

Waka/Jawaka / Jul. 5, 1972 / Rykodisc +++
Recorded by Frank Zappa in the spring of 1972 while he recuperated from the injuries he sustained when he was pushed off the stage of the

Rainbow on Dec. 10, 1971, *Waka/Jawaka* was intended as a followup to his "solo" album, *Hot Rats*. It found him turning away from the comic vocal approach of the Howard Kaylan/Mark Volman edition of the Mothers and more toward a horn-filled, jazz-fusion approach, notably on the title track and "Big Swifty." —*William Ruhlmann*

The Grand Wazoo / Nov. 1972 / Rykodisc ++++
Frank Zappa continued to experiment with an expanded musical unit on this largely instrumental album, which took a big band approach, prominently featuring reeds and horns. —*William Ruhlmann*

☆ **Over-Nite Sensation** / Sep. 1973 / Barking Pumpkin +++++
This is actually Zappa's first new studio album of vocal music in three years, and it finds him with another edition of Mothers (from this point, Mothers group albums and Zappa solo albums become indistinguishable), this time taking the lead vocals himself and writing a new set of catchy, satiric rock-pop songs like "Camarillo Brillo" and "Montana." —*William Ruhlmann*

☆ **Apostrophe** / Mar. 1974 / Barking Pumpkin +++++
Zappa's only gold-selling Top Ten album, featuring the satiric "Don't Eat the Yellow Snow," along with other parodic songs in the same style as *Over-Nite Sensation.* —*William Ruhlmann*

One Size Fits All / Jun. 25, 1975 / Rykodisc +++
The first Mothers of Invention studio album since the group's biggest hit, *Over-Nite Sensation* (although the Zappa solo album *Apostrophe'* and the live group album *Roxy & Elsewhere* came in between), *One Size Fits All* found Frank Zappa retreating from the frontman position he took on the previous album, sharing lead vocals with keyboard player George Duke, reed man Napoleon Murphy Brock, and guitarist Johnny "Guitar" Watson. The lyrics are the usual mix of scorn, absurdity, humor, and local references ("San Ber'dino") and the music leans toward heavy metal and fusion, although with the usual Zappa signature elements of sudden rhythmic changes and short, startling passages, many of them provided by vibes player Ruth Underwood. The album's standout is the stately "Sofa No. 2," which is sung in German. —*William Ruhlmann*

Bongo Fury / Oct. 2, 1975 / Rykodisc +++
A live album recorded with Captain Beefheart on lead vocals, which combines Zappa's provocative songs with Beefheart's peculiar perspective. Contains the should-have-been-a-hit "Carolina Hard-Core Ecstasy." —*William Ruhlmann*

Zoot Allures / Oct. 29, 1976 / Rykodisc +++
Frank Zappa's albums could be incredibly self-indulgent—something that would be offputting coming from others, but worked to the rocker's artistic advantage. Zappa was often so insanely clever and uniquely humorous that one could excuse his excesses (or even enjoy them). *Zoot Allures*, one of the best albums Zappa recorded in the mid-'70s, is about as self-indulgent as it gets. From "The Torture Never Stops" (a very twisted ode to a medieval-type S&M dungeon) to "Disco Boy" (which lampoons disco culture) to the infectious "Ms. Pinky," everything on the album is an eccentric, delightfully unorthodox classic. Zappa was quite a risk-taker, and those risks pay off in a major way on this CD. —*Alex Henderson*

Zappa In New York / Mar. 3, 1978 / Barking Pumpkin +++
This album was recorded in December 1976 at the Palladium in New York and originally intended for release in 1977. It was held up due to arguments between Frank Zappa and his then-record label, Warner Bros. When the two-LP set finally appeared in March 1978, Warner had deleted "Punky's Whips," a song about drummer Terry Bozzio's attraction to Punky Meadows of Angel. When Zappa reacquired the album and released it as a double-CD in 1991, he restored "Punky's Whips" and added four bonus tracks. The Zappa band, which includes bassist Patrick O'Hearn, percussionist Ruth Underwood, and keyboard player Eddie Jobson, along with a horn section including the two Brecker brothers, was one of the bandleader's most accomplished, which it had to be to play songs like "Black Page," even in the "easy" version presented here. Zappa also was at the height of his comic stagecraft, notably on songs like "Titties & Beer," which essentially is a comedy routine between Zappa and Bozzio, and "The Illinois Enema Bandit," which features TV announcer Don Pardo. —*William Ruhlmann*

Studio Tan / Sep. 15, 1978 / Barking Pumpkin ++
The material on this album was intended to be part of a four-record set called *Lather*, for release in 1977. Then Zappa got into a disagreement with Warner Bros., and *Lather* was split up into different releases as part of a contractual agreement. The results were dumped on the market during 1978 and 1979, while Zappa moved on to his own record label. *Studio Tan* contains 4 selections: a 20-minute recitative called "The Adventures Of Greggery Peccary" in the imaginative, comic style of "Billy The Mountain" (who makes an appearance in the narrative), an orchestral instrumental, a pop tune called "Lemme Take You To The Beach," and a rock instrumental. All are typical Zappa, but none are particularly memorable. —*William Ruhlmann*

Joe's Garage: Acts 1-3 / 1979 / Rykodisc ✦✦✦✦
As part of its contract to reissue vintage Frank Zappa material, Rykodisc reissued the two parts of *Joe's Garage*, originally released in 1979, on a double-CD in 1987. The album is a concept piece about a future time when music is illegal. In it, Zappa continued his fascination with ethnic stereotypes ("Catholic Girls") and bathroom activities ("Why Does It Hurt When I Pee?"). But he wasn't able to use it to fulfill a satisfying dramatic function. — *William Ruhlmann*

Sleep Dirt / Jan. 19, 1979 / Barking Pumpkin ✦✦✦
The material on this album originally was intended to be part of a four-record set called *Lather*, prepared for release in 1977. Then Frank Zappa got into a disagreement with his record company, Warner Bros., and *Lather* was split up into several different releases as part of a contractual agreement. The results were dumped on the market during 1978 and 1979, while Zappa moved on to his own record label. *Sleep Dirt* consists of miscellaneous tracks recorded between 1974 and 1976, including "Flambay," "Spider Of Destiny," and "Time Is Money," songs that apparently were part of an unissued Zappa musical/rock opera from 1972 called *Hunchentoot*. They are sung by soprano Thana Harris. It's impossible to say what the entire work would have been like, but this album is little more than musical fragments. — *William Ruhlmann*

Orchestral Favorites / May 4, 1979 / Barking Pumpkin ✦✦✦
The material on this album originally was intended to be part of a four-record set called *Lather*, prepared for release in 1977. Then Frank Zappa got into a disagreement with his record company, Warner Bros., and *Lather* was split up into several different releases as part of a contractual agreement. The results were dumped on the market during 1978 and 1979, while Zappa moved on to his own record label. *Orchestral Favorites* consists of material recorded on September 17 and 18, 1975 with a 37-piece orchestra and includes such familiar Zappa themes as "Duke Of Prunes" (from *Absolutely Free*) and "Strictly Genteel" (from *200 Motels*); "Bogus Pomp" also consisted largely of *200 Motels* music. The themes are melodic and often majestic, with startling juxtapositions and changes. This was the first release of Zappa orchestral material since *Lumpy Gravy* and a precursor of things to come. — *William Ruhlmann*

Return of the Son of Shut Up 'N Play Yer Guitar / May 11, 1981 / Barking Pumpkin ✦✦✦✦
This is the third of three albums of guitar solos by Frank Zappa released simultaneously by his mail order record company, Barking Pumpkin, and subsequently released to retail by Rykodisc on September 1, 1986, as part of a two-CD set called *Shut Up 'N Play Yer Guitar*. The tracks were recorded, mostly in concert, in 1979 and 1980, and they demonstrate Zappa's mastery of the electric guitar, establishing him as the peer of the other guitar heroes of his generation. — *William Ruhlmann*

Tinsel Town Rebellion / May 17, 1981 / Rykodisc ✦✦✦
From the mid-'70s on, Frank Zappa's music divided ever more extremely into complex instrumental passages and broadly satiric songs, which stopped sounding clever and started seeming smutty and sophomoric. There are elements of these excesses on this live double album, but for the most part the appeal of the music and the fine performances overcome objections. There are also remakes of such old favorites as "Brown Shoes Don't Make It." — *William Ruhlmann*

You Are What You Is / Sep. 1981 / Rykodisc ✦✦✦✦
1981 proved to be another prolific year for Frank Zappa, as, counting his three LPs of guitar solos and his two-LP set *Tinsel Town Rebellion*, along with this two-LP set, he released seven LPs' worth of material during the year, just as he had in 1979. The sarcasm was running heavy on this studio album, with Zappa taking off especially on the beauty/fashion industry in songs like "I'm A Beautiful Guy," "Beauty Knows No Pain," and "Charlie's Enormous Mouth" (the last based on a then-current TV commercial for perfume). Elsewhere, Zappa skewered punk ("Mudd Club"), the hesitant ("The Meek Shall Inherit Nothing"), the stupid ("Dumb All Over"), the religious ("Heavenly Bank Account"), and the depressed ("Suicide Chump") for good measure. — *William Ruhlmann*

Ship Arriving Too Late to Save a Drowning Witch / May 1982 / FZ/ Rykodisc ✦✦✦
Ship Arriving Too Late To Save a Drowning Witch features the novelty hit "Valley Girl," with vocals by Zappa's daughter, Moon. (Steve Vai is featured on the appropriately credited "impossible guitar.") — *William Ruhlmann*

Man from Utopia / Mar. 1983 / Barking Pumpkin ✦✦
A rock album featuring one of Zappa's more accomplished bands (Steve Vai plays guitar, Vinnie Colaiuta drums on two tracks), *The Man From Utopia* presents Frank Zappa's standard mixture of bawdy and comic lyrical interests ("Sex," "The Dangerous Kitchen") with complicated musical passages, notably on the instrumentals "Tink Walks Amok," "Moggio," and "We Are Not Alone." Several songs were presented in a jazz vocalese style that was hard to take, but the version of the old hit "Mary Lou" was entertaining. The CD version, released in 1993, differs from the 1983 LP in some respects. The tracks have been edited differ-

ently ("Cocaine Decisions" is almost a minute longer on the CD, "Moggio" is 40 seconds shorter), they have been resequenced, and there is one added track, "Luigi & The Wise Guys." — *William Ruhlmann*

Baby Snakes / Mar. 1983 / Barking Pumpkin ✦✦
This soundtrack to the 1979 movie *Baby Snakes* was belatedly released by Frank Zappa's mail-order record company, Barking Pumpkin, as a picture disc LP. It consists of live recordings made in October 1976, the same kind of material that turned up on the 1978 album *Zappa In New York*, such as "Titties 'N' Beer" and "Punky's Whips," as well as such concert favorites as "Dinah Moe Humm." — *William Ruhlmann*

Them or Us / Oct. 1984 / Rykodisc ✦✦✦
A caution against the dangers of traveling "In France," a tribute to "Sharleena," a cover of the Allman Brothers Band's "Whipping Post," the double-LP set *Them Or Us* (subsequently reissued on a single CD) found Frank Zappa repeating himself with his usual scorn and formidable musicianship, but not breaking any new ground. — *William Ruhlmann*

Thing-Fish / Nov. 1984 / Rykodisc ✦✦✦
A three-record box set (subsequently reissued as a double-CD), *Thing-Fish* purported to be the cast album for an unproduced Broadway show, but was in fact a savage satire on theater and several other things that could not have been produced theatrically. Ike Willis' "Amos 'n' Andy" patois had long since passed into the objectionable by this point, and the composer's preoccupation with sexual and excretory functions had become extreme. This was a culmination of Zappa's tendencies over the last decade, and their most complete expression. Certainly, he retreated from such works in the future, in fact releasing relatively little new material in the last nine years of his life. — *William Ruhlmann*

Shut up 'N Play Yer Guitar / Sep. 1, 1981 / Rykodisc ✦✦✦✦
This is the first of three albums of guitar solos by Frank Zappa released simultaneously by his mail order record company, Barking Pumpkin, and subsequently released to retail by Rykodisc on September, 1, 1986, as part of a two-CD set, also called *Shut Up 'N Play Yer Guitar*. The tracks were recorded, mostly in concert, in 1979 and 1980, and they demonstrate Zappa's mastery of the electric guitar, establishing him as the peer of the guitar heroes of his generation. — *William Ruhlmann*

Shut up 'N Play Yer Guitar Some More / Sep. 1, 1986 / Barking Pumpkin ✦✦✦✦
This is the second of three albums of guitar solos by Frank Zappa released simultaneously by his mail order record company, Barking Pumpkin, and released to retail by Rykodisc on September 1, 1986, as part of a two-CD set called *Shut Up 'N Play Yer Guitar*. This one features "Variations On The Carlos Santana Secret Chord Progression," which should be useful to guitar students everywhere. — *William Ruhlmann*

Jazz from Hell / Nov. 15, 1986 / Rykodisc ✦✦✦✦
This is an album of jazz-rock-oriented instrumental music that, with the exception of the track "St. Etienne," was recorded on the Synclavier music synthesizer. As an expression of Frank Zappa's more popular music styles, it ranks in execution with such albums as *Hot Rats*. It is the winner of a Grammy Award for Best Rock Instrumental Performance (Orchestra Group or Soloist). — *William Ruhlmann*

London Symphony Orchestra 2 / 1987 / Rykodisc ✦✦✦
This is a CD reissue of *Zappa Volume I* with the addition of the 24 1/2-minute "Bogus Pomp" and the deletion of "Pedro's Dowry" and "Envelopes." Common to both LP and CD are "Sad Jane" and "Mo 'N Herb's Vacation." These are orchestral works by Frank Zappa, played by the London Symphony Orchestra, conducted by Kent Nagano. Although Zappa himself has criticized these recordings, they represent the best rendition so far of his orchestral ambitions, more accomplished than *Lumpy Gravy* or *Orchestral Favorites*. The music is moody and ponderous, slow with sudden dramatic passages, in the manner of Stravinsky, and exhibits little of Zappa's usual melodic invention and humor. — *William Ruhlmann*

Guitar / Apr. 1988 / Rykodisc ✦✦✦✦
Frank Zappa's followup to *Shut Up 'N Play Yer Guitar*, this double-CD (there is also a double-LP on Barking Pumpkin with fewer tracks) excerpts Zappa's guitar solos from live performances, recorded between 1979 and 1984. Guitar aficionados will have a field day. (Release date is for the LP; the CD was released on May 23, 1988.) — *William Ruhlmann*

● **You Can't Do That on Stage Anymore, Vol. 1** / May 16, 1988 / Rykodisc ✦✦✦✦
This two-LP set provides a curtain-raiser on the massive *You Can't Do That On Stage Anymore* series and is typical of the approach of the series in that it jumps from one time and band and location to another, leading off, for example, with a version of "Plastic People" recorded by the Mothers of Invention in 1969 and moving immediately to a version of "The Torture Never Stops" by Frank Zappa's band in 1977. Some of Zappa's more entertaining numbers are here, such as "Montana," "King Kong" (a short version from 1982), and "Cosmic Debris," but, as with most of the series, the jumping around gives the album an unfocused feel. — *William Ruhlmann*

You Can't Do That on Stage Anymore, Vol. 2 / Oct. 1988 / Rykodisc ✦✦✦✦

Unlike the other volumes in Frank Zappa's giant reissue series of concert recordings, *Volume 2* chronicles a single performance, "The Helsinki Concert," which occurred on September 22, 1974. At the time, Zappa was leading a relatively small band consisting of himself on guitar and vocals, Napoleon Murphy Brock on sax and vocals, George Duke on keyboard and vocals, Ruth Underwood on percussion, Tom Fowler on bass, and Chester Thompson on drums. "The repertoire is basically the same as the *Roxy* album," Zappa writes in the liner notes, referring to *Roxy & Elsewhere*, which is true, although the 20 tracks include material from earlier (such as "The Idiot Bastard Son") and later, as well as some unreleased material. As Zappa suggests, the band, which had been on the road a year, is tight, and this is a strong, coherent live performance. *— William Ruhlmann*

Broadway the Hardway / Oct. 1988 / Rykodisc ✦✦✦✦
A live album culled from Zappa's final world tour of 1988. It features his comments on Elvis Presley ("Elvis Has Just Left the Building"), televangelists ("Jesus Thinks You're a Jerk"), and other objects of political scorn. *— William Ruhlmann*

You Can't Do That on Stage Anymore, Vol. 3 / Nov. 1989 / Rykodisc ✦✦✦✦

On the third volume of his live reissue series, after devoting *Volume 2* to a single concert, Frank Zappa returned to his policy of mixing times, bands, and repertoire from throughout his career from one track to the next. The first disc, however, is drawn entirely from Zappa's 1984 tour, which gives it more musical coherence than the second disc, which ranges from 1971 to 1984. Many familiar tunes are featured, notably a 24 1/2-minute version of "King Kong" that is edited from performances in 1982 and 1971, and there are several previously unreleased compositions. *— William Ruhlmann*

Frank Zappa Meets the Mothers of Prevention / May 1990 / Rykodisc ✦✦✦
This album mixes the usual Frank Zappa satire with excerpts from Zappa's testimony before Congress in opposition to censorship and to the Parents Music Resource Center (PMRC). The album was issued in three different forms. The US LP version (Barking Pumpkin ST 74203) contains seven tracks. The European LP version (EMI EMC 3507), released in February 1986, eliminated the 12-minute track "Porn Wars" on the grounds that it "would not have been interesting to listeners outside the US," as a sleeve note explained, and substituted three new tracks, "I Don't Even Care," "One Man—One Vote," and "H.R. 2911." The US CD version (Rykodisc RCD 10023), released September 1, 1986, added "I Don't Even Care" and "One Man—One Vote" to the US LP track listing. *— William Ruhlmann*

Tis the Season to Be Jelly / 1991 / Rhino ✦✦✦
Recorded live in Sweden in 1967, this spotlights the humor of the early Mothers on a parody medley of doo-wop and early rock 'n' roll that is both reverent and sardonic. "King Kong" and "It Can't Happen Here," on the other hand, show them equally interested in contemporary avant-garde compositions. *— Richie Unterberger*

The Best Band You Never Heard in Your Life / Apr. 1991 / Barking Pumpkin ✦✦✦✦
This is the second album that Frank Zappa culled from live performances on his final 1988 world tour, the first being *Broadway The Hard Way*. That release contained newly written material; this one, in contrast, contains, as Zappa puts it in his liner notes, "big-band arrangements of concert favorites and obscure album cuts, along with deranged versions of cover tunes and a few premiere recordings." In practice, that means you have the opportunity to hear Zappa treatments of such surprising songs as "Ring Of Fire," "I Left My Heart In San Francisco," "Bolero," "Purple Haze," and "Stairway To Heaven." In other words, even for an idiosyncratic artist, this is an idiosyncratic album. (The title derives from Zappa's note that the band "self-destructed" before most of the US could hear it play.) *— William Ruhlmann*

Make a Jazz Noise Here / Jun. 1991 / Barking Pumpkin ✦✦✦
This is the third album Frank Zappa culled from his final 1988 world tour. The first, *Broadway The Hard Way*, featured new material, and the second, *The Best Band You Never Heard In Your Life*, offered many unusual cover songs. This album displays the band's musical acuity on various demanding Zappa compositions, such as "The Black Page (new age version)," and even includes snatches of Stravinsky and Bartok. *— William Ruhlmann*

You Can't Do That on Stage Anymore, Vol. 4 / Jun. 21, 1991 / Rykodisc ✦✦✦✦
The fourth volume in Frank Zappa's series of CD compilations of live material is typical in that it features recordings made between 1969 and 1988, including such familiar songs as "My Guitar Wants To Kill Your Mama," "Willie The Pimp," and "Disco Boy." There is, however, an unusually large complement of previously unreleased songs here,

including a cover of "Take Me Out To The Ball Game," and the first performance of "The Torture Never Stops," running more than nine minutes, is a highlight. *— William Ruhlmann*

Beat the Boots! [Box] / Jul. 7, 1991 / Rhino ✦✦✦
Frank Zappa frequently has been the victim of bootleggers, and with this release he turns the tables on his tormentors. This boxed eight-cassette set (also available as separate CDs) presents a series of bootlegs as they appeared, without any improvement. Nevertheless, the sound is often surprisingly good, and especially the recordings by the original Mothers (*The Ark*, RHI 70538, for instance) will be of interest to Zappaphiles. (A second version of *Beat the Boots!*, available only as a boxed set, appeared in 1992.) *— William Ruhlmann*

You Can't Do That on Stage Anymore, Vol. 5 / 1992 / Rykodisc ✦✦✦✦
One of Frank Zappa's avowed purposes in compiling his series of archival live recordings under the *You Can't Do That On Stage Anymore* rubric was to demonstrate to fans that, despite what they thought, his bands after the original Mothers of Invention were an improvement over that legendary outfit. On *Volume 5*, however, he seems to have dropped this effort, devoting the first disc to '60s material. And what do you know? It proves him wrong, at least on an emotional level. Maybe the Mothers weren't great technical musicians and maybe these tapes aren't as high-tech as later ones, but the first disc here is more fun than the rest of the series combined. Disc two is given over to a 1982 European concert tour distinguished by Zappa's threat in Geneva to end the concert if anyone else threw something. Can you guess what happened then? *— William Ruhlmann*

Beat the Boots #2 / Jun. 16, 1992 / Rhino ✦✦✦
Frank Zappa followed the release of the first *Beat The Boots!* box set—his own collection of unretouched bootleg albums—with this second set, which contained seven more albums. While the first box set was cassette-only (plus a small run of LPs), with each album also available individually on CD, this box came in a CD version, again with the different albums separately released. Although there are individual selections that might be of interest to more general Zappa fans, the box is, practically by definition, a collector's item. Note, however, that if you buy the box rather than the individual discs, you get a beret and an extensive scrapbook-like booklet containing news reports and interviews spanning Zappa's career. *— William Ruhlmann*

You Can't Do That on Stage Anymore, Vol. 6 / Oct. 23, 1992 / Rykodisc ✦✦✦✦
Frank Zappa ended his series of albums of previously unreleased concert recordings with this volume, which features one disc given over to "songs dealing generally with the topic of sex (safe and otherwise)," as Zappa puts it in the liner notes. Actually, with songs like "Alien Orifice," "Crew Slut," and "Take Your Clothes Off When You Dance," the same theme pervades disc two, also. *— William Ruhlmann*

Ahead of Their Time / Mar. 23, 1993 / Capitol ✦✦✦
This album contains a previously unreleased live concert by the Mothers of Invention recorded October 28, 1968, at the Royal Festival Hall in London. It finds the band still playing some of its familiar repertoire ("Help, I'm A Rock," "Sleeping In A Jar," "Let's Make The Water Turn Black") from its early albums, but also looking forward to the more ambitious *Uncle Meat*, which would be released the following spring ("King Kong"). Members of the BBC Symphony Orchestra accompany the Mothers on some of Frank Zappa's early orchestral efforts. This is a recording from a key point in the Mothers' history. *— William Ruhlmann*

● **Zappa: The Yellow Shark** / Nov. 2, 1993 / Barking Pumpkin ✦✦✦✦
Released only a month before Frank Zappa's death, *The Yellow Shark* is an album of orchestral treatments of Zappa's compositions done by the 25-piece Ensemble Modern orchestra, conducted by Peter Rundel. It features vintage material like "Dog Breath Variations" as well as more recent work, played with more sensitivity and verve than previous orchestras have brought to Zappa's music. Hence, the "pick" notation should alert fans who want to hear the orchestral Zappa—this is the best executed and most varied of the albums Zappa devoted to his "serious" music. *— William Ruhlmann*

● **Strictly Commercial: The Best of Frank Zappa** / Aug. 22, 1995 / Rykodisc ✦✦✦✦
For all of his many attributes, one thing Frank Zappa most certainly was not is commercial. Presumably, the title of this collection is ironic. *Strictly Commercial: The Best of Frank Zappa* is a compilation not of the composer's hits—he only broke the Top 40 on one occasion, with "Valley Girl"—but rather, a collection of his best-known material, from "Don't Eat the Yellow Snow" to "Sexual Harrassment in the Workplace." Zappa's albums often function as individual works, but the disc offers an intelligent selection of songs, serving as an introduction to the maverick musician. *— Stephen Thomas Erlewine*

Lost Episodes / Feb. 27, 1996 / Rykodisc ✦✦✦✦
A 30-track compilation of rarities, spanning much of his career, but in the main confined to the 1960s and early '70s (some date from as early as the late '50s!). Much of it's previously unreleased, or extremely hard to locate. It's not just a collection of fan-oriented odds and ends, though. The material, for one thing, is extremely diverse, ranging from collaborations with Captain Beefheart and primitive teenage garage recordings to comic dialog to progressive instrumentals and orchestral pieces. The pre-*Freak Out* stuff in particular is revelatory, in the sense that it finds Zappa's sophisticated compositional and arrangement skills in full bloom years before he made his proper debut. There's also good old rock and roll, in an early version of "Any Way the Wind Blows," and an early '60s take of "Fountain of Love" with explosive fuzz bass. The cuts range in duration from 11 seconds to 11 minutes, often connected by amusing bits of spoken patter or nifty instrumental links. The effect is somewhat like *Uncle Meat* or *Lumpy Gravy*, meaning that those who appreciate that period of Zappa's evolution will find an immediate affinity with this anthology. —*Richie Unterberger*

Läther / Sep. 24, 1996 / Rykodisc ✦✦✦
The full saga of *Läther* (pronounced leather) is tangled enough to give a migraine to all but the most committed Zappaphiles. Basically, what you need to know is that this project was originally conceived of as a four-record box set. When record-company politics prevented its release in that format, much of the material was spread over the albums *Live in New York*, *Sleep Dirt*, *Studio Tan*, and *Orchestral Favorites*. This three-CD set presents the album as it was originally conceived, with the addition of four bonus tracks at the end. It mixes previously available material, alternate mixes and edits, and previously unissued stuff, though only the most serious Zappa fans will have a good grip on exactly what has appeared where (the liner notes are surprisingly unexact in this regard). And the music? It's almost like a résumé of Zappa's bag of tricks: *Uncle Meat*-like experimentation, intricate jazz-rock, straight hard rock, orchestral composition, and comedy. Some of those comedy tracks became some of his most notorious routines, like "Punky's Whips" and "Titties 'n Beer," which amounted to avant-rock for drunk frat boys and pot-smoking, underachieving junior-high-school students who wanted something to tickle them as they got stoned. The juvenile humor, hamfisted parody of hard rock cliches, and the shaggy-dog opera of the 20-minute "The Adventures of Greggery Peccary" are outshone by the lengthy, more experimental instrumental passages. It's interesting, but exhausting to wade through all at once, and the avant-garde/composerly cuts are not as exceptional as his earlier work in this vein in the late '60s and early '70s. That means that this will appeal far more to the Zappa cultist than the general listener, though the Zappa cult—which has been craving *Läther* in its original format for years—is a pretty wide fan base in and of itself. —*Richie Unterberger*

Have I Offended Someone / Apr. 8, 1997 / Rykodisc ✦✦✦✦
As the title suggests, *Have I Offended Someone?* contains all of Zappa's notoriously tasteless parodies and satires, from "Bobby Brown Goes Down," "Catholic Girls" and "Jewish Princess" to "He's So Gay," "Titties N' Beer," and "Dinah-Moe Humm." Nearly all of the tracks are presented in new remixed versions, and two songs, "Dumb All Over" and "Tinsel-Town Rebellion," have never been released before. Tinkering with the sound of the songs doesn't change their impact at all—this is the material that made Zappa into an adolescent favorite during the late '70s and early '80s and, in a sense, that makes *Have I Offended Someone?* a best-of collection, even though only "Valley Girl" was a hit. In other words, for some Zappa fans, this collection is everything they loved about him, and for most of his detractors, it's everything they always hated about him. —*Stephen Thomas Erlewine*

● **Strictly Genteel: A Classical Introduction** / May 20, 1997 / Rykodisc ✦✦✦✦
A more than adequate introduction to the world of Frank Zappa's instrumental music. A great deal of attention was focused on Zappa's often infantile lyrics, sometimes to the extent that the quality of Zappa's music was ignored. From a performance standpoint, the music was often a challenge (becoming almost impossible once Zappa was composing for the Synclavier); from a compositional standpoint, Zappa's instrumental music shows its twentieth century influences in no uncertain terms. *Strictly Genteel* serves up music performed by orchestral ensembles as well as pieces performed on Synclavier and in a band context, with the common thread being Zappa's brilliance—while sometimes an imperfect composer, his drive and talent resulted in a huge body of work that may one day be appreciated by classicists. —*Steven McDonald*

Warren Zevon

b. Jan. 24, 1947, Chicago, IL
Bass, Guitar, Keyboards, Vocals / Rock & Roll, Singer-Songwriter
One of the most acute and savagely satiric songwriters of his era, Warren Zevon was born in Chicago on January 24, 1947. His formative years were as colorful as the scenarios played out in his music: his father was

a professional gambler, a lifestyle which forced the family to move frequently, and Zevon spent most of his formative years in California and Arizona. He learned to play piano, and focused primarily on classical material, even studying under the tutelage of Igor Stravinsky. However, a disintegrating home life led him into pop music, as well as a few run-ins with the law; after his parents divorced when he was 16 years old, Zevon hopped into the Corvette his father won in a card game and headed for New York to become a folksinger.

His music found little response, however, and he returned to California, eventually releasing his first recordings as part of the duo Lyme and Cybelle. Session work followed before Zevon issued his solo debut *Wanted—Dead or Alive* in 1969; the LP received a poor reception, and so he returned to session work and composing advertising jingles, and also served as the Everly Brothers' pianist before the duo's breakup. Following a 1974 sabbatical to Spain, Zevon returned to Los Angeles, where his longtime friend Jackson Browne had secured him a recording deal; with Browne in the producer's seat, Zevon cut a self-titled offering which was met with lavish critical praise upon its 1976 release. His 1978 follow-up *Excitable Boy* established him as a wholly unique talent, and earned a sizable hit with its wry single "Werewolves of London."

However, Zevon had fallen prey to alcoholism, and his personal demons sidelined him for the next two years; 1980's *Bad Luck Streak in Dancing School* and 1981's live set *Stand in the Fire* marked his gradual return to form, and the promise of his early work was restored in 1982's brilliant release *The Envoy*. The album fared miserably on the charts, however, and Zevon again fell off the wagon. A long period of therapy and counseling followed before, newly sober and revitalized, he issued *Sentimental Hygiene* in 1987, recorded with backing assistance from members of R.E.M. (In 1990, another collection of material from the sessions featuring Zevon and R.E.M.'s Peter Buck, Mike Mills and Bill Berry was released under the name Hindu Love Gods.) He continued his comeback in 1989 with *Transverse City*, a concept record inspired by science fiction's cyberpunk movement, and 1991's *Mr. Bad Example*. In 1993, Zevon issued his second live album, *Learning to Flinch*, followed in 1995 by *Mutineer*. —*Jason Ankeny*

Wanted Dead or Alive / 1969 / One Way ✦✦✦

Warren Zevon / 1976 / Asylum ✦✦✦✦
A beautiful and ambitious debut, it paints a gloomy and cryptic portrait of Hollywood's casualties through gripping songs like "Carmelita," "I'll Sleep When I'm Dead," and "Mohammed's Radio." —*John Floyd*

Excitable Boy / 1978 / Asylum ✦✦✦✦
A disappointing followup, Zevon's sensitivity is sacrificed for mere weirdness. Nevertheless, there's some fine music here. —*John Floyd*

Bad Luck Streak in Dancing School / 1980 / Asylum ✦✦
Warren Zevon's third album *Bad Luck Streak in Dancing School* was a step down from his first two records. Zevon's material either reworks his earlier songs or are flawed attempts to expand his sound, leaving the record a stylistic mess. —*Stephen Thomas Erlewine*

Stand in the Fire / 1981 / Asylum ✦✦✦
This live set rocks harder than his studio discs and also works as a career overview. —*John Floyd*

The Envoy / 1982 / Asylum ✦✦✦
On *The Envoy*, Warren Zevon's reflective side came to the forefront, as he created a set of songs that were more carefully-crafted and subtle than his previous work, particularly the wistful "Looking for the Next Best Thing," but also had time for grinding rockers like "Ain't That Pretty at All." —*Stephen Thomas Erlewine*

A Quiet Normal Life: The Best of Warren Zevon / 1986 / Asylum ✦✦✦✦
This is an adequate but skimpy best-of covering Zevon's best known songs. Though his self-titled album and *Excitable Boy* have a lot of terrific music not represented here, *A Quiet Normal Life* still stands as a good introduction. —*John Floyd*

Sentimental Hygiene / 1987 / Virgin ✦✦✦✦
Warren Zevon returned in 1987 with his first new album in five years, *Sentimental Hygiene*. Featuring musical support by R.E.M., Zevon's songs take on a tough but melodic edge and the songs comprise his most consistent and impressive set since *Excitable Boy*. —*Stephen Thomas Erlewine*

Transverse City / Oct. 1989 / Virgin ✦✦✦
Zevon's attempt to integrate the influence of Stravinsky makes this album a complex, dense but still absorbing blast of jagged rock. —*John Floyd*

Mr. Bad Example / Oct. 15, 1991 / Giant ✦✦
For Zevon, this is a rather tranquil set of soul searchers, but there's still some trenchant humor here. —*John Floyd*

Learning to Flinch / Apr. 13, 1993 / Warner Brothers ✦✦✦
Warren Zevon recorded the acoustic *Learning to Flinch* at various venues all over the world. All of his best-known songs are here, in riveting

rough acoustic forms. Longtime Zevon fans will find this essential and it may win him a few new ones too. — *Stephen Thomas Erlewine*

Mutineer / May 23, 1995 / Giant ♦♦

Recorded at home, the spare instrumentation of *Mutineer* doesn't work in favor of the album. Instead, it emphasizes the pretentious nature of many of the songs, along with their lack of melody, as the dirge-like "Something Bad Happened to a Clown" indicates. — *Stephen Thomas Erlewine*

● **I'll Sleep When I'm Dead (An Anthology)** / Sep. 17, 1996 / Rhino ♦♦♦♦

I'll Sleep When I'm Dead (An Anthology) covers the bulk of Warren Zevon's career, conviently skipping over his long-forgotten first album and concentrating heavily on his Asylum records, as well as his albums for Virgin and Giant. Over the course of the double-disc set's 44 songs, nearly every one of Zevon's greatest songs is featured, including six songs each from *Warren Zevon* and *Excitable Boy*, as well as a number of songs only featured on soundtrack albums, a handful of outtakes, and Hindu Love Gods' cover of Prince's "Raspberry Beret." The quality of Zevon's music declines somewhat as his career progresses, but the compilation captures most of the highlights from his latter-day records. For casual fans that want to dig deeper than *Warren Zevon* or *Excitable Boy, I'll Sleep When I'm Dead (An Anthology)* is an ideal purchase. — *Stephen Thomas Erlewine*

The Zombies

f. 1962, St. Albans, Herts, England, db. 1967
British Invasion, Psychedelic, Pop-Rock

Aside from the Beatles and perhaps the Beach Boys, no mid-'60s rock group wrote melodies as gorgeous as those of the Zombies. Dominated by Colin Blunstone's breathy vocals, choral backup harmonies, and Rod Argent's shining jazz- and classical-influenced organ and piano, the band sounded utterly unique for their era. Indeed, their material—penned by either Argent or guitarist Chris White, with unexpected shifts from major to minor keys—was perhaps too adventurous for the singles market. To this day, they're known primarily for their three big hit singles, "She's Not There" (1964), "Tell Her No" (1965), and "Time of the Season" (1969). Most listeners remain unaware that the group maintained a remarkably high quality of work for several years.

The Zombies formed in the London suburb of St. Albans in the early '60s, and actually didn't entertain serious professional ambitions until they won a local contest, the prize being an opportunity to record a demo for consideration at major labels. Argent's composition "She's Not There" got them a deal with Decca, and the song ended up being their debut release. It was a remarkably confident and original first-time effort, with a great minor melody and the organ, harmonies, and urgent, almost neurotic vocals that would typify much of their work. It did well enough in Britain (making the Top 20), but did even better in the States, where it went to No. 2.

In fact the group would experience a lot more success across the waters than they did at home throughout their career. In early 1965, another piece of classic British Invasion pop, "Tell Her No," went into the Top Ten. Yet that was as much Top 40 success as the group would have for several years.

The tragedy was that throughout 1965 and 1966, the Zombies released a string of equally fine, intricately arranged singles that flopped commercially, at a time in which chart success on 45s was a lot more important to sustain a band's livelihood than it would be a few years down the road. "Remember When I Loved Her," "I Want You Back Again," "Indication," "She's Coming Home," "Whenever You're Ready," "Gotta Get a Hold of Myself," "I Must Move," "Remember You," "Just out of Reach," "How We Were Before"—all are lost classics, some relegated to B-sides, that went virtually unheard, all showing the group eager to try new ideas and expand their approaches. What's worse, the lack of a big single denied the group opportunities to record albums—only one LP, rushed out to capitalize on the success of "She's Not There," would appear before 1968.

Their failure to achieve more widespread success is a bit mystifying, perhaps explained by a few factors. While undeniably pop-based, their original compositions and arrangements were in some senses too adventurous for the radio. "Indication," for instance, winds down with a lengthy, torturous swirl of bitter organ solos and wordless, windblown vocals; "Remember When I Loved Her," despite its beautiful melody, has downbeat lyrics that are almost morbid; "I Want You Back Again" is arranged like a jazz waltz, with the sorts of sudden stops, tempo shifts, and lengthy minor organ solos found in a lot of their tunes. The group were also, perhaps unfairly, saddled with a somewhat square image; much was made of their formidable scholastic record, and they most definitely did not align themselves with the R&B-based school of British bands, preferring more subtle and tuneful territory.

By 1967, the group hadn't had a hit for quite some time, and reckoned it was time to pack it in. Their Decca contract expired early in the year,

and the Zombies signed with CBS for one last album, knowing before the sessions that it was to be their last. A limited budget precluded the use of many session musicians, which actually worked to the band's advantage, as they became among the first to utilize the then-novel Mellotron to emulate strings and horns.

Odessey and Oracle was their only cohesive full-length platter (the first album was largely pasted together from singles and covers). A near-masterpiece of pop/psychedelia, it showed the group reaching new levels of sophistication in composition and performance, finally branching out beyond strictly romantic themes into more varied lyrical territory. The album passed virtually unnoticed in Britain, and was only released in the States after some lobbying from Al Kooper. By this time it was 1968, and the group had split for good.

The Zombies had been defunct for some time when one of the tracks from *Odessey*, "Time of the Season," was released as a single, almost as an afterthought. It took off in early 1969 to become their biggest hit, but the members resisted temptations to reform, leading to a couple of bizarre tours in the late '60s by bogus "Zombies" with no relation to the original group. By this time, Rod Argent was already recording as the leader of Argent, which went in a harder rock direction than the Zombies. After a spell as an insurance clerk, Blunstone had some success (more in Britain than America) in the early '70s as a solo vocalist, with material that often amounted to soft-rock variations on the Zombies sound.

Much more influential than their commercial success would indicate, echoes of the Zombies' innovations can be heard in the Doors, the Byrds, the Left Banke, the Kinks, and many others. After a long period during which most of their work was out of print, virtually all of their recordings have been restored to availability on CD. — *Richie Unterberger*

Odessey & Oracle / 1968 / Rhino ♦♦♦♦

A psychedelic effort whose best song, "Time of the Season," became a monster hit with a sultry, soulful sound not replicated elsewhere on the album. — *Bruce Eder*

Early Days / 1969 / London ♦♦♦

Mish-mash of mid-'60s tracks, including "She's Not There," "Tell Her No," and several fine cuts that had not been available on US LP before. Every song but one ("Kinda Girl") is on *Singles A's & B's*, making this compilation largely obsolete. — *Richie Unterberger*

World of the Zombies / 1970 / Decca ♦♦

Twelve-track hodgepodge of '60s material, surrounding "She's Not There" and "Tell Her No" with some interesting non-hit singles and mediocre cover versions. All the good stuff is available on better, more solidly constructed compilations. — *Richie Unterberger*

Time of the Zombies / 1973 / Epic ♦♦♦

This double LP, containing the entire *Odyssey And Oracle* and another disc of hits and outtakes, is not recommended as an overall sampler; there are other compilations that do a much better job. Zombie collectors, though, will be interested in finding this: Side Two contains eight songs that have rarely been available anywhere else, comprised mostly of late-'60s outtakes and a rare single, some of which may have been recorded in the post-Zombies, pre-Argent days without Blunstone. This material doesn't rank among their best (though Dusty Springfield did cover "If It Don't Work Out" in the mid-'60s), but the piano-dominated "I'll Call You Mine" would have been easily strong enough to fit into *Odyssey And Oracle.* — *Richie Unterberger*

Rock Roots / 1976 / Decca ♦♦♦

Sixteen tracks from 1964-67, including their most popular singles and a couple of LP tracks. It's good material, but it's now available on better, more extensive compilations. — *Richie Unterberger*

Live on the BBC / 1985 / Rhino ♦♦♦

While this compilation of 14 BBC airshots has barely different versions of their self-penned singles "Tell Her No," "Just Out Of Reach," and "Whenever You're Ready," it concentrates on their covers of a surprisingly wide array of soul and R&B standards that the group never released on record. Unlike, say, the Stones, the Zombies were much more noted for their compositional prowess than their original interpretations of American rock and soul; the group's tasteful, melodic restraint could make them sound twee and out of their depth when they tackled chestnuts like "I've Got My Mojo Working" on their first LP. But the covers here, emphasizing the band's harmonies and Rod Argent's keyboards, are well done. Includes songs originally performed by the Isley Brothers, Aretha Franklin, Gene Vincent, the Supremes, Curtis Mayfield, and others, some of them quite obscure even in their original incarnations. Excellent sound rounds off an album that gives some unexpected insight into the Zombies' influences. — *Richie Unterberger*

Best & the Rest of the Zombies / 1986 / Back-Trac ♦♦♦

This half-baked compilation, with only eight songs, is noteworthy only in that it includes three previously unreleased songs, two of which were actually recorded by Rod Argent and Chris White in the late '60s without Colin Blunstone. One of those, "Girl Help Me," is a really fine ballad, and the mid-'60s outtake "I'll Keep Trying" is a decent, characteristic uptempo number. —*Richie Unterberger*

★ **Singles A's & B's** / 1990 / See For Miles ✦✦✦✦✦
While "She's Not There" and "Tell Her No" are the only well-remembered mid-'60s Zombies singles, they recorded quite a few great non-hit 45s as well during this period. This outstanding collection (now available on CD) features all 22 of the sides they released on singles between 1964-67, and shows the group to be among the most superbly inventive pop-rock composers of their era, exploring moody minor-key melodies more than anyone before or since. Colin Blunstone's delicate, neurotic vocals and Rod Argent's biting electric keyboards pace the band on this set, which features the two big hits and such great lost classics as "Remember When I Loved Her," "I Want You Back Again," "I Must Move," "Indication," and "Gotta Get a Hold of Myself." Essential British Invasion music. —*Richie Unterberger*

ZZ Top

f. 1970, El Paso, TX
Group / Rock & Roll, Blues-Rock, Hard Rock, Boogie Rock
This sturdy American blues-rock trio from Texas consists of Billy Gibbons (guitar), Dusty Hill (bass), and Frank Beard (drums). They were formed in 1970 in and around Houston from rival bands the Moving Sidewalks (Gibbons) and the American Blues (Hill and Beard). Their first two albums reflected the strong blues roots and Texas humor of the band. Their third album (*Tres Hombres*) gained them national attention with hit "La Grange," a signature riff tune to this day, based on John Lee Hooker's "Boogie Chillen." Their success continued unabated throughout the '70s, culminating with the year-and-a-half-long Worldwide Texas Tour. Exhausted from the overwhelming work load, they took a three-year break, then switched labels and returned to form with *Deguello* and *El Loco*, both harbingers of what was to come. By their next album, *Eliminator*, and its worldwide smash follow-up, *Afterburner*, they had successfully harnessed the potential of synthesizers to their patented grungy blues-groove, giving their material a more contemporary edge while retaining their patented Texas style. Now sporting long beards, golf hats, and boiler suits, they met the emerging video age head-on, reducing their "message" to simple iconography. Becoming even more popular in the long run, they moved with the times while simultaneously bucking every trend that crossed their path. As genuine roots musicians, they have few peers; Gibbons is one of America's finest blues guitarists working in the arena-rock idiom—both influenced by the originators of the form and British blues-rock guitarists like Peter Green—while Hill and Beard provide the ultimate rhythm section support. The only rock 'n' roll group that's out there with its original members still aboard after 20-plus years, ZZ Top's music is always instantly recognizable, eminently powerful, profoundly soulful, and 100% American in derivation. They have continued to support the blues through various means, perhaps the most visible when they were given a piece of wood from Muddy Waters' shack in Clarksdale, MS. The group members had it made into a guitar, dubbed the "Muddywood," then sent it out on tour to raise money for the Delta Blues Museum. ZZ Top's support and link to the blues remains as rock solid as the music they play. —*Cub Koda*

ZZ Top's First Album / 1970 / Warner Brothers ✦✦✦
This Texas trio's debut was a gritty exercise in bare-boned blues boogie. Tracks like "Brown Sugar," "Neighbor Neighbor," and "Shakin' Your Tree" helped establish them as a regionally successful act in the South. —*Rick Clark*

Rio Grande Mud / 1972 / Warner Brothers ✦✦✦
Rio Grande Mud possessed a beefier sound than its predecessor. The "Brown Sugar"-style "Francine" became their first hit at number 69. Other highlights included "Chevrolet" and "Just Got Paid." —*Rick Clark*

Tres Hombres / 1973 / Warner Brothers ✦✦✦✦
Constant touring and favorable radio exposure made *Tres Hombres* ZZ's first hit album, thanks in no small part to "La Grange," an ode to a whorehouse. By this album, Billy Gibbons had practically perfected his distinctively dirty electric-guitar sound. His riffs and chordal voicings were also more memorable. Highlights included "Beer Drinkers & Hell Raisers," "Precious & Grace," and the twosome "Waitin' for the Bus" and "Jesus Just Left Chicago." —*Rick Clark*

Fandango / 1975 / Warner Brothers ✦✦✦
Fandango is a half-studio/half-live effort. The concert side is a fairly straightahead, no-nonsense affair, which includes a version of "Jailhouse Rock." The studio side featured their first Top 40 hit, "Tush" (No. 20). The hyper-boogie of "Heard It on the X" was another popular track off of this release. —*Rick Clark*

★ **The Best of ZZ Top** / 1977 / Warner Brothers ✦✦✦✦✦
The sound may be a little muddy, but this anthology is still the best representation of ZZ's early work. It contains classic rude, riff-heavy blues-

rockers like "Just Got Paid," "Jesus Just Left Chicago," "Heard It on the X," "Tush," and "La Grange." —*Rick Clark*

Deguello / 1979 / Warner Brothers ✦✦✦✦
Deguello was ZZ's best album from their pre-robotic blues-rock period—the last reminder of what a tough ensemble this trio could be. It was the first time they infused their lunkhead approach to fast cars, kinky girls, and partying with some bizarre humor. Their version of Sam & Dave's "I Thank You" (No. 34) became their first Top 40 hit in five years. Other highlights included the oddball "Manic Mechanic," a rip-roaring version of Elmore James' "Dust My Broom," the funky boogie of "Cheap Sunglasses," and "Fool for Your Stockings," a down-and-dirty fetish blues. —*Rick Clark*

El Loco / 1981 / Warner Brothers ✦✦✦
Not as strong as *Deguello*, *El Loco* vacillates between half-baked ballads ("Leila") and novelty rockers ("Party on the Patio," "Groovy Little Hippie Pad," "Heaven, Hell or Houston"). "Pearl Necklace," with its not-too-subtle sexual double-entendre and Police-inspired groove, was a big AOR hit. —*Rick Clark*

Eliminator / 1983 / Warner Brothers ✦✦✦✦
Hardcore fans might have cried "sellout," but ZZ's introduction of a streamlined synth-heavy sound (and three slickly produced T&A videos) turned this trio from potential blues-rock has-beens to multi-platinum purveyors of space boogie. Most of this album became a staple on album rock radio, with "Gimme All Your Lovin'," "Sharp Dressed Man," and "Legs" becoming the primary hits. —*Rick Clark*

Afterburner / 1985 / Warner Brothers ✦✦✦
Basically a carbon-copy of *Eliminator*, *Afterburner* continued ZZ's winning streak, which includes four hit singles: "Sleeping Bag," "Stages," "Rough Boy," and "Velcro Fly." —*Rick Clark*

Recycler / 1990 / Warner Brothers ✦✦✦
ZZ seemed to be running low on good material as they cranked up the Fairlights for a third go-round. "My Head's in Mississippi," however, is a fine rocker, which synthesized the gritty virtues of their earlier sound with the hi-tech gloss of their later work. *Recycler* also includes "Doubleback," their hit from the movie *Back to the Future—Part III*. —*Rick Clark*

● **Greatest Hits** / Apr. 14, 1992 / Warner Brothers ✦✦✦✦
An 18-song compilation, it features the greatest hits of ZZ Top's MTV era, including "Gimme All Your Lovin'," "Sharp Dressed Man," "Tush," "Pearl Necklace," "Cheap Sunglasses," "Sleeping Bag," "Rough Boy," and a remixed version of "Legs." It's a good, fun collection that should have been sequenced better and, unfortunately, omits a few good songs. —*AMG*

Antenna / Jan. 18, 1994 / RCA ✦✦✦
Like precious few bands from the '70s whose best work is mummified daily thanks to classic rock radio, ZZ Top just keeps rolling on into the next decade. There"s much to love here, from the downright nasty stomp of "Fuzzbox Voodoo," the powerhouse slow blues of "Cover Your Rig," the bass pumping looniness of "Girl in a T-Shirt," to the slow grind of "Breakaway." While Billy Gibbon's guitar tones on this album are highly reminiscent of *Tres Hombres* (an early high-water mark for the band), the high production sheen from their '80s albums remains intact. But Gibbons hasn't played with this much over-the-top abandon since their pre-beard 'n' babes days, and that's what separates this album from the three that came before it. —*Cub Koda*

One Foot in the Blues / Nov. 22, 1994 / Warner ✦✦
Before they sweated their image down to beards, babes and hot rods, ZZ Top were a down 'n' dirty blues-rock trio with a bonafide hot guitar player in Billy Gibbons. On this 14-track offering Warners goes back through the back ZZ catalog and cobbles together an interesting collection of the Texas trio's bluesier sides that originally appeared on their earliest albums. Highlights include "Brown Sugar," "A Fool for Your Stockings," "My Head's in Mississippi," "Apologies to Pearly" and Gibbons' storming stringwork on "Bar-B-Q." —*Cub Koda*

Rhythmeen / Sep. 17, 1996 / RCA ✦✦✦
ZZ Top's long-awaited return to the blues finally arrived in 1996, well over a decade after they abandoned their simple three-chord boogie for a synth and drum machine-driven three-chord boogie. Like *Antenna* before it, *Rhythmeen* is stripped of all the synthizers that characterized the group's albums since *Eliminator* but the key difference between the two albums is how *Rhythmeen* goes for the gut, not the gloss. It's a record that is steeped in the blues and garage rock, one that pounds out its riffs with sweat and feeling. Though ZZ Top sounds reinvigorated, playing with a salacious abandon they haven't displayed since the '70s, they simply haven't come up with enough interesting songs and riffs to make it a true return to form. For dedicated fans, it's a welcome return to their classic "La Grange" sound, but anyone with a just a passing interest in the band will wonder where the hooks went. —*Stephen Thomas Erlewine*

VARIOUS ARTISTS

Ace Story, Vol. 1 / Ace ✦✦✦✦
With five separate volumes, *The Ace Story* is the most comprehensive portrait of the seminal New Orleans R&B record label. Over the course of the series, each of the label's hits are featured, including "Sea Cruise," "Rockin' Pneumonia," "Pop Eye," among others, as well as many lesser-known gems. During the late '50s and early '60s, Ace's roster featured such R&B giants as Huey "Piano" Smith, Eddie Bo, Joe Tex, Lightnin' Hopkins, Charles Brown, Amos Milburn, and Earl King; each artist is featured on at least one disc of *The Ace Story*, along with several acts that didn't have hits, but recorded some outstanding tracks. Start with the first volume, then proceed to the other discs; every one is filled with timeless R&B. —*Stephen Thomas Erlewine*

Ace Story, Vol. 4 / Ace ✦✦✦✦
This fourth entry in chronicling the story of Johnny Vincent's Jackson, Mississippi based Ace Records by the British company that has (legally) used the company logo to become one of the world's largest reissue companies is another fine one. Loaded with 16 tracks of New Orleans styled dynamite from the label's early days, this compilation kicks off with Johnny Angel's "Teenage Wedding," a perfect example of the cross-over sound that Vincent often sought on his releases. Angel, a white Cajun singer, is backed by Huey "Piano" Smith and his band, with the end result being a typical 1950s insert the names of hit songs in the lyrics rocker propelled by a driving Crescent City beat. Soul singer Joe Tex started his early career with Ace and he's represented by one of his most uncharacteristic tracks, "Charlie Brown Got Expelled," an answer record to the Coasters' hit, "Charlie Brown" and a later effort, "Yum Yum Yum." More of the Crescent City alumni saw single releases on the label and are collected here with "Happy Sax" and "Walk On" by saxman Alvin Tyler, "I Wanna Know Why" by Roland Cooke, "Tee-Na-Na" by Dicky Williams and Eddie Bo's "I'll Keep On Trying" being the notable tracks here. And of course, the ever present Huey "Piano" Smith and the Clowns are here with two selections, "Scald Dog" and "Free, Single and Disengaged." Selections from Jesse Allen, Joe & Ann, Floyd Brown, Albert Scott and Frankie Lee Sims (his "Walkin' with Frankie, which, inexplicably, got the 50 something Texas bluesman a shot on *American Bandstand* back then) round out the compilation. No hits aboard, but a great cross section of music, making this a worthy entry in the series. —*Cub Koda*

Acid Visions: Best of Texas Punk/Psychedelic, Vol. 1 / Collectables ✦✦✦✦
One of the very best '60s garage compilations, a high compliment given the thousands of competitors, and the very best Texas '60s garage anthology. With the possible exception of California, Texas was home to more fine obscure garage records than any other state, and these 14 cuts are among the finest. Roy Head delivers a fine Johnny Winter tune, "Easy Lovin' Girl," and Winter himself sings a prime slice of folk-rock-acid-punk, "Birds Can't Row Boats" (this version, incidentally, is much better than the one found on the early Winter compilation of the same name). The other names are totally obscure, and some of the tracks weren't even released until the 1980s. But the Things and the Bad Roads come through with fine pop-punk numbers; and A-440's "Torture," Satori's "Time Machine," and the Pandas' "Walk" have been belatedly recognized as some of the best garage psychedelia ever, combining sharp melodic hooks and songwriting with out-and-out dementia. —*Richie Unterberger*

Across the Tracks: Nashville R&B and Rock'n'roll / 1996 / Ace ✦✦✦
Nashville is now firmly cemented in the collective consciousness as a country capital. But in the '50s and '60s, it did harbor a reasonably active R&B/blues/soul scene. Of the Nashville-based R&B labels, Excello had the highest profile; this compilation gathers 28 late '50s and early '60s tracks from several smaller local competitors (the Champion, Cherokee, Kit, Calvert, Poncello, Spar, and Valdot labels). Few of the performers are

even known on a cult level; Gene Allison (who had a hit with "You Can Make It If You Try," not included here) is about the only one with even modest name recognition value. It's decent but generic early R&B, a bit of gospel, pure soul, or out-and-out Little Richard-like rock'n'roll thrown in, recommended only if early R&B/soul if your main bag. Which isn't to say it's mediocre; there is not, however, a clearly identifiable Nashville R&B sound, as there is for, say, Memphis. The highlights are the most soul-oriented outings from the early '60s (by Lucille & the Strangers, Herbert Hunter, Leevert Allison, and Roscoe Shelton), if only because the tunes are more sophisticated and the production a bit more ambitious. —*Richie Unterberger*

AK79 / 1993 / Flying Nun ✦✦✦✦
AK79 is probably the best compilation of New Zealand's entries for punk rock and new wave of the late '70s. While most of this material was released on small independent labels like Ripper, Propeller, Flying Nun and Mushroom and never saw any exposure outside of New Zealand, the quality of the songs and raw energy behind them should appeal to genre specialists and certainly deserves discovery. Included are rarities from the brilliant yet underrated Swingers, Suburban Reptiles, and Toy Love, among others. —*Chris Woodstra*

All Night Boogie: The Great Atlantic Vocal Groups, Vol. 2 / 1996 / Rhino/Collectors' Choice Music ✦✦✦
Another two-CD, 50-track collection of R&B vocal group (usually doo wop) rarities from the Atlantic vaults, recorded in the 1950s and early '60s. None of these are familiar hits, except for the Coasters' "Yakety Yak" and "Charlie Brown," presented in previously unreleased stereo mixes. It's not recommended if you're not heavily into the genre, but if you're a doo wop specialist, this is one of the best packages of its kind available, with sides (many hard to find) by the Clovers, Cardinals, Penguins, Bobbettes, Sensations, Skyliners, and others. There are also previously unreleased items by the Chords and the Drifters (from both the Clyde McPhatter and Ben E. King lineups), and the original version of "Twist and Shout" (by the Top Notes). —*Richie Unterberger*

American Graffiti Soundtrack, Vol. 1 / 1973 / MCA ✦✦✦✦✦
The soundtrack to the George Lucas film about teenage life in a small California town in the early '60s was probably the best thing about the movie, featuring several dozen outstanding early rock 'n' roll hits. There's nothing terribly obscure here—in fact, most of those were big smashes—but it's a good survey of rock's early days, ranging from super-stars like Buddy Holly, Chuck Berry, Fats Domino, and the Beach Boys to great one-shots like the Monotones, the Tempos, and Buster Brown. Drawbacks: Wolfman Jack talks over the intros of a few songs, and there are a couple things by early-'70s Sha-Na-Na-type revivalists Flash Cadillac. —*Richie Unterberger*

Atlantic R&B—1947-1974 / 1991 / Atlantic ✦✦✦✦✦
Atlantic was one of the most influential independent record labels of the '50s, bringing jazz and R&B to a far larger audience than ever before and making artists like the Drifters, Ray Charles and Aretha Franklin into stars in the process. Originally released as individual volumes, *Atlantic R&B—1947-1974* is an extraordinary eight-disc box set that traces Atlantic's evolution into a pop music powerhouse. Over the course of over 200 songs, *Atlantic R&B* features some of the best and most influential songs in pop music history, illustrating how blues and R&B entered the mainstream. But the set is much more than a history listen—it is vital, exciting listening featuring not only classics, but also a number of forgotten gems that demonstrate the depth of the label's talent. And that roster including, for a brief time, artists on Stax/Volt, was one of the greatest ever assembled, featuring Big Joe Turner, Professor Longhair, LaVern Baker, Coasters, Ruth Brown, Chuck Willis, Clyde McPhatter, Barbara Lewis, Otis Redding, Ben E. King, Solomon Burke, Percy Sledge, Sam & Dave, Wilson Pickett, Joe Tex and the Spinners. Although the set might look like it's designed to appeal only to collec-

tors, *Atlantic R&B* is essential for even casual fans, since it not only offers an abundence of great music, but provides a priceless portrait of the evolution of R&B to soul. — *Stephen Thomas Erlewine*

Beat the Retreat: Songs by Richard Thompson / 1994 / Capitol ✦✦✦
One of the better tribute albums of 1994, *Beat the Retreat* manages to capture not only the dark grace of Richard Thompson, but also his spirit. R.E.M.'s faithful reading of "Wall of Death" is full of beautiful melancholy, while Bob Mould's galloping take on "Turning of the Tide" pays homage to Thompson's breathtaking instrumental skills simply by making the song his own. Most of *Beat the Retreat* works in the same way. The artists' love for the material never shadows their appreciation for Thompson's individuality. Hence, the songs are never replications of the original versions; they are interpretations, which is much more effective. — *Stephen Thomas Erlewine*

Beatle Originals (Original Versions of the Songs the Beatles Made Famous) / 1986 / Rhino ✦✦✦✦
A pretty neat concept for a record: 13 of the *original* versions of the more obscure songs covered by the Beatles on their early albums. The biggest hits that the group interpreted—early Motown songs, Chuck Berry rockers, "Twist and Shout," "Long Tall Sally," "Chains," "Baby It's You"—are not here, on the reasonable grounds that the originals are easily available, and most likely in the collection of many Beatle fans already. Instead it has the less traveled original tracks by Larry Williams and Carl Perkins (three songs apiece), Little Richard's "Kansas City/Hey Hey Hey," Buddy Holly's "Words of Love," Arthur Alexander's "Anna," the Shirelles' "Boys," and Buck Owens' "Act Naturally." The most noteworthy items are the two tracks which even collectors found difficult to locate: the Donays' girl group single "Devil in His Heart," and Dr. Feelgood's "Mr. Moonlight." The material is classic in its own right: equally important, it gives Beatle fans the opportunity to hear original versions that were virtually inaccessible for years, compare them to the (usually great) renditions by the Beatles, and appreciate the well-rounded scope of their influences. Unfortunately, it does not include the prototype versions of "A Taste of Honey" and "Till There Was You," on the debatable premise that they were too pop-oriented to warrant interest. — *Richie Unterberger*

The Berkeley EPs / 1995 / Big Beat [UK] ✦✦✦✦
Essential for '60s San Francisco rock aficionados, this contains four rare indie EPs by four Berkeley bands ranging from famous to obscure: Country Joe & the Fish, Mad River, Frumious Bandersnatch, and Notes from the Underground. The music is quite fine, not just for collector completists. Although the Country Joe songs were re-cut for their official debut LP, these mid-1966 versions are rawer and even more psychedelic; the take of the instrumental "Section 43" ranks not just as one of their greatest moments, but one of the greatest moments in the whole of psychedelic rock. Mad River play two stripped-down versions of songs that were re-recorded for their debut, as well as one they never released elsewhere, the harrowing "Orange Fire," which may be their best composition. The obscure Frumious Bandersnatch, who never released anything other than the EP here (although several members went on to the Steve Miller Band in the 1970s), offer some enticingly delicate and trippy acid guitar interplay and harmonies. Notes from the Underground were the most ordinary of the lot, playing tepid folk/blues/rock; in addition to their EP, three previously unreleased tracks by the band are presented on this compilation. — *Richie Unterberger*

Beserkley's Best / Blackheart ✦✦✦✦
Mainly a revised version of the *Chartbusters* collection, *Beserkley's Best* does a good job of summing up the legendary label's high points with tracks from better known acts like Jonathan Richman and Greg Kihn along with the sorely underated Rubinoos, Earthquake, and the Spitballs (the Beserkley "supergroup"). — *Chris Woodstra*

The Best of Ace Records: The Pop Hits, Vol. 1 / 1992 / Scotti Bros. ✦✦✦
In the late '50s and early '60s, Ace was one of the most successful New Orleans-based rock 'n' roll labels, recording hits by Huey Smith, Frankie Ford, and Jimmy Clanton. This 14-song compilation isn't the best way to hear the Ace catalog, though. Ford and Smith, both of whom have tracks here, are better represented by full compilations of their work; Ford's magnificent "Sea Cruise" is here, but Smith's only big hit, "Don't You Just Know It," is strangely missing in favor of a couple much less renowned tracks. Clanton recorded some nice hits in the teen idol style ("Just a Dream," "Venus in Blue Jeans," and "Go, Jimmy, Go"), all of which are here. But these sound misplaced next to Ford and Smith, and the other Clanton cuts are weak. There's also a rare early single by Joe Tex, "Charlie Brown Got Expelled," an answer record to the Coasters' "Charlie Brown." — *Richie Unterberger*

The Best of Candlelite Records, Vol. 1 / 1993 / Juke Box Treasures ✦✦✦
This is the original installment in this landmark series, collecting 28 obscure doo wop tracks that were originally issued on Wayne Stierle's Candlelite label. The original "Why Don't You Write Me" by the Feathers

is here, along with Jesse Belvin sitting in with them on "Love Song." The crude and crazed "Jeannie" by the Thrashers also makes its first CD appearance, along with the teenage bop of "Come on Baby" by the Five Discs and the dreamy teen sentimentality of "Lost Lover" by the Cameos and "Romance in the Spring" by the Five Roses. An excellent compilation covering the super-obscure side of the genre, and great listening every note of the way. — *Cub Koda*

The Best of House Music, Vol. 1 / 1987-1988 / Profile ✦✦✦
Contrary to popular belief, disco didn't die with the '70s—it simply changed its name to dance music in the '80s and evolved into such forms as European Hi-NRG, so-called "Latin hip-hop/freestyle" and house music (which originated in the nightlife mecca of Chicago and quickly spread to New York, Europe and elsewhere). Like late-'70s disco, house—defined by its tinkling keyboard grooves and thumping bass, among other things—can be either mechanical and formulaic or soulful, enriching and even spiritual. Profile Records' excellent *Best of House Music* series, though far from the last word on house, has done a fine job illustrating house's diversity. This CD ranges from producer-oriented, track-minded club hits like J.M. Silk's "Jack Your Body," Exit's "Let's Work It Out," and Moonfou's abrasive acid-house number "Shut Up" to songs making vocal personality the main attraction, such as Liz Torres' "Can't Get Enough," Ralphi Rosario & Xaviera Gold's "You Used to Hold Me" and Jeanne Harris' "Just Another Man" (a captivating example of deep house, which is essentially an extention of late-'70s Philly disco/soul). Producer Marshall Jefferson, one of house's key figures, is well represented by the insanely catchy "Move Your Body." This compilation's more producer-oriented cuts are enjoyable enough, but ultimately, limited—in the long run, warm and personal singing would do the most to keep house artistically healthy. — *Alex Henderson*

Best of House Music, Vol. 2: Gotta Have House / 1987-1988 / Profile ✦✦✦
House music's detractors vehemently insist that it all sounds alike, which couldn't be farther from the truth. With its second *Best of House Music* compilation, Profile once again showed listeners that house is far from one-dimensional. Those who prefer house's warmer, more vocal-oriented side found much to admire in the inviting and very musical "deep house" of Kechia Jenkins' "I Need Somebody" and remixes of Natalie Cole's hit "Pink Cadillac" and British R&B group Imagination's "Instinctual," while house's more producer-oriented side is exemplified by Royal House's "Can You Party," Jeanette "J.T." Thomas' "Shake Your Body" and Kraze's raucous "The Party." On "I Need Somebody," vocals are everything—whereas on LNR's dissonant and not very musical "Work It to The Bone," it's all about the producer and the track. House fans were already more than familar with most of this material when Profile released this CD in 1988, but for those first exploring house, it served as an engaging and informative introduction. — *Alex Henderson*

Best of House Music, Vol. 3: House Music All Night Long / 1990 / Profile ✦✦✦
House music had become a bit less underground by the time Profile released its third *Best of House* compilation in 1990, the year Madonna gave house a pop hit with "Vogue." Like its predecessors, this CD is an unpredictable release reminding us of house's diversity by including a wide variety of material. Warmth and vocal personality are the main things on Inner City's haunting "Good Life," K-Os' Madonnesque "Definition of Love" and the gutsy Adeva!'s interpretation of the Otis Redding composition/Aretha Franklin hit "Respect." Just how close deep house is to late-'70s Philly disco/soul is hard to miss on Chanelle's sleek, very appealing "One Man." However, the producer, the track and the groove are dominant on Richie Rich and the Jungle Brothers' infectious "I'll House You," Reese & Santonio's "Rock to the Beat" and A Guy Named Gerald's "Voodoo Ray." The latter, in fact, doesn't really have a melody, just a groove and an assertive bass line. Though this approach has its pleasures, it can wear thin quickly—especially outside of a club setting. But that's not the case with the music of Inner City, Chanelle and Adeva!, which has held up quite nicely. — *Alex Henderson*

The Best of New Orleans Rhythm & Blues, Vol. 1 / 1988 / Rhino ✦✦✦✦✦
The Best of New Orleans Rhythm & Blues, Vol. 1 is an incredible collection of 18 of the greatest Crescent City R&B singles ever released. Divided equally between classics ("Mother-In-Law," "It Will Stand," "I Hear You Knocking," "I'm Gonna Be A Wheel Someday," "Lipstick Traces (On A Cigarette)," "A Certain Girl," "One Night," "Ooh Poo Pah Doo (Pt. 1)"), and terrific, but frequently underappreciated singles from the likes of the Spiders, Irma Thomas, Aaron Neville, Earl King and Dave Bartholomew, the collection is a concise and utterly intoxicating overview of New Orleans R&B, one that appeals not only to neophytes, but also to collectors. — *Stephen Thomas Erlewine*

The Best of New Orleans Rhythm & Blues, Vol. 2 / 1988 / Rhino ✦✦✦✦✦
The Best of New Orleans Rhythm & Blues, Vol. 2 is just as thrilling as its predeceessor, featuring 18 tracks of classic, funky R&B from the likes of

Frankie Ford ("Sea Cruise"), Shirley & Lee ("Let the Good Times Roll"), Lee Dorsey ("Ride Your Pony," "Working in a Coal Mine"), the Meters ("Cissy Strut"), Irma Thomas ("Ruler of My Heart," "It's Raining"), the Dixie Cups ("Iko Iko"), Lloyd Price ("Just Because," "Lawdy Miss Clawdy"), Barbara George ("I Know (You Don't Love Me No More)"), Guitar Slim ("The Things That I Used to Do"), Chris Kenner ("I Like It Like That") and Clarence "Frogman" Henry ("Ain't Got No Home"). There are no bad cuts here and nearly every song is a classic, making it an essential edition to any library, as well as one of the definitive overviews of New Orleans R&B. —*Stephen Thomas Erlewine*

Best of Nuggets / Rhino ✦✦✦✦✦
Rhino distilled their multi-volume vinyl *Nuggets* series—which itself was a knock-off of Sire's original double-album set from the early '70s—to a three-volume CD series. The first installment of *Nuggets* contains many of the most familiar garage-rock singles, including the Standells' "Dirty Water," the Seeds' "Pushin' Too Hard" and "Can't Seem to Make You Mine," the Count Five's "Psychotic Reaction," the Easybeats' "Friday On My Mind," the Syndicate Of Sound's "Little Girl," " the Knickerbockers' "Lies," the Beau Brummels' "Just a Little" and "Laugh, Laugh," the Troggs' "Wild Thing" and the Amboy Dukes' "Journey To The Center Of The Mind." It's an excellent overview of the genre, and with its companion *More Nuggets*, it stands as a definitive retrospective for the average listener. —*Stephen Thomas Erlewine*

The Best of the Teen Idols / 1987 / Rhino ✦✦✦✦
The teen idol style probably gets more abuse than any other genre in rock history. But it was a significant, if often lamentable, transitional period in the development of rock 'n' roll. This 14-song compilation presents everything that most listeners will need to know/hear about the teen idols. It has the biggest hits by Fabian, Paul Anka, Frankie Avalon, and Bobby Vee, and one-shots by Tab Hunter and Troy Shondell. There are also dynamic classics by Dion and Del Shannon that are probably too good to be lumped into the teen idol category, but are present because these singers, accurately or inaccurately, were often thought of as teen idols at the peak of their success. There are also excellent liner notes to put the music in its proper context. —*Richie Unterberger*

Beyond the Wall of Sound / Roxy ✦✦✦
Like its sister compilation *Lookin' For Boys*, this is the finest anthology of obscure girl-group singles. *Lookin' For Boys* has the edge for its slightly stronger track selection, but this features several cuts that are almost as great as the best classics of the genre, especially the rarities by Diane Renay ("Watch Out Sally"), Shelley Fabares ("He Don't Love Me"), and Shirley Matthews ("Big Town Boy"). —*Richie Unterberger*

The Big Chill / 1983 / Motown ✦✦✦✦✦
Motown scored big with this album, which contains ten '60s hits, from Marvin Gaye's "I Heard It Through the Grapevine" to Procol Harum's "A Whiter Shade of Pale," just the sort of thing the yuppie thirtysomethings in the movie loved, and music rediscovered by the audience that saw the film. —*William Ruhlmann*

Big in Wigan / 1996 / Kent ✦✦✦
The raison d'être of this disc needs some explanation to North American audiences. Subtitled "collection of shameless oldies played in the golden era of Northern soul," it's an anthology of 20 obscure soul tracks from the mid-'60s to the mid-'70s that have found favor with the cult of obsessive soul listeners in Northern England. There's no real thread connecting the tracks, other than that each one has been selected to represent one of the DJs that spins rare 45s for the dancers who still go to British clubs to hear this music. It's easy to see why these numbers are dancefloor favorites—most have a solidly thumping pop-soul groove conducive to dancing, especially if you're one of those old-fashioned fogies who doesn't want to get blasted into the English Channel with synth-driven rave and techno. It's also, to be harsh, easy to see why they made a beeline for the collector bins rather than the AM airwaves—the material wasn't arresting enough to capture the ears of the masses. Judged solely as a stone-cold home listening experience, it's definitely not an A-list choice for the soul compilation library, even if you're a soul fan. If you're a specialist collector, you may well find it to your liking, populated as it is by obscure names such as Flower Shoppe and the Lovettes, obscure singles by minor soul notables like Bobby Freeman, Millie Jackson, and Leon Haywood, and the primo mod soul of Mickey Lee Lane's "Hey Sah-Lo-Ney," probably the rawest and most compelling track here. —*Richie Unterberger*

Billboard Top Dance Hits: 1976-1980 / 1976 / Rhino ✦✦✦✦
Covering the disco years in detail, Rhino's five-volume *Billboard Top Dance Hits* series is a worthwhile budget retrospective. It isn't as complete or definitive as the label's *Disco Years* series, but it features several tracks that didn't make that series, as well as songs that aren't easily available on other compilations, making it necessary for disco fans. Ten of the top dance hits for each year from 1976 to 1980 are featured on each disc, including such hits as "You Should Be Dancing," "Love Hangover," "Ring My Bell," "You Make Me Feel (Mighty Real)," "Funkytown," "Got to Give It Up," and "Call Me" in their original single form. Unlike

the other *Billboard* series, *Top Dance Hits* actually has liner notes about the songs, not trivia about a particular year. —*Stephen Thomas Erlewine*

Billboard Top Hits: 1975 / 1991 / Rhino ✦✦✦✦
Rhino ended its *Billboard Top Rock & Roll Hits* series with the 1974 volume, replacing it with the *Billboard Top Hits* series beginning with the year 1975. It has the same faults and attributes as the *Rock & Roll* series; the only difference is the fact that it merges R&B hits with the pop singles. Since the late '70s were filled with cheerfully disposable pop singles, each volume differs greatly in quality; the 1978 and 1979 discs are the most consistent, with several soft-rock and disco hits on each album. Rhino's *Have A Nice Day* and *Disco Years* series cover this era in greater detail, with more hits and novelty items on both series; however, these are concise, fun snapshots of a particularly embarrassing and enjoyable moment in pop history. —*Stephen Thomas Erlewine*

Billboard Top Hits: 1980 / 1992 / Rhino ✦✦✦✦
When Rhino's *Billboard Top Hits* series hit the 1980s, the collection began to lose a little steam. From 1980 through 1985, the discs are representative of the pop mainstream, although there were the usual major artists missing. Still, the discs contained plenty of one-hit wonders and classic singles like "Bette Davis Eyes," "Jessie's Girl," "Down Under," "Maneater," and "Centerfold," with the highest concentration of good singles on the 1983 volume. As the series approached the end of the decade, the problem of licensing reared its ugly head; not only were major artists like Madonna, Prince, Phil Collins, and Guns N' Roses unavailable, but smaller artists like Rick Astley, Roxette, Poison, and Michael Damien also don't appear. Although there are a couple of enjoyable period pieces, like Donny Osmond's "Soldier of Love," the bulk of the tracks can't cover the absence of "Never Gonna Give You Up," "Every Rose Has Its Thorn," and "The Look." Perhaps these should have waited a couple of years. —*Stephen Thomas Erlewine*

Billboard Top Hits: 1985 / 1994 / Rhino ✦✦✦
Rhino's most recent collection featuring the top-selling pop singles by decade begins with 1985, and shows that the period's dominant styles included Prince-influenced R&B, synthesizer pop and retro rock. Among the spotlight artists were Mr. Mister, Tears for Fears, REO Speedwagon and John Parr, none of them household names today. The same holds true for Ready for the World, while Starship, Billy Ocean, Glenn Frey, and Jan Hammer have at least retained audience identification, even if they aren't currently issuing songs. This anthology illustrates just how fleeting and transitory fame is in pop music circles. —*Ron Wynn*

Billboard Top Hits: 1986 / 1994 / Rhino ✦✦✦
Aging rockers were still strong on the pop charts in 1986, judging from this 10-track Billboard collection. Robert Palmer, Kenny Loggins, Starship, and Huey Lewis & the News are represented, as well as Eddie Money and Billy Ocean, who weren't exactly fresh faces either. The Bangles, Bananarama, Survivor, and Mr. Mister complete this second disc of mid-'80s pop tunes, showing that at this point pop radio was playing generic, safe material. —*Ron Wynn*

Billboard Top Hits: 1987 / 1994 / Rhino ✦✦✦
There were still no musically significant trends established beyond the rule of generic pop on this third late-'80s Rhino collection. Kim Wilde's remake of the Supremes' "You Keep Me Hangin' On" and Billy Vera's angst hit "At This Moment" struck a blow for the innocence of past eras, as did Bananarama's "I Heard a Rumour" and Starship's "Nothing's Gonna Stop Us Now." The period seems characterized best by Robbie Nevil's "C'est La Vie," an entertaining number that peaked in January and was quickly forgotten, as was Nevil. Only U2, the duo of Aretha Franklin and George Michael, Crowded House, and Belinda Carlisle could be considered significant from a standpoint of longevity, and it's doubtful that any of them would consider these singles their best work. —*Ron Wynn*

Billboard Top Hits: 1988 / 1994 / Rhino ✦✦✦
Some fresh faces and sounds began to emerge in 1988, notably Gloria Estefan & Miami Sound Machine, Expose, Bobby McFerrin, and Terence Trent D'Arby. While D'Arby hasn't yet fulfilled the potential he showed on "Wishing Well," Estefan and McFerrin have become superstars, as has Richard Marx, although in quite different ways and not based solely on chart performances. Will to Power's remake of Peter Frampton's "Baby I Love Your Way" and the Escape Club's "Wild Wild West" were among the year's more left-field hits, while Billy Ocean scored one of his final pop smashes with "Get Outta My Dreams, Get Into My Car." Johnny Hates Jazz enjoyed a brief fling with pop success, while Cheap Trick also joined the hit parade in the summer. —*Ron Wynn*

Billboard Top Hits: 1989 / 1989 / Rhino ✦✦✦
Rock and generic pop dueled for supremacy on the charts in 1989, while R&B was completely shut out except for the light urban influence displayed by New Kids on the Block. Martika, Donny Osmond, and Debbie Gibson represented the non-threatening hit brigade, while Bad English, Tears for Fears, and Warrant checked in for the rockers, and the Bangles, Richard Marx, and Gloria Estefan came in somewhere between these

poles. This 10-track collection shows how stratified and demographically isolated the pop charts were in 1989; they were ripe for the hip-hop and grunge explosions in the 1990s. —*Ron Wynn*

Billboard Top Modern Rock Tracks 1990 / Feb. 18, 1997 / Rhino ◆◆◆

Billboard Top Modern Rock Tracks: 1990 is an uneven but enjoyable 10-track sampler of several of the biggest modern rock and college-radio hits of 1990. Unlike other editions in the *Top Modern Rock Tracks* series, *1990* actually conveys the feeling of the year fairly well, combining classic tracks like the Sundays' "Here's Where the Story Ends," Peter Murphy's "Cuts You Up," Depeche Mode's "Birdhouse in Your Soul," and the Church's "Metropolis," with cuts like INXS' "Suicide Blonde," Concrete Blonde's "Joey," the Heart Throbs' "Dreamtime" and Hothouse Flowers' "Give It Up," which capture the sentiment and popular styles of the post-R.E.M./pre-Nirvana era of alternative rock quite well. —*Stephen Thomas Erlewine*

Billboard Top Modern Rock Tracks 1991 / Feb. 18, 1997 / Rhino ◆◆◆

Considerably more uneven and unfocused than its predecessor, *Billboard Top Modern Rock Tracks: 1991* contains the last gasp of the pre-grunge/pre-dance era of alternative rock. While Primal Scream's "Movin' On Up" points in the direction that English alternative rock would follow over the course of the decade, most of the record is comprised of hits and also-rans from staples of '80s college radio—Siouxsie & the Banshees ("Kiss Them for Me"), the Divinyls ("I Touch Myself"), INXS ("Shining Star"), Daniel Ash ("This Love"), and Big Audio Dynamite II ("Rush"). While all of those selections are wise choices, as is Material Issue's terrific "Valerie Loves Me," the rest of the record is a bit puzzling—nobody has memories of Tin Machine's "One Shot" or the Fixx's "How Much Is Enough," and they also aren't good representations of alternative rock in the early '90s. However, this confused song selection on *1991* demonstrates why modern rock radio was ripe for a breakthrough on the level of Nirvana. —*Stephen Thomas Erlewine*

Billboard Top Modern Rock Tracks 1992 / Feb. 18, 1997 / Rhino ◆◆◆

Billboard Top Modern Rock Tracks: 1992 is the most confused out of all the editions of *Top Modern Rock Tracks*, primarily because modern rock and college radio were coming to grips with grunge over the course of 1992. Consequently, songs like dada's "Dizz Knee Land," Peter Murphy's "The Sweetest Drop," Faith No More's "Midlife Crisis," the Wolfgang Press' "A Girl Like You," INXS' "Not Enough Time," Ocean Blue's "Ballerina Out of Control" and Lou Reed's "What's Good" all sound like they come from a different era—namely 1990, a few years before Nirvana. Many of these songs are good, but songs like Matthew Sweet's "Girlfriend," the Lemonheads' "It's A Shame About Ray" and Teenage Fanclub's "Star Sign" sound like genuine classics of the era. And that means that *1992* is an enjoyable listen, even if it doesn't really feel like 1992. —*Stephen Thomas Erlewine*

Billboard Top R&B Hits: 1955-1974 / 1989 / Rhino ◆◆◆◆◆

Despite its faults, Rhino's *Billboard Top R&B Hits* is one of the finest retrospectives of R&B from 1955 to 1974 ever assembled. The song selection was sometimes puzzling, the liner notes nonexistent, and each disc only had ten tracks, frequently lasting under half an hour. However, the 20-disc series featured most of the major artists and singles of each individual year, as well as providing a rough sketch of the evolution from R&B to soul to disco. For beginners, such an affordable introduction was invaluable; for collectors, the brevity may have been frustrating, but they couldn't argue with the fidelity or the fact that many of these songs were appearing on disc for the first time. Legends like Clyde McPhatter, Little Richard, Jackie Wilson, James Brown, Ben E. King, Brook Benton, Marvin Gaye, Temptations, Supremes, Aretha Franklin, Smokey Robinson, Isley Brothers, Sly Stone, and Curtis Mayfield are featured. The series is currently out of print, but can still be found in cut-out bins. —*Stephen Thomas Erlewine*

Billboard Top Rock & Roll Hits: 1955-1974 / 1988 / Rhino ◆◆◆◆◆

Despite its many faults, Rhino's *Billboard Top Rock & Roll Hits* is as good an introduction to consistently diverse music as possible. It's marred by a confusing song selection, poor liner notes, and brevity, as well as the omission of several important pop, rock, and album-rock artists. However, the series isn't attempting to be comprehensive. Instead, it offers a view of the popular mainstream for each year from 1955 to 1974 at an affordable price. With Elvis, Chuck Berry, Fats Domino, Jerry Lee Lewis, the Everly Brothers, Buddy Holly, and Carl Perkins on the initial '50s volumes, the discs are essential. As the series moves into the '60s, the discs remain remarkably consistent, featuring several Phil Spector hits, the Beach Boys, Dion, and the Kingsmen. It's only in the mid-'60s that the series begins to represent only radio hits, instead of portraying what was really happening during the era. Nevertheless, the 20 discs remain enjoyable listening. —*Stephen Thomas Erlewine*

Birth of Soul / 1996 / Kent ◆◆◆◆

An ingenious mix of 28 pivotal tracks from 1957-1965, mostly from the early '60s, that helped lay the groundwork for soul music. Some heavy-duty collectors may have wished these were all rarities, rather than a blend of hits and rarities. But it must be said that several of the hits here don't turn up on many compilations, like the ones by Inez & Charlie Foxx ("Mockingbird"), the Tams ("Hey Girl Don't Bother Me"), Joe Henderson ("Snap Your Fingers"), Bobby Bland ("Ain't Nothing You Can Do"), and the Marvelows ("I Do"). And there are plenty of nifty collector items as well: outtakes by Otis Redding and Wiliam Bell, "answer" records by Thelma Kilgore and Gloria Lynne, and early Southern soul by Jimmy Hughes. A special treat is the rabble-rousing city soul of Derek Martin's "Daddy Rollin' Stone," which became one of the Who's most obscure tracks when they covered it on the B-side of their second British 45 in 1965. The compilation may fall between the cracks of general soul listeners and soul specialists. But if you don't have most of the tracks yet, it's a good survey of early soul, with an all-encompassing diversity that includes many regional styles, and embraces both "down-home" and "uptown" productions. —*Richie Unterberger*

Blackbox: Wax Trax! Records: The First 13 Years / 1994 / Wax Trax! ◆◆◆◆

Wax Trax was the definitive industrial label and the four-disc box set *Blackbox* is the definitive overview of their peak years. The label's artists—including Ministry, Trent Reznor and KMFDM—developed the corrosive guitars, synths, distorted vocals and jackhammer beats that became the signature sound of industrial. *Blackbox* gathers nearly every worthwhile song to emerge from the Chicago label, including many rare singles, and provides an excellent introduction and summary of the most cutting-edge dance music of the 1980s and '90s. —*Stephen Thomas Erlewine*

Blech / 1996 / Warp ◆◆◆◆

Sparked by Coldcut's highly-rated *Journeys By DJ* mix session, *Blech* is a ransacking of the Warp back-catalog by Coldcut colleagues Strictly Kev and Mr. PC (both of DJ Food), featuring entries from just about every significant Warp artist in the label's eight-plus years in existence. Starting with drum 'n' bass and electro, and moving through just about every flavor of contemporary dance-based experimental electronic music, the cassette-only (natch) release serves equally as an introduction to the Warp discography as it does an up-to-the-minute example of cutting-edge freestyle mixology. —*Sean Cooper*

Blechsdottir / 1996 / Warp ◆◆◆◆

Warp's second label comp in the *Blech* series gets an upgrade to CD and a boost in playing time (up to 70+ minutes!). Once again featuring the nimble deckwork of Strictly and P.C. of DJ Food, *Blechsdottir* includes previously released material from Disjecta, Autechre, Aphex Twin, Nightmares on Wax, B12, Jake Slazenger, Squarepusher, and DJ Mink, as well as a few exclusives (including cuts from Plaid and Mira Calix). The mix is even sturdier this time, with able cutting and scratching and loads of goofy, well-placed needle drop-ins (including Strictly and P.C. on voice synthesizer). Essential. —*Sean Cooper*

Born to Choose / 1993 / Rykodisc ◆◆◆

A benefit album for abortion rights, *Born to Choose* features an almost standard cast of alternative musicians (including R.E.M., Natalie Merchant, Matthew Sweet, Bob Mould, and Soundgarden) supporting the most overtly political of all recent tribute collections. *Born to Choose* would be meaningless if the music was weak. Even though it is the standard mix of outtakes, B-sides, and live tracks, the music is worth the price, with R.E.M. & Natalie Merchant's "Photograph," Pavement's "Greenlander," and Sweet's "She Said, She Said" being the major highlights. —*Stephen Thomas Erlewine*

Bosstown Sound, 1968: The Music & the Time / 1996 / Big Beat ◆◆

The Bosstown (Boston) sound was pushed as a next big thing in the late '60s, but failed to take off, mostly because, as Gertrude Stein might say, there was no "there" there. This double CD features tracks by most of the area's biggest groups—Ultimate Spinach, Orpheus, Earth Opera, Rockin' Ramrods, Bagatelle, Eden's Children—as well as even smaller footnoes, like Ill Wind and Chamaeleon (sic) Church. Mostly it's rather dreary, second-rate psychedelia, heavy on the sub-Cream blues-rock jamming, sub-Airplane mystical riffing, and pretentious wordplay. The poppier acts, in contrast, sound like psychedelicized variants of the Association, a rather ill-advised recipe. Points of interest: Earth Opera's lineup included Peter Rowan and David Grisman (their epic "The American Eagle Tragedy" is featured); the Rockin' Ramrods had a dynamite local pop-rock smash with "Bright Lit Blue Skies" (which has been compiled elsewhere); and the Lost, featuring Willie Alexander and Walter Powers (who would show up in the post-Lou Reed Velvet Underground), offer a couple raw 1965 folk-rockers that aren't bad. —*Richie Unterberger*

Breakbeat Science / Nov. 1996 / Volume [UK] ◆◆◆◆

The best and widest-ranging jungle collection on the market, *Breakbeat Science* alternates tracks from second-wave jungle pioneers with artists both new and more experimental. The best-known names associated with the style—Goldie, LTJ Bukem, Alex Reece—are sadly absent (Goldie does remix one track), but the all-unreleased tracks are very strong nevertheless. Innovators such as 4 Hero, A Guy Called Gerald, Roni Size, Ed Rush and DJ Trace & Nico make appearances, sharing the stage with newer names such as Plug, Boymerang and Spring Heel Jack; New York's illbient scene is represented by Soul Slinger's "The Singer." Among the best tracks on the double-disc set (which comes with a 100-page book) are DJ Trace & Nico's "Area 51," Boymerang's "Blue Note," and A Guy Called Gerald's tribute record, "Fabio." —*John Bush*

The Bridge: A Tribute to Neil Young / 1989 / Caroline ◆◆◆◆
In theory, *The Bridge: A Tribute to Neil Young* was a perfect concept, since most alternative bands of the late '80s owed the singer-songwriter a heavy debt. In practice, it wasn't entirely satisfying. Some groups, like Bongwater's collage of "Mr. Soul," made their interpretations self-consciously distinctive, while others, like Soul Asylum and Loop, played it close to the original. But the best moments came when a band played the song like it was their own. Listen to Sonic Youth's rampaging "Computer Age," Dinosaur Jr.'s faithful "Lotta Love," or the Pixies' gorgeous take on "Winterlong" for proof. —*Stephen Thomas Erlewine*

Brief History of Ambient, Vol. 1 / Feb. 22, 1994 / Virgin ◆◆◆◆
Although it seemed to arrive out of nowhere in the early '90s, ambient music actually has a long and varied history, leading back to Brian Eno and Kraftwerk's electronic experiments in the 1970s right up to Aphex Twin's textural techno soundscapes. As an introduction and history lesson, the two-disc *A Brief History of Ambient Music* can't be beat; it shows that the latest techno trend has roots that most fans wouldn't even realize existed. —*Stephen Thomas Erlewine*

Brill Building Sound / 1993 / Era ◆◆◆◆
Although Phil Spector's songs weren't available due to licensing restrictions, the four-CD box set *The Brill Building Sound* remains an important and entertaining collection, featuring many of the songs that made the Brill Building a pop music institution in the early '60s. —*Stephen Thomas Erlewine*

The British Invasion: History of British Rock, Vols. 1-9 / 1991 / Rhino ◆◆◆◆◆
Rhino's nine-volume *British Invasion: The History of British Rock* is the most exhaustive and essential overview of '60s British pop-rock available. Although the collection doesn't include tracks from the Beatles, the Rolling Stones, the Who, Herman's Hermits, Dave Clark Five and the early Animals, their absence doesn't hurt the series, since it spotlights several artists who never had more than a handful of hits, plus many forgotten gems. And there are plenty of major acts here, as well—the Kinks, Small Faces, Yardbirds, Donovan, Hollies, Zombies, Spencer Davis Group, Searchers, Manfred Mann and Them are all represented by their best-known tracks. The collection runs from the beginnings of Merseybeat to the aftermath of psychedelia, meaning that it chronicles the evolution of British pop-rock quite effectively. But *The History of British Rock* shouldn't be thought of as simply an educational overview of one of the most vital eras of pop—each volume is fun and exciting, and sounds more like a good time than a history lesson. The series is one of the cornerstones of any comprehensive pop-rock collection. —*Stephen Thomas Erlewine*

Broken Dreams, Vol. 1-5 / 1983 / Line ◆◆◆
The *Broken Dreams* series applied the *Pebbles* approach to '60s British rock, assembling dozens of rare tracks in the "beat," mod, R&B, and psychedelic styles for collectors. Since the original release of these albums in the 1980s, a lot of the better songs have been reissued on better compilations, in better fidelity, which diminishes the LPs' value. Based purely on the music itself, these compilations are pretty good, offering an assortment of decent overlooked cuts, with the occasional near-classic by the likes of the Syn or the Poets. There are also rare tracks by relatively well-known acts like the Nashville Teens, the Nice, Genesis, and Chris Farlowe which are hard to find otherwise. —*Richie Unterberger*

The Brunswick Years, Vol. 1 / 1995 / Brunswick ◆◆◆
In the 1960s and early 1970s, the Brunswick label recorded some of the best soul to come out of Chicago. This two-disc, 40-song collection would have ranked higher if the organization was a little less scattered. The cuts by Jackie Wilson, Gene Chandler, Tyrone Davis, Young-Holt Unlimited, and the Chi-Lites are mostly good, but are better heard in the context of those artists' own compilations. Collectors will welcome the presence of rarer items by Barbara Acklin, Billy Butler, the Artistics, Otis Leavill, and Erma Franklin (Aretha's sister), though these tracks are pleasant period fare, not obscure classics. This isn't a bad anthology for those who prefer their vintage soul on the sweet side, but it's probably only worthwhile for specialists. —*Richie Unterberger*

Bubblegum Classics Vol. 1 & 2 / 1995 / Varese Vintage ◆◆◆◆
Although they're missing a few key tracks (notably the Archies' hits and Kasenetz-Katz's "Quick Joey Small"), these are the best collections of late-'60s and early-'70s bubblegum hits ever assembled, including most

of the major hits and a fair number of enticing rarities. In their favor, they encompass not just the most infantile, pre-teen smashes of the genre (1910 Fruitgum Co., Tommy Roe, Bobby Sherman), but also quite a few cuts that could just as easily be classified as enjoyable, highly polished mainstream pop-rock (the Monkees, Tommy James, the Cuff Links, Keith, the Five Americans, the Flying Machine). Running at 20 tracks each, they're maybe a bit much all at once, but they're the best overview of a significant chapter in rock history. —*Richie Unterberger*

Bubblegum Classics, Vol. 3 / Aug. 27, 1996 / Varese ◆◆◆
Bubblegum music could be fun stuff, but it wasn't *that* deep in the content arena, and the third volume of Varese Sarabande's fine series lags a bit behind the first couple in terms of top-notch tunes. It does have some of the core classics of the genre with the Archies' "Sugar, Sugar," Ohio Express' "Chewy, Chewy," and Mac & Katie Kissoon's "Chirpy Chirpy Cheep Cheep." The Monkees (arguably not bubblegum) weigh in with "A Little Bit Me, a Little Bit You," Bobby Sherman represents the teen idol wing with "Little Woman," and Sweet play bubblegum at its hardest and most glam-influenced with "Little Willy." The cuts by the likes of Robin McNamara, Tony Burrows, the Clique, and Salt Water Taffy may be way more obscure, but hearing them all at once is as ill-advised as chewing three packs of the pink stuff a day. Song titles include "Ricky Ticky Ta Ta Ta," "Wham! Bam! Ala Cazam," and Kasenetz-Katz Super Cirkus' immortal "Dong-Dong-Diki-Di-Ki Dong"; they really *don't* write 'em like that anymore. —*Richie Unterberger*

Buddy Holly Sound / 1988 / Rock & Country (Sweden) ◆◆◆
An intriguing compilation of 16 Buddy Holly soundalike singles, circa 1959-1963. With the exception of Tommy Roe's No.1 hit (and "Peggy Sue" ripoff) "Sheila," these are all taken from excruciatingly rare 45s on tiny labels. Of course, this is not a substitute for listening to Buddy himself, but in the spirit of digging the Knickerbockers' superb Beatle knockoff "Lies," this is a nifty sampling of the best Holly imitations, from such never-weres as Bobby Jamesons, Marty Evans, Royce Clark, and Ray Ruff. Not only that, you get several different attempted angles on cornering the Holly sound: rockabilly raveups, sweet orchestrated ballads, easygoing three-chord guitar tunes. Sometimes the similarity is close enough to tell exactly what song they have in mind to evoke, be it "Peggy Sue" (used more than once), "Everyday," or something else. As sub-Buddy Holly attempts go, this anthology is much more successful—and much more enjoyable listening—than the efforts during the same era by the Holly-less Crickets. Besides Roe (who has two obscure cuts in addition to "Sheila"), other names to watch for here are Bobby Fuller, with both sides of his first locally pressed 45 (different than the versions on his *Tapes* reissue), and one David Box, who was briefly the lead singer for the Crickets after Holly died. —*Richie Unterberger*

Carnival Time: The Best of Ric Records, Vol. 1 / 1988 / Rounder ◆◆◆◆
Stomping, romping good time numbers are the menu on this 14-track anthology issued in 1988. Such artists as Joe Jones, Al Johnson, Johnny Adams and Edgar Blanchard were hit acts in New Orleans at the time, but made raw music intended for only for the R&B faithful. While an occasional number like Adams' "I Won't Cry" or Jones' "You Talk Too Much" got a little pop attention, most, like Blanchard's hot "Let's Get It" and Tommy Ridgley's "She's Got What It Takes," didn't move anyone who didn't already have the soul spirit, and that's what made them great. —*Ron Wynn*

Chartbusters: The Best of the Beserkley Years, 1975-1978 / Rhino ◆◆◆◆
Beserkley never scored any chart hits, but they were one of the best American independent record labels of the late '70s and early '80s, featuring such cult favorites as Jonathan Richman and Greg Kihn. *Best of the Beserkley Years* gathers up some of the label's best stripped-down rock 'n' roll, offering a good overview of the indie label. —*Stephen Thomas Erlewine*

Cheatin': From a Man's Point of View / 1995 / Ichiban/Soul Classics ◆◆◆
The companion volume to Ichiban's *Cheatin': From A Woman's Point Of View* offers similar anti-Valentine's Day messages from a variety of soul performers, most recorded between the mid-'60s and mid-'70s. The woman's volume is perhaps more interesting because it assembles more obscurities, but this is another generally worthy collection of non-clichéd soul hits by the Impressions, Little Milton, Johnnie Taylor, Clarence Carter, Luther Ingram, Billy Paul, Don Covay, William Bell, and Z.Z. Hill. Most of them were much bigger R&B sellers than pop ones, and some don't appear on many anthologies. —*Richie Unterberger*

Cheatin': From a Woman's Point of View / 1995 / Ichiban/Soul Classics ◆◆◆
Nifty collection of soul tunes which, just as the title says, deal with cheatin' lovers. Most of these date from the late '60s and early '70s, and while one of these was a Top Ten pop hit (Betty Wright's "Clean Up Woman"), the majority were much bigger on the R&B charts. These include little-anthologized Top Ten R&B hits by Dee Dee Warwick, the

Soul Children, and Barbara Mason. There are also pretty well-known soul classics by Laura Lee ("Dirty Man") and Ann Peebles ("Part Time Love"), one of Gladys Knight's more obscure Motown hits ("I Don't Want To Do Wrong"), and little-heard numbers by Irma Thomas, the Emotions, and Margie Joseph. Shirley Murdock and Millie Jackson offer tracks from the past decade, in contrast to the rest of the set. On the whole, this functions as an excuse to pick up some decent, off-the-beaten-path soul. — *Richie Unterberger*

Chess Rhythm & Roll / 1994 / ✦✦✦✦
A four-disc set chronicling the more rockin' sides in this landmark label's catalog. Here we have the landmark early recordings by Chuck Berry, Bo Diddley, the Moonglows, the Flamingos, marvelous one-shot hit artists like the Monotones ("Book Of Love"), Dale Hawkins ("Susie-Q"), and the Sensations ("Let Me In"), as well as seminal soul sides from Etta James, Billy Stewart and Tommy Tucker's original "High Heel Sneakers." Essential doesn't even begin to describe this box; music from a landmark label that changed the world. — *Cub Koda*

Chess Uptown Soul / Mar. 25, 1997 / Kent ✦✦✦
If you're trying to differentiate what was specifically "uptown" about these '60s Chess soul sides, you're getting into a game of serious hairsplitting. Basically this 24-track compilation offers material—mostly non-hits—from 1963-67 that leans towards sophisticated, brassy soul borrowing much from Motown and Curtis Mayfield, but not matching the peaks of either. It's still pretty enjoyable, if sometimes generic, material, including efforts by some stars (Gene Chandler, Billy Stewart, Etta James, Ramsey Lewis, Little Milton, the Dells, Fontella Bass), Jan Bradley's great one-shot "Mama Didn't Lie," Tony Clarke's fine Top 40 ballad "The Entertainer," and barely heeded names like Jackie Ross, the Radiants, and Marlena Shaw (there's also an early non-hit by Johnny Nash). There's also the occasional song that deserved a much wider hearing than it got, like Nash's "Love Ain't Nothin'," the Radiants' infectious "It Ain't No Big Thing," and Mitty Collier's "I Had a Talk with My Man," which was covered by Dusty Springfield. — *Richie Unterberger*

Chicago Garage Band Greats: The Best of Rembrandt Records 1966-1968 / 1985 / Cicadelic ✦✦✦
The Chicago-based Rembrandt label never had anything remotely resembling a hit, but it did record and release some decent garage pop in the mid-'60s, usually with a cheerier feel than the garage norm. Most of these 14 cuts, actually, were not released at all. It's nothing to make you junk your New Colony Six records, though it's reasonably pleasing. Worth a special mention are the infectiously sunny cuts by the Lemon Drops (who have two albums of their own on Cicadelic), and the Nuchez' zanily inventive "Open Up Your Mind." For years, collectors had thought that the latter tune was a British release, due to its inclusion on the British psych compilation *Chocolate Soup for Diabetics* and its authentic freakbeat feel. — *Richie Unterberger*

Chicago Radio Soul / 1996 / Kent ✦✦✦
The title might be *Chicago Radio Soul,* but it's really a 26-track compilation of soul that was released on Chicago-based Chess Records during the 1960s. Only one of the songs was a big hit (Fontella Bass' "Rescue Me"), though Jackie Ross' "Selfish One" and Mitty Collier's "Sharing You" did well on the R&B charts. There are also little-known singles by Etta James, Little Milton, Billy Stewart, and Denise LaSalle, as well as names that will only be familiar to serious soul fanatics, like the Gems, the Radiants, and Bobby McClure. Chess wasn't as much of a presence in soul as it was in blues, although by the '60s, it was concentrating much more on the soul market. On the whole this is decent if unremarkable '60s soul, showing the influence of both Motown and the crosstown Chicago sound of the Okeh label. High points worth noting by any soul fan are the girl group-tinged "I Can't Help Myself" (the Gems) and Jackie Ross' "Take Me for a Little While," a rare example of a Black soul cover of a single by a white female singer (Evie Sands). — *Richie Unterberger*

Chocolate Soup for Diabetics, Vol. 1-3 / 1980-1982 / Relics ✦✦✦✦
These three volumes of obscure '60s British psychedelic treasures are slightly tainted by dubbed-from-disc sound quality; the transfers also made the records play faster than their actual speed. The music, however, is mostly terrific, the cream of a very fertile UK scene that gave birth to dozens of little-known classics and near classics during its brief apogee in 1966-68. The influence of the Who, Syd Barrett-era Pink Floyd, and 1967 Beatles runs rampant, but most of it's too idiosyncratic to be dismissed as imitative. You could actually say that this was the genre of rock music that most effectively balanced exuberant melodies/harmonies with imaginative experimentation. If that nutshell description sounds appealing, you won't be disappointed by the gems on offer from Tintern Abbey, Dantalian's Chariot, One in a Million, Big Boy Pete, Mike Stuart Span, Syn, and numerous others. A lot of the tracks have been since reissued in better fidelity on sanctioned re-releases, but some are hard to find anywhere else but on these anthologies, which are now themselves sought-after collector's items. — *Richie Unterberger*

Classic Funk, Vol. 1 / Feb. 1996 / React/PolyGram ✦✦✦
Collectors will find little they don't have on this 12-track compilation, which sticks to popular cuts by George Clinton, Parliament, the O'Jays, Kool & the Gang, Ohio Players, the Average White Band, James Brown, and James Brown-associated projects from the early '70s. It's certainly alright as a taster for those who want to start with prime funk before investigating deeper, or those who just want a little of the style in their library. — *Richie Unterberger*

Colpix Dimension Story / 1994 / Rhino ✦✦✦
In the first half of the 1960s, Colpix and Dimension were record label offshoots of Columbia Pictures; Colpix tended toward teen idols, while Dimension was mainly an outlet for the compositions of the Gerry Goffin/Carole King songwriting team. This 40-song double CD includes all the major hits on the labels by the Marcels, James Darren, Shelley Fabares, Paul Petersen, Little Eva, the Cookies, and Carole King herself, as well as quite a few rarities. Although the compilers have done a thorough job, the jumble of disparate styles—sappy teen-idol pop, rhythm and blues, girl groups, soul, even a garage band—makes for tough end-to-end listening. Several of the sides by Darren and Petersen are unbearably cloying; the ones by Fabares, Teddy Randazzo, and Sandy Stewart are barely any better. The hits by Little Eva and the Cookies, on the other hand, are great dynamic girl-group performances. And some of the rarities are pretty cool—Carole King's odd, almost folk-rockish flop single "He's A Bad Boy," Earl-Jean's original version of "I'm Into Something Good" (covered for a hit by Herman's Hermits), the Girlfriends' "My One And Only, Jimmy Boy" (the best Wall of Sound girl-group record not produced by Phil Spector), the little-anthologized Top Ten soul hit "Hey Girl" by Freddie Scott, rare sides by Lou Christie and Duane Eddy, a silly Beatle parody by Sonny Curtis, and extremely rare (if not terribly good) singles by David Jones and Michael Nesmith before they joined The Monkees. — *Richie Unterberger*

Come Together: Motown Sings the Beatles / 1994 / Razor & Tie ✦✦
Motown artists covered Beatle songs fairly often during the 1960s, but the results were among neither the better Motown recordings nor the better Beatle covers. This 15-song compilation has renditions of Lennon-McCartney songs (and George Harrison's solo hit "My Sweet Lord") by most of Motown's biggest stars, including the Supremes, Marvin Gaye, Stevie Wonder, the Four Tops, the Temptations, and Gladys Knight. Most of these were used as album filler in the late 1960s and early 1970s, and favor the too-syrupy style of "sweet soul" production; the Four Tops (who do "Michelle" and "Got to Get You into My Life") fare about the best. In this context, the Supremes' sloppy but energetic 1964 covers of "Can't Buy Me Love" and "A Hard Day's Night" sound better than they really are. This does have the only Beatle song to become a Motown hit (Stevie Wonder's 1971 version of "We Can Work It Out"), another of the highlights on this generally uninspiring collection. — *Richie Unterberger*

Common Ground / Jun. 1996 / EMI ✦✦✦
Assembled by producer Donal Lunny, the loose concept of this compilation was to gather over a dozen Celtic and rock musicians with Irish ancestry to perform Irish traditional music, or original compositions with an Irish traditional flavor. Celtic music fans probably won't be that impressed by the mix of folk and pop tracks; it's kind of an outreach project, designed to broaden the appeal of Irish music without neglecting its truest progenitors. Both folk and rock fans with specialized tastes, however, may appreciate the chance to hear the cuts by Maire Brennan, Paul Brady, Andy Irvine, Christy Moore, and (from the pop world) Elvis Costello, Kate Bush (singing in Gaelic), Sinead O'Connor, Bono & Adam Clayton, and Tim & Neil Finn, none of which are available elsewhere. — *Richie Unterberger*

The Complete Buddah Chart Singles, Vol. 1 / Mar. 26, 1996 / Buddah ✦✦✦
Buddah was one of the prime peddlers of bubblegum during the late '60s, featuring such staples of the genre as 1910 Fruitgum Co., the Lemon Pipers and Ohio Express. *The Complete Buddah Chart Singles, Vol. 1* contains most of the biggest hits from those groups—"Simon Says," "1,2,3 Red Light," "Green Tambourine," "Yummy Yummy Yummy"—plus the Mulberry Fruit Band's "Yes, We Have No Bananas" and the Five Stairsteps & Cubie's "The Shadow of Your Love." So, it does have the bulk of the hits—and those that aren't here are on the second volume—but the lesser-known singles are too sweet and gimmicky for anyone but hardcore bubblegum collectors. — *Stephen Thomas Erlewine*

The Complete Buddah Chart Singles, Vol. 2 / Mar. 26, 1996 / Buddah ✦✦✦
The Complete Buddah Chart Singles, Vol. 2 is actually a stronger collection than its predecessor, even though there aren't as many hits on this disc as there were on *Vol. 1.* This time around, the big hits are from Ohio Express ("Chewy Chewy," "Down at Lulu's"), Kasenetz-Katz Singing Orchestral Circus ("Quick Joey Small (Run Joey Run)"), the 1910 Fruitgum Co. ("Goody Goody Gumdrops"), Brooklyn Bridge's "Worst That Could Happen" and, of course, the infamous Rock 'N' Roll Dubble Bub-

ble Trading Card Co. of Philadelphia—19141, whose "Bubble Gum Music" is perhaps the most infamous single of that genre. The real treat of *Vol. 2*, however, comes from the obscurities like Le Cirque's trippy, faux-psychedelia "Land of Oz" and Zalman Yanovsky's infectious "As Long as You're Here," two songs that are better-written and catchier than the hits themselves, and they are what makes the disc of interest to bubblegum and '60s pop fetishists. —*Stephen Thomas Erlewine*

The Complete Stax-Volt Singles 1959-1968 / 1991 / Atlantic ◆◆◆◆◆
At nine discs and 244 tracks, *The Complete Stax-Volt Singles: 1959-1968* is far too exhaustive for casual fans, but that's not who the set is designed for—it's made for the collector. Featuring every A-side the label released during those nine years, as well as several B-sides, the set is a definitive portrait of gritty, deep Southern soul. Many of the genre's major names—Otis Redding, Sam & Dave, Carla Thomas, Booker T & the MG's, William Bell, Rufus Thomas, the Bar-Kays, Albert King—plus many terrific one-shot wonders are showcased in terrific sound and augmented with an in-depth booklet. For any serious soul or rock collector, it's an essential set, since Stax-Volt was a musically revolutionary label and their roster was deep with talent, which means much of the music on this collection is first-rate. But if you one want the hits, you'll be better off with smaller collection, since too much of this set will sound too similar, and sorting through the nine discs will be a monumental task if you only want to hear Otis, Rufus, Carla and Sam & Dave. —*Stephen Thomas Erlewine*

The Complete Stax-Volt Soul Singles, Vol. 2, 1968-1971 / 1993 / Stax ◆◆◆◆
The first Stax-Volt box was a monolith, standing as the definitive document of the labels and, therefore, gritty Southern soul. Its sequel, *The Complete Stax-Volt Soul Singles, Vol. 2, 1968-1971* is considerably more problematic. Covering only four years compared to its predecessor, which showcased nine years, *Vol. 2* contains 216 tracks, including all of the A and B-sides released during that era. Most critics consider these four years to be substantially less interesting than Stax's earlier years, and in a sense, they're right. There's no Otis Redding or Sam & Dave, and the music doesn't have the same innovative, kinetic spark of the early years. Still, there's a lot of great, great music here, but it's difficult to sort it out among these nine discs. About three or four discs worth of material is truly essential, and it might have been better to boil this era down to a smaller box set, since that would have made for a necessary purchase. As it stands, it's too sprawling and comprehensive to be an essential purchase for anyone other than soul fetishists and hardcore collectors, but those listeners should find much of this fascinating. —*Stephen Thomas Erlewine*

The Complete Stax/Volt Soul Singles, Vol. 3: 1972-1975 / 1994 / Stax ◆◆◆
As the last installment in the three-volume document of the complete Stax-Volt singles, *Vol. 3: 1972-1975* is by far the weakest of the series. During those four years, the label was winding down, since it was unable to successfully make the transition from gritty soul to smooth soul and disco. Their older artists couldn't handle the newer sound, and the newer artists were generally saddled with undistinguished songs. In other words, there weren't many great singles from this era, which is what makes listening to *The Complete Stax-Volt Soul Singles, Vol. 3: 1972-1975* such a chore. While the sound of the set is pleasant, evoking both the funky and smooth soul of the early '70s quite well, the songs and the performances aren't particularly noteworthy. There's about a disc and a half worth of prime material scattered across this set, and only diehard collectors and fetishists will have the patience to find them. Still, those dedicated listeners will find the box to be a nice way to conclude the series, since it is a well-produced and comprehensive set, even if the music itself is uneven. —*Stephen Thomas Erlewine*

Cowabunga! The Surf Box / 1996 / Rhino ◆◆◆◆
Massive, though not quite definitive, four-CD, 82-track box set of surf music. The first three discs are devoted to material from the genre's '60s prime, and the fourth devoted to revivalists from 1977 to 1995. Most listeners are still better off with the several excellent single-disc surf compilations available (the best of which, like this one, are on Rhino). If your interest runs very deep, this should satisfy, placing most of the emphasis on instrumentals rather than vocals (though significant efforts in the latter vein by the Beach Boys, Jan & Dean, and others are included). It has most of the big hits, and quite a few of the ones which were principally popular in Southern California, as well as some neat rarities that are hard to find anywhere, like the Illusions' storming "Jezebel," the Surfmen's "Paradise Cove," the Latin-surf hybrid of Dave Myers' "Moment of Truth," the Sandals' "Theme from Endless Summer," and the Sunrays' pale Beach Boys xerox, "I Live for the Sun." The fourth disc of modern-day revivalists, alas, was probably unnecessary in the minds of everyone except the compilers; it's the first three that really deal with the heart of the matter, with voluminous annotation in the 66-page booklet. —*Richie Unterberger*

Creole Kings of New Orleans / 1992 / Specialty ◆◆◆◆◆
Creole Kings of New Orleans is a splendid 26-track sampler of Specialty Records' numerous R&B legends, including Professor Longhair, Percy Mayfield, Lloyd Price, Joe Liggins, and Guitar Slim. Although only a couple of big hits are included, the material is consistently strong, making the disc an excellent purchase. —*Stephen Thomas Erlewine*

Crescent City Soul: The Sound of New Orleans / Apr. 2, 1996 / EMI ◆◆◆◆◆
The new king of the hill as far as retrospectives of early New Orleans R&B/rock go. This four-CD, 119-song box has hits by all of the major artists, and hits and misses by most of the important minor ones as well. The standards for inclusion are flexible and reasonable: Although New Orleans residents usually carry the day, important records that were recorded in New Orleans by non-natives are also featured. Fats Domino, Little Richard, Irma Thomas, Lee Dorsey, Smiley Lewis, Chris Kenner, Barbara George, Ernie K-Doe, Clarence "Frogman" Henry, Lloyd Price, Aaron Neville, Professor Longhair, Shirley & Lee, and Dr. John are all here, as are one-shots and regional figures like the Showmen, Earl King, Benny Spellman, Dave Bartholomew, and the Spiders. There are plenty of hits, but also plenty of fine songs that most listeners won't be aware of: the original versions of "My Ding-A-Ling" (two of them!), "I'm Gonna Be a Wheel Someday," and "One Night," for instance, which were covered for huge smashes by Fats Domino, Chuck Berry, and Elvis Presley. It's not perfect: the absence of Frankie Ford's "Sea Cruise" is absolutely inexcusable, and the omission of hits like "Blueberry Hill," "Ya Ya," and "Rocking Pneumonia" only slightly less mystifying. It's still the best chunk of New Orleans rock/R&B in one place, with more than enough variety to make the lengthy set a pleasure all the way through. —*Richie Unterberger*

Czechoslovakian Beat, Vol. 1 (65-68) / 1996 / Reverendo Moon ◆◆◆
The title looks like some sort of joke, but this is indeed a collection of 14 garage/punk sides issued in Czechoslovakia in the mid-to-late '60s. Most likely, it's the first compilation of '60s rock of any sort from behind the Iron Curtain. Czech bands, like groups in all Eastern Bloc countries, faced limited recording opportunities, had much more limited access to British and American releases, and had to get along with relatively primitive equipment. It's therefore rather amazing that this sounds more or less like most '60s garage compilations, other than the fact that much of it's sung in Czech. There are the same lo-fi fuzz guitar riffs, cheesy organs, and endearingly clumsy approximations of British Merseybeat, mod, and early psychedelia that you might find in groups from Holland, Spain, or Texas. There's no truly outstanding material, and for English speakers the sound of '60s rock sung in the unfamiliar Czech language is a shock. Its mere existence, however, makes for an intriguing historical document, with the occasional interesting bit of psychedelic weirdness—minor-key folk melodies, strange reverb effects, odd scraping instruments, and such—intruding once in a while, on the tracks by the Juventus especially. —*Richie Unterberger*

D.I.Y.: Anarchy in the UK: UK Punk I (1976-77) / Jan. 19, 1993 / Rhino ◆◆◆◆◆
With the exception of the Clash, who could not be included because of licensing obstacles, this 19-song collection includes all of the major originators of British punk music. The Sex Pistols are here, of course, with somewhat rawer demo versions of "Anarchy In The UK" and "God Save the Queen" that have previously appeared on various quasi-legitimate albums. Otherwise, you get the major singles from a posse of leading bands of the movement, including the Damned, the Saints, the Jam, and the Buzzcocks. Cult acts of nearly equal importance, like X-Ray Spex, the Adverts, the Only Ones, Generation X, and Wire also weigh in with trailblazing singles like "Orgasm Addict" and "One Chord Wonders." Major punk fans and collectors won't find anything here that they don't already have. But for those who didn't pick up everything the first time around, or weren't even around the first time around, it's as ideal an introduction as can be imagined to a sound that totally realigned rock with its emphasis on brittle guitars, amphetamine rhythms, and socially charged songwriting. The booklet includes a lengthy, informative essay by Jon Savage, author of the British punk history *England's Dreaming*. —*Richie Unterberger*

D.I.Y.: Blank Generation: The New York Scene (1975-78) / 1993 / Rhino ◆◆◆◆
From the outset, New York punk rock had more subgenres and styles than its British counterparts. Even the Ramones, who were seemingly the most straightforward band on the scene, had a distinctly arty conceit behind their fusion of garage-rock, bubblegum and pop culture kitsch. Most of their contemporaries had similar attitudes, whether it was Blondie with their sexy, ironic revision of '60s pop, Television's cerebral guitar rock, Richard Hell's jagged atonal rock, Patti Smith's punk poetry, or Suicide's eerie synthesizers. All of those bands are collected in the superb overview *D.I.Y.: Blank Generation: the New York Scene (1975-78)*, along with such cult favorites as the Dictators ("(I Live for) Cars and Girls"), Mink DeVille ("Let Me Dream If I Want To"), Wayne County, the

Dead Boys, the Heartbreakers and the Mumps. While Talking Heads are missing from the collection, *Blank Generation* nevertheless is an accurate and nearly flawless portrait of the heyday of New York punk. —*Stephen Thomas Erlewine*

D.I.Y.: Come out and Play: American Power Pop . . . / 1993 / Rhino
◆◆◆◆◆
Power-pop benefitted from the punk explosion, since it had as much to do with the rock 'n' roll mainstream as the punks. In the wake of the Ramones and Sex Pistols, straightforward, guitar-driven power-pop bands had a greater audience than before, since more listeners were aware of the existence of such a music. And if the ringing pop on *D.I.Y.: Come Out and Play: American Power Pop, Vol. 1* has more to do with the British Invasion than the Damned, it shares the same kinetic energy and vital spirit as punk, especially since many of the bands on this collection were doggedly releasing independent records and touring in the late '70s to a dedicated cult following. There are no hits on *Come Out on Play*—Cheap Trick, the one marquee name on the compilation, is represented by the dynamic album track "Southern Girls"—but that doesn't mean it's a collection of also-rans and mediocrities. Instead, these songs are the foundation of the first wave of power-pop and many of the artists here—Pezband ("Baby It's Cold Outside"), the Nerves ("Hanging on the Telephone"), Artful Dodger ("Wayside"), Chris Stamey ("Summer Sun"), Tommy Hoehn ("Blow Yourself Up"), the Paley Brothers ("Come Out and Play"), Fotomaker ("Where Have You Been All My Life") and Chris Bell ("I Am the Cosmos")—have become legendary in certain circles. As a result, *Come Out and Play* serves as a terrific introduction into the world of power-pop, but it's better seen as a collection of some of the best and catchiest pop singles that slipped through the cracks in the late '70s. —*Stephen Thomas Erlewine*

D.I.Y.: Mass. Ave.: The Boston Scene (1979-83) / 1993 / Rhino ◆◆◆◆
Like the Los Angeles installment of the series, *D.I.Y.: Mass. Ave: The Boston Scene (1979-83)* is weaker than its predecessors because the music it covers simply isn't as diverse, energetic or interesting as the music from New York and England. Boston did have some great bands, yet their second-level groups weren't particularly interesting and they pale considerably when placed next to the paranoid punk of Mission of Burma ("That's When I Reach for My Revolver"), the garage rock of the Lyres ("I Want to Help You Ann"), the rootsy Del Fuegos ("I Always Call Her Back") and the Cars' raw demo of "You're All I've Got Tonight." There are a few cool obscurities, such as Willie Alexander's "Mass. Ave," Nervous Eaters' "Loretta," Unnatural Axe's "They Saved Hitler's Brain," Neighborhood Threat's "No Place Like Home" and the Neats' "Six," but they aren't enough to make *Mass. Ave* worthwhile for anyone but punk and New Wave fetishists. —*Stephen Thomas Erlewine*

D.I.Y.: Shake It up: Americam Power Pop 2 . . . / 1993 / Rhino ◆◆◆◆
In general, the songs on *Shake It Up: American Power Pop, Vol. 2* are a little lighter and bouncier than those on its predecessor *Come out and Play*, but since there was always an element of sweetness in power-pop anyway, that difference will matter to only a handful of listeners. *Shake It Up* still shares many of the same characteristics of *Come out and Play*—namely, it's a collection of 19 dynamic, hook-laden singles from the first wave of American power-pop bands. Again, only a couple of these songs are well-known outside of power-pop circles—the Romantics' "What I Like About You" had become a frat-rock anthem by the end of the '80s—but within those circles, the Rubinoos ("I Wanna Be Your Boyfriend"), Chris Stamey & the dB's ("[I Thought] You Wanted to Know"), the Shoes ("Tomorrow Night," "Too Late"), 20/20 ("Yellow Pills," "Giving It All"), Off Broadway USA ("Stay in Time"), Holly and the Italians ("Tell That Girl to Shut Up") and the Beat ("Work-A-Day World," Walking Out on Love") and their songs became semi-legendary. With the exception of *Come out and Play*, there's no better overview of the early '80s power-pop movement than *Shake It Up*, even with the absence of such major players as Dwight Twilley, Phil Seymour and Great Buildings. —*Stephen Thomas Erlewine*

D.I.Y.: Starry Eyes: UK Pop, Vol. 2 / 1993 / Rhino ◆◆◆◆◆
Picking up where *Teenage Kicks* left off, *D.I.Y.: Starry Eyes: UK Pop, Vol. 2* is even more pop-oriented than its predecessor, and that's taking the Buzzcocks' searing "Ever Fallen in Love (With Someone You Shouldn't Have Fallen In Love With?)" into consideration. Although it includes a handful of great singles from artists that were on *Teenage Kicks* (the Undertones' "Get Over You," XTC's "Life Begins at the Hop," Squeeze's "Up the Junction," the Revillos' "Where's the Boy For Me?"), plus Joe Jackson's familiar "Is She Really Going Out With Him?," *Starry Eyes* shines in how it rounds up terrific singles from underappreciated artists like Bram Tchaikovsky ("Girl of My Dreams"), the Jags ("Back of My Hand (I've Got Your Number)"), the Records ("Starry Eyes"), the Searchers ("Hearts in Her Eyes") and Purple Hearts ("Millions Like Us"). These are sparkling pop songs, with ringing guitars and immediate, catchy melodies. Very few of these songs were actual hits, but they are the cornerstone of British new wave and power-pop, which has rarely sounded as energetic and vital as it does here. —*Stephen Thomas Erlewine*

D.I.Y.: Teenage Kicks: UK Pop (1976-79) / Jan. 19, 1993 / Rhino
◆◆◆◆◆
Punk helped restore a nervy, stripped-down sensibility to rock that was quickly filtered through a number of more pop-oriented bands that were labeled as new wave. Not surprisingly, many of these new wavers were holdovers from pub rock, whose unpretentious, anti-star attitude prophesied punk rock. These pub rockers were devoted to the three-minute pop single, but they also had a biting wit and kinetic energy that separated them from conventional pop-rock bands, and the best of these first wave of new wavers are collected on the dynamic *D.I.Y.: Teenage Kicks: UK Pop (1976-79)*. Beginning with Nick Lowe's explosive "So It Goes," the collection runs through a series of classic singles from Eddie & the Hot Rods ("Do Anything You Wanna Do"), Wreckless Eric ("Whole Wide World"), the Motors ("Dancing the Night Away"), Tom Robinson Band ("2-4-6-8 Motorway"), Squeeze ("Take Me, I'm Yours"), the Only Ones ("Another Girl, Another Planet"), XTC ("This is Pop?"), the Rezillos ("Top of the Pops") and the Undertones ("Teenage Kicks"), throwing in a number of forgotten gems along the way. Although the collection doesn't feature Elvis Costello due to licensing restrictions, he isn't missed—in fact, the collection plays better without him, since focusing on overlooked artists demonstrates what an amazing era for smart, catchy guitar-pop new wave was. Few various-artist collections capture their subject as well, or as infectiously, as *Teenage Kicks* does. —*Stephen Thomas Erlewine*

D.I.Y.: The Modern World: UK Punk 2 (1977-78) / 1993 / Rhino
◆◆◆◆◆
Picking up where the first volume of *D.I.Y.: UK Punk* left off, *D.I.Y.: The Modern World: UK Punk 2 (1977-78)* captures the moment when punk began to fracture into post-punk, hardcore and new wave. There are still some straightforward punk anthems from the Jam ("The Modern World"), the Buzzcocks ("What Do I Get?"), the Rezillos ("My Baby Does) Good Sculptures"), Generation X ("Wild Youth") and Stiff Little Fingers ("Alternative Ulster," "Suspect Device"), but the collection finds punk turning dark, noisy, paranoid and weird through Siouxsie & the Banshees ("Hong Kong Garden"), the Fall ("Bingo Master"), Wire ("I Am the Fly"), X-Ray Spex ("The Day the World Turned Day-Glo"), the Soft Boys ("(I Want to Be an) Angleploise Lamp") and Magazine ("Shot by Both Sides"). There's also some loutish rock from Sham 69 and 999, but *The Modern World* on the whole is much more interesting than that. Despite missing a few major figures like the Clash, it is a definitive portrait of the last days of the original British punk movement and it works both as an introduction and a great, listenable overview. —*Stephen Thomas Erlewine*

D.I.Y.: We're Desperate: the L.A. Scene (1976-79) / 1993 / Rhino
◆◆◆◆
If *D.I.Y.: We're Desperate: The L.A. Scene (1976-79)* is one of the weakest installments in the *D.I.Y.* series, it's only because the Los Angeles scene wasn't nearly as rich and diverse as those in New York and London. New wave pop didn't have a stronghold in the L.A. punk community, which tended to favor raw, hard amateurish punk. Essentially, Los Angeles was one of the first towns to embrace hardcore, and almost all of *We're Desperate* plays as proto-hardcore punk. Of all the bands on the collection, X displays the greatest songcraft and style with their edgy guitars and tag-team vocals. No other group has their finesse, but then again, they don't attempt to write songs, they just want to make noise and on that level the collection works, even if it may get tedious to listeners who have just a passing interest in this style of punk. Still, *We're Desperate* is a good overview of the L.A. scene, featuring its handful of major players—the Germs ("Forming," "Lexicon Devil"), the Dickies ("You Drive Me Ape (You Big Gorilla)"), the Weirdos ("We Got the Neutron Bomb," "A Life of Crime"), the Dils ("I Hate the Rich")—plus many lesser-known acts like the Zeros, the Furys, Eyes, Bags, the Last, Alley Cats, the Plugz and the Dogs, as well as a demo from the Motels. There's not enough variety or substance to make it as essential as the New York and UK collections, but that means *We're Desperate* is an accurate representation of Los Angeles punk. —*Stephen Thomas Erlewine*

Death Row Greatest Hits / Dec. 1996 / Death Row/Priority ◆◆◆◆◆
More than any other label, Death Row defined gangsta rap and hip-hop in the early '90s, and the double-disc *Death Row Greatest Hits* captures nearly all of the label's biggest hits from artists like Dr. Dre, Snoop Doggy Dogg and 2Pac. Although the disc bends some rules by including cuts that weren't released on Death Row and containing an abundance of previously unreleased songs, the compilation sums up the feeling of the early and mid-'90s. A single disc would have provided more consistent thrills—and it would have eliminated the annoying remixes on disc two—but the sprawl is also indicative of the self-indulgence of gangsta rap, which is essential to understanding the genre. And *Death Row Greatest Hits* has a string of great songs—"Let Me Ride," "What's My Name," "Gin and Juice," "Nothin' But a G Thang" (but no "California Love")—making it an excellent summation of gangsta rap's glory days. —*Stephen Thomas Erlewine*

Def Jam Music Group—Ten Year Anniversary / 1995 / Def Jam
✦✦✦✦✦

In the '80s, Def Jam Records became the leading rap and hip-hop label
in America. Featuring a roster filled with superstars—including Public
Enemy, LL Cool J, the Beastie Boys, Slick Rick, and EPMD—Def Jam
released many of the most innovative and groundbreaking records of
the late '80s and, as the four-CD box *Ten Year Anniversary* proves, the
music has lost none of its impact over the years. Over the course of the
four discs, the set runs through a number of hip-hop classics, including
"I Can't Live Without My Radio," "Fight the Power," "(You Gotta) Fight
for Your Right (To Party)," "Slam," "Don't Believe the Hype," "Rock the
Bells," "Regulate," "Crossover," and over 50 other tracks. The one (minor)
drawback of the set is the fact that it isn't sequenced chronologically;
nevertheless, each disc in the box is compulsively listenable. In sheer
musical terms, *Ten Year Anniversary* is one of the best box sets ever
compiled and is essential to any popular music collection. —*Stephen
Thomas Erlewine*

The Del-Fi & Donna Story / 1994 / Ace ✦✦✦

In the late '50s and early '60s, Del-Fi was an interesting, eclectic L.A.-
based independent rock label, recording surf, rockabilly, R&B, and pop,
occasionally landing a national hit. Precisely because of that eclecticism,
though, a survey disc of notable tracks from the Del-Fi vaults isn't the
smoothest listen. This 31-disc compilation does include good sides by
Ritchie Valens, Chan Romero (famous for "Hippy Hippy Shake"), Ron
Holden (who had a one-shot with the New Orleans R&B-like "Love You
So"), teen idol Johnny Crawford, and surf combo the Lively Ones. Serious collectors will also appreciate the CD availability of rare sides by
Dick Dale, Rene Hall (who played guitar on Valens' classic "La Bamba"),
a pre-Bread David Gates, and other unknown tracks in the surf, R&B,
and instrumental vein. Valens, Romero, Crawford, and the Lively Ones
are better appreciated in the context of their own best-of compilations,
however. —*Richie Unterberger*

The Demention of Sound / 1982 / Feedback ✦✦✦✦

If you like your mid-'60s British R&B raw and savage, this is the best
compilation of obscure relics from that era, bar none. None of these
were hits—and, indeed, none of the groups are at all known in the
US—but these guitar-based ravers rock with the authority of the best
early Pretty Things. Standouts include the Syndicat's "Crawdaddy
Simone," with some of the wildest guitar effects ever to grace a mid-'60s
record; Mark Four's "I'm Leaving," with some of the earliest guitar feedback ever recorded (by Eddie Phillips, who along with the rest of the
group would soon become the Creation); and "You've Got What I Want"
by the Sorrows, one of the very best British Invasion bands never to
have a hit in the US. Unfortunately this anthology is very difficult to find
now, although some of the better tracks crop up on other reissues.
—*Richie Unterberger*

Desperate Rock 'n' Roll, Vol. 1 / 1992 / Flame ✦✦✦

This superlative collection compiles 30 tracks, bringing together some
rock 'n' roll, rockabilly, and rhythm & blues tracks that have long been
prized by collectors. The highlights are numerous, as the collection has
no need for filler, pulling singles from labels both reasonably well
known and positively microscopic. "Kiss-A Me Quick," featuring Jackson
Toomb's curiously dispassionate vocal, is highlighted by two scorching
guitar breaks, Terry Dunavan's "Rock It on Mars" features a wildly trem-
oloed guitar break that's both extremely out of tune and perfectly fitting,
while Screamin' Joe Neal lives up to his name on "Rock 'n' Roll Deacon."
Danny Ross' "Go Baby Go" and the Alabama Kid's wild and crudely
played "Rockin' Jalopy" are bare-bones rockabilly that get the job done,
and Mel Smith's "Pretty Plaid Skirt" and the Tempest's "Rockin' Rochester" push the wildness envelope to its extreme. Johnny Watson (no relation to the famous bluesman) checks in with "I'm Not Crazy" which,
along with "Rock Old Sputnick" by Nelson Young and Don Winter's
"Pretty Moon," hold up the hillbilly boogie section of this compilation,
which closes out with a piece of teen garage band mayhem from the
early '60s, the Readymen's rendition of the old folk song "Shortnin'
Bread," which sounds like nothing more than a surf band hopped up on
booze and pills. Also noteworthy are the R&B boogie of Lionel Hampton's Hamptones' "Turkey Hop" and the garage band version of "Johnny
B. Goode" by one Johnny Candles, whose diction makes Chuck Berry's
famous lyrics sound almost as if they're being sung in another language.
If you like your roots rockin' raw and wild, this makes a fine addition to
the collection. —*Cub Koda*

Desperate Rock 'n' Roll, Vol. 2 / Flame ✦✦✦

The second volume in this series highly acclaimed by collectors gathers
up another 30 tracks from the nether regions of rock 'n' roll's early history with several notable examples of the raw and wild aboard. Like the
previous volume, the highlights are plentiful, with rare-as-hen's-teeth
singles like Glen Barber's cleverly written "Ice Cold Water," the voodoo
incantation of "I Want Some of That" by Kai Rai, "She's My Witch" by Kip
Tyler and the Flips (featuring Steve Douglas on sax and Sandy Nelson
on drums), "Long Legged Linda" by the Kids from Texas, and Glenn

Reeves' novelty "Tarzan" (originally issued as "Primitive Love"). The hillbilly rocker side of the equation is well served by "You Ain't No Good for
Me" by Jimmy Lee (eerie falsetto wailing!), Jimmy Johnson's countrified
version of Gene Vincent's "Woman Love," and the proto-rockabilly
sound of Jimmy Symsum's "Big Time Mama." And if you like your early
rock 'n' roll with more than a tint of weirdness to it, by all means check
out the Musical Linn Twins' "Rockin' Out the Blues" and the incredibly
strange "Rockin' 'N' Rollin'" by the mysterious W. L. Horning, a recording that begs the question, "was this guy serious?" Many of the sides
compiled here go for high figures among collectors, and it's great to
have them all collected here, as their scarcity (and lack of master tape
availability) would generally keep them from being anthologized elsewhere. —*Cub Koda*

Didn't It Blow Your Mind! Soul Hits of the '70s / 1995 / Rhino ✦✦✦✦

Soul music began to drift away from gritty deep soul in the late '60s,
moving back toward the smooth, immaculately-produced sounds of
uptown soul, except this time there was a difference. Taking their cue
from the pop-oriented records of Motown, the purveyors of early '70s
soul threw everything in the mix. Not only were there impassioned
vocals and sexy rhythms, there were pop productions, sound effects, psychedelic flourishes, elements of reggae and Latin inflections. It was the
most ambitious soul had been in years, and as the first 15 volumes of
Rhino's multi-disc series *Didn't It Blow Your Mind! Soul Hits of the '70s*
illustrates, it was frequently as good as anything released in the '70s.
Due to contractual reasons, some big names, including Al Green, Stevie
Wonder and Marvin Gaye, aren't included on *Didn't It Blow Your Mind!*,
but they aren't missed because the overall quality of the material is so
shockingly strong. The Spinners establish themselves as the finest vocal
group of the '70s, but the Delfonics, Chi-Lites, the Chairmen of the Board
and many others give them a run for their money. And while Curtis
Mayfield stands out from the competition, that doesn't diminish the
worth of Eddie Holman or Freda Payne. In fact, one of the main pleasures of the set is discovering so many one-hit wonders that released
singles as good as the major artists. There are a few misses on the first
15 volumes, but by and large, each collection is terrific; the curious
should try *Vol. 6* or *Vol. 9*, since they have the highest ratio of classic
material and wonderful forgotten gems. The last five volumes of *Didn't
It Blow Your Mind!* were issued several years after the original 15, which
stopped in 1975. The final five cover the late '70s, which were nowhere
near as consistent, and many of those discs are rather bland, but for the
hardcore collector, it's a nice way to wrap up the series. The average soul
fan should stick to the superb initial volumes, which represent one of
the finest various-artists collections ever assembled. —*Stephen Thomas
Erlewine*

Diggin' Out / 198? / Mr. Manicotti ✦✦✦

When you get into compilations of rare local surf singles from the '60s,
the problem is the same as it is when you get deeper and deeper into
'60s garage compilations, or when you start to plumb the depths of any
genre. The secondary anthologies are rarely as good as those with the
most familiar/best material, and can sound kind of generic taken
together all at once. These 18 sides are undeniably rare—none of these
groups were well known—and the performances are uniformly energetic, with silvery guitar leads, raunchy sax, and middle Eastern/Latin
melodic motifs in abundance. Not much of it is truly mind-blowing,
however; unless surf is one of your specialties, you're better off sticking
with the excellent surf compilations on Rhino. The unquestioned highlight is the Goldtones' "Gutterball/Strike" single, with wild steel guitar
leads from Glenn Campbell, who would later be a key member of the
Misunderstood, one of the greatest unheralded psychedelic bands of the
1960s. —*Richie Unterberger*

The Disco Years / 1990 / Rhino ✦✦✦✦

Rhino's six-volume *The Disco Years* is the best, most comprehensive
overview of disco's late '70s heyday, featuring all of the genre's biggest
hits with the exception of the Bee Gees' singles from *Saturday Night
Fever*. The first four volumes—*Turn the Beat Around, On the Beat,
Boogie Fever* and *Lost In Music*—are essential additions to any com-
prehensive pop library, since they contain the biggest and best hits:
"The Hustle," "Never Can Say Goodbye," "That's the Way (I Like It),"
"Car Wash," "Disco Inferno," "Love Hangover," "Turn the Beat
Around," "Boogie Oogie Oogie," "You Make Me Feel (Mighty Real),"
"Ring My Bell," "I Will Survive," "Funkytown," "Celebration,"
"Y.M.C.A.," "Heart of Glass," "Get Down Tonight," "Macho Man," "Le
Freak," "We Are Family," "Bad Girls," "Hot Stuff," "He's the Greatest
Dancer," "In the Bush" and "Good Times," among others. The next
three—*Must Be the Music, Everybody Dance* and *The Best Disco in
Town*—aren't nearly as consistent, but for listeners with a deep inter-
est in disco, they have enough obscurities and interesting tracks to
make them worthwhile. Still, the first four volumes of *The Disco
Years* is what's really necessary for most listeners, since that's where
all true classics are. —*Stephen Thomas Erlewine*

Don't It Sound Good: the Great Atlantic Vocal Groups / 1995 / Rhino/Collectors' Choice Music ✦✦✦✦
Fifty doo wop cuts from the Atlantic vaults on this double CD, all but one from the 1950s. Divided between hits and rarities, there's no getting around the fact that, due to the factors of both familiarity and quality, the hits are far more interesting to the non-collector. There are quite a few of those here by both the Drifters and the Clovers, as well as the Robins' "Smokey Joe's Cafe," the Chords' "Sh-Boom," and the Cardinals' "Wheel of Fortune." After that it's collector territory, with outfits like the Diamonds (no relation to the white group that had a hit with "Little Darlin'"), the Regals, the Pearls, the Raiders, the Royal Jokers, the Sensations, and others. Characteristically well-done vocal arrangements don't disguise the truth that the material is not as memorable as the hits. Nevertheless, doo wop fans will certainly dig this, as the Atlantic imprint ensured a basic standard of quality. Available by mail-order only, from Collectors' Choice Music (P.O. Box 838, Itasca, IL 60143-0838, 800-923-1122). —*Richie Unterberger*

Doo Wop Box / 1994 / Rhino ✦✦✦✦✦
The four-disc set *The Doo Wop Box* is a superb collection of 101 classic doo wop songs from the genre's golden era. Not only are the classic hit singles presented in crystal clear sound, but so are a number of forgotten treasures. It's the rare box set that's equally appealing to both novices and collectors. —*Stephen Thomas Erlewine*

The Doo Wop Box, Vol. 2: 101 More Vocal Gems / Oct. 1996 / Rhino ✦✦✦✦✦
101 *more* songs, and four *more* hours of doo wop (from 1951-63), from the same concern that brought you the first *Doo Wop Box*. As expected, this delves into less-traveled territory than the first set. It picks up some big chart hits that escaped the first collection, but otherwise the focus is much more on mid-chart items and singles whose impact was primarily local/regional. There are also doo wop efforts by duos and female groups; the first box set had largely passed over those sub-genres in favor of the more classical vocal group prototype. This isn't as essential/definitive as the first volume, simply because the previous anthology collected the overwhelming bulk of made-in-the-shade doo wop classics. The music on *Doo Wop Box II*, however, is almost on the same level, and in some ways more diverse. It encompasses smooth quasi-Ink Spots numbers from the early '50s, Italo-American doo wop from the early '60s, outrageous novelties, funky garage productions, proto-soul, doo wop treatments of pre-rock pop standards, and more. It's pointless to try and recapitulate individual highlights in such a limited space; if you have a taste for the form, you're bound to both re-encounter old favorites and find some lost gems. At the same time, the sheer size of the collection means that mild doo wop enthusiasts are better off just sticking to single-disc collections, or getting the first doo wop box and leaving it at that. The overwhelming quantity also means that it's doubtful that even doo wop fans will love everything here, though every specialized taste will be satisfied by at least some of the selections. —*Richie Unterberger*

Dot Rock & Roll / 1996 / Ace ✦✦✦
The Dot label recorded all kinds of pop in the 1950s; this 28-track compilation focuses on their hardest rocking sides, most of which are rockabilly or rockabilly-related. Dot didn't really have a "house" sound, and what you get here is a trail mix of obscure '50s, mostly white rock 'n' roll, with only a couple of big hits (Sanford Clark's "The Fool" and Nervous Norvus' insane novelty, "Transfusion"). A number of these rarities will have considerable appeal to collectors, like the non-hits by one-hit wonders Robin Luke and Ray Sharpe; the raunchy white Little Richard sounds of Jimmie Dee's "Henrietta" (which was a small hit); a single by Ray Campi (who really didn't become well-known until he became a rockabilly revival artist decades later); a solo outing by ex-Cricket Niki Sullivan; a 1958 Jerry Lee Lewis-clone number by future country star Mickey Gilley; and a rockabilly cut by Mac Wiseman of the Foggy Mountain Boys. It's solid fodder for the most part, though rather middle-of-the-pack as far as vintage rockabilly goes. —*Richie Unterberger*

Dream Babes, Vol. 1: Am I Dreaming? / 1994 / RPM ✦✦✦
The British girl group sound was a different animal than the American article: there was an equal emphasis on production craft, but there was a higher proportion of pop to soul, and a Europop influence in many of the melodies and arrangements. This 24-track compilation gathers rare non-hit singles from 1962 to 1970, and none of the singers will be familiar to US listeners (indeed, most or all of them will be unfamiliar to British ones as well). It's decent but light girl group (or girl group-influenced) '60s pop that could often use more grit; some of it's fairly strong, but there are no melodies or performances that announce "classic" in neon lights. If you're a sucker for the girl group sound, it's an acceptable addition to the library, with some standouts, like Samantha Jones' "Don't Come Any Closer" (covered to greater effect in French by Francoise Hardy), Alma Cogan's "Snakes and Snails," and Carole Deene's goofy "Some People," with a train whistle bleating away in the background. —*Richie Unterberger*

Ear Piercing Punk / Trash ✦✦✦✦
The cover illustration of a class of '77-type punk led some to mistakenly assume this was a modern punk compilation. Actually, it was one of the first '60s garage music anthologies, and remains one of the better ones, despite the lack of liner notes. None of the artists are well known, even by collectors, with the marginal exception of the Mystic Tide and Canada's Ugly Ducklings. But Mile Ends' "Bottle Up and Go," Dean Carter's "Rebel Woman," and especially Keith Kessler's stunning "Don't Crowd Me" are some of the most vicious, compelling '60s garage tunes ever to come storming down the pike. It's not easy to find anymore, but worth searching for if you're a garagehead, especially as many of the tracks have somehow eluded reissue on other compilations. —*Richie Unterberger*

Echoes in Time, Vol. 2 / Solar ✦✦✦
Compared to the first *Echoes in Time* volume, this is a disappointment, with a greater emphasis on conventionally punky '60s rarities, as opposed to spacy psychedelic ones. Not a one of these groups had anything resembling a hit, although SRC and Leviathan have reputations among serious collector circles. It's only fair overall, but Nova Local's "Games" stands out as a white-hot slice of British Invasion-inspired garage pop. One of the true gems in lost '60s rock music, it's only available on this reissue as far as this writer knows. —*Richie Unterberger*

Echoes in Time: Psychedelic Rarities / 1983 / Solar ✦✦✦✦
One of the best compilations of obscure '60s psychedelic music, itself now a collector's item, as it was released in a limited edition of 500 copies. It's worth picking up if you spot one, however, as the cuts by United Travel Service, the Deep, the Human Expression, Fapardokly, and Mother Tucker's Yellow Duck are among the best fusions of trippy experimentation with walking-on-air melodicism. More than any other collector-oriented anthology, this captures psychedelia in its foggiest, most mysterious glory, with melodic harmonies and odd sound/guitar effects given equal weight. A lot of the cuts haven't surfaced on other reissues, either. —*Richie Unterberger*

El Primitivo American Rock'n'roll & Rockabilly / 1993 / Ace ✦✦✦
24 rockabilly tracks recorded in Nashville between 1956 and 1964 under the direction of Murray Nash, who ran the small Do-Ra-Me label. The title doesn't lie. This is raw, and rare; about half of the selections weren't even issued until this CD compilation. Mel Robbins is the most recognizable name here, as some of the tracks were picked up for distribution by Chess, although you'd have a hard time finding anyone familiar with his work other than diehard rockabilly collectors. Mick Farren's liner notes give the impression that you're about to hear a rockabilly Gong Show of sorts, but although the performances are more on the level of inspired amateurism than old Gene Vincent sides, it's rather enjoyable, rarely crossing into ineptitude. You shouldn't get these Elvis-Eddie Cochran-Carl Perkins-et al. derivations unless rockabilly's your main dish, but not everything has to be classic to be good clean fun. That's what's on tap here, offering infectious enthusiasm (if not much originality) and occasional bursts of memorability (as in the Imps' instrumental "Uh Oh," with fuzzy chords reminiscent of vintage Link Wray). —*Richie Unterberger*

Electric Sugar Cube Flashbacks, Vols. 1-4 / AIP ✦✦✦
In comparison to US bands, obscure British groups of the mid- and late '60s have been ill-served by compilations; there are dozens of Pebbles volumes, and hundreds of American garage rock compilations in the same vein, but comparatively few for their British counterparts. There are some, however, and the *Electric Sugar Cube Flashbacks* series is probably the best of them, spotlighting rare early British R&B, "beat," and psychedelic recordings from impossibly rare 45s, many of which were never released in the States. The British bands tended to be somewhat more accomplished, tuneful, and imaginative in their lyrics and arrangements than their American counterparts; those looking for obscure music in the classic British '60s R&B/pop and power-pop style should check these out, with the awareness that they're generally more crudely performed, written, and produced than the material by the British Invasion giants we know and love. As is the case with all AIP series, the volumes tend to get worse as the series progresses; Volume One, if you can find it, is by far the best. —*Richie Unterberger*

Electric Sugar Cube Flashbacks / AIP ✦✦✦✦
When AIP upgrades its catalog to CD, there's a lot of confusion; the same title is usually kept as the vinyl edition, but the tracks are taken from various volumes of a series, and lots of previously uncompiled bonus tracks are tacked on. The CD version of *Electric Sugar Cube Flashbacks* draws from a few volumes of the multi-LP series of British '60s psychedelic rarities that went under that name, especially volume four. About a dozen of the cuts, though (over half the CD), didn't appear on any of the vinyl compilations. There are a few moderately well-known groups among the 21 tracks (the Smoke, Family) and rarities by big-time artists (the Dave Clark Five, Sweet). But mostly these are no-names who caught the lightning for a track or two on hopelessly obscure singles. Not everything here's great, but a lot of it's good, or bet-

ter than that, fusing melodic pop crunch with experimentation better than virtually any other sub-genre of rock. Highlights are the contributions by the Smoke, Big Boy Pete, Andy Ellison, Svensk, and Mike Stuart Span (represented by a rare BBC version of their glorious flop single, "Children of Tomorrow"). —*Richie Unterberger*

Endless Journey, Vol. 1-3 / Psycho ◆◆◆
One of the earlier series of rare psychedelia compilations, *Endless Journey* has lost a little of its luster in subsequent years, as many of the tracks found their way onto better (and official) reissues. The Rising Storm, Moving Sidewalks, Mystic Tide, C.A. Quintet, Faine Jade, and Frumious Bandersnatch tracks are also interesting (and in some cases excellent), but you may as well look for better packages. There are a few items that are hard to find elsewhere, like the Clique's excellent cover of the 13th Floor Elevators' "Splash I," and Strange's stunning "Ruler of the Universe," which has some of the best experimental Hendrix-styled guitar effects ever laid down. —*Richie Unterberger*

English Freakbeat, Vol. 2 / 1996 / AIP ◆◆◆
Another source of discographical confusion from AIP, which upgrades the 1989 vinyl compilation *English Freakbeat Vol. 2* to CD by losing one of the 14 tracks, and adding ten previously uncompiled bonus tracks. Those of you who like rare R&B-influenced British Invasion music and already owned the vinyl will probably have to swallow hard and fork out for the CD, because the ten new tracks are of similar quality. If you're just starting from scratch, this anthology isn't necessarily recommended unless you've got a serious yen for Pretty Things-early Stones-styled R&B/rock raunch. If you specialize in that sort of thing, you'll like a lot of what's here on this erratic but worthwhile compilation of flop singles from the mid-'60s, especially the items by the Kubas, Mickey Finn, the Syndicates (with Steve Howe on guitar), the Wheels, and the Wolf Pack. —*Richie Unterberger*

English Freakbeat, Vol. 5 / 1993 / Voxx ◆◆◆
The *English Freakbeat* series is devoted to unearthing obscure, non-hit treasures of the British Invasion that are known only to obsessive collectors. Truth be told, many of those treasures were obscure for a reason, which makes these anthologies wildly uneven listening, but there are some gems to be found here. The highlights of this 21-song volume include a surprisingly pleasant slice of punk-pop from ex-Beatle drummer Pete Best, "The Way I Feel." Thane Russal's "I Need You" is a first-rate Them imitation, Geoff Goddard's "Sky Man" is a truly inspired piece of Joe Meek-produced lunacy about benign space aliens, and the Greenbeats' Merseyish "You Must Be The One" is undoubtedly the most obscure song that Mick Jagger and Keith Richards wrote in the '60s (no, the Rolling Stones never did get around to recording it). That gives you the flavor of the manic variety on hand here. Some of the cuts are shamelessly derivative early British R&B, and others are simply not as striking as the gushing liner notes would have you believe. The CD also includes some extremely obscure productions by Shel Talmy and Joe Meek, as well as an obscure composition by Jackie DeShannon, that in no way approximates the greatness of their famous work. —*Richie Unterberger*

English Freakbeat, Vols. 1-5 / AIP ◆◆◆
Like its cousin series *Electric Sugar Cube Flashbacks*, this focuses on way-obscure British "beat," R&B, and early psychedelia, circa 1964-1968. There are some great cuts to be found on these, as well as super-rare singles by groups that featured future stars like Steve Howe, Mick Ronson, and Graham Gouldman, and even famous never-weres like Pete Best. They're very uneven anthologies, though, more so than the *Electric Sugar Cube Flashbacks* volumes; one gets the feeling that the tracks were sometimes selected as much or more for their rarity than their actual musical value. —*Richie Unterberger*

Epitaph for a Legend / 1980 / International Artists ◆◆◆◆
The Texas-based International Artists label recorded some intriguing, slightly off-the-wall psychedelic-garage-pop in the 1960s, their most famous act being the 13th Floor Elevators. This is an erratic but extremely interesting double-LP compilation of IA oddities and rarities, much of it previously unreleased. The five Red Krayola demos (some of which would be re-recorded for their first LP) are prime acid folk, especially "Hurricane Fighter Plane," one of the closest American approximations of Syd Barrett-era Pink Floyd. The Chapparrals' "I Tried So Hard" is gutsy punk-pop, Thursday's Children's "A Part of You" is reminiscent of the mid-period Zombies, and the Emperors' "I Want My Woman" is growling garage punk. Side four is devoted entirely to 13th Floor Elevators/Roky Erickson rarities, including a beautiful acoustic version of "Splash I" and the rare single by Roky's pre-Elevators group the Spades. In this company, side three—which has unexceptional straight blues material, including a song by Lightnin' Hopkins—is a misfit, but psychedelic collectors will want the record for the rock material. —*Richie Unterberger*

 Excursions in Ambience: A Collection of Ambient-House Music / 1993 / Plan 9/Caroline ◆◆◆◆
The earliest domestic compilation detailing the ambient-house genre,

EIA is a solid, essential album featuring heavyweights such as Future Sound of London, 777, Ultramarine, and Psychick Warriors Ov Gaia. —*John Bush*

Excursions in Ambience: The Fourth Frontier / Nov. 1995 / Astralwerks ◆◆◆◆
The closest to true ambience of any in the series, this fourth volume includes various artists' exploration of reverb, echo and delay effects. As such, only three tracks have any sort of beat. Though this lack of definition could scare off listeners, the appearance of nontraditional ambient practitioners Flying Saucer Attack and Labradford, along with usual stalwarts 777 and Future Sound of London (as Far-Out Son of Lung), makes for an interesting listening experience. —*John Bush*

Fabulous Flips / 1993 / Ace ◆◆
The concept driving this 26-cut compilation is to take the B-sides of 26 early rock and roll hits from the 1950s and early '60s. Some good songs were placed on these flipsides, and some of the ones anthologized here (Larry Williams' "Slow Down," Jack Scott's rockabilly stormer "Leroy," the Everlys' "I Wonder If I Care As Much," Bobby Day's "Over and Over") made a deservedly substantial impact in their own right. But there's a reason that most B-sides are B-sides; little here stands up to the well-known hits on the top, or is even worthy of belated recognition by collectors. In fact, most of this is formulaic (if spirited) early rock 'n' roll, and the random mix-and-match of rockabilly, doo wop, instrumentals, and R&B by Little Richard, Link Wray, the Skyliners, and a bunch of one-shots makes for jumpy listening. —*Richie Unterberger*

Fabulous Flips, Vol. 3 / Mar. 25, 1997 / Ace ◆◆
It's true that sometimes in rock's early days, songs originally designated as the B-side turned out to be the hits—some quite memorable, at that. That doesn't necessarily mean that the B-sides were as a rule competitive with the plug sides. Here we have 26 B-sides to hits from the late '50s and early '60s, including tracks by Dion & the Belmonts, Fats Domino, Johnny Burnette, Larry Williams, and one-shots like the Shields and the Silhouettes. Besides Benny Spellman's "Fortune Teller" and maybe the Showmen's "Country Fool" (supposedly adapted by High Numbers, later to become the Who, for the B-side of their only single, although the similarity is casual), you'd be hard pressed to call much of this first-rate stuff. The selections by Ray Sharpe, Eugene Church, and a few others aren't bad, but it's more like a nearly random journey through generic early rock 'n' roll than an exhumation of lost treasures. —*Richie Unterberger*

Faster & Louder: Hardcore Punk, Vol. 1 / 1993 / Rhino ◆◆◆◆
Faster & Louder: Hardcore Punk, Vol. 1 overlooks a handful of classic singles in favor of several novelties and rarities, yet the 17-track collection remains a first-rate introduction to hardcore, featuring two absolute classics in the Dead Kennedys' "Holiday in Cambodia" and Bad Brains' "Pay to Cum," plus cuts from such major figures as the Circle Jerks, Suicidal Tendencies, Angry Samoans, Meatmen, Government Issue and Hüsker Dü. —*Stephen Thomas Erlewine*

Faster & Louder: Hardcore Punk, Vol. 2 / 1993 / Rhino ◆◆◆
Considered unimaginably over-the-top and atonal at the time, the early sounds of hardcore punk don't sound nearly as noisy 15 years later. Dare we say, they even sound a bit poppy and tightly conceived in comparison with the uncompromisingly bleak, rushed, and amelodic sounds of today's underground hardcore groups. That's not to take away from the undeniable influence and power of first-generation hardcore. *Faster & Louder: Hardcore Punk, Vol. 2* does a good job of assembling some of the most enduring and accessible moments of the genre's genesis. This 17-song compilation includes the first singles by Hüsker Dü and X, who went on to transcend hardcore's limitations pretty rapidly. It also includes seminal tracks by Agent Orange and Wire, as well as influential bands with smaller cults like the Wipers, the Dils, and Zero Boys, down to nearly forgotten acts (Dys, Stranglehold). The bleakest and most vicious strand of early hardcore is represented by Fear, the Germs, and the Subhumans. Not a bad package for those who want to sample the genre's highlights and limit its representation in their collection to this fairly small and manageable dose. —*Richie Unterberger*

Fire/Fury Records Story / 1993 / Warner Brothers ◆◆◆◆
Although the sequencing is a little too scholarly to be truly compulsive listening, the 51-track, double-disc box set *The Fire/Fury Records Story* contains the majority of the major songs recorded for the seminal blues and R&B label. Apart from Elmore James, Wilbert Harrison, Lightnin' Hopkins, Gladys Knight and Lee Dorsey, King Curtis and Mighty Joe Young, there aren't too many big names here, nor are there many hit singles; only James, Harrison and Dorsey are represented by their best-known songs. Still, the absence of big hits makes the consistently high quality of the set all the more impressive, and serious R&B and blues fans will find it well worth their time. —*Stephen Thomas Erlewine*

Flashback, Vol. 1 / 198? / Flashback ◆◆◆◆
Fine compilation of rare mid-60s psychedelic punk from Texas. A cut above the garage norm, both because of the excellence of much of the

material, and the high level of diversity relative to many garage comps—there's some good pop and folk-rock hooks, not just sludgy bluesy outrage. The Esquires' "Come On, Come On" is garage rock at its most irresistibly frenetic; the Playboys of Edinburgh, the Headstones, and the Floyd Dakil Four are fetchingly Byrdsy, with a bit of country influence even creeping in; and the Trolls ("That's the Way My Love Is") and Finnicum ("Come On Over") offer the kind of raunchy blend of power and finesse that Texas punk is famous for. —*Richie Unterberger*

Flashback, Vol. 2 / 198? / Flashback ✦✦✦✦
Not quite as top-notch as the first *Flashback* volume, but still a well-above-average compilation of Texas psych/punk, more consistent and eclectic than most garage anthologies. The Outcasts' "I'm in Pittsburgh (And It's Raining)" is the closest American approximation of the Pretty Things; the Chevelle V's "Come Back Bird" is the snappiest "Smokestack Lightning" ripoff ever attempted; the Runaways' "18th Floor Girl" has some truly astral guitar scrapes and thunder of doom drumming; and Jimmy Rabbit's "Pushover" is pop-punk of the first order. —*Richie Unterberger*

Flashdance [O.S.T.] / 1983 / Casablanca ✦✦✦✦
Giorgio Moroder's score for this dance fantasy album turned into a blockbuster (five million copies and counting) due to the title track, sung by Irene Cara, Michael Sembello's "Maniac," and a bunch of other modern dance tracks. —*William Ruhlmann*

Flight to Lowland's Paradise: the Netherlands, Part 1 & 2 / Moxie ✦✦✦✦
Pebbles Vol. 15: The Netherlands remains the best compilation of mid-'60s Dutch beat/punk, but these two anthologies, issued in the US in the mid-'80s, are nearly on the same level. Each volume has 16 tracks demonstrating the uniquely brooding Dutch take on British Invasion R&B and mod, with songs by both well-known acts on the scene (the Outsiders, Les Baroques, the Motions, Cuby & the Blizzards) and total unknowns. Good stuff, not mere rare novelties. —*Richie Unterberger*

Footloose / 1984 / CBS ✦✦✦✦
Footloose was a throwback to '50s rock 'n' roll movies, with a silly plot about a town where it is illegal to dance. It was a major hit, as was its soundtrack, which spent a grand total of ten weeks at No. 1 and selling over seven million copies. It's easy to see why—the album delivers its mainstream pop, anthemic rock, and light dance-pop with style and abundance of hooks. Six of the nine tracks became Top 40 hits and three—Kenny Loggins' bouncy title song, the excellent power ballad "Almost Paradise . . . Love Theme From *Footloose*" (a duet between Loverboy's Mike Reno and Heart's Ann Wilson), and Deniece Williams' frothy, charming "Let's Hear It For the Boy"—shot into the Top Ten. The sound and production of *Footloose* has dated badly—there is a reliance on synthesizers and drum machines that instantly announces that the record was made in 1984—but that isn't necessarily a weakness. Not only does it function as a time capsule of a certain moment in pop music history, but many of the songs are catchy enough to transcend their production. There's nothing of substance on the *Footloose* soundtrack, but it's a light, entertaining listen. Sometimes, that can be better than something substantial. —*Stephen Thomas Erlewine*

Frat Rock / 1991 / Rhino ✦✦✦✦✦
Rhino's *Frat Rock* series is an excellent overview of '60s rock 'n' roll and R&B party anthems like the Kingsmen's "Louie Louie," "Double Shot of My Baby's Love" (Swinging Medallions), "La La La La La" (Blendells), "Shout" (Isley Brothers), "Do You Love Me?" (the Contours), and "Money Mony" (Tommy James & the Shondells). —*John Floyd*

Frat Rock: The '70s / 1995 / Rhino ✦✦✦
A fun, but haphazard, collection of album-rock raveups from the '70s, this disc contains highlights like Alice Cooper's "School's Out," Grand Funk Railroad's "We're an American Band," Foreigner's "Hot Blooded," and the Knack's "My Sharona." —*Stephen Thomas Erlewine*

Frat Rock: More of the '70s / 1995 / Rhino ✦✦✦
Like the first volume of *Frat Rock: The '70s, More of the '70s* functions more as a sampler of album-rock hits than frat-house rock, but it still contains a number of good songs, including Golden Earring's "Radar Love," Deep Purple's "Smoke on the Water," the Kinks' "Sleepwalker," Joe Walsh's "Life's Been Good," Foghat's "Slow Ride," Bad Company's "Can't Get Enough," and Gary Glitter's anthemic "Rock and Roll, Part 2." —*Stephen Thomas Erlewine*

Frat Rock: The '80s / 1995 / Rhino ✦✦✦
The '70s editions of the *Frat Rock* series concentrated on album-rock crossover hits. *Frat Rock: The '80s* is more schizophrenic. Most of the disc concentrates on new wave hits like Madness' "Our House," Adam Ant's "Goody Two Shoes," Devo's "Whip It," Stray Cats' "Rock This Town," and Tommy Tutone's "867-5309/Jenny Jenny," but it also has album-rock tracks like the J. Geils Band's "Centerfold" and Top 40 cuts like Robert Palmer's "Addicted to Love," Glenn Frey's "The Heat Is On," and Poison's "Nothin' but a Good Time." —*Stephen Thomas Erlewine*

Freak Beat Phantoms / 1989 / Bam Caruso ✦✦✦✦
If you only want one album of very obscure mid-'60s British rock, you're best advised to track this down. "Freak beat" is the compilers' term for the brand of British rock that was produced circa 1965-67, when the initial impetus of the Merseybeat and R&B bands gave way to wilder mod, power-pop, and early psychedelic sounds. None of these groups "made it" to any degree, but the tuneful crunch (often embellished with distorted guitars) of acts like the Buzz, the Game, Southern Sound, and Fleur De Lys will appeal to anyone who digs the sounds of vintage Who, Yardbirds, and Pretty Things. —*Richie Unterberger*

Friends: Music from the TV Series / Oct. 1995 / Reprise ✦✦✦
Friends successfully targets the same demographic of the television show—twentysomethings that have grown too old for the noise and clutter of college life, yet reluctant to give up the camaraderie (and, indeed, friendship) that stress creates. So, it's a collection of '80s college rock favorites (R.E.M., Paul Westerberg), '80s college rock founding fathers (Pretenders, Lou Reed), and '90s artists that don't really have that much to do with '80s college rock but they're mellow and inoffensive and appear to be genuine since they strum acoustic guitars. In other words, bands like Hootie and the Blowfish. So, most of the album sounds pleasant and upwardly mobile. Apart from the distracting snatches of dialogue, there is nothing to break the flow or engage your attention. —*Stephen Thomas Erlewine*

Funky Broadway Stax Revue Live at the 5/4 Ballroom / 1992 / Stax ✦✦✦✦
Nearly an hour of previously unreleased Stax soul recorded at a Los Angeles venue in August 1965, including cuts by Booker T. & the MGs, Carla Thomas, Rufus Thomas, William Bell, and the Mar-Keys; a couple of relatively little-known Stax vocal groups, the Mad Lads and the Astors, round out the program. This isn't just of interest to soul completists. Good live mid-'60s soul records, in decent fidelity, are fairly rare items. This is genuinely galvanizing stuff, with a rawer, more party-oriented feel than the classic Stax studio sides of the same era. Especially good are Booker T. & the MGs, who really burn through classics like "Green Onions" and "Soul Twist," and Rufus Thomas, who clowns his way through a nine-minute version of "Do the Dog." —*Richie Unterberger*

Funky Stuff: The Best of Funk Essentials / May 18, 1993 / PolyGram ✦✦✦✦
This terrific compilation of the highlights of Mercury's *Funk Essentials* series (which includes individual titles by Parliament, the Bar-Kays, Cameo, and Con Funk Shun) also includes songs from artists that don't have their own CDs. It's essential for anyone curious about the funk. —*AMG*

Funky Tales / 1996 / Ace ✦✦✦✦
Although the Nashville-based Excello label is primarily known for its recordings of Louisiana swamp blues with Slim Harpo, Lazy Lester, and Lightnin' Slim, it moved into soul music pretty aggressively in the late '60s and early '70s. This 24-song compilation of tracks that were cut for the label between 1967 and 1976 offers yet more evidence of how many vital, little-known soul sides were issued during the era by small companies. This is the greasy stuff, too, with no relationship to either "sweet soul" or proto-disco. If you like the sound of the James Brown band circa 1969, or the hardest elements of Stax/Volt, and want more of the same by acts that you never heard on the radio, this is a good investment. Aside from Slim Harpo (represented by a funkish number) and Marva Whitney and Maceo Parker (both of whom recorded for Excello after leaving the James Brown road show), few of these names will ring any bells for all but the most seasoned soul collectors. It's mostly quality, gritty fare, including quite a few percolating instrmentals (the underwater Booker T.-like groove on the Solicitors' "Music for the Brothers" is a highlight). For some quality imitation James Brown arrangements, check out the two previously unissued tracks by the mysterious Little Royal. —*Richie Unterberger*

Get Down Tonight: Best of T.K. Records / 1990 / Rhino ✦✦✦✦
A fine collection of the best tracks from the seminal '70s disco label, including tracks by KC & the Sunshine Band, George McCrae, Gwen McCrae, Betty Wright, Latimore, and Little Beaver. —*Stephen Thomas Erlewine*

Get Hot or Go Home: Vintage RCA Rockabilly '56-'59—Vols. I & II / Country Music Foundation ✦✦✦✦
Get Hot or Go Home: Vintage RCA Rockabilly, '56-'59 is an expertly assembled double-disc collection of rare rockabilly from the RCA vaults. After Elvis Presley became a star, RCA decided to sign a number of new acts to their label, as well as revamp some older country artists to fit the new rockabilly sound. It didn't matter that they bought out Elvis' contract from Sun—they didn't want to risk missing the next Elvis, so they signed anyone they could find. Of course, none of the artists on *Get Hot or Go Home* (including an early Roy Orbison) could have followed Presley's footsteps—they were either too hillbilly (Pee Wee King, Homer & Jethro, Tommy Black) or too slick to cut it. That doesn't mean that the

compilation makes for bad listening; in fact, the unevenness of the material makes the set all the more appealing, because the failures are nearly as entertaining as the successful cuts. Out of all the artists on *Get Hot or Go Home*, only Joe Clay sounds as if he should have had a full-fledged career, but the also-rans, one-hit wonders, and the country guys trying to go rockabilly are all fascinating and frequently fun. It's a great purchase for avid rockabilly and country fans. *— Stephen Thomas Erlewine*

Get Primitive / 1986 / Ubik ✦✦✦✦
The concept here was to offer some of the best tracks from *Pebbles*, the humongous series of '60s garage rock rarities that eventually ran into dozens of volumes. Whether this is the best of the lot is a matter of opinion. The compilers' taste runs toward the rawest and most outrageous items, not necessarily the best. But if you're collecting garage rock anthologies selectively, this is an intelligent investment, featuring such garage favorites as Nobody's Children's "Good Times," the Sparkles' "No Friend of Mine," the Electras' "Action Woman," the Haunted's "1-2-5," and Randy Alvey's infectiously moronic "Green Fuzz." Also worth noting is the original 45 of "Hey Little Bird" by the Barbarians (which wasn't included on their only LP), and the original version of "You're Gonna Miss Me," recorded by the Spades, Roky Erickson's pre-13th Floor Elevators group. *—Richie Unterberger*

Get with the Beat: Mar-Vel' Masters / 1989 / Rykodisc ✦✦✦
Based near Chicago, the Mar-Vel' label recorded lots of regional roots music during the 1950s and early '60s. Although they recorded some R&B and rockabilly, this compilation of 27 cuts by 19 artists—none of whom achieved any national fame whatsoever—leans toward hillbilly, country boogie, and country swing. Though these rarities have their merits, they aren't nearly as good as the classic material by stars mining the same territory. *—Richie Unterberger*

Girl 6 / Mar. 19, 1996 / Warner Bros. ✦✦✦✦
Prince compiled the soundtrack for Spike Lee's phone-sex comedy *Girl 6*, using a handful of new tracks from himself and the New Power Generation, as well as several classic Prince-performed and Prince-produced tracks. If anything, the soundtrack sounds like it was recorded in 1986—nearly every song is about sex and they're all driven by funky keyboards or they're smooth soul ballads. Fortunately, all of Prince's new material comes within shooting distance of standards like "Erotic City," "Adore," and "Girls and Boys," as well as Vanity 6's "Nasty Girl." The New Power Generation tracks fall a little flat in comparison, but *Girl 6* is a fine record, ideal for those pining for Prince's mid-'80s heyday. *— Stephen Thomas Erlewine*

Girl Zone / 1986 / Impact ✦✦
Sixteen tracks in the girl group style (although usually performed by solo singers, not groups), originally released on Decca in the 1960s. Alas, this acts as evidence of how generally inferior British girl group records were to ones being produced across the Atlantic, with occasional exceptions. Much of this is average pop, with decorative flourishes of '60s production the only factors that really distinguish this from pop of any era. Some sparks are kicked up by Beverly (aka Beverly Martyn), Marianne Faithfull's "The Sha La La Song" (one of her better early tracks), and Lulu's smoking cover of Goffin-King's "I Can't Hear You No More," though each of these cuts is available on better compilations. Trainspotter types might want to note the presence of Vashti's "Some Things Just Stick in Your Mind" (one of the least impressive songs that Mick Jagger and Keith Richards donated to other artists), the Orchids' "Mr. Scrooge" (an early Shel Talmy production), and the Vernons Girls' "Only You Can Do It," covered to greater effect by French singer Francoise Hardy. *—Richie Unterberger*

Girls Girls Girls, Vols. 1-14 / Marginal ✦✦✦✦
If you're pretty much done with your bedrock "classic" rock collection and are looking for genres to plumb in greater depth, you should be aware that the girl group style provides a surprisingly deep well of undiscovered recordings. In comparison to, say, rockabilly, doo wop, and garage rock, there have been relatively few reissues of obscure, non-hit early-to-mid-'60s girl group singles. That's beginning to change, with an increasing number of rarity collections. The *Girls Girls Girls* anthologies comprise the most extensive series in this line by far, sort of the *Pebbles* of girl groups—14 volumes' worth by the end of 1995, with more no doubt to come. The focus is not on girl groups per se, but early to mid-'60s female performers who sang in the style; in fact, most of the tracks are by solo female singers, not actual groups. Now, you've got to be pretty committed to go for a complete set of these, as they sell at import prices. If you do want to take the plunge, you won't be disappointed as to the quantity—each volume has 20 tracks (the earliest have 25), meaning that if you get every installment so far, you'll have about 300 rarities. Quality is a different story—like many garage and rockabilly compilations, it's erratic, mixing gems with the routine and humdrum. There *are* some gems, though, which very few people have heard, by the likes of Barbara Dane, Vicki Salee, Ann Cole, Patty Walsh, and Nancy Adams. What is most astonishing, aside from the sheer quantity of material

unearthed, is the considerable range the series encompasses. Extremely Catholic in their tastes, the compilers include just about every permutation of the classic girl group/early '60s female-sung pop-rock sound imaginable: quasi-Spector productions, dippy white teen idols, supper-club ballads, novelties, hard R&B, smoldering near-blues, Motown imitations, New Orleans R&B, Italian and British girl singers, TV/movie celebrities, and early soul. Most of the performers are no-names, but there are also some choice rarities by stars like Mary Wells, Carole King, and Betty Everett, as well as flops by one-hit wonders like Diane Renay, Peggy March, and Dodie Stevens. Which volumes you like the best, and even which tracks strike your fancy, depends on your very individual or idiosyncratic tastes—no one's going to like every cut on any given volume, but the amazing variety is also going to keep most girl group fans from being bored for too long. Oddly, the later volumes seem to feature better material than the first ones; it usually works in exactly the reverse for these sorts of series. Unfortunately, there are no liner notes, though the sound (probably remastered from vinyl copies) is usually pretty good. *—Richie Unterberger*

Girls in the Garage, Vols. 1-7 / Romulan ✦✦✦
Even more than most rock 'n' roll styles, garage rock is thought of as a primarily male terrain, especially given the macho posturing adopted by most of its proponents. *Girls In The Garage* proves that there were also quite a few female groups mining similar territory in the mid-'60s. The compilers have gone far and wide to assemble dozens of doggoned rare singles to fill out these anthologies, and if they don't exactly place among the very top rank of the hundreds of '60s garage rock collections, there's a fair amount of rare stuff to be found here. There simply weren't a lot of females with guitars forming their own groups in the '60s, and so a lot of this material isn't "garage" in the classic sense; a fair amount is raw girl group-style stuff, novelties, or classic garage bands that happened to feature a female singer. Which isn't a drawback, as the collections have more variety than you'll find on your average garage comp. Good liner notes too, although Romulan seems to have resorted to filling out the volumes with some unmemorable, even inept tracks due to the scarcity of source material to choose from. *—Richie Unterberger*

Girls with Guitars / 1989 / Impact ✦✦
Despite what the title might imply, this is not a compilation of self-contained female rock groups (which were a real rarity in the 1960s). It's a selection of 16 of the gutsier mid-'60s British tracks that were sung by UK women, usually in a girl-group type style. It's a good concept for a reissue compilation. The problem was that there isn't a great depth of material to choose from in this arena, most British girl group records being rather timid copies of the American prototypes. Certainly many of the songs here are energetically performed, but the material just isn't very arresting. Goldie & the Gingerbreads (actually an American group based in Britain) were one of the few all-woman bands from the era that played their own instruments, but the two cuts on offer here aren't that special. Lulu, as is often the case on British '60s female rock compilations, takes the honors with her soulful "I'll Come Running Over." A more unlikely highlight is the Vernons Girls' zany update of Bizet-Hammerstein's "Dat's Love." *—Richie Unterberger*

Give Your Body Up: Club Classics & House Foundations / 1996 / Rhino ✦✦✦✦
Rhino's three-volume series *Give Your Body Up: Club Classics & House Foundations* is an excellent overview of the frequently underappreciated dance singles that were made in the years immediately following disco. These records found producers stretching out the disco beat, making it funkier, moving it toward the house music that would dominate late '80s club music. Most of the music on these three discs (available separately) is unknown to most listeners, yet these pioneered techniques that would later become familiar in dance-pop, house and acid house. *—Stephen Thomas Erlewine*

Go Girl! Soul Sisters Tellin' It Like It Is / 1996 / Rhino ✦✦✦✦
The concept here is made plain in the title: tough female soul singers, singing about the hard bumps of romance with toughness and independence. If that's what you want, there's plenty of straight talking here. If you're primarily after good late-'60s/early-'70s soul, it delivers that as well. Aside from Aretha Franklin's "Respect," none of these were big pop hits; many of them didn't even make a splash in the R&B world. It's a good mix of lesser-known tracks by Ann Peebles, Irma Thomas, Betty Wright, and Mable John with ones by singers who are hardly known at all outside of soul aficionados, like Janice Tyrone, Priscilla Price, Jeane & the Darlings, and James Brown protege Lyn Collins. It also has the Velvettes' "Needle in a Haystack," one of the least frequently anthologized mid-'60s Motown singles. *—Richie Unterberger*

Golden Age of American Rock 'n' Roll Vol. 1/ 1991 / Ace (UK) ✦✦✦✦✦
For many years, Original Sound's *Oldies But Goodies* series was acknowledged as the best source for catching up on the many great early rock 'n' roll hits by artists who had only one (or two, or three, or even a few more) classics to offer. Ace's *Golden Age of American Rock 'n'*

Roll series, however, has surpassed *Oldies But Goodies* as the series of choice in the CD age. Even at an import price, they offer better value (with 30 songs each!); they use the best possible available source tapes for remastering; they also offer lengthy, intelligent liner notes and some photos, where Original Sound have historically offered none. Most important, they offer a wealth of great hits from rock 'n' roll's first decade as a widespread phenomenon (1954-63), some of which are very difficult to find on other recordings, CD or not. There are some huge hits represented, but an equal amount of attention is paid to lower-charting items that have fallen out of rotation at oldies stations, as well as some slight/regional hits that you might not have heard even if you grew up during the era. Volume One, like each installment, reflects the incredible diversity and excitement of rock's first decade: doo wop, primitive rockabilly, girl groups, instrumental rock, proto-soul, pop-rock, and more, ranging from famous one-shots (the Jaynetts' "Sally Go Round the Roses," the Penguins' "Earth Angel") to semi-forgotten treasures like the Fendermen's "Mule Skinner Blues" and Toni Fisher's "The Big Hurt." —*Richie Unterberger*

The Golden Age of American Rock'n'roll, Vol. 2 / 1993 / Ace ✦✦✦✦✦
No volume of the *Golden Age of American Rock 'n' Roll* series is more essential than any other one. As all have a good range of styles, and a mix of big and small hits, none is particularly recommended more than others; all are worth acquiring if you want to build a serious rock 'n' roll collection. Volume Two has plenty of classics (the Silhouettes' "Get a Job," Maurice Williams' "Stay," Lonnie Mack's "Memphis," the Rivieras' "California Sun," Link Wray's "Rumble") to go along with some neat one-shots (the Bell-Notes' "I've Had It," Barbara George's "I Know," Harold Dorman's "Mountain of Love"). Just as interesting are the minor hits, like the Eternals' ridiculous "Rockin' in the Jungle" (uptempo doo wop with side-splitting bird calls) and the Gladiolas' original version of "Little Darlin'" (covered with much bigger success by the Diamonds). —*Richie Unterberger*

The Golden Age of American Rock'n'roll, Vol. 3 / 1994 / Ace ✦✦✦✦✦
More good, classic stuff. Everyone will have different favorites according to their tastes, which is an advantage of having such a diverse collection on CD—you can skip around as you like. The roll call here includes many classic one-shots, by Wilbert Harrison ("Kansas City"), Bill Parsons ("The All American Boy," sung by Bobby Bare, although Parsons got the label credit), the Teddy Bears ("To Know Him Is to Love Him," Phil Spector's first classic), the Turbans ("When You Dance"), Skip & Flip ("It Was I"), the Olympics ("Western Movies"), and the Castells ("Sacred"). —*Richie Unterberger*

The Golden Age of American Rock'n'roll, Vol. 4 / 1994 / Ace ✦✦✦✦✦
Another reliably well-packaged collection of major and minor pre-Beatle rock hits. Besides the hits by stars like Dion, Gary US Bonds, Jan & Dean, and Buddy Knox, you have plenty of one-shots by the likes of the Edsels ("Rama Lama Ding Dong"), Little Caesar & the Romans ("Those Oldies But Goodies"), Barbara Lynn ("You'll Lose a Good Thing"), and Ray Sharpe (the classic R&B/jump rocker "Linda Lu"). The further the series goes, the deeper it gets into the lower rungs of the charts, so even rock scholars may not have previously heard cuts by the likes of Nat Kendrick, Nappy Brown, or the Royaltones. Others you may have only heard once or twice, like the ones by Tommy Facenda, the Rip Chords, and Billy & Lillie. —*Richie Unterberger*

The Golden Age of American Rock'n'roll, Vol. 5 / 1995 / Ace ✦✦✦✦✦
It's been said before, but it bears repeating: much of the history (and soul) of early rock 'n' roll resides not only in the recordings of giants like Elvis, Little Richard, Chuck Berry, and Buddy Holly, but in the literally hundreds of acts who managed to produce one or two great singles, in an incredible variety of styles. You can't claim to have a comprehensive rock 'n' roll collection without seeking these out, and you'll have a surprising amount of fun doing so. The fifth volume of the *Golden Age of American Rock'n'Roll* series shows no signs of flagging in its mission to document these important sounds. Big hits by stars (Freddie Cannon, Jan & Dean, Gene Chandler); huge one-shot hits like Dale & Grace's "I'm Leaving It Up to You," Johnnie & Joe's "Over the Mountain, Across the Sea," and Jimmy McCracklin's "The Walk"; treasured cult classics by the Showmen ("It Will Stand") and Eddie Fontaine ("Nothin' Shakin'," covered by the Beatles on *Live at the BBC*); all are here, and more. —*Richie Unterberger*

Golden Age of American Rock'n'roll, Vol. 6 / 1997 / Ace ✦✦✦✦
As this series progresses, there's a higher proportion of obscure material involved. This is both good and bad: it's good to find worthy minor hits that have largely missed the CD revolution, but some of them didn't make it above the 80s on the charts for good reason. Nonetheless, there are some real oodies here, whether hard to find or not: the Del-Vikings' "Come Go with Me," Bobby Freeman's "Do You Want to Dance," the El Dorados' "At My Front Door," the Rivingtons' "Papa-Oom-Mow-Mow," and Joe Bennett's "Black Slacks." Among the rarities, the most interesting items are John Fred's "Shirley" (recorded almost ten years before "Judy in Disguise"), Ronald & Ruby's original version of "Lolli-

pop" (surpassed commercially by the Chordettes' rendition), the Quotations' "Imagination" (top-flight doo wop), and Bunker Hill's "Hide and Go Seek" (described in the liners as "like a gospel holler in a squash court"). Pick find: the Pentagons' "I Wonder," which sounds like a great lost Drifters hit from the early '60s. —*Richie Unterberger*

Golden Groups / 1993 / Specialty ✦✦✦✦
Originally compiled and issued on Relic Records as part of their superlative label-by-label Golden Groups series, this boasts the addition of eight bonus tracks and improved remastering quality. Featuring such wild West Coast gems as the Pentagons' "Silly Dilly" and Tony Allen's "Night Owl," not to mention early recordings by Clydie King and Darlene Love (as part of her first group, the Echoes), this makes a wonderful companion volume to *Hardcore Doo Wop: In the Hallway—Under the Streetlamp.* —*Cub Koda*

Got a Good Thing Going / 1996 / Sequel ✦✦✦✦
Subtitled "25 R&B Radio Hits of the 60s," Billy Vera compiled this with the intention of giving listeners some prime soul singles that weren't huge hits, but also not selected simply on the basis of obscurity. Besides J.J. Jackson's "But It's All Right" and Freddie Scott's "Hey Girl," however, you'd be hard-pressed to recognize any of these, unless you listened to soul stations all the time in the '60s. The attention to quality over rarity, however, has resulted in the one of the finest anthologies of semi-obscure and very obscure '60s soul that you're likely to come across, with lots of diversity, ranging from gospel-tinged shouters to uptown New York productions to exquisite ballads. Almost all of this is very good, and some of it's a lot better than that—the original version of "You're No Good" by Dee Dee Warwick (covered by Betty Everett in the '60s and Linda Ronstadt in the '70s) is a stunner. Little Buster has a fine Sam Cooke soundalike, Jimmy Ricks has a deep croon that sounds like a 45 playing at 33 RPM, Mary Wells offers an overlooked bluesy cut from the late '60s, and Valerie Simpson and Nick Ashford are heard on a rare 1965 single attributed simply to Valerie and Nick. And the mysterious Mighty Hannibal's "Hymn No. 5" is a must-hear for any '60s soul/rock fan, its creepy gospel/soul moan offering one of the best understated protests against the Vietnam War ever recorded. —*Richie Unterberger*

Grace of My Heart / Sep. 1996 / MCA ✦✦✦✦
Alison Anders' film *Grace of My Heart* told the story of a female songwriter whose career closely resembled that of Carole King's. The film followed her as she worked her way through the Brill Building, before going out west to fall in love with a tortured leader of a surf-rock band (a thinly-veiled Brian Wilson and the Beach Boys), before she established herself as a solo artist with an album that recalled *Tapestry*. In order to make the film work, Anders need a collection of new songs that not only recalled classic '60s pop, but also were convincing as hit singles. She assembled an astonishing roster of professional songwriters—including Burt Bacharach, Gerry Goffin, Elvis Costello, David Baerwald, and J. Mascis—that managed to fulfill her goal. The majority of *Grace of My Heart* is astonishing, capturing the feel and sound of classic '60s pop from Phil Spector to the Beach Boys. Occasionally, the lyrics are a little too knowing ("Unwanted Number"), but the songs themselves are wonderful, particularly the Leslie Gore knockoff "My Secret Love" (which was co-written by Gore and sung by Combustible Edison's Elaine Dane), Costello and Bacharach's collaboration "God Give Me Strength" and J. Mascis' bright "Take A Run At the Sun." It's a surprisingly successful and fresh collection, one of the rare soundtracks that is a cohesive as the film itself. And, even more importantly, it's filled with songs that sound like forgotten classics. —*Stephen Thomas Erlewine*

Grandson of Frat Rock / 1991 / Rhino ✦✦✦✦✦
Rhino's *Frat Rock* series is an excellent overview of '60s rock 'n' roll and R&B party anthems like the Kingsmen's "Louie Louie," "Double Shot of My Baby's Love" (Swinging Medallions), "La La La La La" (Blendells), "Shout" (Isley Brothers), "Do You Love Me?" (the Contours), and "Mony Mony" (Tommy James & the Shondells). —*John Floyd*

Growin' up Too Fast: The Girl Group Anthology / 1996 / Mercury ✦✦✦
A two-CD, 50-song collection of girl group hits and misses originally released on the MGM, Smash, Philips, Fontana, 20th Century Fox, and Mercury labels in the early and mid-'60s. It's nice to have some of these rarities easily available in state-of-the-art fidelity, but it's not one of the best girl group compilations around, in terms of either thematic coherence or consistent quality. The hits by the Shangri-Las, Lesley Gore, Dusty Springfield, the Angels, and the Royalettes are good to great, but are better heard in the context of their own compilations. Much of the rest—by obscure singers like Ginny Arnell, the Pixies Three, and Beverly Washburn—is pleasant but rather forgettable. There are some really neat one-shots and lost classics here, though, like Diane Renay's Top Ten hit, "Navy Blue," and her flop follow-up, "Watch Out, Sally!," is one of the toughest white girl group records ever. Also cool are the Secrets' "The Boy Next Door" (an Angels soundalike) and the two songs by Sadina,

which are among the best unknown wall-of-sound-type productions ever. —*Richie Unterberger*

Gulf Coast Grease: The Sandy Story, Vol. 1 / 1996 / Ace ♦♦♦
Based in Mobile, Alabama, the independent Sandy label recorded a bunch of rockabilly/early rock sides in the late '50s, though none of the acts on this 24-song compilation had anything close to a national smash. It's solid, often crudely recorded (in the positive sense of that description) material, perhaps with more of a honky-tonk/swamp flavor than the average rockabilly collection. The highlight may be Jackie Morningstar's "Rockin' in the Graveyard," one of the better overlooked early rock 'n' horror novelties. Ray Sawyer, later to lead Dr. Hook, appears here under his own name on a couple of respectably rockin' early-'60s singles. —*Richie Unterberger*

Gumbo Stew / 1993 / Ace ♦♦♦
In the early 1960s, arranger and multi-instrumentalist Harold Battiste (who had done some A&R for Specialty) formed the New Orleans-based AFO label with the intention of giving local artists a fairer deal via a Black-owned company. Only one true hit resulted, Barbara George's "I Know" (included here), but some solid New Orleans R&B was recorded during its brief time in operation. This is the first of three compilations of AFO material, including a couple of obscure performances by the young Dr. John, sides by second-tier Crescent City artists like Eddie Bo and Alvin Robinson, and several names known only to record collectors. Most of it's from the early '60s, although a few from the late '60s (when Battiste was a successful arranger on the West Coast) also sneak in. This disc isn't up to the level of the classics you'll find on the best vintage New Orleans R&B anthologies, but if you're the kind who plans your vacations around New Orleans music festivals, you won't be disappointed by what's on offer here. —*Richie Unterberger*

Hairspray / 1988 / MCA ♦♦♦♦
John Waters' films may not be to everyone's taste, but give him credit: when it comes to assembling a soundtrack, he uses a lot more imagination than most directors. Set in the early '60s, *Hairspray* has a few hits from the era (Gene Pitney's "Town Without Pity," Barbara Lynn's "You'll Lose a Good Thing," Jan Bradley's "Mama Didn't Lie"). But it's mostly given over to dance/R&B tunes that don't get played on the radio anymore, like the Flares' "Foot Stompin'," the Five Du-Tones' "Shake a Tail Feather," and a couple of the most ridiculous dance tunes ever waxed (Gene and Wendell's "The Roach," Jerry Dallman's "The Bug"). Also included is Toussaint McCall's soulful ballad "Nothing Takes the Place of You," and Little Peggy March's pricelessly silly "I Wish I Were a Princess." Ray Bryant Combo's "The Madison Time" and Rachel Sweet's performance of the movie's theme are a bit incongruous in this company, but as these are the first two tracks on the album, those who are treating this as an oldies collection can easily avoid them. —*Richie Unterberger*

Hardcore Doo-Wop: In the Hallway-Under the Street Lamp / 1993 / Specialty ♦♦♦♦♦
This compact disc collects 25 doo wop collector's classics from a variety of small West Coast R&B labels which dabbled in the genre. The California version of the streetcorner vocal group phenomena had stronger leanings toward bluesier harmonies and vocal performances bordering on madness. As best exemplified here by groups like Arthur Lee Maye & the Crowns and Byron "Slick" Gipson & the Sliders, the West Coast doo wop movement definitely had a sound all its own. —*Cub Koda*

Harlem Shuffle: '60s Soul Classics / Charly ♦♦♦♦
A perfect selection (and disc order) of lesser-known but essential soul hits, including the Barbara Lewis hits "Hello Stranger," "Make Me Your Baby," and "Baby I'm Yours," plus "Oogum Boogum Song" and "Gimme Little Sign" by Brenton Wood, and "Get on up and Get Away" by the Esquires. 21 classic sides in all, every one a delight. An import but worth the trouble to find. —*Michael Erlewine*

Have a Nice Day, Super Hits of the '70s / 1990 / Rhino ♦♦♦♦
Mainstream pop began catching up with the innovations of the late '60s sometime in the early '70s, incorporating watered-downed versions of psychedelia, soul, prog-rock, country-rock and folk-rock. The result was well-produced and crafted schlock that gleefully corrupted the counter-culture values. Along with that schlock was pure trash that ranged from bubblegum epics like "The Night Chicago Died" and "I Think I Love You" to soft-rock ("Precious and Few"), Jesus-rock ("One Toke Over the Line," "Spirit in the Sky"), hard-rock ("Mississippi Queen") and songs like "Gimme Dat Thing" that are simply uncategorizable. What they all had in common was their utter lack of seriousness and big, catchy hooks, which made them perfect singles for AM Radio. Rhino's multi-volume various-artists set *Have a Nice Day: Super Hits of the '70s* (available as individual discs) is an exhaustive overview of such hit singles, containing 12 tracks on each disc. There are some outright dogs on some of these discs, to be sure, but it's remarkable how entertaining the entire series is. Initially, the label intended to only compile 10 or 15 collections, taking the set into the mid-'70s, but *Have a Nice Day* proved so successful that it ran a full 25 volumes and extended right until 1979. Consequently, there's a lot of variety here, and every volume may not be

entertaining to all listeners, especially since Rhino predictably leans a little too heavily on novelties. Still, it's a terrific series to pick and choose from, and each disc has several "classics," as well as several fun obscurities, and it's impossible to imagine a better, more thorough chronicle of this era than *Have a Nice Day*. —*Stephen Thomas Erlewine*

Headz II—Part A / Nov. 1996 / Mo' Wax [UK] ♦♦♦♦
The first of two separately released double-disc sets which document the history of British trip-hop, *Headz II—Part A* includes Mo' Wax stalwarts—DJ Krush, U.N.K.L.E., Solo, RPM—with contributions from artists not directly linked to trip-hop, such as Tortoise, the Beastie Boys, Stereo MCs and Folk Implosion. Other big names include DJ Food (aka Coldcut, PC & Strictly Kev), Massive Attack, Nightmares on Wax, and jungle hero Peshay, who contributes a downtempo rendition of his jungle track, "The Real Thing." —*John Bush*

The Heart of Southern Soul, Vol. 2 / 1996 / Ace ♦♦♦
Stax and Hi weren't the final words in deep Southern soul in the late 1960s; Excello also recorded some solid efforts in the vein. This 24-track compilation accumulates material that appeared on the label and its offshoots from the mid-'60s to the mid-'70s (concentrating on the late '60s) that's only known to serious soul hounds. The Wallace Brothers, Kip Anderson, and Mava Whitney are the most well-known names, to give you an idea of the level of specialization we're talking about here. A lot of this has the churchy, bluesy feel you expect from prime Southern soul, though little if any is truly among the classic cream of the genre. Certainly the swamp blues duet of Dee and Don and the gospel harmonies of the Wallace Brothers are worth hearing by listeners who want to build a large soul collection. Inspirational lyric (from Jerry Washington's "Right Here is Where You Belong"): "He told me I have something worse than cancer. He told me what I have was a very, very bad case of the blues!" —*Richie Unterberger*

Hellbound Hot Rods! / 1995 / Del Fi ♦♦♦
Taken from a bunch of quickie hot rod instrumental LPs that appeared on Del-Fi in the early '60s, there's actually some pretty hot picking to be found on these sides by the Deuce Coupes, De Fenders, and Darts. And there's some historical interest attached to these tracks as well, though the principals may have all but forgotten these skeletons from their closets. The Deuce Coupes feature the guitars of Pat and Lolly Vegas, who would found Redbone in the 1970s; the De Fenders spotlight session guitarist Tommy Tedesco, one of the top L.A. players of the time (who appears on discs by Phil Spector, the Beach Boys, Jan & Dean, and others). Even more surprising is the discovery that the guitarist on the tracks credited to the Darts is none other than Glen Campbell; his whiplash-snappy, concise solos on "Top Eliminator" forever enshrine his rock 'n' roll credentials, whatever you might think of "Gentle on My Mind." The compilation is rounded out by cuts from the Roadstars, the Venturas (Western movie theme-influenced surf), and Opus 1's strange "Back Seat 38 Dodge," where hot rod music meets psychedelia. The disc isn't at the top of the pile for surf and hot rod instrumentals, but if you just want a typically roaring good blast of the genre, it frequently delivers the goods. —*Richie Unterberger*

Here Come the Girls: British Girl Singers of the '60s, Vol. 1 / 1990 / Sequel ♦♦♦♦
The British girl group scene wasn't nearly as vital as the American one, but there were still quite a few fun recordings produced in the style during the mid-'60s. This compilation is a good overview of lesser-known highlights of a sub-genre that is nearly unknown in the US. The emphasis is not on groups, but solo singers in the girl group style; Petula Clark was the only one of these 24 performers to reach stardom Stateside, and only a couple of others (Sandie Shaw, the Honeycombs) became even moderately well-known. In fact, most of these singles flopped in the UK as well. There's still a good amount of sass and sub-New York soul/pop-rock production to be found in the tracks by the Breakaways, Antoinette, Val McKenna, and others. Notable highlights include Sarah Jane's "Listen People" (a ringer for Marianne Faithfull's mid-'60s sound) and Julie Grant's splendidly sultry, operatic "Come to Me." —*Richie Unterberger*

Here Come the Girls, Vol. 6 / 1995 / Sequel ♦♦♦
Twenty-four female-sung British pop-rock singles from 1961-74, some in the girl-group style, some not; originally released on the Pye label, the bulk of them date from the mid-'60s. Not a single one was a big hit, and Petula Clark is the only name that will be familiar to American listeners, although Glenda Collins, Dana Gillespie and Jackie Trent may ring some bells among collectors. This is period British mainstream pop; if you like that style, which is heavy on perky melodies and orchestral arrangements, this is a mid-level journey through some typical material of the genre. If you're being selective about your imports, there aren't any lost gems here, though some of the tunes (by Donna Douglas, the Breakaways and Shirley Abicair) are a bit above average. —*Richie Unterberger*

Hi Times: Hi Records R&B Years [box] / Feb. 21, 1995 / Capitol ♦♦♦♦
Hi Times: Hi Records R&B Years is a superb three-disc box set covering

all of the label's greatest hits, plus a number of forgotten gems. Al Green understandably dominates the set, since he not only was Hi's biggest artist, but also defined the label's sound with his producer Willie Mitchell. As a result, the music on these three discs can sound a little similar at times, but the songwriting and performances from the likes of Green, Ann Peebles and Joe Clay is first-rate, making *Hi Times* a necessary addition to any serious soul collection. —*Stephen Thomas Erlewine*

Highs in the Mid-'60s, Vols. 1-23 / AIP ✦✦✦
A spinoff of the *Pebbles* series, *Highs in the Mid-'60s* assembles yet more rare garage rock recordings, the difference being that each volume focuses upon a city or region such as Los Angeles, Texas, or Michigan. This does provide a public service of sorts by assembling and reissuing hordes of rare singles that would be impossible for any one individual to acquire on his or her own. It must be pointed out, though, that *Pebbles* itself plundered a lot of the prime garage material, and the quality on these supplementary volumes is very patchy. This shouldn't come as that much of a surprise when they include entire LPs devoted to mid-'60s garage-rock recordings from Colorado, two volumes to Wisconsin, or several volumes to L.A.; there just wasn't an infinite supply of great regional bands to go around, and much of the material is annoyingly generic if taken at once, starting to melt into one big sneer and fuzz riff. As is usually the case in these series, the earlier volumes tend to be better. —*Richie Unterberger*

Hip Hop Greats: Classic Raps / Rhino ✦✦✦✦✦
Although it's far from perfect, the 10-track *Hip Hop Greats: Classic Raps* offers a good overview of the first national rap hits. Since it contains the majority of hip-hop's early classics—Sugarhill Gang's "Rapper's Delight," UTFO's "Roxanne, Roxanne," Kurtis Blow's "The Breaks," Run-D.M.C.'s "It's Like That," and both "White Lines (Don't Don't Do It)" and "The Message" from Grandmaster Flash—it's an excellent primer and introduction, even though it's a bit too brief to be a definitive overview. —*Stephen Thomas Erlewine*

History of Cadence Records, Vols. 1-2 / Mar. 26, 1996 / Varese Sarabande ✦✦✦
Cadence was a significant independent label in the 1950s and early '60s, recording hits by the Everly Brothers, Andy Williams, Chordettes, Lenny Welch, and various teen idols and pop vocalists. Putting all of them together on the same retrospective, however, isn't a good idea, unless you're going to concentrate on just the rock, or just the pop vocals. These two collections have plenty of hits by the aforementioned names, as well as one-shots by the likes of Link Wray ("Rumble"). But there's no thematic coherence, other than the fact that they happened to be issued on the same imprint—why you would want to hear the Everlys' classic "(Til) I Kissed You" right after Bill Hayes' corny novelty "The Ballad of Davy Crockett," for instance, is anyone's guess. *Vol. 2* has a good, interesting rare 1961 single by Charlie McCoy (who became one of Nashville's top session musicians), but on the whole you're much better off pursuing compilations of the individual artists represented here than getting these mish-mash samplers. —*Richie Unterberger*

History of Dot Records, Vol. 1: Young Love / Jun. 1996 / Varese Sarabande ✦✦
A couple of nifty rock one-shots (the Hawaiian rockabilly of Robin Luke's 'Susie Darlin',' the lush girl group sound of Robin Ward's "Wonderful Summer") intrude on what's generally a grab bag of easy listening pop hits from the '50s and '60s that happened to come out on the Dot label. Gale Storm, the Fontane Sisters, the Hilltoppers, Pat Boone, Billy Vaughn, and Debbie Reynolds are represented by big and small hits, as are smaller names like Bonnie Guitar. There are also minor chart singles recorded by Jimmie Rodgers and the Mills Brothers way after their commercial primes. Dale Ward's vapid 1963 teen idol hit "Letter From Sherry" doesn't fit in at all. This disc isn't bad if you have a taste for vintage easy listening, but the compilation is so scattershot stylistically that it's hard to see exactly where its audience lies. —*Richie Unterberger*

History of Dot Records, Vol. 2: Come Go with Me / Jun. 1996 / Varese Sarabande ✦✦✦
Much more stylistically consistent than volume one, in that at least this is all rock 'n' roll (or, in Pat Boone and Tab Hunter's cases, teen idol fare that bordered on rock 'n' roll). It's an average collection of oldies from the late '50s and early '60s, unconnected by anything other than the fact that they were released by Dot. There are some classics (the Dell-Vikings' "Come Go with Me", Arthur Alexander's "Anna"), some novelties (Dodie Stevens' "Pink Shoelaces"), some good one-shots (Sanford Clark's early rockabilly hit "The Fool," Travis and Bob's Everlys soundalike "Tell Him No," the Shields' doo wop classic "You Cheated"), and some minor hits (by Carol Jarvis, Nick Todd, and Ronnie Love) that never get played on the radio anymore. As oldies collections go, it's not eye-catching unless you've been trying hard to track down some of the rare cuts on CD. —*Richie Unterberger*

Hitsville USA: The Motown Singles Collection 1959-1971 / 1992 / Motown ✦✦✦✦✦
Instead of following Stax/Volt's pattern and delivering an exhaustive box set containing all of their singles, Motown decided to limit their singles box, *Hitsville USA; The Motown Singles Collection 1959-1971*, to four discs that concentrated on the hits. There are a handful of wonderful lesser-known songs here, such as the Contours' "First I Look at the Purse," but the main strength of the 103-track box is how it features all of the biggest songs from Motown's golden era in one place. Collectors could have used a more comprehensive set, and the box itself could have been packaged with a little more care (there are no artists listed on the back of the individual discs, only songs), but *Hitsville USA* stands as a definitive overview and introduction to one of the most groundbreaking labels in pop music history. —*Stephen Thomas Erlewine*

Hitsville USA, Vol. 2: The Motown Singles Collection (1972-1992) / Oct. 19, 1993 / Motown ✦✦✦
Hitsville USA was such a success that it was little wonder that Motown decided to issue the sequel, *Hitsville USA, Vol. 2: The Motown Singles Collection (1972-1992)*. Certainly, these four discs couldn't help but suffer in comparison to their predecessor—the first volume contained some of the greatest pop singles in history—since Motown was following trends during these 20 years instead of setting them. Nevertheless, there are a surprising number of classic singles here, from "Papa Was A Rolling Stone," "Let's Get It On" and "Dancing Machine" to "Easy," "Brick House" and "Super Freak." Unfortunately, there are too many mediocre songs on this set to make searching for these gems a pleasurable experience. If the compilers had limited themselves to a two-disc set, they would have been able to fit all the highlights on a consistent, listenable collection. As it stands, *Hitsville USA, Vol. 2* simply contains too much middling music to make it useful for anyone but dedicated Motown fans. —*Stephen Thomas Erlewine*

Hollywood Rock & Roll / 1989 / Ace (UK) ✦✦✦
Twelve rare rockabilly tracks from the vaults of Era Records, a minor Hollywood-based label. None of these records (all cut in the late '50s, with the exception of Dorsey Burnette's 1961 effort) came close to being any sort of hits. There wasn't anything particularly special or awful about them, either. Like so much minor-league rockabilly, it's high in energy and not particularly rich in any other department, making for a pleasant and forgettable genre exercise (and a brief one as well, clocking in at a mere 26 minutes). Glen Glenn has half the cuts, and (aside from Burnette) is probably the only vaguely recognizable name. The highlights, though, are actually delivered by Alix Leslie (one of the relatively few Elvis-inspired female singers) and Dick Bush (later to find brief teen idol success as Donnie Brooks), whose self-penned "Hollywood Party" almost sounds like a rockabilly parody with its infectiously inept, gravel-voiced mania. —*Richie Unterberger*

Hot Rod City / 1963 / Sundazed ✦✦
The story behind this 1963 hot rod compilation-exploitation album is rather complicated. Issued at the height of the craze, Vault Records (most famous as the home of the Challengers) wanted to get something on the racks post-haste. Gary Usher was enlisted as co-producer, working with Challengers drummer Richard Delvy. The Challengers played on much of the album, but to foster the illusion that this was a compilation, the tracks were attributed to various bands (the Challengers, the Grand Prix, the Quads, and the Customs). Usher also helped write many of the tunes, all of which had something to do with cars, or racing cars. It's not really worth debating whether (as some have claimed, ridiculously) this is one of rock's first "concept" albums. It's slight, hastily conceived, generic hot rod music, laps behind the Beach Boys and Jan & Dean's efforts in the field, of interest only to hard-core fans and collectors of the style. The CD reissue adds rare bonus tracks of previously unissued cuts, a B-side, and alternate takes, which is really treating this relic with more respect than it deserves. Brian Wilson obsessives may want to be aware of one of those previously unissued tracks, "Ride with Me," which Wilson co-wrote with Roger Christian. —*Richie Unterberger*

How Was the Air up There? / K-Tel ✦✦✦
Compilations of '60s New Zealand rock are still pretty thin on the ground. Back when this came out (it certainly predates the early '80s), it was one of the very few, if not the only one, available. Admittedly there wasn't a huge population pool to draw from, but still, this 22-track compilation is pretty derivative and unimpressive, with too high a percentage of faithful cover versions of American and British hits. Some first-rate cuts break through the sludge: Ray Columbus' "She's a Mod" is a fine early Beatle knockoff, Chants R&B's cover of John Mayall's "I'm a Witchdoctor" is fairly tough, the La De Da's "How Is the Air Up There?" sounds like a good lost Standells single, and Fourmyula's "Nature" is beguiling late-'60s pop-folk-rock. The liner notes are detailed and excellent, but the music's not that durable, making it primarily of historical value. —*Richie Unterberger*

The Hush Records Story / 1997 / Ace ✦✦

Hush, a tiny California label, had one of the biggest one-shot garage hits of the 1960s, the Syndicate of Sound's "Little Girl." Hush didn't only do rock groups—they cut some early sides by soul singer Joe Simon, for instance. But this 24-track compilation concentrates exclusively on garageish bands that the company recorded in the mid-to-late '60s. There wasn't much in the way of a "Hush" sound—this is just average, or sometimes below average, '60s California rock from a variety of young groups, all of it (except "Little Girl") rare, some of it previously unreleased. By far the best of the lot are the Brogues, who included future Quicksilver Messenger Service members Gary Duncan and Greg Elmore. All four of the songs they released (and one alternate take) are here, including an Animals-ish garage classic, "I Ain't No Miracle Worker" (covered by the Chocolate Watch Band), although the Brogues' version has already surfaced on numerous other reissues. Besides that, there's a slew of cuts by the Syndicate of Sound, and some by Wm Penn & the Quakers, the Diminished Fifth, and other unknowns, most in a raw pop-garage vein, none of them especially interesting. —*Richie Unterberger*

I Live for the Sun / 1986 / EMI America ✦✦✦

Patchy compilation of early and mid-'60s surf music from the EMI catalog. The cuts by Jan & Dean and the Beach Boys are great, but hardly obscure, and a lot of the rest is so-so, the instrumental cuts towering over the cheesy vocal numbers. Two fine tunes, though, that are rarely reissued: the Sunrays, a deliberate Beach Boys clone managed by the Wilsons' father Murry, had a hit with their infectious harmonies on "I Live For The Sun," and the Ventures' "The Cruel Sea" is starkly and magnificently powerful. What's most interesting is how many of these acts featured musicians and producers that would play a role in interesting mid- and late-'60s California rock recordings, including Gary Usher, P.F. Sloan, Richie Polodor, and future Blue Cheer guitarist Randy Holden. —*Richie Unterberger*

If You're Ready! the Best of Dunwich Records, Vol. 2 / 1994 / Sundazed ✦✦✦✦

This second volume investigating the history of Chicago's best—and most influential—teen band label of the mid-'60s comes up with 28 tracks of classic Windy City garage band genius with more emphasis on rarities and unissued material than its initial volume, *Oh Yeah!* Dunwich was a small concern, run by three jazz heads, who nonetheless managed to tap into Chicago's fertile teen scene of the mid-'60s and get the very best groups down on tape at the city's best studio, Universal. Although "Gloria" by the Shadows of Knight was their only major national hit, they were one of the few labels that steadily catered to this kind of teenage racket; the quality of their releases was very high and many of them have reached legendary status. The Pride and Joy (actually the Del-Vetts) kick things off with the title track and rare Dunwich 45s from the Shadows of Knight ("I'm Gonna Make You Mine," which starts out with a four-chord guitar blast dripping with reverb, distortion and rock 'n' roll), Things to Come, the Luv'd Ones, Saturday's Children ("You Don't Know Better"), the Rovin' Kind (great covers of "Girl" and John Sebastian's "Didn't Want to Have to Do It") and the Wanderin' Kind all keeping the disc stuck in high gear. Seven of the tracks here are previously unissued masters, and these, along with radio spots by H.P. Lovecraft and the American Breed—one of them for Ban deodorant!—and a rare alternate session take of the Shadows of Knight creaming "I Got My Mojo Working" (originally released on a vinyl album of Dunwich outtakes in the '70s called *Early Chicago*) make this fine collection a worthwhile addition to anyone's '60s garage band collection. This one literally screams of teen clubs, Rickenbacker guitars, and fake IDs. —*Cub Koda*

In Yo' Face! (The History of Funk), Vol. 1 / 1993 / Rhino ✦✦✦✦

Funk fans eagerly anticipated Rhino's five-part series, thinking that they would get something equivalent to the label's wonderful 1970s soul line. While the final results are good, things are not quite as rosy as earlier reports indicated. The most disappointing thing was the decision to settle for single versions of tracks rather than extended ones. This was how the songs sounded on radio, but the results are truncated versions of "Sex Machine" and "Keep On Truckin'," rather than the glorious full cuts with complete musical interludes. Otherwise, most song choices are great, especially the JB's, Funkadelic, and Lyn Collins. —*Ron Wynn*

In Yo' Face! (The History of Funk), Vol. 2 / Rhino ✦✦✦✦

Volume two of Rhino's funk series offers 15 more mostly strong cuts, although it is disappointing to hear edited versions of great anthems. The marvelous trumpet solo and additional chorus from the O'Jays' "For the Love of Money" has been trimmed, and although they don't tell you, only part of B.T. Express' "Do It ('Til You're Satisfied)" is included. There's still plenty of wonderful funk, including classics by Sly & the Family Stone, James Brown, Kool & the Gang, Rufus, Parliament, AWB, and the Temptations. —*Ron Wynn*

In Yo' Face! (The History of Funk), Vol. 3 / Rhino ✦✦✦✦

By the third volume of Rhino's generally solid funk series, it has become apparent who did and did not permit their songs to be licensed.

Once more there are songs from James Brown, Sly & the Family Stone, Parliament, Funkadelic, the O'Jays, and AWB, and it's great that George McRae's delightful "I Get Lifted" made the cut, as well as Graham Central Station's "The Jam." Cameo's "Funk Funk" reveals how close to Parliament they were early in their career, while the Brothers Johnson, Kool and the Gang in their great pre-J.T. Taylor phase, and one-hit wonders Wild Cherry complete the disc. —*Ron Wynn*

In Yo' Face! (The History of Funk), Vol. 4 / 1993 / Rhino ✦✦✦✦

Familiar names comprise the bulk of the final volume in Rhino's funk series. There are more tracks by James Brown, Sly & the Family Stone and AWB, plus numbers from repeat entries the Isley Brothers, Earth, Wind & Fire, Kool & the Gang and Graham Central Station. But new acts offer prototype funk on some smoking numbers such as Slave's "Slide," the Bar-Kays' "Shake Your Rump To The Funk," Brick's "Dazz" and George Duke's "Reach For It." Bootsy's "The Pinocchio Theory" was a classic, and the same is true for Marvin Gaye's "Got to Give It Up, Part 1." Only Brass Construction's "L-O-V-E-U" falls below the standard. —*Ron Wynn*

In Yo' Face! (The History of Funk), Vol. 5 / Rhino ✦✦✦✦

In Yo' Face! (The History of Funk), Vol. 5 admirably wraps up Rhino's funk series by balancing several classic songs—Parliament's "Flashlight," Con Funk Shun's "Ffun," Fatback's "I Like Girls," the Gap Band's "Shake," Zapp's "More Bounce to the Ounce"—with good but lesser-known cuts by Sly & the Family Stone, the Bar-Kays, Bernie Worrell, Ohio Players and Cameo. —*Stephen Thomas Erlewine*

In Yo' Face! (The Roots of Funk), Vol. 1/2 / 1994 / Rhino ✦✦✦✦

Since the five-volume funk series *In Yo' Face* proved successful, Rhino decided to release a collection of gritty, funky R&B and soul from the late '60s and early '70s as *In Yo' Face! (The Roots of Funk), Vol. 1/2*. It's certainly possible to hear the funk in Lowell Fulson's "Tramp," Dyke & the Blazers' "Funky Broadway," Archie Bell's "Tighten Up," the Meters' "Cissy Strut" and Lee Dorsey's "Everything I Do Gonna Be Funky," but what makes this such good listening is the obscurities from the likes of Wilson Pickett, Watts 103rd Street, Laura Lee and Betty Wright, plus lesser-knowns like 8th Day, Fugi, Fantastic Johnny "C" and Tami Lynn. That's what gives the album depth and makes it far more interesting than the average soul or funk collection. —*Stephen Thomas Erlewine*

The International Artists Singles Collection / 1989 / Decal ✦✦✦

The International Artists label retains a legendary aura among '60s collectors as a repository for psych-punk, via releases by the 13th Floor Elevators and several other bands. This is a 15-track collection of material that originally appeared on IA singles; at least some of them never appeared on album, although the total lack of liner notes (other than a complete list of 45s released on IA) make it difficult to determine whether all of them were non-LP. It's a mildly interesting assortment of '60s Texas rock that ranges from more or less straightahead pop-rock to acid-soaked rock, and isn't as mind-blowingly eccentric as you might expect from the label's reputation. Includes cuts by the 13th Floor Elevators, Bubble Puppy, Lost and Found, the weird Endle St. Cloud, and very little-known names like Ginger Valley, Sterling Damon, and the Disciples of Shaftesbury (whose "Times Gone By" may be the catchiest track). International Artists cultists will want this, but non-IA completists will be better off searching for the albums by the label's best artists (the Elevators, Red Krayola, Golden Dawn, and Lost & Found), as well as the fine *Epitaph for a Legend* compilation. —*Richie Unterberger*

It's Bigger Than the Both of Us—N.Z. Singles 1979-82 / 1989 / Festival ✦✦✦

It's Bigger than the Both of Us offers two discs worth of rare singles and stray tracks from New Zealand's often overlooked underground from 1979 to 1981 with releases not only from the better known Flying Nun label but also from Propeller, Ripper, and R.E.M. Featuring some legendary tracks from the Clean, Toy Love, Tall Dwarves, and the Swingers, this is essential listening for anyone interested in the development of New Zealand rock. —*Chris Woodstra*

JS I Love You: Japanese Garage Bands of the 1960s / 1996 / Big Beat ✦✦✦

Japan, like many non-English-speaking countries, was home to a thriving garage/beat band scene in the 1960s. The Japanese scene, at least to Western ears, was more peculiar than most: for one thing, it didn't really kick into gear until 1966, and Japanese groups were still playing in an early British Invasion-influenced style until the end of the decade. Singing in both Japanese and heavily accented English, the guitars (as a result of the Ventures' huge popularity there) were surfish Mosrites, and the material was often a strange fusion of Merseybeat, punk, and over-the-top weirdness. *JS I Love You* is a 28-track compilation of songs originally released on the Crown and Teichiku labels, and while it's no match for the real British groups (or, for that matter, the best beat/punk groups from Holland and Sweden), it's truly like no other '60s rock you've heard. The guitar work is often frenzied and imaginative; the vocals walk the line between tough raunch and low comedy, particularly when they mangle English phonetics (the Swing West's version of Arthur Brown's "Fire," as well as the Out Cast's butchering of "Long Tall Sally," defy printed description). Sound quality and liner notes (in English) are excellent, and cuts like the Blue Jeans' "One More Please" are genuinely good fusions of pop and punk, making this a good pickup for the more adventurous '60s collector. —*Richie Unterberger*

Jungle Exotica / Strip ++++

For every big early rock star, or even one-hit wonder, there were plenty of hopelessly obscure rock 'n' roll singles with no chance of making it big in the marketplace. This didn't stop a lot of people from trying to find the right gimmick. Sometimes that gimmick would involve downright nutty marriages of raw rock 'n' roll with "jungle" rhythms and chants, striptease bump-and-grind cheapness, silly Middle Eastern and Chinese melodies (and accents), and horror movie sound effects and screams. That's what you'll find on this amazing compilation, which has 32 tracks, and nearly 70 minutes, of early rock 'n' roll at its most ridiculously sublime. There's not a star or even a recognizable name in sight on this CD, which rescues impossibly rare singles—known only to the hardest of the hardcore collectors—from oblivion. This is not "exotica" in the Martin Denny easy listening sense of the term. These are early rock 'n' roll novelties that are, without exaggeration, breathtakingly frantic and absurd. The "jungle" culture adopted by a lot of the performers came not from real jungles, but from the jungle as it was pictured in Hollywood movies. As such, the chest-beating ape mating calls and bird noises decorating many of these tracks—not to mention phrases like the fake Chinese "Ah, so!" (which was used as the title for *two* separate songs) or the Bela Lugosi-intoned "come with me to the casbah"—skirt stereotypes that, in later times, would be called politically incorrect. Nonetheless, these cuts are so infectiously silly, and the primeval rock 'n' roll/R&B guitar-and-sax riffing so hot, that you'll have a hard time not laughing at and enjoying this, no matter what your world view is. —*Richie Unterberger*

Just Can't Get Enough: New Wave Hits of the '80s / 1994 / Rhino ++++

New wave was the last great singles era, when the heavy hitters were balanced by a flurry of one-hit wonders that delivered one or two terrific songs and then faded away. Rhino's extensive 15-volume set *Just Can't Get Enough: New Wave Hits of the '80s* (available as individual discs) frequently captures the essence of the era, which saw equal measures of the sublime and the silly. It wisely avoids arty post-punk for most the most part, and due to contractual reasons, it also doesn't include any material from such stars as Elvis Costello, the Clash and the Pretenders, yet they aren't missed since Blondie, the Jam, Duran Duran, ABC and Nick Lowe are here, among many others. Besides, various artists compilations are primarily useful for gathering songs from artists you don't want a full album of, and by that criteria *Just Can't Get Enough* excels, since it contains nearly every one-hit wonder of note. Unfortunately, it contains *way too many* novelties, which should be expected from Rhino, but there simply are so many smarmy, smutty and unworthy obscurities here that they prevent some discs from getting off the ground. Still, there are some terrific novelties and obscurities scattered among the familiar items, making this perfect for the hardcore new wave collector. Casual listeners should pick according to the track listing—the first volumes lean heavily on power-pop, the middle volumes capture the height of synth-pop and New Romantics, as well as selected guitar-pop hits, while the latter volumes showcase MTV stars—since most discs are equally entertaining; the curious should start with either *Vol. 1* or *Vol. 5*, since they are the most consistent. And, despite their flaws, the set is essential to any comprehensive modern rock collection. —*Stephen Thomas Erlewine*

Just Keep on Dancing: Chess Northern Soul / 1996 / Kent +++

Twenty-four slices of mostly upbeat, dance-oriented soul cuts released on Chess between 1961 and 1971, though all but two date from 1964-69. It's peppy, well-produced stuff that, like most of Chess' soul, bears the influence of both Motown and the Windy City productions of Curtis Mayfield and Carl Davis. It'll please Northern soul collectors, though it's more pleasant than compelling. Includes performances by a few big names (Gene Chandler, Billy Stewart, Etta James, the Dells), though most of them are only known to serious soul hounds, and some of the best tracks (James' "Seven Day Fool," Stewart's "A Fat Boy Can Cry") have been readily available on those artists' own compilations. Among the obscurities, Doug Banks' "I Just Kept on Dancing," on which he sounds like he's trying to become the Black Gene Pitney, is worth noting for its sheer oddity value. The Radiants' upbeat sweet soul harmonies on "Hold On" gave them a small R&B hit in 1968, though it has enough pop appeal to sound like a lost Top Ten hit of the late '60s. —*Richie Unterberger*

Kicks / 1984 / Raven +++

To generalize, when it comes to compilations of obscure '60s Australian rock, you're much better off if the collection has a garage-punk-oriented slant, rather than a pop bent. If, just for the heck of it, you want just one

Australian '60s pop-rock anthology, this might be the one to look for. It's not that special, frankly, but it's pretty pleasant, with occasional highlights like the News' accomplished blue-eyed soul treatment of "S.O.S.," the D-Coys' pounding beat rocker "You're Against," and the Playboys' tuneful pop-mod-psych on "Sad." Some of these are merely remakes of American records, though some of those US releases were so little known that all but the most rabid collectors will be unfamiliar with the original versions. Rick Springfield makes a little-noted, not-too-interesting appearance as part of Wickedy Wak. —*Richie Unterberger*

Kill Rock Stars / 1991 / Kill Rock Stars ++++

Kill Rock Stars is an excellent 18-track various-artists collection capturing the essence of early '90s indie-rock pop underground. It's divided equally between amateurish indie-pop, abrasive punk and riot grrrl, featuring many of the best underground bands of that time, including Bratmobile ("Girl Germs"), Mecca Normal ("Narrow"), Bikini Kill ("Feels Blind"), Heavens to Betsy ("My Red Self"), Unwound ("You Speak Jealousy"), Nation of Ulysses ("N.O.U. Cooking with Gas"), Some Velvet Sidewalk ("Loch Ness"), Nirvana ("Beeswax"), and Lois performing under the name Courtney Love ("Don't Mix the Colors"). —*Stephen Thomas Erlewine*

King R&B Box Set / Feb. 27, 1996 / King ++++

An imperfect but nevertheless impressive four-disc overview of King's greatest hits, *The King R&B Box Set* contains signature hits from the like of James Brown, Hank Ballard, the Five Royales and Little Willie John. Many essential items are here, but the sequencing is too scholarly to make the box itself essential, especially since the final disc is comprised of a fairly uninteresting interview. —*Stephen Thomas Erlewine*

Kiss 'n' Tell / 1993 / Ace (UK) +++

Compilation of 30 rare girl group tunes, almost all from the early and mid-'60s, though a couple from the late '60s sneak in. Truth to tell, this is an inoffensive but hardly inspiring compilation of a genre that produced innumerable great records, both famous and obscure. The two famous cuts—Claudine Clark's "Party Lights" and The Donays' "Devil in His Heart" (covered by the Beatles on their second album)—are readily available elsewhere, in better company. Otherwise, there are rare, flop singles, as well as some unissued tracks, by the likes of Earline & Her Girlfriends, Lorraine & the Delights, and the Martin Sisters that simply don't stack up to the cream of the crop. The rare tracks by the Shirelles are pretty good (though already issued on other Ace compilations); Maxine Brown's "Little Girl Lost" is one of the most girl group-oriented singles by a singer who really belongs more in the soul category, and the tracks by Nella Dodds and Dean & Jean are good examples of girl groups' sultriest side. Candy & the Kisses' are good too, although they're more in a Motown vein than a classic girl-group style. The Chiffons are represented by a couple of fairly weak covers and a 1969 tune that barely resembles their girl group origins at all. Annette Funicello weighs in with one of her more standard pop-rock efforts, the unexceptional 1965 single "Better Be Ready." In sum, a pretty erratic compilation with good and unremarkable moments, the balance tilting toward the unremarkable. If you're looking for compilations of interesting non-hit girl-group songs, there are much better (if harder to find) ones about, including *Lookin' For Boys* and *Beyond the Wall of Sound* (both on Roxy) and *Ultimate Girl Groups* (on Goldmine). —*Richie Unterberger*

L.T.J. Bukem Presents Logical Progression / 1996 / Good Looking/London ++++

One of the foremost jungle DJs and owner of his own Good Looking/Looking Good label, L.T.J. Bukem compiled a selection of his label's singles onto a double-disc, double-LP package. Although the LP set is completely unmixed to be DJ-friendly, the CD set's second disc is mixed by Bukem himself. The lengthy and in-depth liner notes go even farther than most jazz LPs in philosophizing about the artists themselves (including Photek, DJ Crystl, Peshay, Wax Doctor, Chameleon and L.T.J. Bukem himself); this is definitely the place for intelligent—yet house-oriented—junglists to call home. —*John Bush*

Later Volume One: Brit Beat / 1996 / Island ++++

Jools Holland's British television show *Later* is known for its musical eclecticism, placing a wide variety of artists on one particular show. Although that commitment to diversity can sometimes make the show appear to be stodgy at a glance, the truth of the matter is that *Later* is one of the finest musical television shows of the mid-'90s. It is a broadminded and thoughtful show, that features everyone from Oasis to Portishead to Robert Plant & Jimmy Page. *Later Volume One: Brit Beat*, the first installment in a six-volume series of discs devoted to the show, concentrates on the Brit-pop movement of the mid-'90s and features nearly every major Brit-pop band, often in compelling, occasionally revelatory performances. Over the course of its 19 tracks, *Later Volume One: Brit Beat* winds through figureheads like Paul Weller, early '90s trendsetters like Suede, Manic Street Preachers and Charlatans, emerging stars like Super Furry Animals and Ash, and the three most popular UK acts of the '90s—Oasis, Blur and Pulp. In between, Supergrass, Elastica, Radiohead, McAlmont/Butler, Ocean Colour Scene, Cast, the Bluetones, the

Auteurs, Edwyn Collins, and Audioweb also get space. The end result is nearly a greatest hits of the '90s. Apart from a couple of unsteady performances (the Charlatans' "Just Lookin'" sounds shaky, Audioweb sounds out of place), *Later Volume One: Brit Beat* is uniformly excellent. For the collector, such rarities as Noel Gallagher's string-augmented take on "Wonderwall" and Pulp's "I Spy" performed with an orchestra make this disc a necessary purchase, but anyone with a passing interest in Brit-pop will enjoy this collection. After all, it plays like the greatest hits of the mid-'90s. — *Stephen Thomas Erlewine*

Later, Vol. 2: Slow Beats / 1996 / Island ✦✦✦
Where the first volume of recordings culled from Jools Holland's late-night musical show concentrated on Brit-pop, *Later, Vol. 2: Slow Beats* is comprised of trip-hop artists like Tricky, Portishead, Bjork and Massive Attack. Generally, this music works better in its original studio incarnation, but *Later, Vol. 2* proves that, given the right artist, it can be electrifying onstage as well. While the album isn't consistently engaging, much of it is entertaining, and for dedicated Brit-pop collectors, it's of interest. Electronica fans won't find it quite as interesting, nor will casual listeners, since above all, *Later, Vol. 2* is a curiosity, not a collection of remixes or hits. — *Stephen Thomas Erlewine*

Let's Go Trippin' / 1996 / Ace ✦✦✦
Thirty surf and hot rod tracks that were released on or distributed by the Dot label in the 1960s; a couple (the Surfaris' "Wipe Out" and the Chantays' "Pipeline") were huge hits, but most of the rest were virtually unknown. It's a grab bag of a set, with further tracks by the Surfaris (a rare 1966 single) and the Chantays, the minor national hit "Boss" by the Rumblers, a strange 1964 minor hit by Pat Boone that found him imitating the Beach Boys with reasonable accuracy ("Beach Girl"), and collector's items by the likes of Don Brandon and Milt Rogers. It's not bad, but the best tracks are available on better surf or single-artist compilations. On the whole it's average surf music, with occasional ear-openers like the Chantays' spooky "Space Probe" or the Rancheros' darkly powerful "Linda's Tune." — *Richie Unterberger*

Live Stiffs / Edsel ✦✦✦✦
In order to promote their label and their roster, Stiff Records devised the Live Stiffs package tour as a way to showcase all of their key artists (Elvis Costello, Nick Lowe, Ian Dury, Wreckless Eric, Lew Lewis & Reformer), as well as themselves. The Live Stiffs shows became notorious for their intoxicatingly (and intoxicated) ragged performances, which the live album *Live Stiffs* captures particularly well. Elvis Costello's torchy version of Bacharach-David's "I Just Don't Know What to Do with Myself" is a highlight, as are Nick Lowe's two cuts, the otherwise-unavailable "Let's Eat" and a rocking version of "I Knew the Bride," which he never released during the late '70s. Dury and Wreckless Eric are nearly as good, and the entire record captures the wild, careening spirit of Stiff—it's fun, trashy rock 'n' roll. — *Stephen Thomas Erlewine*

Living in Oblivion, Vol. 1 / 1993 / Capitol ✦✦✦✦
A somewhat haphazardly assembled retrospective of '80s pop, *Living in Oblivion* contains not only classic new wave cuts, but also features several MTV hits from the mid-'80s and radio hits from the end of the decade. While there are some great songs on every volume, each disc is wildly inconsistent; only the first disc is somewhat coherent. Nevertheless, *Living in Oblivion* captures the fractured mainstream of the decade quite well and manages to include some classic pop songs along the way. — *Stephen Thomas Erlewine*

Living in Oblivion, Vol. 2 / Sep. 7, 1993 / EMI ✦✦✦✦
Like its predecessor, *Living in Oblivion, Vol. 2* is an entertaining but frustrating collection of new wave and MTV hits from the early '80s. A number of great new wave singles are here—"Mickey," "Love Plus One," "Just Got Lucky," "88 Lines About 44 women," "Church of the Poison Mind"—but the album loses momentum by placing slick late '80s MTV hits like T'Pau's "Heart and Soul" and the Power Station's "Bang a Gong (Get It On)" next to non-hits by Debbie Harry and Sigue Sigue Sputnik. Even if it isn't a perfect collection it is fun, and should satisfy casual new wave fans; more serious collectors should purchase these songs on the multi-volume *Just Can't Get Enough*. — *Stephen Thomas Erlewine*

Living in Oblivion, Vol. 3 / 1994 / EMI ✦✦✦
Despite a handful of terrific singles, *Living in Oblivion, Vol. 3* is the weakest entry into the series to date. Placing New Wave hits next to late '80s radio hits prevents the album from gelling, and there are too many bad songs from second-rate acts like Polecats, Jellybean, Device, Ebn-Ozn, So and the Monroes. Still, the handful of good cuts—"(Keep Feeling) Fascination," "Perfect Way," "Cruel Summer," "Life in a Northern Town," "Rock This Town," "Poison Arrow"—almost make it worth acquiring, but they simply don't outweigh the dross on this 19-track collection. — *Stephen Thomas Erlewine*

Living in Oblivion, Vol. 4 / 1994 / Capitol ✦✦✦
Living in Oblivion, Vol. 4 continues the downward spiral of the series. There's little rhyme or reason to the song selection on the disc, as it jumps from New Wave to goth-rock to mainstream rock to alternative.

That scattershot approach prevents the album from becoming a cohesive listen, but the disc does contain several classics, including "Dance Hall Days," "One Thing Leads to Another," "True," "Come on Eileen," "Digging Your Scene," "Under the Milky Way," "Tenderness" and "Mexican Radio." They may be presented in a more logical fashion on other compilations, yet they make *Living in Oblivion, Vol. 4* attractive to undiscriminating collectors. — *Stephen Thomas Erlewine*

The Living in Oblivion: 80's Greatest Hits, Vol. 5 / 1995 / EMI ✦✦✦
Living in Oblivion, Vol. 5 is the most uneven edition of the series, concentrating more on near-hits and never-weres from the likes of Double, Boys Don't Cry, Hipsway and When in Rome, plus minor hits from the likes of ABC, Bananarama and Go West. There are a few good songs here—Peter Schilling's "Major Tom (Coming Home)," Thomas Dolby's "Hyperactive," Naked Eyes' "Hyperactive," OMD's "Enola Gay," Jules Shear's "Steady," DIVInyls' "Pleasure and Pain" and Fun Boy Three's "Our Lips Are Sealed"—but only casual listeners will find this wildly uneven collection worthwhile. — *Stephen Thomas Erlewine*

Lookin' for Boys / 198? / Roxy ✦✦✦✦
Quite simply, this is the best compilation of little-known early- to mid-'60s girl-group singles ever assembled, and proof that quite a few songs never get to be hits for reasons that have nothing to do with their quality. A couple of these (the Girlfriends' "Jimmy Boy" and Earl-Jean's original version of "I'm into Something Good") were small hits, but by and large these were flops. What's amazing is how meticulously produced and tuneful they were; in 1963, the industry was dazzled by Phil Spector's success, and employed quite a few producers and performers that emulated the master very well. Great melodies, harmonies, and Wall-of-Sound Jr. production on most of these, and noted songwriter Ellie Greenwich's dramatic "You Don't Know" is one of the finest obscure mid-'60s rock 'n' roll singles of any genre. — *Richie Unterberger*

Lost Soul / 1994 / Legacy ✦✦✦
These 20 rare cuts, spanning 1961 to 1978, are frankly not so much lost grade-A soul as an exhumation of the CBS vaults. That's not to say soul collectors won't welcome this anthology; there are rare cuts from significant performers such as Don Covay, Howard Tate, Bobby Womack, Brenda & the Tabulations, Z.Z. Hill, Joe Tex, Mavis Staples, and Freddie Scott. Most of this is from the 1970s, dating from either just past or way past soul's heyday, and a good deal tends toward the slicker and softer side. But this is one for the serious soul specialist rather than the general soul fan; the tracks by Staples (a cover of "Crying in the Chapel") and the Drifters-like outing from 1961 by Don Covay are about the best. — *Richie Unterberger*

Lost Treasures! / 1995 / Del Fi ✦✦✦
In the years just prior to the British Invasion, the L.A.-based Del-Fi label was apparently willing to take a chance on almost anything, if the 22 rarities on this CD are any guide. A mixture of *very* rare singles and unissued material, there ain't no hits to be found here, although bongo player Preston Epps did once have a big hit, "Bongo Rock," for another label. Mostly these are gutsy instrumentals in the R&B, surf, and twist styles, or *really* strange novelties, the kind from which even Dr. Demento might shy away. If that sounds like a tall order to fill, check out Bob Ridgley's "The Way Out Mummy," the Bedwells' "Karate," or Yo Yo Hashi's "Yo Yo's Pad," the last of which breaks up standard energetic three-chord instrumental vamps with Asian dialog straight out of your basic Hong Kong exploitation movie—real hitbound stuff, to be sure. Then there's the non-LP B-side by exotica weirdo Eden Ahbez, an instrumental with wacked-out and (for circa 1960) adventurous phasing effects. There are also extremely rare pre-fame appearances by Love's Arthur Lee (as part of the American Four, who offer a sub-Booker T. & the MG's instrumental) and two of the Walker Brothers (who play on the Moongooners' raunchy instrumental, "Moongoon Twist"). These might have been throwaway sessions, but the resulting CD, though certainly geared to a narrow market, isn't a throwaway at all. It's a cool and occasionally glorious reminder of the days when rock 'n' roll indies let the musicians blast away in search of that left-field hit, conventional pop standards of taste and song construction be damned. — *Richie Unterberger*

Louisiana Rockers / 1994 / Ace ✦✦✦
Twenty-four songs from the vaults of Goldband Records in Lake Charles, LA, most from the late '50s and early '60s. Hardly anyone from outside Louisiana will recognize any of these performers; in fact, most people from within the state borders won't either. With an unpolished feel (both in fidelity and performance) that can border on garage sloppiness, this stuff doesn't compare to the Louisiana records of the same era recorded by the Imperial, Specialty, or Minit labels. It's more an illustration of the grass-roots expression of vintage Louisiana rock/R&B, as reflected in the wide range of (usually derivative) approaches. There are Little Richard clones, swamp pop, sub-New Orleans rhythm and blues, and straight rock 'n' roll with equal measures of white and Black influences. There's nothing that announces itself as a hit-that-never-was. But if you want to hear something truly daffy, check out Ray Gerdsen's "Bye

Bye Baby," which is as close as it gets to Dixieland garage rock. —*Richie Unterberger*

Louisiana Saturday Night / 1993 / Ace ✦✦✦
Like its predecessor (*Another Saturday Night*, also on Ace), this is a compilation of Louisiana swamp pop, the admixture of rock, country, blues, pop, and Cajun that continues to thrive in the region. Most of the 26 tracks are vintage sides from the '60s, although there are a few of later origin. Some of the artists are nothing more than names to anyone outside of the state, but actually there are a few more recognizable artists here than on the first volume, including Rusty & Doug Kershaw, Rockin' Sidney, Rod Bernard, Clifton Chenier, and Bobby Charles. It's rock music with an overt good-time flavor, the sonic equivalent of a lazy drawl. In terms of diversity and quality, it actually has a bit of an edge over *Another Saturday Night*, although it isn't truly landmark stuff. Includes Cookie & the Cupcakes' "Mathilda," one of the few national hit singles of the genre (making No. 47 in 1959), and the original version of "You Ain't Nothing but Fine" (by Rockin' Sidney), which would be covered by the Fabulous Thunderbirds. —*Richie Unterberger*

MTV Amp / May 5, 1997 / Caroline ✦✦✦✦
MTV designed the television show *Amp* as a way to showcase electronic dance acts that didn't easily fit into their other specialty shows. Premiering in late 1996, the show quickly became a hit, and it helped ignite the electronica craze of early 1997 by suggesting that American audiences were more interested in techno than many labels previously assumed. Considering its success, it wasn't a great surprise that MTV and Astralwerks assembled the *MTV Amp* compilation to cash in on its success and to provide curious listeners with a one-stop introduction to "electronica." Surprisingly, *MTV Amp* works. Featuring nearly every major electronic artist of the mid-'90s—Daft Punk is missing, but the Chemical Brothers, Underworld, Future Sound of London, Photek, Aphex Twin, Orbital, Goldie, Atari Teenage Riot and Prodigy are all present—the collection illustrates the depth and variety within electronica, alternating between heavy club beats and trance-like drum 'n' bass. For anyone interested in exploring techno, there is no better introduction than *MTV Amp*. —*Stephen Thomas Erlewine*

Mellow Rock Hits of the '70s: Summer Breeze / Feb. 4, 1997 / Rhino ✦✦✦
Rock's long and winding road from Woodstock to the waiting room at the doctor's office was paved with '70s staples such as these. "A Horse with No Name" (America), "Summer Breeze" (Seals & Crofts), "Dreams" (Fleetwood Mac), "How Much I Feel" (Ambrosia)—you get the idea. If you want these for home listening as well, there are some advantages to this 16-track compilation. The liner notes are intelligent and informative, and a bit of sly progressivism sneaks in via the Flying Burrito Bros.' "Hot Burrito No.1." Other artists include James Taylor, Linda Ronstadt and Joe Walsh, as well as vanished easy rockers like Terence Boylan and Jack Tempchin. —*Richie Unterberger*

Mellow Rock Hits of the '70s: Sundown / Feb. 4, 1997 / Rhino ✦✦✦
The most artistically credible volume of Rhino's *Mellow Rock Hits of the '70s* series focuses on male singer-songwriters. Most of these cats have (or had, at any rate) pretty high critical reps, though this tends to be their most familiar/commercial work: Gordon Lightfoot, Don McLean, Kris Kristofferson, Arlo Guthrie, Steve Goodman, John Prine, Steve Forbert. The second tier includes Cat Stevens, Jim Croce, and John David Souther; Gram Parsons slips in, counterbalanced by Breadman David Gates. Some of the merits of these songs have been dulled by overexposure, but it's certainly one of the more respectable anthologies likely to surface for this sort of thing. —*Richie Unterberger*

Mellow Rock Hits of the '70s: Ventura Highway / Feb. 4, 1997 / Rhino ✦✦✦
Mellow rock at its most easygoing and cheerful is the focus of this 16-track compilation, with entries by Seals & Crofts, America, Steve Miller, the Doobie Brothers, and adult-contemporary forerunners that you may not want to revisit: Pure Prairie League's "Amie," Pablo Cruise's "Love Will Find a Way," Player's "Baby Come Back," Orleans' "Still the One." The selections by Little Feat ("Dixie Chicken"), Dr. Hook, and Poco may be a bit unexpected, but aren't nearly radical enough to upset the even-tempered flow of the disc. The crumb tossed to pot-smokers, the Grateful Dead's "Uncle John's Band," is without doubt the CD's highwater mark. —*Richie Unterberger*

Men at Work and Friends / Columbia ✦✦✦
An odd collection, *Men at Work and Friends*, features a handful of the band's hits as well selections from their "friends"—fellow Aussies (and New Zealanders) Tim Finn, Flash and the Pan, Owen Paul, Sherbert, Split Enz, and the Black Sorrows. Also included is a bonus disc which contains two remixes from Flash and the Pan, a remix from Owen Paul (his cover of Marshal Crenshaw's "My Favorite Waste of Time") and a live track from Tim Finn. It's hard to tell the purpose of this release, but it does contain some great music. —*Chris Woodstra*

Mercury R&B Story 1945-55 / Sep. 24, 1996 / Polygram ✦✦✦✦
Mercury R&B Story 1945-55 is a four-disc, 211-track collection covering Mercury's first decade as a label. Each of the four discs are arranged thematically according to regions—East Coast, West Coast, Midwest and Southwest—and each features a number of blues and R&B classics, including cuts from Professor Longhair, Johnny Otis, Eddie "Cleanhead" Vinson, Dinah Washington, Lightnin' Hopkins, Jimmy Witherspoon and Big Bill Broonzy. 22 unreleased performances are mixed into the compilation, making the set enticing for collectors, but the main value of *Mercury R&B Story 1945-55* is as a concise overview of one of the most influential R&B labels in history. —*Stephen Thomas Erlewine*

Message to Love: the 1970 Isle of Wight Festival / 1996 / Columbia/ Legacy ✦✦✦✦
The soundtrack to the documentary film about the 1970 rock festival which was Woodstock-like in size, if not in cultural impact. The musical lineup didn't quite match Woodstock either, but was damn impressive, including Jimi Hendrix, the Doors, the Who, Joni Mitchell, ELP, the Moody Blues, Donovan, Miles Davis, Free, Leonard Cohen, Jethro Tull, and others (how did Kris Kristoferson sneak in?). This double CD has good sound and good (though not landmark) performances. The Who, Hendrix, and Joni Mitchell come off best; odder highlights include Leonard Cohen's ghostly version of "Suzanne," a "Nights in White Satin" from the Moodies that is quite impassioned, and Tiny Tim's "There'll Always be an England." Cinema verité snippets of dialog add to the authenticity, but occasionally detract from the flow. Be aware that Bob Dylan's "Desolation Row" is the 1965 studio recording, not a live performance. —*Richie Unterberger*

Metal Age: The Roots of Metal / 1992 / Rhino ✦✦✦✦
Actually, *Roots of Metal* comes closer to representing the heyday of heavy metal. From Status Quo to Motorhead, all kinds of '70s arena hard rock and metal are covered; over the course of the disc, it becomes clear that metal does *not* all sound the same—there's quite a difference between the thuggish Wishbone Ash, the melodic Cheap Trick, snarling Runaways, and the bloated blues of Beck, Bogert and Appice. Some of it holds up surprisingly well and some of it is embarrassing, but there's no question that it captures its era particularly well. —*Stephen Thomas Erlewine*

Mindrockers, Vol. 1 / 1981 / Line ✦✦✦
When it appeared in the early '80s, *Mindrockers* was one of the more popular series of compilations specializing in obscure '60s rock. Since then its value has diminished considerably, because much of the best material has become available in better sound on domestic reissues. On purely musical grounds, most of the *Mindrockers* volumes are pretty good musically. The first installment features mostly Californian bands, including tracks by the Seeds, the Peanut Butter Conspiracy, the Other Half (raw Haight-Ashbury acid-rock), the Brogues (two of whom would go on to join Quicksilver Messenger Service), and the Jefferson Handkerchief, whose "I'm Allergic to Flowers" is one of the great psychedelic novelties. —*Richie Unterberger*

Mindrockers, Vol. 2 / 1981 / Line ✦✦✦
Fourteen garage-psych numbers from mid-'60s Chicago, originally issued on the Dunwich and USA labels. Much of this has since appeared on domestic reissues that are easier to locate, but there's no denying that this features some of the best raunchy Chicago rock of the period. The Del-Vetts' "Last Time Around" has great crunchy riffs, effective tempo changes, and airy pop hooks; the same goes for Pride & Joy's "If You're Ready," not all that surprising since it's the Del-Vetts after a name change. The Knaves' "The Girl I Threw Away" is sloppy but attractive folk-rock-punk; the Banshees' "Project Blue" is Chicago garage at its most demented. Nothing else here is in this league, and the Shadows of Knight (with "Someone Like Me") are the only well-known group, but it's a solid encapsulation of the rawer side of mid-'60s Chicago rock. —*Richie Unterberger*

Mindrockers, Vol. 3 / 1982 / Line ✦✦✦✦
There seems to have been no concept behind this grouping of songs, other than to gather a bunch of cool rare '60s American rock singles onto one compilation. Usually that means trouble, but sometimes it works out pretty well, and this is an example of the latter. The Myddle Class' "I Happen to Love You" is a great obscure, moody Goffin-King song; the McCoys' "Don't Worry Mother," with flute and psychedelic lyrics, may have been their best track; the Shades' "Ballot Bachs" is a really cool, trippy instrumental; the Next Five's "He Stole My Love" is eerie psych-pop in the style of the Electric Prunes; the Shags' "Hide Away" is outstanding garage pop with Merseybeat harmonies; and the Balloon Farm's "A Question of Temperature," with its exploding balloon sounds, is one of the best entries into the limited field of bubblegum garage. Some of these cuts rarely if ever appear on other compilations, so it can be worth your while to pick this up if you come across it. —*Richie Unterberger*

Mindrockers, Vol. 7 / 1983 / Line ✦✦✦✦
For a major label that, according to some accounts, didn't have much of
an idea of how to record rock 'n' roll, Columbia sure issued a lot of interesting, little-known rock records in the 1960s. This has 14 cuts from
1965-69 and contains some good music, although the best of it has been
subsequently issued on CD. That includes the early dreamy psychedelic
cuts by the Sparrow (who would evolve into Steppenwolf); the blues single by the Rising Sons (with both Taj Mahal and Ry Cooder); and the
inspired R&B/psychedelic fusion of Larry Williams & Johnny Watson's
"Nobody," with backing by Kaleidoscope. More interesting to the collector are the cuts that are hard to find otherwise: the Playboys of Edinburg
(who sound like the *Younger Than Yesterday*-era Byrds with a more
country influence), the propulsive garage punk of the Denims' "I'm Your
Man," and the Dylanish folk-rock of the Bad Seeds' "King of the Soapbox." Future Pure Prairie League member Mike Reilly even makes an
appearance on a 1966 garagey single by the Mark IV. Considering that
Columbia seems in no hurry to issue vault compilations of no-name acts
such as these, this LP is worth picking up if you can find a copy. —*Richie
Unterberger*

Mods Mayday '79 / 1979 / Dojo ✦✦✦✦
Since the British music market was flooded with mod-revivalists in the
late '70s, the only effective way to promote the bands was through package tours—several like-minded (and like-sounding) bands playing short
sets on the same night. *Mods Mayday '79* is a classic collection which
compiles the highlights of one of these tours. Most of the second wave
revivalists—bands who received their inspiration directly from the Jam's
early albums—are represented: Secret Affair, Beggar, Small Hours, the
Mods, Squire, and the Merton Parkas. The one glaring omission is the
Lambrettas, who were unable to attend the tour due to contractual obligations. Nevertheless, this provides the best look at the genre and is the
only place to hear some of the bands who, despite their derivative
nature, wrote some excellent pop songs that hold up pretty well even
when removed from their context. —*Chris Woodstra*

Mods Mayday 2: Modnight at the Bridge / 1997 / Receiver ✦✦✦
Mods Mayday 2: Modnight at the Bridge follows the classic collection
with 15 outtakes presumably from the same show (two of the Merton
Parkas songs were previously added as bonus tracks to the CD version
of *Mods Mayday '79*). Though the recording quality isn't great and the
playing is often amateurish, the conviction and enthusiasm of the bands
more than makes up for their shortcomings, capturing much of the
charm of the movement. A nice companion to the first volume but
essential only for the converted. —*Chris Woodstra*

Monterey International Pop Festival Box Set / Jun. 1967 / Rhino
✦✦✦✦
A sumptuous, four-CD box set with all the deluxe trimmings celebrating the grandaddy of all outdoor rock concerts. With legendary performances by Otis Redding, the Who, Jimi Hendrix, Janis Joplin, the Byrds,
and Paul Butterfield all taken from the mobile-unit multi-track masters
(not to mention an album-sized booklet that'll knock your eyes out), this
box evokes a sound and an era the way few (if any) retrospectives of like
material ever do. Important music from a turning point in rock's history.
—*Cub Koda*

More Gumbo Stew / 1993 / Ace ✦✦✦✦
The second batch of material from the vaults of Harold Battiste's AFO
label is actually a stronger collection than the first (*Gumbo Stew*),
although over half of it was previously unissued. Most of it's good early
'60s New Orleans R&B, with genuine highlights like Prince La La's
"Need You" (a futuristic foreshadowing of the sort of voodoo rock that
Dr. John would play in the late '60s), a couple rambunctious perfor-
mances by the young Dr. John himself ("The Fix" sounds like the early
Animals as played on a department store-quality organ), and the Dr.
John-penned "World of Dreams," sung in heart-tugging fashion by Tami
Lynn. Also includes tracks by Barbara George, Alvin Robinson, Eddie
Bo, and Johnny Adams (a live 1960 performance), as well as Lee
Dorsey's smash "Ya Ya" (not recorded at AFO, but included because AFO
chief Harold Battiste says he produced it). If you've already got the best
New Orleans R&B anthologies and want more of the same, you should
make this one of your next stops. —*Richie Unterberger*

More Hollywood Rock 'n' Roll / 1994 / Ace ✦✦✦
Gene Autry's Challenge label didn't have a lot of big hits, but it sure
released a hell of a lot of rock 'n' roll records of all kinds in the late '50s
and early '60s. Twenty-eight of them are here, including rockabilly,
instrumentals, vocal groups, and a little more. None of them were significant hits, and they didn't necessarily deserve to be. It's average early
rock, appealing more to the collector who wants to hear almost everything than to the learned student looking for genuinely overlooked
important music. There are some interesting odds and ends sprinkled
amidst the Jerry Lee Lewis and Gene Vincent imitations. Big Al Downing pounds some mighty fierce piano on "Down on the Farm," Patsy
Cline (the only well-known singer on the disc) checks in with one of her
infrequent rockabilly attempts ("Gotta Lotta Rhythm in My Soul"), and

the Rip Tides' "Machine Gun" is a tough Bo Diddleyish instrumental.
Kip Tyler's "Jungle Hop" has early appearances by saxophonist Steve
Douglas and pianist Larry Knechtel, both of whom would be among the
most celebrated L.A. session musicians of the 1960s. Weirdest of all is a
rock 'n' roll novelty by actor Scatman Crothers, "Rock Roma Rock It."
—*Richie Unterberger*

Motown's Blue Evolution / Feb. 1996 / Motown ✦✦✦
From the beginning, Motown was almost exclusively devoted to soul.
But they did have a few blues-oriented artists on their roster, especially
in the early 1960s. Truthfully, though, this 20-track compilation isn't
exactly a blues anthology. It's more like a collection of soul cuts with a
bluesy feeling, by performers who had substantial or deep roots in pure
blues. Mable John (Little Willie's sister) and Sammy Ward, for instance,
sing R&B/soul with some bluesy shadings; jump blues veteran Amos
Milburn sings modified earthy R&B, married to Motown's embryonic
production machine; Earl King has a slight New Orleans flavor to his
previously unreleased performances. The unknown Arthur Adams sings
blues/soul crossover; Luther Allison comes by far the closest to real
blues, and is the only one of the artists whose selections date from the
1970s. You can quibble about the accuracy of the compilation's theme,
but it's not a bad excuse to get some interesting Motown performances
out of the vaults and onto CD, though it's not truly top-drawer blues or
soul. Only one of these was even a modest hit (Sammy Ward's 1960 single "Who's the Fool"), and seven tracks were previously unreleased (King
and Adams never even got to officially release anything on Motown), so
even seasoned Motown collectors will find much of interest here.
—*Richie Unterberger*

Movin' on up, Vol. 1: Songs from the Civil Rights Struggle / Feb. 8,
1994 / The Right Stuff ✦✦✦
The civil rights movement of the 1960s found some of its greatest artistic expression through the giants of soul music. The compilation *Movin'
on up* includes 13 of the era's most enduring statements of African-
American pride. While this has a few Top Ten singles, it also brings to
light several strong cuts by superstars like Otis Redding, Stevie Wonder,
Curtis Mayfield, James Brown, and Nina Simone that are not nearly as
well known as their biggest hits. Among the most interesting finds here
are Redding's interpretation of Sam Cooke's heartbreaking ballad "A
Change Is Gonna Come," Stevie Wonder's unexpected cover of Bob
Dylan's "Blowin' in the Wind," James Brown's seven-minute declaration
of Black pride, "I Don't Want Nobody to Give Me Nothing (Open up the
Door, I'll Get It Myself)," Nina Simone's explicitly angry "Mississippi
Goddam," and Donny Hathaway's gospelish version of Simone's compo-
sition "To Be Young, Gifted & Black." Detailed liner notes by R&B writer
David Nathan clarify the connections between the music and the times.
—*Richie Unterberger*

MTV Class of 1983 / 1995 / Rhino ✦✦✦
The double-disc *MTV Class of 1983* attempts to distill the essence of
early MTV to 30 tracks from the biggest names and most popular one-
hit wonders of that year. The approach works remarkably well, as the
compilation features many new wave classics that effortlessly evoke
1983. The sheer size of *MTV Class of 1983* distinguishes it from other
new wave collections, as does the presence of the Pretenders ("Back on
the Chain Gang"), David Bowie ("China Girl"), Talking Heads ("Burning
Down the House") and Herbie Hancock ("Rockit"). However, most new
wave collectors will have this material already, especially if they own
the 15-volume *Just Can't Get Enough*, so it's only appealing to casual
fans. Even so, any new wave or early MTV compilation that doesn't
include Duran Duran could hardly be called definitive. —*Stephen Thomas Erlewine*

MTV's Best of the Buzz Bin, Vol. 1 / Mar. 26, 1996 / Mammoth/Atlan-
tic ✦✦✦
MTV's Best of the Buzz Bin is a curious collection. In one sense, it sums
up the post-Nirvana commercialization of alternative rock quite
well—there's the faux-grunge of Bush ("Everything Zen"), the dippy neo-
hippie rock of Blind Melon ("No Rain"), and the PC jazz/hip-hop fusion
of Us3 ("Cantaloupe") sitting alongside the jazzy folk-rock of the Dave
Matthews Band ("What Would You Say"), the campy metal of White
Zombie ("Thunder Kiss 65"), and the Pearl Jam-as-arena-rock of Stone
Temple Pilots ("Plush"), with Radiohead ("Creep"), the Cranberries
("Zombie"), and Danzig ("Mother") thrown in for good measure. In other
words, it's a bit of a stylistic mess. Nevertheless, most of the bands are
united by an affection for loud, distorted guitars—it makes the light
acoustic rhythms of Dave Matthews seem incongruous. Then again,
mainstream alternative rock—particularly the kind that MTV played
frequently—was dominated by heavy guitar bands. So, while *MTV's Best
of the Buzz Bin* may be lacking both major artists and some interesting
one-hit wonders, it remains a good sampler and there are some great
singles—"Creep," "Thunder Kiss 65," "Plush"—buried amidst some
tracks that are nothing more than artifacts. —*Stephen Thomas Erlewine*

Murder Was the Case / 1994 / Interscope ✦✦✦✦
The soundtrack to an 18-minute film inspired by Snoop Doggy Dogg's "Murder Was the Case" provides more thrills than the average hip-hop release. Again, Dre relies on his standard production tricks and crew, introducing a couple of new members to the mix. But the result sounds anything but stale—it ranks alongside *The Chronic*, *Doggystyle* and *Above the Rim* in terms of quality. In fact, various artist compilations like *Murder Was the Case* are the ideal vehicle for Dr. Dre—they show his versatility. *Murder* has the harrowing title track from Snoop Dogg, as well as the smooth funk of Warren G and the chilling hardcore of "Natural Born Killaz," the first track from Dre's collaboration with Ice Cube. At some point, Dre will need to find some new tricks, but *Murder Was the Case* finds him at the top of his game. —*Stephen Thomas Erlewine*

The Muscle Shoals Sound / Rhino ✦✦✦✦
In a series of nondescript studios in tiny towns tucked in the corner of northwest Alabama, a small band of musicians, singers, and producers sculpted a sound that revolutionized rhythm and blues in the 1960s. Dubbed the "Muscle Shoals Sound" after one of those towns, this region gave birth to the grittiest and funkiest Southern soul music of the era. The 18-song compilation *The Muscle Shoals Sound* presents a cross-section of some of the most influential grooves laid down in these studios during its golden decade (1962-1972). Besides hits by soul giants like Otis Redding, Aretha Franklin, and Wilson Pickett, it includes influential sides by lesser stars like Percy Sledge ("When A Man Loves A Woman"), Etta James ("Tell Mama"), Arthur Conley ("Sweet Soul Music"), and Clarence Carter ("Patches"). It also includes the very first hit cut in the region, Arthur Alexander's "You Better Move On." Behind the scenes, songwriters and musicians like Spooner Oldham, Dan Penn, and Duane Allman were equally important in crafting a style distinguished by rock-solid rhythms and passionate performances. With thorough liner notes about the songs, performers, and musicians, this is a fine introduction to the "deep soul" music that was envied by such heavyweights as the Rolling Stones. —*Richie Unterberger*

Natural Born Killers / 1994 / Interscope ✦✦✦✦
Most soundtracks simply feature the film's incidental music or songs that were heard in the background throughout the movie. Not *Natural Born Killers*. Assembled by Trent Reznor (Nine Inch Nails), the soundtrack to Oliver Stone's brutally warped serial killer saga re-creates the hallucinatory feeling of the film. Snatches of dialogue interweave with song fragments and sound effects, creating a harrowing, violent soundscape, where Leonard Cohen occasionally offers a relief of sorts. In fact, Reznor managed to convey the insanity of the movie's lead characters much more effectively than Stone did with the film itself. —*Stephen Thomas Erlewine*

Naughty Rhythms: The Best of Pub Rock / Apr. 1996 / EMI Premier ✦✦✦✦✦
Pub rock is the frequently forgotten forefather of punk rock, although on the surface the two genres don't appear to have much in common. Punk rock was about revolution and pub rock was about tradition, at least superficially. But place pub rock in its proper context, and it was nearly as revolutionary as punk. In the early '70s, rock 'n' roll was dominated by heavy metal, art-rock, and blues-rock, all genres that required skill. The simple, laidback three-chord shuffles of pub rock—ranging from straightahead rock 'n' roll, to country and blues-rock—didn't require much skill, but it was a working class, do-it-yourself movement that took rock 'n' roll back to its roots, which is essentially what punk rock did. Furthermore, pub rock bands established a circuit of nightclubs within England, which is where all the original punk bands played. *Naughty Rhythms: The Best of Pub Rock* is the first comprehensive colllection of the scene, featuring every major pub rock band, as well as nearly every minor band. Compiled by former Kursaal Flyer Will Birch with Paul Bradshaw, the double-disc set effectively traces the development of the genre, from its country-rock roots with Brinsley Schwarz to the pounding, proto-punk of Eddie & the Hot Rods. In between, there are 34 other songs that cover all the aspects of pub rock, from the relaxed acoustic rock of Eggs Over Easy and the Stonesy groove of Ducks Deluxe and Dr. Feelgood to the commercial gloss of Ace and the eccentric rock of Kilburn and the High Roads. The double-disc set provides all the worthwhile songs from almost every band featured on the collection, with the notable exception of Brinsley Schwarz, who were already represented with five tracks. *Naughty Rhythms* is the definitive document of pub rock and for most listeners, it will be all they need to know. —*Stephen Thomas Erlewine*

New England Teen Scene: Unreleased! 1965-1968 / 1996 / Arf! Arf! ✦✦✦
Even by the standards of '60s garage reissues, we're talking obscure here. None of these 30 tracks were released at the time, and several of the bands represented never managed to issue any official product at all; five of the songs, in fact, are totally uncredited, having been found on undocumented tapes. It's about what you might expect from this sort of project: lots of imitations of the Byrds, Beau Brummels, Zombies, etc., though there's nothing that demands attention, or provides evidence of

woefully undiscovered talent. New England bands in general seemed to favor melodic pop and Zombie-ish keyboards more than groups from other regions, and that's reflected in many of the selections on the disc. If such grave-digging appeals to you, however, you could be a lot worse off. The sound quality is mostly excellent—largely taken from master tapes, it's actually considerably better than the usual garage reissue norm. And while none of this is truly excellent, none of it's truly awful either, most of the acts adhering to basic standards of instrumental competence, and presenting original material rather than overdone covers. —*Richie Unterberger*

New Jack City / 1991 / Giant ✦✦✦✦
This soundtrack, from Mario Van Peebles' hit movie *New Jack City*, is a fairly good cross-section of rap, house and R&B styles, in keeping with the attitude of the movie (a violent cop-vs.-crack-lords drama). There's no "Theme from 'Shaft'" for the '90s here, but there are some slammin' sides all the same—the album kicks right into high gear with Ice-T's "New Jack Hustler (Nino's Theme)," a non-stop barrage of beats, samples and furious rhymes from Ice-T. F.S. Effect manage to convey the same sort of energy and fury with "Get It Together (Black Is a Force)" later in the album. The disappointment in the rap area is the track from 2 Live Crew, with a mix of slightly-better-than-routine beats and samples and some lousy lyrics handled in a lazy throwaway manner. —*Steven McDonald*

New Orleans Ladies: Rhythm & Blues from the Vaults of Ric And Ron / 1988 / Rounder ✦✦✦✦
With the exception of Irma Thomas, this anthology covers female vocalists whose contributions to New Orleans R&B were overlooked or devalued. Both Martha Nelson (Carter) and Leona Buckles were excellent uptempo, dance-oriented vocalists who had no trouble maintaining their vocal authority and clout over driving arrangements, and could also handle steamy ballads or confessional material. Buckles' "I'm Waiting (To Give You My Love)" and "Baby We're Through" were exuberantly sung. The Thomas tracks include her outstanding "Don't Mess With My Man" and three other lesser-known early-'60s numbers that weren't smashes, but displayed the majestic voice and dramatic delivery that ultimately became a dominant part of New Orleans soul. These aren't throwaway numbers, despite their obscurity. —*Ron Wynn*

No Alternative / 1993 / Arista ✦✦✦✦
A mixture of B-sides, outtakes, live tracks, and newly recorded songs, *No Alternative* is the most successful benefit album of 1993, both commercially and artistically. Exceptional songs from Nirvana, Bob Mould, Urge Overkill, Smashing Pumpkins, American Music Club, and Pavement enhance fine outtakes from Buffalo Tom and Matthew Sweet, strengthen Uncle Tupelo and Soul Asylum's strong covers, and make the weak live tracks from the Beastie Boys, Sonic Youth, and the Breeders tolerable. However, nothing can save the Goo Goo Dolls' atrocious pop-metal take on the Rolling Stones' "Bitch." Still, that's only one song out of 19, making *No Alternative* a worthy purchase. —*Stephen Thomas Erlewine*

Northern Soul Spectrum / Apr. 22, 1997 / Kent ✦✦✦✦
Taken from the vaults of EMI Records, *Northern Soul Spectrum* brings together soul styles from the vaults of many of the company's small label holdings, including classics from Roulette, Jubilee, Josie, Port, J2, Satin, Calla and Rust. With 28 tracks covering the years 1962 to 1968 with a stray track from the '70s (Magic Night's soul-disco "If You and I Had Never Met") that atmospherically fits in, this is no mere R&B hodgepodge compilation, but instead a well-programmed and diverse selection of a wide variety of Northern Soul styles. From the pop-flavored offerings of Annabelle Fox's "Lonely Girl" and Frankie & the Classicals' "What Shall I Do" to the minor key Motown-on-fire romp of Brenda Lee Jones' "You're the Love of My Life" to the classic soul balladry of Scotty Williams on "I've Got to Find Her (and Tell Her)," the sheer emotionalism, musicality, and danceability of the genre is here for the listening. For those who want to investigate further than the hit packages of Motown and Stax/Atlantic material, here's a big chunk to digest in one sitting that's grade-A soul music from the classic era. —*Cub Koda*

Nothing but a Man / Mar. 19, 1996 / Motown ✦✦✦✦
This 1996 CD reissue was a surprise, since the 1965 film to which it was attached had only a cult following. Much of the music (Martha & the Vandellas' "Heat Wave," Mary Wells' "You Beat Me to the Punch," the Miracles' "Mickey's Monkey") is available elsewhere, although the producers have used the original master tapes as sources for the CD, so the sound is first rate. And there are two jewels here that have not appeared elsewhere on CD: "You've Really Got a Hold on Me" by the Miracles from their 1963 live album, and "Bye Bye Baby" by Mary Wells from her live album of the same era. The recording on the Miracles live cut leaves something to be desired, but listening to Smokey play the crowd, and the rapture of the audience as the group delivers an impassioned rendition of the song (with a brief foray into Sam Cooke's "Bring It on Home to Me"), all imperfections are forgiven; and the group sounds in great

form. Mary Wells' performance is one of her best on record, a simmering piece of passionate, romantic soul music that rises magnificently to full boil. So why not put both live albums on one CD? —*Bruce Eder*

Nowhere Men: British Beat 64-66 / Beat Club ✦✦✦
This isn't a definitive British Invasion collection, as the title might lead you to believe, but a collection of 16 rare R&B/punk-influenced sides that are coveted by aficionados of the style. In other words, it's only for us geeks who make trips to New York and London and put record-hunting in specialist stores high on the agenda. So this LP might be as noteworthy for its discographical value as its musical merits, including pricy items by the Wheels, the Sorrows, Better Days, Listen (Robert Plant's pre-Led Zep outfit), and the rare fourth single by the Birds (Ron Wood's first band). It's not the greatest collection of overlooked British R&B around, but it's alright, and occasionally torrid (the Wheels and the Sorrows especially). It's also interesting for the inclusion of Shel Naylor's "One Fine Day," written by Dave Davies, but never recorded by the Kinks. —*Richie Unterberger*

Nuggets, Vol. 1: the Hits / 1986 / Rhino ✦✦✦✦✦
A straightforward collection of garage-punk chart successes, including "Psychotic Reaction," "Dirty Water," "Nobody but Me," and "I Had Too Much to Dream Last Night." —*Bruce Eder*

Nuggets, Vol. 2 (More Nuggets) / 1987 / Rhino ✦✦✦✦✦
Picking up where the first *Nuggets* CD left off, *More Nuggets* contains 18 wonderfully raw garage-rockers, which are intercut with some trippy psychedelia and folk-rock. The selection on *More Nuggets* is a little more unpredictable than on its predecessor, since it doesn't just feature hits like "Liar Liar," "I Wonder What She's Doing Tonight," "Talk Talk," "(We Ain't Got) Nothin' Yet," "Western Union" and "The Little Black Egg," but also cult classics from the likes of the Merry-Go-Round ("Live," "You're A Very Lovely Woman"), Captain Beefheart ("Diddy Wah Diddy"), the Chocolate Watch Band ("Are You Gonna Be There (At the Love-In)?," "Sweet Young Thing"), the Left Banke ("Desiree"), the Standells ("Sometimes Good Guys Don't Wear White") and Mouse & the Traps ("A Public Execution"). —*Stephen Thomas Erlewine*

Nuggets, Vol. 3 (Even More Nuggets): Psychedelic / Rhino ✦✦✦✦
Even More Nuggets, the third volume of Rhino's garage rock and psychedelic-pop series, is equally divided between hits ("I Had Too Much to Dream Last Night," "Gloria," "Incense and Peppermints," "Just Dropped in (To See What Condition My Condition Was In)," "Who Do You Love," "Red Rubber Ball," "Time Has Come Today," "Let's Live for Today") and cult favorites from the Barbarians, Third Rail, the Sunshine Company and the E-Types. It doesn't have quite as many classics as its two predecessors, yet it remains one of the more satisfying collections of mainstream garage-rock assembled. —*Stephen Thomas Erlewine*

Nuggets, Vol. 4: Pop, Pt. 2 / 1984 / Rhino ✦✦✦
Most of the acts here take their cues from the lightest aspects of the Beatles. More often than not, the results are pretty infectious. Highlights include the E-Types, the Royal Guardsmen, and the Palace Guard, which featured future Merry-Go-Round leader Emmitt Rhodes. —*Richie Unterberger*

Nuggets, Vol. 5: Pop, Pt. 3 / 1985 / Rhino ✦✦✦
A little sappier than the previous "pop" installments of this series. Highlighted by obscure, minor hit singles by the Strawberry Alarm Clock, the Knickerbockers, the Association, and the Lovin' Spoonful. —*Richie Unterberger*

Nuggets, Vol. 6: Punk, Pt. 2 / 1985 / Rhino ✦✦✦✦
Includes a lot of the greatest regional garage hits of the mid-'60s: the Brogues, We the People, the Unrelated Segments, the Chocolate Watch Band, and Mouse & the Traps all weigh in with strong cuts. Also includes worthy obscurities by Captain Beefheart ("Diddy Wah Diddy") and minor but exciting hits by the Shadows of Knight ("Oh Yeah") and the Electric Prunes (the psychedelic classic "Get Me to the World on Time"). —*Richie Unterberger*

Nuggets, Vol. 7: Early San Francisco / 1985 / Rhino ✦✦✦✦
A fine collection of pre-Summer of Love rarities from the mid-'60s. Besides hits by the Beau Brummels and We Five, it features rarities by the Vejtables, the Great Society (featuring a pre-Jefferson Airplane Grace Slick), and Country Joe & the Fish. —*Richie Unterberger*

Nuggets, Vol. 8: The Northwest / 198? / Rhino ✦✦✦
The Northwest was renowned for some of the rawest, most R&B-grounded garage bands of the '60s. While the region wasn't as studded with riches as Texas and California, this compilation has strong cuts by the Sonics and national hits by the Kingsmen and Paul Revere & the Raiders, as well as decent folk-rock psychedelia by the Daily Flash. —*Richie Unterberger*

Nuggets, Vol. 9: Acid Rock / 198? / Rhino ✦✦✦
Switching to a decidedly heavier mode, this comp includes hits by Love, the Byrds, Steppenwolf, Iron Butterfly, the Chambers Brothers, Vanilla Fudge, and the Strawberry Alarm Clock, as well as worthy lighter,

slightly obscure offerings by the Grass Roots, the Monkees, and the Young Rascals. —*Richie Unterberger*

Nuggets, Vol. 10: Folk Rock / 198? / Rhino ✦✦
One of the weakest offerings in the series, with oft-anthologized hits by the Byrds, Turtles, Scott McKenzie, and Barry McGuire. The non-hit cuts tend toward the lightest, poppiest facets of folk-rock. An exception is the powerful acoustic, original version of "Dazed and Confused" by Jake Holmes, which was transformed into heavy metal by Led Zeppelin. —*Richie Unterberger*

Nuggets, Vol. 11: Pop, Pt. 4 / 198? / Rhino ✦✦✦
Solid collection of slightly psychedelic-influenced, progressive '60s pop. Fine hits by the Left Banke, Fever Tree, and the Grass Roots, neat tracks by the Blues Project, Lee Michaels, and Gene Clark, worthy obscurities by the Magicians, Montage (a Left Banke spinoff), the Critters, and Keith. —*Richie Unterberger*

Nuggets, Vol. 12: Punk, Pt. 3 / 198? / Rhino ✦✦✦
Decent offering of strong cuts by some of the most esteemed regional garage bands of the '60s. The hits by the Hombres, the Syndicate of Sound, and Paul Revere are actually outdone by the tracks from Mouse & the Traps, the Remains, the Unrelated Segments, Kenny & the Kasuals, and the Lollipop Shoppe. Includes the hit "Shape of Things to Come," performed by Max Frost & the Troopers in the psychedelic exploitation film *Wild in the Streets*. —*Richie Unterberger*

Oh Yeah! The Best of Dunwich Records / 1992 / Sundazed ✦✦✦✦
The Chicago-based Dunwich Records was the leading Midwestern garage-rock label, turning out countless great singles from the likes of Shadows of Knight, American Breed, the Rovin' Kind and H.P. Lovecraft. *Oh Yeah! The Best of Dunwich Records* is an excellent 31-track collection that contains the label's best-known hits, plus several fine unreleased cuts, radio commercials and interviews. Anyone that's interested in delving into garage-rock any deeper than the *Nuggets* compilations should start here—it gives a good idea of both the treasures and the mediocrities to be found in the multitiudes of compilations, and few other collections are quite as consistently listenable as this one. —*Stephen Thomas Erlewine*

The OKeh Rhythm & Blues / Apr. 1, 1993 / Columbia ✦✦✦✦
OKeh Records was one of the seminal R&B and blues labels of the '50s, and the three-disc, 78-track box set *OKeh Rhythm & Blues* offers an effective overview of the label's peak years, featuring tracks by the Ravens, Chuck Willis, the Five Scamps, Hadda Brooks, Titus Turner, the Treniers, Paul Gayton and many worthy obscure artists. Although the set is sequenced a little too scholarly to be consistently enjoyable listening, it is a necessary purchase for any serious R&B or blues collector. —*Stephen Thomas Erlewine*

OKeh: A Northern Soul Obsession, Vol. 2 / 1997 / Ace ✦✦✦
Second-division Chicago '60s soul from the genre's pre-eminent label, OKeh. No big hits on this 24-track mix of mid-level names (Larry Williams, Johnny Watson, Major Lance, Walter Jackson, Billy Butler, a 1967 single by Little Richard) and unknowns (Tan Geers, Cookie Jackson, Joyce Davis, and several others). Like most compilations of this nature, it's not recommended unless you're deeply into the genre at hand. If you like the Smokey Robinson-meets-Curtis Mayfield nature of much Chicago soul, and want an intelligently annotated collection of some of the style's harder-to-find sides, this disc does a fine job. —*Richie Unterberger*

Oldies but Goodies, Vol. 1 / Original Sound ✦✦✦
Oldies but Goodies was the first rock 'n' roll anthology, setting the standards for various artists anthologies when it was originally issued in the early '60s. Over the years, the series has held up well in many respects; although there isn't a unifying theme to any of the albums, the music is first-rate, full of popular singles that form the basis of oldies radio stations. However, when the series made its transition to compact disc in 1987, it wasn't nearly as successful. Taken on their own terms, the fidelity of these fourteen discs is quite bad, with muffled, distorted sound on almost every song; compared to CD reissues by other labels, the discs sound positively atrocious. If bad sound doesn't stand in your way, there's plenty of good music to be found on these CDs; the original records remain fine items. —*Stephen Thomas Erlewine*

One Hit Wonders: The '60s, Vol. 1 / Rhino ✦✦✦
One Hit Wonders: The '60s, Vol. 1 collects 12 hit singles from the '60s artists that never had more than one hit, so it's a terrific way to collect a number of wonderful pop singles—"You Were on My Mind," "I Wonder What She's Doing Tonight," "Last Kiss," "Walk Right In," "If You Wanna Be Happy"—that are better heard on a various-artists collection than a greatest-hits compilation. —*Stephen Thomas Erlewine*

One Hit Wonders: The '60s, Vol. 2 / Rhino ✦✦✦✦
If anything, the second volume of *One Hit Wonders: The '60s* is even better than the first, boasting a stronger selection of songs from artists that never had more than one hit, including the Hombres ("Let It Out (Let It All Hang Out)"), Crazy Elephant ("Gimme, Gimme Good Lovin'"), Robert Knight ("Everlasting Love"), Merilee Rush ("Angel of the Morning"),

the Neon Philharmonic ("Morning Girl"), Derek ("Cinnamon"), the Casinos ("Then You Can Tell Me Goodbye") and the McCoys ("Hang on Sloopy"). —*Stephen Thomas Erlewine*

One Last Kiss / 1992 / SpinART ✦✦✦
This, spinART's initial release, fulfilled a very useful function when it appeared. The US indie-pop revolution had been underway for a couple of years, but at that point the bands were still mainly represented (if at all) by small pressings of seven-inch singles or cassettes. This CD collects good songs already released on 45's by other labels, unreleased tracks by established bands and a few debuts. Great tracks by Black Tambourine, Our American Cousins and Jane Pow rub shoulders with offerings from more prominent bands including Velocity Girl, Magnetic Fields, and the Swirlies. The breadth of sounds here shows that while the Americans got a lot of inspiration from their British cousins, they came up with more diversity. —*Michael Ribas*

Pebbles, Vols. 1-28 / ✦✦✦✦
In the early '70s, the *Nuggets* compilation reawakened listeners to the sounds of mid-'60s garage rock. As much of a revelation as that double album was at the time, it only focused on the tip of the iceberg of garage rock. Behind those forgotten hits and semihits lurked hundreds, if not thousands, of regional hits and flops from the same era, most even rawer and cruder. In the late '70s, the Pebbles compilations came along to fill in the gap and then some. Each volume gathered 15-20 obscure 45s—originally issued on tiny labels, and remastered right from the excruciatingly rare original vinyl—of prime mid-'60s garage rock. Sometimes a track by a relatively well-known performer would show up, but by and large these acts were unknown to anyone but collectors and those who happened to have lived in the areas where the bands played. More than any other factor, these compilations were responsible for the resurgence of interest in garage rock, which remains high among collectors to this day. The lyrical attitudes of the bands immortalized on *Pebbles* by and large have to do with cheating girls, adolescent rebellion, and high times. At times downright juvenile and sexist, the lyrics aren't the main attraction so much as the sound and stance, which anticipates the outrage of punk rock, but tempers it with tough British Invasion-inspired melodies, harmonies, and hooks, as well as fuzz-toned guitars, Farfisa organs, and wildly manic songwriting and performances. There are a lot of great unknown songs on *Pebbles*, way too many to cite in a brief review, from all over North America, most from 1965-67. There are also a fair number of generic tunes that have little to recommend beyond an excess of energy, which can make listening to an entire volume at once as much a challenge as a joy. Listeners approaching this series for the first time should search for the first ten volumes; after this initial burst, the well ran increasingly dry, and the later volumes can be a chore. Most of the individual installments don't have themes, but those looking for a concentration of certain items should check out Volume 3 (psychedelia) and Volume 6 (British R&B/mod); Volume 4, devoted to surf, is actually the weakest of the early volumes. Of special interest among the later volumes are installments devoted to obscurities from the European continent. More wide-ranging in style than the typical volume covering US garage, these include albums devoted to '60s rarities from Holland, Sweden, Denmark, and Switzerland; though wildly uneven, they contain some surprisingly strong material. —*Richie Unterberger*

Pebbles, Vol. 8: Southern California, Part 1 / 1996 / AIP ✦✦✦✦
Southern California, and specifically the Los Angeles area, was one of the most active hotbeds of '60s garage punk, both because of its huge size and its flourishing musical and youth culture. Not all L.A. garage rock was great, and this 25-song compilation (much of which has appeared on previous vinyl garage anthologies, *Pebbles* included) is a good way to ferret out some of the better rare singles of the genre. Terry Randall's protest rocker "S.O.S.," the Rumors' "Louie Louie" ripoff "Hold Me Now," Byron & the Mortals' organ-driven "Do You Believe Me," the Dovers' Byrds-meets-the-Zombies "She's Not Just Anybody"—all are among the best garage classics. Most of the rest is pretty good, if a bit generic at times. Lots of informative liner notes, too. —*Richie Unterberger*

Pebbles, Vol. 10 / 1996 / AIP ✦✦✦✦
Twenty-four mid-'60s garage favorites, none available on CD before. It's above the median standard of such compilations, including numerous better cuts from the original vinyl *Pebbles* series: the Leather Boy's truly strange "I'm a Leather Boy," the Clockwork Orange's Electric Prunes-influenced "Your Golden Touch," the Uncalled For's "Do Like Me," and the Others' "I Can't Stand This Love." There are also a number of tracks that are relatively unfamiliar, the most interesting of these being "Leave Me Alone" by the Canadian Squires, who would turn into the Band (yes, the Band) a few years later. —*Richie Unterberger*

The Perfumed Garden, Vols. 1-3 / Reverberation ✦✦✦✦
Originally issued on vinyl in the early '80s and reissued in the mid-'90s (with the addition of an entirely new third volume), *The Perfumed Garden* series presents compilations of excruciatingly rare mid- to late-'60s

British psychedelia, usually from obscure singles. The Groundhogs, Birds, Deviants, and Poets are the most well-known acts included, to give you some idea of the kind of minutiae we're dealing with here. Some very good hard mod pop and trippy Brit-psych, sometimes very imitative of gods like the Who and the Move, but sometimes so good that they're none the worse for that. Some of the hard rock cuts are a bit plodding and turgid, but those who like their psychedelia with whimsy and/or power chords will find a lot to latch onto, although it's a notch below *Freak Beat Phantoms* and *Electric Sugar Cube Flashbacks*, the best compilations of this type. —*Richie Unterberger*

Phat Trax, Vols. 1-5 / 1994 / Rhino ✦✦✦✦✦
Phat Trax is a seven-volume series (all discs are available individually) that chronicles the late '70s and early '80s heyday of funk. Each disc is filled with classic cuts, rarities and 12-inch mixes, giving an excellent overview of every element of funk. The series begins to lose some steam on its later volumes, as it spends too much time with mediocrities, but the set remains the definitive overview of funk. —*Leo Stanley*

Pimps, Players & Private Eyes / Jan. 14, 1992 / Sire ✦✦✦✦
Pimps, Players & Private Eyes gathers 10 theme songs from early '70s Blaxplotation films, including Curtis Mayfield's "Pusherman," Willie Hutch's "Theme of Foxy Brown" and "I Choose You," Isaac Hayes' "Theme from Shaft," Bobby Womack's "Across 110th Street," and Marvin Gaye's "Trouble Man." Although "Superfly" should have been on the album, these funky, soulful cuts effortlessly evoke their era and make for a highly entertaining listen. —*Stephen Thomas Erlewine*

Pittsburgh's Favorite Oldies: At the Hop / Itzy ✦✦✦✦
Pittsburgh was a fertile creative breeding ground for no-holds-barred radio programming from the mid-1950s into the early '60s. The competition between DJs for their share of the audience was fierce and consequently each radio personality played tunes that couldn't be heard anywhere else and certainly nothing that was heard on a national level. This sub series to Itzy's multi-volume *Pittsburgh's Greatest Hits* (this one being subtitled *At The Hop* and split evenly between uptempo selections and ballads) serves up 24 sterling examples of this wide range of programming and shows how it all appealed to the local scene. From wild instrumentals like "The Red Headed Flea" by the Caps and "The Hunch" by Mad Mike and the Maniacs to hard core doo wop obscurities like "Bila" by the Versatones, "True Love Gone" by the Enchanters, and the haunting "A Million Miles Away" by the Uniques to rockers like the original "Charlena" by the Sevilles and Ronnie Haig's "Don't You Hear Me Calling, Baby," the Pittsburgh scene obviously had a built audience for the wild, bluesy, harder sounds being issued at the time. This compilation not only sheds light on an earlier scene, but provides top-notch listening all the way. If you want to proceed past the hits and hear some remarkable music in the bargain, this one is highly recommended. —*Cub Koda*

Pittsburgh's Favorite Oldies: At the Hop, Pt. 2 / Itzy ✦✦✦✦
This second entry into one of Itzy's *Pittsburgh's Best Oldies* subseries is a 24-karat winner all the way. Opening with Frank Motley and His Motley Crew's "Honkin' at Midnight," it becomes apparent that this volume is going to concentrate on uptempo goodies as much as doo wop dreamies. The Ring A Dings' insanely energetic "Snacky Poo" (is this utilizing the same band track as Johnny Faire's rockabilly classic "Bertha Lou"? Too close to call.) sits comfortably alongside Rusty Isabel's piano instrumental "Firewater." And while vocal group classics like Ronnie and the Hi-Lites' "A Slow Dance" and the Royal Jesters' "Love Me" are aboard, they sit right comfortably alongside two or three whoops of novelty trash like the Four Sounds' "Mama Ubangi Bangi," Ronnie Cook's "The Goo Goo Muck" or the slopjar instrumental by the Royal Teens, "Mad Gass." No big hits or really big names on this, but a lot of great music, with all of it just as raw as can be. —*Cub Koda*

Pittsburgh's Favorite Oldies: For Lovers Only / Itzy ✦✦✦✦
The initial entry in this sub-series from Itzy Records chronicling the Pittsburgh scene of the 1950s and early '60s is subtitled *For Lovers Only* and features 24 doo wop obscurities that firmly burrow into the heart of what that city preferred in their hometown sound. Highlights are numerous, but fans of the slow and smooth should take the time to investigate "You" by the Initials, "I Do Love You" by Tex and the Chex, "Oh My Angel" by Bertha Tillman, "I Don't Want Everything" by Jimmy McHugh and "High on a Hill" by Scott English, the closest anything on here comes to being an actual hit. A solid set that's perfect for slow dancing in the kitchen. —*Cub Koda*

Pittsburgh's Greatest Hits, Vol. 1 / 1995 / Itzy ✦✦✦✦
Originally released back in 1966 as a two-record vinyl set, this new edition restores the previous tracks missing from the original compact disc issue of a few years back. Pittsburgh in the late 1950s and early '60s was a musical scene unlike any others; songs that had flopped a year or so back could become "instant oldies" if said record "had the sound." The marketplace also had a penchant for R&B stompers, novelty instrumentals, doo wop smoothies, and proto-soul ravers. All of this is on clear display in the first installment of what has now become a multi-volume

series. Highlights include the Sheppards' "Island of Love," "Fried Onions" by Lord Rockingham, Chuck Edwards' "Bullfight," and the Triumphs' "Draggin' Wagon." An auspicious debut for this very unique and interesting series. —*Cub Koda*

Pittsburgh's Greatest Hits, Vol. 2 / Itzy ♦♦♦♦
While certainly any compilation can be slanted into whatever concept is imaginable, it only takes about three or four tracks into this one that you realize that the music that made the Pittsburgh airwaves and coalesced into local favorites were a breed apart. Raucous, blues-slanted and doo wop-driven, with a penchant for recordings as raw as the performances that lived inside of them, the Pittsburgh crowd was exposed to records far more crude and basic than those in other radio markets. And this excellent series keeps unearthing myriad treasures from that rich vein, bringing records to compact disc that never would have shown up anywhere else. Highlights are indeed plentiful on this generous 28-track collection, but of special note are "Oh but She Did" by the El Capris, the garage band innocence of "Someone" by the Contrails, the rambling soul of the Alma-Keys' "Please Come Back to Me," early Lou Christie with the Classics on "Close Your Eyes," Johnny Jack's classically constructed proto-vocal beauty "Need You," and an early Vogues effort under their original Val Aires handle, "Which One Will It Be." But for sheer curiosity and nutzoid novelty value, nothing tops the inclusion here of a premium 45 issued by Brooke Bond Foods, promoting its TV commercial with the Marquis Chimps masquerading as rock 'n' rollers proselytizing the virtues of Red Rose Tea. This is loose, raw, out of control and slightly demented-sounding; in short, just about everything great we've come to love about this series' concept, of which this edition is a noteworthy addition. —*Cub Koda*

Pittsburgh's Greatest Hits, Vol. 4 / Itzy ♦♦♦♦
The fourth entry into Itzy's main series of local Pittsburgh radio favorites kicks off with a track that virtually defines the series' very strengths and weaknesses. "Cloudburst" by the Orlandos is both—by turns—a doo wop slow classic that's painfully out of tune in spots, whose production values hover somewhere in the one-mike-in-a-broom-closet category while being solidly of one piece, resolutely and defiantly sincere in its spirit. In other words, music of the highest and most immediate warts-and-all reality, a thing to be treasured. That this ragged but right aesthetic would find a place on the radio in a market like Pittsburgh is amazing enough, that it prospered even more amazing. That it pops up again and again on this collection ("Lover's Prayer" by Anne Keith with the Altairs is of massive head-shaking ambience) is even more of a testimony to its uniqueness and vitality. Jewel Akens and the Four Dots' "Pleading for Your Love," the Sabres' jazzy "You Can Depend on Me," the Three Vales' crude blueser "Blue Lights Down Low," and the Contrails' lone instrumental offering of Chet Atkins' "Slinky" are the notable highlights here, but as always, another entry that's of one stylistic big picture, for sure. —*Cub Koda*

Pittsburgh's Greatest Hits, Vol. 5 / Itzy ♦♦♦♦
The fifth entry into the chronicling of the local Pittsburgh radio hit story is another enticing one, with the preponderance of its lineup devoted to local Pittsburgh area artists. As a result, this is one of the few volumes that actually has some tracks that later progressed into national hits, the two notable examples being "Come Go with Me" and "Whispering Bells" by the Dell Vikings, heard here in their original Fee Bee versions, thus bringing some name value to the proceedings. An early vocal effort by George Benson with the Altairs ("If You Love Me") is noteworthy, as are the Marcels' a cappella entry, "Teeter Totter Love," and the loose-as-a-goose, greasepit instrumental by the Vibra-Sonics, "Drag Race." Another solid entry and a lot of unvarnished, raw music in the bargain. —*Cub Koda*

Pittsburgh's Greatest Hits, Vol. 6 / Itzy ♦♦♦♦
This volume is more of a hodgepodge than the other volumes, vacillating between doo wop cookie-cutter sides, New York pop sides, solid efforts from local bigwigs Jimmy Beaumont (a nice take on Percy Mayfield's "Please Send Me Someone to Love"), the Skyliners ("I'll Close My Eyes," the Four Dots ("Peace of Mind"), Lou Christie ("Tomorrow Will Come"), and the stray instrumental here and there. But the musical quotient stays reasonably high, with the original "See You in September" from locals the Tempos and "Blue Moon" by the Marcels being counted up in the mix. But as always with this eccentric series, obscuros like "Christmas Plea" by the Dynamics and "Broken Heart" by the Vel-Tones carry just as much—if not more—musical weight than their better-known counterparts. The instrumental highlight on here goes to local combo the Savoys' "Slappin' Rods and Leaky Oil." —*Cub Koda*

Pittsburgh's Greatest Hits, Vol. 7 / Itzy ♦♦♦♦
This volume keeps the quality up and the pace fairly brisk, combining hard-charging rock 'n' roll turns from Buddy Sharpe ("Linda Lee"), the Shufflers (the previously unreleased instrumental "Soul Shufflin'"), and solid turns from local stars Chuck Jackson ("Come On and Love Me"), the Val Aires (later to become the Vogues and represented here with "Laurie, My Love"), the Caravelles ("Falling in Love"), the Marcels ("Got

a Job"), the Dell Vikings ("You Say You Love Me") and Lou Christie with this volume's lone "real hit," "Two Faces Have I." Closing out this compilation is a delightful bonus track, an a cappella audition tape of the Skyliners working on "Since I Don't Have You," a defining moment in the history of the local scene preserved here, imperfections and all. —*Cub Koda*

Pittsburgh's Greatest Hits, Vol. 8 / Itzy ♦♦♦♦
The eighth volume in the main series (12 in total to date, counting the two sub-series) is another solid one, with this particular volume showing a much higher quotient of what collectors would call "pop doo wop." There's a heavy emphasis this time on showcasing the better white vocal groups that worked the Steel City circuit during the late '50s and early '60s, and classic sides by the Holidays ("Pretend"), the Moonbeams ("Don't Go Away"), the Fenways ("The Number One Song in the Country"), the Five Playboys ("Mr. Echo"), and the Dantes (the Beach Boys-like "Top Down Time"), pepper the sequencing in a most musical way. Other local favorites like the Camelots and the Twilighters add to the musical currency, along with early efforts by Pittsburgh local favorites the Marcels, Jimmy Beaumont ("Everybody's Crying"), Chuck Jackson (a beautiful reading of "Willette"), the Skyliners ("The Loser"), and Lou Christie, who weighs in with the biggest hit here—certainly from a national standpoint—the original "The Gypsy Cried." Solidly in the doo wop corner this time around (with hardly any R&B traces in evidence), here are 25 tracks that prove that the Pittsburgh scene was a musically rich one, indeed. —*Cub Koda*

Pittsburgh's Greatest Oldies: For Lovers Only, Pt. 2 / Itzy ♦♦♦♦
Often what separates a hit from a miss in the doo wop pantheon of rock 'n' roll is a tough and very close call. Surely talent counts for something, but in a genre where the blend and sound are of tantamount importance, one could honestly say that the feel is almost everything. In this regard, the 24 tracks collected here (with many of them being collectors' items worth hundreds of dollars each) shine as classic examples of the form. Johnny Paar's "I Know a Girl," the De Vaurs' "Where Are You," the Fabulaires' "Wedding Song," the Majors' "Les Qua," and the Jaguars' "The Way You Look Tonight" (perhaps the closest to an actual "hit" on this compilation) all have the sound and the style, and why they never became big hits (outside of Pittsburgh, that is) remains a mystery. But few all-slow-song comps sustain a mood and ambience as well as this one does (all of it vocal group to soul-ballad stuff, with the lone ringer slow instrumental "Black and Blue" by the Gigolos being the exception), and even obscure efforts like the Vels' "Mysterious Teenage" (great whistling!), Tony Morra's "I Can't Believe," and mega-buck collector's piece "Searching" by the Tamaneers shine as the true jewels of the genre they are. Another excellent Itzy compilation where—once again—the musical contents belie the lack of hits and big names. —*Cub Koda*

Poptopia! Power Pop Classics of the '70s / May 27, 1997 / Rhino ♦♦♦♦
Named after an annual power-pop festival in the Los Angeles, Rhino's three-disc *Poptopia! Power Pop Classics* series attempts to chronicle power-pop's evolution from its '70s roots to its '90s incarnation as a cult music. Power pop, in many ways, is the ultimate cult music: It has a specific sound, a strict songwriting formula and a small number of classic artists. In other words, it's a genre that lends itself easily to an anthology—it's possible to feature both the classics and a number of obscure gems on one compact disc. The first volume of *Poptopia!* proves this point, as it skillfully balances the familiar with the relatively unknown. Over the course of 18 tracks, the album features all of the key power pop bands, from the Raspberries ("Go All the Way") and Big Star ("September Gurls") to Cheap Trick ("Come on, Come On") and 20/20 ("Yellow Pills"). Nearly every artist is represented in one of their big songs, with the notable exception of Badfinger, whose Capitol material wasn't available due to licensing restrictions. As a result, *Poptopia! Power Pop Classics of the '70s* is a basic primer on the genre, offering every major artist and many of the great songs that provided power pop with its foundation, including Nick Lowe ("Cruel to Be Kind"), the Dwight Twilley Band ("I'm on Fire"), Flamin' Groovies ("Shake Some Action"), Todd Rundgren ("Couldn't I Just Tell You"), the Knack ("Good Girls Don't"), Bram Tchaikovsky ("Girl of My Dreams"), the Shoes ("Too Late"), Pezband ("Baby It's Cold Outside"), the Rubinoos ("I Wanna Be Your Boyfriend") and the Records ("Starry Eyes"). Any serious power pop fan, and many casual listeners as well, will have everything here, but this is where the curious should start. —*Stephen Thomas Erlewine*

Poptopia! Power Pop Classics of the '80s / May 27, 1997 / Rhino ♦♦♦♦
Poptopia! Power Pop Classics of the '70s presented the roots of power-pop and its successor, *Power Pop Classics of the '80s*, finds the genre slowly mutating into a classicist style. In the '80s, power pop didn't have as dedicated an audience as it did in the previous decade (or that it would have in the '90s), and the place to hear catchy guitar-pop was in the ringing jangle-pop of the American underground. As a result, about half of the bands on this collection—including Let's Active, Bangles, the

dB's, Tommy Keene, the Smithereens, Hoodoo Gurus and the La's—had more in common with jangle-pop than power-pop, but they shared the same love of the three-minute single and the pure, catchy melody. Also, their presence makes *Power Pop Classics of the '80s* a bit more diverse than its predecessor, since there's a greater variety of pop styles, from the punchy rock of the Romantics' "What I Like About You" and the British Invasion stylings of the SpongeTones ("She Goes out with Everybody") to the AOR stylings of Utopia ("Crybaby") and the new wave of Holly & the Italians ("Tell That Girl to Shut Up") and the Plimsouls ("A Million Miles Away"). On the whole, the collection doesn't deliver as many thrills as *Power Pop Classics of the '70s*, but that's only by a slight margin, since among these 18 tracks are some of the finest pop singles of the '80s. —*Stephen Thomas Erlewine*

Poptopia! Power Pop Classics of the '90s/ May 27, 1997 / Rhino ✦✦✦
The compilers of *Poptopia!* were on solid ground when they assembled the '70s and '80s editions of their series, since there was already an established canon of power-pop greats for those decades. With *Power Pop Classics of the '90s*, they ran into some problems, the first of which was the fact that the album was released in 1997, three years before the decade was finished. It's quite likely that all the significant power-pop bands of the '90s had already appeared by the time of this collection's release, but the major hurdle the compilers had to face was the possibility that some of the artists they wanted to include might not be available for licensing. That certainly is the case with *Power Pop Classics of the '90s*—there's even a disclaimer in the liner notes that apologizes for the absence of Material Issue, Gin Blossoms and Teenage Fanclub, the Scottish band that defined '90s power-pop along with Matthew Sweet. It's hard to believe that Material Issue and Teenage Fanclub were unavailable, considering that Sweet, the Lemonheads and the Posies, three acts that sold more than those bands, are present, but their absence accentuates how uneven the collection actually is. There are some wonderful songs on *Power Pop Classics of the '90s:* Sweet's "I've Been Waiting" is a classic, the Lemonheads' "Into Your Arms" is charming, Gigolo Aunts find a middle ground between power pop and indie-rock on "Cope," Velvet Crush's "Hold me Up" and P. Hux's "Every Minute" are infectious, Zumpano's "The Party Rages On" is clean, punchy and surprisingly fresh, and Ride's "Twisterella" is superb, even if it only loosely qualifies as power pop. The remainder of the record, however, proves that in the '90s power-pop was a classicist genre, one that cared more about form than content. Most of these songs sound good but they just aren't that memorable, which is especially frustrating in the case of Velocity Girl, the Rembrandts and the Posies, who all have better songs in their catalog. And that draws attention to the fact that many of the livliest and best pop bands of the '90s, from Sloan and Sugar to Cast and Fountains of Wayne, are not here, and consequently, *Power Pop Classics of the '90s* can only be seen as an admirable effort, not a definitive collection. —*Stephen Thomas Erlewine*

Power Chords, Vol. 1 / Apr. 8, 1997 / Hip-O ✦✦✦
The initial entry in this three-volume set starts out admirably enough, with the inclusion of seminal mid-1960s tracks like "Wild Thing" by the Troggs, "You Really Got Me" by the Kinks, "Dirty Water" by the Standells, "Talk Talk" by the Music Machine, "Psychotic Reaction" by the Count Five, "Pushin' Too Hard" by the Seeds, and "I Had Too Much To Dream Last Night" by the Electric Prunes. But the collection quickly short-circuits, including nondescript items like the poppy "Baby, It's You" by Smith, the novelty instrumental "Hocus Pocus" by Focus, and tracks like the James Gang's "The Bomber" best left for other time-frame compilations. While the inclusion of album filler such as Ted Nugent's "Great White Buffalo" is head-scratching enough, even more curious is the absence of the Who, power chord merchants of the highest order. Perhaps a licensing restriction by the group itself, but that still doesn't excuse this shoddy package or its chaotic sequencing, although the inclusion of the Move's original "Do Ya" is a bright spot, fitting the requirements of the compilation like few of the other tracks do. —*Cub Koda*

Power Chords, Vol. 2 / Apr. 8, 1997 / Hip-O ✦✦✦
As chaotic and themeless as the initial volume in this series may be (combining seminal mid-'60s classics with album filler and tracks that just plain *don't fit* the parameters or concept of this collection), the second volume hits the bullseye as its moves into the 1970s, prime territory for this type of rock bombast. Kicking off with the one-two punch of Queen's "Killer Queen" and Lynyrd Skynyrd's "Saturday Night Special," the hits just keep on coming. Counted up in the mix are Sweet's "Ballroom Blitz," Mountain's influential "Mississippi Queen," Bachman-Turner Overdrive's "Let It Ride," Bad Company's "Good Lovin' Gone Bad," the James Gang's "Funk No.49," Joe Walsh's "Rocky Mountain Way," and Edgar Winter's "Frankenstein," classics in this genre by anyone's standards. Also included are great entries from Golden Earring (the long version of "Radar Love"), April Wine, Montrose, and UFO, making this a collection without a bum cut in the batch. If '70s power-chord rock is your thing, this is the one to pick up. —*Cub Koda*

Power Chords, Vol. 3 / Apr. 8, 1997 / Hip-O ✦✦✦
With this third and final volume in the set, we now move into modern-day MTV territory, with a few stragglers thrown in to add ballast to the collection. Everything compiled here was recorded in the 1980s, and although several of the tracks were recorded early in the decade (Donnie Iris' "Ah! Leah!," Aldo Nova's "Fantasy," the Rossington-Collins Band's "Don't Misunderstand Me," Foreigner's "Juke Box Hero" and Blackfoot's "Fly Away" all emanate from 1980-81), the dominant tone of the collection spotlights the hair-band explosion that went hand in hand with the rise of the cable video network MTV. Artists and groups familiar to early *Headbanger's Ball* viewers (Whitesnake, Tesla, Sammy Hagar, and Dio) all weigh in with signature selections loaded with thundering drums, tons of signal processing on the guitars and vocals, and guitar riffing that literally screams of mid-'80s metal excess, spandex, hair mousse and all. There's a fair amount of hits aboard and this makes an admirable entry into the series. —*Cub Koda*

The Psychedelic Snarl: Rubble, Vol. 1 / 1984 / Bam Caruso ✦✦✦
The first volume in the *Rubble* series of British psych-mod rarities is one of the best, with superb slabs of freakbeat from Wimple Winch (three cuts), the Craig's demented "I Must Be Mad," and the Hush's "Grey," one of the best British psychedelic singles with a pop bent. Yet at the same time, about half of this is rather ordinary, and not even especially weird, if that's what you're looking for. The long-deleted *Chocolate Soup for Diabetics* series beats this and every other volume of *Rubble* from all angles, although *Rubble* does offer better sound quality for the cuts that previously appeared on other anthologies. —*Richie Unterberger*

Psychedelic Unknowns / 1979 / Calico ✦✦✦✦
One of the earliest series specializing in unauthorized reissues of rare '60s rock, *Psychedelic Unknowns* was at its beginning of the better ones. The emphasis was on garage-into-psychedelia from approximately 1966-67, and there were 20 tracks on the first volume (although no numeral was actually attached to its title), which was actually a British compilation of two limited edition EPs from America. The Calico Wall's "I'm a Living Sickness" is garage psychedelia at its most apocalyptic; First Crow to the Moon's "Spend Your Life" is great teen Mersey-punk; We the People's "In the Past" is beguiling raga-rock; the Painted Ship's "Frustration" sounds like a more primitive early Doors; and the Squires' "Going All the Way" was anointed as a garage classic back in the early days of the *Pebbles* series (on which it also appeared). By this time most of the best cuts here have appeared on other compilations, but the grouping of songs on this anthology makes for one of the better garage-psych comps you could pick up. —*Richie Unterberger*

Pulp Fiction / 1994 / MCA ✦✦✦✦
The soundtrack to Quentin Tarantino's darkly funny crime classic *Pulp Fiction* manages to re-create the film's wildly careening sense of style, violence and humor by concentrating on the surf music that comprises the bulk of the movie's incidental music and adding a few sexy oldies integral to the film's story ("Let's Stay Together," "Son of a Preacher Man," "You Never Can Tell"). Of course, the inclusion of dialogue and Urge Overkill's seductive cover of Neil Diamond's "Girl, You'll Be a Woman Soon" don't hurt either. —*Stephen Thomas Erlewine*

Punk You, Vol. 1 / 1995 / EMI ✦✦✦✦
No compilation that omits cuts by the Sex Pistols, Clash, and the Jam (to name just the most obvious examples) can claim to be a comprehensive survey of early punk. However, this 17-song collection does have notable songs (usually the most famous/notorious) by the Damned, Generation X, the Buzzcocks, X-Ray Spex, Siouxsie & the Banshees, Wire, Tom Robinson, Stiff Little Fingers, and 999, among others. That makes it a useful enough disc for someone who isn't concerned with building a massive punk collection, although the emphasis is almost totally upon British bands. —*Richie Unterberger*

The R&B Box: 30 Years of Rhythm and Blues / 1994 / Rhino ✦✦✦✦
The concept behind the six-disc *The R&B Box: 30 Years of Rhythm and Blues* is admirable, but it's really too difficult to execute. Rhino wanted to tell the history of R&B's golden era of 1944-1974 by including one cut by each of the major artists in the genre, from Louis Jordan to the Spinners. Licensing restrictions prevented the label from including such heavy hitters as Sam Cooke and Sly Stone, which stops the set from being definitive. They also chose to include questionable cuts by some artists (Smokey Robinson is represented by "Mickey's Monkey"), and the one-song-per-artist rule prevents the collection from being truly representative. That said, *The R&B Box* is still worthwhile for neophytes, since it gives a general idea of the evolution of R&B, and features many great songs in one convenient place. It may leave just as many great songs off, but for listeners unfamiliar with the genre it's a good, if costly, primer. —*Stephen Thomas Erlewine*

Radio Daze: Pop Hits of the 80's, Vols. 1-5 / 1995 / Rhino ✦✦✦✦
Rhino's *Radio Daze: Pop Hits of the 80's* is a five-volume series that culls the hits and highlights from early '80s adult contemporary radio. Each disc is equally divided between guilty pleasures and bland, tedious dreck, but that only means that the series captures the feeling and

sound of adult contemporary radio. In fact, it's surprising how many genuinely good songs are scattered throughout the collection. Although none of the volumes are any better than the next—making any of the five discs an equally representative starting point—there is just as much schlock as there are worthwhile songs and entertaining kitsch on each collection. Because of this, *Radio Daze* may not be consistently entertaining, but it's hard to imagine a better collection of early '80s adult contemporary than this. And that's even acknowledging the absence of Air Supply. —*Stephen Thomas Erlewine*

Radio Tokyo Tapes, Vol. 3 / 1985 / PVC ✦✦✦✦
In the mid-'80s, a bunch of decent underground L.A. groups were playing folk-rock, or at least acoustic-oriented rock. The media never tried to make it a trendy fad, but producer Ethan James was motivated to preserve 16 examples on this interesting compilation. It's certainly diverse. Some of the artists would go on to become reasonably well known with albums of their own (Cindy Lee Berryhill, Phranc, Carmaig de Forest, Balancing Act); others are noisy L.A. post-punks who took the opportunity to do something quieter (the Minutemen's "Time," the Knitters' "Wild Side of Life/Honky Tonk Angels" [an X side project], Henry Rollins' spoken word-oriented "Al Jolson's Bedroom"). Then there's performance artist Linda Albertano, and '60s folk veteran Sandy Bull. Just the rarity value of these compilation appearances alone ensures interest among collectors. But it's also a very solid anthology of acoustic-oriented, oft-melodic alternative rock that doesn't sound revivalist or trendy, including some solid tracks by acts (like Revolver) that never built a reputation with their own releases. —*Richie Unterberger*

Rare 60's Beat Treasures / 1995 / Gone Beat ✦✦✦
Twenty-six British Invasion rarities—the Nashville Teens are the only group that had even one hit, to give you an idea of the obscurity level. This is really aimed more at collectors who want to fill out their discographies than anyone else, and many of the best cuts have already been reissued on AIP compilations like the *English Freakbeat* series. There's some darned good British R&B/pop here, though, like the squirrely vocals of David John; the storming mod/R&B of Miki Dallon and Mickey Finn; the propulsive "That's Alright," by Mickey Most (with Jimmy Page on guitar); and the Syndicats' "Crawdaddy Simone," which has some of the most demented rock guitar soloing of any era. There's also the rare 1963 version of "I Saw Her Standing There" by Duffy Power, which was probably the very first commercially released cover of a Beatles song. —*Richie Unterberger*

Rare on Air, Vol. 1 / 1994 / Mammoth ✦✦✦
A compilation of 16 performances originally broadcast on KCRW, a non-commercial radio station in Los Angeles. This is something of a grab bag of favorites on "AAA" radio, with mildly adventurous artists who are not odd enough to offend the taste of adult, mainstream-grounded listeners, like Tori Amos, Michael Penn, Los Lobos, Lindsey Buckingham, Natalie Merchant, Lucinda Williams, and David Wilcox. It isn't all safe, though; Nick Cave, Beck, John Cale, and Brendan Perry certainly aren't that likely to surface on your local commercial AAA outlet, although these are balanced by conservative choices like Mark Isham and Lindsey Buckingham. Much (though not all) of these tracks have an "unplugged" feel, and there's also the rare duet by Evan Dando (of Lemonheads) and Juliana Hatfield. It's not exceptional enough to be recommended for either its rarity or musical value, though certainly some just-left-of-center listeners will find it satisfying. —*Richie Unterberger*

Rare on Air, Vol. 2 / 1995 / Mammoth ✦✦✦
More live performances from the studios of KCRW in Los Angeles. This has an edgier, more alternative roster than volume one, with contributions by Cibo Matto, Bettie Serveert, Tanya Donnelly, Vic Chesnutt, Sebadoh, and Philip Glass. The presence of Joni Mitchell, J.J. Cale, the Cranberries, Lloyd Cole, and Jackson Browne should rope in all those listeners who usually shy away from something *too* alternative, however. —*Richie Unterberger*

Rare on Air, Vol. 3 / Feb. 11, 1997 / Mammoth ✦✦✦
Rare on Air, Vol. 3: KCRW Performances is a collection of rarities and unreleased live performances from indie and alternative rock bands recorded for the Flagship Public Radio Station. Though the quality of the tracks is a bit uneven, there's a number of highlights on the disc, including cuts by Stereolab, Guided by Voices, Patti Smith, Fiona Apple, the Wallflowers and Ben Folds Five. —*Stephen Thomas Erlewine*

The Raven EP LP, Vol. 1 / 1982 / Raven ✦✦✦✦
These 18 tracks were originally reissued on three Raven EPs, explaining the awkward title. It's an above-average sampler of four '60s Australian garage bands—the Missing Links, the Purple Hearts, the Throb, and the Wild Cherries—who were totally unknown outside of Oz. The Missing Links in particular were an explosive combo, sounding like a mating between the Troggs and the Who with their frenzied feedback guitar breaks and sore-throat vocals. They're represented by six tracks here, including two recorded by an earlier, totally different incarnation of the band, in which they were a bit like a charmingly sloppy Kinks. The rest of the album is more erratic, but still worthwhile. The Purple Hearts play

respectably tough British-style R&B/rock; the Throb do a vicious cover of the folk standard "Black," with shrieking guitar plucks; and the Wild Cherries are the most progressive-oriented (though least interesting) of the lot, with soul and hard rock influences. —*Richie Unterberger*

The Raven EP LP, Vol. 3 / 1984 / Raven ✦✦✦
A compilation of three reissue EPs that had originally appeared on the Raven label a few years previously, containing six or seven tracks apiece by Australian '60s groups Ray Brown, the Groop, and the Pink Finks. These bands weren't terribly similar to each other, which makes it doubtful that many people are going to enjoy the album from start to finish. If you've got a dedicated interest in Australian '60s rock (or in obscure '60s rock in general), there's some decent stuff to investigate here. Ray Brown played in a decent, tough Merseybeat style; the Pink Finks offered fairly raw R&B, though they're no match for the Pretty Things or the Animals. The Groop were by far the weakest of the trio, with anonymous-sounding '60s pop-rock that holds little interest. —*Richie Unterberger*

RCA's Greatest One-Hit Wonders / Jul. 29, 1996 / RCA ✦✦
You'd have to be a pretty strange bird indeed to want to hear classics by the Youngbloods ("Get Together"), Jesse Belvin ("Guess Who"), and Mickey & Sylvia ("Love Is Strange") next to novelties like Lorne Greene's "Ringo," Zager & Evans' "In the Year 2525," Neal Hefti's "Batman Theme," and Marilyn Monroe's "River of No Return." But that's exactly what you'll find on this compilation of 17 cuts from the RCA catalog, mostly from the 1950s and 1960s. True, it's hard to find singles like Tony Perkins' "Moon-Light Swim," Floyd Robinson's "Makin' Love," and (let us not forget) the Pipes & Drums & the Military Band of the Royal Scots Dragoon Guards' bagpipe-driven "Amazing Grace" on CD oldies compilations. But you have to consider that there really hasn't been much of a demand for those items. It's a ridiculously (as in senselessly) eclectic assortment of cuts, of use only to those collectors who have to have every chart hit, regardless of what it sounds like. —*Richie Unterberger*

Rebel Rousers: Southern Rock Classics / Jan. 24, 1992 / Rhino ✦✦✦✦
An audio tour of some of the genre's best moments, featuring seminal tracks by Lynyrd Skynyrd, the Allman Brothers Band, the Outlaws, the Marshall Tucker Band, and .38 Special. Interesting to compare these sides with the early-'90s vogue in country music. —*Cub Koda*

The Red Bird Story / 1991 / Charly ✦✦✦✦
Red Bird was a great label in the mid-'60s, releasing some excellent soul/pop hybrids and some of the greatest girl group records of all time, especially those by the Shangri-Las and the Dixie Cups. This four-CD, 96-track compilation is a frustratingly mixed attempt to enshrine its legacy. There are lots of great sides here: all the Shangri-Las and Dixie Cups hits, many of their rarities, one-shots by the Ad Libs, Jelly Beans, Butterflies, and Tradewinds, and cool rarities by Bessie Banks, Dee Dee Warwick, Evie Sands, Ellie Greenwich, the Soul Brothers, Cathy Saint, Linda Jones, and Andy Kim. But the programming is unnervingly jumpy and haphazard, the liner notes surprisingly fuzzy (no information whatsoever is given about many of the lesser-known artists), and, in the absence of master tapes, some of the cuts were obviously taken from records. And for all its length, it's not even a complete collection of Red Bird's output; some songs that were excluded had even surfaced on previous Charly vinyl anthologies. There's still a lot of great music here, but the execution could have been a lot better. —*Richie Unterberger*

Red Bird Story, Vol. 2 / 1987 / Charly ✦✦✦
A pretty interesting double LP of Red Bird non-hits and rarities, although the diversity of material (and somewhat half-assed sequencing) means that it's more apt to be enjoyed by scholars rather than general listeners. There are three excellent 1966 Shangri-Las tracks; Cathy Saint's "Big Bad World," one of the better non-hit girl group singles; cult soul singer Linda Jones' "Fugitive from Love"; Ellie Greenwich's fabulous dramatic Wall-of-Sound ballad, "You Don't Know"; and rare solo outings by Jeff Barry, Barry Mann, and Shadow Morton, who usually confined their activities to songwriting and production. Most of side four is taken up with previously unreleased extracts from a Jelly Beans session. Much, but not nearly all, of this is on the Charly box set *The Red Bird Story*, so collectors may want to keep an eye out for it. —*Richie Unterberger*

Reservoir Dogs / 1992 / MCA ✦✦✦✦
Only five songs here were featured prominently in Quentin Tarantino's rousing crime film ("Little Green Bag," "Hooked On a Feeling," "I Gotcha," "Stuck In the Middle With You," and "Coconut"), but the record includes Steven Wright's introductions from the film (separately indexed, thankfully), as well as Tarantino's infamous interpretation of the meaning of Madonna's "Like a Virgin" and Harvey Keitel's monologue on how to rob a jewelry store. In total, that's about fifteen to twenty minutes of material. Padding out the rest of the disc are three new songs that were heard in passing in the film—"Fool for Love" is very good, "Harvest Moon" passable, and "Magic Carpet Ride" is abominable. After this, the disc has passed the half hour mark by two minutes.

The amount of music you'll actually want to listen to makes it even shorter, but it is a soundtrack you'll want to return to. —*Stephen Thomas Erlewine*

The Return of the Del-Fi & Donna Story / 1994 / Del-Fi ✦✦✦

Like the first volume (*The Del-Fi & Donna Story*), this has 30-odd cuts from the late '50s-early '60s heyday of Del-Fi, the L.A.-based indie noted for recording Ritchie Valens, Johnny Crawford, and various one-shot artists. The music isn't as strong as the previous disc, but it does go further into the vaults for rarer items (some of which were previously unreleased), although as a whole it's kind of a mish-mash of styles. There are reasonably interesting numbers by the likes of Preston Epps, Ron Holden, Chan Romero (including some of his unreleased demos), doowoppers the Pentagons, the Addrisi Brothers, and a few instrumental acts, though nothing that would appeal to those without a very deep interest in early rock 'n' roll. —*Richie Unterberger*

Return of the DJ / 1996 / Bomb Entertainment ✦✦✦✦

Although vocal rap has become all but synonymous with hip-hop, effectively displacing DJs as the prime movers in determining the music's distinctive aesthetic, a new generation of hip-hop DJs are going it alone, approaching the turntable as an instrument in its own right. San Francisco promoter David Paul's brilliant *Return of the DJ* compilation charts this continuing evolution, with sturdy, mind-bogglingly complex turntable orchestration from such names as Q-Bert, Mixmaster Mike, DJ Disk, the Beat Junkies, New York's X-Men, Z-Trip, and DJ Ghetto, among others. Fluid beats, vast, layered instrumental passages, and tons of deft scratching loosely cement the notion of a restless, DJ-based hip-hop avant-garde craving only one thing: innovation. —*Sean Cooper*

Return of the DJ, Vol. 2 / 1997 / Bomb ✦✦✦✦

The Bomb's second guided tour through the bedrooms of hip-hop's new experimental underground draws this time from an international pool of beat junkies, with tracks checking in from London, New York, Finland, Montreal, Norway, Detroit, and Paris, among others. Names both familiar and unknown– Roc Raider, DJ E.Q., Z-Trip, and Godfather, as well as Kid Koala, Tommy Tee, and Jimmie Jam. The follow-up to the Bomb's scorching debut double-LP, *Return II* features 16 tracks in all of consistently mindblowing (if not quite as innovative) instrumental turntable experiments. —*Sean Cooper*

Risque Rhythm: Nasty 50s R&B / 1991 / Rhino ✦✦✦✦

Risque Rhythm: Nasty 50s R&B contains 18 raw, raunchy R&B and jump blues records from the likes of Moose Jackson, Dinah Washington, the Five Royales, Billy Ward & the Dominoes, Wynonie Harris, Roy Brown and the Swallows. It's remarkable how explicit these double-entrendre-laced singles were, but what really makes *Risque Rhythm* worth acquiring is its gritty, pounding rhythms which are just as sexy as the lyrics. —*Stephen Thomas Erlewine*

Rock Instrumental Classics, Vol. 1 / 1994 / Rhino ✦✦✦✦

Rhino begins yet another concept line with 18 tasty instrumentals from the rock era. It's the first of a five-volume set devoted to this genre, and they certainly picked the right era to launch it. From Duane Eddy's shuddering guitar riffs and Link Wray's rumbling licks to Lee Allen's honking sax lines and bleating phrases, Dave "Baby" Cortez's distorted organ and Ernie Fields' swing/boogie, this anthology shows how early rock 'n' roll emerged through the union of seemingly disparate musical elements. Besides big band jazz and shouting blues, there were also bits of rockabilly, pop, novelty tunes and country, reworked and presented in short, captivating ditties. —*Ron Wynn*

Rock Instrumental Classics, Vol. 2 / 1994 / Rhino ✦✦✦✦

The second release in Rhino's rock instrumentals series moves into the 1960s, again presenting a wide array of material. There's jazz-tinged fare by pianist Ray Bryant, roadhouse blues/boogie from Lonnie Mack, the Ventures' signature surf tune "Walk Don't Run" and another Duane Eddy floor-shaker, "Because They're Young." This collection also shows that the novelty and silly tunes weren't quite as inspired in the 1960s; neither the Fireballs' "Bulldog" nor the T-Bones' "No Matter What Shape (Your Stomach's In)" will ever make anyone forget the Coasters. There are several interesting gimmick and period-piece oddities, from Mason Williams' "Classical Gas" to Jorgen Ingmann's "Apache" and "(Ghost) Riders In The Sky" by the Ramroads. It's shorter than the first volume, and has a bit more fluff, but is still quite valuable. —*Ron Wynn*

Rock Instrumental Classics, Vol. 3 / 1994 / Rhino ✦✦✦

Rhino's third rock instrumentals volume covers the '70s, a period that found disco, funk, and fusion joining the formula alongside one-shot concept works and the usual novelty numbers. The 18 cuts include stomping club/funk from B.T. Express and Brass Construction, King Curtis' updated honking sax cover of Led Zeppelin's "Whole Lotta Love," very stylized material from the Electric Light Orchestra and Deodato, and memorable outings by Billy Preston, Edgar Winter and AWB. Gary Glitter, Edgar Winter, the Chakachas, Rhinoceros, and Van McCoy offer lighter pop variations, and "Sun Goddess" was a musically adventurous excursion into fusion by Earth, Wind & Fire. —*Ron Wynn*

Rock Instrumental Classics, Vol. 4 / 1994 / Rhino ✦✦✦

While the material on volume four of Rhino's rock instrumentals set chronologically preceded what was on the third volume, no soul, R&B or even soul-jazz and funk fan should mind these 18 genuine classics, including two superb numbers from Booker T. and the MGs, seminal tracks by the Mar-Keys, Bar-Kays and Cannonball Adderley, and great Latin tunes from Ray Barretto and Mongo Santamaria. There's absolutely no fluff, and the presence on CD of rare cuts like the Young Holt Trio's "Wack Wack" and Alvin Cash & the Crawlers' "Twine Time" is most welcome. —*Ron Wynn*

Rock Instrumental Classics, Vol. 5 / 1994 / Rhino ✦✦✦✦✦

Rhino closes its five-volume rock instrumentals series with an 18-track outing devoted to surf guitar. This fast-paced, prickly and frequently exciting form may not be among the most diversified structurally, but if does offer some surging playing from its practitioners. They range from founding father Dick Dale to its most popular bands, the Surfaris, Belairs, Ventures and Chantays. While not particularly a hardcore surf collection, this disc certainly outlines its virtues, and the tunes were long enough to display guitar proficiency, but short enough to prevent self-indulgence and repetition. —*Ron Wynn*

Rock This Town: Rockabilly Hits, Vol. 1 / 1991 / Rhino ✦✦✦✦

Rock This Town: Rockabilly Hits, Vol. 1 is a stellar, 18-track collection that contains the bulk of such classic rockabilly singles as Johnny Burnette's "The Train Kept a-Rollin'," Bill Haley's "Rock the Joint," Roy Orbison's "Ooby Dooby," Carl Perkins' "Blue Suede Shoes," Billy Riley's "Red Hot," Dale Hawkins' "Susie-Q," Buddy Knox's "Party Doll," Gene Vincent's "Lotta Lovin'," Buddy Holly's "Oh Boy!," Jerry Lee Lewis' "High School Confidential" and Ritchie Valens' "Come on, Let's Go." Not only does it contain those hits, but there are terrific obscurities from Jimmy Lloyd, Nicky Nelson, Sonnee West, Janis Martin and Sanford Clark, making *Rock This Town* and its companion volume a definitive collection for the average listener. —*Stephen Thomas Erlewine*

Rock This Town: Rockabilly Hits, Vol. 2 / 1991 / Rhino ✦✦✦✦

For its first half, the second volume of *Rock This Town: Rockabilly Hits* is as strong as its predecessor, running through such classic singles as Eddie Cochran's "C'mon Everybody," Wanda Jackson's "Let's Have a Party," Conway Twitty's "Danny Boy," Ronnie Hawkins' "Mary Lou," Johnny Horton's "Honky Tonk Hardwood Floor," Jack Scott's "The Way I Walk" and the Rock-a-Teens' "Woo-Hoo." The latter half contains rockabilly revival numbers ranging from Commander Cody ("Hot Rod Lincoln"), Dave Edmunds ("I Hear You Knocking") and Billy Swan ("I Can Help") to the Blasters ("Flattop Joint"), Robert Gordon ("Red Hot"), and Stray Cats ("Rock This Town"). While these latter-day recordings have merit, they would have been better-heard on a third volume, leaving the second volume to additional cuts from the '50s and '60s. So, that does mean *Rock This Town* is an imperfect collection, but there's enough good stuff to make it necessary for anyone that purchased *Vol. 1*. —*Stephen Thomas Erlewine*

Rockin' from Coast to Coast Vol. 1 / 1996 / Ace ✦✦✦

Garage rock wasn't a concept that originated in the mid-'60s. In the aftermath of the initial rock 'n' roll explosion, young rockabilly and R&B singers brought their unhoned talents into tiny studios throughout the country. This is a compilation of 26 of those efforts, mostly from the late '50s (most from 1958, in fact), and mostly for small independent labels, although some of these were leased to major labels, and a few were even recorded for major labels directly. Only one of these was a chart hit (Freddy Cannon's "Buzz Buzz a-Diddle-It"), and it's easy to see why, from two points of view. The approaches were too uncompromisingly raw, and the production too crude. On the other side of that coin, the songs themselves were rarely anything special, usually being standard three-chord knockoffs with little to make them stand out besides the ferocious energy of the performances. It's not great art, but it's certainly entertaining. That's especially true when the energy spills over to mania, as on the legendary Tyrone Schmidling's shambling sides, the incredibly sloppy rendition of "Good Golly Miss Molly" by Sam Cooke proteges the Valiants, or the echoed-to-infinity Tex-Mex-cum-Jerry Lee Lewis of the Rio Rockers (released on Capitol!). There are some unexpected appearances by stars as well, such as Eddie Cochran (who plays guitar on Lee Denson's "New Shoes"), Brenda Lee (the early rockabilly track "Rock the Bop"), a teenaged Joe South, and Roy Clark (heard as a rockabilly singer). The collection's also educational in its own way, as an illustration of just how extreme and far-flung the rock 'n' roll revolution had become at the grass-roots level just a few years after its birth. —*Richie Unterberger*

Rockin' in the Farmhouse: Original Rockabilly and Chicken Bop, Vol. 2 / 1992 / Sundazed ✦✦✦✦

Rockin' in the Farmhouse—Original Rockabilly and Chicken Bop—Vol. 2 is an excellent 20-track compilation featuring the best of the Roulette label's rarest rockabilly tracks. Highlights include Don "Red" Roberts' "Only One," Jimmy Isle's "Goin' Wild," Jimmy Lloyd's "Rocket in My

Pocket," and five chaotic unissued tracks by the Rock-A-Teens. —*Cub Koda*

Roulette Rock & Roll, Vol. 2: Everybody's Gonna / Jul. 29, 1994 / Sequel ✦✦✦
Although titled *Roulette Rock & Roll* and thus giving off images of a reissue loaded with white rockabilly renegades, this volume is largely a rhythm and blues mix with 11 of its 22 tracks devoted to a pair of Screamin' Jay Hawkins tracks ("The Whammy" and "Strange"), a half-dozen Wynonie Harris numbers (four of them previously unissued) and the four sides the Isley Brothers recorded for Gone and Mark-X. Utilizing the blazing instrumental "7-11" by the Gone All Stars as a midway watershed, the rest of the compilation stays solidly in R&B territory with group offerings from the 4 Chaps (a great 1956 cover of "Roll Over Beethoven"), the DuPonts (the silly but fun "Screamin' Ball at Dracula Hall"), the Cookies ("Hippy Dippy Daddy"), the Emanons ("Hindu Baby"), the Echoes ("Ding Dong"), the Chaperones, and the Valentines with their big hit, "Woo Woo Train." The Cadillacs' sax man and musical director Jesse Powell gets to vocalize with the boys backing him up on "Ain't You Gonna" while Mabel King closes the compilation up nicely singing the virtues of "Alabama Rock and Roll." R&B that tips its hat to both the famous and the undeservedly obscure. —*Cub Koda*

Rutles Highway Revisited / 1990 / Shimmy Disc ✦✦✦✦
Of the hundreds of tribute albums that have been assembled since the mid-'80s, this had one of the most clever concepts: perform a "tribute" to a band that never existed. The Rutles, Eric Idle's spot-on television parody of the Beatles, were never a bonafide unit, but they did record some fine satires for the film's soundtrack, composed by Rutle and ex-Bonzo Dog Band honcho Neil Innes. What we have here are 20 alternative acts of the '90s covering all of the Rutles' songs. Better than most tributes, it still falls prey to the genre's chief pitfalls: compared to the original, it's forced, stiff, and lacking. The best interpretations tend to be the most straightforward, like Syd Straw and Marc Ribot's acoustic "I Must Be in Love"; Shonen Knife's "Goose Step Mama," with its high-pitched vocals and jerky tempos, would have fit easily onto one of their actual albums. Alternative rock collectors may want to pick this up for the otherwise unavailable tracks by Galaxie 500, King Missile, Jellyfish, and Daniel Johnston; there are also some half-famous stalwarts of the indie scene like Das Damen, Unrest, and Peter Stampfel, as well as total obscurities like the Tinklers and Paleface. —*Richie Unterberger*

S.V.R. Rock Hits of the Sixties / 1985 / S.V.R. ✦✦✦
The small Detroit label S.V.R. had a couple of huge local smashes in 1966 (the Tidal Waves' "Farmer John" and the Four Gents' "Soul Sister" both made number one on some Detroit charts, and are both included here). They also recorded some first class garage pop with the Unrelated Segments. This is a good compilation of the label's mid-'60s output, not exclusively garage-oriented; there's also some decent blue-eyed soul, an appealingly limpid white Motown imitation by the Boys, and an instrumental version of "Work Song" (by the Quintette Plus) with endearingly out-of-tune horns. The highlights, though, have to be the Unrelated Segments' singles, wild screamers that nonetheless have good pop hooks, especially "Story of My Life" and "Where You Gonna Go?" —*Richie Unterberger*

The Saint [OST] / Mar. 25, 1997 / Virgin ✦✦✦✦
The soundtrack to the silly Val Kilmer action movie *The Saint* offered a surprisingly effective and useful collection of electronica, offering a good overview and introduction to many of the genre's biggest artists. The Orbital's icy, attractive reworking of "The Saint Theme," Daft Punk's pulsating "Da Funk," Underworld's "Pearl's Girl" and Sneaker Pimps' sexy "6 Underground" stand out, but there are also first-rate cuts from Fluke, Dreadzone, Moby and the Chemical Brothers, who weigh in with an instrumental of "Setting Sun." There's also Everything but the Girl, David Bowie and Luscious Jackson, who find clever ways of balancing pop and techno. *The Saint* still has a few mediocre cuts from the likes of Superior and Duran Duran, but on the whole it's one of the few soundtracks that work better as an album than as a movie. —*Stephen Thomas Erlewine*

Saturday Night Fever / 1977 / PolyGram ✦✦✦✦✦
Saturday Night Fever is where disco turned from a fad into a phenomenon, crossing over into the mainstream and infiltrating every area of pop culture. Based on the film's soundtrack, it's not hard to see why. Where most disco albums were weighed down by endless grooves, *Saturday Night Fever* is relatively concise; only two tracks are longer than five minutes and one of those, the Trampps' "Disco Inferno," actually showed how intoxicatingly good, extended disco could be. But the real key to the album's success isn't "Disco Inferno," or the silly instrumentals "A Fifth of Beethoven" and "Night on Disco Mountain," it's how the Bee Gees were able to mould disco into a pop form on "Stayin' Alive," "How Deep Is Your Love," "Night Fever," "More than a Woman," "Jive Talkin'," "You Should Be Dancing" and Yvonne Elliman's "If I Can't Have You." These are the songs that kept *Saturday Night Fever* on the charts for months on end, and these are the songs that defined an era.

Although portions of *Saturday Night Fever* now sound dated, at its best, it was a peak that most disco albums could not reach. —*Stephen Thomas Erlewine*

The Scepter Records Story / May 26, 1992 / Capricorn ✦✦✦✦✦
During the '50s and early '60s, NYC-based Scepter Records and its subsidiary Wand were part of a group of independents whose artists churned out hit after hit, defining the sound of the day and shaping the sound of the future. The Shirelles, Dionne Warwick, and the Isley Brothers all got their start there; if you love tough, pre-soul-era records like "Will You Still Love Me Tomorrow," "Twist and Shout," and "Walk on By," then this is for you. The label's roster also included singers Chuck Jackson, Maxine Brown, and Tommy Hunt; instrumentalist King Curtis; proto-pop/country artists B.J. Thomas and Ronnie Milsap; and punksters Kingsmen. That's right—"Louie Louie" is here, along with lots of other truly great music. Even though the three discs could have been condensed to a killer two, this box gets high marks. —*Christine Ohlman*

The Scotty Story / 1993 / Arf! Arf! ✦✦✦
Based on Minnesota, the small, independent Scotty company recorded some worthwhile garage rock in the 1960s, with Warren Kendrick acting both as producer and songwriter for many of the acts on his label. While you couldn't say this is an essential release if you're not a garage fan, this is a decent, 30-cut compilation of released and unreleased material from Scotty and its affiliated labels. The Electras in particular have an appealing snarl, best showcased on "Dirty Old Man" and the original, molten-hot version of "Action Woman" (covered by another of Kendrick's acts, the Litter, whose version appears on the *Pebbles* series). The 11 Electras tracks are the most interesting portion of this anthology, but most of the rest of it's reasonably satisfying fuzz-Farfisa garage pop by the Scotsmen, the Victors, the Second Edition, Hope, the Paisleys, and White Lightning, sometimes with pop and/or psychedelic edges. The Scotsmen's "Beer Bust Blues" is frat rock at its grossest; fans of the Litter (by far the most famous group on this compilation) will find a previously unreleased cover of "Hey Joe," as well as a 7-Up commercial. —*Richie Unterberger*

Searchin' for Shakes: Swedish Beat 1965-1968 / 1984 / Amigo [Sweden] ✦✦✦✦
One of the very best compilations of '60s rock from a non-English-speaking country, with excellent fidelity (usually not the case with these productions). With their barely accented English vocals and the heavy mod-rock flavor (with a pinch of Merseybeat thrown in), a bunch of these Swedish bands could pass for overlooked British Invasion groups. The Who's brand of auto-destruct guitar noise seemed to hit home particularly hard in Sweden, and the cuts by the Steampacket II, Lee Kings, Tages, Namelosers, and Bootjacks will appeal to anyone who reveres the early Who and Creation. Other highlights include the Mascots, whose track is one of the best early Merseybeat imitations to be found anywhere, and the Lea Riders, whose "Dom Kellar Dos Mods" (previously issued on a *Pebbles* volume) is one of the prime demented psychedelic obscurities of all time. —*Richie Unterberger*

Searching in the Wilderness / 198? / Muziek Expres ✦✦✦✦
While this compilation might prove mighty hard to track down, it's one of the better anthologies of raw, rare mid-'60s rock, concentrating exclusively on bands from the UK and Europe (i.e., this is not a "garage" compilation in the classic sense). Some of these groups enjoy a cult reputation, especially the Dutch ones (the Outsiders, Q65, Cuby & the Blizzards, the Motions); most will draw blanks even on the faces of specialist record store owners. Still, if you like the R&B/mod of the Pretty Things or the Who and are looking for stuff in that mode that's less polished, this is a good place to land. The Red Squares' "You Can Be My Baby" is as good as the best London 1966 mod; the Buzz's "You're Holding Me Down" is one of British producer Joe Meek's hardest-rocking sessions; Jimmy Page plays a raunchy session guitar lead on Sean Buckley's "Everybody Knows"; and the Outsiders' "Won't You Listen" is one of the wildest, most unhinged beat/punk performances of all time. There's also a rare and basic unreleased mid-'60s song by the Kinks (who are identified as the "Muswell Ravens" on the cover), "All Aboard." —*Richie Unterberger*

Shakin' Fit! / 1992 / Candy ✦✦✦✦
1960s soul music wasn't just Motown, earnest gospel-filled ballads, and dancefloor rabble-rousers. There were also quite a few soul performers who treated the music as fun, first and foremost, taking a somewhat looser and goofier approach than the stars that had long careers. This 29-track CD is a good document of soul music as pure fun, by singers who never had a hit (Don & Dewey are the only marginally recognizable names here), and who owed stronger debts to the honking R&B music of the '50s than most other soul performers. Some of these are downright funny novelties (the Five Du-Tones' "The Chicken Astronaut," Emanual Laskey's "Welfare Cheese"); a great deal of these are novelty-tinged dance tunes that verge on silly, in the best sense of the word ("The Frog," "Skin the Cat," "Sticky Pig Feet," "The Cow," "The Chicken Scratch"). This could have done with some decent liner notes (there are

virtually none), but it's a good deal for soul fans looking for some totally overlooked and fun-filled rarities. —*Richie Unterberger*

Sin Alley / 1985 / Big Daddy ✦✦✦✦
One of the first compilations to apply the *Pebbles* mentality to '50s rock, presenting 18 rare non-hits that were too raw in production and execution to reach a large audience. Most of this is rockabilly, although there's some R&B and straight instrumental rock as well. It's kind of monochrome-toned taken all at once, but it's a good, often funny, smattering of early rock 'n' roll at its most untamed, with uncouth vocals and wild sax and guitar breaks galore. Since no A&R execs were listening anyway, some of the performers felt free to let loose with some pretty over-the-top lyrics, such as Myron Lee's "Homicide," Gradie O'Neal's "The Turkeyneck Stretch," Roy Gaines' "Skippy Is A Sissy," and the Frantic Four's "T.V. Mama," the last of which has some of the most outlandish rock vocals of all time. —*Richie Unterberger*

Singles / Jun. 30, 1992 / Epic ✦✦✦✦
Although Nirvana isn't included, there's no better introduction to the Seattle grunge scene than the *Singles* soundtrack. Most of the significant Seattle bands—Pearl Jam, Mudhoney, Alice In Chains, Screaming Trees, Soundgarden, and Mother Love Bone—are featured, as well as Chicago's Smashing Pumpkins, ex-Replacements leader Paul Westerberg, and Seattle native Jimi Hendrix. "State of Love and Trust" is arguably Pearl Jam's finest moment. Westerberg's first songs since the breakup of the Replacements are here; "Dyslexic Heart" and "Waiting for Somebody" are excellent acoustic-based rockers. Mudhoney's "Overblown," an attack on the marketing of the Seattle scene, is the only true grunge song, with pummeling fuzz guitars and whiny vocals. Competing for top song honors are Alice In Chains' grinding "Would?" and Screaming Trees' pop/psychedelic guitar rave-up "Nearly Lost You." An excellent introduction to the 1990s' alternative rock scene. —*Stephen Thomas Erlewine*

Sixties Rebellion, Vol. 8: Mondo Mutiny #1: Love / 1993 / Music Maniac ✦✦✦
Here's an unusual album concept for you: yet another LP of rare '60s garage singles, the twist being that every single one of them is a cover of a song by famed L.A. psychedelic-folk-rockers Love. If you suspect the source pool is kind of limited, you're right. The compilers managed to come up with 20 tracks, with many multiple versions: four of "Signed D.C.," three of "My Flash On You," three of "Little Red Book" (not written by Love, but popularized by them), three of "7 and 7 Is," etc. And these singles were damned rare and obscure: even the most famous of these groups are known only to specialist collectors (the Sons of Adam, the Other Half, the Rising Storm, the Haunted). But if you're in the rather small sub-group of major Love/'60s garage rock fans, this is kind of a nifty item to have. There's more variation than you might expect, and listenability is maximized by the thoughtful decision to create as much space between multiple cover versions as possible. The arrangements are pleasingly raw, and sometimes done very well indeed (the female folk-rock singer on the Flower Power's "Orange Skies," the apocalyptic crashing folk-rock "Signed D.C." by December's Children Ltd., the Haunted's slowed-down reading of "Message To Pretty"). It also includes a good composition ("Feathered Fish") by Love's principal songwriter, Arthur Lee, that Love never recorded (in versions by both the Sons of Adam and the Other Half). Be aware, though, that the Velvet Underground cover of "She Comes in Colors" is not the famous Velvet Underground, but an unknown Australian pop-rock group that used the same name. —*Richie Unterberger*

Slow Jams: The 60s, Vols. 1 & 2 / The Right Stuff ✦✦✦
There aren't many surprises on these collections of romantic soul ballads from the '60s: lots of fine songs, virtually all of them big hits, nothing obscure in the least. For the general fan who just wants a decently programmed set, it does the job, with cuts by such greats as Percy Sledge, Aretha Franklin, Otis Redding, Dionne Warwick, the Temptations, James Brown, Smokey Robinson, and one-shots like Doris Troy and Barbara Mason, along with good liner notes from soul expert David Nathan. —*Richie Unterberger*

Slow Jams: The 70s, Vols. 1-3 / The Right Stuff ✦✦✦
The *Slow Jams* compilations of romantic soul ballads are obviously not designed for the ravenous collector: there are only ten tracks per disc, the liner notes are informative but basic, and most of the selections are well-known hits. But if you just want some basic highlights of lush '70s soul, or you're giving this to someone with a short attention span, the series does a respectable job. Hits by stars like Al Green, the Stylistics, the Isleys, the O'Jays, and Barry White are mixed with cuts by lesser-known singers like Sylvia, Norman Connors, and Major Harris. —*Richie Unterberger*

Smooth Grooves: A Sensual Collection, Vols. 1-9 / 1995 / Rhino ✦✦✦✦
Rhino's *Smooth Grooves: A Sensual Collection, Vols. 1-9* is an excellent overview of late '70s and early '80s urban R&B ballads—in other words, it features the biggest hits and best-known quiet storm songs. Each disc

contains 12 tracks, some presented in their 12-inch mixes which have never been available on CD before. But the primary strength of *Smooth Grooves* is how it proves that there were many classic soul songs released during this often-overlooked era. While it is true that there a few tediously bland cuts on nearly every volume, there are more keepers than throwaways, including such classics as "Shining Star," "Sexual Healing," "Float On," and "Something He Can Feel." The curious should start with the first volume, which gives an accurate idea of what the series is about, but any quiet storm fan will find every volume worth acquiring. —*Stephen Thomas Erlewine*

Smooth Grooves: The '60s, Vol. 1: Early '60s / Jan. 14, 1997 / Rhino ✦✦✦✦
The first of three chronologically divided compilations of '60s soul ballads has 1960-64 classics by Carla Thomas, Etta James, Ben E. King, Otis Redding, Solomon Burke, James Brown, Bobby Bland, Barbara Lewis, Jerry Butler and others. There are also a few worthy entries from names which won't be familiar to the casual collector, like William Bell, Ketty Lester, and Betty Everett. There's nothing terribly rare here, but it's a first-rate anthology of early soul's smoochiest sides, with thorough liner notes. —*Richie Unterberger*

Smooth Grooves: The '60s, Vol. 2: Mid-'60s / Jan. 14, 1997 / Rhino ✦✦✦✦
The *Smooth Grooves* series moves into the mid-'60s with 16 tracks by both soul giants (Aretha Franklin, Wilson Pickett, Otis Redding, Sam & Dave, the Impressions) and a smattering of performers whose success was primarily confined to the R&B charts (Walter Jackson, Lorraine Ellison, and Howard Tate, who does the original version of "Get It While You Can," covered by Janis Joplin). It's a dependable lineup of some of the best romantic soul of the era; the most obscure cut is Chris Bartley's "The Sweetest Thing This Side of Heaven," written by Van McCoy. —*Richie Unterberger*

Smooth Grooves: The '60s, Vol. 3: Late '60s / Jan. 14, 1997 / Rhino ✦✦✦✦
Of the three *Smooth Grooves* collections devoted to the 1960s, this is the lushest, if a bit slicker and sappier than the others. It also has the most off-the-beaten-track selections, including a pre-Hi single by Al Green ("Back up Train"), and hits by the Dynamics, the Unifics, the Masqueraders, the Moments, and Eddie Floyd that made a much bigger impact on the R&B charts than the pop ones. More familiar cuts are on tap from Aaron Neville ("Tell It like It Is"), Eddie Holman ("Hey There Lonely Girl"), and the Delfonics ("La-La-Means I Love You"). The most valuable treasure may be Toussaint McCall's "Nothing Takes the Place of You," a prime slice of New Orleans sweet soul. —*Richie Unterberger*

Someone to Love / 1996 / Big Beat ✦✦
Thirty-track compilation of early San Francisco rock from the Autumn label, some previously unissued. This disc gets docked a star because it's not the best or most economic way to collect this mid-'60s material, though much of it's of historic interest. The 13 Great Society cuts are all available on Sundazed's domestic *Born to Be Burned* CD; Sundazed has also devoted separate collections to the Mojo Men and the Vejtables, both of whom have songs here. The disc is filled out by unexceptional pop/garage rock by the Tikis and Butch Engle (most previously unissued). The tracks to watch out for, if you're a serious collector of San Francisco rock, are an acoustic, previously unreleased version of "Let's Get Together" by its composer, Dino Valenti, and a previously unissued cut by Mojo Men/Vejtables singer Jan Ashton, "About My Tears." If you're not a completist, you're better off searching for the separate-artist Sundazed comps. In any case, none of this is particularly great by either San Francisco rock or garage rock standards. The Great Society were an excellent and important group (the original version of "Somebody to Love" is here), but the live tapes from a later vintage that were issued on Columbia are far better than the relatively primitive cuts offered here. —*Richie Unterberger*

Songs Lennon & McCartney Gave Away / 1979 / EMI ✦✦✦✦
This British import isn't easy to find these days, but it's essential for Beatles and British Invasion fans, collecting almost every Lennon-McCartney song that was not recorded by the Beatles, but did appear on releases by other artists. The bulk of the material dates from 1963 and 1964, and indeed, most of these were British and/or American hits, some of them quite huge. The tracks by Peter & Gordon and Billy J. Kramer are probably the best known, but you also get the more obscure compositions they donated to Cilla Black, the Applejacks, the Fourmost, P.J. Proby, Tommy Quickly, and Mike Shannon & the Strangers (who?). As in almost everything else they did, John and Paul displayed shrewd judgment in the tracks they passed on to others; most of them are far more lightweight and sappy than the Beatles' typical material. And so are most of the interpretations; in cases where the Beatles recorded unreleased versions (as with "Hello Little Girl," "Love of the Loved," and "That Means a Lot"), the Fab Four's versions are vastly superior. That said, this is irresistibly melodic and jaunty British Invasion pop, with a few late-'60s tracks thrown in by Cilla Black, Carlos Mendes, and Chris

Barber. The only notable absentees are the hits by Mary Hopkin ("Good-bye") and Badfinger ("Come and Get It," which actually bears a McCart-ney solo composition credit). —*Richie Unterberger*

Songs of Protest / 1991 / Rhino ✦✦✦

Of course there are too many noteworthy songs of protest to fit onto one collection, even (or especially) if you're limiting youself to the '60s, as Rhino does on this compilation. Still, it does a good job of mixing mon-ster hits by Barry McGuire, Sonny Bono, Dion, the Kingston Trio, the Temptations, and Edwin Starr with more obscure cuts. Country Joe's "I-Feel-Like-I'm-Fixin'-To-Die Rag" is here, as well as Sonny Bono's self-pitying "Laugh at Me," the pre-electric Donovan's cover of Buffy Saint-Marie's "Universal Soldier," and Manfred Mann's fine, overlooked cover of Dylan's "With God on Our Side." The most hard-to-find songs span the opposite ends of the spectrum. "It's Good News Week," a 1966 hit for the Jonathan King-led group Hedgehoppers Anonymous, is a lightweight catalog of social ills that retains considerable period charm. Far more earnest is Phil Ochs' "I Ain't Marchin' Anymore," represented here by the non-LP, electric folk-rock version released as a single in 1966. Although it made no commercial impact, it holds up to the best protest anthems of the era, both musically and lyrically. —*Richie Unterberger*

Soul Shots, Vol. 1: We Got More Soul (Dance Party) / 1987 / Rhino ✦✦✦✦

The 11-volume *Soul Shots* series, originally issued on vinyl in the late '80s, are the best general overview compilations of soul music. They've since been condensed into a four-CD series which reprises some of the highlights from the records and adds some new tracks. As many of the songs from the original 11-volume set didn't make it onto the CDs, the vinyl editions, which are still easy to find, are still recommended, and even necessary, for the soul connaisseur. *Vol. 1*, with the focus on rau-cous uptempo numbers, has a characteristic mix of stars (James Brown, Jackie Wilson) with important minor figures (Jackie Lee, J.J. Jackson, Dyke & the Blazers, Robert Parker). With thorough liner notes, these compilations are great ways to catch up on a lot of the best one- and two-shot artists of the soul era. —*Richie Unterberger*

Soul Shots, Vol. 2: The "In" Crowd / 1987 / Rhino ✦✦✦✦

"Sweet soul" is not slow ballads, but light-hearted, pop-oriented soul, with the accent on pleasant (often high) vocal arrangements. Not as crit-ically respected as dance soul, deep soul, Motown, or some other sub-genres, there were nonetheless many fine cuts recorded in this style dur-ing soul's heyday. This compilation has a lot of good ones, including Brenton Wood's "Gimme Little Sign," Deon Jackson's "Love Makes the World Go Round," the Esquires' "Get on Up," the Larks' "The Jerk," Bobby Hebb's "Sunny," and several other lesser-known cuts. —*Richie Unterberger*

Soul Shots, Vol. 3: Soul Twist (Soul Instrumentals) / 1987 / Rhino ✦✦✦✦

More than other mid- and late-'60s pop styles, soul lent itself well to instrumentals, both party tunes and slower romantic stuff. This volume has big hits by most of the major soul instrumental stars (Booker T. & the MG's, the Mar-Keys, King Curtis, the Bar-Kays, Young-Holt Unlim-ited, Ramsey Lewis, Hugh Masekela), as well as one-shots like Cliff Nobles ("The Horse") and cuts by Alvin Cash and the Viscounts that rarely get played on oldies radio. —*Richie Unterberger*

Soul Shots, Vol. 4: Tell Mama (Screamin' Soul Sisters) / 1987 / Rhino ✦✦✦✦

One of the best volumes of the series, assembling some of soul's most emotional and expressive female performers. Running from Motown imitations to novelties to pop-soul to raw deep soul to blues-soul, it has outstanding cuts by Etta James, Koko Taylor, Maxine Brown, Fontella Bass, Barbara George, Gloria Jones, and Shirley Ellis. Lorraine Ellison, Linda Jones, and Patti Drew are names only known to serious soul fans, but their tracks are just as fine as the ones by more famous names, and the two selections by Aretha Franklin are among her more obscure ("Lee Cross," from her Columbia era, and the 1968 B-side "You Send Me"). —*Richie Unterberger*

Soul Shots, Vol. 5: La-La Means I Love You / 1987 / Rhino ✦✦✦✦

Another good mixture of stars and one-shots, different regions, and dif-ferent styles. This has cuts by the Impressions, James Carr, Lou Rawls, and Aaron Neville, Philly soul by the Delfonics and Eddie Holman, girl group soul by Barbara Mason, blue-eyed soul by Thee Midniters, New York soul by Garnett Mimms, and eccentric soul by Billy Stewart. All cuts are first-rate slow-tempo smoochers. —*Richie Unterberger*

Soul Shots, Vol. 6: Blue-Eyed Soul / 1988 / Rhino ✦✦✦✦

There weren't a great deal of white performers who sang and wrote soul with authentic conviction—most knew better than to try—but there were a few who not only pulled it off, but did it well, sometimes even crossing over into the Black audience. This LP has many of the more notable blue-eyed soul performers: the Rascals, Tony Joe White, Roy Head, Bill Deal, the Soul Survivors—as well as interesting obscurities in the style by the likes of Bob Kuban and Dean Parrish, and cuts in a blue-

eyed soul vein by performers not strictly associated with the style, like P.J. Proby, Billy Joe Royal, Lonnie Mack, and Wayne Cochran. It's missing major blue-eyed soulsters like the Righteous Brothers, John Fred, and the Box Tops, but those performers have good anthologies of their own. —*Richie Unterberger*

Soul Shots, Vol. 7: Urban Blues / 1988 / Rhino ✦✦✦✦

Another interesting subgenre that doesn't get a lot of critical attention: city blues bearing heavy soul influences. Every one of the performers on this compilation was a blues or soul performer of significance. B.B. King, Junior Wells, Albert King, Buddy Guy, and Otis Rush are bluesmen rep-resented by some of their most soul-soaked cuts; Little Junior Parker, Bobby Bland, Little Milton, and Lowell Fulsom worked the territory between soul, R&B, and blues; Tommy Tucker and Little Johnny Taylor were R&B singers who had hits with heavy blues influences, rounding out the several perspectives of this anthology. —*Richie Unterberger*

Soul Shots, Vol. 8: Sweet Soul Sisters / 1988 / Rhino ✦✦✦✦

They may be sweet in that they sing about love and have a lot of pop appeal, but the female soul singers on this anthology are measurably earthier and heavier than the male "sweet" soul singers spotlighted on Vol. 2 of this series. Jan Bradley, the Jewels, and Betty Everett fall close to the girl group sound; the Sweet Inspirations, led by Cissy Houston (mother of Whitney), take it to the most gospel-flavored extreme. Bar-bara Acklin and Brenda & the Tabulations are among the better-known minor female soul stars; there are also obscure singers like Jackie Ross, Patti Drew, and the Flirtations, whose hit "Nothing but a Heartache" was one of the best soul one-shots of the '60s. For many listeners, the high-light will be Gloria Jones' original version of "Tainted Love," emascu-lated into a synth-pop hit much later by Soft Cell. Jones' rendition isn't exactly sweet soul, but a storming dance number that ranks as one of the great hits-that-never-were of the '60s. —*Richie Unterberger*

Soul Shots, Vol. 9: More Dance Party / 1988 / Rhino ✦✦✦✦

As *Soul Shots* volumes go, this is populated with more obscure perform-ers/songs than usual, enhancing its appeal for collectors without decreasing its accessibility whatsoever. Etta James, Ike & Tina Turner, and Johnnie Taylor are stars, of course; there are also thrilling one-shots by the Capitols ("Cool Jerk"), the Parliaments ("I Wanna Testify," with a lineup including George Clinton), and the Marvelows ("I Do"). Jamo Thomas' "I Spy (For The FBI)" is one of soul's finer novelties, and the compilation also includes the rare original versions of the standards "Shake a Tail Feather" (by the Five Du-Tones) and "Mustang Sally" (by Sir Mack Rice). —*Richie Unterberger*

Soul Shots, Vol. 10: More Sweet Soul / 1988 / Rhino ✦✦✦✦

At least as good, and perhaps better than, the original "Sweet Soul" vol-ume. This has classic hits by Tyrone Davis, Major Lance, James Carr, the Impressions, and the Dells, as well as lesser-known selections by the O'Jays and Eddie Floyd, and hard-to-find items by the likes of the Radi-ants, Tony Clarke, Bobby Moore, and the Poets. The Showmen's "39-21-46," featuring future Chairmen of the Board lead singer General Johnson, is one of early soul's most genuinely eccentric moments. —*Richie Unterberger*

Soul Shots, Vol. 11: More Ballads / 1988 / Rhino ✦✦✦✦

For the soul fan looking to dig a little deeper than established classics, this is probably more exciting than the previous ballad collection in this series. McKinley Mitchell, Spyder Turner, Betty Harris, Jimmy Holi-day—they're all names known primarily to collectors, and they're all represented here. So are stars like the Impressions, Chuck Jackson, the Dells, and O.V. Wright, but the tracks are not among the famous hits. Especially interesting are the original versions of "Get It While You Can" (by Howard Tate), later covered by Janis Joplin, and "You Can Make It if You Try" (by Gene Allison), covered by the Rolling Stones on their first album. Other highlights are Jay Wiggins' "Sad Girl," one of the most haunting soul ballads ever, and Gloria Walker's "Talking About My Baby," one of the most deliciously bitchy and spiteful female soul perfor-mances, despite the fact that it rips off Etta James' "I'd Rather Go Blind." —*Richie Unterberger*

Soul Underground, Vol. 2 / 1995 / Sequel ✦✦✦

One gets the feeling that this 24-song compilation of rare soul sin-gles—originally released on the Roulette, Port, Jubilee, Cat, Alston, Dimension, and Dynovoice labels, mostly in the '60s—was assembled with more of an eye on rarity and collector value than coherence. If there's any thread, it's that they've enjoyed popularity on England's Northern Soul circuit, a school of enthusiasts that is nearly unrivaled for specialist enthusiasm. J.J. Jackson, the Orlons, the Skyliners, Big May-belle, the Clovers, and Esther Phillips are the only names that will be recognizable to most soul fans, and all of the singles by the aforemen-tioned singers are still obscure, usually dating from well past their com-mercial prime. Nevertheless, this is pleasant, danceable pop/soul, usu-ally with uptown production values. But there's not much that truly jumps out and grabs you by the gut, though occasional sides make a more distinct impression, like Beverly Ann Gibson's winning early-'60s pop/soul, June Adams' melodramatic "The Human Race," and J.J. Jackson's hoarse emotion on "It Seems like I've Been Here Before." —*Richie Unterberger*

Soulful Pop / Aug. 27, 1996 / Varese ✦✦✦✦
This is the kind of compilation that doesn't attract much critical attention, but is a pretty nifty concept: 17 songs from 1966-76 that are soul-pop at its poppiest and most commercial, running the scale from R&B-grounded cuts to near-bubblegum. It's a good mix of classics of the micro-genre (the Foundations' "Build Me up Buttercup" and "Baby, Now That I Found You," Jay & the Techniques' "Keep the Ball Rollin'," Maxine Nightingale's "Right Back Where We Started From"), minor half-forgotten hits (James & Bobby Purify's "Let Love Come Between Us," Chairmen of the Board's "You've Got Me Dangling on a String"), singles that were only big in England (Blue Mink's "Melting Pot," the Love Affair's cover of Robert Knight's "Everlasting Love"), and total flops (by the Groove and the Peoples Choice). Especially ingratiating are the Five Stairsteps' "O-oh Child" and Chee-Chee & Peppy's "I Know I'm in Love," a forgotten Jackson 5 imitation (and minor hit) from 1971. —*Richie Unterberger*

The Specialty Story / 1994 / Specialty ✦✦✦✦
Label-owner Art Rupe was a savvy business man who knew the black jukebox industry and what made it tick when he started his Specialty label in the late '40s. This sumptuous five-disc box set contains a bevy of highlights from this seminal R&B/rock 'n' roll label. Over the years, Rupe recorded a little bit of everything; early big band jump (the Liggins brothers), down-home blues and zydeco (Guitar Slim, Frankie Lee Sims, Clifton Chenier), gospel (early Sam Cooke and the Soul Stirrers) and doo wop (the Pentagons, Jesse Belvin). But with the discovery of the label's biggest star, Little Richard, in 1955, here is where the real story of rock 'n' roll begins. A box set that no lover of the real thing can be without. —*Cub Koda*

Stax Presents . . . Sweet Soul Music / 1988 / Stax ✦✦✦
Stax is usually thought of as the gritty alternative to pop/soul, but in its later years it recorded a fair quantity of "sweet soul" more akin to Motown and Gamble-Huff than from Otis Redding and Wilson Pickett. This has 13 Stax productions from the late '60s and early '70s, sung by smooth (and obscure) male groups like the Limitations, the Epsilons, the Lords, the Newcomers, and Fat Larry's Band; the Dramatics and (to a lesser degree) the Mad Lads and the Temprees are the only easily recognizable names to casual soul fans. It's okay, but primarily for collectors. It's pleasantly produced and harmonized, but nothing jumps out as a lost classic, and there are better discs of late-period sweet soul around. —*Richie Unterberger*

The Stax Soul Sisters / 1988 / Stax ✦✦✦
Fourteen cuts of female-sung soul, cut for the Stax label between the late '60s and mid-'70s. It's fair material that will largely appeal to collectors, not being near the top echelon of either soul music or Stax recordings. Carla Thomas, Barbara Lewis, Carla Thomas, Inez Foxx, and Mavis Staples are all represented by little-known tracks; second- or third-division singers like Linda Lyndell, Veda Brown, Mabel John, and Margie Joseph fill out the rest of the disc. The ears only really perk up for Jean Knight's sassy "Mr. Big Stuff," a 1971 No. 2 hit that's available on various other compilations. —*Richie Unterberger*

Stax/Volt Revue, Vol. 3: Live in Europe—Hit the Road Stax / 1992 / Stax ✦✦✦✦
Seventy-two minutes of early 1967 performances from the European tour of the Stax/Volt Revue, recorded in London and Paris, with cuts by Booker T. & the MG's, Carla Thomas, Otis Redding, Eddie Floyd, and the Mar-Keys. Not released until 1992, none of these tracks were included on four previous albums of material from the tour. It's certainly up to the level of those other recordings, in both performance and sound quality, Booker T. & the MG's coming off as especially tight. —*Richie Unterberger*

Step Right Up: The Songs of Tom Waits / 1995 / Virgin ✦✦✦
Fifteen-song tribute album to Waits, dominated by alternative rockers, although a couple of previously released items (Tim Buckley's 1973 cover of "Martha," and 10,000 Maniacs' 1992 cassette single B-side "I Hope That I Don't Fall in Love with You") were licensed for the project. It's above average as tribute discs go, with a diverse lineup (Alex Chilton, Dave Alvin, Pale Saints, Frente!, Archers of Loaf, Pete Shelley, the Wedding Present) taking care to invest their contributions with some imagination. Some Tom Waits fans may find the interpretations too aggressive and arty, and on occasion the approaches are annoying (the Violent Femmes' smirking walk through "Step Right Up," Jeffrey Lee Pierce's white-boy rap on "Pasties and a G-String"). It deserves points for not just throwing together lukewarm variations on the originals, though, but trying to come up with something different, as Drugstore does on its Velvet Underground-like version of "Old Shoes," Other highlights are the Tindersticks' torpid loungeoid cover of "Mockin' Bird," and Magnapop's sultry reading of one of Waits' grimmest pieces, "Christmas Card from a Hooker in Minneapolis." —*Richie Unterberger*

The Stiff Records Box Set / 1992 / Rhino ✦✦✦✦
Stiff Records was a maverick among British independent record labels, partially responsible for starting the punk and new wave revolution of the late '70s. Under the guidance of house producer Nick Lowe, Stiff turned out an enormous number of seminal punk and new wave singles in their first years, including classic tracks by the Damned, Elvis Costello, Graham Parker, the Adverts, Ian Dury, and Lowe himself. But what really gave the label its wild, original flavor were minor artists like Ian Dury, Wreckless Eric, Tenpole Tudor, the Yachts, Lene Lovich, Rachel Sweet, and Mickey Jupp, who turned out a series of raw pop gems that were everything good rock 'n' roll singles should be—catchy, energetic, and memorable. Over 100 of Stiff's finest tracks are collected on this wonderful four-disc box set. While most of these songs weren't hits, they are classic rock 'n' roll. The first three discs are excellent; the fourth disc contains some bright moments, but by that time, their artists were pretty much spent. However, the box remains one of the most compulsively listenable sets ever assembled, providing the definitive retrospective of arguably the most important and influential British record label of the late '70s. —*Stephen Thomas Erlewine*

Still Spicy Gumbo Stew / 1994 / Ace ✦✦✦
The third and last volume of the *Gumbo Stew* series of retrospectives of the New Orleans-based AFO label is perhaps the least impressive of the set. That doesn't mean it's bad, just that much of the 24-song set is rather generic early-'60s Crescent City R&B (with a few cuts dating from the late '60s). However, that's a style which can be both generic and enjoyable, which most of this set is, due to the competence of the singers and players. Barbara George, Alvin Robinson, Eddie Bo, and pianist James Booker (represented by a previously unreleased instrumental) are all here. There are also a couple of enjoyable instrumentals by Dr. John (one previously unissued); "The Point" features some seriously fierce cheese-o organ. Eddie Bo's bouncing "I Found a Little Girl" and Tami Lynn's sultry, soulful ballad "Baby" are also standouts, although on the whole the disc will mostly attract R&B specialists. —*Richie Unterberger*

Street Jams: Back 2 the Old Skool, Vol. 1 / Aug. 20, 1996 / Rhino ✦✦✦✦
The *Back 2 the Old Skool* volumes of Rhino's *Street Jams* series concentrates on late '70s and early '80s funk, always presented in their full-length versions. Where the *Hip-Hop from the Top* and *Street Funk* editions are more closely related to hip-hop, these songs provided the basis for many hip-hop records, either as the source for samples or as the scratched grooves. *Street Jams: Back 2 the Old Skool, Vol. 1* features songs by Bootsy Collins, Dazz, Fatback, and several other artists. Rhino have presented these songs on other collections—most notably *Phat Trax*—before, but *Back 2 the Old Skool* remains an entertaining and informative listen. —*Leo Stanley*

Street Jams: Back 2 the Old Skool, Vol. 2 / Aug. 20, 1996 / Rhino ✦✦✦✦
Like its predecessor, *Back 2 the Old Skool, Vol. 2* concentrates on late '70s and early '80s funk, and if anything, it's an even stronger collection than *Vol. 1*, featuring classic cuts by Funkadelic ("Freak of the Week"), Zapp ("Computer Love"), Brick ("Dusic"), Mtume ("Green Light"), Fatback ("Keep Your Fingers out the Jam") and Slave ("Snap Shot"). —*Leo Stanley*

Street Jams: Back 2 the Old Skool, Vol. 3 / Aug. 20, 1996 / Rhino ✦✦✦✦
Although it isn't quite as consistent as its two predecessors, *Back 2 the Old Skool, Vol. 3* is nevertheless another excellent collection of classic late '70s and early '80s funk, featuring cuts from Chic ("Good Times"), Bootsy's Rubber Band ("Body Slam!"), Mtume ("Juicy Fruit"), Fatback ("On the Floor"), Zapp ("Doo Wa Ditty (Blow That Thing)"), Better Wright ("Tonight is the Night") and Average White Band ("Pick up the Pieces"). —*Leo Stanley*

Street Jams: Electric Funk, Vols. 1-4 / Jul. 16, 1996 / Rhino ✦✦✦
Available either as a box set or as individual discs, *Street Jams: Electric Funk, Vols. 1-4* is an excellent, comprehensive overview of the ground-breaking electro-funk of the early '80s. Over the course of four discs, most of the genre's major players, including Afrika Bambaataa and Grandmaster Flash, are represented by their biggest hits and best-known remixes; many of its one-hit wonders are here as well, adding depth and context. Much of this music is presented in its 12-inch mix, which gives a more accurate portrait of electro-funk and how it stretched and played with rhythms and electronics. For casual listeners, the sheer length of some of these songs may be intimidating—some push the 10-minute mark—but any serious collector or listener of hip-hop, urban R&B, electronica or modern music should be familiar with many of these songs and mixes. —*Stephen Thomas Erlewine*

Street Jams: Hip Hop, Vols. 1-4 / Aug. 20, 1996 / Rhino ✦✦✦✦
Available either as a box set or as four individual discs, *Street Jams: Hip-Hop from the Top, Vols. 1-4* is a superb collection of old-school rap, featuring most of the major singles and artists from the genre's formative years. Over the course of the series, such classics as "Rapper's Delight,"

"The Breaks," "The Message," "It's Like That," "The Roof is on Fire," "Roxanne, Roxanne," "The Real Roxanne," "The Show," "Freaks Come out at Night," "Nightmares" and "La-Di-Da-Di" are presented, usually in their full-length 12-inch mix. It's a comprehensive and surprisingly listenable, illustrating that even from the start all hip-hop did not sound the same. It's an essential collection for any comprehensive urban, rap or pop library. — *Stephen Thomas Erlewine*

Strip Jointz: Hot Songs for Sexy Dancers / Nov. 12, 1996 / Robbins ✦✦✦✦
It may have a silly name, but *Strip Jointz: Hot Songs for Sexy Dancers* is an excellent collection of risque and sexy funk, rap, dance and urban R&B. Instead of concentrating on one era, the album spans over two decades, running from Clarence Carter's "Strokin'," Labelle's "Lady Marmalade," the Commodores' "Brick House" and Rick James' "Superfreak" to Wreckx-N-Effect's "Rump Shaker," R. Kelly's "Bump 'N Grind," 2 in a Room's "Wiggle It," H-Town's "Knockin' Da Boots," the Outhere Brothers' "Boom Boom Boom," 2 Live Crew's "Me So Horny," and Tone Loc's "Wild Thing." *Strip Jointz* is an extremely fun, danceable compilation, with almost no weak tracks, making it a terrific party record. — *Stephen Thomas Erlewine*

Sugarhill Records Story / Feb. 4, 1997 / Rhino ✦✦✦✦✦
Sugarhill Records was the first rap and hip-hop label, giving many listeners their first exposure to the urban rhyming and scratching that transformed pop music during the '80s. Like most indie labels, they had troubles with finances and distribution; eventually, that situation resulted in their records remaining out of print during the rise of hip-hop during the late '80s and '90s. The five-disc *Sugarhill Records Story* remedies this situation by collecting all of the label's classic A-sides, many in their full-length mixes, on one set. Tracks by the Sugarhill Gang, Grandmaster Flash and the Treacherous Three are commonplace and remain excellent, but the true revelation of the box set is how strong largely forgotten cuts by Spoonie Gee, the Funky Four Plus One, Trouble Funk, the Sequence, Super-Wolf and West Street Mob are—these are supremely funky, infectious and inventive cuts, which have been made familiar through samples and quotations on modern rap records. Another surprise is how integrated this music is—male and female rappers trade lines without hesitation, and there is none of the misogyny or violence that characterized gangsta rap. But that doesn't mean the old-school rap on *The Sugarhill Records Story* sounds dated—much of this bright, elastic electro-funk provided the foundation for '90s hits by the likes of the Beastie Boys and Dr. Dre. But the most surprising thing of all is how *The Sugarhill Records Story* barely loses momentum over the course of five discs. There is the occasional dull spot or oddity (check out the bizarre B-52's rip-off "At the Ice Arcade" by the Chilly Kids) that interrupts the flow, but the music is consistently strong, even on the fifth disc. It was inevitable that *The Sugarhill Records Story* would be an important historical document, but what makes it truly essential is how rich, diverse and timeless the music actually is. — *Stephen Thomas Erlewine*

The Sullivan Years: British Invasion / 1990 / TVT ✦✦✦✦
Probably the best of TVT's Sullivan series. Sullivan can actually take a good deal of the credit for breaking the British Invasion in the United States, featuring most of the top bands on his show in the mid-'60s. This compilation has 16 songs from 1964-66 broadcasts by the Searchers, the Animals, Billy J. Kramer, Peter & Gordon, Gerry & the Pacemakers, Herman's Hermits, and Freddie & the Dreamers. Occasionally it's obvious that they're singing to a backing track, but most of the performances are totally live and make for a pleasant listen, though they don't match or redefine the studio versions; the Animals come off the best. Presumably, material by the Beatles, Rolling Stones, and the Dave Clark Five—all of whom played on the show several times—was unavailable for licensing. — *Richie Unterberger*

Sullivan Years: Mod Sound / 1990 / TVT ✦✦✦
This is not so much the "mod" sound of the '60s as the "pop" sound, featuring many of the day's top mainstream pop-rockers: the Mamas & the Papas, Dusty Springfield, Petula Clark, Lulu, Jackie DeShannon, the Seekers, the 5th Dimension, and the Friends of Distinction. Female singers figure prominently on almost all of the tracks, and it's certainly a pleasant enough collection, most of the performances featuring noticeably thinner orchestral arrangements than the hit versions. But it's a souvenir more than anything; you're better off with the originals in every case. — *Richie Unterberger*

The Sullivan Years: Rhythm & Blues Revue / 1993 / TVT ✦✦✦
Ed Sullivan wasn't exactly a champion of R&B, but his show was open to R&B performers at a time when Black entertainers in general had a hard time getting prime-time exposure. This compilation draws almost exclusively from the 1950s, although B.B. King does end the set with a performance of his 1970 hit "The Thrill Is Gone." It also features, in blurry fidelity, cuts by Jackie Wilson, Louis Jordan, the Platters, LaVern Baker, and Brook Benton, sometimes with inappropriately square accompaniment by the show's orchestra. The highlight is Bo Diddley's

1955 rendition of his self-titled debut single; one can only imagine the audience reaction to the fierce rock 'n' roller at a time when Elvis Presley had yet to achieve national success. — *Richie Unterberger*

The Sullivan Years: Rock 'n' Roll Pioneers 1955-1959 / 1993 / TVT ✦✦✦
Live TV spots by Buddy Holly, Bill Haley, Fats Domino, Chubby Checker, Lloyd Price, Gene Vincent, Frankie Lymon, Jerry Lee Lewis, Jimmie Rodgers, Joe Bennett, and the Champs on this compilation. Like the rest of the Sullivan series, it's essentially a collector's item; the performances are spirited, deviate little from the records except that the arrangements are usually thinner, and are exceedingly short (over half the cuts clock in at under two minutes). The Buddy Holly songs are the most valuable, especially considering that barely any live recordings of him survive. The Jerry Lee Lewis medley, incidentally, is from 1969, not the '50s. — *Richie Unterberger*

Sultry Soul Sisters (Wonder Women, Vol. 3) / 1984 / Rhino ✦✦✦✦
Not much of this is rare, but it's an excellent compilation of mid-'60s female-sung soul-pop with a romantic, emotional edge. There are big hits by Dionne Warwick and Barbara Lewis, but there are also excellent sides by Maxine Brown, a pre-Motown Gladys Knight, and Ketty Lester ("Love Letters") that didn't make it into heavy oldies rotation. Bessie Banks' excellent, little-known original version of "Go Now" was copied virtually note-for-note by the Moody Blues, who had a Top Ten hit with it in 1965. Especially great is the original version of "Tainted Love" by Gloria Jones, which was made into a huge international synth-pop smash by Soft Cell in the 1980s. Jones' version, though, is a torrential soul-stomper that rates not just as one of the great lost soul records of all time, but as one of the finest singles of the 1960s that deserved to be a big hit, yet wasn't. — *Richie Unterberger*

Summer of Love / Rhino ✦✦✦
This double album focuses on the sunniest, poppiest aspects of psychedelia. Actually, a lot of this is closer to pure pop than acid, but it has good hits in that vein by Donovan, the Troggs, the Mamas & the Papas, and the Young Rascals. At the rawer end of the spectrum are the Electric Prunes, Strawberry Alarm Clock, and the Byrds; Petula Clark, the 5th Dimension, and the Cowsills, on the other hand, were only as hippie-ish as they needed to be to get in the Top 40 in 1967. — *Richie Unterberger*

Sun & Surf, Cars & Guitars / 1994 / Del-Fi ✦✦✦
Another Del-Fi compilation that mixes up a bunch of rarities into a blender, spitting it out as *Sun & Surf, Cars & Guitars*, an umbrella that doesn't leave much out when you're talking early rock 'n' roll. The lack of liner notes adds to the slapped-together feel, but it's a decent pastiche of material that found a home on the L.A. label in the early half of the '60s, though a good deal of the cuts by the Lively Ones, Bobby Fuller, the Centurions, and others can be found on other Del-Fi comps. As far as enticing collectibles go, the "Twist and Shout" ripoff by the American Four tops the list, as it features a pre-Love Arthur Lee as lead vocalist. There are also three hot rod instrumentals by the Darts with Glen Campbell on guitar, a Buddy Hollyish number by Dick Dale, and future Beach Boy Bruce Johnston's "Do the Surfer Stomp." — *Richie Unterberger*

Sun City / 1985 / Razor & Tie ✦✦✦
Sun City was certainly the most political of all of the charity rock albums of the 1980s. Little Steven organized a number of artists for this protest against apartheid, including such heavyweights as Miles Davis, Bob Dylan, Peter Gabriel, Jimmy Cliff, Bruce Springsteen, Jackson Browne, Run-D.M.C., and Lou Reed. Thankfully, the result was extremely listenable as well as fiercely political; it's one of the few charity or protest albums that stands up to repeated listenings, thanks to the extended instrumental workouts. Arguably the finest moment on the record is one that was added at the last minute—a spare, stripped-down version of U2's "Silver and Gold" by Bono, Keith Richards, and Ron Wood. — *Stephen Thomas Erlewine*

Sun City / 1994 / Rhino ✦✦✦✦✦
There have been a lot of Sun compilations over the years; this three-CD, 74-song compilation strikes the medium ground between abridged single-disc highlights and overkill ten-album box sets. What this means is that you get virtually all the key sides of this vastly influential blues, country, and rockabilly label, including the biggest Sun hits cut by Elvis, Carl Perkins, Jerry Lee Lewis, Johnny Cash, Charlie Rich, and Roy Orbison. There's also a lot of the pioneering electric blues cut by label head Sam Phillips before he made rockabilly Sun's focus, including sides by Howlin' Wolf, B.B. King, Rufus Thomas, Junior Parker, and James Cotton. Then there are the interesting small hits and flops by minor rockabilly figures like Warren Smith, Billy Lee Riley, Malcolm Yelvington, Onie Wheeler, and Carl Mann. There aren't any previously unreleased songs, so the Sun specialist most likely already has everything here; it's a better buy for the avid, knowledgeable fan who isn't a completist. — *Richie Unterberger*

Supernatural Fairy Tales: The Progressive Rock Era / Aug. 20, 1996 / Rhino ✦✦✦

Right down to the Roger Dean-designed sleeve, this five-CD box set overview of progressive rock from 1967-1976 is as grandoise as the music itself—which is not necessarily an unconditional recommendation. But give the compilation points for diversity and thoughtful selection. The expected superstars (Yes, Genesis, ELP, Procol Harum) are usually represented by unexpected cuts which haven't been played to death on FM radio. A lot of ground is covered, from Kraut rock (Can, Amon Duul) and symphonic keyboards (Rare Bird, Argent, the Nice's "America") to the Canterbury sound (Caravan, Hatfield & the North) and pop-hits-with-prog overtones (Traffic's "Paper Sun," Golden Earring's "Radar Love," Roxy Music's "Virginia Plain"). Quite a few of the tracks were never released in the US; a couple were even previously unissued. And a lot of the Continental bands will be fuzzy or unfamiliar names even to progressive rock fans, like Le Orme, Lard Free, Wigwam, Ange, and Samla Mammas Manna—acts which make cult faves like Van Der Graaf Generator, Curved Air, the Pretty Things, Savage Rose, and Gong (all here as well) famous by comparison. Will the music cause those who dislike prog-rock to re-evaluate their feelings? Absolutely not—the more accessible and poppy cuts are balanced by flashy instrumental workouts that, as even the musicians themselves may admit, do not exhibit a trace of humor. And no box that fails to include selections by Pink Floyd, King Crimson, Jethro Tull, Soft Machine, Kraftwerk, Mike Oldfield, early Brian Eno, and Kevin Ayers (in at least some cases for licensing reasons) can claim to be comprehensive. It *is* an interesting, carefully assembled, *extremely* wide-ranging and Catholic survey of the much-maligned genre. It's just a bit too much to take in all at once, and its very eclecticism ensures that many listeners (even dedicated prog fans) will feel the urge to skip around with the remote button to concentrate on the sub-genres they find most appealing. —*Richie Unterberger*

Surf & Drag, Vol. 1 / 1989 / Sundazed ✦✦✦✦

All the great surf and hot-rod sides from the Challenge label. Features Gary Usher, the Four Speeds, the Knickerbockers, Jan & Dean, the Royal Coachmen, Donna Loren, and the Rhythm Rockers. Powerful genre material—this is as good as it gets. —*Cub Koda*

Surf & Drag, Vol. 2 / 1993 / Sundazed ✦✦✦✦

Featuring more rare tracks from the second tier of surf and hot-rod performers, this volume is no less potent than the first. Highlights include the original version of "She Rides with Me" by Paul Petersen, "Bustin' Surfboards" by the Tornadoes, and "GeeTO Tiger" by the Tigers. —*Cub Koda*

Surfin' in the Midwest / 1985 / Unlimited Production ✦✦✦

Although surf music was primarily a Californian phenomenon, there were a lot more surf bands in the Midwest than most listeners would expect. This has 16 rare surf tunes from locales in Minnesota, Wisconsin, Iowa, Kansas, and other Midwest states, recorded between 1963 and 1967. Perhaps there's a tad more of a frat-rock feel to these sides, but generally it sounds quite similar to West Coast surf music; play it to most people, and they would never suspect that it didn't originate in California. It's not incredibly remarkable stuff, but it's solid surf music that will appeal to enthusiasts for the form as much as other mid-level surf compilations dominated by West Coast sides, and includes extremely detailed liner notes. —*Richie Unterberger*

Taste of Doo Wop, Vol. 1 / 1993 / Vee-Jay ✦✦✦✦

No R&B label had more prolific doo wop talent than Vee-Jay, which turned the fertile Chicago area into a goldmine in the '50s and early '60s. This 25-cut anthology contains a healthy sample and thankfully focuses on acts like the 5 Echoes, Orchids, Magnificents, and Rhythm Aces, fine ensembles that didn't score the huge hits of their contemporaries but made several solid records nonetheless. There are also acts that became bigger on other labels, like Sonny Til and his Orioles, the Pips (later Gladys Knight and the Pips), and a funky unreleased version of "The Twist," by the Midnighters (Hank Ballard and company). —*Ron Wynn*

Taste of Doo Wop, Vol. 2 / 1993 / Vee-Jay ✦✦✦✦

The second Vee-Jay various artists anthology showcasing diverse doo wop hits takes the same formula as its predecessor, featuring strong songs by more obscure acts rather than huge hits from established greats. The Kool Gents (a group that once included Dee Clark), the Prodigals, the Hi-Liters, and the El Dorados, plus set one holdovers the Magnificents, 5 Echoes, and Impressions are on hand providing 25 more examples of marvelous harmony singing, jump cuts, and swooning romantic ballads. —*Ron Wynn*

Teen Beat, Vol. 1 / 1993 / Ace ✦✦✦

30 instrumentals from the late '50s and early '60s, the era when instrumental rock was at its peak. Most of these were hits, though a few of them didn't make the Top Twenty, and some didn't even make the Top 100. Hence the selections are often more obscure than what you'll find on Rhino's *Rock Instrumentals* series. The Rhino series, however, remains not only a much better introduction to this nifty genre, but con-

siderably higher in overall quality. The best songs on *Teen Beat* are often as well on the Rhino series as well (the Ventures' "Walk Don't Run," Preston Epps' "Bongo Rock," Link Wray's "Rumble"); the lesser-known ones, though a boon to collectors, simply aren't as good or imaginative. It's a serviceable supplement, though, if you're looking for more of the style, and the best cuts are certainly dynamite. —*Richie Unterberger*

Teen Beat, Vol. 2 / 1994 / Ace ✦✦✦

This digs way deeper into the cobwebs of history than the first volume of the series. Although a few of these were big hits, over half of the 30 tracks didn't even make it into the Top 100. That doesn't mean they should be dismissed. But in the case of these selections at least, they're simply not nearly as memorable as the best early rock 'n' roll instrumentals, whether hits or flops. There are some nifty highlights, like two raw, bluesy '61 cuts by a young Roy Buchanan, uncommonly rocking items by Chet Atkins, and the early Danelectro bass workout by the Fireballs ("Carioca"). But a lot of these are standard-issue three-chord instrumentals by no-names like the Atmospheres, or forgettable flop followups by one-hit wonders like Dave Cortez, Floyd Cramer, and the Champs. The energy level is always high, but that in itself isn't a high recommendation, although devotees of instrumental rock will certainly find a lot of cuts here that are hard to locate on CD. —*Richie Unterberger*

Teen Beat, Vol. 3 / 1996 / Ace ✦✦✦

Devoted wholly to rock instrumentals of the late '50s and early '60s, this 30-track disc is a good investment for collectors looking for hits in the genre that didn't crack the Top 20 (and hence don't get played on oldies radio today), or missed the charts entirely. A couple smashes ("Wipe Out," "Pipeline") slip through, but otherwise there's a variety of forgotten hot wordless platters here, like the Astronauts' "Baja" (some of the best instrumental surf to originate outside out of California), the New Orleans-cum-Philly R&B of saxophonist Lee Allen, the creepy organ of the Wailers' "Mau Mau," the minimalist rockabilly of the Rock-a-Teens' "Woo-Hoo," the Ramrods' wacky adaptation of "Ghost Riders in the Sky," and the hard guitar of Duane Eddy associate Al Casey. When all's said and done, though, these aren't as good as the most famous vintage instrumental hits—stick with the more prominent compilations unless you're deeply into the sound. —*Richie Unterberger*

Teenage Riot! / Atomic Passion ✦✦✦✦

Insanely great rock 'n' roll compilation centered around juvenile-delinquent themes and featuring promo drop-ins from teen-gang movies and anti-rock 'n' roll sermons. Gene Maltais' "Gang War" is not to be missed. —*Cub Koda*

Teenage Rock'n Roll Party / 1995 / Ace (UK) ✦✦✦

This 30-track compilation draws the majority of its contents from 1950s-era West Coast and Southern labels both great and small, including selections from Specialty, Modern, Era, Excello, Goldband, and Johnny Otis' Dig label. While labeled a "rock 'n' roll party," the majority of contents compiled here are straight-up rockin' R&B: "Old Folks' Boogie," by Al Simmons with Slim Green and the Cats From Fresno, takes John Lee Hooker's "Boogie Chillen" and Junior Parker's "Feelin' Good" and reduces them down to a single riff that's even more elemental than those two bare-bones boogies, if such an artistic notion is possible. Several artists right on the edge between rhythm and blues and rock 'n' roll are featured here, including Little Richard, Larry Williams, Young Jessie and Richard Berry, and blues artists with some rockin' in their blood get their due here as well with Slim Harpo, Johnny "Guitar" Watson ("Those Lonely Lonely Nights," with its famous one note solo) and Hop Wilson all making appearances. Honking West Coast sax men Joe Houston and Chuck Higgins contribute a track apiece, while the doo wop side of the equation primarily comes from selections released by the East Coast-based Old Town Records, with the Harptones, Jive 5, and the Cleftones all contributing to the mix. This collection shows considerable depth and breadth, and brings together tracks that seldom make it onto packages like this. Well done. —*Cub Koda*

Tenth Anniversary Rap-A-Lot Records / Nov. 19, 1996 / Virgin ✦✦✦✦

Tenth Anniversary Rap-A-Lot Records is a retrospective of the first decade of the Texas-based hip-hop label, featuring hit singles by the Geto Boys, Scarface, Blac Monks, Raheem, 5th Ward Boyz and Gangsta Nip, among many others. Though some of this material is simply straight-forward gangsta rap, the very best moments here—particularly the Geto Boys' classic "Mind Playin' Tricks on Me"—rank among the best hardcore rap of the late '80s and early '90s, and any dedicated rap fan should explore what it has to offer. —*Stephen Thomas Erlewine*

Texas Music, Vol. 3: Garage Bands & Psychedelia / 1994 / Rhino ✦✦✦

Texas arguably produced the most manic and raunchiest garage rock of any state during the 1960s. While seasoned collectors will find little on this 18-song compilation that they don't already have, it's a decent intro to some of the Lone Star State's shining moments. Long renowned as a melting pot of sounds, Texas groups often flavored their records with R&B, blues, and Tex-Mex, which means that in addition to classic garage sides by the Bobby Fuller Four, the 13th Floor Elevators, Kenny & the Kasuals, and Mouse & the Traps, you get blues-rock (Steve Miller, Johnny Winter), blue-eyed soul (Roy Head's "Treat Her Right"), Tex-Mex-flavored rock (Sam the Sham & the Pharoahs and the Sir Douglas Quintet), and the all-out weirdness of the Legendary Stardust Cowboy ("Paralyzed"). There are also garage singles by the Chessmen, Scotty McKay, and Nobody's Children that were quite rare in their day, though they've appeared on easy-to-find garage compilations. The real find is the Ron-Dels' (featuring Delbert McClinton) "If You Really Want Me To, I'll Go," a country-flavored beat ballad strongly reminiscent of the Beatles' similar material from 1964 and 1965. —*Richie Unterberger*

Texas Punk from the Sixties / 1982 / Eva ✦✦✦
An uneven but worthy collection of 16 mid-'60s Texas garage sides. The Undertakers do a vicious cover of Ray Charles' "Unchain My Heart," as well as a quality spaced-out original with "It's My Time"; the Chessmen's "I Need You There" is Texas punk at its most basic and brutal; the Outcasts' "1523 Blair" is Texas blues-punk at its most berserk. There are a couple of rare (though not great) Mouse & the Traps songs, and much of the rest is just average. Be warned that the two songs by Them are not by the original group, but by a post-Van Morrison edition of the band that found themselves based in Texas for a while. —*Richie Unterberger*

Texas Punk, Vol. 5 / 1985 / Cicadelic ✦✦✦
The small Texas town of McAllen was home to a surprisingly active local scene in the '60s, as evidenced by this compilation. The cuts by the Cavaliers, Christopher & the Souls, Jeanne Hatfield, and the Cavaliers are nothing special, but the ones by the Headstones and the Playboys of Edinburg are on a different level. The Headstones' "Wish She Were Mine" and "24 Hours" are two of the better Texas pop-punk singles, especially the latter, with its bluesy grind. The Playboys of Edinburg, in contrast to the usual Texas group found on these compilations, played tasty Byrds-like folk-rock with nice harmonies and a slight country feel; they were even signed by Columbia, although they never reached a national audience. —*Richie Unterberger*

That Sound from Down Under / Nov. 5, 1996 / Hip-O ✦✦✦
That Sound from Down Under is designed to showcase Australian pop stars from Crowded House and INXS to Kylie Minogue and Jimmy Barnes. The bulk of the collection is comprised of familiar American hits from these artists, but a few obscure acts, like Def FX, are thrown in for good measure. The album is quite diverse stylistically, featuring soft-rock bands like the Little River Band, neo-psychedelia from the Church, hard rock from the Divinyls, and power-pop from Rick Springfield. With such a wide range of styles, it's no surprise that *That Sound from Down Under* is uneven, yet it's an enjoyable sampler, proving that Australia is far from a musical wasteland. —*Stephen Thomas Erlewine*

That Thing You Do / Sep. 24, 1996 / Sony ✦✦✦
The movie's theme song is a thoroughly convincing two minutes of pop glory, more Searchers in its harmonies and instrumental jangle than straight Beatles bop, with a thunderous (by '60s pop conventions) bass drum signature and infectious hand-clap rhythm. As befits a movie about a one-hit-wonder (literally, in case you missed the name's in-joke, the one-hit Wonders), none of the group's other four offerings encroach on the title track's greatness, although "Dance with Me Tonight" is a catchy, early Beatles dance-floor simulation. The Chantrellines' "Hold My Hand, Hold My Heart" covers the conventional mid-'60s girl-group thing while ripping off the central lyric theme from Toni Basil's "Mickey"; Diane Dane offers a sobbing Dusty Springfield-like ballad with "My World Is Over"; the surf/instrumental scene gets checked off with "Voyage Around the Moon" by the Saturn 5 and "Shrimp Shack" by the brilliantly-monickered Cap'n Geech & the Shrimp Shack Shooters. Like the movie itself, there's nothing startlingly original here, but the soundtrack makes for one happy-go-lucky, feel-good way to spend 45 minutes. —*Roch Parisien*

That'll Flat Git It!, Vol. 1 / 1992 / Bear Family ✦✦✦✦
31 tracks of '50s rockabilly-rock 'n' roll tracks culled from the vaults of RCA Victor. Highlights include Joe Clay's "Sixteen Chicks," Joey Castle's "That Ain't Nothin' but Right," and Ric Cartey's ultra-primitive "Heart Throb." —*Cub Koda*

That'll Flat Git It!, Vol. 2: Rockabilly From . . . / 1992 / Bear Family ✦✦✦✦
That'll Flat Git It!, Vol. 2: Rockabilly from the Decca Vaults isn't quite as consistent as its predecessor since Decca's roster wasn't as wild or engaging as RCA's, but there's a number of gems scattered throughout these 30 tracks—including Johnny Carroll's "Wild Wild Women," Don Woody's "You're Barking up the Wrong Tree," Terry Nolan's "Ten Little Women," Buddy Covelle's "Lorraine"—and rarities to make it worthwhile for hardcore rockabilly fetishists. Anyone else will find much of this material a little tedious and repetitive. —*Stephen Thomas Erlewine*

That'll Flat Git It!, Vol. 3: Rockabilly From . . . / 1992 / Bear Family ✦✦✦✦
More raw rockabilly and country bop, this time from the vaults of Capi-

tol Records. While the label had Gene Vincent and Esquerita, a quick listen to these will reveal rockabilly sounds with the accent on the 'billy. Skeets McDonald's "You Oughta See Grandma Rock" goes a long way toward defining the compilation's strengths, and Tommy Sands, long thought of as a teen idol singing pop mush, stokes the fires here with "The Worryin' Kind" and "Playin' the Field." While Ferlin Husky masquerading as Simon Crum on "Bop Cat Bop," the Rio Rockers' "Mexicali Baby" and Bobby Lee Trammell's "You Mostest Girl" show the length and breadth of the genre, perhaps the most fascinating earful of all is the Louvin Brothers testing the waters of rockabilly with "Red Hen Hop" and "Cash on the Barrelhead." —*Cub Koda*

That'll Flat Git It!, Vol. 4 / 1995 / Bear Family ✦✦✦
Like the previous three volumes of Bear Family's *That'll Flat Git It*, the fourth installment contains a wealth of obscure, and frequently bizarre, rockabilly. For *Vol. 4*, Bear Family reached into the vaults of Festival Records, a label that had no stars or hit singles to speak of (although songwriter Otis Blackwell did record a handful of singles for the label). Almost all of this disc is solely of interest to fetishists—after all, it features seven tracks from Billy Barry, five cuts by Charlie Starr, two songs by Ronnie Dio (not to be confused with the metal vocalist of the same name), and "Motorcycle" from one Billy Balls—and even then, much of this music is only of passing interest. While *That'll Flat Git It, Vol. 4* does have a handful of good cuts (Barry's "The Wild One," Starr's "You Ain't My Number One," and Blackwell's "One Broken Heart for Sale"), it remains a lesser entry in the series. —*Stephen Thomas Erlewine*

That'll Flat Git It!, Vol. 7 / 1996 / Bear Family ✦✦✦
Culled from the vaults of MGM Records, *That'll Flat Git It, Vol. 7* is very similar to the Decca volumes in Bear Family's arcane rockabilly series. The disc is divided between rock 'n' rollers who sound like weirder versions of Elvis Presley and country artists trying to hitch their wagons to the rockabilly bandwagon. By and large, the MGM artists aren't as strong as those on Decca, although Marvin Rainwater handled rockabilly better than many of his country counterparts. For fetishists, the bizarre backwoods boogie of Jimmy Swan ("Country Cattin'"), Bernie Early ("Your Kisses Kill Me"), the Berry Kids ("You're My Teen Age Baby"), Ron Hargrave ("Drive-In Movie"), Bob Gallion's "My Square Dancin' Mama," Buck Griffin ("Stutterin' Papa") and Carson Robison ("Rockin' and Rollin' With Grandmaw") is prime material, but the best music on the collection arguably comes from Rainwater and Conway Twitty, who have stronger voices and material than most of their peers on this collection. —*Stephen Thomas Erlewine*

That'll Flat Git It!, Vol. 8 / 1996 / Bear Family ✦✦✦
That'll Flat Git It, Vol. 8 is comprised of offbeat and obscure rockabilly from the Columbia vaults. Unlike their major label peers RCA, Decca and MGM, Columbia didn't push many of their country artists toward rockabilly, so the majority of the compilation is devoted to arcane vocalists like Bolean Barry ("Long Sideburns"), Bobby Lee Trammell ("You Mostest Girl"), Bonnie Guitar ("Frantic Party"), Alvadean Coker ("We're Gonna Bop"), Tom Tall ("That's Alright with Me"), Dickie Podolor ("I Love You Girl"), and Dusty Rose ("Rockin' Maraccas," "Hula Rock"). For the most part, this is the kind of twisted rockabilly that is fun in small doses, unless you're a fetishist, of course. Out of all the songs on *Vol. 8*, only Johnny Horton's pair of songs ("Bawlin' Baby," "Shotgun Boogie") are particularly strong musically—the rest is judged by a different scale, one where rarity and novelty are of greater value than musical worth. For any collector of arcane rockabilly, *Vol. 8* is just as enjoyable as the rest of the discs in the *That'll Flat Git It* series, yet it doesn't offer any truly great rock 'n' roll, which means that it will only appeal to that cult. —*Stephen Thomas Erlewine*

This Are Two Tone / 1983 / Chrysalis ✦✦✦✦
This Are Two Tone is a classic collection of the label's seminal ska-revival hits, highlighted by cuts from Madness ("Madness"), Selecter ("On My Radio," "Too Much Pressure"), the [English] Beat ("Ranking Full Stop," "Tears of a Clown"), Bodysnatchers ("Too Experienced") and several singles from the Specials ("Gangsters," "Rudy, A Message to You," "Stereotype," "Ghost Town"). Although the double-disc *Two Tone Compilation: A Checkered Past* is a more comprehensive set, *This Are Two Tone* remains an excellent, 16-song primer. —*Stephen Thomas Erlewine*

This is Easy / 1996 / Virgin ✦✦✦✦
This is Easy is a stellar double-disc set that combines swinging '60s pop with kitschy film and TV themes, as well as a handful of genuinely strong songs like Aretha Franklin's "I Say a Little Prayer." Although the camp level may be a little too high for some listeners, the set actually contains many of the best-known easy listening and mainstream pop hits from the '60s, from "Raindrops Keep Fallin' on My Head" and Jose Feliciano's "Light My Fire" to the Tijuana Brass' "A Taste of Honey," making it a thoroughly enjoyable guilty pleasure. —*Stephen Thomas Erlewine*

This is Merseybeat / 1989 / Edsel ✦✦✦
At the outset of Beatlemania in July 1963, the tiny UK Oriole label went to Liverpool with a mobile sound unit to record unsigned local beat

groups for a pair of compilation LPs (combined onto this reissue). Only a couple of them (the Nomads, who soon became the Mojos, and the Merseybeats) achieved any British hits. A full 24 of these 28 tunes are covers of US R&B/rock/pop standards. In comparison to the originals they sound pale—the vocals are often especially twee—and the four originals are derivative and unexceptional, a bit cloddish even. This comp illustrates that the Beatles were more a unique product of the Mersey sound than a representative one. —*Richie Unterberger*

This is Mod, Vol. 1: The Rarities 1979-1981 / 1995 / Anagram ♦♦♦
The British mod revival may have been a fad, driven by fashion and most of the time too derivative, but it did produce some fun singles. Since many of the bands that jumped on the bandwagon only released singles or poorly distributed albums for independent labels, much of this music has been hopelessly lost over the years; *This Is Mod, Vol. 1* collects many of the admittedly third-rate (though enjoyable) revival bands for the first time on CD. In 21 tracks, this disc provides the nearly complete recorded output of the Circles, the Amber Squad, the Cigarettes, the Deadbeats, the Letters, the Nips, the Odds, and the Sussed (whose novelty record, "I've Got Me Parka," takes a fun look at the fad)—with each band receiving detailed biographical sketches. For specialists and fetishists, this disc is essential. For most, it's simply excessive. —*Chris Woodstra*

This is Mod, Vol. 2: More Rarities 1979-81 / 1996 / Anagram ♦♦♦♦
The second volume of the *This Is Mod* series covers more mod revivalists: the Killermeters, the Exits, the V.I.P.'s, the Crooks, the Same, Teenage Filmstars, Terry Tonik, and the Purple Hearts. Only the Purple Hearts came close to being major contenders, but all provide a fascinating look at the short-lived genre. —*Chris Woodstra*

This is Mod, Vol. 3: A Diamond Collection / 1996 / Anagram ♦♦♦
Volume three of the *This is Mod Series* focuses on the short-lived Diamond Records, a London-based label which sought to keep the mod revival on life support during the mid-'80s—and nearly all of the label's output is here with the exception (thankfully) of the obscure Oi! band, the Business. Most of the bands, including the Scene, Long Tall Short, the Moment, the B Team, the Way Out, and the Rage, were more '60s purists than the Jam, but it's not much of a stretch to lump these groups in with their late-'70s predecessors. It is, however, hard to believe this stuff was being done as late as 1986. —*Chris Woodstra*

This is Mod, Vol. 4: Modities / 1996 / Anagram ♦♦♦
Modities continues the series' exhaustive mining of mod revival rarities, ranging from the more distinctive and noteworthy Lambrettas, Merton Parkas, and the Accidents to the hopelessly obscure Directions, the Nightriders, the Onlookers, the Reputation, and the Untouchables (UK). As with the first three installments, this may be excessive but it sure is fun. —*Chris Woodstra*

Toes on the Nose: 32 Surf Age Instrumentals / 1996 / Ace ♦♦♦
A stuffed-to-the-max single-disc comp of little-known 1963-65 sides, licensed from the Capitol, Imperial, and Liberty labels. As surf comps go, it's a tad above average, though its appeal is basically limited to those who want to build a deep surf section on their album shelf. It's populated by acts like Eddie & the Showmen, Richie Allen, the Super Stocks, and the Ghouls, none of whom had anything approaching a hit, except for drummer Sandy Nelson, who actually weighs in with the best cut. His "Cashbah" (which was most definitely *not* a hit) is surf at its most evil and middle eastern-influenced, with scorching guitar leads by Richie Podolor and the wildest mid-'60s drumming this side of Keith Moon. Otherwise this reissue's mostly a genre exercise, albeit a fairly good one. Several of the tracks feature the presence of Podolor and Gary Usher, both of whom were among the most important studio architects of the surf sound. Several of the cuts also employ mild space-age gimmicks in the instrumentation or arrangement, though not in truly ear-bending fashions. —*Richie Unterberger*

Too Much Goin' On / 1997 / Candy ♦♦♦♦
Here are 16 tracks that seldom see the compact disc light of day (if they *ever* have as of the time of this writing)—cruder than crude forays into early rock 'n' roll and rhythm and blues definitely not for roots music fans who like their genres presented in a more genteel fashion. Each of the 16 selections is earmarked with a separate dance designation here, with multiple sleaze highlights abounding with the inclusion of Danny Zella and His Zell Rocks' "Black Saxes" (arguably *the* first Detroit rock 'n' roll record), the Monorays' thudding "What's Your Name?," the Hollywood Vines' surf crazy "When Johnny Comes Slidin' Home," Ervin Rucker and the Blues Nighthawks Orchestra's sublimely sloppy, out-of-control, out-of-tune and (therefore) perfect "Done Done the Slop" and Fred Hughes' exercise in leather lung power, "Shout Mama Linda," its dance designation here being described as "stupidity." Comps of old, obscure 45s come and go, but this collection is a true keeper, delivering way more than some folks will be bargaining for in the roots music department. —*Cub Koda*

Totally Wired / Oct. 1995 / Razor & Tie ♦♦♦♦
As the 1970s turned into the 1980s, the first explosion of punk had run its course, and what we now call "post-punk" or "alternative rock" had yet to really coagulate. In the meantime, there were many bands who took their unconventional attitude from the punk era, but sought a more musically diverse format. *Totally Wired* is an 18-song compilation of bands that were staples of college radio during the time, although they were virtually ignored (or scorned) by the mainstream. Featured are key cuts by bands like Gang of Four, the Fall, the Raincoats, the Slits, Joy Division, Bauhaus, Magazine, Au Pairs, and Pylon, as well as even more cultish acts like Delta 5, the Mo-Dettes, and Bush Tetras. Those who followed this fragmented scene at the time won't find much here they're not already familiar with or own. But for others it's a pretty useful intro to acts that embodied an era which has yet to generate much historical commentary or preservation. —*Richie Unterberger*

Trainspotting / Feb. 1996 / EMI Premier ♦♦♦♦
Trainspotting concerns the adventures of a group of young, nearly criminal, drug-addicted Scottish friends. The novel, written by Irvine Welsh, became one of the most popular books in the British indie scene in the early '90s and was adapted to film in 1996 by the makers of *Shallow Grave*. Appropriately, an all-star collection of British pop and techno stars—everyone from Blur, Pulp, and Elastica to Leftfield, Primal Scream, and the Underworld—contributed to the soundtrack, which also features a couple of oldies by veteran punk godfathers like Lou Reed ("Perfect Day") and Iggy Pop ("Lust for Life," "Nightclubbing"). The entire soundtrack holds together surprisingly well, as the techno tracks balance with the pop singles. Every song, whether it's Pulp's deceptively bouncy "Mile End" or Brian Eno's lush "Deep Blue Day," is quite melancholy, creating an effectively bleak, but oddly romantic, atmosphere for the entire record. With the exception of the oldies, every song is rare or especially recorded for the soundtrack, and nearly every one is superb. Primal Scream's title track sees them returning to the dub/dance experiments of *Screamadelica* with grace, while Damon Albarn's first solo song, "Closet Romantic," is as good as any of Blur's waltzes. But the finest new song is Pulp's "Mile End," with its jaunty, neo-dance hall melody and rhythms and Jarvis Cocker's evocative, haunting lyrics. That song, more than anything else on the soundtrack, captures the feeling of the film. —*Stephen Thomas Erlewine*

Trans-World Punk, Vol. 1 / 198? / Crawdad ♦♦♦
As the title implies, the 18 tracks here were recorded in the mid-'60s by beat/garage bands from all over the world, *except* the United States—the UK, Switzerland, New Zealand, Holland, Italy, and Sweden. Collectors have long known that countries from outside America and Britain had pretty fertile scenes, and this is a decent sampler of some of the rawest sounds, usually with a heavy Rolling Stones/Pretty Things/R&B influence. Not every track is notable, but the best hold their own with the best raunchy beat records of the era: the berserk bass runs of Peter & the Blizzards' "Bye Bye Baby," the Dee-Jays' "Blackeyed Woman," and Sons of Fred's "I'll Be There," with its lunar rockabilly riffs. —*Richie Unterberger*

Trans-World Punk, Vol. 2 / 198? / Crawdad ♦♦♦
Sixteen slabs of mid-'60s R&B/punk from all over the world except the US: Britain, Sweden, New Zealand, Italy, Quebec, Denmark, and Spain are all represented. The gap between the good and the bad for this kind of stuff is pretty wide. Much of this is just sloppy, almost inept sub-Pretty Things/Them derivations, the crude energy not nearly enough to make up for the lack of decent songs. There are some good items here, however. The Blue Stars (from New Zealand) work up some stomping rage with their "Social End Product," the Brand whip up a good British R&B frenzy with "Zulu Stomp," and David John's "Pretty Thing" has one of the great discordant guitar solos of all time. —*Richie Unterberger*

Twin Peaks / Sep. 11, 1990 / Warner Brothers ♦♦♦♦
Composer Angelo Badalamenti (*Cousins*) set the tone for David Lynch's bizarre television soap with a haunting theme created from electric piano, synthetic strings and the twangiest guitar this side of Duane Eddy. The love theme, appropriately enough, sounds like a funeral march. (The series' central character was found dead at the beginning of the first episode.) The rest of the music, instantly recognizable to anyone who saw even one episode of the series, borders on fever-dream jazz. Lynch-favorite Julee Cruise sings the only three vocal songs. The music from *Twin Peaks* is dark, cloying and obsessive—and one of the best scores ever written for television. —*Brian Mansfield*

The Two Tone Compilation: Checkered Past / Nov. 16, 1993 / Chrysalis ♦♦♦♦♦
Two Tone Compilation: A Checkered Past is a sublime double-disc set containing all of the ska-revival label's greatest singles, not only from superstars like the Specials, Madness, the [English] Beat, Bodysnatchers and Selecter, but also the Special A.K.A., Swinging Cats, Higsons and Apollinaires. Not one of the label's great songs are missing, and several cuts reveal themselves as forgotten gems. It's a comprehensive and com-

pulsively listenable set, illustrating the kinetic energy of ska-revival as well as the depth of the label's roster. (In England, *A Checkered Past* was released as a four-disc box containing all of the label's A and B-sides.) —*Stephen Thomas Erlewine*

Ugly Things, Vols. 1-3 / Raven ✦✦✦
US and UK audiences were totally unaware at the time, but Australia was home to a thriving garage-punk scene in the mid-'60s. The scope and output of these groups was limited by the country's population, which was only about 15 million or somewhat less, after all. But there was a surprisingly large number of fine singles, some of which measured up to the manic, over-the-top R&B-derived energy of anything coming from Texas, California, or London. *Vol. 1* is by far the best of the series, and indeed, one of the best '60s garage compilations ever, filled with good hooks, screams, and crunching riffs. *Vols. 2* and *3* aren't nearly as good, peppered with undistinguished covers and unmemorable tracks, although some excellent ones do surface, including some from neighboring New Zealand; the best of these two LPs should have been combined into one. Raven has put out a best-of compilation CD from the Ugly Things series that draws from all of the volumes and adds some other cuts. —*Richie Unterberger*

Ultimate Girl Groups / Goldmine ✦✦✦✦
One of the best compilations of obscure girl group singles from the mid-'60s. And we are talking obscure; Diane Renay is the only artist on this 27-track compilation who had a hit of any sort. These actually fall much closer to girl group soul than girl group pop-rock, the influence of Motown being particularly prevalent. These aren't meant as criticisms; these are mostly infectious, well-produced tracks, some of which, like Judy Hughes' "Fine, Fine, Fine," could have been big hits. —*Richie Unterberger*

The Unsung Heroes, 1978-81: The Phase II Mod Collection / 1994 / Unicorn ✦✦✦
Subtitled *The Phase II Mod Collection*, this skimpy 12-track collection offers a scattershot sampling of some of the bright spots in the mod-revival movement of the late '70s and extends into the tail-end of the movement in 1981. A nice addition for the rarities, though far from being a definitive look. —*Chris Woodstra*

Uppers on the South Downs / 1994 / Dojo Limited ✦✦✦
Originally released in the mid-'80s, *Uppers on the South Downs* collects some rarities from the mod-revival, particularly a number of bands from south coast resort towns like Brighton—a favorite mod location and the site of many battles between the mods and the teddy boys. Included are some of the best, though overlooked, bands of the scene: Teenbeats, Missing Persons, Purple Hearts, and the Same. The only questionable inclusion is the South Coast Ska Stars—a mysterious group of old-looking men who dressed in parkas and played ska-revival-style instrumentals. As it turns out, Ray Fenwick, a former member of the Spencer Davis Group who produced the collection, was the founding member. This odd diversion aside, *Uppers on the South Downs* works well as both a nostalgia trip and as enjoyable listening. —*Chris Woodstra*

Vampyros Lesbos: Sexadelic Dance Party / 1995 / Motel ✦✦✦
Around the late '60s, Jess Franco directed three B-movies starring Soledad Miranda that have attracted a following of sorts in the incredibly strange film cult. This is a compilation of music heard in those productions, composed and arranged by Manfred Hubler and Siegfried Schwab, and performed by "the Vampires' Sound Incorporation." It's very much period psychedelic-tinged exploitation soundtrack stuff: fuzzy guitars, occasional odd vocal interjections, jazzy organ runs, sitars for the freak factor, and blaring horn charts. None of these contemporary touches can disguise the fact that this is basically typical gimmicky soundtrack product, altered just enough to be suitable for some mod-psychedelic go-go party-type scenes or seductive encounters. It's just strange enough, though, to find its niche in the exploding easy listening/ space-age pop revival of the mid-'90s. —*Richie Unterberger*

The Vee-Jay Story: 1953-1993 / 1993 / Vee-Jay ✦✦✦✦
For all of its many attributes, the triple-disc *The Vee-Jay Story: 1953-1993* is a severely flawed box set. The music itself is terrific, containing classic blues and R&B songs from the likes of Jimmy Reed, the Impressions, the Spaniels, Gene Chandler, and the Dells. However, the presentation of the box is terrible. All three discs are packaged in clear jewel boxes without liner notes, and the labels on the discs have no songtitles, which means you need the booklet in order to figure out what track is which. That's not just an annoyance—it makes the music much harder to digest, which is unfortunate, since the songs themselves are superb and seminal. Which means that *The Vee-Jay Story* is a worthwhile purchase, even with its major flaws. —*Stephen Thomas Erlewine*

VH1: The Big '80s / 1996 / Rhino ✦✦✦✦
Drawn from the VH1 music video series *The Big '80s*, this single-disc compilation offers a good portrait of the sound of early MTV, even if it doesn't follow any strict generic guidelines. New wavers like Squeeze

("Tempted"), the Go-Go's ("We Got the Beat"), and Gary Numan ("Cars") line up with '70s leftovers like Steve Miller ("Abracadabra") and ABBA's Frida ("I Know There's Something Going On"), as well as pop-metal bands (Night Ranger's "Sister Christian") and power-pop one hit-wonders (Tommy Tutone's "867-5309"). Much of this has appeared on other, more coherent collections, but this has a couple of items that don't show up on many '80s compilations (most notably the Frida track) and it does sound remarkably similar to what MTV actually sounded like in 1983 and 1984. —*Stephen Thomas Erlewine*

Video Soul: Best Soul of the 80's, Vol. 1 / 1995 / Rhino ✦✦✦
Video Soul: Best Soul of the '80s, Vol. 1 is a solid 12-track collection of urban R&B hits from the early '80s that's equally divided between uptempo dance numbers ("Funkytown," "Working My Way Back to You," "He's So Shy") and smooth ballads ("One in a Million You," "Shining Star," "Just the Two of Us"). It's a little brief, but it does capture the feeling of the era, and it, along with its successor, offer a strong overview of early '80s R&B. —*Stephen Thomas Erlewine*

Video Soul: Best Soul of the 80's, Vol. 2 / 1995 / Rhino ✦✦✦
The second volume of *Video Soul: Best Soul of the '80s* follows the same pattern as its predecessor, dividing its time between uptempo dance numbers ("Love on a Two Way Street," "The Other Woman," "Jump to It," "Jump (For My Love)," "Jungle Love," "Lean on Me") and smooth ballads ("Baby Come to Me," "Save the Overtime (For Me)," "Joanna"). This disc covers the mid-'80s, which weren't quite as consistent in terms of material, but there are many of the era's highlights here, and it offers a solid overview of urban R&B during those years. —*Stephen Thomas Erlewine*

Vintage Funk, Vol. 1 / Feb. 1996 / React/PolyGram ✦✦✦
What makes funk "vintage," as opposed to "classic"? In any case, this has a somewhat more interesting track selection than React's similar *Classic Funk, Vol. 1*, although the quality is no better or worse. Along with well-known hits by Charles Wright and Curtis Mayfield, you get tracks by James Brown ("Funky Drummer"), Edwin Starr ("Easin' In"), and Donny Hathaway ("The Ghetto") that don't show up on many anthologies. There are also early-to-mid-'70s cuts by more obscure names like Eddie Harris, and James Brown sidemen Bobby Byrd and Fred Wesley. The short running time (12 songs) and lack of documentation/depth means that this is more useful for the novice than the hardcore funk fan, but it's one of the better introductory samplers of the style. —*Richie Unterberger*

Wail on the Beach! / Satan ✦✦✦
A *Pebbles*-like volume for surf music, meaning that these extremely obscure early-'60s singles were similar to the slightly later garage records in their funky production values and raw performances. Like many garage compilations, it speaks mostly to the converted, with some frenetic playing and wacky sound effects providing more interest than the actual material. It's not bad if you're seriously into surf collecting, with a more frat-rock-influenced sound than the norm, possibly because several of the bands hailed from outside of California. A couple of the more unusual items are Bob Moore's "Trophy Run," with extremely loud Wrayish guitar by a young Roy Buchanan, and Susan Lynne's "Don't Drag No More," a vocal hot-rod death disc. —*Richie Unterberger*

Walkin' Thru the Sleepy City / 1982 / London ✦✦✦
It's never been too easy to find, but this Japanese compilation will intrigue Rolling Stones fans, as it collects 13 singles from the mid-'60s that Mick Jagger and Keith Richards wrote for other artists, rather in the manner of John Lennon and Paul McCartney writing for Peter & Gordon or Billy J. Kramer. About half of the material would eventually turn up on the Stones' releases (sometimes not until the bottom-of-the-barrel mid-'70s compilation *Metamorphosis*); they never released their own versions of the rest. Rather surprisingly, the songs are quite mediocre, lightweight Merseybeat/Beatles-style concoctions. When Jagger and Richards began writing for themselves, it took them a good year or so to lock into a fierce R&B/rock groove, and most of these compositions—some of them quite dreary, actually—date from the era when they were struggling to find their own identity and vocabulary. The most famous tracks, Marianne Faithfull's "As Tears Go By" and "Sister Morphine," and Lulu's "Surprise, Surprise," are easily available elsewhere. The obscurities by George Bean, Adrienne Porter, the Mighty Avengers, Bobby Jameson, Thee, and Vashti are of historical interest only, and the LP doesn't include the relatively decent songs they penned for Gene Pitney ("That Girl Belongs to Yesterday") and the Toggery Five ("I'd Much Rather Be out with the Boys"). —*Richie Unterberger*

Wasted / 1995 / Volume ✦✦✦✦
A two-disc set collecting most of the electronic artists featured in the *Volume* series as of 1995, *Wasted* is an excellent work, including previously unreleased tracks by Aphex Twin, the Orb, Orbital, Underworld, Tricky, LFO, Sabres of Paradise and more. —*John Bush*

Wax 'em Down / Revell ✦✦✦✦
Cool compilation of rare surf tunes, not too hard to find despite appearing on a tiny reissue label. Divided about equally between instrumen-

tals and vocals; the instrumentals, usually featuring magnificent reverb-soaked guitar lines, certainly have the edge. Only a couple of recognizable names here: the Original Surfaris' "Surfari" is the B-side of their well-known "Bombora," and Sandy Nelson's "Casbah" is a great lost treasure, with searing guitar by well-known session player and producer Richie Podolor. Also includes a first-rate surf novelty in Frank Sinatra, Jr's "Beach Girls & the Monster" (included in both vocal and instrumental versions). —*Richie Unterberger*

Wax, Board and Woodie / Jul. 29, 1996 / Varese Sarabande ✦✦✦
Subtitled "a collection of rare and unreleased surf and hot rod songs," this 14-track compilation hits the intended target in a big way. Culling its contents primarily from the MCA/Dot Records vaults, one of the big tickets here is a bone-chilling unreleased moment when we hear the Surfaris attempting to take on the Rolling Stones with their swipe at "Route 66," way cooler than it sounds. A couple of silly but great fun anyway P.F. Sloan sides, including a unreleased sloppy-as-hell song demo, compliment one-off instrumentals like "El Gato" by the Chandelles and "Tremble" by the Galaxies. And in true Dot Records tradition (the label that made their rep inflicting Pat Boone on an unsuspecting world) there's even a "cover" version on here by a Milt Rogers of Dick Dale's "Let's Go Trippin'"!! Not the most essential set of tunes, but one hell of a fun compilation. —*Cub Koda*

We Got a Party: Best of Ron Records, Vol. 1 / 1988 / Rounder ✦✦✦✦
There's something for R&B, blues and soul fans of all persuasions on this anthology spotlighting various New Orleans artists who recorded for the Ron label in the late '50s and early '60s. There were celebrities, like pianist Professor Longhair and the sultry soul queen Irma Thomas, country/rockabilly singers like Warren Lee, novelty specialist Chris Kenner and shouters such as Bobby Mitchell. The 14 tracks on the CD are all good; most are wonderful, even if most of the singers never attained any recognition outside Crescent City R&B circles. —*Ron Wynn*

West Coast Doo-Wop / Ace ✦✦✦✦
Nice collection of vocal group sides from the vaults of Modern Records. Arthur Lee Maye & the Crowns' "Loop-De-Loop-De-Loop" and "Oochie Pachie" are among the numerous highlights. —*Cub Koda*

West Coast Rap: The First Dynasty, Vol. 1 / 1992 / Rhino ✦✦✦✦✦
Although it contains too many obscurities and novelties to make it absolutely essential for casual listeners, *West Coast Rap: The First Dynasty, Vol. 1* is an excellent compilation of early '80s hip-hop from the likes of Ice-T ("The Coldest Rap"), Egyptian Lover ("Egypt, Egypt"), L.A. Dream Team ("Rockberry Jam"), World Class Wrekin' Cru ("Slice"), 2 Live Crew ("2 Live"), and Bobby Jimmy & the Critters ("We Like Ugly Women"). Only Timex Social Club's "Rumors" stands out as a stone-cold classic, but the rest of the record is first-rate old-school rap, and worth the time of any serious hip-hop fan. —*Stephen Thomas Erlewine*

West Coast Rap: The First Dynasty, Vol. 2 / 1992 / Rhino ✦✦✦✦✦
Like its predecessor, *West Coast Rap: The First Dynasty, Vol. 2* is short on indisputable classics, but the overall quality of the material is quite high. Over the course of 13 tracks, *West Coast Rap* runs through several funky old-school highlights from the likes of Ice-T ("Body Rock"), D.J. Matrix ("Feel My Bass"), Kid Frost ("Rough Cut"), L.A. Dream Team ("Calling on the Dream Team"), Darkstar ("Sexybaby"), and Egyptian Lover ("Freak-A-Holic"). Most of this is simply party music, but it's good party music and the collection is worthwhile for any devoted rap listener, even though its momentum occasionally sags. —*Stephen Thomas Erlewine*

West Coast Rap: The First Dynasty, Vol. 3 / 1992 / Rhino ✦✦✦✦✦
Like the other two collections of *West Coast Rap: The First Dynasty, Vol. 3* promises more than it delivers, since it is short on genuine classics and long on novelties. Despite its flaws, *Vol. 3*, like the rest of the *West Coast Rap* series, remains one of the best old-school hip-hop compilations on the market, since it was put together with some care and the overall quality of the music is quite high, even if certain names (Ice-T, Egyptian Lover, Kid Frost, 2 Live Crew, Bobby Jimmy & the Critters) are a little too familiar from the disc's predecessors. Nevertheless, there's enough solid cuts to make this a strong addition to any comprehensive hip-hop collection. —*Stephen Thomas Erlewine*

What a Way to Die / 198? / Satan ✦✦✦✦
One of the very best '60s garage compilations; considering that there are probably over a thousand entries in this field, that's not a light compliment. Many of the best garage-pop treasures are here: the Enfields' "She Already Has Somebody" (which both recalls and stands up to the best of the Zombies), Richard and the Young Lions' odd clash of snotty punk and pop production ("You Can Make It"), Larry & the Loafers' exhilarating frat-rock clarion call "Let's Go to the Beach," and an extremely cool surf rarity by the Standells. Especially great is the single by Detroit's Pleasure Seekers, one of the very few female '60s garage bands, and possibly the best, featuring a teenage Suzi Quatro. "What a Way to Die" is probably the raunchiest female-sung garage record of the 1960s; its flipside, "Never Thought You'd Leave Me," is more subdued and just as

good, showing an unexpected Zombies influence. A nice bonus is the cover shot (of Richard and the Young Lions), one of the best '60s garage band photos ever printed. —*Richie Unterberger*

What's Shakin' / 1966 / Elektra ✦✦✦
An odd, erratic, but interesting anthology of rare performances recorded by Elektra in the mid-'60s, when it was just getting its feet wet with rock. Leading the way are the Paul Butterfield Blues Band, whose five tracks are very much in the style of their first LP; the Butterfield original "Lovin' Cup" is about as good as anything he ever did. Eric Clapton & the Powerhouse are a most interesting aggregation, also featuring Stevie Winwood, Paul Jones, Jack Bruce, and Spencer Davis Group drummer Pete York; their three tracks include early versions of "Steppin' Out" and "Crossroads," which Clapton would record with the Bluesbreakers and Cream, respectively. The Lovin' Spoonful's four tracks date from before reaching stardom with the Kama Sutra label; here they concentrate on blues and early rock 'n' roll-style songs, which frankly don't measure up to their folk-rock. Rare tracks by Tom Rush and Al Kooper (who reworked his contribution, "Can't Keep from Crying Sometimes," with the Blues Project) round out the set. —*Richie Unterberger*

Wild Surf! / 1996 / Del-Fi ✦✦✦
In the early and mid-1960s, Del-Fi recorded a good deal of surf music. This compilation brings together 24 tracks recorded by acts whose impact was strictly regional, including the Lively Ones, the Centurions, Dave Myers, the Sentinals, the Impacts, the Surfman, the Original Surfaris (not the "Wipe Out" guys), the Pharos, and the Gonzos. Some of the best tunes have shown up on surf compilations (like Rhino's *Surf Box*). But if your interest in surf runs deeper than the usual greatest hits collections, this is one of the more solid secondary anthologies out there, many of the tracks exhibiting a distinct Latin influence in the melodies and rhythms. —*Richie Unterberger*

Wild Things: Wild Kiwi Garage 1966-1969 / 1991 / Flying Nun ✦✦✦✦
New Zealand, a tiny country with a population less than the metropolitan San Francisco Bay Area, nevertheless had a fairly prolific and interesting garage/beat scene in the mid-'60s. This collects 16 singles that, with one or two exceptions, were obscure even in the land of their release. Like the bands from neighboring Australia, the Kiwis compensated for their isolation with crude mania, and this has some ferocious sub-Stones pounders from the likes of the La De Da's, Chants R&B, and the Bluestars. An above-average garage collection, well worth checking out by '60s aficionados. —*Richie Unterberger*

Wild Wild Young Women / Rounder ✦✦✦✦
Rockabilly was largely a male domain; except for Wanda Jackson and Brenda Lee, no female rockabilly singers made a notable national impact. But there were a few other women rockabilly vocalists making some good records, and this is the best basic collection of them. Janis Martin, known as "the female Elvis," checks in with three cuts, including "My Boy Elvis"; the Davis Sisters (one of whom was Skeeter Davis) and Rose Maddox are represented by some mid-'50s sides which illustrate rockabilly's close links to country boogie. The Collins Kids recorded some of the most hyper-tempo rockabilly of any sort, and Sparkle Moore, from Nebraska, had a great over-the-top, swooping delivery. You also get some even more obscure, but also worthy, cuts from the Nettles Sisters, Jean Chapel, Joan King, Linda and the Epics, and Alvadean Coker. More sides are available on single-artist compilations by some of these acts, particularly the Collins Kids, the Davis Sisters, Janis Martin, and Rose Maddox, but the compilers have done a good job of selecting first-rate tracks for a general overview. —*Richie Unterberger*

The Wildest from Specialty / 1994 / Specialty ✦✦✦
Excellent 25-track compilation featuring '50s sides that appeared on the Specialty label. Highlights include Jerry Byrne's "Lights Out" and "Carry On" (both featuring a young Dr. John on piano), Bob "Froggy" Landers' surreal "Cherokee Dance," Don and Dewey's original take of "Justine," the Pentagons' "It's Spring Again" and Roddy Jackson's "Moose on the Loose." From the label that brought you Little Richard, this is piano poundin', shack shakin', borderline-nuts first-generation rock 'n' roll. For once, a compilation that truly reflects its title. —*Cub Koda*

Wowie Zowie! World of Progessive Music / 1969 / Decca ✦✦✦

Wrinkles / 1989 / MCA/Chess ✦✦✦
Ten obscure blues, R&B, and rock instrumentals from the Chess label, spanning 1952-63. The Jody Williams track is a scorcher that stands up to Mickey Baker and Otis Rush's best work. Also includes rarities by Chuck Berry, Bo Diddley, Otis Spann, and Little Walter. A ragtag compilation, but a good one. —*Richie Unterberger*

Yellow Pills, Vol. 1 / 1994 / Big Deal ✦✦✦✦
A dynamic power-pop collection featuring new and old tracks by some of the leading groups of the last ten years, including Dwight Twilley, the Shoes, the Rubinoos, and Tommy Keene. The music on *Yellow Pills* is strong enough to convert casual fans into hardcore power-pop fanatics. —*Stephen Thomas Erlewine*

Yellow Pills Vol. 2 / 1994 / Big Deal ✦✦✦✦

Yellow Pills, Vol. 3: More Great Pop / 1995 / Big Deal ✦✦✦✦
The third volume of the newly-recorded power-pop anthology, *Yellow Pills*, is arguably the most interesting and best installment in the series, featuring gems for Paul Collins' Beat, Material Issue, and Greenberry Woods. —*Stephen Thomas Erlewine*

You Can Be Wrong About Boys / 1993 / Sequel ✦✦
Twenty British non-hit singles in the girl group or female solo rock-pop singer styles, mostly from the mid-'60s (although the track dates creep up all the way to 1971). Even by the standards of this fairly narrow sub-genre, it's kind of mediocre and forgettable. Peanut's "Thank Goodness for the Rain" and Barbara Kay's "Someone Has to Cry" have some good Brill Building/Spector touches, but the rest provokes little reaction one way or the other. The only remotely recognizable names are Dana Gillespie, Julie Grant (who had some small British hits), and Swedish actress Britt Ekland, billed simply as Britt on her 1965 single. —*Richie Unterberger*

Youth Gone Wild: Heavy Metal Hits of the '80s, Vol. 1 / Mar. 26, 1996 / Rhino ✦✦✦✦
Rhino's three-volume set *Youth Gone Wild: Heavy Metal Hits of the '80s* nearly chronicles the excesses of '80s metal accurately, but the set falls just short of being definitive. None of the three discs (available separately) has a logical or chronological sequencing, seemingly throwing all of the songs together in random order. Also, several big stars and definitive songs are missing in favor of negligible cult favorties. Even with these two significant flaws, the series is terrific and captures the essence of the era. *Vol. 1* concentrates on early-'80s hits like the Scorpions' "Rock You like a Hurricane," Twisted Sister's "We're Not Gonna Take It," Accept's "Balls to the Wall," Motörhead's "Ace of Spades," Judas Priest's "Parental Guidance," Ratt's "Lay It Down" and Quiet Riot's "Cum on Feel the Noize," throwing in cuts like Poison's "Talk Dirty to Me" for good measure. It might not make for coherent listening, and several cuts (including Krokus' "Screaming in the Night" and Dio's "The Last in Line") have dated poorly, but the set nevertheless has many metal clas-

sics. And if you want to know what mainstream '80s metal and hard rock sounded like, *Youth Gone Wild* can't be beat. —*Stephen Thomas Erlewine*

Youth Gone Wild: Heavy Metal Hits of the '80s, Vol. 2 / Mar. 26, 1996 / Rhino ✦✦✦✦
The second installment of Rhino's *Youth Gone Wild: Heavy Metal Hits Of The '80s* is divided between mid-'80s hits by David Lee Roth ("Goin' Crazy!"), Great White ("Rock Me"), Europe ("The Final Countdown") and Yngwie Malmsteen ("Heaven Tonight") and late-'80s cuts from Winger ("Seventeen"), Vixen ("Edge of a Broken Heart") and Faster Pussycat ("Poison Ivy"). More than any other entry in the series, *Vol. 2* suffers from cutesy, ironic selections—there's no reason Sam Kinison's "Wild Thing" should have been included, and Helloween only gained fame after being showcased on *Beavis & Butt-Head* in the '90s—and a few cuts, like King's X's "Over My Head," appear to be on the disc simply because they were personal favorites of the compilers. Nevertheless, *Youth Gone Wild, Vol. 2* remains a good purchase, especially for fans who want to replace their worn cassettes with only the hits, not full albums. —*Stephen Thomas Erlewine*

Youth Gone Wild: Heavy Metal Hits of the '80s, Vol. 3 / Mar. 26, 1996 / Rhino ✦✦✦✦
The third and final volume of *Youth Gone Wild: Heavy Metal Hits Of The '80s* has fewer hits than either of its predecessors, and it suffers as a result. Of all the cuts, only a handful—Whitesnake's "Still of the Night," Cinderella's "Gypsy Road," White Lion's "Wait," Kingdom Come's "Get it On," Bulletboys' "Smooth up in Ya," Britny Fox's "Girlschool"—were actually hits, while the rest all seem to be randomly selected. Mr. Big's "Addicted to That Rush" has the virtuosity of Paul Gilbert and Billy Sheehan to recommend it, and D.A.D. has some dark glamour, but Bang Tango, Raging Slab, Love/Hate, Dangerous Toys, Fastway and Helix are all faceless and nearly interchangeable, making *Vol. 3* considerably less entertaining than its predecessors. Still, the hits alone make the disc worthwhile for any nostalgic metalhead. —*Stephen Thomas Erlewine*

ESSAYS

Birth of Rock 'n' Roll

For those of us born too late to experience the birth of rock 'n' roll first-hand, an unlikely parallel might be drawn to the Internet. It has been written that no one planned the Internet; it just happened. And the same could be said of rock 'n' roll. No one planned rock 'n' roll, and it overtook the musical culture of America and then the world, with a sudden impact that revolutionized popular music as surely as the Internet is revolutionizing telecommunications.

It has often been said that rock 'n' roll was the result of cross-breeding between rhythm & blues and country & western music. That's a large part of the equation, of course, but hardly the entire picture. Gospel music, swing jazz, jump blues combos, country swing bands, Tin Pan Alley publishers—they were just some of the other key building blocks of the music.

Few would dispute that rock 'n' roll owes most of its origins to the musical traditions of America's Black population. From Africa, Blacks brought a strong oral and musical tradition of music for storytelling, recreation, and work. Continued and modified in the United States under incredibly harsh conditions, these elements would provide the backbone of blues music. As segregated as American society has been, there has been constant personal interchange and cultural exchange between races throughout the nation's history. The white southern population of the United States had its own musical conventions: Anglo-Saxon folk songs, Appalachian music, and religious music for the church. African-Americans absorbed influences from whites in their use of stringed instruments and harmonies. The development of jazz around the turn of the 20th century introduced larger bands and stronger rhythmic elements.

Just as technological developments affected the pace and complexity of life in the early 20th century, so did it accelerate the growth of popular music. The phonograph record enabled artists to reach and influence an exponentially larger audience of listeners and fellow musicians. Huge numbers of Blacks from the South migrated to urban communities, where music and dancing took place in considerably more crowded and hectic environments. And to be heard in those venues, musicians eventually had no choice but to use electronic amplification and, eventually, electric instruments.

As early as the 1930s, strong intimations of rock 'n' roll can be found in rhythmic, increasingly riff-driven swing jazz music, as well as blues-influenced country recordings by the Delmore Brothers, Bob Wills, Jimmie Rodgers, and the Maddox Brothers. Charlie Christian pioneered the use of the electric guitar in the early 1940s, at the same time as jazz musicians like Lionel Hampton were putting out riff-heavy hits like "Flyin' Home." As the '40s progressed, jazz musicians like Illinois Jacquet, Big Joe Turner, Louis Jordan, Jay McShann, and others upped the R&B quotient with honking saxes, "shouter" vocals, and pounding boogie-woogie piano.

Big bands became increasingly less economically viable after the Second World War, and smaller combos became more in vogue. They still had to play just as loudly as ever, though, and riffs, electric guitars, "shouting" R&B vocals, and prominent beats were usually the ticket. So it was that jump blues came into style, paced by Louis Jordan and singers like Wynonie Harris, Tiny Bradshaw, and Roy Brown.

Jump blues itself wasn't far removed from rock 'n' roll, and there were several other major changes afoot as the '50s began. The Delmore Brothers recorded frenetic country-boogie that anticipated the spirit of rockabilly. Vocal groups like the Orioles took the smooth popular stylings of Black harmony ensembles like the Mills Brothers and the Ink Spots and added a more pronounced R&B and gospel feel. After Delta musicians like Muddy Waters amplified their guitars and added rhythm sections, a fullbodied electric blues band sound was born in Chicago,

Memphis, and other urban centers. Fats Domino, Lloyd Price, and others pioneered the keyboard-and-horn driven grooves of New Orleans R&B. Les Paul took electric guitar wattage to new heights with his innovative multi-track recordings.

There were also major rumblings in the music industry and American society itself. Independent companies like Atlantic, King, Sun, Specialty, Chess, and numerous others recorded R&B and hillbilly music, catering to audiences that the major labels deemed too specialized and uncouth to service. Young white listeners began tuning in radio stations that played music for these supposed minority tastes. And the increasingly affluent economy meant that these young listeners had more time and money than ever to spend on records.

These disparate strands began to collide and merge as the '50s progressed. There are a great number of opinions as to what could be called the first "rock 'n' roll" record; indeed, an entire book (the fine *What Was the First Rock 'n' Roll Record?*) has been written on the subject. Certainly, early sides by Jackie Brenston ("Rocket 88"), Bill Haley, Lloyd Price, Hank Ballard, Fats Domino, and others have strong claims. Whatever it was, and whenever it became a style, by 1954 there were several records in the Top 30 that couldn't, from a latter-day vantage point, be called anything but rock 'n' roll: Bill Haley's primitive rockabilly ("Shake, Rattle, and Roll"), the joyous doo wop of the Crows and the Chords ("Gee" and "Sh-Boom"), the saucy R&B of Hank Ballard ("Work with Me Annie"). The music needed a name, and several theories have been advanced as to how the term "rock 'n' roll" came about. Influential Cleveland and New York DJ Alan Freed's claim to have originated the phrase is probably the most widely circulated, though rocking and rolling had long been a euphemism, especially in the Black community, for dancing, partying, and more private pleasures.

In 1955, Bill Haley's "Rock Around the Clock" became the first No. 1 rock 'n' roll hit; Little Richard and Chuck Berry had their first national smashes that year with "Tutti Frutti" and "Maybellene," songs which put electric guitar leads, honking saxes, whooping vocals, and lyrics about cars and girls to the forefront in a glorious package. In early 1956, Elvis Presley's No. 1 hit "Heartbreak Hotel" ended any doubt (or hope by the more conservative factions of the music business) that rock 'n' roll would fade.

An emerging regional sensation, Elvis pioneered rockabilly on his legendary recordings for Sun records in 1954 and 1955 by marrying the feels of the blues and country boogie with his hard-driving rhythms and frenetic vocals. His jump to a major label—and assimilation of slightly more pop-oriented values into his recordings that didn't diminish his genius in the slightest (at least at first)—made rock 'n' roll an international phenomenon. His massive success, and the success of the countless rock 'n' rollers who followed, was the end of the line in the evolution of the forces that gave birth to rock music—and the beginning, of course, of much more.

Recommended Recordings

The Delmore Brothers, *The Best of the Delmore Brothers* (Starday). Country boogie with a reckless feel, close harmonies, and pounding backbeat, separated from rockabilly only by the level of electric instruments and a rhythm section. This collection of their late 1940s sides continues much of their most raucous work.

Bill Haley & His Comets, *Rock the Joint!* (Schoolkids'). A collection of his early 1950s singles, prior to his breakthrough to mass success with "Shake, Rattle, and Roll" and "Rock Around the Clock." The earliest white rock 'n' roll ever recorded, combining country swing, electric guitars, saxophones, and R&B rhythms to come up with something different altogether.

Louis Jordan, *The Best of Louis Jordan* (MCA). A crucial bridge from swing jazz to jump blues, and a major influence upon Chuck Berry.

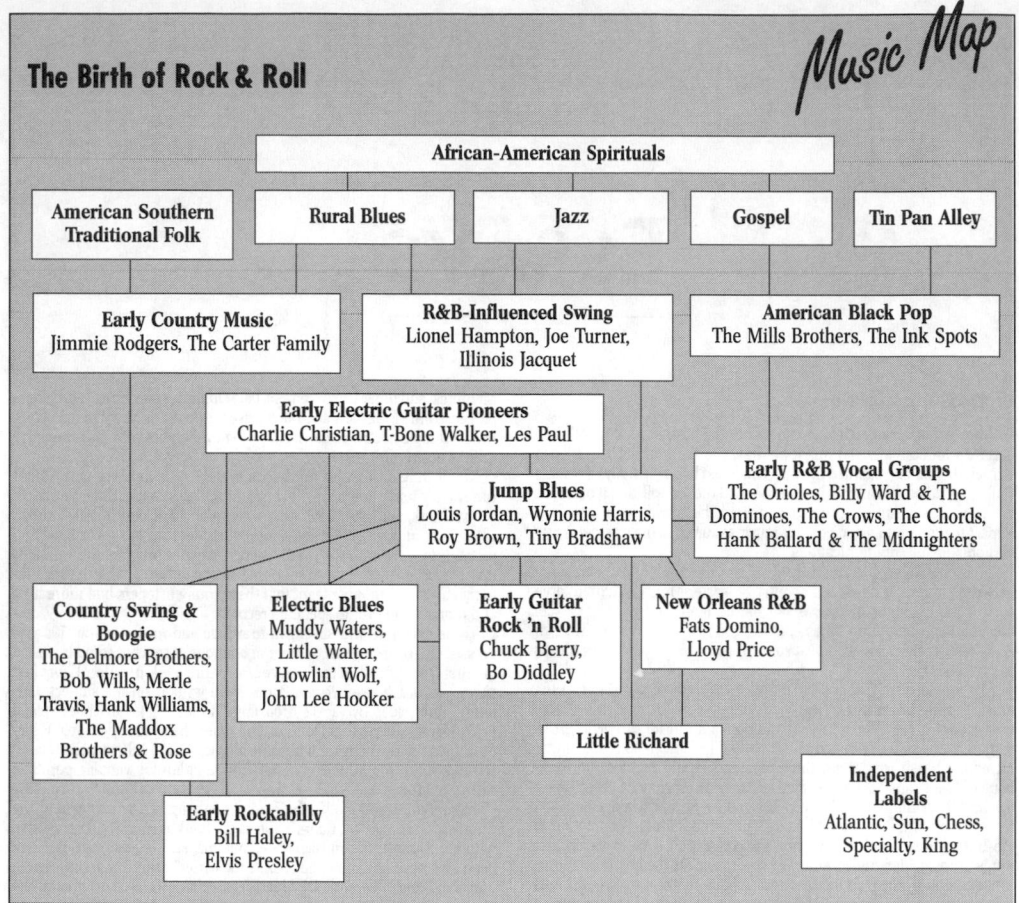

The Birth of Rock & Roll

Music Map

African-American Spirituals

American Southern Traditional Folk · **Rural Blues** · **Jazz** · **Gospel** · **Tin Pan Alley**

Early Country Music
Jimmie Rodgers, The Carter Family

R&B-Influenced Swing
Lionel Hampton, Joe Turner, Illinois Jacquet

American Black Pop
The Mills Brothers, The Ink Spots

Early Electric Guitar Pioneers
Charlie Christian, T-Bone Walker, Les Paul

Jump Blues
Louis Jordan, Wynonie Harris, Roy Brown, Tiny Bradshaw

Early R&B Vocal Groups
The Orioles, Billy Ward & The Dominoes, The Crows, The Chords, Hank Ballard & The Midnighters

Country Swing & Boogie
The Delmore Brothers, Bob Wills, Merle Travis, Hank Williams, The Maddox Brothers & Rose

Electric Blues
Muddy Waters, Little Walter, Howlin' Wolf, John Lee Hooker

Early Guitar Rock 'n Roll
Chuck Berry, Bo Diddley

New Orleans R&B
Fats Domino, Lloyd Price

Little Richard

Early Rockabilly
Bill Haley, Elvis Presley

Independent Labels
Atlantic, Sun, Chess, Specialty, King

The Maddox Brothers & Rose, *Vol. 1* (Arhoolie). Another hillbilly band that anticipated elements of rockabilly with their rumbling boogie and slap-back bass. This has 27 of their songs from 1946-51.

Various Artists, *Hillbilly Music Vol. 1 . . . Thank God!* (Capitol). A double album of rowdy hillbilly music from the late '40s to the mid-'50s, featuring such country giants as Tennessee Ernie Ford, Merle Travis, Buck Owens, and the Louvin Brothers. No other compilation illustrates the white country roots of rock 'n' roll as well.

Various Artists, *Atlantic R&B: 1947-1952* (Atlantic). The Atlantic label was arguably the greatest and most influential record company specializing in rhythm & blues during rock 'n' roll's formative years. This is the first volume of a seven-part series, also available as part of a box set.

Various Artists, *Atlantic R&B: 1952-1955* (Atlantic). More classic performances from the early Atlantic roster, edging closer to rock 'n' roll from its more blues- and R&B-based beginnings.

Various Artists, *Blues Masters Volume 5: Jump Blues Classics* (Rhino). The best jump blues compilation, with classics by Big Jay McNeely, Wynonie Harris, Tiny Bradshaw, Big Joe Turner, and others. A second volume in the *Blues Masters* series (*More Jump Blues Classics*) is of equally high quality.

Various Artists, *Blues Masters Volume 6: Blues Originals* (Rhino). Many of these songs helped form the backbone of the rock repertoire. Often popularized to a larger audience by white performers from Elvis Presley and the Rolling Stones down, here is where you'll find the original versions of classics like "That's All Right," "Back Door Man," "Love in Vain," and a lot of others.

Various Artists, *A History of New Orleans Rhythm and Blues Vol. 1* (Rhino). The first part of this three-volume series features key performances from the early and mid-1950s by artists who laid the foundations for the New Orleans sound, such as Lloyd Price and Guitar Slim.

Billy Ward, *Sixty Minute Men: The Best of Billy Ward & His Dominoes* (Rhino). One of the first great Black harmony groups of rhythm & blues, featuring lead vocals by two singers who would go on to

become early rock 'n' roll stars in their own right, Clyde McPhatter and Jackie Wilson.

Muddy Waters, *The Best of Muddy Waters* (Chess). The cream of the prolific output by the man who did more than any other performer to shape the course of modern electric blues, one of the primary currents feeding into the rock of both the past and present.

Various Artists, *A Sun Blues Collection* (Rhino). Excellent single-disc survey of the electrified country blues that the Sun label specialized in before moving to rockabilly, with great early- and mid-'50s sides by Rufus Thomas, B.B. King, James Cotton, and others.

Various Artists, *A Sun Country Collection* (Rhino). The other side of the Sun equation has the country roots of the southern rockabilly sound, with country hillbilly-verging-on-rockabilly by Johnny Cash, Carl Perkins, Jerry Lee Lewis, Warren Smith, Charlie Feathers, and more obscure performers.

Elvis Presley, *The Complete Sun Sessions* (RCA). The full-fledged birth of rockabilly on Elvis' legendary 1954-55 recordings, which in the eyes of some critics have never been surpassed in the history of rock 'n' roll.

Books

What Was the First Rock 'n' Roll Record?, by Jim Dawson & Steve Propes (1992, Faber & Faber)

Unsung Heroes of Rock 'n' Roll, by Nick Tosches (1984, Charles Scribner's Sons)

The Sound of the City, by Charlie Gillett (1983)

–Richie Unterberger

Early Rhythm & Blues

When rhythm & blues began in the mid-'40s, it didn't even have a name. When the term caught on, though, it caught on in a big way. Right up until the present day, R&B has come to refer to the entire world of Black popular music, although it's mostly identified as R&B—rather than rap, soul, or urban contemporary—by specialized audiences and music industry insiders, not general fans. In its earliest form, rhythm & blues was among the most important precursors of rock 'n' roll, if not THE most important. Early rock 'n' roll is basically R&B blended with country & western and pop influences. R&B wasn't only a crucial bridge between blues and rock 'n' roll, but between blues and soul, R&B's longest-lived and most important offshoot.

The blues, of course, was a big part of rhythm and blues, but jazz was nearly as important. The earliest rhythm & blues artists emerged from the big-band and swing-jazz era. Before World War II, jazz, much more so than today, was a dance-oriented music, often featuring vocalists. Around World War II, many major jazz players began developing bebop and cool jazz, a decidedly less danceable (though equally worthy) style; economic factors, as well as the draft and wartime restrictions on travel, made big bands less viable. Audiences, especially the rapidly growing metropolitan African-American communities, still wanted dance music. The musicians accomodated them by playing louder, more electric instruments, and accentuating riffs, boogies, and vocals.

The first popular style of rhythm & blues is often referred to as "jump" blues. From jazz, jump blues took its horn-driven lineup and swing rhythms; from blues, it took its general riffs and chord structures. Cab Calloway was perhaps the most important precursor of the style, but in jump blues, the vocals were harsher, the rhythms faster. The instrumentation was different, too; the pianos pounded harder, and the saxes didn't just blow, but honked and squealed.

The most important and popular jump blues star was Louis Jordan, whose records, unusually for the era, enjoyed success with both Black and white audiences; he was a big influence on Chuck Berry. Many of the early jump blues performers emerged from Los Angeles, where a large Black community had been growing during the Depression and the war; most other big cities had jump blues stars of their own by the end of the 1940s. Independent labels such as L.A.'s Specialty and Aladdin jump-started their success with the jump blues sound, filling a demand that the majors were basically unaware of. Joe Liggins, Tiny Bradshaw (the original performer of "The Train Kept A-Rollin'"), Amos Milburn, Camille Howard—all are largely forgotten except by record collectors, but all had huge R&B successes in the jump blues style, and ranked among the most popular Black musicians of their time.

Jump blues itself came in several different styles. There were the vocalists that came to be known as the "shouters," adding energy, soul, and gospel to the more restrained brand of big-band singing. Big Joe Turner, who got his start with Kansas City jazz bands, was the most legendary link between the eras, shifting into the R&B era with ease, and even scoring some early rock 'n' roll hits. Wynonie Harris, Roy Brown, Roy Milton, and Nappy Brown were a few of the most popular "shouters" of the late '40s and early '50s, although they aren't nearly as well remembered by history as Turner. There were also showmen, usually saxophonists, whose appeal was primarily instrumental: Big Jay McNeely, Illinois Jacquet, and Joe Houston, all with strong roots in jazz, drove dance crowds crazy with their acrobatic honking. And there were smoother, more urbane singers, like Charles Brown, Percy Mayfield, and Cecil Gant, who were as adept at ballads as uptempo material.

By the time the '50s started, "race" music, as it was known within the industry, had been renamed the more appropriate "rhythm & blues" by *Billboard* magazine staff-member Jerry Wexler. As an A&R man at Atlantic Records, Wexler helped shape jump blues into something with more appeal to pop listeners and teenagers. The recordings by early Atlantic stars like Ruth Brown, LaVern Baker, the first incarnation of the Drifters, and Chuck Willis (who actually began at the OKeh label) retained a strong jump blues flavor, but their rhythms, riffs, and lyrics point more clearly toward rock 'n' roll. Indeed, Baker and Willis managed to enjoy some success in the early rock 'n' roll era with material that was tailored toward a younger audience. As rock 'n' roll began to emerge in the early and mid-'50s, several distinct branches of R&B had developed that would each exert a large influence on popular music in their own rights: doo wop groups, electric blues, and New Orleans rhythm & blues. All of these sub-genres are examined in greater depth in this book in essays of their own, and all would prove to have a greater and more lasting impact on rock 'n' roll than the earlier, jazzier forms of R&B.

Still, there were quite a few performers who survived through the 1950s, and sometimes thrived, recording music that could not be called anything but R&B. Ike Turner, Ivory Joe Hunter, Faye Adams, Wynona Carr, Big Mama Thornton, Big Maybelle—none of these were straight blues artists, but their music wasn't rock 'n' roll either. Blues singers like Bobby "Blue" Bland, Junior Parker, and Little Milton bridged electric blues and soul, but they couldn't be pigeonholed as straight rock 'n' roll singers. Occasionally R&B performers like Johnny Otis, Screamin' Jay Hawkins, and Wilbert Harrison crossed over to the rock 'n' roll audience with their most hook-savvy songs; Harrison's "Kansas City" is largely jump blues with a shuffle beat, at least until it gets to the searing electric guitar break.

Several 1950s singers began as more or less straight R&B performers, but added an earthier, more pronounced gospel and church influence than had ever been heard before. Today, we recognize the greatest of these vocalists—Ray Charles, James Brown, Jackie Wilson, Little Willie John, Johnny Ace, Jessie Belvin, and Clyde McPhatter—as the forefathers of soul. Some of them, like Charles and Brown, would indeed become soul superstars in the '60s. Others, like McPhatter and John, were unable to make the transition, due to a combination of the inability to grow with the times and personal problems that proved insurmountable. R&B, though it has changed greatly since its birth, remains a crucial part of rock, soul, and rap; it's often just below or very much above the surface of the music.

For all of its monumental significance and the vast critical acclaim it has belatedly received, early R&B recordings can be tough to swallow in large lumps for the neophyte. The R&B performers and labels of the '40s and '50s were concerned with entertaining, not establishing diverse artistic oeuvres, and the similar chord patterns and arrangements can be wearing when heard on a compact disc rather than a juke box or dance floor, which is where the songs were often played in their heyday. Those investigating the genre in-depth for the first time are advised to start with some general various artist samplers, and move on from there according to their degrees of interest.

Recommended Recordings

Various Artists, *Blues Masters, Volume 5: Jump Blues Classics* (Rhino). The best jump blues introduction, with key cuts by Joe Turner, Wynonie Harris, Roy Brown, Tiny Bradshaw, Jay McNeely, Big Mama Thornton, Ruth Brown, and others.

Various Artists, *Blues Masters, Volume 14: More Jump Blues* (Rhino). Up to the same level as *Jump Blues Classics*, with tracks by Louis Jordan, LaVern Baker, Big Maybelle, Faye Adams, and many more.

Big Joe Turner, *Big, Bad & Blue: The Big Joe Turner Anthology* (Rhino). As mammoth as the man himself, this three-disc set encompasses several decades, reflecting R&B's evolution from the days of big-band jazz through rock 'n' roll. Too extensive for the casual fan; as alternatives, there are other Turner anthologies that focus on specific phases of his career.

Louis Jordan, *The Best of Louis Jordan* (MCA). Jordan recorded a great deal of material in the 1940s and 1950s, and no collection satisfactorily encompasses all of his classics; this one is the best.

Various Artists, *Atlantic Rhythm & Blues Vol. 1-4* (Atlantic). The most important label in the development of modern R&B, this is part of a seven-volume series that goes up to 1974. There's a whole box set of them if you want to go whole-hog, but the first four cover 1947-1962, before R&B had been fully renamed rock and soul.

Various Artists, *Specialty Story* (Specialty). At five discs, this is too much for non-specialists, if you'll pardon the pun. But it does offer a comprehensive survey of one of early R&B and rock 'n' roll's most important labels, with tracks by such greats as Joe Liggins, Percy Mayfield, Roy Milton, and Lloyd Price, up through early rock stars like Little Richard and Larry Williams.

Ruth Brown, *Rockin' in Rhythm: The Best of Ruth Brown* (Rhino). The singer on whom much of Atlantic's early fortune was built, this disc contains her most popular 1950s sides.

LaVern Baker, *Soul on Fire: The Best of LaVern Baker* (Rhino). One of the most important singers to lead the transition from R&B to rock 'n' roll.

The Drifters, *Let the Boogie-Woogie Roll: Greatest Hits (1953-1958)* (Atlantic). The first lineup of the Drifters, featuring Clyde McPhatter, could be called a doo wop group as well, but also had strong early R&B/jump blues influences.

Ike Turner, *I Like Ike: The Best of Ike Turner* (Rhino). Before joining Tina, Ike was an important talent scout, sideman, and bandleader. This collection of odds 'n' ends is mostly from the 1950s, and often walks the edge between R&B and electric blues.

Ray Charles, *Birth of Soul* (Rhino). Aptly titled three-disc box of Charles' work for Atlantic in the 1950s.

Johnny Otis, *The Capitol Years* (Capitol). An enormously popular figure in R&B as a bandleader, musician, and talent scout, Otis crossed over to success in the rock market in the late '50s by adding a Bo Diddley beat. Although Otis himself preferred straight R&B, this collection of late-'50s sides is his best.

Little Willie John, *Fever: The Best of Little Willie John* (Rhino). One of R&B's most versatile vocalists, and a huge influence on James Brown.

Clyde McPhatter, *Deep Sea Ball: The Best of Clyde McPhatter* (Rhino). His biggest hits for Atlantic in the late '50s, after he left the Drifters.

James Brown, *Roots of a Revolution* (PolyGram). A double-disc retrospective of 1956-1964 recordings, bringing us from hardcore R&B to the verge of the birth of funk.

—Richie Unterberger

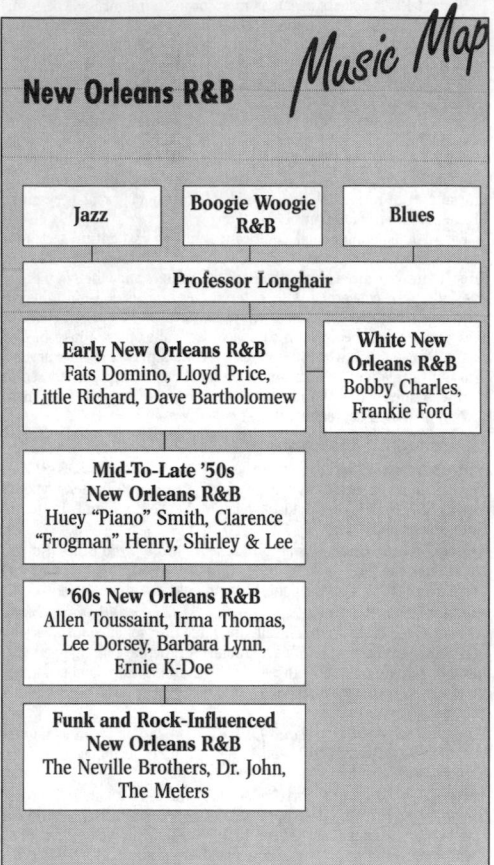

New Orleans R&B — *Music Map*

Jazz | Boogie Woogie R&B | Blues

Professor Longhair

Early New Orleans R&B
Fats Domino, Lloyd Price,
Little Richard, Dave Bartholomew

White New Orleans R&B
Bobby Charles,
Frankie Ford

Mid-To-Late '50s New Orleans R&B
Huey "Piano" Smith, Clarence
"Frogman" Henry, Shirley & Lee

'60s New Orleans R&B
Allen Toussaint, Irma Thomas,
Lee Dorsey, Barbara Lynn,
Ernie K-Doe

Funk and Rock-Influenced New Orleans R&B
The Neville Brothers, Dr. John,
The Meters

New Orleans R&B

When it comes down to naming which American city contributed most to the birth of rock 'n' roll, it really only comes down to two: Memphis and New Orleans. New Orleans, of course, already occupied a rarefied place in the legacy of American popular music for its crucial role in the birth of jazz music. Its contribution to rock 'n' roll was nearly equal in stature, supplying the music with many of its bedrock rhythms, as well as much of its playful humor. Its population, a vibrant mix of Creole, Cajun, Black, and white cultures, cultivated precisely the kind of melting pot of music that led to the early styles of rock 'n' roll.

The early New Orleans sound was characterized by boogie piano, honking saxes, and relaxed, unfettered performances. Pianist Professor Longhair embodies the true sound of New Orleans for some listeners, but it wasn't established as a major commercial force until the emergence of Fats Domino. His 1950 single "The Fat Man" is one of the dozens of performances routinely cited as one of the first rock 'n' roll records. It took a while for Fats to cross over to the pop audience, but once he did, starting with 1955's "Ain't That a Shame," he became one of the most popular early rock 'n' roll performers, rolling off hit after hit for the next half-dozen years.

Another Crescent City candidate for the title of first rock 'n' roll record was Lloyd Price's "Lawdy Miss Clawdy," a 1952 No. 1 R&B hit. Price's late-'50s hits had a much more commercial sound, but his early work was much rawer, and influenced his label, the L.A.-based Specialty Records, to move its focus from jump blues to rock 'n' roll. Their biggest star was Little Richard, a Georgia native who didn't find his groove until he started recording in New Orleans, reeling off a batch of hugely influential hit singles in the mid-'50s that helped define early rock 'n' roll with their wooly vocals, pounding piano, and shrieking horns.

The chief behind-the-scenes architect of the New Orleans sound was Dave Bartholomew, a trumpeter, songwriter, and producer who graced many early classic New Orleans R&B/rock sessions, not the least of which were those of Fats Domino (whose hits Bartholomew co-wrote). Session players like drummer Earl Palmer and saxophonists Alvin "Red" Tyler and Lee Allen also played on numerous sessions, and were

instrumental in putting the stamp on the early New Orleans sound. Little Richard and Fats Domino were the only superstars to emerge from the city's rock 'n' roll scene in the 1950s, but there were also many artists with only one or two national hits that recorded a wealth of fine material (much of which gave them sizable regional hits). Shirley & Lee ("Let the Good Times Roll"), Huey "Piano" Smith ("Rocking Pneumonia & the Boogie-Woogie Flu"), and Clarence "Frogman" Henry ("Ain't Got No Home") all recorded classics which continue to live at the heart of the rock 'n' roll repertoire. Most of the music was recorded by Blacks, but Bobby Charles ("See You Later Alligator") and Frankie Ford ("Sea Cruise") proved that whites could also rock convincingly in the New Orleans style.

In the early '60s, the New Orleans sound was updated slightly to reflect trends in the still-young soul scene. Pianist, songwriter, and producer Allen Toussaint inherited Dave Bartholomew's crown as the city's chief rock 'n' roll visionary. Again, while there were no stars of the magnitude of Fats Domino or Little Richard, there were many classic hits and non-hits by the likes of Ernie K-Doe ("Mother-in-Law"), Chris Kenner ("I Like It Like That"), the Showmen ("It Will Stand"), Barbara George ("I Know"), and Benny Spellman ("Fortune Teller").

Some of the New Orleans performers emerging during this period proved to be durable, though not superstars. Irma Thomas may be the finest female New Orleans R&B singer of all time, not to mention one of the finest soul-R&B singers of any kind; in addition to her classic early New Orleans ballads, she also recorded great pop-rock sides in L.A. and "deep soul" tracks with the Muscle Shoals rhythm section. Lee Dorsey had charming novelty-tinged hits with "Ya Ya," "Working in a Coal Mine," and "Ride Your Pony." Clarence "Frogman" Henry roared back into the charts in the early '60s with several singles in a sort of updated Fats Domino style. The Dixie Cups ran off several great girl group singles in the mid-'60s, one of which, "Iko Iko," was a variation on a traditional Mardi Gras Indian chant. Barbara Lynn recorded many early soul singles, although only one, "You'll Lose a Good Thing," was a big national smash.

After the mid-'60s, national New Orleans R&B hits were relatively rare, although the city continued to house a lively music scene. The most influential latter-day Crescent City performers were the Meters, who mixed New Orleans rhythms with funk; Dr. John, a session player with extensive roots in the New Orleans scene dating back to the late '50s, who created a sort of mystic voodoo-tinged update of the vintage New Orleans sound; and the Neville Brothers, a prodigiously talented family who had been releasing fine R&B and soul records, together and separately, since the mid-'50s.

The New Orleans sound may not be a big commercial presence nowadays—the Neville Brothers are the only big touring act associated with the sound, and they've never delivered the classic record that critics expect of their talents. But truth to tell, the city can carry on its traditions with little help from the rest of the nation, as many R&B musicians continue to base themselves in New Orleans and play to a regional audience. The city also continues to feature dozens of its R&B, blues, and rock performers in the massive New Orleans Jazz Festival, which attracts huge crowds from around the world every year.

Recommended Recordings

Various Artists, *A History of New Orleans Rhythm & Blues Vol. 1-3* (Rhino)
Fats Domino, *My Blue Heaven: Best of Fats Domino* (EMI)
Little Richard, *18 Greatest Hits* (Rhino)
Lee Dorsey, *Holy Cow!: Best of Lee Dorsey* (Arista)
Dr. John, *Anthology* (Rhino)
Irma Thomas, *Time Is on My Side (The Best of Irma Thomas), Vol. 1* (EMI)
Lloyd Price, *Lawdy!* (Specialty)
The Neville Brothers, *Treacherous—A History of the Neville Brothers (1955-1985)* (Rhino)
The Meters, *Funkify Your Life: The Meters Anthology* (Rhino)
Professor Longhair, *Fess: Professor Longhair Anthology* (Rhino)
Dave Bartholomew, *Spirit of New Orleans* (EMI)
Huey "Piano" Smith, *Rock & Roll Revival* (Ace, UK)
Various Artists, *Crescent City Soul: The Sound of New Orleans* (EMI)
—Richie Unterberger

Doo Wop

"Doo wop"—the words bring smiles to the faces of most knowledgeable rock listeners. In some cases, they're smirks of derision, from those who feel that the form exemplifies rock 'n' roll at its most innocuous, silliest, and embarrassingly quaint. From those who grew up during the '50s, it's more likely a smile of pleasure from someone who treasures the exquisite vocal harmonies and mourns the loss of the utter lack of pretension and guile that characterized great doo wop recordings.

Love it or hate it, doo wop is a major part of rock 'n' roll's lexicon. The rhythm & blues ballads and uptempo numbers of doo wop are characterized by those harmonies, of course, but also by the nonsense syllables that often formed the backbone of the backup vocals. "Doo wop" was just one of those common phrases; "bop-bop," "dip-dip," "bomp-a-bomp-bomp-bomp, buh-dang-a-dang-dang," "wah wah, shoop shoop," "dooby dooby doo," and "yip-yip-yip-yip-yip-yip-yip-yip" were just a few of the others. Usually they were love songs, but often they were outrageous comic novelty tunes as well. They were early rock 'n' roll at its most sentimental and humorous. Doo wop—like all great African-American music—has much of its roots in the harmonies and emotive phrasing of gospel. The more pop-oriented side of the equation was provided by the first popular American Black vocal groups, the Ink Spots and the Mills Brothers. Adding a rhythm & blues flavor to this blueprint, as well as a strong "church" feel, the Orioles had a No. 1 R&B hit in 1948 with "It's Too Soon to Know," which is often cited as the first doo wop (and sometimes, even the first rock 'n' roll) record.

Several groups followed in the Orioles' style over the next few years, including the Ravens, the Cardinals, and the Larks (many of the early doo wop acts named themselves after birds). The Clovers drew more explicitly from rhythm & blues, and the snappier rhythms and saucier lyrics of jump blues infiltrated the form in recordings by the Dominoes (featuring Clyde McPhatter) and Hank Ballard & the Midnighters.

By 1954, singles by the Crows ("Gee"), Dominoes, Orioles, and Hank Ballard had crossed over from the R&B market to become bona fide pop chart hits. Numerous urban vocal groups sprang up—a lot of them probably did start on the street corner, as legend would have it—and numerous record companies rushed to get a piece of the action. As rock 'n' roll gained momentum, doo wop become brassier, with more honking sax solos, outrageous stuttering vocal interplay, and more explicitly teenage and young adult themes.

There were probably over a thousand groups that eventually cut a doo wop record over the next decade, leading to a vociferous collector community that probably ranks as the most devoted of its kind in rock 'n' roll. A great many of the records originated in New York, though Los Angeles and Philadelphia were also active centers, and scattered doo wop acts were active, in the studio and otherwise, across the country.

Most of the doo wop groups, if they made it onto the charts at all, were one or two-shot acts, quickly fading into obscurity after failing to secure follow-ups. The Penguins, the Five Satins, the Monotones, the El Dorados, the Dell Vikings, the Silhouettes—these are just a few of those glorious names, though in some cases they recorded some non-hit efforts that were nearly as fine as their smashes. There were also a few groups that managed to maintain a presence on the R&B and pop charts for a few years running, sometimes with numerous personnel changes. The Clovers, the Flamingos, Little Anthony & the Imperials, and the Moonglows were a few of the best. With the Teenagers, Frankie Lymon pioneered a brand of pre-teen soul that was pinpointed as an influence on Michael Jackson when the Jackson 5 emerged many years later. Before Clyde McPhatter left to become a solo act, the first incarnation of the Drifters was one of the most popular R&B acts of the mid-'50s.

At the top of the pyramid were a couple of groups that ranked among the most popular early rock 'n' rollers. The Platters were one of the most pop-oriented of all of the doo wop groups, and appealed to the adult audience more than almost any of the early major rock 'n' roll acts. The Coasters were among the wittiest rock groups of any era, courtesy of Jerry Lieber and Mike Stoller, who penned and produced many classic songs for the singers, including "Searchin'," "Young Blood," "Yakety Yak," and "Poison Ivy."

As the '50s progressed, more and more white performers sang doo wop, sometimes in integrated ensembles (such as the Dell Vikings and the Impalas), sometimes as all-white groups (the Mystics, Dion & the Belmonts). Often Italian-American in origin, by the time the '60s began, these white singers were a major part of the form, which was becoming less of a commercial force.

But before doo wop vanished from the charts altogether, it underwent a revival of sorts in the early '60s, which saw huge doo wop hits by the likes of the Marcels, the Capris, Maurice Williams, and Shep & the Limelites. By the time of the British Invasion, though, there was barely a ripple of pure doo wop to be found on the charts.

Doo wop did not vanish so much as become permanently absorbed into rock and soul. Early soul giants like the Miracles and the Impressions owed huge debts to doo wop; indeed, their early records pretty much are doo wop. A lot of doo wop could be heard in the girl groups of the early '60s. Many hits by the Four Seasons and Dion were doo wop in construction, if not always in production. In vocal surf music, there's no doubt that doo wop was a prime influence on the ensemble singing of the Beach Boys and Jan & Dean. You can also hear it in the early records by the Beatles and several other British Invasion groups, as well as many of Frank Zappa's satirical efforts. Right on up to Boyz II Men, soul music has built upon the harmonies and vocal arrangements of doo wop music.

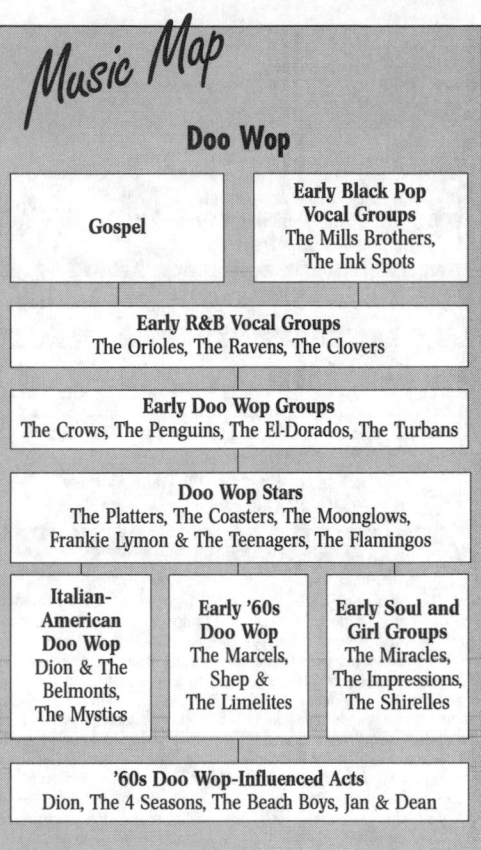

Music Map

Doo Wop

Gospel	Early Black Pop Vocal Groups The Mills Brothers, The Ink Spots

Early R&B Vocal Groups
The Orioles, The Ravens, The Clovers

Early Doo Wop Groups
The Crows, The Penguins, The El-Dorados, The Turbans

Doo Wop Stars
The Platters, The Coasters, The Moonglows, Frankie Lymon & The Teenagers, The Flamingos

Italian-American Doo Wop Dion & The Belmonts, The Mystics	Early '60s Doo Wop The Marcels, Shep & The Limelites	Early Soul and Girl Groups The Miracles, The Impressions, The Shirelles

'60s Doo Wop-Influenced Acts
Dion, The 4 Seasons, The Beach Boys, Jan & Dean

Recommended Recordings

Various Artists, *The Doo Wop Box, Vol. 1-2* (Rhino)

Billy Ward & the Dominoes, *Sixty Minute Men: The Best of Billy Ward His Dominoes* (Rhino)

Hank Ballard & the Midnighters, *Sexy Ways: The Best of Hank Ballard & the Midnighters* (Rhino)

The Drifters, *Let the Boogie Woogie Roll—Greatest Hits (1953- 1958)* (Atlantic)

The Platters, *Magic Touch: An Anthology* (Mercury)

Frankie Lymon & the Teenagers, *Best of Frankie Lymon & the Teenagers* (Rhino)

Dion & the Belmonts, *Everything You Always Wanted to Hear by Dion & the Belmonts* (Laurie)

The Coasters, *50 Coastin' Classics* (Rhino)

The Clovers, *Down in the Alley: The Best of the Clovers* (Atlantic)

The Moonglows, *Blue Velvet: The Ultimate Collection* (Chess)

Various Artists, *The Best of Doo Wop Uptempo Vol. 1-2* (Rhino)

Various Artists, *The Best of Doo Wop Ballads Vol. 1-2* (Rhino)

Books

Doo Wop: The Forgotten Third of Rock 'N Roll, by Dr. Anthony Gribin & Dr. Matthew Shiff (Krause Publications, 1992)

They All Sang on the Corner, by Phillip Groia (Phillie Dee Enterprises, 1983)

—Richie Unterberger

Rockabilly

If rock 'n' roll can be called the child of rhythm and blues and country & western music, no style is a purer blend than rockabilly. The first form of rock 'n' roll performed by white musicians, its duration of mass popularity was brief, but the best of it remains among the most exciting and frenetic rock 'n' roll ever waxed.

Even in the segregated American South of the early 20th century, Blacks and whites often had cause to interact with each other on a daily

Rockabilly

Music Map

Country Swing and Boogie Bob Wills, The Delmore Brothers, The Maddox Brothers & Rose	Jump Blues Shouters Wynonie Harris, Roy Brown	Electric Blues Howlin' Wolf, Junior Parker, Arthur "Big Boy" Crudup

Bill Haley and His Comets

The Sun Sound
Elvis Presley, Carl Perkins, Jerry Lee Lewis, Billy Lee Riley, Roy Orbison

Early Rockabilly Stars Gene Vincent, Buddy Holly, Wanda Jackson, Dale Hawkins, Johnny Burnette	L.A. Rockabilly Eddie Cochran, Ricky Nelson

basis. The interaction carried over to music, and white hillbilly country performers have reflected the influence of the blues and other African-American music since they began recording, as a listen to Jimmie Rodgers will attest to. Just as blues became jazzier, faster, and more electric throughout the 1940s and early '50s, so did country, through swing bands like Bob Wills and the Maddox Brothers. The Delmore Brothers, starting as a more traditional hillbilly harmony act, anticipated much of rockabilly's mania when they added a thumping country boogie beat to the equation on their finest recordings in the late '40s. Nearly forgotten performers like Arthur Smith and Hardrock Gunter laid down country boogie sides that brought the guitar to the forefront.

Considering that most rockabilly musicians of importance came from the South, it's ironic that the first records that could be termed as honest-to-god rockabilly were issued by a northerner, Bill Haley. The Philadelphian had been pursuing a hillbilly career with generally dismal results until 1951, when he covered Jackie Brenston's "Rocket 88" (which is itself often cited as one of the very first rock 'n' roll records). Although they aren't nearly as well known as his huge rock 'n' roll hits like "Rock Around the Clock," the sides he cut for the small Essex label between 1951 and 1954 are groundbreaking early rockabilly; the 1952 single "Rock the Joint," in fact, is almost identical in melody and arrangement to "Rock Around the Clock." Haley was no Elvis vocally, and the steel guitars and jump beats of his Comets betrayed lingering influences of hillbilly and swing music. But he was the first to bring together R&B and C&W with such force, although nobody knew quite what to call the music at the time. There were certainly numerous musicians in the South experimenting with primitive rockabilly-like sounds by mid-1954. Sam Phillips and his Memphis record label, Sun Records, were chiefly responsible for honing the sound and capturing it on vinyl.

Often quoted as having said that he could make a fortune with a white singer who sounded Black (though he has denied saying this in such explicit terms), he found the perfect vehicle for doing so with Elvis Presley, who recorded five singles for Sun between mid-1954 and the end of 1955. Supported by guitarist Scotty Moore and bassist Bill Black, this was rockabilly, if not rock 'n' roll, at its best and purest; as great as his subsequent achievements were, by critical consensus this handful of 45s ranks as Elvis' finest work. Presley didn't set off a mass wave of imitators right away; he was primarily a regional sensation until his contract was bought by RCA. Sam Phillips used the money from the sale to develop his own formidable stable of rockabilly performers. Carl Perkins' "Blue Suede Shoes" almost beat Elvis' "Heartbreak Hotel" to the top of the charts, and although Perkins was never able to duplicate the success, Sun generated a wealth of great rockabilly hits and misses over the next few years by Jerry Lee Lewis, Billy Lee Riley, Sonny Burgess, Carl Mann, and Roy Orbison. The Sun Sound—echo-chamber vocals, crisp electric guitar leads, and slap-back bass—became the standard of rockabilly excellence, often imitated, never recaptured. Presleymania overran the country in 1956, setting off a wave of rockabilly recordings, nationally and (more often) regionally distributed, that was similar in some respects to the garage band explosion of a decade later. Hundreds of performers found their way into studios in Tennessee, Texas, California, and other locales, embracing the new sound with a hepped-up

enthusiasm that often bordered on mania. The singles were usually crudely recorded and extremely basic and derivative, their not inconsiderable saving grace being their infectious energy.

While the Sun Sound was the pinnacle of rockabilly, several performers established legends of their own outside of Sam Phillips' studio. Gene Vincent's 1956 sides, featuring his breathy vocals and the speed-of-light guitar of Cliff Gallup from his backing band the Blue Caps, were usually brilliant. Eddie Cochran brought a sophisticated brand of teenage rebellion to his rockabilly hits, which helped pioneer the use of overdubbed guitars and vocals. Ricky Nelson recorded first-class rockabilly pop in Hollywood with the help of ace guitarist James Burton. Johnny Burnette and his trio recorded some of the raunchiest Elvis-derived rock 'n' roll of the time, including the first rock version of "The Train Kept A-Rollin'." Dale Hawkins cut a crackling classic with "Suzy Q," and Wanda Jackson's raspy rockabilly sides rank as the finest rock 'n' roll recorded by a female singer in the 1950s. Rockabilly began to fade as a commercial force around 1958, not just because of fickle popular taste, but because of the rapid evolution of rock 'n' roll itself. One of the greatest rockabilly singers, Buddy Holly, displayed a facility for melodic invention that branched into all forms of pop-rock, and had a far-reaching influence on all of pop that extended to the British Invasion. Along with the Everly Brothers and Ricky Nelson, he began gravitating towards a more gentle, melodic sound that was not as structurally limited, if not as energetic, as pure rockabilly. Elvis was moving toward more straightforward rock material, and then toward pop after his hitch in the Army.

Those performers that stuck with the basic rockabilly sound faced diminishing returns. Some, like Gene Vincent, simply vanished from the charts, although they maintained loyal audiences, especially overseas. Roy Orbison, never comfortable as a rockabilly singer in the first place, reinvented himself as a masterful crooner of pop-rock ballads. Jerry Lee Lewis' career was crippled by scandal. Eventually he would find success in the country & western mainstream, a path followed by many other singers who had achieved limited success with rockabilly.

Rockabilly never returned to the charts in a significant way after the '50s, though several acts have scored big hits in the style, such as Billy Swan and the Stray Cats. A huge influence on the early Beatles, Creedence Clearwater Revival, and others, rockabilly was instrumental in establishing the focus of rock 'n' roll on the electric guitar-bass-drums combination, with a simple joy and force that has helped inspire generations of musicians.

Recommended Recordings

Elvis Presley, *King of Rock 'n' Roll: Complete '50s Masters* (RCA)
Buddy Holly, *Buddy Holly Collection* (MCA)
Gene Vincent, *The Screamin' End: The Best Of* (Razor & Tie)
Carl Perkins, *Original Sun Greatest Hits* (Rhino)
Jerry Lee Lewis, *18 Original Sun Greatest Hits* (Rhino)
Johnny Burnette, *Tear It Up* (Solid Smoke)
Eddie Cochran, *Legendary Masters* (EMI)
Ricky Nelson, *Legendary Masters* (EMI)
Wanda Jackson, *Rockin' with Wanda* (Capitol)
The Collins Kids, *Introducing Larry and Laurie* (Epic)

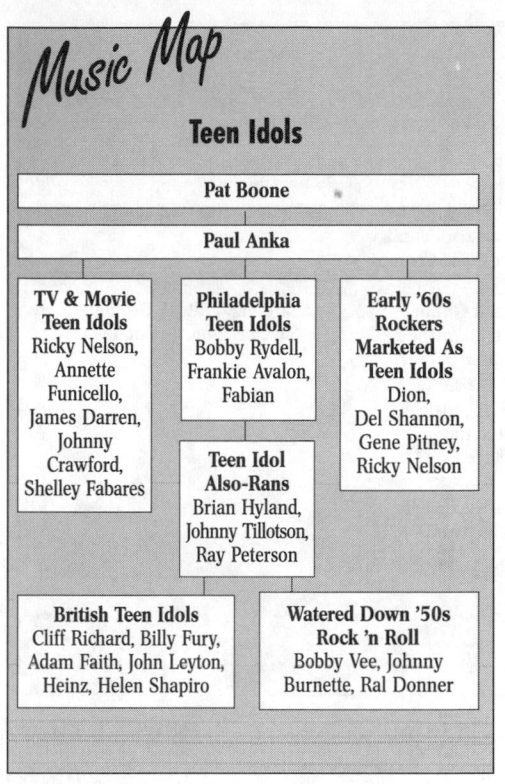

Music Map

Teen Idols

> **Pat Boone**

> **Paul Anka**

TV & Movie Teen Idols Ricky Nelson, Annette Funicello, James Darren, Johnny Crawford, Shelley Fabares	**Philadelphia Teen Idols** Bobby Rydell, Frankie Avalon, Fabian **Teen Idol Also-Rans** Brian Hyland, Johnny Tillotson, Ray Peterson	**Early '60s Rockers Marketed As Teen Idols** Dion, Del Shannon, Gene Pitney, Ricky Nelson

British Teen Idols Cliff Richard, Billy Fury, Adam Faith, John Leyton, Heinz, Helen Shapiro	**Watered Down '50s Rock 'n' Roll** Bobby Vee, Johnny Burnette, Ral Donner

Bill Haley and His Comets, *Rock the Joint!* (School Kids')

Various Artists, *Rock This Town Vol. 1 & 2* (Rhino)

Books

Good Rockin' Tonight: Sun Records and the Birth of Rock 'n' Roll, by Colin Escott with Martin Hawkins (1991, St. Martin's)

Last Train to Memphis, by Peter Guralnick (1994, Little, Brown & Co.)

Elvis: The Illustrated Record, by Roy Carr & Mick Farren (1982, Harmony)

Remembering Buddy: The Definitive Biography of Buddy Holly, by John Goldrosen and John Beecher (1987, Penguin)

The Day the World Turned Blue: A Biography of Gene Vincent, by Britt Hagarty (1984, Blandford Press, UK)

Ricky Nelson: Idol for a Generation, by Joel Selvin (Contemporary, 1990)

                        —*Richie Unterberger*

Teen Idols

To many avid rock historians, the teen idols—who were firmly entrenched on the top of the charts between the death of Buddy Holly and the rise of the Beatles—represent the greatest threat to rock's survival that the music ever weathered. Wimpy, overwhelmingly bland and safe, their connection to rock 'n' roll was often tenuous, and their commercial ascendancy has even been discussed as a conspiracy to rob rock 'n' roll of its vitality.

In retrospect, that seems fairly unlikely, though there's no doubt that the more conservative elements of the entertainment industry and the status quo as a whole felt more comfortable with these performers. Owing as much or more to traditional Tin Pan Alley and middle-of-the-road values than pure rock 'n' roll, their massive success nonetheless didn't come close to stamping out the forces that gave birth to the explosive soul, surf, and British Invasion sounds that reclaimed the airwaves after only a few years.

"Teen idols" were by no means a phenomenon that began with the rock 'n' roll era; bobbysoxers had been pining to the sound of mainstream pop crooners for a good decade or more before Elvis hit the scene. As far as rock was concerned, the original teen idol was Pat Boone, whose first hits were bowdlerized versions of rockers by Little Richard and Fats Domino. As Greg Shaw pointed out in *The Rolling*

Stone Illustrated History of Rock 'n' Roll, Boone "began as a safe alternative to Elvis, and is still a safe alternative to just about everything."

The first two teen idols to achieve mass success after Boone could not have defined the polar extremes of the genre better. There was Paul Anka, whose early hits were mainstream ballads with mild rock 'n' roll trimmings, and who exemplified the style at its most operatic and melodramatic. Then there was Ricky Nelson, whose success was virtually guaranteed by his popular weekly TV series, and whose rockabilly records were better than they had any right to be.

The Philadelphia teen idols of the late '50s—Bobby Rydell, Frankie Avalon, and Fabian—patterned themselves after Anka much more than Nelson. Recorded on the local Cameo-Parkway, Chancellor, and Swan labels, they were launched into national success with regular appearances on American Bandstand, hosted by Dick Clark, who sometimes held financial interests in the record companies of the singers he pushed in this manner. Rydell, at least, could sing; few would contest that Avalon and Fabian were promoted more on their appearance than their limited vocal abilities, and both would move into movies and television work as their chief focus after their initial musical success.

It worked the other way around as well, of course; established teenage television stars with meager vocal abilities were hustled into recording studios to capitalize on their screen images. Ex-Mouseketeer Annette Funicello became one of the first female teen idols in this fashion, and Ed "Kookie" Byrnes, Connie Stevens, Johnny Crawford, James Darren, and Shelley Fabares also got onto the hit parade after they were already established TV performers. Artistically, this was the weakest wing of the teen idol genre; unsuited for singing in the first place, their material often sank to the level of drivel, with a few unexpected choice items thrown in, usually from Brill Building songwriters.

A great many teen idol singers had one or two big hits in this era without establishing a long recording career. Mark Dinning ("Teen Angel") and Ray Peterson ("Tell Laura I Love Her") capitalized on the short-lived vogue for teen death melodrama; Troy Shondell, Johnny Tillotson, Brian Hyland, and even a young Tony Orlando were merely some of the more successful of the legions of young faces who were packaged for the young, middle-class, white, predominantly teenage audience in this era.*j* Then there were the singers who happened to be packaged as teen idols, but who were probably good enough to have succeeded anyway. Dion, Gene Pitney, and Del Shannon, as well as Ricky Nelson, all fall in this category; their music sometimes contained the melodramatic hallmarks of the teen idol style, but were genuine pop-rock innovators each and every one, and have too often been dismissed as superfluous by listeners more concerned with these performers' images than their actual accomplishments.

And there were also teen idols whose music was obviously a watered-down version of early rock 'n' roll forms. Bobby Vee was a transparent Buddy Holly clone, though much softer; Ral Donner was the most accurate Elvis Presley soundalike, though he took after Elvis' pop-rock ballads rather than the King's rockers; and Johnny Burnette had a brief career as a mainstream teen idol after having moderate success as one of the best early rockabilly singers. Finally, there was an entire wing of British teen idols, although they had virtually no success in the States. Cliff Richard was by far the biggest, followed by a stable of singers with unlikely movie-star names, most managed by British impresario Larry Parnes. Billy Fury was the best of them; Adam Faith, John Leyton, Heinz, Helen Shapiro, and others were also big in their homeland before they largely sank into irrelevance after the rise of the Beatles in 1963.

The teen idol style was already on the wane before the Beatles landed in America in early 1964; Motown and other forms of soul music were on the rise, girl groups were big, surf sounds were at their crest. The manufacturing of face and image over content and ability that characterized the teen idol era has repeated itself, to a smaller extent, ever since, though one may call them the preteen idols now. Bobby Sherman and David Cassidy, the Bay City Rollers, Tiffany, Debbie Gibson, Milli Vanilli, New Kids on the Block—all strongly echoed the teen idol era, and sold millions of records despite the wrath of rock critics the world over, as other teen idols will do in the future.

Recommended Recordings

Various Artists, *Teen Idols* (Rhino)

Dion, *24 Golden Greats* (Arista)

Gene Pitney, *Anthology 1961-1968* (Rhino)

Del Shannon, *Greatest Hits* (Rhino)

Pat Boone, *Greatest Hits* (MCA)

Paul Anka, *30th Anniversary Collection* (Rhino)

Ricky Nelson, *The Best of Rick Nelson Vol. 1 & 2* (EMI)

Annette Funicello, *Annette: A Musical Reunion with America's Girl Next Door* (Disney)

Bobby Vee, *Legendary Masters* (EMI)

Ral Donner, *She's Everything* (Murray Hill)

                        —*Richie Unterberger*

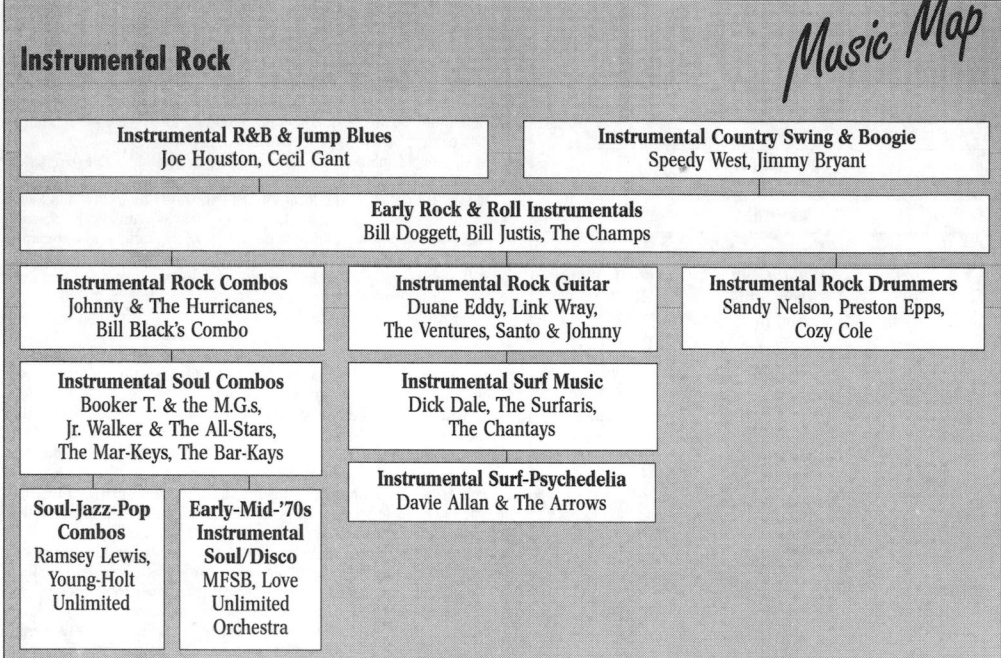

Instrumental Rock

Except for a brief period at the end of the '50s and the early '60s, instrumental rock hasn't been a major commercial force. There have always been instrumental rock hits, of course, and the best instrumental rockers have acted as key inspirations to many of the best rock 'n' roll musicians.

Even before rock 'n' roll became the nation's dominant popular music in the mid-'50s, instrumentals were common in the R&B, jump blues, and country boogie that ranked as rock's chief ancestors. Raunchy R&B saxophonist Joe Houston and lightning-fast country boogie steel guitarist Speedy West were just two of the primarily instrumental musicians who were key influences on first generation rock 'n' rollers. In 1956, organist Bill Doggett's "Honky Tonk" became the first massive instrumental hit of the rock era, although it was more notable for the sax riffs of Clifford Scott than the playing of bandleader Doggett.

The earliest rock 'n' roll instrumental hits, such as the Champs' "Tequila," featured the sax as the lead instrument, but in 1958 Duane Eddy was responsible for changing the emphasis of instrumental rock to the guitar. With his distinctively low, twanging leads (augmented by Steve Douglas' superb saxophone), Eddy was one of the most popular singles artists of his era. His material can sound somewhat repetitious and dated these days, but he was a major influence on the next generation of rock guitarists, from George Harrison on down.

The Ventures were perhaps even more influential, offering a sleek sound with dual lead guitars and crisp drumming. A key building block of instrumental surf music, the group inspired countless nascent guitarists and were extremely popular, especially overseas, where the English language wasn't as key a component of rock music.

Link Wray, although nowhere near as successful as Eddy or the Ventures, may have been the most innovative guitarist of the era. On his 1958 hit "Rumble" and numerous excellent non-hit followups, he pioneered guitar fuzz and distortion on vicious rockers. He was cited as an influence by Pete Townshend, who with several other British guitarists would take Wray's sound a few steps further in the distortion and feedback-riddled guitar leads of British Invasion and psychedelic rock.

In Southern California, Dick Dale developed a reverb-heavy sound with his Fender Telecaster that became known as "surf music." Though relatively few surf instrumentals were big national hits (the Surfaris' "Wipe Out" and the Chantays' "Pipeline" were the biggest), the surf scene was huge in California, and of course a big influence on the Beach Boys, who (along with Jan & Dean) developed a vocal surf sound that became an important part of early- and mid-'60s rock 'n' roll.

The years 1958-1963 were also riddled with many exciting hits, big and small, by performers who were never heard from again, or only managed to run off two or three big tunes. Besides guitarists like Santo

& Johnny and Lonnie Mack, drummers (Sandy Nelson, Preston Epps, Cozy Cole), organists (Dave "Baby" Cortez), saxophone-driven combos (Johnny & the Hurricanes), and even bass players (ex-Elvis Presley sideman Bill Black) got in on the act with memorable hit tunes.

Instrumental rock was already decreasing in popularity when the British Invasion overran the States, making vocalists a near necessity. In the years between the initial rock 'n' roll explosion and the Beatles, however, instrumental performers were responsible for some of the most exciting and gutsy rock 'n' roll available. A key force in the preservation of rock's most exciting elements, instrumental rock was also hugely popular at a local level, and many musicians who wet their chops in instrumental combos went on to join, or develop into, important '60s rock groups. In any case, mid- and late-'60s rock groups never neglected instrumental rock entirely—Paul Butterfield's "East West," the Rolling Stones' "2120 South Michigan Avenue," the Who's "Underture," Quicksilver Messenger Service's "Gold and Silver," the Yardbirds' "Jeff's Boogie," Pink Floyd's "Interstellar Overdrive," and Country Joe & the Fish's "Section 43" are only a few of the great hard rock and psychedelic instrumentals of the era. While the British Invasion is often thought of as a death knell for instrumental rock, instrumentals remained a key strand of soul music for the next decade. The most popular and influential instrumental soul combo were Booker T. & the MG's. In addition to backing most of the greatest performances on the Stax/Volt label, the Memphis group also ran off a long string of marvelously taut instrumental hits of their own. The Mar-Keys and the Bar-Kays were also popular instrumental exponents of the Memphis soul sound. Saxophonist Junior Walker took Motown to its grittiest extremes on his instrumentals (though he often used vocals as well).

There was also no shortage of one-shot soul instrumental hits. Cliff Nobles ("The Horse"), jazzman Hugh Masekela ("Grazing in the Grass"), Billy Preston ("Outa-Space"), Love Unlimited Orchestra ("Love's Theme"), MFSB ("TSOP"), and the Average White Band ("Pick up the Pieces") all had mammoth pop hits with soul instrumentals, although these groups by and large didn't limit their material to instrumentals exclusively. Ramsey Lewis developed a breed of soul-jazz-pop in the mid-'60s, as did his ex-sidemen Young-Holt Unlimited, who hit the Top Ten when they added a lot of straight funk and came up with "Soulful Strut."

While rock and soul instrumentals haven't been nearly as prevalent in the 1980s and '90s as they were in earlier decades, instrumentals will always be a presence in the music, as surprise hit singles and as a testament to the power of guitars, saxophones, drums, and other instruments to move listeners without the benefit of vocals.

Recommended Recordings

Various Artists, *Rock Instrumental Classics, Vol. 1: The '50s* (Rhino)

Various Artists, *Rock Instrumental Classics, Vol. 2: The '60s* (Rhino)
Various Artists, *Rock Instrumental Classics, Vol. 3: The '70s* (Rhino)
Various Artists, *Rock Instrumental Classics, Vol. 4: Soul* (Rhino)
Various Artists, *Rock Instrumental Classics, Vol. 5: Surf* (Rhino)
Duane Eddy, *Twang Thang: The Anthology* (Rhino)
Link Wray, *Rumble! The Best of Link Wray* (Rhino)
The Ventures, *Walk, Don't Run: The Best of the Ventures* (EMI)
Booker T. & the MG's, *The Very Best of Booker T. & the MG's* (Rhino)
Booker T. & the MG's, *Best of Booker T. & the MG's* (Fantasy)
Dick Dale, *King of Surf Guitar: Best of Dick Dale* (Rhino)
Various Artists, *Guitar Player Presents Legends of Guitar, Surf: Vol. 1* (Rhino)

—Richie Unterberger

British Rock 'n' Roll Before the Beatles

For virtually everyone outside the British Isles—and for many who were born and raised there—the story of British rock begins with the Beatles. Britain did have rock 'n' roll performers in the late '50s and early '60s, but they were really no more than a footnote to the real thing, which shook the UK in 1963 as the Beat Boom, and the world in 1964 as the British Invasion. This little-known scene has its interest, though, and even its gems, though they're few and far between.

When rock 'n' roll became an international phenomenon in the mid-'50s, Britain, it would seem, was less equipped to emulate the music on its home shores than almost any other country outside North America. After all, the primary barrier to singing rock 'n' roll is linguistic, and as the second-largest English-speaking nation in the world, Great Britain at least didn't have that particular obstacle to worry about. But the indigenous music of the UK, with the possible exception of British Isles folk, had little parallel with the stew of blues, country, gospel, and Tin Pan Alley pop that gave birth to rock 'n' roll in the States. It took a long time for the country's performers to come to grips with these influences, and master a vocabulary that would enable British rock to hold its own in the international marketplace.

British rock 'n' rollers sprang up almost immediately in the wake of Bill Haley and Elvis Presley; Wee Willie Harris is usually credited as the first, and Tommy Steele was the most successful of the very first batch. The earliest British rock 'n' roll records were, it could be said, hardly rock 'n' roll at all; often they were cover versions of American rock hits that framed the songs in much more conventional and saccharine pop arrangements. In this respect, the British music industry was reacting along similar lines as some American labels, who responded to rock 'n' roll's ascendancy by whitewashing R&B hits with sterile pop covers, or developed teen idols whose music was only marginally connected to the real thing. A more important British development was the popularity of skiffle, principally popularized by Lonnie Donegan, who had first come to prominence as a traditional jazz and blues performer in Chris Barber's band. Skiffle's appeal, in the manner of garage and punk music right to the present day, was that it didn't take a great deal of technical proficiency to perform: you needed a few chords on guitar and banjo, a washboard for percussion, and a repertoire of a few folk songs. Donegan was a hugely successful singer in the late '50s in Britain (his "Rock Island Line" was also a big hit in the States), and many of the skiffle groups he inspired, such as the Quarrymen (soon to become the Beatles), would become key players in the British Invasion. Another Chris Barber sideman, Alexis Korner, would become mentor to key figures of blues and R&B-based rock groups the Rolling Stones, Kinks, Yardbirds, and others, though his contributions really fall beyond the scope of pre-Beatle British rock.

In the meantime, however, the teenagers in these skiffle bands had to suffer through bland pop-rock, or a bland facsimile of such, on their own hit parade. The most popular of the early British rock singers was Cliff Richard, a sort of mini-Elvis who actually managed some respectable rock 'n' roll on his earliest singles in the late '50s, especially on his debut hit, "Move It." He was backed by the Shadows, a tight unit who scored many instrumental hits on their own, emphasizing spare, precise (one might even say clean-cut) riffs. Cliff Richard and the Shadows are remembered fondly by many in British rock circles, and Shadows guitarist Hank Marvin is cited as an influence by many British guitar heroes. But listening to their peak output several decades later, one suspects that this may be due more to nostalgia than quality; the majority of their repertoire consists of watered-down derivations of American pop, pop-rock, and instrumental rock. Shadows bassist Jet Harris, sometimes in collaboration with Shadows drummer Tony Meehan, did have some nifty, growling instrumental hits just before the Beatles broke.

There were quite a few British teen idols in the late '50s and early '60s, usually with fanciful show-business names such as Johnny Gentle, Marty Wilde, Vince Eager, Adam Faith, and Duffy Power (the last of which, surprisingly, turned out to be a decent cult blues-rock performer in the '60s). Like their American cousins, they were innocent and harm-

Music Map

British Rock Before the Beatles

First British Rock Singers
Wee Willie Harris, Tommy Steele, Cliff Richard

British Teen Idols
Billy Fury, John Leyton, Adam Faith, Helen Shapiro

Early '60s British Instrumental Groups	Early '60s British Rockers
The Shadows, The Tornados, The Outlaws	Vince Taylor, Johnny Kidd & The Pirates, Screaming Lord Sutch

Joe Meek Productions
John Leyton, The Tornados, The Outlaws, Screaming Lord Sutch, Mike Berry

less to the point of dopiness. The best of them, Billy Fury, managed to cut some fair, and self-penned, approximations of American rockabilly on his 1960 LP *Sound of Fury* with the help of guitarist Joe Brown (who would have some hits of his own in the early '60s). Fury was also an inspiration to Malcolm McLaren when he was casting about to form the Sex Pistols—but again, one suspects nostalgia as an ingredient for this latter-day respect; Fury was a competent singer, but he too went heavy on the drippy ballads for the hit parade, and as a rockabilly singer, he would have been an also-ran in the States.

Amidst all the dross, there were some genuine fierce British rockers in these dark days. Tony Sheridan, though he never got a chance to adequately showcase his talents on record, was of course an inspiration to the early Beatles, who backed him on several German recordings. Vince Taylor managed several respectable Gene Vincent-type numbers, most notably "Brand New Cadillac."

The best by far, though, and indeed the best pre-Beatle British rockers by a wide margin, were Johnny Kidd & the Pirates. Their late-'50s and early-'60s singles were tough, rockabilly-influenced performances that came off as a cross between Jerry Lee Lewis and Gene Vincent. Kidd was also an underappreciated factor in establishing the dominance of guitar in '60s British rock; several of his songs featured superbly menacing riffs from session players like Joe Moretti that were quite advanced for their time, especially the one from "Shakin' All Over," perhaps the only true pre-Beatle classic of British rock, and the only one which became a rock standard (in versions by the Who, Guess Who, and others). Kidd, alas, was already in a decline phase when the Beat Boom hit, and died in a car crash in 1966.

Besides the Pirates, the hardest rocking British band of the early '60s were Screaming Lord Sutch and the Savages. Sutch—a colorful figure who wore long hair years before it was fashionable, shamelessly emulated Screamin' Jay Hawkins, and ran for Parliament advocating such causes as the right of teenagers to vote and pirate radio—wasn't much of a singer. But his band did play real rock 'n' roll of the hard-driving sort at a time when that was rarely done in the British Isles, and his early-'60s singles (most recorded after the Beatles had debuted), though hardly classics, had a sense of hard-driving reckless fun that anticipated the spirit of the British Invasion. His bands also provided early schooling for such mainstays of British rock as Nicky Hopkins and Ritchie Blackmore (who also recorded some sides as a teenager in the early '60s as part of the instrumental group the Outlaws).

Sutch and the Outlaws were both produced by Joe Meek, a major figure who has merited an entire biography. Meek was the very first British producer to establish his own production company for leasing masters to labels, ensuring control over his product. A legendary eccentric obsessed with the occult and UFOs, Meek imprinted his recordings with as distinctive a sound as any other producer. Compression, sped-up vocals, otherworldly organs, howling wind, and ghostly choruses combined into a sort of space-age sound which was quite futuristic for its era, and is best heard on the Tornados' instrumental "Telstar," which topped the charts on both sides of the Atlantic over a year before the Beatles broke in America.

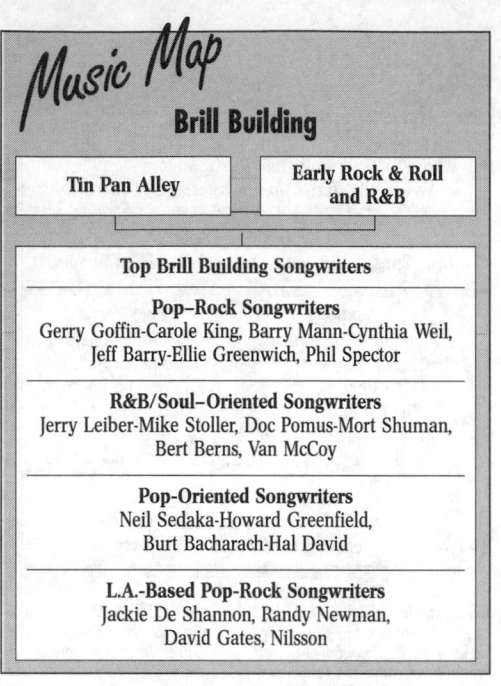

Music Map

Brill Building

Tin Pan Alley	Early Rock & Roll and R&B

Top Brill Building Songwriters

Pop–Rock Songwriters
Gerry Goffin-Carole King, Barry Mann-Cynthia Weil,
Jeff Barry-Ellie Greenwich, Phil Spector

R&B/Soul–Oriented Songwriters
Jerry Leiber-Mike Stoller, Doc Pomus-Mort Shuman,
Bert Berns, Van McCoy

Pop-Oriented Songwriters
Neil Sedaka-Howard Greenfield,
Burt Bacharach-Hal David

L.A.-Based Pop-Rock Songwriters
Jackie De Shannon, Randy Newman,
David Gates, Nilsson

Had Meek only been working with more talented acts and better material, there would be no question of his important stature. As it was, he usually favored simpering teen idols, anonymous instrumental groups, and cringingly dippy material, though he almost always added adventurous production that made the records stand out in the vapid early-'60s British scene. He did manage some tough-rocking sides with the Outlaws, Heinz, Tornados, and especially Screaming Lord Sutch, and sustained his success into the early British Invasion with the Honeycombs. As a producer he was ahead of his time, but his taste in material was rendered hopelessly passé by the Beat Boom, and he died in sordid circumstances (a combination murder-suicide) in early 1967.

The weakness of pre-Beatle rock is reflected in the near-total lack of cover versions of early British rock tunes by British Invasion bands. Though most of those groups' early repertoires were dominated by rock 'n' roll covers, they rarely looked to their own countrymen. *The Complete Beatles Chronicle*, for example, documents the hundreds of songs the group were known to have performed onstage before 1963; only about ten odds and ends by British performers appear, by singers like Lonnie Donegan and Joe Brown.

What was happening, was that it was necessary for an entirely new generation of musicians—one which had grown up listening to and playing rock 'n' roll—to emerge to really play the music properly. The Beatles, and hundreds of other beat combos, looked to the US for inspiration, not their own land. And when they had mastered their instruments, performance, and finally songwriting enough to offer quality material on record, the result turned the British music industry on its head literally within months. The old guard hung on for a few more hits; in some cases, such as Cliff Richard's, they maintained a reasonable degree of popularity.

In the US, British pop hits only crossed over very occasionally. When they did make it into the American hit parade, they tended to be rather quaint pop novelty items, such as Laurie London's "He's Got the Whole World In His Hands," the Caravelles' "You Don't Have to Be a Baby to Cry," and Frank Ifield's "I Remember You" ("Telstar," though near instrumental rock, was also a novelty). Early British rock never meant a thing in the States, and that's why the Beatles and other British groups couldn't get a foothold in the US in 1963; the industry had no reason to expect anything that they couldn't find, cheaper and better, in their own backyard. With "I Want to Hold Your Hand" in early 1964, that all changed—for which we can all be thankful—on both sides of the Atlantic.

Recommended Recordings

Lonnie Donegan, *Collection* (Castle, UK)
Cliff Richard, *20 Rock 'n' Roll Hits* (EMI, UK)
Various Artists, *Roots of British Rock* (Sire)

Billy Fury, *Sound of Fury Plus 10* (PolyGram)
Jet Harris & Tony Meehan, *Diamonds & Other Gems* (Deram, UK)
Johnny Kidd & the Pirates, *Complete Johnny Kidd* (EMI, UK)
Screaming Lord Sutch, *Story* (no label)
The Tornados, *Telstar: The Original Sixties Hits of the Tornados* (Music Club, UK)
The Shadows, *Shadows Are Go!* (Scamp)
The Outlaws, *Ride Again (The Singles As & Bs)* (See for Miles, UK)
Joe Meek, *It's Hard to Believe It: The Amazing World of Joe Meek* (Razor & Tie)

—*Richie Unterberger*

Brill Building Sound

Rock 'n' roll is usually thought of as a hybrid of several types of American roots music—the blues, country and western, R&B, gospel, and others. The influence of mainstream American popular songwriting (embodied by the conglomerate of professional composers and publishers dubbed Tin Pan Alley), on rock's early development is sometimes overlooked. While rock 'n' roll was to a significant degree a reaction against the overly professional, sentimental, and sterile conventions of pre-rock American pop, the best of Tin Pan Alley's melodic and lyrical hallmarks were incorporated into rock 'n' roll to raise the music to new levels of sophistication.

The songwriters most crucial to this process congregated in the early '60s in a New York block known as the Brill Building. Home to leading music industry publishers, it also bred a stable of young songwriters who were just as steeped in rock 'n' roll and rhythm and blues as Tin Pan Alley, if not more so. Several of the most prominent worked for Aldon Music, a publishing firm headed by Al Nevins and Don Kirshner—the same Don Kirshner who would later mastermind the Monkees' hits and act as a legendarily bland master of ceremonies for network TV rock specials.

Many pop-rock songwriters worked in the Brill Building in the early '60s, but several teams carved a legendary legacy, including Gerry Goffin & Carole King, Barry Mann & Cynthia Weil, Jerry Leiber & Mike Stoller, Jeff Barry & Ellie Greenwich, and Doc Pomus & Mort Shuman. Responsible for literally pages worth of hits in the late '50s and first half of the '60s, they matched Tin Pan Alley's highest standards of inventive melodies and lyrics, but they were clearly different from their predecessors. The rock 'n' roll market demanded tunes targeted at teenagers, with earthier concerns than the classics of the '30s and '40s. For many of these songwriters, the task hardly required an adjustment; they were barely out of (or even still in) their teens, and they were going through the pangs of young love and searches for identity themselves. For good measure, Goffin-King, Mann-Weil, and Barry-Greenwich were married to each other, infusing their work with a passion that was actually grounded in their real-life romances.

Brill Building compositions were placed all over the pop-rock map, but had their greatest impact and success with girl groups. It was a heavenly match: girl groups sang about young love with forlorn and passionate innocence, and were largely based near New York City, but very few were songwriters, and they needed suitable material; young Brill Building songwriters wrote about young love with forlorn and passionate innocence, and were largely based near New York City, but needed suitable performers. Most of the classic hits by the Ronettes, Chiffons, Shangri-Las, Dixie Cups, and Little Eva originated at the Brill Building, as well as a few classic one-shots and misses.

Other prime outlets for Brill Building material were teen idols like Connie Francis, Bobby Vee, James Darren, and Neil Sedaka (the last of whom was one of the most successful Brill Building songwriters himself, often in collaboration with Howard Greenfield). These tended to be the most lightweight Brill Building confections, at times even approaching disposable, as a listen to a James Darren greatest hits compilation confirms. Uneven quality couldn't be helped; the songwriters were under tremendous pressure to deliver tunes in a near-assembly-line fashion, and couldn't be expected to come up with "Will You Love Me Tomorrow" or "On Broadway" every time out.

Leiber-Stoller and Pomus-Shuman, however, usually wrote for pop-flavored R&B and early soul acts. Leiber-Stoller wrote (and produced) most of the Coasters' classic comic vignettes, and Pomus-Shuman penned several of the Drifters' hits. Both teams also wrote some of the greatest Elvis Presley songs of the late '50s and early '60s; Goffin-King and Mann-Weil, for their part, would supply songs for the Drifters and Phil Spector's great productions with the best blue-eyed soul act of the '60s, the Righteous Brothers.

Other notable Brill Building mainstays included Phil Spector, a great songwriter and even greater producer; Bert Berns, who also wore both songwriting and production hats, though he worked in a more of a pop-soul vein; and Bacharach-David, who probably owed the most to Tin Pan Alley classic traditions, although that didn't prevent them from writing some great pop-rock songs for the Shirelles, Dionne Warwick, and others. And for every Goffin-King, it must be remembered, there were dozens of much less successful hopefuls scuffling around the edges of the Brill Building crowd, including future folk-rock stars Paul Simon and Jim McGuinn, and future disco king of the "hustle," Van McCoy.

Though Phil Spector is by far the most legendary producer with Brill Building associations, most of the great Brill Building songwriters were also great producers, although they weren't always credited on the label. Several of them were also great performers, and it has been said that the demos they cut were often as good or better than the versions recorded by the performers to whom they were given. Barry Mann, Carole King, and Jeff Barry & Ellie Greenwich (the latter pair as the Raindrops) actually had some hit records on their own, though they much preferred to run things behind the scenes.

There were also quite a few Los Angeles-based songwriters who, though not based at the actual Brill Building, operated in an almost identical fashion. David Gates, Jackie De Shannon, Randy Newman, and Nilsson were some of the best; eventually, each of them would become singing-songwriting stars in their own right.

The British Invasion turned the focus of rock 'n' roll on performers that wrote their own material, and while that didn't spell the end of the success of the great Brill Building songwriters, it meant some adjustments were in order. Girl group records were still hugely successful in 1964, the first year of the British Invasion, but it was soon obvious that their time was coming to an end. The irony was that John Lennon and Paul McCartney owed a great deal to the Brill Building, openly declaring Goffin and King as their greatest songwriting influences, and covering Brill Building classics by the Shirelles, Cookies, and Isley Brothers. Manfred Mann ("Do Wah Diddy Diddy"), Herman's Hermits ("I'm into Something Good"), and other British Invasion groups also took Brill Building covers into the top of the charts.

Occasionally Brill Building songwriters actually managed to supply fresh material to British Invasion groups, as Mann-Weil did with the Animals, and Bert Berns did with Them and Lulu. But inevitably, the proliferation of self-contained rock groups, not to mention soul songwriters who wrote their own material, meant less of a need for professional tunesmiths. And the fact was, both the world and the songwriters were changing as fast as everything else was in the '60s; the composers wanted to express more mature concerns, and much of the rock audience had progressed beyond adolescent love affairs.

The principal architects of the Brill Building coped with these changes in varying fashions. Some became jingle writers; some (Ellie Greenwich) eventually wrote musicals; some (Jeff Barry) wrote and produced bubblegum for the Archies; some (Phil Spector) retired; some (Bacharach-David) moved from pop-rock to MOR pop. The most resourceful became singer-songwriter stars themselves—not only the aforementioned L.A. composers, but also Carole King, who became a superstar as a solo act. The legacy of the Brill Building was enormous, setting the standard for pop-rock songwriting that has been emulated ever since, by everyone from the Beatles on down.

Recommended Recordings

Various Artists, *Brill Building Sound* (Era)

Phil Spector, *Back to Mono* (ABKCO)

The Drifters, *All-Time Greatest Hits & More: 1959-1965* (Atlantic)

The Coasters, *50 Coastin' Classics* (Rhino)

Various Artists, *The Colpix-Dimension Story* (Rhino)

The Shangri-Las, *The Best of the Shangri-Las* (Mercury)

Neil Sedaka, *All-Time Greatest Hits* (RCA)

Various Artists, *The Red Bird Story* (Charly, UK)

Various Artists, *The Best of the Girl Groups, Vol. 1* (Rhino)

Various Artists, *The Best of the Girl Groups, Vol. 2* (Rhino)

—Richie Unterberger

Girl Group

The story of the "girl group" sound—which reached its commercial and artistic peak in the early and mid-'60s—is not just the story of the performers. More than any other style in rock 'n' roll, it was the product of more or less equal partnerships between the singer/performers, songwriters, and producers. The result was one of the most vital links between the birth of rock 'n' roll and the British Invasion, the arrival of which gradually eroded the presence of girl groups on the charts even as it acknowledged enormous debts to the genre.

Girl groups were more polished than the early rock 'n' roll pioneers, more innocent than the soul music that was originating at the same time, and as firmly planted in Tin Pan Alley as rhythm and blues. While it wasn't the rawest or most artistically expressive pop music, few forms of rock were as affecting, romantic, and tuneful. They also provided the forums and mouthpieces for some of pop-rock's most talented songwriting teams, as well as laying the foundation for groundbreaking orchestral production that lent an increased sophistication to rock 'n' roll.

The Chantels, led by the heart-wrenching vocals of Arlene Smith, are generally acknowledged as the first girl group. Their Top 20 hit "Maybe" (1958) had obvious roots in gospel and doo wop, but also displayed yearning, innocent, and vulnerable qualities not apparent in the suaver male doo wop outfits.

It was the Shirelles, however, who really established girl groups as a major force with their No. 1 hit, "Will You Love Me Tomorrow?," in 1960. Significantly, that hit also featured many of the classic girl group trademarks—sweeping orchestral strings, full background harmonies, and a lead vocal that projected soul, warmth, hope, and uncertainty. The Shirelles scored a half-dozen Top 20 singles in the next couple years (along with several memorable lesser hits), and ranked as the most successful female vocal group of the era.

The song was written by Gerry Goffin and Carole King, who would go on to write many girl group classics in the next few years, and were one of the hottest songwriting teams of the Brill Building sound. Named after a complex of music publishing offices on Broadway in New York, it also gave birth to the partnerships between Jeff Barry and Ellie Greenwich, and Barry Mann and Cynthia Weil. These teams were responsible for the lion's share of the best girl group recordings, investing rock 'n' roll with the best melodic and lyrical qualities of classic pop, while retaining a feel for the rhythm and blues roots of the performers. Less celebrated writers like Luther Dixon (who wrote several songs for the Shirelles) and a pre-disco Van McCoy also contributed classics to the genre.

It took Phil Spector to launch the girl group sound to its pinnacle. The producer set material from the cream of the Brill Building crop (as well as his own original compositions) to grandly majestic, orchestral arrangements that achieved an unheard-of density without sacrificing any of the music's passion and melody. The Crystals, the Ronettes, and Darlene Love (who sang uncredited vocals on some of the Crystals' biggest smashes) were the most talented pilots of Spector's grandiose "Wall of Sound" productions, most of which were released on his own label, Philles.

While the Shirelles and Phil Spector's acts were the most prominent girl groups in the years preceding the British Invasion, the sound was emulated by several one- or two-shot groups, and less-celebrated producers, with great success. The Chiffons, Claudine Clark, the Cookies, the Jaynetts, Little Eva, and the Exciters all contributed timeless classics. And there were dozens—if not hundreds—of worthy singles in the style that, for one reason or another, didn't become blockbusters, although they had most or all of the essential elements.

Most of the great girl groups were Black, with clear affinities for R&B and doo wop, but the most innocent qualities of the sound (and occasionally the most soulful ones) were projected in many records by white teen girl singers as well. Lesley Gore was the most renowned of these performers, who also included the Angels, the Raindrops (with Ellie Greenwich on lead vocals), and one-shot artists like Diane Renay and the Murmaids.

While the arrival of the Beatles in 1964 is often thought of as the beginning of the end for the girl groups, girl group records were as successful as ever during that year. The rise of the Red Bird label, featuring the Dixie Cups and the Shangri-Las (who both scored No. 1 hits in 1964), did much to boost the style's commercial fortunes.

Although financial problems caused the Red Bird label to fold within a few years of its founding, the years 1964 and 1965 saw the label shine brightly indeed, and found songwriters like Jeff Barry, Barry Mann, Ellie Greenwich, Jerry Lieber, and Mike Stoller overseeing most of its output from the producer's booth. Producer and songwriter Shadow Morton—almost as idiosyncratic a talent as Phil Spector—created some of the greatest girl group records with the Shangri-Las. These tough-talking but tender-hearted Queens teens may have made the sassiest and most heart-wrenching girl group mini-operas of all.

Although the burgeoning Motown empire wasn't heavily rooted in the girl group sound, 1964 saw the release of break-through discs by Mary Wells, the Supremes, and Martha & the Vandellas that owed heavy debts to the style. Relying heavily on the production and songwriting talents of Smokey Robinson and Berry Gordy, Jr. (among others), their sound was nonetheless grittier and bluesier than the New York school, and their personas (on record and in performance) more distinctive.

There's no doubt that girl groups were among the British Invasion groups' chief influences. John Lennon has stated for the record that he and Paul McCartney hoped to duplicate the success of Goffin and King with their songwriting partnership, and the Beatles' early albums included covers of hits by the Shirelles, the Cookies, and the Marvelettes. Manfred Mann, despite their R&B roots, scored their biggest US hits with covers of songs by the Exciters ("Do Wah Diddy Diddy") and the Shirelles ("Sha La La"), and several other British groups, ranging from Herman's Hermits and the Searchers to the Mindbenders, also made it big with girl group covers. However, the most successful British groups—the Beatles first and foremost among them—were those that relied primarily upon their own material. And it was this shift in

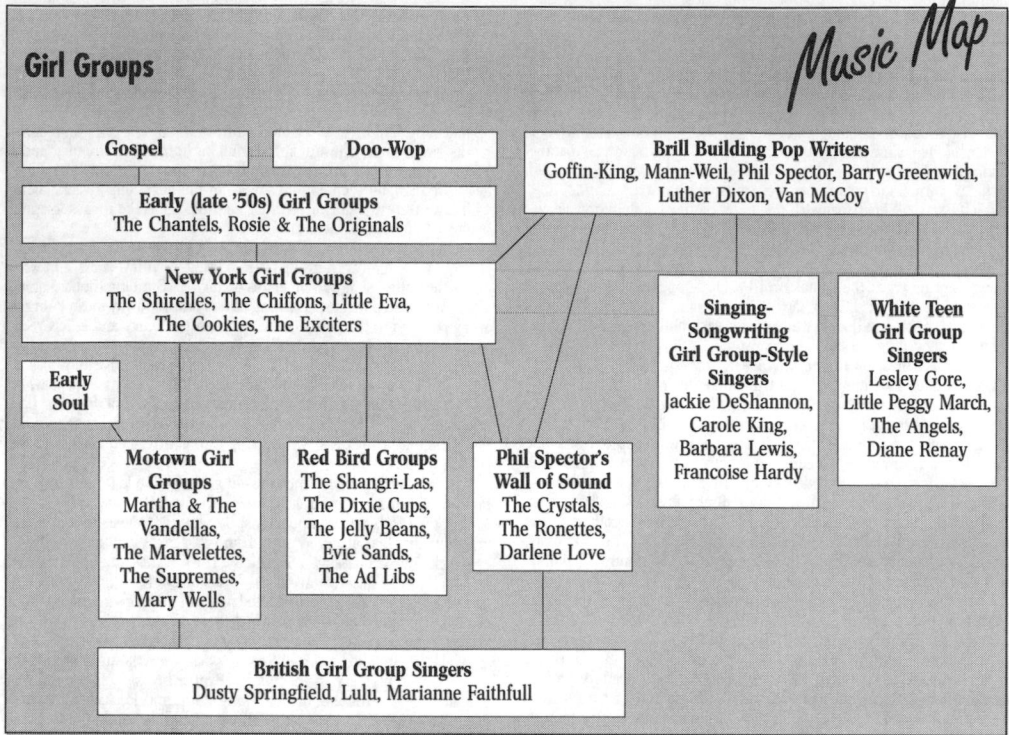

Girl Groups *Music Map*

Gospel	Doo-Wop	**Brill Building Pop Writers** Goffin-King, Mann-Weil, Phil Spector, Barry-Greenwich, Luther Dixon, Van McCoy

Early (late '50s) Girl Groups
The Chantels, Rosie & The Originals

New York Girl Groups
The Shirelles, The Chiffons, Little Eva,
The Cookies, The Exciters

Early Soul

Singing-Songwriting Girl Group-Style Singers
Jackie DeShannon,
Carole King,
Barbara Lewis,
Francoise Hardy

White Teen Girl Group Singers
Lesley Gore,
Little Peggy March,
The Angels,
Diane Renay

Motown Girl Groups
Martha & The Vandellas,
The Marvelettes,
The Supremes,
Mary Wells

Red Bird Groups
The Shangri-Las,
The Dixie Cups,
The Jelly Beans,
Evie Sands,
The Ad Libs

Phil Spector's Wall of Sound
The Crystals,
The Ronettes,
Darlene Love

British Girl Group Singers
Dusty Springfield, Lulu, Marianne Faithfull

emphasis toward self-contained rock groups that played their own instruments that spelled the end of the girl groups as a major force, although singers like Jackie DeShannon, Dusty Springfield, Lulu, Evie Sands, Barbara Lewis, and others continued to produce classic recordings (and sometimes score major hits) in the girl group vein throughout the '60s.

The girl group sound, though, never really went away. You can hear it in many female vocal groups, self-contained and otherwise, through the present day. In the case of some soul groups (such as the Pointer Sisters) or new wave bands (the Bangles, Blondie, and the Go-Go's), the influence is worn quite cheerfully on the sleeve. More subtly, its echoes are heard in all rock that relies upon orchestral production, harmonies, and/or crafty, melodic compositions to send its message.

Recommended Recordings
The Shirelles, *The World's Greatest Girl Group* (Tomato/Rhino)
The Shangri-Las, *It's My Party: Mercury Anthology* (Mercury)
The Shangri-Las, *The Best of the Shangri-Las* (PolyGram)
The Ronettes, *Best of the Ronettes* (ABKCO)
The Crystals, *Best of the Crystals* (ABKCO)
The Chiffons, *Best of the Chiffons* (Laurie)
The Supremes, *Anthology* (Motown)
Martha & the Vandellas, *Live Wire! The Singles 1962-1972* (Motown)
Mary Wells, *Looking Back 1961-1964* (Motown)
Lesley Gore, *It's My Party: Mercury Anthology* (Mercury)
The Marvelettes, *Deliver: The Singles 1961-1971* (Rhino)
Various Artists, *The Best of the Girl Groups, Vol. 1 & 2* (Rhino)
The Exciters, *Tell Him* (EMI)

Books
Girl Groups: The Story of a Sound, by Alan Betrock (Delilah, 1982)
Will You Still Love Me Tomorrow? Girl Groups from the 50s On . . . , by Charlotte Greig (Virago, 1989, UK)

—*Richie Unterbergerj*

Surf
....
In terms of commercial impact, surf music was a short-lived phenomenon. The vast majority of popular surf recordings were waxed between 1961 and 1965; even then, their success was often confined to an isolated region (more often than not, Southern California). Yet its influence upon the sound of the rock 'n' roll guitar is incalculable. Felt by hun-

dreds of artists, it continues to surface, in a much modified form, to this very day.

Between the time when the initial explosion of rock 'n' roll died down in the late '50s and the British Invasion, instrumental rock was more responsible for keeping alive the raunchiest and wildest aspects of the music than any other style. It was also responsible for keeping the electric guitar at the forefront of the music, and surf music was certainly the most guitar-oriented style of instrumental rock 'n' roll, though splashing drums and honking saxes were also prime features of the sound.

Southern California-guitarist Dick Dale is roundly acknowledged as the father of surf music. In the late '50s, he developed its trademark reverb sound. Whether intentionally or otherwise, the "wet," full echo of surf guitars evoked the rides and waves of surfing, which in the early '60s was still an emerging teenage sport that was little known outside of Southern California and Hawaii. Ironically, Jimi Hendrix, who intoned "you'll never hear surf music again" on "Third Stone from the Sun" from his debut album, has been said to have been influenced by Dale, who like Hendrix played his guitar left-handed and upside-down.

"For most surf instrumentals," wrote surf music authority John Blair in his liner notes to *Guitar Player Magazine Presents Legends of Guitar: Surf, Vol. 1,* "a small electronic device called a reverberation unit, or 'reverb' for short, was used to create the distinctive 'surf' guitar sound. Although several companies had reverbs on the market, the one made by the Fender Musical Instrument Company (introduced in the summer of 1961) was the popular choice of most surf bands . . .

"[Dick Dale] used Fender amplifiers and even had the company customize a special left-handed (he played upside-down and left-handed) gold metalflake Stratocaster guitar, which he still plays. In fact, Dale's close association with Fender enabled him to 'roadtest' new equipment for the company. The powerful Dual Showman amplifier, introduced in late 1962, was developed with Dale's help."

On vinyl, the surf craze kicked off with Dale's late-1961 single, "Let's Go Trippin'." Although it was only a regional hit, its influence was tremendous, and within months, dozens of bands—virtually all of them based in Southern California—were playing surf music. Hundreds would record surf singles and albums before the fad started to fade in the mid-'60s. Although they were not Californian, and would certainly not identify themselves as a surf group, the dark, reverberant guitars of the Ventures—then reaching the peak of their massive popularity—were also formidable influences on these groups.

On a national level, the impact of instrumental surf bands was notable, but much slighter. The Chantays ("Pipeline") and the Surfaris ("Wipe

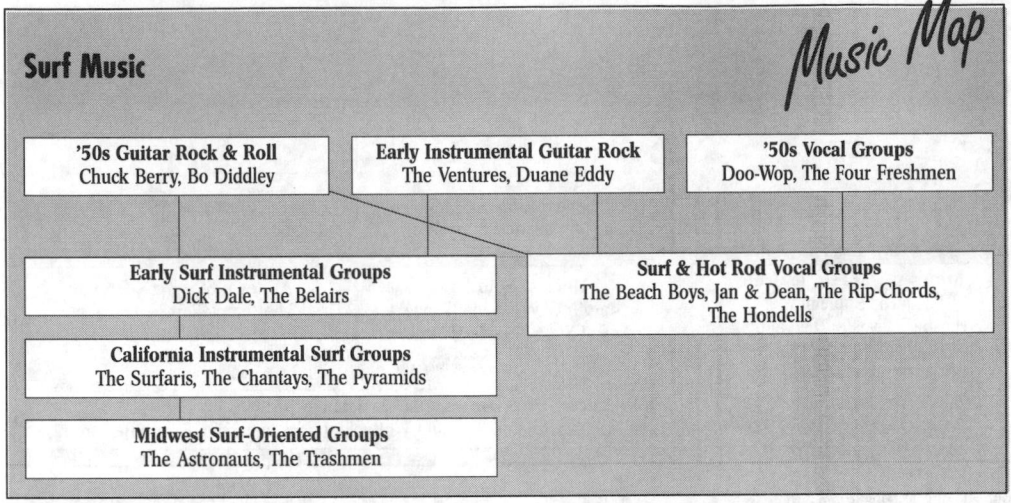

Surf Music

Music Map

'50s Guitar Rock & Roll
Chuck Berry, Bo Diddley

Early Instrumental Guitar Rock
The Ventures, Duane Eddy

'50s Vocal Groups
Doo-Wop, The Four Freshmen

Early Surf Instrumental Groups
Dick Dale, The Belairs

Surf & Hot Rod Vocal Groups
The Beach Boys, Jan & Dean, The Rip-Chords,
The Hondells

California Instrumental Surf Groups
The Surfaris, The Chantays, The Pyramids

Midwest Surf-Oriented Groups
The Astronauts, The Trashmen

Out") scored huge national hits, but few others dented the Top 40, let alone the Top Ten. The Pyramids' early-1964 single "Penetration" was the last big national instrumental surf hit.

While most surf groups were based in Southern California, the genre was not strictly confined to this region. The Astronauts (from Colorado) and the Trashmen (from Minneapolis) were the most successful of the not inconsiderable number of landlocked bands who played surf music, or at least made a few stabs at it. The Trashmen, indeed, went to the Top Five with "Surfin' Bird" in early 1964; only the Beatles, then hitting the US with full force, kept them from the top spot. One of the very best instrumental surf groups, the Atlantics, were not even from the US, but from Australia, where they scored some massive hits in 1963 and 1964.

Surf music would achieve its most lasting influence not with instrumentals, but with vocal groups, in particular the Beach Boys. There's no doubting that Dick Dale was a profound influence on the Hawthorne, CA group, who covered Dale's "Let's Go Trippin'" on their second album, *Surfin' USA*. They recorded a few other surf instrumentals on their first few albums as well, but from the beginning, they were primarily a vocal group, heavily influenced by Chuck Berry, the Four Freshmen, doo wop, and other styles. They were the first group, however, to successfully sing about the surf music phenomenon, adding complex harmonies and clever lyrics to the driving guitars and chugging rhythms. In their wake, some groups like the aforementioned Astronauts and Trashmen tried to play the field with both instrumental and vocal numbers.

Other California vocal acts were quick to jump on the bandwagon, but besides the Beach Boys, only Jan & Dean (who were occasionally beneficiaries of songs and harmonies by Beach Boy-leader Brian Wilson) were a significant success, commercially or artistically. Jan & Dean had been a modestly successful duo for years before latching onto the surf fad, and–like the Beach Boys–they would soon adapt the surf sound to hot rod lyrics emphasizing cars and drag racing. Acts like Ronny & the Daytonas ("G.T.O.") and the Rip Chords ("Hey Little Cobra") hit the Top Ten with one-shot hits in the same style, but were out of their depth when they tried to mine it for memorable follow-ups.

Indeed, after 1963, the Beach Boys–still remembered by many listeners primarily as a surf group–left the subject behind for good. They soon broadened their scope leagues beyond even hot rods and girls to create challenging, personal pop-rock on a competitive level with the British Invasion groups that sounded the death knell for surf music at the beginning of 1964. Even Jan & Dean's hits were not solely limited to surf and hot rod tunes, though their career came to a skidding halt with–ironically–severe injuries suffered by Jan Berry in a car crash in 1966 on Sunset Boulevard in Los Angeles.

The Beach Boys' harmonies, though, left their stamp on countless other groups. The Who's Keith Moon was a huge surf music fan, and the manic splashing of his drum kit owes something to the bashing rumble of surf ensembles; the Who's own harmonies owed surprisingly large debts to the Beach Boys. The lineups of several obscure surf groups included members who went on to fame in surprisingly different contexts. The Crossfires, for example, evolved into the Turtles, and the Jesters, led by Jim Messina, also featured Glenn Frey of the Eagles.

Three decades later, few groups play surf music, although Dick Dale made a surprisingly strong comeback on record and as a national touring act in the early '90s. Echoes of the style, however, live on whenever you heard a reverbed guitar or sweet, high vocal harmonies in a rock 'n' roll song.

Recommended Recordings

The Beach Boys, *Good Vibrations* (Capitol)
The Beach Boys, *Surfin' USA.* (Capitol)
The Beach Boys, *Surfer Girl* (Capitol)
Jan & Dean, *The Legendary Master Series* (EMI)
Dick Dale, *King of the Surf Guitar: The Best of Dick Dale* (Rhino)
The Astronauts, *Surf Party* (RCA)
The Trashmen, *Best of the Trashmen* (Sundazed)
Various Artists, *Guitar Player Presents Legends of Guitar– Surf, Vol. 1* (Rhino)
Various Artists, *The History of Surf Music, Vol. 1* (Rhino)
Various Artists, *Surfin' Hits* (Rhino)
The Atlantics, *The CBS Singles Collection 1963-1965* (Canetoad, Australia)
The Surfaris, *Wipe Out! The Best of the Surfaris* (Varese Sarabande)

Book

The Beach Boys, by David Leaf (1985, Courage)

–Richie Unterberger

Motown

Many labels have left their mark on rock 'n' roll–Sun, Atlantic, Chess, Stax/Volt, Stiff, and lots of others left a permanent imprint on the music's legacy by honing distinctive styles and attitudes. Only one label, however, is immediately identified as a genre of its own. And not just by scholars and record collectors–Motown, to anyone who's listened to popular music since 1960, is not just a label in the middle of a record, but a sound that ranks among the most distinctive in rock history.

In its heyday, the Detroit label was home to the most commercially successful synthesis of R&B and pop ever produced. Motown developed many superstars, but performers were only part of the story. Equally important were the songwriters, including such masters as Smokey Robinson and the Holland-Dozier-Holland team; producers (who often doubled as songwriters); the (often uncredited) backing musicians, like bassist James Jamerson and drummer Benny Benjamin, who gave the music its rock-solid foundation; and the vision of owner Berry Gordy, Jr. You could almost always identify a Motown Record: instantly hummable melodies, pulsing bass lines, punchy tambourines and handclaps, rousing horns and violins, and vocals that evoked a gospel flavor with the call-and-response lines between the lead and backup singers.

The Motown empire, which eventually grew into the biggest Black-owned business in America, was a success story as unlikely as those of Elvis or the Beatles. A former boxer and failed record-store owner, Gordy was a struggling hustler on the edges of the R&B music business in the late '50s, writing some hits for Jackie Wilson. In 1959, he borrowed money from his family to start an independent production company. After leasing hits by Marv Johnson and Barrett Strong to other labels, Gordy formed his own labels. The releases would appear both on Motown and other imprints like Tamla, Gordy, and Soul.

Motown quickly established itself in the early '60s with hits by the Miracles, the Marvelettes, and Mary Wells. It was Gordy's increasingly

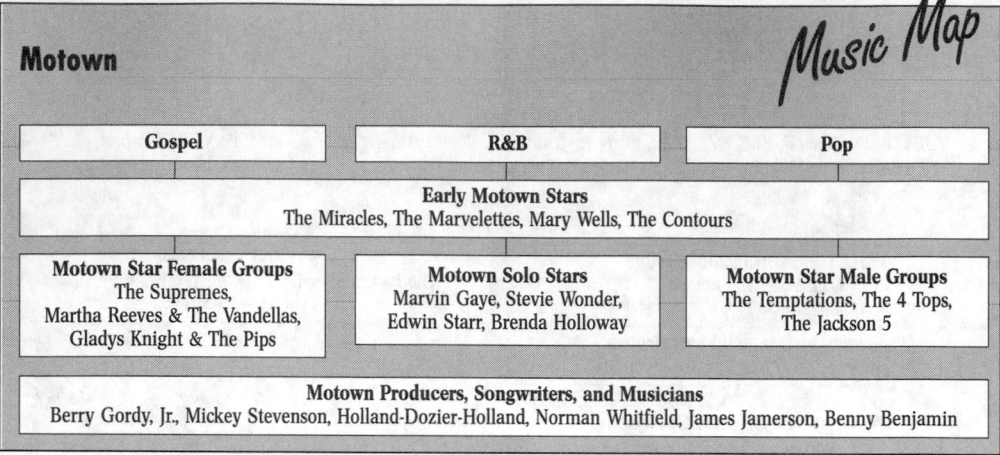

Motown

Music Map

Gospel	R&B	Pop

Early Motown Stars
The Miracles, The Marvelettes, Mary Wells, The Contours

Motown Star Female Groups The Supremes, Martha Reeves & The Vandellas, Gladys Knight & The Pips	**Motown Solo Stars** Marvin Gaye, Stevie Wonder, Edwin Starr, Brenda Holloway	**Motown Star Male Groups** The Temptations, The 4 Tops, The Jackson 5

Motown Producers, Songwriters, and Musicians
Berry Gordy, Jr., Mickey Stevenson, Holland-Dozier-Holland, Norman Whitfield, James Jamerson, Benny Benjamin

refined and systematic production techniques, however, that would ensure that the label continued to succeed and grow. The Motown sound has often been compared to an assembly line, drawing upon the influence of Detroit's automobile plants, with performers, songwriters, producers, and musicians embellishing a basic tried-and-true blueprint. If it were indeed true that Motown's formula was nothing more than an assembly line, it most likely would have exhausted itself quickly. Motown's, and Gordy's, genius was that it was able to spin almost infinite variations on its hugely appealing recipes, while still retaining an instantly recognizable sound, endearing itself to millions of listeners through both innovation and familiarity.

Motown releases might have shared many general similarities, but in time its superstars would develop strong identities of their own. The Miracles, paced by Smokey Robinson (who wrote many of Motown's best songs, both for the Miracles and other artists), handled both romantic ballads and uptempo dance tunes; the Temptations were the most polished soul group of their day; the Four Tops were gritty and emotional; Mary Wells and the Marvelettes recorded the most soulful girl group singles around; child prodigy Stevie Wonder developed into a magnificently gifted songwriter and instrumentalist; Martha Reeves & the Vandellas were Motown at its most feverish and gospel-influenced; Diana Ross & the Supremes were, aside from the Beatles, the most successful pop group of the '60s; Marvin Gaye, along with Stevie Wonder, would prove to be the most eclectic and innovative singer-songwriter on the Motown roster, not even reaching his maturity as an artist (like Wonder) until the 1970s; Junior Walker cut the label's earthiest, most party-oriented R&B.

These were the superstars; there were other fine performers who recorded a notable body of work for Motown in the 1960s, including Gladys Knight, Brenda Holloway, Edwin Starr, Kim Weston, Tammi Terrell, and the Contours. The label's roster was so deep, in fact, that some illustrious artists were neglected; the Spinners didn't do much of anything until they left Motown in the early '70s, the Isley Brothers had only one big hit during their several years there (perhaps because of their inability to truly adapt to the Motown formula), and early-'60s soul star Chuck Jackson had only minimal success after moving to Motown.

Even the stars sometimes expressed dissatisfaction about how they were promoted and directed by Motown, but they most likely knew that their success was at least equally attributable to the label as to their own talents. The point was underscored by Mary Wells' surprise decision to leave Motown in 1964 just after her No. 1 hit, "My Guy." Lured away by a big contract and the promise of a movie career, Wells never had another big hit; without the estimable Motown team, she was just another soul singer. The loss of Wells was covered by the burgeoning careers of other Motown stars, but Gordy faced a much more serious problem in late 1967, when the songwriting and production team of Brian Holland, Lamont Dozier, and Eddie Holland demanded an accounting of their royalties. After initiating a suit against Motown, the trio left the label to establish a company of their own. For a few years, Motown's fortunes were unaffected; they launched the Jackson 5 as superstars, and producers such as Norman Whitfield infused Motown with contemporary funk, psychedelia, and social commentary on tracks like the Temptations' "Cloud Nine," "Psychedelic Shack," and "Ball of Confusion."*j* Motown's golden age truly ended, however, in 1971, when the company moved from Detroit to Los Angeles. Around this time, the careers of some of Motown's mainstays, such as Martha Reeves and the

Marvelettes, had petered out; Diana Ross had already left the Supremes. Marvin Gaye and Stevie Wonder recorded some stupendous album-length statements in the 1970s that showed their full gifts as songwriters and performers for the first time; they also expanded their lyrical concerns beyond the romantic themes that Motown had largely stuck to. But Motown no longer bred scads of stars, or honed a distinctive sound; they were simply a soul/R&B record label, albeit a very big and successful one.

When people talk about the Motown sound, they're referring to those 1960s and early '70s recordings. The most successful label of its day, and the most successful independent label of all time (it's now part of MCA), it was the most influential factor in establishing African-American music as an integral part of mainstream US culture.

Recommended Recordings

Smokey Robinson & the Miracles, *Anthology*
Mary Wells, *Looking Back 1961-1964*
Martha Reeves & the Vandellas, *Live Wire! The Singles 1962-1972*
The Marvelettes, *Marvelettes' Greatest Hits*
Marvin Gaye, *Anthology*
Stevie Wonder, *Looking Back*
The Supremes, *Anthology*
The Temptations, *Emperors of Soul*
The Four Tops, *Anthology*
The Jackson 5, *Anthology*
Junior Walker, *Greatest Hits*
Gladys Knight & the Pips, *Anthology*
Brenda Holloway, *Greatest Hits & Rare Classics*
Edwin Starr, *Motown Superstar Series Vol. 3*
Various Artists, *Hitsville USA: The Motown Singles Collection 1959-1971*

Book

Where Did Our Love Go?: The Rise and Fall of the Motown Sound, by Nelson George (St. Martin's, 1985)

–Richie Unterberger

British Invasion

Of all the movements that have shaken the world of rock 'n' roll in the last 40 years, the British Invasion ranks among the very most exciting and important. Only the music's actual birth as a popular phenomenon with the rise of Elvis Presley is comparable; the punk/new wave explosion of the mid-'70s, while equally unexpected and revolutionary, lacked the British Invasion's across-the-board impact on mainstream popular music and culture.

The British Invasion has sometimes been unfairly disparaged as a bunch of white guitar groups re-selling second-hand, vintage American rock 'n' roll and R&B to a public that had forgotten it, or had never been exposed to it in the first place. While it's true that early American rock and soul were the performers' chief inspirations, the best of the groups broke immense ground as performers, songwriters, and stylists, introducing many of the attitudes and innovations that are taken for granted as part and parcel of rock music today. The British Invasion had its roots in the country's skiffle craze of the mid-'50s, sparked by Lonnie Donegan. Innumerable British teenagers were inspired to form groups based

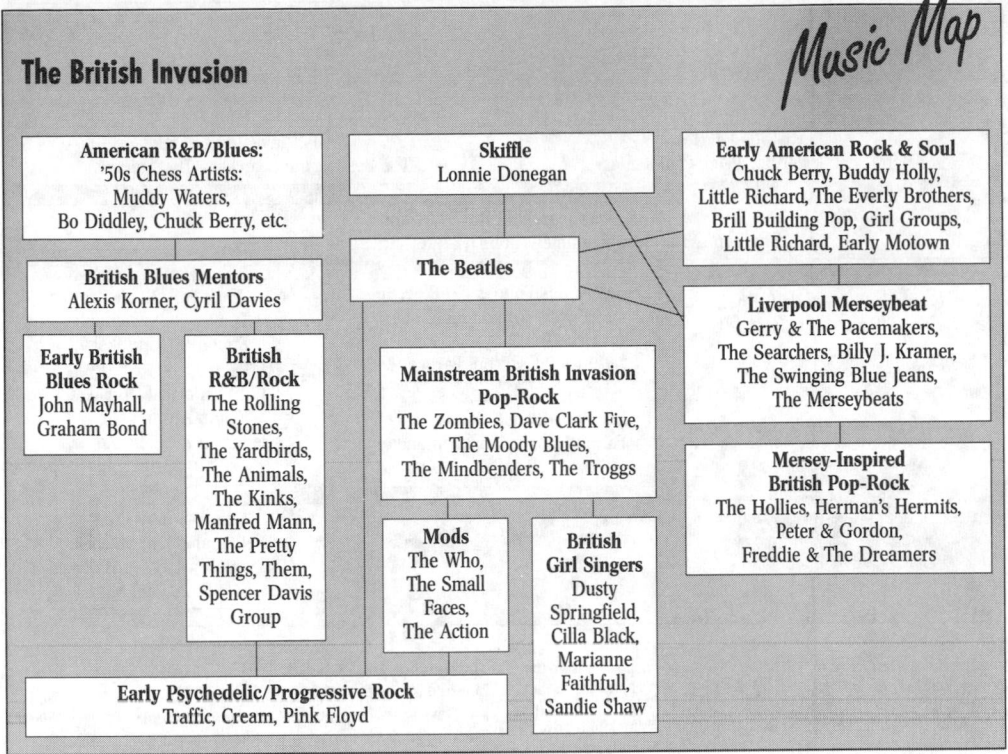

The British Invasion

Music Map

American R&B/Blues:
'50s Chess Artists:
Muddy Waters,
Bo Diddley, Chuck Berry, etc.

Skiffle
Lonnie Donegan

Early American Rock & Soul
Chuck Berry, Buddy Holly,
Little Richard, The Everly Brothers,
Brill Building Pop, Girl Groups,
Little Richard, Early Motown

British Blues Mentors
Alexis Korner, Cyril Davies

The Beatles

Liverpool Merseybeat
Gerry & The Pacemakers,
The Searchers, Billy J. Kramer,
The Swinging Blue Jeans,
The Merseybeats

**Early British
Blues Rock**
John Mayhall,
Graham Bond

**British
R&B/Rock**
The Rolling
Stones,
The Yardbirds,
The Animals,
The Kinks,
Manfred Mann,
The Pretty
Things, Them,
Spencer Davis
Group

**Mainstream British Invasion
Pop-Rock**
The Zombies, Dave Clark Five,
The Moody Blues,
The Mindbenders, The Troggs

**Mersey-Inspired
British Pop-Rock**
The Hollies, Herman's Hermits,
Peter & Gordon,
Freddie & The Dreamers

Mods
The Who,
The Small
Faces,
The Action

**British
Girl Singers**
Dusty
Springfield,
Cilla Black,
Marianne
Faithfull,
Sandie Shaw

Early Psychedelic/Progressive Rock
Traffic, Cream, Pink Floyd

on the simple (and cheap) instrumentation of guitars and washboards. The watered-down folk and blues sound of skiffle can sound unbearably stilted today, but many of those teenage musicians quickly graduated to electric guitars and drums as the focus of their interest shifted to classic early American rock 'n' roll.

There was a homegrown British rock 'n' roll scene in the late '50s and early '60s, but it was overpopulated by pale imitations of American rock, clean-cut instrumentals, and teen idols who offered little more than slightly reworked MOR ballad fare. Tours by American rock 'n' rollers were uncommon, and rock 'n' roll itself was only played on the radio a few hours per week, which meant that young British musicians and listeners devoted to rock 'n' roll had no alternative but to create a grass roots scene themselves. While Liverpool was by far the biggest breeding ground for the Beat Boom, with hundreds of bands in action by the early '60s, groups were sprouting up all over the British Isles—in Manchester, London, Belfast, and elsewhere. While early pioneers of rock were dying, retiring, being crippled by scandal, or falling into commercial disfavor in the United States, these British musicians maintained a fanatical devotion to their idols' music. Chuck Berry and Buddy Holly were arguably the most influential heroes of this generation of musicians, but the British also revered a wide range of other great American performers, including the Everly Brothers, Elvis, Gene Vincent, girl groups, the early Motown acts, and many more.

A listen to the Beatles' early recordings leaves no doubt about their adulation for, and mastery of, the styles of their heroes; but they added a lot more of themselves. They were pioneers in so many areas: writing most of their material at a time when that was rarely done; devising melodies and harmonies that were more inventive than any others that had been used in rock 'n' roll; writing and performing as a self-contained group with distinctive individual talents and personalities, rather than having a star with anonymous backing musicians as their lineup; and embodying the spirit of rebellious youth with their energetic performances, humor, and nonconformist attitudes. They, and the best of their fellow British groups, did this with a giddy exuberance that has rarely been matched in the history of rock 'n' roll.

The impact of Beatlemania—which blanketed Britain in 1963, and the United States the following year—could not be overestimated, not only in terms of commercial success (as in the oft-quoted statistic of how the Beatles claimed the Top Five singles in the US one week in early 1964), but in how it changed rock 'n' roll itself. Sometimes unfairly criticized as a "safe" alternative to the moodier and blacker Rolling Stones,

the Beatles displayed an enormous versatility that refutes such categorizations. They could rock as hard as anyone when that suited them, but more important, they were pop's greatest eclectics, constantly evolving and experimenting in their successful quest to create the most diverse and innovative body of work ever produced by a rock group.

The first flush of "beat" bands, as they were called initially, to overtake Britain and (slightly later) the United States were often from Liverpool, and tended to emulate the Beatles' lightest, most innocuous features. Dubbed "Merseybeat," guitars and harmonies were to the fore, as were bouncy, irresistible melodies (sometimes in the form of actual Lennon-McCartney compositions that the Beatles had rejected for their own recordings). Cute and clean-cut, the recordings of Gerry & the Pacemakers, Billy J. Kramer, Freddie & the Dreamers, and Herman's Hermits have fared poorly in latter-day jaded rock critiques due to their lightweight, at times insipid content. But this shouldn't obscure the glittering harmonies and chiming guitars of the Searchers, the Hollies, and Peter & Gordon, who were probably the best bands that followed the mold of the Beatles' most pop-oriented recordings.

The Beatles' greatest challenge came from the London-based R&B scene, by groups who drew from American electric bluesmen like Muddy Waters and Chess Records rockers like Bo Diddley. Schooled by early British bluesmen like Alexis Korner and Cyril Davies, the Rolling Stones, the Yardbirds, Manfred Mann, the Kinks, the Pretty Things, the Who, and non-London acts like the Animals, the Spencer Davis Group, and Them took the bulk of their early repertoires from obscure blues and R&B recordings, investing them with accelerated tempos and a reckless guitar-based approach. As personalities, they took the Beatles' anti-establishment stance further, rebelling against society more openly and wearing their hair even longer.

The difference between these R&B cultists and the Beatles is not nearly as great as it has sometimes been portrayed. The Beatles and the R&B groups often covered the same songs, not just those by Chuck Berry, but songs by many others; the Beatles, the Stones—and for that matter, Freddie & the Dreamers—all recorded the early Motown tune "Money." The Stones' first big British hit was a cover of Lennon-McCartney's "I Wanna Be Your Man"; their second was a cover of a Buddy Holly song. Manfred Mann covered obscure girl group tunes for their biggest hits, and the Kinks would draw upon British music hall traditions for their most creative work. All the groups from this earthier faction would come to pen their own material, often placing a premium upon melodic invention and harmonies.

Folk Rock

Music Map

Early '60s Folkies	British Invasion Groups
Bob Dylan (acoustic), Peter, Paul & Mary	The Beatles, the Searchers, The Animals

American Folk Rock Groups
The Byrds, The Beau Brummels, Bob Dylan (electric), The Blue Things

Commercial L.A. Folk Rock	Early '60s Folkies Go Electric	New York Folk Rock Groups
The Mamas & the Papas,	Fred Neil, Gordon Lightfoot, Phil Ochs, Ian & Sylvia, Donovan, Richard & Mimi Farina	The Lovin' Spoonful, Simon & Garfunkel

California Folk-Rockers Gone Psychedelic
Jefferson Airplane, Love, Buffalo Springfield

Late '60s British Folk-Rockers
Fairport Convention, Pentangle, Nick Drake

Singer-Songwriters
Neil Young, Joni Mitchell, Tim Buckley, Jackson Browne, Carole King, Paul Simon

Sometimes overlooked in this battle of supposed opposites were the groups that favored neither the R&B nor dippy pop approach, instead focusing their efforts on masterful straightforward rock. The Zombies were probably second only to the Beatles in their breathtakingly adventurous melodies; the Dave Clark Five pounded out tuneful rockers with glorious abandon; the first incarnation of the Moody Blues sang haunting pop-rock tunes that borrowed from R&B, soul, and the Brill Building sound.

In 1964 and 1965, the march of the British Invaders seemed endless, but in the face of a volatile rock scene, it became clear that only the bands that could both write their own material and evolve stylistically would survive. The Beatles, Stones, Who, and Kinks were the only British bands to maintain a high standard of work throughout the '60s, expanding their songwriting talents and instrumental resources at a dizzying pace. Bands like the Yardbirds and Zombies briefly exhibited similar resources for pioneering psychedelia and experimentation before folding due to internal and external pressures. Groups like Gerry & the Pacemakers, the Dave Clark Five, and the Searchers fell off the map commercially due to their inability to write top-notch material or evolve with the times. And a few, like the Hollies and Manfred Mann, survived by incorporating enough progressive elements into their brand of pop-rock to remain hip (and commercially successful).

While a few first-rate bands like the mod Small Faces and the crude Troggs emerged in 1966, that year saw the impetus of the original British Invasion start to fade. A second generation of bands sprang up that took progressive experimentation, cohesive albums, and self-contained songwriting as a given. Some (Traffic, Cream) featured veterans of the first wave of the invasion; others (Pink Floyd) owed little to the movement at all.

In reality, though, the British Invasion has never stopped. Artists from the British Isles continue to invade the American, and indeed the international, audience at a rapid pace, if not nearly as phenomenal a rate as the heady days of 1964 and 1965. Folk-rock, garage-rock, and psychedelia grew directly out of the innovations of the best British Invasion groups. And rock 'n' roll owes much of its climate for artistic freedom and individual expression—not to mention its harmonies, melodies, and guitar-based ensemble sound—to the road paved by the Beatles and their followers.

Recommended Recordings

The Beatles, all of their albums, though *The Beatles 1962-66* (Capitol) has their biggest early hits.

The Rolling Stones, *The Singles Collection* (ABKCO)

The Who, *Meaty, Beaty, Big and Bouncy* (MCA)

The Kinks, *Greatest Hits* (Rhino)

The Yardbirds, *Greatest Hits, Vol. 1* (Rhino)

The Animals, *The Complete Animals* (EMI, UK)

The Zombies, *Singles As & Bs* (See for Miles, UK)

Manfred Mann, *Best of the EMI Years* (Griffin)

The Dave Clark Five, *The History of the Dave Clark Five* (Hollywood)

The Hollies, *30th Anniversary Collection* (EMI)

Them, *Them Featuring Van Morrison* (Parrot)

Various Artists, *The British Invasion Vol. 1-9* (Rhino)

The Pretty Things, *Get a Buzz: The Best of the Fontana Years* (Fontana)

The Small Faces, *The Small Faces* (PolyGram)

The Spencer Davis Group, *The Best of the Spencer Davis Group* (Rhino)

Book

The British Invasion, by Nicholas Schaffner (McGraw Hill)

Videos

A Hard Day's Night (also available as CD-ROM from Voyager)
The Compleat Beatles

—Richie Unterberger

Folk-Rock

In the early '60s, any suggestion that the folk and rock 'n' roll worlds would intertwine to create a hybrid called folk-rock would have met with utter disbelief from both camps. The folk community prided itself on its purity, which meant acoustic instruments and songs of substance; they regarded rock 'n' roll as vulgar and commercial. Rock 'n' rollers, for the most part, were utterly ignorant of folk traditions, and unconcerned with broadening their lyrical content beyond tried-and-true themes of romance and youthful partying. Yet within a few years, folk and rock not only combined into a new form of popular music, but became hugely successful and influential.

By 1964, Bob Dylan had already done much to revolutionize contemporary folk music by singing about topical issues and, (after a couple of years), abstract personal and romantic concerns in a poetic and uniquely expressive fashion. Dylan harbored a secret admiration for the Beatles and other major British Invasion bands, a fascination which was mutual. It was only a matter of time before each started to influence the other.

The roots of folk-rock can be detected in a few pre-1965 recordings by the Searchers and Jackie DeShannon (who helped introduce the ringing, circular 12-string guitar riffs that became one of the music's major trademarks), as well as in that of the Beau Brummels. It is noticeable in the Animals' superb bluesy interpretation of the traditional folk standard "The House of the Rising Sun," and the Beatles' own "I'm a Loser." It took the Byrds, however, to really kick the movement into gear with their electric version of Dylan's "Mr. Tambourine Man," which topped the charts in mid-1965. The first and best folk-rock band, the Byrds may have been comprised of ex-folkies who had only picked up their electric instruments a year or so before they became superstars, but they were, if anything, influenced more by the Beatles than Dylan. They were once quoted as saying (albeit tongue in cheek), that they based their sound on "21% Beatles, 11% Zombies, 8% Dillards, 18% Dylan, 14% Pete Seeger, 16% Searchers, and 12% trial and error/ignorance/accident/originality." Leader Roger McGuinn's chiming 12-string guitar set the sonic standard for the new genre, as did the group's beautiful choral harmonies and superb interpretations of songs by Dylan and Seeger, traditional folk ballads, and their own first-rate original material.

Dylan himself moved into folk-rock around the same time as the Byrds on his *Bringing It All Back Home* album, which was divided into electric and acoustic sides. The subsequent *Highway 61 Revisited* and *Blonde on Blonde* were full-bore electric rock records, marrying Dylan's intense, at times surrealistic poetry to a tough beat, provided by soon-to-be-stars in their own right-musicians such as Mike Bloomfield, Al Kooper, and the Band. His conversion to rock 'n' roll outraged much of his original constituency, which was more than offset by his legions of new fans; indeed, all three of his albums from 1965 and 1966 made the Top Ten, as did the singles "Like a Rolling Stone," "Positively 4th Street," and "Rainy Day Women No.12 & 35."

The success of the Byrds and Dylan ignited a firestorm of emulators and imitators. The Lovin' Spoonful, from Dylan's own stomping ground of Greenwich Village, were the era's greatest exponents of good-time folk-rock; the Mamas & the Papas, led by ex-folkie John Phillips, were at the head of a slickly produced L.A. variation of the sound; Sonny & Cher, the most commercial of the bunch, latched on to a few of folk-rock's most saleable attributes on their first batch of smashes, and went on to highly successful careers in pop's mainstream. Donovan, one of the most talented mid-'60s folkies to follow in Dylan's footsteps, went not only electric, but psychedelic. Producers added 12-string guitars and a rhythm section to an old track by Simon & Garfunkel; after "Sounds of Silence" became a No. 1 hit, the duo became one of the most successful folk-rock acts of all time. Obscure regional groups like the Leaves (from L.A.) and the Blue Things (from Kansas) recorded some wonderful folk-rock singles and even albums that were in the same class as the hits by the top folk-rock stars.

The "rock" in folk-rock was always more prominent than the "folk"; all of the aforementioned acts had a highly commercial sense of melody, grafting guitar patterns and somewhat more personal, topical lyrical concerns from folk music into their own superb pop-rock creations. Performers approaching the hybrid from the folk side were less frequent and less commercially successful, but singer-songwriters like Fred Neil, Phil Ochs, Gordon Lightfoot, Ian & Sylvia, Richard & Mimi Farina, and others proved willing and able to electrify their sound with positive commercial and artistic results.

Folk-rock was not only a tremendous success on the charts in 1965 and 1966, but tremendously influential in expanding the sonic and lyrical vistas of rock as a whole. The Beatles were already addressing more personal concerns on the mid-1965 tunes "Help" and "You've Got to Hide Your Love Away"; *Rubber Soul*, issued at the end of the year, was one of folk-rock's greatest triumphs. Many of the early psychedelic bands from San Francisco were comprised of renegade folkies, and while groups like the Jefferson Airplane and the Beatles themselves would move beyond folk-rock to psychedelia fairly quickly, there's no doubt that folk-rock whetted their appetites for lyrical and instrumental experimentation and innovation.

While folk-rock's commercial heyday was in 1965 and 1966, in truth it has been a strong presence in rock ever since, fading only as a marketing term for a sound that was initially perceived by the industry as a fad, not a permanent addition to the rock 'n' roll lexicon. In 1967, L.A. bands Buffalo Springfield and Love released classic recordings that drew upon folk-rock as their core, adding elements of eclecticism and psychedelia. In the late '60s, British groups like Fairport Convention and Pentangle achieved perhaps the purest folk-rock blend, with nearly equal balances between the electric and the acoustic, and between modern compositions and traditional numbers. The singer-songwriter movement of the late '60s and early '70s was not as prone to electric guitars and group ensembles, perhaps, but also took folk-rock as its chief inspiration. The harmonies, ringing guitars, and chord patterns of classic folk-rock live on in countless contemporary acts, ranging from bands like R.E.M. to singers like Tracy Chapman.

Recommended Recordings

The Byrds, *Mr. Tambourine Man* (Columbia)
The Byrds, *Greatest Hits* (Columbia)
Bob Dylan, *Blonde on Blonde* (Columbia)
Bob Dylan, *Highway 61 Revisited* (Columbia)
The Lovin' Spoonful, *Anthology* (Rhino)
The Beatles, *Rubber Soul* (Capitol)
Donovan, *Troubadour: The Definitive Collection 1964-1976* (Epic)
Simon & Garfunkel, *Collected Works* (Columbia)
Buffalo Springfield, *Buffalo Springfield* (1973 double-LP compilation) (Atco)

Love, *Forever Changes* (Elektra)
The Mamas & the Papas, *Creeque Alley* (MCA)
The Blue Things, *Story Vol. 1-3* (Cicadelic)
The Beau Brummels, *Best of the Beau Brummels* (Rhino)
Richard & Mimi Farina, *The Best of Richard & Mimi Farina* (Vanguard)
The Leaves, *1966* (Panda)

Book

Timeless Flight: The Definitive Biography of the Byrds, by Johnny Rogan (1990, Square One, UK)

–Richie Unterberger

Garage Rock

For those who prize adolescent, primitive energy as one of rock 'n' roll's best features, the garage rock bands of the '60s rank at or near the top of the rock 'n' roll pyramid. Ignored and sometimes scorned by critics in its heyday, garage rock proved an influential inspiration for the punk rock explosion of the '70s. It experienced a renaissance of sorts in the '80s among the rock underground and collector community if nowhere else.

Largely a North American phenomenon, the garage band movement began in the wake of the British Invasion in 1964. There were already plenty of young, white rock groups throughout the US, but they were usually found playing instrumental (sometimes surf) rock or heavily R&B-influenced "frat rock," and were largely unconcerned with writing their own songs or making individualistic, rebellious statements. The Beatles, Rolling Stones, Kinks, Animals, and others changed that overnight. Caught off-guard by this unexpected onslaught, teenage groups put the focus on loud electric guitars and grew their hair long in attempts to emulate their heroes.

What emerged was a distinctly cruder and more adolescent variation of the British Invasion sound (which itself had been largely inspired by American rock and R&B in the first place). It is not accurate to say that the garage groups matched the talents of their British idols, or of American outfits like the Byrds; they were usually considerably younger and less sophisticated, and lacked the songwriting skills or instrumental finesse of the era's major groups. By way of compensation, perhaps, they placed a premium on sheer outrageousness: over-the-top vocal screams and sneers fought it out with loud guitars that almost always had a fuzz-tone attached. Garage bands were so named after the habitual practice space of the musicians, who were overwhelmingly white, suburban, and teenaged. While scattered 1964 recordings by groups like the Gestures and the Barbarians served as early blueprints for the sound, it didn't blanket the country properly until 1965, when virtually every major city (and many minor ones) became home to dozens of new guitar groups hungering for a piece of the action—which meant parties, girls and, of course, records.

These records were usually pressed on tiny local labels, and usually only heard within a 50-100 mile radius (if they were heard on local radio at all). Occasionally they were picked up for nationwide distribution by a larger company; more occasionally still, they became bona fide national hits. The Shadows of Knight, the Count Five, the 13th Floor Elevators, the Standells, the Seeds, ? & the Mysterians, and the Gentrys were among the lucky few who hit this jackpot, although their time in the spotlight was brief.

An enormous amount of records were released by garage bands in the '60s, particularly between 1965 and 1967. California and Texas were probably home to more of these bands per capita than any other state, but the number of groups that recorded, let alone played, was staggering. Detroit, Boston, Chicago, Minneapolis, Seattle, Pittsburgh, Cleveland, Phoenix; they all were home to large local scenes supporting several dozens of bands, much in the manner of today's alternative rock and punk communities. There are a great many generic garage band recordings: fuzzy variations of the "Satisfaction" or "You Really Got Me" riffs, simplistic lyrics about cheating girlfriends, inept guitar solos and cheesy organ riffs. There are also a great many great garage band records by bands that combined their energy with sharp songwriting skills, compelling hooks, or sheer unpredictable mania.

The Texas bands favored galloping rhythms with bigger-than-life fuzztones; the California bands often copped folk-rock and psychedelic licks from their own local heroes; Midwest groups sometimes drew upon trends in soul music; New England groups were more prone to use Zombies-like keyboards and melodies; Cleveland acts showed a strong affinity for Merseybeat and British power pop. But the bands from these territories had a lot more in common than not; all of them kept abreast of the latest trends in British rock, folk-rock, and psychedelic music.

A number of factors conspired to slow the momentum of the garage phenomenon around 1967 and 1968. Facing college, lack of national success, and worst of all, the military draft, many of the bands simply didn't stay together for very long. Increasingly homogenous national radio airplay and distribution meant less of a chance for regional labels to succeed or get their records played, and hence less opportunities for

Garage Rock

Music Map

Instrumental and Surf Groups	British Invasion Groups	Frat Rock Groups
The Ventures, Dick Dale, The Trashmen, The Astronauts	The Beatles, The Rolling Stones, The Animals, The Kinks, The Yardbirds	The Kingsmen, the Rivieras

Early Garage Bands
The Gestures, the Barbarians, the Chartbusters

British Pop-Rock Influenced Garage Bands	Raunchy R&B-Influenced Garage Bands
The Remains, New Colony Six	The Chocolate Watchband, The Standells, The Shadows of Knight, The Count Five

Garage Psychedelia
The Music Machine, The Electric Prunes, The Seeds, The 13th Floor Elevators

---

local talent to enter the studio. And the fact was, a lot of the garage bands were outgrowing the pop-rock of the first wave of the British Invasion, and moving—as their inspirations were—towards more progressive and psychedelic sounds, with lyrics that, for better or worse, addressed more mature concerns than picking up girls and adolescent rebellion. Almost immediately forgotten by rock historians, garage music began its comeback when future Patti Smith Group guitarist Lenny Kaye compiled the original *Nuggets* album in 1972. This double set featured the most popular garage band recordings by the likes of the Standells, Seeds, Chocolate Watch Band, and others; Kaye helped coin the term "punk rock" in his liner notes, in reference to bands such as these that celebrated rock 'n' roll at its most primal and least self-conscious. Adding a measure of contemporary lyrical content and attitude, bands like the Sex Pistols would embellish this prototype and give birth to modern punk rock a few years later.

The *Pebbles* series of the late '70s took the *Nuggets* approach several steps further, unearthing even rarer and rawer garage band recordings from across the nation. Eventually numbering dozens of volumes, *Pebbles* in turn kicked off a deluge of '60s garage band reissues and compilations; often great, sometimes awful, these numbered in the hundreds by the late '80s. Contemporary groups like the Fuzztones, the Pandoras, Thee Fourgiven, and dozens of others played garage revival music in the 1980s, though in truth they never approached the authentic qualities of the best of the '60s garage, and never made a significant impact on either the mainstream or underground rock scenes.

The reissues introduced young and old listeners to scores of fine bands, ironically giving them their greatest international exposure decades after they had broken up. Some, like the Remains or the Music Machine, were arguably too talented and innovative to be lumped in with the garage crowd in the first place. Others, like Zakary Thaks, the Chocolate Watch Band, and the Rising Storm, personified teenage rock 'n' roll at its most enjoyable. All of the above-mentioned groups—and quite a few others—were nearly as good as the more accomplished and more famous British and American hitmaking bands of the era, and deserve belated recognition as first-rate '60s rock 'n' rollers.

Recommended Recordings

Various Artists, *Nuggets Vol. 1-12* (Rhino)
Various Artists, *Pebbles Vol. 1-10* (AIP)
The New Colony Six, *At the River's Edge* (Sundazed)
The Chocolate Watch Band, *Best of the Chocolate Watch Band* (Rhino)
The Standells, *Best of the Standells* (Rhino)
Zakary Thaks, *Texas Band* (Moxie)
The Music Machine, *Best of the Music Machine* (Rhino)
The Rising Storm, *Calm Before* (Arf Arf)
The Remains, *The Remains* (Epic)
We the People, *Declaration of Independence* (Eva, France)
The Shadows of Knight, *Dark Sides: The Best of the Shadows of Knight* (Rhino)
The Mystic Tide, *Solid Sound* (Distortions)
The Lemon Drops, *Crystal Pure* (Cicadelic)

—Richie Unterberger

'60s Rock from Non-English Speaking Territories

Throughout its history, rock 'n' roll has been inextricably linked with the English language—the first tongue, after all, of the nation of its birth, the United States. Up to the present, and most likely for some time to come, the great majority of internationally distributed and acclaimed rock 'n' roll has been produced in English-speaking countries: the US, Canada, and (especially starting with the British Invasion) the United Kingdom, Ireland, Australia, and New Zealand. Almost from the start, however, other countries (mostly in Continental Europe) got in on rock 'n' roll, and it remains a fairly obscure fact that the '60s produced much interesting rock from non-English-speaking countries.

There were already quite a few instrumental rock ensembles recording in Europe, especially in Scandinavia, whose Spotniks (a Ventures-like outfit) had an international reputation; Danish guitarist Jorgen Ingmann had a No. 2 US single with the instrumental "Apache," which was a huge hit for the British group the Shadows in most other territories. Some prominent American and British acts actually boasted key members from the Continent, like the Easybeats (guitarist Harry Vanda, from Holland), the Standells (Tony Valentino, from Italy), the Velvet Underground (Nico, from Germany), and Manfred Mann (Klaus Voormann, a friend of the Beatles from their Hamburg days). The Beatles and the British Invasion had just as immense an impact on most European countries as in the US, and numerous Continental groups launched a beat/R&B/punk response of their own, along the same lines as the garage rock phenomenon in North America.

With rare exceptions, these groups sang in English, even managing the occasional crossover hit in the US; Holland's Shocking Blue ("Venus") and Spain's Los Bravos ("Black Is Black") are two of the most famous examples. It was a measure of just how immense Anglo-American cultural imperialism had become (and so remains) that these groups rarely sang in their native tongue. If they were seeking worldwide demographic audiences, this certainly made sense, English being the most widely understood language in entertainment and international commerce.

Yet given that most of these acts had a miniscule chance of denting non-native charts, it seems unlikely that they catered their material to international tastes. It's more likely that they perceived the English language as an intrinsic element of rock 'n' roll, and would feel foolish translating English songs, or writing rock 'n' roll in a different language. Given that they were not writing in their native tongues, it's impressive how much good original material emerged from some of these groups. In most cases you can hear their indigenous accents awkwardly penetrating their most willing attempts to sound American or English (although in the best groups' cases, these traces are usually slight).

Scandinavian groups usually exhibited the slightest accents and the greatest English proficiency, and it's no surprise that many of the most competent bands emerged from this region, especially Sweden. The Tages, who recorded some excellent mod rock in the British Invasion style, may have been the best of the bunch, and they actually lived and recorded in England for a while in an attempt to break through to a wider market. Many acts recorded one or two fine records, and the best compilation of this vibrant scene is *Searchin' for Shakes: Swedish Beat 1965-1968.*

Swedish groups, generally speaking, were the most able imitators of British Invasion styles while the Dutch bands were more distinctive and idiosyncratic. The raw R&B-rock of the Pretty Things and the Downliners Sect was a surprisingly huge influence on this scene (these two groups were bigger stars on the Continent than the UK). Holland, a small country, gave rise to an astonishing number of groups in the mid- and late-'60s, many of whom harbored a distinctively regional predilection for morose R&B/beat/punk with lingering European folk influences. The Outsiders (no relation to the American pop-rock band of the same name), who recorded a wealth of first-rate original material (both "beat" and psychedelic) in this vein between 1965 and 1969, may have been the very best '60s group to emerge from a non-English-speaking nation, although they remain unknown overseas to all but a small cult. Les Baroques, the pre-hard rock Golden Earrings, and the absurdly sloppy Q65 are also revered by hardcore '60s collectors, and there have been quite a few *Pebbles*-like compilations of Dutch beat-punk.

In general, both the musical quality and English competence drop the further south you travel in Europe when surveying '60s groups—a function of cultural differences that found the youth of these countries less fluent in the language and less exposed to rock culture in general. French and Spanish rock acts, in fact, usually sang in their native language. Many of them were dreadful, but occasionally they were quite good: Los Cheyenes (from Barcelona) laid down some dynamic Kinks-like punk, and Ronnie Bird (from France) was a decent singer in the British mod style with a good band that sometimes featured American expatriate Mickey Baker (of Mickey & Sylvia fame). Be aware that most '60s groups from the European countries where the Romance languages are spoken, particularly from Italy, hold latter-day interest mostly as novelty items. Not at all beat or garage, but definitely worth hearing, is the French chanteuse Francoise Hardy, who wrote and sang some delightful pop-rock (and straight pop), sometimes in a Spectorish girl group or Marianne Faithfull vein. Hardy became a star by singing in French, but made quite a few English recordings as the decade wore on; some were good ("All Over the World" even made the British Top 20 in 1965), but soon she moved to MOR pop.

Germany played more than a minor role in '60s rock, but mostly as a training ground for British bands, particularly in Hamburg, where the Beatles and many others developed their chops in front of rowdy audiences. The homegrown German groups, however, were generally no great shakes, often displaying an awkward martial sense of rhythm and vocal phrasing. To some degree, this crops up in the recordings of the best German beat band, the Lords, who compensated for their shortcomings with a good sense of humor, an unusual reverbed guitar sound run through Lesley amps, and some good original material and remarkably inventive covers.

Go WAY down south, to South America, and you'll find a couple of the best non-Anglo '60s bands. The Shakers (from Uruguay), despite occasional blatant broken accents, were among the best early Beatle imitators; most of their material was original, and unlike most acts attempting to emulate the early Liverpool sound, they went for the gutsier aspects of Merseybeat, not the wimpier ones. Los Mockers were to the Shakers what the Rolling Stones were to the Beatles; phrased differently, the Rolling Stones were to Los Mockers what the Beatles were to the Shakers. These fellow Uruguayans, who wrote most of their own songs, aped the mid-'60s Stones quite well, better in fact than many similarly inclined American garage bands. Surprisingly, material by both Los Mockers and the Shakers is readily available on CD.

While the psychedelic era didn't produce as many notable efforts from non-Anglo groups as the Beat Boom, some odds and ends stand out. Of particular interest were Holland's Group 1850, a weird hybrid of Pink Floyd, the Mothers of Invention, and their own mid-'60s beat-punk roots. Savage Rose, from Denmark, were one of the very few groups of this sort to earn international acclaim; many of their early records also saw release in the United States, where they toured in the early '70s. Featuring the wild range and child-like timbres of lead singer Annisette, they recorded an erratic, but generally intriguing, series of albums in the late '60s and early '70s that rank not only among the most interesting rock records from non-English-speaking countries, but among the most interesting late psychedelic/early progressive rock recordings from anywhere.

Continental rock, indeed, would make a much bigger impact in the progressive rock era in the '70s, via acts like Kraftwerk, Focus, Vangelis (who started in the late-'60s Greek band Aphrodite's Child), and P.F.M. There were also honest-to-god pop stars ABBA, featuring members that had honed their licks in '60s pop-rock bands. The earlier generation of Continental and South American rock, however, remains known only to hard-bitten collectors. For the international audience, though, it's much more accessible today than it was in its heyday, and has been anthologized in numerous *Pebbles*-like compilations (occasionally in the *Pebbles* series itself), which catch up on the dozens of groups that only managed one or two notable songs. For the '60s specialist looking for new artists to collect, it's an area ripe for exploration.

Recommended Recordings

Various Artists, *Searchin' for Shakes: Swedish Beat 1965-1968* (Amigo, Sweden)
The Outsiders, *The Outsiders* (Pseudonym, Holland)
The Outsiders, *CQ* (Pseudonym, Holland)
The Tages, *1964-68* (EMI, Sweden)
Los Mockers, *Los Mockers* (Get Hip)
The Shakers, *All the Best* (EMI, Brazil)
Savage Rose, *The Savage Rose* (Polydor)
Savage Rose, *Dodens Triumf* (Polydor)
Francoise Hardy, *L'Integrale Disques Vogue 1962/1967 (The Complete Vogue Recordings)* (Vogue, France)
Ronnie Bird, *1965* (EMI, France)
Various Artists, *Transworld Punk Vol. 1-2* (Crawdad)
Various Artists, *Pebbles Vol. 15: The Netherlands 1965-1968* (AIP)
Los Cheynes, *Historica de la Musica Pop Española No. 0* (no label)
Group 1850, *1967-1968* (Mercury, Holland)
Various Artists, *Flight to Lowlands Paradise: The Netherlands, Pt. 1 & 2* (Moxie)
Les Baroques, *Such a Cad: The Complete Story of Les Baroques* (Patio Music/Purple Eye)

—*Richie Unterberger*

Psychedelic Rock

Psychedelia represented rock 'n' roll at its most breathtakingly adventurous and innovative—and sometimes, at its most foolish. While the most self-conscious experiments of the mid- and late '60s have dated badly, the best psychedelic rock had an exhilarating recklessness that has been difficult to recapture in the ensuing decades.

Psychedelic music was fed by many sources. The desire to emulate the effect of mind-altering drugs in sound is its most sensational feature. But the musicians who pioneered psychedelia were equally driven by a hunger to expand rock's boundaries and enhance its eclecticism by incorporating influences from Middle Eastern music and improvisational jazz. This went hand-in-hand with exploring the frontiers of amplified sound and instrumental textures (primarily on the electric guitar), as well as lyrics that addressed the burning social and psychological issues of the day.

Trying to pin down the first psychedelic record is nearly as elusive as trying to name the first rock 'n' roll record. Far-fetched claims have been advanced for songs running from the Tornados' futuristic 1962 No. 1 instrumental "Telstar" to the Dave Clark Five's massively reverb-laden "Any Way You Want It." In 1964, the Beatles introduced guitar feedback on "I Feel Fine"; a year later, they introduced the sitar to rock on "Norwegian Wood." But two groups from different sides of the Atlantic with somewhat similar names, the Yardbirds and the Byrds, were really the most responsible for sounding the psychedelic siren.

With their ominous minor key melodies, hyperactive instrumental breaks (called "rave-ups"), unpredictable tempo changes, and use of Gregorian chants (most notably on the single "Still I'm Sad"), the Yardbirds helped define the manic eclecticism that would characterize early psychedelic rock. Jeff Beck's fuzzy, distorted guitar sustain laid the blueprint for psychedelic guitar.

Their early 1966 hit "Shapes of Things" was arguably the first out-and-out psychedelic rock song, with its blistering feedback breaks, veering tempos, and stream-of-consciousness lyrics that owed nothing to traditional romantic themes. The Yardbirds' psychedelic peak was brief, but subsequent 1966 recordings—"Over Under Sideways Down" and "Happenings Ten Years Time Ago" especially—found them approximating speed-of-light trips, drug-induced or otherwise, with nervy but taut daring.

Just a couple months after "Shapes of Things," the Byrds flew into uncharted territory with "Eight Miles High." While the group always claimed that the title referred to an airplane flight, the impressionistic lyrics were taken by many to reflect the psychedelic drug experience, while the furious guitar and bass breaks reflected the group's assimilation of John Coltrane's free jazz and Ravi Shankar's Indian music. The single's B-side ("Why") and many of the songs on their 1966 album *Fifth Dimension* crashed through similar sonic frontiers. Although the Byrds would trade in their spacesuits for cowboy threads in just a couple of years, they continued to produce exciting psychedelic-influenced music through the end of 1967.

Ideas traveled fast in the crucible of 1966 rock, and within a few months many of the era's top bands were flashing psychedelic colors on their recordings. The Beatles' mid-'66 single "Rain" used backwards guitars and vocals, and their *Revolver* album was by far their most eclectic pre-'67 work, imbued with churning, distorted guitars, coy references to drug trips, and even quotes from Timothy Leary's version of the *Tibetan Book of the Dead*. The Rolling Stones used the sitar—perhaps to its greatest effect in a rock 'n' roll song—on "Paint It Black," and constructed

Psychedelic Rock

Music Map

British Invasion Guitar Bands
The Yardbirds, The Who, The Beatles

Jazz & Indian Music
John Coltrane, Ravi Shankar

The Byrds

San Francisco Acid-Rock
Jefferson Airplane, Quicksilver Messenger Service, Grateful Dead, Country Joe & The Fish, Big Brother & The Holding Company

L.A. Psychedelia
The Doors, Love, The Mothers Of Invention, Kaleidoscope

Garage Psychedelia
The Music Machine, The Electric Prunes, The Count Five The 13th floor Elevators

British Acid-Rock
The Jimi Hendrix Experience, Cream, Traffic, Pink Floyd, Soft Machine

The Beatles
(Sgt. Pepper Era)

British Psych-Pop
Donovan, The Zombies (Late Period), Blossom Toes

a dense morass of psychedelic sound and lyrics on "Have You Seen Your Mother, Baby, Standing in the Shadow?" Donovan forsook his acoustic guitar for storybook wanderings in densely orchestrated musical arrangements that drew from both Indian sitars and fog-bound British moors. Garage bands, already attuned to distorted guitars via their attempts to emulate the fuzz riffs on Stones classics like "Satisfaction," went the extra nine yards into all-out freakouts on cuts like the Magic Mushrooms' "It's-A-Happening."

In the United States, psychedelic music took root most firmly in California, particularly San Francisco, where an increasingly large bohemian community had been living the psychedelic lifestyle for a year or two before it infiltrated rock 'n' roll. In 1965 and 1966, disaffected folk musicians formed the Grateful Dead, the Jefferson Airplane, the Charlatans, the Great Society, Country Joe & the Fish, Big Brother & the Holding Company, Quicksilver Messenger Service, and many other less famous combos with equally (for the time) outrageous names. It took them a while to get a handle on their electric instruments, as some of their tentative and awkward pre-'67 recordings can attest to. But after honing their chops on the fertile Haight-Ashbury scene, they introduced a whole new spacy element into the psychedelic brew with their searing guitars and euphoric melodies.

The British strain of psychedelia tended to be more whimsical and fairytale-ish than the West Coast brand of acid-rock. Ethereal organs and mellotrons often set the tone of the generally more symphonic arrangements; the lyrics, occasionally wry to the point of surrealism, were often populated with eccentric British character types, or took a storybook, child's-eye perspective. The Beatles brilliant early-1967 "Strawberry Fields"/"Penny Lane" single was the apex of this genre, and newly emerging bands like Pink Floyd and Traffic, as well as less successful but equally intriguing underground acts like the Soft Machine and Tomorrow, also mined this field with great success.

1967's "Summer of Love" saw psychedelic music at its pinnacle. The Beatles released their definitive psychedelic statement, *Sgt. Pepper*, the San Francisco groups made an international impact via the Monterey Pop Festival; Pink Floyd, the Jefferson Airplane, and Traffic issued their best psychedelic albums. Jimi Hendrix and Cream became international superstars with guitar-based acid-rock that had its roots in the Yardbirds' innovations. The Doors' first album explored the dark and mysterious crannies of psychedelia with an impact that neither they nor anyone else would match. Even the Rolling Stones joined the psychedelic bandwagon, with an underappreciated LP, *Their Satanic Majesties Request*, which was accused by many of being an ersatz *Sgt. Pepper* despite including several first-rate songs.

Psychedelic music was a strong presence in rock 'n' roll throughout the rest of the '60s, but there's no doubt that the genre began to become tired and self-indulgent as the decade approached its end. Following the lead, perhaps, of Bob Dylan's calm and simple *John Wesley Harding*, the Beatles, Byrds, and Rolling Stones all released albums in 1968 with a decidedly earthy and back-to-basics tone (although they didn't eschew

progressive experiments altogether). Cream, Traffic, and the original Jimi Hendrix Experience broke up; Pink Floyd's leader, Syd Barrett, became the era's first acid casualty after their brilliant debut album; the Doors peaked early and couldn't repeat the fluid consistency of their own debut, despite releasing several worthy attempts. Pre-heavy metal groups like Iron Butterfly and Blue Cheer emulated the roar of psychedelic guitar growl without paying any heed to the style's more subtle attractions. And quite a few groups presented psychedelic clichés—long guitar solos, florid lyrics, effects-happy production—without saying much of anything original.

Many of the trimmings of psychedelic rock would form the backbone of progressive rock and heavy metal, which devoted themselves to the most extreme ends of the genre—ambitious, neo-classical epics on the one hand, mind-melting guitar distortion on the other. While groups ranging from Echo & the Bunnymen to Sonic Youth have (usually erroneously) been termed neo-psychedelic at one time or another, psychedelia has retreated from the front of rock's collective consciousness since about 1970 or so.

In its time, however, the psychedelic sound fueled some of the '60s' finest moments, influencing most of the top rock acts to some degree. While groups like the Who, the Beach Boys, Love, and Buffalo Springfield could not exactly be called "psychedelic," some of their finest recordings—"I Can See for Miles," "Good Vibrations," Love's *Forever Changes* LP, Buffalo Springfield's "Expecting to Fly" and "Broken Arrow"—betray a strong psychedelic influence, and could not have been made without the inspiration of their more overtly trippy peers. The intricate arrangements and heavily amplified/distorted guitars of psychedelic productions broke ground that has been utilized routinely in rock recordings from the late '60s to the present day.

Recommended Recordings

The Beatles, *Sgt. Pepper's Lonely Hearts Club Band* (Capitol)
The Beatles, *Magical Mystery Tour* (Capitol)
The Yardbirds, *Roger the Engineer* (Edsel)
The Byrds, *Fifth Dimension* (Columbia)
The Doors, *The Doors* (Elektra)
The Jefferson Airplane, *Jefferson Airplane Loves You* (RCA)
Pink Floyd, *Piper at the Gates Of Dawn* (Capitol)
The Jimi Hendrix Experience, *Are You Experienced?* (Reprise)
The Great Society, *Collector's Item* (Columbia)
The Mothers of Invention, *We're Only in It for the Money* (Rykodisc)
The Rolling Stones, *Their Satanic Majesties Request* (ABKCO)
Donovan, *Sunshine Superman* (Epic)
Cream, *Disraeli Gears* (Polydor)
Traffic, *Mr. Fantasy* (Island)
The Misunderstood, *Before the Dream Faded* (Cherry Red)
—Richie Unterberger

San Francisco Sound

Since the mid-'60s, the San Francisco Bay Area has produced numerous influential and important groups, both mainstream and underground, popular and obscure. When people talk about "The San Francisco Sound," however, they're usually referring to the psychedelic acid rock played by many of the area's bands in the late '60s. Innovative, indulgent, both innocent and ambitious, these groups spread their bohemian, drug-charged messages of peace, love, and musical freedom throughout the world, and retain a vociferous cult following to this day.

In rock 'n' roll's early days, the Bay Area produced some notable rock 'n' roll and R&B singers, such as Bobby Freeman and Jimmy McCracklin, but it was far from a hotbed of either talent or record production. The first self-contained rock group of note to emerge from the city—and indeed, the first American band of note to successfully emulate the sounds of the British Invasion—were the Beau Brummels, who also helped lay the groundwork for folk-rock with their first-rate songwriting and melodic harmonies.

Usually disdained as a teenybopper group of sorts by the underground rock community that emerged a year or two later, the Beau Brummels in fact could rightfully claim to be the true forefathers of the San Francisco scene. Their minor-key melodies, acoustic/electric guitar blends, and soaring harmonies in particular were adopted as key elements by many of the bands that followed in their wake. Other, more commercial folk-rock acts from the Bay Area, such as the Vejtables and the We Five, also recorded underrated prototypes of the early San Francisco sound, especially with regard to the blend of male and female harmonies in the case of the two aforementioned artists.

What made these bands unhip in the eyes of the underground was not so much their sound as their attitude and approach; they had commercial images and aimed for hit singles. In the city's youth culture, particularly in the neighborhood of Haight-Ashbury, a self-consciously bohemian community was emerging, concerned not so much with achieving conventional success as artistic expression, experimental drug use, and the overall exploration of alternatives to "straight" society. The Charlatans are usually credited as the first group to reflect the attitudes of this nascent counterculture.

The Charlatans, truth be told, were much more important as social figures than musical innovators. They helped set the standards of nonconformist images with their attire and loose attitudes, but musically they offered rather unexceptional material, heavy on folk, blues, and jugband influences, and were unable to land a record deal until way past their prime. The scene was developing fast, though, and within a matter of months several important groups emerged that placed a far greater primacy on the sustain-laden electric guitars, soaring harmonies, distortion and feedback, Indian and jazz influences, and stoned romantic whimsy that came to characterize the best San Francisco psychedelic rock. The ingredients varied, but overall it could be said that the bands strove to create, often in a drug-influenced fashion, the musical equivalent of the changes that were expanding their social and personal horizons.

The Jefferson Airplane, featuring a staggering array of vocal and instrumental talent and possessing exceptionally strong folk-rock-derived material, were the best of these groups. They were also the first band to become national stars with their 1967 Top Five album *Surrealistic Pillow*, which contained the hits "Somebody to Love" and "White Rabbit." Both were sung by Grace Slick, who had actually left underrated psychedelic pioneers the Great Society to join the Airplane in 1966. Though not as tight instrumentally as the Airplane, the Great Society featured equally innovative material that made effective, often thrilling use of raga-like guitar lines and improvisations. Grace Slick had sung both "White Rabbit" and "Somebody to Love" with the group before jumping ship for the Airplane; the Society immediately disbanded, though their legacy is preserved on a couple posthumous albums of live material.

In 1966, several groups following the Airplane model began to achieve considerable popularity on the local circuit. The only one to rise to a comparable level of international fame (and then only briefly) were Big Brother & the Holding Company, who would have most likely been also-rans in the psychedelic sweepstakes if not for the addition of Janis Joplin as their lead vocalist. Their (more particularly, Joplin's) electrifying appearance at the Monterey Pop Festival in 1967 vaulted them to stardom almost overnight, but they had trouble both getting along and penning first-rate material, and Joplin left the group to go solo shortly after *Cheap Thrills* topped the charts in 1968.

The Monterey Pop Festival acted as a general lightning rod in drawing attention to the exploding San Francisco scene, which peaked in the summer of 1967, known as the "Summer of Love." Several of the bands performing at the festival already commanded huge local followings before committing their work to vinyl. The Grateful Dead and Quicksilver Messenger Service specialized in both blues-rock and improvised

---

Music Map

The San Francisco Sound

San Francisco Folk Rock
The Beau Brummels, The Vejtables, We Five

Early San Francisco Psychedelic Bands
The Great Society, The Mystery Trend, The Charlatans

San Francisco Acid Rock Stars
The Jefferson Airplane, Big Brother & The Holding Company, Quicksilver Messenger Service, Country Joe & The Fish, The Grateful Dead, Moby Grape, The Steve Miller Band

Late '60s San Francisco Psychedelia
Santana, Mad River
It's A Beautiful Day,
Lee Michaels

Non-Acid Rock '60s San Francisco-Area Rock Superstars
Sly & The Family Stone, Creedence Clearwater Revival

---

jams; both featured virtuoso instrumentalists (particularly lead guitarists Jerry Garcia of the Dead and John Cippolina of Quicksilver), but neither had consistently first-rate songwriters or vocalists. They, and several other San Francisco groups, found it nearly impossible to duplicate their live magic on record, and their late-'60s albums can sound kind of pale and tame in comparison to the glowing memories of their live performances.

A few other major groups of the era took much tighter approaches to their songwriting and recording, without forsaking the loose and joyful ambience that ranked as the San Francisco sound's most ingratiating traits. Country Joe & the Fish wrote both sharp political satire and druggy anthems, although they exhausted their supply of first-rate original material after their fine 1967 debut. Moby Grape were probably the tightest act of the era, at least initially, with three guitarists and five competent songwriters; their debut was an acclaimed collection of fiery straightahead rock with heavy blues and country influences, but their momentum dissipated almost immediately due to severe internal disputes and external pressures. The Steve Miller Band, initially the most blues-oriented of the area's acts, made their mark with psychedelic-tinged, bluesy late-'60s rock.

In addition to these internationally acclaimed bands were several acts that tapped into the San Francisco vibe with erratic, at times enthralling, results. It's a Beautiful Day, Mother Earth, and Lee Michaels (the last of whom is not always strictly identified with the scene) made worthwhile recordings; other decent acts such as the Other Half, Mad River, the Mystery Trend, and Frumious Bandersnatch are nowadays known only to record collectors and those who saw them in their heyday. Sly & the Family Stone and Creedence Clearwater Revival were both superstars, and both plugged into the progressive elements of the San Francisco Sound to some extent, but they were never really considered a big part of it; Sly & the Family Stone drew upon soul as much as psychedelia, and Creedence played rock in a more classic and economic tradition. And there were many obscure bands who played the city's live circuit, or released a record or two of sloppy loud guitars, half-baked psychedelic songwriting, and boring jams, that are deservedly forgotten.

The golden glow of the San Francisco Sound began to rapidly dissipate in the late '60s, principally due to the mundane reasons that erode many important rock genres. Some of the era's best groups, such as the Airplane, Moby Grape, Quicksilver, and Big Brother, suffered important personnel losses, ran short of inspiration and topflight material, and eventually broke up. Haight-Ashbury, originally a haven for youths seeking alternatives to corrupt mainstream society, suffered heavily from some of the same ills as the larger community, such as excessive drug use, crime, and poverty. The bohemian musicians that had emerged from such communities to become stars no longer lived in the neighborhood, and fresh talent didn't emerge to replenish them. The city's live circuit of psychedelic concerts, spearheaded by Chet Helms and Bill Graham, also dried up, fundamentally

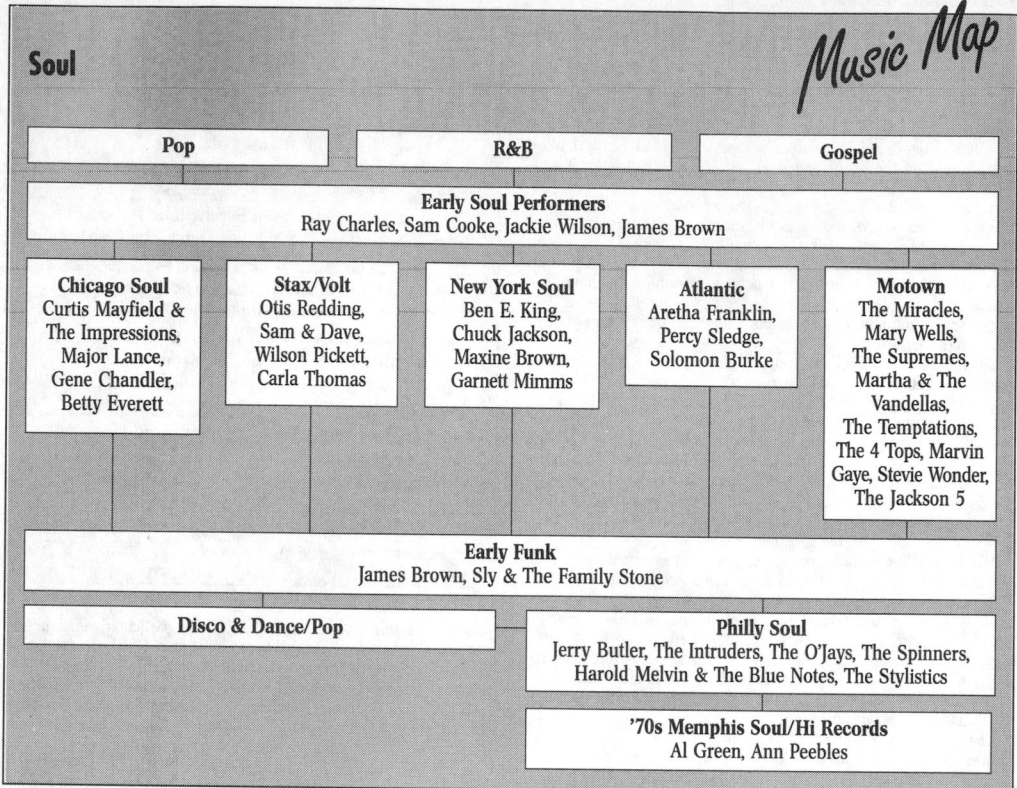

Soul

Music Map

Pop	R&B	Gospel

Early Soul Performers
Ray Charles, Sam Cooke, Jackie Wilson, James Brown

Chicago Soul	Stax/Volt	New York Soul	Atlantic	Motown
Curtis Mayfield & The Impressions, Major Lance, Gene Chandler, Betty Everett	Otis Redding, Sam & Dave, Wilson Pickett, Carla Thomas	Ben E. King, Chuck Jackson, Maxine Brown, Garnett Mimms	Aretha Franklin, Percy Sledge, Solomon Burke	The Miracles, Mary Wells, The Supremes, Martha & The Vandellas, The Temptations, The 4 Tops, Marvin Gaye, Stevie Wonder, The Jackson 5

Early Funk
James Brown, Sly & The Family Stone

Disco & Dance/Pop	Philly Soul
	Jerry Butler, The Intruders, The O'Jays, The Spinners, Harold Melvin & The Blue Notes, The Stylistics

'70s Memphis Soul/Hi Records
Al Green, Ann Peebles

changing the intimate performer-audience relationships that helped make the scene special.

Santana, which combined psychedelic rock with Afro-Latin influences, was the last superstar group to emerge from the San Francisco psychedelic community. By the early '70s, it was basically over, though of course a few of the genre's pioneers—such as Santana, the Grateful Dead, and Steve Miller—enjoyed long, successful, and increasingly mainstream careers. The San Francisco sound was a vital cog in the best psychedelic rock, and, along with the best British Invasion and folk-rock groups, was crucial in establishing rock as a vehicle for literate, self-consciously adventurous expression that drew from all manner of musical and social influences.

Recommended Recordings

Various Artists, *Nuggets Vol. 7: Early San Francisco* (Rhino)

The Beau Brummels, *Best of the Beau Brummels* (Rhino)

The Charlatans, *The Amazing Charlatans* (Big Beat, UK)

The Jefferson Airplane, *Jefferson Airplane Loves You* (RCA)

The Great Society, *Collector's Item* (Columbia)

Janis Joplin, *Janis* (Columbia/Legacy) (box set, includes recordings with Big Brother & the Holding Company)

Country Joe & the Fish, *Electric Music for the Mind and Body* (Vanguard)

Moby Grape, *Vintage: Very Best* (CBS)

Quicksilver Messenger Service, *Quicksilver Messenger Service* (Capitol)

The Grateful Dead, *Live/Dead* (Warner Brothers)

The Steve Miller Band, *Children of the Future* (Capitol)

Santana, *Santana* (Columbia)

Books

Summer of Love, by Joel Selvin (1994, Dutton)

San Francisco Nights, by Gene Sculatti & Davin Seay (1985, St. Martin's)

The Haight-Ashbury, by Charles Perry (1984, Rolling Stone Press)

Grace Slick: The Biography, by Barbara Rowes (1980, Doubleday)

Pearl: The Obsessions and Passions of Janis Joplin, by Ellis Amburn (1992, Warner Books)

—Richie Unterberger

Soul

More than almost any other genre of the rock era, soul is a wide-ranging and immensely diverse style that can only be delineated in the sketchiest manner within a few paragraphs. Peaking in the 1960s, it helped define the African-American experience with a passion, pride, and optimism rare in any art form.

Broadly speaking, soul was the combination of rhythm & blues, gospel, and pop. The gospel ingredient was most evident in the supremely emotional, pleading, and jubilant vocals and harmonies. Rock-solid rhythm sections, punchy horn arrangements, and tight instrumental and vocal ensemble work were also frequent hallmarks of the classic soul sound.

The forefathers of soul were veterans of 1950s rhythm & blues. Ray Charles was perhaps the first to merge gospel, pop, and rhythm and blues in a style that we recognize as a direct ancestor of soul with his 1954 hit "I Got a Woman." Other important pioneers were Jackie Wilson, Sam Cooke, and James Brown. They came from somewhat different backgrounds—Wilson from the R&B vocal group tradition, Cooke from straight gospel as the lead singer of the Soul Stirrers, Brown from the "chitlin" circuit—but they shared an appetite for constantly modernizing their sound with both pop crossover material and R&B-based work that put their emotions at the fore with an arresting grit, naked emotion, and increasingly mature lyrical concerns.

As R&B grew into soul in the early '60s, the arrangements became more intricate, as did the harmonies (though they were often rooted in doo wop, as is obvious from listening to the early work of the Miracles and the Impressions). Romance was usually the subject, but it often was a more complex, adult, and bittersweet form of love than the adolescent fare of much early rock 'n' roll and R&B. Songwriter/performer/producers like Smokey Robinson and Curtis Mayfield put a greater personal stamp on their product than was customary in the 1950s. The session players at labels like Stax/Volt and Motown, though sometimes uncredited on the releases, set a level of instrumental discipline and virtuosity that remains among the benchmark standards of musical excellence in contemporary popular music. Starting with the Drifters, strings were often used to tastefully embellish the material without detracting from the performers' gutsy power.

There were literally hundreds of soul performers who laid down bodies of work that endure several decades later. In many cases, the artists themselves grew enormously over the course of their career, and cannot be conveniently pigeonholed into a certain subgenre or peak output—Marvin Gaye, Aretha Franklin, Curtis Mayfield, and Stevie Wonder are only a few of those. There were certain regional styles that developed, although soul was such a nationwide, overlapping phenomenon that these too cannot be categorized too rigorously, and great acts like the Isley Brothers couldn't be conveniently pigeonholed into any certain school.

By far the most successful style of soul was the kind that came to be identified with Motown Records in Detroit. Emphasizing melodic hooks, bright, clear production, and an extraordinary roster of talented vocalists, Motown was the most successful independent label of its era, crossing over to the pop charts for literally hundreds of Top 20 hits during the 1960s. Instrumental in bringing the sounds of Black America into mainstream American life, Motown has been disdained by some latter-day critics for a formulaic approach, and for appealing to whites, teenagers, and pop listeners more than other kinds of down-home soul music. These are really fairly ridiculous assertions. Motown was if anything more popular with Black audiences than white ones, and its legendary performers—Smokey Robinson, the Temptations, Martha & the Vandellas, Marvin Gaye, Stevie Wonder, the Supremes, Mary Wells, the Four Tops, the Jackson 5, and many others—released an astonishingly large and diverse body of classic work in the 1960s and beyond.

Motown's most serious rival for soul supremacy was the Stax/Volt label, based in Memphis. With Booker T. & the MG's (stars in their own right) usually providing the backing, these records offered a funkier, rootsier brand of soul, with generally rawer vocals and a heavier reliance on horn riffs. Otis Redding, Wilson Pickett, Carla Thomas, and Sam & Dave were the biggest stars to emerge from the Stax/Volt label, which was absorbed into Atlantic in the late '60s. Atlantic Records itself was one of the most influential soul labels, with gritty soul sensations like Solomon Burke and Percy Sledge. A great deal of soul with a similarly down-home Southern sensibility also emerged from the legendary studios in Muscle Shoals, Alabama; Muscle Shoals players backed Aretha Franklin on many of her greatest sides.

In Chicago, performers like the Impressions, Jerry Butler, Betty Everett, Major Lance, and Gene Chandler established their own distinctive regional sound, prominently featuring blaring horn charts and smooth harmonic interplay. New York had a somewhat more pop-oriented, "uptown" sound, typified by Chuck Jackson and Maxine Brown, although as always there were rootsier exceptions that bridged both worlds, like Garnett Mimms, and artists who combined the best of both worlds, like Ben E. King (both as lead singer of the Drifters and as a solo artist). Philadelphia soul records leaned toward doo wop-like group harmonies, eventually evolving into a serious rival of Motown's production machines with the ascendance of Gamble & Huff and Thom Bell.

By the late '60s, soul was changing with the times. Motown-producer Norman Whitfield expanded the label's lyrical scope into psychedelia and social consciousness with songs like the Temptations' "Cloud Nine." James Brown pioneered funk music with his incredible churning rhythms backing increasingly assertive statements of Black pride. Sly & the Family Stone merged hippie concerns and funk on a string of hit singles and albums. In the early '70s, Motown veterans Marvin Gaye and Stevie Wonder broke free of the label's hit-oriented production process to issue vastly influential, album-length statements. The Philadelphia sound, string-drenched and impeccably produced and harmonized, took soul to another level of slickness. In Memphis, Al Green established himself as an heir to Otis Redding with Hi Records and the Memphis Horns.

Soul diminished as a commercial presence in the mid-'70s, as funk and disco began to put more emphasis on danceable rhythms than songwriting and singing. Al Green, seen by some fans as the standardbearer of the classic soul sound, turned to gospel; the once-thriving Stax/Volt empire collapsed in a confusing mess. Much Black soul music became increasingly middle-of-the-road, leading to the new genre of urban contemporary music. Soul is still very much alive, of course, in the harmonies and production that continue to inform contemporary African-American popular music, whether in funk, disco, dance-pop, or rap. The "classic" soul style lives on in different ways—old stars continue to release and record new material for a specialized audience, and veteran performers like Tina Turner and Patti LaBelle have achieved new levels of superstardom with their updated brand of contemporary soul.

Recommended Recordings

Various Artists, *Soul Shots* series (Rhino)
Various Artists, *The Complete Stax-Volt Singles 1959-1968* (Atlantic)
James Brown, *Star Time* (PolyGram)
Otis Redding, *Otis! The Definitive Otis Redding* (Rhino)
Aretha Franklin, *Queen of Soul: The Atlantic Recordings* (Rhino)
Curtis Mayfield & the Impressions, *Anthology 1961-1977* (MCA)
Sam Cooke, *Man & His Music* (RCA)

Music Map
Stax/Volt-Memphis Soul

Early Stax/Volt Stars
Carla Thomas, Rufus Thomas, Booker T. & The MGs

Stars of Stax/ Volt's Prime
Otis Redding, Sam & Dave, Albert King, Eddie Floyd, Johnnie Taylor, William Bell

'60s Stars Inspired By Stax/Volt
Wilson Pickett, Percy Sledge, Arthur Conley, Aretha Franklin

'70s Stax/Volt Stars
Isaac Hayes, The Staple Singers, The Bar-Kays

Goldwax
James Car

Hi Records
Al Green, Ann Peebles, Syl Johnson

Ray Charles, *Birth of Soul* (Rhino)
Ben E. King, *Anthology* (Rhino)
Sly & the Family Stone, *Anthology* (Epic)
Al Green, *Al Green's Greatest Hits* (HI)
The Isley Brothers, *Story, Vol. 1* (Rhino)
Wilson Pickett, *A Man and a Half: The Best of Wilson Pickett* (Rhino)
Jackie Wilson, *Mr. Excitement* (Rhino)
Solomon Burke, *Home in Your Heart* (Rhino)

Books

The Blackwell Guide to Soul Recordings, edited by Robert Pruter (Blackwell, 1993)
Where Did Our Love Go? The Rise and Fall of the Motown Sound, by Nelson George (St. Martin's Press, 1985)
Sweet Soul Music, by Peter Guralnick (Harper & Row, 1986)
Nowhere to Run: The Story of Soul Music, by Gerry Hirshey (Times Books, 1984)

            —Richie Unterberger

Stax/Volt and the Sound of Memphis Soul

Aside from Motown, the Memphis-based Stax label (along with its Volt subsidiary) was the most successful and influential soul record company of the '60s. The comparison shouldn't be taken too far: Motown was far more successful than Stax/Volt, which never crossed over into the pop market nearly as heavily as their Detroit-based competition. In its salad days, the Stax/Volt sound was nearly as identifiable as Motown, and embodied many of the most distinguishing traits of Southern soul, or "deep" soul, as it's sometimes called.

Stax was founded in the early '60s by Jim Stewart and his sister Estelle Axton, shortly after they'd taken teenaged Carla Thomas (daughter of R&B-legend Rufus Thomas) into the Top Ten on the Satellite label with the early soul ballad "Gee Whiz." In the Thomases, Stax already had a couple of first-class R&B/soul singers who would score consistent hits into the early '70s. The next Top Ten hit on Stax, the Mar-Keys' instrumental "Last Night," was a breakthrough on a couple levels. The combination of sleek horn lines, sharp guitar licks, and organ was a blueprint for the Stax soul sound; equally important, some of the Mar-Keys' members eventually formed the nucleus of Booker T. & the MG's, which virtually became Stax's house band for the next decade.

The MG's also ran off a series of instrumental hits that made them stars in their own right. On these, you can hear the sound of Memphis soul stripped down to its essence: the bluesy, surgeon-sharp leads and chords of guitarist Steve Cropper, the choked organ of Booker T. Jones, and the super-tight rhythm section of Duck Dunn and the late Al Jackson. When they played sessions, they were often augmented by the Memphis Horns, whose similarly spare but beefy riffs also came to characterize the Stax/Volt sound. In contrast to the brilliant assembly-line precision of the Motown factory, the Memphis studios created a looser and funkier groove, a reflection of the more casual atmosphere of both the control room and the region itself.

The instrumental backing was just one key part of the Stax/Volt-Memphis equation. The material, penned by such greats as David Porter and Isaac Hayes, had much more of a country influence than most '60s soul. Mind you, you'd never mistake it for Grand Ole Opry fodder, but the melodies, chord changes, and plaintive, emotive tone of much of the material betrayed the melting pot of Black and white southern influences, even in a society as segregated as the American South was in the 1960s. Memphis had been an important blues center for decades, and that influence was also apparent in both the material and the arrangements (with bluesman Albert King, Stax/Volt would successfully merge blues and soul). And the vocals betrayed a strong gospel feel—not that gospel wasn't strongly felt in the soul being produced everywhere else in the United States as well.

Stax/Volt releases were hugely successful in the R&B and soul charts, but not nearly as big with white pop audiences, though there were plenty of Top 40 entries on the label throughout the '60s. Several explanations could be offered for this, none of them necessarily correct or valid; the Stax/Volt sound was certainly grittier, slower, and more R&B-based than the most successful pop-soul of the period. Stax/Volt performers were certainly heroes to many white rock musicians, from the Rolling Stones on down. A 1967 tour of Europe by the Stax/Volt Revue (documented on several recordings) was a huge success, enabling the musicians to realize for the first time just how much of an impact they were making internationally.

The sessionmen and songwriters were crucial cogs in the Stax/Volt machine, but as with Motown, one shouldn't overlook the fact that the singers were the most important factor. Carla Thomas, Rufus Thomas, as well as names which are revered nowadays mostly by hardcore soul fans, such as Johnnie Taylor, Eddie Floyd, and William Bell—all made the songs their own (and often wrote the songs as well). The most popular Stax/Volt acts of the mid-'60s were Sam & Dave, who brought the gospel elements of Memphis soul to the forefront, and Otis Redding, one of the most revered vocalists in rock and soul history. Redding, already a soul superstar, seemed poised for a breakthrough to wide pop stardom after a hugely successful appearance at the Monterey Pop Festival in 1967. It happened, but only after Redding's death, in the wake of which "Dock of the Bay"—a classic which pointed to new introspective and personal directions for both Redding and Stax/Volt—went to No. 1 in early 1968.

Redding's death notwithstanding, Stax/Volt seemed poised to enter an era of great prosperity in the late '60s, but the empire became unraveled in a series of mammoth mishaps which rank it among the most tragic stories in the rock business. In 1968, Stax/Volt ended its partnership with Atlantic, opting for bigger corporate distribution. Atlantic, which had arranged for Wilson Pickett to record a clutch of mid-'60s classics at Stax's studios that were Stax/Volt recordings in all but name, took the Redding and Sam & Dave catalogs with them.

Stax, frustrated by the economics of leasing studio facilities to outside labels and performers, had already restricted itself to in-house projects in 1966. Atlantic's Jerry Wexler responded by approximating the Stax sound (extremely successfully, from both aesthetic and commercial viewpoints) at other southern studios, including Fame and Muscle Shoals in Alabama, and Criteria in Miami. Mid- and late-'60s classics by Percy Sledge, Arthur Conley, Aretha Franklin, and others may not be Stax/Volt recordings, but sonically they would certainly fit into the label's vision comfortably.

Stax continued to score hits well into the 1970s with a vast roster, including several of their most dependable '60s performers, and new additions such as the Staple Singers and Isaac Hayes. With the dissolution of Booker T. & the MG's, the Stax sound grew more diffuse, though it retained much of its earthy identity. But in the mid-'70s, Stax ran into a quagmire of financial troubles that are too labyrinthine to detail in less than a few pages. In early 1976, it was closed by order of a federal bankruptcy court judge.

Stax/Volt, incidentally, didn't have a monopoly on Memphis soul. The small Goldwax label issued releases in the '60s that are coveted by deep soul collectors, particularly those recordings by James Carr, esteemed by some cultists as one of the greatest soul vocalists ever. As noted above, the sound of Stax/Volt was successfully emulated and recreated at other studios. And in the early '70s, Hi Records, featuring the Hi Rhythm Section and, often, musicians who had played at Stax/Volt (such as the Memphis Horns), established itself as a major source of the era's best funky soul. Al Green was the label's only superstar, but other Hi performers like Ann Peebles and Syl Johnson enjoyed a lot of success among the soul audience with recordings that are usually judged superior to the ones issued by Stax/Volt in the early '70s.

When Stax/Volt shut its doors, though, it was a major blow to the city's music scene, eliminating a prime source of work and inspiration for many of the city's brightest talents (some of whom had moved on to other music centers anyway). Arguably, it was a blow from which the region has yet to recover; since the advent of Sun Records, Memphis had been a central location for much of rock, R&B, and soul's finest moments, but today it's somewhat of a musical ghost town in terms of local production. The Stax/Volt story is exhaustively detailed in the liner notes of the three Stax/Volt box sets, and journalist Rob Bowman is currently working on a book about the label.

Recommended Recordings

Various Artists, *The Complete Stax/Volt Soul Singles Vol. 1 1959-1968* (Atlantic)

Various Artists, *The Complete Stax/Volt Soul Singles Vol. 2 1968-1971* (Stax)

Various Artists, *The Complete Stax/Volt Soul Singles Vol. 3 1972-1975* (Stax)

Booker T. & the MG's, *The Very Best of Booker T. & the MG's* (Rhino)

Carla Thomas, *Gee Whiz: The Best of Carla Thomas* (Rhino)

Otis Redding, *Otis! The Definitive Otis Redding* (Rhino)

Wilson Pickett, *The Exciting Wilson Pickett* (Atlantic)

Sam & Dave, *Sweat 'N' Soul* (Rhino/Atlantic)

Johnnie Taylor, *Chronicle* (Stax)

James Carr, *Essential James Carr* (Razor & Tie)

Al Green, *Greatest Hits* (Hi)

Various Artists, *Hi Times: The Hi Records R&B Years* (The Right Stuff)

Rufus Thomas, *The Best of Rufus Thomas* (Rhino)

—*Richie Unterberger*

Blue-Eyed Soul

"Can white men sing the blues?" That's been a point of contention in the worlds of rock and soul since white musicians began singing music with heavy debts to rhythm & blues. White attempts to sing African-American-derived music have often been embarrassing (if sometimes touching in their naivete). But at the same time, some whites have crossed into the world of R&B and soul with a natural ease that proves that music, like all good things in life, is color-blind. During soul music's heyday, a handful of whites handled the challenge with confidence, giving rise to the relatively small but important sub-genre of soul music called blue-eyed soul.

The roots of blue-eyed soul could probably be traced back as far as Elvis Presley's legendary Sun singles, on which he masterfully interpreted a handful of blues and R&B classics. It can also be detected in the many Italian-American doo wop singers during that music's last phase, as well as early '60s acts like Dion and the Four Seasons who borrowed heavily from R&B phrasing and harmonies.

The first of the classic blue-eyed soul acts, and one which was instrumental in defining the genre, were the Righteous Brothers. Hailing from Orange County, CA, of all places, Bill Medley and Bobby Hatfield looked very white, but sounded Black. After teaming up with Phil Spector in the mid-'60s, they reeled off a brief string of huge hits that were soaked with gospel feeling as any African-American soul, but were unable to maintain their artistic or commercial momentum after their association with Spector ended.

The most successful blue-eyed soul group of the '60s were the Rascals. Young veterans of New York's Italian-American rock 'n' roll scene, they flavored their strong (and mostly original) material with horns, harmonies, and a touch of British Invasion energy. Although they worked within the self-contained rock band format, playing their own instruments and writing their own songs, their sound owed as much, if not more, to soul as '60s rock trends. They were also one of the relatively few blue-eyed soul acts to successfully change with the times, writing increasingly reflective and sophisticated material, culminating with the rabble-rousing anthem "People Got to Be Free" in 1968.

Blue-eyed soul acts tended to spring up in the proximity of regions with active soul scenes. Detroit's biggest contribution to the genre were Mitch Ryder and the Detroit Wheels, who served up some of the sweatiest soul-rock hybrids ever waxed. Motown couldn't help but influence a lot of the city's white rock and garage bands, and the Motor City sound is reflected in Michigan's fine regional rock hits of the time by the Rationals and the early singles of Bob Seger.

White southern performers also absorbed the inflections of deep soul into their own earthy sounds. John Fred and Tony Joe White displayed the influence of New Orleans and Louisiana R&B and soul in their brand of swamp pop; Bill Deal and the Rhondels played a kind of soul frat-rock that drew from the "beach music" cult of the Carolinas; Roy Head drew upon the melting pot of Texas blues and R&B for one of the mid-'60s' best one-shot hits, "Treat Her Right." In Memphis, Dan Penn, a white Alabaman who helped write many great deep soul records, produced hits by the Box Tops; teenage lead singer Alex Chilton's vocals were so unnaturally gravelly that many listeners were convinced he was Black. In Los Angeles, there were several Latin soul-rock-R&B acts, the best of which were Thee Midniters (although the group also played convincing Rolling Stones-styled garage rock).

The line between R&B-influenced rock 'n' roll and blue-eyed soul is a thin one that was skirted by many of the British Invasion's finest performers. Certainly Eric Burdon (of the Animals) Stevie Winwood (of the Spencer Davis Group and Traffic), and Van Morrison were extremely soulful singers, even if their material and the sound of their backing groups were more rock-oriented than classic soul grooves. Georgie Fame probably fit the classic blue-eyed soul mold more than any other British Invasion performer, although he also owed quite a bit to Mose Allison's brand of jazz. Dusty Springfield was the best female blue-eyed soul singer of the '60s, though she also sang girl group, rock, and pop ballad material; at the end of the '60s, she traveled to Stax studios in Memphis to cut *Dusty in Memphis*, considered by many listeners as one of the finest white soul albums of all time.

It's worth pointing out that many classic soul records of the '60s by Black performers featured white musicians. Booker T. & the MG's, an integrated ensemble featuring the economic, biting licks of white guitarist Steve Cropper, played on most of the great Stax/Volt soul hits of the '60s, as well as cutting a lot of instrumental soul smashes on their own. Stax/Volt's strongest rival in the field of deep southern soul was the Muscle Shoals Studio in Alabama, which also featured white musicians on many of their sessions, backing soul greats from Aretha Franklin on down. Duane Allman may be mostly known for helping to found Southern-rock with the Allman Brothers, but he also played guitar on sessions by Franklin, Wilson Pickett, Clarence Carter, and King Curtis.

The heyday of blue-eyed soul, like soul music itself, was in the 1960s; after that decade, it was a more scattered presence, although acts like Hall & Oates, the Average White Band, Boz Scaggs, Robert Palmer, David Bowie (in one of his many phases), the latter-day Bee Gees, and Billy Swan all carried the blue-eyed soul torch to large degrees. Contemporary acts like Michael Bolton and George Michael have also been labeled as blue-eyed soul, although their material owes more to classic MOR pop than the original pioneers of the style.

Recommended Recordings

Various Artists, *Soul Shots Vol. 6: Blue-Eyed Soul* (Rhino)
The Righteous Brothers, *Anthology 1962-74* (Rhino)
The Rascals, *Anthology (1965-1972)* (Rhino)
Mitch Ryder, *Rev-Up: The Best of Mitch Ryder & the Detroit Wheels* (Rhino)
The Box Tops, *The Best of the Box Tops: Soul Deep* (Arista)
Dusty Springfield, *Dusty in Memphis* (Rhino)
John Fred & the Playboys, *The History of John Fred & the Playboys* (Paula)
Tony Joe White, *The Best of Tony Joe White* (Warner)
Georgie Fame, *20 Beat Classics* (RSO)
Thee Midniters, *The Best of Thee Midniters* (Rhino)

–Richie Unterberger

Blues-Rock

The blues and rock 'n' roll are often divided by the thinnest of the margins. Blues, more than any other musical style, influenced the birth of rock 'n' roll, and the amplified electric blues of Chicago, Memphis, and other cities during the 1950s was separated from the new music only by its more traditional chord patterns, cruder production values, and narrower market. The term "blues-rock" came into being around the mid-'60s, when white musicians infused electric blues with somewhat louder guitars and flashy images that helped the music make inroads into the white rock audience.

Many of the early blues-rockers were British musicians who had been schooled by Alexis Korner. Helping to organize the first overseas tours by many major American bluesmen, Korner—as well as his former boss Chris Barber, and his early collaborator Cyril Davies—was more responsible than any other musician for introducing the blues to Britain. More important, he acted as a mentor to many younger musicians who would form the R&B-oriented wing of the British Invasion, including Jack Bruce, members of Manfred Mann, Eric Clapton, and, most significantly, the Rolling Stones, whose lead vocalist, Mick Jagger, sang with Korner before the Stones were firmly established.

The Rolling Stones featured a wealth of stone cold blues in their early repertoire. They and other British groups like the Yardbirds and Animals brought a faster and brasher flavor to traditional numbers. They would quickly branch out from 12-bar blues to R&B, soul, and finally, original material of a much more innovative and rock-oriented nature, without ever losing sight of their blues roots.

Several British acts, however, were more steadfast in their devotion to traditional blues, sacrificing commercial success for purism. These included the early Graham Bond Organisation (who featured future Cream members Jack Bruce and Ginger Baker) and, more significantly, John Mayall's Bluesbreakers. In early 1965, Mayall's group provided a refuge for Eric Clapton, who left the Yardbirds on the eve of international success in protest of their forays into pop-rock. His sole album

with Mayall, *Bluesbreakers with Eric Clapton* (1966), was an unexpected Top Ten hit in the UK. Clapton's lightning fast and fluid leads were vastly influential, both on fellow musicians and in introducing tough electric blues to a wide audience.

While Clapton would rapidly depart the Bluesbreakers to form Cream (who took blues-rock to more amplified and psychedelic levels), Mayall continued to be Britain's foremost exponent of blues-rock, as a bandleader of innumerable Bluesbreakers lineups. Many musicians of note were schooled by Mayall, the most prominent being Clapton's successors, Peter Green and future Rolling Stone Mick Taylor. Like Clapton, Green left Mayall after just one album, forming the first incarnation of Fleetwood Mac with a couple of members of Mayall's rhythm section, John McVie and Mick Fleetwood. Under Green's helm, Fleetwood Mac were the finest British blues-rock act of the late '60s. They invested electric Chicago blues with zest and humor, but their own material—featuring Green's icy guitar tone, rich vocals, and personal, often somber lyrics—was more impressive, and extremely successful in Britain, where they racked up several hit albums and singles.

As a bandleader of rotating lineups featuring budding guitar geniuses, Chicago harmonica player Paul Butterfield was Mayall's American counterpart; the two even recorded a rare EP together in the late '60s. The Paul Butterfield Blues Band's first pair of albums featured the sterling guitar duo of Mike Bloomfield and Elvin Bishop, as well as bona fide African-American Chicago bluesmen in the rhythm section. Willing to tackle soul, jazz, and even psychedelic jams in addition to Chicago blues, they were the first American blues-rock band, and perhaps the best.

While blues-rock was less of a commercial or artistic force in the US than the UK, several other American blues-rockers of note emerged in the '60s. Canned Heat were probably the most successful, reaching the Top 20 with "On the Road Again" and an electric update of an obscure rural blues number, "Going up the Country." Steve Miller played mostly blues, with Barry Goldberg and as the leader of his own band, in his early days before tuning into the psychedelic ethos of his adopted base of San Francisco. Captain Beefheart was briefly a white counterpart to Howlin' Wolf before heading off on a furious avant-garde tangent.

In New York, Bob Dylan used Mike Bloomfield on much of his *Highway 61 Revisited* album, and teamed with the Butterfield Band for his enormously controversial electric appearance at the 1965 Newport Folk Festival. John Hammond recorded blues-rock in the mid-'60s with future members of the Band, and Dion cut some overlooked blues-rock sides after being exposed to classic blues by Hammond's father, the legendary Columbia A&R man John Hammond, Sr. The Blues Project, led by Al Kooper, often reworked blues songs with

The following is the content of the Music Map image:

Music Map

Blue-Eyed Soul

R&B	Early Soul

Blue-Eyed Soul Forerunners
Dion, The 4 Seasons

Blue-Eyed Soul Stars
The Righteous Brothers, The Rascals

Detroit Blue-Eyed Soul	Southern Blue-Eyed Soul	British Blue-Eyed Soul
Mitch Ryder, The Rationals	The Boxtops, John Fred, Roy Head, Tony Joe White, Bill Deal & The Rhondels	Georgie Fame, Dusty Springfield

Blue-Eyed Soul of the '70s
Hall & Oates, The Average White Band, Robert Palmer, Boz Scaggs

Blues Rock

Music Map

Post-War Electric Blues
Muddy Waters, Howlin' Wolf, Jimmy Reed, Sonny Boy Williamson, Otis Rush, John Lee Hooker

American Blues Rock
Paul Butterfield, Mike Bloomfield, Elvin Bishop, John Hammond, Jr., Canned Heat, The Blues Project, Steve Miller, Roy Buchanan

British Blues Mentors
Alexis Korner, Chris Barber, Cyril Davies

Early British Blues Rock
John Mayall, Graham Bond

Early British R&B
The Rolling Stones, The Yardbirds, Manfred Mann, The Pretty Things

Southern Blues Rock
The Allman Brothers, Johnny Winter, ZZ Top, Stevie Ray Vaughan

Psychedelic Blues Rock
Cream, Jimi Hendrix

Second Generation Blues Rock
Fleetwood Mac, Ten Years After, Savoy Brown, Chicken Shack, Rory Gallagher

Blues-Influenced British Hard Rock
The Jeff Beck Group, Led Zeppelin, Free

rock arrangements, although their vision was too eclectic to be pigeonholed as blues-rock, also encompassing folk-rock, pop-rock, and psychedelia.

The influence of the first generation of blues-rockers is evident in the early recordings of Jimi Hendrix, and indeed Jimi would always feature a strong element of the blues in his material. Albert King and B.B. King couldn't exactly be called blues-rockers, but their late '60s material betrays contemporary influences from the worlds of rock and soul that found them leaning more in that direction. Early hard rock bands like Led Zeppelin, Free, and the Jeff Beck Group played a great deal of blues, though not enough for purists to consider them actual blues acts.

The blues-rock form became more pedestrian and boogie-oriented as the '60s came to a close. From Britain, Ten Years After, Savoy Brown, Climax Blues Band, Rory Gallagher, Chicken Shack, Juicy Lucy, and Foghat all achieved some success. In the US, blues-rock was the cornerstone of the Allman Brothers' innovative early '70s recordings (which in turned spawned the blues-influenced school of Southern-rock), and Johnny Winter had success with a much more traditional approach.

While blues-rock hasn't been a major commercial force since the late '60s, the style has spawned some hugely successful acts, like ZZ Top and Foghat, as well as influencing all hard rock since the late '60s to some degree. The success of Stevie Ray Vaughan in the 1980s, and groups like Blues Traveler and Spin Doctors in the 1990s, shows that its audience is far from dead. And it is a cliché, but it is often true, that many white listeners would be unaware of Black blues performers if they hadn't been led to them through the work of white blues-rock bands.

Recommended Recordings

John Mayall, *Bluesbreakers with Eric Clapton* (PolyGram)
John Mayall, *London Blues (1964-1969)* (PolyGram)
The Paul Butterfield Blues Band, *East-West* (Elektra)
Fleetwood Mac, *Black Magic Woman* (Epic)
Fleetwood Mac, *Then Play On* (Reprise)
Jimi Hendrix, *Blues* (MCA)
The Graham Bond Organisation, *The Sound of '65* (Edsel)
Canned Heat, *Best of Canned Heat* (EMI)
Cream, *Fresh Cream* (Polydor)
John Hammond, Jr. *So Many Roads* (Vanguard)
The Allman Brothers, *At Fillmore East* (Polydor)
Duffy Power, *Little Boy Blue* (Demon/Edsel)

Books

Blues—The British Connection, by Bob Brunning (1986, Blandford Press)

—*Richie Unterberger*

Country-Rock

Country-rock is one of the hardest rock 'n' roll styles to map and define. Country music, of course, was integral to the birth of rock 'n' roll, and has continued to exert a huge influence on rock until the present. You can find innumerable examples of rock 'n' roll performers that are heavily soaked with country, from Elvis Presley to Elvis Costello. As a label and as a movement, however, country-rock is primarily identified with a school of bands in the late '60s and early '70s that brought the modern and irreverent qualities of rock to the more traditional musical values of country music.

There are many antecedents to country-rock; the close harmonies and acoustic guitars on much of the Everly Brothers' material foreshadows much of it. In the mid-'60s, Del Shannon recorded an entire album of Hank Williams tunes, George Jones and Gene Pitney teamed up for an LP of duets, and the trashy British R&B/punk band the Downliners Sect recorded a bizarre straight country album that was unnoticed commercially and unsuccessful artistically. Several of the '60s top groups dallied successfully with countrified rock 'n' roll at times, such as the Beatles (especially around the *Beatles for Sale* period, on tracks like "I Don't Want to Spoil the Party"), the early Byrds ("Satisfied Mind," "Mr. Spaceman," "Time Between"), and Buffalo Springfield ("Go and Say Goodbye," "Kind Woman"); all of these bands placed a premium on close harmonies, and could incorporate country signatures into their sound with natural ease when the spirit moved them.

The term "country-rock" actually began to get used and thrown around in 1968, when most of the major rock acts were retreating from their psychedelic experiments into a "back-to-basics" approach. Bob Dylan, who had never embraced psychedelia in the first place, led the way with his *John Wesley Harding* album. Dylan had recorded in Nashville before, but this early 1968 effort was far more basic in instrumentation and far more country in tone. In 1969, he would largely eschew his inscrutable wordplay for basic homilies on *Nashville Skyline*, as well as record an entire unreleased LP with one of his chief mentors, Johnny Cash.

The true god of country-rock, though, was guitarist and singer Gram Parsons. As the leader of the International Submarine Band, he recorded an album in 1967, *Safe at Home*, that prominently used pedal steel guitar. The LP is seen by some scholars as the first true country-rock record, although it was little noticed upon its release. Shortly afterwards, Parsons joined the Byrds, and was almost single-handedly responsible for altering the band's focus from folk-rock to country-rock. Byrds leader Roger McGuinn had been entertaining the idea of an ambitious double album with heavy use of electronics, but the project was scuppered in favor of *Sweetheart of the Rodeo*. The 1968 release is almost universally hailed as one of the first and best country-rock efforts.

The Byrds' country-rock era was short; Parsons left the band after a year. Longtime Byrds bassist Chris Hillman left the group around the

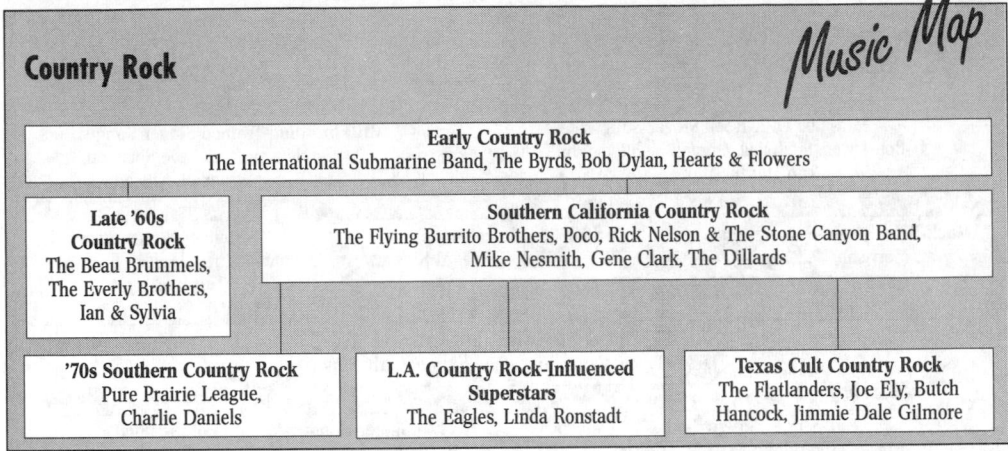

Early Country Rock
The International Submarine Band, The Byrds, Bob Dylan, Hearts & Flowers

Late '60s Country Rock
The Beau Brummels, The Everly Brothers, Ian & Sylvia

Southern California Country Rock
The Flying Burrito Brothers, Poco, Rick Nelson & The Stone Canyon Band, Mike Nesmith, Gene Clark, The Dillards

'70s Southern Country Rock
Pure Prairie League, Charlie Daniels

L.A. Country Rock-Influenced Superstars
The Eagles, Linda Ronstadt

Texas Cult Country Rock
The Flatlanders, Joe Ely, Butch Hancock, Jimmie Dale Gilmore

same time, and the pair quickly teamed to form the nucleus of the Flying Burrito Brothers. Parsons only stayed with the band for a few albums, but these works, also prominently featuring Sneeky Pete Kleinow on pedal steel, are the purest and most influential country-rock hybrids, and rest among the few major country-rock recordings that are not in reality closer to rock than country.

Country music may have sprung from the southern states, but country-rock primarily flourished in Southern California. Other country-rock acts of note in the late '60s included the little-known Hearts & Flowers, who actually surfaced before 1968, but were classified as folk-rock at the time, and Poco, featuring former Buffalo Springfield members Richie Furay and Jim Messina. In northern California, the New Riders of the Purple Sage established themselves as a more countrified and laidback cousin of the Grateful Dead in the early '70s.

Some veteran acts primarily associated with other forms of rock and folk became country-rockers for a time in the late '60s. Folk-rock pioneers the Beau Brummels went to Nashville to record *Bradley's Barn* at the legendary studio of the same name; the Everly Brothers' *Roots* was their most critically acclaimed post-early-'60s work; Ian & Sylvia moved from contemporary folk to country as a duo and leaders of the band Great Speckled Bird; Rick Nelson had an artistic renaissance while fronting the Stone Canyon Band, which featured future Eagle Randy Meisner. Former Byrd Gene Clark recorded country-rock on his own and as part of Dillard & Clark. The Dillards themselves, primarily known as a bluegrass act before the late '60s, had already acted as important figures in folk-rock by helping teach the Byrds harmony vocals, and employing Dewey Martin on drums before he left to join Buffalo Springfield. On 1968's *Wheatstraw Suite*, they became one of the few noted country-rock performers to move into the style from country rather than rock.

Country-rock wasn't big commercially, and may have made its greatest impact in terms of its influence on other performers. The Band, the Grateful Dead, Creedence Clearwater Revival, and George Harrison, for instance, could not be called country-rock performers by any means, but all recorded some impressive country-rock material on their late-'60s and early-'70s albums. Gram Parsons was a big influence on the Rolling Stones around this time, and on Keith Richards in particular, though it should be pointed out that the Stones had fused country and rock as far back as 1966 on "High and Dry." Still, their *Let It Bleed* and *Sticky Fingers* albums had quite a few country licks, most famously on "Wild Horses" (which appeared as a cover by the Flying Burrito Brothers before the Stones released their own version).

Country-rock hasn't gotten much attention as a movement since the early '70s. Commercially, it found its greatest success in the mid-'70s on hits by the Eagles (who featured ex-members of the Burritos, Poco, and the Stone Canyon Band) and Linda Ronstadt, who absorbed country-rock into their brands of soft rock and pop. Southern bands like Pure Prairie League and Charlie Daniels had some success with more southern-fried sounds, and Southern-rock bands like the Allman Brothers, the Ozark Mountain Daredevils, and Lynyrd Skynyrd recorded some country-influenced material, although their focus remained blues-rock and hard rock. In the 1980s and 1990s, it could be argued that Nashville has been a lot more successful in borrowing from rock than the other way around.

Country-rock arguably never recovered from the death of Gram Parsons in 1973, but it's remained alive and kicking, if hardly omnipresent. Elvis Costello made an all-out country album, albeit a commercial flop,

in 1981 with *Almost Blue*, country music informs much of Neil Young's work, in whatever decade that he's working; alternative rockers like the Meat Puppets and the Jayhawks have leaned heavily on country-rock at times. Texas eccentrics Joe Ely, Butch Hancock, and Jimmie Dale Gilmore (all of whom have played with each other at some point) have formed a sort of extended family for their brand of maverick country-rock. Once in a while a country-rock band will get a big push, like Lone Justice, but the hybrid seems to resist huge commercial success.

Recommended Recordings

The Byrds, *Sweetheart of the Rodeo* (Columbia)
The Flying Burrito Brothers, *Farther Along: The Best of the Flying Burrito Brothers* (A&M)
The International Submarine Band, *Safe at Home* (Rhino)
Hearts & Flowers, *Now Is the Time / Of Horses, Kids and Forgotten Things* (Edsel)
The Beau Brummels, *Bradley's Barn* (Edsel, UK)
Poco, *Pickin' up the Pieces* (Epic)
The Everly Brothers, *Roots* (Warner)
The Dillards, *Wheatstraw Suite* (Elektra)
Bob Dylan, *John Wesley Harding* (Columbia)
Various Artists, *Hillbilly Fever Vol. 5* (Rhino)
The Flatlanders, *More a Legend than a Band* (Rounder)
Neil Young, *Harvest Moon* (Reprise)

Books

Gram Parsons: A Music Biography, by Sid Griffin (Sierra, 1985)
Hickory Wind: The Gram Parsons Story, by Ben Fong-Torres
                                              —Richie Unterberger

Singer-Songwriters

The definition of a rock singer-songwriter is elusive. Chuck Berry, the Beatles, Marvin Gaye, Patti Smith, Elvis Costello, Paul Westerberg, Liz Phair—are they not all singers and songwriters of the first degree? Of course they are, but none of them fit the label of a singer-songwriter that has been applied since the form's heyday in the late '60s and early '70s. Generally speaking, singer-songwriters put the emphasis on their material, rather than their vocal delivery, stylistic signatures, or musical backing (although those factors were certainly important). Both the compositions and the arrangements are written primarily as solo vehicles, rather than with full rock 'n' roll bands in mind. Singer-songwriters almost exclusively play guitar and piano; quite a few play both. More than most rock styles, singer/songwriting records draw from folk and acoustic music. There are a higher percentage of women using the singer-songwriter format than you'll find in almost any other form of rock. The material tends toward the introspective, sensitive, romantic, and confessional, though it is not as wholly self-absorbed as some critics claim. They are not singles-oriented artists (though there have been quite a few massive singer-songwriter hit singles), but craft albums as complete, flowing statements.

The golden age of singer-songwriters was in many respects a blend of American contemporary folk and professional pop-rock songcraft. In the early '60s, Bob Dylan was more responsible than any other songwriter for pioneering personal expression and idiosyncratic lyrics; when he moved from acoustic folk arrangements to folk-rock, many of his peers followed. In the mid- and late '60s, Fred Neil, Tim Hardin, Phil

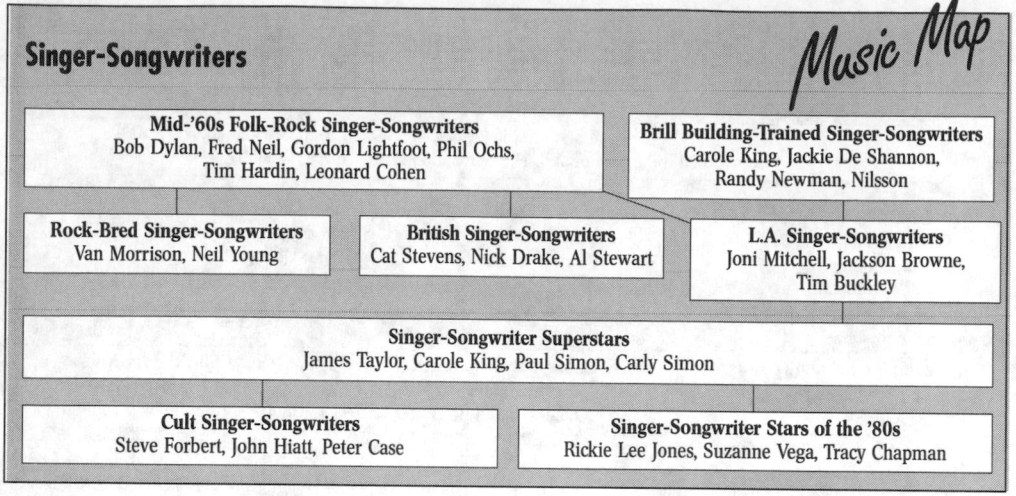

Singer-Songwriters

Music Map

Mid-'60s Folk-Rock Singer-Songwriters
Bob Dylan, Fred Neil, Gordon Lightfoot, Phil Ochs,
Tim Hardin, Leonard Cohen

Brill Building-Trained Singer-Songwriters
Carole King, Jackie De Shannon,
Randy Newman, Nilsson

Rock-Bred Singer-Songwriters
Van Morrison, Neil Young

British Singer-Songwriters
Cat Stevens, Nick Drake, Al Stewart

L.A. Singer-Songwriters
Joni Mitchell, Jackson Browne,
Tim Buckley

Singer-Songwriter Superstars
James Taylor, Carole King, Paul Simon, Carly Simon

Cult Singer-Songwriters
Steve Forbert, John Hiatt, Peter Case

Singer-Songwriter Stars of the '80s
Rickie Lee Jones, Suzanne Vega, Tracy Chapman

Ochs, and Gordon Lightfoot were some of the more notable folkies who followed Dylan into singer-songwriter territory.

There was also a school of songwriters who came to the singer/songwriting camp from the opposite direction of pop-rock. Composers like Randy Newman, Jackie De Shannon, Nilsson, and Carole King began their professional careers primarily as songwriters supplying material for pop acts, not as performers in their own right. De Shannon—an extremely underrated pioneer of the singer-songwriter genre—was the first of these to become a recording star on her own. By the late '60s, many others had stepped out from behind the scenes to begin singing their own songs, even if their voices and images didn't conform to normal commercial music business standards of what was marketable.

Not all came from one wing or the other, of course. Leonard Cohen was already an established poet when he ventured into the musical arena with material that ranks among the most literary rock ever committed to vinyl. Laura Nyro, one of the first critically acclaimed singer-songwriters, drew upon soul and Tin Pan Alley. Neil Young and Van Morrison were seasoned rock 'n' roll performers as members of influential '60s bands, although Young's work has been too eclectic and, at times, fiercely rocking for him to be classified as a singer-songwriter in the classic mold. Paul Simon, as many have pointed out, drew equally from pop and folk traditions, and was a veteran folk-rock star as half of Simon & Garfunkel before moving into more personal territory as a solo act.

Singer-songwriters were overwhelmingly white, middle-class, and well-educated; unsurprisingly, perhaps, many were based in Southern California or the Northeast, particularly Los Angeles or New York City. Los Angeles was always a chief wellspring of folk-rock, and in the late '60s, many talented singer-songwriters emerged that helped define the sound's folk-pop, laidback milieu. The best of these, Joni Mitchell, actually (like Neil Young) hailed from Canada, but was based in L.A. by the time she began recording.

Mitchell's acoustic guitar- and piano-based sound, along with her intimate vocals and largely romantic themes, was a prototype of sorts for the singer-songwriter genre, although she moved on to experiment with jazz in both her vocals and arrangements after reaching superstardom in the mid-'70s.

Other important Southern California singer-songwriters were Randy Newman, who infused the form with humor and (occasionally bitter) satire, and Jackson Browne, whose even-tempoed, easygoing ruminations have defined, for better or worse, the mellow L.A. rock sound in the minds of many listeners. A more eclectic singer-songwriter from the region was Tim Buckley, who dovetailed with psychedelia, jazz, soul, and just plain strange vocal experimentation within the singer-songwriter format.

As far as bringing singer-songwriters to Middle America, no performer was more influential than Carole King, who had already enjoyed a long career dating back to the early '60s as one of America's most successful songwriters. Her 1971 album *Tapestry* remains one of the best-selling recordings of all time. James Taylor, perhaps, was King's closest counterpart; his cover version of King's "You've Got a Friend" (from Tapestry) made it to No. 1, and his 1970 album *Sweet Baby James* epitomized the calming soft rock trends of the early '70s.

Singer-songwriters weren't as big a deal in Britain, but several did emerge that put their own spins on the form. Al Stewart took a more narrative, fanciful, and third-person approach; Nick Drake delved into dark and ambiguous themes that the stars found uncomfortable, or were unwilling to explore. Cat Stevens, the most successful British singer-songwriter of the '70s, was also the most similar in sound and content to his American counterparts.

Singer-songwriters—like almost everything else, but even more so—were a target of early punk and new wave performers, who disdained what they viewed as the genre's self-satisfied, complacent hippie homilies. The style, however, had already crested by the time punk arrived. The huge stars remained popular, sometimes at the same plateau (Paul Simon), more often at steady but diminishing levels. New crops of talent, however, did not arrive; there were occasional waves from performers like Rickie Lee Jones, and critical cults for artists like Steve Forbert, Peter Case, and John Hiatt, whose sheafs of good press never translated into major record sales.

Suzanne Vega and Tracy Chapman were by far the biggest singer-songwriter stars to emerge after 1980, and others like Shawn Colvin, Joe Henry, and Luka Bloom continue to make their mark, although usually more with the critics than the masses. And the influence of the singer-songwriter is strongly felt in dozens, if not hundreds, of artists not strictly identified with the style, ranging from Stevie Wonder and Bruce Springsteen to Mary-Chapin Carpenter and Bob Mould.

Recommended Recordings

Joni Mitchell, *Clouds* (Reprise)

Carole King, *Tapestry* (Epic)

Tim Buckley, *Goodbye & Hello* (Elektra)

Paul Simon, *Negotiations & Love Songs 1971-1986* (Warner Brothers)

Leonard Cohen, *Songs of Leonard Cohen* (CBS)

Nick Drake, *Fruit Tree* (Rykodisc)

James Taylor, *Sweet Baby James* (Warner Brothers)

Jackson Browne, *Late for the Sky* (Asylum)

Randy Newman, *12 Songs* (Reprise)

Neil Young, *After the Gold Rush* (Reprise)

Suzanne Vega, *Suzanne Vega* (A&M)

Tracy Chapman, *Tracy Chapman* (Elektra)

—Richie Unterberger

Art-Rock/Prog-Rock

The names—King Crimson; Renaissance; Van Der Graaf Generator; Magma; Nektar; Barclay James Harvest—seem like echoes out of a distant geological age. Some, like King Crimson and Pink Floyd, have redefined and reinvented themselves with new memberships and sounds. A few, like Yes, Jethro Tull, and the Moody Blues, still tour to sell-out audiences. But for a time, the biggest of them completely ruled the FM airwaves, dominating the radio spectrum as well as filling pages and covers across the rock press. They routinely sold millions of albums, and from 1971 until 1976, they rivaled the success of the pop music's biggest stars. The music is "progressive rock," also sometimes known as "art rock," or "classical rock"—bands playing *suites*, not songs—borrowing riffs from Bach, Beethoven, and Wagner instead of Chuck Berry and Bo Diddley, and using language closer to William Blake or T.S. Eliot than to Carl Perkins or Willie Dixon. It filled the early and mid-1970s with a

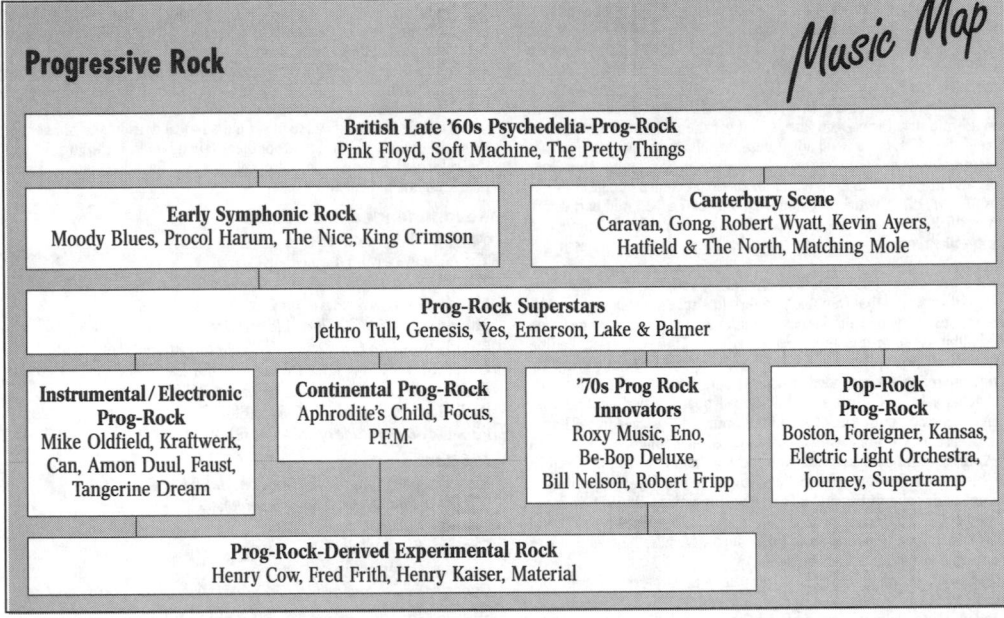

Progressive Rock

Music Map

British Late '60s Psychedelia-Prog-Rock
Pink Floyd, Soft Machine, The Pretty Things

Early Symphonic Rock
Moody Blues, Procol Harum, The Nice, King Crimson

Canterbury Scene
Caravan, Gong, Robert Wyatt, Kevin Ayers,
Hatfield & The North, Matching Mole

Prog-Rock Superstars
Jethro Tull, Genesis, Yes, Emerson, Lake & Palmer

Instrumental / Electronic Prog-Rock
Mike Oldfield, Kraftwerk, Can, Amon Duul, Faust, Tangerine Dream

Continental Prog-Rock
Aphrodite's Child, Focus, P.F.M.

'70s Prog Rock Innovators
Roxy Music, Eno, Be-Bop Deluxe, Bill Nelson, Robert Fripp

Pop-Rock Prog-Rock
Boston, Foreigner, Kansas, Electric Light Orchestra, Journey, Supertramp

Prog-Rock-Derived Experimental Rock
Henry Cow, Fred Frith, Henry Kaiser, Material

phantasmagoric array of sounds and personalities, and carried rock music to levels of sophistication that would've astonished rock 'n' roll's early pioneers. Today, however, progressive rock is the most reviled of all rock genres of the 1960s or 1970s; critics and ordinary listeners still openly snicker at the sight of an ELP or Moody Blues CD. How did a genre once so successful achieve such ignominy in scarcely more than a few years? Progressive rock actually had respectable roots, as a cousin to—and offshoot of—psychedelia. Up until the mid-1960s, rock 'n' roll was considered music for teenagers seeking a good time, usually aimed more at the body than the brain. It was Bob Dylan who made rock 'n' roll grow up, merging folk music's seriousness of purpose with electric instruments into something louder and more cerebral than any music ever before aimed at "kids." There were others who followed in Dylan's wake, most notably the Byrds and Simon & Garfunkel. None of this was lost on the Beatles, who were also expanding their own perceptions of the world; by the time they were working on their second movie, *Help*, John Lennon was already writing more serious, reflective songs like the Dylan-esque "You've Got to Hide Your Love Away." The Beatles also played a key role by introducing to their sound the mellotron, a keyboard instrument originally marketed as a competitor to the Hammond organ, and using tape loops to create the sounds of various combinations of instruments and voices. Other groups had used it, but the Beatles made it the instrument of choice.

It was inevitable that progressive rock would evolve out of this environment. Opening rock 'n' roll to seriousness on any level, and succeeding with it, was like letting a genie out of a bottle; the increasing use of hallucinogenic drugs only heightened the adventurous nature of both bands and their audiences, further increasing the demands placed upon newer bands to look farther and wider for sounds that they could call their own. Classical music was just another source of inspiration, like jazz and blues, when prog-rock began in earnest in June of 1967: rock impressario and ex-Rolling Stones manager Andrew Loog Oldham was getting ready to send his new star, R&B singer P.P. (Pat) Arnold, out on tour and assembled a backing group for her. Christened the Nice, they featured keyboard wizard Keith Emerson, a jazz and classical music aficionado who'd studied music as a boy—something none of the Beatles had done. The Nice soon overwhelmed Arnold, mixing classical music and jazz with Dylan songs ("She Belongs to Me"), Beatles songs ("A Day in the Life"), and even a touch of Italian movie soundtrack composer Ennio Morricone. Soon, P.P. Arnold was largely forgotten, and the Nice's first album, *The Thoughts of Emerlist Davjack*, was released.

While the Nice was still making its name at various festivals, Pink Floyd was making a similar noise, if not the same sound, around the club scene in London, mixing nursery-rhyme style lyrics, high amplification, and extended instrumental jams. Eventually, with the departure of lead singer/guitarist Syd Barrett, the songs became less important than the long jams, and Pink Floyd made the jump from psychedelia to progressive rock. Procol Harum, formed out of the remnants of an R&B-

based band called the Paramounts, rode the charts for months on the single "A Whiter Shade of Pale," adapted from a Bach chorale. The record, a studio creation by the songwriting team of Gary Brooker and Keith Reid, was not fully representative of the sound they finally developed, and the accompanying album had a somewhat different sound, but the single seemed to prime the airwaves for more of the same.

Ironically, they were all beaten to the punch by a group from whom nobody would've expected anything significant, much less a genre-defining record. In 1967, the English Decca label decided to produce an album promoting their advanced stereo system, and needed a band to pair with an orchestra in a rock version of Dvorak's *New World Symphony*. The Moody Blues, a struggling onetime R&B group, were chosen, and in short order, the band and producer Tony Clarke abandoned Dvorak and came up with a lushly orchestrated piece of rock/pop mysticism called *Days of Future Passed*. The LP appeared in the fall of 1967, just in time to attract teens who'd worn out their copies of the Beatles' *Sgt. Pepper* and wanted another album in the same vein, and the Moody Blues soon developed the cosmic consciousness needed to sustain their new sound, making more prominent use of the Mellotron to replace the orchestra. They also served as something of a model for a trio called Giles, Giles & Fripp, who recorded for Decca before re-emerging in 1969 as King Crimson under the leadership of guitarist Robert Fripp. Crimson sounded vaguely like the Moody Blues, but could play circles around them, using the Mellotron almost as a weapon (albeit very skillfully) rather than a backing instrument.

Apart from the Moody Blues, none of these acts were major international successes, however. The Nice got lots of press, but never managed to go over commercially. The group had a couple of built-in problems—their label, Immediate, suffered from major financial difficulties, which precluded any tour support when they played America; also, they were basically an instrumental outfit, lacking a solid lead singer in their lineup. King Crimson also got a lot of press, but the group was already in the process of breaking up by late 1969. Jethro Tull, which had started out doing blues, was still working out whether it was a jazz, folk, or classically-oriented group; Yes, which had been formed in 1968, was still a folk-pop group; and Barclay James Harvest never had a hit during their formative years .

Keith Emerson solved his problem—and progressive rock's larger problem—by breaking up the Nice. He hooked up with King Crimson's Greg Lake and Carl Palmer from the Crazy World of Arthur Brown to form Emerson, Lake & Palmer. If the Nice was progressive rock's first band, ELP was its first supergroup. Their self-titled 1970 debut album, complete with material appropriated from composers Janacek and Bartok, was a hit, and the single "Lucky Man" performed respectably on AM radio. The more ambitious FM outlets were even better served by "Take a Pebble," which regularly took nearly a quarter hour out of many an FM deejay's night-time schedule, while "The Three Fates" and "The Barbarian" showed off organ and synthesizer playing on a level of intensity and volume that few rock listeners had ever heard. There were a lot of efforts in this vein happening around that time. Folk-rockers the Strawbs added a keyboard wizard of their own named Rick Wakeman to the lineup, who, in turn, added extended piano and organ solos to their concerts. Pink Floyd moved back into long form composition with *Atom Heart Mother*, an album with a total of three tracks, one of which ran 25 minutes. Even Deep Purple, not yet the heavy-metal phenomenon of the 1970s but a band adrift in search of a sound, cut its *Concerto for Group and Orchestra*. Yes was already moving in a progressive direction, and ELP's sales made it easier for them to take the plunge with *The Yes Album* (1971), which was dominated by extended multi-part songs. It was during the early stages of recording their next album, *Fragile*, that Rick Wakeman made the leap from the Strawbs, and the classic Yes lineup was in place.

The big success among folk-based bands, however, was Jethro Tull, who, with a sound that combined English folk tunes, scatology, and adolescent sexuality, became heroes to millions of high school boys with their albums *Aqualung* and *Thick as a Brick*. Those albums relied on extended strings of lyrics, in much the same manner that ELP and King Crimson relied on extended instrumentals. Genesis, who came into music as a Moody Blues soundalike, had begun experimenting with longer songs on outre subjects, and their music blossomed in 1971 with the release of *Nursery Cryme;* their two subsequent albums, *Foxtrot* and *Selling England by the Pound*, would carry them into realms of lyrical sophistication that would find them compared to T.S. Eliot and Ezra Pound, and make ELP sound juvenile by comparison. By 1971, with the release of ELP's second album, *Tarkus*, Yes' *The Yes Album*, Procol Harum's *Broken Barricades* and Pink Floyd's *Meddle*, the message was clear: audiences couldn't get enough.

A few American outfits tried to compete in the progressive arena, but mostly prog-rock remained a European phenomenon, and the permutations were fascinating. Germany and France yielded a few competitors in the field, including Kraftwerk, Magma and Nektar (a quartet of Englishmen based in Germany), while Italy's Premiata Forneria Marconi (better known as PFM) was an answer to ELP and King Crimson, with a lighter, less gothic sound than their English counterparts. Some of these groups were genuinely more daring and experimental, and almost deliberately less commercial. A few jazz-based bands, including Soft Machine and Gong, made a strong case for themselves, although their music took some effort and discipline to absorb. Van Der Graaf Generator and their leader Peter Hammill mixed heavy metal intensity with long-form progressive rock and came up with huge sound paintings, sonic murals of considerable beauty. Caravan, by contrast, was almost a folk group, its music quieter but no less compelling, at least for those who got to hear it.

In 1973, Pink Floyd, who'd always sort of been threatening to find a major audience but never had, suddenly did just that. Their album *The Dark Side of the Moon* turned into a sales monster, lingering in the No. 1 spot and the top selling reaches of the US charts for what seemed like forever and remaining on the charts for more than a decade. The problem, finally, was that no one could follow up their work reliably: the *Dark Side* follow-up, *Wish You Were Here*, took three years to be released, while at some point, ELP, King Crimson and Procol Harum, among others, seemed simply to be repeating themselves—albeit in louder, longer, and more ornate form–from album to album. Yes was fortunate in having three writing members and five virtuoso-level players to rely on, and their music advanced significantly from *The Yes Album* to *Fragile* to *Close to the Edge*. Yes' songs also got longer, until their new album for 1974, *Tales from Topographic Oceans*, was a double-LP consisting of four long tracks—they were beautiful songs, but so demanding that even keyboard player Rick Wakeman bailed out after the accompanying tour. The rot started to set in during 1976, the year ELP released their live album *Welcome Back My Friends*. Suffering from poor sound and uninspired playing, this triple album seemed a shadow of the triple-disc Yes live album, *Yessongs*, which had obviously inspired ELP's release. The release of the ELP double-album *Works*, essentially halves of three solo albums with a group effort for the last side, stretched the devotion of fans and critics even thinner. And by this time, even the Moody Blues, the most commercially successful of all of these bands, had split up. The end came quickly: by 1977, the new generation of listeners was even more interested in a good time than the audiences of the early 1960s, and they had no patience for 30 minute prog-rock suites or concept albums based on Tolkien-esque stories. The British punk bands led the charge, condemning Pink Floyd and other arena acts in the progressive rock scene.

Soon, it became clear that prog-rock bands were dinosaurs headed for the boneyard. The artists themselves seemed to bear this out: it was ten years or more past the psychedelic era that had helped spawn progressive rock in the first place, and the members of most of the oldest groups of the scene had been playing and recording professionally for a decade. ELP was barely functioning as a unit, and not producing music

with any energy; Genesis was redefining themselves, in the wake of several lineup changes, as a pop-rock band; and Yes was back to doing songs running four minutes, not 40 minutes, and even releasing singles. By 1980, most of these groups were off the front pages of the rock press and out of the headlines, and their albums sold poorly. Few critics were saying anything kind in the press, and the public no longer really cared. Soon, progressive rock was forgotten, though a few echoes lingered; the metal band Marillion tried to pick up the lyrical density and imagery of Genesis' early work, and a few of the original bands, including Yes and the reformed Moody Blues, also held on. But for all intents and purposes, an era had ended.

Recommended Recordings

Progressive-Psychedelic

The Nice, *Nice No. 3* (Immediate/Charly)
The Nice, *Ars Longa Vita Brevis* (Immediate/Charly)
Moody Blues, *In Search of the Lost Chord* (London)
Moody Blues, *On the Threshold of a Dream* (London)
Moody Blues, *To Our Children's Children's Children* (Threshold)
Giles, Giles & Fripp, *Cheerful Insanity of Giles, Giles & Fripp* (Decca)
Pink Floyd, *Piper at the Gates of Dawn* (EMI)
Pink Floyd, *A Saucerful of Secrets* (EMI)
Pink Floyd, *Dark Side of the Moon* (EMI)

Art-Rock

King Crimson, *Court of the Crimson King* (EG)
King Crimson, *In the Wake of Poseidon* (EG)
Genesis, *Nursery Cryme* (Atlantic)
Genesis, *Foxtrot* (Atlantic)
Genesis, *Genesis Live* – (Atlantic)
Genesis, *Selling England by the Pound* (Atlantic)
Genesis, *The Lamb Lies Down on Broadway* (Atlantic)
Mike Oldfield, *Tubular Bells* (Virgin)
David Bedford, *The Odyssey* (Virgin)
David Bedford, *The Rime of the Ancient Mariner* (Virgin)
King Crimson, *Starless and Bible Black* (EG)
Peter Sinfield, *Still (aka Stillusion)* (Voiceprint)

Classical-Rock

ELP, *Emerson, Lake & Palmer* (Rhino)
ELP, *Works Vol. 1* (Rhino)
Ekseption, *Ekseption 5* (Philips)
Renaissance, *Ashes Are Burning* (One Way)
Renaissance, *Turn of the Cards* (Sire)
Renaissance, *Prologue* (One Way)
Jan Akkerman, *Tabernakel* (Atlantic)
PFM, *Photos of Ghosts* (Great Expectations)*j*

Space-Rock

King Crimson, *Larks' Tongues in Aspic* (EG)
Yes, *Yessongs* (Atlantic)
Yes, *The Yes Album* (Atlantic)
Yes, *Fragile* (Atlantic)
Yes, *Close to the Edge* (Atlantic)
Yes, *Tales from Topographic Oceans* (Atlantic)
ELP, *Brain Salad Surgery* (Rhino)
Peter Banks, *The Two Sides of Peter Banks* (One Way)
Starcastle, *Starcastle* (Epic)
Pink Floyd, *Atom Heart Mother* (EMI)
Nektar, *Remember the Future* (Passport)

Hybrid-Progressive (Jazz/Classical/Folk)

Jethro Tull, *Thick as aBrick* (Chrysalis)
Focus, *Focus III* (Sire/IRS)
King Crimson, *Lizard* (EG)
Strawbs, *Bursting at the Seams* (A&M)
Strawbs, *Grave New World* (A&M)
Strawbs, *From the Witchwood* (A&M)
Gentle Giant, *Acquiring the Taste* (Vertigo)
Gryphon, *Red Queen to Gryphon Three*
Amazing Blondel, *Fantasia Lindum* (Edsel)
Magna Carta, *Seasons* – (Dunhill/Vertigo)

—Bruce Eder

Jazz-Rock

More than most such sub-genres, jazz-rock is a hybrid that has resisted true alchemy. The impulse to blend the basic drive of rock with the improvisational verve and rhythmic complexity of jazz is a challenge that has been taken up by many. Not only has it been successfully faced by few, but the results often prove more weighted toward either rock or

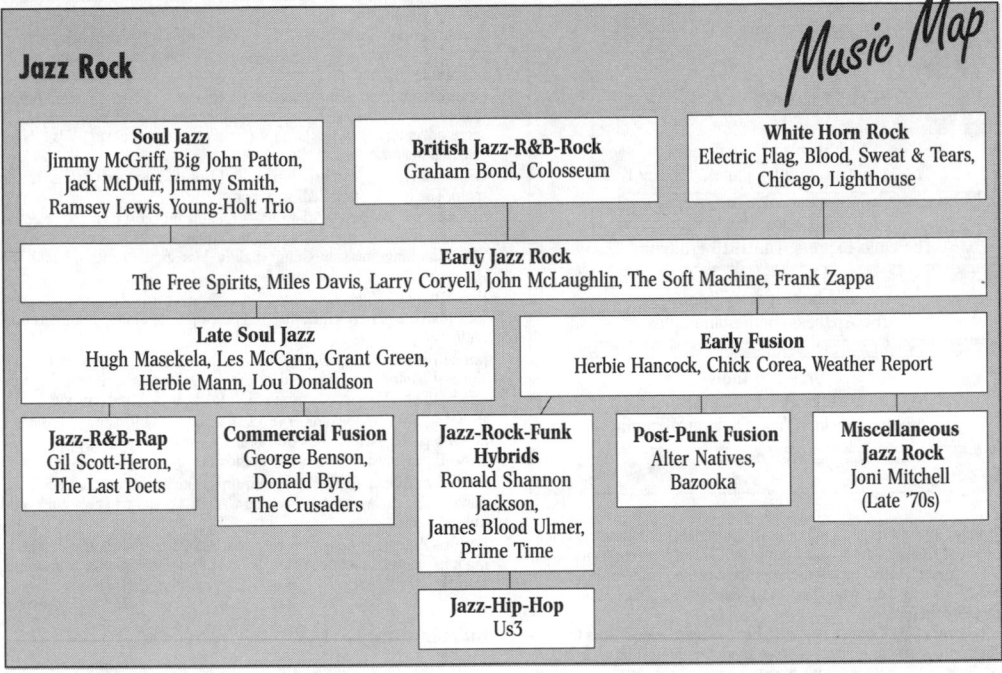

jazz than a true fusion of the styles. Half a century ago, rock and jazz were much more closely intertwined than they are today. In the big-band and swing era, jazz was a much more dance-oriented music; early R&B and jump blues acts that helped lay the foundation for rock 'n' roll drew much of their boogies, riffs, and rhythms (as well as instrumentalists) from jazz. Artists like Joe Turner and Jay McShann could have been classified as either jazz or R&B, but as rock 'n' roll grew into a full-grown giant and jazz evolved toward bebop, the styles took substantially divergent paths.

Jazz's influence on rock 'n' roll during the '50s and '60s wasn't negligible. Lots of R&B and soul bands, including those of Little Richard, Ray Charles, and James Brown, featured musicians from jazz backgrounds. Respected jazz musicians like Barney Kessel played on many rock 'n' roll sessions to help pay the rent, and drummer Cozy Cole crossed over to the rock 'n' roll market with his instrumental smash "Topsy." In the mid-'60s, the Byrds openly credited John Coltrane as an influence on early psychedelic landmarks like "Eight Miles High," and used South African jazz trumpeter Hugh Masekela as a prominent sessionman on a couple of their singles. Notable '60s groups like the Doors, Zombies, Blues Project, Paul Butterfield, Manfred Mann, Traffic, and Santana clearly displayed important secondary jazz influences. Jazz was also an important element in Van Morrison's late-'60s album *Astral Weeks*, which featured the rhythm section of noted jazz players Richard Davis on bass and Connie Kay of the Modern Jazz Quartet on drums.

Not to be overlooked, either, is '60s soul-jazz, a form which attracts little critical attention today, but was quite popular in its day—indeed, it might have been the most popular form of jazz with urban, African-American audiences. Using organs, vocals, and R&B riffs with greater frequency than other jazz musicians, the most popular performers in this sub-genre would include Jimmy Smith, Jimmy McGriff, Big John Patton, and Jack McDuff. Ramsey Lewis and the spinoff combo Young-Holt Trio (later to become Young-Holt Unlimited) had a more pop-oriented take on soul jazz that led to substantial Top 40 success.

"Jazz-rock" as a self-conscious label, however, didn't evolve until the late '60s. The first, and to this day, the most successful, acts to be widely identified as jazz-rock bands weren't so much jazz-rockers as R&B-oriented white rock bands with jazzy horn sections. The Electric Flag, featuring Mike Bloomfield, Buddy Miles, and Nick Gravenites, were the first of these; Blood, Sweat & Tears and Chicago became huge stars, although the MOR nature of their hits led some critics to dub them as "wedding band" or "barmitzvah" soul.

A more ambitious, although obscure, jazz-rock record that predates any of the bands in the above paragraph was the sole album by the New York-based Free Spirits, featuring the young Larry Coryell on guitar. This interesting but erratic effort came much closer to truly striking a

midpoint between rock song forms and jazz instrumentation, although the songs remained in the neighborhood of three minutes, and the vocals were fairly weak. Concentrating more on the jazz and instrumental side of things, Coryell became one of the leading early jazz-rock and fusion performers as the leader of Eleventh House and as a solo artist.

Several British '60s bands featured players that emerged from a jazz background, most notably the Graham Bond Organization. Besides the leader, they featured Jack Bruce and Ginger Baker in their pre-Cream days, and, for a time, guitarist John McLaughlin, although they quickly gravitated toward the R&B and blues sounds of the day. Bruce and Baker have occasionally recorded respectable jazz albums right up to the present, and Bond-John Mayall spinoff-band Colosseum were probably the best jazz-oriented act to emerge from the British R&B-blues scene. The most successful British jazz-rock band of all, and indeed the one act that could be termed to have truly fused the two styles more than any other, were the Soft Machine. Starting as an underground psychedelic group (and a very good one), their late-'60s and early-'70s albums turned toward an increasingly improvisational and instrumental sound, retaining rock elements in Mike Ratledge's buzzing organ and Robert Wyatt's brilliant drumming and soulful vocals.

For most critics, though, the true peak of jazz-rock was reached by Miles Davis on his early-'70s recordings. Impressed by Jimi Hendrix and other late-'60s rock musicians, Davis brought electric guitars and keyboards into his band, culminating in the landmark 1970 LP *Bitches Brew*, roundly acclaimed as one of the most influential jazz recordings of all time. That record featured guitarist John McLaughlin, who would immediately become a leading jazz-rock figure himself, not only as a solo artist, but also with the Mahavishnu Orchestra, and in collaborations with Miles, ex-Davis drummer Tony Williams and Carlos Santana.

Other jazz musicians took the cue from Davis, always a leader and innovator, and added electric instruments and rock-influenced rhythms to their sound. Herbie Hancock, Chick Corea, and Weather Report were the best of these groups, although it's fair to say that, even more than Davis, they were really "rock-influenced jazz," not "jazz-rock." The compositions were usually instrumental, the melodic themes and improvisations clearly from the jazz tradition; the rock influence was felt in the electric instruments and the forceful funk of the arrangements.

Not unsurprisingly, jazz-rock quickly turned in a more commercial, watered-down direction that resulted in the style known as "fusion." As work became harder to find in the struggling jazz scene of the late '60s, notable jazzmen like Lou Donaldson, Herbie Mann, Les McCann, Hugh Masekela, and Grant Green had already been turning in a jazz-soul direction as a means of both broadening their horizons and survival. Many jazz players, usually for brief periods, brought electric instruments and funk rhythms into their arrangements during the 1970s,

Music Map

Bubblegum Music

Bubblegum Forerunners
The Monkees, Tommy James, Tommy Roe

Kasenetz-Katz Productions
The Ohio Express, The 1910 Fruitgum Co.

TV Bubblegum Stars
The Archies, The Banana Splits

Pre-Teen Idols
The Partridge Family, The Osmonds,
Bobby Sherman, The De Franco Family

resulting by and large in unimpressive, at times embarrassing, results. Guitarist George Benson and trumpeter Donald Byrd, to name two of the most obvious examples, found much greater commercial success as pop-fusioneers than with their more critically-respected straight jazz efforts of the '60s.

Jazz-rock hasn't been a big critical or commercial deal since the mid-'70s, but occasional innovators have produced interesting efforts along the lines of the best jazz-rock pioneers. Frank Zappa couldn't properly be considered a jazz-rock musician, but several of his '70s recordings, most notably *Hot Rats*, rank among the most ambitious blends of rock and jazz principles. Guitarist James Blood Ulmer and drummer Ronald Shannon Jackson (whose band, the Decoding Society, featured future Living Colour guitarist Vernon Reid) were both students of the Ornette Coleman school of harmolodics. The best of their records have melded jazz improvisation, funk rhythms, and visceral electric drive as well as anyone. Coleman himself drew on jazz-rock innovations with his Prime Time band. Streetwise jazz poets Gil-Scott Heron and the Last Poets helped lay the foundation for rap music. Defunkt merged jazz and funk rhythms without, at least at the beginning, pandering to watered-down commercial fusion interests. And, most unpredictably, folk-rock star Joni Mitchell delved heavily into jazz improvisation in the late '70s with the help of sidemen Jaco Pastorius and Pat Metheny, and put lyrics to Charles Mingus' last compositions (at his request) on the 1979 album, *Mingus.*

The jazz-rock fusion continues to tempt musicians intermittently in the '90s. Several bands on the alternative rock label SST, most notably Alter Natives and Bazooka, played what was essentially improvisational jazz with fierce electric guitar-driven arrangements. The downtown New York avant-rock-whatchamacallit scene is too eclectic to be figured easily into the jazz-rock equation, but many of its performers are clearly strongly influenced by both worlds. Under the pseudonym Buckshot LeFonque, leading contemporary jazz musician Branford Marsalis took a stab at jazz-funk-R&B-soul-hip-hop. British act Us3 grafted hip-hop samples onto classic Blue Note jazz recordings, sparking some occasionally inspired jazz-hip-hop crossover recordings in the jazz community itself.

Recommended Recordings

Various Artists, *Blue Funk: The History of the Hammond Organ* (Blue Note). More quality soul-jazz was recorded on the Blue Note label than any other, and this compilation includes tracks by most of the biggest stars of the genre: Jimmy Smith, Jimmy McGriff, Jack McDuff, Grant Green, Big John Patton, Lou Donaldson.

The Free Spirits, *Out of Sight, Out of Sound* (ABC). Pretty hard to find these days, this stakes a strong claim as the first jazz-rock record.

The Electric Flag, *A Long Time Comin'* (Columbia). The best of the records by late-'60s white rock groups to be classified as "jazz-rock."

Miles Davis, *Bitches Brew* (Columbia). Still the most influential and respected jazz-rock recording.

The Soft Machine, *3rd* (Columbia). Their most successful pure jazz-rock outing, although their earlier, more psychedelic rock-flavored albums weren't too shabby either.

John McLaughlin, *Devotion* (Restless). It's really a matter of taste as to which early-'70s McLaughlin album stands as his best, but rock listeners

might find this one more approachable, as it uses Jimi Hendrix's Band of Gypsies rhythm section.

Frank Zappa, *Hot Rats* (Rykodisc). One of his most jazz-rock-oriented recordings, this largely instrumental 1970 effort features some of his best guitar playing.

Herbie Hancock, *Head Hunters* (Columbia). The album that broke fusion as a commercial force, though those looking for something a bit more adventurous in the jazz-rock vein might try the early-'70s LPs he released just prior to this effort.

Gil-Scott Heron, *The Revolution Will Not Be Televised* (Flying Dutchman). The leading jazz-R&B-rock poet.

Miles Davis, *Pangaea* (Columbia). Arguably the most recklessly electric of Davis' fusion sessions, featuring the guitar pyrotechnics of Pete Cosey. Those looking for something slightly less experimental should try *Agharta,* recorded on the same day.

Joni Mitchell, *Mingus* (Asylum). The central recording of Mitchell's jazz-rock phase, a period which inspired much debate among both fans and critics.

James Blood Ulmer, *Are You Glad to Be in America?* (Artists House). None of Ulmer's records could exactly be termed as accessible, but this strikes the best balance between funk-R&B grooves and harmolodics.

Ronald Shannon Jackson, *Decode Yourself* (Island). None of Jackson's albums particularly stands out as his most influential; this 1985 Bill Laswell-produced session is one of the more accessible.

Bazooka, *Blowhole* (SST). A group that, like others on the SST label, pursues the elusive goal of wedding Ornette Coleman to post-punk attitude and eclecticism.

Various Artists, *Stolen Moments: Red, Hot & Cool* (GRP). The best jazz-hip-hop compilation, featuring some of the top talents from both worlds.

–Richie Unterberger

Bubblegum

Considering bubblegum's fairly meager legacy—a few dozen hits in the late 1960s and early 1970s—it inspired a lot of heated discussion and revisionism. It arose at a time when the listener demographic for rock was expanding rapidly; originally marketed almost exclusively to teenagers, those teenagers were now growing up, leaving their teens, continuing to buy and play rock 'n' roll. At the same time, the purchasing power of pre-teens was growing. Too young in most cases to appreciate the subtleties of *Tommy* or "Cloud Nine," they needed a simple form of rock 'n' roll to identify with, and bubblegum was created to satisfy their desires.

While 1967 was a year that saw rock and soul shake with paroxysms of change, it also saw million-selling singles by the Monkees, who starred in a show whose audience was composed more of small kids than any other type of viewer. It also saw hits by singers like Tommy James, whose simple but catchy pop-rock was probably vastly more popular with pre-teens than post-adolescents. Although the Monkees' and Tommy James' best work holds up today as outstanding pop-rock, at the time it pointed the way for even more simple and naive music. And although the Monkees eventually played their own instruments on their records, industry insiders were well aware that their early hits were crafted by studio musicians, and knew that bona fide self-contained groups weren't strictly necessary to create smash records.

Most of the early bubblegum records were manufactured at Buddah Records by the production team of Jerry Kasenetz and Jeff Katz. Emphasizing repetitive, throbbing bass lines, simple sing-along lyrics, cheesy organs, and insinuatingly (some would say obnoxiously) catchy melodies, their hit singles by the Ohio Express and the 1910 Fruitgum Co. were played by sessionmen—the "groups" didn't exist outside of the studio. Dubbed "bubblegum" for its childish qualities, mass production values, and instant disposability, it was celebrated as such in the minor 1969 hit single "Bubble Gum Music," released by the unforgettable Rock & Roll Dubble Bubble Trading Card Co. of Philadelphia 19141.

It didn't take long for the Archies, masterminded by brilliant Brill Building tunesmith and producer Jeff Barry, to establish themselves as the most successful bubblegum group. "Jingle Jangle" and particularly the No. 1 hit "Sugar Sugar" were unavoidable if you were within earshot of a radio in 1969; the latter song's qualities were recognized by Wilson Pickett, who made the tune his own in a soul cover version. Another studio-only group, the Archies' records were tied in to a cartoon series based on the famous comic strip, with Archie, Jughead, and the gang playing the songs on the program.

The cross-promotion value of the Monkees' and the Archies' television programs was duplicated by the Partridge Family, the Banana Splits, and to some degree by Bobby Sherman, pre-teen idol. The Partridge Family themselves were picking up a fumble by the Cowsills, a clean-cut pop-rock family act that the Partridges were loosely based upon (although the Cowsills' arrangements were somewhat more sophisticated than the bubblegum norm). When the Partridges peaked, they in turn were supplanted by the Osmonds, a bubblegum version of the Jackson 5 (who, naturally, also had their own TV cartoon series around this time). The Partridges and Osmonds even inspired the briefly successful imitators, the DeFranco Family.

In bubblegum's prime, there were also several huge one-shot hits by "artists" destined never to be heard from again. The Cuff Links' "Tracy," from 1969, featured the same singer who took the lead for the Archies. Daddy Dewdrop ("Chick-A-Boom"), the Pipkins ("Gimme Dat Ding"), and Crazy Elephant ("Gimme Gimme Good Lovin'") were some of the others whose tunes continued to echo in the brain long after their equally silly monikers had faded from memory. A few pop-rock veterans got some mileage out of bubblegum, like Tommy Roe, who cut bubblegum hits with "Dizzy" and "Jam up Jelly Tight"; the Troggs even recorded a bubblegum single, "Hip Hip Hooray," modeled after the Ohio Express.

Bubblegum was savaged by the rock press, who were outraged that simple clap-trap like "Yummy Yummy Yummy"—records by groups that didn't even exist outside of the studio—could sell millions of copies while sensitive, literate efforts of progressive rockers and singer-songwriters struggled to be heard. After bubblegum had faded and punk emerged in the late '70s, some critics took a revisionist stance, hailing bubblegum for its innovative production techniques and for boiling pop-rock down to its irreducible essence. It's often been pointed out that one of the first songs the Talking Heads performed was the 1910 Fruitgum Co.'s "1-2-3 Red Light," and the simple throbbing rhythm and lyrics of numbers like "Psycho Killer" have a distant relation to bubblegum, although no one's going to confuse *Remain in Light* with music aimed at pre-teens.

Bubblegum's influence continues to hover in all music aimed at the record-buying public's youngest segment, who don't care if their heroes wrote the songs or even played on the records. Bubblegum was hardly one of the high points of rock history, but even the most serious-minded listeners are probably fooling themselves if they can't admit to the ingratiating catchiness of hits like "Tracy" and "Sugar, Sugar."

Recommended Recordings

Various Artists, *The Best of the Ohio Express & Other Bubblegum Smashes* (Rhino)

Various Artists, *The Best of the 1910 Fruitgum Company & Other Bubblegum Smashes* (Rhino)

Various Artists, *Bubblegum Classics Vol. 1-3* (Varese Sarabande)

The Archies, *The Archies' Greatest Hits* (Kirshner)

Tommy Roe, *Greatest Hits* (MCA)

—Richie Unterberger

Heavy Metal

Heavy metal is the bastard son of rock 'n' roll. For years, critics tried to ignore its existence, as parents attempted to prevent their children from listening to it. Nevertheless, heavy metal emerged in the early '70s as arguably the most commercially successful form of rock 'n' roll. In the past 25 years, heavy metal has gone in and out of fashion, adapting itself to the times but always remaining near the top of the charts in some form.

At its core, heavy metal is an adolescent experience. Teenagers —primarily white males—form its main audience, buying the records, wearing the bands' T-shirts, and going to the shows. Because of the number of adolescent fans, some critics dismiss heavy metal as simplistic, primal pounding. Certainly, a fair share of metal is nothing but three-chord riffing, yet most metal bands place a premium on technical skill. From Led Zeppelin's Jimmy Page to Eddie Van Halen to Metallica's Kirk Hammett and Soundgarden's Kim Thayil, metal guitarists have always been innovators in technique, speed, and skill. In every subgenre of heavy metal, the guitar is the center of the music. The songs are assembled around the riff, with the guitar solo taking prominence. By and large, heavy metal is rock 'n' roll with all of the roll stripped out—the blues remains, but it doesn't swing. All of the rhythms are fairly rigid, almost military in origin. Bombast is the key—from the drums to the guitars, it's about being as loud as possible.

Most trends in rock 'n' roll last a finite amount of time. Like psychedelia, many listeners expected metal to fade after its initial glory days of the early '70s. And it did fade slightly for a couple of years in the late '70s, but it came back in a newer, tougher form. In each decade, heavy metal always finds its specific audience. In the '70s it was either mystical or boogie-oriented. In the '80s, it was pseudo-glam bubblegum in the mainstream and brutal, fast doom-mongers in the underground. In the '90s, the doom-mongers reigned supreme, as the lines between heavy metal and punk became indistinguishable.

Heavy metal's roots can be traced to the British Invasion, particularly the two-chord opening of the Kinks' "You Really Got Me." "You Really Got Me" didn't swing, it pounded, laying the groundwork for the simplistic hard rock of AC/DC and the scores of boogie bands of the mid-'70s. For all their sheer firepower, the Kinks didn't revel in the pompous,

improvisational instrumental sections that defined metal, as much as the catchy, simplistic riffs. It wasn't until Cream that rock 'n' roll had a band that pushed the boundaries of blues-based rock. Cream attempted to make rock an improvisational art such as jazz. While their records could often be surprisingly pop, the band stretched all rock conventions in concert, spending over ten minutes on one song and letting each instrument improvise. More importantly, they were deafeningly loud. Soon after Cream's debut, Jimi Hendrix appeared and he pushed those boundaries even further, bringing a new sonic vocabulary to rock with distortion and feedback. Although they were nowhere near as accomplished as Cream or Hendrix, Blue Cheer pushed the volume up as far as it could go. The result wasn't much more than volume, yet its primal roar earned the group the distinction of being labeled the first heavy metal band.

The group that wrote the blueprint for the conventional four-piece heavy metal band was the Jeff Beck Group. Keeping the power trio format of Cream and Hendrix, the Jeff Beck Group added a charismatic frontman to the lineup in the person of Rod Stewart. The interplay between the guitarist and the singer became enormously influential, and most heavy metal bands followed the pattern in the following years.

Shortly after the Jeff Beck Group's first album, Led Zeppelin was formed. The Jeff Beck Group may have provided the template, but Led Zeppelin was the definitive heavy metal band. Like the Jeff Beck Group, Led Zeppelin performed blues standards at a crushing volume and featured long trade-offs between vocalist Robert Plant and guitarist Jimmy Page. The band was also made up of superior musicians, as well as songwriters and arrangers, leading the music into a territory that was blues-based but couldn't reasonably be called blues-rock. Zeppelin also brought in touches of British folk, country music, rockabilly and rock 'n' roll to the mix, as well as a lyrical fascination with the occult and medieval imagery that traded time with their sexually oriented songs.

For much of the early '70s, fantastical imagery dominated heavy metal, both through Led Zeppelin and their closest competitors, Black Sabbath. In contrast to the meticulously arranged and surprisingly subtle shifting dynamics of Zeppelin, Sabbath just flailed away at their guitars, creating an impenetrably slow and heavy sludge. Sabbath never sang about sex — they sang of "Warpigs" and "Iron Men." However, their slow beat, gargantuan guitars, and Ozzy Osbourne's wail made them seem grittier and more down to earth. In turn, they would influence nearly as many bands as Led Zeppelin, many of whom forgot about what Sabbath sang about and concentrated on the grimy, dirty riffs.

While Zeppelin and Sabbath ruled the theaters and arenas of America and Britain, they had some competition from the thick boogie of Foghat and Grand Funk Railroad, who attracted legions of fans with their simple, by-the-books, heavy blues-rock. However, Foghat and Grand Funk never had the lasting influence of Alice Cooper. With a stage show designed to shock—filled with fake blood and decapitations—and music to match, Alice Cooper created a grandly theatrical form of heavy metal that also was quite pop-conscious. Not only could the group grind out teenage anthems like "School's Out" and "I'm Eighteen," but they also wrote songs like "No More Mr. Nice Guy" which essentially was a pop song dressed up with loud guitars. Led by the heavily made-up Vincent Furnier (who eventually adopted the name Alice Cooper as his own), the group's flamboyant stage shows and melodic metal set the stage for the pop-metal of the '80s.

Although neither band could officially be termed heavy metal, the New York Dolls and T. Rex had an impact in the metal world. T. Rex's influence wouldn't be felt until the '80s, when a number of bands, particularly Def Leppard, adopted the group's sleek, simple riffs and pretty look. The New York Dolls, however, had immediate impact. Dressing in drag and playing a hard, raunchy variation of the Rolling Stones' swagger, the Dolls never sold many records, but bands such as Aerosmith and Kiss built on the Dolls' trashy retro-chic look and the group's sleazy hard rock. Aerosmith was tamer than the Dolls, never indulging in the group's stylistic excesses, but they made the basic blues-rock of the Stones and the Dolls heavier without losing any of the bluesy swing. Lead vocalist Stephen Tyler was a flamboyant frontman, halfway between Mick Jagger and David Johansen, with a penchant for crude double entendres. Aerosmith's heavy blues-rock didn't quite fit in with the lunkheaded thud of Foghat, and it was much grittier than the mystical visions of Zeppelin and Sabbath. It took the band some time to find an audience, but the proto-power ballad of "Dream On" and the lean *Toys in the Attic* broke the band into the big-time.

Kiss, on the other hand, was all about pure theatrics. Every member of the band was disguised in heavy makeup and ridiculous costumes and was never seen without their makeup. Their stage show was more theatrical than Alice Cooper's, complete with elaborate light shows, dry ice, and fake blood. Accordingly, their music also expanded on Alice Cooper's blueprint, making the heavy guitars heavier and the melodies poppier. For the latter part of the decade, Kiss was among the most popular heavy metal bands in America.

Queen arrived at roughly the same time as Aerosmith and Kiss, although their music could hardly have been more different. Taking their direction from Led Zeppelin's most majestic moments, Queen created a meticulous, multi-layered sound that featured dozens of guitar and vocal overdubs. The band provided a bridge between progressive rock and heavy metal by adopting the pretensions of prog-rock with the melodic sensibilities and loud guitars of metal. Queen was also the most eclectic heavy metal band since Led Zeppelin, adding elements of pop, English music-hall, folk, opera, rockabilly, and, eventually, disco and new wave. That off-kilter musical sensibility was part of the reason the group's music was influential over the years, with bands as diverse as Metallica and Smashing Pumpkins claiming Queen as an inspiration.

AC/DC was the last of the important heavy metal bands to emerge in the mid-'70s, and they were completely different than the orchestrated bombast of Queen. Crude and vulgar, both lyrically and musically, AC/DC were rock hooligans of the highest order; in their own words, they rode the "Highway to Hell." Angus Young's rhythm guitar stripped the riffs down to their barest essentials, while Bon Scott's piercing shriek was positively primal in its power. The rhythm section pounded away, and they had a sense of groove that was missing from most metal bands of their era. But nothing could take away from the all-mighty riff, which was the one important thing in AC/DC's music. With their minimalistic power and working-class image, it could be argued that AC/DC were proto-punks, stripping rock 'n' roll to its core. But neither AC/DC nor any punk rocker would agree.

In the late '70s, heavy metal began to fall out of favor, as disco and punk captured the imaginations of mainstream audiences and critics, respectively. Van Halen helped reverse that trend. Releasing their first album in 1978, the group carried out the metal prototype of a lead singer/lead guitarist interplay to ludicrous extremes. Lead vocalist David Lee Roth treated his frontman role as vaudevillian performance art, while lead guitarist Eddie Van Halen spat out a series of amazingly fast leads. Van Halen's guitar pyrotechnics—which included popularizing the two-handed tapping technique, allowing for guitar licks that sounded faster and more complicated than they actually were—didn't simply expand the boundaries of the instrument, they wrote a whole new book. Throughout the next two decades, most guitarists copied and developed Van Halen's techniques, making his style a familiar part of the musical language. Guitarists from Kirk Hammett through Toto's Steve Lukather to Bon Jovi's Richie Sambora helped incorporate Van Halen's style into speed-metal, pop, and pop-metal.

Van Halen quickly became multi-platinum superstars, capable of selling out arenas. As soon as they reached that status, a new batch of heavy metal bands emerged from the British underground. Dubbed the New Wave of British Heavy Metal, the bands took Sabbath's heaviness, made it leaner and tougher, and dressed it in leather. At first, their lyrical concerns were just as drenched in mysticism as Sabbath, but the groups began singing about death, depression, sex, and life in more realistic terms, at a faster, relentless speed. Judas Priest and Iron Maiden were the leaders of the movement, yet bands like Diamond Head were equally influential among the emerging ranks of speed-metal bands like Metallica and Anthrax. But more than any other band, Motörhead helped create speed-metal—and, in the process, break down the doors between punk and metal. Motörhead took their cues from punk and the Ramones in particular, making their music harder, faster, louder. All of Motörhead's music sounds the same, but that doesn't dilute the impact of its rampaging riffs and Lemmy's bark.

In the early '80s, America developed its own underground metal scene, which expanded on the bleak, hard heavy metal of the New Wave of British Heavy Metal while adding a greater reliance on technical proficiency, and intricate, multi-layered compositions. The band that would bring that movement to popularity was Metallica, a Californian band that emphasized exceptionally tight, fast playing and stark lyrical imagery. *Kill 'Em All*, their 1982 debut, articulated their bleak, percussive vision and caused an instant underground sensation.

However, the group didn't begin to earn mainstream attention until the middle of the decade, when they released their masterpiece, *Master of Puppets*, in 1986. In the meantime, a slicker, more pop-oriented variation of heavy metal began to dominate the pop charts in the early '80s, after new wave began to fade away. AC/DC had their commercial breakthrough in 1980, but that turned out to be a fluke, since no other band followed them to the top of the charts. Quiet Riot's version of Slade's "Cum on Feel the Noize" was a hit in 1983, but what really broke metal into the mainstream was Def Leppard's *Pyromania*.

The rise of pop-metal had a great deal to do with the emergence of MTV. Pop-metal bands tended to be better-looking than the gritty heavy metal bands of the '70s, which made MTV more receptive to their videos. After Def Leppard's success with "Photograph" and Pyromania, legions of pop-metal bands began filtering into MTV and the mainstream. Van Halen had a major hit in 1984 with the aptly titled *1984*, and Mötley Crüe had a Top Ten hit with the sleazy glam-metal of *The-*

atre of Pain in 1985. But it wasn't until Bon Jovi's breakthrough in 1986 that pop-metal became a genuine commercial force.

Like most pop-metal bands—who critics derisively tagged "hair bands" because of their stylized, blow-dried appearance—Bon Jovi emphasized the pop melodies in their music, using loud guitar riffs and solos as an embellishment, not as the primary force. They had slick rockers like "You Give Love a Bad Name" and power ballads like "Wanted: Dead or Alive." A veritable flood of bands followed Bon Jovi through the door, including newer bands like Poison and revamped veteran rockers like Whitesnake. Mötley Crüe managed to straddle the line between pop-metal and sleazy, Los Angeles glam-metal, becoming one of the most popular rock 'n' roll bands of the latter half of the decade. Pop-metal had a prominent place on the pop charts all the way into 1991, when post-punk alternative rock made a commercial break-through with Nirvana's *Nevermind*.

As pop-metal ruled the charts, a dirtier, harder brand of metal came to the forefront, as well. In 1988, the Los Angeles band Guns N' Roses had a hit single with "Sweet Child o' Mine." The band's album had been out for a year, but it immediately began selling following the hit single, eventually hitting No. 1. Guns N' Roses updated the raunchy hard rock of Aerosmith with a nihilistic, punk-rock fervor, opening the doors for the mass commercial acceptance of such speed-metal bands as Metallica, Megadeth, Anthrax, and Slayer. Before, most metal bands were relegated to MTV's Saturday night ghetto, *Headbanger's Ball*, which provided an excellent forum for both new and established bands. Metallica immediately reaped the benefits of the more accommodating airwaves, earning a Grammy nomination and critical acclaim in mainstream publications.

While pop-metal—Guns N' Roses and their offspring, as well as speed-metal bands—became a hot chart item, a handful of bands in the alternative underground were sketching out a brazen fusion of punk and heavy metal, led by the sludgy, heavy riffs of Soundgarden and the pompous art-rock and metal of Jane's Addiction. Both bands received heavy college airplay and positive critical response, earning a small but dedicated following that continued to grow throughout the end of the decade. Jane's Addiction, in particular, became a powerful force in breaking down the barriers between album-rock radio and alternative rock before Nirvana's *Nevermind* in 1991. Not only did the group's second album, 1990's *Ritual de lo Habitual*, receive prominent MTV airplay, but their lead vocalist, Perry Farrell, organized the group's farewell tour, Lollapalooza, as a traveling festival designed to feature alternative bands (most of whom had metal leanings like Jane's themselves), such as Living Colour, Nine Inch Nails, Ice-T's Body Count, and the Rollins Band.

Throughout 1991, metal bands like Skid Row and Mötley Crüe dominated the charts, but it was Metallica's commercial breakthrough, *Metallica*, that signaled the tastes of the mainstream audience were beginning to change. Guns N' Roses delivered their long-awaited second album, *Use Your Illusion I & II*, in the fall of 1991, but they were soon eclipsed by Nirvana's *Nevermind*, as were all of the pop-metal bands that were ruling the singles charts. *Nevermind* not only ushered in alternative rock as a major commercial force, it re-wrote the book for metal bands, forcing all the previous pop-metal groups to toughen up their charts. Most of these efforts were unsuccessful, since there were legions of bands ready to claim the heavy metal audience.

Nirvana was adopted by certain portions of the metal audience, yet they were never really heavy metal. However, their fellow Seattle bands, Alice in Chains and Soundgarden, were decidedly heavy metal and they became genuine arena-rock stars in the early '90s. Alice in Chains fell in between Sabbath and Van Halen, turning out a grinding, heavy rock that was determinedly grim and bleak. Soundgarden recaptured the majestic heaviness of Led Zeppelin and Black Sabbath with 1991's *Badmotorfinger* and 1994's staggering *Superunknown*, which became their commercial breakthrough. More than any other metal band since Metallica, Soundgarden captured the imaginations of both the critics and the audience, establishing themselves as a major force in the '90s. Quasi-metal bands like Smashing Pumpkins had their roots in '70s metal groups like Sabbath and Queen and were quite popular, yet their musical approach and attitude connected them with alternative audiences, not metal. No matter how loud they played, they sounded soft.

While alternative metal had become mainstream, a new underground of heavy metal bands had developed. Inspired by the fast, grim visions of Metallica and Slayer, as well as cult bands like the Accused and Napalm Death, these legions of bands were dubbed death-metal, black-metal, and grindcore, according to the minute variations in their sound. Outsiders could not distinguish between Emperor and Brutal Truth, but there were differences in their music nevertheless. Black-metal, which became the most popular term for the trend, was a defiantly underground phenomenon, with most mainstream publications ignoring it completely; it wasn't allowed any airtime on MTV, since the network cancelled its long-running heavy metal program, *Headbanger's Ball*. Nevertheless, the black-metal cult grew quite large by the middle

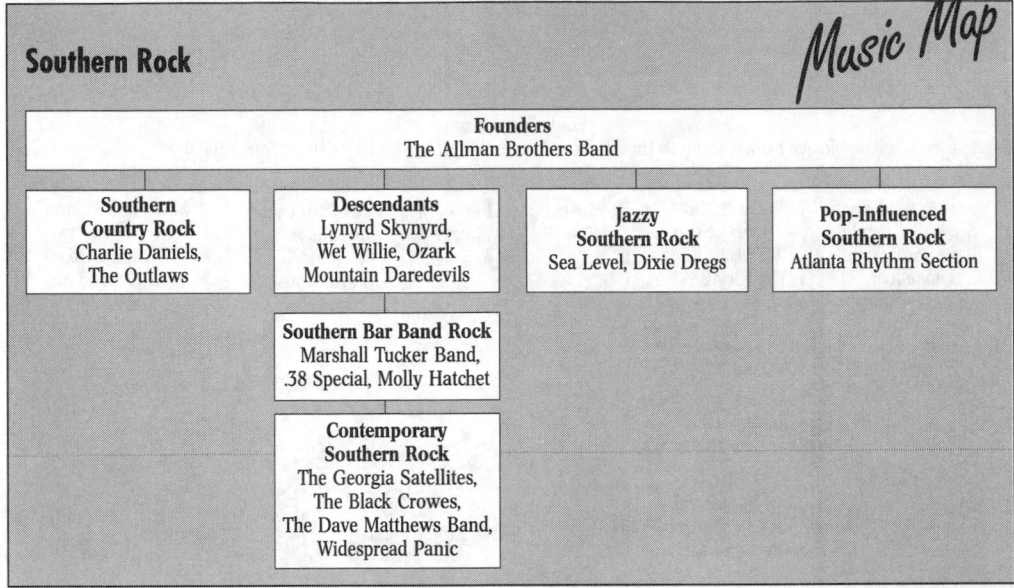

Southern Rock

Music Map

Founders
The Allman Brothers Band

Southern Country Rock
Charlie Daniels, The Outlaws

Descendants
Lynyrd Skynyrd, Wet Willie, Ozark Mountain Daredevils

Jazzy Southern Rock
Sea Level, Dixie Dregs

Pop-Influenced Southern Rock
Atlanta Rhythm Section

Southern Bar Band Rock
Marshall Tucker Band, .38 Special, Molly Hatchet

Contemporary Southern Rock
The Georgia Satellites, The Black Crowes, The Dave Matthews Band, Widespread Panic

of the decade—large enough to make Slayer's 1994 album debut at No. 1. As the rock 'n' roll of the '90s has proven, heavy metal has become part of rock 'n' roll's heritage, working its way into several different forms of pop music. Nevertheless, there's always a metal underground, filled with unrespected and unsavory groups, ready to take over. In addition to the black-metal cult, many of the pop-metal bands of the '80s have retreated to the club circuit, which may mean that they are sowing the seeds of a future comeback. In either case, it's clear that heavy metal will never go away.

Recommended Recordings

Led Zeppelin, *Led Zeppelin II* (Swan Song)
Led Zeppelin, *Led Zeppelin IV* (Swan Song)
Black Sabbath, *Paranoid* (Warner Bros.)
Black Sabbath, *Masters of Reality* (Warner Bros.)
Deep Purple, *Machine Head* (Warner Bros.)
Aerosmith, *Toys in the Attic* (Columbia)
Alice Cooper, *Greatest Hits* (Warner Bros.)
Queen, *Sheer Heart Attack* (Hollywood)
AC/DC, *Highway to Hell* (Atco)
AC/DC, *Back in Black* (Atco)
Motörhead, *The Best of Motörhead* (Roadrunner)
Judas Priest, *British Steel* (Columbia)
Van Halen, *Van Halen* (Warner Bros.)
Def Leppard, *Pyromania* (Mercury)
Metallica, *Kill 'Em All* (Elektra)
Metallica, *Master of Puppets* (Elektra)
Slayer, *Reign in Blood* (Def American)
Guns N' Roses, *Appetite for Destruction* (Geffen)
Mötley Crüe, *Decade of Decadence* (Elektra)
Jane's Addiction, *Ritual de lo Habitual* (Warner Bros.)
Soundgarden, *Superunknown* (A&M)

—*Stephen Thomas Erlewine*

Southern-Rock

While the South, more than any other American region, was responsible for breeding rock 'n' roll, it lacked a readily identifiable white rock band sound after the decline of rockabilly. Southern-rock groups were hardly unknown in the 1960s; John Fred & the Playboys, the Boxtops, and Bill Deal & the Rondels rank among the most talented blue-eyed soul performers, and there were occasional bands following the British Invasion and folk-rock trends, such as the underappreciated Gants. Soul music, of course, thrived in Memphis, New Orleans, and other southern regions throughout the '60s, and white session musicians (especially the white half of Booker T. & the MG's) contributed mightily to the sounds crafted at Stax/Volt Records and the Muscle Shoals and Fame studios.

But Southern-rock, as an identifiable style, didn't come into its own until about 1970. Like many sub-genres of rock 'n' roll, Southern-rock peaked very early in its development. Its story is more tragic than most, perhaps, because it fell from grace not so much from the usual reasons of flagging inspiration and rampant imitation, but from sudden tragedies that tore the heart out of its two flagship groups.

Southern-rock proper began with the Allman Brothers, who had already made some recordings in California as the Hourglass; lead guitarist Duane Allman was a respected session player, contributing to records by Aretha Franklin, Boz Scaggs, and (after the Allmans were established) Eric Clapton. The Allman Brothers established the blueprint for Southern-rock in their heavy debts to roots music forms: the blues was foremost, as were boogie, soul, and hints of country. They weren't at all like either the early rockabilly performers or the contemporary soul musicians, however, in that the guitar-dominated thrust of their arrangements was clearly inspired by the leading hard rock and psychedelic bands of the day, such as Cream and Jimi Hendrix.

While the Allmans were to some degree responsible for some of Southern-rock's lesser attributes—the endless jams, the repetitive boogie riffs—they executed these with more subtlety and polish than any of their descendants, and at their best demonstrated a real facility for combining muscular rock with improvisation. Anchored by Gregg Allman's soulful vocals and the twin lead guitars of Duane Allman and Dickey Betts, the group became stars after the release of the double LP *Live at the Fillmore East*, still one of the most popular live rock recordings of all time. Duane Allman was killed in a motorcycle accident in late 1971, shortly after the release of *Fillmore East*, and bassist Berry Oakley died in eerily similar circumstances a year later. The band has continued to record to the present day, at times with great commercial success, but has never approached the artistic heights of their original lineup.

In the wake of the Allmans' success, several other Southern-rock bands arose to mine the same territory of rootsy boogies and guitar-driven stomp, usually with considerably less subtlety. The most successful, both critically and commercially, were Lynyrd Skynyrd. Attracting important and influential fans in Al Kooper (who produced their debut) and Pete Townshend (who had the group open for the Who during a tour in the early '70s), Lynyrd Skynyrd boasted three lead guitarists. As songwriters and performers, they helped establish the good ol' boy (or, as some would put it less kindly, redneck) image of Southern-rock, and helped define '70s guitar rock with "Freebird," which vies with "Stairway To Heaven" as the most overplayed classic rock song of all time. At the same time, they could show uncommon lyrical subtlety for the genre, as well as economic, hook-savvy smarts. They were one of America's most popular bands by 1977, when lead singer Ronnie Van Zant and guitarist Steve Gaines died in a plane crash. Subseqent recordings by the group, as well as the spinoff Rossington-Collins Band, didn't measure up to those by the Zant-fronted lineup. While no other Southern-rock bands of the '70s approached the Allmans or Lynyrd Skynyrd in popularity or influence, quite a few of them were big. The Charlie Daniels Band and

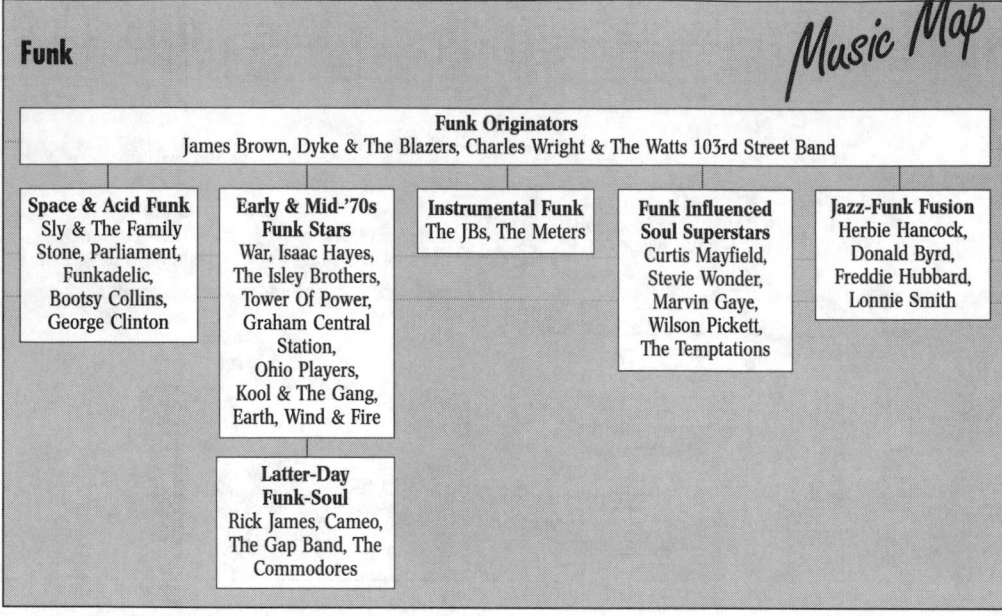

Funk

Music Map

Funk Originators
James Brown, Dyke & The Blazers, Charles Wright & The Watts 103rd Street Band

Space & Acid Funk
Sly & The Family Stone, Parliament, Funkadelic, Bootsy Collins, George Clinton

Early & Mid-'70s Funk Stars
War, Isaac Hayes, The Isley Brothers, Tower Of Power, Graham Central Station, Ohio Players, Kool & The Gang, Earth, Wind & Fire

Instrumental Funk
The JBs, The Meters

Funk Influenced Soul Superstars
Curtis Mayfield, Stevie Wonder, Marvin Gaye, Wilson Pickett, The Temptations

Jazz-Funk Fusion
Herbie Hancock, Donald Byrd, Freddie Hubbard, Lonnie Smith

Latter-Day Funk-Soul
Rick James, Cameo, The Gap Band, The Commodores

---

the Outlaws were the most country-influenced; the Dixie Dregs and Sea Level (both of whom recorded for the Allmans' label, Capricorn) the jazziest; Wet Willie the most R&B and gospel-influenced; the Ozark Mountain Daredevils and the Atlanta Rhythm Section, briefly stars, the most pop-influenced. American blues-rock performers with southern roots like Johnny Winter, Edgar Winter, ZZ Top, and Elvin Bishop were sometimes lumped in the Southern-rock school, although they were really on the edge of the style both geographically and stylistically.

The bar band boogie hallmarks of Southern-rock always go over big live, and several fairly generic bands rose to a level of considerable popularity without offering anything particularly valuable, and, at their worst, perpetuating the worst "redneck rock" stereotypes of brawling, good-time southern boys. Included in this category would be .38 Special and Molly Hatchet. The Marshall Tucker Band, originators of a seemingly endless stream of competently indistinguishable Southern-rock albums, epitomized the common denominator of the genre.

As a big commercial force, Southern-rock didn't last into the 1980s. Many notable alternative rockers, such as R.E.M. and the B-52's, came from the South, but their allegiance was to punk, pop, and new wave, not the blues, country, soul, and hard rock of the '70s Southern-rock groups. The Georgia Satellites and the Black Crowes had big chart albums in the '80s and '90s, though their hard rock was less identifiably Southern than their '70s ancestors. Like most rock styles, Southern-rock will continue to command a significant audience that occasionally results in artists that break out nationally. The mid-'90s success of Widespread Panic and the Dave Matthews Band proved its current viability, though these groups do not so much develop the Southern-rock tradition as keep it alive.

Recommended Recordings

The Allman Brothers Band, *Beginnings* (Polydor)
The Allman Brothers, *Live at the Fillmore East* (Polydor)
Lynyrd Skynyrd, *Gold & Platinum* (MCA)
Various Artists, *Rebel Rousers: Southern Rock Classics* (Rhino)
The Ozark Mountain Daredevils, *The Best* (A&M)
The Dixie Dregs, *The Best of the Dixie Dregs* (Grand Slamm)
The Charlie Daniels Band, *A Decade of Hits* (Epic)
The Atlanta Rhythm Section, *A Rock and Roll Alternative* (Polydor)
Sea Level, *Sea Level* (Capricorn)
Wet Willie, *The Best of Wet Willie* (Polydor)
The Georgia Satellites, *The Georgia Satellites* (Elektra)
The Black Crowes, *Shake Your Money Maker* (Def American)
—Richie Unterberger

Funk

Bridging the classic soul era and the dawn of disco, funk was R&B at its most rhythmic, earthy, and (occasionally) wild and experimental. Not as

hugely successful with the masses as soul or disco, it has proven to be about as influential, strongly affecting not just all post-1970 R&B, but also contemporary rap and alternative rock music.

What exactly puts the "unk" into "funk" can be hard to pigeonhole, but there are some basic traits which distinguish it from mainstream soul and rock music. The emphasis, above all, is on the rhythm, and on the bass and drums of the rhythm section. The accent is often placed on the downbeat, or the first and third beats of 4/4 patterns. The function of the guitar becomes more rhythmic than melodic, often employing what has been called "scratch" or even "chicken scratch" staccato bursts of percussive strings; the horns also take a stronger rhythmic role than in traditional soul music, used for percussive riffing and punctuation as well as taking solos or providing harmonic support.

The rhythms, though, are often anything but simple, building upon each other and playing in counterpoint to build a polyrhythmic drive. Both the lead and backup singers often do their part to add to the excitement with chants, grants, and screams. The lyrics have at times been quite sophisticated and socially conscious, but more often are principally concerned, like the music itself, with stream-of-consciousness grooves, built around slogans and exhortations to dance and party. Adding to the ferment are unpredictable influences from psychedelic and hard guitar rock, Latin music, doo wop, and other elements of the melting pot of American rock, soul, and pop.

Few would dispute that James Brown is not only the Godfather of Soul, but the Godfather of Funk as well. The ignition of the funk explosion can for most intents and purposes be boiled down to his landmark mid-'60s singles "Out of Sight" and especially "Papa's Got a Brand New Bag," the first smashes to incorporate the syncopated horns, stream-of-consciousness lyrics, and staccato guitars that would become funk trademarks. Although it would be a few years before the music began to be called funk, in the last half of the '60s Brown would continue to lay the funk prototype with workouts like "Cold Sweat" and "There Was a Time" that grew increasingly polyrhythmic, jazzy, and improvisational, pushing the melody to the background in favor of the churning beat and Brown's inimitable screams and groans.

The word "funk" itself began to enter the R&B/soul vocabulary with Dyke & the Blazers' R&B dance hit "Funky Broadway." Several theories and explanations of the origins of the actual word "funk" have been offered, the most likely being that, like rock 'n' roll and jazz, it was a euphemism for sexual activity, though "funk" often stood for smelly, gritty, or earthy stuff within the African-American community. By the end of the 1960s, it had come to stand for the greasiest and earthiest variant of soul music.

Although James Brown's early-'70s work was not nearly as commercially successful with the pop audience as the recordings of his 1965-69 peak (though they remained huge R&B sellers), with time they have come to be viewed as nearly as important and influential. These discs found him getting deeper and deeper into the polyrhythmic funk groove, with increasingly basic workouts that in time came to resemble one continuous (if often compelling) performance. His backup band of the era, the JB's, are now recognized as some of funk's greatest musicians, particularly guitarist Jimmy Nolen and horn-players Fred Wesley, Pee Wee Ellis, Maceo Parker, and Clair Pinckney; they also cut many underappreciated instrumental funk workouts on their own.

Another influential Brown sideman, although he was only with the band for a few years, was bassist Bootsy Collins, who was instrumental in boosting his instrument's importance in the funk mix. After leaving Brown in the early '70s, Bootsy teamed up with George Clinton to become a vital cog in what many funk fans regard as the finest exponents of the genre, Parliament-Funkadelic. Clinton was a veteran R&B/soul performer who changed gears radically around 1970, constructing elaborate funk heavily influenced by the acid rock of Jimi Hendrix, as well as touches of jazz and psychedelia. Almost anything went with Clinton and his troops, including spacy jams, inscrutable self-mythologizing and unfathomable concept opuses about spaceships and funk itself, though the bands never lost their slightly absurd sense of humor.

The Parliament-Funkadelic family tree is among the most twisted and difficult to follow in rock history, with a revolving door of musicians who often played in both Parliament and Funkadelic (for tangled contractual reasons, Clinton led similar groups recording under both names, sometimes simultaneously). It grew more complex when Bootsy Collins became a solo star in his own right, with a similarly (perhaps even more excessive) cosmic vision, as a solo act and leader of Bootsy's Rubber Band. Both Clinton and Collins remain active and influential musicians to this day, as both individual artists and collaborators with other heavyweights.

Although they are usually categorized as a soul act rather than a funk one, Sly & the Family Stone also did a great deal to cross-fertilize soul and psychedelia to come up with some of the most adventurous funk of the early '70s. Larry Graham's distinctive finger-popping bass sound has become perhaps THE most single identifying characteristic associated with funk, and Sly Stone's commentaries on racial injustice and people power rank as some of the genre's most sophisticated lyrics. While their early, more soul- and pop-flavored work of the late '60s is equally important, their 1971 album *There's a Riot Goin' On* is their deepest foray into hardcore funk, and remains one of the few funk LPs that hits as deep with its words as its grooves.

The late '60s and early '70s saw several other less important but interesting groups make their mark in the funk parade. Dyke & the Blazers and the Watts 103rd St. Rhythm Band (most famous for "Express Yourself") were among the style's earliest practitioners. After an apprenticeship with Eric Burdon, War stormed the charts in the early and mid-'70s with a series of hits that incorporated Latin rhythms, loose, jazzy grooves, and vague social pontifications. The Meters took the sound of New Orleans R&B, already a bedrock of much post-1950 R&B, soul, and rock, into the funk era, largely on instrumentals (at least at first). Isaac Hayes took endless bubbling funk monologues onto both album and single charts, as his "Shaft" took the wah-wah guitar signatures often found in funk to their limit.

There were also funk classics in the early '70s committed to vinyl by performers who are really best categorized as soul musicians, but were deeply influenced by the funk groove. These years certainly saw some of the best work of soul giants Curtis Mayfield, Stevie Wonder, Wilson Pickett, and Marvin Gaye, all of whom drew heavily upon the expanded lyrical and musical grooves opened up by funk. The Isley Brothers, always one of soul's most eclectic stars, became close to an out-and-out funk band after beefing up their guitars and arrangements under the influence of Jimi Hendrix and Sly Stone. Even more traditional soul vocal groups like the Temptations and O'Jays delved quite heavily into funk for a time to come up with some of their most memorable hits.

Opinions differ on the matter, but it could be argued that the early '70s saw funk at its peak. The music remained extremely popular through the mid-'70s, though, with less sophisticated acts who either concentrated on the dance-and-party element (Kool & the Gang, the Ohio Players, Graham Central Station) or the slicker, more soul- and harmony-influenced variants (Earth, Wind & Fire, the Tower of Power). As for the original innovators, James Brown had seemingly run out of fresh ideas by the middle of the decade, accused even by his backup musicians of not only repeating himself but copying his imitators. Sly Stone fell victim to well-documented substance abuse and financial problems, and the Parliament-Funkadelic clan, while continuing to churn out music at the top of their game, were just too eccentric to truly catch on with the masses.

Disco, although it owed a great deal to funk in its dance rhythms, overran its ancestor in popularity in the mid- and late '70s. Some pop- and dance-oriented acts that owed a debt to funk did enjoy great success in the late '70s and '80s, though, including Rick James, Cameo, the Gap Band, and the Commodores. The influence of funk was also felt in the jazz world with the advent of fusion, particularly in the work of Herbie Hancock, Donald Byrd, Freddie Hubbard, and Lonnie Smith.

If anything, funk has undergone a renaissance in the 1990s. Bootsy Collins and George Clinton are both venerated pioneers who continue to record critically respected albums and draw huge crowds on the club circuit, although they don't chart like they did at their peak. Funk was a big element in the mix of the '80s biggest Black superstars, Michael Jackson and Prince, and funk classics are sampled constantly (some would say excessively) by contemporary rappers. And even some of the biggest white alternative rock acts, such as the Red Hot Chili Peppers, Faith No More, and Primus, draw heavily on funk's rhythms and in-your-face attitudes, if not delivering as much soul as its progenitors.

Recommended Recordings

Various Artists, *In Yo' Face! The Roots of Funk, Vol. 1/2* (Rhino)
[Note: this is volume one-half, or the "prequel" to the *In Yo' Face* History of Funk Series listed below]

Various Artists, *In Yo' Face! The History Of Funk, Vol. 1-5* (Rhino)

James Brown, *Love Power Peace: Live at the Olympia Paris 1971* (PolyGram)

Various Artists, *James Brown's Funky People Parts 1 & 2* (PolyGram)

The JB's, *Funky Good Time* (PolyGram)

Dyke & the Blazers, *Dyke's Greatest Hits* (Original Sound)

Charles Wright & the Watts 103rd Street Band, *Express Yourself: The Best Of* (Warner Brothers)

Sly & the Family Stone, *There's a Riot Goin' On* (Epic)

Parliament, *Tear the Roof Off* (Casablanca)

Funkadelic, *Music for Your Mother* (Westbound)

Bootsy Collins, *Back in the Day: The Best Of* (Warners)

War, *Anthology (1970-1994)* (Rhino)

The Meters, *Funkify Your Life: The Meters Anthology* (Rhino)

Curtis Mayfield, *Superfly* (Curtom)

James Brown, *Foundations of Funk: A Brand New Bag: 1964-1969* (Polydor)

James Brown, *Funk Power 1970: A Brand New Thang* (Polydor)

James Brown, *Make It Funky: The Big Payback: 1971-1975* (Polydor)
—Richie Unterberger

Philly Soul

The last major movement of the classic soul era to make a wide impact, Philadelphia soul represented the style at its sweetest, and soul production at its most sophisticated. Its severest critics would contend that much of the genre was overly slick, the most lightweight of which helped set the ground for the more mechanized elements of disco and urban contemporary. Others would praise the music for almost exactly the same reasons, seeing the Philly sound as soul at its most romantic, ushering in an era of elaborate instrumental and vocal arrangements that continue to play a large part in Black pop music today.

The hallmarks of Philadelphia soul—the lush, buoyant strings and horns, the smooth group harmonies with a touch of street corner *a cappella*, the insistent danceable rhythms and smoldering ballads—were often the handiwork of an extremely small clique of producers. Most of the classic Philly soul recordings of the late '60s and first half of the '70s were devised by the producers Kenny Gamble and Leon Huff (who worked as a team), as well as producer Thom Bell (who sometimes arranged material for Gamble-Huff). Their extremely prolific output, maintaining enough diversity to ensure continuing public interest while stamping each record with distinctive Philly soul qualities, was reminiscent in some respects of Motown's production line during their 1960s' glory days. Gamble & Huff, like Motown, also used a house band of sorts, a core group of musicians that contributed mightily to establishing a sound that could be identified with their records.

None of this could have been accomplished without first-rate singers, both soloists and groups, and the Philly soul stars, like those of Motown, were distinctive talents in their own right. They did differ from their counterparts in that while Motown's stars were largely tapped from their Detroit base, the Philadelphia performers were often (though not by any means always) transplants. Indeed, after the Philly sound had become a major industry force, established soul stars like Wilson Pickett, Dionne Warwick, and Lou Rawls would travel to the city specifically to record with top producers. There was generally less grit involved in the Philadelphia studios, and though it's a matter of conjecture whether the performer's role was more or less limited than it was at Motown or other soul centers, there's no doubt that production was just as important, if not more, as material or performance.

Gamble and Huff were young veterans of the Philly music scene who began scoring their first big national hits in the late '60s with smooth vocal groups like the Intruders and Delfonics and more raucous, dance-oriented records with Archie Bell & the Drells. It was a long-running association with Jerry Butler, already a star with many popular Chicago soul recordings under his belt, that really got them on a roll. The team rode high through the mid-'70s with hits by the aformentioned acts and Joe Simon, Harold Melvin & the Blue Notes (featuring Teddy Pendergrass), and above all the O'Jays, who may have done more than any other act to define the Philadelphia soul sound.

Thom Bell oversaw a smaller roster, and generally pursued a slightly smoother sound. His big acts were the Stylistics, whose creamy harmonies sailed on top of the frothiest Philly soul hits, and the Spinners, who found massive success in Philadelphia studios after years of recording as also-rans for Motown and other labels.

While Gamble-Huff and Bell dominated the Philly scene, they didn't produce every last hit of the era by any means. In particular, Bunny Sigler helped produce some successes for Gamble-Huff's Philadelphia International label, and Peter DeAngelis (who cut his teeth with, of all people, Frankie Avalon and Fabian) arranged and produced Philly soul records for Eddie Holman that both recalled and stood up to the best that Gamble-Huff were churning out at the same time.

Philadelphia soul hits occasionally boasted strong, socially aware lyrics, especially on some of the O'Jays hottest sellers; "Back Stabbers" in particular is often cited as one of the hardest-hitting reflections of urban street life in soul music. By and large, though, they focused on the joys and sorrows of romance, not civil rights or expanding consciousness. That didn't affect commercial sales in the least, but did perhaps limit their impact upon the world of rock at a time when the pressure for lyrical significance was high. David Bowie, always looking for something new to sink his teeth into, brought a lot of Philadelphia soul into his work in the mid-'70s when he unpredictably terminated his arty glam rock phase and traveled to Sigma Sound Studios, where many classic Philly soul hits were recorded, to cut some of his most commercially (though not critically) successful work.

With a rhythmic and elaborate production line already in place, the Philadelphia sound was more equipped than any other soul scene to face the disco era. Indeed, the mid-'70s saw many of the biggest early disco hits emerge from Philadelphia, including recordings which found stalwarts like the O'Jays adapting to the new trend, and new disco acts like the Trammps. Not as critically esteemed as the earlier Philadelphia soul productions, they were nonetheless extremely successful in the marketplace. But the Philadelphia sound, as practiced by Gamble-Huff and their brethren, had spent most of its power as a major artistic force by the end of the '70s, much as Motown lost most of its impetus after the '60s. Unlike Motown, though, the Philadelphia producers didn't maintain a respectable sales profile, largely dropping from sight after the early 1980s. Philadelphia soul lingers, however, in almost all urban contemporary soul and R&B, by veterans like Patti LaBelle and newcomers like Boyz II Men.

Recommended Recordings

The Delfonics, *Best of the Delfonics* (Arista)

The Intruders, *Super Hits* (Philadelphia International)

Archie Bell & the Drells, *The Best Of* (Rhino)

Jerry Butler, *Iceman: The Mercury Years* (PolyGram)

The O'Jays, *The O'Jays in Philadelphia* (Philadelphia International)

Eddie Holman, *I Love You* (Varese Sarabande)

The Stylistics, *Best of the Stylistics* (Amherst)

The O'Jays, *Greatest Hits* (Philadelphia International)

The Spinners, *One of aKind Love Affair—The Anthology* (Atlantic)

Harold Melvin & the Blue Notes, *Collector's Item* (Philadelphia International)

—Richie Unterberger

The Roots of Punk

When punk flowered in the mid-1970s, it took enthusiasts and detractors alike by surprise. It seemed to many that there was no precedent for music so venomous, angry, brittle, fast, and loud. In fact, the elements that would coalesce into punk had been building, on a very underground level, for about a decade before punk became big news with the emergence of Patti Smith, the Ramones, and the Sex Pistols. Often despised and ignored by the masses in their own time, the critical perspective afforded by several decades of hindsight has belatedly anointed these trailblazers—the Velvet Underground, the Stooges, the MC5, Jonathan Richman, and others—as bands whose importance and influence extended way beyond their minimal commercial impact.

Although punk rockers sometimes liked to paint themselves as outcasts who pit themselves in deliberate opposition to all rock 'n' roll traditions, the seeds of punk rock can be traced right back to the birth of rock itself. The wildest early rockabilly and R&B performers sang and played with a shamanistic, primitive abandon that has been matched, but never exceeded. Ditto for the early British Invasion bands, and more specifically the teenage American garage bands that followed in their wake in the mid-'60s. Rock critic (and future Patti Smith Group guitarist) Lenny Kaye helped canonize these groups on his *Nuggets* compilation in the

early 1970s. At the same time, he and other historians like Greg Shaw devised the term "punk" to categorize these kinds of bands, for whom raw energy and sneering attitude were more important than musical virtuosity or sophisticated production.

However, the first group whose work contained demonstrably audible parallels to what we've come to know as the punk/new wave sound were the Velvet Underground. Starting as components of Andy Warhol's traveling pop art/performance ensemble The Exploding Plastic Inevitable, the Velvets were not, as some have implied, totally alienated from the currents affecting music and popular culture in the 1960s. To a large degree, though, they deliberately ran against the grain of both pop-rock and psychedelia. They didn't ignore melody, but placed a higher premium on dense guitar assaults, primitive rock energy, grating feedback/distortion, and occasional willfully atonal excursions into the avant-garde. Lyrically, they took on topics like drug use/abuse, gender confusion, sadomasochism, and urban sleaze that were all but ignored by other rock groups of the day. Much of this commentary was inspired by their New York Lower East Side community, and in fact the Fugs had already begun to document this to an extent (and break similar lyrical taboos) on their early records, although their music did not match the Velvets in lyrical or aural power.

While it's fashionable in some critical circles to pigeonhole the Velvets as loud, defiantly inaccessible outcasts who created the most scabrously sensational sounds they could, in fact that's only part of the picture. Like all truly great rock bands, the Velvets were a versatile bunch, capable of affecting, tuneful folk-rock and tender love songs as well as needle-on-11 screechers such as "Sister Ray" and gothic harbingers of doom such as "Venus in Furs" and "All Tomorrow's Parties." In fact, after the departure of John Cale under tense circumstances in 1968, the Velvets became a considerably more conventional, guitar riff-driven band, though no less powerful or ambitious. The thread that makes their diverse work of a piece is the underlying, unblinking honesty behind the songs and the performances. The Velvets didn't try to sweep conflict under the rug, or wrap their message in feel-good sentiments; they told things as they were, though their grimiest sketches (such as "Heroin") attracted more attention than their not-infrequent joyful rockers.

Two late '60s Detroit bands took the Velvets' primitive aspects to more basic, outrageous, and guitar-dominated extremes. The first to emerge, the MC5, actually had strong roots in the mighty and prolific Ann Arbor, Michigan garage scene. Their early singles for the local A-Square label were one- and two-chord bursts of blurry guitar distortion and shouted vocals; not a totally foreign territory to garage bands, perhaps, but it had never been committed with such metallic mayhem. As if any more outrage were needed, the MC5 began to make their lyrics consciously anarchistic and provocative, reflecting the influence of their manager, noted leftist John Sinclair. The roots of both the Sex Pistols and heavy metal can be heard on their debut album, *Kick out the Jams*, a nonstop (and wearying) assault. While the album actually reached the top 40, management, drug, and personnel problems plagued the group throughout the remainder of their short existence, and they played it much safer on subsequent records before breaking up in the early '70s.

Less political and more minimalist were MC5's Ann Arbor chums, the Stooges, paced by the over-the-top antics of lead singer Iggy Pop. There weren't many sophisticated words, or indeed many words at all, in the Stooges' lyrical vocabulary; that's because, as members of the band have remarked since, they wanted every word to count. The group's first two albums, even more than *Kick out the Jams*, anticipate the Sex Pistols with both the mounds of fuzzy guitar chords and the brooding, nihilistic, shouted/chanted lyrics. With characters as volatile as Iggy and the Gang, long-term stability could have hardly been part of the game plan; the group changed personnel numerous times and struggled with serious drug problems before imploding by the mid-'70s, although they managed to regroup for one more respected recording, *Raw Power*, prior to their final demise.

Historians sometimes paint the Velvets, Stooges, and MC5 as outlaws before their time who were reviled by hippy-dominated audiences that shut their eyes to the realities these brave souls were willing to face. It's certainly true that these bands didn't attain nearly the same level of visibility as the Beatles and Stones, or even Santana and James Taylor. But it isn't true that they went totally unappreciated in their own time. Often they attracted critical raves, not just in underground rock magazines like *Creem*, but *Rolling Stone* as well. Many FM stations played their music, and although their audiences were small (partly because of lackadaisical label promotion), they were devoted, approaching a cult-like fervor. Sometimes members of the audience were inspired to form their own bands, as Velvet Underground fan Jonathan Richman was.

But Richman's band, the Modern Lovers, made barely any impact whatsoever in the early 1970s. That's due, in large part, to the fact that they didn't release any records at the time, although they made some recordings with John Cale and (at separate sessions) Kim Fowley that didn't see the light of day for several years. Time, though, has proven their early work to be nearly as influential as those of the other pre-punk pioneers. The irony is that the Modern Lovers—who also featured future Talking Head Jerry Harrison, and future Car David Robinson—were more accessible than the Stooges. Not nearly as confrontational or dependent upon bludgeoning, over-amped guitars, the Modern Lovers were nonetheless similar in their use of primitive, riff-driven arrangements. And their lyrics, if not as violent, were just as angst-ridden—Richman was not just an outcast, but a neurotic nerd outcast, going on at arresting length about destructive affairs with emotionally disturbed women, abstaining from drugs and sitting in his room, and genuinely torturing himself with alienation. Like the Velvets, though, Richman could be downright jubilant at times, as on his anthemic ode to rock 'n' roll, "Roadrunner." By the time the Modern Lovers' debut was finally released in 1976, the original and best lineup was long gone and the sound tamed. Richman went on to an increasingly strange career of child-like folk/pop that was not without its highlights, but not nearly as nervy as his early material.

The hotbed of American punk was New York City, and most of the first-wave punk/new wave acts, such as Patti Smith, Television, Richard Hell, and Blondie, were performing years before their first official releases. There was one band, though, that had already broken up by the time CBGB's really began hopping. These were the New York Dolls, and in comparison with all the bands mentioned in this piece so far, they can sound the most conventional to latter-day ears. And indeed, at the time, they were more apt to be labeled a glitter band than a punk band (not to mention that the term "punk" was barely even bandied about until years later). The Dolls did adhere to a basic, if somewhat trashy, prototype that placed much more value on attitude and raunch than the players' somewhat limited (though by no means amateurish) abilities. Only managing to record two albums before their breakup, they made little impact beyond New York City (where some critics adored the band). Their long-term impact was substantial; Malcolm McLaren helped manage the Dolls during their dying days, an experience which sparked ideas for molding a band of his own back in London, the Sex Pistols.

While it would be British bands like the Sex Pistols and the Clash that were really responsible for moving punk into high gear, in the early 1970s there were far fewer antecedents for the movement in the UK than in the US. One school of rock that did anticipate some elements of punk's outrageousness and flirtations with decadence was glam rock. As practiced by T. Rex and others, glam did put the focus on earthy expression and basic guitar riffs, features that progressive rockers and singer-songwriters didn't hold nearly as dear. David Bowie is often mentioned as a precursor of sorts to punk, but if that's so, the evidence is much more in his attitude than his meticulously crafted songs and records. But, as Bowie biographers Roy Carr and Charles Shaar Murray once pointed out, Johnny Rotten, Sid Vicious, Siouxsie Sioux, Joe Strummer, Poly Styrene, Elvis Costello, and Billy Idol are "all children of Ziggy Stardust. The punks did as Bowie had done and encouraged Mott the Hoople's Ian Hunter to do: they dropped the all-pervasive fake-American rack 'n rowl voice and sang in the identifiable accents of their hometowns, and they took to the visual vocabulary of Bowie's make-up and costume with a crazed ingenuity."

In his glitter-rock phase, ex-Velvet Underground leader Lou Reed was far more popular in Britain than his native land; the album that broke him in the UK, *Transformer*, was co-produced by none other than Bowie himself. While the solo work of the ex-Velvets could not be said to be nearly as influential as what they recorded together, the individual efforts of Reed, Cale, and Nico were inspirational to all sorts of musicians looking for something expressive and out of the ordinary in the oft-stale musical climate of the early to mid-'70s. Reed's street-talk sing-speak, though muted in much of his early solo albums, was one of the basic models for the punk vocal style, in which it was more important to convey a tough, savvy attitude than sing "well" in the conventional sense. Nico's desolate, moaning ruminations on things metaphysical and inscrutable were an important root of goth-rock (itself an offshoot of punk and new wave). Cale's most important contributions to the birth of punk, in retrospect, were as a producer; he oversaw the most seminal works of the Stooges, the Modern Lovers, Nico, and Patti Smith (*Horses*).

Patti Smith, like Television, Blondie, and Richard Hell, made some recordings before her first widely available full-length release. In each case, these have only been heard by a small clique of hardcore fans, on limited edition independent singles, bootlegs, private tapes, and official CDs that were released long after the acts had passed into legend. In a fashion, these can be considered to show the "roots of punk," although the performers were actually first-wave punk/new wave performers themselves. But anyone with a serious interest in the history of the scene should check these out, the most important of them being Patti Smith's "Hey Joe" single and *Free Music Store* bootleg (taken from a radio broadcast before a drummer had joined her group); Television's "Little Johnny Jewel" single, along with demos from the same mid-'70s period (which appear on the bootleg *Double Exposure*); and Blondie's 1975 demos, finally released officially on 1994's *Platinum Collection*. The most intriguing relics of the lot, though, are the astonishingly abra-

sive cuts recorded in April 1973 by the Neon Boys, who featured both Tom Verlaine and Richard Hell (these were later issued on Hell's *Past And Present* EP).

Other than New York, the only hotbed of pre-punk activity in the United States was Cleveland. The Electric Eels' "Agitated"/"Cyclotron" single (recorded in '75, but not issued until '78) is perhaps the single most modern punk-like record cut before 1976, with ranting, nearly unintelligible lyrics delivered in the most grating way imaginable, while distorted, overmodulated guitars clang chaotically in the background. The tracks on the Eels' posthumous CD collections, issued only in the late '80s and early '90s (some featuring future Cramps drummer Nick Knox), are even less accessible, ranking not just as the most dissonant pre-punk, but as some of the most deliberately alienating and uncommercial rock music ever made; "Agitated"/"Cyclotron" were at least centered around crunching riffs. Other semi-legendary Cleveland bands like Mirrors and the Styrenes did a fair amount of recording, but little has ever been easily available; a cogent collection of mid-'70s Cleveland pre-punk is long overdue. Early demos by mechanical rock pioneers Devo (actually from nearby Akron, Ohio), some dating back as early as 1974, did surface on Rykodisc in the early 1990s.

A final Cleveland band, Rocket from the Tombs, may have been the most interesting of all, featuring David Thomas and Peter Laughner before those two formed Pere Ubu, as well as (for a brief time) future Dead Boy Stiv Bators. While their roots lay in '60s hard rock and heavy metal, what came out was artier, darker, rawer, different, and a definite foreshadowing of punk and new wave in its ominous alienation. Most of their material was original, and indeed several of their stronger compositions would be resuscitated in subsequent years by Pere Ubu ("Thirty Seconds over Tokyo," "Life Stinks," and "Final Solution") and the Dead Boys ("Ain't It Fun"). Nothing was officially released by the group, and even limited edition bootlegs of their tapes (which were actually broadcast on a popular FM Cleveland station in early 1975) are incredibly scarce. These tapes, though not up to "normal" studio standards, are not just some of the most seminal music of the birth of punk/new wave, but some of the most seminal rock music of any sort that has even yet to gain reasonable unofficial availability, though they have circulated among a small group of collectors for years. Thomas and Laughner proceeded along similar but artier directions on their first singles, before Laughner left; he died in 1977, leaving behind some solo recordings in a much folkier vein, wearing a debt to *Berlin*-era Lou Reed on his sleeve.

Part of the problem in classifying and collecting the music that was the roots of punk is that it was not thought of as pre-punk when it was being made, just as the music that led to rock 'n' roll was never labeled as pre-rock until long after the fact. At the time, it was just weird off-shoots of the underground rock scene, some of which got reasonably wide critical attention, some of which was totally ignored, and hardly any of which was seen as part of the same cloth. The first edition of *The Rolling Stone Illustrated History of Rock'n'roll*, for instance, published in 1976 on the eve of punk's birth, covers the Velvet Underground in its chapter on art rock, and the Stooges and MC5 in the heavy metal section. It wasn't until 1976 and 1977 that all of the elements coalesced into a reasonably broad-based movement in both the US and the UK, with the Sex Pistols, the Clash, the Ramones, Patti Smith, and others leading the charge of punk and new wave into the public's consciousness. But like all important "cult" music that was misunderstood or underappreciated in its own era, the pre-punk pioneers—who often owed as much to pre-1970 rock traditions as their own futuristic innovations—have come to be regarded with as much respect as the first bona fide punk rockers.

Recommended Recordings

The Velvet Underground, *Peel Slowly and See* (Polydor)
The Velvet Underground, *1969: Velvet Underground Live* (Mercury)
The Fugs, *The Fugs First Album* (Fantasy)
The Fugs, *The Fugs* (Fantasy)
The MC5, *Babes in Arms* (ROIR)
The MC5, *Kick out the Jams* (Elektra)
The Stooges, *The Stooges* (Elektra)
The Stooges, *Fun House* (Elektra)
The Stooges, *Raw Power* (Elektra)
The Modern Lovers, *The Original Modern Lovers* (Bomp)
Lou Reed, *Transformer* (RCA)
Lou Reed, *Berlin* (RCA)
Nico, *The Marble Index* (Elektra)
The New York Dolls, *New York Dolls* (Mercury)
The New York Dolls, *Too Much, Too Soon* (Mercury)
Various Artists, *The Great New York Singles Scene* (ROIR)
Patti Smith, *Free Music Store* (bootleg)
Television, *Double Exposure* (bootleg)
The Neon Boys, "Love Comes in Spurts"/"That's All I Know (Right Now)" (part of Richard Hell's *Past and Present* EP, Shake)

Rocket From The Tombs, *WMMS Broadcasts* (bootleg tapes)

Books

From Velvets to Voidoids: A Pre-Punk History for a Post-Punk World, by Clinton Heylin (Penguin, 1993)

Up-tight: The Velvet Underground Story, by Victor Bockris (Omnibus, 1993)

Transformer: The Lou Reed Story, by Victor Bockris (Simon & Schuster, 1995)

Nico: The Life & Lies of an Icon, by Richard Witts (Virgin, UK, 1993)

–Richie Unterberger

Pub Rock

Defiantly unpretentious and unfazed by the zeitgeist, pub rock, despite being a short-lived permutation of British rock, was in essence a roots-rock retrenchment that flew in the face of British glam/glitter rock of the early and mid-'70s. Many of pub rock's proponents came from a mixture of mid-'60s British R&B, hippie folk-blues, and country backgrounds, and this conflation of similar styles led to some wonderfully spirited rock 'n' roll that, somewhat unintentionally, turned into a subtle rebellion by musicians against the machinations of the pop music industry. Pub rock never caught on in a big way; in fact some critics assert its heyday was only between 1971-74. Nonetheless, there were plenty of excellent pub rock bands, and many musicians who cut their teeth during this time went on to join some of the seminal English bands of the late '70s.

Although it shares many common elements with American roots-rock, pub rock is distinctly British; the result of a small but supportive community-based scene that focused in pubs around London. The scene coalesced around a former London jazz club, the Tally Ho, and soon spread to dozens of other pubs in the city keen to book rock bands. With glitter/glam rock dominating the British charts, pub rock musicians, fans, and the pub owners who booked them regarded this music as a way to reject the egregious trappings and slavish attempts at pop superstardom for something that was more honest, direct, and communal.

Ironically, the band that gets credit for jumpstarting pub rock is an obscure American R&B band, Eggs over Easy, who in 1972 gigged at the Tally Ho. Despite this jarring piece of history, it should be known that the English musicians inspired by the Eggs had been playing in mid-to-late-'60s blues, folk, and R&B bands such as the Action and Kippington Lodge (the latter featuring Brinsley Schwarz and Nick Lowe). British rock critic Pete Frame, who has written definitively about pub rock, notes three periods in the genre's development roughly spanning the years 1972-1975: first was the early Tally Ho period featuring bands such as Bees Make Honey (their moniker a tribute to Eggs over Easy), Brinsley Schwarz, and Ducks Deluxe; the second wave of bands included Kilburn and the High Roads (featuring Ian Dury), Chilli Willi & the Red Hot Peppers, and Ace; the third and final bunch of pub rockers were led by the Winkies, Sniff & the Tears, and the great Dr. Feelgood.

Of the aforementioned bands, the one perhaps most familiar to American audiences is Brinsley Schwarz. Named after their great lead guitarist, they, more than any other band, defined all that was good about pub rock. And, unlike many of their ilk (up until Dr. Feelgood), had the longest and most successful recording career and managed to get many of their LPs released in America. Despite a storied public-relations disaster wherein the band was flown to the Fillmore East for a showcase gig and slammed by American rock critics (effectively ending stateside interest in pub rock), Brinsley Schwarz set up a two-gigs-a-week residency at the Tally Ho, providing the inspiration for literally every pub rock band that came in their wake. Brinsley Schwarz broke up in 1975, bassist Nick Lowe went on to a solo career, as did guitarist Ian Gomm, while Schwarz and keyboardist Bob Andrews joined forces with ex-Ducks Deluxe guitarist Martin Belmont to form Graham Parker's phenomenal backing band, the Rumour.

Lowe's success and the rise of Graham Parker and the Rumour are a small indication of the kind of influence pub rock had on the next generation of British rock 'n' rollers. After Kilburn and the High Roads, Ian Dury embarked on a wonderful, if inconsistent, solo career; Elvis Costello's earliest musical days were with pub rockers Flip City and he found future Attractions drummer Pete Thomas in Chilli Willi & the Red Hot Peppers; Clash frontman Joe Strummer made his first records in a late-period pub rock band, the 101ers; even enigmatic avant-gardists the Residents had significant musical contributions made to their records by a pub rock vet, the late Phil "Snakefinger" Lithman, another ex-member of Chilli Willi. And lest one think that pub rock had no impact on the American Top Ten, remember the song "How Long," by pub rock veterans Ace, and featuring vocalist/keyboardist Paul Carrack, reached No. 3 in 1975.

Pete Frame argues (and he's right) that after the breakup of Brinsley Schwarz and Ducks Deluxe in 1975, pub rock was, for all intents and purposes, over. However, a wild, high-energy blues/R&B band from

Canvey Island in Essex named Dr. Feelgood was the most vital band of the late pub rock era and served as a crucial link to early punk rock. Fronted by the late great Lee Brilleaux (who succumbed to cancer in 1994), and the inspired guitar playing of Wilko Johnson, the Feelgoods released their first LP, *Down by the Jetty* (recorded in mono) in 1975 and released four great LPs before Johnson's departure in 1977. The band soldiered on until Brilleaux's death (at the end Brilleaux was the lone original member) and made good records, but lacked the panache that Wilko supplied. Important to note is that the members of Feelgood lent the cash for pub rock-fan Dave Robinson to start his great independent label Stiff and give artists like Nick Lowe, Elvis Costello, Ian Dury, Wreckless Eric, the Damned, and Dave Edmunds a place to record.

In many ways, pub rock, because of its insularity, smallness, and disinterest in becoming an international pop phenomenon, was destined to last only a short while. And although it remains somewhat of a mystery to many American ears, the music that resulted from this scene retains its vigorous, incorruptible spirit. It was the music of the moment, played by musicians who cared more about sincerity and less about fame.

Recommended Recordings

Ace, *Five a Side* (Anchor)

Bees Make Honey, *Music Every Night* (EMI)

Brinsley Schwarz, *Brinsley Schwarz* (Capitol) and *Silver Pistol* (Edsel)

Chilli Willi & the Red Hot Peppers, *Bongos over Balham* (Mooncrest)

Ducks Deluxe, *Don't Mind Rockin' Tonight* (RCA)

Dr. Feelgood, *Malpractice* (Columbia) and *Stupidity* (Liberty)

The 101ers, *Elgin Avenue Breakdown* (Andalucia)

The Winkies, *The Winkies* (Chrysalis)

–John Dougan

Punk Music

English critic Jon Savage noted that history is made by those who say "No," and in 1976 there was no louder "No" than that of punk rock. Dismissed by the shortsighted as crude anti-musicality, punk dared to place itself in direct confrontation with the then-ruling rock hegemony: generally thirty-something pop stars content to reinvent and regurgitate clichés in a sort of stylistic stasis, a dire situation exacerbated by the tightly controlled mid-to-late-'70s FM programming style known as AOR (album-oriented rock) and glutted with a seemingly endless array of not-so-hard-rock and not-quite-so-heavy-metal bands that sounded as if they'd been created by record-label marketing departments.

From the start, punk angrily stood in direct contrast to the zeitgeist. Still, as with all rock genres and sub-genres, it was hardly an organic movement. Its antecedents included the noisy primitivism of the Velvet Underground, the mega-loud working-class anger of the Who, the high-energy guitar spuzz of the MC5 and the Stooges, and the androgyny of the New York Dolls (with a few dollops of Bowie and early Roxy Music for good measure). Of course as punk developed (Note: The first known use of "punk rock" as a genre identifier goes back to the early '70s, *Creem* magazine, and critics Dave Marsh and Lester Bangs), it metamorphosed into numerous subgenres that championed a host of influences as disparate as reggae, mid-'60s bubblegum, early psychedelic rock, art-rock, free jazz, and musique concrete. Literally anything fit the equation; it was just a matter of attitude and presentation.

In a purely historical sense, punk's timeline is 1975-1978, and even that's somewhat generous. But with its supernova long since faded and its style coopted by greedy major labels who turned it into the more sanitized "new wave," punk's impact is still being felt in the '90s. It almost singlehandedly revived the independent record-label network and helped start a legitimate network of underground journals and a new style of music criticism. Most importantly, it imbued a younger generation with the spirit that they too could become part of the great rock 'n' roll whatsis, thereby planting the seeds for the future development of many successful US and UK regional alternative rock scenes (e.g., Los Angeles; Minneapolis; Seattle; Athens, GA; Manchester, England). It's hard to imagine bands like the Replacements, Nirvana, and R.E.M. existing without the contributions of the Sex Pistols, Clash, the Ramones, and the Buzzcocks.

These days, the term "punk" seems almost quaint. And truth be told, the story of punk and its pervasive influence is only now being told. But as with rap and current heavy metal (two genres that share punk's attitude), punk always seemed to be about the unencumbered joy of self-expression: total, unequivocal and often unedited. If you listen to a handful of the records listed below, you'll soon hear that, even today, punk never seems too far from the pop zeitgeist, a range of influence far greater than its originators had in mind.

Books

Punk Diary, by George Dimarc (St. Martin's, 1994)

–John Dougan

British Punk

Taking cues from some American bands, as well as the English mini-phenomenon known as "pub rock," English punk transmogrified into an entirely different beast, one that also valued stripped-down, primal guitar rock and a DIY (do it yourself) attitude, but one that openly embraced multiculturalism (e.g., ska and reggae), politics (a dysfunctional late-'70s government), and radical philosophy (e.g., the French Situationists). With the galvanic Sex Pistols leading the way, English rock would never be the same, as the sybaritic excesses of the post-hippie era were replaced by angry kids yelling "no future" and referring to successful rock stars as "boring old farts."

Punk took Great Britain—both its entertainment industry and its general citizenry—by surprise. In the mid-'70s, the massive tornado of the British Invasion was a fading memory whose survivors sat atop the charts with pale echoes of their best work. Disco and soft pop-rock were the trends of the day, as they were in the US. The nation's economy was flailing, and more and more teenagers left school to go straight on the dole (a British equivalent of welfare), with little hope for financial success or social stimulation in the near future.

Malcolm McLaren, who with his wife Vivienne Westwood ran a boutique that catered to an ever-changing clientele seeking alternative fashions, was on the lookout for a band of loutish post-adolescents to use as a platform for his loosely held anarchist and Situationist ideas. He harbored aspirations to take over the New York Dolls' management, but when that band splintered, he looked to even scruffier, younger musicians that frequented his store. In late 1975, the Sex Pistols began to perform, with McLaren as their manager.

An "alternative" scene (though they didn't call it as such at the time) did exist in Britain on a small level, as "pub rock." In truth, bands like Dr. Feelgood, Eggs over Easy, Ducks Deluxe, and even the acclaimed Brinsley Schwarz sound pretty tame and unrevolutionary. What they shared with punk was a disdain for contemporary pop and progressive rock trends, and a love for basic, stripped-down, guitar-oriented music. Besides supplying punk with some of its early figureheads, such as the principal movers of Stiff Records and Joe Strummer (who left his pub rock band the 101ers to join the Clash), the pub rock performance circuit provided crucial live venues for punk acts when the music was struggling to get off the ground. Throughout 1976, the Sex Pistols built up a fierce underground reputation with their incendiary live shows (which were often as not, violence-ridden, chaotic affairs). In late 1976, their debut single "Anarchy in the UK," established punk's modus operandi: scabrous guitars, hyperkinetic rhythms, and inflammatory, venomous lyrics, with crude energy carrying the day.

The Pistols endured a complicated tangle of personnel, management, and label problems in 1977 that kept them from releasing a full-length album for about a year (although a couple more key singles appeared in the meantime). Other groups were already following their blueprint, however, and stepped into the breach that Johnny Rotten had opened. The most famous members of what has come to be called "The Class of '77" include the Damned; the Clash, who infused punk with revolutionary politics and reggae rhythms; the Jam, post-mods who modeled themselves after the early Who; and the Buzzcocks, whose nervous, accelerated rhythms didn't hide a keen grasp of pop hooks.

As with all momentous musical movements, these figureheads (they would have disdained the label "stars" at the time) were the tip of an explosion that saw many minor but important groups adding their voices to the clamor, as well as interesting one and two-shots leaping into the volcano. Generation X, the Adverts, the Vibrators, and the Saints (actually from Australia) recorded important early punk records; X-Ray Spex did a lot to smash rock stereotypes by featuring a half-Black teenage female with braces as their lead singer. Groups like Chelsea, Eater, Johnny Moped, and Slaughter & the Dogs are esteemed by collectors for the one or two memorable songs they had in them.

Today, early British punk records still sound exciting, but hardly the epitome of nihilistic shock. At the time, however, they could not have caused more of a sensation, inspiring equal measures of fervent praise and outright hostility. The tempo was FAST (although hardcore made it go even faster), the guitars and vocals slashing and LOUD, and the lyrics—much, though by no means all, negative in nature—addressed politics, sex, depression, and society with a frank realism that had rarely been heard in pop music, and never as part of a broad-based movement. The performers were not seasoned virtuosos, valuing inspiration and attitude above professionalism. Some listeners viewed the results as unbearably crude; others welcomed them as a necessary shot of air to blast rock 'n' roll out of its complacency.

Punk never took hold in the US as it did in Britain, although those who were converted took up the music with a passion that equaled their UK counterparts. The Sex Pistols found this out the hard way, with John Lydon (nee Rotten) leaving the group in early 1978 after the last show of a brief, legendarily chaotic tour of the States, where their album stopped just short of the Top 100.

Music Map

British Punk

Pub Rock	Early '70s American Proto-Punk

1st Generation British Punk
The Sex Pistols, The Clash, The Jam, The Damned, Generation X, The Buzzcocks

Second Generation British Punk
The Adverts, The Undertones, X-Ray Spex, The Vibrators

Early British New Wave	Arty British Punk/ New Wave
Elvis Costello, Nick Lowe, Tom Robinson	Wire, Joy Division, The Fall, Magazine, Siouxsie & The Banshees

British punk did not so much die out as mutate and diversify, as any vital musical style needs to do in order to survive. As liberating as the first wave of punk was, it was impossible to perform an endless loop of hyper-fast, bile-filled anthems, as the musicians' ambitions broadened and their skills improved. The Jam remained huge stars in their homeland through the early '80s. Like the Clash, who become stars in the US at long last after 1979's *London Calling*, they refined their sound and incorporated R&B, soul, and pop into their compositions without compromising their integrity. While original British punkers like Generation X and Sham 69 played themselves out almost immediately, others went into arty minimalism (Wire, the Fall), post-psychedelia (the Soft Boys), pop-punk (the Undertones, from Northern Ireland), or new wave (Siouxsie & the Banshees)

A fertile, more techno-oriented scene developed in the Buzzcocks' home territory of Manchester, spearheaded by Joy Division and other acts on Factory Records. And pub rock veterans like Nick Lowe, Elvis Costello, and Tom Robinson tapped into punk's energy to midwife new wave, which by 1980 had become the new label for a modified, tamed, but innovative offspring of the original punk explosion.

Recommended Recordings

The Sex Pistols, *Never Mind the Bollocks* (Warner Brothers)
Various Artists, *Anarchy in the UK—UK Punk I (1976-77)* (Rhino)
Various Artists, *The Modern World—UK Punk II (1977-78)* (Rhino)
The Clash, *The Clash* (Epic)
The Jam, *Snap!* (Polydor)
The Buzzcocks, *Singles Going Steady* (IRS)
The Adverts, *Crossing the Sea with the Adverts* (Link Classics, UK)
X-Ray Spex, *Germ-Free Adolescents* (EMI)
The Vibrators, *Power of Money: The Best of the Vibrators* (Continuum)
The Undertones, *The Undertones* (Rykodisc)
Generation X, *Generation X* (Chrysalis)
The Damned, *Damned Damned Damned* (Frontier)

Books

England's Dreaming: Sex Pistols and Punk Rock, by Jon Savage (St. Martin's, 1991)

— *Richie Unterberger & John Dougan*

American Punk Rock

American punk rock was actively brewing years before the UK scene. The trade-off, perhaps, was that it was less explosive, less of a broad-based movement, less confrontational, and less concerned with disowning time-honored rock 'n' roll traditions. Still, it was not only a crucial source of inspiration for Britain's more volatile brand of punk, but a more diverse (though diffuse) movement whose effects were just as influential and long-reaching.

Some have argued that the true source of American punk rock lies in the incredibly active garage rock scene of the mid-'60s, and indeed the term "punk rock" was originally coined by critics like Dave Marsh,

Music Map

American Punk

'60s Proto-Punk Groups
The Velvet Underground, The Stooges, The MC5

Early '70s Proto-Punk Groups
The Modern Lovers, The New York Dolls

CBGB's Groups
The Patti Smith Group, The
Ramones, Television, Blondie,
Richard Hell & The Voidoids,
Talking Heads, The Heartbreakers

Ohio Groups
Pere Ubu, Devo

California Punk
The Avengers,
X, The Dils,
The Germs

New York No-Wave
Suicide, Lydia Lunch,
James Chance,
Glenn Branca

Lester Bangs, and future Patti Smith Group guitarist Lenny Kaye to refer to these bands. In the late '60s, Detroit groups the MC5 and the Stooges played amphetamined rock driven by fuzzed-out guitars and baldly outraged (and outrageous) lyrics that sound all but indistinguishable from early punk records.

An equally important, artier strand of raw rock 'n' roll minimalism was pioneered in New York in the late '60s by the Velvet Underground. Not all of their work foreshadowed punk, but even their songs that didn't feature street-life vignettes and overamped guitars (and there were plenty of both, especially on their early albums) had a no-frills, unembellished attitude that acted as the standard for the many groups, in New York and elsewhere, that looked to them for inspiration.

Two American acts blazed lonely trails in the early '70s that mid-wived the birth of punk. In Boston, the Modern Lovers, led by Jonathan Richman, added youthful naivete to the Velvets' glorious primitivism. Their early '70s recordings rank among the most joyous and affecting proto-punk/new wave efforts, although, tragically, the original and best lineup of the band released nothing during their lifetime. The New York Dolls affected a trashy, sub-early Rolling Stones glam rock image that attracted raves from local critics, but made little national impact, although Malcolm McLaren's brief association with the band in their dying days gave him many ideas to pass on to the Sex Pistols.

The American punk scene coalesced around New York City's Lower East Side and, specifically, at Hilly Kristal's bowery club, CBGB's. By late 1975/early 1976, bands such as the Patti Smith Group, the Ramones, Talking Heads, Blondie, Television, and the Heartbreakers (featuring former New York Doll Johnny Thunders) had pretty much made this dive their home, and complacent old American rock now faced a significant challenge.

Suddenly there was a scene that offered cultural solidarity, if little in the way of stylistic unanimity: the fast, loud, tuneful minimalism of the Ramones was offset by Patti Smith's poetic incantations, Television's spiraling guitar duels, Blondie's sexy neo-Spector pop, the egghead pop of the Talking Heads, and the fierce synthesizer minimalism of Suicide. What connected these bands was a sense of purpose and community; they were angry outsiders who insisted that the only way to change rock 'n' roll was to dismantle it and rebuild it, thereby reclaiming it. That didn't actually mean they weren't cognizant of rock's best traditions: "Hey Joe," "Surfin' Bird," "1-2-3 Red Light," and old songs by the 13th Floor Elevators, Al Green, and Randy & the Rainbows were featured prominently in the early repertoires of one or the other of the bands listed above.

At the outset, these bands were more influential than popular on a national level, though Patti Smith did fairly well, and Blondie and the Talking Heads would eventually break through to superstardom. In fact, Television were far more popular in the UK, where their second album even made the Top Ten. The Ramones were also more popular there, and extremely influential; indeed, their "1-2-3-4!" brand of accelerated rock 'n' roll made them one of the only early CBGB's bands to fit most listeners' basic conceptions of punk rock. It's been claimed that Malcolm

McLaren took the prototype safety pin and torn T-shirt punk look from Richard Hell, who helped ignite the scene with Tom Verlaine in the original Television lineup before fronting the Voidoids. Outside of New York, the US lacked a strong punk scene. With innovative but impossibly uncommercial groups like the Electric Eels, as well as more accessible acts like Rocket from the Tombs and Mirrors, Cleveland had an active proto-punk scene that lacked the exposure, either in a renowned club or on national record labels, necessary to spread its influence. Devo (not actually from Cleveland, but from the Ohio town of Akron) and Pere Ubu eventually broke through to widespread recognition with a style of new wave that was bleaker and more mechanized than most anything happening in New York. Many Boston bands would appear by the late '70s, on the whole more identified with power pop than punk.

In 1977, active punk scenes quickly sprang up in California, particularly in Los Angeles, which owed considerably more to the influence of early British punk—just making its inroads in the States via import records—than the New York bands. Generally, these groups played a harder, nastier, faster, more jaded type of punk. Not as commercial as either the London or New York punk acts—not that any of the California bands would have cared—the Dils, the Germs, the Avengers, and the Dickies laid the foundation for thrash/hardcore. X, very much a part of the early L.A. scene, would be one of the few to break out into any sort of large-scale success, by which time they'd tempered and diversified their original sound.

Isolated pockets of punk activity took hold in quite a few US cities, mainly ones with large youthful, artistic-leaning populations, such as Seattle and Austin. But the fact of the matter is, punk never seized the collective consciousness in the States, partly because of industry resistance to the music, and at least equally because many (perhaps most) rock listeners didn't like it. Nonetheless, American punk bands were a bedrock of much of the music of the 1980s and 1990s: the Athens, GA, new wave scene; alternative rock; the "no-wave" of New York avant-rockers ranging from Lydia Lunch and James Chance to Glenn Branca and Sonic Youth; hardcore; grunge—all of these developments derived key inspiration from the original punk bands.

Recommended Recordings

The Modern Lovers, *Modern Lovers* (Bomp)
The Patti Smith Group, *Horses* (Arista)
The Ramones, *All the Stuff & More, Vol. 1* (Warner Brothers)
Television, *Marquee Moon* (Elektra)
Blondie, *Blondie* (Chrysalis)
The Talking Heads, *Talking Heads '77* (Sire)
Various Artists, *Blank Generation—The New York Scene* (Rhino)
Various Artists, *We're Desperate—The L.A. Scene* (Rhino)
Richard Hell & the Voidoids, *Blank Generation* (Sire)
The Avengers, *Avengers* (CD Presents)
Suicide, *Suicide* (Restless)
Pere Ubu, *Terminal Tower* (Twintone)

Books

From the Velvets to the Voidoids, by Clinton Heylin (Penguin, 1993)
—Richie Unterberger & John Dougan

Post-Punk

For many artists and musicians, punk rock represented the relaxation of artistic conventions and restraints. While some musicians interpreted this relaxation as a cue to be vulgar and anti-social—and thereby laying the groundwork for the nihilistic hardcore movement—just as many interpreted it as a way for them to push musical boundaries. These artists were initially categorized as part of the new wave, but it became clear that the post-punk bands were more ambitious, serious and challenging than the pop-oriented new wave groups. As a result, they rarely had the same commercial success as new wave, but their records received greater critical acclaim and large cult followings that eventually turned into musicians themselves.

Post-punk was artier and darker than punk. It was less concerned with rock, preferring to concentrate on alternately haunting and abrasive textures, incorporating elements of the avant-garde, funk and worldbeat into their minimalistic rock 'n' roll. Essentially, it was assaultive art-rock, one that had little connection with the bloated prog-rock of the '70s, but owed a great deal to the experimental music of the Velvet Underground, the Who, Frank Zappa, the Stooges and Captain Beefheart. This aesthetic was alive and well before the New York strains of punk rock burst to life in the late '70s, as the Cleveland, Ohio-based Pere Ubu illustrates.

Pere Ubu were post-punk before punk even existed. Basing their weird, noisy urban blues-rock on British bands like the Yardbirds and the Who, Pere Ubu moved into dark, claustrophobic and strange directions with their first singles and 1978 debut album *The Modern Dance*. Their music was too odd for most listeners, yet its arty eclecticism and bleak tone set the pace for much of American post-punk, not the least of which were their Akron, Ohio contemporaries Devo. Appearing a few years after Pere Ubu, Devo married their concept of humankind's "devolution" to noisy, herky-jerky synthesized pop and a striking visual style, where the band all looked like robotic clones of each other. Of all the post-punk bands, Devo tended to be a little catchier, yet their hooks were geeky, introverted and entirely arty and claustrophobic.

Since Devo had a clever visual concept, they were able to translate to MTV, thereby giving them a significantly larger audience. Not all of their American peers were as lucky. The Residents' performance-art avant-operas were nearly as old as Pere Ubu, yet they were barely noticed outside of metropolitan circles. All of New York's abrasive, nearly-unlistenable "no wave" scene, led by James Chance & the Contortions, remained obscure outside of the Big Apple. The Feelies were rarely heard outside of underground circles, yet their nervy, jangly pop would have great impact in the American indie-rock world during the '80s. One of the only American post-punk bands to reach both a large cult audience and the mainstream were Talking Heads, who had played both punk and new wave before they worked with Brian Eno on the groundbreaking, African-influenced *Remain in Light.*

On the whole, the Americans were defiantly, self-consciously arty and detachedly intellectual. Their British counterparts were just as arty, yet their music was darker and more emotional; it was angst, not intellectualism. The first wave of post-punks—Gang of Four, Siouxsie & the Banshees, Joy Division, Adam & the Ants—formed immediately after the Sex Pistols, and instead of following through on the Johnny Rotten's unbridled rage, they turned it inward, creating gloomy, atmospheric soundscapes that bristled with tension and claustrophobic angst. Gang of Four's blend of leftist politics, abrasive guitar noise and funk rhythms was invigorating, acclaimed and influential, yet they were rarely heard outside of small circles. Both Siouxsie & the Banshees and Adam & the Ants mined similar territory at first, making records that were dense with dissonant keyboards and angular guitars, and giving theatrical concerts. Joy Division and their lead Ian Curtis weren't as explicitly arty, but their music was even more introverted. Their two haunting, monolithic albums *Unknown Pleasures* and *Closer,* functioned as the touchstone for goth-rock, which was the subgenre that the Cure became known for. Initially, the Cure's music was jagged and fractured, yet quite catchy, but as their career progressed, they slowed their tempos down and began languishing in long, synth-driven soundscapes. But if any band was known for goth, it was Bauhaus, a quartet that specialized in slow, atmospheric textures punctuated by phased guitar and Bowiesque vocals.

By the early '80s, post-punk had distinguished itself from new wave, which had begun to break into the pop mainstream. Post-punk didn't aim for such success, yet it proved to be a mercurial phenomenon anyway. Many of the groups were short-lived, and those that did continue—Talking Heads, Adam & the Ants, Siouxsie & the Banshees, the Cure—altered the sound and attack as they grew artistically. Two other bands, Joy Division and Bauhaus, continued in new guises—New Order and Love & Rockets, respectively—and started to explore new stylistic ground. Most of these groups began moving away from the claustrophobic doom that distinguished early post-punk, moving toward cleaner, dissonant attacks. The Birthday Party and its leader Nick Cave picked up the gloomy slack, but other groups—such as the fractured Fall, the agit-rock Pop Group, the ringingly anthemic U2, the twisted roots-punk of the Mekons and the stark, cool neo-psychedelia of Echo & the Bunnymen and the Teardrop Explodes—fit into the newly redefined sound of post-punk.

Post-punk never died out, but it faded away in the mid-'80s, as its offspring began making records. By that time, the jangle-pop of R.E.M., the post-hardcore punk-pop of Hüsker Dü and the avant-rock of Sonic Youth had all taken center stage in the American underground, while the self-absorbed pop of the Smiths and the swirling noise of the Jesus & Mary Chain divided the British indie scene in two camps. While these groups were active, several of their forefathers were enjoying their greatest success. The Cure, New Order, Siouxsie & the Banshees, Nick Cave, Love & Rockets and the Fall continued to be major players into the early '90s, by which time their music had lost some of its initial shock. Some of the records sound dated and precious, but the best post-punk retains its power, and it's possible to hear its impact throughout contemporary rock, particularly in the epic soundscapes of Radiohead.

Recommended Recordings

Joy Division, *Unknown Pleasures* (Qwest)
Joy Division, *Closer* (Qwest)
The Cure, *Staring at the Sea* (Elecktra)
Pere Ubu, *The Modern Dance* (Blank/Rough Trade)
Talking Heads, *Remain in Light* (Sire)
Adam & the Ants, *Dirk Wears White Socks* (Do It/Epic)
Siouxsie & the Banshees, *Once Upon a Time* (Geffen)
The Feelies, *Crazy Rhythms* (A&M)

Gang of Four, *Entertainment!* (Infinite Zero)
Bauhaus, *In the Flat Field* (4AD)
U2, *Boy* (Island)
The Fall, *458489 A-Sides* (Beggars Banquet)
Birthday Party, *Hits* (4AD)
Mekons, *Mekons Rock & Roll* (A&M)
Echo & the Bunnymen, *Songs to Learn and Sing* (Sire)
New Order, *Movement* (Qwest)
The Pop Group, *The Pop Group* (Radar)
X, *Los Angeles/Wild Gift* (Slash)
The Slits, *Cut* (Antilles)
The Residents, *Meet the Residents* (East Side Digital)
Devo, *Are We Not Men? We Are Devo!* (Warner Brothers)
—Stephen Thomas Erlewine

New Wave

Punk rock may not have had the all-encompassing revolutionary effect that it originally was supposed to—after all, disco and pop still reigned on the charts after the Sex Pistols' disbandment—but it left a number of musical upheavals in its wake. At the time, every musical genre that followed punk was termed "new wave," in homage to the generation of French filmmakers that revolutionized the cinema in the '50s. Many hardline punk fans and critics complained about the term new wave and the music itself, claiming that it was designed to defuse the danger of punk, but in retrospect, the commercialization and broadening of punk culture was inevitable. Also, it seemed that new wave was quite different than post-punk, which tended to be more adventurous and self-consciously arty, as well as hardcore, which took the amateurish, thuggish tendencies of punk to an extreme. So where does that leave new wave? It is a catch-all term, collecting a variety of pop-oriented musics that weren't part of the mainstream, yet were melodic, catchy, idiosyncratic and quirky. new wave applied to everything from synthesized dance-pop to mod and ska-revivalists—as long as it relied on hooks and disregarded the pop mainstream, it was called new wave. There wasn't a specific sound, but there was a sensibility, one that was humorous, quirky and, most of all, not dangerous. It had the left-of-center sensibility, but none of the revolutionary danger, of punk rock.

In America, some of the very first punk bands indicated how the music would transform into new wave. With their ironic reworkings of '60s pop, bubblegum and garage rock, Blondie and the Ramones had the melodic sensibilities, as well as the visual gimmicks that would prove to be key to commercial new wave success. However, Blondie—who were blessed with Debbie Harry's sexy, photogenic looks—made the commercial crossover, and the Ramones remained a cult act, no matter how hard they tried to break into the pop charts with buzzingly catchy rockers like "Sheena is a Punk Rocker" and "Rock N Roll Radio." One of their New York contemporaries, Talking Heads, managed to become stars in the early '80s, after albums like *Talking Heads '77, More Songs About Buildings and Food* and *Remain in Light* had established their geeky, intellectual pop sense. Through these early records, Talking Heads became one of the leading American new wave bands, but their influence was overshadowed by the Athens, Georgia quartet the B-52's and the Boston quintet the Cars.

With their celebration of B-movie kitsch, dissonant harmonies and jerky hooks, the B-52's developed a new rock 'n' roll lexicon. They were defiantly strange and weirdly funny, with distinctive visual gimmicks and aural hooks that were easily as revolutionary as the speedy guitars of the Ramones. Their aesthetic was borrowed by numerous bands, many of which turned out to be one-hit wonders, but there were a handful that took it as a rallying cry. These generally turned out to be bands that were major players in alternative rock—during the late '70s and early '80s, the sound of B-52's was only heard in clubs and colleges, since the mainstream radio accepted new wave in the form of the Cars. For a band that cribbed heavily from the Velvet Underground and Iggy Pop, the Cars were remarkably straightforward; their pulsating, minimal-isitic rock 'n' roll played like arena rock since it emphasized the hook and loud guitars. Following the Cars, album-rock radio and many of its staple artists began incorporating new wave production techniques in an attempt to stay modern, and it resulted in some trashy, fun hits from veteran rockers that were generally clueless about punk. Of course, there were also bands like the Motels, Missing Persons and the Fixx whose sensibility was more akin to AOR than punk, but they were able to co-opt the new wave sound quite successfully. These bands provided the backdrop for the true sound of new wave, the multitudes of quirky, edgy pop singles that incorporated punk sensibility and culture within the confines of a three-minute pop single. The first to essay this idea successfully was Elvis Costello, a pub-rock singer-songwriter that became a sensation with his 1977 debut album *My Aim is True.* A smart, nervy collection of tight pop songs and ballads, *My Aim is True* illustrated that punk's energy could be harnessed in more accessible, straightforward styles and it also established that the music could be the province of geeky outsiders instead of stylish hipsters or brutish thugs. Costello's geeky persona would echo throughout the new wave years, yet his initial impact was how he pushed older pub rockers like Nick Lowe and Graham Parker into the limelight. These pub-rockers, whose initial rejection of rock stardom conventions paved the way for punk, favored pop, rock and folk, and helped usher in an explosive era of singles that covered a wide spectrum of sounds and styles.

During the late '70s and early '80s, there were countless bands that mined the catchy, quirky guitar-pop vein of new wave. There were conventional power-pop bands like Bram Tchaikovsky, the Romantics, 20/20 and the Knack, as well as the revitalized rock 'n' roll of the Pretenders, the jittery pop of XTC, the inspired songcraft of Squeeze, the Police's savvy pop-reggae and the spruced-up retro-rock of Rockpile and its two leaders, Nick Lowe and Dave Edmunds. Almost simultaneously, the ska and mod revivals surfaced in England. The Specials, Madness and the (English) Beat spearheaded the ska revival, which had a stronger dance rhythm than most new wave variations, along with more humor. The Jam updated the stridently British rock of the Who and the Kinks, and countless bands tried to mimic the band's punchy attack and lead singer-songwriter Paul Weller's biting lyricism. Soon, such guitar-oriented bands gave way to the synthesized, danceable territory of synth-pop and New Romantics like ABC, Duran Duran and Spandau Ballet. Inspired by David Bowie and Roxy Music's detached glamor and robotic soul, the New Romantics had cool electronic surfaces, crooning vocals and a distinctive visual style, which incorporated teased hair and flamboyant clothing. Such striking visuals made them naturals for MTV, a cable television network that debuted in 1981.

MTV needed videos to fill their 24 hours of programming, and new wave, particularly New Romantics, became their key to success. Soon, these groups, who had already had significant success in England, began making inroads across America, not only in New York and Los Angeles, but also in the midwest. Elvis Costello, the Clash, the Go-Go's, the Police, the Cars, the Pretenders and Talking Heads became stars thanks to MTV and mainstream radio play, but MTV's most significant contribution was fueling the last great era of one-hit wonders. The network did play the Jam, XTC and the Specials, but these only became major cult acts in America. Instead, the US audience favored A Flock of Seagulls, Haircut 100, the Joboxers, the Buggles—an endless stream of bands that were united only by the fact that they had great videos and one or two hits.

Within a few years, MTV was a major force in the music industry, and they had helped make bands like Duran Duran and the Australian pop-rock combo Men at Work into international stars. But by that point, new wave was beginning to run out of steam. Several major bands, including the Clash, the Specials and the Jam broke up, while others, such as Squeeze, Elvis Costello and Madness had taken time off to restructure their sound. Furthermore, the record industry had pushed too many bands like the Motels that simply co-opted new wave, which helped the public reach a saturation point. Also, MTV began airing videos from veteran stars that successfully negotiated the music video, which meant they didn't have to air new wave all the time. So, new wave quickly disappeared, since only the major players were able to sustain careers. During much of the late '80s, it was ridiculed for its silly fashion and disposable music, but in the mid-'90s, it not only became the subject of a wave of nostalgia, but it became clear that many artists had been inspired by the music. A re-evaluation of the period, however, was far from imminent, since it remained a subject for easy ridicule. That ignores that new wave, for all of its crass tendencies, was a stellar time for pop singles.

Recommended Recordings

Various Artists, *Just Can't Get Enough: New Wave Hits of the '80s, Vols. 1-15* (Rhino)
Various Artists, *DIY: UK Pop, Vols. 1 & 2* (Rhino)
Various Artists, *DIY: US Power Pop, Vol. 1 & 2* (Rhino)
Various Artists, *A Checkered Past: The 2-Tone Story* (Chrysalis/2-Tone)
The Specials, *The Specials* (Chrysalis/2-Tone)
Madness, *Complete Madness* (Stiff)
The Pretenders, *Pretenders* (Sire)
Elvis Costello, *Armed Forces* (Rykodisc)
The Jam, *Snap!* (Polydor)
Squeeze, *Singles: 45's and Under* (A&M)
XTC, *Waxworks* (Geffen)
Talking Heads, *Sand in the Vaseline* (Sire)
Blondie, *Parallel Lines* (Chrysalis)
Duran Duran, *Decade* (Capitol)
Nick Lowe, *Labour of Lust* (Columbia)
The Go-Go's, *Return to the Valley of the Go-Go's* (IRS)
Adam & the Ants, *Antics in the Forbidden Zone* (Epic)
—*Stephen Thomas Erlewine*

Power Pop

While there is nothing inherently wrong with power pop, it's often seen as a post-punk major-label marketing scam, helped along by greedy do-anything-to-make-it musicians who were willing to trade in their spiky haircuts and alienation for skinny ties and sunny dispositions. As true as this is, it represents only a fraction of what can accurately be described as power pop. While it's very easy (and tempting) to dismiss this sub-genre as egregious, market-driven dross, the fact remains that power pop, even at its sleaziest and most manipulative, has a longer history than many people realize, producing some terrific bands and equally terrific music.

The musical sourcepoint for nearly all power pop is: the Beatles. Virtually all stylistic appropriations begin with them: distinctive harmony singing, strong melodic lines, unforgettable guitar riffs, lyrics about boys and girls in love; they created the model that other power-poppers copied for the next few decades. Other profound influences include the Who, the Kinks, and the Move, bands whose aggressive melodies and loud distorted guitars put the "power" in power pop. Actually, in order to be complete, it's safe to say that an authoritative genealogical tree of power-pop influences would include virtually all of the bands of the British Invasion and mod era. Which brings up a subtle, yet essential facet of nearly all (era notwithstanding) American power-pop bands—they seem, vaguely, British. That is, they sing with a slight English lilt to their voices, are likely to cover songs by British bands and, as was the case with many British mod bands, dress up rather than down. Even the most prominent American power-pop influence, the jangly folk-rock of the mid-'60s Byrds, had a British tinge to it *à la* the Searchers and the Hollies.

American power pop's first heyday (ironically, before it was called power pop) was the early '70s. Few American bands encapsulated the commercial popularity and influential cult status of early power pop better than the Raspberries and Big Star. Both recorded great records, and while Big Star's entire recorded output (thanks mainly to the talents of Alex Chilton) remains inarguably the best of the bunch, both bands approached their craft with a similar intent: to write smart, punchy, hook-filled songs. For the Raspberries, a Cleveland-based band built around the Brit-rock obsessions of vocalist Eric Carmen and guitarist Wally Bryson, it was a string of huge hits like "Go All the Way," "Tonight," and the autobiographical "Overnight Sensation (Hit Record)" that made them one of the best commercial rock bands of the early '70s. Granted, their songs were hardly deep, but as heartfelt evocations of romantic teen angst and the naiveté of young love, they remain unbeatable. Memphis natives Big Star, on the other hand, did record deep, emotionally complex songs on three amazing records (*No.1 Record, Radio City* and *Sister Lovers*) that went unheard in their day but contained the best songs of American power pop ("Ballad of El Goodo," "Mod Lang," and the stunning "September Gurls"). Rediscovered by a later generation of pop-loving rockers (most notably the Replacements' Paul Westerberg), Big Star, though never touching the commercial success enjoyed by the Raspberries, became significantly more influential and revered.

By the mid-to-late '70s, power pop's lifeline continued with fluke hits like Dwight Twilley's 1975 Top 20 smash "I'm on Fire." Twilley, a native of Tulsa, OK, along with partner Phil Seymour, recorded a wonderful debut record, *Sincerely*, that along with containing the aforementioned hit, is an excellent example of ebullient, tuneful, rockabilly-tinged power pop. Around the same time, Cheap Trick, a hard rock/pop quartet from Rockford, IL, capitalized on the strong vocals and good looks of lead singer Robin Zander, and the bizarre antics and surreal lyrical narratives of guitarist Rick Neilsen, recording some of the finest pop-rock of the time. After three undeniably great records, the worldwide success of a so-so live album signalled the beginning of the end as Cheap Trick began living up to its name, their greatness reduced to formula.

Power pop, however, was not solely the province of American bands who wanted to sound British; there was a British power-pop "invasion" of sorts in the '70s. Badfinger was the most blatantly Beatles-influenced (they even recorded for the Beatles' Apple label and had Paul McCartney as a producer), but they produced some excellent, occasionally thrilling songs such as "No Matter What," "Baby Blue," and "Day After Day," all three Top 20 hits in 1970-71. Loaded with lush guitars, instantly recognizable melodies and two fine singers in Pete Ham and Joey Molland (a fellow Liverpudlian who bears a strong resemblance to McCartney), Badfinger was the model of a great power-pop band. Sadly, guitarist and songwriter Pete Ham committed suicide in 1975 effectively ending the band's career. By the mid-'70s English power pop was essentially the music of glam rock: stiff, boot-stomping rhythms that sounded like football (i.e. soccer) chants. Glam rock cranked up the guitars while sweetening the melodies, thereby making loud, bubblegum rock fodder perfect for radio. With artists such as Gary Glitter, the Sweet, Slade, and Suzi Quatro (an American who found great success in England) leading the way, glam rock produced a handful of good songs, one great band (Slade) and the obsequious marketing of negligibly talented teen idols (e.g. Bay City Rollers) that would become common practice in the early-'80s power-pop sweepstakes. Power pop's nadir was reached, ironically, during an amazingly fertile period in its history. In the wake of Cheap Trick, excellent Midwestern power-pop bands like the Pezband and the Shoes (both from Illinois) made great records. On the West Coast, Jack Lee, Peter Case and Paul Collins formed the punk-pop Nerves; in Boston, the Real Kids released their debut LP; in Athens, GA, R.E.M. released the *Chronic Town* EP, a gem of Byrdsian power pop; and in New York, Chris Stamey and Peter Holsapple formed the dB's and released two of the smartest and most ambitious power-pop records ever made. Even in England, former pub rocker Will Birch of the Kursaal Flyers formed the Records, a snazzy little combo that released a couple of fine records and an unforgettable single, "Starry Eyes."

However, power pop of the late-'70s/early-'80s is also remembered for the slavish imitators and skinny-tie-wearing no-talents, writing second-generation Raspberries ripoffs, pouting and posing on destined-for-the-cut-out-bin album covers that major labels vomited at an alarming rate. They were faceless hacks like the Cretones, Fotomaker (sadly with ex-Raspberry Wally Bryson), the Producers, Sue Saad and the Next, the Romantics (who had two hit singles and are mostly remembered for their song "What I Like About You"'s use in beer ads), Tattoo, the Tourists (with future- Eurythmics Dave Stewart and Annie Lennox!), the Jags, the Sinceros, the Yachts, Yipes!, and countless other bandwagon jumpers. But, the sine qua non of power-pop condescension and sleaze was without a doubt, the Knack. Fueled by their malodorous 1979 No. 1 single, "My Sharona," the Knack singlehandedly gave power pop its bad name. Unctuous to the nth degree, obvious in their Beatle fakery, the Knack were less a band and more a marketing-department creation, who laughed all the way to the bank, were a trivia question by the mid-'80s, had the audacity to regroup in the early '90s (mainly because Knack leader Doug Feiger is a boyhood friend of hotshot producer Don Was), and recorded another lousy record, which didn't sell.

Although most people are loathe to use the term these days, power pop still exists. Alternarock bands like the Posies, Belly, Throwing Muses, Elastica, Echobelly, Urge Overkill and the Gin Blossoms are not too far removed from the power-pop days of yore. There are flashes of it in Nirvana, and even in retro-punk bands such as the Offspring and Green Day. Inevitably, there are also bands like Material Issue and Jellyfish, who are merely the next generation of Cretones and Jags, fobbing off style and mechanical reproduction as substance. Ultimately power pop is much better than the term implies, and it seems as though it's not willing to go away anytime soon—which is fine, just as long as skinny ties never make a comeback.

Recommended Recordings

Rhino's *DIY American and English Power Pop Anthologies* (Rhino)

Badfinger, *Straight Up* (Capitol)

Big Star, *No.1 Record* and *Radio City* (Stax)

Cheap Trick, *In Color* (Epic)

The dB's, *Stands for Decibels* and *Repercussion* (IRS)

Flamin' Groovies, *Shake Some Action* (Sire)

Go-Go's, *Go-Go's Greatest* (IRS)

Nick Lowe, *Pure Pop for Now People* (Columbia)

Pezband, *30 Seconds over Shaumburg* (PVC)

Raspberries, *The Raspberries' Best (featuring Eric Carmen)* (Capitol)

The Real Kids, *The Real Kids* (Red Star)

The Records, *The Records* (Virgin)

Scruffs, *Wanna Meet the Scruffs?* (Power Play)

Shoes, *Black Vinyl Shoes* (Black Vinyl)

Slade, *Best of Slade* (Polydor)

Sweet, *Best of Sweet* (Capitol)

Dwight Twilley Band, *Sincerely* (OCC)

—John Dougan

Hardcore & Thrash

Few rock listeners have noncommital, or even mixed, opinions about hardcore and thrash. The substantial majority will not only never develop a fondness for the music, but will always view it with active dislike; quite a few figuratively cover their ears and run as fast as they can in the opposite direction. On the other hand, its "core" audience, if you will, forms one of the most fiercely loyal and zealous subcultures in all of rock 'n' roll. The hardcore scene, love it or hate it, has exerted a substantial influence on rock 'n' roll, one that is felt in today's Top 40 more than it was in its early-'80s heyday.

Hardcore, to use what by now has become a cliché, was harder, louder, and faster than its direct ancestor, early punk music. As shocking an assault as first-generation punk was on the heart of the rock industry, hardcore turned on the heat and tightened the screws. Lots of listeners already found the Ramones, Buzzcocks, the Clash, and other early punk giants impossibly fast, loud, and abrasive. Hardcore took the Ramones'

trademark "1-2-3-4!" kickoff countdown and sped up the tempos as much as humanly possible, sticking largely to monochrome guitars, bass, and drums, and favoring half-shouted lyrics venting the most inflammatory sentiments the singers and songwriters could devise.

Hardcore's roots could be traced to the early American reaction to the supernova of 1977 British punk. In somewhat of the same manner as garage bands reacting to the British Invasion in the mid-'60s, American groups came up with a cruder and rawer variation. Many of these bands were based in California, particularly Southern California and the San Francisco Bay Area. Outfits like the Avengers, Dils, and Germs played a more jaded and nastier version of British punk. Shortly afterwards, other bands (who were often peers of the aforementioned acts) went the last nine yards into hardcore, although the line between "straightahead" punk and hardcore/thrash could be (and often still is) thin.

The giants of early hardcore were mostly Californians: the Dead Kennedys, Black Flag, Flipper, the Circle Jerks. Just as almost every city or university town had its punk scene, so they soon had their hardcore bands. Washington, D.C., home of Minor Threat, the Bad Brains, and many other groups, was arguably the biggest hotspot outside of the Golden State, but there were many groups in cities like Vancouver and Boston, to cite just the tip of the iceberg. British hardcore bands were not unknown—early records by Wire and the Fall were certainly hardcore keystones with their melodically minimal, percussive structures, and groups like the Anti-Nowhere League, the Subhumans, G.B.H., the Exploited, and the UK Subs had big international followings. Indeed, there were scads of hardcore bands all over the globe, but North America was always the chief breeding ground. Melody, it's fair to say, wasn't uppermost in the minds of most thrashers. Not infrequently, it wasn't a consideration at all. Energy and, much more often than not, outrage were paramount. As in rap music, the lyrics and the message took precedence, though hardcore never matched the textural and sonic variety of rap. The lyrics were often more pointedly sociopolitical than anything else around, and often pointed fingers: at the government, institutions, teachers, employers, and authority figures of every kind. There was always sexism, racism, the arms race, yuppies, and conformists of all kinds to share the blame as well. A lot of hardcore bands lacked a sense of humor, as people who dwell on such topics are wont to do, but a lot of them could also be quite funny. The Dead Kennedys, Black Flag, Suicidal Tendencies, and many other groups managed the difficult act of lambasting their targets with considerable humor, and songs such as "TV Party" (Black Flag) and "Institutionalized" (Suicidal Tendencies) provoked some honest-to-god belly laughs, and not exclusively from punks.

What is striking when listening to early hardcore is how melodic and poppy it can sound in comparison to later recordings in the genre, although it seemed unimaginably fast and devoid of melody at the time. Hardcore, more than the typical rock genre, didn't require much in the way of traditional instrumental and songwriting skills; virtually all hardcore records were released on small independent labels, often by the bands themselves. Given these low hurdles, the scene was soon crowded with generic bands. Some of the slightly-later-than-first-generation hardcore outfits garnered substantial followings: TSOL, the Wipers, MDC (which stood for Millions of Dead Cops, Multi-Death Corporation, Millions of Damn Christians, and other such phrases during various points in their existence), JFA (an acronym for Jodie Foster's Army), and Redd Kross (barely in their teens when they became nationally known) were some of the most famous. Each month (at its peak, each week) saw cheapo albums, singles, and tapes unleashed on the marketplace, many poorly recorded and virtually indistinguishable from track to track. Any back issue of the international flagship punk zine, *Maximum Rock 'n' Roll*, yields dozens of tiny reviews of bands from all over the place that are virtually forgotten, or were not even known at the time.

Hardcore, even more than most subcultures, was a sea of contradictions. It placed a premium on non-conformism, but a great deal of the music adhered to extremely clichéd conventions (the number of hardcore songs starting with a blast of guitar distortion, a shouted "1, 2, 1-2-3-4," followed by a dog-pulls-the-tablecloth-off-the-kitchen-during-dinner blur of chords, must number in the thousands). Its politics were generally well to the left of center (sometimes openly proclaiming anarchy), yet its fashions and sometimes even music were picked up by some Fascist and neo-Nazi youth. It placed great value on the message of the lyrics, which were often shouted so throatily as to be indecipherable. The music was played violently, confrontationally; the lyrics often preached tolerance, unity, and peace. Laudably, it championed racial and sexual equality; its performers and audience were usually white and male. It preached against apathy, and advocated social change, but often reduced larger society to cartoon stereotypes, and was defiantly inaccessible and uncommercial, ensuring that the vast majority of rock listeners (let alone the population) would never hear the music. And when performers with roots in the thrash community did attract a larger audience, they were invariably accused of selling out by large segments of said community.

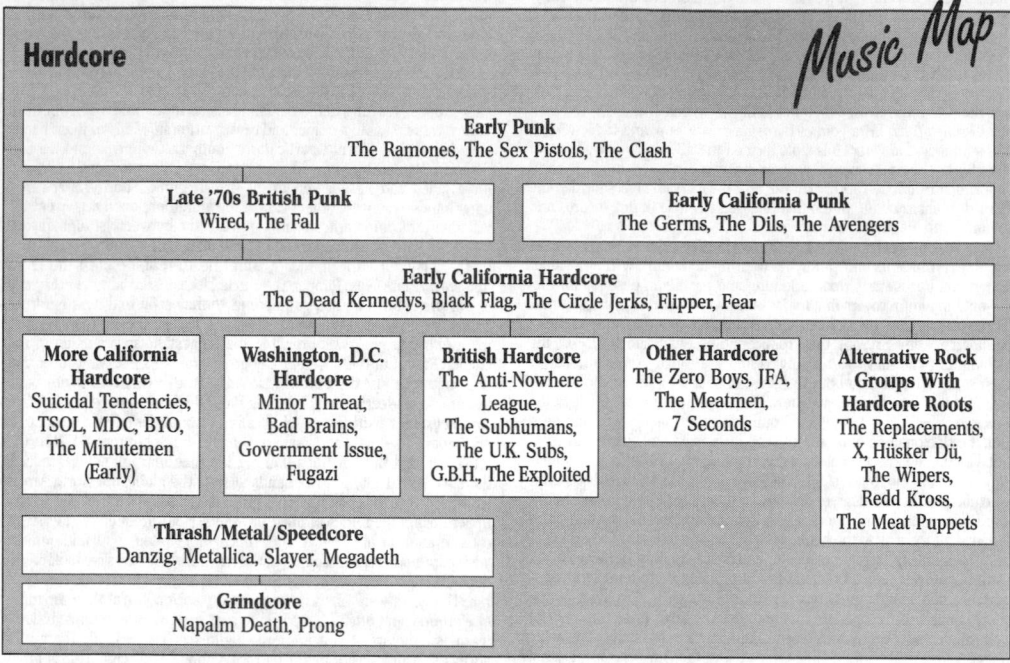

While it may be true that such performers were attracted by the prospects of commercial success, the more difficult truth to swallow was that they also felt constrained by the melodic, lyrical, and stylistic limits of hardcore, which are more severe than most any other subgenre of rock. The Replacements, X, the Meat Puppets, and Hüsker Dü all started out as more or less hardcore acts; none broadened their success beyond a cult level until they broadened the scope of their music (and, it must be pointed out, all eventually betrayed the original punk/hardcore ideal by signing with major labels). All of these groups helped lay the foundation for "alternative rock," although none achieved the multi-platinum success of Green Day and Nirvana, who likely listened to hardcore quite vociferously at some points in their youth. In the mid-'90s, early hardcore "stars" like Henry Rollins (of Black Flag), Bob Mould (of Hüsker Dü), and Mike Watt (of the Minutemen, so-named for the brevity of their songs, and later of fIREHOSE) are genuine rock stars; they don't play hardcore anymore, but their music shows debts to the form, and they've rarely if ever compromised their product in exchange for sales. There are even rare cases of also-ran hardcore bands that radically changed their game plan and hit the commercial jackpot; the Beastie Boys are the example that towers above all others that could be placed in this category.

Unexpectedly, hardcore and thrash also had a substantial influence on some of the '80s and '90s biggest metal bands, who combined the guitar octane of metal with a degree of the faster tempos and lyrical consciousness of hardcore. Metallica, Slayer, Danzig (whose lead singer, Glenn Danzig, started out in the late '70s with punk/hardcore band the Misfits), and Megadeth have all done this to a large degree; the hybrid is sometimes called "thrash-metal," "death-metal" (actually not often an accurate designation), or "speedcore," among other terms. Prong, Napalm Death, and others mixed punky nihilism with grinding metal to come up with "grindcore." Groups like Helmet have achieved critical acclaim with artsy punk-metal blends that, like bleached hair, show hardcore roots if you listen hard enough. On the fairly rare occasions that hardcore stars (like Suicidal Tendencies) or groups with hardcorish leanings (like Social Distortion) were signed to major labels, they probed, or were urged into, a more hard rock, metalish direction.

When the hardcore community is noticed by the outside world, unfortunately, the consequences can be severe. No one knows this more than Dead Kennedys lead singer Jello Biafra, who also helps run the Alternative Tentacles label. In association with a poster included in a Dead Kennedys album, he and others were prosecuted by the Los Angeles City Attorney's office for distributing material harmful to minors. He was eventually acquitted, but the long and exhausting legal defense helped break up the Dead Kennedys.

Hardcore records are all but ignored by the media (even most of the alternative publications), but hardcore has retained a significant audi-

ence in the last decade, linked by a tight (some would say insular) network of zines, skateboarder cliques, and tiny performance spaces. Some acts, like 7 Seconds, the deliberately offensive Meatmen, and the long-gone BYO, were huge within the hardcore community while passing virtually unnoticed by the larger rock world. Very occasionally, bands like Fugazi (led by Ian MacKaye, formerly with "straight-edge" pioneers Minor Threat) achieve wide acclaim in the rock underground by broadening the hardcore base of their sound without alienating the hardcore base of their fans. *Maximum Rock 'n' Roll*, the punk journal, continues to review hardcore recordings by the boatload, and espouse a fervently radical sociopolitical view that some feel to be unhealthily rigid. When Jello Biafra had his leg mangled by slam-dancing thugs (who accused him of being a sellout rock star as they stomped on him) at a Berkeley, CA punk club with strong ties to the magazine in 1994, it was not so much the end of an era as a reflection of the long, strange road this most uncommercial breed of rock music has taken, and the contradictions it continues to embody.

Recommended Recordings

Various Artists, *Faster & Louder: Hardcore Punk, Vol. 1* (Rhino)
Various Artists, *Faster & Louder: Hardcore Punk, Vol. 2* (Rhino)
The Dead Kennedys, *Fresh Fruit for Rotting Vegetables* (IRS)
Black Flag, *The First Four Years* (SST)
The Wipers, *Over the Edge* (Restless)
Bad Brains, *Rock for Light* (Caroline)
Hüsker Dü, *Metal Circus* (SST)
The Replacements, *Sorry Ma, Forgot to Take out the Trash* (Twin/Tone)
The Minutemen, *Double Nickels on the Dime* (SST)
Minor Threat, *Complete* (Dischord)
Suicidal Tendencies, *Suicidal Tendencies* (Frontier)
Fugazi, *Repeater* (Dischord)

—Richie Unterberger

Australian Rock

In 1975, most Americans' relationship with Australian rock consisted of maybe being able to sing the Easybeats' (who weren't native Australians) "Friday on My Mind." A geographically isolated continent, Australia's impact on the global rock 'n' roll market seemed tangential at best; touring was difficult, most people carelessly lumped you in with English bands, and there was a strong feeling that no matter how good you might be, your career was limited to the Western Hemisphere.

In fact, rock 'n' roll has been produced in Australia since the music made its first international impact in the mid-'50s. In 1957, Gene Vincent, Eddie Cochran, and Little Richard became the first rock 'n' roll stars to tour the continent (in fact, it was during this tour that Richard declared his intention to renounce rock 'n' roll for the ministry). Australia had its homegrown rockers in the late '50s and early '60s, like Johnny Rebb, who were unknown elsewhere in the world, and remain little-heard to this day even among rabid collectors and historians. The best of the pre-Beatle groups were the Atlantics, who recorded quite a few storming surf records that match the best instrumental surf music issued in Southern California around the same time.

Beatlemania had as great an impact on Australia as in the UK or US, and after the Beatles swept through Australia on a mid-1964 tour, many British Invasion-inspired combos sprang up throughout the country. One of the first, and the most famous by far, were the Easybeats, who created a mini-Beatlemania of their own (dubbed "Easyfever") on their home turf. Actually composed of musicians who had emigrated from Britain and Holland to Australia during their childhood or teens, the Easybeats boasted prolific writers in guitarists George Young and Harry Vanda. Much of their output during their mid-'60s prime bears a great deal of similarity to the Kinks, Small Faces, and of course the Beatles, with a bouncier, more pop-oriented feel. After moving to Britain in 1966, they had an international smash with "Friday on My Mind," as well as some lesser UK hits, and dabbled in increasingly sophisticated studio concoctions before packing it up at the end of the decade. They ultimately do not measure up to the level of greatness of the best British Invasion bands, but were indisputably the most original and influential Australian group of their time.

Australia was still something of a backwater in the '60s—major American and British groups didn't tour there often, sophisticated equipment and studios were hard to come by, and albums were a rarity, reserved for big stars like the Easybeats. Lacking first-hand exposure to their idols, or easy access to an international audience, Australian groups had to generate their own scene, much in the manner of regional garage groups in the United States. As with the garage bands, the result was often a rawer, less professional variation of the British Invasion sound.

At their best, the Australian garage groups were a match for the best American ones, compensating for their lack of virtuosity with an over-dose of outrage. They're represented on a variety of compilations, which (as with American garage comps) mix gems with tedious genre exercises and unimaginative covers, although *Ugly Things Vol. 1* is recognized as one of the very best '60s garage anthologies from anywhere. Albums and compilations by some of the better and more prolific groups, like the Loved Ones, the Twilights, and the super-raw Missing Links, are spotty, but worth checking out for '60s collectors. The best '60s Australian group bar the Easybeats were the Master's Apprentices, who issued some terrific power-pop-garage singles in their early years, and evolved with the times through psychedelia and progressive rock, attaining some modest recognition in the UK after moving there for a time in the early '70s. Reissues of work by all of the bands mentioned in this paragraph, as well as *Ugly Things* and various other compilations, are available on the Raven label, the company primarily responsible for bringing some measure of belated acclaim to '60s Australian rock. (The Strangeloves, though billed as Australian when they hit with "I Want Candy" in 1965, were not the genuine article; they were in fact New York session musicians/songwriters, using the fake nationality as an attention-grabbing gimmick.)

The most successful Australian rock act of the '60s are not often classified as Australian. The Bee Gees were composed of three brothers who had emigrated from Britain as children; in 1967, they would move to England and successfully invade the British and American markets as lightweight Beatle emulators, becoming even bigger in the 1970s as they moved into disco. They'd been stars in Australia for some time before 1967, though. Their underappreciated 1964-66 work, though rarely heard, reveals them to be among the best British Invasion-wannabes from anywhere in the globe, often recalling the Hollies' best mid-'60s recordings.

Australian rock, like much rock from outside of North America or the British Isles, was extremely derivative and imitative of American and British trends, and the late '60s and early '70s produced many Australian clones of psychedelia, soul, progressive, glam, and other rock trends, almost without exception unworthy of close scrutiny. And Australian bands never rated more than a footnote until ex-Easybeats Harry Vanda and George Young decided to record the band started by George's younger brothers Angus and Malcolm. Ridiculed from the start by critics, and passionately loved by their fans, AC/DC went on to become (and continues to be) a hugely popular heavy metal band. Driven by Angus Young's spastic, mega-loud guitar playing and exhausting stage antics (while dressed up in a schoolboy's uniform), and Bon Scott's screeching tenor voice (Scott died in 1980, his spot filled by Scottish shrieker Brian Johnson), AC/DC stripped away all artifice, laying down a thudding, insistent, riff-driven feral assault that was as catchy as it was simple. In many ways AC/DC's no-frills faster-and-louder approach to rock 'n' roll anticipated what was to be a defining element of the early punk rock scene.

AC/DC, despite a "punky," anti-authoritarian attitude, were never truly a punk band (nor for that matter were they really Australian: Malcolm and Angus, like older brother George, were born in Scotland). They were more precisely the most successful practitioners of Australia's popular working-class hard rock/heavy metal scene, which included influential but lesser known bands such as the Angels (known later as Angel City) and Rose Tattoo. And while the aggressive attitude of these bands made a significant impact on young Australian punks-to-be, another important ingredient precipitating this genesis came in the early '70s when Ann Arbor, MI-native Deniz Tek emigrated to Sydney. A guitarist and fan of the hyped up, loud and direct, proto-punk motor sound of the Stooges and MC5, Tek joined forces with blonde, gruff-voiced Aussie native Rob Younger and formed the seminal (and arguably first) Australian punk band, Radio Birdman. In 1976, Radio Birdman released a scorching EP, *Burn My Eye*, following it up with a terrific steeped-in-the-Stooges debut LP, *Radios Appear* (the title taken from a Blue Öyster Cult song). But despite beating everyone else in getting a record out, and providing the critical impetus that influenced other bands, Radio Birdman were not the center of media attention (especially in the English rock press) for the then nascent Aussie punk movement. That recognition went to a quartet from Brisbane caled the Saints.

Co-led by Ed Kuepper and Chris Bailey, the Saints' debut, *(I'm) Stranded*, was every inch a classic late '70s punk rock record: Bailey's snarling, petulant vocals; the speedy, superdistorted guitars; the (mostly) brief songs; and one of the punk era's best tunes (one that could only be written by an Aussie band) about alienation, "(I'm) Stranded." Because they were the first of their ilk to get to England, the UK pop press enthusiastically dubbed them the Aussie punk band to be reckoned with, thereby cementing their reputation and causing "(I'm) Stranded" to be a hit single. The Saints became the band that (almost) singlehandedly informed the rest of the world that there was a thriving and interesting alternative rock and roll scene in Australia. Unlike Radio Birdman, who were finished by 1981 (Tek did, however, live out a dream by forming the short-lived New Race with ex-Stooges guitarist Ron Asheton and ex-MC5 drummer Dennis Thompson), the Saints (despite Kuepper's departure in 1978 to form the arty, psychedelic Laughing Clowns) continued to record into the '90s as Bailey took them from raw, blitzspeed punk into more deliberate, tuneful, and far less confrontational pop-rock.

As Australia's largest city, Sydney was the putative focal point of the burgeoning Aussie punk scene. However, many interesting, innovative bands were popping up all over the continent. Especially in Melbourne, a city with a rock tradition that went back to the mid-'60s and the much loved Loved Ones. Its large student population formed the sympathetic core for a more arty, avant-garde brand of punk that was less interested in fast guitars, and more interested in free-form musical and literary explorations. Seminal Melbourne underground musicians such as Ollie Olson in his bands Whirlywind and No created a churning din of sound, punctuated by vituperative lyrical broadsides, culminating in extreme performances that sometimes included self-inflicted violence and bloodshed. Still, with much of the student community supporting this sound, Melbourne was soon producing bands unlike anywhere else on the continent. (For an interesting fictional account of the early days of the Melbourne scene see the 1987 film *Dogs in Space*, which surprisingly features a fine performance by INXS lead singer Michael Hutchence.)

Few bands from the Melbourne scene were more interesting, and exhibited more promise, than did the Boys Next Door. Led by the doomy baritone voice and poetically-inclined pen of Jim Morrison acolyte Nick Cave and the twisted, noisy, gnarled guitar playing of Rowland S. Howard, the Boys released *Door Door* in 1979 and almost immediately became one of Melbourne's most influential punk bands. However, Melbourne wasn't big enough, nor centrally located to international audiences, for the Boys. By 1980, they had changed their name to the Birthday Party, moved to London, and became one of the post-punk era's most explosive and copied bands. Cave, after going solo in 1984, has had success that eclipses that of the Birthday Party and the Boys combined. With and without his backing band the Bad Seeds, Cave has pursued the darker impulses of rock 'n' roll, incorporating Delta blues and country music into his cauldron of musical ideas. As of this writing, Cave (with the Bad Seeds) has been a featured act on the Lollapalooza tour, published a novel, become a dad, and kicked a long-standing heroin addiction. He's now at the peak of his popularity, with a career that spans well over a decade and dozens of recordings.

By the early '80s, the punk-inspired deluge of bands had given Australia more musical recognition than ever before. New bands, influenced by Anglo and American punk rock, Radio Birdman, the Saints, and the Melbourne scene, sprang up everywhere, embracing punk's DIY ethos while replicating and reinventing rock 'n' roll. From the remote western city of Perth came the Kim Salmon-led Scientists; '60s psychedelic garage rock was reinterpreted by the Lime Spiders; hook-filled pure pop was the calling card of the Hoodoo Gurus; and a melancholic take on Beatles-inspired pop was offered up by Marty-Willson Piper, Steve Kilbey, and Peter Koppes in the popular Church. There were art-punks

Feedtime (who sounded like Flipper); the Melbourne-influenced King Snake Roost and Hunters and Collectors; the commercial hard rock of the Divinyls (great first record, everything else is worthless); the criminally overlooked Died Pretty; the over-amped pop of the Screaming Tribesmen; the extremely popular, but negligibly interesting, dance-rock of INXS (featuring Michael Hutchence); Rob Younger's post-Birdman outfit, the New Christs; hardcore punks the Cosmic Psychos and the delicately named Hard Ons; Brisbane's brilliant the Go-Betweens, featuring Grant McLennan and Robert Forster; and two very important Sydney-based bands: the Celibate Rifles and Midnight Oil.

Midnight Oil began as a punk-influenced band big with Sydney's sizable surfing community. Led by the imposing figure of surfer/lawyer Peter Garrett, the Oils, as they were affectionately dubbed by fans, began recording in 1978, but it wasn't until five years later, when they released *10, 9, 8, 7, 6, 5, 4, 3, 2, 1*, that (thanks to its huge success in Australia) they established a toehold in the international rock marketplace. Early Oils music is loud, technically adept, and very aggressive, indicative of their fondness for punk. Also it was the kind of assertive, boisterous rock that went down well with the surfer crowds they played to in Sydney-area bars. By the time they recorded *10, 9, 8 . . .* the Oils' music was becoming more polished and pop-oriented, but not so much so that it sacrificed the guitar-driven mania from whence they sprang. Longtime advocates for the environment and aboriginal land rites, and with the articulate Garrett acting as band spokesman, it wasn't long before Midnight Oil became the biggest Aussie rock act since AC/DC. Much of it was due to the enormous success of the single and video "Beds Are Burning" (from the 1987 album *Diesel and Dust*) and ferocious live shows. Although their recent efforts have not yielded a hit single the magnitude of "Beds Are Burning," the Oils have developed a devoted fan base, and continue to make solid, if much less aggressive, records that consistently sell in the millions.

The stripped-down, loud and fast, Ramones-inspired rock of the Celibate Rifles deserves special mention, for this Sydney-based band proved to be the best Australian rock band to emerge from the Radio Birdman/Saints era. With droll, deadpan lead vocals supplied by Damien Lovelock, the core of the Rifles was built around the rampaging guitars of Kent Steedman and Dave Morris. And while they valued power, speed, and volume, they weren't shy about tastefully adding horns, acoustic instruments, and slowing down the tempo. Perhaps too extreme and enigmatic to make a big splash in America, the Rifles did, however, develop a solid, supportive fan base in indie rock circles. However, they toured America sporadically, and as the '80s ended they seemed content to spend much of their time in Australia. Since they released their first EP in 1982, the Rifles' output has been frequently stunning, proving them to be the best Australian rock band you've never heard.

Aussie rock music is more diverse than the hard rock and punk-influenced rock that dominates American and British rock. Unfortunately, there are plenty of standard issue types like gruff-voiced Bob Seger wannabe Jimmy Barnes; hugely popular teenage soap star ("Neighbors") turned sexpot dance-pop singer Kylie Minogue; so-so hard rockers Cold Chisel; worthless, radio/MTV panderers like '80s popular one-shots Men at Work. Far more interesting are recent performers such as blues guitarist Dave Hole and aboriginal singer-songwriter Archie Roach, who have recorded exciting, very different-sounding records than what emanates from both the Aussie mainstream and alternative rock communities. The success of Archie Roach and the band Yothu Yindi (whose influences include mid-'80s aboriginal rock bands such as Goanna and the Warumpi Band) has created a new focus on music made by Australia's aboriginal population, resulting in other established, yet heretofore unknown, Australian performers finding more acceptance (and more fans) in the global pop community, and on previously monochromatic Aussie pop music radio. Artists such as Ruby Hunter, Kev Carmody (the Australian Bob Dylan), and Blek Bela Mujik send a clear signal that there is much more to contemporary Australian rock 'n' roll than simply white boys flailing away at guitars.

As more and more bands have received international acclaim, the Aussie music scene has been accorded more respect and, as a result, is more vigilantly watched by label executives for marketable bands. So, the next generation of Aussie bands, populated by up-and-comers like Silverchair, Spiderbait, the Mark of Cain, and the Joy of Noise, will have a much larger ready-made audience than did their predecessors. Even an old-timer like Deniz Tek has returned to the fray, teaming up with Celibate Rifle Kent Steedman in a part-time project that recaptures the high energy Detroit rock sound that played such a pivotal role in the development of punk and post-punk Australian rock. Despite being on the other side of the planet, the truth is, since the late '70s, rock 'n' roll has helped bring Australia a lot closer to the rest of the world and made it a lot more influential than anyone would have guessed.

Recommended Recordings

The Easybeats, *Absolute Anthology* (EMI, Australia)
Various Artists, *Ugly Things Vol. 1* (Raven, Australia)

The Bee Gees, *The Early Years Vol. 1 & 2* (Excelsior)
The Master's Apprentices, *Hands of Time 1965-72* (Raven, Australia)
AC/DC, *Back in Black* (Atlantic)
Radio Birdman, *Radios Appear* (Sire)
The Saints, *(I'm) Stranded* (Sire)
Midnight Oil, *10, 9, 8, 7, 6, 5, 4, 3, 2, 1* (Columbia)
The Celibate Rifles, *Roman Beach Party* (What Goes On)
The Celibate Rifles, *Blind Ear* (EMI-True Tone, Australia)
Feedtime, *Shovel* (Aberrant/Rough Trade)
The Go-Betweens, *1978-1990* (Beggars Banquet/Capitol)
Divinyls, *Desperate* (Chrysalis)
Archie Roach, *Charcoal Lane* (Hightone)
Yothu Yindi, *Freedom* (Hollywood)
Birthday Party, *Hits* (Warner Brothers)
Nick Cave & the Bad Seeds, *The First Born Is Dead* (Mute)
Died Pretty, *Free Dirt* (What Goes On)
The Hoodoo Gurus, *Stonage Romeos* (A&M)
The Scientists, *Weird Love* (Big Time)

Film
Dogs in Space (1987)

—John Dougan & Richie Unterberger

New Zealand Rock

New Zealand's influence upon the international rock 'n' roll scene has been limited by its size and isolation. The total population of the two islands that comprise the nation is about three million; considerably less than, for instance, the population of the San Francisco Bay Area. The country didn't even have a recording studio until 1948, and as recently as 1989, it took only 7500 units of sales to quality for a gold record. Yet its very size and isolation have also helped foster a brand of rock that may have been too idiosyncratic to flourish elsewhere.

The very first New Zealand rock 'n' roll record was cut way back in August 1955, when John Cooper recorded a version of "Rock Around the Clock." Much in the manner of its much larger neighbor Australia, there was plenty of homegrown Kiwi rock 'n' roll in the late '50s and '60s, especially after the British Invasion sparked the formation of self-contained guitar bands. Some of this was fairly good: Ray Columbus & the Invaders (British Invasion-styled pop) and the La-De-Das (British Invasion-styled R&B/rock) were about the best, and the best of the handful of outrageous New Zealand garage bands can be heard on the compilation *Wild Things*, which holds it own with most international '60s garage reissues of the sort.

The great majority of New Zealand rock and pop, however, was extremely, at times slavishly, derivative of British and American rock trends. To a large degree, this was also characteristic of Australian rock, but the best '60s Australian rock had a more distinctive flavor, and occasional international successes. Few listeners outside the Antipodes heard New Zealand rock until the moderate success of Split Enz, beginning in the mid-'70s.

At various times characterized as art-rock, new wave, or comedy-rock, Split Enz attracted the attention of Roxy Music guitarist Phil Manzanera, who produced one of their early albums. Big stars at home, they also made splashes, in progressively smaller order, in Australia, the UK, and the US. Outside of New Zealand and Australia, they remain very much a cult item, despite their frequent pop-rock focus; listeners tend to either find them intriguingly offbeat, or gimmicky performers who epitomized some of new wave's sillier aspects. In the mid-'80s, Split Enz mainstay Neil Finn (eventually joined by his brother Tim) led Crowded House to international success with tuneful, just-left-of-mainstream pop-rock.

To this day, there continue to be a good many mainstream New Zealand rockers who are popular, or even stars, in their native country. Almost without exception, they are lesser variations on mainstream rock trends originating in the UK or US. There are several bands featuring blends of rock and the music of the indigenous Maori people of the islands, but these are rarely distributed internationally, and often lean more toward the tame pop-rock side of things than ethnic roots. Of much more interest to the inquisitive rock fan are the many alternative Kiwi bands, which emerged from a scene that really didn't get going until the late '70s and early '80s.

If there could be said to be a founding father of New Zealand alternative rock, the title would probably be awarded to Chris Knox. Singer in one of the country's first punk bands, the Enemy, he subsequently fronted the energetic new wave group Toy Love, probably the first alternative rock group of its sort to gain a lot of success in the islands. He subsequently teamed with Alec Bathgate to form half of Tall Dwarfs, who have produced quite a few albums of determinedly individual, eccentric, and funkily recorded punk- and new wave-influenced rock that set the tone for the New Zealand underground of the 1980s. Knox has also recorded some similar albums on his own, and remains quite active in the scene to this day.

Tall Dwarfs were one of the first bands to record for the Flying Nun label, the company which has become almost synonymous with New Zealand underground/alternative rock. The small Kiwi punk scene of the late '70s had given birth to a few independent labels (Ripper and Propeller were the best known); those releases have rarely been heard overseas, and then usually on obscure compilations. Flying Nun, begun in 1981 by record-store manager Roger Shepherd, almost immediately placed several singles on the country's charts, and acted as a magnet for the best non-mainstream Kiwi rock talent. By the late '80s, it seemed as though virtually every alternative Kiwi rock act of note was affiliated with the company.

Although Flying Nun became home to a fairly diverse roster of artists, there are certain attributes which could be broadly applied to their sound, and by association, the New Zealand alternative scene as a whole. The bands were very much of the D.I.Y. generation spawned by punk and new wave, and placed a high premium on tuneful melodies and a sprinkling of pop hooks. They eschewed in-your-face booming hi-tech production, usually sticking to classic guitar-organ-bass-drums line-ups. At the same time, however, they weren't averse to embellishing their products with all manner of odd production touches, often in the four-track manner pioneered by the Tall Dwarfs. Without being slavishly reverent, their music betrayed strong debts to the psychedelia of the '60s, as well as the jangle-pop of the Byrds; the ghost of Syd Barrett's brilliant pop-psychedelia fusions is particularly strong, hovering over many if not most of the NZ groups.

An equally important factor in the warm reception granted New Zealand bands by alternative rock fans worldwide was the innocence, naiveté, and humility of the music. New Zealand is a modern society, but it is the most isolated of the English-speaking territories; overseas records, books, and films take months and years to arrive in the islands, if they become available there at all. In its low-key lifestyle, it's closer to the America of the 1950s than the 1990s. This relative lack of overwhelming outside influence, as well as the tight-knit camaraderie of a scene which remains a minority taste on its home turf, accounts to some degree for the originality of the Flying Nun product, right down to the artful, colorful, at times seemingly hand-drawn sleeves.

One could be forgiven for viewing the Flying Nun label as a sort of extended family of New Zealand rock groups; the groups tend to change personnel quite frequently, often joining or rejoining each other's bands, or forming spin-offs of their own. The label is based in New Zealand's largest city, Auckland, yet many of the musicians hail from the relatively small south island town of Dunedin, as well as its bigger south island neighbor Christchurch. Considering the rather limited population pool, Flying Nun cultivated an impressively lengthy roster of bands that made an international impression of sorts in the 1980s: the Chills, the Bats, the Clean, the Jean-Paul Sartre Experience, the Verlaines, Straightjacket Fits, and Bailter Space, on down to more cultish acts like Able Tasmans, Headless Chickens, and the Cake Kitchen.

On an international level, the most successful of these bands were the Chills, who have gone through a dozen or so lineups under the leadership of Martin Phillipps, and the Bats, whose guitar-dominated sound fit in most readily with the music favored by college radio in the late '80s. The Verlaines, the Jean-Paul Sartre Experience, and Straightjacket Fits also landed overseas licensing deals; Homestead, Rough Trade, and Communion were the prime outlets for NZ product in the US. Since the mid-'80s, appreciation for the Flying Nun sound has grown steadily overseas, especially in the United States. Granted these fans tend to cluster in big cities and university towns; San Francisco has a particularly large clique of Flying Nun aficionados, as do Los Angeles, New York, and Chicago. If one were to judge by the large amounts of ink devoted to Flying Nun bands in underground rock publications and fanzines, one would assume that they were stars. They're not, actually, outside of the fairly small community of listeners who read them. Mainstream audiences have not so much never warmed to these groups as never heard them, although a couple (most notably the Chills) had major-label deals. The bands at least gathered enough of a following to enable them to tour the US, although in most cases these were limited to the East and West Coasts.

Lest one be tempted to think that Flying Nun remains the first and last word in New Zealand indie rock, other Kiwi indies such as Xpressway and IND have also released a few albums that have achieved international recognition, the excruciating noise-rock of the Dead C and the Syd Barrettisms of Alastair Galbraith being two of the more widely known examples. Flying Nun remains as active as ever in the mid-'90s, even though its roster seems increasingly static, the new acts often composed of spin-offs of groups that first recorded with the label in the 1980s. In judging the health of the New Zealand indie scene, one runs up against the isolation problem in reverse: it can take years for bands to get heard overseas, if they get heard at all. The islands can retain considerable pride, though, in schooling a brand of alternative rock that has

rarely bowed to commercial pressures from the mainstream or the underground, while remaining accessible to all who managed to find it.

Recommended Recordings

Various Artists, *Wild Things* (Flying Nun)

Split Enz, *History Never Repeats: The Best of Split Enz* (A&M)

Toy Love, *Toy Love* (WEA, New Zealand)

Various Artists, *Tuatara* (Flying Nun)

The Tall Dwarfs, *Hello Cruel World* (Homestead)

The Chills, *Kaleidoscope World* (Homestead)

The Clean, *Compilation* (Homestead)

The Bats, *The Law of Things* (Communion)

The Jean-Paul Sartre Experience, *Love Songs* (Communion)

The Verlaines, *Juvenilia* (Homestead)

Straightjacket Fits, *Hail* (Flying Nun)

Alastair Galbraith, *Seely Girn* (Feel Good All Over)

Book

Stranded in Paradise: New Zealand Rock 'n' Roll 1955-1988, by John Dix (1988, Paradise Publications, New Zealand)

–Richie Unterberger

Jangle Pop

In the early '80s, once punk rock spawned new wave and launched a move toward mostly English electronic and synth-pop bands, American jangle-rock (the sound characterized by the chiming acoustic and electric guitars of the Beatles, Byrds, Soft Boys and Big Star, and made famous in the 80's by R.E.M.) was the antidotal reaction. A new generation of folk-based guitar bands were born, but commercial radio, a new invention called MTV, and the baby-boomer-dominated staffs at the mainstream rock press were slow to catch on to the sounds. College radio and fanzines were the only available outlets for the new music and consequently, it would take years before the new generation of guitar-wielding musicians would be recognized as cornerstones to the foundation of what would become modern, melody-driven, alternative rock.

The word "jangle" was a reference to Bob Dylan's lyric in the Byrds greatest hit, "Mr. Tambourine Man": "in the jingle-jangle morning." Accompanied by the chiming guitar sound and luscious harmonies, also in evidence in the Byrds' (and Robyn Hitchcock's) version of Pete Seeger's "Bells of Rhymney," the terms "jangling," "ringing" and "chiming" were added to budding rock critic parlance to describe the sound. Fanzines like *The Bob, Matter, Tasty World* and the UK's *Bucketfull of Brains* all paid great attention to covering the genre. It was also the golden age of college radio, independent record stores, and tiny clubs, all of which played a large part in spreading the good word about the R.E.M. and Big Star-related bands (the dB's, Let's Active, Game Theory) and regional artists. The new bands were welcomed into the regional folks' hearts as well as literally into their homes, as the music inspired an unusual passion among record lovers.

R.E.M. were known as the leaders of the movement (if it could be called one) due to their higher profile, and guitarist Peter Buck was free with his endorsements of the aforementioned bands—as he proselytized on his cross-country trips, sleeping on people's couches, granting interviews to small fanzines and combing record stores—telling anyone who would listen about the new guitar rock and the records that excited him, past and present. Independent record stores were the hub of much of this type of exchange as store clerks and owners were also responsible for turning their customers on to the rich guitar-rock canon. Buck's rudimentary style, at his own admission inspired by Roger McGuinn's Rickenbacker, offered the chance to anyone who could hold a guitar the opportunity to play one (not so unlike punk rock) and the ensuing guitar-rock revival was often heralded as the "Return of the Rickenbacker."

It's hard to believe that a little-known band from North Carolina sparked the '80s guitar rock revolution, but all signs point toward the dB's reinventing "jangle-rock," before R.E.M. made it famous. The dB's, led by songwriters Chris Stamey and Peter Holsapple, cut two records (*Stands for Decibels* and *Repercussion,* the latter not coincidentally produced by Scott Litt who would later become R.E.M.'s producer) but had relocated from the South to New York, as regional bands at the time were wont to do. R.E.M. stayed and broke out of the tiny college town of Athens, GA, perhaps making theirs a more interesting story. They recorded their highly praised debut single, "Radio Free Europe," and *Chronic Town* EP at Mitch Easter's Drive-In studio in Winston-Salem, North Carolina, and *Murmur* and *Reckoning* at Reflection Studios in Charlotte. Subsequently, industry attention became focused on the burgeoning scenes that were developing outside of the obvious urban centers and Easter and his recording partner Don Dixon got pretty busy on the heels of R.E.M.'s early, underground success. Though not all of the bands who recorded there—like Easter's own Let's Active, Athens' Art in the Dark, Mississippi's Windbreakers and New York's Bongos —were makers of the shimmering guitar rock, they often got lumped into the category. Basically, anytime a band with a good pop hook added harmonies or acoustic guitars into the mix, they were given the guitar-rock subhead as there was no other place to put these bands during the dawn of MTV and the era of new technology that spawned synth-rock; it was a convenient catch-all.

Consequently, rougher bands like the punk Hüsker Dü and the drunk Replacements were also beneficiaries of the jangle-rock tag from time to time, no doubt due to Buck's perpetual endorsement of their virtues in the press, his guitar work on the 'Mats' jangly 1984 single, "I Will Dare," and Replacement Paul Westerberg's and the Hüskers' Bob Mould's own abilities to write great pop hooks. Early records by singer-songwriters Matthew Sweet and Tommy Keene were also influenced by the R.E.M./ Drive-In sound.

Meanwhile on the West Coast, the Dream Syndicate were experimenting with guitar rock of a different sort, more along the lines of the sonic type as practiced by the Velvet Underground and Neil Young—though both artists held some sway with the janglers; the Velvets' "There She Goes Again" and Young's "Mr. Soul" were covered by bands too numerous to mention. But it was the Syndicate's brethren in the Los Angeles Paisley Underground like the Three O'Clock and Bangles who were paying homage to the soaring, harmony- and guitar-driven sound of Alex Chilton and Big Star's *No. 1 Record* and *Radio City*. L.A.'s the Long Ryders, particularly the group's leader Sid Griffin, were Byrds and Gram Parsons devotees, so country-rock and folk-rock became part of the package, as did good old American rock 'n' roll as played by L.A.'s Green on Red and Nashville's Jason & the Scorchers.

The attendant Hoboken scene sparked by the dB's and revolving around the club Maxwell's included the Richard Barone and James Mastro-led Bongos, and Doug and Janet Wygal's the Individuals. Their forebears in New York-based guitar pop were the Feelies.

Power pop was another crossover influence as groups like the Plimsouls had their greatest success with a shimmering guitar song, "A Million Miles Away," in 1983. Jules & the Polar Bears (Jules Shear), Cheap Trick and Badfinger are cousins to the sound, as on closer inspection, the jangle bands were pulling inspiration from a variety of pure pop sources. For example, the songs Lenny Kaye compiled on the first *Nuggets* record were also informing these bands—if it was guitar-driven and hooky, it qualified, and the pop and garage-rock side of '60s psychedelia was definitely embraced, as heard in L.A.'s Rain Parade and Boston's Lyres.

Perhaps the most significant development of all was that the jangle-rock movement was taking place in America, and the college rock charts were suddenly dominated by homegrown bands as opposed to the UK acts which they'd previously helped introduce to US audiences. (Though early records by Australia's the Church also fit the bill; the Smiths' Johnny Marr jangled, but Morrissey was too English). It also opened the door for local bands in each region that were practicing guitar rock, by garnering them airplay, record contracts and occasionally the ever-so-important Buck endorsement during R.E.M.'s countless cross-country treks. Northern California's Game Theory, New Haven's Miracle Legion and Minneapolis' Reverbs gained notoriety during the second wave of guitar rock. San Francisco's Translator and Wire Train had their jangle moments, particularly Translator with its 1982 college hit, "Everywhere That I'm Not," but faulty production left the bands saddled with the new wave tag. Perhaps they should have checked into the Drive-In.

Jangle-rock finally put to rest the notion that the only rock that emanated from the South was the vaguely racist and sexist blues-derived boogie that bands typically referred to as Southern-rock produced in the '70s. Bands appeared to grow on trees in Athens, like Kilkenny Cats, Oh-OK and Dreams So Real (refer to the soundtrack to the film, *Athens, GA.—Inside/Out*). It also shot down the idea that alternative and underground rock was inaccessible noise; akin to punk rock and not suitable for the masses.

Like punk, mixed gender bands were common as the groups aped the era of the Mamas & the Papas, the Mojo Men and the Velvets and fused the male-dominated '70s rock with female singer-songwriter rock. It's no coincidence that once bands like the Natalie Merchant-led 10,000 Maniacs experienced a modicum of popularity, it made way for the emergence of Suzanne Vega, Tracy Chapman and the Indigo Girls later in the decade, who, in turn, paved the way for the '90s wave of female singer-songwriter rock. Once Peter Case, formerly jangling with his Plimsouls, took a cue from John Hiatt and put down his electric guitar in favor of a subdued, coffeehouse-style delivery, more rockers followed suit and lightened up their attack. The move toward bands performing "unplugged" was partially due to the jangle-rock bands whose folk-rock melodies lent themselves to acoustic renditions that were performed mid-set, at college radio stations and in stores, long before it became the standard (check *Rainy Day*, a 1983 compilation of Paisley Underground-ers doing acoustic covers).

By the mid-'80s, even mainstream rockers like John Mellencamp had incorporated the jangle sound into their music; in particular, Mellencamp's folksy, 1985 *Scarecrow* album, which was arguably influenced by R.E.M. To be fair, there was an exchange going on—R.E.M. recorded *Lifes Rich Pageant* at Mellencamp's Belmont Mall studio the year after, partially inspired by an acoustic version of Mellencamp's "Small Town" which appeared as a B-side. As in any important movement, such exchange is key and leads to a number of other strings and tangents. *Lifes Rich Pageant* was a turning point for R.E.M.; a case could also be made for them borrowing the instrumental border-ska of Camper Van Beethoven (who accompanied them on tour) for their track "Underneath the Bunker" from the same LP. It also had them dabbling in the political-rock arena with their "Flowers of Guatemala."

Lyrics were not exactly at the forefront of jangle (after all, it was named for the guitars), unlike the folk-rock sounds of the '60s—but they weren't as simple and trite as its other cousin, power pop; such timeless rock 'n' roll themes as love and alienation cropped up often. Though their tenure was during the cold Reagan era, few bands engaged in the political arena since mixing politics with rock was considered foolish at the time (perhaps due to a gaffe made by Neil Young who seemingly endorsed Reagan). However, there was an unspoken thread of political correctness that ran throughout—as if to say all jangle-rock devotees came from a left-wing perspective. After keeping their mouths shut for years, R.E.M. became the most cause-concerned band around and their ever-present, offstage green politics contributed toward bands in general becoming more politcally aware.

In addition, Michael Stipe's mumble gave way to a more ethereal sound that was lost in the mix, rather than pointed lyrical accounts. Both factors partially explain why the genre was generally ignored and completely lost on the old-school writers at the mainstream music publications. Few had anything positive to say regarding this portion of the underground, relegating most coverage to fanzines and word of mouth, which is partially why by today's standards it took R.E.M. and others so long to break (in the case of R.E.M. it took six years!). Tight formats at MTV and commercial radio also contributed to the lockout since they did not allow for experimentation. Thus, airplay was confined to specialty programming (like IRS Records' "The Cutting Edge" weekly hour on MTV, wherein bands like R.E.M., Let's Active and Hüsker Dü were allowed to develop previously unseen on-camera personalities. Mid-decade radio opened up to incorporate "modern rock" (which would soon be coined "alternative") programming, but save for the latest records by R.E.M., their playlists were mostly comprised of the synth-pop songs college radio made popular in years prior.

As the decade wore on, it was taken for granted that the guitar had returned as the key instrument in rock 'n' roll and the world at large was ready for the takeover, while the media pretended to have been there all along. By the time Nirvana burst onto the scene, though they'd claimed R.E.M. as a prime influence, Kurt Cobain and other more melodious grunge rockers had turned the form upside down, cashing in the harmonies and delicate vocals, but retaining the guitar-driven spirit behind the melodies. What they also retained was R.E.M.'s take no prisoners, D.I.Y. model of how to be an "alternative" band, by ceaselessly touring, retaining artistic control and supporting humanist causes. Ironically, it was right around this time that R.E.M. became the biggest jangle-rock band in the world with their 1991 single "Losing My Religion" from the *Out of Time* record and subsequently traded in the chime for a darker sound, reclaiming their earliest influences, the Velvet Underground and the Stooges. Entering their second decade as a band, they released the moody *Automatic for the People*, and the thundering, metallic *Monster*.

In the '90s, the Velvets continued to be an overriding influence. However, it was the sound of Big Star's *Third/Sister Lovers* that became favored by former jangler David Roback (Rain Parade) who formed Opal (with the Dream Syndicate's Kendra Smith) then Mazzy Star with Chilton's record as his blueprint. Traces of Chilton's jangle from the first two Big Star albums, along with power pop and hard rock, were heard in the records of the Seattle-based Posies.

The Posies proved their love of jangle when Jon Auer and Ken Stringfellow served as one half of the reformed Big Star with Chilton and Jody Stephens for a 1993 live album *(Columbia)* and tour. Scotland's Teenage Fanclub turned out an album in 1990, *Bandwagonesque*, that was wholly inspired by Big Star, and continue to work and refine their guitar-driven sound. In San Francisco, Scott Miller (ex-Game Theory) still pines at inflecting his music with authentic jangle sounds in his Loud Family.

Brit-pop, though supposedly British to the core, has traces of the jangle. Along with their obvious debt to the Beatles, Oasis' Manchester jangle, inspired by the Smiths, came to them via Marr who probably picked it up from Buck and the Byrds before the Smiths' 1984 debut.

Both the lo-fi and American indie-rock movements of the '90s were heavily indebted to jangle-rock. The three leading figures of lo-fi—Pavement, Sebadoh and Guided by Voices—used jangle as a foundation, capturing its spirit, if not necessarily its sound. Not coincidentally, all three bands were either of college age or in their early twenties during the mid- and late '80s, and they took the do-it-yourself, self-sustained sense of community of jangle-rock to heart, staying on independent labels when they could have moved to the majors.

The Americana, occasionally jangling sounds of Wilco, Son Volt and Jayhawks can be traced immediately back to the Parsons-lovin' Long Ryders and raw, rockin' Jim Dickinson Memphis productions by Green on Red (*Here Come the Snakes*) and the Replacements (*Pleased to Meet Me*). The Gin Blossoms owe a great debt to Paul Westerberg and the Replacements; R.E.M. begat Live and Toad the Wet Sprocket, ad nauseum. But everyone should tip their hat to Bob Dylan, who, though never a favorite among jangle rockers, was the first to fuse rock with folk, and the gave the Byrds "Mr. Tambourine Man" to which to add their chiming harmonies and jangling guitars, making it accessible to the world.

Recommended Recordings

Big Star, *No. 1 Record / Radio City* (Fantasy)
The Soft Boys, *Underwater Moonlight* (Rykodisc)
The dB's, *Repercussion* (I.R.S.)
R.E.M., *Chronic Town* (I.R.S.)
R.E.M., *Murmur* (I.R.S.)
R.E.M., *Reckoning* (I.R.S.)
Let's Active, *Cypress / Afoot* (I.R.S.)
The Plimsouls, *Everywhere at Once* (Geffen)
Bangles, *Bangles* EP (Faulty)
Rain Parade, *Emergency Third Rail Power Trip/Explosions in the Glass Palace* (Enigma)
Dream Syndicate, *Tell Me When It's Over: The Best of the Dream Syndicate* (Rhino)
Three O'Clock, *Baroque Hoedown* EP (Frontier)
Richard Barone/James Mastro, *Nuts and Bolts* (Passport)
Various Artists, *Rainy Day* (Rough Trade)
Long Ryders, *10-5-60* EP (PVC)
The Replacements, *Let It Be* (Twin/Tone)
Robyn Hitchcock & the Egyptians, *Fegmania!* (Rhino)
Game Theory, *Real Nighttime* (Alias)
Camper Van Beethoven, *Telephone Free Landslide Victory* (I.R.S.)
Miracle Legion, *The Backyard* EP (Rough Trade)

—Denise Sullivan

American Alternative Rock

Like new wave before it, "alternative" is basically a meaningless term. Punk, heavy metal, funk, rap, pop, rock 'n' roll, singer-songwriter—everything fits under the term. Essentially, "alternative" is a catch-all for post-punk bands that appeared as new wave began to die out in 1983-84, and runs all the way into 1996, when alternative had become mainstream modern rock. Although there's nothing alternative about Live and Silverchair, their inspiration by R.E.M. and Nirvana were decidedly part of an underground, anti-mainstream rock 'n' roll movement. But what really distinguishes alternative pop-rock is how it reprocesses and reworks rock history, bringing together diverse strands into a whole. Alternative followed somewhat different paths in America and Britain; although the two countries have had bands that were big on both continents, like R.E.M., certain phenomena like Pearl Jam or the Stone Roses haven't translated particularly well. In addition, entire subgenres are isolated to either the US or the UK (funk-metal, for instance, has never been very popular in Britain.)

Alternative pop-rock has its basic roots in punk, new wave and hardcore; it does recall other genres, particularly '60s pop and heavy metal, but the entire subculture first emerged from the punk movement. To over-simplify things, the first American alternative bands were R.E.M. and Hüsker Dü. Both bands formed in the early '80s or late '70s, releasing records on small independent labels before moving to bigger indies and then the majors. In their wake, thousands of bands followed, both musically and ideologically. Hüsker Dü broke up without achieving any mainstream success, while R.E.M. soldiered on into the '90s, becoming one of the most popular rock 'n' roll bands in the world.

For most of the '80s, alternative rock remained the province of small clubs, independent labels, fanzines, and college radio, with the occasional song breaking into MTV and Top 40, or the occasional album receiving critical praise in mainstream publications like *Rolling Stone*. However, the commercial appeal of most alternative bands were nearly nonexistent. Instead, the bands built underground followings by touring constantly and releasing a low-budget album every year. New bands would form in their wake and soon there was a sizable underground circuit in America, with different parts of the country having different scenes.

R.E.M. immediately had the most impact, both commercially and musically. *Murmur*, the band's 1983 debut album, received enormous

critical praise, helping the album chart in the Top 40. Legions of jangling imitators followed, and the group's success helped other southern guitar-pop bands like the dB's and Let's Active get exposure. Also, they helped kick off a group of bands dubbed "The Paisley Underground" that drew from the Velvet Underground and '60s psychedelia. R.E.M. toured non-stop throughout the decade, releasing a record each year and slowly expanding their following, setting the stage for their Top Ten breakthrough in 1987 with *Document* and "The One I Love." By that time, the group's ringing, chiming guitars and Michael Stipe's mumbling vocals had become commonplace on college radio.

While R.E.M.'s success provided a blueprint for many bands of the late '80s and '90s, Hüsker Dü's music had an equally large impact. Starting as a blistering hardcore band, the trio soon moved away from the confines of their subgenre. Without abandoning the loud guitars and furious tempos of hardcore, Hüsker Dü created a music that was both abrasive and melodic, filled with shards of noise and catchy hooks. *Zen Arcade*, a double album released in 1984, was their creative breakthrough, filled with concise pop and noisy, winding instrumental stretches. The group's last album, 1987's *Warehouse: Songs and Stories*, had a more polished sound than their earlier records, but it provided a template for the shiny punk-pop production of Nirvana's seminal *Nevermind*.

Hüsker Dü was signed to SST Records, the label founded by Black Flag leader Greg Ginn in the early '80s. SST was the most influential American independent label of the '80s, not only featuring Black Flag and Hüsker Dü, but also Sonic Youth, the Minutemen, the Meat Puppets, and Dinosaur Jr., among others. While they didn't necessarily pave the way for Sonic Youth—the New York band was already recording when Hüsker Dü came to prominence—Hüsker Dü's albums prepared both critics and audiences for the all-out noise experiments of the group. Sonic Youth was more self-consciously arty than either R.E.M. or Hüsker Dü, with their lyrics sounding like performance-art poetry and their songs essentially being long, winding dissonant soundscapes.

Hüsker Dü were also the leaders of the loose Minneapolis scene, which also included the Replacements and Soul Asylum, who both initially sounded a great deal like the Hüskers. However, the Replacements wound up providing a link between punk and traditional Stones/Faces rock 'n' roll, as well as narrowing the gap between R.E.M.'s pop and Hüsker Dü's noise. At that point in time, Hüsker Dü had broken up, R.E.M. had made a commercial breakthrough, the Minutemen were crippled by the death of D. Boon and Sonic Youth were inactive between 1988 and 1990, as they were preparing to move to a major label. Consequently, several different subgenres that had thrived underneath the reign of the SST bands and R.E.M. came to the forefront. In addition to the loud, sloppy punky rock 'n' roll of the Replacements and Soul Asylum, quirky alternative pop and noisy industrial rock dominated the late '80s American alternative scene.

Much of the alternative guitar-pop of the late '80s had its roots in the awkward, jangly music of the Feelies and the nervous, geeky folk-rock of the Violent Femmes, who both released their debut albums in the early '80s. The Feelies never sold many records at the time, yet their chiming guitar riffs helped pave the way for R.E.M. Unlike R.E.M., the Feelies' melodies and lyrics were twitchy and uptight, quite similar to the songs that Gordon Gano wrote for the Violent Femmes' self-titled debut. Both of the bands began a trend of geeky guitar-pop groups that emphasized their strangeness and bizarre humor. Since they were actively recording and touring at the time quirky guitar-pop became prominent, the Violent Femmes and the Feelies were part of the movement as well as being its forefathers. However, there were many other bands, from the jokey duo They Might Be Giants to the warped eclecticism of Camper Van Beethoven, that kept the music alive on the college charts. A number of off-kilter British guitar-pop bands fit into this trend as well, finding a larger following on American college radio stations than in their homeland. Robyn Hitchcock, the leader of the Soft Boys (who were an acknowledged influence on R.E.M.), was one of the British pop musicians who was warmly welcomed in the US. By this point in their career, XTC had a larger fan base in America than they had in Britain, which meant that their intelligent, meticulously crafted pop was prominently featured on American college radio.

In direct contrast to the good-natured, quirky pop of the Violent Femmes and XTC stood the legions of industrial and post-hardcore noise bands. While many industrial bands had their roots in European electronic groups, both the industrial and post-hardcore bands owed a great debt to Chicago's Big Black. Led by guitarist Steve Albini, Big Black created bleak, scathing, noisy soundscapes with two guitars, a bass, and a drum machine. The group's thin, tinny guitar roar became part of indie-rock's musical vocabulary, as did its shards of white noise. Their records, particularly 1986's *Atomizer*, prepared alternative audiences and college radio audiences for the jarring guitar grind of the Butthole Surfers, Scratch Acid and its offspring, the Jesus Lizard, and countless bands that appropriated the same noise as their own. Most of these bands were also produced by Steve Albini, who continued to be a prominent figure in underground rock into the '90s.

Big Black's records also paved the way for industrial groups that spliced together noisy guitars, dense samples, and relentless drum-machine driven beats. European bands like Front 242, Einstürzende Neubauten, and KMFDM were pioneers in the music and gained a significant amount of American college airplay, but it was Chicago's Ministry that popularized the genre. Originally a synth-pop band in the early '80s, the group, led by guitarist/keyboardist Al Jourgensen, changed direction in the mid-'80s, incorporating elements of dance, heavy metal, electronic music and hip-hop. Ministry's artistic breakthrough, also the record that helped establish industrial music as a staple of alternative rock, was 1988's *The Land of Rape and Honey*. As the years progressed, Ministry began leaning toward heavy metal, helping to make industrial techniques part of mainstream rock. Just as important were Cleveland's Nine Inch Nails, led by Trent Reznor. Nine Inch Nails were more pop-oriented than any other industrial band, which meant they were the ones that brought the music to a wider audience. But by the time that their 1989 debut, *Pretty Hate Machine*, became popular in 1991, industrial music had become passé in most alternative circles.

What had replaced industrial rock as a favored source of noise were revamped versions of Stooges-style punk and heavy metal. After the rise of industrial and quirky guitar pop, the spiky punk-pop of the Pixies and heavy grandeur of Jane's Addiction were the two most popular bands in alternative rock. The Pixies returned a sense of punk brevity to alternative music, as well as working raw noise into pop song structures that were deliberately off-center. Their fractured, stripped-down punk-pop provided a blueprint for groups as diverse as Nirvana, Pavement, Weezer, and Radiohead, who all appropriated portions of the Pixies' music into their rock 'n' roll. Although the Pixies were stars in most of Europe, they never achieved commercial success in America. Jane's Addiction were among the first to break down the walls between alternative and AOR radio, which given their affection for ponderous heavy metal, wasn't surprising. Perry Farrell's lyrics may have had the performance-art shock of Sonic Youth, but the band's music was heavy metal in the vein of Led Zeppelin. Similarly, Seattle's Soundgarden reworked Zeppelin/Black Sabbath heavy metal territory, yet they injected a raw, punkish intensity to the familiar sludge. Both Jane's Addiction and Soundgarden received positive reviews in mainstream publications like *Rolling Stone*, earning them a sizable cult following.

Soundgarden was the first of the Seattle bands to earn wide-spread acclaim in America. In England, Mudhoney was the first Seattle band to earn positive reviews. Mudhoney's Stooges-soaked fuzz-toned 1988 single "Touch Me, I'm Sick," received a significant amount of acclaim in Britain, and the band earned a cult following in the UK by constant touring. To varying degrees, the success of Soundgarden, Mudhoney, the Pixies, and Jane's Addiction, as well as R.E.M., set the stage for Nirvana's breakthrough in late 1991.

Nirvana was the turning point for alternative rock as a commercially viable genre. Other bands had hits before them—particularly R.E.M. and Jane's Addiction—but Nirvana broke down the doors forever with their brand of punk-pop, which took equally from the Pixies, Sonic Youth, Soundgarden, and the Beatles. Following the No. 1 success of *Nevermind*—which symbolically knocked Michael Jackson's *Dangerous* off the top of the charts—bands that had been on the fringe became multi-platinum stars, including the funk-metal of the Red Hot Chili Peppers and Primus, the industrial rock of Ministry and Nine Inch Nails, and the revamped arena-rock of Pearl Jam.

Although Nirvana's success did help send scores of bands, from Pearl Jam and Stone Temple Pilots to Green Day and the Offspring, to the top of the charts, it didn't eliminate the underground—it just gave it more exposure. Initially, this resulted in a flood of Seattle bands achieving considerable commercial success, including Pearl Jam, Alice in Chains, and Offspring. Nirvana's breakthrough also popularized so-called "Generation X" and "slacker" culture. Slackers came in many forms, but no band embodied the aesthetic quite as well as the Beastie Boys. Initially a hardcore band, the Beasties turned to rap in the early '80s, recording *Licensed to Ill*, one of hip-hop's major commercial breakthroughs. In 1989, the group released *Paul's Boutique*, a dense collage of pop and literary references that virtually defined the multi-culturalism and junk culture aesthetic that dominated much of the popular alternative rock of the '90s. However, *Paul's Boutique* was a commercial failure. When the Beastie Boys released *Check Your Head* in 1992, they had returned to playing their instruments and created a record that fused punk culture with hip-hop culture.

While the Beastie Boys presented another commercially successful alternative to heavy alternative rock, a number of female rockers began to gain attention both in the rock press and, occasionally, on MTV. During the '80s, women had prominent roles in important bands like Sonic Youth (bassist Kim Gordon) and the Pixies (bassist Kim Deal). In the late '80s, a number of new female singer-songwriters emerged, particularly Michelle Shocked, Tracy Chapman, Sinéad O'Connor, and Kristin Hersh

of the Throwing Muses. While Shocked and Chapman were essentially folkies, O'Connor and Hersh bent the rules of rock 'n' roll. O'Connor experimented with folk, punk, dance, and art-rock, creating a creative amalgam of styles that paid off with her 1990 commercial breakthrough, *I Do Not Want What I Have Not Got*. Under the direction of Kristin Hersh—and occasionally her step-sister, Tanya Donelly—Throwing Muses created a bracing music that had unpredictable lyrical and song structures which placed the band somewhere between punk, pop and folk.

The late '80s female singer-songwriters prepared the rock media for the onslaught of the early '90s, as well as directly influencing several musicians. In particular, the songs on Liz Phair's 1993 debut *Exile in Guyville* recall music that was made in the late '80s, but her music included elements of rock 'n' roll, power pop, Joni Mitchell-styled folk-rock, and lo-fi alternative rock. There were other singer-songwriters similar to Phair, particularly the blues-punk of England's P.J. Harvey, but most of the female rock 'n' roll acts of the early '90s were punk rock bands, with the occasional fusion of punk and heavy metal which recalled the music of Nirvana and Soundgarden. L7, Babes In Toyland, and Hole fit into this category, but there were underground bands like Bikini Kill and Bratmobile that sketched out an amateurish and politically confrontational form of punk labeled riot grrrl. There were also guitar-pop acts like Belly and Juliana Hatfield which were decidedly sunnier than their counterparts, but there were bands like the Breeders, led by Kim Deal, that straddled the line between arty punk and pop without surrendering to either side.

Because of a media-created desire to lump all of these acts under the banner of "women in rock," most of these bands received a fair amount of press, but only a handful—Belly, Breeders, Hole, and Liz Phair—sold many records. After the initial onslaught of Nirvana, Pearl Jam, Soundgarden, Smashing Pumpkins, and Red Hot Chili Peppers, the groups that sold the most records were neo-punk rockers Green Day and the Offspring. Although it didn't sound much different than their two previous indie releases, Green Day's third album, *Dookie*, and the singles, "Long View" and "Basketcase," sent the group to the top of the charts in the summer of 1994; by the summer of 1995, *Dookie* had sold over eight million copies. Green Day's music essentially was revamped power pop with hints of the Clash and the Jam, but the band's success led to the multi-platinum breakthrough of the metallic punk band the Offspring, who adopted the look of a punk group and the attack of a metal band. In their wake, Green Day and the Offspring focused attention on the hundreds of punk bands that played on the West Coast, particularly Rancid and Pennywise.

For all their ties with independent rock 'n' roll and the underground, Green Day and the Offspring had little to do with alternative music by the time they broke into the mainstream. After Nirvana's breakthrough, the American underground divided into several factions that were all united by their desire to remain underground. There were neo-punk bands like North Carolina's Superchunk which developed devoted followings but never had any desire to break beyond the level of an indie-rock band. There were arty, minimalist pop bands like Unrest which were knowingly clever, post-modern and ironic, but made melodic catchy songs that were never destined to break out of their cult following because the band never intended them for anything larger than their cult audience. There were handfuls of country-rockers like Uncle Tupelo that imploded before they could reach any success.

Most important to the '90s American underground were the group of pop-rockers that were lumped under the "lo-fi" label, named after the poor sound of the band's generally homemade recordings. Beck helped popularize the subgenre with his debut album, *Mellow Gold*. However, *Mellow Gold* was not strictly a lo-fi record—it was too well-produced to fit that label. Nevertheless, Beck acted like a scavenger, much like the Beastie Boys, taking bits and pieces from different musical genres, recording songs that alternately recalled hip-hop, folk, garage-rock, and psychedelia. Beck's other records, the noisy *Stereopathetic Soul Manure* and the folky *One Foot in the Grave*, were genuine lo-fi records, but the success of *Mellow Gold* helped draw attention to the leaders of the movement, Sebadoh and Pavement. Both bands had earned a significant amount of critical acclaim, as well as sizable cult followings, before Beck, but his success began a trend in the rock press to lump all of the bands together. If any band embodies everything that is good and bad about lo-fi, it is Sebadoh. Led by former Dinosaur Jr. member Lou Barlow, Sebadoh isn't so much a band as it is a collective, with each individual member turning in their own songs. Barlow became the figurehead for the lo-fi movement, as he released an amazing amount of recordings in the early '90s under Sebadoh's name, Sentridoh, the Folk Implosion, and his own name. Essentially, Barlow is a post-punk singer-songwriter, writing fairly conventional pop songs that are distinguished by his recording techniques and the occasional burst of pop noise. Nevertheless, the aesthetic is as important as the songs for many lo-fi fans, and Lou Barlow's work provides plenty of good songs and bad songs, all characterized by the thin recording techniques.

The one band that transcends the label of lo-fi is Pavement. What was important about Pavement's music was not the aesthetics, but the concepts. The group reassembled a variety of different rock 'n' roll genres—from noise-rock to country-rock, hitting on power pop, folk-rock, rock 'n' roll, soul, etc. along the way—into a fractured, but tuneful, kaleidoscope of pop music. Unlike Beck's eclecticism, Pavement's songs—mainly written by guitarist/vocalist Stephen Malkmus—not only recontextualize familiar rock genres, they frequently subvert conventional pop structures. Pavement's three albums and numerous singles have earned them a sizable cult following as well as a wealth of critical praise, in effect, establishing the band as a leader of the post-Nirvana American alternative underground. Currently, they don't seem poised for a commercial breakthrough, but many observers felt that way about R.E.M. in 1985.

Recommended Recordings

The Feelies, *Crazy Rhythms* (A&M)

Violent Femmes, *Violent Femmes* (Slash)

R.E.M., *Murmur* (IRS)

Replacements, *Let It Be* (Twin/Tone)

Hüsker Dü, *New Day Rising* (SST)

Big Black, *The Rich Man's Eight-Track* (Touch & Go)

Throwing Muses, *Throwing Muses* (4AD)

Dinosaur Jr., *You're Living All Over Me* (SST)

R.E.M., *Document* (IRS)

10,000 Maniacs, *In My Tribe* (Elektra)

Ministry, *The Land of Rape and Honey* (Sire)

Sonic Youth, *Daydream Nation* (DGC)

Michelle Shocked, *Short Sharp Shocked* (Mercury)

Jane's Addiction, *Nothing's Shocking* (Warner Bros.)

Soundgarden, *Louder than Love* (A&M)

Mudhoney, *Superfuzz Bigmuff* (Sub Pop)

Pixies, *Doolittle* (4AD)

Nine Inch Nails, *Pretty Hate Machine* (TVT)

Nirvana, *Nevermind* (DGC)

Pearl Jam, *Ten* (Epic)

Liz Phair, *Exile in Guyville* (Matador)

Pavement, *Slanted & Enchanted* (Matador)

Beastie Boys, *Check Your Head* (Capitol)

Beck, *Mellow Gold* (DGC)

—Stephen Thomas Erlewine

British Alternative Rock

Two things separate British alternative rock from its American counterpart. By and large, it's considerably more pop-oriented. Of course, there are some exceptions, particularly goth-rock and shoegazing, but most of the bands concentrate on singles as well as albums. Secondly, it acknowledges dance and club culture freely, with pop-rock groups frequently experimenting with dance rhythms and textures. Both of these factors are part of the reason why very few British alternative bands were successful in America between 1984-1995. The other major factor is a tendency to write about specifically British concerns. From the Smiths to Blur, the lyrics of many British groups are dense with British references. However, 1994 and 1995 showed that the success of American alternative rock had begun to break down the barriers in the US for British bands, as Blur had a Top 60 hit, Oasis had a gold album, and Elastica had two charting hits, as well as a prime spot on Lollapalooza.

Like R.E.M. in the US, the Smiths functioned as the turning point between new wave and alternative rock. Hailing from Manchester, the group's layered guitar-pop recalled the Beatles and the Kinks, as well as various girl groups and less-celebrated '60s pop groups. Johnny Marr's innovative, ringing guitar riffs were offset by the literate, self-deprecating and viciously intelligent lyrics of Morrissey. In addition to his distinctive, clever lyrics, Morrissey's voice was unusual, alternating between mild crooning and abrupt yelps, particularly on the band's earlier records. Although the Smiths had only two Top Ten hits, the band's influence loomed large over the next decade, as various bands appropriated Marr's riffs and neo-'60s look. Morrissey's lyrical preoccupations became familiar as well, particularly his tales about English life. The Smiths' lifespan was quite short—their first album was released in 1984, their last in 1987—but no other British band since the Sex Pistols had as large of a musical impact as the Manchester quartet.

For the latter half of the '80s, British alternative pop-rock was dominated by the goth-rock of the Cure, the dance-rock of New Order, and the noisy, neo-psychedelia of the Jesus and Mary Chain. The Cure had formed during the heyday of punk rock, yet their cult began to expand in 1983 and 1984, after which they had a series of best-selling albums and singles. Driven by slow tempos, droning guitars and keyboards, and Robert Smith's self-absorbed, morbid lyrics, the Cure appealed to some

of the Smiths' audience, yet they were decidedly gloomier and less pop-oriented. Bands that copied the music of the Cure and Joy Division were quite popular in the late '80s, particularly Sisters of Mercy and Mission (UK).

Joy Division was arguably more important to goth rock than the Cure, but after the band's lead vocalist, Ian Curtis, committed suicide in 1980, the group moved in a different direction under the name New Order. Instead of relying on rock rhythms, New Order experimented with dance, disco, and club beats, creating a fusion between rock and dance which proved to be commercially successful and musically influential. Although not many bands immediately imitated the sound of the band, it laid the groundwork for the Manchester scene of the early '90s.

Although they used a drum machine on their earliest recordings, the Jesus and Mary Chain were as far away from the dance textures of New Order as possible. Instead, the band unearthed the droning noise of the Velvet Underground, adding more distortion, tighter song structure, and floating harmonies. The Jesus and Mary Chain, along with the gargantuan guitar roar of America's the Pixies and Sonic Youth, instigated a flood of bands in the '90s that relied on shatteringly loud guitars and ethereal, Beach Boys-derived harmonies.

During this time, a number of British acts found greater success in America than they did at home. While artists like the Cure and the Smiths were popular in both countries, certain musicians were virtually ignored in the UK but thrived on American college radio. Foremost among these groups was XTC. Although the group had hits when they first appeared at the height of punk and new wave, they failed to have more than one hit between 1984 and 1989. Nevertheless, the band's late-'80s albums of lush, psychedelic pop found a home in the American alternative scene, particularly 1987's *Skylarking*. Like XTC, Robyn Hitchcock was a new wave survivor, although his former group the Soft Boys were never anywhere near as popular as XTC. However, the Soft Boys' tough, ringing guitar-pop had an influence on many alternative bands of the '80s, particularly R.E.M. Once Hitchcock went solo, he gained a cult following in his native England and America, but had considerably more success in the US, thanks to support from college radio. His 1988 major-label debut, *Globe of Frogs*, marked the peak of his popularity, spending 15 weeks on the American charts. In addition to the off-center pop of XTC and Robyn Hitchcock, there were guitar bands that refined the jangling, multi-layered pop of the Smiths, making it smoother, more laidback and sophisticated. These bands, particularly the Housemartins, managed to sustain popularity on the British charts as well as American college radio.

However, the most significant British band of the late '80s and early '90s was the Stone Roses. Like their fellow Mancunians the Smiths, the Stone Roses specialized in an updated version of '60s guitar-pop. Unlike the Smiths, the Stone Roses were in debt to neo-psychedelic guitar-pop and experimented with club textures, particularly on the singles "Fool's Gold" and "One Love." But the key to the band's success was guitarist John Squire, who crafted songs that sounded like forgotten classics but were driven by an urgent energy and cocksure arrogance. The success of the Stone Roses opened the gates for a flood of bands that reworked the same territory, like the Charlatans and Inspiral Carpets. Of these bands, the Happy Mondays—who were also based in Manchester, giving way to the nickname "Madchester" for the entire pseudo-psychedelic dance scene—were the most noteworthy. Where the Stone Roses only flirted with dance music, the Happy Mondays immersed themselves in it, particularly in the funky rhythms and psychedelic drugs like Ecstasy. Shaun Ryder, the band's lead vocalist, wrote lyrics that were cryptically surreal and melodies that appropriated hooks from other pop songs (the Mondays' "Kinky Afro" had the same melody as Labelle's "Lady Marmalade").

At the beginning of the '90s, it appeared as if the Stone Roses and Happy Mondays would be the leading figures in British pop music for the next few years. However, the Madchester scene quickly collapsed. The Stone Roses became embroiled in a debilitating lawsuit with their record company which took two years to resolve; after the case was settled, they took another three years to deliver a follow-up album, ruining any chances of world domination. The Happy Mondays ran out of steam quickly, mainly due to Ryder's drug addictions. Within a year, British alternative rock was robbed of its two most popular bands, leaving the legions of the Jesus and Mary Chain imitators to come to the forefront. Well, initially they were imitators of the Jesus and Mary Chain. However, by the time the so-called shoegazers—dubbed "shoegazers" by the British music press for their tendency to do nothing but stare at the floor during concerts—came to popularity in 1991, they were mining the territory My Bloody Valentine established in the late '80s.

My Bloody Valentine formed before the Jesus and Mary Chain, but their records didn't gain attention until 1987, when they released a series of EPs, culminating in 1988's album *Isn't Anything*. MBV's music was louder and more ethereal than JMC's records, creating shimmering soundscapes constructed from dissonance and distortion and detached vocals. Soon, the band's influence eclipsed that of the Jesus and Mary

Chain, with numerous bands forming in its wake, including Ride, Lush, and the Boo Radleys. Out of all the shoegazing records released in 1991, My Bloody Valentine's *Loveless* was the one that defined the entire scene.

Apart from shoegazing, the other major British musical development of 1991 was the release of Primal Scream's third album, *Screamadelica*. Compared to *Screamadelica*, the dance-oriented music of the Happy Mondays was positively tentative. Primal Scream employed a number of dance and techno producers, particularly Andrew Weatherall, to help them create their album. The group's basic compositions were clearly rock songs—the single "Movin' on Up" recalled both the Rolling Stones and Stephen Stills' "Love the One You're With"—but the producers took the songs into new territory with the inclusion of dance-club production techniques. The result was one of the most critically acclaimed albums of the year, as well as a commercial hit. More importantly, *Screamadelica* helped open the doors for techno and club music to be discussed seriously in the British music press, which helped the careers of such techno and ambient musicians like the Orb and the Aphex Twin, as well as dance-oriented bands like Massive Attack, Portishead, and Tricky.

However, neither Primal Scream nor the legions of shoegazers provided as much good copy as the Stone Roses and Happy Mondays, which is crucial for an industry with weekly music newspapers. For all of 1991 and most of 1992, the two trends dominated British alternative rock, along with the presence of American groups like Nirvana and Pearl Jam. The arrival of Suede in late 1992 kick-started a revival of British guitar-pop that reached its fruition two years later. Under the leadership of vocalist Brett Anderson and guitarist Bernard Butler, Suede created a pop-savvy fusion of glam-rock and the Smiths' guitar-pop. The band was praised by the music weeklies as the "Best Band in Britain" before their first single was even released, and Morrissey began covering "My Insatiable One" in concert, setting the stage for enormous expectations. By and large, Suede fulfilled the expectations, as they had a series of hit singles that all charted higher than the first, and their 1993 self-titled debut became the fastest-selling record in British history. The band single-handedly knocked the shoegazers off the front cover of the *Melody Maker* and *NME*, setting the stage for British alternative rock's breakthrough into the mainstream in 1994.

Suede may have become British stars in 1993, but they couldn't find a niche in America. During 1994, the band's star began to fade, as Butler left the group before the completion of their second album. That alone wouldn't have been enough to dim their stardom, but the band had created a monster with their debut album that soon outgrew the band itself. Over the course of 1994, no less than three bands emerged as massively popular artists, both commercially and critically. Of these bands, Blur was the first and most successful.

Blur had originally emerged during the height of shoegazing in 1991 with *Leisure*, a record that combined strands of shoegazing with the Madchester craze. Initially, they were popular, but they quickly fell out of favor. The group returned in 1993 with *Modern Life Is Rubbish*, a record that recalled the glory days of British pop, featuring elements of the Kinks, Small Faces, the Jam, and Madness. It was a moderate success, but its performance did nothing to indicate the magnitude of Blur's 1994 breakthrough with *Parklife*. Although it was as fiercely British as its predecessor, *Parklife* was more focused and featured stronger songs, several of which added elements of '80s synth-pop and new wave. "Girls and Boys," the album's opening dance-pop number, entered the charts at No. 5 upon its release in the spring of 1994, opening the doors for a year where British alternative rock became the dominating musical force in the country. By the end of the year, *Parklife* had gone triple platinum in the UK, establishing Blur as arguably the most popular band in the country.

As *Parklife* was beginning to take off in the spring of 1994, a new Manchester-based quintet called Oasis began receiving overwhelmingly positive reviews in the weeklies. By the end of the summer, Oasis had a genuine hit with "Live Forever," and their debut album, *Definitely Maybe*, had unseated Suede as the fastest-selling debut album in UK history. Oasis quickly became as popular as Blur, scoring a No. 1 single in the spring of 1995 with "Some Might Say;" by summer 1995, *Definitely Maybe* had gone triple platinum. In addition to Oasis and Blur, a flood of independent and alternative bands began ruling the British pop charts. The spiky new wave revivalism of Elastica, the elegantly wasted synth-pop of Pulp, the youthful exuberance of Supergrass, the streamlined Smiths guitar-pop of Gene, the Boo Radleys, and Shaun Ryder's new band, Black Grape, all enjoyed Top Ten hits on the pop charts, including several number ones. It was the equivalent of Nirvana's American breakthrough, as nearly every one of Britain's most popular bands had its roots in the alternative pop-rock scene of the past decade.

Recommended Recordings

The Smiths, *Singles* (Reprise)
The Smiths, *The Queen Is Dead* (Sire)
The Cure, *Staring at the Sea* (Elektra)

The Jesus and Mary Chain, *Psychocandy* (Def American)
New Order, *Substance* (Qwest)
XTC, *Skylarking* (Geffen)
Robyn Hitchcock, *Globe of Frogs* (A&M)
The Housemartins, *London 0 Hull 4* (Go!)
The Stone Roses, *The Stone Roses* (London)
The La's, *The La's* (London)
Happy Mondays, *Pills 'n' Thrills & Bellyaches* (Elektra)
My Bloody Valentine, *Loveless* (Sire)
Primal Scream, *Screamadelica* (Sire)
Suede, *Suede* (Columbia)
Blur, *Parklife* (Capitol)
Oasis, *Definitely Maybe* (Epic)

—Stephen Thomas Erlewine

Lo-Fi

Over the last several decades, there's been a more or less ongoing clique of staunch traditionalists who insist that hi-tech, glossy production values are taking the soul and spontaneity out of rock 'n' roll music. As rock heads into the 21st century—in an age where such technology-dependent musics as techno, ambient, and rap are gaining an unstoppable momentum, and multi-track recordings and "punch-in" vocals are standard practice—it's ironic that one of the most influential trends of alternative rock in the '90s has deliberately cast itself in opposition to studio sophistication. Called "lo-fi" artists, more by the rock underground than by themselves, they see simple, even primitive recording quality as an advantage, not a hindrance.

If you're so inclined, you can trace lo-fi right back to the beginning of rock 'n' roll, when thousands of rockabilly and doo wop artists recorded in primitive circumstances, lending to their records a unique naiveté that is impossible to re-create today. The garage bands of the mid-'60s, of course, often recorded in facilities as primitive as the ones they rehearsed in, a quality which was duplicated in the '70s by many of the early punk bands.

The difference between these earlier rock 'n' rollers and today's lo-fi artists is that, in all probability, virtually all of the earlier records sounded primitive due to financial limitations rather than conscious decision. If these rockabilly, garage, and even punks had been asked at the time whether they would like to be recording in more sophisticated facilities, with greater time and budgets at their disposable, the vast majority of them would likely have said yes without a second thought. While today's lo-fi artists are often limited by budgetary constraints as well, the defining difference is that they are by and large making a conscious choice to aim for the spontaneity and distinctive distorted, grainy sonic qualities that can arise from recording quickly on simple, even outdated, equipment.

Again, this approach isn't unique to the '90s, and in fact has pretty deep roots. On their second album, *White Light/White Heat*, the Velvet Underground deliberately turned their amps to 11 and gleefully watched the needles go into the red, ignoring the engineer's pleas to turn down the volume to eliminate distortion. The Beatles deliberately created distortion on tracks like "Revolution"; the Rolling Stones recorded some of "Jumping Jack Flash"'s guitars on cassette to get the right amount of dirt into the sound.

But lo-fi, as the label's applied in 1997, really has its roots in the do-it-yourself ethic that arose from the punk movement in the late '70s. One of its basic (if not always observed) tenets was that anybody could form a band, record their music, and issue it on their own label. By the early '80s, this was taken a step further by some independent artists, who realized that they need not even enter a studio to record their own music, or even "release" it through traditional vinyl means, instead recording at home, dubbing their own cassettes, and selling/trading those at gigs or through the mail. The fuzzy sound, distorted guitars, simple instrumentation, occasional mistakes: these were not viewed as flaws, but as actual enhancements, increasing the most intimate and personal quality of the performances, and the truest representation of the artists' visions. Many alternative acts of the '80s were lo-fi in this classic sense, although the label hadn't been created at the time. Page through any issue of alternative/underground publications such as *Op, Option,* or *Forced Exposure*, and there will be plenty of them, on vinyl, cassette, and eventually, compact disc. The K label, run by Calvin Johnson of Beat Happening, is (in retrospect) the most famous and influential repository of the lo-fi aesthetic. But there were innumerable others following the same path, most (but not all) rock-based, although they didn't achieve even a modicum of mainstream recognition: Jandek, Kath Bloom, Walls of Genius, Linda Smith, and Loren Mazzacane are but a few of the better underappreciated trailblazers of the genre. Content as well as attitude was needed to make this stuff work, as the music of the unspeakably, deliberately awful Happy Flowers, as well as literally thousands of cassette tapes, could attest to.

At the beginning of the 1990s, several alternative rock acts using the lo-fi aesthetic began to rise to levels of attention previously reserved for R.E.M. clones and British gloom-mongers. Chief among these were Sebadoh, formed by Dinosaur, Jr. castoff Lou Barlow; Pavement, a California band that seemed to positively pride itself on non-promotion and an elusive image; and Guided by Voices, an Ohio band that had been releasing their own albums for a good half-dozen years before suddenly getting "discovered" by listeners extending beyond their circle of friends.

Most likely, these bands achieved a level of recognition unattained by previous lo-fi pioneers because of the relatively pop-oriented base of their material. Guided by Voices, for instance, likes nothing more than to be compared to a lost power-pop British Invasion band; Pavement is frequently compared to Lou Reed. Don't be under any illusion, though, that listening to these guys is like putting on a Big Star or Go-Betweens record: there are frequent side trips into experimentalism, free-form song structures, and even downright noise. There's also no doubt of their love for lo-fi textures. Certainly the sound could be "cleaned up" by utilizing moderately more expensive, state-of-the-art studios and equipment, but they realize that deliberate distortion and muffled textures, used purposefully, have desirable aesthetic qualities that would be smothered by more state-of-the-art methods.

The rise of lo-fi brought belated appreciation to some of the progenitors of the genre. The New York noise group Pussy Galore was one of the root bands of lo-fi, especially with their almost legendary (if seldom heard) song-by-song cassette rendition of the Rolling Stones' *Exile on Main Street.* They gave birth to two more accessible, traditionally rock-oriented acts that draw on the lo-fi aesthetic to some degree—the Jon Spencer Blues Explosion and Royal Trux (the latter of whom boasted that they never spent more than $1000 on recording an album until they hooked up with a major label). In New Zealand, Chris Knox, a pivotal figure in that country's punk/new wave scene, recorded intriguing alternative pop both on his own and with his partner Alec Bathgate in Tall Dwarfs, often hastily working on four-track equipment. Many other Kiwi alternative bands, associated with Flying Nun and other labels, prefer to work in similar no-frills fashions; Alastair Galbraith even told *Option* that he intentionally leaves clicks in place when he puts overdubs onto his four-track recordings.

Beat Happening, meanwhile, continue to work today, and Calvin Johnson is still busy organizing and promoting artists working with the lo-fi modus operandi for K records and cassettes with artists like Lois. He also provides an outlet for the less commercial recordings of Beck, who took lo-fi (in a cleaned-up fashion) to the Top 20 with his debut, *Mellow Gold;* his more acoustic-oriented, less-polished efforts can be found on his K release, *One Foot in the Grave.*

The mid-'90s also saw an enormous amount of critical attention lavished upon Jack Logan, discovered in his mid-30s almost by accident after making over 500 home recordings with friends in his small Georgia home. Several dozen of these were culled for a double-CD debut release which made many national critics' Best Of 1994 lists, although it didn't sell more than a few thousand copies. Also hailed by national publications were Palace Brothers, a floating ensemble built around Will Oldham, linking lo-fi to acoustic folk traditions. Palace Brothers are far darker than the relatively cheery and pop-based ruminations of Logan, but are positively jolly when juxtaposed with the more obscure Smog, a *nom de plume* for various projects of the reclusive Bill Callahan, who builds depressing but compelling, gripping soundscapes from the demons troubling his inner psyche. In this respect Smog, Palace Brothers, Beck, and other lo-fi hounds owe an oft-unacknowledged debt to Skip Spence, the brilliant but demented ex-Moby Grape guitarist. Spence's 1969 solo album, *Oar,* anticipated much of the lo-fi aesthetic with its minimal, goofy, and hushed, tormented ambience, constructed primarily as a one-man acoustical band.

One of the greatest lo-fi recordings was never released to the general public. Before gaining instant fame with her 1993 debut *Exile in Guyville,* Phair recorded lo-fi tapes of much of the material that ended up on the record (along with songs she recorded for her second album and ones she never released), using only multi-tracked tapes of her voice and guitar, for limited circulation (primarily to friends and acquaintances). Literally thousands of unauthorized copies of the tapes, dubbed *Girlysound,* have made the rounds with Phair fans, many of whom rank the songs among her best and most unaffected performances, despite the hissy fidelity. Phair is in some important respects a lo-fi anomaly: her two official albums are too elaborately produced to be classified as lo-fi, and *Girlysound* could be categorized with the many excellent bootlegs by famous artists which happen to have primitive sound quality, such as the Beatles' acoustic *White Album* demos. But unlike most of those superstar bootlegs, *Girlysound* has a minimalist and naked D.I.Y. outlook that could only have been produced in the age of lo-fi.

Lo-fi may have a much higher profile than ever as we go to press, but the vast majority of the music is still unheard even by much of the underground—not only by groups that have generated a modest buzz, such as Superchunk, the Grifters, the Silver Jews, and Portastatic, or the

multitudinous and incestuous side projects of many of the top lo-fi bands. The fountain of lo-fi remains the bedrooms and basements of home recording artists, where those who prize feeling over polish pour their hearts out in a format that works in direct opposition to the unwritten rules of today's music studios, equipment manufacturers, and record labels.

Recommended Recordings

Beat Happening, *Dreamy* (Sub Pop)
Pavement, *Westing (By Musket & Sextant)* (Drag City)
Sebadoh, *Smash Your Head on the Punk Rock* (Sub Pop)
Beck, *One Foot in the Grave* (K)
Guided By Voices, *Bee Thousand* (Matador)
Liz Phair, *Girlysound* (bootleg tape)
Alastair Galbraith, *Seely Girn* (Feel Good All Over)
Tall Dwarfs, *Hello Cruel World* (Homestead)
Smog, *Burning Kingdom* (Drag City)
Jack Logan, *Bulk* (Medium Cool)
Lois, *Strumpet* (K)
Palace Brothers, *Palace Brothers* (Drag City)

—Richie Unterberger

Rap

The most popular and influential form of African-American pop music of the 1980s and 1990s, rap is also one of the most controversial styles of the rock era. And not just among the guardians of cultural taste and purity that have always been counted among rock 'n' roll's chief enemies—Black, white, rock, and soul audiences continue to fiercely debate the musical and social merits of rap, whose most radical innovations subverted many of the musical and cultural tenets upon which rock was built.

Antecedents of rap are easy to find in rock and other kinds of music. Music is often used to tell a story, often with spoken rhymes over instruments and rhythms. Talking blues, spoken passages of sanctified prose in gospel, and numerous hits that call out slogans and rhymes, from Bo Diddley's "Say Man" to Shirley Ellis' "The Name Game" to Jerry Reed's "When You're Hot, You're Hot"—you can find pre-raps in material by performers as diverse as Lou Reed, the Shangri-Las, and the Jimmy Castor Bunch, if you want to stretch it.

More direct paths leading to rap, though, can be found in a few of the trends of the late '60s and '70s. In R&B music, funk and disco stripped soul down to its most basic rhythms, foregoing much of the instrumentation and vocals used as embellishments. James Brown in particular is often cited as a forefather in his use of stream-of-consciousness raps over elemental funk backup, and he (and some other funk giants) have been sampled by modern-day rappers on innumerable occasions.

Two much more overlooked influences originated from outside of the R&B and rock mainstream. The Last Poets, Gil Scott-Heron, and Jayne Cortez set highly politicized tales of African-American and urban life against percussive jazz tracks in the early '70s. In reggae, the use of DJs, or "toasters," to rap over basic instrumental backing tracks when they took their mobile sound systems to dances became widespread. New York City, particularly Brooklyn and (more importantly in terms of rap's birth) the Bronx, was home to a large Jamaican community. Jamaican DJs (DJ Kool Herc has been credited as the first) mixed sounds from several turntables, a device which would become one of rap's trademarks.

Although mixing from large sound systems began to be employed at New York house parties in the 1970s, it didn't really emerge as a recorded sound until the Sugarhill Gang's "Rapper's Delight" in 1979. While many critics and listeners shrugged the song aside as a fluke novelty hit, the early rap sound—usually composed of slangy, boastful spoken rhymes over basic bass and percussion grooves—continued to spread in the early '80s, due in large part to the efforts of the Sugarhill label itself. Grandmaster Flash's hard-hitting 1982 single, "The Message," really stands as rap's watershed mark, with a massive impact belied by its relatively modest peak on the pop charts. No longer could rap be ignored as a frivolous micro-genre; here was straight-up social comment, reporting from the front lines of the ghetto with more immediacy than almost any newspaper or television broadcast.

From its inception, rap endured a lot of hostility from listeners—many, but not all, white—who found the music too harsh, monotonous, and lacking in traditional melodic values. However, millions of others—often, though not always, young African-Americans from underprivileged inner-city backgrounds—found an immediate connection with the style. Here was poetry of the street, directly reflecting and addressing the day-to-day reality of the ghetto in a confrontational fashion not found in any other music or media. What's more, you could dance to it, rhyme to it, bring it most anywhere on increasingly ubiquitous portable cassette players (dubbed "ghetto blasters"), and, in the best rock 'n' roll tradition, form your own band without much in the way of formal training.

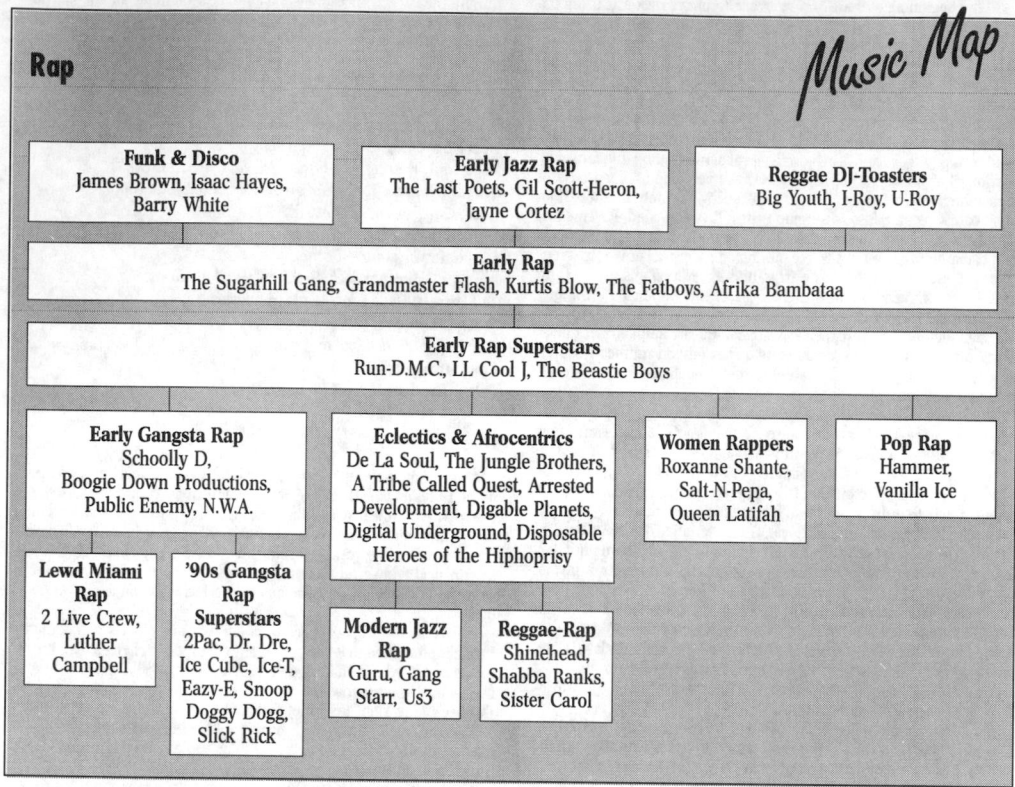

Rap

Music Map

Funk & Disco James Brown, Isaac Hayes, Barry White	Early Jazz Rap The Last Poets, Gil Scott-Heron, Jayne Cortez	Reggae DJ-Toasters Big Youth, I-Roy, U-Roy

Early Rap
The Sugarhill Gang, Grandmaster Flash, Kurtis Blow, The Fatboys, Afrika Bambataa

Early Rap Superstars
Run-D.M.C., LL Cool J, The Beastie Boys

Early Gangsta Rap Schoolly D, Boogie Down Productions, Public Enemy, N.W.A.	Eclectics & Afrocentrics De La Soul, The Jungle Brothers, A Tribe Called Quest, Arrested Development, Digable Planets, Digital Underground, Disposable Heroes of the Hiphoprisy	Women Rappers Roxanne Shante, Salt-N-Pepa, Queen Latifah	Pop Rap Hammer, Vanilla Ice

Lewd Miami Rap 2 Live Crew, Luther Campbell	'90s Gangsta Rap Superstars 2Pac, Dr. Dre, Ice Cube, Ice-T, Eazy-E, Snoop Doggy Dogg, Slick Rick

Modern Jazz Rap Guru, Gang Starr, Us3	Reggae-Rap Shinehead, Shabba Ranks, Sister Carol

The basic workouts of early rappers like Kurtis Blow and the Fat Boys (eventually referred to as "old school" rap) can sound a bit tame today, although the productions of veterans like Afrika Bambaataa and Keith LeBlanc have lost none of their luster. Many were still expecting the music to peter out before Run-D.M.C. came along. Rap was, and to a large degree still is, a singles-oriented medium, but these Queens men proved that rappers could maintain interest and diversity over the course of entire full-length albums. Combining hard beats and innovative production with strong material that emphasized positive social activism without ignoring the cruel realities of urban life, they found as much favor with the critics as the street. Among the first rap groups to climb the pop charts in a big way, they also were among the first to make big inroads into the white and Middle American audiences when they teamed up with Aerosmith's Steven Tyler and Joe Perry for the hit single "Walk This Way."

The mid- and late '80s saw rap continuing to explode in popularity, with the ascendancy of superstars like LL Cool J and Hammer (the latter of whom is often accused of providing a safe rap-pop alternative). Although most early rap productions originated in New York City and its environs, the music took hold as a national phenomenon, with strong scenes developing in other East Coast cities like Philadelphia, as well as West Coast strongholds in Los Angeles and Oakland. Production techniques became increasingly sophisticated; electronics, stop-on-a-dime editing, and—most importantly—sampling from previously recorded sources became prominent (although turntable mixing, along with the "scratching" produced by wiggling records back and forth, continued to be a strong ingredient). The increased emphasis on electronic beats led to the popularization of the term "hip-hop," a designation which is by now used more or less interchangeably with rap. The Beastie Boys, obnoxious white ex-punks from New York, brought rap further into the Middle American mainstream with their vastly popular hybrids of hip-hop, hard rock, and in-your-face braggadocio.

While rap had always forthrightly dealt with urban struggle, the late '80s saw the emergence of a more militant strain of the music. Sometimes dubbed "gangsta-rap," the hotbed of this school was found in the disadvantaged neighborhoods of South Central Los Angeles, although performers like Philadelphia's Schoolly D proved that the genre was not specific to the area. Boogie Down Productions laid down a prototype that was taken to more extreme measures by N.W.A. (Niggaz with Attitude), who reported on the crime, sex, and violence of the ghetto with an explicit verve that some viewed as verging on celebration rather than journalism. Enormously controversial, and enormously popular with record buyers, several N.W.A. members went on to stardom as solo acts, including Ice Cube, Eazy-E, and Dr. Dre. Other boys from their 'hood also made their mark with inflammatory works, such as Ice-T and Snoop Doggy Dogg.

The most popular and controversial of the militant rappers, the New York-based Public Enemy, were perhaps the most political as well. Their brand of activism, like that of Malcolm X's two decades earlier, made a lot of people, including liberals, pretty uncomfortable, with their emphasis upon Black nationalism and careless anti-Semitic, homophobic, and sexist references. Groups such as Public Enemy ignited an ongoing debate in the media. Activist-oriented critics and audiences found a lot to praise in their music: powerful articulations against social and racial injustice, uncompromising portraits of realities that mainstream media shy away from, exhortations to the disadvantaged to empower themselves, and the sometimes overlooked fact that rap generated most of the few massive-selling independent releases produced outside of the corporate major-label machine. At the same time, they could not let the xenophobic tendencies of these acts pass unnoticed, or ignore the frequent quasi-celebration in much rap music of misogyny, drugs, and violence, and the status to be gained in the urban community by the practice thereof. Many rap and rock 'n' roll fans were also concerned parents, torn almost against their will between wanting to support the struggle against race and class oppression, and wanting to protect their children against possible identification with the violence- and obscenity-riddled content of the records themselves. Passionate advocates of civil liberties and free speech wondered, sometimes aloud, whether rappers were taking those privileges too far.

Rap began to lose some of its momentum midway through the '90s, as the genre became mired in copies of Dr. Dre's G-funk, gangsta rap and simpy fusions of R&B and hip-hop. Gangsta continued to rule the charts until 1996, when its sales began to slip. This was partially due to market saturation, but it was also true that gangsta had played itself out, and that it offered few fresh musical ideas. The tragic murders of Tupac Shakur in late 1996 and the Notorious B.I.G. a few months later were the symbolic end to the gangsta generation. Many critics claimed that their deaths would bring about change in the violence-obsessed hip-hop nation, but the truth is changes were brewing in the years that Tupac and Biggie were at their peak.

While gangsta was at the height of its popularity, the funky, hedonisitic bass-music scenes in the southern United States earned large followings, and the jazz-rap of Gangstarr, Us3 and French rapper MC Solaar all earned positive reviews, as did the reggae-rap fusions of Shinehead, Shabba Ranks and Sister Carol. The latter reached its peak on the Fugees' hit 1996 album *The Score*, which not only interlaced reggae rhythms with hip-hop, but also wove in smooth soul and R&B to provide a rich, eclectic music. *The Score* was accessible and clever, but the true innovations in hip-hop were emerging from the underground, most notably in the form of the Wu-Tang Clan. A large, loose-knit crew from Staten Island, the Wu-Tang returned hardcore rap to its edgy, minimalistic roots and under the direction of the RZA, they created a menacing, claustrophobic sound highlighted by scratching strings, disembodied pianos, haunting samples and stark beats. Their 1993 debut *Enter the Wu-Tang (36 Chambers)* became a word-of-mouth hit, and they released no less than six side projects, all coordinated by RZA, before reuniting for the 1997 double album *Wu-Tang Forever*. By that time, it was clear that the group's debut had prophesized a number of musical trends, from Dr. Octagon's strange lo-fi hip-hop to Tricky's hazy, scary soundscapes. In the wake of gangsta's death, the Wu-Tang, Tricky and Dr. Octagon & the Automater, along with the post-hip-hop electronica of the Chemical Brothers and DJ Shadow, illustrated that rap still had the potential to reinvent itself.

Recommended Recordings

Various Artists, *The Sugarhill Records Story* (Rhino)
Various Artists, *Street Jams—Hip-Hop from the Top, Vol. 1-4* (Rhino)
Various Artists, *Street Jams—Electric Funk, Vol. 1-4* (Rhino)
Various Artists, *Hip-Hop Greats—Classic Raps* (Rhino)
Various Artists, *Def Jam Music Group: Ten Year Anniversary* (Def Jam)
Afrika Bambaataa, *Planet Rock* (Tommy Boy)
Run-D.M.C., *Together Forever: Greatest Hits* (Profile)
LL Cool J, *Radio* (Def Jam)
The Beastie Boys, *Licensed to Ill* (Def Jam)
Public Enemy, *It Takes a Nation of Millions to Hold Us Back* (DefJam)
Boogie Down Productions, *Criminal Minded* (Sugar Hill Rap)
N.W.A., *Straight Outta Compton* (Priority)
De La Soul, *Three Feet High & Rising* (Tommy Boy)
Queen Latifah, *All Hail the Queen* (Tommy Boy)
Shinehead, *Unity* (Elektra)
Digable Planets, *Reachin': A New Refutation...* (Pendulum)
Various Artists, *Stolen Moments: Red, Hot + Cool* (GRP)
Ice-T, *O.G. Original Gangster* (Sire)
Salt-N-Pepa, *Blacks' Magic* (London)
Digital Underground, *Sex Packets* (Tommy Boy)
Arrested Development, *Three Years, Five Months & Two Days in the Life Of...* (Chrysalis)
A Tribe Called Quest, *The Low End Theory* (Jive)
Dr. Dre, *The Chronic* (Priority)
Wu-Tang Clan, *Enter the Wu-Tang (36 Chambers)* (Loud/RCA)
Tricky, *Maxinquaye* (Durban Poison/Island)
The Fugees, *The Score* (Ruffhouse)
         —Jimmy James & Stephen Thomas Erlewine

Techno

Although no musical style evolves in a vacuum, techno is one of the few in recent times that appears to have been born almost fully-formed. Typically, that birth is traced to the early '80s and the emaciated inner-city of Detroit, where figures such as Juan Atkins, Derek May, and Kevin Saunderson, among others, fused the quirky machine music of Kraftwerk and Yellow Magic Orchestra with the space-race electric funk of George Clinton, the optimistic futurism of Alvin Toffler's *The Third Wave* (from which the music derived its name), and the emerging electro sound elsewhere being explored by Soul Sonic Force, the Jonzun Crew, Man Parrish, "Pretty" Tony Butler, and L.A.'s Wrecking Cru.

Unlike much electro, however, which playfully explored themes of the video age, space travel, block parties, and b-boy braggadocio, techno's minor-key melodies and spare, repetitive rhythms exhibited a tragic, melancholic edge that seemed to more directly engage the political and cultural issues of late-20th-century urban America. Tracks such as "Clear," "Technicolor," "Night Drive (Thru Babylon)," "Strings of Life," and "Rock to the Beat" often expressed a disdain with the same technology they hoped could deliver a culture in the latter stages of decay. And while techno's concern for the liberatory potential of human-machine interface is often traced back to such European avant-garde figures as Luigi Russolo and Luciano Berio, the music's urban orientation and historical and cultural roots clearly distinguish it sharply from those traditions.

Early techno tracks (on such labels as Metroplex, Transmat, and KMS) were generally produced for limited-run 12-inch release, and although the global popularity of the music in the present day has ensured that many of them have remained in print, techno remained a local phenomenon until the records started showing up on European shores. Consequently, the explosion of techno onto London's emerging acid house scene in the mid- to late-'80s (itself a quixotic mix of Chicago and New York house) meant that many of the music's early creators became bigger "stars" in Europe than in America, a phenomenon that continues to this day (although techno was, and to a certain extent remains, antagonistic toward artist identity and stardom, a function of the music's reaction against certain characteristics of mainstream rock and pop). And while the UK dance music scene, as in America, has retained a decided predilection toward house music (with techno the music of choice in continental locales such as Germany and Belgium), the second phase of the music's evolution has largely taken place there, with labels such as Warp, Rephlex, Infonet, and Rephlex, and artists such as LFO, Richard H. Kirk, Richard James/Aphex Twin, Reload/Link, Germ, B12, and the Black Dog taking the spare electronic experiments of the early Detroit innovators to the next level of abstraction.

Elsewhere, techno's connection to the dancefloor continues to be emphasized, with functional and exploratory approaches that both stick with the music's roots and morph them into a range of related styles, including trance, acid, hardcore and gabber. As stated, techno's sparer, more rugged dancefloor face remains the dance music of choice throughout much of continental Europe (corporate-sponsored raves in Germany and Belgium routinely attract crowds in the tens of thousands), and the number of artists working either in direct tradition of the original Detroit sound or in a regional, often minimalist offshoot thereof remains quite high. Labels such as Tresor, Force Inc., D-Jax Up-Beats, R&S, and Structure/DJ Ungle Fever, among dozens of others, have been most active and influential. Japan has also produced a fair amount of notable techno artists, including Ken Ishii, Sosumo Yakota, and Naohiro Fujikawa, although the scene there is relatively small.

Techno's ongoing status in the United States as a marginal, underground music has meant that the style has been slower to evolve in its birthplace, although third-wave Detroit artists such as Jeff Mills, Stacey Pullen, "Mad" Mike Banks, Drexciya, and AUX 88 (as well as stubborn originators such as Carl Craig and Derrick May) continue to push the style forward. Ironically (or perhaps not so much), it's been the European reinterpretation of techno in electronic hybrids such as trip-hop, jungle, and the so-called "intelligent dance music" of artists such as Autechre, Aphex Twin, and the Black Dog which have opened American ears. Time will tell whether that will translate into what, in Europe and England, has become the next stage of Western pop music.

A BRIEF RUNDOWN OF TECHNO'S MANY FACES

Detroit

Early Detroit techno is characterized by, alternately, a dark, detached, mechanistic vibe, and a smooth, bright, soulful feel (the latter deriving in part from the Motown legacy and the stock-in-trade between early techno and the Chicago-style house developing simultaneously to the south). While essentially designed as dance music meant to uplift, the stark, melancholy edge of early tracks by Cybotron, Model 500, Rhythm Is Rhythm, and Reese also spoke to Detroit's economic collapse in the late '70s following the city's prosperous heyday as the focal point of the American automobile industry.

The music's oft-copied ruddy production and stripped-down aesthetic were largely a function of the limited technology available to the early innovators (records were often mastered from two-track onto cassette); the increasingly sophisticated arrangements of much contemporary techno (on through to hardcore and jungle), conversely, has much to do with the growth and increasing affordability of MIDI-encoded equipment and desktop digital audio. Second- and third-wave Detroit techno, too, has gained considerably in production, although artists such as Derrick May, Juan Atkins, and Kenny Larkin have sought to combine the peerless sheen of the digital arena with the compositional minimalism of their Detroit origins.

No longer simply contained within the 313 area code, Detroit techno has become a global phenomenon (partly as a result of the more widespread acclaim many of the original Detroit artists have found in other countries), buoyed by the fact that many of the classic early tracks remain in print (available through Submerge, at www.submerge.com). Today, Detroit's third wave are re-exploring the aesthetic commitment of the music's early period, with hard-hitting beats (Underground Resistance, Jeff Mills), soulful grooves (Kenny Larkin, Stacey Pullen), and a renewed interest in techno's breakbeat roots (Aux 88, Drexciya, "Mad" Mike, Dopplereffekt).

Although numerous documents of Detroit techno past and present exist, the best introduction to the Motor City sound is undoubtedly *True People: A Detroit Techno Compilation*, a sprawling two-CD set released on React Records in 1995.

Bleep

Generally associated with early Sheffield techno artists such as Robert Gordon, Richard H. Kirk, Forgemasters, and LFO, the bleep moniker was an onomatopoeic attempt to describe the squelching synth noises and quirky MIDI experiments of those artists' early 12-inches for Warp, Network, ZTT, and Vinyl Solution. Bleep is a direct precursor of the electronic listening music characteristic of the GPR and Warp labels (the latter of which Gordon helped found in the early '90s), and has since evolved into the "armchair" or "intelligent" techno of artists such as the Black Dog, Autechre, As One, Aphex Twin, and mu-Ziq.

Acid

Acid music, apart from early techno and electro, has also been America's longest running contribution to the global dance scene, with artists such as Robert Armani, DJ Pierre, Armando, Marshall Jefferson, and Freddie Fresh all being extremely influential in the German and Dutch scenes. The music's name derives less from the drug as from the caustic, abrasive synth squelches associated with the TB-303 synthesizer, the music's most prominent instrumental element.

Trance (also Hard and Goa)

Trance is a superfast offshoot of techno that uses sparse, repetitive structures, dense melodic textures, and high BPMs to induce a sort of mesmerized state. Popular for its psychedelic themes and often used in combination with hallucinogens to enhance the psychotropic effects, the style has been most popular in Germany, where artists such as Hardfloor, DJ Criss, Arpeggiators, and Cygnus X developed a harder-edge style known, appropriately, as hard trance. An increasingly ethnic-infused strain has also evolved through the mid-'90s known as Goa trance, which plays up the spacey, psychedelic side with movie samples and heavy basslines. Hardcore techno artists such as Joey Beltram and Dave Clarke have also helped to blur the line between trance and harder styles of techno, utilizing highly repetitive rhythms layered with slight, slowly morphing electronics.

Intelligent Techno/IDM

Shortform for Intelligent Dance Music, IDM as a musical genre is a relatively recent invention meant to account for new forms of electronic music composition which draw from styles such as house, techno, ambient, and electro while taking them in distinctly different, often more "musical" directions. Although often slighted for its racist connotations (recalling techno's African-American roots and contrasting them with a derivative style largely produced and consumed by white artists and audiences), for better or for worse the term has caught on as a generic placeholder for styles of dance-based electronic music seeking audiences outside the traditional milieu of the DJ and dancefloor. (Artists: Aphex Twin, Orbital, Biosphere, the Black Dog, Autechre, Richard H. Kirk)

Minimal

Minimalist techno, particularly in its European form, involves the stripping away of most of what could be referred to as techno's "musical" side to reveal only the basic pulse of the beat, fitted with a minimum of textural embellishment. Oddly enough, even within this framework, minimalist techno takes on a variety of different faces, from Mike Ink's Studio 1 and Detroit's Basic Channel, to Finland's Sahko label and artists such as ÿ. Variation often comes in the form of vague differences in technology, but usually the motive is the same—to abstract dance music away from the contingency of culture toward something like a "universal groove." The style is probably most popular in Germany, Belgium, and Northern Europe.

—Sean Cooper

Electronica

Electronica has become a manageable, one-word catch-all for a range of music styles which, taken together, many believe represent the next step in the evolution of Western pop. Although what the term actually means tends in large part to depend upon which side of the Atlantic Ocean it's spoken on, electronica in its broadest common significance refers primarily to artists drawing heavily on dance music styles such as house, techno, electro, and EBM (electronic body music) in ways not simply derivative of the dancefloor. Similar in some respects to the early working distinction between rhythm & blues and Rock 'n' roll, electronica tends to involve an adaptation or mutation of dance music compositional elements to other-than-DJ/dancefloor ends; in the context of contemporary electronic dance music, that generally translates into dynamic (rather than static), composed (rather than programmed), listener- (rather than dancer- or DJ-) oriented "songs" (rather than "trax"). If the term's distinction appears to turn only on contrast—that is, by negative comparison to dance music—it's because many of the artists credited with innovating the music (people like the Black Dog, Orbital, Terrace, Speedy J, Richard H. Kirk, the Future Sound Of London, Autechre, and Aphex Twin) saw themselves in contradistinction to dance culture and the limits it placed on its music. These artists were interested in pro-

ducing music designed for other uses—home listening, primarily—which allowed for a wider range of influences (ambient, classical, jazz, non-Western musics, etc.) and a higher index of experimentation. Heavily influenced by the early techno-pop, hip-hop, and electro-funk of Kraftwerk, Cybotron, Man Parrish, Soul Sonic Force, and Ice-T, as well as the first wave techno and Acid House of Detroit and Chicago innovators, these artists brought a penchant for tunefulness and compositional dynamics—elements often lacking in club-borne dance music—to the creative fore.

Original wide-spread use of the term "electronica" derives in part from the influential English experimental techno label New Electronica, which, along with labels such as General Production Recordings, Warp, Evolution, and Rising High, was a leading force in the early 1990s in introducing and supporting dance-based electronic music more oriented toward home listening than dancefloor play. Because of that label's role in the birth of "intelligent techno" (itself a heavily loaded and controversial term referring to electronic listening music rooted in, but not simply reducible to, dancefloor techno), the term in the early part of the 1990s became used to loosely characterize groups such as Orbital, Autechre, Aphex Twin, As One, Global Communication, Sun Electric, the Black Dog, the Orb, Higher Intelligence Agency, Biosphere, etc.—in other words, bands that drew primarily from dancefloor techno in constructing more song-oriented music utilizing similar instrumental elements, compositional techniques, and organizational structures (four-on-the-floor or electronic breakbeats; synth pads and 303, 808, and 909 bass and drum sounds; simple melodies and deep basslines; minor-key chord progressions; etc). As a result, electronica became more or less synonymous with terms such as "intelligent techno," "ambient techno," etc., and was considered distinct from other emerging forms such as jungle and trip-hop, each of which had its own set of defining characteristics (as well as often dauntingly complex litany of terms and microgenres).

A key component in the growth and popularization of the style was the *Artificial Intelligence* series released by the Sheffield-based Warp label starting in 1992, which presented many of the artists now thought to be formative to a wide audience for the first time (including Autechre, Speedy J, Richard H. Kirk, the Black Dog, and Aphex Twin). Previously a source of innovative but nonetheless clearly dancefloor-oriented house and techno (early singles from the label include Nightmares on Wax, Robert Gordon's Forgemasters, and LFO), Warp's two-part compilation series *Artificial Intelligence*, as well as subsequent full-lengths from Kirk, Black Dog Productions, Autechre, and Detroit techno artist Kenny Larkin drew a clear line in the sand between dance music and the "electronic listening music" that would soon become the label's focus. (The first volume of *Artificial Intelligence* pictured a computer rendering of a chrome figure, spliff in hand, reclining before the front-room hi-fi, sleeves of Warp and Pink Floyd records littering the floor.) The series also constituted America's first serious exposure to the new sound; Wax Trax!/TVT licensed the two compilations and have reissued a number of Warp's subsequent full-length releases.

In the United States, electronica has only very recently been appropriated and generalized by the music (and non-music) press to refer to any dance-based electronic music with a potential for pop appeal. As a result, the term has been used to describe everyone from the Chemical Brothers and the Prodigy to Orbital and Tricky, to Alex Reece, Mo'Wax, the Sneaker Pimps, Goldie, and Aphex Twin. Aversions to excessive genrefication notwithstanding, the grouping together of such disparate artists seems symptomatic of larger tendencies within an American music industry which knows little (if anything) about the histories of the various styles these artists represent, a notion which has its antecedents in a largely rock-based music press and its bias—stemming in part from the legacy of disco—against music featuring predominantly electronic instrumentation, as well as a tendency to subsume all potentially significant popular music styles under the category of "rock." Where, in the European usage, the defining feature of electronica was usually its "listenability" (a value gauged within the context of the experimental electronic music underground, which usually had some understanding of the degree to which "song"-y derivatives of the music such as Orbital or Aphex Twin deviated from the more nuts 'n' bolts dancefloor fare of Derrick May, Jeff Mills, and Dave Clarke), in America the distinction seems to turn instead on the music's potential for popularity (read: profitability) via mainstream success: It was only, ironically, when several of these bands began gaining MTV exposure, commercial radio play, and major label recording contracts—despite the fact that the music had been widely popular outside of the US for nearly a decade—that "electronica" as a concrete category in the American music industry gained any viability.

"Electronic listening music" has also, of course, become big business on the other side of the pond as well, with smaller indie releases routinely charting next to their Britpop brethren and artists such as Autechre, the Orb, and the Aphex Twin becoming the closest thing to pop stars the tenets of the genre and the limitations of its audience will allow. The steady adaptation of club culture to the demands of its electronic antagonists, however (as well as the fact that many of the artists and labels—including Scanner, Higher Intelligence Agency, and Coldcut, as well as Warp, Rephlex, Skam, and Leaf—have formed their own clubs), has also (ironically) meant that much of the first wave of dance music dissent has, to a certain extent, been reabsorbed *as* dance music (or at least club music, i.e. music one hears in a club). "Back room" club culture (previously the margin of experimental weirdness relegated to the literal "back rooms" of huge raves and weekly club nights) have also taken on a popular mythos all their own, with the vitality of free-form experimentation associated with them foregrounded in offshoot clubs such as the massive Heavenly club's Sunday Social (and perhaps best embodied by early genrecidal innovators Coldcut's *Journeys by DJ* mix CD, released in 1995). The result has pushed experimentation even further, with the "IDM" of first-wave electronic artists intermingling more directly with hip-hop, funk, industrial, jungle/drum 'n' bass, free jazz, and Indian and Southeast Asian musics, turning up some extremely interesting and innovative hybrids in the offing (from the schizoid electro-jazz/jungle of Atom Heart, Bisk, and Bedouin Ascent to the banging gabber-punk of Alec Empire's Atari Teenage Riot and the paranoid and depressed drum 'n' bass of, alternately, TPower and Panacea). Just how far this dynamic is capable of taking the music remains to be seen.

Several good introductions to the various strains—both hardline and "contemporary"—of electronica's eclectic face exist. An obvious place to start is, of course, New Electronica's early series *Global Electronic Innovations* (which, although heavily oriented toward Detroit techno, include many crucial early cuts), as well as Warp's two-volume *Artificial Intelligence* series. More contemporarily, the German label Studio !K7's two double-CD collections *The Freestyle Files* are excellent cross-sections of the rampant inbreeding of contemporary electronica. Those strapped for cash (most good new-school electronica comps tend to be import-only) should check out Nettwork's "greatest hits" package *Plastic*, as well as the label compilations licensed for stateside release by New York-based Instinct Records, which include Ntone (*Earthrise.Ntone.1*), Em:t (*Em:t 2000* and *Em:t Explorer*), and Compost (two volumes of *The Future Sound of Jazz*). For a taste of now-school breakbeat culture's influence on the music's formerly techno-heavy sound, Rising High's *Further Self-Evident Truths* and *Avant-Gardism*, Blue Planet's *State of the Nu Art*, and the Talvin Singh-compiled *Anohka: Sounds of the Asian Underground* are excellent entrees into electronica's more schizophrenetic offerings.

Recommended Recordings (* Indicates Top 10)

Various Artists, *Artificial Intelligence 2* (TVT/Warp)*
Various Artists, *Journeys by DJ: Coldcut* (JDJ)*
Various Artists, *Objects D'ART 2* (New Electronica)
Various Artists, *The Freestyle Files* (!K7)
Kraftwerk, *Computer World* (Elektra)
808 State, *UTD. 90* (ZTT)*
Aphex Twin, *Selected Ambient Works Vol. 1* (R&S)*
As One, *Reflections* (New Electronica)
Mouse on Mars, *Iaora Tahiti* (American/Too Pure)
Higher Intelligence Agency, *Freefloater* (Beyond)*
Orbital, *In Sides* (Internal)*
Autechre, *Amber* (TVT/Warp)*
Locust, *Truth Is Born of Arguments* (Apollo)
The Black Dog, *Spanners* (EastWest/Warp)*
Future Sound of London, *ISDN* (Astralwerks/Virgin)*
mu-Ziq, *Tango n' Vectif* (Rephlex)
Reload, *A Collection of Short Stories* *
Spacetime Continuum, *Emit Ecaps* (Astralwerks)
Plug, *Drum 'n' Bass for Papa* (Nothing/Blue Planet)
Atom Heart, *HAT* (Rather Interesting)*

—Sean Cooper

Ambient

Ambient music remains something of the scorned, dorky cousin of current electronic music. Dabbled in by scores of artists working primarily in other fields, but still for the most part too esoteric to attract a large audience, the music has been characterized as everything from dolled-up new age, to intellectual, over-indulgent dross, to boring and irrelevant technical noodling. Partly as a function of its relatively limited appeal, the definition of ambient remains extremely vague, a notion also related to the fact that artists considered to be working within its "borders" seem to be drawn from such a wide spectrum of different traditions; more "academic" experimental electronic (Chris Meloche, David Shea, Asmus Tietschens, David Toop, Oval), space music (Robert Rich, Steve Roach, Vidna Obmana, Klaus Shultze, Jeff Greinke, Alio Die), dub (Bill Laswell, the Orb, Mick Harris, Drome, Woob), ethno- or 4th-world electronic music (Jon Hassell, Banco De Gaia, Astralasia), gothic or industrial (Lustmord, Merzbow, Final, Aube, James Plotkin), and the vast

contemporary hybridity of back-room club culture (everything from the KLF, Global Communication, and Mixmaster Morris to Biosphere, Higher Intelligence Agency, and Sun Electric, to Tetsu Inoue, David Moufang, L.T.J. Bukem, and Autechre). As dance-based electronic music has moved increasingly toward the indiscriminant intermingling of influences characteristic of trip-hop, electronica, and jungle/drum 'n' bass, ambient has shifted away from being a concrete genre and more toward a less identifiable (though no less specific) approach to sound, registering its influence in terms of space, color, and texture rather than the presence or absence of a backbeat, recognizable melodic or harmonic structures, etc.

Nonetheless, like other strains of experimental electronic music whose branches stretch into the most complex of arrangements, ambient has its roots, and historical evaluations of ambient music usually begin with Brian Eno. Although Eno's application of the term to his "background" composing of the late '70s itself had precursors in the "furniture music" of Erik Satie, the dadaist and futurist manifestos of Marcel Duchamp and Luigi Russolo, the proto- and high-modernism of Claude Debussy and Igor Stravinsky (as well as in non-Western musical and religious traditions such as Indonesian gamelan and African pygmy chanting), and New York School experimentalists such as John Cage, Morton Feldman, and LaMonte Young, it's with Eno that "ambient" music—i.e. music designed to be heard as an integral part of the environment in which it's played or listened to—first became an end in itself. And his series of recordings bearing the term (and subtitled things like *Music for Airports, Music for Films,* and *On Land*) remain watermarks. Formerly a member of pop/new wave group Roxy Music, Eno was among the first to integrate found sounds and field recordings into the context of the recording studio in order to construct an environment with his music—not necessarily (though in some cases) to re-create existing places, but to build from scratch a music which suggested a sense of context, one which could not only be heard but also experienced by the listener. It's also with Eno that ambient or "environmental" music was approached with predominantly electronic instruments; ambient has few contemporary examples of acoustic-based composers (Pauline Oliveros is one), although the combination of electronics and acoustic-based instruments is common (particularly among so-called electro-acoustic musicians such as Steve Roach, Carl Stone, and Michael Danna).

Of equal influence and importance to Eno's work was that of German synthesist Klaus Schulze, who represents something of the formalist arm of ambient's prehistory. Though aligned more directly with the European classical tradition than Eno (whose background in avant-garde pop and new wave had its consequence in the comparative subtlety and modesty of his music), Schulze's pioneering work in analog synthesis and his extended, highly conceptual compositions based solely on the timbral qualities of electronics were crucial in suggesting new directions for electronic music apart from not only its "pop," but also its academic and classical contexts. Although Schulze's earlier work was more immediately caught up in exploring (and exploiting) the sonic particularities of his medium (a notion which has tended to garner him more criticism than praise), Schulze increasingly sought the fusion of his technical mastery with elements of the lived environment; pieces such as his *Dresden Concert* drew liberally from nature recordings and source tapes which documented the bustle of everyday life, and his mid-'90s recordings with noted new school ambient composer Pete Namlook (of the Frankfurt-based Fax label) brought Schulze's formidable role in forging ambient's early aesthetic full circle.

Although much of the more visible instrumental electronic and electro-acoustic music produced in the late 1970s and early-to-mid-1980s appeared under the aegis of "new age"—a marketing phenomenon more than anything else, applied most often to musics linked by some method or other to relaxation, meditation, and/or escapism—even the overwhelming conservatism of that period had its antithesis in a range of musicians operating at the outer fringes of experimentation, pushing electronics-based composition into ever more challenging, abstract territory. Artists such as Steve Hillage (formerly of Gong), Harold Budd, early Tangerine Dream, Michael Stearns, Robert Rich, and Steve Roach, among others, sought to compose music as free as possible from the weighty baggage of both pop and classical, as well as Western academic and high cultural traditions, turning instead toward methods of composition and performance lacking conventional developmental structure—music which relied instead on programmatic elements such as repetition, texture, alternate tonality, and harmonic and subharmonic relationships (over and against the chordal, melodic, pentatonic, etc. concerns of most Western musical forms). Members of this loose agglomeration of artists often referred to their work as "space music"; not, as is often believed, because it sounded like it was from outer space (although in some cases this was true), but rather since the music tended to refer almost singularly and directly to the space in which it was heard, as well as the inner, more subconscious emotional and contemplative spaces of the listener. Although quite apart from Eno's definition, which sought to locate music in some intermediate between foreground and background, space musicians sought to fuse the two in such a way that the music became the background of its own active exploration; the latter represented an extension of the former, since the relationship between music and the lived environment was the compositional preconception much of the music turned on.

Although the context was in many respects radically different, it was a similar impulse that led to ambient's renaissance in the late-'80s/early-'90s UK rave scene, the source of some of the most exciting innovations in not only the music's sound, but also its presentation. The by-now familiar construct of the "chill space"—that back-room alternative to the high-speed hedonism of main floor raves—was the nexus of that renaissance, with clubs such as Land of Oz (at London's massive weekly Heaven), Telepathic Fish, and Oscillate some of the first blips on the new ambient map. It was at clubs such as these that DJs like Alex Patterson (of the Orb), Mixmaster Morris (of Irresistible Force), and Jonah Sharp (of Spacetime Continuum) began blending together the early ambient experiments of Eno, Schulze, Hillage, Pink Floyd, Robert Rich, and Steve Hillage with everything from stereo test and demonstration records, *Songs of the Humpback Whale* and other nature and field recordings, minimalist classical, non-Western ritual and traditional musics, Jamaican dub, and, eventually, live electronics. As crowds began turning out specifically for chill rooms, all-ambient nights and even weekend-long ambient events became more common, with the appearance of recordings by the KLF (*Chill Out*), the Orb ("A Huge Ever-Growing Brain" and *Adventures Beyond the Ultraworld*, among others), Irresistible Force ("Space Is the Place" and *Flying High*), and the soon-to-be ubiquitous Pete Namlook (*Silence, Air, Dreamfish*) contributing momentum and a growing, non-club-based audience.

The proximity of chill rooms to rave culture meant much of the music reflected elements of acid house and techno, and hybrid terms such as "ambient house," "ambient techno," "ambient dub," etc. began to circulate, serving to differentiate this music not only from the more rigorously environmental experiments of the '70s and '80s, but also (and increasingly) from many parallel contemporary strains of ambient. Including such varied sources as the UK-based Beyond and Rising High labels; the (respectively) Frankfurt and Belgium-based Fax (Pete Namlook's prolific label) and Apollo imprints, as well as the electronic experiments of Mille Plateaux; dark ambient/industrial and isolationist artists such as Coil, Mick Harris, and Aube and labels such as Cold Meat Industries, Projekt, and Staalplaat; ambient soon, as journalist/producer David Toop put it, began taking on the properties of a "glue term," sticking to whatever it was thrown at. But ambient's steady demotion to the status of textual modifier also suggests the increasing fervor with which barriers separating styles were up for dismantling in the atmosphere of the mid-'90s post-rave experimental underground, a process that's given birth to more variations on the theme of electronic dance music in the past five years alone than in the previous two decades. This stylistic deconstruction has given birth to dozens of new genres, subgenres, and sub-subgenres (ambient dub, dark ambient, ambient jungle, electronica, post-rock, etc.) even as it's made the very pursuit of "genre" a mawkishly naive task. This is not to say ambient artists working more or less within the tradition of many of the music's earlier strains have ceased to exist—indeed, ambient's proliferation in the last several years has also contributed a sense of focus to artists pursuing one or another of its mutant strains—but rather that the palette of sounds which constitutes the raw materials of atmospheric or environmental music has broadened to such an extent that many of the definitional criteria of the music (lack of prominent percussion and/or a strong melodic presence, etc.) have been steadily reoriented or altogether abandoned.

Because of the range of musics (to say nothing of the ambiguity) implied by the term, no single, encompassing introduction to ambient exists. However, many good compilations are available which serve to fill in significant portions of the music's historical progression. Virgin's four-part *Ambient* series—each a two-disc set bringing together many of the biggest name artists from the '70s, '80s, and early '90s—is a good place to start. Also released by Virgin is the double-CD *Ocean of Sound*, compiled by musical historian David Toop to accompany his book of the same name (published by Serpent's Tail in 1995), and including everyone from King Tubby to Aphex Twin. Label compilations also provide good reference points (particularly with regard to the music's more recent mutations), with Beyond, Rising High, Instinct, Fax, Apollo, Warp, Silent, and Recycle or Die all reputable sources for high-quality various artist collections.

Recommended Recordings (* Indicates Top 10)

Various Artists, *The Ambient Cookbook* (Fax)*
Various Artists, *Ocean of Sound* (Virgin)
KLF, *Chill Out* (TVT)*
Irresistible Force, *Flying High* (Instinct/Rising High)*
Brian Eno, *Ambient 4: On Land* (EG)*
Pete Namlook, *Air 2* (Fax)

The Orb, *Orbus Terrarum* (Wau!/Mr. Modo)*
Robert Rich & B. Lustmord, *Stalker* (Fathom)*
Tetsu Inoue, *World Receiver* (Instinct)*
Global Communication, *76:14* (Dedicated)*
Vidna Obmana, *The Trilogy* (Relic)
Woob, *1194* (Instinct/Em:t)
Eno & Fripp, *The Essential Fripp & Eno* (Virgin/EG)*
Aphex Twin, *Selected Ambient Works Vol. II* (Sire/Warp)*
Throbbing Gristle, *Second Annual Report* (Mute)

Book
Ocean of Sound, David Toop (Serpent's Tail, 1995)

—*Sean Cooper*

Trip-Hop

Yet another in a long line of plastic place-holders to attach itself to one arm or another of the UK post-acid house dance scene's rapidly mutating experimental underground, "trip-hop" was coined by the English music press in an attempt to characterize a new style of downtempo, jazz-, funk-, and soul-inflected experimental breakbeat music which began to emerge around 1993 in association with labels such as Mo'Wax, Ninja Tune, Cup of Tea, and Wall of Sound. Similar to (though largely without vocals) American hip-hop in its use of sampled drum breaks, typically more experimental, and infused with a high index of ambient-leaning and apparently psychotropic atmospherics (hence "trip"), the term quickly caught on to describe everything from Portishead and Tricky, to DJ Shadow and U.N.K.L.E., to Coldcut, Wagon Christ, and Depth Charge (much to the chagrin of many of these musicians, who saw their music largely as an extension of hip-hop proper, not a gimmicky offshoot). One of the first commericaly signficant hybrids of dance-based listening music to cross over to a more mainstream audience, full-length releases in the style typically top indie charts in the UK and, in artists such as Shadow, Tricky, Morcheeba, the Sneaker Pimps, and Massive Attack, account for a substantial portion of the first wave of "electronica" acts to reach stateside audiences.

With immediate roots in the immensely popular UK acid jazz scene, trip-hop was born out of a dissatisfaction with that scene's creative wane toward the end of the '80s, as well as the increasing influence of the London acid house movement. As many have observed, while the US was steadily separating out the jazz influence from its funk (via Parliament-Funkadelic, the '70s disco-funk of the Gap Band and Zapp & Roger, and the '80s pop-funk of Prince), the UK was reinventing the one through the other, the result being acid jazz: Northern soul (a late-'70s style of dance-based groove music similar to rare groove), jazz instrumentation and voicing, and the solid rhythmic foundation of funk, often with a hip-hop beat. Popularized by labels such as Acid Jazz, Talkin' Loud, and Dorado and artists such as the Young Disciples, Corduroy, Groove Collective, and Incognito, the rise of acid jazz to commercial viability in the UK (as well as in the US; many indie labels were reissuing loads of European releases) was swift and ruthless. Like the latter stages of bebop, the music's polarization into, on the one hand, watered-down commercial accessibility and, on the other, increasingly esoteric chops-based noodling left many unsatisfied.

One way out seemed to be through an engagement of the more soulful possibilities of the acid house underground, a path taken by artists such as Soul II Soul, Galliano, and Massive Attack, many of whom added vocalists and rappers to attract a wider audience. Another way out—and one which appealed to a younger generation who grew up with a different musical perspective—was to focus on the music's hip-hop element, stripping away everything but the essentials and playing up the music's dusty beat. This was the path chosen by a loose affiliate of artists organized by DJ/producer James Lavelle, a DJ/producer and music writer for UK acid jazz mag *Straight No Chaser*. Lavelle sent out a call for demos in his monthly column, citing acid jazz's increasing irrelevance and encouraging hip-hop heads with a taste for experimentation to give him a shout. The first batch of demos he received—instrumental b-boy tracks from the likes of RPM, Palmskin Productions, and La Funk Mobb—became the first series of 12-inches released on his new label, Mo'Wax.

Unlike house and techno, hip-hop (the music, anyway) never really caught fire in England. While a handful of artists have been able to pull it off, melding hip-hop production with an authentically UK lyrical perspective, hip-hop's influence has mostly been in terms of fashion (track suits and fat-laced trainers), graffiti, and electro (the latter particularly among the waves of electronica artists—such as Autechre, the Black Dog, and Reload—who took the style in various new directions). While a large underground of fans of early hip-hop formed in the wake of mid-'80s Wildstyle tour, which brought the various cultural components of hip-hop to a broad British audience for the first time, only a handful of distinctly British hip-hop records were released in subsequent years, and of those only a tiny portion you'd want to hear more than once (some notable exceptions include Underdog and the Brotherhood). While UK sales of American hip-hop records continued to rise (particularly the more musically innovative acts such as Public Enemy and the Beastie Boys), there didn't seem to be an outlet for the growing scene's creative impulse.

This is where Mo'Wax (and, eventually, upstart labels such as Clean Up, D.C., and Represent) came in. While many of the tracks featured on the earliest Mo'Wax releases (and collected on the label's first compilation, *Royalties Overdue*) were in some ways indistinguishable from what was happening at the time in acid jazz, the more experimental B-side tracks—abstract, beat-centric slabs of funky downtempo weirdness with a bare minimum of jerky, effects-laden instrumental samples setting an immersive atmosphere—sounded amazingly fresh and suggested new directions for both acid jazz and instrumental hip-hop. Although it was hard to imagine the music impelling anyone onto the dancefloor, the records were a hit among DJs and bedroom-heads alike.

In retrospect, the pairing of straightahead material with more experimental gear on the flip looks pretty savvy, but the fact was the label (and the burgeoning scene as a whole) was still groping for a sound. Grope became seize, however, when a remix of a little known American rap group called Zimbabwe Legit made its way to Lavelle's record box. The track, "Doin' Damage," had been tearing up the American underground for months, and a remix by an unknown California producer, DJ Shadow, attracted his attention. Lavelle tracked Shadow (aka Josh Davis) down and commissioned a single, "In/Flux," which was released in late '93. A perfect blend of head-bobbing beats and frenetic sample collage, "In/Flux" got the balance of funk, jazz, hip-hop, soul, and stoned out ambience just right, and records nipping at its heels began appearing in droves over the course of the following year.

Mo'Wax's subsequent compilation, *Headz* (released toward the end of 1994 and including the best of the label's catalog to date, as well as a heap of exclusives from Shadow, DJ Krush, Lavelle's U.N.K.L.E. project, and even Autechre), set the watermark, and a scene started growing up around the label and others pursuing a similar sound such as Ninja Tune/Ntone, Wall of Sound, Cup of Tea, Chill Out, and former acid jazz powerhouse Dorado. As "back room" club culture started to shift from the droney bliss of ambient and dub to the free-for-all attitude embodied by the early Sunday Social parties held at London's Heavenly club, more and more beats could be heard issuing from back room bassbins. With more and more records appearing, and more and more one-offs and weeklies forming to promulgate the style, the English press needed a quick, easy reference point for the music. "Trip-hop" fit that bill perfectly.

The term was almost immediately disparaged (Shadow riffs on the dopiness of it in his intro to U.N.K.L.E.'s "Time Has Come," released by Mo'Wax in early '95), not least because its seemed, as usual, that another Black artform had been "discovered" and co-opted by the (predominantly) white music industry. And indeed, it wasn't long before the first wave of pop artists—Portishead, Bjork, Tricky, Massive Attack (although their '91 debut, *Blue Lines*, was also a big influence on Lavelle and company)—began incorporating the sound and hitting pay dirt on the pop charts. But the term's ugly ring had less to do with racial politics than the sense that the artists associated with it (even at the pop level) were trying to move the music forward, not capitalize on its novelty (which, given its etymology, was all the term managed to communicate). Although it remains in use (supplemented by a barrage of similar terms such as Brit-hop, downbeat, amyl house, dub-hop, etc.), for many "trip-hop" has yet to lose its taint of contrivance.

In the UK trip-hop has seen an astonishingly quick ascension to widespread popularity, rivaled perhaps only by jungle and even then exceeding it in terms of audience. Once-fledgling labels such as Mo'Wax, Ninja Tune, and Wall of Sound have since grown into release-a-week powerhouses, often prepping artists for major label success. The music continues to evolve, as well, with the music's early laziness proving little more than a blueprint for artists that have taken the style in any number of directions, fusing it with electro, techno, live funk, jazz, and soul, and drum 'n' bass. Now dabbled in by any number of Brit pop and indie rock artists (from Stereolab and Blur to Arab Strap and Day Behavior), the music has also broken well beyond the clubs (although it continues to thrive there as well).

Trip-hop has also been warmly embraced by both indie and major labels in the American industry, with small name artists (Sneaker Pimps, Baby Fox, Morcheeba, Lamb, Hooverphonic) stumbling into sizable domestic contracts, indie and subsidiary labels focused on promoting the sound (Shadow, Quango, WordSound, Ubiquity), and big players such as Mo'Wax, Cup of Tea, and Ninja Tune piggybacking distribution with majors or setting up shop on North American soil. Along with MTV and alternative radio's expanded coverage of "electronica," many artists have also been appearing (somewhat oddly) on any number of movie soundtrack releases (including *Suburbia*, *The Saint*, *Romeo and Juliet*, and *City of Industry*).

Recommended Recordings (* Indicates Top 10)
Various Artists, *Headz* (Mo'Wax)*

Various Artists, *Ninja Cuts 2: Flexistentialism* (Ninja Tune)
Chemical Brothers, *Exit Planet Dust* (Astralwerks/Junior Boys Own)*
Nightmares on Wax, *Smokers Delight* (TVT/Warp)
Funki Porcini, *Hedphone Sex* (Shadow/Ninja Tune)*
Depth Charge, *Nine Deadly Venoms* (DC Recordings)*
DJ Krush, *Meiso* (FFRR/Mo'Wax)
DJ Shadow, *Endtroducing* (Mo'Wax)*
Wagon Christ, *Throbbing Pouch* (Rising High)
Tricky, *Maxinquaye* (4th & B'way)*
Massive Attack, *Blue Lines* (Virgin)*
DJ Food, *Recipe for Disaster* (Shadow/Ninja Tune)*
Req, *One* (Skint)*
Fila Brazillia, *Mess* (Pork)
Skylab, *No. 1* (Astralwerks/L'Attitude)*
Portishead, *Dummy* (London)

—Sean Cooper

Drum 'n' Bass

While the UK underground dance scene has been both an important point of introduction and a source of almost limitless expansion of American dance music forms such as disco, house, acid, techno, electro, and rare groove, England, it's often been noted, has never really had a dance music of its own. Not, that is, until jungle. Although jungle's most direct roots lie in the hardcore breakbeat style of techno, the music's mutation of hardcore, reggae, ragga, hip-hop, jazz, and dub, as well as its origins in social and economic factors such as race and class oppression, is a distinctly British mix. Born largely in the working-class suburbs of London's East End and the island's Eastern seaboard and now popular throughout England, as well as Europe and North America, jungle has coalesced since its birth into one of the most exciting and distinctive British musical movements since the 1960s rock explosion.

Like American hip-hop (to which it is often compared), jungle (or drum 'n' bass, a stylistic synonym used to describe the music's two main aesthetic components) is an extension of the larger breakbeat heritage which extends back to American funk, soul, and jazz. And like hip-hop, which uses samplers to capture drum break segments from old James Brown, Meters, Jimmy Smith, and Bob James records, jungle uses the beat as a jumping off point, starting with a four- or eight-bar break and cutting, splicing, rearranging, and recombining elements of the beat in almost endless variety. But it's this last element that gives jungle its unique place in the evolution of electronic music; where hip-hop and other sample-based forms of dance music work with beats in a more or less serial fashion (looping, combining, adding, subtracting, etc. rhythmic elements), jungle's approach is nonlinear and, increasingly, polyrhythmic, approaching beats, rhythms, and basslines as more or less malleable raw materials from which new musical ideas can be extracted.

One of the key developments in this approach has been the availability of cheap, relatively easy-to-use sampling technology and desktop digital sequencing tools such as Cubase and Vision, which allow for incredible control and variety. In many respects, these tools have made the music possible, as new techniques such as timestretching (extending a sample's length without altering its pitch) and the music's cut 'n' paste approach to rhythm have only recently been made possible through the explosion and subsequent economic democratization of digital audio.

Although, like most origin mythologies, jungle is fraught with intriguing stories of its birth and etymology (even extending to a street gang in Kingston, Jamaica known as the Junglists), most agree that somewhere down the line "jungle" took on a racist connotation stemming from its popularity among England's inner-city Black population (although, to a far larger extent than in America, England's inner cities are of mixed race and are stratified more by class). True or not, the term has been widely embraced by musicians and audiences alike, and remains a genus-type classification for the dizzying array of species of drum 'n' bass that have popped up in recent times (see below). In an historico-aesthetic sense, jungle's immediate roots lie, of course, in the English underground rave scene of the early '90s, when the repetitive banging of acid house and techno gave way to hardcore breakbeat techno. Although originally referring to a more race-oriented strain of hardcore (so-called "happy hardcore," which translated many of the more escapist elements of acid-house and dancefloor techno into a breakbeat context), a more complex and abrasive strand of "darkside" hardcore soon began to grow in popularity, becoming the post-rave underground music of choice, particularly among urban inner-city and working class youth.

Drawing from the music's audience (and of course the musicians themselves), the music began incorporating more complex beat patterns and elements of reggae, ragga, dub, calypso, and other non-Western Black musics, mutating (through artists such as Rob Playford, 2 Bad Mice, SL2, Acen, and Urban Shakedown) into the high-speed breakbeat madness of jungle's first wave. Though still the soundtrack of the urban English underground, by the time ragga jungle hit, a wider audience had begun to form around the revolutionary new sound, particularly as labels such as Suburban Bass, Kickin', Sound of the Underground, and Moving Shadow began to move into CD-based compilation releases, which helped spread the music into new geographies at a rapid rate. Though the clichés of ragga dated quickly (the booyaka chants, the Scientist samples, etc.), the basic skeleton of the music was refined and elaborated (in a less obvious fashion) in so-called hardstep and darkside, which aimed at preserving the intellectual and emotional impact of the music in a more mature, less gimmicky fashion. The following years would see a dizzying mutation and hybridization of styles, as jungle worked its way into every stylistic context imaginable (from Lee Perry and the Wu-Tang Clan to Soul Coughing and Everything but the Girl), with styles continuing to proliferate to the present day.

Like early hip-hop and, to a large extent, present day house and techno, drum 'n' bass remains primarily a 12-inch culture, with the bulk of artists and musicians engaged in nuts 'n' bolts music-making designed directly for DJs and dancefloors (although, like techno, the gap has begun to close a bit through wider popularity of ambient and "intelligent" styles and large-scale CD production and distribution). The rapid intermixing and evolution of styles is also fueled in part by widespread use of white labels, dubplates, and test pressings, which allow artists and DJs to gauge the popularity of a tune only hours after its been completed in the studio. (Dubplates and test pressings are wax and mylar versions of records—usually only playable ten to fifteen times—cut prior to mass production to insure proper manufacture.) A reasonably reputable DJ may spin anywhere from 10 to 50 percent dubplates in a set, with artists who also DJ often cutting their tunes months in advance of their release (if indeed they're ever released!) to build crowd excitement and anticipation.

As discussed above, like other recent directions in experimental electronic music, jungle has sectioned off into a dizzying array of subgenres and style classes (ragga, hardstep, darkside, jump-up, techstep, ambient) that can make getting a handle on it pretty frustrating. The following is a brief description of many of the most prominent:

Hardcore/Happy Hardcore

An urban working-class offshoot of techno, popular in the late '80s/early '90s, with looping, sped-up breakbeats and dense, angular basslines. A more mainstream, rave-oriented brand of "happy" hardcore remained even truer to the music's acid house roots, drawing wailing divas and upbeat piano and synth lines in close proximity to hardcore's brash rhythms. (Artists: Acen, 2 Bad Mice, SL2)

Ragga

Ragga jungle was one of the earliest and most widely embraced forms of drum 'n' bass not to rely overtly on the clichés of hardcore techno, and was a direct reflection of the rising embrace of drum 'n' bass among the street-level urban population (of which a sizeable portion are of African and Caribbean descent). Ragga jungle is characterized primarily by fast, complex beat patterns, deep, tight bass, and the use of sound system-type MC chanting sampled from old reggae, ragga, and dancehall records. Ragga also makes jungle's connection to African and Caribbean traditional and popular musics most evident, with rhythms recognizably descendent from nyabinghi and calypso-style drumming. (Artists: 2 Bad Mice, Rude Bwoy Monty, Shy FX, Amazon II)

Hardstep/Jump-Up

A spare, limber refinement of hardcore and ragga, which retains the hardness and rhythmic complexity of both while subtracting much of the bonus fat (rude bwoy chatter, excessive samples, etc.). Hardstep also carries more of a sense of progression, varying drum patterns more musically and focusing on bass as a melodic element. Although slight variations exist between hardstep and the more recently-applied jump-up (with the latter generally referring to a sprightlier, more dynamic brand of hardstep), the two are for the most part used interchangeably. (Artists: Ray Keith, DJ SS, Dillinja, DJ Zinc)

Darkside

A somewhat historically rooted term, darkside refers to a sparer, more pessimistic style of hardcore seeking to differentiate itself from the more above-ground, mainstream appeal of rave that by the early '90s was producing only the most repetitive and uncreative of music. Darkside artists stripped the bright melodies and sped-up samples from hardcore and replaced them with gloomy basslines, and less obvious melodic passages more reminiscent of Detroit techno than happy hardcore. Darkside is also something of a bridge between early hardcore and the increasing sophistication of the hardstep and experimental drum 'n' bass of DJ SS, Solo, Source Direct, and the Metalheadz artists.

Techstep

Techstep is similar to hardstep in its beat structures and attitude, but differs in the use of techno-type elements such as bleeps and synth squelches, as well as dense, heavily treated basslines. After the softening of drum 'n' bass in the wake of jungle's first wave of widespread popularity (major label signings, international tours, etc.), darker techstep-type jungle has risen to the fore of the underground, proving one of the most active and interesting splinter styles in its experimentalism. Labels on the bleeding edge of this style include Emotif, No U-Turn, Penny Black, and S.O.U.R., and a good introduction exists in Emotif's label compilation, *Techsteppin'*, as well as S.O.U.R's *Nu Skool Update*. (Artists: Ed Rush, Nico, Solo, Shapeshifter)

Ambient/Intelligent

First used to designate drum 'n' bass styles drawing heavily on atmosphere and environment, the term has come to have something of a negative connotation among the hardcore, referring to loopy, relatively unchallenging rhythmic programming and a predominance of sugary, pop-oriented melodic textures. Most likely the backlash has as much to do with the fact that it was the softer, jazzier ambient style drum 'n' bass that was the first to sever its roots with the underground, gaining popularity among a wide audience. (Artists: TPower, Omni Trio, Source Direct, Photek, 4Hero, Dave Wallace)

—*Sean Cooper*

NON-ROCK STYLES THAT INFLUENCED ROCK

Acoustic Blues

The blues is only one of the foundations of rock 'n' roll music, but it may be the sturdiest and most central. Even in its earliest forms, it pointed toward rock 'n' roll in its reliance upon guitar, piano, and percussion, its raw energy, and its classic chord patterns. Embellished with instruments, fuller arrangements, and electricity, it provided building blocks for jazz, R&B, and electric blues, from which it was just a few more steps to rock music. Rock itself has always looked back to the blues, both electric and acoustic, for inspiration and regeneration.

The history of the blues is a long, complicated, and often fascinating one which has been examined in detail in many scholarly treatises and college courses. It's beyond the scope of this brief overview, in which we'll just note its roots in African chants and rhythms, plantation work songs and field hollers, gospel, ragtime, and minstrel. Largely a southern-based music, it had been around for decades, if not centuries, before it began to be widely recorded in the 1920s. Even then, there were several distinct schools of blues music.

The most popular were the early female blues vocalists, who were closely tied to jazz and even pop/vaudeville. Mamie Smith, Ma Rainey, Bessie Smith, and Victoria Spivey were stars with a wide audience, one which was hardly confined to a rural base, enjoying great popularity in the cities. Not enormously influential on the course of R&B and rock, the singers were nonetheless greatly admired by Janis Joplin and Tracy Nelson (who recorded an entire album of Ma Rainey and Bessie Smith songs in her folkie days), which in turn influenced numerous rock performers who never heard the originals.

After its rediscovery by fanatics in the 1960s, the early blues acquired a romantic image as a musical reflection of suffering and hard times that was unrivaled in its authenticity. It comes as a surprise to some modern listeners to find that there were plenty of early blues performers that didn't conform to that stereotype. There were blues singers with strong shades of ragtime, vaudeville, and gospel. Many were entertainers, able indeed to perform hard-bitten tales of toil when the spirit moved them, but also able to sing all types of music, ranging from country to pop, when their audience required it. There were also quite a few jug bands, several in Memphis alone, frequently using fiddles, banjos, kazoos, and other instruments that hardly fit the blues stereotype.

Unquestionably, however, it was the southern solo guitarists of the first generation of recorded bluesmen that cast the greatest shadow over rock, and held the greatest mystique for listeners that weren't around (or, usually, even born) when the blues first became available on record. Many of them came from the Mississippi Delta— Son House, Charley Patton, Bukka White, Fred McDowell, Skip James and, above all, Robert Johnson have all acquired mythic stature. There were also blues legends active throughout the South, especially Texas (Blind Lemon Jefferson), Atlanta (Blind Willie McTell), and Memphis (Furry Lewis, Memphis Minnie), and southeastern performers who came to be referred to as the Piedmont School (Blind Blake, Blind Boy Fuller).

Not all major blues artists were guitarists—there were also quite a few pianists in the barrelhouse and boogie styles, such as Peetie Wheatstraw, Cow Cow Davenport, and a host of incredibly obscure names that usually only turn up on rare import compilations. But the guitarists, understandably, were the source of greatest influence and fascination for subsequent generations of rock 'n' rollers. The guitar, after all, is rock's premier instrument, and quite a few of the picking styles, riffs, and even songs can be traced directly back to rural blues. Rockers past and present have been equally enamored with its raw vocals and per-

sonal lyrics—a direct, intimate, and supremely earthy expression of their joys and struggles.

Numerous examples could be made of old blues songs that have taken new lives as rock hits. A particularly colorful example is "Matchbox," originally performed by Blind Lemon Jefferson. The song, which may well have been traditional in origin, was spruced up into rockabilly in the mid-'50s by Carl Perkins (who claimed the writing credits); ten years later, it was transformed yet again into full-bore rock 'n' roll by the Beatles, who learned the song from the Perkins version, and may not have even been aware that Jefferson recorded it in the 1920s.

Acoustic blues records were quite popular with Black listeners when they first appeared, but the Depression meant that many of them—poor to begin with—couldn't afford any records at all. Hence many blues performers rarely recorded, or never got to record at all, during much of the 1930s and 1940s. When the blues became popular again, it was a new kind of blues, played with electric guitars and drums, in cities like Chicago and Memphis. Many of these performers, such as Muddy Waters, Elmore James, and Johnny Shines, had moved to the city from the Delta, where they had already perfected their craft as acoustic performers. They electrified as a matter of professional survival, and updated the classical rural guitar blues sound as much as they changed it—you can hear strong echoes of the Delta in everything they did, down to the 12-bar structure that was established as the classic blues form.

Many of the original country blues performers were forgotten until the blues revival of the early 1960s. Not everyone went to the lengths of guitarist John Fahey, who located Bukka White by writing a letter to "Bukka White, Old Blues Singer, c/o General Delivery, Aberdeen, Mississippi" (a town mentioned in one of his songs), but many blues singers, unknown and obscure even in their hometowns, were rediscovered and coaxed out of retirement by white enthusiasts. They found an entire new audience, mostly young and collegiate, waiting for them, and were often, as White was, able to tour and record internationally to considerable acclaim in their remaining years. Singers like Mississippi John Hurt, Skip James, and Fred McDowell may have reached more listeners by touring the folk circuit in the '60s than they did during their prime.

The rediscovery and reappreciation of these early blues legends saw some major rock bands, who had already plundered electric blues for much of their inspiration, going back even further to the earlier acoustic blues. The Rolling Stones were the most successful; their late '60s and early '70s albums often tap into the Delta spirit without sounding like a slavish imitation or bad parody, both on original material like "Salt of the Earth" and covers of classics by Robert Wilkins, Robert Johnson, and Fred McDowell. McDowell himself toured with Bonnie Raitt, who has openly credited the bluesman as a major influence. Canned Heat updated a Henry Thomas panpipe number, "Bull Doze Blues," into the Top 20 single "Going up the Country." The Allman Brothers revived Blind Willie McTell's "Statesboro Blues." Cream recorded exciting electric versions of Skip James' "I'm So Glad" and Robert Johnson's "Crossroads." So it continues until today: Nirvana's posthumous *Unplugged* release included a version of Leadbelly's "Where Did You Sleep Last Night?"

Acoustic blues will always be an element of rock 'n' roll, although not nearly as much as electric blues, both as an influence and as a source of cover material. Acoustic blues itself isn't recorded or performed much these days; it is the modern age, after all, and the great majority of blues performers are working in the electric format both out of choice and necessity. The surprise success of Robert Johnson's 1990 box set, which sold several hundred thousand copies in the days of synthesizers and 64-track production, proves that acoustic blues will always strike listeners with its power and passion, no matter what the era.

Despite its indisputable importance, the unseasoned listener is urged to ease her or his way into the classic blues repertoire. The primitive sound (on which the guitar and vocals sometimes appear to be in the process of being fried on the skillet), the limited melodic variation, and the harsh execution can disappoint those led by enthusiastic critics to expect an instantly transforming experience. Rather than jump into the legacy of legendarily challenging legends like Robert Pete Williams, it might be best to start with more accessible collections, such as the ones listed below.

Recommended Recordings

Various Artists, *Blues Masters, Vol. 10: Blues Roots* (Rhino). Just what it says, focusing on forms like prison songs, work songs, and native African music.

Various Artists, *Blues Masters, Vol. 11: Classic Blues Women* (Rhino). The early female blues stars: Bessie Smith, Mamie Smith, Sippie Wallace, Billie Holiday, Ma Rainey.

Various Artists, *Roots of Robert Johnson* (Yazoo). An interesting concept: the performances that can be seen, with hindsight, to have influenced Johnson, by fellow Mississippi Delta bluesmen like Skip James, Charley Patton, Son House, and Lonnie Johnson.

Various Artists, *Slide Guitar— Bottles Knives & Steel, Vol. 1 & 2* (CBS). The slide guitar is many people's favorite feature of early blues, and these collections have cuts by major practitioners like Bukka White, Tampa Red, Blind Willie Johnson, and Leadbelly.

Skip James, *The Complete Early Recordings* (Yazoo). The most thorough collection of his 1930s sides, including the original version of "I'm So Glad."

Mississippi John Hurt, *1928 Sessions* (Yazoo). One of the finest fingerpicking early blues guitarists. For those who find remastered 78s tough listening, the Vanguard albums he recorded in the 1960s following his rediscovery are a recommended alternative.

Blind Willie McTell, *The Definitive Blind Willie McTell* (Columbia). Double disc of 1929-33 material by the versatile performer, an innovator of 12-string guitar playing.

Leadbelly, *King of the 12-String Guitar* (CBS). Through his popularization of "Goodnight, Irene," "Midnight Special," and others, Leadbelly's influence was also felt in the folk and pop worlds.

Memphis Minnie, *Hoodoo Lady (1933-37)* (CBS). Singer-guitarist roundly considered to be the greatest pre-World War II blueswoman.

Robert Johnson, *The Complete Recordings* (CBS). More may have been written and analyzed about this set of tracks than those found on any other blues collection.

Bukka White, *The Complete Bukka White* (Columbia). One of the most hard-bitten and starkly personal blues singers, these 1937 and 1940 sessions are considered to be his best work.

Muddy Waters, *The Complete Plantation Recordings* (MCA). Recorded for the Library of Congress in the early 1940s, when Muddy lived in Mississippi, and had yet to plug in an electric guitar. A fascinating link between the old and new guard, even if no one could have been aware at the time.

Mississippi Fred McDowell, *Mississippi Delta Blues* (Arhoolie). Although he was born shortly after 1900, this bottleneck slide guitarist wasn't discovered and recorded until 1959; these mid-'60s recordings are considered among his best.

J.B. Lenoir, *Down in Mississippi* (L&R, Germany). A second-division electric Chicago bluesman who recorded for Chess and other labels, Lenoir made a couple little-known European albums in the mid-'60s shortly before his death. These found him expanding the acoustic blues traditions in interesting ways, writing topical songs about contemporary issues like segregation and Vietnam, and using African-derived percussive rhythms. This is recommended above the similar *Alabama Blues* for its greater accessibility.

Ted Hawkins, *Happy Hour* (Rounder). A street performer on the Venice Beach boardwalk in Los Angeles for many years, Hawkins was one of the few acoustic blues musicians to achieve widespread recognition in the 1980s and 1990s, though his material and vocals actually owed as much to soul and R&B as straight blues. Hawkins released his first major label album at the age of 58, shortly before his death in 1995; this 1987 effort uses sparer instrumentation.

Books

Deep Blues, by Robert Palmer (1981, Viking Press)

The Blackwell Guide to Blues Records, edited by Paul Oliver(1989, Blackwell)

The Story of the Blues, by Paul Oliver (Chilton, 1970)

—Richie Unterberger

Gospel
....

Gospel music has rarely been a significant presence in the commercial mainstream, and indeed its fervent religious concerns will most likely always limit it to a specialized audience. Rock and pop fans often find pure gospel rough going, both due to its intensely spiritual focus and its melodic and compositional strictures. Yet even for those rock fans who never develop a passion for the form, it's worth appreciation as one of rock and soul's bedrock influences.

There are strong gospel traditions, reaching back through several centuries, in both the Black and white population of America. The Black tradition, a combination of indigenous African music with Western religious influences, found its expression in both "work songs" and the church, one of the few places where the Black community could openly express itself in the days of segregation. When Black gospel traditions began to mix with the music of the secular world, the combinations that resulted were pivotal in the birth of R&B and soul.

The groaning, moaning, pleading, and supplicating qualities of gospel are easy to hear in the vocals of jump blues artists like Percy Mayfield, Roy Brown, and Wynona Carr, as well as early soul pioneers like Ray Charles, James Brown, Clyde McPhatter, and Little Willie John, even if they may be singing about raucous and romantic joys. Likewise, the harmonies and call-and-response interplay of the classic doo wop groups, from the Orioles through the early work of the Impressions, were refined in the chapel as well as on the street corner.

The connection between gospel and soul, however, is often far more direct. A few of soul's greatest singers, including Wilson Pickett and Little Johnny Taylor, got their starts in gospel quartets. Taylor had been in the Soul Stirrers, also the breeding ground for Sam Cooke, the most famous singer to cross over to pop after establishing himself as a gospel star. Gospel fans were outraged when Cooke abandoned the circuit for pop stardom in the late '50s, but pop and rock fans were enriched immeasurably, as Cooke's work until his death in 1964 was immensely important in paving the road for modern soul music.

Notable female soul and pop singers who began as gospel vocalists include Dionne Warwick and Whitney Houston, whose mother, Cissy, directed the Sweet Inspirations, who sang backup vocals on some of Aretha Franklin's early hits. Franklin herself was the daughter of noted preacher and gospel singer C.L. Franklin, and recorded some gospel as a teenager. When she reached superstardom with a burst of soul smashes in 1967, listeners were responding to a voice letting loose the unbridled passion of gospel on contemporary pop-R&B. Franklin's vision is really too wide to be categorized as a gospel offshoot, but she has always remained cognizant of her roots, occasionally immersing herself in them, as on her acclaimed 1972 album, *Amazing Grace*.

Other notable gospel-soul crossovers include the Chambers Brothers, who were one of the few Black groups to become favorites with the psychedelic crowd; the Edwin Hawkins Singers, who landed a surprise Top Five hit in 1969 with "Oh Happy Day"; and the Staple Singers, whose Memphis soul-gospel approach yielded some of the most inspirational hits of the early '70s. Also from Memphis is Al Green, the most famous singer to travel in the reverse direction, abandoning pop superstardom for gospel. The music world was shocked when Green embraced gospel in the late '70s after a reign of five years or so as soul's most popular performer, and though he's largely a memory for the masses, he's been very active in the studio and as a performer in the gospel world.

In the world of white rock 'n' roll, gospel has been a less prominent but nevertheless important influence. The church was a focal point of white southern rural culture, and often offered the easiest place to sing and play music, as it did in the early African-American community. Most of the first white rock 'n' rollers were southern, and they were also schooled in gospel harmonies and spiritual standards. Many early country acts, like the Carter Family, Bill Monroe, and Tennessee Ernie Ford, took a large part of their repertoire from gospel. The close harmonies of acts like the Delmore Brothers often derived from, and were sometimes actually used on, sacred songs, in turn influencing early rock 'n' rollers who didn't actually perform gospel, the Everly Brothers being the most famous example.

Many early rockabilly stars may have been set on raising hell onstage and in the studio, but gospel was a big part of their background, even in the most unlikely of cases. Jerry Lee Lewis, for instance, is Jimmy Swaggart's cousin, and can be heard debating spiritual matters with Sam Phillips on a famous outtake from Sun Studios. When Lewis, Elvis Presley, Carl Perkins, and others gathered in the same studio in 1956 for the famous Million Dollar Quartet session, they jammed on the songs they all shared and knew by heart—many of which, to the surprise of some latter-day listeners, were gospel tunes. Elvis counted gospel groups like the Statesmen and the Blackwood Brothers among his biggest influences, and employed a gospel group, the Jordanaires, to harmonize and sing backing vocals on most of his biggest hits. He also recorded a good deal of straight gospel himself, from 1957 on through to the 1970s.

Rock stars without direct gospel influences have occasionally called on gospel singers to record appropriate embellishments to particular recordings; Paul Simon was never one to let a good ethnic flavor pass unnoticed, and his use of the Dixie Hummingbirds on the 1973 hit "Loves Me Like a Rock" is one of the most famous examples. Occasionally, rockers have embraced religion long after establishing themselves as secular pop stars, recording gospel-influenced albums that have by and large not been well received, Bob Dylan being the most famous of these. Dylan was outraged at the audience for, as he saw it, dismissing his music because of its religious values; this may have been partly true, but the audiences were also turning a cold shoulder to the records because spiritual music was not his strongest suit, and because they didn't enjoy being hammered over the head with a message, fundamentalist or otherwise. When Violent Femmes leader Gordon Gano recorded a gospel album with his side group the Mercy Seat, the reaction was not so much hostility as indifference, partly because Gano wasn't nearly as mythological a figure as Dylan.

In contemporary music, gospel usually isn't a visible factor, not because its influence is negligible, but because it has permeated the rock and soul mainstream so deeply that it's become permanently absorbed into its structure. It continues to permeate urban contemporary R&B in the smooth harmonies and lead vocals, even if the singers are no longer as directly steeped in the church as they were in the 1950s and 1960s. And there are still instances of singers moving from spiritual music to secular pop-rock, as Amy Grant has done on a superstar level, and singer-songwriter Sam Phillips has done as a cult alternative rock favorite.

Recommended Recordings

Various Artists, *Jubilation Vol. 1-3* (Rhino). Anthologies of classic gospel. The first two volumes cover Black artists like the Soul Stirrers, the Swan Silvertones, Aretha Franklin, Mahalia Jackson, the Staple Singers, and the Five Blind Boys; the third focuses on white country gospel, with sides by the Carter Family, the Louvin Brothers, Kitty Wells, George Jones and Tammy Wynette, Bill Monroe, Johnny Cash, and Hank Williams.

The Soul Stirrers, *The Gospel Soul of Sam Cooke, Vol. 2* (Specialty). An entire disc of Cooke's sides with the gospel group during the first half of the 1950s. Other Soul Stirrers discs, if you want to go further, include performances by Johnnie Taylor and other noteworthy singers who took the leads when Cooke wasn't in the group.

Various Artists, *Something Got a Hold of Me* (RCA). Classic country gospel by the Carter Family, Bill Monroe, the Blue Sky Boys, Uncle Dave Macon, and other less celebrated acts.

Elvis Presley, *The Million Dollar Quartet* (RCA). Actually Elvis, Carl Perkins, and Jerry Lee Lewis plus a few other musicians (Johnny Cash was present for the photo but not for the recording, apparently), jamming on rock, R&B, and not a little gospel. The double-CD *Amazing Grace* is the most wide-ranging compilation of Presley's gospel recordings, but will have considerably less appeal for the rock fan.

Mahalia Jackson, *Gospels, Spirituals & Hymns* (CBS). Often rated as the best gospel singer of all.

arious Artists, *Sam Cooke's SAR Records Story 1959-1965* (ABKCO). Cooke acted as label owner, frequent producer and songwriter for SAR, recording gospel, soul, and combinations of the two by performers like the Womack Brothers, Johnnie Taylor, and the Valentinos.

The Chambers Brothers, *Time Has Come: The Best of the Chambers Brothers* (Columbia). An erratic group whose funk and psychedelic excesses never hid their gospel roots.

The Staple Singers, *Greatest Hits* (Fantasy). A compilation of early-'60s material that gives listeners a sampling of their gospel roots as it was being tempered by contemporary influences. No Staple Singers collection surveys their entire career, which stretches across several decades; try Vee Jay compilations for their earliest and purest gospel material, and *The Best of the Staple Singers* (on Stax) for their soul hits.

Aretha Franklin, *Amazing Grace* (Atlantic). Her 1972 gospel album, also featuring James Cleveland and the Southern California Community Choir.

The Dixie Hummingbirds, *Live* (MCA). A 75-minute live set from the mid-'70s.

Al Green, *The Belle Album* (Hi). His last album (from 1977) before his conversion to full-time gospel, catching him bridging secular soul music with personal spiritual concerns.

Sweet Honey in the Rock, *Live at Carnegie Hall* (Flying Fish). Not purely a gospel group, though heavily gospel-influenced, this all-woman African-American *a cappella* group is proof that music can both draw on gospel traditions and comment on contemporary political, social, and personal concerns. Active since the mid-'70s, with various lineups under the leadership of Bernice Reagon, this is a 1988 concert recording.

—Richie Unterberger

Electric Blues

Of all the many forms of music that contributed to the birth of rock 'n' roll, electric blues has arguably exerted the most fundamental and durable influence. It's not just that electric blues helped establish the prototype of the basic rock lineup—electric guitars and a rhythm section—and that much early rock 'n' roll, from both America and Great Britain, was an embellishment of electric blues with somewhat different rhythms and song construction. It's also that electric blues, in sound, spirit, and execution, is separated from rock 'n' roll by only the thinnest of boundaries. It's rare indeed to find a rock 'n' roll fan who doesn't have the same visceral response to electric blues, even though the music isn't nearly as dominant a presence in the media and the marketplace.

The blues started to become electrified shortly before World War II, as a direct result of major shifts in the lives of millions of African-Americans. Masses of Black migration from rural areas to urban factors, in search of better employment opportunities and living conditions, resulted in a swelling of the Black communities in America's inner cities. A great many of these Blacks came from the South, settling in metropolises like Chicago, St. Louis, Detroit, and Los Angeles. They brought their musical tastes with them, but rural blues had to be adapted to city life to survive. The pace of urban life was faster, the performance venues larger and more lively. To cut through the noise of the crowds, electric instruments and drums were a necessity.

It's unclear exactly who the first electric blues guitarist was, but most likely bluesmen began to try amplified instruments in the late '30s; there have even been rumors that Robert Johnson was playing electric guitar with a band shortly before his death in 1938. Early electric jazz guitar pioneers Eddie Durham and, especially, Charlie Christian mapped out the single-string solo style that early electric blues guitarists would build upon. Guitarist T-Bone Walker, a Texan who relocated to Los Angeles, is almost universally credited as the first electric blues master. Starting around 1940, he combined electric blues with elements of R&B and jazz, enjoying a prolific career that stretched over several decades.

What most people think of as the classic electric blues sound, however, developed in Chicago shortly after World War II. Many of the great Chicago blues musicians had relocated from the Mississippi Delta, long a fountain of great blues performers, and indeed many of the new arrivals had already perfected their craft on acoustic instruments. A brasher, faster electric style was required for professional survival in the Windy City. By the 1950s, Chicago electric blues was thriving, in a small combo format established by bandleaders like Muddy Waters.

Waters was not the most notable electric blues musician in Chicago; John Lee Williamson (the first "Sonny Boy" Williamson), Johnny Shines, and a few others had already used amplification by the time he arrived in the city in 1943. Waters himself was already a blues performer of some note, recording acoustic sessions for the Library of Congress in the early '40s at the Mississippi plantation where he worked. He knew he needed to adapt, though, and assembled a powerhouse band that would, at various points, feature performers who were stars in their own right, including Little Walter, Jimmy Rogers, Otis Spann, Junior Wells, and James Cotton. Driven by compelling riffs on guitar and harmonica, a forceful rhythm section, and strong original material that derived from and updated the classic Delta blues Waters had already mastered, his band was the prototype for Chicago electric blues.

Waters recorded for Chess Records, which quickly became the city's most successful blues and R&B label, with a roster including Little Walter, Howlin' Wolf, Sonny Boy Williamson, and Jimmy Rogers, as well as (for brief periods) Elmore James, John Lee Hooker, Otis Rush, and many interesting minor performers. The Chess sound—spare, clear, and reverberant—did a lot in its own right to refine and solidify the music without sacrificing its raw power. A lot of the credit for Chess' success belongs to arranger, bassist, songwriter, and occasional performer Willie Dixon, who perhaps wrote more classic blues songs than any other songwriter.

A lot of classic Chicago blues from this era was recorded on other labels by greats like Rush, James, Billy Boy Arnold, and Jimmy Reed. And while Chicago had by far the greatest concentration of talent, the blues became electrified in similar patterns in other cities. Memphis had Howlin' Wolf before he moved to Chicago, as well as B.B. King, Ike Turner, and Junior Parker; before he moved into rockabilly, Sam Phillips of Sun Records was often responsible for recording the best Memphis blues musicians. Detroit had John Lee Hooker, the king of boogie; Guitar Slim and Slim Harpo recorded swamp blues in Louisiana; and there were strong scenes in Houston, St. Louis, and California.

Blues didn't only adapt the classic 12-bar, three-chord pattern when it became electrified; it also combined with jazz, pop, and gospel to feed into rhythm and blues, in the form of jump blues "shouters" like Big Joe Turner, Tiny Bradshaw, Ruth Brown, and Jimmy Witherspoon. R&B, of course, eventually fed into rock 'n' roll and early soul pioneers like Ray Charles, James Brown, and Little Willie John, all of whom were strongly influenced by the blues. Bobby "Blue" Bland was the most prominent vocalist who borrowed in fairly equal measures from blues, R&B, and soul. Guitarists like Chuck Berry and Bo Diddley took the electric blues foundation and pioneered rock 'n' roll by adding R&B, jump blues, and pop elements. And ironically (more so considering that Berry and Diddley actually recorded for Chess), rock 'n' roll cut deeply into the blues audience by the end of the 1950s, and electric blues, a huge commercial success on the R&B charts in the early and mid-'50s, was relegated to a small corner of the record-buying public once again.

Electric blues still thrived in the local clubs, and came roaring back into the public consciousness again in the mid-'60s, as British Invasion bands like the Rolling Stones and Yardbirds popularized electric blues classics for the mass audience, and folk festivals and European tours introduced living legends like Waters to white listeners who would never have come across the music otherwise. Some of the best electric blues dates from this decade, when some greats leavened their sound with contemporary R&B and soul influences without removing their blues foundations. Junior Wells, Magic Sam, Buddy Guy, and Albert King recorded their best work in this era; B.B. King even crossed over to the pop charts, a feat that has remained rare for electric blues of all kinds.

It's the Chicago sound of the 1950s that remains the most influential form of electric blues on rock. Jazzed up with faster tempos and more flexible melodies, it was a primary foundation for a great deal of early rockabilly and rock 'n' roll. Many British bands, and a few American ones, built their early chops by covering classics from this time, and constructed their original material around blues riffs (see separate sidebar on blues-rock). Hundreds of classic songs from this era, by Dixon, Waters, James, Reed, and many others, remain at the heart of the rock 'n' roll repertoire.

Blues has not been a significant commercial presence in the past few decades, but continues to thrive, albeit fitfully, on a local level, and via a worldwide network of enthusiasts, festivals, and independent labels. A lot of the Chicago legends are very much alive and active, joined by younger masters like Son Seals and Robert Cray, the latter of whom proved that blues could still sell to the masses on his albums of the late '80s and '90s. Electric blues is a huge and diverse field, with literally hundreds of noteworthy performers. The list below is not meant to be a definitive distillation of the cream of the crop—there are entire books devoted to that purpose—but some top-notch ports of entry.

Recommended Recordings

Various Artists, *Blues Masters, Vol. 1-15* (Rhino). The most comprehensive introductory history to all forms of electric and acoustic blues, including special volumes for Memphis, Texas, Chicago, urban, and jump blues. *Volume 6, Blues Originals,* illustrates the connection between blues and rock most vividly, with original versions of blues classics made popular by rock performers.

T-Bone Walker, *The Complete Capitol/Black & White Recordings* (Capitol). Triple-CD box of 1940s recordings, in which Walker acted as one of the key players in small combo West Coast bands' transition from jazz to a more jump blues/R&B-oriented sound. Alternative Walker compilations include *The Complete Imperial Recordings* (EMI), a double CD of early-'50s sides, and the six-CD *Complete Recordings.*

Muddy Waters, *The Best of Muddy Waters* (Chess). The best single-CD collection; to dip deeper into his huge repertoire, try the three-CD *Chess Box.*

Little Walter, *The Essential Little Walter* (MCA). Double CD of the greatest and most influential blues harmonica player of all time.

Howlin' Wolf, *Howlin' Wolf/Moanin' in the Moonlight* (MCA). This combination of Wolf's first and second albums on one CD is chock full of blues classics that would later become rock 'n' roll staples, including "Little Red Rooster," "Wang Wang Doodle," "Spoonful," and "Back Door Man." Those with a deeper interest and bigger budget should go for the three-CD *Chess Box.*

Elmore James, *The Sky Is Crying* (Rhino). The best single-disc CD of the best blues slide guitarist. This prolific artist has several good compilations available; this is the most wide-ranging, and hence a recommended starting point.

John Lee Hooker, *The Ultimate Collection (1948-90)* (Rhino). The singer whose low, booming voice and stomping rhythms defined electric blues boogie has recorded a staggering quantity of material; this double disc is not so much the best as the most wide-ranging.

Jimmy Reed, *Speak the Lyrics to Me, Mama Reed* (Vee Jay). 25 tracks on a single disc of the singer whose lazy, shuffling blues-R&B yielded several blues-rock classics, including "Big Boss Man," "Baby What You Want Me to Do?," and "Bright Lights, Big City."

Sonny Boy Williamson, *Essential Sonny Boy Williamson* (MCA). Probably the least famous and striking of the four Chess blues superstars (Waters, Little Walter, and Howlin' Wolf were the others), but an outstanding harmonica player and songwriter.

Various Artists, *A Sun Blues Collection* (Rhino). Important early and mid-'50s Memphis blues sides by Howlin' Wolf, Rufus Thomas, Little Milton, James Cotton, Junior Parker, B.B. King, and others.

Otis Rush, *Cobra Recordings, 1956-58* (Flyright). Minor-key blues with a gospel moan and chilling, stinging guitar runs.

Slim Harpo, *The Best of Slim Harpo* (Rhino). The best swamp-bluesman, influential on the Rolling Stones, Kinks, and Yardbirds, including his top 40 hits "Baby, Scratch My Back" and "Rainin' in My Heart," as well as the original versions of "I'm a King Bee" and "Got Love if You Want It."

B.B. King, *Live at the Regal* (MCA). This 1965 album is almost universally regarded as the best live blues recording. The four-CD box set *King of the Blues* is the most comprehensive anthology of this major blues legend.

Bobby "Blue" Bland, *I Pity the Fool* (MCA). Double-CD compilation of the most respected performer to bridge blues with soul and R&B.

Junior Wells, *Hoodoo Man Blues* (Delmark). One of the greatest blues albums, enlivened by soul, R&B, and Latin influences, this enthralling 1965 session also features Buddy Guy on guitar.

Magic Sam, *West Side Soul* (Delmark). The best album by a bluesman who was just reaching his peak when he died at the end of the 1960s.

Koko Taylor, *What It Takes —The Chess Years* (Chess). The best of the early sides by the premier modern female blues singer.

Albert King, *Ultimate Collection* (Rhino). Double CD of the great soul-influenced bluesman, a big influence on Eric Clapton, among others.

Son Seals, *The Son Seals Blues Band* (Alligator). A fiery guitarist, Seals is the most respected Chicago bluesman to achieve national recognition after the 1960s.

Robert Cray, *Strong Persuader* (Mercury). The 1986 album that brought blues back to the commercial spotlight, adding modern rock influences to the classic electric blues prototype.

Books

Deep Blues, by Robert Palmer (1981, Viking Press)

I Am the Blues, by Willie Dixon with Don Snowden (1989, Da Capo)

The Blackwell Guide to Blues Records, edited by Paul Oliver (1989, Blackwell)

—Richie Unterberger

American Folk

American folk music, like most everything else American, is not so much an indigenous sound as it is a melting pot of traditional forms and songs from Europe (especially the British Isles) and Africa, honed in the US, especially in the South, since the 17th century. Usually (but not exclusively) played on acoustic string instruments, the folk repertoire passed from generation to generation, influencing the birth of rock 'n' roll less directly than blues, country, gospel, and jazz, although it was part of the collective consciousness of all American musicians. Folk's revival after the Second World War, culminating in an all-out boom in the early '60s, was safeguarded from commercial corruption by zealous traditionalists, who insisted on reverent interpretation and acoustic instruments—for a while, that is. By the mid-'60s, folk would alter the course of rock and pop in ways that no one forsaw just a few short years earlier.

In the early days of the record business, traditional folk music was a small corner of the market indeed. Certainly the early acoustic blues musicians, and country stars such as Jimmie Rodgers and the Carter Family, owed a great deal to folk music, although they weren't classified and marketed as such. The folk that was recorded was often being preserved for historical, scholarly purposes (as with the extensive Library of Congress catalog), or commercialized almost beyond recognition, or geared toward extremely specialized audiences (as with early Yiddish and Klezmer recordings directed toward the Jewish immigrant community).

Woody Guthrie, more than any other performer, was responsible for linking traditional American folk forms to concerns of the present day. Although he often drew upon classic folk melodies, he was the first major folksinger to develop an extensive repertoire of original material that drew upon his personal experiences and commented directly on contemporary life and social conditions. Contemporaries like Cisco Houston and Oscar Brand also followed this model, but Guthrie, who recorded hundreds of sides in the 1940s and early 1950s, was by far the most influential, on both slightly younger performers like Pete Seeger and Jack Elliott, and singers of the next generation, especially Bob Dylan.

In the late 1940s, the Weavers, a harmonizing folk group featuring Pete Seeger, brought folk to the masses. Although hugely successful—their 1950 No. 1 hit "Goodnight Irene" topped the charts for 13 weeks—their left-leaning politics did not escape the attention of certain government authorities in the Communist-fearing early '50s, and their career was prematurely snuffed by blacklists. In the latter half of the decade, the Weavers resumed activity and, along with other veteran performers and newly emerging interpreters of traditional material like Joan Baez (who was instrumental in exposing Bob Dylan to a wide audience), Dave Van Ronk, and Judy Collins, spearheaded a folk revival.

The folk music that was actually on the charts, however, was usually a highly commercial, watered-down variant of traditional sounds and material. The Kingston Trio, Harry Belafonte, the Rooftop Singers, and the Limeliters were the most popular of these, and they deserve some credit for at least making many Americans aware of folk music in the first place, although they should in no way be taken as its most authentic ambassadors. Other performers, like Bob Gibson and more particularly Peter, Paul & Mary, combined commercial appeal with more passion and material that ran closer to the motherlode of traditional folk.

Small independent labels, chiefly Elektra, Vanguard, and Folkways, did their part to record the era's most earnest interpreters. The audience for these more "authentic" sounds was usually found on campuses and cities with large intellectual, politically progressive populations, like Boston, Berkeley, and New York, where the scene was centered in Greenwich Village. Large festivals, like the ones staged at Newport, were important showcases for the era's best talent. And so the music might have stayed for some time—a popular, if minority, taste, nurtured by a large alternative community—if not for a new generation of performers intent on combining folk with contemporary musical and social influences.

Chief among these was Bob Dylan, who was inspired to become a folk performer after becoming enamored of Woody Guthrie. Dylan assimilated a wide variety of American traditional folk music as well as anyone of his time. His debut album, which consists mostly of folk standards, and the astonishingly extensive repertoire of traditional material that he ran through (and to a large extent continues to run through), in live performances and on oodles of bootlegs, demonstrates this clearly. His second LP, *Freewheelin' Bob Dylan* (1962), was his true groundbreaker, consisting mostly of original material that commented specifically on contemporary political issues and the feelings of his generation.

Dylan was initially embraced as a savior by the folk community, who howled in protest when he quickly moved away from protest material to personal, romantic tunes and surrealistic poems. The howls became battle cries when, with the British Invasion in full swing, he embraced electric instruments and rock 'n' roll, creating the hybrid folk-rock along with the Byrds and Dylan. The old guard crucified Bob as a sellout, but virtually all of his contemporaries—Phil Ochs, Fred Neil, Tim Hardin, Judy Collins, Joan Baez, Gordon Lightfoot, Ian & Sylvia, Buffy Sainte-Marie—followed suit, sooner rather than later. And it wasn't done just to make money and keep pace with the times; to a man and to a woman, every contemporary folk performer knew that original material (or, at least, covers of contemporary songwriters) and electric instruments paved the way for wider expression and, hence, greater art, unfettered by the now outdated demands for purism in the folk community.

All of the performers mentioned in the above paragraph retained a great deal of folk's strength in their folk-rock; the primacy of guitars, the earnest passion and commitment, the incorporation of time-honored American traditional forms—some more than others. Phil Ochs, for instance, inherited Dylan's mantle as the day's premier protest singer, and while he recorded a lot of non-political material, he never wholly abandoned his left-leaning political consciousness. The folk-rock movement is covered in detail in a separate sidebar, but it's important to point out that many of the '60s leading folk-rock and psychedelic musicians were ex-folkies, led back to the rock 'n' roll of their youth by the Beatles and Dylan. The Byrds, the Jefferson Airplane, the Buffalo Springfield, the Grateful Dead, and many others were populated by ex-folk musicians who would have probably remained obscure, and never reached artistic heights of note, if they hadn't realized that the social consciousness of folk could be expressed with far more vitality in rock arrangements.

The interplay between folk and rock has never been nearly as intense as it was in the mid-'60s, probably because the attributes of folk music were absorbed into rock's framework so quickly and deeply. The singer-songwriter movement of the late '60s and early '70s owes a lot to folk music—indeed, some of its most popular practitioners started out as acoustic folkies. But no one would mistake singer-songwriter albums for traditional American folk; the accent was on individual expression and original material, and the arrangements, if somewhat softer than much other rock, did not eschew electric instruments and rhythm sections, although acoustic guitars, harmonicas, and pianos were often prominent in the mix.

While you might hear, say, Nirvana covering a Leadbelly song, or John Cougar Mellencamp and Bruce Springsteen paying lip service to Woody Guthrie, and all manner of bands showing up with acoustic instruments on MTV's *Unplugged* show, the influence of traditional folk on today's rock is pretty small. The "anti-folk" scene of the late 1980s, an attempt by New York musicians to provide an acoustic-based heir of sorts to the hootenannies of the '50s and '60s, had minimal impact; the

Washington Squares, attempting to mimic the "beatnik folk" of Peter, Paul & Mary, were a failure on all counts.

Many fine performers of the last few decades have been labeled as folk because their arrangements are largely acoustic, but really belong more in the singer-songwriter camp than traditional music; their category is often more a function of the audiences they play for, or the fact that acoustic guitars are at the forefront of their arrangements. Hence you might find Kate Wolf, Lucinda Williams, Tish Hinojosa, Mary McCaslin, Peter Stampfel, the McGarrigle Sisters, Townes Van Zandt, and Bill Morrissey in folk sections, although they sing original, at times compelling material about the here and now, and are often not adverse to using some electric instruments. Indeed, the music of the above performers is not terribly dissimilar from some artists commonly marketed as rock and pop musicians, such as Joni Mitchell.

Some performers that are in many respects troubadours in the folk tradition, like Michelle Shocked or Phranc, are marketed as rock because that is where their audience is perceived to be; the Eleventh Dream Day offshoot Freakwater was marketed to alternative/indie rock listeners more because of their pedigree than the music, which hearkens in spirit back to the Carter Family. Nanci Griffith has been increasingly directed towards a country market, although she's as much a contemporary folk singer-songwriter as anything else, and has attracted such decidedly rock fans as Paul Westerberg.

Such separation of performers into folk or non-folk categories approaches arbitrariness at times, which is unfortunate. Contemporary folk continues to produce interesting performers and songwriters that share rock's impulse to reflect and affect the times we live in, although it will often be necessary to check out the folk circuit and the specialized programming of non-commercial and college radio stations to find them.

Recommended Recordings

Various Artists, *The Sounds of the South* (Atlantic). A four-CD box set of field recordings made by premier folklorist Alan Lomax in 1959, this captures the wide variety of American southern folk traditions, white and Black, in about as authentic a context as modern times allow, including Black gospel, white spirituals, Appalachian music, rural blues, and traditional children's songs.

Woody Guthrie, *The Greatest Songs of Woody Guthrie* (Vanguard). Guthrie has many discs available; this 23-song collection has the most famous ones, and is thus the best starting point, though *Dust Bowl Ballads* was the album that specifically inspired Bob Dylan more than any other.

The Weavers, *Weavers at Carnegie Hall* (Vanguard). Their 1955 comeback concert from their McCarthy-imposed hiatus, unfettered by the orchestration that appears on some of their hits.

Various Artists, *Troubadours of the Folk Era, Vols. 1, 2, & 3* (Rhino). Encompassing Woody Guthrie, Pete Seeger, the Weavers, and the Kingston Trio up through '60s singer-songwriters like Tim Hardin, Richard Farina, Fred Neil, and Buffy Sainte-Marie, this is the best delineation of folk's evolution from traditional to modern forms.

Peter, Paul & Mary, *Peter, Paul & Mary* (Warner Brothers). Sounds dated now, but this was the act with the soaring harmonies that was responsible for popularizing folk in the early '60s more than any other, and the first to bring Dylan to the attention of a mass audience via their covers of "Blowin' in the Wind" and other songs.

Joan Baez, *First Ten Years* (Vanguard). Both traditional and contemporary folk material recorded by Baez during the 1960s, remaining her most influential work.

Dave Van Ronk, *Inside Dave Van Ronk* (Fantasy). A CD repackage of two early '60s albums by this gruff and moving acoustic interpreter of traditional blues and folk, whose impassioned delivery was a big influence on Dylan, among others.

Bob Dylan, *Freewheelin' Bob Dylan* (Columbia). Plenty of Bob Dylan albums have a strong folk influence, but this was the one which established his territory as a contemporary songwriter and performer.

Ian & Sylvia, *Greatest Hits* (Vanguard). This Canadian duo played a large, if somewhat unheralded role, in updating traditional folk and paving the way for folk-rock by being among the first to cover material by Dylan and Gordon Lightfoot, as well as using bass on their recordings, and writing strong material of their own, like "You Were on My Mind." Their wide repertoire of original and traditional material, as well as their blend of male and female harmonies, was an overlooked influence on the Jefferson Airplane, the Mamas & the Papas, and Fairport Convention.

Judy Collins, *No. 3* (Elektra). Another overlooked link from folk to folk-rock, this 1963 album mixed standards with covers of material by Dylan, Bob Gibson, Pete Seeger, and Shel Silverstein. Future Byrd Jim McGuinn contributed arrangements, second guitar, and banjo, and may have gotten the idea to revamp Seeger's "Turn! Turn! Turn!" (which was a No. 1 hit for the Byrds in 1966) from Collins, who recorded a fine version on this LP.

John Fahey, *Return of the Repressed* (Rhino). A master of the acoustic guitar, Fahey twisted blues and folk with an adventurous spirit and irreverence that anticipated the innovations of psychedelic rock. This is a double CD of selections from his huge catalog, spanning the late 1950s to the mid-1980s.

Phil Ochs, *Chords of Fame* (A&M). Double-LP compilation of the best acoustic and electric work by the finest topical songwriter of the '60s, at ease in both folk and rock settings.

The Holy Modal Rounders, *The Moray Eels Eat the Holy Modal Rounders* (Elektra). Greenwich village folkies Peter Stampfel and Steve Weber were determined to take acoustic traditional music to its most bizarre limits, and were a chief inspiration for the Fugs (on whose albums the Rounders sometimes played). This late '60s album is perhaps the ultimate psychedelic folk fusion, and while not for everybody (certainly not for traditionalists), is a humorous and vibrant example of the '60s folk scene at its most wacked-out.

Mary McCaslin, *The Best of Mary McCaslin* (Rounder). Not a household name by any means, McCaslin was one of several outstanding folk-based contemporary singer-songwriters to emerge during the '70s, along with Kate Wolf, the McGarrigle Sisters, and several others. This album was selected because she is arguably the most accessible of these to rock listeners, and because she has recorded some of the best Beatle covers with folk arrangements.

Nanci Griffith, *The Last of the True Believers* (Philo). Perhaps the most widely known songwriter of recent years with clear roots in traditional American folk music, her major label albums have been more country-oriented than this 1986 recording, her last before signing with MCA.

Freakwater, *Dancing Underwater* (Thrill Jockey). Featuring Eleventh Dream Day drummer/singer Janet Bean (who primarily plays guitar with Freakwater), this acoustic side project, with Appalachian overtones and close country harmonies, is proof that post-punk alternative rockers can draw upon American folk traditions with conviction. This CD includes both the 1991 album *Dancing Underwater* and their starker, self-titled 1989 debut.

Books

Bringing It All Back Home, by Robbie Wolliver (1986, Pan-theon)

Dylan, by Anthony Scaduto (1971, Grosset & Dunlap)

Death of a Rebel: A Biography of Phil Ochs, by Marc Eliot (1989, Franklin Watts)

—Richie Unterberger

British Isles Folk Music

Since the British began to colonize North America, the indigenous folk music of the British Isles has been a notable factor in American folk music, informing the development of Appalachian and southern folk sounds and thus, by extension, country and rock. Rock wouldn't really feel the direct influence of British folk until the mid-'60s, though, and then primarily on its native soil, although hybrids of British folk and contemporary rock enjoy a strong cult in the US.

In the early '60s, Britain had a traditional folk scene that was comparable to the United States in its strength, though it was smaller. Both communities were increasingly straightjacketed by an overly insular and reverent attitude that demanded traditional instrumentation and interpretation—demands that seemed increasingly stultifying as contemporary society grew increasingly turbulent and electric. The emergence of Bob Dylan, a performer who wrote his own songs and directly commented on the here and now, was welcomed as much in the UK as the US; he toured Britain several times in the early and mid-'60s, and even his acoustic albums were Top Ten sellers.

Dylan himself had been influenced by British Isles folk, as he had been by most kinds of folk music; indeed, the top Irish traditional band, the Clancy Brothers, were pals of Dylan's in his Greenwich Village days. Dylan had also learned some tunes from British guitarist Martin Carthy (he adapted one of them for "Girl from the North Country"), a seminal figure in preserving and arranging tunes from the British folk heritage, and one who remains very much a figurehead of the British folk scene up to the present.

It wasn't long before Britain had produced an answer of sorts to Bob Dylan in Donovan, who made his mark (and even had a few hits) with acoustic material in 1965 before moving into pop-psychedelia. The Scottish singer has been unfairly disparaged by those who remember him primarily as a blissed-out hippie that couldn't match the sophistication of Dylan; his early work was quite bound in British folk, and his earliest albums are littered with old British folk songs made relevant to the day's young generation with lively interpretations.

The earliest records of British folkies of the era like Shirley Collins and Martin Carthy hardly sound groundbreaking several decades later, but they were important in how they opened up the British folk reper-

toire to imaginative interpretations instead of ossifications. Carthy's influence indirectly extended to the masses when Paul Simon moved to Britain for about a year in the mid-'60s, before Simon & Garfunkel had taken off. Carthy taught Simon "Scarborough Fair," which became one of S&G's most popular early tracks.

Simon learned another of his popular early album tracks, "Anji," from guitarist Davey Graham. Though he wasn't much of a vocalist, Graham was vastly influential in synthesizing and extending various traditional folk styles into something new and progressive, though still acoustic, blending blues, folk, jazz, and Middle Eastern music. A more widely heralded British guitarist was Bert Jansch, also a talented songwriter and singer, whose early recordings were reminiscent of the early efforts of fellow Scotsman Donovan. Jansch's presence was also felt on the rock world via his impact on the styles of Neil Young and Jimmy Page, both of whom have cited Jansch as an important influence.

Jansch began recording as a solo artist, but would soon team up with guitarist John Renbourn to form Pentangle. While Pentangle used almost exclusively acoustic instrumentation, they performed, wrote, and interpreted with an energy and flexible imagination that was unquestionably derived, at least in part, from rock, making them one of Britain's greatest folk-rock hybrids. Though they peaked early, it's no exaggeration to note that the talented ensemble were a Beatles of sorts in how their different but complementary talents expanded British folk into uncharted horizons, drawing from jazz, blues, and classical as well as rock.

The British folk community was certainly aware of psychedelia, and though you wouldn't find its performers using mellotrons and backwards tapes, the influence was reflected in their willingness to expand its boundaries and incorporate more adventurous lyrics, arrangements (sometimes electric), and instruments. The most psychedelic-oriented of the British folk acts were the Incredible String Band, a duo of colorful Scotsmen who acted as psychedelic minstrels of sorts with their whimsical songs and unpredictable combinations of sounds, though they remained largely acoustic-based.

For many listeners, the foremost exponents of British folk-rock were Fairport Convention. Starting out as a straight folk-rock group, the group began to veer towards more and more traditional material without altering their forceful electric guitars and rhythm section. Their 1969 album *Liege and Lief* was perhaps the ultimate fusion between electric rock instrumentation and traditional British folk. Equally important, the group acted as the springboard for an astounding range of spin-offs that came to dominate the British folk-rock scene, including Fotheringay, Steeleye Span, the Albion Band, and the solo careers of Richard Thompson, Sandy Denny, and Ian Matthews.

The early half of the 1970s was probably the golden age of British folk-rock. Fairport Convention and their spin-offs, as well as groups like Lindisfarne and the Strawbs, not only continued to electrify British folk fundamentals, but were actually quite commercially successful in the UK, landing several albums in the Top Ten. Their repertoire varied from heavily traditional to mostly self-penned, sharing a general commitment to, as a member of Steeleye Span once said, "put traditional music back into current musical language—to make folk music less esoteric." And this wasn't a scene limited to the young upstarts; veterans Shirley Collins and Martin Carthy showed up for a time in the Albion Band and Steeleye Span. Nick Drake and the solo recordings of Richard Thompson owe more to the singer-songwriter tradition than traditional British Isles fare, but their work did reflect its influence, Thompson's much more so than Drake.

These bands never made it big in the States, although several achieved enough underground acclaim and FM radio exposure to tour there. By the late '70s, they were no longer stars at home, but the musicians, whether they stuck with their bands or headed to other projects, maintained a fairly solid audience.

The British folk-rock scene wasn't moribund as an artistic force, reviving in the 1980s under the banner of "rogue folk." Due to the efforts of Britain's *Folk Roots* magazine and others, appreciation of acoustic and roots music in the UK began to rise. In the mid-'80s, several bona fide stars emerged: the Pogues infused Irish traditional folk with punk energy, and Billy Bragg delivered articulate political and social commentary using (on his early records, at least) little more than a guitar. Bragg's guitar was electric, though, and his rough-hewn attitudes and vocals marked him as a clear product of the post-punk revolution, though he was also a folk troubadour in the best sense of that tradition.

There were other acclaimed "rogue folk" performers that combined folk traditions with modern (often electric) instruments and attitudes, most of whom (unlike Bragg or the Pogues) remain virtually unknown in the States. Scottish guitarist Dick Gaughan sang both traditional material and contemporary political fare, and songwriter Leon Rosselson has been compared to Phil Ochs. The Oyster Band drew from traditional material and contemporary political commentary in their rock-influenced modern folk dance music. In the United States, a society somewhat more removed in everyday life from acoustic musical traditions than the British or Irish, these artists will probably never achieve much more than college and community radio exposure. American bands that actually follow the British folk-rock mold are quite rare; Boiled in Lead, from Minneapolis, is the only one to attain even a modest level of recognition.

On the commercial airwaves, however, you can hear the strains—usually indirect, sometimes fairly evident—of Irish traditional music in that country's most successful rock stars, like Van Morrison, Sinead O'Connor, and U2. The Levellers, stars in the UK and thus far a flop stateside, derive much of their influence from British traditional music. And performers from British folk-rock's most successful phase, such as Richard Thompson and June Tabor, continue to record and tour to considerable acclaim in their middle age.

Recommended Recordings

Donovan, *Spotlight on Donovan* (Pye, UK). Donovan's early mid-'60s acoustic recordings are frustratingly scattered and haphazardly reissued; this double-LP import is the best collection, though it's getting harder to find.

Davey Graham, *Folk Blues and All Points in Between* (See For Miles, UK). A reissue of the eclectic guitarist's groundbreaking 1965 album, with additional bonus cuts from the best of his late '60s recordings.

Bert Jansch, *Bert Jansch/Jack Orion* (Demon/Transatlantic, UK). His first and third albums, from the mid-'60s, combined onto a double CD, demonstrate his facility with both original and traditional material.

The Incredible String Band, *The Hangman's Beautiful Daughter* (Rykodisc). This 1967 album was the ISB's most acclaimed effort. Those looking for a wide-ranging sampler should try to find the two-record *Relics* compilation.

The Pentangle, *Sweet Child* (Reprise). This late-'60s double set, a mixture of studio and live material, is only given the nod because of its length and variety; their self-titled debut and *Basket of Light* are equally worthy.

Fairport Convention, *Liege and Lief* (Hannibal). Not their best album—their previous, more rock-oriented efforts, *What We Did on Our Holidays* and *Unhalfbricking*, were better—but in terms of rock and British folk fusion, this was their most influential. Or, for a compilation with greater breadth, try to find *Chronicles*.

Sandy Denny, *Who Knows Where the Time Goes* (Hannibal). Three-CD box set of Britain's finest folk-rock singer, featuring both solo tracks and performances with Fairport Convention, the Strawbs, and Fotheringay.

Richard Thompson, *Watching the Dark* (Hannibal). Another three-CD compilation, including solo work and cuts with Fairport and his ex-wife Linda.

Steeleye Span, *The Steeleye Span Story: Original Masters* (Chrysalis). Getting harder to find, but this double album is the widest-spanning collection of a prolific group that changed personnel quite a few times.

Clannad, *Clannad* (Boot, Canada). Most of this famous Irish group's releases have leaned towards either the traditional or the pop; on this overlooked 1973 debut, they came off as a sort of Irish Pentangle. Has been issued on different labels, depending upon which country has a copy to be found.

Billy Bragg, *Back to Basics* (Elektra). A compilation of his first two albums, as well as an early EP. Bragg subsequently added fuller rock arrangements without diluting his integrity, but these initial tracks—many only featuring him and his electric guitar—are the recordings most closely tied to British folk sounds.

The Pogues, *Rum, Sodomy & the Lash* (MCA). Their second album, produced by Elvis Costello, blends punk and Irish folk without compromising either form, and includes their best-known tune, a cover of Ewan MacColl's "Dirty Old Town."

The Oyster Band, *From Little Rock to Leipzig* (Rykodisc). With quite a few albums to their credit, it's hard to single out one as the best starting point. This live outing was chosen because it includes versions of material from several of their releases.

The Chieftains, *Long Black Veil* (RCA). The foremost Irish traditional folk band performs folk, pop, and country & western with the Rolling Stones, Sting, Ry Cooder, Marianne Faithfull, Sinead O'Connor, Tom Jones, Mick Jagger, and Van Morrison. In 1988, Morrison recorded an entire album of traditional Irish songs with the Chieftains, *Irish Heartbeat* (Mercury).

June Tabor, *Against the Stream* (Green Linnet). Britain's most acclaimed contemporary folk singer interprets traditional tunes and songs by Richard Thompson and her big fan, Elvis Costello, on this elegantly subdued and moody 1994 record, demonstrating the continued flexibility of modern British folk.

Various Artists, *Troubadours of British Folk Vol. 1-3* (Rhino). Excellent three-volume survey of British folk and folk-rock from the 1950s through the 1980s, from its traditional roots through its electrification, with key cuts from almost all of its major performers (Fairport Conven-

tion, Steeleye Span, Pentangle, the Incredible String Band, Richard Thompson, Nick Drake, Billy Bragg, Oyster Band, etc.)

—Richie Unterberger

Reggae

No form of popular music from the third world has made as much of an international impact as reggae. It has borrowed from rock 'n' roll, and rock in turn has borrowed from it, but it remains a minority, specialty taste for much of the rock audience. That's nothing for reggae proponents to be ashamed of; that the tiny island of Jamaica has produced a wealth of musicians that affected the course of international rock and pop music is astounding.

Reggae had its beginnings in the late '50s, when Jamaican popular musicians combined their indigenous folk music with jazz, African and Caribbean rhythms, and New Orleans rhythm & blues to come up with a music of their own, ska. An oft-repeated folk legend has it that the frenetic, offbeat rhythm was created when islanders listened to New Orleans R&B stations on their transistor radios, the static garbling the rhythms so much that the musicians bastardized the sound into something else altogether when they tried to imitate it. Most likely that's a fanciful tale, but there's no doubt that R&B, particularly the New Orleans variety, was a dominant influence on early ska, and that the ska rhythm never quite locked into a reproduction of its inspiration.

Ska was a relentlessly joyous and upbeat music, finding great popularity not only in Jamaica, but in Britain, which had a large West Indian population. Lots of ska records were imported and licensed for release in Britain, and some British-based musicians recorded ska of their own. One of these productions, Millie Small's "My Boy Lollipop," became a huge hit in both the UK and the US in 1964, bringing ska to an international audience, and remaining—incredibly—one of the very best-selling Jamaican discs ever. This single was produced by white Jamaican expatriate Chris Blackwell, whose label, Island, licensed and produced many ska singles in the '60s, and would be instrumental in exposing reggae to a worldwide audience over the next few decades.

By 1966, the hyper rhythms of ska began to give way to the slower, loping beats of rocksteady. Dreamy and ideal for romantic dancing, harmonies (which had often been a prominent ingredient of ska already) came to the forefront, and the squeaky, jazzy horns that characterized ska were muted and pushed down in the mix. It's obvious from the passionate vocals on classic rocksteady that Jamaican performers of this era were heavily attuned to American soul, as heavy echoes of Motown, Memphis, and harmonizing R&B groups are obvious in the recordings.

Reggae, as much Jamaican popular music came to be known at the end of the 1960s, embellished the bedrock rhythms of ska and rocksteady with political and social lyrics, often informed by Rastafarianism, racial pride, and the turbulent Jamaican political climate. The rhythms ebbed and flowed with the hypnotic, jerky pulse that has become reggae's most identifiable trademark, and the bass and choppy rhythm tracks became not just prominent, but dominant. For many fans, this is reggae's golden age, as many of the music's greatest legends emerged or cut their prime work during this period, including Toots & the Maytals, Burning Spear, and above all the Wailers. The Wailers' Bob Marley would become reggae's towering figure, revered in many Third World countries with a zeal on par with American and British fanaticism for the Beatles; fellow Wailers Peter Tosh and Bunny Wailer also established influential solo careers.

The influence of reggae was felt in rock almost immediately, but usually surfaced as a tangential reference in some stars' isolated songs. The early Beatles song "I Call Your Name," for instance, has a ska break; a few years later, they would appropriate the reggae rhythm for "Ob-La-Di, Ob-La-Da." Jamaican singer Jackie Edwards wrote a few ska-flavored rock-soul hits for the Spencer Davis Group, "Keep on Running" and "Somebody Help Me"; Paul Simon, never one to let a good ethnic sound pass unnoticed, put a reggae beat behind one of his first solo hits, "Mother and Child Reunion." Paul McCartney went full-tilt into reggae on his early solo track "C Moon," and Eric Clapton had a No. 1 hit with his cover of Bob Marley's "I Shot the Sheriff." Stevie Wonder sometimes flirted with reggae rhythms, as on his hit "Boogie on Reggae Woman." But aside from Johnny Nash, a Texan soul singer who actually did some recording in Jamaica and landed big hits with reggae-soul concoctions like "Hold Me Tight," "I Can See Clearly Now," and Marley's "Stir It Up," hardly any rock or soul performers made reggae an integral component of their work.

Occasionally reggae performers would cross over to the rock and pop audience, as with Jimmy Cliff's "Wonderful World, Beautiful People," and Desmond Dekker's "The Israelites," but international reggae hits remained a rare phenomenon. When artists like the Wailers began to get wide international distribution in the early and mid-'70s (usually on Island), the music garnered a sizable cult following on both sides of the Atlantic, primarily with white audiences. Reggae's greatest attributes—its spare power, its outspoken (sometimes militant) commentary on politics, class strife, and religion, its idiosyncratic production flourishes—may also have been what kept it from gaining anything close to the commercial foothold enjoyed by rock and soul.

Reggae itself continued to evolve, not always in accordance with the preferences of its overseas audience. The operators of mobile "sound systems" in Jamaica had often embellished their presentations with voiceovers, and this was eventually practiced in the studio as the art of DJing or toasting, wherein the artist chanted, rhymed, and expounded over a musical backing track. There was also dub music, which erased vocals and stripped tracks to their bones of bass and rhythm, over which all manner of strange and wonderful echo, reverb, and miscellaneous sound effects were overlaid to create spacy and pulsating instrumentals.

Towards the end of the 1970s, reggae's influence made itself felt on a couple of the era's rock and R&B trends. Punk and new wave performers were often big reggae fans, particularly in Britain; the West Indian population was much larger there than in the US, and punks felt a kinship with their struggles as an oppressed minority. The Clash sometimes used reggae rhythms and production touches, even enlisting top dub reggae artist Lee Perry to produce some tracks, and punk bands like the Slits incorporated reggae signatures into their music. Top new wave bands Blondie, and more particularly the Police, built some of their hits around watered-down reggae flourishes. British reggae group Steel Pulse built its following by playing punk venues, and Bob Marley himself encouraged the alliance with a British single, "Punky Reggae Party." The Ruts (who evolved into Ruts D.C.) blended reggae and punk in the late '70s and early '80s, a fusion which the Bad Brains would also attempt throughout the 1980s. In the early '80s, producer Adrian Sherwood used early punk musicians like the Slits, Public Image Ltd., the Raincoats, and the Pop Group to enhance his edgy, hard-to-classify excursions into dub reggae with the New Age Steppers.

At the tail end of the '70s, Britain experienced an all-out ska revival. Bands like the Specials, Madness, the Selecter, and the English Beat enjoyed huge popularity at home—and cult popularity in the US—with their hybrid of ska and new wave. Sometimes called the Two-Tone sound (in honor of the label on which many of the bands appeared), this brand of ska-cum-rock is still kicking today, albeit on a much smaller level.

In the United States around this time, young African-Americans—by and large in New York, home to a fairly large Jamaican community—began to build upon the DJs and toasters to come up with their own stream-of-consciousness poems. The connection between reggae and rap has never gotten a lot of attention, but there's no doubt that reggae contributed to the genesis of what became the most flamboyant African-American music of the 1980s and '90s. Of course, the backing tracks of American rap are usually harsher and starker than reggae, and with isolated exceptions like Shinehead, few have tried to bridge the styles, perhaps because reggae never had an appreciable audience among American Blacks.

With the death of Bob Marley in 1981, as well as the murder of Peter Tosh in 1987, many listeners feel that the golden age of reggae has gone forever. It continues to thrive in Jamaica, where more records are released per capita than any other country in the world. DJ and toasting has produced the spin-off dancehall, which has a more electronic-driven rhythm and, sometimes, risqué or "slack" vocals and lyrics. Reggae itself continues to exert a tangential influence on rock and pop—many stars from the Rolling Stones down have occasionally appropriated reggae rhythms, top Jamaican rhythm section Sly & Robbie guest on albums by major figures like Bob Dylan, and reggae-pop hybrids like UB40 and Aswad even have chart success with pop-conscious adaptations of reggae sounds.

Recommended Recordings

Various Artists, *Tougher than Tough: The Story of Jamaican Music* (Mango). This four-disc box set documents the evolution of reggae from its beginnings to the present, from ska and rocksteady up through dub and dancehall. Of course no box set can cover the music definitively, and this one doesn't claim to, but it's the best retrospective of reggae as a whole, including tracks by most of its major performers.

Various Artists, *Scandal Ska* (Mango). Because it was a soundtrack tie-in to a movie about the 1963 British Profumo scandal, this superb anthology was pretty much ignored by critics. It's probably the best introductory ska sampler, though, with early-'60s sides by Jimmy Cliff, Bob Marley, Desmond Dekker, Laurel Aitken, Ernest Ranglin, Roland Alphonso, and others.

Alton & Hortense Ellis (Heartbeat). There are more wide-ranging rocksteady anthologies available, but this collection of late-'60s sides, featuring solo performances by one of Jamaica's premier vocalists (Alton) and his much less famous but similarly talented sister (Hortense), is enchanting romantic music that makes clear the influence of American '60s soul on reggae.

Johnny Nash, *The Reggae Collection* (Epic/Legacy). 20-track collection spanning the late '60s to the mid-'70s, focusing on the reggae-inspired work of the first (and, still, one of the few) musicians to fuse rock and

soul with reggae for commercial success. Includes the big hits and several less famous songs.

Bob Marley, *Legend* (Tuff Gong). 14 of his most famous tracks. If you want to dig deeper after this, there are many albums to choose from; the Wailers' *Burnin'* and *Catch a Fire* are the most celebrated single LPs, and the four-CD box *Songs of Freedom* the most extensive career retrospective.

Various Artists, *The Harder They Come* (Island). This cult film deserved a lot of credit for introducing worldwide audiences to reggae, both via its gritty picture of Jamaican culture and its top-notch soundtrack, which featured music by Jimmy Cliff (who starred in the film as well), the Maytals, the Melodians, Desmond Dekker, and others.

Toots & the Maytals, *Funky Kingston* (Mango). The most acclaimed album by Toots Hibbert, widely acknowledged as reggae's most soulful singer.

Lee Perry, *The Greatest* (Mango). Vintage productions by dub's top exponent, featuring the Heptones, Junior Murvin, Max Romeo, Prince Jazzbo, and Perry himself. Those looking to go deeper should look for *The Upsetter Compact Set;* actually issued under the name of Perry's studio band, the Upsetters, this is a three-CD package of some of his best work.

Burning Spear, *Marcus Garvey* (Mango). The mid-'70s record that brought them international attention remains one of reggae's most powerful album-length statements.

Various Artists, *The Best of Punky Reggae* (Rhino). 17-track anthology illustrates the cross-fertilization of punk and reggae, with tracks by Patti Smith, Graham Parker, Devo, Pere Ubu, Blondie, Steel Pulse, the Specials, Selecter, the English Beat, UB40, Madness, Keith Levene, and others. Missing influential cuts by the Clash and Bob Marley, presumably because of licensing hurdles.

Various Artists, *Two Tone Compilation: A Checkered Past* (Chrysalis). Double CD of the best tracks from the premier British ska-revival label, including hits by the Specials, the English Beat, Madness, the Selecter, and various spinoffs.

Various Artists, *Inna Reggae Style* (EMI). Not one of the greatest reggae albums of all time, it's included on this list because it illustrates connections between rock and reggae with covers of rock and soul songs by reggae performers like Peter Tosh, the Heptones, and Toots & the Maytals, reggae cuts by rock acts like Blondie and Boy George, pop-reggae hybrids by Aswad, the English Beat, and Third World, and a duet between Peter Tosh and Mick Jagger.

Shinehead, *Unity* (Elektra). The 1988 debut by one of the few performers to successfully bridge reggae with rap.

Divination, *Ambient Dub Vol. 1 & 2* (Subharmonic) Bassist Bill Laswell is the heaviest contributor to these explorations by top experimental rock musicians into dub music, twisting it into more sinister and electronic forms.

Various Artists, *Mash up the Place—The Best of Reggae Dancehall* (Rhino). There are a lot of reggae dancehall compilations; Rhino gets the nod because, typically, it provides the most cohesive and informative packaging. Includes tracks by Shabba Ranks, Ninja Man, Macka B, and others.

—Richie Unterberger

Worldbeat

What "worldbeat" is depends to some degree on who you're asking for a definition, but in general it could be said to refer to contemporary music produced from outside of mainstream American and European rock and pop forms, often incorporating rock, pop, and modern technology into indigenous traditional music. It could be argued that worldbeat has been around as long as rock 'n' roll, or even much longer, but it wasn't until the beginning of the 1980s that world music began to exert a significant influence on Western rock culture.

Western pop has never been closed to music from other climes; many Latin artists enjoyed significant success in the United States from the time hit parades first began to be published. In the early days of rock, Jamaican calypso singer Harry Belafonte was hugely popular; slightly later, South African vocalist Miriam Makeba enjoyed similar success, and bossa nova performers like Astrud Gilberto had big international hits. If you're determined to locate specific traces of world music in rock 'n' roll, you can find them: calypso (Mickey & Sylvia), Latin dance rhythms (the Drifters), Mexican music (Ritchie Valens, early surf instrumentals), Middle Eastern wailing (Gene Pitney's "Mecca").

More direct influences from other shores began to filter into the music in the mid-'60s, around the time that rock started to take itself seriously as an art form. Indian music, particularly the kind associated with the sitar, made a strong impact on the Beatles' mid-'60s recordings, especially George Harrison's compositions. The Byrds, Donovan, the Rolling Stones, and several San Francisco psychedelic groups also made memorable use of the sitar and/or Indian-inspired ragas and melodic lines. With his appearance at the Monterey Pop Festival in 1967, Ravi Shankar became one of the first world musicians to gain a large chunk of the rock audience. In other realms, Simon & Garfunkel, 20 years before it would become fashionable, openly acknowledged the influence of Bulgarian traditional vocals. The Rolling Stones' Brian Jones became fascinated by Moroccan music, recording an album of trance music in the country, and some of the rhythms filtered onto the Stones' controversial *Their Satanic Majesties Request*. Of all the '60s bands, Californian psychedelic-folk-rock group Kaleidoscope were the most proficient at blending Middle Eastern influences into their sound frequently and successfully; their extended jams "Taxim" and "Seven-Ate Sweet" are among the most exciting fusions of Middle Eastern melody and rock energy ever recorded.

Still, throughout the '60s and '70s, most of the rock audience remained unaware of worldbeat, and most rock performers were immune to its influence. This was not because of willful ignorance, but because the music was simply unavailable to most people. The Nonesuch label issued a lot of fine ethnic music recordings, and the explosion of reggae's popularity increased a lot of people's general awareness of music from the Third World, but very few contemporary world music albums were widely distributed in the US (European consumers had somewhat better access to it, especially in Paris, with its large African population).

The conditions did not hold in reverse: the West didn't hear much world music, but the rest of the world heard a lot of Western rock and soul. It had a great impact on musicians from Africa, Brazil, Asia, and other regions, who in turn were not so much inspired to imitate it as borrow from it. What this usually meant was electrifying the instrumentation, adding danceable rhythms, and performing material that addressed a wide range of contemporary concerns (though romance, as in the West, would always be a big topic). Traditional material, melodies, and instruments remained vital ingredients, to varying degrees.

African performers were the first "worldbeat" acts to attract attention, largely in the rock press and alternative/underground community at first. Cameroon's Manu Dibango paved the way with "Soul Makossa," a fluke hit from the early '70s that was also one of the first disco smashes. Fela, from Nigeria, also made a stir with his incendiary brand of funk, and King Sunny Ade catapulted African pop to a new level of recognition with his bubbling, irrepressible highlife. Of course, lumping all of these stars together into a genre is about as appropriate as lumping together the Rolling Stones, the Steve Miller Band, and James Brown; Africa is a huge continent, with an infinite assortment of distinct regional styles. These African stars, however, opened Western ears to a flood of contemporary African pop performers that remains unabated in the mid-'90s; Youssou N'Dour, Ali Farka Toure, Alpha Blondy, Baaba Maal, Angelique Kidjo, and Thomas Mapfumo are just a few of the better-known ones.

South African performers in particular received a good deal of attention after adding much of the flavor to Paul Simon's 1985 megasmash, *Graceland*. Simon was criticized in some quarters for diluting African music, not to mention defying a United Nations decree against recording in South Africa, but there's no question that it opened a lot of ears to previously unheard music by groups like Ladysmith Black Mambazo, who provided many of the album's backup vocals. The South African compilation *The Indestructible Beat of Soweto* made a lot of rock critics' best-of lists, and adventurous listeners were incited to seek out further recordings by other groups from the country, such as Mahlathini and the Mahotella Queens.

Another brand of world music to make an unexpected splash with rock audiences in the 1980s was traditional Bulgarian vocal music, as performed by the Bulgarian State Radio and Television Choir, operating under the *nom de plume* Le Mystère des Voix Bulgares. Touring Europe and North America to great acclaim, their albums actually landed in the Top 200. A left-field hit of even bigger dimensions was scored in 1994 by the Benedictine Monks of Santo Domingo, whose collection of Gregorian Chants went all the way to the Top 20. Less exotic, perhaps, but probably hardly any less expected, was the huge success of Spain's Gipsy Kings, who updated flamenco music into more modern hybrids.

These are just the most successful imports, of course. Zouk, the Israeli pop of Ofra Haza, soca, the Brazilian pop of Gilberto Gil and Caetano Veloso, Astor Piazolla's tangos, Nusrat Fateh Ali Khan, Tuvan throat singers, Indian/Anglo bhangra beat, and lots of other music, way too numerous to summarize in a brief article such as this—all have made big inroads into the Western audience, usually with listeners schooled in rock backgrounds. Large independent companies like Shanachie, Globestyle, and Rykodisc did a great deal to distribute the music in the US and UK; major labels had subsidiaries that specialized in worldbeat releases, such as Mango.

Despite the exceptions listed in the above paragraph, the music did not assume a commercial presence equal to rock, rap, or soul. Foreign language lyrics and non-Western pop structures and rhythms are, and may remain, a large barrier to making world music as successful with the masses as it is with the critics, although it now enjoys one of the largest and most rapidly expanding specialty markets in the industry. A reflection of listeners' increasing tendencies to embrace a more eclectic, multicultural assortment of music, the popularity of world music is also an underrated factor in heightening the prospects for global cooperation and world peace as we prepare to enter the environmental, technological, and sociopolitical chaos of the 21st century.

World music hasn't exerted a deep influence on contemporary rock 'n' roll, although it's become much more common to hear African rhythms or find guest appearances by noted musicians from the third world on rock albums. Occasionally, though, rock stars have borrowed from world music quite heavily—Simon, of course, but also David Byrne, Grateful Dead percussionist Mickey Hart, Dead Can Dance, and Peter Gabriel, who tirelessly champions the real thing via the WOMAD organization and the extensive roster of world music performers on his Real World label. Much in the manner that British Invasion bands were accused of ripping off Black blues and soul artists for a lot of their ideas, these performers are sometimes snubbed for presenting world music in a much more profitable, pop-ready package. A humorous Drew Friedman cartoon a few years ago aptly satirized the situation by presenting Paul Simon and David Byrne, tape recorders in hand, bumping into each other in the deepest depths of the jungle, each searching for suitable ethnic rhythms to plagiarize before the other found them.

Like those old British bands, though, Simon and Byrne are indirectly leading many listeners to the source; and like those old British bands, they aren't exactly making a big secret of their influences. These sources, like old blues records, are more widely available today than ever before. Putting together a list of 15 recommended world music recordings is about as impossible a task as summarizing the Bible in a two-hour movie; the records below should not be treated as an encapsulation of the best world music, but as suggested highlights, illustrations of links between worldbeat and rock, and starting points to an infinite body of work.

Recommended Recordings

Various Artists, *Africa Dances* (Original Music). One of the first widely available compilations of African dance music, this collection, encompassing several regions and spanning the 1950s to the 1970s, displays the roots of today's African pop, as well as being highly enjoyable in its own right.

Joseph Spence, *Happy All the Time* (Carthage). 1964 album by the Bahamian guitarist whose percussive playing and mirthful vocals defied classification, and influenced adventurous rock-oriented guitarists like Ry Cooder and Henry Kaiser.

Hamza El Din, *Music of Nubia* (Vanguard). A Sudanese lute player who was one of the first African musicians to attract wide attention in the West, eventually sharing the stage with the Grateful Dead. This is his 1964 debut.

Kaleidoscope, *Rampe Rampe* (Edsel, UK). The most Middle Eastern-oriented material of the '60s psychedelic band, including their mesmerizing jams "Taxim" and "Seven-Ate Sweet."

Fela Anikulapo Kuti, *Zombie* (Mercury). The father of Afrobeat has dozens of albums; this 1977 recording is one of his most cohesive and most readily available.

The Talking Heads, *Remain in Light* (Sire). With assistance from producer Eno, David Byrne's group recorded one of the first popular rock albums to incorporate Afrobeat rhythms. Byrne delved heavily into Latin and South American music in his solo career, particularly on *Rei Momo*.

King Sunny Ade, *Juju Music* (Mango). The 1982 album that made Ade an international figure.

Various Artists, *The Indestructible Beat of Soweto* (Shanachie). The 1986 compilation of South African music, featuring Ladysmith Black Mambazo, Mahlathini, and others, remains one of the most popular worldbeat releases of all time.

Paul Simon, *Graceland* (Warner Brothers). Whether you love it or not, the most popular album ever released to make extensive use of African rhythms.

Le Mystère des Voix Bulgares, *Le Mystère des Voix Bulgares* (Nonesuch). There are several volumes of this ensemble by now, all consistently beautiful and otherworldly in their polyphonic, multilayered vocals.

The Gipsy Kings, *Gipsy Kings* (Elektra). The 1988 album that broke them in the US market, recommended above subsequent efforts that have tried to broaden their appeal with slicker technology.

Sheila Chandra, *Silk 1983-1990* (Shanachie). As the lead singer of Monsoon and a solo artist, Chandra has been the most successful performer to blend Indian and Western pop-rock music. This compilation was chosen because it draws from several recordings; her approach can vary from dance-pop to traditional to avant-garde. Those seeking the latter should check out her most recent release, 1994's *The Zen Kiss*.

Aisha Kandisha's Jarring Effects, *El Buya* (Barraka El Farnatshi). By far the least well-known album on this list, this Moroccan production from the early '90s is recommended because of its sensational mix of traditional Moroccan music with electronic tweaking, turntable DJing, and dub-like reverb. One of the relatively few African albums that uses modern technology to move indigenous music into new territory without compromising the beauty of the original article in the least.

Dead Can Dance, *Into the Labyrinth* (4AD). Originally affiliated with the gloomy British alternative rock school championed by the 4AD label, they've broadened their approach considerably in the 1990s, incorporating Gregorian chants, European medieval music, and the like so heavily at times that they don't sound like a rock or pop group at all.

Ali Farka Toure & Ry Cooder, *Talking Timbuktu* (Hannibal). From Senegal, Toure is often referred to as the John Lee Hooker of Africa because of his pounding, insistent strumming and vocal phrasing. Although Ry Cooder is co-billed, this is actually much more Toure's show, as the guitarists sympathetically complement each other on a set of material that, from the sound of it, was guided much more by the African than the American.

Books

The Rough Guide to World Music (1994, Rough Guides)
The Virgin Directory to World Music, by Philip Sweeney (1992, Henry Holt)

–Richie Unterberger

Comedy & Rock

Scads of overblown progressive-rock epics aside, rock 'n' roll has always displayed a vivid sense of humor. The humor is usually more subtle than overt, felt in the joy of the singing and instruments, and the celebration of the moment. Often it's quite overt, whether in Chuck Berry and Bo Diddley's narratives about everyday life, the Coasters' jibes about detectives, movies, and teenage gangs, Jan & Dean's goofy little old ladies drag racing in Southern California, the Beatles' obscure B-side lounge lizard cutup "You Know My Name," the Who's fake radio jingles on *The Who Sell Out*, De La Soul's surreal whimsy, and scads of novelty songs from the '50s to the present. Those novelty songs are compiled on many anthologies (there are quite a few collections on the Rhino label alone), or, failing that, the widely syndicated radio show of Dr. Demento (also known as Barry Hansen, one of the leading doo wop experts and rock 'n' roll record collectors alive).

There are relatively few rock acts, however, that base a lengthy and artistically valid career in comedy and satire. It's hard to make good rock 'n' roll music; it's hard to be really, really funny; it's harder still to do both at the same time. The most difficult feat of all, perhaps, is making rock 'n' roll comedy records that stand up to repeated listenings without dating or wearing thin, or indeed even stand up to more than three or four playings before the joke gets stale.

Before rock musicians attempted ambitious, self-consciously satirical works, their trail had been blazed to some extent by non-rock performers of earlier eras. Spike Jones, a brilliant multi-instrumentalist bandleader who lovingly deconstructed and deflated all forms of popular music, is almost universally acknowledged as the most important of these figures. Also influential were Lord Buckley, a jazz beatnik of sorts whose free association ramblings on history were very popular with '60s rock stars when they were coming of age, and Stan Freberg, who, it must be pointed out, directed vicious hatred toward rock 'n' roll in some of his parodies.

The first band to capably combine social satire with rock were the Fugs, formed by Lower East Side New York beat poets Ed Sanders and Tuli Kupferberg. Even more impressively, they managed to take a left-wing perspective and avoid sounding self-important or smug when taking on the CIA, the military-industrial complex, and censorship. Their sexually explicit lyrics were taboo-breaking, but, as Sanders himself admits today, largely juvenile and immature (though it's difficult to resist laughing when they sing cheerily off-key odes to slum goddesses from the Lower East Side). But by and large, their '60s albums, especially their initial pair on the avant-garde ESP label, are still quite ticklish, even if some of the specific issues they were protesting are not in the news anymore (though in a larger sense, the social injustices they were fingering remain very much a part of contemporary life). On their early recordings, the Fugs were aided by New York folkies Peter Stampfel and Steve Weber, who went on to make shambles of folk conventions as the Holy Modal Rounders. Most of their recordings are too shambling to hold up well, but the best, *The Moray Eels Eat the Holy Modal Rounders*, was the greatest bizarrely deluded take on psychedelic folk.

The Mothers of Invention, led by Frank Zappa, were also concerned with social satire, though there are important differences. Unlike the core members of the Fugs, they were accomplished, serious musicians; the issues they satirized tended to be general social conventions, not specific sociopolitical ones; and they simultaneously paid homage to and ripped apart rock 'n' roll genres like love songs and doo wop. Their late-'60s albums on Verve are perhaps the most successful rock satires

ever recorded, losing little or none of their humorous bite when heard in the 1990s; *We're Only in It for the Money*, a vicious send-up of the psychedelic counterculture, is the best album-length concept comedy album of sorts ever produced. While Zappa's early work remains his funniest, he would continue to satirize all manner of sacred cows throughout the rest of his life, in addition to pursuing serious contemporary composition (sometimes doing both at once).

British comedy-rock tended, unsurprisingly, to be droller and subtler, though no less eccentric. The godfather of this genre, Peter Sellers, wasn't a musician exactly, but did record some great musical satires, taking his Shakespearean reading of "A Hard Day's Night" into the British Top 20 in 1965, and even making appearances on tracks by the Hollies and Steeleye Span. Many of his recordings in the '50s and '60s were produced by George Martin, and indeed Martin's association with Sellers helped the Beatles to hit it off with the producer from their very first audition for EMI. The Beatles were great admirers of Sellers and the *Goon Show* radio shows he did with Spike Milligan, and you can hear traces of that humor in their recordings. The Sellers records also required Martin to develop an expertise with sound effects and unusual production methods that served the Beatles well when their recordings became more sophisticated in the late '60s. The Beatles' Christmas records, available only to members of their fan club, were usually sketches that were obviously inspired by the *Goon Show* comic tradition.

The influence of Sellers, the *Goon Show*, and all manner of British music hall and vaudevillian traditions can be heard in a lot of British rock, dating from the Kinks and Syd Barrett to Robyn Hitchcock and XTC (who, of course, recorded an entire psychedelic homage/parody as their alter ego, the Dukes of Stratosphear). The best British comic band, by a long stretch, were the Bonzo Dog Band. Sometimes compared to the Mothers of Invention, their humor was much gentler, if no less side-splitting, and owed more to both vaudevillian traditional jazz and surrealism (their original moniker was the Bonzo Dog Da Da Band, named after the surrealist Dadaist art movement).

The Bonzos were undoubtedly an influence on Monty Python, even working with Pythonites Michael Palin and Terry Jones on a children's TV series shortly before the Pythons premiered their classic show in 1969. Monty Python were themselves sometimes referred to as the Beatles of comedy due to their similar blend of diverse talents into a sum that was bigger than its parts, and towered over everything else in their field. The Beatles were all fans of Monty Python (who frequently used musical bits, rock and otherwise, in their sketches), and in 1978, Python member Eric Idle returned the favor by producing one of the two greatest satirical rock documentaries of all time, *The Rutles* (modeled, obviously, on the Beatle legend). The made-for-TV special starred ex-Bonzo Dog member Neil Innes (in the John Lennon role); Innes also wrote all the brilliant Beatle parodies used on the soundtrack, which itself is perhaps the greatest rock parody ever waxed. All this in turn was a great influence on the other great fake rockumentary, *This Is Spinal Tap*, although the soundtrack to that theatrical release doesn't sound as well on its own as *The Rutles* (although it works brilliantly within the context of the film itself).

There's no parallel in the United States for such a reciprocal relationship between huge rock and comedy stars. One comedy troupe that did plug into a late-'60s countercultural vibe was the Firesign Theatre, who were also quite likely well aware of Zappa's brilliant montages. As has been pointed out elsewhere, the Firesign Theatre were among the few comedians to use the recorded album as their primary vehicle. Their LPs used sound effects and funhouse segues from sketch to sketch with great skill, and their surrealistic (but often quite pointed) observations of contemporary life found a large audience in the rock underground (as did their less subtle peers at the *National Lampoon*, who nonetheless released a brilliant John Lennon parody on one of their albums).

It's all a matter of taste, of course, but one can argue that there haven't been the kind of outstanding symbiotic relationships between rock and comedy in the '80s and '90s as there were in the '60s and '70s. Some of the more notable rock comedians, or comic rockers, depending on how you look at it, would include Mojo Nixon, whose satires on Elvis, MTV VJs, and the like seem to provoke either wild applause or loathing; the Dead Milkmen, the smarmily juvenile punk-new wave smartasses; Gwar, an over-the-top fake metal band whose satire works far better in performance than on record; the Tubes, whose theatrical rock already sounds quite dated, but was quite popular at times; Half Japanese, loony avant-punks that the general rock listener will find infuriatingly irritating; and King Missile (and spin-off Dogbowl), whose wistful but truly demented musings continue the Lower East Side tradition established by the Fugs, minus much of the sociopolitical outrage.

As far as recent rock musicians carrying the banner raised by the Fugs and Zappa long ago, you could turn to Eugene Chadbourne, the experimental guitarist who also skewers all sorts of social institutions from a clever and learned left-wing perspective; he releases too many recordings for his own good, but the best of his work is incisive. The most popular comedy-rock outfit as we go to press are Ween, sometimes compared to Zappa for their accomplished satires of all sorts of social types and most genres of rock music.

They can be pretty juvenile at times, but then again, so could Zappa.

Recommended Recordings

Spike Jones, *Musical Depreciation Revue: The Spike Jones Anthology* (Rhino). There are several worthwhile Jones albums available; as usual, Rhino's double-CD package wins because of its extensive liner notes and the breadth of its coverage.

Lord Buckley, *The Best of Lord Buckley* (Elektra). Not too easy to find, and not as funny as some reviews may lead you to believe, but it was bold for its day, and influential.

Peter Sellers, *A Celebration of Sellers* (EMI). Four-CD box set heavy on the '50s and '60s recordings produced by George Martin, including several Beatles satires.

The Fugs, *Second Album* (Fantasy). Their funniest and most melodic by a wide margin, it includes the classics "Dirty Old Man," "Frenzy," "Kill for Peace," and "Doin' All Right."

The Mothers of Invention, *We're Only in It for the Money* (Rykodisc). The funniest rock satire ever, period.

The Bonzo Dog Band, *The Best of the Bonzo Dog Band* (Rhino). Their first few albums work very well as individual pieces too.

The Beatles, *The Beatles' Christmas Album* (Apple). A compilation of all their fan-club records, mailed only to members in 1971, but widely available as a bootleg ever since. No serious music on these, but a lot of chat and sketches, which grew increasingly elaborate and surrealistic as the '60s progressed.

The Holy Modal Rounders, *The Moray Eels Eat the Holy Modal Rounders* (Elektra). One of the weirdest records of the '60s, which is saying a lot.

Monty Python, *The Instant Monty Python CD Collection* (Virgin). Six CDs, containing eight albums, and it still misses a few of their records. The sketches, of course, work better on film, but the Pythons also devised and recorded a fair amount of material exclusively for record.

The Firesign Theatre, *Don't Crush That Dwarf, Hand Me the Pliers* (Columbia). One of the greatest comedy albums ever, constructed as a marathon late-night flip between TV channels.

The Rutles, *The Rutles* (Rhino). Neil Innes brilliantly parodied all stages of the Beatles' career in song. Get the CD reissue, which has, we kid you not, six bonus tracks heard on the film, but not included on the original LP.

Ween, *Chocolate and Cheese* (Elektra). The most accessible album by the hottest contemporary comedy-rock outfit.

—Richie Unterberger

Spoken Word and Poetry

Many rock performers were attracted to the music in the first place because it provided a means of unconventional artistic expression. It's no surprise, then, that a lot of rock 'n' rollers were similarly fascinated with literature. Just as rock 'n' roll provided an outlet for ideas and emotions that ran against the status quo, so did many authors. When rock 'n' roll lyrics became more self-consciously literary, beginning in the mid-'60s, the influence of many writers and poets was also felt in the music itself. Authors from Homer to Rimbaud have been cited as influences by various songwriters, and it would take at least an entire separate volume to completely examine such threads. As far as an exchange exists between contemporary writers and rock musicians, that can probably be traced to the beat era.

The '50s beats were not rock 'n' roll fans—indeed, their music of choice was jazz, sometimes folk—but their writing evinced a sense of rebellion, waywardness, and personal freedom that appealed to a lot of teenagers and young adults who would become second-generation rock 'n' rollers. Jack Kerouac and Allen Ginsberg were probably the most influential of these beats, both for their writing and personal charisma. Kerouac, ironically, disavowed the hippie generation, but Ginsberg was the type to evolve with the times, and established personal relationships with several notable performers, such as Marianne Faithfull and, especially, Bob Dylan. Dylan was influenced by a lot of musicians and writers, but it's safe to say that Ginsberg (who appears in the Dylan documentaries *Don't Look Back* and *Renaldo and Clara*) was one of the figures who triggered Bob's more ambitious bursts of lyrical free association. Moreover, Ginsberg made guest appearances on a number of rock records, ranging from the extremely obscure early-'80s alternative rock band Start to the Clash, as well as making musical recordings of his own.

Another writer intimate with many of the beats, although he usually is not himself classified as a beat author, is William Burroughs. There may be no other artists who do not sing or play an instrument that have made their presence felt in rock music as much as this ancient, and as of 1997, still-active legend. His novels of the 1950s and 1960s prefigured

the birth of the counterculture, and his 1965 album (featuring readings of passages from his books) circulated around heavyweights like the Beatles and Rolling Stones. His "cut-up" writing and audio techniques influenced the Soft Machine (who took their name from one of his books, and whose original guitarist, David Allen, actually worked on cut-ups with Burroughs in the early '60s) and David Bowie (who wrote some material using the cut-up technique). Burroughs even inadvertently named heavy metal, as the phrase was first lifted from the author and first used in rock by Steppenwolf in their hard rock hit "Born to Be Wild." He's made cameo appearances on recordings by the Soft Machine, Blondie, Ministry, Tom Waits, Kurt Cobain, and others. In the 1990s, producer Hal Willner constructed an album (with some musical arrangements) around Burroughs' readings, as he did around the same time for Allen Ginsberg.

Many notable rock performers had been published writers, or became published writers, including John Lennon, Dylan, Jim Morrison, and Patti Smith. Both Morrison and Smith (on whom Morrison himself was an influence) sometimes included extended spoken-word passages on their actual recordings; Smith's pieces of this sort rank among her most acclaimed work, though Morrison's are generally less well-received. Richard Farina, who formed a fine if not widely heralded folk-rock duo with his wife Mimi (Joan Baez's sister), wrote a novel, *Been Down So Long That It Looks Like Up to Me*, that became a counterculture favorite. The Fugs, older than the typical rock group of the mid-'60s, had their roots in New York's Lower East Side beat scene. Group-mainstays Ed Sanders and Tuli Kupferberg were respected, published poets (and still are), and even set a couple William Blake poems to music on their first album. Leonard Cohen, in a reversal of form, was a poet of international stature before making the first of several esteemed folk-rock albums in the '60s.

It took several Black performers in the 1970s, however, to achieve a truly memorable fusion of music and the power of the spoken word on record. The Last Poets, Gil Scott-Heron, and more obscure performers such as Jayne Cortez voiced the sociopolitical concerns of the African-American, sometimes in a quite militant fashion, against inspired R&B-inflected jazz rhythms. Linton Kwesi Johnson, and other "dub poets" such as Mutabaruka, did the same for Jamaican minorities, using the hypnotic throb of reggae as their backbeat. None of these were "rock" performers per se, but their work would prove vastly influential, as they paved the way for the major African-American popular music of the '80s, rap. (A genre unto its own that owes a great deal, to say the least, to the spoken word, rap is covered in a separate sidebar.)

Like Patti Smith, many punk and post-punk performers were poets and authors; some may well have turned out to be writers had the circumstances been different. John Doe and Exene Cervenka, the (now former) husband-and-wife duo who formed the core of X, met at an alternative writers workshop in Los Angeles. Henry Rollins, the Black Flag singer who has now broadened his audience as the leader of his own band, has published several volumes of his own prose. Jello Biafra, after the Dead Kennedys broke up, became a combination comedian/social commentator/anti-censorship spokesperson, traveling the spoken word/lecture circuit several times since the late '80s. Cervenka, Rollins, and Biafra have all released spoken-word albums on their own.

It's safe to say, though, that none of these spoken-word albums will attain the legendary status of the musical ventures of X, Black Flag, or Dead Kennedys. For one thing, the plain spoken word doesn't lend itself nearly as well to record as music does; or, to phrase it differently, it lends itself better to the printed page, or performance, than tape in most cases.

Another problem is that, unlike Burroughs or Ginsberg, these are musicians, not authors/readers, first. A compelling singer may have a flat spoken delivery; Rollins and Biafra may sound amusing and insightful in print, but can deliver harangues in a fashion that crosses the line from rap to rant when they commit their prose to record. For this reason, compilations of spoken-word performances by musicians (as in the *Giorno Poetry* series), and/or minimal atmospheric musical backing to spoken word pieces, can work better by ensuring more sonic variety and interest.

Popular music, to a great extent, is the poetry of our age, and as long as rock 'n' roll thrives, spoken word will have a presence in the music. Spoken-word performance will rarely be a priority of the major labels, and even less rarely be heard on commercial radio, but small companies such as New Alliance's series and Rhino's Word Beat subsidiary (which plans to release spoken-word material by Robyn Hitchcock) will continue to provide outlets for it.

Recommended Recordings

Jack Kerouac, *The Jack Kerouac Collection* (Rhino). Three-CD set features some musical backing by Steve Allen and jazzmen Al Cohn and Zoot Sims.

Allen Ginsberg, *Holy Soul Jelly Roll: Poems and Songs 1949-1993* (Rhino). Four-CD box covers his career from the '50s to the present, including the epic poem "Howl," collaborations with the Clash and Dylan, and the famous new wave single "Bird Brain."

William Burroughs, *Call Me Burroughs* (Rhino). Originally issued in 1965, this cult album had a wide share of international hipster admirers. Those who prefer some musical variety to spice Burroughs' legendary news announcer style can try the 1990 effort *Dead City Radio,* produced by Hal Willner.

The Last Poets, *Last Poets* (Metrotone). A lot of this prefigures rap, especially the brilliant title track.

Gil Scott-Heron, *The Revolution Will Not Be Televised* (Flying Dutchman). Scott-Heron shares a lot with the Last Poets, though his phrasing is jazzier. He's remained active in the two decades since this 1974 album.

Linton Kwesi Johnson, *Forces of Victory* (Mango). This 1979 album is usually cited as his best.

Various Artists, *Better an Old Demon than a New God* (Giorno Poetry Systems). The Giorno Poetry Systems albums are, to say the least, uneven. Bound to be collector items in the future, they do mix spoken-word performances with tracks by a few leading punk and new wave musicians (who are frequently the speakers as well). This mid-'80s volume has cuts by William Burroughs, Psychic TV, Lydia Lunch, David Johansen, Richard Hell, and Arto Lindsay.

Various Artists, *Neighborhood Rhythms* (Freeway/Rhino). The spoken-word/poetry scene had a fair amount of influence on the L.A. alternative rock community. Not too easy to find these days, this 1984 double album has lots of spoken-word tracks, including performances by Dave Alvin and Exene Cervenka, and is produced more imaginatively than most such sets.

Jello Biafra, *No More Cocoons* (Alternative Tentacles). From 1987, the first of several spoken word releases by the former Dead Kennedys lead singer.

Hakim Bey, *T.A.Z.* (Axiom). One of the most imaginative recent spoken-word projects pits author Bey's readings against trance/world/dub/avant-rock musical backing by Bill Laswell and friends.

—*Richie Unterberger*

Avant-Garde and Contemporary Composition

Until the mid-1960s, avant-garde and contemporary composition had virtually no influence upon rock 'n' roll, or indeed upon any sort of pop music. The opening of its relationship with rock 'n' roll had much to do with changes both in rock itself, and in the kinds of musicians who were making it. The original rock 'n' rollers, whether white or Black, were usually from lower-income backgrounds. Very few of them went to college; many did not finish high school. They may have been committed to the music they were making creatively and spiritually, but they largely viewed their work as entertainment, not art. This is not to say they were any less intelligent or innovative than succeeding generations, but that they formed their music in an age of different expectations.

As it became clear that rock 'n' roll was going to stick around, more and more musicians from educated middle-class backgrounds began to pick up instruments. In their schools and universities, they may have been studying more "respectable" music, but unlike students of previous generations, they had grown up with rock 'n' roll, creating a passion that no discouragement from higher echelons could erase.

Many key figures of the British Invasion—including John Lennon, Keith Richards, Pete Townshend, and members of numerous other fine groups—were art school students before turning professional. They had no less of a feel for pure rock 'n' roll than anyone else, but their background had exposed them to bohemian enclaves and intellectual currents of thought in both art and music. The best of the British Invasion groups were instrumental in turning rock 'n' roll into a more consciously artistic statement that was open to cutting-edge ideas from the art, fashion, literary, and of course non-rock musical worlds.

The Velvet Underground were the first rock band to incorporate many ideas from the musical avant-garde. The pivotal man in establishing this connection was original Velvets bassist/violist/organist John Cale, a Welshman who had studied with experimental composer Cornelius Cardew, and came to the United States under a Leonard Bernstein scholarship to study modern composition with Iannis Xenakis at Tanglewood, MA. Cale actually got a photo spread in the *New York Times* in 1963 after participating in an 18-hour rendition of Erik Satie's "Vexation" with John Cage. Moving to New York, he was a member of the Dream Syndicate with minimalism pioneer LaMonte Young, and other musicians who would play with members of the Velvets before the group had properly formed.

Cale brought the droning textures of Young's work to the Velvet Underground. While Lou Reed was always the group's principal songwriter and visionary, cuts from their first two albums, such as "Black Angel's Death Song," "European Son," "All Tomorrow's Parties," and "Venus in Furs," owe much of their sonic palette to Cale's viola and keyboards. Feedback-ridden freakouts like "I Heard Her Call My Name" and

"Sister Ray" also owe much of their adventurous structure and recklessly abrasive arrangements to ideas from the New York-based avant-garde community. The Velvets also took considerable inspiration for their modern multimedia assault from their first manager, Andy Warhol.

When Cale left the band in 1968, the Velvets became a far more conventional-sounding outfit (though their later work was also hugely important in setting the scene for punk/new wave). In their solo careers, the ex-Velvets continue to be among the most avant-garde-influenced musicians. Cale has collaborated with minimalist Terry Riley, as well as constructed performance art pieces of sorts with Bob Neuwirth and Reed himself. Cale also produced gothic, harmonium-drenched avant-rock albums for original sometime Velvet-vocalist Nico. Although Reed's solo career has run an extremely erratic course that finds him working conventional rock territory more often than not, he has never entirely forsaken his avant-garde roots with the Velvets. His 1975 double album, *Metal Machine Music,* consisting entirely of blistering electronic musique concrete guaranteed to clear the room under any circumstances, ranks as one of the most avant-garde (and uncommercial) records ever released by a rock performer, though opinion remains divided as to whether it was a serious artistic statement, a mean-spirited joke, or a contract-breaker.

Around the same time as the Velvets began recording, Frank Zappa and the Mothers of Invention explored elements of contemporary composition in their early albums. Zappa claimed Edgard Varese as his principal hero (he is even said to have turned on Chicago, the pop-jazz-rock group, to the composer), and his side-long "Help I'm a Rock" (from the Mothers' debut LP, *Freak Out*) was certainly the most avant-garde piece that had been committed to a rock record at that point. Zappa's interest in contemporary composition remained constant throughout his career, although it was the satirical rock that usually brought in the bacon for him; 1967's *Lumpy Gravy* was the first of several serious orchestral works that he released before his death in 1993.

Many psychedelic groups were aware of avant-garde composers, although they used it to pepper their rock compositions, not diving into its rigors nearly as whole-hog as Zappa did. The Beatles, for instance, proclaimed their admiration for Stockhausen; the Grateful Dead's Phil Lesh was well-versed in electronic and "serious" music before joining the band. Sometimes the groups would put bona fide avant-garde sound collages on their albums, as with "Revolution 9" (the Beatles), "What's Become of the Baby" (the Dead), and "A Small Package of Value Will Come to You, Shortly" (the Jefferson Airplane). These were neither extremely well-received by rock listeners and critics, nor especially admired by "serious" musicians, and such efforts were generally viewed as side indulgences. There were rare examples of musicians from the avant-garde community trying their hand at rock; the still-obscure United States of America, led by composer Joseph Byrd and featuring innovative electronic instrumentation, were the best of these.

With the dawn of art-rock, some musicians became more, well, serious in their appropriation of serious music. Spooky Tooth collaborated with composer Pierre Henry, and Pink Floyd's Roger Waters collaborated with composer Ron Geesin for the soundtrack of *The Body.* Geesin would in turn embellish Floyd's *Atom Heart Mother* with orchestral arrangements, and most of the group's late '60s and '70s albums showed considerable familiarity, if not expertise, with elements of electronic composition. Indeed, the Floyd took much of their early inspiration from the British avant-garde ensemble AMM, who (like the early Floyd) were managed by Peter Jenner; Syd Barrett picked up the trick of sliding ball bearings up and down his guitar from them. Brian Eno, after leaving Roxy Music, pioneered ambient music on his '70s solo albums; today he has entirely forsaken the world of pop music, and is recognized as a legitimate major contemporary composer (though he continues to work with many rock groups as a producer). And European art rock groups like Tangerine Dream, Can, and Faust took many of their cues from electronic and experimental music.

Punk often proclaimed its contempt of "serious" rock, but it was hardly bereft of avant-garde influences. It's now a well-known fact that Yoko Ono's caterwauling screams—so ridiculed when she married John Lennon in the late '60s—influenced early new wave singers like the B-52's and Lene Lovich. The Residents' grim sound collages prefigured and reflected punk in its determination to destroy and deconstruct established icons of rock music. The multi-layered minimalism of the electric guitar armies directed by Rhys Chatham and Glenn Branca were vastly influential on Sonic Youth (whose guitarist, Thurston Moore, played in one of Branca's early ensembles). New York no-wavers like Lydia Lunch, Suicide, and DNA also displayed a lot of primal avant-garde angst, carrying over to confrontational performances which bore the influences of the city's performance artists. Performance art and pop would indeed meet halfway with the success of Laurie Anderson in the 1980s.

Almost inevitably, the avant-garde itself began to reflect the influences of rock. Composers like Branca, Chatham, Paul Dresher, John

Oswald, and others don't play rock, but they grew up with it, and the energy of rock informs what they are doing. Serious ensembles like the Kronos Quartet challenged the academic community with their willingness to interpret the works of Jimi Hendrix as well as Webern and other dead composers. Esteemed ambient composer Harold Budd collaborated not only with Eno, but with moody British alternative rock group the Cocteau Twins.

In New York especially, but also in many other communities, musicians are determined to explore the avant-garde with electric instruments; they think of themselves as "rock" musicians sometimes (or, like guitarist Elliott Sharp, either rock or avant-garde depending on whom they're playing with), but they're not interested in constructing their music in accessible, melodically conventional pop forms. John Zorn is probably the best known of these performers, determined to blend the avant-garde with rock and other kinds of popular music, but never in a fashion that will be embraced by the *Billboard* chart listings.

In the 1990s, the influence of the avant-garde is strongly felt in the emerging ambient/techno scene, with its frequent use of dense electronics, found sound, and strategically placed silence. As the 21st century approaches, it's likely that the interchange between rock and the avant-garde will continue to hasten, as younger generations of musicians become increasingly unconcerned with distinctions between genres, and increasingly determined to blur them.

Recommended Recordings

La Monte Young, *The Well-Tuned Piano* (Gramavision). Young, a legendary perfectionist, rarely records; this is his most widely available piece. Neophytes are advised to listen to a copy before buying unheard; comprising five CDs, it's a steeply priced introduction.

Frank Zappa, *Lumpy Gravy* (Verve). From 1967, his first orchestral work.

John Cale & Terry Riley, *Church of Anthrax* (Columbia). Actually, not the highlight of either men's careers; Riley's *In C* and *Rainbow in Curved Air* were his most acclaimed works, and indeed some of the most acclaimed avant-garde works of the '60s.

Roger Waters & Ron Geesin, *Music from the Body* (Harvest). Not so much a collaboration as a complementation, as Waters and Geesin recorded their contributions separately.

Yoko Ono, *Walking on Thin Ice* (Rykodisc). Single-disc compilation focuses on some of her most accessible work; for the blood-curdling epics, go for the six-CD *Onobox,* which will tax the patience of all but the hardiest fans.

Lou Reed, *Metal Machine Music* (RCA). The considerable controversy surrounding this album (described by the *Rolling Stone Album Guide* as a "gigantic 'fuck you' disguised as a groundbreaking experiment") tends to obscure the fact that this is not an uninterrupted burst of amplifier noise, but in fact a genuine composition with different movements and modulations, though none the more accessible for that.

The Residents, *The Residents Present the Third Reich & Roll* (Ralph). Still their most (in)famous work, devoted to side-long medleys of unrecognizable maulings of '60s rock classics.

Brian Eno, *Another Green World* (EG). Caught halfway between the rock and avant-garde, as Eno begins to de-emphasize vocals and pop melodies to concentrate on textures and use of the recording studio as an instrument.

Various Artists, *No New York* (Antilles). The skronk of avant-garde noise-rock, caught in its birth pangs on this 1978 no-wave compilation.

Glenn Branca, *The Ascension* (99). Masses of guitars on one of the most electric contemporary compositional works.

Laurie Anderson, *Big Science* (Warner Bros.). The 1982 album that exposed Anderson to the pop world, although she had already been an established performance artist (and occasional recording artist) for some time. Includes the novelty hit "O Superman."

Harold Budd, Elizabeth Fraser, Robin Guthrie, & Simon Raymonde, *The Moon and the Melodies* (4AD). The ambient composer collaborates with the Cocteau Twins. The result was, perhaps, overly polite, inspiring neither party to work that scaled higher or even different heights than their previous output.

John Zorn, *Naked City* (Nonesuch/Elektra). Zorn actually owes at least as much to jazz as to rock, but he's one of the most popular, if not the most popular, downtown New York avant-garder with the alternative rock audience.

–Richie Unterberger

OTHER ESSAYS, RESOURCES, & REFERENCES

Producers

Since rock began, the role of the producer in rock 'n' roll has both changed a great deal and remained the same in many of its most essential aspects. Production duties vary from artist to artist and record to record, but generally speaking, the producer takes varying degrees of responsibility for shaping the sound of what we hear when discs get into our hands. Arguably, who producers are and what they do matter a lot more to critics and industry types than the average consumer, who is mostly concerned with the sound and image of the artists themselves. But producers have played key roles in rock 'n' roll, at times stamping their records with artistic visions comparable to those of the performers.

A stereotype of the producer, reinforced by some dramatized situations in movies, is that of someone sitting behind a mammoth console, surrounded by reels of tape and equipment, divided from the band only by a thin glass partition. He twiddles knobs, raises and lowers faders, shouts very specific instructions about the performance, and guides the musicians through take after take. Some producers did and do get involved on such a physical level, but in reality their roles are much more diverse, and with increased specialization, much of the hands-on knob-twiddling and microphone placement are handled by engineers and studio technicians, not producers. And, unfortunately, the producer is still, in 1997, almost always a "he"; more than almost any other realm in rock 'n' roll, it remains an almost exclusively male domain.

When rock 'n' roll was born, the term "producer" was not used in the industry as much as the designation "artist and repertoire" staff member, usually shortened to A&R. A&R men were responsible for matching artists on a label's roster with material; in rock's early days, that sometimes meant songs that were actually written by the artists, but more often meant tunes from outside sources. Matching artists with material, or selecting among and suggesting material, from both internal and external sources remains one of the producer's principal activities. A&R staff are generally not found in the studio these days, instead concentrating their efforts on scouting for talent and helping sign artists to labels.

Broadly speaking, production was less sophisticated and much more of a "live" affair in the 1950s. Neither were most artists expected to have a long career, and producers were generally more concerned with finding hit songs and building effective arrangements for them than with building a distinctive sound to complement the artists themselves. There were, of course, many distinct production sounds and innovations during the era: Sam Phillips' "slap-back" echo techniques at Sun Studios did much to define rockabilly, Norman Petty helped craft Buddy Holly's greatest records at a small studio in New Mexico, and Fred Foster of Monument pioneered orchestral pop-rock with Roy Orbison.

It was Phil Spector, though, who really mapped out the potential for rock production for the first time. Utilizing multi-track recording techniques, echo chambers, and scads of session musicians on both traditional rock instruments and full horn and string sections, he created symphonic rock 'n' roll. Also a musician and songwriter of note, Spector, more than any other rock producer before or since, was not just a technician or arranger, but an artist; while his classic singles were performed by the Ronettes, Crystals, Righteous Brothers, and others, they were above all his own work. He was also among the first to establish himself as an independent producer (and record-label owner), not beholden to label superiors when pursuing his muse; British producer Joe Meek blazed a similar trail in Britain, though his material was not nearly in the same league as Spector's.

The soul music of the 1960s was distinguished by production styles specific to certain labels and regions. There were many of these across the United States, but the most famous are the "assembly-line" techniques of Motown Records, the "deep soul" attributed to the Stax/Volt label, and (in the '70s) the lush, string-laden Philly soul sound. Heavily reliant upon the talents of the performers and ace session players, these and other schools of soul had trademark sounds that were instantly identifiable and varied and inspired enough to avoid formulaic repetition, and remain benchmark references for contemporary musicians.

The British Invasion gave rise to self-contained groups, both in the UK and the US, who demanded a much greater voice in their material and, subsequently, production. Buddy Holly had already done much to take the reins of his own sessions before his premature death; Brian Wilson of the Beach Boys took this freedom to new heights by assuming virtual control of his group's production very early on their career (though that often meant recording the Beach Boys' records with session musicians while the rest of the band was on tour). The Beatles, greatly aided by George Martin, were relentless in expanding the horizons of rock production at Abbey Road Studios through both new instruments and experimental production techniques. Other British producers like Shel Talmy (actually an expatriate American) maximized the impact of groups like the Kinks and the Who by helping to craft a more powerful guitar sound than had previously been thought possible on rock records.

In the light of these changes, the role of the producer himself changed to a degree which is still felt in the industry. He was not so much one to delegate and direct sessions as one to work with the musicians, to achieve commercial success certainly, but also to help realize their artistic visions. This didn't so much take the shape of standing behind the board or developing certain kinds of reverb or instrumental balances, which was often the territory of the engineers (some of whom, like Shel Talmy's frequent assistant Glyn Johns, were stars in their own right, eventually assuming the producer's chair). It meant reviewing the material, suggesting modifications for the purpose of achieving the best recorded sound, not the best live sound, and helping to translate the musicians' more ambitious notions via outside horn and string players.

In certain cases, most famously George Martin with the Beatles, the producer sometimes acts as a fifth or sixth member of the band, actually playing instruments on the recording, either to flesh out the arrangements or handle instruments that the band members weren't able to play with the same degree of proficiency. Or sometimes, the producer applies the dictum "less is more," and realizes that his greatest contribution is to stay out of the way and let the musicians be themselves. Occasionally, the producer is not so much the producer in the musical sense as in the financial sense, much like movie producers. Andy Warhol, for instance, made minimal musical contributions to the Velvet Underground's classic first album; he is, however, listed as producer, for the very important reason that he financed the sessions, as well as pretty much carrying the band economically during their early days.

In the modern rock era, to a much greater degree than many listeners realize, the producer is not so much a technician or creative force as a moderator, and a settler of arguments. Decisions about which material to use when more than one bandmember is a songwriter; decisions about whether to use session musicians when a bandmember can't cut it; asking/instructing musicians to put more work into a song before it is deigned complete and ready for recording; putting feet down about kicking out friends, groupies, drug pushers, and other hangers-on slowing down sessions; drawing the line when experimentation is draining the

1174

allotted budget; determining the sound balance when none of the individual musicians are willing to sacrifice their self-interest—it often comes down to the producer to break the stalemate. These can be thankless tasks, and rock musicians are more often than not grudging in their praise of producers. Often their criticisms are justified; just as often, their talents and accompanying egos make it difficult to accept that creative collaboration and restraint is often necessary. In reading rock biographies, one often comes across comments of the sort, "If we had the chance to record it again our way, it would come out so much better. The producer didn't grasp what we were trying to accomplish/was unsympathetic to our ideas/rushed us through the sessions."

What's unspoken here is that if most musicians were allowed to carry on as they wished, the results would often be half-baked and less satisfactory to both the musicians and their audience. It's a difficult task, translating sounds that others hear in their heads, and while some producers do botch the job, in many cases they are arriving at the best possible realization of the musicians' ideas with the available talent, material, and equipment. Of course that hasn't stopped many musicians from taking over production duties, or even production and engineering duties, themselves. Sometimes the results are self-indulgent messes, but performers like Prince, Stevie Wonder, the Rolling Stones, and quite a few others have proved quite able at handling themselves, sometimes down to the smallest detail. We're not going to name any names here, but other artists credit themselves as producers or co-producers when their contribution is relatively minimal, such as helping to select material, approve final mixes, or, yes, finance the sessions in the first place.

In the late '60s and '70s, recording budgets ballooned as artists became more perfectionist, and signed recording contracts granting them specific artistic freedom. Better home-stereo equipment made better technology a concern, and more attention than ever was lavished upon overdubs, multi-track recording, and mixes. Many charged that the soul of the music was being driven out of recorded performance, and the punk/new wave explosion was a reaction against this (and many other things). Many of the seminal punk recordings had a spontaneous, raw, live feel generated by quick, low-budget sessions, but most of the early punk and new wave artists that established career longevity came to appreciate the value of thoughtful, even elaborate production as their music became more diverse. And even the Sex Pistols' *Never Mind the Bollocks* was subject to all sorts of remixing and re-recording until it was finally released after months of sessions, as John Lydon eagerly bitches about to this day.

Some music trends of the 1980s and 1990s have seen the role of the producer further redefined. Rap music demands facility with sampling and stop-on-a-dime editing techniques; rap, and dance music, have brought the roles of the engineer, mixer, and remixer to new levels, as specific sonic textures are created for certain radio and club formats, and the production is sometimes considered of equal or greater importance than the performer or the material. Dub music, in reggae and reggae-rock crossover productions, places greater importance upon sound manipulation and reverb than performance or material. Ambient/techno/rave productions can be more dependent upon manipulation and arrangement of source materials, beats, and samples with synthesizers and other sophisticated electronic equipment than anything else.

All of these developments lead to familiar charges that elaborate production technique from the hands of faceless knob-twiddlers is driving the humanity out of contemporary music, though all of the above genres rank among the fastest-growing styles of rock 'n' roll as the 20th century draws to a close. Those looking for producers who establish their distinctive imprint on the course of rock music with more conventional producer-musician relationships can continue to find many examples, such as Steve Albini, Butch Vig, and Brendan O'Brien (all instrumental in establishing the grunge and post-punk sound which finally translated into mass success in the early '90s), "New Jack Swing" king Teddy Riley, or Bill Laswell, whose production credit seemingly attaches itself to every other experimental rock record.—*Richie Unterberger*

Session Musicians

If one were to write the hidden history of rock 'n' roll, session musicians would have many of the most prominent roles. Often uncredited in the 1950s and 1960s, there are hundreds of musicians who are not stars in their own right, but have done much to shape the course of rock music. Even today, when most session musicians are routinely credited on album jackets, they enjoy far less recognition than the performers they back in the studio. Session musicians, of course, have been used since music began to be recorded for commercial purposes early in the 20th century, and were a feature of pop music long before rock 'n' roll emerged. When rock 'n' roll began to take shape in the late '40s and early '50s, session musicians were already a big part of the game in the studio. A lot of rock 'n' roll singers, regardless of the era, don't play instruments, and while they were sometimes big enough to support touring bands of their own, they didn't always use these bands in the studio. Singers that were just starting out didn't have bands of their own,

and were usually provided with accompaniment from whatever musicians the label could provide. Then as now, a lot of rock 'n' roll musicians who played their own instruments onstage did not, for various reasons, always play their instruments on records.

The session musicians on early rock 'n' roll records would have rarely identified themselves as rock 'n' roll musicians; some would have found the term insulting, but more to the point, the term rock 'n' roll itself hardly existed, and most professional musicians were schooled in different genres of music. In the large urban centers, quite a few of them were jazz musicians making money on the side; guitarists, saxophonists, bassists, and drummers were in demand for both jazz and rock purposes. Also, the musics themselves were both much closer in their evolutionary paths to their blues and R&B roots than they are today, and it wasn't as difficult to switch modes by the day, sometimes by the hour, as it might appear. Other early rock session musicians were conversant with straight pop or even classical; those that recorded for regional independent labels were often from country and blues backgrounds.

It was only decades later, when rock scholarship had grown to a sufficient level, that many of these session players received some measure of public recognition, usually confined to serious fans. While space precludes the listing of every musician who played a great riff or solo, a few of the more notable ones include guitarist Mickey Baker, who played on tons of R&B and rock sessions for Atlantic in addition to gaining stardom as half of Mickey & Sylvia; guitarist James Burton, responsible for the brilliant rockabilly licks on Ricky Nelson's classic singles; guitarist Scotty Moore, who did the same for Elvis Presley's best work; drummer Earl Palmer and saxophonists Lee Allen and Alvin Tyler, responsible for much of what we recognize as the classic New Orleans R&B sound; Willie Dixon, who played bass on many of the great '50s Chess blues and rock 'n' roll sides; and even Chet Atkins, who though identified with country, lent his guitar to some of the Everly Brothers' early material.

Under the guidance of Phil Spector, Brian Wilson, and others, rock production became more sophisticated in the early and mid-'60s. In New York and Los Angeles, session musicians were an important component in the realization of the complex, multitracked sound that such producers were after. Some of these musicians became stars in their own right, within the industry: saxophonist Steve Douglas, bassist Carole Kaye, guitarist Glen Campbell (before stardom as a solo act), and drummer Hal Blaine. These performers were both virtuosos and extremely adaptable to many kinds of material, and their flair for rock 'n' roll did much to establish Los Angeles in particular as a recording center for rock music. Not to be neglected are the backup vocalists for many '60s rock artists, some of whom had a soulfulness on par with the star attractions, especially Darlene Love (who sang uncredited lead vocals on some of the Crystals' hits) and the Sweet Inspirations. Love and the Sweet Inspirations recorded some fine sides on their own, but were never accorded a level of stardom nearly on par with the respect they achieved within the industry.

Session players were extremely important in establishing the success of the day's most popular soul labels, Motown and Stax/Volt. Motown favored an assembly-line approach which gave their records an instantly identifiable appeal, and its musicians, particularly bassist James Jamerson, were worshiped by millions who never knew their names, as they were seldom credited on releases (Berry Gordy, Jr., has pointed out, with some validity, that hardly any labels printed credits in the '60s, and that this wasn't a conscious policy of Motown to keep its hidden assets undiscovered, but simply the status quo of the era). Stax/Volt's most frequent sessionmen, Booker T. & the MG's, were not only not secrets, but stars in their own right. Other Memphis-area session musicians were frequently sought after, such as the Memphis Horns, the Hi Rhythm Section, and the many musicians who worked in nearby Muscle Shoals, Alabama in the Fame Studios. James Brown's pioneering funk bands featured numerous talented musicians, such as Bootsy Collins, Maceo Parker, and Fred Wesley, who are only now starting to get recognition as individual innovators in their own right.

In pre-British Invasion England, session work for rock records was carried out, as it was in the worst American rock 'n' roll records, by bored, middle-aged musicians more conversant with MOR pop. This changed with the Beatles and the British Invasion, as a whole generation of musicians came of age that had grown up with rock 'n' roll, and came by the music naturally. Session musicians continued to be used on many British record dates, and several future guitar heroes, including Jeff Beck, John McLaughlin, and Ritchie Blackmore, gained much of their early recorded experience playing for others.

Before joining the Yardbirds, Jimmy Page was probably THE most active rock 'n' roll session player in all of Britain, gracing countless sides, including major hits by Them, the Who, and the Kinks. Other musicians like drummer Bobby Graham, future Led Zeppelin bassist John Paul Jones (who worked with such pop acts as Herman's Hermits and Lulu), and piano player Nicky Hopkins were guests on numerous records, ranging in Hopkins' case from the Stones to the Who to the Beatles to the Kinks (Ray Davies has been said to have written the Kinks' "Session

Man" about him). And there's the strange case of Ian Stewart, a brilliant keyboard player who was officially kicked out of the Rolling Stones just before the group began recording, but played with them on many of their records and tours, functioning in effect as their sixth member.

The rise of the self-contained rock group was a double-edged sword in some cases. For the bandmembers, there was the increased prestige and creative freedom that comes with playing your own instruments and writing your own material. What the public didn't realize was that many self-contained groups still relied on session players to some extent, leading to some well-publicized controversies when it was revealed that some groups didn't play everything on their records. It has been discovered, for instance, that many of the Beach Boys' greatest records were recorded by Brian Wilson and session musicians while the group was out on tour. The Byrds recorded their breakthrough single "Mr. Tambourine Man" with mostly sessionmen, although, contrary to some accounts, the rest of their classic '60s records featured the group as principal players. Much of the scorn dumped upon the Monkees was generated by the revelation that they didn't play on their early records (though they made no secret of this when confronted with the fact).

While rock groups continued to use session players, they were wary of relying upon them for the bulk of their recorded parts. This hadn't been an issue for most top groups, but they began turning increasingly to friends from other groups, not just professionals assigned to them by labels and/or producers. This was to some degree indicative of the increased self-consciousness and self-sufficiency of the late-'60s rock scene, and while the "heavy friends" syndrome lent itself to some self-indulgent jams, it also produced numerous instances of inspired collaborations which were sparked by the musicians' obvious camaraderie and mutual respect, qualities that would have been absent in many cases if hired hands had been used. Duane Allman's duets with Eric Clapton on Derek and the Dominos' "Layla" is one frequently cited example of such a rapport. (Allman himself was a session player of note before the Allman Brothers became big, contributing notable parts to records by Wilson Pickett, Aretha Franklin, and others.) There were still many solo performers in rock, and many of them couldn't afford to support their own bands, or were not inclined to carry bands to begin with. Many of these were singer-songwriters who had began as solo acoustic acts, and particularly in the early days of folk-rock, giants like Dylan (who used such illustrious musicians as Mike Bloomfield, Al Kooper, the Band, and country harmonica player Charlie McCoy as sidemen in the '60s) were heavily reliant upon session players to effect their transition to electric music. When singer-songwriters became huge in the early '70s, much of their sound was crafted by session musicians, particularly in Los Angeles, leading to a general homogeneity of sound within the Southern Californian rock community as a whole. Such professionalism was attacked by the early punk/new wave groups, yet actually many of them used session musicians to make their material better in the studio.

There have been tons of session players in rock in the last couple of decades, yet in comparison with rock 'n' roll's early days, there are relatively few musicians content to make their living, and their artistic impression, primarily on sessions. This is a reflection of two factors. First, musicians are much more likely to tap members of other groups, or fellow musicians who may be "between" groups or solo acts, rather than professionals who do not choose to record under their own name or affiliate themselves with ongoing recording and touring acts. The second is that instrumentalists themselves are generally much more interested in becoming a member of a group or a solo act than going it alone as a session player. Session players are credited on most album sleeves these days, it's true, but the level of public recognition remains much lower than artists that work under their own name. Equally important, playing sessions affords less chance for the songwriting and creativity that have become de rigeur for most rock musicians since the mid-'60s.

If you're looking for musicians who make a good living primarily as session players, you'll find a lot more of them in MOR rock, or urban contemporary R&B, than most other rock genres. For that matter, you'll find much more of them in Nashville, playing country music, than playing rock music altogether. There do remain respected musicians primarily identified as session players within the rock world, such as drummers Kenny Aronoff and Michael Blair; rhythm section Sly and Robbie (whose bread-and-butter gig remains reggae, as they seemingly appear on every other record released in Jamaica); guitarists Marc Ribot and Robert Quine (rap label Sugar Hill's house band Keith LeBlanc (drums), Doug Wimbish (bass), and Skip McDonald (guitar; they're also members of the groups Tackhead and Little Axe); keyboardist Benmont Tench (also a member of Tom Petty's band), and bassist Bill Laswell (also a prolific producer and recording artist).—*Richie Unterberger*

Independent Labels

The story of rock 'n' roll is not just one of musicians, songwriters, and producers. For many listeners, labels are nothing more than a name in the middle of an album or on the spine of a CD; "major" and "indie" are distinctions that concern serious fans, journalists, and industry insiders.

Rock's ascension as the most popular music of the last half of the 20th century, however, owes much to the pioneering efforts of independent labels, which continue to act as a source of innovation, both on their own and as an influence on "majors," labels run or distributed by major corporations. When rock 'n' roll had its first birth pangs just after World War II, the record industry was dominated by a half-dozen major labels—Capitol, MGM, Decca, Mercury, Columbia, and RCA. By and large they played it safe in the popular music field, leaving the more specialized tastes of the R&B and country & western audiences to smaller, regional companies. Somewhat condescendingly referred to as "race" and "hillbilly" music, the majors felt these markets were too small and crude to cater to, and their A&R departments developed little in the way of talent for their rosters.

This left the field open for smaller enterpreneurs, who faced a much tougher battle in recording their acts, promoting them, and getting them airplay. On the other hand, they were less constrained by established formulas, and able to record more creative and uninhibited performers, satisfying the increasingly hungry demand for raucous R&B and C&W sounds. Charlie Gillett's history of rock 'n' roll, *The Sound of the City*, views the birth of rock 'n' roll as a phenomenon of independent labels developing and marketing music that the majors were ignoring, and does an excellent job of detailing the many influential independent early rock and R&B labels and their rise to commercial success.

It would be a mistake to cast these independent labels as champions of the artistic vanguard, fighting corporate monoliths. Many independent executives treated their artists shoddily, signing them to exploitative contracts, withholding royalties, and casting them aside when they fell from commercial grace. While visionaries such as Sun Records' Sam Phillips and Atlantic's Jerry Wexler were probably motivated as much or more by love of music as profit, many were hustlers seeking a piece of the action by finding whatever niche market they could. Lacking the powerful distribution networks of the majors, all of them were compelled to do things the hard way, driving from town to town to push their latest singles, chatting up and giving gifts to influential DJs in exchange for airplay.

Stations that gave the new sounds such airplay become increasingly plentiful after 1950, and by the mid-'50s the music which was just starting to be called "rock 'n' roll" was becoming an important part of the popular music market. The great majority of the early rock 'n' roll records were released on independent labels, many of which have assumed legendary status in the decades since. Sun, Atlantic, Specialty, Chess, Imperial, Modern, VeeJay, King, Duke/Peacock—all boasted rosters of incredible talent that left permanent imprints on rock 'n' roll. And there were dozens of other independent labels of note, some of which only released one or two hits, some of which released only regional hits, but many of which recorded lasting contributions to rock history.

The majors responded defensively at first, either ignoring rock 'n' roll almost entirely (as Columbia did) or recording watered-down "cover" versions for the pop market. Innovators like Bill Haley and Elvis Presley were signed to major labels and launched to superstardom after establishing themselves on independent labels. The majors vs. indies battle wasn't black-and-white by any means—early greats Gene Vincent and Buddy Holly were signed by major labels without any track record, and went on to record some of the very best rock 'n' roll of the 1950s.

By the end of the 1950s, independents were responsible for about twice as many Top Ten singles as majors, and about three times as many Top Ten rock singles. In the 1960s, major labels didn't so much fight back against indies as adapt to the rock era, starting to focus their energies on developing rock talent rather than more middle-of-the-road sounds. Indies were still a major force in rock 'n' roll; labels like Kama Sutra, Red Bird, Philles, Stax/Volt, and many others developed outstanding rosters, and Motown became the most successful independent label of all time, establishing a commercial presence that rivaled the majors—with the R&B and soul performers that would have been considered a mere "race" market 10-15 years earlier.

In Britain, at the time the Beatles and others claimed a large part of the international pop market, the situation was much more restrictive. Virtually every artist recorded for one of four major companies: EMI, Decca, Pye, and Philips. Somewhat by way of compensation, these labels had huge and varied rosters that were somewhat more adventurous than their US counterparts. In the mid-'60s, several British independents began to make their presence known by recording some of the era's most innovative rock. Encompassing artists like the Small Faces, the Who, Cream, Traffic, Jimi Hendrix, and (in the late '60s) the Beatles, labels like Immediate, Reaction, Track, Island (which began primarily as a ska and bluebeat concern), and the Beatles' Apple unleashed determinedly progressive sounds, although it's important to note that all of those labels benefited from distribution deals with majors. In the US there were also companies that fostered self-consciously progressive rosters, especially Elektra, which hit it big with the Doors and recorded several other influential folk-rock and psychedelic acts.

The 1970s were a time of conglomeration, in which the majors expanded their power by establishing distribution deals with some of the most successful independents. Plenty of independent R&B and Black pop continued to chart, but that genre was increasingly becoming the province of the majors. Mid- and late-'70s punk and new wave bands were often thwarted by industry resistance, which gave birth to the D.I.Y. (do-it-yourself) ethic in both Britain and the US. Realizing that majors weren't going to sign and promote them, or would try to refine their sound, bands put out their own records, formed their own labels, or signed with indies, trading commercial success for artistic freedom. Labels like Britain's Stiff were instrumental in shaping new wave music, though Stiff, like some others, was not averse to major-label distribution to achieve wider exposure.

In the 1980s, the indie ethic became more sociopolitical and divisive. Many performers, critics, label owners, and fans took a virulent anti-major-label stance, seeing major labels as a malignant, homogenizing force that threatened to destroy creativity and hinder artistic expression. The independent/alternative rock network of hundreds of labels, fanzines, and college/community radio stations allowed artists to record and release music that was not only outside of the commercial mainstream, but often actively opposed to it. Labels like SST, Alternative Tentacles, Touch & Go, Sub Pop, and 4AD developed identifiable sounds and styles that constituted artistic visions in and of themselves. Others, like Slash, tried to play it both ways, arranging for distribution deals with majors. The majors tapped into the growing alternative rock market by cutting distribution deals with successful indies, or treating indie labels as farm teams, signing the most successful prospects (bands) after they'd honed their sounds in the minor leagues (which were usually clubs and college radio stations).

Rap was another form of music which encountered some industry resistance, giving rise to many independent rap labels. By and large they weren't as suspicious of mainstream popularity, and many of the most successful indie records of the '80s were rap discs by superstars like Run-D.M.C. and Salt-N-Pepa. Actually, these were among the very few 100% indie productions to become hits; the majors were now composed of six mega-conglomerates, which in the mid-'90s were Sony, CEMA, BMG, PGD, WEA, and UNI (the initials may change according to corporate sales and reorganizations in the future). It's difficult to ascertain an exact figure, but an educated guess would estimate that these labels are responsible for about 90% of the sales in today's market.

The push-and-pull between major and indie labels continues unabated in the mid-'90s. When indie rock superstars like Hüsker Dü leaped to major labels in the mid-'80s, the sales figures were modest. The multi-million-selling success of Nirvana, however, paved the way for grunge music and a wholesale infiltration of the charts by scabrous alternative rockers like Pearl Jam, Nine Inch Nails, Green Day, Liz Phair, and Beck that wouldn't have stood a chance of denting the Top 100 just ten years ago. It's an explosion that wouldn't have been possible without the efforts of independent labels, which were the first to record and develop most of these acts. Indie labels, however, shouldn't be viewed merely as a proving ground for the stars of tomorrow. It's the music that matters, and independent labels continue to house some of the best talent in rock and pop, as well as cultivate some of its most innovative sounds and trends by offering a climate that isn't as obsessed with charts and commercial success. The non-rock music that continues to influence rock—folk, blues, jazz, reggae, worldbeat, the avant-garde—is also usually found on small labels. All indies continue to fight the same obstacles of limited distribution, budgets, and exposure as they did 50 years ago, but they will continue to exert a major influence as long as rock 'n' roll is around.—*Richie Unterberger*

Books

The Sound of the City, by Charlie Gillett (Pantheon, 1970)

Making Tracks: The Story of Atlantic Records, by Charlie Gillett (Souvenir Press, 1974)

Good Rockin' Tonight: Sun Records and the Birth of Rock 'n' Roll, by Colin Escott with Martin Hawkins (St. Martin's, 1991)

Bootleg Overview

Music bootlegs—illegal reproduction and distribution of recordings—have been with us about as long as sound reproduction itself. Few issues in the music industry inspire as much heated debate. A constant irritant to many record companies and musicians, they are a source of pleasure—albeit a bit of a guilty pleasure—to countless fans. Despite periodic efforts by the industry to crack down on manufacturers and retailers of unauthorized recordings, bootlegging continues to persist and make an impact upon a large audience, much as independent labels continue to proliferate even as corporate companies seek to consolidate their domination of the music industry.

There are several kind of bootlegs. There are pirates, which reissue official material (usually rare and out-of-print) without official permission. There are counterfeits, which duplicate the content (and often

sleeve and label) of a record as it appeared in its original release. The most influential and commonly discussed bootlegs collect totally unreleased performances—live concerts, studio outtakes, demos, and radio broadcasts. Bootlegging was hardly unknown in jazz, classical, and other collector recordings before it began to infiltrate the rock audience. A live recording of the Beatles performing "Some Other Guy," a staple of their early sets that they never officially cut in the studio, made the rounds in Liverpool as early as 1963. That same year, the first unauthorized live recording of the Rolling Stones was pressed, giving fans a memento of their heroes before their rapid ascent to international fame.

It was a late-'60s Bob Dylan bootleg, however, that really got the scene rolling. Titled *The Great White Wonder*, this collection of *Basement Tape*-era demos and other odds and ends, packaged in a plain white sleeve, was manna from heaven for Dylan acolytes desperate for any word of his continued existence. And here were a clutch of unreleased, more or less realized studio performances, available for just a bit more than the standard price of an LP. Similarly popular bootlegs of the Beatles' early 1969 *Get Back* sessions and a show from the Rolling Stones' 1969 US tour (*Liver Than You'll Ever Be*) quickly followed. Soon there were live and (considerably less frequently) unreleased studio recordings by most of the major bands (and many minor ones) for purchase on the underground market.

Bootleg product ebbs and flows according to periodic crackdowns by the law and the record industry, but basically it's been uninterrupted. At collector conventions, specialty shops, London flea markets, and the streets of New York, illicit recordings spanning several decades continue to swap hands. Search hard enough for those Liz Phair demos, that Patti Smith broadcast, or last week's Elvis Costello show, and you'll find it, though it may involve considerable expense and mileage. Realizing they were unable to stop the massive circulation of live tapes among Deadheads, the Grateful Dead have more or less condoned the taping and trading of their live performances. Occasionally, a bootleg album slips through this underground web to make an impact upon the mass audience. Such was the case with Prince's unreleased *Black Album* in the late 1980s. Outselling a great deal of its legitimately released competition, it attracted attention and reviews in the mainstream press, and even some airplay on commercial radio stations.

Aesthetically, the most frequent complaint against bootlegs is that they sound terrible. And quite a few of them do, especially the older live ones. But bootleg technology has increased enormously over the last decade. Many boots—perhaps even the majority by now—boast excellent pressings, duplication from first-generation sound board and master tapes, and artwork/packaging that is better than the real thing.

Many labels and performers claim to suffer financial and artistic damage from bootlegs, arguing that they are not being compensated for the sale of their property; that boots are a violation of their artistic wishes; and that unauthorized material damages their artistic reputation. Fans counter that consumers of bootlegs almost invariably own all of the artists' official releases anyway; that many bootlegs expose valuable work to a relatively wide audience and cast new light upon an artist's oeuvre; and that any damage, financial or otherwise, suffered by the artist is compensated for by the free publicity illicit material generates.

From corporate boardrooms to on-line bulletin boards, variations of the above debate rage. And the audience for bootlegs continues to grow. Whatever one's position, it is undeniable that bootleggers have been responsible for bringing many great performances to light. No appraisal of Bob Dylan is complete without listening to his legendary 1966 Albert Hall concert with the Band; no picture of the Beatles complete without hearing their BBC tapes, during which they performed 35 covers (and one original!) never released on their official albums; and no assessment of the Beach Boys made without hearing their legendary unreleased *Smile* album. Indeed, as of mid-1997, several collections of highly touted unreleased material that have circulated as bootlegs for many years have actually gained official release. In late 1994, a double CD of the best Beatle BBC sessions finally appeared on Capitol, and Prince's *Black Album* came out. The Beatles then unveiled three double CDs of previously unreleased material on their *Anthology* series, and *The Rolling Stones Rock and Roll Circus*, a legendary 1968 unreleased TV special, was finally issued (in both video and album formats) after decades of interminable delays. Strong rumors of the imminent appearance of *Smile*, Dylan's Albert Hall concert, and other top-rank archival music indicate that lots of other collections of similar material will be made available to the general public in the near future.—*Richie Unterberger*

Fanzines

Major record labels and the established music press sometime leave little room for innovative ideas and idiosyncratic talents. Just as musicians can choose to work outside the system by recording for independent labels, or their own labels, music fans have their own do-it-yourself alternatives for reading, writing, or publishing about their favorite sounds in fanzines. The term "fanzine" originated among avid science-fiction fans in the 1950s, who would spread news and opinions about their fave works in tiny magazines (or 'zines), which were usually mimeographed and distributed through the mail to other acolytes. These days, fanzines—music and otherwise—are often distributed in stores, and sometimes mushroom into "real" magazines, but remain forums for opinions and information that are impossible to get from the usual sources.

Neither its readers nor its publishers ever thought of it as such, but an argument could be made for citing *Mersey Beat* as the first music fanzine. The tabloid was founded by Bill Harry, an art school chum of John Lennon's and a sci-fi zine reader, in 1961 to fill a void in Liverpool. The burgeoning "beat" music scene had become an explosion numbering several hundred groups and several thousand avid fans, but was virtually uncovered in the region's newspapers, let alone on vinyl or radio.

Launched with 50 pounds and a staff of two (Harry and his girlfriend) to cover the area's groups and music news, *Mersey Beat* was a smash success in its brief heyday (1961-64). John Lennon and Paul McCartney themselves contributed writing to the paper, which—with its comprehensive gigs and entertainment coverage—was something of a forerunner of the "alternative weeklies" of today. Brian Epstein, owner of Liverpool's largest record shop, contributed a regular column for a while in 1961, and it has been theorized that he first found out about the Beatles by reading the publication, though he always claimed otherwise.

In the United States, the first rock 'n' roll fanzine of note was founded by Greg Shaw. Like Harry, Shaw was active in the sci-fi fanzine community, corresponding with future Kiss member Gene Simmons, among others. In the mid-'60s, the teenaged Shaw got the idea to create a rock fanzine. Launched in 1966 in San Francisco's Haight-Ashbury as the Summer of Love was just beginning to bloom, *Mojo Navigator* made the rounds of local record stores, head shops, and other grass-roots channels as a xeroxed paper. Greil Marcus and future Rolling Stone publisher Jann Wenner were among those who helped at the 'zine's collating parties. An excerpt from an early issue, an interview with the then-unsigned and Big Brother & the Holding Company, was reprinted on the insert to the live album *Cheaper Thrills* (recorded in 1966, issued in 1984).

Shaw's next fanzine venture, *Bomp*, would prove considerably more far-reaching and influential. Based in Southern California, it was the first zine to feature the unrestrained rantings of cult critics like Richard Meltzer and Lester Bang. Equally important, it was one of the first rock magazines, if not the first, to cover music of both the past and present, the '60s in particular being Shaw's abiding fascination. From its beginnings as a mimeographed periodical, *Bomp* evolved into a regularly published magazine with a circulation of 30,000 before it folded in 1979.

It was the birth of punk in the mid-'70s, though, that really gave rise to a widespread music fanzine culture. Just as musicians were resorting to pressing their own records and promoting their own gigs to make their presence known, frustrated writers (who were often musicians as well) published their own reviews, features, and diatribes in the absence of any coverage of punk and new wave in slick magazines and newspapers. In keeping with the tone of early punk rock, the writing itself was often far more scathing, not to say scatological, than anything the glossier periodicals would have printed, music-related or not.

Like many punk groups of the time, many of the early zines were short-lived, lasting only an issue or two. Even these productions were viewed as a triumph by the underground, inasmuch as, like groups who said all they could say in a single or two before they broke up or lost inspiration, writers and publishers were sending a message that they could write about what they wanted in the way they wanted—at least, until the money or inspiration ran out. These efforts weren't always short-lived by any means; zines like *Search and Destroy* ran for some time, and the less explicitly punk-oriented and vitriolic *New York Rocker* made it through 52 issues.

Just as the punk scene itself started to fragment and diversify, so did fanzines, moving from the slash 'n' burn style of the mid-'70s to somewhat more professional and readable formats, and a wider scope of subjects, encompassing non-punk rock, '50s and '60s music, individual groups/performers, or even non-rock. Fanzines devoted to blues, reggae, rockabilly, folk, the Velvet Underground, or nursing home residents reviewing records of all kinds (the famous *Duplex Planet*, still active in a modified format) were all fair game.

The '80s saw the fanzine field further diversify and stratify. Some were clearly intended for a local audience or mail distribution to friends, printed in quantities of a few hundred or even less. Productions like *The Offense Newsletter* and *Conflict* were just as uncompromising in their reflection of the authors' tastes, but stirred enough interest to attract national distribution., and at times, actual influence on the larger community: Tim Anstett's *Offense Newsletter* was probably the most important factor in attracting American attention to the British alternative rock label 4AD, and *Conflict* publisher Gerard Cosloy went on to be the A&R honcho of the indie rock labels Homestead and (as of 1995) Matador.

Then there were the bigger, slicker, and more comprehensive zines that became, well, real magazines, and may never have been true zines in the first place, although the grass-roots nature of their coverage and the sensibilities of their audience would not have been possible without the groundwork laid by smaller and less comprising publications. *Op*, which began as a supplement to a program guide of a college radio station in Olympia, Washington, evolved in stages into *Option* magazine; despite its far larger size and glossier appearance, it remains focused on alternative and independent music. *Dirty Linen* began as a Fairport Convention fanzine, and is now the leading folk and world music magazine in the US. In Britain, *Southern Rag* traveled a similar road when it evolved from its zine-like beginnings into *Folk Roots*, the leading folk and roots music magazine in the world. *Trouser Press*, one of the very few nationally distributed publications to cover underground rock upon its inception in the mid-'70s, folded in 1984, but gave birth to the regularly published *Trouser Press Record Guide*, the most definitive guidebook to punk and new wave available.

Then there are the fanzines which manage to be huge, in-depth, painstakingly designed, and totally uncompromising in their championship of the individual tastes of the authors. *Forced Exposure*, dominated by the writing and record collections of editor/publishers Jimmy Johnson and Byron Coley, has defined the most acerbic aspects of the rock underground since the mid-'80s; *Kicks*, run by Billy Miller and Miriam Linna, displays a similar exhaustive devotion to early rockabilly, R&B, surf, and garage rock acts. The specialized tastes (not to mention pointed jabs at anyone who doesn't like what they like) of such zines will prevent them from ever reaching a large readership or even publishing regularly (though they're not especially interested in doing so anyway), but ensures them a far more devoted audience than most publications of any sort, above-ground or underground. Delving into the vast and unpredictable world of fanzines is often as easy as stopping into a few of the hippest record stores in large US or UK cities. Those who don't have the resources to check those out should try reading reviews in *Factsheet Five* (which covers fanzines of all types) or contacting See Hear (59 E. 7th St., NYC 10003), a store which mail-orders a large selection of music zines, magazines, and books.—*Richie Unterberger*

Reissues

Whatever your taste or specialty—doo wop, electric blues, British Invasion, girl group, garage bands, punk, soul, funk, psychedelic—as a record collector, you're in a much better position in 1997 to track down your favorite records than you were even three years ago. Actually, you're in a much better position to track them down than you were when they were actually released, whether they came out in 1985 or 1955. The reissue explosion of the 1980s and 1990s has made more records from more different eras more widely available than any other time in history, and the selection increases daily.

The history of the rock reissue actually goes back nearly as far as rock itself. "Oldies" rock 'n' roll radio formats came into being in the early '60s, and Original Sound's extensive reissue compilation series, eventually numbering over a dozen volumes, helped keep many of rock 'n' roll's earliest and greatest hits relatively accessible. This was a time when little thought was given to preserving rock's heritage—the music hadn't even been around that long to begin with—and while it may have been easier then to buy rare obscurities for a nickel apiece in thrift stores and warehouses, it was much more difficult to find music more than a few years old unless it was recorded by big stars. The 1970s saw the emergence of the first companies dedicated to thoughtful, intelligent compilations of vintage rock 'n' roll. Sire was predominantly a contemporary rock label, handling several influential punk and new wave artists, but it also found time for a series of archival releases for such great acts as the Small Faces, the Troggs, Fleetwood Mac, Del Shannon, and Duane Eddy, as well as issuing the original *Nuggets* compilation. In the UK, Charly became the first of many European labels to plunder rock's history with a fanatical zealousness that, ironically, exceeded anything found in the music's American birthplace. It scored a major coup by licensing the Sun Records catalog, and expanded its focus to most kinds of rock 'n' roll, soul, and R&B music of the '50s and '60s.

Several other British labels followed suit in the 1980s, plundering the vaults of American labels that, again ironically, weren't able to license their material for US release. The biggest of these were Ace (with several subsidiaries, such as Big Beat), and Demon/Edsel, Elvis Costello's British label. Both companies, as well as Charly, are still around and thriving today, joined by others like See for Miles, Sequel, and Beat Goes On, assembling compilations of vintage rock 'n' roll, soul, R&B, British Invasion, and psychedelia whose appeal is probably limited to several thousand buyers worldwide in most cases.

Some authorities have pointed to these reissues, as well as similar compilations of vintage American music from Germany, France, Japan, and even Australia, as proof that great American music is more appreciated overseas than in its birthplace, where the trend-conscious and mindless masses are willfully ignorant of their own heritage. It makes for nice romantic myth, but a more likely explanation is that American companies are more reluctant to reissue obscure, vintage material for small, specialized audiences. The US is home to one of the world's leading reissue labels, Rhino, which has expanded from humble beginnings of novelty records to a catalog of several hundred titles, including many vintage Atlantic releases. The label claims that if your collection consisted of nothing but Rhino releases, you'd still have a damned good collection, and for once, the hype is no empty boast. Through their compilations and single-artist collections, Rhino has repackaged truckloads of classic rock 'n' roll of all types from the last 50 years. It tends not to delve into as obscure artists and vaults as its European counterparts, but even so, it still makes room for compilations of acts like the Shadows of Knight and the New Colony Six that were hardly superstars, as well as assembling little-known work by superstars like David Bowie and Roy Orbison, and previously unreleased material by Tim Buckley and Phil Ochs.

The advent of the CD format in the late '80s spurred reissues further, for reasons not entirely connected to the industry's belated recognition of its massive heritage. Major labels began reissuing their own back catalog, in addition to licensing it, eventually creating entire subsidiaries like Legacy, the Right Stuff, and Polydor Chronicles for that purpose. They realized that many listeners—many, but not all of them, Baby Boomers—were interested in "upgrading" their scratchy vinyl records with CD versions. They also realized that many consumers were interested in buying albums and compilations of artists whose work had lingered out-of-print for quite some time. Relative to new artists, the production, royalty, and promotion costs on reissues were minimal. Many of these reissues added the further enticements of additional bonus tracks (sometimes unreleased, sometimes from rare non-LP singles), remastering and remixing, and scholarly liner notes. For artists with wide appeal, these factors were often combined into box sets, which are discussed in a separate sidebar.

US box sets were often fairly selective in their presentation, and the real fanatics continued to go overseas for boxes that were zealously, sometimes indiscriminately completist. The champion in this department has to be Germany's Bear Family, which has issued box sets of artists like the Browns, Johnny & Jack, Wanda Jackson, and Lefty Frizzell that would be considered impossibly uncommercial in the States. As a whole, Bear Family has been a treasure trove of compilations for American roots music of the '40s, '50s, and (sometimes) '60s, encompassing not just R&B and rockabilly, but country & western, blues, and even an entire box set of music associated with the *Bonanza* TV program, all with exquisitely detailed liner notes. Other overseas companies of note include Germany's Repertoire, with an especially deep '60s catalog, which often adds more bonus tracks than were on the original albums in the first place. Australia's Raven has been crucial in making that country's '60s rock available internationally, and also packages obscure but worthy British and American rock from the same era, as well as sometimes delving into the '50s and '70s. It's still true that many US collectors have to go overseas for a portion, maybe the majority, of their reissue purchases. There are, however, several companies of note besides Rhino that operate in the United States, including Sundazed (specializing in '60s music), One Way, and Collectables (the most R&B-oriented of the trio). All of these reissue material by "cult" artists that Rhino and the majors may pass on because of their relatively limited audiences.

Finding reissues—which by now number in the thousands, produced by hundreds of companies—doesn't require a secret password, but it does require more work and diligence than driving down to the minimall. Collectors are advised to check out *Goldmine* magazine for the best mail-order sources of records that are impossible to find in local stores. Midnight Records (catalog available from P.O. Box 390, Old Chelsea Station, New York, NY 10113-0390) is the most comprehensive of these, although you should check out a few to find what you want and find out what's available on an ongoing basis.—*Richie Unterberger*

The Box Set

Walk past a big record store during the Christmas rush, and you're apt to spy Annette Funicello, Barry Manilow, Janis Joplin, and Led Zeppelin under the same tree. An all-star benefit, perhaps, in which legends agree to return from the dead and set aside their stylistic differences to join their negative mirror images for the sake of some good cause or another? Hardly. It's a phenomenon made possible by the rise of the box set. Literally hundreds of artists have now been anthologized in these lavish packages, which now encompass a smorgasbord of musical eras and styles that was unimaginable a decade ago.

According to Pulse! magazine, over 150 boxed set retrospectives were released in the US and abroad in 1993. (The figure went down slightly in 1994.) If you were to buy all of them at once, that would set you back about $6500. No one's maniacal enough to go to that extreme, but listeners who go beyond the day's current charts to collect their music have more multi-disc options than ever before. The box set has been a feature of the music industry for almost as long as records have been manufactured. Before the introduction of the long-playing record in the late 1940s, several 78 rpm discs were occasionally packaged together in boxes, sometimes in accordion-style binders. Material by superstars like Paul Robeson, Duke Ellington, and Benny Goodman was released in this fashion, although the limitations of the 78 required a good deal more

disc rotation than multiple CD collections do in the digital age. With the LP format, it was possible to release several hours of music within a box at once. The boxed set rapidly became widespread in classical releases, but was used much less often to package jazz or pop music. It was virtually never used to house rock 'n' roll music.

After landmark albums like Dylan's *Blonde on Blonde*, the Mothers of Invention's *Freak Out*, and the Beatles' *White Album* made double LPs acceptable in rock, boxes began to appear—although very rarely—to package multi-disc productions. George Harrison's *All Things Must Pass* and *The Concert for Bangladesh* were a couple of the best-selling examples, but they remained rare events. Eventually, box set collections appeared in small quantities by artists with devoted fan bases like the Beatles, Brian Eno, and Bill Nelson.

The introduction of the compact disc, along with the increasing spending power of Baby Boomers eager to assemble collected works of classic rock and soul musicians, began to spur the production of rock box sets in the mid-1980s. In 1986, Bob Dylan's five-LP *Biograph* set became the first rock retrospective of such size to reach the Top 40 album charts. More importantly, its mix of classic hits, key album cuts, rarities, and previously unreleased material, as well as a lavish booklet, became a model of sorts for the hundreds of rock and pop retrospectives that would follow. Later that year, a five-album box set of live Bruce Springsteen material went to No. 1. Multi-album live boxes didn't sprout in its aftermath; hardly anyone, after all, has as fanatical a following as Springsteen. What it did prove was that fans were willing to pay for such big, lavish packages in much greater force than most people expected.

Within a few years, the box set as concept had picked up a lot of momentum. Most major rock artists—including Elvis Presley, the Rolling Stones, the Who, Pink Floyd, Aerosmith, Aretha Franklin, Otis Redding, and the Beach Boys—have received the box set treatment. In some cases, such as Elvis', there are a few box sets, each devoted to different periods of his career. If your favorite famous artist doesn't have a box set yet, wait a while. It may take a few months or a few years, but odds are that one or several will certainly appear.

The impetus for box set production came from both consumers and the industry. Some music journalists may rant and rave about the ignorance of the great majority of the record-buying public, but the fact is that, on the whole, today's rock 'n' roll buyers are probably more conscious of musical history than ever before, and more willing to revisit past favorites and explore vintage releases that they never became familiar with in the first place. From an industry viewpoint, the CD format has enabled labels to present mammoth quantities of material in a more, well, compact form than was possible with the 12-inch LP.

More cynically, the CD format has generated extensive back catalog reissues because it enables the industry to re-sell albums to consumers that listeners already have in their collection, but may wish to "upgrade" from analog to digital. In comparison with new artists, such back catalog releases require a minimum of fuss in terms of artist development, production, and promotion. Collectors approach box set reissues with a mixture of joy and resentment. Often billed as "remixed" or "digitally remastered from the original tapes" (although the actual sonic differences may be extremely slight or even nonexistent), some listeners welcome the chance to replace their surface-noise-infested vinyl with fresh packages that will not deteriorate over time. Just as often, it seems, some killjoy or other determines that the remastered and remixed versions are actually distinctly inferior to their analog counterparts, sometimes radically so.

For listeners who aren't audiophiles, the issue of value-for-money remains. Who is the typical box set—with its mixture of hits, rarities, and album cuts—really satisfying? The casual fan will be more likely to pick up a greatest hits collection, or one or two LPs, and leave it at that. It's very rare that a box set will feature every last cut by an artist, so it's seldom that it acts as the definitive collection in and of itself. Listeners who are serious fans of an artist, but not unduly concerned with fancy packaging or remastering, find themselves caught in the middle. Enticed by rare and unreleased cuts that appear on almost every one of these sets—but rarely make up the majority of the content—they often find themselves paying quite a few dollars for the five to 15 cuts from a multi-disc box that they really want, and forced to repurchase quite a bit of music that they've already ensconced in their collection, and had no intention of buying again. And it's rare that a record company will accommodate these discerning listeners by issuing a separate collection that only contains the sought-after rarities.

For the truly comprehensive box sets, listeners often need to look to Europe, where reissue labels are truly fanatical about their music. Germany's Bear Family is particularly legendary for its almost humorously exhaustive retrospectives, such as its five-CD Lesley Gore compilation, its four-CD Marvin Rainwater set, and its eight-CD Lonnie Donegan project. These can be just as exhausting as exhaustive—do you really want to hear that Gene Vincent alternate take, or over 200 Fats Domino songs? An essential part of record collecting as the 20th century ends, the box set offers a mixed blessing—access to more rock music than ever before, but at a higher price.—*Richie Unterberger*

Cassette Culture

The punk and new wave explosion of the late '70s is remembered, among other things, for having brought the do-it-yourself ethic into popular music. The formation of numerous independent labels, distribution networks, fanzines, studios, and whatnot were unified not so much by musical style as a determination to do things their way, without concessions to corporate or commercial demands. One application of the DIY ethic that was relatively unheralded, then and now, was the proliferation of independently recorded music distributed by cassette. Perhaps the purest expression of the DIY ethic, its impact upon the commercial scene has been almost nonexistent, even as the number of cassette-only releases has multiplied many times over the last 15 years.

The cassette tape itself is a relatively new technology, only becoming a commonplace household item in the 1970s. It was introduced by the recording industry as a step up from bulky reel-to-reel tapes in portability (if not sound quality), and from the clunky eight-track tapes in both portability and sound quality. In the marketplace, it's been an unqualified success, accounting for more sales than any other format (that statistic can vary according to the source you read). Many listeners turned increased technology to their advantage to tape their friends' records or tape music off the radio, behavior which continues to get the industry up in arms and threatening sales taxes, although the actual impact of such home taping on overall sales is probably pretty slight.

Cassettes, of course, could be used to tape lots of other things besides official releases, including privately performed music. As many channels as the DIY ethic had opened for independent and self-released vinyl (compact discs weren't around then), it didn't necessarily open the door for any old musician who wanted to record and distribute their music. Independent labels still need to be fairly selective about who they sign, and the costs of pressing discs on your own label can be fairly high for those on a tight budget. Releasing music on cassette, though there is a slight drop in sonic quality in comparison to vinyl or compact disc, became an increasingly popular alternative for musicians who were unable to land a record contract, determined to do things exactly their way without the involvement of third parties, or simply wanted to record their own work as an avocation.

The range of cassette-only releases is, to say the least, extremely diverse. There are probably more rock (especially underground rock), experimental, and electronic cassettes than any other, but all types are represented, including traditional folk, world music, jazz, reggae, and what have you. The sound quality can vary from state-of-the-art to absolutely excruciating hiss that challenges the negative standards of the worst bootlegs. The purposes of these cassettes are similarly varied. Some are only meant for circulation to friends and family; some are intended to be taken as legitimate releases, to be judged on the same level as commercially available CDs; some are basically demo tapes, sent to stir up interest from record companies or clubs; some are out-and-out self-indulgent wanking, of no possible interest to anyone other than the perpetrators. Musicians without record deals often have a stock of professionally recorded cassettes of their work to sell at their gigs, or even on the street if they perform there.

A genuine network of musicians and listeners attuned to the cassette-only format didn't begin to evolve until the early '80s, when cassette-only releases received increasing attention in fanzines and national publications, especially the defunct *Op*. Cassette culture continues to get a reasonable amount of attention in underground publications to this day, although there's no central magazine or clearinghouse dealing with the sub-genre; *Option* printed many cassette reviews in its early years, shrinking its coverage of the medium steadily until the present day, when it only reviews such releases rarely. Radio stations (almost exclusively college radio and non-commercial ones) also give cassette releases much more exposure than they did ten to fifteen years ago, occasionally devoting entirely program slots to such items. Just as a glass can be viewed as half empty or half full, there are two valid ways of looking at cassette-only releases. From the most positive viewpoint, no recording medium is as unencumbered by commercial expectations, or as conducive to total artistic freedom. This goes right down to the sleeves, which are often hand-printed or hand-designed. For the increasingly large numbers of musicians who have home studios, or at least enough home studio equipment to record music in some semblance of professional quality, it's the easiest way to record and distribute their music.

A more jaded perspective would point out that the DIY ethic, wonderful in principle, gives voice to many unformed, imitative, repetitious, and downright embarrassing musical ventures through the cassette medium. Just as cassettes enable quality artists to record their music free of commercial pressures, it also enables those without any appreciable talent to record their mediocre, or downright excruciating, music for posterity. Without any professional standards to adhere to, the sound quality on many cassettes is awful, at times absolutely unlistenable. There are even some top-flight cassette artists who abuse the lack of quality-control boards in the medium by flooding the market with dozens of releases, some of them half-baked live performances or studio experi-

ments. Those aiming to take a gander at the world of cassettes should be aware that it's not only a haven for musicians who don't have a home on conventional record labels, but for entire genres of music which only gain CD release very infrequently. Thus there is a high percentage of tape-only releases in the noise/industrial/experimental vein, as well as other fairly esoteric genres like natural sounds and spoken word. That's not to say that the best of these aren't quality work, but that the medium as a whole leans considerably further to the avant-garde end of the spectrum than the larger music community.

Very few artists make significant profits through their cassette-only releases; the great majority are available through the mail only, usually from the musicians themselves, who are often quite amenable to trading for other tapes rather than selling. There are a few artists in cassetteland who have established a reputation, if even a cult one, through the voluminous and high quality of their tapes. R. Stevie Moore, who has made his own tapes since the 1970s (as well as occasional vinyl), is one of the most famous, purveying a sort of avant-garde pop-rock. Underground rock guitarist Eugene Chadbourne, though he's released many "real" albums, has released many more cassettes, often sold on the road at gigs. Experimental musicians Amy Denio and John Oswald, among others, released cassettes before attaining a higher level of visibility within the "new music" community.

Cassette culture's influence upon alternative rock is slight but real. The grand majority of rock bands choosing cassettes as their medium will never be heard by the larger audience, but there are occasional examples of well-known, or somewhat-known, bands like Throwing Muses, Sebadoh, or Pianosaurus who released their own cassettes before landing record deals. Liz Phair's *Girlysound* tapes introduced much of the material to become famous on her first two albums in intimate, low-fi versions, although these were largely intended for friends rather than a general audience; they were instrumental in landing her record deal, and are now among the most popular "unreleased" tapes ever recorded by a major artist. The British band Cleaners from Venus were usually content to release their delightfully eccentric British pop, which held its own with XTC and Robyn Hitchcock, via cassette only. Calvin Johnson's K label introduced notable alternative rock acts like Lois and Johnson's own band, Beat Happening, on cassette releases; the first American Shonen Knife release was on a K cassette (although the music had appeared on vinyl in Japan). Artists like Linda Smith and Jeff Kelly issued high-quality music on cassette that was inferior to "officially" released alternative rock only in its channels of distribution. Occasionally, talented performers who found themselves without a record contract for no apparent reason released their own cassettes to fill the gap, as Penelope Houston did in the early '90s. Most rap music is played and bought on cassette, and the cassette—in the forms of special mixes, self-produced and distributed releases, or (more nefariously) bootlegs—is a big part of rap/hip-hop culture, particularly in New York City, where one can pick up cassette compilations and mixes of hot sounds literally on the street. Oakland rapper Too Short began his climb to platinum with a self-distributed cassette that sold in the thousands before he hooked up with a record label.

There are also a few cassette labels that have carved an identity for themselves as repositories of high quality, non-mainstream music, differing only from similar record companies in their choice of format. Some of the most prominent of these include ROIR, with an extensive catalog of cassette-only releases by big-name alternative rock artists (with occasional detours into other music) such as Television, Richard Hell, and Nico; Tellus, one of the leading experimental/new music labels; and Global Village and Music of the World, both specializing in world music. Several of these labels have switched to the compact disc format, upgrading some or all of their back catalog in the wake of the CD revolution.

It's worth remembering that the cassette remains the primary means of musical distribution, by far, in the Third World. In many of these countries, copyright laws are lax, nonexistent, or unenforced, and pirate tapes are common in markets and stores, ranging from local musicians to superstars like the Beatles, Bob Marley, Dire Straits, and Marvin Gaye. Much of the music from these countries is only in the cassette format, as it's the cheapest medium for populations with lower incomes than the US or Europe, and much fine world music is only available on cassette, only within the performers' native territories. *–Richie Unterberger*

Book

Cassette Mythos, edited by Robin James (1992, Autonomedia)

Reference Books

✦✦✦ **Behind the Hits: Inside Stories of Classic Pop and Rock and Roll** *by Bob Shannon & John Javna* (Warner Books, 1986) Not highbrow stuff, but a pretty fun collection of little-known stories about hit rock records from the '50s to the '80s, weighted considerably toward the '60s and '50s. Grouped by categories like accidental hits, covers, "firsts," novelty tunes, songs inspired by real characters, and classics that came to life in freak studio circumstances, covering over a couple hundred songs. And they choose classics, generally, although occasionally one has cause to wonder whether anyone's interested in the genesis of Toto's "Rosanna" or Henry Gross's "Shannon." Well researched, with lots of fascinating and funny stories from the artists, session musicians, songwriters, DJs, and producers — *Richie Unterberger*

✦✦ **The Billboard Book of Top 40 Hits** *by Joel Whitburn* (Billboard, 1992). One should avoid the temptation to view this as a gospel of pop and rock history, given all the dubious chart measurement standards and payola scandals that have gone down in the rock era. Nevertheless, this fat listing of every single to make the Billboard Top 40 charts from 1955 to mid-1991 is a useful reference work, tracking the most widely used standard of sales and popularity — the charts published in *Billboard* magazine. Every listing includes the single's peak position, date of entry, and weeks on the chart, along with the label and catalog number. Arranged by artist, every song title is indexed in the back. The personnel listings, birthdates, and other trivia that accompany many of the entries can be useful, but be aware that they contain a surprising number of errors. — *Richie Unterberger*

✦✦ **The Blackwell Guide To Blues Records** *edited by Paul Oliver* (Blackwell, 1989) The most comprehensive reference book of its sort, not to say that it's even close to perfect, but there's really not much competition. The Blackwell layout is daunting for the novice: lots of essays of varying quality on regional styles, tons of song listings, and many fine capsule reviews of albums, ranging from famous to very, very obscure. Divided into chapters covering both regions (such as postwar Chicago) and styles (piano blues, "downhome postwar blues"), it also covers subgenres like rhythm and blues and soul blues that some purists would have regarded as too diluted and commercial to include. It's not the kind of thing you can read in a few sittings, but if you have patience, there's a lot of valuable information here, and the authors are good at pinpointing the best anthologies and starting points. — *Richie Unterberger*

✦✦ **The Blackwell Guide to Soul Recordings** *edited by Robert Pruter* (Blackwell, 1993) As books, the Blackwell Guides aren't the greatest; the essays sometimes cover such wide territory that they lose readers who aren't familiar with the subject, the writing can be dry, and the interspersion of reviews, essays, and discographical data is a bit of a jumble. Still, this is the best survey of soul recordings, divided by region, covering the music from its '50s R&B beginnings through "funk and later trends," as the last chapter is titled. In addition to all the expected big names, there are reviews of quite a few performers known primarily to the soul collector community, such as McKinley Mitchell, Lorraine Ellison, Shorty Long, Howard Tate, and Betty Harris. The book might benefit from focusing more on the concise reviews, which are usually quite good, but in any case this has info on a lot of performers that aren't reviewed in the more famous record guides. Inevitably, it misses a lot of reissues from the last two or three years that have been generated from the compact disc explosion. — *Richie Unterberger*

✦✦✦ **Blues: The British Connection** *by Bob Brunning* (Blanford Press, 1986) Brunning is not only an authority on British blues-rock, he was there: he played bass in the first lineup of Fleetwood Mac before John McVie joined, and went on to play with Savoy Brown and other blues-rock groups. This is a good survey of British blues-rock from the days of Alexis Korner through the 1980s, concentrating mostly on the 1960s, when the form was in its heyday. There are chapters devoted to all the major groups: the Yardbirds, John Mayall, Pretty Things, Spencer Davis, Manfred Mann, Graham Bond, Fleetwood Mac, Groundhogs, Ten Years After, Chicken Shack, Rory Gallagher, producer Mike Vernon. A lot of them are spiced by first hand recollections from band members; the ones missing these are considerably weaker. The sections on minor figures like Dave Kelly, Savoy Brown, and the Blues Band hold considerably less interest than the ones on the more important musicians, but it does give a pretty complete picture of the scene. — *Richie Unterberger*

✦✦✦✦ **Bootleg: The Secret History of the Other Recording Industry** *by Clinton Heylin* (St. Martin's, 1995) The inner machinations of the rock bootleg industry, responsible for literally thousands of important recordings that have never surfaced via official music business channels, have remained shadowy and murky even to many bootleg enthusiasts. This book doesn't solve all of the mysteries, but it's an often fascinating document of the growth of bootlegs since the late '60s, when unreleased recordings by Dylan, the Beatles, and the Stones gave them a jump start. Heylin talks to many of the principal bootleggers of the past and present (going on the record, necessarily, anonymously). This sheds valuable light on how the industry grew — the often farcical circumstances under which bootlegs were clandestinely manufactured and distributed, about absorbing anecdotes behind the acquisition of rare studio tapes, the mechanics of unauthorized live taping, the vehement attempts by the international record industry to eliminate bootlegs from public access. There are also discussions of the musical content of dozens of the most crucial bootlegs, investigations of music industry claims that they are financially harmful and artistically inferior, and evaluations of the importance of material archived on bootleg and the public's right to hear it. The lengthy passages detailing copyrights and legalities may be too dry for the music-oriented reader, and I would have preferred more extensive comments about the music itself (though there's a fair amount of that). But it's a valuable window into a previously hush-hush topic, and even those opposed to bootlegs will find much to think about in Heylin's persuasive arguments that unauthorized recordings represent no threat to the above-ground industry or artists' livelihood (the average bootleg title sells well under 5000 units), and have brought to light recordings of immense importance. — *Richie Unterberger*

✦✦✦ **Bringing It All Back Home** *by Robbie Woliver* (Pantheon, 1986) Ostensibly built around the New York club Folk City, this is really a story of the music scene of Greenwich Village, which has been crucial to the folk, folk-rock, and singer/songwriter scenes since the early '60s. Most of the book is oral history, with Woliver providing brief narrative links. Dozens of interviewees get space to tell stories, and the list covers just about everybody who was anybody who was based in New York (and some who weren't) and participated in the scene: Dylan, Roger McGuinn, Joan Baez, Judy Collins, Arlo Guthrie, John Sebastian, Dave Van Ronk, Peter Stampfel, Mary Travers, Lenny Kaye, Steve Forbert, Pete Seeger, and Suzanne Vega, among many others, on down to fairly obscure, if influential, figures like Carolyn Hester, Jean Ritchie, and Buzzy Linhart. The book losesf continuity in the last sections, as the scene expanded to include punk and new wave acts like Patti Smith, Talking Heads, the Ramones, the Violent Femmes, and so forth who couldn't be considered part of the folk and folk-rock lineage. But it still contains a great deal of lore that will interest almost any folk and rock fan. An identical version of the book was issued by St. Martin's under the title *Hoot!: A 25-Year History of the Greenwich Village Music Scene.* — *Richie Unterberger*

✦✦✦✦✦ **The British Invasion** *by Nicholas Schaffner* (McGraw-Hill, 1982) By far the best account of the '60s musical movement that, more than virtually any other, changed the face of rock music. A combination reference work and general interest account, with the accent on the general interest, Schaffner devotes entire chapters to the Beatles, Rolling Stones, Who, Pink Floyd, Kinks, T. Rex, and David Bowie, adding an overview of the punk/new wave explosion. These performers have been written about at great length elsewhere, to be sure, but Schaffner uncovers a great deal of obscure information and quotes from old reviews while telling their stories in an entertaining and critically acute fashion. There are also brief but info-packed one- and two-page sketches of 100 of the most notable British rockers, from 1964 to 1980. It includes a wealth of photos and chart information as well. — *Richie Unterberger*

✦✦ **Call Up the Groups!** *by Alan Clayson* (Blandford Press, 1985) Dedicated to "The Golden Age of British Beat 1962-67," this is a 200-page collection of profiles of virtually every U.K. group to land a British or American hit during the British Invasion, as well as a few who didn't. As a reference book, it has shortcomings. Clayson's writing is erratic, both in quality and depth. Many entries stick to dry, bare-bones facts without offering insightful description or critiques of the performers' music; others have some colorful commentary about their stage presence or behavior without really conveying a sense of what they sounded like, or assessing their significance to the British rock scene. And there are no essays covering the development of the British Invasion as a whole, or putting its various sub genres and styles into some kind of context. Stick with Nicholas Schaffner's The British Invasion for the best document of the movement, but those who want to dig deeper will find a lot of details on more obscure acts (although the coverage could be a lot better), as well as a wealth of photos. — *Richie Unterberger*

✦✦✦✦ **Christgau's Record Guide: Rock Albums of the '70s** *by Robert Christgau* (Da Capo Press, 1990) As the longtime rock critic for the *Village Voice*, Christgau is one of the most famous American rock journalists. In a monthly column, he offers paragraph-long reviews of recent significant releases, assigning each of them a grade, from A to E. This is a book-length compilation, almost 500 pages worth, of such reviews from the '70s, refurbished a bit from their original publication. Very few people feel neutral about Christgau; the blunt viciousness of some of his putdowns is bound to make all of his readers angry at some point or another, and the academic obtuseness of some of his evaluations can be infuriating. As a reference, though, this is pretty valuable, covering just about every release of major significance from the decade, and quite a few of minor significance. You will often disagree with him, but he almost always knows what he's talking about, and most of the pithy reviews convey the essential characteristics of the disc, even if you find his "grade" incorrect. Covers rock and soul, and a fair number of reggae, jazz, and other sundry non-rock releases as well. — *Richie Unterberger*

✦✦✦✦ **Christgau's Record Guide: The '80s** *by Robert Christgau* (Pantheon, 1990) 500 more pages, in exactly the same format as his compilation of '70s reviews, this time covering the following decade. All of the comments for his '70s volume apply here, though it seems as though there's a higher percentage of frustratingly obtuse reviews. Again, covers all kinds of aboveground and underground rock and soul, as well as plenty of world music, reggae, country, and other kinds of non-rock. The most significant gap is the absence of quite a few indie alternative rock records; as Christgau himself notes in his opening essays, the '80s were categorized by fragmentation and increasing diversity, and he drew the line at absorbing and reviewing a lot of records he might have found time for in previous years. For those, we'll have to look in *The Trouser Press Record Guide* and *Option*. Includes extensive introductory remarks about '80s rock. —*Richie Unterberger*

✦✦✦✦ **Country on Compact Disc** *by the Country Music Foundation,* edited by *Paul Kingsbury* (1993, Grove Press) There's a major shortage of good critical reference works on country records — country of all kinds, encompassing traditional sounds, bluegrass, and Nashville. This is by far the best, strongly resembling the *Rolling Stone Album Guide* in format, with its one-to-five star rating system and combination career/discography overviews. The writing's very good — a rarity in country journalism — and very catholic in taste, viewing Jimmie Rodgers and Garth Brooks as part of the same spectrum, in the manner that rock critics can view Elvis Presley and Madonna as part of the same phenomenon. Some might find their assessments of the current Nashville crop too generous, but in treating the so-called "Hats" with seriousness, they are according them respectful evaluations that are merited by the fact that much of mainstream America listens to such music more than anything else. The chief flaw is the limited scope of the volume — as the title implies, only albums which have been issued on compact disc are reviewed, which makes the guide extremely strong on records of the late '80s and early '90s, but omits quite a few vintage albums that hadn't come out on CD by 1993. —*Richie Unterberger*

✦✦✦✦ **Deep Blues** *by Robert Palmer* (Viking Press, 1981). Renowned critic, and sometime musician, Palmer traces the evolution of a major (perhaps THE major) strain of blues, from rural Mississippi Delta acoustic forms through its move to the cities, particularly Chicago, where it became amplified and provided a bedrock foundation for rock 'n' roll. There are more comprehensive, scholarly analyses of the blues available, but this is the most readable and accessible by a wide margin, with plenty of first hand recollections from Muddy Waters, Robert Lockwood, Jr., Sam Phillips, and others. —*Richie Unterberger*

✦✦✦✦✦ **England's Dreaming** *by Jon Savage* (Faber & Faber, 1991) A mammoth, absorbing history of the birth of British punk, focusing primarily on the Sex Pistols, but including lots of coverage of early pioneers such as the Clash and the Buzzcocks, as well as the accompanying birth of a punk subculture as reflected through fanzines and the music's audience. Packed with great stories about the group's unlikely birth and success, peppered with succinct social analysis and recollections from a lot of those who were there at the time. Even if you don't care for punk, this is fascinating reading, exploring the birth of a movement that upset the industry, and the public at large, to an almost unimaginable extent. Sometimes the focus rambles, and sometimes the sociopolitical analysis gets a trifle too weighty, but these are minor quibbles. Includes a huge discography, with critical commentary, on almost every early punk record of note. — *Richie Unterberger*

✦✦✦✦ **Feel Like Going Home** *by Peter Guralnick* (Vintage, 1971) Guralnick is one of America's premier writers and critics of roots music, and this collection of his early essays is an important work, offering sensitive and in-depth portraits of a gaggle of major early rock and blues stars: Jerry Lee Lewis, Howlin' Wolf, Charlie Rich, Muddy Waters, Skip James, Johnny Shines, and the owners of Sun and Chess Records. Guralnick spent a lot of time with each of his subjects, often observing them at home or on stage; in some cases, he was apparently the first journalist to treat the musician as a serious artist. Perhaps as a result, he landed some poignant and personal material, the kind that publicists shield from serious but inquisitive writers. Guralnick tends to romanticize his heroes as artists who have never received their just due, but this is one of the best books of its kind. — *Richie Unterberger*

✦✦✦✦✦ **From the Velvets to the Voidoids: A Pre-punk History for a Post-Punk World** *by Clinton Heylin* (Penguin, 1993) The definitive history of early American punk and new wave, focusing mostly upon the New York scene clustered around CBGB's, as well as some Cleveland artists (the groups that sprang up in the wake of the early punk explosion in California and other areas are not covered). Alternating between Heylin's text and dozens of fascinating quotes and recollections from key players like Patti Smith, Tom Verlaine, and David Johansen, this has lots of little-heard stories of punk's evolution in the early and mid-'70s. Patti Smith, Television, Blondie, the Ramones, the New York Dolls, the Talking Heads, Suicide, Richard Hell, and Pere Ubu are all covered exhaustively, and the early chapters document such important pre-punk pioneers as the Velvet Underground, the MC5, the Stooges, and the Modern Lovers. A large critical discography covers both released material and bootlegs. Combined with Jon Savage's British punk history, *England's Dreaming*, it's the best document of early punk to date. —*Richie Unterberger*

✦✦ **Fortunate Son: The Best of Dave Marsh** *by Dave Marsh* (Random House, 1985) Probably America's most famous rock critic, Dave Marsh has often ranked among the nation's best, though his reputation has suffered in the past decade or so due to his idoltry of Bruce Springsteen, the hectoring tone of his publication, *Rock 'n' Roll Confidential*, and his

inability to fully come to grips with alternative rock and other recent trends. This anthology covers roughly 15 years of his writing, and doesn't dig beyond the mainstream too much. That's not a flaw; there are dozens of interesting, at times insightful, pieces here on many of the most worthy rock icons, including Marvin Gaye, Muddy Waters, Elvis Presley, Sly & the Family Stone, and the Rolling Stones, in addition to essays on general developments in soul, disco, and punk, as well as probes into film, books, and aspects of the rock business. Sometimes his opinions are didactic, and he's as much bewildered by punk and post-early '70s underground rock as excited by it. But this collection is worth reading, highlighted perhaps by passionate musings on heroes from his Detroit hometown (Mitch Ryder, Bob Seger, Iggy Pop, the MC5). —*Richie Unterberger*

✦✦✦✦✦ **Girl Groups: The Story of a Sound** *by Alan Betrock* (Delilah, 1982) Definitive and entertaining history of the early '60s girl groups, covering all of the keystones of the style: the singers, the producers, and the songwriters. It has in-depth histories of all of the major girl group performers: the Chantels, the Shirelles, the Shangri-Las, Lesley Gore, Mary Wells, Martha & the Vandellas, the Supremes, the Ronettes, the Crystals, the Chiffons, the Dixie Cups, the Angels, and more. But it's not a reference book: it's written as a story, with large sections on the Brill Building songwriters who wrote many girl group classics, Phil Spector, and the Red Bird label (home of several of the best girl groups). With first-hand memories from many of the principal singers and songwriters, lots of photos, and penetrating commentary about the reasons for the style's vast success and swift downfall in the mid-'60s, this is one of the best rock 'n' roll books. —*Richie Unterberger*

✦✦✦✦✦ **Good Rockin' Tonight: Sun Records and the Birth of Rock 'n' Roll** *by Colin Escott with Martin Hawkins* (St. Martin's Press, 1991) Excellent history of what was, in the final estimation, the label most responsible for launching rock 'n' roll, although the contributions of other indies like Atlantic were also immensely important. Includes chapters on all the major Sun stars: Elvis, Johnny Cash, Carl Perkins, Jerry Lee Lewis, and Roy Orbison. Of equal interest, though, are the descriptions of owner/producer Sam Phillips's slap-echo studio sound and distinctive artistic vision, which also encompassed a wealth of blues and country music. Besides first- and second-hand interviews with the most famous characters in the Sun story, you also hear from more obscure performers and sidemen, and get profiles of relatively unheralded artists like Warren Smith and Junior Parker. Fascinating stuff, this is an updated version of a history first published around 1980, and includes a good deal of new information and many great photos. —*Richie Unterberger*

✦✦ **The Haight-Ashbury** *by Charles Perry* (Rolling Stone Press, 1984) Not a rock book, this is nonetheless recommended reading for anyone interested in late-'60s rock in general, and in San Francisco psychedelic rock in particular. The interplay between counterculture and music was more fervid in San Francisco's Haight-Ashbury in the mid- and late '60s than almost any other scene. Perry was there, and he chronicles the period with detail, covering the psychedelic drug culture, community organizations, local press, live performance spaces, clashes between youth and authority, and the music. — *Richie Unterberger*

✦✦ **The History of Scottish Rock and Pop: All That Ever Mattered** *by Brian Hogg* (Guinness Publishing, UK, 1993) Like Ireland, Scotland, a tiny country (a little over five million people), has made impressive contributions to rock history way out of proportion to its actual size. The problem in assembling a history of Scottish rock for this volume, a companion to a BBC television series, is that it (like Irish rock, for that matter) lacks strong unifying stylistic elements. Lulu, Alex Harvey, the Bay City Rollers, Donovan, the Average White Band, the Incredible String Band, Gerry Rafferty, Simple Minds, the Jesus & Mary Chain, Primal Scream, Teenage Fanclub—yes, all have made an international impact, but they haven't exactly sprung from similar musical schools. And while most rock fans will be interested in the histories of a few of these performers, very few will be interested in all of them, which makes this quite a jumpy read, no matter what your taste. The 400 pages contain a lot of information, much of it quite obscure, and as such, it's a reasonably valuable reference, but general readers are advised to go for the chapters or sections covering performers they're interested in, and not feel guilty about skipping chunks altogether. — *Richie Unterberger*

✦✦✦ **Hollywood Rock** *by Marshall Crenshaw* (Harper Perennial, 1994) "A guide to rock 'n' roll in the movies," this falls second to the best reference book to rock films, *Rock on Film*, despite covering movies through 1993 (*Rock on Film* only got to the beginning of the 1980s). The reviews are longer, but the writing isn't quite as good, and it fails to mention some interesting items entirely that made it into *Rock on Film*. There aren't any separate essays to put the whole rock film genre into context, and more importantly, the reviewers often demonstrate a weakness for schlock, giving too many four- and five-star ratings to silly beach and exploitation films, as fun as those might be if you're in a certain mood. Still, a useful guide to have around, including about 300 reviews, and capsule descriptions of a few hundred more. — *Richie Unterberger*

✦✦✦✦ Incredibly Strange Music, Vol. 1 & 2 (RE/SEARCH, 1993 & 1994). For all the tens of thousands of albums covered by current reference books music recordings, there are tens of thousands of others that never get covered. These are the kind of albums and singles that populate thrift shops, garage sales, and attics: exotica, novelty, soundtracks, unknown regional 45s of all styles. These fat volumes consist primarily of fascinating interviews with major record collectors, talking about their weirdest obscure albums. And these are plenty weird, ranging from inept musical excursions by celebrities to a choir of ex-drug addicts to fusions of psychedelia and muzak. Several of these collectors are musical celebrities in their own right, such as Jello Biafra, the Cramps, and *Kicks* magazine publishers Billy Miller and Miriam Linna; there are also interviews with cult artists like exotica king Martin Denny, spoken word master Ken Nordine, and Robert Moog. Judging from the compilation of music that Caroline put out to accompany the first volume, a lot of this stuff might not be as mindbendingly strange and exciting as it seems from the descriptions. Still, for anyone interested in record collecting or musical/pop culture of all sorts, this is real edge-of-the-chair reading, with hundreds of great reproductions of some of the strangest album sleeves you'll ever see. — *Richie Unterberger*

✦✦✦✦ Krautrocksampler *by Julian Cope* (Head Heritage, 1995) A passionate survey of "Krautrock," the German synthesis of progressive/psychedelic rock with contemporary classical and electronics, by cult rocker Julian Cope. After a bit of general background, Cope zooms right into enthusiastic, chapter-long appreciations of Krautrock's heavy hitters: Can, Faust, Neu!, Ash Ra Tempel, Tangerine Dream, and Amon Duul. There are also detailed reviews of Cope's 50 favorite Krautrock albums, including his favorite works by the artists mentioned above, as well as ones by Popol Vuh, Cluster and Klaus Schultze, on down to trivia questions like Guru Guru. Cope's a funny writer, describing his records with such zeal that you can get caught up in the text without having heard them (and most people *haven't* heard them). His enthusiasm might be over-the-top: numerous records are described as one-of-a-kind, incomparable to anything else ever done, or the best example of (fill in the blank) in the entire history of rock 'n' roll. But considering how little has been written about the subject, it's a valuable reference guide, with a sense of humor that much Krautrock itself lacks. Also includes color reproductions of Cope's favorite Krautrock album sleeves. — *Richie Unterberger*

✦✦ The L.A. Musical History Tour *by Art Fein* (Faber & Faber, 1991) "A guide to the rock and roll landmarks of Los Angeles," this has photos and entertaining capsule descriptions of over 200 local homes, studios, clubs, record stores, hotels, restaurants, album cover sites, gravestones, and other locations that made their mark on rock 'n' roll history. Fein's a witty and knowledgeable writer, as interested in Eddie Cochran's gravestone or the canyon where the Rolling Stones were photographed for the *High Tide* sleeve as world-famous images like the Capitol Records Tower and the Whisky-A-Go-Go. Full of interesting trivia, this is a frivolous project, yes, but a highly enjoyable one. — *Richie Unterberger*

✦✦✦✦ Lost Highway *by Peter Guralnick* (Vintage, 1979) Like his previous *Feel Like Going Home*, these are more first-rate, human portrayals of major American roots musicians, going heavier on the country & western this time around (though blues and early rock musicians are also included). Many musicians of the first echelon and a few more obscure noteworthies are included in this gallery of portraits, including Ernest Tubb, Hank Snow, Rufus Thomas, Bobby Bland, Scotty Moore, Charlie Feathers, Mickey Gilley, Waylon Jennings, Merle Haggard, James Talley, Joe Turner, Howlin' Wolf, and Otis Spann. — *Richie Unterberger*

✦✦✦ Louie, Louie *by Dave Marsh* (Hyperion, 1993) An unusual idea for a rock book, done well. "Louie Louie" is the quintessential garage rock tune, and has been covered by more artists than almost any other rock 'n' roll song. Marsh traces its genesis through the decades, from the original 1956 version by unsung L.A. R&B singer Richard Berry (who himself based it on a riff from an obscure cha cha number). A regional hit that was pretty much left for dead, it was revived a few years later by several Northwest bands, culminating in the unlikely number two national hit by the Kingsmen in 1963. Its classic three-chord riff came to ensure its place as a rock 'n' roll standard, after overcoming a ludicrous FBI investigation into the supposed lewdness of its lyrics. Eventually it inspired "Louie Louie" radio marathons, and campaigns to adopt it as the official Washington State song. Marsh follows the trail all the way (the description of the early-'60s Northwest rock 'n' roll scene, a forerunner of garage rock and punk, is especially interesting), ending with the rights to the composition finally getting restored to its rightful owner, Richard Berry. Some of Marsh's recent work has been heavy-handed, but this study, if it can be called that, combines an appropriate sense of humor and affection with its scholarly detail.

✦✦✦ Making Tracks *by Charlie Gillett* (1974, Souvenir Press) Gillett is the author of the first comprehensive (and still one of the most acclaimed) rock 'n' roll histories, *The Sound of the City*. This is his history of Atlantic Records, the most successful independent to survive from rock 'n' roll's earliest days. More a history of the music than the business, anyone who's interested in early R&B and rock will find a lot of absorbing reading here. Gillett interviewed Atlantic principals Ahmet Ertegun and (to a significantly greater degree) Jerry Wexler extensively, yielding a lot of first-hand recollections about the early careers of such important artists as Ruth Brown, Clyde McPhatter, Joe Turner, Ray Charles, Solomon Burke, Otis Redding, and Aretha Franklin. Important ancillary figures like Jesse Stone, songwriters Jerry Leiber and Mike Stoller, and Rick Hall of Fame Studios in Muscle Shoals, AL, also get a chance to speak. Gillett is principally an R&B and soul man, so Atlantic's ventures into pop, white rock, and British rock are covered in considerably less depth, although they aren't neglected. — *Richie Unterberger*

✦✦ Music Man *by Dorothy Wade & Justine Picardie* (1990, W.W. Norton) Atlantic Records chief Ahmet Ertegun may have been a more conscientious guy, and more knowledgeable musical authority, than most of the other figureheads of independent companies that helped launch rock 'n' roll. He still had to play the music business game to survive and thrive, especially in the early days, when that meant courting favor with disc jockeys or wangling complicated and tense deals to ensure the company's success. Knowledge of this underbelly of intrigue behind rock 'n' roll is valuable, if fairly depressing in its low premium upon ethics. The book details the machinations behind a big record label fairly well at times, but suffers from two problems. First, it can't decide whether to be a specific history of Ertegun/Atlantic or of rock 'n' roll wheeling and dealing as a whole, veering off into tangents about such avaricious early rock businessmen as Morris Levy and Alan Freed, and throwing in bits of history about other independent labels and scandalous behavior in the music industry. Second, little sense of Ertegun/Atlantic's specific vision, which saw them launch or sustain the careers of such giants as Ray Charles, Aretha Franklin, Led Zeppelin, Crosby, Stills & Nash, and the Rolling Stones, emerges. For that tale, as well as a much more focused read, seek out Charlie Gillett's *Making Tracks*, a fine history of Atlantic from a more musical perspective. — *Richie Unterberger*

✦✦ Off The Record: An Oral History Of Popular Music *by Joe Smith, edited by Mitchell Fink* (1988, Warner Books) As a DJ, and more especially as a high-ranking executive for Warner Brothers, Elektra/Asylum, and Capitol, Joe Smith has been an important figure in the music business. Over the course of four decades or so, he's met most of the major players, and this 430-page volume has oral histories from over 200 of them; musicians mostly, but also important producers, songwriters, and industry moguls. Breadth is not the problem here; the majority of the major rock legends are present, from Dylan and members of the Beatles and Stones down. Each history, though, runs only a page or two, so this could hardly be considered an in-depth or satisfying work, though plenty of interesting morsels and trivia emerge. — *Richie Unterberger*

✦✦✦✦✦ The Penguin Guide To Jazz On CD, LP & Cassette *by Richard Cook & Brian Morton* (1994, Penguin) One of the most impressive musical reference books of any sort, this has 1,400 pages of informed, detailed criticism of several thousands of jazz albums of every stripe. The authors really know their stuff, and rate each record on a scale from one to four stars. Some minor reservations: the listings, as mammoth as they are, include only albums that are in print, excluding quite a few noteworthy, even classic, works; the writing can be a bit obtuse; and the entries usually plunge right into reviews of specific albums, without supplying thumbnail biographical data or a summary/perspective of the artists' significance and their overall contribution to jazz. It's still an essential reference, one which no jazz fan should be without. — *Richie Unterberger*

✦✦✦ Pete Frame's Rock Family Trees *by Pete Frame* (1979, Quick Fox) If your collection is big enough, chances are you've got some Pete Frame family trees residing in your liner notes. Rock fanatic and graphic artist Frame specializes in family trees detailing a band's evolution, through the years and different lineups; he'll often group several bands of a particular region or style together to illustrate the incestuous trades and comings-and-goings. Alongside the "trees," in tiny print, is commentary not only explaining who played what and when, and why people came and left, but also featuring some fascinating trivia and critical comments. This volume gathers together a few dozen of his best trees, encompassing many of the major bands of the '60s and '70s, and is both a fun read and a valuable resource work. A second volume documents the trees of less interesting artists, and is much less essential; both volumes were recently combined into one book and reissued. — *Richie Unterberger*

✦✦✦ Punk Diary 1970-1979 *by George Gimarc* (1994, St. Martin's) Not a personal diary, but a comprehensive diary of notable record releases, live shows, band personnel changes, and other noteworthy developments in early punk rock, concentrating of course much more heavily on 1976-79 than 1970-75, arranged by exact date. This is somewhat more developed than an assemblage of raw data, but somewhat less than a work of prose. Gimarc condenses the events into matter-of-fact sentences and paragraphs, drawing heavily from quotes and articles that appeared at the time in magazines like *NME*, peppering the entries with reproductions of record sleeves and promotional posters. It's only recommended to serious punk fans, but those will find it a valuable reference work, if a bit on the dry side. —*Richie Unterberger*

✦✦✦ **Rhythm Oil** by *Stanley Booth* (1991, Pantheon) He hasn't written prolifically, and he hasn't written much about music that was performed after the early '70s, but Memphis writer Booth is one of the best chroniclers of blues, soul, and rock that draws upon those influences. This collection of essays, often drawn from first-person experiences with the musicians at recording sessions, concerts, and their homes, includes good pieces on Otis Redding, Furry Lewis, B.B. King, Elvis, Janis Joplin, Al Green, James Brown, and little-known but widely respected Memphis jazz pianist Phineas Newborn. An adept critic, Booth's special skill is drawing upon the cultural ambience of the music—often Memphis, almost always the American South—to give a deeper understanding of how their environment, professional and personal, informs their art. —*Richie Unterberger*

✦✦✦**Rock: The Rough Guide** edited by *Johathan Buckley and Mark Ellingham*(Rough Guides, 1996)
Rock: The Rough Guide is a rarity among books of its kind; instead of the usual critics and pop historians, it's written entirely by fans, its biographies of musicians commissioned initially via newspaper and magazine advertisements and later over the *Rough Guide's* internet site. The result is an admirably democratic volume, but also a schizophrenic and often puzzling one: as is expected, the writing ranges from the professional to the amateurish, and while none of the entries lack enthusiasm, many are strangely incomplete and littered with errors, especially odd given that the biographies are, at least in theory, written by major fans of the given artists. Additionally, the book is rather self-indulgent, skipping over a number of major mainstream performers in favor of cult fetishes—one-hit wonders James Jones and the La's make the cut, for example, but stalwart pop stars Billy Joel and Huey Lewis are nowhere in sight; even more curious is the inclusion of minor figures Balaam and the Angel, Honeycrack and Salad. Finally, critical analysis is kept to a minimum, with only a handful of reviews accompanying each biography—not even the Beatles and Bob Dylan are given a thorough appraisal. While a fascinating undertaking, *Rock: The Rough Guide* is too flawed to be of interest or value to most readers. — *Jason Ankeny*

✦✦ **Rock Around The Bloc** by *Timothy W. Ryback* (1990, Oxford University Press) Ever since rock began, it's been received with vociferous enthusiasm in Eastern Europe and the former Soviet Union, and, until the recent thaw of the cold war, met with equally zealous official oppression. This is an extremely thorough, if a bit dry, history of the music in the region. As a basic informational source, it's a useful volume, drawing upon hundreds of sources to present events and developments that were rarely reported in the West. The rare concerts behind the Iron Curtain by Western performers, ranging from the Rolling Stones to Uriah Heep, almost always provoked a brouhaha of sorts (even those by such relatively mild acts as the Nitty Gritty Dirt Band), and these are detailed as well. Readable despite its somewhat academic treatment, it gives us a lot of the what, but not enough of the how and why. Lots of musicians and listeners went to considerable risk to hear and play rock in the Eastern Bloc; in the late '50s, rock 'n' roll records were pirated onto the emulsion of discarded X-ray plates, and Czechoslavakia's Plastic People were imprisoned for playing their music. But the actual Eastern Bloc rock community doesn't tell its story here, and the music that Eastern Bloc performers created is not analyzed in great critical depth (although many of them never got to record). —*Richie Unterberger*

✦✦✦ **Rock 'n' Roll Road Trip** by *A.M. Nolan* (1992, Pharos) Subtitled "the ultimate guide to the sites, the shrines and the legends across America," and lives up to its billing. This has the addresses and succinct, informative capsule descriptions of clubs and concert halls (many still active), birthplaces, studios, record stores, gravesites, album cover landmarks, and various other sites of interest to devoted rock fans throughout America. Including lots of photos, the book's strength is that it's not a mere collection of listings. Nolan also tells the stories behind the places, and what makes their history interesting, which makes for good reading even if you don't do a lot of traveling. —*Richie Unterberger*

✦✦✦ **Rock On Film** by *David Ehrenstein & Bill Reed* (1982, Delilah) It only goes up to the beginning of the 1980s, but this is the best book about, well, rock on film. A combination reference book/critical study, it lists nearly 500 films — documentaries, festivals, fiction films starring rock musicians in prominent roles, fiction films in which rock music is a central or vital ingredient, films which feature memorable cameo musical performances by notable rock musicians, films for which major rock musicians provided the soundtrack, and more. Each entry is accompanied by a pithy capsule summary/critique. The listings are preceded by 100 pages of good critical essays about various subgenres like the rockumentary, the Beatles on film, beach movies, and rock soundtracks. —*Richie Unterberger*

✦✦✦ **Rolling Stone Album Guide** edited by *Anthony DeCurtis & James Henke with Holly George-Warren* (Straight Arrow, 1992). There's a lot to criticize about this 800+ page reference work, if you're so inclined. Many worthwhile performers are not listed, particularly alternative and independent rock artists; the reviewers are sometimes brief to a fault; they are often churlish, even brutally nasty, in their assessment of some acts that do not measure up to current standards of hipness. The fact remains, though, that this is the best overall guide to rock recordings available. The writing is informed and passionate, if occasionally smug; virtually all artists of truly major significance are included; the discographies are pretty thorough, with a handy (if unavoidably inconsistent) rating system ranging from one to five stars. Incidentally, this is the third edition of the book, completely revised from the original 1979 volume, which was edited by Dave Marsh. That red-covered edition, called *The Rolling Stone Record Guide*, is worth picking up if you find it used; the reviews are entirely different, and the entries cover quite a few artists and out-of-print albums that didn't make it into the current revision. The second edition (identifiable by its blue cover), from the mid-1980s, is dispensable. —*Richie Unterberger*

✦✦✦✦ **The Rolling Stone Illustrated History Of Rock & Roll** by *Anthony DeCurtis & James Henke with Holly George-Warren* (Straight Arrow, 1992). Still the best general history of rock music, comprising about 100 succinct essays on rock's most important performers and most important genres. Many of the best rock journalists contribute to this volume, including Greil Marcus, Dave Marsh, Peter Guralnick, Robert Palmer, Robert Christgau, Lester Bangs, and Greg Shaw. It is packed with both critical insight and historical detail, with excellent discographies and many wonderful photos. Only two flaws to consider: unavoidably, a lot of interesting performers were omitted (you'd need several volumes of this size to satisfactorily cover every worthwhile rock musician). More seriously, the coverage is heavily weighted towards, and much stronger on, pre-1980 rock; it really seems to run out of steam, in both breadth and quality, when it approaches the modern era. Hold on to the original mid-'70s edition as well, if you still have it; many photos were reproduced in larger formats in that volume, and some essays that appeared in the initial version have been excised or revised for no good reason. —*Richie Unterberger*

✦✦✦ **The Rolling Stone Interviews, Vol. 1** (1971, Straight Arrow) Rolling Stone was the first American publication to treat rock 'n' roll musicians as cultural and artistic figures of major significance. The musicians were thankful to have a forum to express their views and opinions with seriousness, and in its early years, the magazine ran many fascinating, extremely lengthy (by 1990s standards) interviews with most of the period's leading rockers. Their first interview anthology, long out of print but easy to find as a cheap used paperback, was the best, containing almost 500 pages of Q & A's with John Lennon, Eric Clapton, Jim Morrison, Grace Slick, Mick Jagger, Phil Spector, John Fogerty, Bob Dylan, Pete Townshend, Chuck Berry, Little Richard, David Crosby, Frank Zappa, and others. —*Richie Unterberger*

✦✦✦✦ **The Rough Guide To World Music** (1994, Rough Guides) Easily the best reference book currently available for world music, which in the editors' terms covers everything except western classical music and Anglo-American rock, soul, rap, jazz, and country. That leaves 700 pages covering traditional and popular sounds from all continents, from Celtic folk to Indonesian pop to soukous and zouk to reggae and gamelan to flamenco and Indian film music. The chapters are divided into lengthy scene overviews, with sidebars covering musical terms, notable festivals, and portraits of/interviews with important performers like Youssou N'Dour, Baaba Maal, Ruben Blades, Caetano Veloso, and many others. The variety of focus, skilled, passionate writing, and plenty of photos make this a much more enjoyable experience than the typical reference work. It's not a discography or compendium of record reviews, if that's what you're looking for, although there are numerous brief capsule descriptions of the most essential recordings of each region/country/genre. —*Richie Unterberger*

✦✦✦ **San Francisco Nights: The Psychedelic Music Trip 1965-1968** by *Gene Sculatti & Davin Seay* (1985, St. Martin's) Not as comprehensive as Joel Selvin's more recent *Summer of Love*, and more anecdotal in approach, but a more enjoyable read, overall. Selvin's book was written as a recreation of events; Sculatti and Seay take a lot of first-hand memories and quotes from such key figures as Quicksilver Messenger Service's John Cipollina and Big Brother's Peter Albin. Focuses very much on the birth of the scene and its early days, with attention paid to the biggest groups like the Airplane and Dead, but a fair amount is also told of the Mystery Trend and the Charlatans as well. Also a lot of history of the early psychedelic concert circuit, with plenty of photos and concert posters from the scene's halcyon days. —*Richie Unterberger*

✦✦✦✦ **The Sound Of The City** by *Charlie Gillett* (1970, Pantheon) Originating as a university thesis, this was the first attempt to write a comprehensive history of rock 'n' roll, dealing with the form primarily in musical terms, not celebrity or popular culture ones. It's still one of the best, although the coverage only extends into the early '70s. Gillett's scholarship, though quite readable, is intensely detailed, accurately describing the cross-fertilization of vocal, instrumental, and production styles from the mid-'40s through the next several decades. He views the struggle of independent labels, as well as the struggle of major labels to come to terms with rock's popularity, as one of the most important undercurrents of rock; hence the performers are often discussed in terms of their labels and producers, as well as their regions or styles. Gillett's tastes run towards R&B and roots-rock, and singles rather than album-length statements; some readers may be taken aback by his clinical, not-wholly-enthusiastic assessments of the Beatles, Jimi Hendrix, Elvis Presley, and other major rock deities. The focus, concerned with what's in the grooves rather than personality and attitude, may strike some as too detached and analytical. Gillett covered an enormous amount with this volume, though, intelligently and objectively, and this remains an important foundation of rock scholarship. The Pantheon revised edition adds a little material to the 1970 printing, just extending the coverage a year or two into the 1970s. —*Richie Unterberger*

♦♦ **Starmakers And Svengalis** *by Johnny Rogan* (1988, Queen Anne Press, UK) Rogan is one of Britain's most dedicated rock scribes, penning lengthy histories of the Byrds, the Smiths, the Kinks, and Neil Young, among others. This collection of profiles of Britain's most famous rock and pop managers, never issued in the States, deserves points for broaching unusual subject matter, but doesn't stand up as well as his other bios. Not through much fault of Rogan's: he does his usual thorough research and first-hand interviews, profiling the most famous (Brian Epstein, Andrew Oldham, Malcolm McLaren) along with names that are less familiar to Americans (Don Arden, Reg Calvert, early Bowie mentor Kenneth Pitt). Concentrating more on the business/professional side of things than the artistic one, the subjects of these profiles are, to put it simply, generally, less interesting than musicians, and it's debatable how many readers are concerned with reading about someone like Gordon Mills (whose prior clients were Tom Jones, Engelbert Humperdinck, and Gilbert O'Sullivan). There are anecdotes concerning most major, and many minor, British acts of the '60s and '70s (not as many, or as interesting, as you might expect). The chapters on Larry Parnes and Reg Calvert provide glimpses into the little-documented world of pre-Beatles British rock and pop, but by the end of the book, one has tired of reading about the ego battles and business headaches that afflict, in similar fashions, most successful rock acts. —*Richie Unterberger*

♦♦♦♦ **Stranded** *edited by Greil Marcus* (1979, Alfred A. Knopf) Marcus' question: If you were stranded on a desert island, what record would you take with you? He asked 20 writers, including such noted rock critics as Dave Marsh, Robert Christgau, Jim Miller, Simon Frith, Nick Tosches, Ellen Willis, Lester Bangs, Ed Ward, and John Rockwell, to produce chapter-length essays on their choice. How much you enjoy the result depends to a large degree on what chapter you're on, and how much you like the album in question, as the picks covered a fairly wide range of critics' pets (Jackson Browne, Van Morrison, the Ramones, the New York Dolls, the Kinks, the Rolling Stones, the Velvet Underground, Captain Beefheart), with some surprises (the Ronettes, Little Willie John, Huey "Piano" Smith, the 5 Royales). Interesting, but generally overwrought, at times taxing; it could also be fairly asked exactly how many people are really interested in reading ten-to-twenty-page exegeses of the Eagles' *Desperado* and Linda Ronstadt's *Living in the U.S.A.* Marcus' 45-page discography of his personal faves, with pithy critical comments, is the best section of the book. Published in 1979, so no records from the '80s or '90s are covered. —*Richie Unterberger*

♦♦♦ **Stranded In Paradise: New Zealand Rock 'n' Roll 1955-1988** *by John Dix* (1988, Paradise Publications, New Zealand) Not too easy to hunt down by any means, but this 354-page history of Kiwi rock is not only the definitive word on the subject, but one of the best volumes ever devoted to a pretty obscure sub-branch of rock music. Rock 'n' roll was present in New Zealand from 1955, when Johnny Cooper recorded a cover of "Rock Around the Clock," and the country produced its share of rockabilly singers, British Invasion-type acts, psychedelia, and blue-eyed soulsters. Here are the detailed stories of local heroes like rockabilly wildman Johnny Devlin, garage/R&B band the La-De-Das, mod/beat rockers Ray Columbus & the Invaders, and many others. The story continues through the '70s success of Split Enz (the first N.Z. band to attract significant international attention), the punk/new wave scene, the reggae and Maori-influenced Polynesian rock, and the rise of the Flying Nun label, one of the most respected alternative rock companies in the world. Along the way there are plenty of interesting (and some not so interesting) stories of little-known performers, both mainstream and underground, who never made the slightest impression outside of the country. Dix also places the music in context with the times and the industry, covering rock journalism, rock festivals, radio, and record companies as well. A great deal of New Zealand rock, particularly in its early days, was derivative of British and American forms, and if there's a fault to this volume, it's that a lot of the acts fall into this category, and don't merit in-depth discussion. Still, serious rock fanatics should pick this up

if they can find it; it's crammed with well-written anecdotes and facts and fine photos, and gorgeously designed. —*Richie Unterberger*

♦♦♦ **Summer Of Love** *by Joel Selvin* (1994, Dutton) Not necessarily the best, but the most wide-ranging and comprehensive history of the San Francisco psychedelic rock scene in the late '60s. Selvin constructs the book as interweaving stories of the principal bands of the area: the Jefferson Airplane, Big Brother/Janis Joplin, and the Grateful Dead especially, and also Quicksilver Messenger Service, Country Joe & the Fish, Moby Grape, Santana, the Charlatans, and Hot Tuna. Other important bands like the Great Society, Steve Miller, and Creedence Clearwater Revival are covered in less depth; minor ones like It's a Beautiful Day, Sons of Champlin, and Cold Blood are only touched upon, and the Beau Brummels, the first San Francisco band of note, are barely mentioned. The straight musical coverage is spiced with lots of anecdotes about the general acid-soaked Haight-Ashbury milieu and the city's live concert scene, sparked by Chet Helms and dominated by promoter Bill Graham. More material on the less famous artists might have been nice, but as it is this covers the most essential players fairly well, from the mid-'60s birth pangs of the Charlatans in the Haight-Ashbury to the general dissolution of the golden era in the early '70s. —*Richie Unterberger*

♦♦♦♦♦ **Sweet Soul Music** *by Peter Guralnick* (1986, Harper & Row) What "deep soul" actually means is a matter of varying opinions, but whatever it is, this is the best history of it, covering the evolution of much Southern-based soul (along with a few northern performers with clear ties to the style) in the 1960s. Besides entire chapters on such giants as James Brown, Otis Redding, Aretha Franklin, and Solomon Burke, there's a wealth of material—much gleaned from first-hand interviews—with the dozens of songwriters, label executives, session players, producers, and minor performers that made the music happen. Lots of coverage of the Stax/Volt/Atlantic axis and the Muscle Shoals studio in particular, and anecdote upon anecdote from such legendary behind-the-scenes figures as songwriter Dan Penn. Guralnick also takes a wider perspective than an in-depth musical account, illustrating how the music could not have reached the heights it did without collaboration between Blacks and whites—a symbiosis which was still highly fraught with tension in the American South of the 1960s. If there's a major fault to be found, it's that the breadth of focus, as wide as it is, is fairly arbitrary—what, for example, makes Ray Charles worthy of inclusion, but not Curtis Mayfield? — *Richie Unterberger*

♦♦ **'Til The Cows Come Home: Rock 'n' Roll Nebraska** *by Bart Becker* (1985, Real Gone) Granted the audience for this—an actual history of rock 'n' roll in Nebraska from the early '50s through the mid-'80s — will be small. Also granted that Nebraska is not one of the leading hotbeds of rock 'n' roll, though it, like almost every state of the union, has spawned some notable performers, and many also-rans. This is a pretty neat project, though, well-written and laid out, with great pictures and expert commentary. It's not a dry archival guide: there are detailed rundowns on some pretty interesting performers, like early woman rockabilly singer Sparkle Moore, definitive one-shot wonders Zager & Evans ("In the Year 2525"), R&B/jazzman Preston Love, and local garage bands like the Rumbles and the Coachmen. Including introductory history, alphabetical entries for performer bios, and discography, the serious rock fan will find this worth searching for. —*Richie Unterberger*

♦♦♦♦ **Trouser Press Guide to '90s Rock** *edited by Ira Robbins and David Sprague* (Fireside/Simon & Schuster, 1997) The all-new fifth edition of Ira Robbins' *Trouser Press Record Guide* firmly re-establishes the book as one of the finest overviews of alternative music on the market. The previous volume in the series appeared in 1991, a.k.a. "the year punk broke;" as a result, the book appeared too early to note the release of Nirvana's *Nevermind*, let alone to take stock of the subsequent mainstream explosion enjoyed by onetime underground acts ranging from Soundgarden to the Red Hot Chili Peppers. Wisely, this new book, published in early 1997, does not replace earlier editions, and for the most part skips over music released prior to 1991 (and already covered in earlier volumes); instead, the focus is almost solely on the alternative music of the 1990s, spanning from grunge to electronica and from major-label superstars to indie-label cult heroes. Written primarily by Robbins and David Sprague, the book is informative and all-inclusive, its reviews thoughtful and concise (although occasionally an entire artist's output is dismissed outright, simply because the given writer dislikes them -- not helpful for any pre-existing fan wondering which of their records to buy next). Ultimately, the major pitfall of *The Trouser Press Guide to '90s Rock* is its overall lack of biographical information; apart from a general sense of who a performer is, there's very little here beyond critical analysis. Still, as a consumer handbook, it's one of the best. —*Jason Ankeny*

♦♦♦♦ **The Trouser Press Record Guide** *edited by Ira A. Robbins* (Collier, 1991). A necessary supplement to the more mainstream *Rolling Stone* guides, this 750-page volume focuses almost entirely on post-1975 punk, new wave, and alternative rock (a little rap, reggae, and other odds and ends slip in). Reviewing about 2,500 artists and almost 10,000 records, it covers a great many indies and imports. The writing could be better; the assessments are sometimes lacking in precise descriptive detail, and the evaluations are on the whole too nondescript and generous. Nonetheless, it's easily the best (and one of the few) reference works of its kind. —*Richie Unterberger*

✦✦✦ **Unsung Heroes Of Rock 'n' Roll** by *Nick Tosches* (1984, Charles Scribner's Sons) Brief profiles of 25 pioneers of rock 'n' roll, mostly from the decade before rock 'n' roll was widely known (1945-55). Some are extremely famous (Nat King Cole, Louis Jordan, Big Joe Turner, Bill Haley), but most are known these days to collectors (Stick McGhee, Cecil Gant, Skeets McDonald, Hardrock Gunter); most are early R&B performers, a few are hillbilly C&W singers. Tosches' style is not for everybody, emphasizing lewd and suggestive angles that some may find offensive. He is also of the unequivocal conviction that rock 'n' roll peaked, in essence, before it really started, and his biases can be irritating. Still, this is a handy primer that illustrates how deep rock 'n' roll's roots lie in the most energetic R&B and C&W of the late '40s and early '50s, although the mid-'50s are commonly thought of as the music's true starting point. The lengthy final section includes a chronology of the development of rock 'n' roll from 1945 to 1955, and discographies for all of the performers profiled. —*Richie Unterberger*

✦✦✦ **The Virgin Directory Of World Music** by *Philip Sweeney* (1991, Owl) Much less lively and more outdated than *The Rough Guide to World Music*, but still worth picking up as a decent world music reference book. This has useful overviews of the regional music of a little over 100 countries, covering general stylistic developments and key performers, and listing (but not reviewing) the essential recordings at the end of each chapter. Each section has an introductory essay by a notable world music personality; these include Manu Dibango, Peter Gabriel, British DJ Andy Kershaw, and Gilberto Gil. —*Richie Unterberger*

✦✦✦✦✦ **What Was The First Rock 'n' Roll Record?** by *Jim Dawson & Steve Propers* (1992, Faber & Faber) Everyone can agree that rock 'n' roll came into being sometime in the decade after World War II, but its exact origins can be hard to pinpoint. This is an absolutely fascinating study of 50 key records which pointed the way for rock 'n' roll, or popularized it, between 1944 and 1956. It doesn't so much answer the question posed by the title as illustrate how many divergent strands of music were involved in rock's conception, and what a fascinating and exciting process it was. Major singles by Louis Jordan, John Lee Hooker, Fats Domino, Muddy Waters, Bill Haley, and Elvis are discussed in depth, as are ones by much more obscure artists such as Hardrock Gunter, Big Boy Crudup, Stick McGhee, Jackie Brenston, and Arkie Shibley. Besides explaining the significance of each record with detailed musical analysis, the authors tracked down key artists, session musicians, and producers for their comments, unearthing a wealth of compelling anecdotes. Essential for anyone interested in rock's birth. —*Richie Unterberger*

✦✦✦ **Where Are You Now, Bo Diddley?** by *Edward Kiersh* (1986, Doubleday) In the 1980s, Kiersh tracked down over 40 rock 'n' roll legends from the past, primarily from the 1960s, although a few from the '50s and '70s appear as well. Each one gets a few pages to reminisce about their ups and downs—the ups, unsurprisingly, were considerably briefer in duration than the downs. Equally unsurprisingly, it's somewhat suffused with nostalgia—a lot of these people are has-beens, even if they were great for a time, and many display a mystification at the changing and fickle music business trends that effectively put them out to the pasture after a year or ten of outrageous success. And it seems like quite a few interviewees claim that, at one point, there was no one bigger than they except the Beatles. If such occasional sentiments don't bother you, it's still a pretty fun read, covering the gamut of rock 'n' roll, from James Brown and Dave Clark to Donovan and Fabian, from Tommy James and Robbie Robertson to the Fugs and Janis Ian, although one sometimes wishes the more interesting subjects had more than ten or so pages to tell their stories. —*Richie Unterberger*

✦✦✦✦✦ **Where Did Our Love Go?** by *Nelson George* (1985, St. Martin's) Absolutely the best, by a wide margin, of the several histories of Motown Records. One of the leading authorities on R&B music, and one of the finest contemporary music journalists, George rightfully focuses on Motown's golden decade, the '60s, though some attention is given to its far less fascinating (though commercially successful) phase after its move from Detroit to L.A. The history of Motown, for all its greatness, was shrouded with a sort of mystery and vagueness. George discusses all the big stars, but he views the company as a team effort of performers, songwriters, producers, session players, and label boss Berry Gordy, Jr., that concocted something far greater than the sum of the parts. In his determination to examine all cogs of the machine, he uncovers previously untold stories and unheralded figures that do not diminish the company's achievements, or the beauty and clarity of its vision, in the least. Combining a wealth of information with acute critical passion, this is necessary reading for the serious rock fan. —*Richie Unterberger*

✦✦✦ **The Wicked Ways Of Malcolm McLaren** by *Craig Bromberg* (1989, Harper & Row) If you're primarily concerned with learning about the Sex Pistols, that story has been better told elsewhere, particularly in Jon Savage's *England's Dreaming*. This is a worthwhile complement, though, written straightforwardly, exhaustively researched, and drawing

upon material from dozens of McLaren's associates, including Steve Jones and Glen Matlock. Besides interesting stories about the Pistols' early days, there's coverage of the other notable, if not always important, acts he had a hand in, including the New York Dolls, Bow Bow Bow, and (before they became stars) Boy George and Adam Ant. McLaren comes off as a con man, albeit one who has anticipated and helped midwife some notable musical trends, more concerned with his ego and commercial fortunes than the anti-establishment statements he often purports to be making, and whose principal talent is obtaining advances for ideas which are usually not finished or realized. —*Richie Unterberger*

✦✦✦ **Will You Still Love Me Tomorrow?: Girl Groups From The '50s On** by *Charlotte Greig* (1989, Virago) For Greig, "girl groups" are not specifically identified with the early and mid-'60s, in the common use of the term within rock criticism. There's a lot of coverage of the classic "girl group" sound within this volume, but it's just one section of the book, which covers groups of female singers working within the pop/rock/R&B mainstream from the '50s through the '80s. For those looking for straight historical coverage, there are a lot of first-hand interviews with major performers like the Shirelles, the Supremes, Ellie Greenwich, Sister Sledge, and Salt-n-Pepa. The main thrust though, is social criticism: Greig analyzes the lyrics and attitudes (which, much more often than not, are concerned with romance) quite seriously, without investing them with unwarranted significance. This doesn't come at the expense of readability, and the post-1970 material in particular covers quite a few artists, along the lines of Honey Cone, the Three Degrees, the Emotions, the Pointer Sisters, and Vanity 6, with considerably more depth and seriousness than they're accorded elsewhere. Those interested in a more musical account of the classic girl group sound are directed toward Alan Betrock's fine *Girl Groups*, but this is worthy reading for a more wide-ranging and scholarly viewpoint. —*Richie Unterberger*

Catalogs

CD International • This is the most complete catalog of CDs in print we have yet seen. A recent edition has 73,116 album titles on 120,827 discs (popular music only). For each title, the label and number are given for that release (if available) in the U.S., U.K., Germany, Japan, and Canada. This is the catalog of choice among the music pros, and the only one that lets you see what is available in other countries at a glance. The format is 8 1/2 x 11; 650 pages. For more information, write to CDI Publishing Corp., P.O. Box 22014, Milwaukie, OR 97222 — *JME*

CD International (American Guide) • CD International offers an additional volume that contains only American CDs — some 21,369 discs. Similar format to the above and about 300 pages long. For many of these discs, individual track listings and playing times (track by track) are included. CDI Publishing Corporation can be reached at P.O. Box 22014 Milwaukie, OR 97222. — *JME*

Record Roundup • This is the grandfather of companies offering music by mail with reviews. Started in 1979 as an offshoot of Rounder Records, Record Roundup issues a 70-page newsletter free of charge several times a year. Each issue is chock-full of reviews and comments about the quality of the recordings offered. P.O. Box 154, North Cambridge, MA 02140; (617) 661-6308 (customer service) or (800) 44-DISCS (credit card orders). — *Michael Erlewine*

Roots & Rhythm • (Down Home Music) If Record Roundup started it all, then the Roots & Rhythm catalog (begun in 1978) has perfected the art of catalog/album reviews. Originally called Down Home Music, and affiliated with the Arhoolie record label, Roots & Rhythm reads more like a magazine of reviews than a catalog. Each issue is filled with expert opinion, comment, and reviews on the latest in domestic and imported releases. The latest catalog, between 60 and 100 pages, is free. In addition to providing information on domestic labels, Roots & Rhythm stocks and reviews a great number of imported albums that are available nowhere else. Certainly this company deserves some sort of award for the groundbreaking work they have done and the example they have set for catalogs with music reviews. Roots & Rhythm can be reached at 6921 Stockton Ave., El Cerrito, CA 94530; (510) 525-1494. — *Michael Erlewine*

SKR Classical • If you don't have a good classical record/CD shop in your town, you may be interested in SKR Classical mail-order. Here is a well-stocked classical store that is staffed by some of the most knowledgeable and approachable staff that I have yet met. Not only do they have comparative listening down pat, but they are experienced in mail-order. I often use them myself. — *Michael Erlewine*

SKR Classical
539 E. Liberty Street
Ann Arbor, MI 48104
(800) 272-4506

Schoolkid's Records • Not everyone has a well-stocked record store in their town. For those who do not, here is a record store that has not only a great stock but also a very knowledgeable staff that can talk to you about the music you are interested in. They are experienced in mail-order, have the best stuff always in stock, and can get anything else for you in a short time. I have shopped with them for many years. — *Michael Erlewine*

Schoolkid's Records
523 E. Liberty Street
Ann Arbor, MI 48104
(800) 445-2361

J&R Music World • An established catalog of both audio equipment and recorded music, all discounted. You can get a free catalog via their 800 number. — *AMG*

J&R Music World
59-50 Queens-Midtown Expressway
Maspeth, NY 11378-9896
(800) 221-8180
FAX (718) 497-1791

Bose Express Music • This is one of the larger and better-known of the mail-order companies. They carry all kinds of music and offer a 300-page catalog (70,000 CDs and cassettes) and a year's subscription to their monthly newsletter for $6. Each newsletter offers about 1000 CDs on special sale. They carry no vinyl but do offer a variety of accessories (CD racks, tapes, etc.). If a title is not in stock, Bose will find that CD you are looking for and ship it to you. Visa, M/C, AmEx. — *Michael Erlewine*

Bose Express Music
The Mountain
Framingham, MA 01701
(800) 451-BOSE
FAX (508) 875 0604

Music Master • This is the largest music service company in Great Britain, similar to Phonlog (Trade Service, Inc.) in the U.S. They offer a variety of publications that may interest some of our readers:

Music Master
Unit 4
Durham Road
Boreham Wood
Herts WD6 1LW
England
(081) 953-5433
FAX (081) 207-5814
Music Master Subscription Package: Includes a large and exhaustive listing of over 200,000 recordings. Monthly supplements.

Magazines and Newsletters

Alternative Press • The writing and production quality aren't up to the level of *Option*, but this monthly offers comprehensive coverage of the alternative rock scene, focusing almost wholly on the bands to be found on college radio stations. Given over almost entirely to features, interviews, and reviews, it's a barometer of sorts as to what's getting played and listened to by the alternative rock crowd. Not as slick or imaginative as some of the competition, but there's a lot of info here. It's stuck to a regular publishing schedule for a long time (a rare feat in the alternative rock world), and it's steadily improved over the years. (P.O. Box 17136, N. Hollywood, CA 91615-9817) — *Richie Unterberger*

Both Sides Now Newsletter • This is the quarterly newsletter from which *Both Sides Now* is assembled. It covers both CDs and vinyl and includes interviews with the people who put together oldies reissue packages, previously unpublished discographies, and all kinds of information. Write to Both Sides Now, Box 384, Fairfax Station, VA 22039. (*Both Sides Now* is also a book.) — *JME*

C-Bub Productions • Specializing in back issues of music magazines from the past 35 years, C-Bub provides collectors and researchers with information on the values of magazines and rock memorabilia, provides sources for buying and selling and resources for magazines and articles from rare and long out-of-print music magazines. If you"re looking for the *Rolling Stone* with John Lennon on the cover or the first time Nirvana appeared on the cover of *Circus* magazine, C-Bub can help you. For a free list contact C-Bub with the artists or groups you are interested in.. (C-Bub Productions, P.O. Box 83812-MG, Portland, OR 97283-0812 (503) 735-0934 Fax: (503) 735-9876.

Country Music • Country may be the most popular music in the land bar rock, but the quality of journalistic coverage and criticism given to the music is poor. *Country Music* is the best national publication devoted to the style. In fact, it is the only country magazine worth recommending, and the only one to offer intelligent, knowledgeable criticism. Adhering mostly to the standard feature/ interview/ review format, it covers the entire spectrum of country: the Nashville superstars, of course, get a bigger chunk than anyone else, but there's also a goodly amount of space for more rootsy and acoustic-based performers, independent label releases, vintage reissues, and hillbilly. Includes contributions from renowned writers like Rich Kienzle and John Morthland. (329 Riverside Ave., Westport, CT 06880) — *Richie Unterberger*

Dirty Linen • The leading American magazine devoted to "folk, electric folk, traditional and world music," by a long shot. This bi-monthly has

plenty of features, oodles of CD, tape, video, concert, and book reviews, roundups of neglected genres and old recordings, listings of new releases, and lots of news. Also offers tour information via several online services. Not as glossy, well-written, or wide-ranging as *Folk Roots*, but almost as informative, complementing that British magazine's coverage. (P.O. Box 66600, Baltimore, MD 21239-6600) — *Richie Unterberger*

Discoveries Magazine • Like *Goldmine*, this is a tabloid-size magazine (published monthly) devoted to record collectors and record collecting. And also like *Goldmine*, it is filled with articles (and discographies) on artists and groups that will interest non-collectors. The two magazines differ somewhat in the music and forms they try to cover. *Goldmine* is geared to rock 'n' roll, blues, and R&B, both on vinyl and CDs, while *Discoveries* is oriented more toward vinyl, focusing on earlier rock and even some traditional popular music. In addition, *Discoveries* encourages readers to communicate with each other about various music trivia and record questions through their mail-box. Write to them, mention the All Music Guide, and receive a free sample issue. P.O. Box 255, Port Townsend, WA 98368;/ (206) 385-1200. — *JME*

Forced Exposure • While its sporadic publishing schedule qualifies this underground rock journal as a fanzine, its 100+ page length and professional layout are of magazine quality. Principally edited and written by famed critics and gargantuan record collectors Jimmy Johnson and Byron Coley, this is rock journalism at its most uncompromising: the authors write about what they like and little else, enthuse wildly and denigrate viciously, and aren't apologetic in the least. Each issue includes massive interviews with underground rock heroes, fiction and essays by underground rock musicians and other noted counterculture authors, and a huge review section which includes many imports, bootlegs, reissues, and obscurities that you're not going to read about anywhere else. (Box 9102, Waltham, MA 02254) — *Richie Unterberger*

Goldmine Magazine • Published since 1974, *Goldmine* is just that — a goldmine of discographical information, extended articles, and great album reviews. Nowhere else will you find in-depth articles on individual artists and groups of this length and breadth. And almost every article is accompanied by a complete discography. *Goldmine* is geared to the record collector. In fact, a good part of each issue is filled with the ads of collectors. Reading through these is an experience in itself. Those of us who don't collect may have little idea of the amount of activity in out-of-print and hard-to-find albums. Thanks to these folks, it is possible to find almost any hard-to-find album. *Goldmine* has some of the best writers in the business, and almost every major freelance writer has written for them at one time or another. It is a tabloid-size magazine of about 170 pages published bi-weekly! There is a lot of information here. If you have never browsed through a copy, you have an experience in store for you. It's an eye-opener. Write to them and mention the *All Music Guide* for a free sample issue. 700 E. State St., Iola, WI 54990; (715)445-2214 — *JME*

ICE • Steeply priced ($3.95 for 20-page issues), but this newsletter is extremely useful for the hard-bitten record collector, as well as for those involved in the music industry at almost any level. Includes the most comprehensive schedule of upcoming releases, both new and reissues; lots of news about in-the-works projects and reissue packages; items about hard-to-find imports; a column devoted to complaints about inadequate CD remastering, track selection, or packaging, featuring responses from the labels themselves; and listings (with brief comments) of CD bootlegs. Most interesting are the feature stories about major reissues, box sets, or new releases, which often highlight in-depth, inside scoops from the label, compilers, or artists themselves. Mostly rock-oriented, with some coverage of jazz, country, blues, and other genres. (P.O. Box 3043, Santa Monica, CA 90408). — *Richie Unterberger*

Living Blues • Absolutely the best blues publication available, and in fact one of the best specialized music magazines of any kind. Features huge, definitive interviews with major and minor blues performers, a big review section that covers almost every blues release available (lots of imports included), news, obituaries, and miscellaneous other features. It's upgraded its production values recently without sacrificing the depth and integrity of the content. Well-written and accessible to the general reader, not just a scholarly publication for blues fanatics. (Center for the Study of Southern Culture, The University of Mississippi, University, MS 38677-9836) — *Richie Unterberger*

Musician • Perhaps the most intelligent and well-written mainstream U.S. music publication, with the emphasis on long (but not exhausting) features and interviews. Leans a bit toward the classic rock side of the coin, or new performers in the classic rock mold, but there's reasonable coverage of alternative rock, as well as some jazz and other music (hip-hop and Black pop gets a pretty thin slice). Also a fair amount of technology info, including equipment reviews and details of specific musicians' instruments, along with comments about them from the artists themselves. —*Richie Unterberger*

Mojo • Fat, glossy general interest British monthly rock magazine with more of a historical perspective than most. Coverage is about equally divided between current acts and artists from the past, with a bit (not much) of a bias toward "classic rock." The in-depth interviews, historical surveys, and eyewitness recollections of interesting star and cult rock icons of the past are often fascinating, and usually considerably more well-written and less oriented toward collector details than those that appear in *Goldmine*. Also includes record and book reviews, news bits, and other interesting columns. (Tower House, Sovereign Park, Lathkill St., Market Harborough, Leics. LE 16 9EF, U.K.) — *Richie Unterberger*

New Musical Express • This weekly tabloid remains the most widely read and circulated British music publication. Resolutely trendy, NME is so eager to find and hype The Next Big Thing that there's a breathless tone to the coverage, with fickle, mercurial critical evaluations that can run from gushing praise to merciless putdowns within weeks. Americans may find the prose difficult to follow at times, occasionally approaching impenetrability. They may also be surprised at the importance attached to musicians' opinions on all sorts of matters not strictly musical, including politics, sex, personal relationships, and other bands. That said, it's the best source for keeping up with the volatile U.K. music scene, including scads of reviews, and many profiles of bands (or even stars) months and years before they become known, or release records, on U.S. shores. (P.O. Box 272, Haywards Heath, West Sussex RH16 3ZA, England) — *Richie Unterberger*

Option • The production values have gotten steadily slicker in the decade since this bi-monthly started, and the coverage of widely known, major label acts has expanded, with a corresponding (but slighter) decrease in the articles about total unknowns. Still, it's the leading international publication devoted to coverage of alternative and indie music of all kinds, and there's still plenty of space for way-underground acts in both the features and reviews sections. Reviews about 200 releases, mostly independent, in every issue, and contains columns devoted to alternative music industry trends and developments, other media, and miscellaneous news. — *Richie Unterberger*

Q • This glossy British monthly is probably the best general interest rock and pop music publication. The review section of each issue covers literally hundreds of new releases, including a lot of British imports and reissues. In-depth features on major performers covering the entire rock and pop spectrum, departments for up-and-coming bands and gossip, book and movie reviews, cool "where are they now?" reports, and eyewitness recollections of major moments in rock history. The writing is much more straightforward and accessible to Yankee readers than the more whimsical and personality-oriented British rock weeklies. Expensive, but worth it, and widely distributed in the U.S. (Tower Publishing Services Ltd., Tower House, Lathkill St., Sovereign Park, Market Harborough LE16 9EF, U.K.) — *Richie Unterberger*

Rap Pages • Not as good or as in-depth as *The Source*, but worth reading by rap fans. Nothing remarkable about the format, but has its share of reviews, articles, and interviews. (LFP Inc., 9171 Wilshire Blvd., Suite 300, Beverly Hills, CA 90210) — *Richie Unterberger*

Rolling Stone • Still the most widely circulated music-oriented publication in the United States. At this point, it's pretty widely disdained by the alternative community for moving squarely into the mainstream of the marketplace. As one staff member admitted in a book about the magazine, it has become a tracker of American taste, rather than a pacesetter of American taste. There are still plenty of well-written features about both established and emerging performers, and a small review section with in-depth evaluations of noteworthy new releases. It has given more space to alternative rock of late, though that may be as much of a reflection of that style's radically increased commercial presence as a conscious decision. — *Richie Unterberger*

The Source • "The magazine of hip-hop music, culture & politics" has experienced some well-circulated internal conflicts of late, but remains the most in-depth rap magazine. The writing is erratic, and those who are not immersed in this aspect of African-American culture will find the lingo that peppers much of the writing occasionally difficult to understand impenetrable at times. But it gets the interviews with a lot of performers who are hard to read about elsewhere, not shying away from controversial gangsta rappers, and includes departments for record reviews, radio, film/TV, and gossip. (P.O. Box 586, Mt. Morris, IL 61054) — *Richie Unterberger*

Spin • Launched as the principal competitor to Rolling Stone in the mid-'80s, *Spin* is clearly here to stay, after some wobbly crises in its early days. Covers alternative rock much more aggressively than its rival, ranging from the very popular to the absolutely unknown, and everything in between, though pieces on historical figures and classic rock are seldom presented. Considering its high profile as the second largest music publication in the United States, the writing and focus remain surprisingly erratic. Much more personality-oriented (both in terms of the acts it covers and the writers themselves) than the other big rock magazine in New York, which leads to both liveliness and self-indulgence. Also includes a fair amount of coverage of politics and popular culture. — *Richie Unterberger*

Urb • Devoted mostly to dance music, usually of Black origin, but not always. Covers hip-hop, acid house, acid jazz, club music, some soul, reg-

gae, and rock. Consisting mostly of reviews, features, and interviews, it's distinguished from the somewhat overlapping coverage of *The Source* and *Rap Pages* by a wider scope, more readable format, higher production values, and better writing. (1680 N. Vine, Suite 1012, Los Angeles, CA 90028) — *Richie Unterberger*

Ugly Things • Issued approximately once a year, this is essential for '60s specialists, especially British Invasion and garage rock enthusiasts. Contains fascinating, minutely detailed interviews with both legends and obscure collector cult figures of the time, ranging from the Pretty Things and the Monks to the Music Machine, the Leaves, Tomorrow, the Downliners Sect, and many others. Well written and laid out, with a large review section (principally for reissues). (405 W. Washington St. #237, San Diego, CA 92103) — *Richie Unterberger*

Vibe • Certainly the slickest and biggest magazine devoted to African-American music, this monthly covers Black pop of all sorts – urban contemporary, soul, hip-hop, dance, and more. Usually fairly mainstream in its coverage, but there are plenty of deviations into emerging and more obscure acts, as well as rock releases that have heavy debts to R&B, funk, and hip-hop. Also includes coverage of African-American popular culture. — *Richie Unterberger*

Wired • Not a music magazine, although it has a tiny review section, and occasionally features stories about musicians making use of technology in cutting-edge fashions. This is the most comprehensive and readable general interest magazine about "the information superhighway" and the accompanying technological developments. Every issue has news about CD-ROM, online, and other technologies that may change the way music is listened to and distributed in the near future. (520 3rd St., 4th Floor, San Francisco, CA 94107) — *Richie Unterberger*

Mail Order

For those millions of us unlucky enough to reside in places outside the realm of superstores (in other words, most folks), trying to find even the lastest hyped major label jazz item in a mall store, standard retail outlet or neighborhood mom-and-pop one-stop can be disastrous. Assuming the clerk even knows what you're talking about "Duke who?", you've got a better chance of striking oil in the back yard than you do of finding much jazz. Thus, you're inevitably forced to the option of mail order. Granted, there are many disadvantages to this. For one, unless you're a preferred customer, by the time you find out about sales, most of the prime items are gone. Frequently you send the money in for six titles and two weeks later get four, with either a refund check or an inquiry asking if you want to back order. Plus, nothing's preferable to walking into a store, browsing, winnowing down a pile of potential buys and finally walking out with records (discs/tapes) in hand. Anyway, here are a few places that we've personally dealt with over the years without problems. This means they have reasonable shipping rates, will actually send you what you order, the product arrives in playable shape, and they issue catalogs in a timely manner. By no means are these the only options available: such magazines as *Goldmine*, *Record Collector* and *Discoveries* are full of ads for stores that deal in jazz mail order; there are also many collectors nationwide who regularly hold auctions and set sales. But, if you have never ventured into the wild world of mail order, here are some good places to start. The following is just a selection of some of the longest-lived and most extensive mail-order outfits specializing in rock recordings (and often, those of rock-related genres). Note that this listing just covers a few of the many useful companies of this sort; listeners should also check the advertisements in collector-oriented magazines, especially *Goldmine*, the leader in that field. Most mail-order operations will send their catalog for a small fee, or for free.

Midnight Records • The world's largest mail-order company specializing in independent and reissued rock CDs and LPs. Astonishing depth of selection, with thousands of imports from all over the world in addition to domestic titles. Especially strong in '50s and '60s rock and independent alternative rock, but also good in vintage soul, blues, some '50s pop. They also have a long list of out-of-print rarities. P.O. Box 390, New York, NY 10113-390; (212)675-2768.

Wayside Music • The most extensive selection of avant garde/ experimental/progressive rock music by mail. P.O. Box 8427, Silver Spring, MD 20907-8427.

Metro Music • A similar focus as Midnight, on '60s reissues and new independent rock, lots of imports. Not as deep a selection as Midnight, but always offers some stuff no one else has, and has a large list of out-of-print LPs and 45s. P.O. Box 10004, Silver Spring, MD 20904-0004; (301)622-2473.

Eurock • Archie Patterson, a journalist for more than 20 years, started Eurock Ltd. in 1973 to promote and distribute electronic and progressive music from around the world. He's written about some of today's name artists, before they broke into the mainstream and continues today exploring the far corners of the globe for adventurous new music. Eurock, P.O. Box 13718, Portland, OR 97213; (503)281-0247.

INDEX

Balin, Marty 475, 476, 477, 621
Ball, David 736, 859
Ball, Lucille 265
Ballard, Florence 351, 790, 916, 934
Ballard, Glen 9, 181, 629
Ballard, Hank **46**, 46, 124, 1093, 1099, 1103
Ballard, Hank & the Midnighters 177, 1103
Ballard, John 5
Ballard, Russ 26, 103, 791, 806, 948
Balloon Farm 1079
Bama Band 16
Bambaataa, Afrika **46**, 125, 126, 499, 524, 1153, 1155
Bambaataa, Afrika & the Soul Sonic Force 47
Bamonte, Perry 233, 234
Banana Splits **47**, 1130
Bananarama **47**, 47, 48, 318, 361, 407, 1062
Band 44, **48**, 48, 49, 82, 100, 122, 152, 153, 186, 218, 258, 291, 293, 351, 371, 417, 540, 546, 601, 618, 687, 777, 887, 1022, 1033, 1083, 1115, 1123, 1125, 1176, 1177
Band Aid 111, 977
Band of Gypsies 423, 805, 1130
Band of Joy 533
Band of Susans 422
Bang Tango 1098
Bangham, Kid 323, 324
Bangles **49**, 49, 61, 84, 363, 431, 436, 503, 751, 827, 948, 1036, 1062, 1110, 1148, 1149
Bangs, Lester 350, 432
Banks, "Mad" Mike 1155
Banks, Bessie 1086, 1092
Banks, Nick 741
Banks, Peter 1043, 1044, 1128
Banks, Ron 284
Banks, Tony 377
Banton, Hugh 982
Barbarians **49**, 50, 1072, 1115
Barbarossa, Dave 114
Barbata, John 475, 476
Barbe, David 637, 911
Barber, Chris 275, 1089, 1107, 1123
Barber, Glenn 1068
Barbero, Lori 38
Barbieri, Richard 472, 473
Barclay James Harvest **50**, 1126, 1127
Barclay, Michael 504
Bardens 154
Bardens, Pete 154
Bardot, Brigitte 366, 565
Bare, Bobby 1049, 1073
Barge, Gene 1021
Bargeld, Blixa 166, 304
Barham, Meriel 566, 685
Bar-Kays **51**, 51, 155, 579, 589, 672, 762, 1106, 1071, 1076, 1087, 1090
Barker, Phil 144
Barlow, Barriemore 481
Barlow, Bruce 207
Barlow, Lou 265, 266, 573, 584, 817, 818, 841, 1150, 1152
Barnes, Don 943
Barnes, James 698
Barnes, Jimmy 1094, 1146
Barnes, Patrick 269
Barnes, Phil 24

Barnes, Prentiss 628
Barnes, Sidney 791
Barnstorm 470, 1002
Barone, Richard 108, 109, 1148, 1149
Baroques 1071
Barre, Martin 480, 481, 482
Barrere, Paul 549, 550
Barret 339
Barrett, Marcia 108
Barrett, Richard 170
Barrett, Syd 13, 35, 36, **52**, 52, 103, 182, 193, 214, 215, 239, 315, 382, 429, 430, 492, 618, 654, 683, 706, 707, 708, 709, 729, 760, 860, 870, 943, 945, 948, 963, 1033, 1065, 1070, 1118, 1127, 1147, 1170, 1172
Barretto, Ray 1087
Barri, Steve 390, 471, 847, 967
Barrow, Geoff 178, 720, 801
Barry & the Remains 50, **52**, 53
Barry, Jeff 26, 387, 471, 511, 528, 537, 624, 625, 788, 824, 1086, 1108, 1109, 1130
Barry, John 6, 168, 951
Barry, Len 567
Barson, Mike 569, 570
Bart, Lionel 849
Bartel, Beate 304
Barthol, Bruce 219
Bartholomew, Dave **53**, 53, 128, 277, 545, 551, 730, 828, 1066, 1102
Bartholomew, Simon 119
Bartley, Chris 1089
Bartley, Jock 336, 337
Bartok, Bela 1056
Barton, Lou Ann 316, 323, 985
Barton, Steve 958
Bartos, Karl 307, 545
Barwell, Buzz 273
Base, Rob **53**, 53
Basement Wall **53**
Bash & Pop 769
Basic Channel 1156
Basie, Count 965
Basil, Toni 404, 1094
Baskin, Don 923
Baskin, Richard 905
Bass, Colin 154
Bass, Fontella **53**, 54, 1065, 1090
Bass, Martha and Fontella 53
Bassey, Shirley 1043
Bateman, Bill 92
Bates, Martyn 810
Bathgate, Alec 522, 926, 1146, 1153
Batiste, Alvin 1074
Bators, Stiv 245, 1137
Bats **54**, 54, 192, 573, 841, 1147
Batt, Mike 371
Battin, Skip 347, 348
Battiste, Harold 274, 379, 1074, 1080
Baughan, David 596
Bauhaus **54**, 54, 55, 231, 472, 558, 641, 1095, 1141
Baumann, Peter 425, 927
Baxter, Jeff 281, 888
Bay City Rollers **55**, 55, 396, 1105, 1142, 1182
Baylor, Helen 310
Baylor, John 454
Bazalgette, Edward 985
Bazooka 1130
Bazz, John 92
BBM 628

Beach Boys 25, 30, 33, **55**, 56, 57, 58, 59, 65, 78, 110, 120, 132, 139, 145, 153, 158, 179, 182, 229, 237, 238, 255, 260, 265, 295, 301, 305, 332, 343, 345, 396, 428, 429, 441, 471, 557, 584, 639, 646, 650, 674, 688, 697, 705, 711, 733, 761, 785, 791, 830, 869, 917, 980, 987, 1031, 1047, 1058, 1060, 1063, 1066, 1074, 1075, 1076, 1078, 1084, 1092, 1103, 1106, 1111, 1118, 1151, 1174, 1176, 1177, 1179
Beach-Nuts 900
Beale Streeters 5
Bean, George 1096
Bean, Janet Beveridge 307, 357, 1166
Bear, Booga 178
Beard 1059
Beard, Annette 580, 581, 815
Beard, Michael 51
Beastie Boys 23, 31, **60**, 60, 61, 177, 310, 381, 408, 466, 565, 566, 571, 622, 676, 796, 857, 942, 961, 995, 1068, 1074, 1081, 1144, 1150, 1151, 1154, 1155, 1158
Beat **61**, 61, 311, 648, 1142
Beat Farmers **61**, 61, 62, 662
Beat Happening **62**, 62, 565, 1008, 1152, 1153, 1180
Beat Rodeo **62**, 62, 63
Beatles 11, 16, 17, 22, 25, 30, 42, 43, 47, 51, 53, 55, 56, 57, **63**, 64, 65, 66, 67, 68, 70, 71, 72, 74, 78, 79, 84, 86, 90, 91, 100, 108, 109, 111, 112, 118, 132, 140, 145, 147, 161, 163, 164, 168, 170, 174, 175, 176, 177, 182, 188, 189, 195, 196, 197, 198, 199, 206, 215, 217, 225, 226, 227, 228, 231, 236, 237, 239, 248, 255, 262, 277, 279, 280, 290, 295, 297, 298, 306, 313, 319, 328, 334, 336, 340, 341, 343, 349, 352, 353, 355, 356, 358, 361, 364, 367, 370, 371, 379, 380, 381, 382, 385, 388, 396, 397, 402, 406, 412, 413, 416, 419, 420, 425, 427, 431, 432, 433, 436, 437, 440, 441, 458, 460, 467, 473, 478, 482, 484, 487, 490, 492, 507, 511, 512, 513, 514, 519, 520, 522, 524, 525, 532, 533, 535, 536, 538, 539, 540, 549, 550, 551, 565, 575, 578, 583, 590, 591, 592, 593, 599, 607, 611, 622, 623, 625, 638, 639, 642, 643, 646, 647, 650, 658, 659, 660, 663, 667, 674, 675, 677, 678, 690, 696, 697, 698, 699, 703, 705, 713, 714, 718, 721, 722, 727, 729, 735, 737, 745, 754, 756, 767, 770, 771, 772, 773, 777, 782, 783, 785, 787, 791, 792, 796, 797, 799, 800, 815, 816, 819, 825, 826, 828, 829, 840, 847, 850, 856, 869, 874, 876, 877, 880, 883, 885, 886, 887, 900, 903, 915, 916, 917, 919, 920, 921, 928, 930, 931, 932, 942, 948, 954, 958, 959, 967, 968, 971, 972, 980, 999, 1004, 1005, 1009, 1015, 1018, 1019, 1022, 1028, 1030, 1031, 1032, 1038, 1042, 1058, 1061, 1064, 1065, 1070, 1073, 1075, 1077, 1082, 1086, 1088, 1089, 1092,

1094, 1095, 1096, 1103, 1104, 1105, 1106, 1107, 1108, 1109, 1111, 1112, 1113, 1114, 1115, 1116, 1117, 1118, 1124, 1125, 1127, 1136, 1142, 1143, 1144, 1145, 1147, 1148, 1150, 1151, 1152, 1153, 1161, 1165, 1166, 1167, 1168, 1170, 1171, 1172, 1174, 1175, 1176, 1177, 1178, 1179, 1180, 1181, 1183, 1184, 1185, 1186
Beatmasters 28
Beats International 439
Beatty, Warren 571
Beau Brummels **68**, 68, 145, 320, 390, 561, 562, 848, 853, 987, 1081, 1082, 1114, 1115, 1119, 1120, 1125, 1185
Beau, Richard 753
Beauford, Carter 583
Beaumont, Jimmy 843, 1084
Beautiful South **69**, 69, 439, 547
Beauvoir, Jean 711
BeBop Deluxe **69**, 69, 70, 842
Bechirian, Roger 881, 882
Beck **70**, 70, 71, 72, 408, 418, 578, 912, 1086, 1150, 1151, 1153, 1177
Beck, Billy 815
Beck, Bogert, Appice 71, 1079
Beck, Jeff 48, **70**, 71, 72, 279, 280, 341, 423, 466, 487, 534, 617, 618, 701, 745, 815, 894, 917, 935, 1007, 1031, 1041, 1042, 1117, 1175
Beck, Jeff Group 71, 72, 442, 893, 1030, 1042, 1124, 1131
Becker, Jozef 963
Becker, Walter 324, 474, 494, 495, 715, 887, 888, 889, 904
Beckett, Barry 44, 666, 806, 858, 958
Beckett, Larry 133
Beckley, Gerry 17
Bedford, David 35, 1128
Bedford, Mark 569
Bedouin Ascent 954, 1157
Bee Gees **72**, 72, 73, 74, 105, 106, 162, 348, 377, 395, 564, 565, 584, 826, 904, 905, 918, 948, 984, 1004, 1123, 1145, 1146
Bee, Barry 846
Beebe, David 499
Beefeaters 145, 147
Been, Michael 153
Beers, Gary 455
Bees Make Honey 1138
Beethoven, Ludwig van 60
BEF 421, 826, 966
Beggar 1080
Beggs, Nick 501
Beginning 510
Behler, Chuck 600
Beiderbecke, Bix 211
Beinhorn, Michael 47, 682
Bel Canto **74**, 74
Belafonte, Harry 177, 190, 1165, 1168
BelAirs 169, 1087
Beland, John 347, 348
Belew, Adrian 19, 116, 659, 926
Belfast Gypsies 939
Bell 672
Bell & Arc 354
Bell Biv Devoe **74**, 74, 118, 123, 652
Bell Notes 1073
Bell, Al 347, 884, 885
Bell, Andy 314, 315, 775, 776

When it comes to music, we wrote the book

All Music Guide
The Best CDs, Albums & Tapes—Third Edition

Edited by Michael Erlewine, Chris Woodstra & Vladimir Bogdanov

This fascinating reference leads readers to the best recordings of 4,000-plus artists and groups. From rock to rap, classical to country and everything in between, more than 21,000 recordings in 20 categories are reviewed and rated by 150 top music critics. Includes artist bios, music timelines, and more.

Softcover, 1,500pp, 6-1/8 x 9-1/4, ISBN 0-87930-423-5, $27.95

All Music Guide to The Blues
The Experts' Guide to the Best Blues Recordings

Edited by Michael Erlewine, Chris Woodstra, Vladimir Bogdanov, and Cub Koda

This easy-to-use and fun-to-browse book is a crucial companion for anyone who listens to the blues. It features reviews and ratings of over 2,600 recordings and profiles of over 560 musicians.

Softcover, 432pp, 6-1/8 x 9-1/4, ISBN 0-87930-424-3, $17.95

All Music Guide to Jazz
The Best CDs, Albums & Tapes—Second Edition

Edited by Michael Erlewine, Chris Woodstra, Vladimir Bogdanov, and Scott Yanow

The essential reference for starting, expanding, or fine-tuning a prime jazz collection. Noted jazz critics profile the lives and work of 1,400 key artists, and review and rate each one's superior recordings—more than 13,000 in all.

Softcover, 900pp, 6-1/8 x 9-1/4, ISBN 0-87930-407-3, $24.95

All Music Guide to Country
The Experts's Guide to the Best Country Recordings

Edited by Michael Erlewine, Chris Woodstra, Vladimir Bogdanov and Stephen Thomas Erlewine

The only complete guide to country music, performers, and first-rate recordings. For 5,500 CDs, albums and tapes by 1,000 artists—from the 1920s hillbilly to today's crossovers with rock and pop— concise reviews, expert ratings and revealing career profiles, plus historical music maps and dozens of essays on styles and influences.

Softcover, 640pp, 6-1/8 x 9-1/4, ISBN 0-87930-475-8, $22.95

All Music Book of Hit Albums
The Top 10 US & UK Album Charts from 1960 to the Present Day • Compiled by Dave McAleer

From the birth of album charts in 1960, this unique book lists the Top 10 albums in both the US and the UK through the present. Also filled with photos and fascinating trivia.

Softcover, 352pp, 8 x 8-1/2, ISBN 0-87930-393-X, $22.95

All Music Book of Hit Singles
Top Twenty Charts from 1954 to the Present Day • Second Edition• Compiled by Dave McAleer

This musical time capsule compares U.S. and U.K. Top 20 charts for the past 40 years. The book is studded with photos, trivia and chart-facts featuring the stars and styles of pop music.

Softcover, 432pp, 8 x 8-1/2, ISBN 0-87930-425-1, $22.95

The Musician's Home Recording Handbook
Practical Techniques for Recording Great Music at Home
By Ted Greenwald

This easy-to-follow, practical guide to setting up a home recording studio will help any musician who wants to get the best results from the equipment already at hand.

Softcover, 176pp, 8-1/2 x 11, ISBN 0-87930-237-2, $19.95

The Musician's Guide to Reading & Writing Music
By Dave Stewart

For the brand new rocker, the seasoned player or the pro who could use new problem-solving methods, this is a clear and practical guide to learning written music notation. "Essential reading for hitherto lazy rock musicians!" —*Keyboard*

Softcover, 112pp, 6 x 9, ISBN 0-87930-273-9, $9.95

Making Music Your Business
A Guide for Young Musicians
By David Ellefson

This book is designed to help young musicians understand how to manage the business side of their career. David Ellefson, bassist for Megadeth, draws on nearly 20 years of recording and touring experience to share his hands-on knowledge about how the music industry works—from the musician's perspective.

Softcover, 144pp, 6 x 9-1/4, ISBN 0-87930-460-X, $14.95

How to Play Guitar
The Basics & Beyond–Chords, Scales, Tunes & Tips
By the Editors of Guitar Player

For anyone learning to play acoustic or electric guitar, this book and CD set is packed with music, licks, and lessons from the pros. The CD guides readers through nine lessons.

Softcover, 80 pp, 8-1/2 x 11, ISBN 0-87930-399-9, $14.95

How to Play Rock Guitar
By the Editors of Guitar Player

Like a private lesson with Eric Clapton or Eddie Van Halen, this book and CD reveal the styles, licks, tips, and secrets of top rock guitar masters. The CD lets players hear exactly how they should sound.

Softcover, 80 pp, 8-1/2 x 11, ISBN 0-87930-403-0, $14.95

Hot Guitar
Rock Soloing, Blues Power, Rapid-Fire Rockabilly, Slick Turnarounds, and Cool Licks • By Arlen Roth

This collection of hot techniques and cool licks includes detailed instruction and hundreds of musical examples. This book covers string bending, slides, picking and fingering techniques, soloing, and rock, blues, and country licks.

Softcover, 130pp, 8-1/2 x 11, ISBN 0-87930-276-3, $19.95

The Hammond Organ
Beauty in the B
By Mark Vail

This book celebrates the rich history of the Hammond B-3 tone-wheel organ; its right-hand man, the whirling Leslie speaker; and their combined influence on gospel, blues, jazz, and rock since the '50s. It also covers other famous Hammond models, and includes photos and performance tips from B-3 stars, plus tips on buying and maintaining a B-3.

Softcover, 240pp, 8-1/2 x 11, 200 photos, ISBN 0-87930-459-6, $24.95

Rock Hardware
40 Years of Rock Instrumentation
By Tony Bacon

This richly illustrated book chronicles the development of the great instruments of rock, how they are used, and how they shape the sound of popular music. It covers guitars, keyboards, synthesizers, drums, brass, recording gear, and more.

Softcover, 144pp, 8-1/2 x 11, 200 color photos, ISBN 0-87930-428-6, $24.95

Miller Freeman Books

Available at fine book and music stores, or contact: **Miller Freeman Books,** 6600 Silacci Way, Gilroy, CA 95020
Phone (800) 848-5594 • Fax (408) 848-5784 • E-Mail: mfbooks@mfi.com
World Wide Web: http://www.books.mfi.com

When it comes to music, we wrote the book

The Fender Amp Book
A Complete History of Fender Amplifiers
By John Morrish

Before Fender electric guitars became household words, Fender amplifiers were already making the scene. Here is the absorbing tale of how Fender fame spread via one of the company's most important product lines.

Hardcover, 96pp, 4-1/2 x 9-1/8, ISBN 0-87930-345-X, $17.95

Electric Guitars and Basses
A Photographic History
By George Gruhn and Walter Carter

This striking, full-color companion volume to Gruhn and Carter's acclaimed book on acoustics traces the technical and aesthetic development of American electric guitars and their manufacturers from 1935 to the present.

Hardcover, 256pp, 8-3/4 x 11-1/2, ISBN 0-87930-328-X, $39.95

Classic Guitars of the '50s
The Electric Guitar and the Musical Revolution of the '50s
Edited by Tony Bacon

This spectacular book explores the electric guitar's growth in the magical decade of the '50s, when rock was born and popular culture changed forever. It features color photos of dozens of 1950s electric guitars made by the great manufacturers. Insightful essays place the guitar in the musical and cultural context of this fascinating decade.

Hardcover, 88pp, 10 x 12-3/4, 200 color photos ISBN 0-87930-427-8, $29.95

The Story of the Fender Stratocaster
"Curves, Contours and Body Horns"
A Celebration of the World's Greatest Guitar
By Ray Minhinnett and Bob Young

This loving profile of the American electric guitar that gave us rock 'n' roll and changed pop culture forever features exclusive interviews and color photos of the legendary Strat, its creators, and famous players.

Hardcover, 128pp, 9-1/6 x 11, ISBN 0-87930-349-2, $24.95

Guitar Player Repair Guide
How to Set Up, Maintain, and Repair Electrics and Acoustics —Second Edition
By Dan Erlewine

Whether you're a player, collector, or repairperson, this hands-on guide provides all the essential information on caring for guitars and electric basses. Includes hundreds of photos and drawings detailing techniques for guitar care and repair.

Softcover, 309pp, 8-1/2 x 11, ISBN 0-87930-291-7, $22.95

Vintage Synthesizers
Groundbreaking Instruments and Pioneering Designers of Electronic Music Synthesizers
By Mark Vail

Focuses on the modern history of the electronic synthesizer (1962-1992), including in-depth interviews with pioneering synth designers and users, performance techniques, buying tips, and production and pricing information.

Softcover, 299pp, 8-1/2 x 11, ISBN 0-87930-275-5, $22.95

1000 Great Guitarists
By Hugh Gregory

Profiling the world's outstanding guitarists from A to Z, this inviting "encyclopedia" covers all kinds of guitar music. Superstars and lesser-knowns are listed with full details on their styles, guitars, best recordings, and more. Includes 10-song CD.

Softcover, 164pp, 7-1/4 x 9-1/2, ISBN 0-87930-416-2, $24.95

The Fender Book
A Complete History of Fender Electric Guitars
By Tony Bacon and Paul Day

This is the fascinating story of Fender electric guitars, from the classic 1950s Telecaster and Stratocaster to current models. The genius of Leo Fender comes to life through unique color photos of outstanding Fender models.

Hardcover, 96pp, 7-1/2 x 9-3/4, ISBN 0-87930-259-3, $22.95

The Rickenbacker Book
A Complete History of Rickenbacker Guitars
By Tony Bacon and Paul Day

The technical and artistic elegance of this electric guitar is as distinctive as its manufacturer's development. This entertaining narrative includes 100 exclusive photos of outstanding "Rickys," plus specifications for every model from 1953 to 1994.

Hardcover, 96pp, 7-1/2 x 9-3/4, ISBN 0-87930-329-8, $19.95

The Gibson Les Paul Book
A Complete History of Les Paul Guitars
By Tony Bacon and Paul Day

Here's the history of Gibson's best-selling guitar model, from its introduction in 1952 in collaboration with the country's most popular guitarist to the present. This book describes all Les Paul guitars and offers color photos of famous ones owned by influential players.

Hardcover, 96pp, 7-1/2 x 9-3/4, ISBN 0-87930-289-5, $22.95

Do-It-Yourself Projects for Guitarists
35 Useful, Inexpensive Electronic Projects to Help Unlock Your Instrument's Potential
By Craig Anderton

A step-by-step guide for electric guitarists who want to create maximum personalized sound with minimum electronic problems, and get the satisfaction of achieving all this themselves.

Softcover, 171pp, 7-3/8 x 10-7/8, ISBN 0-87930-359-X, $19.95

The Bass Book
A Complete Illustrated History of Bass Guitars
By Tony Bacon and Barry Moorhouse

Celebrating the electric bass and its revolutionary impact on popular music worldwide, this richly colorful history features rare, classic and modern basses, plus exclusive quotes from Paul McCartney, Stanley Clarke, and other bass greats.

Hardcover, 108pp, 7-1/2 x 9-3/4, ISBN 0-87930-368-9, $22.95

Secrets from the Masters
40 Great Guitar Players
Edited by Don Menn

Featuring the most influential guitarists of the past 25 years: Jimi Hendrix, Les Paul, Eric Clapton, Eddie Van Halen, Chuck Berry, Andrés Segovia, Pete Townshend and more. Combines personal biography, career history, and playing techniques.

Softcover, 300 pp, 8-1/2 x 11, ISBN 0-87930-260-7, $19.95

 **Miller Freeman Books**

Available at fine book and music stores, or contact:

Miller Freeman Books, 6600 Silacci Way, Gilroy, CA 95020
Phone (800) 848-5594 • Fax (408) 848-5784 • E-Mail: mfbooks@mfi.com
World Wide Web: http://www.books.mfi.com